AHA

AHA Guide

American Hospital Association Guide to the Health Care Field

1987 Edition

Annual directory of hospitals, multihospital systems, and health-related organizations

American Hospital Association Guide to the Health Care Field

1987 Edition

American Hospital Association
840 North Lake Shore Drive
Chicago, Illinois 60611

AHA members $60
Nonmembers $150
AHA catalog no. G01-010087
Telephone orders 1-800-AHA-2626

ISSN 0094-8969
ISBN 0-87258-452-6

840 North Lake Shore Drive
Chicago, Illinois 60611

Contents

Section

Health Organizations, Agencies and Providers

Indexes

The *American Hospital Association Guide to the Health Care Field* is published annually by the American Hospital Association, Carol M. McCarthy, Ph.D., J.D., President.

Division of Marketing Services

Directory Publications Department
Elliot Howes Gage, Manager
Ralph H. Saunders, Production Coordinator
Kim Mallery, Production Staff
Stella Durango, Production Staff
Carolyn Bowyer, Production Staff
Eleanor Law, Production Staff
Karen Abee, Production Staff
Ingrid Lindberg, Secretary

Production Department
Gale E. Petersen, Manager

Design/Planning Department
Michael S. Brierton, Manager
Ken Pagni, Designer
Katherine Stoepel, Designer
David A. Prihoda, Designer
Sherry LaPorte, Designer

Marketing Research Department
Michael A. Pajor, Manager
Michael J. Walsdorf, Research Specialist
Joel H. Landry, Programmer

Director, John M. Bisinger

Membership Department
Judy Williams, Manager
Deborah Maxey-Strong, Administrative Assistant
Stella Hines, Secretary
Hannah Jackson, Supervisor
Juanita King, Supervisor
Donna Houston, Senior Membership Services Representative
Jolanta Lukasiewicz, Membership Services Representative
Debra McNeil, Membership Services Representative
Dessiree Paschal, Membership Services Representative
Aletha Moore-Pointer, Membership Services Representative
Yvette Revis, Membership Services Representative
Elsa Romero, Membership Services Representative
Hortense Simons, Membership Services Representative
Narcisa Vicencio, Senior Membership Services Representative

Order Services
Ruby Paprocki, Manager
Rose Armstrong, Supervisor Customer Service
Audrine Piediscalzi, Senior Customer Service Representative
Grace McKeever, Customer Service Representative
Lillian Pagan, Customer Service Representative
Leesa Terzulli, Customer Service Representative
Cindy Wrobbel, Customer Service Representative
Betty Johnson, Customer Service Representative
Willetta Thomas, Customer Service Representative
Judy Cutler, Customer Service Representative
Dorothy Tifsky, Customer Service Representative
Mary Fialkowski, Supervisor Order Entry
Lettie DeJesus, Senior Order Entry Assistant
Sylvia Pagan, Order Entry Assistant
Diane Minnice, Order Entry Assistant
Beatrice Spears, Order Entry Assistant
Doreen Foster, Order Entry Assistant
Brenda Ford, Senior Correspondent
Josefina Benito, Microfilm Equipment Operator

AHA Warehouse
John Rose, Supervisor
William Hafley, Warehouseman
Dean Jones, Warehouseman
Vincent Ellison, Shipping Clerk

Director, Wayne W. Orlowski
Margery Bahde, Secretary

Mailing Department
Vito A. Benigno, Director
Frank Minnice, Supervisor
Ralph Armstrong, Senior Machine Operator
Mildred Brown, Senior Mail Clerk
Willie Williams, Machine Operator
James Jancich, Machine Operator

Division of Health Economic Studies and Hospital Data Center

AHA Annual Survey of Hospitals
Roy A. Clark, Manager
Dorothy McNeil, Government Hospitals Outside the U.S.
Steve Reczynski, Project Director
Elaine R. Smith, Project Director
Mary T. Krzywicki, Research Assistant
Michael J. Jankowiak, Senior Programmer
Angeline Choate, Data Analyst
Rita DeGonia, Data Analyst
Carol Dunlap, Data Analyst
Pamela Y. Edmon, Data Analyst
Leslie D. Ferguson, Data Analyst
Andrew J. Garfield, Data Analyst
Clisby Jackson, Data Analyst
Dorian McCraney, Data Analyst
Frederick J. Tauber, Data Analyst
Doris D. Valdez, Data Analyst
Gerald K. Vasily, Data Analyst

Director, Hospital Data Center, Peter D. Kralovec

Director, Joseph R. Martin

Office of Constituency Sections

Section for Multihospital Systems
Dorothy L. Cobbs, Staff Specialist
Elworth Taylor, Senior Staff Specialist

Director, Maria Miragliotta

Vice President, Shirley Ann Munroe

Division of Operational Support Services

Lucille Bye, Production Control, Supervisor
Vicki Battles, Control Coordinator
Darlene Spears, Control Coordinator
James O'Connor, Supervisor, Computer Operations
Genie Allen, Computer Operations
Barbara Green, Computer Operations
Sek Jay, Computer Operations
Jairam Koorasingh, Computer Operations
Ernest Nemours, Computer Operations
Anthea Rachwal, Computer Operations
Stanley Zimla, Computer Operations
Bob Jancich, Manager

Director, George P. Young

Division of Information Systems Development

Thomas R. Crissey, Project Manager
Elizabeth P. Joly, Senior Programmer
L. John Haugen, Systems Analyst
Brian M. Clifford, Manager

Director, John F. Wood

Vice President, Corporate Information Systems, Daniel L. Dudek

For Further Information

Section A:

Statistical information and facility codes: Peter Kralovec, 312/280-6523

Institutional identification and approval codes: Judy Williams, 312/280-5972

Government hospitals outside U.S.: Dorothy McNeil, 312/280-6525

Accredited long-term care facilities: JCAH, 312/642-6061

Section B: Dorothy L. Cobbs, 312/280-6392

Sections C & E: Elliot Gage, 312/280-6712

Section D: Hannah Jackson, 312/280-6038

Data tapes of Annual Survey information: Hospital Information Services, 312/280-6197

Order fulfillment: 1-800-AHA-2626
AHA Services, Inc.
P.O. Box 99376
Chicago, IL 60693

Cartography by
J. D. S. Knight
P.O. Box 1334
Evanston, IL 60204

Computer typesetting provided by
Graphic Image Corporation
300 W. Grand Avenue
Chicago, IL 60610

Printed provided by
Banta Company
Menasha, Wisconsin

Introduction

How to use the *AHA Guide to the Health Care Field*

The data published here should be used with the following advisements: The data are based on replies to an annual survey that seeks a variety of information, not all of which is published in this book. The information gathered by the survey includes specific services, but not all of each hospital's services. Therefore, the data do not reflect an exhaustive list of all services offered by all hospitals. For information on the availability of additional data, please call Hospital Information Services, American Hospital Association, at 312/280-6197. Also see Hospital Statistics, *1987 edition, AHA catalog number HO1-082087, for aggregate hospital data.*

The American Hospital Association does not assume responsibility for the accuracy of information voluntarily reported by the individual institutions surveyed. The purpose of this publication is to provide basic data reflecting the delivery of health care in the United States and associated territories; it is not intended to serve as an official and all-inclusive list of services offered by individual hospitals.

Acknowledgement

This year, we wish to recognize Lucille Bye for her long-standing contribution to the *AHA Guide*. In her position of production control supervisor in the Division of Operation Support Services, Lucille Bye is the principle link between the AHA's computer system and its users including the processing and typesetting of the *AHA Guide*. For 19 years, Lucille's integrity, knowledge, and special dedication has been essential in the creation of the high quality for which the *AHA Guide* is known. Although the *AHA Guide* is only one of her projects, Lucille's concern for detail and desire to go the extra mile sets a fine example for AHA staff, and provides a valuable service to AHA members.

What's new

The *American Hospital Association Guide to the Health Care Field* is a central reference source for information on health care institutions, on the American Hospital Association, on organizations and agencies in the health field, and on national hospital statistical data. This is the 42nd volume in a series that started in 1945 with the publication of the first *American Hospital Directory*.

In this year's directory you'll find a number of enhancements. Although each annual *AHA Guide* follows the general pattern established by its predecessors, each year brings innovations as the editors attempt to increase the usefulness of the book. This year is no different. The American Hospital Association has worked to make the *AHA Guide* more reflective of the health care industry.

New lists of Health Maintenance Organizations, freestanding Ambulatory Surgery Centers, Hospices, JCAH accredited Substance Abuse Programs, and Health Care Coalitions have been developed. These lists are found in section E, the salmon pages, of the 1987 *AHA Guide*. The list of state government agencies, also in section E, has been greatly expanded. Section E now serves to make the *AHA Guide* a more complete reference tool for the health care industry.

A new section, section B with green pages, has been added on Multihospital Systems and Alliances. Previously, this information has been published in the AHA's *Directory of Multihospital Systems, Multistate Alliances and Networks*. Now this directory has been merged into the *AHA Guide*. Section B also lists alliances and networks along with their member hospitals.

The *AHA Guide* also now contains maps showing the number of hospitals in each city in the United States. These maps use the listing of hospitals in section A as their legend.

With the addition of the new section on Multihospital Systems and Alliances, the maps, and the new lists of health care providers, the 1987 *AHA Guide* continues to be the complete information source for the health care field.

General format

Each major section begins with its own table of contents and pertinent definitions or other explanatory information. The sections are color coded for easy identification.

Health care institutions

(section A)
This section contains lists of (1) AHA-registered and osteopathic hospitals in the United States and associated areas, by state and area, (2) U.S. government hospitals outside the United States, (3) all U.S. hospitals, alphabetically, (4) headquarters of multihospital systems, and (5) accredited long-term care facilities. Three of the lists of U.S. hospitals serve as a roster of AHA member hospitals, which are identified by a star (★). Hospitals accredited under one of the programs of the Joint Commission on Accreditation of Hospitals are identified by a hollow square (□).

AHA-registered hospitals.—Preceding the lists of hospitals is a statement of the formal requirements for registration by the AHA.

The lists themselves provide a variety of information about each hospital, including the administrator's name; various approvals; selected services and facilities; relationship to a multihospital system; classification by control, service, and length of stay; and selected statistical data from AHA's 1986 Annual Survey of Hospitals.

Some of this information is coded. Included are *approval, facility,* and *multihospital system* codes immediately following the hospital identification, and *classification* codes, tabulated on the right side of the page, preceding the statistical data. Pages A2-4 explain the various codes and define the categories of data.

Approval codes refer to approvals held by a hospital; they represent information supplied by various national approving and reporting bodies. For example, code A-1 indicates accreditation under one of the programs of the Joint Commission on Accreditation of Hospitals—formal evidence that a hospital meets established standards for quality of patient care.

Facility codes refer to facilities and services available within the hospital. For easy reference, both numerical and alphabetical lists of the 54 codes are provided.

Multihospital system codes refer to specific headquarters of multihospital systems. Inclusion of one of these codes indicates that the hospital belongs to a multihospital system and identifies the system to which the hospital belongs. Absence of one of these codes indicates that the hospital does not belong to a multihospital system. Information on the type of control, that is, whether the hospital is owned, leased, sponsored, or contract-managed by the system, is provided in section B of the *AHA Guide*.

For easy reference, system codes are listed both numerically and alphabetically.

Classification codes indicate the type of organization that controls or operates the hospital, the type of service, and the predominant length of stay. The major categories of the *control* codes are as follows: code numbers in the 10s denote nonfederal (state and local) government hospitals; in the 20s, nongovernment not-for-profit hospitals; in the 30s, investor-owned hospitals; in the 40s, federal hospitals; and in the 60s and 70s, nonregistered osteopathic hospitals.

Among the *service* codes, the most common is code 10, indicating a general hospital. Other numbers designate various special services. For example, code 22 indicates a psychiatric hospital, and codes in the 50s indicate children's hospitals. There are two codes for lengths of stay: *S* denotes short-term stay, and *L* denotes long-term stay.

Osteopathic hospitals.—Interfiled in the list of hospitals are the names of osteopathic hospitals, furnished by the American Osteopathic Hospital Association. Codes and symbols identifying these institutions are explained on pages A2-4 and in the headnote at the top of each page of the list of hospitals.

U.S. government hospitals outside the United States.—Institutions marked with a star (★) in this section are AHA associate members.

All U.S. hospitals, alphabetically.—This list consists of all U.S. hospitals listed alphabetically by hospital name. The city and state of each hospital are also included. This list enables a reader to determine the location of a hospital for which only the name is known. Once the city and state are known, additional information about the hospital can be found in the section A list "Hospitals in the United States, by State."

Accredited long-term care facilities.—This list is supplied by the Joint Commission on Accreditation of Hospitals. An explanatory statement precedes the list. Institutions that are members of the AHA are identified by a star (★) preceding the name.

Multihospital systems, multistate alliances and networks

(section B)

There are three types of lists in this section.

Beginning on page B3 is an alphabetical list of multihospital systems and their hospitals. Data on bed size for each hospital in the system are provided along with an indication of whether the hospital is owned, leased, sponsored or contract-managed.

Following this the headquarters of multihospital systems are indexed three ways: by system code number including system name, telephone number, and chief executive officer; alphabetically, by system name; and geographically, by state and city. These indices are useful for cross-referencing the system codes included in the hospital listings "Hospitals in the United States, by State" in section A.

The final type of list in section B provides information on multistate alliances and networks and their members.

Maps of hospital distribution

(section C)

This section consists of a series of maps depicting the distribution of cities with hospitals in the United States. Maps are provided for each of the 50 states and Puerto Rico as well as for the 20 metropolitan areas with the greatest density of hospitals. The listing of hospitals beginning on page A15 serves as the legend for these maps.

The maps are further described on page C2.

AHA membership

(section D)

This section contains lists of AHA institutional members not shown elsewhere in the *Guide* and lists of associate members and personal members. The list of institutional members includes Canadian hospitals, hospital schools of nursing, and provisional members; the list of associate members includes extended care facilities, ambulatory centers and home care agencies, Blue Cross plans, health maintenance organizations, shared services organizations, health planning agencies, and schools of health services administration.

Page D3 provides a key to AHA membership categories. Page D4 gives reference information on AHA offices, officers, and historical data, including winners of various awards and the sites and dates of all AHA annual conventions since the year 1899.

Health organizations and agencies

(section E)

There are four categories in this section.

The first category includes international, national, and regional organizations. Many voluntary organizations that are interested in, or of interest to, the health field are included. The list is alphabetical.

The second category lists United States government agencies.

The third category presents a list of state and provincial organizations and government agencies. The lists for states and provinces include Blue Cross and Blue Shield plans, health systems agencies, hospital associations and councils, hospital licensure agencies, medical and nursing licensure agencies, peer review organizations, state health planning and development agencies, state departments of health and welfare and other related agencies,statewide health coordinating councils, and healthcare coalitions.

The fourth category consists of

lists of various healthcare providers including JCAH accredited substance abuse programs, hospices, freestanding ambulatory surgery centers, and Health Maintenance Organizations. Also listed here are the state agencies one should contact for more information regarding these facilities and organizations.

Index

(section F)

The detailed index helps the reader to locate specific information quickly. It lists alphabetically the subjects covered in the various sections and indicates where they can be found.

Abbreviations

(page F2)

This page is an alphabetical list of all abbreviations used in the *Guide*. In some cases an abbreviation may stand for two or more words or terms or for variants of the same word. In such cases, the meaning will be determined by the context.

Acknowledgments

The editorial staff of the *AHA Guide* acknowledges the cooperation given by many professional groups and government agencies in the health field, particularly the following: American College of Surgeons; American Medical Association; American Osteopathic Hospital Association; Blue Cross-Blue Shield Association; Council of Teaching Hospitals of the Association of American Medical Colleges; Joint Commission on Accreditation of Hospitals; National League for Nursing, Inc.; and various offices within the U.S. Department of Health and Human Services. ■

A

Health Care Institutions

*AHA-registered hospitals in the United States and associated areas are approved for registration by the Executive Committee of the Board of Trustees of the American Hospital Association. This list of registered hospitals is complete as of June 1, 1987. The list of osteopathic hospitals, interfiled in this section, is supplied by the American Osteopathic Hospital Association.

†List supplied by the Joint Commission on Accreditation of Hospitals.

Explanation of Hospital Listings

Hospital, Address, Telephone, Administrator, Approval and Facility Codes, Multihospital System Code	Classification Codes				Inpatient Data				Newborn Data		Expense (thousands of dollars)		
★ American Hospital Association (AHA) membership □ Joint Commission on Accreditation of Hospitals (JCAH) accreditation + American Osteopathic Hospital Association (AOHA) membership ○ American Osteopathic Association (AOA) accreditation Δ Commission on Accreditation of Rehabilitation Facilities (CARF) accreditation Control codes 61, 63, 64, 71, 72 and 73 indicate hospitals listed by AOHA, but not registered by AHA. For definition of numerical codes, see page A2	Control	Service	Stay	Facilities	Beds	Admissions	Census	Occupancy (percent)	Bassinets	Births	Total	Payroll	Personnel
ANYTOWN—Universal County													
★ COMMUNITY HOSPITAL, First St. and Main Ave., Zip 62835; tel. 204/391-2345; John Doe, adm. **A** 1 2 3 4 6 9 10 **F** 1 2 3 4 5 6 8 9 10 11 12 13 14 15 16 17 18 19 23 24 34; **S** 1234	23	10	S	TF	346	10778	284	82.1	45	1693	20695	9973	796
				H	266	10619	209	—	45	1693	19169	9132	751

1 (A 1 2 3 4 6 9 10) 2 (F 1 2 3 4 5 6 8 9 10 11 12 13 14 15 16 17 18 19 23 24 34)

1 Approval Codes

Reported by the approving bodies specified, as of the dates noted.

1 Accreditation under one of the programs of the Joint Commission on Accreditation of Hospitals (Feb. 1987):
1a Acute care hospital accreditation
1b Psychiatric hospital accreditation (includes one or more of the following programs: child, adolescent, or adult psychiatric; community mental health; or alcohol and drug abuse) Requests for more specific information should be directed to the JCAH.
2 Cancer program approved by American College of Surgeons (Nov. 1986).
3 Approval to participate in residency training, by the Accreditation Council for Graduate Medical Education (Jan. 1987). As of June 30, 1975, internship (formerly code 4) was included under residency, code 3.
5 Medical school affiliation, reported to the American Medical Association (Jan. 1987).
6 Hospital-controlled professional nursing school, reported by National League for Nursing (Jan. 1987).
7 Accreditation by Commission on Accreditation of Rehabilitation Facilities (Jan. 1987).
8 Member of Council of Teaching Hospitals of the Association of American Medical Colleges (Jan. 1987).
9 Hospital contracting or participating in Blue Cross Plan, reported by Blue Cross Association (Feb. 1986).
10 Certified for participation in the Health Insurance for the Aged (Medicare) Program by the U.S. Department of Health and Human Services (Jan. 1987).
11 Accreditation by American Osteopathic Association (Jan. 15, 1987).
12 Internship approved by American Osteopathic Association (Jan. 15, 1987).
13 Residency approved by American Osteopathic Association (Jan. 15, 1987).

Nonreporting indicates that the 1986 Annual Survey questionnaire for the hospital had not been received by April 30, 1987, the cutoff date for statistical processing.
Newly Registered indicates that the hospital was registered after the mailing of the 1986 Annual Survey.
Data Not Available indicates that the hospital returned a questionnaire but its statistics were combined with non-hospital data, incomplete, or otherwise unusable.

2 Facility Codes

Actually available within, and reported by, the institution; for definitions, see page A5.

(Numerical Order)

1 Ambulatory surgery services
2 Intensive care unit (cardiac care only)
3 Intensive care unit (mixed or other)
4 Open-heart surgery facilities
5 Trauma center
6 Ultrasound
7 X-ray radiation therapy
8 Megavoltage radiation therapy
9 Radioactive implants
10 Diagnostic radioisotope facility
11 Therapeutic radioisotope facility
12 Histopathology laboratory
13 Organ transplant
14 Blood bank
15 Health promotion services
16 Respiratory therapy services
17 Magnetic resonance imaging (nuclear magnetic resonance)
18 Self-care unit
19 Skilled nursing or other long-term care unit
20 Hemodialysis
21 Hospice
22 Burn care unit
23 Physical therapy services
24 Occupational therapy services
25 Rehabilitation inpatient unit
26 Rehabilitation outpatient services
27 Psychiatric inpatient unit
28 Psychiatric outpatient services
29 Psychiatric partial hospitalization program
30 Psychiatric emergency services
31 Psychiatric foster and/or home care program
32 Psychiatric consultation and education services
33 Clinical psychology services
34 Organized outpatient department
35 Emergency department
36 Birthing room
37 Family planning services
38 Genetic counseling services
39 Extracorporeal shock wave lithotripter (ESWL)
40 Obstetrics
41 Home care program
42 Recreational therapy
43 Day hospital
44 Speech pathology services
45 Hospital auxiliary
46 Volunteer services department
47 Patient representative services
48 Alcoholism/chemical dependency inpatient unit
49 Alcoholism/chemical dependency outpatient services
50 Geriatric services
51 Neonatal intensive care unit
52 Pediatric inpatient unit
53 CT scanner
54 Cardiac catheterization laboratory

Hospital, Address, Telephone, Administrator, Approval and Facility Codes, Multihospital System Code	Classification Codes				Inpatient Data				Newborn Data		Expense (thousands of dollars)		
★ American Hospital Association (AHA) membership □ Joint Commission on Accreditation of Hospitals (JCAH) accreditation + American Osteopathic Hospital Association (AOHA) membership ○ American Osteopathic Association (AOA) accreditation Δ Commission on Accreditation of Rehabilitation Facilities (CARF) accreditation Control codes 61, 63, 64, 71, 72 and 73 indicate hospitals listed by AOHA, but not registered by AHA. For definition of numerical codes, see page A2	Control	Service	Stay	Facilities	Beds	Admissions	Census	Occupancy (percent)	Bassinets	Births	Total	Payroll	Personnel
ANYTOWN—Universal County													
★ COMMUNITY HOSPITAL, First St. and Main Ave., Zip 62835; tel. 204/391-2345; John Doe,	23	10	S	TF	346	10778	284	82.1	45	1693	20695	9973	796
adm. **A** 1 2 3 4 6 9 10 **F** 1 2 3 4 5 6 8 9 10 11 12 13 14 15 16 17 18 19 23 24 34; **S**1234				H	266	10619	209	—	45	1693	19169	9132	751

2 Facility codes (continued)

(Alphabetical Order)

Alcoholism/chemical dependency inpatient unit **48**
Alcoholism/chemical dependency outpatient services **49**
Ambulatory surgery services **1**
Birthing room **36**
Blood bank **14**
Burn care unit **22**
Cardiac catheterization laboratory **54**
Clinical psychology services **33**
CT scanner **53**
Day hospital **43**
Diagnostic radioisotope facility **10**
Emergency department **35**
Extracorporeal shock wave lithotripter (ESWL) **39**
Family-planning services **37**
Genetic counseling service **38**
Geriatric services **50**
Health promotion services **15**
Hemodialysis **20**
Histopathology laboratory **12**
Home care program **41**
Hospice **21**
Hospital auxiliary **45**
Intensive care unit (cardiac care only) **2**
Intensive care unit (mixed or other) **3**
Magnetic resonance imaging (nuclear magnetic resonance) **17**
Megavoltage radiation therapy **8**
Neonatal intensive care unit **51**
Obstetrics **40**
Occupational therapy services **24**
Open-heart surgery facilities **4**
Organ transplant **13**
Organized outpatient department **34**
Patient representative services **47**
Pediatric inpatient unit **52**
Physical therapy services **23**
Psychiatric consultation and education services **32**
Psychiatric emergency services **30**
Psychiatric foster and/or home care program **31**
Psychiatric inpatient unit **27**
Psychiatric outpatient services **28**
Psychiatric partial hospitalization program **29**
Radioactive implants **9**
Recreational therapy **42**
Rehabilitation inpatient unit **25**
Rehabilitation outpatient services **26**
Respiratory therapy services **16**
Self-care unit **18**
Skilled nursing or other long-term care unit **19**
Speech pathology services **44**
Therapeutic radioisotope facility **11**
Trauma center **5**
Ultrasound **6**
Volunteer services department **46**
X-ray radiation therapy **7**

3 Multihospital System Code

A code number has been assigned to each multihospital system headquarters. The inclusion of one of these codes (1) indicates that the hospital belongs to a multihospital system and (2) identifies the specific system to which the hospital belongs. For easy reference, the multihospital systems are listed by code number in section A.

4 Classification Codes

Control

Government, nonfederal
12 State
13 County
14 City
15 City-county
16 Hospital district or authority

Nongovernment not-for-profit
21 Church operated
23 Other

Investor-owned (for-profit)
31 Individual
32 Partnership
33 Corporation

Government, federal
41 Air Force
42 Army
43 Navy
44 Public Health Service other than 47
45 Veterans Administration
46 Federal other than 41-45, 47-48
47 Public Health Service Indian Service
48 Department of Justice

Osteopathic*
61 Church operated
63 Other not-for-profit
64 Other
71 Individual for-profit
72 Partnership for-profit
73 Corporation for-profit

*Control codes 61, 63, 71, 72 and 73 indicate hospitals listed by the AOHA but not registered by AHA.

Hospital, Address, Telephone, Administrator, Approval and Facility Codes, Multihospital System Code	Classification Codes				Inpatient Data				Newborn Data		Expense (thousands of dollars)		
★ American Hospital Association (AHA) membership □ Joint Commission on Accreditation of Hospitals (JCAH) accreditation + American Osteopathic Hospital Association (AOHA) membership ○ American Osteopathic Association (AOA) accreditation Δ Commission on Accreditation of Rehabilitation Facilities (CARF) accreditation Control codes 61, 63, 64, 71, 72 and 73 indicate hospitals listed by AOHA, but not registered by AHA. For definition of numerical codes, see page A2	Control	Service	Stay	Facilities	Beds	Admissions	Census	Occupancy (percent)	Bassinets	Births	Total	Payroll	Personnel
ANYTOWN—Universal County													
★ COMMUNITY HOSPITAL, First St. and Main Ave., Zip 62835; tel. 204/391-2345; John Doe, adm. **A** 1 2 3 4 6 9 10 **F** 1 2 3 4 5 6 8 9 10 11 12 13 14 15 16 17 18 19 23 24 34; **S** 1234	23	10	S	TF	346	10778	284	82.1	45	1693	20695	9973	796
				H	266	10619	209	—	45	1693	19169	9132	751

5

4 Classification Codes (continued)

Service

10 General medical and surgical
11 Hospital unit of an institution (prison hospital, college infirmary, etc.)
12 Hospital unit within an institution for the mentally retarded
22 Psychiatric
33 Tuberculosis and other respiratory diseases
44 Obstetrics and gynecology
45 Eye, ear, nose, and throat
46 Rehabilitation
47 Orthopedic
48 Chronic disease
49 Other specialty†
50 Children's general
51 Children's hospital unit of an institution
52 Children's psychiatric
53 Children's tuberculosis and other respiratory diseases
55 Children's eye, ear, nose, and throat
56 Children's rehabilitation
57 Children's orthopedic
58 Children's chronic disease
59 Children's other specialty†
62 Institution for mental retardation
82 Alcoholism and other chemical dependency

†When a hospital restricts its service to a specialty not defined by a specific code, it is coded 49 (59 if a children's hospital) and the specialty is indicated in parentheses following the name of the hospital.

Stay

S Short-term—average length of stay for all patients is less than 30 days or over 50 percent of all patients are admitted to units where average length of stay is less than 30 days.

L—Long-term—average length of stay for all patients is 30 days or more or over 50 percent of all patients are admitted to units where average length of stay is 30 days or more.

5 Headings

Definitions are based on the American Hospital Association's Hospital Administration Terminology, *catalog no. 097101. Where a 12-month period is specified, hospitals were requested to report on the Annual Survey of Hospitals for the 12 months ending Sept. 30, 1986. Hospitals reporting for less than a 12-month period are so designated.*

Facilities: For those institutions that include nursing home-type units, two lines of data are provided: total facility (TF), which includes hospital data and nursing home-type unit data, and hospital (H), which includes hospital data only. Nursing home-type data can be obtained by subtracting the hospital line from the total facility line. Prior to the 1984 edition, only one line of data, total facility, was provided in the *Guide*. For those institutions without nursing home-type units, only one line of data is provided.

Inpatient Data:
Beds—Number of beds, cribs, and pediatric and neonatal bassinets regularly maintained (set up and staffed for use) for inpatients as of the close of the reporting period; does not include bassinets for normal newborn infants.
Admissions—Number of patients accepted for inpatient service during a 12-month period; does not include newborn. Because of internal transfers, hospital admissions may be greater than total facility admissions.
Census—Average number of inpatients receiving care each day during the 12-month reporting period; does not include newborn.
Occupancy—Ratio of average daily census to the average number of beds (statistical beds) maintained during the 12-month reporting period. (Note that the number of these "statistical beds" may differ from the bed count at the close of the reporting period.)
Newborn Data: Bassinets—Number of bassinets normally available for newborn infants. **Births**—Number of infants born in the hospital and accepted for service in a newborn infant bassinet during a 12-month period; excludes stillbirths.
Expense: Expense for a 12-month period; both total expense and payroll components are shown. Payroll expenses include all salaries and wages except those paid to medical and dental interns and residents, and other trainees (e.g., medical technology trainees, x-ray therapy trainees, administrative residents, etc.).
Personnel: Includes persons on payroll on Sept. 30, 1986; includes full-time equivalents of part-time personnel, but excludes medical and dental interns and residents and other trainees. Full-time equivalents were calculated on the basis that two part-time persons equal one full-time person.

Annual Survey

Each year, an annual survey of hospitals is conducted by the Hospital Data Center of the American Hospital Association (AHA).

Until the 1981 edition, this publication included a copy of both the Annual Survey and the instructions and definitions that accompanied the survey instrument. However, because of their size, the questionnaire and associated definitions are no longer reproduced. The definitions of facility codes are presented instead.

The American Hospital Association Guide to the Health Care Field *does not include all data collected from the 1986 Annual Survey. Requests for purchasing other Annual Survey data should be directed to Hospital Information Services, American Hospital Association, at 312/280-6197.*

Definitions of Facility Codes

1. **Ambulatory surgery services** Scheduled surgical services provided to patients who do not remain in the hospital overnight. The surgery may be performed in operating suites also used for inpatient surgery, specially designated surgical suites for ambulatory surgery, or procedure rooms within an ambulatory care facility.

2. **Intensive care unit (cardiac care only)** Provides patient care of a more specialized nature than the usual medical and surgical care, on the basis of physicians' orders and approved nursing care plans. The unit is staffed with specially trained nursing personnel and contains monitoring and specialized support or treatment equipment for patients who, because of heart seizure, open-heart surgery, or other life-threatening conditions, require intensified, comprehensive observation and care. May include myocardial infarction, pulmonary care, and heart transplant units. Beds must be set up and staffed in a unit(s) specifically designated for this service.

3. **Intensive care unit (mixed or other)** Provides nursing care to adult and/or pediatric patients of a more intensive nature than the usual medical, surgical, pediatric, and/or psychiatric care on the basis of physicians' orders and approved nursing care plans. Included are medical-surgical, pediatric, and psychiatric (isolation) units. These units are staffed with specially trained nursing personnel and contain monitoring and specialized support equipment for patients who, because of shock, trauma, or life-threatening conditions, require intensified, comprehensive observation and care. These units may also include cardiac care when such services are not provided in a distinct cardiac care unit.

4. **Open-heart surgery facilities** The equipment and staff necessary to perform open-heart surgery.

5. **Trauma center** Provides emergency and specialized intensive care to critically injured patients.

6. **Ultrasound** The use of acoustic waves above the range of 20,000 cycles per second to visualize internal body structures for diagnostic purposes.

7. **X-ray radiation therapy** The treatment of disease by roentgen rays or other radiant energy, with the exception of radium, cobalt, or radioisotopes.

8. **Megavoltage radiation therapy** The use of specialized equipment in the supervoltage and megavoltage (above 1 million volts) ranges for deep therapy treatment of cancer. This would include cobalt units, linear accelerators with or without electron beam therapy capability, betatrons, and Van de Graff machines.

9. **Radioactive implants** The use of radioactive material (radium, cobalt-60, cesium-137, or iridium-192 implants) for the treatment of malignancies.

10. **Diagnostic radioisotope facility** The use of radioactive isotopes (radiopharmaceuticals), as tracers or indicators, to detect an abnormal condition or disease.

11. **Therapeutic radioisotope facility** The use of radioactive isotopes (radiopharmaceuticals) for the treatment of malignancies.

12. **Histopathology laboratory** A laboratory in which tissue specimens are examined by a qualified pathologist.

13. **Organ transplant** The necessary staff and equipment to perform the surgical removal of a viable human organ, other than a kidney, from a donor, either alive or just deceased, and the surgical grafting of the organ to a suitably evaluated and prepared patient.

14. **Blood bank** A medical facility with the responsibility for each of the following: blood procurement, drawing, processing, and distribution.

15. **Health promotion services** Education and/or other supportive services that are planned and coordinated by the hospital and that will assist individuals or groups to adopt healthy behaviors and/or reduce health risks, increase self-care skills, improve management of common minor ailments, use health care services effectively, and/or improve understanding of medical procedures and therapeutic regimens. Includes the following specific activities:

    Educational activities. Written goals and objectives for the patient and/or family related to therapeutic regimens, medical procedures, and self care; takes place at the hospital.

    Community health promotion. Similar to educational activities, but for individuals in the community not within a place of employment or as a patient.

    Worksite health promotion. Similar to educational activities, but for employees of a company implemented by the hospital and sponsored by their employer.

16. **Respiratory therapy services** The equipment and staff necessary for the administration of oxygen and certain potent drugs through inhalation or positive pressure.

17. **Magnetic resonance imaging (nuclear magnetic resonance)** The use of a uniform magnetic field and radio frequencies to study tissue and structure of the body. This procedure enables the visualization of biochemical activity of the cell *in vivo* without the use of ionizing radiation, radioisotopic substances, or high-frequency sound.

18. **Self-care unit** Provides minimal nursing care to ambulatory patients who must remain hospitalized. Beds must be set up and staffed in a unit specifically designated for this service.

19. **Skilled nursing or other long-term care unit** Provides physician services and continuous professional nursing supervision to patients who are not in the acute phase of illness and who currently require primarily convalescent rehabilitative and/or restorative services. May include extended care units. Can include, but not restricted to, Medicare/Medicaid certified skilled nursing care. May also include intermediate, residential, or other long-term care units. Beds must be set up and staffed in a unit(s) specifically designated for this service.

20. **Hemodialysis** Provision of equipment and personnel for the treatment of renal insufficiency, on an inpatient or outpatient basis.

21. **Hospice** A program providing palliative care, chiefly medical relief of pain and supportive services, to terminally ill patients and assistance to their families in adjusting to the patient's illness and death.

22. **Burn care unit** Provides more intensive care to severely burned patients than the usual acute nursing care provided in medical and surgical units. Beds must be set up and staffed in a unit specifically designated for this service.

23. **Physical therapy services** Facilities for the provision of physical therapy services prescribed by physicians and administered by, or under the direction of, a qualified physical therapist.

24. **Occupational therapy services** Facilities for the provision of occupational therapy services prescribed by physicians and administered by, or under the direction of, a qualified occupational therapist.

25. **Rehabilitation inpatient unit** Provides coordinated multidisciplinary physical restorative services to inpatients under the direction of a physician knowledgeable and experienced in rehabilitative medicine. Beds must be set up and staffed in a unit specifically designated for this service.

26. **Rehabilitation outpatient services** Provision of coordinated multidisciplinary physical restorative services to ambulatory patients under the direction of a physician knowledgeable and experienced in rehabilitation medicine.

27. **Psychiatric inpatient unit** Provides acute care to emotionally disturbed patients, including patients admitted for diagnosis and those admitted for treatment of psychiatric problems, on the basis of physicians' orders and approved nursing care plans. May also include the provision of medical care, nursing services, and supervision to the chronically mentally ill, mentally disordered, or other mentally incompetent persons. Beds must be set up and staffed in a unit(s) specifically designated for this service.

28. **Psychiatric outpatient services** Hospital services for the diagnosis and treatment of psychiatric outpatients.

29. **Psychiatric partial hospitalization program** Organized hospital facilities and services for day care and/or night care of psychiatric patients who do not require inpatient care 24 hours a day.

30. **Psychiatric emergency services** Hospital facilities for the provision of unscheduled outpatient care to psychiatric patients whose conditions are considered to require immediate care. Staff must be available 24 hours a day.

31. **Psychiatric foster and/or home care program** Planned postdischarge psychiatric observation and care in the patient's place of residence or in an approved foster home.

32. **Psychiatric consultation and education services** Provision of interpretive psychiatric consultation and education services to community agencies and workers such as schools, police, courts, public health nurses, welfare agencies, clergy, and so forth. The purpose is to expand the mental health knowledge and competence of personnel not working in the mental health field and to promote good mental health through improved understanding, attitudes, and behavioral patterns.

33. **Clinical psychology services** One or more clinical psychologists who provide diagnostic or therapeutic services on a regular full-time schedule or intermittently.

34. **Organized outpatient department** Organized hospital services (or clinics) for the provision of nonemergency medical and/or dental services for ambulatory patients.

35. **Emergency department** Organized hospital facilities for the provision of unscheduled outpatient services to patients whose conditions are considered to require immediate care. Must be staffed 24 hours a day.

36. **Birthing room** A hospital-managed combination labor and delivery unit with a homelike setting for mothers and fathers who have completed a specified childbirth course.

37. Family planning services Includes any or all of the following:

Contraceptive care. A family planning service with full range of fertility control methods including education and counseling on all options of contraception.

Fertility services. A unit which counsels and educates on infertility problems. Includes laboratory and surgical workup and management on infertility to individuals having problems conceiving children.

Sterilization. A service with capacity to perform total occlusion or ligation, as appropriate, for women and vasectomy for men.

38. Genetic counseling service A service, directed by a qualified physician, equipped with adequate laboratory facilities, to advise parents and prospective parents on potential problems in cases of genetic defects.

39. Extracorporeal shock wave lithotripter (ESWL) A medical device used for treating stones in the kidney or ureter. The device disintegrates kidney stones, noninvasively, through the transmission of acoustic shock waves directed at the stones.

40. Obstetrics unit Provides care to mothers following delivery, on the basis of physicians' orders and approved nursing care plans. Beds must be set up and staffed in a unit specifically designated for this service.

41. Home care program An organized program, administered by the hospital, that provides medical, nursing, other treatment, and social services to patients in their places of residence.

42. Recreational therapy Facilities for the provision of recreational therapy services prescribed by physicians and administered by or under the direction of a qualified recreational therapist.

43. Day hospital Provides diagnostic, treatment, and rehabilitative services to patients who spend the major portion of the day at the hospital but who do not require care 24 hours a day. More intensive care than provided in an outpatient clinic and of a limited duration.

44. Speech pathology services Personnel available on a routine basis to provide speech therapy for inpatients or outpatients.

45. Hospital auxiliary A volunteer community organization formed to assist the institution in carrying out its purpose and to serve as a link between the institution and the community.

46. Volunteer services department An organized hospital department responsible for coordinating the services of volunteers working within the institution.

47. Patient representative services Organized hospital services providing personnel through whom patients and staff can seek solutions to institutional problems affecting the delivery of high-quality care and services.

48. Alcoholism/chemical dependency inpatient unit Provides medical care and/or rehabilitative services to patients for whom the primary diagnosis is alcoholism or other chemical dependency. Beds must be set up and staffed in a unit specifically designated for this service.

49. Alcoholism/chemical dependency outpatient services Hospital services for the medical care and/or rehabilitative treatment of outpatients for whom the primary diagnosis is alcoholism or other chemical dependency.

50. Geriatric services Includes any or all of the following:

Comprehensive geriatric assessment services. Services that determine geriatric patients' long-term care service needs. Includes the assessment of medical conditions, functional activities, mental and emotional conditions, individual and family preferences, and financial status.

Geriatric acute care unit. Provides acute care to elderly patients in specially designed medical and surgical units. These services may have trained staff in geriatrics, architectural adaptations designed to accommodate the decreased sensory perception of older adults, or age 65 + eligibility requirements.

Satellite geriatric clinics. Clinics or centers which are geographically located at some distance from the hospital and provide health and related services to older adults. Common locations are in senior citizens' centers or senior housing complexes.

51. Neonatal intensive care unit Provides newborn infants with more intensive care than the usual nursing care provided in newborn acute care units, on the basis of physicians' orders and approved nursing care plans. Beds must be set up and staffed in a unit specifically designated for this service.

52. Pediatric inpatient unit Provides acute care to pediatric patients on the basis of physicians' orders and approved nursing care plans. Beds must be set up and staffed in a unit specifically designated for this service.

53. CT scanner Computed tomographic scanners for head and/or whole body scans.

54. Cardiac catheterization laboratory Provides special diagnostic procedures necessary for the care of patients with cardiac conditions. Available procedures include introduction of a catheter into the interior of the heart through a vein or artery or by direct needle puncture.

Headquarters of Multihospital Systems

Alphabetically

9355 Adventist Health System-Eastern and Middle America
4165 Adventist Health System-Sunbelt Health Care Corporation
0235 Adventist Health System-West
0225 Alameda County Health Care Services Agency
0065 Alexian Brothers Health Systems Inc.
1385 Allegany Health System
2565 Alliance Health System
0045 American Health Group International, Inc.
0075 American Healthcare Corporation
1375 American Healthcare Management, Inc.
0195 American Medical Centers
0125 American Medical International
0985 Amerihealth, Inc.
0135 Ancilla Systems, Inc.
0145 Appalachian Regional Healthcare
0205 Asc Health System
0865 Atlantic Health Systems, Inc.
0305 Baptist Health Care Corporation
0315 Baptist Healthcare, Inc.
8810 Baptist Hospital and Health Systems
0345 Baptist Medical Centers
0355 Baptist Medical System
1625 Baptist Memorial Healthcare Development Corporation
0265 Baptist Memorial Hospital System
0185 Baptist Regional Health Services, Inc.
1935 Basic American Medical, Inc.
0095 Baylor Health Care System
1095 Baystate Health Systems, Inc.
0515 Benedictine Health System
1635 Benedictine Health System
0505 Benedictine Sisters
0535 Benedictine Sisters
0545 Benedictine Sisters of the Annunciation
0745 Berkshire Health Systems
0285 Bernardine Sisters of the 3rd Order of St. Francis
0415 Bethesda Hospital, Inc.
5085 Bon Secours Health System, Inc.
0585 Brim and Associates, Inc.
9305 Bromenn Healthcare
0595 Bronson Healthcare Group, Inc.
6665 Brunswick Hospital Center
0955 Camcare, Inc.
9855 Camelback Hospitals, Inc.
5175 Catholic Health Corporation
5205 Catholic Healthcare West
5805 Central Management Corporation
0665 Century Healthcare Corporation
0705 Charlotte-Mecklenburg Hospital Authority
0695 Charter Medical Corporation
0565 Christian Health Services Development Corporation
0735 Church-Charity Foundation of Long Island
8805 Columbus-Cuneo-Cabrini Medical Center
0215 Community Care Systems, Inc.
0875 Community Health Systems, Inc.
1085 Community Hospitals of Central California
0785 Community Psychiatric Centers
0275 Comprehensive Care Corporation
5695 Congregation of St. Agnes
0245 Continental Medical, Inc.
5885 Covenant Health Systems, Inc.
5435 CSJ Health System of Wichita
1885 Daughters of Charity Health Systems-West
1885 Daughters of Charity Health Systems-East Central, Inc.
1885 Daughters of Charity Health Systems East
1885 Daughters of Charity National Health Systems-West Central
1885 Daughters of Charity National Health System
6995 Department of Health and Hospitals, Hospital Services Division
0845 Devereux Foundation
1435 Doctor John McDonald Health Systems
1045 Doctors Hospital
1195 Dominican Sisters Congregation of the Most Holy Name
1295 Dominican Sisters Congregation of Our Lady of the Sacred Heart
1895 East Texas Hospital Foundation
3595 Eastern Mercy Health System
0945 Empire Health Services
0885 Erlanger Health Services
1255 Escambia County Health Care Authority
1215 Eskaton
1225 Evangelical Health Systems
1305 Fairfax Hospital Association
1325 Fairview Hospital and Healthcare Services
1345 Felician Healthcare Systems, Inc.
1275 First Health, Inc.
0295 First Hospital Corporation
1355 Forbes Healthmark
0655 Forest Health Systems, Inc.
0905 Forum Health Investors, Inc.
1455 Franciscan Health Advisory Services, Inc.
5325 Franciscan Health System
9650 Franciscan Health System, Inc.
1475 Franciscan Missionaries of Our Lady Provincial House
5375 Franciscan Services Corporation
1395 Franciscan Sisters Health Care
1415 Franciscan Sisters Health Care Corporation
5705 Franciscan Sisters of Perpetual Adoration
1485 Franciscan Sisters of the Poor Health Systems, Inc.
1425 Fulton-De Kalb Hospital Authority
0495 Gateway Medical Systems
5570 Geisinger System Services
0775 General Health, Inc.
0645 Glenbeigh, Inc.
1495 Grandcor
1535 Great Plains Health Alliance, Inc.
1155 Greenleaf Health Systems, Inc.
1555 Greenville Hospital System
5885 Grey Nuns Health Systems, Inc.
9995 Group Health Cooperative of Puget Sound
0675 Guthrie Medical Center
1655 Harper-Grace Hospitals
2345 Harris Methodist Health System
1865 HCA Oklahoma Health Network
5415 Health and Hospital Services
5945 Health Care Corporation of the Sisters of St. Joseph of Carondelet
6545 Health Corporation of the Archdiocese of Newark
0965 Health Dimensions, Inc.
1905 Health Management Services
8865 Health Management Services, Inc.
0395 Healthcare International, Inc.
1585 Healthcare Management Group, Inc.
0405 Healthcare Services of America
1695 Healtheast, Inc.
2755 Healthlink
0955 Healthnet, Inc.
6235 HealthOne Corporation
2595 Healthshare, Inc.
1365 Healthstar Corporation
6905 Healthwest Foundation
6905 Healthwest Medical Centers
2195 Hei Corporation
3535 Hendrick Medical Development Corporation
0725 Hermann Affiliated Hospital Systems
1525 Hillsborough County Hospital Authority
3395 Hitchcock Alliance
5585 Holy Cross Health System Corporation
5855 Holy Cross Life Care Systems, Inc.
6005 Holy Family of Nazareth Health System
1025 Horizon Health System, Inc.
1035 Horizon Health Systems
1755 Hospital Corporation of America
1775 Hospital Management Associates
2495 Hospital Management Professionals, Inc.
5355 Hospital Sisters Health System-Hospital Sisters of the Third Order of St. Francis-American Province
1235 Humana Inc.
5645 Humility of Mary Health Care Corporation
5565 Incarnate Word Health Services
8855 Intercare Health Systems
1815 Intermountain Health Care, Inc.
1595 Iowa Methodist Health System
1015 Johns Hopkins Health System
0435 Jupiter Hospital Corporation
2105 Kaiser Foundation Hospitals
0995 Kennestone Regional Health Care Systems
2245 LHS Corporation
2295 Little Company of Mary Sisters Healthcare Systems
5755 Los Angeles County-Department of Health Services
6295 Lutheran General Health Care Systems
2245 Lutheran Hospital Society of Southern California
2235 Lutheran Hospitals and Homes Society of America
7775 Main Line Health, Inc.
1335 Mease Health Care
1135 Mediplex Group, Inc.
3825 Mediq, Inc.
6615 Medlantic Healthcare Group
2645 Memorial Care Systems
5155 Mercy Health Care System
5195 Mercy Health Care System
5545 Mercy Health System of Western New York
5215 Mercy-Chicago Province Healthcare Systems
0685 Merritt Peralta Medical Center
7235 Methodist Health Care Network
8875 Methodist Health Services Corporation
2715 Methodist Health System
9345 Methodist Health Systems, Inc.
9335 Methodist Hospital of Indiana
2735 Methodist Hospitals of Dallas
7995 Metropolitan Hospital
2755 Metropolitan Hospitals, Inc.
1615 Mid Florida Medical Services
6975 Mills-Peninsula Hospitals
3775 Milwaukee County Department of Health and Human Services
2855 Missionary Benedictine Sisters American Province
2475 Mississippi County Hospital System
6555 Multicare Medical Center
5895 National Healthcare, Inc.
3015 National Medical Enterprises
9265 Nebraska Methodist Health System, Inc.
3175 Neponset Valley Health System
3075 New York City Health and Hospital Corporation
0465 Nexus Healthcare Corporation
3115 North Broward Hospital District
3165 North Central Health Services
7555 Northern San Diego County Hospital District
1805 Numed Hospitals, Inc.
0455 Numed Psychiatric, Inc.
0715 Office of Hospitals
3315 Ohio Valley Health Services and Education Corporation
3355 Orlando Regional Medical Center
7555 Palomar Pomerado Hospital District
5765 Paracelsus Healthcare
3455 Pennsylvania Hospital
3465 Peoples Community Hospital Authority
1130 Presbyterian Healthcare Systems
5255 Presentation Health System
1315 Recovery Centers of America
1065 Regent Health Systems, Inc.
3615 Religious Hospitallers of St. Joseph, Province of St. Joseph
6525 Republic Health Corporation
8815 Research Health Services
4810 Riverside Healthcare Association, Inc.
0070 Roanoke Hospital Association
8495 Rushmore National Health Systems
5395 Sacred Heart Corporation
8985 Safecare Company, Inc/Safecare Health Service, Inc.
4045 Samaritan Health Service
1055 Samissa Health Care Corporation
7895 Santa Fe Healthcare
0605 SCH Health Care System
0575 Schick Laboratories, Inc.
1505 Scripps Memorial Hospitals
4025 Servantcor
4125 Shriners Hospitals for Crippled Children
5995 Sisters of Charity Center
5115 Sisters of Charity Health Care Systems, Inc.
6095 Sisters of Charity Health Care Systems Corporation
5095 Sisters of Charity of Leavenworth Health Services Corporation
3045 Sisters of Charity of Nazareth Health Corporation
5745 Sisters of Charity of Our Lady of Mercy
5125 Sisters of Charity of St. Augustine Health and Human Services
5815 Sisters of Charity of St. Elizabeth
5985 Sisters of Mercy
5165 Sisters of Mercy Health Corporation
5185 Sisters of Mercy Health Systems-St. Louis
6015 Sisters of Mercy of the Union-Province of Baltimore
5275 Sisters of Providence
5285 Sisters of Providence Health and Human Service
5265 Sisters of Providence-Province of St. Ignatius
5685 Sisters of St. Casimir
5345 Sisters of St. Francis Health Services, Inc.
5925 Sisters of St. Francis of the Mission of the Immaculate Virgin
5365 Sisters of St. Francis of the Province of God
5975 Sisters of St. Francis-Immaculate Heart of Mary-Province of Hankinson
5715 Sisters of St. Francis-3rd Order Regular of Buffalo
5935 Sisters of St. Joseph
5555 Sisters of St. Joseph Health System

5435 Sisters of St. Joseph Health Systems of Wichita
5615 Sisters of St. Joseph of Chambery-North American Province
5445 Sisters of St. Joseph-3rd Order of St. Francis
5455 Sisters of St. Mary
5575 Sisters of the Holy Family of Nazareth-Sacred Heart Province
5235 Sisters of the Pallottine Missionary Society
5255 Sisters of the Presentation of the Blessed Virgin Mary
5305 Sisters of the Sorrowful Mother-Ministry Corporation
5875 Sisters of the Sorrowful Mother-Tulsa Provincialate
5955 Sisters of the 3rd Franciscan Order-Minor Conventuals
5335 Sisters of the 3rd Order of St. Francis
4155 South Carolina Baptist Hospitals
1605 Southeast Community Health Services
4175 Southern Illinois Hospital Services
3505 Southwest Community Health Services
2395 Southwest Health System
4195 Spartanburg Hospital System
0825 Specialty Hospital Division of Nme
0365 Springhill Health Services
5455 SSM Health Care System
9650 St. Francis Health Corporation
5425 St. Joseph Health System
7675 St. Luke's Health System
5845 St. Luke's Regional Medical Center
3555 State of Hawaii, Department of Health
0805 Stormont-Vail Health Services Corporation
8835 Strategic Health Systems
3025 Summit Health, Ltd.
0025 SunHealth Corporation
8795 Sutter Community Hospitals
8795 Sutter Health System
9255 Truman Medical Center
9095 U. S. Health Corporation
9905 United Health Services, Inc.
0335 United Healthcare, Inc.
6345 United Hospitals, Inc.
9605 United Medical Corporation
9555 Universal Health Services, Inc.
9105 University of Alabama Hospitals
6405 University of California-Systemwide Administration
6415 University of Washington Hospitals
8895 Vista Hill Foundation
6705 Wake Medical Center
6615 Washington Healthcare Corporation
6725 West Jersey Health System
0615 Western Hospital Corporation
7005 Western Reserve Care System
9795 Westworld Community Healthcare, Inc.
6745 Wheaton Franciscan Services, Inc.
9575 William Beaumont Hospital Corporation
0015 Zurbrugg Memorial Hospital

★Indicates Type III membership in the American Hospital Association.

By System Code

0015 ★ZURBRUGG MEMORIAL HOSPITAL, Hospital Plaza, Riverside, NJ 08075; tel. 609/461-6700; George D. Hartnett, pres.

0025 ★SUNHEALTH CORPORATION, 4501 Charlotte Park Dr., Box 668800, Charlotte, NC 28266; tel. 704/529-3300; Ben W. Latimer, pres.

0045 AMERICAN HEALTH GROUP INTERNATIONAL, INC., 401 Park Pl., Suite 500, Kirkland, WA 98033; tel. 206/827-1195; Michael D. Drobot, pres.

0065 ★ALEXIAN BROTHERS HEALTH SYSTEMS INC. (Formerly Alexian Brothers of America, Inc.), 600 Alexian Way, Elk Grove Village, IL 60007; tel. 312/640-7550; Bruce Fisher, exec. vice-pres.

0070 ROANOKE HOSPITAL ASSOCIATION, Box 13367, Roanoke, VA 24033; tel. 703/981-7347; Thomas L. Robertson, pres.

0075 AMERICAN HEALTHCARE CORPORATION, 21 W. End Ave., Suite 1100, Nashville, TN 37203; tel. 615/327-2200; Don R. Abercrombie, pres., chm. & chief exec. off.

0095 BAYLOR HEALTH CARE SYSTEM, 3201 Worth St., P O Box 26265, Dallas, TX 75226; tel. 214/820-2891; Boone Powell Jr., pres.

0125 ★AMERICAN MEDICAL INTERNATIONAL, 414 N. Camden Dr., Beverly Hills, CA 90210; tel. 213/278-6200; Walter Weisman, pres. & chief exec. off.

0135 ANCILLA SYSTEMS, INC. (Formerly Ancilla Domini Health Services, Inc.), 1100 Elmhurst Rd., Elk Grove Village, IL 60007; tel. 312/694-4210; Edwin W. Murphy, pres.

0145 ★APPALACHIAN REGIONAL HEALTHCARE, Box 8086, Lexington, KY 40533; tel. 606/255-4431; Robert L. Johnson, pres.

0185 ★BAPTIST REGIONAL HEALTH SERVICES, INC., P O Box 17500, Pensacola, FL 32522; tel. 904/434-4805; James F. Vickery, pres.

0195 AMERICAN MEDICAL CENTERS (Formerly Listed Under Nashville), P O Box 2526, Norcross, GA 30071; tel. 615/244-8410; Paul T. Agee, sr. vice-pres. & chief exec. off.

0205 ★ASC HEALTH SYSTEM, 3 Eagle Center, Suite 1, P O Box 568, O'Fallon, IL 62269; tel. 618/632-1284; Joseph B. Ahlschier, pres.

0215 COMMUNITY CARE SYSTEMS, INC., 210 Lincoln St., Boston, MA 02111; tel. 617/451-0300; Frederick J. Thacher, pres.

0225 ALAMEDA COUNTY HEALTH CARE SERVICES AGENCY, 499 Fifth St., Oakland, CA 94607; tel. 415/268-2722; David J. Kears, dir.

0235 ADVENTIST HEALTH SYSTEM-WEST, P O Box 619002, Roseville, CA 95661; tel. 916/781-2000; Frank F. Dupper, pres.

0245 CONTINENTAL MEDICAL, INC., 880 Johnson Ferry Rd. N.E., 260, Atlanta, GA 30342; tel. 404/255-8220; Richard V. Urquhart, pres.

0265 BAPTIST MEMORIAL HOSPITAL SYSTEM, 111 Dallas St., San Antonio, TX 78286; tel. 512/222-8431; David Garrett, pres. & chief exec. off.

0275 COMPREHENSIVE CARE CORPORATION, 18551 Von Karman Ave., Irvine, CA 92715; tel. 714/851-2273; Richard Santoni PhD, pres.

0285 BERNARDINE SISTERS OF THE 3RD ORDER OF ST. FRANCIS, 647 Springmill Rd.-Maryview, Villanova, PA 19085; tel. 215/525-2686; Sr. M. Gerald, supr. gen.

0295 FIRST HOSPITAL CORPORATION, World Trade Ctr, Suite 870, Norfolk, VA 23510; tel. 804/622-3034; Ronald I. Dozoretz MD, chm.

0305 ★BAPTIST HEALTH CARE CORPORATION, 7428 Nicholson Dr., Oklahoma City, OK 73132; tel. 405/721-6504; Joe L. Ingram MD, pres.

0315 ★BAPTIST HEALTHCARE, INC. (Formerly Baptist Hospitals, Inc.), 4007 Kresgee Way, Louisville, KY 40207; tel. 502/561-3277; Ben R. Brewer, pres.

0335 UNITED HEALTHCARE, INC., 4015 Travis Dr., Nashville, TN 37211; tel. 615/833-1077; Jerry E. Gilliland, pres. & chief exec. off.

0345 ★BAPTIST MEDICAL CENTERS, 2700 U. S. Hwy. 280, P O Box 30040, Birmingham, AL 35222; tel. 205/322-9319; Emmett Johnson, pres.

0355 ★BAPTIST MEDICAL SYSTEM, 9601 Interstate 630, Exit 7, Little Rock, AR 72205; tel. 501/227-2000; Russell D. Harrington Jr., pres.

0365 SPRINGHILL HEALTH SERVICES, 3715 Dauphin St., Mobile, AL 36608; tel. 205/342-3300; Bill A. Mason, pres.

0395 HEALTHCARE INTERNATIONAL, INC., 9737 Great Hills Trail, P O Box 4008, Austin, TX 78759; tel. 512/346-4300; James L. Fariss, bd. chm.

0405 HEALTHCARE SERVICES OF AMERICA, 2000 Southbridge Pkwy., Suite 200, Birmingham, AL 35209; tel. 205/879-8970; Charles A. Speir, bd. chm. & chief exec. off.

0415 ★BETHESDA HOSPITAL, INC., 619 Oak St., Cincinnati, OH 45206; tel. 513/569-6111; L. Thomas Wilburn Jr., chm. & chief exec. off.

0435 JUPITER HOSPITAL CORPORATION, 249 E. Ocean Blvd., Long Beach, CA 90802; tel. 213/437-7717; Bernard Broermann, chm.

0455 NUMED PSYCHIATRIC, INC. (Formerly Maxim Healthcare Corporation), 1265 Drummers Lane, Suite 107, P O Box 754, Valley Forge, PA 19482; tel. 215/687-5151; Edmund Bujalski, pres. & chief exec. off.

0465 ★NEXUS HEALTHCARE CORPORATION, Madison Ave., Summey Bldg., Suite 201, Mount Holly, NJ 08060; tel. 609/261-7011; Chester B. Kaletkowski, pres.

0495 GATEWAY MEDICAL SYSTEMS (Formerly Listed Under St. Louis, Missouri), 2351 Bolton Rd. N.W., Third Fl, Atlanta, GA 30318; tel. 404/351-9611; James R. Cheek, bd. chm.

0505 BENEDICTINE SISTERS, Priory of St. Gertrude, Box 107, Cottonwood, ID 83522; tel. 208/962-3224; Sr. Mary Matthew Geis

0515 BENEDICTINE HEALTH SYSTEM (Formerly Benedictine Sisters), 1028 E. Eighth St., Duluth, MN 55805; tel. 218/722-4799; Sr. Rebecca Wright, pres.

0535 BENEDICTINE SISTERS, St. Benedicts Convent, St. Joseph, MN 56374; tel. 612/362-5100; Sr. Katherine Howard

0545 BENEDICTINE SISTERS OF THE ANNUNCIATION, 7520 University Dr., Bismarck, ND 58501; tel. 701/255-1520; Sr. Susan Lardy, prioress

0565 ★CHRISTIAN HEALTH SERVICES DEVELOPMENT CORPORATION, 11155 Dunn Rd., St. Louis, MO 63136; tel. 314/355-0095; Fred L. Brown, pres. & chief exec. off.

0575 SCHICK LABORATORIES, INC., 1901 Ave. of the Stars, Los Angeles, CA 90067; tel. 213/553-3366; Patrick J. Frawley Jr., chm.

0585 BRIM AND ASSOCIATES, INC., 177 N. E. 102nd Ave., Portland, OR 97220; tel. 503/256-2070; A. E. Brim, pres.

0595 ★BRONSON HEALTHCARE GROUP, INC., One Healthcare Plaza, Kalamazoo, MI 49007; tel. 616/344-5222; Russell P. Kneen, chm. & chief exec. off.

0605 ★SCH HEALTH CARE SYSTEM, 6400 Lawndale Ave., Houston, TX 77023; tel. 713/928-2931; Sr. Carmella O'Donoghue, pres.

0615 WESTERN HOSPITAL CORPORATION, 1124 Ballena Blvd., Alameda, CA 94501; tel. 415/521-4110; Harvey W. Glasser MD, pres.

0645 GLENBEIGH, INC., 1001 N. U. S. Hwy., Suite 8, Jupiter, FL 33458; tel. 305/747-6565; G. Norman McCann, pres.

0655 FOREST HEALTH SYSTEMS, INC., 555 Wilson Lane, Des Plains, IL 60016; tel. 312/635-4100; Morris B. Squire, pres.

0665 CENTURY HEALTHCARE CORPORATION, 7615 E. 63rd Pl., Suite 200, Tulsa, OK 74133; tel. 918/250-9651; Jerry D. Dillon, pres. & chief exec. off.

0675 GUTHRIE MEDICAL CENTER, Guthrie Square, Sayre, PA 18840; tel. 717/888-6666; Ralph H. Meyer, pres.

0685 MERRITT PERALTA MEDICAL CENTER, Hawthorne Ave. & Webster St., Oakland, CA 94609; tel. 415/451-4900; Richard J. McCann, pres. & chief exec. off.

0695 ★CHARTER MEDICAL CORPORATION, 577 Mulberry St., 31202; Mailing Address P O Box 209, Macon, GA Zip 31298; tel. 912/742-1161; William A. Fickling Jr., chm. & chief exec. off.

0705 CHARLOTTE-MECKLENBURG HOSPITAL AUTHORITY, Box 32861, Charlotte, NC 28232; tel. 704/338-2145; Harry A. Nurkin PhD, pres.

0715 OFFICE OF HOSPITALS, P O Box 44215, Baton Rouge, LA 70804; tel. 504/342-2595; Jack Edwards, dep. asst.

0725 HERMANN AFFILIATED HOSPITAL SYSTEMS, 1020 Holcombe, Suite 900, Houston, TX 77030; tel. 713/796-0891; William E. Young Jr., chief exec. off.

0735 ★CHURCH-CHARITY FOUNDATION OF LONG ISLAND, 393 Front St., Hempstead, NY 11550; tel. 516/560-6460; Alexander H. Williams III, exec. vice-pres.

0745 ★BERKSHIRE HEALTH SYSTEMS, Sixth & Spruce, West Reading, PA 19603; tel. 215/378-6257; James B. Gronseth, chief exec. off.

0775 GENERAL HEALTH, INC., 5757 Corporate Blvd., Suite 202, Baton Rouge, LA 70808; tel. 504/924-4324; Thomas H. Sawyer, pres.

0785 COMMUNITY PSYCHIATRIC CENTERS, 2204 E. Fourth St., Santa Ana, CA 92705; tel. 714/835-4535; James W. Conte, pres. & chief exec. off.

0805 STORMONT-VAIL HEALTH SERVICES CORPORATION, 1500 Southwest Tenth St., Topeka, KS 66604; tel. 913/354-6112; Howard M. Chase, chief exec. off.

0825 SPECIALTY HOSPITAL DIVISION OF NME, 1010 Wisconsin Ave. N.W., Suite 900, Washington, DC 20007; tel. 202/337-5600; Norman A. Zober, pres.

0845 ★DEVEREUX FOUNDATION, 19 S. Waterloo Rd., Devon, PA 19333; tel. 215/964-3050; Ronald P. Burd, pres.

0865 ★ATLANTIC HEALTH SYSTEMS, INC., 466 Southern Blvd., Chatham, NJ 07928; tel. 201/514-1993; Thomas J. Foley, pres. & chief exec. off.

0875 COMMUNITY HEALTH SYSTEMS, INC., 14550 Torrey Chase Blvd., 450, Houston, TX 77014; tel. E. Thomas Chaney, pres.

0885 ERLANGER HEALTH SERVICES, 6400 Lee Hwy., Suite 106, Chattanooga, TN 37421; Ron Williams, pres.

0905 FORUM HEALTH INVESTORS, INC., 401 W. Peachtree N.W., 1600, Atlanta, GA 30308; tel. 404/688-9019; J. Dennis Meaders, chief exec. off.

0945 ★EMPIRE HEALTH SERVICES, S. 400 Jefferson St., Suite 333, Spokane, WA 99204; tel. 509/458-7965; Jon K. Mitchell, pres. & chief exec. off.

0955 ★CAMCARE, INC. (Formerly Healthnet, Inc.), Box 1547, Charleston, WV 25326; tel. 304/348-7627; James C. Crews, pres. & chief exec. off.

0965 ★HEALTH DIMENSIONS, INC., 2005 Hamilton Ave., Suite 300, San Jose, CA 95125; tel. 408/599-2701; Robert K. Kirk, pres.

0985 AMERIHEALTH, INC., 2849 Paces Ferry Rd., Suite 790, Atlanta, GA 30339; tel. 404/435-1776; William G. White, pres.

0995 ★KENNESTONE REGIONAL HEALTH CARE SYSTEMS, 677 Church St., Marietta, GA 30060; tel. 404/428-2000; Bernard L. Brown Jr., exec. dir.

1015 ★JOHNS HOPKINS HEALTH SYSTEM, 600 N. Wolfe St., Baltimore, MD 21205; tel. 301/955-1488; Robert M. Heyssel MD, pres.

1025 ★HORIZON HEALTH SYSTEM, INC., 60 W. Broad St., Suite 201, Bethlehem, PA 18018; tel. 215/865-9988; William P. Koughan, pres.

1035 ★HORIZON HEALTH SYSTEMS, 21700 Greenfield Rd., Oak Park, MI 48237; tel. 313/968-2800; James L. Rieder, pres. & chief exec. off.

1045 DOCTORS HOSPITAL, 1087 Dennison Ave., Columbus, OH 43215; tel. 614/297-4000; Richard L. Sims, pres.

1055 SAMISSA HEALTH CARE CORPORATION, 3340 Ocean Park Blvd., Suite 3060, Santa Monica, CA 90405; tel. 213/450-3637; Barry Fireman MD, pres.

1065 REGENT HEALTH SYSTEMS, INC., Liberty St., P O Box 8754, Clinton, LA 70722; tel. 504/683-3319; Charles J. Mueller, pres.

1085 COMMUNITY HOSPITALS OF CENTRAL CALIFORNIA, Fresno & R Sts., P O Box 1232, Fresno, CA 93715; tel. 209/442-6000; James D. Helzer, pres. & chief exec. off.

1095 ★BAYSTATE HEALTH SYSTEMS, INC., 759 Chestnut St., Springfield, MA 01199; tel. 413/787-3345; Michael J. Daly, pres. & chief exec. off.

1130 ★PRESBYTERIAN HEALTHCARE SYSTEMS (Formerly Presbyterian Medical Center), 8220 Walnut Hill Lane, Suite 700, Dallas, TX 75231; tel. 214/696-8500; Douglas D. Hawthorne, pres.

1135 MEDIPLEX GROUP, INC., 15 Walnut St., Wellesley, MA 02181; tel. 617/446-6900; Joseph N. Cassese, pres.

1155 GREENLEAF HEALTH SYSTEMS, INC., Two Northgate Park, Chattanooga, TN 37415; tel. 615/870-5110; Dan B. Page, pres.

1195 DOMINICAN SISTERS CONGREGATION OF THE MOST HOLY NAME, Dominican Convent-San Rafael, San Rafael, CA 94901; tel. 415/454-9221; Sr. Jeremy

1215 ESKATON, 5105 Manzanita Ave., Carmichael, CA 95608; tel. 916/334-0810; Jack Billingsley, pres.

1225 ★EVANGELICAL HEALTH SYSTEMS, 2025 Windsor Dr., Oak Brook, IL 60521; tel. 312/572-9393; John G. King, pres. & chief exec. off.

1235 ★HUMANA INC., 500 W. Main St., Humana Bldg., Box 1438, Louisville, KY 40201; tel. 502/580-1000; David A. Jones, bd. chm. & chief exec. off.; H. Wendell Cherry, pres. & chief oper. off.

1255 ESCAMBIA COUNTY HEALTH CARE AUTHORITY (Formerly Escambia County Hospital Board), Brewton, AL 36426; tel. 205/867-8061; B. J. Griffin, adm.

1275 FIRST HEALTH, INC., 107 Public Square, Batesville, MS 38606; tel. 601/563-7676; David A. Vance, pres.

1295 DOMINICAN SISTERS CONGREGATION OF OUR LADY OF THE SACRED HEART, 1237 W. Monroe St., Springfield, IL 62704; tel. 217/787-0481; Sr. M. Dominica Brennan

1305 ★FAIRFAX HOSPITAL ASSOCIATION, 8001 Braddock Rd., Springfield, VA 22151; tel. 703/321-4213; J. Knox Singleton, pres.

1315 RECOVERY CENTERS OF AMERICA, 1010 Wisconsin Ave., Washington, DC 20007; tel. 202/298-3230; Thomas J. Doherty, exec. vice-pres.

1325 ★FAIRVIEW HOSPITAL AND HEALTHCARE SERVICES (Formerly Fairview Community Hospitals), 2312 S. Sixth St., Minneapolis, MN 55454; tel. 612/371-6300; Carl N. Platou, pres.

1335 MEASE HEALTH CARE, 833 Milwaukee Ave., P O Box 760, Dunedin, FL 33528; tel. 813/733-1111; Donald M. Schroder, pres. & chief exec. off.

1345 ★FELICIAN HEALTHCARE SYSTEMS, INC., 1325 Enfield St., Enfield, CT 06082; tel. 203/745-2542; M. Augustine Kloza, pres.

1355 ★FORBES HEALTHMARK, 500 Finley St., Pittsburgh, PA 15206; tel. 412/665-3565; George H. Schmitt, chm.

1365 HEALTHSTAR CORPORATION, 3555 Timmons Lane, Suite 700, Houston, TX 77027; tel. 713/627-2145; Hugh M. Morrison, bd. chm. & pres.

1375 AMERICAN HEALTHCARE MANAGEMENT, INC., 14160 Dallas Pkwy., Suite 900, Dallas, TX 75240; tel. 214/385-7000; John A. Bradley PhD, bd. chm. & chief exec. off.

1385 ★ALLEGANY HEALTH SYSTEM, 11300 Fourth St. N., Suite 220, St. Petersburg, FL 33702; tel. 813/577-9363; James E. Grobmyer, pres.

1395 ★FRANCISCAN SISTERS HEALTH CARE, 116 S.E. Eighth Ave., Little Falls, MN 56345; tel. 612/632-3601; Sr. Felix Mushel, pres.

1415 ★FRANCISCAN SISTERS HEALTH CARE CORPORATION, St. Francis Woods, Rte. 4, Mokena, IL 60448; tel. 815/469-4888; Sr. Dismas Janssen, bd. chm. & pres.

1425 FULTON-DE KALB HOSPITAL AUTHORITY, 80 Butler St. S.E., Atlanta, GA 30335; tel. 404/589-4307; J. W. Pinkston, exec. dir.

1435 DOCTOR JOHN MCDONALD HEALTH SYSTEMS, 5000 University Dr., P O Box 141739, Coral Gables, FL 33114; tel. 305/666-2111; William H. Comte, pres.

1455 ★FRANCISCAN HEALTH ADVISORY SERVICES, INC., 2409 S. Alverno Rd., Manitowoc, WI 54220; tel. 414/684-7071; Sr. Laura Wolf, pres.

1475 FRANCISCAN MISSIONARIES OF OUR LADY PROVINCIAL HOUSE, 4200 Essen Lane, Baton Rouge, LA 70809; tel. 504/927-7481; Sr. Brendan M. Ronayne

1485 FRANCISCAN SISTERS OF THE POOR HEALTH SYSTEMS, INC., 186 Joralemon St., Brooklyn, NY 11201; tel. 718/625-6530; Sr. Joanne Schuster, pres.

1495 GRANDCOR, 405 Grand Ave., Dayton, OH 45405; tel. 513/222-7990; Richard J. Minor, pres. & chief exec. off.

1505 ★SCRIPPS MEMORIAL HOSPITALS, 9888 Genesee Ave., La Jolla, CA 92038; tel. 619/457-4123; Ames S. Early, pres.

1525 HILLSBOROUGH COUNTY HOSPITAL AUTHORITY, Davis Island, Administrative Bldg., Tampa, FL 33607; tel. 813/251-7383; Newell E. France, mng. dir.

1535 GREAT PLAINS HEALTH ALLIANCE, INC. (Formerly Great Plains Lutheran Hospitals), Box 366, Phillipsburg, KS 67661; tel. 913/543-2111; Curtis Erickson, pres. & chief exec. off.

1555 ★GREENVILLE HOSPITAL SYSTEM, 701 Grove Rd., Greenville, SC 29605; tel. 803/242-7000; Jack A. Skarupa, pres.

1585 HEALTHCARE MANAGEMENT GROUP, INC., 146 Sylvan Dr., Jackson, GA 30233; tel. 205/979-0805; Earl Bonds Jr., chief exec. off.

1595 ★IOWA METHODIST HEALTH SYSTEM, 1200 Pleasant St., Des Moines, IA 50308; tel. 515/283-6201; David S. Ramsey, pres.

1605 SOUTHEAST COMMUNITY HEALTH SERVICES, 1433 Miccosukee Rd., Tallahassee, FL 32308; tel. 904/681-5675; Keith Gilles, chief oper. off.

1615 MID FLORIDA MEDICAL SERVICES, 200 Ave. F N.E., Winter Haven, FL 33880; tel. 813/293-8226; Lance W. Annstasio, pres. & chief exec. off.

1625 BAPTIST MEMORIAL HEALTHCARE DEVELOPMENT CORPORATION, 899 Madison Ave., Memphis, TN 38146; Bobby Hancock, sr. vice-pres. asst.

1635 BENEDICTINE HEALTH SYSTEM, 1005 W. Eighth St., Yankton, SD 57078; tel. 605/668-1511; Sr. Rosaria Kranz, pres.

1655 ★HARPER-GRACE HOSPITALS, 3990 John R St., Detroit, MI 48201; tel. 313/745-9375; Michael H. Fritz, pres. & chief exec. off.

1695 ★HEALTHEAST, INC., 337 N. West St., Allentown, PA 18102; tel. 215/778-2950; David P. Buchmueller, pres. & chief exec. off.

1755 ★HOSPITAL CORPORATION OF AMERICA, One Park Plaza, Box 550, Nashville, TN 37202; tel. 615/327-9551; Thomas F. Frist Jr. MD, chm.

1775 HOSPITAL MANAGEMENT ASSOCIATES, 800 Laurel Oak Dr., Naples, FL 33963; tel. 813/598-3104; William J. Schoen, bd. chm., pres. & chief exec. off.

1805 NUMED HOSPITALS, INC. (Formerly Numed, Inc.), 16633 Ventura Blvd., 13th Floor, Encino, CA 91436; tel. 818/990-2000; Stephen Bowles, pres. & chief exec. off.

1815 ★INTERMOUNTAIN HEALTH CARE, INC., 36 S. State, 22nd Floor, Salt Lake City, UT 84111; tel. 801/533-8282; Scott S. Parker, pres.

1865 HCA OKLAHOMA HEALTH NETWORK, 1601 N.W. Expwy., Suite 2200, Oklahoma City, OK 73118; tel. 405/840-2284; Bruce Perry, pres.

1885 DAUGHTERS OF CHARITY NATIONAL HEALTH SYSTEM, 7806 National Bridge Rd., P.O. Drawer 5730, St. Louis, MO 63121; 314/389-8900; Sr. Irene Kraus, pres.

1895 EAST TEXAS HOSPITAL FOUNDATION, P O Drawer 6400, Tyler, TX 75711; tel. 214/597-0351; Elmer G. Ellis, pres.

1905 HEALTH MANAGEMENT SERVICES, 5793 Widewaters Pkwy., Syracuse, NY 13214; tel. 315/445-2082; James W. Krembs, pres.

1935 BASIC AMERICAN MEDICAL, INC., 4000 E. Southport Rd., Indianapolis, IN 46237; tel. 317/783-5461; Brady R. Justice Jr., pres.

2105 ★KAISER FOUNDATION HOSPITALS, One Kaiser Plaza, Oakland, CA 94612; tel. 415/271-5910; James A. Vohs, chm. & pres.

2195 HEI CORPORATION, 7676 Woodway, Suite 112, Houston, TX 77063; tel. 713/780-7802; George G. Alexander MD, chm. & chief exec. off.

2235 ★LUTHERAN HOSPITALS AND HOMES SOCIETY OF AMERICA, 1202 Westrac Dr., Box 2087, Fargo, ND 58107; tel. 701/293-9053; Michael O. Bice, pres. & chief exec. off.

2245 ★LHS CORPORATION (Formerly Lutheran Hospital Society of Southern California), 1423 S. Grand Ave., Los Angeles, CA 90015; tel. 213/748-0191; Samuel J. Tibbitts, pres.

2295 ★LITTLE COMPANY OF MARY SISTERS HEALTHCARE SYSTEMS, 9350 S. California Ave., Evergreen Park, IL 60642; tel. 312/422-6200; Sr. Sharon Ann Walsh, prov. supr.

2345 ★HARRIS METHODIST HEALTH SYSTEM, 1325 Pennsylvania Ave., Eighth Fl, Fort Worth, TX 76104; tel. 817/878-5973; Ronald L. Smith, pres.

2395 ★SOUTHWEST HEALTH SYSTEM, 133 Donohoe Rd., Greensburg, PA 15601; tel. 412/836-6820; Joseph J. Peluso, pres. & chief exec. off.

2475 MISSISSIPPI COUNTY HOSPITAL SYSTEM, Box 108, Blytheville, AR 72315; tel. 501/762-3300; William E. Peaks, adm.

2495 ★HOSPITAL MANAGEMENT PROFESSIONALS, INC., 5200 Maryland Way, Suite 103, Brentwood, TN 37027; tel. 615/373-8830; Michael W. Barton, pres.

2565 ★ALLIANCE HEALTH SYSTEM, 18 Koger Executive Center, Suite 202, Norfolk, VA 23502; tel. 804/466-6000; Glenn R. Mitchell, pres.

2595 HEALTHSHARE, INC., 501 W. Mitchell St., Suite 300, Petoskey, MI 49770; tel. 616/348-4567; John Rasmussen, pres.

2645 MEMORIAL CARE SYSTEMS, 7777 Southwest Fwy, Suite 100, Houston, TX 77074; tel. 713/776-6992; Dan S. Wilford, pres.

2715 METHODIST HEALTH SYSTEM (Formerly Methodist Hospital, Inc.), 580 W. Eighth St., Jacksonville, FL 32209; tel. 904/798-8000; Marcus Drewa, pres.

2735 ★METHODIST HOSPITALS OF DALLAS, 301 W. Colorado Blvd., 75208; Mailing Address P O Box 655999, Dallas, TX Zip 75265; tel. 214/944-8137; David H. Hitt, pres. & chief exec. off.

2755 ★HEALTHLINK (Formerly Metropolitan Hospitals, Inc.), 500 N.E. Multnomah St., Portland, OR 97232; tel. 503/234-4500; G. Rodney Wolford, pres.

2855 MISSIONARY BENEDICTINE SISTERS AMERICAN PROVINCE, 300 N. 18th St., Norfolk, NE 68701; tel. 402/371-3438; Sr. Matilda Handl

3015 NATIONAL MEDICAL ENTERPRISES, 11620 Wilshire Blvd., P O Box 25980, Los Angeles, CA 90025; tel. 213/479-5526; Richard K. Eamer, chm. & chief exec. off.; Leonard Cohen, pres. & chief oper. off.

3025 SUMMIT HEALTH, LTD., 1800 Ave. of the Stars, Los Angeles, CA 90067; tel. 213/201-4000; William L. Pierpoint, pres. & chief exec. off.

3045 ★SISTERS OF CHARITY OF NAZARETH HEALTH CORPORATION, 9300 Shelbyville Rd., Suite 501, Louisville, KY 40222; tel. 502/429-5055; Sr. Jane Frances Kennedy, pres.

3075 NEW YORK CITY HEALTH AND HOSPITAL CORPORATION, 125 Worth St., New York, NY 10013; tel. 212/566-8038; Jo Ivey Boufford MD, actg. pres.

3115 NORTH BROWARD HOSPITAL DISTRICT, 1625 S.E. Third Ave., Fort Lauderdale, FL 33316; tel. 305/355-4400; Robert L. Kennedy, exec. dir.

3165 NORTH CENTRAL HEALTH SERVICES, 930 Tenth Ave., Spearfish, SD 57783; tel. 605/642-2744; Larry Marshall, vice-pres.

3175 NEPONSET VALLEY HEALTH SYSTEM, 800 Washington St., Norwood, MA 02062; tel. 617/769-4000; Frank S. Crane III, pres.

3315 ★OHIO VALLEY HEALTH SERVICES AND EDUCATION CORPORATION, 90 N. Fourth St., Martins Ferry, OH 43935; tel. 304/234-8765; David J. Campbell, vice chm. & chief exec. off.

3355 ORLANDO REGIONAL MEDICAL CENTER, 1414 S. Kuhl Ave., Orlando, FL 32806; tel. 305/841-5111; J. Gary Strack, pres.

3395 ★HITCHCOCK ALLIANCE, P O Box 1001, Hanover, NH 03755; tel. 603/646-8150; James W. Varnum, pres.

3455 PENNSYLVANIA HOSPITAL (Formerly Pennsylvania Hospital Corporation), Eighth & Spruce Sts., Philadelphia, PA 19107; tel. 215/829-3312; H. Robert Cathcart, pres.

3465 ★PEOPLES COMMUNITY HOSPITAL AUTHORITY, 33000 Annapolis Ave., Wayne, MI 48184; tel. 313/467-4600; Fred E. Blair, chief exec. off.

3505 ★SOUTHWEST COMMUNITY HEALTH SERVICES, 6100 Pan American Freeway N.E., 87109; Mailing Address P O Box 26666, Albuquerque, NM Zip 87125; tel. 505/823-8313; Richard Barr, pres.

3535 HENDRICK MEDICAL DEVELOPMENT CORPORATION (Formerly Hendrick Medical Center), 19th & Hickory St., Abilene, TX 79601; tel. 915/677-3551; Michael C. Waters, pres.

3555 STATE OF HAWAII, DEPARTMENT OF HEALTH, P O Box 3378, Honolulu, HI 96801; tel. 808/548-7402; Jerry Walker, dep. dir.

3595 ★EASTERN MERCY HEALTH SYSTEM, Scott Plaza Two, Suite 403, Philadelphia, PA 19113; tel. 215/521-4500; Daniel F. Russell, pres. & chief exec. off.

3615 RELIGIOUS HOSPITALLERS OF ST. JOSEPH, PROVINCE OF ST. JOSEPH, 16 Manitou Crescent E., Kingston, Ont., Canada; tel. 613/389-0275

3775 MILWAUKEE COUNTY DEPARTMENT OF HEALTH AND HUMAN SERVICES (Formerly Milwaukee County Institute and Departments), 8731 Watertown Plank Rd., Milwaukee, WI 53226; tel. 414/257-6489; James W. Wahner, dir.

3825 MEDIQ, INC., One Mediq Plaza, Pennsauken, NJ 08110; tel. 609/665-9300; Bernard Korman, pres.

4025 ★SERVANTCOR, 175 S. Wall St., Kankakee, IL 60901; tel. 815/937-2034; Joseph S. Feth, pres.

4045 ★SAMARITAN HEALTH SERVICE, 1410 N. Third St., Phoenix, AZ 85004; tel. 602/239-4106; David Reed, pres.

4125 ★SHRINERS HOSPITALS FOR CRIPPLED CHILDREN (Formerly Shriner's Childrens Hospitals), Box 25356, Tampa, FL 33622; tel. 813/885-2575; Jack D. Hoard, exec. adm.

4155 ★SOUTH CAROLINA BAPTIST HOSPITALS, 1333 Taylor St., Columbia, SC 29201; tel. 803/771-5046; William A. Boyce, pres.

4165 ★ADVENTIST HEALTH SYSTEM-SUNBELT HEALTH CARE CORPORATION, 2400 Bedford Rd., Orlando, FL 32803; tel. 305/897-1919; Mardian J. Blair, pres.

4175 ★SOUTHERN ILLINOIS HOSPITAL SERVICES, 608 E. College St., P O Box 522, Carbondale, IL 62903; tel. 618/457-7833; Jerry A. Hickam, pres.

4195 ★SPARTANBURG HOSPITAL SYSTEM, 101 E. Wood St., Spartanburg, SC 29303; tel. 803/591-6107; Charles C. Boone, pres.

4810 RIVERSIDE HEALTHCARE ASSOCIATION, INC. (Formerly Riverside Hospital), 606 Denbigh Blvd., Suite 601, Newport News, VA 23602; tel. 804/875-7500; Nelson L. St. Clair, pres.

5085 ★BON SECOURS HEALTH SYSTEM, INC., 5457 Twin Knolls Rd., Suite 300, Columbia, MD 21045; tel. 301/992-7330; John P. Brozovich, pres. & chief exec. off. oper.

5095 ★SISTERS OF CHARITY OF LEAVENWORTH HEALTH SERVICES CORPORATION, 4200 S. Fourth St., Leavenworth, KS 66048; tel. 913/682-1338; Sr. Macrina Ryan, pres.

5115 ★SISTERS OF CHARITY HEALTH CARE SYSTEMS, INC., 345 Neeb Rd., Cincinnati, OH 45238; tel. 513/922-9775; Sr. Celestia Koebel, pres.

5125 ★SISTERS OF CHARITY OF ST. AUGUSTINE HEALTH AND HUMAN SERVICES, 5232 Broadview Rd., Richfield, OH 44286; tel. 216/659-9283; Sr. Mary Patricia Barrett, pres.

5155 ★MERCY HEALTH CARE SYSTEM, 2303 Grandview Ave., Cincinnati, OH 45206; tel. 513/221-2736; Sr. M. Michaeleen, pres. & chief exec. off.

5165 ★SISTERS OF MERCY HEALTH CORPORATION, 28550 Eleven Mile Rd., Farmington Hills, MI 48018; tel. 313/478-9900; Sr. Mary Corita Heid, pres.

5175 ★CATHOLIC HEALTH CORPORATION, 920 S. 107th Ave., Omaha, NE 68114; tel. 402/393-7661; Diane Moeller, pres.

5185 ★SISTERS OF MERCY HEALTH SYSTEMS-ST. LOUIS (Formerly Sisters of Mercy of the Union-Province of St. Louis), 2039 N. Geyer Rd., St. Louis, MO 63131; tel. 314/965-6100; Sr. Mary R. Rocklage, chief exec. off. & chairperson

5195 ★MERCY HEALTH CARE SYSTEM, Mercy Center, Lake St., Box 370, Dallas, PA 18612; tel. 717/675-3535; William D. McGuire, pres. & chief exec. off.

5205 ★CATHOLIC HEALTHCARE WEST (Formerly Mercy Health Systems), 2300 Adeline Dr., Burlingame, CA 94010; tel. 415/340-7470; Robert C. Densmore, pres.

5215 MERCY-CHICAGO PROVINCE HEALTHCARE SYSTEMS (Formerly Listed Under Chicago), 1s450 Summit Ave., Oakbrook Terrace, IL 60181; tel. 312/953-2970; Catherine C. Gallagher, exec. dir.

5235 ★SISTERS OF THE PALLOTTINE MISSIONARY SOCIETY, 2900 First Ave., Huntington, WV 25702; tel. 304/696-2550; James Spencer, dir. finance

5255 ★PRESENTATION HEALTH SYSTEM (Formerly Sisters of the Presentation of the Blessed Virgin Mary), 1301 S. Ninth Ave., Suite 102, Mailing Address , Sioux Falls, SD Zip 57105; tel. 605/331-4999; Sr. Colman Coakley, pres.

5265 ★SISTERS OF PROVIDENCE-PROVINCE OF ST. IGNATIUS, 9 E. Ninth Ave., Spokane, WA 99202; tel. 509/455-4879; Sr. Barbara Ann Brenner, chief exec. off.

5275 ★SISTERS OF PROVIDENCE (Formerly Sisters of Providence Health Care Corporations), 520 Pike St., P O Box C11038, Seattle, WA 98111; tel. 206/464-3355; Donald A. Brennan, pres.

5285 ★SISTERS OF PROVIDENCE HEALTH AND HUMAN SERVICE (Formerly Listed Under Holyoke), 209 Carew St., Springfield, MA 01104; tel. 413/536-7511; Sr. Catherine Laboure, pres.

5305 ★SISTERS OF THE SORROWFUL MOTHER-MINISTRY CORPORATION, 6618 N. Teutonia Ave., Milwaukee, WI 53209; tel. 414/352-4056; Sr. M. Lois Bush, pres. & chief exec. off.

5325 ★FRANCISCAN HEALTH SYSTEM, Brandywine 1 Bldg., Suite 301, Rtes. 1 & 202, Chadds Ford, PA 19317; tel. 215/358-3950; Ronald R. Aldrich, pres.

5335 ★SISTERS OF THE 3RD ORDER OF ST. FRANCIS, 1124 N. Berkley Ave., Peoria, IL 61603; tel. 309/655-2850; Sr. Frances Marie, exec. vice-pres.

5345 ★SISTERS OF ST. FRANCIS HEALTH SERVICES, INC., 1515 Dragoon Trail, P O Box 1290, Mishawaka, IN 46544; tel. 219/256-3935; Sr. M. Theresa Solbach, pres.

5355 ★HOSPITAL SISTERS HEALTH SYSTEM-HOSPITAL SISTERS OF THE THIRD ORDER OF ST. FRANCIS-AMERICAN PROVINCE, Sangamon Ave. Rd., Box 19431, Springfield, IL 62794; tel. 217/522-6969; Sr. Marianna Kosior, pres.

5365 SISTERS OF ST. FRANCIS OF THE PROVINCE OF GOD, Grove & McRoberts Rds., Pittsburgh, PA 15234; tel. 412/882-9911; Sr. Marietta Zvirblis, coor.

5375 ★FRANCISCAN SERVICES CORPORATION, 6832 Convent Blvd., Sylvania, OH 43560; tel. 419/882-8373; John W. O'Connell, pres.

5395 ★SACRED HEART CORPORATION (Formerly Sisters of St. Francis of Penance and Christian Charity-Sacred Heart Province), 2861 W. 52nd Ave., Denver, CO 80221; tel. 303/458-8611; Sr. Christina Oleske, pres.

5415 ★HEALTH AND HOSPITAL SERVICES, 1715 114th Ave. S.E., Suite 110, Bellevue, WA 98004; tel. 206/454-8068; Sr. Joan M. McInnes, pres.

5425 ★ST. JOSEPH HEALTH SYSTEM, 440 S. Batavia St., Orange, CA 92668; tel. 714/997-7690; Robert W. O'Leary, pres.

5435 ★CSJ HEALTH SYSTEM OF WICHITA (Formerly Sisters of St. Joseph Health Systems of Wichita), 3720 E. Bayley, Wichita, KS 67218; tel. 316/686-7171; Sr. Antoinette Yelek, pres.; Gregory G. Guntly, chief exec. off.

5445 SISTERS OF ST. JOSEPH-3RD ORDER OF ST. FRANCIS, 105 E. Jefferson, P O Box 688, South Bend, IN 46624; tel. 219/233-1166; Sr. Adalbert Stal, central treas.; Sr. Joanne Skalski, dir. inst sponsorship bd.

5455 ★SSM HEALTH CARE SYSTEM (Formerly Sisters of St. Mary), 1031 Bellevue Ave., St. Louis, MO 63117; tel. 314/768-1600; Sr. Mary Jean Ryan, pres. & chief exec. off.

5545 MERCY HEALTH SYSTEM OF WESTERN NEW YORK (Formerly Sisters of Mercy), 565 Abbott Rd., Buffalo, NY 14220; tel. 716/827-2375; Sr. Mary Annunciate Kelleher, pres.

5555 ★SISTERS OF ST. JOSEPH HEALTH SYSTEM, 3427 Gull Rd., Nazareth, MI 49074; tel. 616/381-2500; Sr. Irene Waldmann, pres.

5565 ★INCARNATE WORD HEALTH SERVICES, 303 W. Sunset Rd., San Antonio, TX 78209; tel. 512/828-1733; Sr. Nora Marie Walsh, pres.

5570 GEISINGER SYSTEM SERVICES, N. Academy Ave., Danville, PA 17822; tel. 717/271-6631; Frank J. Trembulak, pres.

5575 SISTERS OF THE HOLY FAMILY OF NAZARETH-SACRED HEART PROVINCE, 353 N. River Rd., Des Plaines, IL 60016; tel. 312/298-6760; Sr. M. Loretta Markiewicz, prov. supr.

5585 ★HOLY CROSS HEALTH SYSTEM CORPORATION, 3606 E. Jefferson Blvd., South Bend, IN 46615; tel. 219/233-8558; William A. Himmelsbach Jr., pres. & chief exec. off.

5615 SISTERS OF ST. JOSEPH OF CHAMBERY-NORTH AMERICAN PROVINCE, 27 Park Rd., West Hartford, CT 06119; tel. 203/233-5126; Sr. Jean Sauntry, supr.

5645 ★HUMILITY OF MARY HEALTH CARE CORPORATION (Formerly Sisters of the Humility of Mary), P O Box 841, Lorain, OH 44052; tel. 216/871-0971; Sr. Frances Flanigan, chief exec. off.

5685 SISTERS OF ST. CASIMIR, 2601 W. Marquette Rd., Chicago, IL 60629; tel. 312/434-6700; Sr. M. Joanella Fayert, pres.

5695 ★CONGREGATION OF ST. AGNES, 475 Gillett St., Fond Du Lac, WI 54935; tel. 414/923-2121; Sr. Mary Mollison, corp dir.

5705 FRANCISCAN SISTERS OF PERPETUAL ADORATION, 912 Market St., La Crosse, WI 54601; tel. 608/782-5610; Sr. Patricia Alden, pres.

5715 ★SISTERS OF ST. FRANCIS-3RD ORDER REGULAR OF BUFFALO, 400 Mill St., Williamsville, NY 14221; tel. 716/632-2155; Sr. Maureen Ann, gen. minister

5745 SISTERS OF CHARITY OF OUR LADY OF MERCY, Box 12410, Charleston, SC 29412; tel. 803/795-6083; Sr. Anne Francis Campbell

5755 LOS ANGELES COUNTY-DEPARTMENT OF HEALTH SERVICES (Formerly County of Los Angeles-Department of Health Services), 313 N. Figueroa St., Room 936, Los Angeles, CA 90012; tel. 213/974-8101; Robert C. Gates, dir. health

5765 PARACELSUS HEALTHCARE (Formerly Paracelsus Hospital Corporation), 155 N. Lake Ave., Suite 1100, Pasadena, CA 91101; tel. 818/792-8600; R. J. Messenger, pres. & chief oper. off.

5805 ★CENTRAL MANAGEMENT CORPORATION, 112-114 Roberts St., Suite 208, Fargo, ND 58102; tel. 701/237-9290; James Dunne, pres.

5815 ★SISTERS OF CHARITY OF ST. ELIZABETH (Formerly Listed Under Jersey City), 49 Demarest Rd., Paramus, NJ 07652; tel. 201/539-1600; Sr. Ellen L. Joyce, gen. superior

5845 ST. LUKE'S REGIONAL MEDICAL CENTER, 2720 Stone Park Blvd., Sioux City, IA 51104; tel. 712/279-3500; David O. Biorn, pres. & chief exec. off.

5855 ★HOLY CROSS LIFE CARE SYSTEMS, INC. (Formerly Sisters of Mercy of the Holy Cross-Province of the U. S.), 1500 O'Day St., Merrill, WI 54452; tel. 715/536-5101; Robert E. Wulff, adm. & chief exec. off.

5875 SISTERS OF THE SORROWFUL MOTHER-TULSA PROVINCIALATE, 17600 E. 51st St. S., Broken Arrow, OK 74012; tel. 918/355-5595; Sr. M. Julietta Mendoza, prov.

5885 ★COVENANT HEALTH SYSTEMS, INC. (Formerly Grey Nuns Health Systems, Inc.), 10 Pelham Rd., Lexington, MA 02173; tel. 617/862-1634; Sr. Dorothy Cooper, pres. & chief exec. off.

5895 NATIONAL HEALTHCARE, INC., 444 N. Oates St., P O Box 1649, Dothan, AL 36302; tel. 205/793-2399; Steve L. Phelps, pres. & chief exec. off.

5925 SISTERS OF ST. FRANCIS OF THE MISSION OF THE IMMACULATE VIRGIN, Immaculate Conception Motherhouse, Hastings On Hudson, NY 10706; tel. 914/478-3910; Sr. Mary Paul, supr. gen.

5935 SISTERS OF ST. JOSEPH, Rural Rte. 3, Box 291a, Tipton, IN 46072; tel. 317/456-5300; Sr. Veronica Baumgartner, pres.

5945 ★HEALTH CARE CORPORATION OF THE SISTERS OF ST. JOSEPH OF CARONDELET, 77 W. Port Plaza, Suite 222, St. Louis, MO 63146; tel. 314/576-5562; Sr. Mary K. Ford, pres.

5955 SISTERS OF THE 3RD FRANCISCAN ORDER-MINOR CONVENTUALS, 100 Michaels Ave., Syracuse, NY 13208; tel. 315/425-0115; Sr. M. Aileen Griffin, supr. gen.

5975 SISTERS OF ST. FRANCIS-IMMACULATE HEART OF MARY-PROVINCE OF HANKINSON, St. Francis Convent, Hankinson, ND 58041; tel. 701/242-7197; Sr. Mary Louise Jundt, dir.

5985 SISTERS OF MERCY, Sacred Heart Convent, Belmont, NC 28012; tel. 704/825-2011; Sr. Jeanne Margaret McNally, supr. gen.

5995 SISTERS OF CHARITY CENTER, Mount St. Vincent On Hudson, Bronx, NY 10471; tel. 212/549-9200; Sr. Agnes Connolly, pres.

6005 ★HOLY FAMILY OF NAZARETH HEALTH SYSTEM (Formerly Sisters of the Holy Family of Nazareth-Vice Provincialate), 1814 Egyptian Way, 75051; Mailing Address Box 530959, Grand Prairie, TX Zip 75053; tel. 214/641-4496; Sr. M. Beata, pres.

6015 SISTERS OF MERCY OF THE UNION-PROVINCE OF BALTIMORE, P O Box 11448, Baltimore, MD 21239; tel. 301/435-4400; Sr. Angela Marie Ebberwein

6095 ★SISTERS OF CHARITY HEALTH CARE SYSTEMS CORPORATION, 355 Bard Ave., Staten Island, NY 10310; tel. 212/390-1650; John J. Depierro, pres. & chief exec. off.

6235 ★HEALTHONE CORPORATION, 2810 57th Ave. N., Minneapolis, MN 55430; tel. 612/333-1711; Richard S. Blair, interim pres. & chief exec. off.

6295 ★LUTHERAN GENERAL HEALTH CARE SYSTEMS (Formerly Lutheran Institute of Human Ecology), 1775 Dempster St., Park Ridge, IL 60068; tel. 312/696-5600; George B. Caldwell, pres.

6345 UNITED HOSPITALS, INC., 100 W. Laurel Ave., Cheltenham, PA 19012; tel. 215/663-5400; Myles G. Turtz MD, chm. & chief exec. off.

6405 UNIVERSITY OF CALIFORNIA-SYSTEMWIDE ADMINISTRATION, 764 University Hall, Berkeley, CA 94720; tel. 415/642-5192; C. L. Hopper MD, vice-pres. health affairs

6415 ★UNIVERSITY OF WASHINGTON HOSPITALS, Sc-61 University of Washington, Seattle, WA 98195; tel. 206/548-6364; Robert Muilenburg, exec. dir.

6525 ★REPUBLIC HEALTH CORPORATION, 15303 Dallas Pkwy., Suite 1400, Dallas, TX 75248; tel. 214/851-3100; James E. Buncher, pres. & chief exec. off.

6545 ★HEALTH CORPORATION OF THE ARCHDIOCESE OF NEWARK, 41 Centre St., Newark, NJ 07102; tel. 201/596-3900; Margaret J. Straney, pres.

6555 ★MULTICARE MEDICAL CENTER (Formerly Consolidated Hospitals), 409 S. J St., P O Box 5277, Tacoma, WA 98405; tel. 206/594-1251; W. Barry Connoley, pres. & chief exec. off.

6615 ★MEDLANTIC HEALTHCARE GROUP (Formerly Washington Healthcare Corporation), 100 Irving St. N.W., Washington, DC 20010; tel. 202/541-6006; John P. McDaniel, pres.

6665 BRUNSWICK HOSPITAL CENTER, 366 Broadway, Amityville, NY 11701; tel. 516/789-7000; Benjamin M. Stein MD, pres.

6705 WAKE MEDICAL CENTER (Formerly Wake County Hospital Systems), 3000 New Bern Ave., Raleigh, NC 27610; tel. 919/755-8112; Raymond L. Champ, pres.

6725 ★WEST JERSEY HEALTH SYSTEM, Mount Ephraim & Atlantic Aves., Camden, NJ 08104; tel. 609/342-4600; Barry D. Brown, pres.; William Michael Tomlinson, exec. vice-pres.

6745 ★WHEATON FRANCISCAN SERVICES, INC., 26w171 Roosevelt Rd., P O Box 667, Wheaton, IL 60189; tel. 312/462-9271; Willis F. Fry, pres. & chief exec. off.

6905 ★HEALTHWEST MEDICAL CENTERS (Formerly Healthwest Foundation), 21800 Oxnard St., Suite 550, Woodland Hills, CA 91367; tel. 818/716-2777; Roger H. Drue, pres.

6975 MILLS-PENINSULA HOSPITALS, 50 S. San Mateo Dr., San Mateo, CA 94401; tel. 415/579-2190; Charles H. Mason Jr., pres. & chief exec. off.

6995 DEPARTMENT OF HEALTH AND HOSPITALS, HOSPITAL SERVICES DIVISION, 818 Harrison Ave., Boston, MA 02118; tel. 617/424-5365; Lewis Pollack, comr.

7005 ★WESTERN RESERVE CARE SYSTEM, 345 Oak Hill Ave., Youngstown, OH 44501; tel. 216/747-9727; James E. Michels, pres.

7235 ★METHODIST HEALTH CARE NETWORK, 5615 Kirby Dr., Suite 800, Houston, TX 77005; tel. 713/831-2900; Michael Williamson, pres. & chief oper. off.; Larry L. Mathis, bd. chm. & chief exec. off.

7555 PALOMAR POMERADO HOSPITAL DISTRICT (Formerly Northern San Diego County Hospital District), 215 S. Hickory St., Suite 310, Escondido, CA 92025; tel. 619/489-4860; Robert M. Edwards, pres. & chief exec. off.

7675 ★ST. LUKE'S HEALTH SYSTEM, 5025 E. Washington, Suite 200, Phoenix, AZ 85034; tel. 602/231-0017; Brian C. Lockwood, pres.

7775 ★MAIN LINE HEALTH, INC. (Formerly Listed Under Philadelphia), 259 Radnor-Chester Rd., Suite 290, Radnor, PA 19087; tel. 215/254-8840; Ralph F. Moriarty, pres.

7895 ★SANTA FE HEALTHCARE (Formerly Santa Fe Healthcare System, Inc.), 720 S.W. Second Ave., P O Box 749, Gainesville, FL 32602; tel. 904/375-4321; Edward C. Peddie, pres.

7995 METROPOLITAN HOSPITAL, 801 Arch St., Fifth Floor, Philadelphia, PA 19107; tel. 215/238-6700; Jack R. Dyson, actg. chief oper. off.

8495 RUSHMORE NATIONAL HEALTH SYSTEMS, P O Box 2720, Rapid City, SD 57709; tel. 605/341-8100; Gary Riedmann, pres.

8795 SUTTER HEALTH SYSTEM (Formerly Sutter Community Hospitals), 1111 Howe Ave., Suite 600, Sacramento, CA 95825; tel. 916/927-5211; Patrick G. Hays, pres. & chief exec. off.

8805 ★COLUMBUS-CUNEO-CABRINI MEDICAL CENTER, 676 N. St. Clair, Suite 1900, Chicago, IL 60611; tel. 312/943-1333; James P. Hamill, chief exec. off.

8810 ★BAPTIST HOSPITAL AND HEALTH SYSTEMS, 2224 W. Northern Ave., Suite D-300, Phoenix, AZ 85021; tel. 602/864-1184; J. Barry Johnson, pres.

8815 ★RESEARCH HEALTH SERVICES, 6400 Prospect Ave., Kansas City, MO 64132; tel. 816/276-9167; E. Wynn Presson, pres.

8835 ★STRATEGIC HEALTH SYSTEMS, 767 Beta Dr., Suite E., Mayfield Village, OH 44143; tel. 216/449-7710; Robert Moss, pres.

8855 ★INTERCARE HEALTH SYSTEMS, 98 James St., Mediplex Suite 400, Edison, NJ 08820; tel. 201/632-1500; Michael T. Kornett, pres. & chief exec. off.

8865 HEALTH MANAGEMENT SERVICES, INC., 340 E. Town St., Suite 7-800, Columbus, OH 43215; tel. 614/461-3401; Ned Boatright, pres.

8875 ★METHODIST HEALTH SERVICES CORPORATION, 221 N.E. Glen Oak Ave., Peoria, IL 61636; tel. 309/672-4826; James K. Knoble, pres.; Daniel P. Chonowski, exec. vice-pres.

8895 ★VISTA HILL FOUNDATION, 3420 Camino Del Rio N., Suite 100, San Diego, CA 92108; tel. 619/563-1770; Ronald E. Fickle, pres. & chief exec. off.

8985 SAFECARE COMPANY, INC/SAFECARE HEALTH SERVICE, INC., 900 Fourth Ave., Suite 800, P O Box 21485, Seattle, WA 98111; tel. 206/223-4560; Stephen R. Jepson, sr. vice-pres. & pres.

9095 ★U. S. HEALTH CORPORATION, 3555 Olentangy River Rd., Suite 4000, Columbus, OH 43214; tel. 614/261-5902; Erie Chapman III, pres. & chief exec. off.

9105 ★UNIVERSITY OF ALABAMA HOSPITALS, 619 S. 19th St., Birmingham, AL 35233; tel. 205/934-4011; James E. Moon, adm.

9255 ★TRUMAN MEDICAL CENTER, 2301 Holmes, Kansas City, MO 64108; tel. 816/556-3153; James J. Mongan MD, exec. dir.

9265 NEBRASKA METHODIST HEALTH SYSTEM, INC., 8303 Dodge St., Omaha, NE 68114; tel. 402/390-4844; John W. Estabrook, pres. & chief exec. off.

9305 BROMENN HEALTHCARE, 807 N. Main St., Bloomington, IL 61702; tel. 309/827-4321; Jeffrey B. Schaub, pres.

9335 METHODIST HOSPITAL OF INDIANA, 1701 N. Senate Blvd., Indianapolis, IN 46202; tel. 317/929-8510; Frank P. Lloyd MD, pres.

9345 ★METHODIST HEALTH SYSTEMS, INC., 1211 Union Ave., Suite 700, Memphis, TN 38104; tel. 901/726-2300; John T. Casey, pres.

9355 ★ADVENTIST HEALTH SYSTEM-EASTERN AND MIDDLE AMERICA, 8800 W. 75th St., Shawnee Mission, KS 66204; tel. 913/677-8000; J. Russell Shawver, pres.

9555 UNIVERSAL HEALTH SERVICES, INC., 367 S. Gulph Rd., King of Prussia, PA 19406; tel. 215/768-3300; Alan B. Miller, pres.

9575 ★WILLIAM BEAUMONT HOSPITAL CORPORATION, 3601 W. Thirteen Mile Rd., Royal Oak, MI 48072; tel. 313/288-8000; Kenneth E. Myers, pres.; Ted D. Wasson, exec. vice-pres.

9605 UNITED MEDICAL CORPORATION, 20 N. Orange Ave., Suite 1600, Orlando, FL 32801; tel. 305/423-2200; Donald R. Dizney, chm.; James E. English, pres.

9650 ★FRANCISCAN HEALTH SYSTEM, INC. (Formerly St. Francis Health Corporation), 615 S. Tenth St., La Crosse, WI 54601; tel. 608/785-0940; Stewart W. Laird, pres.

9795 WESTWORLD COMMUNITY HEALTHCARE, INC., 23832 Rockfield Rd., Lake Forest, CA 92630; tel. 714/768-2981; Stephen F. Arterburn, pres. & chief exec. off.

9855 ★CAMELBACK HOSPITALS, INC., 7447 E. Earll Dr., Scottsdale, AZ 85251; tel. 602/941-7660; Daniel W. Capps, pres. & chief exec. off.

9905 ★UNITED HEALTH SERVICES, INC., 1200 S. Columbia Rd., P O Box 6002, Grand Forks, ND 58201; tel. 701/780-5200; Robert M. Jacobson, pres.

9995 ★GROUP HEALTH COOPERATIVE OF PUGET SOUND, 300 Elliott Ave. W., Seattle, WA 98119; tel. 206/326-6844; Mr. Gail L. Warden, pres. & chief exec. off.

Registration Requirements

This directory includes hospitals registered by the American Hospital Association and osteopathic hospitals listed by the American Osteopathic Association. Identification codes for both types of hospitals are explained fully on pages A2-4. For the reader's convenience, the codes for osteopathic hospitals are also summarized in the notes at the top of each page of this section. Beginning in November 1970, osteopathic hospitals became eligible to apply for registration with the American Hospital Association. Registered osteopathic hospitals carry the same codes as all other hospitals registered by the American Hospital Association.

The following requirements were approved by the Executive Committee of the Board of Trustees, May 13, 1986.

AHA-Registered Hospitals

Any institution that can be classified as a hospital according to the requirements may be registered if it so desires. Membership in the American Hospital Association is not a prerequisite.

The American Hospital Association may, at the sole discretion of the Executive Committee of the Board of Trustees, grant, deny, or withdraw the registration of an institution.

An institution may be registered by the American Hospital Association as a hospital if it is accredited by the Joint Commission on Accreditation of Hospitals or is certified as a provider of acute services under Title 18 of the Social Security Act and has provided the Association with documents verifying the accreditation or certification.

In lieu of the preceding accreditation or certification, an institution licensed as a hospital by the appropriate state agency may be registered by AHA as a hospital by meeting the following alternative requirements:

Function: The primary function of the institution is to provide patient services, diagnostic and therapeutic, for particular or general medical conditions.

1. The institution shall maintain at least six inpatient beds, which shall be continuously available for the care of patients who are nonrelated and who stay on the average in excess of 24 hours per admission.
2. The institution shall be constructed, equipped, and maintained to ensure the health and safety of patients and to provide uncrowded, sanitary facilities for the treatment of patients.
3. There shall be an identifiable governing authority legally and morally responsible for the conduct of the hospital.
4. There shall be a chief executive to whom the governing authority delegates the continuous responsibility for the operation of the hospital in accordance with established policy.
5. There shall be an organized medical staff of fully licensed physicians* that may include other licensed individuals permitted by law and by the hospital to provide patient care services independently in the hospital. The medical staff shall be accountable to the governing authority for maintaining proper standards of medical care, and it shall be governed by bylaws adopted by said staff and approved by the governing authority.
6. Each patient shall be admitted on the authority of a member of the medical staff who has been granted the privilege to admit patients to inpatient services in accordance with state law and criteria for standards of medical care established by the individual medical staff. Each patient's general medical condition is the responsibility of a qualified physician member of the medical staff. When nonphysician members of the medical staff are granted privileges to admit patients, provision is made for prompt medical evaluation of these patients by a qualified physician. Any graduate of a foreign medical school who is permitted to assume responsibilities for patient care shall possess a valid license to practice medicine, or shall be certified by the Educational Commission for Foreign Medical Graduates, or shall have qualified for and have successfully completed an academic year of supervised clinical training under the direction of a medical school approved by the Liaison Committee on Medical Education of the American Medical Association and the Association of American Medical Colleges.
7. Registered nurse supervision and other nursing services are continuous.
8. A current and complete‡ medical record shall be maintained by the institution for each patient and shall be available for reference.
9. Pharmacy service shall be maintained in the institution and shall be supervised by a registered pharmacist.
10. The institution shall provide patients with food service that meets their nutritional and therapeutic requirements; special diets shall also be available.

*Physician—Term used to describe an individual with an MD or DO degree who is fully licensed to practice medicine in all its phases.

‡The completed records in general shall contain at least the following: the patient's identifying data and consent forms, medical history, record of physical examination, physicians' progress notes, operative notes, nurses' notes, routine x-ray and laboratory reports, doctors' orders, and final diagnosis.

Types of Hospitals

In addition to meeting these 10 general registration requirements, hospitals are registered as one of four types of hospitals: general, special, rehabilitation and chronic disease, or psychiatric. The following definitions of function by type of hospital and special requirements for registration are employed:

General

The primary function of the institution is to provide patient services, diagnostic and therapeutic, for a variety of medical conditions. A general hospital also shall provide:

- diagnostic x-ray services with facilities and staff for a variety of procedures
- clinical laboratory service with facilities and staff for a variety of procedures and with anatomical pathology services regularly and conveniently available
- operating room service with facilities and staff.

Special

The primary function of the institution is to provide diagnostic and treatment services for patients who have specified medical conditions, both surgical and nonsurgical. A special hospital also shall provide:

- such diagnostic and treatment services as may be determined by the Executive Committee of the Board of Trustees of the American Hospital Association to be appropriate for the specified medical conditions for which medical services are provided shall be maintained in the institution with suitable facilities and staff. If such conditions do not normally require diagnostic x-ray service, laboratory service, or operating room service, and if any such services are therefore not maintained in the institution, there shall be written arrangements to make them available to patients requiring them.
- clinical laboratory services capable of providing tissue diagnosis when offering pregnancy termination services.

Rehabilitation and Chronic Disease

The primary function of the institution is to provide diagnostic and treatment services to handicapped or disabled individuals requiring restorative and adjustive services. A rehabilitation and chronic disease hospital also shall provide:

- arrangements for diagnostic x-ray services, as required, on a regular and conveniently available basis
- arrangements for clinical laboratory service, as required, on a regular and conveniently available basis
- arrangements for operating room service, as required, on a regular and conveniently available basis
- a physical therapy service with suitable facilities and staff in the institution
- an occupational therapy service with suitable facilities and staff in the institution
- arrangements for psychological and social work services on a regular and conveniently available basis
- arrangements for educational and vocational services on a regular and conveniently available basis
- written arrangements with a general hospital for the transfer of patients who require medical, obstetrical, or surgical services not available in the institution.

Psychiatric

The primary function of the institution is to provide diagnostic and treatment services for patients who have psychiatric-related illnesses. A psychiatric hospital also shall provide:

- arrangements for clinical laboratory service, as required, on a regular and conveniently available basis
- arrangements for diagnostic x-ray services, as required, on a regular and conveniently available basis
- psychiatric, psychological, and social work service with facilities and staff in the institution
- arrangements for electroencephalograph services, as required, on a regular and conveniently available basis
- written arrangements with a general hospital for the transfer of patients who require medical, obstetrical, or surgical services not available in the institution.

The American Hospital Association may, at the sole discretion of the Executive Committee of the Board of Trustees, grant, deny, or withdraw the registration of an institution.

AOHA-Listed Hospitals

The list of osteopathic hospitals includes both members and nonmembers of the American Osteopathic Hospital Association.

*Physician—Term used to describe an individual with an MD or DO degree who is fully licensed to practice medicine in all its phases.

‡The completed records in general shall contain at least the following: the patient's identifying data and consent forms, medical history, record of physical examination, physicians' progress notes, operative notes, nurses' notes, routine x-ray and laboratory reports, doctors' orders, and final diagnosis.

Hospitals in the United States, by State

Hospital, Address, Telephone, Administrator, Approval and Facility Codes, Multihospital System Code

- ★ American Hospital Association (AHA) membership
- □ Joint Commission on Accreditation of Hospitals (JCAH) accreditation
- + American Osteopathic Hospital Association (AOHA) membership
- ○ American Osteopathic Association (AOA) accreditation
- Δ Commission on Accreditation of Rehabilitation Facilities (CARF) accreditation

Control codes 61, 63, 64, 71, 72 and 73 indicate hospitals listed by AOHA, but not registered by AHA. For definition of numerical codes, see page A2

Alabama

Hospital, Address, Telephone, Administrator, Approval and Facility Codes, Multihospital System Code	Classification Codes				Inpatient Data				Newborn Data		Expense (thousands of dollars)		
	Control	Service	Stay	Facilities	Beds	Admissions	Census	Occupancy (percent)	Bassinets	Births	Total	Payroll	Personnel
ABBEVILLE—Henry County													
HENRY COUNTY HOSPITAL AND NURSING HOME, 212 Dothan Rd., P O Box 639, Zip 36310; tel. 205/585-2241; Ann S. Medley, adm. (Total facility includes 60 beds in nursing home-type unit) **A**9 10 **F**1 12 14 19 35; **S**1935	33	10	S	TF	108	904	72	66.7	10	1	3054	1234	98
				H	48	834	12	—	10	1	2153	752	52
ALABASTER—Shelby County													
★□ SHELBY MEDICAL CENTER, 1000 First St. N., Box 488, Zip 35007; tel. 205/663-8100; Charles L. Denton, adm. **A**1a 9 10 **F**1 3 6 10 14 16 23 27 30 32 33 34 35 45 46 53 54	13	10	S		170	5761	83	51.9	0	0	19516	7400	407
ALEXANDER CITY—Tallapoosa County													
★□ RUSSELL HOSPITAL, U. S. 280 By-Pass, P O Box 939, Zip 35010; tel. 205/329-7100; James W. Brown Jr., adm. **A**1a 9 10 **F**1 3 6 10 12 14 15 16 23 35 36 40 43 46 47 52 53	23	10	S		75	3097	39	52.0	12	341	6981	3268	224
ANDALUSIA—Covington County													
□ COLUMBIA REGIONAL MEDICAL CENTER (Formerly Columbia General Hospital), 200 Hillcrest Dr., Zip 36420; tel. 205/222-4141; Larry L. Ruggles, adm. (Total facility includes 48 beds in nursing home-type unit) **A**1a 9 10 **F**1 3 6 10 12 14 16 17 19 23 35 46 52	33	10	S	TF	137	727	58	42.3	0	0	—	—	74
				H	89	693	11	—	0	0	—	—	—
COMMUNITY HOSPITAL OF ANDALUSIA, See HCA Andalusia Hospital													
★□ HCA ANDALUSIA HOSPITAL (Formerly Community Hospital of Andalusia), S. Three Notch St., Box 760, Zip 36420; tel. 205/222-8466; Alease H. Daniel, adm. **A**1a 9 10 **F**1 3 6 10 12 14 15 16 23 30 35 40 45 46 47 53; **S**1755	33	10	S		77	2571	35	45.5	10	236	5999	2660	167
ANNISTON—Calhoun County													
★□ NORTHEAST ALABAMA REGIONAL MEDICAL CENTER, 400 E. Tenth St., Box 2208, Zip 36202; tel. 205/235-5121; Allen Fletcher, pres. **A**1a 3 5 9 10 **F**1 3 5 6 7 8 9 10 11 12 14 15 16 20 23 27 28 30 32 33 34 35 40 41 42 45 46 48 49 52 53 54	23	10	S		306	12104	197	66.8	38	1278	33745	15744	864
★□ STRINGFELLOW MEMORIAL HOSPITAL, 301 E. 18th St., Zip 36201; tel. 205/235-8000; George Simpson, adm. **A**1a 9 10 **F**1 3 6 10 11 12 14 15 16 21 23 24 26 35 41 44 45 46 47 53	23	10	S		92	2734	52	50.5	0	0	10638	4966	245
ARAB—Marshall County													
★□ ARAB HOSPITAL, 200 S. Main St., Zip 35016; tel. 205/586-4181; Jesse G. Brown, adm. **A**1a 9 10 **F**1 3 6 12 14 15 16 23 34 35 36 37 40 43 45 46 47 53	13	10	S		48	1682	20	41.7	8	195	3734	1560	104
ASHLAND—Clay County													
★□ CLAY COUNTY HOSPITAL AND NURSING HOME, 544 E. First Ave., Box 277, Zip 36251; tel. 205/354-2131; Joe M. McCaig, adm. (Total facility includes 63 beds in nursing home-type unit) **A**1a 9 10 **F**1 3 6 12 14 16 19 34 35 40 45	13	10	S	TF	116	2167	91	78.4	6	122	5002	2113	180
				H	53	2122	29	—	6	122	4047	1689	137
ATHENS—Limestone County													
□ ATHENS-LIMESTONE HOSPITAL, 700 W. Market St., Box 999, Zip 35611; tel. 205/729-9292; Philip E. Dotson, chief exec. off. **A**1a 9 10 **F**1 3 6 9 10 12 14 15 16 20 23 35 36 40 45 46 52 53	15	10	S		91	3994	58	63.7	18	395	9379	4177	263
ATMORE—Escambia County													
★□ GREENLAWN HOSPITAL, 401 S. Eighth Ave., P O Drawer 1147, Zip 36504; tel. 205/368-2500; Joseph W. Henry Sr., adm. **A**1a 9 10 **F**1 3 6 14 16 23 35 36 40 45 46 47; **S**1255	13	10	S		51	1410	17	33.3	10	189	3038	1546	109
BAY MINETTE—Baldwin County													
□ NORTH BALDWIN HOSPITAL, 1815 Hand Ave., Box 790, Zip 36507; tel. 205/937-5521; Gary W. Farrow, adm. **A**1a 9 10 **F**1 3 6 10 15 16 17 23 34 35 36 40 45 46 53	13	10	S		55	1390	19	34.5	9	110	2916	1448	94
BESSEMER—Jefferson County													
★□ BESSEMER CARRAWAY MEDICAL CENTER, U. S. Hwy. 11 S., Zip 35020; Mailing Address Box 847, Zip 35021; tel. 205/426-7000; Dan M. Eagar Jr., adm. **A**1a 9 10 **F**1 2 3 6 7 14 15 16 20 23 24 28 30 32 33 35 36 40 44 45 47 49 53	23	10	S		180	6080	104	57.8	14	125	22835	—	522
BIRMINGHAM—Jefferson County													
★□ AMI BROOKWOOD MEDICAL CENTER (Formerly Brookwood Medical Center), 2010 Brookwood Medical Center Dr., Zip 35259; tel. 205/877-1000; Gregory H. Burfitt, pres. (Nonreporting) **A**1a 2 9 10; **S**0125	33	10	S		586	—	—	—	—	—	—	—	—
★□ BAPTIST MEDICAL CENTER-MONTCLAIR, 800 Montclair Rd., Zip 35213; tel. 205/592-1000; Dennis A. Hall, pres. **A**1a 2 3 5 9 10 **F**1 2 3 4 5 6 7 8 9 10 11 12 14 15 16 20 21 23 26 27 30 32 33 34 35 36 37 40 42 45 46 47 48 49 50 52 53 54; **S**0345	21	10	S		591	17429	356	60.2	51	794	80202	30653	1663
★□ BAPTIST MEDICAL CENTER-PRINCETON, 701 Princeton Ave. S.W., Zip 35211; tel. 205/783-3000; Byron Harrell, pres. **A**1a 2 3 5 9 10 **F**1 2 3 4 6 7 8 9 10 11 12 13 14 15 16 20 21 23 24 27 32 33 34 35 40 42 45 46 53 54; **S**0345	21	10	S		443	16218	318	71.8	32	456	65579	25883	1359
BROOKWOOD MEDICAL CENTER, See AMI Brookwood Medical Center													
★□ CARRAWAY METHODIST MEDICAL CENTER, 1600 N. 26th St., Zip 35234; tel. 205/226-6000; James D. Hallmark, adm. **A**1a 2 3 5 8 9 10 **F**1 2 3 4 5 6 7 8 9 10 11 12 14 15 16 20 23 24 26 27 30 33 35 36 40 42 44 47 52 53 54	21	10	S		395	14565	324	72.6	24	915	78547	38253	1872
★□ CHILDREN'S HOSPITAL OF ALABAMA, 1600 Seventh Ave. S., Zip 35233; tel. 205/939-9100; Jon H. Vance, exec. dir. **A**1a 3 5 9 10 **F**1 3 5 6 10 12 13 14 15 16 20 22 23 24 27 30 32 33 34 35 42 44 45 46 47 53	23	50	S		160	7689	128	80.0	0	0	37393	16581	892
COMMUNITY HOSPITAL, See Medical Park West													
★□ COOPER GREEN HOSPITAL, 1515 Sixth Ave. S., Zip 35233; tel. 205/934-7900; John O. Rohde, chief exec. off. **A**1a 3 5 9 10 **F**1 3 5 6 10 12 14 15 26 34 35 37 40 45 46	13	10	S		190	6901	97	51.1	60	1859	31693	10693	622
★□ EYE FOUNDATION HOSPITAL, 1720 University Blvd., Zip 35233; tel. 205/325-8100; Gordon L. Smith, adm. **A**1a 3 5 9 10 **F**1 12 13 14 16 34 35	23	45	S		91	1680	11	12.1	0	0	7663	2667	146
HILL CREST HOSPITAL, See HSA Hill Crest Sunrise Hospital													
★□ HSA HILL CREST SUNRISE HOSPITAL (Formerly Hill Crest Hospital), 6869 Fifth Ave. S., Box 2896, Zip 35212; tel. 205/833-9000; Isaac W. Ferniany PhD, adm. **A**1b 9 10 **F**23 24 28 30 32 34 42 44 49; **S**0405	32	22	S		119	1228	70	53.8	0	0	9592	3467	178

★ American Hospital Association (AHA) membership
□ Joint Commission on Accreditation of Hospitals (JCAH) accreditation
+ American Osteopathic Hospital Association (AOHA) membership
○ American Osteopathic Association (AOA) accreditation
Δ Commission on Accreditation of Rehabilitation Facilities (CARF) accreditation
Control codes 61, 63, 64, 71, 72 and 73 indicate hospitals listed by AOHA, but not registered by AHA.
For definition of numerical codes, see page A2

Hospital, Address, Telephone, Administrator, Approval and Facility Codes, Multihospital System Code	Classification Codes				Inpatient Data				Newborn Data		Expense (thousands of dollars)		
	Control	Service	Stay	Facilities	Beds	Admissions	Census	Occupancy (percent)	Bassinets	Births	Total	Payroll	Personnel
★□ LAKESHORE HOSPITAL, 3800 Ridgeway Dr., Zip 35209; tel. 205/868-2000; Michael E. Stephens, pres. & chief exec. off. (Total facility includes 36 beds in nursing home-type unit) **A**1a 9 10 **F**16 19 23 24 26 33 34 42 44 46 47	23	46	S	TF H	136 100	1514 1244	109 83	80.1 —	0 0	0 0	11159 —	5532 —	277 —
★□ LLOYD NOLAND HOSPITAL AND HEALTH CENTERS (Formerly Listed Under Fairfield), 701 Ridgeway Rd., P O Box 538, Zip 35064; tel. 205/783-5121; Gary M. Glasscock, adm. **A**1a 3 5 9 10 **F**1 2 3 6 10 12 14 15 16 23 26 27 28 30 32 33 34 35 40 44 45 46 47 48 49 50 52 53 54	23	10	S		252	7227	168	63.6	17	288	41231	19412	704
★□ MEDICAL CENTER EAST, 50 Medical Park East Dr., Zip 35235; tel. 205/838-3000; Robert C. Chapman, pres. & chief exec. off. **A**1a 3 5 9 10 **F**1 2 3 4 6 10 11 12 14 15 16 17 20 23 24 25 26 30 32 33 34 35 36 40 41 42 44 45 46 47 52 53 54	23	10	S		282	10824	168	59.6	22	535	36816	12961	848
★□ MEDICAL PARK WEST (Formerly Community Hospital), 1915 19th St., Ensley, Zip 35218; tel. 205/783-1000; Lewis Mashburn, adm. **A**1a 9 10 **F**1 3 6 10 16 23 34 35; **S**0885	23	10	S		83	1100	28	35.4	12	61	—	—	110
★□ SOUTH HIGHLANDS HOSPITAL, 1127 S. 12th St., Zip 35205; tel. 205/930-7000; Dennis H. Descher, chief exec. off. **A**1a 9 10 **F**1 3 6 10 12 14 15 16 20 23 32 34 35 44 46 53 54; **S**1755	23	10	S		179	4682	99	54.1	0	0	23496	9705	445
★□ ST. VINCENT'S HOSPITAL, 2701 Ninth Court S., Zip 35205; Mailing Address P O Box 915, Zip 35201; tel. 205/939-7000; Sr. Almeda Golson, pres. **A**1a 6 9 10 **F**1 2 3 6 7 8 9 10 11 12 14 15 16 17 20 23 24 26 30 34 35 40 45 46 47 51 53 54; **S**1885	21	10	S		325	13959	227	69.8	42	2526	44640	19107	1026
★□ UNIVERSITY OF ALABAMA HOSPITAL, 619 S. 19th St., Zip 35233; tel. 205/934-4011; James E. Moon, adm. **A**1a 2 3 5 8 9 10 **F**1 2 3 4 5 6 7 8 9 10 11 12 13 14 15 16 17 19 20 21 22 23 24 25 26 27 28 29 32 33 35 36 37 38 40 41 42 44 45 46 47 50 53 54; **S**9105	12	10	S		774	28193	630	79.7	70	2167	187601	75676	4586
★□ VETERANS ADMINISTRATION MEDICAL CENTER, 700 S. 19th St., Zip 35233; tel. 205/933-8101; Hugh R. Vickerstaff, dir. **A**1a b 2 3 5 8 **F**2 3 6 10 12 14 15 16 20 23 24 25 26 28 29 30 32 33 34 35 38 41 42 43 44 46 49 50 53 54	45	10	S		414	13858	273	65.9	0	0	67709	32443	1302
BOAZ—Marshall County													
★□ BOAZ-ALBERTVILLE MEDICAL CENTER (Formerly Boaz-Albertville Hospital), U. S. Hwy. 431 N., Drawer Z, Zip 35957; tel. 205/593-8310; Marlin Hanson, adm. **A**1a 9 10 **F**1 3 6 10 16 23 30 35 36 40 45 47 53	13	10	S		102	4235	64	62.7	12	323	13157	5448	310
BREWTON—Escambia County													
★□ D. W. MCMILLAN MEMORIAL HOSPITAL, 1301 Belleville Ave., Zip 36426; Mailing Address Drawer 908, Zip 36427; tel. 205/867-8061; Billy J. Griffin, adm. **A**1a 9 10 **F**1 3 6 8 10 16 35 36 40 45 52 53; **S**1255	13	10	S		91	3595	49	53.8	9	254	6924	3323	218
BRIDGEPORT—Jackson County													
□ NORTH JACKSON HOSPITAL, Rte. 1, Box 88, Zip 35740; tel. 205/437-2101; John D. Foster, adm. **A**1a 9 10 **F**1 6 14 15 16 23 35 37 40 45	13	10	S		58	1507	19	32.8	8	68	2536	1019	75
BUTLER—Choctaw County													
★ RUSH HOSPITAL-BULTER, Hwy. 10 E., P O Box 518, Zip 36904; tel. 205/459-2461; Paul E. May, adm. **A**9 10 **F**1 6 14 16 23 35 45 46 47	23	10	S		65	1582	19	29.2	0	0	—	—	94
CAMDEN—Wilcox County													
J. PAUL JONES HOSPITAL, McWilliams Ave., Drawer B, Zip 36726; tel. 205/682-4131; James O. Graham, adm. (Nonreporting) **A**9 10; **S**1585	15	10	S		30	—	—	—	—	—	—	—	—
CARROLLTON—Pickens County													
★□ PICKENS COUNTY MEDICAL CENTER (Formerly Pickens County Hospital), Rte. 2, P O Box 478, Zip 35447; tel. 205/367-8111; James R. Griffin, adm. **A**1a 9 10 **F**3 6 12 14 16 17 23 35 40 45 46 47 53	21	10	S		116	4103	55	47.4	13	453	10660	4505	251
CENTRE—Cherokee County													
★□ BAPTIST MEDICAL CENTER-CHEROKEE, 400 Northwood Dr., Box 150, Zip 35960; tel. 205/927-5531; Barry S. Cochran, exec. dir. **A**1a 9 10 **F**1 3 6 9 10 14 16 17 23 35 36 40 45 53; **S**0345	23	10	S		60	1347	18	30.0	7	76	—	—	108
CENTREVILLE—Bibb County													
□ BIBB MEDICAL CENTER, 163 Pierson Ave., Zip 35042; tel. 205/926-4881; Terry J. Smith, adm. (Total facility includes 103 beds in nursing home-type unit) **A**1a 9 10 **F**6 16 19 23 45 46	13	10	S	TF H	128 25	879 782	111 10	86.7 —	6 6	41 41	3156 2312	1684 1015	140 79
CHATOM—Washington County													
WASHINGTON COUNTY HOSPITAL, St. Stephens Ave., Box 597, Zip 36518; tel. 205/847-2223; Mary Coffey, adm. **A**9 10 **F**35	13	10	S		30	644	8	26.7	6	1	—	—	48
CLANTON—Chilton County													
★□ CENTRAL ALABAMA COMMUNITY HOSPITAL (Formerly Baptist Medical Center-Chilton), 1010 Lay Dam Rd., Zip 35045; tel. 205/755-2500; Michael C. Marshman, adm. **A**1a 9 10 **F**1 3 6 10 14 15 16 23 34 35 45 47 53; **S**5895	33	10	S		60	1675	20	33.3	0	146	4572	1700	89
COURTLAND—Lawrence County													
FIRST HEALTH COURTLAND (Formerly Community Hospital of Courtland), 101 Madison St., Box 466, Zip 35618; tel. 205/637-2721; Carl J. Velte, adm. (Nonreporting) **A**9 10; **S**1275	33	10	S		35	—	—	—	—	—	—	—	—
CULLMAN—Cullman County													
★□ CULLMAN MEDICAL CENTER, 401 Arnold St. N.E., P O Box 1108, Zip 35056; tel. 205/734-1210; Larry W. Throneberry, adm. **A**1a 9 10 **F**1 3 6 10 12 14 15 16 23 26 35 37 40 44 45 46 47 48 53; **S**0345	13	10	S		169	6065	87	51.5	24	772	15137	6920	423
★□ WOODLAND COMMUNITY HOSPITAL, 1910 Cherokee Ave. S.W., Zip 35055; tel. 205/739-3500; Harry Alvis, adm. **A**1a 9 10 **F**1 3 6 9 10 12 14 16 23 34 41 44 45 46 47	33	10	S		100	2153	31	31.0	0	0	7531	2523	125
DADEVILLE—Tallapoosa County													
★ LAKESHORE COMMUNITY HOSPITAL, Rte. 4, Box 8, Zip 36853; tel. 205/825-7821; Nancy Klinger, adm. **A**9 10 **F**1 2 15 16 23 26 28 29 30 32 33 34 35 45 47 48 49; **S**5895	33	10	S		46	918	15	32.6	0	0	2664	1932	71
DECATUR—Morgan County													
★□ CHARTER RETREAT HOSPITAL AND RECOVERY CENTER, 2205 Beltline Rd. S.W., P O Box 1230, Zip 35602; tel. 205/350-1450; Pamela W. McCullough, adm. (Nonreporting) **A**1b 9 10; **S**0695	33	22	S		104	—	—	—	—	—	—	—	—
★□ DECATUR GENERAL HOSPITAL, 1201 Seventh St. S.E., Zip 35601; Mailing Address Box 2239, Zip 35602; tel. 205/552-0055; Robert L. Smith, adm. **A**1a 9 10 **F**1 2 3 5 6 10 12 14 15 16 20 23 24 27 29 33 35 40 45 46 47 52 53	15	10	S		222	8703	134	60.4	47	1618	22701	9862	654
★□ PARKWAY MEDICAL CENTER HOSPITAL, 1874 Beltline Rd. S.W., Zip 35601; Mailing Address P O Box 2211, Zip 35602; tel. 205/350-2211; Eric Freeburg, adm. **A**1a 9 10 **F**1 3 6 10 14 15 16 23 35 41 45 46 47 50 53	33	10	S		120	3350	58	48.3	0	0	10418	4239	226
DEMOPOLIS—Marengo County													
★□ BRYAN W. WHITFIELD MEMORIAL HOSPITAL, Hwy. 80, Box 890, Zip 36732; tel. 205/289-4000; Charles E. Nabors, adm. **A**1a 9 10 **F**1 3 6 10 14 23 35 36 40 45 46 53	14	10	S		99	4463	66	66.7	10	374	8268	3750	241

★ American Hospital Association (AHA) membership
□ Joint Commission on Accreditation of Hospitals (JCAH) accreditation
+ American Osteopathic Hospital Association (AOHA) membership
○ American Osteopathic Association (AOA) accreditation
Δ Commission on Accreditation of Rehabilitation Facilities (CARF) accreditation
Control codes 61, 63, 64, 71, 72 and 73 indicate hospitals listed by AOHA, but not registered by AHA.
For definition of numerical codes, see page A2

Hospital, Address, Telephone, Administrator, Approval and Facility Codes, Multihospital System Code	Classification Codes				Inpatient Data				Newborn Data		Expense (thousands of dollars)		
	Control	Service	Stay	Facilities	Beds	Admissions	Census	Occupancy (percent)	Bassinets	Births	Total	Payroll	Personnel
DOTHAN—Houston County													
★□ CHARTER WOODS HOSPITAL, 700 Cottonwood Rd., P O Box 6138, Zip 36301; tel. 205/793-6660; Allen W. Moon, adm. **A**1a 9 10 **F**12 15 23 24 28 32 33 34 42 44 48 49; **S**0695	33	22	S		75	684	44	58.7	0	0	—	—	96
★□ FLOWERS HOSPITAL, 3228 W. Main St., Zip 36301; Mailing Address Box 6907, Zip 36302; tel. 205/793-5000; L. Keith Granger, adm. **A**1a 9 10 **F**1 2 3 4 5 6 9 10 12 14 16 20 23 34 35 36 40 46 52 53 54; **S**1755	33	10	S		200	10637	166	83.0	20	977	32426	12150	737
★□ SOUTHEAST ALABAMA MEDICAL CENTER, Hwy. 84 E., P O Drawer 6987, Zip 36302; tel. 205/793-8111; James R. Blackmon, adm. **A**1a 9 10 **F**1 2 3 4 5 6 7 8 9 10 11 12 14 15 16 20 23 24 34 35 36 40 45 46 47 52 53 54; **S**5895	13	10	S		400	16496	256	64.0	31	1199	44407	20785	1169
ELBA—Coffee County													
ELBA GENERAL HOSPITAL, 987 Drayton St., P O Drawer G, Zip 36323; tel. 205/897-2257; Donna Etheridge, chief financial off. (Total facility includes 79 beds in nursing home-type unit) **A**9 10 **F**1 6 14 15 16 19 35 47 53; **S**5895	33	10	S	TF	122	1348	89	73.0	0	1	3662	—	129
				H	43	1254	13	—	0	1	—	—	65
ENTERPRISE—Coffee County													
★□ ENTERPRISE HOSPITAL, Dothan Hwy., Zip 36330; Mailing Address Box 1220, Zip 36331; tel. 205/347-9541; J. Alan Kent, adm. (Total facility includes 150 beds in nursing home-type unit) **A**1a 9 10 **F**1 14 16 19 20 23 26 34 46 47; **S**1755	14	10	S	TF	197	1209	161	81.7	0	0	4385	2065	189
				H	47	888	15	—	0	0	2636	1233	—
★□ HUMANA HOSPITAL -ENTERPRISE, 400 N. Edwards St., Zip 36330; tel. 205/347-0584; Wendell W. Briggs, exec. dir. **A**1a 9 10 **F**1 3 6 10 14 16 23 34 35 40 47 53; **S**1235	33	10	S		120	3760	51	42.5	11	414	10853	3430	223
EUFAULA—Barbour County													
★□ LAKEVIEW COMMUNITY HOSPITAL, 820 W. Washington St., Zip 36027; tel. 205/687-5761; Ron Dyer, adm. **A**1a 9 10 **F**1 3 6 10 14 15 16 23 34 35 45 46 47; **S**5895	33	10	S		74	2599	32	43.2	16	242	5701	2700	137
EUTAW—Greene County													
GREENE COUNTY HOSPITAL, 509 Wilson Ave., Zip 35462; tel. 205/372-3388; Ron Smith, adm.; R. J. Coker Jr., asst. adm. & contr. **A**9 10 **F**14 34 35 37 40 46 52	13	10	S		20	486	5	25.0	5	178	—	—	37
FAIRFIELD—Jefferson County													
LLOYD NOLAND HOSPITAL AND HEALTH CENTERS, See Birmingham													
FAIRHOPE—Baldwin County													
★□ THOMAS HOSPITAL, 750 Morphy Ave., Drawer 929, Zip 36533; tel. 205/928-2375; Robert W. Young, adm. **A**1a 9 10 **F**1 3 6 10 12 15 16 27 30 33 34 35 36 40 45 53	13	10	S		120	3836	52	57.8	14	635	10702	4160	269
FAYETTE—Fayette County													
★□ FAYETTE COUNTY HOSPITAL, 1653 Temple Ave. N., P O Drawer 878, Zip 35555; tel. 205/932-5966; John Lucas, chief exec. off. (Total facility includes 101 beds in nursing home-type unit) **A**1a 9 10 **F**1 3 6 10 12 14 15 16 19 23 24 26 34 35 37 42 44 46	16	10	S	TF	162	1858	120	74.1	0	121	5118	2464	165
				H	61	1759	21	—	0	121	3738	1951	121
FLOMATON—Escambia County													
□ ABERNETHY MEMORIAL HOSPITAL, Drawer A, Zip 36441; tel. 205/296-2427; Donny P. Myers, adm. **A**1a 9 10 **F**10 12 15 16 17 23 35 53; **S**1255	13	10	S		30	507	8	26.7	0	0	1432	623	49
FLORALA—Covington County													
FLORALA MEMORIAL HOSPITAL, E. Fifth Ave. & Sixth St., Box 206, Zip 36442; tel. 205/858-3287; James York, adm. (Nonreporting) **A**9 10	23	10	S		23	—	—	—	—	—	—	—	—
FLORENCE—Lauderdale County													
★□ ELIZA COFFEE MEMORIAL HOSPITAL (Includes Mitchell-Hollingsworth Annex), 205 Marengo St., Zip 35630; Mailing Address Box 818, Zip 35631; tel. 205/767-9191; Richard H. Peck, adm. (Total facility includes 202 beds in nursing home-type unit) **A**1a 9 10 **F**1 2 3 4 6 8 10 12 14 15 16 19 23 27 28 29 30 33 35 36 40 46 52 53 54	15	10	S	TF	536	12807	466	86.9	42	1483	32774	19176	1204
				H	334	12656	267	—	42	1483	29710	17111	1013
★□ HUMANA HOSPITAL -FLORENCE, 2111 Cloyd Blvd., Box 2010, Zip 35631; tel. 205/767-8700; William M. Donohoo, exec. dir. **A**1a 9 10 **F**1 3 6 10 11 12 14 15 16 23 26 32 33 35 37 43 53; **S**1235	33	10	S		155	4219	78	50.3	0	0	—	4541	271
FOLEY—Baldwin County													
★□ SOUTH BALDWIN HOSPITAL, 1613 N. McKenzie St., Zip 36535; tel. 205/943-5051; Sandy D. McGill, adm. **A**1a 9 10 **F**1 3 5 6 10 14 16 23 34 35 37 40 45 46 52 53	13	10	S		82	3543	45	54.9	13	268	6383	2846	188
FORT MCCLELLAN—Calhoun County													
★□ NOBLE ARMY COMMUNITY HOSPITAL, Zip 36205; tel. 205/238-2232; Col. Roger V. Codal MC, cmdr. **A**1a **F**6 12 14 23 28 33 34 35 37 40 46 47	42	10	S		100	4142	45	45.0	10	333	20430	16182	499
FORT PAYNE—De Kalb County													
★□ BAPTIST MEDICAL CENTER-DEKALB, 200 Medical Center Dr., P O Box 778, Zip 35967; tel. 205/845-3150; William Hynson, adm. **A**1a 9 10 **F**1 3 6 10 12 14 16 23 35 40 46 52 53; **S**0345	21	10	S		116	4162	56	48.3	13	427	10798	5260	251
FORT RUCKER—Dale County													
★□ U. S. LYSTER ARMY HOSPITAL, U. S. Army Aeromedical Center, Zip 36362; tel. 205/255-7360; Col. Elray Jenkins MC, cmdr. **A**1a **F**1 3 6 12 14 15 16 23 24 28 30 33 34 35 36 37 40 41 46 47 52	42	10	S		65	2450	27	41.5	10	491	17768	—	488
GADSDEN—Etowah County													
★□ BAPTIST MEMORIAL HOSPITAL, 1007 Goodyear Ave., Zip 35999; tel. 205/543-4983; Charles Roe, pres.; Robert J. Corey, exec. dir. & adm. **A**1a 2 3 5 9 10 **F**1 2 3 5 6 10 12 14 15 16 23 24 26 27 30 34 35 36 40 45 47 52 53	23	10	S		251	9660	168	61.5	31	1099	36601	15716	736
★□ HOLY NAME OF JESUS MEDICAL CENTER (Formerly Holy Name of Jesus Hospital), Moragne Park, P O Box 268, Zip 35902; tel. 205/543-5200; Sr. James Cecilia, adm. **A**1a 6 9 10 **F**1 2 3 4 5 6 9 10 11 12 14 15 16 20 23 26 28 30 32 33 35 36 40 41 44 46 49 52 53 54	23	10	S		251	7180	136	61.0	16	476	20395	—	557
★ MOUNTAIN VIEW BAPTIST HOSPITAL, 3001 Scenic Hwy., Zip 35901; tel. 205/546-9265; John C. Hamiter Jr., adm. **A**9 10 **F**24 30 32 33 42 44 48	23	22	L		68	510	42	61.8	0	0	3528	879	107
GENEVA—Geneva County													
★□ WIREGRASS HOSPITAL, 1200 W. Maple Ave., Zip 36340; tel. 205/684-3655; Roger H. Mayers, adm. (Nonreporting) **A**1a 9 10; **S**1755	13	10	S		169	—	—	—	—	—	—	—	—
GEORGIANA—Butler County													
GEORGIANA COMMUNITY HOSPITAL, Jones & Miranda Sts., Box 548, Zip 36033; tel. 205/376-2205; John Atchison, adm. **A**9 10 **F**1 6 14 16 19 35 42; **S**1935	33	10	S		22	735	11	50.0	0	0	2854	857	57
GRAYSVILLE—Jefferson County													
★□ LONGVIEW GENERAL HOSPITAL, 1100 Bankhead Hwy. S.W., Zip 35073; tel. 205/674-9422; David L. Noland, adm. **A**1a 9 10 **F**1 6 23 35	33	10	S		50	910	17	34.0	0	0	3045	1188	75
GREENSBORO—Hale County													
★ HALE COUNTY HOSPITAL, First & Greene Sts., Zip 36744; tel. 205/624-3024; William L. Lemley, adm. **A**9 10 **F**1 6 14 15 23 34 35 40	13	10	S		28	662	9	32.1	8	137	1081	530	42
GREENVILLE—Butler County													
★□ L. V. STABLER MEMORIAL HOSPITAL OF GREENVILLE, Hwy. 10 W., Box 1000, Zip 36037; tel. 205/382-2671; Thomas E. Hoerl, adm. **A**1a 9 10 **F**1 3 6 10 14 15 16 23 26 35 43	33	10	S		74	2220	36	48.6	0	0	—	—	127

Hospital, Address, Telephone, Administrator, Approval and Facility Codes, Multihospital System Code	Classification Codes				Inpatient Data				Newborn Data		Expense (thousands of dollars)		
★ American Hospital Association (AHA) membership ☐ Joint Commission on Accreditation of Hospitals (JCAH) accreditation + American Osteopathic Hospital Association (AOHA) membership ○ American Osteopathic Association (AOA) accreditation Δ Commission on Accreditation of Rehabilitation Facilities (CARF) accreditation Control codes 61, 63, 64, 71, 72 and 73 indicate hospitals listed by AOHA, but not registered by AHA. For definition of numerical codes, see page A2	Control	Service	Stay	Facilities	Beds	Admissions	Census	Occupancy (percent)	Bassinets	Births	Total	Payroll	Personnel
GROVE HILL—Clarke County													
★☐ GROVE HILL MEMORIAL HOSPITAL, Jackson Hwy., P O Box 935, Zip 36451; tel. 205/275-3191; John Henry Luff, adm. **A**1a 9 10 **F**1 12 16 35 40 45	14	10	S		46	1261	17	37.0	9	119	2559	—	85
GUNTERSVILLE—Marshall County													
★☐ GUNTERSVILLE HOSPITAL, 2067 Gunter Ave., P O Box 640, Zip 35976; tel. 205/582-9194; Jesse G. Brown, adm. **A**1a 9 10 **F**1 6 16 17 23 34 35 45 46 53	13	10	S		56	2630	33	56.9	14	284	4863	2086	154
HALEYVILLE—Winston County													
★☐ BURDICK-WEST MEMORIAL HOSPITAL, Hwy. 195 E., Box 780, Zip 35565; tel. 205/486-5213; Tillman L. Hill, adm. **A**1a 9 10 **F**1 3 6 15 16 17 23 35	13	10	S		47	2821	40	44.9	0	0	5093	2493	149
HAMILTON—Marion County													
★☐ MARION COUNTY GENERAL HOSPITAL, 1315 Military St. S., Zip 35570; tel. 205/921-7861; W. Douglas Arnold, adm. (Nonreporting) **A**1a 9 10; **S**5895	33	10	S		126	—	—	—	—	—	—	—	—
HARTSELLE—Morgan County													
★☐ HARTSELLE MEDICAL CENTER, 300 W. Pine St., P O Box 969, Zip 35640; tel. 205/773-6511; Ronald L. Sparkman, adm. **A**1a 9 10 **F**1 6 14 15 16 23 26 34 35 45 46 53	33	10	S		150	2952	50	33.3	0	0	8595	3447	158
HEFLIN—Cleburne County													
CLEBURNE COMMUNITY MEDICAL CENTER AND NURSING HOME (Formerly Cleburne Hospital), 411 Ross St. S., Box 398, Zip 36264; tel. 205/463-2121; William B. Ross, adm. (Total facility includes 40 beds in nursing home-type unit) **A**9 10 **F**1 6 14 16 19 23 26 35 42 45 46 47 53; **S**1935	33	10	S	TF	70	635	49	70.0	0	0	—	—	38
				H	30	538	11	—	0	0	—	—	—
HUNTSVILLE—Madison County													
★☐ CRESTWOOD HOSPITAL, One Hospital Dr., Zip 35801; tel. 205/882-3100; N. A. Thompson, adm. **A**1a 9 10 **F**1 3 6 7 9 10 12 14 15 16 23 34 35 42 46 47 48 49; **S**1755	33	10	S		120	3975	79	65.8	0	0	13124	4737	293
FOX ARMY COMMUNITY HOSPITAL, See Redstone Arsenal													
★☐ HUMANA HOSPITAL-HUNTSVILLE, 911 Big Cove Rd. S.E., Zip 35801; tel. 205/532-5712; Patricia A. Davis, exec. dir. **A**1a 9 10 **F**1 2 3 6 9 10 11 12 14 16 20 23 34 35 40 45 46 47 53 54; **S**1235	33	10	S		323	11225	206	63.8	29	1090	37632	14041	747
★☐ HUNTSVILLE HOSPITAL, 101 Sivley Rd., Zip 35801; tel. 205/533-8020; Edward D. Boston, chief exec. off. **A**1a 3 5 9 10 **F**1 2 3 4 5 6 7 8 9 10 11 12 14 15 16 20 23 24 27 30 32 33 34 35 36 37 40 41 42 43 44 45 46 47 50 51 52 54	14	10	S		513	20073	375	73.1	78	2792	64010	27113	1530
JACKSON—Clarke County													
CLARKE HOSPITAL, 220 Hospital Dr., Box 428, Zip 36545; tel. 205/246-9021; Sam H. Hughston, adm. (Nonreporting) **A**9 10	33	10	S		35	—	—	—	—	—	—	—	—
JACKSONVILLE—Calhoun County													
JACKSONVILLE HOSPITAL, S. Pelham Rd., Box 999, Zip 36265; tel. 205/435-4970; R. Michael Limerick, adm. **A**9 10 **F**1 3 6 10 14 16 23 35 40 45 46	14	10	S		56	2129	33	58.9	6	293	6144	2766	168
JASPER—Walker County													
★☐ WALKER REGIONAL MEDICAL CENTER, 3400 Hwy. 78 E., Zip 35501; Mailing Address Box 3547, Zip 35502; tel. 205/387-4000; James L. Armour, pres. **A**1a 9 10 **F**1 3 6 10 12 14 15 16 23 26 27 32 35 40 45 46 47 48 53	23	10	S		227	11783	165	72.7	25	767	30453	11090	641
LAFAYETTE—Chambers County													
★ CHAMBERS COUNTY HOSPITAL, 404 Ninth Ave. S.W., Zip 36862; tel. 205/864-8844; Gil McKenzie, adm. **A**9 10 **F**1 3 14 16 35 46	13	10	S		38	730	9	23.7	10	25	1588	674	57
LANGDALE—Chambers County													
GEORGE H. LANIER MEMORIAL HOSPITAL AND NURSING HOME, See Valley													
LESTER—Limestone County													
☐ FIRST HEALTH JACKSON (Formerly D. E. Jackson Memorial Hospital), Ivy Point Rd., Drawer A, Zip 35647; tel. 205/232-7511; Joe Gregory, adm. **A**1a 9 10 **F**1 6 16 23 35 50 52; **S**1275	33	10	S		38	373	5	13.2	0	0	—	—	33
LIVINGSTON—Sumter County													
☐ LIVINGSTON-TOMBIGBEE REGIONAL MEDICAL CENTER, Hwy. 11 N., P O Drawer AA, Zip 35470; tel. 205/652-9511; Paul E. Majors Jr., adm. **A**1a 9 10 **F**47 48; **S**9795	33	10	S		72	703	14	19.4	6	15	—	—	95
LUVERNE—Crenshaw County													
☐ CRENSHAW COUNTY HOSPITAL, S. Forrest Ave., Box 432, Zip 36049; tel. 205/335-3374; John Lee, adm. **A**1a 9 10 **F**1 3 6 14 16 24 27 30 32 33 35 36 37 42 45 46 48 49	13	10	S		65	1801	30	46.2	9	339	3405	1651	122
MARION—Perry County													
PERRY COMMUNITY HOSPITAL, E. Lafayette St., P O Box 149, Zip 36756; tel. 205/683-6111; Marshall L. Nero, adm. (Total facility includes 31 beds in nursing home-type unit) **A**9 10 **F**10 14 19 23 35 45; **S**1935	33	10	S	TF	67	703	35	52.2	0	0	—	—	60
				H	36	649	15	—	0	0	—	—	42
MAXWELL AIR FORCE BASE—Montgomery County													
★☐ U. S. AIR FORCE REGIONAL HOSPITAL MAXWELL, Zip 36112; tel. 205/293-7801; Col. Robert T. Jones MC USAF, cmdr.; Col. John Vanherpen, adm. (Nonreporting) **A**1a	41	10	S		117	—	—	—	—	—	—	—	—
MOBILE—Mobile County													
★☐ CHARTER SOUTHLAND HOSPITAL, 5800 Southland Dr., P O Box 9699, Zip 36609; tel. 205/666-7900; James F. Button, adm. **A**1b 9 10 **F**12 28 30 32 33 42; **S**0695	33	22	S		84	655	44	52.4	0	0	—	—	91
★☐ DOCTORS HOSPITAL OF MOBILE, 1700 Center St., Zip 36604; Mailing Address Box 1708, Zip 36633; tel. 205/438-4551; Stephen C. Loescher, adm. **A**1a b 9 10 **F**1 2 3 6 10 12 14 16 23 24 26 28 29 30 32 33 35 41 42 45 46 47 53; **S**1755	33	10	S		159	3338	88	55.3	0	0	—	—	297
★☐ KNOLLWOOD PARK HOSPITAL, 5600 Girby Rd., Zip 36609; Mailing Address P O Box 9753, Zip 36691; tel. 205/661-5020; Stephen C. Loescher, adm. **A**1a 9 10 **F**1 3 6 12 14 15 16 23 30 33 35 46 47 53; **S**1755	33	10	S		100	3538	56	56.0	0	0	—	—	232
★☐ MOBILE INFIRMARY MEDICAL CENTER (Formerly Mobile Infirmary), 5 Mobile Infirmary Circle, Box 2144, Zip 36652; tel. 205/431-2400; John O. Tucker, pres. & chief exec. off. **A**1a 2 9 10 **F**1 2 3 4 6 7 8 9 10 11 12 14 16 17 20 23 25 27 35 36 40 45 46 52 53 54	23	10	S		654	25581	458	71.1	50	1801	95717	38824	2243
★☐ PROVIDENCE HOSPITAL, 1504 Springhill Ave., Zip 36604; Mailing Address Box 3201, Zip 36652; tel. 205/438-7611; Sr. Elise Boudreaux, pres. **A**1a 9 10 **F**1 2 3 6 7 8 9 10 11 12 14 15 16 20 23 24 26 27 30 32 34 35 36 40 42 45 46 47 48 49 52 53 54; **S**1885	21	10	S		349	9346	186	53.3	34	1303	37765	17274	892
ROTARY REHABILITATION HOSPITAL, 1874 Pleasant Ave., Zip 36607; tel. 205/431-3400; E. Chandler Bramlett, pres. **A**9 10 **F**15 23 24 26 33 34 42 44 45 46 47	23	46	S		50	659	45	90.0	0	0	5850	2978	210
☐ SPRINGHILL MEMORIAL HOSPITAL, 3719 Dauphin St., Box 8246, Zip 36608; tel. 205/344-9630; Donald O. Bedsole MD, bd. chm. **A**1a 9 10 **F**1 3 6 10 11 14 16 17 23 34 35 39 40 45 46 47 52 53; **S**0365	33	10	S		252	10664	161	63.9	30	1563	38779	11842	575
★☐ UNIVERSITY OF SOUTH ALABAMA MEDICAL CENTER, 2451 Fillingim St., Zip 36617; tel. 205/471-7110; Stephen H. Simmons, actg. adm. **A**1a 2 3 5 8 9 10 **F**1 2 3 4 5 6 7 8 9 10 11 12 14 15 16 23 24 26 27 28 30 32 33 35 36 37 38 40 42 45 46 47 50 51 52 53 54	12	10	S		394	14862	277	70.5	26	2895	56763	23724	1161

★ American Hospital Association (AHA) membership
☐ Joint Commission on Accreditation of Hospitals (JCAH) accreditation
\+ American Osteopathic Hospital Association (AOHA) membership
○ American Osteopathic Association (AOA) accreditation
Δ Commission on Accreditation of Rehabilitation Facilities (CARF) accreditation
Control codes 61, 63, 64, 71, 72 and 73 indicate hospitals listed by AOHA, but not registered by AHA. For definition of numerical codes, see page A2

Hospital, Address, Telephone, Administrator, Approval and Facility Codes, Multihospital System Code	Classification Codes				Inpatient Data				Newborn Data		Expense (thousands of dollars)		
	Control	Service	Stay	Facilities	Beds	Admissions	Census	Occupancy (percent)	Bassinets	Births	Total	Payroll	Personnel
MONROEVILLE—Monroe County													
★☐ MONROE COUNTY HOSPITAL, Hwy. 21, Box 886, Zip 36461; tel. 205/575-3111; Michael S. Potter, adm. **A**1a 9 10 **F**1 3 6 14 15 16 23 28 34 35 36 45 46 47 50 52 53; **S**1755	13	10	S		94	3290	41	43.6	12	385	6025	2829	179
MONTGOMERY—Montgomery County													
★☐ BAPTIST MEDICAL CENTER, 2105 E. South Blvd., Box 11010, Zip 36198; tel. 205/288-2100; W. Taylor Morrow, pres. **A**1a 3 5 9 10 **F**1 2 3 6 7 8 9 10 11 12 14 15 16 21 23 24 26 27 28 30 32 33 34 35 36 40 41 42 44 45 46 48 49 51 52 53	21	10	S		434	15024	250	57.6	40	2699	42565	18231	962
★☐ HUMANA HOSPITAL -EAST MONTGOMERY, Taylor Rd., Box 17720, Zip 36193; tel. 205/277-8330; John W. Melton, exec. dir. **A**1a 9 10 **F**1 2 6 10 12 14 16 17 20 23 34 35 46 48 53 54; **S**1235	33	10	S		150	3972	62	41.3	0	0	14811	4590	269
★☐ JACKSON HOSPITAL AND CLINIC, 1235 Forest Ave., Zip 36106; tel. 205/293-8000; Donald M. Ball, adm. **A**1a 3 5 9 10 **F**1 2 3 6 7 8 9 10 11 12 14 15 16 23 24 27 30 32 33 34 35 40 46 52 53	23	10	S		378	14061	249	65.9	25	991	39530	17940	1041
★☐ ST. MARGARET'S HOSPITAL, 301 S. Ripley, Box 311, Zip 36101; tel. 205/269-8000; Matthias D. Maguire, pres. **A**1a 3 5 9 10 **F**1 2 3 4 6 7 8 9 10 11 12 14 15 16 20 23 24 26 34 35 36 40 41 42 45 46 47 48 52 53 54; **S**1885	21	10	S		230	9705	161	70.0	15	1139	33630	13587	769
U. S. AIR FORCE REGIONAL HOSPITAL MAXWELL, See Maxwell Air Force Base													
★☐ VETERANS ADMINISTRATION MEDICAL CENTER, 215 Perry Hill Rd., Zip 36193; tel. 205/272-4670; Roy C. McCracken, dir. **A**1a **F**1 3 6 12 14 15 16 23 26 34 44 46 47	45	10	S		200	3281	143	71.5	0	0	21985	11786	409
MOULTON—Lawrence County													
☐ LAWRENCE COUNTY HOSPITAL, 202 Hospital St., Zip 35650; tel. 205/974-2200; Richard Stroud, adm. **A**1a 9 10 **F**1 3 6 14 15 16 23 34 35 45 46 47 53	13	10	S		98	2993	41	41.8	0	0	4863	2248	182
MOUNT VERNON—Mobile County													
SEARCY HOSPITAL, Zip 36560; tel. 205/829-9411; John T. Bartlett, dir. **A**3 5 **F**31 33 42 46	12	22	L		650	800	639	97.3	0	0	21880	13957	759
MUSCLE SHOALS—Colbert County													
★☐ HUMANA HOSPITAL -SHOALS (Formerly Listed Under Sheffield), 201 Avalon Ave., P O Box 3359, Zip 35661; tel. 205/386-1600; Charles P. Stokes, exec. dir. **A**1a 9 10 **F**1 3 6 10 15 16 23 35 46 48 49 53; **S**1235	33	10	S		128	3160	60	46.9	0	0	11823	4143	234
NORTHPORT—Tuscaloosa County													
★☐ AMI WEST ALABAMA HOSPITAL (Formerly AMI West Alabama General Hospital), 2700 11th Ave., Zip 35476; tel. 205/339-5100; Steve Scully, pres. (Nonreporting) **A**1a b 9 10; **S**0125	33	10	S		156	—	—	—	—	—	—	—	—
ONEONTA—Blount County													
★ BLOUNT MEMORIAL HOSPITAL, 1000 Lincoln Ave., Box 220, Zip 35121; tel. 205/625-3511; Thomas A. Hackney, adm. **A**9 10 **F**3 6 14 16 34 35 52	13	10	S		101	3149	50	49.5	0	0	—	—	148
OPELIKA—Lee County													
★☐ EAST ALABAMA MEDICAL CENTER, 2000 Pepperell Pkwy., Zip 36802; tel. 205/749-3411; Terry A. Andrus, adm. **A**1a 9 10 **F**1 2 3 5 6 7 8 9 10 11 14 15 16 20 23 27 30 32 33 35 36 40 45 46 47 52 53 54; **S**5895	13	10	S		311	11008	203	65.3	19	1221	32664	13076	858
OPP—Covington County													
★ MIZELL MEMORIAL HOSPITAL, 702 Main St., Box 429, Zip 36467; tel. 205/493-3541; Don Nelson, adm. **A**9 10 **F**1 3 6 10 15 16 23 35 40 45 46 47 53; **S**0185	23	10	S		99	2901	43	42.2	9	214	5186	2457	160
OZARK—Dale County													
☐ DALE COUNTY HOSPITAL, 510 James St., Box 1149, Zip 36360; tel. 205/774-2601; Robert J. Humphrey, adm. **A**1a 9 10 **F**1 3 6 12 14 15 16 23 35 40 45 46 47; **S**0025	16	10	S		89	2851	41	46.1	0	0	—	—	196
PELL CITY—St. Clair County													
★ ST. CLAIR REGIONAL HOSPITAL (Formerly St. Clair County Hospital), 2805 Hospital Dr., Zip 35125; tel. 205/338-3301; C. M. Jones, adm. **A**9 10 **F**3 6 12 14 16 34 35 40 45 53; **S**9105	13	10	S		72	2022	35	48.6	12	161	6485	2719	150
PHENIX CITY—Russell County													
★☐ HOMER D. COBB MEMORIAL HOSPITAL, 1707 21st Ave., Box 190, Zip 36867; tel. 205/298-7811; J. Stuart Mitchell, adm. **A**1a 9 10 **F**1 2 3 6 7 9 10 11 12 14 15 16 20 23 26 35 40 44 45 46 47 48 52 53	14	10	S		234	6626	134	57.3	8	304	—	—	614
PIEDMONT—Calhoun County													
PIEDMONT HOSPITAL AND NURSING HOME, Calhoun St., Box 330, Zip 36272; tel. 205/447-6041; James M. Jumper, adm. (Nonreporting) **A**9 10; **S**1935	14	10	S		78	—	—	—	—	—	—	—	—
PRATTVILLE—Autauga County													
AUTAUGA MEDICAL CENTER, 124 S. Memorial Dr., Zip 36067; tel. 205/365-0651; Willis S. Sanders, chief exec. off. **A**9 10 **F**1 5 6 10 12 14 15 16 23 26 33 34 35 37 45 46 47 53; **S**0985	33	10	S		62	2135	33	53.2	0	0	6382	2037	162
RED BAY—Franklin County													
★ RED BAY HOSPITAL, 211 Hospital Rd., Box 490, Zip 35582; tel. 205/356-9532; Jane Williams, adm. **A**9 10 **F**1 3 15 16 35 46	14	10	S		33	1210	16	48.5	0	0	1910	838	64
REDSTONE ARSENAL—Madison County													
★☐ FOX ARMY COMMUNITY HOSPITAL, Zip 35809; tel. 205/876-4147; Col. A. T. Hadley III MD, cmdr. **A**1a **F**1 3 6 16 23 33 34 35	42	10	S		42	1846	23	54.8	0	0	8045	—	418
ROANOKE—Randolph County													
★☐ RANDOLPH COUNTY HOSPITAL, 1000 Wadley Hwy., Box 669, Zip 36274; tel. 205/863-4111; Kevin E. Beightol, adm. **A**1a 9 10 **F**1 3 6 10 11 14 16 23 35 40 45 46 47 53	13	10	S		74	2046	33	44.6	10	202	4188	1892	144
RUSSELLVILLE—Franklin County													
★☐ HUMANA HOSPITAL -RUSSELLVILLE, Hwy. 43 By-Pass, Box 1089, Zip 35653; tel. 205/332-1611; Bradley K. Grover Sr., exec. dir. **A**1a 9 10 **F**1 6 10 14 16 23 34 35 46 53; **S**1235	33	10	S		100	3629	55	55.0	8	296	—	—	212
SATSUMA—Mobile County													
☐ NORTH MOBILE COMMUNITY HOSPITAL, Hartley & Baker Rds., Box 518, Zip 36572; tel. 205/675-1541; John V. Oliver, exec. dir. (Nonreporting) **A**1a 9 10	33	10	S		38	—	—	—	—	—	—	—	—
SCOTTSBORO—Jackson County													
☐ JACKSON COUNTY HOSPITAL, Woods Cove Rd., Box 1050, Zip 35768; tel. 205/259-4444; James K. Mason, adm. (Total facility includes 50 beds in nursing home-type unit) **A**1a 9 10 **F**1 3 6 10 12 14 16 19 23 33 34 35 36 37 45 46 53	13	10	S	TF	182	4612	120	65.9	20	436	10164	4680	312
				H	132	4575	71	—	20	436	9511	4367	281
SELMA—Dallas County													
★☐ SELMA MEDICAL CENTER, 1015 Medical Center Pkwy., Zip 36701; tel. 205/872-8461; Robert F. Letson, adm. **A**1a 2 3 5 9 10 **F**1 2 3 5 6 7 8 10 11 14 15 16 20 23 24 26 27 30 32 33 34 35 44 45 46 47 53; **S**1755	33	10	S		180	6483	120	66.7	0	0	—	—	405
★☐ VAUGHAN REGIONAL MEDICAL CENTER, W. Dallas Ave., Box 328, Zip 36702; tel. 205/872-0411; Frank R. Gannon, adm. **A**1a 3 5 9 10 **F**1 3 6 10 14 16 23 34 35 40 45 46 52 53	23	10	S		101	4824	62	61.4	24	1303	10024	4327	278

★ American Hospital Association (AHA) membership
□ Joint Commission on Accreditation of Hospitals (JCAH) accreditation
+ American Osteopathic Hospital Association (AOHA) membership
○ American Osteopathic Association (AOA) accreditation
Δ Commission on Accreditation of Rehabilitation Facilities (CARF) accreditation
Control codes 61, 63, 64, 71, 72 and 73 indicate hospitals listed by AOHA, but not registered by AHA.
For definition of numerical codes, see page A2

Hospital, Address, Telephone, Administrator, Approval and Facility Codes, Multihospital System Code	Classification Codes				Inpatient Data				Newborn Data		Expense (thousands of dollars)		
	Control	Service	Stay	Facilities	Beds	Admissions	Census	Occupancy (percent)	Bassinets	Births	Total	Payroll	Personnel
SHEFFIELD—Colbert County													
★□ HELEN KELLER MEMORIAL HOSPITAL, 1300 S. Montgomery Ave., Box 610, Zip 35660; tel. 205/386-4196; Ralph Clark Jr., pres. **A**1a 9 10 **F**1 2 3 6 10 12 14 15 16 17 23 34 35 40 45 46 47 52 53	13	10	S		185	6453	115	62.2	24	588	19313	8427	454
HUMANA HOSPITAL -SHOALS, See Muscle Shoals													
SYLACAUGA—Talladega County													
★□ SYLACAUGA HOSPITAL, W. Hickory St., Zip 35150; tel. 205/249-4921; Steven M. Johnson, adm. (Total facility includes 52 beds in nursing home-type unit) **A**1a 6 9 10 **F**1 3 6 10 12 14 15 16 19 23 30 35 40 45 52 53	14	10	S	TF	185	5003	123	69.5	25	283	12811	5322	384
				H	133	4958	72	—	25	283	12078	4955	352
TALLADEGA—Talladega County													
★□ CITIZENS HOSPITAL, 604 Stone Ave., P O Box 888, Zip 35160; tel. 205/362-8111; Jack B. Hethcox, adm. **A**1a 9 10 **F**1 3 6 10 14 16 23 35 40 46 47 48 53	23	10	S		122	4175	59	48.4	15	533	8776	3668	253
TALLASSEE—Elmore County													
★□ COMMUNITY HOSPITAL, Friendship Rd., Box 707, Zip 36078; tel. 205/283-6541; K. Byron Lowery, adm. **A**1a 9 10 **F**1 3 6 10 12 14 15 16 23 35 40 45	23	10	S		77	2806	45	58.4	0	0	5282	2294	180
THOMASVILLE—Clarke County													
□ THOMASVILLE HOSPITAL, Hwy. 43 N., Drawer 429, Zip 36784; tel. 205/636-4431; Benny Ray Stephens, adm. (Nonreporting) **A**1a 9 10; **S**1935	33	10	S		43	—	—	—	—	—	—	—	—
TROY—Pike County													
□ EDGE MEMORIAL HOSPITAL, Hwy. 231 By-Pass, Box 667, Zip 36081; tel. 205/566-0140; Willis Dale Walley, adm. **A**1a 9 10 **F**1 3 6 12 14 16 23 35 40 45 46 47	14	10	S		97	4184	63	64.9	5	365	8373	2731	264
TUSCALOOSA—Tuscaloosa County													
BRYCE HOSPITAL, 200 University Blvd., Zip 35401; tel. 205/759-0799; Charles A. Fetner, dir. (Nonreporting)	12	22	L		1395	—	—	—	—	—	—	—	—
★□ DCH REGIONAL MEDICAL CENTER (Formerly Druid City Hospital Regional Medical Center), 809 University Blvd. E., Zip 35403; tel. 205/759-7111; J. H. Ford Jr., adm. **A**1a 3 5 9 10 **F**1 2 3 4 5 6 7 8 9 10 11 12 14 15 16 20 23 24 26 27 28 30 32 33 34 35 36 40 41 42 44 46 47 51 52 53 54	16	10	S		570	22093	424	74.4	36	2616	72614	34122	1860
★□ DCH REHABILITATION PAVILION, 1101 Sixth Ave. E., Zip 35401; tel. 205/759-7375; A. Lamar Tanner, adm. **A**1a 9 10 **F**1 15 16 23 24 25 26 32 33 34 37 42 44 48 49	23	10	S		54	627	27	50.0	0	0	3494	2089	101
DRUID CITY HOSPITAL REGIONAL MEDICAL CENTER, See Dch Regional Medical Center													
★□ VETERANS ADMINISTRATION MEDICAL CENTER, Loop Rd., Zip 35404; tel. 205/553-3760; Robert P. Blair, dir. (Total facility includes 120 beds in nursing home-type unit) **A**1a **F**4 5 10 14 16 17 19 23 24 29 30 32 33 42 44 45 46 47 50	45	22	L	TF	702	3741	593	84.5	0	0	34044	23461	1189
				H	582	3678	478	—	0	0	29619	19982	1104
TUSKEGEE—Macon County													
★□ VETERANS ADMINISTRATION MEDICAL CENTER, Zip 36083; tel. 205/727-0550; Jimmie Clay, dir. (Total facility includes 112 beds in nursing home-type unit) **A**1a 2 **F**1 2 3 6 10 12 14 15 16 19 21 23 24 25 26 27 28 30 31 32 33 34 41 42 44 46 48 49 50 53	45	10	S	TF	834	5947	706	84.7	0	0	47963	34728	1313
				H	722	5933	600	—	0	0	—	—	1234
TUSKEGEE INSTITUTE—Macon County													
JOHN A. ANDREW COMMUNITY HOSPITAL, Zip 36088; tel. 205/727-9375; R. Roland Bradford, adm. **A**9 10 **F**1 6 14 16 23 26 35 36 40 46 47 52; **S**0885	23	10	S		59	1893	23	43.4	12	451	3647	1385	92
UNION SPRINGS—Bullock County													
★ BULLOCK COUNTY HOSPITAL, 102 W. Conecuh Ave., Zip 36089; tel. 205/738-2140; Rodney Watford, adm. (Total facility includes 32 beds in nursing home-type unit) **A**9 10 **F**6 14 19 35 50	23	10	S	TF	59	719	36	61.0	0	0	—	—	78
				H	27	697	7	—	0	0	—	—	51
VALLEY—Chambers County													
★□ GEORGE H. LANIER MEMORIAL HOSPITAL AND NURSING HOME (Formerly Listed Under Langdale), 4800 48th St., Zip 36854; tel. 205/756-3111; Howard D. Clem Sr., adm. (Total facility includes 75 beds in nursing home-type unit) **A**1a 9 10 **F**1 2 3 6 10 12 14 15 16 19 23 35 40 44 45 46 47 52; **S**9105	23	10	S	TF	192	5094	140	72.9	14	358	13920	5906	384
				H	117	4965	72	—	14	358	12876	5334	334
VERNON—Lamar County													
★ LAMAR REGIONAL HOSPITAL (Formerly LaMar Carraway Medical Center), 507 Fifth St. S.W., Box 308, Zip 35592; tel. 205/695-7111; Donald B. Hatcher, adm. (Nonreporting) **A**9 10; **S**5895	21	10	S		70	—	—	—	—	—	—	—	—
WEDOWEE—Randolph County													
□ WEDOWEE HOSPITAL, 301 N. Main St., Box 307, Zip 36278; tel. 205/357-2111; Kerlene Mitchell, adm. **A**1a 9 10 **F**3 14 16 34 35 39 45 47; **S**1935	33	10	S		34	444	5	14.7	0	0	—	—	22
WETUMPKA—Elmore County													
★□ ELMORE COUNTY HOSPITAL, 1201 Company St., P O Box 120, Zip 36092; tel. 205/567-4311; Christine Trumble, adm. **A**1a 9 10 **F**1 3 6 10 14 15 16 20 23 35 37 45 48 49	13	10	S		58	1242	23	35.9	0	0	3683	1825	110
WINFIELD—Marion County													
★□ WINFIELD CARRAWAY HOSPITAL, Hwy. 78 W., Box 130, Zip 35594; tel. 205/487-4234; Terry Blackwood, adm. **A**1a 9 10 **F**1 3 6 10 12 14 15 16 23 34 35 40 43 46 47 52	23	10	S		68	2145	30	44.1	12	151	5492	2221	154
YORK—Sumter County													
□ RUSH-HILL HOSPITAL OF YORK, 751 Derby Dr., Zip 36925; tel. 205/392-5263; Lowry Rush III, adm. **A**1a 9 10 **F**1 6 14 16 35 45 46 47	23	10	S		33	1341	15	45.5	6	173	—	—	81

Hospital, Address, Telephone, Administrator, Approval and Facility Codes, Multihospital System Code	Classification Codes				Inpatient Data				Newborn Data		Expense (thousands of dollars)		
★ American Hospital Association (AHA) membership ☐ Joint Commission on Accreditation of Hospitals (JCAH) accreditation + American Osteopathic Hospital Association (AOHA) membership ○ American Osteopathic Association (AOA) accreditation Δ Commission on Accreditation of Rehabilitation Facilities (CARF) accreditation Control codes 61, 63, 64, 71, 72 and 73 indicate hospitals listed by AOHA, but not registered by AHA. For definition of numerical codes, see page A2	Control	Service	Stay	Facilities	Beds	Admissions	Census	Occupancy (percent)	Bassinets	Births	Total	Payroll	Personnel

Alaska

Hospital	Control	Service	Stay	Facilities	Beds	Admissions	Census	Occupancy (percent)	Bassinets	Births	Total	Payroll	Personnel
ANCHORAGE—Judicial Division 2													
☐ ALASKA PSYCHIATRIC INSTITUTE, 2900 Providence Dr., Zip 99508; tel. 907/561-1633; Alvin D. Finneseth, adm. **A**1b 9 **F**15 24 32 33 42 46 47	12	22	L		174	1138	162	93.1	0	0	13731	9037	298
★☐ CHARTER NORTH HOSPITAL, 2530 Debarr Rd., Zip 99508; tel. 907/258-7575; Steven D. Berkshire, adm. **A**1b 9 10 **F**15 24 28 29 30 32 33 42 45 47 48 49; **S**0695	33	22	S		80	766	51	63.8	0	0	—	—	110
★ HORIZON RECOVERY CENTER, 1650 S. Bragaw, Zip 99508; tel. 907/277-1522; Gloria Heatherington, adm. (Nonreporting) **A**9; **S**6525	33	82	S		34	—	—	—	—	—	—	—	—
★☐ HUMANA HOSPITAL -ALASKA, 2801 Debarr Rd., Zip 99508; Mailing Address P O Box 143889, Zip 99514; tel. 907/276-1131; Mary D. Willis, exec. dir. **A**1a 9 10 **F**1 2 3 6 10 12 14 15 16 17 20 23 24 25 26 30 34 35 36 37 40 42 44 45 46 47 52 53 54; **S**1235	33	10	S		238	6972	97	42.9	20	1561	—	—	515
★☐ PROVIDENCE HOSPITAL, 3200 Providence Dr., Zip 99508; Mailing Address P O Box 196604, Zip 99519; tel. 907/562-2211; Al M. Camosso, chief exec. off. **A**1a 9 10 **F**1 2 3 4 6 7 8 9 10 11 12 15 16 17 20 22 23 24 25 26 27 28 29 30 32 33 34 35 36 40 41 42 44 45 46 47 51 52 53 54; **S**5275	21	10	S		324	13545	232	78.6	24	2319	82232	40103	1232
U. S. AIR FORCE REGIONAL HOSPITAL ELMENDORF, See Elmendorf Air Force Base													
★☐ U. S. PUBLIC HEALTH SERVICE ALASKA NATIVE MEDICAL CENTER, Third & Gambell Sts., Box 7-741, Zip 99510; tel. 907/279-6661; Richard Mandsager MD, dir. (Nonreporting) **A**1a 10	47	10	S		170	—	—	—	—	—	—	—	—
BARROW—Judicial Division 4													
★☐ U. S. PUBLIC HEALTH SERVICE ALASKA NATIVE HOSPITAL, Zip 99723; tel. 907/852-4611; Carolyn McClintock, serv. unit dir. **A**1a 10 **F**6 12 14 34 35 37 40	47	10	S		14	722	5	35.7	5	96	—	—	46
BETHEL—Judicial Division 1													
★☐ U. S. PUBLIC HEALTH SERVICE YUKON-KUSKOKWIM DELTA REGIONAL HOSPITAL, Zip 99559; tel. 907/543-2251; Delbert Nutter, adm. **A**1a 10 **F**6 12 14 15 23 34 35 37 40 45 46 52	47	10	S		51	2076	21	41.2	7	472	11221	—	142
CORDOVA—Judicial Division 2													
★ CORDOVA COMMUNITY HOSPITAL, 602 Chase St., Box 160, Zip 99574; tel. 907/424-7551; Edward Zeine, adm. (Nonreporting) **A**9 10	14	10	S		18	—	—	—	—	—	—	—	—
DILLINGHAM—Judicial Division 1													
★☐ KANAKANAK HOSPITAL, P O Box 3050, Zip 99576; tel. 907/842-5201; G. Robert Appel, adm. **A**1a 9 10 **F**1 6 15 28 29 30 32 33 34 35 36 37 40 43 47 49 52	23	10	S		15	472	4	14.3	3	94	6361	3487	60
ELMENDORF AIR FORCE BASE—Judicial Division 2													
★☐ U. S. AIR FORCE REGIONAL HOSPITAL ELMENDORF, Zip 99506; tel. 907/552-3500; Col. William E. Palma, cmdr. **A**1a **F**1 3 6 12 14 15 21 23 24 27 28 29 30 32 33 34 35 36 37 40 46 47 52	41	10	S		90	5344	63	70.0	22	994	—	—	680
FAIRBANKS—Judicial Division 1													
BASSETT ARMY COMMUNITY HOSPITAL, See Fort Wainwright													
★☐ FAIRBANKS MEMORIAL HOSPITAL, 1650 Cowles St., Zip 99701; tel. 907/452-8181; Philip Koon, adm. **A**1a 2 9 10 **F**1 3 6 10 12 14 15 16 20 23 24 26 27 30 32 35 36 40 41 45 46 47 51 52 53; **S**2235	23	10	S		156	6837	93	66.9	16	1553	31641	17333	474
FORT WAINWRIGHT—Judicial Division 1													
★☐ BASSETT ARMY COMMUNITY HOSPITAL, Zip 99703; tel. 907/353-5108; Col. Lionel E. Waldman MD, cmdr.; Lt. Col. John R. Mohn, dep. cmdr. adm. **A**1a **F**1 3 6 12 14 15 16 23 28 29 30 32 33 34 35 36 37 40 46 47 49	42	10	S		85	1865	20	23.5	15	447	22015	17705	349
HOMER—Judicial Division 3													
★ SOUTH PENINSULA HOSPITAL, 4300 Bartlett St., Zip 99603; tel. 907/235-8101; Michael Herring, adm. (Total facility includes 16 beds in nursing home-type unit) **A**9 10 **F**1 3 10 14 17 19 23 35 36 40 43 45	23	10	S	TF	38	1114	24	61.5	6	177	6157	2950	—
				H	22	1105	10	—	6	177	—	—	—
JUNEAU—Judicial Division 3													
★ BARTLETT MEMORIAL HOSPITAL, 3260 Hospital Dr., Zip 99801; tel. 907/586-2611; William M. Selvey Jr., adm. **A**9 10 **F**1 3 5 6 10 14 15 16 17 23 35 36 37 40 45 46 47 53	23	10	S		38	1114	24	61.5	6	177	6157	2950	—
KETCHIKAN—Judicial Division 3													
★☐ KETCHIKAN GENERAL HOSPITAL (Includes Island View Manor), 3100 Tongass Ave., Zip 99901; tel. 907/225-5171; Sr. Barbara Haase, adm. (Total facility includes 44 beds in nursing home-type unit) **A**1a 9 10 **F**1 3 6 10 14 16 19 23 30 34 35 36 40 42 45; **S**5415	23	10	S	TF	83	1578	55	66.3	6	314	8959	5115	190
				H	39	1520	15	—	6	314	6724	4491	165
KODIAK—Judicial Division 2													
★ KODIAK ISLAND HOSPITAL, 1915 E. Rezanoff Dr., Zip 99615; tel. 907/486-3281; James H. Gingerich, adm. (Total facility includes 19 beds in nursing home-type unit) **A**9 10 **F**1 3 6 10 14 15 16 23 27 28 30 34 35 36 37 40 44 45 46 47 50; **S**2235	23	10	S	TF	44	1258	26	59.1	7	262	5601	3390	83
				H	25	1230	—	—	7	262	4541	2782	—
KOTZEBUE—Judicial Division 4													
★☐ U. S. PUBLIC HEALTH SERVICE ALASKA NATIVE HOSPITAL, Zip 99752; tel. 907/442-3321; Frank H. Williams, serv. unit dir. **A**1a 10 **F**1 6 14 15 16 28 32 34 35 36 37 40 47 52	47	10	S		31	773	7	22.6	6	131	—	—	66
NOME—Judicial Division 4													
★☐ NORTON SOUND REGIONAL HOSPITAL, Bering St., Box 966, Zip 99762; tel. 907/443-5411; Richard Conti, adm. (Nonreporting) **A**1a 9 10	23	10	S		21	—	—	—	—	—	—	—	—
PALMER—Judicial Division 2													
★ VALLEY HOSPITAL, 515 E. Dahlia St., P O Box 1687, Zip 99645; tel. 907/745-4813; James G. Walsh, exec. dir. **A**9 10 **F**1 3 6 14 15 16 23 33 35 37 40 41 52	23	10	S		36	1969	21	58.3	8	572	9856	4785	169
PETERSBURG—Judicial Division 3													
★ PETERSBURG GENERAL HOSPITAL AND LONG TERM CARE FACILITY, 103 Fram St., Box 589, Zip 99833; tel. 907/772-4291; Gary W. Grandy, adm. (Total facility includes 12 beds in nursing home-type unit) **A**9 10 **F**1 3 6 14 16 19 23 29 34 35 36 40 42 45 50	15	10	S	TF	22	234	12	54.5	5	47	2416	1097	34
				H	10	219	1	—	5	47	2077	812	24
SEWARD—Judicial Division 2													
★ SEWARD GENERAL HOSPITAL, 521 First Ave., Box 365, Zip 99664; tel. 907/224-5205; C. Keith Campbell, pres. & chief exec. off. **A**9 10 **F**1 3 12 14 16 23 30 34 35 36 40 45 52	23	10	S		32	456	3	9.4	4	47	1872	957	36

Hospital, Address, Telephone, Administrator, Approval and Facility Codes, Multihospital System Code	Classification Codes				Inpatient Data				Newborn Data		Expense (thousands of dollars)		
★ American Hospital Association (AHA) membership □ Joint Commission on Accreditation of Hospitals (JCAH) accreditation + American Osteopathic Hospital Association (AOHA) membership ○ American Osteopathic Association (AOA) accreditation Δ Commission on Accreditation of Rehabilitation Facilities (CARF) accreditation Control codes 61, 63, 64, 71, 72 and 73 indicate hospitals listed by AOHA, but not registered by AHA. For definition of numerical codes, see page A2	Control	Service	Stay	Facilities	Beds	Admissions	Census	Occupancy (percent)	Bassinets	Births	Total	Payroll	Personnel
SITKA—Judicial Division 3													
★□ MOUNT EDGECUMBE HOSPITAL (Formerly U. S. Public Health Service Alaska Native Hospital), 222 Tongass Dr., Zip 99835; tel. 907/966-2411; Arthur C. Willman, vice-pres. oper. **A**1a 10 **F**1 14 15 19 23 28 29 30 32 33 34 35 40 45 47 48 52	47	10	S		78	1361	36	46.2	3	93	—	—	185
★□ SITKA COMMUNITY HOSPITAL, 209 Moller Ave., Zip 99835; tel. 907/747-3241; Edward Malewski, adm. & chief exec. off. **A**1a 9 10 **F**1 3 6 14 16 23 35 36 41 45 46	14	10	S		24	643	7	29.2	6	95	4014	1803	64
SOLDOTNA—Judicial Division 3													
★ CENTRAL PENINSULA GENERAL HOSPITAL, 250 Hospital Pl., Zip 99669; tel. 907/262-4404; Michael J. Lockwood, adm. **A**9 10 **F**1 3 6 14 15 16 23 34 35 36 40 45 47 49 52; **S**2235	23	10	S		46	2306	23	50.0	8	510	8473	4548	141
VALDEZ—Judicial Division 3													
★ VALDEZ COMMUNITY HOSPITAL, 911 Meals Ave., Box 550, Zip 99686; tel. 907/835-2249; Cathy Ringstad Winfree, adm. **A**9 10 **F**1 6 14 34 35 43 45; **S**2235	23	10	S		15	155	1	6.7	5	61	1265	761	22
WRANGELL—Judicial Division 3													
★ WRANGELL GENERAL HOSPITAL AND LONG TERM CARE FACILITY, First Ave. & Bennett St., Box 80, Zip 99929; tel. 907/874-3356; John Vowell, adm. (Nonreporting) **A**9 10	14	10	S		23	—	—	—	—	—	—	—	—

Hospital, Address, Telephone, Administrator, Approval and Facility Codes, Multihospital System Code

★ American Hospital Association (AHA) membership
□ Joint Commission on Accreditation of Hospitals (JCAH) accreditation
+ American Osteopathic Hospital Association (AOHA) membership
○ American Osteopathic Association (AOA) accreditation
Δ Commission on Accreditation of Rehabilitation Facilities (CARF) accreditation
Control codes 61, 63, 64, 71, 72 and 73 indicate hospitals listed by AOHA, but not registered by AHA.
For definition of numerical codes, see page A2

Arizona

Hospital, Address, Telephone, Administrator, Approval and Facility Codes, Multihospital System Code	Classification Codes				Inpatient Data				Newborn Data		Expense (thousands of dollars)		
	Control	Service	Stay	Facilities	Beds	Admissions	Census	Occupancy (percent)	Bassinets	Births	Total	Payroll	Personnel
BENSON—Cochise County													
□ BENSON HOSPITAL, 475 S. Ocotillo St., P O Box 2290, Zip 85602; tel. 602/586-2261; Ronald A. McKinnon, adm. (Nonreporting) **A**1a 9 10	23	10	S		22	—	—	—	—	—	—	—	—
BISBEE—Cochise County													
□ COPPER QUEEN COMMUNITY HOSPITAL, Cole Ave. & Bisbee Rd., Zip 85603; tel. 602/432-5383; John Houston, adm. (Total facility includes 21 beds in nursing home-type unit) **A**1a 9 10 **F**1 3 10 14 15 16 19 23 35 36 40 41 42 45 53	23	10	S	TF	49	881	29	59.2	4	81	3238	1586	97
				H	28	850	9	—	4	81	3033	1414	87
BULLHEAD CITY—Mohave County													
★ BULLHEAD COMMUNITY HOSPITAL, 2735 Silver Creek Rd., Zip 86442; tel. 602/763-2273; Joseph P. Harrington, vice-pres. & adm. **A**9 10 **F**1 3 5 6 16 23 26 35 41 45 46 53; **S**8810	23	10	S		36	2151	22	61.1	2	14	—	—	158
CASA GRANDE—Pinal County													
★□ CASA GRANDE REGIONAL MEDICAL CENTER, 1800 E. Florence Blvd., Zip 85222; tel. 602/426-6300; Robert C. Benjamin, pres. **A**1a 9 10 **F**1 3 6 12 14 15 16 23 26 30 35 36 40 45 46 47 53	23	10	S		100	3720	43	33.9	8	513	12122	3813	192
CHANDLER—Maricopa County													
□ CHANDLER COMMUNITY HOSPITAL, 475 S. Dobson Rd., Zip 85224; tel. 602/963-4561; Kaylor Shemberger, pres. & chief exec. off. **A**1a 9 10 **F**1 3 6 10 14 15 16 20 23 24 26 30 35 36 40 42 44 45 48 49 52 53	23	10	S		120	4261	56	55.4	8	575	18321	6410	315
CHINLE—Apache County													
★ CHINLE COMPREHENSIVE HEALTH CARE FACILITY, Zip 86503; tel. 602/674-5281; Bob Stopp, serv. unit dir. **A**10 **F**1 3 5 6 14 15 16 20 23 28 30 32 33 34 35 36 37 40 42 43 44 52	47	10	S		58	2801	34	59.6	14	807	13752	8219	371
COTTONWOOD—Yavapai County													
★□ MARCUS J. LAWRENCE MEMORIAL HOSPITAL, 202 S. Willard St., Box 548, Zip 86326; tel. 602/634-2251; Reid M. Wood, pres. **A**1a 9 10 **F**1 3 6 10 12 14 16 21 23 24 26 35 36 40 41 43 44 45 52 53	23	10	S		104	3748	47	45.2	8	335	11943	4918	268
DAVIS MONTHAN AIR FORCE BASE—Pima County													
□ U. S. AIR FORCE HOSPITAL, Zip 85707; tel. 602/748-5533; Lt. Col. Lawrence W. Ciminelli MSC USAF, adm. (Nonreporting) **A**1a	41	10	S		70	—	—	—	—	—	—	—	—
DOUGLAS—Cochise County													
□ SOUTHEAST ARIZONA MEDICAL CENTER, Rural Rte. 1, Box 30, Zip 85607; tel. 602/364-7931; Steve Jackson, adm. **A**1a 9 10 **F**1 3 6 14 15 16 19 23 26 35 36 40 41 42 45 46 50; **S**8985	23	10	S		75	1423	48	64.0	10	219	4679	1956	107
FLAGSTAFF—Coconino County													
★□ FLAGSTAFF MEDICAL CENTER, 1215 N. Beaver St., P O Box 1268, Zip 86002; tel. 602/779-3366; Jeff Comer, pres. & chief exec. off. **A**1a 9 10 **F**1 3 6 7 8 9 10 11 12 15 16 23 24 25 26 29 30 34 35 36 37 40 41 44 45 46 52 53	23	10	S		110	5961	68	61.8	20	1058	17295	8346	415
FLORENCE—Pinal County													
□ PINAL GENERAL HOSPITAL, Adamsville Rd., Box 789, Zip 85232; tel. 602/868-5841; Mary A. Fields, adm. (Nonreporting) **A**1a 9 10	13	10	S		88	—	—	—	—	—	—	—	—
FORT DEFIANCE—Apache County													
★□ U. S. PUBLIC HEALTH SERVICE INDIAN HOSPITAL, Box 649, Zip 86504; tel. 602/729-5741; Catherine E. Hanley, actg. serv. unit dir. (Nonreporting) **A**1a 10	47	10	S		68	—	—	—	—	—	—	—	—
FORT HUACHUCA—Cochise County													
★□ RAYMOND W. BLISS ARMY COMMUNITY HOSPITAL, Zip 85613; tel. 602/538-2026; Col. Warren A. Todd Jr., CO **A**1a **F**1 3 6 12 14 16 23 27 28 30 32 33 34 35 40 46 47 49 52	42	10	S		73	3036	36	42.9	15	426	15808	11635	435
GANADO—Apache County													
□ SAGE MEMORIAL HOSPITAL, Box 457, Zip 86505; tel. 602/755-3411; Jeffrey J. Hamblen, chief exec. off. **A**1a 9 10 **F**14 15 34 35 36 40 41 46 50 52	23	10	S		45	993	11	24.4	10	109	4802	2561	160
GLENDALE—Maricopa County													
★□ THUNDERBIRD SAMARITAN HOSPITAL AND HEALTH CENTER, 5555 W. Thunderbird Rd., Zip 85306; tel. 602/588-5555; Charles H. Welliver, chief exec. off. **A**1a 9 10 **F**1 3 6 10 12 14 15 16 20 23 24 26 33 34 35 36 37 40 43 44 46 47 50 53 54; **S**4045	23	10	S		210	9278	123	59.1	19	1353	41565	14406	677
U. S. AIR FORCE HOSPITAL LUKE, See Luke Air Force Base													
★ WEST VALLEY CAMELBACK HOSPITAL, 5625 W. Thunderbird Rd., Zip 85306; tel. 602/588-4700; Dale Rinard, chief exec. off. **A**9 10 **F**24 30 32 33 42 49; **S**9855	23	22	S		84	748	43	66.2	0	0	6466	1956	103
GLOBE—Gila County													
★□ GILA COUNTY GENERAL HOSPITAL, 1100 Monroe St., Zip 85501; tel. 602/425-5721; Elton Somers, adm. (Total facility includes 59 beds in nursing home-type unit) **A**1a 9 10 **F**1 3 10 12 14 16 19 23 30 35 40 45 46 47 50 52	13	10	S	TF	113	1060	71	62.8	8	159	—	—	194
				H	54	1038	13	—	8	159	—	—	—
HOLBROOK—Navajo County													
NORTHLAND MEDICAL CENTER, 500 E. Iowa, Zip 86025; tel. 602/524-3913; Bill Ward, adm. (Nonreporting) **A**9 10	23	10	S		23	—	—	—	—	—	—	—	—
KEAMS CANYON—Navajo County													
★□ U. S. PUBLIC HEALTH SERVICE, KEAMS CANYON INDIAN HOSPITAL AND CLINICS, Box 98, Zip 86034; tel. 602/738-2211; Terry Pourier, dir. **A**1a 10 **F**6 14 15 34 35 37 40 52	47	10	S		26	1080	10	38.5	6	159	—	—	118
KEARNY—Pinal County													
★□ KENNECOTT SAMARITAN HOSPITAL, 100 Tilbury Dr., P O Box 368, Zip 85237; tel. 602/363-5573; Glenda K. Hatfield, adm. **A**1a 9 10 **F**1 6 16 23 24 26 35 36 40 45 46 47; **S**4045	23	10	S		20	527	7	35.0	6	34	—	—	49
KINGMAN—Mohave County													
★□ KINGMAN REGIONAL HOSPITAL, 3269 Stockton Hill Rd., Zip 86401; tel. 602/757-2101; Donald J. Logue, pres. & chief exec. off. **A**1a 9 10 **F**1 2 6 10 12 14 15 16 23 27 30 34 35 40 41 45 46 47 52 53	16	10	S		83	4280	51	61.4	14	481	10931	5388	309
LAKE HAVASU CITY—Mohave County													
★□ HAVASU REGIONAL HOSPITAL, 101 Civic Center Lane, Zip 86403; tel. 602/855-8185; Dennis G. Zielinski, adm. **A**1a 9 10 **F**1 3 5 6 10 12 16 23 24 35 40 41 44 45 47 52 53; **S**4045	23	10	S		88	3029	39	44.3	6	412	11148	4507	209
LUKE AIR FORCE BASE—Maricopa County													
□ U. S. AIR FORCE HOSPITAL LUKE, Zip 85309; tel. 602/856-7501; Lt. Col. Charles Hare, adm. **A**1a **F**1 3 6 12 15 16 21 23 28 30 32 33 34 35 36 37 40 45 46 47 52	41	10	S		96	4545	51	60.7	14	556	19971	13819	507

★ American Hospital Association (AHA) membership
□ Joint Commission on Accreditation of Hospitals (JCAH) accreditation
+ American Osteopathic Hospital Association (AOHA) membership
○ American Osteopathic Association (AOA) accreditation
Δ Commission on Accreditation of Rehabilitation Facilities (CARF) accreditation
Control codes 61, 63, 64, 71, 72 and 73 indicate hospitals listed by AOHA, but not registered by AHA. For definition of numerical codes, see page A2

Hospital, Address, Telephone, Administrator, Approval and Facility Codes, Multihospital System Code	Classification Codes				Inpatient Data				Newborn Data		Expense (thousands of dollars)		
	Control	Service	Stay	Facilities	Beds	Admissions	Census	Occupancy (percent)	Bassinets	Births	Total	Payroll	Personnel
MESA—Maricopa County													
★□ DESERT SAMARITAN HOSPITAL AND HEALTH CENTER, 1400 S. Dobson Rd., Zip 85202; tel. 602/835-3000; George A. Zara, chief exec. off. **A**1a 2 9 10 **F**1 3 4 6 7 8 9 10 15 16 20 23 24 27 28 30 32 33 34 35 36 40 45 46 47 52 53 54; **S**4045	23	10	S		343	19639	280	81.6	44	4428	73596	25282	1126
□ ○ MESA GENERAL HOSPITAL MEDICAL CENTER, 515 N. Mesa Dr., Zip 85201; tel. 602/969-9111; Mark Werber, exec. dir. **A**1a 9 10 11 12 **F**1 3 6 10 12 14 15 16 23 24 26 34 35 36 40 41 42 46 52 54; **S**3025	33	10	S		115	4267	60	52.2	9	761	—	—	298
★□ MESA LUTHERAN HOSPITAL, 525 W. Brown Rd., Zip 85201; tel. 602/834-1211; Richard Probst, chief exec. off. **A**1a 2 9 10 **F**1 3 4 6 9 10 11 12 14 15 16 17 20 21 23 24 25 26 27 30 33 34 35 40 41 42 44 45 46 52 53; **S**2235	23	10	S		375	11739	203	54.1	22	1453	50824	23567	1192
★□ VALLEY LUTHERAN HOSPITAL, 6644 Baywood Ave., Zip 85206; tel. 602/981-2000; Charles R. Brackney, adm. **A**1a 10 **F**1 3 5 6 10 12 15 16 20 23 24 30 34 35 44 45 46 47 53; **S**2235	23	10	S		120	5244	90	75.0	0	0	25959	8811	496
MIAMI—Gila County													
□ MIAMI INSPIRATION HOSPITAL, Drawer M, Zip 85539; tel. 602/425-3261; Mary Anne Moreno, adm. **A**1a 9 10 **F**1 5 12 14 23 26 40	23	10	S		49	1097	16	32.7	11	89	6817	2034	97
MORENCI—Greenlee County													
□ MORENCI HOSPITAL, Zip 85540; tel. 602/865-4511; Eddie W. Arnold, adm.; Benviendo Dayao MD, med. dir. (Nonreporting) **A**1a 9 10	33	10	S		49	—	—	—	—	—	—	—	—
NOGALES—Santa Cruz County													
★□ HOLY CROSS HOSPITAL AND HEALTH CENTER, 1230 Target Range Rd., Zip 85621; tel. 602/287-2771; Walt Connolly, adm. (Total facility includes 31 beds in nursing home-type unit) **A**1a 9 10 **F**1 3 6 7 10 12 14 15 16 17 19 21 23 35 40 46 47 50 52; **S**5945	21	10	S	TF	80	1474	61	76.3	10	346	—	—	173
				H	49	1440	13	—	10	346	—	—	128
PAGE—Coconino County													
★□ PAGE HOSPITAL, N. Navajo Dr. & Vista Ave., Box 1447, Zip 86040; tel. 602/645-2424; Kevin Poorten, adm. **A**1a 9 10 **F**1 10 12 14 15 16 17 23 24 26 34 35 40 42 45 49 52; **S**4045	23	10	S		25	619	6	24.0	8	131	2242	1111	52
PARKER—La Paz County													
★ ○ + PARKER COMMUNITY HOSPITAL, Mohave Rd., Box 1149, Zip 85344; tel. 602/669-9201; William G. Coe, adm. **A**9 10 11 12 **F**1 6 10 12 14 16 23 30 35 45 47; **S**7675	23	10	S		39	1322	15	38.5	0	0	5193	1625	96
★□ U. S. PUBLIC HEALTH SERVICE INDIAN HOSPITAL, Zip 85344; tel. 602/669-2137; David Morgan, serv. unit dir. **A**1a 10 **F**15 34 35 37	47	10	S		20	544	9	45.0	0	0	2365	1619	64
PAYSON—Gila County													
★□ LEWIS R. PYLE MEMORIAL HOSPITAL, 807 S. Ponderosa, Zip 85541; tel. 602/474-3222; Lowell Horning, chief exec. off. **A**1a 9 10 **F**1 6 12 14 16 17 23 35 36 40 41 45 52	23	10	S		44	602	19	43.2	2	115	4120	1675	111
PHOENIX—Maricopa County													
□ ARIZONA STATE HOSPITAL, 2500 E. Van Buren St., Zip 85008; tel. 602/244-1331; Glenn Lippman MD, supt. **A**1b 10 **F**15 23 24 30 32 33 42 44 46	12	22	L		506	598	485	95.8	0	0	33157	16769	787
□ ○ COMMUNITY HOSPITAL MEDICAL CENTER, 6501 N. 19th Ave., Zip 85015; tel. 602/249-3434; Robert Cannon, exec. dir. **A**1a 9 10 11 **F**3 6 10 12 14 16 23 24 34 35 44 45 46; **S**3025	33	10	S		75	1590	22	29.3	0	0	—	—	144
★□ Δ GOOD SAMARITAN MEDICAL CENTER, 1111 E. McDowell Rd., Zip 85006; Mailing Address Box 2989, Zip 85062; tel. 602/239-2000; Richard B. Uhrich MD, chief exec. off. **A**1a 2 3 5 7 8 9 10 **F**1 2 3 4 5 6 7 8 9 10 11 12 13 14 15 16 17 20 23 24 25 26 27 28 30 32 33 34 35 36 37 38 40 41 42 43 44 45 46 47 49 50 53 54; **S**4045	23	10	S		640	28226	482	74.2	58	6292	176803	64961	3020
★□ HUMANA HOSPITAL -DESERT VALLEY, 3929 E. Bell Rd., Zip 85032; tel. 602/867-5600; Kenneth A. Levin, exec. dir. **A**1a 9 10 **F**1 3 6 7 8 9 10 11 12 14 15 16 23 24 26 30 32 33 34 35 36 37 39 40 43 44 46 47 50 53; **S**1235	33	10	S		117	6289	69	59.0	21	917	—	—	266
★□ HUMANA HOSPITAL -PHOENIX, 1947 E. Thomas Rd., Zip 85016; tel. 602/241-7600; Raymond A. Rouleau Jr., exec. dir. (Nonreporting) **A**1a 9 10; **S**1235	33	10	S		314	—	—	—	—	—	—	—	—
★□ JOHN C. LINCOLN HOSPITAL AND HEALTH CENTER, 9211 N. Second St., Zip 85020; tel. 602/943-2381; Robert J. Langlais, exec. vice-pres. & adm. **A**1a 9 10 **F**1 3 5 6 9 10 11 12 14 15 16 20 23 24 26 28 29 30 32 34 35 36 37 40 41 42 44 45 46 47 48 49 50 52 53 54	23	10	S		282	8310	133	47.2	23	1195	44836	17812	795
★□ MARICOPA MEDICAL CENTER, 2601 E. Roosevelt St., Zip 85008; Mailing Address P O Box 5099, Zip 85010; tel. 602/267-5011; Philip Hamilton, dir. **A**1a 2 3 5 8 9 10 **F**1 2 3 5 6 9 10 11 12 14 15 16 20 22 23 24 26 27 28 29 30 31 32 33 34 35 37 38 43 44 45 46 47 51 52 53 54	13	10	S		524	19990	299	57.1	69	5549	95609	46498	1671
★□ MARYVALE SAMARITAN HOSPITAL, 5102 W. Campbell Ave., Zip 85031; tel. 602/848-5000; Melvin E. Cunningham, vice-pres. & chief exec. off. **A**1a 3 9 10 **F**1 3 6 7 8 9 10 11 12 14 15 16 20 23 24 26 27 28 29 30 32 33 35 36 40 42 44 45 46 47 52 53; **S**4045	23	10	S		238	8772	140	58.8	20	1137	38825	14384	605
★□ PHOENIX BAPTIST HOSPITAL AND MEDICAL CENTER, 6025 N. 20th Ave., Zip 85015; tel. 602/249-0212; James E. Bagley, sr. exec. vice-pres. **A**1a 3 5 9 10 **F**1 3 4 6 9 10 12 14 15 16 23 24 26 27 30 32 33 34 35 36 40 44 45 46 47 52 53; **S**8810	23	10	S		241	9845	145	60.2	16	1200	43852	17430	756
★□ PHOENIX CAMELBACK HOSPITAL, 5055 N. 34th St., Zip 85018; tel. 602/955-6200; Beryl Janick, vice-pres. & chief exec. off. **A**1b 9 10 **F**24 30 32 33 42 46 47; **S**9855	23	22	L		89	754	70	78.7	0	0	7327	3785	171
★□ PHOENIX CHILDREN'S HOSPITAL, 1111 E. McDowell Rd., 1300 N. 12th St., Suite 404, Zip 85006; tel. 602/239-5920; Daniel T. Cloud MD, pres. & chief exec. off. **A**1a 3 9 **F**1 4 12 13 15 20 25 27 28 30 32 33 34 41 45 46 47 51 54	23	50	S		160	5561	120	79.5	0	0	43880	14252	541
★ ○ + PHOENIX GENERAL HOSPITAL, 1950 W. Indian School Rd., Box 21331, Zip 85036; tel. 602/279-4411; Harold R. Huebner, chief exec. off. **A**9 10 11 12 13 **F**1 3 4 6 7 10 11 12 14 15 16 20 23 24 25 26 33 34 35 36 40 44 46 47 48 49 52 54	23	10	S		239	8661	129	54.0	16	847	40683	17051	769
★□ PHOENIX INDIAN MEDICAL CENTER, 4212 N. 16th St., Zip 85016; tel. 602/263-1200; Rice C. Leach MD, serv. unit dir. **A**1a 3 10 **F**1 3 6 12 14 15 16 23 28 32 33 34 35 37 38 40 44 45 46 47 50 52	47	10	S		143	6221	114	75.5	12	882	22658	16370	615
★□ PHOENIX MEMORIAL HOSPITAL, 1201 S. Seventh Ave., Zip 85007; Mailing Address Box 21207, Zip 85036; tel. 602/258-5111; Joseph McKinley, exec. vice-pres. (Total facility includes 14 beds in nursing home-type unit) **A**1a 2 9 10 **F**1 3 5 6 7 8 9 10 11 12 14 15 16 19 20 23 24 26 28 30 32 33 34 35 36 37 38 40 41 42 43 44 45 46 47 49 50 52 53	23	10	S	TF	178	8227	110	64.0	12	1542	40037	13193	675
				H	164	8086	105	—	12	1542	39601	13036	662
★□ Δ ST. JOSEPH'S HOSPITAL AND MEDICAL CENTER, 350 W. Thomas Rd., Zip 85013; Mailing Address Box 2071, Zip 85001; tel. 602/285-3000; John J. Buckley Jr., pres. **A**1a 3 5 7 8 9 10 **F**1 2 3 4 5 6 7 8 9 10 11 12 13 14 15 16 17 20 23 24 25 26 27 28 29 30 32 33 34 35 36 37 38 39 40 41 42 43 44 45 46 47 51 52 53 54; **S**5205	21	10	S		656	28403	531	80.9	30	4606	153258	68039	3236
★□ ST. LUKE'S BEHAVIORAL HEALTH CENTER (Psychiatric, Chemical Dependency, Behavorial Medicine), 1800 E. Van Buren, Zip 85006; tel. 602/251-8100; Robert A. Rundio, pres. **A**1b 10 **F**3 15 24 27 28 29 30 32 33 34 42 44 46 47 48 49; **S**7675	23	49	S		150	2369	121	80.7	0	0	17095	6998	288

Hospital, Address, Telephone, Administrator, Approval and Facility Codes, Multihospital System Code	Classification Codes: Control	Service	Stay	Facilities	Inpatient Data: Beds	Admissions	Census	Occupancy (percent)	Newborn Data: Bassinets	Births	Expense (thousands of dollars): Total	Payroll	Personnel
★ American Hospital Association (AHA) membership □ Joint Commission on Accreditation of Hospitals (JCAH) accreditation + American Osteopathic Hospital Association (AOHA) membership ○ American Osteopathic Association (AOA) accreditation Δ Commission on Accreditation of Rehabilitation Facilities (CARF) accreditation Control codes 61, 63, 64, 71, 72 and 73 indicate hospitals listed by AOHA, but not registered by AHA. For definition of numerical codes, see page A2													
★□ ST. LUKE'S MEDICAL CENTER, 1800 E. Van Buren St., Zip 85006; tel. 602/251-8100; Brian C. Lockwood, pres. **A**1a 9 **F**1 3 4 6 9 10 11 12 13 14 15 16 19 20 23 24 26 34 35 42 43 44 45 46 47 48 50 53 54; **S**7675	23	10	S		241	7245	147	57.0	0	0	49587	19512	705
★□ VETERANS ADMINISTRATION MEDICAL CENTER, Seventh St. & Indian School Rd., Zip 85012; tel. 602/277-5551; Ray L. Bourne, dir. (Total facility includes 120 beds in nursing home-type unit) **A**1a b 2 3 5 **F**1 2 3 6 10 12 15 16 19 20 23 24 25 26 27 28 29 30 32 33 34 42 43 44 45 46 47 48 49 50 53	45	10	S	TF	590	12119	441	74.7	0	0	63759	35026	1307
				H	470	11991	325	—	0	0	59301	31888	1151
PRESCOTT—Yavapai County													
★□ VETERANS ADMINISTRATION MEDICAL CENTER, Zip 86313; tel. 602/445-4860; Virgil I. McIntyre, dir. (Total facility includes 214 beds in nursing home-type unit) **A**1a **F**1 3 6 10 12 14 15 16 19 23 24 25 26 28 30 32 33 34 42 44 46 48 49	45	10	S	TF	380	3521	287	71.0	0	0	18300	13100	472
				H	166	3176	100	—	0	0	—	—	464
★□ YAVAPAI REGIONAL MEDICAL CENTER, 1003 Willow Creek Rd., Zip 86301; tel. 602/445-2700; Michael R. Vitek, chief exec. off. **A**1a 9 10 **F**1 2 3 6 9 10 12 14 15 16 23 24 26 27 30 32 33 35 36 37 40 41 42 45 46 47 50 52 53	23	10	S		113	5392	69	61.1	12	621	15396	7730	426
SACATON—Pinal County													
★□ U. S. PUBLIC HEALTH SERVICE INDIAN HOSPITAL, Gila River Indian Reservation, Zip 85247; tel. 602/562-3321; Gary W. Thompson, serv. unit dir. (Nonreporting) **A**1a 10	47	10	S		20	—	—	—	—	—	—	—	—
SAFFORD—Graham County													
★□ MOUNT GRAHAM COMMUNITY HOSPITAL, 1600 20th Ave., P O Box 1019, Zip 85548; tel. 602/428-1171; Lloyd L. Jackson, adm. **A**1a 9 10 **F**1 6 14 23 34 35 40 45 46	23	10	S		42	1948	18	42.9	6	403	3723	1728	101
SAN CARLOS—Gila County													
★□ U. S. PUBLIC HEALTH SERVICE INDIAN HOSPITAL, P O Box 208, Zip 85550; tel. 602/475-2381; George W. Lefebvre, dir. **A**1a 10 **F**6 14 15 28 32 33 34 35 37 40 49 52	47	10	S		28	1015	11	33.3	4	144	3080	2238	112
SAN MANUEL—Pinal County													
SAN MANUEL DIVISION HOSPITAL, MAGMA COPPER COMPANY, McNab Pkwy. & County Rd., Box L, Zip 85631; tel. 602/385-3412; Sandra Payne, adm. (Nonreporting)	33	10	S		30	—	—	—	—	—	—	—	—
SCOTTSDALE—Maricopa County													
★□ SCOTTSDALE CAMELBACK HOSPITAL, 7575 E. Earll Dr., Zip 85251; tel. 602/941-7500; Frank Adame Jr., chief exec. off. **A**1b 9 10 **F**24 28 29 30 32 33 41 42 43 46 49 50; **S**9855	23	22	S		98	1175	72	77.4	0	0	7996	3807	181
□ ○ + SCOTTSDALE COMMUNITY HOSPITAL, 8435 E. McDowell Rd., Zip 85257; tel. 602/945-7600; Ross J. Monaco, pres. **A**1a 9 10 11 **F**1 3 6 10 12 14 15 16 20 23 35 45 46 53	73	10	S		37	710	9	24.3	0	0	4193	1462	77
★□ SCOTTSDALE MEMORIAL HOSPITAL, 7400 E. Osborn Rd., Zip 85251; tel. 602/994-9616; James L. Schamadan MD, pres. & chief exec. off. **A**1a 2 3 5 9 10 **F**1 3 4 5 6 9 10 11 12 13 14 15 16 17 20 23 24 26 28 30 32 33 34 35 36 37 40 41 44 49 52 53	23	10	S		336	14262	228	67.9	24	1498	—	—	—
SELLS—Pima County													
★□ U. S. PUBLIC HEALTH SERVICE INDIAN HOSPITAL, Box 548, Zip 85634; tel. 602/383-7251; Ernest J. Johnson MD, dir. **A**1a 10 **F**6 14 15 16 20 23 26 28 29 30 32 34 35 36 37 40 43 50 52	47	10	S		40	1370	27	67.5	4	90	—	—	137
SHOW LOW—Navajo County													
★□ NAVAPACHE HOSPITAL, 2200 Show Low Lake Rd., Zip 85901; tel. 602/537-4375; Jim Marovich, adm. **A**1a 9 10 **F**1 6 14 15 16 19 23 34 35 40 44 45 47; **S**0585	23	10	S		29	2257	19	59.4	8	376	5668	2179	114
SIERRA VISTA—Cochise County													
★□ SIERRA VISTA COMMUNITY HOSPITAL, 300 El Camino Real S.E., Zip 85635; tel. 602/458-4641; Dale A. Decker, adm. **A**1a 9 10 **F**3 6 10 12 14 16 23 24 26 34 35 41 44 45 46 47 53	23	10	S		55	3039	32	58.2	7	474	—	—	155
SPRINGERVILLE—Apache County													
★□ WHITE MOUNTAIN COMMUNITIES HOSPITAL, Box 471, Zip 85938; tel. 602/333-4368; Dennis Silva, exec. dir. **A**1a 9 10 **F**1 6 10 14 15 16 22 23 34 35 36 40 45 46 53; **S**4045	23	10	S		25	917	9	36.0	5	199	3626	1659	73
SUN CITY—Maricopa County													
★□ WALTER O. BOSWELL MEMORIAL HOSPITAL, 10401 Thunderbird Blvd., Box 1690, Zip 85351; tel. 602/977-7211; W. A. Turner, pres. & chief exec. off.; V. Grace Jones, exec. vice-pres. **A**1a 9 10 **F**1 2 3 4 6 9 10 11 12 15 16 20 23 24 25 26 32 33 35 37 41 44 45 46 47 50 53	23	10	S		355	12569	265	74.6	0	0	60272	24699	1191
TEMPE—Maricopa County													
★□ TEMPE ST. LUKE'S HOSPITAL, 1500 S. Mill Ave., Zip 85281; tel. 602/968-9411; Earl J. Motzer PhD, pres. & chief exec. off. **A**1a 9 10 **F**1 3 6 10 12 14 15 16 20 23 24 26 32 33 34 35 36 37 40 43 44 45 46 47 48 49 52 53; **S**7675	23	10	S		77	3212	39	50.6	9	325	12860	4479	208
TUBA CITY—Coconino County													
★□ U. S. PUBLIC HEALTH SERVICE INDIAN HOSPITAL, Zip 86045; tel. 602/283-6211; Phillip L. Smith MD, serv. unit dir. (Nonreporting) **A**1a 10	47	10	S		101	—	—	—	—	—	—	—	—
TUCSON—Pima County													
★□ EL DORADO HOSPITAL AND MEDICAL CENTER, 1400 N. Wilmot, Zip 85712; Mailing Address Box 13070, Zip 85732; tel. 602/886-6361; Roger L. Snapp, adm. **A**1a 9 10 **F**1 2 3 4 6 10 12 14 15 16 17 20 23 24 25 26 35 44 45 46 47; **S**1755	33	10	S		146	6719	102	69.9	0	0	—	—	541
★□ KINO COMMUNITY HOSPITAL, 2800 E. Ajo Way, Zip 85713; tel. 602/294-4471; Arthur A. Gonzalez, adm. **A**1a 3 5 9 10 **F**1 3 5 6 10 12 14 15 16 23 24 26 27 28 29 30 31 32 33 34 35 36 37 40 42 43 44 45 46 47 49 50 53; **S**1755	13	10	S		93	4274	62	66.7	17	949	26252	11507	616
★□ NORTHWEST HOSPITAL, 6200 N. La Cholla Blvd., Zip 85741; tel. 602/742-9000; R. John Harris, chief exec. off. (Nonreporting) **A**1a 9 10; **S**1755	33	10	S		63	—	—	—	—	—	—	—	—
★□ PALO VERDE HOSPITAL, 2695 N. Craycroft, Zip 85712; Mailing Address Box 40030, Zip 85717; tel. 602/795-4357; Robert J. Edison, adm. **A**1a 3 5 9 10 **F**15 24 28 29 30 32 33 34 35 41 42 43 46 50	23	22	S		62	1279	52	83.9	0	0	7378	3666	197
★□ Δ ST. JOSEPH'S HOSPITAL AND HEALTH CENTER (Formerly St. Joseph's Hospital and Health Care Center), 350 N. Wilmot Rd., Zip 85711; Mailing Address Box 12069, Zip 85732; tel. 602/296-3211; Sr. St. Joan Willert, pres. & chief exec. off. **A**1a 3 7 9 10 **F**1 2 3 4 6 10 12 13 14 15 16 20 23 24 25 26 30 33 34 35 36 37 41 43 44 45 46 47 48 49 52 53 54; **S**5945	21	10	S		305	12598	197	64.6	25	1943	47791	21593	1068
★□ Δ ST. MARY'S HOSPITAL AND HEALTH CENTER, 1601 W. St. Mary's Rd., Zip 85745; Mailing Address Box 5386, Zip 85703; tel. 602/622-5833; Sr. St. Joan Willert, pres. & chief exec. off. **A**1a 7 9 10 **F**1 2 3 4 6 10 12 13 14 15 16 20 21 22 23 24 25 26 27 28 29 30 32 33 34 35 37 41 43 44 45 46 47 52 53 54; **S**5945	21	10	S		332	13587	260	78.3	0	0	61446	27883	1516
★ ○ TUCSON GENERAL HOSPITAL (Includes Westcenter Alcoholic Detoxification Adult and Adolescent), 3838 N. Campbell Ave., Zip 85719; tel. 602/327-5431; Ken Seidel, exec. dir. (Nonreporting) **A**9 10 11 12 13; **S**3025	23	10	S		157	—	—	—	—	—	—	—	—
★□ TUCSON MEDICAL CENTER, 5301 E. Grant Rd., Box 42195, Zip 85733; tel. 602/327-5461; William Hansen, sr. vice-pres. fin **A**1a 2 3 5 8 9 10 **F**1 2 3 4 5 6 9 10 12 14 15 16 17 20 23 24 25 26 34 35 36 37 40 41 42 44 45 46 47 51 52 53 54	23	10	S		562	23746	360	64.1	56	5257	97340	45773	2037

Hospital, Address, Telephone, Administrator, Approval and Facility Codes, Multihospital System Code	Classification Codes			Facilities	Inpatient Data				Newborn Data		Expense (thousands of dollars)		Personnel
★ American Hospital Association (AHA) membership ☐ Joint Commission on Accreditation of Hospitals (JCAH) accreditation + American Osteopathic Hospital Association (AOHA) membership ○ American Osteopathic Association (AOA) accreditation Δ Commission on Accreditation of Rehabilitation Facilities (CARF) accreditation Control codes 61, 63, 64, 71, 72 and 73 indicate hospitals listed by AOHA, but not registered by AHA. For definition of numerical codes, see page A2	Control	Service	Stay	Facilities	Beds	Admissions	Census	Occupancy (percent)	Bassinets	Births	Total	Payroll	Personnel
☐ TUCSON PSYCHIATRIC INSTITUTE, 355 N. Wilmot Rd., Zip 85711; tel. 602/745-5100; Tommie Duncan, adm. (Nonreporting) **A**1a 9 10; **S**0825	33	22	S		38	—	—	—	—	—	—	—	—
U. S. AIR FORCE HOSPITAL, See Davis Monthan Air Force Base													
⊞ UNIVERSITY MEDICAL CENTER, 1501 N. Campbell Ave., Zip 85724; tel. 602/626-0111; Alethea O. Caldwell, chief exec. off. **A**1a 2 3 5 8 10 **F**1 2 3 4 5 6 7 8 9 10 11 12 13 14 15 16 20 23 24 30 32 34 35 39 40 45 46 47 51 52 53 54	23	10	S		241	10802	174	71.3	15	1777	73997	30863	1454
⊞ VETERANS ADMINISTRATION MEDICAL CENTER, Zip 85723; tel. 602/792-1450; Gaylord V. Morton, dir. (Total facility includes 41 beds in nursing home-type unit) **A**1a 3 5 8 **F**1 2 3 4 6 10 11 12 13 14 15 16 19 20 23 24 26 27 28 30 32 33 34 35 37 41 42 44 45 46 47 48 49 50 53 54	45	10	S	TF H	344 303	10214 10140	246 208	71.5 —	0 0	0 0	56575 53355	30740 29165	1078 1051
WHITERIVER—Navajo County													
⊞ U. S. PUBLIC HEALTH SERVICE INDIAN HOSPITAL, Box 860, Zip 85941; tel. 602/338-4911; Carla Alchesay-Nachu, dir. (Nonreporting) **A**1a	47	10	S		47	—	—	—	—	—	—	—	—
WICKENBURG—Maricopa County													
⊞ COMMUNITY HOSPITAL, 111 Rose Lane, Box 1388, Zip 85358; tel. 602/684-5421; Glenn D. Jones, adm. (Total facility includes 40 beds in nursing home-type unit) **A**1a 9 10 **F**1 3 6 12 14 15 16 19 23 35 40 42 44 45 46 47 50 52	23	10	S	TF H	74 34	735 667	46 9	62.2 —	4 4	53 53	3000 2283	1617 1180	93 64
WILLCOX—Cochise County													
☐ NORTHERN COCHISE COMMUNITY HOSPITAL, 901 W. Rex Allen Dr., Zip 85643; tel. 602/384-3541; Joseph Carpenter, adm. (Nonreporting) **A**1a 9 10	16	10	S		48	—	—	—	—	—	—	—	—
WILLIAMS AIR FORCE BASE—Maricopa County													
U. S. AIR FORCE HOSPITAL, Zip 85240; tel. 602/988-6615; Maj. Richard C. Storey Jr., adm.; Capt. Donna D. Hume, pat aff off. **F**1 6 14 15 23 33 34 35 40 46 47	41	10	S		25	1879	17	65.4	10	335	—	—	277
WINSLOW—Navajo County													
★ WINSLOW MEMORIAL HOSPITAL, 1501 Williamson Ave., Zip 86047; tel. 602/289-4691; Kent M. Aland, adm. **A**9 10 **F**1 6 14 16 23 35 37 40 45 46 47 50 52	23	10	S		42	1094	15	35.7	6	227	2331	1128	67
YOUNGTOWN—Maricopa County													
⊞ VALLEY VIEW COMMUNITY HOSPITAL, 12207 N. 113th Ave., Zip 85363; tel. 602/933-0155; Larry A. Mullins, exec. vice-pres. (Nonreporting) **A**1a 9 10; **S**8810	23	10	S		104	—	—	—	—	—	—	—	—
YUMA—Yuma County													
U. S. PUBLIC HEALTH SERVICE INDIAN HOSPITAL, See Winterhaven, Calif.													
⊞ YUMA REGIONAL MEDICAL CENTER, 2400 Ave. A, Zip 85364; tel. 602/344-2000; Ronald D. Morton, chief exec. off. **A**1a 9 10 **F**1 3 6 9 10 11 12 15 16 23 27 30 32 33 34 35 36 40 45 46 47 52 53	23	10	S		235	11876	161	68.5	16	1922	35447	16234	796

Hospital, Address, Telephone, Administrator, Approval and Facility Codes, Multihospital System Code	Classification Codes				Inpatient Data				Newborn Data		Expense (thousands of dollars)		
★ American Hospital Association (AHA) membership □ Joint Commission on Accreditation of Hospitals (JCAH) accreditation + American Osteopathic Hospital Association (AOHA) membership ○ American Osteopathic Association (AOA) accreditation Δ Commission on Accreditation of Rehabilitation Facilities (CARF) accreditation Control codes 61, 63, 64, 71, 72 and 73 indicate hospitals listed by AOHA, but not registered by AHA. For definition of numerical codes, see page A2	Control	Service	Stay	Facilities	Beds	Admissions	Census	Occupancy (percent)	Bassinets	Births	Total	Payroll	Personnel

Arkansas

Hospital	Control	Service	Stay	Facilities	Beds	Admissions	Census	Occupancy (percent)	Bassinets	Births	Total	Payroll	Personnel
ARKADELPHIA—Clark County													
⊞ TWIN RIVERS MEDICAL CENTER, 3050 Twin Rivers Dr., Box 98, Zip 71923; tel. 501/246-9801; Dan Gathright, sr. vice-pres. **A**1a 9 10 **F**1 3 5 6 10 14 16 23 35 36 40 45 46; **S**0355	23	10	S		57	2166	24	42.1	8	229	—	—	141
ASHDOWN—Little River County													
LITTLE RIVER MEMORIAL HOSPITAL, Fifth & Locke Sts., Box 577, Zip 71822; tel. 501/898-5011; Shirley Eaton, adm. **A**9 10 **F**1 3 16 23 34 45	13	10	S		42	975	15	35.7	0	0	2119	763	79
BATESVILLE—Independence County													
GRAY'S HOSPITAL, 477 E. Main St., Box 2437, Zip 72501; tel. 501/793-2321; James R. Crews, adm. (Nonreporting) **A**9 10	33	10	S		51	—	—	—	—	—	—	—	—
⊞ WHITE RIVER MEDICAL CENTER, 1710 Harrison St., Zip 72501; Mailing Address P O Box 2197, Zip 72503; tel. 501/793-1200; Steven B. Lampkin, adm. **A**1a 9 10 **F**1 3 6 10 12 14 15 16 23 24 30 32 34 36 40 45 53 54; **S**0355	23	10	S		97	4791	72	74.2	10	441	11772	4190	309
BENTON—Saline County													
⊞ SALINE MEMORIAL HOSPITAL, N. East at McNeil Sts., Zip 72015; tel. 501/776-0611; Lonnie Busby, adm. (Total facility includes 14 beds in nursing home-type unit) **A**1a 9 10 **F**1 3 6 10 11 15 16 19 23 34 35 36 40 41 45 47 52 53; **S**2495	13	10	S	TF	113	4055	59	52.2	10	276	11635	6023	314
				H	99	3954	57	—	10	276	11565	5963	307
BENTONVILLE—Benton County													
⊞ BATES MEMORIAL HOSPITAL, 602 N. Walton Blvd., Zip 72712; tel. 501/273-2481; Wayne E. Lawson, adm. **A**1a 9 10 **F**1 3 6 12 14 15 16 23 34 35 37 44 45 46 53	23	10	S		40	1624	22	55.0	6	6	4670	2030	122
BERRYVILLE—Carroll County													
CARROLL GENERAL HOSPITAL, 214 Carter St., Zip 72616; tel. 501/423-6951; Paul Z. Strahl, adm. **A**9 10 **F**1 3 5 6 15 16 23 34 35 40 45 47	13	10	S		50	1631	21	42.0	6	197	3587	1873	—
BLYTHEVILLE—Mississippi County													
⊞ MISSISSIPPI COUNTY HOSPITALS-BLYTHEVILLE (Formerly Chickasawba Hospital), Division & Highland Sts., Box 108, Zip 72315; tel. 501/762-3300; William Peaks, adm. **A**1a 9 10 **F**1 3 6 10 12 14 15 16 19 23 26 33 35 40 43 44 46 53; **S**2475	13	10	S		168	4788	70	41.7	10	759	11412	4653	301
U. S. AIR FORCE HOSPITAL, See Blytheville Air Force Base													
BLYTHEVILLE AIR FORCE BASE—Mississippi County													
U. S. AIR FORCE HOSPITAL, Zip 72317; tel. 501/762-7351; Maj. John F. McMahon MSC USAF, adm. (Nonreporting)	41	10	S		37	—	—	—	—	—	—	—	—
BOONEVILLE—Logan County													
★ BOONEVILLE CITY HOSPITAL, 1200 W. Main, Rte. 4, Box 19, Zip 72927; tel. 501/675-2800; Robert E. Baumann, adm. **A**9 10 **F**1 3 6 15 16 35 40 45	14	10	S		43	972	15	34.9	6	60	1803	879	69
BRINKLEY—Monroe County													
DELTA MEDICAL CENTER (Includes St. Joseph Home), 505 S. New York St., Zip 72021; tel. 501/734-4141; Alan C. Spears, adm. (Nonreporting) **A**9 10; **S**9795	33	10	S		40	—	—	—	—	—	—	—	—
BULL SHOALS—Marion County													
BULL SHOALS COMMUNITY HOSPITAL AND CLINIC, Box 356, Zip 72619; tel. 501/445-4292; Abija Hughes, adm. (Nonreporting) **A**9 10	33	10	S		48	—	—	—	—	—	—	—	—
CALICO ROCK—Izard County													
MEDICAL CENTER OF CALICO ROCK, Box 438, Zip 72519; tel. 501/297-3726; John L. Grasse, chief exec. off. **A**9 10 **F**6 14 23 34 35 37 41 45	33	10	S		26	855	12	46.2	3	93	1462	570	48
CAMDEN—Ouachita County													
⊞ OUACHITA HOSPITAL, 638 California St., Box 797, Zip 71701; tel. 501/836-1000; C. C. McAllister, adm. (Total facility includes 10 beds in nursing home-type unit) **A**1a 9 10 **F**1 3 6 10 12 14 15 16 19 21 23 33 35 36 40 41 44 45 46 47 48 53; **S**1755	13	10	S	TF	150	4360	58	38.7	17	348	8106	3886	290
				H	140	4269	55	—	17	348	—	—	—
CLARKSVILLE—Johnson County													
★ JOHNSON COUNTY REGIONAL HOSPITAL, 1100 Poplar St., P O Box 738, Zip 72830; tel. 501/754-2060; Jerry Campbell, exec. dir. **A**9 10 **F**1 3 5 6 7 10 14 15 16 23 26 33 34 35 36 41 43 45 46 47 49; **S**2495	13	10	S		68	2133	30	44.1	10	210	4958	2396	169
CLINTON—Van Buren County													
VAN BUREN COUNTY MEMORIAL HOSPITAL, Rte. 1, Box 206, Zip 72031; tel. 501/745-2401; Greg R. McNeil, adm. (Nonreporting) **A**9 10	23	10	S		102	—	—	—	—	—	—	—	—
CONWAY—Faulkner County													
⊞ CONWAY REGIONAL HOSPITAL (Formerly Conway Memorial Hospital), College & Western Aves., Zip 72032; tel. 501/329-3831; Bill Langford, exec. dir. **A**1a 9 10 **F**1 3 6 7 11 15 16 23 24 33 35 36 40 41 44 46 50 53	23	10	S		114	3268	47	41.2	12	450	9483	4270	272
CORNING—Clay County													
⊞ CORNING COMMUNITY HOSPITAL, Hospital Dr., Box 158, Zip 72422; tel. 501/857-6961; Donald F. Henry, adm. **A**1a 9 10 **F**1 6 14 16 23 33 34 35 41 45 46 47 48 53; **S**0335	33	10	S		40	667	15	37.5	6	4	2661	954	79
CROSSETT—Ashley County													
⊞ ASHLEY MEMORIAL HOSPITAL, 400 Main St., Box 400, Zip 71635; tel. 501/364-4111; Steve Reeder, adm. **A**1a 9 10 **F**1 3 6 14 16 19 23 35 45 50; **S**1755	23	10	S		61	1523	20	32.8	6	93	3101	1394	94
DANVILLE—Yell County													
★ YELL COUNTY HOSPITAL, Hwy. 10 at Detroit, P O Box 580, Zip 72833; tel. 501/495-2241; J. G. Jirinec, adm. **A**9 10 **F**1 6 10 16 23 35 40 45	13	10	S		49	897	14	28.6	0	0	1788	891	80
DARDANELLE—Yell County													
DARDANELLE HOSPITAL, 200 N. Third St., Box T, Zip 72834; tel. 501/229-4677; Mike Oliver, adm. **A**9 10 **F**1 3 6 16 23 35 36 44 45	13	10	S		44	1191	13	29.5	6	82	2020	884	70
DE QUEEN—Sevier County													
★ COMMUNITY HOSPITAL OF DE QUEEN, Hwy. 70 W., Box 346, Zip 71832; tel. 501/584-4111; Jim Pearce, adm. **A**9 10 **F**1 3 6 10 12 14 16 23 35 36 40 41 43 44 45; **S**1755	33	10	S		122	2088	31	25.4	12	223	5521	2560	164
DE WITT—Arkansas County													
DEWITT CITY HOSPITAL, Hwy. 1 & Madison St., Box 32, Zip 72042; tel. 501/946-3571; Clayton Eddleman, adm. **A**9 10 **F**1 6 14 16 23 34 35 45	14	10	S		34	893	12	35.3	7	53	1999	809	63
DERMOTT—Chicot County													
⊞ DERMOTT-CHICOT MEMORIAL HOSPITAL, 700 W. Gaines St., Zip 71638; tel. 501/538-5242; Charles S. Covington, adm. (Nonreporting) **A**1a 9 10	13	10	S		29	—	—	—	—	—	—	—	—

★ American Hospital Association (AHA) membership
□ Joint Commission on Accreditation of Hospitals (JCAH) accreditation
+ American Osteopathic Hospital Association (AOHA) membership
○ American Osteopathic Association (AOA) accreditation
Δ Commission on Accreditation of Rehabilitation Facilities (CARF) accreditation
Control codes 61, 63, 64, 71, 72 and 73 indicate hospitals listed by AOHA, but not registered by AHA.
For definition of numerical codes, see page A2

Hospital, Address, Telephone, Administrator, Approval and Facility Codes, Multihospital System Code	Classification Codes				Inpatient Data				Newborn Data		Expense (thousands of dollars)		
	Control	Service	Stay	Facilities	Beds	Admissions	Census	Occupancy (percent)	Bassinets	Births	Total	Payroll	Personnel
DUMAS—Desha County													
★□ DELTA MEMORIAL HOSPITAL, 300 E. Pickens St., Box 126, Zip 71639; tel. 501/382-4303; S. Howard Johnson, adm. **A**1a 9 10 **F**1 3 6 10 14 15 16 23 34 35 37 45 47	23	10	S		50	1663	21	42.0	10	156	2525	1156	77
EL DORADO—Union County													
★□ UNION MEDICAL CENTER, 700 W. Grove St., Zip 71730; tel. 501/864-3200; Cary M. Dougherty Jr., adm. **A**1a 3 5 9 10 **F**1 3 5 6 9 11 12 14 15 16 23 28 29 30 32 33 34 35 40 41 44 45 46 47 52	13	10	S		106	5204	72	67.9	18	740	12429	5318	313
★□ WARNER BROWN HOSPITAL, 460 W. Oak St., Zip 71730; tel. 501/863-2000; Phillip K. Gilmore, pres. & adm. **A**1a 3 5 9 10 **F**1 2 3 5 6 9 10 11 12 14 15 16 20 23 24 26 27 28 29 30 31 32 33 34 35 40 41 42 44 45 50 52	23	10	S		169	4568	74	43.8	6	322	14254	6426	313
EUREKA SPRINGS—Carroll County													
EUREKA SPRINGS HOSPITAL, 24 Norris St., Zip 72632; tel. 501/253-9727; Anita Wise, adm. (Nonreporting) **A**9 10	33	10	S		22	—	—	—	—	—	—	—	—
FAYETTEVILLE—Washington County													
★□ CHARTER VISTA HOSPITAL, 4253 Crossover Rd., Zip 72702; tel. 501/521-5731; Dan Johnson, group adm. (Nonreporting) **A**1a 9 10; **S**0695	33	22	L		65	—	—	—	—	—	—	—	—
FAYETTEVILLE CITY HOSPITAL, 221 S. School St., Zip 72701; Mailing Address Box 1743, Zip 72702; tel. 501/442-5100; Alan Prather, adm. (Total facility includes 103 beds in nursing home-type unit) **A**9 10 **F**1 6 14 15 16 19 23 24 26 34 37 41 45 46 50	23	10	S	TF	138	754	98	71.0	0	0	4356	2211	209
				H	35	710	13	—	0	0	—	—	123
★□ VETERANS ADMINISTRATION MEDICAL CENTER, 1100 N. College Ave., Zip 72701; tel. 501/443-4301; Dan G. Kadrovach, dir. **A**1a **F**1 3 6 12 14 15 16 23 26 30 32 33 34 44 46 49	45	10	S		187	4589	113	60.4	0	0	18784	11891	456
★□ WASHINGTON REGIONAL MEDICAL CENTER, 1125 N. College Ave., Zip 72701; tel. 501/442-1000; Earl W. Eddins, adm. **A**1a 2 3 5 9 10 **F**1 2 3 5 6 7 9 10 11 12 14 15 16 17 20 21 23 24 34 35 36 40 42 43 44 45 46 47 51 52 53 54	13	10	S		172	9057	123	71.5	24	1444	25270	11493	655
FORDYCE—Dallas County													
DALLAS COUNTY HOSPITAL, 201 Clifton St., Zip 71742; tel. 501/352-3155; Curt Moberg, exec. dir. (Nonreporting) **A**9 10; **S**5895	13	10	S		79	—	—	—	—	—	—	—	—
FORREST CITY—St. Francis County													
★□ BAPTIST MEMORIAL HOSPITAL-FORREST CITY, I-40 at State Rd. 284, Box 667, Zip 72335; tel. 501/633-2020; Thomas F. Kennedy, adm. **A**1a 9 10 **F**1 3 6 10 12 14 15 16 23 26 34 35 36 40 41 45 47 53; **S**1625	21	10	S		112	3758	47	42.0	12	526	7341	3380	184
FORT SMITH—Sebastian County													
□ HARBOR VIEW MERCY HOSPITAL, 10301 Mayo Rd., Zip 72902; tel. 501/484-5550; Sr. Judith Marie Keith, chief exec. off. **A**1a 9 10 **F**15 23 24 26 28 32 33 42 44 45 46 49 50	21	22	S		80	1013	46	68.7	0	0	3009	1403	101
★□ SPARKS REGIONAL MEDICAL CENTER, 1311 S. I St., Zip 72901; tel. 501/441-4000; Charles R. Shuffield, pres. **A**1a 2 3 5 9 10 **F**1 2 3 4 6 7 9 10 12 14 15 16 20 21 23 25 27 30 33 34 35 36 37 40 41 45 46 48 50 51 52 53 54	23	10	S		466	17439	314	67.4	40	1630	52199	25641	1338
★□ ST. EDWARD MERCY MEDICAL CENTER, 7301 Rogers Ave., Zip 72903; Mailing Address P O Box 2405, Zip 72902; tel. 501/484-6000; Sr. Judith Marie Keith, chief exec. off. **A**1a 2 3 5 9 10 **F**1 3 5 6 10 11 12 14 15 16 20 23 24 25 30 34 35 36 40 41 44 45 46 47 52 53 54; **S**5185	21	10	S		343	14334	229	66.8	25	1499	30128	14259	760
GRAVETTE—Benton County													
GRAVETTE MEDICAL CENTER HOSPITAL, P O Box 470, Zip 72736; tel. 501/787-5291; John R. Rhine MD, adm. **A**9 10 **F**1 3 6 10 16 23 34 35 37 40 45	23	10	S		99	2102	32	32.3	6	281	4129	1949	155
GURDON—Clark County													
GURDON MUNICIPAL HOSPITAL, Third & Walnut Sts., Zip 71743; tel. 501/353-4401; Jeffrey O'Brien, adm. (Nonreporting) **A**9 10; **S**9795	23	10	S		28	—	—	—	—	—	—	—	—
HARDY—Sharp County													
BAPTIST MEMORIAL HOSPITAL-EASTERN OZARKS, S. Allegheny Dr., Zip 72543; tel. 501/257-4101; Ted Spurlock, adm. **A**9 **F**1 3 14 16 34 35 41 45; **S**1625	21	10	S		25	651	10	40.0	0	0	2468	790	57
HARRISON—Boone County													
★ NORTH ARKANSAS MEDICAL CENTER (Formerly Boone County Hospital), 620 N. Willow St., Zip 72601; tel. 501/365-2000; Franklin E. Wise, adm. **A**9 10 **F**1 2 3 6 7 8 9 10 12 14 15 16 19 23 30 35 40 41 44 45 46 52 53	13	10	S		174	5474	85	48.9	16	491	12078	5421	443
HEBER SPRINGS—Cleburne County													
□ CLEBURNE COUNTY HOSPITAL, Hwy. 110 W., P O Box 510, Zip 72543; tel. 501/362-3121; George S. Fray, adm. **A**1a 9 10 **F**1 3 6 14 15 16 17 23 35 40 45 53	13	10	S		49	1057	12	24.5	5	60	—	—	71
HELENA—Phillips County													
★□ HELENA HOSPITAL, Newman Dr., Box 788, Zip 72342; tel. 501/338-6411; Raymond L. Board, adm. **A**1a 9 10 **F**1 3 5 6 10 12 14 15 16 17 23 30 32 34 35 36 40 45 46 52; **S**1755	14	10	S		155	4275	56	36.1	18	644	10667	4941	300
HOPE—Hempstead County													
★□ AMI MEDICAL PARK HOSPITAL (Formerly Medical Park Hospital), 2001 S. Main St., Box 460, Zip 71801; tel. 501/777-2323; Donald G. Carney, exec. dir. (Nonreporting) **A**1a 9 10; **S**0125	33	10	S		75	—	—	—	—	—	—	—	—
HOT SPRINGS—Garland County													
★□ AMI NATIONAL PARK MEDICAL CENTER (Formerly National Park Medical Center), 3110 Malvern Rd., Box 1137, Zip 71901; tel. 501/321-1000; Warner N. Kass, exec. dir. (Total facility includes 10 beds in nursing home-type unit) **A**1a 9 10 **F**1 3 5 6 10 12 14 15 16 19 20 23 29 34 35 36 40 45 46 52 53 54; **S**0125	33	10	S	TF	155	6339	88	56.8	16	1008	19179	5165	340
				H	145	6261	85	—	16	1008	—	—	—
HOT SPRINGS NATIONAL PARK—Garland County													
LEO N. LEVI NATIONAL ARTHRITIS HOSPITAL, See Levi Arthritis Hospital													
★□ LEVI ARTHRITIS HOSPITAL (Formerly Leo N. Levi National Arthritis Hospital), 300 Prospect Ave., Box 850, Zip 71901; tel. 501/624-1281; Rosalie Reynolds, adm. **A**1a 9 10 **F**15 23 24 25 26 34 45 46	23	49	S		62	741	26	41.9	0	0	3067	1756	141
★□ ST. JOSEPH'S REGIONAL HEALTH CENTER, 100 Whittington Ave., Zip 71901; tel. 501/624-5451; Sr. Mary Werner, pres. **A**1a 9 10 **F**1 2 3 4 6 7 8 9 10 11 12 14 15 16 17 20 23 24 25 28 30 32 34 35 41 44 45 46 53 54; **S**5185	21	10	S		267	9342	174	65.2	0	0	24993	12491	752
HUNTSVILLE—Madison County													
HUNTSVILLE MEMORIAL HOSPITAL (Includes Meadowview Lodge), Hwy. 68 W., Drawer E, Zip 72740; tel. 501/738-2125; George W. Johnson, adm. (Nonreporting) **A**9 10	23	10	S		34	—	—	—	—	—	—	—	—
JACKSONVILLE—Pulaski County													
★□ REBSAMEN REGIONAL MEDICAL CENTER, 1400 Braden St., Box 159, Zip 72076; tel. 501/982-9515; Robert L. Green, adm. **A**1a 9 10 **F**1 3 6 10 11 12 15 16 23 33 35 36 40 45 46 53 54; **S**1755	14	10	S		93	3731	45	48.4	12	388	9301	3617	227
U. S. AIR FORCE HOSPITAL, See Little Rock Air Force Base													
JONESBORO—Craighead County													
★□ METHODIST HOSPITAL OF JONESBORO, 3024 Stadium Blvd., Zip 72401; tel. 501/972-7000; Philip H. Walkley Jr., adm. **A**1a 5 9 10 **F**1 3 6 10 12 14 15 16 23 26 30 32 33 34 35 36 37 41 44 45 46 50 53; **S**9345	21	10	S		98	4122	68	69.4	8	390	10963	3463	225

Hospital, Address, Telephone, Administrator, Approval and Facility Codes, Multihospital System Code	Classification Codes				Inpatient Data				Newborn Data		Expense (thousands of dollars)		
★ American Hospital Association (AHA) membership ☐ Joint Commission on Accreditation of Hospitals (JCAH) accreditation + American Osteopathic Hospital Association (AOHA) membership ○ American Osteopathic Association (AOA) accreditation Δ Commission on Accreditation of Rehabilitation Facilities (CARF) accreditation Control codes 61, 63, 64, 71, 72 and 73 indicate hospitals listed by AOHA, but not registered by AHA. For definition of numerical codes, see page A2	Control	Service	Stay	Facilities	Beds	Admissions	Census	Occupancy (percent)	Bassinets	Births	Total	Payroll	Personnel
☐ ST. BERNARD'S REGIONAL MEDICAL CENTER, 224 E. Matthews St., Zip 72401; tel. 501/972-4284; Ben E. Owens, adm. **A**1a 3 5 9 10 **F**1 3 4 6 7 8 10 11 12 14 15 16 20 23 24 26 32 33 35 36 40 41 44 45 46 47 52 53 54	21	10	S		281	12691	222	79.0	24	1025	30436	11935	729
LAKE VILLAGE—Chicot County													
☐★ CHICOT MEMORIAL HOSPITAL, Hwys. 65 & 82, Box 512, Zip 71653; tel. 501/265-5351; Daniel R. Smigelski, adm. **A**1a 9 10 **F**1 3 6 14 15 16 17 23 34 35 45 46 47 53; **S**1755	13	10	S		62	2524	31	50.0	7	214	4519	2096	127
LEWISVILLE—Lafayette County													
★ LAFAYETTE COUNTY MEMORIAL HOSPITAL, 1105 Chestnut St., Zip 71845; tel. 501/921-5751; Kaye Cheatham, actg. adm. **A**9 10 **F**1 3 16 23 35 45	13	10	S		38	785	10	26.3	0	0	1252	701	44
LITTLE ROCK—Pulaski County													
☐★ ARKANSAS CHILDREN'S HOSPITAL, 800 Marshall St., Zip 72202; tel. 501/370-1100; Randall L. O'Donnell PhD, chief exec. off. **A**1a 3 5 8 9 10 **F**1 2 4 6 10 12 13 14 15 16 20 22 23 24 26 27 32 33 34 35 38 44 45 46 47 51 53 54	23	50	S		188	6973	139	73.9	0	0	47709	23348	1176
☐★ ARKANSAS REHABILITATION INSTITUTE, 9601 Interstate 630, Exit 7, Zip 72205; tel. 501/223-7578; Robin H. Hagaman, sr. vice-pres. & adm. **A**1a 3 9 10 **F**15 16 23 24 26 28 32 33 34 42 43 44 45 46 48; **S**0355	23	46	S		110	1395	82	74.5	0	0	—	—	259
☐ ARKANSAS STATE HOSPITAL, 4313 W. Markham St., Zip 72205; tel. 501/664-4500; Richard E. Maxwell, dir. (Nonreporting) **A**1a 3 5 9	12	22	S		386	—	—	—	—	—	—	—	—
☐★ BAPTIST MEDICAL CENTER, 9601 Interstate 630, Exit 7, Zip 72205; tel. 501/227-2000; Dale Collins, sr. vice-pres. **A**1a 3 5 6 10 **F**1 2 3 4 5 6 9 10 11 12 14 15 16 17 20 21 23 24 27 30 33 35 36 37 40 41 44 45 46 51 52 53 54; **S**0355	23	10	S		617	24226	478	77.5	30	2375	95366	43258	2290
☐★ DOCTORS HOSPITAL, 6101 W. Capitol, Zip 72205; tel. 501/661-4000; W. Perry Kinder, adm. **A**1a 9 10 **F**1 2 3 6 10 12 14 15 16 20 23 35 36 37 40 45 46 47 54; **S**1755	33	10	S		310	8671	132	43.3	51	1958	—	—	575
☐★ JOHN L. MCCLELLAN MEMORIAL VETERANS HOSPITAL (Includes Little Rock Division, 4300 W. Seventh St., Zip 72205; tel. 501/661-1202; North Little Rock Division, North Little Rock, Zip 72114; tel. 501/661-1202), Vincent J. Parrish, dir. (Total facility includes 200 beds in nursing home-type unit) **A**1a b 2 3 5 8 **F**1 3 4 5 6 9 10 11 12 15 16 19 20 21 23 24 26 27 28 29 30 31 32 33 34 35 41 42 43 44 45 46 47 48 49 50 53 54	45	10	S	TF	1505	21422	1117	74.2	0	0	127351	73293	2923
				H	1305	21305	928	—	0	0	125613	72124	2699
☐★ RIVERVIEW HOSPITAL, 1310 Cantrell Rd., Zip 72201; tel. 501/375-5381; Lavon Henley, adm. (Nonreporting) **A**1a 10; **S**8985	23	10	S		60	—	—	—	—	—	—	—	—
☐★ ST. VINCENT INFIRMARY, Two St. Vincent Circle, Zip 72205; tel. 501/660-3000; Sr. Margaret Vincent Blandford, chief exec. off.; A. Jack Reynolds, pres. **A**1a 3 5 9 10 **F**1 2 3 4 6 9 10 12 14 15 16 20 23 24 26 27 30 34 35 39 45 46 47 51 52 53 54; **S**3045	21	10	S		591	22229	467	81.5	0	0	99696	43746	2198
☐★ UNIVERSITY HOSPITAL OF ARKANSAS (Formerly University Hospital and Ambulatory Care Center), 4301 W. Markham St., Zip 72205; tel. 501/661-5000; Richard Pierson, exec. dir. **A**1a 8 9 10 **F**1 2 3 4 5 6 9 10 11 12 13 14 15 16 17 20 23 24 26 27 28 29 30 32 33 34 35 36 37 38 40 44 45 46 50 51 53 54	12	10	S		327	13959	241	73.7	55	3512	86214	—	1456
LITTLE ROCK AIR FORCE BASE—Pulaski County													
☐ U. S. AIR FORCE HOSPITAL, Zip 72099; tel. 501/988-7411; Col. David J. O'Mara MC, cmdr. **A**1a **F**1 6 15 23 34 35 40 46 47 49	41	10	S		56	1831	16	28.6	16	376	—	—	396
MAGNOLIA—Columbia County													
☐★ MAGNOLIA HOSPITAL, 101 Hospital Dr., Box 629, Zip 71753; tel. 501/235-3000; William D. Hedden, adm. **A**1a 9 10 **F**1 3 6 10 15 16 19 34 35 36 40 44 45 46 53	14	10	S		86	2462	36	41.9	10	265	5362	2840	201
MALVERN—Hot Spring County													
★ HOT SPRING COUNTY MEMORIAL HOSPITAL, 1001 Schneider Dr., Zip 72104; tel. 501/337-4911; Michael E. Henze, adm. **A**9 10 **F**1 3 6 10 12 14 15 16 19 23 35 40 44 45	13	10	S		77	2564	35	45.5	10	140	5297	2433	155
MARIANNA—Lee County													
★ LEE MEMORIAL HOSPITAL, 528 W. Chestnut St., Drawer 567, Zip 72360; tel. 501/295-2524; Carl Brown, adm. (Nonreporting) **A**9; **S**1755	13	10	S		25	—	—	—	—	—	—	—	—
MCCRORY—Woodruff County													
WOODRUFF COUNTY HOSPITAL, Box 407, Zip 72101; tel. 501/731-2543; C. L. Cross, adm. (Nonreporting) **A**9 10	13	10	S		139	—	—	—	—	—	—	—	—
MCGEHEE—Desha County													
☐★ MCGEHEE-DESHA COUNTY HOSPITAL, Box 351, Zip 71654; tel. 501/222-5600; Talmadge Robertson, adm. **A**1a 9 10 **F**1 6 10 14 15 16 23 26 35 41 45 46	13	10	S		34	918	14	41.2	6	34	1935	1096	86
MENA—Polk County													
☐★ WILHELMINA MEDICAL CENTER, N. Morrow St., Zip 71953; tel. 501/394-6100; Michael Lee, adm. **A**1a 9 10 **F**1 3 6 16 23 34 35 36 45; **S**1755	23	10	S		57	1010	11	19.3	8	102	3107	1216	102
MONTICELLO—Drew County													
☐ DREW MEMORIAL HOSPITAL, 778 Scogin Dr., Box 538, Zip 71655; tel. 501/367-2411; James M. Gathings, adm. (Nonreporting) **A**1a 9 10	13	10	S		50	—	—	—	—	—	—	—	—
MORRILTON—Conway County													
☐★ CONWAY COUNTY HOSPITAL, 4 Hospital Dr., Box 31, Zip 72110; tel. 501/354-3512; Johnson L. Smith, adm. **A**1a 9 10 **F**1 3 6 10 15 16 19 23 34 35 36 40 44 45 46 47	21	10	S		84	2367	32	38.1	10	201	5027	2595	149
MOUNTAIN HOME—Baxter County													
☐★ BAXTER COUNTY REGIONAL HOSPITAL, Hospital Dr., P O Box 746, Zip 72653; tel. 501/425-3141; H. William Anderson, adm. **A**1a 9 10 **F**1 3 6 10 12 14 15 16 19 20 21 23 26 34 35 36 40 41 43 45 46 47 49 50 53	23	10	S		151	5063	80	56.7	10	425	16381	5564	350
MOUNTAIN VIEW—Stone County													
STONE COUNTY MEDICAL CENTER (Formerly Mountain View General Hospital), Hwy. 14 E., Box 510, Zip 72560; tel. 501/269-4361; Bobby Justus, adm. **A**9 10 **F**1 3 14 15 16 35 40	33	10	S		48	854	12	25.0	6	20	—	—	—
NASHVILLE—Howard County													
★ HOWARD MEMORIAL HOSPITAL (Formerly Howard County Memorial Hospital), Box 381, Zip 71852; tel. 501/845-4400; Lewis T. Peeples, adm. **A**9 10 **F**1 3 6 10 12 14 15 16 23 33 34 35 36 40 45 47 53; **S**1755	13	10	S		63	1384	20	30.3	7	47	3455	1589	109
NEWPORT—Jackson County													
☐★ HARRIS HOSPITAL (Formerly Harris Hospital and Clinic), 1205 McLain St., Zip 72112; tel. 501/523-8911; Jim Seward, exec. dir. (Nonreporting) **A**1a 9 10; **S**5895	33	10	S		89	—	—	—	—	—	—	—	—
HARRIS HOSPITAL AND CLINIC, See Harris Hospital													
★ NEWPORT HOSPITAL AND CLINIC, 2000 McLain, Zip 72112; tel. 501/523-6721; Eugene Zuber, adm. **A**10 **F**1 3 6 10 12 14 15 16 23 26 32 34 35 37 43 44 46; **S**1755	33	10	S		86	3003	47	54.7	6	73	7812	2176	177
NORTH LITTLE ROCK—Pulaski County													
☐ BPIDGEWAY, 21 Bridgeway Rd., Zip 72118; tel. 501/771-1500; Sharon Stevens, mng. dir. **A**1b 9 10 **F**12 23 24 30 32 33 42	33	22	S		60	410	42	70.0	0	0	5978	2000	94

Hospital, Address, Telephone, Administrator, Approval and Facility Codes, Multihospital System Code	Classification Codes				Inpatient Data				Newborn Data		Expense (thousands of dollars)		
★ American Hospital Association (AHA) membership □ Joint Commission on Accreditation of Hospitals (JCAH) accreditation + American Osteopathic Hospital Association (AOHA) membership ○ American Osteopathic Association (AOA) accreditation Δ Commission on Accreditation of Rehabilitation Facilities (CARF) accreditation Control codes 61, 63, 64, 71, 72 and 73 indicate hospitals listed by AOHA, but not registered by AHA. For definition of numerical codes, see page A2	Control	Service	Stay	Facilities	Beds	Admissions	Census	Occupancy (percent)	Bassinets	Births	Total	Payroll	Personnel
★□ MEMORIAL HOSPITAL, One Pershing Circle, Zip 72114; tel. 501/771-3000; Harrison M. Dean, sr. vice-pres. & adm. **A**1a 9 10 **F**1 2 3 6 9 10 11 14 15 16 23 24 30 33 35 36 40 44 45 46 52 53 54; **S**0355	23	10	S		186	8289	134	78.4	22	662	—	—	632
VETERANS ADMINISTRATION HOSPITAL, NORTH LITTLE ROCK DIVISION, See Veterans Administration Medical Center, Little Rock													
OSCEOLA—Mississippi County													
★□ OSCEOLA MEMORIAL HOSPITAL, 611 W. Lee Ave., Box 607, Zip 72370; tel. 501/563-7000; Tommy L. Hatcher, vice-pres. & chief oper. off. **A**1a 9 10 **F**1 2 6 14 15 16 23 34 35 45 46 53; **S**2475	13	10	S		82	2361	26	31.7	10	170	5176	1752	134
OZARK—Franklin County													
TURNER MEMORIAL HOSPITAL, 801 W. River, Box 527, Zip 72949; tel. 501/667-4138; Jonah Ted Yates, adm. (Nonreporting) **A**9 10	23	10	S		39	—	—	—	—	—	—	—	—
PARAGOULD—Greene County													
★□ ARKANSAS METHODIST HOSPITAL, 900 W. Kingshighway, Box 339, Zip 72450; tel. 501/239-7000; T. Dale Christian, adm. **A**1a 9 10 **F**1 3 6 8 12 14 15 16 23 26 34 35 40 41 44 45 46 53	23	10	S		129	6002	84	65.1	20	473	10173	4947	339
PIGGOTT—Clay County													
★ PIGGOTT COMMUNITY HOSPITAL, 1206 Hwy. 62 W., Zip 72454; tel. 501/598-3881; Betty J. Reams, exec. dir. **A**9 10 **F**1 6 16 23 34 35 41 45	14	10	S		35	1094	18	51.4	3	35	2238	966	65
PINE BLUFF—Jefferson County													
★□ JEFFERSON REGIONAL MEDICAL CENTER, 1515 W. 42nd Ave., Zip 71603; tel. 501/541-7100; Larry Barton, adm. (Total facility includes 100 beds in nursing home-type unit) **A**1a 3 5 6 9 10 **F**1 2 3 6 7 8 9 10 11 12 14 15 16 19 20 23 24 27 32 34 35 36 37 40 41 45 46 47 50 52 53 54	23	10	S	TF	500	14454	316	63.2	50	1467	43154	19396	1198
				H	400	14411	217	—	50	1467	41595	18249	1127
POCAHONTAS—Randolph County													
□ RANDOLPH COUNTY MEDICAL CENTER, 2801 Medical Center Dr., Zip 72455; tel. 501/892-4511; Hank Fender, exec. dir. (Nonreporting) **A**1a 9 10; **S**5895	33	10	S		50	—	—	—	—	—	—	—	—
PRESCOTT—Nevada County													
★ SOUTHWEST MEDICAL CENTER, Hwy. 67 N., Box 717, Zip 71857; tel. 501/887-2681; Richard C. Bright, adm. (Total facility includes 13 beds in nursing home-type unit) **A**9 10 **F**3 14 15 16 19 23 34 35 45	13	10	S	TF	65	1009	14	21.5	6	67	2459	827	72
				H	52	955	11	—	6	67	—	—	70
ROGERS—Benton County													
★□ ST. MARY-ROGERS MEMORIAL HOSPITAL, 1200 W. Walnut St., Zip 72756; tel. 501/636-0200; Sr. Rosanne Timmerman, adm. (Total facility includes 10 beds in nursing home-type unit) **A**1a 2 9 10 **F**1 3 6 10 12 14 15 16 23 33 34 35 36 40 44 45 46 51 52 53; **S**1295	21	10	S	TF	146	5642	79	54.1	8	753	13439	5941	383
				H	136	5556	76	—	8	753	—	—	—
RUSSELLVILLE—Pope County													
★□ AMI ST. MARY'S HOSPITAL (Formerly St. Mary's Hospital), 1808 W. Main St., Zip 72801; tel. 501/968-2841; Jerry D. Mabry, exec. dir. **A**1a 9 10 **F**1 3 6 10 12 14 15 16 19 20 23 24 30 35 36 37 40 41 44 45 46 47 53 54; **S**0125	33	10	S		144	6113	87	60.4	14	675	16186	4089	291
SALEM—Fulton County													
FULTON COUNTY HOSPITAL, Hwy. 9, Zip 72576; tel. 501/895-2691; Howard Campbell, adm. **A**9 10 **F**1 3 6 14 19 23 35 45	13	10	S		70	1869	29	41.4	6	169	2828	1533	119
SEARCY—White County													
★□ AMI CENTRAL ARKANSAS GENERAL HOSPITAL (Formerly Central Arkansas General Hospital), 1200 S. Main, Zip 72143; tel. 501/268-7171; David C. Laffoon, chief exec. off. **A**1a 9 **F**1 6 12 14 15 16 19 23 34 35 36 41 45 46 50 53 54; **S**0125	33	10	S		113	5075	74	65.5	11	371	12472	3735	210
CENTRAL ARKANSAS GENERAL HOSPITAL, See AMI Central Arkansas General Hospital													
★□ WHITE COUNTY MEMORIAL HOSPITAL, 3214 E. Race St., Box 809, Zip 72143; tel. 501/268-6121; Albert Pilkington, adm. **A**1a 9 10 **F**1 3 6 10 15 24 34 35 37 42 44 45 47 53 54	13	10	S		128	4241	57	44.5	16	431	8623	4028	305
SILOAM SPRINGS—Benton County													
★□ MEMORIAL HOSPITAL, 205 E. Jefferson St., Zip 72761; tel. 501/524-4141; Larry N. Winder, adm. **A**1a 9 10 **F**1 3 6 10 12 15 16 23 34 35 36 37 40 45 46 47; **S**1755	14	10	S		73	1991	24	32.9	9	199	4029	1759	128
SPRINGDALE—Washington County													
★□ SPRINGDALE MEMORIAL HOSPITAL, 607 Maple St., Zip 72764; tel. 501/751-5711; Hugh D. Means, adm. **A**1a 3 5 9 10 **F**1 2 3 4 6 9 10 12 14 15 16 21 23 24 26 27 30 32 33 34 35 36 37 40 44 45 47 52 53 54	21	10	S		205	6117	99	48.3	12	560	16021	7585	526
STUTTGART—Arkansas County													
★□ STUTTGART MEMORIAL HOSPITAL, Rte. 1, Box 21-C, Zip 72160; tel. 501/673-3511; Jim E. Bushmiaer, adm. & chief exec. off. (Nonreporting) **A**1a 9 10	23	10	S		99	—	—	—	—	—	—	—	—
TEXARKANA—Miller County													
★□ ST. MICHAEL HOSPITAL, Sixth & Hazel Sts., Zip 75502; tel. 501/774-2121; Thomas G. Byrne, adm. **A**1a 9 10 **F**1 3 4 5 6 7 8 9 10 11 12 14 15 16 20 23 24 25 35 44 45 46 47 52 53 54; **S**0605	21	10	S		254	9300	192	75.6	0	0	29156	11568	702
VAN BUREN—Crawford County													
★□ CRAWFORD COUNTY MEMORIAL HOSPITAL, E. Main & S. 20th Sts., Box 409, Zip 72956; tel. 501/474-3401; Jeanne Bouxsein Parham, adm. **A**1a 9 10 **F**1 3 6 15 16 21 23 24 32 33 34 35 41 45 53; **S**6525	33	10	S		70	1815	26	37.1	0	0	7451	2228	121
WALDRON—Scott County													
★ MERCY HOSPITAL AND PINEWOOD NURSING HOME, Highways 71 & 80, Box Q, Zip 72958; tel. 501/637-4135; Sr. Donald Mary, adm. **A**9 10 **F**1 14 16 34 35 45 46; **S**5185	21	10	S		26	763	11	42.3	0	88	1584	598	30
WALNUT RIDGE—Lawrence County													
□ LAWRENCE MEMORIAL HOSPITAL (Includes Lawrence Hall Nursing Home), 1309 Hwy. 25 W., Zip 72476; tel. 501/886-1200 (Total facility includes 122 beds in nursing home-type unit) **A**1a 9 10 **F**1 3 6 10 15 16 17 19 23 34 35 43 50	13	10	S	TF	170	1394	136	84.0	0	0	4889	2113	164
				H	48	1329	25	—	0	0	3560	1597	98
WARREN—Bradley County													
★□ BRADLEY COUNTY MEMORIAL HOSPITAL, 404 S. Bradley St., Zip 71671; tel. 501/226-3731; Harry Stevens, adm. **A**1a 9 10 **F**1 3 14 16 34 35 36 45 50	13	10	S		49	2485	37	75.5	10	199	3762	1995	174
WEST MEMPHIS—Crittenden County													
□ CRITTENDEN MEMORIAL HOSPITAL, 200 Tyler St., Box 2248, Zip 72301; tel. 501/735-1500; J. Michael Rayburn, pres. & chief exec. off. **A**1a 9 10 **F**1 3 6 10 12 14 16 20 23 35 36 40 44 45 46 47 53	23	10	S		142	5543	84	59.2	18	687	15907	7156	396
WYNNE—Cross County													
★ CROSS COUNTY HOSPITAL, 310 S. Falls Blvd., Box H, Zip 72396; tel. 501/238-3300; Carl Barker, adm. **A**9 10 **F**1 3 6 14 16 23 30 35 37 41 45 46 53	13	10	S		41	2299	29	70.7	10	195	3847	1941	135
YELLVILLE—Marion County													
CENTRAL OZARKS MEDICAL CENTER, Drawer 219, Zip 72687; tel. 501/449-6211; Ronald E. Hand, adm. (Nonreporting) **A**9 10	33	10	S		59	—	—	—	—	—	—	—	—

Hospital, Address, Telephone, Administrator, Approval and Facility Codes, Multihospital System Code	Classification Codes				Inpatient Data				Newborn Data		Expense (thousands of dollars)		
★ American Hospital Association (AHA) membership □ Joint Commission on Accreditation of Hospitals (JCAH) accreditation + American Osteopathic Hospital Association (AOHA) membership ○ American Osteopathic Association (AOA) accreditation Δ Commission on Accreditation of Rehabilitation Facilities (CARF) accreditation Control codes 61, 63, 64, 71, 72 and 73 indicate hospitals listed by AOHA, but not registered by AHA. For definition of numerical codes, see page A2	Control	Service	Stay	Facilities	Beds	Admissions	Census	Occupancy (percent)	Bassinets	Births	Total	Payroll	Personnel

California

Hospital	Control	Service	Stay	Facilities	Beds	Admissions	Census	Occupancy (percent)	Bassinets	Births	Total	Payroll	Personnel
ALAMEDA—Alameda County													
★□ ALAMEDA HOSPITAL, 2070 Clinton Ave., Zip 94501; tel. 415/522-3700; William J. Dal Cielo, chief exec. off. **A**1a 9 10 **F**1 3 5 6 9 10 12 14 15 16 20 23 26 35 36 37 40 44 45 46 47 50 53	23	10	S		98	3995	61	62.2	10	406	21008	8927	367
ALHAMBRA—Los Angeles County													
★□ ALHAMBRA COMMUNITY HOSPITAL, 100 S. Raymond Ave., Box 510, Zip 91802; tel. 818/570-1606; Ronald E. Dahlgren, chief exec. off. & adm. (Nonreporting) **A**1a 2 9 10	23	10	S		125	—	—	—	—	—	—	—	—
ALTURAS—Modoc County													
MODOC MEDICAL CENTER (Formerly Mercy-Modoc Medical Center), 228 McDowell St., Zip 96101; tel. 916/233-5131; Everett L. Beck, adm. (Nonreporting) **A**9 10	13	10	S		28	—	—	—	—	—	—	—	—
ANAHEIM—Orange County													
★□ ANAHEIM GENERAL HOSPITAL, 3350 W. Ball Rd., Zip 92804; tel. 714/827-6700; Brad H. Jeffrey, exec. dir. **A**1a 9 10 **F**3 6 10 12 16 23 24 26 34 35 36 40 41 44 46 47 52 53; **S**0435	33	10	S		99	2645	40	40.4	18	469	15119	4018	204
★□ ANAHEIM MEMORIAL HOSPITAL, 1111 W. La Palma Ave., Box 3005, Zip 92803; tel. 714/774-1450; Robert M. Sloane, pres. & chief exec. off. **A**1a 2 9 10 **F**1 3 4 6 9 10 12 14 15 16 23 24 26 34 35 42 43 44 45 46 47 48 49 53 54	23	10	S		186	6700	123	65.4	0	0	47499	18382	813
★□ HUMANA HOSPITAL -WEST ANAHEIM, 3033 W. Orange Ave., Box 2097, Zip 92804; tel. 714/827-3000; John W. Hanshaw, exec. dir. **A**1a 2 9 10 **F**1 3 6 10 12 15 16 23 26 35 36 40 45 49 52 53; **S**1235	33	10	S		243	5353	79	32.5	12	975	—	—	403
★□ KAISER FOUNDATION HOSPITAL, 441 N. Lakeview Ave., Zip 92807; tel. 714/978-4000; Patricia B. Siegel, adm. **A**1a 3 9 10 **F**1 2 3 6 10 12 14 15 16 20 23 24 26 30 34 35 36 37 40 41 42 44 46 47 51 52 53 54; **S**2105	23	10	S		178	10316	126	72.0	32	2820	—	—	798
★□ MARTIN LUTHER HOSPITAL MEDICAL CENTER, 1830 W. Romneya Dr., Zip 92801; Mailing Address Box 3304, Zip 92803; tel. 714/491-5200; George H. Mack, pres. & exec. dir. **A**1a 2 9 10 **F**1 2 3 6 8 9 10 11 12 14 15 16 21 23 24 26 34 35 36 37 38 40 44 45 46 47 48 49 50 51 53; **S**2245	23	10	S		200	7981	114	57.0	35	2510	38278	17966	725
□ WESTERN MEDICAL CENTER ANAHEIM, 1025 S. Anaheim Blvd., Zip 92805; tel. 714/533-6220; Carolyn Gillespie, exec. dir. **A**1a 9 10 **F**1 3 4 6 10 12 14 15 16 23 24 26 27 28 29 30 32 33 35 41 42 44 45 46 47 48 49 53 54	23	10	S		206	4029	108	52.4	0	0	29451	10192	569
ANTIOCH—Contra Costa County													
□ DELTA MEMORIAL HOSPITAL, 3901 Lone Tree Way, P O Box 1469, Zip 94509; tel. 415/757-1700; Lee Domanico, pres. & chief exec. off. **A**1a 9 10 **F**1 3 6 10 14 15 16 23 24 35 36 37 40 41 43 44 45 47 49 52 53; **S**0685	23	10	S		53	2946	37	69.8	12	512	16108	7342	257
APPLE VALLEY—San Bernardino County													
★□ ST. MARY DESERT VALLEY HOSPITAL, 18300 Hwy. 18, Box 1225, Zip 92307; tel. 619/242-2311; Beatrice Weiskopf, pres. & chief exec. off. **A**1a 2 9 10 **F**1 3 6 9 10 11 15 16 20 23 24 33 35 36 39 40 41 45 52 53	21	10	S		97	6743	77	79.4	16	1297	22254	9668	405
ARCADIA—Los Angeles County													
★□ METHODIST HOSPITAL OF SOUTHERN CALIFORNIA, 300 W. Huntington Dr., Box 418, Zip 91006; tel. 818/445-4441; Frederick C. Meyer, pres. & chief exec. off. **A**1a 2 9 10 **F**1 3 5 6 7 8 9 10 11 12 14 15 16 23 24 25 26 27 28 29 30 32 33 34 35 36 37 40 42 43 44 45 46 47 50 52 53	23	10	S		305	11177	189	62.0	30	1019	54524	26134	1050
ARCATA—Humboldt County													
□ MAD RIVER COMMUNITY HOSPITAL, 3800 Janes Rd., P O Box 1115, Zip 95521; tel. 707/822-3621; Michael Young, adm. (Nonreporting) **A**1a 9 10	33	10	S		78	—	—	—	—	—	—	—	—
ARROYO GRANDE—San Luis Obispo County													
★□ AMI ARROYO GRANDE COMMUNITY HOSPITAL (Formerly Arroyo Grande Community Hospital), 345 S. Halcyon Rd., Zip 93420; tel. 805/482-4261; Richard N. Woolslayer exec. dir. **A**1a 9 10 **F**1 3 6 10 12 15 16 23 24 26 34 35 44 45 46 47 53; **S**0125	33	10	S		79	2377	36	45.6	0	0	12495	4462	178
ARTESIA—Los Angeles County													
□ PIONEER HOSPITAL, 17831 S. Pioneer Blvd., Zip 90701; tel. 213/865-6291; John S. McDonald, adm. (Nonreporting) **A**1a 9 10	32	10	S		99	—	—	—	—	—	—	—	—
ATASCADERO—San Luis Obispo County													
□ ATASCADERO STATE HOSPITAL, 10333 El Camino Real, Drawer A, Zip 93422; tel. 805/461-2000; Sidney F. Herndon, exec. dir. (Nonreporting) **A**1b	12	22	L		973	—	—	—	—	—	—	—	—
ATWATER—Merced County													
□ BLOSS MEMORIAL DISTRICT HOSPITAL, 1691 Third St., Zip 95301; tel. 209/358-8201; Joseph N. Wierzba, adm. (Nonreporting) **A**1a 9 10; **S**5585	16	10	S		23	—	—	—	—	—	—	—	—
AUBURN—Placer County													
★□ AUBURN FAITH COMMUNITY HOSPITAL, 11815 Education St., Box 8992, Zip 95604; tel. 916/885-7201; Benjamin E. McGlaughlin, adm. **A**1a 9 10 **F**1 3 6 10 16 21 23 24 26 34 36 37 40 45 46 47 53	23	10	S		102	4520	62	60.8	6	650	21735	10400	464
AVALON—Los Angeles County													
AVALON MUNICIPAL HOSPITAL, 100 Falls Canyon Rd., Box 1563, Zip 90704; tel. 213/510-0700; Lew Gillette, adm. (Nonreporting) **A**9 10	14	10	S		12	—	—	—	—	—	—	—	—
AVENAL—Kings County													
□ AVENAL DISTRICT HOSPITAL, 317 Alpine St., Zip 93204; tel. 209/386-5278; Sherman J. Hansen, adm. **A**1a 9 10 **F**1 14 34 35 43 46; **S**5585	16	10	S		28	854	8	28.6	0	0	2049	872	52
AZUSA—Los Angeles County													
□ SIERRA ROYALE HOSPITAL, 125 W. Sierra Madre Ave., Zip 91702; tel. 818/334-0351; Diana Goulet, adm. **A**1b 9 10 **F**23 24 28 29 32 33 42 43 44 47 49; **S**0825	33	22	L		50	443	38	76.0	0	0	4526	1648	83
BAKERSFIELD—Kern County													
★□ BAKERSFIELD COMMUNITY HOSPITAL, 901 Olive Dr., Zip 93308; Mailing Address P O Box 5900, Zip 93388; tel. 805/399-4461; Roy D. Friedlos, adm. **A**1a 9 10 **F**3 35 37; **S**6525	23	10	S		64	1745	27	42.2	0	0	9420	3278	182
★□ BAKERSFIELD MEMORIAL HOSPITAL (Formerly Greater Bakersfield Memorial Hospital), 420 34th St., Zip 93301; Mailing Address Box 1888, Zip 93303; tel. 805/327-1792; C. Larry Carr, pres. **A**1a 9 10 **F**1 3 6 10 12 15 16 20 23 24 35 36 40 41 44 45 47 52 53	23	10	S		208	10503	122	58.7	50	3027	36618	18191	840
GREATER BAKERSFIELD MEMORIAL HOSPITAL, See Bakersfield Memorial Hospital													
★□ KERN MEDICAL CENTER, 1830 Flower St., Zip 93305; tel. 805/326-2000; Sally Brewer, interim chief exec. off. **A**1a 2 3 5 8 9 10 **F**1 3 5 6 9 10 11 12 14 16 20 23 24 27 30 32 33 34 35 36 37 38 40 45 50 51 52 53	13	10	S		236	13501	166	70.3	30	4281	57113	28170	1061

★ American Hospital Association (AHA) membership
☐ Joint Commission on Accreditation of Hospitals (JCAH) accreditation
+ American Osteopathic Hospital Association (AOHA) membership
○ American Osteopathic Association (AOA) accreditation
Δ Commission on Accreditation of Rehabilitation Facilities (CARF) accreditation
Control codes 61, 63, 64, 71, 72 and 73 indicate hospitals listed by AOHA, but not registered by AHA. For definition of numerical codes, see page A2

Hospital, Address, Telephone, Administrator, Approval and Facility Codes, Multihospital System Code	Classification Codes				Inpatient Data				Newborn Data		Expense (thousands of dollars)		
	Control	Service	Stay	Facilities	Beds	Admissions	Census	Occupancy (percent)	Bassinets	Births	Total	Payroll	Personnel
☐ KERN VIEW HOSPITAL (Formerly Kern View Community Mental Health Center and Hospital), 3600 San Dimas St., Zip 93301; tel. 805/327-7621; Walter Reid, chief exec. off. **A**1b 9 10 **F**15 24 28 29 32 33 34 42 43 46 48 49	23	22	S		44	410	27	81.8	0	0	4279	2267	118
★☐ MERCY HOSPITAL, 2215 Truxtun Ave., Zip 93301; Mailing Address Box 119, Zip 93302; tel. 805/327-3371; Sr. Phyllis Hughes, pres. (Total facility includes 50 beds in nursing home-type unit) **A**1a 9 10 **F**1 2 3 6 10 12 14 15 16 19 20 23 24 26 34 35 41 44 45 46 52 53; **S**5205	21	10	S	TF H	276 226	10172 10086	222 173	80.4 —	0 0	0 0	52297 50697	27081 26252	1170 1128
★☐ SAN JOAQUIN COMMUNITY HOSPITAL, 2615 Eye St., Zip 93301; Mailing Address Box 2615, Zip 93303; tel. 805/327-1711; Terry Burns, interim adm. **A**1a 2 9 10 **F**1 4 6 9 10 11 12 15 16 20 23 24 35 36 40 44 45 46 52 54	23	10	S		174	7067	120	69.0	10	41	34772	14633	686
BALDWIN PARK—Los Angeles County													
★☐ TERRACE PLAZA MEDICAL CENTER, 14148 Francisquito Ave., Zip 91706; tel. 213/338-1101; Rolland E. Wick, exec. dir. (Nonreporting) **A**1a 9 10; **S**1805	33	10	S		95	—	—	—	—	—	—	—	—
BANNING—Riverside County													
★☐ MEMORIAL HOSPITAL OF SAN GORGONIO PASS (Formerly San Gorgonio Pass Memorial Hospital), 600 N. Highland Springs Ave., Zip 92220; tel. 714/845-1121; William Sheldon, adm. **A**1a 9 10 **F**1 3 6 10 12 14 15 16 17 23 35 40 45 52 53	16	10	S		68	2971	44	64.7	10	342	11777	4892	228
BARSTOW—San Bernardino County													
★☐ BARSTOW COMMUNITY HOSPITAL, 555 S. Seventh St., Zip 92311; tel. 619/256-1761; Patricia Carey, adm. **A**1a 9 10 **F**1 3 6 12 14 16 35 40 45; **S**1755	14	10	S		56	3278	38	67.9	10	459	11504	5064	190
BEALE AIR FORCE BASE—Yuba County													
U. S. AIR FORCE HOSPITAL BEALE, Zip 95903; tel. 916/634-2871; Lt. Col. Fred Hight, adm. (Nonreporting)	41	10	S		30	—	—	—	—	—	—	—	—
BELLFLOWER—Los Angeles County													
☐ BELLFLOWER DOCTORS HOSPITAL, 9542 E. Artesia Blvd., Zip 90706; tel. 213/925-8355; Dennis Cheshire, adm. (Nonreporting) **A**1a 9 10; **S**0435	33	10	S		163	—	—	—	—	—	—	—	—
☐ BELLWOOD GENERAL HOSPITAL, 10250 E. Artesia Blvd., Zip 90706; tel. 213/866-9028; Joseph B. Courtney, reg. vice-pres. **A**1a 2 9 10 **F**1 3 6 9 10 11 12 14 16 20 23 35 37 40 45 50 53; **S**5765	33	10	S		85	3522	55	64.7	10	636	—	—	199
★☐ KAISER FOUNDATION HOSPITAL (Includes Kaiser Foundation Hospital, Norwalk), 9400 E. Rosecrans Ave., Zip 90706; tel. 213/920-4321; Charles W. Washington Jr., adm. **A**1a 2 9 10 **F**1 2 3 6 10 12 14 15 16 20 21 23 24 30 32 33 35 40 41 44 46 51 52 53; **S**2105	23	10	S		364	21084	261	70.7	48	4673	—	—	1197
BELMONT—San Mateo County													
☐ CPC BELMONT HILLS HOSPITAL (Formerly Belmont Hills Psychiatric Center), 1301 Ralston Ave., Zip 94002; tel. 415/593-2143; Patrick D. Cecil, adm. (Nonreporting) **A**1b 10; **S**0785	33	22	S		54	—	—	—	—	—	—	—	—
BERKELEY—Alameda County													
★☐ ALTA BATES HOSPITAL, 3001 Colby St., Zip 94705; tel. 415/540-0337; Eleanor G. Claus, pres. **A**1a 2 9 10 **F**1 3 4 6 7 8 9 10 11 12 14 15 16 20 21 22 23 24 26 32 34 35 36 37 38 40 42 44 46 48 51 53 54	23	10	S		256	13323	201	78.5	73	4014	83667	33213	1176
★☐ ERNEST V. COWELL MEMORIAL HOSPITAL, University of California, Zip 94720; tel. 415/642-6621; James R. Brown MD, dir. **A**1a **F**1 15 23 28 32 33 34 37 46 49; **S**6405	23	11	S		20	332	3	15.0	0	0	7547	4423	127
★☐ HERRICK HOSPITAL AND HEALTH CENTER, 2001 Dwight Way, Zip 94704; tel. 415/845-0130; John E. Martin, pres. (Nonreporting) **A**1a 2 9	23	10	S		179	—	—	—	—	—	—	—	—
BIG BEAR LAKE—San Bernardino County													
☐ BEAR VALLEY COMMUNITY HOSPITAL, 41870 Garstin Rd., Box 1732, Zip 92315; tel. 714/866-6501; L. Wayne Sasser, exec. dir. (Nonreporting) **A**1a 9 10; **S**9795	33	10	S		28	—	—	—	—	—	—	—	—
BISHOP—Inyo County													
★☐ NORTHERN INYO HOSPITAL, 150 Pioneer Lane, Zip 93514; tel. 619/873-5811; Herman J. Spencer, adm. **A**1a 9 10 **F**1 3 5 6 12 14 15 16 21 23 27 30 32 34 35 36 40 45 52 53	16	10	S		59	2061	24	40.7	6	343	10016	4721	203
BLYTHE—Riverside County													
☐ PALO VERDE HOSPITAL, 250 N. First St., Drawer Z, Zip 92226; tel. 619/922-4115; Richard L. Henson, adm. **A**1a 9 10 **F**1 3 10 16 17 23 28 35 40 45	23	10	S		55	1939	18	32.7	10	390	5751	2337	140
BRAWLEY—Imperial County													
★☐ PIONEERS MEMORIAL HOSPITAL, 207 W. Legion Rd., Zip 92227; tel. 619/344-2120; Willis D. Cox, adm. **A**1a 9 10 **F**1 3 6 10 14 15 16 20 23 35 36 40 45 46 52 53; **S**0585	16	10	S		78	3816	45	57.7	8	959	13645	6266	365
BREA—Orange County													
☐ BREA COMMUNITY HOSPITAL, 380 W. Central Ave., Zip 92621; tel. 714/529-0211; Thomas E. Du Boise, adm. **A**1a 9 10 **F**1 2 3 6 10 12 14 15 16 23 34 35 43 45 46 52	33	10	S		162	5526	73	45.1	0	0	22827	7934	320
★ BREA HOSPITAL-NEUROPSYCHIATRIC CENTER, 875 N. Brea Blvd., Zip 92621; tel. 714/529-4963; David J. Delmastro, vice-pres. & exec. dir. **A** 9 10 **F**3 15 24 29 30 32 33 42 45 46 47; **S**0275	33	22	S		142	1567	117	82.4	0	0	13087	4296	148
BRIDGEPORT—Mono County													
★☐ MONO GENERAL HOSPITAL, Twin Lakes Rd., Box 536, Zip 93517; tel. 619/932-7011; Marguerite S. Ivey, adm. **A**1a 9 10 **F**30 35 45	13	10	S		10	185	7	70.0	0	7	1606	685	41
BUENA PARK—Orange County													
BEACH COMMUNITY HOSPITAL, See Buena Park Doctors Hospital													
☐ BUENA PARK COMMUNITY HOSPITAL, 6850 Lincoln Ave., Zip 90620; tel. 714/827-1161; Paul R. Schmidt, adm. **A**1a 9 10 **F**1 3 6 10 14 15 16 23 34 35 46 49 53; **S**5765	33	10	S		66	1330	21	31.8	0	0	7264	2593	165
☐ BUENA PARK DOCTORS HOSPITAL (Formerly Beach Community Hospital), 5742 Beach Blvd., Zip 90621; tel. 714/521-4770; David A. Robinson, adm. (Nonreporting) **A**1a 9 10; **S**0435	33	10	S		58	—	—	—	—	—	—	—	—
BURBANK—Los Angeles County													
★☐ + BURBANK COMMUNITY HOSPITAL, 466 E. Olive Ave., Zip 91501; Mailing Address P O Box 4501, Zip 91503; tel. 818/953-6500; J. C. P. Rhee, adm. **A**1a 9 10 12 **F**1 3 6 10 12 14 15 16 21 23 24 25 26 33 34 35 37 40 42 44 45 46 47 48 50 53	23	10	S		103	2239	45	43.7	10	263	13109	6276	260
★☐ ST. JOSEPH MEDICAL CENTER, Buena Vista & Alameda Sts., Zip 91505; tel. 818/843-5111; James E. Sauer Jr., adm. (Total facility includes 149 beds in nursing home-type unit) **A**1a 2 9 10 **F**1 2 3 4 5 6 7 8 9 10 11 12 14 15 16 19 20 21 23 24 26 34 35 36 39 40 41 42 44 45 46 47 48 49 51 52 53 54; **S**5275	23	10	S	TF H	586 437	19704 18671	467 332	79.8 —	29 29	2281 2281	111258 —	52207 —	2039 1865
BURLINGAME—San Mateo County													
★☐ PENINSULA HOSPITAL AND MEDICAL CENTER, 1783 El Camino Real, Zip 94010; tel. 415/872-5400; Charles H. Mason Jr., pres. & chief exec. off. **A**1a 2 9 10 **F**1 2 3 4 6 7 8 9 10 11 12 15 16 20 23 24 26 27 28 29 30 32 33 35 36 40 42 44 45 46 47 48 49 52 53 54; **S**6975	23	10	S		310	9740	189	61.0	14	750	58554	31667	766
CALABASAS—Los Angeles County													
★☐ WOODVIEW-CALABASAS HOSPITAL, 25100 Calabasas Rd., Zip 91302; tel. 818/888-7500; Robert Trostler, adm. (Nonreporting) **A**1a 9 10; **S**1755	32	22	L		102	—	—	—	—	—	—	—	—

Hospital, Address, Telephone, Administrator, Approval and Facility Codes, Multihospital System Code	Classification Codes				Inpatient Data				Newborn Data		Expense (thousands of dollars)		
★ American Hospital Association (AHA) membership □ Joint Commission on Accreditation of Hospitals (JCAH) accreditation + American Osteopathic Hospital Association (AOHA) membership ○ American Osteopathic Association (AOA) accreditation Δ Commission on Accreditation of Rehabilitation Facilities (CARF) accreditation Control codes 61, 63, 64, 71, 72 and 73 indicate hospitals listed by AOHA, but not registered by AHA. For definition of numerical codes, see page A2	Control	Service	Stay	Facilities	Beds	Admissions	Census	Occupancy (percent)	Bassinets	Births	Total	Payroll	Personnel
CALEXICO—Imperial County													
□ CALEXICO HOSPITAL, 450 Birch St., Zip 92231; tel. 619/357-1191; Arthur Simmons, adm. **A**1a 9 10 **F**1 3 14 16 23 26 34 35 36 45 46 52 53; **S**3015	16	10	S		34	919	11	32.4	8	76	3453	1413	71
CAMARILLO—Ventura County													
CAMARILLO STATE HOSPITAL AND DEVELOPMENT CENTER (Formerly Camarillo State Hospital), Zip 93010; Mailing Address Box A, Zip 93011; tel. 805/484-3661; Frank Turley PhD, exec. dir. (Nonreporting) **A**3 9 10 **F**1 23 24 30 32 33 35 42 44	12	22	L		1315	1495	1167	88.0	0	0	—	—	2142
★□ PLEASANT VALLEY HOSPITAL, 2309 Antonio, Zip 93010; tel. 805/484-2831; Wanda S. Gravett, exec. vice-pres. (Total facility includes 99 beds in nursing home-type unit) **A**1a 9 10 **F**1 3 6 9 10 12 15 16 19 21 23 24 26 35 36 40 45 46 47 52 53	23	10	S	TF H	180 81	4264 4119	79 57	61.2 —	10 10	600 600	18328 —	7245 —	381 323
CAMP PENDLETON—San Diego County													
★□ NAVAL HOSPITAL, Zip 92055; tel. 619/725-1288; Capt. R. W. Higgins, CO **A**1a 3 5 **F**3 6 10 12 14 15 16 23 24 27 28 29 30 32 33 34 35 36 37 40 43 44 45 46 47 48 49 52 53	43	10	S		151	7225	91	60.3	36	1107	—	—	1161
CAMPBELL—Santa Clara County													
CHEMICAL DEPENDENCY INSTITUTE OF NORTHERN CALIFORNIA, 3333 S. Bascom Ave., Zip 95008; tel. 408/559-2000; Roy R. Shelden, adm. & chief exec. off. (Nonreporting) **A** 9; **S**8985	33	82	S		40	—	—	—	—	—	—	—	—
CARMICHAEL—Sacramento County													
★□ AMERICAN RIVER HOSPITAL (Formerly Eskaton American River Hospital), 4747 Engle Rd., Zip 95608; tel. 916/486-3211; Merle E. Wolf, pres. & chief exec. off. **A**1a 9 10 **F**1 3 6 10 11 12 14 15 16 23 24 25 26 27 28 30 32 33 35 36 37 40 42 44 45 52 53 54; **S**1215	23	10	S		221	9503	154	69.7	25	1035	46443	17561	745
ESKATON AMERICAN RIVER HOSPITAL, See American River Hospital													
★□ MERCY SAN JUAN HOSPITAL, 6501 Coyle Ave., P O Box 479, Zip 95608; tel. 916/537-5000; Gregg R. Schnepple, pres. **A**1a 9 10 **F**1 2 3 6 10 12 14 15 16 17 21 23 35 36 40 41 45 52 53; **S**5205	21	10	S		211	10368	152	72.0	31	1456	47717	18733	796
CASTLE AIR FORCE BASE—Merced County													
U. S. AIR FORCE HOSPITAL-CASTLE, Zip 95342; tel. 209/384-4127; Lt. Col. Lloyd E. Dodd Jr., cmdr. (Nonreporting)	41	10	S		20	—	—	—	—	—	—	—	—
CASTRO VALLEY—Alameda County													
★□ EDEN HOSPITAL MEDICAL CENTER (Formerly Eden Hospital), 20103 Lake Chabot Rd., Zip 94546; tel. 415/537-1234; Dev Mahadevan, pres. & chief exec. off. **A**1a 2 9 10 **F**1 2 3 5 6 7 8 9 10 12 14 15 16 20 22 23 24 26 27 33 35 36 40 41 44 45 46 47 53	16	10	S		223	7517	123	56.2	20	1033	42843	19566	570
□ LAUREL GROVE HOSPITAL, 19933 Lake Chabot Rd., Zip 94546; tel. 415/538-6464; I. D. Howard, adm. **A**1a 9 10 **F**1 3 6 10 12 14 15 16 23 25 45 46	33	10	S		78	1011	20	25.6	0	0	8611	3012	102
CERES—Stanislaus County													
MEMORIAL HOSPITAL CERES, See Memorial Hospital Association, Modesto													
CERRITOS—Los Angeles County													
□ COLLEGE HOSPITAL, 10802 College Pl., Zip 90701; tel. 213/924-9581; Barry J. Weiss, exec. dir.; Kent Dunlap, adm. **A**1b 9 10 **F**15 24 26 28 29 30 32 33 34 42 44 48 49	33	22	S		125	1024	102	91.1	0	0	21753	7106	347
CHESTER—Plumas County													
SENECA DISTRICT HOSPITAL, Brentwood Dr., Box 737, Zip 96020; tel. 916/258-2151; Claire Kuczkowski, adm. (Nonreporting) **A**9 10	16	10	S		26	—	—	—	—	—	—	—	—
CHICO—Butte County													
★□ CHICO COMMUNITY HOSPITAL, 560 Cohasset Rd., Zip 95926; tel. 916/896-5000; Daniel Chesanow, chief exec. off. **A**1a 9 10 **F**1 3 5 6 12 14 15 16 22 23 24 25 26 30 34 35 42 44 45 46 52 53; **S**5765	33	10	S		135	3508	71	52.6	0	0	24312	9105	374
★□ N. T. ENLOE MEMORIAL HOSPITAL, Fifth Ave. & Esplanade, Zip 95926; tel. 916/891-7300; James P. Sweeney, exec. dir. **A**1a 2 9 10 **F**1 2 3 4 5 6 7 8 9 10 11 12 15 16 17 20 21 23 24 26 33 34 35 36 37 40 41 44 45 46 51 52 53 54	23	10	S		196	9691	162	85.7	18	1395	53026	24510	1038
CHINO—San Bernardino County													
★□ CHINO COMMUNITY HOSPITAL, 5451 Walnut Ave., Zip 91710; tel. 714/627-6111; Dennis Bruns, adm. **A**1a 9 10 **F**1 3 14 15 16 23 35 41 45 46 48 49 52; **S**1755	33	10	S		118	2905	41	34.7	0	0	—	—	231
HOSPITAL OF THE CALIFORNIA INSTITUTION FOR MEN, 14901 Central Ave., Box 128, Zip 91710; tel. 714/597-1821; W. E. Sigurdson MD, adm. (Nonreporting)	12	10	S		81	—	—	—	—	—	—	—	—
CHOWCHILLA—Madera County													
CHOWCHILLA DISTRICT MEMORIAL HOSPITAL, 1104 Ventura Ave., Box 1027, Zip 93610; tel. 209/665-3781; Norma Lewis, adm. (Nonreporting) **A**9 10	16	10	S		23	—	—	—	—	—	—	—	—
CHULA VISTA—San Diego County													
★□ COMMUNITY HOSPITAL OF CHULA VISTA, 751 Medical Center Ct., Zip 92010; Mailing Address Box 1297, Zip 92012; tel. 619/421-6110; Robert D. Hansen, exec. dir. (Total facility includes 98 beds in nursing home-type unit) **A**1a 9 10 **F**1 3 6 10 12 14 16 19 23 24 26 35 45 46 52	23	10	S	TF H	229 131	4938 4730	112 77	48.9 —	0 0	0 0	15987 —	7247 —	383 328
★□ SCRIPPS MEMORIAL HOSPITAL-CHULA VISTA, 435 H St., Zip 92012; Mailing Address Box 1537, Zip 92010; tel. 619/691-7000; Jeff K. Bills, vice-pres. & adm. **A**1a 9 10 **F**1 3 6 10 12 14 15 16 17 20 23 24 32 33 34 35 36 40 41 44 45 46 47 52 53; **S**1505	23	10	S		159	9849	120	75.5	20	2982	33060	15983	574
★□ SOUTHWOOD PSYCHIATRIC HOSPITAL (Includes Adolescent Residential Treatment Facilities), 950 Third Ave., Zip 92011; tel. 619/426-6310; Allan Kydd, adm. **A**1b 9 10 **F**3 15 24 28 29 30 32 33 34 42 48 49	33	52	L		40	309	37	92.5	0	0	4231	2093	86
★□ VISTA HILL HOSPITAL, 730 Medical Center Ct., Zip 92010; tel. 619/421-6900; Ruth Dundon, adm. **A**1b 9 10 **F**15 24 28 29 30 31 32 33 42 43 46 48 49; **S**8895	23	22	S		58	783	47	81.0	0	0	5160	2638	121
CLEARLAKE—Lake County													
★□ REDBUD COMMUNITY HOSPITAL, Box 6720, Zip 95422; tel. 707/994-6486; Rusty Shelton, exec. dir. **A**1a 9 10 **F**1 6 10 11 14 15 16 23 34 35 36 37 41 46 47 53; **S**0585	16	10	S		40	1568	16	40.0	0	95	—	—	59
CLOVIS—Fresno County													
□ CLOVIS COMMUNITY HOSPITAL, 88 N. Dewitt Ave., Zip 93612; tel. 209/298-8041; James D. Helzer, pres. & chief exec. off.; Norm Andrews, vice-pres. & chief oper. off. (Nonreporting) **A**1a 9 10; **S**1085	23	10	S		63	—	—	—	—	—	—	—	—
COALINGA—Fresno County													
□ COALINGA DISTRICT HOSPITAL, 10 Washington St., Zip 93210; tel. 209/935-2051; Ted Kittell, adm. **A**1a 9 10 **F**1 6 14 23 30 33 35 41 45 46	16	10	S		26	601	5	19.2	0	1	3247	1233	67
COLUSA—Colusa County													
□ COLUSA COMMUNITY HOSPITAL, 199 E. Webster St., P O Box 331, Zip 95932; tel. 916/458-5821; Ken Smith, adm. **A**1a 9 10 **F**1 3 6 10 14 16 23 34 35 36 40 41 43 45 53; **S**8985	23	10	S		56	1020	12	21.4	2	129	4341	1572	88
CONCORD—Contra Costa County													
★□ MT. DIABLO HOSPITAL MEDICAL CENTER, 2540 East St., Zip 94520; tel. 415/674-2002; Michael L. Wall, chief exec. off. **A**1a 2 9 10 **F**1 2 3 4 6 7 8 9 10 11 12 14 15 16 17 20 21 23 24 26 35 36 40 41 42 43 44 45 46 47 48 49 52 53 54	16	10	S		303	9481	172	56.8	31	835	68817	32246	1012

★ American Hospital Association (AHA) membership
□ Joint Commission on Accreditation of Hospitals (JCAH) accreditation
+ American Osteopathic Hospital Association (AOHA) membership
○ American Osteopathic Association (AOA) accreditation
Δ Commission on Accreditation of Rehabilitation Facilities (CARF) accreditation
Control codes 61, 63, 64, 71, 72 and 73 indicate hospitals listed by AOHA, but not registered by AHA.
For definition of numerical codes, see page A2

Hospital, Address, Telephone, Administrator, Approval and Facility Codes, Multihospital System Code	Classification Codes				Inpatient Data				Newborn Data		Expense (thousands of dollars)		
	Control	Service	Stay	Facilities	Beds	Admissions	Census	Occupancy (percent)	Bassinets	Births	Total	Payroll	Personnel
CORCORAN—Kings County													
□ CORCORAN DISTRICT HOSPITAL, 1310 Hanna Ave., Box 758, Zip 93212; tel. 209/992-5051; Don N. Larkin, chief exec. off. **A**1a 9 10 **F**1 5 6 12 14 15 16 23 24 26 34 35 36 40 44 45 46 50 52 53	16	10	S		32	956	9	28.1	6	93	3030	—	88
CORNING—Tehama County													
□ CORNING MEMORIAL HOSPITAL, 275 Solano St., Zip 96021; tel. 916/824-5451; Bridget Simone, adm. (Nonreporting) **A**1a 9 10	33	10	S		30	—	—	—	—	—	—	—	—
CORONA—Riverside County													
★□ AMI CIRCLE CITY HOSPITAL (Formerly Circle City Hospital), 730 Old Magnolia Ave., P O Box 310, Zip 91719; tel. 714/736-7252; Henry Gothelf, exec. dir. **A**1a 9 10 **F**1 3 6 12 14 15 16 21 23 32 34 35 36 40 41 45 46 47 52 53; **S**0125	33	10	S		99	4980	57	57.6	9	662	21684	7567	308
★□ CHARTER GROVE HOSPITAL, 2005 Kellogg Ave., Zip 91719; tel. 714/735-2910; James P. Fridlington, adm. (Nonreporting) **A**1b 9 10; **S**0695	33	22	S		82	—	—	—	—	—	—	—	—
CIRCLE CITY HOSPITAL, See AMI Circle City Hospital													
★□ Δ CORONA COMMUNITY HOSPITAL, 800 S. Main St., Zip 91720; tel. 714/737-4343; Byron Streifling, pres. **A**1a 7 9 10 **F**1 3 6 10 12 14 15 16 21 23 24 25 26 34 35 40 41 42 43 44 45 46 47 50 52 53	23	10	S		148	5069	72	48.6	8	713	23212	8884	458
CORONADO—San Diego County													
★□ CORONADO HOSPITAL, 250 Prospect Pl., Zip 92118; tel. 619/435-6251; R. Jay Comstock, adm. (Total facility includes 51 beds in nursing home-type unit) **A**1a 9 10 **F**1 3 6 10 12 15 16 19 23 24 26 30 34 35 36 37 41 42 44 45 46 47 48 49	23	10	S	TF	115	2873	80	69.6	11	741	13611	5656	308
				H	64	2801	38	—	11	741	13080	5248	283
COSTA MESA—Orange County													
□ COSTA MESA MEDICAL CENTER HOSPITAL, 301 Victoria St., Zip 92627; tel. 714/642-2734; Lawrence J. Anderson, adm. **A**1a 9 10 **F**1 3 6 10 14 15 16 23 24 34 35 42 44 45 46 47 52 53	33	10	S		99	1798	33	33.3	0	0	—	—	183
COVINA—Los Angeles County													
★□ CHARTER OAK HOSPITAL, 1161 E. Covina Blvd., Zip 91724; tel. 818/966-1632; Barbara Cech Noblet, adm. **A**1b 9 10 **F**24 28 29 30 32 33 42 43 46; **S**0695	33	22	S		83	770	72	86.7	0	0	—	—	146
□ INTER-COMMUNITY MEDICAL CENTER, 303 N. Third Ave., Zip 91723; tel. 818/331-7331; Duane A. Carlberg, exec. vice-pres. & dir. **A**1a 2 9 10 **F**1 2 3 4 6 7 8 9 10 11 12 14 15 16 21 23 24 26 27 30 32 33 35 36 40 41 42 44 45 46 52 53 54	23	10	S		274	9880	142	51.8	32	593	41454	18938	734
CRESCENT CITY—Del Norte County													
□ SUTTER COAST HOSPITAL (Formerly Seaside Hospital and Medical Clinic), 100 A St., Zip 95531; tel. 707/464-8511; John E. Menaugh, adm. **A**1a 9 10 **F**1 6 14 15 16 23 26 35 36 40 44 45 46 47 53; **S**8795	23	10	S		56	1856	22	39.3	12	246	—	—	193
CULVER CITY—Los Angeles County													
BROTMAN MEDICAL CENTER, See HCA Brotman Medical Center													
★□ HCA BROTMAN MEDICAL CENTER (Formerly Brotman Medical Center), 3828 Delmas Terr., Box 2459, Zip 90231; tel. 213/836-7000; Donald Bernstein DDS, adm. **A**1a 9 10 **F**1 2 3 4 6 7 8 9 10 11 12 14 15 16 17 20 22 23 24 25 26 27 33 34 35 36 40 42 44 45 46 47 48 49 50 53 54; **S**1755	33	10	S		327	10358	237	72.5	8	617	—	—	1277
□ WASHINGTON MEDICAL CENTER, 12101 W. Washington Blvd., Box 2787, Zip 90231; tel. 213/391-0601; David A. Levinsohn, adm. **A**1a 9 10 **F**1 3 6 12 14 15 16 17 23 24 35 41 44 46 53	33	10	S		99	2082	35	35.4	0	0	16186	5505	239
DALY CITY—San Mateo County													
★□ SETON MEDICAL CENTER, 1900 Sullivan Ave., Zip 94015; tel. 415/992-4000; Frank C. Hudson, pres. & chief exec. off. (Total facility includes 23 beds in nursing home-type unit) **A**1a 3 5 9 10 **F**1 2 3 4 5 6 7 8 9 10 11 12 14 15 16 19 20 21 23 24 26 27 30 31 32 34 35 36 40 41 42 44 46 49 52 53 54; **S**1885	21	10	S	TF	295	11116	185	66.1	35	924	—	—	1327
				H	272	11065	183	—	35	924	—	—	1308
DANA POINT—Orange County													
□ CAPISTRANO BY THE SEA HOSPITAL, 33915 Del Obispo St., Box 398, Zip 92629; tel. 714/496-5702; Harvey H. Hanemoto, adm. (Nonreporting) **A**1b 9 10	33	22	S		82	—	—	—	—	—	—	—	—
DAVIS—Yolo County													
★□ COWELL HOSPITAL AND STUDENT HEALTH CENTER, University of California-Davis, Zip 95616; tel. 916/752-2300; William C. Waid, adm.; William E. Bittner MD, actg. med. staff dir. **A**1a **F**1 15 23 28 30 34 35 37; **S**6405	23	11	S		10	348	2	20.0	0	0	4595	2900	105
□ SUTTER DAVIS HOSPITAL, Rd. 99 at Covell Blvd., Zip 95616; Mailing Address P O Box 1617, Zip 95617; tel. 916/756-6440; Patrick R. Brady, adm. **A**1a 9 10 **F**1 3 6 14 15 16 20 23 24 26 34 35 44 45 46 47 53; **S**8795	23	10	S		48	1479	18	37.5	0	0	6784	2911	138
DEER PARK—Napa County													
□ ST. HELENA HOSPITAL AND HEALTH CENTER, P O Box 250, Zip 94576; tel. 707/963-3611; Leonard Yost, pres. **A**1a 9 10 **F**1 3 4 6 10 12 14 15 16 20 21 23 24 26 27 28 30 32 33 34 35 39 40 41 42 44 45 46 47 48 53 54; **S**0235	21	10	S		165	4499	93	56.4	10	288	33056	14077	503
DELANO—Kern County													
□ DELANO REGIONAL MEDICAL CENTER, 1401 Garces Hwy., Zip 93215; Mailing Address Box 460, Zip 93216; tel. 805/725-4800; Wesley Bilson, pres. (Total facility includes 62 beds in nursing home-type unit) **A**1a 9 10 **F**1 3 6 10 12 14 15 16 19 23 35 36 40 44 45 46 47 50 53	33	10	S	TF	120	3615	97	80.8	10	682	12527	5329	324
				H	58	3380	40	—	10	682	—	—	284
DINUBA—Tulare County													
□ ALTA DISTRICT HOSPITAL (Formerly Alta Hospital District), 500 Adelaide Way, Zip 93618; tel. 209/591-4171; Robert M. Montion, adm. **A**1a 9 10 **F**1 6 10 12 14 15 16 23 34 35 40 45 46 53	16	10	S		50	1982	19	38.0	11	261	5009	2330	121
DOS PALOS—Merced County													
DOS PALOS MEMORIAL HOSPITAL, 2118 Marguerite St., Zip 93620; tel. 209/392-6106; Howard Sager, interim adm. (Nonreporting) **A**10	23	10	S		15	—	—	—	—	—	—	—	—
DOWNEY—Los Angeles County													
★□ DOWNEY COMMUNITY HOSPITAL, 11500 Brookshire Ave., Caller 7010, Zip 90241; tel. 213/806-5000; Allen R. Korneff, chief exec. off. **A**1a 2 9 10 **F**1 3 6 10 12 14 15 16 17 20 23 24 26 33 35 36 40 41 44 45 50 53	23	10	S		170	7146	123	72.4	25	732	41710	19579	750
★□ Δ LAC-RANCHO LOS AMIGOS MEDICAL CENTER (Formerly Rancho Los Amigos Medical Center), 7601 E. Imperial Hwy., Zip 90242; tel. 213/940-7022; Armando Lopez Jr., exec. dir. (Total facility includes 40 beds in nursing home-type unit) **A**1a 3 5 7 9 10 **F**1 3 6 10 12 14 15 16 19 23 24 25 26 28 32 33 34 42 44 46 47 50 52 53; **S**5755	13	10	S	TF	435	4949	427	98.2	0	0	111570	56279	—
				H	395	4908	389	—	0	0	—	—	—
★□ ○ RIO HONDO MEMORIAL HOSPITAL, 8300 E. Telegraph Rd., Zip 90240; Mailing Address Caller 7020, Zip 90241; tel. 213/806-1821; Patrick A. Petre, adm. **A**1a 9 10 11 12 **F**1 3 7 8 9 11 12 14 15 16 34 35 40 43 45 46 47 48 49 52; **S**6525	33	10	S		146	3927	64	43.8	16	564	18133	7980	267
DUARTE—Los Angeles County													
★□ CITY OF HOPE NATIONAL MEDICAL CENTER (Cancer, Genetic, Respiratory, Blood Dyscrasia and Metabolic Diseases), 1500 E. Duarte Rd., Zip 91010; tel. 818/359-8111; Sanford M. Shapero, chief exec. off. **A**1a 2 3 5 9 10 **F**1 3 6 7 8 9 10 11 12 14 15 16 23 24 26 34 38 41 42 43 44 45 46 47 52 53 54	23	49	S		132	4940	117	58.8	0	0	73936	37107	1210

Hospital, Address, Telephone, Administrator, Approval and Facility Codes, Multihospital System Code

★ American Hospital Association (AHA) membership
□ Joint Commission on Accreditation of Hospitals (JCAH) accreditation
+ American Osteopathic Hospital Association (AOHA) membership
○ American Osteopathic Association (AOA) accreditation
Δ Commission on Accreditation of Rehabilitation Facilities (CARF) accreditation
Control codes 61, 63, 64, 71, 72 and 73 indicate hospitals listed by AOHA, but not registered by AHA.
For definition of numerical codes, see page A2

Hospital, Address, Telephone, Administrator, Approval and Facility Codes, Multihospital System Code	Classification Codes				Inpatient Data				Newborn Data		Expense (thousands of dollars)		
	Control	Service	Stay	Facilities	Beds	Admissions	Census	Occupancy (percent)	Bassinets	Births	Total	Payroll	Personnel
★□ SANTA TERESITA HOSPITAL, 1210 Royal Oaks Dr., P O Box I, Zip 91010; tel. 818/359-3243; Sr. Vincent Marie Finnegan, pres. & chief exec. off. (Total facility includes 133 beds in nursing home-type unit) **A**1a 2 9 10 **F**1 2 3 6 10 12 14 15 16 19 23 35 36 40 45 46 47 50 53	21	10	S	TF H	283 150	2969 2918	174 44	61.5 —	20 20	619 619	18590 16995	9314 7932	445 367
EDWARDS AIR FORCE BASE—Kern County													
U. S. AIR FORCE HOSPITAL -EDWARDS, Zip 93523; tel. 805/277-2010; Col. Darvin K. Suter, cmdr.; Maj. Joseph L. McGraw, adm. (Nonreporting)	41	10	S		36	—	—	—	—	—	—	—	—
EL CAJON—San Diego County													
★□ AMI VALLEY MEDICAL CENTER (Formerly El Cajon Valley Hospital), 1688 E. Main St., Zip 92021; tel. 619/440-1122; Jerry Gillman, exec. dir. (Nonreporting) **A**1a 9 10; **S**0125	33	10	S		189	—	—	—	—	—	—	—	—
KAISER FOUNDATION HOSPITAL, See Kaiser Foundation Hospital, San Diego													
★□ RANCHO PARK HOSPITAL, 109 E. Chase Ave., Zip 92020; tel. 213/579-1666; Kathleen Burns, chief exec. off. **A**1a 9 10 **F**30 32 33	32	22	L		30	187	20	66.7	0	0	3081	1338	127
EL CENTRO—Imperial County													
★□ EL CENTRO REGIONAL MEDICAL CENTER (Formerly El Centro Community Hospital), 1415 Ross Ave., Zip 92243; tel. 619/339-7100; Norm Martin, adm. **A**1a 9 10 **F**1 3 6 7 8 9 10 11 12 14 15 16 17 23 24 26 34 35 37 39 40 43 44 45 46 47 52 53	14	10	S		100	5443	72	72.0	4	1109	21091	—	336
ELDRIDGE—Sonoma County													
SONOMA DEVELOPMENTAL CENTER (Formerly Sonoma State Hospital), Zip 95431; tel. 707/938-6000; Thomas A. Gillons, adm. **A**10 **F**14 16 19 23 24 29 31 32 33 42 44 45 46 47	12	62	L		1423	97	1329	93.4	0	0	77040	48485	2182
ENCINITAS—San Diego County													
□ CPC SAN LUIS REY HOSPITAL (Formerly San Luis Rey Hospital), 1015 Devonshire Dr., Zip 92024; tel. 619/753-1245; William T. Sparrow, adm. (Nonreporting) **A**1b 9; **S**0785	33	22	S		83	—	—	—	—	—	—	—	—
SAN LUIS REY HOSPITAL, See CPC San Luis Rey Hospital													
★□ SCRIPPS MEMORIAL HOSPITAL-ENCINITAS, 354 Santa Fe Dr., P O Box 817, Zip 92024; tel. 619/753-6501; Steven J. Goe, vice-pres. & adm. **A**1a 9 10 **F**1 3 6 9 10 12 15 16 20 23 24 26 30 33 35 37 41 44 45 46 53 54; **S**1505	23	10	S		93	4212	59	63.4	0	0	20709	8805	258
ESCONDIDO—San Diego County													
★□ PALOMAR MEMORIAL HOSPITAL, 555 E. Valley Pkwy., Zip 92025; tel. 619/489-4864; Robert M. Edwards, pres. & chief exec. off.; Robert J. Harenski, exec. vice-pres. & adm. **A**1a 2 9 10 **F**3 5 6 7 10 11 14 16 20 23 24 27 34 35 36 40 44 46 50 52 53; **S**7555	16	10	S	TF H	267 0	13404 —	214 —	80.1 —	24 24	1939 1939	57635 56933	22021 21729	1372 1320
EUREKA—Humboldt County													
□ GENERAL HOSPITAL, 2200 Harrison Ave., Zip 95501; tel. 707/445-5111; Vern Reed, chief exec. off. (Data for 273 days) **A**1a 9 10 **F**1 3 6 12 15 16 17 21 23 24 30 35 36 37 40 44 45 51 53; **S**0585	33	10	S		84	2003	29	34.5	15	607	9045	3692	211
★□ ST. JOSEPH HOSPITAL, 2700 Dolbeer St., Zip 95501; tel. 707/443-8051; Peter W. Kriger, pres. & chief exec. off. **A**1a 9 10 **F**1 3 6 7 8 9 10 11 12 15 16 17 19 23 24 35 43 44 45 46 53; **S**5425	21	10	S		69	3790	49	71.0	0	0	20292	8194	283
EXETER—Tulare County													
★□ MEMORIAL HOSPITAL AT EXETER, 215 Crespi Ave., Zip 93221; tel. 209/592-2151; Melba Jeffress, interim adm. (Total facility includes 21 beds in nursing home-type unit) **A**1a 9 10 **F**1 6 7 8 9 10 11 12 15 16 19 23 35 40 43 45 53; **S**1755	23	10	S	TF H	74 53	1109 1024	35 15	47.3 —	12 12	137 137	4580 4274	1933 1693	140 121
FAIRFIELD—Solano County													
DAVID GRANT U. S. AIR FORCE MEDICAL CENTER, See Travis Air Force Base													
★□ NORTHBAY MEDICAL CENTER (Formerly Intercommunity Hospital), 1800 Pennsylvania Ave., Zip 94533; tel. 707/429-3600; Gary J. Passama, adm. & chief exec. off. **A**1a 9 10 **F**1 2 3 5 6 9 10 12 16 17 20 23 24 30 35 37 40 41 44 45 47 51 52 53	23	10	S		111	5882	78	70.3	10	1036	28210	12997	451
FALL RIVER MILLS—Shasta County													
MAYERS MEMORIAL HOSPITAL, Hwy. 299 E., Box 459, Zip 96028; tel. 916/336-5511; Everett L. Beck, adm. (Nonreporting) **A**9 10	16	10	S		56	—	—	—	—	—	—	—	—
FALLBROOK—San Diego County													
□ FALLBROOK HOSPITAL DISTRICT, 624 E. Elder St., Zip 92028; tel. 619/728-1191; William E. Smikahl, adm. **A**1a 9 **F**1 3 6 10 12 15 16 23 24 26 29 32 35 36 37 40 42 44 45 46 47 53	16	10	S		50	3025	32	64.0	8	879	10179	5277	167
FOLSOM—Sacramento County													
★□ MERCY HOSPITAL OF FOLSOM, 223 Fargo Way, Zip 95630; tel. 916/985-4441; J. R. Eason, adm. **A**1a 9 10 **F**1 3 6 10 12 14 16 23 35 45; **S**5205	21	10	S		34	1188	19	55.9	0	0	6187	2429	103
FONTANA—San Bernardino County													
★□ KAISER FOUNDATION HOSPITAL, 9961 Sierra Ave., Zip 92335; tel. 714/829-5000; Susan E. Garrison, adm. (Total facility includes 30 beds in nursing home-type unit) **A**1a 2 3 5 9 10 **F**1 3 6 10 11 12 14 15 16 19 20 21 23 24 25 26 34 35 37 40 41 42 44 46 47 48 49 51 52 53; **S**2105	23	10	S	TF H	436 406	21333 21070	352 329	80.7 —	85 85	3692 3692	— —	— —	1845 1818
FORT BRAGG—Mendocino County													
□ MENDOCINO COAST DISTRICT HOSPITAL, 700 River Dr., Zip 95437; tel. 707/961-1234; Dorel Freeman, adm. **A**1a 9 10 **F**1 3 6 10 12 14 16 21 23 24 30 32 35 36 40 41 44 45 46 47 50 53	16	10	S		54	1947	26	48.1	9	279	8139	3940	141
FORT IRWIN—San Bernardino County													
★□ WEED ARMY COMMUNITY HOSPITAL, Zip 92310; tel. 619/386-3108; Lt. Col. L. Patrick McKelvey, exec. off. **A**1a **F**1 6 15 16 23 28 34 35 37 40 45 46 47 49	42	10	S		26	1859	13	50.0	7	217	—	—	287
FORT ORD—Monterey County													
★□ SILAS B. HAYS ARMY COMMUNITY HOSPITAL, Zip 93941; tel. 408/242-6005; Col. Cecil B. Harris MC USAF, deputy cmdr. adm. (Nonreporting) **A**1a 3 5	42	10	S		168	—	—	—	—	—	—	—	—
FORTUNA—Humboldt County													
★□ REDWOOD MEMORIAL HOSPITAL, 3300 Renner Dr., Zip 95540; tel. 707/725-3361; Willard G. Foote, pres. & chief exec. off. **A**1a 9 10 **F**1 3 6 9 10 12 14 15 16 23 24 32 34 35 36 40 43 44 45 50 52 53; **S**5425	21	10	S		47	2215	22	46.8	8	554	7364	2791	127
FOUNTAIN VALLEY—Orange County													
□ FOUNTAIN VALLEY REGIONAL HOSPITAL AND MEDICAL CENTER (Formerly Fountain Valley Community Hospital), 17100 Euclid, Zip 92708; tel. 714/979-1211; Craig G. Myers, adm. **A**1a 2 9 10 **F**1 3 4 5 6 10 12 14 15 16 20 23 24 34 35 36 37 40 41 44 45 46 47 49 51 52 53 54	33	10	S		287	15050	208	72.5	24	4014	84877	29524	1008
FOWLER—Fresno County													
FOWLER MUNICIPAL HOSPITAL, 420 E. Merced St., Zip 93625; tel. 209/834-5321; Temen J. Conley, adm. **A**9 10 **F**1 12 35	14	10	S		12	322	4	33.3	0	0	1015	340	31
FREMONT—Alameda County													
★□ WASHINGTON HOSPITAL, 2000 Mowry Ave., Zip 94538; tel. 415/797-1111; Richard M. Warren, chief exec. off. & adm. (Nonreporting) **A**1a 9 10	16	10	S		231	—	—	—	—	—	—	—	—

Hospital, Address, Telephone, Administrator, Approval and Facility Codes, Multihospital System Code	Classification Codes				Inpatient Data				Newborn Data		Expense (thousands of dollars)		
★ American Hospital Association (AHA) membership □ Joint Commission on Accreditation of Hospitals (JCAH) accreditation + American Osteopathic Hospital Association (AOHA) membership ○ American Osteopathic Association (AOA) accreditation Δ Commission on Accreditation of Rehabilitation Facilities (CARF) accreditation Control codes 61, 63, 64, 71, 72 and 73 indicate hospitals listed by AOHA, but not registered by AHA. For definition of numerical codes, see page A2	Control	Service	Stay	Facilities	Beds	Admissions	Census	Occupancy (percent)	Bassinets	Births	Total	Payroll	Personnel
FRESNO—Fresno County													
★□ Δ FRESNO COMMUNITY HOSPITAL AND MEDICAL CENTER, Fresno & R Sts., Box 1232, Zip 93715; tel. 209/442-6000; James D. Helzer, pres. & chief exec. off.; Bryan Ballard, vice-pres. & chief oper. off. **A**1a 2 7 9 10 **F**1 2 3 4 5 6 7 8 9 10 11 12 13 15 16 17 20 23 24 25 26 27 28 29 30 32 33 35 36 37 40 41 42 44 45 46 47 48 49 52 53 54; **S**1085	23	10	S		458	21068	323	70.5	30	4985	89420	38935	1866
FRESNO CONVALESCENT HOSPITAL, See Sierra Hospital													
★□ SIERRA COMMUNITY HOSPITAL (Includes Fresno Convalescent Hospital), 2025 E. Dakota Ave., Zip 93726; tel. 209/221-5600; John W. Frye Jr., vice-pres. & chief oper. off. **A**1a 9 10 **F**1 2 3 6 10 12 14 15 16 20 23 24 26 28 29 32 33 34 35 45 46 47 53; **S**1085	23	10	S		77	2834	39	50.6	0	0	16870	5900	305
★□ ST. AGNES HOSPITAL AND MEDICAL CENTER, 1303 E. Herndon, Zip 93710; tel. 209/449-3000; Sr. Ruth Marie Nickerson, pres. & chief exec. off. **A**1a 9 10 **F**1 2 3 4 6 9 10 11 12 14 15 16 17 20 21 23 24 26 34 35 36 37 40 41 42 43 44 45 46 47 50 53 54; **S**5585	23	10	S		320	18253	243	75.9	22	2312	77464	36126	1621
★□ VALLEY CHILDREN'S HOSPITAL, 3151 N. Millbrook, Zip 93703; tel. 209/225-3000; James D. Northway MD, pres. & chief exec. off. **A**1a 2 3 5 9 10 **F**1 4 6 10 12 14 15 16 23 24 25 26 28 30 32 33 34 35 37 38 42 43 44 45 46 47 51 52 53 54	23	50	S		127	5595	87	68.5	0	0	39811	18880	873
★□ VALLEY MEDICAL CENTER OF FRESNO, 445 S. Cedar Ave., Zip 93702; tel. 209/453-4000; Manuel L. English PhD, adm. (Total facility includes 20 beds in nursing home-type unit) **A**1a 3 5 8 9 10 **F**1 2 3 5 6 7 8 9 10 11 12 14 16 19 20 21 22 23 24 26 27 28 30 34 35 36 40 42 44 45 46 47 51 52 53 54	13	10	S	TF H	271 251	16257 16075	255 230	94.1 —	18 18	3086 3086	82168 —	35648 —	1339 1319
★□ VETERANS ADMINISTRATION MEDICAL CENTER, 2615 E. Clinton Ave., Zip 93703; tel. 209/225-6100 (Total facility includes 60 beds in nursing home-type unit) **A**1a 2 3 5 8 **F**1 3 6 10 12 14 15 16 19 23 26 27 28 29 30 32 33 34 35 41 42 44 46 48 49 50 53 54	45	50	S	TF H	278 218	4770 4650	191 139	68.7 —	0 0	0 0	33521 —	22570 —	736 699
FULLERTON—Orange County													
★□ Δ ST. JUDE HOSPITAL-FULLERTON, 101 E. Valencia Mesa Dr., Zip 92635; Mailing Address Box 4138, Zip 92634; tel. 714/871-3280; Sr. Jane Frances, pres. **A**1a 2 7 9 10 **F**1 2 3 4 6 7 8 9 10 11 12 15 16 21 23 24 25 26 33 35 36 40 41 42 44 45 46 47 52 53 54; **S**5425	21	10	S		301	11017	190	63.1	32	1753	61009	25998	1152
GARBERVILLE—Humboldt County													
□ SOUTHERN HUMBOLDT COMMUNITY HOSPITAL DISTRICT, 733 Cedar St., Zip 95440; tel. 707/923-3921; Dian Pecora, adm. **A**1a 9 10 **F**1 15 16 35 36 40 45	16	10	S		18	483	4	22.2	2	86	1951	734	43
GARDEN GROVE—Orange County													
★□ AMI MEDICAL CENTER OF GARDEN GROVE (Formerly Medical Center of Garden Grove), 12601 Garden Grove Blvd., Zip 92643; tel. 714/537-5160; Mark Meyers, exec. dir. **A**1a 9 10 **F**1 3 6 12 14 15 16 23 24 26 34 35 36 37 40 45 46 47 53; **S**0125	33	10	S		175	4167	69	39.4	18	629	28839	8306	324
GARDENA—Los Angeles County													
★□ COMMUNITY HOSPITAL OF GARDENA, 1246 W. 155th St., Box 2106, Zip 90247; tel. 213/323-5330; James Sato, adm. **A**1a 9 10 **F**1 3 6 10 12 14 15 16 20 23 24 34 44 47; **S**1755	33	10	S		55	961	15	27.3	0	0	—	—	110
★□ MEMORIAL HOSPITAL OF GARDENA, 1145 W. Redondo Beach Blvd., Zip 90247; tel. 213/532-4200; Seth Ellis, adm. **A**1a 9 10 **F**1 3 6 7 8 9 10 11 12 14 15 16 17 20 23 24 26 34 35 36 37 40 41 42 44 45 46 47 53 54; **S**6525	33	10	S		131	4690	55	42.0	24	1501	21599	7830	286
GEORGE AIR FORCE BASE—San Bernardino County													
U. S. AIR FORCE HOSPITAL, Zip 92394; tel. 619/269-3060; Lt. Col. Fred Huberty MSC USAF, adm. **F**1 3 6 14 23 34 35 37 40 46	41	10	S		30	2435	21	70.0	9	466	—	—	264
GILROY—Santa Clara County													
★□ WHEELER HOSPITAL, 651 Sixth St., Zip 95020; tel. 408/842-5621; Mort G. Walser, adm. **A**1a 9 10 **F**1 3 6 10 12 15 16 23 34 35 36 40 44 45 46 47 53; **S**0965	23	10	S		56	2962	26	46.4	12	606	11399	4683	178
GLENDALE—Los Angeles County													
□ Δ GLENDALE ADVENTIST MEDICAL CENTER, 1509 Wilson Terr., Zip 91206; tel. 818/409-8000; Bob Scott, pres. **A**1a 2 3 5 7 9 10 **F**1 2 3 4 6 7 8 9 10 11 12 14 15 16 17 23 24 25 26 27 28 29 30 32 33 34 35 36 37 39 40 42 44 45 46 47 48 49 51 53 54; **S**0235	21	10	S		604	15256	378	62.6	30	2314	108014	44948	1871
★□ Δ GLENDALE MEMORIAL HOSPITAL AND HEALTH CENTER (Formerly Memorial Hospital of Glendale), 1420 S. Central Ave., Zip 91204; tel. 818/502-1900; William D. Parente, pres. (Nonreporting) **A**1a 2 7 9 10	23	10	S		310	—	—	—	—	—	—	—	—
MEMORIAL HOSPITAL OF GLENDALE, See Glendale Memorial Hospital and Health Center													
★□ VERDUGO HILLS HOSPITAL, 1812 Verdugo Blvd., Zip 91208; Mailing Address Box 1431, Zip 91209; tel. 818/790-7100; Ronald J. Davey, pres. **A**1a 9 10 **F**1 3 6 10 12 14 15 16 20 23 24 26 34 35 36 40 41 43 44 45 46 49 53	23	10	S		150	5815	85	56.7	17	876	32620	14365	510
GLENDORA—Los Angeles County													
★□ AMI GLENDORA COMMUNITY HOSPITAL (Formerly Glendora Community Hospital), 150 W. Alosta Ave., Zip 91740; tel. 818/335-0231; Joe Gagliardi, exec. dir. **A**1a 2 9 **F**1 6 10 12 14 15 16 17 20 23 34 35 36 37 40 41 45 46 50 52 53; **S**0125	33	10	S		143	4008	51	35.7	10	869	16628	5846	261
★□ FOOTHILL PRESBYTERIAN HOSPITAL-MORRIS L. JOHNSTON MEMORIAL, 250 S. Grand Ave., Zip 91740; tel. 818/963-8411; Donald D. Hitt, pres. **A**1a 2 9 10 **F**1 2 3 6 10 12 14 15 16 23 24 34 35 36 39 40 41 44 45 46 47 52 53	23	10	S		123	4001	50	40.7	8	517	20254	7777	356
GLENDORA COMMUNITY HOSPITAL, See AMI Glendora Community Hospital													
GOLETA—Santa Barbara County													
DEVEREUX FOUNDATION-CALIFORNIA, See Santa Barbara													
GRASS VALLEY—Nevada County													
★□ SIERRA NEVADA MEMORIAL HOSPITAL, 155 Glasson Way, Box 1029, Zip 95945; tel. 916/273-7221; Lloyd Hamilton, chief exec. off. **A**1a 9 10 **F**1 3 6 10 12 15 16 23 35 36 41 45 46 52 53	23	10	S		124	4723	61	49.2	10	707	22783	8724	380
GREENVILLE—Plumas County													
INDIAN VALLEY HOSPITAL DISTRICT, 174 Hot Springs Rd., Box 9, Zip 95947; tel. 916/284-7191; Claire Kuczkowski, adm. (Nonreporting) **A**9 10	16	10	S		26	—	—	—	—	—	—	—	—
GRIDLEY—Butte County													
★□ BIGGS-GRIDLEY MEMORIAL HOSPITAL, 240 Spruce St., Box 97, Zip 95948; tel. 916/846-5671; Charles B. Norton, adm. (Nonreporting) **A**1a 9 10	23	10	S		55	—	—	—	—	—	—	—	—
HANFORD—Kings County													
□ HANFORD COMMUNITY HOSPITAL, 450 Greenfield Ave., Zip 93230; Mailing Address Box 240, Zip 93232; tel. 209/582-9000; Fred Manchur, pres. (Nonreporting) **A**1a 9 10; **S**0235	21	10	S		50	—	—	—	—	—	—	—	—
★□ SACRED HEART HOSPITAL, 1025 N. Douty St., Box 480, Zip 93232; tel. 209/582-2551; Matt Luebbers, interim adm. **A**1a 9 10 **F**1 3 5 6 10 12 14 15 16 20 23 34 35 36 40 45 46 47 52 53; **S**5175	21	10	S		88	3328	40	45.5	11	609	11877	5508	292
HAWAIIAN GARDENS—Los Angeles County													
★□ CHARTER COMMUNITY HOSPITAL, 21530 S. Pioneer Blvd., Zip 90716; tel. 213/860-0401; Wendy Bardet, adm. (Nonreporting) **A**1a 9 10; **S**0695	33	10	S		150	—	—	—	—	—	—	—	—

Hospital, Address, Telephone, Administrator, Approval and Facility Codes, Multihospital System Code

- ★ American Hospital Association (AHA) membership
- □ Joint Commission on Accreditation of Hospitals (JCAH) accreditation
- \+ American Osteopathic Hospital Association (AOHA) membership
- ○ American Osteopathic Association (AOA) accreditation
- Δ Commission on Accreditation of Rehabilitation Facilities (CARF) accreditation

Control codes 61, 63, 64, 71, 72 and 73 indicate hospitals listed by AOHA, but not registered by AHA. For definition of numerical codes, see page A2

Hospital, Address, Telephone, Administrator, Approval and Facility Codes, Multihospital System Code	Classification Codes				Inpatient Data				Newborn Data		Expense (thousands of dollars)		
	Control	Service	Stay	Facilities	Beds	Admissions	Census	Occupancy (percent)	Bassinets	Births	Total	Payroll	Personnel
HAWTHORNE—Los Angeles County													
★□ HAWTHORNE HOSPITAL (Formerly Memorial Hospital of Hawthorne), 13300 S. Hawthorne Blvd., Zip 90250; tel. 213/679-3321; R. Kupferstein, adm. (Nonreporting) **A**1a 9 10; **S**0435	33	10	S		73	—	—	—	—	—	—	—	—
MEMORIAL HOSPITAL OF HAWTHORNE, See Hawthorne Hospital													
★□ ROBERT F. KENNEDY MEDICAL CENTER, 4500 W. 116th St., Zip 90250; tel. 213/970-0601; Robert C. Shaw, pres. & chief exec. off. **A**1a 2 9 10 **F**1 2 3 6 10 12 14 15 16 20 23 24 27 30 33 34 35 41 42 44 45 46 47 48 53	23	10	S		226	6611	136	60.2	0	0	38129	16178	792
HAYWARD—Alameda County													
★□ HAYWARD HOSPITAL (Formerly Hayward Vesper Hospital), 22455 Maple Ct., Zip 94541; tel. 415/886-9500; Ken Breaux, adm. (Nonreporting) **A**1a 9 10; **S**6525	33	10	S		166	—	—	—	—	—	—	—	—
HAYWARD VESPER HOSPITAL, See Hayward Hospital													
★□ KAISER FOUNDATION HOSPITAL, 27400 Hesperian Blvd., Zip 94545; tel. 415/784-4000; Ivan Fawley, adm. **A**1a 10 **F**1 3 5 6 9 12 15 16 21 23 26 28 33 34 35 40 41 43 46 49 51 52; **S**2105	23	10	S		230	12112	153	75.0	32	2914	—	—	—
★□ ST. ROSE HOSPITAL, 27200 Calaroga Ave., Zip 94545; tel. 415/782-6200; Dean Van Metre, pres. & chief exec. off. (Total facility includes 46 beds in nursing home-type unit) **A**1a 9 10 **F**1 3 5 6 10 12 14 15 16 19 20 23 24 26 34 35 36 40 41 42 44 45 46 48 49 53; **S**5435	21	10	S	TF	175	6849	114	65.1	23	1163	33362	17117	583
				H	129	6408	89	—	23	1163	—	—	476
HEALDSBURG—Sonoma County													
★□ AMI HEALDSBURG GENERAL HOSPITAL (Formerly Healdsburg General Hospital), 1375 University St., Box 696, Zip 95448; tel. 707/433-4461; Duane M. Kenward, exec. dir. (Nonreporting) **A**1a 9 10; **S**0125	33	10	S		49	—	—	—	—	—	—	—	—
HEMET—Riverside County													
★□ HEMET VALLEY HOSPITAL DISTRICT, 1117 E. Devonshire Ave., Zip 92343; tel. 714/652-2811; Thomas J. Broderick, adm. (Nonreporting) **A**1a 9 10	16	10	S		238	—	—	—	—	—	—	—	—
HOLLISTER—San Benito County													
HAZEL HAWKINS CONVALESCENT HOSPITAL, See San Benito Hospital District													
HAZEL HAWKINS MEMORIAL HOSPITAL, See San Benito Hospital District													
★□ SAN BENITO HOSPITAL DISTRICT (Includes Hazel Hawkins Memorial Hospital, 911 Sunset Dr., Zip 95023; tel. 408/637-5711; Thomas J. Harn, adm.; Hazel Hawkins Convalescent Hospital, 3110 Southside Rd., Zip 95023; tel. 408/637-5711), Mailing Address 911 Sunset Dr., Zip 95023; tel. 408/637-5711; Thomas Harn, adm. (Total facility includes 52 beds in nursing home-type unit) **A**1a 9 10 **F**1 3 6 15 16 19 23 24 33 34 35 36 40 42 44 45 46 47 50 53	16	10	S	TF	101	1729	67	66.3	10	406	7854	3244	172
				H	49	1675	16	—	10	406	6790	2681	132
HOOPA—Humboldt County													
KLAMATH-TRINITY COMMUNITY HOSPITAL, Box 1328, Zip 95546; tel. 916/625-4225; Jansen N. Blanton, adm. (Nonreporting) **A**10	33	10	S		16	—	—	—	—	—	—	—	—
HUNTINGTON BEACH—Orange County													
★□ HUMANA HOSPITAL -HUNTINGTON BEACH, 17772 Beach Blvd., Zip 92647; tel. 714/842-1473; Mark Aanonson, exec. dir. **A**1a 9 **F**1 2 3 6 12 14 15 16 23 27 30 32 33 35 36 40 45 46 47 52 53; **S**1235	33	10	S		141	4577	68	48.2	26	619	—	—	318
□ PACIFICA COMMUNITY HOSPITAL, 18792 Delaware St., Zip 92648; tel. 714/842-0611; Philip P. Gustafson, exec. dir. **A**1a 2 9 10 **F**1 3 6 12 15 16 20 23 27 28 30 32 33 34 35 45 46 49 53; **S**0045	33	10	S		109	3195	58	53.2	0	0	20979	6169	228
HUNTINGTON PARK—Los Angeles County													
□ COMMUNITY HOSPITAL OF HUNTINGTON PARK, 2623 E. Slauson Ave., Zip 90255; tel. 213/583-1931; Peter J. S. Friedman, adm. **A**1a 9 10 **F**1 3 10 12 16 17 20 23 35 52 53; **S**1375	33	10	S		56	2245	27	48.2	0	0	8366	3437	72
□ MISSION HOSPITAL, 3111 E. Florence Ave., Zip 90255; tel. 213/582-8261; Robert P. Hutchins, adm. (Nonreporting) **A**1a 9 10; **S**1375	33	10	S		127	—	—	—	—	—	—	—	—
IMOLA—Napa County													
NAPA STATE HOSPITAL, See Napa													
INDIO—Riverside County													
□ JOHN F. KENNEDY MEMORIAL HOSPITAL, 47-111 Monroe St., Zip 92201; Mailing Address P O Drawer LLLL, Zip 92202; tel. 619/347-6191; Fredrick W. Hodges, chief exec. off. **A**1a 2 9 10 **F**1 3 6 10 12 14 15 16 20 23 24 26 34 35 36 40 44 45 46 52 53; **S**3015	33	10	S		131	5651	66	50.4	24	1412	24460	9008	369
INGLEWOOD—Los Angeles County													
★□ Δ CENTINELA HOSPITAL MEDICAL CENTER, 555 E. Hardy St., Zip 90301; Mailing Address Box 720, Zip 90307; tel. 213/673-4660; Russell S. Stromberg, pres. **A**1a 2 3 7 9 10 **F**1 3 4 6 7 8 9 10 12 14 15 16 17 20 23 24 25 26 34 35 36 40 41 42 44 45 46 47 48 49 51 52 53 54	23	10	S		375	10704	221	58.9	31	1473	74779	34493	1291
★□ Δ DANIEL FREEMAN MEMORIAL HOSPITAL, 333 N. Prairie Ave., Zip 90301; Mailing Address Box 100, Zip 90306; tel. 213/674-7050; Sr. Regina Clare Salazar, pres. **A**1a 2 7 9 10 **F**1 2 3 4 5 6 7 8 9 10 11 12 14 15 16 17 20 23 24 25 26 34 35 37 41 42 44 45 46 47 52 53 54; **S**5945	21	10	S		395	10994	265	66.6	0	204	93861	38047	1738
□ INGLEWOOD GENERAL HOSPITAL, 426 E. 99th St., Zip 90301; tel. 213/674-5971; John R. Edwards, adm. (Nonreporting) **A**1a 9 10	33	10	S		28	—	—	—	—	—	—	—	—
JACKSON—Amador County													
□ AMADOR HOSPITAL, 810 Court St., Zip 95642; tel. 209/223-6600; Cliff D. Richards, adm. (Total facility includes 44 beds in nursing home-type unit) **A**1a 9 10 **F**1 3 6 10 12 14 15 16 19 23 24 35 36 37 40 45 46 50 53; **S**0615	13	10	S	TF	87	1537	61	70.1	5	149	7529	3459	156
				H	43	1484	18	—	5	149	6889	2980	125
JOSHUA TREE—San Bernardino County													
□ HI-DESERT MEDICAL CENTER, 6601 Whitefeather Rd., Zip 92252; tel. 619/366-3711; Joann O'Boyle, adm. **A**1a 9 10 **F**1 3 6 10 12 14 15 16 17 23 24 30 32 34 35 41 44 45 46 47 50 53	16	10	S		56	2386	36	64.3	0	0	10297	3445	144
KENTFIELD—Marin County													
★□ KENTFIELD MEDICAL HOSPITAL, 1125-B Sir Francis Drake Blvd., Zip 94904; tel. 415/456-9680; James R. Belding, adm. **A**1a 9 10 **F**16 23 24 26 34 42 44 45 46 50; **S**0615	33	46	S		48	333	26	54.2	0	0	6447	3279	126
KING CITY—Monterey County													
□ GEORGE L. MEE MEMORIAL HOSPITAL, 300 Canal St., Zip 93930; tel. 408/385-5491; Arthur Marcello, adm. **A**1a 9 10 **F**1 3 6 19 40 43 45 46 47; **S**0585	23	10	S		42	1148	11	26.2	9	230	4300	1895	101
KINGSBURG—Fresno County													
□ KINGSBURG GENERAL HOSPITAL, 1200 Smith St., Zip 93631; tel. 209/897-5841; Owen Shafner, interim adm. (Nonreporting) **A**1a 9 10; **S**9795	16	10	S		38	—	—	—	—	—	—	—	—
LA HABRA—Orange County													
★□ LA HABRA COMMUNITY HOSPITAL, 1251 W. Lambert Rd., Zip 90631; tel. 213/694-3838; Raymond C. Webb Jr., adm. **A**1a 9 10 **F**1 3 6 7 10 11 12 14 15 16 17 27 30 32 33 34 35 43 45 46 47 48 49 50 52; **S**1755	33	10	S		299	2528	61	20.4	0	0	—	—	277

Hospital, Address, Telephone, Administrator, Approval and Facility Codes, Multihospital System Code	Classification Codes				Inpatient Data				Newborn Data		Expense (thousands of dollars)		
★ American Hospital Association (AHA) membership □ Joint Commission on Accreditation of Hospitals (JCAH) accreditation + American Osteopathic Hospital Association (AOHA) membership ○ American Osteopathic Association (AOA) accreditation Δ Commission on Accreditation of Rehabilitation Facilities (CARF) accreditation Control codes 61, 63, 64, 71, 72 and 73 indicate hospitals listed by AOHA, but not registered by AHA. For definition of numerical codes, see page A2	Control	Service	Stay	Facilities	Beds	Admissions	Census	Occupancy (percent)	Bassinets	Births	Total	Payroll	Personnel
LA JOLLA—San Diego County													
CECIL H. AND IDA M. GREEN HOSPITAL OF SCRIPPS CLINIC, See Green Hospital of Scripps Clinic													
[★] GREEN HOSPITAL OF SCRIPPS CLINIC (Formerly Cecil H. and Ida M. Green Hospital of Scripps Clinic), 10666 N. Torrey Pines Rd., Zip 92037; tel. 714/455-9100; Richard M. Bracken, exec. dir. & adm. **A**1a 2 3 5 9 **F**1 3 6 8 9 10 11 12 14 16 23 24 33 39 44 46 53; **S**1755	33	10	S		158	6574	93	58.9	0	0	—	—	503
[★] Δ SCRIPPS MEMORIAL HOSPITAL-LA JOLLA, 9888 Genesee Ave., Zip 92037; Mailing Address Box 28, Zip 92038; tel. 619/457-4123; Martin Buser, sr. vice-pres. & adm. **A**1a b 2 7 9 10 **F**1 2 3 4 5 6 7 8 9 10 11 12 15 16 20 23 24 34 35 36 39 40 41 44 45 46 47 48 49 52 53 54; **S**1505	23	10	S		375	13892	251	66.9	27	1670	78186	33656	1088
LA MESA—San Diego County													
[★] GROSSMONT DISTRICT HOSPITAL, 5555 Grossmont Center Dr., Box 158, Zip 92042; tel. 619/465-0711; Michael H. Erne, chief exec. off. **A**1a 2 9 10 **F**1 2 3 4 6 9 10 11 12 14 15 16 20 23 24 25 26 27 28 29 30 32 33 34 35 36 37 38 40 41 42 44 45 46 47 51 52 53 54	16	10	S		402	17761	289	71.9	24	3208	80632	42875	1822
LA MIRADA—Los Angeles County													
[★] Δ MEDICAL CENTER OF LA MIRADA (Formerly La Mirada Community Hospital), 14900 E. Imperial Hwy., Zip 90637; tel. 213/941-2251; Noel Hecht, exec. dir. (Nonreporting) **A**1a 7 9 10; **S**1805	33	10	S		141	—	—	—	—	—	—	—	—
LA PALMA—Orange County													
[★] Δ LA PALMA INTERCOMMUNITY HOSPITAL, 7901 Walker St., Zip 90623; Mailing Address P O Box 5850, Buena Park, Zip 90622; tel. 714/670-7400; John R. Cochran III, chief exec. off. & adm. **A**1a 2 7 9 10 **F**1 2 3 6 10 12 14 15 16 17 23 24 25 26 30 32 33 34 35 36 40 42 44 45 46 47 48 49 53; **S**6905	23	10	S		136	3684	64	47.1	12	288	20136	7594	337
LAGUNA HILLS—Orange County													
□ SADDLEBACK COMMUNITY HOSPITAL, 24451 Health Center Dr., Zip 92653; tel. 714/837-4500; James L. Ray, exec. vice-pres. **A**1a 2 9 10 **F**1 2 3 4 5 6 9 10 11 12 15 16 21 23 24 25 26 33 35 38 41 42 44 45 46 47 53 54	23	10	S		175	7506	144	82.3	0	0	46042	19163	769
LAKE ARROWHEAD—San Bernardino County													
□ MOUNTAINS COMMUNITY HOSPITAL, Box 70, Zip 92352; tel. 714/336-3651; Joel Hile, adm. **A**1a 9 10 **F**1 6 12 14 15 16 23 24 26 34 35 36 40 42 43 48 49 52; **S**9795	33	10	S		28	952	15	46.9	0	110	7011	2541	111
LAKE ELSINORE—Riverside County													
INLAND VALLEY REGIONAL MEDICAL CENTER, See Wildomar													
LAKE ISABELLA—Kern County													
[★] KERN VALLEY HOSPITAL, 6412 Laurel Ave., Rte. 1, Box 152, Zip 93240; tel. 619/379-2681; D. E. Naworski, adm. **A**1a 9 10 **F**1 3 6 10 12 16 17 23 35 41 44 45 52 53	16	10	S		27	1275	17	63.0	0	1	4638	2360	135
LAKEPORT—Lake County													
[★] LAKESIDE COMMUNITY HOSPITAL, 5176 Hill Rd. E., P O Box 729, Zip 95453; tel. 707/263-5651; Will Sellers, adm. **A**1a 9 10 **F**1 3 6 10 15 16 23 24 26 34 35 44 46 47 53; **S**2245	23	10	S		35	1557	21	63.6	0	4	9419	3102	173
LAKEWOOD—Los Angeles County													
DOCTORS HOSPITAL OF LAKEWOOD-CLARK, 5300 Clark Ave., Zip 90712; tel. 213/866-9711; Michael Kerr, chief exec. off. & exec. dir. (Nonreporting) **A**9 10; **S**0825	33	82	S		90	—	—	—	—	—	—	—	—
□ DOCTORS HOSPITAL OF LAKEWOOD-SOUTH STREET, 3700 E. South St., Zip 90712; tel. 213/531-2550; Michael Kerr, chief exec. off. & exec. dir. **A**1a 2 9 10 **F**1 2 3 5 6 9 10 11 12 14 15 16 17 20 21 23 24 26 34 35 36 40 41 43 44 45 46 47 49 50 53 54; **S**3015	33	10	S		162	6468	98	60.5	16	594	—	—	452
LANCASTER—Los Angeles County													
[★] ANTELOPE VALLEY HOSPITAL MEDICAL CENTER, 1600 W. Ave. J, Zip 93534; tel. 805/949-5000; John T. Evans Jr., adm. **A**1a 9 10 **F**1 2 3 5 6 9 10 11 12 14 15 16 23 24 26 27 28 30 32 33 35 40 44 45 46 47 48 49 52 53	16	10	S		184	9598	149	81.0	10	2368	44131	21231	849
[★] LAC-HIGH DESERT HOSPITAL, 44900 N. 60th St. W., Zip 93536; tel. 805/945-8461; A. R. Fleischman, adm. (Total facility includes 72 beds in nursing home-type unit) **A**1a 9 10 **F**1 3 6 12 14 16 19 23 24 26 34 42 44; **S**5755	13	10	S	TF H	135 63	1700 1506	102 30	76.7 —	0 0	0 0	20584 —	10846 —	503 436
□ LANCASTER COMMUNITY HOSPITAL, 43830 N. Tenth St. W., Zip 93534; tel. 805/948-4781; Steven C. Schmidt, adm. (Nonreporting) **A**1a 9 10; **S**5765	33	10	S		132	—	—	—	—	—	—	—	—
LEMOORE—Kings County													
[★] NAVAL HOSPITAL, Zip 93246; tel. 209/998-4201; Capt. R. H. Brant MSC USN, CO **A**1a **F**1 6 10 23 28 32 34 35 37 40 45 46 47	43	10	S		27	1947	14	51.9	10	484	2849	—	242
LINDSAY—Tulare County													
[★] LINDSAY HOSPITAL MEDICAL CENTER, 740 N. Sequoia Ave., Box 1297, Zip 93247; tel. 209/562-4955; Frank F. Guyton, adm. (Total facility includes 51 beds in nursing home-type unit) **A**1a 9 10 **F**1 6 10 12 14 15 16 19 23 24 35 36 40 43 44 46 52; **S**6905	23	10	S	TF H	97 46	2134 2080	71 21	73.2 —	7 7	666 666	8648 6971	3537 2921	199 171
LIVERMORE—Alameda County													
[★] VALLEY MEMORIAL HOSPITAL, 1111 E. Stanley Blvd., Zip 94550; tel. 415/447-7000; Robert H. Fish, pres. & chief exec. off. **A**1a 9 10 **F**1 3 6 10 12 14 15 16 23 24 26 33 35 36 40 41 43 45 46 52 53	23	10	S		110	5170	59	53.6	8	932	26384	11446	349
[★] VETERANS ADMINISTRATION MEDICAL CENTER, 4951 Arroyo Rd., Zip 94550; tel. 415/447-2560; Marvin E. O'Rear, dir. (Total facility includes 120 beds in nursing home-type unit) **A**1a 2 **F**1 3 6 10 12 14 15 16 19 23 24 25 26 28 32 33 34 42 44 46 47 50 53	45	10	S	TF H	284 164	1952 1866	201 94	70.8 —	0 0	0 0	21080 15665	13965 10190	525 421
LODI—San Joaquin County													
[★] COMMUNITY HOSPITAL OF LODI (Formerly Lodi Community Hospital), 800 S. Lower Sacramento Rd., Zip 95242; tel. 209/333-0211; James T. Lassiter, adm. (Nonreporting) **A**1a 9 10; **S**5765	31	10	S		93	—	—	—	—	—	—	—	—
LODI COMMUNITY HOSPITAL, See Community Hospital of Lodi													
[★] LODI MEMORIAL HOSPITAL, 975 S. Fairmont Ave., Call Box 3004, Zip 95241; tel. 209/334-3411; Richard E. Sandford, adm. **A**1a 9 10 **F**1 3 6 9 10 12 15 16 23 24 34 35 36 37 39 40 41 44 45 46 50 52 53	23	10	S		99	4893	63	63.6	16	837	19725	9594	350
LOMA LINDA—San Bernardino County													
[★] JERRY L. PETTIS MEMORIAL VETERANS HOSPITAL, 11201 Benton St., Zip 92357; tel. 714/825-7084; John F. Hickman, dir. (Total facility includes 60 beds in nursing home-type unit) **A**1a b 3 5 8 **F**1 2 3 6 10 12 15 16 19 20 23 24 25 26 27 28 29 30 31 32 33 34 35 41 42 43 44 46 47 48 49 50 53 54	45	10	S	TF H	462 402	10028 9892	402 345	87.0 —	0 0	0 0	60330 —	35906 —	1231 1201
[★] LOMA LINDA COMMUNITY HOSPITAL, 25333 Barton Rd., Zip 92354; tel. 714/796-0167; Everett J. Gooch, pres. **A**1a 9 10 **F**1 3 6 10 16 20 23 35 46 47 48 52 53	21	10	S		120	3865	61	50.8	0	0	17770	6545	326

★ American Hospital Association (AHA) membership
□ Joint Commission on Accreditation of Hospitals (JCAH) accreditation
+ American Osteopathic Hospital Association (AOHA) membership
○ American Osteopathic Association (AOA) accreditation
Δ Commission on Accreditation of Rehabilitation Facilities (CARF) accreditation
Control codes 61, 63, 64, 71, 72 and 73 indicate hospitals listed by AOHA, but not registered by AHA.
For definition of numerical codes, see page A2

Hospital, Address, Telephone, Administrator, Approval and Facility Codes, Multihospital System Code	Classification Codes				Inpatient Data				Newborn Data		Expense (thousands of dollars)		
	Control	Service	Stay	Facilities	Beds	Admissions	Census	Occupancy (percent)	Bassinets	Births	Total	Payroll	Personnel
□★ LOMA LINDA UNIVERSITY MEDICAL CENTER, 11234 Anderson St., Box 2000, Zip 92354; tel. 714/796-7311; John D. Ruffcorn, pres. **A**1a 2 3 5 8 9 10 **F**1 2 3 4 5 6 7 8 9 10 11 12 13 14 15 16 17 20 23 24 25 26 27 28 30 33 34 35 37 38 39 40 41 42 44 45 46 47 51 52 53 54	21	10	S		525	20520	445	84.8	12	1768	189122	73703	—
LOMPOC—Santa Barbara County													
□ LOMPOC DISTRICT HOSPITAL, 508 E. Hickory St., Zip 93436; Mailing Address Box 1058, Zip 93438; tel. 805/735-3351; Joseph P. Diruscio, adm. (Nonreporting) **A**1a 9 10	16	10	S		170	—	—	—	—	—	—	—	—
U. S. AIR FORCE HOSPITAL, See Vandenberg Air Force Base													
U. S. PENITENTIARY HOSPITAL, Zip 93436; tel. 805/735-2771; J. Van Tassel, adm. **F**1 23 33 34 35	46	10	S		25	113	2	8.0	0	0	—	—	18
LONE PINE—Inyo County													
□ SOUTHERN INYO HOSPITAL, 501 E. Locust St., Box 1009, Zip 93545; tel. 619/876-5501 (Nonreporting) **A**1a 9 10	16	10	S		35	—	—	—	—	—	—	—	—
LONG BEACH—Los Angeles County													
□★ CHARTER HOSPITAL OF LONG BEACH (Formerly Charter Baywood Hospital), 6060 Paramount Blvd., Zip 90805; tel. 213/634-9102; James Sholes, chief exec. off. **A**1a 9 10 **F**24 30 32 33 42 44 45 46; **S**0695	33	22	S		187	1922	117	62.6	0	0	—	—	224
□ DOMINGUEZ MEDICAL CENTER (Formerly Dominguez Valley Hospital), 171 W. Bort St., P O Box 5806, Zip 90805; tel. 213/639-5151; Lorraine P. Auerbach, chief exec. off. (Nonreporting) **A**1a 9 10; **S**3015	33	10	S		250	—	—	—	—	—	—	—	—
DOMINGUEZ VALLEY HOSPITAL, See Dominguez Medical Center													
□★ LONG BEACH COMMUNITY HOSPITAL, 1720 Termino Ave., Zip 90804; Mailing Address Box 2587, Zip 90801; tel. 213/498-1000; Paul S. Viviano, exec. vice-pres. & chief exec. off. **A**1a 2 9 10 **F**1 2 3 4 6 7 8 9 10 11 12 14 16 17 20 21 23 24 26 27 29 34 35 36 40 41 42 43 44 45 46 47 48 49 50 53 54; **S**6905	23	10	S		284	9210	139	49.1	28	2282	42280	18928	993
□★ LONG BEACH HOSPITAL, 1725 Pacific Ave., Zip 90813; tel. 213/599-3551; Dick W. Dillingham, adm. **A**1a 9 10 **F**1 3 12 16 20 23	33	10	S		43	1232	18	41.9	0	0	4779	2044	110
□ LOS ALTOS HOSPITAL AND MENTAL HEALTH CENTER (Formerly Los Altos Hospital), 3340 Los Coyotes Diagonal, Box 8000, Zip 90808; tel. 213/421-9311; Thomas R. Mesa, adm. (Nonreporting) **A**1a 2 9; **S**0825	33	10	S		97	—	—	—	—	—	—	—	—
□★ MEMORIAL MEDICAL CENTER, 2801 Atlantic Ave., Box 1428, Zip 90801; tel. 213/595-2311; Darrell Brownell, exec. vice-pres. & chief oper. off. **A**1a 2 3 5 8 10 **F**1 2 3 4 5 6 7 8 9 10 11 12 14 15 16 17 21 23 24 25 26 27 32 33 34 35 36 38 39 40 41 42 44 45 46 48 50 51 52 53 54	23	10	S		848	33364	643	75.8	65	5454	180795	82644	2892
□★ NAVAL HOSPITAL (Includes Medical Clinic, Marine Corp Air Sta., El Toro, Zip 92709; tel. 714/651-3158), Zip 90822; tel. 213/420-5201; RADM M. F. Hall, CO **A**1a **F**1 6 10 12 14 15 16 23 28 32 33 34 37 44 46 47 48 49 52 53	43	10	S		166	5111	100	60.2	0	142	22457	—	1076
□ ○ PACIFIC HOSPITAL OF LONG BEACH, 2776 Pacific Ave., P O Box 1268, Zip 90801; tel. 213/595-1911; Gerald S. Goldberg, adm. & chief exec. off. **A**1a 9 10 11 12 13 **F**1 3 6 8 9 10 11 12 15 16 17 20 21 23 24 25 26 34 35 36 38 40 44 45 46 48 53	23	10	S		208	4842	76	36.5	11	465	22561	9704	460
★ REDGATE MEMORIAL HOSPITAL, 1775 Chestnut Ave., Zip 90813; tel. 213/599-8444; Elizabeth Stanley, adm. (Nonreporting) **A**9	23	82	S		75	—	—	—	—	—	—	—	—
□★ ST. MARY MEDICAL CENTER, 1050 Linden Ave., Box 887, Zip 90801; tel. 213/491-9000; Sr. Mary Lucille Desmond, adm. (Nonreporting) **A**1a 2 3 5 9 10; **S**0605	21	10	S		431	—	—	—	—	—	—	—	—
□★ VETERANS ADMINISTRATION MEDICAL CENTER, 5901 E. Seventh St., Zip 90822; tel. 213/494-2611; Dean R. Stordahl, dir. (Total facility includes 270 beds in nursing home-type unit) **A**1a 2 3 5 **F**1 2 3 4 6 7 8 9 10 11 12 14 15 16 19 20 23 24 25 26 27 28 29 30 32 33 34 35 41 42 44 45 46 47 48 49 50 53 54	45	10	S	TF H	1166 896	18146 17910	938 673	79.0 —	0 0	0 0	133860 —	91453 —	3088 3003
□ WOODRUFF COMMUNITY HOSPITAL, 3800 Woodruff Ave., Zip 90808; tel. 213/421-8241; Maryann J. Greenwell, adm. **A**1a 9 10 **F**1 3 6 12 14 15 16 19 23 24 35 44 45 46; **S**1375	33	10	S		99	1489	26	26.3	0	0	7861	3168	178
LOS ALAMITOS—Orange County													
□ LOS ALAMITOS MEDICAL CENTER, 3751 Katella Ave., Zip 90720; tel. 213/598-1311; Nicholas V. McClure, exec. dir. **A**1a 2 9 10 **F**1 3 6 7 8 9 10 11 12 14 15 16 17 20 21 23 35 36 40 45 46 47 52 53; **S**3015	33	10	S		173	7565	83	48.0	13	515	23859	8772	437
LOS ANGELES—Los Angeles County													
□★ AMI MEDICAL CENTER OF NORTH HOLLYWOOD, 12629 Riverside Dr., Zip 91607; tel. 818/984-1165; Michael Weinstein, pres. & chief exec. off. (Nonreporting) **A**1a 9 10; **S**0125	33	10	S		182	—	—	—	—	—	—	—	—
□★ AMI RANCHO ENCINO HOSPITAL (Formerly Rancho Encino Hospital), 5333 Balboa Blvd., Zip 91316; tel. 818/788-4400; Frank Montague, chief exec. off. **A**1a 10 **F**1 3 6 7 8 9 10 11 12 15 16 20 23 24 32 34 35 37 44 45 46 50 53; **S**0125	33	10	S		102	2525	35	34.3	0	0	14976	4843	180
□★ AMI TARZANA REGIONAL MEDICAL CENTER (Formerly Medical Center of Tarzana Hospital), 18321 Clark St., Zip 91356; tel. 818/881-0800; Arnold N. Kimmel, exec. dir. **A**1a 2 9 10 **F**1 2 3 6 7 9 10 11 12 14 15 16 17 23 24 35 36 37 39 40 46 47 51 52 53 54; **S**0125	33	10	S		212	9378	126	59.4	28	1942	53993	18503	627
□ BARLOW HOSPITAL, 2000 Stadium Way, Zip 90026; tel. 213/250-4200; Hans E. Einstein MD, med. dir. **A**1a 9 10 **F**3 16 19 23 24 25 26 33 34 44 46	23	23	L		63	303	40	63.5	0	0	12453	5292	211
□★ BAY HARBOR HOSPITAL, 1437 W. Lomita Blvd., Zip 90710; tel. 213/325-1221; Joel J. Prell, chief exec. off. & adm. (Total facility includes 212 beds in nursing home-type unit) **A**1a 2 9 10 **F**1 2 3 6 9 10 11 12 14 15 16 17 19 20 21 23 24 25 26 34 35 36 37 40 41 43 44 45 46 47 52 53	23	10	S	TF H	353 141	5692 4791	248 77	70.3 —	9 9	804 804	30239 24513	13719 10901	— —
BEVERLY GLEN HOSPITAL (Substance Abuse), 10361 W. Pico Blvd., Zip 90064; tel. 213/277-5111; Philip Herschman PhD, adm. (Nonreporting) **A** 9 10	33	49	S		80	—	—	—	—	—	—	—	—
□★ BEVERLY HILLS MEDICAL CENTER, 1177 S. Beverly Dr., Zip 90035; tel. 213/553-5155; Jeffrey P. Winter, adm. (Nonreporting) **A**1a 9 10; **S**6525	33	10	S		241	—	—	—	—	—	—	—	—
BRENTWOOD VETERANS ADMINISTRATION DIVISION, See Veterans Administration Medical Center-West Los Angeles													
CALIFORNIA HOSPITAL MEDICAL CENTER, See California Medical Center-Los Angeles													
□★ CALIFORNIA MEDICAL CENTER-LOS ANGELES (Formerly California Hospital Medical Center), 1414 S. Hope St., Zip 90015; tel. 213/748-2411; William F. Haug, pres. **A**1a 2 3 5 9 10 **F**1 3 6 7 8 9 10 12 14 15 16 19 23 24 26 34 35 36 37 38 40 44 45 46 50 51 52 53; **S**2245	23	10	S		278	12293	191	68.7	30	2891	58558	26523	869
□ CANOGA PARK HOSPITAL, 20800 Sherman Way, Zip 91306; tel. 818/348-0200; Barbara Meyers, adm. (Nonreporting) **A**1a 9 10	32	10	S		72	—	—	—	—	—	—	—	—
□ CAREUNIT BEHAVIORAL CENTER LOS ANGELES (Formerly Care Unit Hospital of Los Angeles), 5035 Coliseum St., Zip 90016; tel. 213/295-6441; Gregory L. McAllester, adm. **A**1b 9 10 **F**15 16 17 23 24 27 29 31 32 42 44 46 49; **S**0275	33	82	S		104	822	48	46.2	0	0	7392	2551	132

★ American Hospital Association (AHA) membership
□ Joint Commission on Accreditation of Hospitals (JCAH) accreditation
+ American Osteopathic Hospital Association (AOHA) membership
○ American Osteopathic Association (AOA) accreditation
Δ Commission on Accreditation of Rehabilitation Facilities (CARF) accreditation
Control codes 61, 63, 64, 71, 72 and 73 indicate hospitals listed by AOHA, but not registered by AHA.
For definition of numerical codes, see page A2

Hospital, Address, Telephone, Administrator, Approval and Facility Codes, Multihospital System Code	Classification Codes				Inpatient Data				Newborn Data		Expense (thousands of dollars)		
	Control	Service	Stay	Facilities	Beds	Admissions	Census	Occupancy (percent)	Bassinets	Births	Total	Payroll	Personnel
★□ CEDARS-SINAI MEDICAL CENTER, 8700 Beverly Blvd., Box 48750, Zip 90048; tel. 213/855-5000; Stuart J. Marylander, pres.; Thomas M. Priselac, sr. vice-pres. oper. **A**1a 2 3 5 8 9 10 **F**1 2 3 4 5 6 7 8 9 10 11 12 13 14 15 16 17 20 21 23 24 25 26 27 28 29 30 31 32 33 34 35 36 37 38 40 41 42 43 44 45 46 47 48 49 50 51 52 53 54	23	10	S		1013	39256	724	71.5	57	6422	288415	132361	4954
□ CENTURY CITY HOSPITAL, 2070 Century Park E., Zip 90067; tel. 213/201-6610; Joel Bergenfeld, exec. dir. (Nonreporting) **A**1a 9 10; **S**3015	33	10	S		195	—	—	—	—	—	—	—	—
CENTURY COMMUNITY HOSPITAL, 9500 S. Broadway, Zip 90003; tel. 213/777-7663; Robert Bourseau, adm. (Nonreporting) **A**9; **S**3015	32	10	S		50	—	—	—	—	—	—	—	—
★□ CHILDRENS HOSPITAL OF LOS ANGELES, 4650 Sunset Blvd., Box 54700, Zip 90054; tel. 213/660-2450; Jane Hurd, chief exec. off. **A**1a 2 3 5 8 9 10 **F**1 3 4 5 6 7 8 9 10 11 12 13 14 15 16 20 23 24 28 32 33 34 35 37 42 44 45 46 47 51 53 54	23	50	S		331	11501	232	70.1	0	0	124216	63250	2216
□ CIGNA HOSPITAL OF LOS ANGELES, 1711 W. Temple St., Zip 90026; tel. 213/413-1313; Lawrence Robinow, vice-pres. (Total facility includes 28 beds in nursing home-type unit) **A**1a 9 10 **F**1 3 6 9 10 16 19 20 23 24 44 46 47 53	33	10	S	TF	145	5438	93	64.1	0	0	23972	7182	308
				H	117	5116	74	—	0	0	—	—	292
★ COLDWATER CANYON HOSPITAL, 6421 Coldwater Canyon, Zip 91606; tel. 818/769-1000; John M. Wilson, adm. **A**10 **F**24 29 32 33 42 48; **S**6905	23	22	L		70	511	47	67.1	0	0	7576	2711	113
□ CPC WESTWOOD HOSPITAL, 2112 S. Barrington Ave., Zip 90025; tel. 213/479-4281; Sue L. Blackburn, adm. **A**1a 9 10 **F**24 32 40 42 43 45 47 49; **S**0785	33	22	L		94	538	40	43.0	0	0	—	—	80
□ CRENSHAW CENTER HOSPITAL, 3831 Stocker St., Zip 90008; tel. 213/292-0221; Robert Shell, adm. (Nonreporting) **A**1a 9 10; **S**0615	33	10	S		48	—	—	—	—	—	—	—	—
★□ CROSSROADS HOSPITAL, 6323 Woodman Ave., Zip 91401; tel. 818/782-2470; Rebecca Highman, adm. (Nonreporting) **A**1a 9; **S**0275	33	52	L		43	—	—	—	—	—	—	—	—
★□ DANIEL FREEMAN MARINA HOSPITAL, 4650 Lincoln Blvd., Zip 90291; tel. 213/823-8911; Stephen L. Packwood, adm. **A**1a 9 10 **F**1 2 3 6 12 14 15 16 23 24 25 26 30 32 33 35 44 45 46 47 48 49 53; **S**5945	21	10	S		203	4130	84	41.4	0	0	34365	10081	323
□ EAST LOS ANGELES DOCTORS HOSPITAL, 4060 Whitter Blvd., Zip 90023; tel. 213/268-5514; T. R. Estrada, chief exec. off.; Luana D. Murphy, adm. **A**1a 9 10 **F**1 3 6 10 12 14 16 23 34 35 40 53	23	10	S		128	4067	55	43.0	8	582	14064	4798	229
□ EDGEMONT HOSPITAL, 4841 Hollywood Blvd., Zip 90027; tel. 213/666-5252; Nancy Decoster RN, adm. **A**1b 9 10 **F**3 23 24 28 30 32 33 42 44 47	33	22	S		55	622	32	58.2	0	0	6080	2191	99
★□ ENCINO HOSPITAL, 16237 Ventura Blvd., Zip 91436; tel. 818/995-5003; Stephen Bernstein, adm. **A**1a 2 9 10 **F**1 2 3 4 6 9 10 12 14 16 20 23 24 25 26 35 44 46 47 53 54; **S**1755	33	10	S		189	4044	67	35.4	0	0	—	—	371
★ ESTELLE DOHENY EYE HOSPITAL, 1537 Norfolk St., Zip 90033; tel. 213/224-5000; Paul J. Hensler, adm. **A**9 10 **F**1 6 13 16 34; **S**1755	23	45	S		35	1113	10	28.6	0	0	5754	1783	73
□ FEDERAL CORRECTIONAL INSTITUTION, Terminal Island, Zip 90731; tel. 213/831-8961; Walter G. Bunselmeyer, adm. off. **A**1a **F**1 15 16 23 24 26 27 28 29 30 32 33 34 35 37 42 43 49 50	48	11	S		37	194	32	86.5	0	0	1536	791	32
★□ FRENCH HOSPITAL OF LOS ANGELES, 531 W. College St., Zip 90012; tel. 213/624-8411; Donald W. Carrico, chief exec. off. **A**1a 9 10 **F**1 3 6 10 12 14 15 16 23 35 37 40 41 43 45 46 47	23	10	S		125	5319	82	65.6	16	995	18688	8553	314
GATEWAYS HOSPITAL AND MENTAL HEALTH CENTER, 1891 Effie St., Zip 90026; tel. 213/666-0171; Al Sorkin, adm. (Nonreporting) **A** 9 10	23	22	S		154	—	—	—	—	—	—	—	—
★□ GRANADA HILLS COMMUNITY HOSPITAL, 10445 Balboa Blvd., Zip 91344; tel. 818/360-1021; Dennis E. Coleman, chief exec. off. **A**1a 2 9 10 **F**1 3 4 6 10 12 14 16 20 23 24 26 34 35 40 43 44 45 46 53 54	23	10	S		201	5580	88	43.8	16	1110	35221	12253	594
□ HOLLYWOOD COMMUNITY HOSPITAL, 6245 De Longpre Ave., Zip 90028; tel. 213/462-2271; Rodger L. Morrison, adm. (Nonreporting) **A**1a 9 10; **S**5765	33	10	S		99	—	—	—	—	—	—	—	—
□ HOLLYWOOD PRESBYTERIAN MEDICAL CENTER, 1300 N. Vermont Ave., Zip 90027; tel. 213/660-3530; Allene Nungasser, chief exec. off. (Total facility includes 57 beds in nursing home-type unit) **A**1a 2 3 5 9 10 **F**1 2 3 4 5 6 7 8 10 11 12 14 16 19 20 23 24 26 34 35 36 40 41 43 44 45 46 47 53 54	23	10	S	TF	291	11500	217	73.3	34	2194	68859	28626	1216
				H	234	11154	183	—	34	2194	67908	27951	1188
★□ HOLY CROSS HOSPITAL, 15031 Rinaldi St., Zip 91345; tel. 818/365-8051; Sr. M. Carolita, pres. & chief exec. off. (Total facility includes 88 beds in nursing home-type unit) **A**1a 10 **F**1 3 5 6 10 12 15 16 17 19 20 23 24 26 34 35 36 38 40 41 44 45 46 48 49 52 53 54; **S**5585	21	10	S	TF	311	10645	226	72.7	31	2368	44742	17353	732
				H	223	10111	148	—	31	2368	43694	16713	656
□ HOSPITAL DEL PUEBLO, 5425 E. Pomona Blvd., Zip 90022; tel. 213/738-7331; Tim Kollars, adm. (Nonreporting) **A**1a	33	10	S		61	—	—	—	—	—	—	—	—
★□ HOSPITAL OF THE GOOD SAMARITAN, 616 S. Witmer St., Zip 90017; tel. 213/977-2121; John H. Westerman, pres. & chief exec. off. **A**1a 2 3 5 8 9 10 **F**1 3 4 6 7 8 9 10 11 12 14 15 16 17 20 23 24 25 26 28 32 33 34 35 37 38 41 42 44 45 46 47 50 53 54	23	10	S		282	9593	196	67.1	0	0	70573	31011	1215
★□ HUMANA HOSPITAL -WEST HILLS, 7300 Medical Center Dr., Zip 91307; tel. 818/712-4110; Michael B. McCallister, exec. dir. **A**1a 9 10 **F**1 2 3 4 6 10 12 14 15 16 17 23 24 30 35 36 40 44 45 46 47 48 49 50 51 52 53 54; **S**1235	33	10	S		236	7355	107	45.3	12	1106	—	—	544
★□ KAISER FOUNDATION HOSPITAL-HARBOR CITY, 25825 S. Vermont Ave., Zip 90710; tel. 213/325-5111; James C. Heidenreich, adm. **A**1a 2 9 10 **F**1 2 3 6 9 10 12 14 16 20 23 24 35 36 40 41 44 50 52 53; **S**2105	23	10	S		231	11121	175	75.8	27	2020	—	—	883
★□ KAISER FOUNDATION HOSPITAL-PANORAMA CITY, 13652 Cantara St., Zip 91402; tel. 818/908-2000; Nancy A. Nightingale, adm. (Total facility includes 46 beds in nursing home-type unit) **A**1a 2 3 5 9 10 **F**1 2 3 6 10 12 14 15 16 19 20 21 23 24 30 32 33 35 40 41 42 44 46 47 51 52 53; **S**2105	23	10	S	TF	331	14670	240	72.5	32	2617	—	—	1127
				H	285	14169	198	—	32	2617	—	—	1057
★□ KAISER FOUNDATION HOSPITAL-SUNSET, 4867 Sunset Blvd., Zip 90027; tel. 213/667-4011; Joseph William Hummel, adm. (Total facility includes 46 beds in nursing home-type unit) **A**1a 2 3 5 9 10 **F**1 2 3 4 6 7 8 9 10 11 12 13 14 15 16 19 20 21 23 24 26 35 40 41 42 44 46 47 51 52 53 54; **S**2105	23	10	S	TF	613	26053	439	71.3	64	4423	—	—	2086
				H	567	25540	412	—	64	4423	—	—	2032
★□ KAISER FOUNDATION HOSPITAL-WEST LOS ANGELES, 6041 Cadillac Ave., Zip 90034; tel. 213/857-2201; Ophelia Long RN, adm. **A**1a 2 3 5 9 10 **F**1 3 6 10 12 14 15 16 20 23 24 30 35 36 37 40 41 42 44 46 51 52 53 54; **S**2105	23	10	S		220	11768	179	81.4	41	2311	—	—	548
★□ KAISER FOUNDATION MENTAL HEALTH CENTER, 765 W. College St., Zip 90012; tel. 213/250-8500; Jose A. Samartin, adm. **A**1b 10 **F**24 32 33 42; **S**2105	23	22	S		55	1547	45	81.8	0	0	—	—	133
★□ LAC COUNTY-KING-DREW MEDICAL CENTER, 12021 S. Wilmington Ave., Zip 90059; tel. 213/603-5201; William A. Delgardo, adm. **A**1a 2 3 5 8 9 10 **F**1 3 4 5 6 10 12 14 15 16 20 23 24 26 27 28 29 30 31 32 33 34 35 36 37 38 40 42 44 45 46 50 51 52 53 54; **S**5755	13	10	S		396	24899	377	95.9	26	8321	149411	64183	2727
★□ LAC-UNIVERSITY OF SOUTHERN CALIFORNIA MEDICAL CENTER (Includes General Hospital, 1200 N. State St., Zip 90033; Pediatric Pavilion, 1129 N. State St., Zip 90033; Psychiatric Hospital, 1934 Hospital Pl., Zip 90033; Women's Hospital, 1240 N. Mission Rd., P O Box 1938, Zip 90033), 1200 N. State St., Zip 90033; tel. 213/226-2345; J. L. Buckingham, exec. dir. **A**1a b 2 3 5 6 8 9 10 **F**1 2 3 4 5 6 7 8 9 10 11 12 13 14 15 16 20 22 23 24 26 27 28 29 30 32 33 34 35 36 37 38 40 41 42 43 44 45 46 47 49 50 51 52 53 54; **S**5755	13	10	S		1454	80298	1232	84.7	140	17371	418722	193654	7210

Hospital, Address, Telephone, Administrator, Approval and Facility Codes, Multihospital System Code	Classification Codes				Inpatient Data				Newborn Data		Expense (thousands of dollars)		
★ American Hospital Association (AHA) membership □ Joint Commission on Accreditation of Hospitals (JCAH) accreditation + American Osteopathic Hospital Association (AOHA) membership ○ American Osteopathic Association (AOA) accreditation Δ Commission on Accreditation of Rehabilitation Facilities (CARF) accreditation Control codes 61, 63, 64, 71, 72 and 73 indicate hospitals listed by AOHA, but not registered by AHA. For definition of numerical codes, see page A2	Control	Service	Stay	Facilities	Beds	Admissions	Census	Occupancy (percent)	Bassinets	Births	Total	Payroll	Personnel
LINCOLN HOSPITAL MEDICAL CENTER, 443 S. Soto St., Zip 90033; tel. 213/261-1181; Tim Kollars, adm. (Nonreporting) **A**9	33	10	S		47	—	—	—	—	—	—	—	—
□ LINDA VISTA COMMUNITY HOSPITAL (Formerly Santa Fe Community Hospital), 610 S. St. Louis St., Zip 90023; tel. 213/265-0789; Louis Rubino, adm. **A**1a 9 10 **F**1 3 14 16 23 34 35; **S**1375	33	10	S		150	950	18	12.0	0	0	8514	2711	122
□ LOS ANGELES COMMUNITY HOSPITAL, 4081 E. Olympic Blvd., Zip 90023; tel. 213/267-0477; Kenneth H. Madfes, adm. **A**1a 9 10 **F**3 6 10 14 16 20 23 24 26 35 44 53; **S**5765	33	10	L		142	4000	46	32.0	16	840	—	—	165
LOS ANGELES COUNTY CENTRAL JAIL HOSPITAL, 441 Bauchet St., Zip 90012; tel. 213/974-5045; William H. Kern, dir. (Nonreporting)	13	11	S		346	—	—	—	—	—	—	—	—
□ MAXICARE MEDICAL CENTER, 5525 W. Slauson Ave., Zip 90056; tel. 213/410-0999; Richard Feldman, exec. dir. **A**1a 9 10 **F**1 3 6 10 14 15 16 20 23 34 36 37 40 47 51 53	33	10	S		76	3930	39	51.3	24	1337	19608	7308	215
METROPOLITAN HOSPITAL, 2001 S. Hoover St., Zip 90007; tel. 213/748-0211; Victoria M. Carbon, adm. (Nonreporting) **A**9	33	10	S		50	—	—	—	—	—	—	—	—
□ MIDWAY HOSPITAL MEDICAL CENTER, 5925 San Vicente Blvd., Zip 90019; Mailing Address Box 35909, Zip 90035; tel. 213/938-3161; Philip A. Cohen, reg. vice-pres. (Nonreporting) **A**1a 9; **S**3025	33	10	S		230	—	—	—	—	—	—	—	—
★ MOTION PICTURE AND TELEVISION HOSPITAL, 23388 Mulholland Dr., Zip 91364; tel. 818/347-1591; John M. Pavlik, exec. dir.; Robert D. Tonry, adm. & dir. health serv. **A**1a 9 10 **F**1 3 6 9 12 14 15 16 19 21 23 24 26 28 32 33 34 37 42 43 46 47 50 53	23	10	S		170	761	142	83.5	0	0	18095	11412	495
★ Δ NORTHRIDGE HOSPITAL MEDICAL CENTER, 18300 Roscoe Blvd., Zip 91328; tel. 818/885-8500; Daniel F. Adams, exec. vice-pres. & chief exec. off. **A**1a 2 3 5 7 9 10 **F**1 3 4 5 6 7 8 9 10 11 12 14 15 16 17 20 21 23 24 25 26 27 28 29 30 32 33 34 35 36 37 40 41 42 43 44 45 46 47 49 50 51 52 53 54; **S**6905	23	10	S		345	11996	282	81.7	16	2456	78948	33839	1405
★ NU-MED REGIONAL MEDICAL CENTER-WEST VALLEY (Includes Nu-Med Regional Medical Center West Valley-North Campus, 22141 Roscoe Blvd., Zip 91304; tel. 213/340-0580; George Rooth, chief exec. off.; Nu-Med Regional Medical Center West Valley-South Campus, 7011 Shoup Ave., Zip 91307; tel. 818/348-0500; Claudia Haynes-Streaty, adm). 22141 Roscoe Blvd., Zip 91304; tel. 818/340-0580; George Rooth, Exec. Dir. **A**1a 9 10 **F**1 3 6 12 14 15 16 21 23 24 35 36 40 43 45 46 48 49 53 54	33	10	S		159	2377	37	23.3	13	238	20053	5506	382
★ ORTHOPAEDIC HOSPITAL, 2400 S. Flower St., Zip 90007; Mailing Address Box 60132, Terminal Annex, Zip 90060; tel. 213/742-1000; Jeffrey S. Kirschner, pres. & chief exec. off. **A**1a 2 3 5 9 10 **F**1 3 6 10 12 14 15 16 23 24 26 28 32 33 34 35 38 42 44 45 46 47 50 52	23	47	S		105	3483	60	49.6	0	0	40650	16039	691
□ PANORAMA COMMUNITY HOSPITAL, 14850 Roscoe Blvd., Zip 91402; tel. 818/787-2222; Charlotte McGuire, mng. dir. **A**1a 9 10 **F**3 6 10 12 14 16 23 25 35 46 49 53; **S**9555	33	10	S		96	2701	46	47.9	0	0	18526	6852	237
★ QUEEN OF ANGELS MEDICAL CENTER, 2301 Bellevue Ave., Zip 90026; tel. 213/413-3000; Richard F. Smith, pres. & chief exec. off. (Total facility includes 31 beds in nursing home-type unit) **A**1a 2 9 10 **F**1 3 6 9 10 11 12 14 15 16 19 23 24 35 36 40 44 45 46 47 53; **S**1885	21	10	S	TF	226	7690	172	76.4	30	1936	43801	19425	670
				H	195	7349	150	—	30	1936	—	—	—
★ SAN PEDRO PENINSULA HOSPITAL, 1300 W. Seventh St., Zip 90732; tel. 213/832-3311; Rodney J. Aymond, pres. (Total facility includes 128 beds in nursing home-type unit) **A**1a 2 3 9 10 **F**1 2 3 6 7 8 9 10 11 12 14 15 16 17 19 20 21 23 24 25 26 27 28 29 30 32 33 34 35 36 37 38 40 41 42 43 44 45 46 47 48 49 50 52 53 54	23	10	S	TF	436	7233	214	49.1	18	684	47985	21387	795
				H	308	6724	127	—	18	684	44654	19808	643
SANTA FE COMMUNITY HOSPITAL, See Linda Vista Community Hospital													
□ SANTA MARTA HOSPITAL, 319 N. Humphreys Ave., Zip 90022; tel. 213/266-6500; Walter S. Becker, adm. **A**1a 2 10 **F**1 2 6 10 12 14 15 16 23 34 35 37 40 45 46 47 53	21	10	S		110	3634	46	41.8	15	1705	15383	6000	308
★ SERRA MEMORIAL HEALTH CENTER, 9449 San Fernando Rd., Zip 91352; tel. 818/767-3310; Jerry Hawley, adm. & chief oper. off. (Nonreporting) **A**1a 9 10; **S**0045	33	10	S		232	—	—	—	—	—	—	—	—
★ SHERMAN OAKS COMMUNITY HOSPITAL, 4929 Van Nuys Blvd., Zip 91403; tel. 818/981-7111; M. Marc Goldberg, chief exec. off. (Nonreporting) **A**1a 9 10; **S**1805	33	10	S		156	—	—	—	—	—	—	—	—
★ SHRINERS HOSPITALS FOR CRIPPLED CHILDREN, 3160 Geneva St., Zip 90020; tel. 213/388-3151; Paul D. Hargis, adm. **A**1a 3 **F**15 23 24 26 34 42 46 52; **S**4125	23	57	S		60	653	41	68.3	0	0	—	—	120
★ ST. VINCENT MEDICAL CENTER, 2131 W. Third St., P O Box 57992, Zip 90057; tel. 213/484-7111; Vincent F. Guinan, pres. **A**1a 2 9 10 **F**1 2 3 4 6 9 10 11 12 13 14 15 16 17 20 21 23 24 26 33 43 44 45 46 47 53 54; **S**1885	21	10	S		313	11323	217	69.3	0	0	70855	29540	1308
□ TEMPLE COMMUNITY HOSPITAL, 235 N. Hoover St., Zip 90004; tel. 213/382-7252; Herbert G. Needman, adm. & chief exec. off. **A**1a 9 10 **F**1 3 6 9 10 11 12 14 15 16 20 23 24 44 46 50 53	33	10	S		142	3238	68	47.9	0	0	17483	5423	242
★ UNIVERSITY OF CALIFORNIA AT LOS ANGELES MEDICAL CENTER, 10833 Le Conte Ave., Zip 90024; tel. 213/825-9111; Raymond G. Schultze MD, dir. **A**1a 2 3 5 8 9 10 **F**1 2 3 4 5 6 7 8 9 10 11 12 13 14 16 17 20 23 24 34 35 37 38 39 40 44 45 46 47 50 51 52 53 54; **S**6405	23	10	S		652	24362	445	68.3	30	2538	236898	104465	3735
★ UNIVERSITY OF CALIFORNIA AT LOS ANGELES NEUROPSYCHIATRIC HOSPITAL, 760 Westwood Plaza, Zip 90024; tel. 213/825-9548; Don A. Rockwell MD, dir. **A**1b 3 5 8 9 10 **F**24 27 28 32 33 34 42 44 45 46 50; **S**6405	23	49	S		161	1822	115	71.4	0	0	33298	16832	603
★ UNIVERSITY OF SOUTHERN CALIFORNIA-KENNETH NORRIS JR. CANCER HOSPITAL, 1441 Eastlake Ave., P O Box 33804, Zip 90033; tel. 213/224-6600; G. Peter Shostak, adm. **A**1a 3 10 **F**1 3 6 7 8 9 10 11 12 14 15 16 34 43 45 46 47 53; **S**2245	23	10	S		45	1838	33	84.6	0	0	23288	7087	309
★ Δ VALLEY HOSPITAL MEDICAL CENTER, 14500 Sherman Circle, Zip 91405; tel. 213/997-0101; David Gustafson, exec. vice-pres. & chief exec. off. **A**1a 7 9 10 **F**1 3 6 9 10 12 14 15 16 19 23 24 25 26 27 28 30 32 33 34 35 36 40 42 44 46 47 53 54; **S**6905	23	10	S		198	4626	110	54.5	12	0	30699	12883	523
★ VALLEY PRESBYTERIAN HOSPITAL, 15107 Vanowen St., Zip 91405; tel. 818/782-6600; Robert C. Bills, pres. **A**1a 2 3 9 **F**3 4 6 7 8 9 10 11 12 14 16 19 20 23 24 32 34 35 36 40 44 45 46 47 48 49 51 52 53	23	10	S		363	16145	218	61.9	23	2691	44170	30990	1183
□ VAN NUYS COMMUNITY HOSPITAL, 14433 Emelita St., P O Box 2698, Zip 91401; tel. 818/787-1511; Joseph Sharp, adm. (Nonreporting) **A**1a 9 10; **S**5765	33	10	S		63	—	—	—	—	—	—	—	—
□ VAN NUYS HOSPITAL, 15220 Vanowen St., Zip 91405; tel. 818/787-0123; David R. Green, adm. **A**1b 9 10 **F**24 28 29 30 32 33 34 42 44 46 47	33	22	S		41	521	35	85.4	0	0	3474	1570	96
★ VETERANS ADMINISTRATION MEDICAL CENTER-SEPULVEDA, 16111 Plummer St., Zip 91343; tel. 818/891-7711; Norman Hensley, dir. (Total facility includes 200 beds in nursing home-type unit) **A**1a 3 5 8 **F**1 2 3 6 10 12 14 15 16 19 20 23 24 25 26 27 28 29 30 32 33 34 35 42 43 44 46 47 48 49 50 53 54	45	10	S	TF	743	11059	525	70.7	0	0	72596	45117	1730
				H	543	10776	341	—	0	0	—	—	1619

Hospital, Address, Telephone, Administrator, Approval and Facility Codes, Multihospital System Code	Classification Codes			Facilities	Inpatient Data				Newborn Data		Expense (thousands of dollars)		Personnel
★ American Hospital Association (AHA) membership □ Joint Commission on Accreditation of Hospitals (JCAH) accreditation + American Osteopathic Hospital Association (AOHA) membership ○ American Osteopathic Association (AOA) accreditation Δ Commission on Accreditation of Rehabilitation Facilities (CARF) accreditation Control codes 61, 63, 64, 71, 72 and 73 indicate hospitals listed by AOHA, but not registered by AHA. For definition of numerical codes, see page A2	Control	Service	Stay		Beds	Admissions	Census	Occupancy (percent)	Bassinets	Births	Total	Payroll	
★□ VETERANS ADMINISTRATION MEDICAL CENTER-WEST LOS ANGELES (Includes Brentwood Veterans Administration Division; Wadsworth Veterans Administration Division), Wilshire & Sawtelle Blvds, Zip 90073; tel. 213/478-3711; William K. Anderson, dir. (Total facility includes 120 beds in nursing home-type unit) **A**1a b 3 5 8 **F**2 3 4 6 7 8 9 10 11 12 14 15 16 19 20 21 23 24 25 26 27 28 30 32 33 34 35 42 43 44 45 46 47 48 49 50 53 54	45	10	S	TF	1345	20168	995	74.0	0	0	175089	103075	3818
				H	1225	20140	939	—	0	0	171595	100601	3701
WADSWORTH VETERANS ADMINISTRATION DIVISION, See Veterans Administration Medical Center-West Los Angeles													
□ WEST HOLLYWOOD HOSPITAL, 1233 N. La Brea Ave., Zip 90038; tel. 213/874-6111; Jerry L. Dollison, adm. (Nonreporting) **A**1a 9 10; **S**5765	33	10	S		44	—	—	—	—	—	—	—	—
WEST PARK HOSPITAL, See Northwestern University-MEDX Medical Center-West Valley													
★□ WESTSIDE HOSPITAL, 910 S. Fairfax Ave., Zip 90036; tel. 213/938-3431; Michael Weinstein, exec. dir. **A**1a 9 10 **F**1 3 6 12 14 16 20 23 26 34 35 43 45	33	10	S		91	2181	33	36.3	0	0	9938	3994	134
★□ Δ WHITE MEMORIAL MEDICAL CENTER, 1720 Brooklyn Ave., Zip 90033; tel. 213/268-5000; Michael H. Jackson, pres. **A**1a 2 3 5 7 9 10 **F**1 2 3 4 6 7 8 9 10 11 12 14 15 16 23 24 25 26 34 35 36 37 40 42 44 45 46 47 51 52 53 54; **S**0235	21	10	S		247	12378	189	76.5	32	4686	76016	31328	1222
LOS BANOS—Merced County													
□ LOS BANOS COMMUNITY HOSPITAL, 520 W. I St., Zip 93635; tel. 209/826-0591; Lee Ashjian, adm. (Nonreporting) **A**1a 9 10; **S**8795	23	10	S		48	—	—	—	—	—	—	—	—
LOS GATOS—Santa Clara County													
□ COMMUNITY HOSPITAL AND REHABILITATION CENTER OF LOS GATOS-SARATOGA, 815 Pollard Rd., Zip 95030; tel. 408/378-6131 **A**1a 9 10 **F**1 2 3 6 10 12 14 16 17 20 23 24 25 26 33 34 35 36 39 40 42 43 44 45 46 47 48 49 51 52; **S**3015	33	10	S		208	5147	81	40.1	14	740	29917	13534	458
□ MISSION OAKS HOSPITAL (Formerly Valley West General Hospital), 15891 Los Gatos-Almaden Rd., Zip 95030; tel. 408/356-4111; Lee McLendon, adm. (Nonreporting) **A**1a 9 10; **S**8985	33	10	S		54	—	—	—	—	—	—	—	—
VALLEY WEST GENERAL HOSPITAL, See Mission Oaks Hospital													
LOYALTON—Sierra County													
SIERRA VALLEY COMMUNITY HOSPITAL (Formerly Sierra Valley District Hospital), 309 W. Third St., Box 178, Zip 96118; tel. 916/993-1225; James C. Thomas, adm. (Total facility includes 30 beds in nursing home-type unit) **A**9 10 **F**1 16 19 23 34 35 43 44 45 46 50	33	10	S	TF	40	212	23	57.5	1	4	—	—	58
				H	10	128	1	—	1	4	—	—	—
LYNWOOD—Los Angeles County													
★□ ST. FRANCIS MEDICAL CENTER, 3630 E. Imperial Hwy., Zip 90262; tel. 213/603-6000; Sr. Elizabeth Joseph Keaveney, pres. & chief exec. off. **A**1a 2 9 **F**1 3 4 6 7 8 9 10 11 12 14 15 16 17 20 23 24 25 26 27 30 32 34 35 40 44 45 46 47 50 51 52 53 54; **S**1885	21	10	S		426	12303	259	60.8	12	1643	64164	32294	1292
MADERA—Madera County													
□ MADERA COMMUNITY HOSPITAL, 1250 E. Almond Ave., Box 1328, Zip 93639; tel. 209/673-5101; K. S. Ellis, adm. (Nonreporting) **A**1a 9 10	23	10	S		83	—	—	—	—	—	—	—	—
MAMMOTH LAKES—Mono County													
□ CENTINELA MAMMOTH HOSPITAL, 85 Sierra Park Rd., P O Box 660, Zip 93546; tel. 619/934-3311; Thomas P. Jacobsen, adm. (Nonreporting) **A**1a 9 10	23	10	S		15	—	—	—	—	—	—	—	—
MANTECA—San Joaquin County													
□ DOCTORS HOSPITAL OF MANTECA (Formerly Manteca Hospital), 1205 E. North St., Box 191, Zip 95336; tel. 209/823-3111; Woody Laughnan Jr., adm. **A**1a 9 10 **F**1 3 6 12 14 15 16 23 24 26 34 35 36 37 40 44 45 46 47 53; **S**3015	33	10	S		49	2260	27	55.1	5	160	—	—	176
MARCH AIR FORCE BASE—Riverside County													
□ U. S. AIR FORCE REGIONAL HOSPITAL, Zip 92518; tel. 714/655-4461; Col. Charles R. Terry, adm. (Nonreporting) **A**1a	41	10	S		115	—	—	—	—	—	—	—	—
MARIPOSA—Mariposa County													
JOHN C. FREMONT HOSPITAL, 5189 Hospital Rd., Box 216, Zip 95338; tel. 209/966-3631; David W. Goger, chief exec. off. (Total facility includes 10 beds in nursing home-type unit) **A**9 10 **F**1 12 15 19 24 34 35 36 40 45 46 50; **S**0585	16	10	S	TF	34	464	17	50.0	6	53	2156	900	—
				H	24	457	7	—	6	53	—	—	—
MARTINEZ—Contra Costa County													
★□ KAISER FOUNDATION HOSPITAL, 200 Muir Rd., Zip 94553; tel. 415/372-1000; Donald D. Nesbit, adm. **A**1a 10 **F**1 3 6 12 14 15 16 23 27 28 29 30 31 32 33 34 35 37 41 45 46 47 53; **S**2105	23	10	S		113	3796	92	81.4	0	0	—	—	—
□ MERRITHEW MEMORIAL HOSPITAL, 2500 Alhambra Ave., Zip 94553; tel. 415/372-4200; Frank J. Puglisi Jr., exec. dir. **A**1a 3 5 10 **F**1 3 6 12 14 15 16 21 23 24 25 26 27 28 29 30 32 33 34 35 36 40 41 42 44 45 46 47 50 52 53; **S**1805	13	10	S		190	7264	110	57.9	16	898	52613	28089	796
★□ VETERANS ADMINISTRATION MEDICAL CENTER, 150 Muir Rd., Zip 94553; tel. 415/228-6800; Clarence H. Nixon, dir. **A**1a b 2 3 5 8 **F**1 2 3 6 7 8 9 10 11 12 14 15 16 20 23 24 26 27 28 30 32 33 34 35 37 42 43 44 46 48 49 50 53 54	45	10	S		402	7755	295	73.4	0	0	61378	32968	1140
MARYSVILLE—Yuba County													
□ RIDEOUT MEMORIAL HOSPITAL, 726 Fourth St., Box 2128, Zip 95901; tel. 916/742-7381; Thomas P. Hayes, adm. **A**1a 9 10 **F**1 3 5 12 14 15 16 19 23 24 35 43 44 45 46 50 52 53 54	23	10	S		124	4693	74	59.7	0	0	17264	7673	363
MATHER AIR FORCE BASE—Sacramento County													
□ U. S. AIR FORCE HOSPITAL, Zip 95655; tel. 916/364-2114; Col. William B. Moore, cmdr. (Nonreporting) **A**1a	41	10	S		103	—	—	—	—	—	—	—	—
MERCED—Merced County													
□ MERCED COMMUNITY MEDICAL CENTER, 301 E. 13th St., Box 231, Zip 95340; tel. 209/385-7000; Kenneth E. Monfore Jr., chief exec. off. **A**1a 3 5 9 10 **F**1 2 3 6 9 10 12 14 15 16 20 23 24 26 30 34 35 36 37 39 40 41 42 44 45 46 47 48 49 52 53 54; **S**0585	13	10	S		158	6945	101	63.9	16	1504	28565	11772	694
★□ MERCY HOSPITAL, 2740 M St., Zip 95340; tel. 209/384-6444; Louis J. Carlentine, chief exec. off. **A**1a 9 10 **F**1 3 6 10 15 16 20 23 35 36 40 45 46 47 53; **S**5175	21	10	S		93	4605	58	62.4	14	864	16270	7432	336
MISSION VIEJO—Orange County													
□ MISSION COMMUNITY HOSPITAL, 27700 Medical Center Rd., Zip 92691; tel. 714/831-2300; George McLay, exec. dir. (Nonreporting) **A**1a 2 9 10	33	10	S		123	—	—	—	—	—	—	—	—
MODESTO—Stanislaus County													
□ DOCTORS MEDICAL CENTER, 1441 Florida Ave., Box 4138, Zip 95352; tel. 209/578-1211; J. Douglas Dent, exec. dir. **A**1a 9 10 **F**1 2 3 4 6 9 10 11 12 14 15 16 17 20 23 24 26 32 34 35 36 40 41 43 44 45 46 47 52 53 54; **S**3015	33	10	S		298	10302	168	56.4	22	1245	49986	19145	920
MEMORIAL HOSPITAL MEDICAL CENTER, See Memorial Hospitals Association													
★□ MEMORIAL HOSPITALS ASSOCIATION (Includes Memorial Hospital Ceres, 1905 Memorial Dr., Zip 95307, Mailing Address Modesto; Memorial Hospital Medical Center, 1700 Coffee Rd., Zip 95355), Mailing Address Box 942, Zip 95353; tel. 209/526-4500; William K. Piche, pres. & chief exec. off. (Total facility includes 48 beds in nursing home-type unit) **A**1a 2 9 10 **F**1 2 3 6 7 8 9 10 11 12 15 16 19 20 23 24 27 30 33 35 36 37 40 42 44 45 47 48 49 52 53	23	10	S	TF	290	10620	192	67.8	14	1426	43587	19527	1002
				H	242	10402	150	—	14	1426	40288	17894	923

Hospital, Address, Telephone, Administrator, Approval and Facility Codes, Multihospital System Code	Classification Codes				Inpatient Data				Newborn Data		Expense (thousands of dollars)		
★ American Hospital Association (AHA) membership ☐ Joint Commission on Accreditation of Hospitals (JCAH) accreditation + American Osteopathic Hospital Association (AOHA) membership ○ American Osteopathic Association (AOA) accreditation Δ Commission on Accreditation of Rehabilitation Facilities (CARF) accreditation Control codes 61, 63, 64, 71, 72 and 73 indicate hospitals listed by AOHA, but not registered by AHA. For definition of numerical codes, see page A2	Control	Service	Stay	Facilities	Beds	Admissions	Census	Occupancy (percent)	Bassinets	Births	Total	Payroll	Personnel
☐ MODESTO CITY HOSPITAL, 730 17th St., Zip 95354; Mailing Address P O Box 700, Zip 95353; tel. 209/577-2100; Hal Chilton, adm. **A**1a 9 10 **F**1 3 6 10 12 14 15 16 23 34 35 36 37 40 46 48 49 51 52 53; **S**3015	33	10	S		121	5918	78	64.5	30	2282	20486	10461	374
★☐ SCENIC GENERAL HOSPITAL, 830 Scenic Dr., Box 3271, Zip 95353; tel. 209/571-6296; Phillipp K. Wessels, adm. (Nonreporting) **A**1a 3 5 9 10; **S**1755	13	10	S		117	—	—	—	—	—	—	—	—
MONROVIA—Los Angeles County													
☐ MONROVIA COMMUNITY HOSPITAL, 323 S. Heliotrope Ave., Box 707, Zip 91016; tel. 818/359-8341; Dennis Cheshire, adm. (Nonreporting) **A**1a 9 10; **S**5765	33	10	S		49	—	—	—	—	—	—	—	—
MONTCLAIR—San Bernardino County													
☐ DOCTORS' HOSPITAL OF MONTCLAIR, 5000 San Bernardino St., Zip 91763; tel. 714/625-5411; Richard Forrester, adm. (Nonreporting) **A**1a 9 10; **S**3015	33	10	S		99	—	—	—	—	—	—	—	—
MONTEBELLO—Los Angeles County													
★☐ BEVERLY HOSPITAL, 309 W. Beverly Blvd., Zip 90640; tel. 213/726-1222; K. E. Blake, adm. **A**1a 2 9 10 **F**1 2 3 4 6 7 9 10 11 12 14 15 16 23 24 26 35 40 44 45 53 54	23	10	S		212	10736	142	67.0	30	1704	40793	19358	799
MONTEREY—Monterey County													
★☐ COMMUNITY HOSPITAL OF THE MONTEREY PENINSULA, 23625 Holman Hwy., Zip 93940; Mailing Address Box HH, Zip 93942; tel. 408/624-5311; Thomas E. Tonkin, pres. **A**1a 9 10 **F**1 2 3 6 7 8 9 10 11 12 14 15 16 17 23 24 27 28 29 30 32 33 34 35 36 40 45 46 47 52 53	23	10	S		170	11169	143	84.1	24	1708	51773	25476	845
MONTEREY PARK—Los Angeles County													
☐ GARFIELD MEDICAL CENTER, 525 N. Garfield Ave., Zip 91754; tel. 818/573-2222; Roger W. Wessels, exec. dir. **A**1a 2 9 10 **F**1 2 3 4 6 7 9 10 11 12 14 16 20 23 24 35 36 40 42 44 45 46 51 52 54; **S**3015	33	10	S		229	8402	114	49.8	28	3037	31163	13148	588
★☐ MONTEREY PARK HOSPITAL, 900 S. Atlantic Blvd., Zip 91754; tel. 818/570-9000; Reggie Panis, adm. (Nonreporting) **A**1a 2 9 10; **S**1375	33	10	S		96	—	—	—	—	—	—	—	—
MORGAN HILL—Santa Clara County													
★☐ MONTE VILLA HOSPITAL, 17925 Hale Ave., Box 947, Zip 95037; tel. 408/779-4151; Ronald M. Davis, adm. **A**1a 9 **F**24 28 30 32 33 42 44 48 49	21	22	S		52	813	32	61.5	0	0	—	—	90
MOSS BEACH—San Mateo County													
★☐ ST. CATHERINE HOSPITAL ON HALF MOON BAY, Marine Blvd. & Etheldore St., Zip 94038; tel. 415/728-5521; Frank C. Hudson, pres. & chief exec. off.; Anna C. Mullins, exec. vice-pres. pat serv. & oper. (Total facility includes 81 beds in nursing home-type unit) **A**1a 9 10 **F**1 12 14 15 16 19 23 24 34 35 42 45 46 47 48 50	21	10	S	TF H	112 31	403 355	91 11	81.3 —	0 0	0 0	5443 —	2551 —	— —
MOUNT SHASTA—Siskiyou County													
★☐ MERCY MEDICAL CENTER MOUNT SHASTA (Formerly Mount Shasta Community Hospital), 914 Pine St., P O Box 239, Zip 96067; tel. 916/926-6111; James R. Hoss, adm. **A**1a 9 10 **F**1 3 6 12 14 15 16 23 35 36 40 41 45 46 47; **S**5205	21	10	S		33	1433	17	51.5	6	168	5762	2212	131
MOUNTAIN VIEW—Santa Clara County													
★☐ EL CAMINO HOSPITAL, 2500 Grant Rd., Zip 94042; Mailing Address P O Box 7025, Zip 94039; tel. 415/940-7000; Neilson S. Buchanan, chief exec. off. **A**1a 9 10 **F**1 2 3 4 5 6 8 9 10 11 12 14 15 16 17 20 23 24 27 29 30 33 35 36 40 41 42 44 45 47 48 49 52 53 54	16	10	S		362	17563	238	60.3	52	3171	79736	43074	1269
NAPA—Napa County													
☐ NAPA STATE HOSPITAL (Formerly Listed Under Imola), 2100 Napa-Vallejo Hwy., Zip 94558; tel. 707/253-5454; Richard P. Friday, interim exec. dir. **A**1a b 2 3 10 **F**1 3 12 15 16 19 23 24 30 32 33 42 44 46 47 50	12	22	L		1600	1202	1284	77.0	0	0	90868	59381	2230
★☐ QUEEN OF THE VALLEY HOSPITAL, 1000 Trancas St., Box 2340, Zip 94558; tel. 707/252-4411; Sr. Ann McGuinn, pres. & chief exec. off. **A**1a 2 9 10 **F**1 3 5 6 7 8 9 10 11 12 15 16 17 19 20 23 24 26 28 30 34 35 36 37 39 40 41 44 45 47 52 53 54; **S**5425	21	10	S		180	7660	123	68.3	10	924	46447	18257	934
NATIONAL CITY—San Diego County													
☐ Δ PARADISE VALLEY HOSPITAL, 2400 E. Fourth St., Zip 92050; tel. 619/267-9500; Fred M. Harder, adm. (Nonreporting) **A**1a 7 9 10; **S**0235	21	10	S		210	—	—	—	—	—	—	—	—
NEEDLES—San Bernardino County													
★☐ NEEDLES-DESERT COMMUNITIES HOSPITAL, 1401 Bailey Ave., Zip 92363; tel. 619/326-4531; Hank N. Fishman, adm. (Nonreporting) **A**1a 9 10; **S**9795	16	10	S		39	—	—	—	—	—	—	—	—
NEWHALL—Los Angeles County													
★ NEWHALL COMMUNITY HOSPITAL, 24237 San Fernando Rd., Box 730, Zip 91321; tel. 805/259-6300; Bienvenido Tan MD, adm. (Nonreporting) **A**9	33	10	S		9	—	—	—	—	—	—	—	—
NEWMAN—Stanislaus County													
☐ WEST SIDE COMMUNITY HOSPITAL DISTRICT, 151 S. Hwy. 33, Zip 95360; tel. 209/862-2951; Thomas E. Carter, adm. **A**1a 9 10 **F**1 6 10 16 23 24 35 44 45	16	10	S		22	296	5	22.7	0	0	1360	492	25
NEWPORT BEACH—Orange County													
★☐ HOAG MEMORIAL HOSPITAL PRESBYTERIAN, 301 Newport Blvd., Box Y, Zip 92658; tel. 714/645-8600; Michael D. Stephens, pres. & chief exec. off. **A**1a 2 9 10 **F**1 2 3 4 6 7 8 9 10 11 12 14 15 16 17 20 23 24 26 27 28 29 30 32 33 34 35 36 37 40 42 44 45 46 47 51 52 53 54	23	10	S		375	16889	265	67.9	40	2344	99453	38677	1703
☐ NEWPORT HARBOR PSYCHIATRIC INSTITUTE, 1501 E. 16th St., Zip 92663; tel. 714/642-9310; Tom Heitman, adm. (Nonreporting) **A**1b 9; **S**0665	33	52	S		34	—	—	—	—	—	—	—	—
NORWALK—Los Angeles County													
★☐ COAST PLAZA MEDICAL CENTER, 13100 Studebaker Rd., Zip 90650; tel. 213/868-3751; Arthur Gerrick, exec. dir. **A**1a 9 10 **F**1 3 6 10 12 14 15 16 19 20 23 24 35 43 44 45 46 53; **S**1805	33	10	S		62	2755	47	75.8	0	0	—	—	223
KAISER FOUNDATION HOSPITAL, See Kaiser Foundation Hospital, Bellflower													
METROPOLITAN STATE HOSPITAL, 11400 Norwalk Blvd., Zip 90650; tel. 213/863-7011; George Siela, adm. (Nonreporting)	12	22	L		1030	—	—	—	—	—	—	—	—
☐ NORWALK COMMUNITY HOSPITAL, 13222 Bloomfield Ave., Zip 90650; tel. 213/863-4763; Paul Strom, adm. **A**1a 9 10 **F**1 3 6 12 14 16 23 35 47; **S**5765	33	10	S		50	1771	24	48.0	0	0	—	—	—
NOVATO—Marin County													
★☐ NOVATO COMMUNITY HOSPITAL, 1625 Hill Rd., P O Box 1108, Zip 94947; tel. 415/897-3111; Joel Grey, adm. **A**1a 9 10 **F**1 3 6 10 12 14 15 16 21 23 34 35 36 37 40 43 45 46 52 53; **S**8795	23	10	S		52	1794	22	42.3	6	78	10794	4588	183
OAKDALE—Stanislaus County													
☐ OAK VALLEY DISTRICT HOSPITAL, 350 S. Oak St., P O Box 1508, Zip 95361; tel. 209/847-3011; Margaret Williams RN, interim adm. **A**1a 9 10 **F**1 3 6 15 16 23 34 35 36 37 40 41 45 46	16	10	S		39	1813	21	53.8	4	127	6766	2751	164
OAKLAND—Alameda County													
CALIFORNIA SURGICAL CENTER HOSPITAL, WOMEN'S HOSPITAL OF OAKLAND, 400 40th St., Zip 94609; tel. 415/655-8727; E. Pederren, bd. chm. (Nonreporting)	23	10	S		34	—	—	—	—	—	—	—	—
★☐ CHILDREN'S HOSPITAL MEDICAL CENTER OF NORTHERN CALIFORNIA, 747 52nd St., Zip 94609; tel. 415/428-3000; Antoine H. Paap, pres. & chief exec. off. **A**1a 3 5 9 10 **F**1 4 5 6 10 12 15 16 23 24 26 28 32 33 34 35 37 38 42 43 44 45 46 51 53 54	23	50	S		149	6459	136	95.1	0	0	77732	—	1210

★ American Hospital Association (AHA) membership
□ Joint Commission on Accreditation of Hospitals (JCAH) accreditation
\+ American Osteopathic Hospital Association (AOHA) membership
○ American Osteopathic Association (AOA) accreditation
Δ Commission on Accreditation of Rehabilitation Facilities (CARF) accreditation
Control codes 61, 63, 64, 71, 72 and 73 indicate hospitals listed by AOHA, but not registered by AHA. For definition of numerical codes, see page A2

Hospital, Address, Telephone, Administrator, Approval and Facility Codes, Multihospital System Code	Classification Codes				Inpatient Data				Newborn Data		Expense (thousands of dollars)		
	Control	Service	Stay	Facilities	Beds	Admissions	Census	Occupancy (percent)	Bassinets	Births	Total	Payroll	Personnel
★□ EVERETT A. GLADMAN MEMORIAL HOSPITAL, 2633 E. 27th St., Zip 94601; tel. 415/536-8111; Joan A. Bero, adm. **A**1b 9 10 **F**12 28 29 30 32	33	22	S		92	1618	54	58.7	0	0	7669	4097	186
□ HIGHLAND GENERAL HOSPITAL, 1411 E. 31st St., Zip 94602; tel. 415/534-8055; Joyce Berger, dir. (Nonreporting) **A**1a 3 5 10; **S**0225	13	10	S		244	—	—	—	—	—	—	—	—
★□ KAISER FOUNDATION HOSPITAL, 280 W. MacArthur Blvd., Zip 94611; tel. 415/428-5000; Thomas DeMartino, adm. **A**1a 3 5 10 **F**1 3 6 9 10 12 14 15 16 21 23 30 32 35 36 40 41 46 47 51 52 53; **S**2105	23	10	S		245	14307	206	84.1	46	3005	—	—	—
★□ NAVAL HOSPITAL, Zip 94627; tel. 415/633-5019; Capt. Jack W. Bartlett MSC USN, dir. adm. **A**1a 2 3 5 **F**1 2 3 6 7 8 9 10 11 12 14 16 20 23 24 27 28 30 32 33 34 35 36 37 40 44 46 47 48 49 51 52 53	43	10	S		263	12320	189	67.0	23	1223	89248	—	1765
□ OAKLAND HOSPITAL, 2648 E. 14th St., Zip 94601; tel. 415/532-3300; Walter J. Filkowski, adm. (Nonreporting) **A**1a 9 10; **S**5765	33	10	S		90	—	—	—	—	—	—	—	—
★□ PERALTA HOSPITAL, 450 30th St., Zip 94609; Mailing Address P O Box 23010, Zip 94623; tel. 415/451-4900; Ronald A. Pavellas, adm. **A**1a 9 10 **F**1 3 6 7 8 9 11 12 14 15 16 17 20 23 24 34 35 37 41 44 46 47 49 53 54; **S**0685	23	10	S		86	3848	60	69.8	0	0	28217	10648	400
★□ PROVIDENCE HOSPITAL, 3100 Summit St., Zip 94609; Mailing Address Box 23020, Zip 94623; tel. 415/835-4500; Sr. Dona Taylor, adm. **A**1a 9 10 **F**1 2 3 6 9 10 12 15 16 20 23 24 27 28 30 32 33 34 35 36 40 44 45 46 50 53; **S**5275	21	10	S		230	8890	181	78.7	15	7	57916	26040	770
□ SAMUEL MERRITT HOSPITAL, Hawthorne Ave. & Webster St., Zip 94609; tel. 415/655-4000; Ronald A. Pavellas, adm. **A**1a 2 3 5 9 10 **F**1 2 3 4 6 7 8 9 10 11 14 15 16 17 20 23 24 34 35 36 37 40 41 43 44 46 47 49 53 54; **S**0685	23	10	S		256	11228	173	67.6	27	1874	80460	32222	1110
OCEANSIDE—San Diego County													
★□ TRI-CITY MEDICAL CENTER (Formerly Tri-City Hospital), 4002 Vista Way, Zip 92056; tel. 619/940-3348; Richard A. Hachten II, chief exec. off. **A**1a 2 9 10 **F**1 2 3 4 6 7 8 9 10 11 12 14 15 16 17 20 21 23 24 25 26 27 30 32 33 34 35 36 37 40 41 42 44 45 46 47 52 53 54	16	10	S		434	15273	255	78.9	26	2898	69155	35317	1351
OJAI—Ventura County													
□ OJAI VALLEY COMMUNITY HOSPITAL, 1306 Maricopa Hwy., Zip 93023; tel. 805/646-1401; Larry L. Meyer, adm. (Total facility includes 42 beds in nursing home-type unit) **A**1a 9 10 **F**1 3 6 12 14 16 19 35 36 40 43 45 48	33	10	S	TF	97	1957	68	70.1	7	296	—	—	193
				H	55	1885	30	—	7	296	—	—	156
ONTARIO—San Bernardino County													
□ ○ ONTARIO COMMUNITY HOSPITAL, 550 N. Monterey, Zip 91764; tel. 714/984-2201; John W. Packard, adm. **A**1a 9 10 11 13 **F**1 3 6 14 15 16 17 20 23 24 35 43 44 45 46 47 48 49 52 53; **S**3015	33	10	S		99	2360	48	48.5	0	0	12287	5181	197
ORANGE—Orange County													
★□ CAREUNIT HOSPITAL OF ORANGE, 401 S. Tustin Ave., Zip 92666; tel. 714/633-9582; Richard Tradewell, adm. **A**1b 9 10 **F**24 30 32 33 42 45 46 47 48; **S**0275	33	22	S		103	1354	88	91.7	0	0	—	—	174
□ CHAPMAN GENERAL HOSPITAL, 2601 E. Chapman Ave., Zip 92669; tel. 714/633-0011; Daryl S. Crane Jr., adm. **A**1a 9 10 **F**1 3 6 9 10 11 12 14 16 20 23 24 35 36 40 44 45 53; **S**1375	33	10	S		99	3742	41	41.4	16	1103	—	—	232
★□ CHILDRENS HOSPITAL OF ORANGE COUNTY, 455 S. Main St., Zip 92668; Mailing Address P O Box 5700, Zip 92613; tel. 714/997-3000; Harold W. Wade, chief exec. off. **A**1a 2 3 5 9 10 **F**1 15 16 33 34 38 41 42 43 45 46 51	23	50	S		155	6316	110	72.4	0	0	44080	17793	801
★□ ST. JOSEPH HOSPITAL, 1100 W. Stewart Dr., Zip 92668; tel. 714/633-9111; Walter W. Noce Jr., pres. & chief exec. off. **A**1a 2 3 5 9 10 **F**1 2 3 4 6 7 8 9 10 11 12 13 14 15 16 20 21 23 24 26 27 28 29 30 32 33 34 35 36 40 41 45 46 47 48 49 53 54; **S**5425	21	10	S		409	20156	313	76.5	49	4990	98081	58477	1889
★□ UNIVERSITY OF CALIFORNIA IRVINE MEDICAL CENTER, 101 the City Dr., Zip 92668; tel. 714/634-5678; Leon M. Schwartz, dir. **A**1a 2 3 5 8 9 10 **F**1 2 3 4 5 6 7 8 9 10 11 12 13 14 15 16 17 20 22 23 24 25 26 27 28 30 32 33 34 35 37 38 40 42 43 44 45 46 47 50 51 52 53 54; **S**6405	23	10	S		382	16230	299	80.6	34	3438	121080	52952	2069
OROVILLE—Butte County													
□ OROVILLE HOSPITAL, 2767 Olive Hwy., Zip 95966; tel. 916/533-8500; Arden Bennett, adm. **A**1a 9 10 **F**1 3 5 6 9 10 12 14 15 16 23 24 34 35 40 44 45 53	23	10	S		99	4076	68	68.7	10	494	20387	8843	417
OXNARD—Ventura County													
★□ CHANNEL ISLANDS COMMUNITY HOSPITAL, 540 Hobson Way, Zip 93030; Mailing Address Box 1148, Zip 93032; tel. 805/487-7941; Emma Mayer Orr, adm. **A**1a 9 10 **F**1 3 6 12 14 15 16 23 24 35 42 44 45 46 47 48; **S**6525	33	10	S		85	1815	35	41.2	0	0	9353	3370	142
★ CHANNEL ISLANDS COMMUNITY HOSPITAL-CARE UNIT, 2130 N. Ventura Rd., Zip 93030; tel. 805/487-5358; Emma Mayer Orr, adm. (Nonreporting) **A** 9 10	33	82	S		37	—	—	—	—	—	—	—	—
★□ ST. JOHN'S REGIONAL MEDICAL CENTER, 333 N. F St., Zip 93030; tel. 805/988-2500; Daniel R. Herlinger, pres. (Total facility includes 12 beds in nursing home-type unit) **A**1a 2 9 10 **F**1 2 3 4 6 7 8 9 10 11 12 15 16 17 19 20 21 23 24 25 26 32 33 34 35 36 40 44 45 46 47 52 53 54; **S**5205	21	10	S	TF	260	11491	173	66.8	24	2009	50381	25154	931
				H	248	11302	162	—	24	2009	50113	24893	918
PALM SPRINGS—Riverside County													
★□ DESERT HOSPITAL, 1150 N. Indian Ave., Zip 92262; Mailing Address Box 1627, Zip 92263; tel. 714/323-6511; Larry N. Minden, pres. & chief exec. off. **A**1a 2 9 10 **F**1 2 3 5 6 7 8 10 11 12 15 16 17 20 21 23 24 25 26 27 29 30 32 33 34 35 36 40 41 42 44 45 46 47 50 52 53 54	16	10	S		330	12730	220	66.7	20	1897	65420	30924	1253
PALMDALE—Los Angeles County													
□ PALMDALE HOSPITAL MEDICAL CENTER (General Medical and Psychiatric), 1212 E. Ave. S, Zip 93550; tel. 805/273-2211; Reid Anderson, exec. dir. (Nonreporting) **A**1a 9 10; **S**0045	33	49	S		123	—	—	—	—	—	—	—	—
PALO ALTO—Santa Clara County													
★□ CHILDREN'S HOSPITAL AT STANFORD, 520 Sand Hill Rd., Zip 94304; tel. 415/327-4800; John R. Williams, exec. dir. **A**1a 3 5 9 10 **F**6 15 16 23 24 28 32 33 34 42 43 44 45 46 47	23	50	S		60	1707	37	61.7	0	0	24068	10785	365
★□ VETERANS ADMINISTRATION MEDICAL CENTER, 3801 Miranda Ave., Zip 94304; tel. 415/493-5000; James C. Deniro, dir. (Total facility includes 150 beds in nursing home-type unit) **A**1a 2 3 5 8 **F**1 3 4 6 9 10 11 12 14 15 16 19 20 21 23 24 25 26 27 28 29 30 31 32 33 34 35 41 42 43 44 46 47 48 49 50 53 54	45	10	S	TF	1428	14216	1152	80.7	0	0	119007	70825	2431
				H	1278	13513	1010	—	0	0	113551	66456	2360
PARADISE—Butte County													
□ FEATHER RIVER HOSPITAL, 5974 Pentz Rd., Zip 95969; tel. 916/877-9361; George Pifer, pres. **A**1a 9 10 **F**1 3 6 10 15 16 23 24 35 36 40 44 45 46 47 48; **S**0235	21	10	S		125	3902	55	44.0	10	611	16827	7086	350
PARAMOUNT—Los Angeles County													
★□ CHARTER SUBURBAN HOSPITAL -PARAMOUNT (Formerly Charter Suburban Hospital), 16453 S. Colorado Ave., Zip 90723; tel. 213/531-3110; Gary W. Turner, adm. (Nonreporting) **A**1a 9 10; **S**0695	33	10	S		184	—	—	—	—	—	—	—	—

Hospital, Address, Telephone, Administrator, Approval and Facility Codes, Multihospital System Code	Classification Codes				Inpatient Data				Newborn Data		Expense (thousands of dollars)		
★ American Hospital Association (AHA) membership □ Joint Commission on Accreditation of Hospitals (JCAH) accreditation + American Osteopathic Hospital Association (AOHA) membership ○ American Osteopathic Association (AOA) accreditation Δ Commission on Accreditation of Rehabilitation Facilities (CARF) accreditation Control codes 61, 63, 64, 71, 72 and 73 indicate hospitals listed by AOHA, but not registered by AHA. For definition of numerical codes, see page A2	Control	Service	Stay	Facilities	Beds	Admissions	Census	Occupancy (percent)	Bassinets	Births	Total	Payroll	Personnel
PASADENA—Los Angeles County													
★□ HUNTINGTON MEMORIAL HOSPITAL, 100 Congress St., Zip 91105; tel. 818/440-5000; Allen W. Mathies Jr. MD, pres. & chief exec. off.; Stephen A. Ralph, vice-pres. adm. **A**1a 2 3 5 8 9 10 **F**1 2 3 4 5 6 7 8 9 10 11 12 14 15 16 17 20 23 24 25 26 32 33 34 35 36 37 39 40 42 43 44 45 46 47 50 51 52 53 54	23	10	S		546	20331	399	73.1	32	3639	126216	62447	2363
★□ LAS ENCINAS HOSPITAL, 2900 E. Del Mar Blvd., Zip 91107; tel. 818/795-9901; Rachel S. Crenwelge, exec. dir. **A**1a 9 10 **F**3 15 19 23 24 28 29 30 32 33 34 42 43 46 47 48 49; **S**1755	33	22	L		140	1187	102	72.9	0	0	14498	6091	240
★ PASADENA COMMUNITY HOSPITAL, 1845 N. Fair Oaks Ave., Zip 91103; tel. 818/798-7811; Kimberly Rocha, actg. adm. **A**9 10 **F**15 20 23 24 32 33 34 42; **S**6905	23	82	S		66	324	34	51.5	0	0	6545	2434	116
★□ ST. LUKE MEDICAL CENTER (Formerly St. Luke Hospital), 2632 E. Washington Blvd., Bin 7021, Zip 91109; tel. 818/797-1141; Harry F. Adams, exec. dir. (Data for 102 days) **A**1a 2 9 10 **F**1 2 3 6 10 12 14 15 16 20 23 34 35 44 45 46 49 53; **S**3025	33	10	S		107	871	67	62.6	0	0	6182	2599	386
PATTERSON—Stanislaus County													
□ DEL PUERTO HOSPITAL, Box 187, Zip 95363; tel 209/892-8782; Thomas Avery, adm. **A**1a 9 10 **F**1 12 14 15 16 19 23 26 35 36 37 40 45 46 48 49 50	16	10	S		43	693	17	39.5	6	104	3929	1317	50
PATTON—San Bernardino County													
PATTON STATE HOSPITAL, 3102 E. Highland Ave., Zip 92369; tel. 714/862-8121; Donald G. Stockman, exec. dir. (Total facility includes 39 beds in nursing home-type unit) **F**10 19 23 24 30 32 33 34 37 44 46	12	22	L	TF	1166	741	1034	91.2	0	0	55186	34944	1372
				H	1127	731	1010	—	0	0	—	—	1340
PETALUMA—Sonoma County													
□ PETALUMA VALLEY HOSPITAL, 400 N. McDowell Blvd., Zip 94952; tel. 707/778-1111; Charles E. Cowen, adm. (Nonreporting) **A**1a 9 10	16	10	S		99	—	—	—	—	—	—	—	—
PICO RIVERA—Los Angeles County													
□ PICO RIVERA COMMUNITY HOSPITAL, 5216 S. Rosemead Blvd., Box 788, Zip 90660; tel. 213/948-1121; Rendel Levonian MD, adm. (Nonreporting) **A**1a 9 10	33	10	S		95	—	—	—	—	—	—	—	—
PINOLE—Contra Costa County													
□ DOCTORS HOSPITAL OF PINOLE, 2151 Appian Way, Zip 94564; tel. 415/724-5000; Danny N. Mar, adm. (Data not available) **A**1a 9 10 **F**1 3 6 10 12 15 16 17 20 23 24 26 34 35 41 42 44 45 46 47 49 53; **S**3015	33	10	S		137	—	—	—	—	—	—	—	—
PITTSBURG—Contra Costa County													
□ LOS MEDANOS COMMUNITY HOSPITAL (Formerly Los Medanos Community Hospital District), 2311 Loveridge Rd., Zip 94565; tel. 415/432-2200; Efton Hall Jr., chief exec. off. & adm. **A**1a 9 10 **F**1 3 6 10 12 14 15 16 20 23 24 34 35 36 40 41 44 45 46 47 53	23	10	S		81	3706	49	60.5	7	579	20814	9042	344
PLACENTIA—Orange County													
□ PLACENTIA-LINDA COMMUNITY HOSPITAL, 1301 Rose Dr., Zip 92670; tel. 714/993-2000; Gary Fybel, adm. **A**1a 9 10 **F**1 3 6 10 12 14 15 16 23 26 34 35 36 40 43 46 48 49 52 53; **S**3015	33	10	S		114	3741	53	46.5	12	259	17675	7283	285
PLACERVILLE—El Dorado County													
★□ MARSHALL HOSPITAL, Marshall Way, Zip 95667; tel. 916/622-1441; Frank Nachtman, adm. **A**1a 9 10 **F**1 3 6 10 12 14 16 23 32 35 40 41 44 45 46 47 53	23	10	S		90	3802	49	54.4	10	650	15024	5970	265
POMONA—Los Angeles County													
★□ Δ CASA COLINA HOSPITAL FOR REHABILITATIVE MEDICINE, 255 E. Bonita Ave., Zip 91767; tel. 714/593-7521; Steve Duvall, vice-pres. & adm. **A**1a 7 9 **F**15 23 24 26 33 34 42 43 44 45 46 47 50	23	46	S		64	547	46	71.9	0	0	14353	6927	379
□ CPC HORIZON HOSPITAL (Formerly Horizon Hospital), 566 N. Gordon St., Zip 91768; tel. 714/629-4011; Marnell R. Davis, sr. adm. **A**1a 9 10 **F**24 29 32 33 42 43; **S**0785	33	22	S		79	1028	51	64.6	0	0	—	—	77
HORIZON HOSPITAL, See CPC Horizon Hospital													
□ Δ LANTERMAN DEVELOPMENTAL CENTER (Formerly Lanterman State Hospital and Developmental Center), 3530 W. Pomona Blvd., P O Box 100, Zip 91769; tel. 714/595-1221; Rowena J. Taylor, exec. dir. **A**1a 7 10 **F**16 23 24 32 33 42 44 45 46 47 52	12	62	L		1127	65	1063	91.2	0	0	63534	38446	1631
★□ POMONA VALLEY COMMUNITY HOSPITAL, 1798 N. Garey Ave., Zip 91767; tel. 714/865-9500; Robert W. Burwell, pres. **A**1a 2 9 10 **F**1 2 3 5 6 7 8 9 10 11 12 14 16 17 23 34 35 36 39 40 45 46 47 48 49 51 52 53	23	10	S		389	15762	276	71.0	24	2902	82413	39610	1562
PORT HUENEME—Ventura County													
□ ANACAPA ADVENTIST HOSPITAL (Formerly Port Hueneme Adventist Hospital), 307 E. Clara St., Zip 93041; tel. 805/488-3661; Darwin Remboldt, pres. (Nonreporting) **A**1a 9 10; **S**0235	21	10	S		49	—	—	—	—	—	—	—	—
PORTERVILLE—Tulare County													
□ PORTERVILLE DEVELOPMENTAL CENTER (Formerly Porterville State Hospital), Box 2000, Zip 93258; tel. 209/782-2222; James T. Shelton MD, exec. dir. **A**1a 10 **F**12 16 23 24 30 32 33 42 44 46 50 52	12	62	L		1286	43	1241	91.1	0	0	56979	42445	1816
PORTERVILLE STATE HOSPITAL, See Porterville Developmental Center													
□ SIERRA VIEW DISTRICT HOSPITAL, 465 W. Putnam Ave., Zip 93257; tel. 209/784-1110; Roger S. Good, adm. **A**1a 9 10 **F**1 2 3 6 15 16 35 36 40 43 45 47 52 53	16	10	S		93	4645	57	70.4	5	680	13614	6866	314
PORTOLA—Plumas County													
EASTERN PLUMAS DISTRICT HOSPITAL, 500 First Ave., Box 1075, Zip 96122; tel. 916/832-4277; Ronald E. Scovill, reg. adm. **A**10 **F**1 6 14 15 16 23 34 35 36 37 41 44 45 46	23	10	S		24	546	5	20.8	2	53	2570	1087	65
POWAY—San Diego County													
□ POMERADO HOSPITAL, 15615 Pomerado Rd., Zip 92064; tel. 619/485-6511; Robert M. Edwards, pres. & chief exec. off.; Victoria Penland, exec. vice-pres. & adm. **A**1a 2 9 10 **F**1 3 6 9 10 11 12 14 15 16 21 23 24 26 35 36 40 41 44 45 48 53; **S**7555	16	10	S		130	5316	70	53.8	16	1105	21776	8246	403
QUINCY—Plumas County													
□ PLUMAS DISTRICT HOSPITAL, 1065 Bucks Lake Rd., Zip 95971; tel. 916/283-2121; William Setterlund, adm. **A**1a 9 10 **F**1 6 16 23 27 35 36 41 45 46 53	16	10	S		34	916	8	23.5	4	103	3486	1446	73
RANCHO MIRAGE—Riverside County													
□ EISENHOWER MEDICAL CENTER, 39000 Bob Hope Dr., Zip 92270; tel. 619/340-3911; Michael A. Rembis, adm. **A**1a 2 9 10 **F**1 2 3 4 6 7 8 9 10 11 12 15 16 17 20 23 24 26 32 33 34 35 41 42 44 45 46 47 52 53 54	23	10	S		239	9060	155	76.0	0	0	60613	25071	1385
RED BLUFF—Tehama County													
★□ ST. ELIZABETH COMMUNITY HOSPITAL, 2550 Sister Mary Columba Dr., Zip 96080; tel. 916/527-2112; R. Michael Barry, pres. & chief exec. off. **A**1a 9 10 **F**1 3 6 10 12 14 15 16 21 23 24 26 35 36 40 41 42 44 45 46 47 49 50 53; **S**5175	21	10	S		76	2892	36	46.8	6	563	13388	6307	322
REDDING—Shasta County													
★□ MERCY MEDICAL CENTER, Clairmont Hts., Zip 96001; Mailing Address Box 6009, Zip 96099; tel. 916/243-2121; George A. Govier, chief exec. off. **A**1a 2 3 9 10 **F**1 2 3 5 6 7 8 9 10 11 12 14 15 16 20 21 23 24 35 36 40 41 45 46 47 51 52 53; **S**5205	21	10	S		188	8881	123	62.4	20	991	33755	14951	763
□ REDDING MEDICAL CENTER, 1100 Butte St., Zip 96001; Mailing Address Box 2458, Zip 96099; tel. 916/244-5400; Gerald E. Knepp, adm. **A**1a 9 10 **F**1 2 3 5 6 10 12 13 14 15 16 17 20 23 24 26 34 35 37 42 43 44 45 48 53 54; **S**3015	33	10	S		132	4602	57	43.2	0	0	20595	7804	369

Hospital, Address, Telephone, Administrator, Approval and Facility Codes, Multihospital System Code	Classification Codes: Control	Service	Stay	Facilities	Inpatient Data: Beds	Admissions	Census	Occupancy (percent)	Newborn Data: Bassinets	Births	Expense (thousands of dollars): Total	Payroll	Personnel
★□ SHASTA GENERAL HOSPITAL, 2630 Hospital Lane, P O Box 6050, Zip 96099; tel. 916/241-3232; Jo-Ann Castrina-Hanula, adm. (Nonreporting) **A**1a 3 5 9 10; **S**1755	13	10	S		73	—	—	—	—	—	—	—	—
REDLANDS—San Bernardino County													
★□ REDLANDS COMMUNITY HOSPITAL, 350 Terracina Blvd., Box 3391, Zip 92373; tel. 714/793-3101; George A. DeLange, pres. **A**1a 2 9 10 **F**1 3 6 9 10 12 14 15 16 21 23 24 26 32 35 36 40 43 44 45 46 47 48 52 53; **S**2245	23	10	S		195	7481	104	53.3	16	1690	31911	12229	561
REDONDO BEACH—Los Angeles County													
★□ AMI SOUTH BAY HOSPITAL (Formerly South Bay Hospital), 514 N. Prospect Ave., Zip 90277; tel. 213/376-9474; Lynn C. Orfgen, exec. dir. (Nonreporting) **A**1a 2 9 10; **S**0125	33	10	S		203	—	—	—	—	—	—	—	—
REDWOOD CITY—San Mateo County													
★□ KAISER FOUNDATION HOSPITAL, 1150 Veterans Blvd., Zip 94063; tel. 415/780-2000; Carolyn Kever, adm. **A**1a 3 10 **F**1 3 6 10 12 15 16 23 24 28 32 33 35 37 40 41 52 53; **S**2105	23	10	S		150	7368	112	74.7	24	1758	—	—	—
★□ SEQUOIA HOSPITAL DISTRICT, Whipple & Alameda, Zip 94062; tel. 415/369-5811; Richard R. Daniels, adm. (Total facility includes 48 beds in nursing home-type unit) **A**1a 2 3 9 10 **F**1 2 3 4 6 7 8 9 10 11 12 14 15 16 17 19 20 21 23 24 26 27 28 29 30 32 33 35 36 37 40 42 43 44 45 48 49 50 52 53 54	16	10	S	TF H	301 253	11920 11041	217 172	64.6 —	8 8	1070 1070	76338 74668	30624 29833	— —
□ WOODSIDE WOMEN'S HOSPITAL, 1600 Gordon St., Zip 94061; tel. 415/368-4134; Jacquelyn Thompson Aker, adm. **A**1a b 9 **F**28 29 32 33 48; **S**1055	33	22	S		24	224	14	58.3	0	0	2442	937	54
REEDLEY—Fresno County													
★□ KINGS VIEW HOSPITAL, 42675 Rd. 44, Zip 93654; tel. 209/638-2505; Roger D. Miller, adm. **A**1b 3 10 **F**15 24 28 29 30 32 33 34 42 43 49	23	22	L		55	177	54	98.2	0	0	7858	4295	199
★□ SIERRA-KINGS DISTRICT HOSPITAL, 372 W. Cypress Ave., Zip 93654; tel. 209/638-8155; Jerry Sullivan, adm. **A**1a 9 10 **F**1 6 16 23 35 37 40 45 53; **S**1085	16	10	S		36	1402	13	36.1	8	464	3554	1631	88
RICHMOND—Contra Costa County													
★□ KAISER FOUNDATION HOSPITAL, 1330 Cutting Blvd., Zip 94804; tel. 415/231-4600; John Rawls, adm. **A**1a 10 **F**1 3 6 15 16 23 26 34 35 45 46 47; **S**2105	23	10	S		40	896	21	48.8	0	0	—	—	—
RIDGECREST—Kern County													
★□ RIDGECREST COMMUNITY HOSPITAL, 1081 N. China Lake Blvd., Zip 93555; tel. 619/446-3551; David A. Mechtenberg, adm. **A**1a 9 10 **F**1 3 6 10 12 16 21 23 35 40 41 45 46 52	23	10	S		78	2984	45	57.7	8	489	10261	5293	250
RIVERSIDE—Riverside County													
★□ PARKVIEW COMMUNITY HOSPITAL, 3865 Jackson St., Zip 92503; tel. 714/688-2211; Kenneth L. Willes, pres. **A**1a 2 9 10 **F**1 3 6 9 10 12 14 15 16 23 35 36 40 45 46 47 48	23	10	S		156	5833	75	48.1	16	1342	24202	9233	399
★□ RIVERSIDE COMMUNITY HOSPITAL, 4445 Magnolia Ave., Zip 92501; Mailing Address Box 1669, Zip 92502; tel. 714/788-3000; David W. Patton, pres. **A**1a 2 9 10 **F**1 2 3 5 6 8 9 10 11 12 14 15 16 20 23 24 25 26 28 29 30 32 34 35 36 40 41 42 43 44 45 46 47 48 49 50 52 54	23	10	S		363	12430	185	51.0	18	1872	45839	21139	911
□ RIVERSIDE COMMUNITY HOSPITAL-KNOLLWOOD CENTER, 5900 Brockton Ave., Zip 92506; Mailing Address Box 1669, Zip 92502; tel. 714/788-3500; David W. Patton, pres. **A**1a 9 10 **F**1 16 23 24 27 28 29 30 32 33 34 41 42 43 44 45 46 47 49	23	10	S		70	569	22	31.4	0	0	2776	1323	34
★□ RIVERSIDE GENERAL HOSPITAL-UNIVERSITY MEDICAL CENTER, 9851 Magnolia Ave., Zip 92503; tel. 714/351-7100; Kenneth B. Cohen, adm. **A**1a 2 3 5 8 9 10 **F**1 3 5 6 10 12 15 16 20 23 24 27 29 30 34 35 37 40 41 43 45 46 47 51 52 53	44	10	S		312	16500	220	70.5	13	2484	63307	27337	1214
U. S. AIR FORCE REGIONAL HOSPITAL, See March Air Force Base													
ROSEMEAD—Los Angeles County													
□ CPC ALHAMBRA HOSPITAL, 4619 N. Rosemead Blvd., P O Box 369, Zip 91770; tel. 818/286-1191; Margaret Minnick, adm. **A**1a 9 10 **F**24 28 29 30 32 33 42 43 47; **S**0785	33	22	S		98	1274	59	60.2	0	0	—	—	91
★□ INGLESIDE HOSPITAL, 7500 E. Hellman Ave., Zip 91770; tel. 818/288-1160; W. H. Newell, pres. **A**1b 9 10 **F**12 23 24 28 29 30 32 33 42 45 46 47	23	22	S		130	1238	70	53.8	0	0	9065	4231	174
ROSEVILLE—Placer County													
★□ ROSEVILLE COMMUNITY HOSPITAL, 333 Sunrise Ave., Zip 95661; tel. 916/781-1200; Kenneth M. Kelley, pres. & chief exec. off. **A**1a 9 10 **F**1 3 6 7 8 9 10 11 12 14 15 16 17 20 21 23 24 30 34 35 36 37 40 41 43 45 47 48 49 52 53 54	23	10	S		234	8625	144	61.5	15	1363	39181	19617	643
ROSS—Marin County													
★□ ROSS GENERAL HOSPITAL, 1150 Sir Francis Drake Blvd., P O Box Cs 6001, Zip 94957; tel. 415/453-7800; Roger W. Moore, adm. (Nonreporting) **A**1a 9 10; **S**6525	33	10	S		147	—	—	—	—	—	—	—	—
SACRAMENTO—Sacramento County													
★□ COMMUNITY HOSPITAL OF SACRAMENTO, 2251 Hawthorne St., Zip 95815; tel. 916/929-2333; Howard J. Wooling, adm. (Nonreporting) **A**1a 9 10; **S**6525	33	10	S		100	—	—	—	—	—	—	—	—
★□ KAISER FOUNDATION HOSPITAL, 2025 Morse Ave., Zip 95825; tel. 916/973-5000; Jerry Newman, adm. **A**1a 3 5 10 **F**1 2 3 6 9 10 11 12 15 16 21 23 28 32 33 34 35 36 37 38 40 41 45 46 47 49 51 52 53; **S**2105	23	10	S		336	20051	255	75.9	60	4300	—	—	—
★□ MERCY HOSPITAL OF SACRAMENTO, 4001 J St., Zip 95819; tel. 916/453-4545; Sr. Bridget McCarthy, pres. & chief exec. off. (Total facility includes 50 beds in nursing home-type unit) **A**1a 2 9 10 **F**1 2 3 4 6 7 8 9 10 11 12 14 15 16 17 19 20 21 23 24 25 34 35 36 40 42 45 46 47 52 53 54; **S**5205	21	10	S	TF H	385 335	12988 12334	255 212	68.9 —	16 16	1060 1060	78234 76868	35429 34426	1355 1326
□ METHODIST HOSPITAL, 7500 Timberlake Way, Zip 95823; tel. 916/423-3000; Stanley C. Oppegard, pres. & chief exec. off. **A**1a 9 10 **F**1 3 6 10 12 16 21 23 34 35 36 40 44 45 52 53	23	10	S		150	5575	76	50.7	21	781	28017	11925	455
★□ SUTTER COMMUNITY HOSPITALS (Includes Sutter General Hospital, 2820 L St., Zip 95816; tel. 916/454-2222; J. F. Riley, adm.; Sutter Memorial Hospital, 52nd & F Sts., Zip 95819; tel. 916/454-3333; M. J. Cohill, adm.), 1111 Howe Ave., Suite 600, Zip 95825; tel. 916/927-5211; Patrick G. Hays, pres. & chief exec. off. (Total facility includes 132 beds in nursing home-type unit) **A**1a 2 3 5 9 **F**1 2 3 4 6 10 11 12 13 14 15 16 19 20 21 23 24 27 28 29 32 33 34 35 36 37 40 42 43 44 45 46 47 51 52 53 54; **S**8795	23	10	S	TF H	723 591	28028 28006	510 488	70.5 —	52 52	5436 5436	151104 150622	77887 77655	3061 2940
SUTTER GENERAL HOSPITAL, See Sutter Community Hospitals													
SUTTER MEMORIAL HOSPITAL, See Sutter Community Hospitals													
★□ UNIVERSITY OF CALIFORNIA DAVIS MEDICAL CENTER, 2315 Stockton Blvd., Zip 95817; tel. 916/453-3096; Frank J. Loge, dir. **A**1a 2 3 5 8 9 10 **F**1 2 3 4 5 6 10 12 13 14 15 16 20 21 22 23 24 25 26 27 28 30 32 33 34 35 37 38 40 44 45 46 47 50 51 52 53 54; **S**6405	12	10	S		439	16604	349	79.5	16	1308	146939	71140	2527
SALINAS—Monterey County													
ALISAL COMMUNITY HOSPITAL, See Community Hospital of Salinas													
★□ COMMUNITY HOSPITAL OF SALINAS (Formerly Alisal Community Hospital), 970 Circle Dr., Zip 93905; tel. 408/424-0381; James R. Schlaak, adm. **A**1a 9 10 **F**1 3 6 15 20 33 34 37 45 48 49 50; **S**0585	23	10	S		42	912	17	40.5	0	0	4043	1816	92

★ American Hospital Association (AHA) membership
□ Joint Commission on Accreditation of Hospitals (JCAH) accreditation
\+ American Osteopathic Hospital Association (AOHA) membership
○ American Osteopathic Association (AOA) accreditation
Δ Commission on Accreditation of Rehabilitation Facilities (CARF) accreditation
Control codes 61, 63, 64, 71, 72 and 73 indicate hospitals listed by AOHA, but not registered by AHA.
For definition of numerical codes, see page A2

★ American Hospital Association (AHA) membership
□ Joint Commission on Accreditation of Hospitals (JCAH) accreditation
\+ American Osteopathic Hospital Association (AOHA) membership
○ American Osteopathic Association (AOA) accreditation
Δ Commission on Accreditation of Rehabilitation Facilities (CARF) accreditation
Control codes 61, 63, 64, 71, 72 and 73 indicate hospitals listed by AOHA, but not registered by AHA.
For definition of numerical codes, see page A2

Hospital, Address, Telephone, Administrator, Approval and Facility Codes, Multihospital System Code	Classification Codes				Inpatient Data				Newborn Data		Expense (thousands of dollars)		
	Control	Service	Stay	Facilities	Beds	Admissions	Census	Occupancy (percent)	Bassinets	Births	Total	Payroll	Personnel
⊞ NATIVIDAD MEDICAL CENTER, 1330 Natividad Rd., Zip 93902; Mailing Address Box 81611, Zip 93912; tel. 408/757-0200; James H. Youree, adm. (Total facility includes 52 beds in nursing home-type unit) **A**1a 3 5 9 10 **F**1 3 6 12 14 16 19 20 23 24 26 27 29 30 32 33 34 35 36 37 40 42 43 44 46 49 50 52 53; **S**0585	13	10	S	TF	173	5820	108	62.4	18	1298	27015	13170	551
				H	121	5624	59	—	18	1298	—	—	—
⊞ SALINAS VALLEY MEMORIAL HOSPITAL, 450 E. Romie Lane, Zip 93901; tel. 408/757-4333; Samuel W. Downing, exec. dir. **A**1a 9 10 **F**1 2 3 6 10 12 14 15 16 17 20 21 23 34 35 36 37 40 45 46 47 52 53	16	10	S		211	10156	151	71.6	33	1711	39435	16740	735
SAN ANDREAS—Calaveras County													
□ ST. JOSEPH'S-MARK TWAIN HOSPITAL (Formerly Mark Twain Hospital District), 768 Mountain Ranch Rd., Zip 95249; tel. 209/754-3521; Richard Wing, adm. (Nonreporting) **A**1a 9 10	16	10	S		49	—	—	—	—	—	—	—	—
SAN BERNARDINO—San Bernardino County													
□ SAN BERNARDINO COMMUNITY HOSPITAL, 1500 W. 17th St., Zip 92411; tel. 714/887-6333; Robert S. Lund, adm. (Total facility includes 99 beds in nursing home-type unit) **A**1a 2 9 10 **F**1 2 3 6 9 10 12 14 15 16 19 23 24 25 26 27 28 30 33 34 35 36 37 40 42 44 45 46 47 48 49 52 53	23	10	S	TF	421	8356	256	65.3	36	1480	38308	18570	1009
				H	322	8284	187	—	36	1480	37013	18011	935
⊞ SAN BERNARDINO COUNTY MEDICAL CENTER, 780 E. Gilbert St., Zip 92404; tel. 714/387-8111; Charles R. Jervis, dir. **A**1a 2 3 5 9 10 **F**1 3 5 6 7 9 10 11 12 13 15 16 22 23 24 27 30 32 33 34 35 36 37 40 41 46 50 51 52 53 54	13	10	S		286	12986	200	69.9	23	1699	63016	23533	1073
⊞ ST. BERNARDINE MEDICAL CENTER (Formerly St. Bernardine Hospital), 2101 N. Waterman Ave., Zip 92404; tel. 714/883-8711; Sr. M. Nora Dwan, adm. **A**1a 2 9 10 **F**1 2 3 4 6 9 10 12 14 15 16 17 21 23 24 26 27 28 29 30 35 40 41 42 44 45 46 47 50 52 53 54; **S**0605	21	10	S		311	12580	200	64.3	19	2100	50736	22301	1082
SAN CLEMENTE—Orange County													
□ SAN CLEMENTE GENERAL HOSPITAL, 654 Camino De Los Mares, Zip 92672; tel. 714/661-4402; Thomas W. McClintock, adm. (Nonreporting) **A**1a 2 9 10; **S**1375	33	10	S		116	—	—	—	—	—	—	—	—
SAN DIEGO—San Diego County													
□ ALVARADO HOSPITAL MEDICAL CENTER (Formerly Alvarado Community Hospital), 6655 Alvarado Rd., Zip 92120; tel. 619/287-3270; Daniel P. McLean, exec. dir. **A**1a 9 10 **F**1 3 4 6 8 9 10 11 12 14 15 16 20 23 24 26 30 33 34 35 37 42 44 45 46 53 54; **S**3015	33	10	S		214	7131	110	51.4	0	0	39243	15554	595
⊞ AMI CLAIREMONT COMMUNITY HOSPITAL (Formerly Clairemont Community Hospital), 5255 Mount Etna Dr., Zip 92117; tel. 619/278-8100; Steve Hall, exec. dir. **A**1a 9 10 **F**1 3 6 10 12 14 16 23 24 27 33 35 37 42 44 45 46 47 53; **S**0125	33	10	S		136	1935	40	29.4	0	0	15674	4837	180
⊞ AMI MISSION BAY HOSPITAL (Formerly Mission Bay Memorial Hospital), 3030 Bunker Hill St., Zip 92109; tel. 619/274-7721; Steve Hall, exec. dir. **A**1a 9 **F**1 3 6 9 10 12 14 16 20 23 24 30 33 34 35 43 44 45 46 47 48 50 53; **S**0125	33	10	S		150	4166	61	40.7	0	0	20788	5390	288
⊞ CHILDREN'S HOSPITAL AND HEALTH CENTER, 8001 Frost St., Zip 92123; tel. 619/576-1700; Blair L. Sadler, pres. **A**1a 2 3 5 9 10 **F**1 5 12 15 16 17 23 24 26 34 37 38 42 44 45 46 47 51	23	50	S		107	6163	97	90.7	0	0	58108	25903	1140
CLAIREMONT COMMUNITY HOSPITAL, See AMI Clairemont Community Hospital													
⊞ HARBOR VIEW MEDICAL CENTER, 120 Elm St., Zip 92101; tel. 619/232-4331; Margareta Norton, adm. **A**1a 10 **F**1 2 3 6 10 12 16 23 24 27 33 34 35 42 43 46 47 50; **S**6525	33	10	S		176	1827	56	31.8	0	0	12100	5700	203
⊞ ○ + HILLSIDE HOSPITAL, 1940 El Cajon Blvd., Zip 92104; tel. 619/297-2251; Robert C. Gordon Jr., adm. **A**1a 9 10 11 12 **F**1 3 6 10 12 15 16 19 20 23 32 33 35 44 45 48 49 50 53	23	10	S		133	2606	47	35.3	0	0	12803	5128	284
⊞ KAISER FOUNDATION HOSPITAL (Includes Kaiser Foundation Hospital, 203 Travelodge Dr., El Cajon, Zip 92020; tel. 619/584-5000), 4647 Zion Ave., Zip 92120; tel. 619/584-5000; Kenneth F. Colling, adm. **A**1a 2 3 5 9 10 **F**1 3 6 7 9 10 11 12 14 15 16 20 21 23 24 35 36 37 38 40 41 44 45 50 51 52 53; **S**2105	23	10	S		281	16303	212	77.4	58	4381	—	—	1092
⊞ MERCY HOSPITAL AND MEDICAL CENTER, 4077 Fifth Ave., Zip 92103; tel. 619/294-8111; Richard L. Keyser, pres. & chief exec. off. **A**1a 3 5 8 9 10 **F**1 3 4 5 6 9 10 12 14 15 16 17 20 23 24 26 27 28 30 32 33 34 35 36 40 41 42 44 45 46 47 50 51 52 53 54; **S**5205	21	10	S		416	19649	304	70.4	44	3539	95198	45470	1641
⊞ MESA VISTA HOSPITAL, 7850 Vista Hill Ave., Zip 92123; tel. 619/694-8300; Donald K. Allen, adm. & chief exec. off. **A**1b 9 10 **F**15 24 29 30 31 32 33 42 43 45 46 49 50; **S**8895	23	22	S		150	2212	125	83.3	0	0	13166	6935	230
MISSION BAY MEMORIAL HOSPITAL, See AMI Mission Bay Hospital													
⊞ NAVAL HOSPITAL, Zip 92134; tel. 619/233-2413; CDR L. G. Seible MSC USN, dir. adm. **A**1a 2 3 5 **F**1 2 3 4 6 7 8 9 10 11 12 14 15 16 18 20 23 27 28 29 30 32 33 34 35 36 37 38 40 44 46 47 48 49 50 51 52 53 54	43	10	S		566	24398	398	70.3	52	2713	140729	—	2852
SAN DIEGO COUNTY HILLCREST MENTAL HEALTH FACILITY, 345 W. Dickinson St., Zip 92103; Mailing Address P O Box 85524, Zip 92138; tel. 619/236-4960; Eric Eliason, adm. **A**9 10 **F**24 28 30 32 33 42 46 47	13	22	S		60	1568	59	95.2	0	0	15770	8356	218
SAN DIEGO COUNTY LOMA PORTAL MENTAL HEALTH FACILITY, 3485 Kenyon St., Zip 92110; Mailing Address Box 85524, Zip 92138; tel. 714/236-4960; Eric Eliason, adm. **F**15 24 28 29 30 32 33 34 42 43 46 47	13	22	S		58	577	46	79.3	0	0	11197	5469	163
□ SAN DIEGO PHYSICIANS AND SURGEONS HOSPITAL, 446 26th St., Zip 92102; tel. 619/234-4341; Scott Rhine, chief exec. off. (Total facility includes 78 beds in nursing home-type unit) **A**1a 9 10 **F**1 3 6 10 12 14 16 19 20 23 34 35 42 45 46 48; **S**3015	33	10	S	TF	156	2917	135	86.5	0	0	17124	5874	285
				H	78	2784	49	—	0	0	—	—	239
⊞ SHARP CABRILLO HOSPITAL, 3475 Kenyon St., Zip 92110; tel. 619/221-3500; Harold W. Hartman, sr. vice-pres. & adm. **A**1a 9 10 **F**1 3 6 9 10 12 15 16 20 23 24 25 28 29 32 33 34 35 42 44 45 46 47 48 49 50 53	23	10	S		250	6452	121	48.4	0	0	34614	13187	514
⊞ SHARP MEMORIAL HOSPITAL (Includes Donald N. Sharp Rehabilitation Center), 7901 Frost St., Zip 92123; tel. 619/541-3400; Charles S. Koch, sr. vice-pres. & adm. **A**1a 2 9 10 **F**1 2 3 4 5 6 9 10 12 13 15 16 20 23 24 25 26 33 34 35 36 37 38 40 41 42 44 45 46 47 51 53 54	23	10	S		415	21002	337	81.2	40	6590	121831	57293	1689
⊞ UNIVERSITY OF CALIFORNIA SAN DIEGO MEDICAL CENTER, 225 Dickinson St., Zip 92103; tel. 619/294-6222; Michael R. Stringer, dir. **A**1a 2 3 5 8 9 10 **F**1 2 3 4 5 6 8 9 10 11 12 14 15 16 17 20 22 23 24 26 27 28 30 32 33 34 35 36 37 38 39 40 41 42 44 45 46 47 50 51 52 53 54; **S**6405	12	10	S		406	17855	315	77.6	24	3651	139678	59049	2405
⊞ VETERANS ADMINISTRATION MEDICAL CENTER, 3350 Lajolla Village Dr., Zip 92161; tel. 619/453-7500; Barbara A. Small, dir. (Total facility includes 60 beds in nursing home-type unit) **A**1a 3 5 8 **F**1 2 3 4 6 9 10 11 12 14 15 16 19 20 23 24 25 26 27 28 29 30 31 32 33 34 35 41 42 44 46 47 48 49 50 53 54	45	10	S	TF	622	14061	386	62.1	0	0	75708	42213	1551
				H	562	13838	334	—	0	0	73877	40861	1518
⊞ VILLAVIEW COMMUNITY HOSPITAL, 5550 University Ave., P O Box 5587, Zip 92105; tel. 619/582-3516; T. N. Pendleton, pres. **A**1a 9 10 **F**1 3 6 10 12 14 15 16 23 27 30 32 33 35 42 45 48 49 50; **S**8810	23	10	S		100	2180	58	58.0	0	0	12606	5726	323

★ American Hospital Association (AHA) membership
□ Joint Commission on Accreditation of Hospitals (JCAH) accreditation
+ American Osteopathic Hospital Association (AOHA) membership
○ American Osteopathic Association (AOA) accreditation
Δ Commission on Accreditation of Rehabilitation Facilities (CARF) accreditation
Control codes 61, 63, 64, 71, 72 and 73 indicate hospitals listed by AOHA, but not registered by AHA.
For definition of numerical codes, see page A2

Hospital, Address, Telephone, Administrator, Approval and Facility Codes, Multihospital System Code	Classification Codes				Inpatient Data				Newborn Data		Expense (thousands of dollars)		
	Control	Service	Stay	Facilities	Beds	Admissions	Census	Occupancy (percent)	Bassinets	Births	Total	Payroll	Personnel
SAN DIMAS—Los Angeles County													
★□ AMI SAN DIMAS COMMUNITY HOSPITAL (Formerly San Dimas Community Hospital), 1350 W. Covina Blvd., Zip 91773; tel. 714/599-6811; Ruben Fernandez, exec. dir. **A**1a 2 9 10 **F**3 40 52; **S**0125	33	10	S		99	3932	47	47.5	15	839	22978	8578	236
SAN FERNANDO—Los Angeles County													
□ SAN FERNANDO COMMUNITY HOSPITAL, 700 Chatsworth Dr., Zip 91340; tel. 818/361-7331; George Riesz, chief exec. off. **A**1a 9 10 **F**1 3 10 12 15 16 23 27 30 32 33 35 43 45 46	23	10	S		69	734	12	22.6	0	0	4612	1938	108
SAN FRANCISCO—San Francisco County													
CALIFORNIA PODIATRY HOSPITAL, See Pacific Coast Hospital													
★□ CHILDREN'S HOSPITAL OF SAN FRANCISCO, 3700 California St., Zip 94118; Mailing Address Box 3805, Zip 94119; tel. 415/387-8700; Charles F. Cross, actg. chief exec. off. & vice-pres. adm. **A**1a 2 3 5 8 9 10 **F**1 2 3 6 7 8 9 10 11 12 14 15 16 20 23 24 26 28 30 32 33 34 35 36 37 38 40 42 45 46 47 50 51 52 53	23	10	S		245	12033	179	73.1	44	3627	77300	30586	1277
★□ CHINESE HOSPITAL, 845 Jackson St., Zip 94133; tel. 415/982-2400; Paul M. Rader, chief exec. off. **A**1a 9 10 **F**1 3 6 10 11 12 14 16 17 23 34 36 40 45 46 53	23	10	S		59	2079	39	66.1	6	274	11259	5128	173
★□ FRENCH HOSPITAL, 4131 Geary Blvd., Zip 94118; Mailing Address Box 7883, Zip 94120; tel. 415/386-9000; Leslie R. Smith, chief exec. off. (Total facility includes 50 beds in nursing home-type unit) **A**1a 2 9 10 **F**1 2 3 6 10 12 14 15 16 19 20 23 24 26 27 28 30 32 33 34 35 39 42 44 45 46 47 49 53	23	10	S	TF	234	4470	99	42.3	0	0	48099	20047	656
				H	184	3972	71	—	0	0	46202	19205	627
GARDEN-SULLIVAN HOSPITAL, See Pacific Medical Center													
★□ KAISER FOUNDATION HOSPITAL, 2425 Geary Blvd., Zip 94115; tel. 415/929-4000; Frank D. Alvarez, adm. **A**1a 3 5 8 10 **F**1 2 3 4 6 10 12 14 15 16 20 23 24 30 32 33 35 36 37 38 40 41 43 44 46 47 50 51 52 53 54; **S**2105	23	10	S		273	15245	232	85.0	33	3063	—	—	—
★ LAGUNA HONDA HOSPITAL AND REHABILITATION CENTER, 375 Laguna Honda Blvd., Zip 94116; tel. 415/664-1580; Ben Abramovice, exec. adm. (Total facility includes 1082 beds in nursing home-type unit) **A**9 10 **F**1 15 16 19 23 24 25 26 33 42 44 46 50	15	48	L	TF	1106	1219	1058	95.7	0	0	55795	36106	1386
				H	24	332	9	—	0	0	2031	1449	—
★□ LANGLEY PORTER PSYCHIATRIC INSTITUTE-HOSPITALS AND CLINICS, 401 Parnassus Ave., Zip 94143; tel. 415/476-7000; Fariborz Amini MD, adm. **A**1b 3 5 10 **F**24 28 29 32 33 42 46 47; **S**6405	23	22	S		70	680	55	78.6	0	0	11914	7599	192
★□ LETTERMAN ARMY MEDICAL CENTER, Presidio of San Francisco, Zip 94129; tel. 415/561-2231; Col. Paul Shetler, cmdr. **A**1a 2 3 5 **F**1 2 3 4 6 7 8 9 10 11 12 14 15 16 20 23 24 26 27 28 30 31 32 33 34 35 36 37 38 40 41 42 43 44 45 46 47 49 50 51 52 53 54	42	10	S		380	10135	275	72.4	8	575	94452	—	1714
★□ MARSHAL HALE MEMORIAL HOSPITAL, 3773 Sacramento St., Zip 94118; tel. 415/386-7000; Robert B. Duncan, pres. **A**1a 2 3 9 10 **F**1 3 6 10 12 15 16 19 20 23 24 34 35 42 43 44 45 47 48 49 53	23	10	S		154	2711	73	47.4	0	0	20464	10435	339
MEDICAL CENTER AT THE UNIVERSITY OF CALIFORNIA, See University of California, San Francisco Medical Center													
★□ MOUNT ZION HOSPITAL AND MEDICAL CENTER, 1600 Divisadero St., Zip 94115; Mailing Address Box 7921, Zip 94120; tel. 415/567-6600; Martin H. Diamond, pres. & chief exec. off. **A**1a 2 3 5 8 9 10 **F**1 3 4 6 7 8 9 10 11 12 13 14 16 19 20 23 24 25 26 27 28 29 30 32 33 34 35 36 38 40 41 42 44 45 46 47 50 52 53 54	23	10	S		298	9438	185	62.1	18	1162	85285	44521	1440
★□ PACIFIC COAST HOSPITAL (Formerly California Podiatry Hospital), 1210 Scott St., Zip 94115; Mailing Address Box 7855, Rincon Annex, Zip 94120; tel. 415/563-3444; Richard H. Lanham Jr., pres. **A**1a 9 10 **F**1 15 23 26 34	23	49	S		28	648	5	17.9	0	0	—	—	81
PACIFIC PRESBYTERIAN HOSPITAL, See Pacific Presbyterian Medical Center													
★□ PACIFIC PRESBYTERIAN MEDICAL CENTER (Formerly Pacific Medical Center) (Includes Garden-Sullivan Hospital, 2750 Geary Blvd., Zip 94118; tel. 415/921-6171; Mitchell Fox, adm.; Pacific Presbyterian Hospital, 2333 Buchanan St., Zip 94115; tel. 415/563-4321; Robert Merwin, adm. & chief oper. off.), Clay at Buchanan St., Zip 94115; Mailing Address Box 7999, Zip 94120; tel. 415/563-4321; B. E. Spivey MD, pres. **A**1a 2 3 5 8 9 10 **F**1 2 3 4 6 10 12 13 15 16 17 19 20 21 23 24 25 26 27 28 29 33 34 35 41 42 44 45 46 47 48 49 50 52 53 54	23	10	S		391	11220	257	63.3	0	0	103369	47730	1548
★□ RALPH K. DAVIES MEDICAL CENTER-FRANKLIN HOSPITAL, Castro & Duboce Sts., Zip 94114; tel. 415/565-6779; George D. Monardo, pres. **A**1a 2 3 5 9 10 **F**1 2 3 6 7 8 9 10 11 12 15 16 17 19 20 23 24 25 26 32 33 34 35 39 41 42 43 44 45 50 53; **S**2245	23	10	S		161	4823	128	79.5	0	0	43146	21193	704
□ SAN FRANCISCO GENERAL HOSPITAL MEDICAL CENTER, 1001 Potrero Ave., Zip 94110; tel. 415/821-8200; Phillip E. Sowa, exec. dir. (Nonreporting) **A**1a 3 5 8 9 10	15	10	S		444	—	—	—	—	—	—	—	—
★□ SHRINERS HOSPITAL FOR CRIPPLED CHILDREN, 1701 19th Ave., Zip 94122; tel. 415/665-1100; Ronald J. Castagno, adm. **A**1a 3 5 **F**15 19 23 24 26 34 38 42 46; **S**4125	23	57	S		48	416	20	41.7	0	0	—	—	117
★□ ST. FRANCIS MEMORIAL HOSPITAL, 900 Hyde St., Zip 94109; Mailing Address Box 7726, Zip 94120; tel. 415/775-4321; John G. Williams, pres. & chief exec. off. **A**1a 2 3 9 10 **F**1 2 3 6 7 8 9 10 11 12 15 16 20 22 23 24 25 26 27 30 32 33 34 35 41 42 44 45 46 47 53 54	23	10	S		328	6971	157	47.9	0	0	52000	22466	894
★□ ST. LUKE'S HOSPITAL, 3555 Army St., Zip 94110; tel. 415/641-6666; Earl A. Simendinger PhD, pres. & chief exec. off. **A**1a 2 9 10 **F**1 3 6 10 12 14 15 16 19 20 23 24 27 30 32 33 34 35 36 37 40 41 44 45 46 47 52 53	23	10	S		209	7244	109	59.9	25	1332	37639	19156	508
★□ ST. MARY'S HOSPITAL AND MEDICAL CENTER, 450 Stanyan St., Zip 94117; tel. 415/668-1000; James E. Metcalfe, pres. (Total facility includes 33 beds in nursing home-type unit) **A**1a 2 3 5 8 9 10 **F**1 3 4 6 7 8 9 10 11 12 14 15 16 19 20 23 24 25 26 27 28 29 30 32 33 34 35 36 37 39 40 41 42 43 44 45 46 47 48 49 52 53 54; **S**5205	21	10	S	TF	489	10206	293	59.9	20	706	85132	46896	1255
				H	456	9747	270	—	20	706	—	—	1133
★□ UNIVERSITY OF CALIFORNIA, SAN FRANCISCO MEDICAL CENTER (Formerly Medical Center at the University of California), Zip 94143; tel. 415/476-1401; William B. Kerr, dir. **A**1a 2 3 5 8 9 10 **F**1 2 3 4 6 7 8 9 10 11 12 13 14 15 16 17 20 23 24 34 35 36 37 38 39 40 41 42 44 45 46 47 51 52 53 54; **S**6405	23	10	S		560	18972	377	67.3	31	1561	166949	78355	2652
★□ VETERANS ADMINISTRATION MEDICAL CENTER, 4150 Clement St., Zip 94121; tel. 415/221-4810; John W. Ditzler MD, dir. **A**1a 3 5 8 **F**1 2 3 4 6 9 10 11 12 14 15 16 17 20 23 24 26 27 28 29 30 32 33 34 35 41 42 44 46 47 48 49 50 53 54	45	10	S		354	11545	221	62.4	0	0	87519	44530	1182
SAN GABRIEL—Los Angeles County													
★□ SAN GABRIEL VALLEY MEDICAL CENTER (Formerly Community Hospital of San Gabriel), 218 S. Santa Anita St., Zip 91776; Mailing Address P O Box 1507, Zip 91778; tel. 818/289-5454; Makoto Nakayama, exec. dir. (Total facility includes 6 beds in nursing home-type unit) **A**1a 2 9 10 **F**1 2 3 6 7 8 9 10 11 12 14 15 16 19 20 23 24 26 28 29 33 34 35 37 41 43 44 45 46 47 49 50 52 53 54	23	10	S	TF	184	5799	111	60.3	0	0	35687	15492	—
				H	178	5797	111	—	0	0	35684	15490	—
SAN JOSE—Santa Clara County													
★□ ALEXIAN BROTHERS HOSPITAL OF SAN JOSE, 225 N. Jackson Ave., Zip 95116; tel. 408/259-5000; Dean Grant, pres. & chief exec. off. **A**1a 9 10 **F**1 3 6 10 12 14 16 23 24 35 36 40 41 44 45 47 52 53; **S**0065	21	10	S		204	7960	105	51.5	24	1638	41532	18672	489

★ American Hospital Association (AHA) membership
☐ Joint Commission on Accreditation of Hospitals (JCAH) accreditation
+ American Osteopathic Hospital Association (AOHA) membership
○ American Osteopathic Association (AOA) accreditation
Δ Commission on Accreditation of Rehabilitation Facilities (CARF) accreditation
Control codes 61, 63, 64, 71, 72 and 73 indicate hospitals listed by AOHA, but not registered by AHA.
For definition of numerical codes, see page A2

Hospital, Address, Telephone, Administrator, Approval and Facility Codes, Multihospital System Code	Classification Codes				Inpatient Data				Newborn Data		Expense (thousands of dollars)		
	Control	Service	Stay	Facilities	Beds	Admissions	Census	Occupancy (percent)	Bassinets	Births	Total	Payroll	Personnel
⊞ GOOD SAMARITAN HOSPITAL OF SANTA CLARA VALLEY, 2425 Samaritan Dr., Zip 95124; tel. 408/559-2011; Richard E. Herington, adm. **A**1a 2 9 10 **F**1 2 3 4 6 10 12 14 15 16 17 20 21 23 24 27 28 29 30 32 33 34 35 36 37 40 41 42 44 45 46 47 48 51 52 53 54; **S**0965	23	10	S		388	16870	239	61.6	45	3888	82015	40191	1118
⊞ O'CONNOR HOSPITAL (Includes St. Vincent Pavilion, 455 O'Connor Dr., Zip 95128), 2105 Forest Ave., Zip 95128; tel. 408/947-2500; William C. Finlayson, pres. & chief exec. off.; Robert G. Brueckner, exec. vice-pres. **A**1a 2 9 10 **F**1 2 3 4 6 7 8 9 10 11 12 15 16 20 23 24 34 35 36 37 40 41 44 45 46 47 48 49 52 53 54; **S**1885	21	10	S		285	12975	197	69.1	25	2346	81289	37775	939
⊞ SAN JOSE HOSPITAL, 675 E. Santa Clara St., Zip 95112; tel. 408/998-3212; John C. Aird, pres.; Robert G. Brueckner, exec. vice-pres. **A**1a 2 3 5 9 10 **F**1 2 3 4 5 6 7 8 9 10 11 12 14 16 17 20 23 24 25 26 27 30 32 33 35 36 39 40 42 44 45 46 47 48 52 53 54; **S**0965	23	10	S		289	12026	201	69.6	32	1571	68619	33853	1109
⊞ Δ SANTA CLARA VALLEY MEDICAL CENTER, 751 S. Bascom Ave., Zip 95128; tel. 408/299-6827; Robert Sillen, exec. dir. **A**1a 2 3 5 7 8 10 **F**1 3 4 5 6 7 8 9 10 11 12 13 15 16 17 22 23 24 25 26 27 28 29 30 32 33 34 35 37 38 39 40 42 44 45 46 47 51 52 53 54	13	10	S		480	15530	346	77.2	16	2581	141530	65299	2800
⊞ SANTA TERESA COMMUNITY HOSPITAL, 250 Hospital Pkwy., Zip 95119; tel. 408/972-7000; John H. Chappell, adm. **A**1a 9 10 **F**1 2 3 6 10 12 14 15 16 20 23 30 35 36 38 40 46 47 52 54; **S**2105	23	10	S		222	12241	141	64.7	44	2863	—	—	—
ST. VINCENT PAVILION, See O'Connor Hospital													
SAN LEANDRO—Alameda County													
★ ESTUDILLO HOSPITAL, 345 Estudillo Ave., Zip 94577; tel. 415/483-5114; Lynne W. Tully, adm. (Nonreporting) **A**9 10	33	10	S		6	—	—	—	—	—	—	—	—
☐ FAIRMONT HOSPITAL, 15400 Foothill Blvd., Zip 94578; tel. 415/667-7820; Neil R. Petersen, actg. adm. (Total facility includes 134 beds in nursing home-type unit) **A**1a 9 **F**6 15 16 19 23 24 25 26 34 35 37 42 44 45 46 47 53; **S**0225	13	10	S	TF	249	1925	208	83.5	0	0	32425	16885	680
				H	115	1351	78	—	0	0	—	—	596
⊞ HUMANA HOSPITAL -SAN LEANDRO, 13855 E. 14th St., Zip 94578; tel. 415/357-6500; Doris I. Porth, exec. dir. **A**1a 9 10 **F**1 3 6 10 12 14 15 16 20 23 34 35 37 44 45 46 49 53; **S**1235	33	10	S		136	4281	67	49.3	0	0	22935	9878	367
⊞ MEMORIAL HOSPITAL-SAN LEANDRO, 2800 Benedict Dr., Zip 94577; tel. 415/357-8300; Phillip J. Mazzuca, exec. dir. (Nonreporting) **A**1a 9 10; **S**6525	33	10	S		142	—	—	—	—	—	—	—	—
SAN LUIS OBISPO—San Luis Obispo County													
AMI SIERRA VISTA HOSPITAL, See AMI Sierra Vista Regional Medical Center													
⊞ AMI SIERRA VISTA REGIONAL MEDICAL CENTER (Formerly AMI Sierra Vista Hospital), 1010 Murray Ave., Zip 93401; Mailing Address Box 1367, Zip 93406; tel. 805/546-7600; Glenn D. Carlson, chief exec. off. **A**1a 9 10 **F**1 3 6 7 8 9 10 11 12 14 16 23 24 35 36 40 44 45 46 47 52 53; **S**0125	33	10	S		175	6422	95	54.3	12	629	27299	9336	425
CALIFORNIA MENS COLONY HOSPITAL, Zip 93409; tel. 805/543-2700 (Nonreporting)	12	11	S		38	—	—	—	—	—	—	—	—
⊞ FRENCH HOSPITAL MEDICAL CENTER (Formerly French Hospital), 1911 Johnson Ave., Zip 93401; tel. 805/543-5353; Jim Gstettenbauer, exec. dir. (Data for 84 days) **A**1a 9 10 **F**1 3 4 6 10 12 14 15 16 23 24 26 34 35 44 46 47 48 49 52 53 54; **S**3025	33	10	S		125	761	49	39.5	0	0	3938	1533	268
☐ SAN LUIS OBISPO GENERAL HOSPITAL, 2180 Johnson Ave., Zip 93406; Mailing Address Box 8113, Zip 93403; tel. 805/543-1500; George B. Rowland MD, dir. **A**1a 9 10 **F**1 3 6 12 16 20 23 27 28 29 30 31 32 33 34 35 36 40 45 46	10	10	S		69	2816	33	47.8	17	1331	12953	4623	246
SAN MATEO—San Mateo County													
☐ HAROLD D. CHOPE COMMUNITY HOSPITAL, 222 W. 39th Ave., Zip 94403; tel. 415/573-2222; Lola Thompson, actg. dir. (Total facility includes 124 beds in nursing home-type unit) **A**1a 3 9 10 **F**1 3 5 6 10 12 16 20 23 24 25 26 27 28 29 30 32 33 34 35 37 42 43 44 45 46 47 49 50 52 53	13	10	S	TF	240	3744	197	82.1	0	1	42766	18385	761
				H	116	3543	78	—	0	1	35900	14874	608
⊞ MILLS MEMORIAL HOSPITAL, 100 S. San Mateo Dr., Zip 94401; tel. 415/579-2000; Charles H. Mason Jr., pres. (Total facility includes 75 beds in nursing home-type unit) **A**1a 9 10 **F**1 2 3 6 10 12 15 16 19 20 23 24 25 26 30 34 35 36 40 42 44 45 46 47 48 49 51 52 53; **S**6975	23	10	S	TF	344	8906	228	63.7	25	1129	57003	28525	1044
				H	269	8620	156	—	25	1129	55082	27782	987
SAN PABLO—Contra Costa County													
☐ BROOKSIDE HOSPITAL, 2000 Vale Rd., Zip 94806; tel. 415/235-7000; John P. Friel, chief exec. off. (Total facility includes 24 beds in nursing home-type unit) **A**1a 2 9 10 **F**1 2 3 6 7 8 9 10 11 12 16 19 22 23 24 26 34 35 36 37 40 46 47 52 53 54	16	10	S	TF	222	6577	108	44.6	24	934	40053	19886	653
				H	198	6545	107	—	24	934	—	—	633
SAN QUENTIN—Marin County													
CHARLES L. NEUMILLER MEMORIAL HOSPITAL, California State Prison, Zip 94964; tel. 415/454-1460; William G. Ham, adm. **F**1 16 23 28 30 33 34	12	11	S		54	564	38	70.4	0	0	—	—	84
SAN RAFAEL—Marin County													
⊞ KAISER FOUNDATION HOSPITAL-SAN RAFAEL (Formerly Listed Under Terra Linda), 99 Montecillo Rd., Zip 94903; tel. 415/499-2000; Patrice Dowd, adm. **A**1a 10 **F**3 6 12 14 15 16 23 26 30 34 35 41 45 46 47 52; **S**2105	23	10	S		119	5467	85	71.4	0	0	—	—	1020
⊞ MARIN GENERAL HOSPITAL, 250 Bon Air Rd., Box 8010, Zip 94912; tel. 415/925-7000; Henry J. Buhrmann, pres. & chief exec. off. **A**1a 2 9 10 **F**1 2 3 6 7 8 9 10 11 12 14 15 16 20 23 24 27 28 29 30 32 34 35 36 37 40 42 43 44 45 46 48 49 50 51 52 53 54	23	10	S		255	8861	123	48.2	23	1218	45029	21388	682
SANGER—Fresno County													
☐ SANGER HOSPITAL, 2558 Jensen Ave., Zip 93657; tel. 209/875-6571; Richard Harris PhD, adm. **A**1a 9 10 **F**1 6 10 12 16 34 40	31	10	S		49	1098	11	22.4	8	420	—	—	78
SANTA ANA—Orange County													
⊞ COASTAL COMMUNITIES HOSPITAL (Formerly Mercy General Hospital), 2701 S. Bristol, Zip 92704; tel. 714/754-5454; Elizabeth J. Stark, adm. (Nonreporting) **A**1a 9 10; **S**6525	33	10	S		215	—	—	—	—	—	—	—	—
☐ CPC SANTA ANA PSYCHIATRIC HOSPITAL (Formerly Santa Ana Psychiatric Hospital), 2212 E. Fourth St., Zip 92705; tel. 714/543-8481; Al Smith, adm. **A**1b 9 10 **F**15 24 29 30 32 33 42 43; **S**0785	33	22	S		32	617	37	75.5	0	0	—	—	46
☐ DOCTORS HOSPITAL OF SANTA ANA, 1901 N. College Ave., Zip 92706; tel. 714/547-2565; Robert J. Trautman, exec. dir. **A**1a 9 10 **F**1 3 6 14 15 16 20 23 24 26 34 35 41 44 46 47; **S**3025	33	10	S		54	2602	34	63.0	0	0	11564	3963	178
⊞ SANTA ANA HOSPITAL MEDICAL CENTER, 1901 N. Fairview St., Zip 92706; tel. 714/554-1653; Thomas A. Salerno, exec. dir. **A**1a 9 10 **F**1 3 6 10 14 15 16 17 20 23 24 26 34 35 36 40 41 44 46 47 53; **S**3025	33	10	S		83	4064	56	67.5	6	1094	17660	5861	227
SANTA ANA PSYCHIATRIC HOSPITAL, See CPC Santa Ana Psychiatric Hospital													
⊞ WESTERN MEDICAL CENTER, 1001 N. Tustin Ave., Zip 92705; tel. 714/835-3555; Wayne D. Schroeder, pres. & exec. dir. **A**1a 2 10 **F**1 2 3 4 5 6 7 8 9 10 11 12 14 15 16 17 20 23 24 26 30 32 33 34 35 36 37 38 40 41 42 44 45 46 47 50 51 52 53 54	23	10	S		327	12354	179	54.7	16	2275	75177	25600	1720

Hospital, Address, Telephone, Administrator, Approval and Facility Codes, Multihospital System Code	Classification Codes				Inpatient Data				Newborn Data		Expense (thousands of dollars)		
★ American Hospital Association (AHA) membership □ Joint Commission on Accreditation of Hospitals (JCAH) accreditation + American Osteopathic Hospital Association (AOHA) membership ○ American Osteopathic Association (AOA) accreditation Δ Commission on Accreditation of Rehabilitation Facilities (CARF) accreditation Control codes 61, 63, 64, 71, 72 and 73 indicate hospitals listed by AOHA, but not registered by AHA. For definition of numerical codes, see page A2	Control	Service	Stay	Facilities	Beds	Admissions	Census	Occupancy (percent)	Bassinets	Births	Total	Payroll	Personnel
SANTA BARBARA—Santa Barbara County													
★□ DEVEREUX FOUNDATION-CALIFORNIA (Formerly Devereux Foundation-California Treadway Division, Goleta), Box 1079, Zip 93102; tel. 805/968-2525; Thomas P. McCool, dir. (Nonreporting) **A**1b ; **S**0845	23	22	L		56	—	—	—	—	—	—	—	—
★□ GOLETA VALLEY COMMUNITY HOSPITAL, 351 S. Patterson Ave., Box 6306, Zip 93160; tel. 805/967-3411; David C. Bigelow, adm. **A**1a 2 9 10 **F**1 3 4 6 10 12 14 15 16 23 35 36 39 40 42 43 45 48 49 53 54	23	10	S		113	3536	53	46.9	10	692	17679	—	307
MEMORIAL HOSPITAL OF SANTA BARBARA, See Rehabilitation Institute of Santa Barbara													
□ PINECREST HOSPITAL (General Medical and Surgical, Alcoholism and Chemical Dependency, and Short-Term and Long-Term Skilled Nursing), 2415 De La Vina St., Zip 93105; tel. 805/682-2511; Virginia J. Lutz, vice-pres. (Total facility includes 40 beds in nursing home-type unit) **A**1a 9 10 **F**15 16 19 23 24 28 29 32 33 34 42 44 46 49	23	82	S	TF	72	748	48	66.7	0	0	5517	2205	98
				H	32	452	20	—	0	0	3334	1332	—
□ REHABILITATION INSTITUTE OF SANTA BARBARA (Formerly Memorial Hospital of Santa Barbara), 427 Camino Del Remedio, Zip 93110; tel. 805/683-3788; Scott Glenn, chief exec. off. **A**1a 9 10 **F**15 16 23 24 26 33 34 42 43 44 46 47	23	46	L		46	382	35	76.1	0	0	7966	3687	173
★□ SANTA BARBARA COTTAGE HOSPITAL, Pueblo at Bath St., Box 689, Zip 93102; tel. 805/682-7111; James L. Ash, pres. & chief exec. off. **A**1a 2 3 5 9 10 **F**1 2 3 4 6 8 10 12 14 15 16 20 23 24 27 28 29 30 32 34 35 36 40 41 42 43 44 45 46 52 53 54	23	10	S		345	14060	232	67.2	32	1936	65017	28387	1312
★□ SCHICK SHADEL HOSPITAL, 45 E. Alamar, Zip 93105; tel. 805/687-2411; Richard J. Callanan, adm. **A**1a 9 10 **F**15 26 28 30 31 32 33 34 47 49; **S**0575	33	82	S		30	1431	23	76.7	0	0	5158	1366	64
★□ ST. FRANCIS HOSPITAL OF SANTA BARBARA, 601 E. Micheltorena St., Zip 93103; tel. 805/962-7661; James A. Keens, adm. **A**1a 2 9 10 **F**1 3 6 12 14 15 16 23 24 26 34 35 44 45 46 53; **S**1415	21	10	S		110	3003	46	41.8	0	0	17128	7815	333
SANTA CLARA—Santa Clara County													
★□ KAISER FOUNDATION HOSPITAL, 900 Kiely Blvd., Zip 95051; tel. 408/985-4000; Thomas R. Seifert, adm. **A**1a 3 5 10 **F**1 2 3 6 10 12 14 15 16 21 23 24 34 35 37 40 41 43 50 51 52; **S**2105	23	10	S		320	13897	204	63.8	46	3367	—	—	—
SANTA CRUZ—Santa Cruz County													
★□ AMI COMMUNITY HOSPITAL OF SANTA CRUZ (Formerly Community Hospital of Santa Cruz), 610 Frederick St., Zip 95062; tel. 408/426-3282; Ann Klein, exec. dir. **A**1a 9 10 **F**1 3 5 6 10 12 14 15 16 20 23 26 34 35 36 37 40 43 44 45 46 50 53 54; **S**0125	33	10	S		180	3982	50	27.8	16	1092	16431	6592	272
COMMUNITY HOSPITAL OF SANTA CRUZ, See AMI Community Hospital of Santa Cruz													
★□ DOMINICAN SANTA CRUZ HOSPITAL, 1555 Soquel Dr., Zip 95065; tel. 408/462-7700; Sr. Julie Hyer, pres. & chief exec. off. (Total facility includes 37 beds in nursing home-type unit) **A**1a 2 9 10 **F**1 2 3 6 10 12 14 16 17 19 20 23 24 27 35 36 40 44 45 47 48 51 52 53	21	10	S	TF	247	10022	171	69.8	16	1208	41923	19312	—
				H	210	9700	147	—	16	1208	—	—	—
SANTA MARIA—Santa Barbara County													
★□ MARIAN MEDICAL CENTER, 1400 E. Church St., Zip 93454; Mailing Address Box 1238, Zip 93456; tel. 805/922-5811; Charles J. Cova, adm. (Total facility includes 10 beds in nursing home-type unit) **A**1a 9 10 **F**1 3 4 6 7 10 12 14 15 16 19 20 23 24 26 34 35 36 40 41 42 43 44 45 46 47 49 52 53	21	10	S	TF	130	6240	78	60.0	24	1017	25829	10249	—
				H	120	6228	76	—	24	1017	—	—	—
□ VALLEY COMMUNITY HOSPITAL, 505 E. Plaza Dr., Zip 93454; tel. 805/925-0935; Bryan D. Burklow, exec. dir. (Nonreporting) **A**1a 9 10; **S**3025	33	10	S		48	—	—	—	—	—	—	—	—
SANTA MONICA—Los Angeles County													
★□ SAINT JOHN'S HOSPITAL AND HEALTH CENTER, 1328 22nd St., Zip 90404; tel. 213/829-5511; Sr. Marie Madeleine, pres. **A**1a 2 9 10 **F**1 2 3 4 6 7 8 9 10 11 12 14 15 16 23 24 26 27 28 29 30 32 33 34 35 36 40 42 44 45 46 48 49 52 53 54; **S**5095	21	10	S		551	15673	289	52.5	30	1632	92072	45796	1692
★□ SANTA MONICA HOSPITAL MEDICAL CENTER, 1225 15th St., Zip 90404; tel. 213/319-4000; Leonard Labella Jr., pres. & exec. dir. **A**1a 2 3 5 9 10 **F**1 2 3 4 5 6 7 8 9 10 11 12 14 15 16 20 23 24 26 34 35 36 37 40 41 44 45 46 47 52 53 54; **S**2245	23	10	S		285	10585	177	62.1	20	1938	66224	30529	1154
SANTA PAULA—Ventura County													
□ SANTA PAULA MEMORIAL HOSPITAL, 825 N. Tenth St., P O Box 270, Zip 93060; tel. 805/252-7171; James W. Knight, adm. (Data not available) **A**1a 9 10 **F**1 3 6 10 12 14 15 16 23 35 36 40 43 45 53	23	10	S		60	—	—	—	—	—	—	—	—
SANTA ROSA—Sonoma County													
BROOKWOOD HOSPITAL, See North Coast Rehabilitation Center													
□ COMMUNITY HOSPITAL, 3325 Chanate Rd., Zip 95404; tel. 707/544-3340; Larry E. Hood, adm. **A**1a 3 5 9 10 **F**1 2 3 6 9 10 12 15 16 23 24 34 35 40 44 45 46 51 52 53; **S**0585	13	10	S		145	8126	94	64.8	16	3191	—	—	663
□ NORTH COAST REHABILITATION CENTER (Formerly Brookwood Hospital), 151 Sotoyome St., Zip 95405; tel. 707/542-2771; Pamela Killian, adm. **A**1a 9 10 **F**15 16 19 23 24 26 27 28 29 30 32 33 34 42 44 46 50; **S**0585	33	46	S		61	834	38	62.3	0	0	5296	2768	146
★□ SANTA ROSA MEMORIAL HOSPITAL, 1165 Montgomery Dr., Zip 95405; Mailing Address Box 522, Zip 95402; tel. 707/546-3210; George L. Heidkamp, pres. & chief exec. off. **A**1a 9 10 **F**1 2 3 4 6 9 10 12 13 14 15 16 20 23 24 34 35 36 40 41 45 46 47 48 49 50 51 52 53 54; **S**5425	21	10	S		240	11690	181	75.4	16	1089	63666	29252	912
□ WARRACK MEDICAL CENTER HOSPITAL, 2449 Summerfield Rd., Zip 95405; tel. 707/542-9030; Dale E. Iversen, adm. & vice-pres. (Nonreporting) **A**1a 9 10	33	10	S		79	—	—	—	—	—	—	—	—
SCOTTS VALLEY—Santa Cruz County													
★□ STAR LODGE HOSPITAL, 5271 Scotts Valley Dr., P O Box 66798, Zip 95066; tel. 408/438-2090; Jan Spangler, adm. **A**1a 9 **F**33 42	33	82	S		27	317	16	59.3	0	0	2363	928	32
SEBASTOPOL—Sonoma County													
★□ PALM DRIVE HOSPITAL, 501 Petaluma Ave., Zip 95472; tel. 707/823-8511; Vance Fager, adm. **A**1a 9 10 **F**1 3 6 9 10 12 15 16 23 35 45 46; **S**1755	33	10	S		56	2295	30	53.6	0	0	—	—	196
SELMA—Fresno County													
★□ SELMA DISTRICT HOSPITAL, 1141 Rose Ave., Zip 93662; tel. 209/891-1000; Jack Waller, chief exec. off. **A**1a 9 10 **F**1 6 15 35 40 45 46 47 52 53; **S**1805	16	10	S		65	2776	31	47.7	12	489	7354	3566	143
SIMI VALLEY—Ventura County													
□ MOUNTAIN VIEW MEDICAL CENTER (Formerly Simi Valley Community Hospital), 1575 Erringer Rd., Zip 93065; tel. 805/527-9383; James Pappas, exec. dir. (Nonreporting) **A**1a 9 10; **S**0235	33	10	S		70	—	—	—	—	—	—	—	—
★□ SIMI VALLEY ADVENTIST HOSPITAL, 2975 N. Sycamore Dr., Box 819, Zip 93062; tel. 805/527-2462; Darwin R. Remboldt, pres. (Nonreporting) **A**1a 9 10; **S**0235	21	10	S		139	—	—	—	—	—	—	—	—
SIMI VALLEY COMMUNITY HOSPITAL, See Mountain View Medical Center													
SOLVANG—Santa Barbara County													
★□ SANTA YNEZ VALLEY HOSPITAL, 700 Alamo Pintado Rd., Zip 93463; tel. 805/688-6431; Baxter F. Black, adm. **A**1a 9 10 **F**1 3 6 15 16 23 34 35 45 46	23	10	S		30	610	8	26.7	6	4	3896	1607	74
SONOMA—Sonoma County													
★□ SONOMA VALLEY HOSPITAL, 347 Andrieux St., Box 600, Zip 95476; tel. 707/938-4545; Robert M. Baden, adm. & chief exec. off. **A**1a 9 10 **F**1 3 6 9 10 12 14 15 16 20 21 23 24 33 34 35 36 37 40 41 43 44 45 46 47 48	16	10	S		68	2577	41	60.3	2	168	13880	6339	209

Hospital, Address, Telephone, Administrator, Approval and Facility Codes, Multihospital System Code	Classification Codes				Inpatient Data				Newborn Data		Expense (thousands of dollars)		
★ American Hospital Association (AHA) membership ☐ Joint Commission on Accreditation of Hospitals (JCAH) accreditation + American Osteopathic Hospital Association (AOHA) membership ○ American Osteopathic Association (AOA) accreditation Δ Commission on Accreditation of Rehabilitation Facilities (CARF) accreditation Control codes 61, 63, 64, 71, 72 and 73 indicate hospitals listed by AOHA, but not registered by AHA. For definition of numerical codes, see page A2	Control	Service	Stay	Facilities	Beds	Admissions	Census	Occupancy (percent)	Bassinets	Births	Total	Payroll	Personnel
SONORA—Tuolumne County													
SIERRA HOSPITAL, See Sonora Community Hospital													
☐ SONORA COMMUNITY HOSPITAL (Includes Sierra Hospital, 179 S. Fairview Lane, Zip 95370; tel. 209/532-7181), 1 S. Forest Rd., Zip 95370; tel. 209/532-3161; Stan B. Berry, pres. (Total facility includes 32 beds in nursing home-type unit) **A**1a 9 10 **F**1 3 6 10 15 16 19 23 24 26 35 36 37 40 44 45 46 53 54; **S**0235	21	10	S	TF H	104 72	3361 3241	57 38	54.8 —	7 7	598 598	15806 15328	6108 5785	283 262
☐ TUOLUMNE GENERAL HOSPITAL, 101 E. Hospital Rd., Zip 95370; tel. 209/532-3401; Lawrence C. Long, adm. (Total facility includes 32 beds in nursing home-type unit) **A**1a 9 10 **F**1 3 6 14 15 16 19 23 34 35 45 50 53; **S**0585	13	10	S	TF H	64 32	1342 1274	49 17	76.6 —	0 0	0 0	7137 6739	2864 2567	158 139
SOUTH EL MONTE—Los Angeles County													
☐ GREATER EL MONTE COMMUNITY HOSPITAL, 1701 S. Santa Anita Ave., Zip 91733; tel. 818/579-7777; Kenneth R. Dillard, chief exec. off. **A**1a 9 10 **F**1 3 6 10 14 16 23 35 40 41 53; **S**1375	33	10	S		115	4323	49	42.6	10	1074	—	—	255
SOUTH LAGUNA—Orange County													
★☐ SOUTH COAST MEDICAL CENTER, 31872 Coast Hwy., Zip 92677; tel. 714/499-1311; Paul McQuade, pres. **A**1a 2 9 10 **F**1 3 6 7 8 9 10 11 12 14 15 16 20 23 24 26 27 28 30 32 33 34 35 36 37 40 41 42 44 45 48 49 52 53	23	10	S		150	3898	79	52.7	18	471	26333	12541	427
SOUTH LAKE TAHOE—El Dorado County													
☐ BARTON MEMORIAL HOSPITAL, Fourth & South Sts., Box 9578, Zip 95731; tel. 916/541-3420; Jonathon W. Baker, adm. **A**1a 9 10 **F**1 3 6 10 12 14 15 21 34 35 36 40 41 45 46 53	23	10	S		81	4287	35	43.2	8	651	13622	5397	315
SOUTH SAN FRANCISCO—San Mateo County													
★☐ KAISER FOUNDATION HOSPITAL, 1200 El Camino Real, Zip 94080; tel. 415/742-2547; Joseph L. Meresman, adm. (Nonreporting) **A**1a 10; **S**2105	23	10	S		120	—	—	—	—	—	—	—	—
STANFORD—Santa Clara County													
★☐ STANFORD UNIVERSITY HOSPITAL, Zip 94305; tel. 415/723-5222; Sheldon S. King, pres. **A**1a 3 5 8 9 10 **F**1 2 3 4 5 6 7 8 9 10 11 12 13 14 15 16 20 21 23 24 27 29 30 33 35 36 37 40 41 42 44 45 46 47 48 49 51 52 53 54	23	10	S		597	22996	409	69.7	34	3480	190770	96043	2604
STANTON—Orange County													
★☐ MIDWOOD COMMUNITY HOSPITAL, 7770 Katella Ave., Zip 90680; tel. 714/898-0300; Doris Confer, adm. (Nonreporting) **A**1a 9 10	33	10	S		110	—	—	—	—	—	—	—	—
STOCKTON—San Joaquin County													
★☐ DAMERON HOSPITAL, 525 W. Acacia St., Zip 95203; tel. 209/944-5550; Luis Arismendi MD, adm. **A**1a 2 9 10 **F**1 2 3 4 6 9 10 12 15 16 22 23 24 35 40 41 43 45 47 52 53 54	23	10	S		142	9550	110	76.4	22	2447	32880	15913	677
★☐ SAINT JOSEPH'S MEDICAL CENTER OF STOCKTON (Formerly St. Joseph's Hospital of Stockton), 1800 N. California St., Zip 95204; tel. 209/943-2000; Sr. Mary Gabriel, pres.; Edward G. Schroeder, chief exec. off. **A**1a 2 9 10 **F**1 2 3 4 5 6 7 8 9 10 11 12 14 15 16 20 23 24 26 27 28 30 32 35 36 40 41 42 43 44 45 52 53 54; **S**1195	21	10	S		311	14260	227	73.0	16	1423	70230	36004	1276
☐ Δ SAN JOAQUIN GENERAL HOSPITAL, P O Box 1020, Zip 95201; tel. 209/468-6600; Michael N. Smith, dir. **A**1a 3 5 7 9 10 **F**1 3 5 6 10 12 15 16 20 23 24 25 26 30 32 33 34 35 37 38 40 42 44 45 46 47 51 52 53 54	13	10	S		226	7204	128	56.6	30	2089	45782	23230	1092
ST. JOSEPH'S OAK PARK HOSPITAL, 2510 N. California St., Zip 95204; tel. 209/948-2100; Gary L. Spaugh, adm.; Kathryn Konklin Yarbrough, asst. adm. **A**9 10 **F**1 10 14 16 23 24 42 43 48; **S**1195	21	10	S		43	686	24	55.8	0	0	3423	1235	47
SUSANVILLE—Lassen County													
☐ LASSEN COMMUNITY HOSPITAL, 560 Hospital Lane, Zip 96130; tel. 916/257-5325; John H. Loftus, chief exec. off. (Nonreporting) **A**1a 9 10; **S**1215	23	10	S		59	—	—	—	—	—	—	—	—
SYLMAR—Los Angeles County													
★☐ LOS ANGELES COUNTY-OLIVE VIEW MEDICAL CENTER, 14445 Olive View Dr., Zip 91342; tel. 818/364-1555; Douglas D. Bagley, adm. **A**1a 3 5 9 10 **F**1 3 6 10 11 12 14 16 23 24 26 27 30 33 34 35 37 38 42 44 45 46 49 50 52 54; **S**5755	13	10	S		126	5702	116	92.1	0	0	62205	30402	1405
TAFT—Kern County													
☐ WEST SIDE DISTRICT HOSPITAL, 110 E. North St., Zip 93268; tel. 805/763-4211; Terence Henry, adm. **A**1a 9 10 **F**1 6 16 35 36 40 41 45 47	16	10	S		43	722	7	16.3	9	171	4334	2008	86
TEHACHAPI—Kern County													
★☐ TEHACHAPI HOSPITAL, 115 W. E St., Box 648, Zip 93561; tel. 805/822-3241; Larry E. Clements, adm. (Nonreporting) **A**1a 9 10	16	10	S		22	—	—	—	—	—	—	—	—
TEMPLETON—San Luis Obispo County													
☐ TWIN CITIES COMMUNITY HOSPITAL, 1100 Las Tablas Rd., Zip 93465; tel. 805/434-2813; Floyd H. Anderson, adm. **A**1a 9 10 **F**1 3 6 12 13 14 15 16 23 34 35 36 40 45 50 53; **S**3015	33	10	S		84	3484	43	51.2	4	430	—	—	243
TERRA LINDA—Marin County													
KAISER FOUNDATION HOSPITAL-SAN RAFAEL, See San Rafael													
THOUSAND OAKS—Ventura County													
★☐ LOS ROBLES REGIONAL MEDICAL CENTER, 215 W. Janss Rd., Zip 91360; tel. 805/497-2727; Robert Quist, adm. **A**1a 2 9 10 **F**1 2 3 4 6 10 12 14 15 16 20 23 24 26 34 35 40 44 46 47 52 53 54; **S**1755	33	10	S		212	7541	112	52.8	34	1242	—	—	629
TORRANCE—Los Angeles County													
★☐ AMI DEL AMO HOSPITAL (Formerly Del Amo Psychiatric Hospital), 23700 Camino Del Sol, Zip 90505; tel. 213/530-1151; William H. Bennett Jr., exec. dir. **A**1b 9 10 **F**24 29 32 42 43 47; **S**0125	33	22	L		166	1065	121	72.9	0	0	16787	6744	281
★☐ CHARTER PACIFIC HOSPITAL, 4025 W. 226th St., Zip 90505; tel. 213/373-7733; Steven Hirsch, adm. **A**1a 9 **F**24 29 32 33 42 44 47 48 49; **S**0695	33	22	S		63	351	40	63.5	0	0	—	—	90
★☐ LAC-HARBOR-UNIVERSITY OF CALIFORNIA AT LOS ANGELES MEDICAL CENTER, 1000 W. Carson St., Zip 90509; tel. 213/533-2101; Edward J. Foley, adm. **A**1a 2 3 5 8 9 10 **F**2 3 4 5 6 7 8 9 10 11 12 13 14 15 16 20 23 24 26 27 28 30 32 33 34 35 37 38 40 42 44 45 46 47 51 52 53 54; **S**5755	13	10	S		502	25482	421	84.5	64	6485	158990	73136	2715
★☐ LITTLE COMPANY OF MARY HOSPITAL, 4101 Torrance Blvd., Zip 90503; tel. 213/540-7676; James C. Lester, pres. **A**1a 2 9 10 **F**1 2 3 4 6 9 10 11 12 14 15 16 20 23 24 26 35 36 40 41 44 45 46 47 51 52 53 54; **S**2295	21	10	S		239	11884	166	65.9	30	2366	63036	30841	1166
★☐ TORRANCE MEMORIAL HOSPITAL MEDICAL CENTER, 3330 Lomita Blvd., Zip 90505; tel. 213/325-9110; George Graham, pres. **A**1a 2 9 10 **F**1 3 4 5 6 7 8 9 10 11 12 13 14 15 16 17 20 22 23 24 26 30 34 35 40 43 44 45 46 47 52 53 54	23	10	S		286	13297	183	64.0	28	2679	65686	28440	1102
TRACY—San Joaquin County													
★☐ TRACY COMMUNITY MEMORIAL HOSPITAL, 1450 N. Tracy Blvd., Zip 95376; tel. 209/835-1500; Terry Mack, adm. **A**1a 9 10 **F**1 3 6 10 13 14 15 16 20 23 35 36 40 41 43 45 46 53	23	10	S		59	3142	39	66.1	12	269	12504	5620	215
TRAVIS AIR FORCE BASE—Solano County													
☐ DAVID GRANT U. S. AIR FORCE MEDICAL CENTER, Zip 94535; tel. 707/428-8000; Col. Charles W. Brown, adm. (Nonreporting) **A**1a 2 3 5	41	10	S		310	—	—	—	—	—	—	—	—

★ American Hospital Association (AHA) membership
☐ Joint Commission on Accreditation of Hospitals (JCAH) accreditation
+ American Osteopathic Hospital Association (AOHA) membership
○ American Osteopathic Association (AOA) accreditation
Δ Commission on Accreditation of Rehabilitation Facilities (CARF) accreditation
Control codes 61, 63, 64, 71, 72 and 73 indicate hospitals listed by AOHA, but not registered by AHA.
For definition of numerical codes, see page A2

Hospital, Address, Telephone, Administrator, Approval and Facility Codes, Multihospital System Code	Classification Codes: Control	Service	Stay	Facilities	Inpatient Data: Beds	Admissions	Census	Occupancy (percent)	Newborn Data: Bassinets	Births	Expense (thousands of dollars): Total	Payroll	Personnel
TRUCKEE—Nevada County													
☐ TAHOE FOREST HOSPITAL DISTRICT, Tahoe Dr. & Pine Ave., Box 759, Zip 95734; tel. 916/587-6011; James Maki, adm. (Total facility includes 28 beds in nursing home-type unit) **A**1a 9 10 **F**1 2 6 14 16 19 21 23 35 36 40 41 42 44 45 46 47 50	16	10	S	TF	70	2084	21	30.0	6	327	10437	4499	230
				H	42	2071	21	—	6	327	10385	4468	211
TULARE—Tulare County													
☐ TULARE DISTRICT HOSPITAL (Includes Tulare View), 869 Cherry St., Zip 93274; tel. 209/688-0821; Jerry W. Boyter, adm. **A**1a 9 10 **F**3 27 40 45 46 47 52	16	10	S		97	4993	64	66.0	17	877	15073	7875	350
TURLOCK—Stanislaus County													
★☐ EMANUEL MEDICAL CENTER, 825 Delbon Ave., Zip 95380; Mailing Address Box 2120, Zip 95381; tel. 209/667-4200; Robert A. Moen, pres. & chief exec. off. (Total facility includes 145 beds in nursing home-type unit) **A**1a 9 10 **F**1 3 6 10 12 15 19 21 23 24 26 34 35 36 40 41 44 45 46 48 49 52 53	21	10	S	TF	319	7133	271	85.0	12	984	28208	11365	644
				H	174	6971	126	—	12	984	25663	10142	527
TUSTIN—Orange County													
☐ HEALTHCARE MEDICAL CENTER OF TUSTIN, 14662 Newport Ave., Zip 92680; tel. 714/838-9600; Douglas Wilson Jr., exec. dir. (Nonreporting) **A**1a 9 10; **S**0395	33	10	S		150	—	—	—	—	—	—	—	—
UKIAH—Mendocino County													
☐ MENDOCINO COMMUNITY HOSPITAL, 860 N. Bush St., Zip 95482; tel. 707/463-4010; Ramona Edwards, adm. (Nonreporting) **A**1a 9 10	13	10	S		50	—	—	—	—	—	—	—	—
★☐ UKIAH ADVENTIST HOSPITAL, 275 Hospital Dr., Box 859, Zip 95482; tel. 707/462-6631; Edwin L. Ermshar, pres. **A**1a 9 10 **F**1 3 6 10 15 16 23 24 26 35 43 46 52 53; **S**0235	21	10	S		43	2073	30	69.8	0	0	9369	3521	173
★☐ UKIAH GENERAL HOSPITAL, 1120 S. Dora St., Box 3900, Zip 95482; tel. 707/462-3866; Kelly C. Morgan, adm. **A**1a 9 10 **F**1 3 6 9 10 12 15 16 23 35 36 40 45 46 47 52; **S**1755	33	10	S		45	2866	29	64.4	10	1017	—	—	170
UPLAND—San Bernardino County													
★☐ SAN ANTONIO COMMUNITY HOSPITAL, 999 San Bernardino Rd., Box 5001, Zip 91786; tel. 714/985-2811; Ronald L. Sackett, pres. **A**1a 2 9 10 **F**1 2 3 5 6 7 8 9 10 11 12 14 15 16 17 20 23 24 26 27 30 32 33 34 35 36 40 41 42 45 46 52 53	23	10	S		302	14060	203	66.6	34	2597	58286	28036	1152
VACAVILLE—Solano County													
CALIFORNIA MEDICAL FACILITY, Zip 95696; tel. 707/448-6841; Miguel Nieves Jr., med. dir.; Eddie Ylst, supt. (Nonreporting)	12	22	L		84	—	—	—	—	—	—	—	—
VALENCIA—Los Angeles County													
★☐ HENRY MAYO NEWHALL MEMORIAL HOSPITAL, 23845 W. McBean Pkwy., Zip 91355; tel. 805/253-8000; Duffy Watson, pres. **A**1a 9 10 **F**1 3 5 6 10 12 14 16 20 23 24 26 35 36 40 44 45 46 47 53; **S**2245	23	10	S		133	6489	97	72.9	10	961	35246	13022	442
VALLEJO—Solano County													
★☐ KAISER FOUNDATION HOSPITAL AND REHABILITATION CENTER, 975 Sereno Dr., Zip 94589; tel. 707/648-6000; Steve Williams, adm. **A**1a 10 **F**1 3 6 10 12 14 15 16 23 24 25 26 28 30 32 33 34 35 37 40 41 44 45 46 47 49 52 53; **S**2105	23	10	S		231	11834	167	72.3	21	2331	—	—	—
★☐ SUTTER SOLANO MEDICAL CENTER, 300 Hospital Dr., Zip 94589; Mailing Address P O Box 3189, Zip 94590; tel. 707/554-4444; Joseph A. Stewart, adm. **A**1a 9 10 **F**1 3 6 10 12 16 20 23 34 35 36 40 44 45 46 47 53; **S**8795	23	10	S		97	3626	51	52.6	9	403	18836	8642	257
VANDENBERG AIR FORCE BASE—Santa Barbara County													
☐ U. S. AIR FORCE HOSPITAL, Zip 93437; tel. 805/866-6726; Lt. Col. William W. Dick, chief exec. off. (Nonreporting) **A**1a	41	10	S		45	—	—	—	—	—	—	—	—
VENTURA—Ventura County													
★☐ COMMUNITY MEMORIAL HOSPITAL OF SAN BUENAVENTURA, Loma Vista Rd. at Brent, Zip 93003; tel. 805/652-5011; Michael D. Bakst PhD, exec. dir. (Total facility includes 34 beds in nursing home-type unit) **A**1a 9 10 **F**1 2 3 4 6 9 10 12 14 15 16 17 19 21 23 24 34 35 36 37 40 44 45 47 52 53 54	23	10	S	TF	226	8336	131	58.2	20	1517	32276	16041	684
				H	192	8003	111	—	20	1517	—	—	654
☐ CPC VISTA DEL MAR HOSPITAL, 801 Seneca St., Zip 93001; tel. 805/653-6434; Jack Peters, adm. (Nonreporting) **A**1b 9 10	33	22	L		41	—	—	—	—	—	—	—	—
☐ VENTURA COUNTY MEDICAL CENTER, 3291 Loma Vista Rd., Zip 93003; tel. 805/652-6058; John Puryear, adm. **A**1a 3 9 10 **F**1 2 3 5 6 10 12 14 15 16 20 23 24 27 28 29 30 32 33 34 35 37 40 43 44 45 46 47 50 51 52 53	13	10	S		211	10750	145	72.1	14	2470	—	—	635
VICTORVILLE—San Bernardino County													
U. S. AIR FORCE HOSPITAL, See George Air Force Base													
★☐ VICTOR VALLEY COMMUNITY HOSPITAL, 15248 11th St., Zip 92392; tel. 619/245-8691 (Nonreporting) **A**1a 2 9 10; **S**0585	23	10	S		91	—	—	—	—	—	—	—	—
VISALIA—Tulare County													
★☐ KAWEAH DELTA DISTRICT HOSPITAL, 400 W. Mineral King St., Zip 93291; tel. 209/625-2211; Thomas M. Johnson, exec. dir. **A**1a 2 9 10 **F**1 3 5 6 10 15 16 17 20 21 23 24 35 36 40 41 44 45 46 49 51 52 53 54	16	10	S		230	12017	166	72.2	16	1966	40050	16118	950
★☐ VISALIA COMMUNITY HOSPITAL, 1633 S. Court St., Box 911, Zip 93277; tel. 209/733-1333; Larry C. Andrews, exec. dir. **A**1a 9 10 **F**1 3 5 6 10 14 15 16 23 26 32 34 35 36 40 45 46 50 53; **S**0125	33	10	S		52	2392	27	51.9	8	612	9723	3402	168
WALNUT CREEK—Contra Costa County													
☐ CPC WALNUT CREEK HOSPITAL (Formerly Walnut Creek Hospital), 175 La Casa Via, Zip 94598; tel. 415/933-7990; Kenneth W. Pearce, adm. **A**1b 10 **F**10 24 29 30 31 33 42 43 47; **S**0785	33	22	S		108	1191	64	59.3	0	0	—	—	130
☐ JOHN MUIR MEMORIAL HOSPITAL, 1601 Ygnacio Valley Rd., Zip 94598; tel. 415/939-3000; J. Kendall Anderson, pres. & chief exec. off. **A**1a 2 9 10 **F**1 2 3 4 5 6 9 10 12 14 15 16 17 20 23 24 25 26 34 35 36 37 38 40 41 42 44 45 46 51 52 54	23	10	S		267	12434	165	61.8	22	1620	66993	32441	1058
★☐ KAISER FOUNDATION HOSPITAL, 1425 S. Main St., Zip 94596; tel. 415/943-2000; Kenneth P. Kentch, adm. **A**1a 3 10 **F**1 2 3 6 10 12 14 15 16 21 23 24 32 35 40 46 47 52 53; **S**2105	23	10	S		179	9808	126	70.4	30	3065	—	—	—
WALNUT CREEK HOSPITAL, See CPC Walnut Creek Hospital													
WASCO—Kern County													
★ NORTH KERN HOSPITAL, 2101 Seventh St., Zip 93280; tel. 805/758-5123; Scott Griffith, chief exec. off. (Nonreporting) **A**9 10; **S**9795	31	10	S		25	—	—	—	—	—	—	—	—
WATSONVILLE—Santa Cruz County													
★☐ WATSONVILLE COMMUNITY HOSPITAL, Green Valley & Holohan Rds., Zip 95076; Mailing Address Box 310, Zip 95077; tel. 408/724-4741; William W. Carpenter, chief exec. off. **A**1a 9 10 **F**1 3 6 9 10 12 15 16 17 20 23 24 26 35 36 40 44 45 48 49 53 54	23	10	S		96	5638	76	79.2	12	1091	26414	12541	472
WEAVERVILLE—Trinty County													
TRINITY GENERAL HOSPITAL, N. Taylor St., P O Box 1229, Zip 96093; tel. 916/623-5541; Patricia Menning, adm. (Total facility includes 42 beds in nursing home-type unit) **A**9 10 **F**1 6 15 16 19 23 24 28 30 32 33 34 35 36 41 42 45 46 47 48 49 50 53	33	10	S	TF	71	633	50	70.4	2	62	7520	2046	119
				H	29	594	7	—	2	62	5398	1432	69

Hospital, Address, Telephone, Administrator, Approval and Facility Codes, Multihospital System Code	Classification Codes				Inpatient Data				Newborn Data		Expense (thousands of dollars)		
★ American Hospital Association (AHA) membership □ Joint Commission on Accreditation of Hospitals (JCAH) accreditation + American Osteopathic Hospital Association (AOHA) membership ○ American Osteopathic Association (AOA) accreditation Δ Commission on Accreditation of Rehabilitation Facilities (CARF) accreditation Control codes 61, 63, 64, 71, 72 and 73 indicate hospitals listed by AOHA, but not registered by AHA. For definition of numerical codes, see page A2	Control	Service	Stay	Facilities	Beds	Admissions	Census	Occupancy (percent)	Bassinets	Births	Total	Payroll	Personnel
WEST COVINA—Los Angeles County													
□ COVINA VALLEY COMMUNITY HOSPITAL, 845 N. Lark Ellen Ave., Zip 91791; tel. 818/339-5451; David L. Hendry, adm. **A**1a 9 10 **F**3 6 16 23 24 35 44 46 47 53; **S**0585	32	10	S		76	2582	41	53.9	0	0	9794	4915	152
★□ QUEEN OF THE VALLEY HOSPITAL, 1115 S. Sunset Ave., Zip 91790; Mailing Address Box 1980, Zip 91793; tel. 818/962-4011; James E. Haden, pres. & chief exec. off. **A**1a 2 9 10 **F**1 2 3 5 6 12 14 15 16 21 23 24 25 26 30 33 34 35 36 40 44 45 46 47 51 52	23	10	S		268	14143	193	72.3	42	3790	62824	30780	1204
□ WEST COVINA HOSPITAL, 725 S. Orange Ave., Zip 91790; tel. 818/338-8481; John Hogue, adm. (Nonreporting) **A**1a 2 9 10; **S**5765	33	10	S		60	—	—	—	—	—	—	—	—
WESTLAKE VILLAGE—Los Angeles County													
□ WESTLAKE COMMUNITY HOSPITAL, 4415 S. Lakeview Canyon Rd., Zip 91361; tel. 818/706-8000; Douglass D. Dailey, dir. **A**1a 9 10 **F**1 3 5 6 10 12 14 15 16 17 20 23 24 34 35 36 40 43 44 45 46 52 53 54; **S**9555	33	10	S		98	3503	44	44.9	14	625	18112	6679	213
WESTMINSTER—Orange County													
★□ HUMANA HOSPITAL -WESTMINSTER, 200 Hospital Circle, Zip 92683; tel. 714/896-9239; Debra Gray Mathias, exec. dir. **A**1a 9 **F**1 3 6 10 12 14 15 16 23 24 35 36 40 43 44 45 46 52 53; **S**1235	33	10	S		182	5423	60	33.0	24	736	—	—	373
WHITTIER—Los Angeles County													
★□ PRESBYTERIAN INTERCOMMUNITY HOSPITAL, 12401 E. Washington Blvd., Zip 90602; tel. 213/698-0811; Lowell W. Smith, pres. & chief exec. off. **A**1a 2 3 5 9 10 **F**1 3 4 5 6 7 8 9 10 11 12 13 14 15 16 20 23 24 26 27 28 29 30 32 33 34 35 36 37 38 40 44 45 46 48 49 50 51 52 53 54	23	10	S		330	13310	213	64.5	17	1969	77043	32228	1130
□ WHITTIER HOSPITAL MEDICAL CENTER, 15151 Janine Dr., Zip 90605; tel. 213/945-3561; David A. Bianchi, exec. dir. **A**1a 9 10 **F**1 2 3 6 9 10 12 14 15 16 17 20 23 24 26 34 35 36 37 38 40 41 45 46 47 50 52 53; **S**3025	33	10	S		179	9756	114	63.7	25	2320	36038	13184	652
WILDOMAR—Riverside County													
□ INLAND VALLEY REGIONAL MEDICAL CENTER (Formerly Mission Valley Medical Center, Lake Elsinore), 36485 Inland Valley Dr., Zip 92395; tel. 714/677-8671; Dan C. McLaughlin, mng. dir. **A**1a 9 10 **F**1 3 6 10 12 16 23 35 45 46 47 53; **S**9555	33	10	S		62	2512	36	58.1	0	0	10596	3959	181
WILLITS—Mendocino County													
□ FRANK R. HOWARD MEMORIAL HOSPITAL, Madrone & Manzanita Sts., Box 1430, Zip 95490; tel. 707/459-6801; Robert J. Walker, adm. **A**1a 9 10 **F**3 6 12 16 21 23 35 44 45 46 47; **S**0235	23	10	S		38	1030	11	26.2	0	0	4000	2000	84
WILLOWS—Glenn County													
□ VALLEY COMMUNITY HOSPITAL (Formerly Glenn General Hospital), 1133 W. Sycamore St., P O Box 948, Zip 95988; tel. 916/934-3351; Andrew Radoszewski, adm. **A**1a 9 10 **F**1 3 6 16 23 34 35 45 46; **S**8985	23	10	S		62	809	10	16.1	0	0	4832	1994	107
WINTERHAVEN—Imperial County													
★□ U. S. PUBLIC HEALTH SERVICE FORT YUMA INDIAN HOSPITAL, Zip 92283; Mailing Address P O Box 1368, Yuma, Ariz., Zip 85364; tel. 619/572-0217; Lance Hodahkwen Sr., actg. dir. (Nonreporting) **A**1a 10	47	10	S		17	—	—	—	—	—	—	—	—
WOODLAND—Yolo County													
★□ WOODLAND MEMORIAL HOSPITAL, 1325 Cottonwood St., Zip 95695; tel. 916/662-3961; Jack Hudock, adm. **A**1a 9 10 **F**1 3 5 6 10 12 15 16 17 23 24 26 27 29 30 31 32 33 34 35 36 40 41 42 43 44 45 47 52 54	23	10	S		122	6183	74	60.7	14	1597	20857	9484	410
★□ YOLO GENERAL HOSPITAL, 170 W. Beamer St., Zip 95695; tel. 916/666-8950; Thom M. Corbin, adm. **A**1a 9 10 **F**3 6 12 14 16 19 23 24 27 29 30 32 34 35 42 44 45 46 49	13	10	S		118	1584	80	67.8	0	0	10886	—	183
YORBA LINDA—Orange County													
★ ST. JUDE HOSPITAL YORBA LINDA, 16850 E. Bastanchury Rd., Box 69, Zip 92686; tel. 714/993-3000; Gayle N. Bullock, pres. & chief exec. off. **A**9 **F**1 3 6 10 12 14 15 16 21 23 24 35 36 40 41 45 46 47 49; **S**5425	21	10	S		106	1781	27	25.5	12	468	13581	4153	180
YOUNTVILLE—Napa County													
★□ VETERANS HOME OF CALIFORNIA, Veterans Home Sta., Zip 94599; tel. 707/944-4200; Charles H. Pedri, adm. (Total facility includes 756 beds in nursing home-type unit) **A**1a 10 **F**1 3 12 14 16 19 21 23 24 26 27 28 29 33 34 42 44 46 47 49 50	12	10	S	TF	802	2232	678	84.5	0	0	37113	21197	932
				H	46	1035	25	—	0	0	5623	3149	—
YREKA—Siskiyou County													
□ SISKIYOU GENERAL HOSPITAL, 818 S. Main St., Zip 96097; tel. 916/842-4121; O. B. Parks, chief exec. off. **A**1a 10 **F**3 10 12 16 23 34 35 36 45 46 47 53	23	10	S		57	1852	23	40.4	4	219	7167	—	155
YUBA CITY—Sutter County													
□ FREMONT MEDICAL CENTER, 970 Plumas St., Zip 95991; tel. 916/671-2220; J. P. Hanks Jr., chief exec. off. **A**1a 9 10 **F**1 3 6 14 15 16 23 24 34 35 40 44 45 47 52	23	10	S		128	6919	88	68.8	16	1827	16932	7947	402

Hospital, Address, Telephone, Administrator, Approval and Facility Codes, Multihospital System Code	Classification Codes				Inpatient Data				Newborn Data		Expense (thousands of dollars)		
★ American Hospital Association (AHA) membership □ Joint Commission on Accreditation of Hospitals (JCAH) accreditation + American Osteopathic Hospital Association (AOHA) membership ○ American Osteopathic Association (AOA) accreditation Δ Commission on Accreditation of Rehabilitation Facilities (CARF) accreditation Control codes 61, 63, 64, 71, 72 and 73 indicate hospitals listed by AOHA, but not registered by AHA. For definition of numerical codes, see page A2	Control	Service	Stay	Facilities	Beds	Admissions	Census	Occupancy (percent)	Bassinets	Births	Total	Payroll	Personnel

Colorado

Hospital	Control	Service	Stay	Facilities	Beds	Admissions	Census	Occupancy (percent)	Bassinets	Births	Total	Payroll	Personnel
AKRON—Washington County													
★ WASHINGTON COUNTY PUBLIC HOSPITAL, 465 Main St., Zip 80720; tel. 303/345-2211; Terry Hoffart, adm. **A**9 10 **F**1 16 23 35 36 45 46; **S**2235	23	10	S		19	227	2	10.5	3	25	839	383	23
ALAMOSA—Alamosa County													
⊞ ALAMOSA COMMUNITY HOSPITAL, 106 Blanca Ave., Zip 81101; tel. 303/589-2511; Paul Herman, adm. **A**1a 9 10 **F**1 3 6 10 12 15 16 23 34 35 36 37 40 47 50 53	21	10	S		70	1896	17	24.3	13	435	4405	1915	127
ASPEN—Pitkin County													
⊞ ASPEN VALLEY HOSPITAL DISTRICT, 0200 Castle Creek Rd., Zip 81611; tel. 303/925-1120 (Nonreporting) **A**1a 9 10	16	10	S		49	—	—	—	—	—	—	—	—
AURORA—Arapahoe County													
⊞ AMI PRESBYTERIAN AURORA HOSPITAL, 700 Potomac St., Zip 80011; tel. 303/363-7200; H. Phil Herre, exec. dir. **A**1a 9 **F**1 3 6 10 12 15 16 20 23 24 26 34 35 36 40 44 45 46 47 52 53; **S**0125	33	10	S		106	6371	76	71.7	0	0	25682	9461	342
⊞ FITZSIMONS ARMY MEDICAL CENTER, Zip 80045; tel. 303/361-8223; Brig. Gen. Thomas M. Geer, adm. (Nonreporting) **A**1a 2 3 5	42	10	S		422	—	—	—	—	—	—	—	—
⊞ HUMANA HOSPITAL -AURORA, 1501 S. Potomac, Zip 80012; tel. 303/695-2600; Timothy L. Austin, exec. dir. **A**1a 9 10 **F**1 3 5 6 10 12 14 15 16 23 24 26 34 35 36 40 44 46 52 53; **S**1235	33	10	S		200	10316	87	43.5	30	2147	24566	9692	437
BOULDER—Boulder County													
⊞ BOULDER COMMUNITY HOSPITAL, N. Broadway & Balsam, P O Box 9019, Zip 80301; tel. 303/440-2273; John C. McFetridge, pres. **A**1a 9 10 **F**1 2 3 5 6 9 10 11 12 14 15 16 20 21 23 24 27 28 29 30 32 33 34 35 36 37 40 41 43 44 45 46 47 53	23	10	S		147	7061	83	59.7	24	2232	24153	11361	531
⊞ Δ BOULDER MEMORIAL HOSPITAL, 311 Mapleton Ave., Zip 80302; tel. 303/443-0230; Warren M. Clark, pres. **A**1a 7 9 10 **F**1 3 12 15 16 21 23 24 25 26 34 35 41 42 44 45 46 47 48 52 54; **S**9355	21	10	S		87	2583	52	59.8	0	0	18163	9055	384
□ BOULDER PSYCHIATRIC INSTITUTE, 4390 Baseline Rd., 777 29th St., Zip 80303; tel. 303/447-2900; Andrew L. Braun, adm. **A**1b 9 10 **F**24 29 32 33 42 43 47 48 49; **S**0825	33	22	L		64	436	49	76.6	0	0	5999	2670	124
WARDENBURG STUDENT HEALTH SERVICE, University of Colorado, Campus Box 119, Zip 80309; tel. 303/492-5101; H. Rolan Zick MD, dir. (Nonreporting)	12	11	S		11	—	—	—	—	—	—	—	—
BRIGHTON—Adams County													
⊞ PLATTE VALLEY MEDICAL CENTER, 1850 Egbert St., P O Box 98, Zip 80601; tel. 303/659-1531; Harold A. Buck, adm. **A**1a 9 10 **F**1 3 6 10 12 14 15 16 21 22 23 24 26 34 35 36 40 41 44 45 46 47 50 52 53; **S**9355	23	10	S		58	2028	22	37.9	6	387	8236	3503	167
BROOMFIELD—Boulder County													
⊞ Δ CLEO WALLACE CENTER HOSPITAL, 8405 W. 100th, Box 345, Zip 80020; tel. 303/466-7391; James Cole, pres. & chief exec. off. (Data for 229 days) (Total facility includes 108 beds in nursing home-type unit) **A**1b 7 9 **F**19 24 29 30 31 32 33 42 44 47	23	22	L	TF	128	190	128	100.0	0	0	5845	3434	300
				H	20	58	17	—	0	0	—	—	—
BRUSH—Morgan County													
★ EAST MORGAN COUNTY HOSPITAL, 2400 Edison St., Box 565, Zip 80723; tel. 303/842-5151; Keith Mesmer, adm. **A**9 10 **F**1 2 3 6 15 16 23 34 35 36 40 44 45 46 47 49; **S**2235	23	10	S		29	580	7	24.1	6	78	1807	897	49
BURLINGTON—Kit Carson County													
★ HI-PLAINS HEALTH CENTER (Formerly Kit Carson County Memorial Hospital), 286 16th St., tel. 303/346-5311; William M. Gartner, chief exec. off. **A**9 10 **F**1 3 6 10 14 16 23 34 35 36 40 41 45 46 47	13	10	S		24	625	7	29.2	8	135	1745	—	54
CANON CITY—Fremont County													
⊞ ST. THOMAS MORE HOSPITAL AND PROGRESSIVE CARE CENTER, 1019 Sheridan St., Zip 81212; tel. 303/275-3381; Sr. Judith Kuhn, adm. (Total facilitv includes 120 beds in nursing home-type unit) **A**1a 9 10 **F**1 3 6 10 12 14 15 16 19 21 23 24 25 26 30 33 34 35 36 40 41 42 43 44 45 46 47 53; **S**1635	21	10	S	TF	201	2319	118	58.7	8	222	8322	4097	293
				H	81	2014	27	—	8	222	6542	3508	239
CHEYENNE WELLS—Cheyenne County													
⊞ ST. JOSEPH HOSPITAL OF THE PLAINS, 602 N. Sixth St. W., P O Box 578, Zip 80810; tel. 303/767-5661; James L. Giedd, chief exec. off. **A**1a 9 10 **F**1 6 16 23 26 34 35 40 45; **S**5445	21	10	S		32	231	5	15.6	3	18	806	444	36
COLORADO SPRINGS—El Paso County													
CEDAR SPRINGS PSYCHIATRIC HOSPITAL, 2135 Southgate Rd., Zip 80906; Mailing Address Box 640, Zip 80901; tel. 303/633-4114; Richard A. Bangert, chief exec. off. **A**9 10 **F**15 24 29 30 32 33 42 44 47 48; **S**0395	33	22	S		100	642	39	41.5	0	0	—	—	142
○ + EISENHOWER MEDICAL CENTER, 33 Barnes Ave., Zip 80909; tel. 303/475-2111; Joe O'Neill, exec. dir. (Nonreporting) **A**9 10 11 12; **S**3025	33	10	S		122	—	—	—	—	—	—	—	—
⊞ MEMORIAL HOSPITAL, 1400 E. Boulder St., Zip 80909; Mailing Address Box 1326, Zip 80901; tel. 303/475-5000; J. Robert Peters, exec. dir. **A**1a 6 9 10 **F**1 2 3 4 5 6 10 12 14 15 16 20 23 24 26 30 33 34 35 36 37 38 40 41 43 44 45 46 47 50 51 52 53 54	14	10	S		342	11063	156	45.6	24	2612	47830	24494	1150
PENROSE CANCER HOSPITAL, See Penrose Hospitals													
PENROSE COMMUNITY HOSPITAL, See Penrose Hospitals													
⊞ Δ PENROSE HOSPITALS (Includes Penrose Community Hospital, 3205 N. Academy Blvd., Zip 80917; tel. 303/591-3000; Douglas M. Farnham Jr., adm.; Penrose Cancer Hospital, 2215 N. Cascade Ave., P O Box 7021, Zip 80907; tel. 303/630-3300; Jan Bastian, adm. dir.), 2215 N. Cascade Ave., P O Box 7021, Zip 80933; tel. 303/630-5111; Sr. Myra James, pres. (Total facility includes 22 beds in nursing home-type unit) **A**1a 2 3 5 7 9 10 **F**1 3 4 6 7 8 9 10 11 12 14 15 16 19 20 22 23 24 25 26 27 28 29 30 32 33 34 35 36 38 40 41 42 43 44 45 46 47 48 49 52 53 54; **S**5115	21	10	S	TF	460	16335	284	61.7	30	1893	72507	34741	1812
				H	438	15861	268	—	30	1893	72215	34461	1721
⊞ ST. FRANCIS HOSPITAL SYSTEMS, E. Pikes Peak at Prospect, Zip 80903; tel. 303/636-8800; Al Farr, pres. & chief exec. off. (Total facility includes 15 beds in nursing home-type unit) **A**1a 9 10 **F**1 3 5 6 10 12 14 15 16 19 20 23 24 26 27 30 32 33 34 35 36 40 42 45 46 47 50 52 53 54; **S**5115	21	10	S	TF	204	6860	102	50.0	13	1026	28417	12505	579
				H	189	6542	92	—	13	1026	—	—	—
UNION PRINTERS HOME, Pikes Peak Ave. & Union Blvd., Box 817, Zip 80901; tel. 303/634-3711; Donald M. Fifield, adm. (Total facility includes 162 beds in nursing home-type unit) **A**10 **F**18 19 35	23	10	S	TF	168	57	144	85.7	0	0	2504	1462	101
				H	6	11	0	—	0	0	—	—	—

Hospital, Address, Telephone, Administrator, Approval and Facility Codes, Multihospital System Code	Classification Codes				Inpatient Data				Newborn Data		Expense (thousands of dollars)		
	Control	Service	Stay	Facilities	Beds	Admissions	Census	Occupancy (percent)	Bassinets	Births	Total	Payroll	Personnel
CORTEZ—Montezuma County													
★□ SOUTHWEST MEMORIAL HOSPITAL, 1311 N. Mildred Rd., Zip 81321; tel. 303/565-6666; Tyler A. Erickson, adm. (Total facility includes 76 beds in nursing home-type unit) **A**1a 10 **F**1 3 6 10 12 14 15 19 21 23 35 36 37 40 42 45 46 47 52 53; **S**1755	16	10	S	TF	137	2120	96	70.1	8	245	6896	3277	182
				H	61	2081	22	—	8	245	5473	2414	142
CRAIG—Moffat County													
★□ MEMORIAL HOSPITAL, 785 Russell St., Zip 81625; tel. 303/824-9411; Berend Roeters, adm. (Nonreporting) **A**1a 9 10	13	10	S		42	—	—	—	—	—	—	—	—
DEL NORTE—Rio Grande County													
★ ST. JOSEPH HOSPITAL, 1280 Grande Ave., Box 248, Zip 81132; tel. 303/657-3311; Edwin L. Medford, pres. & chief exec. off. (Total facility includes 33 beds in nursing home-type unit) **A**9 10 **F**1 3 6 14 15 16 19 23 24 26 30 32 35 36 40 42 43 45 46 47 50 52; **S**5435	21	10	S	TF	73	933	43	58.9	4	73	2513	1197	86
				H	40	926	10	—	4	73	2316	1024	69
DELTA—Delta County													
★□ DELTA COUNTY MEMORIAL HOSPITAL, 100 Stafford Lane, Zip 81416; tel. 303/874-7681; Ken Moore, adm. **A**1a 9 10 **F**1 3 6 14 15 16 21 23 24 26 34 35 36 40 41 42 44 45 46 47; **S**3505	16	10	S		52	2021	21	40.4	8	267	6458	3135	150
DENVER—Denver and Adams Counties													
★□ AMI PRESBYTERIAN-DENVER HOSPITAL, 1719 E. 19th Ave., Zip 80218; tel. 303/839-6100; Donald Lenz, exec. dir. (Total facility includes 22 beds in nursing home-type unit) **A**1a 2 3 5 8 9 10 **F**1 3 4 6 7 8 9 10 11 12 15 16 17 19 20 23 24 27 28 32 34 39 42 43 44 45 46 47 53 54; **S**0125	33	10	S	TF	223	9176	191	87.2	0	0	52441	19208	751
				H	201	9114	172	—	0	0	—	—	719
★□ AMI PRESBYTERIAN-ST. LUKE'S MEDICAL CENTER, 601 E. 19th Ave., Zip 80203; tel. 303/839-1000; Donald W. Lenz, exec. dir. **A**1a 2 3 5 8 9 10 **F**1 3 4 5 6 7 8 9 10 11 12 13 14 15 16 17 20 23 24 25 26 27 30 32 33 34 35 36 37 38 40 41 42 44 45 46 47 48 49 50 53 54; **S**0125	33	10	S		366	9857	231	64.5	0	0	57179	21417	733
★□ BETH ISRAEL HOSPITAL, 1601 Lowell Blvd., Zip 80204; tel. 303/825-2190; Francisco D. Sabichi, pres. & adm. (Total facility includes 145 beds in nursing home-type unit) **A**1a 9 10 **F**1 6 10 12 14 15 16 19 23 24 26 33 34 35 37 41 42 43 44 45 46 47 50 53 54	23	10	S	TF	262	2825	205	78.2	0	0	21547	11259	576
				H	117	2777	69	—	0	0	18079	9735	477
★□ BETHESDA PSYCHEALTH SYSTEM (Formerly Bethesda Hospital and Community Mental Health Center), 4400 E. Iliff Ave., Zip 80222; tel. 303/758-1514; Jerry Dykman, chief exec. off. **A**1a 9 10 **F**24 28 29 30 31 32 33 34 42 43 45 46 47 49 50	23	22	L		70	641	58	82.9	0	0	9252	5719	222
★□ CHILDREN'S HOSPITAL, 1056 E. 19th Ave., Zip 80218; tel. 303/861-8888; Lua R. Blankenship Jr., pres. **A**1a 3 5 9 10 **F**1 4 6 10 12 14 15 16 21 23 24 26 27 28 29 32 33 34 35 38 41 42 43 44 45 46 47 51 52 53 54	23	50	S		182	6603	130	81.3	0	0	63001	30490	1303
★□ DENVER HEALTH AND HOSPITALS, 777 Bannock St., Zip 80204; tel. 303/893-6000; Joyce J. Neville, mgr. **A**1a 10 **F**1 2 3 5 6 10 11 12 14 15 16 19 23 24 25 26 27 29 30 32 33 34 35 37 40 42 44 46 47 48 49 51 52 53 54	15	10	S		326	17207	237	72.7	24	2971	95809	53605	1878
□ FORT LOGAN MENTAL HEALTH CENTER, 3520 W. Oxford Ave., Zip 80236; tel. 303/761-0220 **A**1b 9 10 **F**15 23 24 28 29 31 32 33 34 42 43 44 45 46 47 50	12	22	L		357	711	303	86.1	0	0	19580	14201	543
HIGHLAND CENTER HOSPITAL, 1920 High St., Zip 80218; tel. 303/320-5871; Tom Beisler, adm. (Nonreporting) **A**9 10	33	10	S		130	—	—	—	—	—	—	—	—
★ HORIZON HOSPITAL (Formerly Horizon Recovery Hospital) (Includes Adult Chemical Dependency Unit, Adolescent Psychiatric Unit), 1920 High St., Zip 80218; tel. 303/388-2491; Bruce B. McBogg, adm. **A** 9 10 **F**27 33 42; **S**6525	33	82	S		53	328	18	36.7	0	0	1832	761	44
HUMANA HOSPITAL-MOUNTAIN VIEW, See Thornton													
★□ MERCY MEDICAL CENTER, 1650 Fillmore St., Zip 80206; tel. 303/393-3000; Daniel Aten, pres. **A**1a 3 5 9 10 **F**1 3 4 6 9 10 12 14 15 16 23 24 32 33 34 35 36 40 41 42 44 45 46 47 48 50 52 53 54; **S**5175	21	10	S		386	7407	171	44.3	25	689	46308	20426	752
★ MOUNT AIRY PSYCHIATRIC CENTER, 4455 E. 12th Ave., Zip 80220; tel. 303/322-1803; Dana B. Prince, adm. **A** 9 10 **F**3 19 24 28 29 30 32 42 45 47 49	23	22	S		100	973	77	77.0	0	0	10163	6285	270
★□ NATIONAL JEWISH CENTER FOR IMMUNOLOGY AND RESPIRATORY MEDICINE (Formerly National Jewish Hospital and Research Center-National Asthma Center), 1400 Jackson St., Zip 80206; tel. 303/388-4461; Michael K. Schonbrun, pres. **A**1a 3 5 8 9 10 **F**3 16 23 24 26 27 28 32 33 34 42 45 46 47 52	23	49	S		105	1075	80	76.2	0	0	43924	28192	868
★□ PORTER MEMORIAL HOSPITAL, 2525 S. Downing St., Zip 80210; tel. 303/778-1955; Donald L. Hanson, pres. **A**1a 2 3 9 10 **F**1 2 3 4 6 7 8 9 10 11 12 13 14 15 16 20 21 23 24 26 27 28 29 30 32 33 34 35 36 37 41 42 43 44 45 46 47 49 50 52 53 54; **S**9355	21	10	S		347	13417	217	62.5	0	0	70501	31630	1407
○ + Δ ROCKY MOUNTAIN HOSPITAL, 4701 E. Ninth Ave., Zip 80220; tel. 303/393-5700; Keith Baldwin, adm. **A**7 9 10 11 12 13 **F**1 3 6 9 10 12 14 16 19 20 23 24 26 27 28 33 34 35 36 40 42 43 45 46 47 50; **S**1755	23	10	S		109	2065	47	43.1	8	218	12323	5595	244
★□ ROSE MEDICAL CENTER, 4567 E. Ninth Ave., Zip 80220; tel. 303/320-2121; Jeffrey A. Dorsey, exec. vice-pres. & adm.; Joel Edelman, pres. **A**1a 2 3 5 9 10 **F**1 2 3 4 6 10 12 14 15 16 20 21 23 24 25 26 32 33 34 35 36 37 38 40 41 42 43 44 45 46 47 51 53 54; **S**1755	23	10	S		318	13405	202	63.5	37	3657	63789	31175	1351
★□ SAINT JOSEPH HOSPITAL, 1835 Franklin St., Zip 80218; tel. 303/837-7111; Sr. Mary Andrew, pres. **A**1a 2 3 5 9 10 **F**1 2 3 4 6 7 8 9 10 11 12 14 15 16 20 23 24 25 26 27 30 32 33 34 35 36 40 43 44 45 46 47 53 54; **S**5095	21	10	S		565	25624	382	67.6	44	5194	90768	47668	1777
★□ Δ SPALDING REHABILITATION HOSPITAL, 1919 Ogden St., Zip 80218; tel. 303/861-0504; John Hershberger, exec. dir. **A**1a 7 9 10 **F**15 16 23 24 26 29 32 33 34 41 42 44 45 46 47 49	21	46	S		80	968	54	67.5	0	0	9973	5697	220
ST. ANTHONY HOSPITAL CENTRAL, See St. Anthony Hospital Systems													
★□ ST. ANTHONY HOSPITAL SYSTEMS (Includes St. Anthony Hospital Central, 4231 W. 16th Ave., Zip 80204; tel. 303/629-3511; E. V. Kuhlman, pres.; St. Anthony Hospital North, 2551 W. 84th Ave., Westminster, Zip 80030; tel. 303/426-2151; Joann Corn, dir.), 4231 W. 16th Ave., Zip 80204; tel. 303/629-3511; Douglas R. Cook, pres. **A**1a 2 3 5 9 10 **F**1 2 3 4 5 6 7 8 9 10 11 12 14 15 16 17 19 23 24 27 30 32 34 35 36 40 42 44 45 46 47 50 52 53 54; **S**5115	21	10	S		557	21603	331	56.1	0	0	106121	50724	2058
★□ UNIVERSITY HOSPITAL, 4200 E. Ninth Ave., Zip 80262; tel. 303/394-8446; Robert M. Dickler, dir. **A**1a 2 3 5 8 9 10 **F**1 2 3 4 5 6 7 8 9 10 11 12 13 15 16 17 20 22 23 24 26 34 35 37 38 40 41 42 43 44 45 46 47 50 51 52 53 54	12	10	S		322	14382	229	71.6	40	2653	85509	42165	1451
★□ VETERANS ADMINISTRATION MEDICAL CENTER, 1055 Clermont St., Zip 80220; tel. 303/399-8020; Fred Salas, dir. (Total facility includes 60 beds in nursing home-type unit) **A**1a b 2 3 5 8 **F**1 2 3 4 6 10 11 12 14 15 16 19 20 21 23 24 26 27 28 29 30 32 33 34 35 41 42 43 44 46 47 48 49 50 53 54	45	10	S	TF	378	11112	288	86.2	0	0	71823	35476	1291
				H	318	10877	240	—	0	0	68296	33221	1249
DURANGO—La Plata County													
□ LA PLATA COMMUNITY HOSPITAL, 3801 N. Main Ave., Zip 81301; tel. 303/259-1110; Tom Galbraith, adm. **A**1a b 9 10 **F**1 3 6 7 8 9 10 11 12 14 15 16 23 24 27 28 29 30 31 32 33 34 35 36 37 40 42 43 44 45 49 50	16	10	S		51	1401	18	35.3	6	192	4337	2151	120

★ American Hospital Association (AHA) membership
□ Joint Commission on Accreditation of Hospitals (JCAH) accreditation
+ American Osteopathic Hospital Association (AOHA) membership
○ American Osteopathic Association (AOA) accreditation
Δ Commission on Accreditation of Rehabilitation Facilities (CARF) accreditation
Control codes 61, 63, 64, 71, 72 and 73 indicate hospitals listed by AOHA, but not registered by AHA.
For definition of numerical codes, see page A2

Hospital, Address, Telephone, Administrator, Approval and Facility Codes, Multihospital System Code	Classification Codes				Inpatient Data				Newborn Data		Expense (thousands of dollars)		
★ American Hospital Association (AHA) membership □ Joint Commission on Accreditation of Hospitals (JCAH) accreditation + American Osteopathic Hospital Association (AOHA) membership ○ American Osteopathic Association (AOA) accreditation Δ Commission on Accreditation of Rehabilitation Facilities (CARF) accreditation Control codes 61, 63, 64, 71, 72 and 73 indicate hospitals listed by AOHA, but not registered by AHA. For definition of numerical codes, see page A2	Control	Service	Stay	Facilities	Beds	Admissions	Census	Occupancy (percent)	Bassinets	Births	Total	Payroll	Personnel
⊞ MERCY MEDICAL CENTER, 375 E. Park Ave., Zip 81301; tel. 303/247-4311; Michael J. Lawler, pres. (Total facility includes 11 beds in nursing home-type unit) **A**1a 9 10 **F**1 3 5 6 7 8 9 10 11 12 14 15 16 19 21 23 24 26 28 30 32 33 34 35 36 37 38 39 40 41 42 43 44 45 46 47 51 52 53; **S**5175	21	10	S	TF	101	3823	48	47.5	12	641	13401	6433	262
				H	90	3693	44	—	12	641	—	—	256
EADS—Kiowa County													
★ WEISBROD MEMORIAL HOSPITAL, 1208 Luther St., P O Box 817, Zip 81036; tel. 303/438-5401; Andrew Wills, adm. (Total facility includes 34 beds in nursing home-type unit) **A**9 10 **F**1 16 19 23 35 37 40 45 50; **S**0585	16	10	S	TF	42	118	29	69.0	2	12	997	481	38
				H	8	96	1	—	2	12	642	337	19
ENGLEWOOD—Arapahoe County													
⊞ Δ CRAIG HOSPITAL, 3425 S. Clarkson, Zip 80110; tel. 303/789-8000; Dennis O'Malley, pres. **A**1a 7 9 10 **F**1 3 23 24 26 33 34 39 42 44 45 46 47	23	49	L		80	694	70	87.5	0	0	15201	7601	377
⊞ SWEDISH MEDICAL CENTER, 501 E. Hampden Ave., Zip 80110; tel. 303/788-5000; Lowell E. Palmquist, pres. & chief exec. off.; John D. Oswald, exec. vice-pres. & adm. **A**1a 2 9 10 **F**1 3 5 6 9 10 12 14 15 16 20 23 24 30 34 35 36 37 38 40 41 43 44 45 46 47 50 51 53	23	10	S		305	15088	217	71.1	40	3274	63833	30403	1352
ESTES PARK—Larimer County													
⊞ ESTES PARK MEDICAL CENTER, 555 Prospect, Box 2740, Zip 80517; tel. 303/586-2317; Karen I. Spotts, chief exec. off. (Total facility includes 60 beds in nursing home-type unit) **A**1a 9 10 **F**1 6 14 15 16 19 23 24 30 34 35 36 41 43 44 45 46 47 50; **S**0125	16	10	S	TF	76	664	51	67.1	4	58	3452	1521	89
				H	16	580	5	—	4	58	2276	1041	51
FLORENCE—Fremont County													
⊞ ST. JOSEPH HOSPITAL, 600 W. Third St., Zip 81226; tel. 303/784-4891; Thomas W. Laux, exec. vice-pres. & adm. (Total facility includes 43 beds in nursing home-type unit) **A**1a 9 10 **F**1 3 14 15 16 19 23 26 34 35 36 40 42 43 45 46 47 52; **S**5115	21	10	S	TF	77	569	45	58.4	6	55	2750	1282	88
				H	34	501	7	—	6	55	2018	984	60
FORT CARSON—El Paso County													
⊞ U. S. ARMY COMMUNITY HOSPITAL, Zip 80913; tel. 303/579-7200; Col. Freeman Howard, cmdr. **A**1a 2 3 **F**1 2 3 12 14 15 16 23 24 26 28 30 32 33 34 35 37 40 41 46 47 49 52 53	42	10	S		195	6753	84	60.0	36	858	42684	—	941
FORT COLLINS—Larimer County													
⊞ POUDRE VALLEY HOSPITAL, 1024 Lemay Ave., Zip 80524; tel. 303/482-4111; Robert L. Bakken, adm. **A**1a 2 3 5 9 10 **F**1 2 3 4 5 6 9 10 12 14 15 16 20 23 24 25 26 27 30 32 33 34 35 36 37 40 41 42 43 44 45 46 47 52 53 54	16	10	S		215	11604	131	62.7	24	2127	38720	20170	793
FORT LYON—Bent County													
★ VETERANS ADMINISTRATION MEDICAL CENTER, Zip 81038; tel. 303/456-1260; Robert E. Lee, dir. (Total facility includes 37 beds in nursing home-type unit) **F**1 15 16 19 23 24 26 28 29 32 33 34 42 45 46 47 48 50	45	22	L	TF	372	1292	342	91.9	0	0	23767	14729	604
				H	335	1275	306	—	0	0	22236	13678	584
FORT MORGAN—Morgan County													
□ FORT MORGAN COMMUNITY HOSPITAL, 1000 Lincoln St., Zip 80701; tel. 303/867-5671; Gary J. Guidetti, chief exec. off. (Nonreporting) **A**1a 9 10; **S**0585	23	10	S		40	—	—	—	—	—	—	—	—
FRUITA—Mesa County													
FAMILY HEALTH WEST, 228 N. Cherry St., Box 668, Zip 81521; tel. 303/858-9871; Carroll E. Rushold, exec. dir. (Nonreporting) **A**9 10	23	10	S		140	—	—	—	—	—	—	—	—
GLENWOOD SPRINGS—Garfield County													
⊞ VALLEY VIEW HOSPITAL, 1906 Blake Ave., Box 1970, Zip 81602; tel. 303/945-6535; John Johnson, adm. **A**1a 9 10 **F**1 3 5 6 10 12 14 15 16 23 35 36 40 45 46 47 53; **S**1755	23	10	S		57	2631	26	45.6	10	441	8776	3768	160
GRAND JUNCTION—Mesa County													
○ + COMMUNITY HOSPITAL, 2021 N. 12th St., Zip 81501; tel. 303/242-0920; Roger C. Zumwalt, exec. dir. **A**9 10 11 **F**1 3 6 10 12 15 16 23 30 32 33 34 35 36 37 40 45 46 47 52 53	23	10	S		45	2049	21	31.8	8	352	7060	3369	177
MESA MEMORIAL HOSPITAL, See St. Mary's Hospital and Medical Center													
⊞ ST. MARY'S HOSPITAL AND MEDICAL CENTER (Includes Mesa Memorial Hospital, 405 N. Tenth St., Zip 81501; Mailing Address Box 1628, Zip 81502; tel. 303/243-1331), Seventh St. & Patterson Rd., P O Box 1628, Zip 81501; tel. 303/244-2273; Sr. Marianna Bauder, pres. **A**1a 3 5 9 10 **F**1 2 3 5 6 7 8 9 10 11 12 14 15 16 20 23 24 26 27 30 34 35 36 40 41 43 44 45 46 47 51 52 53 54; **S**5095	21	10	S		190	8592	113	59.5	20	1157	33607	15673	688
⊞ VETERANS ADMINISTRATION MEDICAL CENTER, 2121 North Ave., Zip 81501; tel. 303/242-0731; A. Bourret, dir. (Total facility includes 42 beds in nursing home-type unit) **A**1a **F**1 3 6 10 12 15 16 19 23 24 26 27 28 30 33 34 42 44 45 46 48 49 50	45	10	S	TF	157	2793	106	67.5	0	0	11374	7386	308
				H	115	2761	67	—	0	0	9519	6131	293
GREELEY—Weld County													
○ + MEMORIAL HOSPITAL, 928 12th St., Zip 80631; tel. 303/352-3123; W. Dale Ferguson, chief exec. off. (Nonreporting) **A**9 10 11; **S**1495	23	10	S		34	—	—	—	—	—	—	—	—
⊞ NORTH COLORADO MEDICAL CENTER, 1801 16th St., Zip 80631; tel. 303/352-4121; Richard H. Stenner, pres. **A**1a 2 3 5 9 10 **F**1 2 3 4 5 6 7 8 9 10 11 12 14 15 16 20 22 23 24 25 26 27 28 29 30 32 33 34 35 36 37 40 41 42 44 45 46 47 49 52 53 54	23	10	S		326	11033	153	47.7	23	1657	42637	20285	919
GUNNISON—Gunnison County													
GUNNISON VALLEY HOSPITAL (Formerly Gunnison County Public Hospital), 214 E. Denver Ave., Zip 81230; tel. 303/641-1456; Robert S. Austin, adm. **A**9 10 **F**1 3 6 14 15 16 23 26 29 30 34 35 40 44 45 46	13	10	S		24	665	5	20.8	6	145	1931	817	50
HAXTUN—Phillips County													
★ HAXTUN HOSPITAL DISTRICT, W. Fletcher St., Box 308, Zip 80731; tel. 303/774-6123; Doug McMillan, adm. (Nonreporting) **A**9 10	16	10	S		33	—	—	—	—	—	—	—	—
HOLYOKE—Phillips County													
★ MELISSA MEMORIAL HOSPITAL, 505 S. Baxter Ave., Zip 80734; tel. 303/854-2241; Hildegarde T. Hassler, chief exec. off. **A**9 10 **F**1 6 15 23 34 35 37 40 43 45 52	16	10	S		18	225	2	10.0	5	42	915	437	40
HUGO—Lincoln County													
★ LINCOLN COMMUNITY HOSPITAL AND NURSING HOME, 111 Sixth St., Box 248, Zip 80821; tel. 303/743-2421; Delores Nance, chief exec. off. (Total facility includes 35 beds in nursing home-type unit) **A**9 10 **F**1 6 14 15 16 19 23 24 34 35 36 40 41 42 44 45 46 47 50	13	10	S	TF	56	385	35	62.5	4	87	1232	597	28
				H	21	368	4	—	4	87	708	309	—
JULESBURG—Sedgwick County													
★ SEDGWICK COUNTY HOSPITAL, 900 Cedar St., Zip 80737; tel. 303/474-3323; Richard L. Scott, adm. (Total facility includes 32 beds in nursing home-type unit) **A**9 10 **F**1 3 6 14 15 16 19 23 35 40 41 46 52; **S**9355	13	10	S	TF	52	319	33	63.5	4	25	1282	593	46
				H	20	295	3	—	4	25	804	327	21
KREMMLING—Grand County													
★ KREMMLING MEMORIAL HOSPITAL, Fourth & Grand Ave., Box 398, Zip 80459; tel. 303/724-3442; Pamela Meyer, adm. (Total facility includes 2 beds in nursing home-type unit) **A**9 10 **F**1 3 6 10 14 15 16 19 23 26 34 35 36 37 40 41 43 44 45 46 47 53	16	10	S	TF	21	516	7	35.0	4	112	2059	384	42
				H	19	516	6	—	4	112	—	—	40

Hospital, Address, Telephone, Administrator, Approval and Facility Codes, Multihospital System Code	Classification Codes				Inpatient Data				Newborn Data		Expense (thousands of dollars)		
★ American Hospital Association (AHA) membership □ Joint Commission on Accreditation of Hospitals (JCAH) accreditation + American Osteopathic Hospital Association (AOHA) membership ○ American Osteopathic Association (AOA) accreditation Δ Commission on Accreditation of Rehabilitation Facilities (CARF) accreditation Control codes 61, 63, 64, 71, 72 and 73 indicate hospitals listed by AOHA, but not registered by AHA. For definition of numerical codes, see page A2	Control	Service	Stay	Facilities	Beds	Admissions	Census	Occupancy (percent)	Bassinets	Births	Total	Payroll	Personnel
LA JARA—Conejos County													
★□ CONEJOS COUNTY HOSPITAL, Box 639, Zip 81140; tel. 303/274-5121; Calvin C. Graber, adm. (Total facility includes 16 beds in nursing home-type unit) **A**1a 9 10 **F**1 3 6 12 14 15 16 19 21 23 26 34 35 36 37 40 41 42 43 44 45 46 47 50 52	16	10	S	TF	43	800	22	51.2	6	95	2005	856	48
				H	27	705	6	—	6	95	1717	734	39
LA JUNTA—Otero County													
★□ ARKANSAS VALLEY REGIONAL MEDICAL CENTER (Formerly La Junta Medical Center), 1100 Carson Ave., Zip 81050; tel. 303/384-5412; Elbert Detwiler, adm. (Total facility includes 145 beds in nursing home-type unit) **A**1a 9 10 **F**1 3 6 10 12 14 15 16 19 23 25 26 30 34 35 36 37 40 44 45 47 50 53	21	10	S	TF	206	2450	174	84.5	12	372	9911	5003	315
				H	61	2382	33	—	12	372	8426	4017	240
LA JUNTA MEDICAL CENTER, See Arkansas Valley Regional Medical Center													
LAKEWOOD—Jefferson County													
★□ AMC CANCER RESEARCH CENTER, 1600 Pierce St., Zip 80214; tel. 303/233-6501; Marvin A. Rich MD, pres. & dir. (Total facility includes 20 beds in nursing home-type unit) **A**1a 2 10 **F**1 15 17 19 23 26 34 41 45 46 47	23	49	S	TF	32	206	16	50.0	0	0	9419	3180	141
				H	12	73	1	—	0	0	8887	2781	127
LAMAR—Prowers County													
★□ PROWERS MEDICAL CENTER, 2101 S. Memorial Dr., Zip 81052; tel. 303/336-4343; Murry A. Carter, adm. **A**1a 9 10 **F**1 3 6 10 12 14 15 16 23 35 36 40 43 45 46 47 50	16	10	S		40	1286	12	30.0	10	306	3109	1581	86
LEADVILLE—Lake County													
★□ ST. VINCENT GENERAL HOSPITAL, W. Fourth & Washington Sts., Zip 80461; tel. 303/486-0230; Robert L. Woodward, adm. **A**1a 9 10 **F**1 3 6 10 12 14 15 16 23 35 36 37 40 42 45 52 53	23	10	S		22	898	10	45.5	5	97	2922	1489	73
LONGMONT—Boulder County													
★□ LONGMONT UNITED HOSPITAL, 1950 W. Mountain View Ave., Box 1659, Zip 80501; tel. 303/651-5111; Kenneth R. Huey, adm. **A**1a 2 9 10 **F**1 3 5 6 9 10 11 12 14 15 16 21 23 24 27 30 32 33 35 36 40 41 42 44 45 46 47 52 53	23	10	S		128	5790	74	57.8	13	826	17933	8403	415
LOVELAND—Larimer County													
★□ MCKEE MEDICAL CENTER, 2000 Boise Ave., Zip 80537; tel. 303/669-4640; Craig J. Broman, adm. **A**1a 9 10 **F**1 3 6 7 9 10 12 15 16 20 21 23 24 25 26 34 35 36 37 40 41 44 45 46 47 49 52 53; **S**2235	23	10	S		105	4581	56	55.4	16	725	15945	7054	340
MEEKER—Rio Blanco County													
★ PIONEERS HOSPITAL OF RIO BLANCO COUNTY (Includes Walbridge Memorial Convalescent Wing), 345 Cleveland St., Zip 81641; tel. 303/878-5047; Hugh Sargent, chief exec. off. (Nonreporting) **A**9 10	13	10	S		42	—	—	—	—	—	—	—	—
MONTE VISTA—Rio Grande County													
★□ MONTE VISTA COMMUNITY HOSPITAL, 95 W. First Ave., Zip 81144; tel. 303/852-3541; Dennis R. Turney, adm. **A**1a 9 10 **F**1 3 14 16 21 23 27 29 30 32 34 35 36 40 41 43 45 52; **S**1755	23	10	S		39	557	9	23.1	6	87	1818	1057	55
MONTROSE—Montrose County													
★□ MONTROSE MEMORIAL HOSPITAL, 800 S. Third St., Zip 81401; tel. 303/249-2211; Stephen T. Scott, adm. **A**1a 2 9 10 **F**1 3 6 10 12 14 15 16 23 24 26 28 30 32 33 34 35 36 42 44 45 46 47 48 49 50 53	13	10	S		75	2539	32	42.7	8	261	9045	4277	225
PUEBLO—Pueblo County													
□ COLORADO STATE HOSPITAL, 1600 W. 24th St., Zip 81003; tel. 303/546-4147; Haydee Kort MD, supt. **A**1b 9 10 **F**1 12 14 16 23 24 28 29 32 33 34 35 42 44 45 46 47 48	12	22	L		716	3037	651	90.9	0	0	44766	—	—
★□ PARKVIEW EPISCOPAL MEDICAL CENTER, 400 W. 16th St., Zip 81003; tel. 303/584-4000; Michael D. Pugh, pres. & chief exec. off. **A**1a 9 10 **F**1 3 4 5 6 10 11 12 14 15 16 23 24 26 27 28 29 30 32 33 34 35 36 37 39 40 41 42 44 45 46 47 48 49 52 53 54; **S**1755	23	10	S		239	6947	128	50.4	16	672	28728	12215	628
★□ ST. MARY-CORWIN HOSPITAL REGIONAL MEDICAL AND HEALTH CENTER, 1008 Minnequa Ave., Zip 81004; tel. 303/560-4000; Edmond T. Doyle, pres. & chief exec. off. (Total facility includes 16 beds in nursing home-type unit) **A**1a 2 3 5 9 10 **F**1 2 3 4 6 7 8 9 10 11 12 14 15 16 19 20 21 23 24 25 26 27 28 29 30 32 33 34 35 36 37 38 40 41 42 43 44 45 46 47 50 51 52 53 54; **S**5115	21	10	S	TF	307	10274	186	60.6	25	1232	48052	21016	926
				H	291	9977	175	—	25	1232	47756	20727	910
RANGELY—Rio Blanco County													
★ RANGELY DISTRICT HOSPITAL, 511 S. White Ave., Zip 81648; tel. 303/675-5011; Russell McDaniel, exec. dir. **A**9 10 **F**1 6 14 16 23 34 35 36 40	16	10	S		19	161	2	10.5	4	27	1712	726	41
RIFLE—Garfield County													
★□ CLAGETT MEMORIAL HOSPITAL (Includes E. Dene Moore Memorial Home), 701 E. Fifth St., P O Box 912, Zip 81650; tel. 303/625-1510; Edwin A. Gast, adm. (Total facility includes 57 beds in nursing home-type unit) **A**1a 9 10 **F**1 3 6 12 14 15 16 19 21 23 24 34 35 37 40 41 42 44 45 49 50	16	10	S	TF	89	499	66	74.2	4	56	2815	1532	90
				H	32	482	9	—	4	56	1836	897	54
SALIDA—Chaffee County													
□ SALIDA HOSPITAL, First & B Sts., Box 429, Zip 81201; tel. 303/539-6661; Tim Crowley, chief exec. off. **A**1a 9 10 **F**1 3 6 10 15 16 23 24 35 36 40 41 44 45 47 53; **S**2495	16	10	S		38	1403	17	44.7	7	202	3627	1786	121
SPRINGFIELD—Baca County													
★ SOUTHEAST COLORADO HOSPITAL, 373 E. Tenth Ave., Zip 81073; tel. 303/523-4501; Edna Chenoweth, adm. (Total facility includes 40 beds in nursing home-type unit) **A**9 10 **F**6 14 16 19 23 35 40 45	16	10	S	TF	65	545	46	70.8	2	29	1561	707	61
				H	25	526	9	—	2	29	897	384	33
STEAMBOAT SPRINGS—Routt County													
★□ ROUTT MEMORIAL HOSPITAL, 80 Park Ave., Zip 80487; tel. 303/879-1322; John Richwagen, adm. (Total facility includes 50 beds in nursing home-type unit) **A**1a 9 10 **F**1 3 6 10 15 16 19 23 35 36 40 43 45 47	23	10	S	TF	72	1100	51	70.8	4	223	4333	2162	134
				H	22	1051	10	—	4	223	3339	1542	83
STERLING—Logan County													
★□ LOGAN COUNTY HOSPITAL, 615 Fairhurst St., Box 3500, Zip 80751; tel. 303/522-0122; Brian C. Larson, adm. (Nonreporting) **A**1a 9 10; **S**2235	13	10	S		98	—	—	—	—	—	—	—	—
THORNTON—Denver and Adams Counties													
★□ HUMANA HOSPITAL-MOUNTAIN VIEW (Formerly Valley View Hospital and Medical Center, Denver), 9191 Grant St., Zip 80229; tel. 303/451-7800; Jack Shapiro, exec. dir. **A**1a 9 10 **F**1 3 6 10 12 14 15 16 20 23 34 35 36 37 40 45 46 47 52 53; **S**1235	33	10	S		172	5579	73	39.5	31	683	23940	8972	375
TRINIDAD—Las Animas County													
★□ MOUNT SAN RAFAEL HOSPITAL, 410 Benedicta Ave., Zip 81082; tel. 303/846-9213; Ron Shafer, adm. **A**1a 9 10 **F**1 3 6 12 14 15 16 34 35 37 40 45 46 47 52	23	10	S		66	1211	18	27.3	4	161	3734	1644	120
USAF ACADEMY—El Paso County													
★□ U. S. AIR FORCE ACADEMY HOSPITAL, Zip 80840; tel. 303/472-5101; Col. Robert D. Iott, adm. **A**1a **F**1 3 6 10 12 14 15 16 23 28 30 33 34 35 36 37 40 43 46 47 49 52 53	41	10	S		80	4299	51	63.8	18	604	—	—	495
VAIL—Eagle County													
★□ VAIL VALLEY MEDICAL CENTER, 181 W. Meadow Dr., Zip 81657; tel. 303/476-2451; Ray McMahan, adm. **A**1a 9 10 **F**1 6 14 15 16 23 32 35 36 40 43 45; **S**0125	23	10	S		19	1438	12	63.2	6	343	5802	2380	109

Hospital, Address, Telephone, Administrator, Approval and Facility Codes, Multihospital System Code	Classification Codes				Inpatient Data				Newborn Data		Expense (thousands of dollars)		
★ American Hospital Association (AHA) membership □ Joint Commission on Accreditation of Hospitals (JCAH) accreditation + American Osteopathic Hospital Association (AOHA) membership ○ American Osteopathic Association (AOA) accreditation Δ Commission on Accreditation of Rehabilitation Facilities (CARF) accreditation Control codes 61, 63, 64, 71, 72 and 73 indicate hospitals listed by AOHA, but not registered by AHA. For definition of numerical codes, see page A2	Control	Service	Stay	Facilities	Beds	Admissions	Census	Occupancy (percent)	Bassinets	Births	Total	Payroll	Personnel
WALSENBURG—Huerfano County													
□ HUERFANO MEMORIAL HOSPITAL, 900 E. Indiana Ave., Box 443, Zip 81089; tel. 303/738-2621; William B. Watts, adm. **A**1a 9 10 **F**1 6 14 15 16 23 24 34 35 36 37 40 41 43 45 47	16	10	S		38	582	10	26.3	4	35	2207	951	79
WALSH—Baca County													
WALSH DISTRICT HOSPITAL, 150 Nevada St., Box 206, Zip 81090; tel. 303/324-5262; Luann Weldon, adm. (Total facility includes 8 beds in nursing home-type unit) **A**9 10 **F**1 6 16 19 23 34 35 36 40 50	16	10	S	TF	25	221	11	44.0	3	11	1058	434	40
				H	17	202	4	—	3	11	831	347	22
WESTMINSTER—Denver and Adams Counties													
ST. ANTHONY HOSPITAL NORTH, See St. Anthony Hospital Systems, Denver													
WHEAT RIDGE—Jefferson County													
★□ LUTHERAN MEDICAL CENTER, 8300 W. 38th Ave., Zip 80033; tel. 303/425-4500; James D. Willard, pres. **A**1a 2 10 **F**1 2 3 5 6 9 10 12 14 15 16 17 21 23 24 25 26 30 34 35 36 37 40 41 43 45 46 47 51 52•53	23	10	S		380	17663	258	67.4	31	2079	67268	35339	1454
WRAY—Yuma County													
★ WRAY COMMUNITY DISTRICT HOSPITAL, 340 Birch St., Box 65, Zip 80758; tel. 303/332-4811; Steve A. Thomas, adm. **A**9 10 **F**1 6 14 15 23 26 34 35 40 41 43	16	10	S		25	413	5	20.0	4	56	1057	536	34
YUMA—Yuma County													
YUMA DISTRICT HOSPITAL, 910 S. Main St., Zip 80759; tel. 303/848-5405; James Naeve, adm. **A**9 10 **F**14 16 23 35 36 40 41 44 45; **S**0585	16	10	S		18	296	4	20.0	4	41	968	518	34

Hospital, Address, Telephone, Administrator, Approval and Facility Codes, Multihospital System Code	Classification Codes				Inpatient Data				Newborn Data		Expense (thousands of dollars)		
★ American Hospital Association (AHA) membership □ Joint Commission on Accreditation of Hospitals (JCAH) accreditation + American Osteopathic Hospital Association (AOHA) membership ○ American Osteopathic Association (AOA) accreditation Δ Commission on Accreditation of Rehabilitation Facilities (CARF) accreditation Control codes 61, 63, 64, 71, 72 and 73 indicate hospitals listed by AOHA, but not registered by AHA. For definition of numerical codes, see page A2	Control	Service	Stay	Facilities	Beds	Admissions	Census	Occupancy (percent)	Bassinets	Births	Total	Payroll	Personnel

Connecticut

Hospital	Control	Service	Stay	Facilities	Beds	Admissions	Census	Occupancy (percent)	Bassinets	Births	Total	Payroll	Personnel
BETHLEHEM—Litchfield County													
★□ WELLSPRING FOUNDATION, 21 Arch Bridge Rd., P O Box 370, Zip 06751; tel. 203/266-7235; W. J. Genovese, bus. adm. (Nonreporting) **A**1b	23	22	L		8	—	—	—	—	—	—	—	—
BRIDGEPORT—Fairfield County													
★□ BRIDGEPORT HOSPITAL, 267 Grant St., P O Box 5000, Zip 06610; tel. 203/384-3000; Michael E. Schrader, pres. **A**1a 2 3 5 6 8 9 10 **F**1 2 3 4 5 6 7 8 9 10 11 12 14 15 16 22 25 27 29 30 32 34 35 36 37 38 40 41 43 45 46 47 49 50 51 52 53 54	23	10	S		537	21637	410	77.5	36	2682	89620	46309	1938
★□ GREATER BRIDGPORT COMMUNITY MENTAL HEALTH CENTER, 1635 Central Ave., Box 5117, Zip 06610; tel. 203/579-6646; Melodie Peet, dir. (Newly Registered) **A**1b 9 **F**24 28 30 32 33 34 42 43 45 46 47 48 49	12	22	S		66	1495	55	83.3	0	0	10571	3916	255
★□ PARK CITY HOSPITAL, 695 Park Ave., Zip 06604; tel. 203/579-5000; Bruce J. Markowitz, pres. & chief exec. off. **A**1a 2 9 10 **F**1 3 6 7 10 12 14 15 16 20 23 24 25 26 27 28 30 32 33 34 35 36 37 40 42 43 44 45 46 47 52 53	23	10	S		155	7250	93	60.0	23	790	27790	13116	521
★□ ST. VINCENT'S MEDICAL CENTER, 2800 Main St., Zip 06606; tel. 203/576-6000; William J. Riordan, pres. & chief exec. off. **A**1a 2 3 5 6 8 9 10 **F**1 2 3 4 5 6 7 8 9 10 11 12 14 15 16 20 23 24 26 27 28 29 30 32 34 35 36 40 41 42 43 44 45 46 47 48 50 52 53 54; **S**1885	21	10	S		362	13693	294	78.2	32	1320	65942	32318	1351
BRISTOL—Hartford County													
★□ BRISTOL HOSPITAL, Brewster Rd., Zip 06010; tel. 203/589-2000; Richard F. Peterson, actg. pres. **A**1a 2 9 10 **F**1 3 6 10 12 14 15 16 23 24 26 27 28 30 32 33 34 35 36 40 41 42 44 45 46 47 49 50 52 53	23	10	S		210	8289	166	79.0	12	870	36267	20965	709
DANBURY—Fairfield County													
★□ DANBURY HOSPITAL, 24 Hospital Ave., Zip 06810; tel. 203/797-7000; Gerard D. Robilotti, pres. **A**1a 2 3 5 8 9 10 **F**1 2 3 5 6 7 8 9 10 11 12 14 15 16 20 23 24 25 26 27 28 29 30 32 33 34 35 36 37 38 40 42 43 44 45 46 47 48 49 50 52 53 54	23	10	S		366	16460	321	87.7	26	2257	87551	37122	1742
DERBY—New Haven County													
★□ GRIFFIN HOSPITAL, 130 Division St., Zip 06418; tel. 203/735-7421; John Bustelos Jr., pres. & chief exec. off. **A**1a 2 3 5 9 10 **F**1 3 6 10 12 14 15 16 20 23 24 26 27 28 29 30 32 33 34 35 36 37 40 41 43 44 45 46 47 49 52 53	23	10	S		217	6586	141	65.0	20	588	37160	18976	816
FARMINGTON—Hartford County													
★□ UNIVERSITY OF CONNECTICUT HEALTH CENTER, JOHN DEMPSEY HOSPITAL, Zip 06032; tel. 203/674-2000; Helen L. Smits MD, interim dir. **A**1a 2 3 5 8 9 10 **F**1 3 5 6 7 8 9 10 11 12 14 15 16 20 23 24 26 27 28 29 30 32 33 34 35 37 38 40 41 42 43 44 46 47 48 49 51 52 53 54	12	10	S		232	6863	159	68.5	20	656	60636	23616	1063
GREENWICH—Fairfield County													
★□ GREENWICH HOSPITAL, 5 Perryridge Rd., Zip 06830; tel. 203/863-3000; Edward M. Kenney, pres. (Nonreporting) **A**1a 2 3 5 9 10	23	10	S		230	—	—	—	—	—	—	—	—
GROTON—New London County													
★□ NAVAL HOSPITAL, Zip 06349; tel. 203/449-3261; Capt. Hugh P. Scott MC USN, CO **A**1a **F**1 3 6 10 12 14 16 23 28 30 32 33 34 35 37 40 43 46 47 48 52	43	10	S		60	3570	34	56.7	30	591	15181	7482	505
HARTFORD—Hartford County													
★□ HARTFORD HOSPITAL, 80 Seymour St., Zip 06115; tel. 203/524-3011 ; John J. Meehan, exec. vice-pres. (Total facility includes 90 beds in nursing home-type unit) **A**1a 2 3 5 8 9 10 **F**1 2 3 4 5 6 7 8 9 10 11 12 13 14 15 16 19 20 21 23 24 26 27 28 29 30 32 33 34 35 36 37 40 42 43 44 45 46 49 50 51 52 53 54	23	10	S	TF	993	33654	786	79.2	66	4261	187450	95794	3784
				H	903	33149	702	—	66	4261	183314	93434	3671
★□ HEBREW HOME AND HOSPITAL (Geriatric and Chronic Disease), 615 Tower Ave., Zip 06112; tel. 203/242-6207; Irving Kronenberg, pres. & exec. dir. (Total facility includes 270 beds in nursing home-type unit) **A**1a 9 10 **F**16 19 23 24 30 32 42 44 45 46 47 50	23	49	L	TF	315	305	306	97.1	0	0	11167	6744	327
				H	45	65	2	—	0	0	—	—	—
★□ INSTITUTE OF LIVING, 400 Washington St., Zip 06106; tel. 203/241-8000; William L. Webb Jr. MD, pres. & psych.-in-chief (Nonreporting) **A**1a 3 5 9 10	23	22	L		401	—	—	—	—	—	—	—	—
★□ MOUNT SINAI HOSPITAL, 500 Blue Hills Ave., Zip 06112; tel. 203/242-4431; Robert B. Bruner, pres. & exec. dir. **A**1a 2 3 5 8 9 10 **F**1 2 3 6 10 12 14 15 16 20 23 24 25 26 27 28 29 30 32 33 34 35 36 37 38 40 41 42 43 44 45 46 47 50 51 52 53 54	23	10	S		306	12121	233	75.2	28	1831	75249	40068	1667
★□ SAINT FRANCIS HOSPITAL AND MEDICAL CENTER, 114 Woodland St., Zip 06105; tel. 203/548-4000; Sr. Francis Marie Garvey, pres. & treas. **A**1a 2 3 5 6 8 9 10 **F**1 2 3 4 5 6 7 8 9 10 11 12 14 15 16 20 23 24 25 26 27 28 30 32 33 34 35 36 40 41 44 45 46 47 49 50 51 52 53 54; **S**5615	21	10	S		569	21916	449	77.8	31	2557	110946	57626	2301
LITCHFIELD—Litchfield County													
★□ COUNTRY PLACE, E. Litchfield Rd., Box 668, Zip 06759; tel. 203/567-8763; Renee Nell EdD, exec. dir. (Nonreporting) **A**1b 9	33	22	L		27	—	—	—	—	—	—	—	—
MANCHESTER—Hartford County													
★□ MANCHESTER MEMORIAL HOSPITAL, 71 Haynes St., Zip 06040; tel. 203/646-1222; Warren L. Prelesnik, pres. **A**1a 9 10 **F**1 3 6 10 12 14 15 16 23 24 25 26 27 28 29 30 32 33 35 36 40 41 42 44 45 46 49 52 53	23	10	S		303	9532	166	54.8	34	1356	39954	21255	889
MANSFIELD—Tolland County													
NATCHAUG HOSPITAL, See Mansfield Center													
MANSFIELD CENTER—Tolland County													
□ NATCHAUG HOSPITAL (Formerly Listed Under Mansfield), 189 Storrs Rd., Zip 06250; tel. 203/423-2514; Robert Spagnuolo, chief exec. off. **A**1b 3 9 10 **F**15 23 24 28 29 30 32 33 34 42 43 49	23	22	L		60	621	56	93.3	0	0	5867	3467	159
MERIDEN—New Haven County													
□ HENRY D. ALTOBELLO CHILDREN AND YOUTH CENTER, Undercliff Rd., P O Box 902, Zip 06450; tel. 203/238-6054; Judith Normandin, supt. (Nonreporting) **A**1b 9	12	52	L		57	—	—	—	—	—	—	—	—
★□ MEMORIAL HOSPITAL, 883 Paddock Ave., Zip 06450; tel. 203/237-5531; Thomas E. Wilhelmsen Jr., adm. **A**1a 9 10 **F**1 3 6 10 12 14 15 16 20 23 24 26 27 30 32 33 34 35 39 41 42 45 46 50 53	23	10	S		92	3006	68	73.9	0	0	15605	7619	357
★□ MERIDEN-WALLINGFORD HOSPITAL, 181 Cook Ave., Zip 06450; tel. 203/238-8200; Theodore H. Horwitz, pres. & chief exec. off. **A**1a 2 9 10 **F**1 2 3 6 7 9 10 12 14 15 16 20 23 24 26 28 29 30 32 33 34 35 36 37 40 41 42 43 44 45 46 47 48 49 50 52 53	23	10	S		170	7672	119	70.0	20	994	38204	18328	779
MIDDLETOWN—Middlesex County													
★□ Δ CONNECTICUT VALLEY HOSPITAL, Silver St., Box 351, Zip 06457; tel. 203/344-2666; Vincenzo Cocilovo MD, supt. **A**1b 3 5 7 9 10 **F**15 23 24 26 28 30 32 33 34 42 44 45 46 47 48 50	12	22	L		658	2924	637	96.8	0	0	32808	26434	1008

★ American Hospital Association (AHA) membership
☐ Joint Commission on Accreditation of Hospitals (JCAH) accreditation
+ American Osteopathic Hospital Association (AOHA) membership
○ American Osteopathic Association (AOA) accreditation
Δ Commission on Accreditation of Rehabilitation Facilities (CARF) accreditation
Control codes 61, 63, 64, 71, 72 and 73 indicate hospitals listed by AOHA, but not registered by AHA.
For definition of numerical codes, see page A2

Hospital, Address, Telephone, Administrator, Approval and Facility Codes, Multihospital System Code	Classification Codes				Inpatient Data				Newborn Data		Expense (thousands of dollars)		
	Control	Service	Stay	Facilities	Beds	Admissions	Census	Occupancy (percent)	Bassinets	Births	Total	Payroll	Personnel
★☐ MIDDLESEX MEMORIAL HOSPITAL, 28 Crescent St., Zip 06457; tel. 203/347-9471; Gordon B. McWilliams, pres. **A**1a 2 3 5 6 9 10 **F**1 3 5 6 7 8 9 10 11 12 14 15 16 20 21 23 24 26 27 28 29 30 32 33 34 35 36 37 40 41 42 43 44 45 46 49 53	23	10	S		264	11704	203	75.2	20	1039	53573	28676	1172
☐ RIVERVIEW HOSPITAL FOR CHILDREN, River Rd., Box 621, Zip 06457; tel. 203/344-2700; Richard J. Wiseman PhD, supt. **A**1a 9 **F**29 30 32 33 42 44 46 47	12	52	L		57	134	46	80.7	0	0	3908	3397	124
MILFORD—New Haven County													
★☐ MILFORD HOSPITAL, 2047 Bridgeport Ave., Zip 06460; tel. 203/878-3551; Paul E. Moss, adm. **A**1a 9 10 **F**1 3 6 10 12 14 15 16 34 35 36 40 45 46 52 53	23	10	S		149	4634	79	53.0	12	597	18466	9740	451
NEW BRITAIN—Hartford County													
★☐ NEW BRITAIN GENERAL HOSPITAL, 100 Grand St., Zip 06050; tel. 203/224-5011; Laurence A. Tanner, pres. & chief exec. off. **A**1a 3 5 8 9 10 **F**1 3 5 6 7 8 9 10 11 12 14 15 16 20 23 24 26 27 28 29 30 32 33 34 35 36 37 40 41 42 43 44 45 46 47 49 50 51 53 54	23	10	S		350	15223	266	70.0	32	2172	61386	33968	1354
★☐ NEW BRITAIN MEMORIAL HOSPITAL, 2150 Corbin Ave., Zip 06053; tel. 203/223-2761; Katherine C. Ill MD, pres. & med. dir. **A**1a 9 10 **F**6 15 16 23 24 25 26 32 33 34 42 44 45 47	23	48	L		200	283	178	89.0	0	0	14160	8839	463
NEW CANAAN—Fairfield County													
★ SILVER HILL FOUNDATION HOSPITAL, 208 Valley Rd., Box 1177, Zip 06840; tel. 203/966-3561 **A** 9 10 **F**23 24 28 29 32 33 34 42 43 44 45 46 48 49	23	22	L		77	496	68	88.3	0	0	8229	4913	190
NEW HAVEN—New Haven County													
★☐ CONNECTICUT MENTAL HEALTH CENTER, 34 Park St., Zip 06519; Mailing Address Box 1842, Zip 06508; tel. 203/789-7291; Boris M. Astrachan MD, dir. **A**1a 3 5 9 **F**15 24 26 28 29 30 32 33 34 43 47 49	12	22	S		47	684	42	93.3	0	0	14040	9788	416
★☐ HOSPITAL OF SAINT RAPHAEL, 1450 Chapel St., Zip 06511; tel. 203/789-3000; Robert T. Beeman, pres. **A**1a 2 3 5 8 9 10 **F**1 2 3 4 5 6 7 8 9 10 11 12 14 15 16 20 23 24 25 26 27 28 30 32 33 34 35 36 40 41 42 44 45 46 47 50 52 53 54; **S**5815	21	10	S		441	17364	371	82.1	22	1135	93723	41958	1858
☐ YALE PSYCHIATRIC INSTITUTE, Huntington & Prospect Sts., Box 12a, Yale Sta., Zip 06520; tel. 203/432-1030; Gary L. Tischler MD, dir. **A**1b 3 5 9 **F**24 28 29 30 33 34 42 43 47	23	22	L		61	52	56	91.8	0	0	—	—	158
YALE UNIVERSITY HEALTH SERVICES (Formerly Yale University Health Services Center), 17 Hillhouse Ave., Zip 06520; tel. 203/436-3298; Daniel S. Rowe MD, dir. (Nonreporting)	23	11	S		38	—	—	—	—	—	—	—	—
★☐ YALE-NEW HAVEN HOSPITAL, 20 York St., Zip 06504; tel. 203/785-4242; C. Thomas Smith, pres. **A**1a 2 3 5 8 9 10 **F**1 2 3 4 5 6 7 8 9 10 11 12 13 14 15 16 17 20 23 24 26 27 28 30 32 33 34 35 36 37 38 40 41 44 45 46 47 50 51 52 53 54	23	10	S		829	31004	643	77.8	46	5776	187744	89804	3715
NEW LONDON—New London County													
★☐ LAWRENCE AND MEMORIAL HOSPITAL, 365 Montauk Ave., Zip 06320; tel. 203/442-0711; John F. Mirabito, pres. & chief exec. off. **A**1a 9 10 **F**1 2 3 6 10 12 14 15 16 20 21 23 24 25 26 27 28 29 30 32 33 34 35 36 37 39 40 41 43 44 45 46 47 52 53 54	23	10	S		325	12723	225	69.2	28	1658	52568	29477	1114
NEW MILFORD—Litchfield County													
★☐ NEW MILFORD HOSPITAL, 21 Elm St., Zip 06776; tel. 203/355-2611; Richard E. Pugh, pres. **A**1a 9 10 **F**1 3 6 10 12 14 15 16 23 26 28 30 32 33 35 36 40 44 45 46 50 52 53	23	10	S		85	3786	57	67.1	10	394	15181	7482	337
NEWINGTON—Hartford County													
☐ CEDARCREST REGIONAL HOSPITAL, 525 Russell Rd., Zip 06111; tel. 203/666-4613; Carl A. Cappello, supt. **A**1a 9 10 **F**24 30 32 33 42 45 46 47	12	22	L		95	972	92	96.8	0	0	9823	7323	287
★☐ NEWINGTON CHILDREN'S HOSPITAL, 181 E. Cedar St., Zip 06111; tel. 203/667-5200; A. John Menichetti, pres. & chief exec. off. **A**1a 3 5 9 10 **F**1 6 14 15 16 23 24 25 26 27 28 29 32 33 34 37 38 42 43 44 45 46 53	23	50	S		98	2520	56	57.1	0	0	23021	13793	543
★☐ VETERANS ADMINISTRATION MEDICAL CENTER, 555 Willard Ave., Zip 06111; tel. 203/666-6951; Robert K. Davenport, dir. **A**1a 3 5 8 **F**1 2 3 6 9 10 12 14 15 16 20 23 24 26 27 28 30 32 33 34 35 42 45 46 48 49	45	10	S		186	3344	132	71.0	0	0	31075	14338	464
NEWTOWN—Fairfield County													
★☐ FAIRFIELD HILLS HOSPITAL, Box W, Zip 06470; tel. 203/426-2531; Dennis E. Angelini PhD, supt. **A**1b 9 10 **F**15 19 23 24 31 32 33 34 42 46 47 48 50	12	22	L		733	2675	711	97.0	0	0	34005	17646	1057
☐ HOUSATONIC ADOLESCENT HOSPITAL, Box W, Zip 06470; tel. 203/426-2531; Leonard Suchotliff PhD, supt. (Nonreporting) **A**1b 9	12	52	L		35	—	—	—	—	—	—	—	—
NORWALK—Fairfield County													
★☐ Δ NORWALK HOSPITAL, Maple St., Zip 06856; tel. 203/852-2000; David W. Osborne, pres. & chief exec. off. **A**1a 2 3 5 7 8 9 10 **F**1 3 5 6 7 8 9 10 11 12 14 15 16 17 20 23 24 25 26 27 28 29 30 32 33 34 35 36 37 38 40 41 42 43 44 45 46 47 48 49 50 51 52 53 54	23	10	S		437	14910	305	69.8	24	1676	81216	42969	1974
NORWICH—New London County													
★☐ NORWICH HOSPITAL, Rte. 12, Box 508, Zip 06360; tel. 203/889-7361; Garrell S. Mullaney, supt. **A**1b 3 9 10 **F**12 23 24 32 33 42 44 45 46 47 48 50	12	22	L		649	2852	614	94.6	0	0	42268	25222	1070
★☐ UNIVERSITY OF CONNECTICUT HEALTH CENTER, UNCAS ON THAMES HOSPITAL (Oncology), W. Thames St., Zip 06360; tel. 203/889-1321; Thomas W. Redding, supt. **A**1a 3 9 10 **F**7 8 9 10 23 45 46	12	49	S		28	246	13	46.4	0	0	5971	3664	148
★☐ WILLIAM W. BACKUS HOSPITAL, 326 Washington St., Zip 06360; tel. 203/889-8331; Michael T. Moore, chief exec. off. **A**1a 3 9 10 **F**1 3 5 6 10 12 14 15 16 20 23 24 26 27 28 29 30 32 35 36 38 40 41 42 45 46 52 53	23	10	S		211	10465	155	69.5	28	1169	35137	18712	780
PORTLAND—Middlesex County													
☐ ELMCREST PSYCHIATRIC INSTITUTE, 25 Marlborough St., Zip 06480; tel. 203/342-0480 **A**1b 9 10 **F**15 24 26 28 29 30 32 33 34 41 42 46 47 49 50; **S**0825	32	22	L		105	943	105	100.0	0	0	11880	5885	277
PUTNAM—Windham County													
★☐ DAY KIMBALL HOSPITAL, 320 Pomfret St., Zip 06260; tel. 203/928-6541; Charles F. Schneider, exec. dir. **A**1a 9 10 **F**1 3 6 9 10 12 14 15 16 21 23 24 28 29 30 31 32 33 34 35 36 37 40 42 43 44 45 46 47 49 52 53	23	10	S		148	5211	77	52.0	18	720	22238	11246	481
ROCKVILLE—Tolland County													
★☐ ROCKVILLE GENERAL HOSPITAL, 31 Union St., Zip 06066; tel. 203/872-0501; Robert C. Boardman, exec. dir. **A**1a 9 10 **F**1 2 3 6 10 12 14 15 16 20 23 24 30 34 35 36 37 40 41 43 44 45 46 47 49 52 53	23	10	S		102	5747	64	62.7	12	674	19137	9297	412
ROCKY HILL—Hartford County													
☐ VETERANS HOME AND HOSPITAL, 287 West St., Zip 06067; tel. 203/529-2571; Maj. David B. McQuillan, actg. comdt. & adm. **A**1a 10 **F**12 14 15 16 23 24 32 35 42 44 46 50	12	48	L		350	508	309	88.3	0	0	15142	11473	490
SHARON—Litchfield County													
★☐ SHARON HOSPITAL, W. Main St., Zip 06069; tel. 203/364-5511; Paul W. Sternlof, pres. & chief exec. off. **A**1a 2 9 10 **F**1 3 6 10 12 14 15 16 21 23 30 32 33 34 35 36 40 44 45 46 47 49 52 53	23	10	S		92	3167	52	56.5	8	425	14127	7211	306

Hospital, Address, Telephone, Administrator, Approval and Facility Codes, Multihospital System Code	Classification Codes				Inpatient Data				Newborn Data		Expense (thousands of dollars)		
★ American Hospital Association (AHA) membership □ Joint Commission on Accreditation of Hospitals (JCAH) accreditation + American Osteopathic Hospital Association (AOHA) membership ○ American Osteopathic Association (AOA) accreditation Δ Commission on Accreditation of Rehabilitation Facilities (CARF) accreditation Control codes 61, 63, 64, 71, 72 and 73 indicate hospitals listed by AOHA, but not registered by AHA. For definition of numerical codes, see page A2	Control	Service	Stay	Facilities	Beds	Admissions	Census	Occupancy (percent)	Bassinets	Births	Total	Payroll	Personnel
SOMERS—Tolland County													
CONNECTICUT DEPARTMENT OF CORRECTION'S HOSPITAL, Box 100, Zip 06071; tel. 203/232-8182; Edward A. Blanchette MD, dir. (Nonreporting)	12	11	S		60	—	—	—	—	—	—	—	—
SOUTHINGTON—Hartford County													
⊞ BRADLEY MEMORIAL HOSPITAL, Meriden Ave., Zip 06489; tel. 203/621-3661; John F. Mullett, pres. **A**1a 9 10 **F**1 3 6 10 12 14 15 16 23 26 30 32 35 45 46 47	23	10	S		62	3071	49	79.0	0	0	13302	6846	286
STAFFORD SPRINGS—Tolland County													
⊞ JOHNSON MEMORIAL HOSPITAL, 230 Chestnut Hill Rd., P O Drawer 860, Zip 06076; tel. 203/684-4251; Alfred A. Lerz, pres. **A**1a 9 10 **F**1 3 6 10 12 14 15 16 23 26 34 35 45 46 47 52 53	23	10	S		78	2468	42	53.8	0	0	11684	6025	242
STAMFORD—Fairfield County													
⊞ ST. JOSEPH MEDICAL CENTER (Formerly St. Joseph Hospital), 128 Strawberry Hill Ave., Box 1222, Zip 06904; tel. 203/327-3500; Sr. Daniel Marie McCabe, pres. & chief exec. off. **A**1a 2 3 5 9 10 **F**1 3 6 9 10 11 12 14 15 16 20 21 23 24 25 26 30 33 34 35 36 40 41 44 45 46 49 52 53 54; **S**5615	21	10	S		200	5581	119	59.5	10	339	26888	14114	589
⊞ STAMFORD HOSPITAL, Shelburne Rd. & W. Broad St., P O Box 9317, Zip 06904; tel. 203/325-7000; Philip D. Cusano, pres. & chief exec. off. **A**1a 2 3 5 8 9 10 **F**1 3 5 6 7 8 9 10 11 12 14 15 16 20 21 23 24 25 26 27 28 29 30 32 33 34 35 36 37 38 40 41 42 43 44 45 46 47 49 51 52 53 54	23	10	S		289	10253	205	71.9	25	1536	52587	25481	929
TORRINGTON—Litchfield County													
⊞ CHARLOTTE HUNGERFORD HOSPITAL, 540 Litchfield St., Box 988, Zip 06790; tel. 203/496-6666; Robert J. Summa, pres. **A**1a 2 9 10 **F**1 3 6 7 8 10 11 12 14 15 16 20 23 24 26 27 28 29 30 31 32 33 34 35 36 40 41 43 44 45 46 49 52 53	23	10	S		188	7077	129	68.6	20	718	26163	14526	624
WALLINGFORD—New Haven County													
ARCHBOLD HOSPITAL, Choate Rosemary Hall, P O Box 788, Zip 06492; Leonard S. Krassner MD, dir. (Data for 225 days) **F**15 23 28 29 30 32 33 34 37 43 49	23	11	S		15	415	3	20.0	0	0	268	163	18
⊞ Δ GAYLORD HOSPITAL, Gaylord Farm Rd., Box 400, Zip 06492; tel. 203/269-3344; Curtland C. Brown Jr. MD, pres. **A**1a 7 9 10 **F**15 16 23 24 26 33 34 42 44 45 46 47 48	23	46	L		121	1066	110	90.9	0	0	15323	9019	391
★ MASONIC HOME AND HOSPITAL (Formerly Masonic Hospital), Masonic Ave., Box 70, Zip 06492; tel. 203/265-0931; Edgar G. Kilby, exec. dir. **A**9 10 **F**6 16 19 21 23 24 32 33 36 41 42 44	23	49	L	TF	538	173	498	93.0	0	0	15415	9152	521
				H	100	45	93	—	0	0	3853	2288	—
WATERBURY—New Haven County													
⊞ ST. MARY'S HOSPITAL, 56 Franklin St., Zip 06702; tel. 203/574-6000; Sr. Marquerite Waite, exec. dir. **A**1a 2 3 5 6 8 9 10 **F**1 2 3 5 6 7 8 9 10 11 12 14 15 16 20 23 24 26 27 28 30 32 33 34 35 36 38 40 44 45 46 49 53 54; **S**5615	21	10	S		301	13040	251	77.2	32	1488	65233	34168	1265
⊞ WATERBURY HOSPITAL, 64 Robbins St., Zip 06721; tel. 203/573-6000; John H. Tobin, pres. **A**1a 2 3 5 8 9 10 **F**1 3 5 6 7 8 9 10 11 12 14 15 16 20 21 23 27 28 29 30 32 33 35 36 37 38 40 44 45 46 52 53 54	23	10	S		273	10477	220	72.8	0	1073	64642	33225	1129
WEST HAVEN—New Haven County													
⊞ VETERANS ADMINISTRATION MEDICAL CENTER, W. Spring St., Zip 06516; tel. 203/932-5711; Albert M. Blecich, dir. (Total facility includes 90 beds in nursing home-type unit) **A**1a 3 5 8 **F**1 2 3 4 6 7 9 10 12 14 15 16 19 20 23 24 26 27 28 29 30 32 33 34 35 42 43 44 46 47 48 49 50 53 54	45	10	S	TF	731	10341	447	61.1	0	0	61237	35187	1237
				H	641	10306	363	—	0	0	58624	33418	1176
WESTPORT—Fairfield County													
⊞ HALL-BROOKE HOSPITAL, A DIVISION OF HALL-BROOKE FOUNDATION, 47 Long Lots Rd., Zip 06881; tel. 203/227-1251; Bennett Rosner MD, med. dir. **A**1b 9 10 **F**24 28 29 30 32 33 34 42 43 46 47 48	23	22	L		78	828	71	91.0	0	0	8885	5278	225
WILLIMANTIC—Windham County													
⊞ WINDHAM COMMUNITY MEMORIAL HOSPITAL, 112 Mansfield Ave., Zip 06226; tel. 203/423-9201; John E. Peck, adm. **A**1a 9 10 **F**1 2 3 6 10 12 14 15 16 21 23 24 25 26 30 32 33 34 35 36 38 40 41 44 45 46 47 49 52 53 54	23	10	S		175	4885	81	46.3	20	417	23633	12153	538
WINSTED—Litchfield County													
⊞ WINSTED MEMORIAL HOSPITAL, 115 Spencer St., P O Box 749, Zip 06098; tel. 203/379-3351; Paul E. Graff, pres. (Nonreporting) **A**1a 9 10	23	10	S		49	—	—	—	—	—	—	—	—

Hospital, Address, Telephone, Administrator, Approval and Facility Codes, Multihospital System Code

- ★ American Hospital Association (AHA) membership
- □ Joint Commission on Accreditation of Hospitals (JCAH) accreditation
- \+ American Osteopathic Hospital Association (AOHA) membership
- ○ American Osteopathic Association (AOA) accreditation
- Δ Commission on Accreditation of Rehabilitation Facilities (CARF) accreditation

Control codes 61, 63, 64, 71, 72 and 73 indicate hospitals listed by AOHA, but not registered by AHA. For definition of numerical codes, see page A2

Delaware

Hospital, Address, Telephone, Administrator, Approval and Facility Codes, Multihospital System Code	Classification Codes				Inpatient Data				Newborn Data		Expense (thousands of dollars)		
	Control	Service	Stay	Facilities	Beds	Admissions	Census	Occupancy (percent)	Bassinets	Births	Total	Payroll	Personnel
DOVER—Kent County													
★□ KENT GENERAL HOSPITAL, 640 S. State St., Zip 19901; tel. 302/674-7000; Dennis E. Klima, pres. **A**1a 2 9 10 **F**1 3 6 10 12 14 15 16 20 23 27 28 30 33 35 36 40 41 44 45 46 47 52 53	23	10	S		174	7653	133	76.4	21	1147	28202	14116	755
U. S. AIR FORCE HOSPITAL DOVER, See Dover Air Force Base													
DOVER AIR FORCE BASE—Kent County													
U. S. AIR FORCE HOSPITAL DOVER, Zip 19902; tel. 302/735-2525; Maj. Richard T. Chamberlain, adm. **F**1 6 14 15 23 28 30 32 33 34 35 37 40 46 47	41	10	S		30	2078	22	62.9	14	463	—	—	313
LEWES—Sussex County													
★□ BEEBE HOSPITAL OF SUSSEX COUNTY, 424 Savannah Rd., Zip 19958; tel. 302/645-3300; Gilbert L. Cook, adm. **A**1a 2 6 9 10 **F**1 2 3 6 10 12 14 15 16 23 27 28 29 30 32 33 35 36 37 40 41 45 46 47 49 50 52 53	23	10	S		124	5018	102	82.3	20	361	17238	9008	513
MILFORD—Sussex County													
★□ MILFORD MEMORIAL HOSPITAL, Clarke Ave., Box 199, Zip 19963; tel. 302/422-3311; L. Glenn Davis, adm. **A**1a 9 10 **F**1 3 6 10 11 12 14 15 16 21 23 26 33 35 40 41 45 46 52 53	23	10	S		139	6595	99	53.5	12	812	17782	8202	485
NEW CASTLE—New Castle County													
□ DELAWARE STATE HOSPITAL, Dupont Hwy., Zip 19720; tel. 302/421-6011; Robert Davidson, dir. **A**1a 3 5 9 10 **F**19 23 24 32 33 42 46	12	22	L		468	1943	491	97.2	0	0	23226	12062	—
SEAFORD—Sussex County													
★□ NANTICOKE MEMORIAL HOSPITAL, 801 Middleford Rd., Zip 19973; tel. 302/629-6611; Edward H. Hancock, pres. **A**1a 9 10 **F**1 3 5 6 10 12 14 15 16 20 21 23 26 35 36 37 40 41 44 45 46 52 53	23	10	S		119	5414	79	66.4	13	553	19213	6146	384
SMYRNA—Kent County													
DELAWARE HOSPITAL FOR THE CHRONICALLY ILL, Zip 19977; tel. 302/653-8556; Arnold Budin, actg. dir. **F**15 19 23 42 44 45 46 47 50	12	48	L		536	262	521	93.5	0	0	16921	10416	696
WILMINGTON—New Castle County													
★□ ALFRED I. DUPONT INSTITUTE, 1600 Rockland Rd., Box 269, Zip 19899; tel. 302/651-4000; Thomas P. Ferry, adm. **A**1a 3 5 9 **F**1 6 10 12 14 16 23 24 25 26 28 32 33 34 38 41 42 44 45 46 52 53	23	57	S		97	1575	56	57.7	0	0	36524	13757	619
CHRISTIANA HOSPITAL, See Wilmington Medical Center													
EUGENE DUPONT MEMORIAL HOSPITAL, See Wilmington Medical Center													
★□ MEDICAL CENTER OF DELAWARE (Includes Christiana Hospital; Eugene Dupont Memorial Hospital; Wilmington Hospital), 501 W. 14th St., Box 1668, Zip 19899; tel. 302/428-1212; Allen L. Johnson, pres. & chief oper. off. **A**1a 2 3 8 9 10 **F**1 2 3 4 5 6 7 8 9 10 11 12 14 15 16 19 23 24 25 26 27 29 30 32 33 34 35 36 37 38 40 41 43 44 45 46 47 51 52 53 54	23	10	S		1090	38201	739	67.8	57	5975	183403	89334	4113
★ ○ + RIVERSIDE HOSPITAL, 700 Lea Blvd., Box 845, Zip 19899; tel. 302/764-6120; Norval R. Copeland, exec. dir. **A**9 10 11 **F**1 3 6 10 12 15 16 20 23 26 30 34 35 44 45 46 47 53	23	10	S		75	2330	42	56.0	0	1	11595	5849	302
★□ ROCKFORD CENTER, 1605 N. Broom St., Zip 19806; tel. 302/652-3892; Joseph F. Barszczewski, adm. **A**1a 9 10 **F**32 33 42; **S**1755	33	22	S		58	713	45	77.6	0	0	—	—	95
★□ ST. FRANCIS HOSPITAL, Seventh & Clayton Sts., Zip 19805; tel. 302/421-4100; Paul C. King Jr., pres. & chief exec. off. **A**1a 2 3 5 9 10 **F**1 3 6 12 14 15 16 23 24 26 27 30 32 33 34 35 36 40 41 42 45 46 50 52 53; **S**5325	21	10	S		331	12206	236	71.3	12	740	48529	22800	1045
★□ VETERANS ADMINISTRATION MEDICAL CENTER, 1601 Kirkwood Hwy., Zip 19805; tel. 302/994-2511; Wilfred E. Kingsley, dir. (Total facility includes 60 beds in nursing home-type unit) **A**1a 3 5 **F**1 3 6 9 10 12 14 15 16 19 23 24 26 28 30 31 32 33 34 42 44 45 46 47	45	10	S	TF	316	4598	213	61.2	0	0	33228	19568	644
				H	256	4475	156	—	0	0	—	—	617
WILMINGTON HOSPITAL, See Wilmington Medical Center													

Hospital, Address, Telephone, Administrator, Approval and Facility Codes, Multihospital System Code	Classification Codes				Inpatient Data				Newborn Data		Expense (thousands of dollars)		
★ American Hospital Association (AHA) membership ☐ Joint Commission on Accreditation of Hospitals (JCAH) accreditation + American Osteopathic Hospital Association (AOHA) membership ○ American Osteopathic Association (AOA) accreditation Δ Commission on Accreditation of Rehabilitation Facilities (CARF) accreditation Control codes 61, 63, 64, 71, 72 and 73 indicate hospitals listed by AOHA, but not registered by AHA. For definition of numerical codes, see page A2	Control	Service	Stay	Facilities	Beds	Admissions	Census	Occupancy (percent)	Bassinets	Births	Total	Payroll	Personnel

District of Columbia

Hospital	Control	Service	Stay	Facilities	Beds	Admissions	Census	Occupancy (percent)	Bassinets	Births	Total	Payroll	Personnel
WASHINGTON—													
★☐ CAPITOL HILL HOSPITAL, 700 Constitution Ave. N.E., Zip 20002; tel. 202/269-8000; William J. Haire, pres. & chief exec. off. **A**1a 9 10 **F**1 3 5 6 10 12 14 15 16 17 20 23 35 41 44 45 46 47 53; **S**6615	23	10	S		250	6831	175	70.0	0	0	38179	17108	701
★☐ CHILDREN'S HOSPITAL NATIONAL MEDICAL CENTER, 111 Michigan Ave. N.W., Zip 20010; tel. 202/745-5000; Donald Brown, pres. & chief exec. off. **A**1a 3 5 8 9 **F**1 2 3 4 5 6 12 13 14 15 16 20 22 23 24 26 27 28 30 32 33 34 35 37 38 41 43 44 45 46 47 51 52 53 54	23	49	S		279	9772	196	70.3	0	0	83097	40352	2330
★☐ COLUMBIA HOSPITAL FOR WOMEN MEDICAL CENTER, 2425 L St. N.W., Zip 20037; tel. 202/293-6500; G. Patrick Kane, pres. **A**1a 3 5 9 10 **F**1 3 6 12 14 15 16 34 36 37 38 40 41 43 45 46 47 51; **S**6615	23	44	S		189	16467	133	70.4	48	4723	35077	16948	694
★☐ DISTRICT OF COLUMBIA GENERAL HOSPITAL, 19th St. & Massachusetts Ave. S.E., Zip 20003; tel. 202/675-5404; John Dandridge Jr., chief exec. off. **A**1a 3 5 8 9 10 **F**1 2 3 5 6 7 8 9 10 11 12 14 15 16 20 23 24 25 26 33 34 35 36 37 40 44 46 47 48 50 51 52 53 54	14	10	S		440	13860	315	73.1	25	1807	100587	57567	2031
★☐ GEORGE WASHINGTON UNIVERSITY HOSPITAL, 901 23rd St. N.W., Zip 20037; tel. 202/676-6000; Michael M. Barch, adm. **A**1a 3 5 8 9 10 **F**1 2 3 4 5 6 7 8 9 10 11 12 13 14 15 16 20 23 24 25 26 27 28 29 30 32 33 34 35 36 37 38 40 42 44 45 47 49 53 54	23	10	S		511	16280	371	72.6	56	1396	124615	56928	2804
★☐ GEORGETOWN UNIVERSITY MEDICAL CENTER, 3800 Reservoir Rd. N.W., Zip 20007; tel. 202/625-7001; Charles M. O'Brien Jr., adm. **A**1a 2 3 5 8 9 10 **F**1 2 3 4 5 6 7 8 9 10 11 12 13 14 15 16 20 23 24 26 27 28 30 32 33 34 35 36 37 38 39 40 42 43 44 45 46 47 49 50 51 52 53 54	21	10	S		539	18059	407	75.5	24	1442	119381	56389	2387
★☐ GREATER SOUTHEAST COMMUNITY HOSPITAL, 1310 Southern Ave. S.E., Zip 20032; tel. 202/574-6611; Thomas W. Chapman, pres. **A**1a 2 3 5 9 10 **F**1 3 5 6 10 11 12 15 16 20 23 24 25 26 27 28 30 32 33 35 36 40 41 42 44 45 46 47 50 51 52 53	23	10	S		460	16185	375	81.5	34	1806	80067	40379	1305
★☐ HADLEY MEMORIAL HOSPITAL, 4601 Martin Luther King Jr Ave. S.W., Zip 20032; tel. 202/574-5700; Albert Dudley, pres. **A**1a 9 10 **F**1 3 6 10 14 15 16 23 26 35 37 53; **S**9355	21	10	S		76	2232	55	76.4	0	0	14434	6183	261
★☐ HOSPITAL FOR SICK CHILDREN, 1731 Bunker Hill Rd. N.E., Zip 20017; tel. 202/832-4400; Constance U. Battle MD, med. dir. & chief exec. off. **A**1a 9 **F**16 19 23 24 33 42 44	23	56	L		80	99	70	87.5	0	0	8272	4841	242
★☐ HOWARD UNIVERSITY HOSPITAL, 2041 Georgia Ave. N.W., Zip 20060; tel. 202/745-6100; Haynes Rice, dir. **A**1a 2 3 5 8 9 10 **F**1 3 4 5 6 7 8 9 10 11 12 13 14 16 20 23 24 27 28 30 32 33 34 35 36 38 40 42 44 45 46 47 52 53 54	23	10	S		515	13133	378	73.7	35	1121	121774	63475	2558
MALCOLM GROW U. S. AIR FORCE MEDICAL CENTER, See Camp Springs, Md.													
★☐ PROVIDENCE HOSPITAL, 1150 Varnum St. N.E., Zip 20017; tel. 202/269-7000; Sr. Catherine Norton, pres. **A**1a 3 5 9 10 **F**1 3 6 10 11 12 14 15 16 20 23 24 26 27 30 34 35 36 37 40 41 42 44 45 46 47 48 49 53; **S**1885	21	10	S		342	10879	272	79.5	26	1440	56535	26249	1242
☐ PSYCHIATRIC INSTITUTE OF WASHINGTON, 4460 McArthur Blvd. N.W., Zip 20007; tel. 202/944-3400; Howard Hoffman MD, chief exec. off. **A**1a 9 10 **F**3 19 24 28 29 30 32 33 42 46 47 48 49; **S**0825	33	22	L		201	1716	145	72.1	0	0	—	—	333
★☐ SAINT ELIZABETHS HOSPITAL, 2700 Martin Luther King Jr Ave. S.E., Zip 20032; tel. 202/373-7166; William G. Prescott MD, supt. (Nonreporting) **A**1b 3 5 10	44	22	L		1633	—	—	—	—	—	—	—	—
★☐ SIBLEY MEMORIAL HOSPITAL, 5255 Loughboro Rd. N.W., Zip 20016; tel. 202/537-4000; Robert L. Sloan, chief exec. off. **A**1a 3 5 9 10 **F**1 3 6 7 8 9 10 12 14 15 16 19 20 23 24 26 27 30 32 34 35 36 37 40 42 45 46 50 52 53	23	10	S		362	13551	262	72.4	24	1645	55631	27116	1103
★☐ VETERANS ADMINISTRATION MEDICAL CENTER, 50 Irving St. N.W., Zip 20422; tel. 202/745-8000; Joseph P. Travers, dir. (Total facility includes 116 beds in nursing home-type unit) **A**1a 2 3 5 8 **F**1 3 4 6 7 8 10 11 12 14 15 16 19 20 23 24 26 27 28 32 33 34 35 41 42 44 45 46 47 48 49 50 53 54	45	10	S	TF	718	16310	590	87.0	0	0	90194	60855	1829
				H	602	16191	520	—	0	0	—	—	—
★☐ WALTER REED ARMY MEDICAL CENTER, Zip 20307; tel. 202/576-3501; Maj. Gen. Lewis A. Mologne, Cmdg. gen. **A**1a 2 3 5 **F**1 2 3 4 6 7 8 9 10 11 12 13 14 15 16 17 20 23 24 25 26 27 28 30 32 33 34 35 36 37 38 40 42 44 45 46 47 49 51 52 53 54	42	10	S		889	24782	698	77.1	20	1302	245800	175900	5439
★☐ WASHINGTON HOSPITAL CENTER, 110 Irving St. N.W., Zip 20010; tel. 202/541-0500; Dunlop Ecker, pres. **A**1a 2 3 5 8 9 10 **F**1 2 3 4 5 6 7 8 9 10 11 12 13 14 15 16 17 20 22 23 24 25 26 27 28 30 32 33 34 35 36 37 40 42 44 45 46 47 48 50 51 53 54; **S**6615	23	10	S		784	30497	702	89.5	37	3150	202070	99851	3726

Hospital, Address, Telephone, Administrator, Approval and Facility Codes, Multihospital System Code	Classification Codes				Inpatient Data				Newborn Data		Expense (thousands of dollars)		
★ American Hospital Association (AHA) membership □ Joint Commission on Accreditation of Hospitals (JCAH) accreditation + American Osteopathic Hospital Association (AOHA) membership ○ American Osteopathic Association (AOA) accreditation Δ Commission on Accreditation of Rehabilitation Facilities (CARF) accreditation Control codes 61, 63, 64, 71, 72 and 73 indicate hospitals listed by AOHA, but not registered by AHA. For definition of numerical codes, see page A2	Control	Service	Stay	Facilities	Beds	Admissions	Census	Occupancy (percent)	Bassinets	Births	Total	Payroll	Personnel

Florida

Hospital	Control	Service	Stay	Facilities	Beds	Admissions	Census	Occupancy (percent)	Bassinets	Births	Total	Payroll	Personnel
ALTAMONTE SPRINGS—Seminole County													
FLORIDA HOSPITAL-ALTAMONTE, See Florida Hospital Medical Center, Orlando													
APALACHICOLA—Franklin County													
GEORGE E. WEEMS MEMORIAL HOSPITAL, Washington Square, Zip 32320; tel. 904/653-8853; Henry D. Shiver, adm. (Nonreporting) **A**9; **S**1935	13	10	S		29	—	—	—	—	—	—	—	—
APOPKA—Orange County													
FLORIDA HOSPITAL-APOPKA, See Florida Hospital Medical Center, Orlando													
ARCADIA—De Soto County													
⊞ DESOTO MEMORIAL HOSPITAL, P O Box 2180, Zip 33821; tel. 813/494-3535; Richard M. Irwin Jr., pres. **A**1a 9 10 **F**1 3 6 14 15 16 23 24 35 36 40 43 44 45 52 53	23	10	S		69	2626	33	47.8	14	465	6554	2842	180
G. PIERCE WOOD MEMORIAL HOSPITAL, State Hwy. 31, Rte. 1, Box 189, Zip 33821; tel. 813/494-3323; Richard L. Insley, adm. **A**10 **F**15 19 23 24 30 32 33 35 37 42 44 46 50	12	22	L		925	904	814	81.9	0	0	24609	15258	1098
ATLANTIS—Palm Beach County													
⊞ JOHN F. KENNEDY MEMORIAL HOSPITAL, 4800 S. Congress Ave., Zip 33462; Mailing Address Box 1489, Lake Worth, Zip 33460; tel. 305/965-7300; James K. Johnson, adm. (Nonreporting) **A**1a 10; **S**6525	23	10	S		369	—	—	—	—	—	—	—	—
AUBURNDALE—Polk County													
★ MORROW MEMORIAL HOSPITAL, 105 Ariana Blvd., Box 277, Zip 33823; tel. 813/967-8511; Laurie McCraney, adm. (Nonreporting) **A**9 10; **S**1615	21	10	S		40	—	—	—	—	—	—	—	—
AVON PARK—Highlands County													
□ FLORIDA ALCOHOLISM TREATMENT CENTER, 100 W. College Dr., Zip 33825; tel. 813/453-3151; Glenn Rohrer PhD, supt. **A**1b 9 **F**24 33 42 46	12	82	S		58	796	55	94.8	0	0	2053	1276	78
⊞ WALKER MEMORIAL HOSPITAL, U. S. Hwy. 27 N., P O Box 1200, Zip 33825; tel. 813/453-7511; William C. Sager, pres. **A**1a 9 10 **F**1 3 6 12 14 15 16 23 35 36 40 45 46 47 53; **S**4165	21	10	S		122	5683	81	66.4	11	453	15312	7309	353
BARTOW—Polk County													
⊞ BARTOW MEMORIAL HOSPITAL, 1239 E. Main St., Box 1050, Zip 33830; tel. 813/533-8111; Stephen D. Mason, adm. **A**1a 9 10 **F**1 2 6 10 14 16 23 29 34 35 36 37 40 43 45 53	23	10	S		56	1631	19	33.9	10	258	5297	2138	127
⊞ POLK GENERAL HOSPITAL (Includes Rohr Nursing Home), 2010 E. Georgia St., Box 816, Zip 33830; tel. 813/533-1111; Lisle T. Lenny, adm. (Total facility includes 60 beds in nursing home-type unit) **A**1a 9 10 **F**1 3 6 10 12 14 15 19 23 27 30 32 33 34 35 40 44 45 52	13	10	S	TF	220	6230	151	68.6	24	2279	17112	9960	536
				H	160	6209	92	—	24	2279	16128	9396	494
BAY PINES—Pinellas County													
⊞ VETERANS ADMINISTRATION MEDICAL CENTER, Zip 33504; tel. 813/398-6661; Richard F. McElligott, dir. (Nonreporting) **A**1a	45	10	S		1088	—	—	—	—	—	—	—	—
BELLE GLADE—Palm Beach County													
⊞ GLADES GENERAL HOSPITAL, 1201 S. Main St., Box 9900, Zip 33430; tel. 305/996-6571; Patrick Lennon, adm. **A**1a 9 10 **F**1 3 6 15 16 34 35 37 45 52	16	10	S		64	2305	32	50.0	0	0	10299	3845	214
BLOUNTSTOWN—Calhoun County													
⊞ CALHOUN GENERAL HOSPITAL (Formerly Calhoun Hospital), 424 Burns Ave., Zip 32424; tel. 904/674-5411; Floyd Miller, chief oper. off. **A**1a 9 10 **F**1 6 12 15 16 34 37 38 40 45 52	23	10	S		36	756	8	22.2	10	131	1925	686	42
BOCA RATON—Palm Beach County													
⊞ BOCA RATON COMMUNITY HOSPITAL, 800 Meadows Rd., Zip 33432; tel. 305/395-7100; Stephen J. Ladika, pres. **A**1a 2 9 10 **F**1 2 3 6 7 8 9 10 11 12 14 15 16 20 23 24 26 30 35 41 43 44 45 46 47 52 53	23	10	S		390	14936	302	77.4	0	0	62843	29911	1304
BONIFAY—Holmes County													
□ DOCTORS MEMORIAL HOSPITAL, 401 E. Byrd Ave., Box 188, Zip 32425; tel. 904/547-4271; Robert R. Reddish, adm. (Nonreporting) **A**1a 9 10; **S**5895	16	10	S		34	—	—	—	—	—	—	—	—
BOYNTON BEACH—Palm Beach County													
⊞ BETHESDA MEMORIAL HOSPITAL, 2815 S. Seacrest Blvd., Zip 33435; tel. 305/737-7733; Russell T. Clayton, pres. **A**1a 9 10 **F**1 2 3 6 7 8 9 10 11 12 14 15 16 20 23 24 26 34 35 36 37 38 40 41 42 43 44 45 46 47 52	23	10	S		350	11109	171	48.9	33	2806	44614	18771	917
BRADENTON—Manatee County													
⊞ Δ L. W. BLAKE MEMORIAL HOSPITAL, 2020 59th St. W., Zip 33529; Mailing Address P O Box 25004, Zip 33506; tel. 813/792-6611; Lindell W. Orr, adm. **A**1a 7 9 10 **F**1 3 6 7 8 9 10 11 12 15 16 20 23 24 25 26 35 41 43 44 45 53; **S**1755	33	10	S		383	11102	231	60.3	0	0	49555	19205	1032
⊞ MANATEE MEMORIAL HOSPITAL, 206 Second St. E., Zip 33508; tel. 813/746-5111; Gerald L. Wissink, chief exec. off. (Nonreporting) **A**1a 2 9 10; **S**8810	23	10	S		512	—	—	—	—	—	—	—	—
BRANDON—Hillsborough County													
⊞ HUMANA HOSPITAL -BRANDON, 119 Oakfield Dr., Zip 33511; tel. 813/681-5551; William R. Heburn, exec. dir. **A**1a 9 10 **F**1 2 3 5 6 9 10 12 15 16 17 20 23 24 26 34 35 36 37 38 40 44 45 47 52 53; **S**1235	33	10	S		220	10425	161	73.2	19	1396	31996	11439	551
BROOKSVILLE—Hernando County													
⊞ LYKES MEMORIAL HOSPITAL, 100 S. State Rd. 700, Box 37, Zip 34298; tel. 904/796-5111; Alan Chapman, exec. dir. (Nonreporting) **A**1a 9 10	23	10	S		166	—	—	—	—	—	—	—	—
BUNNELL—Flagler County													
⊞ COASTAL COMMUNITIES HOSPITAL, Star Rte. 1, Box 2, Zip 32010; tel. 904/437-2211; Douglas W. Parker, adm. **A**1a 9 10 **F**1 3 6 10 14 15 16 23 34 35 45 46; **S**0335	33	10	S		81	1198	19	23.5	0	0	—	—	111
BUSHNELL—Sumter County													
□ KOALA CENTER, State Rd. 476 W., P O Box 250, Zip 33513; tel. 904/793-6000; Susan A. Yates, exec. dir. (Nonreporting) **A**1a 9	33	82	L		160	—	—	—	—	—	—	—	—
CAPE CORAL—Lee County													
⊞ CAPE CORAL HOSPITAL, 636 Del Prado Blvd., Zip 33904; tel. 813/574-2323; J. Michael Ward, pres. **A**1a 9 10 **F**1 3 6 9 10 12 14 15 16 20 23 24 34 35 43 45 46 47	23	10	S		174	5787	108	62.1	0	0	29330	11105	725
CHATTAHOOCHEE—Gadsden County													
FLORIDA STATE HOSPITAL, Box 156, Zip 32324; tel. 904/663-7536; Robert B. Williams, adm. (Total facility includes 225 beds in nursing home-type unit) **A**10 **F**16 19 23 24 33 34 35 42 44 46 50	12	22	L	TF	1349	899	1259	84.7	0	0	63133	39941	2752
				H	1124	554	1083	—	0	0	58418	36481	2493

★ American Hospital Association (AHA) membership
□ Joint Commission on Accreditation of Hospitals (JCAH) accreditation
+ American Osteopathic Hospital Association (AOHA) membership
○ American Osteopathic Association (AOA) accreditation
Δ Commission on Accreditation of Rehabilitation Facilities (CARF) accreditation
Control codes 61, 63, 64, 71, 72 and 73 indicate hospitals listed by AOHA, but not registered by AHA.
For definition of numerical codes, see page A2

Hospital, Address, Telephone, Administrator, Approval and Facility Codes, Multihospital System Code	Classification Codes				Inpatient Data				Newborn Data		Expense (thousands of dollars)		
	Control	Service	Stay	Facilities	Beds	Admissions	Census	Occupancy (percent)	Bassinets	Births	Total	Payroll	Personnel
CHIPLEY—Washington County													
★□ FLORIDA COMMUNITY HOSPITAL (Formerly Washington County Hospital), Hwy. 77 & 280, Box K, Zip 32428; tel. 904/638-1610; J. Glenn Brown Jr., adm. **A**1a 9 10 **F**1 3 5 6 10 14 15 16 23 34 35 45 47 52; **S**5895	33	10	S		45	1762	24	53.3	0	2	4424	1875	116
CITRA—Marion County													
★□ HCA GRANT CENTER HOSPITAL OF NORTH FLORIDA (Formerly Grant Center Hospital -Ocala), U. S. Hwy. 301, P O Box 100, Zip 32627; tel. 904/595-3500; James Laws, adm. **A**1b 9 10 **F**15 24 28 29 30 32 33 42 47; **S**1755	33	22	L		120	217	72	60.0	0	0	—	—	146
CLEARWATER—Pinellas County													
★□ AMI CLEARWATER COMMUNITY HOSPITAL (Formerly Clearwater Community Hospital), 1521 E. Druid Rd., Zip 33516; tel. 813/447-4571; Reynold Jennings, exec. dir. **A**1a 9 10 **F**1 3 6 12 14 15 16 23 24 34 35 44 45 53; **S**0125	33	10	S		120	5048	91	75.8	0	0	—	—	—
CLEARWATER COMMUNITY HOSPITAL, See AMI Clearwater Community Hospital													
★□ HORIZON HOSPITAL, 11300 U. S. 19 S., Zip 33546; tel. 813/541-2646; Tracy Thomas Payne, adm. & chief exec. off. **A**1a 9 10 **F**15 24 32 33 42 49 50	33	22	S		200	2190	130	65.0	0	0	14802	5966	275
★□ MORTON F. PLANT HOSPITAL, 323 Jeffords St., Box 210, Zip 33517; tel. 813/462-7000; Duane T. Houtz, pres. & chief exec. off. (Total facility includes 124 beds in nursing home-type unit) **A**1a 2 9 10 **F**1 2 3 4 6 7 8 9 10 11 12 15 16 19 20 23 24 26 27 30 32 33 34 35 36 40 41 42 43 44 45 47 50 51 52 53 54	23	10	S	TF	738	23314	608	76.5	25	2130	86706	42191	1964
				H	614	22713	492	—	25	2130	83390	40158	1850
CLERMONT—Lake County													
★□ SOUTH LAKE MEMORIAL HOSPITAL, 847 Eighth St., Zip 32711; tel. 904/394-4071; Steven A. Grimm, adm. & chief exec. off. (Nonreporting) **A**1a 9 10; **S**1755	16	10	S		68	—	—	—	—	—	—	—	—
CLEWISTON—Hendry County													
★□ HENDRY GENERAL HOSPITAL, 524 W. Sagamore St., Zip 33440; tel. 813/983-9121; Joseph C. Greene Jr., adm. (Nonreporting) **A**1a 9 10; **S**1775	16	10	S		66	—	—	—	—	—	—	—	—
COCOA BEACH—Brevard County													
★□ CAPE CANAVERAL HOSPITAL, State Rd. 520 Causeway, Box 69, Zip 32931; tel. 305/799-7111; Larry F. Garrison, pres. **A**1a 9 10 **F**1 3 5 6 9 10 12 14 15 16 17 20 21 23 26 29 30 32 33 34 35 36 38 40 41 43 44 45 46 47 50 53	23	10	S		150	5454	87	58.0	14	782	18925	7826	408
CORAL GABLES—Dade County													
★□ CORAL GABLES HOSPITAL, 3100 Douglas Rd., Zip 33134; tel. 305/445-8461; Anthony M. Degina Jr., adm. (Nonreporting) **A**1a 9 10; **S**6525	33	10	S		226	—	—	—	—	—	—	—	—
★□ DOCTORS' HOSPITAL, 5000 University Dr., P O Box 14-1739, Zip 33114; tel. 305/666-2111; William H. Comte, pres. (Nonreporting) **A**1a 9 10; **S**1435	23	10	S		260	—	—	—	—	—	—	—	—
□ NORTH GABLES HOSPITAL, 5190 S.W. Eighth St., Zip 33134; tel. 305/445-1364; William P. Rauschberg, adm. (Nonreporting) **A**1a 9 10; **S**0985	23	10	S		53	—	—	—	—	—	—	—	—
CRESTVIEW—Okaloosa County													
★□ HCA NORTH OKALOOSA MEDICAL CENTER (Formerly Crestview Community Hospital), 151 Redstone Ave. S.E., Zip 32536; tel. 904/682-9731; James E. Rogers, adm. **A**1a 9 10 **F**1 3 6 7 8 10 12 14 15 16 23 34 35 45 46 53; **S**1755	33	10	S		110	2908	52	47.3	0	0	10003	3430	183
CRYSTAL RIVER—Citrus County													
□ SEVEN RIVERS COMMUNITY HOSPITAL, 6201 N. Suncoast Blvd., Zip 32629; tel. 904/795-6560; Michael Heindel, adm. (Nonreporting) **A**1a 9 10; **S**3015	33	10	S		90	—	—	—	—	—	—	—	—
DADE CITY—Pasco County													
★□ HUMANA HOSPITAL -PASCO, 1550 Fort King Hwy., Zip 33525; tel. 904/567-6726; Sandra J. Jones, exec. dir. **A**1a 9 10 **F**1 3 6 12 14 16 23 26 35 36 40 45 46 47 53; **S**1235	33	10	S		120	3240	53	44.2	4	255	12737	4197	216
DAYTONA BEACH—Volusia County													
★□ HALIFAX HOSPITAL MEDICAL CENTER, 303 N. Clyde Morris Blvd., Zip 32014; Mailing Address Box 1990, Zip 32015; tel. 904/254-4000; Ron R. Rees, adm. **A**1a 2 3 5 9 10 **F**1 2 3 5 6 7 8 9 10 11 12 14 15 16 17 20 21 23 24 26 27 32 33 34 35 36 37 39 40 41 42 43 44 45 46 47 50 51 52 53 54	16	10	S		529	17633	344	65.0	24	2299	71447	29737	1773
★□ HUMANA HOSPITAL -DAYTONA BEACH, 400 N. Clyde Morris Blvd., Box 9000, Zip 32020; tel. 904/239-5000; William W. Ward, exec. dir. **A**1a 9 10 **F**1 3 10 12 14 15 16 17 20 23 24 26 27 28 30 33 35 37 38 42 44 45 47 48 49; **S**1235	33	10	S		214	4232	101	47.2	0	0	17775	7004	368
DE FUNIAK SPRINGS—Walton County													
□ VALLEY SPRINGS COMMUNITY HOSPITAL, 21 College Ave., Zip 32433; tel. 904/892-5171; Arthur D. Hatten Jr., adm. **A**1a 9 10 **F**1 3 10 14 16 34 35 45	23	10	S		50	1353	18	36.0	0	0	4229	1608	94
DE LAND—Volusia County													
★□ FISH MEMORIAL HOSPITAL AT DELAND, 245 E. New York Ave., Zip 32724; Mailing Address P O Box 167, Zip 32721; tel. 904/734-2323; Thomas C. Dandridge, adm. **A**1a 9 10 **F**1 3 6 12 14 15 16 23 24 26 32 34 35 44 45 47 53; **S**1755	31	10	S		71	3137	49	69.0	0	0	11586	4107	218
★□ WEST VOLUSIA MEMORIAL HOSPITAL, Stone & Plymouth Sts., Box 509, Zip 32720; tel. 904/734-3320; Lawrence A. Welch, adm. **A**1a 9 10 **F**1 3 6 9 10 12 14 15 16 17 23 24 27 30 34 35 36 40 41 44 45 52 53	16	10	S		162	5450	76	46.9	18	1089	20196	9577	475
DELRAY—Palm Beach County													
□ PINECREST REHABILITATION HOSPITAL AT DELRAY, 5360 Linton Blvd., Zip 33445; tel. 305/495-0400; Kenneth Esrig, adm. (Newly Registered) **A**1a 9 10	33	46	S		60	—	—	—	—	—	—	—	—
DELRAY BEACH—Palm Beach County													
□ DELRAY COMMUNITY HOSPITAL, 5352 Linton Blvd., Zip 33445; tel. 305/498-4440; John D. Bartlett, exec. dir. (Nonreporting) **A**1a 9 10; **S**3015	33	10	S		211	—	—	—	—	—	—	—	—
DUNEDIN—Pinellas County													
★□ MEASE HOSPITAL DUNEDIN (Formerly Mease Health Care), 833 Milwaukee Ave., Zip 33528; Mailing Address P O Box 760, Zip 34296; tel. 813/733-1111; Charles T. Frock, vice-pres. & adm. **A**1a 2 9 10 **F**1 2 3 6 9 10 11 12 14 15 16 20 23 24 26 27 30 32 35 36 40 44 45 46 47 52 53; **S**1335	23	10	S		199	9326	150	75.4	20	1630	40295	17579	858
EGLIN AIR FORCE BASE—Okaloosa County													
★□ U. S. AIR FORCE REGIONAL HOSPITAL, Boatner Rd., Zip 32542; tel. 904/885-3222; Col. Thomas F. Treat, adm. **A**1a 3 5 **F**1 3 6 12 14 15 23 24 27 28 30 33 34 35 37 40 42 46 47 48 49	41	10	S		155	8001	117	75.5	35	970	—	—	961
EUSTIS—Lake County													
★□ WATERMAN MEDICAL CENTER, 201 N. Eustis, Zip 32726; Mailing Address P O Box B, Zip 32727; tel. 904/589-3333; Carl J. Bender Jr., chief exec. off. (Total facility includes 29 beds in nursing home-type unit) **A**1a 9 10 **F**1 3 5 6 9 10 12 15 16 19 23 24 26 34 35 36 37 40 41 42 43 44 45 46 47 50 53	23	10	S	TF	182	10667	98	57.0	9	922	21774	8504	509
				H	153	6261	87	—	9	922	—	—	489
FERNANDINA BEACH—Nassau County													
★□ NASSAU GENERAL HOSPITAL, 1700 E. Lime St., Zip 32034; tel. 904/261-3627; Hugh R. White, adm. **A**1a 9 10 **F**1 3 6 10 14 16 23 35 36 40 45; **S**1755	13	10	S		54	1418	18	33.3	6	157	5634	2123	124
FORT LAUDERDALE—Broward County													
AMI NORTH RIDGE GENERAL HOSPITAL, See AMI North Ridge Medical Center													
★□ AMI NORTH RIDGE MEDICAL CENTER (Formerly AMI North Ridge General Hospital), 5757 N. Dixie Hwy., Zip 33334; tel. 305/776-6000; Don Steigman, exec. dir. **A**1a 9 10 **F**1 2 3 4 6 10 12 14 15 16 20 23 24 35 43 44 45 46 53 54; **S**0125	33	10	S		278	8448	179	64.4	0	0	—	—	—

Hospital, Address, Telephone, Administrator, Approval and Facility Codes, Multihospital System Code	Classification Codes			Facilities	Inpatient Data				Newborn Data		Expense (thousands of dollars)		
★ American Hospital Association (AHA) membership □ Joint Commission on Accreditation of Hospitals (JCAH) accreditation + American Osteopathic Hospital Association (AOHA) membership ○ American Osteopathic Association (AOA) accreditation Δ Commission on Accreditation of Rehabilitation Facilities (CARF) accreditation Control codes 61, 63, 64, 71, 72 and 73 indicate hospitals listed by AOHA, but not registered by AHA. For definition of numerical codes, see page A2	Control	Service	Stay	Facilities	Beds	Admissions	Census	Occupancy (percent)	Bassinets	Births	Total	Payroll	Personnel
⊠ BROWARD GENERAL MEDICAL CENTER, 1600 S. Andrews Ave., Zip 33316; tel. 305/355-4400; Richard J. Stull II, adm. **A**1a 2 3 9 10 **F**1 2 3 4 6 7 8 9 10 11 12 14 16 23 24 26 27 30 34 35 37 40 42 44 45 46 47 51 52 54; **S**3115	16	10	S		681	25906	536	78.7	68	5720	109523	51752	2180
⊠ CORAL RIDGE PSYCHIATRIC HOSPITAL, 4545 N. Federal Hwy., Zip 33308; tel. 305/771-2711; Michael J. Held, adm. **A**1b 9 **F**15 24 28 29 31 32 33 34 42 48 49	31	22	L		86	305	52	60.5	0	0	3815	2150	126
□ CPC FORT LAUDERDALE HOSPITAL (Formerly Fort Lauderdale Hospital), 1601 E. Las Olas Blvd., Zip 33301; tel. 305/463-4321; Robert Heyman, adm. **A**1b 9 10 **F**15 29 32 33 42 48; **S**0785	33	22	S		100	989	53	53.0	0	0	5000	2500	97
⊠ FLORIDA MEDICAL CENTER HOSPITAL, 5000 W. Oakland Park Blvd., Zip 33313; tel. 305/735-6000; Edward A. Dauer MD, pres. **A**1a 9 10 **F**1 2 3 4 6 7 10 12 14 16 20 23 24 27 34 35 42 45 46 47 53 54	33	10	S		459	11129	267	58.2	0	0	—	—	1148
FORT LAUDERDALE HOSPITAL, See CPC Fort Lauderdale Hospital													
⊠ HCA NORTH BEACH HOSPITAL (Formerly North Beach Community Hospital), 2835 N. Ocean Blvd., Zip 33308; tel. 305/565-3381; Lenore D. Robins, adm. (Nonreporting) **A**1a 9 10; **S**1755	33	10	S		153	—	—	—	—	—	—	—	—
⊠ HOLY CROSS HOSPITAL, 4725 N. Federal Hwy., Zip 33308; Mailing Address Box 23460, Zip 33307; tel. 305/771-8000; Sr. M. Mercy McGrady, exec. vice-pres. **A**1a 9 10 **F**1 2 3 4 6 7 8 9 10 11 12 14 15 16 20 21 23 24 25 26 30 32 33 34 35 40 42 44 45 46 47 51 52 53; **S**3595	21	10	S		360	14718	296	80.7	26	1446	72777	31275	1483
⊠ IMPERIAL POINT MEDICAL CENTER, 6401 N. Federal Hwy., Zip 33308; tel. 305/776-8500; Thomas J. Corder, adm. **A**1a 9 10 **F**1 3 6 10 11 12 14 15 16 21 23 24 26 27 30 32 33 34 35 42 44 45 46 47 53; **S**3115	16	10	S		204	5426	129	63.2	0	0	28418	12977	546
LAS OLAS COMMUNITY HOSPITAL, 1516 E. Las Olas Blvd., Zip 33301; Mailing Address Box 030400, Zip 33303; tel. 305/764-8900; Robert D. Kerley, adm. **A**9 10 **F**1 3 6 12 14 16 23 33 43 45 53; **S**0435	33	10	S		64	1430	28	43.8	0	0	6722	2366	125
NORTH BEACH COMMUNITY HOSPITAL, See HCA North Beach Hospital													
FORT MYERS—Lee County													
⊠ CHARTER GLADE HOSPITAL, 3550 Colonial Blvd., P O Box 06120, Zip 33906; tel. 813/939-0403; Stanley G. Hilliard, adm. (Nonreporting) **A**1a b 9 10; **S**0695	33	22	S		104	—	—	—	—	—	—	—	—
FORT MYERS COMMUNITY HOSPITAL, See Southwest Florida Regional Medical Center													
⊠ LEE MEMORIAL HOSPITAL, 2776 Cleveland Ave., Drawer 2218, Zip 33902; tel. 813/332-1111; James R. Nathan, pres. (Nonreporting) **A**1a 9 10	16	10	S		457	—	—	—	—	—	—	—	—
□ SOUTHWEST FLORIDA REGIONAL MEDICAL CENTER (Formerly Fort Myers Community Hospital), 3785 Evans Ave., Box 7146, Zip 33901; tel. 813/939-1147; Herbert F. Dorsett, pres. (Nonreporting) **A**1a 9 10; **S**1935	33	10	S		400	—	—	—	—	—	—	—	—
FORT PIERCE—St. Lucie County													
⊠ HARBOUR SHORES HOSPITAL OF LAWNWOOD, 1860 N. Lawnwood Circle, P O Box 1540, Zip 33454; tel. 305/466-1500; Frederick L. Stevens Jr. PhD, adm. **A**1b **F**15 23 24 30 32 33 42 50; **S**1755	33	22	S		60	490	33	55.0	0	0	3547	1425	91
INDIAN RIVER COMMUNITY MENTAL HEALTH CENTER, 800 Ave. H, Zip 33450; tel. 305/464-8111; Richard L. Mills, exec. dir. (Nonreporting) **A**9	23	22	S		15	—	—	—	—	—	—	—	—
⊠ LAWNWOOD REGIONAL MEDICAL CENTER, 1700 S. 23rd St., Zip 33450; Mailing Address Box 188, Zip 33454; tel. 305/461-4000; Nicholas T. Carbone, adm. **A**1a 9 10 **F**1 3 5 6 7 8 10 11 12 16 20 23 26 34 35 36 40 45 46 47 52 53; **S**1755	33	10	S		225	10014	173	76.9	22	1753	—	—	687
FORT WALTON BEACH—Okaloosa County													
⊠ HUMANA HOSPITAL-FORT WALTON BEACH, 1000 Mar-Walt Dr., Zip 32548; tel. 904/862-1111; J. Michael Mastej, exec. dir. **A**1a 9 10 **F**1 2 3 5 6 10 12 14 15 16 20 23 24 27 33 34 35 36 37 40 42 44 45 52 53 54; **S**1235	33	10	S		236	8971	146	61.9	22	1122	30205	9583	558
GAINESVILLE—Alachua County													
⊠ ALACHUA GENERAL HOSPITAL, 801 S.W. Second Ave., P O Box Agh, Zip 32602; tel. 904/372-4321; Wassie Griffin, chief oper. off. **A**1a 3 5 9 10 **F**1 3 4 5 6 9 10 12 14 15 16 20 21 23 24 26 27 28 29 30 32 33 34 35 36 40 41 42 43 44 45 46 47 52 53 54; **S**7895	23	10	S		415	13877	223	53.7	32	2295	45569	17401	768
⊠ HCA NORTH FLORIDA REGIONAL MEDICAL CENTER (Formerly North Florida Regional Hospital), State Rd. 26 at I-75, Box Nfr, Zip 32602; tel. 904/377-8511; Eugene C. Fleming, adm. **A**1a 9 10 **F**1 3 4 6 10 12 14 15 16 20 23 24 26 34 35 44 46 53 54; **S**1755	33	10	S		247	11333	193	76.6	0	0	40479	13664	656
NORTH FLORIDA REGIONAL HOSPITAL, See HCA North Florida Regional Medical Center													
⊠ SHANDS HOSPITAL AT THE UNIVERSITY OF FLORIDA, 1600 Archer Rd., Zip 32610; tel. 904/395-0111; John E. Ives, exec. vice-pres. **A**1a 2 3 5 8 9 10 **F**1 2 3 4 5 6 7 8 9 10 11 12 13 14 15 16 17 20 22 23 24 27 30 35 36 39 40 42 44 45 46 47 51 52 53 54	23	10	S		464	19290	396	85.3	20	2944	124799	50148	2991
⊠ VETERANS ADMINISTRATION MEDICAL CENTER, Archer Rd., Zip 32602; tel. 904/376-1611; Malcom Randall, dir. (Total facility includes 120 beds in nursing home-type unit) **A**1a3 5 8 **F**1 3 4 6 10 12 14 15 16 19 20 23 24 26 27 28 29 30 32 33 34 41 42 44 46 47 48 49 50 53 54	45	10	S	TF	598	12056	480	80.3	0	0	75273	37503	1439
				H	478	11954	366	—	0	0	71607	34832	1321
GRACEVILLE—Jackson County													
★ CAMPBELLTON GRACEVILLE HOSPITAL, 1305 College Dr., Zip 32440; tel. 904/263-4431; Douglas J. Hammond, adm. **A**9 10 **F**10 14 15 16 34 35 45 46 50 52; **S**1935	33	10	S		50	944	13	26.0	0	5	1251	—	45
GREEN COVE SPRINGS—Clay County													
⊠ CLAY MEMORIAL HOSPITAL, Oak & Green Sts., Box 808, Zip 32043; tel. 904/284-3072; Thomas Lafferty, adm. (Nonreporting) **A**1a 9 10; **S**2715	16	10	S		60	—	—	—	—	—	—	—	—
GULF BREEZE—Santa Rosa County													
⊠ GULF BREEZE HOSPITAL, 1110 Gulf Breeze Pkwy., P O Box 159, Zip 32561; tel. 904/934-2000; Richard C. Fulford, adm. **A**1a 9 10 **F**1 3 6 10 14 15 16 23 24 34 35 44 45 46 47 53; **S**0185	23	10	S		29	903	13	44.8	0	0	6378	1657	102
⊠ THE FRIARY, 4400 Hickory Shores Blvd., Zip 32561; tel. 904/932-9375; Gayle Piret, exec. dir. **A**1b **F**15 19 26 33 42 46 47 49	33	82	S		24	153	11	50.0	0	0	—	—	34
HAINES CITY—Polk County													
⊠ HEART OF FLORIDA HOSPITAL, Tenth St. & Wood Ave., Box 67, Zip 33844; tel. 813/422-4971; Mary T. Erde, adm. (Nonreporting) **A**1a 9 10; **S**1615	23	10	S		51	—	—	—	—	—	—	—	—
HIALEAH—Dade County													
⊠ AMI PALMETTO GENERAL HOSPITAL (Formerly Palmetto General Hospital), 2001 W. 68th St., Zip 33016; tel. 305/823-5000; Edward Tudanger, exec. dir. **A**1a 9 10 **F**1 2 3 6 10 12 14 15 16 23 24 26 27 33 35 45 46 47 53; **S**0125	33	10	S		360	9720	172	47.8	0	0	51990	16382	820
⊠ HIALEAH HOSPITAL, 651 E. 25th St., Zip 33013; tel. 305/693-6100; Terry M. Carson, pres. **A**1a 9 10 **F**1 2 3 6 10 12 14 15 16 20 23 24 29 30 32 34 35 36 40 41 42 44 45 46 51 52 53	23	10	S		411	10684	200	48.7	35	2198	53776	24179	1082
⊠ PALM SPRINGS GENERAL HOSPITAL, 1475 W. 49th St., Box 2804, Zip 33012; tel. 305/558-2500; Manuel Fernandez, exec. vice-pres. (Nonreporting) **A**1a 9 10	33	10	S		250	—	—	—	—	—	—	—	—
PALMETTO GENERAL HOSPITAL, See AMI Palmetto General Hospital													

Hospital, Address, Telephone, Administrator, Approval and Facility Codes, Multihospital System Code	Classification Codes: Control	Service	Stay	Facilities	Inpatient Data: Beds	Admissions	Census	Occupancy (percent)	Newborn Data: Bassinets	Births	Expense (thousands of dollars): Total	Payroll	Personnel
★ American Hospital Association (AHA) membership □ Joint Commission on Accreditation of Hospitals (JCAH) accreditation + American Osteopathic Hospital Association (AOHA) membership ○ American Osteopathic Association (AOA) accreditation Δ Commission on Accreditation of Rehabilitation Facilities (CARF) accreditation Control codes 61, 63, 64, 71, 72 and 73 indicate hospitals listed by AOHA, but not registered by AHA. For definition of numerical codes, see page A2													
HOLLY HILL—Volusia County													
○ + UNIVERSITY HOSPITAL (Formerly Daytona Beach General Hospital), 1340 Ridgewood Ave., Zip 32017; tel. 904/677-5100; Robert Helms, pres. (Nonreporting) **A**9 10 11; **S**3015	33	10	S		97	—	—	—	—	—	—	—	—
HOLLYWOOD—Broward County													
□ DOCTORS HOSPITAL OF HOLLYWOOD, 1859 Van Buren St., Box 1220, Zip 33022; tel. 305/920-9000; Alex Spinos, adm.; Kenneth Berg, exec. dir. (Nonreporting) **A**1a 9 10; **S**9555	33	10	S		124	—	—	—	—	—	—	—	—
□ HOLLYWOOD MEDICAL CENTER, 3600 Washington St., Zip 33021; tel. 305/966-4500; Calvin K. Knight, exec. dir. (Nonreporting) **A**1a 9 10; **S**3015	33	10	S		334	—	—	—	—	—	—	—	—
□ HOLLYWOOD PAVILION, 1201 N. 37th Ave., Zip 33021; tel. 305/962-1355; Karen Kallen, adm. **A**1a b 9 10 **F**24 32 33 42 44	33	22	S		46	481	25	54.3	0	0	1740	—	47
★□ ○ + HUMANA HOSPITAL -SOUTH BROWARD, 5100 W. Hallandale Beach Blvd., Zip 33023; tel. 305/966-8100; Stephen L. Sutherlin, exec. dir. **A**1a 9 10 11 12 **F**1 3 6 10 12 14 15 16 17 20 23 34 35 36 37 40 43 44 46 47 48 53; **S**1235	33	10	S		256	3233	71	27.7	8	228	—	—	332
★□ MEMORIAL HOSPITAL, 3501 Johnson St., Zip 33021; tel. 305/987-2000; S. A. Mudano, adm. **A**1a b 3 9 10 **F**1 3 4 6 7 8 9 10 11 12 14 15 16 17 20 23 24 25 26 27 30 32 33 34 35 40 42 43 44 45 46 47 48 49 51 52 53 54	16	10	S		737	24650	526	71.4	60	4093	98499	45787	2085
HOMESTEAD—Dade County													
★□ JAMES ARCHER SMITH HOSPITAL, 160 N.W. 13th St., Zip 33030; tel. 305/248-3232; Joseph P. Jacobs, adm. **A**1a 9 10 **F**1 2 3 6 10 12 14 15 16 23 34 35 40 44 45 46 47 53	14	10	S		120	3900	67	55.8	12	555	14673	6927	350
U. S. AIR FORCE HOSPITAL, See Homestead Air Force Base													
HOMESTEAD AIR FORCE BASE—Dade County													
□ U. S. AIR FORCE HOSPITAL, Zip 33039; tel. 305/257-7578; Col. Brian J. Duffy, adm. **A**1a **F**1 6 12 14 15 16 23 28 32 34 35 36 40 46 47	41	10	S		65	4134	49	71.0	18	561	—	—	450
HUDSON—Pasco County													
★□ HCA BAYONET POINT-HUDSON REGIONAL MEDICAL CENTER (Formerly Bayonet Point-Hudson Regional Medical Center), 14000 Fivay Rd., Zip 33567; tel. 813/863-2411; Dan Chambers Jr., adm. (Nonreporting) **A**1a 9 10; **S**1755	33	10	S		200	—	—	—	—	—	—	—	—
INVERNESS—Citrus County													
★□ CITRUS MEMORIAL HOSPITAL, 502 Highland Blvd., Zip 32652; tel. 904/726-1551; Charles A. Blasband, chief exec. off. **A**1a 9 10 **F**1 3 6 10 12 14 15 16 20 21 23 34 35 36 41 43 45 46 47 53	16	10	S		171	7004	100	67.6	8	863	18842	7387	449
JACKSONVILLE—Duval County													
★□ BAPTIST MEDICAL CENTER, 800 Prudential Dr., Zip 32207; tel. 904/393-2000; William C. Mason, pres. **A**1a 3 5 9 10 **F**1 2 3 4 5 6 7 8 9 10 11 12 14 15 16 17 20 21 23 24 26 27 30 32 33 34 35 36 38 39 40 41 42 44 45 46 47 50 51 52 53 54	23	10	S		531	20875	368	69.3	33	2291	91112	35040	2142
★ CAREUNIT OF JACKSONVILLE BEACH, 1320 Roberts Dr., Zip 32250; tel. 904/241-5133; Joe H. McWaters, adm. (Nonreporting) **S**0275	33	82	S		84	—	—	—	—	—	—	—	—
□ CPC ST. JOHNS RIVER HOSPITAL (Formerly St. Johns River Hospital), 6300 Beach Blvd., Zip 32216; tel. 904/724-9202; Patrick G. Kelly, adm. (Nonreporting) **A**1b 9 10; **S**0785	33	22	S		99	—	—	—	—	—	—	—	—
★□ ○ + JACKSONVILLE MEDICAL CENTER, 4901 Richard St., Box 10398, Zip 32207; tel. 904/737-3120; Hany Mounib, exec. dir. **A**1a 9 10 11 12 13 **F**1 3 6 10 12 14 15 16 23 30 32 34 35 43 46 50 53	23	10	S		107	2847	48	44.9	0	0	13557	4812	273
★□ MEMORIAL MEDICAL CENTER OF JACKSONVILLE, 3627 University Blvd. S., Box 16325, Zip 32216; tel. 904/399-6918; E. K. Prentice, pres.; Mark A. Mrozek, adm. **A**1a 9 10 **F**1 3 4 5 6 10 12 14 15 16 20 34 35 36 37 38 40 43 45 46 47 51 53 54	23	10	S		353	15856	261	73.9	10	2473	73870	27538	1543
★ Δ MEMORIAL REGIONAL REHABILITATION CENTER, 3599 University Blvd. S., P O Box 16406, Zip 32216; tel. 904/399-6123; Stephen K. Wilson, adm. **A**7 10 **F**23 24 26 34 42 44	23	46	S		80	596	54	67.5	0	0	7524	3849	147
★□ METHODIST HOSPITAL, 580 W. Eighth St., Zip 32209; tel. 904/798-8000; Marcus E. Drewa, pres. **A**1a b 9 10 **F**1 3 5 6 9 10 12 15 16 20 21 23 24 34 35 36 37 40 41 47 53; **S**2715	23	10	S		244	8138	172	70.5	13	62	38613	17344	981
★□ NAVAL HOSPITAL, Zip 32214; tel. 904/777-7300; Capt. L. U. Pulicicchio, MC USN **A**1a 2 3 5 **F**1 3 6 10 12 14 15 16 23 27 28 30 32 33 34 35 37 40 46 47 52 53 , 37	43	10	S		178	9217	103	55.4	36	1309	57124	41450	962
★□ RIVERSIDE HOSPITAL, 2033 Riverside Ave., Zip 32204; tel. 904/387-7000; Suzan V. David, exec. vice-pres. & chief oper. off. **A**1a 9 10 **F**1 3 6 9 10 11 12 15 16 20 23 24 27 29 33 35 36 40 42 45 50 53	23	10	S		183	6191	103	56.3	10	865	24313	10217	464
ST. JOHNS RIVER HOSPITAL, See CPC St. Johns River Hospital													
★□ ST. LUKE'S HOSPITAL, 4201 Belfort Rd., Zip 32216; tel. 904/739-3700; Robert C. Harrison, pres. **A**1a 9 10 **F**1 2 3 4 5 6 12 14 15 16 17 20 23 24 32 35 43 44 45 46 53 54	23	10	S		168	6325	108	64.3	0	0	41883	14302	749
★□ ST. VINCENT'S MEDICAL CENTER, 1800 Barrs St., Box 2982, Zip 32203; tel. 904/387-7300; Sr. Mary Clare Hughes, pres. **A**1a 2 3 5 9 10 **F**1 2 3 4 5 6 7 8 9 10 11 12 13 14 15 16 20 23 24 26 27 30 31 33 34 35 36 40 41 42 44 45 46 47 52 53 54; **S**1885	21	10	S		528	19993	369	69.9	25	1730	87004	34794	1455
□ UNIVERSITY HOSPITAL OF JACKSONVILLE, 655 W. Eighth St., Zip 32209; tel. 904/350-6899; John F. Gregg, pres. **A**1a 2 3 5 8 9 10 **F**1 3 4 5 6 8 9 10 11 12 14 15 16 17 20 23 24 27 28 29 30 32 33 34 35 36 37 38 40 42 45 46 47 50 51 52 53 54	23	10	S		464	18446	340	73.3	60	4352	88599	35484	2004
JACKSONVILLE BEACH—Duval County													
★□ BEACHES HOSPITAL, 1430 16th Ave. S., Zip 32250; tel. 904/246-6731; Bart A. Hove, adm. **A**1a 9 10 **F**1 3 6 10 12 14 15 16 23 24 26 30 34 35 42 44 45 52 53; **S**1755	16	10	S		82	2054	30	36.6	0	0	7387	2926	135
JASPER—Hamilton County													
★ HAMILTON COUNTY MEMORIAL HOSPITAL, Sixth Ave. & Fourth St. N.W., Box 1300, Zip 32052; tel. 904/792-2101; Robert B. Marvin, adm. **A**9 10 **F**1 3 6 12 14 15 16 23 28 30 34 35 37 40 45 47 49 50	13	10	S		42	1402	21	50.0	2	145	3038	1395	94
JAY—Santa Rosa County													
★ JAY HOSPITAL, 221 S. Alabama St., Zip 32565; tel. 904/675-4532; Grady D. Ivey, adm. **A**9 10 **F**1 3 6 10 12 14 16 23 35 46 53; **S**0185	23	10	S		52	767	13	25.0	0	0	3052	1224	57
JUPITER—Palm Beach County													
★□ JUPITER HOSPITAL, 1210 S. Old Dixie Hwy., Zip 33458; tel. 305/747-2234; Dino P. Cagni, exec. dir. **A**1a 9 10 **F**1 3 6 8 10 12 16 23 24 35 41 44 45 46 47 53; **S**1755	23	10	S		156	4950	87	55.8	0	0	21787	7750	471
KEY WEST—Monroe County													
DE POO MEMORIAL DOCTORS HOSPITAL, 1200 Kennedy Dr., Box 690, Zip 33040; tel. 305/294-4692; Larry Melby, adm. **A**9 10 **F**1 3 6 12 14 15 16 23 26 34 35 44 45 47; **S**6525	33	10	S		34	1555	25	73.5	0	0	7000	—	134
★□ FLORIDA KEYS MEMORIAL HOSPITAL, 5900 Junior College Rd., Zip 33040; tel. 305/294-5531; George Avery, adm. **A**1a 9 10 **F**1 3 6 12 14 15 16 20 23 30 33 35 36 40 45 46 48 49 53; **S**1755	16	10	S		120	2776	38	31.7	12	789	11219	5286	211

★ American Hospital Association (AHA) membership
□ Joint Commission on Accreditation of Hospitals (JCAH) accreditation
+ American Osteopathic Hospital Association (AOHA) membership
○ American Osteopathic Association (AOA) accreditation
Δ Commission on Accreditation of Rehabilitation Facilities (CARF) accreditation
Control codes 61, 63, 64, 71, 72 and 73 indicate hospitals listed by AOHA, but not registered by AHA.
For definition of numerical codes, see page A2

Hospital, Address, Telephone, Administrator, Approval and Facility Codes, Multihospital System Code	Classification Codes				Inpatient Data				Newborn Data		Expense (thousands of dollars)		
	Control	Service	Stay	Facilities	Beds	Admissions	Census	Occupancy (percent)	Bassinets	Births	Total	Payroll	Personnel
KISSIMMEE—Osceola County													
★☐ HUMANA HOSPITAL -KISSIMMEE, 700 W. Oak St., Zip 32741; Mailing Address P O Box 2589, Zip 32742; tel. 305/933-3601; James A. Shanks, exec. dir. **A**1a 9 10 **F**1 3 6 9 10 12 14 15 16 20 23 26 34 35 36 37 40 45 46 47 53 54; **S**1235	33	10	S		169	7424	106	62.7	16	1115	—	—	371
□ KISSIMMEE MEMORIAL HOSPITAL, 200 Hilda St., Zip 32741; Mailing Address P O Box 2108, Zip 32742; tel. 305/846-4343; Denny W. Powell, pres. **A**1a 9 10 **F**1 3 6 10 12 14 15 16 20 23 24 26 32 34 35 37 44 45 46 50 52 53; **S**1935	33	10	S		120	3409	56	46.7	0	0	12968	4558	284
LAKE BUTLER—Union County													
RECEPTION AND MEDICAL CENTER HOSPITAL, Box 628, Zip 32054; tel. 904/496-2222; Ronald Rice, adm. **F**1 6 15 16 23 27 28 29 30 32 33 34 35 43	12	11	S		153	2064	95	62.1	0	0	17937	7066	220
LAKE CITY—Columbia County													
★☐ AMI LAKE CITY MEDICAL CENTER (Formerly Lake City Medical Center), 1701 W. Duval St., Zip 32055; tel. 904/752-2922; Steve Chapman, chief exec. off. **A**1a 9 10 **F**1 3 6 10 16 27 34 46 53; **S**0125	33	10	S		75	2200	34	45.3	0	0	7485	2163	133
LAKE CITY MEDICAL CENTER, See AMI Lake City Medical Center													
★☐ LAKE SHORE HOSPITAL, 560 E. Franklin St., Box 1989, Zip 32055; tel. 904/755-3200; Jeffrey M. Judd, dir. **A**1a 9 10 **F**1 3 6 10 15 16 23 34 35 41 45 53	16	10	S		128	4241	60	46.9	10	519	12251	5284	308
★☐ VETERANS ADMINISTRATION MEDICAL CENTER, 801 S. Marion St., Zip 32055; tel. 904/755-3016; Howard M. Ruppen, dir. (Nonreporting) **A**1a 3 5	45	10	S		449	—	—	—	—	—	—	—	—
LAKE WALES—Polk County													
★☐ LAKE WALES HOSPITAL, 410 S. 11th St., P O Box 3460, Zip 33859; tel. 813/676-1433; Joe Connell, adm. **A**1a 9 10 **F**1 3 6 12 14 16 23 35 36 40 43 45 46 53	23	10	S		154	3706	48	31.2	13	391	8487	4468	300
LAKE WORTH—Palm Beach County													
DOCTORS HOSPITAL OF LAKE WORTH, See HCA Doctors Hospital													
★☐ HCA DOCTORS HOSPITAL (Formerly Doctors Hospital of Lake Worth), 2829 Tenth Ave. N., Box 1649, Zip 33460; tel. 305/967-7800; Rodney F. Dorsette, adm. **A**1a 9 10 **F**1 3 6 10 12 15 16 23 24 26 35 44 45 46 50 53; **S**1755	33	10	S		200	5197	101	50.5	0	0	—	—	375
□ LAKE HOSPITAL OF THE PALM BEACHES, 1710 Fourth Ave. N., Box 1668, Zip 33460; tel. 305/588-7341; Mark E. Schneider, chief exec. off.; Irl Extein MD, med. dir. **A**1b 9 10 **F**24 28 29 30 32 33 42 44 48 49 50; **S**0825	33	22	L		72	644	60	83.3	0	0	6292	2062	138
LAKELAND—Polk County													
★☐ LAKELAND REGIONAL MEDICAL CENTER, Lakeland Hills Blvd., Drawer 448, Zip 33802; tel. 813/687-1100; Jack T. Stephens Jr., pres. & chief exec. off. **A**1a 9 10 **F**1 2 3 4 6 7 8 9 10 11 12 15 16 20 23 24 27 30 34 35 36 40 42 45 46 48 51 52 53 54	23	10	S		637	26672	481	76.3	30	1604	88884	41931	2129
★☐ PALMVIEW HOSPITAL, 2510 N. Florida Ave., Zip 33805; tel. 813/682-6105; Ryan Beaty, interim adm. (Nonreporting) **A**1b 10; **S**1775	33	22	S		66	—	—	—	—	—	—	—	—
LAND'O'LAKES—Hillsborough County													
★☐ FLORIDA CAMELOT (Formerly Camelot Care Center) (Formerly listed under Lutz), Mailing Address P O Box 1101, Lutz, Zip 33549; tel. 813/949-7491; James E. Spicer PhD, exec. dir. **A**1b **F**24 30 31 32 33 42	33	52	L		32	51	24	100.0	0	0	1254	672	41
LARGO—Pinellas County													
★☐ HCA LARGO MEDICAL CENTER HOSPITAL (Formerly Largo Medical Center Hospital), 201 14th St. S.W., Zip 33540; Mailing Address P O Box 2905, Zip 34294; tel. 813/586-1411; Winston Rushing, adm. **A**1a 2 9 10 **F**1 2 3 4 6 7 9 10 11 12 14 15 16 20 23 24 26 34 35 42 43 44 45 46 47 52 54; **S**1755	33	10	S		256	9011	173	67.6	0	0	39972	11832	603
LARGO MEDICAL CENTER HOSPITAL, See HCA Largo Medical Center Hospital													
□ MEDFIELD CENTER, 12891 Seminole Blvd., Zip 33544; tel. 813/581-8757; Sherrie Klein, adm. (Nonreporting) **A**1b 9 10; **S**0825	33	22	S		32	—	—	—	—	—	—	—	—
○ + SUN COAST HOSPITAL, 2025 Indian Rocks Rd., Zip 33544; Mailing Address Box 2025, Zip 34294; tel. 813/581-9474; William P. Smith, chief exec. off. **A**9 10 11 12 13 **F**1 3 6 7 8 9 10 11 12 15 16 23 24 27 32 34 35 37 39 40 42 43 44 45 46 47 48 52 53	23	10	S		241	7366	170	70.5	6	690	27310	11383	618
LEESBURG—Lake County													
□ LAKE MEDICAL CENTER (Formerly Lake Community Hospital), 200 N. Blvd. E., Zip 32748; Mailing Address Box 750, Zip 32749; tel. 904/787-6881; Joseph P. Lyons, exec. dir. **A**1a 9 10 **F**1 3 6 10 12 16 23 35 40 44 45 53; **S**1805	33	10	S		162	3900	60	37.0	11	349	16509	4253	210
★☐ LEESBURG REGIONAL MEDICAL CENTER, 600 E. Dixie Ave., Zip 32748; tel. 904/787-7222; Frederick D. Woodrell, pres.; Lynn Burnseo, exec. vice-pres. **A**1a 9 10 **F**1 3 5 6 9 10 12 15 16 20 23 26 34 35 41 45 46 47 53; **S**1755	23	10	S		132	6486	115	87.1	0	0	17827	6920	369
LEHIGH ACRES—Lee County													
★☐ HCA EAST POINTE HOSPITAL (Formerly East Pointe Hospital), 1500 Lee Blvd., Zip 33936; tel. 813/369-2101; Richard W. Klusmann, adm. (Nonreporting) **A**1a 9 10; **S**1755	33	10	S		88	—	—	—	—	—	—	—	—
LIVE OAK—Suwannee County													
★☐ SUWANNEE HOSPITAL (Formerly Suwannee County Hospital), Fifth St., P O Drawer 1149, Zip 32060; tel. 904/362-1413; C. Elwin O'Steen, chief oper. off. (Nonreporting) **A**1a 9 10; **S**7895	16	10	S		50	—	—	—	—	—	—	—	—
LONGWOOD—Seminole County													
★☐ WEST LAKE HOSPITAL, 589 W. State Rd. 434, Zip 32750; tel. 305/260-1900; Dennis Menard, adm. **A**1b 9 10 **F**24 30 32 33 42 44 47 48 50; **S**1755	33	22	L		80	507	49	61.3	0	0	5539	1954	124
LUTZ—Hillsborough County													
CAMELOT CARE CENTER, See Florida Camelot, Land-O-Lakes													
MACCLENNY—Baker County													
★ ED FRASER MEMORIAL HOSPITAL, 159 N. Third St., Zip 32063; tel. 904/259-3151; C. V. Stotler, exec. adm. (Total facility includes 68 beds in nursing home-type unit) **A**9 10 **F**1 6 19 23 34 35 45	16	10	S	TF	93	720	75	80.6	0	0	3295	1285	100
				H	25	699	8	—	0	0	2506	761	57
NORTHEAST FLORIDA STATE HOSPITAL, Hwy. 121, Zip 32063; tel. 904/259-6211 **A**10 **F**14 15 19 23 24 30 32 33 35 37 42 44 46 47 50	12	22	L		722	507	656	86.3	0	0	27705	16588	1106
MACDILL AIR FORCE BASE—Hillsborough County													
□ U. S. AIR FORCE REGIONAL HOSPITAL MACDILL, Zip 33608; tel. 813/830-3258; Col. Mervin T. Avants MSC USAF, adm. **A**1a **F**1 3 6 12 14 15 16 23 28 30 32 33 34 35 36 37 40 43 45 46 47 49 52 53	41	10	S		96	4080	48	50.0	19	515	—	—	469
MADISON—Madison County													
MADISON COUNTY MEMORIAL HOSPITAL, 201 E. Marion St., P O Box 390, Zip 32340; tel. 904/973-2271; Jeannie Baker, adm. (Nonreporting) **A**9 10	13	10	S		42	—	—	—	—	—	—	—	—
MARATHON—Monroe County													
□ FISHERMEN'S HOSPITAL, 3301 Overseas Hwy., Zip 33050; tel. 305/743-5533; Ray G. Musselman, adm. **A**1a 9 10 **F**1 3 6 10 12 15 16 23 34 35 39 45 53; **S**1775	33	10	S		58	1223	21	36.2	0	1	6445	2464	117
MARGATE—Broward County													
★☐ HCA NORTHWEST REGIONAL HOSPITAL (Formerly Northwest Regional Hospital), 5801 Colonial Dr., P O Box 639002, Zip 33063; tel. 305/974-0400; Joseph Feith, adm. **A**1a 9 10 **F**1 3 6 9 10 12 14 15 16 20 23 35 36 37 40 45 46 50 52 53; **S**1755	33	10	S		150	5821	100	66.7	20	681	26804	8613	382

Hospital, Address, Telephone, Administrator, Approval and Facility Codes, Multihospital System Code

- ★ American Hospital Association (AHA) membership
- □ Joint Commission on Accreditation of Hospitals (JCAH) accreditation
- + American Osteopathic Hospital Association (AOHA) membership
- ○ American Osteopathic Association (AOA) accreditation
- Δ Commission on Accreditation of Rehabilitation Facilities (CARF) accreditation

Control codes 61, 63, 64, 71, 72 and 73 indicate hospitals listed by AOHA, but not registered by AHA. For definition of numerical codes, see page A2

Hospital, Address, Telephone, Administrator, Approval and Facility Codes, Multihospital System Code	Classification Codes				Inpatient Data				Newborn Data		Expense (thousands of dollars)		
	Control	Service	Stay	Facilities	Beds	Admissions	Census	Occupancy (percent)	Bassinets	Births	Total	Payroll	Personnel
MARIANNA—Jackson County													
⊠ JACKSON HOSPITAL, 800 Hospital Dr., P O Box 1608, Zip 32446; tel. 904/526-2200; Chuck Ellis, adm. **A**1a 9 10 **F**1 3 6 10 12 14 16 23 34 35 36 40 41 45 47 53; **S**1755	16	10	S		107	4146	61	57.0	10	404	9839	4115	246
MELBOURNE—Brevard County													
□ BREVARD MENTAL HEALTH CENTER, 400 E. Sheridan Rd., Zip 32901; tel. 305/723-3910; James B. Whitaker, exec. dir. (Data not available) **A**1a 10 **F**24 28 29 30 31 32 33 42 43 49	23	22	S		48	—	—	—	—	—	—	—	—
⊠ HOLMES REGIONAL MEDICAL CENTER, 1350 S. Hickory St., Zip 32901; tel. 305/727-7000; Ned B. Wilford, pres. **A**1a 9 10 **F**1 2 3 4 6 7 8 9 10 11 12 14 15 20 21 23 24 26 35 36 39 40 41 44 45 46 52 53 54	23	10	S		447	19156	327	73.2	34	1934	67399	28709	1516
MIAMI—Dade County													
AMERICAN HOSPITAL OF MIAMI, See AMI Kendall Regional Medical Center													
⊠ AMI KENDALL REGIONAL MEDICAL CENTER (Formerly American Hospital of Miami), 11750 Bird Rd., Zip 33175; tel. 305/223-3000; Larry E. Hanan, exec. dir. (Nonreporting) **A**1a 9 10; **S**0125	33	10	S		314	—	—	—	—	—	—	—	—
⊠ Δ BAPTIST HOSPITAL OF MIAMI, 8900 N. Kendall Dr., Zip 33176; tel. 305/596-6503; Brian Keeley, pres. & chief exec. off. (Nonreporting) **A**1a 2 7 9 10	23	10	S		371	—	—	—	—	—	—	—	—
⊠ BASCOM PALMER EYE INSTITUTE AND ANNE BATES LEACH EYE HOSPITAL, 900 N.W. 17th St., Zip 33136; tel. 305/326-6000; William F. Nowak, adm. **A**1a 3 5 9 10 **F**1 5 12 15 34 35 45 46 47; **S**1755	23	49	S		100	2185	18	18.0	0	0	16968	—	337
⊠ CEDARS MEDICAL CENTER, 1400 N.W. 12th Ave., Zip 33136; tel. 305/325-5770; Daniel L. Stickler, exec. dir. **A**1a 2 9 10 **F**1 2 3 4 6 7 8 9 10 11 12 14 15 16 17 20 23 24 26 27 28 30 32 33 34 37 42 44 45 46 47 50 53 54	23	10	S		404	11962	280	69.3	0	0	74191	31254	1380
⊠ CORAL REEF HOSPITAL, 9333 S.W. 152nd St., Zip 33157; tel. 305/251-2500; C. William Nordwall, chief exec. off. (Nonreporting) **A**1a 9 10; **S**0365	32	10	S		190	—	—	—	—	—	—	—	—
DODGE HOSPITAL, See Harbor View													
⊠ GRANT CENTER HOSPITAL, 20601 S.W. 157th Ave., Zip 33187; Mailing Address Box 1159, Zip 33197; tel. 305/251-0710; Walter Grono, adm. **A**1b **F**15 24 29 30 32 33 42 43 44; **S**1755	33	52	L		140	270	74	54.0	0	0	10102	4252	159
□ HARBOR VIEW (Formerly Dodge Hospital), 1861 N.W. South River Dr., Zip 33125; tel. 305/642-3555; John Picciano, adm **A**1a 9 10 **F**24 30 32 33 42 48	33	22	S		80	984	54	60.0	0	0	6777	2714	100
⊠ HIGHLAND PARK HOSPITAL (Formerly Highland Park General Hospital), 1660 N.W. Seventh Ct., Zip 33136; tel. 305/324-8111; Alan Markowitz PhD, adm. **A**1b 9 10 **F**24 28 30 31 32 42 47 48 49 50; **S**1755	33	22	S		106	861	63	59.4	0	0	5320	2122	108
⊠ HUMANA HOSPITAL -BISCAYNE, 20900 Biscayne Blvd., Zip 33180; tel. 305/932-0250; Robert M. Krieger, exec. dir. (Nonreporting) **A**1a 10; **S**1235	33	10	S		458	—	—	—	—	—	—	—	—
⊠ Δ JAMES M. JACKSON MEMORIAL HOSPITAL, 1611 N.W. 12th Ave., Zip 33136; tel. 305/325-7429; Fred J. Cowell, pres. **A**1a 2 3 5 6 7 8 9 **F**1 2 3 4 5 6 7 8 9 10 11 12 13 15 16 20 22 23 24 26 27 28 29 30 32 33 34 35 36 37 40 41 42 44 45 46 47 49 51 52 53 54; **S**1565	13	10	S		1197	48876	1057	88.6	92	12084	293109	132981	5495
⊠ MERCY HOSPITAL, 3663 S. Miami Ave., Zip 33133; tel. 305/854-4400; Edward J. Rosasco Jr., pres. & chief exec. off. **A**1a 9 10 **F**1 2 3 4 6 7 8 9 10 11 12 14 15 16 20 23 24 26 27 29 32 33 34 35 36 40 43 44 46 47 53 54	21	10	S		361	15450	295	74.7	33	2064	76355	32551	1343
⊠ MIAMI CHILDREN'S HOSPITAL, 6125 S.W. 31st St., Zip 33155; tel. 305/666-6511; Thomas F. Jones, pres. & chief exec. off. **A**1a 3 5 9 10 **F**1 4 5 6 10 12 14 16 17 20 23 24 26 27 28 29 30 32 33 34 35 38 44 45 46 47 51 53 54	23	50	S		188	6883	135	71.8	0	0	43751	20628	1048
⊠ MIAMI GENERAL HOSPITAL, 17300 N.W. Seventh Ave., Zip 33169; tel. 305/652-4200; Carlos G. Padron, adm. **A**1a 9 10 **F**1 6 10 14 15 16 20 23 24 30 33 34 35 44 47 52 53	33	10	S		270	8749	161	59.6	0	0	40557	14574	665
⊠ NORTH SHORE MEDICAL CENTER, 1100 N.W. 95th St., Zip 33150; tel. 305/835-6000; Richard A. Pakan, pres. & chief exec. off. **A**1a 2 9 10 **F**1 2 3 6 8 9 10 12 14 15 16 20 21 23 24 26 27 34 35 36 37 40 44 45 46 47 51 52 53	23	10	S		318	10622	178	56.2	28	1957	52120	20204	960
⊠ PAN AMERICAN HOSPITAL, 5959 N.W. Seventh St., Zip 33126; tel. 305/264-1000; James Yeagley, adm. **A**1a 9 10 **F**1 2 3 6 10 12 14 16 20 23 34 35 44 46 47 53	23	10	S		146	4654	93	63.7	0	0	19236	7588	471
⊠ UNIVERSITY OF MIAMI HOSPITAL AND CLINICS-NCCH, 1475 N.W. 12th Ave., Zip 33136; tel. 305/547-6418; Murray S. Zacharia, adm. **A**1a 3 5 9 10 **F**1 6 10 15 16 17 23 24 26 28 32 34 44 46 47 53; **S**1565	23	10	S		40	1541	36	75.0	0	0	12717	4212	199
⊠ VETERANS ADMINISTRATION MEDICAL CENTER, 1201 N.W. 16th St., Zip 33125; tel. 305/324-4455; Thomas C. Doherty, dir. (Total facility includes 120 beds in nursing home-type unit) **A**1a b 3 5 8 **F**1 2 3 4 6 7 8 9 10 11 12 14 15 16 19 20 23 24 25 26 27 28 29 30 31 33 34 41 42 44 46 47 48 49 50 53 54	45	10	S	TF	771	16371	573	70.9	0	0	106123	56983	2252
				H	651	16240	464	—	0	0	—	—	2155
⊠ VICTORIA HOSPITAL, 955 N.W. Third St., Zip 33128; P O Box 016216, Flagler Sta., Zip 33101, tel. 305/545-8050, Charles Jenkins Sweat, pres. (Data not available) **A**1a 9 10 **F**1 6 10 12 14 15 16 20 24 32 34 49 53	23	10	S		201	—	—	—	—	—	—	—	—
★ ○ + WESTCHESTER GENERAL HOSPITAL, 2500 S.W. 75th Ave., Zip 33155; tel. 305/264-5252; Sylvia Urlich, chief exec. off. (Nonreporting) **A**9 10 11 12	33	10	S		50	—	—	—	—	—	—	—	—
MIAMI BEACH—Dade County													
⊠ MIAMI HEART INSTITUTE, 4701 N. Meridian Ave., Zip 33140; tel. 305/674-3044; John P. Lauri, adm. **A**1a 9 10 **F**1 3 4 6 9 10 11 12 14 15 16 17 20 23 24 29 32 34 37 44 45 46 47 50 53 54	23	10	S		258	6957	183	70.9	0	0	59567	23273	1067
⊠ MOUNT SINAI MEDICAL CENTER, 4300 Alton Rd., Zip 33140; tel. 305/674-2121; Fred D. Hirt, pres. & chief exec. off. **A**1a 2 3 5 8 9 10 **F**1 3 4 5 6 7 8 9 10 11 12 14 15 16 17 20 23 24 25 26 28 30 32 33 34 35 36 37 38 40 41 42 44 45 46 47 48 49 50 52 53 54	23	10	S		699	19884	487	69.7	35	1940	139186	67800	2710
⊠ SOUTH SHORE HOSPITAL AND MEDICAL CENTER, 630 Alton Rd., Zip 33139; tel. 305/672-2100; William Zubkoff PhD, exec. dir. **A**1a 9 10 **F**1 3 6 10 12 14 15 16 20 23 24 26 27 29 32 33 34 35 43 44 45 46 47 50	23	10	S		140	3259	91	65.0	0	0	17910	7029	428
⊠ ST. FRANCIS HOSPITAL, 250 W. 63rd St., Zip 33141; tel. 305/868-5000; Sr. Margaret McManus, pres. & chief exec. off. **A**1a 9 10 **F**1 2 3 4 6 9 10 12 14 15 16 20 23 24 26 27 28 30 32 33 34 35 41 42 44 45 46 47 50 53 54; **S**1385	21	10	S		273	6143	151	55.3	0	0	42979	15219	755
MILTON—Santa Rosa County													
⊠ HCA SANTA ROSA MEDICAL CENTER (Formerly Santa Rosa Hospital), 1450 Berryhill Rd., Zip 32570; Mailing Address P O Box 648, Zip 32572; tel. 904/623-9741; Jon C. Trezona, adm. **A**1a 9 10 **F**1 3 6 10 12 14 15 16 23 26 30 32 34 35 36 37 40 43 45 46 52; **S**1755	33	10	S		74	3295	46	50.0	20	667	—	—	238
NAPLES—Collier County													
⊠ NAPLES COMMUNITY HOSPITAL, 350 Seventh St. N., Zip 33940; Mailing Address Box 2507, Zip 33939; tel. 813/262-3131; William G. Crone, pres. **A**1a 2 9 10 **F**1 3 6 7 8 9 10 11 12 14 15 16 20 23 24 26 27 29 30 33 34 35 36 40 42 44 45 46 52 53	23	10	S		391	15075	258	66.3	28	1753	57027	24863	1304
★ NAPLES RESEARCH AND COUNSELING CENTER, 9001 Tamiami Trail E., Zip 33962; tel. 813/775-4500; Marcus Zillman, exec. dir. **A** 9 **F**15 19 28 32 33 42 46 47 48 49	33	49	S		92	767	44	47.8	0	0	—	—	85

Hospital, Address, Telephone, Administrator, Approval and Facility Codes, Multihospital System Code	Classification Codes				Inpatient Data				Newborn Data		Expense (thousands of dollars)		
★ American Hospital Association (AHA) membership □ Joint Commission on Accreditation of Hospitals (JCAH) accreditation + American Osteopathic Hospital Association (AOHA) membership ○ American Osteopathic Association (AOA) accreditation Δ Commission on Accreditation of Rehabilitation Facilities (CARF) accreditation Control codes 61, 63, 64, 71, 72 and 73 indicate hospitals listed by AOHA, but not registered by AHA. For definition of numerical codes, see page A2	Control	Service	Stay	Facilities	Beds	Admissions	Census	Occupancy (percent)	Bassinets	Births	Total	Payroll	Personnel
NEW PORT RICHEY—Pasco County													
COMMUNITY HOSPITAL, See HCA New Port Richey Hospital													
★□ HCA NEW PORT RICHEY HOSPITAL (Formerly Community Hospital), 205 High St., Box 996, Zip 33552; tel. 813/848-1733; Andrew Oravec Jr., adm. (Nonreporting) **A**1a 9 10; **S**1755	33	10	S		414	—	—	—	—	—	—	—	—
★ RIVERSIDE HOSPITAL, 500 Indiana Ave., Zip 33552; tel. 813/842-8468; Bradley Reid, adm. (Nonreporting) **A**9 10; **S**1375	33	10	S		100	—	—	—	—	—	—	—	—
NEW SMYRNA BEACH—Volusia County													
★□ FISH MEMORIAL HOSPITAL, 401 Palmetto, Zip 32069; tel. 904/427-3401; William J. Schneider, adm. **A**1a 9 10 **F**1 3 6 12 15 16 21 23 26 35 36 40 41 45 46 53	16	10	S		116	3252	48	41.4	10	310	12093	5675	279
NICEVILLE—Okaloosa County													
★□ TWIN CITIES HOSPITAL, Hwy. 85 N. & College Blvd., Zip 32578; tel. 904/678-4131; Glen Jones, adm. (Nonreporting) **A**1a 9 10; **S**1755	33	10	S		75	—	—	—	—	—	—	—	—
NORTH MIAMI—Dade County													
★□ Δ BON SECOURS HOSPITAL, 1050 N.E. 125th St., Zip 33161; tel. 305/891-8850; Warren R. Slavin, exec. vice-pres. (Total facility includes 212 beds in nursing home-type unit) **A**1a 7 9 10 **F**16 19 23 24 26 33 34 42 44 45 46; **S**5085	23	46	S	TF H	272 60	1127 510	230 45	84.6 —	0 0	0 0	12703 —	6141 —	357 168
★□ NORTH MIAMI MEDICAL CENTER (Formerly North Miami General Hospital), 1701 N.E. 127th St., Zip 33261; tel. 305/891-3550; Ed Goffinett, adm. (Nonreporting) **A**1a 9 10; **S**6525	33	10	S		278	—	—	—	—	—	—	—	—
NORTH MIAMI BEACH—Dade County													
★□ Δ AMI PARKWAY REGIONAL MEDICAL CENTER (Formerly Parkway Regional Medical Center), 160 N.W. 170th St., Zip 33169; tel. 305/651-1100; Jay S. Weinstein, assoc. exec. dir. (Nonreporting) **A**1a 7 9 10; **S**0125	33	10	S		412	—	—	—	—	—	—	—	—
★ ○ + AMI SOUTHEASTERN MEDICAL CENTER (Formerly Southeastern Medical Center), 1750 N.E. 167th St., Zip 33162; tel. 305/945-5400; Neil Natkow DO, exec. dir. **A**9 10 11 12 13 **F**1 3 6 7 8 10 11 12 14 15 16 17 23 24 34 35 36 37 40 44 45 46 47 53; **S**0125	33	10	S		224	5321	101	45.1	13	538	32436	8963	385
PARKWAY REGIONAL MEDICAL CENTER, See AMI Parkway Regional Medical Center													
SOUTHEASTERN MEDICAL CENTER, See AMI Southeastern Medical Center													
OCALA—Marion County													
★□ CHARTER SPRINGS HOSPITAL, 3130 S.W. 27th Ave., P O Box 3338, Zip 32678; tel. 904/237-7293; Gregory A. Williams, adm. (Data for 349 days) **A**1b 9 10 **F**15 24 28 29 32 33 34 42 43 48 49; **S**0695	33	22	S		68	460	25	36.8	0	0	3015	881	75
★□ MARION COMMUNITY HOSPITAL, 1431 S.W. First Ave., Box 2200, Zip 32670; tel. 904/732-2700; Terry Upton, adm. (Nonreporting) **A**1a 2 9 10; **S**1755	33	10	S		190	—	—	—	—	—	—	—	—
★□ MUNROE REGIONAL MEDICAL CENTER, 131 S.W. 15th St., Zip 32670; Mailing Address Box 6000, Zip 32678; tel. 904/351-7200; Dyer T. Michell, adm. **A**1a 2 9 10 **F**1 3 5 6 12 15 16 20 23 24 26 27 29 30 32 34 35 36 40 42 44 45 46 50 52 53	23	10	S		248	10899	168	67.7	24	1928	42632	16446	942
OKEECHOBEE—Okeechobee County													
★□ HCA RAULERSON HOSPITAL (Formerly H. H. Raulerson Jr. Memorial Hospital), 1796 Hwy. 441 N., Box 1307, Zip 33472; tel. 813/763-2151; Roy C. Vinson, adm. **A**1a 9 10 **F**1 3 6 10 12 15 16 17 23 26 34 45 47 52; **S**1755	33	10	S		93	3218	59	63.4	0	0	—	—	219
ORANGE PARK—Clay County													
★□ HUMANA HOSPITAL -ORANGE PARK, 2001 Kingsley Ave., P O Box 2000, Zip 32067; tel. 904/272-8500; Lee R. Ledbetter, exec. dir. **A**1a 9 10 **F**1 2 3 6 9 10 12 14 15 16 20 23 26 34 35 36 40 43 44 45 46 52 53; **S**1235	33	10	S		196	8522	128	65.3	22	1173	29329	9264	571
ORLANDO—Orange County													
★□ AMI BROOKWOOD COMMUNITY HOSPITAL (Formerly Brookwood Community Hospital), 1800 Mercy Dr., P O Box 15400, Zip 32808; tel. 305/295-5151; Gary L. Rowe, chief exec. off. (Nonreporting) **A**1a 10; **S**0125	32	10	S		153	—	—	—	—	—	—	—	—
BROOKWOOD COMMUNITY HOSPITAL, See AMI Brookwood Community Hospital													
★□ Δ FLORIDA HOSPITAL MEDICAL CENTER (Includes Florida Hospital-Altamonte, 601 E. Altamonte, Altamonte Springs, Zip 32701; tel. 305/830-4321; Florida Hospital-Apopka, 201 N. Park Ave., Apopka, Zip 32703; tel. 305/889-2566), 601 E. Rollins St., Zip 32803; tel. 305/896-6611; Thomas L. Werner, pres. (Nonreporting) **A**1a 3 5 7 9 10; **S**4165	21	10	S		1071	—	—	—	—	—	—	—	—
HOLIDAY DIVISION, See Orlando Regional Medical Center													
★□ Δ HUMANA HOSPITAL -LUCERNE, 818 S. Main Lane, Zip 32801; tel. 305/237-6111; Jeffrey E. Green, exec. dir. **A**1a 7 9 10 **F**1 2 3 4 6 10 12 13 14 15 16 17 20 23 24 25 34 35 39 42 43 44 45 46 47 53 54; **S**1235	33	10	S		267	10369	188	70.4	0	0	48340	15214	740
★□ NAVAL HOSPITAL, Zip 32813; tel. 305/646-4900; Capt. D. D. Palmer MSC USN, CO **A**1a **F**1 3 6 10 12 14 15 16 23 27 28 30 32 33 34 35 37 40 46 47	43	10	S		114	4266	72	56.7	12	462	35315	26059	941
ORANGE MEMORIAL DIVISION, See Orlando Regional Medical Center													
□ ○ + ORLANDO GENERAL HOSPITAL, 7727 Lake Underhill Dr., Zip 32872; tel. 305/277-8110; Walter J. Wozniak, pres. **A**1a 9 10 11 12 **F**1 3 5 6 12 14 15 16 17 20 23 29 30 32 33 34 35 36 37 40 41 44 45 46 47 48 49 53	23	10	S		197	5088	99	50.3	6	447	22490	8394	473
★□ Δ ORLANDO REGIONAL MEDICAL CENTER (Includes Holiday Division; Orange Memorial Division), 1414 S. Kuhl Ave., Zip 32806; tel. 305/841-5111; J. Gary Strack, pres. & chief exec. off. **A**1a 2 3 5 7 8 9 10 **F**1 2 3 4 5 6 7 8 9 10 11 12 14 15 16 17 20 21 22 23 24 25 26 27 28 29 32 33 34 35 36 37 38 39 40 41 42 44 45 46 47 51 52 53 54; **S**3355	23	10	S		781	29342	556	70.6	68	5803	136569	57080	2977
ORMOND BEACH—Volusia County													
★□ MEMORIAL HOSPITAL, 875 Sterthaus Ave., Zip 32074; tel. 904/677-6900; Richard A. Lind, adm. **A**1a 9 10 **F**1 3 4 5 6 12 14 15 16 20 23 26 34 35 45 46 47 53 54	23	10	S		205	6318	124	60.5	0	0	29385	12326	649
□ ○ + PENINSULA MEDICAL CENTER, 264 S. Atlantic Ave., Zip 32074; tel. 904/672-4161; Terry Hilker, adm. **A**1a 9 10 11 12 **F**1 3 6 10 12 14 15 16 23 26 34 35 43 44 46 47 50 53; **S**5765	33	10	S		119	2767	51	47.2	0	0	—	—	187
PAHOKEE—Palm Beach County													
★□ EVERGLADES MEMORIAL HOSPITAL, 200 S. Barfield Hwy., Box 659, Zip 33476; tel. 305/924-5201; Donald A. Anderson, adm. **A**1a 9 10 **F**1 3 6 14 15 16 34 35 36 40 45 46 47 52	16	10	S		63	3797	42	66.7	20	1162	9325	3455	225
PALATKA—Putnam County													
★□ PUTNAM COMMUNITY HOSPITAL, Hwy. 20 W., Zip 32077; Mailing Address P O Drawer 778, Zip 32078; tel. 904/328-5711; Michael S. Boggs, adm. **A**1a 9 10 **F**1 3 6 10 12 15 16 23 35 36 40 44 45 46 47 53; **S**1755	33	10	S		120	6181	90	75.0	12	504	14361	5526	311
PALM BEACH GARDENS—Palm Beach County													
★□ AMI PALM BEACH GARDENS MEDICAL CENTER (Formerly Palm Beach Gardens Medical Center), 3360 Burns Rd., Zip 33410; tel. 305/622-1411; Jack Barto, exec. dir. (Nonreporting) **A**1a 9 10; **S**0125	33	10	S		204	—	—	—	—	—	—	—	—

Hospital, Address, Telephone, Administrator, Approval and Facility Codes, Multihospital System Code

- ★ American Hospital Association (AHA) membership
- □ Joint Commission on Accreditation of Hospitals (JCAH) accreditation
- + American Osteopathic Hospital Association (AOHA) membership
- ○ American Osteopathic Association (AOA) accreditation
- Δ Commission on Accreditation of Rehabilitation Facilities (CARF) accreditation

Control codes 61, 63, 64, 71, 72 and 73 indicate hospitals listed by AOHA, but not registered by AHA. For definition of numerical codes, see page A2

Hospital, Address, Telephone, Administrator, Approval and Facility Codes, Multihospital System Code	Classification Codes				Inpatient Data				Newborn Data		Expense (thousands of dollars)		
	Control	Service	Stay	Facilities	Beds	Admissions	Census	Occupancy (percent)	Bassinets	Births	Total	Payroll	Personnel
PANAMA CITY—Bay County													
★□ BAY MEDICAL CENTER, 615 N. Bonita Ave., P O Box 2515, Zip 32401; tel. 904/769-1511; A. Gary Muller, adm. **A**1a 9 10 **F**1 3 4 6 7 8 9 10 11 12 14 15 16 17 20 21 23 24 27 30 32 33 34 35 36 39 40 41 43 44 45 46 47 52 53 54	13	10	S		279	11519	220	78.3	28	1087	40899	17452	943
GULF COAST COMMUNITY HOSPITAL, See HCA Gulf Coast Hospital													
★□ HCA GULF COAST HOSPITAL (Formerly Gulf Coast Community Hospital), 449 W. 23rd St., Zip 32405; tel. 904/769-8341; Donald E. Butts, adm. **A**1a 9 10 **F**1 3 6 10 12 14 15 16 20 23 34 35 40 46 47 53; **S**1755	33	10	S		176	7254	112	63.6	16	879	—	—	449
U. S. AIR FORCE HOSPITAL, See Tyndall Air Force Base													
PATRICK AIR FORCE BASE—Brevard County													
U. S. AIR FORCE HOSPITAL, Zip 32925; tel. 305/494-8102 (Nonreporting)W. 23rd	41	10	S		25	—	—	—	—	—	—	—	—
PEMBROKE PINES—Broward County													
□ PEMBROKE PINES GENERAL HOSPITAL, 2301 University Dr., Zip 33024; tel. 305/962-9650; Edward Maas, exec. dir. **A**1a 9 10 **F**1 2 3 6 10 12 14 15 16 23 24 34 35 44 45 46 47 53; **S**1805	33	10	S		301	5667	111	36.9	0	0	29292	8680	474
PENSACOLA—Escambia County													
★□ BAPTIST HOSPITAL, Box 17500, Zip 32522; tel. 904/434-4011; John N. Robbins, adm. (Total facility includes 62 beds in nursing home-type unit) **A**1a 2 3 5 9 10 **F**1 2 3 5 6 7 8 9 10 11 12 14 15 16 17 19 20 23 24 26 27 28 30 32 33 34 35 36 37 39 40 41 42 44 45 46 47 48 49 50 53 54; **S**0185	23	10	S	TF	520	12038	276	53.1	16	1011	54478	21575	1293
				H	458	11695	247	—	16	1011	53519	21070	1257
★□ NAVAL HOSPITAL, Zip 32512; tel. 904/452-6611; Capt. L. F. Raymond MSC USN, CO **A**1a 2 3 5 **F**1 3 6 10 12 14 15 16 23 28 30 33 34 35 37 38 40 46 47 48 52	43	10	S		119	6198	84	70.6	31	936	49334	33765	1068
REHABILITATION INSTITUTE OF WEST FLORIDA, See West Florida Regional Medical Center													
★□ SACRED HEART HOSPITAL OF PENSACOLA, 5151 N. Ninth Ave., Zip 32513; tel. 904/474-7000; Sr. Virginia Cotter, pres. **A**1a 3 5 9 10 **F**1 2 3 4 5 6 10 12 14 15 16 23 24 34 35 36 38 40 43 44 45 46 47 50 51 52 53 54; **S**1885	21	10	S		380	14300	240	63.2	20	1891	56945	23862	1334
THE PAVILION, See West Florida Regional Medical Center													
□ UNIVERSITY HOSPITAL AND CLINIC, 1200 W. Leonard St., Zip 32501; tel. 904/436-9011; Gib Newsome, adm. (Nonreporting) **A**1a 9 10; **S**9555	13	10	S		130	—	—	—	—	—	—	—	—
WEST FLORIDA HOSPITAL, See West Florida Regional Medical Center													
★□ Δ WEST FLORIDA REGIONAL MEDICAL CENTER (Includes Rehabilitation Institute of West Florida, 8391 N. Davis Hwy., P O Box 18900, Zip 32523; tel. 904/434-3481; Andrew H. Dearth, adm.; West Florida Hospital, 8383 N. Davis Hwy., Zip 32514; tel. 904/478-4460; John Kausch, adm.; The Pavilion, 8383 N. Davis Hwy., P O Box 18900, Zip 32523; tel. 904/478-4460; John Kausch, adm.), 8383 N. David Hwy., P O Box 18900, Zip 32523; tel. 904/478-4460; John Kausch, adm. **A**1a 2 7 9 10 **F**1 2 3 4 5 6 7 8 9 10 11 12 14 15 16 17 19 20 23 24 25 26 27 30 32 33 34 35 36 39 40 42 43 44 46 48 49 53 54; **S**1755	33	10	S		547	12190	278	50.8	15	558	61333	22538	1139
PERRY—Taylor County													
★□ DOCTORS MEMORIAL HOSPITAL, 407 E. Ash St., P O Box 1090, Zip 32347; tel. 904/584-0800; William H. Anderson, adm. **A**1a 9 10 **F**1 3 6 10 16 23 35 36 47; **S**1605	23	10	S		48	1405	14	29.2	8	126	4475	1770	95
PINELLAS PARK—Pinellas County													
○ + METROPOLITAN GENERAL HOSPITAL, 7950 66th St. N., Box 30, Zip 33565; tel. 813/546-9871; D. William Adams, exec. dir. (Nonreporting) **A**9 10 11 12	23	10	S		154	—	—	—	—	—	—	—	—
PLANT CITY—Hillsborough County													
★□ SOUTH FLORIDA BAPTIST HOSPITAL, 301 N. Alexander St., Drawer H, Zip 34289; tel. 813/757-1200; Dale E. Howard, adm. **A**1a 9 10 **F**1 3 6 10 12 14 15 16 20 23 35 36 37 40 45 47 52 53	23	10	S		114	4781	76	66.7	11	91	12780	5590	322
PLANTATION—Broward County													
□ ○ DOCTORS GENERAL HOSPITAL, 6701 W. Sunrise Blvd., Zip 33313; tel. 305/581-7800; William C. Gompers, chief exec. off. **A**1a 9 10 11 12 **F**1 3 6 10 12 15 16 20 23 34 35 36 40 44 46 50 52 53; **S**9555	32	10	S		159	5662	101	63.5	4	151	24145	8640	353
★□ HUMANA HOSPITAL -BENNETT, 8201 W. Broward Blvd., Zip 33324; tel. 305/476-3915; H. Rex Etheredge, exec. dir. **A**1a 10 **F**1 3 6 10 11 12 14 15 16 20 23 34 35 45 46 53; **S**1235	33	10	S		204	8142	140	68.6	0	0	29429	10266	500
★□ PLANTATION GENERAL HOSPITAL, 401 N.W. 42nd Ave., Zip 33317; tel. 305/587-5010; James Sample, adm. **A**1a 9 10 **F**1 2 3 6 10 12 14 15 16 20 23 26 34 35 40 42 46 51 52 53 54; **S**1755	33	10	S		264	9978	145	54.9	23	2483	35595	14851	678
POMPANO BEACH—Broward County													
★□ HUMANA HOSPITAL -CYPRESS, 600 S.W. Third St., Zip 33060; tel. 305/786-5030; Stephen P. Dexter, exec. dir. **A**1a 9 10 **F**1 2 3 6 10 12 14 16 20 23 35 41 43 45 46 47 53; **S**1235	33	10	S		273	5181	100	36.6	0	0	21616	8579	378
★□ NORTH BROWARD MEDICAL CENTER, 201 Sample Rd., Zip 33064; tel. 305/941-8300; Thomas J. Corder, adm. **A**1a 9 10 **F**1 2 3 6 7 8 9 10 11 12 14 15 16 20 23 24 26 34 35 43 44 45 46 47 52 53 54; **S**3115	16	10	S		347	11125	243	74.3	0	0	51798	23854	1038
PORT CHARLOTTE—Charlotte County													
□ FAWCETT MEMORIAL HOSPITAL, 21298 Olean Blvd., Zip 33952; tel. 813/629-1181; R. Wayne Cole, pres. (Nonreporting) **A**1a 9 10; **S**1935	33	10	S		254	—	—	—	—	—	—	—	—
★□ ST. JOSEPH HOSPITAL, 2500 Harbor Blvd., Zip 33952; tel. 813/625-4122; Col. Russel L. Bryant, actg. adm. **A**1a 9 10 **F**1 3 6 10 12 14 15 16 23 24 26 34 35 36 40 44 45 46 47 52 53; **S**1345	21	10	S		212	6063	104	49.1	10	661	23583	8610	531
PORT ST. JOE—Gulf County													
GULF PINES HOSPITAL, 102 20th St., P O Box 40, Zip 32456; tel. 904/227-1121; David Odum, adm. (Nonreporting) **A**9 10; **S**1935	23	10	S		45	—	—	—	—	—	—	—	—
PORT ST. LUCIE—St. Lucie County													
★□ HCA MEDICAL CENTER OF PORT ST. LUCIE (Formerly Port St. Lucie Hospital), 1800 S.E. Tiffany Ave., Zip 33452; tel. 305/335-4000; C. Robert Benson, adm. **A**1a 9 10 **F**1 3 6 10 12 14 15 16 23 30 34 35 45 46 47 53; **S**1755	33	10	S		150	4369	78	52.0	0	0	17237	5769	312
PUNTA GORDA—Charlotte County													
★□ MEDICAL CENTER HOSPITAL, 809 E. Marion Ave., Zip 33950; tel. 813/639-3131; Valgene Devitt, pres. **A**1a 9 10 **F**1 3 6 9 10 11 12 14 15 16 23 24 26 27 29 30 32 33 34 35 41 42 43 44 45 46 47 48 49 50 52 53 54; **S**4165	21	10	S		208	5073	101	48.6	0	0	22117	9413	534
QUINCY—Gadsden County													
□ GADSDEN MEMORIAL HOSPITAL, Hwy. 90 E., Box 819, Zip 32351; tel. 904/875-1100; Steven D. Patonai, adm. **A**1a 9 10 **F**1 6 15 23 26 34 35 36 40 45 46 50; **S**1605	23	10	S		51	1822	22	43.1	12	265	4724	1697	128
ROCKLEDGE—Brevard County													
★□ WUESTHOFF MEMORIAL HOSPITAL, 110 Longwood Ave., Box 6, Zip 32955; tel. 305/636-2211; Robert Carman, pres. **A**1a 9 10 **F**1 3 6 9 10 12 14 15 16 17 20 21 23 24 26 27 32 33 34 35 36 39 40 41 45 46 47 52 53 54	23	10	S		264	11999	207	82.8	17	992	43854	18843	966

Hospital, Address, Telephone, Administrator, Approval and Facility Codes, Multihospital System Code	Classification Codes			Facilities	Inpatient Data				Newborn Data		Expense (thousands of dollars)		Personnel
★ American Hospital Association (AHA) membership □ Joint Commission on Accreditation of Hospitals (JCAH) accreditation + American Osteopathic Hospital Association (AOHA) membership ○ American Osteopathic Association (AOA) accreditation Δ Commission on Accreditation of Rehabilitation Facilities (CARF) accreditation Control codes 61, 63, 64, 71, 72 and 73 indicate hospitals listed by AOHA, but not registered by AHA. For definition of numerical codes, see page A2	Control	Service	Stay		Beds	Admissions	Census	Occupancy (percent)	Bassinets	Births	Total	Payroll	
SAFETY HARBOR—Pinellas County													
MEASE HOSPITAL COUNTRYSIDE, 3231 McMullen-Booth Rd., Zip 33572; tel. 813/725-6222; Richard H. Katzeff, vice-pres. (Newly Registered) **A**9 10 **F**1 3 6 9 10 11 12 14 15 16 20 23 24 26 30 32 35 36 44 45 46 47 53; **S**1335	23	10	S		70	3026	46	65.7	0	0	12800	4781	286
SANFORD—Seminole County													
★□ CENTRAL FLORIDA REGIONAL HOSPITAL, 1401 W. Seminole Blvd., Zip 32771; tel. 305/321-4500; James D. Tesar, adm. (Nonreporting) **A**1a 9 10; **S**1755	33	10	S		226	—	—	—	—	—	—	—	—
SARASOTA—Sarasota County													
★□ DOCTORS HOSPITAL, 2750 Bahia Vista St., Zip 33579; tel. 813/366-1411; H. Allen Williams, adm. (Nonreporting) **A**1a b 9 10; **S**1755	33	10	S		168	—	—	—	—	—	—	—	—
MEMORIAL HOSPITAL, See Sarasota Memorial Hospital													
★□ SARASOTA MEMORIAL HOSPITAL (Formerly Memorial Hospital), 1700 S. Tamiami Trail, Zip 33579; tel. 813/955-1111; Philip K. Beauchamp, pres. **A**1a 9 10 **F**1 2 3 4 5 6 9 10 11 12 15 16 17 20 23 24 26 27 28 29 30 32 33 34 35 36 40 41 42 43 44 45 46 48 52 53 54	16	10	S		642	22115	458	71.3	30	2332	95987	39065	1969
□ SARASOTA PALMS HOSPITAL, 1650 S. Osprey Ave., Zip 33579; tel. 813/366-6070; Robert J. Constantine PhD, adm. (Nonreporting) **A**1b 9 10; **S**0825	33	22	S		90	—	—	—	—	—	—	—	—
SEBASTIAN—Indian River County													
★□ HUMANA HOSPITAL -SEBASTIAN, 13695 N. U. S. Hwy. 1, Box 838, Zip 32958; tel. 305/589-3186; Mitchell B. Smith, exec. dir. **A**1a 9 10 **F**1 3 6 10 12 15 16 23 30 32 33 34 35 36 40 44 45 46 47 48 50 53; **S**1235	33	10	S		133	3896	88	66.2	8	232	—	—	249
SEBRING—Highlands County													
★□ HIGHLANDS REGIONAL MEDICAL CENTER (Formerly Highlands General Hospital), 3600 S. Highlands Ave., Drawer 2066, Zip 33870; tel. 813/385-6101; Joe D. Pinion, exec. dir. (Nonreporting) **A**1a 9 10; **S**1775	16	10	S		99	—	—	—	—	—	—	—	—
SEMINOLE—Pinellas County													
□ LAKE SEMINOLE HOSPITAL, 9675 Seminole Blvd., P O Box 4001, Zip 33542; tel. 813/393-4646; Dan F. Ausman, adm. **A**1a 9 10 **F**1 3 6 9 10 12 14 15 16 23 34 35 45 46 47 53; **S**0875	33	10	S		99	2558	54	54.5	0	0	—	—	202
□ ○ UNIVERSITY GENERAL HOSPITAL, 10200 Seminole Blvd., Zip 33544; tel. 813/397-5511; Frank W. Harris, adm. **A**1a 9 10 11 12 13 **F**1 3 6 10 12 14 15 16 20 23 24 33 34 35 37 42 43 44 46 50; **S**0875	33	10	S		140	2952	59	42.1	0	0	13606	4540	200
SOUTH MIAMI—Dade County													
★□ LARKIN GENERAL HOSPITAL, 7031 S.W. 62nd Ave., Zip 33243; tel. 305/666-6500; William H. Comte, pres. **A**1a 9 10 **F**1 3 6 10 12 14 15 16 20 23 24 26 27 29 34 35 42 44 45 46 53; **S**1435	32	10	S		112	2628	43	46.2	0	0	13077	5276	294
★□ SOUTH MIAMI HOSPITAL, 7400 S.W. 62nd Ave., Zip 33143; tel. 305/661-4611; M. W. Crews, pres. **A**1a b 2 9 10 **F**1 2 3 4 5 6 10 11 12 15 16 20 21 23 24 25 26 34 35 36 37 40 42 44 45 46 47 48 49 50 51 53 54	23	10	S		406	15264	299	73.6	30	2861	73850	36360	1644
SPRING HILL—Hernando County													
★□ HCA OAK HILL HOSPITAL (Formerly Oak Hill Community Hospital), 11375 Cortez Blvd., P O Box 5300, Zip 33526; tel. 904/596-6632; Dennis Taylor, adm. **A**1a 9 10 **F**1 3 6 15 16 20 23 24 34 35 44 45 46 47 53; **S**1755	33	10	S		96	3511	60	62.5	0	0	—	—	264
ST. AUGUSTINE—St. Johns County													
★□ FLAGLER HOSPITAL, 159 Marine St., Box 100, Zip 32084; tel. 904/824-8411; James D. Conzemius, pres. **A**1a 9 10 **F**1 3 6 10 12 15 16 20 21 23 27 30 32 33 34 35 36 40 41 45 46 47 52 53	23	10	S		131	4124	68	51.9	12	495	12285	5435	350
★□ ST. AUGUSTINE GENERAL HOSPITAL, U. S. 1 S., Zip 32084; Mailing Address Drawer 2208, Zip 32085; tel. 904/824-8431; Raymond M. Johnson, adm. **A**1a 9 10 **F**1 3 6 10 15 16 20 23 35 43 45 46 47 52 53; **S**1755	33	10	S		115	2564	50	43.5	0	0	—	—	265
ST. CLOUD—Osceola County													
★□ ORLANDO REGIONAL MEDICAL CENTER ST. CLOUD, 2906 17th St., Zip 32769; tel. 305/892-2135; Jim Norris, adm. **A**1a 9 10 **F**1 3 6 12 14 15 16 23 35 45 53; **S**3355	23	10	S		68	2479	39	57.4	0	0	7856	2758	188
ST. PETERSBURG—Pinellas County													
★□ ALL CHILDREN'S HOSPITAL, 801 Sixth St. S., Zip 33701; tel. 813/898-7451; J. Dennis Sexton, pres. **A**1a 3 5 9 10 **F**1 3 4 6 12 14 15 16 20 23 24 33 34 42 44 45 46 51 54	23	50	S		103	3964	82	82.0	0	0	29944	12896	657
★□ BAYFRONT MEDICAL CENTER, 701 Sixth St. S., Zip 33701; tel. 813/893-6111; Theodor L. Jacobsen, pres. **A**1a 3 5 8 9 10 **F**1 2 3 5 6 7 8 9 10 11 12 14 15 16 17 20 23 24 25 26 32 33 34 35 36 37 40 41 42 44 45 46 47 53	23	10	S		276	16000	256	80.3	59	3804	56043	24172	1292
EDWARD H. WHITE II MEMORIAL HOSPITAL, See HCA Edward White Hospital													
□ ○ + HARBORSIDE HOSPITAL, 401 15th St. N., Zip 33705; Mailing Address P O Box 11748, Zip 33733; tel. 813/821-2021; Lynn C. Orfgen, adm. **A**1a 9 10 11 12 **F**1 3 6 7 8 10 12 16 23 24 27 30 33 34 35 44 46 53; **S**1375	33	10	S		143	1813	49	34.3	0	0	11423	3808	173
★□ HCA EDWARD WHITE HOSPITAL (Formerly Edward H. White Ii Memorial Hospital), 2323 Ninth Ave. N., Zip 33713; Mailing Address P O Box 12018, Zip 33733; tel. 813/323-1111; Bruce A. Klockars, adm. **A**1a 9 10 **F**1 3 6 10 12 14 15 16 23 34 35 37 46 47; **S**1755	33	10	S		167	3379	72	43.1	0	0	19281	6117	310
★□ HUMANA HOSPITAL -ST. PETERSBURG, 6500 38th Ave. N., Zip 33710; Mailing Address Box 13096, Zip 33733; tel. 813/384-1414; David K. Donin, exec. dir. **A**1a 9 10 **F**1 3 6 9 10 11 12 14 15 16 20 23 26 32 33 34 35 45 46 47 53; **S**1235	33	10	S		219	6128	133	61.0	0	0	29593	9565	474
★□ HUMANA HOSPITAL -SUN BAY, 3030 Sixth St. S., Zip 33705; tel. 813/823-1122; John B. Wheatley Jr., exec. dir. (Nonreporting) **A**1a 9 10; **S**1235	33	10	S		200	—	—	—	—	—	—	—	—
★□ HUMANA HOSPITAL-NORTHSIDE, 6000 49th St. N., Zip 33709; tel. 813/521-5000; Donald A. Shaffett, exec. dir. **A**1a 9 10 **F**1 2 3 5 6 10 11 12 15 16 20 23 24 34 35 44 46 53; **S**1235	33	10	S		188	4817	95	50.5	0	0	23000	7353	393
□ PALMS OF PASADENA HOSPITAL, 1501 Pasadena Ave. S., Zip 33707; Mailing Address Box 6158, Zip 33736; tel. 813/381-1000; Erwin E. Abrams, adm. **A**1a 9 10 **F**1 2 3 6 7 8 9 10 11 12 14 15 16 20 23 32 34 35 44 46 47 53; **S**3015	33	10	S		310	7335	166	53.5	0	0	—	—	608
★□ ST. ANTHONY'S HOSPITAL, 601 12th St. N., Zip 33705; tel. 813/825-1100; Daniel T. McMurray, pres. (Nonreporting) **A**1a 9 10; **S**1385	21	10	S		434	—	—	—	—	—	—	—	—
STARKE—Bradford County													
★□ BRADFORD HOSPITAL, 922 E. Call St., P O Box 1210, Zip 32091; tel. 904/964-6000; Tim Rearick, chief oper. off. **A**1a 9 10 **F**1 6 14 15 16 23 34 35 45; **S**7895	23	10	S		30	1338	18	60.0	0	0	3313	1169	72
STUART—Martin County													
★□ MARTIN MEMORIAL HOSPITAL, Hospital Dr., Zip 33494; Mailing Address P O Bin 2396, Zip 33495; tel. 305/287-5200; Guy N. Cromwell, exec. vice-pres. **A**1a 9 10 **F**1 3 6 7 8 9 10 11 12 14 15 16 20 21 23 24 29 30 34 35 36 40 41 44 45 46 47 52 53	23	10	S		308	11924	202	64.1	16	1065	45563	20191	1015
SUN CITY CENTER—Hillsborough County													
★ HCA SUN CITY HOSPITAL (Formerly Sun City Regional Medical Center), 4016 State Rd. 674, Zip 33570; tel. 813/634-3301; W. Harold O'Neal, adm. (Nonreporting) **A**9 10; **S**1755	33	10	S		73	—	—	—	—	—	—	—	—

Hospital, Address, Telephone, Administrator, Approval and Facility Codes, Multihospital System Code	Classification Codes				Inpatient Data				Newborn Data		Expense (thousands of dollars)		
★ American Hospital Association (AHA) membership □ Joint Commission on Accreditation of Hospitals (JCAH) accreditation + American Osteopathic Hospital Association (AOHA) membership ○ American Osteopathic Association (AOA) accreditation Δ Commission on Accreditation of Rehabilitation Facilities (CARF) accreditation Control codes 61, 63, 64, 71, 72 and 73 indicate hospitals listed by AOHA, but not registered by AHA. For definition of numerical codes, see page A2	Control	Service	Stay	Facilities	Beds	Admissions	Census	Occupancy (percent)	Bassinets	Births	Total	Payroll	Personnel
TALLAHASSEE—Leon County													
⊞ TALLAHASSEE COMMUNITY HOSPITAL, 2626 Capital Medical Blvd., Zip 32308; tel. 904/656-5000; Kenneth J. Newell, adm. **A**1a 9 10 **F**1 3 5 6 10 12 14 15 16 20 23 24 26 32 33 35 36 37 38 40 42 44 45 47 49 53 54; **S**1755	33	10	S		180	6151	90	50.0	25	1143	19966	6446	390
⊞ TALLAHASSEE MEMORIAL REGIONAL MEDICAL CENTER, Miccosukee Rd. & Magnolia Dr., Zip 32308; tel. 904/681-5385; Middleton T. Mustian, pres. & chief exec. off. (Total facility includes 113 beds in nursing home-type unit) **A**1a 2 3 9 10 **F**1 2 3 4 5 6 7 8 9 10 11 12 13 15 16 17 19 20 21 23 24 26 27 30 33 34 35 36 37 39 40 41 42 44 45 46 47 50 52 53 54	23	10	S	TF H	771 658	22076 21564	434 332	56.3 —	51 51	2301 2301	85464 —	35986 —	1824 1735
TAMARAC—Broward County													
⊞ UNIVERSITY COMMUNITY HOSPITAL, 7201 N. University Dr., Zip 33321; tel. 305/721-2200; Lawrence L. Pieretti, adm. **A**1a 9 10 **F**1 3 6 7 8 9 10 11 12 14 16 23 24 26 34 35 37 46 47 52 53; **S**1755	33	10	S		236	8430	159	71.3	0	0	—	—	475
TAMPA—Hillsborough County													
⊞ AMI MEMORIAL HOSPITAL OF TAMPA (Formerly Memorial Hospital of Tampa), 2901 Swann Ave., Zip 33609; Mailing Address Box 18054, Zip 33679; tel. 813/877-0441; Keith Henthorne, chief exec. off.; Vincent Nico, asst. adm. (Nonreporting) **A**1a 9 10; **S**0125	32	10	S		158	—	—	—	—	—	—	—	—
⊞ AMI TOWN AND COUNTRY MEDICAL CENTER (Formerly Town and Country Hospital), 6001 Webb Rd., Zip 33615; tel. 813/885-6666; Gerald McAteer, exec. dir. (Nonreporting) **A**1a 9 10; **S**0125	33	10	S		201	—	—	—	—	—	—	—	—
□ ○ + CARROLLWOOD COMMUNITY HOSPITAL, 7171 N. Dale Mabry Hwy., Zip 33614; tel. 813/935-1191; Mary A. Reese, adm. **A**1a 9 10 11 **F**1 3 6 10 12 15 16 23 32 33 34 35 44 46 50 53	33	10	S		120	4315	56	46.7	0	0	18817	5220	251
⊞ CENTRO ASTURIANO HOSPITAL, 1302 21st Ave., Zip 33605; tel. 813/247-4771; John Fernandez Jr., adm. **A**1a 9 10 **F**1 3 6 14 15 16 20 23 26 35 44 45 46 53	33	10	S		144	2285	59	41.0	0	0	10772	4531	225
★ CENTRO ESPANOL MEMORIAL HOSPITAL, 4801 N. Howard Ave., Zip 33603; tel. 813/879-1550; Robert M. Velarde, chief exec. off. **A**9 10 **F**1 3 10 15 16 17 28 35 37 45	23	10	S		102	2201	45	44.1	0	0	—	—	154
⊞ CHARTER HOSPITAL OF TAMPA BAY (Formerly Tampa Heights Hospital), 4004 N. Riverside Dr., Zip 33603; tel. 813/238-8671; James P. Hackett Jr., adm. **A**1b 9 10 **F**24 28 29 32 33 42 48; **S**0695	33	22	S		133	1511	88	66.2	0	0	—	—	152
⊞ HILLSBOROUGH COUNTY HOSPITAL (Special Medical and Psychiatric), 5906 N. 30th St., P O Box 11912, Zip 33680; tel. 813/239-1186; Lanny W. Erickson, adm. **A**1a 3 5 9 10 **F**12 14 16 23 24 27 28 29 30 32 33 34 42 50; **S**1525	13	49	S		137	1518	71	56.8	0	0	—	—	260
⊞ HUMANA WOMEN'S HOSPITAL -TAMPA, 3030 W. Buffalo Ave., Zip 33607; tel. 813/879-4730; William A. Marek, exec. dir. **A**1a 9 10 **F**1 6 12 14 15 16 34 36 37 40 45 46 51; **S**1235	33	44	S		219	9753	119	54.3	84	5814	30956	11777	596
⊞ JAMES A. HALEY VETERANS HOSPITAL, 13000 Bruce B Downs Blvd., Zip 33612; tel. 813/972-2000; Richard A. Silver, dir. (Nonreporting) **A**1a b 3 5 8	45	10	S		817	—	—	—	—	—	—	—	—
MEMORIAL HOSPITAL OF TAMPA, See AMI Memorial Hospital of Tampa													
★ SHRINERS HOSPITALS FOR CRIPPLED CHILDREN, 12502 N. Pine Dr., Zip 33612; tel. 813/972-2250; Gene Yeazell, adm. (Data for 352 days) **A**9 **F**23 24 33 34 42 46; **S**4125	23	47	S		60	598	20	33.3	0	0	—	—	179
⊞ ST. JOSEPH'S HOSPITAL, 3001 W. Buffalo Ave., Zip 33607; Mailing Address Box 4227, Zip 33677; tel. 813/870-4000; Sr. Marie Celeste Sullivan, pres. **A**1a 2 3 5 9 10 **F**1 2 3 4 5 6 7 8 9 10 11 12 13 15 16 20 23 24 26 27 28 29 30 32 34 35 42 43 44 45 46 47 52 53 54; **S**1385	21	10	S		649	25341	491	75.7	0	0	95596	44712	2313
□ TAMPA BAY COMMUNITY HOSPITAL, 4555 S. Manhattan Ave., Zip 33611; tel. 813/839-6341; Stephen H. Noble, exec. dir. (Nonreporting) **A**1a 9 10; **S**9605	32	10	S		73	—	—	—	—	—	—	—	—
⊞ Δ TAMPA GENERAL HOSPITAL, Davis Islands, Zip 33606; Mailing Address P O Box 1289, Zip 33601; tel. 813/253-0711; Newell E. France, pres. **A**1a 2 3 5 7 8 9 10 **F**1 2 3 4 5 6 7 8 9 10 11 12 13 14 15 16 17 20 22 23 24 25 26 27 29 32 33 34 35 36 37 40 42 43 44 45 46 47 51 52 53 54; **S**1525	16	10	S		596	22670	479	80.4	48	5328	139528	58426	2409
TAMPA HEIGHTS HOSPITAL, See Charter Hospital of Tampa Bay													
TOWN AND COUNTRY HOSPITAL, See AMI Town and Country Medical Center													
U. S. AIR FORCE REGIONAL HOSPITAL MACDILL, See MacDill Air Force Base													
⊞ UNIVERSITY COMMUNITY HOSPITAL, 3100 E. Fletcher Ave., Zip 33613; tel. 813/971-6000; Terry L. Jones, adm. (Nonreporting) **A**1a 2 9 10	23	10	S		321	—	—	—	—	—	—	—	—
TARPON SPRINGS—Pinellas County													
⊞ AMI ANCLOTE MANOR PSYCHIATRIC HOSPITAL (Formerly AMI Anclote Manor Hospital), 1527 Riverside Dr., Zip 33589; tel. 813/937-4211; Walter Wellborn MD, exec. dir. (Nonreporting) **A**1b 5 9; **S**0125	23	22	L		100	—	—	—	—	—	—	—	—
⊞ TARPON SPRINGS GENERAL HOSPITAL, 1395 S. Pinellas Ave., Zip 33589; tel. 813/937-3201; Joseph N. Kiefer, adm. **A**1a 9 10 **F**1 2 3 6 10 15 16 23 24 34 35 44 45 46 52 53	23	10	S		150	4980	96	64.0	0	0	17039	6006	339
TAVERNIER—Monroe County													
□ MARINERS HOSPITAL, 50 High Point Rd., Zip 33070; tel. 305/852-9222; Howard C. Andersen, adm. **A**1a 9 10 **F**1 3 10 12 16 17 23 24 35 44 45 46 47 53	23	10	S		42	1134	18	42.9	0	0	4531	1844	126
TITUSVILLE—Brevard County													
⊞ JESS PARRISH MEMORIAL HOSPITAL, 951 N. Washington Ave., Zip 32796; Mailing Address Drawer W, Zip 32780; tel. 305/268-6000; Rod Baker, adm. **A**1a 9 10 **F**1 3 6 9 10 12 14 15 16 23 24 26 30 32 33 34 35 36 37 40 44 45 46 47 52 53	16	10	S		210	8727	133	63.3	20	720	27648	11737	619
TYNDALL AIR FORCE BASE—Bay County													
□ U. S. AIR FORCE HOSPITAL, Zip 32403; tel. 904/283-7515; Col. Paul V. Humbert MC, cmdr. (Nonreporting) **A**1a	41	10	S		50	—	—	—	—	—	—	—	—
VENICE—Sarasota County													
⊞ VENICE HOSPITAL, 540 the Rialto, Zip 33595; tel. 813/485-7711; Ronald T. Hanson, pres. **A**1a 9 10 **F**1 3 6 10 12 14 15 16 20 23 24 26 28 30 33 34 35 36 40 43 45 46 47 53 54	23	10	S		312	10576	201	64.4	5	238	37692	15584	777
VERO BEACH—Indian River County													
⊞ INDIAN RIVER MEMORIAL HOSPITAL, 1000 36th St., Zip 32960; tel. 305/567-4311; Michael J. O'Grady, pres. **A**1a 9 10 **F**1 3 6 10 12 14 15 16 20 23 24 26 33 34 35 36 40 44 45 46 47 48 50 53; **S**0025	23	10	S		293	10445	177	60.4	21	844	36225	15417	862
TREASURE COAST REHABILITATION HOSPITAL, 1600 37th St., Zip 32960; tel. 305/778-2100; Lester J. Perling, adm. & chief exec. off. (Data for 90 days) **A**9 **F**16 23 24 26 33 34 42 44 46 47	33	46	S		40	54	14	35.0	0	0	—	—	—
WAUCHULA—Hardee County													
⊞ HARDEE MEMORIAL HOSPITAL, 533 W. Carlton St., Box 1058, Zip 33873; tel. 813/773-3101; Terry D. Miller, adm. **A**1a 9 10 **F**1 6 12 14 23 34 35 45	16	10	S		50	1178	13	26.0	0	0	3302	1403	102
WEST HOLLYWOOD—Broward County													
SOUTH FLORIDA STATE HOSPITAL, 1000 S.W. 84th Ave., Zip 33025; tel. 305/983-4321; Nancy L. Dion, adm. **A**10 **F**23 24 32 33 42 46 47 50	12	22	L		573	308	569	95.2	0	0	25117	14929	855

Hospital, Address, Telephone, Administrator, Approval and Facility Codes, Multihospital System Code	Classification Codes				Inpatient Data				Newborn Data		Expense (thousands of dollars)		
★ American Hospital Association (AHA) membership □ Joint Commission on Accreditation of Hospitals (JCAH) accreditation + American Osteopathic Hospital Association (AOHA) membership ○ American Osteopathic Association (AOA) accreditation Δ Commission on Accreditation of Rehabilitation Facilities (CARF) accreditation Control codes 61, 63, 64, 71, 72 and 73 indicate hospitals listed by AOHA, but not registered by AHA. For definition of numerical codes, see page A2	Control	Service	Stay	Facilities	Beds	Admissions	Census	Occupancy (percent)	Bassinets	Births	Total	Payroll	Personnel
WEST PALM BEACH—Palm Beach County													
★□ FORTY-FIFTH STREET MENTAL HEALTH CENTER, 1041 45th St., Zip 33407; tel. 305/844-9741; Terry H. Allen, exec. dir. (Nonreporting) **A**1b	23	22	S		39	—	—	—	—	—	—	—	—
★□ GOOD SAMARITAN HOSPITAL, Flagler Dr. at Palm Beach Lakes Blvd., Box 3166, Zip 33402; tel. 305/655-5511; Kenneth A. Weda, pres. **A**1a 9 10 **F**1 3 6 7 8 9 10 11 12 14 15 16 20 23 24 30 34 35 36 37 40 45 46 47 51 52 53	23	10	S		285	11924	183	64.2	32	2392	43069	18964	969
★□ ○ HUMANA HOSPITAL -PALM BEACHES, 2201 45th St., Zip 33407; tel. 305/863-3801; Niels P. Vernegaard, exec. dir. (Nonreporting) **A**1a 9 10 11 12 13; **S**1235	33	10	S		250	—	—	—	—	—	—	—	—
★□ ST. MARY'S HOSPITAL, 901 45th St., Zip 33407; tel. 305/844-6300; John E. Fidler, pres. **A**1a 9 10 **F**1 2 3 6 7 8 9 10 11 12 15 16 17 20 23 24 30 35 36 40 41 44 45 46 51 52 53; **S**1385	23	10	S		358	14447	266	74.3	24	3028	55273	23930	1063
WILLISTON—Levy County													
★□ WILLISTON MEMORIAL HOSPITAL, 125 S.W. Seventh St., P O Drawer 550, Zip 32696; tel. 904/528-2801; John T. Myles, chief oper. off. **A**1a 9 10 **F**1 3 12 14 15 16 34 35 43 45 47; **S**7895	23	10	S		40	861	15	37.5	0	0	3218	1189	66
WINTER GARDEN—Orange County													
★□ WEST ORANGE MEMORIAL HOSPITAL, 555 N. Dillard St., P O Box 1107, Zip 32787; tel. 305/656-1244; Mark E. Robitaille, adm. **A**1a 9 10 **F**1 3 6 10 12 14 15 16 23 24 26 34 35 37 40 41 42 43 44 45 46 47 52 53	16	10	S		141	3387	42	29.8	7	373	12763	5568	295
WINTER HAVEN—Polk County													
★□ WINTER HAVEN HOSPITAL, 200 Ave. F N.E., Zip 33881; tel. 813/293-1121; Lance W. Anastasio, adm. (Total facility includes 100 beds in nursing home-type unit) **A**1a 9 10 **F**1 2 3 5 6 7 8 9 10 11 12 14 15 16 17 19 20 21 23 24 26 27 28 29 30 32 33 34 35 36 40 41 42 43 44 45 46 47 50 52 53; **S**1615	23	10	S	TF	392	14857	269	68.6	35	1304	48813	23597	1559
				H	292	14550	243	—	35	1304	47577	23166	1506
WINTER PARK—Orange County													
★□ WINTER PARK MEMORIAL HOSPITAL, 200 N. Lakemont Ave., Zip 32792; tel. 305/646-7000; Willard E. Wisler, pres. **A**1a 9 10 **F**1 2 3 5 6 10 12 15 16 17 23 33 34 35 36 40 44 45 46 47 50 52 53 54	23	10	S		301	12966	198	65.8	25	1563	37763	16558	888
ZEPHYRHILLS—Pasco County													
★□ EAST PASCO MEDICAL CENTER, 2500 N. Hwy. 301, Zip 34248; tel. 813/788-0411; Bob Dodd, adm. (Nonreporting) **A**1a 10; **S**4165	21	10	S		85	—	—	—	—	—	—	—	—

Hospital, Address, Telephone, Administrator, Approval and Facility Codes, Multihospital System Code	Classification Codes				Inpatient Data				Newborn Data		Expense (thousands of dollars)		
★ American Hospital Association (AHA) membership ☐ Joint Commission on Accreditation of Hospitals (JCAH) accreditation + American Osteopathic Hospital Association (AOHA) membership ○ American Osteopathic Association (AOA) accreditation Δ Commission on Accreditation of Rehabilitation Facilities (CARF) accreditation Control codes 61, 63, 64, 71, 72 and 73 indicate hospitals listed by AOHA, but not registered by AHA. For definition of numerical codes, see page A2	Control	Service	Stay	Facilities	Beds	Admissions	Census	Occupancy (percent)	Bassinets	Births	Total	Payroll	Personnel

Georgia

Hospital	Control	Service	Stay	Facilities	Beds	Admissions	Census	Occupancy (percent)	Bassinets	Births	Total	Payroll	Personnel
ADEL—Cook County													
MEMORIAL HOSPITAL OF ADEL, 706 N. Parrish Ave., Box 677, Zip 31620; tel. 912/896-2251; James E. Cunningham, adm. (Nonreporting) **A**9 10	33	10	S		142	—	—	—	—	—	—	—	—
ALBANY—Dougherty County													
★☐ HCA PALMYRA MEDICAL CENTERS (Formerly Palmyra Medical Centers), 2000 Palmyra Rd., Box 1908, Zip 31703; tel. 912/888-3800; Douglas M. Parker, adm. **A**1a 9 10 **F**1 2 3 5 6 10 11 12 14 15 16 23 24 26 34 35 44 46 47 53; **S**1755	33	10	S		172	6557	108	52.0	0	0	—	—	498
★☐ PHOEBE PUTNEY MEMORIAL HOSPITAL, 417 Third Ave., Box 1828, Zip 31703; tel. 912/883-1800; Duncan Moore, adm. **A**1a 9 10 **F**1 2 3 4 5 6 7 8 9 10 11 12 14 15 16 20 21 23 27 33 35 37 39 40 42 45 46 47 48 51 52 53 54	16	10	S		384	15793	271	70.6	68	2569	42148	20896	1202
ALMA—Bacon County													
BACON COUNTY HOSPITAL, 302 S. Wayne St., P O Box 745, Zip 31510; tel. 912/632-8961; Jeff Kinlawa, adm. **A**9 10 **F**1 6 14 15 16 34 35 45	16	10	S		50	1295	15	30.0	8	67	2706	1168	87
AMERICUS—Sumter County													
★☐ SUMTER REGIONAL HOSPITAL, 100 Wheatley Dr., Zip 31709; tel. 912/924-6011; James R. Griffith Jr., adm. **A**1a 2 9 10 **F**1 2 3 6 7 8 10 11 12 14 15 16 20 23 24 26 27 30 34 35 36 40 41 42 45 52 53	16	10	S		164	6456	96	58.5	14	842	14658	6534	464
ARLINGTON—Calhoun County													
CALHOUN MEMORIAL HOSPITAL, Academy & Carswell Sts., Drawer R, Zip 31713; tel. 912/725-4272; Newana Williams, adm. (Nonreporting) **A**9 10	16	10	S		84	—	—	—	—	—	—	—	—
ASHBURN—Turner County													
TURNER COUNTY HOSPITAL, 615 E. Washington St., Zip 31714; tel. 912/567-4305; Vernon L. Griffin, adm. **A**9 10 **F**1 14 16 35 40 46	16	10	S		40	604	7	17.5	5	88	981	485	40
ATHENS—Clarke County													
★☐ ATHENS REGIONAL MEDICAL CENTER (Formerly Athens General Hospital), 1199 Prince Ave., Zip 30613; tel. 404/549-9977; John A. Drew, pres. **A**1a 9 10 **F**1 2 3 6 7 8 9 10 11 12 14 15 16 20 23 24 26 27 29 30 32 34 35 36 37 40 42 44 45 46 47 48 49 51 52 53 54	16	10	S		295	12315	197	67.5	14	1205	39446	17523	972
★☐ CHARTER WINDS HOSPITAL, 240 Mitchell Bridge Rd., P O Box 6297, Zip 30604; tel. 404/546-7277; Elbert T. McQueen, adm. (Nonreporting) **A**1a 9 10; **S**0695	33	22	S		65	—	—	—	—	—	—	—	—
★☐ ST. MARY'S HOSPITAL, 1230 Baxter St., Zip 30613; tel. 404/548-7581; Edward J. Fechtel Jr., adm. **A**1a 9 10 **F**1 3 6 10 11 12 14 15 16 20 23 24 26 34 35 40 41 43 44 45 47 51 52 53	23	10	S		204	9502	132	64.7	12	904	30927	14672	873
☐ UNIVERSITY HEALTH SERVICE, UNIVERSITY OF GEORGIA, Zip 30602; tel. 404/542-1162; Jacquelyn S. Kinder, dir. (Nonreporting) **A**1a 9	12	11	S		30	—	—	—	—	—	—	—	—
ATLANTA—Fulton and De Kalb Counties													
☐ ANCHOR HOSPITAL, 5454 Yorktowne Dr., Zip 30349; tel. 404/991-6044; Benjamin H. Underwood, chief exec. off. & adm. (Newly Registered) (Data for 266 days) **A**1b 9 **F**15 25 32 42 47	33	82	S		60	215	20	33.3	0	0	1902	—	55
☐ ATLANTA HOSPITAL (Formerly Atlanta Community Hospital), 705 Juniper St. N.E., Zip 30365; tel. 404/873-2871; Lewis A. Ransdell, adm. (Nonreporting) **A**1a 9 10; **S**0435	33	10	S		72	—	—	—	—	—	—	—	—
★☐ CHARTER PEACHFORD HOSPITAL, 2151 Peachford Rd., Zip 30338; tel. 404/455-3200; James W. Eyler, adm. **A**1b 9 10 **F**28 30 32 33 48 49; **S**0695	33	22	L		214	1895	170	79.4	0	0	—	—	352
☐ CPC PARKWOOD HOSPITAL (Formerly Peachtree-Parkwood Hospital), 1999 Cliff Valley Way N.E., Zip 30329; tel. 404/633-8431; Ronald E. Yates, adm. & chief exec. off. (Nonreporting) **A**1b 9; **S**0785	33	22	L		130	—	—	—	—	—	—	—	—
★☐ CRAWFORD LONG HOSPITAL OF EMORY UNIVERSITY (Formerly Crawford W. Long Memorial Hospital), 550 Peachtree St. N.E., Zip 30365; tel. 404/892-4411; John D. Henry, adm. **A**1a 2 3 5 6 8 9 10 **F**1 2 3 4 5 6 7 8 9 10 11 12 14 16 20 23 34 35 37 40 45 51 52 53 54	21	10	S		478	17081	309	64.6	24	2047	80612	40137	1918
☐ DOCTORS MEMORIAL HOSPITAL, 20 Linden Ave. N.E., Zip 30308; tel. 404/881-8400; Reynold Jennings, adm. (Nonreporting) **A**1a 9 10	33	10	S		76	—	—	—	—	—	—	—	—
★☐ Δ EMORY UNIVERSITY HOSPITAL, 1364 Clifton Rd. N.E., Zip 30322; tel. 404/727-7021; Paul B. Hofmann, exec. dir. **A**1a 2 3 5 7 8 9 10 **F**1 2 3 4 6 10 11 12 13 14 15 16 17 20 23 24 25 26 27 29 33 37 39 42 44 45 46 53 54	23	10	S		555	20505	464	82.4	0	0	130936	59622	2494
★☐ GEORGIA BAPTIST MEDICAL CENTER, 300 Boulevard N.E., Zip 30312; tel. 404/653-4200; William C. Brown, pres. & chief exec. off. **A**1a 2 3 5 6 9 10 **F**1 2 3 4 5 6 7 8 9 10 11 12 14 15 16 17 20 23 24 25 26 27 29 30 31 32 33 34 35 36 39 40 41 42 44 45 46 47 48 49 50 51 52 53 54	21	10	S		483	20486	354	79.7	32	2985	98649	48459	2263
☐ GEORGIA MENTAL HEALTH INSTITUTE, 1256 Briarcliff Rd. N.E., Zip 30306; tel. 404/894-5911; B. C. Robbins, supt. (Nonreporting) **A**1b 3 5 10	12	22	S		212	—	—	—	—	—	—	—	—
★☐ GRADY MEMORIAL HOSPITAL, 80 Butler St. S.E., Zip 30335; tel. 404/589-4252; J. W. Pinkston Jr., exec. dir. **A**1a 2 3 5 8 9 **F**1 2 3 4 5 6 7 8 9 10 11 12 13 14 15 16 18 20 21 22 23 24 25 26 27 28 29 30 32 33 34 35 36 37 38 40 42 43 44 46 47 51 52 53 54; **S**1425	16	10	S		918	40819	717	78.1	116	7478	167891	84287	4157
★☐ HCA WEST PACES FERRY HOSPITAL (Formerly West Paces Ferry Hospital), 3200 Howell Mill Rd. N.W., Zip 30327; tel. 404/351-0351; Chip Caldwell, adm. **A**1a 2 9 10 **F**1 3 6 9 10 11 12 14 15 16 20 23 24 25 26 27 28 29 30 32 33 34 35 36 40 42 43 44 45 46 48 49 50 53 54; **S**1755	33	10	S		294	9609	178	60.5	20	1258	—	—	588
★☐ HENRIETTA EGLESTON HOSPITAL FOR CHILDREN, 1405 Clifton Rd. N.E., Zip 30322; tel. 404/325-6000; Selena D. Dunn, adm. **A**1a 3 5 8 9 10 **F**1 2 4 5 6 10 12 13 14 16 20 23 24 26 32 33 35 42 44 45 46 47 51 54	23	50	S		165	6516	133	80.6	0	0	39307	19979	865
☐ HUGHES SPALDING MEDICAL CENTER, 35 Butler St. S.E., Zip 30335; tel. 404/222-2200; T. L. Collier, actg. adm. **A**1a 9 10 **F**1 3 6 12 14 16 20 23 27 29 35 42; **S**1425	16	10	S		66	1835	41	49.4	0	0	7716	4177	184
★☐ JESSE PARKER WILLIAMS HOSPITAL, 542 Peachtree St. N.E., Zip 30365; tel. 404/881-6167; Freda M. Moss, adm. **A**1a 9 10 **F**52	23	10	S		50	1629	36	72.0	0	0	6310	20	1
JOSEPH B. WHITEHEAD MEMORIAL INFIRMARY, GEORGIA INSTITUTE OF TECHNOLOGY, 275 Fifth St. N.W., Zip 30318; tel. 404/894-2584; John A. Wilhelm MD, dir. (Nonreporting)	12	11	S		70	—	—	—	—	—	—	—	—
★☐ METROPOLITAN HOSPITAL, 3223 Howell Mill Rd. N.W., Zip 30327; tel. 404/351-0500; Richard F. Jensen, adm. (Nonreporting) **A**1a 9 10; **S**0695	33	45	S		64	—	—	—	—	—	—	—	—
MIDTOWN HOSPITAL (Reproductive Health), 144 Ponce De Leon Ave. N.E., Zip 30308; tel. 404/875-3411; Ignatius Deblasi, adm. **F**1 6 14 15 34 37 43	32	49	S		19	778	2	10.5	0	0	—	—	50

★ American Hospital Association (AHA) membership
☐ Joint Commission on Accreditation of Hospitals (JCAH) accreditation
+ American Osteopathic Hospital Association (AOHA) membership
○ American Osteopathic Association (AOA) accreditation
Δ Commission on Accreditation of Rehabilitation Facilities (CARF) accreditation
Control codes 61, 63, 64, 71, 72 and 73 indicate hospitals listed by AOHA, but not registered by AHA.
For definition of numerical codes, see page A2

Hospital, Address, Telephone, Administrator, Approval and Facility Codes, Multihospital System Code	Classification Codes				Inpatient Data				Newborn Data		Expense (thousands of dollars)		
	Control	Service	Stay	Facilities	Beds	Admissions	Census	Occupancy (percent)	Bassinets	Births	Total	Payroll	Personnel
☒ NORTHSIDE HOSPITAL, 1000 Johnson Ferry Rd. N.E., Zip 30042; tel. 404/851-8000; W. Christopher Clark, pres. (Nonreporting) **A**1a 2 9 10	16	10	S		375	—	—	—	—	—	—	—	—
PEACHTREE-PARKWOOD HOSPITAL, See CPC Parkwood Hospital													
☐ PHYSICIANS AND SURGEONS HOSPITAL, 2355 Bolton Rd. N.W., Zip 30381; tel. 404/352-1200; Nolan Simmons, adm.; Julius D. Spears Jr., adm. (Nonreporting) **A**1a 9 10; **S**0495	33	10	S		181	—	—	—	—	—	—	—	—
☒ PIEDMONT HOSPITAL, 1968 Peachtree Rd. N.W., Zip 30309; tel. 404/350-2222; Hulett D. Sumlin, adm. (Data not avaliable) **A**1a 2 3 5 9 10 **F**1 2 3 5 8 9 10 11 12 13 14 15 16 17 19 20 21 23 24 26 34 35 36 37 40 51 52 53 54	23	10	S		490	—	—	—	—	—	—	—	—
☐ PSYCHIATRIC INSTITUTE OF ATLANTA, 811 Juniper St. N.E., Zip 30308; tel. 404/881-5800; Mark A. Gould MD, chief exec. off. **A**1a b 9 10 **F**15 24 30 32 33 42 44; **S**0825	33	22	S		33	449	26	78.8	0	0	3021	1064	50
☒ SAINT JOSEPH'S HOSPITAL, 5665 Peachtree Dunwoody Rd. N.E., Zip 30342; tel. 404/851-7001; Kenneth E. Wheeler, pres. & chief exec. off. **A**1a 2 9 10 **F**1 2 3 4 6 7 8 9 10 11 12 13 14 15 16 20 23 24 26 34 35 44 45 46 47 53 54; **S**3595	21	10	S		295	12893	225	76.3	0	0	58785	24156	1427
☒ SCOTTISH RITE CHILDREN'S HOSPITAL, 1001 Johnson Ferry Rd. N.E., Zip 30363; tel. 404/256-5252; James E. Tally PhD, adm. **A**1a 3 5 9 **F**1 5 6 10 14 15 16 23 24 32 33 34 35 41 42 44 45 46 53	23	50	S		86	5038	63	72.4	0	0	25455	11014	593
☐ SHEPHERD SPINAL CENTER (Long Term Acute Care, Rehabilitation and Spinal Cord Patients), 2020 Peachtree Rd. N.W., Zip 30309, tel. 404/352-2020; James B. Collins, adm. (Newly Registered) **A**1a 9 10 **F**3 15 23 24 25 26 42 45 46 47	23	49	L		80	505	66	82.5	0	0	13247	5984	282
☒ SOUTHWEST HOSPITAL AND MEDICAL CENTER (Formerly Southwest Community Hospital), 501 Fairburn Rd. S.W., Zip 30331; tel. 404/699-1111; William L. Jackson, adm. **A**1a 3 5 9 10 **F**1 3 6 10 12 14 15 16 17 20 21 23 35 36 40 46 47 52 53	23	10	S		121	3338	59	48.8	22	339	14737	6012	323
U. S. PENITENTIARY HOSPITAL, 601 McDonough Blvd. S.E., Zip 30315; tel. 404/622-6241 **F**5 7 23 24 27 28 29 30 32 33 34 42 43 44	48	11	S		39	517	20	51.3	0	0	—	—	38
WEST PACES FERRY HOSPITAL, See HCA West Paces Ferry Hospital													
AUGUSTA—Richmond County													
☐ GEORGIA REGIONAL HOSPITAL AT AUGUSTA, 3405 Old Savannah Rd., Zip 30906; Mailing Address P O Box 327, Gracewood, Zip 30812; tel. 404/790-2600; Everett C. Kuglar MD, supt. **A**1a 3 10 **F**18 19 23 24 29 30 32 33 42 46 48	12	22	L		289	2405	256	88.6	0	0	13917	8745	496
☒ HUMANA HOSPITAL -AUGUSTA, 3651 Wheeler Rd., Zip 30910; tel. 404/863-3232; G. Wayne Peloquin, exec. dir. **A**1a 9 10 **F**1 3 6 10 12 14 15 16 20 22 23 24 26 27 30 32 34 35 36 40 42 44 45 46 47 52 53 54; **S**1235	33	10	S		374	8997	178	47.6	21	602	—	—	810
☒ MEDICAL COLLEGE OF GEORGIA HOSPITAL AND CLINICS, 1120 15th St., Zip 30912; tel. 404/828-0211; R. Edward Howell, exec. dir. **A**1a 2 3 5 8 9 10 **F**1 3 4 5 6 9 10 11 12 13 14 15 16 17 20 22 23 24 27 28 30 32 33 34 35 36 37 38 40 42 44 46 49 51 52 53 54	12	10	S		516	17584	385	75.9	28	2209	96367	47831	2666
☒ ST. JOSEPH HOSPITAL, 2260 Wrightsboro Rd., Zip 30910; tel. 404/737-7400; William Sherwood Atkinson, pres.; Vincent Caponi, adm. **A**1a 9 10 **F**1 3 6 10 12 14 15 16 20 21 23 24 25 26 34 35 36 40 41 44 45 46 52 53 54; **S**5945	21	10	S		235	9393	154	65.5	30	1241	32786	15080	766
☒ UNIVERSITY HOSPITAL, 1350 Walton Way, Zip 30910; tel. 404/826-8866; Edward M. Gillespie, pres. **A**1a 2 3 5 9 10 **F**1 2 3 4 6 10 12 13 14 15 16 17 20 23 24 26 27 28 30 32 34 35 36 37 39 40 41 42 44 45 46 47 48 51 52 53 54	23	10	S		708	26655	558	78.8	60	3562	117338	58870	3159
☒ VETERANS ADMINISTRATION MEDICAL CENTER, Zip 30910; tel. 404/724-5116; Donald E. Burnette, dir. (Total facility includes 40 beds in nursing home-type unit) **A**1a 3 5 8 **F**1 2 3 4 6 10 12 14 15 16 19 20 23 24 26 27 28 30 31 32 33 34 35 38 41 42 44 46 47 48 49 50 53 54	45	10	S	TF	1094	11041	841	76.5	0	0	81758	51037	2013
				H	1054	11003	804	—	0	0	80186	49922	1990
AUSTELL—Cobb County													
☒ COBB GENERAL HOSPITAL, 3950 Austell Rd., Zip 30001; tel. 404/944-5000; Richard B. Hubbard, adm. (Nonreporting) **A**1a 2 9 10	16	10	S		237	—	—	—	—	—	—	—	—
BAINBRIDGE—Decatur County													
☒ MEMORIAL HOSPITAL, 1500 E. Shotwell St., Zip 31717; tel. 912/246-3500; Raymond W. Wright, exec. dir. (Total facility includes 107 beds in nursing home-type unit) **A**1a 9 10 **F**1 3 6 14 15 17 19 23 34 35 36 40 45 46 52 53	16	10	S	TF	187	3741	148	79.1	14	388	7939	3121	279
				H	80	3718	41	—	14	388	6255	2419	207
BAXLEY—Appling County													
APPLING GENERAL HOSPITAL, 301 E. Tollison St., Zip 31513; tel. 912/367-9841; Meredith Smith, adm. **A**9 10 **F**1 3 6 12 16 35 36	16	10	S		40	1840	22	55.0	7	88	3298	1658	112
BLACKSHEAR—Pierce County													
PIERCE COUNTY HOSPITAL, Carter Ave., Box 32, Zip 31516; tel. 912/449-6631; William V. Maxwell, adm. (Data for 181 days) (Total facility includes 29 beds in nursing home-type unit) **A**9 10 **F**10 16 19 35 40 45 52	16	10	S	TF	64	421	39	37.9	8	61	884	413	74
				H	35	416	10	—	8	61	643	287	53
BLAIRSVILLE—Union County													
★ UNION GENERAL HOSPITAL, Rte. 8, Box 8403, Zip 30512; tel. 404/745-2111; Leon Davenport, adm. (Total facility includes 96 beds in nursing home-type unit) **A**9 10 **F**1 3 6 10 14 16 19 35 45	16	10	S	TF	141	2005	127	90.1	8	110	5255	2613	180
				H	45	1960	31	—	8	110	3737	1742	112
BLAKELY—Early County													
☒ EARLY MEMORIAL HOSPITAL, 630 Columbia St., Zip 31723; tel. 912/723-4241; Robert E. Tiner, adm. (Total facility includes 127 beds in nursing home-type unit) **A**1a 9 10 **F**1 6 12 14 15 16 19 35 36 40 47	16	10	S	TF	176	1691	132	75.0	5	135	4371	2080	183
				H	49	1621	19	—	5	135	2554	1408	117
BLUE RIDGE—Fannin County													
☐ FANNIN REGIONAL HOSPITAL, Hwy. 5 N., Box 1549, Zip 30513; tel. 404/632-3711; Emil Miller, adm. (Nonreporting) **A**1a 9 10; **S**0875	33	10	S		51	—	—	—	—	—	—	—	—
BOWDON—Carroll County													
BOWDON AREA HOSPITAL, 501 Mitchel Ave., Zip 30108; tel. 404/258-7207; Robert C. Eaton, adm. **A**9 10 **F**1 3 6 12 14 15 16 23 35 43 45 53	33	10	S		41	1333	14	34.1	0	0	2260	829	54
BREMEN—Haralson County													
★ HIGGINS GENERAL HOSPITAL, 200 Allen Memorial Dr., Box 745, Zip 30110; tel. 404/537-2315; Robin Smith, adm. **A**9 10 **F**1 2 6 12 14 15 16 23 35 37 45 50; **S**1755	15	10	S		59	2025	27	45.8	0	0	3659	1746	118
BRUNSWICK—Glynn County													
☒ GLYNN-BRUNSWICK MEMORIAL HOSPITAL, 3100 Kemble Ave., Zip 31520; Mailing Address Box 1518, Zip 31521; tel. 912/264-6960; David Dunham, adm. **A**1a 9 10 **F**1 2 3 6 7 10 11 12 14 15 16 23 26 30 35 37 40 45 46 47 52 53 54; **S**0585	16	10	S		340	11637	202	59.4	29	1178	31626	13981	816
BUENA VISTA—Marion County													
MARION MEMORIAL HOSPITAL, Hwy. 41, Box 197, Zip 31803; tel. 912/649-2331; L. E. Peace III, adm. (Nonreporting) **A**9 10; **S**1935	16	10	S		80	—	—	—	—	—	—	—	—
BUFORD—Gwinnett County													
BUFORD HOSPITAL, See Gwinnett Hospital Systems, Lawrenceville													
CAIRO—Grady County													
GRADY GENERAL HOSPITAL, 1155 Fifth St. S.E., Zip 31728; tel. 912/377-1150; Elmo Elrod, adm. **A**9 10 **F**1 3 6 16 23 35 36 40 45 46 52	23	10	S		60	1686	26	43.3	6	146	3394	1485	113

Hospital, Address, Telephone, Administrator, Approval and Facility Codes, Multihospital System Code	Classification Codes: Control	Service	Stay	Facilities	Inpatient Data: Beds	Admissions	Census	Occupancy (percent)	Newborn Data: Bassinets	Births	Expense (thousands of dollars): Total	Payroll	Personnel
CALHOUN—Gordon County													
★□ GORDON HOSPITAL, Red Bud Rd., P O Box 938, Zip 30701; tel. 404/629-2895; Robert E. Trimble, pres. (Nonreporting) **A**1a 9 10; **S**4165	21	10	S		65	—	—	—	—	—	—	—	—
CAMILLA—Mitchell County													
□ MITCHELL COUNTY HOSPITAL, 90 Stevens St., Zip 31730; tel. 912/336-5284; Jim Butler Jr., adm. (Nonreporting) **A**1a 9 10	16	10	S		161	—	—	—	—	—	—	—	—
CANTON—Cherokee County													
★□ R. T. JONES MEMORIAL HOSPITAL, 201 Hospital Rd., Box 906, Zip 30114; tel. 404/479-1941; Neil Copelan, exec. dir. **A**1a 9 10 **F**1 3 6 10 12 14 15 16 17 23 24 34 35 37 45 46 53	16	10	S		64	3022	45	70.3	13	20	8152	3359	219
CARROLLTON—Carroll County													
★□ TANNER MEDICAL CENTER, 705 Dixie St., Zip 30117; tel. 404/836-9666; James R. Giffin, adm. **A**1a 9 10 **F**1 2 3 6 10 12 14 15 16 20 23 24 33 35 36 40 43 44 45 46 47 48 49 50 52 53; **S**1755	16	10	S		222	8150	129	60.3	19	931	21690	8532	530
CARTERSVILLE—Bartow County													
★□ HUMANA HOSPITAL-CARTERSVILLE (Formerly Sam Howell Memorial Hospital), Rte. 7, Hwy. 41 N., Box 1008, Zip 30120; tel. 404/382-1530; Keith Sandlin, exec. dir. (Nonreporting) **A**1a 9 10; **S**1235	33	10	S		80	—	—	—	—	—	—	—	—
CEDARTOWN—Polk County													
★□ POLK GENERAL HOSPITAL, 424 N. Main St., Zip 30125; tel. 404/748-2500; Elder B. Perdue, adm. (Nonreporting) **A**1a 9 10	16	10	S		60	—	—	—	—	—	—	—	—
CHAMBLEE—De Kalb County													
★□ SHALLOWFORD HOSPITAL (Formerly Shallowford Community Hospital), 4575 N. Shallowford Rd., Box 80846, Zip 30338; tel. 404/455-6000; Erich J. Wolters, adm. **A**1a 9 10 **F**1 2 3 6 10 12 14 16 20 23 24 26 34 35 36 37 40 42 44 45 46 53; **S**0695	33	10	S		157	8408	99	63.1	21	2041	—	—	408
CLAXTON—Evans County													
★□ EVANS MEMORIAL HOSPITAL, 200 N. River St., Box 518, Zip 30417; tel. 912/739-2611; Eston Price Jr., adm. **A**1a 9 10 **F**1 6 14 16 23 24 35 45 50	16	10	S		36	1201	13	31.0	4	27	3536	1709	99
CLAYTON—Rabun County													
★ RABUN COUNTY MEMORIAL HOSPITAL, S. Main St., Box 705, Zip 30525; tel. 404/782-4233; Richard B. Wallace, adm. **A**9 10 **F**1 3 6 14 16 23 35 40 44 45	16	10	S		26	641	6	23.1	8	64	1012	567	46
★□ RIDGECREST HOSPITAL, Hwy. 76 W. Germany Rd., Box 376, Zip 30525; tel. 404/782-4297; Richard J. Turner Jr., adm. **A**1a 9 10 **F**3 6 14 16 17 23 34 35 45 46 47 53; **S**0985	33	10	S		45	1097	17	37.8	0	0	2183	1046	75
□ WOODRIDGE HOSPITAL, Germany Rd., P O Box 1764, Zip 30525; tel. 404/782-3100; Richard J. Turner MD, proj. dir. (Newly Registered) **A**1b 9 10 **F**5 15 19 28 32 33 34 40 42	31	82	S		32	262	15	46.9	0	0	1568	374	30
COCHRAN—Bleckley County													
★ BLECKLEY MEMORIAL HOSPITAL, Peacock St., Box 536, Zip 31014; tel. 912/934-6211; Richard Gamber, adm. **A**9 10 **F**1 3 6 15 16 23 34 35 45 47 52	16	10	S		45	1591	21	46.7	0	0	3368	1426	65
COLQUITT—Miller County													
MILLER COUNTY HOSPITAL, 209 N. Cuthbert St., Zip 31737; tel. 912/758-3385; Edd W. Johnson, adm. (Total facility includes 83 beds in nursing home-type unit) **A**9 10 **F**1 14 16 19 35 40	16	10	S	TF	121	1322	97	80.2	5	125	2897	1542	134
				H	38	1274	14	—	5	125	1653	898	72
COLUMBUS—Muscogee County													
★□ BRADLEY CENTER, 2000 16th Ave., Zip 31993; tel. 404/324-4882; Michael W. Wolfe, adm. oper.; Molly Mitchell Jones, adm. finance **A**1b 9 10 **F**3 24 28 29 30 31 32 33 42 43 49	23	22	L		64	398	36	56.3	0	0	5122	2996	156
★□ DOCTORS HOSPITAL, 616 19th St., Zip 31993; Mailing Address P O Box 2188, Zip 31902; tel. 404/571-4262; Ronald A. Schwartz, adm. **A**1a 9 10 **F**1 3 6 9 12 13 14 16 20 23 24 34 35 39 42 43 44 45 46 47 52 53; **S**1755	32	10	S		252	4926	83	32.9	0	0	—	—	339
★□ HUGHSTON SPORTS MEDICINE HOSPITAL, 6260 Hamilton Rd., Zip 31905; Mailing Address P O Box 2319, Zip 31902; tel. 404/576-2100; Charles Keaton, adm. **A**1a 10 **F**1 12 14 15 16 23 24 25 26 42 43 44 53; **S**1755	33	47	S		100	3625	58	58.0	0	0	13351	3443	283
★□ MEDICAL CENTER, 710 Center St., Zip 31901; Mailing Address Box 951, Zip 31994; tel. 404/571-1000; Larry S. Sanders, pres. & chief exec. off. **A**1a 2 3 5 8 9 10 **F**1 3 5 6 7 8 9 10 11 12 14 15 16 17 20 21 23 24 26 27 28 30 32 33 34 35 36 37 38 40 41 42 43 44 45 46 47 50 51 52 53 54	23	10	S		457	14526	233	51.0	48	3391	51375	18748	1201
★□ ST. FRANCIS HOSPITAL, Expwy. & Woodruff Rd., Box 7000, Zip 31995; tel. 404/322-8281; Sr. Patricia Garrigan, adm. (Nonreporting) **A**1a 9 10	21	10	S		264	—	—	—	—	—	—	—	—
COMMERCE—Jackson County													
★ BANKS-JACKSON-COMMERCE HOSPITAL, 655 Hospital Rd., Zip 30529; tel. 404/335-3181; Willene G. Dyer, chief exec. off. (Total facility includes 72 beds in nursing home-type unit) **A**9 10 **F**1 12 14 19 23 35 40 45	16	10	S	TF	138	2665	105	76.1	12	302	6046	2750	232
				H	66	2624	33	—	12	302	4905	2304	186
CONYERS—Rockdale County													
□ ROCKDALE HOSPITAL (Formerly Rockdale County Hospital), 1412 Milstead Ave. N.E., Zip 30207; tel. 404/922-8901; Archer R. Rose, exec. dir. **A**1a 2 9 10 **F**1 3 6 10 14 15 16 23 35 36 39 40 44 45	16	10	S		100	3949	45	45.0	10	615	12205	5223	324
CORDELE—Crisp County													
□ CRISP COUNTY HOSPITAL, 906 Fifth St. N., Box 709, Zip 31015; tel. 912/273-4211; D. Wayne Martin, adm. **A**1a 9 10 **F**1 3 5 6 10 12 14 15 16 23 34 35 40 52	16	10	S		70	3521	48	68.6	12	428	8313	3615	259
COVINGTON—Newton County													
★□ NEWTON GENERAL HOSPITAL, 5126 Hospital Dr., Zip 30209; tel. 404/786-7053; James F. Weadick, adm. **A**1a 9 10 **F**1 3 6 10 12 14 15 16 23 26 34 35 36 40 43 45 46 53	16	10	S		90	3483	42	46.7	13	505	10238	4553	237
CUMMING—Forsyth County													
□ LAKESIDE COMMUNITY HOSPITAL (Formerly Forsyth County Hospital), 133 Samaritan Dr., Box 768, Zip 30130; tel. 404/887-2355; Steven E. Hitt, adm. **A**1a 9 10 **F**1 3 6 10 12 14 15 16 23 34 35 45 46 47 53	33	10	S		36	1586	17	47.2	0	0	4614	1412	69
CUTHBERT—Randolph County													
★ PATTERSON HOSPITAL, 109 Randolph St., Zip 31740; tel. 912/732-2181; David J. Carney, adm. (Total facility includes 80 beds in nursing home-type unit) **A**9 10 **F**1 14 16 19 35 40 45	16	10	S	TF	120	809	91	75.8	10	104	2638	1424	132
				H	40	790	12	—	10	104	1455	800	78
DAHLONEGA—Lumpkin County													
★□ SAINT JOSEPH'S HOSPITAL OF DAHLONEGA (Formerly Lumpkin County Hospital), 1111 Mountain Dr., Zip 30533; tel. 404/864-6136; Tommy G. Reddin, sr. vice-pres. & chief oper. off. **A**1a 9 10 **F**1 3 6 10 15 16 23 34 35 40 44 45 52; **S**3595	23	10	S		46	1416	16	34.8	12	142	3432	1830	125
DALLAS—Paulding County													
★□ PAULDING MEMORIAL MEDICAL CENTER (Formerly Paulding Memorial Hospital), 600 W. Memorial Dr., Zip 30132; tel. 404/445-4411; Ray C. Brees, adm. (Total facility includes 136 beds in nursing home-type unit) **A**1a 9 10 **F**1 2 6 10 12 15 16 19 23 34 35 43 46 53	16	10	S	TF	206	2486	166	80.6	0	0	8126	3893	269
				H	70	2445	31	—	0	0	6861	3167	201

★ American Hospital Association (AHA) membership
□ Joint Commission on Accreditation of Hospitals (JCAH) accreditation
+ American Osteopathic Hospital Association (AOHA) membership
○ American Osteopathic Association (AOA) accreditation
Δ Commission on Accreditation of Rehabilitation Facilities (CARF) accreditation
Control codes 61, 63, 64, 71, 72 and 73 indicate hospitals listed by AOHA, but not registered by AHA.
For definition of numerical codes, see page A2

Hospital, Address, Telephone, Administrator, Approval and Facility Codes, Multihospital System Code	Classification Codes				Inpatient Data				Newborn Data		Expense (thousands of dollars)		
★ American Hospital Association (AHA) membership □ Joint Commission on Accreditation of Hospitals (JCAH) accreditation + American Osteopathic Hospital Association (AOHA) membership ○ American Osteopathic Association (AOA) accreditation Δ Commission on Accreditation of Rehabilitation Facilities (CARF) accreditation Control codes 61, 63, 64, 71, 72 and 73 indicate hospitals listed by AOHA, but not registered by AHA. For definition of numerical codes, see page A2	Control	Service	Stay	Facilities	Beds	Admissions	Census	Occupancy (percent)	Bassinets	Births	Total	Payroll	Personnel
DALTON—Whitfield County													
★□ HAMILTON MEDICAL CENTER, Memorial Dr., Box 1168, Zip 30720; tel. 404/278-2105; Norman D. Burkett, pres. & chief exec. off. (Nonreporting) **A**1a 2 9 10	23	10	S		237	—	—	—	—	—	—	—	—
DAWSON—Terrell County													
TERRELL COUNTY HOSPITAL, Cinderella Lane, Box 150, Zip 31742; tel. 912/995-2121; Kenneth W. Hamilton, adm. (Nonreporting) **A**9 10; **S**1935	13	10	S		34	—	—	—	—	—	—	—	—
DECATUR—De Kalb County													
★□ DECATUR HOSPITAL, 450 N. Candler St., Zip 30030; Mailing Address Box 40, Zip 30031; tel. 404/377-0221; Dewey A. Greene, adm. (Nonreporting) **A**1a 9 10; **S**6525	33	10	S		120	—	—	—	—	—	—	—	—
★□ DEKALB GENERAL HOSPITAL, 2701 N. Decatur Rd., Zip 30033; tel. 404/297-2700; Charles B. Eberhart, adm. (Total facility includes 50 beds in nursing home-type unit) **A**1a 2 9 10 **F**1 2 3 6 7 8 9 10 11 12 14 15 16 19 20 23 24 26 27 29 30 32 34 35 36 37 40 44 45 46 47 51 53	16	10	S	TF H	478 428	18913 18736	354 306	74.1 —	36 36	2924 2924	65793 —	34837 —	1738 1708
□ GEORGIA REGIONAL HOSPITAL AT ATLANTA, 3073 Panthersville Rd., Zip 30034; tel. 404/242-2100; Richard A. Fields MD, supt. (Nonreporting) **A**1b 10	12	22	S		345	—	—	—	—	—	—	—	—
★□ VETERANS ADMINISTRATION MEDICAL CENTER ATLANTA, 1670 Clairmont Rd., Zip 30033; tel. 404/321-6111; Glenn Alred Jr., dir. (Total facility includes 120 beds in nursing home-type unit) **A**1a 2 3 5 8 **F**1 2 3 6 7 8 12 14 15 16 19 20 23 24 25 26 27 28 29 30 33 34 35 41 42 43 44 46 47 49 50 53 54	45	10	S	TF H	613 493	12965 12897	482 372	78.6 —	0 0	0 0	75401 —	44044 —	1506 1431
DEMOREST—Habersham County													
★□ HABERSHAM COUNTY MEDICAL CENTER, Hwy. 441, Box 37, Zip 30535; tel. 404/754-2161; Michael R. Blackburn, adm. (Total facility includes 84 beds in nursing home-type unit) **A**1a 9 10 **F**1 3 6 12 14 15 16 19 23 26 34 35 36 40 45 46 53; **S**1755	16	10	S	TF H	143 59	2159 2138	111 27	77.6 —	7 7	139 139	7193 5754	3185 2356	223 163
DONALSONVILLE—Seminole County													
DONALSONVILLE HOSPITAL, Hospital Circle, Box 677, Zip 31745; tel. 912/524-5217; Millie W. Trulock, adm. **A**9 10 **F**1 6 14 16 35 40 46	23	10	S		61	1928	25	41.0	6	109	3649	1213	98
DOUGLAS—Coffee County													
★□ COFFEE REGIONAL HOSPITAL, W. Ward St., Box 1248, Zip 31533; tel. 912/384-1900; Charles E. Hill, adm. (Nonreporting) **A**1a 9 10	16	10	S		157	—	—	—	—	—	—	—	—
DOUGLASVILLE—Douglas County													
★□ ANNEEWAKEE HOSPITAL, 4771 Anneewakee Rd., Zip 30135; tel. 404/942-2391; Henry Evans, adm. (Nonreporting) **A**1b	23	52	L		383	—	—	—	—	—	—	—	—
□ DOUGLAS GENERAL HOSPITAL, 8954 Hospital Dr., Zip 30134; Mailing Address Box 1098, Zip 30133; tel. 404/949-1500; William W. Ragland, adm. **A**1a 9 10 **F**1 3 6 10 12 14 16 20 23 32 35 36 40 43 45 46 52 53	16	10	S		96	4445	52	54.2	11	602	12523	5699	306
DUBLIN—Laurens County													
★□ FAIRVIEW PARK HOSPITAL, 200 Industrial Blvd., Box 1408, Zip 31021; tel. 912/275-2000; Dominic Ingrando, adm. **A**1a 9 10 **F**1 3 6 10 12 14 15 16 23 30 35 36 39 40 45 52 53; **S**1755	33	10	S		190	9753	138	72.6	23	941	—	—	464
★□ VETERANS ADMINISTRATION MEDICAL CENTER, U. S. Hwy. 80, Zip 31021; tel. 912/272-1210; William O. Edgar, dir. (Nonreporting) **A**1a	45	10	S		388	—	—	—	—	—	—	—	—
DULUTH—Gwinnett County													
JOAN GLANCY MEMORIAL HOSPITAL, See Gwinnett Hospital Systems, Lawrenceville													
EAST POINT—Fulton County													
★□ SOUTH FULTON HOSPITAL, 1170 Cleveland Ave., Zip 30344; tel. 404/669-4000; Clyde E. Maxwell Jr., adm. **A**1a 2 9 10 **F**1 2 3 6 7 8 9 10 11 12 14 15 16 19 20 23 24 29 32 33 35 36 37 40 44 45 46 49 50 52 53	16	10	S		427	12344	200	46.8	30	1291	37679	20002	981
EASTMAN—Dodge County													
□ DODGE COUNTY HOSPITAL, 715 Griffin St., Box 706, Zip 31023; tel. 912/374-3491; Richard D. Osmus, adm. **A**1a 9 10 **F**1 3 6 10 16 23 34 35 40 45 47; **S**2495	16	10	S		87	2636	36	41.4	8	125	4864	2297	165
EATONTON—Putnam County													
PUTNAM GENERAL HOSPITAL, Greensboro Hwy., Box 32, Zip 31024; tel. 404/485-2711; Lavilla P. Bryan, adm. (Nonreporting) **A**9 10	16	10	S		50	—	—	—	—	—	—	—	—
ELBERTON—Elbert County													
★□ ELBERT MEMORIAL HOSPITAL (Formerly Elberton-Elbert County Hospital), 4 Medical Dr., Zip 30635; tel. 404/283-3151; Victor M. Ribeiro, adm. (Nonreporting) **A**1a 9 10	16	10	S		55	—	—	—	—	—	—	—	—
ELLIJAY—Gilmer County													
★ NORTH GEORGIA MEDICAL CENTER (Formerly Watkins Memorial Hospital) (Includes Gilmer Nursing Home), Jasper Rd., Box 346, Zip 30540; tel. 404/276-4741; John J. Downs, adm. (Nonreporting) **A**9 10	21	10	S		100	—	—	—	—	—	—	—	—
FITZGERALD—Ben Hill County													
★□ DORMINY MEDICAL CENTER (Formerly Dorminy Memorial Hospital), Perry House Rd., Drawer 989, Zip 31750; tel. 912/423-5431; Charles Y. Davis, adm. (Nonreporting) **A**1a 9 10	16	10	S		75	—	—	—	—	—	—	—	—
FOLKSTON—Charlton County													
★ CHARLTON MEMORIAL HOSPITAL, 1203 Third St., Box 188, Zip 31537; tel. 912/496-2531; Charles Mitchener, adm. **A**9 10 **F**1 3 6 12 14 16 23 35; **S**1755	16	10	S		46	898	12	26.1	0	0	2446	858	73
FORSYTH—Monroe County													
MONROE COUNTY HOSPITAL, Culloden Rd., Box 1068, Zip 31029; tel. 912/994-2521; Richard Von Seeberg, adm. (Nonreporting) **A**9 10	16	10	S		40	—	—	—	—	—	—	—	—
FORT BENNING—Chattahoochee County													
★□ MARTIN ARMY COMMUNITY HOSPITAL, Zip 31905; tel. 404/544-2041 (Nonreporting) **A**1a 2 3 5	42	10	S		278	—	—	—	—	—	—	—	—
FORT GAINES—Clay County													
FORT GAINES HOSPITAL, Clay County, Box 160, Zip 31751; tel. 912/768-2521; William B. Ross, adm. (Nonreporting) **A**9 10; **S**1935	16	10	S		84	—	—	—	—	—	—	—	—
FORT GORDON—Richmond County													
★□ DWIGHT DAVID EISENHOWER ARMY MEDICAL CENTER, Zip 30905; tel. 404/791-2620; Brig. Gen. Frederick N. Bussey MD, cmdr.; Col. Robert T. Maruca, chief exec. off. **A**1a 2 3 5 **F**1 3 6 10 12 14 15 16 20 23 24 26 27 28 29 30 32 33 34 35 36 37 38 40 41 42 43 44 46 47 48 49 50 52 53 54	42	10	S		385	14519	321	83.4	25	847	106123	—	1659
FORT OGLETHORPE—Catoosa County													
★□ GREENLEAF CENTER, 500 Greenleaf Circle, Zip 30742; tel. 404/861-4357; Jimmie W. Harden, adm. **A**1b 10 **F**15 30 32 33 42 48; **S**1155	33	22	S		60	893	51	85.0	0	0	4397	1778	125
★□ HUTCHESON MEDICAL CENTER, 100 Gross Crescent Circle, Zip 30742; tel. 404/866-2121; W. Leonard Fant, pres. (Total facility includes 25 beds in nursing home-type unit) **A**1a 9 10 **F**1 3 5 6 10 12 14 15 16 19 20 21 23 34 35 36 40 41 43 44 45 46 47 52 53 54	16	10	S	TF H	247 222	9617 9514	169 145	68.4 —	18 18	858 858	30888 30602	13178 12913	876 856

Hospital, Address, Telephone, Administrator, Approval and Facility Codes, Multihospital System Code	Classification Codes				Inpatient Data				Newborn Data		Expense (thousands of dollars)		
★ American Hospital Association (AHA) membership □ Joint Commission on Accreditation of Hospitals (JCAH) accreditation + American Osteopathic Hospital Association (AOHA) membership ○ American Osteopathic Association (AOA) accreditation Δ Commission on Accreditation of Rehabilitation Facilities (CARF) accreditation Control codes 61, 63, 64, 71, 72 and 73 indicate hospitals listed by AOHA, but not registered by AHA. For definition of numerical codes, see page A2	Control	Service	Stay	Facilities	Beds	Admissions	Census	Occupancy (percent)	Bassinets	Births	Total	Payroll	Personnel
FORT STEWART—Liberty County													
⊞ WINN ARMY COMMUNITY HOSPITAL, Zip 31314; tel. 912/767-6001 **A**1a **F**1 3 6 12 14 15 16 23 24 27 28 29 30 32 33 34 35 37 40 46 47 49 52	42	10	S		116	5693	78	67.2	22	968	26924	21787	652
FORT VALLEY—Peach County													
⊞ PEACH COUNTY HOSPITAL, 601 N. Camellia Blvd., Zip 31030; tel. 912/825-8691 (Nonreporting) **A**1a 9 10; **S**1755	16	10	S		75	—	—	—	—	—	—	—	—
GAINESVILLE—Hall County													
⊞ LANIER PARK HOSPITAL, 675 White Sulphur Rd., Zip 30501; Mailing Address P O Box 1354, Zip 30503; tel. 404/531-2301; T. Marvin Goldman, adm. **A**1a 9 10 **F**1 3 6 10 12 14 15 16 23 35 46 47 53; **S**1755	33	10	S		124	4773	71	57.3	0	0	—	—	286
⊞ NORTHEAST GEORGIA MEDICAL CENTER, 743 Spring St. N.E., Zip 30505; tel. 404/535-3553; John A. Ferguson Jr., pres. **A**1a 2 9 10 **F**1 2 3 5 6 7 8 9 10 11 12 14 15 16 20 21 23 24 26 27 28 30 32 33 34 35 36 37 39 40 41 42 44 45 46 47 48 49 52 53 54	23	10	S		332	15941	248	74.7	40	2086	48571	22868	1255
GLENWOOD—Wheeler County													
WHEELER COUNTY HOSPITAL, Third St., Box 398, Zip 30428; tel. 912/523-5113; David P. Crowson, adm. (Nonreporting) **A**9 10; **S**1935	33	10	S		40	—	—	—	—	—	—	—	—
GRACEWOOD—Richmond County													
GRACEWOOD STATE SCHOOL AND HOSPITAL, Zip 30812; tel. 404/790-2030; Joanne P. Miklas PhD, supt. (Total facility includes 654 beds in nursing home-type unit) **F**19 23 24 38 42 43 44 46	12	12	S	TF	679	452	661	97.3	0	0	39385	24615	1404
				H	25	355	11	—	0	0	627	459	24
GREENSBORO—Greene County													
★ MINNIE G. BOSWELL MEMORIAL HOSPITAL, Siloam Rd., P O Box 329, Zip 30642; tel. 404/453-7331; Richard M. Yaun, adm. (Nonreporting) **A**9 10; **S**0025	16	10	S		29	—	—	—	—	—	—	—	—
GRIFFIN—Spalding County													
⊞ AMI GRIFFIN-SPALDING HOSPITAL (Formerly Griffin-Spalding County Hospital), S. Eighth St., P O Drawer V, Zip 30224; tel. 404/228-2721; Thomas A. Gordy, exec. dir. (Nonreporting) **A**1a 9 10; **S**0125	16	10	S		173	—	—	—	—	—	—	—	—
HAHIRA—Lowndes County													
SMITH HOSPITAL, 117 E. Main St., Zip 31632; tel. 912/794-2502; Lucilla Acree, adm. (Nonreporting) **A**9 10; **S**0195	33	10	S		71	—	—	—	—	—	—	—	—
HARTWELL—Hart County													
⊞ HART COUNTY HOSPITAL, Gibson & Cade Sts., Zip 30643; tel. 404/376-3921; Darrell M. Oglesby, adm. **A**1a 9 10 **F**1 6 10 14 15 16 23 35 37 40 45 50 53	16	10	S		57	1399	20	35.1	13	71	3538	1546	98
HAWKINSVILLE—Pulaski County													
⊞ R. J. TAYLOR MEMORIAL HOSPITAL, Macon Hwy., Zip 31036; tel. 912/783-0200; Dan S. Maddock, pres. (Nonreporting) **A**1a 9 10	23	10	S		55	—	—	—	—	—	—	—	—
HAZLEHURST—Jeff Davis County													
★ JEFF DAVIS HOSPITAL, 1215 S. Tallahassee St., Box 1200, Zip 31539; tel. 912/375-7781; James G. Peak, adm. **A**9 10 **F**1 6 10 12 14 16 23 34 35 40 43 45 46	16	10	S		56	1625	17	30.4	8	132	2999	1626	85
HIAWASSEE—Towns County													
★ TOWNS COUNTY HOSPITAL, Main St., Box 509, Zip 30546; tel. 404/896-2222; Jack P. Story Jr., adm. (Nonreporting) **A**9 10	16	10	S		42	—	—	—	—	—	—	—	—
HINESVILLE—Liberty County													
LIBERTY MEMORIAL HOSPITAL, Box 232, Zip 31313; tel. 912/876-3511; Anton F. Jeselnik, adm. **A**9 10 **F**1 6 14 15 16 30 33 35	16	10	S		33	1937	19	57.6	8	163	4079	2035	119
HOMERVILLE—Clinch County													
★ CLINCH MEMORIAL HOSPITAL, Carswell St., P O Box 516, Zip 31634; tel. 912/487-5211; R. E. Cagle, adm. **A**9 10 **F**1 14 15 16 23 34 35 36 37 40 45 50 52	16	10	S		56	1326	20	35.7	8	101	2587	1272	94
JACKSON—Butts County													
SYLVAN GROVE HOSPITAL, 1050 McDonough Rd., Zip 30233; tel. 404/775-7861; Jack F. Frayer, pres. (Nonreporting) **A**9 10; **S**1585	16	10	S		28	—	—	—	—	—	—	—	—
JASPER—Pickens County													
★ PICKENS GENERAL HOSPITAL, 1301 Church St., Zip 30143; tel. 404/692-2441; Fred M. Walker Jr., adm. (Nonreporting) **A**9 10	13	10	S		36	—	—	—	—	—	—	—	—
JESUP—Wayne County													
⊞ WAYNE MEMORIAL HOSPITAL, 865 S. First St., Box 408, Zip 31545; tel. 912/427-6811; Charles R. Morgan II, adm. **A**1a 9 10 **F**1 3 6 9 10 12 14 15 16 23 35 37 40 45 46 53; **S**1755	16	10	S		123	4320	71	57.7	15	465	10919	5002	295
KENNESAW—Cobb County													
⊞ DEVEREUX CENTER-GEORGIA BRANCH, 1980 Stanley Rd., Zip 30144; tel. 404/427-0147; Ralph L. Comerford, adm. (Nonreporting) **A**1b ; **S**0845	23	52	L		82	—	—	—	—	—	—	—	—
LA GRANGE—Troup County													
⊞ WEST GEORGIA MEDICAL CENTER, 1514 Vernon Rd., Box 1567, Zip 30240; tel. 404/882-1411; Charles L. Foster Jr., adm. (Total facility includes 150 beds in nursing home-type unit) **A**1a 2 9 10 **F**1 2 3 5 6 7 8 9 10 11 12 14 15 16 19 20 21 23 28 34 35 36 37 40 41 44 45 46 50 51 52 53 54	15	10	S	TF	397	9069	297	74.8	16	1005	30165	14558	991
				H	247	8975	148	—	16	1005	27450	12976	872
LAKELAND—Lanier County													
⊞ LOUIS SMITH MEMORIAL HOSPITAL, 852 W. Thigpen Rd., Box 306, Zip 31635; tel. 912/482-3110; Paul Massengill, pres. **A**1a 9 10 **F**1 3 6 14 16 23 35 36 45 46 47; **S**4165	21	10	S		40	1581	20	50.0	5	110	2500	1087	90
LAWRENCEVILLE—Gwinnett County													
⊞ GWINNETT HOSPITAL SYSTEM (Includes Buford Hospital, 55 Morningside Dr., Buford, Zip 30518; tel. 404/932-4000; Gwinnett Medical Center, Box 348, Zip 30246; tel. 404/955-4321; Joan Glancy Memorial Hospital, McClure Bridge Rd., Duluth, Zip 30136; tel. 404/497-4800), Highways 316 & 120, Box 348, Zip 30245; tel. 404/995-4321; Franklin Rinker, pres. **A**1a 9 10 **F**1 2 3 5 6 9 10 12 14 15 16 20 23 24 35 36 37 40 44 45 46 47 48 49 52 53	16	10	S		281	11798	180	65.9	24	1396	42226	18894	1010
GWINNETT MEDICAL CENTER, See Gwinnett Hospital Systems													
LITHIA SPRINGS—Douglas County													
⊞ HCA PARKWAY MEDICAL CENTER (Formerly Parkway Regional Hospital), 1000 Thornton Rd., P O Box 570, Zip 30057; tel. 404/944-4141; Sonny Boggus Jr., adm. **A**1a 9 10 **F**1 3 6 8 9 10 11 12 14 15 16 20 23 27 30 32 33 35 36 40 45 46 47 52 54; **S**1755	33	10	S		226	6535	114	50.4	18	861	23774	7296	420
LOUISVILLE—Jefferson County													
□ JEFFERSON HOSPITAL, 1067 Peachtree St., Zip 30434; tel. 912/625-7000; C. James Allen, adm. **A**1a 9 10 **F**1 6 14 16 23 35 40 43 45 46 50 52	15	10	S		50	933	12	24.0	0	0	3087	1327	89
MACON—Bibb County													
⊞ CHARTER LAKE HOSPITAL (Psychiatric and Chemical Dependency), 3500 Riverside Dr., P O Box 7067, Zip 31209; tel. 912/474-6200; Olivia E. Cunningham, adm. **A**1a 9 10 **F**15 24 30 33 42 48 50; **S**0695	33	22	S		80	970	66	82.5	0	0	—	—	118

★ American Hospital Association (AHA) membership
☐ Joint Commission on Accreditation of Hospitals (JCAH) accreditation
+ American Osteopathic Hospital Association (AOHA) membership
○ American Osteopathic Association (AOA) accreditation
Δ Commission on Accreditation of Rehabilitation Facilities (CARF) accreditation
Control codes 61, 63, 64, 71, 72 and 73 indicate hospitals listed by AOHA, but not registered by AHA.
For definition of numerical codes, see page A2

Hospital, Address, Telephone, Administrator, Approval and Facility Codes, Multihospital System Code	Classification Codes				Inpatient Data				Newborn Data		Expense (thousands of dollars)		
	Control	Service	Stay	Facilities	Beds	Admissions	Census	Occupancy (percent)	Bassinets	Births	Total	Payroll	Personnel
⊞ CHARTER NORTHSIDE HOSPITAL (Formerly Charter Northside Community Hospital), 400 Charter Blvd., P O Box 4627, Zip 31210; tel. 912/477-9520; Darrell Lumpkin, adm. (Nonreporting) **A**1a 9 10; **S**0695	33	10	S		103	—	—	—	—	—	—	—	—
COLISEUM PSYCHIATRIC HOSPITAL, See HCA Coliseum Psychiatric Hospital													
⊞ HCA COLISEUM MEDICAL CENTERS (Formerly Coliseum Park Hospital), 350 Hospital Dr., Zip 31213; tel. 912/745-9461; Charles T. Neal, adm. (Nonreporting) **A**1a 9 10; **S**1755	33	10	S		250	—	—	—	—	—	—	—	—
⊞ HCA COLISEUM PSYCHIATRIC HOSPITAL (Formerly Coliseum Psychiatric Hospital), 340 Hospital Dr., Zip 31201; Mailing Address Box 4366, Zip 31208; tel. 912/741-1355; Barbara D. Simpson, adm. (Nonreporting) **A**1b 10; **S**1755	33	22	S		76	—	—	—	—	—	—	—	—
⊞ MEDICAL CENTER OF CENTRAL GEORGIA, 777 Hemlock St., Box 6000, Zip 31208; tel. 912/744-1000; Damon D. King, adm. **A**1a 3 5 9 10 **F**1 2 3 4 6 10 12 14 15 16 20 23 24 26 27 30 33 34 35 36 37 38 40 42 45 46 47 51 52 53 54	16	10	S		505	19005	365	72.3	25	2296	82237	37390	1879
⊞ MIDDLE GEORGIA HOSPITAL, 888 Pine St., Box 6278, Zip 31297; tel. 912/743-1551; Paul D. Vogen, adm. **A**1a 9 10 **F**1 3 6 10 12 14 15 16 20 23 43 53 54; **S**0695	33	10	S		119	4591	80	67.2	0	0	—	—	333
MADISON—Morgan County													
MORGAN MEMORIAL HOSPITAL, Canterbury Park, Box 860, Zip 30650; tel. 404/342-1666; Bob Baldwin, adm. **A**9 10 **F**1 14 15 16 35 37; **S**1585	16	10	S		26	971	9	34.6	5	90	1717	690	40
MARIETTA—Cobb County													
⊞ KENNESTONE HOSPITAL, 677 Church St., Zip 30060; tel. 404/428-2000; Bernard L. Brown Jr., adm. **A**1a 9 10 **F**1 2 3 5 6 7 8 9 10 11 12 14 15 16 17 18 19 20 21 23 24 25 26 27 32 34 35 36 39 40 41 42 44 45 46 47 51 52 53 54; **S**0995	16	10	S		517	23864	386	74.7	48	2975	69840	31921	1941
⊞ KENNESTONE HOSPITAL AT WINDY HILL, 2540 Windy Hill Rd., Zip 30067; tel. 404/951-3100; John Richards, adm. **A**1a 9 10 **F**1 3 6 10 12 14 16 20 23 26 29 30 32 33 35 37 46 47 53; **S**0995	16	10	S		85	3935	51	60.0	0	0	13425	5608	311
MCRAE—Telfair County													
★ THREE RIVERS HOSPITAL AND MEDICAL CENTER, U. S. 341 S., Rte. 1, Box 5, Zip 31055; tel. 912/868-5621; Gary D. Ballard, adm. (Nonreporting) **A**9 10; **S**1935	23	10	S		48	—	—	—	—	—	—	—	—
METTER—Candler County													
★ CANDLER COUNTY HOSPITAL, Cedar Rd., Box 597, Zip 30439; tel. 912/685-5741; J. C. Rivenbark, adm. **A**9 10 **F**1 3 6 14 16 20 23 34 35 36 40 43 45 46 47 52	16	10	S		54	1443	23	42.6	8	136	3736	1749	124
MILLEDGEVILLE—Baldwin County													
⊞ BALDWIN COUNTY HOSPITAL, 1957 N. Cobb St., Box 690, Zip 31061; tel. 912/453-8441; Norman T. Neder, adm. **A**1a 9 10 **F**1 3 6 7 9 10 11 12 14 15 16 23 30 32 35 36 40 44 45 46 47 52 53	16	10	S		145	5889	96	66.2	24	627	21328	8932	456
☐ Δ CENTRAL STATE HOSPITAL, Zip 31062; tel. 912/453-4128; Myers R. Kurtz, supt. (Total facility includes 381 beds in nursing home-type unit) **A**1a b 7 10 **F**1 3 6 10 12 14 16 18 19 23 24 26 30 33 34 35 42 44 46 47 48	12	22	L	TF	2003	3876	1832	91.0	0	1	100058	61556	3589
				H	1622	3830	1471	—	0	1	—	—	2430
MILLEN—Jenkins County													
★ JENKINS COUNTY HOSPITAL, 515 E. Winthrop Ave., Zip 30442; tel. 912/982-4221; Douglas Reid Sasser, adm. **A**9 10 **F**1 12 14 16 34 35 40	16	10	S		38	1374	13	34.2	8	58	1897	922	74
MONROE—Walton County													
⊞ WALTON COUNTY HOSPITAL AND WALTON COUNTY HOSPITAL CONVALESCENT WING, 330 Alcova St., Box 1346, Zip 30655; tel. 404/267-8461; Raymond McCulloch, adm. (Total facility includes 58 beds in nursing home-type unit) **A**1a 9 10 **F**1 3 6 9 12 14 16 19 23 35 36 37 42 45	16	10	S	TF	159	3137	81	50.9	15	276	10670	4572	281
				H	101	3056	36	—	15	276	10275	4225	251
MONTEZUMA—Macon County													
★ MACON COUNTY MEDICAL CENTER, 509 Sumter St., Box 574, Zip 31063; tel. 912/472-2311; George L. Long, adm. (Data for 273 days) **A**9 10 **F**1 3 5 6 12 14 15 16 23 28 30 32 33 34 35 45 46 53; **S**5765	33	10	S		50	942	15	30.0	0	0	2728	733	63
MONTICELLO—Jasper County													
JASPER MEMORIAL HOSPITAL, 898 College St., Zip 31064; tel. 404/468-6411; Phillip Jordan, adm. (Nonreporting) **A**9 10	16	10	S		68	—	—	—	—	—	—	—	—
MOODY AIR FORCE BASE—Lowndes County													
U. S. AIR FORCE HOSPITAL MOODY, Zip 31699; tel. 912/333-3772; Col. Robert D. Kabo MC USAF, cmdr. (Nonreporting)	41	10	S		25	—	—	—	—	—	—	—	—
MOULTRIE—Colquitt County													
⊞ COLQUITT REGIONAL MEDICAL CENTER, Thomasville Hwy., Zip 31768; Mailing Address Box 40, Zip 31776; tel. 912/985-3420; James R. Lowry, adm. **A**1a 9 10 **F**1 3 5 6 10 12 14 15 16 20 23 24 34 35 37 40 41 44 45 53	16	10	S		155	4717	64	41.3	12	515	11951	5493	338
☐ TURNING POINT CARE CENTER, 319 By-Pass, P O Box 1177, Zip 31768; tel. 912/985-4815; Gary Bulkin, mng. dir. (Nonreporting) **A**1b 9	33	82	L		54	—	—	—	—	—	—	—	—
NASHVILLE—Berrien County													
☐ BERRIEN COUNTY HOSPITAL, 1221 E. McPherson St., P O Box 665, Zip 31639; tel. 912/686-7471; Dale C. Armstrong, adm. **A**1a 9 10 **F**1 3 6 14 15 16 23 34 35 43 45 46 47; **S**5895	33	10	S		60	2101	27	45.0	0	0	—	—	88
NEWNAN—Coweta County													
⊞ HUMANA HOSPITAL -NEWNAN, 60 Hospital Rd., Zip 30263; Mailing Address Box 2228, Zip 30264; tel. 404/253-1912; Jack D. Davis PhD, exec. dir. **A**1a 9 10 **F**1 3 6 10 12 14 15 16 23 26 35 36 37 40 45 46 47 52 53; **S**1235	33	10	S		144	4201	52	36.1	14	555	12792	4540	279
⊞ NEWNAN HOSPITAL, 80 Jackson St., Zip 30263; Mailing Address Box 997, Zip 30264; tel. 404/253-2330; Ken Ford, adm. **A**1a 9 10 **F**1 3 6 10 12 14 15 16 23 35 36 40 45 52	23	10	S		100	4313	67	67.0	12	199	13865	6112	335
OCILLA—Irwin County													
IRWIN COUNTY HOSPITAL, 710 N. Irwin Ave., Zip 31774; tel. 912/468-7411; Nellie Jo Spicer, adm. (Nonreporting) **A**9 10	16	10	S		64	—	—	—	—	—	—	—	—
PERRY—Houston County													
⊞ PERRY HOSPITAL (Formerly Perry Houston County Hospital), 1120 Morningside Dr., Drawer 1004, Zip 31069; tel. 912/987-3600; Sidney Oglesby, adm. (Nonreporting) **A**1a 9 10	13	10	S		45	—	—	—	—	—	—	—	—
REYNOLDS—Taylor County													
SAMS AND WHATLEY HOSPITAL, Zip 31076; tel. 912/847-4125; F. H. Sams Jr., adm. (Nonreporting)	33	10	S		13	—	—	—	—	—	—	—	—
RIVERDALE—Clayton County													
⊞ CLAYTON GENERAL HOSPITAL, 11 S.W. Upper Riverdale Rd., Box 328, Zip 30274; tel. 404/991-8000; Dennis K. Scheidt, adm. **A**1a 9 10 **F**1 2 3 6 7 10 12 14 15 16 20 23 26 27 30 32 34 35 36 37 40 41 45 46 47 52 53 54	16	10	S		304	16630	251	80.2	30	1370	47203	23283	1279
ROBINS AIR FORCE BASE—Houston County													
⊞ U. S. AIR FORCE HOSPITAL ROBINS, Zip 31098; tel. 912/926-6397; Lt. Col. James J. Gallman MSC USAF, adm. **A**1a **F**1 6 14 15 23 33 34 35 37 40 46 49	41	10	S		30	1190	12	40.0	12	144	—	—	382

Hospital, Address, Telephone, Administrator, Approval and Facility Codes, Multihospital System Code	Classification Codes				Inpatient Data				Newborn Data		Expense (thousands of dollars)		
★ American Hospital Association (AHA) membership ☐ Joint Commission on Accreditation of Hospitals (JCAH) accreditation + American Osteopathic Hospital Association (AOHA) membership ○ American Osteopathic Association (AOA) accreditation Δ Commission on Accreditation of Rehabilitation Facilities (CARF) accreditation Control codes 61, 63, 64, 71, 72 and 73 indicate hospitals listed by AOHA, but not registered by AHA. For definition of numerical codes, see page A2	Control	Service	Stay	Facilities	Beds	Admissions	Census	Occupancy (percent)	Bassinets	Births	Total	Payroll	Personnel
ROCKMART—Polk County													
ROCKMART-ARAGON HOSPITAL, N. Piedmont Ave., Box B, Zip 30153; tel. 404/684-6506; Stevan C. Sluder, adm. **A**9 10 **F**1 14 15 16 23 35 37 45 46 47	23	10	S		44	1009	12	27.3	0	0	1886	916	73
ROME—Floyd County													
⊞ FLOYD MEDICAL CENTER, Turner McCall Blvd., Box 233, Zip 30161; tel. 404/295-5500; Bill G. Waters, pres. **A**1a 2 3 9 10 **F**1 2 3 5 6 9 10 11 12 14 15 16 23 24 26 27 28 30 32 33 34 35 36 37 40 41 44 45 46 47 48 49 52 53	16	10	S		314	12038	183	58.3	36	2127	32832	15020	915
☐ NORTHWEST GEORGIA RÉGIONAL HOSPITAL, 1305 Redmond Circle, Zip 30161; tel. 404/295-6246; Robert L. Pulliam, supt. (Total facility includes 98 beds in nursing home-type unit) **A**1a b 9 10 **F**3 19 24 27 30 32 33 42 44 46 47 48	12	49	S	TF	373	3537	368	98.7	0	0	19531	15021	804
				H	275	3529	270	—	0	0	—	—	674
⊞ REDMOND PARK HOSPITAL, 501 Redmond Rd., Box 4077, Zip 30161; tel. 404/291-0291; William Paul Rutledge, adm. **A**1a 9 10 **F**1 3 6 10 12 14 15 16 20 23 34 35 43 46 47 53 54; **S**1755	33	10	S		201	7995	111	55.2	0	0	—	—	404
ROSWELL—Fulton County													
⊞ AMI NORTH FULTON MEDICAL CENTER (Formerly North Fulton Medical Center), 11585 Alpharetta St., Zip 30076; tel. 404/475-5552; Frederick Bailey, exec. dir. **A**1a 9 10 **F**1 3 5 6 10 12 14 15 16 23 24 25 26 34 35 36 40 42 44 46 47 51 53 54; **S**0125	33	10	S		147	4690	38	25.0	10	624	19604	7339	307
ROYSTON—Franklin County													
⊞ COBB MEMORIAL HOSPITAL (Includes Brown Memorial Convalescent Center), 577 Franklin Springs St., Box 8, Zip 30662; tel. 404/245-5034; H. Thomas Brown, adm. (Total facility includes 144 beds in nursing home-type unit) **A**1a 9 10 **F**1 3 6 14 15 16 19 23 33 34 35 40 45 47 52 53	23	10	S	TF	212	2854	188	85.1	8	202	7344	3417	278
				H	68	2799	44	—	8	202	5140	2236	176
SANDERSVILLE—Washington County													
★ MEMORIAL HOSPITAL OF WASHINGTON COUNTY, 610 Sparta Hwy., Box 636, Zip 31082; tel. 912/552-3901; Larry W. Anderson, adm. (Total facility includes 50 beds in nursing home-type unit) **A**9 10 **F**1 2 6 14 16 19 30 35 44 45 46 47	16	10	S	TF	106	1956	81	76.4	0	0	6500	2292	160
				H	56	1902	28	—	0	0	5882	1869	133
SAVANNAH—Chatham County													
⊞ Δ CANDLER GENERAL HOSPITAL, 5353 Reynolds St., Box 9787, Zip 31412; tel. 912/354-9211; John T. Carpenter, pres. **A**1a 7 9 10 **F**1 2 3 6 10 12 14 15 16 20 23 24 25 26 30 32 33 34 35 36 40 43 44 45 46 50 53	23	10	S		335	14050	273	81.5	48	2129	54019	24309	1358
⊞ CHARTER BROAD OAKS HOSPITAL, 5002 Waters Ave., Zip 31406; Mailing Address P O Box 13604, Zip 31416; tel. 912/354-3911; John M. Stribling, exec. dir. **A**1b 9 10 **F**15 24 28 29 30 32 33 34 42 43 49; **S**0695	33	22	S		88	1046	61	69.3	0	0	6069	1998	118
☐ GEORGIA REGIONAL HOSPITAL AT SAVANNAH, Eisenhower Dr. at Varnedoe, Zip 31406; Mailing Address Box 13607, Zip 31416; tel. 912/356-2045; Galen C. Huffman MD, supt. (Nonreporting) **A**1b 10	12	22	S		282	—	—	—	—	—	—	—	—
⊞ MEMORIAL MEDICAL CENTER, 4700 Waters Ave., Zip 31404; Mailing Address Box 23089, Zip 31403; tel. 912/356-8000; Kenneth W. Wood, pres. & chief exec. off. **A**1a 2 3 5 8 9 10 **F**1 2 3 4 5 6 7 8 9 10 11 12 14 15 16 17 20 23 24 25 26 27 28 33 34 35 36 38 39 40 42 45 46 47 51 52 53 54; **S**1755	23	10	S		487	18998	419	86.4	40	2569	94935	39308	1733
☐ ST. JOSEPH'S HOSPITAL, 11705 Mercy Blvd., Zip 31419; tel. 912/925-4100; Sr. M. Faith McKean, pres. **A**1a 9 10 **F**1 2 3 4 5 6 10 12 15 16 20 23 24 26 34 35 40 43 44 45 46 47 53 54; **S**6015	21	10	S		311	9461	186	59.8	14	270	36789	17432	1048
SMYRNA—Cobb County													
⊞ BRAWNER PSYCHIATRIC INSTITUTE, 3180 Atlanta St. S.E., Zip 30080; tel. 404/436-0081; Brent J. Bryson, adm. **A**1a b 9 10 **F**24 29 30 32 33 42 43 44 48 49; **S**0825	33	22	S		89	927	76	93.8	0	0	8823	3073	195
⊞ RIDGEVIEW INSTITUTE, 3995 S. Cobb Dr., Zip 30080; tel. 404/434-4567; Edward J. Osborne, exec. vice-pres. **A**1b 9 10 **F**15 28 29 30 32 33 42 48 49	23	22	L		200	1634	181	90.5	0	0	16523	6859	440
⊞ SMYRNA HOSPITAL, 3949 S. Cobb Dr., Zip 30080; tel. 404/434-0710; James McAlvin, pres. (Nonreporting) **A**1a 9 10; **S**4165	21	10	S		100	—	—	—	—	—	—	—	—
SNELLVILLE—Gwinnett County													
⊞ HUMANA HOSPITAL -GWINNETT, 2160 Fountain Dr., Box 587, Zip 30278; tel. 404/979-0200; David L. Harris, exec. dir. **A**1a 9 10 **F**1 2 3 6 9 10 12 14 15 16 20 23 24 33 35 36 43 44 46 53; **S**1235	33	10	S		120	5760	61	50.8	17	1055	—	—	294
SPARTA—Hancock County													
HANCOCK MEMORIAL HOSPITAL, 453 Boland St., Zip 31087; tel. 404/444-5232; Fuller G. Marshall, adm. (Nonreporting) **A**9 10	16	10	S		52	—	—	—	—	—	—	—	—
SPRINGFIELD—Effingham County													
⊞ EFFINGHAM COUNTY HOSPITAL AND EXTENDED CARE FACILITY, Box 386, Zip 31329; tel. 912/754-6451; Norma J. Morgan, adm. (Total facility includes 56 beds in nursing home-type unit) **A**1a 9 10 **F**1 6 14 15 16 19 21 23 34 35 43 44 45	16	10	S	TF	94	718	66	70.2	0	0	2205	1062	94
				H	38	705	12	—	0	0	1462	817	53
ST. MARYS—Camden County													
★ GILMAN HOSPITAL, 805 Dilworth St., Box 805, Zip 31558; tel. 912/882-5426; Charles W. Baker, adm. (Nonreporting) **A**9 10	23	10	S		33	—	—	—	—	—	—	—	—
ST. SIMONS ISLAND—Glynn County													
⊞ CHARTER BY-THE-SEA HOSPITAL, 2927 Demere Rd., Zip 31522; tel. 912/638-1999; James R. Thomas, adm. (Nonreporting) **A**1b 9 10; **S**0695	33	82	S		60	—	—	—	—	—	—	—	—
STATESBORO—Bulloch County													
⊞ BULLOCH MEMORIAL HOSPITAL, 500 E. Grady St., Box 1048, Zip 30458; tel. 912/764-6671; William T. Richardson, adm. **A**1a 2 9 10 **F**1 3 6 10 12 15 16 23 24 26 35 36 37 40 45 46 47 50 52 53	16	10	S		119	5577	74	62.2	20	675	12893	5425	366
⊞ WILLINGWAY HOSPITAL, 311 Jones Mill Rd., Zip 30458; tel. 912/764-6236; Wyman H. Hunt, adm. **A**1b **F**16 21 41 42	33	82	L		40	426	40	100.0	0	0	5301	2021	134
STOCKBRIDGE—Henry County													
⊞ HENRY GENERAL HOSPITAL, 1133 Hudson Bridge Rd., Zip 30281; tel. 404/389-2200; Joseph G. Brum, adm. **A**1a 9 10 **F**1 2 3 6 10 12 14 15 16 23 28 30 33 34 35 37 40 45 46 49 52 53	16	10	S		102	5533	76	74.5	10	492	16713	7107	378
SUMMERVILLE—Chattooga County													
★ CHATTOOGA COUNTY HOSPITAL, Highland Ave., Box 449, Zip 30747; tel. 404/857-4761; Betty R. Wollstein, exec. dir. (Total facility includes 90 beds in nursing home-type unit) **A**9 10 **F**16 19 35	16	10	S	TF	121	934	100	82.6	0	0	2284	1182	108
				H	31	880	11	—	0	0	1369	725	66
SWAINSBORO—Emanuel County													
⊞ EMANUEL COUNTY HOSPITAL, Kite Rd., Box 7, Zip 30401; tel. 912/237-9911; Leland E. Farnell, adm. (Nonreporting) **A**1a 9 10; **S**1755	16	10	S		118	—	—	—	—	—	—	—	—
SYLVANIA—Screven County													
⊞ SCREVEN COUNTY HOSPITAL, 215 Mims Rd., Zip 30467; tel. 912/564-7426; Al Strickland, adm. (Nonreporting) **A**1a 9 10	16	10	S		54	—	—	—	—	—	—	—	—
SYLVESTER—Worth County													
⊞ WORTH COMMUNITY HOSPITAL, Camilla Hwy., Box 545, Zip 31791; tel. 912/776-6961; John Smithhisler, adm. **A**1a 9 10 **F**3 6 12 14 16 23 26 34 35 40 45 46 47 48 49 52; **S**1755	33	10	S		50	1433	19	38.0	12	132	3065	1281	82

Hospital, Address, Telephone, Administrator, Approval and Facility Codes, Multihospital System Code	Classification Codes			Facilities	Inpatient Data				Newborn Data		Expense (thousands of dollars)		
★ American Hospital Association (AHA) membership □ Joint Commission on Accreditation of Hospitals (JCAH) accreditation + American Osteopathic Hospital Association (AOHA) membership ○ American Osteopathic Association (AOA) accreditation Δ Commission on Accreditation of Rehabilitation Facilities (CARF) accreditation Control codes 61, 63, 64, 71, 72 and 73 indicate hospitals listed by AOHA, but not registered by AHA. For definition of numerical codes, see page A2	Control	Service	Stay		Beds	Admissions	Census	Occupancy (percent)	Bassinets	Births	Total	Payroll	Personnel
THOMASTON—Upson County													
★□ UPSON COUNTY HOSPITAL, 801 W. Gordon St., Box 1059, Zip 30286; tel. 404/647-8111; Ernest H. Borders, adm. **A**1a 9 10 **F**1 3 6 10 12 14 15 16 23 24 35 40 45 52 53; **S**1755	16	10	S		119	4780	57	47.9	21	759	11292	4991	307
THOMASVILLE—Thomas County													
★□ JOHN D. ARCHBOLD MEMORIAL HOSPITAL, Gordon Ave. & Mimosa Dr., Zip 31792; tel. 912/228-2000; Ken B. Beverly, pres. & chief exec. off. **A**1a 9 10 **F**1 2 3 5 6 7 8 9 10 11 12 14 15 16 17 20 23 24 26 27 28 29 30 31 32 33 34 35 36 37 38 40 41 42 43 44 45 46 47 49 50 53 54	23	10	S		246	10504	162	65.9	28	949	27973	12662	845
THOMSON—McDuffie County													
★ MCDUFFIE COUNTY HOSPITAL, 521 Hill St. S.W., Zip 30824; tel. 404/595-1411; Inez R. Lemke, adm. **A**9 10 **F**1 6 14 16 23 34 35 45 46 50 52	16	10	S		33	118	1	3.0	0	0	3148	1411	100
TIFTON—Tift County													
★□ TIFT GENERAL HOSPITAL, 901 E. 18th St., Drawer 747, Zip 31793; tel. 912/382-7120; Roger W. Long, adm. **A**1a 9 10 **F**1 3 6 12 14 15 16 20 21 23 34 35 40 45 46 47 53	16	10	S		168	7974	103	61.3	24	828	19581	7950	526
TOCCOA—Stephens County													
★□ STEPHENS COUNTY HOSPITAL, Falls Rd., Box 947, Zip 30577; tel. 404/886-6841; James E. Lathren, adm. **A**1a 2 9 10 **F**1 3 6 10 12 14 15 16 23 24 34 35 36 40 41 45 46 52 53	16	10	S		99	3615	47	47.5	9	320	8855	4175	258
TUCKER—De Kalb County													
★ ○ + DOCTORS HOSPITAL, 2160 Idlewood Rd., Zip 30084; tel. 404/496-6740; Frank B. Murphy, adm. **A**9 10 11 12 13 **F**1 2 3 6 10 12 14 15 16 23 26 30 32 33 34 35 36 37 40 46 47 52 53; **S**1755	33	10	S		143	4212	54	37.8	8	211	—	—	281
VALDOSTA—Lowndes County													
★□ GREENLEAF CENTER (Formerly Valdosta Center), 2209 Pineview Dr., Zip 31602; tel. 912/247-4357; Allen R. Vessels, adm. (Nonreporting) **A**1b 10; **S**1155	33	22	S		70	—	—	—	—	—	—	—	—
★□ SOUTH GEORGIA MEDICAL CENTER, Pendleton Park, Zip 31602; Mailing Address Box 1727, Zip 31603; tel. 912/333-1000; John S. Bowling, adm. **A**1a 2 9 10 **F**1 3 5 6 8 9 10 11 12 14 15 16 20 23 24 26 27 30 32 33 34 35 36 37 42 43 44 45 46 47 52 53 54	16	10	S		259	12832	202	78.0	22	1373	35771	15472	982
U. S. AIR FORCE HOSPITAL MOODY, See Moody Air Force Base													
VALDOSTA CENTER, See Greenleaf Center													
VIDALIA—Toombs County													
★ DR. JOHN M. MEADOWS MEMORIAL HOSPITAL, 1703 Meadows Lane, Box 1048, Zip 30474; tel. 912/537-8921; Weston Bergman Jr., adm. & chief exec. off. **A**9 10 **F**1 3 6 10 12 14 15 16 23 24 35 36 40 45 52; **S**2495	16	10	S		81	2915	44	54.3	8	441	8497	3431	214
VIENNA—Dooly County													
□ DOOLY MEDICAL CENTER, Pitts Rd., Box 278, Zip 31092; tel. 912/268-4141; Mark Phillips, adm. (Nonreporting) **A**1a 9 10; **S**5895	33	10	S		43	—	—	—	—	—	—	—	—
VILLA RICA—Carroll County													
★ TANNER MEDICAL CENTER-VILLA RICA (Formerly Villa Rica City Hospital), 601 Dallas Rd., Box 638, Zip 30180; tel. 404/459-3681; J. M. McCollum, adm. **A**9 10 **F**1 2 6 12 14 16 35 45 46; **S**1755	16	10	S		54	1814	18	33.3	6	206	3613	1778	100
WARM SPRINGS—Meriwether County													
★ MERIWETHER MEMORIAL HOSPITAL, Box 8, Zip 31830; tel. 404/655-3331; George T. Hudson, adm. (Nonreporting) **A**9 10	16	10	S		36	—	—	—	—	—	—	—	—
★□ Δ ROOSEVELT WARM SPRINGS INSTITUTE FOR REHABILITATION, P O Box 1000, Zip 31830; tel. 404/655-2000; Frank C. Ruzycki, exec. dir.; Paul E. Peach MD, med. dir. (Nonreporting) **A**1a 7 9 10	12	46	S		73	—	—	—	—	—	—	—	—
WARNER ROBINS—Houston County													
★□ HOUSTON MEDICAL CENTER (Formerly Medical Center of Houston County), 1601 Watson Blvd., Box 2886, Zip 31093; tel. 912/922-4281; Oscar K. Weinmeister Jr., exec. dir. **A**1a 9 10 **F**1 3 6 12 14 16 23 24 27 34 35 36 40 45 46 47 51 52 53	16	10	S		180	8085	125	67.9	20	1067	26069	11208	760
WASHINGTON—Wilkes County													
★□ WILLS MEMORIAL HOSPITAL, Gordon St., Box 370, Zip 30673; tel. 404/678-2151; Hugh P. Warren, adm. **A**1a 9 10 **F**1 3 15 16 20 23 34 35 40 43 45 47	16	10	S		60	1671	23	38.3	13	52	3739	1882	113
WAYCROSS—Ware County													
★□ MEMORIAL HOSPITAL (Includes Riverside Nursing Home), 410 Darling Ave., Zip 31501; Mailing Address P O Box 139, Zip 31502; tel. 912/283-3030; H. Virgil Parker, exec. dir. **A**1a 9 10 **F**1 2 3 6 10 11 12 14 15 16 20 23 35 36 39 40 45 46 47 51 53	16	10	S		171	6626	93	54.4	32	786	18619	9165	500
WAYNESBORO—Burke County													
★□ BURKE COUNTY HOSPITAL, 351 Liberty St., Zip 30830; tel. 404/554-4435; James R. Emery, adm. **A**1a 9 10 **F**1 3 6 14 16 20 34 35 36 45; **S**0025	16	10	S		40	1499	17	36.2	9	129	3770	1626	99
WINDER—Barrow County													
★□ AMI BARROW MEDICAL CENTER (Formerly Barrow Medical Center), 1035 N. Broad St., Box 768, Zip 30680; tel. 404/867-3400; Gerald Trevisol, exec. dir. (Nonreporting) **A**1a 9 10; **S**0125	33	10	S		60	—	—	—	—	—	—	—	—
WOODSTOCK—Cherokee County													
★ WOODSTOCK HOSPITAL (Formerly Cherokee Atomedic Hospital), 103 Arnold Mill Rd., Zip 30188; tel. 404/926-5351; Julia Ellis, adm. (Nonreporting) **A**9 10	33	10	S		21	—	—	—	—	—	—	—	—

Hospital, Address, Telephone, Administrator, Approval and Facility Codes, Multihospital System Code

★ American Hospital Association (AHA) membership
□ Joint Commission on Accreditation of Hospitals (JCAH) accreditation
+ American Osteopathic Hospital Association (AOHA) membership
○ American Osteopathic Association (AOA) accreditation
Δ Commission on Accreditation of Rehabilitation Facilities (CARF) accreditation
Control codes 61, 63, 64, 71, 72 and 73 indicate hospitals listed by AOHA, but not registered by AHA.
For definition of numerical codes, see page A2

Hawaii

Hospital, Address, Telephone, Administrator, Approval and Facility Codes, Multihospital System Code	Classification Codes: Control	Service	Stay	Facilities	Inpatient Data: Beds	Admissions	Census	Occupancy (percent)	Newborn Data: Bassinets	Births	Expense (thousands of dollars): Total	Payroll	Personnel
HANA—Maui County													
HANA MEDICAL CENTER, See Maui Memorial Hospital, Wailuku													
HILO—Hawaii County													
□★ HILO HOSPITAL, 1190 Waianuenue Ave., Zip 96720; tel. 808/969-4111; Jerry E. Merrill, adm. (Total facility includes 108 beds in nursing home-type unit) **A**1a 10 **F**1 3 5 6 7 8 9 10 11 12 14 15 16 19 23 24 26 27 29 30 32 34 35 37 40 41 42 44 45 46 47 49 50 52 53; **S**3555	12	10	S	TF	274	6996	188	68.6	14	1113	25964	11153	580
				H	166	6743	89	—	14	1113	—	—	513
HONOKAA—Hawaii County													
★ HONOKAA HOSPITAL, Box 237, Zip 96727; tel. 808/775-7211; Yoshito Iwamoto, adm. **A**10 **F**1 3 14 19 23 24 35 36 37 40 46 52; **S**3555	12	10	S		30	485	12	40.0	5	75	1850	927	45
HONOLULU—Honolulu County													
□★ KAISER FOUNDATION HOSPITAL, 3288 Moanalua Rd., Zip 96819; tel. 808/834-5333; Ronald J. Mikolajczyk, adm. **A**1a 2 3 5 10 **F**1 3 6 9 10 14 15 16 23 26 28 32 33 34 35 36 37 40 45 46 47 50 51 52 53 54; **S**2105	23	10	S		158	8631	130	82.3	32	1671	—	—	722
□★ KAPIOLANI MEDICAL CENTER FOR WOMEN AND CHILDREN (Formerly Kapiolani Women's and Children's Medical Center) (Obstetrics, Gynecology and Pediatrics), 1319 Punahou St., Zip 96826; tel. 808/947-8511; Richard Davi, pres. **A**1a 3 5 10 **F**1 3 5 6 12 14 15 16 23 24 26 28 30 32 33 34 35 36 37 40 42 44 45 46 47 51 52 53	23	49	S		226	13512	161	71.2	90	6441	51157	24442	1117
□★ KUAKINI MEDICAL CENTER (Includes Hale Pulama Mau), 347 N. Kuakini St., Zip 96817; tel. 808/536-2236; Masaichi Tasaka, pres. **A**1a 2 3 5 10 **F**1 3 4 5 6 7 8 9 10 11 12 14 15 16 20 23 24 34 35 45 46 47 53 54	23	10	S		249	7658	177	71.1	0	0	47673	24849	1127
★ LEAHI HOSPITAL, 3675 Kilauea Ave., Zip 96816; tel. 808/734-0221; Abraham L. Choy, adm. (Total facility includes 140 beds in nursing home-type unit) **A**10 **F**12 15 19 23 24 26 34 42 44 45 46 47 50; **S**3555	12	49	L	TF	166	116	142	85.5	0	0	8705	4827	—
				H	26	41	7	—	0	0	811	346	—
□★ QUEEN'S MEDICAL CENTER, 1301 Punchbowl St., Zip 96813; tel. 808/538-9011; Fred A. Pritchard, pres. & chief exec. off.; John V. Schleif, exec. vice-pres. & chief oper. off. **A**1a 2 3 5 10 **F**1 2 3 4 5 6 7 8 9 10 11 12 14 15 16 17 20 21 23 24 26 27 28 29 30 31 32 33 34 35 36 37 39 40 41 42 43 44 45 46 47 49 53 54	23	10	S		437	17422	360	82.9	35	1292	—	—	1768
□★ Δ REHABILITATION HOSPITAL OF THE PACIFIC, 226 N. Kuakini St., Zip 96817; tel. 808/531-3511; Patrick J. Duarte, pres. & chief exec. off. **A**1a 7 10 **F**15 16 23 24 34 42 44 45 46	23	46	L		100	700	68	68.0	0	0	—	—	360
□★ SHRINERS HOSPITAL FOR CRIPPLED CHILDREN, 1310 Punahou St., Zip 96826; tel. 808/941-4466; Allan D. Robb, adm. **A**1a 3 5 **F**15 23 24 26 34 42 46; **S**4125	23	57	L		40	304	34	85.0	0	0	—	—	92
□★ ST. FRANCIS MEDICAL CENTER (Formerly St. Francis Hospital), 2230 Liliha St., Zip 96817; tel. 808/547-6011; Sr. Maureen Keleher, chief exec. off. (Total facility includes 52 beds in nursing home-type unit) **A**1a 2 3 5 10 **F**1 3 4 5 6 7 8 9 10 11 12 13 14 15 16 19 20 21 23 24 26 28 29 30 32 33 34 35 41 42 44 45 46 47 49 53 54; **S**5955	21	10	S	TF	233	783	201	100.0	0	0	49685	23893	1240
				H	181	6225	150	—	0	0	47048	22732	1200
□ STRAUB CLINIC AND HOSPITAL, 888 S. King St., Zip 96813; tel. 808/523-2311; Tom L. Battisto, exec. adm. **A**1a 2 3 5 10 **F**1 2 3 6 9 10 11 12 14 15 16 20 21 22 23 24 26 28 30 32 33 34 35 37 38 41 45 46 47 50 53 54	33	10	S		159	7461	124	78.0	0	0	41915	13814	918
□★ TRIPLER ARMY MEDICAL CENTER, Zip 96859; tel. 808/433-6661 (Nonreporting) **A**1a 2 3 5	42	10	S		555	—	—	—	—	—	—	—	—
KAHUKU—Honolulu County													
□ KAHUKU HOSPITAL, Box 218, Zip 96731; tel. 808/293-9221; Rikio Tanji, chief exec. off. (Nonreporting) **A**1a 10	23	10	S		26	—	—	—	—	—	—	—	—
KAILUA—Honolulu County													
□★ CASTLE MEDICAL CENTER, 640 Ulukahiki St., Zip 96734; tel. 808/263-5500; Terry W. White, pres. & adm. **A**1a 10 **F**1 3 5 6 10 12 15 16 23 24 27 30 32 33 34 35 36 44 45 46 47 48 49 53; **S**0235	21	10	S		156	6068	106	67.9	20	639	21310	10185	413
KANEOHE—Honolulu County													
HAWAII STATE HOSPITAL, 45-710 Keaahala Rd., Zip 96744; tel. 808/247-2191; Howard Gudeman PhD, adm. **A**3 5 10 **F**15 23 24 32 33 42 45 46 47	12	22	L		231	783	263	100.0	0	0	13195	7912	407
KAPAA—Kauai County													
★ SAMUEL MAHELONA MEMORIAL HOSPITAL, 4800 Kawaihau Rd., Zip 96746; tel. 808/822-4961; John M. English, adm. **A**10 **F**3 19 23 24 27 30 42 46; **S**3555	12	48	L		76	297	64	84.2	0	0	4517	2512	137
KAUNAKAKAI—Maui County													
□★ MOLOKAI GENERAL HOSPITAL, Box 408, Zip 96748; tel. 808/553-5331; Herbert K. Yim, pres. & adm. **A**1a 10 **F**1 15 16 19 23 24 30 34 35 36 37 40	23	10	S		30	457	17	56.3	4	69	—	—	42
KEALAKEKUA—Hawaii County													
□★ KONA HOSPITAL, Box 69, Zip 96750; tel. 808/322-9311; Jennie Wung, adm. (Total facility includes 17 beds in nursing home-type unit) **A**1a 10 **F**1 3 6 12 14 16 19 23 24 30 35 36 40 42 45 46 50 52; **S**3555	12	10	S	TF	59	2842	41	69.5	10	477	8763	3996	205
				H	42	2783	28	—	10	477	—	—	195
KOHALA—Hawaii County													
★ KOHALA HOSPITAL, Mailing Address Box 10, Kapaau, Zip 96755; tel. 808/889-6211; Jack O. Halstead, adm. (Total facility includes 16 beds in nursing home-type unit) **A**10 **F**15 19 24 35 40 45 46 50; **S**3555	12	10	L	TF	26	179	17	65.4	4	2	1619	788	32
				H	10	159	—	—	4	2	—	—	—
KULA—Maui County													
KULA GENERAL HOSPITAL, See Kula Hospital													
★ KULA HOSPITAL (Includes Kula General Hospital), 204 Kula Hwy., Zip 96790; tel. 808/878-1221; Romel Dela Cruz, adm. **A**10 **F**19 23 24 34 44 45 46 50; **S**3555	12	48	L		105	144	94	89.5	0	0	6020	2793	169
LANAI CITY—Maui County													
★ LANAI COMMUNITY HOSPITAL, 628 Seventh St., Box 797, Zip 96763; tel. 808/565-6411; Monica L. Borges, adm. **A**10 **F**3 27 30 34 35 36 40 45 46 50; **S**3555	12	10	S		14	118	8	57.1	2	17	909	463	23
LIHUE—Kauai County													
□★ G. N. WILCOX MEMORIAL HOSPITAL (Formerly G. N. Wilcox Memorial Hospital and Health Center), 3420 Kuhio Hwy., Zip 96766; tel. 808/245-1100; Phil Palmer, chief exec. off. (Total facility includes 80 beds in nursing home-type unit) **A**1a 2 10 **F**1 3 6 10 11 12 15 16 19 23 24 26 35 36 37 40 45 50 53	23	10	S	TF	155	3908	114	73.5	10	574	15147	7243	415
				H	75	3709	38	—	10	574	12707	6512	373
PAHALA—Hawaii County													
★ KAU HOSPITAL, Box 40, Zip 96777; tel. 808/928-8331; Kenji Nagao, adm. **A**10 **F**3 19 23 24 35 40 42 46 50; **S**3555	12	10	L		15	82	7	46.7	2	19	1344	703	36

- ★ American Hospital Association (AHA) membership
- □ Joint Commission on Accreditation of Hospitals (JCAH) accreditation
- + American Osteopathic Hospital Association (AOHA) membership
- ○ American Osteopathic Association (AOA) accreditation
- Δ Commission on Accreditation of Rehabilitation Facilities (CARF) accreditation

Control codes 61, 63, 64, 71, 72 and 73 indicate hospitals listed by AOHA, but not registered by AHA. For definition of numerical codes, see page A2

Hospital, Address, Telephone, Administrator, Approval and Facility Codes, Multihospital System Code	Classification Codes				Inpatient Data				Newborn Data		Expense (thousands of dollars)		
	Control	Service	Stay	Facilities	Beds	Admissions	Census	Occupancy (percent)	Bassinets	Births	Total	Payroll	Personnel
WAHIAWA—Honolulu County													
⊞ WAHIAWA GENERAL HOSPITAL, 128 Lehua St., Box 580, Zip 96786; tel. 808/621-8411; Kenam Kim, pres. (Total facility includes 93 beds in nursing home-type unit) **A**1a 10 **F**1 3 6 12 15 16 19 23 24 26 34 35 36 40 41 42 45 46 50 53	23	10	S	TF	162	2846	137	84.6	15	507	14521	6360	330
				H	69	2786	46	—	15	507	11265	5512	272
WAIAKOA—Maui County													
KULA HOSPITAL, See Kula													
WAILUKU—Maui County													
MAUI MEMORIAL HOSPITAL, See Maui Community Hospital													
⊞ MAUI MEMORIAL HOSPITAL (Includes Hana Medical Center, Hana; Maui Memorial Hospital), 221 Mahalani St., Zip 96793; tel. 808/244-9056; Frederick M. Burkle Jr. MD, adm. **A**1a 2 10 **F**1 3 6 10 12 14 16 23 24 27 34 35 36 40 45 46 52 53; **S**3555	12	10	S		145	7512	98	67.6	18	1324	19927	8903	466
WAIMEA—Kauai County													
⊞ KAUAI VETERANS MEMORIAL HOSPITAL, Waimea Canyon Rd., Box 337, Zip 96796; tel. 808/338-9431; Janet Kawamura, actg. adm. (Total facility includes 6 beds in nursing home-type unit) **A**1a 2 10 **F**1 3 6 14 15 16 19 20 23 24 35 36 37 40 46 50; **S**3555	12	10	S	TF	50	1011	19	38.0	10	138	5397	2410	117
				H	44	1004	13	—	10	138	5015	2246	—

Hospital, Address, Telephone, Administrator, Approval and Facility Codes, Multihospital System Code

- ★ American Hospital Association (AHA) membership
- □ Joint Commission on Accreditation of Hospitals (JCAH) accreditation
- + American Osteopathic Hospital Association (AOHA) membership
- ○ American Osteopathic Association (AOA) accreditation
- Δ Commission on Accreditation of Rehabilitation Facilities (CARF) accreditation

Control codes 61, 63, 64, 71, 72 and 73 indicate hospitals listed by AOHA, but not registered by AHA. For definition of numerical codes, see page A2

Idaho

Hospital, Address, Telephone, Administrator, Approval and Facility Codes, Multihospital System Code	Classification Codes: Control	Service	Stay	Facilities	Inpatient Data: Beds	Admissions	Census	Occupancy (percent)	Newborn Data: Bassinets	Births	Expense (thousands of dollars): Total	Payroll	Personnel
AMERICAN FALLS—Power County													
★ HARMS MEMORIAL HOSPITAL, Gifford at Roosevelt, P O Box 420, Zip 83211; tel. 208/226-2327; Francis X. McNamara, adm. (Total facility includes 20 beds in nursing home-type unit) **A**9 10 **F**1 3 14 16 19 34 35 45 46 52	16	10	S	TF	41	281	22	53.7	6	13	1620	764	61
				H	21	241	2	—	6	13	—	—	29
ARCO—Butte County													
★ LOST RIVERS DISTRICT HOSPITAL (Formerly Lost Rivers Hospital), 551 Highland Dr., P O Box 145, Zip 83213; tel. 208/527-8206; Martha Danz, adm. (Total facility includes 10 beds in nursing home-type unit) **A**9 10 **F**1 3 14 15 16 19 34 35 37 40 43 45 50	16	10	S	TF	24	289	13	54.2	4	35	736	379	39
				H	14	264	—	—	4	35	639	281	29
ASHTON—Fremont County													
ASHTON MEMORIAL HOSPITAL, 801 Main St., P O Box An, Zip 83420; tel. 208/652-7461; Ann C. P. Stivers, adm. (Total facility includes 12 beds in nursing home-type unit) **A**9 10 **F**1 5 12 14 15 16 19 21 23 26 34 35 36 37 41 42 43 44 45 46 47 49 50	23	10	S	TF	24	319	16	66.7	3	14	—	—	35
				H	12	294	3	—	3	14	—	—	—
BLACKFOOT—Bingham County													
⊞ BINGHAM MEMORIAL HOSPITAL (Includes Bingham County Nursing Home), 98 Poplar St., Zip 83221; tel. 208/785-4100; Carl Staley, adm. (Total facility includes 56 beds in nursing home-type unit) **A**1a 2 9 10 **F**1 3 5 6 10 12 14 15 16 19 23 24 35 36 37 40 44 46 50	13	10	S	TF	110	1650	70	63.6	12	431	5934	2863	184
				H	54	1595	16	—	12	431	5251	2415	152
STATE HOSPITAL SOUTH, E. Alice St., Box 400, Zip 83221; tel. 208/785-1200; George W. Bachik, adm. dir. **F**12 19 23 24 30 32 33 42 44 45 47 50	12	22	L		179	489	159	88.8	0	0	7767	4743	268
BOISE—Ada County													
□ CPC INTERMOUNTAIN HOSPITAL OF BOISE, 303 N. Allumbaugh St., Zip 83704; tel. 208/377-8400; Paul Logan, adm. **A**1b 9 10 **F**3 15 24 30 32 33 42 47; **S**0785	33	22	S		75	587	27	36.0	0	0	—	—	—
★ Δ IDAHO ELKS REHABILITATION HOSPITAL, 204 Fort Pl., Zip 83702; Mailing Address Box 1100, Zip 83701; tel. 208/343-2583; Richard L. Williams, adm. **A**7 9 10 **F**16 23 24 26 44 45	23	46	S		50	655	43	86.0	0	0	5593	3586	171
⊞ SAINT ALPHONSUS REGIONAL MEDICAL CENTER, 1055 N. Curtis Rd., Zip 83706; tel. 208/378-2121; Sr. Patricia Vandenberg, pres. **A**1a 2 3 5 9 10 **F**1 3 5 6 10 12 13 14 15 16 17 20 23 24 26 27 28 30 32 33 35 36 40 41 42 43 44 45 50 53 54; **S**5585	21	10	S		246	9864	157	60.9	12	152	40147	16735	830
⊞ ST. LUKE'S REGIONAL MEDICAL CENTER, 190 E. Bannock St., Zip 83712; tel. 208/386-2222; Elbert E. Gilbertson, pres.; Edwin E. Dahlberg, exec. vice-pres. **A**1a 2 3 5 9 10 **F**1 2 3 4 6 7 8 9 10 11 12 14 15 16 17 21 23 24 26 34 35 36 37 40 41 43 44 45 46 47 50 51 52 53 54	23	10	S		252	13885	173	68.7	41	2931	53776	23312	1205
⊞ VETERANS ADMINISTRATION MEDICAL CENTER, 500 W. Fort St., Zip 83702; tel. 208/336-5100; James A. Goff, dir. (Total facility includes 60 beds in nursing home-type unit) **A**1a 3 5 8 **F**1 3 6 10 12 14 15 16 19 20 21 23 24 26 27 28 29 30 31 32 33 34 35 42 44 46 47 48 49 50 53	45	10	S	TF	222	3965	158	71.2	0	0	28084	14461	595
				H	162	3747	107	—	0	0	25765	12623	523
BONNERS FERRY—Boundary County													
★ COMMUNITY HOSPITAL (Includes Boundary County Nursing Home), 551 Kaniksu St., Box 1449, Zip 83805; tel. 208/267-3141; E. Louis Keller, adm. (Total facility includes 26 beds in nursing home-type unit) **A**9 10 **F**1 2 3 12 14 15 16 19 23 24 26 29 34 35 36 40 42 44 45 46 47 49 50 52	13	10	S	TF	52	404	35	67.3	4	40	1841	998	77
				H	26	337	10	—	4	40	1550	770	44
BURLEY—Cassia County													
⊞ CASSIA MEMORIAL HOSPITAL AND MEDICAL CENTER, 2303 Park Ave., Box 489, Zip 83318; tel. 208/678-4444; Richard Packer, adm. (Total facility includes 34 beds in nursing home-type unit) **A**1a 2 9 10 **F**1 3 6 10 12 14 15 16 19 23 24 26 34 35 37 40 41 42 44 45 46 50; **S**1815	23	10	S	TF	87	2338	56	64.4	10	543	6647	3227	232
				H	53	2268	26	—	10	543	5830	2986	215
CALDWELL—Canyon County													
⊞ WEST VALLEY MEDICAL CENTER (Formerly Caldwell Memorial Hospital), 1717 Arlington, Zip 83605; tel. 208/459-4641; Robert G. Conrad, adm. **A**1a 9 10 **F**1 3 6 10 12 14 15 16 21 23 24 27 28 29 30 32 33 34 35 36 40 41 42 43 45 46 49 52 53; **S**1755	33	10	S		133	4249	63	47.4	12	466	—	—	342
CASCADE—Valley County													
VALLEY COUNTY HOSPITAL, Zip 83611; tel. 208/382-4242; Gerald L. Hart, adm. (Nonreporting) **A**9 10; **S**5585	13	10	S		10	—	—	—	—	—	—	—	—
COEUR D'ALENE—Kootenai County													
⊞ KOOTENAI MEDICAL CENTER, 2003 Lincoln Way, Zip 83814; tel. 208/667-6441; Joseph E. Morris, adm. **A**1a 9 10 **F**1 3 5 6 10 12 14 15 16 23 24 25 26 30 33 34 35 36 40 43 44 45 46 47 51 52 53	16	10	S		168	7289	88	52.4	18	965	22771	9680	409
COTTONWOOD—Idaho County													
ST. MARY'S HOSPITAL, Lewiston & North Sts., P O Box 137, Zip 83522; tel. 208/962-3251; John R. Hull, adm. (Total facility includes 6 beds in nursing home-type unit) **A**9 10 **F**1 16 19 23 35 36 45; **S**0505	21	10	S	TF	28	492	9	32.1	6	47	1328	546	46
				H	22	455	5	—	6	47	—	—	44
COUNCIL—Adams County													
COMMUNITY HOSPITAL, 205 N. Berkley St., Zip 83612; tel. 208/253-4242; Marv Schultz, adm. (Data for 316 days) **A**9 10 **F**3 14 15 16 23 34 35 36 43 45 46	16	10	S		20	265	3	15.0	4	17	596	—	29
DOWNEY—Bannock County													
MARSH VALLEY HOSPITAL, Zip 83234; tel. 208/897-5281; Wiley C. Watkins, adm. **A**9 10 **F**1 5 15 16 23 34 35 36 45 46 50	16	10	S		17	185	1	5.9	4	17	—	—	17
DRIGGS—Teton County													
TETON VALLEY HOSPITAL, Box 460, Zip 83422; tel. 208/354-2383; Susan Kunz, adm. (Data for 273 days) **A**9 10 **F**1 3 6 12 14 34 35 36 40 43	13	10	S		13	200	4	30.8	3	20	375	220	19
EMMETT—Gem County													
□ WALTER KNOX MEMORIAL HOSPITAL, 1202 E. Locust St., Zip 83617; tel. 208/365-3561; Newton H. States, adm. **A**1a 9 10 **F**1 6 12 14 15 23 27 30 35 36 40 41 44 45 46 52	13	10	S		31	835	7	19.4	8	92	1610	932	60
GOODING—Gooding County													
⊞ GOODING COUNTY MEMORIAL HOSPITAL, 1120 Montana St., Zip 83330; tel. 208/934-4433; Duane E. Cutright, adm. **A**1a 9 10 **F**1 12 15 16 23 24 25 34 35 41 44 45	13	10	S		49	645	16	32.7	6	5	—	—	45
GRANGEVILLE—Idaho County													
SYRINGA GENERAL HOSPITAL, W. Main & B Sts., Zip 83530; tel. 208/983-1700; Donald L. Harris, adm. (Nonreporting) **A**9 10	16	10	S		27	—	—	—	—	—	—	—	—

Hospital, Address, Telephone, Administrator, Approval and Facility Codes, Multihospital System Code	Classification Codes				Inpatient Data				Newborn Data		Expense (thousands of dollars)		
★ American Hospital Association (AHA) membership □ Joint Commission on Accreditation of Hospitals (JCAH) accreditation + American Osteopathic Hospital Association (AOHA) membership ○ American Osteopathic Association (AOA) accreditation Δ Commission on Accreditation of Rehabilitation Facilities (CARF) accreditation Control codes 61, 63, 64, 71, 72 and 73 indicate hospitals listed by AOHA, but not registered by AHA. For definition of numerical codes, see page A2	Control	Service	Stay	Facilities	Beds	Admissions	Census	Occupancy (percent)	Bassinets	Births	Total	Payroll	Personnel
HAILEY—Blaine County													
BLAINE COUNTY MEDICAL CENTER, Box 927, Zip 83333; tel. 208/788-2222; David D. Farnes, pres. (Nonreporting) **A**9 10; **S**5585	13	10	S		40	—	—	—	—	—	—	—	—
IDAHO FALLS—Bonneville County													
★□ EASTERN IDAHO REGIONAL MEDICAL CENTER, 3100 Channing Way, P O Box 2077, Zip 83403; tel. 208/529-6111; Max Lauderdale, adm. (Data for 303 days) (Total facility includes 92 beds in nursing home-type unit) **A**1a 9 10 **F**1 3 5 6 10 12 14 15 16 19 20 23 24 26 27 28 30 32 33 34 35 36 37 40 42 43 44 45 46 49 50 51 52 53 54; **S**1755	23	10	S	TF	334	11276	251	73.2	33	1526	29892	13855	785
				H	242	11140	166	—	33	1526	28833	13146	746
JEROME—Jerome County													
★□ ST. BENEDICT'S FAMILY MEDICAL CENTER (Formerly St. Benedict's Hospital), 709 N. Lincoln Ave., Box 586, Zip 83338; tel. 208/324-4301; Robert D. Campbell, chief exec. off. (Total facility includes 40 beds in nursing home-type unit) **A**1a 9 10 **F**1 3 6 10 15 16 19 20 23 24 34 35 36 40 41 44 45; **S**0505	21	10	S	TF	80	1469	50	62.5	4	240	5583	2624	174
				H	40	1396	12	—	4	240	5159	2294	149
KELLOGG—Shoshone County													
★□ SHOSHONE MEDICAL CENTER, Jacobs Gulch, Zip 83837; tel. 208/784-1221; Langford W. Palmer, adm. (Total facility includes 10 beds in nursing home-type unit) **A**1a 9 10 **F**1 3 6 12 14 16 19 23 24 28 34 35 36 40 44 46 52	16	10	S	TF	42	785	11	26.2	4	43	2252	1083	57
				H	32	767	10	—	4	43	—	—	56
LEWISTON—Nez Perce County													
★□ ST. JOSEPH REGIONAL MEDICAL CENTER (Formerly St. Joseph's Hospital), 415 Sixth St., Box 816, Zip 83501; tel. 208/743-2511; Howard A. Hayes, adm. **A**1a 2 9 10 **F**1 3 5 6 10 12 14 15 16 21 23 26 30 34 35 36 40 41 44 45 46 47 49 50 52 53; **S**5945	21	10	S		139	6805	86	61.9	15	849	22014	9297	434
MALAD CITY—Oneida County													
ONEIDA HOSPITAL, 150 North 200 West, Box 126, Zip 83252; tel. 208/766-2231; Jim L. Russell, adm. (Total facility includes 24 beds in nursing home-type unit) **A**9 10 **F**1 16 19 23 34 35 43 45 46 50	13	10	S	TF	35	302	23	65.7	3	16	—	—	48
				H	11	234	2	—	3	16	—	—	31
MCCALL—Valley County													
MCCALL MEMORIAL HOSPITAL, Forest & State Sts., Box 906, Zip 83638; tel. 208/634-2221; Karen Kellie, adm. **A**9 10 **F**1 3 6 14 15 16 21 23 34 35 40 41 45 52; **S**5585	16	10	S		21	513	4	19.0	3	90	1220	609	40
MONTPELIER—Bear Lake County													
★ BEAR LAKE MEMORIAL HOSPITAL, 164 S. Fifth St., Zip 83254; tel. 208/847-1630; Rod Jacobson, adm. (Total facility includes 37 beds in nursing home-type unit) **A**9 10 **F**1 3 15 16 19 23 35 41	13	10	S	TF	64	776	36	56.3	5	89	1873	998	81
				H	27	700	6	—	5	89	1234	590	52
MOSCOW—Latah County													
★□ GRITMAN MEMORIAL HOSPITAL, 715 S. Washington St., Zip 83843; tel. 208/882-4511; Robert A. Colvin, adm. **A**1a 9 10 **F**1 3 6 10 12 15 16 23 30 35 36 40 41 45 46 53; **S**1755	23	10	S		48	1976	19	38.8	8	358	5071	2621	134
MOUNTAIN HOME—Elmore County													
★ ELMORE MEDICAL CENTER (Formerly Elmore Memorial Hospital), 895 N. Sixth East St., Drawer H, Zip 83647; tel. 208/587-8401; Jan G. Cox, adm. (Total facility includes 55 beds in nursing home-type unit) **A**9 10 **F**1 2 6 12 14 15 16 19 23 35 40 45 46; **S**5585	13	10	S	TF	83	1229	64	77.1	6	218	3484	1466	95
				H	28	1199	12	—	6	218	—	—	74
MOUNTAIN HOME AIR FORCE BASE—Elmore County													
U. S. AIR FORCE HOSPITAL MOUNTAIN HOME, Zip 83648; tel. 208/828-2505; Maj. John D. Hilburn, adm. (Nonreporting)	41	10	S		28	—	—	—	—	—	—	—	—
NAMPA—Canyon County													
IDAHO STATE SCHOOL AND HOSPITAL, 3100 11th Ave. N., Zip 83651; tel. 208/466-9255; Dan Fazzini PhD, adm. dir. (Nonreporting) **A**9 10	12	12	S		34	—	—	—	—	—	—	—	—
★□ MERCY MEDICAL CENTER, 1512 12th Avenue Rd., Zip 83651; tel. 208/467-1171; C. Kregg Hanson, pres. & chief exec. off. **A**1a 2 9 10 **F**1 3 6 10 11 12 14 15 16 21 23 24 25 26 34 35 36 40 41 43 44 45 46 48 49 52 53; **S**5175	21	10	S		85	6118	85	53.1	8	1091	18172	9184	455
OROFINO—Clearwater County													
★ CLEARWATER VALLEY HOSPITAL, 301 Cedar, Zip 83544; tel. 208/476-4555; M. Merle Loseth, adm. **A**9 10 **F**1 3 16 21 23 35 40 41 45 46	13	10	S		26	641	7	26.9	8	54	1929	1037	60
STATE HOSPITAL NORTH, Box 672, Zip 83544; tel. 208/476-4511; Marvin Lambrecht, adm. dir. **F**24 29 30 32 33 42	12	22	S		32	299	25	78.1	0	0	1091	554	40
POCATELLO—Bannock County													
★□ BANNOCK REGIONAL MEDICAL CENTER, Memorial Dr., Zip 83201; tel. 208/232-6150; Alan Stevenson, adm. **A**1a 2 9 10 **F**1 2 3 6 7 8 9 10 11 12 14 15 16 21 23 35 36 37 40 45 46 47 51 52 53	13	10	S		147	5551	69	46.9	22	1493	19360	8456	454
★□ POCATELLO REGIONAL MEDICAL CENTER, 777 Hospital Way, Zip 83201; tel. 208/234-0777; Richard M. Cagen, adm. **A**1a 2 9 10 **F**1 2 3 5 6 10 12 14 15 16 20 23 24 25 26 34 35 43 44 45 46 47 53; **S**1815	23	10	S		110	3557	62	56.4	0	0	16678	6680	329
PRESTON—Franklin County													
FRANKLIN COUNTY MEDICAL CENTER, 44 N. First East St., Zip 83263; tel. 208/852-0137; Michael G. Andrus, adm. (Total facility includes 45 beds in nursing home-type unit) **A**9 10 **F**1 15 16 19 23 34 35 45 47	13	10	S	TF	65	465	42	64.6	8	90	1967	800	66
				H	20	419	3	—	8	90	—	509	27
REXBURG—Madison County													
★ MADISON MEMORIAL HOSPITAL, 400 E. Main, Box 526, Zip 83440; tel. 208/356-3691; Keith M. Steiner, chief exec. off. (Nonreporting) **A**9 10	13	10	S		54	—	—	—	—	—	—	—	—
RUPERT—Minidoka County													
★ MINIDOKA MEMORIAL HOSPITAL, 1224 Eighth St., Zip 83350; tel. 208/436-0481; Ed Richardson, adm. (Total facility includes 78 beds in nursing home-type unit) **A**9 10 **F**1 3 6 10 12 14 15 16 19 23 26 34 35 37 40 44 45 50	13	10	S	TF	105	1005	81	76.4	8	99	4572	2152	145
				H	27	935	11	—	8	99	3207	1333	106
SALMON—Lemhi County													
★ STEELE MEMORIAL HOSPITAL, Main & Daisy Sts., Box 700, Zip 83467; tel. 208/756-4291; Kay H. Springer, adm. **A**9 10 **F**1 3 6 16 23 34 35 36 40 46	13	10	S		35	911	10	28.6	6	103	1777	897	53
SANDPOINT—Bonner County													
★□ BONNER GENERAL HOSPITAL, 520 N. Third Ave., Box 1448, Zip 83864; tel. 208/263-1441; Gene Tomt, adm. **A**1a 9 10 **F**1 3 6 14 15 16 21 23 24 26 28 29 30 32 34 35 36 40 44 45 46 47	23	10	S		53	2399	24	45.3	5	434	6247	2916	146
SILVERTON—Shoshone County													
★ EAST SHOSHONE HOSPITAL, Box 87, Zip 83867; tel. 208/752-1248; John VanDyke, adm. **A**9 10 **F**1 3 6 14 15 16 23 24 35 36 40 41 44 52	16	10	S		40	852	9	22.5	6	60	2469	1239	74
SODA SPRINGS—Caribou County													
★ CARIBOU MEMORIAL HOSPITAL AND NURSING HOME, 300 S. Third West St., Zip 83276; tel. 208/547-3341; Dell L. Maughan, adm. (Total facility includes 37 beds in nursing home-type unit) **A**9 10 **F**1 3 16 19 23 42 45	13	10	S	TF	66	461	39	59.1	6	97	1951	1008	65
				H	29	413	4	—	6	97	1275	588	44
ST. MARIES—Benewah County													
BENEWAH COMMUNITY HOSPITAL, 229 S. Seventh St., Zip 83861; tel. 208/245-5551; B. D. Jackson, adm. **A**9 10 **F**1 3 5 14 16 23 34 35 36 37 45	13	10	S		33	1050	11	33.3	5	90	1851	959	63

Hospital, Address, Telephone, Administrator, Approval and Facility Codes, Multihospital System Code	Classification Codes				Inpatient Data				Newborn Data		Expense (thousands of dollars)		
★ American Hospital Association (AHA) membership □ Joint Commission on Accreditation of Hospitals (JCAH) accreditation + American Osteopathic Hospital Association (AOHA) membership ○ American Osteopathic Association (AOA) accreditation Δ Commission on Accreditation of Rehabilitation Facilities (CARF) accreditation Control codes 61, 63, 64, 71, 72 and 73 indicate hospitals listed by AOHA, but not registered by AHA. For definition of numerical codes, see page A2	Control	Service	Stay	Facilities	Beds	Admissions	Census	Occupancy (percent)	Bassinets	Births	Total	Payroll	Personnel
SUN VALLEY—Blaine County													
★ MORITZ COMMUNITY HOSPITAL, Box 86, Zip 83353; tel. 208/622-3323; Raymond T. Hino, adm. **A**9 10 **F**1 3 6 16 23 35 36 45 52	14	10	S		27	1187	10	37.0	4	130	—	—	68
TWIN FALLS—Twin Falls County													
★□ MAGIC VALLEY REGIONAL MEDICAL CENTER, 650 Addison Ave. W., Zip 83301; Mailing Address Box 409, Zip 83303; tel. 208/737-2000; John Bingham, adm. **A**1a 2 9 10 **F**1 3 5 6 10 12 14 15 16 21 23 24 35 36 40 41 44 45 46 47 51 52 53; **S**1755	13	10	S		152	6121	78	51.3	22	1161	22118	7134	409
TWIN FALLS CLINIC HOSPITAL, 666 Shoshone St. E., Box 1233, Zip 83301; tel. 208/733-3700; Marley D. Jackman, adm. (Nonreporting) **A**9 10	33	10	S		40	—	—	—	—	—	—	—	—
WEISER—Washington County													
★ MEMORIAL HOSPITAL, 645 E. Fifth St., Box 550, Zip 83672; tel. 208/549-0370; Byron Quinton, exec. dir. (Nonreporting) **A**9 10; **S**0585	15	10	S		27	—	—	—	—	—	—	—	—

Hospital, Address, Telephone, Administrator, Approval and Facility Codes, Multihospital System Code	Classification Codes				Inpatient Data				Newborn Data		Expense (thousands of dollars)		
★ American Hospital Association (AHA) membership ☐ Joint Commission on Accreditation of Hospitals (JCAH) accreditation + American Osteopathic Hospital Association (AOHA) membership ○ American Osteopathic Association (AOA) accreditation Δ Commission on Accreditation of Rehabilitation Facilities (CARF) accreditation Control codes 61, 63, 64, 71, 72 and 73 indicate hospitals listed by AOHA, but not registered by AHA. For definition of numerical codes, see page A2	Control	Service	Stay	Facilities	Beds	Admissions	Census	Occupancy (percent)	Bassinets	Births	Total	Payroll	Personnel

Illinois

Hospital	Control	Service	Stay	Facilities	Beds	Admissions	Census	Occupancy (percent)	Bassinets	Births	Total	Payroll	Personnel
ALEDO—Mercer County													
★ MERCER COUNTY HOSPITAL, 409 N.W. Ninth Ave., Zip 61231; tel. 309/582-5301; Phillip C. Forslund, adm. **A**9 10 **F**1 3 6 14 15 16 23 34 35 36 40 41 45	13	10	S		53	1904	22	41.5	5	121	5022	2140	106
ALTON—Madison County													
☐ ALTON MEMORIAL HOSPITAL, One Memorial Dr., Zip 62002; tel. 618/463-7311; Ronald B. McMullen, pres. (Nonreporting) **A**1a 9 10	21	10	S		165	—	—	—	—	—	—	—	—
☐ ALTON MENTAL HEALTH CENTER, 4500 College Ave., Zip 62002; tel. 618/465-5593; Thomas M. Richards, dir. **A**1b 10 **F**30 32 33 42 44 46 47	12	22	L		298	876	258	86.6	0	0	11483	7941	365
★☐ SAINT ANTHONY'S HOSPITAL, Saint Anthony's Way, Zip 62002; tel. 618/465-2571; Sr. M. Theotima, pres. (Total facility includes 30 beds in nursing home-type unit) **A**1a 9 10 **F**1 3 6 10 12 14 15 16 19 21 23 24 27 30 32 33 34 35 41 42 44 45 46 52 53	21	10	S	TF	206	4168	108	52.4	0	0	17885	8048	469
				H	176	3875	83	—	0	0	16588	7594	440
★☐ ST. JOSEPH'S HOSPITAL, 915 E. Fifth St., Zip 62002; tel. 618/463-5151; Sr. Barbara Jean Donovan, pres. **A**1a 9 10 **F**1 3 6 7 8 9 10 11 12 14 15 16 23 34 35 36 40 41 44 45 46 48 49 52 53; **S**5365	21	10	S		165	5140	82	41.4	20	755	18253	7853	376
ANNA—Union County													
☐ ANNA MENTAL HEALTH AND DEVELOPMENTAL CENTER (Psychiatric and Mental Retardation), 1000 N. Main St., Zip 62906; tel. 618/833-5161; Ronald G. Bittle PhD, actg. supt. **A**1b 10 **F**23 24 29 32 33 42 44 46	12	22	L		495	876	438	88.5	0	0	18305	13473	684
★☐ UNION COUNTY HOSPITAL, 517 N. Main St., Zip 62906; tel. 618/833-5155; E. A. Helfrich, adm. (Total facility includes 60 beds in nursing home-type unit) **A**1a 9 10 **F**1 3 6 10 16 19 23 35 44 45 53	16	10	S	TF	100	1494	77	77.0	0	0	5147	2590	196
				H	40	1439	19	—	0	0	4222	2009	151
ARLINGTON HEIGHTS—Cook County													
★☐ NORTHWEST COMMUNITY HOSPITAL, 800 W. Central Rd., Zip 60005; tel. 312/259-1000; Malcolm D. McCoun, pres. **A**1a 2 9 10 **F**1 2 3 5 6 7 8 9 10 11 12 14 15 16 20 23 24 27 30 33 34 35 36 40 41 44 45 46 47 52 53	23	10	S		420	22729	364	86.7	36	2549	74737	34780	1422
AURORA—Kane County													
★☐ COPLEY MEMORIAL HOSPITAL, Lincoln & Weston Aves., Zip 60505; tel. 312/844-1000; Gregory W. Lintjer, pres. **A**1a 2 9 10 **F**1 3 5 6 7 8 9 10 11 12 14 15 16 20 23 24 26 34 35 36 37 40 44 45 46 47 49 52 53 54	23	10	S		212	8485	124	58.2	40	1573	30249	14472	700
★☐ MERCY CENTER FOR HEALTH CARE SERVICES, 1325 N. Highland Ave., Zip 60506; tel. 312/859-2222; Sr. Rita Meagher, pres. (Nonreporting) **A**1a 2 9 10; **S**5215	21	10	S		334	—	—	—	—	—	—	—	—
AVON—Warren County													
SAUNDERS HOSPITAL, Box 250, Zip 61415; tel. 309/465-3171; Margaret Repp, adm. (Nonreporting) **A**9 10	23	10	S		20	—	—	—	—	—	—	—	—
BARRINGTON—Lake County													
★☐ GOOD SHEPHERD HOSPITAL, 450 W. Hwy. 22, Zip 60010; tel. 312/381-9600; Russell Feurer, vice-pres. **A**1a 9 10 **F**1 3 6 10 12 14 15 16 23 24 30 34 35 36 40 41 44 45 46 52 53; **S**1225	21	10	S		166	7213	102	61.4	20	1353	30931	12191	469
BELLEVILLE—St. Clair County													
★☐ MEMORIAL HOSPITAL, 4501 N. Park Dr., Zip 62223; tel. 618/233-7750; Harry R. Maier, pres. (Total facility includes 108 beds in nursing home-type unit) **A**1a 3 5 9 10 **F**1 3 5 6 7 8 9 10 11 12 14 16 19 21 23 24 27 30 34 35 36 40 41 42 44 45 46 47 52 53 54	23	10	S	TF	499	14348	370	74.1	32	1800	53831	27152	1392
				H	391	14086	265	—	32	1800	51168	25554	1321
★☐ ST. ELIZABETH'S HOSPITAL, 211 S. Third St., Zip 62222; tel. 618/234-2120; Gerald M. Harman, exec. vice-pres. **A**1a 2 3 5 9 10 **F**1 3 6 7 8 9 10 11 12 14 15 16 20 23 24 25 26 27 30 35 36 40 42 44 45 46 48 52 53 54; **S**5355	21	10	S		447	14235	310	72.1	30	1047	49508	24358	1319
BELVIDERE—Boone County													
★☐ HIGHLAND HOSPITAL, 1625 S. State St., Zip 61008; tel. 815/547-5441; Frank Baker, adm. **A**1a 9 10 **F**1 3 6 14 15 16 23 35 45 46 48 49 52 53	23	10	S		69	1462	17	30.4	0	56	3727	1874	123
☐ ST. JOSEPH'S HOSPITAL, 1005 Julien St., Zip 61008; tel. 815/544-3411; W. Daniel Cobbs, adm. (Nonreporting) **A**1a 9 10; **S**1375	33	10	S		60	—	—	—	—	—	—	—	—
BENTON—Franklin County													
★☐ FRANKLIN HOSPITAL AND SKILLED NURSING CARE UNIT, 201 Bailey Lane, Zip 62812; tel. 618/439-3161; Margaret V. Walton RN, adm. (Total facility includes 78 beds in nursing home-type unit) **A**1a 9 10 **F**1 3 6 7 10 12 14 15 16 19 23 29 35 36 40 41 44 45 50	16	10	S	TF	191	2283	96	50.3	9	102	7648	3974	269
				H	113	1947	30	—	9	102	6361	3374	219
BERWYN—Cook County													
★☐ MACNEAL HOSPITAL, 3249 S. Oak Park Ave., Zip 60402; tel. 312/795-9100; Luke McGuinness, pres. **A**1a 2 3 5 8 9 10 **F**1 2 3 6 10 11 12 14 15 16 20 23 24 26 27 29 30 32 33 34 35 36 37 38 40 41 44 45 46 47 48 49 52 53	23	10	S		427	12007	221	51.8	30	1486	69386	—	986
BLOOMINGTON—McLean County													
☐ MENNONITE HOSPITAL, 807 N. Main St., Zip 61702; tel. 309/827-4321; David A. Schertz, chief oper. off. (Total facility includes 95 beds in nursing home-type unit) **A**1a 9 10 **F**1 3 5 6 9 10 12 13 14 15 16 19 21 23 24 26 34 35 41 43 44 45 46 47 50 53; **S**9305	21	10	S	TF	221	3970	155	70.1	0	0	23418	9983	602
				H	126	3820	70	—	0	0	—	—	541
★☐ ST. JOSEPH'S HOSPITAL MEDICAL CENTER, 2200 E. Washington St., Box 1287, Zip 61701; tel. 309/662-3311; Kenneth J. Natzke, adm. **A**1a 9 10 **F**1 3 5 6 7 8 9 10 11 12 14 15 16 23 24 26 34 35 36 40 41 44 45 46 52 53 54; **S**5335	21	10	S		149	4903	72	51.4	18	630	16302	7604	416
BLUE ISLAND—Cook County													
★☐ ST. FRANCIS HOSPITAL, 12935 S. Gregory St., Zip 60406; tel. 312/597-2000; Bryant R. Hanson, exec. dir. **A**1a 2 9 10 **F**1 3 4 6 10 12 14 15 16 23 26 35 36 40 41 45 46 47 51 52 53 54; **S**5455	21	10	S		401	17270	294	73.3	24	1237	64389	30216	942
BREESE—Clinton County													
★☐ ST. JOSEPH'S HOSPITAL, Jamestown Rd., Zip 62230; tel. 618/526-4511; Sr. Mary Anthony Menting, exec. vice-pres. **A**1a 9 10 **F**1 3 6 12 14 15 16 21 23 35 40 45 46 52; **S**5355	21	10	S		93	2888	50	53.8	6	374	7639	3882	206
CANTON—Fulton County													
★☐ GRAHAM HOSPITAL, 210 W. Walnut St., Zip 61520; tel. 309/647-5240; Kenneth C. Etcheson, pres. **A**1a 6 9 10 **F**1 3 5 6 10 12 14 15 16 23 30 34 35 36 40 41 44 45 46 47 53	23	10	S		124	5050	78	55.3	12	325	17356	7603	386
CARBONDALE—Jackson County													
★☐ MEMORIAL HOSPITAL, 404 W. Main St., Box 481, Zip 62901; tel. 618/549-0721; George Maroney, adm. **A**1a 2 3 5 9 10 **F**1 3 5 6 10 12 14 15 16 20 23 34 35 36 37 40 41 44 45 46 52 53; **S**4175	23	10	S		151	7119	93	61.6	17	1282	21303	9332	512

★ American Hospital Association (AHA) membership
□ Joint Commission on Accreditation of Hospitals (JCAH) accreditation
+ American Osteopathic Hospital Association (AOHA) membership
○ American Osteopathic Association (AOA) accreditation
Δ Commission on Accreditation of Rehabilitation Facilities (CARF) accreditation
Control codes 61, 63, 64, 71, 72 and 73 indicate hospitals listed by AOHA, but not registered by AHA.
For definition of numerical codes, see page A2

Hospital, Address, Telephone, Administrator, Approval and Facility Codes, Multihospital System Code	Classification Codes				Inpatient Data				Newborn Data		Expense (thousands of dollars)		
	Control	Service	Stay	Facilities	Beds	Admissions	Census	Occupancy (percent)	Bassinets	Births	Total	Payroll	Personnel
CARLINVILLE—Macoupin County													
□★ CARLINVILLE AREA HOSPITAL, 1001 E. Morgan St., Zip 62626; tel. 217/854-3141; Robert W. Porteus, chief exec. off. **A**1a 9 10 **F**1 15 23 35 41 45 46	23	10	S		54	1885	24	44.4	0	2	4428	2366	123
CARMI—White County													
□★ CARMI TOWNSHIP HOSPITAL, Plum & Webb Sts., Zip 62821; tel. 618/382-4171; Michael C. O'Brien, adm. **A**1a 9 10 **F**1 3 6 10 12 14 15 16 23 35 44 45 52 53	16	10	S		50	1783	31	62.0	0	0	3601	1976	138
CARROLLTON—Greene County													
★ THOMAS H. BOYD MEMORIAL HOSPITAL (Includes Reisch Memorial Nursing Home), 800 School St., Zip 62016; tel. 217/942-6946; Thomas J. McKula, adm. (Total facility includes 40 beds in nursing home-type unit) **A**9 10 **F**1 14 16 19 35 45 52	23	10	S	TF	73	547	47	64.4	0	0	1842	720	79
				H	33	532	8	—	0	0	1253	468	55
CARTHAGE—Hancock County													
□★ MEMORIAL HOSPITAL, S. Adams St., Zip 62321; tel. 217/357-3131; Steven T. Moburg, adm. **A**1a 9 10 **F**1 3 6 10 12 14 15 16 23 34 35 40 45 46	23	10	S		67	1675	23	34.3	8	119	4483	2103	144
CENTRALIA—Marion and Clinton Counties													
□★ ST. MARY'S HOSPITAL, 400 N. Pleasant Ave., Zip 62801; tel. 618/532-6731; Sr. Mary Clarette Stryzewski, pres. & chief exec. off. **A**1a 2 9 **F**1 3 6 7 8 9 10 11 12 13 14 15 16 24 27 29 30 32 33 35 40 42 43 44 45 46 47 48 49 52 53; **S**1345	21	10	S		256	9131	162	63.8	18	811	22782	10622	685
CENTREVILLE—St. Clair County													
□★ CENTREVILLE TOWNSHIP HOSPITAL, 5900 Bond Ave., Zip 62207; tel. 618/332-3060; Carl G. Jaeger, adm. **A**1a 9 10 **F**1 3 6 10 11 12 14 15 16 23 34 35 40 45 46 47 52	16	10	S		189	4647	59	31.2	20	1185	8632	4064	253
CHAMPAIGN—Champaign County													
□★ BURNHAM HOSPITAL, 407 S. Fourth St., Zip 61820; tel. 217/337-2500; Peter E. Goschy, chief exec. off. **A**1a 2 9 10 **F**1 3 4 5 6 10 12 14 15 16 20 23 24 26 30 32 33 34 35 36 37 40 41 43 44 45 46 47 50 52 53 54	14	10	S		190	6051	90	47.4	10	526	27173	12245	685
□ COLE HOSPITAL, 809 W. Church St., P O Box 598, Zip 61820; tel. 217/351-7200; Gary Callahan, adm. (Nonreporting) **A**1a 9 10; **S**9555	23	10	S		65	—	—	—	—	—	—	—	—
CHANUTE AIR FORCE BASE—Champaign County													
□ U. S. AIR FORCE HOSPITAL CHANUTE, Zip 61868; tel. 217/495-3510; Lt. Col. Herbert A. Turk Jr., adm. **A**1a **F**1 6 12 14 15 16 23 28 30 32 33 34 35 36 37 40 45 46 49 53	41	10	S		35	2068	24	69.4	5	365	14500	10955	351
CHESTER—Randolph County													
□ CHESTER MENTAL HEALTH CENTER, Box 31, Zip 62233; tel. 618/826-4571; Stephen L. Hardy PhD, supt. (Nonreporting) **A**1b	12	22	L		250	—	—	—	—	—	—	—	—
□★ MEMORIAL HOSPITAL, 1900 State St., Box 609, Zip 62233; tel. 618/826-4581; William W. Vonderlage, adm. **A**1a 9 10 **F**1 6 10 12 14 16 21 23 40 44 45 46 52 53	16	10	S		76	2153	36	47.4	10	144	5349	2647	176
CHICAGO—Cook County													
ALBERT MERRITT BILLINGS HOSPITAL, See University of Chicago Hospitals													
□★ AUGUSTANA HOSPITAL AND HEALTH CARE CENTER, 2035 N. Lincoln Ave., Zip 60614; tel. 312/975-5000; David Jensen, pres. **A**1a 6 9 10 **F**1 3 6 8 9 10 11 12 14 15 16 23 24 26 34 35 36 37 40 41 42 44 45 46 47 49 53; **S**6295	21	10	S		330	4599	112	33.9	20	410	29941	12791	592
□ BELMONT COMMUNITY HOSPITAL, 4058 W. Melrose St., Zip 60641; tel. 312/736-7000; John W. McCracken, exec. dir. (Nonreporting) **A**1a 9 10; **S**9555	33	10	S		134	—	—	—	—	—	—	—	—
□★ BETHANY HOSPITAL, 3435 W. Van Buren, Zip 60624; tel. 312/265-7700; A. Kenneth Peterson, chief exec. off. **A**1a 10 **F**1 3 6 10 12 14 15 16 20 23 24 27 32 33 34 35 36 40 45 46 52; **S**1225	21	10	S		194	8268	138	71.1	22	736	32538	13143	557
BETHANY METHODIST HOSPITAL, See Methodist Hospital of Chicago													
□ BETHESDA HOSPITAL, 2451 W. Howard St., Zip 60645; tel. 312/761-6000; Richard A. Snow, mng. dir. **A**1a 9 10 **F**1 3 6 9 10 12 15 16 20 23 33 35 37 46; **S**9555	33	10	S		129	1586	34	26.4	0	0	—	—	184
BOBS ROBERTS MEMORIAL HOSPITAL FOR CHILDREN, See University of Chicago Hospitals													
□★ CENTRAL COMMUNITY HOSPITAL, 5701 S. Wood St., Zip 60636; tel. 312/737-4600; Patrick S. Demoon, adm. **A**1a 2 9 10 **F**1 3 6 10 12 15 16 23 26 30 32 33 35 45 46 47 48 49 50	23	10	S		114	2306	59	51.8	0	0	13790	5624	341
CHARLES GILMAN SMITH HOSPITAL, See University of Chicago Hospitals and Clinics													
★ CHARTER BARCLAY HOSPITAL, 4700 N. Clarendon Ave., Zip 60640; tel. 312/728-7100; Edward M. Goldberg, adm. **A** 9 10 **F**15 24 28 30 32 33 42 47 49; **S**0695	33	22	L		118	1301	111	94.1	0	0	—	—	208
□★ CHICAGO LAKESHORE HOSPITAL, 4840 N. Marine Dr., Zip 60640; tel. 312/878-9700; Jerome R. Kearney, adm. **A**1b 9 10 **F**15 24 32 33 42 48 49; **S**1755	33	22	L		104	743	76	73.1	0	0	8008	3768	157
CHICAGO LYING-IN HOSPITAL, See University of Chicago Hospitals													
○ + CHICAGO OSTEOPATHIC MEDICAL CENTERS, 5200 S. Ellis Ave., Zip 60615; tel. 312/947-3000; L. U. Haspel DO, exec. vice-pres. **A**9 10 11 12 13 **F**1 2 6 8 9 10 11 12 14 15 16 20 23 24 26 27 28 29 30 32 33 34 35 36 37 40 41 42 43 44 45 46 47 48 49 50 51 52 53	23	10	S		276	8544	152	55.1	22	992	46912	19949	808
CHICAGO WESLEY MEMORIAL HOSPITAL, See Northwestern Memorial Hospital													
□ CHICAGO-READ MENTAL HEALTH CENTER, 4200 N. Oak Park Ave., Zip 60634; tel. 312/794-4000; Kris B. Lall MD, dir. **A**1b 10 **F**15 24 27 30 33 45 46 47	12	22	S		605	6677	432	71.0	0	0	27208	18620	886
□★ CHILDREN'S MEMORIAL HOSPITAL, 2300 Childrens Plaza, Zip 60614; tel. 312/880-4000; Earl J. Frederick, pres. **A**1a 2 3 5 8 9 10 **F**1 3 4 5 6 10 12 13 14 15 16 20 23 24 26 27 28 30 32 33 34 35 38 42 43 44 45 46 47 51 53 54	23	50	S		254	13131	214	84.3	0	0	92728	39870	1913
CLARISSA C. PECK PAVILION OF THE CHICAGO HOME FOR INCURABLES, See University of Chicago Hospitals													
□★ COLUMBUS HOSPITAL, 2520 N. Lakeview Ave., Zip 60614; tel. 312/883-7300; William R. Blanchard, chief oper. off. **A**1a 2 3 5 9 10 **F**1 3 4 6 7 8 9 10 11 12 14 15 16 21 23 24 26 28 30 32 33 34 35 36 38 40 41 42 43 44 45 46 47 50 51 52 53 54; **S**8805	21	10	S		330	13119	260	72.8	28	1896	62925	28765	1712
□★ COOK COUNTY HOSPITAL, 1835 W. Harrison St., Zip 60612; tel. 312/633-6000; Terrence M. Hansen, dir. **A**1a 2 3 5 8 9 10 **F**1 3 5 6 7 9 10 11 12 14 16 20 22 23 24 28 33 34 35 37 40 44 45 46 47 49 51 52 53 54	13	10	S		1092	38919	742	66.1	129	5260	246759	147022	5619
COUNTRY HOME FOR CONVALESCENT CHILDREN, See University of Chicago Hospitals													
□★ EDGEWATER HOSPITAL, 5700 N. Ashland Ave., Zip 60660; tel. 312/878-6000; Frank J. Reichert, adm. **A**1a 2 3 9 10 **F**1 2 3 4 6 7 8 9 10 11 12 14 15 16 20 23 24 26 33 34 35 36 40 44 45 46 47 52 53 54	23	10	S		431	8413	177	41.1	20	608	45452	—	1065
FORKOSH MEMORIAL HOSPITAL, See Lincoln West Hospital													
FOSTER G. MCGAW HOSPITAL, LOYOLA UNIVERSITY OF CHICAGO, See Maywood													
□★ FRANK CUNEO MEMORIAL HOSPITAL, 750 W. Montrose Ave., Zip 60613; tel. 312/883-8300; Barbara Runyen, chief oper. off. **A**1a 3 9 10 **F**1 3 6 12 14 15 16 23 24 25 26 34 35 42 45 46 47 48 49; **S**8805	21	10	S		100	3196	95	74.2	0	0	16251	7899	274
□★ FRANKLIN BOULEVARD COMMUNITY HOSPITAL, 3240 W. Franklin Blvd., Zip 60624; tel. 312/722-3020; Patrick A. Demoon, chief exec. off. **A**1a 2 9 10 **F**1 3 6 12 14 15 16 23 34 35 41 43 45 46 47 48 49	23	10	S		96	2229	33	34.4	0	0	8579	3536	192

Hospital, Address, Telephone, Administrator, Approval and Facility Codes, Multihospital System Code	Classification Codes				Inpatient Data				Newborn Data		Expense (thousands of dollars)		
★ American Hospital Association (AHA) membership □ Joint Commission on Accreditation of Hospitals (JCAH) accreditation + American Osteopathic Hospital Association (AOHA) membership ○ American Osteopathic Association (AOA) accreditation Δ Commission on Accreditation of Rehabilitation Facilities (CARF) accreditation Control codes 61, 63, 64, 71, 72 and 73 indicate hospitals listed by AOHA, but not registered by AHA. For definition of numerical codes, see page A2	Control	Service	Stay	Facilities	Beds	Admissions	Census	Occupancy (percent)	Bassinets	Births	Total	Payroll	Personnel
FRANKLIN MCLEAN MEMORIAL RESEARCH INSTITUTE, See University of Chicago Hospitals													
GERTRUDE DUNN HICKS MEMORIAL HOSPITAL, See University of Chicago Hospitals													
★□ GRANT HOSPITAL OF CHICAGO, 550 W. Webster Ave., Zip 60614; tel. 312/883-2000; Richard J. Brennan, pres. & chief exec. off. **A**1a b 3 5 9 10 **F**1 2 3 4 6 9 10 11 12 14 15 16 20 23 24 25 26 27 30 32 33 34 35 36 37 38 40 44 45 46 48 49 50 52 53 54	23	10	S		416	12548	296	71.2	32	1074	69007	33473	1342
★□ HARTGROVE HOSPITAL, 520 N. Ridgeway Ave., Zip 60624; tel. 312/722-3113; Katherine B. Wade, adm. **A**1b 9 10 **F**24 30 32 33 42 44; **S**0455	33	22	L		99	675	70	70.7	0	0	—	—	200
★□ Δ HOLY CROSS HOSPITAL, 2701 W. 68th St., Zip 60629; tel. 312/471-8000; Sr. Teresa Mary Clarkson, pres. **A**1a 2 7 9 10 **F**1 2 3 6 7 9 10 11 12 14 15 16 20 23 24 25 26 28 30 32 33 34 35 36 40 41 42 44 45 46 47 49 52 53 54; **S**5685	23	10	S		365	11559	269	73.7	30	318	58167	30984	1390
HOME FOR DESTITUTE CRIPPLED CHILDREN, See University of Chicago Hospitals													
★□ HOSPITAL OF ENGLEWOOD, 6001 S. Green St., Zip 60621; tel. 312/962-5000; Dennis L. King, chief exec. off. (Nonreporting) **A**1a 9 10	23	10	S		121	—	—	—	—	—	—	—	—
★□ HYDE PARK HOSPITAL (Formerly Hyde Park Community Hospital), 5800 S. Stony Island Ave., Zip 60637; tel. 312/643-9200; Jon W. Gepford, pres. (Nonreporting) **A**1a 3 5 9 10; **S**9355	23	10	S		184	—	—	—	—	—	—	—	—
★□ ILLINOIS MASONIC MEDICAL CENTER, 836 W. Wellington Ave., Zip 60657; tel. 312/975-1600; Gerald W. Mungerson, exec. dir. (Total facility includes 330 beds in nursing home-type unit) **A**1a 2 3 5 6 8 9 10 **F**1 3 4 5 6 7 8 9 10 11 12 14 15 16 19 20 21 23 24 26 27 28 30 32 33 34 35 36 37 38 40 41 42 43 44 45 46 50 52 53 54	23	10	S	TF	701	15098	594	84.7	24	2208	102214	44573	2580
				H	371	14472	282	—	24	2208	94502	40948	2282
□ ILLINOIS STATE PSYCHIATRIC INSTITUTE, 1601 W. Taylor St., Zip 60612; tel. 312/996-1000; James T. Barter MD, dir. **A**1b 3 5 10 **F**19 24 28 30 32 33 42 44	12	22	L		197	1394	185	93.9	0	0	15205	—	473
INSTITUTE OF PSYCHIATRY, See Northwestern Memorial Hospital													
★□ JACKSON PARK HOSPITAL, 7531 S. Stony Island Ave., Zip 60649; tel. 312/947-2840; John R. Haugabrook, exec. vice-pres. (Nonreporting) **A**1a 2 3 5 9 10	23	10	S		254	—	—	—	—	—	—	—	—
★□ JOHN F. KENNEDY MEDICAL CENTER (Formerly Northwest Hospital), 5645 W. Addison St., Zip 60634; tel. 312/282-7000; Peter Rusin, adm. & chief exec. off. **A**1a 9 10 **F**1 3 5 6 7 8 12 14 15 16 19 20 23 34 35 36 40 42 43 44 45 46 47 52 53 54	23	10	S		417	10585	275	63.1	25	411	55454	25085	1192
JOHNSTON R. BOWMAN HEALTH CENTER, See Rush-Presbyterian-St. Luke's Medical Center													
★□ LA RABIDA CHILDREN'S HOSPITAL AND RESEARCH CENTER (Pediatric Chronic Disease), E. 65th St. at Lake Michigan, Zip 60649; tel. 312/363-6700; Arthur F. Kohrman MD, dir. **A**1a 3 5 9 10 **F**16 23 24 26 33 34 35 44 46 47 52	23	59	S		77	1522	49	63.6	0	0	11114	5957	272
★□ LAKESIDE COMMUNITY HOSPITAL, 255 W. Cermak Rd., Zip 60616; tel. 312/225-4500; Thomas A. Madeja, adm. (Nonreporting) **A**1a 10	23	10	S		124	—	—	—	—	—	—	—	—
□ LINCOLN WEST HOSPITAL (Formerly Forkosh Memorial Hospital), 2544 W. Montrose Ave., Zip 60618; tel. 312/267-2200; Stephen M. Weinstein, chief exec. off. (Nonreporting) **A**1a 9 10; **S**0905	33	10	S		201	—	—	—	—	—	—	—	—
★□ LORETTO HOSPITAL, 645 S. Central Ave., Zip 60644; tel. 312/626-4300; Sr. Marion, pres. & chief exec. off. **A**1a 9 10 **F**1 3 6 10 11 12 15 16 23 24 27 28 30 32 33 34 35 42 46 47 48 49 52 53; **S**5685	21	10	S		212	5560	146	68.9	0	0	24663	12802	692
★□ LOUIS A. WEISS MEMORIAL HOSPITAL, 4646 N. Marine Dr., Zip 60640; tel. 312/878-8700; James E. Champer, pres. **A**1a 2 3 5 9 10 **F**1 3 5 6 7 8 9 10 11 12 14 15 16 20 23 26 32 33 34 35 36 37 40 43 44 45 46 47 48 49 50 53	23	10	S		275	9175	199	76.0	21	440	51871	27153	1082
★□ MARTHA WASHINGTON HOSPITAL, 4055 N. Western Ave., Zip 60618; tel. 312/583-9000; Jerold A. Nelson, adm. **A**1a 9 10 **F**1 2 3 6 10 12 15 16 23 25 33 35 42 43 45 47 48 49 50	23	10	S		200	4003	106	53.0	0	0	23200	10783	491
★□ MARY THOMPSON HOSPITAL, 140 N. Ashland Ave., Zip 60607; tel. 312/666-7373; Ivette Estrada, adm. **A**1a 2 9 10 **F**1 3 6 14 15 16 17 23 34 35 40 45 46 47 52	23	10	S		203	5361	99	48.8	10	241	19358	7613	372
★□ MERCY HOSPITAL AND MEDICAL CENTER, Stevenson Expwy. at King Dr., Zip 60616; tel. 312/567-2000; Sr. Sheila Lyne, pres. **A**1a 2 3 5 8 9 10 **F**1 2 3 4 6 7 8 9 10 11 12 14 15 16 20 23 24 25 26 27 28 29 30 32 33 34 35 36 37 38 40 41 44 46 48 49 50 52 53 54; **S**5215	21	10	S		502	14288	339	67.0	30	1297	89109	46146	2050
★□ METHODIST HOSPITAL OF CHICAGO (Formerly Bethany Methodist Hospital), 5025 N. Paulina St., Zip 60640; tel. 312/271-9040; Stephen A. Dahl, pres. & chief exec. off. **A**1a 2 9 10 **F**1 3 6 10 12 14 15 16 23 24 26 32 33 34 35 41 44 46 50 53	23	10	S		163	4498	99	55.3	0	0	19897	8580	425
★□ Δ MICHAEL REESE HOSPITAL AND MEDICAL CENTER, Lake Shore Dr. at 31st St., Zip 60616; tel. 312/791-2000; Marvin B. Klein, pres. **A**1a 2 3 5 7 8 9 10 **F**1 2 3 4 5 6 7 8 9 10 11 12 15 16 20 23 24 25 26 27 28 30 32 33 34 35 36 37 38 39 40 42 44 45 46 47 51 52 53 54	23	10	S		689	25368	504	73.9	53	3379	184604	92188	3387
★□ MOUNT SINAI HOSPITAL MEDICAL CENTER OF CHICAGO, California Ave. & 15th St., Zip 60608; tel. 312/542-2000; Ruth M. Rothstein, pres. **A**1a 2 3 5 8 9 10 **F**1 2 3 4 6 7 8 9 10 11 12 14 15 16 20 23 24 27 28 29 30 31 32 33 34 35 36 37 38 40 41 42 43 45 46 48 49 50 51 52 53 54	23	10	S		379	13830	271	71.5	24	1927	68624	33981	1600
NANCY ADELE MCELWEE MEMORIAL HOSPITAL, See University of Chicago Hospitals													
NATHAN GOLDBLATT MEMORIAL HOSPITAL AND GOLDBLATT PAVILION, See University of Chicago Hospitals													
NORTHWEST HOSPITAL, See John F. Kennedy Medical Center													
★□ NORTHWESTERN MEMORIAL HOSPITAL (Includes Chicago Wesley Memorial Hospital; Institute of Psychiatry; Passavant Memorial Hospital; Prentice Women's Hospital), Superior St. & Fairbanks Ct., Zip 60611; tel. 312/908-2000; Gary A. Mecklenburg, pres. & chief exec. off. **A**1a 2 3 5 8 9 10 **F**1 2 3 4 5 6 7 8 9 10 11 12 13 14 15 16 17 20 23 24 26 27 28 29 30 32 33 34 35 36 37 38 39 40 41 42 44 45 46 47 48 49 50 51 53 54	23	10	S		735	26519	585	79.6	93	4252	221707	89901	3883
□ NORWEGIAN-AMERICAN HOSPITAL, 1044 N. Francisco Ave., Zip 60622; tel. 312/278-8800; William Leyhe, adm. **A**1a 9 10 **F**1 3 6 10 12 14 15 16 23 24 34 35 40 44 45 46 50 51 52 53; **S**0585	23	10	S		230	9293	121	52.6	26	2066	23920	12278	514
PASSAVANT MEMORIAL HOSPITAL, See Northwestern Memorial Hospital													
PHILIP D. ARMOUR CLINICAL RESEARCH BUILDING, See University of Chicago Hospitals													
PRENTICE WOMEN'S HOSPITAL, See Northwestern Memorial Hospital													
★□ PROVIDENT MEDICAL CENTER, 500 E. 51st St., Zip 60615; tel. 312/285-5300 (Nonreporting) **A**1a 9 10	23	10	S		180	—	—	—	—	—	—	—	—
★□ RAVENSWOOD HOSPITAL MEDICAL CENTER, 4550 N. Winchester Ave., Zip 60640; tel. 312/878-4300; Henry J. Kutsch, pres. (Total facility includes 38 beds in nursing home-type unit) **A**1a 2 3 5 6 9 10 **F**1 2 3 6 9 10 11 12 14 15 16 19 20 23 24 25 26 27 28 29 30 32 33 34 35 36 37 38 40 41 42 43 44 45 46 47 50 52 53 54	23	10	S	TF	350	10217	252	71.4	22	1731	58308	27654	1191
				H	312	9939	219	—	22	1731	—	—	—

Hospital, Address, Telephone, Administrator, Approval and Facility Codes, Multihospital System Code

★ American Hospital Association (AHA) membership
□ Joint Commission on Accreditation of Hospitals (JCAH) accreditation
+ American Osteopathic Hospital Association (AOHA) membership
○ American Osteopathic Association (AOA) accreditation
Δ Commission on Accreditation of Rehabilitation Facilities (CARF) accreditation
Control codes 61, 63, 64, 71, 72 and 73 indicate hospitals listed by AOHA, but not registered by AHA.
For definition of numerical codes, see page A2

Hospital, Address, Telephone, Administrator, Approval and Facility Codes, Multihospital System Code	Classification Codes				Inpatient Data				Newborn Data		Expense (thousands of dollars)		
	Control	Service	Stay	Facilities	Beds	Admissions	Census	Occupancy (percent)	Bassinets	Births	Total	Payroll	Personnel
★□ Δ REHABILITATION INSTITUTE OF CHICAGO, 345 E. Superior St., Zip 60611; tel. 312/908-6000; Edward M. Stein Jr., pres. **A**1a 3 5 7 9 10 **F**6 23 24 26 33 34 42 43 44 45 46	23	46	L		176	1472	144	81.8	0	0	39271	21690	874
★□ RESURRECTION HOSPITAL, 7435 W. Talcott Ave., Zip 60631; tel. 312/774-8000; Sr. Bonaventure, pres. (Total facility includes 295 beds in nursing home-type unit) **A**1a 2 3 5 9 10 **F**1 2 3 5 6 7 8 9 10 11 12 14 15 16 19 20 23 24 30 32 33 35 36 40 41 44 45 46 47 48 49 52 53	21	10	S	TF	749	17517	597	79.7	40	1502	76980	34392	1899
				H	454	16767	324	—	40	1502	69204	30671	1649
★□ ROSELAND COMMUNITY HOSPITAL, 45 W. 111th St., Zip 60628; tel. 312/995-3000; Denise R. Williams, pres. **A**1a 9 10 **F**1 3 6 10 12 14 15 16 35 36 40 43 45 53	23	10	S		168	7220	124	73.8	11	655	22661	11461	550
★□ RUSH-PRESBYTERIAN-ST. LUKE'S MEDICAL CENTER (Includes Johnston R. Bowman Health Center, 700 S. Paulina, Zip 60612; tel. 312/942-7000; Ernest Crane, asst. vice-pres. & adm. dir.; Sheridan Road Hospital, 6130 N. Sheridan Rd., Zip 60660; tel. 312/743-2600; Lewis Lippner, asst. vice-pres. & adm.), 1653 W. Congress Pkwy., Zip 60612; tel. 312/942-5492; Leo M. Henikoff MD, pres. (Total facility includes 44 beds in nursing home-type unit) **A**1a 2 3 5 8 9 10 **F**1 3 4 6 7 8 9 10 11 12 13 14 15 16 17 19 20 23 24 25 26 27 28 29 30 32 33 34 35 36 37 38 39 40 41 42 43 44 45 46 47 48 49 50 51 52 53 54	23	10	S	TF	1068	30241	809	76.0	31	2773	390589	173909	7501
				H	1024	29696	776	—	31	2773	386099	173272	—
★□ SAINT MARY OF NAZARETH HOSPITAL CENTER, 2233 W. Division St., Zip 60622; tel. 312/770-2000; Sr. Stella Louise, pres. **A**1a 2 3 5 8 9 10 **F**1 2 3 4 6 7 8 9 10 11 12 14 15 16 20 23 24 25 26 27 28 29 30 32 33 34 35 40 41 42 43 44 45 46 47 49 52 53 54; **S**5575	21	10	S		490	11473	241	49.2	32	1148	69452	35298	1434
★□ Δ SCHWAB REHABILITATION CENTER, 1401 S. California Blvd., Zip 60608; tel. 312/522-2010; Ruth M. Rothstein, pres.; Kathleen Yosko, vice-pres. **A**1a 3 5 7 8 9 10 **F**15 23 24 26 32 33 42 44 46 47	23	46	L		70	748	55	78.6	0	0	8019	4001	168
SHERIDAN ROAD HOSPITAL, See Rush-Presbyterian-St. Luke's Medical Center													
★□ SHRINERS HOSPITALS FOR CRIPPLED CHILDREN, 2211 N. Oak Park Ave., Zip 60635; tel. 312/622-5400; Vernon C. Showalter, adm. **A**1a 3 5 **F**12 15 16 19 23 24 26 34 38 42 44 46 53; **S**4125	23	57	S		60	1318	43	71.7	0	0	—	—	223
SILVAIN AND ARMA WYLER CHILDREN'S HOSPITAL, See University of Chicago Hospitals													
★□ SOUTH CHICAGO COMMUNITY HOSPITAL, 2320 E. 93rd St., Zip 60617; tel. 312/978-2000; Harlan H. Newkirk, pres. & chief exec. off. **A**1a 2 6 9 10 **F**1 3 6 10 12 13 14 15 16 23 26 35 36 37 40 45 46 47 48 49 50 52 53	23	10	S		440	14075	270	61.4	37	1654	54321	25578	1181
★□ SOUTH SHORE HOSPITAL, 8015 S. Luella Ave., Zip 60617; tel. 312/768-0810; John D. Harper, adm. **A**1a 9 10 **F**1 3 6 10 12 14 15 16 20 23 26 34 35 37 44 45 46 47 52 53	23	10	S		170	5613	103	60.6	0	0	18851	9360	478
★□ ST. ANNE'S HOSPITAL, 4950 W. Thomas St., Zip 60651; tel. 312/378-7100; Reginald P. Gibson, assoc. exec. dir. **A**1a 2 6 9 10 **F**1 3 9 10 12 14 15 16 20 23 24 26 27 28 30 32 33 35 36 40 42 43 44 46 52 53; **S**0135	21	10	S		239	8112	164	68.6	20	626	34086	16641	724
★□ ST. ANTHONY HOSPITAL, 2875 W. 19th St., Zip 60623; tel. 312/521-1710; Timothy P. Selz, pres. **A**1a 9 **F**1 3 6 10 12 14 15 16 20 23 24 35 40 44 46 47 52 53; **S**1415	21	10	S		183	6336	105	57.4	18	792	23403	10452	441
★□ ST. BERNARD HOSPITAL, 64th & Dan Ryan Expwy., Zip 60621; tel. 312/962-3900; David Kannankeril, pres. & chief exec. off. **A**1a 9 10 **F**1 3 6 10 12 14 15 16 20 23 34 35 40 45 46 50 52 53; **S**3615	21	10	S		217	8190	169	77.9	26	1111	28930	13919	693
□ ST. ELIZABETH'S HOSPITAL, 1431 N. Claremont Ave., Zip 60622; tel. 312/278-2000; Bernard Dickens Sr., chief exec. off. (Total facility includes 28 beds in nursing home-type unit) **A**1a 2 3 9 10 **F**1 2 3 6 10 12 14 15 16 19 20 23 33 34 35 42 43 45 46 47 48 50 52 53; **S**0135	21	10	S	TF	277	8878	180	65.0	0	0	34819	15456	628
				H	249	8859	179	—	0	0	—	—	612
★ ST. FRANCES XAVIER CABRINI HOSPITAL, 811 S. Lytle St., Zip 60607; tel. 312/883-4343; Lawrence A. Biro EdD, chief oper. off. **A**3 9 10 **F**1 3 6 12 14 15 16 23 34 35 40 45 46 47 52; **S**8805	21	10	S		201	8632	141	72.7	24	978	24614	9850	385
★□ ST. JOSEPH HOSPITAL AND HEALTH CARE CENTER (Formerly St. Joseph Hospital), 2900 N. Lake Shore Dr., Zip 60657; tel. 312/975-3000; Michael Connelly, pres. **A**1a 2 3 5 8 9 10 **F**1 2 3 4 6 7 8 9 10 11 12 15 16 20 21 23 24 26 27 29 30 32 33 34 35 36 37 38 39 40 43 44 45 46 47 50 52 53 54; **S**1885	21	10	S		312	12527	251	80.4	33	1304	71753	35397	1691
★□ SWEDISH COVENANT HOSPITAL, 5145 N. California Ave., Zip 60625; tel. 312/878-8200; James B. McCormick MD, pres. & chief exec. off. **A**1a 2 3 5 9 10 **F**1 3 6 7 8 10 11 12 14 15 16 20 23 24 25 26 28 30 32 33 34 35 36 40 41 44 45 46 47 50 52 53	21	10	S		247	9641	195	78.9	26	1071	45418	18921	950
★□ THOREK HOSPITAL AND MEDICAL CENTER, 850 W. Irving Park Rd., Zip 60613; tel. 312/525-6780; Jon Gepford, pres. **A**1a 9 10 **F**1 3 6 7 9 10 11 12 14 15 16 20 23 24 26 34 35 43 44 46 47 53; **S**9355	21	10	S		218	6096	119	54.6	0	0	24886	9259	418
★□ UNIVERSITY OF CHICAGO HOSPITALS (Includes Albert Merritt Billings Hospital; Bobs Roberts Memorial Hospital for Children; Charles Gilman Smith Hospital; Chicago Lying-in Hospital; Clarissa C. Peck Pavilion of the Chicago Home for Incurables; Country Home for Convalescent Children; Franklin McLean Memorial Research Institute; Gertrude Dunn Hicks Memorial Hospital; Home for Destitute Crippled Children; Nancy Adele McElwee Memorial Hospital; Nathan Goldblatt Memorial Hospital and Goldblatt Pavilion; Philip D. Armour Clinical Research Building; Silvain and Arma Wyler Children's Hospital; Surgery-Brain Research Institute), 5841 S. Maryland, Zip 60637; tel. 312/702-1000; Ralph Muller, pres. **A**1a 2 3 5 8 9 10 **F**1 2 3 4 5 6 7 8 9 10 11 12 13 14 15 16 20 22 23 24 26 27 28 29 30 32 33 34 35 36 37 38 39 40 41 42 43 44 45 46 47 50 51 52 53 54	23	10	S		515	21185	449	81.9	47	2541	187642	75960	2787
★□ UNIVERSITY OF ILLINOIS HOSPITAL, 1740 W. Taylor St., Zip 60612; Mailing Address P O Box 6998, Zip 60680; tel. 312/996-3900; James M. Malloy, dir. **A**1a 2 3 5 8 9 10 **F**1 2 3 4 6 7 8 9 10 11 12 13 14 15 16 17 20 23 24 25 26 27 28 30 32 33 34 35 36 37 38 40 42 44 45 46 47 50 51 52 53 54	12	10	S		530	19053	372	70.2	53	3852	130381	63218	2784
★□ VETERANS ADMINISTRATION LAKESIDE MEDICAL CENTER, 333 E. Huron St., Zip 60611; tel. 312/943-6600; Joseph L. Moore, dir. **A**1a 3 5 8 **F**1 2 3 6 7 8 10 11 12 14 15 16 20 23 24 25 26 27 28 30 32 33 34 35 42 44 45 46 47 53 54	45	10	S		446	12082	277	62.0	0	0	54292	29533	1028
★□ VETERANS ADMINISTRATION WEST SIDE MEDICAL CENTER, 820 S. Damen Ave., Zip 60612; Mailing Address Box 8195, Zip 60680; tel. 312/666-6500; Paul R. Stanford Jr., dir. **A**1a 2 3 5 8 **F**1 3 4 6 9 10 11 12 14 15 16 20 23 24 25 26 27 28 29 30 32 33 34 35 38 41 42 43 44 45 46 47 48 49 50 53 54	45	10	S		484	12789	364	75.2	0	0	81022	33544	1598
CHICAGO HEIGHTS—Cook County													
★□ ST. JAMES HOSPITAL MEDICAL CENTER (Formerly St. James Hospital), Chicago Rd. at Lincoln Hwy., Zip 60411; tel. 312/756-1000; Sr. Antoinette Marie Van Der Werf, pres. **A**1a 2 9 10 **F**1 2 3 5 6 7 8 10 11 12 14 15 16 23 24 34 35 36 40 41 44 45 46 47 51 52 53; **S**5345	21	10	S		365	13762	232	61.2	28	1446	55207	26945	1202

Hospital, Address, Telephone, Administrator, Approval and Facility Codes, Multihospital System Code	Classification Codes				Inpatient Data				Newborn Data		Expense (thousands of dollars)		
★ American Hospital Association (AHA) membership □ Joint Commission on Accreditation of Hospitals (JCAH) accreditation + American Osteopathic Hospital Association (AOHA) membership ○ American Osteopathic Association (AOA) accreditation Δ Commission on Accreditation of Rehabilitation Facilities (CARF) accreditation Control codes 61, 63, 64, 71, 72 and 73 indicate hospitals listed by AOHA, but not registered by AHA. For definition of numerical codes, see page A2	Control	Service	Stay	Facilities	Beds	Admissions	Census	Occupancy (percent)	Bassinets	Births	Total	Payroll	Personnel
CLIFTON—Iroquois County													
★□ CENTRAL COMMUNITY HOSPITAL, 335 E. Fifth Ave., Box 68, Zip 60927; tel. 815/694-2392; Dianne Soucie, adm. (Nonreporting) **A**1a 9 10; **S**4025	23	10	S		32	—	—	—	—	—	—	—	—
CLINTON—De Witt County													
★ DR. JOHN WARNER HOSPITAL, 422 W. White St., Zip 61727; tel. 217/935-9571; Marjorie June Hein RN, adm. **A**9 10 **F**1 3 6 10 15 16 23 24 26 30 35 36 40 44 45 53	14	10	S		52	1801	24	46.2	4	66	4936	2281	157
DANVILLE—Vermilion County													
★□ LAKEVIEW MEDICAL CENTER, 812 N. Logan Ave., Zip 61832; tel. 217/443-5000; Richard V. Livengood, pres. **A**1a 2 6 9 10 **F**1 3 6 8 9 10 11 12 15 16 19 20 21 23 24 26 35 36 40 41 42 44 45 46 47 48 49 52 53	23	10	S		188	7473	124	66.0	10	861	33149	12517	648
★□ ST. ELIZABETH HOSPITAL, 600 Sager Ave., Zip 61832; tel. 217/442-6300; David T. Ochs, pres. (Nonreporting) **A**1a 2 9 10; **S**1415	21	10	S		236	—	—	—	—	—	—	—	—
★□ VETERANS ADMINISTRATION MEDICAL CENTER, 1900 E. Main St., Zip 61832; tel. 217/442-8000; Donald Riedl, dir. (Total facility includes 120 beds in nursing home-type unit) **A**1a 3 5 **F**1 3 6 10 11 12 15 16 19 23 24 26 27 28 29 30 31 32 33 34 35 42 44 45 46 47 48 49 50 54	45	10	L	TF	980	7340	710	72.4	0	0	51422	33661	1474
				H	860	6919	598	—	0	0	46029	30709	1404
DE KALB—De Kalb County													
★□ KISHWAUKEE COMMUNITY HOSPITAL, Bethany Rd., Box 707, Zip 60115; tel. 815/756-1521; Wayne Fesler, pres. **A**1a 2 9 10 **F**1 3 5 6 10 12 15 16 23 24 26 27 28 30 32 33 35 36 40 44 45 46 47 48 49 50 52 53	23	10	S		132	4095	59	44.7	14	557	14071	5809	363
DECATUR—Macon County													
□ ADOLF MEYER MENTAL HEALTH AND DEVELOPMENTAL CENTER, 2310 E. Mound Rd., Zip 62526; tel. 217/877-3410; Christopher T. Power PhD, facility dir. **A**1b **F**15 24 32 33 42 44 46 47	12	22	L		160	354	144	93.5	0	0	7065	4910	216
★□ DECATUR MEMORIAL HOSPITAL, 2300 N. Edward St., Zip 62526; tel. 217/877-8121; Donald I. Gent, pres. & chief exec. off. (Total facility includes 54 beds in nursing home-type unit) **A**1a 2 3 5 9 10 **F**1 3 5 6 7 8 9 10 11 12 15 16 19 20 21 23 24 26 33 34 35 36 37 38 40 41 42 43 44 45 46 47 50 51 52 53 54	23	10	S	TF	370	17727	267	72.2	36	813	41937	19758	1145
				H	316	17515	216	—	36	813	41242	19201	1087
★□ ST. MARY'S HOSPITAL, 1800 E. Lake Shore Dr., Zip 62525; tel. 217/429-2966; Terence J. Schuessler, exec. vice-pres. & chief exec. off. (Total facility includes 40 beds in nursing home-type unit) **A**1a 2 3 5 9 10 **F**1 3 6 9 10 11 12 14 15 16 19 23 24 26 27 28 30 32 33 35 36 40 42 44 45 46 48 49 52 53; **S**5355	21	10	S	TF	377	13070	260	71.4	27	1292	41723	22017	1200
				H	337	12968	243	—	27	1292	41323	21656	1170
DES PLAINES—Cook County													
★□ FOREST HOSPITAL, 555 Wilson Lane, Zip 60016; tel. 312/635-4100; Mary Jane Such, adm. **A**1b 9 **F**15 28 30 32 33 34 49; **S**0655	33	22	L		160	1231	133	83.1	0	0	—	—	339
★□ HOLY FAMILY HOSPITAL, 100 N. River Rd., Zip 60016; tel. 312/297-1800; Sr. Patricia Ann, pres. **A**1a 2 9 10 **F**1 2 3 6 10 11 12 14 15 16 20 21 23 24 34 35 36 40 41 44 45 46 53; **S**5575	23	10	S		246	7988	146	59.3	14	633	43262	18813	897
DIXON—Lee County													
★□ KATHERINE SHAW BETHEA HOSPITAL, 403 E. First St., Zip 61021; tel. 815/288-5531; James O. Dague, pres. **A**1a 2 9 10 **F**1 3 6 10 12 14 15 16 20 23 24 26 27 28 29 30 32 33 34 35 36 40 41 42 44 45 46 47 50 52 53	23	10	S		121	4154	71	58.7	17	395	15032	6569	319
DOWNERS GROVE—Du Page County													
★□ GOOD SAMARITAN HOSPITAL, 3815 Highland Ave., Zip 60515; tel. 312/963-5900; David M. McConkey, vice-pres. & chief exec. **A**1a 2 9 10 **F**1 3 6 9 10 12 14 15 16 20 23 24 27 30 34 35 36 40 42 44 45 46 50 52 53 54; **S**1225	21	10	S		287	12402	216	75.3	20	2123	56826	22580	1029
DU QUOIN—Perry County													
★□ MARSHALL BROWNING HOSPITAL, 900 N. Washington St., Box 192, Zip 62832; tel. 618/542-2146; David R. Hosler, chief exec. off. **A**1a 9 10 **F**1 12 15 16 23 26 35 40 45	23	10	S		60	1602	22	36.7	10	233	4403	2153	124
EAST ST. LOUIS—St. Clair County													
COMMUNITY HOSPITAL, See Gateway Community Hospital													
□ GATEWAY COMMUNITY HOSPITAL (Formerly Community Hospital), 1509 Martin Luther King Dr., Zip 62201; tel. 618/874-7076; Christian C. Kolom, adm. (Nonreporting) **A**1a 9; **S**0495	23	10	S		217	—	—	—	—	—	—	—	—
□ ST. MARY'S HOSPITAL, 129 N. Eighth St., Zip 62201; tel. 618/274-1900; Philip J. Karst PhD, exec. dir. **A**1a 9 10 **F**1 3 5 6 7 8 10 11 12 14 15 16 19 21 23 26 27 30 32 33 34 35 41 42 46 49 50 53; **S**0135	21	10	S		273	8891	184	70.0	0	0	24075	11950	694
EFFINGHAM—Effingham County													
★□ ST. ANTHONY'S MEMORIAL HOSPITAL, 503 Maple St., Zip 62401; tel. 217/342-2121; Gregory A. Voss, adm. **A**1a 2 9 10 **F**1 3 5 6 10 12 14 15 16 23 24 26 35 36 40 42 44 45 52 53; **S**5355	21	10	S		146	5952	88	60.3	16	906	16300	7944	400
ELDORADO—Saline County													
FERRELL HOSPITAL, 1201 Pine St., Zip 62930; tel. 618/273-3361; E. T. Seely, actg. adm. (Nonreporting) **A**9 10	33	10	S		47	—	—	—	—	—	—	—	—
★□ PEARCE HOSPITAL, 1901 Organ St., Zip 62930; tel. 618/273-2411; Ann Pulliam, adm. (Nonreporting) **A**1a 9 10	23	10	S		72	—	—	—	—	—	—	—	—
ELGIN—Kane County													
ELGIN MENTAL HEALTH CENTER, 750 S. State St., Zip 60123; tel. 312/742-1040; Roalda J. Alderman, dir. **A**10 **F**3 12 15 16 23 24 30 32 33 35 37 42 44 46 47 50	12	22	L		830	1608	818	99.8	0	0	37083	27096	1206
★□ SAINT JOSEPH HOSPITAL, 77 N. Airlite St., Zip 60123; tel. 312/695-3200; Robert J. Mohalski, pres. **A**1a 2 9 10 **F**1 3 6 7 8 9 10 11 12 14 15 16 23 24 26 27 28 30 32 33 35 36 40 42 44 45 46 47 52 53 54; **S**1415	21	10	S		280	7892	172	61.4	22	583	31608	15424	686
★□ SHERMAN HOSPITAL, 934 Center St., Zip 60120; tel. 312/742-9800; John A. Graham, pres. **A**1a 2 9 10 **F**1 2 3 4 5 6 10 12 14 15 16 20 23 24 26 34 35 36 40 41 44 45 46 47 52 53 54	23	10	S		418	14052	243	58.1	47	1756	56135	27339	1259
ELK GROVE VILLAGE—Cook County													
★□ Δ ALEXIAN BROTHERS MEDICAL CENTER, 800 W. Biesterfield Rd., Zip 60007; tel. 312/437-5500; Brother Philip Kennedy, pres. & chief exec. off. **A**1a 2 7 9 10 **F**1 3 6 10 12 14 15 16 20 21 23 24 25 26 27 28 29 30 32 33 34 35 36 37 40 41 42 43 44 45 46 47 48 49 52 53 54; **S**0065	21	10	S		370	12374	280	75.7	32	1461	67113	33386	1418
ELMHURST—Du Page County													
★□ ELMHURST MEMORIAL HOSPITAL, 200 Berteau Ave., Zip 60126; tel. 312/833-1400; Robert M. Magnuson, pres. **A**1a 2 9 10 **F**1 2 3 4 5 6 7 8 9 10 11 12 14 15 16 20 23 24 26 27 30 32 34 35 36 40 42 43 44 46 48 52 53 54	23	10	S		384	15549	290	78.0	40	1660	66301	33335	1449
EUREKA—Woodford County													
□ EUREKA COMMUNITY HOSPITAL (Formerly Eureka Hospital), 101 S. Major St., Zip 61530; tel. 309/467-2371; Kay Schraith, adm. (Nonreporting) **A**1a 9 10; **S**9305	21	10	S		35	—	—	—	—	—	—	—	—
EVANSTON—Cook County													
★□ Δ EVANSTON HOSPITAL (Includes Glenbrook Hospital, 2100 Pfingsten Rd., Glenview, Zip 60025; tel. 312/729-8800), 2650 Ridge Ave., Zip 60201; tel. 312/492-2000; Bernard J. Lachner, pres. & chief exec. off. **A**1a 2 3 5 7 8 9 10 **F**1 2 3 4 6 7 8 9 10 11 12 13 14 15 16 20 23 24 25 26 27 28 29 30 32 33 34 35 36 37 38 40 41 42 43 44 45 46 47 48 49 50 51 52 53 54	23	10	S		543	21612	441	81.2	34	3154	128455	54938	2406

Hospital, Address, Telephone, Administrator, Approval and Facility Codes, Multihospital System Code	Classification Codes				Inpatient Data				Newborn Data		Expense (thousands of dollars)		
★ American Hospital Association (AHA) membership □ Joint Commission on Accreditation of Hospitals (JCAH) accreditation + American Osteopathic Hospital Association (AOHA) membership ○ American Osteopathic Association (AOA) accreditation Δ Commission on Accreditation of Rehabilitation Facilities (CARF) accreditation Control codes 61, 63, 64, 71, 72 and 73 indicate hospitals listed by AOHA, but not registered by AHA. For definition of numerical codes, see page A2	Control	Service	Stay	Facilities	Beds	Admissions	Census	Occupancy (percent)	Bassinets	Births	Total	Payroll	Personnel
NORTHWESTERN UNIVERSITY STUDENT HEALTH SERVICE HOSPITAL, 633 Emerson St., Zip 60201; tel. 312/491-8100; Helen M. Wilks MD, med. dir. **F**15 28 32 33 34 37	23	11	S		23	231	2	8.7	0	0	2225	1165	57
⊞ ST. FRANCIS HOSPITAL, 355 Ridge Ave., Zip 60202; tel. 312/492-4000; Sr. M. Alfreda Bracht, pres. **A**1a 2 3 5 6 9 10 **F**1 2 3 4 6 7 8 9 10 11 12 14 15 16 20 23 24 26 28 30 32 33 34 35 36 37 38 39 40 41 42 44 45 46 49 50 52 53 54; **S**5345	21	10	S		469	13099	281	59.9	24	1207	76290	31667	1423
EVERGREEN PARK—Cook County													
⊞ LITTLE COMPANY OF MARY HOSPITAL, 2800 W. 95th St., Zip 60642; tel. 312/422-6200; Paul R. Wozniak, pres. **A**1a 2 3 5 9 10 **F**1 2 3 6 7 8 9 10 11 12 15 16 20 21 23 24 27 33 35 36 40 41 42 44 45 46 47 49 51 52 53; **S**2295	21	10	S		386	15532	289	73.4	36	1607	81978	36355	1689
FAIRBURY—Livingston County													
⊞ FAIRBURY HOSPITAL (Includes Helen Lewis Smith Pavilion), 519 S. Fifth St., Zip 61739; tel. 815/692-2346; John L. Tummons PhD, adm. (Total facility includes 49 beds in nursing home-type unit) **A**1a 9 10 **F**1 6 10 14 16 19 23 34 35 36 40 45 46 50; **S**8875	23	10	S	TF	117	1223	75	64.1	4	61	—	—	164
				H	68	1214	27	—	4	61	—	—	137
FAIRFIELD—Wayne County													
⊞ FAIRFIELD MEMORIAL HOSPITAL, N.W. 11th St., Zip 62837; tel. 618/842-2611; C. F. Kerchner, adm. (Total facility includes 23 beds in nursing home-type unit) **A**1a 9 10 **F**1 3 6 10 12 14 16 19 23 35 36 40 44 45 46 53	23	10	S	TF	72	1549	20	26.7	7	106	3371	1696	117
				H	49	1449	15	—	7	106	3300	1627	110
FLORA—Clay County													
⊞ CLAY COUNTY HOSPITAL, 700 N. Mill St., Zip 62839; tel. 618/662-2131; John E. Monnahan, adm. **A**1a 9 10 **F**1 6 14 15 16 23 34 35 36 40 45 46 47; **S**0565	13	10	S		40	925	11	27.5	6	151	2972	1362	94
FOREST PARK—Cook County													
⊞ HCA RIVEREDGE HOSPITAL (Formerly Riveredge Hospital), 8311 W. Roosevelt Rd., Zip 60130; tel. 312/771-7000; Joyce W. Washington, exec. dir. **A**1b 9 10 **F**24 29 32 33 42 44 46 47 48 49; **S**1755	33	22	L		204	1489	172	84.3	0	0	—	—	327
FREEPORT—Stephenson County													
⊞ FREEPORT MEMORIAL HOSPITAL, 1045 W. Stephenson St., Zip 61032; tel. 815/235-4131; Dennis L. Hamilton, pres. (Total facility includes 24 beds in nursing home-type unit) **A**1a 9 10 **F**1 3 6 9 10 11 12 14 15 16 19 23 24 35 36 40 44 45 46 52 53	23	10	S	TF	180	6295	110	61.1	16	774	19078	8587	500
				H	156	6290	92	—	16	774	18820	8348	482
GALENA—Jo Daviess County													
⊞ GALENA-STAUSS HOSPITAL, 215 Summit St., Zip 61036; tel. 815/777-1340; Roger D. Hervey, adm. (Total facility includes 34 beds in nursing home-type unit) **A**1a 9 10 **F**1 6 16 19 23 30 40 45	16	10	S	TF	63	566	40	63.5	4	45	1921	906	70
				H	29	552	7	—	4	45	—	—	48
GALESBURG—Knox County													
⊞ GALESBURG COTTAGE HOSPITAL, 695 N. Kellogg St., Zip 61402; tel. 309/343-8131; Steven J. West, pres. & chief exec. off. **A**1a 9 10 **F**1 2 3 5 6 10 12 14 15 16 20 23 24 27 30 33 35 36 40 43 44 45 46 48 52 53	23	10	S		203	6535	106	52.2	20	455	23242	9578	487
⊞ ST. MARY'S HOSPITAL, 3333 N. Seminary St., Zip 61401; tel. 309/344-3161; Richard S. Kowalski, adm. **A**1a 2 9 10 **F**1 3 5 6 10 12 15 16 19 23 24 33 34 35 36 40 41 44 45 46 47 52 53; **S**5335	21	10	S		159	5811	92	57.9	20	446	19166	9205	429
GENESEO—Henry County													
⊞ HAMMOND-HENRY HOSPITAL, 210 W. Elk St., Zip 61254; tel. 309/944-6431; Paul Gurgel, pres. & chief exec. off. (Total facility includes 60 beds in nursing home-type unit) **A**1a 9 10 **F**1 3 6 10 14 15 16 19 23 34 35 36 40 42 43 44 45 46	16	10	S	TF	105	1717	68	64.8	10	290	5633	3092	180
				H	45	1563	17	—	10	290	4591	2414	151
GIBSON CITY—Ford County													
⊞ GIBSON COMMUNITY HOSPITAL (Includes Gibson Community Hospital Annex), 1120 N. Melvin St., P O Box 429, Zip 60936; tel. 217/784-4251; Terry Thompson, adm. (Total facility includes 26 beds in nursing home-type unit) **A**1a 9 10 **F**1 3 6 10 12 14 15 16 19 23 35 36 40 41 43 45 53; **S**2495	23	10	S	TF	81	1201	48	59.3	10	100	4647	2149	155
				H	55	1100	13	—	10	100	3500	1608	119
GLENDALE HEIGHTS—Du Page County													
⊞ GLENDALE HEIGHTS COMMUNITY HOSPITAL, 1505 Jill Ct., Zip 60139; tel. 312/858-9700; A. A. Chacon, pres. **A**1a 9 10 **F**1 3 5 6 7 9 10 11 12 14 15 16 23 24 27 28 29 30 32 33 34 35 36 37 40 42 44 45 46 47 49 50 53; **S**9355	21	10	S		186	3504	77	41.4	24	301	24331	7750	346
GLENVIEW—Cook County													
GLENBROOK HOSPITAL, See Evanston Hospital, Evanston													
GRANITE CITY—Madison County													
⊞ ST. ELIZABETH MEDICAL CENTER, 2100 Madison Ave., Zip 62040; tel. 618/798-3000; Ted Eilerman, pres. **A**1a 2 9 10 **F**1 3 5 6 7 8 9 10 11 12 14 15 16 17 19 20 21 23 24 26 27 28 30 31 33 34 35 36 40 41 42 44 45 46 47 48 49 50 52 53	21	10	S		389	9661	201	51.7	10	766	40831	19616	1029
GREAT LAKES—Lake County													
⊞ NAVAL HOSPITAL, Zip 60088; tel. 312/688-4560 **A**1a 2 3 5 **F**1 3 6 8 10 11 12 14 15 16 23 27 28 30 32 33 34 35 37 40 46 47 48 49 52	43	10	S		173	6405	111	64.2	10	811	53413	28121	1063
GREENVILLE—Bond County													
⊞ EDWARD A. UTLAUT MEMORIAL HOSPITAL (Includes Fair Oaks), Health Care Dr., Zip 62246; tel. 618/664-1230; Donald R. Wise, adm. (Total facility includes 144 beds in nursing home-type unit) **A**1a 9 10 **F**1 6 10 12 14 15 16 19 23 34 35 40 45 47 52 53	23	10	S	TF	201	1409	144	71.6	7	136	5617	3008	232
				H	57	1239	16	—	7	136	3466	1686	157
HARRISBURG—Saline County													
□ HARRISBURG MEDICAL CENTER, 17 Country Club Ct., Box 428, Zip 62946; tel. 618/253-7671; John R. Denbo, adm. **A**1a 9 10 **F**1 6 10 12 14 15 16 23 34 35 36 40 41 45 52	23	10	S		85	3083	41	48.2	8	474	7440	3503	238
HARVARD—McHenry County													
⊞ HARVARD COMMUNITY MEMORIAL HOSPITAL, Grant & McKinley Sts., Zip 60033; tel. 815/943-5431; John M. Seegers, adm. **A**1a 9 10 **F**1 3 6 10 12 14 15 16 23 26 34 35 40 45 46 53	16	10	S		46	1126	13	28.3	10	147	3169	1624	102
HARVEY—Cook County													
⊞ INGALLS MEMORIAL HOSPITAL, One Ingalls Dr., Zip 60426; tel. 312/333-2300; Robert L. Harris, pres. **A**1a 2 9 10 **F**1 2 3 6 7 8 9 10 11 12 14 15 16 20 23 24 26 27 30 32 33 35 36 40 41 42 44 45 46 47 48 49 52 53 54	23	10	S		554	22803	448	81.0	41	2460	94540	48116	1959
HAVANA—Mason County													
⊞ MASON DISTRICT HOSPITAL, 520 E. Franklin St., Box 529, Zip 62644; tel. 309/543-4431; Emerson H. Teveit, adm. **A**1a 9 10 **F**1 3 6 16 23 35 41 45 53	16	10	S		36	993	18	50.0	0	0	4635	1975	140
HAZEL CREST—Cook County													
⊞ SOUTH SUBURBAN HOSPITAL, 178th St. & Kedzie Ave., Zip 60429; tel. 312/799-8000; Robert Rutkowski, exec. vice-pres. **A**1a 9 10 **F**1 3 6 9 10 12 14 15 16 23 24 26 34 35 36 40 41 44 45 46 47 52 53	23	10	S		217	9003	153	68.3	20	787	37889	17339	761
HERRIN—Williamson County													
★ HERRIN HOSPITAL, 201 S. 14th St., Zip 62948; tel. 618/942-2171; Larry Feil, adm. **A**9 10 **F**1 3 6 9 10 12 14 15 16 20 23 34 35 36 40 41 44 45 46 53; **S**4175	23	10	S		98	4196	77	78.6	6	181	11320	5277	322

Hospital, Address, Telephone, Administrator, Approval and Facility Codes, Multihospital System Code	Classification Codes				Inpatient Data				Newborn Data		Expense (thousands of dollars)		
★ American Hospital Association (AHA) membership □ Joint Commission on Accreditation of Hospitals (JCAH) accreditation + American Osteopathic Hospital Association (AOHA) membership ○ American Osteopathic Association (AOA) accreditation Δ Commission on Accreditation of Rehabilitation Facilities (CARF) accreditation Control codes 61, 63, 64, 71, 72 and 73 indicate hospitals listed by AOHA, but not registered by AHA. For definition of numerical codes, see page A2	Control	Service	Stay	Facilities	Beds	Admissions	Census	Occupancy (percent)	Bassinets	Births	Total	Payroll	Personnel
HIGHLAND—Madison County													
★□ ST. JOSEPH'S HOSPITAL, 1515 Main St., Zip 62249; tel. 618/654-7421; Mark W. Reifsteck, exec. vice-pres. **A**1a 9 10 **F**1 3 6 10 12 14 15 16 19 21 23 24 34 35 41 44 45 46 52 53; **S**5355	21	10	S		106	1749	37	34.9	0	0	7695	3900	188
HIGHLAND PARK—Lake County													
★□ HIGHLAND PARK HOSPITAL, 718 Glenview Ave., Zip 60035; tel. 312/432-8000; Ronald G. Spaeth, pres. & chief exec. off. (Total facility includes 18 beds in nursing home-type unit) **A**1a 2 9 10 **F**1 2 3 6 10 11 12 14 15 16 19 20 21 23 24 26 27 28 30 32 33 34 35 36 37 40 41 42 44 45 46 47 48 49 52 53	23	10	S	TF	280	8703	167	62.5	16	1049	44883	19542	894
				H	262	8651	163	—	16	1049	44514	19385	878
HILLSBORO—Montgomery County													
□ HILLSBORO HOSPITAL, 1200 E. Tremont St., Zip 62049; tel. 217/532-6111; Brian J. McDermott, adm. (Total facility includes 40 beds in nursing home-type unit) **A**1a 9 10 **F**1 3 6 10 12 14 15 16 19 23 34 35 36 37 40 43 44 45 46 47 50	23	10	S	TF	100	2274	49	49.0	6	157	5246	2678	173
				H	60	2036	23	—	6	157	4861	2329	148
HINES—Cook County													
□ JOHN J. MADDEN MENTAL HEALTH CENTER, 1200 S. First Ave., Zip 60141; tel. 312/345-9870; Glenn J. Grzonka, dir. **A**1b 10 **F**24 32 33 42 44 46	12	22	S		269	4184	256	95.2	0	0	13439	9889	366
★□ VETERANS ADMINISTRATION HOSPITAL, Fifth Ave. & Roosevelt Rd., Zip 60141; tel. 312/261-6700; John R. Fears, dir. (Total facility includes 179 beds in nursing home-type unit) **A**1a3 5 8 **F**1 2 3 4 6 7 8 9 10 11 12 13 14 15 16 19 20 21 23 24 25 26 27 28 30 32 33 34 35 41 42 44 45 46 47 48 49 50 53 54	45	10	S	TF	1343	25784	897	67.5	0	0	138830	82092	3377
				H	1164	25488	785	—	0	0	—	—	3182
HINSDALE—Du Page and Cook Counties													
★□ HINSDALE HOSPITAL, 120 N. Oak St., Zip 60521; tel. 312/887-2400; Ken Bauer, pres. **A**1a 2 3 5 9 10 **F**1 2 3 6 7 8 9 10 11 12 14 15 16 23 24 25 26 27 28 29 30 32 34 35 36 37 38 40 41 42 43 44 45 46 47 48 49 52 53 54; **S**9355	21	10	S		468	16517	329	70.3	48	3310	89331	40945	1680
□ SUBURBAN HOSPITAL AND SANITARIUM OF COOK COUNTY, 55th St. & County Line Rd., Zip 60521; tel. 312/323-5800; William R. Sittler, exec. vice-pres. & chief exec. off. **A**1a 9 10 **F**1 2 3 6 10 12 14 15 16 20 23 24 26 34 35 43 44	16	10	S		122	1713	42	34.4	0	0	14252	7415	222
HOFFMAN ESTATES—Cook County													
★□ HUMANA HOSPITAL -HOFFMAN ESTATES, 1555 N. Barrington Rd., Zip 60194; tel. 312/843-2000; Donald L. Maloney II, exec. dir. **A**1a 9 10 **F**1 3 6 10 12 14 15 16 20 23 24 34 35 36 40 44 46 47 52 53; **S**1235	33	10	S		216	10175	143	66.2	32	2426	38400	12631	654
HOOPESTON—Vermilion County													
□ HOOPESTON REGIONAL HOSPITAL (Formerly Hoopeston Community Memorial Hospital), 701 E. Orange St., Zip 60942; tel. 217/283-5531; Daniel G. Van Wieringen, adm. (Nonreporting) **A**1a 9 10; **S**9795	23	10	S		94	—	—	—	—	—	—	—	—
HOPEDALE—Tazewell County													
□ HOPEDALE HOSPITAL, Zip 61747; tel. 309/449-3321; L. J. Rossi MD, med. dir. (Nonreporting) **A**1a 9 10	23	10	S		62	—	—	—	—	—	—	—	—
JACKSONVILLE—Morgan County													
★□ PASSAVANT AREA HOSPITAL, 1600 W. Walnut St., Zip 62650; tel. 217/245-9541; Clarence E. Lay, chief exec. off. **A**1a 9 10 **F**1 3 5 6 10 12 15 16 23 26 35 36 40 45 46 47 53	23	10	S		168	6256	100	59.5	18	534	18875	9168	515
JERSEYVILLE—Jersey County													
★□ JERSEY COMMUNITY HOSPITAL, 400 Maple Summit Rd., Zip 62052; tel. 618/498-6402; Sylvia Kallal, interim adm. **A**1a 9 10 **F**1 3 6 10 12 14 15 16 23 35 36 40 45 46 47 52 53	16	10	S		67	2350	36	53.7	8	380	6136	3530	169
JOLIET—Will County													
★□ SILVER CROSS HOSPITAL, 1200 Maple Rd., Zip 60432; tel. 815/740-1100; Keyton H. Nixon, pres. **A**1a 9 10 **F**1 3 5 6 8 9 10 11 12 14 15 16 20 21 23 24 34 35 36 37 40 41 44 46 48 49 50 52 53	23	10	S		276	13862	229	83.0	26	1347	42305	21465	909
★□ ST. JOSEPH MEDICAL CENTER, 333 N. Madison St., Zip 60435; tel. 815/725-7133; Edward J. Schlicksup Jr., pres. **A**1a 2 6 9 10 **F**1 2 3 5 6 7 8 9 10 11 12 15 16 21 23 24 25 26 27 28 29 30 32 33 35 36 40 42 43 44 45 46 47 48 49 50 52 53 54; **S**1415	21	10	S		531	18187	377	71.0	60	1925	63396	31874	1427
STATEVILLE CORRECTIONAL CENTER HOSPITAL, Box 112, Zip 60434; tel. 815/727-3607; William M. Reger III, adm. (Nonreporting)	12	11	S		86	—	—	—	—	—	—	—	—
KANKAKEE—Kankakee County													
★□ Δ RIVERSIDE MEDICAL CENTER, 350 N. Wall St., Zip 60901; tel. 815/933-1671; Robert G. Miller, pres. (Total facility includes 15 beds in nursing home-type unit) **A**1a 7 9 10 **F**1 2 3 5 6 9 10 12 14 15 16 19 23 24 25 26 27 28 30 31 32 33 34 35 36 37 40 41 42 44 45 46 47 48 49 50 52 53	23	10	S	TF	311	9133	196	63.0	30	1174	34462	16597	812
				H	296	8930	185	—	30	1174	—	—	804
★□ ST. MARY'S HOSPITAL OF KANKAKEE, 500 W. Court St., Zip 60901; tel. 815/937-2490; Michael K. Winthrop, pres. (Total facility includes 15 beds in nursing home-type unit) **A**1a 2 9 10 **F**1 3 5 6 7 8 9 10 11 12 14 15 16 19 20 23 24 26 30 34 35 36 40 44 45 46 52 53; **S**4025	21	10	S	TF	250	8697	151	60.4	12	416	30764	13628	702
				H	235	8597	145	—	12	416	—	—	696
KEWANEE—Henry County													
★□ KEWANEE PUBLIC HOSPITAL, 719 Elliott St., Zip 61443; tel. 309/853-3361; Glenn A. Doyle, adm. **A**1a 9 10 **F**1 3 6 10 12 14 15 16 23 34 35 36 37 40 41 44 45 46 52 53; **S**2495	23	10	S		111	2966	37	33.3	9	216	8740	3846	229
LA GRANGE—Cook County													
★□ LA GRANGE MEMORIAL HOSPITAL (Formerly Community Memorial General Hospital), 5101 Willow Springs Rd., Zip 60525; tel. 312/352-1200; Joseph P. Calandra, pres. **A**1a 2 3 5 9 10 **F**1 2 3 6 10 12 14 15 16 34 35 36 40 45 46 47 52 53 54	23	10	S		247	9674	164	67.2	32	1122	47976	20100	819
LA HARPE—Hancock County													
LA HARPE HOSPITAL, B St. & Archer Ave., Box 547, Zip 61450; tel. 217/659-3011; Richard Miller, adm. (Total facility includes 49 beds in nursing home-type unit) **A**9 10 **F**15 19 23 24 34 35 42 44 45 46 47	23	10	S	TF	64	198	56	87.5	0	0	—	—	52
				H	15	165	8	—	0	0	—	—	27
LAKE FOREST—Lake County													
★□ Δ LAKE FOREST HOSPITAL, 660 N. Westmoreland Rd., Zip 60045; tel. 312/234-5600; William G. Ries, pres. & chief exec. off. (Total facility includes 82 beds in nursing home-type unit) **A**1a 2 7 9 10 **F**1 3 6 7 8 10 11 13 14 15 16 17 19 21 23 24 34 35 36 37 40 41 42 44 45 46 47 50 52 53	23	10	S	TF	239	7450	185	78.1	23	1640	32637	14208	712
				H	157	7235	105	—	23	1640	29355	12774	644
LAWRENCEVILLE—Lawrence County													
★ LAWRENCE COUNTY MEMORIAL HOSPITAL, W. State St., Zip 62439; tel. 618/943-2381; Wendell C. Trent, pres. **A**9 10 **F**1 2 3 6 12 14 15 16 23 26 28 29 30 32 33 35 40 46 47 50 53	13	10	S		65	1812	24	36.9	10	152	4302	2112	136
LIBERTYVILLE—Lake County													
★□ CONDELL MEMORIAL HOSPITAL, 900 Garfield, Zip 60048; tel. 312/362-2900; Eugene Pritchard, pres. **A**1a 2 9 10 **F**1 3 6 10 12 14 15 16 23 24 26 34 35 36 37 40 41 42 44 45 46 47 52 53	23	10	S		181	6852	106	58.6	12	951	26488	11810	555

Hospital, Address, Telephone, Administrator, Approval and Facility Codes, Multihospital System Code	Classification Codes			Facilities	Inpatient Data				Newborn Data		Expense (thousands of dollars)		
★ American Hospital Association (AHA) membership □ Joint Commission on Accreditation of Hospitals (JCAH) accreditation + American Osteopathic Hospital Association (AOHA) membership ○ American Osteopathic Association (AOA) accreditation Δ Commission on Accreditation of Rehabilitation Facilities (CARF) accreditation Control codes 61, 63, 64, 71, 72 and 73 indicate hospitals listed by AOHA, but not registered by AHA. For definition of numerical codes, see page A2	Control	Service	Stay		Beds	Admissions	Census	Occupancy (percent)	Bassinets	Births	Total	Payroll	Personnel
LINCOLN—Logan County													
★□ ABRAHAM LINCOLN MEMORIAL HOSPITAL, 315 Eighth St., Zip 62656; tel. 217/732-2161; D. David Sniff, pres. & chief exec. off. **A**1a 9 10 **F**1 3 5 6 10 12 14 15 16 23 26 30 35 36 40 44 45 46 52 53	23	10	S		80	2936	41	45.1	18	201	10402	4887	264
LINCOLN DEVELOPMENTAL CENTER, 861 S. State St., Zip 62656; tel. 217/735-2361; Linda K. Gustafson PhD, dir. **F**19 23 24 33 42 44 46	12	62	L		530	20	498	94.0	0	0	19763	12072	704
LITCHFIELD—Montgomery County													
★□ ST. FRANCIS HOSPITAL, 1215 E. Union Ave., Zip 62056; tel. 217/324-2191; Sr. Mary Ann Laxen, exec. vice-pres. **A**1a 9 10 **F**1 3 5 6 10 12 14 15 16 23 24 35 36 40 41 44 45 46 53; **S**5355	21	10	S		138	3936	51	37.0	12	365	10051	5175	271
MACOMB—McDonough County													
★□ MCDONOUGH DISTRICT HOSPITAL, 525 E. Grant St., Zip 61455; tel. 309/833-4101; Stephen R. Hopper, pres. & chief exec. off. **A**1a 2 9 10 **F**1 3 5 6 10 12 14 15 16 21 23 24 35 36 40 41 44 45 46 47 52 53	16	10	S		155	5578	82	52.9	10	448	15807	7360	417
MARION—Williamson County													
★□ MARION MEMORIAL HOSPITAL, 917 W. Main St., Zip 62959; tel. 618/997-5341; Merle L. Aukamp, adm. **A**1a 9 10 **F**1 3 5 6 10 12 14 15 16 23 26 32 34 35 36 37 40 45 46 50	14	10	S		120	4055	67	55.8	10	234	11611	6114	355
★□ VETERANS ADMINISTRATION MEDICAL CENTER, 2401 W. Main St., Zip 62959; tel. 618/997-5311; Robert T. Patton, dir. (Total facility includes 60 beds in nursing home-type unit) **A**1a **F**1 3 6 12 14 15 16 19 23 24 28 32 33 34 35 42 44 46 47 50	45	10	S	TF	231	5421	181	78.4	0	0	21527	13528	484
				H	171	5333	128	—	0	0	18408	11367	430
MARYVILLE—Madison County													
★□ ANDERSON HOSPITAL (Formerly Oliver C. Anderson Hospital), Rte. 162, Zip 62062; tel. 618/288-5711; R. Coert Shepard, pres. **A**1a 9 10 **F**1 3 6 10 12 14 15 16 23 30 35 36 40 45 53	23	10	S		140	4487	72	51.4	16	675	16796	7285	366
MATTOON—Coles County													
★□ SARAH BUSH LINCOLN HEALTH CENTER, Rte. 16, Box 372, Zip 61938; tel. 217/258-2525; Gerald Dooley, chief exec. off. **A**1a 9 10 **F**1 3 5 6 10 12 14 16 23 24 27 33 34 35 36 40 44 45 52 53	23	10	S		171	8872	119	63.3	19	885	26152	12983	586
MAYWOOD—Cook County													
★□ FOSTER G. MCGAW HOSPITAL, LOYOLA UNIVERSITY OF CHICAGO, 2160 S. First Ave., Zip 60153; tel. 312/531-3000; Robert S. Condry, dir. **A**1a 2 3 5 8 9 10 **F**2 3 4 5 6 7 8 9 10 11 12 13 14 15 16 17 20 22 23 24 26 27 28 30 32 33 35 36 40 42 43 44 46 47 51 52 53 54	23	10	S		512	18677	429	83.8	25	1056	158488	47361	2234
MCHENRY—McHenry County													
★□ Δ NORTHERN ILLINOIS MEDICAL CENTER, 4201 Medical Center Dr., Zip 60050; tel. 815/344-5000; Paul E. Laudick, pres. **A**1a 2 7 9 10 **F**1 3 5 6 10 12 14 15 16 23 24 25 30 32 33 34 35 36 40 41 44 45 46 47 52 53	23	10	S		152	6653	114	75.0	12	498	31060	11635	576
MCLEANSBORO—Hamilton County													
★□ HAMILTON MEMORIAL HOSPITAL, 611 S. Marshall Ave., Zip 62859; tel. 618/643-2361; Michael C. Karcher, adm. (Total facility includes 60 beds in nursing home-type unit) **A**1a 9 10 **F**1 12 14 16 19 23 35 41 45 46	16	10	S	TF	108	1533	84	77.8	0	0	3845	2070	161
				H	48	1511	25	—	0	0	3012	1557	113
MELROSE PARK—Cook County													
★□ GOTTLIEB MEMORIAL HOSPITAL, 701 W. North Ave., Zip 60160; tel. 312/681-3200; Ira H. Goldberg, pres. (Total facility includes 34 beds in nursing home-type unit) **A**1a 9 10 **F**1 2 3 6 10 12 14 15 16 19 23 24 28 30 32 34 35 36 40 41 42 44 45 46 49 50 52 53 54	23	10	S	TF	275	9170	178	64.7	35	781	42234	18793	925
				H	241	8590	155	—	35	781	—	—	917
★□ WESTLAKE COMMUNITY HOSPITAL, 1225 Lake St., Zip 60160; tel. 312/681-3000; Leonard J. Muller, pres. **A**1a 9 10 **F**1 3 5 6 7 12 14 15 16 21 23 24 25 26 27 32 33 34 36 37 40 41 42 44 45 46 47 48 49 52 53 54	23	10	S		261	9853	208	79.7	18	716	41918	18052	722
MENDOTA—La Salle County													
★□ MENDOTA COMMUNITY HOSPITAL, 1315 Memorial Dr., Zip 61342; tel. 815/539-7461; E. E. Williams, adm. **A**1a 9 10 **F**1 3 14 16 23 34 35 36 40 45 46 49	23	10	S		72	2263	31	43.1	8	176	5368	2810	135
METROPOLIS—Massac County													
★□ MASSAC MEMORIAL HOSPITAL, Memorial Hts., Zip 62960; tel. 618/524-2176; Loren L. Erwin, adm. (Nonreporting) **A**1a 9 10	16	10	S		57	—	—	—	—	—	—	—	—
MOLINE—Rock Island County													
★□ LUTHERAN HOSPITAL, 501 Tenth Ave., Zip 61265; tel. 309/757-2611; Kenneth D. Moburg, pres. **A**1a 2 6 9 10 **F**1 2 3 5 6 7 8 9 10 11 12 15 16 21 23 24 30 33 35 37 42 43 44 45 46 52 53	21	10	S		197	6854	116	58.9	0	0	28037	11142	589
★□ MOLINE PUBLIC HOSPITAL, 635 Tenth Ave., Zip 61265; tel. 309/757-3131; Tyler B. Schoenherr, adm. & chief exec. off. **A**1a 6 9 10 **F**1 3 5 6 9 10 12 14 15 16 19 20 23 24 34 35 36 37 40 44 45 50 53 54	14	10	S		160	5760	74	46.3	25	1034	22241	10697	545
MONMOUTH—Warren County													
★□ COMMUNITY MEMORIAL HOSPITAL, 1000 W. Harlem Ave., Zip 61462; tel. 309/734-3141; David M. Coates PhD, pres. **A**1a 9 10 **F**1 3 6 10 14 16 19 23 35 36 40 45 46 52; **S**8875	14	10	S		86	2586	35	40.7	10	189	6417	2749	173
MONTICELLO—Platt County													
★□ JOHN AND MARY KIRBY HOSPITAL, 1111 N. State St., Zip 61856; tel. 217/762-2115; Thomas D. Dixon, adm. **A**1a 9 10 **F**1 6 14 15 16 23 24 30 35 41 43 44 45 47 50	23	10	S		22	555	9	40.9	0	0	1807	793	60
MORRIS—Grundy County													
★□ MORRIS HOSPITAL, 150 W. High St., Zip 60450; tel. 815/942-2932; Frederick E. Butts, pres. (Nonreporting) **A**1a 9 10	23	10	S		94	—	—	—	—	—	—	—	—
MORRISON—Whiteside County													
★ MORRISON COMMUNITY HOSPITAL, 303 N. Jackson St., Zip 61270; tel. 815/772-4003; Kent L. Brown, adm. (Total facility includes 38 beds in nursing home-type unit) **A**9 10 **F**1 3 6 12 14 16 19 23 24 35 40 42 44 45 46 52	16	10	S	TF	86	890	41	47.7	9	102	3009	1706	84
				H	48	640	8	—	9	102	2091	1116	63
MOUNT CARMEL—Wabash County													
★□ WABASH GENERAL HOSPITAL DISTRICT, 1418 College Dr., Zip 62863; tel. 618/262-8621; Bill Vokonas, adm. **A**1a 9 10 **F**1 3 10 12 16 23 35 36 40 41 45 46; **S**1755	16	10	S		64	2038	27	42.2	8	212	5978	2293	128
MOUNT VERNON—Jefferson County													
CROSSROADS COMMUNITY HOSPITAL (Formerly Mount Vernon Hospital), 8 Doctors Park, Zip 62864; tel. 618/244-5500; Ron Wolff, adm. **A**9 10 **F**1 3 10 12 16 20 23 35 41 45; **S**5895	33	10	S		55	1627	26	47.3	0	0	—	—	103
★□ GOOD SAMARITAN HOSPITAL, 605 N. 12th St., Zip 62864; tel. 618/242-4600; Herbert H. Bell, pres. **A**1a 9 10 **F**1 2 3 5 6 9 12 14 15 16 20 21 23 24 26 30 32 33 35 36 40 41 44 45 46 47 52 53; **S**5365	21	10	S		188	7332	129	68.6	8	709	23644	11470	654
MOUNT VERNON HOSPITAL, See Crossroads Community Hospital													

Hospital, Address, Telephone, Administrator, Approval and Facility Codes, Multihospital System Code	Classification Codes				Inpatient Data				Newborn Data		Expense (thousands of dollars)		
★ American Hospital Association (AHA) membership □ Joint Commission on Accreditation of Hospitals (JCAH) accreditation + American Osteopathic Hospital Association (AOHA) membership ○ American Osteopathic Association (AOA) accreditation Δ Commission on Accreditation of Rehabilitation Facilities (CARF) accreditation Control codes 61, 63, 64, 71, 72 and 73 indicate hospitals listed by AOHA, but not registered by AHA. For definition of numerical codes, see page A2	Control	Service	Stay	Facilities	Beds	Admissions	Census	Occupancy (percent)	Bassinets	Births	Total	Payroll	Personnel
MURPHYSBORO—Jackson County													
★□ ST. JOSEPH MEMORIAL HOSPITAL, 800 N. Second St., P O Box 588, Zip 62966; tel. 618/684-3156; John D. Groves, pres. & chief exec. off. **A**1a 9 10 **F**1 6 14 15 23 35 40 45 46 52; **S**0205	23	10	S		62	2579	37	59.7	12	242	5716	2750	169
NAPERVILLE—Du Page County													
★□ EDWARD HOSPITAL, 801 S. Washington St., Zip 60566; tel. 312/355-0450; John R. Whitcomb, pres. **A**1a 2 9 10 **F**1 3 6 10 12 15 16 23 32 35 36 37 40 44 45 46 52 53; **S**2495	23	10	S		163	6764	95	58.3	24	768	27235	12432	515
NASHVILLE—Washington County													
★□ WASHINGTON COUNTY HOSPITAL, 603 S. Grand St., Zip 62263; tel. 618/327-8236; Thomas K. Janssen, adm. **A**1a 9 10 **F**1 3 6 10 15 16 21 23 35 40 41 45 53	16	10	S		68	1344	18	26.5	6	127	3421	1631	101
NORMAL—McLean County													
□ BROKAW HOSPITAL, Virginia & Franklin Sts., Zip 61761; tel. 309/454-1400 (Nonreporting) **A**1a 9 10; **S**9305	23	10	S		213	—	—	—	—	—	—	—	—
NORTH CHICAGO—Lake County													
★□ VETERANS ADMINISTRATION MEDICAL CENTER, 3001 Green Bay Rd., Zip 60064; tel. 312/688-1900; Lawrence C. Stewart, dir. (Total facility includes 190 beds in nursing home-type unit) **A**1a 3 5 8 **F**1 3 6 10 12 14 15 16 19 23 24 25 26 27 28 29 30 31 32 33 34 35 42 44 46 47 48 49 50	45	10	L	TF H	1254 1064	6315 6225	906 729	72.2 —	0 0	0 0	81043 —	49381 —	1794 1715
NORTHLAKE—Cook County													
□ ST. ANNE'S HOSPITAL-WEST, 365 E. North Ave., Zip 60164; tel. 312/345-8100; Bernard Dickens Sr., chief exec. off. **A**1a 9 10 **F**1 3 6 10 12 14 15 16 20 23 24 26 30 34 35 44 46 50 52; **S**0135	21	10	S		78	1385	19	24.4	0	0	9296	2903	100
OAK FOREST—Cook County													
★□ Δ OAK FOREST HOSPITAL OF COOK COUNTY, 15900 S. Cicero Ave., Zip 60452; tel. 312/928-4200; Edmund G. Lawler, dir. **A**1a 7 10 **F**1 3 6 10 12 14 15 16 19 20 23 24 25 26 32 33 34 35 37 42 44 46 47	13	48	L		1054	1540	929	88.1	0	0	68250	39527	1968
OAK LAWN—Cook County													
★□ Δ CHRIST HOSPITAL AND MEDICAL CENTER (Formerly Christ Hospital), 4440 W. 95th St., Zip 60453; tel. 312/425-8000; Joseph W. Beard, vice-pres. & chief exec. **A**1a 2 3 5 6 7 8 9 10 **F**1 2 3 4 5 6 7 8 9 10 11 12 14 15 16 20 23 24 26 27 29 30 32 33 34 35 36 37 38 40 42 43 44 45 46 47 48 49 50 51 52 53 54; **S**1225	21	10	S		873	26065	579	66.3	40	3728	142324	64066	2707
OAK PARK—Cook County													
★□ OAK PARK HOSPITAL, 520 S. Maple Ave., Zip 60304; tel. 312/383-9300; Jacolyn Schlautman, actg. pres. **A**1a 9 10 **F**1 2 3 6 7 8 9 10 11 12 14 15 16 17 20 21 23 26 28 32 35 36 40 43 44 45 46 52 53 54; **S**6745	21	10	S		305	7712	162	53.1	24	194	33684	14882	682
★□ WEST SUBURBAN HOSPITAL MEDICAL CENTER, Erie at Austin, Zip 60302; tel. 312/383-6200; Norman B. Goodman, pres. & chief exec. off. **A**1a 2 3 5 8 9 10 **F**1 2 3 6 7 8 9 10 11 12 14 15 16 20 23 26 30 33 34 35 36 37 38 40 41 44 45 46 52 53 54	23	10	S		372	9849	178	48.1	22	1307	58503	23967	1347
OLNEY—Richland County													
★□ RICHLAND MEMORIAL HOSPITAL, 800 E. Locust St., Zip 62450; tel. 618/395-2131; Harvey H. Pettry, adm. **A**1a 2 9 10 **F**1 3 5 6 10 11 12 14 15 16 23 26 27 30 32 33 35 36 40 41 45 46 47 52 53	13	10	S		146	4551	69	47.3	8	457	14808	5825	371
OLYMPIA FIELDS—Cook County													
○ + OLYMPIA FIELDS OSTEOPATHIC MEDICAL CENTER, 20201 Crawford Ave., Zip 60461; tel. 312/747-4000; Lawrence U. Haspel DO, exec. vice-pres. **A**9 11 12 13 **F**1 2 3 4 6 9 10 12 14 15 16 23 24 25 26 27 28 30 32 33 34 35 36 37 38 40 41 42 44 45 46 49 50 51 52 53 54	23	10	S		173	7063	120	69.4	15	607	45241	18400	720
OTTAWA—La Salle County													
★□ COMMUNITY HOSPITAL OF OTTAWA, 1100 E. Norris Dr., Zip 61350; tel. 815/433-3100; Yale M. Wolk, pres. & chief exec. off. **A**1a 9 10 **F**1 3 6 10 12 14 15 16 21 23 26 27 29 30 34 35 36 40 41 42 44 45 48 49 52 53	23	10	S		155	4334	68	43.9	16	411	13268	6016	350
PALOS HEIGHTS—Cook County													
★□ PALOS COMMUNITY HOSPITAL, 12251 S. 80th Ave., Zip 60463; tel. 312/361-4500; Sr. Margaret Wright, pres. **A**1a 9 10 **F**1 2 3 6 7 9 10 11 12 14 15 16 23 24 26 27 28 30 32 33 34 35 36 40 41 42 44 45 46 48 49 52 53 54	23	10	S		409	15586	287	70.2	32	1784	72063	36314	1454
PANA—Christian County													
★□ PANA COMMUNITY HOSPITAL, S. Locust St., Zip 62557; tel. 217/562-2131; John Mauldin, adm. **A**1a 9 10 **F**1 3 6 10 12 14 15 16 23 34 35 37 41 43 44 45 47 53; **S**1755	23	10	S		60	1749	20	33.3	0	0	3576	1594	102
PARIS—Edgar County													
★□ PARIS COMMUNITY HOSPITAL, E. Court St., Zip 61944; tel. 217/465-4141; Lawrence Wills, adm. **A**1a 9 10 **F**1 3 6 10 12 14 15 16 17 23 35 37 40 44 45 47 50; **S**2495	23	10	S		98	2007	30	30.6	12	196	5721	3005	176
PARK RIDGE—Cook County													
LUTHERAN CENTER-SUBSTANCE ABUSE, See Parkside Lutheran Hospital													
★□ Δ LUTHERAN GENERAL HOSPITAL, 1775 Dempster St., Zip 60068; tel. 312/696-2210; Roger S. Hunt, pres. & chief exec. off. **A**1a 2 3 5 6 7 8 9 10 **F**1 2 3 4 5 6 7 8 9 10 11 12 14 15 16 20 23 24 25 26 27 28 29 30 32 33 34 35 36 37 38 40 42 43 44 45 46 47 51 52 53 54; **S**6295	21	10	S		587	22269	481	79.0	44	3704	143738	64928	2535
★□ PARKSIDE LUTHERAN HOSPITAL (Formerly Lutheran Center-Substance Abuse), 1700 Luther Lane, Zip 60068; tel. 312/696-6050; Rev. John E. Keller, exec. dir. (Nonreporting) **A**1b ; **S**6295	23	82	S		88	—	—	—	—	—	—	—	—
PAXTON—Ford County													
□ PAXTON COMMUNITY HOSPITAL, 651 E. Pells St., P O Box 22, Zip 60957; tel. 217/379-4811; Edward T. McGrath, exec. dir. (Nonreporting) **A**1a 9 10; **S**9795	23	10	S		29	—	—	—	—	—	—	—	—
PEKIN—Tazewell County													
★□ PEKIN MEMORIAL HOSPITAL, Court & 14th Sts., Zip 61554; tel. 309/347-1151; Norman F. Webb II, pres. **A**1a 9 10 **F**1 3 5 6 10 12 14 15 16 21 23 24 26 34 35 36 37 40 41 44 45 46 47 48 49 52 53 54	23	10	S		202	5732	103	51.0	20	432	19620	9980	479
PEORIA—Peoria County													
□ GEORGE A. ZELLER MENTAL HEALTH CENTER, 5407 N. University St., Zip 61614; tel. 309/693-5000; Robert W. Vyverberg EdD, supt. **A**1b 10 **F**16 19 24 32 33 46 47	12	22	L		252	1174	224	96.6	0	0	10623	7773	354
★□ METHODIST MEDICAL CENTER OF ILLINOIS, 221 N.E. Glen Oak Ave., Zip 61636; tel. 309/672-5522; James K. Knoble, pres. **A**1a 2 3 5 6 9 10 **F**1 2 3 4 5 6 7 8 9 10 11 12 14 15 16 17 20 21 23 24 25 26 27 30 32 33 34 35 36 37 40 41 42 44 45 46 47 52 53 54; **S**8875	21	10	S		479	18494	372	77.7	32	1823	84780	38293	2052
★□ PROCTOR COMMUNITY HOSPITAL, 5409 N. Knoxville Ave., Zip 61614; tel. 309/691-1000; Norman H. Laconte, pres. & chief exec. off. **A**1a 9 10 **F**1 3 6 10 12 14 15 16 23 24 26 33 34 35 36 40 44 45 46 47 48 49 52 53 54	23	10	S		244	7375	138	56.1	12	535	30772	14435	706

Hospital, Address, Telephone, Administrator, Approval and Facility Codes, Multihospital System Code	Classification Codes				Inpatient Data				Newborn Data		Expense (thousands of dollars)		
★ American Hospital Association (AHA) membership □ Joint Commission on Accreditation of Hospitals (JCAH) accreditation + American Osteopathic Hospital Association (AOHA) membership ○ American Osteopathic Association (AOA) accreditation Δ Commission on Accreditation of Rehabilitation Facilities (CARF) accreditation Control codes 61, 63, 64, 71, 72 and 73 indicate hospitals listed by AOHA, but not registered by AHA. For definition of numerical codes, see page A2	Control	Service	Stay	Facilities	Beds	Admissions	Census	Occupancy (percent)	Bassinets	Births	Total	Payroll	Personnel
★□ SAINT FRANCIS MEDICAL CENTER, 530 N.E. Glen Oak Ave., Zip 61637; tel. 309/655-2000; Sr. M. Canisia, adm. **A**1a 2 3 5 6 8 9 10 **F**1 2 3 4 5 6 9 10 11 12 13 14 15 16 17 20 21 23 24 25 26 27 28 29 30 32 34 35 36 39 40 41 42 45 46 47 51 52 53 54; **S**5335	21	10	S		855	22446	487	57.0	55	2409	121726	57603	2691
PERU—La Salle County													
★□ ILLINOIS VALLEY COMMUNITY HOSPITAL, 925 West St., Zip 61354; tel. 815/223-3300; Ralph B. Berkley, adm. **A**1a 9 10 **F**1 3 5 6 10 12 16 21 23 24 35 36 40 41 44 45 46 52 53; **S**8875	23	10	S		108	4420	57	51.4	12	462	12433	5775	289
PINCKNEYVILLE—Perry County													
★□ PINCKNEYVILLE COMMUNITY HOSPITAL, 101 N. Walnut St., Zip 62274; tel. 618/357-2187; George W. Ranta, adm. (Total facility includes 32 beds in nursing home-type unit) **A**1a 9 10 **F**1 5 6 12 14 15 16 19 23 24 26 30 34 35 40 42 44 45	16	10	S	TF	84	1610	55	65.5	10	104	4281	2305	134
				H	52	1506	25	—	10	104	3885	1947	107
PITTSFIELD—Pike County													
★□ ILLINI COMMUNITY HOSPITAL, 640 W. Washington St., Zip 62363; tel. 217/285-2113; Kathleen Wegener, adm. **A**1a 9 10 **F**1 3 6 12 16 23 34 35 36 40 43 44 46 50 52 53; **S**1755	23	10	S		59	1725	26	44.1	5	131	4678	2184	116
PONTIAC—Livingston County													
PONTIAC CORRECTIONAL CENTER, 701 Vermillion St., Box 99, Zip 61764; tel. 815/842-2816; Vickie Bybee, adm. (Nonreporting)	12	11	S		35	—	—	—	—	—	—	—	—
★□ SAINT JAMES HOSPITAL, 610 E. Water St., Zip 61764; tel. 815/842-2828; Steve L. Urosevich, adm. (Total facility includes 14 beds in nursing home-type unit) **A**1a 2 9 10 **F**1 3 5 6 10 12 14 16 19 23 28 34 35 36 40 45 53; **S**5335	21	10	S	TF	91	3455	57	62.6	10	282	9870	4603	244
				H	77	3270	47	—	10	282	9343	4432	236
PRINCETON—Bureau County													
★□ PERRY MEMORIAL HOSPITAL, 530 Park Ave. E., Zip 61356; tel. 815/875-2811; William H. Spitler III, pres. **A**1a 9 10 **F**1 3 6 10 12 15 16 23 35 36 40 45	14	10	S		97	3560	50	51.5	10	287	8854	4307	225
QUINCY—Adams County													
★□ BLESSING HOSPITAL, Broadway at 11th St., Zip 62301; tel. 217/223-5811; Lawrence L. Swearingen, pres. (Total facility includes 24 beds in nursing home-type unit) **A**1a 2 3 5 6 9 10 **F**1 2 3 5 6 7 8 9 10 11 12 14 15 16 19 20 21 23 24 25 26 28 29 30 32 34 35 36 40 41 42 44 45 46 47 50 52 53 54	23	10	S	TF	265	8429	188	70.9	25	790	26116	12842	754
				H	241	8432	165	—	25	790	25877	12606	737
★□ ST. MARY HOSPITAL, 1415 Vermont St., Zip 62301; tel. 217/223-1200; Roland D. Olen, pres. **A**1a 2 3 5 9 10 **F**1 3 5 6 10 11 12 14 15 16 23 24 27 30 32 33 34 35 36 40 41 42 44 45 46 48 50 52 53; **S**1485	21	10	S		222	6164	128	58.4	10	469	22514	9382	539
RANTOUL—Champaign County													
U. S. AIR FORCE HOSPITAL CHANUTE, See Chanute Air Force Base													
RED BUD—Randolph County													
★□ ST. CLEMENT HOSPITAL, 325 Spring St., Zip 62278; tel. 618/282-3831; Harlow J. Herman, pres. **A**1a 9 10 **F**1 3 5 6 12 14 15 16 23 34 35 36 40 45 52 53; **S**0205	21	10	S		105	2593	39	37.1	8	204	7039	3362	205
ROBINSON—Crawford County													
★□ CRAWFORD MEMORIAL HOSPITAL, 1000 N. Allen St., Zip 62454; tel. 618/544-3131; Merle Hansen, adm. (Total facility includes 40 beds in nursing home-type unit) **A**1a 9 10 **F**1 3 6 12 14 15 16 19 23 34 35 36 40 41 44 45 47 53; **S**1755	16	10	S	TF	105	2839	67	63.8	8	184	6284	2728	176
				H	65	2763	32	—	8	184	5989	2505	160
ROCHELLE—Ogle County													
★□ ROCHELLE COMMUNITY HOSPITAL, 900 N. Second St., Zip 61068; tel. 815/562-2181; Robert G. Knapp, adm. **A**1a 9 10 **F**1 3 6 10 15 16 23 35 36 40 45	23	10	S		42	1375	17	40.5	8	172	3800	1776	102
ROCK ISLAND—Rock Island County													
★□ Δ FRANCISCAN MEDICAL CENTER, 2701 17th St., Zip 61201; tel. 309/793-2121; Michael A. Turner, exec. vice-pres. & chief exec. off. **A**1a 7 9 10 **F**1 3 6 10 12 14 15 16 22 23 24 25 26 27 28 29 30 31 32 33 34 35 36 40 43 44 45 46 47 49 53 54	23	10	S		265	7259	127	47.9	36	657	33087	15893	758
ROCKFORD—Winnebago County													
□ H. DOUGLAS SINGER MENTAL HEALTH AND DEVELOPMENTAL CENTER, 4402 N. Main St., Box 62, Zip 61105; tel. 815/987-7096; Richard F. Kunnert, fac dir. **A**1b 10 **F**15 19 23 24 29 32 33 42 43 44 46 50	12	22	L		219	734	208	95.0	0	0	10078	—	301
★□ Δ ROCKFORD MEMORIAL HOSPITAL, 2400 N. Rockton Ave., Zip 61103; tel. 815/968-6861; H. W. Maysent, pres. **A**1a 2 3 5 6 7 9 10 **F**1 2 3 4 5 6 7 8 9 10 11 12 14 15 16 17 20 23 24 25 26 30 33 34 35 36 37 38 40 42 43 44 45 46 47 48 49 51 52 53 54	23	10	S		396	14904	274	68.8	33	2126	65944	31275	1373
★□ SAINT ANTHONY MEDICAL CENTER (Formerly St. Anthony Hospital-Medical Center), 5666 E. State St., Zip 61101; tel. 815/226-2000; Kevin D. Schoeplein, adm. (Nonreporting) **A**1a 2 3 5 6 9 10; **S**5335	21	10	S		258	—	—	—	—	—	—	—	—
★□ SWEDISHAMERICAN HOSPITAL, 1400 Charles St., Zip 61108; tel. 815/968-4400; Robert A. Henry MD, pres. & chief exec. off.; Robert B. Klint, exec. vice-pres. & chief oper. off. **A**1a 2 3 5 9 10 **F**1 3 4 5 6 7 8 9 10 11 12 14 15 16 17 23 24 26 27 29 30 32 33 34 35 36 37 40 41 42 43 44 45 46 47 50 52 53 54	23	10	S		393	13729	251	63.9	31	1695	54633	24078	1329
ROSICLARE—Hardin County													
★□ HARDIN COUNTY GENERAL HOSPITAL, Ferrell Rd., Zip 62982; tel. 618/285-6634; Roby D. Williams, adm. **A**1a 9 10 **F**6 15 16 35 45	23	10	S		48	1689	27	56.3	0	0	2481	1148	111
RUSHVILLE—Schuyler County													
★ SARAH D. CULBERTSON MEMORIAL HOSPITAL, 238 S. Congress St., Zip 62681; tel. 217/322-4321; Charles Berry Jr., adm. (Total facility includes 20 beds in nursing home-type unit) **A**9 10 **F**1 3 6 12 16 19 23 35 40 44 45 46	16	10	S	TF	70	1527	32	46.4	8	122	2811	1358	112
				H	50	1476	26	—	8	122	2763	1322	89
SALEM—Marion County													
★□ PUBLIC HOSPITAL OF THE TOWN OF SALEM, Bryan Memorial Park, Zip 62881; tel. 618/548-3194; Charles D. Roberts, adm. **A**1a 9 10 **F**1 6 12 14 16 23 35 41 44 45; **S**0565	23	10	S		64	2111	26	40.6	6	8	4868	2381	136
SANDWICH—De Kalb County													
★□ SANDWICH COMMUNITY HOSPITAL, 11 E. Pleasant Ave., Zip 60548; tel. 815/786-8484; Marvin D. Tice, pres. **A**1a 9 10 **F**1 3 6 10 12 14 15 16 23 35 40 45 46 52 53	23	10	S		53	1844	26	45.6	8	145	4884	2178	121
SAVANNA—Carroll County													
SAVANNA CITY HOSPITAL, 1125 N. Fifth St., Zip 61074; tel. 815/273-7751; Richard D. Phillips, adm. **A**9 10 **F**1 6 14 16 23 35 37 40 43 45 52; **S**5165	14	10	S		34	698	8	23.5	6	38	1681	740	55
SCOTT AIR FORCE BASE—St. Clair County													
★□ U. S. AIR FORCE MEDICAL CENTER, Zip 62225; tel. 618/256-1170; Col. Michael J. Torma MC USAF, cmdr. (Nonreporting) **A**1a 3	41	10	S		165	—	—	—	—	—	—	—	—
SHELBYVILLE—Shelby County													
★□ SHELBY MEMORIAL HOSPITAL, S. First & Cedar Sts., Zip 62565; tel. 217/774-3961; Garland Strohl, adm. **A**1a 9 10 **F**1 3 6 14 15 16 23 24 35 44 45 46 52	23	10	S		51	1816	23	45.1	0	0	3931	1973	156
SILVIS—Rock Island County													
★□ ILLINI HOSPITAL, 801 Hospital Rd., Zip 61282; tel. 309/792-9363; Gary E. Larson, adm. **A**1a 9 10 **F**1 3 6 10 12 15 16 23 35 40 43 45 46 47 52 53	16	10	S		150	5441	70	46.7	24	543	16988	8651	384

Hospital, Address, Telephone, Administrator, Approval and Facility Codes, Multihospital System Code	Classification Codes				Inpatient Data				Newborn Data		Expense (thousands of dollars)		
★ American Hospital Association (AHA) membership ☐ Joint Commission on Accreditation of Hospitals (JCAH) accreditation + American Osteopathic Hospital Association (AOHA) membership ○ American Osteopathic Association (AOA) accreditation Δ Commission on Accreditation of Rehabilitation Facilities (CARF) accreditation Control codes 61, 63, 64, 71, 72 and 73 indicate hospitals listed by AOHA, but not registered by AHA. For definition of numerical codes, see page A2	Control	Service	Stay	Facilities	Beds	Admissions	Census	Occupancy (percent)	Bassinets	Births	Total	Payroll	Personnel
SKOKIE—Cook County													
☐ CPC OLD ORCHARD HOSPITAL, 9700 Kenton St., Zip 60076; tel. 312/676-7600; Phil Donahue, adm. **A**1b 9 10 **F**24 28 29 30 32 33 34 42 43; **S**0785	33	22	L		99	637	71	71.7	0	0	—	—	134
★☐ SKOKIE VALLEY HOSPITAL, 9600 Gross Point Rd., Zip 60076; tel. 312/677-9600; Ralph G. Hutchins, pres. **A**1a b 2 9 10 **F**1 3 6 10 12 14 15 16 20 23 35 36 37 40 44 45 46 47 48 49 52	23	10	S		218	6600	133	61.0	26	558	29247	13959	647
SPARTA—Randolph County													
★☐ SPARTA COMMUNITY HOSPITAL, 818 E. Broadway St., Zip 62286; tel. 618/443-2177; William H. Nehrt, adm. **A**1a 9 10 **F**1 12 14 15 23 35 36 37 40 45 46	16	10	S		53	1662	20	37.7	8	96	3880	1727	114
SPRING VALLEY—Bureau County													
★☐ ST. MARGARET'S HOSPITAL, 600 E. First St., Zip 61362; tel. 815/664-5311; Kelby K. Krabbenhoft, pres. **A**1a 9 10 **F**1 3 6 7 9 10 12 14 15 16 21 23 32 34 35 36 40 45 46 47 52 53; **S**5805	21	10	S		100	4175	59	39.1	16	280	12134	5208	288
SPRINGFIELD—Sangamon County													
☐ ANDREW MCFARLAND MENTAL HEALTH CENTER, 901 Southwind Rd., Zip 62703; tel. 217/786-6994; Nieves Tan-Lachica MD, supt. **A**1a b 3 5 **F**33 46 47	12	22	L		146	449	132	90.4	0	0	6366	4647	196
★☐ HUMANA HOSPITAL -SPRINGFIELD, 5230 S. Sixth St., Frontage Rd., Zip 62703; tel. 217/529-7151; Austin D. Edwards, exec. dir. (Nonreporting) **A**1a 9 10; **S**1235	33	10	S		100	—	—	—	—	—	—	—	—
★☐ Δ MEMORIAL MEDICAL CENTER, 800 N. Rutledge St., Zip 62781; tel. 217/788-3000; Robert T. Clarke, pres. & chief exec. off. **A**1a 2 3 5 7 8 9 10 **F**1 2 3 4 6 7 8 9 10 11 12 13 14 15 16 20 21 22 23 24 25 26 27 28 29 30 31 32 33 34 35 36 39 40 41 42 44 45 46 47 52 53 54	23	10	S		566	19494	449	79.0	26	1580	99934	48506	2282
★☐ ST. JOHN'S HOSPITAL, 800 E. Carpenter St., Zip 62769; tel. 217/544-6464; Sr. Ann Pitsenberger, exec. vice-pres. (Total facility includes 67 beds in nursing home-type unit) **A**1a 2 3 5 6 8 9 10 **F**1 3 4 5 6 7 8 9 10 11 12 14 15 16 17 19 20 21 23 24 26 27 30 31 32 33 35 36 37 38 40 41 42 43 44 45 46 47 48 49 50 51 52 53 54; **S**5355	21	10	S	TF H	744 677	27288 26613	607 560	81.9 —	24 24	2294 2294	111560 107243	58137 55451	2806 2646
ST. CHARLES—Kane County													
★☐ DELNOR COMMUNITY HOSPITAL (Includes Community Hospital, 416 S. Second St., Geneva, Zip 60134, tel. 312/232-0771; Delnor Hospital; 975 N. Fifth Ave., Zip 60174; tel. 312/584-3300), 975 N. Fifth Ave., Zip 60174; tel. 312/584-3300; Craig A. Livermore, pres & chief exec. off. **A**1a 9 10 **F**1 3 6 9 10 11 12 14 15 16 23 26 30 34 35 36 37 38 40 41 45 46 47 52 53	23	10	S		200	7096	99	47.8	17	1538	27257	13119	671
STAUNTON—Macoupin County													
★☐ COMMUNITY MEMORIAL HOSPITAL, 216 W. Pennsylvania St., Zip 62088; tel. 618/635-2200; Patrick B. Heise, exec. dir. **A**1a 9 10 **F**1 3 6 10 12 14 15 16 23 34 35 40 41 44 45 46 52 53	23	10	S		59	1499	21	35.6	7	96	4559	2192	112
STERLING—Whiteside County													
★☐ COMMUNITY GENERAL HOSPITAL, 1601 First Ave., Zip 61081; tel. 815/625-0400; Darryl Wahler, chief exec. off. **A**1a 2 9 10 **F**1 3 5 6 10 12 14 15 16 23 24 26 34 35 36 40 44 45 46 52 53	14	10	S		129	5620	73	54.9	15	658	15320	7109	387
STREATOR—La Salle County													
★☐ ST. MARY'S HOSPITAL, 111 E. Spring St., Zip 61364; tel. 815/673-2311; Jim Lansford, actg. adm. **A**1a 9 10 **F**1 3 6 7 8 9 10 11 12 14 15 16 23 24 26 32 33 34 35 36 40 41 43 44 45 46 49 52 53; **S**5355	21	10	S		164	5560	95	57.9	28	385	16673	8788	473
SYCAMORE—De Kalb County													
★☐ SYCAMORE HOSPITAL (Formerly Sycamore Municipal Hospital), 225 Edward St., Zip 60178; tel. 815/895-2144; Martin Losoff, adm. **A**1a 9 10 **F**1 6 9 10 11 12 14 15 16 23 24 34 35 36 40 43 44 45 46 47 53	33	10	S		50	1152	15	30.0	12	224	3870	1737	95
TAYLORVILLE—Christian County													
★☐ ST. VINCENT MEMORIAL HOSPITAL, 201 E. Pleasant St., Zip 62568; tel. 217/824-3331; Robert B. Cooper, pres. (Total facility includes 30 beds in nursing home-type unit) **A**1a 9 10 **F**1 3 6 12 14 15 16 19 23 24 26 30 35 36 40 41 43 44 45 46 50 52 53; **S**0205	21	10	S	TF H	167 137	4099 3978	73 55	43.7 —	8 8	197 197	9445 9190	4959 4735	273 255
TINLEY PARK—Cook County													
☐ TINLEY PARK MENTAL HEALTH CENTER, 7400 W. 183rd St., Zip 60477; tel. 312/532-7000; Abdul Basit PhD, supt. **A**1b 10 **F**12 24 33 42	12	22	S		365	5130	349	100.0	0	0	15044	12030	524
TUSCOLA—Douglas County													
★☐ DOUGLAS COUNTY JARMAN MEMORIAL HOSPITAL, 704 N. Main St., Zip 61953; tel. 217/253-3361; Mark F. Fedyk, adm. **A**1a 9 10 **F**1 3 6 10 16 23 24 34 35 40 42 43 44 45 46 47 52	13	10	S		43	1085	15	34.9	7	144	—	—	89
URBANA—Champaign County													
★☐ CARLE FOUNDATION HOSPITAL, 611 W. Park St., Zip 61801; tel. 217/337-3311; Charles B. Van Vorst, pres. & chief exec. off. (Total facility includes 200 beds in nursing home-type unit) **A**1a 2 3 5 8 9 10 **F**1 3 15 16 19 23 24 26 30 32 35 36 37 40 41 44 45 46 47 51 52 54	23	10	S	TF H	483 283	12471 11989	316 181	65.4 —	20 20	1287 1287	46101 42929	18837 17511	1069 950
MCKINLEY MEMORIAL HOSPITAL, 1109 S. Lincoln Ave., Zip 61801; tel. 217/333-0180; Robert F. Mangan, adm. (Nonreporting) **A**9	12	11	S		16	—	—	—	—	—	—	—	—
★☐ Δ MERCY HOSPITAL, 1400 W. Park Ave., Zip 61801; tel. 217/337-2233; William Casey, pres. & chief exec. off. **A**1a 2 3 5 7 8 9 10 **F**1 2 3 4 6 7 8 9 10 11 12 14 15 16 20 21 23 24 25 26 27 30 33 34 35 36 40 42 44 45 46 47 52; **S**4025	21	10	S		222	7369	128	57.7	16	1135	34753	14499	741
VANDALIA—Fayette County													
★☐ FAYETTE COUNTY HOSPITAL, Seventh & Taylor Sts., Zip 62471; tel. 618/283-1231; M. Jean Chambless, adm. (Total facility includes 134 beds in nursing home-type unit) **A**1a 9 10 **F**1 3 6 15 16 19 23 26 34 35 40 44 45 50; **S**1755	16	10	S	TF H	182 48	1623 1442	148 20	81.3 —	8 8	149 149	6873 4798	3329 2007	224 146
WATSEKA—Iroquois County													
★☐ IROQUOIS MEMORIAL HOSPITAL AND RESIDENT HOME, 200 Fairman St., Zip 60970; tel. 815/432-5201; Paul F. Wenz, chief exec. off. (Total facility includes 51 beds in nursing home-type unit) **A**1a 9 10 **F**1 3 6 10 12 14 15 16 19 23 34 35 36 37 40 44 45 46 50	23	10	S	TF H	119 68	2462 2347	76 34	50.3 —	9 9	232 232	8080 7069	4295 3718	258 227
WAUKEGAN—Lake County													
★☐ SAINT THERESE MEDICAL CENTER, 2615 Washington St., Zip 60085; tel. 312/249-3900; Nora C. O'Malley, pres. (Total facility includes 40 beds in nursing home-type unit) **A**1a 2 9 10 **F**1 3 5 6 9 10 11 12 14 15 16 19 21 23 24 26 27 30 32 33 34 35 36 40 41 42 44 45 46 47 50 52 53	21	10	S	TF H	326 286	12160 11760	203 190	62.3 —	18 18	1315 1315	45281 44839	21739 21375	1063 1049
★☐ VICTORY MEMORIAL HOSPITAL, 1324 N. Sheridan Rd., Zip 60085; tel. 312/360-3000; Donald Wasson, pres. **A**1a 2 9 10 **F**1 3 6 9 10 11 12 14 15 16 20 23 24 35 36 37 40 41 44 45 46 48 49 50 52 53	23	10	S		315	9650	194	61.6	41	811	40219	20566	930
WEST FRANKFORT—Franklin County													
WEST FRANKFORT UNITED MINE WORKERS OF AMERICA UNION HOSPITAL, 507 W. St. Louis St., Zip 62896; tel. 618/932-2155; William D. Palmer, adm. **A**9 10 **F**1 6 14 15 16 23 34 35 36 37 40 43 45 52	23	10	S		42	2141	35	48.6	6	186	5295	2851	168

Hospital, Address, Telephone, Administrator, Approval and Facility Codes, Multihospital System Code	Classification Codes				Inpatient Data				Newborn Data		Expense (thousands of dollars)		
★ American Hospital Association (AHA) membership □ Joint Commission on Accreditation of Hospitals (JCAH) accreditation + American Osteopathic Hospital Association (AOHA) membership ○ American Osteopathic Association (AOA) accreditation Δ Commission on Accreditation of Rehabilitation Facilities (CARF) accreditation Control codes 61, 63, 64, 71, 72 and 73 indicate hospitals listed by AOHA, but not registered by AHA. For definition of numerical codes, see page A2	Control	Service	Stay	Facilities	Beds	Admissions	Census	Occupancy (percent)	Bassinets	Births	Total	Payroll	Personnel
WHEATON—Du Page County													
★□ Δ MARIANJOY REHABILITATION CENTER, 26 W. 171 Roosevelt Rd., P O Box 795, Zip 60189; tel. 312/462-4000; Bruce A. Schurman, pres. **A**1a 7 9 10 **F**16 23 24 26 32 33 42 43 44 45 46 47; **S**6745	21	46	L		91	1035	81	89.0	0	0	19013	9530	457
WHITE HALL—Greene County													
WHITE HALL HOSPITAL, 407 N. Main St., Zip 62092; tel. 217/374-2121; Lawrence P. Bear, adm. **A**9 10 **F**1 12 14 15 16 23 35 36 37 38 40 42 43 45 46 47 50	23	10	S		30	925	16	53.3	4	5	2003	878	73
WINFIELD—Du Page County													
★□ CENTRAL DUPAGE HOSPITAL, 25 N. Winfield Rd., Zip 60190; tel. 312/682-1600; George G. Holzhauer, pres. **A**1a 2 9 10 **F**1 2 3 4 5 6 9 10 12 14 15 16 20 23 24 26 27 28 30 31 32 33 35 36 40 41 42 44 45 46 47 50 52 53 54	23	10	S		330	15239	232	68.8	40	2787	56784	25559	1029
WOOD RIVER—Madison County													
★□ WOOD RIVER TOWNSHIP HOSPITAL, Edwardsville Rd., Zip 62095; tel. 618/254-3821; W. Eugene Cowsert, pres. **A**1a 9 10 **F**1 3 5 6 10 11 12 14 15 16 21 23 24 25 26 27 30 32 33 35 40 42 43 44 45 46 52 53	16	10	S		155	4948	104	67.1	6	191	19256	8570	446
WOODSTOCK—McHenry County													
★□ MEMORIAL HOSPITAL FOR MCHENRY COUNTY, 527 W. South St., Zip 60098; tel. 815/338-2500; Philip G. Dionne, chief exec. off. **A**1a 9 10 **F**1 3 6 10 12 14 15 16 23 24 27 30 32 33 35 36 37 40 44 45 46 47 48 52 53; **S**1755	23	10	S		123	4933	86	69.9	13	729	18827	8249	409
ZION—Lake County													
□ AMERICAN INTERNATIONAL HOSPITAL, Emmaus & Shiloh Blvd., Zip 60099; tel. 312/872-4561; Kenneth F. Sample, adm. **A**1a 9 10 **F**1 3 6 10 12 14 15 16 23 30 32 33 34 35 44 46 53; **S**0585	33	10	S		95	2267	52	54.7	0	0	17285	6016	271

Hospital, Address, Telephone, Administrator, Approval and Facility Codes, Multihospital System Code

- ★ American Hospital Association (AHA) membership
- ☐ Joint Commission on Accreditation of Hospitals (JCAH) accreditation
- \+ American Osteopathic Hospital Association (AOHA) membership
- ○ American Osteopathic Association (AOA) accreditation
- Δ Commission on Accreditation of Rehabilitation Facilities (CARF) accreditation

Control codes 61, 63, 64, 71, 72 and 73 indicate hospitals listed by AOHA, but not registered by AHA. For definition of numerical codes, see page A2

Indiana

Hospital, Address, Telephone, Administrator, Approval and Facility Codes, Multihospital System Code	Classification Codes: Control	Service	Stay	Facilities	Inpatient Data: Beds	Admissions	Census	Occupancy (percent)	Newborn Data: Bassinets	Births	Expense (thousands of dollars): Total	Payroll	Personnel
ANDERSON—Madison County													
☐★ COMMUNITY HOSPITAL OF ANDERSON AND MADISON COUNTY, 1515 N. Madison Ave., Zip 46012; tel. 317/642-8011; Stephen L. Abbott, pres. **A**1a 9 10 **F**1 3 6 10 12 14 15 16 21 23 24 27 28 30 32 33 35 36 37 40 43 44 45 47 52 53	23	10	S		207	6664	104	50.2	20	684	24465	10464	550
☐★ ST. JOHN'S HEALTHCARE CORPORATION (Formerly St. John's Medical Center), 2015 Jackson St., Zip 46014; tel. 317/649-2511; James H. Stephens, pres. & chief exec. off. **A**1a 9 10 **F**1 3 6 7 8 9 10 11 12 14 15 16 21 23 24 26 27 30 32 34 35 36 40 41 44 45 46 48 52 53; **S**5585	21	10	S		371	10145	187	50.4	25	832	40719	15490	876
ANGOLA—Steuben County													
★ CAMERON MEMORIAL COMMUNITY HOSPITAL, 416 E. Maumee St., Zip 46703; tel. 219/665-2141; Joe Hochderffer, adm. **A**9 10 **F**1 3 14 16 21 23 35 36 40 41 45 46 47 48 52	23	10	S		61	1779	28	45.9	10	272	4777	2033	119
AUBURN—De Kalb County													
★ DEKALB MEMORIAL HOSPITAL, E. Seventh St., P O Box 542, Zip 46706; tel. 219/925-4600; Jack M. Corey, pres. **A**9 10 **F**1 3 6 10 12 15 16 23 30 34 35 36 40 41 45 46	23	10	S		77	2565	33	41.8	10	440	6957	3354	209
BATESVILLE—Ripley County													
☐★ MARGARET MARY COMMUNITY HOSPITAL, 321 Mitchell Ave., Zip 47006; tel. 812/934-6624; James K. Stroebel, chief exec. off. (Total facility includes 35 beds in nursing home-type unit) **A**1a 9 10 **F**1 3 6 10 12 14 15 16 19 23 33 34 35 36 40 41 42 44 45 48 49 52	23	10	S	TF	120	2056	68	56.7	10	387	5579	2698	187
				H	85	2023	36	—	10	387	5331	2485	—
BEDFORD—Lawrence County													
☐★ BEDFORD MEDICAL CENTER, 2900 W. 16th St., Zip 47421; tel. 812/279-3581; Donald W. Dodds, chief exec. off. **A**1a 9 10 **F**1 3 6 10 12 14 15 16 21 23 26 29 32 33 34 35 36 40 41 44 45 46 48 49 53	23	10	S		117	3669	54	46.2	14	396	10514	4689	249
☐★ DUNN MEMORIAL HOSPITAL, 1616 23rd St., Zip 47421; tel. 812/275-3331; Richard Hahn, exec. dir. **A**1a 9 10 **F**1 3 5 6 10 12 15 16 18 20 21 23 24 28 29 30 32 33 34 35 36 40 41 43 44 45 46 50 52 53	13	10	S		137	3170	44	32.1	16	300	10238	4780	284
BEECH GROVE—Marion County													
☐★ ST. FRANCIS HOSPITAL CENTER, 1600 Albany St., Zip 46107; tel. 317/787-3311; Paul J. Stitzel, pres. & chief exec. off. **A**1a 3 5 8 9 10 **F**1 2 3 4 6 7 8 9 10 11 12 14 15 16 20 23 24 27 28 30 32 35 36 40 41 42 44 45 46 47 49 50 51 52 53 54; **S**5345	21	10	S		470	17086	330	70.2	24	2057	70429	34812	1842
BLOOMINGTON—Monroe County													
☐★ BLOOMINGTON HOSPITAL, 605 W. Second St., Box 1149, Zip 47402; tel. 812/336-6821; Roland E. Kohr, pres. **A**1a 9 10 **F**1 3 6 7 8 9 10 11 12 14 15 16 23 24 27 30 34 35 36 40 41 44 45 46 52 53 54	23	10	S		339	11928	180	59.8	35	1624	42184	19024	1035
BLUFFTON—Wells County													
☐★ CAYLOR-NICKEL HOSPITAL, One Caylor-Nickel Square, Zip 46714; tel. 219/824-3500; William F. Brockmann, pres. **A**1a 2 9 10 **F**1 2 3 5 6 7 8 9 10 11 12 14 15 16 21 23 24 26 27 28 29 30 32 33 34 35 36 40 41 42 43 44 46 47 49 52 53 54	23	10	S		188	4640	86	45.7	10	411	19774	8363	504
☐★ WELLS COMMUNITY HOSPITAL, 1100 S. Main St., Zip 46714; tel. 219/824-3210; Paul L. Bender, adm. **A**1a 9 10 **F**1 3 6 10 12 14 15 16 21 23 30 33 34 35 36 40 41 45 47	13	10	S		45	1381	19	42.2	8	210	4408	1912	129
BOONVILLE—Warrick County													
☐★ WARRICK HOSPITAL, 1116 Millis Ave., Box 629, Zip 47601; tel. 812/897-4800; Sr. Renee Rose, adm. & chief exec. off. **A**1a 9 10 **F**1 5 6 12 14 15 16 23 35 45 46; **S**1885	23	10	S		48	1421	21	43.8	0	0	5531	2540	167
BRAZIL—Clay County													
☐★ CLAY COUNTY HOSPITAL, 1206 E. National Ave., Zip 47834; tel. 812/448-2675; Richard Denney, adm. **A**1a 9 10 **F**1 3 6 10 12 14 15 16 23 26 35 36 40 44 45 46 53	13	10	S		78	1716	24	30.4	9	180	5697	1964	—
BREMEN—Marshall County													
★ COMMUNITY HOSPITAL OF BREMEN (Formerly Community Hospital of German Township), 411 S. Whitlock St., Zip 46506; tel. 219/546-2211; Jerome J. Bozek, adm. **A**9 10 **F**1 14 15 16 23 35 40 44 45 46; **S**0135	23	10	S		28	798	13	46.4	6	150	1612	887	51
BROOK—Newton County													
★ GEORGE ADE MEMORIAL HOSPITAL, Indiana Hwy. 16, Zip 47922; tel. 219/275-2531; George Hyde, adm. (Total facility includes 23 beds in nursing home-type unit) **A**9 10 **F**1 6 12 16 19 35 40 43 45	13	10	S	TF	63	572	38	60.3	8	56	2007	1088	75
				H	40	468	15	—	8	56	—	—	60
BUTLERVILLE—Jennings County													
MUSCATATUCK STATE DEVELOPMENTAL CENTER (Formerly Muscatatuck State Hospital and Training Center), Box 77, Zip 47223; tel. 812/346-4401; Don G. Polly, supt. (Nonreporting)	12	62	L		790	—	—	—	—	—	—	—	—
CARMEL—Hamilton County													
ST. VINCENT CARMEL HOSPITAL, See St. Vincent Hospital and Healthcare Center, Indianapolis													
CHARLESTOWN—Clark County													
☐★ HCA NORTH CLARK COMMUNITY HOSPITAL (Formerly North Clark Community Hospital), 2200 Market St., Zip 47111; tel. 812/256-3301; Aaron R. Hazzard, adm. **A**1a 9 10 **F**1 3 6 14 15 16 23 34 35 45 46 53; **S**1755	33	10	S		96	1851	31	32.3	0	0	7222	3005	146
CLINTON—Vermillion County													
☐★ VERMILLION COUNTY HOSPITAL, 801 S. Main St., Zip 47842; tel. 317/832-2451; Donald Brawley, adm. **A**1a 9 10 **F**1 3 6 10 12 14 15 16 23 34 35 40 44 45 46 47 52 53	13	10	S		56	2024	31	55.4	6	183	5833	2463	175
COLUMBIA CITY—Whitley County													
☐★ WHITLEY COUNTY MEMORIAL HOSPITAL, 353 N. Oak St., Zip 46725; tel. 219/244-6191; John M. Hatcher, pres. **A**1a 9 10 **F**1 3 6 10 15 16 23 24 34 35 36 40 41 43 45 46 47 49	13	10	S		80	2847	39	48.8	8	328	8215	3875	230
COLUMBUS—Bartholomew County													
☐★ BARTHOLOMEW COUNTY HOSPITAL, 2400 E. 17th St., Zip 47201; tel. 812/379-4441; John C. McGinty Jr., pres. & chief exec. off. **A**1a 2 9 10 **F**1 3 6 7 8 9 10 11 12 14 15 16 23 24 25 27 28 29 30 32 35 36 37 40 42 44 45 46 47 52 53	13	10	S		215	10582	137	63.4	37	1264	31593	15727	778
KOALA CENTER, 2223 Poshard Dr., Zip 47201; tel. 812/376-1711; Ann V. Miller, exec. dir. (Nonreporting) **A** 9	33	82	S		60	—	—	—	—	—	—	—	—
CONNERSVILLE—Fayette County													
☐★ FAYETTE MEMORIAL HOSPITAL, 1941 Virginia Ave., Zip 47331; tel. 317/825-5131; Jack A. Peters, exec. dir. **A**1a 9 10 **F**1 3 6 10 12 14 15 16 23 26 34 35 36 40 41 44 45 46 47 52 53	23	10	S		93	4109	46	49.5	16	262	9853	4533	271

★ American Hospital Association (AHA) membership
□ Joint Commission on Accreditation of Hospitals (JCAH) accreditation
+ American Osteopathic Hospital Association (AOHA) membership
○ American Osteopathic Association (AOA) accreditation
Δ Commission on Accreditation of Rehabilitation Facilities (CARF) accreditation
Control codes 61, 63, 64, 71, 72 and 73 indicate hospitals listed by AOHA, but not registered by AHA.
For definition of numerical codes, see page A2

Hospital, Address, Telephone, Administrator, Approval and Facility Codes, Multihospital System Code	Classification Codes				Inpatient Data				Newborn Data		Expense (thousands of dollars)		
	Control	Service	Stay	Facilities	Beds	Admissions	Census	Occupancy (percent)	Bassinets	Births	Total	Payroll	Personnel
CORYDON—Harrison County													
⊞ HARRISON COUNTY HOSPITAL, 245 Atwood St., Zip 47112; tel. 812/738-4251; William Childers, exec. dir. **A**1a 9 10 **F**1 3 6 15 16 23 34 35 36 37 40 47 53	13	10	S		68	2069	24	35.3	10	275	5165	2235	151
CRAWFORDSVILLE—Montgomery County													
⊞ AMI CULVER UNION HOSPITAL (Formerly Culver Union Hospital), 1710 Lafayette Rd., Zip 47933; tel. 317/362-2800; Michael L. Collins, exec. dir. **A**1a 9 10 **F**1 3 6 14 15 16 23 34 35 36 40 45 46 47 50 53; **S**0125	33	10	S		120	3404	42	35.0	11	340	12846	3180	190
CROWN POINT—Lake County													
⊞ ST. ANTHONY MEDICAL CENTER, Main St. & Franciscan Rd., Zip 46307; tel. 219/738-2100; Stephen O. Leurck, pres. **A**1a 9 10 **F**1 2 3 4 5 6 7 8 9 10 11 12 14 15 16 17 20 23 24 25 26 30 33 34 35 36 40 41 42 44 45 46 47 50 52 53 54	21	10	S		342	8649	165	46.7	22	604	49512	21412	917
DANVILLE—Hendricks County													
⊞ HENDRICKS COUNTY HOSPITAL, 1000 E. Main St., P O Box 409, Zip 46122; tel. 317/745-4452; Dennis W. Dawes, adm. **A**1a 9 10 **F**1 3 6 10 12 14 15 16 21 23 24 27 30 33 34 35 36 40 41 44 45 46 47 53	13	10	S		127	4153	63	49.6	20	411	15553	6527	387
DECATUR—Adams County													
★ ADAMS COUNTY MEMORIAL HOSPITAL, 805 High St., Zip 46733; tel. 219/724-2145; Andrew J. Barrett II, exec. dir. **A**9 10 **F**1 3 6 10 14 15 16 23 24 26 27 30 32 34 35 36 40 41 42 44 45 50 52 53	13	10	S		87	2124	33	37.9	13	345	5698	2644	161
DYER—Lake County													
⊞ OUR LADY OF MERCY HOSPITAL, U. S. Hwy. 30, Zip 46311; tel. 219/865-2141; J. Donald Manchak, pres. **A**1a 9 10 **F**1 3 6 10 12 14 15 16 23 24 27 30 32 33 34 35 42 44 45 46 48 49 53; **S**5165	21	10	S		264	6173	167	63.3	0	0	37050	13749	621
EAST CHICAGO—Lake County													
⊞ ST. CATHERINE HOSPITAL OF EAST CHICAGO, 4321 Fir St., Zip 46312; tel. 219/392-1700; John R. Birdzell, chief exec. off. **A**1a 2 9 10 **F**1 3 4 6 7 8 9 10 11 12 14 15 16 17 20 23 24 27 30 32 34 35 40 44 45 46 47 52 53 54; **S**0135	21	10	S		409	9207	197	48.2	30	422	51252	24552	1191
ELKHART—Elkhart County													
⊞ ELKHART GENERAL HOSPITAL, 600 East Blvd., Box 1329, Zip 46515; tel. 219/294-2621; Raymond Budrys, pres. **A**1a 3 5 9 10 **F**1 3 6 7 9 10 11 12 14 15 16 21 23 24 26 27 29 30 33 34 35 36 40 44 45 46 47 48 49 52 53	23	10	S		354	12078	219	61.9	37	1629	36511	17059	855
ELWOOD—Madison County													
⊞ MERCY HOSPITAL, 1331 S. A St., Zip 46036; tel. 317/552-3336; James E. Baer, adm. **A**1a 9 10 **F**1 3 6 12 15 16 23 24 34 35 40 43 44 46 53; **S**5935	21	10	S		49	1812	28	57.1	7	165	5027	2066	116
EVANSVILLE—Vanderburgh County													
⊞ DEACONESS HOSPITAL, 600 Mary St., Zip 47747; tel. 812/426-3000; Thomas H. Kramer, pres. **A**1a 2 3 5 6 9 10 **F**1 2 3 4 5 6 7 8 9 10 11 12 14 15 16 20 23 24 25 26 27 30 31 32 33 34 35 36 37 38 40 41 42 44 45 46 47 48 49 52 53 54	23	10	S		596	16948	314	52.7	34	988	67696	34891	1561
□ EVANSVILLE STATE HOSPITAL, 3400 Lincoln Ave., Zip 47715; tel. 812/473-2222; John Hedges, supt. (Nonreporting) **A**1b 9	12	22	L		503	—	—	—	—	—	—	—	—
⊞ ST. MARY'S MEDICAL CENTER OF EVANSVILLE, 3700 Washington Ave., Zip 47750; tel. 812/479-4000; Sr. Xavier Ballance, pres. **A**1a 2 3 5 9 10 **F**1 3 4 6 7 8 9 10 11 12 14 15 16 20 23 24 26 29 32 33 34 35 36 40 45 46 47 48 49 50 51 52 53 54; **S**1885	21	10	S		526	16725	282	53.6	26	2156	72124	32457	1557
⊞ Δ WELBORN MEMORIAL BAPTIST HOSPITAL, 401 S.E. Sixth St., Zip 47713; tel. 812/426-8000; Marjorie Soyugenc, pres. **A**1a 2 7 9 10 **F**1 2 3 4 5 6 7 8 9 10 11 12 14 15 16 20 23 24 25 26 27 28 29 30 32 33 34 35 36 40 42 43 44 45 46 47 48 49 50 51 52 53 54	23	10	S		372	11226	213	57.3	17	1198	40407	20518	1056
FORT BENJAMIN HARRISON—Marion County													
⊞ HAWLEY U. S. ARMY COMMUNITY HOSPITAL, Zip 46216; tel. 317/542-5153; Lt. Col. Robert T. Hawkins, dep. cmdr. adm. **A**1a **F**12 14 15 23 24 30 33 34 35 37 46 47	42	10	S		20	886	8	40.0	0	0	—	—	233
FORT WAYNE—Allen County													
⊞ CHARTER BEACON (Formerly Charter Beacon Hospital), 1720 Beacon St., Zip 46805; tel. 219/423-3651; Gerald H. Wallman, adm. **A**1b 9 10 **F**15 23 24 32 33 42 44 48; **S**0695	33	22	S		65	338	52	80.0	0	0	5793	1754	115
FORT WAYNE STATE HOSPITAL AND TRAINING CENTER, 4900 St. Joe Rd., Zip 46815; tel. 219/485-7554; Ora R. Ackerman EdD, supt. (Nonreporting)	12	62	L		731	—	—	—	—	—	—	—	—
⊞ LUTHERAN HOSPITAL OF FORT WAYNE, 3024 Fairfield Ave., Zip 46807; tel. 219/458-2001; Frederick H. Kerr, pres. & chief exec. off. **A**1a 3 5 6 9 10 **F**1 2 3 4 6 7 8 9 10 11 12 13 14 15 16 17 20 21 23 24 27 30 32 34 35 36 40 44 45 46 47 51 52 53 54	21	10	S		403	15867	328	81.4	16	1582	69091	31912	1565
⊞ Δ PARKVIEW MEMORIAL HOSPITAL, 2200 Randallia Dr., Zip 46805; tel. 219/484-6636; Mark Slen, pres. **A**1a 3 5 6 7 9 10 **F**1 2 3 4 5 6 7 8 9 10 11 12 14 15 16 17 20 21 23 24 25 26 27 28 29 30 32 33 35 38 40 41 42 44 45 46 47 48 49 51 52 53 54	23	10	S		649	24278	502	76.4	36	3090	100435	46023	2185
⊞ ST. JOSEPH'S MEDICAL CENTER (Formerly St. Joseph's Hospital), 700 Broadway, Zip 46802; tel. 219/425-3000; Stanley A. Abramowski, exec. dir. **A**1a 3 5 6 9 10 **F**1 2 3 4 5 6 7 8 10 11 12 14 15 16 17 20 21 22 23 24 26 27 30 34 35 36 40 41 42 44 45 46 47 48 52 53 54; **S**0135	21	10	S		327	9319	216	66.1	36	768	45543	21297	1098
⊞ VETERANS ADMINISTRATION MEDICAL CENTER, 1600 Randallia Dr., Zip 46805; tel. 219/426-5431; Raymond C. Sullivan, dir. (Total facility includes 54 beds in nursing home-type unit) **A**1a **F**1 3 6 10 12 14 15 16 19 23 24 27 28 30 32 34 35 42 44 46 47 49	45	10	S	TF	230	3708	169	73.5	0	0	16924	9818	386
				H	176	3685	117	—	0	0	14927	8659	335
FRANKFORT—Clinton County													
⊞ CLINTON COUNTY HOSPITAL, 1300 S. Jackson St., Zip 46041; tel. 317/659-4731; Brian R. Zeh, exec. dir. **A**1a 9 10 **F**1 3 6 14 15 16 23 26 32 34 35 36 40 44 45 52 53	13	10	S		66	2076	26	39.4	11	216	6212	2645	155
FRANKLIN—Johnson County													
⊞ JOHNSON COUNTY MEMORIAL HOSPITAL, 1125 W. Jefferson St., P O Box 549, Zip 46131; tel. 317/736-3300; Norbert Smith, adm. (Nonreporting) **A**1a 9 10	13	10	S		136	—	—	—	—	—	—	—	—
GARY—Lake County													
⊞ Δ METHODIST HOSPITALS NORTHWEST INDIANA (Includes Northlake Campus, 600 Grant St., Zip 46402; tel. 219/886-4000; Southlake Campus, 8701 Broadway, Merrillville, Zip 46410; tel. 219/738-5500), John H. Betjemann, pres. **A**1a 2 3 5 7 9 10 **F**1 3 4 5 6 7 8 9 10 11 12 15 16 20 23 24 25 26 27 32 33 34 35 36 40 42 44 45 46 47 48 49 50 52 53 54	23	10	S		666	21820	458	68.8	70	3001	99857	49229	2100
⊞ ST. MARY MEDICAL CENTER (Includes St. Mary Medical Center, 1500 S. Lake Park Ave., Hobart, Zip 46342; tel. 219/942-0551), 540 Tyler St., Zip 46402; tel. 219/882-9411; John Birdzell, chief exec. off. **A**1a 9 10 **F**1 3 5 6 7 9 10 12 14 15 16 23 24 27 34 35 42 44 45 46 47 48 49 52 53; **S**0135	21	10	S		349	12209	255	76.8	0	0	58721	26178	1036
GOSHEN—Elkhart County													
⊞ GOSHEN GENERAL HOSPITAL, 200 High Park Ave., Zip 46526; tel. 219/533-2141; Frank N. Yaggi, pres. **A**1a 9 10 **F**1 3 6 10 12 14 15 16 21 23 34 35 36 40 41 44 45 46 47 52 53	23	10	S		160	6163	85	53.1	20	1209	16609	7969	414

Hospital, Address, Telephone, Administrator, Approval and Facility Codes, Multihospital System Code	Classification Codes				Inpatient Data				Newborn Data		Expense (thousands of dollars)		
★ American Hospital Association (AHA) membership ☐ Joint Commission on Accreditation of Hospitals (JCAH) accreditation + American Osteopathic Hospital Association (AOHA) membership ○ American Osteopathic Association (AOA) accreditation Δ Commission on Accreditation of Rehabilitation Facilities (CARF) accreditation Control codes 61, 63, 64, 71, 72 and 73 indicate hospitals listed by AOHA, but not registered by AHA. For definition of numerical codes, see page A2	Control	Service	Stay	Facilities	Beds	Admissions	Census	Occupancy (percent)	Bassinets	Births	Total	Payroll	Personnel
GREENCASTLE—Putnam County													
☐ PUTNAM COUNTY HOSPITAL, 1542 Bloomington St., Zip 46135; tel. 317/653-5121; John D. Fajt, exec. dir. **A**1a 9 10 **F**1 3 6 10 12 14 15 16 23 26 34 35 36 37 40 44 45 46 52 53; **S**9335	13	10	S		85	2532	33	38.8	12	223	6632	2926	196
GREENFIELD—Hancock County													
★☐ HANCOCK MEMORIAL HOSPITAL, 801 N. State St., Box 827, Zip 46140; tel. 317/462-5544; Fuad Hammoudeh, pres. **A**1a 9 10 **F**1 3 6 9 10 12 14 15 16 23 24 33 34 35 36 37 40 41 43 44 45 46 53	13	10	S		120	3570	54	45.0	16	396	11737	5938	321
GREENSBURG—Decatur County													
★☐ DECATUR COUNTY MEMORIAL HOSPITAL, 720 N. Lincoln St., Zip 47240; tel. 812/663-4331; David Trexler, exec. dir. **A**1a 9 10 **F**1 3 6 10 14 15 16 23 34 35 37 40 41 43 44 45 46 50 52 53	13	10	S		115	1915	28	24.3	14	109	6514	2766	167
GREENWOOD—Johnson County													
☐ CPC VALLE VISTA HOSPITAL, 898 E. Main St., P O Box 304, Zip 46142; tel. 317/887-1348; Frederick Mirmelstein, adm. (Data not available) **A**1a 9 10 **F**15 28 29 30 32 33 49	33	22	S		120	—	—	—	—	—	—	—	—
HAMMOND—Lake County													
★☐ ST. MARGARET HOSPITAL, 5454 Hohman Ave., Zip 46320; tel. 219/932-2300; Sr. Jane Marie Klein, pres. **A**1a 2 9 10 **F**1 2 3 6 7 8 9 10 11 12 14 15 16 20 23 24 25 26 33 34 35 36 40 41 44 45 46 47 51 52 53 54; **S**5345	21	10	S		487	15158	261	53.6	40	1038	62340	30990	1385
HARTFORD CITY—Blackford County													
★ BLACKFORD COUNTY HOSPITAL, 503 E. Van Cleve St., Zip 47348; tel. 317/348-0300; R. Gladys Phemister, adm. **A**9 10 **F**1 3 6 10 12 16 23 24 34 35 40 44 45 47	13	10	S		47	1226	16	34.0	8	118	2987	1332	95
HOBART—Lake County													
ST. MARY MEDICAL CENTER, See St. Mary Medical Center, Gary													
HUNTINGBURG—Dubois County													
★☐ ST. JOSEPH'S HOSPITAL, Leland Hts., P O Box 148, Zip 47542; tel. 812/683-2121; Sr. Jeanne Roach, pres. & chief exec. off. **A**1a 9 10 **F**1 3 6 10 12 14 15 16 23 26 30 34 35 36 39 40 43 45 46 48 49 50 52	21	10	S		87	2524	32	36.8	12	290	7106	3381	199
HUNTINGTON—Huntington County													
★☐ HUNTINGTON MEMORIAL HOSPITAL, 1215 Etna Ave., Zip 46750; tel. 219/356-3000; L. K. McCoy, pres. **A**1a 9 10 **F**1 3 6 15 16 21 23 35 40 41 44 45 46 48 52	13	10	S		69	2207	35	49.3	16	349	7622	3699	210
INDIANAPOLIS—Marion County													
CENTRAL STATE HOSPITAL, 3000 W. Washington St., Zip 46222; tel. 317/639-3600; Ruth Stanley, supt. **A**9 **F**23 24 33 42 44 46 47 48	12	22	L		520	551	469	90.2	0	0	17850	12313	668
★☐ Δ COMMUNITY HOSPITALS OF INDIANA (Formerly Community Hospital of Indianapolis), 1500 N. Ritter Ave., Zip 46219; tel. 317/353-1411; William E. Corley, pres. & adm. **A**1a 2 3 5 7 9 10 **F**1 2 3 4 6 7 8 9 10 11 12 13 14 15 16 20 23 24 25 26 28 29 30 31 32 33 34 35 36 37 40 41 42 43 44 45 46 47 49 50 51 52 53 54	23	10	S		565	22047	447	73.8	35	2161	—	—	2574
☐ FAIRBANKS HOSPITAL, 8102 Clearvista Pkwy., Zip 46256; tel. 317/849-8222; Thomas W. Brink, adm. **A**1b 9 10 **F**28 33 42 46 49	23	82	S		96	1092	69	71.9	0	0	4113	2434	133
HAWLEY U. S. ARMY COMMUNITY HOSPITAL, See Fort Benjamin Harrison													
★☐ HUMANA WOMEN'S HOSPITAL-INDIANAPOLIS, 8111 Township Line Rd., Zip 46260; tel. 317/872-1803; Jay W. Williams, exec. dir. **A**1a 9 10 **F**1 6 12 14 15 16 34 36 37 40 46 51; **S**1235	33	44	S		108	5334	45	41.7	34	1855	15804	4782	225
★☐ INDIANA UNIVERSITY HOSPITALS (Includes James Whitcomb Riley Hospital; Robert W. Long Hospital; University Hospital), 1100 W. Michigan St., Zip 46223; tel. 317/274-5000; David J. Handel, dir. **A**1a 3 5 8 9 10 **F**1 2 3 4 5 6 7 8 9 10 11 12 13 14 15 16 17 20 22 23 24 26 27 28 30 32 33 34 35 36 37 38 40 41 42 44 45 46 47 51 52 53 54	12	10	S		573	18170	451	78.7	30	973	142864	60261	2976
JAMES WHITCOMB RILEY HOSPITAL, See Indiana University Hospitals													
☐ LARUE D. CARTER MEMORIAL HOSPITAL, 1315 W. Tenth St., Zip 46202; tel. 317/634-8401; Clare M. Assue MD, supt. & med. dir. **A**1b 3 5 9 10 **F**24 28 29 30 32 33 34 42 46	12	22	L		151	368	110	72.8	0	0	11259	7983	368
★☐ METHODIST HOSPITAL OF INDIANA, 1701 N. Senate Blvd., P O Box 1367, Zip 46206; tel. 317/924-6411; Frank Lloyd MD, pres. & chief exec. off. **A**1a 2 3 5 8 9 10 **F**1 2 3 4 5 6 7 8 9 10 11 12 13 14 16 17 18 20 21 23 24 25 26 27 28 29 30 32 33 34 35 36 37 39 40 42 44 46 47 51 52 53 54; **S**9335	21	10	S		1130	38768	768	68.0	55	3905	196038	94168	4345
★☐ RICHARD L. ROUDEBUSH VETERANS ADMINISTRATION MEDICAL CENTER, 1481 W. Tenth St., Zip 46202; tel. 317/635-7401; Terrence L. Johnson, dir. (Total facility includes 60 beds in nursing home-type unit) **A**1a 3 5 8 **F**1 2 3 4 6 10 12 14 15 16 19 20 21 23 24 26 27 28 30 31 32 33 34 35 41 42 44 45 46 47 48 49 50 53 54	45	10	S	TF	525	14584	407	77.5	0	0	71584	37394	1453
				H	465	14389	353	—	0	0	—	—	1426
ROBERT W. LONG HOSPITAL, See Indiana University Hospitals													
★☐ ST. VINCENT HOSPITAL AND HEALTH CARE CENTER (Includes St. Vincent Carmel Hospital, 13500 N. Meridian, Carmel, Zip 46032; tel. 317/573-7000; Frank Magliery, adm.; St. Vincent Stress Center, 8401 Harcourt Rd., Zip 46260; tel 317/875-4600; Lawrence Ulrich, adm.), 2001 W. 86th St., P O Box 46240, Zip 46240; tel. 317/871-2345; Bain J. Farris, pres. & chief exec. off. **A**1a 2 3 5 8 9 10 **F**1 2 3 4 6 7 8 9 10 11 12 14 15 16 17 18 20 21 23 24 27 30 32 33 34 35 36 40 41 42 43 44 45 46 47 48 49 51 52 53 54	21	10	S		820	31414	580	74.2	36	3384	152029	65869	3128
ST. VINCENT STRESS CENTER, See St. Vincent Hospital and Health Care Center													
★☐ UNIVERSITY HEIGHTS HOSPITAL, 1402 E. County Line Rd. S., Box 27010, Zip 46227; tel. 317/887-7111; George W. Poor, pres. **A**1a 9 10 **F**1 3 6 12 14 15 16 23 24 35 44 45 46 48 52 53	23	10	S		140	3786	66	52.8	0	0	18881	7097	384
UNIVERSITY HOSPITAL, See Indiana University Hospitals													
○ + WESTVIEW HOSPITAL, 3630 Guion Rd., Box 22650, Zip 46222; tel. 317/924-6661; James F. Knopp, pres. **A**9 10 11 12 13 **F**1 3 6 10 14 15 16 23 34 35 43 45 46 47	23	10	S		90	3112	54	60.0	0	0	13726	5436	242
★☐ WILLIAM N. WISHARD MEMORIAL HOSPITAL, 1001 W. Tenth St., Zip 46202; tel. 317/639-6671; William T. Paynter MD, dir. **A**1a 3 5 8 9 10 **F**1 2 3 5 6 10 12 14 15 16 22 23 24 26 27 28 29 30 32 33 34 35 37 38 40 42 44 45 46 47 49 50 52 53	15	10	S		415	15968	307	74.0	45	2986	89694	42113	2508
★☐ WINONA MEMORIAL HOSPITAL, 3232 N. Meridian St., Zip 46208; tel. 317/924-3392; Howard W. Watts, adm. (Data for 243 days) **A**1a 9 10 **F**1 3 6 7 10 11 12 14 15 16 21 23 24 25 27 28 32 33 34 35 44 45 46 47 48 49 53 54; **S**6525	32	10	S		237	4376	137	57.8	0	0	25150	9166	620
JASPER—Dubois County													
★☐ MEMORIAL HOSPITAL AND HEALTH CARE CENTER, 800 W. Ninth St., Zip 47546; tel. 812/482-2345; Herman Kohlman, pres. **A**1a 9 10 **F**1 3 5 6 9 10 12 14 15 16 23 24 26 27 29 30 35 36 40 45 46 53; **S**2295	21	10	S		131	3950	60	45.8	10	524	11263	5744	301
JEFFERSONVILLE—Clark County													
★☐ CLARK COUNTY MEMORIAL HOSPITAL, 1220 Missouri Ave., Box 69, Zip 47131; tel. 812/282-6631; Merle E. Stepp, chief exec. off. **A**1a 9 10 **F**1 3 6 9 10 11 12 14 15 16 21 23 24 25 26 35 40 44 45 46 47 52 53	13	10	S		232	7102	122	52.6	17	474	23132	12112	644

Hospital, Address, Telephone, Administrator, Approval and Facility Codes, Multihospital System Code	Classification Codes				Inpatient Data				Newborn Data		Expense (thousands of dollars)		
★ American Hospital Association (AHA) membership □ Joint Commission on Accreditation of Hospitals (JCAH) accreditation + American Osteopathic Hospital Association (AOHA) membership ○ American Osteopathic Association (AOA) accreditation Δ Commission on Accreditation of Rehabilitation Facilities (CARF) accreditation Control codes 61, 63, 64, 71, 72 and 73 indicate hospitals listed by AOHA, but not registered by AHA. For definition of numerical codes, see page A2	Control	Service	Stay	Facilities	Beds	Admissions	Census	Occupancy (percent)	Bassinets	Births	Total	Payroll	Personnel
□ LIFESPRING MENTAL HEALTH SERVICES (Formerly Southern Indiana Mental Health and Guidance Center), 207 W. 13th St., Zip 47130; tel. 812/283-4491; John R. Case, adm. **A**1b 10 **F**28 29 30 31 32 33 43 46 49	23	22	S		47	869	39	83.0	0	0	5784	3367	165
KENDALLVILLE—Noble County													
★□ MCCRAY MEMORIAL HOSPITAL, Hospital Dr., Box 249, Zip 46755; tel. 219/347-1100; Jennifer L. Smith, adm. **A**1a 9 10 **F**1 2 12 14 16 21 23 30 32 33 34 35 36 37 40 41 44 45 46; **S**1755	15	10	S		66	2365	30	45.5	15	387	6924	2785	141
KNOX—Starke County													
★ STARKE MEMORIAL HOSPITAL, 102 E. Culver Rd., Zip 46534; tel. 219/772-6231; Spencer L. Grover, exec. dir. **A**9 10 **F**1 3 6 10 15 16 21 23 24 34 35 40 41 44 45 52 53; **S**2495	13	10	S		55	2575	33	60.0	8	165	6116	2828	168
KOKOMO—Howard County													
★□ HOWARD COMMUNITY HOSPITAL, 3500 S. La Fountain St., Zip 46902; tel. 317/453-0702; George R. Banjak, pres. & chief exec. off. **A**1a 9 10 **F**1 3 6 8 9 10 11 12 14 15 16 23 24 26 27 28 29 30 32 33 35 36 40 41 42 44 45 46 47 48 49 53	13	10	S		216	5283	100	46.3	22	418	21879	10511	508
★□ SAINT JOSEPH HOSPITAL AND HEALTH CENTER (Formerly St. Joseph Memorial Hospital), 1907 W. Sycamore St., Zip 46901; tel. 317/452-5611; Sr. M. Martin McEntee, pres. **A**1a 9 10 **F**1 3 5 6 7 8 9 10 11 12 14 15 16 21 23 24 26 32 35 36 40 41 43 44 45 46 47 53; **S**5935	21	10	S		152	7749	110	66.7	16	1090	27175	12556	540
ST. JOSEPH MEMORIAL HOSPITAL, See Saint Joseph Hospital and Health Center													
LAFAYETTE—Tippecanoe County													
★□ LAFAYETTE HOME HOSPITAL, 2400 South St., Zip 47904; tel. 317/447-6811; Franklin E. Simek, pres. (Total facility includes 71 beds in nursing home-type unit) **A**1a 9 10 **F**1 2 3 5 6 10 12 14 15 16 19 20 23 24 26 28 30 32 33 34 35 36 40 41 42 44 45 46 47 51 52 53	23	10	S	TF	377	11907	237	62.9	23	2046	40105	18740	1019
				H	306	11562	172	—	23	2046	38405	17979	972
PURDUE UNIVERSITY STUDENT HOSPITAL, See West Lafayette													
★□ ST. ELIZABETH HOSPITAL MEDICAL CENTER, 1501 Hartford St., Zip 47904; Mailing Address Box 7501, Zip 47903; tel. 317/423-6011; Paul E. Hess, pres. **A**1a 2 6 9 10 **F**1 2 3 4 5 6 7 8 9 10 11 12 14 15 16 20 21 23 24 30 33 34 35 36 40 44 45 46 50 52 53 54; **S**5345	21	10	S		257	8686	149	56.9	15	604	40016	17498	935
LAGRANGE—Lagrange County													
LAGRANGE HOSPITAL, Rte. 5, Box 79, Zip 46761; tel. 219/463-2143; Steve Malcolm, adm. (Nonreporting) **A**9 10	13	10	S		62	—	—	—	—	—	—	—	—
LAPORTE—La Porte County													
★□ LAPORTE HOSPITAL, State & Madison Sts., Box 250, Zip 46350; tel. 219/326-1234; Leigh E. Morris, pres. (Total facility includes 26 beds in nursing home-type unit) **A**1a 9 10 **F**1 3 6 10 12 14 15 16 19 23 24 25 26 27 28 29 30 32 33 34 35 36 40 42 44 45 46 47 49 50 52 53 54	23	10	S	TF	227	6271	114	55.3	20	725	23348	9915	591
				H	201	6226	111	—	20	725	23217	9789	574
LAWRENCEBURG—Dearborn County													
★□ DEARBORN COUNTY HOSPITAL, 600 Wilson Creek Rd., Zip 47025; tel. 812/537-8200; Russell C. Dean Jr., exec. dir. **A**1a 9 10 **F**1 3 6 10 12 15 16 21 23 35 36 40 41 44 45 52 53	13	10	S		131	4342	69	51.5	14	408	13999	6568	323
LEBANON—Boone County													
□ WITHAM MEMORIAL HOSPITAL, 1124 N. Lebanon St., Zip 46052; tel. 317/482-2700; John B. Riekena, adm. (Nonreporting) **A**1a 9 10	13	10	S		80	—	—	—	—	—	—	—	—
LINTON—Greene County													
★□ GREENE COUNTY GENERAL HOSPITAL, Rural Rte. 1, Box 453, Zip 47441; tel. 812/847-2281; Jonas S. Uland, exec. dir. **A**1a 9 10 **F**1 3 6 10 12 14 15 16 23 34 35 37 40 41 44 45 52 53	13	10	S		76	2232	31	40.8	14	163	5300	3028	159
LOGANSPORT—Cass County													
LOGANSPORT STATE HOSPITAL, Rural Rte. 2, Zip 46947; tel. 219/722-4141; Jeffrey H. Smith PhD, supt. (Nonreporting) **A**9	12	22	L		735	—	—	—	—	—	—	—	—
★□ MEMORIAL HOSPITAL, 1101 Michigan Ave., Zip 46947; tel. 219/753-7541; Herbert L. Fromm, exec. dir. **A**1a 9 10 **F**1 3 6 10 12 16 21 23 35 36 40 41 44 45 47 52 53	13	10	S		125	3555	46	36.8	12	575	11086	4845	278
MADISON—Jefferson County													
★□ KING'S DAUGHTERS' HOSPITAL, 112 Presbyterian Ave., Box 447, Zip 47250; tel. 812/265-5211; Darrel J. Scott, pres. **A**1a 9 10 **F**1 3 6 10 12 14 16 23 35 36 40 41 44 45 46 52 53	23	10	S		142	5862	96	67.6	15	434	14449	5938	355
★□ MADISON STATE HOSPITAL, Cragmont St., Zip 47250; tel. 812/265-2611; Jerry Thaden, supt. **A**1b 9 10 **F**19 23 33 42 44 46 47 48 50	12	22	L		464	450	399	83.0	0	0	16093	9934	568
MARION—Grant County													
★□ MARION GENERAL HOSPITAL, Wabash & Euclid Aves., Zip 46952; tel. 317/662-1441; John W. Green, adm. **A**1a 9 10 **F**1 2 3 5 6 10 12 14 16 21 23 24 26 35 36 40 44 46 47 49 52 53	23	10	S		250	10213	154	61.6	24	1077	29839	14601	748
★□ VETERANS ADMINISTRATION MEDICAL CENTER, Zip 46952; tel. 317/674-3321; A. G. Branch, dir. (Nonreporting) **A**1b	45	22	L		802	—	—	—	—	—	—	—	—
MARTINSVILLE—Morgan County													
★ MORGAN COUNTY MEMORIAL HOSPITAL, 2209 John R Wooden Dr., P O Box 1717, Zip 46151; tel. 317/342-8441; S. Dean Melton, adm. **A**9 10 **F**1 3 6 10 12 14 15 16 23 26 35 36 40 45 46 53	13	10	S		108	3006	48	44.4	18	305	10228	4488	262
MERRILLVILLE—Lake County													
SOUTHLAKE CAMPUS, See Methodist Hospital of Gary, Gary													
MICHIGAN CITY—La Porte County													
□ KINGWOOD HOSPITAL (Formerly Walters Hospital Foundation), 3714 S. Franklin St., Zip 46360; tel. 219/872-0531; Mary Lou Saxon, adm. (Nonreporting) **A**1a 9 10; **S**0825	23	10	S		89	—	—	—	—	—	—	—	—
★□ MEMORIAL HOSPITAL OF MICHIGAN CITY, Fifth & Pine Sts., Zip 46360; tel. 219/879-0202; Norman Steider, pres. **A**1a 9 10 **F**1 3 6 9 10 12 14 15 16 23 24 33 35 36 40 44 45 46 48 49 52 53	23	10	S		102	2997	67	65.7	16	296	11551	4457	249
★□ ST. ANTHONY HOSPITAL, 301 W. Homer St., Zip 46360; tel. 219/879-8511; Kevin D. Leahy, pres. **A**1a 9 10 **F**1 3 6 10 11 12 15 16 23 24 25 26 34 35 36 40 41 44 45 46 52 53; **S**5345	21	10	S		190	6073	106	55.8	20	483	22408	10265	535
WALTERS HOSPITAL FOUNDATION, See Kingwood Hospital													
MISHAWAKA—St. Joseph County													
□ SAINT JOSEPH HOSPITAL, 215 W. Fourth St., Zip 46544; tel. 219/259-2431; Allen V. Rupiper, exec. dir. **A**1a 3 9 10 **F**1 3 6 10 15 16 23 30 32 33 34 35 36 40 43 45 46 47 50 52 53; **S**0135	21	10	S		117	4636	66	56.4	16	620	14365	5497	291
MONTICELLO—White County													
★□ WHITE COUNTY MEMORIAL HOSPITAL, 1101 O'Connor Blvd., Zip 47960; tel. 219/583-7111; Ed Pfeiffer, adm. **A**1a 9 10 **F**1 3 6 10 14 16 23 34 35 40 44 45 46 53; **S**2495	13	10	S		59	2014	26	44.1	13	208	5711	2646	172

Hospital, Address, Telephone, Administrator, Approval and Facility Codes, Multihospital System Code	Classification Codes				Inpatient Data				Newborn Data		Expense (thousands of dollars)		
★ American Hospital Association (AHA) membership □ Joint Commission on Accreditation of Hospitals (JCAH) accreditation + American Osteopathic Hospital Association (AOHA) membership ○ American Osteopathic Association (AOA) accreditation Δ Commission on Accreditation of Rehabilitation Facilities (CARF) accreditation Control codes 61, 63, 64, 71, 72 and 73 indicate hospitals listed by AOHA, but not registered by AHA. For definition of numerical codes, see page A2	Control	Service	Stay	Facilities	Beds	Admissions	Census	Occupancy (percent)	Bassinets	Births	Total	Payroll	Personnel
MOORESVILLE—Morgan County													
★□ KENDRICK MEMORIAL HOSPITAL (Colorectal, Proctology Orthopaedic Surgery), 1201 Hadley Rd. N.W., Zip 46158; tel. 317/831-1160; Charles D. Swisher, exec. dir. **A**1a 9 10 **F**1 23 34 46	23	49	S		60	1321	16	26.7	0	0	3622	1398	124
MUNCIE—Delaware County													
★□ BALL MEMORIAL HOSPITAL, 2401 University Ave., Zip 47303; tel. 317/747-3111; Robert Brodhead, pres. **A**1a 3 5 9 10 **F**1 2 3 4 5 6 7 8 9 10 11 12 14 15 16 20 21 23 24 25 26 27 30 32 34 35 36 38 40 41 42 44 45 46 47 48 49 51 52 53 54	23	10	S		532	17745	357	65.3	40	1817	70230	36267	1549
MUNSTER—Lake County													
□ COMMUNITY HOSPITAL, 901 MacArthur Blvd., Zip 46321; tel. 219/836-1600; Edward P. Robinson, adm. (Nonreporting) **A**1a 9 10	23	10	S		245	—	—	—	—	—	—	—	—
NEW ALBANY—Floyd County													
★□ FLOYD MEMORIAL HOSPITAL (Formerly Memorial Hospital), 1850 State St., Zip 47150; tel. 812/944-7701; John B. White, pres. **A**1a 2 9 10 **F**1 3 5 6 7 8 10 11 12 14 15 16 21 23 24 26 35 36 37 40 41 44 45 46 47 48 49 52 53	13	10	S		270	9039	145	58.5	16	726	27469	12865	683
NEW CASTLE—Henry County													
★□ HENRY COUNTY MEMORIAL HOSPITAL, 1000 N. 16th St., Box 490, Zip 47362; tel. 317/521-0890; Jack Basler, pres. **A**1a 9 10 **F**1 3 6 10 12 14 16 23 35 36 40 44 45 46 52 53	13	10	S		117	4143	61	57.5	10	374	13868	6029	369
NOBLESVILLE—Hamilton County													
★□ RIVERVIEW HOSPITAL, 395 Westfield Rd., P O Box 220, Zip 46060; tel. 317/773-0760; Bruce Carter, adm. **A**1a 9 10 **F**1 3 6 14 15 16 23 24 34 35 36 37 40 41 44 45 46 47 52 53	13	10	S		128	5418	72	50.7	16	464	14466	7348	366
NORTH VERNON—Jennings County													
★□ JENNINGS COMMUNITY HOSPITAL, 301 Henry St., Zip 47265; tel. 812/346-6200; Lou Vaught, adm. (Nonreporting) **A**1a 9 10	23	10	S		48	—	—	—	—	—	—	—	—
OAKLAND CITY—Gibson County													
○ + WIRTH OSTEOPATHIC HOSPITAL, Hwy. 64 W., Zip 47660; tel. 812/749-6111; John R. Webb, adm. **A**9 10 11 **F**14 16 19 23 35 40 45 46	23	10	S		39	699	12	30.8	5	42	2124	1077	66
PAOLI—Orange County													
★□ ORANGE COUNTY HOSPITAL, R R 3, Box 74, Zip 47454; tel. 812/723-2811; W. Lavelle Garritson, exec. dir. **A**1a 9 10 **F**1 3 6 12 14 16 23 30 32 34 35 40 45 46	13	10	S		52	1555	20	38.5	9	185	4317	1925	141
PERU—Miami County													
★□ DUKES MEMORIAL HOSPITAL, Grant & Boulevard, Zip 46970; tel. 317/473-6621; Robert L. Allman, exec. dir. **A**1a 9 10 **F**1 3 6 10 14 15 16 23 34 35 40 44 45 46 47 52	13	10	S		110	2847	40	36.4	10	401	8553	4162	263
PLYMOUTH—Marshall County													
★□ HOLY CROSS PARKVIEW HOSPITAL, 1915 Lake Ave., P O Box 670, Zip 46563; tel. 219/936-3181; David Baytos, pres. & chief oper. off. **A**1a 9 10 **F**1 3 6 10 12 14 15 16 23 34 35 36 40 41 45 46 53; **S**5585	21	10	S		58	2289	28	48.3	10	342	5971	2995	157
PORTLAND—Jay County													
★□ JAY COUNTY HOSPITAL, 500 W. Votaw St., P O Box 1069, Zip 47371; tel. 219/726-7131; Charles S. Wohl, adm. **A**1a 9 10 **F**1 3 6 10 12 14 15 16 23 34 35 36 40 41 45 46 53	13	10	S		65	2209	34	52.3	8	223	6399	2538	161
PRINCETON—Gibson County													
★□ GIBSON GENERAL HOSPITAL, 1808 Sherman Dr., Zip 47670; tel. 812/385-3401; William D. Gibson, adm. (Total facility includes 45 beds in nursing home-type unit) **A**1a 9 10 **F**1 3 6 12 14 16 17 19 23 34 35 36 40 42 45 52 53	23	10	S	TF	118	2148	70	59.3	16	171	6636	3648	231
				H	73	2003	30	—	16	171	6141	3215	203
RENSSELAER—Jasper County													
★ JASPER COUNTY HOSPITAL, 1104 E. Grace St., Zip 47978; tel. 219/866-5141; Timothy M. Schreeg, exec. dir. **A**9 10 **F**1 3 6 14 16 18 19 21 23 34 35 40 41 45 49 52 53	13	10	S		73	2082	26	32.9	15	203	6267	2863	197
RICHMOND—Wayne County													
★□ REID MEMORIAL HOSPITAL, 1401 Chester Blvd., Zip 47374; tel. 317/983-3000; Kenneth R. Spoon, pres. (Total facility includes 58 beds in nursing home-type unit) **A**1a 9 10 **F**1 2 3 6 7 8 9 10 11 12 14 16 19 21 23 24 27 35 36 40 41 42 44 45 46 48 50 52 53	23	10	S	TF	349	9779	221	64.6	36	1121	37967	16411	692
				H	291	9758	166	—	36	1121	36297	15808	669
RICHMOND STATE HOSPITAL, N.W. 18th St., Zip 47374; tel. 317/966-0511; Gene Darby, supt. **A**9 10 **F**15 23 24 32 33 42 43 46 47 48 50	12	22	L		602	638	470	78.1	0	0	17449	10672	662
ROCHESTER—Fulton County													
★ WOODLAWN HOSPITAL, 1400 E. Ninth St., Zip 46975; tel. 219/223-3141; Michael L. Gordon, exec. dir. **A**9 10 **F**1 3 6 10 12 14 15 16 23 34 35 40 41 44 45 46 53	13	10	S		49	2165	33	67.3	6	177	6238	2793	187
RUSHVILLE—Rush County													
★ RUSH MEMORIAL HOSPITAL, 1300 N. Main St., Zip 46173; tel. 317/932-4111; Steven L. Taylor, exec. dir. **A**9 10 **F**1 3 6 10 12 14 15 16 23 26 30 34 35 40 43 45 46 47 50	13	10	S		38	1047	15	36.6	6	102	3894	1655	102
SALEM—Washington County													
★□ WASHINGTON COUNTY MEMORIAL HOSPITAL, 911 N. Shelby St., Box 171, Zip 47167; tel. 812/883-5881; Rodney M. Coats, exec. dir. **A**1a 9 10 **F**1 3 6 12 14 16 23 34 35 36 37 40 43 45 47	13	10	S		75	1736	24	32.0	8	235	4721	2192	148
SCOTTSBURG—Scott County													
★□ SCOTT COUNTY MEMORIAL HOSPITAL, Rte. 1, Hwy. 31 N., Box 456, Zip 47170; tel. 812/752-3456; Arthur B. Allaben, adm. **A**1a 9 10 **F**1 6 16 17 23 34 35 40 45 46 47 52 53	13	10	S		107	2511	31	29.0	12	119	4918	2264	173
SEYMOUR—Jackson County													
★ JACKSON COUNTY SCHNECK MEMORIAL HOSPITAL, 200 S. Walnut St., Zip 47274; tel. 812/522-2349; George H. James, adm. **A**9 10 **F**1 3 6 10 12 14 15 16 23 33 34 35 36 40 41 44 45 46 47 52	13	10	S		106	4295	59	55.7	15	539	10523	4968	295
SHELBYVILLE—Shelby County													
★□ MAJOR HOSPITAL, 150 W. Washington St., Box 10, Zip 46176; tel. 317/392-3211; Frank H. Learned, adm. **A**1a 9 10 **F**1 3 6 12 14 15 23 34 35 36 40 45 46 47 53	15	10	S		89	2975	51	57.3	13	328	8666	3668	226
SOUTH BEND—St. Joseph County													
★ HEALTHWIN HOSPITAL, 20531 Darden Rd., Zip 46637; tel. 219/272-0100; Michael Roman, adm. (Total facility includes 124 beds in nursing home-type unit) **A**9 10 **F**15 19 23 24 26 33 34 42 44 45 46 50	13	48	L	TF	156	147	146	93.6	0	0	5860	3482	243
				H	32	23	25	—	0	0	2787	1627	166
★□ MEMORIAL HOSPITAL OF SOUTH BEND, 615 N. Michigan St., Zip 46601; tel. 219/234-9041; Stephen L. Ummel, pres. **A**1a 2 3 5 6 9 10 **F**1 2 3 4 5 6 7 8 9 10 11 15 16 23 24 25 26 27 32 34 35 36 38 40 41 42 44 45 46 47 48 49 51 52 53 54	23	10	S		475	18259	333	66.9	38	2997	80409	36265	1554
○ + MICHIANA COMMUNITY HOSPITAL (Formerly South Bend Osteopathic Hospital), 2515 E. Jefferson Blvd., Zip 46615; tel. 219/288-8311; David S. Anderson, pres. **A**9 10 11 12 13 **F**1 3 6 9 10 12 14 15 16 23 35 36 40 45 46 52 53	23	10	S		107	3839	51	47.7	8	447	12429	5429	279
SOUTH BEND OSTEOPATHIC HOSPITAL, See Michiana Community Hospital													

Hospital, Address, Telephone, Administrator, Approval and Facility Codes, Multihospital System Code	Classification Codes			Facilities	Inpatient Data				Newborn Data		Expense (thousands of dollars)		
★ American Hospital Association (AHA) membership □ Joint Commission on Accreditation of Hospitals (JCAH) accreditation + American Osteopathic Hospital Association (AOHA) membership ○ American Osteopathic Association (AOA) accreditation Δ Commission on Accreditation of Rehabilitation Facilities (CARF) accreditation Control codes 61, 63, 64, 71, 72 and 73 indicate hospitals listed by AOHA, but not registered by AHA. For definition of numerical codes, see page A2	Control	Service	Stay		Beds	Admissions	Census	Occupancy (percent)	Bassinets	Births	Total	Payroll	Personnel
★□ ST. JOSEPH'S MEDICAL CENTER, 811 E. Madison St., Box 1935, Zip 46634; tel. 219/237-7111; Don Larimore, pres. **A**1a 2 3 5 9 10 **F**1 2 3 6 7 8 9 10 11 12 14 15 16 20 23 24 25 26 34 35 42 43 44 45 46 47 49 50 52 53 54; **S**5585	21	10	S		339	11195	224	66.1	0	0	56582	18851	1328
SULLIVAN—Sullivan County													
★□ MARY SHERMAN HOSPITAL, 320 N. Section St., Zip 47882; tel. 812/268-4311; Alan L. Martinez, adm. **A**1a 9 10 **F**1 3 6 10 12 14 15 16 23 34 35 37 40 44 46 47	13	10	S		50	1749	26	52.0	7	181	4112	2189	150
TELL CITY—Perry County													
PERRY COUNTY MEMORIAL HOSPITAL, 1 Hospital Rd., Zip 47586; tel. 812/547-7011; Anthony J. Nasralla, adm. & chief exec. off. (Nonreporting) **A**9 10	13	10	S		75	—	—	—	—	—	—	—	—
TERRE HAUTE—Vigo County													
□ HAMILTON CENTER, 620 Eighth Ave., Zip 47804; tel. 812/231-8323; Donald E. Foltz, dir. **A**1b 10 **F**15 24 29 30 31 32 33 34 35 41 42 44 48 49	23	22	S		49	1401	34	69.4	0	0	7122	3054	224
★□ TERRE HAUTE REGIONAL HOSPITAL, 601 Hospital Lane, Zip 47802; tel. 812/232-0021; William C. Giermak, adm. (Nonreporting) **A**1a 2 9 10; **S**1755	33	10	S		284	—	—	—	—	—	—	—	—
★□ UNION HOSPITAL, 1606 N. Seventh St., Zip 47804; tel. 812/238-7000; Frank Shelton, pres. **A**1a 2 3 5 9 10 **F**1 2 3 5 6 10 11 12 14 15 16 20 23 24 26 30 34 35 36 37 38 40 41 43 44 45 46 47 48 51 52 53 54	23	10	S		286	11930	212	74.1	32	1617	41631	18235	1079
TIPTON—Tipton County													
★□ TIPTON COUNTY MEMORIAL HOSPITAL, 1000 S. Main St., Zip 46072; tel. 317/675-8500; James C. Talley, adm. **A**1a 9 10 **F**1 3 6 10 11 12 14 16 23 24 27 33 35 36 40 44 45 47 50 53	13	10	S		136	2626	39	28.7	17	162	8231	4040	264
UNION CITY—Randolph County													
★ UNION CITY MEMORIAL HOSPITAL, 900 N. Columbia St., Zip 47390; tel. 317/964-6222; Cecily Fultz, adm. (Nonreporting) **A**9 10	23	10	S		30	—	—	—	—	—	—	—	—
VALPARAISO—Porter County													
★□ PORTER MEMORIAL HOSPITAL, 814 La Porte Ave., Zip 46383; tel. 219/464-8611; Arthur S. Malasto, adm. **A**1a 9 10 **F**1 3 5 6 9 10 11 12 14 15 16 20 23 24 26 34 35 36 40 43 44 45 51 52 53	13	10	S		401	13815	240	59.9	36	1547	40422	20411	1082
VINCENNES—Knox County													
★□ GOOD SAMARITAN HOSPITAL, 520 S. Seventh St., Zip 47591; tel. 812/882-5220; John Hidde, exec. dir. **A**1a 2 9 10 **F**1 3 6 7 8 9 10 11 12 14 16 20 23 24 26 27 28 29 30 31 32 33 34 35 36 40 42 44 45 46 49 52 53	13	10	S		289	10812	194	67.1	16	721	34684	15606	904
WABASH—Wabash County													
★□ WABASH COUNTY HOSPITAL, 670 N. East St., Box 548, Zip 46992; tel. 219/563-3131; C. Wayne Hendrix, exec. dir. **A**1a 9 10 **F**1 3 6 10 11 12 15 16 21 23 26 34 35 36 40 41 44 45 46 47 48 49 52 53	13	10	S		114	3276	42	36.8	8	398	9459	4430	268
WARSAW—Kosciusko County													
★□ KOSCIUSKO COMMUNITY HOSPITAL, 2101 E. Dubois Dr., Zip 46580; tel. 219/267-3200; L. Milton Holmgrain, pres. **A**1a 9 10 **F**1 3 6 10 12 15 16 23 34 35 36 40 45 53	23	10	S		113	3923	50	44.2	9	603	11104	4773	245
WASHINGTON—Daviess County													
★□ DAVIESS COUNTY HOSPITAL, 1314 Grand Ave., P O Box 760, Zip 47501; tel. 812/254-2760; Michael Shaffer, adm. (Nonreporting) **A**1a 9 10	13	10	S		136	—	—	—	—	—	—	—	—
WEST LAFAYETTE—Tippecanoe County													
□ PURDUE UNIVERSITY STUDENT HOSPITAL (Formerly Listed Under Lafayette), Zip 47907; tel. 317/494-1700; Thomas A. Schott, adm. **A**1a 9 10 **F**23 28 29 30 32 33 34 35 37	12	11	S		23	221	2	8.7	0	0	2840	1948	69
★ WABASH VALLEY HOSPITAL (Formerly Wabash Valley Hospital Mental Health Center), 2900 N. River Rd., Zip 47906; tel. 317/463-2555; Donald R. Kinzer, adm. **A**9 10 **F**15 19 28 29 30 31 32 33 42 43 45 46 47 48 49	23	22	S		71	739	55	77.5	0	0	6335	3897	191
WILLIAMSPORT—Warren County													
★ COMMUNITY HOSPITAL, 412 N. Monroe St., Zip 47993; tel. 317/762-2496; Phillip D. Marlott, adm. **A**9 10 **F**1 3 6 12 14 15 16 21 23 24 34 35 41 42 44 45 46 47 50 52 53	23	10	S		35	750	10	28.6	0	0	2250	1077	60
WINAMAC—Pulaski County													
★□ PULASKI MEMORIAL HOSPITAL, 616 E. 13th St., Zip 46996; tel. 219/946-6131; Richard H. Mynark, adm. **A**1a 9 10 **F**1 3 6 12 14 15 16 23 35 36 40 41 44 45 46 53	13	10	S		47	1862	24	49.0	6	217	4536	2062	132
WINCHESTER—Randolph County													
RANDOLPH COUNTY HOSPITAL, Oak St. & Greenville Ave., Zip 47394; tel. 317/584-9001; James N. Harness, exec. dir. **A**9 10 **F**1 6 12 16 23 35 40 41 45 46	13	10	S		29	1169	14	48.3	12	113	3355	1584	95

★ American Hospital Association (AHA) membership
☐ Joint Commission on Accreditation of Hospitals (JCAH) accreditation
+ American Osteopathic Hospital Association (AOHA) membership
○ American Osteopathic Association (AOA) accreditation
Δ Commission on Accreditation of Rehabilitation Facilities (CARF) accreditation
Control codes 61, 63, 64, 71, 72 and 73 indicate hospitals listed by AOHA, but not registered by AHA.
For definition of numerical codes, see page A2

Iowa

Hospital, Address, Telephone, Administrator, Approval and Facility Codes, Multihospital System Code	Classification Codes				Inpatient Data				Newborn Data		Expense (thousands of dollars)		
	Control	Service	Stay	Facilities	Beds	Admissions	Census	Occupancy (percent)	Bassinets	Births	Total	Payroll	Personnel
AKRON—Plymouth County													
AKRON HOSPITAL, Zip 51001; tel. 712/568-2422; Jerold J. Dykstra, adm. (Total facility includes 45 beds in nursing home-type unit) **A**9 **F**1 14 15 16 19 23 26 35 40 45 46 47 50	14	10	S	TF	61	131	52	85.2	0	2	912	501	45
				H	16	61	1	—	0	2	542	294	24
ALBIA—Monroe County													
MONROE COUNTY HOSPITAL, R.F.D. 3 Avery Rd., Zip 52531; tel. 515/932-2134; Ronald Davis, adm. **A**9 10 **F**1 15 16 23 34 35 36 40 45	13	10	S		46	839	19	41.3	4	39	3043	1193	78
ALGONA—Kossuth County													
★ KOSSUTH COUNTY HOSPITAL, Hwy. 169 S., Zip 50511; tel. 515/295-2451; David Schultz, adm. **A**9 10 **F**1 6 14 15 16 23 30 35 40 41 45; **S**5165	13	10	S		40	1066	14	35.0	6	150	2480	1204	78
AMES—Story County													
★☐ MARY GREELEY MEDICAL CENTER, 117 11th St., Zip 50010; tel. 515/239-2011; John D. Worley Jr., pres. & chief oper. off. **A**1a 9 10 **F**1 3 6 7 8 9 10 11 12 14 15 16 20 21 23 24 25 26 27 28 29 30 33 34 35 36 37 40 41 42 44 45 46 47 49 51 52 53	14	10	S		217	8584	130	59.9	22	1262	23079	12178	654
ANAMOSA—Jones County													
★☐ ANAMOSA COMMUNITY HOSPITAL, 104 Broadway Pl., Zip 52205; tel. 319/462-3588; Sara Miller, adm. **A**1a 9 10 **F**1 15 23 24 34 35 36 37 40 41 45 46 47	23	10	S		38	634	10	26.3	8	56	1291	636	58
ATLANTIC—Cass County													
★☐ CASS COUNTY MEMORIAL HOSPITAL, 1501 E. Tenth St., Zip 50022; tel. 712/243-3250; Dennis J. Renander, adm. (Total facility includes 16 beds in nursing home-type unit) **A**1a 9 10 **F**1 3 6 10 12 15 16 19 21 23 34 35 40 41 42 43 44 45 53	13	10	S	TF	76	2082	30	39.5	10	303	5893	3060	170
				H	60	1994	26	—	10	303	5580	2889	160
AUDUBON—Audubon County													
☐ AUDUBON COUNTY MEMORIAL HOSPITAL, 515 Pacific St., Zip 50025; tel. 712/563-2611; Jerry Klein, adm. **A**1a 9 10 **F**1 6 16 23 34 35 37 40 44 45 53	13	10	S		29	307	6	20.7	6	53	1207	571	34
BELMOND—Wright County													
★☐ BELMOND COMMUNITY HOSPITAL, 403 First St. S.E., P O Box 326, Zip 50421; tel. 515/444-3223; James R. Hovelson, adm. **A**1a 9 10 **F**1 2 16 23 35 40 45; **S**5165	14	10	S		22	272	6	27.3	4	17	884	438	28
BLOOMFIELD—Davis County													
DAVIS COUNTY HOSPITAL, 507 N. Madison St., Zip 52537; tel. 515/664-2145; William H. Koellner, adm. (Total facility includes 28 beds in nursing home-type unit) **A**9 10 **F**1 3 10 12 15 16 19 23 34 35 40 42 45 50	13	10	S	TF	76	1521	44	64.7	6	61	4215	2079	132
				H	48	1410	19	—	6	61	3974	1875	115
BOONE—Boone County													
★☐ BOONE COUNTY HOSPITAL, 1015 Union St., Zip 50036; tel. 515/432-3140; Terry Gott, adm. **A**1a 9 10 **F**1 3 6 10 12 14 15 16 23 34 35 36 37 40 41 44 45 46 47 53	13	10	S		57	2101	29	50.9	12	171	6411	2817	221
BRITT—Hancock County													
★☐ HANCOCK COUNTY MEMORIAL HOSPITAL, 531 Second St. N.W., Box 68, Zip 50423; tel. 515/843-3801; Lawrence N. Crail, adm. **A**1a 9 10 **F**1 6 15 16 23 24 34 35 36 37 40 43 44 45 46; **S**5165	13	10	S		30	512	8	26.7	12	97	1521	746	43
BURLINGTON—Des Moines County													
★☐ BURLINGTON MEDICAL CENTER (Includes F. Albert Klein Unit, 2910 Madison Rd., Zip 52601; tel. 319/752-5461), 602 N. Third St., Zip 52601; tel. 319/753-3011; Glen L. Heagle, pres. & chief exec. off. (Total facility includes 149 beds in nursing home-type unit) **A**1a 9 10 **F**1 3 5 6 7 8 9 10 11 12 14 15 16 19 20 23 24 25 26 27 30 32 35 36 37 40 41 42 44 45 46 47 48 49 50 52 53 54	23	10	S	TF	388	8421	269	69.3	16	789	32395	13464	764
				H	239	7772	128	—	16	789	28968	12133	698
F. ALBERT KLEIN UNIT, See Burlington Medical Center													
CARROLL—Carroll County													
★☐ ST. ANTHONY REGIONAL HOSPITAL, S. Clark St., Zip 51401; tel. 712/792-3581; Robert D. Blincow, adm. (Total facility includes 79 beds in nursing home-type unit) **A**1a 9 10 **F**1 3 6 10 12 14 15 16 19 23 35 38 40 44 45 52 53; **S**5705	21	10	S	TF	132	1973	104	78.8	10	322	6665	2841	188
				H	53	1920	27	—	10	322	5719	2336	155
CEDAR FALLS—Black Hawk County													
★☐ SARTORI MEMORIAL HOSPITAL, Sixth & College Sts., Zip 50613; tel. 319/266-3584; Duane R. Vorseth, chief exec. off. (Total facility includes 18 beds in nursing home-type unit) **A**1a 9 10 **F**1 3 5 6 12 14 15 16 19 21 23 24 30 34 35 36 40 41 42 44 45 47 53	14	10	S	TF	101	2688	36	35.6	10	382	10584	4373	238
				H	83	2528	30	—	10	382	—	—	227
CEDAR RAPIDS—Linn County													
★☐ MERCY HOSPITAL (Includes Hallmar), 701 Tenth St. S.E., Zip 52403; tel. 319/398-6011; A. James Tinker, adm. (Total facility includes 76 beds in nursing home-type unit) **A**1a3 9 10 **F**1 3 5 6 7 8 9 10 11 12 14 15 16 17 19 20 21 23 27 28 30 32 33 34 35 36 38 40 41 45 46 47 48 49 50 52 53 54	21	10	S	TF	429	11860	288	67.1	24	624	40511	20416	1213
				H	353	11284	206	—	24	624	38358	19575	1199
★☐ Δ ST. LUKE'S METHODIST HOSPITAL, 1026 A Ave. N.E., Zip 52402; tel. 319/369-7211; Samuel T. Wallace, pres. **A**1a 3 5 6 7 9 10 **F**1 2 3 4 5 6 9 10 11 12 14 15 16 17 20 23 24 26 27 28 29 30 32 33 34 35 36 37 38 40 42 44 45 46 47 51 52 53 54	23	10	S		455	16833	296	64.2	42	2250	54905	26476	1469
CENTERVILLE—Appanoose County													
★☐ ST. JOSEPH'S MERCY HOSPITAL, Rte. 3, Zip 52544; tel. 515/437-4111; Kenneth L. Smithmier, chief exec. off. (Total facility includes 19 beds in nursing home-type unit) **A**1a 9 10 **F**1 3 6 10 14 15 16 19 23 34 35 40 44 47 53; **S**5175	21	10	S	TF	55	1247	40	72.7	8	139	4184	2030	111
				H	36	1237	21	—	8	139	4034	1879	105
CHARITON—Lucas County													
★ LUCAS COUNTY HEALTH CENTER (Formerly Lucas County Memorial Hospital), 1200 N. Seventh St., Rte. 3, Box 43-A, Zip 50049; tel. 515/774-2181; Randy Richards, chief exec. off. **A**9 10 **F**1 3 6 15 16 23 35 40 45 50 53	13	10	S		56	1012	16	28.6	6	23	3901	1627	101
CHARLES CITY—Floyd County													
★☐ FLOYD COUNTY MEMORIAL HOSPITAL, 11th & S. Main Sts., Zip 50616; tel. 515/228-6830; James D. Schneckloth, adm. **A**1a 9 10 **F**1 3 6 15 16 23 35 37 40 41 45 52	13	10	S		55	1582	22	40.0	6	143	4108	1775	115
CHEROKEE—Cherokee County													
☐ MENTAL HEALTH INSTITUTE, 1200 W. Cedar St., Zip 51012; tel. 712/225-2594; E. A. Kjenaas MD, supt. **A**1b 3 5 9 10 **F**15 23 24 28 29 30 31 32 33 34 35 41 42 43 44 45 46 47 49 50	12	22	L		264	1414	240	90.9	0	0	11307	7824	385
★ SIOUX VALLEY MEMORIAL HOSPITAL, 300 Sioux Valley Dr., Zip 51012; tel. 712/225-5101; Kenneth R. Hobson, adm. **A**9 10 **F**1 2 6 14 15 16 23 24 26 35 40 44 52 53	23	10	S		67	1560	23	34.3	14	162	3505	2011	138

Hospital, Address, Telephone, Administrator, Approval and Facility Codes, Multihospital System Code	Classification Codes				Inpatient Data				Newborn Data		Expense (thousands of dollars)		
★ American Hospital Association (AHA) membership □ Joint Commission on Accreditation of Hospitals (JCAH) accreditation + American Osteopathic Hospital Association (AOHA) membership ○ American Osteopathic Association (AOA) accreditation Δ Commission on Accreditation of Rehabilitation Facilities (CARF) accreditation Control codes 61, 63, 64, 71, 72 and 73 indicate hospitals listed by AOHA, but not registered by AHA. For definition of numerical codes, see page A2	Control	Service	Stay	Facilities	Beds	Admissions	Census	Occupancy (percent)	Bassinets	Births	Total	Payroll	Personnel
CLARINDA—Page County													
★□ CLARINDA MUNICIPAL HOSPITAL, 17th & Wells Sts., P O Box 217, Zip 51632; tel. 712/542-2176; Richard C. Hamilton, adm. **A**1a 9 10 **F**1 6 10 12 14 15 16 17 23 35 40 44 45 46 47 52 53	14	10	S		47	973	12	25.5	8	132	2128	1111	69
□ MENTAL HEALTH INSTITUTE, Box 338, Zip 51632; tel. 712/542-2161; Mark Lund, supt. **A**1a 9 10 **F**15 23 24 28 30 32 33 34 35 42 48 49 50	12	22	L		120	750	129	100.0	0	0	6054	4189	209
CLARION—Wright County													
□ COMMUNITY MEMORIAL HOSPITAL, 1316 S. Main St., Zip 50525; tel. 515/532-2811; Paul Hurd, adm. **A**1a 9 10 **F**1 3 6 16 23 34 35 36 37 40 45	14	10	S		33	674	14	42.4	5	97	1935	802	57
CLINTON—Clinton County													
★□ JANE LAMB HEALTH CENTER, 638 S. Bluff Blvd., Zip 52732; tel. 319/243-1131; Mark Richardson, pres. (Total facility includes 18 beds in nursing home-type unit) **A**1a 9 10 **F**1 3 6 7 10 11 12 15 16 19 23 24 27 29 30 32 33 34 35 36 40 44 45 46 50 52 53	23	10	S	TF	148	3305	58	39.2	12	328	10886	4993	283
				H	130	3091	45	—	12	328	10642	4761	270
★□ ST. JOSEPH MERCY HOSPITAL, 1410 N. Fourth St., Zip 52732; tel. 319/243-5900; Sr. Mary Margaret Westrick, pres. & chief exec. off. **A**1a 9 10 **F**1 3 6 10 12 15 16 19 23 24 35 36 40 41 45 49 50 52 53; **S**5165	21	10	S		141	3985	66	45.8	12	305	12502	6428	335
CORNING—Adams County													
★□ MERCY HOSPITAL (Formerly Rosary Hospital), Rosary Dr., Box 368, Zip 50841; tel. 515/322-3121; James C. Ruppert, adm. **A**1a 9 10 **F**1 6 15 16 23 35 41 43 45 53; **S**5175	21	10	S		35	470	9	25.7	6	40	1536	812	56
CORYDON—Wayne County													
★ WAYNE COUNTY HOSPITAL, 417 S. E. St., Zip 50060; tel. 515/872-2260; C. James Platt, adm. **A**9 10 **F**1 3 6 15 16 23 34 35 40 45 53	13	10	S		28	799	13	46.4	6	59	1967	864	58
COUNCIL BLUFFS—Pottawattamie County													
★□ JENNIE EDMUNDSON MEMORIAL HOSPITAL, 933 E. Pierce St., Zip 51501; tel. 712/328-6000; Edward R. Lynn, adm. (Total facility includes 17 beds in nursing home-type unit) **A**1a 6 9 10 **F**1 2 3 5 6 7 8 9 10 11 12 14 15 16 17 19 20 23 24 26 27 28 29 30 32 33 35 36 40 42 44 45 46 47 49 52 53	23	10	S	TF	176	6493	148	84.1	20	619	24858	12475	578
				H	159	6274	136	—	20	619	24197	12236	—
★□ MERCY HOSPITAL, 800 Mercy Dr., Box 1c, Zip 51502; tel. 712/328-5000; Mervin M. Riepe, pres. **A**1a 9 10 **F**1 2 3 6 12 14 16 19 23 24 27 28 29 30 34 35 36 40 42 44 45 46 47 48 49 50 52 53; **S**5175	21	10	S		284	7079	153	53.9	16	345	24655	11460	546
CRESCO—Howard County													
★□ HOWARD COUNTY HOSPITAL, 235 Eighth Ave. W., Zip 52136; tel. 319/547-2101; Steven B. Reiter, adm. **A**1a 9 10 **F**1 3 14 15 16 21 23 34 35 36 40 41 42 45 46; **S**5165	13	10	S		42	822	12	28.6	8	134	2330	1124	72
CRESTON—Union County													
★□ GREATER COMMUNITY HOSPITAL, Cottonwood & Townline, Zip 50801; tel. 515/782-7091; Richard Gamel, adm. **A**1a 9 10 **F**1 3 6 7 8 12 14 15 16 21 23 24 28 30 32 33 34 35 36 40 41 43 44 45	13	10	S		68	1830	25	36.8	10	228	5019	2506	156
DAVENPORT—Scott County													
○ + DAVENPORT MEDICAL CENTER, 1111 W. Kimberly Rd., Zip 52806; tel. 319/391-2020; Jeff Burres, exec. dir. (Nonreporting) **A**9 10 11 12 13; **S**3025	33	10	S		150	—	—	—	—	—	—	—	—
★□ Δ MERCY HOSPITAL, W. Central Park at Marquette, Box 4110, Zip 52804; tel. 319/383-1000; H. Gerald Smith, pres. & chief exec. off. **A**1a 3 5 7 9 10 **F**1 3 5 6 10 12 14 15 16 23 24 25 26 27 30 32 33 34 35 36 40 42 44 45 48 49 50 52 53 54; **S**5215	21	10	S		265	9328	181	68.3	20	733	35347	16209	831
★□ ST. LUKE'S HOSPITAL, 1227 E. Rusholme St., Zip 52803; tel. 319/326-6512; James R. Stuhler, pres. **A**1a 3 5 9 10 **F**1 3 4 6 7 8 10 12 14 15 16 20 21 23 24 26 34 35 36 37 40 41 45 46 47 51 52 53 54	23	10	S		238	8542	127	53.4	24	1429	31963	13486	670
DE WITT—Clinton County													
★□ DEWITT COMMUNITY HOSPITAL, 1118 11th St., Zip 52742; tel. 319/659-3241; Bruce A. Marlowe, adm. (Total facility includes 50 beds in nursing home-type unit) **A**1a 9 10 **F**1 2 6 14 15 16 19 30 35 40 45 46 47 50	23	10	S	TF	74	733	61	82.4	4	46	2251	1126	100
				H	24	684	13	—	4	46	1609	877	78
DECORAH—Winneshiek County													
★□ WINNESHIEK COUNTY MEMORIAL HOSPITAL, 901 Montgomery St., Zip 52101; tel. 319/382-2911; Paul Anderson, adm. **A**1a 9 10 **F**1 3 6 10 12 14 15 16 23 26 35 36 40 41 42 44 45 53	13	10	S		83	1973	28	33.7	10	297	4733	2433	130
DENISON—Crawford County													
★□ CRAWFORD COUNTY MEMORIAL HOSPITAL, 2020 First Ave. S., Zip 51442; tel. 712/263-5021; Terry R. Magden, adm. **A**1a 9 10 **F**3 6 10 12 14 16 23 35 40 44 45 49 53	13	10	S		92	1965	26	28.3	5	236	3586	2027	126
DES MOINES—Polk County													
★□ BROADLAWNS MEDICAL CENTER, 18th St. & Hickman Rd., Zip 50314; tel. 515/282-2200; William L. Meyer, exec. dir. (Total facility includes 78 beds in nursing home-type unit) **A**1a 3 5 9 10 **F**1 3 6 12 14 15 16 19 23 24 26 27 28 29 30 32 33 34 35 36 37 40 42 43 45 46 48 49 52	13	10	S	TF	294	5878	215	73.1	14	613	30273	15135	708
				H	216	5853	139	—	14	613	28527	14180	652
★□ CHARTER COMMUNITY HOSPITAL OF DES MOINES (Formerly Charter Community Hospital), 1818 48th St., Zip 50310; tel. 515/271-6000; Dennis Janssen, adm. **A**1a 9 10 **F**1 3 6 10 12 14 15 16 23 24 27 30 32 34 35 37 42 45 46; **S**0695	33	10	S		118	1561	30	25.4	0	0	7730	3170	177
★ ○ + DES MOINES GENERAL HOSPITAL, 603 E. 12th St., Zip 50307; tel. 515/263-4200; William I. Cairns, pres. **A**9 10 11 12 13 **F**1 3 4 6 10 12 14 16 19 20 23 32 34 35 36 40 41 42 44 45 46 48 52 54	23	10	S		241	6147	119	48.6	10	428	31648	12549	669
HELEN POWELL CONVALESCENT CENTER, See Iowa Methodist Medical Center													
★□ IOWA LUTHERAN HOSPITAL, University at Penn, Zip 50316; tel. 515/263-5612; Marlin J. Stirm, adm. (Total facility includes 16 beds in nursing home-type unit) **A**1a 3 5 9 10 **F**1 2 3 4 5 6 9 10 11 12 14 15 16 19 20 23 24 26 27 28 30 32 33 34 36 37 40 42 44 45 46 47 48 52 53 54; **S**1325	23	10	S	TF	365	9237	230	63.0	24	1090	47829	21443	1091
				H	349	9045	221	—	24	1090	—	—	1082
★□ IOWA METHODIST MEDICAL CENTER (Includes Helen Powell Convalescent Center; Raymond Blank Memorial Hospital for Children; Younker Memorial Rehabilitation Center), 1200 Pleasant St., Zip 50308; tel. 515/283-6212; David S. Ramsey, pres. **A**1a 2 3 5 6 8 9 10 **F**1 2 3 4 5 6 7 8 9 10 11 12 13 14 15 16 17 22 23 24 25 26 27 30 33 34 35 36 37 38 39 40 41 42 44 45 46 47 48 49 50 51 52 53 54; **S**1595	23	10	S		680	16770	438	64.4	30	1971	98854	47559	2431
★□ Δ MERCY HOSPITAL MEDICAL CENTER, Sixth & University Ave., Zip 50314; tel. 515/247-3121; Sr. Patricia Clare Sullivan, pres. **A**1a 2 6 7 9 10 **F**1 2 3 4 5 6 10 12 13 14 15 16 20 21 23 24 26 28 30 32 33 34 35 36 39 40 41 42 43 44 45 46 47 48 49 50 52 53 54; **S**5175	21	10	S		500	22897	411	82.2	37	2419	97332	41917	2060
RAYMOND BLANK MEMORIAL HOSPITAL FOR CHILDREN, See Iowa Methodist Medical Center													
★□ VETERANS ADMINISTRATION MEDICAL CENTER, 30th & Euclid Ave., Zip 50310; tel. 515/255-2173; Wayne Maddocks, dir. **A**1a 2 3 5 **F**1 3 6 10 12 14 15 16 23 24 26 28 30 32 33 34 35 44 46 47 49 50 53 54	45	10	S		273	5648	149	54.6	0	0	31989	19961	704
YOUNKER MEMORIAL REHABILITATION CENTER, See Iowa Methodist Medical Center													

★ American Hospital Association (AHA) membership
□ Joint Commission on Accreditation of Hospitals (JCAH) accreditation
+ American Osteopathic Hospital Association (AOHA) membership
○ American Osteopathic Association (AOA) accreditation
Δ Commission on Accreditation of Rehabilitation Facilities (CARF) accreditation
Control codes 61, 63, 64, 71, 72 and 73 indicate hospitals listed by AOHA, but not registered by AHA. For definition of numerical codes, see page A2

Hospital, Address, Telephone, Administrator, Approval and Facility Codes, Multihospital System Code	Classification Codes				Inpatient Data				Newborn Data		Expense (thousands of dollars)		
	Control	Service	Stay	Facilities	Beds	Admissions	Census	Occupancy (percent)	Bassinets	Births	Total	Payroll	Personnel
DUBUQUE—Dubuque County													
★□ FINLEY HOSPITAL, 350 N. Grandview Ave., Zip 52001; tel. 319/582-1881; Stephen C. Hanson, pres. (Total facility includes 17 beds in nursing home-type unit) **A**1a 6 9 10 **F**1 3 5 6 7 8 9 10 11 12 14 15 16 19 20 23 30 33 35 36 37 38 40 41 43 45 46 47 52 53	23	10	S	TF	158	5417	89	56.3	12	454	20968	9565	454
				H	141	5095	76	—	12	454	20430	9153	434
★□ MERCY HEALTH CENTER (Includes St. Joseph's Unit, Mercy Dr., Zip 52001; tel. 319/589-8000; St. Mary's Unit, 1111 Third St. S.W., Dyersville, Zip 52040; tel. 319/875-7101), Mercy Dr., Zip 52001; Sr. Helen Huewe, pres. (Total facility includes 60 beds in nursing home-type unit) **A**1a 9 10 **F**1 3 4 5 6 10 11 12 14 15 16 19 23 24 25 26 27 28 29 30 32 33 34 35 36 40 41 42 43 44 45 46 47 48 49 50 51 52 53 54; **S**5165	21	10	S	TF	400	11012	242	60.5	30	1315	41661	21938	1047
				H	340	10660	188	—	30	1315	41016	21335	1025
DYERSVILLE—Dubuque County													
ST. MARY'S UNIT, See Mercy Health Center, Dubuque													
ELDORA—Hardin County													
★ ELDORA REGIONAL MEDICAL CENTER (Formerly Eldora Community Hospital), 2413 Edgington Ave., Zip 50627; tel. 515/858-5416; Jonathan Goble, adm. **A**9 10 **F**1 3 6 15 16 23 24 26 34 35 36 40 44 45 48 52; **S**5165	14	10	S		24	385	10	41.7	4	25	1500	565	40
ELKADER—Clayton County													
★ CENTRAL COMMUNITY HOSPITAL, 901 Davidson St. N.W., Zip 52043; tel. 319/245-2250; Samuel J. Curnow, adm. **A**9 10 **F**1 6 10 15 16 23 24 34 35 36 37 40 44 45	23	10	S		27	626	12	44.4	5	61	1693	809	57
EMMETSBURG—Palo Alto County													
PALO ALTO COUNTY HOSPITAL, W. First St., Zip 50536; tel. 712/852-2434; Darrell E. Vondrak, adm. (Total facility includes 22 beds in nursing home-type unit) **A**9 10 **F**1 3 6 14 15 16 19 23 34 35 36 37 40 44 45 47	13	10	S	TF	54	1066	19	46.3	6	169	2816	1399	72
				H	32	1018	14	—	6	169	2680	1356	64
ESTHERVILLE—Emmet County													
★□ HOLY FAMILY HOSPITAL, 826 N. Eighth St., Zip 51334; tel. 712/362-2631; Donald M. Schmaus, pres. **A**1a 9 10 **F**1 3 6 10 12 14 15 16 21 23 35 40 41 42 44 45 48 49 53; **S**5305	21	10	S		58	1331	28	48.3	10	114	4478	1980	128
FAIRFIELD—Jefferson County													
★ JEFFERSON COUNTY HOSPITAL, 400 Highland St., Box 588, Zip 52556; tel. 515/472-4111; Walter W. Brownlee, adm. (Total facility includes 16 beds in nursing home-type unit) **A**9 10 **F**1 3 6 10 12 14 15 16 19 23 34 35 36 40 43 45	13	10	S	TF	67	1687	45	67.2	5	195	3777	2136	142
				H	51	1683	29	—	5	195	3635	2000	133
FOREST CITY—Winnebago County													
FOREST CITY COMMUNITY HOSPITAL, Hwy. 9 E., Box 470, Zip 50436; tel. 515/582-3113; Gregory E. Patten, adm. **A**9 10 **F**1 15 16 23 35 36 40 45 48 52; **S**5165	14	10	S		45	668	23	51.1	5	98	1569	700	62
FORT DODGE—Webster County													
★□ TRINITY REGIONAL HOSPITAL, S. Kenyon Rd., Zip 50501; tel. 515/573-3101; Tom Tibbits, pres. **A**1a 9 10 **F**1 3 5 6 9 10 11 12 14 15 16 19 20 23 26 27 28 29 30 34 35 36 40 41 42 45 46 48 49 52 53 54	23	10	S		194	6047	102	52.6	24	636	20275	10290	571
FORT MADISON—Lee County													
★□ FORT MADISON COMMUNITY HOSPITAL, 2210 Ave. H, Zip 52627; tel. 319/372-6530; Stephen R. Schoaps, chief exec. off. **A**1a 9 10 **F**1 3 6 10 12 14 15 16 23 26 28 30 32 34 35 36 37 40 43 45 46 48 49 53; **S**1755	23	10	S		95	2078	33	34.7	10	170	5847	2675	142
GLENWOOD—Mills County													
GLENWOOD STATE HOSPITAL SCHOOL, Zip 51534; tel. 712/527-4811; William E. Campbell PhD, supt. **F**15 23 24 26 29 30 32 33 34 37 38 42 43 44 45 46 50	12	62	L		668	29	670	94.1	0	0	29856	20347	1166
GREENFIELD—Adair County													
ADAIR COUNTY MEMORIAL HOSPITAL, 609 S.E. Kent St., Rural Rte. 3, Box 100, Zip 50849; tel. 515/743-2123; Joseph Rivera, adm. (Nonreporting) **A**9 10	13	10	S		31	—	—	—	—	—	—	—	—
GRINNELL—Poweshiek County													
★□ GRINNELL GENERAL HOSPITAL, 210 Fourth Ave., Zip 50112; tel. 515/236-7511; Bruce C. Jensen, chief exec. off. **A**1a 9 10 **F**1 3 6 10 12 15 16 21 23 24 30 34 35 37 40 41 43 44 45 46 50 53	23	10	S		53	2485	37	69.8	10	231	8353	3451	205
GRUNDY CENTER—Grundy County													
GRUNDY COUNTY MEMORIAL HOSPITAL, E. J Ave., Zip 50638; tel. 319/824-5421; Lowell M. Honson, adm. (Total facility includes 55 beds in nursing home-type unit) **A**9 10 **F**1 3 14 15 16 19 23 34 35 40 42 45 52	13	10	S	TF	88	171	58	65.9	7	13	1898	873	56
				H	33	122	4	—	7	13	1233	551	29
GUTHRIE CENTER—Guthrie County													
★ GUTHRIE COUNTY HOSPITAL, 710 N. 12th St., Zip 50115; tel. 515/747-2201; Lois E. Hall, adm. **A**9 10 **F**1 3 14 15 23 35 40 42 44 45	13	10	S		25	593	8	32.0	5	43	1269	633	39
GUTTENBERG—Clayton County													
★ GUTTENBERG MUNICIPAL HOSPITAL, Second & Main St., Box A, Zip 52052; tel. 319/252-1121 **A**9 10 **F**1 3 15 16 23 35 36 40 45 52; **S**5805	14	10	S		37	622	9	24.3	6	56	1472	711	44
HAMBURG—Fremont County													
★ GRAPE COMMUNITY HOSPITAL-SOUTHWEST IOWA MEDICAL CENTER (Formerly Grape Community Hospital), Hwy. 275 N., P O Box 246, Zip 51640; tel. 712/382-1515; K. E. Moyer, adm. **A**9 10 **F**1 6 14 15 16 29 34 35 41 43 45	23	10	S		49	860	13	26.5	4	140	3691	1610	129
HAMPTON—Franklin County													
★ FRANKLIN GENERAL HOSPITAL, 1720 Central Ave. E., Zip 50441; tel. 515/456-4721; Gary Busack, adm. (Total facility includes 52 beds in nursing home-type unit) **A**9 10 **F**1 3 6 10 14 15 16 19 23 24 32 33 34 35 36 40 42 44 45; **S**5165	13	10	S	TF	92	732	63	68.5	4	93	3486	1818	113
				H	40	690	12	—	4	93	2624	1244	89
HARLAN—Shelby County													
★□ MYRTUE MEMORIAL HOSPITAL (Formerly Shelby County Myrtue Memorial Hospital), 1213 Garfield Ave., Zip 51537; tel. 712/755-5161; Eugene Leblond, adm. **A**1a 9 10 **F**1 2 6 15 16 23 33 34 35 36 40 44 45 50 53	13	10	S		52	1790	25	48.1	6	162	4056	2047	126
HARTLEY—O'Brien County													
COMMUNITY MEMORIAL HOSPITAL (Includes Mann Memorial Wing), P O Box 188, Zip 51346; tel. 712/728-2428; Madonna M. Towne RN, adm. (Total facility includes 43 beds in nursing home-type unit) **A**9 10 **F**1 3 6 16 19 23 26 30 35 40 41 43 45 47 50	23	10	S	TF	63	221	48	76.2	4	17	1155	624	47
				H	20	186	7	—	4	17	704	352	26
HAWARDEN—Sioux County													
HAWARDEN COMMUNITY HOSPITAL, 1111 11th St., Zip 51023; tel. 712/552-1121; Earl J. Steinhoff, adm. **A**9 10 **F**1 3 6 14 15 16 21 23 34 35 40 45 49 50 52	14	10	S		27	371	4	14.8	6	41	716	399	25
HUMBOLDT—Humboldt County													
★□ HUMBOLDT COUNTY MEMORIAL HOSPITAL, 1000 N. 15th St., Box 587, Zip 50548; tel. 515/332-4200; Richard L. Abrahamson, adm. **A**1a 9 10 **F**1 6 14 15 16 23 34 35 40 43 45; **S**1595	13	10	S		49	847	20	40.8	6	99	2561	1241	75
IDA GROVE—Ida County													
★ HORN MEMORIAL HOSPITAL, E. Second St., Zip 51445; tel. 712/364-3311; John Blanco, adm. **A**9 10 **F**1 3 6 12 14 15 16 17 23 34 35 37 40 41 42 45 53	23	10	S		42	922	13	31.0	6	150	1713	871	51

Hospital, Address, Telephone, Administrator, Approval and Facility Codes, Multihospital System Code	Classification Codes				Inpatient Data				Newborn Data		Expense (thousands of dollars)		
★ American Hospital Association (AHA) membership □ Joint Commission on Accreditation of Hospitals (JCAH) accreditation + American Osteopathic Hospital Association (AOHA) membership ○ American Osteopathic Association (AOA) accreditation Δ Commission on Accreditation of Rehabilitation Facilities (CARF) accreditation Control codes 61, 63, 64, 71, 72 and 73 indicate hospitals listed by AOHA, but not registered by AHA. For definition of numerical codes, see page A2	Control	Service	Stay	Facilities	Beds	Admissions	Census	Occupancy (percent)	Bassinets	Births	Total	Payroll	Personnel
INDEPENDENCE—Buchanan County													
□ MENTAL HEALTH INSTITUTE, Box 111, Zip 50644; tel. 319/334-2583; B. J. Dave MD, supt. **A**1b 9 10 **F**24 28 29 30 32 33 34 35 42 43 45 46 47 48 49 50	12	22	L		282	1658	243	83.8	0	0	11656	8248	397
★ PEOPLE'S MEMORIAL HOSPITAL, 1600 First St. E., Zip 50644; tel. 319/334-6071; Robert J. Richard, adm. (Total facility includes 59 beds in nursing home-type unit) **A**9 10 **F**1 6 15 16 19 21 23 26 35 36 40 45 46 53	13	10	S	TF	109	1119	67	61.5	6	96	3112	1774	126
				H	50	1041	11	—	6	96	2355	1235	81
IOWA CITY—Johnson County													
⊞ MERCY HOSPITAL, 500 Market St., Zip 52240; tel. 319/337-0500; Sr. Mary Venarda, chief exec. off. **A**1a 3 5 9 10 **F**1 3 5 6 9 10 11 12 14 15 16 23 26 28 29 30 32 33 34 35 36 40 41 44 45 46 51 52 53; **S**5215	21	10	S		240	8545	132	55.0	23	1323	27367	11438	516
PSYCHIATRIC HOSPITAL, See University of Iowa Hospitals and Clinics													
UNIVERSITY HOSPITAL SCHOOL, See University of Iowa Hospitals and Clinics													
⊞ UNIVERSITY OF IOWA HOSPITALS AND CLINICS (Includes Chemical Dependency Center, Oakdale, Zip 52319; tel. 319/353-4966; Psychiatric Hospital, 500 Newton Rd., Zip 52242; tel. 319/353-3234; University Hospital School, Zip 52242; tel. 319/353-4131), 650 Newton Rd., Zip 52242; tel. 319/356-1616; John W. Colloton, dir. & asst. to vice-pres. **A**1a 2 3 5 8 9 10 **F**1 2 3 4 5 6 7 8 9 10 11 12 13 14 15 16 17 18 19 20 22 23 24 27 28 30 32 33 34 35 36 37 38 39 40 42 44 46 47 48 49 50 51 52 53 54	12	10	S		899	34620	700	78.7	23	2461	180733	81092	4309
⊞ VETERANS ADMINISTRATION MEDICAL CENTER, Hwy. 6 W., Zip 52240; tel. 319/338-0581; Gary L. Wilkinson, dir. **A**1a 3 5 8 **F**1 2 3 6 9 10 12 13 14 15 16 20 23 24 27 28 29 33 34 41 42 44 46 47 53 54	45	10	S		291	9488	216	74.2	0	0	48422	21884	939
IOWA FALLS—Hardin County													
⊞ ELLSWORTH MUNICIPAL HOSPITAL, 110 Rocksylvania Ave., Zip 50126; tel. 515/648-4631; Daniel T. Meyer, adm. **A**1a 9 10 **F**1 3 15 16 23 26 34 35 36 40 45; **S**5165	14	10	S		42	1033	15	35.7	6	140	3053	1230	82
JEFFERSON—Greene County													
⊞ GREENE COUNTY MEDICAL CENTER, 1000 W. Lincolnway, Zip 50129; tel. 515/386-2114; Roger W. Lenz, pres. (Total facility includes 74 beds in nursing home-type unit) **A**1a 9 10 **F**1 3 6 15 16 19 23 34 35 36 40 41 45 50 52 53	13	10	S	TF	127	1097	94	74.0	6	113	4422	2377	163
				H	53	1032	23	—	6	113	3231	1735	113
KEOKUK—Lee County													
⊞ KEOKUK AREA HOSPITAL, 1600 Morgan St., Zip 52632; tel. 319/524-7150; Greg R. Miller, chief exec. off. (Total facility includes 12 beds in nursing home-type unit) **A**1a 9 10 **F**1 3 6 10 12 14 15 16 19 23 24 27 29 30 32 33 34 35 36 37 40 41 42 44 45 47 52 53	23	10	S	TF	117	3914	65	55.6	12	227	11258	5213	305
				H	105	3681	56	—	12	227	11146	5104	—
KEOSAUQUA—Van Buren County													
VAN BUREN COUNTY MEMORIAL HOSPITAL, Rural Rte. 1, Box 70, Zip 52565; tel. 319/293-3171; Ronald J. Volk, adm. **A**9 10 **F**1 16 23 34 35 36 40 44 45 52; **S**5805	13	10	S		40	727	16	40.0	7	83	1699	852	61
KNOXVILLE—Marion County													
★ KNOXVILLE AREA COMMUNITY HOSPITAL, 1002 S. Lincoln St., Zip 50138; tel. 515/842-2151; David Christiansen, adm. **A**9 10 **F**1 3 6 10 15 16 21 23 26 33 34 35 40 44 45 46 47 53; **S**1755	23	10	S		59	1923	31	52.5	4	117	4338	1480	99
⊞ VETERANS ADMINISTRATION MEDICAL CENTER, W. Pleasant St., Zip 50138; tel. 515/842-3101; Donald D. Ziska, dir. (Total facility includes 200 beds in nursing home-type unit) **A**1a **F**15 16 19 23 24 25 26 28 31 33 34 42 43 44 46 47 48 49 50	45	22	L	TF	656	3200	510	77.7	0	0	32516	22490	926
				H	456	3143	317	—	0	0	24320	16808	811
LAKE CITY—Calhoun County													
⊞ STEWART MEMORIAL COMMUNITY HOSPITAL, 1200 W. Monroe, Zip 51449; tel. 712/464-3171; Edward R. Maahs, adm. **A**1a 9 10 **F**1 3 6 15 16 21 23 26 30 34 35 40 41 44 45 46 53	23	10	S		26	1875	25	96.2	4	163	3357	1482	98
LE MARS—Plymouth County													
FLOYD VALLEY HOSPITAL, Hwy. 3 E., P O Box 10, Zip 51031; tel. 712/546-7871; J. Dwight Gray, adm. **A**9 10 **F**1 3 6 14 15 16 23 34 35 37 40 42 44 45 47 52; **S**5845	14	10	S		44	1426	21	47.7	6	191	2734	1335	72
LEON—Decatur County													
⊞ DECATUR COUNTY HOSPITAL, 1405 N.W. Church St., Zip 50144; tel. 515/446-4871; John Myers, adm. **A**1a 9 10 **F**1 3 6 10 15 16 23 35 37 40 45 46 53	13	10	S		54	1171	17	31.5	7	136	2926	1276	93
MANCHESTER—Delaware County													
DELAWARE COUNTY MEMORIAL HOSPITAL, 709 W. Main St., Zip 52057; tel. 319/927-3232; Paul Albright, adm. (Total facility includes 37 beds in nursing home-type unit) **A**9 10 **F**1 3 6 10 12 14 15 19 21 34 35 37 40 45	13	10	S	TF	90	1218	52	57.8	10	214	4148	1909	133
				H	53	1189	16	—	10	214	3614	1695	115
MANNING—Carroll County													
MANNING GENERAL HOSPITAL, 410 Main St., Zip 51455; tel. 712/653-2072; Greg Hanson, adm. (Total facility includes 12 beds in nursing home-type unit) **A**9 10 **F**1 6 10 15 16 19 23 29 30 32 33 34 35 36 37 40 41 42 44 45 48 49 50 53	23	10	S	TF	41	594	24	58.5	2	41	1941	888	80
				H	29	592	13	—	2	41	—	828	73
MAQUOKETA—Jackson County													
⊞ JACKSON COUNTY PUBLIC HOSPITAL, 700 W. Grove St., Zip 52060; tel. 319/652-2474; Karl C. Schroeder, exec. dir. (Total facility includes 16 beds in nursing home-type unit) **A**1a 9 10 **F**1 3 6 10 12 15 16 19 23 34 35 36 37 40 41 44 45 46 47	13	10	S	TF	59	1820	35	58.3	4	229	5557	2782	171
				H	43	1631	20	—	4	229	5364	2595	160
MARENGO—Iowa County													
MARENGO MEMORIAL HOSPITAL, 300 May St., Box 228, Zip 52301; tel. 319/642-5543; John J. Henderson, pres. **A**9 10 **F**1 12 14 15 16 23 34 35 40 42 43 50 52	14	10	S		44	408	30	68.2	8	10	1491	744	38
MARSHALLTOWN—Marshall County													
⊞ MARSHALLTOWN MEDICAL AND SURGICAL CENTER, 3 S. Fourth Ave., Zip 50158; tel. 515/754-5151; Omar L. Voran, adm. (Total facility includes 26 beds in nursing home-type unit) **A**1a 9 10 **F**1 3 6 10 12 14 15 16 19 23 24 27 30 34 35 36 40 42 43 45 47 52 53	23	10	S	TF	176	5801	93	52.8	22	690	17456	8964	444
				H	150	5519	79	—	22	690	16946	8614	429
MASON CITY—Cerro Gordo County													
⊞ NORTH IOWA MEDICAL CENTER, 910 N. Eisenhower Ave., Zip 50401; tel. 515/424-0440; Ronald O. Ebersole, exec. dir. **A**1a 2 9 10 **F**1 3 6 12 15 16 23 35 41 45 46; **S**6235	23	10	S		64	2539	42	65.6	0	0	9336	4015	234
⊞ ST. JOSEPH MERCY HOSPITAL, 84 Beaumont Dr., Zip 50401; tel. 515/424-7211; David H. Vellinga, pres. & chief exec. off. **A**1a 2 3 5 9 10 **F**1 2 3 5 6 7 8 9 10 11 12 14 15 16 23 24 26 27 28 30 32 33 34 35 36 40 42 44 45 46 51 52 53; **S**5165	21	10	S		318	9718	148	46.5	16	1103	31431	14293	788
MISSOURI VALLEY—Harrison County													
⊞ COMMUNITY MEMORIAL HOSPITAL, 631 N. Eighth St., Zip 51555; tel. 712/642-2784; James A. Seymour, adm. **A**1a 9 10 **F**1 2 3 12 15 16 23 32 33 35 40 45	23	10	S		56	859	12	21.4	10	30	2445	1142	55
MONTICELLO—Jones County													
★ JOHN MCDONALD HOSPITAL, W. First St., Zip 52310; tel. 319/465-3511; Sally Miller, adm. **A**9 10 **F**1 3 14 15 16 23 28 34 35 37 40 45 48	23	10	S		38	529	15	39.5	3	23	1497	459	36
MOUNT AYR—Ringgold County													
RINGGOLD COUNTY HOSPITAL, 211 Shellway Dr., Zip 50854; tel. 515/464-3226; Michael Lanctot, adm. **A**9 10 **F**1 6 14 16 23 27 34 35 36 37 45	13	10	S		40	643	18	45.0	4	45	2260	965	53

Hospital, Address, Telephone, Administrator, Approval and Facility Codes, Multihospital System Code	Classification Codes			Facilities	Inpatient Data				Newborn Data		Expense (thousands of dollars)		
★ American Hospital Association (AHA) membership □ Joint Commission on Accreditation of Hospitals (JCAH) accreditation + American Osteopathic Hospital Association (AOHA) membership ○ American Osteopathic Association (AOA) accreditation Δ Commission on Accreditation of Rehabilitation Facilities (CARF) accreditation Control codes 61, 63, 64, 71, 72 and 73 indicate hospitals listed by AOHA, but not registered by AHA. For definition of numerical codes, see page A2	Control	Service	Stay	Facilities	Beds	Admissions	Census	Occupancy (percent)	Bassinets	Births	Total	Payroll	Personnel
MOUNT PLEASANT—Henry County													
★ HENRY COUNTY HEALTH CENTER, Saunders Park, Zip 52641; tel. 319/385-3141; Robert Miller, chief exec. off. (Total facility includes 29 beds in nursing home-type unit) **A**9 10 **F**1 3 5 6 10 12 14 15 16 19 20 23 26 34 35 36 40 41 42 43 44 45 46 47 50	13	10	S	TF	79	1281	50	63.3	8	190	4850	2395	147
				H	50	1256	21	—	8	190	4375	2101	135
□ MENTAL HEALTH INSTITUTE, 1200 E. Washington St., Zip 52641; tel. 319/385-7231; David J. Scurr, supt. **A**1b 9 10 **F**16 30 32 33 46 47 48 50	12	22	L		165	840	144	87.3	0	0	6115	3903	182
MUSCATINE—Muscatine County													
⊞ MUSCATINE GENERAL HOSPITAL, 1518 Mulberry Ave., Zip 52761; tel. 319/264-9100; A. W. Zastrow, chief exec. off. (Total facility includes 8 beds in nursing home-type unit) **A**1a 9 10 **F**1 3 5 6 10 12 14 15 16 19 21 23 24 26 28 30 32 33 35 36 37 40 41 44 45 49 50 52 53	13	10	S	TF	80	2750	37	46.3	12	417	8761	4039	—
				H	72	2744	34	—	12	417	—	—	225
NEVADA—Story County													
★ STORY COUNTY HOSPITAL AND HEALTH CARE FACILITY, 630 Sixth St., Zip 50201; tel. 515/382-2111; John J. Kaduce, adm. (Total facility includes 80 beds in nursing home-type unit) **A**9 10 **F**1 3 6 14 15 16 19 23 28 33 34 35 36 40 42 44 45 46 47 50	13	10	S	TF	122	656	89	73.0	4	21	3005	1552	116
				H	42	583	12	—	4	21	1930	1161	82
NEW HAMPTON—Chickasaw County													
⊞ ST. JOSEPH COMMUNITY HOSPITAL, 308 N. Maple Ave., Zip 50659; tel. 515/394-4121; Vincent T. Morrissey, pres. & chief exec. off. **A**1a 9 10 **F**1 3 15 16 23 33 35 40 43 45	21	10	S		49	1160	16	32.7	6	137	2969	1432	88
NEWTON—Jasper County													
⊞ SKIFF MEDICAL CENTER (Formerly Mary Frances Skiff Memorial Hospital), 204 N. Fourth Ave. E., Zip 50208; tel. 515/792-1273; Ronald R. Ross, adm. **A**1a 9 10 **F**1 3 6 12 15 16 19 23 24 27 28 29 30 35 36 40 41 44 45 53	14	10	S		61	2055	39	63.9	8	177	6136	3314	186
OAKDALE—Johnson County													
CHEMICAL DEPENDENCY CENTER, See University of Iowa Hospitals and Clinics, Iowa City													
□ IOWA MEDICAL AND CLASSIFICATION CENTER (Formerly Iowa Security and Medical Facility), Zip 52319; tel. 319/626-2391; D. E. Brookhart, supt. (Nonreporting) **A**1b	12	22	L		80	—	—	—	—	—	—	—	—
OELWEIN—Fayette County													
⊞ MERCY HOSPITAL OF FRANCISCAN SISTERS, 201 Eighth Ave. S.E., Zip 50662; tel. 319/283-2314; Andrew J. Huff, pres. **A**1a 9 10 **F**1 3 6 15 16 23 35 36 40 45 50 52 53; **S**6745	21	10	S		49	993	12	24.5	8	91	1963	1122	69
ONAWA—Monona County													
⊞ BURGESS MEMORIAL HOSPITAL, 1600 Diamond Ave., Zip 51040; tel. 712/423-2311; Karmon T. Bjella, pres. **A**1a 9 10 **F**1 3 6 12 15 16 23 26 33 34 35 40 41 45 46	23	10	S		48	1275	17	35.4	6	97	2850	1461	87
ORANGE CITY—Sioux County													
ORANGE CITY MUNICIPAL HOSPITAL, 115 Fourth St. N.W., Zip 51041; tel. 712/737-4984; J. Dwight Gray, adm. **A**9 10 **F**1 3 6 16 23 24 35 40 44 45; **S**5845	14	10	S		43	808	29	72.5	4	126	2198	1054	71
OSAGE—Mitchell County													
⊞ MITCHELL COUNTY MEMORIAL HOSPITAL, 616 N. Eighth St., Zip 50461; tel. 515/732-3781; David M. Smith, adm. **A**1a 9 10 **F**1 3 6 14 15 16 23 35 36 37 40 44 45	13	10	S		40	1101	16	40.0	9	136	2507	1217	79
OSCEOLA—Clarke County													
★ CLARKE COUNTY PUBLIC HOSPITAL, 800 S. Fillmore St., Zip 50213; tel. 515/342-2184; Timothy F. Weyers, adm. **A**9 10 **F**1 6 16 23 34 35 36 45; **S**1595	13	10	S		48	524	33	68.8	8	51	1798	816	58
OSKALOOSA—Mahaska County													
□ MAHASKA COUNTY HOSPITAL, 1229 C Ave. E., Zip 52577; tel. 515/673-3431; David E. Rutter, adm. **A**1a 9 10 **F**1 3 6 10 12 14 16 23 29 30 35 40 42 44 45 47; **S**1595	13	10	S		53	1729	21	39.6	14	226	3868	2138	134
OTTUMWA—Wapello County													
⊞ OTTUMWA REGIONAL HEALTH CENTER, 1001 E. Pennsylvania Ave., Zip 52501; tel. 515/682-7511; Clarence Cory, pres. (Total facility includes 10 beds in nursing home-type unit) **A**1a 9 10 **F**1 3 5 6 7 8 9 10 11 15 16 17 19 23 24 26 27 28 30 32 34 35 36 37 40 41 42 44 45 47 50 51 52 53	23	10	S	TF	155	5196	91	58.7	10	703	17168	7595	445
				H	145	5080	87	—	10	703	17063	7495	—
⊞ ST. JOSEPH HEALTH AND REHABILITATION CENTER (Formerly St. Joseph Hospital), 312 E. Alta Vista Ave., Zip 52501; tel. 515/684-4651; Sr. Pauline Tursi, pres. & chief exec. off. (Total facility includes 8 beds in nursing home-type unit) **A**1a 9 10 **F**1 3 6 12 14 15 16 19 23 24 34 35 41 43 44 45 46 49 50; **S**5175	21	10	S	TF	90	2346	50	55.6	0	0	7500	3493	229
				H	82	2245	45	—	0	0	7244	3318	—
ST. JOSEPH HOSPITAL, See St. Joseph Health and Rehabilitation Center													
PELLA—Marion County													
★ PELLA COMMUNITY HOSPITAL, 404 Jefferson St., Zip 50219; tel. 515/628-3150; John Harmeling, adm. (Total facility includes 61 beds in nursing home-type unit) **A**9 10 **F**1 3 6 10 12 14 15 16 19 23 24 29 32 33 34 35 37 40 42 44 45 46 47 53	23	10	S	TF	108	1176	89	82.4	10	224	4252	2028	131
				H	47	1138	29	—	10	224	3425	1493	84
PERRY—Dallas County													
⊞ DALLAS COUNTY HOSPITAL, Tenth & Iowa Sts., Zip 50220; tel. 515/465-3547; William M. Deets, adm. **A**1a 9 10 **F**1 3 6 16 23 26 35 40 44 45 46; **S**1595	13	10	S		53	919	12	22.6	6	76	3276	1338	79
POCAHONTAS—Pocahontas County													
POCAHONTAS COMMUNITY HOSPITAL, 606 N.W. Seventh, Zip 50574; tel. 712/335-3501; Carolyn K. Hess, adm. **A**9 10 **F**1 3 6 12 14 15 23 35 37 40 41 44 45 47	14	10	S		36	520	7	19.4	6	77	1284	622	48
POSTVILLE—Allamakee County													
COMMUNITY MEMORIAL HOSPITAL, Oak Dr. & Hospital Rd., Zip 52162; tel. 319/864-7431; John C. Meyer, adm. (Total facility includes 8 beds in nursing home-type unit) **A**9 10 **F**1 6 10 12 14 15 16 19 21 23 24 34 35 36 40 41 42 44 45 53	14	10	S	TF	26	466	10	38.5	3	55	1011	534	48
				H	18	422	5	—	3	55	859	460	40
PRIMGHAR—O'Brien County													
⊞ BAUM HARMON MEMORIAL HOSPITAL, 255 N. Welch Ave., Zip 51245; tel. 712/757-3905; Marlys Scherlin, adm. **A**1a 9 10 **F**1 3 6 14 15 16 23 26 33 34 35 40 44 45 53	14	10	S		19	575	6	31.6	4	56	1011	395	34
RED OAK—Montgomery County													
⊞ MONTGOMERY COUNTY MEMORIAL HOSPITAL, 1201 Highland Ave., Zip 51566; tel. 712/623-2541; Allen E. Pohren, adm. **A**1a 9 10 **F**1 6 10 12 14 15 16 23 34 35 36 40 44 45 52 53	13	10	S		49	2061	32	54.2	8	127	5117	2773	154
ROCK RAPIDS—Lyon County													
MERRILL PIONEER COMMUNITY HOSPITAL, 801 S. Greene St., Zip 51246; tel. 712/472-2591; Vince Schleusner, adm. **A**9 10 **F**1 6 23 35 45	23	10	S		30	553	8	26.7	12	68	1056	—	34
ROCK VALLEY—Sioux County													
HEGG MEMORIAL HEALTH CENTER (Formerly Hegg Memorial Hospital), 1200 21st Ave., Zip 51247; tel. 712/476-5305; Justin E. Cassel, adm. (Total facility includes 94 beds in nursing home-type unit) **A**9 10 **F**1 3 14 15 16 19 23 24 30 34 35 36 40 41 42 43 44 45 46 47 50 52; **S**5165	23	10	S	TF	122	496	100	82.0	4	82	2144	1197	91
				H	28	466	8	—	4	82	1179	559	34

Hospital, Address, Telephone, Administrator, Approval and Facility Codes, Multihospital System Code	Classification Codes				Inpatient Data				Newborn Data		Expense (thousands of dollars)		
★ American Hospital Association (AHA) membership □ Joint Commission on Accreditation of Hospitals (JCAH) accreditation + American Osteopathic Hospital Association (AOHA) membership ○ American Osteopathic Association (AOA) accreditation Δ Commission on Accreditation of Rehabilitation Facilities (CARF) accreditation Control codes 61, 63, 64, 71, 72 and 73 indicate hospitals listed by AOHA, but not registered by AHA. For definition of numerical codes, see page A2	Control	Service	Stay	Facilities	Beds	Admissions	Census	Occupancy (percent)	Bassinets	Births	Total	Payroll	Personnel
SAC CITY—Sac County													
★ LORING HOSPITAL, Highland Ave., Zip 50583; tel. 712/662-7105; Terry Dejong, chief exec. off. (Total facility includes 21 beds in nursing home-type unit) **A**9 10 **F**1 2 6 14 15 16 19 21 23 24 28 30 35 36 40 41 44 45 46 47 49 50	23	10	S	TF	54	647	29	53.7	8	49	1538	890	65
				H	33	630	9	—	8	49	1425	777	55
SHELDON—O'Brien County													
⊞ NORTHWEST IOWA HEALTH CENTER (Formerly Community Memorial Hospital and Nursing Home), 118 N. Seventh Ave., Zip 51201; tel. 712/324-5041; Mark V. Dagoberg, chief exec. off. (Total facility includes 54 beds in nursing home-type unit) **A**1a 9 10 **F**1 3 6 10 12 14 15 16 19 23 24 28 34 35 36 37 40 41 44 45 46 47 50 53	23	10	S	TF	88	828	63	71.6	6	130	2554	1331	99
				H	34	793	11	—	6	130	1869	839	58
SHENANDOAH—Page County													
★ SHENANDOAH MEMORIAL HOSPITAL, 300 Pershing Ave., Zip 51601; tel. 712/246-1230; David Drew, adm. (Total facility includes 61 beds in nursing home-type unit) **A**9 10 **F**1 3 6 10 12 15 16 18 19 23 33 34 35 44 45 47 53	23	10	S	TF	105	1366	73	69.5	4	100	5206	2176	156
				H	44	1333	17	—	4	100	4399	1808	123
SIBLEY—Osceola County													
★ OSCEOLA COMMUNITY HOSPITAL, Ninth Ave. N., Zip 51249; tel. 712/754-2574; Frederick W. Haack, chief exec. off. **A**9 10 **F**1 3 6 12 14 15 16 23 35 36 40 41 44 45 46 53	23	10	S		32	747	11	34.4	5	108	1384	676	42
SIGOURNEY—Keokuk County													
KEOKUK COUNTY HEALTH CENTER (Formerly Keokuk County Hospital), Rural Rte. 3, Box 286, Zip 52591; tel. 515/622-2720; Douglas A. Sheetz, chief exec. off. **A**9 10 **F**1 14 15 34 35 40	13	10	S		33	344	12	36.4	6	15	1173	620	43
SIOUX CENTER—Sioux County													
SIOUX CENTER COMMUNITY HOSPITAL, 605 S. Main Ave., Zip 51250; tel. 712/722-1271 (Total facility includes 69 beds in nursing home-type unit) **A**9 10 **F**1 3 6 12 15 19 34 35 36 40 41 42 44 45 46 47	23	10	S	TF	90	721	76	84.4	6	219	2645	1147	113
				H	21	652	7	—	6	219	2258	808	—
SIOUX CITY—Woodbury County													
⊞ MARIAN HEALTH CENTER (Includes North Campus, 2101 Court St., Zip 51104), 801 Fifth St., Zip 51101; Mailing Address Box 3168, Zip 51102; tel. 712/279-2010; Sr. Elizabeth Mary Burns, pres. & chief exec. off. **A**1a 2 3 5 6 9 10 **F**1 2 3 4 5 6 7 8 9 10 11 12 14 15 16 20 21 23 24 26 27 28 30 32 33 34 35 36 40 41 42 45 46 47 48 52 53 54; **S**5165	21	10	S		484	10870	265	54.8	18	663	56111	24383	1235
⊞ ST. LUKE'S REGIONAL MEDICAL CENTER, 2720 Stone Park Blvd., Zip 51104; tel. 712/279-3500; David O. Biorn, pres. **A**1a 2 3 5 6 9 10 **F**1 2 3 5 6 7 8 9 10 11 12 14 15 16 20 22 23 27 28 30 33 34 35 36 37 38 40 45 46 47 49 51 52 53; **S**5845	23	10	S		371	12210	223	60.1	30	1635	45746	21522	1114
SPENCER—Clay County													
★ SPENCER MUNICIPAL HOSPITAL, 114 E. 12th St., Zip 51301; tel. 712/264-6198; James Striepe, adm. (Total facility includes 14 beds in nursing home-type unit) **A**9 10 **F**1 3 6 10 15 16 19 21 23 24 27 30 34 35 40 41 44 45 46 47	14	10	S	TF	91	3125	42	46.2	14	301	7935	4044	224
				H	77	2883	37	—	14	301	7557	3822	—
SPIRIT LAKE—Dickinson County													
□ DICKINSON COUNTY MEMORIAL HOSPITAL, Hwy. 71 S., Box AB, Zip 51360; tel. 712/336-1230; William M. Deets, adm. **A**1a 9 10 **F**1 3 6 10 15 16 23 28 32 35 37 40 45 46 53	13	10	S		53	1297	18	35.3	8	144	3766	1720	100
STORM LAKE—Buena Vista County													
⊞ BUENA VISTA COUNTY HOSPITAL, 1525 W. Fifth St., Zip 50588; tel. 712/732-4030; James O. Nelson, adm. **A**1a 9 10 **F**1 3 5 6 14 15 16 23 29 30 32 34 35 36 40 41 45 46 49 50 53	13	10	S		70	2259	32	45.7	10	362	5025	2393	150
STORY CITY—Story County													
★ STORY CITY MEMORIAL HOSPITAL, 812 Elm St., Zip 50248; tel. 515/733-5121; Steven T. Carter, adm. (Total facility includes 11 beds in nursing home-type unit) **A**9 10 **F**1 3 15 19 23 26 34 35 37 40 43 45 50	14	10	S	TF	36	573	22	61.1	6	31	1392	795	55
				H	25	556	12	—	6	31	—	742	51
SUMNER—Bremer County													
COMMUNITY MEMORIAL HOSPITAL, 909 W. First St., Box 148, Zip 50674; tel. 319/578-3275; Ronald D. Waggoner, adm. & chief exec. off. **A**9 10 **F**1 6 15 16 19 34 35 40 41 42 44 45	23	10	S		29	550	6	20.7	4	31	1240	605	42
VINTON—Benton County													
★ VIRGINIA GAY HOSPITAL, 502 N. Ninth Ave., Zip 52349; tel. 319/472-2348; Mark Hearn, adm. (Total facility includes 58 beds in nursing home-type unit) **A**9 10 **F**1 5 6 15 16 19 23 26 30 32 33 34 35 36 37 40 41 42 44 45 46 50 53	23	10	S	TF	89	837	68	76.4	4	42	2551	1161	97
				H	31	720	10	—	4	42	2056	890	62
WASHINGTON—Washington County													
★ WASHINGTON COUNTY HOSPITAL, 400 E. Polk St., P O Box 909, Zip 52353; tel. 319/653-5481; Gary Kluber, adm. (Total facility includes 30 beds in nursing home-type unit) **A**9 10 **F**1 3 12 15 16 19 23 40 44 45 46	13	10	S	TF	70	799	36	51.4	9	155	3116	1748	133
				H	40	761	11	—	9	155	2579	1402	114
WATERLOO—Black Hawk County													
⊞ ALLEN MEMORIAL HOSPITAL, 1825 Logan Ave., Zip 50703; tel. 319/235-3941; Larry W. Pugh, pres. (Total facility includes 20 beds in nursing home-type unit) **A**1a 3 5 6 9 10 **F**1 3 4 5 6 9 10 12 14 15 16 19 20 21 23 24 26 27 28 29 30 32 33 34 35 36 37 40 41 42 43 44 45 46 47 49 52 53 54	23	10	S	TF	196	7313	129	65.8	15	460	27528	13468	707
				H	176	6928	116	—	15	460	27185	13137	690
⊞ Δ COVENANT MEDICAL CENTER (Includes Covenant Medical Center-St. Francis, 3421 W. Ninth St., Zip 50702; tel. 319/236-4111; Covenant Medical Center-Schoitz, 2101 Kimball Ave., Zip 50702; tel. 319/291-3131), 3421 W. Ninth St., Zip 50702; tel. 319/236-4111; Raymond F. Burfeind, pres. & chief exec. off. **A**1a 3 5 7 9 10 **F**1 3 5 6 7 8 9 10 11 12 14 15 16 17 19 20 21 23 24 25 26 27 28 29 30 32 33 34 35 36 40 41 42 43 44 45 46 47 48 49 50 51 52 53; **S**6745	21	10	S		410	14595	245	58.5	20	1608	23378	10689	1155
WAUKON—Allamakee County													
□ VETERANS MEMORIAL HOSPITAL, Golf View Addition, Zip 52172; tel. 319/568-3411; Kenneth A. Ewen, chief exec. off. **A**1a 9 10 **F**1 3 6 15 16 23 26 35 40 44 45 47	14	10	S		40	913	13	32.5	4	126	2033	1031	66
WAVERLY—Bremer County													
⊞ WAVERLY MUNICIPAL HOSPITAL, 312 Ninth St. S.W., Zip 50677; tel. 319/352-4120; Arnold Flessner, adm. **A**1a 9 10 **F**1 6 14 15 16 21 23 34 35 36 37 40 44 45 46	14	10	S		45	1160	15	33.3	8	180	2419	1135	71
WEBSTER CITY—Hamilton County													
⊞ HAMILTON COUNTY PUBLIC HOSPITAL, 800 Ohio St., Zip 50595; tel. 515/832-3431; Lawrence Massa, adm. **A**1a 9 10 **F**1 3 6 16 17 21 23 26 34 35 36 40 43 45 46 52 53	13	10	S		65	1751	22	33.8	7	109	3821	1932	118
WEST UNION—Fayette County													
⊞ PALMER MEMORIAL HOSPITAL, 112 Jefferson St., Box 476, Zip 52175; tel. 319/422-3812; Jeanine Matt, adm. **A**1a 9 10 **F**1 3 6 10 14 15 16 21 23 24 26 28 32 35 36 44 45 46	14	10	S		30	859	13	43.3	8	118	2283	929	64
WINTERSET—Madison County													
□ MADISON COUNTY MEMORIAL HOSPITAL, 300 Hutchings St., Zip 50273; tel. 515/462-2373; Mary Sue Fountain, adm. **A**1a 9 10 **F**1 3 6 14 16 21 23 24 34 35 36 40 42 44 45	13	10	S		35	621	8	22.9	6	31	2105	935	53
WOODWARD—Boone County													
WOODWARD STATE HOSPITAL-SCHOOL, Zip 50276; tel. 515/438-2600; Michael J. Davis PhD, supt. **F**19 23 24 33 35 42 44 46	12	62	L		498	76	483	89.4	0	0	25376	18698	960

Hospital, Address, Telephone, Administrator, Approval and Facility Codes, Multihospital System Code	Classification Codes				Inpatient Data				Newborn Data		Expense (thousands of dollars)		
★ American Hospital Association (AHA) membership □ Joint Commission on Accreditation of Hospitals (JCAH) accreditation + American Osteopathic Hospital Association (AOHA) membership ○ American Osteopathic Association (AOA) accreditation Δ Commission on Accreditation of Rehabilitation Facilities (CARF) accreditation Control codes 61, 63, 64, 71, 72 and 73 indicate hospitals listed by AOHA, but not registered by AHA. For definition of numerical codes, see page A2	Control	Service	Stay	Facilities	Beds	Admissions	Census	Occupancy (percent)	Bassinets	Births	Total	Payroll	Personnel

Kansas

Hospital	Control	Service	Stay	Facilities	Beds	Admissions	Census	Occupancy (percent)	Bassinets	Births	Total	Payroll	Personnel
ABILENE—Dickinson County													
★□ MEMORIAL HOSPITAL, 511 N.E. Tenth St., Zip 67410; tel. 913/263-2100; Leon J. Boor, adm. **A**1a 9 10 **F**1 6 10 16 21 23 24 26 34 35 36 40 41 44 52 53	16	10	S		69	1009	15	21.7	9	109	3258	1704	87
ANTHONY—Harper County													
★ HOSPITAL DISTRICT NUMBER SIX OF HARPER COUNTY (Formerly Anthony Hospital and Clinic), 1101 E. Spring St., Zip 67003; tel. 316/842-5111; Jay P. Jolly, adm. **A**9 10 **F**1 6 16 23 35 37 44 45 47	16	10	S		26	542	12	46.2	2	34	1469	802	60
ARKANSAS CITY—Cowley County													
★□ ARKANSAS CITY MEMORIAL HOSPITAL, 216 W. Birch Ave., Zip 67005; tel. 316/442-2500; Robert J. King, adm. **A**1a 9 10 **F**1 3 6 10 12 14 15 16 23 26 35 36 40 41 45 46 47 48 52 53; **S**2495	14	10	S		69	2237	30	43.5	10	280	7235	3092	186
ASHLAND—Clark County													
ASHLAND DISTRICT HOSPITAL, 709 Oak St., Zip 67831; tel. 316/635-2241; Hazel Thomas, adm. **A**9 10 **F**1 16 28 33 34 35 37 43 50	16	10	S		16	102	1	6.3	3	11	520	269	16
ATCHISON—Atchison County													
★□ ATCHISON HOSPITAL, 1301 N. Second St., Zip 66002; tel. 913/367-2131; James A. Asher, adm. (Total facility includes 45 beds in nursing home-type unit) **A**1a 9 10 **F**1 3 6 10 14 15 16 19 23 26 34 35 36 37 40 43 45 46 47 52 53	23	10	S	TF	141	2251	57	40.4	17	301	5532	2727	162
				H	96	2193	26	—	17	301	5300	2501	148
ATTICA—Harper County													
ATTICA DISTRICT HOSPITAL ONE, 302 N. Botkin St., Box 268, Zip 67009; tel. 316/254-7253; Ron McCoy, adm. (Nonreporting) **A**9 10	16	10	S		47	—	—	—	—	—	—	—	—
ATWOOD—Rawlins County													
★ RAWLINS COUNTY HOSPITAL, 707 Grant St., Box 47, Zip 67730; tel. 913/626-3211; Pamela Thomas, adm. **A**9 10 **F**1 15 16 21 23 35 44 45; **S**1535	23	10	S		27	594	10	37.0	4	42	1411	656	50
AUGUSTA—Butler County													
AUGUSTA MEDICAL COMPLEX, 2101 Dearborn St., Box 430, Zip 67010; tel. 316/775-5421; Larry Wilkerson, adm. (Nonreporting) **A**9 10	23	10	S		147	—	—	—	—	—	—	—	—
BAXTER SPRINGS—Cherokee County													
★ BAXTER MEMORIAL HOSPITAL, Tenth St. & Washington Ave., Zip 66713; tel. 316/856-2314; Phil Unruh, adm. **A**9 10 **F**1 3 6 10 16 23 34 35 40 41 43 45 48 49	14	10	S		45	900	17	37.8	5	29	2393	1125	64
BELLEVILLE—Republic County													
★□ REPUBLIC COUNTY HOSPITAL, Zip 66935; tel. 913/527-2255; Bonnie Elliott, adm. (Total facility includes 38 beds in nursing home-type unit) **A**1a 9 10 **F**1 6 10 12 14 15 16 19 23 24 26 34 35 42 43 50; **S**1535	23	10	S	TF	86	1193	53	61.6	8	114	2828	1379	102
				H	48	1161	16	—	8	114	—	—	86
BELOIT—Mitchell County													
★□ MITCHELL COUNTY COMMUNITY HOSPITAL, Eighth & Lincoln Aves., Zip 67420; tel. 913/738-2266; Jeffrey S. Tarrant, adm. (Total facility includes 40 beds in nursing home-type unit) **A**1a 9 10 **F**1 6 14 15 16 19 21 23 35 36 45; **S**1535	23	10	S	TF	89	1370	60	67.4	6	128	4216	2164	131
				H	49	1325	21	—	6	128	—	—	110
BURLINGTON—Coffey County													
COFFEY COUNTY HOSPITAL, Fourth & Garretson Sts., Box 189, Zip 66839; tel. 316/364-2121; James M. Cazier, adm. **A**9 10 **F**1 2 6 12 14 16 23 34 35	13	10	S		26	620	8	30.8	7	26	2620	1187	66
CALDWELL—Sumner County													
★ HOSPITAL DISTRICT ONE OF SUMNER COUNTY, 601 S. Osage St., Zip 67022; tel. 316/845-6492; Eugene M. Horak, adm. **A**9 10	16	10	S		27	421	6	22.2	3	10	915	483	29
CANEY—Montgomery County													
★ CANEY MUNICIPAL HOSPITAL, Box 325, Zip 67333; tel. 316/879-2182; Susan Barrett, adm. **A**9 10 **F**1 6 41	14	10	S		24	347	7	29.2	4	21	729	344	30
CEDAR VALE—Chautauqua County													
CEDAR VALE REGIONAL HOSPITAL, 501 Cedar St., Box 398, Zip 67024; tel. 316/758-2266; Jack F. Lewis, adm. **A**10 **F**1 3 12 14 15 16 23 30 32 34 35 37 40 42 48 49 52	33	10	S		35	779	21	60.0	3	10	3597	1943	83
CHANUTE—Neosho County													
★□ NEOSHO MEMORIAL HOSPITAL, 629 S. Plummer, Box 426, Zip 66720; tel. 316/431-4000; Murray L. Brown, adm. **A**1a 9 10 **F**1 3 6 10 15 16 23 34 35 36 40 41 44 45 46 52 53	13	10	S		62	2081	30	48.4	8	249	6140	2817	172
CLAY CENTER—Clay County													
★□ CLAY COUNTY HOSPITAL, 617 Liberty St., Zip 67432; tel. 913/632-2144; Jon J. Robison, chief exec. off. **A**1a 9 10 **F**1 3 6 15 16 21 23 24 35 36 40 43 44 45 47 53	13	10	S		30	872	13	43.3	4	78	2523	1123	72
COFFEYVILLE—Montgomery County													
★□ COFFEYVILLE REGIONAL MEDICAL CENTER, 1400 W. Fourth, Zip 67337; tel. 316/251-1200; Raymond M. Dunning Jr., adm. **A**1a 9 10 **F**1 3 6 7 8 9 10 11 12 14 15 16 23 24 26 27 30 32 33 35 36 40 41 45 53; **S**1755	14	10	S		83	3609	60	72.3	14	331	11061	4826	289
COLBY—Thomas County													
★□ CITIZENS MEDICAL CENTER, 100 E. College Dr., Zip 67701; tel. 913/462-7511; Ross Schultz, adm. **A**1a 9 10 **F**1 3 10 14 15 16 23 26 34 35 36 40 41 45 46 47	23	10	S		40	1183	14	35.0	6	171	4135	1493	90
COLDWATER—Comanche County													
COMANCHE COUNTY HOSPITAL, Second & Frisco Sts., Zip 67029; tel. 316/582-2144; LaNell Wagnon, adm. **A**9 10 **F**1 6 24 33 34 35 43 45	13	10	S		19	148	2	10.5	6	15	517	277	30
COLUMBUS—Cherokee County													
★ MAUDE NORTON MEMORIAL CITY HOSPITAL, 220 N. Pennsylvania St., Zip 66725; tel. 316/429-2545; Imogene Sandella, adm. **A**9 10 **F**6 14 16 23 24 35 40 41 44 45 46 53	14	10	S		39	573	10	25.6	6	28	1420	670	48
CONCORDIA—Cloud County													
★□ ST. JOSEPH HOSPITAL, 1100 Highland Dr., Zip 66901; tel. 913/243-1234; Sr. Elizabeth Stover, pres. **A**1a 9 10 **F**1 3 6 7 8 9 10 11 12 14 15 16 23 26 27 28 29 30 32 33 34 35 36 40 41 42 43 45 46 47 52 53; **S**5435	21	10	S		53	1851	34	64.2	7	94	5435	3159	150
COUNCIL GROVE—Morris County													
MORRIS COUNTY HOSPITAL, 600 N. Washington St., P O Box 275, Zip 66846; tel. 316/767-5151; Ron Thompson, adm. (Nonreporting) **A**9 10	13	10	S		28	—	—	—	—	—	—	—	—
DIGHTON—Lane County													
★ LANE COUNTY HOSPITAL, 243 S. Second, Box 969, Zip 67839; tel. 316/397-5321; Donna McGowan RN, adm. (Total facility includes 21 beds in nursing home-type unit) **A**9 10 **F**19 21 35 45; **S**1535	13	10	S	TF	31	76	21	67.7	0	0	855	476	35
				H	10	64	2	—	0	0	—	—	—

Hospital, Address, Telephone, Administrator, Approval and Facility Codes, Multihospital System Code	Classification Codes				Inpatient Data				Newborn Data		Expense (thousands of dollars)		
★ American Hospital Association (AHA) membership □ Joint Commission on Accreditation of Hospitals (JCAH) accreditation + American Osteopathic Hospital Association (AOHA) membership ○ American Osteopathic Association (AOA) accreditation Δ Commission on Accreditation of Rehabilitation Facilities (CARF) accreditation Control codes 61, 63, 64, 71, 72 and 73 indicate hospitals listed by AOHA, but not registered by AHA. For definition of numerical codes, see page A2	Control	Service	Stay	Facilities	Beds	Admissions	Census	Occupancy (percent)	Bassinets	Births	Total	Payroll	Personnel
DODGE CITY—Ford County													
★□ HUMANA HOSPITAL -DODGE CITY, 3001 Ave. A, Box 1478, Zip 67801; tel. 316/225-9050; I. Lynn Jeane, exec. dir. **A**1a 9 10 **F**1 3 6 10 12 14 16 23 26 35 40 43 45 50 51 53; **S**1235	33	10	S		110	5389	60	54.5	12	593	12523	4182	209
EL DORADO—Butler County													
★□ SUSAN B. ALLEN MEMORIAL HOSPITAL, 720 W. Central Ave., Zip 67042; tel. 316/321-3300; Jim Wilson, adm. **A**1a 9 10 **F**1 3 10 16 17 19 23 24 28 35 41 44 45 46 47	23	10	S		103	2224	44	42.7	6	208	8067	4123	206
ELKHART—Morton County													
★ MORTON COUNTY HOSPITAL, 445 Hilltop St., Box 937, Zip 67950; tel. 316/697-2141; Jack Vallandingham, chief exec. off. (Total facility includes 60 beds in nursing home-type unit) **A**9 10 **F**1 3 6 16 19 23 29 32 35 40 41 45	13	10	S	TF H	83 23	802 771	48 9	57.8 —	8 8	51 51	3115 2409	1572 1139	99 67
ELLINWOOD—Barton County													
★ ELLINWOOD DISTRICT HOSPITAL, 605 N. Main St., Zip 67526; tel. 316/564-2548; Gordon L. Ensley, area dir. **A**9 10 **F**1 14 15 16 23 35 45 50; **S**1535	23	10	S		24	244	3	12.5	0	0	631	311	18
ELLSWORTH—Ellsworth County													
ELLSWORTH COUNTY VETERANS MEMORIAL HOSPITAL, 300 Kingsley St., Drawer F, Zip 67439; tel. 913/472-3111; Hugh E. Adams, chief exec. off. & adm. (Nonreporting) **A**9 10	23	10	S		22	—	—	—	—	—	—	—	—
□ ST. FRANCIS AT ELLSWORTH, P O Box 127, Zip 67439; tel. 913/472-4453; Rev. Canon N. Kenneth Yates, pres. **A**1b 9 **F**31 32 33 42 44 46	23	22	L		26	19	25	96.2	0	0	562	17	35
EMPORIA—Lyon County													
★□ NEWMAN MEMORIAL COUNTY HOSPITAL, 12th & Chestnut Sts., Zip 66801; tel. 316/343-6800; Thomas McCall, adm. (Total facility includes 16 beds in nursing home-type unit) **A**1a 6 9 10 **F**1 3 6 10 12 14 16 19 23 26 27 30 32 33 35 36 40 41 43 44 45 46 47 49 50 52; **S**1755	13	10	S	TF H	178 162	3663 3507	65 56	36.5 —	15 15	733 733	12835 —	5927 —	279 271
★□ ST. MARY'S HEALTH CENTER (Formerly St. Mary's Hospital), 15th Ave. & State St., Zip 66801; tel. 316/342-2450; Mark I. Barnett, chief exec. off. **A**1a 9 10 **F**1 3 6 10 12 14 15 16 23 24 32 35 41 43 44 45 53; **S**5435	21	10	S		44	1115	18	39.1	0	0	4573	1951	128
EUREKA—Greenwood County													
★ GREENWOOD COUNTY HOSPITAL, 100 W. 16th St., Zip 67045; tel. 316/583-7451; Nancy McKenzie, adm. **A**9 10 **F**1 6 12 14 15 16 23 24 34 35 41 43 44 45 50; **S**1535	23	10	S		46	1177	18	39.1	9	54	2528	1257	84
FORT LEAVENWORTH—Leavenworth County													
★□ MUNSON ARMY COMMUNITY HOSPITAL, Zip 66027; tel. 913/684-5401; Col. James E. Pryor, CO; Col. Chauncy P. Brothers Jr., dep. cmdr. adm. (Nonreporting) **A**1a	42	10	S		39	—	—	—	—	—	—	—	—
FORT RILEY—Geary County													
★□ IRWIN ARMY COMMUNITY HOSPITAL, Zip 66442; tel. 913/239-7101; Col. Hylan C. Moore MC USA, cmdr. (Nonreporting) **A**1a 2	42	10	S		145	—	—	—	—	—	—	—	—
FORT SCOTT—Bourbon County													
★□ MERCY HOSPITALS OF KANSAS, 821 Burke St., Zip 66701; tel. 316/223-2200; Andrew B. Lorimer, chief exec. off. (Total facility includes 20 beds in nursing home-type unit) **A**1a 9 10 **F**1 3 6 7 10 11 12 14 15 16 19 23 24 35 36 40 42 44 45 46 47 53; **S**5185	21	10	S	TF H	162 142	4496 4136	74 61	45.7 —	16 16	483 483	11538 10889	6541 6318	276 262
FREDONIA—Wilson County													
★□ FREDONIA REGIONAL HOSPITAL, 1527 Madison St., Box 579, Zip 66736; tel. 316/378-2121; Richard Carter, chief oper. off. **A**1a 9 10 **F**1 6 9 10 14 16 23 34 35 41 45; **S**1755	14	10	S		32	660	10	31.3	0	0	1972	970	59
GARDEN CITY—Finney County													
★□ ST. CATHERINE HOSPITAL, 608 N. Fifth St., Zip 67846; tel. 316/275-6111; Steven D. Wilkinson, pres. & chief exec. off. **A**1a 9 10 **F**1 3 6 7 8 10 11 12 13 14 16 23 24 27 28 29 30 32 33 35 40 41 42 43 45 46 47 52; **S**5175	21	10	S		112	4139	63	56.3	8	910	15636	7690	378
GARDNER—Johnson County													
★ MEADOWBROOK HOSPITAL (Formerly Gardner Community Medical Center), 427 W. Main St., Zip 66030; tel. 913/884-8711; Brian K. Morris, adm. (Nonreporting) **A**9	33	10	S		85	—	—	—	—	—	—	—	—
GARNETT—Anderson County													
ANDERSON COUNTY HOSPITAL, 421 S. Maple, Box 309, Zip 66032; tel. 913/448-3131; Orlin E. Cunningham, adm. (Nonreporting) **A**9 10; **S**1535	13	10	S		72	—	—	—	—	—	—	—	—
GIRARD—Crawford County													
★ CRAWFORD COUNTY HOSPITAL DISTRICT ONE, W. St. John St. & Hospital Rd., Rural Rte. 2, Box 5a, Zip 66743; tel. 316/724-8291; Barbara Lohmeyer RN, adm. **A**9 10 **F**1 3 16 23 35 44 45 53	16	10	S		25	830	13	52.0	4	91	2028	1032	53
GOODLAND—Sherman County													
★ NORTHWEST KANSAS REGIONAL MEDICAL CENTER, First & Sherman Sts., Box 540, Zip 67735; tel. 913/899-3625; Rick Ketchum, adm. **A**9 10 **F**1 3 6 10 12 14 16 23 26 30 32 33 34 35 40 41 43 44 45 48 49 50 52; **S**9355	13	10	S		49	827	22	44.9	7	94	3848	1603	90
GREAT BEND—Barton County													
★□ CENTRAL KANSAS MEDICAL CENTER, 3515 Broadway St., Zip 67530; tel. 316/792-2511; Sr. Philomena Hrencher, pres. **A**1a 9 10 **F**1 3 6 7 8 10 11 12 15 16 23 24 27 28 30 33 35 36 39 40 45 46 47 52 53; **S**5175	21	10	S		135	4382	70	51.9	12	605	13367	7208	339
GREENSBURG—Kiowa County													
★ KIOWA COUNTY MEMORIAL HOSPITAL, 501 S. Walnut St., Zip 67054; tel. 316/723-3341; Don Klassen, adm. **A**9 10 **F**1 14 16 23 34 35 43 45	21	10	S		24	615	11	45.8	6	62	1306	705	53
HALSTEAD—Harvey County													
★□ HALSTEAD HOSPITAL, 328 Poplar St., Zip 67056; tel. 316/835-2651; Richard L. Nierman, pres. **A**1a 9 10 **F**1 3 4 5 15 16 23 24 27 30 34 35 45 46; **S**5435	21	10	S		190	4395	91	47.9	0	0	19142	5811	296
HANOVER—Washington County													
WASHINGTON COUNTY HOSPITAL, DISTRICT ONE, Hanover & Washington Sts., Box 38, Zip 66945; tel. 913/337-2214; Roger D. Warren MD, adm. (Total facility includes 32 beds in nursing home-type unit) **A**9 10 **F**14 19 23 30 35 48	16	10	S	TF H	50 18	357 308	30 5	60.0 —	0 0	28 28	1229 1107	641 523	59 44
HARPER—Harper County													
★ HOSPITAL DISTRICT NUMBER FIVE OF HARPER COUNTY, 12th & Maple Sts., Zip 67058; tel. 316/896-7324; Marshall P. Ray, adm. **A**10 **F**1 3 15 16 23 35 36 37 41 45 46 50	16	10	S		29	652	9	31.0	5	55	1796	880	54
HAYS—Ellis County													
★□ HADLEY REGIONAL MEDICAL CENTER, 201 E. Seventh St., Zip 67601; tel. 913/628-8251; David R. Carpenter, pres. & chief exec. off. **A**1a 2 9 10 **F**1 3 6 10 15 16 23 24 25 26 27 29 30 34 35 36 40 41 45 46 52 53	21	10	S		125	3322	61	48.8	9	274	11920	6013	313
★□ ST. ANTHONY HOSPITAL, 2220 Canterbury Rd., Zip 67601; tel. 913/625-7301; Oren M. Windholz, pres. (Nonreporting) **A**1a 2 9 10; **S**5695	21	10	S		116	—	—	—	—	—	—	—	—
HERINGTON—Dickinson County													
HERINGTON MUNICIPAL HOSPITAL, 100 E. Helen St., Zip 67449; tel. 913/258-2207; Larry Landers, adm. **A**9 10 **F**1 6 10 14 15 16 23 35 37 41 44 45	14	10	S		32	655	12	37.5	6	31	2095	981	62

Hospital, Address, Telephone, Administrator, Approval and Facility Codes, Multihospital System Code	Classification Codes				Inpatient Data				Newborn Data		Expense (thousands of dollars)		
★ American Hospital Association (AHA) membership □ Joint Commission on Accreditation of Hospitals (JCAH) accreditation + American Osteopathic Hospital Association (AOHA) membership ○ American Osteopathic Association (AOA) accreditation Δ Commission on Accreditation of Rehabilitation Facilities (CARF) accreditation Control codes 61, 63, 64, 71, 72 and 73 indicate hospitals listed by AOHA, but not registered by AHA. For definition of numerical codes, see page A2	Control	Service	Stay	Facilities	Beds	Admissions	Census	Occupancy (percent)	Bassinets	Births	Total	Payroll	Personnel
HIAWATHA—Brown County													
⊞ HIAWATHA COMMUNITY HOSPITAL, 300 Utah St., Zip 66434; tel. 913/742-2131; J. Michael Frost, adm. (Nonreporting) **A**1a 9 10; **S**0805	23	10	S		32	—	—	—	—	—	—	—	—
HILL CITY—Graham County													
★ GRAHAM COUNTY HOSPITAL, 304 W. Prout St., P O Box 339, Zip 67642; tel. 913/674-2121; Virgil J. Aldridge, adm. **A**9 10 **F**1 6 16 23 36 41 43 45	13	10	S		42	855	15	35.7	6	26	2167	1108	73
HILLSBORO—Marion County													
★ SALEM HOSPITAL, 701 S. Main St., Zip 67063; tel. 316/947-3114; John F. Wiebe, adm. (Total facility includes 74 beds in nursing home-type unit) **A**9 10 **F**1 6 15 16 19 23 24 32 36 37 41 43 44	21	10	S	TF	100	506	70	70.0	6	41	2040	1077	82
				H	26	465	6	—	6	41	1146	591	35
HOISINGTON—Barton County													
⊞ HOISINGTON LUTHERAN HOSPITAL, 250 W. Ninth St., Zip 67544; tel. 316/653-2114; Angeline C. Deutsch RN, adm. **A**1a 9 10 **F**1 6 14 16 23 24 33 35 44 45 48 49	21	10	S		48	795	21	43.8	8	37	2010	913	55
HOLTON—Jackson County													
HOLTON CITY HOSPITAL, 510 Kansas Ave., Zip 66436; tel. 913/364-2116; Bill Gartner, adm. **A**9 10 **F**1 23 26 35 41 45	14	10	S		27	499	12	44.4	6	32	1027	488	39
HORTON—Brown County													
★ HORTON COMMUNITY HOSPITAL, 240 W. 18th St., Zip 66439; tel. 913/486-2642; F. Edward Berger, adm. **A**9 10 **F**1 3 14 15 16 23 24 26 30 34 35 37 40 41 42 44 45 46 47	23	10	S		35	1167	18	51.4	5	43	2565	1076	66
HOXIE—Sheridan County													
⊞ SHERIDAN COUNTY HOSPITAL, 826 18th St., P O Box 167, Zip 67740; tel. 913/675-3281; Larry L. Baecht, adm. (Nonreporting) **A**1a 9 10	13	10	S		60	—	—	—	—	—	—	—	—
HUGOTON—Stevens County													
★ STEVENS COUNTY HOSPITAL, 1006 S. Jackson St., Box 10, Zip 67951; tel. 316/544-8511; Carlyle Kiehne, adm. **A**9 10 **F**1 6 16 23 28 30 34 35 37 40 41 45	23	10	S		22	405	5	22.7	4	33	1256	480	30
HUTCHINSON—Reno County													
⊞ HUTCHINSON HOSPITAL CORPORATION, 1701 E. 23rd St., Zip 67502; tel. 316/665-2000; Gene E. Schmidt, pres.; Alvin Penner, exec. vice-pres. (Total facility includes 20 beds in nursing home-type unit) **A**1a 9 10 **F**1 3 6 8 9 10 11 12 14 16 19 23 24 26 27 28 30 32 33 34 35 36 40 42 43 44 45 46 47 49 52 53	23	10	S	TF	230	7657	119	51.7	30	935	21119	10611	563
				H	210	7399	106	—	30	935	20554	10402	548
INDEPENDENCE—Montgomery County													
⊞ MERCY HOSPITALS OF KANSAS, 800 W. Myrtle St., Box 388, Zip 67301; tel. 316/331-2200; Jerry Stevenson, vice-pres. & chief oper. off. (Total facility includes 14 beds in nursing home-type unit) **A**1a 9 10 **F**1 3 6 10 14 15 16 19 23 24 26 34 35 36 40 41 44 45 53; **S**5185	21	10	S	TF	93	2394	36	38.7	10	175	6316	3286	136
				H	79	2206	29	—	10	175	5876	3160	129
IOLA—Allen County													
⊞ ALLEN COUNTY HOSPITAL, 101 S. First St., Box 540, Zip 66749; tel. 316/365-3131; Bill May, chief exec. off. **A**1a 9 10 **F**1 3 5 6 10 11 12 14 15 16 23 24 26 35 36 40 41 44 45 46 47 53; **S**8815	13	10	S		45	1508	21	33.3	5	190	4362	1695	107
JETMORE—Hodgeman County													
★ HODGEMAN COUNTY HEALTH CENTER, Zip 67854; tel. 316/357-8361; Robert A. Cuthbertson, adm. (Total facility includes 35 beds in nursing home-type unit) **A**9 10 **F**1 6 15 16 23 30 32 33 34 35 44 48	13	10	S	TF	51	149	36	69.2	5	20	1180	697	50
				H	16	135	4	—	5	20	—	—	34
JOHNSON—Stanton County													
★ STANTON COUNTY HOSPITAL AND LONG TERM CARE UNIT, 404 N. Chestnut St., Box E, Zip 67855; tel. 316/492-6250; David A. James, adm. (Total facility includes 28 beds in nursing home-type unit) **A**9 10 **F**1 14 15 19 23 34 35 42 45; **S**1535	13	10	S	TF	46	335	26	56.5	4	62	1109	616	48
				H	18	326	3	—	4	62	—	—	31
JUNCTION CITY—Geary County													
⊞ GEARY COMMUNITY HOSPITAL, 1102 St. Marys Rd., Box 490, Zip 66441; tel. 913/238-4131; Gerald G. Geringer, adm. **A**1a 9 10 **F**1 3 5 10 15 16 23 35 37 40 45	13	10	S		92	1913	27	29.3	12	245	5676	2911	155
KANSAS CITY—Wyandotte County													
⊞ Δ BETHANY MEDICAL CENTER, 51 N. 12th St., Zip 66102; tel. 913/281-8400; John L. Millard, pres. (Total facility includes 40 beds in nursing home-type unit) **A**1a 2 3 5 7 9 10 **F**1 3 4 6 7 8 9 10 11 12 14 15 16 19 20 23 24 25 26 27 33 35 36 40 41 42 43 44 45 46 47 48 49 50 52 53 54	23	10	S	TF	359	10575	238	66.1	24	1074	46156	21066	1112
				H	319	10184	208	—	24	1074	44655	20370	1083
⊞ PROVIDENCE-ST. MARGARET HEALTH CENTER, 8929 Parallel Pkwy., Zip 66112; tel. 913/596-4000; James J. O'Connell, exec. dir. **A**1a 2 9 10 **F**1 2 3 4 6 9 10 11 12 15 16 20 23 24 26 30 34 35 36 37 40 43 44 45 46 47 52 53 54	23	10	S		276	9097	172	62.3	16	997	37132	16617	807
⊞ Δ UNIVERSITY OF KANSAS HOSPITAL (Formerly University of Kansas College of Health Sciences and Bell Memorial Hospital), 39th St. & Rainbow Blvd., Zip 66103; tel. 913/588-5000; Eugene L. Staples, vice chancellor **A**1a 2 3 5 7 8 9 10 **F**1 3 4 5 6 7 8 9 10 11 12 13 14 16 17 20 22 23 24 25 26 27 28 30 32 33 34 35 37 38 39 40 42 44 45 46 47 49 51 52 53 54	12	10	S		500	15870	346	69.2	24	1481	96003	—	2109
KINGMAN—Kingman County													
★ KINGMAN COMMUNITY HOSPITAL, 750 Ave. D W., Zip 67068; tel. 316/532-3147; Leon McDaniel, adm. **A**9 10 **F**1 3 6 10 14 15 16 23 35 36 40 43 48 49 50	23	10	S		49	946	19	38.8	8	158	2051	949	66
KINSLEY—Edwards County													
EDWARDS COUNTY HOSPITAL, 620 W. Eighth St., Box 99, Zip 67547; tel. 316/659-3621; Donald G. Larson, adm. **A**9 10 **F**6 12 14 16 23 35 40 41 45	21	10	S		49	484	8	16.3	6	44	1473	735	39
KIOWA—Barber County													
★ KIOWA DISTRICT HOSPITAL, 810 Drumm St., Zip 67070; tel. 316/825-4131; Buck McKinney, adm. (Nonreporting) **A**9 10	16	10	S		24	—	—	—	—	—	—	—	—
LA CROSSE—Rush County													
★ RUSH COUNTY MEMORIAL HOSPITAL, Eighth & Locust Sts., P O Box 520, Zip 67548; tel. 913/222-2545; Carol Larkin, adm. (Nonreporting) **A**9 10	13	10	S		50	—	—	—	—	—	—	—	—
LAKIN—Kearny County													
★ KEARNY COUNTY HOSPITAL, Thorpe Ave., Box 744, Zip 67860; tel. 316/355-7111; Steven S. Reiner, adm. **A**9 10 **F**1 6 10 14 15 16 35 36 40 43 52	13	10	S		20	485	5	25.0	4	82	1357	568	37
LARNED—Pawnee County													
□ LARNED STATE HOSPITAL, Rural Rte. 3, P O Box 89, Zip 67550; tel. 316/285-2131; G. W. Getz MD, supt. & clin. dir. **A**1b 9 10 **F**24 33 42 44 46 47 48	12	22	L		488	1184	488	100.0	0	0	20918	15377	818
⊞ ST. JOSEPH MEMORIAL HOSPITAL, 923 Carroll Ave., Zip 67550; tel. 316/285-3161; Garrett E. Colquette, chief oper. off. **A**1a 9 10 **F**1 14 16 23 24 35 36 40 43 44 45 46 48 49; **S**5175	21	10	S		68	899	31	45.6	3	59	3522	1095	73
LAWRENCE—Douglas County													
⊞ LAWRENCE MEMORIAL HOSPITAL, 325 Maine, Zip 66044; tel. 913/749-6100; Robert B. Ohlen, exec. dir. (Nonreporting) **A**1a 9 10	14	10	S		180	—	—	—	—	—	—	—	—
WATKINS MEMORIAL HOSPITAL, University of Kansas, Zip 66045; tel. 913/843-4455; James E. Strobl, dir. (Nonreporting) **A**9	12	10	S		35	—	—	—	—	—	—	—	—

Hospital, Address, Telephone, Administrator, Approval and Facility Codes, Multihospital System Code	Classification Codes				Inpatient Data				Newborn Data		Expense (thousands of dollars)		
★ American Hospital Association (AHA) membership ☐ Joint Commission on Accreditation of Hospitals (JCAH) accreditation + American Osteopathic Hospital Association (AOHA) membership ○ American Osteopathic Association (AOA) accreditation Δ Commission on Accreditation of Rehabilitation Facilities (CARF) accreditation Control codes 61, 63, 64, 71, 72 and 73 indicate hospitals listed by AOHA, but not registered by AHA. For definition of numerical codes, see page A2	Control	Service	Stay	Facilities	Beds	Admissions	Census	Occupancy (percent)	Bassinets	Births	Total	Payroll	Personnel
LEAVENWORTH—Leavenworth County													
⊞ CUSHING MEMORIAL HOSPITAL, 623 Marshall St., Zip 66048; tel. 913/682-8000; Charles L. Rogers, adm. (Nonreporting) **A**1a 9 10	23	10	S		110	—	—	—	—	—	—	—	—
⊞ ST. JOHN HOSPITAL, 3500 S. Fourth St., Zip 66048; tel. 913/682-3721; Sr. Mary Aloys Powell, exec. dir. **A**1a 9 10 **F**1 3 6 10 16 23 24 26 34 35 36 40 41 44 45 46 48 52 53; **S**5095	21	10	S		76	1936	29	38.2	10	222	7352	3791	199
U. S. PENITENTIARY, HOSPITAL UNIT, Zip 66048; tel. 913/682-8700; W. C. Gaunce, adm. **F**1 5 10 15 26 28 30 32 33 34 35 37 43 49	48	11	S		20	220	4	20.0	0	0	—	—	26
⊞ VETERANS ADMINISTRATION MEDICAL CENTER, Zip 66048; tel. 913/682-2000; James H. Cuer, dir. (Total facility includes 45 beds in nursing home-type unit) **A**1a **F**1 3 6 10 12 14 15 16 19 23 24 25 26 27 28 30 32 33 34 35 42 44 45 46 47 48 49 50	45	10	S	TF H	482 437	4548 4528	352 309	73.0 —	0 0	0 0	42523 —	29130 —	984 —
LEOTI—Wichita County													
★ WICHITA COUNTY HOSPITAL, 211 E. Earl, Zip 67861; tel. 316/375-2233; Roger Pearson, adm. **A**9 10 **F**1 15 16 23 24 35 37 44; **S**1535	13	10	S		13	209	3	23.1	4	34	632	299	23
LIBERAL—Seward County													
⊞ SOUTHWEST MEDICAL CENTER, W. 15th St., Box 1340, Zip 67901; tel. 316/624-1651; Paul Dougherty, adm. **A**1a 9 10 **F**1 3 6 7 8 10 11 12 14 15 16 17 23 34 35 36 37 40 41 45 52	13	10	S		93	3289	43	46.2	14	631	9821	4461	239
LINCOLN—Lincoln County													
LINCOLN COUNTY HOSPITAL, 624 N. Second St., P O Box 406, Zip 67455; tel. 913/524-4403; Jolene Yager, adm. (Total facility includes 20 beds in nursing home-type unit) **A**9 10 **F**6 15 16 19 23 35 45; **S**1535	13	10	S	TF H	34 14	312 285	22 3	64.7 —	4 4	7 7	928 —	451 —	41 23
LINDSBORG—McPherson County													
★ LINDSBORG COMMUNITY HOSPITAL, 605 W. Lincoln St., Zip 67456; tel. 913/227-3308; Bob Jones, adm. **A**9 10 **F**1 6 14 15 16 23 35 41 45 46; **S**1535	23	10	S		39	624	11	28.2	4	17	1529	796	57
LYONS—Rice County													
★ HOSPITAL DISTRICT NUMBER ONE OF RICE COUNTY, 619 S. Clark St., Zip 67554; tel. 316/257-5173; Robert L. Mullen, adm. **A**9 10 **F**1 16 23 24 35 44 45	16	10	S		44	849	13	29.5	10	142	1848	893	56
MANHATTAN—Riley County													
LAFENE STUDENT HEALTH CENTER AND UNIVERSITY HOSPITAL, Zip 66506; tel. 913/532-6544; Robert C. Tout MD, dir. (Data for 349 days) **F**15 23 26 28 29 30 32 33 34 35 37 43 47	12	11	S		10	128	1	10.0	0	0	2266	1645	63
⊞ MEMORIAL HOSPITAL, Sunset Ave. & Claflin Rd., Box 1208, Zip 66502; tel. 913/776-3300; E. Michael Nunamaker, chief exec. off. **A**1a 9 10 **F**1 3 6 10 14 15 16 23 30 34 35 36 40 45 46 51 52; **S**6235	23	10	S		74	1930	21	28.4	21	940	4469	2295	122
⊞ ST. MARY HOSPITAL, 1823 College Ave., Box 1047, Zip 66502; tel. 913/776-3322; Daniel P. Broyles, pres. & adm. **A**1a 9 10 **F**1 3 5 6 12 14 15 16 23 24 26 30 33 34 35 42 43 44 45 46 47 52; **S**5435	21	10	S		100	2234	36	36.0	0	0	7944	3993	217
MANKATO—Jewell County													
JEWELL COUNTY HOSPITAL, 100 Crest Vue, Box 327, Zip 66956; tel. 913/378-3137; Doris Hancock, adm. (Nonreporting) **A**9 10	13	10	S		61	—	—	—	—	—	—	—	—
MARION—Marion County													
★ ST. LUKE HOSPITAL, 1014 E. Melvin St., Zip 66861; tel. 316/382-2179; Craig J. Hanson, adm. **A**9 10 **F**1 3 5 6 15 16 23 26 34 35 36 41 45 46 53; **S**2235	23	10	S		25	656	10	40.0	4	40	1518	700	53
MARYSVILLE—Marshall County													
★ COMMUNITY MEMORIAL HOSPITAL, 708 N. 18th St., Zip 66508; tel. 913/562-2311; Harley B. Appel, adm. **A**9 10 **F**1 3 6 14 15 16 23 26 35 37 40 41 44 45 46 47 53	23	10	S		61	1167	21	34.4	8	113	3444	1421	88
MCCONNELL AIR FORCE BASE—Sedgwick County													
☐ U. S. AIR FORCE HOSPITAL, Zip 67221; tel. 316/652-5000; Maj. Raymond Williams III, adm. **A**1a **F**1 6 14 15 23 28 30 32 33 34 35 37 46 47	41	10	S		15	989	9	60.0	0	0	—	—	202
MCPHERSON—McPherson County													
⊞ MEMORIAL HOSPITAL, 1000 Hospital Dr., Zip 67460; tel. 316/241-2250; Stan Regehr, pres. & chief exec. off. **A**1a 9 10 **F**1 3 9 10 16 23 35 36 40 41 44 45 46 47 53	23	10	S		45	1720	23	51.1	12	240	4800	2562	135
MEADE—Meade County													
★ MEADE DISTRICT HOSPITAL, 510 E. Carthage St., Box 680, Zip 67864; tel. 316/873-2141; Michael P. Thomas, adm. **A**9 10 **F**1 5 6 14 16 23 24 34 35 43 44 50	21	10	S		26	460	8	30.8	6	59	1208	541	34
MEDICINE LODGE—Barber County													
★ MEDICINE LODGE MEMORIAL HOSPITAL, 710 N. Walnut St., P O Drawer C, Zip 67104; tel. 316/886-3771; Kevin White, adm. **A**9 10 **F**1 14 15 16 23 35 45; **S**1535	16	10	S		28	929	12	42.9	5	72	3652	1353	77
MINNEAPOLIS—Ottawa County													
★ OTTAWA COUNTY HOSPITAL, Box 209, Zip 67467; tel. 913/392-2122; Joy Reed RN, adm. (Total facility includes 19 beds in nursing home-type unit) **A**9 10 **F**12 14 15 16 19 23 35 41 46 50; **S**1535	23	10	S	TF H	39 20	489 482	35 16	89.7 —	0 0	0 0	1212 —	672 —	56 —
MINNEOLA—Clark County													
★ MINNEOLA DISTRICT HOSPITAL, 212 Main St., Zip 67865; tel. 316/885-4264; Blaine K. Miller, adm. **A**9 10 **F**1 6 15 16 23 24 35 37 44; **S**1535	16	10	S		15	366	7	46.7	6	30	1014	396	25
MOUNDRIDGE—McPherson County													
★ MERCY HOSPITAL, 218 E. Pack St., Box 180, Zip 67107; tel. 316/345-6391; Doyle K. Johnson, adm. (Total facility includes 6 beds in nursing home-type unit) **A**9 10 **F**1 19 23 24 34 35 40 44 52	21	10	S	TF H	27 21	419 355	8 5	29.6 —	5 5	37 37	676 —	365 —	26 —
NEODESHA—Wilson County													
WILSON COUNTY HOSPITAL, 205 Mill St., Box 360, Zip 66757; tel. 316/325-2611; Rick E. Wulf, adm. **A**9 10 **F**1 6 14 16 23 28 30 32 34 35 36 40 41 43 45 48 49	13	10	S		38	616	15	39.5	6	63	1935	840	66
NESS CITY—Ness County													
⊞ NESS COUNTY HOSPITAL DISTRICT NUMBER TWO, 312 E. Custer St., Zip 67560; tel. 913/798-2291; Clyde T. McCracken, adm. (Total facility includes 27 beds in nursing home-type unit) **A**1a 9 10 **F**1 14 15 16 19 23 34 35 36 37 45	16	10	S	TF H	56 29	631 621	33 7	58.9 —	5 5	53 53	1913 1712	963 807	65 43
NEWTON—Harvey County													
⊞ AXTELL CHRISTIAN HOSPITAL, 209 E. Broadway St., Zip 67114; tel. 316/283-5200; W. Charles Waters, adm. **A**1a 9 10 **F**1 3 6 12 14 15 16 23 26 35 40 44 45 46 47 50 52 53	21	10	S		79	1660	25	30.1	8	125	5049	2482	133
⊞ BETHEL DEACONESS HOSPITAL, 411 S.E. Second St., Box 868, Zip 67114; tel. 316/283-2700; Marvin H. Ewert, pres. (Total facility includes 12 beds in nursing home-type unit) **A**1a 9 10 **F**1 3 7 8 10 11 14 16 19 23 24 35 36 40 44 45 46 53	23	10	S	TF H	70 58	2060 1875	31 22	44.3 —	12 12	391 391	6042 —	3055 —	168 —
☐ PRAIRIE VIEW MENTAL HEALTH CENTER, 1901 E. First St., Box 467, Zip 67114; tel. 316/283-2400; Larry W. Nikkel, exec. dir. (Nonreporting) **A**1b 9 10	21	22	L		43	—	—	—	—	—	—	—	—
NORTON—Norton County													
★ NORTON COUNTY HOSPITAL, 102 E. Holme, P O Box 250, Zip 67654; tel. 913/877-3351; Richard Miller, adm. **A**9 10 **F**1 6 15 16 23 35 40 43 44 46	13	10	S		43	791	12	27.9	4	84	1886	1019	72
NORTON STATE HOSPITAL, Zip 67654; tel. 913/877-3301; John C. Adams, actg. supt. **F**33 42 44 45 46 47	12	62	L		167	5	145	86.8	0	0	6135	—	240

Hospital, Address, Telephone, Administrator, Approval and Facility Codes, Multihospital System Code	Classification Codes				Inpatient Data				Newborn Data		Expense (thousands of dollars)		
★ American Hospital Association (AHA) membership ☐ Joint Commission on Accreditation of Hospitals (JCAH) accreditation + American Osteopathic Hospital Association (AOHA) membership ○ American Osteopathic Association (AOA) accreditation Δ Commission on Accreditation of Rehabilitation Facilities (CARF) accreditation Control codes 61, 63, 64, 71, 72 and 73 indicate hospitals listed by AOHA, but not registered by AHA. For definition of numerical codes, see page A2	Control	Service	Stay	Facilities	Beds	Admissions	Census	Occupancy (percent)	Bassinets	Births	Total	Payroll	Personnel
OAKLEY—Logan County													
LOGAN COUNTY HOSPITAL, 211 Cherry St., Zip 67748; tel. 913/672-3211; Rodney Bates, adm. (Total facility includes 18 beds in nursing home-type unit) **A**9 10 **F**1 3 6 14 16 19 34 35 36 40	13	10	S	TF	39	421	13	33.3	6	61	1147	620	41
				H	21	395	6	—	6	61	—	—	—
OBERLIN—Decatur County													
★ DECATUR COUNTY HOSPITAL, 810 W. Columbia St., Zip 67749; tel. 913/475-2208; Charles P. Myers, adm. (Total facility includes 38 beds in nursing home-type unit) **A**9 10 **F**1 14 16 19 23 34 35 44; **S**2235	23	10	S	TF	62	811	54	87.1	4	63	2253	1146	84
				H	24	787	17	—	4	63	1661	776	59
OLATHE—Johnson County													
☐ KANSAS INSTITUTE, 555 E. Santa Fe, P O Box 2230, Zip 66061; tel. 913/782-7000; Eugene Hastings, adm. (Nonreporting) **A**1a b 9 10	23	22	L		37	—	—	—	—	—	—	—	—
★☐ OLATHE MEDICAL CENTER (Formerly Olathe Community Hospital), 215 W. 151st St., Zip 66061; tel. 913/782-1451; Frank H. Devocelle, adm. **A**1a 9 10 **F**1 3 5 6 7 9 10 12 14 15 16 21 23 34 35 36 40 45 46 47 52 53	23	10	S		100	5366	73	73.0	10	560	16258	7438	389
ONAGA—Pottawatomie County													
COMMUNITY HOSPITAL-ONAGA (Formerly Community Hospital District Number One), 120 W. Eighth St., Zip 66521; tel. 913/889-4272; Joseph T. Engelken, adm. (Nonreporting) **A**9 10	16	10	S		20	—	—	—	—	—	—	—	—
OSAWATOMIE—Miami County													
☐ OSAWATOMIE STATE HOSPITAL, Box 500, Zip 66064; tel. 913/755-3151; Norma J. Stephens, supt. **A**1b 9 10 **F**15 23 24 32 33 37 42 46 47 48 50	12	22	L		416	1626	336	80.8	0	0	15352	10759	613
OSBORNE—Osborne County													
★ OSBORNE COUNTY MEMORIAL HOSPITAL, 424 W. New Hampshire St., P O Box 70, Zip 67473; tel. 913/346-2121; Jeff Lebeda, adm. (Nonreporting) **A**9 10	23	10	S		29	—	—	—	—	—	—	—	—
OSWEGO—Labette County													
OSWEGO CITY HOSPITAL, 900 Barker Dr., Rural Rte. 2, Box 10a, Zip 67356; tel. 316/795-2921; James E. Vietti, adm. (Nonreporting) **A**9 10	14	10	S		18	—	—	—	—	—	—	—	—
OTTAWA—Franklin County													
★☐ RANSOM MEMORIAL HOSPITAL, 13th & S. Main Sts., Zip 66067; tel. 913/242-3344; Dennis George, actg. adm. **A**1a 9 10 **F**1 3 6 14 16 23 24 26 34 35 40 44 45 46 47 53	13	10	S		65	1453	19	29.2	5	130	4129	2050	130
OVERLAND PARK—Johnson County													
★☐ HUMANA HOSPITAL -OVERLAND PARK, 10500 Quivira Rd., P O Box 15959, Zip 66215; tel. 913/541-5000; Prosser Lee Ashbury Jr., exec. dir. (Nonreporting) **A**1a 9 10; **S**1235	33	10	S		400	—	—	—	—	—	—	—	—
PAOLA—Miami County													
★ MIAMI COUNTY HOSPITAL, 501 S. Hospital Dr., Box 365, Zip 66071; tel. 913/294-2327; Robert E. Johnson, adm. **A**9 10 **F**1 6 12 14 16 23 34 35 36 41 43 45 46	13	10	S		28	524	8	28.6	4	56	2306	1048	61
PARSONS—Labette County													
★☐ LABETTE COUNTY MEDICAL CENTER, S. 21st St., P O Box 956, Zip 67357; tel. 316/421-4880; Jerry D. Lilley, adm. **A**1a 9 10 **F**1 3 6 10 14 15 16 23 34 35 36 40 43 45 53	13	10	S		109	4008	58	53.2	16	430	11123	5639	274
PARSONS STATE HOSPITAL AND TRAINING CENTER, 26th & Gabriel Sts., Box 738, Zip 67357; tel. 316/421-6550; Gary J. Daniels PhD, supt. (Nonreporting) **A**9	12	62	L		339	—	—	—	—	—	—	—	—
PHILLIPSBURG—Phillips County													
★ PHILLIPS COUNTY HOSPITAL, 1150 State St., Box 607, Zip 67661; tel. 913/543-5226; Joanne Johnson RN, adm. (Total facility includes 33 beds in nursing home-type unit) **A**9 10 **F**1 6 15 16 19 23 35 36 43 45 46; **S**1535	23	10	S	TF	62	1227	47	75.8	8	83	3222	1447	104
				H	29	1178	15	—	8	83	—	—	84
PITTSBURG—Crawford County													
★☐ MOUNT CARMEL MEDICAL CENTER, Centennial & Rouse Sts., Zip 66762; tel. 316/231-6100; Dan Lingor, pres. & chief exec. off. **A**1a 9 10 **F**3 6 7 8 9 10 11 12 14 16 21 23 24 27 30 32 33 34 35 36 40 41 42 45 48 52 53; **S**5435	23	10	S		163	4478	89	54.6	12	206	12873	6279	314
PLAINVILLE—Rooks County													
PLAINVILLE RURAL HOSPITAL DISTRICT, 304 S. Colorado Ave., Zip 67663; tel. 913/434-4553; Robert H. Lane, adm. **A**10 **F**1 6 34 35 36 40 41 44	16	10	S		25	453	5	20.0	5	46	1094	583	40
PRATT—Pratt County													
★☐ PRATT REGIONAL MEDICAL CENTER, 200 Commodore St., Zip 67124; tel. 316/672-6476; Roland G. Walsh, pres. & chief exec. off. (Total facility includes 15 beds in nursing home-type unit) **A**1a 9 10 **F**1 3 6 10 11 14 16 19 23 33 34 35 36 40 41 45 46 48 52 53; **S**5435	13	10	S	TF	84	1814	28	33.3	6	115	6567	2823	170
				H	69	1743	26	—	6	115	6516	2776	160
QUINTER—Gove County													
GOVE COUNTY HOSPITAL, Fifth & Garfield Sts., Zip 67752; tel. 913/754-3341; Paul Davis, adm. (Nonreporting) **A**9 10	13	10	S		64	—	—	—	—	—	—	—	—
RANSOM—Ness County													
★ GRISELL MEMORIAL HOSPITAL DISTRICT ONE, P O Box 268, Zip 67572; tel. 913/731-2231; Fern Mishler, adm. (Total facility includes 33 beds in nursing home-type unit) **A**9 10 **F**1 16 19 23 35 36 45; **S**1535	16	10	S	TF	51	222	36	70.6	4	19	1271	712	50
				H	18	212	3	—	4	19	—	—	36
RUSSELL—Russell County													
★☐ RUSSELL CITY HOSPITAL, 200 S. Main St., Zip 67665; tel. 913/483-3131; Thomas J. Earley, pres. & chief exec. off. **A**1a 9 10 **F**1 3 6 10 12 14 15 16 23 34 35 36 40 41 44 45 53	14	10	S		37	1014	14	30.4	6	60	3223	1638	73
SABETHA—Nemaha County													
★ SABETHA COMMUNITY HOSPITAL, 14th & Oregon Sts., P O Box 229, Zip 66534; tel. 913/284-2121; Rita Becker, adm. **A**9 10 **F**1 12 14 15 16 23 24 26 34 35 36 43 45 50; **S**1535	23	10	S		27	575	8	29.6	6	69	1288	602	37
SALINA—Saline County													
★☐ ASBURY HOSPITAL, 400 S. Santa Fe Ave., Box 1760, Zip 67402; tel. 913/827-4411; Clay D. Edmands, pres. **A**1a 3 5 6 9 10 **F**1 3 6 9 10 11 12 14 15 16 21 23 24 27 30 32 33 35 36 37 39 40 44 45 46 47 50 52 53	23	10	S		178	6671	110	61.8	20	1077	17799	9173	464
☐ ST. FRANCIS AT SALINA, 5097 Cloud St., Zip 67401; tel. 913/825-0563; Rev. Canon N. Kenneth Yates, pres. **A**1b 9 **F**31 32 33 42 44 46	23	22	L		26	22	23	88.5	0	0	535	305	33
★☐ ST. JOHN'S HOSPITAL, 139 N. Penn St., Zip 67401; Mailing Address P O Box 5201, Zip 67402; tel. 913/827-5591; Roy E. White, adm. **A**1a 3 9 10 **F**1 3 6 7 8 9 10 11 12 14 15 16 21 23 24 26 32 35 42 43 44 45 46 48 49 50 52; **S**5435	21	10	S		204	4147	122	61.3	0	0	17179	7867	476
SATANTA—Haskell County													
★ SATANTA DISTRICT HOSPITAL, Box 159, Zip 67870; tel. 316/649-2761; T. G. Lee, adm. (Total facility includes 24 beds in nursing home-type unit) **A**9 10 **F**1 6 12 15 16 19 23 24 35 37 41 44 45; **S**1535	23	10	S	TF	38	384	29	76.3	5	24	1693	912	60
				H	14	372	5	—	5	24	—	—	43
SCOTT CITY—Scott County													
★ SCOTT COUNTY HOSPITAL, 310 E. Third St., Zip 67871; tel. 316/872-5811; Jackie John, adm. **A**9 10 **F**1 6 15 16 23 24 35 37 44 45 46; **S**1535	23	10	S		27	767	15	55.6	6	93	1886	891	66

Hospital, Address, Telephone, Administrator, Approval and Facility Codes, Multihospital System Code	Classification Codes				Inpatient Data				Newborn Data		Expense (thousands of dollars)		
★ American Hospital Association (AHA) membership □ Joint Commission on Accreditation of Hospitals (JCAH) accreditation + American Osteopathic Hospital Association (AOHA) membership ○ American Osteopathic Association (AOA) accreditation Δ Commission on Accreditation of Rehabilitation Facilities (CARF) accreditation Control codes 61, 63, 64, 71, 72 and 73 indicate hospitals listed by AOHA, but not registered by AHA. For definition of numerical codes, see page A2	Control	Service	Stay	Facilities	Beds	Admissions	Census	Occupancy (percent)	Bassinets	Births	Total	Payroll	Personnel
SEDAN—Chautauqua County													
SEDAN CITY HOSPITAL, 300 North St., Box C, Zip 67361; tel. 316/725-3115; Gary Martin, adm. **A**9 10 **F**1 12 14 34 35 36 40 48 49 50	14	10	S		38	250	10	23.3	3	14	972	549	39
SENECA—Nemaha County													
★ NEMAHA VALLEY COMMUNITY HOSPITAL, 604 Nemaha St., Zip 66538; tel. 913/336-6181; Helen A. McGinty RN, adm. **A**9 10 **F**1 6 16 23 24 34 35 36 37 44 45 50	23	10	S		31	952	12	38.7	6	109	1628	840	58
SHAWNEE MISSION—Johnson County													
★□ SHAWNEE MISSION MEDICAL CENTER, 9100 W. 74th St., Zip 66201; tel. 913/676-2000; Cleo Johnson, pres. **A**1a 2 9 10 **F**1 3 4 6 10 12 15 16 20 23 26 27 30 33 34 35 36 40 44 45 46 47 48 49 52 53 54; **S**9355	21	10	S		383	14762	260	67.9	34	2132	67281	30545	1289
SMITH CENTER—Smith County													
★□ SMITH COUNTY MEMORIAL HOSPITAL, S. Main St., P O Box 349, Zip 66967; tel. 913/282-6661; J. H. Seitz, area dir. (Total facility includes 26 beds in nursing home-type unit) **A**1a 9 10 **F**1 6 15 16 17 19 23 35 36 43; **S**1535	23	10	S	TF	52	973	39	75.0	8	48	1935	1027	87
				H	26	952	12	—	8	48	—	—	73
SPEARVILLE—Ford County													
SPEARVILLE DISTRICT HOSPITAL, Zip 67876; tel. 316/385-2662; Robert P. Renick, adm. **A**9 10 **F**1 6 16 23 35 45	16	10	S		16	57	6	37.5	4	3	534	247	28
ST. FRANCIS—Cheyenne County													
★ CHEYENNE COUNTY HOSPITAL, 210 W. First St., P O Box 547, Zip 67756; tel. 913/332-2104; Shirley Billiar Adams RN, adm. **A**9 10 **F**1 15 16 23 35 45; **S**1535	23	10	S		23	155	2	8.7	3	22	474	244	18
ST. JOHN—Stafford County													
★ ST. JOHN DISTRICT HOSPITAL, E. First & Santa Fe Sts., Zip 67576; tel. 316/549-3255; Joyce Schulte, adm. (Total facility includes 10 beds in nursing home-type unit) **A**9 10 **F**1 15 16 19 23 32 35 41 42 45 47	16	10	S	TF	30	326	7	23.3	0	4	1030	486	33
				H	20	299	3	—	0	4	—	—	—
STAFFORD—Stafford County													
□ STAFFORD DISTRICT HOSPITAL NUMBER FOUR, 502 S. Buckeye St., Box 190, Zip 67578; tel. 316/234-5221; Jeff Reinert, adm. **A**1a 9 10 **F**1 3 6 16 23 35 44 45 46	16	10	S		25	508	9	36.0	0	10	1417	616	45
SYRACUSE—Hamilton County													
HAMILTON COUNTY HOSPITAL, E. Ave. G & Huser St., Box 909, Zip 67878; tel. 316/384-7461; Marvin E. Graber, adm. (Nonreporting) **A**9 10	13	10	S		56	—	—	—	—	—	—	—	—
TOPEKA—Shawnee County													
★□ C. F. MENNINGER MEMORIAL HOSPITAL, 5800 W. Sixth St., Zip 66606; Mailing Address Box 829, Zip 66601; tel. 913/273-7500; Edward J. Zoble PhD, adm. **A**1b 3 9 10 **F**24 28 29 30 31 32 33 42 43 48 49	23	22	L		166	472	150	90.4	0	0	21993	10155	386
CHILDRENS DIVISION OF MENNINGER FOUNDATION, Box 829, Zip 66601; tel. 913/273-7500; Leland Koon, adm. **A**3 9 **F**15 28 29 31 32 33 34 42 43 44 49	23	52	L		69	51	65	94.2	0	0	9227	4355	192
★□ COLMERY-O'NEIL VETERANS ADMINISTRATION MEDICAL CENTER, 2200 Gage Blvd., Zip 66622; tel. 913/272-3111; Paul K. Kennedy, dir. (Total facility includes 79 beds in nursing home-type unit) **A**1a 3 5 **F**1 3 6 10 12 14 15 16 19 23 24 25 26 27 28 29 30 31 32 33 34 42 44 46 47 48 49 50 53	45	10	L	TF	887	5913	656	74.0	0	0	45898	29564	1221
				H	808	5892	581	—	0	0	43406	27819	1142
KANSAS NEUROLOGICAL INSTITUTE, 3107 W. 21st St., Zip 66604; tel. 913/296-5389; Ann Marshall-Levine PhD, supt. (Nonreporting)	12	12	S		18	—	—	—	—	—	—	—	—
★□ MEMORIAL HOSPITAL CORPORATION OF TOPEKA, 600 Madison, Zip 66607; tel. 913/354-5100; Charles E. Beall, pres. & chief exec. off. **A**1a 9 10 **F**1 3 6 10 12 14 15 16 23 24 26 27 28 29 30 31 32 33 34 35 39 43 44 45 46 47 53 54	23	10	S		132	2857	61	47.3	0	0	17393	8213	411
★□ ST. FRANCIS HOSPITAL AND MEDICAL CENTER, 1700 W. Seventh St., Zip 66606; tel. 913/295-8000; Sr. Ann Marita Loosen, pres. **A**1a 2 9 10 **F**1 2 3 4 6 7 8 9 10 11 12 13 15 16 20 21 23 24 25 26 30 33 34 35 36 40 41 43 45 46 47 48 49 52 53 54; **S**5095	21	10	S		311	10351	185	59.5	38	1115	49623	22658	1149
★□ STORMONT-VAIL REGIONAL MEDICAL CENTER, 1500 W. Tenth St., Zip 66604; tel. 913/354-6000; Howard M. Chase, pres. & chief exec. off. **A**1a 3 5 6 9 10 **F**1 2 3 4 5 6 9 10 11 12 15 16 23 24 26 27 30 31 32 34 35 36 37 38 40 41 42 43 45 46 47 48 51 52 53 54; **S**0805	23	10	S		338	11996	234	74.1	24	1699	57262	27491	1354
□ TOPEKA STATE HOSPITAL, 2700 W. Sixth St., Zip 66606; tel. 913/296-4596; E. G. Burdzik MD, supt. **A**1b 3 9 10 **F**19 24 30 32 33 42 44 46	12	22	L		403	1260	380	94.3	0	0	17003	10893	656
TRIBUNE—Greeley County													
★ GREELEY COUNTY HOSPITAL, 506 Third St., Box 338, Zip 67879; tel. 316/376-4221; Irene Pierce RN, adm. **A**9 10 **F**1 14 15 16 35; **S**1535	23	10	S		18	269	3	16.7	4	63	727	350	23
ULYSSES—Grant County													
★ BOB WILSON MEMORIAL GRANT COUNTY HOSPITAL, 415 N. Main St., Zip 67880; tel. 316/356-1266; Wally Boyd, adm. **A**9 10 **F**1 3 6 10 14 15 16 23 33 34 35 40 41 45 47 52; **S**1535	13	10	S		42	1062	16	38.1	7	108	2894	1346	65
WAKEENEY—Trego County													
★ TREGO COUNTY-LEMKE MEMORIAL HOSPITAL, 320 13th St., Zip 67672; tel. 913/743-2182; James Wahlmeier, adm. (Total facility includes 36 beds in nursing home-type unit) **A**9 10 **F**1 15 16 19 23 35 36 45; **S**1535	23	10	S	TF	64	731	46	71.9	7	33	2055	1062	91
				H	28	680	12	—	7	33	—	—	53
WAMEGO—Pottawatomie County													
WAMEGO CITY HOSPITAL, 711 Genn Dr., Zip 66547; tel. 913/456-2295; Lannie Zweimiller, adm. **A**9 10 **F**1 6 12 14 15 16 23 24 33 34 35 36 40 41 42 44; **S**0805	14	10	S		26	595	6	23.1	4	125	1338	650	45
WASHINGTON—Washington County													
★ WASHINGTON COUNTY HOSPITAL, 304 E. Third St., Zip 66968; tel. 913/325-2211; Beth Koch RN, adm. **A**9 10 **F**1 3 10 14 16 23 24 35 40 43 44 45 52	13	10	S		27	343	3	11.1	8	23	1029	453	38
WELLINGTON—Sumner County													
ST. LUKES HOSPITAL, 1323 N. A St., Zip 67152; tel. 316/326-7451; James Gallemore, adm. (Total facility includes 18 beds in nursing home-type unit) **A**9 10 **F**1 3 6 10 14 19 23 34 35 40 45 48	14	10	S	TF	80	1306	21	26.3	6	123	3650	1843	123
				H	62	1229	16	—	6	123	3492	1710	113
+ WELLINGTON HOSPITAL AND CLINIC, 924 S. Washington, Zip 67152; tel. 316/326-3353; Terry Deschaine, adm. (Nonreporting) **A**9 10	31	10	S		37	—	—	—	—	—	—	—	—
WESTMORELAND—Pottawatomie County													
DECHAIRO HOSPITAL, Zip 66549; tel. 913/457-3311; Donn Demaree, adm. **A**9 10 **F**1 2 6 14 23 34 35 50; **S**0805	33	10	S		20	319	4	20.0	0	0	809	408	28
WICHITA—Sedgwick County													
○ + RIVERSIDE HOSPITAL, 2622 W. Central St., Zip 67203; tel. 316/945-9161; S. Lee Baker, adm. **A**9 10 11 12 13 **F**1 3 6 10 12 14 15 16 23 33 34 35 36 40 44 45 46 47 48 52 53	23	10	S		90	2326	32	36.8	8	120	9817	4857	248
★□ ST. FRANCIS REGIONAL MEDICAL CENTER, 929 N. St. Francis Ave., Zip 67214; tel. 316/268-5000; Sr. M. Sylvia Egan, pres. & chief exec. off. **A**1a b 2 3 5 8 9 10 **F**1 2 3 4 5 6 7 8 9 10 11 12 13 14 15 16 17 20 22 23 24 26 27 28 30 32 33 34 35 36 37 40 41 42 43 44 45 46 47 49 51 52 53 54; **S**5305	21	10	S		570	20540	389	68.2	30	1519	120853	57206	2487
★□ Δ ST. JOSEPH MEDICAL CENTER, 3600 E. Harry St., Zip 67218; tel. 316/685-1111; Gerald S. Cambron, pres. & chief exec. off.; Sr. Mary Alice Girrens, exec. vice-pres. & chief oper. off. **A**1a b 2 3 5 7 8 9 10 **F**1 2 3 4 5 6 7 8 9 10 11 12 14 15 16 17 20 23 24 25 26 27 29 30 33 34 35 36 40 41 42 43 44 45 46 47 48 49 50 51 52 53 54; **S**5435	23	10	S		473	15410	337	67.8	23	1523	71691	35835	1464

Hospital, Address, Telephone, Administrator, Approval and Facility Codes, Multihospital System Code	Classification Codes				Inpatient Data				Newborn Data		Expense (thousands of dollars)		
★ American Hospital Association (AHA) membership □ Joint Commission on Accreditation of Hospitals (JCAH) accreditation + American Osteopathic Hospital Association (AOHA) membership ○ American Osteopathic Association (AOA) accreditation Δ Commission on Accreditation of Rehabilitation Facilities (CARF) accreditation Control codes 61, 63, 64, 71, 72 and 73 indicate hospitals listed by AOHA, but not registered by AHA. For definition of numerical codes, see page A2	Control	Service	Stay	Facilities	Beds	Admissions	Census	Occupancy (percent)	Bassinets	Births	Total	Payroll	Personnel
U. S. AIR FORCE HOSPITAL, See McConnell Air Force Base													
★□ VETERANS ADMINISTRATION MEDICAL CENTER, 901 George Washington Blvd., Zip 67211; tel. 316/685-2221; Robert F. Pelka, dir. (Total facility includes 60 beds in nursing home-type unit) **A**1a 3 5 **F**1 3 6 10 12 14 15 16 19 20 23 24 26 27 28 29 30 32 33 34 35 41 42 43 44 46 49 50	45	10	S	TF H	218 158	4359 4161	180 123	82.6 —	0 0	0 0	26435 23247	14257 12946	501 469
★□ Δ WESLEY MEDICAL CENTER, 550 N. Hillside Ave., Zip 67214; tel. 316/688-2468; A. B. Davis Jr., chm. & chief exec. off.; Donald M. Stewart, pres. & chief oper. off. **A**1a 2 3 5 7 8 9 10 **F**1 2 3 4 5 6 7 8 9 10 11 12 14 15 16 17 20 23 24 26 27 30 32 34 35 36 37 38 39 40 41 42 43 44 45 46 47 50 51 52 53 54; **S**1755	33	10	S		601	26215	420	69.9	48	5069	—	—	2490
WINCHESTER—Jefferson County													
JEFFERSON COUNTY MEMORIAL HOSPITAL (Includes Jefferson County Memorial Hospital Geriatrics Center), Rural Rte. 1, Box 1, Zip 66097; tel. 913/774-4340; Gary Fowler, adm. (Total facility includes 100 beds in nursing home-type unit) **A**9 10 **F**1 2 6 10 15 16 19 23 24 34 35 40 42 44 45 46 50	23	10	S	TF H	136 36	604 535	100 10	73.5 —	6 6	45 45	2501 1365	1347 857	123 56
WINFIELD—Cowley County													
★□ WILLIAM NEWTON MEMORIAL HOSPITAL, 1300 E. Fifth St., Zip 67156; tel. 316/221-2300; Harold W. Steadham, adm. (Total facility includes 14 beds in nursing home-type unit) **A**1a 9 10 **F**1 3 6 10 12 14 15 16 19 20 23 28 30 34 35 36 37 40 41 43 44 45 46 47 53	14	10	S	TF H	99 85	2452 2310	41 36	41.4 —	12 12	341 341	6917 6767	3591 3459	219 214
WINFIELD STATE HOSPITAL AND TRAINING CENTER, Rte. 1, Box 123, Zip 67156; tel. 316/221-1200; Michael L. Dey PhD, supt. **F**16 23 24 33 42 44 46 47	12	62	L		510	11	485	93.4	0	0	18503	12519	677

Hospital, Address, Telephone, Administrator, Approval and Facility Codes, Multihospital System Code

★ American Hospital Association (AHA) membership
□ Joint Commission on Accreditation of Hospitals (JCAH) accreditation
+ American Osteopathic Hospital Association (AOHA) membership
○ American Osteopathic Association (AOA) accreditation
Δ Commission on Accreditation of Rehabilitation Facilities (CARF) accreditation
Control codes 61, 63, 64, 71, 72 and 73 indicate hospitals listed by AOHA, but not registered by AHA.
For definition of numerical codes, see page A2

Kentucky

Hospital, Address, Telephone, Administrator, Approval and Facility Codes, Multihospital System Code	Classification Codes: Control	Service	Stay	Facilities	Inpatient Data: Beds	Admissions	Census	Occupancy (percent)	Newborn Data: Bassinets	Births	Expense (thousands of dollars): Total	Payroll	Personnel
ALBANY—Clinton County													
CLINTON COUNTY WAR MEMORIAL HOSPITAL, 723 Burkesville Rd., Zip 42602; tel. 606/387-6421; Eddy R. Stockton, actg. adm. (Nonreporting) **A**9 10	23	10	S		42	—	—	—	—	—	—	—	—
ASHLAND—Boyd County													
FEDERAL CORRECTIONAL INSTITUTE HOSPITAL, Zip 41101; tel. 606/928-6414; William A. Trzetziak, adm. (Nonreporting)	48	11	S		10	—	—	—	—	—	—	—	—
★□ KING'S DAUGHTERS' MEDICAL CENTER, 2201 Lexington Ave., Zip 41101; Mailing Address P O Box 151, Zip 41105; tel. 606/329-2133; C. Timothy Maloney, pres. (Total facility includes 10 beds in nursing home-type unit) **A**1a 9 10 **F**1 3 6 9 10 11 12 14 15 16 19 23 24 25 26 27 30 32 33 34 35 37 40 41 42 44 45 46 52 53	23	10	S	TF	315	12034	190	60.3	25	1182	39522	17416	817
				H	305	12012	189	—	25	1182	39492	17386	809
ASHLAND—Greenup County													
★□ OUR LADY OF BELLEFONTE HOSPITAL, St. Christopher Dr., P O Box 789, Zip 41101; tel. 606/836-0231; W. Leon Hisle, pres. & chief exec. off.; Sr. Mary Lawrence VanderBurg, exec. vice-pres. **A**1a 9 10 **F**1 3 6 8 9 10 12 14 15 16 20 23 24 26 30 34 35 41 42 44 45 46 48 49 52 53; **S**1485	21	10	S		127	6139	122	100.0	0	0	22988	9217	447
BARBOURVILLE—Knox County													
★□ KNOX COUNTY GENERAL HOSPITAL, Broadway & High Sts., Zip 40906; tel. 606/546-4175; Ray B. Canady, adm. **A**1a 9 10 **F**1 3 6 14 16 23 30 35 37 40 45 46	13	10	S		58	2971	39	67.2	9	249	3763	1790	131
BARDSTOWN—Nelson County													
★□ FLAGET MEMORIAL HOSPITAL, 201 Cathedral Manor, Zip 40004; tel. 502/348-3923; Michael McAndrew, pres. **A**1a 9 10 **F**1 6 14 15 16 23 26 34 35 45 46 52 53; **S**3045	21	10	S		52	2080	25	48.1	8	144	3945	1860	107
BENTON—Marshall County													
★□ MARSHALL COUNTY HOSPITAL, 503 George McClain Dr., Zip 42025; tel. 502/527-1336; Andrew J. Hetrick, adm. (Nonreporting) **A**1a 9 10; **S**2495	13	10	S		80	—	—	—	—	—	—	—	—
BEREA—Madison County													
★□ BEREA HOSPITAL, Estill St., Box 128, Zip 40403; tel. 606/986-3151; David E. Burgio, adm. (Total facility includes 37 beds in nursing home-type unit) **A**1a 9 10 **F**1 3 6 14 15 16 19 23 30 32 33 34 35 43 45 46 47 53	23	10	S	TF	110	2642	65	59.1	0	0	7882	2970	177
				H	73	2414	31	—	0	0	6964	2579	147
BEVERLY—Bell County													
RED BIRD MOUNTAIN MEDICAL CENTER (Formerly Red Bird Hospital), Hc 69, Box 700, Zip 40913; tel. 606/598-5135; Gerald Kinney, interim exec. dir. (Nonreporting) **A**9 10	21	10	S		21	—	—	—	—	—	—	—	—
BOWLING GREEN—Warren County													
GREENVIEW HOSPITAL, See HCA Greenview Hospital													
★□ HCA GREENVIEW HOSPITAL (Formerly Greenview Hospital), 1801 Ashley Circle, Box 370, Zip 42101; tel. 502/781-4330; James C. Barnett, adm. **A**1a 9 10 **F**3 5 6 10 12 14 15 16 23 26 34 35 46 47 53 54; **S**1755	33	10	S		211	7574	133	63.0	0	0	—	—	467
★□ MEDICAL CENTER AT BOWLING GREEN, 250 Park St., Box 56, Zip 42101; tel. 502/781-2150; John C. Desmarais, pres. **A**1a 9 10 **F**1 2 3 5 6 7 8 9 10 11 12 14 15 16 20 23 24 26 27 28 29 30 32 33 34 35 36 37 38 40 41 42 43 44 46 47 48 49 50 51 52 53 54	23	10	S		312	10439	171	54.8	19	1690	33855	13523	724
BURKESVILLE—Cumberland County													
★ CUMBERLAND COUNTY HOSPITAL, P O Box 280, Zip 42717; tel. 502/864-2511; Randel Flowers, adm. **A**9 10 **F**6 12 14 15 16 35 36	13	10	S		31	2139	28	90.3	6	74	2345	1045	117
CADIZ—Trigg County													
★ TRIGG COUNTY HOSPITAL, Hwy. 68 E., Box 312, Zip 42211; tel. 502/522-3215; David W. Shore, adm. **A**9 10 **F**1 3 6 14 16 34 35 40 45 46 47 52	15	10	S		40	846	10	25.0	4	21	2153	960	64
CALHOUN—McLean County													
MCLEAN COUNTY GENERAL HOSPITAL, Hwy. 81, Zip 42327; tel. 502/273-5252; Jim McMahon, adm. (Nonreporting) **A**9 10	13	10	S		26	—	—	—	—	—	—	—	—
CAMPBELLSVILLE—Taylor County													
★□ TAYLOR COUNTY HOSPITAL, 1700 Old Lebanon Rd., Zip 42718; tel. 502/465-3561; David R. Hayes, adm. **A**1a 9 10 **F**1 3 6 14 15 16 23 32 35 36 37 40 41 45 46 53	16	10	S		90	3470	46	51.1	10	375	8152	3306	238
CARLISLE—Nicholas County													
NICHOLAS COUNTY HOSPITAL (Includes Johnson-Mathers Nursing Home), Rte. 2, Box 232, Zip 40311; tel. 606/289-7181; Robert Hester, adm. (Total facility includes 55 beds in nursing home-type unit) **A**9 10 **F**1 6 10 14 15 16 19 23 34 35 44 46	13	10	S	TF	83	1735	72	86.7	6	76	3583	1559	135
				H	28	1635	20	—	6	76	—	—	90
CARROLLTON—Carroll County													
★ CARROLL COUNTY MEMORIAL HOSPITAL, 309 11th St., Zip 41008; tel. 502/732-4321; John Dillon, adm. (Nonreporting) **A**9 10	13	10	S		54	—	—	—	—	—	—	—	—
COLUMBIA—Adair County													
□ WESTLAKE CUMBERLAND HOSPITAL, Westlake Dr., P O Box 468, Zip 42728; tel. 502/384-4753; Rex A. Tungate, adm. **A**1a 9 10 **F**1 3 6 10 12 14 16 23 34 35 40 41 44 45 46 53	16	10	S		65	3252	50	76.9	3	102	6397	2837	199
CORBIN—Whitley County													
★□ BAPTIST REGIONAL MEDICAL CENTER (Formerly Southeastern Kentucky Baptist Hospital), 1 Trillium Way, Zip 40701; tel. 606/528-1212; Kerry G. Gillihan, adm. **A**1a 9 10 **F**1 3 6 7 10 12 14 15 16 23 24 26 27 28 29 30 32 33 34 35 36 37 40 42 43 45 46 52 53; **S**0315	23	10	S		210	7792	133	85.3	15	619	15882	7099	505
COVINGTON—Kenton County													
□ CHILDREN'S PSYCHIATRIC HOSPITAL OF NORTHERN KENTUCKY, 502 Farrell Dr., Box 2680, Zip 41012; tel. 606/331-1900; Luke J. Dober, adm. **A**1a b 9 10 **F**24 30 32 33 42 45 46	23	52	L		51	121	43	84.3	0	0	3768	1871	115
★□ ST. ELIZABETH MEDICAL CENTER-NORTH (Includes St. Elizabeth Medical Center-South, 1 Medical Village Dr., Edgewood, Zip 41017; tel. 606/344-2000), 401 E. 20th St., Zip 41011; tel. 606/292-4000; Joseph W. Gross, pres. & chief exec. off. **A**1a 3 5 9 10 **F**1 2 3 4 5 6 7 8 9 10 11 12 14 15 16 20 21 23 24 27 34 35 36 40 41 42 44 45 46 48 49 51 52 53 54	21	10	S		623	20633	414	65.5	30	2093	80442	38466	1852
CYNTHIANA—Harrison County													
★□ HARRISON MEMORIAL HOSPITAL, Rte. 4, P O Box 250, Zip 41031; tel. 606/234-2300; James R. Farris, adm. (Total facility includes 24 beds in nursing home-type unit) **A**1a 9 10 **F**1 3 6 10 14 15 16 19 23 34 35 36 40 45 46 50 52 53	23	10	S	TF	99	2833	63	63.6	6	302	6296	2908	203
				H	75	2772	40	—	6	302	—	—	183

Hospital, Address, Telephone, Administrator, Approval and Facility Codes, Multihospital System Code	Classification Codes				Inpatient Data				Newborn Data		Expense (thousands of dollars)		
★ American Hospital Association (AHA) membership □ Joint Commission on Accreditation of Hospitals (JCAH) accreditation + American Osteopathic Hospital Association (AOHA) membership ○ American Osteopathic Association (AOA) accreditation Δ Commission on Accreditation of Rehabilitation Facilities (CARF) accreditation Control codes 61, 63, 64, 71, 72 and 73 indicate hospitals listed by AOHA, but not registered by AHA. For definition of numerical codes, see page A2	Control	Service	Stay	Facilities	Beds	Admissions	Census	Occupancy (percent)	Bassinets	Births	Total	Payroll	Personnel
DANVILLE—Boyle County													
★□ EPHRAIM MCDOWELL REGIONAL MEDICAL CENTER (Formerly Ephraim McDowell Memorial Hospital), 217 S. Third St., Zip 40422; tel. 606/236-4121; Thomas W. Smith, pres. & chief exec. off. **A**1a 9 10 **F**1 3 6 10 12 14 15 16 23 34 35 36 37 40 44 45 46 47 52 53	23	10	S		120	5662	80	66.7	17	647	13968	6324	349
EDGEWOOD—Kenton County													
ST. ELIZABETH MEDICAL CENTER-SOUTH, See St. Elizabeth Medical Center-North, Covington													
ELIZABETHTOWN—Hardin County													
★□ HARDIN MEMORIAL HOSPITAL, N. Dixie Hwy. 31 W., Zip 42701; tel. 502/737-1212; Warner Butters, adm. **A**1a 9 10 **F**1 2 3 5 6 10 11 12 14 15 16 21 23 27 30 32 33 34 35 37 40 43 44 45 46 47 50 52 53; **S**1755	13	10	S		235	11496	177	75.3	25	1184	28688	12831	723
FLEMINGSBURG—Fleming County													
★□ FLEMING COUNTY HOSPITAL, 920 Elizaville Ave., Box 388, Zip 41041; tel. 606/849-2351; Lee Ben Clarke, adm. **A**1a 9 10 **F**1 3 6 10 14 16 23 26 35 45 46; **S**1755	13	10	S		52	2082	32	61.5	6	3	3929	1825	116
FLORENCE—Boone County													
★□ SALVATION ARMY WILLIAM BOOTH MEMORIAL HOSPITAL, 7380 Turfway Rd., P O Box 6095, Zip 41042; tel. 606/525-5200; Ronald Lyons, adm. **A**1a 9 10 **F**1 2 3 6 10 12 14 15 16 23 24 27 28 30 32 33 34 35 42 45 46 47 52 53	21	10	S		161	6471	130	80.7	0	0	25003	11645	587
FORT CAMPBELL—Christian County													
★□ COLONEL FLORENCE A. BLANCHFIELD ARMY COMMUNITY HOSPITAL, Zip 42223; tel. 502/798-8040; Col. Richardo Alba MSC USAF, dep. cmdr. adm. **A**1a 2 **F**1 3 6 12 14 15 16 23 24 27 28 29 30 32 33 34 35 36 37 38 40 45 46 47 49 52	42	10	S		141	8312	115	81.6	16	1707	40251	—	958
FORT KNOX—Hardin County													
★□ U. S. IRELAND ARMY COMMUNITY HOSPITAL, 851 Ireland Loop, Zip 40121; tel. 502/624-9222; Col. Phillip Dorsey, adm. **A**1a **F**1 3 6 10 11 12 14 15 16 23 24 27 28 30 32 33 34 35 37 40 41 44 46 47 49 52 53	42	10	S		232	10339	141	60.8	17	1269	—	—	1113
FORT THOMAS—Campbell County													
★□ ST. LUKE HOSPITAL, 85 N. Grand Ave., Zip 41075; tel. 606/572-3100; John D. Hoyle, pres. **A**1a 2 9 10 **F**1 2 3 6 8 9 10 11 12 14 15 16 23 26 29 30 32 34 35 36 37 40 44 45 46 47 48 49 52 53	23	10	S		346	10130	203	58.7	36	1529	40519	17619	882
FRANKFORT—Franklin County													
★□ KING'S DAUGHTERS MEMORIAL HOSPITAL, King's Daughters Dr., Zip 40601; tel. 502/875-5240; Ronald T. Tyrer, adm. **A**1a 9 10 **F**1 3 5 6 10 12 15 16 23 30 34 35 36 37 40 44 45 46 47 53; **S**1755	33	10	S		125	5103	74	59.2	20	614	14808	5860	319
FRANKLIN—Simpson County													
★ FRANKLIN-SIMPSON MEMORIAL HOSPITAL, Brookhaven Rd., Zip 42134; tel. 502/586-3253; Rita J. Wilder, adm. **A**9 10 **F**14 16 23 35 40 45 47; **S**1755	13	10	S		50	1014	14	28.0	0	3	2125	973	75
FULTON—Fulton County													
★ PARKWAY REGIONAL HOSPITAL (Formerly Fulton Hospital), 2000 Holiday Lane, Zip 42041; tel. 502/472-2522; Michael J. McLaren, adm. **A**9 10 **F**1 3 14 15 23 26 35 36 41 45; **S**0335	33	10	S		70	1906	25	45.5	6	8	—	—	90
GEORGETOWN—Scott County													
★ SCOTT GENERAL HOSPITAL, 1140 Lexington Rd., Zip 40324; tel. 502/863-2141; Larry Kloess, adm. **A**9 10 **F**1 3 6 12 14 15 16 23 26 34 35 36 40 44 45 46 47; **S**1755	33	10	S		75	1422	18	24.0	13	168	—	—	91
GLASGOW—Barren County													
★□ T. J. SAMSON COMMUNITY HOSPITAL, N. Race St., Box 257, Zip 42141; tel. 502/651-6171; H. Glenn Joiner, adm. **A**1a 9 10 **F**1 3 6 10 12 14 15 16 23 27 28 30 33 34 35 37 40 41 45 47 51 52 53	23	10	S		174	8772	134	68.4	20	936	17121	8239	540
GREENSBURG—Green County													
★ JANE TODD CRAWFORD MEMORIAL HOSPITAL, 202 Milby St., P O Box 220, Zip 42743; tel. 502/932-4211; William E. Dowe, adm. (Total facility includes 26 beds in nursing home-type unit) **A**9 10 **F**1 3 6 12 14 15 16 19 23 32 33 34 35 42 44 45 46 48 49 53	13	10	S	TF	70	1125	36	51.4	8	19	3123	1644	113
				H	44	1031	15	—	8	19	2325	1160	81
GREENVILLE—Muhlenberg County													
★□ MUHLENBERG COMMUNITY HOSPITAL, 440 Hopkinsville St., P O Box 387, Zip 42345; tel. 502/338-4211; Charles J. Perry, adm. (Total facility includes 30 beds in nursing home-type unit) **A**1a 9 10 **F**1 3 6 10 12 14 16 19 23 35 36 40 41 45 46 47 52; **S**1755	23	10	S	TF	135	3802	70	51.9	10	428	11489	4325	287
				H	105	3640	48	—	10	428	11097	4025	268
HARDINSBURG—Breckinridge County													
★ BRECKINRIDGE MEMORIAL HOSPITAL, U. S. Hwy. 60, Rte. 1, Box 133a, Zip 40143; tel. 502/756-2124; George E. Walz, adm. **A**9 10 **F**1 5 6 10 14 15 16 23 26 35 41 44 45 46 47	23	10	S		45	2040	24	53.3	10	79	3903	1668	91
HARLAN—Harlan County													
★□ HARLAN APPALACHIAN REGIONAL HOSPITAL, Martins Fork Rd., Zip 40831; tel. 606/573-1400; Ray G. Roberts, adm. **A**1a 9 10 **F**1 3 5 6 10 12 14 15 16 23 28 29 30 32 34 35 36 37 40 41 44 45 47 52; **S**0145	23	10	S		110	5491	67	60.9	20	618	12474	5463	238
HARRODSBURG—Mercer County													
★ JAMES B. HAGGIN MEMORIAL HOSPITAL, 464 Linden Ave., Zip 40330; tel. 606/734-5441; William O. Leach, adm.; John W. Landrum, bd. chm. **A**9 10 **F**1 3 6 10 14 15 16 23 32 34 35 36 37 40 43 46	23	10	S		80	1753	26	32.5	10	90	3553	2002	149
HARTFORD—Ohio County													
★□ OHIO COUNTY HOSPITAL, 1211 Main St., Zip 42347; tel. 502/298-7411; Blaine Pieper, adm. **A**1a 9 10 **F**1 3 6 15 16 23 32 34 36 45 46 47; **S**1755	23	10	S		68	2302	33	48.5	9	64	4825	2396	139
HAZARD—Perry County													
★□ ARH REGIONAL MEDICAL CENTER (Formerly Hazard Appalachian Regional Hospital), P O Box 7000, Zip 41701; tel. 606/439-1331; Russ D. Sword, adm. **A**1a 9 10 **F**1 3 6 10 12 14 15 16 20 23 26 27 30 34 35 37 38 39 40 41 44 45 46 51 52 53; **S**0145	23	10	S		156	5799	84	53.8	16	309	13890	6412	297
HENDERSON—Henderson County													
★□ COMMUNITY METHODIST HOSPITAL, 1305 N. Elm St., Box 48, Zip 42420; tel. 502/826-6251; Charles R. Chapman, exec. dir. **A**1a 9 10 **F**1 3 6 10 12 14 15 16 23 27 30 35 36 40 41 45 46 51 52 53	21	10	S		213	9870	137	64.3	8	892	22271	10960	581
HOPKINSVILLE—Christian County													
★□ JENNIE STUART MEDICAL CENTER, 320 W. 18th St., Zip 42240; tel. 502/886-5221; J. H. Walker, adm. **A**1a 9 10 **F**1 2 3 6 7 8 9 10 11 12 14 16 20 23 35 36 40 45 46 47 51 52 53	23	10	S		222	6710	110	49.5	20	370	19525	7308	506
□ WESTERN STATE HOSPITAL, Russellville Rd., Box 2200, Zip 42240; tel. 502/886-4431; Gary H. Latham, fac dir. (Nonreporting) **A**1b 9 10	12	22	L		425	—	—	—	—	—	—	—	—

★ American Hospital Association (AHA) membership
☐ Joint Commission on Accreditation of Hospitals (JCAH) accreditation
+ American Osteopathic Hospital Association (AOHA) membership
○ American Osteopathic Association (AOA) accreditation
Δ Commission on Accreditation of Rehabilitation Facilities (CARF) accreditation
Control codes 61, 63, 64, 71, 72 and 73 indicate hospitals listed by AOHA, but not registered by AHA.
For definition of numerical codes, see page A2

Hospital, Address, Telephone, Administrator, Approval and Facility Codes, Multihospital System Code	Classification Codes				Inpatient Data				Newborn Data		Expense (thousands of dollars)		
	Control	Service	Stay	Facilities	Beds	Admissions	Census	Occupancy (percent)	Bassinets	Births	Total	Payroll	Personnel
HORSE CAVE—Hart County													
★ CAVERNA MEMORIAL HOSPITAL, Hwy. 31w S., P O Box 120, Zip 42749; tel. 502/786-2191; Russell C. Hackley, adm. **A**9 10 **F**1 3 6 16 35 46	23	10	S		30	1304	15	50.0	7	45	1843	887	60
HYDEN—Leslie County													
⊞ MARY BRECKINRIDGE HOSPITAL (Formerly Mary Breckinridge Hospital-Frontier Nursing Service), Hospital Dr., Zip 41749; tel. 606/672-2901; Douglas Taylor, adm. **A**1a 9 10 **F**1 6 15 16 34 35 36 37 40 41 43 45 46 47 52	23	10	S		40	2012	20	50.0	10	498	7199	3398	140
IRVINE—Estill County													
★ MARCUM AND WALLACE MEMORIAL HOSPITAL, 201 Richmond Rd., Zip 40336; tel. 606/723-2115; Daniel F. Sheehan, adm. (Nonreporting) **A**9 10; **S**5155	21	10	S		26	—	—	—	—	—	—	—	—
JENKINS—Letcher County													
☐ FIRST HEALTH JENKINS (Formerly Jenkins Community Hospital), Main St., Drawer 472, Zip 41537; tel. 606/832-2171; Glenn R. Sago, adm. (Nonreporting) **A**1a 9 10; **S**1275	33	10	S		60	—	—	—	—	—	—	—	—
LA GRANGE—Oldham County													
⊞ CHARTERTON HOSPITAL, 507 Yager Ave., P O Box 400, Zip 40031; tel. 502/222-7148; Ralph E. Suratt, adm. (Nonreporting) **A**1b 10; **S**0695	33	82	S		66	—	—	—	—	—	—	—	—
LANCASTER—Garrard County													
⊞ GARRARD COUNTY MEMORIAL HOSPITAL, 308 W. Maple Ave., Zip 40444; tel. 606/792-2112; W. David MacCool, chief exec. off. (Total facility includes 98 beds in nursing home-type unit) **A**1a 9 10 **F**1 6 15 16 19 22 23 26 34 35 37 48	13	10	S	TF	129	1251	94	72.9	9	12	3279	1948	124
				H	31	1019	14	—	9	12	2147	1246	120
LEBANON—Marion County													
⊞ HCA SPRING VIEW HOSPITAL (Formerly Spring View Hospital), St. Mary Rd., Zip 40033; tel. 502/692-3161; Robert E. Garrison, adm. (Total facility includes 38 beds in nursing home-type unit) **A**1a 9 10 **F**1 3 5 6 10 12 14 15 16 19 21 23 26 34 35 36 37 40 45 46 47 50; **S**1755	33	10	S	TF	113	2477	61	54.0	14	334	5029	2294	180
				H	75	2436	26	—	14	334	4756	2076	162
LEITCHFIELD—Grayson County													
★ GRAYSON COUNTY HOSPITAL, 910 Wallace Ave., Zip 42754; tel. 502/259-3134; Stephen L. Meredith, adm. **A**9 10 **F**1 3 6 14 16 23 34 35 36 40 41 45 46 47	23	10	S		75	3241	47	62.7	10	199	6172	2657	180
LEXINGTON—Fayette County													
★ Δ CARDINAL HILL HOSPITAL, 2050 Versailles Rd., Zip 40504; tel. 606/254-5701; Lyman Ginger EdD, exec. dir. **A**3 5 7 9 10 **F**15 23 24 25 26 33 34 42 44 45 46 47	23	49	S		67	813	54	71.1	0	0	7912	5201	304
⊞ CENTRAL BAPTIST HOSPITAL, 1740 S. Limestone St., Zip 40503; tel. 606/278-3411; Dan H. Akin, pres. **A**1a 2 3 5 9 10 **F**1 2 3 4 6 7 8 10 11 12 14 15 16 20 23 24 26 34 35 36 37 40 41 45 46 47 51 53 54; **S**0315	23	10	S		338	14209	226	66.9	34	2731	41521	16775	768
⊞ CHARTER RIDGE HOSPITAL, 3050 Rio Dosa Dr., Zip 40509; tel. 606/269-2325; Stuart Dinney, adm. (Nonreporting) **A**1a 9 10; **S**0695	33	22	S		80	—	—	—	—	—	—	—	—
☐ EASTERN STATE HOSPITAL, 627 W. Fourth St., Zip 40508; tel. 606/255-1431; Donald Ralph, dir. (Nonreporting) **A**1b 9 10	12	22	L		276	—	—	—	—	—	—	—	—
⊞ GOOD SAMARITAN HOSPITAL, 310 S. Limestone St., Zip 40508; tel. 606/252-6612; J. J. Purvis, pres. & chief exec. off. **A**1a 2 9 10 **F**1 2 3 6 9 10 12 15 16 20 23 24 27 30 32 33 34 35 36 37 40 42 44 45 46 47 53 54	23	10	S		315	10562	188	59.7	19	644	33585	14604	726
★ HUMANA HOSPITAL -LEXINGTON, 150 N. Eagle Creek Dr., P O Box 23260, Zip 40523; tel. 606/268-4800; David L. Miller, exec. dir. **A**10 **F**1 3 6 10 11 12 14 15 16 23 35 36 40 46 52 53 54; **S**1235	33	10	S		162	5981	81	50.0	20	653	18899	6364	360
⊞ SHRINERS HOSPITALS FOR CRIPPLED CHILDREN, 1900 Richmond Rd., Zip 40502; tel. 606/266-2101; Bobbie P. Spradlin RN, adm. **A**1a 3 5 **F**15 23 24 26 34 42 46; **S**4125	23	57	S		36	906	29	59.2	0	0	—	—	123
⊞ ST. JOSEPH HOSPITAL, One St. Joseph Dr., Zip 40504; tel. 606/278-3436; Sr. Michael Leo Mullaney, pres. **A**1a 3 5 9 10 **F**1 2 3 4 5 6 9 10 12 14 15 16 20 23 24 27 28 30 32 33 35 44 45 46 47 48 49 50 52 53 54; **S**3045	21	10	S		468	15729	328	70.1	0	0	58834	26574	1272
⊞ UNIVERSITY HOSPITAL, 800 Rose St., Zip 40536; tel. 606/233-5000; Frank Butler, dir. **A**1a 2 3 5 8 9 10 **F**1 2 3 4 5 6 7 8 9 10 11 12 13 14 15 16 17 20 22 23 24 27 28 30 32 33 34 35 37 38 40 41 42 44 45 46 47 49 50 51 52 53 54	12	10	S		433	15451	313	69.7	21	1731	74512	35681	1864
⊞ VETERANS ADMINISTRATION MEDICAL CENTER, Leestown Pike, Zip 40511; tel. 606/233-4511; John R. Rowan, dir. (Nonreporting) **A**1a b 3 5 8	45	10	S		1004	—	—	—	—	—	—	—	—
LIBERTY—Casey County													
CASEY COUNTY WAR MEMORIAL HOSPITAL, Wolford St., Rte. 2, Box 569a, Zip 42539; tel. 606/787-6275; Roger Williams, adm. **A**9 10 **F**1 15 16 23 30 35 45	16	10	S		22	761	9	40.9	0	0	1488	626	51
LONDON—Laurel County													
☐ MARYMOUNT HOSPITAL, E. Ninth St., Zip 40741; tel. 606/878-6520; Lowell Jones, adm. (Nonreporting) **A**1a 9 10; **S**1375	33	10	S		55	—	—	—	—	—	—	—	—
LOUISA—Lawrence County													
⊞ HUMANA HOSPITAL -LOUISA, Hwy. 644, Box 769, Zip 41230; tel. 606/638-9451; James Ellison, exec. dir. **A**1a 9 10 **F**1 3 6 12 14 15 16 23 34 35 40 43; **S**1235	33	10	S		90	2673	39	43.3	6	204	6451	2853	164
LOUISVILLE—Jefferson County													
AMELIA BROWN FRAZIER REHAB CENTER, See Frazier Rehab Center													
BAPTIST HOSPITAL EAST, See Louisville Baptist Hospitals													
BAPTIST HOSPITAL HIGHLANDS, See Louisville Baptist Hospitals													
☐ CENTRAL STATE HOSPITAL, Lagrange Rd., Zip 40223; tel. 502/245-4121; Johnny L. Clayton, dir. **A**1b **F**15 23 24 33 42 46 50	12	22	L		158	1855	153	96.8	0	0	9745	3949	412
★ Δ FRAZIER REHAB CENTER (Formerly Amelia Brown Frazier Rehab Center), 220 Abraham Flexner Way, Zip 40202; tel. 502/582-7400; William A. Brown, pres.; David Watkins MD, actg. med. dir. **A**3 5 7 9 10 **F**15 23 24 26 33 34 42 44 46	23	46	S		64	867	59	92.2	0	0	6790	3400	174
⊞ HUMANA HOSPITAL -AUDUBON, One Audubon Plaza Dr., Box 17555, Zip 40217; tel. 502/636-7111; Bruce W. MacLeod, exec. dir. **A**1a 9 10 **F**1 2 3 4 5 6 7 8 9 10 11 12 13 14 15 16 17 20 23 24 26 34 35 36 37 40 44 46 47 51 52 53 54; **S**1235	33	10	S		484	21335	325	67.1	42	2048	64446	26626	1220
⊞ HUMANA HOSPITAL -SOUTHWEST, 9820 Third St. Rd., Zip 40272; tel. 502/933-2110; Max K. Harder, exec. dir. (Nonreporting) **A**1a 9 10; **S**1235	33	10	S		150	—	—	—	—	—	—	—	—
⊞ HUMANA HOSPITAL -SUBURBAN, 4001 Dutchmans Lane, Zip 40207; tel. 502/893-1000; Jeff Holland, chief exec. off. **A**1a 9 10 **F**1 2 3 6 10 11 12 14 16 23 34 35 37 39 45 46 47 53; **S**1235	33	10	S		380	13074	215	56.6	0	0	—	—	933
⊞ HUMANA HOSPITAL -UNIVERSITY, 530 S. Jackson St., Zip 40202; tel. 502/562-4000; David G. Laird, exec. dir.; Sam Holtzman, adm. **A**1a 2 3 5 8 9 10 **F**1 3 4 5 6 9 10 11 12 13 14 16 17 20 22 23 24 26 27 30 32 33 34 35 37 40 44 45 46 47 50 51 53 54; **S**1235	33	10	S		404	16022	305	75.5	45	2774	79786	28772	1337
⊞ JEWISH HOSPITAL, 217 E. Chestnut St., Zip 40202; tel. 502/587-4011; Henry C. Wagner, pres. & chief exec. off.; Douglas E. Shaw, senior vice-pres. & chief oper. off. **A**1a 3 5 9 10 **F**3 4 5 6 9 10 12 13 14 15 16 20 23 26 35 45 46 47 50 53 54	23	10	S		442	14797	305	67.2	0	0	79438	32683	1436
⊞ KMI MEDICAL CENTER, 8521 Old Lagrange Rd., Zip 40223; tel. 502/426-6380; Steve Miller, exec. dir. (Nonreporting) **A**1b 9 10; **S**9605	33	22	S		69	—	—	—	—	—	—	—	—

Hospital, Address, Telephone, Administrator, Approval and Facility Codes, Multihospital System Code	Classification Codes				Inpatient Data				Newborn Data		Expense (thousands of dollars)		
★ American Hospital Association (AHA) membership ☐ Joint Commission on Accreditation of Hospitals (JCAH) accreditation + American Osteopathic Hospital Association (AOHA) membership ○ American Osteopathic Association (AOA) accreditation Δ Commission on Accreditation of Rehabilitation Facilities (CARF) accreditation Control codes 61, 63, 64, 71, 72 and 73 indicate hospitals listed by AOHA, but not registered by AHA. For definition of numerical codes, see page A2	Control	Service	Stay	Facilities	Beds	Admissions	Census	Occupancy (percent)	Bassinets	Births	Total	Payroll	Personnel
☐ KOSAIR-CHILDREN HOSPITAL, 982 Eastern Pkwy., Zip 40217; Mailing Address Box 37370, Zip 40233; tel. 502/562-6000; E. M. Schottland, sr. vice-pres. (Nonreporting) **A**1a 2 3 5 9	23	57	S		59	—	—	—	—	—	—	—	—
⊞ Δ LOUISVILLE BAPTIST HOSPITALS (Includes Baptist Hospital East, 4000 Kresge Way, Zip 40207; tel. 502/897-8100; Baptist Hospital Highlands, 810 Barret Ave., Zip 40204; tel. 502/561-3100; Bernard Tamme, exec. vice-pres.), Tommy J. Smith, pres. **A**1a 2 7 9 10 **F**1 2 3 6 10 12 14 15 16 23 24 25 27 28 29 30 34 35 36 40 41 42 45 46 47 48 49 50 53; **S**0315	21	10	S		545	15148	316	58.0	38	2083	57828	26846	1390
⊞ METHODIST EVANGELICAL HOSPITAL, 315 E. Broadway, Box 843, Zip 40201; tel. 502/585-2241; E. Dean Grout, pres. & chief exec. off. **A**1a 9 10 **F**1 2 3 6 7 10 12 14 15 16 20 23 26 34 35 36 37 39 40 45 46 47 53	21	10	S		363	13786	230	63.4	50	1783	47098	22247	1116
⊞ NKC HOSPITALS (Includes Kosair/Children's Hospital, Zip 40202; Mailing Address Box 35070, Zip 40232; tel. 502/562-6000; E. M. Schottland, sr. vice-pres.; Norton Hospital, P O Box 35070, Zip 40232; tel. 502/562-8000; F. V. Murphy, sr. vice-pres.), 200 E. Chestnut St., Zip 40202; Mailing Address Box 35070, Zip 40232; tel. 502/562-8000; James R. Petersdorf, pres. **A**1a 2 3 5 9 10 **F**1 2 3 4 5 6 9 10 11 12 13 14 15 16 20 22 23 27 28 29 30 32 33 34 35 36 37 38 40 42 45 46 47 49 51 52 53 54	23	10	S		518	20029	403	77.8	30	2520	89863	39763	2077
NORTON HOSPITAL, See NKC Hospitals													
☐ OUR LADY OF PEACE HOSPITAL, 2020 Newburg Rd., Zip 40205; tel. 502/451-3330; Thomas M. Keefe, pres. (Nonreporting) **A**1b 9 10	21	22	S		370	—	—	—	—	—	—	—	—
⊞ SAINTS MARY AND ELIZABETH HOSPITAL, 4400 Churchman Ave., Zip 40215; tel. 502/361-6011; A. Jack Reynolds, interim pres. **A**1a 9 10 **F**1 2 3 6 10 12 14 15 16 20 23 35 41 44 45 46 53; **S**3045	21	10	S		331	8949	183	55.3	0	0	38684	17896	760
⊞ ST. ANTHONY MEDICAL CENTER (Formerly St. Anthony Hospital), 1313 St. Anthony Pl., Zip 40204; tel. 502/587-1161; Michael Budnick, adm. **A**1a 3 5 9 10 **F**1 2 3 6 7 8 9 10 11 12 14 15 16 23 35 36 40 45 46 52 53; **S**5345	21	10	S		237	9546	227	91.2	40	1293	34954	18152	948
⊞ VETERANS ADMINISTRATION MEDICAL CENTER, 800 Zorn Ave., Zip 40202; tel. 502/895-3401; Russell B. Wimmer, dir. **A**1a 2 3 5 8 **F**1 2 3 6 12 14 15 16 23 24 26 27 28 33 34 35 42 43 44 46 47 48 49 50 53 54	45	10	S		316	8426	259	82.0	0	0	45671	26119	960
MADISONVILLE—Hopkins County													
⊞ REGIONAL MEDICAL CENTER, Hospital Dr., Zip 42431; tel. 502/825-5100; Richard A. Byrnes, pres. **A**1a 2 3 5 9 10 **F**1 2 3 4 5 6 7 8 9 10 11 12 14 15 16 20 21 23 24 26 27 30 35 36 37 40 41 46 47 48 49 51 52 53 54	23	10	S		410	11761	202	49.3	24	977	38801	17151	927
MANCHESTER—Clay County													
★ MEMORIAL HOSPITAL, 401 Memorial Dr., Zip 40962; tel. 606/598-5104; D. Thomas Amos, pres. (Total facility includes 11 beds in nursing home-type unit) **A**9 10 **F**1 3 6 14 15 16 19 23 34 35 36 40 46 47; **S**4165	21	10	S	TF H	63 52	3546 3504	47 37	74.6 —	8 8	352 352	5656 5292	2450 2312	159 —
MARION—Crittenden County													
⊞ CRITTENDEN COUNTY HOSPITAL, Hwy. 60 S., Box 386, Zip 42064; tel. 502/965-5281; John J. Morris, adm. **A**1a 9 10 **F**1 2 6 14 15 16 35 40 41 45 47	23	10	S		37	1932	26	70.3	6	78	3328	1568	101
MARTIN—Floyd County													
⊞ OUR LADY OF THE WAY HOSPITAL, Rte. 1428, Box 910, Zip 41649; tel. 606/285-5181; Sr. Monica Justinger, adm. **A**1a 9 10 **F**1 14 15 16 35 36 40 46; **S**5115	21	10	S		39	2740	32	82.1	5	263	4685	2217	124
MAYFIELD—Graves County													
⊞ COMMUNITY HOSPITAL, 206 W. South St., Zip 42066; tel. 502/247-5211; John Sullivan, adm. **A**1a 9 10 **F**1 3 6 10 11 12 14 15 16 23 34 35 36 40 41 44 46 53; **S**1755	33	10	S		89	4112	64	71.9	10	256	9146	3713	236
MAYSVILLE—Mason County													
⊞ MEADOWVIEW REGIONAL HOSPITAL, 989 W. Hwy. 10, Zip 41056; tel. 606/759-5311; Gary J. Herbek, adm. **A**1a 9 10 **F**1 3 6 12 14 15 16 23 35 36 40 44 45 46 47 52; **S**1755	33	10	S		111	3589	55	49.5	11	408	—	—	225
MCDOWELL—Floyd County													
⊞ MCDOWELL APPALACHIAN REGIONAL HEALTH CARE (Formerly McDowell Appalachian Regional Hospital), Rte. 122, Box 247, Zip 41647; tel. 606/377-2411; Edward V. Collins, adm. **A**1a 9 10 **F**1 3 6 12 14 16 23 35 41 45 46 52 53; **S**0145	23	10	S		60	2554	36	60.0	0	0	5461	2405	122
MIDDLESBORO—Bell County													
⊞ MIDDLESBORO APPALACHIAN REGIONAL HOSPITAL, 3600 W. Cumberland Ave., Box 340, Zip 40965; tel. 606/248-3300; John I. Frederick, adm. **A**1a 9 10 **F**1 3 6 10 15 16 23 35 36 37 40 41 44 45 52; **S**0145	23	10	S		96	6120	69	71.9	14	419	9425	4276	237
MONTICELLO—Wayne County													
☐ WAYNE COUNTY HOSPITAL, Rte. 4, Box 56b, Zip 42633; tel. 606/348-9343; J. Edward Cooper, adm. **A**1a 9 10 **F**1 6 12 16 23 34 35 36 47	23	10	S		30	1063	13	43.3	0	0	2202	916	72
MOREHEAD—Rowan County													
⊞ ST. CLAIRE MEDICAL CENTER, 222 Medical Circle, Zip 40351; tel. 606/784-6661; Sr. Mary Jeanette, adm. **A**1a 9 10 **F**1 3 6 10 12 14 15 16 21 23 26 27 28 29 30 31 32 33 34 35 36 40 41 42 44 45 46 52 53	21	10	S		133	5992	90	67.7	10	634	14722	7065	394
MORGANFIELD—Union County													
⊞ VALLEY VIEW MEDICAL CENTER, Rte. 4, Box 62h, Zip 42437; tel. 502/389-3030; Patrick Donahue, adm. **A**1a 9 10 **F**1 3 6 10 14 16 35 40 45 47 53	33	10	S		54	1374	14	25.9	7	31	2701	1241	75
MOUNT STERLING—Montgomery County													
⊞ MARY CHILES HOSPITAL, Sterling Ave., P O Box 7, Zip 40353; tel. 606/498-1220; R. Alan Newberry, adm. (Total facility includes 40 beds in nursing home-type unit) **A**1a 9 10 **F**1 3 6 10 12 14 15 16 19 23 24 26 34 35 37 40 42 44 45 46 50	23	10	S	TF H	103 63	2784 2583	67 34	65.0 —	13 13	243 243	7177 —	3052 2740	187 162
MOUNT VERNON—Rockcastle County													
ROCKCASTLE HOSPITAL (Formerly Rockcastle County Hospital), Newcomb Ave., Rte. 4, Box 28, Zip 40456; tel. 606/256-2195; Wayne Stewart, adm. (Nonreporting) **A**9 10	23	10	S		58	—	—	—	—	—	—	—	—
MURRAY—Calloway County													
⊞ MURRAY-CALLOWAY COUNTY HOSPITAL, 803 Poplar St., Zip 42071; tel. 502/753-5131; Stuart Poston, adm. (Total facility includes 40 beds in nursing home-type unit) **A**1a 9 10 **F**1 3 6 10 12 14 15 16 19 21 23 29 30 35 36 40 41 44 45 46 47 52 53	15	10	S	TF H	218 178	5632 5535	121 84	55.5 —	17 17	663 663	13980 13105	6633 6209	427 404
OWENSBORO—Daviess County													
⊞ MERCY HOSPITAL, 1006 Ford Ave., Zip 42301; Mailing Address P O Box 2839, Zip 42302; tel. 502/685-5181; Gerald J. Lagesse, pres. **A**1a 9 10 **F**1 3 6 12 15 16 23 30 35 45 46 52 53; **S**5155	23	10	S		125	5384	84	67.2	0	0	15578	6378	353
⊞ OWENSBORO-DAVIESS COUNTY HOSPITAL, Center & Pearl Sts., Zip 42301; Mailing Address Box 2799, Zip 42302; tel. 502/926-3030; J. D. Collins, adm. **A**1a 9 10 **F**1 2 3 6 7 8 9 10 11 12 14 15 16 19 20 23 27 35 40 41 44 45 46 47 52 53 54	15	10	S		465	15213	289	62.2	39	1956	39091	20351	1224

★ American Hospital Association (AHA) membership
☐ Joint Commission on Accreditation of Hospitals (JCAH) accreditation
+ American Osteopathic Hospital Association (AOHA) membership
○ American Osteopathic Association (AOA) accreditation
Δ Commission on Accreditation of Rehabilitation Facilities (CARF) accreditation
Control codes 61, 63, 64, 71, 72 and 73 indicate hospitals listed by AOHA, but not registered by AHA.
For definition of numerical codes, see page A2

Hospital, Address, Telephone, Administrator, Approval and Facility Codes, Multihospital System Code	Classification Codes				Inpatient Data				Newborn Data		Expense (thousands of dollars)		
	Control	Service	Stay	Facilities	Beds	Admissions	Census	Occupancy (percent)	Bassinets	Births	Total	Payroll	Personnel
★☐ VALLEY INSTITUTE OF PSYCHIATRY, 1000 Industrial Dr., P O Box 4010, Zip 42302; tel. 502/686-8477; Alvin R. Freedman PhD, adm. (Newly Registered) **A**1b 9	23	52	L		56	—	—	—	—	—	—	—	—
OWENTON—Owen County													
OWEN COUNTY MEMORIAL HOSPITAL, 330 Roland Ave., Zip 40359; tel. 502/484-3441; Alan S. Cross, adm. **A**9 10 **F**1 6 12 15 16 23 26 32 33 34 35 46 47 50	13	10	S		50	781	10	20.0	0	0	1414	617	46
PADUCAH—McCracken County													
★☐ LOURDES HOSPITAL, 1530 Lone Oak Rd., Zip 42001; Mailing Address P O Box 7100, Zip 42002; tel. 502/444-2102; John Sullivan, pres. & chief exec. off. **A**1a 9 10 **F**1 3 6 10 11 12 14 15 16 20 21 23 24 25 26 27 28 30 32 33 34 35 41 42 44 45 52 53	23	10	S		352	12230	277	78.7	0	0	41805	19055	1039
★☐ WESTERN BAPTIST HOSPITAL, 2501 Kentucky Ave., Zip 42001; tel. 502/575-2100; H. Earl Feezor, pres. **A**1a 9 10 **F**1 2 3 4 5 6 7 8 9 10 11 12 14 15 16 23 26 33 34 35 36 40 45 47 52 53 54; **S**0315	21	10	S		344	13449	261	75.9	36	1628	41573	18626	970
PAINTSVILLE—Johnson County													
☐ PAUL B. HALL REGIONAL MEDICAL CENTER, 104 James S. Trimble Blvd., P O Box 1487, Zip 41240; tel. 606/789-3511; Samuel P. Fowler, adm. **A**1a 9 10 **F**1 3 6 14 16 23 34 35 40 46; **S**1775	33	10	S		72	3097	39	54.2	10	276	8442	1932	128
PARIS—Bourbon County													
★☐ HCA BOURBON GENERAL HOSPITAL (Formerly Bourbon General Hospital), 9 Linville Dr., Zip 40361; tel. 606/987-3600; Gerald Fornoff, adm. **A**1a 9 10 **F**1 3 6 12 14 15 16 21 23 34 35 44 46 47 53; **S**1755	33	10	S		60	1460	20	33.3	0	0	4563	1571	104
PIKEVILLE—Pike County													
★☐ METHODIST HOSPITAL OF KENTUCKY, 911 S. Bypass, Zip 41501; tel. 606/437-9621; Lee D. Keene, adm. **A**1a 9 10 **F**1 3 6 7 8 9 10 11 12 14 16 23 35 36 40 45 46 52 53	21	10	S		183	11097	146	79.8	29	1184	18854	8902	526
PINEVILLE—Bell County													
★☐ PINEVILLE COMMUNITY HOSPITAL, Riverview Ave., Zip 40977; tel. 606/337-3051; James K. Wilson, adm. **A**1a 9 10 **F**1 3 6 10 12 14 16 23 26 30 35 40 41 45 46 52	23	10	S		155	5750	98	63.2	10	344	10725	4981	317
PRESTONSBURG—Floyd County													
★☐ HIGHLANDS REGIONAL MEDICAL CENTER, U. S. 23 N., Box 668, Zip 41653; tel. 606/886-8511; Clarence Traum, adm. **A**1a 9 10 **F**1 3 5 6 12 14 16 23 30 32 34 35 36 40 45 46 53	23	10	S		184	7585	102	55.4	10	638	16946	6739	420
PRINCETON—Caldwell County													
★☐ CALDWELL COUNTY HOSPITAL, 101 Hospital Dr., Box 410, Zip 42445; tel. 502/365-0300; Jeffrey L. Buckley, chief exec. off. **A**1a 9 10 **F**1 3 6 10 12 14 15 16 21 23 35 37 40 41 45 46 47	13	10	S		58	1957	27	46.6	7	236	4817	2453	152
RICHMOND—Madison County													
★☐ PATTIE A. CLAY HOSPITAL, Eastern By-Pass, Zip 40475; tel. 606/623-3131; Richard M. Thomas, adm. **A**1a 9 10 **F**1 3 6 10 14 15 16 23 34 35 36 37 40 41 45 46 47 50 53	23	10	S		105	5400	71	67.6	22	810	11873	5709	320
RUSSELL SPRINGS—Russell County													
RUSSELL COUNTY HOSPITAL, Dowell Rd., P O Box 147, Zip 42642; tel. 502/866-4141; O. G. Bottom, adm. **A**9 10 **F**1 3 6 12 14 15 16 23 34 35 45 46 47	16	10	S		45	1250	19	42.2	4	11	3282	1132	92
RUSSELLVILLE—Logan County													
★☐ HCA LOGAN MEMORIAL HOSPITAL (Formerly Logan County Hospital), 1625 S. Nashville Rd., P O Box 10, Zip 42276; tel. 502/726-4011; Michael L. Graue, adm. **A**1a 9 10 **F**1 3 6 14 23 34 35 36 40 45 46; **S**1755	33	10	S		100	2363	38	38.0	9	191	7022	2770	145
SALEM—Livingston County													
★ LIVINGSTON COUNTY HOSPITAL, Hwy. 60 E., Box 138, Zip 42078; tel. 502/988-2299; Benedict Hesen, exec. dir. **A**9 10 **F**1 6 15 16 35 41 45	23	10	S		26	1328	15	57.7	0	0	2219	1151	77
SCOTTSVILLE—Allen County													
★☐ ALLEN COUNTY WAR MEMORIAL HOSPITAL, Box 485, Zip 42164; tel. 502/237-3131; Scott M. Landrum, adm. **A**1a 9 10 **F**1 3 6 14 16 23 35 40 45 47 52	13	10	S		53	1136	17	32.1	8	50	2009	970	70
SHELBYVILLE—Shelby County													
KING'S DAUGHTERS HOSPITAL, See United Medical Center Shelbyville													
★☐ UNITED MEDICAL CENTER SHELBYVILLE (Formerly King's Daughters Hospital), 727 Hospital Dr., P O Box 849, Zip 40065; tel. 502/633-2345; Steve Corso, adm. **A**1a 9 10 **F**1 3 6 14 15 23 26 34 35 36 40 47; **S**9605	33	10	S		76	3011	45	59.2	10	280	7570	2978	186
SOMERSET—Pulaski County													
★☐ HUMANA HOSPITAL -LAKE CUMBERLAND, 305 Langdon St., Box 620, Zip 42501; tel. 606/679-7441; Derek W. Cimala, exec. dir. (Nonreporting) **A**1a 9 10; **S**1235	33	10	S		183	—	—	—	—	—	—	—	—
SOUTH WILLIAMSON—Pike County													
★☐ WILLIAMSON APPALACHIAN REGIONAL HOSPITAL, 2000 Central Ave., Zip 41503; tel. 606/237-1010; W. D. Crosley, adm. **A**1a 9 10 **F**1 6 11 12 14 15 16 23 35 36 40 41 43 45 46 52 53; **S**0145	23	10	S		143	5934	84	46.4	10	381	13268	5791	263
STANFORD—Lincoln County													
★☐ FORT LOGAN HOSPITAL, 124 Portman Ave., Box 447, Zip 40484; tel. 606/365-2187; Terry C. Powers, adm. (Total facility includes 30 beds in nursing home-type unit) **A**1a 9 10 **F**1 6 14 15 16 19 23 26 35 36 42 44 45 46	23	10	S	TF	73	1567	50	68.5	2	65	3751	1571	132
				H	43	1466	23	—	2	65	2878	1197	90
TOMPKINSVILLE—Monroe County													
★ MONROE COUNTY MEDICAL CENTER, Cap Harlan Rd., Zip 42167; tel. 502/487-9231; Lance C. Labine, adm. **A**9 10 **F**1 6 14 15 16 23 26 34 35 41 45; **S**1755	23	10	S		49	2301	29	59.2	8	1	3288	1276	103
VERSAILLES—Woodford County													
★☐ WOODFORD MEMORIAL HOSPITAL, 360 Amsden Ave., Zip 40383; tel. 606/873-3111; Edward J. Quinn Jr., adm. **A**1a 9 10 **F**1 3 6 10 12 14 16 23 35 36 40 45 50	23	10	S		60	1417	21	35.0	8	163	4949	2179	115
WEST LIBERTY—Morgan County													
★☐ MORGAN COUNTY APPALACHIAN REGIONAL HOSPITAL, Wells Hill Rd., Box 579, Zip 41472; tel. 606/743-3186; Raymond Rowlett, adm. (Total facility includes 15 beds in nursing home-type unit) **A**1a 9 10 **F**1 6 14 16 19 34 35 40 41 45 46 52; **S**0145	23	10	S	TF	45	1887	33	73.3	6	37	4248	1906	93
				H	30	1837	22	—	6	37	—	—	92
WHITESBURG—Letcher County													
★☐ WHITESBURG APPALACHIAN REGIONAL HOSPITAL, 550 Jenkins Rd., Zip 41858; tel. 606/633-2211; Paul V. Miles, adm. **A**1a 9 10 **F**1 3 6 10 12 14 15 16 23 26 34 35 36 37 40 41 44 45 52; **S**0145	23	10	S		71	4444	49	69.0	9	462	7992	3619	170
WILLIAMSTOWN—Grant County													
★☐ GRANT COUNTY HOSPITAL, 238 Barnes Rd., Zip 41097; tel. 606/823-5051; Rodney Battles, adm. (Nonreporting) **A**1a 9 10	13	10	S		30	—	—	—	—	—	—	—	—
WINCHESTER—Clark County													
★☐ CLARK COUNTY HOSPITAL, W. Lexington Ave., P O Box B, Zip 40391; tel. 606/744-3261; Thomas O. Logue Jr. EdD, adm. **A**1a 9 10 **F**3 6 10 12 14 15 16 21 23 33 35 40 45 46 53	23	10	S		100	3306	50	50.0	12	259	8663	3633	217

★ American Hospital Association (AHA) membership
□ Joint Commission on Accreditation of Hospitals (JCAH) accreditation
+ American Osteopathic Hospital Association (AOHA) membership
○ American Osteopathic Association (AOA) accreditation
Δ Commission on Accreditation of Rehabilitation Facilities (CARF) accreditation
Control codes 61, 63, 64, 71, 72 and 73 indicate hospitals listed by AOHA, but not registered by AHA.
For definition of numerical codes, see page A2

Louisiana

Hospital, Address, Telephone, Administrator, Approval and Facility Codes, Multihospital System Code	Classification Codes				Inpatient Data				Newborn Data		Expense (thousands of dollars)		
	Control	Service	Stay	Facilities	Beds	Admissions	Census	Occupancy (percent)	Bassinets	Births	Total	Payroll	Personnel
ABBEVILLE—Vermilion Parish													
★□ ABBEVILLE GENERAL HOSPITAL, 118 N. Hospital Dr., Drawer 580, Zip 70510; tel. 318/893-5466; John H. Matthews, adm. **A**1a 9 10 **F**1 3 6 10 14 15 16 23 35 36 40 41 53	16	10	S		97	3592	51	52.6	12	260	11872	4467	250
ALEXANDRIA—Rapides Parish													
★□ RAPIDES GENERAL HOSPITAL, 211 Fourth St., Box 30101, Zip 71301; tel. 318/473-3150; Julius R. McLaurin, pres. **A**1a 2 9 10 **F**1 3 4 5 6 7 8 9 10 11 12 14 15 16 21 23 35 37 40 41 43 44 45 46 47 48 49 52 53 54	23	10	S		309	13087	191	61.8	29	1333	43293	17860	1043
★□ ST. FRANCES CABRINI HOSPITAL, 3330 Masonic Dr., Zip 71301; tel. 318/487-1122; Jon C. Hilsabeck, adm. **A**1a 2 9 10 **F**1 3 4 5 6 7 8 10 11 12 13 15 16 23 26 34 35 36 40 45 46 47 51 52 54; **S**0605	23	10	S		232	9017	149	64.2	24	826	39360	13479	677
★□ VETERANS ADMINISTRATION MEDICAL CENTER, Zip 71301; tel. 318/473-0010; Charles C. Freeman, dir. (Total facility includes 93 beds in nursing home-type unit) **A**1a 3 5 **F**1 3 6 10 12 14 15 16 19 23 24 26 27 28 30 32 33 34 42 44 46 47 49 50 53	45	10	S	TF H	414 321	6437 6414	355 270	85.7 —	0 0	0 0	28944 27311	18673 17428	724 691
AMITE—Tangipahoa Parish													
★ HOOD MEMORIAL HOSPITAL, 301 W. Walnut St., Zip 70422; tel. 504/748-9485; A. D. Richardson, adm. (Total facility includes 10 beds in nursing home-type unit) **A**9 10 **F**1 6 10 12 14 16 19 35 41	16	10	S	TF H	45 35	1255 1169	19 17	42.2 —	0 0	0 0	2792 2677	1364 1261	92 85
ARCADIA—Bienville Parish													
★ BIENVILLE GENERAL HOSPITAL, 810 Pine St., Drawer 599, Zip 71001; tel. 318/263-2044; Hoye A. Bowman, adm. **A**9 10 **F**1 6 16 35	16	10	S		30	973	12	40.0	0	0	2484	1229	62
ARNAUDVILLE—St. Landry Parish													
★□ ST. LUKE GENERAL HOSPITAL, Guidroz St., P O Box 110, Zip 70512; tel. 318/754-5112; Tom McElree, adm. (Nonreporting) **A**1a 9 10	16	10	S		33	—	—	—	—	—	—	—	—
BARKSDALE AIR FORCE BASE—Caddo Parish													
□ U. S. AIR FORCE HOSPITAL, Zip 71110; tel. 318/456-2365; Lt. Col. P. E. Jacobson Jr., adm. (Nonreporting) **A**1a	41	10	S		60	—	—	—	—	—	—	—	—
BASTROP—Morehouse Parish													
★□ MOREHOUSE GENERAL HOSPITAL, 323 W. Walnut St., Box 1060, Zip 71221; tel. 318/281-2431; William W. Bing, adm. (Nonreporting) **A**1a 9 10	16	10	S		107	—	—	—	—	—	—	—	—
BATON ROUGE—East Baton Rouge Parish													
★□ BATON ROUGE GENERAL MEDICAL CENTER, 3600 Florida St., P O Box 2511, Zip 70821; tel. 504/387-7767; Edgar H. Silvey, chief exec. off. (Nonreporting) **A**1a 6 9 10; **S**0775	23	10	S		420	—	—	—	—	—	—	—	—
□ CPC MEADOW WOOD HOSPITAL, 9032 Perkins Rd., Zip 70810; tel. 504/766-8553; Theodore S. Johnson, adm. (Nonreporting) **A**1b 9 10	33	22	S		85	—	—	—	—	—	—	—	—
□ EARL K. LONG MEMORIAL HOSPITAL, 5825 Airline Hwy., P O Box 52999, Zip 70805; tel. 504/356-3361; William C. Bankston, dir. **A**1a 3 5 9 10 **F**1 3 5 6 9 10 12 14 15 16 20 23 24 26 34 35 37 40 45 46 47 51 52; **S**0715	12	10	S		174	10809	167	96.0	43	3342	27714	15676	753
★ MEDICAL CENTER OF BATON ROUGE, 17000 Medical Center Dr., Zip 70816; tel. 504/922-4800; Jerry G. Moeller, adm. (Nonreporting) **A**9 10; **S**1755	33	10	S		78	—	—	—	—	—	—	—	—
★□ OUR LADY OF THE LAKE REGIONAL MEDICAL CENTER, 500 Hennessy Blvd., Zip 70809; tel. 504/765-6565; Robert C. Davidge, exec. dir. **A**1a 6 9 10 **F**1 2 3 4 5 6 10 12 14 15 16 19 23 24 25 26 30 34 35 39 41 42 43 44 45 46 47 49 52 53 54; **S**1475	21	10	S		683	23957	424	62.1	0	0	87763	38175	1854
★ PARKLAND HOSPITAL, 2414 Bunker Hill Dr., Zip 70808; tel. 504/927-9050; Ralph J. Waite III, adm. **A**9 10 **F**15 16 24 29 30 32 33 42 43 45 46 47 48 49 50; **S**1755													
★□ WOMAN'S HOSPITAL, Goodwood at Airline, Box 95009, Zip 70895; tel. 504/927-1300; Thomas R. Hightower, adm. **A**1a 9 10 **F**1 6 9 10 12 14 16 23 34 36 38 40 41 43 45 46 51	23	44	S		205	13181	190	92.7	80	7149	28935	14866	668
BAYOU VISTA—St. Mary Parish													
★ FAIRVIEW HOSPITAL, 915 Southeast Blvd., Zip 70380; tel. 504/395-6701; L. G. Turner, adm. (Nonreporting) **A**9 10	16	10	S		49	—	—	—	—	—	—	—	—
BERNICE—Union Parish													
TRI-WARD GENERAL HOSPITAL, First St., P O Box 697, Zip 71222; tel. 318/285-9066; William A. Colvin III, adm. **A**9 10 **F**35	16	10	S		25	565	9	36.0	0	0	946	502	39
BOGALUSA—Washington Parish													
★□ BOGALUSA COMMUNITY MEDICAL CENTER, 433 Plaza St., Box 940, Zip 70427; tel. 504/732-7122; Benjamin R. Light, adm. (Total facility includes 28 beds in nursing home-type unit) **A**1a 9 10 **F**1 3 6 10 16 19 23 34 35 40 41 45 46 47 48 52 53	23	10	S	TF H	126 98	3192 2921	68 54	54.0 —	12 12	205 205	7758 7285	— —	309 278
□ WASHINGTON-ST. TAMMANY CHARITY HOSPITAL, 400 Memphis St., Box 40, Zip 70427; tel. 504/735-1322; Bill Mohon, adm. **A**1a 3 5 9 10 **F**1 6 14 15 16 27 29 30 34 35 37 40 45 47 49 52; **S**0715	12	10	S		68	2999	37	54.4	10	672	5679	3028	175
BOSSIER CITY—Bossier Parish													
★□ BOSSIER MEDICAL CENTER, 2105 Airline Dr., Zip 71111; tel. 318/227-6113; David A. Bird, exec. dir. **A**1a 9 10 **F**1 3 6 9 10 12 14 15 16 19 20 23 30 33 34 35 40 41 43 44 45 46 47 53 54	14	10	S		175	6762	94	53.7	23	861	18946	8119	434
★□ RIVERSIDE COMMUNITY HOSPITAL, 4900 Medical Dr., Zip 71112; tel. 318/747-9500; Joseph D. Grau, exec. dir. **A**1a 9 10 **F**1 3 6 10 14 16 19 23 35 46 53	33	10	S		102	1759	28	27.5	0	0	9857	2530	123
BREAUX BRIDGE—St. Martin Parish													
★□ GARY MEMORIAL HOSPITAL, Box 357, Zip 70517; tel. 318/332-2178; James C. Morrogh, chief exec. off. **A**1a 9 10 **F**1 6 10 12 14 16 23 34 35 37 41 43 45 46 47	16	10	S		30	857	9	30.0	5	83	2096	1034	67
BUNKIE—Avoyelles Parish													
★□ BUNKIE GENERAL HOSPITAL, Evergreen Hwy., Box 380, Zip 71322; tel. 318/346-6681; Ray A. Lemoine, adm. **A**1a 9 10 **F**1 3 5 6 15 16 23 34 35 41 45 47 52	16	10	S		49	1504	19	38.8	6	90	3010	1370	78
CAMERON—Cameron Parish													
★ SOUTH CAMERON MEMORIAL HOSPITAL, Rte. 1, Box 277, Zip 70631; tel. 318/542-4111; Kenneth H. Hopper, adm. **A**9 10 **F**16 35	16	10	S		27	404	6	22.2	0	0	1466	615	46

Hospital, Address, Telephone, Administrator, Approval and Facility Codes, Multihospital System Code	Classification Codes				Inpatient Data				Newborn Data		Expense (thousands of dollars)		
★ American Hospital Association (AHA) membership □ Joint Commission on Accreditation of Hospitals (JCAH) accreditation + American Osteopathic Hospital Association (AOHA) membership ○ American Osteopathic Association (AOA) accreditation Δ Commission on Accreditation of Rehabilitation Facilities (CARF) accreditation Control codes 61, 63, 64, 71, 72 and 73 indicate hospitals listed by AOHA, but not registered by AHA. For definition of numerical codes, see page A2	Control	Service	Stay	Facilities	Beds	Admissions	Census	Occupancy (percent)	Bassinets	Births	Total	Payroll	Personnel
CARVILLE—Iberville Parish													
□ GILLIS W. LONG HANSEN'S DISEASE CENTER (Formerly National Hansen's Disease Center), River Rd., Zip 70721; tel. 504/642-7771; John R. Trautman MD, dir. **A**1a **F**1 12 15 16 19 23 24 26 33 34 35 42 46 47 49 50	44	48	L		316	168	219	69.1	0	0	15230	9854	316
CHALMETTE—St. Bernard Parish													
□ CHALMETTE GENERAL HOSPITAL, 801 Virtu St., Zip 70043; tel. 504/277-7711; William E. Price, mng. dir. **A**1a 9 10 **F**1 3 6 10 12 14 15 16 17 20 23 24 26 34 35 39 43 46 47 53; **S**9555	33	10	S		108	3257	68	63.0	0	0	—	—	253
□ DE LA RONDE HOSPITAL, 9001 Patricia St., Zip 70043; tel. 504/277-8011; William E. Price, mng. dir. (Nonreporting) **A**1a 9 10; **S**9555	33	10	S		118	—	—	—	—	—	—	—	—
CHURCH POINT—Acadia Parish													
□ ACADIA-ST. LANDRY HOSPITAL, 810 S. Broadway St., Zip 70525; tel. 318/684-5435; Alcus Trahan, adm. (Nonreporting) **A**1a 9 10	16	10	S		30	—	—	—	—	—	—	—	—
CLINTON—East Feliciana Parish													
REGENT HOSPITAL FELICIANA (Formerly Feliciana Medical Center), Liberty St., Box 927, Zip 70722; tel. 504/683-5109; Charles J. Mueller, chief exec. off. (Nonreporting) **A**10; **S**1065	33	10	S		36	—	—	—	—	—	—	—	—
COLUMBIA—Caldwell Parish													
CALDWELL MEMORIAL HOSPITAL, 410 Main St., Box 899, Zip 71418; tel. 318/649-6111; Faye Long, adm. (Nonreporting) **A**9 10	33	10	S		50	—	—	—	—	—	—	—	—
COUSHATTA—Red River Parish													
L. S. HUCKABAY MD MEMORIAL HOSPITAL, Box 369, Zip 71019; tel. 318/932-5784; Ronnie Cox, adm. (Nonreporting) **A**9 10	33	10	S		74	—	—	—	—	—	—	—	—
COVINGTON—St. Tammany Parish													
⊞ AMI HIGHLAND PARK HOSPITAL (Formerly Highland Park Hospital), One Park Pl., Drawer 1269, Zip 70433; tel. 504/892-5900; Gerald Peterman, exec. dir. (Nonreporting) **A**1a 9 10; **S**0125	33	10	S		104	—	—	—	—	—	—	—	—
⊞ DEPAUL NORTHSHORE HOSPITAL, Depaul Northshore Dr., P O Box 2439, Zip 70434; tel. 504/893-9200; Patrick J. Canal, adm. (Nonreporting) **A**1b 10; **S**1755	33	22	S		64	—	—	—	—	—	—	—	—
HIGHLAND PARK HOSPITAL, See AMI Highland Park Hospital													
⊞ HSA GREENBRIER HOSPITAL, Greenbrier Blvd., P O Box 1836, Zip 70434; tel. 504/893-2970; Dominic R. Catalano, adm. (Nonreporting) **A**1a b 10; **S**0405	33	22	S		56	—	—	—	—	—	—	—	—
⊞ ST. TAMMANY PARISH HOSPITAL, 1202 S. Tyler St., Zip 70433; tel. 504/892-3380; Chip Faircloth, adm. **A**1a 9 10 **F**1 3 6 10 12 14 16 23 35 36 40 41 44 45 46 52 53	16	10	S		128	5131	80	62.5	18	396	14240	6721	377
CROWLEY—Acadia Parish													
⊞ AMERICAN LEGION HOSPITAL, 1305 E. Hwy. 90, Zip 70526; tel. 318/783-3222; Leonard J. Spears, adm. **A**1a 9 10 **F**1 3 10 12 16 17 23 34 35 40 45	23	10	S		70	3041	35	46.1	10	435	6099	2922	139
DE QUINCY—Calcasieu Parish													
DEQUINCY MEMORIAL HOSPITAL, 110 W. Fourth St., Box 1166, Zip 70633; tel. 318/786-1200; Luther J. Lewis, adm. **A**10 **F**1 15 16 23 34 35 45 46; **S**1585	14	10	S		49	1220	16	32.0	3	8	2655	1063	57
DE RIDDER—Beauregard Parish													
⊞ BEAUREGARD MEMORIAL HOSPITAL, 600 S. Pine St., P O Box 730, Zip 70634; tel. 318/462-0376; Ted Badger, adm. **A**1a 9 10 **F**1 3 6 10 14 15 16 23 35 40 41 45 47 52 53	16	10	S		102	4408	61	59.8	8	354	9614	4475	278
DELHI—Richland Parish													
□ RICHLAND PARISH HOSPITAL-DELHI, 507 Cincinnati, Zip 71232; tel. 318/878-5171; Michael E. Cooper, adm. (Nonreporting) **A**1a 9 10	16	10	S		42	—	—	—	—	—	—	—	—
DENHAM SPRINGS—Livingston Parish													
□ DIXON MEMORIAL HOSPITAL, 10123 Florida Blvd., Zip 70726; tel. 504/665-8211; Lonnie C. Graeber, adm. (Total facility includes 8 beds in nursing home-type unit) **A**1a 9 10 **F**1 3 6 10 15 16 19 23 35 45 47; **S**0775	23	10	S	TF	52	1519	22	42.3	0	0	5409	2358	97
				H	44	1457	20	—	0	0	5334	2283	91
DONALDSONVILLE—Ascension Parish													
⊞ PREVOST MEMORIAL HOSPITAL, Memorial Dr., Box 186, Zip 70346; tel. 504/473-7931; Harold J. Ramirez, adm. **A**1a 9 10 **F**1 6 14 16 19 23 35 45	16	10	S		35	737	9	25.7	0	0	2375	987	61
ENGLAND AIR FORCE BASE—Rapides Parish													
★ U. S. AIR FORCE HOSPITAL, Zip 71311; tel. 318/448-5342; Maj. Richard J. Febuary, adm. **F**1 14 15 16 23 33 34 35 37 45 46 47	41	10	S		25	1396	14	56.0	0	0	—	—	230
ERATH—Vermilion Parish													
□ REGENT HOSPITAL -ACADIANA (Formerly Regent Hospital), 504 N. Broadway St., Zip 70533; tel. 318/937-5851; James L. Wentz, vice-pres. (Nonreporting) **A**1a 9 10; **S**1065	33	10	S		63	—	—	—	—	—	—	—	—
EUNICE—St. Landry Parish													
⊞ MOOSA MEMORIAL HOSPITAL, Moosa Blvd., Box 1026, Zip 70535; tel. 318/457-5244; Douglas C. Longman, adm. (Nonreporting) **A**1a 9 10	16	10	S		92	—	—	—	—	—	—	—	—
FARMERVILLE—Union Parish													
UNION GENERAL HOSPITAL, 901 James Ave., Zip 71241; tel. 318/368-9751; Chuck Hall, actg. adm. (Nonreporting) **A**9 10	16	10	S		35	—	—	—	—	—	—	—	—
FERRIDAY—Concordia Parish													
★ RIVERLAND MEDICAL CENTER (Formerly Concordia Parish Hospital), E. E. Wallace Blvd., Box 111, Zip 71334; tel. 318/757-6551; Vernon Stevens Jr., adm. (Total facility includes 7 beds in nursing home-type unit) **A**9 10 **F**1 3 5 6 12 14 16 19 23 32 34 35 37 40 41 43 53	16	10	S	TF	49	1918	26	53.1	8	289	5374	2313	137
				H	42	1845	22	—	8	289	—	—	—
FORT POLK—Vernon Parish													
⊞ BAYNE-JONES ARMY COMMUNITY HOSPITAL, Zip 71459; tel. 318/537-3102; Col. Robert E. Wright, dep. cmdr. & adm. **A**1a **F**2 3 6 12 14 15 16 23 24 27 28 29 30 31 32 33 34 35 37 40 44 45 46 47 52 53	42	10	S		139	5452	74	53.2	22	1116	33419	26177	833
FRANKLIN—St. Mary Parish													
⊞ FRANKLIN FOUNDATION HOSPITAL, 1501 Hospital Ave., Box 577, Zip 70538; tel. 318/828-0760; Kyle J. Viator, adm. **A**1a 9 10 **F**1 3 6 10 12 16 23 35 45 47; **S**1755	16	10	S		48	1969	22	44.9	12	218	5755	2397	120
FRANKLINTON—Washington Parish													
⊞ RIVERSIDE MEDICAL CENTER, Enon Hwy., Box 528, Zip 70438; tel. 504/839-4431; James Branon, adm. **A**1a 3 9 10 **F**1 3 6 10 14 15 16 20 23 24 35 37 41 44 45 53; **S**8985	16	10	S		48	1809	28	58.3	6	3	5843	2680	146
GALLIANO—Lafourche Parish													
⊞ LADY OF THE SEA GENERAL HOSPITAL, Box 68, Zip 70354; tel. 504/632-6401; Barney T. Falgout, adm. **A**1a 9 10 **F**1 6 10 12 14 16 23 35 45 53	16	10	S		45	1413	17	37.8	6	32	5732	2209	102
GONZALES—Ascension Parish													
⊞ EAST ASCENSION GENERAL HOSPITAL, 615 E. Worthy Rd., Zip 70737; Mailing Address P O Box 1029, Zip 70707; tel. 504/647-2891; Keith Rush, adm. (Nonreporting) **A**1a 9 10	16	10	S		50	—	—	—	—	—	—	—	—
GREENSBURG—St. Helena Parish													
★ ST. HELENA PARISH HOSPITAL, Box 337, Zip 70441; tel. 504/222-6111; John M. Nolan, adm. (Nonreporting) **A**9 10; **S**0775	16	10	S		35	—	—	—	—	—	—	—	—

★ American Hospital Association (AHA) membership
□ Joint Commission on Accreditation of Hospitals (JCAH) accreditation
+ American Osteopathic Hospital Association (AOHA) membership
○ American Osteopathic Association (AOA) accreditation
Δ Commission on Accreditation of Rehabilitation Facilities (CARF) accreditation
Control codes 61, 63, 64, 71, 72 and 73 indicate hospitals listed by AOHA, but not registered by AHA.
For definition of numerical codes, see page A2

Hospital, Address, Telephone, Administrator, Approval and Facility Codes, Multihospital System Code	Classification Codes			Facilities	Inpatient Data				Newborn Data		Expense (thousands of dollars)		Personnel
	Control	Service	Stay		Beds	Admissions	Census	Occupancy (percent)	Bassinets	Births	Total	Payroll	
GREENWELL SPRINGS—East Baton Rouge Parish													
□ GREENWELL SPRINGS HOSPITAL, Greenwell Springs Rd., P O Box 549, Zip 70739; tel. 504/261-2730; Mark T. Ott, chief exec. off. **A**1a 9 10 **F**19 24 32 33 42 44 45 46 47 48	12	22	L		128	1482	116	80.0	0	0	7058	4405	272
GRETNA—Jefferson Parish													
□ MEADOWCREST HOSPITAL, 2500 Belle Chasse Hwy., Zip 70056; tel. 504/392-3131; Mark F. Keiser, exec. dir. (Nonreporting) **A**1a 9 10; **S**3015	33	10	S		169	—	—	—	—	—	—	—	—
GUEYDAN—Vermilion Parish													
GUEYDAN MEMORIAL HOSPITAL, 710 Fifth St., Box K, Zip 70542; tel. 318/536-9400; Keith Lamm, adm. **A**9 10 **F**1 16 34 37 41	23	10	S		21	556	6	28.6	2	23	1120	510	42
HAMMOND—Tangipahoa Parish													
□★ AMI WESTPARK COMMUNITY HOSPITAL (Formerly Westpark Community Hospital), 1900 S. Morrison Blvd., Zip 70403; Mailing Address P O Box 2608, Zip 70404; tel. 504/542-7777; Steve Turner, pres. & chief exec. off. **A**1a 10 **F**1 3 6 12 15 16 21 23 24 34 35 41 46 47 53; **S**0125	33	10	S		50	2369	31	62.0	0	0	8194	2609	117
□★ SEVENTH WARD GENERAL HOSPITAL, Hwy. 51 S., Box 2668, Zip 70404; tel. 504/345-2700; James E. Cathey Jr., adm. **A**1a 9 10 **F**1 3 6 10 12 14 15 16 19 20 23 24 34 36 39 40 42 43 44 46 47 52 53; **S**2495	16	10	S		196	7126	112	57.1	20	1040	25381	9893	552
WESTPARK COMMUNITY HOSPITAL, See AMI Westpark Community Hospital													
HARAHAN—Orleans Parish													
□★ RIVER OAKS HOSPITAL (Formerly Listed Under New Orleans), 1525 River Oaks Rd. W., Zip 70123; tel. 504/734-1740; Gregory P. Roth, adm. (Nonreporting) **A**1b 3 9; **S**8985	33	22	L		124	—	—	—	—	—	—	—	—
HAYNESVILLE—Claiborne Parish													
NORTH CLAIBORNE HOSPITAL, Hwy. 79, Drawer 431, Zip 71038; tel. 318/624-0441; Helen M. Sharp, adm. **A**9 10 **F**1 16 23 35	16	10	S		32	595	8	25.0	5	9	1439	653	54
HOMER—Claiborne Parish													
★ HOMER MEMORIAL HOSPITAL, E. College St., Box 809, Zip 71040; tel. 318/927-2024; Jacqueline Foster, adm. (Nonreporting) **A**9 10	14	10	S		57	—	—	—	—	—	—	—	—
HOUMA—Terrebonne Parish													
HSA BAYOU OAKS HOSPITAL, 934 E. Main St., Zip 70360; tel. 504/872-2020; Wallace E. Smith PhD, adm. (Nonreporting) **A**9 10	33	22	S		76	—	—	—	—	—	—	—	—
□★ TERREBONNE GENERAL MEDICAL CENTER, 936 E. Main St., Box 6037, Zip 70361; tel. 504/873-4141; Alex B. Smith, adm. (Total facility includes 16 beds in nursing home-type unit) **A**1a 9 10 **F**1 3 5 6 10 12 14 15 16 19 20 34 35 36 40 45 46 47 52 53 54; **S**0025	16	10	S	TF	219	9653	126	55.0	35	886	36236	12648	673
				H	203	9590	124	—	35	886	36182	12598	665
INDEPENDENCE—Tangipahoa Parish													
□ LALLIE KEMP CHARITY HOSPITAL, P O Box 70, Zip 70443; tel. 504/878-9421; Thomas W. Landry, adm. **A**1a 3 5 9 10 **F**1 3 5 6 10 12 14 15 16 34 35 37 40 46 52; **S**0715	12	10	S		74	3230	49	58.3	15	806	8973	4521	280
JACKSON—East Feliciana Parish													
EAST LOUISIANA STATE HOSPITAL, P O Box 498, Zip 70748; tel. 504/634-2651 **A**9 10 **F**15 16 19 23 24 30 32 33 37 42 44 45 46 47 48 50	12	22	L		452	2094	423	93.6	0	0	21090	13339	787
VILLA FELICIANA GERIATRIC HOSPITAL, Box 438, Zip 70748; tel. 504/634-7793; John A. London, adm. (Nonreporting) **A**10; **S**0715	12	48	L		490	—	—	—	—	—	—	—	—
JENA—La Salle Parish													
□★ LA SALLE GENERAL HOSPITAL, Hwy. 84, P O Box 1388, Zip 71342; tel. 318/992-8231; L. Paul Grummer, adm. (Total facility includes 18 beds in nursing home-type unit) **A**1a 9 10 **F**1 6 14 16 17 19 23 34 35 41 45	16	10	S	TF	67	1877	35	52.2	0	0	5223	2230	141
				H	49	1706	29	—	0	0	—	—	—
JENNINGS—Jefferson Davis Parish													
□★ JENNINGS AMERICAN LEGION HOSPITAL, Hwy. 26, Box 1027, Zip 70546; tel. 318/824-2490; Terry J. Terrebonne, adm. (Nonreporting) **A**1a 9 10	23	10	S		55	—	—	—	—	—	—	—	—
JONESBORO—Jackson Parish													
□ JACKSON PARISH HOSPITAL, 600 Beech Springs Rd., Box 685, Zip 71251; tel. 318/259-4435; Larry J. Ayres, adm. (Nonreporting) **A**1a 9 10	16	10	S		66	—	—	—	—	—	—	—	—
JONESVILLE—Catahoula Parish													
★ CATAHOULA MEMORIAL HOSPITAL (Formerly Catahoula Parish Hospital), 2801 Fourth St., P O Box 739, Zip 71343; tel. 318/339-7961; George E. Tosspon Jr., adm. (Nonreporting) **A**10	16	10	S		49	—	—	—	—	—	—	—	—
KAPLAN—Vermilion Parish													
★ ABROM KAPLAN MEMORIAL HOSPITAL, 1310 W. Seventh St., Zip 70548; tel. 318/643-8300; Lawson K. Woods, adm. **A**9 10 **F**3 6 14 15 16 23 35 36 40 52	16	10	S		40	1685	20	50.0	8	245	3647	2200	97
KENNER—Jefferson Parish													
★ AMI ST. JUDE MEDICAL CENTER, 180 W. Esplanade Ave., Zip 70065; tel. 504/468-8600; John W. McDaniel, pres. & chief exec. off. **A**9 10 **F**1 3 4 6 9 10 12 14 15 16 20 23 26 30 35 36 37 40 46 47 51 52 53 54; **S**0125	33	10	S		149	4026	66	44.3	24	459	41518	8747	359
KENTWOOD—Tangipahoa Parish													
★ E. S. PIKE MEMORIAL HOSPITAL, Hwy. 38 W., Box 89, Zip 70444; tel. 504/229-7313; Shirley B. Frazier, adm. (Nonreporting) **A**9 10	33	10	S		26	—	—	—	—	—	—	—	—
KINDER—Allen Parish													
★ ALLEN PARISH HOSPITAL, Box 1670, Zip 70648; tel. 318/738-2527; Joseph R. Darbone Jr., adm.; Sybil Thompson RN, asst. adm. **A**9 10 **F**1 6 16 34 35 37 43 45 46	13	10	S		25	961	11	44.0	6	145	2146	984	55
LAFAYETTE—Lafayette Parish													
□ CDU OF ACADIANA, P O Box 91526, Zip 70509; tel. 318/234-5614; Ronald E. Weller, adm. (Newly Registered) **A**1b 9	23	82	S		52	—	—	—	—	—	—	—	—
★ CYPRESS HOSPITAL, 302 Dulles Dr., Zip 70506; tel. 318/233-9024; Robert Leven, adm. **A** 10 **F**3 15 19 24 30 32 33 34 42 47 48 49; **S**1755	33	22	S		94	943	60	63.8	0	0	5421	2481	125
★ HAMILTON MEDICAL CENTER HOSPITAL, 2810 Ambassador Caffery Pkwy., Zip 70506; tel. 318/981-2949; Thomas M. Weiss, adm. **A**10 **F**1 3 6 9 10 12 14 15 16 23 24 35 36 40 43 46 53 54; **S**1755	33	10	S		67	4460	57	85.1	13	622	—	—	333
□★ INSIGHT HOSPITAL, 310 Youngsville Hwy., Zip 70508; tel. 318/837-8787; Kenneth O'Rourke, adm. **A**1b **F**15 26 28 30 32 33 34 42 49;	33	22	S		34	416	32	94.1	0	0	—	—	47
□★ LAFAYETTE GENERAL MEDICAL CENTER (Formerly Lafayette General Hospital), 1214 Coolidge Ave., Box 52009 OCS, Zip 70505; tel. 318/261-7991; John J. Burdin Jr., exec. vice-pres. **A**1a 9 10 **F**1 3 4 5 6 7 8 9 10 11 12 14 15 16 17 19 20 23 24 25 26 34 35 36 40 41 44 45 46 47 51 52 53 54; **S**7235	23	10	S		214	11250	161	80.9	16	618	46547	18933	849
□★ Δ OUR LADY OF LOURDES REGIONAL MEDICAL CENTER, 611 St. Landry St., Zip 70506; Mailing Address Box 4027c, Zip 70502; tel. 318/234-7381; Dudley Romero, chief exec. off. **A**1a 7 9 10 **F**1 3 4 6 7 9 12 14 15 16 17 19 23 24 25 26 34 35 41 42 44 45 46 52 53 54; **S**1475	21	10	S		315	11658	192	58.5	0	0	42138	17198	879
□ UNIVERSITY MEDICAL CENTER, 2390 W. Congress St., P O Box 4016-C, Zip 70502; tel. 318/261-6000; Gerry Morris, adm. **A**1a 2 3 5 10 **F**1 3 6 10 12 14 16 20 23 34 35 40 45 46 48 51 52 54; **S**0715	12	10	S		168	10854	145	82.9	16	3122	25040	11821	692

★ American Hospital Association (AHA) membership
□ Joint Commission on Accreditation of Hospitals (JCAH) accreditation
+ American Osteopathic Hospital Association (AOHA) membership
○ American Osteopathic Association (AOA) accreditation
Δ Commission on Accreditation of Rehabilitation Facilities (CARF) accreditation
Control codes 61, 63, 64, 71, 72 and 73 indicate hospitals listed by AOHA, but not registered by AHA.
For definition of numerical codes, see page A2

Hospital, Address, Telephone, Administrator, Approval and Facility Codes, Multihospital System Code	Classification Codes				Inpatient Data				Newborn Data		Expense (thousands of dollars)		
	Control	Service	Stay	Facilities	Beds	Admissions	Census	Occupancy (percent)	Bassinets	Births	Total	Payroll	Personnel
★□ WOMEN'S AND CHILDREN'S HOSPITAL (Formerly Woman's Hospital of Acadiana), 4600 Ambassador Caffery Pkwy., Zip 70508; tel. 318/981-9100; Karen Poole, adm. **A**1a 10 **F**1 6 12 15 16 34 36 37 38 40 46 51; **S**1755	33	44	S		89	3363	37	41.6	45	2168	—	—	212
LAKE CHARLES—Calcasieu Parish													
□ DR. WALTER OLIN MOSS REGIONAL HOSPITAL, 1000 Walters St., Zip 70605; tel. 318/477-3350; Edward G. Poor, dir. **A**1a 3 5 9 10 **F**1 3 6 12 14 16 19 30 34 35 37 40 43 45 46 47 48 50 52; **S**0715	12	10	S		108	5733	68	63.0	20	1264	12874	6585	380
★ HUMANA HOSPITAL -LAKE CHARLES, 4200 Nelson Rd., Zip 70605; tel. 318/474-6370; Davis Walton, exec. dir. **A**10 **F**1 6 12 14 15 16 34 36 37 40 46 47 51; **S**1235	33	44	S		90	2410	25	27.8	30	1131	9758	3243	144
★□ LAKE CHARLES MEMORIAL HOSPITAL, 1701 Oak Park Blvd., Zip 70601; Mailing Address Drawer M, Zip 70602; tel. 318/494-3000; Elton L. Williams Jr., exec. dir. **A**1a 9 10 **F**1 3 5 6 12 14 15 16 20 23 24 26 34 35 36 40 42 43 44 45 46 47 52 53 54	23	10	S		257	10065	148	57.6	34	851	35858	12978	540
★□ ST. PATRICK HOSPITAL, 524 S. Ryan St., Zip 70601; tel. 318/436-2511; Sr. Mary Fatima McCarthy, adm. **A**1a 2 9 10 **F**1 3 4 5 6 7 8 9 10 11 12 15 16 20 21 23 24 26 34 35 36 40 41 43 44 45 46 47 48 49 52 53 54; **S**0605	21	10	S		273	10383	180	65.9	10	202	38525	14597	703
LAKE PROVIDENCE—East Carrol Parish													
REGENT HOSPITAL -EAST CARROLL (Formerly East Carroll Parish Hospital), 226 N. Hood St., Zip 71254; tel. 318/559-2441; Shirley M. Sikes, adm. (Nonreporting) **A**9; **S**1065	16	10	S		29	—	—	—	—	—	—	—	—
LAPLACE—St. John the Baptist Parish													
□ RIVER PARISHES MEDICAL CENTER, 500 Rue De Sante, Zip 70068; tel. 504/652-7000; George J. Foss, mng. dir. **A**1a 10 **F**1 3 6 10 12 14 15 16 20 23 26 34 35 36 40 43 45 46 47 50 53; **S**9555	33	10	S		102	2976	41	40.2	6	322	12104	3879	193
LEESVILLE—Vernon Parish													
★□ BYRD MEMORIAL HOSPITAL, 1020 Port Arthur Blvd., Zip 71446; tel. 318/239-9041; Greg Griffith, exec. dir. (Nonreporting) **A**1a 9 10	33	10	S		70	—	—	—	—	—	—	—	—
□ LEESVILLE GENERAL HOSPITAL, Kurthwood Rd., Zip 71446; tel. 318/239-3801; William W. Speaker, adm. (Nonreporting) **A**1a 9 10; **S**1065	33	10	S		28	—	—	—	—	—	—	—	—
LULING—St. Charles Parish													
★ ST. CHARLES HOSPITAL, Paul Maillard Rd., Box 87, Zip 70070; tel. 504/785-6242; Fred Martinez Jr., adm. **A**9 10 **F**1 3 6 10 15 16 20 23 35 45 53	16	10	S		50	1432	18	36.0	0	0	5755	1925	121
LUTCHER—St. James Parish													
★ ST. JAMES PARISH HOSPITAL, Box 430, Zip 70071; tel. 504/869-5512; Roy L. Mohon, adm. (Nonreporting) **A**9 10	16	10	S		36	—	—	—	—	—	—	—	—
MAMOU—Evangeline Parish													
★□ SAVOY MEMORIAL HOSPITAL, 801 Poinciana Ave., Zip 70554; tel. 318/468-5261; J. E. Richardson, adm. (Total facility includes 82 beds in nursing home-type unit) **A**1a 9 10 **F**1 3 6 10 15 16 19 23 24 34 35 37 41 43 44 46 53 54	23	10	S	TF	213	4216	132	75.0	7	255	14375	6043	418
				H	131	4169	63	—	7	255	13567	5556	376
MANDEVILLE—St. Tammany Parish													
□ BOWLING GREEN INN, 701 Florida Ave., P O Box 417, Zip 70448; tel. 504/626-5661; Bob Alario, exec. dir. (Nonreporting) **A**1b	33	82	S		44	—	—	—	—	—	—	—	—
□ SOUTHEAST LOUISIANA HOSPITAL, Box 3850, Zip 70448; tel. 504/626-8161; Gary A. Sneed MD, chief exec. off. **A**1b 5 9 10 **F**15 24 30 32 33 42 44 45 46 48	12	22	L		483	1799	448	92.8	0	0	16372	10011	647
MANSFIELD—De Soto Parish													
★□ DE SOTO GENERAL HOSPITAL, 207 Jefferson St., P O Box 672, Zip 71052; tel. 318/872-4610; Robert R. Taylor, pres. **A**1a 9 10 **F**1 3 6 16 23 35 45	23	10	S		72	1379	21	29.2	0	1	3768	1483	97
MANY—Sabine Parish													
MANY HOSPITAL, 923 Highland Dr., Box 821, Zip 71449; tel. 318/256-9292; Mike McCallister, adm. (Nonreporting)	33	10	S		34	—	—	—	—	—	—	—	—
SABINE MEDICAL CENTER, 923 Highland Dr., Box 971, Zip 71449; tel. 318/256-5691; George McGowan, adm. **A**10 **F**1 6 16 23 34 35 37 41 44 45 46 47	33	10	S		68	1654	19	27.9	5	87	2549	942	83
MARKSVILLE—Avoyelles Parish													
★□ HUMANA HOSPITAL -MARKSVILLE, Box 255, Zip 71351; tel. 318/253-8611; Lloyd C. Dupuy, exec. dir. **A**1a 9 10 **F**1 3 6 14 16 23 35 46 47; **S**1235	33	10	S		55	1237	16	29.1	9	18	—	—	99
MARRERO—Jefferson Parish													
★□ WEST JEFFERSON MEDICAL CENTER (Formerly West Jefferson General Hospital), 1101 Ave. D, Zip 70072; tel. 504/347-5511; David M. Smith, dir. **A**1a 9 10 **F**1 2 3 4 5 6 7 8 10 11 12 14 15 16 20 22 23 24 27 35 40 41 44 45 46 47 52 53 54	16	10	S		418	12084	219	52.4	30	712	55652	23012	1369
MERRYVILLE—Beauregard Parish													
MERRYVILLE GENERAL HOSPITAL, Bryan St., Drawer C, Zip 70653; tel. 318/825-6181; D. W. Nichols, adm. (Total facility includes 50 beds in nursing home-type unit) **A**9 10 **F**1 6 16 19 23 34 35 43 45 53; **S**1585	16	10	S	TF	74	498	53	71.6	0	0	2139	758	69
				H	24	476	5	—	0	0	1561	507	43
METAIRIE—Jefferson Parish													
★□ DOCTORS HOSPITAL OF JEFFERSON, 4320 Houma Blvd., Zip 70006; tel. 504/456-5657; Robert L. Kinneberg Jr., Adm., adm. (Nonreporting) **A**1a 9 10; **S**1755	33	10	S		77	—	—	—	—	—	—	—	—
★□ EAST JEFFERSON GENERAL HOSPITAL, 4200 Houma Blvd., Zip 70011; tel. 504/454-4000; Peter J. Betts, pres. & chief exec. off. **A**1a 9 10 **F**1 2 3 4 6 9 12 14 15 16 17 19 20 21 23 24 25 27 30 33 34 35 36 40 41 45 46 47 48 52 53 54	16	10	S		456	16481	319	68.9	19	1134	71471	31356	1398
★□ LAKESIDE HOSPITAL, 4700 I-10 Service Rd., Zip 70001; tel. 504/885-3333; Gerald L. Parton, adm. (Nonreporting) **A**1a 9 10; **S**1755	33	10	S		209	—	—	—	—	—	—	—	—
MINDEN—Webster Parish													
□ MINDEN MEDICAL CENTER, 1 Medical Plaza, Zip 71055; tel. 318/377-2321; George E. French III, adm. (Nonreporting) **A**1a 10; **S**1375	33	10	S		108	—	—	—	—	—	—	—	—
MONROE—Ouachita Parish													
□ E. A. CONWAY MEMORIAL HOSPITAL, 4801 S. Grand St., Box 1881, Zip 71201; tel. 318/387-8460; Roy D. Bostick, dir. **A**1a 3 5 9 10 **F**1 3 5 12 14 15 16 19 23 34 35 40 45 46 52; **S**0715	12	10	S		181	8857	128	70.7	49	2329	16947	9625	585
★□ NORTH MONROE COMMUNITY HOSPITAL, 3421 Medical Park Dr., Zip 71203; tel. 318/388-1946; Arlen Reynolds, adm. (Nonreporting) **A**1a 10; **S**1755	33	10	S		110	—	—	—	—	—	—	—	—
★□ ST. FRANCIS MEDICAL CENTER, 309 Jackson St., Zip 71201; Mailing Address Box 1901, Zip 71210; tel. 318/362-4000; Sr. Anne Marie Twohig, chief exec. off. **A**1a 9 10 **F**1 2 3 4 5 6 7 8 9 10 11 14 15 16 19 21 23 24 25 26 27 29 30 32 33 34 35 36 38 40 41 42 43 44 45 46 48 50 51 52 53 54; **S**1475	21	10	S		449	14957	262	58.4	37	892	46250	20492	1213
MORGAN CITY—St. Mary Parish													
★□ LAKEWOOD HOSPITAL, 1125 Marguerite St., Zip 70380; Mailing Address Drawer 2308, Zip 70381; tel. 504/384-2200; Joe L. Germany, adm. **A**1a 9 10 **F**1 3 6 10 12 15 16 23 35 36 44 45 48 49	16	10	S		93	3559	43	42.6	14	408	12841	5029	287
NAPOLEONVILLE—Assumption Parish													
★□ ASSUMPTION GENERAL HOSPITAL, Whitaker Lane, P O Drawer 546, Zip 70390; tel. 504/369-7241; Jean-Paul Lejeune, adm. **A**1a 9 10 **F**1 6 12 14 16 23 35 45	13	10	S		26	721	9	34.6	0	0	1934	925	52
NATCHITOCHES—Natchitoches Parish													
★□ NATCHITOCHES PARISH HOSPITAL, 501 Keyser Ave., Box 2009, Zip 71457; tel. 318/352-1200; Eugene Spillman, exec. dir. (Nonreporting) **A**1a 9 10	16	10	S		167	—	—	—	—	—	—	—	—

Hospital, Address, Telephone, Administrator, Approval and Facility Codes, Multihospital System Code	Classification Codes				Inpatient Data				Newborn Data		Expense (thousands of dollars)		
★ American Hospital Association (AHA) membership ☐ Joint Commission on Accreditation of Hospitals (JCAH) accreditation + American Osteopathic Hospital Association (AOHA) membership ○ American Osteopathic Association (AOA) accreditation Δ Commission on Accreditation of Rehabilitation Facilities (CARF) accreditation Control codes 61, 63, 64, 71, 72 and 73 indicate hospitals listed by AOHA, but not registered by AHA. For definition of numerical codes, see page A2	Control	Service	Stay	Facilities	Beds	Admissions	Census	Occupancy (percent)	Bassinets	Births	Total	Payroll	Personnel
NEW IBERIA—Iberia Parish													
★☐ DAUTERIVE HOSPITAL, 600 N. Lewis St., P O Box 430, Zip 70560; tel. 318/365-7311; Clay Hurley, adm. (Nonreporting) **A**1a 9 10; **S**1755	33	10	S		116	—	—	—	—	—	—	—	—
★☐ IBERIA GENERAL HOSPITAL AND MEDICAL CENTER, 2315 E. Main St., Box 1450, Zip 70560; tel. 318/364-0441; Donald R. Hebert, exec. dir. **A**1a 9 10 **F**1 3 6 10 12 16 20 23 35 36 37 40 45 46 52 53 54	16	10	S		125	3640	48	38.4	15	558	—	—	237
NEW ORLEANS—Orleans Parish													
★☐ CHARITY HOSPITAL AT NEW ORLEANS, 1532 Tulane Ave., Zip 70140; tel. 504/568-3202; Elliott C. Roberts Sr., chief exec. off. **A**1a b 2 3 5 6 8 9 10 **F**1 3 5 6 7 8 9 10 11 12 13 14 15 16 20 23 24 25 26 27 30 32 33 34 35 37 38 40 42 44 46 47 48 51 52 53 54	12	10	S		986	32763	824	83.6	68	5989	151118	76098	4044
★☐ CHILDREN'S HOSPITAL (Children's General Medical and Surgical, and Rehabilitation), 200 Henry Clay Ave., Zip 70118; tel. 504/899-9511; Steve Worley, actg. exec. dir. **A**1a 3 5 8 9 10 **F**1 6 10 12 14 16 23 24 25 26 33 34 35 38 42 44 45 46 52 53	23	59	S		122	3312	66	54.1	0	0	—	—	538
COLISEUM MEDICAL CENTER, See CPC Coliseum Medical Center													
★☐ CPC COLISEUM MEDICAL CENTER (Formerly Coliseum Medical Center), 3601 Coliseum St., Zip 70115; tel. 504/897-9700; John R. Wastak, adm. (Total facility includes 42 beds in nursing home-type unit) **A**1b 9 10 **F**15 16 19 23 24 26 29 32 33 42 43 44 49 50; **S**0785	33	22	L	TF H	164 122	1125 695	86 54	52.4 —	0 0	0 0	— —	— —	156 —
CPC EAST LAKE HOSPITAL, 5650 Read Blvd., Zip 70127; tel. 504/241-0888; Stuart Podolnick, adm. (Newly Registered); **S**0785	33	22	S		60	—	—	—	—	—	—	—	—
★ DE PAUL HOSPITAL, 1040 Calhoun St., Zip 70118; tel. 504/899-8282; Sal A. Barbera, exec. dir. (Nonreporting) **A** 10; **S**1755	33	22	L		314	—	—	—	—	—	—	—	—
☐ EYE, EAR, NOSE AND THROAT HOSPITAL, 145 Elk Pl., Zip 70112; tel. 504/595-6100; Donald E. Patterson, chief exec. off. **A**1a 3 5 9 10 **F**1 12 15 34 45 46; **S**6525	23	45	S		47	1262	8	17.0	0	0	9143	1521	163
★ Δ F. EDWARD HEBERT HOSPITAL, 1 Sanctuary Dr., Zip 70114; tel. 504/363-2200; Raymond J. Osbun, adm. (Nonreporting) **A**7	33	46	S		200	—	—	—	—	—	—	—	—
★☐ HOTEL DIEU HOSPITAL, 2021 Perdido St., Zip 70112; Mailing Address Box 61262, Zip 70161; tel. 504/588-3000; Sr. Marie Breitling, pres. **A**1a 3 5 9 10 **F**1 3 4 6 9 10 13 15 16 20 21 23 24 26 34 35 40 41 43 44 45 46 47 50 52 53 54; **S**1885	21	10	S		283	9543	176	62.2	15	1216	49885	20949	827
★☐ HUMANA HOSPITAL -NEW ORLEANS (Formerly Humana Women's Hospital-East Orleans), 6000 Bullard Rd., Zip 70128; Mailing Address P O Box 29504, Zip 70189; tel. 504/245-4851; James Le Doux, exec. dir. (Nonreporting) **A**1a 10; **S**1235	33	10	S		150	—	—	—	—	—	—	—	—
☐ JO ELLEN SMITH MEDICAL CENTER, 4444 General Meyer Ave., Zip 70114; tel. 504/363-7011; Ronald J. Ensor, adm. **A**1a 9 10 **F**1 3 5 6 9 10 11 12 13 14 15 16 20 23 24 26 30 34 35 37 42 43 44 45 46 47 50 52 54; **S**3015	33	10	S		164	4597	83	50.6	0	0	23281	10200	434
★☐ MERCY HOSPITAL OF NEW ORLEANS, 301 N. Jefferson Davis Pkwy., Zip 70119; tel. 504/486-7361; Sr. Barbara Grant, chief oper. off. **A**1a 9 10 **F**1 3 6 7 8 9 10 11 12 14 15 16 19 23 24 34 35 41 45 46 49 53; **S**5185	21	10	S		248	6919	145	58.5	0	0	32634	12772	651
★ MONTELEPRE MEMORIAL HOSPITAL, 3125 Canal St., Zip 70119; tel. 504/822-8222; W. Clark Wherritt, adm. (Nonreporting) **A**9 10	33	10	S		64	—	—	—	—	—	—	—	—
★ NEW ORLEANS GENERAL HOSPITAL, 625 Jackson Ave., Zip 70130; tel. 504/587-0100; Patricia A. Beggs, adm. (Nonreporting) **A**10; **S**0495	23	10	S		109	—	—	—	—	—	—	—	—
★☐ OCHSNER FOUNDATION HOSPITAL, 1516 Jefferson Hwy., Zip 70121; tel. 504/838-3000; David R. Page, exec. vice-pres. & dir. **A**1a 2 3 5 8 9 10 **F**1 2 3 4 6 7 8 9 10 11 12 13 14 15 16 17 19 20 21 23 24 25 26 27 28 30 32 33 34 35 36 37 38 39 40 41 42 44 46 48 49 51 52 53 54	23	10	S		511	17156	328	64.1	20	748	115496	47000	2394
★☐ PENDLETON MEMORIAL METHODIST HOSPITAL, 5620 Read Blvd., Zip 70127; tel. 504/244-5100; Fred Young, pres. **A**1a 9 10 **F**1 2 3 5 6 7 9 10 12 14 15 16 23 24 30 34 35 36 40 41 44 45 46 47 52 53 54	23	10	S		201	7849	157	46.0	58	590	41433	17942	760
RIVER OAKS HOSPITAL, See Harahan													
★☐ SOUTHERN BAPTIST HOSPITAL, 2700 Napoleon Ave., Zip 70115; tel. 504/899-9311; Nelson Toebbe, pres. **A**1a 3 5 9 10 **F**1 2 3 4 5 6 9 10 12 13 14 15 16 17 19 20 23 24 26 27 29 30 33 34 35 36 40 41 42 44 45 46 51 52 53 54	23	10	S		463	13658	259	55.9	46	1872	82836	33622	1602
☐ ST. CHARLES GENERAL HOSPITAL, 3700 St. Charles Ave., Zip 70115; tel. 504/899-7441; Richard Freeman, adm. **A**1a 10 **F**1 3 6 16 20 23 35 45 46 47 50; **S**3015	33	10	S		161	5946	125	77.6	0	0	—	—	357
★☐ TOURO INFIRMARY, 1401 Foucher St., Zip 70115; tel. 504/897-7011; Barth A. Weinberg, exec. dir. **A**1a 2 3 5 6 8 9 10 **F**1 3 4 6 7 8 9 10 11 12 14 15 16 19 20 23 24 25 26 27 28 29 30 31 32 33 34 35 36 37 40 42 44 45 46 47 53 54	23	10	S		405	12701	273	67.4	22	1262	76627	33339	1487
★☐ TULANE UNIVERSITY HOSPITAL AND CLINICS, 1415 Tulane Ave., Zip 70112; tel. 504/588-5471; Charley O. Trimble, vice-pres. hosp. & clinic affairs **A**1a 3 5 9 10 **F**1 2 3 4 6 9 10 12 13 14 15 16 20 23 24 26 27 28 29 30 31 32 33 34 35 36 37 38 41 42 44 45 46 47 50 51 52 53 54	23	10	S		290	9743	203	70.0	5	318	79997	31200	1554
☐ UNITED MEDICAL CENTER NEW ORLEANS, 3419 St. Claude Ave., Zip 70117; tel. 504/948-8200; Mark A. Meyers, exec. dir. (Nonreporting) **A**1a 9 10; **S**9605	33	10	S		136	—	—	—	—	—	—	—	—
★☐ VETERANS ADMINISTRATION MEDICAL CENTER, 1601 Perdido St., Zip 70146; tel. 504/568-0811; Gregory J. Haag, dir. **A**1a 2 3 5 8 **F**1 3 4 6 9 10 12 13 14 15 16 19 20 23 24 26 27 28 29 30 31 32 33 34 35 37 38 41 42 43 44 45 46 47 48 49 53 54	45	10	S		401	12219	366	86.9	0	0	76224	40911	1576
NEW ROADS—Pointe Coupee Parish													
★☐ POINTE COUPEE GENERAL HOSPITAL, 2202 False River Dr., P O Box 578, Zip 70760; tel. 504/638-6331; Jerry Marquette, adm. **A**1a 9 10 **F**1 6 15 16 23 34 35 41 43 44 45 49; **S**1755	16	10	S		27	1617	21	40.4	6	130	5818	2616	137
NEWELLTON—Tensas Parish													
TENSAS MEMORIAL HOSPITAL, 903 Verona St., P O Box 665, Zip 71357; tel. 318/467-5421; Daryl Doir, adm. (Nonreporting) **A**9 10	23	10	S		30	—	—	—	—	—	—	—	—
OAK GROVE—West Carroll Parish													
☐ WEST CARROLL MEMORIAL HOSPITAL, Ross St., Box 748, Zip 71263; tel. 318/428-3237; Ben Snead, adm. (Nonreporting) **A**1a 9 10	23	10	S		52	—	—	—	—	—	—	—	—
OAKDALE—Allen Parish													
★☐ HUMANA HOSPITAL -OAKDALE, 130 N. Hospital Dr., Box 629, Zip 71463; tel. 318/335-3700; Louis J. Deumite, exec. dir. (Nonreporting) **A**1a 9 10; **S**1235	33	10	S		61	—	—	—	—	—	—	—	—
OLLA—La Salle Parish													
★☐ HARDTNER MEDICAL CENTER, P O Box 1218, Zip 71465; tel. 318/495-3131; Malcolm L. Barksdale, adm. **A**1a 9 10 **F**1 6 14 16 23 26 34 35 45	16	10	S		47	1472	21	43.8	6	11	2798	1157	59
OPELOUSAS—St. Landry Parish													
★☐ AMI DOCTORS' HOSPITAL OF OPELOUSAS (Formerly Doctors' Hospital of Opelousas), 5101 Hwy. 167 S., Zip 70570; tel. 318/948-2100; Brian Riddle, chief exec. off. **A**1a 10 **F**1 3 6 10 12 14 15 16 23 24 26 30 34 35 36 37 45 46 50; **S**0125	32	10	S		81	3004	39	48.1	0	0	11818	3323	136
DOCTORS' HOSPITAL OF OPELOUSAS, See AMI Doctors' Hospital of Opelousas													

Hospital, Address, Telephone, Administrator, Approval and Facility Codes, Multihospital System Code	Classification Codes			Facilities	Inpatient Data				Newborn Data		Expense (thousands of dollars)		Personnel
★ American Hospital Association (AHA) membership □ Joint Commission on Accreditation of Hospitals (JCAH) accreditation + American Osteopathic Hospital Association (AOHA) membership ○ American Osteopathic Association (AOA) accreditation Δ Commission on Accreditation of Rehabilitation Facilities (CARF) accreditation Control codes 61, 63, 64, 71, 72 and 73 indicate hospitals listed by AOHA, but not registered by AHA. For definition of numerical codes, see page A2	Control	Service	Stay	Facilities	Beds	Admissions	Census	Occupancy (percent)	Bassinets	Births	Total	Payroll	Personnel
★□ OPELOUSAS GENERAL HOSPITAL, 520 Prudhomme Lane, Box 1208, Zip 70571; tel. 318/948-3011; J. Michael Douthitt, adm. **A**1a 9 10 **F**1 3 6 10 15 16 23 35 36 37 40 44 46 47 48 49 52 53; **S**2495	16	10	S		183	5878	82	44.8	28	1008	16632	6773	402
PINEVILLE—Rapides Parish													
□ CENTRAL LOUISIANA STATE HOSPITAL, W. Shamrock Ave., Zip 71360; Mailing Address P O Box 5031, Zip 71361; tel. 318/484-6200; Roy D. Hill MD, chief exec. off. **A**1b 9 10 **F**15 24 25 30 32 33 42 46 47	12	22	L		570	2142	487	85.4	0	0	21655	14564	805
□ HUEY P. LONG MEMORIAL HOSPITAL, Hospital Blvd., Zip 71360; Mailing Address Box 5352, Zip 71361; tel. 318/448-0811; James E. Morgan, adm. **A**1a 3 5 9 10 **F**1 3 5 6 12 14 16 23 34 35 40 43 48 52; **S**0715	12	10	S		137	6466	88	64.2	38	1544	15444	7941	436
PINECREST STATE SCHOOL HOSPITAL, Box 191, Zip 71360; tel. 318/640-0754; L. J. Credeur MD, med. dir. (Nonreporting)	12	62	L		1652	—	—	—	—	—	—	—	—
□ WOODVIEW REGIONAL HOSPITAL (Formerly Listed Under Tioga), 5505 Shreveport Hwy., Zip 71360; tel. 318/640-0222; Robert R. Bash, adm. (Nonreporting) **A**1a 9 10; **S**5895	33	10	S		53	—	—	—	—	—	—	—	—
PLAQUEMINE—Iberville Parish													
★□ RIVER WEST MEDICAL CENTER, 1725 River W. Dr., Zip 70764; tel. 504/687-9222; Roger A. Snell, exec. dir. **A**1a 9 10 **F**1 3 6 12 14 23 35 36 40 41 45	33	10	S		100	2586	40	40.0	7	162	9837	3373	158
PLEASANT HILL—Sabine Parish													
PLEASANT HILL GENERAL HOSPITAL, 212 Pearl St., Box 66, Zip 71065; tel. 318/796-3311; James Spann, adm. (Nonreporting) **A**9 10	33	10	S		30	—	—	—	—	—	—	—	—
PORT SULPHUR—Plaquemines Parish													
★ PLAQUEMINES PARISH GENERAL HOSPITAL, Civic Dr., Rte. 2, Box 105, Zip 70083; tel. 504/564-3346; Judi Guthrie, adm. **A**9 10 **F**1 3 6 14 16 23 35 41 44 49; **S**1755	16	10	S		39	838	11	28.2	0	0	3932	1612	84
RACELAND—Lafourche Parish													
★□ ST. ANNE GENERAL HOSPITAL, Hwy. 1 & Twin Oaks Dr., Box 440, Zip 70394; tel. 504/537-6841; Bernard J. Boyne, chief exec. off. (Total facility includes 20 beds in nursing home-type unit) **A**1a 9 10 **F**1 3 6 10 12 14 16 19 23 35 41 45 53	16	10	S	TF	75	3047	37	49.3	18	440	8787	4303	251
				H	55	2928	33	—	18	440	—	—	—
RAYNE—Acadia Parish													
★□ RAYNE-BRANCH HOSPITAL, 301 S. Chevis St., Box 427, Zip 70578; tel. 318/334-4217; H. Dale Moore, adm. **A**1a 9 10 **F**1 3 6 10 12 14 15 16 17 23 34 35 45 46 53	16	10	S		35	1772	23	43.4	8	135	3874	1790	97
RAYVILLE—Richland Parish													
□ RICHLAND PARISH HOSPITAL-RAYVILLE, Box 388, Zip 71269; tel. 318/728-4181; Michael E. Cooper, adm. (Nonreporting) **A**1a 9 10	16	10	S		75	—	—	—	—	—	—	—	—
RUSTON—Lincoln Parish													
★□ LINCOLN GENERAL HOSPITAL, White St., P O Drawer 1368, Zip 71273; tel. 318/255-5780; Ronald K. Rooney, adm. **A**1a 9 10 **F**1 3 6 10 12 14 15 16 23 30 34 35 36 40 45 53 54; **S**2495	23	10	S		130	6336	82	63.1	14	380	14347	6848	416
SAINT FRANCISVILLE—West Feliciana Parish													
★□ WEST FELICIANA PARISH HOSPITAL, Box 368, Zip 70775; tel. 504/635-3811; Virginia Satterfield, adm. **A**1a 9 10 **F**1 12 16 23 30 35	16	10	S		22	551	6	27.3	0	0	1244	794	47
SHREVEPORT—Caddo Parish													
□ DOCTORS' HOSPITAL, 1130 Louisiana Ave., Box 1526, Zip 71165; tel. 318/227-1211; Charles E. Boyd, adm. (Nonreporting) **A**1a 9 10; **S**9555	33	10	S		157	—	—	—	—	—	—	—	—
★□ HIGHLAND HOSPITAL, 1006 Highland Ave., Zip 71101; tel. 318/227-2221; Ronald J. Elder, adm. **A**1a 9 10 **F**1 3 6 7 8 9 10 11 14 15 16 20 23 24 34 35 36 40 42 44 53; **S**1755	33	10	S		130	4667	62	47.7	15	568	—	—	257
★□ HUMANA HOSPITAL -BRENTWOOD, 1800 Irving Pl., Zip 71101; tel. 318/424-6761; Raymond Bane, exec. dir. **A**1b 9 10 **F**24 28 30 32 33 42 46 47 48 49; **S**1235	33	22	S		174	1074	66	37.9	0	0	6120	2421	141
□ LOUISIANA STATE UNIVERSITY HOSPITAL, 1541 Kings Hwy., Box 33932, Zip 71130; tel. 318/674-5000; Gene L. Hammett, adm. **A**1a 2 3 5 8 9 10 **F**1 3 4 5 6 7 8 9 10 11 12 13 14 15 16 20 22 23 24 26 27 30 33 34 35 37 38 40 44 46 47 51 52 53 54	12	10	S		472	20337	374	82.0	47	4329	114749	63492	1879
★□ Δ PHYSICIANS AND SURGEONS HOSPITAL, 1530 Line Ave., Zip 71104; Mailing Address Box 4466, Zip 71134; tel. 318/227-3950; Jonathan W. Farr, adm. **A**1a 7 9 10 **F**1 3 5 6 12 14 15 16 20 21 23 24 25 26 34 35 36 37 40 41 42 44 45 46 53	33	10	S		183	4184	74	33.6	12	194	—	—	299
★□ SCHUMPERT MEDICAL CENTER, 915 Margaret Pl., Box 21976, Zip 71120; tel. 318/227-4500; Sr. M. Agnesita Brosnan, adm. **A**1a 3 5 9 10 **F**1 3 4 6 7 8 9 10 11 12 13 14 15 16 17 20 21 23 24 26 27 28 29 30 32 34 35 36 40 41 42 43 44 45 46 47 48 49 51 52 53 54; **S**0605	21	10	S		625	21803	402	64.3	33	1136	80191	37285	2054
★□ SHRINERS HOSPITALS FOR CRIPPLED CHILDREN, 3100 Samford Ave., Zip 71103; tel. 318/222-5704; Gwendolyn McRae RN, adm. **A**1a 3 5 **F**23 24 26 34 42 46; **S**4125	23	57	S		45	583	17	41.5	0	0	—	—	104
U. S. AIR FORCE HOSPITAL, See Barksdale Air Force Base													
★□ VETERANS ADMINISTRATION MEDICAL CENTER, 510 E. Stoner Ave., Zip 71130; tel. 318/221-8411; Donald A. Pabst, dir. **A**1a 2 3 5 8 **F**1 3 6 9 10 11 12 15 16 23 24 26 27 28 30 31 32 33 34 35 42 44 46 48 49 53	45	10	S		350	9381	262	69.5	0	0	45000	22935	927
★□ Δ WILLIS-KNIGHTON MEDICAL CENTER, 2600 Greenwood Rd., Zip 71103; tel. 318/632-4600; James K. Elrod, pres. (Nonreporting) **A**1a 7 9 10	23	10	S		426	—	—	—	—	—	—	—	—
SLIDELL—St. Tammany Parish													
NORTH SHORE PSYCHIATRIC HOSPITAL, 104 Medical Center Dr., Zip 70461; tel. 504/643-1100; Robert Hall, adm. (Newly Registered) **A**10	33	22	S		28	—	—	—	—	—	—	—	—
★□ SLIDELL MEMORIAL HOSPITAL, 1001 Gause Blvd., Zip 70458; tel. 504/643-2200; Robert P. Atkinson, chief exec. off. (Nonreporting) **A**1a 9 10	16	10	S		173	—	—	—	—	—	—	—	—
SPRINGHILL—Webster Parish													
★□ HUMANA HOSPITAL -SPRINGHILL, 1001 Humana Dr., Box 917, Zip 71075; tel. 318/539-9161; Ronald P. O'Neal, exec. dir. **A**1a 9 10 **F**3 6 15 16 35 40 41 45 46 47 52; **S**1235	33	10	S		86	2102	35	40.7	10	50	—	—	135
STERLINGTON—Ouachita Parish													
STERLINGTON MEMORIAL HOSPITAL, Hwy. 2, P O Box 567, Zip 71280; Larry A. Jones, adm. **A**9 10 **F**12 17 23 34 43	33	10	S		23	1024	15	65.2	0	0	1761	784	58
SULPHUR—Calcasieu Parish													
★□ WEST CALCASIEU-CAMERON HOSPITAL, Cypress St., P O Box 2269, Zip 70664; tel. 318/527-7035; Frank R. Gayle, dir. **A**1a 9 10 **F**1 3 6 10 12 14 15 16 23 35 39 40 41 45 52 53	16	10	S		115	4820	71	61.7	10	325	14638	7543	386
TALLULAH—Madison Parish													
MADISON PARISH HOSPITAL, 900 Johnson St., Zip 71282; Mailing Address P O Box 1559, Zip 71284; tel. 318/574-2374; Woodrow N. Burke, adm. (Nonreporting) **A**9 10	13	10	S		25	—	—	—	—	—	—	—	—
THIBODAUX—Lafourche Parish													
★□ THIBODAUX GENERAL HOSPITAL, 602 N. Acadia Rd., Zip 70301; Mailing Address Box 1118, Zip 70302; tel. 504/447-5500; Joel J. Champagne, adm. **A**1a 9 10 **F**1 3 6 9 10 11 12 14 15 16 19 34 35 40 41 43 45 46 47 51 52 53	16	10	S		149	5409	72	48.3	15	832	15288	6918	459

Hospital, Address, Telephone, Administrator, Approval and Facility Codes, Multihospital System Code

- ★ American Hospital Association (AHA) membership
- □ Joint Commission on Accreditation of Hospitals (JCAH) accreditation
- + American Osteopathic Hospital Association (AOHA) membership
- ○ American Osteopathic Association (AOA) accreditation
- Δ Commission on Accreditation of Rehabilitation Facilities (CARF) accreditation

Control codes 61, 63, 64, 71, 72 and 73 indicate hospitals listed by AOHA, but not registered by AHA.
For definition of numerical codes, see page A2

Hospital, Address, Telephone, Administrator, Approval and Facility Codes, Multihospital System Code	Classification Codes				Inpatient Data				Newborn Data		Expense (thousands of dollars)		
	Control	Service	Stay	Facilities	Beds	Admissions	Census	Occupancy (percent)	Bassinets	Births	Total	Payroll	Personnel
TIOGA—Rapides Parish													
WOODVIEW REGIONAL HOSPITAL, See Pineville													
VILLE PLATTE—Evangeline Parish													
⊞ HUMANA HOSPITAL -VILLE PLATTE, 800 E. Main St., Box 349, Zip 70586; tel. 318/363-5684; James C. Colligan, exec. dir. (Nonreporting) **A**1a 9 10; **S**1235	33	10	S		124	—	—	—	—	—	—	—	—
VIVIAN—Caddo Parish													
⊞ NORTH CADDO MEMORIAL HOSPITAL, 1000 S. Spruce St., Box 792, Zip 71082; tel. 318/375-3235; Phillip Randy Hartline, adm. **A**1a 9 10 **F**10 15 16 19 35	16	10	S		33	1187	20	60.6	0	0	—	—	76
WELSH—Jefferson Davis Parish													
WELSH GENERAL HOSPITAL, 410 Simmons St., P O Box 918, Zip 70591; tel. 318/734-2555; Ron Piccione, adm. (Nonreporting) **A**9 10	14	10	S		81	—	—	—	—	—	—	—	—
WEST MONROE—Ouachita Parish													
□ GLENWOOD REGIONAL MEDICAL CENTER, 925 McMillan Rd., Box 35805, Zip 71294; tel. 318/329-4200; Larry D. Rentfro, pres. & chief exec. off. (Total facility includes 12 beds in nursing home-type unit) **A**1a 9 10 **F**1 2 3 6 7 8 9 10 11 12 14 15 16 19 21 23 24 34 35 36 37 40 41 44 45 46 48 49 52 53	23	10	S	TF	197	9325	127	65.1	17	639	25270	11135	582
				H	185	9095	120	—	17	639	25006	10912	—
★ WOODLAND HILLS HOSPITAL, 6100 Cypress St., P O Box 1436, Zip 71294; tel. 318/396-5900; Betty Abanto, adm. (Nonreporting) **A**9 10; **S**6525	33	82	S		90	—	—	—	—	—	—	—	—
WINNFIELD—Winn Parish													
⊞ HUMANA HOSPITAL -WINN PARISH, 301 W. Boundary St., Box 152, Zip 71483; tel. 318/628-2721; Donald L. Kannady, exec. dir. **A**1a 9 10 **F**1 3 10 12 14 15 34 35 43 45 46 53; **S**1235	33	10	S		98	1921	39	39.8	0	0	—	—	149
WINNSBORO—Franklin Parish													
FRANKLIN PARISH HOSPITAL, 2106 Loop Rd., Zip 71295; tel. 318/435-9411; John A. Cuny, adm. (Nonreporting) **A**9 10	16	10	S		55	—	—	—	—	—	—	—	—
ZACHARY—East Baton Rouge Parish													
⊞ LANE MEMORIAL HOSPITAL, 6300 Main St., Zip 70791; tel. 504/654-4511; Charlie L. Massey, adm. (Total facility includes 38 beds in nursing home-type unit) **A**1a 9 10 **F**1 3 6 10 12 14 15 16 19 23 34 35 36 40 41 45 46 50 52 53; **S**2495	16	10	S	TF	135	3930	90	66.7	14	305	13193	6035	320
				H	97	3921	53	—	14	305	12885	5740	303

Hospital, Address, Telephone, Administrator, Approval and Facility Codes, Multihospital System Code	Classification Codes: Control	Service	Stay	Facilities	Inpatient Data: Beds	Admissions	Census	Occupancy (percent)	Newborn Data: Bassinets	Births	Expense (thousands of dollars): Total	Payroll	Personnel

★ American Hospital Association (AHA) membership
□ Joint Commission on Accreditation of Hospitals (JCAH) accreditation
\+ American Osteopathic Hospital Association (AOHA) membership
○ American Osteopathic Association (AOA) accreditation
Δ Commission on Accreditation of Rehabilitation Facilities (CARF) accreditation
Control codes 61, 63, 64, 71, 72 and 73 indicate hospitals listed by AOHA, but not registered by AHA.
For definition of numerical codes, see page A2

Maine

Hospital	Control	Service	Stay	Facilities	Beds	Admissions	Census	Occupancy (percent)	Bassinets	Births	Total	Payroll	Personnel
AUGUSTA—Kennebec County													
□ AUGUSTA MENTAL HEALTH INSTITUTE, Arsenal St., Box 724, Zip 04330; tel. 207/622-3751; William C. Daumueller, supt. (Nonreporting) **A**1b 9 10	12	22	L		353	—	—	—	—	—	—	—	—
★□ KENNEBEC VALLEY MEDICAL CENTER, 6 E. Chestnut St., Zip 04330; tel. 207/626-1000; Warren C. Kessler, pres. **A**1a 2 3 5 9 10 **F**1 2 3 6 7 8 9 10 11 12 14 15 16 23 24 25 26 27 28 30 32 33 34 35 36 37 40 44 45 46 52 53	23	10	S		201	8414	125	62.2	20	650	26017	12464	642
BANGOR—Penobscot County													
□ BANGOR MENTAL HEALTH INSTITUTE, 656 State St., Box 926, Zip 04401; tel. 207/941-4000; Charles Meredith MD, supt. (Total facility includes 130 beds in nursing home-type unit) **A**1b 9 10 **F**15 19 23 24 30 32 33 42 46 47 50	12	22	L	TF	294	384	280	95.2	0	0	13721	9689	540
				H	164	301	155	—	0	0	—	—	—
★□ EASTERN MAINE MEDICAL CENTER (Includes Ross Skilled Nursing Facility), 489 State St., Zip 04401; tel. 207/945-7000; Robert Brandow, pres. (Total facility includes 15 beds in nursing home-type unit) **A**1a 2 3 5 9 10 **F**1 2 3 5 6 7 8 9 10 11 12 15 16 19 20 21 23 24 25 26 27 28 30 32 33 34 35 36 37 38 40 42 44 45 46 47 48 49 52 53 54	23	10	S	TF	409	14479	328	80.2	26	1630	73354	34389	1697
				H	394	14242	316	—	26	1630	72907	34020	—
★□ ST. JOSEPH HOSPITAL, 297 Center St., Zip 04401; tel. 207/947-8311; Sr. Mary Norberta, pres. **A**1a 9 10 **F**1 3 5 6 10 11 12 14 15 16 21 23 24 26 29 30 32 33 34 35 41 43 44 45 46 47 49 52 53; **S**1345	21	10	S		130	3135	59	45.4	0	0	16155	7608	451
○ + TAYLOR HOSPITAL (Formerly James A. Taylor Osteopathic Hospital) (Includes Memorial Pavilion Intermediate Care Facility), 268 Stillwater Ave., Zip 04401; tel. 207/942-5286; Philip J. Stoner, adm. (Total facility includes 38 beds in nursing home-type unit) **A**9 10 11 **F**1 3 15 16 19 23 33 35 36 40 45 46 47	23	10	S	TF	87	719	51	54.3	6	34	4052	1902	116
				H	49	701	13	—	6	34	—	—	97
BAR HARBOR—Hancock County													
★□ MOUNT DESERT ISLAND HOSPITAL, Wayman Lane, Zip 04609; tel. 207/288-5081; James A. Mroch, pres. **A**1a 9 10 **F**1 3 6 10 14 16 23 35 36 40 45 49	23	10	S		49	1788	27	54.0	4	95	4936	2886	148
BATH—Sagadahoc County													
★□ BATH MEMORIAL HOSPITAL, 1356 Washington St., Zip 04530; tel. 207/443-5524; J. Neil Bassett, pres. **A**1a 9 10 **F**1 3 6 10 12 15 16 23 24 35 36 37 40 45 46 48 52	23	10	S		59	1676	22	37.3	10	260	6448	3402	180
BELFAST—Waldo County													
★□ WALDO COUNTY GENERAL HOSPITAL, Northport Ave., P O Box 287, Zip 04915; tel. 207/338-2500; Mark A. Biscone, exec. dir. **A**1a 9 10 **F**1 3 6 12 15 16 23 24 26 34 35 36 38 40 43 44 45 46 47 49 53	23	10	S		49	1854	25	51.0	10	213	6037	3003	174
BIDDEFORD—York County													
★□ SOUTHERN MAINE MEDICAL CENTER (Formerly Webber Hospital Association), 1 Mountain Rd., P O Box 626, Zip 04005; tel. 207/283-3663; Philip K. Reiman, exec. dir. **A**1a 9 10 **F**1 3 6 10 12 14 15 16 23 24 27 29 30 35 36 40 44 45 46 52 53	23	10	S		150	4861	108	72.0	16	500	20342	10007	469
BLUE HILL—Hancock County													
★□ BLUE HILL MEMORIAL HOSPITAL, Water St., Box S, Zip 04614; tel. 207/374-2836; Ronald Pond, adm. **A**1a 9 10 **F**1 3 6 15 16 21 23 28 30 32 33 34 35 36 37 40 41 45 47 49	23	10	S		26	1326	16	61.5	5	285	5448	2116	135
BOOTHBAY HARBOR—Lincoln County													
★□ ST. ANDREWS HOSPITAL, 3 St. Andrews Lane, Zip 04538; tel. 207/633-2121; Shirleyann Davison, chief exec. off. **A**1a 9 10 **F**1 6 15 16 23 30 34 35 36 40 41 43 45	23	10	S		32	674	9	28.1	6	29	2196	1244	71
BRIDGTON—Cumberland County													
★□ NORTHERN CUMBERLAND MEMORIAL HOSPITAL, S. High St., P O Box 230, Zip 04009; tel. 207/647-8841; Raymond J. Laplante, chief exec. off. **A**1a 9 10 **F**1 3 6 10 14 15 16 21 23 35 36 40 45 46	23	10	S		40	1905	29	72.5	4	112	5978	3006	163
BRUNSWICK—Cumberland County													
★□ PARKVIEW MEMORIAL HOSPITAL, 329 Maine St., Zip 04011; tel. 207/729-1641; Kurt K. Ganter, pres. **A**1a 9 10 **F**1 3 5 6 12 14 15 16 23 26 34 35 36 40 43 45 46 47; **S**9355	21	10	S		55	2513	30	54.5	14	860	6484	3111	169
★□ REGIONAL MEMORIAL HOSPITAL, 58 Baribeau Dr., Zip 04011; tel. 207/729-0181; Herbert Paris, adm. (Total facility includes 8 beds in nursing home-type unit) **A**1a 9 10 **F**1 3 6 12 15 16 19 23 24 27 30 32 33 34 35 37 45 46 47 52 53	23	10	S	TF	98	3057	53	54.1	0	0	8710	4481	241
				H	90	3002	46	—	0	0	8510	4322	235
CALAIS—Washington County													
★□ CALAIS REGIONAL HOSPITAL, 50 Franklin St., Zip 04619; tel. 207/454-7521; Ray H. Davis Jr., pres. **A**1a 9 10 **F**1 3 6 10 14 15 16 23 24 28 30 35 36 37 40 43 47 49 52	23	10	S		77	1564	20	26.0	8	120	5420	2520	153
CARIBOU—Aroostook County													
★□ CARY MEDICAL CENTER, Mra Van Buren Rd., Box 37, Zip 04736; tel. 207/498-3111; John J. McCormack, exec. dir. (Nonreporting) **A**1a 9 10; **S**1755	14	10	S		65	—	—	—	—	—	—	—	—
CASTINE—Hancock County													
★ CASTINE COMMUNITY HOSPITAL, Ct. St., Box 198, Zip 04421; tel. 207/326-4348; Donald S. Clark, adm. **A**9 10 **F**6 14 15 16 23 34 35 37 43 45 46 50	23	10	S		12	222	3	25.0	0	0	750	398	33
DAMARISCOTTA—Lincoln County													
★□ MILES MEMORIAL HOSPITAL, Bristol Rd., Box 019, Zip 04543; tel. 207/563-1234; Clarence R. Laliberty Jr., adm. (Total facility includes 41 beds in nursing home-type unit) **A**1a 9 10 **F**1 3 6 15 16 19 21 23 34 35 36 40 41 45 46	23	10	S	TF	68	1307	55	80.9	4	138	4675	2234	146
				H	27	1266	16	—	4	138	3502	1748	106
DOVER-FOXCROFT—Piscataquis County													
★□ MAYO REGIONAL HOSPITAL, 75 W. Main St., Zip 04426; tel. 207/564-8401; Robert McReavy, adm. **A**1a 9 10 **F**1 3 6 15 16 23 33 34 35 36 45 46 47 49 53; **S**1755	16	10	S		52	2683	34	65.4	8	268	6542	3070	178
ELLSWORTH—Hancock County													
★□ MAINE COAST MEMORIAL HOSPITAL, 50 Union St., Zip 04605; tel. 207/667-5311; Richard P. Fredericks, pres. **A**1a 9 10 **F**1 3 6 14 15 16 21 23 33 34 35 36 37 40 45 46 47 49 53	23	10	S		64	2175	30	46.9	12	167	6612	3314	185
FARMINGTON—Franklin County													
★□ FRANKLIN MEMORIAL HOSPITAL, One Hospital Dr., Zip 04938; tel. 207/778-6031; James T. Bowse, pres. **A**1a 9 10 **F**1 3 6 10 12 14 15 16 21 23 24 29 30 32 33 34 35 36 40 43 44 45 46 47 49 53	23	10	S		70	3337	44	62.9	10	492	10291	4872	269
FORT KENT—Aroostook County													
★□ NORTHERN MAINE MEDICAL CENTER, 143 E. Main St., Zip 04743; tel. 207/834-3155; Martin B. Bernstein, exec. dir. **A**1a 9 10 **F**1 3 6 10 12 14 15 16 23 33 34 35 36 37 40 41 45 46 47 53	23	10	S		70	1710	28	40.0	12	97	5061	2501	154
GREENVILLE—Piscataquis County													
CHARLES A. DEAN MEMORIAL HOSPITAL, See Mid-Maine Medical Center, Waterville													

★ American Hospital Association (AHA) membership
□ Joint Commission on Accreditation of Hospitals (JCAH) accreditation
+ American Osteopathic Hospital Association (AOHA) membership
○ American Osteopathic Association (AOA) accreditation
Δ Commission on Accreditation of Rehabilitation Facilities (CARF) accreditation
Control codes 61, 63, 64, 71, 72 and 73 indicate hospitals listed by AOHA, but not registered by AHA. For definition of numerical codes, see page A2

Hospital, Address, Telephone, Administrator, Approval and Facility Codes, Multihospital System Code	Classification Codes				Inpatient Data				Newborn Data		Expense (thousands of dollars)		
	Control	Service	Stay	Facilities	Beds	Admissions	Census	Occupancy (percent)	Bassinets	Births	Total	Payroll	Personnel
HOULTON—Aroostook County													
⊞ HOULTON REGIONAL HOSPITAL, 20 Hartford St., Zip 04730; tel. 207/532-9471; Bradley C. Bean, adm. (Total facility includes 24 beds in nursing home-type unit) **A**1a 9 10 **F**1 3 6 10 14 15 16 19 23 24 34 35 45 46 47 48; **S**1755	23	10	S	TF	89	2342	54	60.7	10	218	8906	3885	232
				H	65	2197	32	—	10	218	8591	3627	200
JACKMAN—Somerset County													
JACKMAN REGION HEALTH CENTER, See Mid-Maine Medical Center, Waterville													
LEWISTON—Androscoggin County													
⊞ CENTRAL MAINE MEDICAL CENTER, 300 Main St., Zip 04240; tel. 207/795-0111; William W. Young Jr., pres. **A**1a 2 3 5 9 10 **F**1 2 3 5 6 7 8 9 10 11 12 13 14 15 16 20 23 24 25 26 34 35 36 38 40 43 44 45 46 47 51 52 53 54	23	10	S		250	8811	162	64.8	19	1046	33006	16623	851
⊞ ST. MARY'S GENERAL HOSPITAL, 45 Golder St., P O Box 291, Zip 04240; tel. 207/786-2901; Andrew J. Riddell, pres. & chief exec. off. **A**1a 2 6 9 10 **F**1 3 5 6 10 11 12 14 15 16 23 24 25 26 27 28 30 32 34 35 36 40 42 43 45 46 47 49 52 53	21	10	S		233	6360	139	59.7	24	573	25878	12621	626
LINCOLN—Penobscot County													
⊞ PENOBSCOT VALLEY HOSPITAL, Transalpine Rd., Zip 04457; tel. 207/794-3321; Ronald D. Victory, adm. **A**1a 9 10 **F**1 3 6 14 15 16 23 34 35 36 40 45 46 47 52 53; **S**1755	16	10	S		44	1228	17	38.6	5	110	—	—	114
MACHIAS—Washington County													
⊞ DOWN EAST COMMUNITY HOSPITAL, Upper Ct. St., Rural Rte. 1, Box 11, Zip 04654; tel. 207/255-3356; Donald S. Clark III, adm. **A**1a 9 10 **F**1 14 15 16 23 35 36 40 45 49	23	10	S		38	1484	28	73.7	8	172	—	—	151
MILLINOCKET—Penobscot County													
⊞ MILLINOCKET REGIONAL HOSPITAL, 200 Somerset St., Zip 04462; tel. 207/723-5161; James J. Morrissey Jr., exec. dir. **A**1a 9 10 **F**1 3 6 10 15 16 23 35 36 40 45 46 49 52	23	10	S		50	1933	23	46.0	10	152	6294	2945	170
NEW GLOUCESTER—Cumberland County													
PINELAND CENTER, See Pownal													
NORWAY—Oxford County													
⊞ STEPHENS MEMORIAL HOSPITAL, 80 Main St., Zip 04268; tel. 207/743-5933; Harrison F. Hahn, exec. dir. **A**1a 9 10 **F**1 3 6 10 12 14 15 16 23 26 35 36 40 45 53	23	10	S		50	2661	39	78.0	6	316	8280	3880	201
PITTSFIELD—Somerset County													
⊞ SEBASTICOOK VALLEY HOSPITAL, Grove Hill, Zip 04967; tel. 207/487-5141; Ann Morrison RN, pres. **A**1a 9 10 **F**1 3 14 15 16 21 23 24 34 35 45 46; **S**1755	23	10	S		30	1096	13	41.9	0	8	3398	1704	88
PORTLAND—Cumberland County													
⊞ MAINE MEDICAL CENTER, 22 Bramhall St., Zip 04102; tel. 207/871-0111; Edward C. Andrews Jr. MD, pres. **A**1a 2 3 5 8 9 10 **F**1 2 3 4 5 6 7 8 9 10 11 12 13 14 15 16 20 22 23 24 26 27 28 29 30 31 32 33 34 35 36 37 38 40 42 44 45 46 47 49 51 52 53 54	23	10	S		591	21746	505	83.1	42	2854	124531	59599	2801
⊞ MERCY HOSPITAL, 144 State St., Zip 04101; tel. 207/879-3000; Howard R. Buckley, pres. **A**1a 3 6 9 10 **F**1 2 3 6 10 11 12 14 15 16 23 24 26 32 34 35 36 40 44 45 46 47 48 53; **S**3595	21	10	S		200	7405	168	84.0	14	672	30250	13259	712
○ + OSTEOPATHIC HOSPITAL OF MAINE, 335 Brighton Ave., Zip 04102; tel. 207/774-3921; Gary Barnett, exec. dir. **A**9 10 11 12 13 **F**1 3 6 10 12 14 15 16 23 24 26 34 35 36 40 42 44 45 46 47 52 53	23	10	S		135	5762	112	75.7	10	424	23581	11544	614
POWNAL—Cumberland County													
□ PINELAND CENTER (Formerly Listed Under New Gloucester), Rte. 231, Zip 04260; Mailing Address Box E., Zip 04069; tel. 207/688-4811; Spencer A. Moore EdD, supt. **A**1b 10 **F**23 24 32 33 42 44 45 46 47	12	62	L		292	115	275	94.2	0	0	17919	11253	687
PRESQUE ISLE—Aroostook County													
⊞ AROOSTOOK MEDICAL CENTER (Includes Arthur R. Gould Memorial Hospital, Academy St., Box 151, Zip 04769; tel. 207/768-4000; Aroostook Health Center, Highland Ave., Mars Hill, Zip 04758; tel. 207/768-4900; Community General Hospital, 3 Green St., Fort Fairfield, Zip 04742; tel. 207/768-4700), Box 151, Zip 04769; David A. Peterson, pres. & chief exec. off. (Total facility includes 96 beds in nursing home-type unit) **A**1a 2 9 10 **F**1 3 5 6 7 8 10 12 14 15 16 19 23 24 25 26 27 28 30 32 33 34 35 36 37 38 40 43 44 45 46 49 52 53	23	10	S	TF	223	3293	158	70.9	12	306	18225	8197	519
				H	127	3215	63	—	12	306	16220	6996	441
ROCKPORT—Knox County													
⊞ PENOBSCOT BAY MEDICAL CENTER, Mailing Address Glen Cove, Rockland, Zip 04841; tel. 207/594-9511; Jerry S. Koontz, pres. (Total facility includes 44 beds in nursing home-type unit) **A**1a 2 9 10 **F**1 3 6 10 12 14 15 16 23 24 26 27 35 36 37 40 44 45 46 52 53	23	10	S	TF	150	4741	127	84.7	17	496	18569	8921	513
				H	106	4709	83	—	17	496	17464	8294	463
RUMFORD—Oxford County													
⊞ RUMFORD COMMUNITY HOSPITAL, 420 Franklin St., Zip 04276; tel. 207/364-4581; Ashley L. O'Brien, exec. dir. **A**1a 2 9 10 **F**1 3 6 10 12 14 15 16 23 29 34 35 36 37 40 43 45 46 49 50 52 53	23	10	S		97	2115	36	37.1	11	104	8480	4109	259
SANFORD—York County													
⊞ HENRIETTA D. GOODALL HOSPITAL, 25 June St., Zip 04073; tel. 207/324-4310; Peter G. Booth, adm. (Total facility includes 102 beds in nursing home-type unit) **A**1a 9 10 **F**1 3 6 15 16 19 23 26 35 36 40 42 45 46 52	23	10	S	TF	175	2869	146	83.4	12	430	12214	5622	354
				H	73	2803	49	—	12	430	9908	4439	274
SKOWHEGAN—Somerset County													
⊞ REDINGTON-FAIRVIEW GENERAL HOSPITAL, Fairview Ave., Box 468, Zip 04976; tel. 207/474-5121; Benjamin W. Mac Arthur, exec. dir. **A**1a 2 9 10 **F**1 3 6 10 12 14 15 16 21 23 24 30 33 34 35 36 40 44 45 47 50 52 53	23	10	S		92	2992	41	44.6	10	157	8648	4878	263
SOUTH PORTLAND—Cumberland County													
□ JACKSON BROOK INSTITUTE, 175 Running Hill Rd., Zip 04106; tel. 207/761-2200; Dennis P. King, pres. **A**1a b 9 10 **F**24 30 32 33 42 48	33	22	S		81	906	55	67.9	0	0	7656	2727	162
TOGUS—Kennebec County													
⊞ VETERANS ADMINISTRATION MEDICAL CENTER (General Medical, Surgical and Psychiatric), Zip 04330; tel. 207/623-8411; Thomas A. Holthaus, dir. (Total facility includes 60 beds in nursing home-type unit) **A**1a 2 **F**1 3 6 10 11 12 14 15 16 19 20 23 24 26 27 28 30 31 32 33 34 42 44 46 47 48 49 50	45	49	S	TF	468	6508	358	76.5	0	0	29243	22728	956
				H	408	6417	302	—	0	0	26699	20737	927
VAN BUREN—Aroostook County													
⊞ VAN BUREN COMMUNITY HOSPITAL, 2 Main St., Zip 04785; tel. 207/868-2796; Romeo J. Parent, chief exec. off. (Nonreporting) **A**1a 9 10	23	10	S		29	—	—	—	—	—	—	—	—
WATERVILLE—Kennebec County													
⊞ MID-MAINE MEDICAL CENTER (Includes Charles A. Dean Memorial Hospital, Greenville, Zip 04441; Jackman Region Health Center, Jackman), North St., Zip 04901; tel. 207/872-1000; William P. Spolyar, pres. (Total facility includes 54 beds in nursing home-type unit) **A**1a 2 3 5 9 10 **F**1 3 5 6 7 8 9 10 11 12 14 15 16 19 20 23 24 25 26 27 30 32 33 34 35 36 40 42 44 45 46 47 48 49 52 53	23	10	S	TF	316	9753	226	71.5	21	1129	39315	20001	1113
				H	262	9704	173	—	21	1129	38646	19550	1041
★ ○ + WATERVILLE OSTEOPATHIC HOSPITAL, Kennedy Memorial Dr., Zip 04901; tel. 207/873-0731; Stanley L. Stanczak, chief exec. off. **A**9 10 11 12 13 **F**1 3 6 10 12 14 15 16 23 28 30 33 34 35 36 37 40 44 45 46 47 52 53	23	10	S		78	2795	45	57.7	6	138	9437	4546	281

Hospital, Address, Telephone, Administrator, Approval and Facility Codes, Multihospital System Code	Classification Codes				Inpatient Data				Newborn Data		Expense (thousands of dollars)		
★ American Hospital Association (AHA) membership □ Joint Commission on Accreditation of Hospitals (JCAH) accreditation + American Osteopathic Hospital Association (AOHA) membership ○ American Osteopathic Association (AOA) accreditation Δ Commission on Accreditation of Rehabilitation Facilities (CARF) accreditation Control codes 61, 63, 64, 71, 72 and 73 indicate hospitals listed by AOHA, but not registered by AHA. For definition of numerical codes, see page A2	Control	Service	Stay	Facilities	Beds	Admissions	Census	Occupancy (percent)	Bassinets	Births	Total	Payroll	Personnel
WESTBROOK—Cumberland County													
WESTBROOK COMMUNITY HOSPITAL, 40 Park Rd., Zip 04092; tel. 207/854-8464; Paul H. Schreiber, adm. **A**9 10 **F**1 14 35 45 49	23	10	S		30	659	10	33.3	6	22	1523	807	39
YORK—York County													
★□ YORK HOSPITAL, 15 Hospital Dr., Zip 03909; tel. 207/363-4321; Jud Knox, adm. (Total facility includes 18 beds in nursing home-type unit) **A**1a 9 10 **F**1 3 6 14 15 16 19 21 23 24 26 35 42 44 45 46 47 49 53 54	23	10	S	TF	86	2646	58	67.4	0	0	9885	4536	241
				H	68	2580	43	—	0	0	9538	4331	228

★ American Hospital Association (AHA) membership
□ Joint Commission on Accreditation of Hospitals (JCAH) accreditation
+ American Osteopathic Hospital Association (AOHA) membership
○ American Osteopathic Association (AOA) accreditation
Δ Commission on Accreditation of Rehabilitation Facilities (CARF) accreditation
Control codes 61, 63, 64, 71, 72 and 73 indicate hospitals listed by AOHA, but not registered by AHA.
For definition of numerical codes, see page A2

Maryland

Hospital, Address, Telephone, Administrator, Approval and Facility Codes, Multihospital System Code	Classification Codes				Inpatient Data				Newborn Data		Expense (thousands of dollars)		
	Control	Service	Stay	Facilities	Beds	Admissions	Census	Occupancy (percent)	Bassinets	Births	Total	Payroll	Personnel
ANDREWS AIR FORCE BASE—Prince Georges County													
★ □ MALCOLM GROW U. S. AIR FORCE MEDICAL CENTER, Mailing Address Washington, D.C., Zip 20331; tel. 202/981-3001 **A**1a 3 5 **F**1 3 6 10 11 12 14 15 16 19 20 23 24 27 28 30 32 33 34 35 37 40 46 48 50 51 52 53	41	10	S		339	9191	201	61.1	26	1070	—	—	1336
ANNAPOLIS—Anne Arundel County													
★ □ ANNE ARUNDEL GENERAL HOSPITAL, Franklin & Cathedral Sts., Zip 21401; tel. 301/267-1000; Carl A. Brunetto, adm. **A**1a 2 9 10 **F**1 2 3 6 10 12 14 15 16 20 21 23 27 30 32 35 36 40 41 45 46 52 53	23	10	S		303	14201	220	72.6	35	2214	40211	20289	1125
BALTIMORE—Independent City													
★ □ BON SECOURS HOSPITAL, 2000 W. Baltimore St., Zip 21223; tel. 301/362-3000; Victor A. Broccolino, chief exec. off. & exec. vice-pres. (Nonreporting) **A**1a 9 10; **S**5085	23	10	S		202	—	—	—	—	—	—	—	—
★ □ CHILDREN'S HOSPITAL, 3825 Greenspring Ave., Zip 21211; tel. 301/462-6800; Stephen C. Loescher, chief exec. off. **A**1a 3 5 9 10 **F**1 3 16 23 24 34 44 46; **S**1755	23	49	S		106	1870	31	29.2	0	0	9682	3589	217
★ □ CHURCH HOSPITAL CORPORATION, 100 N. Broadway, Zip 21231; tel. 301/522-8000; T. Gillam Whedbee Jr., pres. **A**1a 9 10 **F**1 2 3 6 10 12 14 15 16 21 23 24 28 30 32 34 35 37 41 44 45 46 47 53	23	10	S		196	7351	160	81.6	0	0	39004	16689	865
★ DEATON HOSPITAL AND MEDICAL CENTER OF CHRIST LUTHERAN CHURCH, 611 S. Charles St., Zip 21230; tel. 301/547-8500; Noel Kroncke, chief exec. off. (Nonreporting) **A**9 10	23	48	L		230	—	—	—	—	—	—	—	—
★ □ FRANCIS SCOTT KEY MEDICAL CENTER, 4940 Eastern Ave., Zip 21224; tel. 301/955-0120; Ronald R. Peterson, pres. (Total facility includes 218 beds in nursing home-type unit) **A**1a b 3 5 8 9 10 **F**1 2 3 5 6 10 12 13 14 15 16 17 19 20 21 22 23 24 26 27 28 29 30 32 33 34 35 36 37 40 41 42 43 44 46 47 48 49 50 52 53 54; **S**1015	23	10	S	TF	602	12796	477	78.7	20	1079	77383	30738	1787
				H	384	12510	268	—	20	1079	70513	27930	1605
★ □ FRANKLIN SQUARE HOSPITAL, 9000 Franklin Square Dr., Zip 21237; tel. 301/682-7262; Michael R. Merson, pres. & chief exec. off. **A**1a b 3 5 8 9 10 **F**1 2 3 6 10 12 14 15 16 20 23 27 28 30 34 35 37 38 40 41 44 45 46 48 49 50 52 53 54	23	10	S		461	19360	337	73.1	35	3284	70299	36612	1804
★ □ Δ GOOD SAMARITAN HOSPITAL OF MARYLAND, 5601 Loch Raven Blvd., Zip 21239; tel. 301/323-2200; James A. Oakey, pres. **A**1a 3 5 7 9 10 **F**1 2 3 6 10 11 12 14 15 16 20 23 24 25 26 32 33 34 35 41 44 45 46 47 53	23	10	S		259	6217	192	74.1	0	0	35115	17856	860
★ □ GREATER BALTIMORE MEDICAL CENTER, 6701 N. Charles St., Zip 21204; tel. 301/828-2000; Robert P. Kowal, pres. **A**1a 3 5 8 9 10 **F**1 2 3 6 7 8 9 10 11 12 14 15 16 20 23 24 30 32 34 35 36 37 38 40 41 42 44 45 46 47 49 50 51 52 53 54	23	10	S		424	18475	269	63.4	40	3577	64658	32603	1433
□ GUNDRY HOSPITAL, 2 N. Wickham Rd., Zip 21229; tel. 301/644-9917; Nathan Miller, adm. (Nonreporting) **A**1a b 9 10	33	22	L		35	—	—	—	—	—	—	—	—
★ □ JAMES LAWRENCE KERNAN HOSPITAL, 2200 N. Forest Park Ave., Zip 21207; tel. 301/448-2500; William D. Currie, exec. dir. **A**1a 3 5 9 10 **F**1 3 14 16 23 24 26 34 42 45 46	23	47	S		90	1365	21	23.3	0	0	8431	3906	199
★ □ JOHNS HOPKINS HOSPITAL, 600 N. Wolfe St., Zip 21205; tel. 301/955-5000; Albert H. Owens Jr. MD, pres. **A**1a 2 3 5 8 9 10 **F**1 2 3 4 5 6 7 8 9 10 11 12 13 14 15 16 17 19 20 23 24 26 27 28 29 30 32 33 34 35 36 37 38 40 41 42 43 45 46 47 49 50 51 52 53 54; **S**1015	23	10	S		940	35293	797	86.1	36	2691	233055	103279	5123
★ □ KENNEDY INSTITUTE FOR HANDICAPPED CHILDREN, 707 N. Broadway, Zip 21205; tel. 301/522-5407; Ann A. Jones PhD, adm. **A**1a 9 10 **F**3 15 23 24 26 28 32 33 34 42 44 46	23	59	S		40	436	29	72.5	0	0	14892	8087	323
★ KESWICK-HOME FOR INCURABLES OF BALTIMORE CITY, 700 W. 40th St., Zip 21211; tel. 301/235-8860; Brooks R. Major, exec. dir. (Total facility includes 176 beds in nursing home-type unit) **A**9 10 **F**19 23 24 32 42 44 45 46 47	23	48	L	TF	216	74	214	99.1	0	0	7113	3925	291
				H	40	15	40	—	0	0	—	—	—
★ □ LEVINDALE HEBREW GERIATRIC CENTER AND HOSPITAL, 2434 W. Belvedere Ave., Zip 21215; tel. 301/466-8700; Stanford A. Alliker, pres. (Total facility includes 253 beds in nursing home-type unit) **A**1a 9 10 **F**15 16 19 21 23 24 25 32 34 42 43 44 45 46 50	23	49	L	TF	306	334	289	94.4	0	0	10303	5174	349
				H	53	274	39	—	0	0	—	—	—
★ □ LIBERTY MEDICAL CENTER, 2600 Liberty Hts. Ave., Zip 21215; tel. 301/578-2295; William L. Jews, pres. & chief exec. off. (Nonreporting) **A**1a 3 5 8 9 10	23	10	S		304	—	—	—	—	—	—	—	—
★ □ MARYLAND GENERAL HOSPITAL, 827 Linden Ave., Zip 21201; tel. 301/225-8000; James R. Wood, pres. **A**1a 3 5 6 9 10 **F**1 2 3 6 7 9 10 11 12 14 15 16 20 23 24 26 27 30 32 33 34 35 36 37 40 41 42 44 45 46 47 52 53 54	23	10	S		229	7837	156	68.1	17	1168	41197	22415	849
★ □ MERCY HOSPITAL, 301 St. Paul Pl., Zip 21202; tel. 301/332-9000; Sr. Mary Thomas, pres. **A**1a 3 5 9 10 **F**1 2 3 6 10 11 12 14 15 16 20 23 26 28 30 32 33 34 35 36 40 41 45 46 47 49 50 51 52 53 54; **S**6015	21	10	S		290	10966	219	75.5	21	1511	54254	24837	1250
★ □ Δ MONTEBELLO REHABILITATION HOSPITAL (Formerly Montebello Hospital), 2201 Argonne Dr., Zip 21218; tel. 301/554-5200; James P. G. Flynn MD, chief exec. off. **A**1a 3 7 10 **F**16 23 24 26 32 33 42 44 45 46	12	46	L		153	768	134	88.2	0	0	15676	9924	519
★ □ Δ MOUNT WASHINGTON PEDIATRIC HOSPITAL (Pediatric Post-Acute and Rehabilitation), 1708 W. Rogers Ave., Zip 21209; tel. 301/578-8600; Frank A. Pommett, pres.; Paulette Harar MD, med. dir. **A**1a 7 9 10 **F**16 23 24 26 33 41 42 44 46 47 52	23	59	L		67	205	63	94.0	0	0	8264	4495	238
★ □ NORTH CHARLES HOSPITAL (Formerly North Charles General Hospital), 2724 N. Charles St., Zip 21218; tel. 301/338-2000; Irwin P. Bloom, pres. **A**1a 9 10 **F**1 2 3 6 10 11 12 13 14 15 16 23 24 26 27 28 29 30 32 33 34 35 37 41 42 43 46 47 48 50 53 54; **S**1015	23	10	S		182	6294	137	75.3	0	0	29254	14689	663
★ □ SHEPPARD AND ENOCH PRATT HOSPITAL (Formerly Listed Under Towson), 6501 N. Charles St., Box 6815, Zip 21285; tel. 301/823-8200; Robert Gibson MD, pres. & chief exec. off. **A**1b 3 5 9 10 **F**15 24 28 29 30 32 33 34 42 43 45 46 48 49 50	23	22	L		312	1360	289	92.6	0	0	33738	18716	899
★ □ Δ SINAI HOSPITAL OF BALTIMORE, Belvedere Ave. at Greenspring, Zip 21215; tel. 301/578-5678; B. Stanley Cohen MD, pres. **A**1a 2 3 5 7 8 9 10 **F**1 2 3 5 6 7 8 9 10 11 12 14 15 16 17 20 21 23 24 25 26 27 28 29 30 32 33 34 35 36 37 38 40 41 42 44 45 46 47 49 50 51 52 53 54	23	10	S		569	18316	357	62.7	32	3998	103607	51860	2204
★ □ SOUTH BALTIMORE GENERAL HOSPITAL, 3001 S. Hanover St., Zip 21230; tel. 301/347-3200; L. Barney Johnson, pres. & chief exec. off. **A**1a 2 3 5 6 9 10 **F**1 3 6 10 12 14 15 16 23 26 30 34 35 36 40 41 44 45 46 47 49 52 53	23	10	S		324	13693	254	73.2	28	1946	46144	22603	1130
SPRING GROVE HOSPITAL CENTER, See Catonsville													
★ □ ST. AGNES HOSPITAL OF THE CITY OF BALTIMORE, 900 Caton Ave., Zip 21229; tel. 301/368-6000; Sr. Mary Louise Lyons, pres. **A**1a 2 3 5 9 10 **F**1 2 3 6 10 12 14 16 20 21 23 24 28 30 32 33 34 35 36 40 41 44 45 46 47 49 51 52 53 54; **S**1885	21	10	S		480	18804	359	74.8	38	2681	77873	39002	2021

Hospital, Address, Telephone, Administrator, Approval and Facility Codes, Multihospital System Code	Classification Codes				Inpatient Data				Newborn Data		Expense (thousands of dollars)		
★ American Hospital Association (AHA) membership □ Joint Commission on Accreditation of Hospitals (JCAH) accreditation + American Osteopathic Hospital Association (AOHA) membership ○ American Osteopathic Association (AOA) accreditation Δ Commission on Accreditation of Rehabilitation Facilities (CARF) accreditation Control codes 61, 63, 64, 71, 72 and 73 indicate hospitals listed by AOHA, but not registered by AHA. For definition of numerical codes, see page A2	Control	Service	Stay	Facilities	Beds	Admissions	Census	Occupancy (percent)	Bassinets	Births	Total	Payroll	Personnel
ST. JOSEPH HOSPITAL, See Towson													
[★] UNION MEMORIAL HOSPITAL, 201 E. University Pkwy., Zip 21218; tel. 301/554-2000; Charles D. Jenkins, pres. **A**1a 3 5 6 9 10 **F**1 2 3 5 6 9 10 11 12 14 15 16 17 20 21 23 24 26 30 34 35 36 37 40 41 44 45 46 50 52 53 54	23	10	S		383	15405	282	73.6	18	1721	68433	35127	1745
[★] UNIVERSITY OF MARYLAND MEDICAL SYSTEMS, 22 S. Greene St., Zip 21201; tel. 301/328-6294; Morton I. Rapoport MD, chief exec. off. **A**1a 2 3 5 8 9 10 **F**1 2 3 4 5 6 7 8 9 10 11 12 13 14 15 16 17 20 23 24 26 27 28 30 32 33 34 35 36 37 38 40 42 43 44 45 46 47 50 51 52 53 54	23	10	S		703	21748	539	76.7	35	1983	163083	73927	3244
[★] VETERANS ADMINISTRATION MEDICAL CENTER, 3900 Loch Raven Blvd., Zip 21218; tel. 301/467-9932; James A. Christian, dir. **A**1a 3 5 8 **F**1 2 3 6 10 12 14 15 16 21 23 26 27 28 29 30 31 32 33 34 35 38 41 42 43 46 47 48 49 50 53 54	45	10	S		265	6352	170	63.2	0	0	41646	23449	748
[★] WYMAN PARK MEDICAL CENTER (Formerly Wyman Park Health Systems), 3100 Wyman Park Dr., Zip 21211; tel. 301/338-3000; Patrick H. Mattingly MD, pres. **A**1a 3 5 9 10 **F**1 3 6 10 12 14 15 16 23 24 26 27 28 29 30 32 33 34 35 37 42 43 44 45 46 47 48 49 50; **S**1015	23	10	S		135	3849	71	52.6	0	0	29799	14257	483
BEL AIR—Harford County													
□ NEW BEGINNING AT HIDDEN BROOK, 522 Thomas Run Rd., Zip 21014; tel. 301/836-7490; Michael A. Barbieri, exec. dir. (Nonreporting) **A**1b 9; **S**1315	33	82	S		52	—	—	—	—	—	—	—	—
BETHESDA—Montgomery County													
[★] CLINICAL CENTER, NATIONAL INSTITUTES OF HEALTH (Biomedical Research), 9000 Rockville Pike, Zip 20892; tel. 301/496-4114; John L. Decker MD, dir. **A**1a 8 **F**1 2 3 4 6 7 8 9 10 11 12 14 15 16 17 23 24 26 27 34 38 42 44 46 47 53 54	44	49	S		502	8839	298	59.4	0	0	114016	51991	1973
[★] NAVAL HOSPITAL, Zip 20814; tel. 301/295-2266; Capt. E. S. Amis Jr., CO **A**1a b 2 3 5 8 **F**1 2 3 4 6 7 8 9 10 12 14 15 16 20 23 24 27 28 30 32 33 34 35 36 37 38 40 43 44 45 46 47 48 49 51 52 53 54	43	10	S		468	16160	360	75.2	12	1537	40520	12976	620
[★] SUBURBAN HOSPITAL, 8600 Old Georgetown Rd., Zip 20814; tel. 301/530-3100; Joan Finnerty, adm. **A**1a 3 5 9 10 **F**1 3 5 6 10 11 12 14 15 16 20 23 24 26 27 30 33 35 37 42 44 45 46 47 48 49 50 53 54	23	10	S		360	11335	238	63.5	0	0	45523	23372	1162
CAMBRIDGE—Dorchester County													
[★] DORCHESTER GENERAL HOSPITAL, 300 Byrn St., Box 439, Zip 21613; tel. 301/228-5511; Alan B. Malnak Jr., adm. **A**1a 9 10 **F**1 3 6 10 12 14 16 21 23 35 36 40	23	10	S		135	3304	59	43.7	13	308	10451	4660	330
□ EASTERN SHORE HOSPITAL CENTER, Box 800, Zip 21613; tel. 301/228-0800; David W. Leap, adm. **A**1b 10 **F**23 24 31 32 33 42 45 46 47	12	22	L		198	529	132	66.7	0	0	12507	8212	411
CAMP SPRINGS—Prince Georges County													
MALCOLM GROW U. S. AIR FORCE MEDICAL CENTER, See Andrews Air Force Base													
CATONSVILLE—Baltimore County													
SPRING GROVE HOSPITAL CENTER (Formerly Listed Under Baltimore), Wade Ave., Zip 21228; tel. 301/455-7181; Bruce L. Regan MD, supt. (Nonreporting) **A**3 5	12	22	L		541	—	—	—	—	—	—	—	—
CHESTERTOWN—Kent County													
[★] KENT AND QUEEN ANNE'S HOSPITAL, Brown St., Zip 21620; tel. 301/778-3300; William R. Kirk, chief exec. off. **A**1a 9 10 **F**1 3 6 10 12 14 15 16 23 30 35 36 37 40 45 46 52	23	10	S		86	3368	46	53.5	6	202	7071	3353	206
CHEVERLY—Prince Georges County													
[★] PRINCE GEORGE'S HOSPITAL CENTER (Formerly Prince George's General Hospital and Medical Center), One Hospital Dr., Zip 20785; tel. 301/341-3300; Richard Graham, chief exec. off. (Total facility includes 100 beds in nursing home-type unit) **A**1a 3 5 9 10 **F**1 2 3 5 6 10 12 14 15 16 19 20 23 24 26 27 28 30 32 34 35 36 37 40 42 44 45 46 47 48 50 52 53; **S**1755	23	10	S	TF	558	17546	443	75.6	48	3222	75882	36867	1248
				H	458	17435	345	—	48	3222	73159	35242	1184
CLINTON—Prince Georges County													
CLINTON COMMUNITY HOSPITAL, See Parkwood Hospital													
□ PARKWOOD HOSPITAL (Formerly Clinton Community Hospital), 8910 Woodyard Rd., Zip 20735; tel. 301/868-2700; May Sarmiento RN, adm. (Nonreporting) **A**1a 9 10	33	10	S		33	—	—	—	—	—	—	—	—
[★] SOUTHERN MARYLAND HOSPITAL, 7503 Surratts Rd., Zip 20735; tel. 301/868-8000; Francis P. Chiaramonte MD, chief exec. off. **A**1a 9 10 **F**1 2 3 5 6 7 8 9 10 11 12 14 15 16 20 23 24 27 30 32 33 34 35 36 40 41 42 44 46 47 49 50 52 53	33	10	S		308	13931	283	91.9	16	1532	48306	18176	1046
COLUMBIA—Howard County													
[★] HOWARD COUNTY GENERAL HOSPITAL, 5755 Cedar Lane, Zip 21044; tel. 301/740-7890; Donald J. Jacobs, pres. **A**1a 9 10 **F**1 3 6 10 12 14 15 16 23 24 27 30 32 34 35 36 37 42 45 46 50 53	23	10	S		173	9099	148	85.5	21	1644	28980	12727	694
CRISFIELD—Somerset County													
[★] EDWARD W. MCCREADY MEMORIAL HOSPITAL (Includes Alice Byrd Tawes Nursing Home), 201 Hall Hwy., Zip 21817; tel. 301/968-1200; Rod Williams, adm. (Nonreporting) **A**1a 9 10	23	10	S		104	—	—	—	—	—	—	—	—
CROWNSVILLE—Anne Arundel County													
□ CROWNSVILLE HOSPITAL CENTER, Zip 21032; tel. 301/987-6200; Denise E. Holland MD, clin. dir. (Nonreporting) **A** 1b 10	12	22	L		535	—	—	—	—	—	—	—	—
CUMBERLAND—Allegany County													
[★] MEMORIAL HOSPITAL, Memorial Ave., Zip 21502; tel. 301/777-4000; Donald C. McAneny, pres. **A**1a 9 10 **F**1 3 5 6 9 10 12 14 15 16 19 20 23 24 26 30 32 33 34 35 36 37 40 41 44 45 46 52 53 54	23	10	S		247	9062	165	66.8	17	751	31356	14557	735
[★] SACRED HEART HOSPITAL, 900 Seton Dr., Zip 21502; tel. 301/759-4200; Sr. Cecilia Rose, pres. **A**1a 2 9 10 **F**1 3 6 7 8 9 10 11 12 14 15 16 20 21 23 24 26 27 30 34 35 36 37 40 41 42 44 45 46 49 52 53; **S**1885	21	10	S		240	8658	172	71.7	16	640	27446	14213	803
□ THOMAS B. FINAN CENTER, Country Club Rd., Box 1722, Zip 21502; tel. 301/777-2200; Robert R. Grooms PhD, dir. (Nonreporting) **A**1b 10	12	22	L		166	—	—	—	—	—	—	—	—
EAST NEW MARKET—Dorchester County													
[★] NEW BEGINNINGS-WARWICK MANOR, Rte. 1, Box 178, Zip 21631; tel. 301/943-8108; Breck Stringer, exec. dir. (Nonreporting) **A**1b ; **S**1315	33	82	L		39	—	—	—	—	—	—	—	—
EASTON—Talbot County													
[★] MEMORIAL HOSPITAL AT EASTON MARYLAND, 219 S. Washington St., Zip 21601; tel. 301/822-1000; Nick Rajacich, pres. (Total facility includes 33 beds in nursing home-type unit) **A**1a 6 9 10 **F**1 3 6 7 10 11 12 14 15 16 19 20 23 24 26 32 33 34 35 36 40 44 45 46 47 48 50 52 53	23	10	S	TF	213	8477	180	84.5	24	985	27083	12948	727
				H	180	8359	150	—	24	985	—	—	708
ELKTON—Cecil County													
[★] UNION HOSPITAL OF CECIL COUNTY, Bow St., Zip 21921; tel. 301/398-4000; David W. Grupenhoff, adm. **A**1a 9 10 **F**1 3 6 10 12 15 16 23 24 28 30 32 33 35 36 40 44 45 46 48 49 52 53	23	10	S		142	6212	93	57.1	14	402	17059	9251	501
ELLICOTT CITY—Howard County													
□ TAYLOR MANOR HOSPITAL, College Ave., Box 396, Zip 21043; tel. 301/465-3322; Morris L. Scherr, adm. **A**1b 9 **F**15 24 28 29 32 33 34 42 46 47 48 49	33	22	L		166	720	125	78.6	0	0	—	—	284

Hospital, Address, Telephone, Administrator, Approval and Facility Codes, Multihospital System Code	Classification Codes				Inpatient Data				Newborn Data		Expense (thousands of dollars)		
★ American Hospital Association (AHA) membership □ Joint Commission on Accreditation of Hospitals (JCAH) accreditation + American Osteopathic Hospital Association (AOHA) membership ○ American Osteopathic Association (AOA) accreditation Δ Commission on Accreditation of Rehabilitation Facilities (CARF) accreditation Control codes 61, 63, 64, 71, 72 and 73 indicate hospitals listed by AOHA, but not registered by AHA. For definition of numerical codes, see page A2	Control	Service	Stay	Facilities	Beds	Admissions	Census	Occupancy (percent)	Bassinets	Births	Total	Payroll	Personnel
EMMITSBURG—Frederick County													
MOUNTAIN MANOR TREATMENT CENTER FOR ALCOHOLISM, Rte. 15, Box 126, Zip 21727; tel. 301/447-2361; Bernard McMonigle, dir. (Nonreporting)	33	82	S		80	—	—	—	—	—	—	—	—
FALLSTON—Harford County													
★□ FALLSTON GENERAL HOSPITAL, 200 Milton Ave., Zip 21047; tel. 301/877-3700; Chester L. Price, pres. & chief exec. off. (Nonreporting) **A**1a 9 10	33	10	S		219	—	—	—	—	—	—	—	—
FORT GEORGE G. MEADE—Anne Arundel County													
★□ KIMBROUGH ARMY COMMUNITY HOSPITAL, Zip 20755; tel. 301/677-4171; Col. Robert B. McLean, CO; Col. Edward H. Uemura, dep. cmdr. adm. (Nonreporting) **A**1a	42	10	S		52	—	—	—	—	—	—	—	—
FORT HOWARD—Baltimore County													
★□ VETERANS ADMINISTRATION MEDICAL CENTER, Zip 21052; tel. 301/477-1800; Philip S. Elkins, dir. (Total facility includes 47 beds in nursing home-type unit) **A**1a b 3 5 **F**1 3 6 10 14 15 16 19 20 23 24 25 26 28 32 33 34 35 42 44 46 47 48 49 50	45	49	L	TF	262	2016	217	82.8	0	0	19593	13944	477
				H	215	2004	172	—	0	0	—	—	460
FREDERICK—Frederick County													
★□ FREDERICK MEMORIAL HOSPITAL, 400 W. Seventh St., Zip 21701; tel. 301/698-3300; James K. Kluttz, pres. **A**1a 2 9 10 **F**1 3 6 10 11 12 14 15 16 20 23 24 26 30 32 33 35 36 37 39 40 41 44 45 46 47 52 53	23	10	S		187	10091	151	80.7	32	1440	27821	13583	799
FROSTBURG—Allegany County													
★□ FROSTBURG COMMUNITY HOSPITAL, 48 Tarn Terr., Zip 21532; tel. 301/689-3411; G. William Udovich, adm. **A**1a 9 10 **F**1 3 6 15 16 23 24 30 34 35 44 45 46 47	23	10	S		50	1165	22	44.0	0	0	3925	1799	105
GLEN BURNIE—Anne Arundel County													
★□ NORTH ARUNDEL HOSPITAL, 301 Hospital Dr., Zip 21061; tel. 301/787-4000; Alfred J. Bryan Jr., exec. dir. **A**1a 9 10 **F**1 2 3 6 9 10 11 12 14 15 16 23 32 34 35 41 45 46 48 49 52 53 54	23	10	S		329	12786	239	72.6	0	0	36889	18624	914
HAGERSTOWN—Washington County													
□ BROOK LANE PSYCHIATRIC CENTER, Box 1945, Zip 21742; tel. 301/733-0330; David F. Rutherford, exec. dir. (Nonreporting) **A**1b 9 10	23	22	L		40	—	—	—	—	—	—	—	—
★□ WASHINGTON COUNTY HOSPITAL, 251 E. Antietam St., Zip 21740; tel. 301/824-8000; H. W. Murphy, pres. **A**1a 9 10 **F**1 3 5 6 7 8 9 10 11 12 14 15 16 20 21 23 24 27 28 30 33 34 35 36 40 41 44 45 46 48 49 50 52 53	23	10	S		277	12886	210	75.8	41	1493	45523	22102	1171
□ WESTERN MARYLAND CENTER, 1500 Pennsylvania Ave., Zip 21740; tel. 301/791-4410; Carl A. Fischer MD, dir. (Total facility includes 58 beds in nursing home-type unit) **A**1a 9 10 **F**3 12 16 19 20 23 24 25 26 34 42 43 44 45 46 47	12	48	L	TF	175	248	162	92.6	0	0	10848	6523	356
				H	117	242	108	—	0	0	9783	5740	318
HAVRE DE GRACE—Harford County													
★□ HARFORD MEMORIAL HOSPITAL, 501 S. Union Ave., Zip 21078; tel. 301/939-2400; Leonard E. Cantrell Jr., pres. & chief exec. off. **A**1a 9 10 **F**1 2 3 6 10 12 14 16 20 23 32 35 36 40 45 46 52 53 54	23	10	S		205	7574	105	51.2	32	878	20160	9281	479
JESSUP—Howard County													
□ CLIFTON T. PERKINS HOSPITAL CENTER, Dorsey Run Rd., Zip 20794; tel. 301/792-4022; Stuart B. Silver MD, supt. (Nonreporting) **A**1b	12	22	L		246	—	—	—	—	—	—	—	—
LA PLATA—Charles County													
★□ PHYSICIANS MEMORIAL HOSPITAL, 701 E. Charles St., Zip 20646; tel. 301/645-0100; Robert T. Jetland, adm. **A**1a 9 10 **F**1 3 6 10 12 14 16 20 23 35 36 40 45 46 52 53	23	10	S		98	5046	77	78.6	12	461	14080	6428	329
LANHAM—Prince Georges County													
★□ AMI DOCTORS' HOSPITAL (Formerly Doctors' Hospital of Prince George's County), 8118 Good Luck Rd., Zip 20706; tel. 301/552-9400; Phil Down, exec. dir. **A**1a 9 10 **F**1 2 3 6 10 15 16 20 23 24 35 41 46 53; **S**0125	33	10	S		250	9832	199	79.6	0	0	41934	16272	615
LAUREL—Prince Georges County													
★□ GREATER LAUREL BELTSVILLE HOSPITAL, 7100 Contee Rd., Zip 20707; tel. 301/725-4300; Gary M. Stein, adm. **A**1a 9 10 **F**1 2 3 6 10 12 14 15 16 21 23 24 26 27 29 30 32 33 34 35 37 44 45 46 48 49 53; **S**1755	23	10	S		180	5547	120	66.7	0	0	21675	10165	409
LEONARDTOWN—St. Marys County													
★□ ST. MARY'S HOSPITAL, 234 Jefferson St., P O Box 527, Zip 20650; tel. 301/475-8981; Peter B. Lambert, adm. **A**1a 9 10 **F**1 3 6 10 12 14 15 16 21 23 30 34 35 37 40 46 47 52 53	23	10	S		114	4672	71	62.3	16	585	12486	5480	285
OAKLAND—Garrett County													
★□ GARRETT COUNTY MEMORIAL HOSPITAL, 251 N. Fourth St., Zip 21550; tel. 301/334-2155; Larry M. Beck, pres. **A**1a 9 10 **F**1 3 6 10 14 15 16 21 23 35 36 40 41 45 46 52	23	10	S		76	3361	53	69.7	12	368	8970	4007	239
OLNEY—Montgomery County													
★□ MONTGOMERY GENERAL HOSPITAL, 18101 Prince Philip Dr., Zip 20832; tel. 301/774-7800; Frank R. Gabor, pres. **A**1a 2 9 10 **F**1 2 3 6 10 12 14 15 16 20 23 24 27 28 30 32 33 35 36 40 42 44 46 47 48 49 52	23	10	S		229	7797	135	61.4	18	979	27708	14557	692
PATUXENT RIVER—St. Marys County													
★□ NAVAL HOSPITAL, Zip 20670; tel. 301/863-1460 **A**1a **F**1 12 14 15 23 33 34 35 46 47	43	10	S		13	1033	9	39.1	0	235	3004	—	210
PERRY POINT—Cecil County													
★□ VETERANS ADMINISTRATION MEDICAL CENTER, Zip 21902; tel. 301/642-2411; Barbara L. Gallagher, dir. (Nonreporting) **A**1a	45	22	L		853	—	—	—	—	—	—	—	—
PRINCE FREDERICK—Calvert County													
★□ CALVERT MEMORIAL HOSPITAL, Rte. 4, Zip 20678; tel. 301/535-4000; Constance F. Row, pres. **A**1a 9 10 **F**1 3 6 12 14 15 16 23 24 26 27 30 32 33 34 35 36 37 40 42 45 46 52	23	10	S		130	5280	87	69.6	12	567	14779	7075	367
RANDALLSTOWN—Baltimore County													
★□ BALTIMORE COUNTY GENERAL HOSPITAL, 5401 Old Court Rd., Zip 21133; tel. 301/521-2200; Robert W. Fischer, exec. vice-pres. **A**1a 9 10 **F**1 3 6 10 12 14 15 16 20 23 29 30 32 35 37 45 46 47 50 53	23	10	S		220	9017	191	86.8	0	0	34706	16340	849
RIVERDALE—Prince Georges County													
★□ LELAND MEMORIAL HOSPITAL, 4401 E.-W. Hwy., Zip 20737; tel. 301/699-2000; Charley O. Eldridge, pres. **A**1a 9 10 **F**1 3 6 10 12 14 15 16 23 24 26 27 30 32 35 42 45 46 53; **S**9355	21	10	S		120	3363	89	69.5	0	0	16042	6686	329
ROCKVILLE—Montgomery County													
★□ CHESTNUT LODGE HOSPITAL (Formerly Chestnut Lodge), 500 W. Montgomery Ave., Zip 20850; tel. 301/424-8300; Dexter M. Bullard Jr. MD, med. dir. & pres. **A**1a 3 **F**24 26 28 29 32 33 34 42 43	33	22	L		117	64	107	91.5	0	0	12374	7601	280
□ PSYCHIATRIC INSTITUTE OF MONTGOMERY COUNTY, 14901 Broschart Rd., Zip 20850; tel. 301/251-4500; John Meeks MD, chief exec. off. (Nonreporting) **A**1b 9 10; **S**0825	33	22	L		75	—	—	—	—	—	—	—	—
★□ SHADY GROVE ADVENTIST HOSPITAL, 9901 Medical Center Dr., Zip 20850; tel. 301/279-6000; Bryan L. Breckenridge, pres. **A**1a 9 10 **F**1 3 6 10 12 14 15 16 19 20 23 24 34 35 36 37 40 43 44 45 46 47 52 53; **S**9355	21	10	S		224	11658	158	70.5	22	2772	40567	17593	925

Hospital, Address, Telephone, Administrator, Approval and Facility Codes, Multihospital System Code	Classification Codes				Inpatient Data				Newborn Data		Expense (thousands of dollars)		
★ American Hospital Association (AHA) membership □ Joint Commission on Accreditation of Hospitals (JCAH) accreditation + American Osteopathic Hospital Association (AOHA) membership ○ American Osteopathic Association (AOA) accreditation Δ Commission on Accreditation of Rehabilitation Facilities (CARF) accreditation Control codes 61, 63, 64, 71, 72 and 73 indicate hospitals listed by AOHA, but not registered by AHA. For definition of numerical codes, see page A2	Control	Service	Stay	Facilities	Beds	Admissions	Census	Occupancy (percent)	Bassinets	Births	Total	Payroll	Personnel
SALISBURY—Wicomico County													
□ DEER'S HEAD CENTER, Box 2018, Zip 21801; tel. 301/543-4000; Edward G. Phoebus, dir. (Total facility includes 14 beds in nursing home-type unit) **A**1a 10 **F**15 16 19 20 21 23 24 25 26 32 33 42 44 45 46 47	12	48	L	TF	137	407	132	91.7	0	0	9858	6162	303
				H	123	407	112	—	0	0	9451	5855	287
★□ PENINSULA GENERAL HOSPITAL MEDICAL CENTER, 100 E. Carroll St., Zip 21801; tel. 301/546-6400; John B. Stevens Jr., pres. **A**1a 2 9 10 **F**1 2 3 4 5 6 7 8 9 10 12 14 15 16 20 23 30 33 34 35 36 40 43 45 46 47 49 50 52 53 54	23	10	S		368	18067	314	87.2	28	2026	50671	22002	1368
SILVER SPRING—Montgomery County													
★□ HOLY CROSS HOSPITAL OF SILVER SPRING, 1500 Forest Glen Rd., Zip 20910; tel. 301/565-0100; Sr. Jean Louise, pres. **A**1a 3 5 8 9 10 **F**1 6 10 12 14 15 16 17 20 21 23 24 26 29 30 32 34 35 36 41 42 44 45 46 47 53; **S**5585	21	10	S		460	19936	319	69.3	40	4532	64706	28616	1940
SYKESVILLE—Carroll County													
SPRINGFIELD HOSPITAL CENTER, Zip 21784; tel. 301/795-2100; Bruce Hershfield MD, actg. supt. **A**3 5 10 **F**12 15 16 23 24 30 31 32 33 37 42 45 46 47 50	12	22	L		1023	1995	908	91.9	0	0	46686	39561	1511
TAKOMA PARK—Montgomery County													
★□ WASHINGTON ADVENTIST HOSPITAL, 7600 Carroll Ave., Zip 20912; tel. 301/891-7600; Ronald D. Marx, pres. **A**1a 2 9 10 **F**1 3 4 6 7 8 9 10 11 12 14 15 16 20 23 24 26 27 29 33 35 36 37 40 42 44 45 46 47 48 49 50 53 54; **S**9355	21	10	S		300	12637	246	82.0	34	2087	56684	23810	1115
TOWSON—Baltimore County													
SHEPPARD AND ENOCH PRATT HOSPITAL, See Baltimore													
★□ ST. JOSEPH HOSPITAL (Formerly Listed Under Baltimore), 7620 York Rd., Zip 21204; tel. 301/337-1000; Sr. Marie Cecilia Irwin, pres. & chief exec. off. **A**1a 6 9 10 **F**1 2 3 4 6 15 16 20 21 23 24 27 34 35 36 37 40 41 44 45 46 48 49 52 53 54; **S**5325	21	10	S		349	16450	310	88.8	20	1712	67703	33981	1508
WESTMINSTER—Carroll County													
★□ CARROLL COUNTY GENERAL HOSPITAL, Memorial Ave., Zip 21157; tel. 301/848-3000; Charles R. Graf, exec. vice-pres. **A**1a 9 10 **F**1 2 3 6 10 12 14 15 16 23 26 30 35 36 45 46 52 53	23	10	S		159	5943	89	56.0	15	708	17661	8888	506

Hospital, Address, Telephone, Administrator, Approval and Facility Codes, Multihospital System Code

- ★ American Hospital Association (AHA) membership
- □ Joint Commission on Accreditation of Hospitals (JCAH) accreditation
- \+ American Osteopathic Hospital Association (AOHA) membership
- ○ American Osteopathic Association (AOA) accreditation
- Δ Commission on Accreditation of Rehabilitation Facilities (CARF) accreditation

Control codes 61, 63, 64, 71, 72 and 73 indicate hospitals listed by AOHA, but not registered by AHA. For definition of numerical codes, see page A2

Massachusetts

Hospital, Address, Telephone, Administrator, Approval and Facility Codes, Multihospital System Code	Classification Codes				Inpatient Data				Newborn Data		Expense (thousands of dollars)		
	Control	Service	Stay	Facilities	Beds	Admissions	Census	Occupancy (percent)	Bassinets	Births	Total	Payroll	Personnel
AMESBURY—Essex County													
★□ AMESBURY HOSPITAL, Morrill Pl., Zip 01913; tel. 617/388-5060; Robert Ponticelli, adm. **A**1a 9 10 **F**1 3 6 10 14 15 16 23 24 26 28 29 30 32 33 34 35 44 45 46 47 50 52	14	10	S		63	1971	38	60.3	0	0	7501	3562	174
AMHERST—Hampshire County													
□ UNIVERSITY HEALTH SERVICES, University of Massachusetts, Zip 01003; tel. 413/549-2671; David P. Kraft MD, exec. dir. (Nonreporting) **A**1a 10	12	11	S		24	—	—	—	—	—	—	—	—
ANDOVER—Essex County													
ISHAM INFIRMARY, Phillips Academy, Zip 01810; tel. 617/475-3400; E. Coolidge-Stolz, adm. (Data for 235 days) **F**15 33 34 37	23	11	S		20	633	5	25.0	0	0	—	—	25
ARLINGTON—Middlesex County													
SYMMES HOSPITAL, See Choate-Symmes Hospitals, Woburn													
ASHBURNHAM—Worcester County													
NAUKEAG HOSPITAL, 216 Lake Rd., Zip 01430; tel. 617/827-5115; James W. Murphy, exec. dir. (Nonreporting)	33	82	S		26	—	—	—	—	—	—	—	—
ATHOL—Worcester County													
★□ ATHOL MEMORIAL HOSPITAL, 2033 Main St., Zip 01331; tel. 617/249-3511; William Difederico, pres. (Nonreporting) **A**1a 9 10; **S**1755	23	10	S		81	—	—	—	—	—	—	—	—
ATTLEBORO—Bristol County													
★□ STURDY MEMORIAL HOSPITAL, 211 Park St., Zip 02703; tel. 617/222-5200; Linda Shyavitz, pres. & chief exec. off. **A**1a 9 10 **F**1 3 6 10 12 14 15 16 23 35 36 40 45 46 47 52 53	23	10	S		176	7572	138	68.7	28	1029	25950	14805	669
AYER—Middlesex County													
★□ NASHOBA COMMUNITY HOSPITAL, 200 Groton Rd., Zip 01432; tel. 617/772-0200; Roland E. Larson, pres. & chief exec. off. **A**1a 9 10 **F**1 3 6 10 12 14 15 16 20 23 26 28 30 32 34 35 37 43 44 45 46 52 53	23	10	S		102	3287	55	53.9	0	0	13444	6498	317
BALDWINVILLE—Worcester County													
TEMPLETON COLONY, See Walter E. Fernald State School, Waltham													
BEDFORD—Middlesex County													
★□ EDITH NOURSE ROGERS MEMORIAL VETERANS HOSPITAL, 200 Springs Rd., Zip 01730; tel. 617/275-7500; Michael J. Kane, dir. (Total facility includes 162 beds in nursing home-type unit) **A**1a 3 5 **F**1 3 6 10 12 14 15 16 19 23 24 26 28 29 30 31 33 34 35 41 42 43 44 45 46 47 48 49 50	45	22	L	TF	895	3267	820	91.6	0	0	49299	32968	1288
				H	733	3191	669	—	0	0	41971	28023	1226
BELMONT—Middlesex County													
★□ MCLEAN HOSPITAL, 115 Mill St., Zip 02178; tel. 617/855-2000; Francis De Marneffe MD, gen. dir. **A**1a 3 5 8 9 10 **F**23 24 26 28 30 32 33 34 42 45 46 47 49	23	22	L		328	1352	293	89.3	0	0	58820	34539	1386
BEVERLY—Essex County													
★□ BEVERLY HOSPITAL, Herrick St., Zip 01915; tel. 617/922-3000; Robert R. Fanning Jr., pres. **A**1a 2 9 10 **F**1 2 3 6 10 12 14 15 16 20 23 24 26 27 28 30 32 33 34 35 36 37 40 42 44 45 46 50 52 53	23	10	S		238	8210	171	71.8	16	1416	39344	21880	826
BOSTON—Suffolk County													
★□ BETH ISRAEL HOSPITAL, 330 Brookline Ave., Zip 02215; tel. 617/735-2000; Mitchell T. Rabkin MD, pres. **A**1a 3 5 8 9 10 **F**1 2 3 4 5 6 7 8 9 10 11 12 13 14 15 16 18 20 23 24 26 27 28 30 32 33 34 35 36 37 40 41 44 45 46 50 53 54	23	10	S		472	20831	416	90.0	42	4490	172205	67939	3668
□ BOSTON CITY HOSPITAL, 818 Harrison Ave., Zip 02118; tel. 617/424-5000; Lewis W. Pollack, comr. **A**1a 2 3 5 9 10 **F**1 2 3 5 6 9 10 11 12 14 15 16 19 20 23 24 26 28 30 33 34 35 37 38 40 42 44 46 49 50 51 52 53; **S**6995	14	10	S		391	15041	277	70.8	18	1738	117749	53336	2661
BOSTON HOSPITAL FOR WOMEN, See Brigham and Women's Hospital													
★□ BRIGHAM AND WOMEN'S HOSPITAL (Includes Boston Hospital for Women; Peter Bent Brigham Hospital; Robert B. Brigham Hospital), 75 Francis St., Zip 02115; tel. 617/732-5500; H. Richard Nesson MD, pres. **A**1a 2 3 5 8 10 **F**1 2 3 4 5 6 7 8 9 11 12 13 14 15 16 17 20 22 23 24 26 30 32 34 35 36 37 38 40 44 45 46 47 49 50 51 53 54	23	10	S		720	32154	597	82.9	89	9844	240380	103161	5601
★□ CARNEY HOSPITAL, 2100 Dorchester Ave., Dorchester, Zip 02124; tel. 617/296-4000; John W. Logue, pres. **A**1a 2 3 5 8 9 10 **F**1 2 3 6 10 11 12 14 15 16 20 23 24 27 28 30 32 33 34 35 42 43 44 45 46 47 49 50 52 53 54; **S**1885	21	10	S		416	10012	270	64.4	0	0	63577	32683	1402
★□ CHILDREN'S HOSPITAL, 300 Longwood Ave., Zip 02115; tel. 617/735-6000; David S. Weiner, pres. & dir. **A**1a 2 3 5 8 9 **F**1 4 5 6 10 12 13 14 15 16 20 23 24 28 30 32 33 34 35 37 38 42 44 45 46 47 51 53 54	23	50	S		339	13801	266	78.5	0	0	177515	84877	3155
★□ DANA-FARBER CANCER INSTITUTE, 44 Binney St., Zip 02115; tel. 617/732-3000; John W. Pettit, chief adm. off. (Nonreporting) **A**1a 3 8 10	23	49	S		57	—	—	—	—	—	—	—	—
DORCHESTER MENTAL HEALTH CENTER, 591 Morton St., Dorchester, Zip 02124; tel. 617/436-6000; Lawrence D. Art, actg. area dir. (Nonreporting) **A**9	12	22	L		50	—	—	—	—	—	—	—	—
★□ FAULKNER HOSPITAL, 1153 Centre St., Jamaica Plain, Zip 02130; tel. 617/522-5800; Elaine S. Ullian, pres. **A**1a 2 3 5 8 9 10 **F**1 2 3 6 10 12 14 15 16 20 23 24 26 27 28 29 30 32 33 34 35 42 43 44 45 46 47 49 53	23	10	S		259	7366	177	68.3	0	0	44894	20296	908
★□ HAHNEMANN HOSPITAL, 1515 Commonwealth Ave., Brighton, Zip 02135; tel. 617/254-1100; Joanna B. Kennedy, chief exec. off. **A**1a 9 10 **F**1 6 14 15 16 24 30 32 33 34 46 47 50; **S**0215	23	10	S		65	1808	44	67.7	0	0	7684	3454	167
★□ HEBREW REHABILITATION CENTER FOR AGED, 1200 Centre St., Roslindale, Zip 02131; tel. 617/325-8000; Maurice I. May, chief exec. off. **A**1a 10 **F**16 23 24 32 42 45 46 47 50	23	48	L		725	153	703	97.0	0	0	24429	13983	667
★□ JEWISH MEMORIAL HOSPITAL, 59 Townsend St., Zip 02119; tel. 617/442-8760; Stanley M. Fertel, exec. dir. **A**1a 9 10 **F**15 16 19 23 24 26 32 33 34 41 42 44 45 46 47 50	23	49	L		207	354	174	84.1	0	0	14835	8802	422
★□ Δ JOSEPH P. KENNEDY JR. MEMORIAL HOSPITAL (Children's General Medical and Surgical and Rehabilitation), 30 Warren St., Brighton, Zip 02135; tel. 617/254-3800; Sr. Mary Ann Loughlin, pres. **A**1a 7 9 10 **F**1 6 14 15 16 23 24 25 26 29 32 33 34 35 38 42 44 47 52	21	59	S		100	713	62	62.0	0	0	14514	9042	432
□ LEMUEL SHATTUCK HOSPITAL, 170 Morton St., Jamaica Plain, Zip 02130; tel. 617/522-8110; Ira G. Shimp, exec. dir. (Nonreporting) **A**1a 3 5 9 10	12	10	L		252	—	—	—	—	—	—	—	—
□ LONG ISLAND HOSPITAL (Formerly Listed Under Quincy), Boston Harbor, Zip 02169; tel. 617/328-1371; Meribah Stanton, dir. **A**1a 9 10 **F**12 16 23 24 32 42 44 45 46; **S**6995	14	48	L		193	156	184	95.3	0	0	—	—	384

Hospital, Address, Telephone, Administrator, Approval and Facility Codes, Multihospital System Code

- ★ American Hospital Association (AHA) membership
- ☐ Joint Commission on Accreditation of Hospitals (JCAH) accreditation
- \+ American Osteopathic Hospital Association (AOHA) membership
- ○ American Osteopathic Association (AOA) accreditation
- Δ Commission on Accreditation of Rehabilitation Facilities (CARF) accreditation

Control codes 61, 63, 64, 71, 72 and 73 indicate hospitals listed by AOHA, but not registered by AHA. For definition of numerical codes, see page A2

Hospital	Classification Codes: Control	Service	Stay	Facilities	Inpatient Data: Beds	Admissions	Census	Occupancy (percent)	Newborn Data: Bassinets	Births	Expense (thousands of dollars): Total	Payroll	Personnel
[★] MASSACHUSETTS EYE AND EAR INFIRMARY, 243 Charles St., Zip 02114; tel. 617/523-7900; Ephraim Friedman MD, pres. **A**1a 3 5 8 9 10 **F**1 5 6 12 13 15 26 34 35 38 44 46 53	23	45	S		174	9720	93	53.4	0	0	46689	21959	1099
[★] MASSACHUSETTS GENERAL HOSPITAL (Includes Vincent Memorial Hospital), 32 Fruit St., Zip 02114; tel. 617/726-2000; J. Robert Buchanan MD, dir. **A**1a 2 3 5 8 9 10 **F**1 2 3 4 5 6 7 8 9 10 11 12 13 14 15 16 17 20 22 23 24 26 27 28 30 32 33 34 35 37 38 39 42 43 44 45 46 47 49 51 52 53 54	23	10	S		1082	34116	860	79.5	0	0	309899	147647	6200
★ MASSACHUSETTS MENTAL HEALTH CENTER, 74 Fenwood Rd., Zip 02115; tel. 617/734-1300; Miles F. Shore MD, supt. (Nonreporting) **A**3 5	12	22	S		35	—	—	—	—	—	—	—	—
○ + MASSACHUSETTS OSTEOPATHIC HOSPITAL AND MEDICAL CENTER, 222 S. Huntington Ave., Jamaica Plain, Zip 02130; tel. 617/522-4300; William J. Trifone, adm. **A**9 10 11 12 **F**1 6 12 14 15 16 23 24 26 28 29 32 33 34 39 44 49 50	63	10	S		63	952	21	32.3	0	0	6352	2992	151
[★] MATTAPAN HOSPITAL, 249 River St., Zip 02126; tel. 617/298-7900; Katherine K. Domoto MD, med. dir. (Nonreporting) **A**1a 9 10; **S**6995	14	48	L		165	—	—	—	—	—	—	—	—
[★] NEW ENGLAND BAPTIST HOSPITAL, 91 Parker Hill Ave., Zip 02120; tel. 617/738-5800; Raymond C. McAfoose, pres. **A**1a 3 5 6 9 10 **F**1 3 6 10 14 16 20 23 24 26 34 45 46 53 54	23	10	S		245	6692	160	65.3	0	0	45185	21682	968
[★] NEW ENGLAND DEACONESS HOSPITAL, 185 Pilgrim Rd., Zip 02215; tel. 617/732-7000; Laurens MacLure, pres. **A**1a 2 3 5 6 8 9 10 **F**1 2 3 4 6 7 8 9 10 11 12 13 14 15 16 20 23 24 26 27 28 32 33 34 41 42 43 45 46 47 53 54	23	10	S		489	13916	387	79.1	0	0	128997	59212	2544
[★] Δ NEW ENGLAND MEDICAL CENTER, 750 Washington St., Zip 02111; tel. 617/956-5000; Jerome H. Grossman MD, chm. & chief exec. off. **A**1a 3 5 7 8 9 10 **F**1 2 3 4 5 6 7 8 9 10 11 12 13 14 15 16 17 23 24 25 26 27 28 29 30 31 32 33 34 35 37 38 42 43 44 46 47 49 51 52 53 54	23	10	S		453	15367	393	89.5	0	0	178748	64065	2517
[★] SHRINERS BURNS INSTITUTE, 51 Blossom St., Zip 02114; tel. 617/722-3000; Salvatore P. Russo PhD, adm. **A**1a **F**15 22 23 24 33 34 42 46 47; **S**4125	23	59	S		30	584	17	56.7	0	0	—	—	198
[★] Δ SPAULDING REHABILITATION HOSPITAL, 125 Nashua St., Zip 02114; tel. 617/720-6400; Manuel J. Lipson MD, exec. dir. **A**1a 7 9 10 **F**1 6 7 15 16 23 24 26 28 31 32 33 34 41 42 44 45 46 47 48 49 52	23	46	L		284	3111	265	93.3	0	0	—	—	855
[★] ST. ELIZABETH'S HOSPITAL OF BOSTON, 736 Cambridge St., Brighton, Zip 02135; tel. 617/789-3000; William J. Skerry, pres. **A**1a 2 3 5 6 8 9 10 **F**1 2 3 4 5 6 7 8 10 11 12 14 15 16 20 23 24 26 27 28 30 32 33 34 35 36 40 41 42 43 45 46 47 48 49 52 53 54	21	10	S		385	12771	281	73.0	30	1061	93146	43895	1767
[★] ST. JOHN OF GOD HOSPITAL, 296 Allston St., 296 Allston St., Brighton, Zip 02146; tel. 617/277-5750; Sr. Clarisse Correia, pres. **A**1a 9 10 **F**16 23 24 29 30 32 33 42 44 45 46 47 50	21	48	L		64	170	60	93.8	0	0	5982	2972	138
[★] ST. MARGARET'S HOSPITAL FOR WOMEN, 90 Cushing Ave., Dorchester, Zip 02125: tel. 617/436-8600; Linda B. Caliga, pres. **A**1a 3 5 8 9 10 **F**1 6 12 14 15 16 23 34 36 40 45 46 47 51	21	44	S		152	6239	98	64.5	49	3706	24799	13162	561
[★] THE ARBOUR, 49 Robinwood Ave., Jamaica Plain, Zip 02130; tel. 617/522-4400; Roy A. Ettlinger, chief exec. off. **A**1b 9 10 **F**15 24 28 29 32 33 42 47; **S**9555	33	22	S		118	2131	108	91.5	0	0	12167	5515	235
[★] UNIVERSITY HOSPITAL, 75 E. Newton St., Zip 02118; tel. 617/638-8000; J. Scott Abercrombie Jr. MD, pres. **A**1a 2 3 5 8 9 10 **F**1 2 3 4 5 6 7 8 9 10 11 12 13 14 15 16 17 20 23 24 26 27 28 29 30 32 33 34 35 37 41 42 43 44 45 46 50 53 54	23	10	S		379	9639	300	79.2	0	0	93640	45221	1449
[★] VETERANS ADMINISTRATION MEDICAL CENTER, 150 S. Huntington Ave., Jamaica Plain, Zip 02130; tel. 617/232-9500; Jerry B. Boyd, dir. **A**1a 2 3 5 8 **F**1 2 3 6 7 8 9 10 11 12 13 14 15 16 20 23 24 25 26 27 28 30 31 32 33 34 35 41 42 43 44 46 47 48 49 50 53 54	45	10	S		616	15108	479	71.9	0	0	76966	43671	1565
VETERANS ADMINISTRATION MEDICAL CENTER, See Boockton-West Roxbury Veterans Administration Medical Center													
VINCENT MEMORIAL HOSPITAL, See Massachusetts General Hospital													
BOYLSTON—Worcester County													
WORCESTER COUNTY HOSPITAL, Paul Ware Dr., Zip 01505; tel. 617/852-1533; C. Vincent Shea, adm. **A**9 10 **F**12 16 23 24 42 46 50	13	48	L		122	85	94	77.0	0	0	6041	3573	158
BRAINTREE—Norfolk County													
[★] Δ BRAINTREE HOSPITAL, 250 Pond St., Zip 02184; tel. 617/848-5353; Ernest J. Broadbent, pres. **A**1a 7 9 10 **F**15 21 23 24 28 32 33 34 37 42 44 46 47	33	46	L		150	1317	128	85.3	0	0	22308	13335	593
[★] NORFOLK COUNTY HOSPITAL, 2001 Washington St., Zip 02184; tel. 617/843-0690; John A. Barmack, adm. **A**1a 9 10 **F**14 15 16 19 23 24 26 34 42 44 47; **S**1755	13	49	L		98	503	90	91.8	0	0	11202	6255	290
BRIDGEWATER—Plymouth County													
BRIDGEWATER STATE HOSPITAL (Correctional Institution), Administration Rd., Box 366, Zip 02324; tel. 617/697-6941; Charles W. Gaughan, supt. (Nonreporting)	12	11	L		480	—	—	—	—	—	—	—	—
BRIGHTON—Suffolk County See Boston													
BROCKTON—Plymouth County													
[★] BROCKTON HOSPITAL, 680 Centre St., Zip 02402; tel. 617/586-2600; Wayne M. Henry, pres. **A**1a 2 3 5 6 9 10 **F**1 2 3 6 7 8 9 10 11 12 14 15 16 20 23 24 27 30 32 33 34 35 36 37 40 44 45 46 47 50 52 53	23	10	S		301	10251	245	81.4	29	1240	54007	22718	1026
★ BROCKTON-WEST ROXBURY VETERANS ADMINISTRATION MEDICAL CENTER (Includes Veterans Administration Medical Center, 940 Belmont St., Zip 02401; tel. 617/583-4500; Veterans Administration Medical Center, 1400 Veterans of Foreign Wars Pkwy., West Roxbury, Boston, Zip 02132; tel. 617/323-7700), 940 Belmont St., Zip 02401; tel. 617/583-4500; Smith Jenkins, dir. (Total facility includes 100 beds in nursing home-type unit) **A**3 5 8 **F**1 3 4 6 10 12 14 15 16 19 23 24 25 26 27 28 29 30 31 32 33 34 35 41 42 43 44 48 49 50 54	45	10	L	TF	1029	7205	870	84.5	0	0	95684	58029	2200
				H	929	7167	775	—	0	0	93324	56288	2144
[★] CARDINAL CUSHING GENERAL HOSPITAL, 235 N. Pearl St., Zip 02401; tel. 617/588-4000; Peter J. Heffernan, pres. **A**1a 2 3 5 9 10 **F**1 2 3 5 6 10 11 12 14 15 16 20 23 24 26 30 33 34 35 44 45 46 47 50 52 53	23	10	S		275	7675	187	68.0	0	0	35644	17421	828
VETERANS ADMINISTRATION MEDICAL CENTER, See Brockton-West Roxbury Veterans Administration Medical Center													
BROOKLINE—Norfolk County													
☐ BOURNEWOOD HOSPITAL, 300 South St., Zip 02167; tel. 617/469-0300; Nasir A. Khan MD, dir. **A**1b 10 **F**24 28 29 30 32 33 42 44	33	22	S		90	949	66	73.3	0	0	6527	3712	173
[★] BROOKLINE HOSPITAL, 165 Chestnut St., Zip 02146; tel. 617/734-1330; Raymond D. Sanzone, dir. **A**1a 9 10 **F**1 3 6 12 14 16 23 24 43 44 45 46 50	23	10	S		109	1319	15	13.8	0	0	9587	4710	208
☐ HUMAN RESOURCE INSTITUTE, 227 Babcock St., Zip 02146; tel. 617/731-3200; Joseph W. Nolan, mng. dir. (Nonreporting) **A**1b 9 10; **S**9555	33	22	S		68	—	—	—	—	—	—	—	—
BROOKLINE—Suffolk County													
ST. JOHN OF GOD HOSPITAL, See Boston													
BURLINGTON—Norfolk County													
[★] LAHEY CLINIC HOSPITAL, 41 Mall Rd., Zip 01805; tel. 617/273-5100; Robert E. Wise MD, chief exec. off. **A**1a 2 10 **F**1 2 3 6 7 8 9 10 11 12 13 14 16 17 20 23 24 26 30 35 37 39 44 47 50 53 54	23	10	S		200	9776	192	96.0	0	0	76117	28616	1580

Hospital, Address, Telephone, Administrator, Approval and Facility Codes, Multihospital System Code

★ American Hospital Association (AHA) membership
□ Joint Commission on Accreditation of Hospitals (JCAH) accreditation
+ American Osteopathic Hospital Association (AOHA) membership
○ American Osteopathic Association (AOA) accreditation
Δ Commission on Accreditation of Rehabilitation Facilities (CARF) accreditation
Control codes 61, 63, 64, 71, 72 and 73 indicate hospitals listed by AOHA, but not registered by AHA.
For definition of numerical codes, see page A2

Hospital	Classification Codes				Inpatient Data				Newborn Data		Expense (thousands of dollars)		
	Control	Service	Stay	Facilities	Beds	Admissions	Census	Occupancy (percent)	Bassinets	Births	Total	Payroll	Personnel
CAMBRIDGE—Middlesex County													
[★] CAMBRIDGE HOSPITAL, 1493 Cambridge St., Zip 02139; tel. 617/498-1000; John O'Brien, adm. **A**1a 3 5 9 10 **F**3 6 10 12 14 15 16 23 27 28 29 30 32 33 34 35 36 37 40 44 48 49 52 53	14	10	S		152	4857	116	65.5	24	574	32926	17038	728
□ M. I. T. MEDICAL DEPARTMENT, 77 Massachusetts Ave., Zip 02139; tel. 617/253-4487; Arnold N. Weinberg MD, med. dir. (Nonreporting) **A**1a	23	11	S		18	—	—	—	—	—	—	—	—
[★] MOUNT AUBURN HOSPITAL, 330 Mount Auburn St., Zip 02238; tel. 617/492-3500; Francis P. Lynch, pres. (Nonreporting) **A**1a 2 3 5 8 9 10	23	10	S		305	—	—	—	—	—	—	—	—
OTIS HOSPITAL, 85 Otis St., Zip 02141; tel. 617/864-8300; Lawrence J. Hesenius, adm. (Nonreporting) **A**10	33	48	L		109	—	—	—	—	—	—	—	—
[★] SANCTA MARIA HOSPITAL, 799 Concord Ave., Zip 02238; tel. 617/868-2200; Sr. Mary Mark Pizzotti, pres. **A**1a 9 10 **F**1 3 6 10 12 15 16 20 23 26 35 42 44 45 46 50 53	21	10	S		100	3239	73	54.9	0	0	16921	8789	421
□ STILLMAN INFIRMARY, HARVARD UNIVERSITY HEALTH SERVICES, 75 Mount Auburn St., Zip 02138; tel. 617/495-2010; Warren E. C. Wacker MD, dir. **A**1a 9 10 **F**1 6 21 23 28 30 33 34 35 41 45 46 47	23	11	S		34	1110	14	41.2	0	0	13620	7313	229
[★] Δ YOUVILLE REHABILITATION AND CHRONIC DISEASE HOSPITAL, 1575 Cambridge St., Zip 02138; tel. 617/876-4344; Sr. Annette Caron, pres. & chief exec. off. **A**1a 7 9 10 **F**6 12 15 16 23 24 25 26 32 33 42 44 45 46; **S**5885	21	49	L		305	553	299	98.0	0	0	26115	16840	748
CANTON—Norfolk County													
[★] MASSACHUSETTS HOSPITAL SCHOOL, 3 Randolph St., Zip 02021; tel. 617/828-2440; John H. Britt, chief exec. off. (Nonreporting) **A**1a 3 5 10	12	57	L		161	—	—	—	—	—	—	—	—
CHELSEA—Suffolk County													
[★] LAWRENCE F. QUIGLEY MEMORIAL HOSPITAL (General Medical, Surgical and Geriatric), 91 Crest Ave., Zip 02150; tel. 617/884-5660; Maurice V. Gordon Jr., comdt. (Nonreporting) **A**1a 2 3 5 9 10	12	49	S		159	—	—	—	—	—	—	—	—
CHESTNUT HILL—Norfolk County													
BOURNEWOOD HOSPITAL, See Brookline													
CLINTON—Worcester County													
[★] CLINTON HOSPITAL, 201 Highland St., Zip 01510; tel. 617/365-4531; Frederick R. Boss, pres. **A**1a 9 10 **F**1 6 12 14 15 16 17 23 24 26 34 35 42 43 44 45 46 52 53	23	10	S		80	1451	26	32.5	0	0	6144	3248	176
CONCORD—Middlesex County													
[★] EMERSON HOSPITAL, Old Rd. to Nine Acre Corner, Zip 01742; tel. 617/369-1400; Rina K. Spence, pres. & chief exec. off. **A**1a 2 9 10 **F**1 3 6 10 12 14 15 16 21 23 24 26 27 28 29 30 32 33 34 35 36 40 41 42 43 44 45 46 47 49 52 53	23	10	S		221	8852	146	66.1	24	1855	34147	18009	806
DANVERS—Essex County													
[★] HUNT MEMORIAL HOSPITAL, Lindall St., Zip 01923; tel. 617/774-4400; Edward F. Kittredge, adm. **A**1a 2 9 10 **F**1 3 6 10 14 15 16 23 30 35 36 40 45 46 52 53; **S**1755	14	10	S		142	4548	91	64.1	15	660	24160	11107	473
EVERETT—Middlesex County													
[★] WHIDDEN MEMORIAL HOSPITAL, 103 Garland St., Zip 02149; tel. 617/389-6270; Rocco C. Mittica, exec. vice-pres. **A**1a 9 10 **F**1 3 6 10 12 14 15 16 21 23 24 26 30 32 33 34 35 41 44 45 46 47 52 53	23	10	S		173	5285	136	78.6	0	0	26442	12538	580
FALL RIVER—Bristol County													
[★] CHARLTON MEMORIAL HOSPITAL, 363 Highland Ave., Zip 02720; tel. 617/679-3131; Frederic C. Dreyer Jr., pres. **A**1a 2 9 10 **F**1 3 6 10 11 12 14 15 16 23 24 26 30 34 35 36 40 44 45 46 47 50 53	23	10	S		383	11934	274	71.5	38	1977	55289	25381	1122
[★] ST. ANNE'S HOSPITAL, 795 Middle St., Zip 02721; tel. 617/674-5741; Alan D. Knight, pres. **A**1a 2 9 10 **F**1 3 6 7 8 9 10 11 12 14 15 16 21 23 30 32 33 34 35 38 41 44 45 46 47 49 50 52 53	21	10	S		182	6383	127	69.8	0	0	27988	11421	567
FALMOUTH—Barnstable County													
[★] FALMOUTH HOSPITAL, Ter Heun Dr., Zip 02540; tel. 617/548-5300; Roy A. Hitchings Jr., pres. & chief exec. off. **A**1a 9 10 **F**1 3 6 10 12 14 15 16 21 23 24 26 30 34 35 36 37 40 42 43 44 45 46 47 50 52 53	23	10	S		130	5177	84	64.6	12	518	19801	9522	437
FITCHBURG—Worcester County													
[★] BURBANK HOSPITAL, Nichols Rd., Zip 01420; tel. 617/343-5000; William J. Williams, pres. **A**1a 3 5 9 10 **F**1 3 5 6 9 10 11 12 14 15 16 20 23 24 26 27 29 30 32 33 34 35 36 37 40 41 42 44 45 46 47 50 52 53	23	10	S		226	6642	120	53.1	20	918	28764	14405	598
FORT DEVENS—Worcester County													
[★] CUTLER ARMY HOSPITAL (Formerly Cutler Army Community Hospital), Zip 01433; tel. 617/796-6745; Col. Phillip Breunle MSC USA, deputy cDR adm. **A**1a **F**1 6 12 15 16 23 28 30 32 33 34 35 37 43 45 46 47 49 52	42	10	S		68	2565	31	45.6	0	0	9321	4216	432
FRAMINGHAM—Middlesex County													
□ BETHANY HOSPITAL, 97 Bethany Rd., Zip 01701; tel. 617/872-6750; Sr. Blanche Larose, adm. **A**1a 9 10 **F**15 16 23 24 26 28 34 42 46 47 50	23	48	L		93	106	87	93.5	0	0	3152	1581	154
□ CUSHING HOSPITAL (General Medical and Geriatric Long Term Care), Dudley Rd., Box 190, Zip 01701; tel. 617/872-4301; John S. Gracey, supt. **A**1a 9 10 **F**19 21 23 24 32 33 42 45 46 47 50	12	49	L		350	51	343	90.0	0	0	13976	11142	590
[★] FRAMINGHAM UNION HOSPITAL, 115 Lincoln St., Zip 01701; tel. 617/879-7111; James W. Walckner, exec. vice-pres. **A**1a 2 3 5 6 9 10 **F**1 2 3 5 6 7 10 11 12 14 15 16 20 23 24 27 30 32 33 34 35 36 37 40 44 45 46 47 52 53 54	23	10	S		311	10865	209	67.2	50	2151	56896	26133	1098
GARDNER—Worcester County													
[★] HENRY HEYWOOD MEMORIAL HOSPITAL, 242 Green St., Zip 01440; tel. 617/632-3420; Paul E. Corcoran, adm. **A**1a 9 10 **F**1 3 6 10 12 14 16 23 24 27 30 32 33 35 40 44 45 46 47 49 52 53	23	10	S		153	4907	91	59.5	14	241	17246	8358	423
GEORGETOWN—Essex County													
★ BALDPATE HOSPITAL, Baldpate Rd., Zip 01833; tel. 617/352-2131; Lucille M. Batal, adm. (Nonreporting) **A**9	33	22	S		59	—	—	—	—	—	—	—	—
GLOUCESTER—Essex County													
[★] ADDISON GILBERT HOSPITAL, 298 Washington St., Zip 01930; tel. 617/283-4000; Theodore A. Scharfenstein, pres. **A**1a 2 9 10 **F**1 3 6 10 14 15 16 23 24 26 27 30 32 33 35 36 40 43 44 45 46 47 50 52 53	23	10	S		124	4107	94	75.8	14	306	17898	8895	456
GREAT BARRINGTON—Berkshire County													
[★] FAIRVIEW HOSPITAL, 29 Lewis Ave., Zip 01230; tel. 413/528-0790; Richard Rose, pres. & chief exec. off. **A**1a 9 10 **F**1 3 6 10 12 14 15 16 23 24 26 35 36 40 45 46 53	23	10	S		41	1710	29	56.9	9	142	—	—	221
GREENFIELD—Franklin County													
[★] FRANKLIN MEDICAL CENTER, 164 High St., Zip 01301; tel. 413/772-0211; Richard Harris, pres. **A**1a 2 9 10 **F**1 3 6 10 12 14 15 16 20 21 23 24 27 28 30 32 33 34 35 36 40 42 44 45 46 47 49 52 53 54; **S**1095	23	10	S		142	5173	77	50.0	20	864	19565	10086	437
HANSON—Plymouth County													
□ PLYMOUTH COUNTY HOSPITAL, High St., P O Box 628, Zip 02341; tel. 617/293-6322; Alvin R. Haase, dir. **A**1a 9 10 **F**23 24 34 42 44 45 46	13	48	L		72	35	68	100.0	0	0	4353	2514	149

★ American Hospital Association (AHA) membership
☐ Joint Commission on Accreditation of Hospitals (JCAH) accreditation
+ American Osteopathic Hospital Association (AOHA) membership
○ American Osteopathic Association (AOA) accreditation
Δ Commission on Accreditation of Rehabilitation Facilities (CARF) accreditation
Control codes 61, 63, 64, 71, 72 and 73 indicate hospitals listed by AOHA, but not registered by AHA.
For definition of numerical codes, see page A2

Hospital, Address, Telephone, Administrator, Approval and Facility Codes, Multihospital System Code	Classification Codes				Inpatient Data				Newborn Data		Expense (thousands of dollars)		
	Control	Service	Stay	Facilities	Beds	Admissions	Census	Occupancy (percent)	Bassinets	Births	Total	Payroll	Personnel
HATHORNE—Essex County													
DANVERS STATE HOSPITAL, P O Box 100, Zip 01937; tel. 617/774-5000; William Bonnes, chief oper. off. **A**3 9 **F**24 33 42 46 47	12	22	L		280	1248	261	94.2	0	0	11121	8274	455
HAVERHILL—Essex County													
★☐ HAVERHILL MUNICIPAL-HALE HOSPITAL, 140 Lincoln Ave., Zip 01830; tel. 617/374-2000; Thomas Sager, adm. **A**1a 9 10 **F**1 3 6 10 12 14 16 23 34 35 36 40 45 46 52 53	14	10	S		188	6414	137	72.1	17	627	35724	14195	590
★ WHITTIER REHABILITATION HOSPITAL, 76 Summer St., Zip 01830; tel. 617/372-8000; X. L. Papaioanou MD, adm. (Nonreporting) **A**9 10; **S**1755	33	46	L		112	—	—	—	—	—	—	—	—
HOLDEN—Worcester County													
★☐ HOLDEN HOSPITAL, Boyden Rd., Zip 01520; tel. 617/829-6721; Daniel P. Moen, pres. **A**1a 9 10 **F**1 3 6 10 12 14 15 16 23 24 30 32 33 34 35 41 44 45 46 52 53	23	10	S		82	2376	42	51.2	0	0	10012	4601	248
HOLYOKE—Hampden County													
★☐ HOLYOKE HOSPITAL, 575 Beech St., Zip 01040; tel. 413/534-2500; Hank J. Porten, chief exec. off. **A**1a 2 9 10 **F**1 3 6 9 10 11 12 14 15 16 20 21 23 24 26 30 32 34 35 44 45 46 47 49 52 53	23	10	S		232	7548	191	78.9	0	0	31621	16113	763
★☐ PROVIDENCE HOSPITAL, 1233 Main St., Zip 01040; tel. 413/536-5111; William J. Laffey, pres. **A**1a 2 9 10 **F**1 2 3 6 10 12 14 15 16 23 24 26 34 35 36 37 40 44 45 46 47 49 50 52 53; **S**5285	21	10	S		247	6192	121	49.0	26	1240	25936	14602	714
★☐ SOLDIERS' HOME IN HOLYOKE, Cherry St., Zip 01040; tel. 413/532-9475; James K. Kelly, supt. (Total facility includes 309 beds in nursing home-type unit) **A**1a 9 10 **F**1 10 12 19 23 24 34 42 43 44 46	12	11	L	TF	336	205	267	79.5	0	0	10433	6729	362
				H	27	120	15	—	0	0	—	—	—
HYANNIS—Barnstable County													
★☐ CAPE COD HOSPITAL, 27 Park St., Zip 02601; tel. 617/771-1800; James F. Lyons, pres. **A**1a 2 9 10 **F**1 2 3 5 6 7 8 9 10 11 12 14 15 16 20 23 24 26 30 34 35 36 37 38 40 44 45 46 47 50 52 53	23	10	S		228	11602	194	85.1	23	1222	45533	23926	900
HYDE PARK—Suffolk County See Boston													
JAMAICA PLAIN—Suffolk County See Boston													
LAKEVILLE—Plymouth County													
★☐ Δ LAKEVILLE HOSPITAL, Main St., Zip 02347; tel. 617/947-1231; John R. Pratt, exec. dir. (Nonreporting) **A**1a 7 9 10	12	46	L		80	—	—	—	—	—	—	—	—
LAWRENCE—Essex County													
★☐ LAWRENCE GENERAL HOSPITAL, One General St., Zip 01842; tel. 617/683-4000; Thomas F. Hennessey, pres. & chief exec. off. **A**1a 9 10 **F**1 2 3 5 6 12 14 15 16 21 23 24 26 34 35 36 37 40 43 44 45 46 47 52 53	23	10	S		337	11767	253	75.1	38	1670	43137	20210	1082
LEEDS—Hampshire County													
HAMPSHIRE COUNTY LONG TERM CARE FACILITY, River Rd., Zip 01053; tel. 413/584-8457; Edwin C. Warner, adm. (Nonreporting) **A**9	13	48	L		120	—	—	—	—	—	—	—	—
LEOMINSTER—Worcester County													
★☐ LEOMINSTER HOSPITAL, Hospital Rd., Zip 01453; tel. 617/537-4811; Carl N. Wathne, pres. & chief exec. off. **A**1a 6 9 10 **F**1 3 6 10 12 14 15 16 23 24 26 30 32 33 34 35 36 40 44 45 46 52 53	23	10	S		118	4974	82	67.8	21	1126	19699	9864	408
LOWELL—Middlesex County													
☐ H. C. SOLOMON MENTAL HEALTH CENTER, 391 Varnum Ave., Zip 01854; tel. 617/454-8851; Fernando A. Duran; area dir. & supt. (Nonreporting) **A**1b 9 10	12	22	L		46	—	—	—	—	—	—	—	—
★☐ LOWELL GENERAL HOSPITAL, 295 Varnum Ave., Zip 01854; tel. 617/937-6000; Robert A. Donovan, pres. **A**1a 2 9 10 **F**1 3 5 6 7 8 9 10 11 12 14 15 16 20 23 24 26 27 30 32 33 34 35 36 37 40 41 43 44 45 46 48 49 52 53	23	10	S		293	10673	179	61.1	40	2258	33434	17391	893
★☐ ST. JOHN'S HOSPITAL, Hospital Dr., P O Box 30, Zip 01853; tel. 617/458-1411; Sr. Maria Loyola, pres. **A**1a 2 9 10 **F**1 3 6 9 10 12 14 15 16 20 23 24 35 38 41 44 45 46 52 53	21	10	S		254	7186	163	64.2	0	0	31519	16158	730
★☐ ST. JOSEPH'S HOSPITAL, 220 Pawtucket St., Zip 01854; tel. 617/453-1761; James H. Frame, pres. **A**1a 2 9 10 **F**1 3 6 10 12 14 15 16 20 23 24 34 35 36 40 44 45 46 47 52	23	10	S		232	5482	107	46.1	23	396	27532	14131	704
LUDLOW—Hampden County													
★☐ LUDLOW HOSPITAL, 14 Chestnut Pl., Zip 01056; tel. 413/583-8361; John Kirby, exec. dir. **A**1a 10 **F**1 3 6 10 12 14 15 16 23 34 35 44 45 46 53	23	10	S		76	1675	32	42.1	0	0	—	—	208
LYNN—Essex County													
★☐ ATLANTICARE MEDICAL CENTER (Includes Lynn Hospital, 212 Boston St., Zip 01904; tel. 617/598-5100; Edward F. Kittredge, pres.; Union Hospital, 500 Lynnfield St., Zip 01904; tel. 617/581-9200; Peter B. Davis, pres.), 212 Boston St., Zip 01904; tel. 617/596-2500; Bernard A. Mulhall, pres. **A**1a 2 3 5 9 10 **F**1 2 3 5 6 7 8 9 10 11 12 14 15 16 23 24 26 27 28 29 30 32 33 34 35 36 40 44 45 46 47 49 50 52 53	23	10	S		511	13744	288	56.4	31	945	—	—	1508
LYNN HOSPITAL, See Atlanticare Medical Center													
★☐ MOUNT PLEASANT HOSPITAL, 60 Granite St., Zip 01904; tel. 617/581-5600; A. Daniel Rubenstein MD, adm. **A**1b 9 **F**10 16 24 28 32 33 34 42 46 49	33	82	S		88	2643	66	75.0	0	0	4844	1996	101
UNION HOSPITAL, See Atlanticare Medical Center													
MALDEN—Middlesex County													
★☐ MALDEN HOSPITAL, Hospital Rd., Zip 02148; tel. 617/322-7560; Stanley W. Krygowski, pres. **A**1a 2 3 5 6 9 10 **F**1 3 6 10 12 14 15 16 21 23 24 26 28 34 35 36 37 40 45 46 53	23	10	S		241	7012	143	59.3	36	2123	38151	16485	765
MARLBOROUGH—Middlesex County													
★☐ MARLBOROUGH HOSPITAL, 57 Union St., Zip 01752; tel. 617/485-1121; Matthew O. Anderson, pres. & chief exec. off. **A**1a 9 10 **F**1 3 6 10 12 14 15 16 21 23 24 27 28 29 30 32 33 34 35 37 41 42 44 45 46 47 48 49 50 52 53	23	10	S		164	5361	93	56.7	0	0	22400	11928	548
MATTAPAN—Suffolk County See Boston													
MEDFIELD—Norfolk County													
MEDFIELD STATE HOSPITAL, 45 Hospital Rd., Zip 02052; tel. 617/359-7312 (Nonreporting) **A**9	12	22	L		257	—	—	—	—	—	—	—	—
MEDFORD—Middlesex County													
★☐ LAWRENCE MEMORIAL HOSPITAL OF MEDFORD, 170 Governors Ave., Zip 02155; tel. 617/396-9250; Charles F. Johnson, pres. **A**1a 3 5 6 9 **F**1 3 6 12 14 15 16 23 24 26 34 35 41 44 45 46 50 52 53	23	10	S		200	4183	110	55.0	0	0	25232	12844	520
MELROSE—Middlesex County													
★☐ MELROSE-WAKEFIELD HOSPITAL ASSOCIATION, 585 Lebanon St., Zip 02176; tel. 617/662-7200; Richard S. Quinlan, pres. **A**1a 2 9 10 **F**1 3 6 10 12 14 15 16 21 23 24 27 28 29 30 32 33 35 36 40 41 43 44 45 46 52 53	23	10	S		253	9034	181	71.5	28	1306	33346	16630	736
METHUEN—Essex County													
★☐ BON SECOURS HOSPITAL OF METHUEN, 70 East St., Zip 01844; tel. 617/687-0151; William L. Lane, pres. & chief exec. off. **A**1a 9 10 **F**1 2 3 6 7 8 9 10 11 12 14 15 16 17 20 23 24 26 27 28 30 32 33 34 35 36 40 42 45 46 47 52 53	21	10	S		329	10628	238	72.3	30	1230	38279	21349	1075

Hospital, Address, Telephone, Administrator, Approval and Facility Codes, Multihospital System Code	Classification Codes				Inpatient Data				Newborn Data		Expense (thousands of dollars)		
★ American Hospital Association (AHA) membership ☐ Joint Commission on Accreditation of Hospitals (JCAH) accreditation + American Osteopathic Hospital Association (AOHA) membership ○ American Osteopathic Association (AOA) accreditation Δ Commission on Accreditation of Rehabilitation Facilities (CARF) accreditation Control codes 61, 63, 64, 71, 72 and 73 indicate hospitals listed by AOHA, but not registered by AHA. For definition of numerical codes, see page A2	Control	Service	Stay	Facilities	Beds	Admissions	Census	Occupancy (percent)	Bassinets	Births	Total	Payroll	Personnel
MIDDLEBORO—Plymouth County													
★☐ ST. LUKES HOSPITAL OF MIDDLEBOROUGH, 52 Oak St., Zip 02346; tel. 617/947-6000; Peter W. Brown, pres. **A**1a 9 10 **F**1 3 6 10 12 14 15 16 23 34 35 41 43 44 45 46 52	23	10	S		66	2082	41	62.1	0	0	9812	5005	247
MILFORD—Worcester County													
★☐ MILFORD-WHITINSVILLE REGIONAL HOSPITAL (Includes Whitinsville Division, 18 Granite St., Whitinsville, Zip 01588; tel. 617/234-6311), 14 Prospect St., Zip 01757; tel. 617/473-1190; Kenneth Luke, adm. **A**1a 9 10 **F**1 3 6 10 12 14 15 16 23 24 27 30 32 33 35 40 42 44 45 46 47 52 53; **S**1755	23	10	S		183	6387	126	68.9	16	468	29797	14463	642
MILTON—Norfolk County													
★☐ MILTON MEDICAL CENTER, 92 Highland St., Zip 02186; tel. 617/696-4600; George A. Geary, pres. **A**1a 9 10 **F**1 3 6 10 12 14 15 16 23 24 26 30 34 35 44 45 46 47 53	23	10	S		161	4927	103	64.0	0	0	21586	9207	453
MONTAGUE—Franklin County													
★☐ FARREN MEMORIAL HOSPITAL, 56 Main St., Mailing Address Turners Falls, Zip 01376; tel. 413/774-3111; Alan J. Labonte, adm. **A**1a 2 9 10 **F**1 3 6 12 14 15 16 21 23 26 33 34 35 45 46 47 52 53; **S**5285	23	10	S		72	1891	34	47.2	0	0	10134	5216	262
NANTUCKET—Nantucket County													
★☐ NANTUCKET COTTAGE HOSPITAL, S. Prospect St., Zip 02554; tel. 617/228-1200; Nathaniel Bond, adm. **A**1a 9 10 **F**1 3 6 14 16 20 21 23 26 28 34 35 36 40 41 46 47 52	23	10	S		39	872	12	30.0	5	81	4071	2019	80
NATICK—Middlesex County													
★☐ LEONARD MORSE HOSPITAL, 67 Union St., Zip 01760; tel. 617/653-3400; Janice B. Wyatt, pres. & chief exec. off. **A**1a 2 9 10 **F**1 2 3 6 10 12 14 15 16 20 23 24 27 28 30 32 33 35 36 40 42 44 45 46 48 50 52 53; **S**3015	23	10	S		259	7580	169	65.3	16	709	36388	18156	769
NEEDHAM—Norfolk County													
★☐ GLOVER MEMORIAL HOSPITAL, 148 Chestnut St., Zip 02192; tel. 617/444-5600; Frank A. Niro III, adm. (Nonreporting) **A**1a 2 9 10	14	10	S		95	—	—	—	—	—	—	—	—
NEW BEDFORD—Bristol County													
★☐ FRANCES P. MEMORIAL HOSPITAL, 1074 Pleasant St., Zip 02740; tel. 617/997-1211; Eli Nochimow MD, med. dir. (Nonreporting) **A**1a 9 10	33	48	L		60	—	—	—	—	—	—	—	—
☐ PARKWOOD HOSPITAL, 4499 Acushnet Ave., Box L-8, Zip 02745; tel. 617/995-4400; Robert F. Davis, exec. dir. (Nonreporting) **A**1a 10	33	10	S		100	—	—	—	—	—	—	—	—
★☐ ST. LUKE'S HOSPITAL OF NEW BEDFORD, 101 Page St., Zip 02740; Mailing Address Box H3003, Zip 02741; tel. 617/997-1515; John P. Bihldorff, pres. & chief exec. off. **A**1a 9 10 **F**1 3 6 10 11 12 14 15 16 20 21 23 24 26 30 33 34 35 36 37 40 41 44 45 46 47 50 52 53	23	10	S		433	15955	317	73.2	44	2015	54865	29656	1417
NEWBURYPORT—Essex County													
★☐ ANNA JAQUES HOSPITAL, 25 Highland Ave., Zip 01950; tel. 617/462-6600; Allan L. DesRosiers, pres. & chief exec. off. **A**1a 9 10 **F**1 3 6 10 12 14 15 16 23 27 34 35 36 40 44 45 46 50 52 53	23	10	S		156	5687	106	67.9	12	827	23282	12027	519
NEWTON—Middlesex County													
★☐ NEWTON-WELLESLEY HOSPITAL (Formerly Listed Under Newton Lower Falls), 2014 Washington St., Zip 02162; tel. 617/243-6000; Barry M. Spero, pres. & chief exec. off. **A**1a 2 3 5 8 9 10 **F**1 3 5 6 10 12 14 15 16 20 23 24 26 27 28 29 30 31 32 33 34 35 36 37 40 42 43 44 45 46 47 52 53	23	10	S		299	11979	233	80.3	40	2470	62539	32742	1283
NEWTON LOWER FALLS—Middlesex County													
NEWTON-WELLESLEY HOSPITAL, See Newton													
NORFOLK—Norfolk County													
☐ SOUTHWOOD COMMUNITY HOSPITAL, 111 Dedham St., tel. 617/668-0385; John D. Dalton, adm. (Nonreporting) **A**1a 2 10; **S**3175	23	10	S		183	—	—	—	—	—	—	—	—
NORTH ADAMS—Berkshire County													
★☐ NORTH ADAMS REGIONAL HOSPITAL, Hospital Ave., Zip 01247; tel. 413/663-3701; Bernard Shapiro, pres. **A**1a 2 9 10 **F**1 2 3 6 10 12 14 15 16 23 35 36 40 44 45 46 47 52 53	23	10	S		172	4148	85	49.4	12	379	17569	9906	454
NORTHAMPTON—Hampshire County													
★☐ COOLEY DICKINSON HOSPITAL, 30 Locust St., Zip 01060; tel. 413/584-4090; Willis H. Brucker, pres. & chief exec. off. **A**1a 2 9 10 **F**1 3 6 7 8 9 10 11 12 14 15 16 21 23 24 26 34 35 36 37 40 41 44 45 46 47 50 52 53	23	10	S		189	8047	133	68.9	19	1129	26357	15188	676
NORTHAMPTON STATE HOSPITAL, Prince & West Sts., Zip 01060; tel. 413/584-1644; Donald C. Siddell, chief oper. off. **A**9 **F**23 24 32 33 42	12	22	L		225	864	188	83.6	0	0	13730	9494	438
★☐ VETERANS ADMINISTRATION MEDICAL CENTER, Berkshire Trail, Zip 01060; tel. 413/584-4040; Hugh M. Ferguson Jr., dir. (Total facility includes 40 beds in nursing home-type unit) **A**1a **F**1 3 6 10 12 15 16 17 19 23 24 25 26 28 30 33 34 35 42 44 46 48 49 50	45	22	L	TF H	540 500	2574 2552	500 451	86.4 —	0 0	0 0	34365 —	24874 —	871 845
NORWOOD—Norfolk County													
★☐ NORWOOD HOSPITAL, 800 Washington St., Zip 02062; tel. 617/769-4000; Frank S. Crane III, chief exec. off. (Nonreporting) **A**1a 2 9 10; **S**3175	23	10	S		302	—	—	—	—	—	—	—	—
OAK BLUFFS—Dukes County													
★☐ MARTHA'S VINEYARD HOSPITAL, Linton Lane, Box 1477, Zip 02557; tel. 617/693-0410; David F. Federowicz, pres. (Total facility includes 41 beds in nursing home-type unit) **A**1a 9 10 **F**1 3 6 10 14 16 19 23 26 29 30 35 36 37 40 42 45 46 47 49 50	23	10	S	TF H	80 39	1583 1560	65 24	81.3 —	6 6	113 113	8461 7922	3924 3450	160 86
PALMER—Hampden County													
★☐ WING MEMORIAL HOSPITAL AND MEDICAL CENTERS (Formerly Wing Memorial Hospital), Wright St., Zip 01069; tel. 413/283-7651; Richard H. Scheffer, pres. **A**1a 2 9 10 **F**1 3 6 10 12 14 15 16 23 24 26 27 28 30 32 33 34 35 42 44 45 46 49 50 52 53	23	10	S		80	2263	43	53.8	0	0	11518	6140	282
PEABODY—Essex County													
★☐ JOSIAH B. THOMAS HOSPITAL, 15 King St., Zip 01960; tel. 617/531-2900; Sheldon B. Aronson, pres. **A**1a 9 10 **F**1 3 6 12 14 15 23 28 30 35 41 46	14	10	S		86	2242	57	66.3	0	0	12847	6875	276
PEMBROKE—Plymouth County													
★☐ AMI PEMBROKE HOSPITAL, 199 Oak St., Zip 02359; tel. 617/826-8161; Sherwin Z. Goodblatt, exec. dir. (Newly Registered) **A**1a 3 **F**23 24 32 33 42; **S**0125	33	22	S		100	1152	86	86.0	0	0	10712	3275	177
PITTSFIELD—Berkshire County													
★☐ Δ BERKSHIRE MEDICAL CENTER, 725 North St., Zip 01201; tel. 413/499-4161; John C. Johnson, pres. **A**1a 2 3 5 7 8 9 10 **F**1 2 3 5 6 7 9 10 12 14 15 16 17 20 23 24 25 26 27 28 30 33 34 35 36 37 40 44 45 46 47 50 52 53 54	23	10	S		369	11057	215	58.3	36	1386	53978	27910	1001
★☐ HILLCREST HOSPITAL, 165 Tor Ct., Box 1155, Zip 01201; tel. 413/443-4761; Eugene A. Dellea, adm. **A**1a 9 10 **F**1 3 6 10 12 14 15 16 23 24 28 30 33 35 37 42 45 46 47 48 49 50 52 53	23	10	S		130	4040	79	60.8	0	0	16667	8980	401
PLYMOUTH—Plymouth County													
★☐ JORDAN HOSPITAL, 275 Sandwich St., Zip 02360; tel. 617/746-2000; Peter A. Chapman, pres. **A**1a 2 9 10 **F**1 2 3 6 10 12 14 15 16 20 23 24 26 30 32 33 35 36 40 44 45 46 47 52 53; **S**1755	23	10	S		147	6794	107	72.8	12	813	24166	12621	487

Hospital, Address, Telephone, Administrator, Approval and Facility Codes, Multihospital System Code	Classification Codes				Inpatient Data				Newborn Data		Expense (thousands of dollars)		
★ American Hospital Association (AHA) membership □ Joint Commission on Accreditation of Hospitals (JCAH) accreditation + American Osteopathic Hospital Association (AOHA) membership ○ American Osteopathic Association (AOA) accreditation Δ Commission on Accreditation of Rehabilitation Facilities (CARF) accreditation Control codes 61, 63, 64, 71, 72 and 73 indicate hospitals listed by AOHA, but not registered by AHA. For definition of numerical codes, see page A2	Control	Service	Stay	Facilities	Beds	Admissions	Census	Occupancy (percent)	Bassinets	Births	Total	Payroll	Personnel
POCASSET—Barnstable County													
★□ BARNSTABLE COUNTY HOSPITAL, 870 County Rd., Zip 02559; tel. 617/563-5941; Edward J. Clark, adm. (Nonreporting) **A**1a 9 10	13	48	L		56	—	—	—	—	—	—	—	—
QUINCY—Norfolk County													
LONG ISLAND HOSPITAL, See Boston													
★□ QUINCY CITY HOSPITAL, 114 Whitwell St., Zip 02169; tel. 617/773-6100; Mark J. Mundy, dir. **A**1a 9 10 **F**1 3 5 6 10 12 14 15 16 20 23 24 26 30 32 33 34 35 36 37 40 44 45 46 47 50 52 53; **S**1755	14	10	S		303	9739	213	70.3	36	868	40618	21742	861
REVERE—Suffolk County													
GROVER MANOR HOSPITAL, 405 Washington Ave., Zip 02151; tel. 617/284-7990; Dorothy N. Fletcher, adm. (Nonreporting) **A**9 10	33	48	L		161	—	—	—	—	—	—	—	—
ROSLINDALE—Suffolk County See Boston													
ROXBURY—Suffolk County See Boston													
RUTLAND—Worcester County													
★□ Δ RUTLAND HEIGHTS HOSPITAL, Maple Ave., Zip 01543; tel. 617/886-4711; William D. Thompson, exec. dir. (Nonreporting) **A**1b 7 9 10	12	48	L		248	—	—	—	—	—	—	—	—
SALEM—Essex County													
★□ Δ DR. J. ROBERT SHAUGHNESSY CHRONIC DISEASE-REHABILITATION HOSPITAL, Dove Ave., Zip 01970; tel. 617/745-9000; James A. Lomastro PhD, exec. dir. (Nonreporting) **A**1a 7 10	14	46	L		160	—	—	—	—	—	—	—	—
★□ NORTH SHORE CHILDREN'S HOSPITAL, 57 Highland Ave., Zip 01970; tel. 617/745-2100; Barbara A. Betts, adm. (Nonreporting) **A**1a 3 5 9	23	50	S		50	—	—	—	—	—	—	—	—
★□ SALEM HOSPITAL, 81 Highland Ave., Zip 01970; tel. 617/741-1200; Michael J. Geaney Jr., pres. **A**1a 2 3 5 9 10 **F**1 2 3 5 6 7 8 9 10 11 12 14 15 16 20 23 24 26 27 28 29 30 32 33 34 35 36 37 40 44 45 46 47 48 49 50 53 54	23	10	S		342	11343	246	71.7	49	1407	58692	32907	1366
SOMERVILLE—Middlesex County													
□ CENTRAL HOSPITAL, 26 Central St., Zip 02143; tel. 617/625-8900; Marvin Stern, adm. (Nonreporting) **A**1a 9 10; **S**0075	33	10	S		99	—	—	—	—	—	—	—	—
★□ SOMERVILLE HOSPITAL, 230 Highland Ave., Zip 02143; tel. 617/666-4400; Normand E. Girard, pres. **A**1a 6 9 10 **F**1 3 6 10 12 14 15 16 23 24 26 34 35 37 45 46 47 50	23	10	S		138	3244	70	50.7	0	0	20363	9483	443
SOUTH ATTLEBORO—Bristol County													
★□ FULLER MEMORIAL HOSPITAL, 231 Washington St., Zip 02703; tel. 617/761-8500; Ronald C. Brown, pres. **A**1a 9 10 **F**23 24 28 32 33 34 42 48 49; **S**9355	21	22	S		82	1168	57	69.5	0	0	6589	3213	160
SOUTH BOSTON—Suffolk County See Boston													
SOUTH WEYMOUTH—Norfolk County													
★□ SOUTH SHORE HOSPITAL, 55 Fogg Rd., Zip 02190; tel. 617/337-7011; Alvin S. Topham, exec. vice-pres. & chief oper. off. **A**1a 2 9 10 **F**1 3 5 6 9 10 12 14 15 16 20 21 23 24 26 28 30 32 33 34 35 36 37 38 40 41 44 45 46 50 52 53	23	10	S		280	12627	250	89.3	44	2015	51998	25984	1236
SOUTHBRIDGE—Worcester County													
★□ HARRINGTON MEMORIAL HOSPITAL, 100 South St., Zip 01550; tel. 617/765-9771; Richard M. Mangion, exec. vice-pres. & adm. **A**1a 9 10 **F**1 3 6 10 12 14 15 16 23 24 26 27 28 29 30 33 34 35 36 37 40 41 43 44 45 46 49 52 53 54	23	10	S		121	4969	87	71.9	11	560	18061	8661	428
SPRINGFIELD—Hampden County													
★□ BAYSTATE MEDICAL CENTER (Includes Springfield Hospital; Wesson Memorial Hospital; Wesson Women's Hospital), 759 Chestnut St., Zip 01199; tel. 413/787-2500; Michael J. Daly, pres. **A**1a 2 3 5 6 8 9 10 **F**1 2 3 4 5 6 7 8 9 10 11 12 14 16 20 21 23 24 27 28 30 33 34 35 36 37 38 40 43 44 45 46 47 51 52 53 54; **S**1095	23	10	S		741	30080	586	76.1	99	5640	141140	74932	3199
★□ Δ MERCY HOSPITAL, 271 Carew St., Zip 01101; Mailing Address Box 9012, Zip 01102; tel. 413/781-9100; Sr. Mary Caritas, pres. **A**1a 2 7 9 10 **F**1 3 6 10 11 12 14 15 16 17 23 24 26 30 33 35 42 43 44 45 46 47 52 53; **S**5285	21	10	S		322	10929	232	72.0	0	0	45513	22742	1124
★□ SHRINERS HOSPITALS FOR CRIPPLED CHILDREN, 516 Carew St., Zip 01104; tel. 413/781-6750; Edwin C. Thorn, adm. **A**1a 3 5 **F**15 23 32 33 34 38 42 46 47; **S**4125	23	57	S		60	594	31	51.7	0	0	—	—	137
SPRINGFIELD HOSPITAL, See Baystate Medical Center													
SPRINGFIELD MUNICIPAL HOSPITAL, 1400 State St., Zip 01109; tel. 413/787-6700; Theresa M. Theroux, dir. **A**9 10 **F**12 15 16 23 24 25 42 44 45 46 47 50	14	48	L		438	216	376	85.9	0	0	13339	8816	541
WESSON MEMORIAL HOSPITAL, See Baystate Medical Center													
WESSON WOMEN'S HOSPITAL, See Baystate Medical Center													
STOCKBRIDGE—Berkshire County													
★□ AUSTEN RIGGS CENTER, Main St., Zip 01262; tel. 413/298-5511; Michael T. Zanin, adm. **A**1a 3 5 **F**24 29 32 33 47	23	22	L		47	32	43	91.5	0	0	3333	1387	69
STONEHAM—Middlesex County													
★□ NEW ENGLAND MEMORIAL HOSPITAL, 5 Woodland Rd., Zip 02180; tel. 617/665-1740; Wolfgang Von Maack, pres. **A**1a 2 3 5 9 10 **F**1 2 3 6 10 11 12 14 15 16 23 24 26 27 30 32 33 34 35 36 37 40 42 44 45 46 47 48 49 50 52 53; **S**9355	21	10	S		301	6534	172	57.1	18	853	36229	18978	1051
STOUGHTON—Norfolk County													
★□ GODDARD MEMORIAL HOSPITAL, 909 Sumner St., Zip 02072; tel. 617/344-5100; William B. Sheehan, pres. **A**1a 2 9 10 **F**1 2 3 5 6 9 10 12 14 15 16 20 23 24 26 33 35 36 37 38 40 42 44 45 46 47 50 52 53	23	10	S		236	10676	182	77.1	40	2264	35721	16392	756
★□ Δ NEW ENGLAND SINAI HOSPITAL (Chronic Disease and Rehabilitation), 150 York St., Zip 02072; tel. 617/364-4850; Donald H. Goldberg, exec. dir. **A**1a 7 9 10 **F**15 16 23 24 25 26 32 33 34 42 43 44 45 46	23	49	L		200	349	195	97.5	0	0	20290	11197	517
TAUNTON—Bristol County													
★□ MORTON HOSPITAL AND MEDICAL CENTER (Formerly Morton Hospital), 88 Washington St., Zip 02780; tel. 617/824-6911; Lawrence E. Ross, pres. **A**1a 9 10 **F**1 3 6 10 12 14 15 16 20 21 23 24 33 34 35 36 38 40 44 45 46 52 53	23	10	S		207	6437	142	68.6	22	650	33664	15699	720
TAUNTON STATE HOSPITAL, Hodges Ave. Ext., Box 151, Zip 02780; tel. 617/824-7551; W. Walter Sowyrda, dir. (Nonreporting) **A**9 10	12	22	L		293	—	—	—	—	—	—	—	—
TEWKSBURY—Middlesex County													
★□ TEWKSBURY HOSPITAL, East St., Zip 01876; tel. 617/851-7321; Aldo A. Caira, actg. supt. **A**1a 10 **F**16 23 24 42 46	12	48	L		730	170	734	100.0	0	0	27846	17788	955
TURNERS FALLS—Franklin County													
FARREN MEMORIAL HOSPITAL, See Montague													
WALTHAM—Middlesex County													
★ METROPOLITAN STATE HOSPITAL, 475 Trapelo Rd., Zip 02154; tel. 617/894-3600; Audrey Y. Deloffi, chief oper. off. **A**3 5 9 **F**32 33 46	12	22	L		430	1447	379	94.0	0	0	—	—	733
□ MIDDLESEX COUNTY HOSPITAL, 775 Trapelo Rd., Zip 02254; tel. 617/894-4600; Alfred Smialek, dir.; David Takvoryan MD, med. dir. **A**1a 9 10 **F**12 14 16 23 24 32 33 34 42 44 46 47 49 50	13	48	L		170	224	129	75.9	0	0	12445	6826	368
WALTER E. FERNALD STATE SCHOOL (Includes Templeton Colony, Baldwinville), 200 Trapelo Rd., Zip 02154; Mailing Address Box 158, Belmont, Zip 02178; tel. 617/894-3600; Peter O'Meara, supt. (Nonreporting)	12	62	L		940	—	—	—	—	—	—	—	—

Hospital, Address, Telephone, Administrator, Approval and Facility Codes, Multihospital System Code	Classification Codes				Inpatient Data				Newborn Data		Expense (thousands of dollars)		
★ American Hospital Association (AHA) membership □ Joint Commission on Accreditation of Hospitals (JCAH) accreditation + American Osteopathic Hospital Association (AOHA) membership ○ American Osteopathic Association (AOA) accreditation Δ Commission on Accreditation of Rehabilitation Facilities (CARF) accreditation Control codes 61, 63, 64, 71, 72 and 73 indicate hospitals listed by AOHA, but not registered by AHA. For definition of numerical codes, see page A2	Control	Service	Stay	Facilities	Beds	Admissions	Census	Occupancy (percent)	Bassinets	Births	Total	Payroll	Personnel
★□ WALTHAMWESTON HOSPITAL AND MEDICAL CENTER, Hope Ave., Zip 02254; tel. 617/647-6000; Richard A. Rielly, pres. & chief exec. off. **A**1a 2 3 9 10 **F**1 2 3 6 7 8 10 11 12 14 15 16 20 21 23 24 27 28 30 32 33 34 35 36 37 40 41 44 45 46 47 49 52 53	23	10	S		305	8460	171	56.1	30	814	43605	22003	859
WARE—Hampshire County													
★□ MARY LANE HOSPITAL, 85 South St., Zip 01082; tel. 413/967-6211; William J. Zwemke, pres. **A**1a 9 10 **F**1 6 10 12 14 15 16 21 23 24 28 32 35 36 39 40 41 43 44 45 46 47 49 52 53	23	10	S		78	2154	34	43.6	9	243	6809	3416	201
WAREHAM—Plymouth County													
★□ TOBEY HOSPITAL, 43 High St., Zip 02571; tel. 617/295-0880; Charles S. Kinney, pres. **A**1a 9 10 **F**1 3 6 10 12 14 16 21 23 24 26 32 34 35 36 40 43 44 45 46 52	23	10	S		89	3445	56	62.9	9	294	11762	6584	305
WAVERLEY—Middlesex County													
WALTER E. FERNALD STATE SCHOOL, See Waltham													
WEBSTER—Worcester County													
★□ HUBBARD REGIONAL HOSPITAL, 340 Thompson Rd., Zip 01570; tel. 617/943-2600; Richard L. Cunningham, adm. **A**1a 9 10 **F**1 3 6 10 12 14 15 16 23 24 25 26 28 30 32 33 34 35 37 43 44 45 47 49; **S**1755	23	10	S		82	2144	44	53.7	0	0	9786	4707	234
WELLESLEY—Norfolk County													
★□ CHARLES RIVER HOSPITAL, 203 Grove St., Zip 02181; tel. 617/235-8400; Joel Rosenhaus, pres. & chief exec. off. (Nonreporting) **A**1a b 3 5 9; **S**0215	33	22	S		58	—	—	—	—	—	—	—	—
SIMPSON INFIRMARY, WELLESLEY COLLEGE, Zip 02181; tel. 617/235-0320; Thomas J. Keighley MD, dir. health serv. (Data for 245 days) **A**9 **F**15 28 29 30 32 33 37	23	11	S		21	316	3	14.3	0	0	—	—	14
WEST ROXBURY—Suffolk County See Boston													
WESTBOROUGH—Worcester County													
WESTBOROUGH STATE HOSPITAL, Lyman St., Box 288, Zip 01581; tel. 617/727-5506; Alan Zampini, chief oper. off. **A**9 **F**23 24 29 30 32 33 42 45 46 47 50	12	22	L		423	557	308	87.3	0	0	14607	9306	422
WESTFIELD—Hampden County													
★□ NOBLE HOSPITAL, 115 W. Silver St., Box 870, Zip 01086; tel. 413/568-2811; Scott B. Bullock, pres. **A**1a 9 10 **F**1 3 6 10 12 14 15 16 23 24 27 29 32 33 35 41 45 46 47 52 53	23	10	S		162	3960	102	63.0	0	0	18122	9283	437
□ WESTERN MASSACHUSETTS HOSPITAL, 91 E. Mountain Rd., Zip 01085; tel. 413/562-4131; Blake M. Molleur, exec. dir. (Nonreporting) **A**1a 9 10	12	48	L		102	—	—	—	—	—	—	—	—
WESTWOOD—Norfolk County													
★□ AMI WESTWOOD LODGE HOSPITAL (Formerly Westwood Lodge Hospital), 45 Clapboardtree St., Zip 02090; tel. 617/762-7764; Sherwin Z. Goodblatt, exec. dir. **A**1a b 3 9 **F**23 24 32 33 42 47; **S**0125	33	22	S		75	882	73	97.3	0	0	11179	4592	160
WHITINSVILLE—Worcester County													
WHITINSVILLE DIVISION, See Milford-Whitinsville Regional Hospital, Milford													
WINCHESTER—Middlesex County													
★□ WINCHESTER HOSPITAL, 41 Highland Ave., Zip 01890; tel. 617/729-9000; Eugene E. Loubier, pres. **A**1a 2 9 10 **F**1 3 6 12 14 15 16 23 24 26 28 32 33 35 36 40 43 44 45 46 47 50 52 53	23	10	S		223	7848	126	56.5	36	1408	29133	12950	666
WINTHROP—Suffolk County													
★□ WINTHROP HOSPITAL, 40 Lincoln St., Zip 02152; tel. 617/846-2600; Gerard H. Nocton, exec. dir. **A**1a 9 10 **F**1 3 6 10 11 12 14 15 16 23 24 26 27 28 30 32 33 34 35 41 45 46 47 50 53	23	10	S		110	2626	77	70.0	0	0	14820	6947	340
WOBURN—Middlesex County													
CHOATE MEMORIAL HOSPITAL, See Choate-Symmes Hospitals													
★□ CHOATE-SYMMES HOSPITALS (Includes Choate Memorial Hospital, 21 Warren Ave., Zip 01801; tel. 617/933-6700; Symmes Hospital, Hospital Rd., Arlington, Zip 02174; tel. 617/646-1500), 21 Warren Ave., Zip 01801; tel. 617/933-6700; Paul L. Downey, pres. **A**1a 2 9 10 **F**1 3 6 10 12 14 15 16 23 24 26 27 29 30 35 44 45 46 50 52	23	10	S		305	7961	173	56.7	0	0	46075	22024	1161
★□ Δ NEW ENGLAND REHABILITATION HOSPITAL, Two Rehabilitation Way, Zip 01801; tel. 617/935-5050; Gerald Borgal, chief exec. off. **A**1a 7 9 10 **F**15 23 24 26 28 32 33 34 42 44 45 46	33	46	L		198	2170	184	92.9	0	0	21509	12126	555
WORCESTER—Worcester County													
□ DOCTORS HOSPITAL OF WORCESTER (Comprehensive Alcohol and Drug Services), 107 Lincoln St., Zip 01605; tel. 617/799-9000; David W. Hillis, pres. (Nonreporting) **A**1a 9 10	33	82	S		88	—	—	—	—	—	—	—	—
□ FAIRLAWN HOSPITAL, 189 May St., Zip 01602; tel. 617/791-6351; Francis P. Kirley, pres. (Nonreporting) **A**1a 9 10	23	10	S		104	—	—	—	—	—	—	—	—
★□ SAINT VINCENT HOSPITAL, 25 Winthrop St., Zip 01604; tel. 617/798-1234; William D. Harkins, pres. & chief exec. off. **A**1a 2 3 5 6 8 9 10 **F**1 2 3 4 6 7 8 9 10 11 12 14 15 16 20 23 24 26 27 28 30 32 33 34 35 36 40 41 42 44 45 46 47 49 52 53 54	23	10	S		504	18397	376	74.2	40	1809	76775	41110	1827
★□ UNIVERSITY OF MASSACHUSETTS MEDICAL CENTER (Formerly University of Massachusetts Medical School and Teaching Hospital), 55 Lake Ave. N., Zip 01605; tel. 617/856-0011; Keith J. Waterbrook, vice chancellor & dir. **A**1a 2 3 5 8 9 10 **F**1 2 3 4 5 6 7 8 9 10 11 12 13 14 15 16 20 21 23 24 26 27 28 29 30 32 33 34 35 37 38 44 46 47 50 52 53 54	12	10	S		348	11116	276	79.3	0	0	102110	47615	1964
□ WORCESTER CITY HOSPITAL, 26 Queen St., Zip 01610; tel. 617/799-8000; Thomas E. Cummings, adm. **A**1a 3 5 6 10 **F**1 3 6 7 8 9 10 11 12 14 15 16 21 22 23 24 26 28 32 34 35 37 45 46 47 48 49 50 52 53; **S**1755	14	10	S		300	4725	131	43.2	0	0	32650	16436	813
WORCESTER COUNTY HOSPITAL, See Boylston													
★□ WORCESTER HAHNEMANN HOSPITAL, 281 Lincoln St., Zip 01605; tel. 617/792-8000; Robert M. Barry, pres. **A**1a 3 5 6 9 10 **F**1 3 6 10 11 12 14 15 16 20 23 24 26 30 34 35 36 37 40 41 43 44 45 46 50 52 53	23	10	S		252	8600	135	53.6	30	1110	31548	18164	814
★□ WORCESTER MEMORIAL HOSPITAL, 119 Belmont St., Zip 01605; tel. 617/793-6611; David A. Barrett, pres. & chief exec. off. **A**1a 2 3 5 8 9 10 **F**1 2 3 6 7 8 9 10 11 12 14 15 16 20 23 24 26 27 28 30 32 33 34 35 36 37 38 40 45 46 50 53 54	23	10	S		315	14000	268	84.5	24	3135	62558	31087	1316
WORCESTER STATE HOSPITAL, 305 Belmont St., Zip 01604; tel. 617/752-4681; Edward A. Riquier, chief oper. off. **A**3 5 9 10 **F**23 24 33 42 46 47 50	12	22	L		418	1791	399	91.3	0	0	17917	13570	711

Hospital, Address, Telephone, Administrator, Approval and Facility Codes, Multihospital System Code

- ★ American Hospital Association (AHA) membership
- □ Joint Commission on Accreditation of Hospitals (JCAH) accreditation
- \+ American Osteopathic Hospital Association (AOHA) membership
- ○ American Osteopathic Association (AOA) accreditation
- Δ Commission on Accreditation of Rehabilitation Facilities (CARF) accreditation

Control codes 61, 63, 64, 71, 72 and 73 indicate hospitals listed by AOHA, but not registered by AHA. For definition of numerical codes, see page A2

Michigan

Hospital, Address, Telephone, Administrator, Approval and Facility Codes, Multihospital System Code	Classification Codes				Inpatient Data				Newborn Data		Expense (thousands of dollars)		
	Control	Service	Stay	Facilities	Beds	Admissions	Census	Occupancy (percent)	Bassinets	Births	Total	Payroll	Personnel
ADDISON—Lenawee County													
□ ADDISON COMMUNITY HOSPITAL AUTHORITY, 421 N. Steer St., Zip 49220; tel. 517/547-6151; John F. Beaudrie, chief exec. off. **A**1a 9 10 **F**1 6 10 12 14 15 16 23 32 35 44 47 50 52	16	10	S		24	588	8	33.3	0	0	2853	1224	62
ADRIAN—Lenawee County													
★□ EMMA L. BIXBY HOSPITAL, 818 Riverside Ave., Zip 49221; tel. 517/263-0711; Douglas W. McNeill, pres. **A**1a 9 10 **F**1 3 6 7 8 9 10 11 12 14 15 16 23 24 34 35 36 40 43 44 45 46 47 48 49 52 53 54	23	10	S		172	6233	79	45.9	25	965	17682	9569	451
ALBION—Calhoun County													
★□ ALBION COMMUNITY HOSPITAL, 809 W. Erie St., Zip 49224; tel. 517/629-2191; Richard C. Hoeth, pres. **A**1a 9 10 **F**1 3 6 10 12 14 15 16 23 28 33 34 35 36 37 40 42 45 46 47 52; **S**2495	14	10	S		55	2526	31	53.4	12	237	7375	2845	190
ALLEGAN—Allegan County													
★□ ALLEGAN GENERAL HOSPITAL, 555 Linn St., Zip 49010; tel. 616/673-8424; Jack L. Denton, pres. **A**1a 9 10 **F**1 3 6 10 14 15 16 23 24 27 28 29 30 32 33 34 35 36 40 42 43 44 45 46 47 48 52	23	10	S		75	2561	41	54.7	14	255	10887	5413	248
ALLEN PARK—Wayne County													
★□ VETERANS ADMINISTRATION MEDICAL CENTER, Southfield & Outer Dr., Zip 48101; tel. 313/562-6000; James H. Stephens, dir. (Total facility includes 162 beds in nursing home-type unit) **A**1a b 2 3 5 8 **F**1 3 6 7 10 11 12 14 15 16 19 20 21 23 24 26 27 28 29 30 32 33 34 35 41 42 43 44 46 47 48 49 53 54	45	10	S	TF	611	13974	473	77.4	0	0	77089	40238	1546
				H	449	13793	329	—	0	0	—	—	1522
ALMA—Gratiot County													
★□ GRATIOT COMMUNITY HOSPITAL, 300 S. Warwick Dr., Zip 48801; tel. 517/463-1101; Philip H. Kell, pres. **A**1a 9 10 **F**1 3 6 10 12 15 16 20 23 27 30 32 33 35 36 40 41 42 43 44 45 46 47 49 52	23	10	S		151	5312	79	52.3	20	725	20005	9697	429
ALMONT—Macomb County													
ST. JOSEPH'S-ALMONT COMMUNITY HOSPITAL, See St. Joseph Hospital, Mount Clemens													
ALPENA—Alpena County													
★□ ALPENA GENERAL HOSPITAL, 1501 W. Chisholm St., Zip 49707; tel. 517/356-7390; John A. McVeety, adm. **A**1a 9 10 **F**1 3 6 10 12 14 15 16 23 24 27 28 34 35 36 40 42 45 46 47 48 52	13	10	S		169	5080	91	53.8	15	552	21178	9499	428
ANN ARBOR—Washtenaw County													
★□ CATHERINE MCAULEY HEALTH CENTER (Includes Mercywood Hospital, 5361 McAuley Dr., Box 1127, Zip 48106; tel. 313/572-5678; St. Joseph Mercy Hospital, 5301 E. Huron River Dr., Box 995, Zip 48106; tel. 313/572-3456), Robert E. Laverty, pres. **A**1a 3 5 8 9 10 **F**1 2 3 4 6 7 8 9 10 11 12 14 15 16 19 20 23 24 25 30 32 33 34 35 36 40 42 44 45 46 47 48 49 53 54; **S**5165	21	10	S		614	24020	469	80.3	61	3843	150118	61100	2172
★□ UNIVERSITY OF MICHIGAN HOSPITALS, 300 N. Ingalls, Zip 48109; tel. 313/936-4000; John D. Forsyth, exec. dir. **A**1a 2 3 5 8 9 **F**1 2 3 4 5 6 7 8 9 10 11 12 13 14 15 16 17 20 22 23 24 25 26 27 28 29 30 32 33 34 35 36 37 38 39 40 41 42 43 44 45 46 47 49 50 51 52 53 54	23	10	S		852	27989	704	81.1	28	1657	281876	124951	5627
★□ VETERANS ADMINISTRATION MEDICAL CENTER, 2215 Fuller Rd., Zip 48105; tel. 313/769-7100; Ronald F. Lipp, dir. (Nonreporting) **A**1a 3 5 8	45	10	S		410	—	—	—	—	—	—	—	—
BAD AXE—Huron County													
★□ HURON MEMORIAL HOSPITAL, 1100 S. Van Dyke St., Zip 48413; tel. 517/269-9521; James B. Gardner, adm. **A**1a 9 10 **F**1 3 6 10 12 15 16 23 24 34 35 37 40 44 45 52	23	10	S		93	3112	41	44.1	10	270	9317	4760	227
BATTLE CREEK—Calhoun County													
★□ BATTLE CREEK ADVENTIST HOSPITAL, 165 N. Washington Ave., Zip 49016; tel. 616/964-7121; Teddric J. Mohr, pres. **A**1a 10 **F**12 14 16 23 24 28 29 30 32 33 42 43 45 46 48 49; **S**9355	21	22	S		136	1425	93	67.9	0	0	10804	6276	284
★□ COMMUNITY HOSPITAL ASSOCIATION, 183 West St., Zip 49016; tel. 616/964-5880; C. Dennis Barr, pres. & chief exec. off. **A**1a 9 10 **F**1 3 5 6 10 12 14 15 16 20 30 33 34 35 36 37 40 45 46 47 52 53	23	10	S		210	7647	115	54.8	32	1419	30046	14974	704
★□ LEILA HOSPITAL AND HEALTH CENTER, 300 North Ave., Zip 49016; tel. 616/966-8002; Donald F. Ryan, pres. & chief exec. off. **A**1a 2 9 10 **F**1 3 6 7 8 9 10 11 12 14 15 16 23 33 34 35 45 46 52 53; **S**5165	21	10	S		209	6484	120	57.4	0	0	29394	14379	641
★ Δ SOUTHWESTERN MICHIGAN REHABILITATION HOSPITAL, 183 West St., Zip 49017; tel. 616/965-3206; L. M. Mullins, pres. **A**7 9 10 **F**23 24 26 32 33 34 42 44 46 47	23	46	S		29	244	19	65.5	0	0	3043	1400	64
★□ VETERANS ADMINISTRATION MEDICAL CENTER, Zip 49016; tel. 616/966-5600; Viola V. Johnson, dir. (Total facility includes 205 beds in nursing home-type unit) **A**1a **F**3 12 15 16 19 23 24 26 28 29 30 31 32 33 34 41 42 44 45 46 47 48 49 50	45	22	L	TF	991	5286	864	87.2	0	0	52373	34172	1344
				H	786	5168	666	—	0	0	44922	29297	1271
BAY CITY—Bay County													
★□ BAY MEDICAL CENTER (Includes Samaritan Health Center, 713 Ninth St., Zip 48708; tel. 517/894-3799), 1900 Columbus Ave., Zip 48708; tel. 517/894-6465; Anthony W. Armstrong, pres. **A**1a b 2 9 10 **F**1 3 5 6 10 11 12 15 16 19 23 24 26 27 32 33 34 35 36 37 38 40 42 44 45 46 47 48 49 50 52 53	23	10	S		378	14616	243	64.3	40	1146	56699	28305	1223
○ + BAY OSTEOPATHIC HOSPITAL, 3250 E. Midland Rd., Zip 48706; tel. 517/686-2920; John J. Mills, pres. **A**9 10 11 12 13 **F**1 3 6 10 14 16 23 34 35 36 40 41 45 46 49	23	10	S		86	2837	39	45.3	10	353	10940	3854	179
SAMARITAN HEALTH CENTER, See Bay Medical Center													
BELDING—Ionia County													
★ ○ + ORCHARD HILLS HOSPITAL (Formerly Belding Community Hospital), 1534 W. State St., Zip 48809; tel. 616/794-0400; Robert F. Jernigan Jr., adm. **A**9 10 11 **F**1 6 10 14 15 16 23 34 35 40 52; **S**1755	23	10	S		56	768	7	12.5	5	64	2513	1053	50
BENTON HARBOR—Berrien County													
MERCY HOSPITAL, See Southwestern Michigan Health Care Association, St. Joseph													
BERRIEN CENTER—Berrien County													
★□ BERRIEN GENERAL HOSPITAL, 6418 Dean's Hill Rd., Zip 49102; tel. 616/471-7761; Sandra Bruce, pres. (Total facility includes 187 beds in nursing home-type unit) **A**1a 9 10 **F**1 3 6 12 14 15 16 19 23 33 34 35 36 40 42 44 45 46 52	13	10	S	TF	248	3383	216	87.1	10	1103	11936	6020	431
				H	61	3048	35	—	10	1103	8551	4847	324
BIG RAPIDS—Mecosta County													
★□ MECOSTA COUNTY GENERAL HOSPITAL, 405 Winter Ave., Zip 49307; tel. 616/796-8691; Karl E. Stomner, pres. **A**1a 9 10 **F**1 3 6 10 12 14 15 16 23 24 26 34 35 37 40 44 45 46 47 52	13	10	S		74	2719	34	45.9	12	522	10864	5432	268

Hospital, Address, Telephone, Administrator, Approval and Facility Codes, Multihospital System Code	Classification Codes				Inpatient Data				Newborn Data		Expense (thousands of dollars)		
★ American Hospital Association (AHA) membership ☐ Joint Commission on Accreditation of Hospitals (JCAH) accreditation + American Osteopathic Hospital Association (AOHA) membership ○ American Osteopathic Association (AOA) accreditation Δ Commission on Accreditation of Rehabilitation Facilities (CARF) accreditation Control codes 61, 63, 64, 71, 72 and 73 indicate hospitals listed by AOHA, but not registered by AHA. For definition of numerical codes, see page A2	Control	Service	Stay	Facilities	Beds	Admissions	Census	Occupancy (percent)	Bassinets	Births	Total	Payroll	Personnel
BRIGHTON—Livingston County													
⊞ BRIGHTON HOSPITAL, 12851 E. Grand River Rd., Zip 48116; tel. 313/227-1211; Ivan C. Harner, pres. **A**1b 9 **F**10 32 33 46 49	23	82	S		63	1035	61	96.8	0	0	4563	2002	109
BUCHANAN—Berrien County													
★ ○ + VISITORS HOSPITAL, 15198 N. Main St., Zip 49107; tel. 616/695-3851; Pam Leiter, adm. & chief oper. off. **A**9 10 11 **F**1 14 16 23 24 26 32 33 34 42 44 45 46 52	33	10	S		42	245	7	16.7	0	0	2502	1016	94
CADILLAC—Wexford County													
⊞ MERCY HOSPITAL, 400 Hobart St., Zip 49601; tel. 616/779-7200; Robert Maher, pres. **A**1a 9 10 **F**1 3 6 10 12 14 15 16 20 23 24 28 30 32 33 34 35 36 40 44 45 46 47 52; **S**5165	21	10	S		174	6174	87	49.7	22	730	18377	8533	482
CARO—Tuscola County													
⊞ CARO COMMUNITY HOSPITAL, 401 N. Hooper St., P O Box 71, Zip 48723; tel. 517/673-3141; William P. Miller, chief exec. off. **A**1a 9 10 **F**1 6 12 15 16 21 23 26 28 30 34 35 37 40 44 45 46 47 52	14	10	S		50	1026	12	24.0	0	56	3828	1800	102
CARO REGIONAL MENTAL HEALTH CENTER, Box A, Zip 48723; tel. 517/673-3191; Marlin H. Roll PhD, dir. **A**9 10 **F**15 23 24 27 30 31 32 33 34 35 38 42 43 44 45 47 50	12	62	L		502	544	449	89.3	0	0	25674	16563	706
CARSON CITY—Montcalm County													
○ + CARSON CITY HOSPITAL, Elm at Third St., Zip 48811; tel. 517/584-3131; Bruce L. Traverse, pres. **A**9 10 11 12 **F**1 3 6 10 12 15 16 23 34 35 36 40 41 44 45 46 52	23	10	S		65	2302	31	30.1	11	301	8619	4388	253
CASS CITY—Tuscola County													
⊞ HILLS AND DALES GENERAL HOSPITAL, 4675 Hill St., Zip 48726; tel. 517/872-2121; Ken E. Jensen, adm. **A**1a 9 10 **F**1 6 14 15 16 23 35 36 40 44 45 46 47 52	23	10	S		65	1892	25	38.5	11	193	5006	2279	117
CHARLEVOIX—Charlevoix County													
⊞ CHARLEVOIX AREA HOSPITAL, Lake Shore Dr., Zip 49720; tel. 616/547-4024; Richard L. Krueger, adm. **A**1a 9 10 **F**1 3 6 14 15 16 23 24 34 35 40 44 45 46 52	23	10	S		44	1549	20	45.5	9	209	4590	2268	118
CHARLOTTE—Eaton County													
⊞ HAYES-GREEN-BEACH MEMORIAL HOSPITAL, 321 E. Harris St., Zip 48813; tel. 517/543-1050; Stephen W. Mapes, pres. **A**1a 9 10 **F**1 6 15 16 34 35 36 40 45 52	23	10	S		46	1384	19	41.3	9	133	5213	2498	156
CHEBOYGAN—Cheboygan County													
⊞ COMMUNITY MEMORIAL HOSPITAL, 748 S. Main St., P O Box 419, Zip 49721; tel. 616/627-5601; Howard J. Purcell Jr., pres. (Total facility includes 50 beds in nursing home-type unit) **A**1a 9 10 **F**1 2 6 10 12 14 15 16 19 21 23 35 40 45 46 52	23	10	S	TF H	129 79	2756 2718	85 36	65.9 —	6 6	301 301	8994 —	4836 —	255 221
CHELSEA—Washtenaw County													
⊞ Δ CHELSEA COMMUNITY HOSPITAL, 775 S. Main St., Zip 48118; tel. 313/475-1311; Willard H. Johnson, pres. **A**1a b 3 5 7 9 10 **F**1 3 6 10 15 16 19 21 23 24 25 26 27 28 29 32 33 34 35 41 42 43 44 45 46 47 48 49	23	10	S		137	2968	82	61.7	0	0	16203	7378	417
CLARE—Clare County													
★ ○ CLARE COMMUNITY HOSPITAL, 104 W. Sixth St., Zip 48617; tel. 517/386-9951; Lawrence F. Barco, pres. **A**9 10 11 **F**1 2 6 10 16 23 24 35 36 42 44 45 46 47 50	23	10	S		64	2072	24	37.5	7	305	6890	3006	169
COLDWATER—Branch County													
⊞ COMMUNITY HEALTH CENTER OF BRANCH COUNTY, 274 E. Chicago St., Zip 49036; tel. 517/278-7361; David J. Ameen, pres. **A**1a 9 10 **F**1 3 6 10 12 14 15 16 20 23 34 35 36 37 40 41 44 45 46 47 49 52	13	10	S		130	4419	59	45.4	20	545	15607	8218	332
CRYSTAL FALLS—Iron County													
★ CRYSTAL FALLS COMMUNITY HOSPITAL, Michigan Ave. & Third St., Zip 49920; tel. 906/875-6661; Harry B. Purdy, adm. **A**9 10 **F**1 2 12 16 20 35 40 45	14	10	S		35	627	11	31.4	5	31	2100	1045	56
DEARBORN—Wayne County													
DEARBORN MEDICAL CENTRE HOSPITAL, See Oakwood Springwells Health Center													
⊞ OAKWOOD HOSPITAL, 18101 Oakwood Blvd., P O Box 2500, Zip 48123; tel. 313/593-7000; Gerald D. Fitzgerald, pres. **A**1a 2 3 5 8 9 10 **F**1 2 3 6 7 8 9 10 11 12 14 15 16 17 20 23 24 26 27 29 30 32 33 34 35 36 40 42 44 45 46 47 51 52 53 54	23	10	S		615	24128	494	80.3	66	4259	127205	57667	2210
⊞ OAKWOOD SPRINGWELLS HEALTH CENTER (Formerly Dearborn Medical Centre Hospital), 10151 Michigan Ave., Zip 48126; tel. 313/584-4770; William T. Harris PhD, adm. **A**1a 9 10 **F**1 15 16 23 24 34	23	10	S		45	353	5	11.1	0	0	2666	1208	59
DECKERVILLE—Sanilac County													
⊞ DECKERVILLE COMMUNITY HOSPITAL, 3559 Pine St., Zip 48427; tel. 313/376-2835; David L. Corteville, adm. **A**1a 9 10 **F**1 2 3 6 14 15 16 23 24 30 34 35 44 45 52	23	10	S		25	693	9	36.0	6	106	2033	1069	58
DETROIT—Wayne County													
⊞ BRENT GENERAL HOSPITAL, 16260 Dexter, Zip 48221; tel. 313/862-3400; Danford L. Wilson, chief exec. off. **A**1a 9 10 **F**1 3 7 9 10 11 12 14 16 28 31 33 34 37 47 48 49 50	23	10	S		116	1134	23	20.0	0	0	6592	2725	125
⊞ CHILDREN'S HOSPITAL OF MICHIGAN, 3901 Beaubien, Zip 48201; tel. 313/745-5437; Paul L. Broughton, pres. & chief exec. off. **A**1a 3 5 8 9 10 **F**1 4 5 6 10 12 13 14 15 16 20 22 23 24 26 28 32 33 34 35 38 42 44 45 46 47 51 53 54	23	50	S		250	12628	191	76.4	0	0	71907	39192	1454
DETROIT OSTEOPATHIC HOSPITAL, See Highland Park													
⊞ DETROIT RECEIVING HOSPITAL AND UNIVERSITY HEALTH CENTER (Emergency Trauma), 4201 St. Antoine, Zip 48201; tel. 313/745-3000; Edward S. Thomas, pres. **A**1a 3 5 8 10 **F**3 5 6 12 14 16 22 23 24 27 28 30 32 33 34 35 44 46 47 53	23	49	S		322	10166	262	81.9	0	0	94106	34136	1744
⊞ DETROIT-MACOMB HOSPITAL CORPORATION (Includes Macomb Hospital, 11800 E. Twelve Mile Rd., Warren, Zip 48093; tel. 313/573-5000; Richard T. Young, adm.; Detroit Riverview Hospital, 7733 E. Jefferson Ave., Zip 48214; tel. 313/499-3000; Gareth H. Mitchell, adm.), 7815 E. Jefferson Ave., Zip 48214; tel. 313/821-6000; Jack Ryan MD, pres. & chief exec. off. **A**1a 2 3 9 **F**1 2 3 5 6 8 9 10 11 12 14 15 16 23 24 25 26 27 30 32 33 34 35 36 37 40 42 44 45 46 49 52 53	23	10	S		656	19863	434	66.2	70	3269	95001	50964	2120
⊞ DOCTORS HOSPITAL, 2730 E. Jefferson Ave., Zip 48207; tel. 313/259-3050; William N. Hettiger, pres. **A**1a b 9 10 **F**1 3 6 10 12 14 15 16 23 26 28 29 32 33 34 35 44 45 46 47 49 50	23	10	S		101	2254	63	62.4	0	0	10841	5201	250
⊞ GRACE HOSPITAL, 18700 Meyers Rd., Zip 48235; tel. 313/966-3111; George P. Caralis, adm. **A**1a 2 3 5 8 9 10 **F**1 2 3 6 7 8 9 10 11 12 14 15 16 23 26 34 35 36 37 40 41 44 45 46 47 50 51 53 54; **S**1655	23	10	S		303	12209	227	74.9	34	2589	71555	33908	1478
⊞ HARPER HOSPITAL, 3990 John R St., Zip 48201; tel. 313/745-8111; Albert L. Greene, adm. **A**1a 2 3 5 8 9 10 **F**1 2 3 4 6 7 8 9 10 11 12 13 14 15 16 17 20 23 24 27 28 29 32 33 34 42 43 44 45 46 47 48 49 50 53 54; **S**1655	23	10	S		709	19704	585	82.5	0	0	194190	—	—
⊞ HENRY FORD HOSPITAL, 2799 W. Grand Blvd., Zip 48202; tel. 313/876-2600; Douglas S. Peters, pres. **A**1a 2 3 5 6 8 9 10 **F**1 2 3 4 5 6 7 8 9 10 11 12 13 14 15 16 17 20 23 24 26 27 28 30 32 33 34 35 36 37 38 39 40 41 42 44 46 47 48 49 50 51 52 53 54	23	10	S		837	32917	712	81.3	37	2281	389777	199084	6884
⊞ HOLY CROSS HOSPITAL, 4777 E. Outer Dr., Zip 48234; tel. 313/369-9100; Gerald E. Moore, pres. **A**1a 9 10 **F**1 3 6 12 14 15 16 23 24 26 34 35 40 44 45 46 52 53 54; **S**5375	23	10	S		365	7924	155	42.5	35	600	40140	19077	715

Hospital, Address, Telephone, Administrator, Approval and Facility Codes, Multihospital System Code	Classification Codes				Inpatient Data				Newborn Data		Expense (thousands of dollars)		
★ American Hospital Association (AHA) membership □ Joint Commission on Accreditation of Hospitals (JCAH) accreditation + American Osteopathic Hospital Association (AOHA) membership ○ American Osteopathic Association (AOA) accreditation Δ Commission on Accreditation of Rehabilitation Facilities (CARF) accreditation Control codes 61, 63, 64, 71, 72 and 73 indicate hospitals listed by AOHA, but not registered by AHA. For definition of numerical codes, see page A2	Control	Service	Stay	Facilities	Beds	Admissions	Census	Occupancy (percent)	Bassinets	Births	Total	Payroll	Personnel
★□ HUTZEL HOSPITAL, 4707 St. Antoine Blvd., Zip 48201; tel. 313/745-7174; Frank P. Iacobell, pres. **A**1a b 3 5 8 9 10 **F**1 3 6 9 10 11 12 13 14 15 16 20 23 24 26 30 32 33 34 35 36 37 38 40 41 42 44 45 46 47 48 49 51 53 54	23	10	S		385	19237	347	91.1	86	6579	96546	44818	1869
□ LAFAYETTE CLINIC, 951 E. Lafayette St., Zip 48207; tel. 313/256-9350; Samuel Gershon MD, dir. **A**1b 3 5 10 **F**3 12 15 24 28 29 31 32 33 34 38 42 43 46 47 50	12	22	L		128	467	101	78.9	0	0	19593	—	332
LAKESHORE HOSPITAL, See Michigan Osteopathic Medical Center													
○ + MICHIGAN OSTEOPATHIC MEDICAL CENTER (Includes Lakeshore Hospital, 3245 E. Jefferson, Zip 48207; tel. 313/259-4141; Tom Johnson, adm.), 2700 Martin Luther King Jr Blvd., Zip 48208; tel. 313/361-8000; Mary-Jane Trimner, vice-pres. & adm. (Nonreporting) **A**9 10 11 12 13	23	10	S		197	—	—	—	—	—	—	—	—
★□ MOUNT CARMEL MERCY HOSPITAL, 6071 W. Outer Dr., Zip 48235; tel. 313/927-7000; LeRoy D. Fahle, pres. **A**1a 3 5 8 9 10 **F**1 3 5 6 7 8 9 10 11 12 13 14 15 16 20 23 24 26 27 28 29 30 32 33 34 35 43 44 45 46 47 49 52 53 54; **S**5165	21	10	S		347	14117	312	80.0	0	0	98239	42261	1588
★□ NEW CENTER HOSPITAL, 801 Virginia Park, Zip 48202; tel. 313/874-2800; James J. Polonis, chief adm. off. (Nonreporting) **A**1a 9 10	23	10	S		145	—	—	—	—	—	—	—	—
★□ NORTH DETROIT GENERAL HOSPITAL, 3105 Carpenter Ave., Zip 48212; tel. 313/369-3000; Jerry A. Frohlich, adm. **A**1a 9 10 **F**1 2 3 6 10 12 14 15 16 23 24 27 30 32 33 35 42 44 46 47 53	23	10	S		319	6061	170	53.3	0	0	29518	15861	734
○ + NORTHWEST GENERAL HOSPITAL, 8741 W. Chicago Blvd., Zip 48204; tel. 313/934-3030; Johnny C. Brown, adm. **A**9 10 11 12 **F**1 6 10 12 14 16 17 23 28 32 34 35 44 52	23	10	S		104	2322	48	46.2	0	0	12085	5419	238
★□ REHABILITATION INSTITUTE, 261 Mack Blvd., Zip 48201; tel. 313/745-9731; Leonard F. Bender, pres. **A**1a 3 5 9 10 **F**23 24 26 34 42 44 45 46 47	23	46	L		173	2004	141	81.0	0	0	25130	13304	551
★□ SAMARITAN HEALTH CENTER, 5555 Conner Ave., Zip 48213; tel. 313/579-4000; Robert Peoples, pres. **A**1a 3 9 10 **F**1 2 3 6 10 12 14 15 16 20 23 24 27 28 29 30 32 33 34 35 36 37 40 42 44 45 46 47 48 49 52 53; **S**5165	21	10	S		375	9334	233	62.1	32	851	77563	28706	1265
★□ SARATOGA COMMUNITY HOSPITAL, 15000 Gratiot Ave., Zip 48205; tel. 313/245-1200; K. Rand Dykman, exec. dir. **A**1a 9 10 **F**1 3 6 10 12 15 16 23 24 25 26 34 35 37 43 44 45 46 47 50 53	23	10	S		200	4999	109	62.6	0	0	30687	13348	633
★□ Δ SINAI HOSPITAL OF DETROIT, 6767 W. Outer Dr., Zip 48235; tel. 313/493-6824; Irving A. Shapiro, exec. vice-pres. **A**1a 3 5 7 8 9 10 **F**1 2 3 4 6 7 8 9 10 11 12 14 15 16 23 24 25 26 27 28 29 30 31 34 35 36 37 38 40 42 43 44 45 46 47 51 53 54	23	10	S		545	22039	475	87.2	57	4267	146654	67210	2994
★□ SOUTHWEST DETROIT HOSPITAL, 2401 20th St., Zip 48216; tel. 313/496-7710; Reginald P. Ayala, pres. & chief exec. off.; Betty Fry, exec. vice-pres. & chief oper. off. **A**1a 9 10 **F**1 3 10 12 15 16 23 24 26 32 33 34 35 37 38 42 43 44 45 46 47 52 53	23	10	S		217	3861	95	59.4	0	0	25288	10694	554
★□ ST. JOHN HOSPITAL, 22101 Moross Rd., Zip 48236; tel. 313/343-4000; Glenn A. Wesselmann, pres. & chief exec. off. **A**1a 3 5 8 9 10 **F**1 2 3 4 5 6 7 8 9 10 11 12 14 15 16 23 24 26 34 35 36 37 40 41 44 45 46 47 51 52 53 54; **S**5555	21	10	S		568	22214	443	79.7	52	3011	129104	51762	2236
DOWAGIAC—Cass County													
★□ LEE MEMORIAL HOSPITAL, 420 W. High St., Zip 49047; tel. 616/782-8681; Roman I. Borszcz, adm. **A**1a 9 10 **F**1 3 6 12 14 15 16 23 30 35 36 40 44 45 46 52; **S**5555	21	10	S		74	2801	37	50.0	12	183	7755	3407	196
EATON RAPIDS—Eaton County													
★□ EATON RAPIDS COMMUNITY HOSPITAL, 1500 S. Main St., Zip 48827; tel. 517/663-2671; James N. Miller, pres. & chief exec. off. **A**1a 9 10 **F**1 6 12 14 15 16 23 34 35 40 45 46	23	10	S		41	1317	16	39.0	6	112	5055	1881	143
EDMORE—Montcalm County													
★□ TRI-COUNTY COMMUNITY HOSPITAL, 1131 E. Howard City & Edmore Rd., Zip 48829; tel. 517/427-5116; Darwin Finkbeiner, pres. **A**1a b 9 10 **F**1 14 16 23 35 36 40 48 49; **S**9355	23	10	S		44	749	22	50.0	5	2	2012	1071	65
ELOISE—Wayne County													
WALTER P. REUTHER PSYCHIATRIC HOSPITAL, See Westland													
ESCANABA—Delta County													
★□ ST. FRANCIS HOSPITAL, 3401 Ludington St., Zip 49829; tel. 906/786-3311; Robert Clark, adm. **A**1a 9 10 **F**1 2 3 6 10 12 14 15 16 17 23 32 34 35 40 43 44 45 46 47; **S**5335	21	10	S		110	3643	54	44.6	16	543	11931	6708	322
FARMINGTON HILLS—Oakland County													
★ ○ + BOTSFORD GENERAL HOSPITAL-OSTEOPATHIC, 28050 Grand River Ave., Zip 48024; tel. 313/471-8000; Gerson I. Cooper, pres. **A**9 10 11 12 13 **F**2 3 4 5 7 10 15 16 17 20 24 28 33 34 36 40 42 43 44 45 46 48 49 52 53	23	10	S		300	10461	199	66.3	36	1123	56422	26723	1180
FERNDALE—Oakland County													
★□ KINGSWOOD HOSPITAL, 10300 W. Eight Mile Rd., Zip 48220; tel. 313/398-3200; Ralph A. Stromberg, adm. **A**1a 9 10 **F**15 24 42 47	23	22	S		91	1031	61	67.0	0	0	6684	3719	182
FLINT—Genesee County													
○ + FLINT OSTEOPATHIC HOSPITAL, 3921 Beecher Rd., Zip 48502; tel. 313/762-4000; Gerald C. Selke, pres. **A**9 10 11 12 13 **F**1 3 5 6 10 11 12 15 16 20 23 24 34 35 40 44 45 46 47 50 52 53	23	10	S		359	15476	227	63.2	30	1717	58199	27478	1017
★□ GENESEE MEMORIAL HOSPITAL, 702 S. Ballenger Hwy., Zip 48502; tel. 313/239-1481; Homer W. Read, pres. **A**1a 9 10 **F**1 6 10 12 14 15 16 23 34 45 46	23	10	S		95	1344	12	12.6	0	0	10304	4566	152
★□ HURLEY MEDICAL CENTER, One Hurley Plaza, Zip 48502; tel. 313/257-9000; Phillip C. Dutcher, dir. **A**1a b 2 3 5 6 8 9 10 **F**1 2 3 5 6 7 8 9 10 11 12 13 14 15 16 20 21 22 23 24 27 29 30 32 33 34 35 40 41 42 44 45 46 47 49 50 51 52 53 54	14	10	S		502	19983	370	73.7	40	2903	109478	59804	2371
★□ Δ MCLAREN GENERAL HOSPITAL, 401 S. Ballenger Hwy., Zip 48502; tel. 313/762-2000; Gary R. Peterson, pres. **A**1a 3 5 7 9 10 **F**1 2 3 4 6 7 9 10 11 12 14 15 16 23 24 25 26 27 32 33 34 35 37 40 42 44 45 46 52 53 54	23	10	S		362	13605	289	79.8	44	1029	72879	38533	1415
★□ ST. JOSEPH HOSPITAL, 302 Kensington Ave., Zip 48502; tel. 313/762-8000; Young S. Suh, pres. **A**1a 2 3 5 9 10 **F**1 2 3 4 5 6 7 8 9 10 11 12 14 15 16 20 23 24 26 32 34 35 36 40 44 45 46 50 52 53 54; **S**5555	21	10	S		423	15487	260	61.5	39	1682	64418	30912	1430
FRANKFORT—Benzie County													
★□ PAUL OLIVER MEMORIAL HOSPITAL, 224 Park Ave., Zip 49635; tel. 616/352-9621; Davis D. Skinner, adm. **A**1a 9 10 **F**1 3 14 15 16 23 34 35 36 40 45 46 49 52	23	10	S		48	923	15	31.3	6	54	4081	1673	91
FREMONT—Newaygo County													
★□ GERBER MEMORIAL HOSPITAL, 212 S. Sullivan St., Zip 49412; tel. 616/924-3300; Ned B. Hughes Jr., pres. **A**1a 9 10 **F**1 2 3 6 14 15 23 35 36 40 45 46	23	10	S		82	2246	24	29.3	14	380	6717	2911	171
GARDEN CITY—Wayne County													
○ + GARDEN CITY OSTEOPATHIC HOSPITAL, 6245 N. Inkster Rd., Zip 48135; tel. 313/421-3300; Allan L. Breakie, pres. **A**9 10 11 12 13 **F**1 6 10 11 12 14 15 16 21 23 24 33 34 35 36 40 41 44 45 46 47 49 52 53	23	10	S		349	9805	184	52.7	30	1168	41488	21160	803
GAYLORD—Otsego County													
★□ OTSEGO MEMORIAL HOSPITAL (Includes McReynolds Hall), 825 N. Center St., Zip 49735; tel. 517/732-1731; Robert J. Kemp, adm. (Total facility includes 34 beds in nursing home-type unit) **A**1a 9 10 **F**1 3 6 12 16 19 23 25 34 35 40 45 46 47 48 49 52	23	10	S	TF	111	2165	61	62.9	8	244	6805	3218	191
				H	77	2096	29	—	8	244	5960	2681	169

Hospital, Address, Telephone, Administrator, Approval and Facility Codes, Multihospital System Code	Classification Codes			Facilities	Inpatient Data				Newborn Data		Expense (thousands of dollars)		Personnel
★ American Hospital Association (AHA) membership □ Joint Commission on Accreditation of Hospitals (JCAH) accreditation + American Osteopathic Hospital Association (AOHA) membership ○ American Osteopathic Association (AOA) accreditation Δ Commission on Accreditation of Rehabilitation Facilities (CARF) accreditation Control codes 61, 63, 64, 71, 72 and 73 indicate hospitals listed by AOHA, but not registered by AHA. For definition of numerical codes, see page A2	Control	Service	Stay		Beds	Admissions	Census	Occupancy (percent)	Bassinets	Births	Total	Payroll	
GLADWIN—Gladwin County													
★□ GLADWIN AREA HOSPITAL, 455 S. Quarter St., Box 594, Zip 48624; tel. 517/426-9286; Joseph M. Smith, pres. **A**1a 9 10 **F**1 15 16 23 34 35 45 52	23	10	S		42	1430	23	54.8	0	0	4731	2042	89
GOODRICH—Genesee County													
★□ WHEELOCK MEMORIAL HOSPITAL, 7280 State Rd., Zip 48438; tel. 313/636-2221; Norma J. Murphy, chief exec. off. **A**1a 9 10 **F**1 6 14 15 16 21 23 35 45; **S**5555	23	10	S		31	958	10	32.3	0	0	3867	1947	104
GRAND HAVEN—Ottawa County													
★□ NORTH OTTAWA COMMUNITY HOSPITAL, 1309 Sheldon Rd., Zip 49417; tel. 616/842-3600; Ronald G. Czarneke, pres. **A**1a 9 10 **F**1 3 5 6 10 12 14 16 21 23 24 26 30 33 34 35 36 40 41 44 45 46 52	16	10	S		104	3523	46	44.2	18	568	14161	6731	330
GRAND RAPIDS—Kent County													
★□ BLODGETT MEMORIAL MEDICAL CENTER, 1840 Wealthy St. S.E., Zip 49506; tel. 616/774-7444; Terrence M. O'Rourke, pres. **A**1a 2 3 5 6 8 9 10 **F**1 3 4 5 6 7 8 9 10 11 12 14 16 22 23 24 26 34 35 36 37 38 40 42 43 44 45 46 52 53 54	23	10	S		407	14424	243	59.7	57	2225	68489	30992	1371
★□ BUTTERWORTH HOSPITAL, 100 Michigan St. N.E., Zip 49503; tel. 616/774-1774; William G. Gonzalez, pres. & chief exec. off. **A**1a 2 3 5 8 9 10 **F**1 3 4 5 6 7 8 9 10 11 12 14 15 16 23 24 30 34 35 36 40 43 44 45 46 51 52 53 54	23	10	S		529	22752	416	78.6	77	4490	97791	50910	2369
★□ FERGUSON HOSPITAL (Colon-Rectal), 72 Sheldon Blvd. S.E., Zip 49503; tel. 616/456-0202; Jack B. Carter, pres. **A**1a 2 3 5 9 10 **F**1 3 6 12 14 15 16 21 34 47	23	49	S		105	2387	39	37.1	0	0	8790	4344	220
□ FOREST VIEW PSYCHIATRIC HOSPITAL, 1055 Medical Park Dr. S.E., Zip 49506; tel. 616/942-9610; Stan A. Mills, mng. dir. (Nonreporting) **A**1a 9; **S**9555	33	22	L		62	—	—	—	—	—	—	—	—
★□ KENT COMMUNITY HOSPITAL COMPLEX (Includes Kent Community Hospital, 750 Fuller Ave. N.E., Zip 49503; tel. 616/774-3300; Howard S. Claus, exec. dir.; Kent Oaks Hospital, 1330 Bradford St. N.E., Zip 49503; tel. 616/774-3450; Patrick D. Waugh, adm.), 750 Fuller Ave. N.E., Zip 49503; tel. 616/774-3300; Howard S. Claus, exec. dir. (Total facility includes 338 beds in nursing home-type unit) **A**1a 9 10 **F**16 19 23 24 26 27 29 33 42 44 45 46 48	13	10	S	TF	534	2959	434	81.3	0	0	18297	9824	571
				H	196	1974	111	—	0	0	—	—	331
★□ Δ MARY FREE BED HOSPITAL AND REHABILITATION CENTER, 235 Wealthy S.E., Zip 49503; tel. 616/242-0300; William H. Blessing, pres. **A**1a 7 9 10 **F**15 23 24 26 32 33 34 42 44 46	23	46	L		80	583	65	81.3	0	0	11798	6998	382
○ + METROPOLITAN HOSPITAL, 1919 Boston St. S.E., Zip 49506; tel. 616/247-7200; Francis J. McCarthy, pres. **A**9 10 11 12 13 **F**1 3 6 10 12 14 15 16 19 23 24 25 26 30 32 33 34 35 36 37 40 44 45 46 47 49 52 53 54	23	10	S		222	8844	135	62.2	24	981	35418	16335	663
★□ PINE REST CHRISTIAN HOSPITAL, 300 68th St. S.E., Zip 49508; tel. 616/455-5000; Ronald L. Stuursma, exec. dir. **A**1b 5 9 10 **F**24 28 29 32 33 42 44 45 46 47	23	22	L		220	1193	193	87.7	0	0	21210	14013	680
★□ ST. MARY'S HEALTH SERVICES (Formerly St. Mary's Hospital), 200 Jefferson St. S.E., Zip 49503; tel. 616/774-6090; Stephen A. Robbins, actg. pres. & chief exec. off. **A**1a 2 3 5 8 9 10 **F**1 3 6 7 8 9 10 11 12 13 14 15 16 20 23 24 26 34 35 36 40 42 43 44 45 46 52 53; **S**5165	21	10	S		370	13055	206	55.7	37	2637	66309	29083	1234
GRAYLING—Crawford County													
★□ MERCY HOSPITAL, 1100 Michigan Ave., Zip 49738; tel. 517/384-5461; Robert J. Maher, pres. & chief exec. off. (Total facility includes 40 beds in nursing home-type unit) **A**1a 9 10 **F**1 3 6 10 14 15 16 19 23 24 34 35 36 40 44 45 46 47 52; **S**5165	21	10	S	TF	104	3035	81	77.9	8	275	12375	5313	292
				H	64	2938	45	—	8	275	10995	4890	265
GREENVILLE—Montcalm County													
★□ UNITED MEMORIAL HOSPITAL, 615 S. Bower St., P O Box 430, Zip 48838; tel. 616/754-4691; Frederic W. Brown Jr., adm. (Total facility includes 40 beds in nursing home-type unit) **A**1a 9 10 **F**1 3 6 10 16 19 23 24 35 36 40 44 45 46 52	23	10	S	TF	92	1602	50	54.3	15	252	5057	2637	177
				H	52	1415	13	—	15	252	4624	2257	149
GROSSE POINTE—Wayne County													
★□ BON SECOURS HOSPITAL, 468 Cadieux Rd., Zip 48230; tel. 313/343-1000; Christopher M. Carney, exec. dir. & chief exec. off. **A**1a 3 5 9 10 **F**1 2 3 6 10 12 14 15 16 21 23 26 34 35 36 40 41 44 45 46 47 52 53; **S**5085	21	10	S		311	13076	234	75.2	30	1821	49781	23457	999
GROSSE POINTE FARMS—Wayne County													
★□ COTTAGE HOSPITAL OF GROSSE POINTE, 159 Kercheval Ave., Zip 48236; tel. 313/884-8600; Ralph L. Wilgarde, exec. vice-pres. **A**1a 9 10 **F**1 3 6 10 15 16 20 21 23 24 26 27 29 30 33 35 42 44 45 46 47 53	23	10	S		195	4723	121	62.1	0	0	28280	13275	575
HANCOCK—Houghton County													
★□ PORTAGE VIEW HOSPITAL, 200 Michigan St., Zip 49930; tel. 906/482-1122; Dave Woodland, adm. (Total facility includes 30 beds in nursing home-type unit) **A**1a 9 10 **F**1 3 5 6 10 12 14 16 19 23 34 35 36 40 44 45 46 54; **S**2495	23	10	S	TF	85	2292	66	77.6	10	372	8748	4469	212
				H	55	2272	36	—	10	372	7863	4179	194
HARBOR BEACH—Huron County													
★□ HARBOR BEACH COMMUNITY HOSPITAL, Broad & First Sts., Zip 48441; tel. 517/479-3201; Pauline Siemen RN, adm. (Total facility includes 40 beds in nursing home-type unit) **A**1a 9 10 **F**1 6 14 16 19 23 24 34 35 40 42 44 45 46 47 52	23	10	S	TF	67	673	47	70.1	6	34	2694	1520	92
				H	27	639	8	—	6	34	1691	861	69
HART—Oceana County													
★□ OCEANA HOSPITAL, 611 E. Main St., Zip 49420; tel. 616/873-2131; Paul J. Ivkovich, exec. dir. **A**1a 9 10 **F**1 3 14 15 16 34 35 45 52	23	10	S		36	526	6	16.7	0	0	2013	911	50
HASTINGS—Barry County													
★□ PENNOCK HOSPITAL, 1009 W. Green St., Zip 49058; tel. 616/945-3451; Daniel Hamilton, pres. **A**1a 9 10 **F**1 3 6 10 12 14 15 16 21 23 24 30 33 34 35 40 41 43 44 45 46 47 52	23	10	S		92	3409	48	52.2	14	406	12495	6007	350
HIGHLAND PARK—Wayne County													
★ ○ + DETROIT OSTEOPATHIC HOSPITAL (Formerly Listed Under Detroit), 12523 Third Ave., Zip 48203; tel. 313/252-4556; Chris Allen, vice-pres. & adm. **A**9 10 11 12 13 **F**1 2 3 4 6 7 8 9 10 11 12 14 16 20 23 24 27 32 33 34 42 44 45 46 47 48 53 54; **S**1035	23	10	S		203	5727	152	74.9	0	0	42491	—	687
HILLSDALE—Hillsdale County													
★□ HILLSDALE COMMUNITY HEALTH CENTER, 168 S. Howell St., Zip 49242; tel. 517/437-4451; Gordon Beem, adm. & chief oper. off. **A**1a 9 10 **F**1 2 3 6 10 14 15 16 23 24 28 30 32 33 34 35 36 37 40 44 45 46 52	14	10	S		86	2839	33	38.4	10	381	8231	3600	164
HOLLAND—Ottawa County													
★□ HOLLAND COMMUNITY HOSPITAL, 602 Michigan Ave., Zip 49423; tel. 616/392-5141; David Andersen, pres. **A**1a 9 10 **F**1 3 6 10 12 14 15 16 23 24 26 27 28 29 30 32 33 35 36 40 41 42 44 45 46 52 53	16	10	S		209	7588	105	50.2	24	1326	25173	11973	553
HOWELL—Livingston County													
★□ MCPHERSON COMMUNITY HEALTH CENTER, 620 Byron Rd., Zip 48843; tel. 517/546-1410; Peter J. Schonfeld, chief exec. off. **A**1a b 9 10 **F**1 3 6 12 14 15 16 23 24 34 35 36 37 40 41 43 44 45 46 48 50 52	23	10	S		127	4300	63	49.6	16	571	16056	8366	374
HUDSON—Lenawee County													
★□ THORN HOSPITAL, 458 Cross St., Zip 49247; tel. 517/448-2371; Dennis C. White, interim adm. **A**1a 9 10 **F**1 14 16 23 35 44 45	14	10	S		22	460	6	27.3	0	0	1685	888	39

Hospital, Address, Telephone, Administrator, Approval and Facility Codes, Multihospital System Code	Classification Codes				Inpatient Data				Newborn Data		Expense (thousands of dollars)		
★ American Hospital Association (AHA) membership □ Joint Commission on Accreditation of Hospitals (JCAH) accreditation + American Osteopathic Hospital Association (AOHA) membership ○ American Osteopathic Association (AOA) accreditation Δ Commission on Accreditation of Rehabilitation Facilities (CARF) accreditation Control codes 61, 63, 64, 71, 72 and 73 indicate hospitals listed by AOHA, but not registered by AHA. For definition of numerical codes, see page A2	Control	Service	Stay	Facilities	Beds	Admissions	Census	Occupancy (percent)	Bassinets	Births	Total	Payroll	Personnel
IONIA—Ionia County													
★□ IONIA COUNTY MEMORIAL HOSPITAL, 479 Lafayette St., Box 1001, Zip 48846; tel. 616/527-4200; Martin E. Anderson, adm. **A**1a 9 10 **F**1 2 3 6 12 14 15 16 23 35 40 45 52	14	10	S		77	1856	22	28.6	12	233	5243	2834	154
IRON MOUNTAIN—Dickinson County													
★□ DICKINSON COUNTY HOSPITALS (Includes Anderson Memorial Hospital, Main St., Norway, Zip 49870; tel. 906/563-9243), 400 Woodward Ave., Zip 49801; tel. 906/774-1313; Marvin L. Dehne, pres. **A**1a 9 10 **F**1 2 5 6 10 12 14 15 16 23 26 34 35 36 40 43 45 46 47 52	13	10	S		107	4423	64	53.8	13	499	12090	6462	337
★□ VETERANS ADMINISTRATION MEDICAL CENTER, H St., Zip 49801; tel. 906/774-3300; Joseph S. Spurgas Jr., dir. (Total facility includes 40 beds in nursing home-type unit) **A**1a **F**1 3 6 10 12 14 15 16 19 20 21 23 26 27 28 30 32 34 35 42 44 46 50	45	10	S	TF	245	5809	163	66.5	0	0	17975	10360	415
				H	205	5621	124	—	0	0	—	—	395
IRON RIVER—Iron County													
★□ IRON COUNTY GENERAL HOSPITAL, 1400 W. Ice Lake Rd., Zip 49935; tel. 906/265-6121; Jerry Miller, adm. **A**1a 9 10 **F**1 3 6 10 14 15 23 30 35 36 40 43 44; **S**1755	13	10	S		36	1103	15	41.7	5	112	3554	1558	89
IRONWOOD—Gogebic County													
★□ GRAND VIEW HOSPITAL, N10561 Grand View Lane, Zip 49938; tel. 906/932-2525; Wayne P. Hellerstedt, exec. dir. **A**1a 9 10 **F**1 2 6 12 14 15 16 34 35 36 40 45 52	13	10	S		72	1959	22	30.6	8	180	5850	2716	132
ISHPEMING—Marquette County													
□ FRANCIS A. BELL MEMORIAL HOSPITAL, 101 S. Fourth St., Zip 49849; tel. 906/486-4431; Timothy P. Healey, exec. dir. **A**1a 9 10 **F**1 3 6 10 11 12 15 16 23 24 33 35 36 40 45 52	23	10	S		99	2692	46	41.8	12	247	8926	4334	200
JACKSON—Jackson County													
○ + JACKSON OSTEOPATHIC HOSPITAL, 110 N. Elm Ave., Zip 49202; tel. 517/787-1440; Lee F. Sayre, adm. **A**9 10 11 **F**1 3 6 10 12 15 16 23 34 37 45 46 47 52	23	10	S		75	1826	26	34.7	0	0	7650	3011	153
★□ W. A. FOOTE MEMORIAL HOSPITAL, 205 N. East Ave., Zip 49201; tel. 517/788-4800; Paul Tejada, pres. **A**1a 9 10 **F**1 2 3 5 6 9 10 11 12 14 15 16 20 23 24 26 27 30 32 33 34 35 36 37 40 42 45 46 47 48 52 53	23	10	S		387	15597	241	62.3	52	1907	60144	27095	1354
K I SAWYER AIR FORCE BASE—Marquette County													
U. S. AIR FORCE HOSPITAL, Zip 49843; tel. 906/346-2236; Maj. Jack Gupton, adm. **F**1 5 6 12 14 15 23 24 28 29 30 32 33 34 35 36 37 40 42 43 46 47 52	41	10	S		15	1193	9	47.4	8	371	—	—	247
KALAMAZOO—Kalamazoo County													
★□ BORGESS MEDICAL CENTER, 1521 Gull Rd., Zip 49001; tel. 616/383-7000; R. Timothy Stack, pres. **A**1a 2 3 5 8 9 10 **F**1 2 3 4 5 6 7 8 9 10 11 12 13 14 15 16 20 23 24 26 27 28 29 30 31 32 33 34 35 36 40 42 45 46 47 48 49 50 52 53 54; **S**5555	21	10	S		462	17760	334	72.3	32	1307	115983	52826	2242
★□ BRONSON METHODIST HOSPITAL, 252 E. Lovell St., Zip 49007; tel. 616/383-7654; Peter W. Froyd, pres. **A**1a 2 3 5 6 10 **F**1 2 3 4 5 6 7 8 9 10 11 12 14 15 16 19 20 22 23 24 26 30 33 34 35 36 37 40 43 45 46 47 51 52 53 54; **S**0595	23	10	S		456	16467	296	65.8	48	3181	95578	49382	1909
□ KALAMAZOO REGIONAL PSYCHIATRIC HOSPITAL, 1312 Oakland Dr., Box A, Zip 49008; tel. 616/385-1200 **A**1b 9 **F**24 30 32 33 42 45 46 47 50	12	22	L		645	809	575	88.6	0	0	39544	22541	817
KALKASKA—Kalkaska County													
★ KALKASKA MEMORIAL HOSPITAL, 419 Coral St., Zip 49646; tel. 616/258-9142; Harvey W. Norris, adm. (Total facility includes 8 beds in nursing home-type unit) **A**9 10 **F**15 16 19 23 35 45	16	10	S	TF	21	437	12	57.1	0	4	1863	836	58
				H	13	333	4	—	0	4	—	—	—
L'ANSE—Baraga County													
★ BARAGA COUNTY MEMORIAL HOSPITAL, 770 N. Main St., Zip 49946; tel. 906/524-6166; John P. Tembreull, adm. (Total facility includes 28 beds in nursing home-type unit) **A**9 10 **F**1 6 12 14 15 16 19 23 26 34 35 40 42 43 44 45 52	13	10	S	TF	67	1329	44	65.7	6	88	4484	2406	126
				H	39	1317	17	—	6	88	3588	2125	115
LAKEVIEW—Montcalm County													
★□ KELSEY MEMORIAL HOSPITAL, 418 Washington Ave., Zip 48850; tel. 517/352-7211; Melvin R. Creeley, exec. dir. (Total facility includes 42 beds in nursing home-type unit) **A**1a 9 10 **F**1 12 14 15 16 19 23 24 35 36 40 42 44 46 52	23	10	S	TF	94	1204	52	55.3	7	173	4357	2289	121
				H	52	1113	11	—	7	173	3188	1876	95
LANSING—Ingham County													
★□ EDWARD W. SPARROW HOSPITAL, 1215 E. Michigan Ave., P O Box 30480, Zip 48909; tel. 517/483-2700; F. K. Neumann, pres. & chief exec. off. **A**1a 2 3 5 8 9 10 **F**1 2 3 5 6 7 8 9 10 11 12 13 14 15 16 20 22 23 24 26 32 34 35 36 37 40 42 43 44 45 46 48 51 52 53	23	10	S		522	21549	310	60.5	60	4258	91149	43762	1941
★□ INGHAM MEDICAL CENTER, 401 W. Greenlawn Ave., Zip 48910; tel. 517/374-2121; Edward B. McRee, pres. **A**1a 3 5 9 10 **F**1 2 3 4 6 10 12 14 15 16 23 24 26 27 34 35 44 45 46 52 53 54	13	10	S		258	10419	166	64.6	0	0	59914	28934	1293
★ ○ + LANSING GENERAL HOSPITAL, 2727 S. Pennsylvania Ave., Zip 48910; tel. 517/372-8220; Robert E. Miller, pres. **A**9 10 11 12 13 **F**1 3 6 10 12 14 15 16 23 24 25 26 32 34 35 36 37 40 41 44 45 46 47 49 50 52 53	23	10	S		177	7160	106	59.9	30	1193	36064	17079	746
★□ ○ + ST. LAWRENCE HOSPITAL, 1210 W. Saginaw St., Zip 48915; tel. 517/372-3610; Arthur Knueppel, pres. (Total facility includes 171 beds in nursing home-type unit) **A**1a 3 5 9 10 11 **F**1 3 5 6 12 14 15 16 19 21 23 24 27 28 29 30 32 33 34 35 36 40 41 44 45 46 47 48 49 50 53; **S**5165	21	10	S	TF	451	8800	353	69.1	27	997	51247	23771	873
				H	280	8457	192	—	27	997	48601	22088	792
LAPEER—Lapeer County													
★□ LAPEER GENERAL HOSPITAL (Formerly Lapeer County General Hospital), 1375 N. Main St., Zip 48446; tel. 313/664-8511; Thomas H. Keesling, chief exec. off. **A**1a b 9 10 **F**1 2 3 6 10 11 12 14 15 16 21 23 24 26 27 30 32 33 34 35 37 40 41 44 45 46 47 48 49 50 52	13	10	S		184	7216	98	55.4	25	872	24012	11333	555
LAURIUM—Houghton County													
★□ CALUMET PUBLIC HOSPITAL, 205 Osceola St., Zip 49913; tel. 906/337-3100; Dion Paquette, adm. **A**1a 9 10 **F**1 3 6 10 12 14 16 23 35 36 40 45 52	23	10	S		48	1408	24	50.0	8	102	5154	2620	143
LINCOLN PARK—Wayne County													
LYNN HOSPITAL, See Oakwood Downriver Medical Center													
★□ OAKWOOD DOWNRIVER MEDICAL CENTER (Formerly Lynn Hospital), 25750 W. Outer Dr., Zip 48146; tel. 313/383-6000; Michael E. Cassidy, pres. & chief exec. off. **A**1a 9 10 **F**1 3 10 14 15 16 23 26 34 35 37 46 48	23	10	S		72	1083	20	27.8	0	0	7504	3323	161
★□ OUTER DRIVE HOSPITAL, 26400 W. Outer Dr., Zip 48146; tel. 313/594-6000; Oliver G. Crump, adm. **A**1a b 9 10 **F**1 3 6 10 12 14 15 16 19 23 24 26 29 30 33 34 35 36 40 41 42 44 45 46 47 49 50 53; **S**3465	16	10	S		253	5774	116	45.8	18	647	27016	14207	564
LIVONIA—Wayne County													
★□ ARDMORE ACRES HOSPITAL, 19810 Farmington Rd., Zip 48152; tel. 313/474-3500; E. R. Schweier, adm. **A**1b 9 **F**24 42 47	33	22	S		50	751	38	76.0	0	0	—	—	125
★□ ST. MARY HOSPITAL, 36475 Five Mile Rd., Zip 48154; tel. 313/464-4800; Sr. Mary Modesta, pres. & chief exec. off. **A**1a 9 10 **F**1 2 3 5 6 9 10 11 12 14 15 16 20 23 24 26 27 30 32 33 34 35 36 40 42 44 46 47 49 53; **S**1345	21	10	S		304	10679	222	73.0	30	918	47125	23842	921

Hospital, Address, Telephone, Administrator, Approval and Facility Codes, Multihospital System Code

- ★ American Hospital Association (AHA) membership
- □ Joint Commission on Accreditation of Hospitals (JCAH) accreditation
- \+ American Osteopathic Hospital Association (AOHA) membership
- ○ American Osteopathic Association (AOA) accreditation
- Δ Commission on Accreditation of Rehabilitation Facilities (CARF) accreditation

Control codes 61, 63, 64, 71, 72 and 73 indicate hospitals listed by AOHA, but not registered by AHA. For definition of numerical codes, see page A2

Hospital, Address, Telephone, Administrator, Approval and Facility Codes, Multihospital System Code	Classification Codes: Control	Service	Stay	Facilities	Inpatient Data: Beds	Admissions	Census	Occupancy (percent)	Newborn Data: Bassinets	Births	Expense (thousands of dollars): Total	Payroll	Personnel
LUDINGTON—Mason County													
⊞ MEMORIAL MEDICAL CENTER OF WEST MICHIGAN, One Atkinson Dr., Zip 49431; tel. 616/843-2591; Robert C. Marquardt, adm. **A**1a 9 10 **F**1 3 6 9 10 12 14 15 16 23 35 36 40 41 45 46	23	10	S		81	3385	49	57.6	16	411	10731	4926	263
MADISON HEIGHTS—Oakland County													
⊞ MADISON COMMUNITY HOSPITAL, 30671 Stephenson Hwy., P O Box E., Zip 48071; tel. 313/588-8000; Charles F. Pinkerman, adm. **A**1a 9 10 **F**1 6 10 12 14 15 16 23 24 35 42 45 46	23	10	S		36	1032	17	47.2	0	0	6584	2718	122
○ + OAKLAND GENERAL HOSPITAL OSTEOPATHIC, 27351 Dequindre, Zip 48071; tel. 313/967-7000; Anthony R. Tersigni, pres. & chief exec. off. **A**9 10 11 12 13 **F**1 3 6 12 14 15 16 23 24 30 32 34 35 44 46 47 52 53 54	23	10	S		162	5220	107	69.0	0	0	33221	12150	546
MANISTEE—Manistee County													
⊞ WEST SHORE HOSPITAL, 1465 E. Parkdale Ave., Zip 49660; tel. 616/723-3501; Burton O. Parks, adm. **A**1a 9 10 **F**1 3 6 9 10 12 14 15 16 23 24 26 34 35 40 44 45 46 52	13	10	S		57	2256	36	63.2	11	202	8375	4322	188
MANISTIQUE—Schoolcraft County													
⊞ SCHOOLCRAFT MEMORIAL HOSPITAL, 500 Main St., Zip 49854; tel. 906/341-2163; David B. Jahn, adm. **A**1a 9 10 **F**1 6 12 14 15 16 23 30 33 34 35 37 40 43 44 45 47 52	13	10	S		47	1331	14	29.8	12	154	4431	2201	108
MARLETTE—Sanilac County													
⊞ MARLETTE COMMUNITY HOSPITAL, 2770 Main St., Zip 48453; tel. 517/635-7491; Darwin Root, adm. (Total facility includes 43 beds in nursing home-type unit) **A**1a 9 10 **F**1 3 6 10 14 15 16 21 23 24 26 32 34 35 44 45 46 50 52; **S**2495	23	10	S	TF H	91 48	1249 1157	58 15	63.7 —	0 0	0 0	4684 3407	2446 2043	165 137
MARQUETTE—Marquette County													
⊞ MARQUETTE GENERAL HOSPITAL, 420 W. Magnetic St., Zip 49855; tel. 906/228-9440; Robert C. Neldberg, exec. dir. **A**1a b 2 3 5 9 10 **F**1 2 3 4 5 6 7 8 9 10 11 12 14 15 16 17 20 23 24 25 27 30 32 33 34 35 36 37 40 42 44 45 46 47 48 49 51 52 53 54	23	10	S		306	10536	219	71.6	12	627	43384	20251	985
MARSHALL—Calhoun County													
⊞ OAKLAWN HOSPITAL, 200 N. Madison St., Zip 49068; tel. 616/781-4271; Rob Covert, adm. **A**1a 9 10 **F**1 3 6 10 12 14 15 16 23 24 26 30 32 33 34 35 36 37 40 41 42 44 45 46 49 50 52	23	10	S		77	2704	41	53.2	12	400	9241	4751	231
MENOMINEE—Menominee County													
⊞ BAY AREA MEDICAL CENTER-MENOMINEE (Formerly Menominee County Lloyd Hospital), 1110 Tenth Ave., Zip 49858; tel. 906/863-5571; Thomas K. Prusak, chief exec. off. **A**1a 9 10 **F**1 3 6 10 14 15 16 23 34 45 52; **S**2495	23	10	S		78	2280	30	38.5	0	0	6680	3137	144
MIDLAND—Midland County													
⊞ MIDLAND HOSPITAL CENTER, 4005 Orchard Dr., Zip 48670; tel. 517/839-3000; David A. Reece, pres. (Total facility includes 48 beds in nursing home-type unit) **A**1a 2 3 5 9 10 **F**1 2 3 6 7 8 9 10 12 14 15 16 19 23 24 26 27 30 33 35 36 37 40 42 44 45 46 47 50 52 53	23	10	S	TF H	307 259	10175 9899	210 169	68.4 —	32 32	1379 1379	48449 46514	24622 24032	977 949
MONROE—Monroe County													
⊞ MERCY MEMORIAL HOSPITAL, 718 N. Macomb St., P O Box 67, Zip 48161; tel. 313/241-1700; Richard S. Hiltz, pres. **A**1a 9 10 **F**1 3 6 10 12 14 15 16 23 24 26 27 30 32 33 35 37 40 41 42 44 45 46 47 52 53	23	10	S		179	7991	130	72.6	32	998	28274	13418	660
MORENCI—Lenawee County													
★ MORENCI AREA HOSPITAL, 13101 Sims Hwy., Zip 49256; tel. 517/458-2236; Walter E. Teeter, adm. **A**9 10 **F**1 6 12 16 23 35 37 44 45	14	10	S		31	856	8	25.8	7	37	1938	842	54
MOUNT CLEMENS—Macomb County													
⊞ ○ HARRISON COMMUNITY HOSPITAL, 26755 Ballard Rd., Zip 48045; tel. 313/465-5501; David Sessions, adm. **A**1a 9 10 11 **F**1 3 6 10 14 15 16 23 24 26 32 33 34 35 37 42 43 44 46 48 52; **S**5555	23	10	S		96	2032	39	40.6	0	0	9354	3881	225
○ + MOUNT CLEMENS GENERAL HOSPITAL, 1000 Harrington Blvd., Zip 48043; tel. 313/466-8000; Jack Weiner, adm. **A**9 10 11 12 13 **F**1 3 5 6 10 12 14 16 20 23 35 36 40 46 47 52 53 54	23	10	S		288	9785	166	57.6	24	1107	44754	20339	978
⊞ ST. JOSEPH'S HOSPITAL CENTER (Formerly St. Joseph Hospitals) (Includes St. Joseph Hospital East, 215 North Ave., Zip 48043; tel. 313/466-9300; St. Joseph Hospital West, 15855 19 Mile Rd., Zip 48044; tel. 313/263-2300; St. Joseph's-Almont Community Hospital, 80650 N. Van Dyke, Almont, Zip 48003; tel. 313/798-8551), Mailing Address 15855 19 Mile Rd., Zip 48044; tel. 313/263-2300; Mark L. Penkhus, pres. & chief exec. off. **A**1a 9 10 **F**1 2 3 6 9 10 11 12 14 15 16 21 23 24 26 27 28 30 32 33 34 35 36 39 40 41 44 45 46 47 48 49 50 52 53; **S**5115	23	10	S		535	17716	308	57.6	25	1232	70738	33584	1544
MOUNT PLEASANT—Isabella County													
⊞ CENTRAL MICHIGAN COMMUNITY HOSPITAL, 1221 South Dr., Zip 48858; tel. 517/772-6700; Paul K. Halverson, pres. & chief exec. off. **A**1a 9 10 **F**1 3 6 10 11 12 14 15 16 27 30 32 33 35 36 40 45 47 52; **S**6235	23	10	S		123	4643	75	61.0	24	555	17055	7744	360
MUNISING—Alger County													
⊞ MUNISING MEMORIAL HOSPITAL, Sand Point Rd., Rte. 1, Box 501, Zip 49862; tel. 906/387-4110; Allan Gearig, adm. **A**1a 9 10 **F**1 6 14 15 16 23 26 34 35 36 37 43 45 46 47 52	23	10	S		40	753	9	22.5	3	55	1843	951	44
MUSKEGON—Muskegon County													
⊞ HACKLEY HOSPITAL, 1700 Clinton St., Zip 49443; tel. 616/726-3511; Gordon A. Mudler, pres. **A**1a 2 9 10 **F**1 2 3 5 6 7 8 9 10 11 12 14 15 16 23 24 26 27 32 34 35 36 40 43 44 45 46 47 52 53	23	10	S		358	8991	152	42.6	46	1411	40547	18847	903
★ MERCY HOSPITAL, 1500 E. Sherman Blvd., P O Box 358, Zip 49443; tel. 616/739-9341; Alan J. Reberg, pres. & chief exec. off. **A**1a 9 10 **F**1 2 3 4 5 6 10 12 14 15 16 20 23 24 26 34 35 41 45 46 49 50 52 53 54; **S**5165	23	10	S		228	6928	115	50.4	0	0	37784	15326	696
○ + MUSKEGON GENERAL HOSPITAL, 1700 Oak Ave., Zip 49442; tel. 616/773-3311; Raymond G. Bishop, pres. **A**9 10 11 12 13 **F**1 3 6 10 12 14 15 16 23 24 26 34 35 36 40 41 44 45 46 47 50 52	23	10	S		127	4043	62	48.8	20	888	18605	7572	365
MUSKEGON HEIGHTS—Muskegon County													
□ + HERITAGE HOSPITAL, 3020 Peck St., Zip 49444; tel. 616/739-7141; Gary Arbon, adm. (Nonreporting) **A**1a 9 10	23	10	S		46	—	—	—	—	—	—	—	—
NEW BALTIMORE—Macomb County													
★ PSYCHIATRIC CENTER OF MICHIGAN, 35031 23 Mile Rd., Zip 48047; tel. 313/725-5777; Raymond Buck MD, chief exec. off.(Nonreporting) **A**,9 10; **S**0825	32	22	S		48	—	—	—	—	—	—	—	—
NEWBERRY—Luce County													
□ HELEN NEWBERRY JOY HOSPITAL (Includes Helen Newberry Joy Hospital Annex), 502 W. Harrie St., Zip 49868; tel. 906/293-5181; Thomas Hicks, adm. (Total facility includes 31 beds in nursing home-type unit) **A**1a 9 10 **F**1 15 16 19 23 35 37 40 45 52	13	10	S	TF H	74 43	761 753	42 11	56.8 —	4 4	70 70	2661 2101	1538 1174	123 68

Hospital, Address, Telephone, Administrator, Approval and Facility Codes, Multihospital System Code

- ★ American Hospital Association (AHA) membership
- □ Joint Commission on Accreditation of Hospitals (JCAH) accreditation
- \+ American Osteopathic Hospital Association (AOHA) membership
- ○ American Osteopathic Association (AOA) accreditation
- Δ Commission on Accreditation of Rehabilitation Facilities (CARF) accreditation

Control codes 61, 63, 64, 71, 72 and 73 indicate hospitals listed by AOHA, but not registered by AHA. For definition of numerical codes, see page A2

Hospital	Classification Codes: Control	Service	Stay	Facilities	Inpatient Data: Beds	Admissions	Census	Occupancy (percent)	Newborn Data: Bassinets	Births	Expense (thousands of dollars): Total	Payroll	Personnel
NEWBERRY REGIONAL MENTAL HEALTH CENTER (Psychiatric and Developmental Disabilities), 3001 S. Newberry Ave., Zip 49868; tel. 906/293-5121; Albert L. Meuli, dir. (Total facility includes 210 beds in nursing home-type unit) **A**9 **F**16 19 23 24 27 31 33 42 44 46 47 50	12	49	L	TF	252	221	225	88.6	0	0	17298	9066	344
				H	42	201	33	—	0	0	—	—	—
NILES—Berrien County													
★□ PAWATING HOSPITAL, 31 N. St. Joseph Ave., Zip 49120; tel. 616/683-5510; Robert P. Harrison, pres. & chief exec. off. **A**1a 9 10 **F**1 6 10 12 14 15 16 23 24 26 34 35 37 40 44 45 46 52	23	10	S		174	5059	76	43.7	20	399	16123	8700	451
NORTHPORT—Leelanau County													
★□ LEELANAU MEMORIAL HOSPITAL, Zip 49670; tel. 616/386-5101; Kathleen Putnam RN, adm. (Total facility includes 61 beds in nursing home-type unit) **A**1a 9 10 **F**1 6 14 15 16 19 23 35 36 40 43 44 45 52	23	10	S	TF	87	526	62	71.3	4	19	3253	1589	114
				H	26	459	5	—	4	19	1891	852	53
NORTHVILLE—Wayne County													
□ HAWTHORN CENTER, 18471 Haggerty Rd., Zip 48167; tel. 313/349-3000; Harold L. Wright Jr. MD, dir. **A**1b 3 5 9 **F**3 28 29 32 33 34 43	12	52	L		136	166	101	74.3	0	0	16807	9791	329
NORTHVILLE REGIONAL PSYCHIATRIC HOSPITAL, 41001 W. Seven Mile Rd., Zip 48167; tel. 313/349-1800; Richard Fletcher, adm. off. **A**3 5 **F**10 15 23 24 28 32 33 34 42 46	12	22	L		1171	3675	886	75.7	0	0	63482	—	1565
NORWAY—Dickinson County													
ANDERSON MEMORIAL HOSPITAL, See Dickinson County Hospitals, Iron Mountain													
ONAWAY—Presque Isle County													
★ RUSSELL MEMORIAL HOSPITAL, 201 N. Pine St., Zip 49765; tel. 517/733-8541; Marion Lyon, adm. **A**9 10 **F**1 16 34 35 40 45 52	23	10	S		17	544	7	41.2	3	13	1079	563	39
ONTONAGON—Ontonagon County													
★□ ONTONAGON MEMORIAL HOSPITAL, 601 Seventh St., Zip 49953; tel. 906/884-4134; Russell V. Onken, adm. (Total facility includes 46 beds in nursing home-type unit) **A**1a 9 10 **F**1 6 15 16 19 23 34 35 36 40 52	14	10	S	TF	87	1406	63	72.4	6	79	3964	1997	124
				H	41	1322	18	—	6	79	3189	1498	80
OSCODA—Iosco County													
U. S. AIR FORCE HOSPITAL, See Wurtsmith Air Force Base													
OWOSSO—Shiawassee County													
★□ MEMORIAL HOSPITAL, 826 W. King St., Zip 48867; tel. 517/723-5211; Hugh D. Witham, pres. **A**1a 9 10 **F**1 3 9 10 12 15 16 17 20 21 23 24 26 27 28 29 30 31 33 34 35 36 37 40 41 44 45 46 47 48 52 53	23	10	S		171	5481	95	57.2	23	735	20182	10515	523
PAW PAW—Van Buren County													
★□ LAKE VIEW COMMUNITY HOSPITAL, 408 Hazen St., Box 209, Zip 49079; tel. 616/657-3141; James R. Phillippe, adm. (Total facility includes 120 beds in nursing home-type unit) **A**1a 9 10 **F**1 6 16 19 23 34 35 36 40 45; **S**2495	16	10	S	TF	159	1904	138	82.1	6	202	8338	3959	232
				H	39	1792	20	—	6	202	6495	2997	146
PETOSKEY—Emmet County													
LITTLE TRAVERSE DIVISION, See Northern Michigan Hospitals													
LOCKWOOD-MACDONALD DIVISION, See Northern Michigan Hospitals													
★□ NORTHERN MICHIGAN HOSPITALS (Includes Little Traverse Division, 416 Connable Ave., Zip 49770; Lockwood-MacDonald Division, 1 MacDonald Dr., Zip 49770), 416 Connable St., Zip 49770; tel. 616/348-4000; James E. Raney, pres. **A**1a 2 9 10 **F**1 3 4 5 7 8 9 10 11 12 14 15 16 20 23 24 27 29 30 32 33 34 35 36 37 38 40 45 46 51 52 53 54; **S**2595	23	10	S		260	9797	178	68.5	20	822	43510	20903	943
PIGEON—Huron County													
★□ SCHEURER HOSPITAL, 170 N. Caseville Rd., Zip 48755; tel. 517/453-3223; George D. Desmarais, adm. (Total facility includes 19 beds in nursing home-type unit) **A**1a 9 10 **F**1 6 12 15 16 19 23 24 26 30 34 35 37 40 43 44 45 46 47	23	10	S	TF	47	1177	36	76.6	7	69	3983	1954	104
				H	28	1145	15	—	7	69	3793	1807	93
PLAINWELL—Allegan County													
★□ PIPP COMMUNITY HOSPITAL, 411 Naomi St., Zip 49080; tel. 616/685-6811; Fritz Fahrenbacher, adm. **A**1a 9 10 **F**1 3 6 12 14 15 16 23 24 26 30 33 34 35 37 40 43 44 45 46 52	23	10	S		43	1652	18	41.9	7	157	5407	2774	139
PONTIAC—Oakland County													
CLINTON VALLEY CENTER, 140 Elizabeth Lake Rd., Zip 48053; tel. 313/338-7241; Anthony D. Drabik, dir. (Nonreporting) **A**3	12	22	L		502	—	—	—	—	—	—	—	—
★□ PONTIAC GENERAL HOSPITAL, Seminole at W. Huron St., Zip 48053; tel. 313/857-7200; James M. Wright, pres. **A**1a 3 5 9 10 **F**1 2 3 5 6 7 8 9 10 11 12 14 15 16 20 23 24 27 28 30 32 33 34 35 36 40 41 42 44 45 46 47 51 52 53	14	10	S		302	11350	209	61.3	43	1598	56010	27375	1217
○ + PONTIAC OSTEOPATHIC HOSPITAL, 50 N. Perry St., Zip 48058; tel. 313/338-5000; Jack H. Whitlow, exec. dir. (Nonreporting) **A**9 10 11 12 13	63	10	S		314	—	—	—	—	—	—	—	—
★□ ST. JOSEPH MERCY HOSPITAL, 900 Woodward Ave., Zip 48053; tel. 313/858-3000; John P. Cullen, pres. & chief exec. off. **A**1a 3 5 8 9 10 **F**1 2 3 4 5 6 9 10 12 14 15 16 20 23 24 25 26 27 28 29 30 32 33 34 35 36 37 38 40 42 43 44 45 46 47 48 49 52 53 54; **S**5165	21	10	S		531	21368	424	79.8	60	2282	101370	48529	2039
★□ WOODSIDE MEDICAL, 845 S. Woodward Ave., Zip 48053; tel. 313/338-7144; Jim W. Albright, adm. **A**1a 9 **F**24 29 32 33 42 48	33	22	S		54	912	40	74.1	0	0	3928	—	146
PORT HURON—St. Clair County													
★□ MERCY HOSPITAL, 2601 Electric Ave., Zip 48061; tel. 313/985-1500; Robert Beyer, pres. **A**1a 9 10 **F**1 3 5 6 7 8 9 10 11 12 14 15 16 20 23 24 26 34 35 42 44 45 46 47; **S**5165	21	10	S		119	3274	64	53.8	0	0	22299	8328	366
★□ PORT HURON HOSPITAL, 1001 Kearney St., P O Box 5011, Zip 48061; tel. 313/987-5000; Charles W. McKinley, pres. **A**1a 9 10 **F**1 3 6 10 12 14 15 16 23 24 26 27 30 32 33 34 35 36 37 38 41 44 45 46 47 48 49 51 52 53	23	10	S		253	10673	191	77.0	32	1541	39444	17809	833
REDFORD—Wayne County													
★□ REDFORD COMMUNITY HOSPITAL, 25210 Grand River Ave., Zip 48240; tel. 313/531-6200; Robert Laible, pres. & chief exec. off. **A**1a 10 **F**1 3 6 10 12 14 16 23 24 30 35 44 47	23	10	S		72	1361	28	38.9	0	0	6858	2610	159
REED CITY—Osceola County													
★□ REED CITY HOSPITAL, 7665 Patterson Rd., Zip 49677; tel. 616/832-3271; Jack L. Haybarker, adm. (Total facility includes 54 beds in nursing home-type unit) **A**1a 9 10 **F**1 3 6 14 15 16 19 23 26 34 35 37 40 42 45 46 52	14	10	S	TF	110	2312	78	70.9	6	184	6923	3428	224
				H	56	2161	25	—	6	184	5560	2640	187
RIVER ROUGE—Wayne County													
★□ MILTON COMMUNITY HOSPITAL, 234 S. B Milton Dr., Zip 48218; tel. 313/388-2000; H. Benford Milton, adm. (Nonreporting) **A**1a 9 10	23	10	S		88	—	—	—	—	—	—	—	—
RIVERVIEW—Wayne County													
MARIAN MANOR MEDICAL CENTER, 18591 Quarry Rd., Zip 48192; tel. 313/282-2100; Margaret Adams, adm. (Nonreporting) **A**9	33	82	S		57	—	—	—	—	—	—	—	—
ROCHESTER—Oakland County													
★□ CRITTENTON HOSPITAL, 1101 W. University Dr., Zip 48063; tel. 313/652-5000; Richard J. Zunker, pres. **A**1a 2 9 10 **F**1 2 3 6 9 10 12 14 15 16 23 24 26 33 35 36 40 41 42 44 45 46 47 52 53 54	23	10	S		246	13026	188	76.4	42	2406	50481	24819	1126

Hospital, Address, Telephone, Administrator, Approval and Facility Codes, Multihospital System Code

★ American Hospital Association (AHA) membership
□ Joint Commission on Accreditation of Hospitals (JCAH) accreditation
\+ American Osteopathic Hospital Association (AOHA) membership
○ American Osteopathic Association (AOA) accreditation
Δ Commission on Accreditation of Rehabilitation Facilities (CARF) accreditation
Control codes 61, 63, 64, 71, 72 and 73 indicate hospitals listed by AOHA, but not registered by AHA.
For definition of numerical codes, see page A2

Hospital, Address, Telephone, Administrator, Approval and Facility Codes, Multihospital System Code	Classification Codes				Inpatient Data				Newborn Data		Expense (thousands of dollars)		
	Control	Service	Stay	Facilities	Beds	Admissions	Census	Occupancy (percent)	Bassinets	Births	Total	Payroll	Personnel
ROGERS CITY—Presque Isle County													
⊞ ROGERS CITY HOSPITAL (Includes Presque Isle Extended Care Facility), 555 N. Bradley Hwy., Zip 49779; tel. 517/734-2151; Samuel S. Gregory, adm. (Total facility includes 49 beds in nursing home-type unit) **A**1a 9 10 **F**1 3 5 6 12 14 15 16 19 23 35 40 42 44 45 50 52; **S**1755	14	10	S	TF H	94 45	1012 993	60 12	63.8 —	4 4	79 79	4595 4110	2240 1851	124 —
ROYAL OAK—Oakland County													
⊞ WILLIAM BEAUMONT HOSPITAL, 3601 W. Thirteen Mile Rd., Zip 48072; tel. 313/288-8000; Kenneth J. Matzick, dir. **A**1a 2 3 5 9 10 **F**1 2 3 4 5 6 7 8 9 10 11 12 13 14 15 16 20 23 24 25 26 27 28 30 32 33 34 35 36 37 38 39 40 42 43 44 45 46 47 51 52 53 54; **S**9575	23	10	S		929	39686	701	75.5	74	5899	210578	90073	4504
SAGINAW—Saginaw County													
⊞ SAGINAW COMMUNITY HOSPITAL (General Medical, Rehabilitation, Alcoholism, Psychiatric and Long term care), 3340 Hospital Rd., Box 2089, Zip 48605; tel. 517/790-1234; Robert A. Clowater MD, pres. & chief exec. off. (Total facility includes 217 beds in nursing home-type unit) **A**1a 9 10 **F**19 23 24 25 26 27 32 33 34 42 44 45 46 47 48	13	49	S	TF H	323 106	1560 1285	288 73	89.2 —	0 0	0 0	15334 7974	9000 —	480 —
⊞ SAGINAW GENERAL HOSPITAL, 1447 N. Harrison St., Zip 48602; tel. 517/771-4000; Donald E. Juenemann, pres. **A**1a 3 5 9 10 **F**1 2 3 6 10 15 16 20 23 24 27 30 32 33 34 35 36 37 40 42 45 46 47 49 50 51 53	23	10	S		352	12720	204	57.6	45	3499	43822	20544	987
⊞ ST. LUKE'S HOSPITAL, 705 Cooper St., Zip 48602; tel. 517/771-6000; Spencer Maidlow, pres. **A**1a 3 5 9 10 **F**1 2 3 5 6 10 15 16 19 23 24 26 34 35 37 45 46 52 53	23	10	S		282	9105	147	52.1	0	0	39880	18876	852
⊞ ST. MARY'S HOSPITAL, 830 S. Jefferson Ave., Zip 48601; tel. 517/776-8000; Edward Cook, pres. & chief exec. off. **A**1a 2 3 5 9 10 **F**1 2 3 4 5 6 7 8 9 10 11 12 14 15 16 21 22 23 24 26 30 33 34 35 44 45 46 47 49 52 53 54; **S**1885	21	10	S		238	10044	181	76.1	0	0	51050	23771	1168
⊞ VETERANS ADMINISTRATION MEDICAL CENTER, 1500 Weiss St., Zip 48602; tel. 517/793-2340; Jonathan P. Hawk, dir. (Total facility includes 30 beds in nursing home-type unit) **A**1a 3 5 **F**1 3 6 12 14 15 16 19 23 24 26 28 30 32 33 34 42 44 45 46	45	10	S	TF H	185 155	3631 3492	137 107	74.1 —	0 0	0 0	18348 —	10863 —	403 388
SALINE—Washtenaw County													
⊞ SALINE COMMUNITY HOSPITAL, 400 W. Russell St., Zip 48176; tel. 313/429-1500; William Lavery, adm. **A**1a 9 10 **F**1 3 6 12 14 15 16 23 24 26 28 30 32 33 35 44 45 46 48 49 50	23	10	S		58	2013	34	58.6	0	0	11085	4978	233
SANDUSKY—Sanilac County													
⊞ MCKENZIE MEMORIAL HOSPITAL, 120 Delaware St., Zip 48471; tel. 313/648-3770; Joseph W. Weiler, adm. **A**1a 9 10 **F**1 3 6 15 16 23 24 30 34 35 40 44 45 46 52	23	10	S		38	1394	15	39.5	6	102	4495	1858	114
SAULT STE MARIE—Chippewa County													
★ WAR MEMORIAL HOSPITAL, 500 Osborn Blvd., Zip 49783; tel. 906/635-4350; Ronald L. Bodary, adm. (Total facility includes 51 beds in nursing home-type unit) **A**9 10 **F**1 3 6 10 12 14 15 16 19 23 24 33 34 35 36 40 42 45 49 50; **S**1755	23	10	S	TF H	138 87	3867 3821	100 50	71.9 —	19 19	313 313	10687 —	6271 —	297 267
SHELBY—Oceana County													
□ LAKESHORE COMMUNITY HOSPITAL, 72 S. State St., Zip 49455; tel. 616/861-2156; William H. Yeager, adm. (Nonreporting) **A**1a 9 10	23	10	S		35	—	—	—	—	—	—	—	—
SHERIDAN—Montcalm County													
○ + SHERIDAN COMMUNITY HOSPITAL, 301 N. Main St., Zip 48884; tel. 517/291-3261; John R. Hudson, adm. **A**9 10 11 **F**1 3 6 12 14 15 16 23 35 36 40 45 52	23	10	S		42	990	12	28.6	5	92	3363	1477	93
SOUTH HAVEN—Van Buren County													
⊞ SOUTH HAVEN COMMUNITY HOSPITAL, 955 S. Bailey Ave., Box 489, Zip 49090; tel. 616/637-5271; Robert M. Irwin, adm. **A**1a 9 10 **F**1 2 6 14 15 24 34 36 37 40 41 42 44 45 46 52	16	10	S		82	2211	31	37.8	12	220	7344	3542	197
SOUTHFIELD—Oakland County													
⊞ PROVIDENCE HOSPITAL, 16001 W. Nine Mile Rd., Zip 48075; Mailing Address Box 2043, Zip 48037; tel. 313/424-3000; Brian M. Connolly, pres. **A**1a 2 3 5 8 9 10 **F**1 2 3 5 6 7 8 9 10 11 12 14 15 16 20 23 24 26 27 28 29 30 32 33 34 35 36 38 40 42 43 44 45 46 47 49 51 52 53 54; **S**1885	21	10	S		457	19040	378	82.7	80	3794	—	—	2539
○ + Δ SOUTHFIELD REHABILITATION HOSPITAL (Formerly Southfield Rehabilitation Center), 22401 Foster Winter Dr., Zip 48075; tel. 313/423-1409; Marcia T. Brown, adm. (Nonreporting) **A**7 11 13	73	46	L		108	—	—	—	—	—	—	—	—
⊞ STRAITH MEMORIAL HOSPITAL, 23901 Lahser Rd., Zip 48034; tel. 313/357-3360; Gregory R. Hoose, assc adm. **A**1a 9 10 **F**1 11 13 34 37 52	23	10	S		34	1304	7	20.6	0	0	6993	2614	109
ST. CLAIR—St. Clair County													
⊞ RIVER DISTRICT HOSPITAL, 4100 S. River Rd., Zip 48079; tel. 313/329-7111; William B. Leaver, adm. **A**1a 9 10 **F**1 3 6 14 15 16 23 24 26 28 32 33 34 35 36 37 40 42 44 45 46 47 49 52; **S**5555	16	10	S		68	2464	38	55.9	12	171	9357	4557	202
ST. IGNACE—Mackinac County													
MACKINAC STRAITS HOSPITAL AND HEALTH CENTER, 220 Burdette St., Zip 49781; tel. 906/643-8585; John Taylor, actg. adm. **A**9 10 **F**14 16 30 34 35 52; **S**2595	16	10	S		15	189	2	10.0	0	0	827	507	22
ST. JOHNS—Clinton County													
⊞ CLINTON MEMORIAL HOSPITAL, 805 S. Oakland St., Zip 48879; tel. 517/224-6881; Paul E. McNamara, pres. **A**1a 9 10 **F**1 3 6 14 15 16 21 23 24 26 34 35 36 40 41 44 45 46 52	23	10	S		48	1893	24	50.0	12	221	7867	3956	182
ST. JOSEPH—Berrien County													
MEMORIAL HOSPITAL, See Southwestern Michigan Health Care Association													
⊞ MERCY MEMORIAL MEDICAL CENTER (Includes Memorial Hospital, 2611 Morton Ave., Zip 49085; tel. 616/983-8300; Joseph A. Wasserman, exec. vice-pres.; Mercy Hospital, 960 Agard St., Benton Harbor, Zip 49022; tel. 616/927-5100), 2611 Morton Ave., Zip 49085; tel. 616/983-8300; Joseph A. Wasserman, pres. **A**1a 9 10 **F**1 3 4 5 6 8 9 10 12 14 15 16 20 23 24 27 30 34 35 36 40 42 44 45 46 52 53 54	23	10	S		285	11764	182	65.0	32	1182	43417	19773	981
STANDISH—Arenac County													
⊞ STANDISH COMMUNITY HOSPITAL, 805 W. Cedar St., Zip 48658; tel. 517/846-4521; Gordon C. Tolodziecki, adm. (Total facility includes 44 beds in nursing home-type unit) **A**1a 9 10 **F**1 2 5 6 10 15 16 19 23 24 33 34 35 40 42 44 45 50	23	10	S	TF H	81 37	1159 1047	51 14	63.0 —	6 6	1 1	4299 3128	2096 1525	159 133
STANWOOD—Mecosta County													
NORTHLAND MEDICAL CENTER (Formerly Mecosta Memorial Hospital), 18087 Pierce Rd., Zip 49346; tel. 616/823-2071; Jerry M. Bogart, adm. (Nonreporting) **A**9	23	10	S		36	—	—	—	—	—	—	—	—
STURGIS—St. Joseph County													
⊞ STURGIS HOSPITAL, 916 Myrtle, Zip 49091; tel. 616/651-7824; Patrick A. Hite, adm. **A**1a 9 10 **F**1 3 6 10 12 14 15 16 23 26 34 35 36 40 41 45 52	14	10	S		94	2220	23	24.5	12	450	9003	4190	183
TAWAS CITY—Iosco County													
⊞ TAWAS ST. JOSEPH HOSPITAL, 200 Hemlock, P O Box 659, Zip 48764; tel. 517/362-3411; Michael Jones, pres. **A**1a 9 10 **F**1 3 6 10 12 14 16 23 34 35 36 40 45 46 52; **S**5555	23	10	S		65	2972	41	63.1	6	310	10496	4762	261
TAYLOR—Wayne County													
⊞ HERITAGE HOSPITAL, 24775 Haig Ave., Zip 48180; tel. 313/295-5000; H. Arthur Sugarman, adm. **A**1a 10 **F**1 3 6 12 14 15 16 23 24 26 27 29 30 32 33 35 41 42 44 45 46 47 49 52 53; **S**3465	16	10	S		281	8583	194	72.1	0	0	38500	19834	893

Hospital, Address, Telephone, Administrator, Approval and Facility Codes, Multihospital System Code	Classification Codes				Inpatient Data				Newborn Data		Expense (thousands of dollars)		
★ American Hospital Association (AHA) membership □ Joint Commission on Accreditation of Hospitals (JCAH) accreditation + American Osteopathic Hospital Association (AOHA) membership ○ American Osteopathic Association (AOA) accreditation Δ Commission on Accreditation of Rehabilitation Facilities (CARF) accreditation Control codes 61, 63, 64, 71, 72 and 73 indicate hospitals listed by AOHA, but not registered by AHA. For definition of numerical codes, see page A2	Control	Service	Stay	Facilities	Beds	Admissions	Census	Occupancy (percent)	Bassinets	Births	Total	Payroll	Personnel
TECUMSEH—Lenawee County													
⊞ HERRICK MEMORIAL HOSPITAL, 500 E. Pottawatamie St., Zip 49286; tel. 517/423-2141; Phillip Sullivan, adm. **A**1a 9 10 **F**1 3 6 10 12 14 15 16 23 24 26 27 29 30 32 33 34 35 36 37 40 41 42 43 44 45 52 53	14	10	S		91	1925	35	38.5	9	187	8952	3978	235
THREE RIVERS—St. Joseph County													
⊞ THREE RIVERS AREA HOSPITAL, 214 Spring St., Zip 49093; tel. 616/278-1145; James P. Perricone, pres. **A**1a 9 10 **F**1 3 6 14 15 16 23 35 40 45 52; **S**1755	16	10	S		72	2052	28	38.9	10	307	6788	3343	156
TRAVERSE CITY—Grand Traverse County													
⊞ MUNSON MEDICAL CENTER, 1105 Sixth St., Zip 49684; tel. 616/922-9000; John C. Bay, pres. **A**1a 9 10 **F**1 2 3 5 6 7 8 9 10 11 12 14 15 16 21 23 24 25 26 27 28 29 30 34 35 36 37 40 41 43 44 45 46 48 49 50 51 52 53 54	23	10	S		289	13162	219	76.3	19	1386	45405	22663	1070
○ + TRAVERSE CITY OSTEOPATHIC HOSPITAL, 550 Munson Ave., Zip 49684; tel. 616/922-8400; Bruce G. Krider, pres. **A**9 10 11 12 **F**1 3 6 10 12 14 15 16 21 23 26 34 35 36 40 44 45 46 52	23	10	S		81	3337	52	64.2	10	421	12580	6491	360
□ TRAVERSE CITY REGIONAL PSYCHIATRIC HOSPITAL, Elmwood & 11th Sts., Box C, Zip 49684; tel. 616/922-5200; Martin J. Nolan II, dir. **A**1b 9 **F**15 24 32 33 42 46 50	12	22	L		154	366	135	74.6	0	0	13008	8010	290
TRENTON—Wayne County													
★ ○ + RIVERSIDE OSTEOPATHIC HOSPITAL, 150 Truax St., Zip 48183; tel. 313/676-4200; Patrick L. Muldoon, vice-pres. & adm. **A**9 10 11 12 13 **F**1 3 6 10 12 14 15 16 23 26 34 35 36 40 41 44 45 46 47 52 53; **S**1035	23	10	S		188	6971	118	62.8	25	1215	33458	13448	517
⊞ SEAWAY HOSPITAL, 5450 Fort St., Zip 48183; tel. 313/671-3800; Edward V. Slingerland, adm. **A**1a b 9 10 **F**1 3 9 10 12 15 16 17 20 23 24 26 28 34 35 41 44 45 47 49 50 52 53; **S**3465	16	10	S		206	3424	57	27.7	0	0	20409	10870	426
TROY—Oakland County													
⊞ WILLIAM BEAUMONT HOSPITAL-TROY, 44201 Dequindre Rd., Zip 48098; tel. 313/828-5100; John D. Labriola, vice-pres. & dir. **A**1a 3 5 9 10 **F**1 2 3 6 9 10 12 14 15 16 20 23 24 26 32 34 35 44 45 46 47 52 53 54; **S**9575	23	10	S		189	9652	138	73.0	0	0	47994	20703	886
VICKSBURG—Kalamazoo County													
⊞ BRONSON VICKSBURG HOSPITAL (Formerly Franklin Community Hospital), 13326 N. Boulevard, Zip 49097; tel. 616/649-2321; Edward Spartz, pres. **A**1a 9 10 **F**1 15 16 23 24 26 33 34 35 42 44 45 52; **S**0595	23	10	S		41	399	12	29.3	0	0	3395	1232	60
WARREN—Macomb County													
★ ○ + BI-COUNTY COMMUNITY HOSPITAL, 13355 E. Ten Mile Rd., Zip 48089; tel. 313/759-7300; Gary W. Popiel, vice-pres. & adm. **A**9 10 11 12 13 **F**1 3 6 10 12 14 15 16 20 23 34 35 36 40 41 44 45 46 47 49 52 53; **S**1035	23	10	S		247	7630	162	65.6	35	864	41618	17057	695
⊞ GLEN EDEN HOSPITAL, 6902 Chicago Rd., Zip 48092; tel. 313/264-8875; Dennis G. Chenail, adm. **A**1b 9 **F**15 24 29 32 33 42 43	33	22	S		126	1862	102	81.0	0	0	—	—	247
⊞ MONSIGNOR CLEMENT KERN HOSPITAL FOR SPECIAL SURGERY, 21230 Dequindre, Zip 48091; tel. 313/759-4520; Gary R. Snyder, exec. vice-pres. **A**1a 10 **F**1	23	49	S		46	574	4	8.7	0	0	4929	2158	98
SOUTH MACOMB HOSPITAL, See Detroit-Macomb Hospital Corporation, Detroit													
WATERVLIET—Berrien County													
⊞ COMMUNITY HOSPITAL, Medical Park, Box 158, Zip 49098; tel. 616/463-3111; Robert I. Schmelter, adm. **A**1a 9 10 **F**1 2 6 12 14 15 16 21 23 34 35 45 46 47 52; **S**1755	23	10	S		70	2393	32	45.7	0	0	6973	2910	142
WAYNE—Wayne County													
⊞ ANNAPOLIS HOSPITAL, 33155 Annapolis Rd., Zip 48184; tel. 313/467-4000; Wade C. Adams, adm. **A**1a 9 10 **F**1 2 3 6 12 14 15 16 23 24 26 32 33 35 37 40 41 44 45 46 47 49 52 53 54; **S**3465	16	10	S		276	11898	195	70.7	40	959	39152	20860	857
WEST BRANCH—Ogemaw County													
⊞ TOLFREE MEMORIAL HOSPITAL, 335 E. Houghton Ave., Zip 48661; tel. 517/345-3660; Douglas E. Pattullo, chief exec. off. **A**1a 9 10 **F**1 3 6 12 14 16 23 34 35 36 40 44 45 46 52	14	10	S		92	3745	51	55.4	12	404	9733	5159	275
WESTLAND—Wayne County													
□ WALTER P. REUTHER PSYCHIATRIC HOSPITAL (Formerly Listed Under Eloise), 30901 Palmer Rd., Zip 48185; tel. 313/722-4500; John Reynolds, dir. **A**1b 9 **F**16 23 24 30 33 42 45 46 47	12	22	L		302	171	290	96.0	0	0	17821	10044	386
⊞ WESTLAND MEDICAL CENTER, 2345 Merriman Rd., Zip 48185; tel. 313/467-2840; Richard Lane, exec. vice-pres. & chief oper. off. **A**1a 3 10 **F**1 2 3 6 10 12 14 16 23 24 26 27 31 34 35 37 40 42 44 46 47 52 53 54	23	10	S		356	3647	71	22.9	20	219	35951	11987	495
WHITE PINE—Ontonagon County													
□ LACROIX HOSPITAL, Main St., Box 157, Zip 49971; tel. 906/885-5311; Roger J. Pakonen, adm. (Nonreporting) **A**1a 9 10	23	10	S		36	—	—	—	—	—	—	—	—
WURTSMITH AIR FORCE BASE—Iosco County													
U. S. AIR FORCE HOSPITAL, Zip 48753; tel. 517/747-6032; Maj. Jimmy C. Brown, adm. **F**1 6 14 15 16 23 28 30 32 33 34 35 37 40 46 47 52	41	10	S		20	1289	11	55.0	10	325	—	—	224
WYANDOTTE—Wayne County													
⊞ Δ WYANDOTTE GENERAL HOSPITAL, 2333 Biddle Ave., Zip 48192; tel. 313/284-2400; John C. Fitch, exec. vice-pres. **A**1a 7 9 10 **F**1 3 6 12 14 15 16 23 24 25 26 27 28 29 30 32 33 35 36 40 42 43 44 45 46 52 53	14	10	S		359	10904	285	79.4	33	1189	54772	29556	1406
YALE—St. Clair County													
⊞ YALE COMMUNITY HOSPITAL, 420 North St., Zip 48097; tel. 313/387-3211; Fredrick W. Spaven, adm. **A**1a 9 10 **F**1 6 12 14 23 35 40 43 45 52	23	10	S		39	810	9	23.1	6	14	1567	767	42
YPSILANTI—Washtenaw County													
⊞ BEYER MEMORIAL HOSPITAL, 135 S. Prospect St., Zip 48198; tel. 313/484-2200; Jane G. McCormick, adm. **A**1a 9 10 **F**1 3 6 10 12 14 15 16 23 24 26 32 35 36 40 41 44 45 46 49 52; **S**3465	16	10	S		169	5158	77	45.6	32	422	20970	11252	467
□ YPSILANTI REGIONAL PSYCHIATRIC HOSPITAL, 3501 Willis Rd., Box A, Zip 48197; tel. 313/434-3400; Joy Holland, dir. **A**1b 9 **F**15 16 24 30 31 32 33 42 44 46 47	12	22	L		684	1342	513	75.0	0	0	—	—	796
ZEELAND—Ottawa County													
⊞ ZEELAND COMMUNITY HOSPITAL, 129 S. Taft St., Zip 49464; tel. 616/772-4644; Henry A. Veenstra, adm. **A**1a 9 10 **F**1 3 6 12 14 15 16 23 34 35 40 43 45 46 52	23	10	S		61	2095	26	42.6	15	501	6164	3160	167

Hospital, Address, Telephone, Administrator, Approval and Facility Codes, Multihospital System Code	Classification Codes				Inpatient Data				Newborn Data		Expense (thousands of dollars)		
	Control	Service	Stay	Facilities	Beds	Admissions	Census	Occupancy (percent)	Bassinets	Births	Total	Payroll	Personnel

★ American Hospital Association (AHA) membership
□ Joint Commission on Accreditation of Hospitals (JCAH) accreditation
+ American Osteopathic Hospital Association (AOHA) membership
○ American Osteopathic Association (AOA) accreditation
Δ Commission on Accreditation of Rehabilitation Facilities (CARF) accreditation
Control codes 61, 63, 64, 71, 72 and 73 indicate hospitals listed by AOHA, but not registered by AHA.
For definition of numerical codes, see page A2

Minnesota

Hospital	Control	Service	Stay	Facilities	Beds	Admissions	Census	Occupancy (percent)	Bassinets	Births	Total	Payroll	Personnel
ADA—Norman County													
★ ADA MUNICIPAL HOSPITAL (Includes John Wimmer Memorial Home), 405 E. Second Ave., Zip 56510; tel. 218/784-2561; Robert Cameron, adm. (Total facility includes 53 beds in nursing home-type unit) **A**9 10 **F**1 6 10 14 15 19 23 35 36 45 53	14	10	S	TF	81	400	55	67.9	6	12	1714	1067	80
				H	28	372	5	—	6	12	821	424	41
ADRIAN—Nobles County													
ARNOLD MEMORIAL HOSPITAL, 601 Louisiana Ave., Box 279, Zip 56110; tel. 507/483-2668; Charlotte Heitkamp, adm. (Total facility includes 41 beds in nursing home-type unit) **A**9 10 **F**1 16 19 35 40 41 45 52	14	10	S	TF	58	494	47	81.0	6	6	—	657	45
				H	17	477	6	—	6	6	—	—	16
AITKIN—Aitkin County													
★ AITKIN COMMUNITY HOSPITAL, 301 Minnesota Ave. S., Zip 56431; tel. 218/927-2121; Patrick B. Renner, adm. (Total facility includes 48 beds in nursing home-type unit) **A**9 10 **F**1 3 6 10 14 16 19 23 34 35 42 45 46 53	23	10	S	TF	84	998	53	63.1	6	79	3615	2099	133
				H	36	903	11	—	6	79	3114	1651	98
ALBANY—Stearns County													
★□ ALBANY AREA HOSPITAL (Formerly Albany Community Hospital), Box 370, Zip 56307; tel. 612/845-2121; William F. Lindberg, adm. **A**1a 9 10 **F**1 3 6 15 23 34 35 40 41 44 45	14	10	S		26	545	6	23.1	5	91	1538	827	41
ALBERT LEA—Freeborn County													
★□ NAEVE HOSPITAL, 404 Fountain St., Zip 56007; tel. 507/373-2384; Terry R. Maxhimer, exec. dir. **A**1a 9 10 **F**1 3 6 8 10 11 12 14 15 16 20 21 23 35 41 45 46 47 48 53	23	10	S		115	3766	58	50.4	17	578	10087	4830	293
ALEXANDRIA—Douglas County													
★□ DOUGLAS COUNTY HOSPITAL, 111 17th Ave. E., Zip 56308; tel. 612/762-1511; William G. Flaig, adm. **A**1a 9 10 **F**1 3 6 10 12 14 15 16 23 24 26 28 30 32 33 34 35 36 40 44 45 46 52 53	13	10	S		130	3565	48	36.9	14	494	14051	6723	315
ANOKA—Anoka County													
ANOKA-METROPOLITAN REGIONAL TREATMENT CENTER (Formerly Anoka State Hospital), 3300 Fourth Ave. N., Zip 55303; tel. 612/422-4150; Jonathan A. Balk, chief exec. off. **A**9 10 **F**15 24 32 33 45 46 47 48	12	22	L		337	1270	312	92.6	0	0	12963	9584	364
APPLETON—Swift County													
★ APPLETON MUNICIPAL HOSPITAL AND NURSING HOME, 30 S. Behl St., Zip 56208; tel. 612/289-2422; Mark E. Paulson, adm. (Total facility includes 84 beds in nursing home-type unit) **A**9 10 **F**15 16 19 23 35 40 44 45 46	14	10	S	TF	107	522	87	81.3	4	13	2219	1076	78
				H	23	477	6	—	4	13	965	424	27
ARLINGTON—Sibley County													
★□ ARLINGTON MUNICIPAL HOSPITAL, 601 W. Chandler St., Zip 55307; tel. 612/964-2271; Larry A. Schulz, adm. **A**1a 9 10 **F**1 6 14 15 16 21 23 34 35 36 37 41 45 46	14	10	S		17	516	8	47.1	5	42	976	465	30
AURORA—St. Louis County													
★ WHITE COMMUNITY HOSPITAL, 320 Hwy. 110 E., Zip 55705; tel. 218/229-2211; A. J. Briggs, adm. (Total facility includes 69 beds in nursing home-type unit) **A**9 10 **F**1 14 19 23 35 46 50	23	10	S	TF	85	370	70	82.4	4	24	1882	1196	77
				H	16	292	3	—	4	24	828	745	53
AUSTIN—Mower County													
★□ ST. OLAF HOSPITAL, 300 N.W. Eighth Ave., Zip 55912; tel. 507/437-4551; Donald R. Brezicka, adm. **A**1a 9 10 **F**1 3 5 6 10 12 14 15 16 23 24 26 27 28 29 30 32 33 34 35 36 40 41 44 45 46 47 48 49 52 53	23	10	S		138	3537	51	37.0	18	454	10513	5418	271
BAGLEY—Clearwater County													
★□ CLEARWATER COUNTY MEMORIAL HOSPITAL, 505 N. Bagley Ave., Box P, Zip 56621; tel. 218/694-6501; Randy Beck, adm. (Nonreporting) **A**1a 9 10	13	10	S		48	—	—	—	—	—	—	—	—
BAUDETTE—Lake of the Woods County													
★ TRINITY HOSPITAL, Main Ave. & Fifth St., Box E., Zip 56623; tel. 218/634-2120; David A. Nelson, pres. & chief exec. off. **A**9 10 **F**1 6 14 15 17 23 34 35 40 41 45 52 53; **S**1395	21	10	S		34	497	5	14.7	5	70	1241	581	37
BEMIDJI—Beltrami County													
★□ NORTH COUNTRY HOSPITAL, 1100 W. 38th St., Zip 56601; tel. 218/751-5430; Leon C. Swanson, pres. **A**1a 9 10 **F**1 3 6 10 12 14 15 16 21 23 24 26 35 36 37 40 41 44 45 46 53	23	10	S		89	4499	57	64.0	12	803	11986	5927	285
BENSON—Swift County													
★□ SWIFT COUNTY-BENSON HOSPITAL, 1815 Wisconsin Ave., Zip 56215; tel. 612/843-4232; Steven L. Hilpipre, adm. **A**1a 9 10 **F**1 3 6 14 15 16 17 23 24 35 36 40 41 44 45 52	15	10	S		31	775	14	45.2	7	68	2134	1055	58
BIGFORK—Itasca County													
★ NORTHERN ITASCA DISTRICT HOSPITAL AND CONVALESCENT AND NURSING CARE UNIT, Zip 56628; tel. 218/743-3177; Lillian Krueger, adm. (Total facility includes 40 beds in nursing home-type unit) **A**9 10 **F**1 6 10 14 15 19 21 23 24 26 34 35 36 37 40 43 44 45 50 52	16	10	S	TF	56	394	41	73.2	4	36	1984	1085	63
				H	16	364	4	—	4	36	1208	—	41
BLUE EARTH—Faribault County													
★□ UNITED HOSPITAL DISTRICT, 515 S. Moore St., Zip 56013; tel. 507/526-3273; Frank Lawatsch, adm. **A**1a 9 10 **F**1 3 6 12 15 16 23 26 32 34 35 36 37 40 43 45 47	16	10	S		43	1158	16	37.2	4	121	3746	1563	91
BRAINERD—Crow Wing County													
□ BRAINERD REGIONAL HUMAN SERVICES CENTER (Formerly Brainerd State Hospital), 1777 Hwy. 18 E., Zip 56401; tel. 218/828-2201; Elmer Davis, actg. chief exec. off. & adm. **A**1b 9 10 **F**3 15 19 23 24 27 32 33 42 44 46 47 49	12	82	L		504	1368	398	79.0	0	0	21425	15315	612
★□ ST. JOSEPH'S MEDICAL CENTER, 523 N. Third St., Zip 56401; tel. 218/829-2861; James E. Koerper, pres. **A**1a 9 10 **F**1 2 6 10 12 14 15 16 21 23 24 32 33 34 35 36 40 41 43 45 46 47 48 49 52 53; **S**0515	21	10	S		162	5697	84	51.9	15	633	18686	8987	402
BRECKENRIDGE—Wilkin County													
★□ ST. FRANCIS MEDICAL CENTER, 415 Oak St., Zip 56520; tel. 218/643-3000; Mark C. McNelly, pres. **A**1a 9 10 **F**1 3 6 9 10 12 14 15 16 21 23 26 30 33 35 36 40 41 45 46 47 49 52 53; **S**1395	21	10	S		60	2804	32	53.3	12	377	7765	3895	176
BROWERVILLE—Todd County													
□ ST. JOHN'S HOSPITAL, 540 Eighth St. W., Zip 56438; tel. 612/594-2204; Debra M. Noble, adm. **A**1a 9 10 **F**1 6 14 15 16 17 23 34 35 36 40 45 50 52; **S**1375	33	10	S		32	249	3	9.4	4	28	—	—	19
BUFFALO—Wright County													
BUFFALO MEMORIAL HOSPITAL, See Health Central of Buffalo													
★□ HEALTH CENTRAL OF BUFFALO (Formerly Buffalo Memorial Hospital), 303 Catlin St., Zip 55313; tel. 612/682-1212; Steven P. Bresnahan, chief exec. off. **A**1a 9 10 **F**1 3 6 10 14 15 16 23 28 35 36 40 44 45 48 49 53; **S**6235	23	10	S		30	1712	21	32.3	10	389	6708	2661	100

★ American Hospital Association (AHA) membership
□ Joint Commission on Accreditation of Hospitals (JCAH) accreditation
+ American Osteopathic Hospital Association (AOHA) membership
○ American Osteopathic Association (AOA) accreditation
Δ Commission on Accreditation of Rehabilitation Facilities (CARF) accreditation
Control codes 61, 63, 64, 71, 72 and 73 indicate hospitals listed by AOHA, but not registered by AHA.
For definition of numerical codes, see page A2

Hospital, Address, Telephone, Administrator, Approval and Facility Codes, Multihospital System Code	Classification Codes				Inpatient Data				Newborn Data		Expense (thousands of dollars)		
	Control	Service	Stay	Facilities	Beds	Admissions	Census	Occupancy (percent)	Bassinets	Births	Total	Payroll	Personnel
BURNSVILLE—Hennepin County													
★ FAIRVIEW RIDGES HOSPITAL, 201 E. Nicollet Blvd., Zip 55337; tel. 612/892-2100; Mark M. Enger, vice-pres. adm. (Nonreporting) **A**10; **S**1325	23	10	S		97	—	—	—	—	—	—	—	—
CALEDONIA—Houston County													
★ CALEDONIA HEALTH CARE CENTER, 425 N. Badger, Zip 55921; tel. 507/724-3351; Sr. Elizabeth Amman, adm. (Data for 264 days) (Total facility includes 74 beds in nursing home-type unit) **A**9 10 **F**1 19 23 24 34 35 44 45 46 47; **S**9650	23	10	S	TF	92	211	74	80.4	6	27	1310	733	78
				H	18	177	3	—	6	27	446	220	37
CAMBRIDGE—Isanti County													
⊞ MEMORIAL HOSPITAL, 725 S. Dellwood St., Zip 55008; tel. 612/689-1500; Clayton R. Peterson, chief exec. off. & adm. **A**1a 9 10 **F**1 3 6 14 15 16 21 23 34 35 36 37 40 41 45 46 47 48 49 52	23	10	S		86	3291	40	46.5	8	465	8951	4831	227
CANBY—Yellow Medicine County													
⊞ CANBY COMMUNITY HOSPITAL DISTRICT ONE (Includes Senior Haven Convalescent and Nursing Care Unit), 112 St. Olaf Ave., Zip 56220; tel. 507/223-7277; Robert J. Salmon, adm. (Total facility includes 75 beds in nursing home-type unit) **A**1a 9 10 **F**1 2 6 10 15 16 19 23 34 35 36 40 41 44 45 46 47 50 52 53	16	10	S	TF	98	564	80	81.6	8	82	2324	1339	99
				H	23	528	7	—	8	82	1082	825	51
CANNON FALLS—Goodhue County													
★ COMMUNITY HOSPITAL, 1116 W. Mill St., Zip 55009; tel. 507/263-4221; Donald J. Finn, adm. (Nonreporting) **A**9 10	16	10	S		21	—	—	—	—	—	—	—	—
CASS LAKE—Cass County													
⊞ U. S. PUBLIC HEALTH SERVICE INDIAN HOSPITAL, Third Ave. W. & Seventh St., Zip 56633; tel. 218/335-2293; Jerry C. Fagerstrom, serv. unit dir. **A**1a 10 **F**15 34 35 40 43 52	47	10	S		19	520	5	26.3	2	0	3147	1592	61
CHISAGO CITY—Chisago County													
⊞ CHISAGO HEALTH SERVICES (Formerly Chisago Lakes Hospital and Skilled Nursing Unit), Zip 55013; tel. 612/257-2500; Scott Wordelman, pres. & chief exec. off. (Total facility includes 40 beds in nursing home-type unit) **A**1a 9 10 **F**1 3 15 16 19 23 26 35 36 37 40 41 43 45 47	23	10	S	TF	89	1383	53	59.6	8	209	5238	2524	229
				H	49	1337	14	—	8	209	4131	2134	198
CLOQUET—Carlton County													
⊞ COMMUNITY MEMORIAL HOSPITAL AND CONVALESCENT AND NURSING CARE SECTION, Skyline Blvd., Zip 55720; tel. 218/879-4641; James J. Carroll, adm. (Total facility includes 88 beds in nursing home-type unit) **A**1a 9 10 **F**1 3 6 12 14 15 16 19 23 26 34 35 36 37 40 41 43 44 45 46 47 50 53 54	23	10	S	TF	165	1585	101	61.2	16	180	6385	3471	183
				H	77	1491	15	—	16	180	4337	2558	91
COMFREY—Brown County													
COMFREY HOSPITAL, Zip 56019; tel. 507/877-3211; Elaine Dutcher, adm. **A**9 10 **F**1 6 14 16 23 34 35 40 45 52	23	10	S		8	199	2	25.0	4	10	425	227	18
COOK—St. Louis County													
★ COOK COMMUNITY HOSPITAL, Third St. & Cedar Ave., Zip 55723; tel. 218/666-5945; Lineta Scott RN, adm. (Total facility includes 41 beds in nursing home-type unit) **A**9 10 **F**12 14 15 16 19 23 24 26 31 33 35 41 42 44 45 46 47 50	14	10	S	TF	55	279	44	80.0	8	19	1849	1038	71
				H	14	254	3	—	8	19	927	520	39
COON RAPIDS—Anoka County													
MERCY MEDICAL CENTER, See Health Central, Minneapolis													
CROOKSTON—Polk County													
⊞ RIVERVIEW HOSPITAL ASSOCIATION, 323 S. Minnesota St., Zip 56716; tel. 218/281-4682; Thomas C. Lenertz, exec. vice-pres. (Total facility includes 100 beds in nursing home-type unit) **A**1a 9 10 **F**1 3 6 10 12 14 15 16 19 21 23 24 26 34 35 36 37 40 44 45 46 47 53	23	10	S	TF	149	1788	118	79.2	10	184	7702	3888	246
				H	49	1704	22	—	10	184	5563	2751	126
CROSBY—Crow Wing County													
★ CUYUNA RANGE DISTRICT HOSPITAL, Zip 56441; tel. 218/546-5147; Thomas F. Reek, adm. (Total facility includes 130 beds in nursing home-type unit) **A**9 10 **F**1 3 14 15 16 19 20 23 34 35 36 40 41 43 45	16	10	S	TF	172	1488	141	82.0	7	142	6461	3382	204
				H	42	1276	16	—	7	142	4708	2429	115
DAWSON—Lac Qui Parle County													
JOHNSON MEMORIAL HOSPITAL AND HOME, Walnut St. & Memorial Pl., Zip 56232; tel. 612/769-4323; Mark Rinehardt, adm. (Nonreporting) **A**9 10	16	10	S		94	—	—	—	—	—	—	—	—
DEER RIVER—Itasca County													
★ COMMUNITY MEMORIAL HOSPITAL OF DEER RIVER, Box 488, Zip 56636; tel. 218/246-8245; David J. McClure, adm. (Nonreporting) **A**9 10	23	10	S		70	—	—	—	—	—	—	—	—
DETROIT LAKES—Becker County													
□ ST. MARY'S HOSPITAL AND NURSING HOME, 1014 Lincoln Ave., Zip 56501; tel. 218/847-5611; Barry B. Fewson, adm. (Total facility includes 100 beds in nursing home-type unit) **A**1a 9 10 **F**1 3 6 10 14 15 16 19 23 24 26 30 35 36 40 44 45 46 47 50 53; **S**1375	33	10	S	TF	153	2332	120	78.4	16	410	7594	3555	186
				H	53	2183	26	—	16	410	5430	2428	—
DULUTH—St. Louis County													
⊞ Δ MILLER-DWAN MEDICAL CENTER, 502 E. Second St., Zip 55805; tel. 218/727-8762; William Palmer, adm. **A**1a 3 5 7 9 10 **F**1 3 7 8 9 10 11 12 14 15 20 22 24 25 27 28 30 32 33 34 37 42 45 46 47 49	14	10	S		129	2724	73	56.6	0	0	17701	8358	444
⊞ ST. LUKE'S HOSPITAL, 915 E. First St., Zip 55805; tel. 218/726-5555; E. Thompson Evans Jr., adm. **A**1a 3 5 9 10 **F**1 2 3 5 6 10 12 14 15 16 21 23 24 26 27 28 29 30 32 33 34 35 36 40 41 43 44 45 46 50 52 53	23	10	S		231	8840	136	56.9	18	832	36022	19252	810
⊞ ST. MARY'S MEDICAL CENTER, 407 E. Third St., Zip 55805; tel. 218/726-4000; Sr. Kathleen Hofer, pres. **A**1a 3 5 9 10 **F**1 2 3 4 5 6 9 10 11 12 14 15 16 23 24 26 30 34 35 36 40 41 45 46 47 51 52 53 54; **S**0515	21	10	S		303	12893	204	65.6	18	1548	47197	25669	1141
EDINA—Hennepin County													
FAIRVIEW SOUTHDALE HOSPITAL, See Minneapolis													
ELBOW LAKE—Grant County													
★ GRANT COUNTY HOSPITAL, Box 5052, Zip 56531; tel. 218/685-4462; Wayne Hendrickson, adm. (Nonreporting) **A**9 10	13	10	S		32	—	—	—	—	—	—	—	—
ELY—St. Louis County													
★ ELY-BLOOMENSON COMMUNITY HOSPITAL, 328 W. Conan St., Zip 55731; tel. 218/365-3271; Vearl V. Nelson, adm. (Total facility includes 99 beds in nursing home-type unit) **A**9 10 **F**1 3 6 14 15 16 19 21 23 26 35 36 40 41 44 45 50 52	23	10	S	TF	138	851	109	79.0	3	75	4848	2790	154
				H	39	748	8	—	3	75	2810	1414	97
EVELETH—St. Louis County													
★ EVELETH FITZGERALD COMMUNITY HOSPITAL, 227 McKinley Ave., Zip 55734; tel. 218/744-1950; Rosalyn Karosich, adm. (Total facility includes 24 beds in nursing home-type unit) **A**9 10 **F**1 14 19 34 35 42 45 46 47	23	10	S	TF	50	159	26	52.0	0	0	865	540	45
				H	26	147	2	—	0	0	442	327	—
FAIRMONT—Martin County													
⊞ FAIRMONT COMMUNITY HOSPITAL, 835 Johnson St., P O Box 835, Zip 56031; tel. 507/238-4254; Gerry Gilbertson, adm. (Total facility includes 40 beds in nursing home-type unit) **A**1a 9 10 **F**1 3 6 12 16 19 23 26 33 35 45 53	23	10	S	TF	114	2150	59	51.8	16	357	6046	2931	144
				H	74	2027	25	—	16	357	5686	2579	121
FARIBAULT—Rice County													
CONSTANCE BULTMAN WILSON CENTER FOR ADOLESCENT PSYCHIATRY, See Wilson Center for Adolescent Psychiatry													

Hospital, Address, Telephone, Administrator, Approval and Facility Codes, Multihospital System Code

★ American Hospital Association (AHA) membership
☐ Joint Commission on Accreditation of Hospitals (JCAH) accreditation
+ American Osteopathic Hospital Association (AOHA) membership
○ American Osteopathic Association (AOA) accreditation
Δ Commission on Accreditation of Rehabilitation Facilities (CARF) accreditation
Control codes 61, 63, 64, 71, 72 and 73 indicate hospitals listed by AOHA, but not registered by AHA.
For definition of numerical codes, see page A2

Hospital, Address, Telephone, Administrator, Approval and Facility Codes, Multihospital System Code	Classification Codes				Inpatient Data				Newborn Data		Expense (thousands of dollars)		
	Control	Service	Stay	Facilities	Beds	Admissions	Census	Occupancy (percent)	Bassinets	Births	Total	Payroll	Personnel
FARIBAULT REGIONAL CENTER (Formerly Faribault State Hospital), 802 Circle Dr., Zip 55021; tel. 507/332-3000; W. C. Saufferer, chief exec. off. (Total facility includes 35 beds in nursing home-type unit) **A**9 **F**15 16 19 23 24 29 30 32 33 34 35 42 43 44 45 46 47 50	12	62	L	TF	748	19	621	82.1	0	0	31959	22939	1030
				H	713	9	591	—	0	0	30399	21819	985
★☐ RICE COUNTY DISTRICT ONE HOSPITAL, 631 S.E. First St., Zip 55021; tel. 507/334-6451; Gaylord J. Bridge, exec. dir. **A**1a 9 10 **F**1 3 6 12 14 15 16 23 24 33 35 36 40 44 45 52	16	10	S		84	2527	37	44.0	16	390	7072	3627	161
WILSON CENTER FOR ADOLESCENT PSYCHIATRY (Formerly Constance Bultman Wilson Center for Adolescent Psychiatry), Box 917, Zip 55021; tel. 507/334-5561; Kevin J. Mahoney, chief oper. off. (Nonreporting)	33	22	L		71	—	—	—	—	—	—	—	—
FARMINGTON—Dakota County													
★☐ SANFORD MEMORIAL HOSPITAL AND NURSING HOME, 913 Main St., Zip 55024; tel. 612/463-7825; Robert D. Johnson, adm. (Total facility includes 65 beds in nursing home-type unit) **A**1a 9 10 **F**1 3 6 10 14 15 16 19 21 23 34 35 36 40 41 43 44 45 46 47 50 52 53	23	10	S	TF	79	598	70	88.6	5	209	3570	1940	110
				H	14	559	6	—	5	209	2077	1125	—
FERGUS FALLS—Otter Tail County													
☐ FERGUS FALLS REGIONAL TREATMENT CENTER (Formerly Fergus Falls State Hospital) (Psychiatric, Chemical Dependency and Mental Retardation), Fir & Union Aves., Box 157, Zip 56537; tel. 218/739-7200; Elaine J. Timmer, chief exec. off. **A**1b 9 10 **F**12 23 24 27 32 33 42 44 46 47	12	82	L		499	1898	436	84.0	0	0	18910	17182	559
★☐ LAKE REGION HOSPITAL AND NURSING HOME, 712 S. Cascade St., Zip 56537; tel. 218/736-5475; Edward J. Mehl, adm. (Total facility includes 44 beds in nursing home-type unit) **A**1a 9 10 **F**1 3 6 7 10 11 12 14 15 16 19 20 23 24 26 35 36 37 40 41 42 45 46 50 52 53	23	10	S	TF	144	3470	84	58.3	10	450	12778	6170	329
				H	100	3204	45	—	10	450	11476	5615	259
FOREST LAKE—Washington County													
★☐ DISTRICT MEMORIAL HOSPITAL, 246 11th Ave. S.E., Zip 55025; tel. 612/464-3341; Terrence J. Brenny, adm. **A**1a 9 10 **F**1 3 15 16 35 36 40 41 45 46 49 50 52	16	10	S		49	1310	14	28.6	8	176	3964	1855	91
FOSSTON—Polk County													
★ FOSSTON MUNICIPAL HOSPITAL, 900 S. Hilligoss Blvd. E., Zip 56542; tel. 218/435-1133; David Hubbard, adm. (Total facility includes 50 beds in nursing home-type unit) **A**9 10 **F**1 14 15 19 23 34 35 36 40 41 42 45 46 52	23	10	S	TF	93	814	55	59.1	7	79	2605	1276	87
				H	43	762	9	—	7	79	1747	962	59
FRIDLEY—Anoka County													
UNITY MEDICAL CENTER, See Health Central, Minneapolis													
GAYLORD—Sibley County													
★ GAYLORD COMMUNITY HOSPITAL, 640 Third St., Box 386, Zip 55334; tel. 612/237-2905; Richard C. Kons, adm. (Total facility includes 58 beds in nursing home-type unit) **A**9 10 **F**1 6 10 15 16 19 23 24 34 35 42 43 45 46 49 50	14	10	S	TF	82	219	61	74.4	5	18	1661	748	55
				H	24	203	3	—	5	18	—	299	20
GLENCOE—McLeod County													
★☐ GLENCOE AREA HEALTH CENTER, 705 E. 18th St., Zip 55336; tel. 612/864-3121; John Robson, exec. dir. (Total facility includes 110 beds in nursing home-type unit) **A**1a 9 10 **F**1 2 3 6 14 15 16 19 23 24 26 34 35 36 40 42 44 45 46 50 53 54	14	10	S	TF	159	1264	121	76.1	5	122	5836	2443	146
				H	49	1154	13	—	5	122	3213	1675	96
GLENWOOD—Pope County													
★☐ GLACIAL RIDGE HOSPITAL, 10 Fourth Ave. S.E., Zip 56334; tel. 612/634-4521; Jerry G. Marks, adm. **A**1a 9 10 **F**1 3 14 15 16 21 34 35 36 37 40 41 43 45 46 52	16	10	S		34	609	8	23.5	4	66	1395	676	47
GOLDEN VALLEY—Hennepin County													
GOLDEN VALLEY HEALTH CENTER, See Health Central, Minneapolis													
GRACEVILLE—Big Stone County													
★☐ HOLY TRINITY HOSPITAL, 115 W. Second St., Zip 56240; tel. 612/748-7223; Sr. M. Paula Leick, adm. **A**1a 9 10 **F**1 6 15 16 19 21 23 33 35 40 43 45 52 53; **S**2855	21	10	S		40	1041	15	38.5	6	64	1714	779	52
GRAND MARAIS—Cook County													
COOK COUNTY NORTH SHORE HOSPITAL, Zip 55604; tel. 218/387-1500; Craig Kantos, adm. (Total facility includes 47 beds in nursing home-type unit) **A**9 10 **F**1 6 14 19 23 34 35 36 42 43 45 46 49	13	10	S	TF	63	394	49	77.8	4	30	2213	1252	72
				H	16	367	4	—	4	30	1257	697	38
GRAND RAPIDS—Itasca County													
★☐ ITASCA MEMORIAL HOSPITAL, 126 First Ave. S.E., Zip 55744; tel. 218/326-3401; Gene Hanson, adm. (Total facility includes 35 beds in nursing home-type unit) **A**1a 2 9 10 **F**1 3 6 10 12 14 15 16 17 19 21 23 24 27 30 32 33 34 35 36 40 44 45 47 53	13	10	S	TF	143	3589	74	51.7	16	436	10868	6032	278
				H	108	3235	41	—	16	436	9487	5256	250
GRANITE FALLS—Yellow Medicine County													
★☐ GRANITE FALLS MUNICIPAL HOSPITAL AND MANOR, 345 Tenth Ave., Zip 56241; tel. 612/564-3111; George Gerlach, adm. (Total facility includes 64 beds in nursing home-type unit) **A**1a 9 10 **F**1 3 14 15 16 19 23 35 37 41 44 45 46; **S**6235	14	10	S	TF	94	1075	78	83.0	6	113	4373	2078	128
				H	30	1053	14	—	6	113	2990	1305	68
GREENBUSH—Roseau County													
★ GREENBUSH COMMUNITY HOSPITAL AND CONVALESCENT AND NURSING CARE UNIT, Zip 56726; tel. 218/782-2131; Maurice A. Bertilrud, adm. (Total facility includes 60 beds in nursing home-type unit) **A**9 10 **F**1 19 23 35	23	10	S	TF	87	282	59	67.8	5	25	1414	858	57
				H	27	215	3	—	5	25	636	369	35
HALLOCK—Kittson County													
★ KITTSON MEMORIAL HOSPITAL, Zip 56728; tel. 218/843-3612; Bruce Berg, adm. (Total facility includes 95 beds in nursing home-type unit) **A**10 **F**1 2 19 23 40 45	23	10	S	TF	131	317	92	70.2	8	31	2107	1086	89
				H	36	271	4	—	8	31	826	315	46
HARMONY—Fillmore County													
HARMONY COMMUNITY HOSPITAL, 815 S. Main Ave., Rte. 1, Box 173, Zip 55939; tel. 507/886-6544; Greg Braun, adm. (Nonreporting) **A**10	23	10	S		59	—	—	—	—	—	—	—	—
HASTINGS—Dakota County													
★☐ REGINA MEDICAL COMPLEX (Formerly Regina Memorial Hospital), 1260 Nininger Rd., Zip 55033; tel. 612/437-3121; John W. Junkman, adm. (Total facility includes 61 beds in nursing home-type unit) **A**1a 9 10 **F**1 3 6 12 14 15 19 23 34 35 36 40 42 45 46 47 50	21	10	S	TF	141	1896	76	53.9	12	343	7718	4129	205
				H	80	1874	18	—	12	343	6195	3515	168
HENDRICKS—Lincoln County													
★☐ HENDRICKS COMMUNITY HOSPITAL, E. Lincoln St., Zip 56136; tel. 507/275-3134; Steven L. Midjaune, adm. (Total facility includes 70 beds in nursing home-type unit) **A**1a 9 10 **F**1 3 12 15 19 23 24 34 35 40 41 45 46 47	23	10	S	TF	96	397	75	78.1	6	42	1540	874	82
				H	26	379	6	—	6	42	—	535	55
HERON LAKE—Jackson County													
HERON LAKE MUNICIPAL HOSPITAL, Zip 56137; tel. 507/793-2346; Mike Dulaney, adm. (Total facility includes 47 beds in nursing home-type unit) **A**9 10 **F**19 35 45	14	10	S	TF	63	223	48	76.2	0	4	960	—	42
				H	16	209	2	—	0	4	355	—	15
HIBBING—St. Louis County													
★☐ MESABI REGIONAL MEDICAL CENTER, 750 E. 34th St., Zip 55746; tel. 218/262-4881; David M. Beach, chief exec. off. **A**1a 9 10 **F**1 3 6 10 12 14 15 16 20 23 24 26 27 28 29 30 31 32 33 34 35 36 37 40 41 43 44 45 46 47 48 49 50 53; **S**6235	23	10	S		175	3234	56	32.0	16	390	13296	6327	260

Hospital, Address, Telephone, Administrator, Approval and Facility Codes, Multihospital System Code

- ★ American Hospital Association (AHA) membership
- □ Joint Commission on Accreditation of Hospitals (JCAH) accreditation
- + American Osteopathic Hospital Association (AOHA) membership
- ○ American Osteopathic Association (AOA) accreditation
- Δ Commission on Accreditation of Rehabilitation Facilities (CARF) accreditation

Control codes 61, 63, 64, 71, 72 and 73 indicate hospitals listed by AOHA, but not registered by AHA. For definition of numerical codes, see page A2

Hospital	Classification Codes: Control	Service	Stay	Facilities	Inpatient Data: Beds	Admissions	Census	Occupancy (percent)	Newborn Data: Bassinets	Births	Expense (thousands of dollars): Total	Payroll	Personnel
HUTCHINSON—McLeod County													
★□ HUTCHINSON COMMUNITY HOSPITAL, 1095 Hwy. 15 S., Zip 55350; tel. 612/587-2148; Philip G. Graves, adm. **A**1a 10 **F**1 3 6 15 16 23 24 27 28 29 30 33 35 36 37 40 42 45 49 52 53	14	10	S		67	2130	24	35.8	6	361	4934	2775	131
INTERNATIONAL FALLS—Koochiching County													
★ INTERNATIONAL FALLS MEMORIAL HOSPITAL, 1800 Third St., Zip 56649; tel. 218/283-4481; Randall M. Olson, adm. **A**9 10 **F**1 3 6 14 15 23 34 35 40 45 46 47 48 49 53; **S**1755	23	10	S		64	1410	17	26.6	11	138	3861	2105	119
IVANHOE—Lincoln County													
★□ DIVINE PROVIDENCE HOSPITAL AND HOME, Zip 56142; tel. 507/694-1414; Sr. Mariette Ketterer, adm. (Total facility includes 51 beds in nursing home-type unit) **A**1a 9 10 **F**1 3 10 14 15 16 19 23 24 26 30 33 35 40 41 43 45 46 50 52; **S**5175	23	10	S	TF	79	457	55	69.6	6	21	1622	903	65
				H	28	425	6	—	6	21	875	628	48
JACKSON—Jackson County													
★ JACKSON MUNICIPAL HOSPITAL AND NURSING HOME, North Hwy., Zip 56143; tel. 507/847-2420; Sr. Maureen McDonald, adm. (Total facility includes 21 beds in nursing home-type unit) **A**9 10 **F**1 3 15 19 23 35 37 40 41 45 52	14	10	S	TF	41	650	27	65.9	2	50	1560	847	57
				H	20	643	7	—	2	50	1426	716	46
KARLSTAD—Kittson County													
★ KARLSTAD MEMORIAL HOSPITAL, Third & Washington, Box I, Zip 56732; tel. 218/436-2141; Jerry D. Peak, adm. **A**9 10 **F**1 6 12 14 23 34 35 36 40 45 53; **S**9355	14	10	S		19	646	7	36.8	6	52	1419	561	39
LAKE CITY—Wabasha County													
★□ LAKE CITY HOSPITAL, 904 S. Lakeshore Dr., Zip 55041; tel. 612/345-3321; Thomas Rasmussen, adm. **A**1a 9 10 **F**1 6 15 16 23 35 37 40 45	14	10	S		49	838	11	22.4	8	83	1817	1055	64
LAKEFIELD—Jackson County													
LAKEFIELD MUNICIPAL HOSPITAL, Second Ave. & Milwaukee St., P O Box 0638, Zip 56150; tel. 507/662-5295; Patrick McNeil, adm. **A**9 10 **F**1 6 14 16 23 35 40 45	14	10	S		18	202	2	11.1	4	15	781	354	21
LE SUEUR—Le Sueur County													
★ MINNESOTA VALLEY MEMORIAL HOSPITAL (Includes Garden View Nursing Home), 621 S. Fourth St., Zip 56058; tel. 612/665-3375; John K. McLain, adm. (Nonreporting) **A**9 10	23	10	S		109	—	—	—	—	—	—	—	—
LITCHFIELD—Meeker County													
★ MEEKER COUNTY MEMORIAL HOSPITAL, 612 S. Sibley Ave., Zip 55355; tel. 612/693-3242; Ronald E. Johnson, adm. **A**9 10 **F**1 3 6 10 12 14 23 35 40 45 46 47 52 53	13	10	S		48	1348	19	39.6	8	151	3401	1783	90
LITTLE FALLS—Morrison County													
★□ ST. GABRIEL'S HOSPITAL, 815 Second St. S.E., Zip 56345; tel. 612/632-5441; Gerald K. Spinner, pres. (Total facility includes 159 beds in nursing home-type unit) **A**1a 9 10 **F**1 3 5 6 10 12 14 15 16 19 20 21 23 28 30 32 33 34 35 36 40 43 45 46 49; **S**1395	21	10	S	TF	255	2863	182	65.9	20	414	12517	5817	331
				H	96	2706	35	—	20	414	9491	4274	220
LONG PRAIRIE—Todd County													
★□ LONG PRAIRIE MEMORIAL HOSPITAL, 20 Ninth St. S.E., Zip 56347; tel. 612/732-2141; Kevin J. Smith, exec. vice-pres. (Nonreporting) **A**1a 9 10; **S**6235	23	10	S		157	—	—	—	—	—	—	—	—
LUVERNE—Rock County													
COMMUNITY HOSPITAL, 305 E. Luverne St., Zip 56156; tel. 507/283-2321; Joseph A. McFadden, adm. **A**9 10 **F**1 16 23 35 37 40 43 45	14	10	S		38	1008	17	44.7	10	162	2071	996	66
MADELIA—Watonwan County													
★□ MADELIA COMMUNITY HOSPITAL, 121 Drew Ave. S.E., Zip 56062; tel. 507/642-3255; Emily E. Kunz RN, adm. **A**1a 9 10 **F**1 6 10 14 15 16 23 24 35 36 40 41 42 43 44 45	23	10	S		25	573	7	26.9	7	71	924	487	33
MADISON—Lac Qui Parle County													
★ MADISON HOSPITAL, 820 Third Ave., B0x 184, Zip 56256; tel. 612/598-7556; Richard Range, adm. **A**9 10 **F**1 3 16 23 24 35 36 40 41 43 44 45 47 50	23	10	S		21	434	6	28.6	4	37	1189	552	36
MAHNOMEN—Mahnomen County													
MAHNOMEN COUNTY AND VILLAGE HOSPITAL AND NURSING CENTER, Box 396, Zip 56557; tel. 218/935-2511; Wallace M. Eid, adm. (Nonreporting) **A**9 10	15	10	S		66	—	—	—	—	—	—	—	—
MANKATO—Blue Earth County													
★□ IMMANUEL-ST. JOSEPH'S HOSPITAL, 325 Garden Blvd., Zip 56001; Mailing Address P O Box 8673, Zip 56002; tel. 507/625-4031; Jerome A. Crest, pres. **A**1a 2 9 10 **F**1 2 3 5 6 7 8 9 10 11 12 14 15 16 20 21 23 24 26 27 28 30 32 33 34 35 36 37 40 41 42 43 45 46 47 48 49 52 53	23	10	S		184	8365	121	65.4	26	1148	22348	11650	523
MARSHALL—Lyon County													
★□ WEINER MEMORIAL MEDICAL CENTER, 300 S. Bruce St., Zip 56258; tel. 507/532-9661; Ronald Jensen, adm. (Total facility includes 76 beds in nursing home-type unit) **A**1a 9 10 **F**1 3 6 12 14 15 16 19 23 30 35 36 40 41 43 44 45 46 50 52 53	14	10	S	TF	138	1932	96	69.6	8	347	7020	3489	192
				H	62	1859	22	—	8	347	5363	2842	152
MELROSE—Stearns County													
★ MELROSE HOSPITAL AND PINE VILLA CONVALESCENT AND NURSING CARE UNIT, 11 N. Fifth Ave. W., Zip 56352; tel. 612/256-4231; Julia M. Westendorf, adm. (Total facility includes 75 beds in nursing home-type unit) **A**9 10 **F**1 3 6 14 15 19 23 35 36 40 41 45 46 53	14	10	S	TF	103	646	81	78.6	6	125	2599	1472	101
				H	28	623	7	—	6	125	1386	780	59
MILACA—Mille Lacs County													
□ MILACA FAIRVIEW HOSPITAL (Formerly Milaca Area District Hospital), 150 N.W. Tenth St., Zip 56353; tel. 612/983-3131; Eleanor Starr, adm. (Nonreporting) **A**1a 9 10; **S**1325	16	10	S		41	—	—	—	—	—	—	—	—
MINNEAPOLIS—Hennepin County													
★□ Δ ABBOTT-NORTHWESTERN HOSPITAL (Includes Sister Kenny Institute), 800 E. 28th St. at Chicago, Zip 55407; tel. 612/874-4000; Gordon M. Sprenger, pres. **A**1a b 2 3 5 7 9 10 **F**1 2 3 4 5 6 7 8 9 10 11 12 13 14 15 16 17 20 21 23 24 25 26 27 28 29 30 31 32 33 34 35 36 37 38 40 41 42 43 44 45 46 47 48 49 50 53 54	23	10	S		734	25025	524	71.4	32	2927	165500	78952	3438
★□ CARONDELET COMMUNITY HOSPITALS (Includes St. Joseph's Division, 69 W. Exchange St., St. Paul, Zip 55102; tel. 612/291-3000; St. Mary's Division, 2414 S. Seventh St., Zip 55454; tel. 612/338-2229), Mailing Address 2414 S. Seventh St., Zip 55454; John R. McIntire, pres. (Total facility includes 64 beds in nursing home-type unit) **A**1b 2 3 5 9 10 **F**1 2 3 4 6 7 8 9 10 11 12 14 15 16 17 19 20 21 23 24 25 26 27 28 30 32 33 34 35 36 37 40 41 42 44 45 46 47 48 49 50 53 54; **S**5945	21	10	S	TF	645	18802	420	65.1	58	3805	86030	40294	—
				H	581	18274	385	—	58	3805	83184	38844	—
★□ FAIRVIEW DEACONESS CENTER (Formerly Fairview Deaconess Hospital), 1400 E. 24th St., Zip 55404; tel. 612/721-9100; Daniel K. Anderson, vice-pres. & adm. (Nonreporting) **A**1a 6 9; **S**1325	23	49	L		128	—	—	—	—	—	—	—	—
★□ FAIRVIEW RIVERSIDE HOSPITAL (Formerly Fairview Hospital), 2312 S. Sixth St., Zip 55454; tel. 612/371-6300; Pamela L. Tibbetts, vice-pres. adm. **A**1a 3 5 9 10 **F**1 2 3 6 7 8 9 10 11 12 14 15 16 17 19 20 21 23 24 25 26 27 28 29 30 31 32 33 34 35 36 37 40 42 43 44 45 46 47 48 49 52 53; **S**1325	23	10	S		492	13994	308	62.6	49	3117	61844	28567	1263
★□ FAIRVIEW SOUTHDALE HOSPITAL (Formerly Listed Under Edina), 6401 France Ave. S., Zip 55435; tel. 612/924-5000; Douglas N. Robinson, vice-pres. adm. (Nonreporting) **A**1a 9 10; **S**1325	23	10	S		390	—	—	—	—	—	—	—	—

Hospital, Address, Telephone, Administrator, Approval and Facility Codes, Multihospital System Code	Classification Codes: Control	Service	Stay	Facilities	Inpatient Data: Beds	Admissions	Census	Occupancy (percent)	Newborn Data: Bassinets	Births	Expense (thousands of dollars): Total	Payroll	Personnel
★ American Hospital Association (AHA) membership ☐ Joint Commission on Accreditation of Hospitals (JCAH) accreditation + American Osteopathic Hospital Association (AOHA) membership ○ American Osteopathic Association (AOA) accreditation Δ Commission on Accreditation of Rehabilitation Facilities (CARF) accreditation Control codes 61, 63, 64, 71, 72 and 73 indicate hospitals listed by AOHA, but not registered by AHA. For definition of numerical codes, see page A2													
⊞ HEALTH CENTRAL METROPOLITAN HOSPITALS (Includes Golden Valley Health Center, 4101 Golden Valley Rd., Golden Valley, Zip 55422; tel. 612/588-2771; Steven R. Kamber, chief exec. off.; Mercy Medical Center, 4050 Coon Rapids Blvd., Coon Rapids, Zip 55433; tel. 612/427-2200; William J. Macnally, exec. vice-pres. & chief exec. off.; Unity Medical Center, 550 Osborne Rd. N.E., Fridley, Zip 55432; tel. 612/786-2200; John Haines, exec. vice-pres.), 2810 57th Ave. N., Zip 55430; tel. 612/574-7800; William Kreykes, pres. (Total facility includes 129 beds in nursing home-type unit) **A**1a 2 9 10 **F**1 3 5 6 9 10 12 14 15 16 17 19 20 21 23 24 26 27 28 29 30 32 33 34 35 36 37 40 42 43 44 45 46 47 48 49 50 52 53 54; **S**6235	23	10	S	TF	834	24067	559	67.0	64	4045	99592	48832	2108
				H	705	24001	434	—	64	4045	96977	47008	2011
⊞ HENNEPIN COUNTY MEDICAL CENTER, 701 Park Ave. S., Zip 55415; tel. 612/347-2342; Daniel B. McLaughlin, adm. **A**1a 2 3 5 8 9 10 **F**1 2 3 4 5 6 12 13 14 15 16 20 22 23 24 26 27 28 30 32 33 34 35 36 37 40 42 44 45 46 47 50 51 52 53 54	13	10	S		377	15833	283	75.1	20	1534	124948	—	1734
METHODIST HOSPITAL, See St. Louis Park													
⊞ Δ METROPOLITAN MEDICAL CENTER, 900 S. Eighth St., Zip 55404; tel. 612/347-4444; Frank J. Larkin, pres. & chief exec. off. **A**1a b 2 3 5 7 9 10 **F**1 2 3 4 6 7 8 9 10 11 12 13 14 15 16 19 21 23 24 25 26 27 28 29 30 32 33 34 35 36 39 40 42 43 44 45 46 47 48 49 52 53 54; **S**6235	23	10	S		506	13375	263	52.0	24	1062	82406	35872	1500
⊞ MINNEAPOLIS CHILDREN'S MEDICAL CENTER, 2525 Chicago Ave., Zip 55404; tel. 612/863-6112; Patricia Klauck, pres. **A**1a 2 3 5 9 10 **F**1 3 4 6 12 14 15 16 23 28 30 32 33 34 35 37 41 43 44 45 46 51	23	50	S		122	4951	87	71.3	0	0	39063	20997	810
⊞ MOUNT SINAI HOSPITAL, 2215 Park Ave., Zip 55404; tel. 612/871-3700; Warren A. Green, adm. **A**1a 3 5 9 10 **F**1 2 3 4 6 12 14 16 20 23 24 26 30 32 33 34 35 41 45 46 47 53 54; **S**1755	23	10	S		173	6848	90	52.0	0	0	31562	15868	713
NORTH MEMORIAL MEDICAL CENTER, See Robbinsdale													
⊞ SHRINERS HOSPITALS FOR CRIPPLED CHILDREN, 2025 E. River Rd., Zip 55414; tel. 612/339-6711; Roberta Antoine Dressen, adm. **A**1a 3 **F**1 15 23 26 33 34 42 45 46 47 52; **S**4125	23	57	S		40	813	25	62.5	0	0	—	—	101
SISTER KENNY INSTITUTE, See Abbott-Northwestern Hospital Corporation													
ST. MARY'S DIVISION, See Carondelet Community Hospitals													
⊞ UNIVERSITY OF MINNESOTA HOSPITAL AND CLINIC, Harvard St. at E. River Rd., Zip 55455; tel. 612/626-3000; Gregory Hart, interim dir. **A**1a 3 5 8 9 10 **F**1 3 4 5 6 7 8 9 10 11 12 13 14 15 16 17 20 23 24 25 26 27 28 29 30 31 32 33 34 35 36 37 38 39 40 41 42 44 45 46 47 49 51 52 53 54	12	10	S		591	17381	397	68.2	8	433	194909	83614	3581
⊞ VETERANS ADMINISTRATION MEDICAL CENTER, 54th St. & 48th Ave. S., Zip 55417; tel. 612/725-6767; Thomas P. Mullon, dir.; Wallace M. Hopkins, assoc. dir. **A**1a 2 3 5 8 **F**1 3 4 6 7 8 9 10 11 12 13 14 15 16 20 23 24 25 26 27 28 29 30 32 33 34 35 41 42 43 44 46 47 48 49 50 53 54	45	10	S		711	19443	530	74.5	0	0	132327	60598	2353
MONTEVIDEO—Chippewa County													
CHIPPEWA COUNTY MONTEVIDEO HOSPITAL, 824 N. 11th St., Zip 56265; tel. 612/269-8878; Fred Knutson, adm. (Nonreporting) **A**9 10	15	10	S		35	—	—	—	—	—	—	—	—
MONTICELLO—Wright County													
⊞ MONTICELLO-BIG LAKE COMMUNITY HOSPITAL, 1013 Hart Blvd., Box 480, Zip 55362; tel. 612/295-2945; Barbara Schwientek, exec. dir. (Total facility includes 91 beds in nursing home-type unit) **A**1a 9 10 **F**1 3 6 14 15 16 19 21 26 34 35 36 40 42 44 45 46 47 49 50; **S**6235	16	10	S	TF	130	1104	89	73.6	9	160	5313	2609	145
				H	39	1058	10	—	9	160	4497	2099	72
MOORHEAD—Clay County													
⊞ ST. ANSGAR HOSPITAL, 715 N. 11th St., Zip 56560; tel. 218/299-2200 **A**1a 2 9 10 **F**1 3 9 10 12 14 15 16 23 24 27 28 29 30 32 33 34 35 36 40 41 42 43 44 45 46 47 53; **S**1395	21	10	S		69	3029	59	85.5	12	269	12868	5782	302
MOOSE LAKE—Carlton County													
⊞ MERCY HOSPITAL, Zip 55767; tel. 218/485-4481; William F. Zellmann, adm. (Nonreporting) **A**1a 9 10	16	10	S		129	—	—	—	—	—	—	—	—
☐ MOOSE LAKE STATE HOSPITAL, 1000 Lake Shore Dr., Zip 55767; tel. 218/485-4411; Frank R. Milczark, chief exec. off. (Nonreporting) **A**1b 9 10	12	22	L		662	—	—	—	—	—	—	—	—
MORA—Kanabec County													
⊞ KANABEC HOSPITAL, 300 Clark St., Zip 55051; tel. 612/679-1212; John A. Kayfes, adm. **A**1a 9 10 **F**1 2 3 6 14 15 16 23 24 34 35 36 40 44 45 46 47 52 53	13	10	S		54	1285	14	25.0	8	228	3039	1608	79
MORRIS—Stevens County													
★ STEVENS COMMUNITY MEMORIAL HOSPITAL, 400 E. First St., Zip 56267; tel. 612/589-1313; Ronald L. Jacobson, chief exec. off. **A**9 10 **F**1 2 6 14 15 16 21 23 24 28 30 32 33 34 35 36 37 40 41 44 45 46 47 48 49 53	23	10	S		54	1014	16	29.6	5	159	3037	1584	74
MOUNTAIN LAKE—Cottonwood County													
MOUNTAIN LAKE COMMUNITY HOSPITAL, 801 Third Ave., Zip 56159; tel. 507/427-2511; Roxann A. Wellman, adm. **A**9 10 **F**1 3 6 10 15 23 35 37 40 45 46 47 48	14	10	S		26	380	5	19.2	8	38	1085	518	31
NEW PRAGUE—Le Sueur and Scott Counties													
⊞ QUEEN OF PEACE HOSPITAL, 301 Second St. N.E., Zip 56071; tel. 612/758-4431; Sr. Jean Juenemann, chief exec. off. **A**1a 9 10 **F**1 3 6 14 15 16 23 24 28 32 33 34 35 36 40 41 44 45 46 53; **S**0535	23	10	S		56	1446	17	30.4	8	228	4571	2009	106
NEW ULM—Brown County													
⊞ SIOUX VALLEY HOSPITAL, 1324 Fifth North St., Box 577, Zip 56073; tel. 507/354-2111; Robert Stevens, adm. **A**1a 9 10 **F**1 3 6 10 12 14 15 16 21 23 35 36 40 41 44 45 46 48 49 53; **S**6235	23	10	S		85	2062	31	36.5	12	386	7233	3051	152
NORTHFIELD—Rice County													
⊞ NORTHFIELD HOSPITAL (Formerly Northfield City Hospital) (Includes H. O. Dilley Skilled Nursing Facility), 80 W. First St., Zip 55057; tel. 507/645-6661; Cliff Christiansen, adm. (Total facility includes 40 beds in nursing home-type unit) **A**1a 9 10 **F**1 3 6 10 14 15 16 19 21 23 24 26 34 35 36 40 41 45 46 50 52	14	10	S	TF	86	1677	50	58.1	12	245	—	—	147
				H	46	1617	11	—	12	245	—	—	138
OLIVIA—Renville County													
⊞ RENVILLE COUNTY HOSPITAL, 611 E. Fairview Ave., Zip 56277; tel. 612/523-1261; Jerry Popowski, adm. **A**1a 9 10 **F**1 3 15 23 34 35 36 40 45 50	13	10	S		35	788	10	28.6	6	124	1708	864	49
ONAMIA—Mille Lacs County													
⊞ MILLE LACS HOSPITAL (Formerly Community Mercy Hospital), Zip 56359; tel. 612/532-3154; Gene M. Helle, adm. (Total facility includes 80 beds in nursing home-type unit) **A**1a 9 10 **F**1 3 5 6 10 14 15 16 17 19 20 23 24 26 34 35 36 37 41 45 46 47 49 50 53; **S**1395	23	10	S	TF	108	965	91	84.3	3	92	4052	1989	112
				H	28	934	12	—	3	92	2480	1405	76
ORTONVILLE—Big Stone County													
★ ORTONVILLE AREA HEALTH SERVICES, 750 Eastvold Ave., Zip 56278; tel. 612/839-2502; Richard G. Slieter, adm. (Total facility includes 74 beds in nursing home-type unit) **A**9 10 **F**1 6 10 15 16 19 23 26 35 37 41 45 46 53	14	10	S	TF	105	658	81	77.1	4	104	3045	1556	96
				H	31	643	8	—	4	104	1654	767	43

Hospital, Address, Telephone, Administrator, Approval and Facility Codes, Multihospital System Code	Classification Codes				Inpatient Data				Newborn Data		Expense (thousands of dollars)		
	Control	Service	Stay	Facilities	Beds	Admissions	Census	Occupancy (percent)	Bassinets	Births	Total	Payroll	Personnel
OWATONNA—Steele County													
★□ HEALTH CENTRAL OF OWATONNA (Formerly Owatonna City Hospital), 903 S. Oak, Zip 55060; tel. 507/451-3850; Richard G. Slieter, chief exec. off. **A**1a 9 10 **F**1 3 6 14 15 16 23 24 27 29 30 32 33 34 35 36 40 44 45 52; **S**6235	23	10	S		77	2183	24	31.2	16	370	5909	2819	136
PARK RAPIDS—Hubbard County													
★□ ST. JOSEPH'S HOSPITAL, 600 Pleasant Ave., Zip 56470; tel. 218/732-3311; David R. Hove, pres. & chief exec. off. **A**1a 9 10 **F**1 3 6 10 14 16 23 35 36 40 45 52 53; **S**1395	21	10	S		50	1908	26	52.0	10	215	5456	2507	132
PARKERS PRAIRIE—Otter Tail County													
PARKERS PRAIRIE DISTRICT HOSPITAL, Zip 56361; tel. 218/338-4011; James J. Talley, adm. (Nonreporting) **A**9 10	16	10	S		18	—	—	—	—	—	—	—	—
PAYNESVILLE—Stearns County													
★ PAYNESVILLE COMMUNITY HOSPITAL, 200 First St. W., Zip 56362; tel. 612/243-3767; William M. LaCroix, adm. (Total facility includes 64 beds in nursing home-type unit) **A**9 10 **F**1 3 6 10 14 15 16 19 23 24 34 35 36 40 43 45 46 47 53	14	10	S	TF	94	879	72	76.6	9	121	3581	1592	108
				H	30	828	10	—	9	121	2211	816	68
PELICAN RAPIDS—Otter Tail County													
★ PELICAN VALLEY HEALTH CENTER, 211 E. Mill St., Zip 56572; tel. 218/863-3111; Charles F. Harms, adm. (Total facility includes 46 beds in nursing home-type unit) **A**9 10 **F**1 6 15 16 19 23 34 35 41 45 46; **S**2235	16	10	S	TF	59	346	47	79.7	0	1	1828	921	66
				H	13	305	3	—	0	1	1093	452	—
PERHAM—Otter Tail County													
□ MEMORIAL HOSPITAL AND HOME (Includes Memorial Nursing Home), 665 Third St. S.W., Zip 56573; tel. 218/346-4500; Richard J. Failing, adm. (Total facility includes 102 beds in nursing home-type unit) **A**1a 9 10 **F**1 3 6 14 15 16 19 23 24 34 35 36 40 41 43 45 46	16	10	S	TF	131	720	108	82.4	3	119	4071	2101	124
				H	29	671	8	—	3	119	2462	1359	72
PIPESTONE—Pipestone County													
★□ PIPESTONE COUNTY MEDICAL CENTER, 911 Fifth Ave. S.W., P O Box 370, Zip 56164; tel. 507/825-5811; Allan J. Christensen, adm. (Total facility includes 43 beds in nursing home-type unit) **A**1a 9 10 **F**1 3 6 14 15 16 19 23 35 36 40 41 45 50 52 53; **S**9355	13	10	S	TF	87	950	50	57.5	12	137	3103	1561	110
				H	44	850	11	—	12	137	2609	1191	82
PRINCETON—Mille Lacs County													
★□ FAIRVIEW PRINCETON HOSPITAL, 704 First St., Zip 55371; tel. 612/389-1313; Glenn G. Erickson, reg. adm. **A**1a 9 10 **F**1 3 6 14 15 23 24 26 34 35 36 40 41 42 44 45 46 47 52 53; **S**1325	23	10	S		35	1290	13	37.1	9	202	3952	1781	73
RED WING—Goodhue County													
★□ ST. JOHN'S HOSPITAL, 1407 W. Fourth St., Zip 55066; tel. 612/388-6721; Jeffrey B. Stevenson, adm. **A**1a 9 10 **F**1 3 6 11 12 14 15 16 23 24 26 34 35 36 37 40 41 43 44 45 46 47 48 49 52 53	23	10	S		84	3186	34	42.5	14	446	9454	4235	210
REDLAKE—Beltrami County													
★□ U. S. PUBLIC HEALTH SERVICE INDIAN HOSPITAL, Zip 56671; tel. 218/679-3912; John M. Kutch Jr., serv. unit dir. **A**1a 10 **F**1 15 23 34 35 36 40 41 46 47 52	47	10	S		23	932	9	39.1	7	51	5775	1796	109
REDWOOD FALLS—Redwood County													
★□ REDWOOD FALLS MUNICIPAL HOSPITAL, 100 Fallwood Rd., Zip 56283; tel. 507/637-2907; James E. Schulte, adm. **A**1a 9 10 **F**1 2 6 14 15 16 21 35 36 40 43 45	14	10	S		42	1259	14	33.0	10	201	2444	1233	68
ROBBINSDALE—Hennepin County													
★□ NORTH MEMORIAL MEDICAL CENTER (Formerly Listed Under Minneapolis), 3300 Oakdale N., Zip 55422; tel. 612/520-5200; Scott R. Anderson, pres. **A**1a 2 3 5 9 10 **F**1 2 3 4 5 6 7 9 10 11 12 14 15 16 17 20 21 23 24 25 26 27 30 32 33 34 35 36 37 40 41 44 45 46 47 50 51 52 53 54	23	10	S		334	18172	242	72.5	32	2840	84293	41928	1709
ROCHESTER—Olmsted County													
★□ OLMSTED COMMUNITY HOSPITAL, 1650 Fourth St. S.E., Zip 55904; tel. 507/285-8485; Robert L. Brandt, adm. **A**1a 9 10 **F**1 3 6 14 15 16 23 26 34 36 40 41 43 45 46 47	13	10	S		45	1707	18	40.0	18	734	5856	3159	134
★□ ROCHESTER METHODIST HOSPITAL, 201 W. Center St., Zip 55902; tel. 507/286-7890; James G. Anderson, chief exec. off. **A**1a 3 5 9 10 **F**1 2 3 6 13 15 16 20 23 24 32 35 36 40 44 45 46 47 48 52	23	10	S		701	23872	516	73.6	32	1943	77511	40625	1691
★□ Δ ST. MARYS HOSPITAL OF ROCHESTER, 1216 Second St. S.W., Zip 55902; tel. 507/285-5123; Michael J. Myers, chief exec. off. **A**1a 3 5 7 8 9 10 **F**1 2 3 4 5 6 9 10 11 12 13 14 15 16 17 20 23 24 25 26 27 29 30 32 33 34 35 38 39 42 44 45 51 52 53 54	23	10	S		1002	32824	765	75.7	0	0	108412	60643	2649
ROSEAU—Roseau County													
★□ ROSEAU AREA HOSPITAL, 715 Third Ave. S.E., Zip 56751; tel. 218/463-2500; David F. Hagen, adm. (Total facility includes 64 beds in nursing home-type unit) **A**1a 9 10 **F**1 3 6 10 15 16 19 23 30 35 36 42 45	16	10	S	TF	109	1143	78	71.6	7	192	3628	2004	129
				H	45	1125	15	—	7	192	2620	1572	94
RUSH CITY—Chisago County													
★□ RUSH CITY HOSPITAL, Zip 55069; tel. 612/358-4708; Joel Hanson, adm. (Nonreporting) **A**1a 10	14	10	S		29	—	—	—	—	—	—	—	—
SANDSTONE—Pine County													
□ SANDSTONE AREA HOSPITAL AND NURSING HOME, 317 Court St., Zip 55072; tel. 612/245-2212; James G. Blum, exec. dir. (Nonreporting) **A**1a 9 10	13	10	S		111	—	—	—	—	—	—	—	—
SAUK CENTRE—Stearns County													
★□ ST. MICHAEL'S HOSPITAL, 425 N. Elm St., Zip 56378; tel. 612/352-2221; Roy Provo, adm. (Total facility includes 60 beds in nursing home-type unit) **A**1a 9 10 **F**1 3 6 14 15 16 19 23 26 34 35 36 45 46 47 49 50 53	14	10	S	TF	106	890	68	64.2	8	126	3048	1789	119
				H	46	849	10	—	8	126	2451	1316	81
SHAKOPEE—Scott County													
★□ ST. FRANCIS REGIONAL MEDICAL CENTER, 325 W. Fifth Ave., Zip 55379; tel. 612/445-2322; Sr. M. Agnes Otting, pres. & chief exec. off. **A**1a 9 10 **F**1 3 6 10 12 14 15 16 21 23 24 26 28 30 32 33 34 35 36 40 41 43 44 45 46 47 49 52 53	21	10	S		112	3315	32	28.6	11	736	10997	5495	236
SLAYTON—Murray County													
MURRAY COUNTY MEMORIAL HOSPITAL, 2042 Juniper Ave., Zip 56172; tel. 507/836-6111; Jerry Bobeldyk, adm. **A**9 10 **F**1 3 16 23 35 40 45 47 52	13	10	S		35	728	10	28.6	5	63	1570	660	42
SLEEPY EYE—Brown County													
SLEEPY EYE MUNICIPAL HOSPITAL, 400 Fourth Ave. N.W., Zip 56085; tel. 507/794-3571; Scott E. Morin, adm. **A**9 10 **F**1 6 12 14 15 16 23 34 35 42 43 44 45 46 52	14	10	S		24	864	9	37.5	6	84	1720	823	54
SOUTH ST. PAUL—Dakota County													
□ DIVINE REDEEMER MEMORIAL HOSPITAL, 724 19th Ave. N., Zip 55075; tel. 612/450-4500; Drew Haynes, adm. **A**1a 9 10 **F**1 3 5 6 12 15 16 23 24 26 27 35 45 47 48 53; **S**1375	33	10	S		82	2147	31	37.8	0	0	11724	4814	221
SPRING GROVE—Houston County													
TWEETEN-LUTHERAN HEALTH CARE CENTER (Formerly Tweeten Memorial Hospital and Convalescent Home), 125 Fifth Ave. S.E., Zip 55974; tel. 507/498-3211 (Total facility includes 79 beds in nursing home-type unit) **A**9 10 **F**15 19 34 42 45 46 50	23	10	S	TF	89	66	77	86.5	4	3	1247	756	64
				H	10	26	0	—	4	3	—	—	37

★ American Hospital Association (AHA) membership
□ Joint Commission on Accreditation of Hospitals (JCAH) accreditation
\+ American Osteopathic Hospital Association (AOHA) membership
○ American Osteopathic Association (AOA) accreditation
Δ Commission on Accreditation of Rehabilitation Facilities (CARF) accreditation
Control codes 61, 63, 64, 71, 72 and 73 indicate hospitals listed by AOHA, but not registered by AHA.
For definition of numerical codes, see page A2

Hospital, Address, Telephone, Administrator, Approval and Facility Codes, Multihospital System Code	Classification Codes				Inpatient Data				Newborn Data		Expense (thousands of dollars)		
★ American Hospital Association (AHA) membership □ Joint Commission on Accreditation of Hospitals (JCAH) accreditation + American Osteopathic Hospital Association (AOHA) membership ○ American Osteopathic Association (AOA) accreditation Δ Commission on Accreditation of Rehabilitation Facilities (CARF) accreditation Control codes 61, 63, 64, 71, 72 and 73 indicate hospitals listed by AOHA, but not registered by AHA. For definition of numerical codes, see page A2	Control	Service	Stay	Facilities	Beds	Admissions	Census	Occupancy (percent)	Bassinets	Births	Total	Payroll	Personnel
SPRING VALLEY—Fillmore County													
★ COMMUNITY MEMORIAL HOSPITAL AND NURSING HOME, 800 Memorial Dr., Zip 55975; tel. 507/346-7381; David Herder, adm. (Total facility includes 50 beds in nursing home-type unit) **A**9 10 **F**1 3 14 15 16 19 21 23 24 35 40 41 42 43 45 46 50 52	23	10	S	TF	79	369	55	69.6	5	5	2112	1163	74
				H	29	347	5	—	5	5	1063	530	38
SPRINGFIELD—Brown County													
★ SPRINGFIELD COMMUNITY HOSPITAL, 625 N. Jackson, Box 146, Zip 56087; tel. 507/723-6201; Michael Milbrath, adm. **A**9 10 **F**1 6 15 16 23 34 35 36 40 41 45	14	10	S		24	566	7	29.2	6	97	1003	495	31
ST. CLOUD—Stearns County													
⊞ ST. CLOUD HOSPITAL, 1406 Sixth Ave. N., Zip 56301; tel. 612/251-2700; John R. Frobenius, exec. vice-pres. **A**1a 6 9 10 **F**1 2 3 5 6 7 8 9 10 11 12 14 15 16 20 21 23 24 25 26 27 28 30 32 33 34 35 36 40 41 42 43 44 45 46 47 48 49 52 53 54; **S**0535	21	10	S		360	13717	231	62.6	40	2196	48746	25977	1048
⊞ VETERANS ADMINISTRATION MEDICAL CENTER, Zip 56301; tel. 612/252-1670; Ralph W. Knoebel, dir. (Total facility includes 130 beds in nursing home-type unit) **A**1a **F**3 14 16 19 21 23 24 28 29 30 32 33 42 43 44 46 47 48 49 50	45	22	L	TF	829	3007	461	71.7	0	0	37789	24648	977
				H	699	2888	417	—	0	0	35826	23183	891
ST. JAMES—Watonwan County													
□ WATONWAN MEMORIAL HOSPITAL, 1207 Sixth Ave. S., Zip 56081; tel. 507/375-3261; Donald Loren Johnson, adm. **A**1a 9 10 **F**1 6 15 16 21 23 28 32 33 34 35 37 40 41 43 44 45 47 49 50	23	10	S		31	659	7	22.6	10	95	1545	663	40
ST. LOUIS PARK—Hennepin County													
⊞ METHODIST HOSPITAL (Formerly Listed Under Minneapolis), 6500 Excelsior Blvd., Mailing Address Box 650, Minneapolis, Zip 55426; tel. 612/932-5000; Terry Finzen, pres. & chief exec. off. (Total facility includes 35 beds in nursing home-type unit) **A**1a 2 5 9 10 **F**1 2 3 4 5 6 7 8 9 10 11 12 14 15 16 19 20 21 23 24 25 26 30 34 35 36 37 40 41 42 44 45 46 47 50 52 53 54	23	10	S	TF	411	18903	261	64.3	36	3450	74787	35988	1541
				H	376	18221	231	—	36	3450	73878	35217	1515
ST. PAUL—Ramsey County													
★ BAPTIST HOSPITAL FUND (Includes Midway Hospital, 1700 University Ave., Zip 55104; tel. 612/641-5500; Ann M. Schrader, adm.; Mounds Park Hospital, 200 Earl St., Zip 55106; tel. 612/774-5901; William Knutson, adm.), 1700 University Ave., Zip 55104; tel. 612/641-5100 (Total facility includes 39 beds in nursing home-type unit) **A**9 **F**1 2 3 6 7 8 9 10 11 12 14 15 16 19 21 23 24 26 27 28 29 30 31 32 34 35 36 37 40 41 43 45 46 47 48 49 50 53	23	10	S	TF	303	11282	186	49.9	40	1398	40831	21476	951
				H	264	10971	178	—	40	1398	—	—	924
⊞ BETHESDA LUTHERAN MEDICAL CENTER, 559 Capitol Blvd., Zip 55103; tel. 612/221-1754; Donald C. Mills, pres. & chief exec. off. (Total facility includes 138 beds in nursing home-type unit) **A**1a 3 5 9 10 **F**1 3 6 10 11 12 15 16 19 21 23 24 26 27 28 29 30 32 33 34 35 36 37 40 41 42 43 44 45 46 47 49 52 53 54	21	10	S	TF	278	6576	235	84.5	11	761	33302	15594	810
				H	140	6418	99	—	11	761	30159	13983	718
⊞ CHILDREN'S HOSPITAL, 345 N. Smith Ave., Zip 55102; tel. 612/298-8666; Brock D. Nelson, adm. (Nonreporting) **A**1a 3 5 9 10; **S**6235	23	50	S		105	—	—	—	—	—	—	—	—
□ GILLETTE CHILDREN'S HOSPITAL (Neuromuscular, Skeletal and Developmental Disabilities), 200 University Ave. E., Zip 55101; tel. 612/291-2848; Norman Allan, adm. **A**1a 3 5 9 **F**1 3 15 23 24 26 33 34 42 44 45 46 47 52	16	59	S		54	939	23	42.6	0	0	10323	5307	236
MIDWAY HOSPITAL, See Baptist Hospital Fund													
MOUNDS PARK HOSPITAL, See Baptist Hospital Fund													
□ SAMARITAN HOSPITAL, 1515 Charles Ave., Zip 55104; tel. 612/645-9111; Joel B. Warner, adm. **A**1a 9 10 **F**1 3 6 10 12 14 15 16 19 23 24 30 35 37 44 45 46 47 49 53; **S**1375	33	10	S		98	1094	22	22.2	0	0	—	—	147
⊞ ST. JOHN'S EASTSIDE HOSPITAL (Formerly St. John's Hospital), 403 Maria Ave., Zip 55106; tel. 612/772-5500; John Reiling, pres. & chief exec. off. **A**1a 3 5 9 10 **F**1 3 5 6 10 12 14 15 16 21 23 24 26 34 35 36 40 42 44 45 46 47 52 53	23	10	S		223	9794	139	64.4	37	1864	46821	21134	879
ST. JOSEPH'S DIVISION, See Carondelet Community Hospitals, Minneapolis													
⊞ ST. PAUL-RAMSEY MEDICAL CENTER, 640 Jackson St., Zip 55101; tel. 612/221-3456; Marlene E. Marschall, pres. **A**1a 2 3 5 8 9 10 **F**1 2 3 4 5 6 9 10 11 12 14 15 16 20 22 23 24 25 26 27 28 30 32 33 34 35 37 38 40 42 43 44 45 46 47 48 49 50 51 52 53 54	16	10	S		304	13637	230	75.7	12	1209	88912	49151	1710
⊞ UNITED HOSPITAL, 333 N. Smith Ave., Zip 55102; tel. 612/298-8888; Thomas H. Rockers, pres. **A**1a 3 5 9 10 **F**1 2 3 4 5 6 9 10 11 12 14 15 16 20 23 24 25 26 27 28 29 30 32 33 34 35 36 37 38 40 42 43 44 46 47 50 54; **S**6235	23	10	S		326	14879	259	79.4	38	3329	77843	36690	1531
ST. PETER—Nicollet County													
★ COMMUNITY HOSPITAL AND HEALTH CARE CENTER, 618 W. Broadway, Zip 56082; tel. 507/931-2200; David Larson, adm. (Total facility includes 85 beds in nursing home-type unit) **A**9 10 **F**1 3 14 15 16 19 21 23 24 35 36 40 42 44 45 46 47 50 52	14	10	S	TF	121	1023	96	79.3	8	120	4181	2471	157
				H	36	983	12	—	8	120	2147	1228	74
□ ST. PETER REGIONAL TREATMENT CENTER, 100 Freeman Dr., Zip 56082; tel. 507/931-7100; Joseph W. Solien, chief exec. off. (Nonreporting) **A**1b 10	12	22	L		419	—	—	—	—	—	—	—	—
STAPLES—Wadena County													
★ UNITED DISTRICT HOSPITAL AND HOME, 401 Prairie Ave. N., Zip 56479; tel. 218/894-1515; Tim Rice, adm. (Total facility includes 100 beds in nursing home-type unit) **A**9 10 **F**1 3 6 14 15 19 21 23 34 35 36 40 41 42 43 45 46 47 49 50 53	16	10	S	TF	140	1003	110	78.6	4	127	5114	2637	156
				H	40	957	11	—	4	127	4324	2041	102
STARBUCK—Pope County													
★ MINNEWASKA DISTRICT HOSPITAL, 610 W. Sixth St., Zip 56381; tel. 612/239-2201; Glenn Christian, adm. **A**9 10 **F**1 15 21 35 45 46 47	16	10	S		19	619	8	42.1	4	44	1166	587	27
STILLWATER—Washington County													
⊞ LAKEVIEW MEMORIAL HOSPITAL, 919 W. Anderson St., Zip 55082; tel. 612/439-5330; Dale C. Mattison, adm. **A**1a 9 10 **F**1 6 10 15 16 23 35 36 40 45 53	23	10	S		82	2787	30	36.6	12	496	7019	3576	160
THIEF RIVER FALLS—Pennington County													
⊞ NORTHWEST MEDICAL CENTER (Formerly Northwestern Hospital Services), 120 LaBree Ave. S., Zip 56701; tel. 218/681-4240; Richard A. Spyhalski, pres. (Total facility includes 90 beds in nursing home-type unit) **A**1a 9 10 **F**1 3 6 11 12 15 16 19 23 24 27 28 29 30 32 33 35 36 40 42 43 45 46 52; **S**6235	23	10	S	TF	189	2967	131	69.3	20	325	10452	5818	310
				H	99	2876	44	—	20	325	8626	5099	269
TRACY—Lyon County													
⊞ TRACY MUNICIPAL HOSPITAL, Fifth St. E., Zip 56175; tel. 507/629-3200; Omer J. Eischens, adm. **A**1a 9 10 **F**1 3 6 16 23 35 40 43 45 52	14	10	S		37	788	9	24.3	5	38	1348	752	38
TRIMONT—Martin County													
⊞ TRIMONT COMMUNITY HOSPITAL, Box H, Zip 56176; tel. 507/639-2911; Thomas A. Tallant, adm. **A**1a 9 10 **F**1 6 15 35 40 45 52	23	10	S		24	406	6	25.0	4	10	869	455	31
TWO HARBORS—Lake County													
★ LAKE VIEW MEMORIAL HOSPITAL, 11th Ave. & Fourth St., Zip 55616; tel. 218/834-2211; Michael E. Walke, adm. (Total facility includes 50 beds in nursing home-type unit) **A**9 10 **F**1 5 6 14 16 19 23 24 30 35 36 40 42 44 45 46 49	23	10	S	TF	80	653	55	68.8	3	87	2431	1469	80
				H	30	598	7	—	3	87	1347	835	44
TYLER—Lincoln County													
★ A. L. VADHEIM MEMORIAL HOSPITAL, 240 Willow St., Zip 56178; tel. 507/247-5521; Pamela J. Gilchrist, adm. (Total facility includes 43 beds in nursing home-type unit) **A**9 10 **F**1 6 14 16 23 35 36 37 41 42 45; **S**5255	23	10	S	TF	67	558	51	76.1	5	30	2017	905	69
				H	24	537	8	—	5	30	1336	507	46

Hospital, Address, Telephone, Administrator, Approval and Facility Codes, Multihospital System Code	Classification Codes				Inpatient Data				Newborn Data		Expense (thousands of dollars)		
★ American Hospital Association (AHA) membership □ Joint Commission on Accreditation of Hospitals (JCAH) accreditation + American Osteopathic Hospital Association (AOHA) membership ○ American Osteopathic Association (AOA) accreditation Δ Commission on Accreditation of Rehabilitation Facilities (CARF) accreditation Control codes 61, 63, 64, 71, 72 and 73 indicate hospitals listed by AOHA, but not registered by AHA. For definition of numerical codes, see page A2	Control	Service	Stay	Facilities	Beds	Admissions	Census	Occupancy (percent)	Bassinets	Births	Total	Payroll	Personnel
VIRGINIA—St. Louis County													
⊞ VIRGINIA REGIONAL MEDICAL CENTER, 901 Ninth St. N., Zip 55792; tel. 218/741-3340; John A. Tucker, adm. (Total facility includes 122 beds in nursing home-type unit) **A**1a 9 10 **F**1 3 5 6 10 12 14 15 16 19 21 27 29 30 33 34 35 36 40 41 45 46 50 52 53; **S**2495	14	10	S	TF H	295 173	4313 4167	161 47	54.6 —	22 22	467 467	13373 11193	7246 6088	344 280
WABASHA—Wabasha County													
⊞ ST. ELIZABETH HOSPITAL, 1200 Fifth Grant Blvd. W., Zip 55981; tel. 612/565-4531; Thomas Crowley, adm. (Total facility includes 52 beds in nursing home-type unit) **A**1a 9 10 **F**1 12 14 15 16 19 23 35 36 40 42 43 50; **S**5305	21	10	S	TF H	97 45	909 865	58 11	59.8 —	4 4	121 121	2943 —	1880 —	110 83
WACONIA—Carver County													
⊞ WACONIA RIDGEVIEW HOSPITAL, 500 S. Maple St., Zip 55387; tel. 612/442-2191; John P. Devins, exec. dir. **A**1a 9 10 **F**1 5 6 9 10 12 14 15 16 23 30 35 36 37 40 41 44 45 46 52 53	14	10	S		109	4495	47	43.1	20	740	14398	7814	327
WADENA—Wadena County													
⊞ TRI-COUNTY HOSPITAL, 418 Jefferson St. N., Zip 56482; tel. 218/631-3510; James G. Lawson, adm. **A**1a 9 10 **F**1 3 6 10 14 15 16 23 26 34 35 36 37 40 45 46 47 52	23	10	S		56	2140	38	67.9	8	240	5170	2565	138
WARREN—Marshall County													
★ WARREN COMMUNITY HOSPITAL, 109 S. Minnesota St., Zip 56762; tel. 218/745-4211; Gordon Sommers, adm. **A**9 10 **F**1 3 15 16 21 23 26 35 36 37 40 45 46 52	23	10	S		41	484	8	19.5	11	36	1010	515	27
WASECA—Waseca County													
⊞ WASECA AREA MEMORIAL HOSPITAL, 100 Fifth Ave. N.W., Zip 56093; tel. 507/835-1210; Dennis C. Miley, adm. **A**1a 9 10 **F**1 3 12 14 15 23 26 28 34 35 36 40 41 45 49 52; **S**1325	23	10	S		19	884	9	45.0	6	194	2225	1200	64
WELLS—Faribault County													
★ WELLS HOSPITAL (Formerly Wells Municipal Hospital), 400 Fourth Ave. S.W., Zip 56097; tel. 507/553-3111; Charisse Oland, adm. **A**10 **F**1 3 15 35 43 45 47	14	10	S		28	301	4	14.3	8	33	698	345	25
WESTBROOK—Cottonwood County													
DR. HENRY SCHMIDT MEMORIAL HOSPITAL, 920 Bell Ave., Zip 56183; tel. 507/274-6121; Jeffery J. Rotert, adm. **A**10 **F**1 6 10 15 16 34 35 43 45	23	10	S		12	136	2	16.7	6	11	445	216	16
WHEATON—Traverse County													
★ WHEATON COMMUNITY HOSPITAL, 401 12th St. N., Zip 56296; tel. 612/563-8226; William C. Buchholz, adm. **A**9 10 **F**1 14 15 23 35 36 40 45 52	14	10	S		35	809	12	34.3	8	76	1808	853	49
WILLMAR—Kandiyohi County													
⊞ RICE MEMORIAL HOSPITAL, 301 Becker Ave. S.W., Zip 56201; tel. 612/235-4543; Hans A. Dahl, adm. **A**1a 9 10 **F**1 3 5 6 7 8 9 10 11 12 14 15 16 20 21 23 24 27 28 29 30 32 33 34 35 36 40 42 43 44 45 46 47 52 53	14	10	S		164	6321	87	53.0	20	856	19509	9236	437
□ WILLMAR REGIONAL TREATMENT CENTER (Formerly Willmar State Hospital), Box 1128, Zip 56201; tel. 612/231-5100; Gregory G. Spartz, chief exec. off. **A**1b 9 10 **F**15 19 23 24 33 42 46 47 48 49 50	12	22	L		621	1285	510	82.1	0	0	19864	14229	604
WINDOM—Cottonwood County													
⊞ WINDOM AREA HOSPITAL, Highways 60 & 71 N., Box 339, Zip 56101; tel. 507/831-2400; Vern B. Pytleski, adm. (Nonreporting) **A**1a 9 10	14	10	S		35	—	—	—	—	—	—	—	—
WINONA—Winona County													
⊞ COMMUNITY MEMORIAL HOSPITAL AND CONVALESCENT AND REHABILITATION UNIT, 855 Mankato Ave., Zip 55987; tel. 507/454-3650; Roger L. Metz, adm. (Total facility includes 104 beds in nursing home-type unit) **A**1a 9 10 **F**1 3 6 10 12 14 15 16 19 20 21 23 24 26 27 30 32 33 35 36 37 40 41 42 44 45 46 53	23	10	S	TF H	224 120	4361 4099	153 56	66.5 —	21 21	538 538	12890 10827	7354 5941	350 300
WINSTED—McLeod County													
⊞ ST. MARY'S HOSPITAL AND HOME, 551 Fourth St. N., P O Box 750, Zip 55395; tel. 612/485-2151; Jeanne Johnson, chief exec. off. (Nonreporting) **A**1a 9 10; **S**6235	23	10	S		120	—	—	—	—	—	—	—	—
WORTHINGTON—Nobles County													
□ WORTHINGTON REGIONAL HOSPITAL, 1018 Sixth Ave., Zip 56187; tel. 507/372-2941; David P. Gehant, adm. (Total facility includes 5 beds in nursing home-type unit) **A**1a 9 10 **F**1 3 6 7 9 10 11 12 14 15 16 19 20 23 24 27 29 30 33 35 36 40 41 42 44 45 53	14	10	S	TF H	99 94	2731 2642	37 34	37.4 —	12 12	374 374	6888 6746	3892 3788	172 —
ZUMBROTA—Goodhue County													
⊞ ZUMBROTA COMMUNITY HOSPITAL, 383 W. Fifth St., Zip 55992; tel. 507/732-5131; Jeffrey Robertson, adm. **A**1a 9 10 **F**1 6 14 15 16 23 24 34 35 41 45 46	23	10	S		19	604	7	36.8	4	65	1420	729	42

Hospital, Address, Telephone, Administrator, Approval and Facility Codes, Multihospital System Code

- ★ American Hospital Association (AHA) membership
- □ Joint Commission on Accreditation of Hospitals (JCAH) accreditation
- \+ American Osteopathic Hospital Association (AOHA) membership
- ○ American Osteopathic Association (AOA) accreditation
- Δ Commission on Accreditation of Rehabilitation Facilities (CARF) accreditation

Control codes 61, 63, 64, 71, 72 and 73 indicate hospitals listed by AOHA, but not registered by AHA. For definition of numerical codes, see page A2

Mississippi

Hospital	Classification Codes: Control	Service	Stay	Facilities	Inpatient Data: Beds	Admissions	Census	Occupancy (percent)	Newborn Data: Bassinets	Births	Expense (thousands of dollars): Total	Payroll	Personnel
ABERDEEN—Monroe County													
ABERDEEN-MONROE COUNTY HOSPITAL, 400 S. Chestnut St., Box 747, Zip 39730; tel. 601/369-2455; Donald L. Ray, adm. **A**9 10 **F**3 6 16 23 35	15	10	S		84	1412	19	22.6	10	3	—	—	80
ACKERMAN—Choctaw County													
CHOCTAW COUNTY HOSPITAL, W. Cherry St., Zip 39735; tel. 601/285-6235; Robert B. Hughes, adm. (Total facility includes 32 beds in nursing home-type unit) **A**9 10 **F**6 14 16 19 23 35 41 50 53	13	10	S	TF	60	1092	47	78.3	5	95	2162	1107	86
				H	28	1083	15	—	5	95	1789	840	58
AMORY—Monroe County													
⊠ GILMORE MEMORIAL HOSPITAL, S. Boulevard Dr., Zip 38821; tel. 601/256-7111; Clay M. McCluskey, adm. **A**1a 9 10 **F**1 2 3 6 10 12 14 15 16 35 36 37 40 47 51 52 53	23	10	S		103	4095	49	47.6	20	1020	8036	4671	258
BATESVILLE—Panola County													
SOUTH PANOLA COMMUNITY HOSPITAL, Hospital Dr., Box 433, Zip 38606; tel. 601/563-5611; Doyle Atchley, adm. **A**9 10 **F**1 6 10 16 23 35 45 46 47 53	13	10	S		70	1817	22	31.4	6	234	—	—	131
BAY SPRINGS—Jasper County													
⊠ JASPER GENERAL HOSPITAL (Includes Jasper County Nursing Home), Sixth St., Box 527, Zip 39422; tel. 601/764-2101; Jackie M. Belding, adm. (Total facility includes 61 beds in nursing home-type unit) **A**1a 9 10 **F**6 10 16 19 23 26 35 41 47	13	10	S	TF	110	562	69	62.7	0	0	—	—	127
				H	49	541	8	—	0	0	—	—	81
BAY ST. LOUIS—Hancock County													
⊠ HANCOCK MEDICAL CENTER (Formerly Hancock General Hospital), 149 Drinkwater Blvd., Zip 39520; tel. 601/467-9081; Phillip R. Wolfe, adm. **A**1a 9 10 **F**1 3 14 15 16 23 26 34 35 45 47 53; **S**1755	13	10	S		56	2515	33	58.9	7	137	6093	2453	147
BELZONI—Humphreys County													
★ HUMPHREYS COUNTY MEMORIAL HOSPITAL, 501 First St., P O Box 510, Zip 39038; tel. 601/247-3831; Alvin Word III, adm. (Total facility includes 7 beds in nursing home-type unit) **A**9 10 **F**14 16 19 23 35 47	13	10	S	TF	32	794	11	34.4	0	0	1599	663	46
				H	25	718	—	—	0	0	—	545	34
BILOXI—Harrison County													
⊠ BILOXI REGIONAL MEDICAL CENTER, 300 Reynoir St., Box 128, Zip 39533; tel. 601/432-1571; James D. Baker, exec. dir. **A**1a 2 9 10 **F**1 3 6 7 8 9 10 12 14 15 16 20 23 34 35 36 37 40 43 45 46 52 53; **S**1775	23	10	S		188	5054	85	40.9	28	713	—	—	313
□ GULF COAST COMMUNITY HOSPITAL (Includes Gulf Oaks Hospital and Clinic, 4645 W. Beach Blvd., Zip 39531; tel. 601/388-0650; Raymond Butler, adm.), 4642 W. Beach Blvd., Zip 39535; Mailing Address Box 4518, Zip 39531; tel. 601/388-6711; Albert A. Brust III, exec. dir. **A**1a 9 10 **F**1 2 3 6 10 12 14 15 16 21 23 35 45 52 53; **S**9555	33	10	S		185	5214	88	64.3	0	0	—	—	333
GULF OAKS HOSPITAL AND CLINIC, See Gulf Coast Community Hospital													
U. S. AIR FORCE MEDICAL CENTER KEESLER, See Keesler Air Force Base													
⊠ VETERANS ADMINISTRATION MEDICAL CENTER, Zip 39531; tel. 601/388-5541; J. H. Caldwell Jr., dir. (Total facility includes 78 beds in nursing home-type unit) **A**1a 2 3 5 **F**1 2 3 5 6 10 11 12 14 15 16 19 23 24 25 26 27 28 30 31 32 33 34 35 42 44 46 47 48 49 50	45	10	S	TF	574	9954	515	94.5	0	0	—	—	1638
				H	496	9880	453	—	0	0	—	—	—
BOONEVILLE—Prentiss County													
⊠ BAPTIST MEMORIAL HOSPITAL-BOONEVILLE, Washington & Second Sts., Zip 38829; tel. 601/728-5331; John Tompkins, adm. **A**1a 9 10 **F**1 2 6 10 12 14 15 16 23 35 45 46 47 50 52 53; **S**1625	21	10	S		78	2532	41	47.7	0	0	6787	2361	156
BRANDON—Rankin County													
⊠ RANKIN GENERAL HOSPITAL, 350 Crossgate Blvd., Zip 39042; tel. 601/825-2811; Thomas Wiman, adm. **A**1a 9 10 **F**1 3 5 6 10 12 14 15 16 20 23 34 35 44 45 46 47 50 53	13	10	S		90	2877	49	54.4	0	0	9875	5036	302
BROOKHAVEN—Lincoln County													
⊠ KING'S DAUGHTERS HOSPITAL, Hwy. 51 N., P O Box 558, Zip 39601; tel. 601/833-6011; G. Richard Borgmann, exec. dir. **A**1a 9 10 **F**1 2 6 10 12 14 15 16 20 21 23 34 35 41 45 46 47 53	23	10	S		135	3167	57	42.2	20	27	8047	3397	222
CALHOUN CITY—Calhoun County													
HILLCREST HOSPITAL, Box 770, Zip 38916; tel. 601/628-6611; Gene Wayne Schuler, adm. **A**9 10 **F**1 6 10 13 14 15 16 23 35 43 45 47; **S**5895	14	10	S		30	705	9	30.0	0	0	—	—	47
CANTON—Madison County													
★ MADISON GENERAL HOSPITAL, Country Club Rd., Box 281, Zip 39046; tel. 601/859-1331; S. L. Whittington, exec. dir. (Total facility includes 60 beds in nursing home-type unit) **A**9 10 **F**1 6 12 14 16 19 23 35 46 47 50	13	10	S	TF	127	2174	85	66.9	10	189	3892	2423	176
				H	67	2143	25	—	10	189	2936	1840	120
CARTHAGE—Leake County													
LEAKE COUNTY MEMORIAL HOSPITAL, 300 Ellis St., Box 557, Zip 39051; tel. 601/267-4511; Joe Hugh Cooper, adm. (Total facility includes 37 beds in nursing home-type unit) **A**9 10 **F**6 12 14 16 19 23 35	13	10	S	TF	72	635	52	72.2	7	1	—	—	88
				H	35	318	15	—	7	1	—	—	63
CENTREVILLE—Wilkinson County													
□ FIELD MEMORIAL COMMUNITY HOSPITAL, Main St., Box 639, Zip 39631; tel. 601/645-5221; Brock A. Slabach, adm. **A**1a 9 10 **F**1 6 15 16 23 34 35 40 43 45	13	10	S		66	2057	24	36.4	6	198	—	—	86
CHARLESTON—Tallahatchie County													
□ TALLAHATCHIE GENERAL HOSPITAL, Box F, Zip 38921; tel. 601/647-5535; F. W. Ergle Jr., adm. (Total facility includes 40 beds in nursing home-type unit) **A**1a 9 10 **F**1 6 10 14 16 19 23 35 44 45 47	13	10	S	TF	75	1051	50	66.7	10	119	2298	1148	105
				H	35	1032	11	—	10	119	1853	825	76
CHUNKY—Lauderdale County													
PINE FOREST SANITARIUM AND HOSPITAL, Zip 39323; tel. 601/655-8229; Raymond Harold RN, adm. **A**9	23	48	L		35	45	33	94.3	0	0	—	—	38
CLARKSDALE—Coahoma County													
□ NORTHWEST MISSISSIPPI REGIONAL MEDICAL CENTER, Hospital Dr., Box 1218, Zip 38614; tel. 601/627-3211; Clifford L. Johnson Jr., exec. dir. **A**1a 9 10 **F**1 3 6 10 11 12 14 16 20 23 35 45 53	13	10	S		194	8425	130	67.0	23	1221	17196	8419	532
CLEVELAND—Bolivar County													
⊠ BOLIVAR COUNTY HOSPITAL, Hwy. 8 E., P O Box 1380, Zip 38732; tel. 601/846-0061; Noel W. Hart, adm. (Total facility includes 33 beds in nursing home-type unit) **A**1a 9 10 **F**1 3 6 12 14 16 19 23 35 40 45 46 47 52	13	10	S	TF	187	5172	110	58.8	16	641	—	—	387
				H	154	5161	78	—	16	641	—	—	358
COLLINS—Covington County													
□ COVINGTON COUNTY HOSPITAL, Box 1149, Zip 39428; tel. 601/765-6711; Irving Hitt, adm. **A**1a 9 10 **F**1 2 6 10 14 15 16 21 23 34 35 37 41 44 45 46 47	13	10	S		49	1553	23	34.3	6	179	3921	1736	112

Hospital, Address, Telephone, Administrator, Approval and Facility Codes, Multihospital System Code	Classification Codes				Inpatient Data				Newborn Data		Expense (thousands of dollars)		
★ American Hospital Association (AHA) membership □ Joint Commission on Accreditation of Hospitals (JCAH) accreditation + American Osteopathic Hospital Association (AOHA) membership ○ American Osteopathic Association (AOA) accreditation Δ Commission on Accreditation of Rehabilitation Facilities (CARF) accreditation Control codes 61, 63, 64, 71, 72 and 73 indicate hospitals listed by AOHA, but not registered by AHA. For definition of numerical codes, see page A2	Control	Service	Stay	Facilities	Beds	Admissions	Census	Occupancy (percent)	Bassinets	Births	Total	Payroll	Personnel
COLUMBIA—Marion County													
□ MARION COUNTY GENERAL HOSPITAL, 1560 Sumrall Rd., Box 630, Zip 39429; tel. 601/736-6303; John W. Reynolds, adm. **A**1a 9 10 **F**1 3 6 8 10 11 14 15 16 23 26 34 35 37 40 41 45 46 47 50 52 53; **S**1755	13	10	S		90	3251	44	48.9	10	117	—	—	250
COLUMBUS—Lowndes County													
★ COLUMBUS HOSPITAL, 525 Willowbrook Rd., Zip 39701; Mailing Address Box 991, Zip 39703; tel. 601/327-2950; Thomas F. Wolford II, pres. **A**9 10 **F**1 3 5 14 15 16 23 27 28 30 32 33 35 37 47 48 49	23	10	S		92	2902	62	67.4	0	0	—	—	242
★□ GOLDEN TRIANGLE REGIONAL MEDICAL CENTER, 2520 Fifth St. N., Box 1307, Zip 39701; tel. 601/243-1000; Charles A. Faulkner, adm. **A**1a 9 10 **F**1 3 5 6 9 13 14 15 16 20 21 23 35 36 37 40 43 45 46 47 52 53	13	10	S		247	7996	117	47.4	20	935	20474	8914	573
U. S. AIR FORCE HOSPITAL, See Columbus Air Force Base													
COLUMBUS AIR FORCE BASE—Lowndes County													
U. S. AIR FORCE HOSPITAL, Zip 39701; tel. 601/434-9521; Maj. John R. Gaddis, adm. **F**1 14 15 23 28 34 35 36 37 40 46 47 52	41	10	S		15	903	8	42.1	7	132	—	—	228
CORINTH—Alcorn County													
★□ MAGNOLIA HOSPITAL, Alcorn Dr., Zip 38834; tel. 601/286-6961; W. C. Whitfield, adm. **A**1a 9 10 **F**1 3 6 10 12 14 15 16 23 35 36 40 41 43 44 45 46 53 54	15	10	S		114	5280	83	75.5	14	381	—	—	449
DE KALB—Kemper County													
★ RILEY-KEMPER COMMUNITY HOSPITAL (Formerly Kemper County Hospital), Box 246, Zip 39328; tel. 601/743-5851; Art M. Nester, adm. **A**9 10 **F**15 16 35 42 46 50	23	10	S		35	453	6	17.1	0	0	—	—	45
DURANT—Holmes County													
★ DISTRICT TWO COMMUNITY HOSPITAL, 603 N. West Ave., Zip 39063; tel. 601/653-3151; Joe McLellan, adm. **A**9 10 **F**1 6 16 23 34 44 45 46 47	13	10	S		29	513	9	31.0	3	7	—	—	39
ELLISVILLE—Jones County													
ELLISVILLE MUNICIPAL HOSPITAL, Ivy St., Zip 39437; tel. 601/477-9381; Meredith L. Nichols, adm. **A**9 10 **F**6 14 16 35	14	10	S		17	273	4	23.5	0	0	512	248	18
EUPORA—Webster County													
WEBSTER GENERAL HOSPITAL, 500 Hwy. 9 S., Zip 39744; tel. 601/258-6221; Harold H. Whitaker, exec. dir. **A**9 10 **F**1 6 9 10 14 16 23 35 45 47 53	15	10	S		55	2296	30	54.5	7	85	3447	1755	125
FAYETTE—Jefferson County													
★ JEFFERSON COUNTY HOSPITAL, 809 S. Main St., Box 577, Zip 39069; tel. 601/786-3401; Ann Brown, adm. **A**9 10 **F**6 14 16 23 35 44	13	10	S		30	1326	18	60.0	6	0	4168	1039	80
FOREST—Scott County													
★ S. E. LACKEY MEMORIAL HOSPITAL, 330 N. Broad St., Box 428, Zip 39074; tel. 601/469-4151; E. Tyler Zeigler, adm. (Total facility includes 30 beds in nursing home-type unit) **A**9 10 **F**6 14 16 19 35 47 53	13	10	S	TF	74	902	38	51.4	10	2	—	—	80
				H	44	875	12	—	10	2	—	—	59
FULTON—Itawamba County													
ITAWAMBA COUNTY HOSPITAL, Box 759, Zip 38843; tel. 601/862-3183; Elizabeth Roberts, actg. adm. **A**9 10 **F**1 16 23 35 44 45	13	10	S		49	872	16	25.8	5	0	2021	793	67
GREENVILLE—Washington County													
★□ DELTA MEDICAL CENTER, 1400 E. Union St., Box 5247, Zip 38701; tel. 601/378-3783; William H. Sellers, adm. **A**1a 9 10 **F**1 2 3 6 7 8 10 11 12 14 15 16 20 22 23 24 27 30 34 35 40 41 44 45 46 47 48 49 52 53	13	10	S		268	5679	114	42.5	20	749	20013	8125	546
★□ KING'S DAUGHTERS HOSPITAL, 339 Arnold Ave., Zip 38702; Mailing Address Box 1857, Zip 38701; tel. 601/378-2020; Donald Joe Fisher, exec. dir. **A**1a 9 10 **F**1 3 6 10 12 14 15 16 23 40 44 45 47 52	23	10	S		137	4031	60	43.8	19	645	—	—	315
GREENWOOD—Leflore County													
□ GREENWOOD LEFLORE HOSPITAL, River Rd., Drawer 1410, Zip 38930; tel. 601/459-9751; Thomas Luster Askew, exec. dir. **A**1a 9 10 **F**1 3 6 10 12 14 15 16 20 23 34 35 37 40 46 47 50 52 53	15	10	S		260	8864	130	53.9	25	965	—	—	495
GRENADA—Grenada County													
★□ GRENADA LAKE MEDICAL CENTER (Formerly Grenada County Hospital), 960 Avent Dr., Zip 38901; tel. 601/226-8111; Paul Johnson Wood Sr., exec. dir. **A**1a 9 10 **F**1 2 6 10 11 12 16 23 35 41 44 45	13	10	S		86	4377	57	66.3	14	680	9571	4795	315
GULFPORT—Harrison County													
★□ AMI GARDEN PARK COMMUNITY HOSPITAL (Formerly Garden Park Community Hospital), 1520 Broad Ave., Zip 39501; tel. 601/864-4210; L. V. Johnston, exec. dir. **A**1a 9 10 **F**1 3 6 10 12 14 15 16 23 26 34 35 37 44 45 47 53; **S**0125	33	10	S		120	3076	53	44.2	0	0	13916	3365	245
□ CPC SAND HILL HOSPITAL (Formerly Sand Hill Hospital), 12222 Hwy. 49 N., Zip 39503; tel. 601/831-1700; Phillip W. Langston, adm. **A**1b 10 **F**15 24 30 32 33 42 48; **S**0785	33	22	L		60	166	16	26.7	0	0	—	—	27
GARDEN PARK COMMUNITY HOSPITAL, See AMI Garden Park Community Hospital													
★□ MEMORIAL HOSPITAL AT GULFPORT, 4500 13th St., Box 1810, Zip 39501; tel. 601/863-1441; Ronald Burton, adm. **A**1a 2 9 10 **F**1 3 6 7 8 9 10 11 12 14 15 16 20 23 27 30 33 34 35 36 37 40 45 46 47 50 52 53	15	10	S		281	11719	181	64.4	40	1717	37830	15785	841
HATTIESBURG—Forrest County													
★□ FORREST COUNTY GENERAL HOSPITAL, 400 S. 28th Ave., Zip 39401; Mailing Address P O Box 16389, Zip 39404; tel. 601/264-7000; Lowery A. Woodall, exec. dir. **A**1a 2 9 10 **F**1 2 3 4 6 7 8 9 10 11 12 14 15 16 20 23 24 27 30 32 33 34 35 37 40 41 42 43 44 46 47 48 51 52 53 54	13	10	S		443	16884	300	67.7	20	2428	47320	20311	1243
★□ METHODIST HOSPITAL OF HATTIESBURG (Formerly Methodist Hospital), 5001 W. Hardy St., Zip 39401; Mailing Address Box 16509, Zip 39404; tel. 601/268-8000; William K. Ray, pres. **A**1a 2 9 10 **F**1 3 6 9 10 11 15 16 20 23 34 35 45 46 47	23	10	S		201	8284	137	68.2	0	0	23811	7968	604
HAZELHURST—Copiah County													
★□ HARDY WILSON MEMORIAL HOSPITAL, 233 Magnolia St., P O Box 889, Zip 39083; tel. 601/894-4541; Pat Moreland, adm. **A**1a 9 10 **F**1 6 14 15 16 23 35 37 40 42 44 46 50	13	10	S		49	1697	23	46.9	8	203	—	—	126
HOLLANDALE—Washington County													
SOUTH WASHINGTON COUNTY HOSPITAL, Hwy. 61 S., Box 398, Zip 38748; tel. 601/827-2231; Adrian McKinley, adm. **A**9 10 **F**1 6 14 15 16 23 35 50	13	10	S		40	810	17	42.5	0	0	1845	839	54
HOLLY SPRINGS—Marshall County													
MARSHALL COUNTY HOSPITAL, 1430 E. Salem, Zip 38635; tel. 601/252-1212; R. J. Mincey, actg. adm. **A**9 10 **F**1 6 14 16 35 53	13	10	S		40	1501	21	52.5	0	5	2784	994	83
HOUSTON—Chickasaw County													
★□ HOUSTON COMMUNITY HOSPITAL, Hwy. 8 E., Zip 38851; tel. 601/456-3701; David A. Wiley, adm. (Total facility includes 66 beds in nursing home-type unit) **A**1a 9 10 **F**1 3 6 10 16 23 34 35 45 46 47 53; **S**5895	33	10	S	TF	150	2131	94	62.7	11	58	5688	2390	105
				H	84	2105	28	—	11	58	4633	1881	—
INDIANOLA—Sunflower County													
□ SOUTH SUNFLOWER COUNTY HOSPITAL, 121 E. Baker St., Zip 38751; tel. 601/887-3113; H. J. Blessitt, adm. **A**1a 9 10 **F**2 6 10 14 16 23 35 36 45	13	10	S		69	2906	34	49.3	10	439	4211	1901	134

Hospital, Address, Telephone, Administrator, Approval and Facility Codes, Multihospital System Code	Classification Codes: Control	Service	Stay	Facilities	Inpatient Data: Beds	Admissions	Census	Occupancy (percent)	Newborn Data: Bassinets	Births	Expense (thousands of dollars): Total	Payroll	Personnel
IUKA—Tishomingo County													
□ TISHOMINGO HOSPITAL (Formerly Tishomingo County Hospital), 1410 W. Quitman, Zip 38852; tel. 601/423-6051; William E. Rutledge, adm. **A**1a 9 10 **F**1 2 3 6 10 12 15 16 23 35 53	13	10	S		105	2253	37	35.2	0	29	—	—	126
JACKSON—Hinds County													
★□ CHARTER HOSPITAL OF JACKSON (Formerly Riverside Hospital), Box 4297, Zip 39216; tel. 601/939-9030; Jim Johnson, adm. **A**1a 9 10 **F**12 16 30 32 33 42 44	33	22	S		108	1062	68	63.0	0	0	—	—	139
□ DOCTORS HOSPITAL, 2969 University Dr., Box 4783, Zip 39216; tel. 601/982-8321; Ronald T. Seal, adm. **A**1a 9 10 **F**1 2 3 6 12 14 15 16 23 33 34 43 45 47 48 49 53; **S**1375	33	10	S		162	1766	37	22.8	0	0	—	—	174
★□ HINDS GENERAL HOSPITAL, 1850 Chadwick Dr., Zip 39204; tel. 601/376-1000; Robert G. Wilson, adm. **A**1a 3 5 9 10 **F**1 2 3 6 9 10 12 14 15 16 20 23 34 35 36 37 40 44 45 46 47 51 52 53	13	10	S		290	12723	220	75.9	14	726	35196	16428	931
★□ MISSISSIPPI BAPTIST MEDICAL CENTER, 1225 N. State St., Zip 39202; tel. 601/968-1000; Paul J. Pryor, exec. dir. **A**1a 2 3 5 9 10 **F**1 2 3 4 5 6 8 9 10 11 12 14 15 16 20 23 33 34 35 36 40 44 45 46 47 48 49 50 51 52 53 54	21	10	S		612	24695	472	77.1	32	2026	70705	33311	2095
★□ MISSISSIPPI METHODIST HOSPITAL AND REHABILITATION CENTER, 1350 Woodrow Wilson Dr., Box 4878, Fondren Sta., Zip 39216; tel. 601/981-2611; J. Michael Ainsworth, pres. **A**1a 9 10 **F**1 12 14 16 23 24 26 34 41 42 44 45 46 47	23	46	S		114	1293	83	77.6	0	0	18826	8069	421
★ RIVER OAKS HOSPITAL, 1030 River Oaks Dr., P O Box 5100, Zip 39216; tel. 601/932-1030; Timothy R. Gompf, exec. dir. **A**9 10 **F**1 3 6 10 12 14 15 16 23 34 35 37 43 45 46 47 53	33	10	S		100	3816	48	48.0	0	0	—	—	153
RIVERSIDE HOSPITAL, See Charter Hospital of Jackson													
★□ ST. DOMINIC-JACKSON MEMORIAL HOSPITAL, 969 Lakeland Dr., Zip 39216; tel. 601/364-6848; Sr. John Vianney, pres. **A**1a 9 10 **F**1 2 3 4 6 10 12 14 15 16 20 23 26 27 28 29 30 32 33 35 39 42 43 45 46 53 54; **S**1295	23	10	S		358	13729	272	76.0	0	0	33778	16264	1072
★□ UNIVERSITY HOSPITAL, 2500 N. State St., Zip 39216; tel. 601/984-4100; David E. Bussone, dir. **A**1a 2 3 5 8 9 10 **F**1 2 3 4 5 6 8 9 10 11 12 13 14 15 16 20 23 24 27 28 30 32 33 34 35 37 38 40 44 45 46 47 49 50 51 52 53 54; **S**1755	12	10	S		501	21916	407	81.4	64	4624	74361	30603	1613
★□ VETERANS ADMINISTRATION MEDICAL CENTER, 1500 E. Woodrow Wilson Dr., Zip 39216; tel. 601/362-4471; J. L. Warnock, dir. (Total facility includes 120 beds in nursing home-type unit) **A**1a 2 3 5 8 **F**1 2 3 6 10 11 12 14 15 16 19 20 23 24 26 27 28 30 32 33 34 41 42 44 46 47 48 49 50 53 54	45	10	S	TF	573	14268	439	80.4	0	0	54127	30029	1184
				H	453	14167	327	—	0	0	49028	27026	1130
WOMAN'S HOSPITAL, P O Box 4546, Zip 39216; tel. 601/932-1000; Thomas E. Fitz Jr., exec. dir. **A**9 10 **F**1 6 12 14 15 16 23 24 36 37 40 45 46 50 51; **S**5765	33	10	S		111	3573	43	38.7	40	1780	—	—	207
KEESLER AIR FORCE BASE—Harrison County													
★□ U. S. AIR FORCE MEDICAL CENTER KEESLER, Zip 39534; tel. 601/377-6012; Col. Gilbert R. Inman, adm. **A**1a 2 3 5 **F**1 2 3 4 5 6 7 8 9 10 11 12 14 15 16 18 20 23 24 27 28 30 32 33 34 35 37 38 40 42 44 46 47 49 51 52 53 54	41	10	S		329	11586	242	73.6	18	1159	—	—	1386
KILMICHAEL—Montgomery County													
★ KILMICHAEL HOSPITAL, Lamar St., P O Box 188, Zip 39747; tel. 601/262-4311; Barbara S. Moore, adm. **A**9 10 **F**15 34 35 36	16	10	S		19	988	13	68.4	4	34	—	—	46
KOSCIUSKO—Attala County													
MONTFORT JONES MEMORIAL HOSPITAL, Hwy. 12 W., Box 677, Zip 39090; tel. 601/289-4311; Thomas Bland, adm. **A**9 10 **F**1 2 6 10 15 16 23 35 37 40 50 53	13	10	S		78	2154	28	35.9	12	124	—	—	124
LAUREL—Jones County													
★□ JONES COUNTY COMMUNITY HOSPITAL, Jefferson St. & 13th Ave., Box 607, Zip 39440; tel. 601/649-4000; Terry G. Whittington, exec. dir. **A**1a 9 10 **F**1 2 3 5 6 8 10 11 12 14 15 16 23 26 34 35 36 40 43 44 45 46 52 53	13	10	S		255	9488	156	61.2	20	645	—	—	732
□ SOUTH MISSISSIPPI STATE HOSPITAL, 100 Buchanan St., Box 929, Zip 39441; tel. 601/649-4730; Russell M. Carlos, adm. **A**1a 9 10 **F**14 23 34 35 40 45 46 47 52	12	10	S		95	3074	35	36.8	15	659	3556	2159	132
LEAKESVILLE—Greene County													
GREENE COUNTY HOSPITAL AND EXTENDED CARE FACILITY, Box 39, Zip 39451; tel. 601/394-2371; Judy H. Thurman, adm. (Total facility includes 24 beds in nursing home-type unit) **A**9 10 **F**14 16 19 23 35 36 44 46 50	13	10	S	TF	40	547	29	72.5	5	22	—	—	61
				H	16	538	5	—	5	22	—	—	46
LEXINGTON—Holmes County													
★ METHODIST HOSPITAL OF MIDDLE MISSISSIPPI (Formerly Holmes County Hospital), Box 641, Zip 39095; tel. 601/834-1321; Frank Jones, adm. **A**9 10 **F**1 3 6 10 14 15 16 23 34 35 37 40 46; **S**9345	23	10	S		84	2663	36	42.9	12	238	—	—	121
LOUISVILLE—Winston County													
□ WINSTON COUNTY COMMUNITY HOSPITAL AND NURSING HOME, Hwy. 14 E., Box 670, Zip 39339; tel. 601/773-6211; Paul J. Wood, adm. (Total facility includes 82 beds in nursing home-type unit) **A**1a 9 10 **F**1 2 3 6 10 14 16 19 23 34 35 44 45 47 53	13	10	S	TF	147	2006	111	75.5	7	165	—	—	183
				H	65	1991	29	—	7	165	—	—	132
LUCEDALE—George County													
GEORGE COUNTY-MOBILE INFIRMARY (Formerly George County Hospital), 305 S. Winter St., P O Box 607, Zip 39452; tel. 601/947-3161; Rupert J. Ingram, adm. **A**9 10 **F**1 3 6 10 12 14 15 16 23 35 45	23	10	S		53	1364	16	30.2	6	106	—	—	107
LUMBERTON—Lamar County													
★ LUMBERTON CITIZENS HOSPITAL, 600 11th Ave., Box 193, Zip 39455; tel. 601/796-2681; Howard Beall, adm. (Data for 84 days) **A**9 10 **F**6 14 16 35 50	14	10	S		23	135	7	30.4	6	4	—	—	32
MACON—Noxubee County													
NOXUBEE GENERAL HOSPITAL, Jefferson St., Box 480, Zip 39341; tel. 601/726-4231; Richard W. Manning, adm. **A**9 10 **F**1 6 14 15 16 23 35 40 44 46	13	10	S		49	1287	20	40.8	8	136	2314	1137	83
MADDEN—Leake County													
THAGGARD HOSPITAL, Box 157, Zip 39109; tel. 601/267-4562; Ronald Yarborogh, adm. **A**9 10 **F**6 16 23 35; **S**0075	33	10	S		22	945	12	54.5	0	0	—	—	39
MAGEE—Simpson County													
MAGEE GENERAL HOSPITAL, 300 S.E. Third Ave., Zip 39111; tel. 601/849-5070; Katherine C. Magee, adm. **A**9 10 **F**1 6 10 16 35 37	23	10	S		44	2072	35	79.5	7	53	—	—	106
MAGNOLIA—Pike County													
BEACHAM MEMORIAL HOSPITAL, N. Cherry St., Zip 39652; tel. 601/783-2351; William E. Shanks, adm. **A**9 10 **F**1 6 14 16 23 35	23	10	S		37	1175	18	48.6	0	0	1734	822	63
MARKS—Quitman County													
QUITMAN COUNTY HOSPITAL, 340 Getwell Dr., Zip 38646; tel. 601/326-8031; David W. Fuller, exec. dir. (Total facility includes 60 beds in nursing home-type unit) **A**9 10 **F**1 6 10 14 16 19 23 34 35 45 46 47 50	13	10	S	TF	96	1391	78	81.3	0	59	—	—	101
				H	36	1361	18	—	0	59	—	—	72
MCCOMB—Pike County													
★□ SOUTHWEST MISSISSIPPI REGIONAL MEDICAL CENTER, 215 Marion Dr., Zip 39648; tel. 601/684-7361; Norman Price, adm. **A**1a 9 10 **F**1 3 5 6 10 12 14 15 16 23 34 35 37 40 41 45 47 53	15	10	S		158	7748	110	69.6	26	1339	15405	7228	437
MEADVILLE—Franklin County													
★□ FRANKLIN COUNTY MEMORIAL HOSPITAL, Box 428, Zip 39653; tel. 601/384-5801; Bill B. Martin, exec. dir. **A**1a 9 10 **F**1 2 6 14 16 23 26 35 36 53	13	10	S		53	748	10	18.9	4	0	—	—	71

Legend:
★ American Hospital Association (AHA) membership
□ Joint Commission on Accreditation of Hospitals (JCAH) accreditation
+ American Osteopathic Hospital Association (AOHA) membership
○ American Osteopathic Association (AOA) accreditation
Δ Commission on Accreditation of Rehabilitation Facilities (CARF) accreditation
Control codes 61, 63, 64, 71, 72 and 73 indicate hospitals listed by AOHA, but not registered by AHA.
For definition of numerical codes, see page A2

- ★ American Hospital Association (AHA) membership
- □ Joint Commission on Accreditation of Hospitals (JCAH) accreditation
- + American Osteopathic Hospital Association (AOHA) membership
- ○ American Osteopathic Association (AOA) accreditation
- Δ Commission on Accreditation of Rehabilitation Facilities (CARF) accreditation

Control codes 61, 63, 64, 71, 72 and 73 indicate hospitals listed by AOHA, but not registered by AHA. For definition of numerical codes, see page A2

Hospital, Address, Telephone, Administrator, Approval and Facility Codes, Multihospital System Code	Classification Codes				Inpatient Data				Newborn Data		Expense (thousands of dollars)		
	Control	Service	Stay	Facilities	Beds	Admissions	Census	Occupancy (percent)	Bassinets	Births	Total	Payroll	Personnel
MENDENHALL—Simpson County													
SIMPSON GENERAL HOSPITAL, 931 Jackson Ave., Zip 39114; tel. 601/847-2221; B. L. Lott, adm. **A**9 10 **F**1 6 12 14 15 16 23 35 37 45 46 47 50 53	13	10	S		49	1328	21	42.9	6	6	—	—	106
MERIDIAN—Lauderdale County													
★ EAST MISSISSIPPI STATE HOSPITAL, State Blvd., Box 4128, West Sta., Zip 39302; tel. 601/482-6186; Pablo Hernandez MD, dir. (Total facility includes 181 beds in nursing home-type unit) **A**9 **F**3 15 19 24 28 29 30 31 32 33 42 46 48 50	12	22	L	TF H	595 414	1178 1173	464 295	75.2 —	0 0	0 0	14397 11058	8244 7057	690 576
F. G. RILEY MEMORIAL HOSPITAL, See Riley Memorial Hospital													
★□ JEFF ANDERSON REGIONAL MEDICAL CENTER, 2124 14th St., Zip 39301; tel. 601/483-8811; Mark D. McPhail, chief exec. off. **A**1a 9 10 **F**1 2 3 5 6 9 10 11 12 14 15 16 23 35 36 40 45 46 47 51 53 54	23	10	S		250	8846	136	54.4	27	821	—	—	494
□ MATTY HERSEE HOSPITAL, Eighth Street Rd., P O Box 4192, W. Sta., Zip 39301; tel. 601/482-2434; Sam Rogers, adm. **A**1a 9 10 **F**1 6 15 16 34 35 36 37 40 46 50 52	12	10	S		66	2463	30	45.5	19	880	—	—	116
★□ MERIDIAN REGIONAL HOSPITAL, Hwy. 39 N., Zip 39301; tel. 601/483-6211; Wallace H. Cooper Jr., adm. **A**1a 10 **F**1 5 6 9 10 12 15 16 23 24 26 27 30 32 33 34 35 37 42 45 47 49 50 53; **S**6525	33	10	S		154	2697	66	42.9	0	0	—	—	210
★□ RILEY MEMORIAL HOSPITAL (Formerly F. G. Riley Memorial Hospital), 1102 21st Ave., Box 1810, Zip 39301; tel. 601/693-2511; Thomas Montgomery, exec. dir. **A**1a 9 10 **F**1 2 5 6 10 11 14 15 16 20 23 26 34 35 41 45 46 47 50 52 53	23	10	S		162	6206	105	64.0	0	0	18174	8445	440
★□ RUSH FOUNDATION HOSPITAL, 1314 19th Ave., Zip 39301; tel. 601/483-0011; J. C. McElroy Jr., dir. **A**1a 9 10 **F**1 2 3 5 6 10 11 12 15 16 23 34 35 40 46 47 52 53	23	10	S		205	9561	150	73.2	10	452	24791	8725	551
MONTICELLO—Lawrence County													
LAWRENCE COUNTY HOSPITAL, Hwy. 84 E., Box 788, Zip 39654; tel. 601/587-4051; C. W. Nelson, adm. **A**9 10 **F**1 2 6 10 11 14 15 16 35 41 47	13	10	S		53	1646	24	40.7	0	51	3146	1436	105
NATCHEZ—Adams County													
★□ HUMANA HOSPITAL -NATCHEZ, 129 Jefferson Davis Blvd., Box 1203, Zip 39120; tel. 601/446-7711; Thomas E. Casaday, exec. dir. **A**1a 9 10 **F**1 3 6 10 12 14 16 23 34 35 43 45 46 47 48 53; **S**1235	33	10	S		101	2394	37	36.6	0	0	—	—	143
★□ JEFFERSON DAVIS MEMORIAL HOSPITAL, Seargent S. Prentiss Dr., Box 1488, Zip 39120; tel. 601/442-2871; William G. Mitchell, exec. dir. **A**1a 9 10 **F**1 2 3 5 6 7 9 10 11 12 14 16 20 23 24 34 35 36 37 40 45 46 47 50 51 52 53	13	10	S		205	7872	102	49.8	24	1041	16549	8393	480
NEW ALBANY—Union County													
★□ UNION COUNTY GENERAL HOSPITAL, Hwy. 30 W., Zip 38652; tel. 601/534-7631; Robert N. Fulghum, adm. **A**1a 9 10 **F**1 3 6 10 12 14 15 16 23 35 45 46 47 53	13	10	S		125	6523	84	67.2	12	590	11339	6279	376
NEWTON—Newton County													
RUSH HOSPITAL-NEWTON, S. Main St., P O Box 299, Zip 39345; tel. 601/683-2031; Dan M. Harrison, adm. **A**9 10 **F**1 15 16 23 34 35 37 45 46 47 50	23	10	S		49	777	11	22.4	8	59	1955	801	61
OKOLONA—Chickasaw County													
★ OKOLONA COMMUNITY HOSPITAL (Includes Shearer-Richardson Memorial Nursing Home), Rockwell Dr., P O Box 420, Zip 38860; tel. 601/447-3311; D. R. Pounds, adm. (Total facility includes 60 beds in nursing home-type unit) **A**9 10 **F**14 19 23 35	13	10	S	TF H	77 17	443 427	49 6	54.4 —	0 0	0 0	798 —	449 —	66 40
OXFORD—Lafayette County													
★□ OXFORD-LAFAYETTE MEDICAL CENTER (Formerly Oxford-Lafayette County Hospital), 2301 S. Lamar Blvd., Box 946, Zip 38655; tel. 601/234-6721; Jerry L. Lee, adm. **A**1a 2 9 10 **F**1 3 4 5 6 8 10 11 12 14 15 16 23 27 35 36 45 47 52 53 54	15	10	S		147	5313	77	52.4	14	292	12878	5434	430
PASCAGOULA—Jackson County													
★□ SINGING RIVER HOSPITAL SYSTEM (Includes Singing River Hospital and Ocean Springs Hospital), 2809 Denny Ave., Zip 39567; tel. 601/938-5000; Robert L. Lingle, exec. dir. **A**1a 2 9 10 **F**1 3 5 6 10 11 12 14 15 16 20 23 24 27 32 33 34 35 36 37 40 44 45 47 48 49 51 52 53	13	10	S		329	14439	243	74.1	29	1281	50746	23817	1060
PHILADELPHIA—Neshoba County													
★□ CHOCTAW HEALTH CENTER, Rte. 7, Box R-50, Zip 39350; tel. 601/656-2211; James M. Cox, exec. dir. **A**1a 10 **F**6 15 28 30 32 33 34 35 37 47 49 52	47	10	S		35	770	8	22.9	5	4	5422	2287	123
PICAYUNE—Pearl River County													
□ LUCIUS OLEN CROSBY MEMORIAL HOSPITAL, 801 Goodyear Blvd., Box 909, Zip 39466; tel. 601/798-4711; Tim F. Crowley, pres. **A**1a 9 10 **F**1 3 6 10 12 14 15 16 23 35 37 40 41 45 46 50 53	23	10	S		95	4062	52	54.7	11	396	8532	3893	254
PONTOTOC—Pontotoc County													
★ PONTOTOC COMMUNITY HOSPITAL AND EXTENDED CARE FACILITY, 176 S. Main St., Zip 38863; tel. 601/489-5510; William R. Currie, exec. dir. (Total facility includes 44 beds in nursing home-type unit) **A**9 10 **F**3 6 12 14 15 16 19 23 35 36 46 50	13	10	S	TF H	102 58	1784 1750	66 23	64.7 —	8 8	51 51	3227 2759	1470 1206	152 103
POPLARVILLE—Pearl River County													
PEARL RIVER COUNTY HOSPITAL, W. Moody St., Box 392, Zip 39470; tel. 601/795-4543; Dorothy C. Bilbo, adm. (Total facility includes 40 beds in nursing home-type unit) **A**9 10 **F**1 6 14 16 19 23 35 37 45	13	10	S	TF H	70 30	1251 1237	54 14	77.1 —	6 6	128 128	2039 1474	954 747	87 60
PORT GIBSON—Claiborne County													
★ CLAIBORNE COUNTY HOSPITAL, McComb Ave., P O Drawer D, Zip 39150; tel. 601/437-5141; Debra L. Griffin, adm. **A**9 10 **F**6 14 15 16 23 34 35 37	13	10	S		32	621	6	18.8	6	89	1721	1004	48
PRENTISS—Jefferson Davis County													
JEFFERSON DAVIS COUNTY HOSPITAL, Berry St., Drawer P, Zip 39474; tel. 601/792-4276; W. Dale Saulters, adm. (Total facility includes 60 beds in nursing home-type unit) **A**9 10 **F**6 16 19 35	13	10	S	TF H	101 41	712 694	70 10	69.3 —	8 8	1 1	— —	— —	106 58
QUITMAN—Clarke County													
★□ H. C. WATKINS MEMORIAL HOSPITAL, 605 S. Archusa Ave., Zip 39355; tel. 601/776-6925; Charles W. Shepherd, pres. & chief exec. off. **A**1a 9 10 **F**1 3 6 10 14 15 16 23 35 50 53	23	10	S		50	1583	19	38.0	0	0	3145	1317	89
RICHTON—Perry County													
★ PERRY COUNTY GENERAL HOSPITAL, 206 Bay St., Drawer Y, Zip 39476; tel. 601/788-6316; George G. Posey, adm. **A**9 10 **F**6 23 35 41	13	10	S		44	720	12	27.3	8	39	1945	896	58
RIPLEY—Tippah County													
★□ TIPPAH COUNTY HOSPITAL, 1005 Hwy. 15 N., Zip 38663; tel. 601/837-9221; Jerry Green, adm. **A**1a 9 10 **F**2 6 10 14 15 16 35 45 53	13	10	S		106	2887	51	48.1	15	60	5556	2855	210
RULEVILLE—Sunflower County													
★□ NORTH SUNFLOWER COUNTY HOSPITAL, 840 N. Oak Ave., Zip 38771; tel. 601/756-2711; Earnest L. Dorrough, adm. **A**1a 9 10 **F**1 6 14 16 35 41 47	16	10	S		82	1098	20	24.4	7	93	2402	1248	77
SARDIS—Panola County													
□ NORTH PANOLA REGIONAL HOSPITAL AND NURSING CENTER, Drawer 160, Zip 38666; tel. 601/487-2720; Melvin E. Walker, adm. (Total facility includes 60 beds in nursing home-type unit) **A**1a 9 10 **F**6 9 10 14 16 19 35	15	10	S	TF H	114 54	1172 1145	73 14	64.0 —	9 9	186 186	— —	— —	128 88
STARKVILLE—Oktibbeha County													
□ OKTIBBEHA COUNTY HOSPITAL, Hospital Rd., Drawer 1506, Zip 39759; tel. 601/323-4320; Arthur C. Kelly, dir. **A**1a 9 10 **F**1 2 3 6 9 10 11 14 15 16 23 35 37 45 53	13	10	S		96	3880	47	49.0	12	880	8983	4031	282

Hospital, Address, Telephone, Administrator, Approval and Facility Codes, Multihospital System Code	Classification Codes				Inpatient Data				Newborn Data		Expense (thousands of dollars)		
★ American Hospital Association (AHA) membership ☐ Joint Commission on Accreditation of Hospitals (JCAH) accreditation + American Osteopathic Hospital Association (AOHA) membership ○ American Osteopathic Association (AOA) accreditation Δ Commission on Accreditation of Rehabilitation Facilities (CARF) accreditation Control codes 61, 63, 64, 71, 72 and 73 indicate hospitals listed by AOHA, but not registered by AHA. For definition of numerical codes, see page A2	Control	Service	Stay	Facilities	Beds	Admissions	Census	Occupancy (percent)	Bassinets	Births	Total	Payroll	Personnel
TUNICA—Tunica County													
TUNICA COUNTY HOSPITAL, Box 428, Zip 38676; tel. 601/363-1311; Barbara Henderson, exec. dir. **A**9 10 **F**14 35 40 41	23	10	S		22	704	7	31.8	4	23	1228	448	32
TUPELO—Lee County													
★☐ NORTH MISSISSIPPI MEDICAL CENTER, 830 S. Gloster St., Zip 38801; tel. 601/841-3000; John D. Hicks, pres. **A**1a 2 9 10 **F**1 3 4 5 6 8 9 10 11 12 14 15 16 20 21 23 24 27 28 30 32 33 34 35 36 40 41 42 45 46 47 48 49 51 52 53 54	23	10	S		585	24725	427	73.0	48	2498	—	—	1858
TYLERTOWN—Walthall County													
WALTHALL COUNTY GENERAL HOSPITAL, 100 Hospital Dr., Zip 39667; tel. 601/876-2122; Jimmy Graves, adm. **A**9 10 **F**6 14 16 23 35 45 46	13	10	S		49	1963	25	51.0	0	1	3849	1793	112
UNION—Newton County													
☐ LAIRD HOSPITAL, Peachtree St. & Old Jackson Rd., Zip 39365; tel. 601/774-8214; Margaret E. Muse, adm. **A**1a 10 **F**6 10 15 16 23 34 35 41 45 46 47 53	33	10	S		41	1956	25	61.0	4	11	3835	1641	139
VICKSBURG—Warren County													
☐ KUHN MEMORIAL STATE HOSPITAL, 1422 Openwood St., Zip 39180; tel. 601/636-8921; Ralph L. Burroughs, adm. **A**1a 9 10 **F**1 6 14 15 16 34 35 37 38 40 45 46 50 52	12	10	S		84	2656	32	38.1	16	760	3895	2320	102
★☐ MERCY REGIONAL MEDICAL CENTER, 100 McAuley Dr., Box 271, Zip 39180; tel. 601/631-2131; James S. Kaigler, adm. & chief oper. off. (Total facility includes 28 beds in nursing home-type unit) **A**1a 2 9 10 **F**1 3 6 10 12 14 15 16 19 23 26 34 35 36 40 41 43 44 45 46 48 49 52 53; **S**5185	23	10	S	TF	225	4400	88	39.1	18	229	17040	6806	351
				H	197	4346	72	—	18	229	16768	6570	337
★☐ VICKSBURG MEDICAL CENTER, 3311 Frontage Rd., Zip 39180; tel. 601/636-2611; Wendell H. Baker Jr., adm. **A**1a 9 10 **F**1 3 5 6 10 11 12 14 15 16 20 23 34 35 36 37 40 43 45 46 47 50 53; **S**1755	33	10	S		144	4259	74	51.4	20	281	—	—	219
WATER VALLEY—Yalobusha County													
YALOBUSHA GENERAL HOSPITAL, Hwy. 7 S., Box 728, Zip 38965; tel. 601/473-1411; James H. Ivy, adm. (Total facility includes 42 beds in nursing home-type unit) **A**9 10 **F**1 2 6 10 14 15 16 19 34 35 43 45 46 50	13	10	S	TF	91	989	58	63.7	0	0	—	—	122
				H	49	983	16	—	0	0	—	—	86
WAYNESBORO—Wayne County													
WAYNE GENERAL HOSPITAL, 950 Matthew Dr., Box 590, Zip 39367; tel. 601/735-5151; Donald Hemeter, adm. (Nonreporting) **A**9 10	13	10	S		80	—	—	—	—	—	—	—	—
WEST POINT—Clay County													
CLAY COUNTY MEDICAL CENTER, 835 Medical Center Dr., Zip 39773; tel. 601/494-2321; David M. Reid, adm. **A**9 10 **F**1 3 6 9 14 15 16 23 34 35 36 43 44 45 46 47 50 53	23	10	S		60	2218	27	45.0	8	264	—	—	119
WHITFIELD—Rankin County													
★ MISSISSIPPI STATE HOSPITAL, Zip 39193; tel. 601/939-1221; James C. Stubbs, adm. & dir. (Total facility includes 1249 beds in nursing home-type unit) **A**3 5 9 **F**19 24 32 33 42 46 47 48 50	12	22	L	TF	1646	1902	1411	85.7	0	0	32307	17733	1599
				H	397	1359	278	—	0	0	—	—	1360
WHITFIELD MEDICAL SURGICAL HOSPITAL, Zip 39193; tel. 601/939-1221; Jeff D. Caples, adm. **A**10 **F**12 14 34 50	12	10	S		39	573	18	46.2	0	0	—	—	92
WIGGINS—Stone County													
★☐ METHODIST HOSPITAL OF STONE COUNTY (Formerly Stone County Hospital), Rte. 1, Box 48, Zip 39577; tel. 601/928-5251; Richard J. Hightower, exec. dir. **A**1a 9 10 **F**1 6 10 15 16 23 34 35 41 43 45 46	23	10	S		49	1218	16	32.7	0	0	2153	810	96
WINONA—Montgomery County													
☐ TYLER HOLMES MEMORIAL HOSPITAL, Tyler Holmes Dr., Zip 38967; tel. 601/283-4114; James F. Dorris, adm. **A**1a 9 10 **F**1 6 10 15 16 23 35 40 44 45 53	13	10	S		49	1822	27	55.1	7	123	3020	1225	109
YAZOO CITY—Yazoo County													
★ KING'S DAUGHTERS HOSPITAL, 823 Grand Ave., Box 328, Zip 39194; tel. 601/746-2261; Joe Dan Edwards, adm. **A**9 10 **F**1 6 10 14 15 16 23 34 35 45 47 50	23	10	S		88	2273	33	37.5	15	108	4168	2129	144

Hospital, Address, Telephone, Administrator, Approval and Facility Codes, Multihospital System Code	Classification Codes				Inpatient Data				Newborn Data		Expense (thousands of dollars)		
★ American Hospital Association (AHA) membership □ Joint Commission on Accreditation of Hospitals (JCAH) accreditation + American Osteopathic Hospital Association (AOHA) membership ○ American Osteopathic Association (AOA) accreditation Δ Commission on Accreditation of Rehabilitation Facilities (CARF) accreditation Control codes 61, 63, 64, 71, 72 and 73 indicate hospitals listed by AOHA, but not registered by AHA. For definition of numerical codes, see page A2	Control	Service	Stay	Facilities	Beds	Admissions	Census	Occupancy (percent)	Bassinets	Births	Total	Payroll	Personnel

Missouri

Hospital	Control	Service	Stay	Facilities	Beds	Admissions	Census	Occupancy (percent)	Bassinets	Births	Total	Payroll	Personnel
ALBANY—Gentry County													
★ GENTRY COUNTY MEMORIAL HOSPITAL, Clark & College Sts., Zip 64402; tel. 816/726-3941; John W. Richmond, adm. **A**9 10 **F**1 3 6 10 12 15 16 23 24 26 34 35 36 37 40 41 44 45 47 50 53	23	10	S		43	1006	17	39.5	6	98	2534	1381	94
APPLETON CITY—St. Clair County													
★ ELLETT MEMORIAL HOSPITAL, 610 N. Ohio Ave., Zip 64724; tel. 816/476-2111; Willard W. Daugherty, adm. & chief exec. off. **A**9 10 **F**1 6 16 23 35 46 53	16	10	S		25	519	7	28.0	0	0	1046	517	46
AURORA—Lawrence County													
★ AURORA COMMUNITY HOSPITAL, 500 Porter St., Zip 65605; tel. 417/678-2122; David W. Phillipi, adm. **A**9 10 **F**1 3 5 6 10 14 15 16 23 26 34 35 36 37 40 41 45 46 53	14	10	S		49	1866	25	51.0	8	157	3780	1962	121
BELTON—Cass County													
★ RESEARCH BELTON HOSPITAL, 17065 S. 71 Hwy., Zip 64012; tel. 816/348-1200; Daryl W. Thornton, adm. **A**9 **F**1 3 6 10 12 14 16 23 24 33 34 35 37 44 45 46 47; **S**8815	23	10	S		40	1402	18	45.0	0	0	6768	2409	107
BETHANY—Harrison County													
★ NOLL MEMORIAL HOSPITAL, Hwy. 69 & 136, Box 428, Zip 64424; tel. 816/425-2211; Mark Van Fleet, adm. **A**9 10 **F**1 3 6 10 15 16 23 26 34 35 36 37 40 44 45 53	23	10	S		37	647	5	13.5	8	36	—	—	49
BLUE SPRINGS—Jackson County													
★□ ST. MARY'S HOSPITAL OF BLUE SPRINGS, 201 W. R D Mize Rd., Zip 64015; tel. 816/228-5900; N. Gary Wages, exec. dir. **A**1a 9 10 **F**1 3 6 10 14 15 16 20 23 24 34 35 41 44 45 46 52 53; **S**5455	23	10	S		72	3115	52	72.2	0	0	14908	5307	273
BOLIVAR—Polk County													
□ CITIZENS MEMORIAL HOSPITAL, 1500 N. Oakland, Zip 65613; tel. 417/326-6000; Donald J. Babb, chief exec. off. **A**1a 9 10 **F**1 3 6 10 14 15 16 23 30 35 37 40 41 44 45 46 47	16	10	S		53	2256	32	60.4	6	216	6594	2822	193
BONNE TERRE—St. Francois County													
★□ BONNE TERRE HOSPITAL, 10 Lake Dr., Zip 63628; tel. 314/358-2211; Daniel L. Gantz, adm. **A**1a 9 10 **F**1 3 12 15 16 20 23 24 26 35 41 42 44 45; **S**0565	23	10	S		56	1428	22	36.1	0	0	3797	1751	122
BOONVILLE—Cooper County													
★□ COOPER COUNTY MEMORIAL HOSPITAL, Rural Rte. 1, Box 88, Zip 65233; tel. 816/882-7461; Hugh Arant, adm. **A**1a 9 10 **F**1 3 6 12 14 15 16 23 24 26 34 35 40 41 42 43 44 45 46 47 50 53	13	10	S		53	898	15	28.3	8	20	3801	1869	120
BRANSON—Taney County													
★ SKAGGS COMMUNITY HOSPITAL, Cahill Rd., Box 650, Zip 65616; tel. 417/334-3155; Larry S. Goodloe, adm. (Total facility includes 14 beds in nursing home-type unit) **A**10 **F**1 3 5 10 12 15 16 19 23 26 32 35 36 37 40 41 43 53	23	10	S	TF	68	3246	47	56.0	6	220	8718	3603	225
				H	54	2954	38	—	6	220	8571	3464	216
BRIDGETON—St. Louis County													
★□ DEPAUL HEALTH CENTER (Includes DePaul General Hospital Division; St. Vincent's Psychiatric Division), 12303 Depaul Dr., Zip 63044; tel. 314/344-6000; Frank A. Petrich, pres. (Total facility includes 100 beds in nursing home-type unit) **A**1a b 10 **F**1 2 3 4 5 6 7 8 9 10 11 12 13 14 15 16 17 19 20 23 24 25 26 27 29 30 31 32 33 34 35 36 40 42 44 45 46 47 48 50 52 53 54; **S**1885	23	10	S	TF	563	16224	452	80.3	27	1640	80468	38692	1689
				H	463	15883	365	—	27	1640	—	—	1629
ST. VINCENT'S PSYCHIATRIC DIVISION, See DePaul Community Health Center													
BROOKFIELD—Linn County													
□ GENERAL JOHN J. PERSHING MEMORIAL HOSPITAL, 130 E. Lockling Ave., Box 160, Zip 64628; tel. 816/258-2222; Don L. Sipes, adm. **A**1a 9 10 **F**1 3 6 10 16 23 34 35 40 41 44 45 47	23	10	S		57	1415	18	31.6	8	128	2898	1643	97
BUTLER—Bates County													
□ BATES COUNTY MEMORIAL HOSPITAL, 615 W. Nursery St., Zip 64730; tel. 816/679-4135; James W. Baldwin Jr., adm. **A**1a 9 10 **F**1 3 6 10 14 15 16 23 26 34 35 36 37 40 45 46 47 50 52 53	13	10	S		37	1782	30	81.1	10	53	4543	2280	136
CAMERON—Clinton County													
CAMERON COMMUNITY HOSPITAL, 1015 W. Fourth St., Zip 64429; tel. 816/632-2101; Robert A. Goldsbury, adm. **A**9 10 **F**1 3 6 10 16 23 24 26 35 40 41 44 45 46 52 53	23	10	S		28	1348	18	64.3	4	51	4062	1912	118
CAPE GIRARDEAU—Cape Girardeau County													
★□ SOUTHEAST MISSOURI HOSPITAL, 1701 Lacey St., Zip 63701; tel. 314/334-4822; O. D. Niswonger, adm. **A**1a 2 10 **F**1 2 3 4 5 6 7 8 9 10 11 12 14 15 16 17 20 21 23 24 26 27 32 33 34 35 36 37 40 41 44 45 46 51 52 53 54	23	10	S		276	9414	153	55.4	23	1532	36184	15604	921
★□ ST. FRANCIS MEDICAL CENTER, 211 St. Francis Dr., Zip 63701; tel. 314/335-1251; John J. Keusenkothen, pres. **A**1a 2 10 **F**1 3 5 6 10 12 14 15 16 23 24 25 26 27 29 30 32 33 34 35 41 42 44 45 46 47 48 49 52 53 54; **S**6745	23	10	S		264	10254	200	75.8	0	0	37555	17009	1027
CARROLLTON—Carroll County													
CARROLL COUNTY MEMORIAL HOSPITAL, 1502 N. Jefferson St., Zip 64633; tel. 816/542-1695; Jack L. Tindle, chief exec. off. **A**9 10 **F**1 6 12 14 16 23 24 35 41 44 45 47	23	10	S		33	607	10	30.3	0	0	1575	828	52
CARTHAGE—Jasper County													
★ MCCUNE-BROOKS HOSPITAL, 627 W. Centennial Ave., Zip 64836; tel. 417/358-8121; James W. McPheeters, adm. **A**10 **F**1 3 6 10 15 16 23 35 37 40 41 45 52 53	14	10	S		68	2145	31	45.6	10	207	6100	3059	216
CASSVILLE—Barry County													
SOUTH BARRY COUNTY MEMORIAL HOSPITAL, 87 Gravel St., Zip 65625; tel. 417/847-4115; James Ford, adm. **A**9 10 **F**1 23 24 35 37 41 42 44 45 46 50	16	10	S		18	605	9	50.0	3	26	1068	610	44
CHAFFEE—Scott County													
CHAFFEE GENERAL HOSPITAL, 537 W. Yoakum Ave., Drawer C, Zip 63740; tel. 314/887-3573; Ben Felton, adm. **A**9 10 **F**1 6 12 14 16 23 34 43 45 46 53	33	10	S		41	712	11	25.0	0	27	2194	1143	68
CHESTERFIELD—St. Louis County													
★ ST. LUKE'S HOSPITAL, 232 S. Woods Mill Rd., Zip 63017; tel. 314/434-1500; Paul H. Wunderlich, pres. & chief exec. off. **A**6 9 10 **F**1 2 3 4 5 6 8 9 10 11 12 14 15 16 20 21 23 24 25 26 27 30 32 33 34 35 36 37 40 41 44 45 46 47 53 54	23	10	S		368	14227	271	73.6	36	2207	77509	41501	1680
CHILLICOTHE—Livingston County													
★□ HEDRICK MEDICAL CENTER, 100 Central St., Zip 64601; tel. 816/646-1480; Mark E. Marley, adm. **A**1a 9 10 **F**1 3 6 10 15 16 23 26 34 35 37 40 41 43 45 46 53; **S**0565	23	10	S		62	1760	24	38.7	9	357	3735	1426	113
CLINTON—Henry County													
★□ GOLDEN VALLEY MEMORIAL HOSPITAL, Junction Hwy. 7 & 13 N., Zip 64735; tel. 816/885-5511; Edward Farnsworth, adm. (Total facility includes 12 beds in nursing home-type unit) **A**1a 9 10 **F**1 3 5 6 10 12 14 15 16 19 23 24 26 32 34 35 36 37 40 41 42 44 45 46 53	16	10	S	TF	99	4340	69	56.6	13	401	9976	5326	281
				H	87	4109	60	—	13	401	—	—	268

Hospital, Address, Telephone, Administrator, Approval and Facility Codes, Multihospital System Code	Classification Codes				Inpatient Data				Newborn Data		Expense (thousands of dollars)		
★ American Hospital Association (AHA) membership □ Joint Commission on Accreditation of Hospitals (JCAH) accreditation + American Osteopathic Hospital Association (AOHA) membership ○ American Osteopathic Association (AOA) accreditation Δ Commission on Accreditation of Rehabilitation Facilities (CARF) accreditation Control codes 61, 63, 64, 71, 72 and 73 indicate hospitals listed by AOHA, but not registered by AHA. For definition of numerical codes, see page A2	Control	Service	Stay	Facilities	Beds	Admissions	Census	Occupancy (percent)	Bassinets	Births	Total	Payroll	Personnel
COLUMBIA—Boone County													
⊞ AMI COLUMBIA REGIONAL HOSPITAL (Formerly Columbia Regional Hospital), 404 Keene St., Zip 65201; tel. 314/875-9000; Ed Clawson, chief exec. off. (Total facility includes 16 beds in nursing home-type unit) **A**1a 2 9 10 **F**1 3 6 9 10 11 12 14 15 16 17 19 23 24 26 27 28 29 30 32 34 35 37 41 43 44 46 53 54; **S**0125	33	10	S	TF	286	7557	167	58.4	0	0	33331	10954	639
				H	270	7366	159	—	0	0	—	—	626
⊞ BOONE HOSPITAL CENTER, 1600 E. Broadway, Zip 65201; tel. 314/875-4545; John O'Shaughnessy, pres. **A**1a 2 9 10 **F**1 3 4 5 6 7 8 9 10 11 12 14 15 16 17 20 23 24 26 27 28 31 32 33 35 36 40 42 44 45 46 52 53 54	13	10	S		312	9597	184	62.8	30	1599	51392	23992	942
COLUMBIA REGIONAL HOSPITAL, See AMI Columbia Regional Hospital													
□ ELLIS FISCHEL ST. CANCER CENTER, 115 Business Loop 70 W., Zip 65203; tel. 314/875-2100; Ronald G. Vincent MD, dir. **A**1a 2 5 9 10 **F**1 3 6 7 8 9 10 11 12 14 15 16 23 26 28 32 33 34 37 45 46 47 50 53	12	49	S		68	1357	28	41.2	0	0	9192	5271	238
⊞ HARRY S. TRUMAN MEMORIAL VETERANS HOSPITAL, 800 Hospital Dr., Zip 65201; tel. 314/443-2511; J. L. Kurzejeski, dir. (Total facility includes 54 beds in nursing home-type unit) **A**1a 3 5 8 **F**2 3 4 6 9 10 11 14 15 16 19 23 24 25 26 27 29 31 32 33 34 35 41 42 44 46 48 49 53 54	45	10	S	TF	352	7324	282	73.2	0	0	43233	23580	913
				H	298	7307	230	—	0	0	41123	21865	887
□ MID MISSOURI MENTAL HEALTH CENTER, 3 Hospital Dr., Zip 65201; tel. 314/449-2511; A. E. Daniel MD, supt. **A**1b 3 5 10 **F**24 28 30 31 32 33 42 44 46 48 49	12	22	S		75	1020	68	90.7	0	0	9338	5673	289
⊞ Δ UNIVERSITY OF MISSOURI-COLUMBIA HOSPITAL AND CLINICS, One Hospital Dr., Zip 65212; tel. 314/882-4141; Robert B. Smith, exec. dir. **A**1a 2 3 5 7 8 9 10 **F**1 2 3 4 5 6 7 8 9 10 11 12 13 14 15 16 20 22 23 24 25 26 34 35 36 37 38 40 42 43 44 45 46 47 51 52 53 54	12	10	S		431	13057	294	68.2	14	1514	95903	43721	2015
CREVE COEUR—St. Louis County													
FAITH HOSPITAL, See St. Louis													
CRYSTAL CITY—Jefferson County													
⊞ JEFFERSON MEMORIAL HOSPITAL, P O Box 350, Zip 63019; tel. 314/933-1000; Bill M. Seek, chief exec. off. **A**1a 9 10 **F**1 3 5 6 10 11 12 14 15 16 23 29 30 31 34 35 36 40 41 45 46 52 53	23	10	S		206	5372	101	49.0	15	391	22655	10237	512
DEXTER—Stoddard County													
□ DEXTER MEMORIAL HOSPITAL, 1200 N. One Mile Rd., P O Box 279, Zip 63841; tel. 314/624-5566; Nolan O. England, adm. **A**1a 9 10 **F**1 3 6 10 14 15 16 23 34 35 37 40 41 43 44 45 46 50 53	23	10	S		42	1360	15	35.7	8	100	3720	1633	95
DONIPHAN—Ripley County													
RIPLEY COUNTY MEMORIAL HOSPITAL, Grand & Plumb Sts., Zip 63935; tel. 314/996-2141; Ray Freeman, adm. **A**9 10 **F**1 3 6 15 16 23 24 35 40 41 42 50	13	10	S		30	791	14	46.7	5	26	1725	724	54
EL DORADO SPRINGS—Cedar County													
CEDAR COUNTY MEMORIAL HOSPITAL, 1401 S. Park St., Zip 64744; tel. 417/876-2511; Arlene Moomaw, adm. **A**9 10 **F**1 15 16 23 35 36 40 41 45	13	10	S		34	1132	15	44.1	8	105	2142	1137	78
ELLINGTON—Reynolds County													
REYNOLDS COUNTY MEMORIAL HOSPITAL, Box 250, Zip 63638; tel. 314/663-2511; Warren R. Betts, adm. **A**9 10 **F**1 6 14 16 23 35 40 45; **S**0565	16	10	S		29	402	4	13.8	4	36	—	—	26
ELLISVILLE—St. Louis County													
FORUM HOSPITAL (Formerly Horizon Hospital), 15623 Manchester Rd., Zip 63011; tel. 314/227-4400; Nancy J. Regelsperger, adm. **A** 9 10 **F**32 49	33	82	S		36	137	8	22.2	0	0	—	—	23
EXCELSIOR SPRINGS—Clay County													
□ EXCELSTOR SPRINGS CITY HOSPITAL AND CONVALESCENT CENTER, 1700 Rainbow Blvd., Box 398, Zip 64024; tel. 816/637-6081; Jack L. Ferguson, chief exec. off. (Total facility includes 60 beds in nursing home-type unit) **A**1a 9 10 **F**1 3 6 15 16 19 23 24 34 35 36 37 40 41 44 45 46 49 50	14	10	S	TF	91	1382	71	78.0	7	120	6140	2920	201
				H	31	1221	14	—	7	120	4962	2314	152
FAIRFAX—Atchison County													
★ COMMUNITY HOSPITAL, Hwy. 59, Zip 64446; tel. 816/686-2211; Lewis I. Alley, adm. **A**9 10 **F**1 3 5 6 14 15 16 23 24 34 35 37 40 44 45 46 47 53; **S**1755	23	10	S		51	1157	18	35.3	4	142	2960	1388	74
FARMINGTON—St. Francois County													
⊞ FARMINGTON COMMUNITY HOSPITAL, 1101 W. Liberty, Zip 63640; tel. 314/756-6451; William D. Blair, adm. **A**1a 9 10 **F**1 3 6 15 16 23 36 37 40 41 44 52 53	23	10	S		130	3109	42	32.3	14	378	7115	3777	261
FARMINGTON STATE HOSPITAL, Zip 63640; tel. 314/756-6792; Fred McDaniel, supt. **A**10 **F**15 21 23 24 28 29 30 31 32 33 42 44 46 50	12	22	L		318	913	266	78.9	0	0	—	—	741
○ + MINERAL AREA OSTEOPATHIC HOSPITAL, 1212 Weber Rd., Zip 63640; tel. 314/756-4581; Kenneth West, adm. **A**9 10 11 12 **F**1 3 5 6 10 12 14 15 16 23 35 37 40 43 45 46 47 49 53	23	10	S		145	3480	45	31.0	8	473	8023	3720	288
FAYETTE—Howard County													
ALBERT M. KELLER MEMORIAL HOSPITAL, 600 W. Morrison St., Zip 65248; tel. 816/248-2261; William V. Ayres, adm. (Total facility includes 26 beds in nursing home-type unit) **A**9 10 **F**1 6 12 14 16 19 23 24 35 36 37 40 42 43 44 45 46 50	13	10	S	TF	75	779	23	30.7	10	100	—	—	95
				H	49	677	9	—	10	100	—	—	81
FLORISSANT—St. Louis County													
CHRISTIAN HOSPITAL NORTHWEST, See Christian Hospitals Northeast-Northwest, St. Louis													
FORT LEONARD WOOD—Pulaski County													
⊞ GENERAL LEONARD WOOD ARMY COMMUNITY HOSPITAL, Zip 65473; tel. 314/368-9131; Col. Ronald G. Williams, cmdr. **A**1a 2 **F**1 3 5 6 10 12 14 15 16 23 24 27 28 29 30 32 33 34 35 36 37 40 41 42 46 47 49 52 53	42	10	S		148	9264	120	76.4	23	487	37730	28799	960
FREDERICKTOWN—Madison County													
⊞ MADISON MEMORIAL HOSPITAL, W. College Ave., Box 431, Zip 63645; tel. 314/783-3341; O. Douglas Taylor, adm. (Total facility includes 121 beds in nursing home-type unit) **A**1a 9 10 **F**1 3 6 10 14 15 16 19 23 24 26 35 42 44 45 46 50; **S**2495	13	10	S	TF	163	1521	104	63.8	10	156	—	—	227
				H	42	1471	18	—	10	156	—	—	129
FULTON—Callaway County													
★ CALLAWAY COMMUNITY HOSPITAL, 10 S. Hospital Dr., Zip 65251; tel. 314/642-3376; G. S. Curtis Jr., adm. **A**9 10 **F**1 3 6 14 15 16 23 24 26 34 35 36 40 44 45; **S**8985	23	10	S		46	1144	12	26.1	5	100	4204	1595	87
□ FULTON STATE HOSPITAL, E. Fifth St., Zip 65251; tel. 314/642-3311; John H. Mayfield, supt. **A**1b 10 **F**3 15 23 24 28 30 32 33 34 42 44 46 47 50	12	22	L		528	598	480	90.4	0	0	30121	18683	1142
HANNIBAL—Marion County													
⊞ LEVERING HOSPITAL, 1734 Market St., Zip 63401; tel. 314/221-6511; Woodrow Lee, adm. (Total facility includes 25 beds in nursing home-type unit) **A**1a 9 10 **F**1 3 5 6 12 14 15 16 19 23 35 36 37 40 43 44 45 47 50 52 53	23	10	S	TF	102	2612	60	58.8	12	289	6909	3490	232
				H	77	2545	39	—	12	289	—	—	218
⊞ ST. ELIZABETH'S HOSPITAL, 109 Virginia St., Box 551, Zip 63401; tel. 314/221-0414; Edson E. Swift, exec. dir. **A**1a 9 10 **F**1 3 5 6 10 11 14 15 16 23 27 28 29 30 32 33 35 36 40 44 45 46 47 52 53; **S**5455	23	10	S		99	3608	57	57.6	15	384	9568	4368	231

★ American Hospital Association (AHA) membership
□ Joint Commission on Accreditation of Hospitals (JCAH) accreditation
+ American Osteopathic Hospital Association (AOHA) membership
○ American Osteopathic Association (AOA) accreditation
Δ Commission on Accreditation of Rehabilitation Facilities (CARF) accreditation
Control codes 61, 63, 64, 71, 72 and 73 indicate hospitals listed by AOHA, but not registered by AHA.
For definition of numerical codes, see page A2

Hospital, Address, Telephone, Administrator, Approval and Facility Codes, Multihospital System Code	Classification Codes				Inpatient Data				Newborn Data		Expense (thousands of dollars)		
	Control	Service	Stay	Facilities	Beds	Admissions	Census	Occupancy (percent)	Bassinets	Births	Total	Payroll	Personnel
HARRISONVILLE—Cass County													
★□ CASS MEDICAL CENTER, 1800 E. Mechanic St., Zip 64701; tel. 816/884-3291; David G. Couser, chief exec. off. **A**1a 9 10 **F**1 3 6 10 15 16 23 24 34 35 40 44 45 46 47; **S**8815	13	10	S		50	1425	19	38.0	8	134	—	—	127
HAYTI—Pemiscot County													
★□ PEMISCOT COUNTY MEMORIAL HOSPITAL, E. Reed St. & Hwy. 61, Box 489, Zip 63851; tel. 314/359-1372; Glenn D. Haynes, adm. (Total facility includes 60 beds in nursing home-type unit) **A**1a 9 10 **F**1 3 6 14 16 19 23 24 34 35 40 41 43 44 45 46 47 50 52 53	13	10	S	TF	185	3360	99	53.5	12	379	7028	3541	245
				H	125	3325	41	—	12	379	6697	3229	216
HERMANN—Gasconade County													
★ + HERMANN AREA DISTRICT HOSPITAL, Rte. 1, Box 30, Zip 65041; tel. 314/486-2191; William G. Wilson, adm. **A**9 10 **F**1 3 6 10 15 16 23 35 37 40 41 45 52 53	16	10	S		46	889	15	32.6	7	88	3581	1596	96
HOUSTON—Texas County													
TEXAS COUNTY MEMORIAL HOSPITAL, 1333 Sam Houston Blvd., Box 260, Zip 65483; tel. 417/967-3311; Edward Riley, adm. **A**9 10 **F**1 3 5 6 15 16 21 23 34 35 40 41 45 46 47	13	10	S		53	1880	25	47.2	8	151	4800	2354	155
INDEPENDENCE—Jackson County													
★□ INDEPENDENCE REGIONAL HEALTH CENTER (Formerly Independence Sanitarium and Hospital), 1509 W. Truman Rd., Zip 64050; tel. 816/836-8100; Joseph E. Lammers, pres. (Total facility includes 60 beds in nursing home-type unit) **A**1a 9 10 **F**1 2 3 5 6 7 9 10 11 12 14 15 16 19 21 23 24 26 27 30 32 33 34 35 36 37 40 41 42 43 44 45 46 47 48 49 50 52 53 54	23	10	S	TF	289	9278	188	65.1	15	592	37894	17259	1038
				H	229	8424	144	—	15	592	—	—	—
★□ MEDICAL CENTER OF INDEPENDENCE, 17203 E. 23rd St., Zip 64057; tel. 816/373-2300; Harold H. Kaseff, adm. **A**1a 9 10 **F**1 3 5 6 10 12 14 15 16 20 23 24 26 27 29 30 31 32 33 34 35 36 37 40 42 44 45 46 47 52 53; **S**1755	23	10	S		185	5428	97	52.4	17	975	21344	9593	614
JEFFERSON CITY—Cole County													
○ + CHARLES E. STILL OSTEOPATHIC HOSPITAL, 1125 Madison St., Box 1128, Zip 65102; tel. 314/635-7141; James P. Cox, adm. (Total facility includes 21 beds in nursing home-type unit) **A**9 10 11 12 13 **F**1 3 5 6 8 10 11 12 14 15 16 19 23 24 25 26 28 29 31 32 33 34 35 36 37 39 40 41 42 44 45 47 48 49 50 52	23	10	S	TF	184	5418	99	53.8	8	368	18024	8453	530
				H	163	5256	90	—	8	368	17792	8233	518
★□ MEMORIAL COMMUNITY HOSPITAL, 1432 Southwest Blvd., Zip 65101; Mailing Address Box 1067, Zip 65102; tel. 314/635-6811; Gordon H. Butler, adm. **A**1a 2 9 10 **F**1 3 5 6 10 11 12 14 15 16 21 23 24 26 32 33 34 35 37 41 44 45 46	23	10	S		96	3320	60	62.5	0	2	11985	—	305
MISSOURI STATE PENITENTIARY HOSPITAL, State & Lafayette Sts., Zip 65101; Mailing Address P O Box 597, Zip 65102; tel. 314/751-3224; Richard K. Bowers DO, chief med. adm. (Data not available) **F**14 19 23 26 27 31 33 35 37 43 50	12	11	S		134	—	—	—	—	—	—	—	—
★□ ST. MARY'S HEALTH CENTER, 610 W. Elm St., Zip 65101; tel. 314/635-7642; Charles M. Harris, exec. dir. **A**1a 9 10 **F**1 3 5 6 10 12 14 15 16 23 24 26 27 30 32 35 36 40 44 45 46 50 52; **S**5455	23	10	S		130	4507	64	49.2	14	1000	14876	5966	313
JOPLIN—Jasper County													
★□ FREEMAN HOSPITAL, 1102 W. 32nd St., Zip 64801; tel. 417/623-2801; Richard E. Long, pres. **A**1a 9 10 **F**1 3 5 6 10 12 13 14 15 16 23 24 34 35 36 37 40 41 45 46 48 50 51 52 53	23	10	S		167	7183	93	55.7	30	1697	21934	9130	456
○ + OAK HILL HOSPITAL, 932 E. 34th St., Zip 64804; tel. 417/623-4640; Keith Adams, adm. **A**9 10 11 12 **F**1 3 5 6 10 12 14 16 23 34 35 36 37 40 41 45 53 54	23	10	S		105	3506	55	52.4	8	310	11863	5605	325
★□ Δ ST. JOHN'S REGIONAL MEDICAL CENTER, 2727 McClelland Blvd., Zip 64804; tel. 417/781-2727; Robert J. Fanning, pres. & chief exec. off. **A**1a 2 7 9 10 **F**1 2 3 4 5 6 8 9 10 11 12 14 15 16 20 21 23 24 25 26 27 29 31 32 33 34 35 41 44 52 53 54; **S**5175	23	10	S		345	12273	246	71.3	0	0	54531	21591	1058
KANSAS CITY—Jackson County													
★□ BAPTIST MEDICAL CENTER, 6601 Rockhill Rd., Zip 64131; tel. 816/361-3500; Dan H. Anderson, pres. (Total facility includes 17 beds in nursing home-type unit) **A**1a 2 3 5 9 10 **F**1 2 3 4 5 6 10 11 12 14 15 16 19 20 23 24 25 26 27 28 30 31 34 35 37 41 42 44 45 46 47 48 49 52 53 54	21	10	S	TF	324	9303	226	69.8	0	0	48645	20203	967
				H	307	9012	212	—	0	0	48353	19947	953
★□ CHILDREN'S MERCY HOSPITAL, 24th at Gillham Rd., Zip 64108; tel. 816/234-3000; Lawrence McAndrews, pres. & chief exec. off. **A**1a 2 3 5 9 10 **F**1 4 5 6 10 12 14 15 16 18 20 22 23 24 26 28 29 30 31 32 34 35 38 42 43 44 45 46 47 51 53 54	23	50	S		158	6520	115	72.8	0	0	46549	24700	1150
□ CRITTENTON CENTER, 10918 Elm Ave., Zip 64134; tel. 816/765-6600; Gary D. Baker, pres. **A**1b **F**15 19 24 28 30 31 32 33 34 42 43 46	23	52	L		67	124	64	95.5	0	0	4674	2603	158
○ + LAKESIDE HOSPITAL, 8701 Troost Ave., Zip 64131; tel. 816/995-2000; James A. Barber, adm. (Total facility includes 15 beds in nursing home-type unit) **A**9 10 11 12 13 **F**1 3 6 9 10 12 14 15 16 19 23 24 26 31 34 35 37 40 41 46 47 48 49 52 53	23	10	S	TF	98	2843	46	46.9	5	126	8597	4281	222
				H	83	1966	37	—	5	126	—	—	221
★□ MENORAH MEDICAL CENTER, 4949 Rockhill Rd., Zip 64110; tel. 816/276-8000; Sol Schaengold, pres. **A**1a 2 3 5 9 10 **F**1 2 3 4 5 6 7 8 9 10 11 12 14 15 16 20 21 23 24 26 27 29 30 31 32 33 34 35 36 37 40 41 42 44 45 46 47 52 53 54	23	10	S		298	12121	231	77.5	28	2007	52555	26457	1081
○ + PARK LANE MEDICAL CENTER, 5151 Raytown Rd., Zip 64133; tel. 816/358-8000; James K. Johnson, pres. & chief exec. off. **A**9 10 11 12 **F**1 3 5 6 7 10 12 14 15 16 20 23 24 29 32 35 44 45 46 52 53	23	10	S		44	2772	47	42.7	0	0	16411	6263	319
Δ REHABILITATION INSTITUTE, 3011 Baltimore Ave., Zip 64108; tel. 816/756-2250; George Gutknecht, exec. dir. **A**7 9 10 **F**15 23 24 26 31 32 34 42 44 45	23	46	L		40	176	16	40.0	0	0	5743	3533	82
★□ RESEARCH MEDICAL CENTER, 2316 E. Meyer Blvd., Zip 64132; tel. 816/276-4000; Richard W. Brown, pres. **A**1a 3 5 9 10 **F**1 3 4 5 6 7 8 9 10 11 12 13 14 15 16 19 20 23 24 25 26 32 33 34 35 36 37 40 42 43 44 45 46 47 51 52 53 54; **S**8815	23	10	S		477	16789	325	68.1	32	1893	89878	42904	2001
★□ RESEARCH PSYCHIATRIC CENTER, 2323 E. 63rd St., Zip 64130; tel. 816/444-8161; Gail M. Oberta, adm. **A**1b 9 10 **F**28 31 32 33 42 46 47 48 50; **S**1755	33	22	S		100	1128	69	69.0	0	0	7140	2699	118
★□ SAINT JOSEPH HEALTH CENTER OF KANSAS CITY (Formerly Saint Joseph Hospital of Kansas City), 1000 Carondelet Dr., Zip 64114; tel. 816/942-4400; Richard M. Abell, pres. **A**1a 2 9 10 **F**1 3 4 5 6 10 12 14 15 16 20 23 24 26 34 35 40 44 45 46 51 52 53 54; **S**5945	23	10	S		279	11735	191	68.5	22	1541	51795	23926	1111
★□ ST. LUKE'S HOSPITAL, 44th & Wornall, P O Box 119000, Zip 64111; tel. 816/932-2000; Charles C. Lindstrom, chief exec. off. **A**1a 2 3 5 8 9 10 **F**1 2 3 4 5 6 7 8 9 10 11 12 13 14 15 16 17 20 21 23 24 25 26 34 35 36 37 38 40 42 44 45 46 47 50 51 52 53 54	23	10	S		604	23326	467	77.3	26	2895	127652	58439	2490
★□ ST. MARY'S HOSPITAL, 2800 Main St., Zip 64108; tel. 816/753-5700; William P. Thompson, exec. dir. (Total facility includes 10 beds in nursing home-type unit) **A**1a 3 5 9 10 **F**1 3 5 6 7 8 9 10 11 12 15 16 19 20 23 24 26 27 29 30 31 32 33 34 35 36 40 41 42 43 45 46 47 48 49 50 53 54; **S**5455	23	10	S	TF	264	5582	153	58.0	20	218	34025	15530	709
				H	254	5345	145	—	20	218	33743	15295	701
★ SWOPE RIDGE REHABILITATION HOSPITAL, 5900 Swope Pkwy., Zip 64130; tel. 816/333-2700; Charles C. Nigro, exec. dir. (Total facility includes 186 beds in nursing home-type unit) **A**10 **F**16 19 23 24 26 27 29 32 34 42 44 45 46 50	23	46	L	TF	234	318	181	77.4	0	0	6313	4551	223
				H	48	96	8	—	0	0	—	—	91

★ American Hospital Association (AHA) membership
□ Joint Commission on Accreditation of Hospitals (JCAH) accreditation
+ American Osteopathic Hospital Association (AOHA) membership
○ American Osteopathic Association (AOA) accreditation
Δ Commission on Accreditation of Rehabilitation Facilities (CARF) accreditation
Control codes 61, 63, 64, 71, 72 and 73 indicate hospitals listed by AOHA, but not registered by AHA.
For definition of numerical codes, see page A2

Hospital, Address, Telephone, Administrator, Approval and Facility Codes, Multihospital System Code	Classification Codes				Inpatient Data				Newborn Data		Expense (thousands of dollars)		
	Control	Service	Stay	Facilities	Beds	Admissions	Census	Occupancy (percent)	Bassinets	Births	Total	Payroll	Personnel
★□ TRINITY LUTHERAN HOSPITAL, 3030 Baltimore Ave., Zip 64108; tel. 816/753-4600; Patrick R. Garrett, chief exec. off. (Total facility includes 19 beds in nursing home-type unit) **A**1a 2 3 5 9 10 **F**1 2 3 4 5 6 7 8 9 10 11 12 13 14 15 16 19 20 23 24 26 27 28 32 34 35 37 41 42 43 45 46 47 52 53 54	21	10	S	TF	301	6510	154	51.2	0	0	40633	17081	854
				H	282	6225	142	—	0	0	40294	16774	842
★□ Δ TRUMAN MEDICAL CENTER-EAST, 7900 Lee's Summit Rd., Zip 64139; tel. 816/373-4415; Clifford Browne Jr., adm. (Total facility includes 226 beds in nursing home-type unit) **A**1a 2 3 7 9 10 **F**1 6 14 15 16 19 23 24 25 26 27 31 32 33 34 35 37 40 42 44 45 46 47 50; **S**9255	23	10	S	TF	300	3405	273	91.0	14	1038	19401	10265	598
				H	74	3187	56	—	14	1038	—	—	474
★□ TRUMAN MEDICAL CENTER-WEST, 2301 Holmes St., Zip 64108; tel. 816/556-3000; Daniel M. Couch, adm. & dep. exec. dir. **A**1a 3 5 8 9 10 **F**1 3 5 6 10 12 14 15 16 20 23 24 26 34 35 36 37 38 39 40 44 45 46 47 51 53 54; **S**9255	23	10	S		271	12490	240	90.9	49	2892	54656	26192	1407
○ + UNIVERSITY OF HEALTH SCIENCES, UNIVERSITY HOSPITAL, 2105 Independence Blvd., Zip 64124; tel. 816/283-2000; Rudolph S. Bremen, adm. **A**9 10 11 12 13 **F**1 3 4 5 6 10 12 13 14 15 16 23 24 26 30 34 35 36 37 38 40 46 49 50 51 52 53 54	23	10	S		175	3374	64	36.6	30	625	—	11063	663
★□ VETERANS ADMINISTRATION MEDICAL CENTER, 4801 Linwood Blvd., Zip 64128; tel. 816/861-4700; Daniel H. Winship MD, dir. **A**1a 3 5 8 **F**2 3 6 10 12 14 15 16 20 23 24 25 26 27 28 29 32 33 34 35 41 42 43 44 46 49 50 53 54	45	10	S		401	10487	361	90.0	0	0	64091	35041	1233
□ WESTERN MISSOURI MENTAL HEALTH CENTER, 600 E. 22nd St., Zip 64108; tel. 816/471-3000; Morty Lebedun PhD, supt. **A**1b 3 5 9 10 **F**15 24 28 29 30 31 32 33 34 35 42 43 45 46 47 49	12	22	S		224	3190	213	95.1	0	0	19248	10809	635
KENNETT—Dunklin County													
□ TWIN RIVERS REGIONAL MEDICAL CENTER, 1301 First St., P O Box 787, Zip 63857; tel. 314/888-4522; Warren N. Kerber, adm. **A**1a 9 10 **F**1 3 5 6 10 14 15 16 23 34 35 37 40 43 45 46 47 53; **S**8985	33	10	S		116	4231	58	50.0	12	181	8938	3411	231
KIRKSVILLE—Adair County													
GRIM-SMITH HOSPITAL AND CLINIC, 112 E. Patterson Ave., Zip 63501; tel. 816/665-7241; Steven E. Clark, adm. **A**9 10 **F**1 3 6 12 13 15 16 23 28 35 40 46 53	33	10	S		75	2843	41	54.7	9	315	9020	3069	219
○ + KIRKSVILLE OSTEOPATHIC MEDICAL CENTER (Includes Laughlin Pavilion, 900 E. Laharpe St., Zip 63501; tel. 816/665-5171), 800 W. Jefferson, Zip 63501; tel. 816/626-2121; Edward R. Balotsky, exec. dir. (Data for 304 days) **A**9 10 11 12 13 **F**1 3 5 6 10 12 14 15 16 20 23 24 26 27 28 29 30 32 33 34 35 36 37 40 41 42 43 44 45 46 47 48 49 50 52 53 54; **S**3015	33	10	S		228	3347	97	42.5	19	190	18331	6191	406
LAUGHLIN PAVILION, See Kirksville Osteopathic Health Center													
KIRKWOOD—St. Louis County													
★□ ST. JOSEPH HOSPITAL (Formerly Listed Under St. Louis), 525 Couch Ave., Kirkwood, Zip 63122; tel. 314/966-1500; Sr. Catherine Durr, pres. (Total facility includes 20 beds in nursing home-type unit) **A**1a 9 10 **F**1 3 4 5 6 7 9 10 11 12 14 15 16 17 19 20 21 23 24 26 35 36 40 41 44 45 46 49 52 53 54; **S**5945	23	10	S	TF	332	10537	193	58.1	25	1222	42584	20391	990
				H	312	10308	183	—	25	1222	42257	20157	978
LAMAR—Barton County													
BARTON COUNTY MEMORIAL HOSPITAL, Second & Gulf Sts., Zip 64759; tel. 417/682-5535; Elden S. Selves, adm. **A**9 10 **F**1 3 6 10 12 14 15 16 23 35 37 40 41 43 45 46 47 53	13	10	S		49	1334	21	42.9	10	83	3118	1549	95
LEBANON—Laclede County													
□ BREECH MEDICAL CENTER, 305 Harwood Ave., P O Box N., Zip 65536; tel. 417/532-2136; Drew Hartman, adm. **A**1a 9 10 **F**1 3 6 10 12 15 16 23 24 34 35 40 41 44 45 46 52 53	23	10	S		53	2141	29	54.7	6	179	4589	1997	163
LEES SUMMIT—Jackson County													
★□ LEE'S SUMMIT COMMUNITY HOSPITAL, 530 N. Murray, P O Box 767, Zip 64063; tel. 816/525-2950; David J. Maschger, chief exec. off. **A**1a 9 10 **F**1 3 6 12 14 15 16 23 24 26 33 35 44 45 46 47 53; **S**1755	23	10	S		92	2795	56	60.9	0	0	12721	5251	224
LEXINGTON—Lafayette County													
★□ LAFAYETTE REGIONAL HEALTH CENTER, 15th & State St., Zip 64067; tel. 816/259-2203; Frank I. Luddington, adm. **A**1a 9 10 **F**1 3 6 10 15 16 23 24 26 34 35 36 40 41 43 44 45 46 53; **S**8815	23	10	S		38	908	10	26.3	6	116	3637	1460	86
LIBERTY—Clay County													
★□ LIBERTY HOSPITAL, 2525 Glenn Hendren Dr., Zip 64068; tel. 816/781-7200; Jim D. Redding, adm. (Total facility includes 20 beds in nursing home-type unit) **A**1a 9 10 **F**1 3 5 6 9 11 12 14 15 16 19 20 21 23 24 26 35 37 41 42 44 45 46 50 53	16	10	S	TF	150	5303	92	61.3	0	0	20350	8428	503
				H	130	5030	80	—	0	0	19119	8195	485
LOCKWOOD—Dade County													
★ DADE COUNTY MEMORIAL HOSPITAL, 1005 S. Main St., Zip 65682; tel. 417/232-4567; Allen Hackbirth, adm. **A**9 10 **F**6 14 15 16 23 24 35 43 44 45 50 53	16	10	S		21	405	9	42.9	0	0	1119	574	37
LOUISIANA—Pike County													
★□ PIKE COUNTY MEMORIAL HOSPITAL, 2305 W. Georgia St., Zip 63353; tel. 314/754-5531; Richard L. Conklin, adm. **A**1a 9 10 **F**1 3 6 10 12 14 15 16 23 24 28 29 33 34 35 36 37 40 42 44 45 49 50; **S**0565	13	10	S		54	1323	17	24.6	10	73	4263	488	115
MACON—Macon County													
SAMARITAN MEMORIAL HOSPITAL, Hwy. 63, Zip 63552; tel. 816/385-3151; Bernard A. Orman Jr., adm. **A**9 10 **F**1 6 14 15 16 23 24 26 34 35 36 40 44 45	13	10	S		48	1099	17	35.4	6	80	—	—	59
MANSFIELD—Wright County													
★ MERCY HOSPITAL (Formerly Mercy Hospital-Tri County), Hwy. 60 & 5 N., Box 528, Zip 65704; tel. 417/924-3281; Mark E. Cross, adm. **A**10 **F**1 3 6 14 15 16 23 34 35 36 40 41 44 45 53; **S**5185	21	10	S		51	1351	17	33.3	6	184	2390	997	80
MARCELINE—Linn County													
★□ ST. FRANCIS HOSPITAL, 225 W. Hayden St., Zip 64658; tel. 816/376-3521; Terry L. Watson, exec. dir. (Total facility includes 42 beds in nursing home-type unit) **A**1a 9 10 **F**1 3 6 14 15 16 19 23 26 32 35 36 40 42 44 45 50 52; **S**5455	23	10	S	TF	95	811	51	53.7	4	66	3399	1741	149
				H	53	771	13	—	4	66	3023	1434	76
MARSHALL—Saline County													
★ JOHN FITZGIBBON MEMORIAL HOSPITAL, 868 S. Brunswick Ave., Box 250, Zip 65340; tel. 816/886-7431; Gaylon C. Lowery, chief exec. off. **A**9 10 **F**1 3 5 6 10 12 14 15 16 23 24 34 35 36 37 40 43 44 45 52 53	23	10	S		72	1960	26	36.1	8	116	4378	2295	110
MARSHALL HABILITATION CENTER, E. Slater & Lincoln, Box 190, Zip 65340; tel. 816/886-2202; Adrienne D. McKenna, supt. (Nonreporting)	12	62	L		620	—	—	—	—	—	—	—	—
MARYVILLE—Nodaway County													
□ ST. FRANCIS HOSPITAL, 1802 S. Main St., Zip 64468; tel. 816/562-2600; Gregory B. Vinardi, pres. **A**1a 9 10 **F**1 3 5 6 10 12 14 15 16 23 26 35 36 40 41 43 44 45 48 49 53	23	10	S		89	1970	34	44.2	9	206	6462	2961	211
MEMPHIS—Scotland County													
★ ○ + SCOTLAND COUNTY MEMORIAL HOSPITAL, Sigler Ave., Rte. 1, Box 53, Zip 63555; tel. 816/465-8511; William C. Assell, adm. **A**9 10 11 **F**1 3 14 15 16 23 26 35 40 42 43 44 45 50 52	23	10	S		27	463	8	29.6	6	41	1389	694	54

Hospital, Address, Telephone, Administrator, Approval and Facility Codes, Multihospital System Code	Classification Codes				Inpatient Data				Newborn Data		Expense (thousands of dollars)		
★ American Hospital Association (AHA) membership □ Joint Commission on Accreditation of Hospitals (JCAH) accreditation + American Osteopathic Hospital Association (AOHA) membership ○ American Osteopathic Association (AOA) accreditation Δ Commission on Accreditation of Rehabilitation Facilities (CARF) accreditation Control codes 61, 63, 64, 71, 72 and 73 indicate hospitals listed by AOHA, but not registered by AHA. For definition of numerical codes, see page A2	Control	Service	Stay	Facilities	Beds	Admissions	Census	Occupancy (percent)	Bassinets	Births	Total	Payroll	Personnel
MEXICO—Audrain County													
⊞ AUDRAIN MEDICAL CENTER, 620 E. Monroe St., Zip 65265; tel. 314/581-1760; Charles P. Jansen, adm. (Total facility includes 19 beds in nursing home-type unit) **A**1a 9 10 **F**1 3 5 6 9 10 11 12 14 15 16 19 20 23 24 26 27 28 29 30 31 32 33 35 36 37 40 43 44 45 46 49 50 53	13	10	S	TF	135	5231	91	62.3	18	332	17750	8891	474
				H	116	4841	79	—	18	332	17425	8579	458
MILAN—Sullivan County													
SULLIVAN COUNTY MEMORIAL HOSPITAL, 630 W. Third St., Zip 63556; tel. 816/265-4212; David Watt, adm. **A**9 10 **F**3 6 10 14 16 26 35 40 43 45	13	10	S		47	399	8	17.0	8	13	2024	870	59
MOBERLY—Randolph County													
⊞ + MOBERLY REGIONAL MEDICAL CENTER, 1515 Union St., P O Box 3000, Zip 65270; tel. 816/263-8400; James C. Culpepper, adm. **A**1a 9 10 **F**1 3 5 6 10 14 15 16 23 35 36 40 43 44 52; **S**9355	23	10	S	TF	115	3702	66	57.4	8	330	15209	5563	326
				H	0	3575	—	—	8	330	—	—	—
MONETT—Barry County													
□ ST. VINCENT'S HOSPITAL, 801 Lincoln Ave., Zip 65708; tel. 417/235-3144; Sr. Marita Pozek, chief exec. off. **A**1a 9 10 **F**1 3 6 12 15 16 23 24 35 40 41 44 45 46 53	21	10	S		53	2333	34	47.2	6	50	4277	2391	151
MOUNT VERNON—Lawrence County													
□ MISSOURI REHABILITATION CENTER (Formerly Missouri State Chest Hospital), 600 N. Main, Zip 65712; tel. 417/466-3711; Don Lamkins, adm. **A**1a 10 **F**3 6 10 12 14 15 16 23 24 26 41 42 44 46 53	12	46	L		182	896	80	44.0	0	0	11698	6529	413
MOUNTAIN VIEW—Howell County													
⊞ ST. FRANCIS HOSPITAL, Hwy. 60, Zip 65548; tel. 417/934-2246; Sr. Mary Cornelia, adm. **A**1a 9 10 **F**1 6 14 15 16 23 34 35 40 41 44 45 46 47 53	23	10	S		45	1033	14	31.1	5	113	—	—	67
NEOSHO—Newton County													
SALE HOSPITAL (Formerly Sale Memorial Hospital), 113 W. Hickory St., Zip 64850; tel. 417/451-1234; George Olive MD, adm. **A**10 **F**1 3 6 10 34 35 36 37 40 41 43 46 53	33	10	S		67	2280	42	62.7	6	79	—	—	225
NEVADA—Vernon County													
HSA HEARTLAND HOSPITAL, Ashland & Prewitt St., Zip 64772; tel. 417/667-2666; James E. Ferguson, chief exec. off. **A**9 10 **F**15 24 26 28 31 32 33 42 44; **S**0405	33	22	L		66	316	51	82.3	0	0	—	—	194
★ NEVADA CITY HOSPITAL, 800 S. Ash St., Zip 64772; tel. 417/667-3355; Albert Ban Jr., adm. (Total facility includes 10 beds in nursing home-type unit) **A**9 10 **F**1 3 6 10 12 14 15 16 19 23 24 26 32 34 35 36 40 41 44 45 46 47 48 49 52 53	14	10	S	TF	97	2490	35	36.1	10	247	6201	3026	190
				H	87	2330	28	—	10	247	—	—	179
NEVADA STATE HOSPITAL, N. Ash St., Zip 64772; tel. 417/667-7833; Harold W. Wilson, supt. **A**9 **F**15 24 30 31 32 33 34 35 38 41 42 46 49	12	22	L		155	480	158	100.0	0	0	4858	3512	202
NORTH KANSAS CITY—Clay County													
⊞ NORTH KANSAS CITY HOSPITAL (Formerly North Kansas City Memorial Hospital), 2800 Hospital Dr., Zip 64116; tel. 816/346-7000; D. L. Haymons, pres. **A**1a 9 10 **F**1 2 3 5 6 10 12 14 15 16 23 24 26 27 28 29 30 32 33 34 35 36 37 40 42 43 44 45 46 48 49 50 53 54	14	10	S		326	11824	222	78.4	20	1375	45346	22684	963
OSAGE BEACH—Camden County													
⊞ LAKE OF THE OZARKS GENERAL HOSPITAL, Box 187-Cb, Zip 65065; tel. 314/348-3181; Andrew Talley, adm. **A**1a 9 10 **F**1 3 5 6 10 12 14 15 16 23 34 35 36 40 44 45 47 53	23	10	S		99	3726	48	48.5	7	357	9717	3957	249
OSCEOLA—St. Clair County													
⊞ SAC-OSAGE HOSPITAL, Junction Highways 13 & 82, Box 426, Zip 64776; tel. 417/646-8181; Terry E. Erwine, adm. **A**1a 9 10 **F**3 6 10 12 15 16 23 24 35 37 40 45 53	16	10	S		47	1337	22	46.8	5	67	2629	1314	94
PERRYVILLE—Perry County													
□ PERRY COUNTY MEMORIAL HOSPITAL, N. West St., Zip 63775; tel. 314/547-2536; Louis G. Schilly, adm. **A**1a 9 10 **F**1 3 6 14 15 16 23 34 35 36 40 41 44 45 53	13	10	S		55	1494	24	43.6	6	123	5048	2230	141
PILOT KNOB—Iron County													
⊞ ARCADIA VALLEY HOSPITAL, Hwy. 21, Zip 63663; tel. 314/546-3924; Kerry Noble, exec. dir. (Total facility includes 24 beds in nursing home-type unit) **A**1a 9 10 **F**1 3 6 12 14 15 16 19 23 24 33 35 41 42 44 45 46 50; **S**5455	23	10	S	TF	50	1138	40	80.0	0	0	3541	1655	113
				H	26	1128	19	—	0	0	—	—	95
POPLAR BLUFF—Butler County													
⊞ AMI LUCY LEE HOSPITAL (Formerly Lucy Lee Hospital), 2620 Westwood Blvd., Zip 63901; tel. 314/785-7721; William L. Bradley, exec. dir. (Total facility includes 16 beds in nursing home-type unit) **A**1a 10 **F**1 3 5 6 7 9 10 11 12 14 15 16 19 23 24 34 35 36 37 40 41 43 50 52 53; **S**0125	33	10	S	TF	168	5461	86	51.2	17	639	17836	4942	342
				H	152	5205	77	—	17	639	—	—	—
□ DOCTORS REGIONAL MEDICAL CENTER, 621 Pine Blvd., Zip 63901; tel. 314/686-4111; Harold Boyer, adm. **A**1a 2 9 10 **F**1 3 5 6 10 12 14 15 16 23 27 32 33 34 35 36 39 40 41 42 43 45 46 47 48 50 53; **S**5895	33	10	S		194	6733	109	56.2	16	599	—	—	339
LUCY LEE HOSPITAL, See AMI Lucy Lee Hospital													
⊞ VETERANS ADMINISTRATION MEDICAL CENTER, 1500 N. Westwood Blvd., Zip 63901; tel. 314/686-4151; W. H. Bonner, dir. (Total facility includes 49 beds in nursing home-type unit) **A**1a **F**1 3 6 10 12 14 15 16 19 23 26 29 32 33 34 35 41 42 44 45 46 47 49	45	10	S	TF	225	3854	160	71.1	0	0	15587	9437	375
				H	176	3829	114	—	0	0	—	—	358
POTOSI—Washington County													
WASHINGTON COUNTY MEMORIAL HOSPITAL, 300 Henry Bub Dr., Zip 63664; tel. 314/438-5451; John Bennett, adm. **A**9 10 **F**1 3 6 16 23 24 35 37 40 41 44 45 46 47	13	10	S		48	1401	17	35.4	8	124	2978	782	94
RICHMOND—Ray County													
RAY COUNTY MEMORIAL HOSPITAL, Hwy. 13 S., Rte. 4, Box 45, Zip 64085; tel. 816/776-5432; Tommy L. Hicks, adm. (Total facility includes 11 beds in nursing home-type unit) **A**9 10 **F**1 3 6 14 16 19 23 24 35 36 37 40 41 44 45 46 47 53	13	10	S	TF	54	1405	24	44.4	6	94	4110	2399	156
				H	43	1343	21	—	6	94	4011	2316	154
ROLLA—Phelps County													
⊞ ○ PHELPS COUNTY REGIONAL MEDICAL CENTER, 1000 W. Tenth St., Zip 65401; tel. 314/364-3100; Glen Marshall, adm. (Total facility includes 32 beds in nursing home-type unit) **A**1a 9 10 11 12 **F**1 3 5 6 10 12 15 16 19 23 24 26 27 28 30 32 33 35 36 37 40 45 46 48 50 52 53; **S**2495	13	10	S	TF	200	7149	151	75.5	23	992	15202	6777	591
				H	168	7124	120	—	23	992	—	—	567
SALEM—Dent County													
□ SALEM MEMORIAL DISTRICT HOSPITAL, Hwy. 72 N., Box 774, Zip 65560; tel. 314/729-6626; Edward Browning, adm. **A**1a 9 10 **F**1 6 10 14 15 16 17 20 23 24 26 34 35 37 40 41 42 43 44 45 47 50	16	10	S		55	1228	20	36.4	4	1	4137	1900	113
SEDALIA—Pettis County													
⊞ BOTHWELL REGIONAL HEALTH CENTER, 601 E. 14th St., P O Box 1706, Zip 65301; tel. 816/826-8833; L. Don Feeback, adm. **A**1a 9 10 **F**1 3 6 8 10 12 14 15 16 20 23 34 35 36 37 40 41 43 44 45 47 52 53	14	10	S		185	7023	125	67.6	20	673	18490	9303	544
SIKESTON—Scott County													
⊞ MISSOURI DELTA MEDICAL CENTER (Formerly Missouri Delta Community Hospital), 1008 N. Main St., Zip 63801; tel. 314/471-1600; Harold L. Jones, adm. (Total facility includes 14 beds in nursing home-type unit) **A**1a 2 9 10 **F**1 3 5 6 7 8 9 10 11 12 14 16 19 20 23 26 35 36 37 40 45 46 47 52 53	23	10	S	TF	153	6316	96	63.2	16	732	17233	7292	455
				H	139	6154	89	—	16	732	17055	7131	443

★ American Hospital Association (AHA) membership
□ Joint Commission on Accreditation of Hospitals (JCAH) accreditation
\+ American Osteopathic Hospital Association (AOHA) membership
○ American Osteopathic Association (AOA) accreditation
Δ Commission on Accreditation of Rehabilitation Facilities (CARF) accreditation
Control codes 61, 63, 64, 71, 72 and 73 indicate hospitals listed by AOHA, but not registered by AHA.
For definition of numerical codes, see page A2

Hospital, Address, Telephone, Administrator, Approval and Facility Codes, Multihospital System Code	Classification Codes				Inpatient Data				Newborn Data		Expense (thousands of dollars)		
	Control	Service	Stay	Facilities	Beds	Admissions	Census	Occupancy (percent)	Bassinets	Births	Total	Payroll	Personnel
SMITHVILLE—Clay County													
★□ SPELMAN MEMORIAL HOSPITAL, 601 S. 169 Hwy., Zip 64089; tel. 816/532-3700; Gene Meyer, chief exec. off. **A**1a 9 10 **F**1 3 5 6 10 11 12 15 16 21 23 24 25 26 29 30 32 34 35 36 40 41 44 45 46 53	23	10	S		128	3141	48	37.5	10	431	12346	5785	267
SPRINGFIELD—Greene County													
★□ LESTER E. COX MEDICAL CENTERS (Includes Lester E. Cox Medical Center-North, 1423 N. Jefferson Ave., Zip 65802; tel. 417/836-3000; Lester E. Cox Medical Center South, 3801 S. National Ave., Zip 65807; tel. 417/885-6000), 1423 N. Jefferson St., Zip 65802; tel. 417/836-3000; Charles M. Edwards, exec. adm. & chief exec. off. (Total facility includes 26 beds in nursing home-type unit) **A**1a 6 10 **F**1 2 3 4 5 6 7 8 9 10 11 12 14 15 16 19 20 21 23 24 25 26 27 30 33 34 35 37 40 41 42 44 45 46 47 48 49	23	10	S	TF	775	23037	445	53.0	60	3148	90053	39807	2187
				H	749	22668	426	—	60	3148	—	—	2171
○ + SPRINGFIELD GENERAL HOSPITAL, 2828 N. National St., Box 783, Jewell Sta., Zip 65801; tel. 417/869-5571; Kenneth L. Clark, adm. **A**10 11 **F**1 3 6 12 15 16 23 26 35 36 40 41 45 46 47 53	63	10	S		75	2533	35	46.7	4	254	7684	2827	209
□ SPRINGFIELD PARK CENTRAL HOSPITAL, 440 S. Market Ave., Zip 65806; Mailing Address P O Box 1715, SSS, Zip 65805; tel. 417/865-5581; Beverly J. Lawlor, adm. **A**1a 9 10 **F**1 3 6 10 14 15 16 23 29 30 31 32 33 35 37 41 42 44 48 49 50 53; **S**0655	33	22	S		149	1713	83	55.7	0	0	9494	3859	238
★□ ST. JOHN'S REGIONAL HEALTH CENTER, 1235 E. Cherokee St., Zip 65804; tel. 417/885-2000; James W. Swift, pres. **A**1a 6 10 **F**1 2 3 4 5 6 7 8 9 10 11 12 14 15 16 20 22 23 24 25 26 27 28 29 30 31 32 33 35 36 37 39 40 41 42 44 45 46 48 49 51 52 53 54; **S**5185	21	10	S		880	27770	582	66.1	30	1392	97480	47806	2603
□ U. S. MEDICAL CENTER FOR FEDERAL PRISONERS, 1900 W. Sunshine St., Zip 65802; tel. 417/862-7042; C. A. Turner, warden **A**1a **F**1 3 6 14 15 16 20 23 24 26 27 28 29 32 33 34 35 42 44 50	48	11	L		631	2258	436	69.1	0	0	—	—	231
ST. CHARLES—St. Charles County													
□ CPC WELDON SPRING HOSPITAL (Formerly Weldon Spring Hospital), 5931 Hwy. 94 S., Zip 63303; tel. 314/441-7300; Ina Watts, adm. **A**1b 9 10 **F**15 24 29 30 31 32 42 43 46 48 49; **S**0785	33	52	L		104	552	49	47.1	0	0	5567	1778	80
★□ ST. JOSEPH HEALTH CENTER, 300 First Capitol Dr., Zip 63301; tel. 314/947-5000; Martin J. Strussion, exec. dir. **A**1a 9 10 **F**1 2 3 4 5 6 7 9 10 11 12 14 15 16 20 21 23 24 25 26 27 28 29 30 31 32 33 34 35 36 37 38 40 41 42 43 44 45 46 47 49 50 52 53 54; **S**5455	23	10	S		402	12818	223	55.5	37	1725	49378	21140	1078
ST. JOSEPH—Buchanan County													
★□ HEARTLAND HOSPITAL EAST (Formerly St. Joseph Hospital), 5325 Faraon St., Zip 64506; tel. 816/271-6000; Charles A. Lynn Jr., adm. **A**1a 9 10 **F**1 3 5 6 9 10 11 12 14 15 16 20 23 24 26 33 35 44 45 46 53	23	10	S		205	8159	147	71.7	0	0	29081	12137	586
★□ HEARTLAND HOSPITAL WEST (Formerly Methodist Medical Center), 801 Faraon St., Zip 64501; tel. 816/271-7201; Gary M. White, exec. vice-pres. (Total facility includes 159 beds in nursing home-type unit) **A**1a 2 6 9 10 **F**1 2 3 5 6 9 10 11 12 14 15 16 19 20 21 23 24 25 26 27 31 32 34 35 36 37 40 41 42 43 44 45 46 48 49 50 52 53	23	10	S	TF	469	9564	273	58.2	29	1728	40171	18460	989
				H	310	8904	152	—	29	1728	35184	16731	914
METHODIST MEDICAL CENTER, See Heartland Hospital West													
ST. JOSEPH HOSPITAL, See Heartland Hospital East													
ST. JOSEPH STATE HOSPITAL, 3400 Frederick Ave., P O Box 263, Zip 64502; tel. 816/232-8431; Hildreth Hultine, supt. **A**9 10 **F**18 23 24 28 31 32 42 43 45 46 47 48 50	12	22	L		318	1054	262	81.1	0	0	18676	12435	767
ST. LOUIS—Independent City													
★□ ALEXIAN BROTHERS HOSPITAL, 3933 S. Broadway, Zip 63118; tel. 314/865-3333; Deno Fabbre, pres. & chief exec. off. (Total facility includes 23 beds in nursing home-type unit) **A**1a 9 10 **F**1 3 6 10 12 14 15 16 19 20 23 24 26 27 29 31 33 34 35 41 42 44 45 46 47 53; **S**0065	21	10	S	TF	181	5083	124	68.5	0	0	25263	11509	575
				H	158	4781	109	—	0	0	24891	11223	560
BARNARD FREE SKIN AND CANCER HOSPITAL, See Barnes Hospital													
★□ BARNES HOSPITAL (Includes Barnard Free Skin and Cancer Hospital; Queeny Tower; Rand-Johnson; The Pavilion; Wohl-Washington University Clinics), Barnes Hospital Plaza, Zip 63110; tel. 314/362-5000; Max Poll, pres. & chief exec. off. **A**1a 2 3 5 6 8 9 10 **F**1 2 3 4 5 7 8 9 11 12 13 14 15 16 20 21 22 23 24 25 26 27 29 31 33 34 35 36 37 38 39 40 41 42 44 45 46 47 54	23	10	S		1054	35565	849	79.5	59	3060	222894	89875	4510
★□ BETHESDA GENERAL HOSPITAL (Includes Bethesda-Dilworth Memorial Home), 3655 Vista Ave., Zip 63110; tel. 314/772-9200; John F. Norwood, pres. (Total facility includes 29 beds in nursing home-type unit) **A**1a 9 10 **F**1 3 13 14 15 16 19 23 26 34 35 37 41 42 43 47 50	23	10	S	TF	122	2149	59	49.6	0	0	20854	9315	657
				H	93	1869	38	—	0	0	9846	4599	251
★□ CARDINAL GLENNON CHILDREN'S HOSPITAL, 1465 S. Grand Blvd., Zip 63104; tel. 314/577-5600; Douglas A. Ries, exec. dir. **A**1a 3 5 9 10 **F**1 4 5 6 12 13 14 15 16 20 23 24 29 30 31 32 33 34 35 38 42 44 45 46 47 51 53 54; **S**5455	23	50	S		190	7828	135	71.1	0	0	49444	23143	1117
★□ CAREUNIT HOSPITAL OF ST. LOUIS, 1755 S. Grand Blvd., Zip 63104; tel. 314/771-0500; Vincent B. Sullivan, adm. **A**1b 9 **F**15 23 24 29 34 42 46 48 49; **S**0275	33	22	S		144	1487	109	75.7	0	0	10087	3470	110
□ CENTRAL MEDICAL CENTER HOSPITAL, 4411 N. Newstead Ave., Zip 63115; tel. 314/382-7979; Wilbur A. Smith, adm. **A**1a 9 10 **F**1 6 10 12 14 15 16 23 26 31 32 33 35 37 42 44 45 46 47 49 53	23	10	S		194	5900	99	51.0	28	648	18844	6601	300
★□ CHILDREN'S HOSPITAL, 400 S. Kingshighway Blvd., Zip 63110; tel. 314/454-6000; Ronald G. Evens MD, pres. & chief exec. off. **A**1a 3 5 8 9 10 **F**1 4 5 6 10 13 14 15 16 17 20 23 24 27 30 31 32 33 34 35 38 42 44 45 46 51 53 54	23	50	S		235	7609	148	63.0	0	0	64513	20041	1007
CHRISTIAN HOSPITAL NORTHEAST, See Christian Hospitals Northeast-Northwest													
★□ CHRISTIAN HOSPITALS NORTHEAST-NORTHWEST (Includes Christian Hospital Northeast, 11133 Dunn Rd., Zip 63136; tel. 314/355-2300; Christian Hospital Northwest, 1225 Graham Rd., Florissant, Zip 63031; tel. 314/839-3800), 11133 Dunn Rd., Zip 63136; tel. 314/355-2300; Fred L. Brown, pres. & chief exec. off. (Total facility includes 16 beds in nursing home-type unit) **A**1a b 2 9 10 **F**1 3 4 5 9 10 12 14 15 16 19 20 21 23 24 25 26 27 30 32 33 35 36 37 40 41 42 43 44 45 46 47 48 49 52 53 54; **S**0565	23	10	S	TF	646	19560	444	68.7	30	1228	99631	47423	2279
				H	630	19343	434	—	30	1228	99486	47291	2269
★□ DEACONESS HOSPITAL, 6150 Oakland Ave., Zip 63139; tel. 314/768-3000; Richard P. Ellerbrake, pres. **A**1a 2 3 5 6 9 10 **F**1 2 3 6 7 8 9 10 11 12 14 15 16 20 21 23 24 25 26 27 28 29 30 32 33 34 35 36 37 40 41 42 44 45 46 48 49 52 53	23	10	S		527	16099	343	65.1	35	2099	74735	36558	1772
EDGEWOOD CHEMICAL DEPENDENCY UNIT, See St. John's Mercy Medical Center													
★□ FAITH HOSPITAL, Olive & Mason Rds., Zip 63141; tel. 314/434-0600; Andrew J. Signorelli, adm. **A**1a 9 10 **F**1 3 6 12 14 16 23 34 35 53	23	10	S		124	1495	28	22.6	0	0	—	—	147
★□ INCARNATE WORD HOSPITAL, 3545 Lafayette Ave., Zip 63104; tel. 314/664-6500; James R. Kaskie, pres. & chief exec. off. (Total facility includes 42 beds in nursing home-type unit) **A**1a 9 10 **F**1 3 6 9 10 11 12 14 15 16 19 23 24 25 34 35 41 42 43 44 45 46 47 53; **S**5565	21	10	S	TF	236	6340	156	66.1	0	0	30653	14641	776
				H	194	6066	140	—	0	0	29359	13639	758

Hospital, Address, Telephone, Administrator, Approval and Facility Codes, Multihospital System Code

★ American Hospital Association (AHA) membership
☐ Joint Commission on Accreditation of Hospitals (JCAH) accreditation
\+ American Osteopathic Hospital Association (AOHA) membership
○ American Osteopathic Association (AOA) accreditation
Δ Commission on Accreditation of Rehabilitation Facilities (CARF) accreditation
Control codes 61, 63, 64, 71, 72 and 73 indicate hospitals listed by AOHA, but not registered by AHA.
For definition of numerical codes, see page A2

Hospital, Address, Telephone, Administrator, Approval and Facility Codes, Multihospital System Code	Classification Codes				Inpatient Data				Newborn Data		Expense (thousands of dollars)		
	Control	Service	Stay	Facilities	Beds	Admissions	Census	Occupancy (percent)	Bassinets	Births	Total	Payroll	Personnel
★☐ JEWISH HOSPITAL OF ST. LOUIS, 216 S. Kingshighway Blvd., Zip 63110; Mailing Address Box 14109, Zip 63178; tel. 314/454-7000; David A. Gee, pres. **A**1a 2 3 5 6 8 9 10 **F**1 3 4 6 7 8 9 10 11 12 14 15 16 20 21 23 24 25 26 27 28 29 31 32 33 34 35 36 37 38 40 41 42 43 44 45 46 47 49 50 53 54	23	10	S		550	16647	388	70.5	25	1865	120813	57511	2383
★☐ LINDELL HOSPITAL, 4930 Lindell Blvd., Zip 63108; tel. 314/367-3770; James F. Schmidt, adm. **A**1a 9 10 **F**1 3 6 14 16 23 24 27 32 33 34 35 48 49	23	10	S		51	1519	36	55.4	0	0	—	—	135
☐ LUTHERAN MEDICAL CENTER, 2639 Miami St., Zip 63118; tel. 314/772-1456; Harry J. Carr, exec. dir. **A**1a 3 6 9 10 **F**1 3 6 7 8 9 10 11 12 14 15 16 21 23 24 26 27 30 32 33 35 36 37 40 41 42 44 48 49 50 53; **S**3015	33	10	S		278	8227	169	60.8	30	2525	34353	13724	695
☐ MALCOLM BLISS MENTAL HEALTH CENTER, 1420 Grattan St., Zip 63104; tel. 314/241-7600; Robert O. Muether, supt. **A**1b 3 5 10 **F**24 28 29 30 31 32 33 42 43 45 46	12	22	S		150	1487	133	88.7	0	0	15321	9573	524
★☐ MISSOURI BAPTIST HOSPITAL, 3015 N. Ballas Rd., Zip 63131; tel. 314/432-1212; Norman E. McCann, pres. **A**1a 6 9 10 **F**1 2 3 4 6 7 8 9 10 11 12 14 15 16 17 20 23 24 26 27 28 33 34 35 36 37 40 41 42 44 45 46 47 53 54	23	10	S		403	11844	272	67.5	42	997	65235	33745	1506
NORMANDY OSTEOPATHIC HOSPITAL-NORTH, See Normandy Osteopathic Medical Center													
NORMANDY OSTEOPATHIC HOSPITAL-SOUTH, See Normandy Osteopathic Medical Center													
★ ○ + NORMANDY OSTEOPATHIC MEDICAL CENTER (Includes Normandy Osteopathic Hospital-North, 7840 Natural Bridge Rd., Zip 63121; tel. 314/389-0015; Normandy Osteopathic Hospital-South, 530 Des Peres Rd. at Dougherty Ferry Rd., Zip 63131; tel. 314/821-5850), 8225 Florissant Rd., Zip 63121; tel. 314/524-8480; Warren A. Brucker, second vice-pres. & chief exec. off. **A**9 10 11 12 13 **F**1 5 6 10 12 14 15 16 23 24 26 27 30 33 34 35 36 37 40 44 45 46 52 53 54	23	10	S		306	10163	185	60.5	26	898	45594	21239	907
QUEENY TOWER, See Barnes Hospital													
RAND-JOHNSON, See Barnes Hospital													
SAINT LOUIS MEMORIAL HOSPITAL, 1027 Bellevue Ave., Zip 63117; tel. 314/781-9997; Don M. Chase, adm. **A**9 10 **F**1 15 16 23 37 52; **S**6525	32	10	S		40	1315	14	35.0	0	0	7748	2231	74
★☐ SHRINERS HOSPITALS FOR CRIPPLED CHILDREN, 2001 S. Lindbergh Blvd., Zip 63131; tel. 314/432-3600; A. Duane Seabury Jr., adm. **A**1a 3 5 **F**23 24 26 34 42; **S**4125	23	57	S		80	1595	44	55.0	0	0	—	—	176
★☐ ST. ANTHONY'S MEDICAL CENTER, 10010 Kennerly Rd., Zip 63128; tel. 314/525-1000; Richard Grisham, pres. & chief exec. off. (Total facility includes 335 beds in nursing home-type unit) **A**1a 2 9 10 **F**1 2 3 5 6 7 8 10 11 12 14 15 16 17 19 20 23 24 26 27 30 31 32 33 34 35 36 40 41 42 44 45 46 47 48 49 50 53	23	10	S	TF	707	18615	485	72.9	44	1281	68543	30160	1316
				H	372	14821	255	—	44	1281	—	—	1285
★☐ Δ ST. JOHN'S MERCY MEDICAL CENTER (Includes St. John's Mercy Medical Center, 615 S. New Ballas Rd., Zip 63141; tel. 314/569-6000; St. John's Mercy Hospital, 200 Madison Ave., Washington, Zip 63090; tel. 314/239-7711; Edgewood Chemical Dependency Unit, 615 S. New Ballas Rd., Zip 63141; tel. 314/569-6500), John T. Farrell, pres. & chief exec. off. (Total facility includes 20 beds in nursing home-type unit) **A**1a b 2 3 5 7 8 9 10 **F**1 2 3 4 5 6 7 8 9 10 11 12 14 15 16 17 19 20 21 22 23 24 25 26 27 28 29 30 32 33 34 35 36 37 38 40 41 42 43 44 45 46 47 48 49 50 51 52 53 54; **S**5185	21	10	S	TF	911	35283	694	76.2	94	6534	142031	73470	3123
				H	891	34978	681	—	94	6534	141751	73199	3107
ST. JOSEPH HOSPITAL, See Kirkwood													
★☐ ST. LOUIS REGIONAL MEDICAL CENTER (Formerly St. Luke's Hospital), 5535 Delmar Blvd., Zip 63112; tel. 314/361-1212; Robert B. Johnson, chief exec. off. **A**1a 3 5 6 9 10 **F**1 3 6 10 11 12 14 16 20 23 24 26 34 35 37 41 42 44 45 46 47 52 53; **S**0585	23	10	L		231	7493	173	74.9	0	0	55447	19047	1170
☐ ST. LOUIS STATE HOSPITAL COMPLEX, 5400 Arsenal St., Zip 63139; tel. 314/644-8000; Milton T. Fujita MD, supt. (Total facility includes 25 beds in nursing home-type unit) **A**1b 9 10 **F**3 12 14 15 19 23 24 28 29 30 31 32 33 34 35 41 42 43 45 46 47 48 49 50	12	22	L		469	3111	417	87.1	0	0	29799	15116	948
★☐ ST. MARY'S HEALTH CENTER, 6420 Clayton Rd., Zip 63117; tel. 314/768-8000; Sr. Betty Brucker, exec. dir. **A**1a 2 3 5 8 9 10 **F**1 2 3 4 6 7 8 9 10 11 12 14 15 16 20 21 23 24 25 26 27 30 32 33 34 35 36 38 40 41 42 43 44 45 46 47 48 53 54; **S**5455	23	10	S		482	17110	374	71.8	42	2947	88417	38523	1654
THE PAVILION, See Barnes Hospital													
★☐ UNIVERSITY HOSPITAL, ST. LOUIS UNIVERSITY MEDICAL CENTER (Formerly St. Louis University Hospitals), 1325 S. Grand Blvd., Zip 63104; tel. 314/577-8000; Herbert B. Schneiderman, exec. dir. & chief oper. off. **A**1a 3 5 8 9 10 **F**1 2 3 4 5 6 7 8 9 10 11 12 13 14 15 16 20 23 24 26 27 29 31 32 33 34 35 37 38 41 42 44 45 46 47 53 54	23	10	S		294	10316	242	82.0	0	0	74769	27336	1421
★☐ VETERANS ADMINISTRATION MEDICAL CENTER, Zip 63125; tel. 314/487-0400; John T. Carson, dir. (Total facility includes 93 beds in nursing home-type unit) **A**1a 2 3 5 8 **F**1 2 3 6 7 8 9 10 11 12 13 15 16 17 19 20 23 24 26 27 28 29 31 32 33 34 35 41 42 43 44 46 48 49 50 53 54	45	10	S	TF	932	18608	703	75.4	0	0	111897	71201	2174
				H	839	18491	612	—	0	0	—	—	2129
WOHL-WASHINGTON UNIVERSITY CLINICS, See Barnes Hospital													
ST. PETERS—St. Charles County													
★☐ ST. PETERS COMMUNITY HOSPITAL, 10 Hospital Dr., Zip 63376; tel. 314/447-6600; Fred Woody, adm. **A**1a 9 10 **F**1 3 6 10 12 14 15 16 23 26 32 34 35 43 45 46 47 50 53; **S**1755	33	10	S		102	4227	68	66.7	0	0	18326	6730	295
STE GENEVIEVE—Ste. Genevieve County													
STE GENEVIEVE COUNTY MEMORIAL HOSPITAL, Box 468, Zip 63670; tel. 314/883-2751; Stephen L. Crain, adm. **A**9 10 **F**1 3 6 10 14 15 16 23 35 37 40 41 45 53	13	10	S		51	1114	15	29.4	9	164	3278	1606	98
SULLIVAN—Franklin County													
★ SULLIVAN COMMUNITY HOSPITAL, 751 Sappington Bridge Rd., Zip 63080; tel. 314/468-4186; Dave Rose, chief exec. off. **A**9 10 **F**1 3 6 10 12 14 23 34 35 37 40 43 44 45 46; **S**2195	33	10	S		73	1891	24	32.9	10	105	4631	1573	97
SWEET SPRINGS—Saline County													
SWEET SPRINGS COMMUNITY HOSPITAL, 701 Bridge St., P O Box 206, Zip 65351; tel. 816/335-6311; Marshall C. Parsons, adm. **A**9 10 **F**1 6 15 16 23 24 26 35 37 40 41 44 45 50	23	10	S		31	448	7	22.6	6	35	1370	731	48
TRENTON—Grundy County													
WRIGHT MEMORIAL HOSPITAL, 701 E. First St., Zip 64683; tel. 816/359-5621; James C. Cox, interim adm. **A**9 10 **F**1 3 6 16 23 26 34 35 36 40 41 45	23	10	S		53	1503	20	37.7	8	188	3474	1588	110
TROY—Lincoln County													
LINCOLN COUNTY MEMORIAL HOSPITAL, 1000 E. Cherry, Zip 63379; tel. 314/528-8551; William B. Haden, adm. **A**9 10 **F**1 3 5 6 10 12 15 16 23 34 35 37 40 41 44 45 46 52 53	13	10	S		88	3049	49	48.0	10	164	9425	3179	252
WARRENSBURG—Johnson County													
★☐ WESTERN MISSOURI MEDICAL CENTER (Formerly Johnson County Memorial Hospital), Burkarth Rd. & E. Gay St., Zip 64093; tel. 816/747-2500; Louis E. Gordon, pres. (Total facility includes 12 beds in nursing home-type unit) **A**1a 9 10 **F**1 3 6 7 10 14 15 16 19 23 35 36 40 45 46 53	13	10	S	TF	78	2726	41	52.6	18	313	8105	3526	221
				H	66	2535	34	—	18	313	—	—	210

Hospital, Address, Telephone, Administrator, Approval and Facility Codes, Multihospital System Code	Classification Codes			Facilities	Inpatient Data				Newborn Data		Expense (thousands of dollars)		Personnel
★ American Hospital Association (AHA) membership □ Joint Commission on Accreditation of Hospitals (JCAH) accreditation + American Osteopathic Hospital Association (AOHA) membership ○ American Osteopathic Association (AOA) accreditation Δ Commission on Accreditation of Rehabilitation Facilities (CARF) accreditation Control codes 61, 63, 64, 71, 72 and 73 indicate hospitals listed by AOHA, but not registered by AHA. For definition of numerical codes, see page A2	Control	Service	Stay	Facilities	Beds	Admissions	Census	Occupancy (percent)	Bassinets	Births	Total	Payroll	Personnel
WASHINGTON—Franklin County													
ST. JOHN'S MERCY HOSPITAL, See St. John's Mercy Medical Center, St. Louis													
WAVERLY—Lafayette County													
KELLING HOSPITAL, Box 155, Zip 64096; tel. 816/493-2251; Jerry Dollison, adm. (Nonreporting) **A**9 10	33	10	S		54	—	—	—	—	—	—	—	—
WEST PLAINS—Howell County													
★ OZARKS MEDICAL CENTER, 1103 Alaska Ave., P O Box 1007, Zip 65775; tel. 417/256-9111; Colin C. Collins PhD, adm. (Total facility includes 14 beds in nursing home-type unit) **A**10 **F**1 3 5 6 10 15 16 19 23 34 35 37 40 41 43 45 46 47 52 53	23	10	S	TF H	100 86	3970 3699	59 50	59.0 —	12 12	526 526	— —	— —	297 286
WHITEMAN AIR FORCE BASE—Johnson County													
U. S. AIR FORCE HOSPITAL WHITEMAN, Zip 65305; tel. 816/687-2109; Capt. Frank H. Weigelt, adm. **F**1 6 12 15 23 28 29 32 34 35 37 40 45 46 47	41	10	S		34	1977	17	50.0	11	315	—	—	232

Hospital, Address, Telephone, Administrator, Approval and Facility Codes, Multihospital System Code

★ American Hospital Association (AHA) membership
□ Joint Commission on Accreditation of Hospitals (JCAH) accreditation
+ American Osteopathic Hospital Association (AOHA) membership
○ American Osteopathic Association (AOA) accreditation
Δ Commission on Accreditation of Rehabilitation Facilities (CARF) accreditation
Control codes 61, 63, 64, 71, 72 and 73 indicate hospitals listed by AOHA, but not registered by AHA.
For definition of numerical codes, see page A2

Montana

Hospital, Address, Telephone, Administrator, Approval and Facility Codes, Multihospital System Code	Classification Codes: Control	Service	Stay	Facilities	Inpatient Data: Beds	Admissions	Census	Occupancy (percent)	Newborn Data: Bassinets	Births	Expense (thousands of dollars): Total	Payroll	Personnel
ANACONDA—Deer Lodge County													
★ COMMUNITY HOSPITAL OF ANACONDA, 401 W. Penn Ave., Zip 59711; tel. 406/563-5261; Manuel Ortiz, adm. (Total facility includes 68 beds in nursing home-type unit) **A**9 10 **F**1 3 6 12 16 19 23 27 35 40 45	23	10	S	TF	110	1426	80	72.7	6	70	4603	2493	136
				H	42	1354	17	—	6	70	3452	1840	98
BAKER—Fallon County													
FALLON MEMORIAL HOSPITAL, 320 Hospital Dr., Drawer 820, Zip 59313; tel. 406/778-3331 (Total facility includes 32 beds in nursing home-type unit) **A**9 10 **F**3 19 35 40 45 52	23	10	S	TF	51	250	27	52.9	3	21	1136	675	45
				H	19	219	2	—	3	21	613	332	19
BIG SANDY—Chouteau County													
BIG SANDY MEDICAL CENTER, Box 530, Zip 59520; tel. 406/378-2188; Jay L. Toth, chief exec. off. (Total facility includes 20 beds in nursing home-type unit) **A**9 10 **F**19 24 35 40	16	10	S	TF	29	174	2	6.9	1	1	409	269	32
				H	9	166	1	—	1	1	327	215	25
BIG TIMBER—Sweet Grass County													
SWEET GRASS COMMUNITY HOSPITAL, Fifth & Hooper Sts., Box 430, Zip 59011; tel. 406/932-5917; Karen Herman, adm. **A**9 10 **F**1 3 6 23 24 35 40 45	23	10	S		17	130	5	29.4	0	16	557	299	12
BILLINGS—Yellowstone County													
BILLINGS DEACONESS HOSPITAL, See Deaconess Medical Center													
★□ DEACONESS MEDICAL CENTER (Formerly Billings Deaconess Hospital), 2813 Ninth Ave. N., Zip 59101; Mailing Address Box 2547, Zip 59103; tel. 406/657-4000; Lane W. Basso, pres. **A**1a 9 10 **F**1 2 3 4 6 8 9 10 11 12 14 16 20 23 24 27 28 29 30 31 32 33 35 44 45 46 47 52 53 54	23	10	S		253	9291	176	70.4	0	0	42040	17065	773
★□ SAINT VINCENT HOSPITAL AND HEALTH CENTER, P O Box 35200, Zip 59107; tel. 406/657-7101; William M. Murray, pres. **A**1a 9 10 **F**1 3 6 7 9 10 11 12 14 16 21 23 24 25 30 33 34 35 40 44 45 46 51 52 53 54; **S**5095	21	10	S		313	11424	165	52.9	28	2225	40983	18617	895
BOZEMAN—Gallatin County													
★ BOZEMAN DEACONESS HOSPITAL, 915 Highland Blvd., Zip 59715; tel. 406/585-5000; Gary Kenner, adm. (Total facility includes 60 beds in nursing home-type unit) **A**10 **F**1 3 6 7 9 10 12 14 16 19 23 34 35 40 41 45 46	23	10	S	TF	132	4350	90	68.2	14	700	10306	4999	249
				H	72	4016	37	—	14	700	8768	4406	193
BROWNING—Glacier County													
★□ U. S. PUBLIC HEALTH SERVICE INDIAN HOSPITAL, Zip 59417; tel. 406/338-6150; Randy Webb, actg. dir. **A**1a 10 **F**6 15 23 28 30 34 35 37 40 52	47	10	S		27	1598	13	43.3	6	130	4839	2578	149
BUTTE—Silver Bow County													
★□ ST. JAMES COMMUNITY HOSPITAL, 400 S. Clark St., Zip 59701; tel. 406/782-8361; Sr. Loretto Marie Colwell, pres. **A**1a 9 10 **F**3 8 9 10 12 16 19 23 27 30 32 33 35 40 45 46 48 51 52; **S**5095	21	10	S		274	6886	111	40.5	12	657	25974	12403	624
CHESTER—Liberty County													
★ LIBERTY COUNTY HOSPITAL AND NURSING HOME, Zip 59522; tel. 406/759-5181; Richard O. Brown, adm. (Total facility includes 40 beds in nursing home-type unit) **A**9 10 **F**16 19 23 40 44 45	13	10	S	TF	51	342	41	80.4	4	32	1628	901	67
				H	11	300	4	—	4	32	750	362	23
CHOTEAU—Teton County													
★ TETON MEDICAL CENTER, 915 Fourth St. N.W., Box 820, Zip 59422; tel. 406/466-5763; Richard P. Spilovoy, adm. (Total facility includes 24 beds in nursing home-type unit) **A**9 10 **F**1 3 16 19 34 35 45 46 47 52; **S**2235	16	10	S	TF	46	411	34	73.9	4	46	1482	803	60
				H	22	402	10	—	4	46	1081	550	37
CIRCLE—McCone County													
MCCONE COUNTY HOSPITAL, Box 195, Zip 59215; tel. 406/485-2063; Jim Adams, adm. (Total facility includes 40 beds in nursing home-type unit) **A**9 10 **F**14 19 35 40 45 52	23	10	S	TF	60	254	43	71.7	6	15	1270	725	40
				H	20	236	4	—	6	15	533	319	22
COLUMBUS—Stillwater County													
STILLWATER COMMUNITY HOSPITAL, 44 W. Fourth Ave. N., Box 959, Zip 59019; tel. 406/322-5316; John Bartos, adm. **A**9 10 **F**1 3 6 14 23 34 35 40 41 52	23	10	S		27	543	10	37.0	5	48	1122	650	36
CONRAD—Pondera County													
★□ PONDERA MEDICAL CENTER, 805 Sunset Blvd., Box 757, Zip 59425; tel. 406/278-3211; Norman R. Campeau, adm. (Total facility includes 78 beds in nursing home-type unit) **A**1a 9 10 **F**1 3 10 16 19 23 33 35 40 44 45 47; **S**2235	23	10	S	TF	112	562	73	65.2	6	57	2688	1412	98
				H	34	479	4	—	6	57	1473	628	35
CROW AGENCY—Big Horn County													
★□ U. S. PUBLIC HEALTH SERVICE INDIAN HOSPITAL, Box 9, Zip 59022; tel. 406/638-2626; Duane L. Jeanotte, serv. unit dir. **A**1a 10 **F**6 15 23 28 30 34 35 37 40 52	47	10	S		34	1308	13	38.2	4	153	4332	2496	127
CULBERTSON—Roosevelt County													
ROOSEVELT MEMORIAL HOSPITAL, Zip 59218; tel. 406/787-6621; Mike Schafer, adm. (Total facility includes 40 beds in nursing home-type unit) **A**9 10 **F**3 12 14 19 23 34 35 40 52 53	16	10	S	TF	54	431	44	81.5	3	24	1313	672	51
				H	14	380	5	—	3	24	788	324	20
CUT BANK—Glacier County													
GLACIER COUNTY MEDICAL CENTER, 802 Second St. S.E., Zip 59427; tel. 406/873-2251; Gerald E. Hughes, adm. (Total facility includes 39 beds in nursing home-type unit) **A**9 10 **F**1 3 16 19 35 40 45 52	13	10	S	TF	59	600	39	66.1	4	52	2095	1145	79
				H	20	533	6	—	4	52	1693	826	52
DEER LODGE—Powell County													
★□ POWELL COUNTY MEMORIAL HOSPITAL, 1101 Texas Ave., Zip 59722; tel. 406/846-2212; Jon Frantsvog, adm. (Total facility includes 12 beds in nursing home-type unit) **A**1a 9 10 **F**1 3 6 7 16 19 23 33 35 40 41 45 47 52; **S**2235	23	10	S	TF	35	553	9	30.0	6	26	1332	671	37
				H	23	501	6	—	6	26	1248	627	30
DILLON—Beaverhead County													
★ BARRETT MEMORIAL HOSPITAL, 1260 S. Atlantic St., Zip 59725; tel. 406/683-2324; Myron Mortier, exec. dir. **A**9 10 **F**3 6 16 23 34 35 40 41 44 52; **S**0585	16	10	S		31	1020	9	29.0	6	120	2364	1032	56
EKALAKA—Carter County													
DAHL MEMORIAL HOSPITAL, Zip 59324; tel. 406/775-8730; Randall G. Holom, adm. (Total facility includes 21 beds in nursing home-type unit) **A**9 10 **F**3 19 34 35 40 45	23	10	S	TF	36	84	20	55.6	4	1	670	378	24
				H	15	59	0	—	4	1	114	64	6
ENNIS—Madison County													
MADISON VALLEY HOSPITAL, Box 397, Zip 59729; tel. 406/682-4222; J. Page Puckett, adm. **A**9 10 **F**3 16 35 40 45 52	16	10	S		13	307	3	23.1	3	20	428	216	14
FORSYTH—Rosebud County													
ROSEBUD COMMUNITY HOSPITAL, 383 N. 17th Ave., Zip 59327; tel. 406/356-2161; Joyce Asay, adm. (Total facility includes 55 beds in nursing home-type unit) **A**9 10 **F**3 7 14 16 19 23 35 40 45 47 52; **S**0585	23	10	S	TF	75	470	55	73.3	2	30	1657	895	67
				H	20	390	4	—	2	30	1009	549	19

Hospital, Address, Telephone, Administrator, Approval and Facility Codes, Multihospital System Code	Classification Codes: Control	Service	Stay	Facilities	Inpatient Data: Beds	Admissions	Census	Occupancy (percent)	Newborn Data: Bassinets	Births	Expense (thousands of dollars): Total	Payroll	Personnel
FORT BENTON—Chouteau County													
CHOUTEAU COUNTY DISTRICT HOSPITAL, 1501 St. Charles St., Box 249, Zip 59442; tel. 406/622-3331; Robert E. Smith, adm. (Total facility includes 22 beds in nursing home-type unit) **A**9 10 **F**19 23 35 40 41 45 46	16	10	S	TF	39	234	23	59.0	5	8	1089	663	44
				H	17	224	3	—	5	8	560	338	26
FORT HARRISON—Lewis and Clark County													
★☐ VETERANS ADMINISTRATION HOSPITAL, Zip 59636; tel. 406/442-6410; Frank W. Caldwell, dir. **A**1a **F**1 3 6 12 14 15 16 19 23 28 30 32 33 34 46 50	45	10	S		150	3264	106	70.7	0	0	16440	8278	311
GLASGOW—Valley County													
★☐ FRANCES MAHON DEACONESS HOSPITAL, 621 Third St. S., Zip 59230; tel. 406/228-4351; Kyle Hopstad, adm. (Total facility includes 6 beds in nursing home-type unit) **A**1a 9 10 **F**1 3 6 10 12 14 16 19 23 24 34 35 41 45 52	23	10	S	TF	54	987	11	20.4	10	143	3510	1553	107
				H	48	948	9	—	10	143	3503	1545	106
GLENDIVE—Dawson County													
★☐ GLENDIVE COMMUNITY HOSPITAL, Prospect & Ames, Zip 59330; tel. 406/365-3306; John Solheim, chief exec. off. (Total facility includes 75 beds in nursing home-type unit) **A**1a 9 10 **F**1 3 10 14 16 19 23 35 40 45	23	10	S	TF	121	1192	95	78.5	6	121	4391	2265	145
				H	46	1174	20	—	6	121	2642	1349	104
GREAT FALLS—Cascade County													
★☐ COLUMBUS HOSPITAL, 500 15th Ave. S., Box 5013, Zip 59403; tel. 406/727-3333; William J. Downer Jr., pres. **A**1a 2 9 10 **F**1 3 6 8 9 10 11 12 14 16 20 21 23 24 25 26 32 33 34 35 40 41 44 45 46 47 52 53 54; **S**5265	21	10	S		198	6308	98	49.5	11	324	25780	13305	622
★☐ Δ MONTANA DEACONESS MEDICAL CENTER, 1101 26th St. S., Zip 59405; tel. 406/761-1200; David R. Cornell, pres. (Total facility includes 124 beds in nursing home-type unit) **A**1a 7 9 10 **F**1 2 3 4 6 7 10 12 14 16 19 23 24 25 26 27 28 30 33 34 35 40 41 44 45 46 47 48 49 51 52 53 54	23	10	S	TF	412	8820	274	66.5	18	964	40461	23102	1033
				H	288	8644	156	—	18	964	37647	21650	951
HAMILTON—Ravalli County													
★ MARCUS DALY MEMORIAL HOSPITAL, 1200 Westwood Dr., Zip 59840; tel. 406/363-2211; Richard C. Atkins, chief exec. off. **A**9 10 **F**3 6 10 14 16 23 27 35 40 45 46 52	23	10	S		48	2060	21	43.8	7	202	3484	1793	123
HARDIN—Big Horn County													
BIG HORN COUNTY MEMORIAL HOSPITAL, 17 N. Miles St., Zip 59034; tel. 406/665-2310; Mike N. Sinclair, exec. dir. (Total facility includes 34 beds in nursing home-type unit) **A**9 10 **F**14 16 19 23 34 35 45 47; **S**0585	23	10	S	TF	50	657	38	76.0	5	99	1790	857	61
				H	16	600	6	—	5	99	1096	532	23
HARLEM—Blaine County													
★☐ U. S. PUBLIC HEALTH SERVICE INDIAN HOSPITAL, Rural Rte. 1, Box 67, Zip 59526; tel. 406/353-2651; Don Ade, serv. unit dir. **A**1a 10 **F**1 6 15 28 30 34 35 37 40 52	47	10	S		18	447	5	27.8	0	2	2637	1290	64
HARLOWTON—Wheatland County													
★ WHEATLAND MEMORIAL HOSPITAL, 530 Third St. N.W., Box 287, Zip 59036; tel. 406/632-4351; John H. Johnson, adm. (Total facility includes 33 beds in nursing home-type unit) **A**9 10 **F**1 3 6 16 19 23 34 35 45 49; **S**2235	23	10	S	TF	56	267	29	51.8	5	19	1180	626	43
				H	23	235	2	—	5	19	769	362	20
HAVRE—Hill County													
★☐ NORTHERN MONTANA HOSPITAL, 30 13th St., Box 1231, Zip 59501; tel. 406/265-2211; Gerald W. Bibo, pres. (Total facility includes 20 beds in nursing home-type unit) **A**1a 9 10 **F**3 6 10 11 12 14 16 19 23 30 33 34 35 40 41 44 45 46 52 53	23	10	S	TF	120	3598	56	46.7	10	495	9599	4519	228
				H	100	3527	39	—	10	495	9344	4357	218
HELENA—Lewis and Clark County													
★ SHODAIR CHILDREN'S HOSPITAL, 840 Helena Ave., P O Box 5539, Zip 59604; tel. 406/442-1980; Daniel L. Yazak, adm. **A**9 10 **F**1 16 33 34 35 38 48 49	23	50	S		8	657	8	27.6	0	0	3753	2432	107
★☐ ST. PETER'S COMMUNITY HOSPITAL, 2475 Broadway, Zip 59601; tel. 406/442-2480; John A. Guy, pres. **A**1a 9 10 **F**3 6 10 12 14 16 20 21 23 24 27 28 30 33 34 35 40 44 45 46 52 53 54	23	10	S		103	5493	68	70.1	17	850	16463	8276	402
KALISPELL—Flathead County													
★☐ KALISPELL REGIONAL HOSPITAL, 310 Sunnyview Lane, Zip 59901; tel. 406/751-5111; Eugene G. Johnson, pres. & adm. **A**1a 9 10 **F**3 6 9 10 12 14 16 20 23 24 30 35 38 40 44 45 46 47 52 53	23	10	S		104	5667	73	70.2	12	740	15847	7451	396
LEWISTOWN—Fergus County													
★☐ CENTRAL MONTANA HOSPITAL, 408 Wendell Ave., Box 580, Zip 59457; tel. 406/538-7711; Gary Fletcher, adm. & exec. off. (Total facility includes 70 beds in nursing home-type unit) **A**1a 9 10 **F**1 3 6 10 11 12 14 16 19 21 23 34 35 40 41 44 45	23	10	S	TF	111	1490	85	75.2	5	188	5491	2675	152
				H	41	1421	16	—	5	188	3869	1789	107
LIBBY—Lincoln County													
☐ ST. JOHN'S LUTHERAN HOSPITAL, 350 Louisiana Ave., Zip 59923; tel. 406/293-7761; Raymond Bergroos, adm. **A**1a 9 10 **F**1 3 6 14 16 23 26 32 35 40 44 45 47 52; **S**0585	23	10	S		29	1353	14	48.3	6	183	3023	1352	79
LIVINGSTON—Park County													
★ LIVINGSTON MEMORIAL HOSPITAL, 504 S. 13th St., Zip 59047; tel. 406/222-3541; Richard V. Brown, adm. **A**9 10 **F**1 3 6 10 12 14 16 23 24 34 35 40 44 45 46 53	23	10	S		33	1453	18	40.9	8	167	3477	1875	92
MALMSTROM AIR FORCE BASE—Cascade County													
U. S. AIR FORCE HOSPITAL, Zip 59402; tel. 406/731-3863; Roger D. Delffs, adm. **F**1 6 15 23 28 29 30 32 33 34 35 37 46 47 49	41	10	S		20	1508	13	65.0	10	373	—	—	236
MALTA—Phillips County													
PHILLIPS COUNTY HOSPITAL, 417 S. Fourth St. E., Box 640, Zip 59538; tel. 406/654-1100; Leslie O. Urvand, adm. **A**9 10 **F**1 3 6 35 40 52	23	10	S		30	679	7	23.3	5	45	917	496	29
MILES CITY—Custer County													
★☐ HOLY ROSARY HOSPITAL, 2101 Clark St., Zip 59301; tel. 406/232-2540; Michael R. Piper, exec. dir. **A**1a 9 10 **F**1 3 6 10 12 14 16 21 23 24 27 28 30 32 33 35 40 41 44 45 46 52 53; **S**5255	21	10	S		109	2585	31	28.4	13	381	7066	3653	199
★☐ VETERANS ADMINISTRATION MEDICAL CENTER, 210 S. Winchester Ave., Zip 59301; tel. 406/232-3060; James A. Huff, dir. (Total facility includes 26 beds in nursing home-type unit) **A**1a **F**1 3 10 14 15 16 19 23 26 32 34 42 45 46 47 49 50	45	10	S	TF	117	1567	72	61.5	0	0	—	—	199
				H	91	1541	47	—	0	0	—	—	185
MISSOULA—Missoula County													
★☐ Δ MISSOULA COMMUNITY HOSPITAL, 2827 Fort Missoula Rd., Zip 59801; tel. 406/728-4100; Grant M. Winn, exec. dir. **A**1a 7 9 10 **F**1 3 6 9 10 12 14 16 23 24 25 26 33 34 35 38 40 41 44 45 46 51 52 53; **S**0585	23	10	S		125	5797	76	60.8	30	1650	21627	10937	488
☐ MISSOULA GENERAL HOSPITAL, 902 N. Orange St., Zip 59802; tel. 406/542-2191; Karen Foster, adm. **A**1a 9 10 **F**1 3 6 12 16 23 30 34 35 44 45 46 47; **S**1375	33	10	S		50	926	10	21.3	0	0	4695	1307	65
★☐ ST. PATRICK HOSPITAL, 500 W. Broadway, Box 4587, Zip 59806; tel. 406/543-7271; Lawrence L. White Jr., pres. **A**1a 9 10 **F**1 3 4 6 8 9 10 11 12 14 16 20 21 23 24 27 28 29 30 32 33 35 41 44 45 46 49 52 53 54; **S**5265	21	10	S		213	7742	126	59.2	0	0	33524	13358	634
PHILIPSBURG—Granite County													
GRANITE COUNTY MEMORIAL HOSPITAL AND NURSING HOME, Box 729, Zip 59858; tel. 406/859-3271; Mike Kahoe, adm. (Total facility includes 13 beds in nursing home-type unit) **A**9 10 **F**19 24 34 44 45	13	10	S	TF	23	132	13	56.5	0	3	645	382	17
				H	10	118	2	—	0	3	464	275	5

Legend:
- ★ American Hospital Association (AHA) membership
- ☐ Joint Commission on Accreditation of Hospitals (JCAH) accreditation
- + American Osteopathic Hospital Association (AOHA) membership
- ○ American Osteopathic Association (AOA) accreditation
- Δ Commission on Accreditation of Rehabilitation Facilities (CARF) accreditation
- Control codes 61, 63, 64, 71, 72 and 73 indicate hospitals listed by AOHA, but not registered by AHA.
- For definition of numerical codes, see page A2

Hospital, Address, Telephone, Administrator, Approval and Facility Codes, Multihospital System Code

- ★ American Hospital Association (AHA) membership
- ☐ Joint Commission on Accreditation of Hospitals (JCAH) accreditation
- + American Osteopathic Hospital Association (AOHA) membership
- ○ American Osteopathic Association (AOA) accreditation
- Δ Commission on Accreditation of Rehabilitation Facilities (CARF) accreditation

Control codes 61, 63, 64, 71, 72 and 73 indicate hospitals listed by AOHA, but not registered by AHA. For definition of numerical codes, see page A2

Hospital, Address, Telephone, Administrator, Approval and Facility Codes, Multihospital System Code	Classification Codes				Inpatient Data				Newborn Data		Expense (thousands of dollars)		
	Control	Service	Stay	Facilities	Beds	Admissions	Census	Occupancy (percent)	Bassinets	Births	Total	Payroll	Personnel
PLAINS—Sanders County CLARK FORK VALLEY HOSPITAL, Box 768, Zip 59859; tel. 406/826-3601; Michael Billing, chief exec. off. (Total facility includes 28 beds in nursing home-type unit) **A**9 10 **F**3 6 12 14 16 19 23 30 33 34 35 41 44 45 52; **S**0585	33	10	S	TF	44	714	35	79.5	0	35	2222	1083	56
				H	16	675	7	—	0	35	1591	761	35
PLENTYWOOD—Sheridan County SHERIDAN MEMORIAL HOSPITAL, 440 W. Laurel Ave., Zip 59254; tel. 406/765-1420; Jerry Beaudette, adm. (Total facility includes 65 beds in nursing home-type unit) **A**9 10 **F**1 6 10 14 19 23 24 34 35 40 41 45	23	10	S	TF	86	786	77	89.5	4	70	2179	1287	81
				H	21	732	15	—	4	70	919	488	46
POLSON—Lake County ⊞ ST. JOSEPH HOSPITAL, Skyline Dr., Box 1010, Zip 59860; tel. 406/883-5377; E. R. Testerman, adm. **A**1a 9 10 **F**3 6 12 14 16 21 23 24 35 41 44 45 46 52; **S**5255	21	10	S		40	937	7	17.5	8	100	2176	1073	75
POPLAR—Roosevelt County COMMUNITY HOSPITAL, Zip 59255; tel. 406/768-3452; Jay Pottenger, adm. (Total facility includes 22 beds in nursing home-type unit) **A**9 10 **F**3 6 10 12 19 35 40 52	16	10	S	TF	44	790	25	56.8	6	94	1441	853	55
				H	22	750	7	—	6	94	929	592	34
RED LODGE—Carbon County ★ CARBON COUNTY MEMORIAL HOSPITAL, 600 W. 20th St., Box 580, Zip 59068; tel. 406/446-2345; Mark Teckmeyer, adm. (Total facility includes 24 beds in nursing home-type unit) **A**9 10 **F**2 6 14 19 23 32 35 40 45; **S**2235	23	10	S	TF	52	641	33	63.5	8	31	1294	673	32
				H	28	628	9	—	8	31	938	468	23
RONAN—Lake County ★ ST. LUKE COMMUNITY HOSPITAL, 901 26th St., Box J, Zip 59864; tel. 406/676-4441; James T. Oliverson, adm. (Total facility includes 43 beds in nursing home-type unit) **A**9 10 **F**1 6 16 19 23 35 40 45	23	10	S	TF	67	935	49	73.1	4	66	2615	1634	86
				H	24	854	7	—	4	66	2157	1266	59
ROUNDUP—Musselshell County ROUNDUP MEMORIAL HOSPITAL, 1202 Third St. W., P O Box 627, Zip 59072; tel. 406/323-2302; Fern E. Mikkelson, exec. dir. (Total facility includes 16 beds in nursing home-type unit) **A**10 **F**6 14 16 19 23 35 40 45; **S**0585	23	10	S	TF	33	315	21	63.6	6	25	1086	587	47
				H	17	284	6	—	6	25	813	463	20
SCOBEY—Daniels County DANIELS MEMORIAL HOSPITAL, Main & Fifth Sts., Box 400, Zip 59263; tel. 406/487-2296; Curtis Leibrand, adm. (Total facility includes 42 beds in nursing home-type unit) **A**9 10 **F**3 6 12 19 35	16	10	S	TF	50	216	33	62.3	6	23	955	472	41
				H	8	166	2	—	6	23	389	189	12
SHELBY—Toole County ★ TOOLE COUNTY HOSPITAL AND NURSING HOME, 640 Park Dr., P O Box P, Zip 59474; tel. 406/434-5536; Todd Hansen, adm. (Total facility includes 43 beds in nursing home-type unit) **A**9 10 **F**1 3 6 12 14 16 19 23 34 35 40 44 45 46	13	10	S	TF	63	1027	54	85.7	4	113	2787	1185	92
				H	20	1015	11	—	4	113	1955	754	49
SHERIDAN—Madison County RUBY VALLEY HOSPITAL, 220 E. Crofoot St., Box 336, Zip 59749; tel. 406/842-5778; M. Jane Evans, adm. **A**9 10 **F**3 35 40 45	16	10	S		18	212	2	11.1	4	10	458	269	14
SIDNEY—Richland County ★ COMMUNITY MEMORIAL HOSPITAL, 216 14th Ave. S.W., Box 1690, Zip 59270; tel. 406/482-2120; Peter Wise, adm. & chief exec. off. **A**9 10 **F**1 3 6 10 12 16 23 24 30 32 33 34 35 40 41 45 46	23	10	S		55	1813	20	36.4	10	226	5757	2246	126
ST. IGNATIUS—Lake County MISSION VALLEY HOSPITAL, Mission Dr., P O Box 310, Zip 59865; tel. 406/745-2700; J. T. Oliverson, adm. (Total facility includes 11 beds in nursing home-type unit) **A**9 10 **F**16 19 23 35 40 45 52	23	10	S	TF	29	547	4	16.0	4	70	1256	592	40
				H	18	526	4	—	4	70	1236	573	32
SUPERIOR—Mineral County MINERAL COUNTY HOSPITAL, Roosevelt & Brooklyn, Box 66, Zip 59872; tel. 406/822-4841; Madelyn Faller, exec. dir. (Total facility includes 20 beds in nursing home-type unit) **A**9 10 **F**1 3 6 12 14 16 19 23 35 45; **S**0585	23	10	S	TF	30	337	23	76.7	4	21	1217	635	42
				H	10	315	4	—	4	21	864	472	23
TERRY—Prairie County ★ PRAIRIE COMMUNITY HOSPITAL, 312 S. Adams Ave., Box 156, Zip 59349; tel. 406/637-5511; Earl K. Paulson, adm. (Total facility includes 14 beds in nursing home-type unit) **A**9 10 **F**19 35 45 46; **S**2235	16	10	S	TF	20	91	15	75.0	4	4	617	363	25
				H	6	83	2	—	4	4	319	177	11
TOWNSEND—Broadwater County BROADWATER COMMUNITY HOSPITAL, 100 N. Oak St., Zip 59644; tel. 406/266-3186; Barbara Kysar, adm. **A**9 10 **F**1 3 14 16 23 35 40 52	23	10	S		10	325	3	15.8	3	34	770	384	22
WARM SPRING—Deer Lodge County MONTANA STATE HOSPITAL, Zip 59756; tel. 406/693-2221; Jane Edwards, supt. **A**9 **F**12 14 16 24 32 42 48 50	12	12	S		32	1797	16	50.0	0	0	1329	848	61
WHITE SULPHUR SPRINGS—Meagher County MOUNTAINVIEW MEMORIAL HOSPITAL, 16 W. Main St., Box Q, Zip 59645; tel. 406/547-3321; M. E. Bedsaul, adm. (Total facility includes 31 beds in nursing home-type unit) **A**9 10 **F**1 3 14 19 23 35 40 41 45 52; **S**2235	23	10	S	TF	37	184	24	64.9	2	10	981	436	36
				H	6	161	1	—	2	10	393	174	28
WHITEFISH—Flathead County ★ NORTH VALLEY HOSPITAL, 6575 Hwy. 93 S., Zip 59937; tel. 406/862-2501; Dale Jessup, adm. (Total facility includes 56 beds in nursing home-type unit) **A**9 10 **F**1 3 6 14 16 19 21 23 35 40 44 45 47 53; **S**0585	23	10	S	TF	100	2094	70	70.0	7	324	5481	2911	175
				H	44	1981	21	—	7	324	4128	2440	116
WOLF POINT—Roosevelt County TRINITY HOSPITAL, 315 K St., Zip 59201; tel. 406/653-2100 **A**9 10 **F**3 6 14 16 19 28 30 34 35 40 41 45 47 48 52; **S**0585	23	10	S		42	1119	11	26.2	5	136	1894	1037	46

Hospital, Address, Telephone, Administrator, Approval and Facility Codes, Multihospital System Code	Classification Codes: Control	Service	Stay	Facilities	Inpatient Data: Beds	Admissions	Census	Occupancy (percent)	Newborn Data: Bassinets	Births	Expense (thousands of dollars): Total	Payroll	Personnel

★ American Hospital Association (AHA) membership
□ Joint Commission on Accreditation of Hospitals (JCAH) accreditation
+ American Osteopathic Hospital Association (AOHA) membership
O American Osteopathic Association (AOA) accreditation
Δ Commission on Accreditation of Rehabilitation Facilities (CARF) accreditation
Control codes 61, 63, 64, 71, 72 and 73 indicate hospitals listed by AOHA, but not registered by AHA. For definition of numerical codes, see page A2

Nebraska

Hospital	Control	Service	Stay	Facilities	Beds	Admissions	Census	Occupancy (percent)	Bassinets	Births	Total	Payroll	Personnel
AINSWORTH—Brown County													
BROWN COUNTY HOSPITAL, 945 E. Zero, Zip 69210; tel. 402/387-2800; Richard W. Martin, adm. **A**9 10 **F**1 6 16 23 34 35 37 44 45 50	13	10	S		25	380	7	28.0	4	28	965	527	37
ALBION—Boone County													
BOONE COUNTY COMMUNITY HOSPITAL, 723 W. Fairview St., P O Box 151, Zip 68620; tel. 402/395-2191; Jean Garten, adm. **A**9 10 **F**1 3 6 12 14 15 16 23 24 26 34 35 36 40 41 42 43 44 45 46 49 52	13	10	S		34	571	9	26.5	5	39	1269	548	43
ALLIANCE—Box Butte County													
□ BOX BUTTE GENERAL HOSPITAL, 2101 Box Butte Ave., P O Box 810, Zip 69301; tel. 308/762-6660; Mark E. Shellabarger, adm. **A**1a 9 10 **F**1 3 6 10 14 15 16 23 35 36 40 45	13	10	S		44	1570	17	37.0	6	255	2871	1475	90
ALMA—Harlan County													
★□ HARLAN COUNTY HOSPITAL, Zip 68920; tel. 308/928-2151; Ladonna Robison RN, adm. **A**1a 9 10 **F**1 16 23 35 41 45; **S**1535	13	10	S		25	491	8	32.0	4	40	1010	482	33
ATKINSON—Holt County													
WEST HOLT MEMORIAL HOSPITAL, Pearl St., Zip 68713; tel. 402/925-2811; Dwight P. Daniels, adm. **A**9 10 **F**1 6 15 23 35 36 41 45	23	10	S		18	727	7	38.9	8	134	958	450	33
AUBURN—Nemaha County													
★□ NEMAHA COUNTY HOSPITAL, 2022 13th St., Zip 68305; tel. 402/274-4366; Glen Krueger, adm. **A**1a 9 10 **F**1 3 6 14 16 23 34 35 40 45 50	13	10	S		42	1029	17	40.5	4	85	1618	881	59
AURORA—Hamilton County													
★□ MEMORIAL HOSPITAL, 1423 Seventh St., Zip 68818; tel. 402/694-3171; Eldon A. Wall, adm. (Total facility includes 45 beds in nursing home-type unit) **A**1a 9 10 **F**1 6 16 19 20 23 34 35 36 40 45 46	23	10	S	TF	86	1122	56	65.1	8	143	2857	1368	103
				H	41	1074	14	—	8	143	2308	987	70
BASSETT—Rock County													
ROCK COUNTY HOSPITAL, Zip 68714; tel. 402/684-3366; Alma Sandall, adm. (Nonreporting) **A**9 10	13	10	S		20	—	—	—	—	—	—	—	—
BEATRICE—Gage County													
★□ BEATRICE COMMUNITY HOSPITAL AND HEALTH CENTER, 1110 N. Tenth St., Zip 68310; tel. 402/228-3344; Kenneth J. Zimmerman, adm. (Total facility includes 87 beds in nursing home-type unit) **A**1a 9 10 **F**1 3 6 10 14 15 16 19 21 23 24 30 33 34 35 40 41 44 45 46 47 48 50	23	10	S	TF	183	2119	114	62.3	8	289	7577	3814	272
				H	96	2081	33	—	8	289	—	—	225
BENKELMAN—Dundy County													
DUNDY COUNTY HOSPITAL, Hospital Rd., Box 626, Zip 69021; tel. 308/423-2670; Daniel L. Dennis, adm. (Nonreporting) **A**9 10	13	10	S		28	—	—	—	—	—	—	—	—
BLAIR—Washington County													
★□ MEMORIAL COMMUNITY HOSPITAL, 810 N. 22nd St., Zip 68008; tel. 402/426-2182; Gareth D. Weeks, adm. **A**1a 9 10 **F**1 3 10 12 14 15 16 23 24 34 35 36 41 44 45 46	23	10	S		46	1280	17	37.0	8	137	3387	1946	109
BRIDGEPORT—Morrill County													
★ MORRILL COUNTY COMMUNITY HOSPITAL, 1313 S. St., Zip 69336; tel. 308/262-1616; Julie Garsha, adm. (Nonreporting) **A**9 10	13	10	S		23	—	—	—	—	—	—	—	—
BROKEN BOW—Custer County													
JENNIE M. MELHAM MEMORIAL MEDICAL CENTER, Zip 68822; tel. 308/872-6891; Michael Steckler, adm. (Total facility includes 70 beds in nursing home-type unit) **A**9 10 **F**1 3 6 12 14 16 19 21 23 24 34 35 36 40 41 44 45	23	10	S	TF	113	836	80	70.8	6	123	—	—	111
				H	43	772	11	—	6	123	—	—	62
BURWELL—Garfield County													
COMMUNITY MEMORIAL HOSPITAL, Zip 68823; tel. 308/346-4440; Wilber Kizer, adm. (Total facility includes 58 beds in nursing home-type unit) **A**9 10 **F**1 3 6 14 19 34 35 40 46	23	10	S	TF	88	354	50	56.8	6	14	931	526	59
				H	30	283	3	—	6	14	536	255	27
CALLAWAY—Custer County													
CALLAWAY HOSPITAL DISTRICT, 211 Kimball, Box 248, Zip 68825; tel. 308/836-2228; Marvin Neth, adm. **A**9 10 **F**1 3 14 16 34 35 43 45	16	10	S		12	345	5	41.7	5	26	753	352	22
CAMBRIDGE—Furnas County													
★ CAMBRIDGE MEMORIAL HOSPITAL, W. Hwy. 6 & 34, Zip 69022; tel. 308/697-3329; Don Harpst, adm. (Total facility includes 36 beds in nursing home-type unit) **A**9 10 **F**1 6 14 15 16 19 21 23 24 30 33 35 37 40 41 44 45 52; **S**2235	23	10	S	TF	67	482	46	68.7	6	36	1731	868	72
				H	31	452	12	—	6	36	1256	601	54
CENTRAL CITY—Merrick County													
LITZENBERG MEMORIAL COUNTY HOSPITAL, 1715 26th St., Zip 68826; tel. 308/946-3015; William L. Ferguson, adm. (Nonreporting) **A**9 10	13	10	S		79	—	—	—	—	—	—	—	—
CHADRON—Dawes County													
★ CHADRON COMMUNITY HOSPITAL, 821 Morehead St., Zip 69337; tel. 308/432-5586; Richard L. Terry, adm. (Nonreporting) **A**9 10	23	10	S		42	—	—	—	—	—	—	—	—
COLUMBUS—Platte County													
★□ COLUMBUS COMMUNITY HOSPITAL, 3111 19th St., Zip 68601; tel. 402/564-7118; Donald H. Zornes, adm. (Total facility includes 13 beds in nursing home-type unit) **A**1a 9 10 **F**1 3 6 10 14 15 16 19 23 34 35 40 41 45	23	10	S	TF	81	2901	35	43.2	13	578	6117	3002	178
				H	68	2887	35	—	13	578	6103	2990	170
COZAD—Dawson County													
COZAD COMMUNITY HOSPITAL, P O Box 108, Zip 69130; tel. 308/784-2261; Harold Lewis, adm. **A**9 10 **F**1 2 21 23 35 36 40 41 45 52	16	10	S		30	491	6	20.0	6	68	1323	—	59
CRAWFORD—Dawes County													
COMMUNITY MEMORIAL HOSPITAL, 11 Paddock St., P O Box 272, Zip 69339; tel. 308/665-1770; M. A. Anderson, actg. adm. (Nonreporting) **A**9 10	23	10	S		20	—	—	—	—	—	—	—	—
CREIGHTON—Knox County													
★□ LUNDBERG MEMORIAL HOSPITAL, Box 167, Zip 68729; tel. 402/358-3322; Linda J. Neese, adm. **A**1a 9 10 **F**1 6 16 23 24 35 40 41 44 45; **S**2235	23	10	S		38	428	7	18.4	8	45	1285	608	43
CRETE—Saline County													
★ CRETE MUNICIPAL HOSPITAL, 1500 Grove Sts., Zip 68333; tel. 402/826-2154; Kenneth M. Bors, adm. (Total facility includes 22 beds in nursing home-type unit) **A**9 10 **F**1 6 12 14 15 19 23 35 40 45	14	10	S	TF	57	836	40	70.2	8	66	1631	912	65
				H	35	829	19	—	8	66	1292	774	54
DAVID CITY—Butler County													
★ BUTLER COUNTY HOSPITAL, 372 S. Ninth St., Zip 68632; tel. 402/367-3115; Joellen Vrbka, adm. **A**9 10 **F**1 6 15 16 23 41 44	13	10	S		34	969	17	50.0	8	130	1801	1004	63

Hospital, Address, Telephone, Administrator, Approval and Facility Codes, Multihospital System Code	Classification Codes				Inpatient Data				Newborn Data		Expense (thousands of dollars)		
★ American Hospital Association (AHA) membership □ Joint Commission on Accreditation of Hospitals (JCAH) accreditation + American Osteopathic Hospital Association (AOHA) membership ○ American Osteopathic Association (AOA) accreditation Δ Commission on Accreditation of Rehabilitation Facilities (CARF) accreditation Control codes 61, 63, 64, 71, 72 and 73 indicate hospitals listed by AOHA, but not registered by AHA. For definition of numerical codes, see page A2	Control	Service	Stay	Facilities	Beds	Admissions	Census	Occupancy (percent)	Bassinets	Births	Total	Payroll	Personnel
FAIRBURY—Jefferson County													
★□ JEFFERSON COUNTY MEMORIAL HOSPITAL, 2200 N. H St., Box 277, Zip 68352; tel. 402/729-3351; Verlyn Foster, adm. (Total facility includes 42 beds in nursing home-type unit) **A**1a 9 10 **F**1 3 12 14 15 19 23 26 30 35 40 41 45	23	10	S	TF H	91 49	1097 1072	51 11	56.0 —	8 8	82 82	2325 1809	1147 809	72 59
FALLS CITY—Richardson County													
★ COMMUNITY HOSPITAL, 2307 Barada St., Zip 68355; tel. 402/245-2428; Victor Lee, adm. **A**9 10 **F**1 3 6 10 11 16 23 35 36 40 44 45 46; **S**1535	23	10	S		49	1136	16	32.7	8	117	1923	939	57
FRANKLIN—Franklin County													
★ FRANKLIN COUNTY MEMORIAL HOSPITAL, 1406 Q St., Box 127, Zip 68939; tel. 308/425-6221; John M. Ramsay, adm. **A**9 10 **F**1 14 15 16 30 35	13	10	S		20	285	4	20.0	4	19	684	335	32
FREMONT—Dodge County													
★□ MEMORIAL HOSPITAL OF DODGE COUNTY (Includes Memorial Hospital Annex), 450 E. 23rd St., Zip 68025; tel. 402/721-1610; Vincent J. O'Connor Jr., pres. (Total facility includes 133 beds in nursing home-type unit) **A**1a 9 10 **F**1 3 6 10 12 15 16 19 23 26 34 35 40 41 44 45 47 52 53	13	10	S	TF H	245 112	4719 4550	190 63	77.6 —	17 17	573 573	16245 15217	8370 7492	447 373
FRIEND—Saline County													
WARREN MEMORIAL HOSPITAL, 905 Second St., Zip 68359; tel. 402/947-2541; Michael R. Bowman, adm. (Nonreporting) **A**9 10	14	10	S		15	—	—	—	—	—	—	—	—
FULLERTON—Nance County													
★ FULLERTON MEMORIAL HOSPITAL, 903 Broadway, P O Box 370, Zip 68638; tel. 308/536-2474; Judy L. Palmer, adm. (Nonreporting) **A**9 10	14	10	S		20	—	—	—	—	—	—	—	—
GENEVA—Fillmore County													
FILLMORE COUNTY HOSPITAL, 1325 H St., Zip 68361; tel. 402/759-3167; Larry Warrelmann, adm. (Total facility includes 20 beds in nursing home-type unit) **A**9 10 **F**1 6 15 19 23 26 34 35 36 37 41 44 45 49	13	10	S	TF H	59 39	814 789	33 14	55.9 —	8 8	77 77	1738 —	913 —	74 61
GENOA—Nance County													
GENOA COMMUNITY HOSPITAL, 706 Ewing Ave., Zip 68640; tel. 402/993-2283; Neal Simley, adm. (Nonreporting) **A**9 10	33	10	S		20	—	—	—	—	—	—	—	—
GORDON—Sheridan County													
★ GORDON MEMORIAL HOSPITAL DISTRICT, 300 E. Eighth St., Zip 69343; tel. 308/282-0401; Charles R. Miller, adm. **A**9 10 **F**1 3 6 12 14 15 16 23 34 35 40 41 45 46 47	16	10	S		45	1136	17	37.8	5	157	2159	1101	90
GOTHENBURG—Dawson County													
GOTHENBURG MEMORIAL HOSPITAL, 910 20th St., Zip 69138; tel. 308/537-3661; Roger Heidebrink, adm. (Total facility includes 28 beds in nursing home-type unit) **A**9 10 **F**1 6 14 19 23 35 45	16	10	S	TF H	48 20	616 591	33 7	68.8 —	6 6	80 80	1495 1110	852 597	71 40
GRAND ISLAND—Hall County													
★□ SAINT FRANCIS MEDICAL CENTER, 2620 W. Faidley Ave., Box 2118, Zip 68802; tel. 308/384-4600; Cale E. Neal, pres. **A**1a 9 10 **F**1 3 5 10 12 14 15 16 21 23 30 33 35 36 38 40 41 44 45 46 47 52 53; **S**5115	21	10	S		131	4396	68	51.9	17	802	14671	6282	357
★□ VETERANS ADMINISTRATION MEDICAL CENTER, 2201 N. Broadwell Ave., Zip 68803; tel. 308/382-3660; Margaret D. Etheridge, dir. (Total facility includes 42 beds in nursing home-type unit) **A**1a **F**1 3 10 12 14 15 16 19 20 23 24 26 28 30 32 33 34 35 42 44 46 48 49 50	45	10	S	TF H	204 162	3098 2984	130 95	63.7 —	0 0	0 0	13244 —	8506 —	339 322
GRANT—Perkins County													
PERKINS COUNTY COMMUNITY HOSPITAL (Includes Golden Ours Convalescent Home), 902 Central Ave., Zip 69140; tel. 308/352-4391; Donald Benge, adm. (Nonreporting) **A**9 10	13	10	S		84	—	—	—	—	—	—	—	—
HASTINGS—Adams County													
HASTINGS REGIONAL CENTER (Psychiatric, Alcoholism and Other Chemical Dependency), Box 579, Zip 68901; tel. 402/463-2471; Michael Sheehan, chief exec. off. **A**9 10 **F**15 24 27 28 30 32 33 34 42 44 46 48	12	49	L		232	1354	223	90.7	0	0	10793	7681	419
★□ MARY LANNING MEMORIAL HOSPITAL, 715 N. St. Joseph Ave., Zip 68901; tel. 402/463-4521; James W. Kenney, adm. **A**1a 2 6 9 10 **F**1 3 5 6 7 8 9 10 11 12 14 15 16 21 23 35 36 37 38 40 41 44 45 51 52 53	23	10	S		195	5319	77	39.5	12	616	16653	8769	570
HEBRON—Thayer County													
★ THAYER COUNTY MEMORIAL HOSPITAL, 120 Park Ave., P O Box 49, Zip 68370; tel. 402/768-6041; Marilyn N. Cooper, adm. **A**9 10 **F**1 6 15 35 40 45 47; **S**2235	23	10	S		18	364	4	22.2	6	32	814	350	26
HENDERSON—York County													
HENDERSON COMMUNITY HOSPITAL, 1621 Front St., Zip 68371; tel. 402/723-4512; Stan Voth, adm. (Nonreporting) **A**9 10	23	10	S		56	—	—	—	—	—	—	—	—
HOLDREGE—Phelps County													
★□ PHELPS MEMORIAL HEALTH CENTER, 1220 Miller St., P O Box 630, Zip 68949; tel. 308/995-2211; Rex J. Kelly, adm. **A**1a 9 10 **F**1 3 6 12 14 15 16 23 34 35 40 44 45	23	10	S		55	1993	30	51.7	7	120	4111	2043	119
HUMBOLDT—Richardson County													
COMMUNITY MEMORIAL HOSPITAL, 1128 Grand Ave., Zip 68376; tel. 402/862-2231; John L. Fischer, adm. (Nonreporting) **A**9 10	23	10	S		35	—	—	—	—	—	—	—	—
IMPERIAL—Chase County													
CHASE COUNTY COMMUNITY HOSPITAL, 600 W. 12th St., Zip 69033; tel. 308/882-7111; William K. McCamley, adm. (Nonreporting) **A**9 10	13	10	S		26	—	—	—	—	—	—	—	—
KEARNEY—Buffalo County													
★□ GOOD SAMARITAN HOSPITAL, 31st St. & Central Ave., Zip 68847; tel. 308/236-8511; LeRoy E. Rheault, pres. **A**1a 2 9 10 **F**1 3 6 7 8 9 10 11 12 14 15 16 20 21 23 24 26 27 30 34 35 36 40 41 43 44 45 46 47 48 49 51 52 53; **S**5115	21	10	S		185	7001	121	65.4	12	808	24264	9874	487
KIMBALL—Kimball County													
KIMBALL COUNTY HOSPITAL, 505 S. Burg St., Zip 69145; tel. 308/235-3621; Barbara Rosendahl RN, adm. **A**9 10 **F**1 2 6 14 15 16 19 23 34 35 37 40 41 43 45 50 52	13	10	S		30	668	11	36.7	4	57	1265	637	44
LEXINGTON—Dawson County													
★□ TRI-COUNTY AREA HOSPITAL, 13th & Erie Sts., P O Box 980, Zip 68850; tel. 308/324-5651; Calvin A. Hiner, adm. **A**1a 9 10 **F**1 6 12 14 15 16 21 23 26 35 36 45 50	16	10	S		40	1426	14	35.0	8	165	2496	1279	75
LINCOLN—Lancaster County													
★□ BRYAN MEMORIAL HOSPITAL, 1600 S. 48th St., Zip 68506; tel. 402/489-0200; R. Lynn Wilson, pres. **A**1a 2 3 5 6 9 10 **F**1 2 3 4 6 9 10 13 15 16 20 23 27 33 35 36 37 40 45 46 52 53 54	21	10	S		270	11461	189	70.0	20	870	52273	21907	1152
★□ LINCOLN GENERAL HOSPITAL, 2300 S. 16th St., Zip 68502; tel. 402/475-1011; Arlan L. Stromberg, adm. **A**1a 2 3 5 9 10 **F**1 3 5 6 7 8 9 10 11 12 14 15 16 20 23 27 28 29 30 32 33 34 35 36 37 40 42 43 45 46 47 48 49 50 52 53	14	10	S		290	8198	159	55.0	36	694	31701	14219	770
□ LINCOLN REGIONAL CENTER, Folsom & Van Dorn Sts., Box 94949, Zip 68509; tel. 402/471-4444; Klaus Hartmann MD, supt.; Don F. Wermers, dir. support servs **A**1b 3 5 9 10 **F**15 24 29 30 32 33 42 43 46 47	12	22	L		233	552	221	94.8	0	0	10724	7113	439

Hospital, Address, Telephone, Administrator, Approval and Facility Codes, Multihospital System Code	Classification Codes				Inpatient Data				Newborn Data		Expense (thousands of dollars)		
★ American Hospital Association (AHA) membership □ Joint Commission on Accreditation of Hospitals (JCAH) accreditation + American Osteopathic Hospital Association (AOHA) membership ○ American Osteopathic Association (AOA) accreditation Δ Commission on Accreditation of Rehabilitation Facilities (CARF) accreditation Control codes 61, 63, 64, 71, 72 and 73 indicate hospitals listed by AOHA, but not registered by AHA. For definition of numerical codes, see page A2	Control	Service	Stay	Facilities	Beds	Admissions	Census	Occupancy (percent)	Bassinets	Births	Total	Payroll	Personnel
★ Δ MADONNA CENTERS, 2200 S. 52nd St., Zip 68506; tel. 402/489-7102; Sr. Phyllis Hunhoff, chief exec. off. (Total facility includes 208 beds in nursing home-type unit) **A**7 10 **F**3 15 19 23 24 26 33 34 42 44 45 46 47 50	21	46	L	TF H	252 44	1007 346	242 38	96.0 —	0 0	0 0	9986 3666	6603 2668	465 —
⊞ ST. ELIZABETH COMMUNITY HEALTH CENTER, 555 S. 70th St., Zip 68510; tel. 402/489-7181; Robert J. Lanik, pres. **A**1a 2 3 5 9 10 **F**1 3 6 9 10 15 16 20 22 23 26 34 35 36 40 41 45 46 47 51 52 53; **S**5115	21	10	S		218	8723	113	51.8	30	1924	30108	13304	714
UNIVERSITY HEALTH CENTER, UNIVERSITY OF NEBRASKA, 15th & U. Sts., Zip 68588; tel. 402/472-2102; Gerald J. Fleischli MD, med. dir. & interim adm. (Nonreporting)	12	11	S		14	—	—	—	—	—	—	—	—
⊞ VETERANS ADMINISTRATION MEDICAL CENTER, 600 S. 70th St., Zip 68510; tel. 402/489-3802; Max L. Lybarger, dir. **A**1a 2 3 5 **F**1 2 3 6 10 12 14 15 16 20 23 24 26 27 28 29 30 32 33 34 35 42 44 46 48 49	45	10	S		180	4121	119	66.1	0	0	18674	12356	434
LYNCH—Boyd County													
NIOBRARA VALLEY HOSPITAL, Zip 68746; tel. 402/569-2451; Douglas E. Maw, adm. **A**9 10 **F**1 14 16 23 34 36 45	23	10	S		29	349	4	13.8	2	7	—	—	37
MCCOOK—Red Willow County													
⊞ COMMUNITY HOSPITAL, 1301 E. H St., P O Box 310, Zip 69001; tel. 308/345-2650; Gary Bieganski, pres. **A**1a 9 10 **F**1 3 6 10 14 15 16 23 35 40 44 45 46 47 52	23	10	S		56	1780	22	39.3	6	223	4975	2162	132
MINDEN—Kearney County													
★ KEARNEY COUNTY COMMUNITY HOSPITAL, 727 E. First St., Zip 68959; tel. 308/832-1440; Marcia Shannon, adm. (Total facility includes 50 beds in nursing home-type unit) **A**9 10 **F**1 16 19 23 24 26 34 35 36 42 44 45 46	13	10	S	TF H	80 30	500 469	56 6	70.0 —	7 7	52 52	— —	— —	56 —
NEBRASKA CITY—Otoe County													
⊞ ST. MARY'S HOSPITAL, 1314 Third Ave., Zip 68410; tel. 402/873-3321; Michael Atkins, adm. **A**1a 9 10 **F**1 3 6 10 11 14 15 16 23 35 41 44 45 46 49	21	10	S		49	1154	16	32.0	10	115	3051	1316	82
NELIGH—Antelope County													
★ ANTELOPE MEMORIAL HOSPITAL, 102 W. Ninth St., Zip 68756; tel. 402/887-4151; Jack W. Green, adm. **A**9 10 **F**1 6 14 15 16 23 26 34 35 37 41 44 45 46	23	10	S		49	846	12	24.5	5	88	1736	910	58
NORFOLK—Madison County													
⊞ LUTHERAN COMMUNITY HOSPITAL, 2700 Norfolk Ave., Box 869, Zip 68701; tel. 402/371-4880; Daryl Mackender, adm. **A**1a 9 10 **F**1 3 6 15 16 20 23 35 36 37 40 41 45	23	10	S		78	2800	36	46.2	12	487	7563	3491	208
□ NORFOLK REGIONAL CENTER, 1700 N. Victory Rd., Box 1209, Zip 68701; tel. 402/371-4343; Allen E. McElravy, adm. **A**1b 9 **F**15 19 23 24 30 32 33 42 44 46 50	12	22	L		140	437	134	95.7	0	0	6665	4505	276
⊞ OUR LADY OF LOURDES HOSPITAL, 1500 Koenigstein Ave., Zip 68701; tel. 402/371-3402; Carl I. Maltas, adm. (Total facility includes 12 beds in nursing home-type unit) **A**1a 9 10 **F**1 3 6 10 15 19 35 36 40 45 46 53; **S**2855	21	10	S	TF H	83 71	2300 2182	38 29	45.8 —	12 12	322 322	6903 —	2920 —	190 —
NORTH PLATTE—Lincoln County													
⊞ GREAT PLAINS REGIONAL MEDICAL CENTER, 601 W. Leota St., Box 1167, Zip 69101; tel. 308/534-9310; Cindy Bradley, adm. **A**1a 9 10 **F**1 3 6 10 12 14 15 16 20 21 24 27 30 32 33 35 40 41 42 44 45 46 51 52 53; **S**1755	23	10	S		130	4696	64	49.2	15	598	13158	5585	312
O'NEILL—Holt County													
⊞ ST. ANTHONY'S HOSPITAL, Second & Adams Sts., Zip 68763; tel. 402/336-2611; Larry W. Veitz, adm. **A**1a 10 **F**1 6 14 15 16 23 34 35 40 45 46; **S**5395	21	10	S		44	1011	16	36.4	10	121	2461	1095	64
OAKLAND—Burt County													
★ OAKLAND MEMORIAL HOSPITAL, 601 E. Second St., Zip 68045; tel. 402/685-5601; Craig Hanson, adm. **A**9 10 **F**1 15 16 23 35 36 37 40 45 52; **S**2235	23	10	S		23	325	4	17.4	4	18	774	381	29
OFFUTT AIR FORCE BASE—Sarpy County													
□ EHRLING BERGQUIST U. S. AIR FORCE REGIONAL HOSPITAL, Zip 68113; tel. 402/294-7312; Col. Duane W. Newton, adm. **A**1a **F**3 6 12 14 15 16 23 28 34 35 37 40 46 47	41	10	S		111	5808	61	52.6	26	878	—	—	704
OGALLALA—Keith County													
OGALLALA COMMUNITY HOSPITAL, 300 E. Tenth St., Zip 69153; tel. 308/284-4011; Robert W. Cottrell, adm. (Nonreporting) **A**9 10	23	10	S		49	—	—	—	—	—	—	—	—
OMAHA—Douglas County													
⊞ AMI SAINT JOSEPH HOSPITAL (Formerly Saint Joseph Hospital), 601 N. 30th St., Zip 68131; tel. 402/449-4000; Kenneth G. Hermann, exec. dir. **A**1a b 2 3 5 8 10 **F**1 3 4 5 6 7 8 9 10 11 12 13 14 15 16 17 20 23 24 26 34 35 36 40 45 46 51 52 53 54; **S**0125	33	10	S		293	12583	208	71.2	16	1251	88818	30367	1498
★ AMI ST. JOSEPH CENTER FOR MENTAL HEALTH (Formerly St. Joseph Center for Mental Health), 819 Dorcas, Zip 68108; tel. 402/449-4653; Johanna M. Anderson RN, exec. dir. **A**9 **F**24 28 29 30 32 33 42 46 49; **S**0125	33	22	S		131	1666	101	80.8	0	0	10510	4474	197
⊞ ARCHBISHOP BERGAN MERCY HOSPITAL, 7500 Mercy Rd., Zip 68124; tel. 402/398-6060; Larry C. Rennecker, pres. (Total facility includes 250 beds in nursing home-type unit) **A**1a 2 3 5 9 10 **F**1 3 5 6 7 8 9 10 11 12 14 15 16 17 19 20 21 23 24 26 35 36 40 41 44 45 46 47 50 51 52 53 54; **S**5175	21	10	S	TF H	619 369	14849 13909	454 241	81.2 —	48 48	2146 2146	— —	— —	1302 1111
⊞ BISHOP CLARKSON MEMORIAL HOSPITAL, Dewey Ave. & 44th St., Zip 68105; tel. 402/559-2000; D. Max Francis, adm. **A**1a 2 3 5 9 10 **F**1 2 3 4 6 7 8 9 10 11 12 13 14 15 16 20 21 23 24 26 33 35 36 37 40 44 46 50 53 54	23	10	S		371	13171	242	61.9	36	553	70180	30105	1477
□ BOYS TOWN NATIONAL INSTITUTE FOR COMMUNICATION DISORDERS IN CHILDREN, 555 N. 30th St., Zip 68131; tel. 402/449-6511; Jack R. McCullough, adm. (Nonreporting) **A**1a 9 10	23	50	S		16	—	—	—	—	—	—	—	—
⊞ CHILDRENS MEMORIAL HOSPITAL, 8301 Dodge St., Zip 68114; tel. 402/390-5400; Gary A. Perkins, pres. **A**1a 3 5 9 10 **F**1 4 6 10 12 14 15 16 23 24 33 34 35 38 42 44 45 46 51 53 54	23	50	S		100	3842	50	50.0	0	0	17813	6676	274
DOUGLAS COUNTY HOSPITAL, 4102 Woolworth Ave., Zip 68105; tel. 402/444-7000; Helen Bergstrom, adm. (Nonreporting) **A**9 10	13	49	S		329	—	—	—	—	—	—	—	—
EHRLING BERGQUIST U. S. AIR FORCE REGIONAL HOSPITAL, See Offutt Air Force Base													
⊞ Δ IMMANUEL MEDICAL CENTER, 6901 N. 72nd St., Zip 68122; tel. 402/572-2121; Charles J. Marr, pres. & chief exec. off. (Total facility includes 200 beds in nursing home-type unit) **A**1a 2 7 9 10 **F**1 2 3 4 5 6 7 8 9 10 11 12 14 15 16 19 20 23 24 25 26 27 28 29 30 32 33 34 35 36 40 42 44 45 46 47 48 49 50 52 53 54	21	10	S	TF H	601 401	9824 9731	437 241	72.7 —	24 24	720 720	56122 51769	26457 24169	1396 1256
LUTHERAN GENERAL HOSPITAL, See Lutheran Medical Center													
⊞ LUTHERAN MEDICAL CENTER (Includes Lutheran General Hospital; Richard H. Young Memorial Hospital), Harney at 26th St., Zip 68105; Mailing Address Box 3434, Zip 68103; tel. 402/536-6600; Sandra Carson, adm. **A**1a b 2 9 10 **F**1 3 6 7 8 10 11 12 14 15 16 20 23 24 26 27 28 30 32 33 34 35 41 42 45 46 48 50 53	21	10	S		258	4163	153	67.1	0	0	23687	10412	558
⊞ METHODIST HOSPITAL (Includes Methodist Midtown), 8303 Dodge St., Zip 68114; tel. 402/390-4000; Stephen D. Long, pres. & chief exec. off. **A**1a 2 3 5 6 9 10 **F**1 2 3 4 6 7 8 9 10 11 12 14 15 16 17 19 23 24 25 26 34 35 36 37 39 40 41 42 43 44 45 46 47 48 49 50 53 54; **S**9265	21	10	S		667	15809	310	43.5	32	2791	67475	30962	1454

Hospital, Address, Telephone, Administrator, Approval and Facility Codes, Multihospital System Code	Classification Codes				Inpatient Data				Newborn Data		Expense (thousands of dollars)		
★ American Hospital Association (AHA) membership □ Joint Commission on Accreditation of Hospitals (JCAH) accreditation + American Osteopathic Hospital Association (AOHA) membership ○ American Osteopathic Association (AOA) accreditation Δ Commission on Accreditation of Rehabilitation Facilities (CARF) accreditation Control codes 61 63, 64, 71, 72 and 73 indicate hospitals listed by AOHA, but not registered by AHA. For definition of numerical codes, see page A2	Control	Service	Stay	Facilities	Beds	Admissions	Census	Occupancy (percent)	Bassinets	Births	Total	Payroll	Personnel
RICHARD H. YOUNG MEMORIAL HOSPITAL, See Lutheran Medical Center													
SAINT JOSEPH HOSPITAL, See AMI Saint Joseph Hospital													
ST. JOSEPH CENTER FOR MENTAL HEALTH, See AMI St. Joseph Center for Mental Health													
★□ UNIVERSITY HOSPITAL -UNIVERSITY OF NEBRASKA (Includes University Psychiatric Serivces, 602 S. 45th St., Zip 68106; tel. 402/559-5000; Brent R. Stevenson, interim dir.), 42nd St. & Dewey Ave., Zip 68105; tel. 402/559-4000; Brent R. Stevenson, interim dir. **A**1a b 2 3 5 8 9 10 **F**1 3 4 5 6 7 8 9 10 11 12 13 14 15 16 17 21 23 24 26 27 28 30 32 33 34 35 36 37 38 40 41 42 44 45 46 47 50 51 52 53 54	12	10	S		356	9526	227	63.8	18	1076	74647	31967	1727
UNIVERSITY PSYCHIATRIC SERIVCES, See University Hospital-University of Nebraska													
★□ VETERANS ADMINISTRATION MEDICAL CENTER, 4101 Woolworth Ave., Zip 68105; tel. 402/346-8800; Roderick L. Turcotte, dir. **A**1a 3 5 8 **F**1 3 6 9 10 11 12 14 15 16 20 23 24 26 27 28 29 30 32 33 34 42 43 44 46 48 49 53 54	45	10	S		374	8296	258	69.0	0	0	44464	23422	931
ORD—Valley County													
VALLEY COUNTY HOSPITAL, 217 Westridge Dr., Zip 68862; tel. 308/728-3211; Ronald Edzards, adm. (Total facility includes 73 beds in nursing home-type unit) **A**9 10 **F**1 14 15 19 34 35 36 45	13	10	S	TF	99	832	78	78.8	8	106	1678	944	94
				H	26	741	7	—	8	106	—	—	44
OSCEOLA—Polk County													
ANNIE JEFFREY MEMORIAL COUNTY HOSPITAL, Zip 68651; tel. 402/747-2031; Don Buller, adm. (Nonreporting) **A**9 10	13	10	S		36	—	—	—	—	—	—	—	—
OSHKOSH—Garden County													
GARDEN COUNTY HOSPITAL, Zip 69154; tel. 308/772-3283; Donna I. Fiesterman, adm. (Total facility includes 40 beds in nursing home-type unit) **A**9 10 **F**1 2 6 16 19 23 34 35 40 44 45 50	13	10	S	TF	60	471	38	63.3	3	30	1133	645	53
				H	20	390	4	—	3	30	720	391	37
OSMOND—Pierce County													
★ OSMOND GENERAL HOSPITAL, Zip 68765; tel. 402/748-3393; Leonard R. Frodyma, adm. **A**9 10 **F**1 6 14 15 16 23 35 40 41 45 50	23	10	S		30	935	15	50.0	6	118	1347	750	46
OXFORD—Furnas County													
★ FRITZER MEMORIAL HOSPITAL, 811 Howell St., Box 128, Zip 68967; tel. 308/824-3271; Susan Peterson, interim adm. **A**9 10 **F**1 6 12 14 15 16 23 24 35 37 41 42 43 44 45	23	10	S		20	324	4	20.0	6	6	607	303	15
PAPILLION—Sarpy County													
★□ MIDLANDS COMMUNITY HOSPITAL, 11111 S. 84th St., Zip 68046; tel. 402/593-3000; Don M. Chase, adm. **A**1a 10 **F**1 3 6 10 11 12 14 15 16 27 30 32 34 35 36 40 42 45 46 48 49 52 53; **S**1755	23	10	S		155	3697	75	48.4	18	445	14893	6320	370
PAWNEE CITY—Pawnee County													
PAWNEE COUNTY MEMORIAL HOSPITAL, Zip 68420; tel. 402/852-2231; James A. Kubik, adm. **A**9 10 **F**1 15 16 23 30 34 35 37 44 45	13	10	S		23	388	5	21.7	6	38	916	424	35
PENDER—Thurston County													
★ PENDER COMMUNITY HOSPITAL, 603 Earl St., Box 100, Zip 68047; tel. 402/385-3083; Kenneth D. Olsson, adm. **A**9 10 **F**1 3 6 10 14 16 23 26 35 40 41 42 44 45 47; **S**2235	23	10	S		39	835	11	26.2	7	96	1738	858	50
PLAINVIEW—Pierce County													
□ PLAINVIEW PUBLIC HOSPITAL, Zip 68769; tel. 402/582-4245; Vernon Minnis, adm. **A**1a 9 10 **F**1 6 16 23 35 45	14	10	S		29	571	7	24.1	8	38	798	387	28
RED CLOUD—Webster County													
WEBSTER COUNTY COMMUNITY HOSPITAL, Sixth Ave. & Franklin St., Zip 68970; tel. 402/746-2291; Roy M. Vap, adm. (Nonreporting) **A**9 10	13	10	S		24	—	—	—	—	—	—	—	—
SARGENT—Custer County													
SARGENT DISTRICT HOSPITAL, Zip 68874; tel. 308/527-3414; Audrey M. Peterson, adm. **A**9 10 **F**1 6 14 23 35 41	16	10	S		18	259	3	16.7	2	15	—	—	30
SCHUYLER—Colfax County													
★□ MEMORIAL HOSPITAL, 104 W. 17th St., Zip 68661; tel. 402/352-2441; Lynn Wattier, adm. (Nonreporting) **A**1a 9 10	23	10	S		26	—	—	—	—	—	—	—	—
SCOTTSBLUFF—Scotts Bluff County													
★□ WEST NEBRASKA GENERAL HOSPITAL, 4021 Ave. B, Zip 69361; tel. 308/635-3711; David M. Nitschke, pres. **A**1a 2 6 9 10 **F**1 3 5 6 7 8 9 10 11 12 15 16 20 21 23 24 26 27 28 30 32 34 35 36 38 40 41 44 45 46 47 48 49 50 52 53	21	10	S		228	8328	151	66.2	20	800	28217	11887	645
SEWARD—Seward County													
MEMORIAL HOSPITAL, 300 N. Columbia Ave., Zip 68434; tel. 402/643-2971; Douglas W. Ellis, adm. (Total facility includes 12 beds in nursing home-type unit) **A**9 10 **F**1 6 10 12 16 19 23 30 35 41 44 46	23	10	S	TF	49	1775	20	40.8	6	100	—	—	78
				H	37	1709	11	—	6	100	—	—	—
SIDNEY—Cheyenne County													
MEMORIAL HOSPITAL AND HOME, Seventh & Osage Sts., Zip 69162; tel. 308/254-5825; Robert L. Driewer, chief exec. off. (Total facility includes 52 beds in nursing home-type unit) **A**9 10 **F**1 3 6 12 16 19 23 24 34 35 41 42 43 45 46 47	23	10	S	TF	115	1695	66	57.4	6	179	3920	2152	158
				H	63	1658	20	—	6	179	3441	1900	135
ST. PAUL—Howard County													
★ HOWARD COUNTY COMMUNITY HOSPITAL, 1102 Kendall St., Box 374, Zip 68873; tel. 308/754-4421; Russell W. Swigart, adm. **A**9 10 **F**1 6 15 16 23 35 37 44 45	13	10	S		36	542	16	44.4	7	55	1126	611	45
SUPERIOR—Nuckolls County													
★□ BRODSTONE MEMORIAL NUCKOLLS COUNTY HOSPITAL, Tenth & Idaho Sts., P O Box 187, Zip 68978; tel. 402/879-3281; Mike Oglevie, adm. **A**1a 9 10 **F**1 3 6 15 16 23 34 35 36 40 45 52	23	10	S		49	1115	15	30.6	8	86	2287	1067	78
SYRACUSE—Otoe County													
COMMUNITY MEMORIAL HOSPITAL, 1579 Midland St., Zip 68446; tel. 402/269-2011; Ron Anderson, adm. (Nonreporting) **A**9 10	16	10	S		25	—	—	—	—	—	—	—	—
TECUMSEH—Johnson County													
JOHNSON COUNTY HOSPITAL, 202 High St., Zip 68450; tel. 402/335-3361; Lavonne M. Rowe, adm. **A**9 10 **F**1 3 6 14 16 23 35 36 40 45 47	13	10	S		30	791	13	43.3	5	33	1355	552	47
TILDEN—Antelope County													
TILDEN COMMUNITY HOSPITAL, Box 340, Zip 68781; tel. 402/368-5343; Nila Brandner, adm. (Nonreporting) **A**9 10	23	10	S		26	—	—	—	—	—	—	—	—
VALENTINE—Cherry County													
CHERRY COUNTY HOSPITAL, Hwy. 12 & Green St., Zip 69201; tel. 402/376-2525; Brent Peterson, adm. **A**9 10 **F**1 3 6 15 16 23 34 35 40 45 47 52	13	10	S		33	720	9	27.3	8	120	1311	633	39
WAHOO—Saunders County													
SAUNDERS COUNTY COMMUNITY HOSPITAL, 805 W. Tenth St., P O Box 249, Zip 68066; tel. 402/443-4191; Stephen L. Spence, adm. **A**9 10 **F**1 12 14 15 16 23 29 35 36 40 45	13	10	S		30	407	9	30.0	5	9	1054	522	29
WAKEFIELD—Dixon County													
WAKEFIELD HEALTHCARE CENTER, 306 Ash St., Zip 68784; tel. 402/287-2244; John Viken, adm. (Nonreporting) **A**9 10	14	10	S		87	—	—	—	—	—	—	—	—

Hospital, Address, Telephone, Administrator, Approval and Facility Codes, Multihospital System Code	Classification Codes			Facilities	Inpatient Data				Newborn Data		Expense (thousands of dollars)		
★ American Hospital Association (AHA) membership □ Joint Commission on Accreditation of Hospitals (JCAH) accreditation + American Osteopathic Hospital Association (AOHA) membership ○ American Osteopathic Association (AOA) accreditation Δ Commission on Accreditation of Rehabilitation Facilities (CARF) accreditation Control codes 61, 63, 64, 71, 72 and 73 indicate hospitals listed by AOHA, but not registered by AHA. For definition of numerical codes, see page A2	Control	Service	Stay		Beds	Admissions	Census	Occupancy (percent)	Bassinets	Births	Total	Payroll	Personnel
WAYNE—Wayne County													
PROVIDENCE MEDICAL CENTER, 1200 Providence Rd., Zip 68787; tel. 402/375-3800; Marcile Thomas, adm. **A**9 10 **F**15 16 23 35 45; **S**2855	21	10	S		31	708	16	51.6	6	133	1686	684	45
WEST POINT—Cuming County													
★ ST. FRANCIS MEMORIAL HOSPITAL, 430 N. Monitor St., Zip 68788; tel. 402/372-2404; Sr. Emy Beth Furrer, pres. **A**9 10 **F**1 6 14 15 16 23 26 34 35 40 45 52; **S**1455	21	10	S		49	896	12	24.5	10	126	2280	1146	60
WINNEBAGO—Thurston County													
★□ U. S. PUBLIC HEALTH SERVICE INDIAN HOSPITAL, Zip 68071; tel. 402/878-2231; John W. Williams, serv. unit dir.; Lee A. Craig MD, clin. dir. **A**1a 10 **F**14 32 33 34 35 37 40 42 48 49 52	47	10	S		38	931	18	47.4	3	1	2529	1714	81
YORK—York County													
YORK GENERAL HOSPITAL, 2222 Lincoln Ave., Zip 68467; tel. 402/362-6671; Al Klaasmeyer, adm. **A**9 10 **F**1 3 6 15 16 23 24 34 35 40 41 45 46	23	10	S		70	1487	19	27.1	8	239	3103	1623	111

★ American Hospital Association (AHA) membership
□ Joint Commission on Accreditation of Hospitals (JCAH) accreditation
+ American Osteopathic Hospital Association (AOHA) membership
○ American Osteopathic Association (AOA) accreditation
Δ Commission on Accreditation of Rehabilitation Facilities (CARF) accreditation
Control codes 61, 63, 64, 71, 72 and 73 indicate hospitals listed by AOHA, but not registered by AHA.
For definition of numerical codes, see page A2

Nevada

Hospital, Address, Telephone, Administrator, Approval and Facility Codes, Multihospital System Code	Classification Codes				Inpatient Data				Newborn Data		Expense (thousands of dollars)		
	Control	Service	Stay	Facilities	Beds	Admissions	Census	Occupancy (percent)	Bassinets	Births	Total	Payroll	Personnel
BATTLE MOUNTAIN—Lander County													
★ BATTLE MOUNTAIN GENERAL HOSPITAL, Sixth & Humboldt, P O Box 460, Zip 89820; tel. 702/635-2550; Seleta Zoe Hines, adm. **A**10 **F**2 14 16 19 35 45	16	10	S		15	144	6	40.0	0	1	1007	520	29
BOULDER CITY—Clark County													
★ BOULDER CITY HOSPITAL, 901 Adams Blvd., Zip 89005; tel. 702/293-4111; John Pfeffer, actg. adm. (Nonreporting) **A**9 10	23	10	S		38	—	—	—	—	—	—	—	—
CARSON CITY—Ormsby County													
★□ CARSON TAHOE HOSPITAL, 775 Fleischmann Way, Box 2168, Zip 89701; tel. 702/882-1361; C. Thomas Collier, adm. **A**1a 10 **F**1 2 6 10 12 14 15 16 23 24 27 30 32 33 34 35 36 37 40 43 44 45 46 47 52	15	10	S		108	4858	50	48.1	10	892	16040	7457	328
ELKO—Elko County													
★□ ELKO GENERAL HOSPITAL, 1297 College Ave., Zip 89801; tel. 702/738-5151; Bill M. Welch, adm. **A**1a 10 **F**3 6 10 11 15 16 23 35 40 45 52 53	13	10	S		52	2241	25	48.1	7	417	6437	3078	137
ELY—White Pine County													
★□ WILLIAM BEE RIRIE HOSPITAL, 1500 Ave. H, Zip 89301; tel. 702/289-3001; Jack T. Wood, adm. **A**1a 10 **F**1 3 6 14 15 16 23 27 34 35 40 45 46 54	13	10	S		40	668	8	20.0	10	110	—	—	65
FALLON—Churchill County													
★ CHURCHILL REGIONAL MEDICAL CENTER, 155 N. Taylor St., Box 1240, Zip 89406; tel. 702/423-3151; Thomas F. Grimes, adm. **A**10 **F**1 6 14 34 35 36 40 42 43 44 45 46 47; **S**1195	23	10	S		40	1432	16	40.0	8	320	—	—	103
HAWTHORNE—Mineral County													
★ MOUNT GRANT GENERAL HOSPITAL, P O Box 1510, Zip 89415; tel. 702/945-2461; Richard Munger, adm. (Nonreporting) **A**10	13	10	S		53	—	—	—	—	—	—	—	—
HENDERSON—Clark County													
★□ ST. ROSE DE LIMA HOSPITAL, 102 Lake Mead Dr., Zip 89015; tel. 702/564-2622; David B. Coats, pres. & chief exec. off. **A**1a 9 10 **F**1 3 5 6 10 12 14 15 16 23 34 35 36 40 44 45 46	21	10	S		74	2377	30	40.5	12	394	10454	4286	186
INCLINE VILLAGE—Washoe County													
□ LAKESIDE COMMUNITY HOSPITAL, 880 Alder Ave., P O Box 8160, Zip 89450; tel. 702/831-5755; M. J. Madden, interim adm. **A**1a 10 **F**1 3 6 14 16 23 34 35 40 45 46 47 49 52	23	10	S		29	586	6	20.7	1	6	4859	1340	56
LAS VEGAS—Clark County													
★ CHARTER HOSPITAL OF LAS VEGAS, 7000 W. Spring Mountain Rd., Zip 89180; tel. 702/876-4357; David Richardson, adm. (Nonreporting) **A**9 10; **S**0695	33	22	S		80	—	—	—	—	—	—	—	—
★□ DESERT SPRINGS HOSPITAL, 2075 E. Flamingo Rd., Zip 89119; Mailing Address P O Box 19204, Zip 89132; tel. 702/733-8800; Thomas L. Koenig, adm. **A**1a 9 10 **F**1 3 4 5 6 11 12 14 15 16 20 23 34 35 37 43 44 45 46 47 53 54; **S**0695	33	10	S		225	6197	106	47.1	0	0	—	—	465
★□ HUMANA HOSPITAL -SUNRISE, 3186 Maryland Pkwy., Zip 89109; Mailing Address Box 14157, Zip 89114; tel. 702/731-8000; Donald L. Stewart, exec. dir.; Dan Brothman, adm. **A**1a 2 9 10 **F**1 4 5 6 9 10 11 12 14 15 16 20 23 24 28 29 30 32 33 34 35 36 37 42 43 44 45 46 47 49 53 54; **S**1235	33	10	S		679	19260	301	44.3	35	2581	—	—	1522
★□ MONTEVISTA CENTRE, 5900 W. Rochelle Ave., P O Box 26874, Zip 89126; tel. 702/364-1111; James T. Harper, adm. **A**1b 10 **F**15 23 24 32 33 42 44 45 48 49 50; **S**1755	33	22	S		80	940	47	58.8	0	0	—	—	89
SOUTHERN NEVADA MEMORIAL HOSPITAL, See University Medical Center of Southern Nevada													
U. S. AIR FORCE HOSPITAL, See Nellis Air Force Base													
★□ UNIVERSITY MEDICAL CENTER OF SOUTHERN NEVADA (Formerly Southern Nevada Memorial Hospital), 1800 W. Charleston Blvd., Zip 89102; tel. 702/383-2000; Richard J. Coughlin, adm. **A**1a 2 3 5 8 9 **F**1 2 3 4 5 6 8 9 10 11 12 14 15 16 20 22 23 24 25 26 27 30 34 35 36 39 40 42 44 45 46 47 52 53 54; **S**1755	15	10	S		436	14987	264	64.7	25	3007	72379	32403	1373
□ VALLEY HOSPITAL MEDICAL CENTER, 620 Shadow Lane, Zip 89106; tel. 702/388-4000; Claus Eggers, adm. (Nonreporting) **A**1a 9 10; **S**9555	33	10	S		310	—	—	—	—	—	—	—	—
□ WOMENS HOSPITAL, 2025 E. Sahara Ave., Box 43417, Zip 89116; tel. 702/735-7106; Ed Martinez, adm. (Nonreporting) **A**1a 3 5 9 10; **S**5765	33	44	S		61	—	—	—	—	—	—	—	—
LOVELOCK—Pershing County													
PERSHING GENERAL HOSPITAL, 855 Sixth Ave., Box 661, Zip 89419; tel. 702/273-2621; Myra Garland, adm. (Nonreporting) **A**10	13	10	S		49	—	—	—	—	—	—	—	—
NELLIS AIR FORCE BASE—Clark County													
□ U. S. AIR FORCE HOSPITAL, Zip 89191; tel. 702/643-4077; Lt. Col. H. B. Nicholson Jr., adm. **A**1a **F**6 14 15 23 28 30 32 33 34 35 37 40 46 47 49	41	10	S		45	3244	31	63.3	20	656	—	—	419
NORTH LAS VEGAS—Clark County													
□ COMMUNITY HOSPITAL OF NORTH LAS VEGAS, 1409 E. Lake Mead Blvd., Zip 89030; tel. 702/649-7711; Victor Brewer, adm. **A**1a 9 10 **F**1 3 5 6 12 14 15 16 17 23 34 35 45 46 47 48 50 52 53; **S**1375	33	10	S		163	2459	49	30.1	0	0	15678	4508	190
OWYHEE—Elko County													
★ U. S. PUBLIC HEALTH SERVICE OWYHEE COMMUNITY HEALTH FACILITY, Box 130, Zip 89832; tel. 702/757-2415; Wally Paisano, serv. unit dir. (Nonreporting) **A**10	47	10	S		15	—	—	—	—	—	—	—	—
RENO—Washoe County													
NEVADA MENTAL HEALTH INSTITUTE, See Sparks													
★□ ST. MARY'S HOSPITAL, 235 W. Sixth St., Zip 89520; tel. 702/323-2041; W. J. Van Ry, chief exec. off. **A**1a 10 **F**1 2 3 5 6 10 12 14 15 16 21 23 24 25 26 34 35 36 37 39 40 41 42 43 44 45 46 47 48 49 50 51 52 53 54; **S**1195	21	10	S		370	13392	189	51.9	53	2539	67461	31746	1302
★□ TRUCKEE MEADOWS HOSPITAL, 1240 E. Ninth St., Zip 89512; Mailing Address P O Box 30012, Zip 89520; tel. 702/323-0478; Laura Thomas, adm. **A**1b 10 **F**15 23 24 26 28 29 30 32 33 34 42 44 47; **S**1755	33	22	L		95	512	62	65.3	0	0	—	—	125
★□ VETERANS ADMINISTRATION MEDICAL CENTER, 1000 Locust St., Zip 89520; tel. 702/786-7200; Mary Ann Coffey, dir. (Total facility includes 60 beds in nursing home-type unit) **A**1a 3 5 **F**1 3 6 10 12 14 15 16 19 23 24 26 27 28 30 32 33 34 41 42 44 46 48 49 50	45	10	S	TF	216	5047	171	79.2	0	0	31613	17867	648
				H	156	4828	115	—	0	0	—	—	614
★□ WASHOE MEDICAL CENTER, 77 Pringle Way, Zip 89520; tel. 702/785-4100; James A. Lamb, adm. **A**1a 2 3 5 10 **F**1 2 3 4 5 6 7 8 9 10 11 12 14 15 16 20 23 24 25 26 27 29 30 32 33 34 35 36 37 40 44 45 46 50 51 52 53 54	23	10	S		537	18556	270	50.3	18	1412	93690	38234	1534

Hospital, Address, Telephone, Administrator, Approval and Facility Codes, Multihospital System Code	Classification Codes				Inpatient Data				Newborn Data		Expense (thousands of dollars)		
★ American Hospital Association (AHA) membership ☐ Joint Commission on Accreditation of Hospitals (JCAH) accreditation + American Osteopathic Hospital Association (AOHA) membership ○ American Osteopathic Association (AOA) accreditation Δ Commission on Accreditation of Rehabilitation Facilities (CARF) accreditation Control codes 61, 63, 64, 71, 72 and 73 indicate hospitals listed by AOHA, but not registered by AHA. For definition of numerical codes, see page A2	Control	Service	Stay	Facilities	Beds	Admissions	Census	Occupancy (percent)	Bassinets	Births	Total	Payroll	Personnel
SCHURZ—Mineral County													
★☐ U. S. PUBLIC HEALTH SERVICE INDIAN HOSPITAL, P O Box Drawer A, Zip 89427; tel. 702/773-2345; Elmer Brewster, serv. unit dir. (Nonreporting) **A**1a 10	47	10	S		14	—	—	—	—	—	—	—	—
SPARKS—Washoe County													
☐ NEVADA MENTAL HEALTH INSTITUTE (Formerly Listed Under Reno), 480 Galletti Way, Zip 89431; tel. 702/322-6961; Norton A. Roitman MD, dir. **A**1b 10 **F**24 28 29 30 31 32 33 34 35 42 43 46 47 50	12	22	S		98	1232	81	86.2	0	0	8759	5353	238
TONOPAH—Nye County													
NYE GENERAL HOSPITAL, 825 Erie Main, Box 391, Zip 89049; tel. 702/482-6233; Larry Higginbotham, adm. (Total facility includes 24 beds in nursing home-type unit) **A**10 **F**1 3 6 12 14 16 19 34 35 37 40 50	13	10	S	TF	45	724	24	53.3	2	52	2758	1040	69
				H	21	683	5	—	2	52	—	—	57
WINNEMUCCA—Humboldt County													
★ HUMBOLDT GENERAL HOSPITAL, 118 E. Haskell St., Zip 89445; tel. 702/623-5222; E. J. Hanssen, adm. (Total facility includes 14 beds in nursing home-type unit) **A**10 **F**1 6 12 14 16 19 23 30 35 37 40 45 47 49 50	16	10	S	TF	32	632	18	56.3	6	105	2205	1026	73
				H	18	608	5	—	6	105	—	—	—
YERINGTON—Lyon County													
★ SOUTH LYON COMMUNITY HOSPITAL (Formerly Lyon Health Center), Surprize at Whitacre Ave., Box 940, Zip 89447; tel. 702/463-2301; R. Duane Nimke, adm. (Nonreporting) **A**10	21	10	S		46	—	—	—	—	—	—	—	—

Hospital, Address, Telephone, Administrator, Approval and Facility Codes, Multihospital System Code	Classification Codes				Inpatient Data				Newborn Data		Expense (thousands of dollars)		
★ American Hospital Association (AHA) membership □ Joint Commission on Accreditation of Hospitals (JCAH) accreditation + American Osteopathic Hospital Association (AOHA) membership ○ American Osteopathic Association (AOA) accreditation Δ Commission on Accreditation of Rehabilitation Facilities (CARF) accreditation Control codes 61, 63, 64, 71, 72 and 73 indicate hospitals listed by AOHA, but not registered by AHA. For definition of numerical codes, see page A2	Control	Service	Stay	Facilities	Beds	Admissions	Census	Occupancy (percent)	Bassinets	Births	Total	Payroll	Personnel

New Hampshire

Hospital	Control	Service	Stay	Facilities	Beds	Admissions	Census	Occupancy (percent)	Bassinets	Births	Total	Payroll	Personnel
BERLIN—Coos County													
★□ ANDROSCOGGIN VALLEY HOSPITAL, 59 Page Hill Rd., Zip 03570; tel. 603/752-2200; Donald Saunders, pres. **A**1a 9 10 **F**1 3 5 6 10 14 15 16 23 24 26 27 30 32 34 35 36 43 44 45 46 50 53	23	10	S		92	2586	43	46.7	9	184	8511	4134	211
CLAREMONT—Sullivan County													
★□ VALLEY REGIONAL HOSPITAL, 243 Elm St., Zip 03743; tel. 603/542-7771; Donald R. Holl, pres. **A**1a 9 10 **F**1 3 6 9 10 11 12 14 15 16 23 26 34 35 36 37 39 40 43 44 45 46 50 53	23	10	S		71	2543	37	52.1	12	397	10778	4752	263
COLEBROOK—Coos County													
★□ UPPER CONNECTICUT VALLEY HOSPITAL, Corliss Lane, R.F.D. 2, Box 13, Zip 03576; tel. 603/237-4971; James M. Fallon, adm. **A**1a 9 10 **F**1 3 5 6 14 16 35 37 40 45	23	10	S		31	827	10	32.3	6	74	1988	879	77
CONCORD—Merrimack County													
★□ CONCORD HOSPITAL, 250 Pleasant St., Zip 03301; tel. 603/225-2711; Richard G. Warner, pres. **A**1a 2 6 9 10 **F**1 3 5 6 10 11 12 14 15 16 20 23 24 26 30 34 35 36 37 39 40 42 44 45 46 47 48 53	23	10	S		214	10859	174	72.2	31	1574	39356	17694	875
□ NEW HAMPSHIRE HOSPITAL, 105 Pleasant St., Zip 03301; tel. 603/224-6531; Jack E. Melton PhD, supt. (Total facility includes 258 beds in nursing home-type unit) **A**1b 3 10 **F**15 19 23 24 30 32 33 42 44 46 47 50	12	22	L	TF	432	733	400	87.1	0	0	24156	16313	909
				H	174	700	160	—	0	0	—	—	705
DERRY—Rockingham County													
★□ PARKLAND MEDICAL CENTER, One Parkland Dr., Zip 03038; tel. 603/432-1500; Steven R. Gordon, adm. **A**1a 9 10 **F**1 3 6 10 14 15 16 23 24 26 34 35 36 40 44 46 53; **S**1755	33	10	S		58	3202	41	70.7	8	458	12662	4590	247
DOVER—Strafford County													
★□ SEABORNE HOSPITAL, Seaborne Dr., Zip 03820; tel. 603/742-9300; Luther A. Cloud MD, dir. med. servs **A**1b **F**15 33 42 47 49	33	82	S		65	701	41	63.1	0	0	3156	1246	74
★□ WENTWORTH-DOUGLASS HOSPITAL, 789 Central Ave., Zip 03820; tel. 603/742-5252; William C. Richwagen, exec. dir. **A**1a 2 9 10 **F**1 3 5 6 8 9 10 11 12 14 15 16 23 24 26 30 34 35 36 37 38 40 44 45 46 52 53	23	10	S		158	7016	106	67.1	18	885	25173	12505	586
DUBLIN—Cheshire County													
★□ BEECH HILL HOSPITAL, New Harrisville Rd., Box 254, Zip 03444; tel. 603/563-8511; John H. Valentine, pres. **A**1b **F**15 33 42 49; **S**9355	21	82	S		140	2305	68	90.7	0	0	7556	2954	137
EXETER—Rockingham County													
★□ EXETER HOSPITAL, 10 Buzell Ave., Zip 03833; tel. 603/778-7311; Barbara A. Grillo, exec. dir. **A**1a 2 9 10 **F**1 3 5 6 15 16 23 24 26 30 34 35 36 40 44 45 46 47 52 53	23	10	S		100	5773	76	76.0	10	939	19485	8423	342
LAMONT INFIRMARY, Phillips Exeter Academy, Zip 03833; tel. 603/772-4311; Janet Corson-Rikert MD, med. dir. **F**1 15 23 26 29 30 32 33 34 35 37 43	23	11	S		17	401	2	11.8	0	0	—	—	—
FRANKLIN—Merrimack County													
★□ FRANKLIN REGIONAL HOSPITAL, Aiken Ave., Zip 03235; tel. 603/934-2060; H. Rudolph Wirth, exec. dir. **A**1a 9 10 **F**1 3 5 6 10 12 14 15 16 23 24 34 35 36 37 40 44 45 46 47 49 53	23	10	S		49	1825	32	65.3	8	150	6105	3120	174
GREENFIELD—Hillsborough County													
Δ CROTCHED MOUNTAIN REHABILITATION CENTER, Verney Dr., Zip 03047; tel. 603/547-3311; David A. Jordan, pres. (Newly Registered) **A**7 9 10	23	46	L		66	—	—	—	—	—	—	—	—
HANOVER—Grafton County													
★ DICK HALL'S HOUSE, 7 Rope Ferry Rd., Zip 03755; tel. 603/646-5433; Robert A. Black, adm. **A**9 **F**15 28 29 30 32 33 34 37 47 49	23	11	S		10	356	4	40.0	0	0	2043	—	44
★□ MARY HITCHCOCK MEMORIAL HOSPITAL, 2 Maynard St., Zip 03756; tel. 603/646-5000; James W. Varnum, pres. **A**1a 2 3 5 8 9 10 **F**1 2 3 4 5 6 7 8 9 10 11 12 14 16 17 20 23 24 26 27 28 29 30 32 33 35 36 38 39 40 41 42 43 44 45 46 51 52 53 54; **S**3395	23	10	S		378	14058	303	80.2	18	938	80143	38101	1881
KEENE—Cheshire County													
★□ CHESHIRE MEDICAL CENTER, 580 Court St., Zip 03431; tel. 603/352-4111; John T. Foster, pres. **A**1a 2 9 10 **F**1 3 5 6 8 9 10 11 12 14 15 16 23 24 26 27 30 32 33 35 36 40 41 42 44 45 46 47 52 53	23	10	S		173	6374	105	60.7	20	546	20400	10293	552
□ WHISPERING PINES HOSPITAL, Rte. 9, Zip 03782; tel. 603/357-2307; James F. O'Neill, pres. (Newly Registered) **A**1a 9	33	82	L		80	—	—	—	—	—	—	—	—
LACONIA—Belknap County													
★□ LAKES REGION GENERAL HOSPITAL, Highland St., Zip 03246; tel. 603/524-3211; Wallace W. Smith, pres. **A**1a 2 9 10 **F**1 3 5 6 7 12 14 15 16 23 24 26 27 30 32 33 34 35 36 40 43 44 45 46 50 52 53	23	10	S		157	6026	82	52.2	16	721	16048	8062	425
LANCASTER—Coos County													
★□ WEEKS MEMORIAL HOSPITAL, Middle St., Zip 03584; tel. 603/788-4911; G. A. Desrochers, adm. (Total facility includes 10 beds in nursing home-type unit) **A**1a 9 10 **F**1 3 6 10 12 14 16 19 23 24 33 34 35 36 40 45 46 47 53	23	10	S	TF	59	1802	34	57.6	7	147	5202	2655	143
				H	49	1684	26	—	7	147	5044	2538	139
LEBANON—Grafton County													
★□ ALICE PECK DAY MEMORIAL HOSPITAL, 125 Mascoma St., Zip 03766; tel. 603/448-3121; Robert Mesropian, exec. dir. (Total facility includes 46 beds in nursing home-type unit) **A**1a 9 10 **F**1 6 14 15 16 19 23 24 26 34 35 36 37 40 42 43 44 45 48 49; **S**3395	23	10	S	TF	78	1071	54	69.2	12	271	4465	2542	139
				H	32	949	14	—	12	271	3947	2101	112
LITTLETON—Grafton County													
★□ LITTLETON HOSPITAL, 107 Cottage St., Zip 03561; tel. 603/444-7731; LeRoy Deabler, pres. **A**1a 2 9 10 **F**1 3 6 10 12 14 15 16 23 24 28 35 40 44 45 46 52 53 54; **S**1755	23	10	S		54	2455	31	57.4	5	261	6956	3389	191
MANCHESTER—Hillsborough County													
★□ Δ CATHOLIC MEDICAL CENTER, 100 McGregor St., Zip 03102; tel. 603/668-3545; Charles F. Whittemore, pres. **A**1a 2 7 9 10 **F**1 3 4 6 12 14 15 16 20 23 24 25 26 27 30 32 35 36 37 38 40 42 44 45 46 48 50 52 53 54	23	10	S		330	10528	208	63.0	12	932	42934	19630	929
★□ ELLIOT HOSPITAL, 955 Auburn St., Zip 03103; tel. 603/669-5300; Francis J. Cronin, pres. **A**1a 2 9 10 **F**1 3 5 6 7 8 9 10 11 12 14 15 16 17 20 21 23 24 25 26 27 30 31 32 33 34 35 36 37 39 40 41 42 43 44 45 46 52 53 54	23	10	S		273	9765	169	61.9	26	1474	37766	16399	799
★ LAKE SHORE HOSPITAL, 200 Zachary Rd., Zip 03103; tel. 603/645-6700; Ronald C. Andrews, pres. **A**9 10 **F**24 30 32 33 42 46 47 48; **S**0215	33	22	S		90	449	27	41.5	0	0	4474	1693	132

Hospital, Address, Telephone, Administrator, Approval and Facility Codes, Multihospital System Code

- ★ American Hospital Association (AHA) membership
- ☐ Joint Commission on Accreditation of Hospitals (JCAH) accreditation
- \+ American Osteopathic Hospital Association (AOHA) membership
- ○ American Osteopathic Association (AOA) accreditation
- Δ Commission on Accreditation of Rehabilitation Facilities (CARF) accreditation

Control codes 61, 63, 64, 71, 72 and 73 indicate hospitals listed by AOHA, but not registered by AHA. For definition of numerical codes, see page A2

Hospital	Classification Codes: Control	Service	Stay	Facilities	Inpatient Data: Beds	Admissions	Census	Occupancy (percent)	Newborn Data: Bassinets	Births	Expense (thousands of dollars): Total	Payroll	Personnel
★☐ VETERANS ADMINISTRATION MEDICAL CENTER, 718 Smyth Rd., Zip 03104; tel. 603/624-4366; William H. Kelleher, dir. (Total facility includes 120 beds in nursing home-type unit) **A**1a b 2 3 5 **F**1 3 6 12 14 15 16 19 20 23 24 26 27 28 30 32 33 34 42 44 45 46 47 48 49	45	10	S	TF	284	4164	224	78.9	0	0	27804	14925	608
				H	164	3867	120	—	0	0	—	—	559
NASHUA—Hillsborough County													
MEMORIAL HOSPITAL, See Nashua Memorial Hospital													
NASHUA BROOKSIDE HOSPITAL, 11 Northwest Blvd., Zip 03063; tel. 603/886-5000; Kenneth F. Courage Jr., adm. (Newly Registered) **A**10 **F**15 24 29 30 31 33 34 42 48 49	33	22	S		90	684	48	53.3	0	0	7442	2614	270
★☐ NASHUA MEMORIAL HOSPITAL (Formerly Memorial Hospital), 8 Prospect St., Box 2014, Zip 03061; tel. 603/883-5521; William T. Christopher Jr., pres. **A**1a 9 10 **F**1 3 5 6 10 12 14 15 16 20 21 23 24 26 27 29 30 34 35 36 40 44 45 46 47 52 53	23	10	S		173	8123	116	67.1	24	1817	26704	13907	723
★☐ ST. JOSEPH HOSPITAL, 172 Kinsley St., Caller Service 2013, Zip 03061; tel. 603/889-6681; Peter B. Davis, pres. **A**1a 9 10 **F**1 3 5 6 12 14 16 23 24 25 35 36 37 40 44 45 46 48 49 52 53; **S**5885	21	10	S		218	7819	145	66.5	36	805	32010	16545	717
NEW LONDON—Merrimack County													
★☐ NEW LONDON HOSPITAL, County Rd., Zip 03257; tel. 603/526-2911; Harry M. Lowd III, dir. (Total facility includes 52 beds in nursing home-type unit) **A**1a 9 10 **F**1 3 6 14 15 16 19 23 24 26 29 30 32 33 34 35 36 40 41 42 43 44 45 46 49 50 53	23	10	S	TF	87	1112	60	69.0	8	79	6731	3386	199
				H	35	981	16	—	8	79	—	2865	163
NEWPORT—Sullivan County													
★☐ NEWPORT HOSPITAL, 167 Summer St., Zip 03773; tel. 603/863-1123; Clinton G. Cooper, pres. **A**1a 9 10 **F**1 15 16 30 35 43 45 46 50	23	10	S		27	807	13	48.1	0	0	3196	1503	81
NORTH CONWAY—Carroll County													
★☐ MEMORIAL HOSPITAL, Intervale Rd., Zip 03860; tel, 603/356-5461; Gary R. Poquette, exec. dir. (Total facility includes 21 beds in nursing home-type unit) **A**1a 9 10 **F**1 3 6 10 14 15 16 19 21 23 30 35 36 40 46 47 52 53	23	10	S	TF	56	1471	39	69.6	6	237	5458	2419	128
				H	35	1463	18	—	6	237	5145	2196	113
PEASE AIR FORCE BASE—Rockingham County													
★☐ U. S. AIR FORCE HOSPITAL PEASE, Zip 03803; tel. 603/430-2775; Allen Middleton, adm. **A**1a **F**1 14 15 16 23 28 32 34 35 40 46 49 52	41	10	S		45	2806	43	86.0	14	528	—	—	368
PETERBOROUGH—Hillsborough County													
★☐ MONADNOCK COMMUNITY HOSPITAL, Old Street Rd., Zip 03458; tel. 603/924-7191; Alvin D. Felgar, adm. **A**1a 9 10 **F**1 3 6 12 15 16 23 24 26 35 36 37 40 42 44 45 46 47 52	23	10	S		67	2192	33	49.3	10	439	6638	3266	195
PLYMOUTH—Grafton County													
★☐ SPEARE MEMORIAL HOSPITAL (Formerly Sceva Speare Memorial Hospital), Hospital Rd., Zip 03264; tel. 603/536-1120; David L. Pearse, adm. **A**1a 9 10 **F**1 3 6 10 14 15 16 23 24 35 36 37 40 44 45 46 47 50 53	23	10	S		47	1329	22	46.8	7	93	4606	2349	128
PORTSMOUTH—Rockingham County													
★☐ PORTSMOUTH REGIONAL HOSPITAL (Formerly Portsmouth Hospital), 333 Borthwick Ave., Zip 03801; tel. 603/436-5110; William J. Schuler, adm. **A**1a 2 9 10 **F**1 3 5 6 10 11 12 14 15 16 23 24 26 27 28 30 32 33 34 35 36 40 41 42 44 45 46 47 49 52 53 54; **S**1755	33	10	S		106	4643	71	67.0	18	737	19984	7881	382
U. S. AIR FORCE HOSPITAL PEASE, See Pease Air Force Base													
ROCHESTER—Strafford County													
★☐ FRISBIE MEMORIAL HOSPITAL, Whitehall Rd., Zip 03867; tel. 603/332-5211; Vincent J. DeNobile, pres. **A**1a 2 9 10 **F**1 3 6 10 12 15 16 23 24 27 34 35 36 40 45 46 48 50 52 53	23	10	S		116	4448	72	63.2	10	623	17370	7150	393
SPOFFORD—Cheshire County													
★☐ SPOFFORD HALL HOSPITAL (Formerly Spofford Hall), Rte. 9a, Box 225, Zip 03462; tel. 603/363-4545; William Hawthorne MD, exec. dir. **A**1b **F**15 32 33 42 49; **S**1135	33	82	S		143	1724	136	100.0	0	0	—	—	186
SUNAPEE—Sullivan County													
☐ SEMINOLE POINT HOSPITAL (Formerly Seminole Point), Woodland Rd., Box 1000, Zip 03782; tel. 603/763-2545; James F. O'Neill, pres. **A**1b 9 **F**15 24 26 32 33 38 42 49	33	82	S		72	875	58	80.6	0	0	4760	1159	73
WOLFEBORO—Carroll County													
★☐ HUGGINS HOSPITAL, Box 912, Zip 03894; tel. 603/569-2150; Leslie N. H. MacLeod, pres. (Total facility includes 21 beds in nursing home-type unit) **A**1a 9 10 **F**1 3 6 10 12 15 16 17 19 23 24 26 35 36 37 40 42 44 46 53	23	10	S	TF	82	2347	46	56.1	7	110	6326	3232	185
				H	61	2199	36	—	7	110	6102	3041	178
WOODSVILLE—Grafton County													
★☐ COTTAGE HOSPITAL, Swiftwater Rd., Zip 03785; tel. 603/747-2761; David J. Moore, adm. **A**1a 2 9 10 **F**1 3 6 12 14 16 23 28 35 36 40 44 45 52	23	10	S		48	1149	14	29.2	9	86	3715	2025	97

Hospital, Address, Telephone, Administrator, Approval and Facility Codes, Multihospital System Code	Classification Codes				Inpatient Data				Newborn Data		Expense (thousands of dollars)		
★ American Hospital Association (AHA) membership □ Joint Commission on Accreditation of Hospitals (JCAH) accreditation + American Osteopathic Hospital Association (AOHA) membership ○ American Osteopathic Association (AOA) accreditation Δ Commission on Accreditation of Rehabilitation Facilities (CARF) accreditation Control codes 61, 63, 64, 71, 72 and 73 indicate hospitals listed by AOHA, but not registered by AHA. For definition of numerical codes, see page A2	Control	Service	Stay	Facilities	Beds	Admissions	Census	Occupancy (percent)	Bassinets	Births	Total	Payroll	Personnel

New Jersey

Hospital	Control	Service	Stay	Facilities	Beds	Admissions	Census	Occupancy (percent)	Bassinets	Births	Total	Payroll	Personnel
ATLANTIC CITY—Atlantic County													
★□ ATLANTIC CITY MEDICAL CENTER, 1925 Pacific Ave., Zip 08401; tel. 609/441-8020; George F. Lynn, pres. **A**1a 2 3 5 9 10 **F**1 2 3 5 6 7 8 9 10 11 12 14 15 16 20 21 23 27 28 30 32 35 36 37 38 40 45 46 47 50 52 53	23	10	S		615	20351	385	62.6	44	2310	79417	41079	1553
★□ CHILDREN'S SEASHORE HOUSE, 4100 Atlantic Ave., Zip 08404; tel. 609/345-5191; Richard W. Shepherd, adm. **A**1a 9 10 **F**16 23 24 25 26 28 33 34 42 44 45 46	23	50	L		94	541	54	57.4	0	0	12384	6432	293
BAYONNE—Hudson County													
★□ BAYONNE HOSPITAL, 29 E. 29th St., Zip 07002; tel. 201/858-5000; Dennis J. Bruschi, chief exec. off. **A**1a 6 9 10 **F**1 3 6 10 12 14 15 16 23 24 27 30 32 33 34 35 40 44 45 46 52 53	23	10	S		299	10162	249	83.3	30	504	35481	16859	791
BELLE MEAD—Somerset County													
★□ CARRIER FOUNDATION, Box 147, Zip 08502; tel. 201/874-4000; Stanley Birch Jr., pres. **A**1a 9 10 **F**3 23 24 28 30 32 33 34 42 45 46 47 48 49 50	23	22	L		269	2730	225	83.6	0	0	20260	12510	660
BELLEVILLE—Essex County													
★□ CLARA MAASS MEDICAL CENTER, One Franklin Ave., Zip 07109; tel. 201/450-2000; Robert S. Curtis, pres. & exec. dir. **A**1a 2 6 9 10 **F**1 3 6 7 8 9 10 11 12 14 15 16 23 26 27 32 34 35 36 40 42 44 45 46 47 52 53	23	10	S		575	17772	352	61.2	54	1647	49716	25158	1174
BERKELEY HEIGHTS—Union County													
★□ JOHN E. RUNNELLS HOSPITAL OF UNION COUNTY (Alcoholism, Chronic Disease, Psychiatric and Rehabilitation and Skilled Nursing), Zip 07922; tel. 201/322-7240; Kathleen S. Hoza, adm. (Total facility includes 251 beds in nursing home-type unit) **A**1a 9 10 **F**15 16 19 23 24 25 26 27 32 34 42 44 46 48 49 50	13	48	L	TF	309	786	259	83.8	0	0	16115	9993	454
				H	58	263	28	—	0	0	—	—	—
BERLIN—Camden County													
★□ WEST JERSEY HOSPITAL SOUTHERN DIVISION, Townsend Ave. & White Horse Pike, Zip 08009; tel. 609/768-6000; R. Ronald Lawson, exec. dir. **A**1a 9 **F**1 3 6 15 16 23 26 34 35; **S**6725	23	10	S		95	3016	74	77.9	0	0	—	—	224
BLACKWOOD—Camden County													
□ CAMDEN COUNTY HEALTH SERVICES CENTER (Formerly Listed Under Lakeland) (Includes Psychiatric Division, Evergreen Manor and Red Oak Manor) (Psychiatric, Skilled Nursing and Long-Term Care), Zip 08012; tel. 609/227-3000; Frank J. Kelly MD, exec. dir. (Nonreporting) **A**1b 3 10	13	49	L		507	—	—	—	—	—	—	—	—
BOONTON—Morris County													
RIVERSIDE HOSPITAL, See St. Clare's-Riverside Medical Center, Denville													
BRIDGETON—Cumberland County													
★□ BRIDGETON HOSPITAL, Manheim & Irving, Zip 08302; tel. 609/451-6600; Paul S. Cooper, pres. **A**1a 9 10 **F**1 3 6 10 12 14 15 16 20 26 27 28 32 33 34 35 36 37 40 42 45 46 52 53	23	10	S		252	7288	172	68.3	21	920	24735	11232	550
BROWNS MILLS—Burlington County													
★□ DEBORAH HEART AND LUNG CENTER, Trenton Rd., Zip 08015; tel. 609/893-6611; Sergius B. Gambal, exec. vice-pres. **A**1a 9 10 **F**3 4 6 10 12 14 16 17 20 23 34 42 45 46 47 52 54	23	49	S		155	4874	102	65.8	0	0	47504	23998	837
CAMDEN—Camden County													
★□ COOPER HOSPITAL-UNIVERSITY MEDICAL CENTER, One Cooper Plaza, Zip 08103; tel. 609/342-2000; Kevin G. Halpern, pres. & chief exec. off. **A**1a 3 5 8 9 10 **F**1 2 3 4 5 6 7 8 9 10 11 12 14 15 16 17 20 23 24 26 27 28 29 30 32 33 34 35 36 37 38 40 43 44 45 46 47 49 51 52 53 54	23	10	S		496	17575	416	83.9	24	2027	99392	40910	1962
★□ Δ OUR LADY OF LOURDES MEDICAL CENTER, 1600 Haddon Ave., Zip 08103; tel. 609/757-3500; Sr. Elizabeth Corry, pres. & chief exec. off. **A**1a 3 5 6 7 9 10 **F**1 2 3 4 6 10 11 12 13 14 15 16 20 23 24 25 26 27 30 32 33 34 35 36 38 40 41 42 44 45 46 47 51 52 53 54; **S**1385	23	10	S		398	12015	295	74.1	32	2098	54434	24677	1291
★□ WEST JERSEY HOSPITAL, NORTHERN DIVISION, Mount Ephraim & Atlantic Aves., Zip 08104; tel. 609/342-4000; Michael P. Dennis, exec. dir. **A**1a 2 6 9 10 **F**1 3 6 10 14 15 16 23 34 35 45 46 47 48 49 53; **S**6725	23	10	S		224	8524	177	79.0	0	0	109115	46370	860
CAPE MAY COURT HOUSE—Cape May County													
★□ BURDETTE TOMLIN MEMORIAL HOSPITAL, Stone Harbor Blvd., Zip 08210; tel. 609/465-2000; William H. Waldron III, pres. (Nonreporting) **A**1a 9 10	23	10	S		239	—	—	—	—	—	—	—	—
CEDAR GROVE—Essex County													
□ ESSEX COUNTY HOSPITAL CENTER, 125 Fairview Ave., Zip 07009; tel. 201/228-8000; Arthur N. Avella MD, med. dir. & actg. div dir. **A**1b 9 10 **F**23 24 28 32 33 34 42 44 46 47	13	22	L		672	673	623	87.5	0	0	49179	31705	1144
CHERRY HILL—Camden County													
CHERRY HILL DIVISION, See Kennedy Memorial Hospitals-University Medical Center													
CHESTER—Morris County													
★□ Δ WELKIND REHABILITATION HOSPITAL, Pleasant Hill Rd., Zip 07930; tel. 201/584-8145; Donald J. Mueller, chief exec. off. **A**1a 7 10 **F**15 16 23 24 26 33 34 42 44 45 46 47 50	23	46	L		72	349	56	77.8	0	0	8525	4048	211
DENVILLE—Morris County													
★□ ST. CLARE'S -RIVERSIDE MEDICAL CENTER (Includes Riverside Hospital, Powerville Rd., Boonton, Zip 07005; St. Clare's Hospital, Pocono Rd., Zip 07834), Pocono Rd., Zip 07834; tel. 201/625-6000; Kenneth M. Courey, pres. & chief exec. off. (Nonreporting) **A**1a 2 9 10	21	10	S		401	—	—	—	—	—	—	—	—
ST. CLARE'S HOSPITAL, See St. Clare's-Riverside Medical Center													
DOVER—Morris County													
★□ DOVER GENERAL HOSPITAL AND MEDICAL CENTER, Jardine St., Zip 07801; tel. 201/989-3000; Wayne C. Schiffner, pres. & chief exec. off. **A**1a 2 9 10 **F**1 3 5 6 7 8 9 10 11 12 15 16 23 24 26 34 35 36 37 38 40 41 42 43 44 45 46 47 50 52 53	23	10	S		360	10336	207	57.5	28	906	43337	20187	1037
EAST ORANGE—Essex County													
★□ EAST ORANGE GENERAL HOSPITAL, 300 Central Ave., Zip 07019; tel. 201/672-8400; Laurence M. Merlis, pres. & chief exec. off. **A**1a 9 10 **F**1 3 6 10 12 14 15 16 20 24 26 27 28 30 31 32 33 34 35 37 42 44 45 46 47 49 50 52	23	10	S		277	6433	195	70.4	0	0	28152	13497	643
★□ VETERANS ADMINISTRATION MEDICAL CENTER, Tremont Ave. & S. Centre St., Zip 07019; tel. 201/676-1000; Peter Baglio, dir. (Total facility includes 60 beds in nursing home-type unit) **A**1a 2 3 5 8 **F**1 2 3 6 7 8 9 10 11 12 14 15 16 19 20 23 24 25 26 27 28 29 30 32 33 34 35 41 42 44 46 47 48 49 53 54	45	10	S	TF	805	16043	666	82.7	0	0	97143	54058	1858
				H	745	15988	609	—	0	0	94371	52085	1831

Hospital, Address, Telephone, Administrator, Approval and Facility Codes, Multihospital System Code	Classification Codes				Inpatient Data				Newborn Data		Expense (thousands of dollars)		
★ American Hospital Association (AHA) membership □ Joint Commission on Accreditation of Hospitals (JCAH) accreditation + American Osteopathic Hospital Association (AOHA) membership ○ American Osteopathic Association (AOA) accreditation Δ Commission on Accreditation of Rehabilitation Facilities (CARF) accreditation Control codes 61, 63, 64, 71, 72 and 73 indicate hospitals listed by AOHA, but not registered by AHA. For definition of numerical codes, see page A2	Control	Service	Stay	Facilities	Beds	Admissions	Census	Occupancy (percent)	Bassinets	Births	Total	Payroll	Personnel
EDISON—Middlesex County													
JOHN F. KENNEDY COMMUNITY HOSPITAL, See John F. Kennedy Medical Center													
★□ Δ JOHN F. KENNEDY MEDICAL CENTER (Formerly John F. Kennedy Community Hospital), 59 James St., Zip 08818; tel. 201/321-7000 **A**1a 3 5 7 9 10 **F**2 3 6 7 8 9 10 11 12 14 15 16 20 23 24 25 26 28 30 32 33 34 35 36 40 42 43 44 45 46 47 49 50 52 53; **S**8855	23	10	S		380	19380	357	93.9	48	1720	58518	32346	1417
★ ROBERT WOOD JOHNSON JR. REHABILITATION INSTITUTE, James St., Zip 08818; tel. 201/321-7050; Scott Gephard, adm. **A**9 **F**6 15 23 24 25 28 30 32 33 34 35 42 44 45 46 47; **S**8855	23	46	L		74	660	71	95.8	0	0	13120	6715	338
★□ ROOSEVELT HOSPITAL, Mailing Address P O Box 151, Metuchen, Zip 08840; tel. 201/321-6800; Man Wah Cheung MD, supt. & med. dir. (Total facility includes 250 beds in nursing home-type unit) **A**1a 9 10 **F**3 15 16 19 23 24 33 34 35 42 44 45 46 47 49	13	48	L	TF H	558 308	574 424	530 283	95.0 —	0 0	0 0	29295 15380	16966 9060	914 447
ELIZABETH—Union County													
★□ ALEXIAN BROTHERS HOSPITAL, 655 E. Jersey St., Zip 07206; tel. 201/351-9000; Michael J. Schwartz, pres. & chief exec. off. **A**1a 9 10 **F**1 2 3 6 10 12 14 15 16 20 21 24 26 34 35 44 45 46 53; **S**0065	23	10	S		190	6751	156	82.1	0	0	33156	13644	604
★□ ELIZABETH GENERAL MEDICAL CENTER, 925 E. Jersey St., Zip 07201; tel. 201/289-8600; George F. Billington, pres. **A**1a 2 3 5 6 9 10 **F**1 3 6 10 12 14 15 16 23 27 28 29 30 32 33 34 35 36 37 38 40 42 43 45 46 49 50 52 53	23	10	S		382	15331	255	66.8	36	1552	46652	26298	1246
★□ ST. ELIZABETH HOSPITAL, 225 Williamson St., Zip 07207; tel. 201/527-5000; Sr. Elizabeth Ann Maloney, exec. dir. **A**1a 2 3 5 9 10 **F**1 3 6 7 8 9 10 11 12 14 15 16 21 32 34 35 36 37 38 40 44 45 46 48 53 54; **S**5815	21	10	S		328	10662	223	68.0	26	987	40488	18281	858
ELMER—Salem County													
★□ ELMER COMMUNITY HOSPITAL, W. Front St., Zip 08318; tel. 609/358-2341; John H. Wisda, adm. **A**1a 9 10 **F**1 3 6 10 12 14 15 23 35 43 44 45 46 53	23	10	S		91	3241	55	60.4	0	0	11263	4753	255
ENGLEWOOD—Bergen County													
★□ ENGLEWOOD HOSPITAL, 350 Engle St., Zip 07631; tel. 201/894-3000; Ronald C. Dematteo, pres. **A**1a 2 3 5 6 9 10 **F**1 2 3 5 6 7 8 9 10 11 12 14 15 16 17 20 21 23 24 26 27 28 30 32 34 35 36 37 38 40 41 44 45 46 47 52 53 54; **S**1935	23	10	S		547	21552	420	76.8	44	2383	67756	32736	1626
FLEMINGTON—Hunterdon County													
★□ HUNTERDON MEDICAL CENTER, Rte. 31, Zip 08822; tel. 201/788-6100; Donald W. Davis, pres. **A**1a 3 5 9 10 **F**1 3 6 7 10 11 12 14 15 16 24 26 27 28 29 30 32 33 34 35 36 37 38 40 41 44 45 46 47 49 50 52 53	23	10	S		182	8862	127	69.8	22	1037	30763	15911	706
FORT DIX—Burlington County													
★□ WALSON ARMY COMMUNITY HOSPITAL, Zip 08640; tel. 609/562-2852; Col. Albert C. Molnar MD, cmdr. **A**1a **F**3 6 12 14 15 16 23 24 27 28 30 32 33 34 35 37 46 47 52	42	10	S		175	7365	106	60.6	0	0	29461	21762	943
FORT MONMOUTH—Monmouth County													
★□ PATTERSON ARMY COMMUNITY HOSPITAL (Formerly Patterson U. S. Army Community Hospital), Zip 07703; tel. 201/532-1341; Col. Doyle Driver Jr. MC, CO **A**1a **F**6 10 12 14 15 16 23 34 35 37 41 44 46 47 52	42	10	S		49	1470	15	30.6	0	0	15781	10231	395
FREEHOLD—Monmouth County													
★□ FREEHOLD AREA HOSPITAL, W. Main St., Zip 07728; tel. 201/431-2000; Jack De Cerce, pres. **A**1a 9 10 **F**1 2 3 6 9 10 11 12 14 15 16 21 24 26 28 30 32 33 34 35 37 40 42 44 45 46 47 49 50 52 53	23	10	S		248	13376	193	77.8	18	1169	33525	15935	934
GREYSTONE PARK—Morris County													
GREYSTONE PARK PSYCHIATRIC HOSPITAL, Zip 07950; tel. 201/538-1800; Michael Ross, chief exec. off. **A** 9 10 **F**12 23 24 30 32 33 42 44 45 46 47	12	22	L		829	692	844	96.0	0	0	44987	31263	1392
HACKENSACK—Bergen County													
★□ HACKENSACK MEDICAL CENTER, 30 Prospect Ave., Zip 07601; tel. 201/441-2000; John P. Ferguson, pres. & chief exec. off. **A**1a 2 3 5 8 9 10 **F**1 3 4 5 6 7 8 9 10 11 12 13 14 15 16 20 21 23 24 26 27 28 30 32 33 34 35 36 37 38 41 42 44 45 46 47 49 50 51 52 53 54	23	10	S		510	19792	423	82.9	40	2179	93671	42848	2168
HACKETTSTOWN—Warren County													
★□ HACKETTSTOWN COMMUNITY HOSPITAL, 651 Willow Grove St., Zip 07840; tel. 201/852-5100; Gene C. Milton, pres. & chief exec. off. **A**1a 2 9 10 **F**1 3 6 10 12 14 15 16 23 26 34 35 36 40 45 46 47 49 53; **S**9355	21	10	S		106	4758	57	53.8	12	593	13434	6129	306
HAMILTON—Mercer County													
★□ HAMILTON HOSPITAL, Whitehorse-Hamilton Square Rd., Zip 08690; tel. 609/586-7900; J. Austin White, pres. (Nonreporting) **A**1a 9 10	23	10	S		166	—	—	—	—	—	—	—	—
HAMMONTON—Camden County													
★□ ANCORA PSYCHIATRIC HOSPITAL, Hammonton Post Office, Zip 08037; tel. 609/561-1700; Thomas M. Osborn, actg. chief exec. off. **A**1b 3 5 9 10 **F**12 14 23 24 26 32 33 35 37 42 44 50	12	22	L		654	1108	616	81.2	0	0	39370	26336	1266
HAMMONTON—Atlantic County													
★□ WILLIAM B. KESSLER MEMORIAL HOSPITAL, White Horse Pike & Central Ave., Zip 08037; tel. 609/561-6700; Warren E. Gager, adm. **A**1a 9 10 **F**1 3 6 10 12 14 15 16 23 35 41 45 46 47 52	23	10	S		125	4183	90	72.0	0	0	13886	7511	396
HASBROUCK HEIGHTS—Bergen County													
□ SOUTH BERGEN HOSPITAL, 214 Terrace Ave., Zip 07604; tel. 201/288-0800; Sr. Claire Tynan, actg. adm. (Nonreporting) **A**1a 9 10	23	10	S		40	—	—	—	—	—	—	—	—
HOBOKEN—Hudson County													
★□ ST. MARY HOSPITAL, 308 Willow Ave., Zip 07030; tel. 201/792-8000; Bruce Smith, adm. **A**1a 3 9 10 **F**1 3 6 10 12 14 15 16 24 26 27 28 30 32 33 34 35 36 40 42 43 44 45 46 49 52 53; **S**1485	21	10	S		330	11044	235	71.2	25	779	38381	18405	784
HOLMDEL—Monmouth County													
★□ BAYSHORE COMMUNITY HOSPITAL, 727 N. Beers St., Zip 07733; tel. 201/739-5900; Thomas Goldman, pres. **A**1a 9 10 **F**1 3 6 10 12 14 15 16 21 23 24 26 28 30 32 33 34 35 42 43 44 45 46 47 49 50 52 53	23	10	S		218	8943	187	85.8	0	0	25039	11999	668
IRVINGTON—Essex County													
★□ IRVINGTON GENERAL HOSPITAL, 832 Chancellor Ave., Zip 07111; tel. 201/399-6000; Louis A. Ditzel Jr., pres. & chief exec. off. **A**1a 9 10 **F**1 3 6 10 12 14 15 16 23 24 26 34 35 44 45 46 47 53	23	10	S		115	4467	111	96.5	0	0	17997	8721	427
JERSEY CITY—Hudson County													
★□ CHRIST HOSPITAL, 176 Palisade Ave., Zip 07306; tel. 201/795-8200; Lloyd R. Currier, pres. (Nonreporting) **A**1a 6 9 10	23	10	S		367	—	—	—	—	—	—	—	—
★□ GREENVILLE HOSPITAL, 1825 Kennedy Blvd., Zip 07305; tel. 201/547-6100; Lawrence P. Ward, adm. **A**1a 9 10 **F**1 2 6 10 12 14 15 16 23 34 35 45 46 47	23	10	S		86	2949	72	69.9	0	0	9699	5076	219
□ JERSEY CITY MEDICAL CENTER, 50 Baldwin Ave., Zip 07304; tel. 201/451-9800; Harvey A. Holzberg, exec. dir. **A**1a 3 5 9 10 **F**1 2 3 5 6 12 14 15 16 20 23 26 27 28 29 30 32 33 34 35 36 37 38 40 46 47 50 51 52 53	16	10	S		447	15691	379	84.8	32	2776	72772	37500	1760

Hospital, Address, Telephone, Administrator, Approval and Facility Codes, Multihospital System Code	Classification Codes				Inpatient Data				Newborn Data		Expense (thousands of dollars)		
★ American Hospital Association (AHA) membership □ Joint Commission on Accreditation of Hospitals (JCAH) accreditation + American Osteopathic Hospital Association (AOHA) membership ○ American Osteopathic Association (AOA) accreditation Δ Commission on Accreditation of Rehabilitation Facilities (CARF) accreditation Control codes 61, 63, 64, 71, 72 and 73 indicate hospitals listed by AOHA, but not registered by AHA. For definition of numerical codes, see page A2	Control	Service	Stay	Facilities	Beds	Admissions	Census	Occupancy (percent)	Bassinets	Births	Total	Payroll	Personnel
★□ JEWISH HOSPITAL AND REHABILITATION CENTER OF NEW JERSEY, 198 Stevens Ave., Zip 07305; tel. 201/451-9000; Charles P. Berkowitz, exec. vice-pres. (Nonreporting) **A**1a 9 10	23	48	L		450	—	—	—	—	—	—	—	—
★□ ST. FRANCIS HOSPITAL, 25 McWilliams Pl., Zip 07302; tel. 201/795-7000; Thomas A. Schember, pres.; Thomas F. Zenty, sr. vice-pres. **A**1a 6 9 10 **F**1 2 3 6 9 10 12 14 15 16 23 26 27 30 32 34 35 42 44 45 46 47 50 52 53; **S**1485	21	10	S		254	8303	213	83.9	0	0	29428	14090	680
KEARNY—Hudson County													
★□ WEST HUDSON HOSPITAL, 206 Bergen Ave., Zip 07032; tel. 201/955-7000; Frank P. Smilari, chief exec. off. (Total facility includes 46 beds in nursing home-type unit) **A**1a 9 10 **F**1 3 5 6 10 12 14 15 16 19 21 23 24 26 30 34 35 41 42 44 45 46 47 50 52 53	23	10	S	TF	218	5935	162	74.3	0	0	22824	10594	557
				H	172	5804	123	—	0	0	22291	10071	526
LAKELAND—Camden County													
CAMDEN COUNTY HEALTH SERVICES CENTER, See Blackwood													
LAKEWOOD—Ocean County													
★□ KIMBALL MEDICAL CENTER, 600 River Ave., Zip 08701; tel. 201/363-1900; Joseph Segalla, pres. & chief exec. off. **A**1a 9 10 **F**1 3 6 10 12 14 15 16 20 21 23 26 27 30 32 34 35 36 40 44 45 46 47 49 52 53	23	10	S		307	9867	262	85.3	24	906	42228	17595	934
LAWRENCEVILLE—Mercer County													
★□ Δ ST. LAWRENCE REHABILITATION CENTER, 2381 Lawrenceville Rd., Zip 08648; tel. 609/896-9500; S. Janet Henry, adm. (Total facility includes 66 beds in nursing home-type unit) **A**1a 7 9 10 **F**15 19 21 24 26 33 34 42 44 50; **S**5325	21	46	S	TF	142	1094	77	54.2	0	0	7882	4176	203
				H	76	755	56	—	0	0	6037	3121	—
LIVINGSTON—Essex County													
★□ ST. BARNABAS MEDICAL CENTER, Old Short Hills Rd., Zip 07039; tel. 201/533-5000; Ronald Del Mauro, pres. & chief exec. off. **A**1a 2 3 5 8 9 10 **F**1 2 3 6 7 8 9 10 11 12 13 14 15 16 17 20 22 23 24 26 27 30 32 33 34 35 36 38 40 41 44 45 46 47 49 51 52 53 54	23	10	S		705	26731	485	68.8	36	3690	107537	43044	1822
□ ○ + WEST ESSEX GENERAL HOSPITAL, 204 Hillside Ave., Zip 07039; tel. 201/992-6550; Valeris Glesnes-Anderson, actg. pres. **A**1a 9 10 11 12 **F**1 3 6 10 12 14 15 16 23 26 35 37 44 45 46	23	10	S		94	2391	49	52.1	0	0	9106	4507	224
LONG BRANCH—Monmouth County													
★□ MONMOUTH MEDICAL CENTER, 300 Second Ave., Zip 07740; tel. 201/222-5200; Charles R. Blatchley, chief exec. off. (Nonreporting) **A**1a 2 3 5 8 9 10	23	10	S		506	—	—	—	—	—	—	—	—
LYONS—Somerset County													
★□ VETERANS ADMINISTRATION MEDICAL CENTER, Zip 07939; tel. 201/647-0180; A. Paul Kidd, dir. (Total facility includes 90 beds in nursing home-type unit) **A**1a b **F**3 6 12 14 15 16 19 23 24 25 26 27 28 29 30 31 32 33 34 42 44 46 47 48 49 50	45	10	L	TF	1134	4101	1015	87.5	0	0	55490	42853	1629
				H	1044	4025	927	—	0	0	—	—	1592
MANAHAWKIN—Ocean County													
★ SOUTHERN OCEAN COUNTY HOSPITAL, 1140 W. Bay Ave., Zip 08050; tel. 609/597-6011; David P. Laskowski, adm. (Nonreporting) **A**9 10; **S**0465	23	10	S		100	—	—	—	—	—	—	—	—
MARLBORO—Monmouth County													
★□ MARLBORO PSYCHIATRIC HOSPITAL, Sta. A, Zip 07746; tel. 201/946-8100; David A. Sorensen PhD, chief exec. off. **A**1b 9 10 **F**23 24 33 42 44	12	22	L		845	1769	826	95.3	0	0	42755	29111	1437
MARLTON—Burlington County													
★□ WEST JERSEY HOSPITAL GARDEN STATE DIVISION (Formerly West Jersey Health Systems, Garden State Community Hospital Division), Rte. 73 & Brick Rd., Zip 08053; tel. 609/596-3500; Kevin M. Manley, exec. dir. **A**1a 9 10 **F**1 6 10 12 14 15 16 23 32 33 34 35 43 45 46 47 52; **S**6725	23	10	S		204	8367	160	78.4	24	1514	—	—	523
MILLVILLE—Cumberland County													
★□ MILLVILLE HOSPITAL, High & Harrison Ave., Zip 08332; tel. 609/825-3500; Hal T. McMillen, adm. **A**1a 9 10 **F**1 3 6 7 8 9 10 11 12 14 15 16 23 34 35 45 46 52 53	23	10	S		100	3532	78	78.0	0	0	14532	6579	349
MONTCLAIR—Essex County													
★□ MONTCLAIR COMMUNITY HOSPITAL, 120 Harrison Ave., Zip 07042; tel. 201/744-7300; Emilie M. Murphy, adm. **A**1a 9 10 **F**1 3 6 10 12 14 15 16 23 26 35 37 44 45 46	23	10	S		100	3669	61	61.0	0	0	10033	5107	243
★□ MOUNTAINSIDE HOSPITAL, Bay & Highland Aves., Zip 07042; tel. 201/429-6000; Bernard G. Koval, pres. & chief exec. off. **A**1a 2 3 5 6 9 10 **F**1 2 3 7 8 9 11 12 14 15 16 20 24 26 28 34 35 36 37 40 41 44 45 46 47 48 49 52 54	23	10	S		419	13552	292	69.7	34	959	53095	27935	1281
MORRISTOWN—Morris County													
★□ MORRISTOWN MEMORIAL HOSPITAL (Includes Mount Kemble Division), 100 Madison Ave., Zip 07960; tel. 201/540-5000; Donald A. Bradley, pres. **A**1a 2 3 5 8 9 10 **F**1 2 3 5 6 7 8 9 10 11 12 14 15 16 19 20 23 24 25 26 27 28 30 32 33 34 35 36 37 38 40 42 44 45 46 47 50 52 53 54; **S**0865	23	10	S		606	20783	428	70.6	37	2594	91059	43290	1863
MOUNT HOLLY—Burlington County													
★□ MEMORIAL HOSPITAL OF BURLINGTON COUNTY, 175 Madison Ave., Zip 08060; tel. 609/267-0700; Geoffrey Stone, adm. **A**1a 2 3 5 9 10 **F**1 3 6 7 8 9 10 11 12 14 15 16 20 23 24 26 27 30 32 33 34 35 36 37 38 40 42 44 45 46 47 50 52 53; **S**0465	23	10	S		322	14337	264	82.0	50	2043	54599	23240	1232
MOUNTAINSIDE—Union County													
★□ Δ CHILDREN'S SPECIALIZED HOSPITAL, New Providence Rd., Zip 07091; tel. 201/233-3720; Richard B. Ahlfeld, pres.; Ilana W. Zarafu MD, med. dir. **A**1a 7 10 **F**15 16 24 26 33 34 41 42 44 45 46	23	56	L		60	271	57	95.0	0	0	11315	6713	281
NEPTUNE—Monmouth County													
★□ JERSEY SHORE MEDICAL CENTER, 1945 Corlies Ave., Zip 07753; tel. 201/775-5500; John K. Lloyd, pres. **A**1a 2 3 5 6 8 9 10 **F**1 2 3 5 6 7 8 9 10 11 12 14 15 16 20 21 24 26 27 28 29 30 32 33 34 35 36 37 38 40 41 42 43 44 45 46 47 49 50 51 52 53 54	23	10	S		494	18437	383	77.5	35	1496	66797	32301	1548
NEW BRUNSWICK—Middlesex County													
HURTADO HEALTH CENTER, 11 Bishop Pl., Zip 08903; tel. 201/932-7401; Robert H. Bierman MD, med. dir. **F**2 3 15 18 19 21 22 25 27 28 30 32 34 37 40 46 47 48 51 52	12	11	S		26	544	1	10.9	0	0	1011	929	49
MIDDLESEX GENERAL-UNIVERSITY HOSPITAL, See Robert Wood Johnson University Hospital													
★□ ROBERT WOOD JOHNSON UNIVERSITY HOSPITAL (Formerly Middlesex General-University Hospital), 1 Robert Wood Johnson Pl., Zip 08901; tel. 201/828-3000; G. Bruce McFadden, pres. **A**1a 2 3 5 8 9 10 **F**1 2 3 4 5 6 10 12 14 15 16 20 23 24 26 28 30 32 33 34 35 36 37 38 40 41 44 45 46 47 50 52 53 54	23	10	S		353	12731	263	74.5	24	921	81932	31814	1341
★□ ST. PETER'S MEDICAL CENTER, 254 Easton Ave., Zip 08901; tel. 201/745-8600; Sr. Marie De Pazzi, pres.; John E. Matuska, exec. vice-pres. **A**1a 2 3 5 6 8 9 10 **F**1 3 6 7 8 9 10 11 12 14 15 16 17 21 23 26 30 32 34 35 36 37 38 40 44 45 46 47 49 50 51 52 53 54	21	10	S		424	22581	362	85.0	50	4095	65860	31533	1269
NEW LISBON—Burlington County													
BUTTONWOOD HOSPITAL OF BURLINGTON COUNTY (Formerly Evergreen Park Psychiatric Hospital), Pemberton-Browns Mills Rd., Zip 08064; tel. 609/894-2235; Lynn C. O'Connor, adm. **F**12 15 19 23 24 27 32 33 42 46 47 50	13	48	L	TF	255	400	203	79.6	0	0	6541	3872	290
				H	30	171	76	—	0	0	—	—	—

★ American Hospital Association (AHA) membership
□ Joint Commission on Accreditation of Hospitals (JCAH) accreditation
+ American Osteopathic Hospital Association (AOHA) membership
○ American Osteopathic Association (AOA) accreditation
Δ Commission on Accreditation of Rehabilitation Facilities (CARF) accreditation
Control codes 61, 63, 64, 71, 72 and 73 indicate hospitals listed by AOHA, but not registered by AHA.
For definition of numerical codes, see page A2

Hospital, Address, Telephone, Administrator, Approval and Facility Codes, Multihospital System Code	Classification Codes				Inpatient Data				Newborn Data		Expense (thousands of dollars)		
	Control	Service	Stay	Facilities	Beds	Admissions	Census	Occupancy (percent)	Bassinets	Births	Total	Payroll	Personnel
NEWARK—Essex County													
CHILDREN'S HOSPITAL OF NEW JERSEY, See United Hospitals Medical Center													
★□ COLUMBUS HOSPITAL, 495 N. 13th St., Zip 07107; tel. 201/268-1400; John G. Magliaro, adm. **A**1a 9 10 **F**1 3 6 10 12 14 15 16 23 30 34 35 40 45 46 47 52	23	10	S		206	7854	132	64.1	15	666	21055	10020	515
★□ NEWARK BETH ISRAEL MEDICAL CENTER, 201 Lyons Ave., Zip 07112; tel. 201/926-7000; Lester M. Bornstein, pres. **A**1a 2 3 5 8 9 10 **F**1 3 4 6 7 8 9 10 11 12 13 14 15 16 20 23 24 26 27 28 29 30 31 32 33 34 35 36 37 38 40 41 42 43 44 45 46 47 50 51 52 53 54	23	10	S		545	23281	452	82.9	32	2221	101845	47024	2300
NEWARK EYE AND EAR INFIRMARY, See United Hospitals Medical Center													
ORTHOPEDIC UNIT, See United Hospitals Medical Center													
PRESBYTERIAN UNIT, See United Hospitals Medical Center													
★□ SAINT JAMES HOSPITAL OF NEWARK, 155 Jefferson St., Zip 07105; tel. 201/465-2707; Charles L. Brennan, pres. **A**1a 3 9 10 **F**1 3 6 10 12 14 15 16 20 26 34 35 40 44 45 46 50 52; **S**6545	21	10	S		206	8599	149	72.3	30	613	21974	11248	524
★□ SAINT MICHAEL'S MEDICAL CENTER, 268 Dr. Martin Luther King Jr Blvd., Zip 07102; tel. 201/877-5000; William J. Cornetta Jr., actg. pres. (Nonreporting) **A**1a 3 5 8 9 10; **S**6545	21	10	S		411	—	—	—	—	—	—	—	—
□ UNITED HOSPITALS MEDICAL CENTER (Includes Children's Hospital of New Jersey; Newark Eye and Ear Infirmary; Orthopedic Unit; Presbyterian Unit), 15 S. Ninth St., Zip 07107; tel. 201/268-8000; James R. Cowan MD, pres. & chief exec. off. **A**1a 3 5 9 10 **F**1 3 4 6 8 9 10 12 14 16 19 23 24 26 30 32 34 35 42 44 45 46 47 50 51 52 53 54	23	10	S		429	14615	315	73.4	0	0	75900	43176	1457
★□ UNIVERSITY OF MEDICINE AND DENTISTRY OF NEW JERSEY-UNIVERSITY HOSPITAL, 150 Bergen St., Zip 07103; tel. 201/456-4300; Marc H. Lory, chief exec. off. & vice-pres. **A**1a 2 3 5 8 10 **F**1 3 5 6 7 8 9 10 11 12 14 15 16 20 23 24 26 27 30 32 33 34 35 36 37 38 40 41 43 44 45 46 47 49 51 52 53 54; **S**1755	12	10	S		501	15404	408	81.4	32	2170	119834	55711	2110
NEWTON—Sussex County													
★□ Δ NEWTON MEMORIAL HOSPITAL, 175 High St., Zip 07860; tel. 201/383-2121; Wendel J. Schmitt, pres. **A**1a 2 7 9 10 **F**1 3 6 10 12 14 15 16 21 23 24 25 26 27 28 29 30 32 33 34 35 36 37 40 41 42 43 44 49 52 53	23	10	S		168	7949	126	75.0	24	1049	23224	11323	585
NORTH BERGEN—Hudson County													
★□ PALISADES GENERAL HOSPITAL, 7600 River Rd., Zip 07047; tel. 201/854-5000; Harry Berkowitz, pres. (Nonreporting) **A**1a 9 10; **S**1755	23	10	S		202	—	—	—	—	—	—	—	—
ORANGE—Essex County													
★□ HOSPITAL CENTER AT ORANGE (Includes New Jersey Orthopaedic Hospital Unit; Orange Memorial Hospital Unit), 188 S. Essex Ave., Zip 07051; tel. 201/266-2000; Arthur T. Dunn, pres. & chief exec. off. **A**1a 2 3 5 6 9 10 **F**1 2 3 5 6 7 8 9 10 11 12 14 15 16 23 24 26 34 35 37 40 41 42 44 45 46 47 52 53	23	10	S		332	11142	226	68.1	23	789	39253	20578	983
NEW JERSEY ORTHOPAEDIC HOSPITAL UNIT, See Hospital Center at Orange													
ORANGE MEMORIAL HOSPITAL UNIT, See Hospital Center at Orange													
★□ ST. MARY'S HOSPITAL, 135 S. Center St., Zip 07050; tel. 201/266-3000; Sr. Mary Fidelise, pres. (Nonreporting) **A**1a 9 10; **S**6545	21	10	S		228	—	—	—	—	—	—	—	—
PARAMUS—Bergen County													
★□ BERGEN PINES COUNTY HOSPITAL, E. Ridgewood Ave., Zip 07652; tel. 201/967-4000; Frank Kopczynski, interim chief exec. off. **A**1a 3 5 9 10 **F**1 3 6 8 10 12 15 16 19 23 24 25 27 28 30 32 33 34 35 42 43 44 46 47 48 49 50; **S**0585	13	10	L		1045	6136	952	91.1	0	0	66409	42099	2026
PASSAIC—Passaic County													
★□ BETH ISRAEL HOSPITAL, 70 Parker Ave., Zip 07055; tel. 201/365-5000; Jeffrey S. Moll, exec. dir. & chief exec. off. **A**1a 2 9 10 **F**1 3 6 7 8 9 10 11 12 14 15 16 21 23 24 26 34 35 37 41 43 44 45 46 47 49 50 52 53	23	10	S		223	6183	140	62.8	0	0	27136	12119	611
★□ GENERAL HOSPITAL CENTER AT PASSAIC (Formerly Passaic General Hospital), 350 Boulevard, Zip 07055; tel. 201/365-4300; Daniel Marcantuono, pres. **A**1a 9 10 **F**1 3 4 5 6 10 12 14 15 16 17 26 34 35 36 40 43 52 53 54	23	10	S		303	12900	229	75.6	25	1134	50908	21758	1009
PASSAIC GENERAL HOSPITAL, See General Hospital Center at Passaic													
★□ ST. MARY'S HOSPITAL, 211 Pennington Ave., Zip 07055; tel. 201/470-3000; Hugh Quigley, adm. **A**1a 9 10 **F**1 2 3 6 14 15 16 26 27 28 29 30 34 35 37 40 42 43 45 46 47 52 53; **S**5815	21	10	S		222	8125	167	75.2	34	660	28220	14282	676
PATERSON—Passaic County													
★□ BARNERT MEMORIAL HOSPITAL CENTER, 680 Broadway, Zip 07514; tel. 201/977-6600; Bruce M. Topolosky, pres. & chief exec. off. **A**1a 9 10 **F**1 2 3 6 8 10 12 14 16 23 24 26 27 28 29 30 32 33 34 35 36 40 42 43 44 45 46 49 50 52 53	23	10	S		212	10231	175	79.5	25	997	30509	15195	756
★□ ST. JOSEPH'S HOSPITAL AND MEDICAL CENTER, 703 Main St., Zip 07503; tel. 201/977-2000; Sr. Jane Frances Brady, pres. (Total facility includes 135 beds in nursing home-type unit) **A**1a 2 3 5 8 9 10 **F**1 2 3 4 5 6 7 8 9 10 11 12 14 15 16 19 20 23 24 26 27 28 29 30 31 32 33 34 35 36 37 38 40 42 43 44 45 46 47 51 52 53 54; **S**5815	21	10	S	TF	701	22815	642	91.6	30	2455	104651	54741	2526
				H	566	22778	509	—	30	2455	101080	52478	2349
PEAPACK—Somerset County													
★ MATHENY SCHOOL, Main St., Zip 07977; tel. 201/234-0011; Elaine Baumeister, dir. **A**10 **F**19 23 24 25 33 42 44	23	59	L		102	23	70	68.6	0	0	5091	3206	55
PERTH AMBOY—Middlesex County													
OLD BRIDGE DIVISION, See Raritan Bay Medical Center													
PERTH AMBOY DIVISION, See Raritan Bay Medical Center													
★□ RARITAN BAY MEDICAL CENTER (Includes Old Bridge Division; Perth Amboy Division), 530 New Brunswick Ave., Zip 08861; tel. 201/442-3700; Keith H. McLaughlin, pres. & chief exec. off. **A**1a 3 5 6 9 10 **F**1 2 3 5 6 9 10 12 14 15 16 20 21 23 24 26 27 30 32 34 35 36 37 40 42 43 44 45 46 48 49 50 52 53	23	10	S		539	16015	353	65.5	45	1329	65508	33918	1553
PHILLIPSBURG—Warren County													
★□ WARREN HOSPITAL, 185 Roseberry St., Zip 08865; tel. 201/859-6700; John A. Demarrais, adm. **A**1a 2 3 5 9 10 **F**1 3 6 10 11 12 14 15 16 24 27 30 32 34 35 36 40 42 44 45 46 47 49 50 52 53	23	10	S		250	8213	159	63.6	15	595	25156	11551	594
PLAINFIELD—Union County													
★□ MUHLENBERG REGIONAL MEDICAL CENTER (Formerly Muhlenberg Hospital), Park Ave. & Randolph Rd., Box 1272, Zip 07061; tel. 201/668-2000; David M. Ridgway, pres. **A**1a 3 5 6 8 9 10 **F**1 2 3 5 6 7 8 9 10 11 12 14 15 16 20 21 24 26 27 28 30 32 34 35 36 37 39 40 41 43 44 45 46 47 50 52 53	23	10	S		424	16676	309	72.9	43	1897	62742	29237	1481
POINT PLEASANT—Ocean County													
★□ NORTHERN OCEAN HOSPITAL SYSTEM (Includes Brick Hospital Division, 425 Jack Martin Blvd., Brick Township, Zip 08724; tel. 201/840-2200; Richard J. Leone, pres.; Point Pleasant Hospital Division, 2121 Edgewater Pl., Zip 08742; tel. 202/892-1100; Richard J. Leone, pres.), 2121 Edgewater Pl., Zip 08742; tel. 201/892-1100; Richard J. Leone, pres. **A**1a 9 10 **F**1 2 3 5 6 10 12 14 15 16 20 21 23 24 26 34 35 36 40 41 44 45 46 47 49 50 52 53	23	10	S		384	15224	342	85.1	23	1484	55396	25058	1288

Hospital, Address, Telephone, Administrator, Approval and Facility Codes, Multihospital System Code	Classification Codes				Inpatient Data				Newborn Data		Expense (thousands of dollars)		
★ American Hospital Association (AHA) membership □ Joint Commission on Accreditation of Hospitals (JCAH) accreditation + American Osteopathic Hospital Association (AOHA) membership ○ American Osteopathic Association (AOA) accreditation Δ Commission on Accreditation of Rehabilitation Facilities (CARF) accreditation Control codes 61, 63, 64, 71, 72 and 73 indicate hospitals listed by AOHA, but not registered by AHA. For definition of numerical codes, see page A2	Control	Service	Stay	Facilities	Beds	Admissions	Census	Occupancy (percent)	Bassinets	Births	Total	Payroll	Personnel
POMONA—Atlantic County													
[★] Δ BETTY BACHARACH REHABILITATION HOSPITAL, Jim Leeds Rd., Zip 08240; tel. 609/652-7000; Joseph C. Affanato, adm. **A**1a 7 9 10 **F**15 16 24 26 32 33 34 41 42 44 45 46 47 50	23	46	L		80	715	68	85.0	0	0	8428	4598	238
POMPTON PLAINS—Morris County													
[★] CHILTON MEMORIAL HOSPITAL, 97 W. Parkway, Zip 07444; tel. 201/831-5000; Gerald M. Krantz, pres. & chief exec. off. **A**1a 9 10 **F**1 3 6 10 12 14 15 16 23 24 27 30 32 33 34 35 36 37 40 43 44 50 52 53	23	10	S		243	13206	191	78.6	25	1468	36952	16631	751
PRINCETON—Mercer County													
[★] MEDICAL CENTER AT PRINCETON (Includes Acute General Hospital Unit, Merwick Unit-Extended Care and Rehabilitation, Princeton House Unit-Community Mental Health); 253 Witherspoon St., Zip 08540; tel. 609/921-7700; Dennis W. Doody, pres. (Total facility includes 160 beds in nursing home-type unit) **A**1a 2 3 5 9 10 **F**1 2 3 6 7 8 9 10 11 12 14 15 16 19 21 24 25 26 27 28 30 32 33 34 35 36 37 40 41 42 44 45 46 47 48 49 50 52 53	23	10	S	TF	427	16526	316	74.0	24	1744	—	—	1249
				H	267	15170	187	—	24	1744	—	—	890
PRINCETON UNIVERSITY HEALTH SERVICES, MCCOSH HEALTH CENTER, Zip 08544; tel. 609/452-3129; Louis A. Pyle Jr. MD, dir. (Nonreporting)	23	11	S		21	—	—	—	—	—	—	—	—
RAHWAY—Union County													
[★] RAHWAY HOSPITAL, 865 Stone St., Zip 07065; tel. 201/381-4200; John L. Yoder, pres. (Total facility includes 10 beds in nursing home-type unit) **A**1a 9 10 **F**1 2 3 5 6 9 10 12 14 15 16 19 21 23 24 28 29 30 32 34 35 36 37 40 42 43 44 45 46 47 50 52 53	23	10	S	TF	253	10896	190	75.1	30	954	33353	16477	733
				H	243	10839	185	—	30	954	33213	16368	—
RED BANK—Monmouth County													
[★] Δ RIVERVIEW MEDICAL CENTER, 35 Union St., Zip 07701; tel. 201/741-2700; John K. Pawlowski, pres. **A**1a 2 7 9 10 **F**1 2 3 6 7 8 9 10 11 12 14 16 21 23 24 25 27 28 29 30 32 34 35 36 40 42 44 45 46 47 48 49 52 53	23	10	S		507	16092	377	74.4	48	2327	60247	24357	1548
RIDGEWOOD—Bergen County													
[★] VALLEY HOSPITAL, Linwood & N. Van Dien Aves., Zip 07451; tel. 201/447-8000; Michael W. Azzara, pres. **A**1a 2 9 10 **F**1 2 3 6 7 8 9 10 11 12 14 15 16 20 21 23 24 26 27 28 30 32 34 35 37 40 41 42 44 45 46 47 49 50 52 53 54	23	10	S		387	25368	326	84.2	43	2875	59067	31716	1416
RIVERSIDE—Burlington County													
[★] ZURBRUGG MEMORIAL HOSPITAL-RIVERSIDE DIVISION, Hospital Plaza, Zip 08075; tel. 609/461-6700; John Tegley, sr. vice-pres. (Nonreporting) **A**1a 9 10; **S**0015	23	10	S		173	—	—	—	—	—	—	—	—
SADDLE BROOK—Bergen County													
□ ○ + KENNEDY MEMORIAL HOSPITALS AT SADDLE BROOK (Formerly Saddle Brook General Hospital), 300 Market St., Zip 07662; tel. 201/368-6000; Paul R. Cardillo, exec. dir. **A**1a 9 10 11 12 13 **F**1 3 6 10 12 14 15 16 23 34 35 37 43 46 47 50	23	10	S		112	3749	68	89.5	0	0	15318	6928	518
SALEM—Salem County													
[★] MEMORIAL HOSPITAL OF SALEM COUNTY (Formerly Salem County Memorial Hospital), Salem Woodstown Rd., Zip 08079; tel. 609/935-1000; Jos Michael Galvin Jr., pres. **A**1a 9 10 **F**1 3 6 10 12 14 15 16 23 34 35 36 37 40 41 45 46 50 52 53	23	10	S		152	5863	114	75.0	16	496	20103	9318	427
SECAUCUS—Hudson County													
HUDSON COUNTY MEADOWVIEW HOSPITAL, 595 County Ave., Zip 07094; tel. 201/863-5100; Joseph G. Mraz, supt. (Nonreporting) **A**9 10	13	49	L		640	—	—	—	—	—	—	—	—
□ MEADOWLANDS HOSPITAL MEDICAL CENTER (Formerly Riverside General Hospital), Meadowland Pkwy., Zip 07094; tel. 201/392-3100; Paul V. Cavalli MD, pres. & chief exec. off.; Helen M. Kennedy, exec. vice-pres. & adm. (Nonreporting) **A**1a 9 10; **S**6905	32	10	S		200	—	—	—	—	—	—	—	—
RIVERSIDE GENERAL HOSPITAL, See Meadowlands Hospital Medical Center													
SOMERS POINT—Atlantic County													
[★] SHORE MEMORIAL HOSPITAL, E. New York Ave., Zip 08244; tel. 609/653-3500; Richard A. Pitman, exec. vice-pres. **A**1a 9 10 **F**1 2 3 6 10 12 14 15 16 20 23 24 35 36 40 41 42 44 45 46 49 52 53	23	10	S		285	12084	228	80.6	28	1259	47165	19819	937
SOMERVILLE—Somerset County													
[★] SOMERSET MEDICAL CENTER, Rehill Ave., Zip 08876; tel. 201/685-2200; William J. Monagle, pres. **A**1a 2 3 5 9 10 **F**1 2 3 6 7 9 10 11 12 14 15 16 20 21 24 25 26 27 28 29 30 32 33 34 35 36 37 40 41 42 43 44 45 46 47 49 50 52 53	23	10	S		377	12583	238	63.1	35	1254	43961	23268	1046
SOUTH AMBOY—Middlesex County													
[★] SOUTH AMBOY MEMORIAL HOSPITAL AND COMMUNITY MENTAL HEALTH CENTER, 540 Bordentown Ave., Zip 08879; tel. 201/721-1000; Irv J. Diamond, chief exec. off. **A**1a 9 10 **F**1 3 6 10 12 14 15 16 23 26 27 28 29 30 31 32 33 34 35 44 45 46 47 49 53	23	10	S		144	5234	109	75.7	0	0	18539	10312	461
STRATFORD—Camden County													
★ ○ + KENNEDY MEMORIAL HOSPITALS UNIVERSITY MEDICAL CENTER (Includes Cherry Hill Division, Chapel Ave. & Cooper Landing Rd., Cherry Hill, Zip 08002; Mailing Address P O Box 5009, Cherry Hill, Zip 08034; tel. 609/488-6500; Andrew E. Harris, adm.; Washington Township Division, Hurffville-Cross Keys Rd., Turnersville, Zip 08012; tel. 609/582-2500; Kenneth Kozloff, adm.), 113 E. Laurel Rd., Zip 08084; tel. 609/784-4000; Augustine R. Pirolli, pres. **A**9 10 11 12 13 **F**1 3 6 9 10 12 14 15 16 21 23 24 27 28 30 32 33 34 35 36 37 38 40 41 42 43 44 45 46 47 52 53 54	23	10	S		607	23895	400	65.9	41	2220	82016	33127	1605
SUMMIT—Union County													
□ FAIR OAKS HOSPITAL, 19 Prospect St., Zip 07901; tel. 201/522-7000; William A. Howe, adm. (Nonreporting) **A**1b 9 10; **S**0825	33	22	L		144	—	—	—	—	—	—	—	—
[★] OVERLOOK HOSPITAL, 99 Beauvoir Ave. at Sylvan Rd., Zip 07901; tel. 201/522-2000; Thomas J. Foley, pres. & chief exec. off. (Nonreporting) **A**1a 2 3 5 8 9 10; **S**0865	23	10	S		564	—	—	—	—	—	—	—	—
SUSSEX—Sussex County													
[★] WALLKILL VALLEY GENERAL HOSPITAL, 20 Walnut St., Zip 07461; tel. 201/875-4121; John J. Farley, pres. (Nonreporting) **A**1a 2 9 10	23	10	S		106	—	—	—	—	—	—	—	—
TEANECK—Bergen County													
[★] HOLY NAME HOSPITAL, 718 Teaneck Rd., Zip 07666; tel. 201/833-3000; Sr. Patricia A. Lynch, adm. **A**1a 2 3 6 9 10 **F**1 3 5 6 9 10 12 14 15 16 18 20 23 24 26 27 29 30 32 34 35 36 37 41 42 43 44 45 46 47 49 52 53	21	10	S		377	14541	266	70.6	34	1387	50056	25262	1169
TOMS RIVER—Ocean County													
[★] COMMUNITY MEMORIAL HOSPITAL, Hwy. 37 W., Cn 2002, Zip 08753; tel. 201/349-8000; James P. Schuessler, pres. **A**1a 9 10 **F**1 2 3 6 7 8 9 10 11 12 14 15 16 20 21 23 24 26 34 35 36 37 38 40 41 44 45 46 47 52 53	23	10	S		460	16496	414	90.0	20	1279	69485	30027	1502
[★] Δ GARDEN STATE REHABILITATION HOSPITAL, 14 Hospital Dr., Zip 08753; tel. 201/244-3100; H. P. Thesingh, chief exec. off. & adm. (Total facility includes 92 beds in nursing home-type unit) **A**1a 7 10 **F**15 16 19 23 24 26 28 32 33 34 42 44 46 47 50; **S**0825	33	46	L	TF	146	710	131	89.7	0	0	10090	5140	332
				H	54	589	50	—	0	0	—	—	220

Hospital, Address, Telephone, Administrator, Approval and Facility Codes, Multihospital System Code

- ★ American Hospital Association (AHA) membership
- □ Joint Commission on Accreditation of Hospitals (JCAH) accreditation
- + American Osteopathic Hospital Association (AOHA) membership
- ○ American Osteopathic Association (AOA) accreditation
- Δ Commission on Accreditation of Rehabilitation Facilities (CARF) accreditation

Control codes 61, 63, 64, 71, 72 and 73 indicate hospitals listed by AOHA, but not registered by AHA. For definition of numerical codes, see page A2

Hospital, Address, Telephone, Administrator, Approval and Facility Codes, Multihospital System Code	Classification Codes				Inpatient Data				Newborn Data		Expense (thousands of dollars)		
	Control	Service	Stay	Facilities	Beds	Admissions	Census	Occupancy (percent)	Bassinets	Births	Total	Payroll	Personnel
TRENTON—Mercer County													
★□ HELENE FULD MEDICAL CENTER, 750 Brunswick Ave., Zip 08638; tel. 609/394-6000; William K. Hogan, chief exec. off. **A**1a 3 5 6 9 10 **F**1 3 4 5 6 10 11 12 14 15 16 20 23 24 26 27 28 29 30 31 32 33 34 35 36 37 38 40 41 42 43 44 45 46 49 50 52 53 54	23	10	S		327	9587	222	64.9	40	809	43613	20711	1008
★□ MERCER MEDICAL CENTER, 446 Bellevue Ave., Box 1658, Zip 08607; tel. 609/394-4000; Charles E. Baer, pres. **A**1a 2 6 9 10 **F**1 2 3 6 7 8 9 10 11 12 14 15 16 24 28 32 34 36 37 38 40 44 45 46 47 52 53	23	10	S		336	13105	235	69.9	36	2375	45253	21488	1073
NEW JERSEY STATE PRISON HOSPITAL, Third & Federal Sts., Zip 08611; Mailing Address Drawer N, Zip 08625; tel. 609/292-7456; Brigetta Mitchell, adm. (Nonreporting)	12	11	S		23	—	—	—	—	—	—	—	—
★□ ST. FRANCIS MEDICAL CENTER, 601 Hamilton Ave., Zip 08629; tel. 609/599-5000; Patrick F. Roche, pres. **A**1a 2 3 5 6 9 10 **F**1 2 3 5 6 7 8 9 10 11 12 14 15 16 17 20 26 27 28 29 30 34 35 36 38 40 43 44 45 46 50 52 53 54; **S**5325	23	10	S		409	15597	323	79.0	35	603	53684	23898	1251
★□ TRENTON PSYCHIATRIC HOSPITAL, Mailing Address Box 7500, West Trenton, Zip 08628; tel. 609/633-1500; Frank G. Cuomo, chief exec. off. (Nonreporting) **A**1b 3 5 9 10	12	22	L		473	—	—	—	—	—	—	—	—
TURNERSVILLE—Gloucester County													
WASHINGTON TOWNSHIP DIVISION, See Kennedy Memorial Hospitals-University Medical Center													
UNION—Union County													
★ ○ + UNION HOSPITAL (Formerly Memorial General Hospital), 1000 Galloping Hill Rd., Zip 07083; tel. 201/687-1900; Victor J. Fresolone, pres. **A**9 10 11 12 13 **F**1 3 5 6 8 9 10 11 12 14 15 16 21 23 26 27 30 32 33 34 35 41 45 46 47 48 49 50 53	23	10	S		201	7629	146	72.6	0	0	27458	11400	446
VINELAND—Cumberland County													
★□ NEWCOMB MEDICAL CENTER, 65 S. State St., Zip 08360; tel. 609/691-9000; Dan L. Rex, pres. & chief exec. off. **A**1a 9 10 **F**1 3 5 6 10 12 14 15 16 23 24 26 34 35 36 37 40 42 44 45 46 47 52 53	23	10	S		243	7473	139	57.2	21	1367	26032	13427	640
□ VINELAND DEVELOPMENT CENTER HOSPITAL, 1676 E. Landis Ave., Zip 08360; tel. 609/696-6200; Bernardo O. Peralta MD, med. dir. **A**1b 10 **F**3 12 14 15 16 24 26 28 30 32 33 34 35 42 44	12	12	S		110	994	65	59.1	0	0	—	—	279
VOORHEES—Camden County													
★□ WEST JERSEY HOSPITAL, EASTERN DIVISION, Evesham Rd., Zip 08043; tel. 609/772-5000; Thomas H. Litz, exec. dir. **A**1a 3 5 9 **F**1 3 6 9 10 11 12 14 15 16 23 26 34 35 36 37 40 45 46 47 51 52 53; **S**6725	23	10	S		246	10880	193	80.1	40	1659	—	—	618
WAYNE—Passaic County													
★□ WAYNE GENERAL HOSPITAL, 224 Hamburg Turnpike, Zip 07470; tel. 201/942-6900; Justin E. Doheny, pres. **A**1a 9 10 **F**1 3 6 7 9 10 11 12 14 15 16 23 26 28 29 30 31 32 33 34 35 36 37 40 45 46 47 49 53	23	10	S		189	9022	173	81.2	27	681	29590	14462	719
WEST ORANGE—Essex County													
★□ Δ KESSLER INSTITUTE FOR REHABILITATION (Includes East Orange Facility, West Orange Facility and Saddle Brook Facility), 1199 Pleasant Valley Way, Zip 07052; tel. 201/731-3600; Kenneth W. Aitchison, pres.; Joel A. Delisa MD, med. dir. **A**1a 3 5 7 10 **F**6 15 16 23 24 26 33 34 42 44 45 46	23	46	L		178	1329	146	82.1	0	0	—	—	611
WESTWOOD—Bergen County													
★□ PASCACK VALLEY HOSPITAL, Old Hook Rd., Zip 07675; tel. 201/358-3000; Louis R. Ycre Jr., exec. dir. **A**1a 2 9 10 **F**1 3 6 9 10 12 14 15 16 23 24 26 34 35 36 37 40 44 45 46 52 53	23	10	S		256	12613	198	77.3	18	1120	36328	17714	821
WILLINGBORO—Burlington County													
★□ ZURBRUGG MEMORIAL HOSPITAL, RANCOCAS VALLEY DIVISION, Sunset Rd., Zip 08046; tel. 609/835-2900; George Hartnett, pres. (Nonreporting) **A**1a ; **S**0015	23	10	S		318	—	—	—	—	—	—	—	—
WOODBINE—Cape May County													
WOODBINE DEVELOPMENTAL CENTER, De Hirsch Ave., Zip 08270; tel. 609/861-2164; Bernard B. Blanks, supt. **F**23 24 33 42 43 44 46 47 50	12	62	L		750	16	11	—	0	0	—	—	164
WOODBRIDGE—Middlesex County													
WOODBRIDGE DEVELOPMENT CENTER, Rahway Ave., P O Box 189, Zip 07095; tel. 201/636-3400; Amy R. Bailon MD, med. dir. (Nonreporting)	12	12	S		125	—	—	—	—	—	—	—	—
WOODBURY—Gloucester County													
★□ UNDERWOOD-MEMORIAL HOSPITAL, 509 N. Broad St., P O Box 359, Zip 08096; tel. 609/845-0100; William D. Thompson, pres. **A**1a 3 5 9 10 **F**1 2 3 6 10 12 14 15 16 18 23 24 26 27 30 32 35 36 40 44 45 46 52 53	23	10	S		339	13375	249	73.5	32	1528	39879	19840	1029
WYCKOFF—Bergen County													
□ CHRISTIAN HEALTH CARE CENTER, 301 Sicomac Ave., Zip 07481; tel. 201/848-0300; Robert Van Dyk, exec. dir. (Total facility includes 120 beds in nursing home-type unit) **A**1b 9 **F**19 24 28 30 32 33 42 45 46 49	23	22	L	TF	228	131	223	97.8	0	0	—	—	233
				H	108	88	103	—	0	0	—	—	106

★ American Hospital Association (AHA) membership
□ Joint Commission on Accreditation of Hospitals (JCAH) accreditation
\+ American Osteopathic Hospital Association (AOHA) membership
○ American Osteopathic Association (AOA) accreditation
Δ Commission on Accreditation of Rehabilitation Facilities (CARF) accreditation
Control codes 61, 63, 64, 71, 72 and 73 indicate hospitals listed by AOHA, but not registered by AHA.
For definition of numerical codes, see page A2

New Mexico

Hospital, Address, Telephone, Administrator, Approval and Facility Codes, Multihospital System Code	Classification Codes: Control	Service	Stay	Facilities	Inpatient Data: Beds	Admissions	Census	Occupancy (percent)	Newborn Data: Bassinets	Births	Expense (thousands of dollars): Total	Payroll	Personnel
ALAMOGORDO—Otero County													
★□ GERALD CHAMPION MEMORIAL HOSPITAL, 1209 Ninth St., Box 597, Zip 88310; tel. 505/437-3770; Carl W. Mantey, adm. **A**1a 9 10 **F**1 3 6 12 14 15 16 23 34 35 36 40 45; **S**1755	23	10	S		59	3591	39	65.0	10	455	9097	4052	192
ALBUQUERQUE—Bernalillo County													
★ CARRIE TINGLEY HOSPITAL (Formerly Carrie Tingley Crippled Children's Hospital), 1127 University Blvd. N.E., Zip 87102; tel. 505/841-5000; Linda Worley, adm. **A**3 5 9 10 **F**15 16 23 24 26 32 34 38 42 44 45 46 47 52	12	57	S		30	465	9	31.0	0	0	5877	1913	115
★□ ○ + HEIGHTS GENERAL HOSPITAL, 4701 Montgomery N.E., Zip 87109; tel. 505/888-7800; Polly Pine, adm. **A**1a 9 10 11 12 13 **F**1 3 6 10 12 14 15 16 17 21 23 24 35 36 40 45 46 47 50 53	23	10	S		80	3728	41	51.3	10	379	15629	5896	251
★□ HEIGHTS PSYCHIATRIC HOSPITAL, 103 Hospital Loop N.E., Zip 87109; tel. 505/883-8777; Andrea Brightwell, adm. **A**1b 9 10 **F**15 24 28 29 30 32 33 42 43 44 47; **S**1755	33	22	S		80	569	43	53.8	0	0	4926	2051	118
★ KASEMAN PRESBYTERIAN HOSPITAL, 8300 Constitution Ave. N.E., Zip 87110; tel. 505/291-2000; Phillip J. Todd, adm. **A**9 10 **F**1 3 6 9 10 12 14 15 16 20 23 24 26 27 30 32 33 34 35 42 45 46 47 52 53; **S**3505	23	10	S		192	7497	125	68.7	0	0	24935	9440	448
★□ LOVELACE MEDICAL CENTER, 5400 Gibson Blvd. S.E., Zip 87108; tel. 505/262-7000; Richard E. Gillock, vice-pres. & adm. **A**1a 2 3 5 9 10 **F**1 3 4 5 6 10 11 12 14 15 16 17 20 23 24 28 30 31 32 33 34 35 36 37 38 40 41 43 44 45 46 47 48 50 52 53 54; **S**1755	33	10	S		177	9533	115	65.0	16	1462	83469	26922	1420
★ NORTHSIDE PRESBYTERIAN HOSPITAL, 5901 Harper Dr. N.E., Zip 87109; tel. 505/823-8500; Gordon R. Aird, adm. **A**9 10 **F**1 3 6 9 10 11 14 15 16 23 24 34 35 37 43 44 45 46 47 48 49 52 53; **S**3505	23	10	S		57	1063	24	42.1	0	0	7953	2646	152
★□ PRESBYTERIAN HOSPITAL, P O Box 26666, Zip 87125; tel. 505/841-1443; Robert Luther, adm. **A**1a 2 3 5 9 10 **F**1 2 3 4 6 10 11 12 13 14 15 16 20 21 23 24 34 35 36 37 40 41 44 45 46 47 50 51 52 53 54; **S**3505	23	10	S		413	20749	279	67.6	47	3894	77992	26900	1647
★□ ST. JOSEPH HEALTH CARE CORPORATION (Formerly St. Joseph Hospital), 400 Walter St. N.E., Zip 87102; tel. 505/848-8000; John M. Kirk, pres. **A**1a 2 9 10 **F**1 3 5 6 7 8 9 10 11 12 14 15 16 23 24 25 26 34 35 36 40 42 43 44 45 46 47 52 53; **S**5115	23	10	S		377	11361	190	50.4	12	630	60014	25980	1376
★□ U. S. PUBLIC HEALTH SERVICE INDIAN HOSPITAL, 801 Vassar Dr. N.E., Zip 87106; tel. 505/262-6325; Raymond L. Rodgers, serv. ut dir. **A**1a 10 **F**1 6 15 24 28 32 33 34 35 37 44 49 52	47	10	S		36	1218	19	52.8	0	0	5729	4339	163
★□ UNIVERSITY OF NEW MEXICO HOSPITAL-BERNALILLO COUNTY MEDICAL CENTER, 2211 Lomas Blvd. N.E., Zip 87106; tel. 505/843-2111; William H. Johnson Jr., chief exec. off. **A**1a 2 3 5 8 9 **F**1 3 4 5 6 12 13 14 15 16 22 23 24 26 32 33 34 35 36 37 38 40 41 45 46 47 51 52 53 54	12	10	S		275	14460	210	76.4	19	2875	61354	29408	1501
★ UNIVERSITY OF NEW MEXICO MENTAL HEALTH CENTER, 2600 Marble N.E., Zip 87106; tel. 505/843-2811; Juan Vigil, adm. (Total facility includes 16 beds in nursing home-type unit) **A**9 10 **F**19 28 29 30 31 32 33 34 35 45 46 48 49	13	22	S	TF	95	1979	85	89.5	0	0	13635	8628	417
				H	79	1939	67	—	0	0	—	—	408
★□ VETERANS ADMINISTRATION MEDICAL CENTER, 2100 Ridgecrest Dr. S.E., Zip 87108; tel. 505/265-1711; Andrew Montano, dir. (Total facility includes 47 beds in nursing home-type unit) **A**1a 2 3 5 8 **F**1 3 4 6 9 10 11 12 14 15 16 19 20 23 24 26 27 28 29 30 31 32 33 34 41 42 43 44 46 47 48 49 50 53 54	45	10	S	TF	447	10013	309	70.4	0	0	72009	31021	1218
				H	400	9826	262	—	0	0	—	—	1191
★□ VISTA SANDIA HOSPITAL, 501 Alameda Blvd. N.E., Zip 87113; tel. 505/823-2000; Audrey M. Worrell MD, chief exec. off. & med. dir. **A**1b 9 10 **F**15 24 28 29 30 32 33 34 42 43 44 48 49; **S**8895	23	22	S		92	601	39	42.4	0	0	3531	1771	93
ARTESIA—Eddy County													
★□ ARTESIA GENERAL HOSPITAL, 702 N. 13th St., Zip 88210; tel. 505/748-3333; Joe Abrutz, adm. **A**1a 9 10 **F**1 6 16 23 34 35 36 37 40 43 45 52; **S**3505	16	10	S		36	1289	14	38.9	6	161	3319	1329	73
BELEN—Valencia County													
★ VALENCIA PRESBYTERIAN HOSPITAL, 609 S. Christopher Rd., Zip 87002; tel. 505/864-2221; John Zondlo, adm. **A**9 10 **F**1 6 12 14 15 16 23 30 35 36 37 40 41 45 46 47 52 53; **S**3505	23	10	S		25	1684	18	72.0	6	156	3041	1158	66
CANNON AIR FORCE BASE—Curry County													
U. S. AIR FORCE HOSPITAL, Zip 88103; tel. 505/784-4582; Maj. Michael S. Waters, adm. (Nonreporting)	41	10	S		40	—	—	—	—	—	—	—	—
CARLSBAD—Eddy County													
★□ GUADALUPE MEDICAL CENTER, 2430 W. Pierce St., Zip 88220; tel. 505/887-6633; Donald E. Barton, adm. **A**1a 9 10 **F**1 3 6 12 14 15 16 20 21 23 24 26 27 28 29 30 31 32 33 34 35 40 41 42 43 44 45 51 52 53 54; **S**1755	33	10	S		144	5560	77	53.5	12	672	17192	6271	340
CLAYTON—Union County													
★ UNION COUNTY GENERAL HOSPITAL, 301 Harding St., Box 489, Zip 88415; tel. 505/374-2585; Doris B. Turgeon, adm. **A**9 10 **F**1 3 14 15 16 35 36 40 45 52; **S**2235	23	10	S		30	783	7	23.3	4	67	1585	680	45
CLOVIS—Curry County													
★□ CLOVIS HIGH PLAINS HOSPITAL, 2100 N. Thomas St., Box 1688, Zip 88101; tel. 505/769-2141; Phillip J. Todd, adm. **A**1a 9 10 **F**1 3 6 7 10 12 14 15 16 20 23 26 34 36 40 41 45 46 49 52 53; **S**3505	23	10	S		106	4935	81	76.4	13	321	13324	4905	275
CROWNPOINT—McKinley County													
★□ U. S. PUBLIC HEALTH SERVICE INDIAN HOSPITAL, Box 358, Zip 87313; tel. 505/786-5291; Rosalyn T. Curtis, serv. unit dir. **A**1a 10 **F**6 14 15 23 28 30 32 33 34 35 37 40 52	47	10	S		28	966	11	39.3	7	115	—	—	104
CUBA—Bernalillo County													
CUBA HOSPITAL, State Hwy. 44, Box 638, Zip 87013; tel. 505/289-3291; H. Donald Alexander, adm. (Nonreporting) **A**9 10	23	10	S		9	—	—	—	—	—	—	—	—
DEMING—Luna County													
★ MIMBRES MEMORIAL HOSPITAL, 900 W. Ash St., Zip 88030; tel. 505/546-2761; Roy Rumbaugh, adm. (Total facility includes 70 beds in nursing home-type unit) **A**9 10 **F**1 3 6 16 19 34 35 40 45 52	13	10	S	TF	118	2446	93	78.8	10	312	4600	2437	174
				H	48	2384	26	—	10	312	3555	1785	119
ESPANOLA—Rio Arriba County													
★□ ESPANOLA HOSPITAL, 1010 Spruce St., Zip 87532; tel. 505/753-7111; Grant H. Nelson, adm. **A**1a 9 10 **F**1 6 10 12 14 15 16 23 34 35 36 40 41 43 45 46 47 52 53; **S**3505	23	10	S		80	3611	34	42.5	10	415	9104	3613	194

★ American Hospital Association (AHA) membership
□ Joint Commission on Accreditation of Hospitals (JCAH) accreditation
+ American Osteopathic Hospital Association (AOHA) membership
○ American Osteopathic Association (AOA) accreditation
Δ Commission on Accreditation of Rehabilitation Facilities (CARF) accreditation
Control codes 61, 63, 64, 71, 72 and 73 indicate hospitals listed by AOHA, but not registered by AHA.
For definition of numerical codes, see page A2

Hospital, Address, Telephone, Administrator, Approval and Facility Codes, Multihospital System Code	Classification Codes				Inpatient Data				Newborn Data		Expense (thousands of dollars)		
	Control	Service	Stay	Facilities	Beds	Admissions	Census	Occupancy (percent)	Bassinets	Births	Total	Payroll	Personnel
FARMINGTON—San Juan County													
★□ SAN JUAN REGIONAL MEDICAL CENTER, 801 W. Maple St., Zip 87401; tel. 505/325-5011; Donald R. Carlson, exec. dir. **A**1a 9 10 **F**1 3 5 6 9 12 14 15 16 23 24 26 30 34 35 36 37 39 40 42 44 45 46 52 53	23	10	S		118	5958	69	56.1	16	1153	19607	9674	443
FORT BAYARD—Grant County													
FORT BAYARD MEDICAL CENTER, Box 219, Zip 88036; tel. 505/537-3302; Arthur E. Salas, adm. (Nonreporting) **A**9	12	82	S		233	—	—	—	—	—	—	—	—
GALLUP—McKinley County													
★□ GALLUP INDIAN MEDICAL CENTER, E. Nizhoni Blvd., Box 1337, Zip 87301; tel. 505/722-1403; Timothy G. Fleming MD, serv. unit dir. **A**1a 10 **F**1 3 6 12 14 15 16 23 26 27 28 29 30 32 33 34 35 36 37 40 41 46 50 52 53	47	10	S		138	6685	87	63.0	18	1293	15643	11992	526
★ REHOBOTH MCKINLEY CHRISTIAN HOSPITAL, 1901 Red Rock Dr., Zip 87301; tel. 505/863-6832; Virginia W. Goodrich, adm. **A**9 10 **F**1 3 6 12 14 15 16 17 20 23 26 34 35 40 45 46 47 50 52	23	10	S		71	2655	31	43.7	18	422	9182	3286	181
GRANTS—Cibola County													
★□ CIBOLA GENERAL HOSPITAL, 1212 Bonita Ave., Zip 87020; tel. 505/287-4446; Donald L. Caughron, adm. **A**1a 9 10 **F**1 3 16 17 23 35 36 40 45 52 53; **S**1755	23	10	S		39	1304	14	35.9	10	186	3263	1556	79
HOBBS—Lea County													
★□ LEA REGIONAL HOSPITAL, Lovington Hwy. 18, Box 3000, Zip 88240; tel. 505/392-6581; R. Gordon Taylor, adm. **A**1a 9 10 **F**1 3 5 6 10 12 14 15 16 23 27 30 32 33 34 35 40 42 44 45 46 47 48 52 53; **S**1755	33	10	S		216	6964	109	50.5	18	1142	21012	7570	403
HOLLOMAN AIR FORCE BASE—Otero County													
U. S. AIR FORCE HOSPITAL, AFM 4801, Bldg. 15, Zip 88330; tel. 505/479-6511; Maj. Nancy L. McDaniel, adm. **F**1 3 6 15 23 33 34 35 40 45 46 47 52	41	10	S		30	2246	20	57.1	10	500	—	—	327
KIRTLAND AIR FORCE BASE—Bernalillo County													
□ U. S. AIR FORCE HOSPITAL-KIRTLAND, Zip 87117; tel. 505/844-8276; Col. Frederic H. Brown USAF, Cmdr. **A**1a 3 5 **F**1 3 6 12 14 15 16 23 28 30 32 33 34 35 40 45 46	41	10	S		40	2754	27	67.5	13	501	—	—	403
LAS CRUCES—Dona Ana County													
★□ MEMORIAL GENERAL HOSPITAL, Telshor & University Sts., Zip 88001; tel. 505/522-8641; Kevin R. Andrews, adm. **A**1a 9 10 **F**1 3 5 6 10 12 15 16 20 23 27 32 33 34 35 36 40 45 47 52 53	15	10	S		239	12084	169	70.7	34	1883	31227	14443	758
LAS VEGAS—San Miguel County													
LAS VEGAS MEDICAL CENTER, Hot Springs Blvd., Box 1388, Zip 87701; tel. 505/425-6711; Tom Delker, adm.; Ann Hughes MD, clin. dir. (Nonreporting) **A**9 10	12	22	L		626	—	—	—	—	—	—	—	—
★□ NORTHEASTERN REGIONAL HOSPITAL, 1235 Eighth St., Box 238, Zip 87701; tel. 505/425-6751; Larry Thompson, adm. (Nonreporting) **A**1a 9 10; **S**0585	23	10	S		62	—	—	—	—	—	—	—	—
LOS ALAMOS—Los Alamos County													
★□ LOS ALAMOS MEDICAL CENTER, 3917 West Rd., Zip 87544; tel. 505/662-4201; Paul J. Wilson, adm. **A**1a 9 10 **F**1 3 6 10 12 14 16 24 26 35 36 40 44 45 52; **S**2235	23	10	S		80	2388	25	31.3	12	373	8598	3155	168
LOS LUNAS—Valencia County													
★ LOS LUNAS HOSPITAL AND TRAINING SCHOOL, Box 1269, Zip 87031; tel. 505/865-9611; Mark A. Delgado, adm. (Nonreporting)	12	62	L		375	—	—	—	—	—	—	—	—
LOVINGTON—Lea County													
★□ NOR-LEA GENERAL HOSPITAL, 1600 N. Main, Zip 88260; tel. 505/396-6611; Nancy McIlwaine, adm. **A**1a 9 10 **F**1 6 12 14 15 16 23 26 34 37 42 43 45 46 47 50; **S**3505	16	10	S		28	462	7	25.0	0	0	2321	817	40
MESCALERO—Otero County													
★□ U. S. PUBLIC HEALTH SERVICE INDIAN HOSPITAL, Box 210, Zip 88340; tel. 505/671-4441 **A**1a 10 **F**15 32 33 34 35 37 40 41 43 46 50 52	47	10	S		15	452	4	26.7	0	0	—	—	33
PORTALES—Roosevelt County													
★□ ROOSEVELT GENERAL HOSPITAL, 1700 S. Ave. O, P O Box 60, Zip 88130; tel. 505/356-4411; George McGowan, exec. dir. (Total facility includes 49 beds in nursing home-type unit) **A**1a 9 10 **F**1 3 6 14 15 16 19 23 26 34 35 36 40 41 42 43 45 46 47 50 52; **S**0045	13	10	S	TF	99	2007	71	71.7	14	506	5215	2518	155
				H	50	1967	22	—	14	506	—	—	132
RATON—Colfax County													
COLFAX HEALTH CARE SYSTEMS, See Miners' Colfax Medical Center													
★ MINERS' COLFAX MEDICAL CENTER (Formerly Miners' Hospital of New Mexico), Hospital Dr., Box 1067, Zip 87740; tel. 505/445-3661; Marquita George, chief exec. off. (Total facility includes 35 beds in nursing home-type unit) **A**9 10 **F**1 12 14 15 16 19 34 35 37 42 43 46 50 53	12	10	S	TF	45	450	35	77.8	0	0	4062	1603	103
				H	10	432	5	—	0	0	3714	1321	80
★ MINERS' COLFAX MEDICAL CENTER (Formerly Colfax Health Care Systems) (Includes Colfax General Hospital, 615 Prospect Ave., P O Box 458, Springer, Zip 87747; tel. 505/483-2443), Hospital Dr., Zip 87740; tel. 505/445-3661; John E. Saint, adm. (Total facility includes 30 beds in nursing home-type unit) **A**9 10 **F**1 6 12 14 16 19 23 35 45; **S**3505	13	10	S	TF	60	1453	41	68.3	5	224	3909	1712	115
				H	30	1394	17	—	5	224	3289	1337	—
ROSWELL—Chaves County													
★□ EASTERN NEW MEXICO MEDICAL CENTER, 405 W. Country Club Rd., Zip 88201; tel. 505/622-8170; James D'Agostino, exec. dir. **A**1a 9 10 **F**1 3 6 9 10 11 12 14 15 16 20 23 28 29 30 34 35 36 40 43 44 45 47 51 52	13	10	S		95	4177	51	53.7	18	1033	9322	4661	259
□ Δ NEW MEXICO REHABILITATION CENTER, 31 Gail Harris Ave., Zip 88201; tel. 505/347-5491; Irvin E. Ashley Jr. EdD, exec. dir. **A**1a 7 9 10 **F**23 24 26 33 34 44 45 46 47	12	46	S		25	223	16	64.0	0	0	2783	1695	84
★□ ST. MARY'S REGIONAL HEALTH CENTER (Formerly St. Mary's Hospital) (Includes Casa Maria Health Care Centre), S. Main & Chisum Sts., Box 1938, Zip 88201; tel. 505/622-1110; George S. Macko, chief exec. off. (Total facility includes 120 beds in nursing home-type unit) **A**1a 9 10 **F**1 3 5 6 7 8 9 10 11 14 15 16 19 21 23 35 42 44 45 48 52 53; **S**5875	21	10	S	TF	238	2937	178	74.8	0	0	15435	7317	490
				H	118	2845	61	—	0	0	13661	6164	419
RUIDOSO—Lincoln County													
★□ LINCOLN COUNTY MEDICAL CENTER (Formerly Ruidoso Hondo Valley Hospital), 211 Sudderth Dr., P O Drawer 3c/d, Hollywood Sta., Zip 88345; tel. 505/257-7381; Steve Keller, adm. (Nonreporting) **A**1a 9 10; **S**3505	23	10	S		39	—	—	—	—	—	—	—	—
SAN FIDEL—Valencia County													
★□ ACOMA-CANONCITO-LAGUNA HOSPITAL, P O Box 130, Zip 87049; tel. 505/552-6634; James L. Toya, adm. **A**1a 10; **F**6 15 16 33 34 35 37 44 47 49	47	10	S		25	536	9	35.4	0	0	—	—	135
SANTA FE—Santa Fe County													
★□ ST. VINCENT HOSPITAL, 455 St. Michael's Dr., P O Box 2107, Zip 87501; tel. 505/983-3361; Hugh R. Hallgren, pres. **A**1a 9 10 **F**1 2 3 5 6 7 8 9 10 11 12 14 15 16 20 21 23 24 26 27 28 29 30 32 33 34 35 36 37 38 40 41 42 43 44 45 47 48 49 50 52 53	23	10	S		268	10394	152	56.7	24	1386	35778	17072	743
★□ U. S. PUBLIC HEALTH SERVICE INDIAN HOSPITAL, 1700 Cerrillos Rd., Zip 87501; tel. 505/988-9821; Joseph A. Moquino, dir. (Nonreporting) **A**1a 10	47	10	S		39	—	—	—	—	—	—	—	—
SHIPROCK—San Juan County													
★□ U. S. PUBLIC HEALTH SERVICE INDIAN HOSPITAL, Box 160, Zip 87420; tel. 505/368-4971; Taylor McKenzie MD, serv. unit dir. **A**1a 10 **F**1 3 6 14 15 16 23 28 29 30 32 33 34 35 36 37 40 43 45 46 49 52	47	10	S		50	3427	38	76.0	14	968	—	—	264

★ American Hospital Association (AHA) membership
□ Joint Commission on Accreditation of Hospitals (JCAH) accreditation
\+ American Osteopathic Hospital Association (AOHA) membership
○ American Osteopathic Association (AOA) accreditation
Δ Commission on Accreditation of Rehabilitation Facilities (CARF) accreditation
Control codes 61, 63, 64, 71, 72 and 73 indicate hospitals listed by AOHA, but not registered by AHA.
For definition of numerical codes, see page A2

Hospital, Address, Telephone, Administrator, Approval and Facility Codes, Multihospital System Code	Classification Codes				Inpatient Data				Newborn Data		Expense (thousands of dollars)		
	Control	Service	Stay	Facilities	Beds	Admissions	Census	Occupancy (percent)	Bassinets	Births	Total	Payroll	Personnel
SILVER CITY—Grant County													
[★] GILA REGIONAL MEDICAL CENTER, 1313 E. 32nd St., Zip 88061; tel. 505/388-1591; Ronald L. McArthur, adm. **A**1a 9 10 **F**1 3 6 10 12 14 15 16 23 24 27 28 29 30 32 33 34 35 36 40 41 44 45 53; **S**1755	13	10	S		68	3168	36	58.1	10	514	8036	3188	194
SOCORRO—Socorro County													
[★] SOCORRO GENERAL HOSPITAL, U. S. Hwy. 60 W., Box 1009, Zip 87801; tel. 505/835-1140; Jeffrey M. Dye, adm. **A**1a 9 10 **F**1 6 14 16 23 35 36 40 41 45 47 52; **S**3505	23	10	S		32	1231	11	34.4	2	190	3880	1228	68
SPRINGER—Colfax County													
COLFAX GENERAL HOSPITAL, See Colfax Health Care System, Raton													
TAOS—Taos County													
□ HOLY CROSS HOSPITAL, Santa Fe Rd., Box Dd, Zip 87571; tel. 505/758-8883; Leigh Cox, adm. **A**1a 9 10 **F**1 3 6 12 14 15 16 23 32 35 36 40 52; **S**0585	23	10	S		33	2078	21	63.6	10	261	—	—	122
TRUTH OR CONSEQUENCES—Sierra County													
[★] SIERRA VISTA HOSPITAL, 800 E. Ninth Ave., Zip 87901; tel. 505/894-2111; Domenica Rush RN, pres. (Nonreporting) **A**1a 9 10; **S**4165	21	10	S		34	—	—	—	—	—	—	—	—
TUCUMCARI—Quay County													
★ DR. DAN C. TRIGG MEMORIAL HOSPITAL, 301 E. Miel De Luna Ave., P O Box 608, Zip 88401; tel. 505/461-0141; Gary Little, adm. **A**9 10 **F**6 16 23 35 40 41 45 47 52; **S**3505	23	10	S		42	1183	13	31.0	2	134	2488	927	58
ZUNI—McKinley County													
[★] U. S. PUBLIC HEALTH SERVICE INDIAN HOSPITAL, P O Box 467, Zip 87327; tel. 505/782-4431; Milton G. Poola, serv. unit dir. **A**1a 10 **F**1 6 14 15 20 23 26 28 30 32 33 34 35 37 38 40 41 43 46 49 50 52	47	10	S		45	1077	13	28.9	8	165	4018	2716	114

Hospital, Address, Telephone, Administrator, Approval and Facility Codes, Multihospital System Code

★ American Hospital Association (AHA) membership
☐ Joint Commission on Accreditation of Hospitals (JCAH) accreditation
+ American Osteopathic Hospital Association (AOHA) membership
○ American Osteopathic Association (AOA) accreditation
Δ Commission on Accreditation of Rehabilitation Facilities (CARF) accreditation
Control codes 61, 63, 64, 71, 72 and 73 indicate hospitals listed by AOHA, but not registered by AHA.
For definition of numerical codes, see page A2

New York

Hospital, Address, Telephone, Administrator, Approval and Facility Codes, Multihospital System Code	Classification Codes: Control	Service	Stay	Facilities	Inpatient Data: Beds	Admissions	Census	Occupancy (percent)	Newborn Data: Bassinets	Births	Expense (thousands of dollars): Total	Payroll	Personnel
ALBANY—Albany County													
★☐ ALBANY MEDICAL CENTER HOSPITAL, New Scotland Ave., Zip 12208; tel. 518/445-3125; Michael Vanko PhD, gen. dir. **A**1a 2 3 5 6 8 9 10 **F**1 2 3 4 5 6 7 8 9 10 11 12 13 14 15 16 17 20 23 24 25 26 27 30 32 33 34 35 36 37 40 42 44 45 46 47 51 52 53 54	23	10	S		689	19731	555	79.4	20	2342	118677	52093	2907
★☐ CAPITAL DISTRICT PSYCHIATRIC CENTER, 75 New Scotland Ave., Zip 12208; tel. 518/447-9611; Jesse Nixon Jr. PhD, dir. **A**1b 3 5 10 **F**15 28 29 30 31 32 33 34 42 45 46 47 53	12	22	L		212	1370	237	100.0	0	0	—	—	559
★☐ CHILD'S HOSPITAL, 25 Hackett Blvd., Zip 12208; tel. 518/462-4211; William Madden, exec. dir. **A**1a 3 5 9 10 **F**1 6 12 14 15 16 23 34 37 43 44 45 46 47	21	10	S		35	1564	11	24.4	0	0	6587	2806	120
★☐ MEMORIAL HOSPITAL, 600 Northern Blvd., Zip 12204; tel. 518/471-3221; J. Clark Winslow, chief exec. off. **A**1a 6 9 10 **F**1 2 3 6 10 11 12 14 16 20 23 24 26 32 34 35 39 41 44 45 46 53	23	10	S		233	6043	197	84.5	0	0	30323	15344	727
★☐ ST. PETER'S HOSPITAL, 315 S. Manning Blvd., Zip 12208; tel. 518/454-1550; Sr. Ellen Lawlor, pres. **A**1a b 3 5 9 10 **F**1 2 3 6 8 10 12 14 15 16 20 21 23 24 25 26 30 33 34 35 40 41 44 45 46 47 48 49 52 53 54; **S**3595	23	10	S		437	17028	400	90.5	60	2981	58101	29864	1659
★☐ VETERANS ADMINISTRATION MEDICAL CENTER, 113 Holland Ave., Zip 12208; tel. 518/462-3311; Clark C. Graninger, dir. (Total facility includes 100 beds in nursing home-type unit) **A**1a 2 3 5 8 **F**1 2 3 6 7 8 9 10 11 12 14 15 16 19 20 21 23 24 25 26 27 28 29 30 31 32 33 34 35 39 41 42 43 44 46 47 48 49 50 53 54	45	10	S	TF H	616 516	9591 9382	523 424	87.3 —	0 0	0 0	68796 64400	43301 41001	1478 1422
ALBION—Orleans County													
★☐ ARNOLD GREGORY MEMORIAL HOSPITAL AND SKILLED NURSING FACILITIES, 243 S. Main St., Zip 14411; tel. 716/589-4422; William P. Gillick, adm. (Total facility includes 30 beds in nursing home-type unit) **A**1a 9 10 **F**1 3 6 12 14 15 16 19 23 26 35 40 45 46	23	10	S	TF H	78 48	1291 1303	51 22	65.4 —	10 10	80 80	4750 3853	2374 1805	169 147
ALEXANDRIA BAY—Jefferson County													
★☐ E. J. NOBLE HOSPITAL OF ALEXANDRIA BAY, 19 Fuller St., Zip 13607; tel. 315/482-2511; F. Joseph Kehoe, adm. (Total facility includes 17 beds in nursing home-type unit) **A**1a 9 10 **F**1 3 6 14 15 16 19 23 24 35 42 44 45 46 47	23	10	S	TF H	52 35	867 856	40 24	76.9 —	0 0	0 0	3293 —	1735 —	116 —
AMITYVILLE—Suffolk County													
★☐ BRUNSWICK GENERAL HOSPITAL, 366 Broadway, Zip 11701; tel. 516/789-7000; Benjamin M. Stein MD, pres. (Nonreporting) **A**1a 9 10; **S**6665	33	10	S		255	—	—	—	—	—	—	—	—
★☐ BRUNSWICK HALL, 80 Louden Ave., Zip 11701; tel. 516/789-7100; Benjamin M. Stein MD, pres.; Harold Lasker MD, med. dir. (Nonreporting) **A**1b 10; **S**6665	33	22	L		122	—	—	—	—	—	—	—	—
★ BRUNSWICK HOUSE ALCOHOLISM TREATMENT CENTER, 81 Louden Ave., Zip 11701; tel. 516/789-7361; Barbara L. McGinley, exec. dir.; Joseph D. Beasley MD, med. dir. (Nonreporting); **S**6665	33	82	S		76	—	—	—	—	—	—	—	—
★ BRUNSWICK PHYSICAL MEDICINE AND REHABILITATION HOSPITAL (Formerly Brunswick Rehabilitation Hospital), 366 Broadway, Zip 11701; tel. 516/789-7000; Benjamin M. Stein MD, pres.; Eduardo Rodriguez MD, med. dir. (Nonreporting) **A**10; **S**6665	33	46	L		64	—	—	—	—	—	—	—	—
★☐ SOUTH OAKS HOSPITAL, 400 Sunrise Hwy., Zip 11701; tel. 516/264-4000; Leonard W. Krinsky PhD, exec. dir. **A**1a 10 **F**15 23 24 28 29 32 33 34 42 43 48 49 50	33	22	L		334	2302	277	82.9	0	0	—	—	628
AMSTERDAM—Montgomery County													
★☐ AMSTERDAM MEMORIAL HOSPITAL, Upper Market St., Zip 12010; tel. 518/842-3100; Edwin B. Bolz, pres. & chief exec. off. (Total facility includes 61 beds in nursing home-type unit) **A**1a 9 10 **F**1 3 6 10 12 14 15 16 19 23 24 26 34 35 37 40 42 44 45 46 50 52 53	23	10	S	TF H	176 115	3867 3836	144 83	80.4 —	10 10	218 218	14913 12507	7548 6938	415 376
★☐ ST. MARY'S HOSPITAL, 427 Guy Park Ave., Zip 12010; tel. 518/842-1900; Peter E. Capobianco, adm. **A**1a 6 9 10 **F**1 3 6 12 15 16 23 24 27 29 30 31 32 33 34 35 40 42 45 46 47 49 52 53; **S**5945	23	10	S		148	5506	120	81.1	9	500	17256	8800	496
AUBURN—Cayuga County													
★☐ AUBURN MEMORIAL HOSPITAL, Lansing St., Zip 13021; tel. 315/255-7226; Christopher J. Rogers, adm. **A**1a 9 10 **F**1 2 3 6 9 10 16 23 27 30 35 36 40 45 46 50 52 53	23	10	S		266	8394	207	75.8	24	889	27301	13911	712
BATAVIA—Genesee County													
★☐ GENESEE MEMORIAL HOSPITAL, 127 North St., Zip 14020; tel. 716/343-6030; F. James Murphy, adm. **A**1a 9 10 **F**1 3 6 10 12 15 16 23 35 36 40 45 47 52	23	10	S		94	4258	78	83.0	24	673	9941	4839	333
★☐ ST. JEROME HOSPITAL, 16 Bank St., Zip 14020; tel. 716/343-3131; Sr. Margaret Mary, adm. **A**1a 9 10 **F**1 2 3 6 12 14 15 16 23 35 44 52 53; **S**5545	21	10	S		106	2818	78	72.2	0	0	9276	4916	289
★☐ VETERANS ADMINISTRATION MEDICAL CENTER, Redfield Pkwy., Zip 14020; tel. 716/343-7500; R. L. Wickham, dir. (Total facility includes 52 beds in nursing home-type unit) **A**1a **F**1 3 6 10 12 14 15 16 19 23 24 25 26 28 32 33 34 42 44 46 49 50	45	48	L	TF H	219 167	1430 1361	160 126	76.2 —	0 0	0 0	19674 —	11624 —	469 429
BATH—Steuben County													
★☐ IRA DAVENPORT MEMORIAL HOSPITAL, Rte. 54, Box 350, Zip 14810; tel. 607/776-2141; Merrill A. Frank, adm. **A**1a 10 **F**1 3 6 10 12 14 15 16 21 23 35 36 37 40 44 45 46 52 53	23	10	S		66	1986	44	66.7	12	258	5933	3575	190
★☐ VETERANS ADMINISTRATION MEDICAL CENTER, Zip 14810; tel. 607/776-2111; Mel A. Gores, dir. **A**1a **F**3 12 14 15 16 19 23 24 26 27 28 30 33 34 35 42 44 46 49 50	45	10	L		208	2130	188	90.4	0	0	25646	15969	637
BAY SHORE—Suffolk County													
★☐ SOUTHSIDE HOSPITAL, Montauk Hwy., Zip 11706; tel. 516/968-3001; Theodore A. Jospe, pres. **A**1a 3 5 9 10 **F**1 2 3 6 7 8 9 12 14 16 19 23 24 27 34 35 36 37 41 43 44 45 46 47 48 50 52 53 54	23	10	S		493	19404	364	73.8	44	2164	59043	31046	1289
BEACON—Dutchess County													
★☐ CRAIG HOUSE HOSPITAL, Howland Ave., Zip 12508; tel. 914/831-1200; Constantine Vardopoulos MD, pres. (Nonreporting) **A**1b	33	22	L		49	—	—	—	—	—	—	—	—
ST. FRANCIS HOSPITAL, See St. Francis Hospital, Poughkeepsie													
BELLEROSE—Queens County See New York City													
BETHPAGE—Nassau County													
★☐ MID-ISLAND HOSPITAL, 4295 Hempstead Turnpike, Zip 11714; tel. 516/579-6000; James J. Dickson, adm. **A**1a 9 10 **F**1 3 6 7 8 9 10 11 12 14 16 19 23 35 46 47 52 53	31	10	S		223	12140	178	76.7	21	1214	30744	13684	569
BINGHAMTON—Broome County													
BINGHAMTON GENERAL HOSPITAL, See United Health Services													
☐ BINGHAMTON PSYCHIATRIC CENTER, 425 Robinson St., Zip 13901; tel. 607/724-1391; Louis Dozoretz MD, dir. **A**1b 10 **F**12 16 19 23 24 26 28 29 30 31 32 33 34 41 42 43 44 45 46 47 50	12	22	L		673	760	617	90.6	0	0	27382	24685	1039

Hospital, Address, Telephone, Administrator, Approval and Facility Codes, Multihospital System Code	Classification Codes				Inpatient Data				Newborn Data		Expense (thousands of dollars)		
★ American Hospital Association (AHA) membership □ Joint Commission on Accreditation of Hospitals (JCAH) accreditation + American Osteopathic Hospital Association (AOHA) membership ○ American Osteopathic Association (AOA) accreditation Δ Commission on Accreditation of Rehabilitation Facilities (CARF) accreditation Control codes 61, 63, 64, 71, 72 and 73 indicate hospitals listed by AOHA, but not registered by AHA. For definition of numerical codes, see page A2	Control	Service	Stay	Facilities	Beds	Admissions	Census	Occupancy (percent)	Bassinets	Births	Total	Payroll	Personnel
★ OUR LADY OF LOURDES MEMORIAL HOSPITAL, 169 Riverside Dr., Zip 13905; tel. 607/798-5111; Sr. Margaret Tuley, pres. & chief exec. off. **A**1a 2 9 10 **F**1 3 6 7 8 9 10 11 12 14 15 16 21 23 24 26 30 33 34 35 36 37 38 40 41 42 44 45 46 47 52 53; **S**1885	21	10	S		267	11557	199	73.2	25	1771	42036	21449	1194
★ UNITED HEALTH SERVICES (Formerly Listed Under Johnson City) (Includes Binghamton General Hospital, Mitchell Ave., Zip 13903; tel. 607/771-2200; Matthew Salanger, dir.; Charles S. Wilson Memorial Hospital, 33-57 Harrison St., Johnson City, Zip 13790; tel. 607/770-6726; Kay Boland, dir.), Mitchell Ave., Zip 13903; tel. 607/770-6140; Gennaro J. Vasile, pres. & chief exec. off. (Total facility includes 100 beds in nursing home-type unit) **A**1a 2 3 5 8 10 **F**1 2 3 6 9 11 12 15 16 19 20 23 24 25 26 27 28 30 32 33 34 35 36 40 41 42 44 45 46 47 48 49 50 51 52 53 54	23	10	S	TF	626	21333	516	77.8	40	2016	89318	44208	2070
				H	526	21187	418	—	40	2016	87666	43142	1950
BROCKPORT—Monroe County													
★ LAKESIDE MEMORIAL HOSPITAL, West Ave., Zip 14420; tel. 716/637-3131; Robert W. Harris, chief exec. off. **A**1a 9 10 **F**1 3 5 6 15 16 23 34 36 37 40 45 46	23	10	S		72	2383	41	56.9	20	488	6962	3602	233
BRONX—Bronx County See New York City													
BRONXVILLE—Westchester County													
★ LAWRENCE HOSPITAL, 55 Palmer Ave., Zip 10708; tel. 914/337-7300; Roger G. Dvorak, pres. **A**1a 2 9 10 **F**1 3 6 10 12 14 15 16 20 23 32 34 35 36 38 40 44 45 46 52 53	23	10	S		280	9842	214	76.4	14	1145	38555	19435	849
BROOKLYN—Kings County See New York City													
BUFFALO—Erie County													
□ BRY-LIN HOSPITAL, 1263 Delaware Ave., Zip 14209; tel. 716/886-8200; Leonard Pleskow, pres. & chief exec. off. (Nonreporting) **A**1b 9 10	32	22	S		96	—	—	—	—	—	—	—	—
BUFFALO COLUMBUS HOSPITAL, 300 Niagara St., Zip 14201; tel. 716/845-4300; Sushil Sharma, pres. **A**9 10 **F**12 14 16 23 43 44 45 46 47	23	10	S		58	1372	33	51.6	0	0	5229	3215	351
★ BUFFALO GENERAL HOSPITAL (Includes Deaconess Hospital Division), 100 High St., Zip 14203; tel. 716/845-5600; William V. Kinnard Jr. MD, pres. (Total facility includes 108 beds in nursing home-type unit) **A**1a 3 5 6 8 9 10 **F**1 2 3 4 5 6 7 8 9 10 11 12 13 14 15 16 19 20 21 23 24 26 27 28 29 30 31 32 33 34 35 36 37 38 39 40 41 42 43 44 45 46 47 49 50 52 53 54	23	10	S	TF	1058	25669	740	69.9	44	1248	106660	57045	3271
				H	950	25577	632	—	44	1248	102737	54966	3088
★ BUFFALO PSYCHIATRIC CENTER, 400 Forest Ave., Zip 14213; tel. 716/885-2261; Patricia T. Oulton, exec. dir. **A**1b 10 **F**15 19 23 24 26 28 29 31 32 33 34 42 45 46 47	12	22	L		985	834	727	73.8	0	0	41262	28974	1141
□ CHILDREN'S HOSPITAL (Children's General Medical and Surgical, and Maternity), 219 Bryant St., Zip 14222; tel. 716/878-7000; J. E. Stibbards, pres. **A**1a 3 5 9 10 **F**1 4 6 10 12 13 14 15 16 17 20 23 24 26 28 30 32 33 34 35 36 37 38 40 41 42 43 44 46 47 51 52 53 54	23	50	S		313	15948	—	—	64	4810	60007	29584	1594
DEACONESS HOSPITAL DIVISION, See Buffalo General Hospital													
★ ERIE COUNTY MEDICAL CENTER, 462 Grider St., Zip 14215; tel. 716/898-4048; George H. McCoy, chief exec. off. (Total facility includes 120 beds in nursing home-type unit) **A**1a 3 5 8 9 10 **F**1 2 3 4 5 6 7 8 9 10 11 12 13 14 16 19 20 23 24 25 26 27 28 30 32 33 34 35 37 42 44 45 46 47 48 49 52 53 54	13	10	S	TF	661	14713	533	79.8	0	0	104608	44625	2094
				H	541	14623	413	—	0	0	102611	43103	1997
★ MERCY HOSPITAL, 565 Abbott Rd., Zip 14220; tel. 716/826-7000; Sr. Sheila Marie, adm. (Total facility includes 60 beds in nursing home-type unit) **A**1a 3 5 9 10 **F**1 2 3 6 10 12 14 15 16 19 23 24 25 26 34 35 36 40 41 42 44 45 46 50 52 53; **S**5545	21	10	S	TF	453	16842	400	88.3	60	2474	42501	21020	1416
				H	393	16797	341	—	60	2474	40648	20424	1373
★ MILLARD FILLMORE HOSPITAL (Includes Millard Fillmore Suburban Hospital, 1540 Maple Rd., Williamsville, Zip 14221; tel. 716/688-3100), 3 Gates Circle, Zip 14209; tel. 716/887-4600; Jan Jennings, pres. (Total facility includes 41 beds in nursing home-type unit) **A**1a 3 5 6 8 9 10 **F**1 2 3 4 6 12 13 14 15 16 17 19 20 23 24 26 34 35 36 40 44 45 46 47 50 53 54	23	10	S	TF	629	22290	560	77.9	46	2182	85143	38478	2053
				H	588	22269	519	—	46	2182	84540	38056	2019
★ ROSWELL PARK MEMORIAL INSTITUTE (Cancer Research Treatment and Education), 666 Elm St., Zip 14263; tel. 716/845-2300; Robert Lawson, dir. **A**1a 2 3 5 9 10 **F**1 3 6 7 8 9 10 11 12 14 15 16 23 24 26 32 33 34 42 44 46 47 52 53	12	49	S		273	8146	187	68.5	0	0	53805	31619	1448
★ SHEEHAN MEMORIAL HOSPITAL (Formerly Sheehan Emergency Hospital), 425 Michigan Ave., Zip 14203; tel. 716/842-2200; James Glair, adm. **A**1a 9 10 **F**1 3 6 10 12 14 16 22 23 24 34 35 45 46 47	23	10	S		90	2690	76	82.6	0	0	12492	5496	327
★ SISTERS OF CHARITY HOSPITAL, 2157 Main St., Zip 14214; tel. 716/862-2000; Sr. Angela Bontempo, pres. (Total facility includes 80 beds in nursing home-type unit) **A**1a 3 5 6 9 10 **F**1 2 3 6 9 10 11 12 14 15 16 19 23 24 26 30 32 33 34 35 36 37 40 41 42 44 45 46 47 49 50 52 53; **S**1885	21	10	S	TF	530	15216	440	83.0	60	2434	45455	23906	1429
				H	450	15167	361	—	60	2434	44307	23040	1373
★ ST. FRANCIS HOSPITAL OF BUFFALO, 2787 Main St., Zip 14214; tel. 716/837-4200; Sr. Jeanne Weisbeck, adm. **A**1a 9 10 **F**1 3 6 14 15 16 23 34 35 37 45; **S**5715	21	10	S		75	2160	39	52.0	0	0	4603	2336	158
★ VETERANS ADMINISTRATION MEDICAL CENTER, 3495 Bailey Ave., Zip 14215; tel. 716/834-9200; Joseph Paris, dir. (Total facility includes 36 beds in nursing home-type unit) **A**1a 2 3 5 8 **F**1 2 3 4 6 7 8 9 10 11 12 13 14 15 16 19 20 23 24 25 26 27 28 29 30 31 32 33 34 35 37 41 42 43 44 45 46 47 48 49 50 53 54	45	10	S	TF	770	15151	668	86.8	0	0	77055	46307	1741
				H	734	15072	634	—	0	0	75189	—	1687
CAMBRIDGE—Washington County													
□ MARY MCCLELLAN HOSPITAL, Zip 12816; tel. 518/677-2611; John R. Remillard, adm. (Total facility includes 39 beds in nursing home-type unit) **A**1a 9 10 **F**1 3 6 10 12 14 15 16 19 23 24 26 34 35 36 37 40 44 45 46	23	10	S	TF	113	1914	79	69.9	11	177	7649	3939	257
				H	74	1893	40	—	11	177	—	3513	225
CANANDAIGUA—Ontario County													
★ CANANDAIGUA VETERANS ADMINISTRATION MEDICAL CENTER, Fort Hill Ave., Zip 14424; tel. 716/394-2000; Dewayne C. Robertson, dir. (Total facility includes 100 beds in nursing home-type unit) **A**1a **F**1 3 6 12 14 15 16 19 23 24 26 27 28 30 31 32 33 34 35 41 42 43 44 46 47 48 49 50	45	49	L	TF	1006	1904	855	83.6	0	0	40871	28916	1266
				H	906	1850	759	—	0	0	37904	26778	1199
★ FREDERICK FERRIS THOMPSON HOSPITAL, 350 Parrish St., Zip 14424; tel. 716/394-1100; Steven P. Boyle, adm. **A**1a 9 10 **F**1 3 6 10 12 14 16 23 24 35 40 44 45 46	23	10	S		121	4059	98	81.0	18	549	11996	6366	371
CARMEL—Putnam County													
★ ARMS ACRES, Seminary Hill Rd., P O Box X, Zip 10512; tel. 914/225-3400; Mark Schottinger, exec. dir. (Nonreporting) **A**1b	33	82	S		65	—	—	—	—	—	—	—	—
★ PUTNAM HOSPITAL CENTER, Stoneleigh Ave., Zip 10512; tel. 914/279-5711; William R. Wedral, pres.; Peter L. Gosline, assoc. adm. **A**1a 9 10 **F**1 3 6 10 12 14 15 16 23 26 35 36 40 41 44 45 46 47 52 53	23	10	S		156	5514	114	73.1	14	479	19732	10195	449
CARTHAGE—Jefferson County													
★ CARTHAGE AREA HOSPITAL, W. Street Rd., Zip 13619; tel. 315/493-1000; Jeffrey Drop, chief exec. off. (Total facility includes 30 beds in nursing home-type unit) **A**1a 9 10 **F**1 12 14 15 16 19 23 26 34 35 37 40 41 42 45 54; **S**1905	23	10	S	TF	78	1648	59	75.6	6	96	4864	2740	155
				H	48	1619	29	—	6	96	4587	2473	135
CASTLE POINT—Dutchess County													
★ VETERANS ADMINISTRATION MEDICAL CENTER, Zip 12511; tel. 914/831-2000; Richard S. Droske, dir. (Total facility includes 148 beds in nursing home-type unit) **A**1a 3 5 **F**1 6 12 14 15 19 23 24 25 26 32 33 34 41 42 44 46 47 50	45	10	S	TF	404	3584	321	79.5	0	0	28839	17251	701
				H	256	3480	181	—	0	0	20522	10853	624

Hospital, Address, Telephone, Administrator, Approval and Facility Codes, Multihospital System Code	Classification Codes				Inpatient Data				Newborn Data		Expense (thousands of dollars)		
★ American Hospital Association (AHA) membership □ Joint Commission on Accreditation of Hospitals (JCAH) accreditation + American Osteopathic Hospital Association (AOHA) membership ○ American Osteopathic Association (AOA) accreditation Δ Commission on Accreditation of Rehabilitation Facilities (CARF) accreditation Control codes 61, 63, 64, 71, 72 and 73 indicate hospitals listed by AOHA, but not registered by AHA. For definition of numerical codes, see page A2	Control	Service	Stay	Facilities	Beds	Admissions	Census	Occupancy (percent)	Bassinets	Births	Total	Payroll	Personnel
CATSKILL—Greene County													
★□ MEMORIAL HOSPITAL AND NURSING HOME OF GREENE COUNTY, 159 Jefferson Hts., Zip 12414; tel. 518/943-2000; Gerald R. Fitzgibbon, adm. (Total facility includes 120 beds in nursing home-type unit) **A**1a 9 10 **F**1 3 6 10 12 14 16 19 23 24 26 34 35 36 37 40 41 44 45 46 52	13	10	S	TF H	205 85	3095 3048	177 60	83.5 —	5 5	322 322	13554 9699	6349 4426	429 282
CENTRAL ISLIP—Suffolk County													
★□ CENTRAL ISLIP PSYCHIATRIC CENTER, Carleton Ave., Zip 11722; tel. 516/234-6262; James E. Ramseur, exec. dir. **A**1b 10 **F**6 12 14 23 24 28 30 31 32 33 34 42 44 46 50	12	22	L		1224	601	1232	90.5	0	0	57891	38877	1508
CENTRAL VALLEY—Orange County													
□ FALKIRK HOSPITAL, Falkirk Pl., Box 194, Zip 10917; tel. 914/928-2256; Theodore Neumann Jr. MD, dir. **A**1a **F**15 24 29 31 32 42 47 49	33	22	L		60	278	39	65.0	0	0	—	—	170
CHEEKTOWAGA—Erie County													
★□ ST. JOSEPH INTERCOMMUNITY HOSPITAL, 2605 Harlem Rd., Zip 14225; tel. 716/896-6300; Sr. Mary Jan Nasiadka, adm. **A**1a 9 10 **F**1 3 6 10 12 14 15 16 20 23 35 44 45 46 47 50 53	21	10	S		213	6935	165	77.5	0	0	21002	9819	583
CLIFTON SPRINGS—Ontario County													
★□ CLIFTON SPRINGS HOSPITAL AND CLINIC, 2 Coulter Rd., Zip 14432; tel. 315/462-9561; Robert Mincemoyer, exec. dir. (Total facility includes 40 beds in nursing home-type unit) **A**1a 9 10 **F**1 3 6 7 8 9 10 11 12 14 15 16 19 23 24 27 28 29 32 33 35 42 44 45 46 47 48 49 50 53; **S**1755	23	10	S	TF H	178 138	3253 3209	135 95	75.8 —	0 0	0 0	17453 16019	7900 7504	509 476
COBLESKILL—Schoharie County													
★□ COMMUNITY HOSPITAL SCHOHARIE COUNTY, Grandview Dr., Zip 12043; tel. 518/234-2511; Howard J. Archer, adm. **A**1a 2 9 10 **F**1 3 6 10 12 14 16 23 29 30 34 35 36 40 43 45 46 47 50	23	10	S		70	1523	36	51.4	12	111	6777	2940	195
COHOES—Albany County													
□ COHOES MEMORIAL HOSPITAL, Columbia St., Zip 12047; tel. 518/237-5630 (Nonreporting) **A**1a 9 10	23	10	S		103	—	—	—	—	—	—	—	—
COLD SPRING—Putnam County													
□ JULIA L. BUTTERFIELD MEMORIAL HOSPITAL, Paulding Ave., Zip 10516; tel. 914/265-3642; Robert I. Miller, chief oper. off. **A**1a 9 10 **F**1 12 14 15 23 26 35 36 40 44 45 46 47	23	10	S		36	1748	26	72.2	7	210	—	—	80
COOPERSTOWN—Otsego County													
□ MARY IMOGENE BASSETT HOSPITAL AND CLINICS, Atwell Rd., Zip 13326; tel. 607/547-3100; William F. Streck MD, pres. & chief exec. off. **A**1a 2 3 5 8 10 **F**1 3 5 6 7 8 9 10 11 12 14 16 20 23 24 27 28 29 30 32 33 34 35 36 37 40 42 44 45 46 47 49 52 53 54	23	10	S		180	6124	140	77.8	9	339	34787	17147	1069
CORINTH—Saratoga County													
□ ADIRONDACK REGIONAL HOSPITAL, 200 Smith Dr., Zip 12822; tel. 518/654-9041; Timothy Reardon, chief exec. off. **A**1a 9 10 **F**12 14 15 16 23 34 35 45 46 47	15	10	S		30	738	15	50.0	0	0	2834	1333	75
CORNING—Steuben County													
★□ CORNING HOSPITAL, 176 Denison Pkwy. E., Zip 14830; tel. 607/937-7200; John E. Pignatore, exec. dir. (Total facility includes 120 beds in nursing home-type unit) **A**1a 9 10 **F**1 2 3 6 10 12 14 16 19 21 23 24 35 36 40 42 44 45 46 52 53	23	10	S	TF H	278 158	5854 5808	234 115	84.2 —	24 24	482 482	19840 16571	10943 8900	612 463
CORNWALL—Orange County													
★□ CORNWALL HOSPITAL, Laurel Ave., Zip 12518; tel. 914/534-7711; Val S. Gray, adm. **A**1a 9 10 **F**1 3 6 10 12 14 15 16 23 35 44 45 46 52	23	10	S		127	3948	89	70.1	0	0	13501	6625	325
CORTLAND—Cortland County													
★□ CORTLAND MEMORIAL HOSPITAL, 134 Homer Ave., Zip 13045; tel. 607/756-7525; Robert M. Lovell, pres. & chief exec. off. **A**1a 9 10 **F**1 3 6 10 12 14 15 16 23 24 26 27 30 32 33 34 35 36 37 40 41 42 44 45 46 52	23	10	S		177	7169	141	79.7	15	673	17694	8817	548
CUBA—Allegany County													
★□ CUBA MEMORIAL HOSPITAL, 140 W. Main St., Zip 14727; tel. 716/968-2000; Timothy M. Callaghan, adm. (Total facility includes 30 beds in nursing home-type unit) **A**1a 9 10 **F**1 3 15 16 19 23 35 42 44 45	23	10	S	TF H	69 39	1255 1228	52 23	68.4 —	0 0	0 0	5019 —	2426 —	161 137
DANSVILLE—Livingston County													
★□ NICHOLAS H. NOYES MEMORIAL HOSPITAL, 111 S. Clara Barton St., Zip 14437; tel. 716/335-6001; Richard S. Warren, adm. **A**1a 9 10 **F**1 3 6 10 12 14 16 23 26 28 30 32 33 35 36 40 44 45 46 47	23	10	S		85	3457	61	71.8	10	378	8419	4240	278
DELHI—Delaware County													
★□ A. LINDSAY AND OLIVE B. O'CONNOR HOSPITAL, Andes Rd., Rte. 28, Zip 13753; tel. 607/746-2371; Richard L. Dewey, adm. **A**1a 9 10 **F**6 7 12 14 15 16 23 35 45 46 47	23	10	S		30	1195	21	70.0	0	0	3145	1648	102
DOBBS FERRY—Westchester County													
★□ DOBBS FERRY HOSPITAL, 128 Ashford Ave., Zip 10522; tel. 914/693-0700; John T. Macca, exec. dir. **A**1a 9 10 **F**1 6 14 15 16 23 35 44 45 46 52	23	10	S		25	843	16	64.0	0	0	3094	1669	75
DUNKIRK—Chautauqua County													
★□ BROOKS MEMORIAL HOSPITAL, 529 Central Ave., Zip 14048; tel. 716/366-1111; Richard H. Ketcham, exec. dir. **A**1a 9 10 **F**1 3 6 12 14 15 16 23 26 35 36 40 41 44 45 46 52 53; **S**1755	23	10	S		133	5727	103	60.6	26	464	15106	6677	385
EAST MEADOW—Nassau County													
□ NASSAU COUNTY MEDICAL CENTER, 2201 Hempstead Turnpike, Zip 11554; tel. 516/542-0123; Donald H. Eisenberg, exec. dir. **A**1a 2 3 5 8 9 10 **F**3 4 5 6 7 8 9 10 11 12 14 15 16 20 21 22 23 24 25 27 28 29 30 32 33 34 35 36 38 40 42 43 44 45 46 47 48 49 51 52 53	13	10	S		615	20990	518	84.2	36	2526	157512	83563	3000
ELIZABETHTOWN—Essex County													
★□ ELIZABETHTOWN COMMUNITY HOSPITAL, Park St., Zip 12932; tel. 518/873-6377; Judith Hathaway, adm. **A**1a 9 10 **F**1 3 6 15 16 23 26 34 35 44 45 46	23	10	S		25	662	14	56.0	0	0	2481	1285	64
ELLENVILLE—Ulster County													
★□ ELLENVILLE COMMUNITY HOSPITAL, Rte. 209, P O Box 668, Zip 12428; tel. 914/647-6400; Richard F. Spreer, exec. vice-pres. **A**1a 9 10 **F**1 6 10 14 16 23 35 45 46 52	23	10	S		63	2144	41	65.1	0	0	4363	2040	138
ELMIRA—Chemung County													
★□ ARNOT-OGDEN MEMORIAL HOSPITAL, 600 Roe Ave., Zip 14905; tel. 607/737-4100; Anthony J. Cooper Jr., pres. & chief exec. off. (Total facility includes 40 beds in nursing home-type unit) **A**1a 2 6 10 **F**1 3 4 5 6 7 8 9 10 11 12 14 15 16 17 19 20 23 34 35 36 37 40 43 45 46 47 51 53 54	23	10	S	TF H	296 256	8004 7991	223 183	75.3 —	30 30	1225 1225	42138 41574	21025 20538	1094 1064
□ ELMIRA PSYCHIATRIC CENTER, 100 Washington St., Caller 1527, Zip 14902; tel. 607/737-4739; Bert W. Pyle Jr., dir. **A**1b 10 **F**15 24 28 29 30 31 32 33 42 43 46 47	12	22	L		215	766	200	93.0	0	0	12134	7053	478

Hospital, Address, Telephone, Administrator, Approval and Facility Codes, Multihospital System Code	Classification Codes: Control	Service	Stay	Facilities	Inpatient Data: Beds	Admissions	Census	Occupancy (percent)	Newborn Data: Bassinets	Births	Expense (thousands of dollars): Total	Payroll	Personnel
★ □ Δ ST. JOSEPH'S HOSPITAL (Includes Twin Tiers Rehabilitation Center), 555 E. Market St., Zip 14902; tel. 607/733-6541; Sr. Martha Gersbach, pres. (Total facility includes 31 beds in nursing home-type unit) **A**1a 2 6 7 9 10 **F**1 3 5 6 10 12 14 16 19 21 22 23 24 25 26 27 32 33 34 35 36 40 42 44 45 46 47 49 52	21	10	S	TF	270	6107	188	69.6	16	352	—	—	1106
				H	239	6090	158	—	16	352	—	—	1086
FAR ROCKAWAY—Queens County See New York City													
FLUSHING—Queens County See New York City													
FREEPORT—Nassau County													
★ □ FREEPORT HOSPITAL, 267 S. Ocean Ave., Zip 11520; tel. 516/378-0800; James Heckler, exec. dir. **A**1b 10 **F**32 49	32	82	S		52	1500	24	46.2	0	0	—	—	54
FULTON—Oswego County													
★ □ ALBERT LINDLEY LEE MEMORIAL HOSPITAL, 510 S. Fourth St., Zip 13069; tel. 315/592-2224; Dennis A. Casey, exec. dir. **A**1a 9 10 **F**3 12 14 15 16 23 35 45 46	23	10	S		67	2498	44	65.7	0	0	6846	3592	200
GENEVA—Ontario County													
★ □ GENEVA GENERAL HOSPITAL, 196 North St., Zip 14456; tel. 315/789-4222; James J. Dooley, pres. & chief exec. off. (Total facility includes 42 beds in nursing home-type unit) **A**1a 9 10 **F**1 3 6 10 12 14 15 16 19 23 24 26 33 34 35 36 37 40 42 44 45 46 47 50 52 53	23	10	S	TF	174	4949	138	79.3	20	1061	19138	9181	545
				H	132	4927	96	—	20	1061	18540	8753	516
GLEN COVE—Nassau County													
★ □ COMMUNITY HOSPITAL AT GLEN COVE, St. Andrews Lane, Zip 11542; tel. 516/676-5000; Walter R. Rentschler, pres. & chief exec. off. **A**1a 2 3 5 9 10 **F**1 2 3 6 7 8 9 10 11 12 14 15 16 20 21 23 24 26 27 30 31 32 33 34 35 36 37 40 42 44 45 46 49 50 52 53	23	10	S		278	8425	199	71.6	20	752	40741	21996	816
GLEN OAKS—Queens County See New York City													
GLENS FALLS—Warren County													
★ □ GLENS FALLS HOSPITAL, 100 Park St., Zip 12801; tel. 518/792-3151; William E. Philion, pres. **A**1a 9 10 **F**1 2 3 6 8 9 10 11 12 14 16 20 22 23 24 27 28 29 30 32 33 34 35 36 40 44 45 46 47 49 50 52 53	23	10	S		408	15722	329	80.6	37	1531	51918	27297	1383
GLOVERSVILLE—Fulton County													
★ □ NATHAN LITTAUER HOSPITAL, 99 E. State St., Zip 12078; tel. 518/725-8621; Thomas J. Dowd, exec. dir. **A**1a 9 10 **F**1 3 6 10 12 14 15 16 23 35 36 40 41 45 46 47 52 53	23	10	S		124	4447	83	66.9	18	471	16797	8551	421
GOSHEN—Orange County													
★ □ ARDEN HILL HOSPITAL, Harriman Dr., Zip 10924; tel. 914/294-5441; A. Gordon McAleer, exec. dir. **A**1a 9 10 **F**1 3 6 10 14 16 18 23 27 30 32 33 35 36 40 44 45 46 49 50 52	23	10	S		165	7334	151	91.5	14	893	21208	10574	573
GOUVERNEUR—St. Lawrence County													
□ EDWARD JOHN NOBLE HOSPITAL OF GOUVERNEUR, 77 W. Barney St., Zip 13642; tel. 315/287-1000; Michael Delarm, adm. **A**1a 10 **F**1 3 6 14 16 23 35 40 42 45 52; **S**1905	23	10	S		47	1256	20	42.6	4	217	3408	1927	175
GOWANDA—Cattaraugus County													
★ □ TRI-COUNTY MEMORIAL HOSPITAL, 100 Memorial Dr., Zip 14070; tel. 716/532-3377; Thomas Brunelle, chief exec. off. **A**1a 9 10 **F**1 3 6 12 14 15 16 23 35 36 40 45 46	23	10	S		61	2080	34	55.7	8	266	4534	2142	99
GRANVILLE—Washington County													
★ □ EMMA LAING STEVENS HOSPITAL, Rural Delivery 1, Zip 12832; tel. 518/642-2345; Douglas E. Cosey, adm. **A**1a 9 10 **F**6 23 35 45 47	23	10	S		25	222	8	32.0	0	0	1893	830	68
GREENPORT—Suffolk County													
★ □ EASTERN LONG ISLAND HOSPITAL, 201 Manor Pl., Zip 11944; tel. 516/477-1000; Anne T. Dixon, exec. vice-pres. **A**1a 9 10 **F**1 3 6 9 10 12 14 15 16 23 24 27 30 34 35 45 46 47 52	23	10	S		60	1966	58	67.4	0	0	10837	5375	201
GRIFFISS AIR FORCE BASE—Oneida County													
U. S. AIR FORCE HOSPITAL, Zip 13441; tel. 315/330-7711; Maj. Thomas A. Rupp, adm. **F**1 6 14 15 23 28 30 33 34 35 37 40 46 49	41	10	S		20	1483	13	65.0	10	384	—	—	278
HAMILTON—Madison County													
★ □ COMMUNITY MEMORIAL HOSPITAL, Broad St., Zip 13346; tel. 315/824-1100; David Felton, adm. (Total facility includes 40 beds in nursing home-type unit) **A**1a 9 10 **F**1 3 6 12 14 15 16 19 23 26 35 36 37 40 42 44 45 47 50 52 53	23	10	S	TF	89	2559	73	84.9	8	393	6538	3061	166
				H	49	2525	33	—	8	393	—	—	139
HARRIS—Sullivan County													
★ □ COMMUNITY GENERAL HOSPITAL OF SULLIVAN COUNTY (Includes Harris Division and Grover M. Hermann Division), Bushville Rd., P O Box 800, Zip 12742; tel. 914/794-3300; Martin I. Richman, exec. dir. **A**1a 9 10 **F**1 6 14 15 16 19 23 24 26 27 34 35 36 42 43 44 45 46 47 48 49 52 53	23	10	S		310	8674	249	80.3	22	671	35204	16052	830
HARRISON—Westchester County													
ST. VINCENT'S HOSPITAL AND MEDICAL CENTER OF NEW YORK, WESTCHESTER BRANCH, See St. Vincent's Hospital and Medical Center of New York, New York City													
HELMUTH—Erie County													
★ □ GOWANDA PSYCHIATRIC CENTER, Zip 14079; tel. 716/532-3311; John R. Collier, exec. dir. **A**1b 10 **F**12 14 15 23 24 28 30 31 32 33 34 42 44 46 47 50	12	22	L		541	558	496	91.7	0	0	28445	20197	758
HEMPSTEAD—Nassau County													
★ □ HEMPSTEAD GENERAL HOSPITAL MEDICAL CENTER, 800 Front St., Zip 11551; tel. 516/560-1200; Joseph F. Turner Jr., exec. dir. **A**1a 9 10 **F**1 2 3 6 10 12 14 15 16 23 24 26 27 30 32 33 34 35 37 42 46 53	32	10	S		213	7989	179	80.6	0	0	27189	14872	523
HORNELL—Steuben County													
★ □ ST. JAMES MERCY HOSPITAL, 411 Canisteo St., Zip 14843; tel. 607/324-3900; Sr. Mary Rene McNiff, adm. **A**1a 6 9 10 **F**1 2 3 6 10 14 15 16 20 21 23 24 26 27 28 29 30 32 35 36 40 42 43 44 45 46 47 49 52; **S**3595	23	10	S		169	5300	125	80.6	12	498	15108	7999	560
HUDSON—Columbia County													
★ □ COLUMBIA MEMORIAL HOSPITAL, 71 Prospect Ave., Zip 12534; tel. 518/828-7601; Alexander Stetynski, pres. **A**1a 9 10 **F**1 3 6 8 9 10 11 12 15 16 23 24 26 30 32 35 36 37 40 43 44 45 52 53	23	10	S		160	5874	125	78.1	12	567	17970	10717	478
HUNTINGTON—Suffolk County													
★ □ HUNTINGTON HOSPITAL, 270 Park Ave., Zip 11743; tel. 516/351-2000; Elwood A. Opstad, exec. dir. **A**1a 3 5 9 10 **F**1 2 3 6 7 8 9 10 11 12 14 15 16 20 23 26 27 30 32 35 36 40 42 45 46 50 52 53	23	10	S		424	17582	365	86.1	30	1813	54426	27803	1180
ILION—Herkimer County													
★ □ MOHAWK VALLEY GENERAL HOSPITAL, 295 W. Main St., Zip 13357; tel. 315/895-7474; Nicholas B. Munhofen II, adm. **A**1a 9 10 **F**1 3 6 14 16 23 24 26 32 35 36 40 44 45 46 52; **S**1755	15	10	S		83	3738	59	71.1	13	507	8303	3968	299
IRVING—Chautauqua County													
□ LAKE SHORE HOSPITAL, 845 Rte. 5 & 20, Zip 14081; tel. 716/934-2654; James B. Foster, adm. (Total facility includes 80 beds in nursing home-type unit) **A**1a 9 10 **F**1 3 6 12 14 15 16 19 23 34 35 41 45 46 47	23	10	S	TF	124	1835	115	92.0	0	0	6014	2920	167
				H	44	1795	37	—	0	0	5442	2431	136

Legend:
- ★ American Hospital Association (AHA) membership
- □ Joint Commission on Accreditation of Hospitals (JCAH) accreditation
- + American Osteopathic Hospital Association (AOHA) membership
- ○ American Osteopathic Association (AOA) accreditation
- Δ Commission on Accreditation of Rehabilitation Facilities (CARF) accreditation
- Control codes 61, 63, 64, 71, 72 and 73 indicate hospitals listed by AOHA, but not registered by AHA.
- For definition of numerical codes, see page A2

Hospital, Address, Telephone, Administrator, Approval and Facility Codes, Multihospital System Code	Classification Codes				Inpatient Data				Newborn Data		Expense (thousands of dollars)		
★ American Hospital Association (AHA) membership □ Joint Commission on Accreditation of Hospitals (JCAH) accreditation + American Osteopathic Hospital Association (AOHA) membership ○ American Osteopathic Association (AOA) accreditation Δ Commission on Accreditation of Rehabilitation Facilities (CARF) accreditation Control codes 61, 63, 64, 71, 72 and 73 indicate hospitals listed by AOHA, but not registered by AHA. For definition of numerical codes, see page A2	Control	Service	Stay	Facilities	Beds	Admissions	Census	Occupancy (percent)	Bassinets	Births	Total	Payroll	Personnel
ITHACA—Tompkins County													
★□ TOMPKINS COMMUNITY HOSPITAL, 1285 Trumansburg Rd., Zip 14850; tel. 607/274-4011; Bonnie H. Howell, adm. **A**1a 2 9 10 **F**1 3 6 10 12 14 15 16 23 24 26 27 30 32 34 35 36 37 40 42 43 44 45 46 53	23	10	S		191	8535	149	78.0	22	1214	23096	11042	652
JAMAICA—Queens County See New York City													
JAMESTOWN—Chautauqua County													
★□ JAMESTOWN GENERAL HOSPITAL, 51 Glasgow Ave., Zip 14701; tel. 716/484-1161; Ronald J. Fryzel, adm. **A**1a 9 10 **F**1 3 6 10 12 14 15 16 23 24 27 30 32 33 34 35 37 45 46 47	14	10	S		107	3812	85	75.2	0	0	14566	6400	372
★□ WOMAN'S CHRISTIAN ASSOCIATION HOSPITAL, 207 Foote Ave., Zip 14701; tel. 716/487-0141; Murray S. Marsh, adm. **A**1a 2 9 10 **F**1 2 3 5 6 7 8 10 11 12 14 15 16 20 21 23 24 26 30 32 33 35 36 40 43 44 45 46 52 53	23	10	S		251	11132	202	80.5	38	1317	26797	13757	856
JOHNSON CITY—Broome County													
CHARLES S. WILSON MEMORIAL HOSPITAL, See United Health Services, Binghamton													
UNITED HEALTH SERVICES, See Binghamton													
JOHNSTOWN—Fulton County													
★□ JOHNSTOWN HOSPITAL, 201 S. Melcher St., Zip 12095; tel. 518/762-3161; Robert C. Winfrey, chief exec. off. **A**1a 9 10 **F**1 3 6 10 12 16 34 35 45 47; **S**1755	23	10	S		39	1229	29	54.7	0	0	4555	2051	140
KATONAH—Westchester County													
★□ FOUR WINDS HOSPITAL, 800 Cross River Rd., Zip 10536; tel. 914/763-8151; Samuel C. Klagsbrun MD, med. dir. **A**1a 10 **F**19 24 33 42 47	33	22	L		160	401	128	90.8	0	0	—	—	577
KENMORE—Erie County													
★□ KENMORE MERCY HOSPITAL, 2950 Elmwood Ave., Zip 14217; tel. 716/879-6100; Sr. Mary Joel, adm. (Total facility includes 80 beds in nursing home-type unit) **A**1a 9 10 **F**1 3 6 10 12 14 15 16 19 23 24 34 35 36 40 42 44 45 46 47 53; **S**5545	21	10	S	TF H	324 244	9394 9339	277 197	85.5 —	20 20	827 827	25245 22920	12416 11498	857 778
KINGS PARK—Suffolk County													
★□ KINGS PARK PSYCHIATRIC CENTER, Box A, Zip 11754; tel. 516/544-2957; Stephen Goldstein, exec. dir. **A**1b 10 **F**12 15 23 24 28 29 31 32 33 34 37 42 43 44 46 47 50	12	22	L		2481	2184	2060	83.0	0	0	79818	73506	2960
KINGSTON—Ulster County													
★□ BENEDICTINE HOSPITAL, 105 Marys Ave., Zip 12401; tel. 914/338-2500; Sr. Mary Charles McCarthy, pres.; Thomas H. Fletcher, exec. vice-pres. **A**1a 3 5 9 10 **F**3 5 6 7 10 11 12 14 16 23 27 30 32 34 35 36 40 44 45 46 47 49 52 53	21	10	S		222	8312	190	85.6	32	1055	29879	13024	718
□ KINGSTON HOSPITAL, 396 Broadway, Zip 12401; tel. 914/331-3131; Anthony R. Triulzi, chief exec. off. **A**1a 3 5 9 10 **F**1 3 5 8 10 15 16 23 24 35 36 37 40 42 45 46 47 53	23	10	S		140	5647	127	90.7	32	328	—	—	437
LACKAWANNA—Erie County													
★□ OUR LADY OF VICTORY HOSPITAL, 55 Melroy & Ridge Rd., Zip 14218; tel. 716/825-8000; Albert L. Condino, adm. **A**1a 9 10 **F**1 2 3 10 12 14 15 16 17 23 32 35 44 45 46 53	21	10	S		216	7702	209	96.8	0	0	25206	11369	659
LAKE PLACID—Essex County													
★□ PLACID MEMORIAL HOSPITAL, Church St., Zip 12946; tel. 518/523-3311; David Davis, pres. (Total facility includes 15 beds in nursing home-type unit) **A**1a 9 10 **F**1 12 14 19 23 35 45 46	23	10	S	TF H	44 29	728 726	28 13	63.6 —	0 0	0 0	2892 2685	1650 1466	101 88
LEWISTON—Niagara County													
★□ MOUNT ST. MARY'S HOSPITAL OF NIAGARA FALLS, 5300 Military Rd., Zip 14092; tel. 716/297-4800; Richard B. Russell, adm. **A**1a 9 10 **F**1 3 6 10 11 12 14 15 16 23 26 29 30 32 35 40 45 46 47 52 53; **S**5715	21	10	S		204	6521	130	63.7	22	416	18154	9060	512
LITTLE FALLS—Herkimer County													
★□ LITTLE FALLS HOSPITAL, 140 Burwell St., Zip 13365; tel. 315/823-1000; David S. Armstrong Jr., adm. (Total facility includes 34 beds in nursing home-type unit) **A**1a 9 10 **F**1 2 3 6 14 16 17 19 23 24 35 36 40 44 45 46 52	23	10	S	TF H	150 116	3811 3800	120 87	80.0 —	12 12	264 264	10225 9873	5522 5177	372 345
LOCKPORT—Niagara County													
★□ LOCKPORT MEMORIAL HOSPITAL, 521 East Ave., Zip 14094; tel. 716/434-9111; N. Donald Peifer, pres. **A**1a 9 10 **F**1 3 6 10 12 14 15 16 23 35 36 40 46 52	23	10	S		134	5095	85	62.0	12	386	16877	6694	369
LONG BEACH—Nassau County													
★□ LONG BEACH MEMORIAL HOSPITAL, 455 E. Bay Dr., Zip 11561; tel. 516/432-8000; Martin F. Nester Jr., chief exec. off. (Total facility includes 200 beds in nursing home-type unit) **A**1a 9 10 **F**1 2 3 6 9 10 11 12 14 15 16 19 20 23 24 26 28 30 32 33 34 35 37 41 42 44 45 46 47 49 50 52 53	23	10	S	TF H	370 170	5615 5443	322 123	87.0 —	0 0	0 0	32154 23997	16542 12435	677 490
LONG ISLAND CITY—Queens County See New York City													
LOWVILLE—Lewis County													
□ LEWIS COUNTY GENERAL HOSPITAL, N. State St., Zip 13367; tel. 315/376-5200; Edward Sieber Jr., adm. (Total facility includes 120 beds in nursing home-type unit) **A**1a 9 10 **F**1 3 12 14 16 19 23 24 26 35 36 40 42 43 44 45 46 47 50; **S**1905	13	10	S	TF H	174 54	2117 2071	165 46	84.6 —	12 12	298 298	10287 7114	5058 3318	325 241
MALONE—Franklin County													
★□ ALICE HYDE HOSPITAL ASSOCIATION, Park St., Zip 12953; tel. 518/483-3000; Norman M. Gervais, exec. vice-pres. (Total facility includes 75 beds in nursing home-type unit) **A**1a 9 10 **F**1 3 6 12 14 15 16 19 23 26 30 35 36 40 45 46 47 53	23	10	S	TF H	155 80	4094 4064	142 67	86.6 —	8 8	421 421	9629 —	5626 —	316 255
MANHASSET—Nassau County													
★□ NORTH SHORE UNIVERSITY HOSPITAL, 300 Community Dr., Zip 11030; tel. 516/562-0100; John S. T. Gallagher, exec. vice-pres. & chief exec. off. **A**1a 2 3 5 8 9 10 **F**1 2 3 4 5 6 8 9 10 11 12 14 15 16 17 20 23 24 27 28 29 30 32 33 34 35 36 37 38 40 41 42 44 45 46 47 49 51 52 53 54	23	10	S		614	27255	598	97.4	50	4456	184056	92861	3212
MARGARETVILLE—Delaware County													
★□ MARGARETVILLE MEMORIAL HOSPITAL, Rte. 28, Zip 12455; tel. 914/586-2631; David A. Summers, adm. (Total facility includes 31 beds in nursing home-type unit) **A**1a 9 10 **F**3 14 16 19 23 24 26 35 42 45 46 47	23	10	S	TF H	53 22	868 837	45 14	84.9 —	0 0	0 0	— —	— —	130 —
MASSENA—St. Lawrence County													
□ MASSENA MEMORIAL HOSPITAL, One Hospital Dr., Zip 13662; tel. 315/764-1711; William S. Abbott, adm. **A**1a 9 10 **F**1 3 6 12 14 16 23 26 35 36 40 45 52 53; **S**1755	14	10	S		60	2840	41	68.3	12	233	7756	4170	219
MEDINA—Orleans County													
★□ MEDINA MEMORIAL HOSPITAL, 500 Ohio St., Zip 14103; tel. 716/798-2000; Richard W. Petersen, adm. (Total facility includes 30 beds in nursing home-type unit) **A**1a 9 10 **F**1 3 6 10 12 14 16 19 23 35 36 40 44 45 46 52	23	10	S	TF H	101 71	2649 2604	67 38	66.3 —	15 15	322 322	6193 —	3323 —	241 222
MELVILLE—Suffolk County													
★□ SAGAMORE CHILDREN'S PSYCHIATRIC CENTER (Formerly Sagamore Children's Center), 197 Half Hollow Rd., Zip 11747; tel. 516/673-7700; Robert Schweitzer EdD, dir. **A**1b **F**15 28 31 32 33 41 42 43 44 46 47	12	52	L		84	324	85	100.0	0	0	9666	7283	264
MIDDLETOWN—Orange County													
★□ HORTON MEMORIAL HOSPITAL, 60 Prospect Ave., Zip 10940; tel. 914/343-2424; John W. Norton, pres. **A**1a 9 **F**1 2 3 5 6 7 8 9 10 11 12 14 15 16 20 23 24 26 28 30 35 36 37 38 40 41 42 44 45 46 47 49 52 53	23	10	S		301	11214	251	83.4	24	1205	38921	19836	964

Hospital, Address, Telephone, Administrator, Approval and Facility Codes, Multihospital System Code

★ American Hospital Association (AHA) membership
□ Joint Commission on Accreditation of Hospitals (JCAH) accreditation
\+ American Osteopathic Hospital Association (AOHA) membership
○ American Osteopathic Association (AOA) accreditation
Δ Commission on Accreditation of Rehabilitation Facilities (CARF) accreditation
Control codes 61, 63, 64, 71, 72 and 73 indicate hospitals listed by AOHA, but not registered by AHA.
For definition of numerical codes, see page A2

Hospital	Classification Codes				Inpatient Data				Newborn Data		Expense (thousands of dollars)		
	Control	Service	Stay	Facilities	Beds	Admissions	Census	Occupancy (percent)	Bassinets	Births	Total	Payroll	Personnel
★□ MIDDLETOWN PSYCHIATRIC CENTER, 141 Monhagen Ave., Box 1453, Zip 10940; tel. 914/342-5511; Helen M. Houston, chief exec. off. **A**1b 3 10 **F**15 23 24 28 29 30 31 32 33 34 37 42 43 46 50	12	22	L		894	647	853	95.4	0	0	41407	27508	1125
MINEOLA—Nassau County													
★□ WINTHROP-UNIVERSITY HOSPITAL, 259 First St., Zip 11501; tel. 516/663-0333; S. Stephen Bonadonna, exec. vice-pres. **A**1a 2 3 5 8 10 **F**1 2 3 4 5 6 7 8 9 10 11 12 14 15 16 20 23 24 27 30 32 33 34 35 36 37 38 40 41 42 44 45 46 47 49 51 52 53 54	23	10	S		548	19257	484	88.3	33	2722	94351	45879	1816
MONTICELLO—Sullivan County													
HAMILTON AVENUE HOSPITAL, 17 Hamilton Ave., Zip 12701; tel. 914/794-5550; Carl K. Heins MD, exec. dir. (Nonreporting)	32	10	S		68	—	—	—	—	—	—	—	—
MONTOUR FALLS—Schuyler County													
★□ SCHUYLER HOSPITAL, Zip 14865; tel. 607/535-7121; Robert M. Swinnerton, adm. (Total facility includes 40 beds in nursing home-type unit) **A**1a 9 10 **F**1 3 6 12 14 15 16 19 23 26 34 35 36 40 42 45 46 47 50	23	10	S	TF	89	1833	73	82.0	6	70	8834	4549	230
				H	49	1815	33	—	6	70	8231	4175	200
MONTROSE—Westchester County													
★□ FRANKLIN DELANO ROOSEVELT VETERANS ADMINISTRATION HOSPITAL, Zip 10548; tel. 914/737-4400; Dewey Robbiano Jr. MD, dir. (Total facility includes 122 beds in nursing home-type unit) **A**1a **F**3 6 10 12 14 15 16 19 23 24 25 26 28 29 30 31 32 33 34 41 42 43 45 46 47 48 49 50	45	22	L	TF	1195	3803	973	75.5	0	0	57445	44998	1628
				H	1073	3725	861	—	0	0	—	—	1589
MOUNT KISCO—Westchester County													
★□ NORTHERN WESTCHESTER HOSPITAL CENTER, 400 Main St., Zip 10549; tel. 914/666-1200; Peter H. Wade, pres. **A**1a 2 9 10 **F**1 3 5 6 8 9 10 11 12 14 15 16 23 24 27 30 32 33 34 35 36 37 40 42 44 45 46 47 50 52 53	23	10	S		259	9782	201	77.6	27	1696	44789	21370	910
MOUNT VERNON—Westchester County													
★□ MOUNT VERNON HOSPITAL, 12 N. Seventh Ave., Zip 10550; tel. 914/664-8000; Joseph L. Stile, dir. **A**1a 2 3 5 6 9 10 **F**1 2 3 5 6 10 12 14 15 16 23 24 26 34 35 36 37 38 40 42 44 45 46 47 49 53	23	10	S		225	7996	181	80.4	24	866	37938	18623	772
NEW HARTFORD—Oneida County													
★□ ST. LUKE'S MEMORIAL HOSPITAL CENTER (Includes Allen-Calder Skilled Nursing Facility), Zip 13413; Mailing Address P O Box 479, Utica, Zip 13503; tel. 315/798-6000; Andrew E. Peterson, exec. dir. (Total facility includes 76 beds in nursing home-type unit) **A**1a 9 10 **F**1 2 3 6 10 12 14 15 16 19 20 23 24 34 35 36 37 40 42 44 45 46 47 50 52 54	23	10	S	TF	338	10576	292	86.4	36	1444	34998	16974	892
				H	262	10516	216	—	36	1444	33985	16084	834
NEW ROCHELLE—Westchester County													
★□ NEW ROCHELLE HOSPITAL MEDICAL CENTER, 16 Guion Pl., Zip 10802; tel. 914/632-5000; George A. Vecchione, pres. **A**1a 2 3 5 8 9 10 **F**1 2 3 5 6 9 10 12 14 15 16 20 23 24 26 28 30 32 33 34 35 36 37 38 40 41 44 45 46 47 50 52 53	23	10	S		311	10515	259	83.3	20	781	54087	24800	1061
NEW YORK CITY (Includes all hospitals located within the five Boroughs)													
BRONX—Bronx County (Mailing Address-Bronx)													
BROOKLYN—Kings County (Mailing Address-Brooklyn)													
MANHATTAN—New York County (Mailing Address-New York)													
QUEENS—Queens County (Mailing Addresses Astoria, Edgemere, Elmhurst, Far Rockaway, Flushing, Forest Hills, Glen Oaks, Hollis, Jackson Heights, Jamaica, Kew Gardens, Little Neck, Long Island City, Queens Village, St. Albans and Whitestone)													
RICHMOND—Richmond County (Mailing Address-Staten Island)													
ABRAHAM JACOBI GENERAL CARE AND PSYCHIATRIC UNITS, See Bronx Municipal Hospital Center													
□ ASTORIA GENERAL HOSPITAL, 25-10 30th Ave., Long Island City, Zip 11102; tel. 718/932-1000; Henry Olshin, adm. (Nonreporting) **A**1a 9 10	33	10	S		235	—	—	—	—	—	—	—	—
□ ○ BAPTIST MEDICAL CENTER OF NEW YORK, 2749 Linden Blvd., Brooklyn, Zip 11208; tel. 718/277-5100; Solomon Kalish, exec. dir. (Total facility includes 140 beds in nursing home-type unit) **A**1a 9 10 11 12 13 **F**3 5 10 12 14 16 19 20 23 24 27 35 42 45 46 47	23	10	S	TF	347	6290	297	85.6	0	0	27859	15054	652
				H	207	6181	158	—	0	0	—	—	543
★□ BAYLEY SETON HOSPITAL, Bay St. & Vanderbilt Ave., Staten Island, Zip 10304; tel. 718/390-6000; Andrew J. Passeri, vice-pres. & dir. **A**1a 2 3 5 10 **F**1 2 3 6 10 12 14 15 16 20 23 24 27 28 29 30 32 33 34 35 44 45 46 47 48 49 53; **S**6095	21	10	S		204	6895	148	72.5	0	0	46188	20509	735
★□ BELLEVUE HOSPITAL CENTER (Includes Bellevue General Care Unit, Bellevue General Physical Medicine and Rehabilitation Unit, Bellevue Psychiatric Unit, and Bellevue Tuberculosis Unit), First Ave. & 27th St., Zip 10016; tel. 212/561-4141; Harriet Dronska, exec. dir. **A**1a 2 3 5 8 9 10 **F**1 2 3 4 5 6 9 10 11 12 14 16 20 23 24 25 26 27 28 29 30 32 33 34 35 36 38 40 42 43 44 45 46 48 49 50 51 52 53 54; **S**3075	14	10	S		1197	26217	887	74.1	40	1853	229855	131667	4706
★□ BETH ISRAEL MEDICAL CENTER, First Ave. & 16th St., Zip 10003; tel. 212/420-2000; Robert G. Newman MD, pres. **A**1a 2 3 5 8 9 10 **F**1 2 3 6 7 8 9 10 11 12 14 15 16 17 20 21 23 24 25 26 27 28 29 30 32 33 34 35 36 37 38 40 41 42 44 46 47 48 49 50 51 52 53 54	23	10	S		908	31265	788	86.8	56	3540	214511	106989	4353
★□ BOOTH MEMORIAL MEDICAL CENTER, Main St. at Booth Memorial Ave., Flushing, Zip 11355; tel. 718/670-1021; Lt. Col. Thomas E. Adams, exec. dir. **A**1a 2 3 5 8 9 10 **F**1 2 3 5 6 7 8 9 10 11 12 14 16 20 23 24 26 27 28 30 32 33 34 35 36 38 40 41 42 44 45 46 47 48 49 52 53	21	10	S		467	18608	426	91.2	42	2878	100479	45454	1773
□ BOULEVARD HOSPITAL, 46-04 31st Ave., Long Island City, Zip 11103; tel. 212/204-3300; Claude A. Moldaver, adm. (Nonreporting) **A**1a	32	10	S		234	—	—	—	—	—	—	—	—
□ BRONX CHILDREN'S PSYCHIATRIC CENTER, 1000 Waters Pl., Bronx, Zip 10461; tel. 212/892-0808; E. Richard Feinberg MD, dir. **A**1b **F**26 28 29 30 31 32 33 41 42 43 44 45 46 47	12	52	L		75	125	78	100.0	0	0	8675	7877	265
★□ BRONX MUNICIPAL HOSPITAL CENTER (Includes Abraham Jacobi General Care and Psychiatric Units; Nathan B. Van Etten General Care Hospital), Pelham Pkwy. S. & Eastchester Rd., Zip 10461; tel. 212/430-8141; Harold A. Levine, actg. exec. dir. **A**1a 3 5 8 9 10 **F**1 3 5 6 10 12 14 15 16 22 23 24 25 26 27 28 29 30 32 33 34 35 37 38 40 41 42 43 44 45 46 47 48 49 52 53; **S**3075	14	10	S		811	23957	654	78.8	49	2755	167512	90698	3525
BRONX PSYCHIATRIC CENTER, 1500 Waters Pl., Bronx, Zip 10461; tel. 212/931-0600; Robert T. Hettenbach, exec. dir. (Nonreporting) **A**3 5	12	22	L		781	—	—	—	—	—	—	—	—
★□ BRONX-LEBANON HOSPITAL CENTER (Includes Concourse Division, 1650 Grand Concourse, Zip 10457; tel. 212/588-7000; Fulton Division, 1276 Fulton Ave., Zip 10456; tel. 212/588-7000), Fred Silverman, pres. **A**1a 2 3 5 8 9 10 **F**1 3 6 7 8 9 10 11 12 14 16 20 23 24 27 28 29 30 32 33 34 35 37 40 42 43 44 45 46 49 50 51 52 53 54	23	10	S		565	24775	506	89.6	49	2723	110164	60584	2410
★□ BROOKDALE HOSPITAL MEDICAL CENTER, Linden Blvd. & Brookdale Plaza, Brooklyn, Zip 11212; tel. 718/240-5000; Charles H. Meyer, pres. & chief exec. off. **A**1a 2 3 5 8 9 10 **F**1 3 5 6 7 8 9 10 11 12 13 14 15 16 20 23 24 26 27 28 29 30 31 32 33 34 35 36 37 38 40 41 42 43 44 45 46 47 50 52 53 54	23	10	S		803	29140	701	87.2	59	5049	159691	76280	3224
BROOKLYN HOSPITAL, See Brooklyn Hospital-Caledonian Hospital													

Hospital, Address, Telephone, Administrator, Approval and Facility Codes, Multihospital System Code	Classification Codes				Inpatient Data				Newborn Data		Expense (thousands of dollars)		
★ American Hospital Association (AHA) membership ☐ Joint Commission on Accreditation of Hospitals (JCAH) accreditation + American Osteopathic Hospital Association (AOHA) membership ○ American Osteopathic Association (AOA) accreditation Δ Commission on Accreditation of Rehabilitation Facilities (CARF) accreditation Control codes 61, 63, 64, 71, 72 and 73 indicate hospitals listed by AOHA, but not registered by AHA. For definition of numerical codes, see page A2	Control	Service	Stay	Facilities	Beds	Admissions	Census	Occupancy (percent)	Bassinets	Births	Total	Payroll	Personnel
★ BROOKLYN HOSPITAL-CALEDONIAN HOSPITAL (Includes Brooklyn Hospital, 121 DeKalb Ave., Zip 11201; tel. 718/403-8000; Caledonian Hospital, 10 St. Paul's Pl., Zip 11226; tel. 718/469-1000), 121 DeKalb Ave., Zip 11201; tel. 718/403-8005; Frederick D. Alley, pres. & chief exec. off. **A**1a 2 3 5 8 9 10 **F**1 2 3 6 7 8 9 10 11 12 14 15 16 20 23 24 26 30 33 34 35 37 38 40 41 42 44 45 46 47 51 52 53 54	23	10	S		634	21495	575	90.7	48	2963	115159	60407	2164
★ CABRINI MEDICAL CENTER, 227 E. 19th St., Zip 10003; tel. 212/725-6000; Sr. Josephine Tsuei, pres. **A**1a 2 3 5 8 9 10 **F**1 2 3 6 7 8 9 10 11 12 14 15 16 20 21 23 24 27 29 30 32 33 35 41 43 44 45 46 47 50 53 54	21	10	S		493	14411	437	88.6	0	0	76280	34693	1450
CALEDONIAN HOSPITAL, See Brooklyn Hospital-Caledonian Hospital													
★ CALVARY HOSPITAL (Advanced Cancer), 1740-70 Eastchester Rd., Bronx, Zip 10461; tel. 212/863-6900; Frank A. Calamari, pres. & exec. dir. **A**1a 9 10 **F**8 14 16 23 24 32 34 41 42 44 45 46 47	21	49	L		200	1294	173	86.5	0	0	25284	14797	568
★ CATHOLIC MEDICAL CENTER OF BROOKLYN AND QUEENS (Includes Hospital of the Holy Family, 155 Dean St., Brooklyn, Zip 11217; tel. 718/875-9200; Paul Ciaramella, exec. dir.; Mary Immaculate Hospital, 152-11 89th Ave., Zip 11432; tel. 718/291-3300; Thomas P. Dailey, exec. dir.; St. John's Queens Hospital, 90-02 Queens Blvd., Elmhurst, Zip 11373; tel. 718/457-1300; Sr. Helen Faulds, exec. dir.; St. Joseph's Hospital, 158-40 79th Ave., Flushing, Zip 11366; tel. 212/591-1000; Michael Marigliano, exec. dir.; St. Mary's Hospital, 170 Buffalo Ave., Brooklyn, Zip 11213; tel. 718/774-3600; Bernard M. McCaffrey, exec. dir.), 88-25 153rd St., Zip 11432; tel. 718/657-6800; Alvin J. Conway, pres. **A**1a 2 3 5 8 9 10 **F**1 2 3 6 7 8 9 10 11 12 14 15 16 20 23 26 28 30 32 33 34 35 36 38 40 41 44 45 46 47 49 51 52	21	10	S		1161	41967	981	84.5	81	4848	253632	149527	4562
★ Δ CITY HOSPITAL CENTER AT ELMHURST, 79-01 Broadway, Elmhurst Sta., Zip 11373; tel. 718/830-1515; Alan H. Channing, exec. dir. (Total facility includes 72 beds in nursing home-type unit) **A**1a 2 3 5 7 8 10 **F**1 3 5 6 10 11 12 14 15 16 19 20 23 24 25 26 27 28 30 32 33 34 35 36 37 38 40 41 42 44 45 46 47 48 49 50 51 52 53 54; **S**3075	14	10	S	TF	761	18968	663	86.4	31	2328	143292	83912	3083
				H	689	18864	591	—	31	2328	142065	82795	3031
★ COLER MEMORIAL HOSPITAL, Franklin D Roosevelt Island, Zip 10044; tel. 212/688-9400; Mark J. Kator, exec. dir. (Total facility includes 775 beds in nursing home-type unit) **A**1a 9 **F**3 6 10 12 14 16 19 23 24 25 42 44 45 46 47; **S**3075	14	48	L	TF	1045	1034	961	92.0	0	0	68985	44821	1875
				H	270	631	198	—	0	0	—	—	578
★ COMMUNITY HOSPITAL OF BROOKLYN, 2525 Kings Hwy., Brooklyn, Zip 11229; tel. 718/377-7900; Louise Kane, exec. dir. **A**1a 9 10 **F**1 3 6 10 12 14 15 16 23 35 37 46 47	23	10	S		134	5544	109	81.3	0	0	—	—	301
CONCOURSE DIVISION, See Bronx-Lebanon Hospital Center													
★ ○ CONEY ISLAND HOSPITAL, 2601 Ocean Pkwy., Brooklyn, Zip 11235; tel. 718/615-4000; Howard C. Cohen, exec. dir. **A**1a 2 3 5 9 10 11 12 **F**1 2 3 6 10 12 14 15 16 20 23 24 25 26 27 28 29 30 32 33 34 35 37 38 40 42 43 44 45 46 47 48 49 50 52 53 54; **S**3075	14	10	S		445	17251	388	87.2	28	1439	113680	65417	2428
★ CREEDMOOR PSYCHIATRIC CENTER, 80-45 Winchester Blvd., Queens Vlg., Zip 11427; tel. 718/464-7500; Barbara Sacco, actg. exec. dir. **A**1b 3 10 **F**12 19 23 24 28 29 30 31 32 33 42 44 46 47 50	12	22	L		1262	3161	1265	100.0	0	0	—	—	2217
☐ DEEPDALE GENERAL HOSPITAL, 55-15 Little Neck Pkwy., Little Neck, Zip 11362; tel. 718/428-3000; Mark Rosenblatt, exec. dir. (Nonreporting) **A**1a 9 10	32	10	S		195	—	—	—	—	—	—	—	—
★ DOCTORS HOSPITAL, 170 East End Ave., Zip 10128; tel. 212/870-9000; John C. Donaher Jr., exec. vice-pres. **A**1a 9 10 **F**1 2 3 6 9 10 12 14 15 16 20 23 26 35 37 44 46 47 53	23	10	S		263	8361	176	66.9	0	0	45063	20561	677
★ DOCTORS' HOSPITAL OF STATEN ISLAND, 1050 Targee St., Staten Island, Zip 10304; tel. 718/981-1400; Stephen N. F. Anderson, exec. dir. **A**1a 2 9 10 **F**1 3 6 10 12 14 15 16 20 23 32 35 46 53	33	10	S		129	4159	102	76.1	0	0	15769	8163	350
★ FLUSHING HOSPITAL AND MEDICAL CENTER, Parsons Blvd. & 45th Ave., Flushing, Zip 11355; tel. 212/670-5000; Michael S. Kaminski, pres. & chief exec. off. **A**1a 2 3 5 6 9 10 **F**1 2 3 6 7 8 9 10 11 12 14 15 20 23 26 28 33 34 35 36 37 38 40 41 44 45 46 47 51 52 53	23	10	S		424	15346	371	87.5	32	2703	74551	34695	1450
FULTON DIVISION, See Bronx-Lebanon Hospital Center													
★ GOLDWATER MEMORIAL HOSPITAL, Franklin D Roosevelt Island, Zip 10044; tel. 212/750-6800; I. Bernard Hirsch, exec. dir. (Total facility includes 412 beds in nursing home-type unit) **A**1a 3 5 9 10 **F**3 6 12 14 16 19 23 24 25 32 33 42 44 45 46 47 50; **S**3075	14	48	L	TF	912	932	857	94.0	0	0	63518	39798	2106
				H	500	708	453	—	0	0	—	—	1785
★ GRACIE SQUARE HOSPITAL, 420 E. 76th St., Zip 10021; tel. 212/988-4400; Robert J. Campbell MD, dir. **A**1b 9 10 **F**23 24 30 32 33 42 47 48	33	22	S		220	2809	169	76.8	0	0	18698	9241	320
★ Δ HARLEM HOSPITAL CENTER (Includes Harlem General Care Unit, Harlem Psychiatric Unit, and Harlem Tuberculosis Unit), 506 Lenox Ave., Zip 10037; tel. 212/491-1234; Charles E. Windsor, exec. dir. **A**1a 2 3 5 7 8 9 10 **F**1 3 5 6 7 8 9 10 11 12 14 16 20 22 23 24 25 27 28 29 30 31 32 33 34 35 36 37 40 41 42 43 44 45 46 47 48 49 50 52 53 54; **S**3075	14	10	S		725	20983	560	77.2	45	2732	165511	77145	4084
HEBREW HOSPITAL FOR CHRONIC SICK, 2200 Givan Ave., Bronx, Zip 10475; tel. 212/379-5020; Richard Shedlovsky, exec. dir. **F**19 23 24 32 41 42 44 45 46 47 50	23	48	L		480	192	466	97.1	0	0	21900	16400	447
HENRY AND LUCY MOSES DIVISION AND LOEB CENTER SKILLED NURSING FACILITY, See Montefiore Medical Center													
HILLSIDE DIVISION, See Long Island Jewish-Hillside Medical Center													
★ Δ HOSPITAL FOR JOINT DISEASES ORTHOPAEDIC INSTITUTE, 301 E. 17th St., Zip 10003; tel. 212/598-6000; Harvey Machaver, exec. dir. **A**1a 3 5 7 8 9 **F**1 12 14 16 23 24 26 34 42 44 45 46 47 50 53	23	47	S		230	6339	175	76.1	0	0	61933	28426	960
★ HOSPITAL FOR SPECIAL SURGERY, 535 E. 70th St., Zip 10021; tel. 212/606-1000; Donald S. Broas, vice-pres. & exec. dir. **A**1a 3 5 8 9 10 **F**1 6 10 12 14 15 16 23 24 26 28 33 34 42 44 45 46 47 53	23	47	S		192	5140	157	81.8	0	0	54915	25187	948
☐ INTERFAITH MEDICAL CENTER (Includes St. John's Episcopal, Brooklyn Jewish) (Includes Interfaith Medical Center-Brooklyn Jewish Division, 555 Prospect Pl., Zip 11238; tel. 718/935-7000; St. John's Episcopal Division, 1545 Atlantic Ave., Zip 11213; tel. 718/935-7000), 555 Prospect Pl., Zip 11238; tel. 718/935-7000; Theodore R. Jamison, pres. **A**1a 2 3 5 9 10 **F**6 7 8 9 10 11 12 14 16 20 23 24 26 27 28 29 30 31 32 33 34 35 36 40 41 42 44 45 46 47 48 49 51 52 53	23	10	S		620	24557	519	83.7	50	1952	130328	94936	2637
INTERFAITH MEDICAL CENTER-BROOKLYN JEWISH DIVISION, See Interfaith Medical Center													
JACK D. WEILER HOSPITAL OF EINSTEIN COLLEGE OF MEDICINE, See Montefiore Medical Center													
★ JAMAICA HOSPITAL, 89th Ave. & Van Wyck Expwy., Jamaica, Zip 11418; tel. 718/657-1800; David P. Rosen, pres. **A**1a 2 3 5 9 10 **F**1 3 6 10 12 14 15 16 20 23 26 34 35 40 45 46 52 53	23	10	S		282	9876	207	73.4	40	1355	46983	23163	993
☐ JOINT DISEASES NORTH GENERAL HOSPITAL, 1919 Madison Ave., Zip 10035; tel. 212/650-4000; Eugene McCabe, pres. **A**1a 3 5 10 **F**1 3 6 7 8 10 11 12 14 15 16 23 24 26 28 30 32 33 34 35 37 46 47 48 49 50 52	23	10	S		190	6401	168	88.4	0	0	—	—	—

★ American Hospital Association (AHA) membership
□ Joint Commission on Accreditation of Hospitals (JCAH) accreditation
+ American Osteopathic Hospital Association (AOHA) membership
○ American Osteopathic Association (AOA) accreditation
Δ Commission on Accreditation of Rehabilitation Facilities (CARF) accreditation
Control codes 61, 63, 64, 71, 72 and 73 indicate hospitals listed by AOHA, but not registered by AHA.
For definition of numerical codes, see page A2

Hospital, Address, Telephone, Administrator, Approval and Facility Codes, Multihospital System Code	Classification Codes				Inpatient Data				Newborn Data		Expense (thousands of dollars)		
	Control	Service	Stay	Facilities	Beds	Admissions	Census	Occupancy (percent)	Bassinets	Births	Total	Payroll	Personnel
★ KINGS COUNTY HOSPITAL CENTER, 451 Clarkson Ave., Brooklyn, Zip 11203; tel. 718/735-3131; Ira C. Clark, chief exec. off. & reg. adm. **A**1a b 2 3 5 8 9 10 **F**2 3 5 6 7 8 10 11 12 14 15 16 19 20 21 22 23 24 25 26 27 28 29 30 32 33 34 35 36 37 38 40 42 43 44 45 46 47 48 49 50 52 53; **S**3075	14	10	S		1221	35936	1094	86.4	80	5110	169437	—	5668
□ KINGS HIGHWAY HOSPITAL CENTER, 3201 Kings Hwy., Brooklyn, Zip 11234; tel. 718/252-3000; S. Berson MD, exec. dir. (Nonreporting) **A**1a 9 10	33	10	S		212	—	—	—	—	—	—	—	—
★ KINGSBORO PSYCHIATRIC CENTER, 681 Clarkson Ave., Brooklyn, Zip 11203; tel. 212/735-1700; Ella A. Curry PhD, exec. dir. (Nonreporting) **A**1b 3 5 10	12	22	L		870	—	—	—	—	—	—	—	—
★ Δ KINGSBROOK JEWISH MEDICAL CENTER, 585 Schenectady Ave., Brooklyn, Zip 11203; tel. 718/604-5000; Harold A. Schneider, exec. dir. **A**1a 3 5 7 9 10 **F**3 6 7 8 10 11 12 14 15 16 20 23 24 25 26 28 32 33 34 35 38 41 42 44 45 46 50 52 53	23	10	S		343	9167	287	83.7	0	0	53269	27235	1747
★ LAGUARDIA HOSPITAL, 102-01 66th Rd., Forest Hills, Zip 11375; tel. 718/830-4000; Leon N. Cohen, bd. chm. & chief corp off.; Arnold E. Rosenblum, chief hosp. off. (Nonreporting) **A**1a 2 3 5 10	23	10	S		302	—	—	—	—	—	—	—	—
★ LENOX HILL HOSPITAL, 100 E. 77th St., Zip 10021; tel. 212/439-2345; Allan C. Anderson, pres. **A**1a 3 5 8 9 10 **F**1 2 3 4 6 7 8 9 10 11 12 14 15 16 20 23 24 26 28 30 32 33 34 35 36 37 38 40 41 42 44 45 46 47 50 51 52 53 54	23	10	S		698	25350	562	80.5	33	2879	131465	67233	2618
★ LINCOLN MEDICAL AND MENTAL HEALTH CENTER, 234 E. 149th St., Bronx, Zip 10451; tel. 212/579-5000; Angel Quinones, exec. dir. **A**1a 3 5 9 10 **F**1 2 3 5 6 7 8 9 10 11 12 14 15 16 20 23 24 26 27 28 29 30 32 33 34 35 36 37 38 40 41 42 44 45 46 47 49 50 51 52 53 54; **S**3075	14	10	S		571	26742	557	98.8	60	4690	167781	87620	2459
★ LONG ISLAND COLLEGE HOSPITAL, Brooklyn, Zip 11201; tel. 718/780-1000; Harold L. Light, pres. & chief exec. off. **A**1a 2 3 5 8 9 10 **F**1 3 6 7 8 9 10 11 12 14 16 20 23 24 25 26 28 29 34 35 36 38 40 41 42 44 45 46 47 48 49 52 53 54	23	10	S		567	22710	485	85.5	42	2610	139924	65386	2437
★ LONG ISLAND JEWISH MEDICAL CENTER (Formerly Long Island Jewish-Hillside Medical Center) (Includes Hillside Division, Glen Oaks, tel. 212/470-2000; Henry Hoffman, adm.; Long Island Jewish-Hillside Medical Center-Manhasset Division, Manhasset, tel. 516/627-9000), Mailing Address New Hyde Park, Zip 11042; tel. 212/470-2000; Robert K. Match MD, pres. **A**1a 2 3 5 8 9 10 **F**1 3 4 6 7 8 9 10 11 12 14 15 16 17 20 21 23 24 26 27 28 29 30 31 32 33 34 35 36 37 38 40 41 42 43 44 45 46 47 49 50 52 53 54	23	10	S		806	27776	757	92.3	42	4141	252245	134897	4910
★ LUTHERAN MEDICAL CENTER, 150 55th St., Brooklyn, Zip 11220; tel. 718/630-7000; George Adams, pres. **A**1a 2 3 5 9 10 **F**1 2 3 6 7 8 9 10 11 12 14 15 16 20 23 24 25 26 28 33 34 35 37 38 40 44 45 46 47 49 50 52 53	23	10	S		526	15576	414	78.7	40	2020	79917	35739	1844
★ MAIMONIDES MEDICAL CENTER, 4802 Tenth Ave., Brooklyn, Zip 11219; tel. 212/270-7679; Lee W. Schwenn, exec. vice-pres. **A**1a 2 3 5 8 9 10 **F**1 2 3 4 5 6 9 10 11 12 14 15 16 20 23 24 26 27 28 29 30 32 33 34 35 36 37 38 40 41 42 43 44 45 46 47 50 51 52 53 54	23	10	S		700	24806	646	92.3	60	3743	148618	75334	2530
★ MANHATTAN EYE, EAR AND THROAT HOSPITAL, 210 E. 64th St., Zip 10021; tel. 212/838-9200; George A. Sarkar PhD, exec. dir. **A**1a 2 3 5 10 **F**1 11 12 15 34 35 44 45 46 47	23	45	S		150	12515	97	64.7	0	0	36981	15711	626
★ MANHATTAN PSYCHIATRIC CENTER-WARD'S ISLAND, 600 E. 125th St., Zip 10035; tel. 212/369-0500; Michael H. Ford MD, exec. dir. **A**1b 3 5 **F**23 24 28 29 30 32 33 42 43 44 46 47	12	22	L		1139	1259	1178	100.0	0	0	67246	45571	1943
□ MEDICAL ARTS CENTER HOSPITAL, 57 W. 57th St., Zip 10019; tel. 212/755-0200; Norman J. Sokolow, dir. **A**1a 9 10 **F**3 10 12 14 16 23 35 48	33	10	S		77	3626	46	59.7	0	0	6666	3800	150
★ MEMORIAL HOSPITAL FOR CANCER AND ALLIED DISEASES, 1275 York Ave., Zip 10021; tel. 212/794-7722; Peter J. Hughes, exec. vice-pres. **A**1a 2 3 5 8 9 10 **F**3 6 7 8 9 10 11 12 13 14 16 17 20 23 24 28 32 33 34 39 42 43 45 46 47 52 53	23	49	S		565	17915	499	88.3	0	0	265000	144000	4000
★ METHODIST HOSPITAL, 506 Sixth St., Brooklyn, Zip 11215; tel. 718/780-3000; Don A. Rece, exec. dir. **A**1a 2 3 5 8 9 10 **F**1 3 6 7 8 9 10 11 12 14 16 20 23 24 25 26 27 28 30 33 34 35 36 37 40 41 44 45 46 47 50 51 52 53	23	10	S		514	16500	416	80.9	42	1996	99724	45637	1768
★ METROPOLITAN HOSPITAL CENTER (Includes Metropolitan General Care Unit, Metropolitan Drug Detoxification and Metropolitan Psychiatric Unit), 1901 First Ave., Zip 10029; tel. 212/360-6262; Stephen N. Lenhardt, actg. exec. dir. **A**1a 3 5 8 9 10 **F**1 3 6 10 12 14 15 16 20 23 24 25 26 27 28 29 30 32 33 34 35 37 38 40 41 42 43 44 45 46 47 49 52 53 54; **S**3075	14	10	S		598	16529	510	85.3	33	2177	137980	58264	2946
★ MONTEFIORE MEDICAL CENTER (Includes Henry and Lucy Moses Division and Loeb Center Skilled Nursing Facility, 111 E. 210th St., Zip 10467; tel. 212/920-4321; Robert J. Henkel, vice-pres. oper.; Jack D. Weiler Hospital of Einstein College of Medicine, 1825 Eastchester Rd., Zip 10461; tel. 212/430-2000; James E. Romer, vice-pres. oper.), Mailing Address 111 E. 210th St., Zip 10467; tel. 212/920-6701; Spencer Foreman MD, pres.; Nathan G. Kase MD, actg. chief exec. off. **A**1a 2 3 5 8 9 10 **F**1 2 3 4 6 7 8 9 10 11 12 13 14 15 16 17 19 20 23 24 25 26 27 28 30 32 33 34 35 36 37 38 40 41 42 44 45 46 47 50 52 53 54	23	10	S		1242	41255	1127	89.3	37	3115	419640	160926	6073
★ MOUNT SINAI MEDICAL CENTER (Formerly Mount Sinai Hospital), One Gustave L Levy Pl., Zip 10029; tel. 212/650-8888; James F. Glenn MD, pres.; Nathan G. Kase MD, actg. chief exec. off. **A**1a b 3 5 8 9 10 **F**1 2 3 4 6 7 8 9 10 11 12 13 14 15 16 17 20 23 24 26 27 28 29 30 32 33 34 35 36 37 38 39 40 41 42 43 44 45 46 47 49 50 51 52 53 54	23	10	S		1112	33537	940	81.0	81	3625	275501	—	4774
NATHAN B. VAN ETTEN GENERAL CARE HOSPITAL, See Bronx Municipal Hospital Center													
★ NEW YORK EYE AND EAR INFIRMARY, 310 E. 14th St., Zip 10003; tel. 212/598-1313; Paul R. Kessler, assoc. vice-pres. **A**1a 3 5 9 10 **F**1 5 12 15 34 35 45 46	23	45	S		147	11762	84	57.1	0	0	25964	12774	586
NEW YORK HOSPITAL, See Society of the New York Hospital													
□ NEW YORK INFIRMARY-BEEKMAN DOWNTOWN HOSPITAL, 170 William St., Zip 10038; tel. 212/312-5000; Joseph Sherber, exec. vice-pres. & chief exec. off. **A**1a 2 3 5 9 10 **F**1 3 5 6 7 8 10 12 14 16 20 23 24 34 35 36 37 38 40 41 44 45 46 47 52 53	23	10	S		324	11008	281	86.7	24	1556	56007	26715	949
□ NEW YORK STATE PSYCHIATRIC INSTITUTE, 722 W. 168th St., Zip 10032; tel. 212/960-2200; Herbert Pardes MD, dir. (Nonreporting) **A**1b 3 5 10	12	22	L		64	—	—	—	—	—	—	—	—
★ Δ NEW YORK UNIVERSITY MEDICAL CENTER (Includes Rusk Institute, 400 E. 34th St., Zip 10016; University Hospital, 560 First Ave., Zip 10016), 550 First Ave., Zip 10016; tel. 212/340-5111; James J. Quinn MD, vice-pres. oper. **A**1a 2 3 5 7 8 9 10 **F**1 3 4 6 7 8 9 10 11 12 14 15 16 17 20 23 24 25 26 27 30 32 33 35 37 38 39 40 42 44 45 46 47 50 51 52 53 54	23	10	S		878	27161	794	90.4	40	2310	208086	—	3132
★ NORTH CENTRAL BRONX HOSPITAL, 3424 Kossuth Ave., Bronx, Zip 10467; tel. 212/920-7171; A. Richard Plaatsman, exec. dir. **A**1a 3 5 9 10 **F**1 3 6 10 12 14 15 16 23 24 25 26 27 28 30 32 33 34 35 37 40 42 44 45 46 47 51 52; **S**3075	14	10	S		353	13761	298	79.7	30	2658	105404	57127	1960
★ OUR LADY OF MERCY MEDICAL CENTER, 600 E. 233rd St., Bronx, Zip 10466; tel. 212/920-9000; Kevin W. Ryan, pres. **A**1a 2 3 5 8 10 **F**1 2 3 5 6 7 8 9 10 11 12 14 15 16 20 23 24 26 27 28 30 32 33 34 35 40 41 42 44 45 46 47 49 50 51 52 53	21	10	S		422	14507	310	73.5	36	2403	81303	38237	1401

Hospital, Address, Telephone, Administrator, Approval and Facility Codes, Multihospital System Code	Classification Codes				Inpatient Data				Newborn Data		Expense (thousands of dollars)		
★ American Hospital Association (AHA) membership □ Joint Commission on Accreditation of Hospitals (JCAH) accreditation + American Osteopathic Hospital Association (AOHA) membership ○ American Osteopathic Association (AOA) accreditation Δ Commission on Accreditation of Rehabilitation Facilities (CARF) accreditation Control codes 61, 63, 64, 71, 72 and 73 indicate hospitals listed by AOHA, but not registered by AHA. For definition of numerical codes, see page A2	Control	Service	Stay	Facilities	Beds	Admissions	Census	Occupancy (percent)	Bassinets	Births	Total	Payroll	Personnel
★□ PARKWAY HOSPITAL, 70-35 113th St., Forest Hills, Zip 11375; tel. 718/990-4100; Robert S. Goodman, chief exec. off. **A**1a 10 **F**1 2 3 6 10 12 14 16 20 23 35 37 43 46	32	10	S		227	7823	173	76.2	0	0	—	—	—
□ PARSONS HOSPITAL, 35-06 Parsons Blvd., Flushing, Zip 11354; tel. 212/353-7100; Dermot J. Browner, adm. **A**1a 9 10 **F**3 12 14 16 23 35 37 44 46 53	33	10	S		100	3018	73	67.6	0	0	—	—	236
PAYNE WHITNEY PSYCHIATRIC CLINIC, See Society of the New York Hospital													
★□ PELHAM BAY GENERAL HOSPITAL, 1870 Pelham Pkwy. S., Bronx, Zip 10461; tel. 212/430-6000; John P. Albanese MD, chief exec. off. **A**1a 9 10 **F**3 6 10 12 14 16 23 24 35 46 47 50	32	10	S		183	3931	112	61.2	0	0	11182	6063	297
□ PENINSULA HOSPITAL CENTER, 51-15 Beach Channel Dr., Far Rockaway, Zip 11691; tel. 718/945-7100; Irwin M. Langer, adm. **A**1a 3 5 9 10 **F**2 3 6 7 8 9 10 11 12 14 15 16 20 23 24 26 33 34 35 42 44 45 46 47 50 52 53	23	10	S		272	7666	228	83.8	0	0	35834	19037	860
□ PHYSICIANS HOSPITAL, 34-01 73rd St., Zip 11372; tel. 212/446-1100; Silvio R. Lamattina, adm. (Nonreporting) **A**1a 10	33	10	S		142	—	—	—	—	—	—	—	—
★□ Δ PRESBYTERIAN HOSPITAL IN THE CITY OF NEW YORK, Columbia-Presby Med. Ctr, Zip 10032; tel. 212/305-2500; Thomas Q. Morris MD, pres. **A**1a 2 3 5 7 8 9 10 **F**1 2 3 4 6 7 8 9 10 11 12 13 14 15 16 17 20 23 24 25 26 27 28 30 32 33 34 35 37 38 40 42 44 45 46 47 49 51 52 53 54	23	10	S		1291	44319	1138	88.1	59	4297	296461	146276	5898
QUEENS CHILDREN'S PSYCHIATRIC CENTER, 74-03 Commonwealth Blvd., Bellerose, Zip 11426; tel. 212/464-2900; Gloria Faretra MD, dir. (Nonreporting)	12	52	L		173	—	—	—	—	—	—	—	—
★□ QUEENS HOSPITAL CENTER (Includes Queens General Hospital and Triboro Hospital), 82-68 164th St., Jamaica, Zip 11432; tel. 718/990-3377; Lorraine Tregde, exec. dir. **A**1a 2 3 5 9 10 **F**3 6 10 12 14 15 16 19 20 23 24 25 26 27 28 29 30 32 33 34 35 36 37 38 40 42 43 44 45 46 47 48 49 50 51 52 53; **S**3075	14	10	S		551	18411	447	77.7	34	2218	139201	78859	2933
□ REGENT HOSPITAL, 425 E. 61st St., Zip 10021; tel. 212/935-3400; Ben Farbman, adm.; A. Carter Pottash MD, med. dir. (Nonreporting) **A**1b ; **S**0825	33	22	L		29	—	—	—	—	—	—	—	—
□ RICHMOND MEMORIAL HOSPITAL AND HEALTH CENTER, 375 Seguine Ave., Staten Island, Zip 10309; tel. 718/317-2000; Anthony J. Succo, exec. vice-pres. (Data for 273 days) **A**1a 9 10 **F**1 3 6 10 12 14 16 20 23 28 34 35 44 45 46 47 49 50 53	23	10	S		115	5213	115	69.3	0	56	19924	9758	529
□ ROCKEFELLER UNIVERSITY HOSPITAL (General Medical and Clinical Research), 1230 York Ave., Zip 10021; tel. 212/570-8000; Kathy Kleinbard, adm. **A**1a 3 9 10 **F**34 42	23	49	S		30	420	23	76.7	0	0	4562	2400	65
ROOSEVELT HOSPITAL, See St. Luke's-Roosevelt Hospital Center													
RUSK INSTITUTE, See New York University Medical Center													
★□ SOCIETY OF THE NEW YORK HOSPITAL (Includes New York Hospital; New York Hospital, Westchester Division, White Plains; Payne Whitney Psychiatric Clinic), 525 E. 68th St., Zip 10021; tel. 212/472-5454; David D. Thompson MD, dir. **A**1a b 3 5 8 10 **F**2 3 4 5 6 7 8 9 10 11 12 13 14 15 16 17 20 22 23 24 26 27 29 30 32 33 34 35 36 37 38 39 40 41 42 43 44 45 46 47 49 50 51 52 53 54	23	10	S		1418	41920	1287	90.8	44	3080	309000	166135	5309
□ SOUTH BEACH PSYCHIATRIC CENTER, 777 Seaview Ave., Staten Island, Zip 10305; tel. 212/667-2300; Lucy Sarkis MD, exec. dir. **A**1b 10 **F**15 24 28 29 30 31 32 33 34 41 42 43 45 46 47 50	12	22	L		371	3209	416	100.0	0	0	47961	31898	1130
★□ ST. BARNABAS HOSPITAL, 183rd St. & Third Ave., Bronx, Zip 10457; tel. 212/960-6101; Ronald Gade MD, pres. **A**1a 3 5 9 10 **F**1 3 6 10 12 14 15 16 20 23 24 25 26 27 29 32 33 34 35 44 45 46 47 48 50	23	10	S		406	11550	329	81.0	0	0	56360	25485	1054
□ ST. CLARE'S HOSPITAL AND HEALTH CENTER, 415 W. 51st St., Zip 10019; tel. 212/586-1500 **A**1a 10 **F**1 3 6 10 12 14 15 16 20 23 24 26 27 32 33 34 35 42 44 45 46 47 50	23	10	S		250	5433	177	70.8	0	0	34469	18745	682
ST. JOHN'S EPISCOPAL DIVISION, See Interfaith Medical Center													
★□ ST. JOHN'S EPISCOPAL HOSPITAL-SOUTH SHORE, 327 Beach 19th St., Far Rockaway, Zip 11691; tel. 212/917-3000; Keith F. Safian, adm. **A**1a 3 9 **F**1 2 3 5 6 10 12 14 15 16 20 23 24 26 27 30 31 32 33 34 35 36 37 38 40 42 44 45 46 47 48 49 50 52 53; **S**0735	21	10	S		300	10894	259	86.3	34	1244	59072	27437	1054
ST. LUKE'S HOSPITAL CENTER, See St. Luke's-Roosevelt Hospital Center													
★□ ST. LUKE'S-ROOSEVELT HOSPITAL CENTER (Includes Roosevelt Hospital, 428 W. 59th St., Zip 10019; tel. 212/554-7000; St. Luke's Hospital Center, Amsterdam Ave. & 114th St., Zip 10025; tel. 212/870-6000; Woman's Hospital, Amsterdam Ave. & 113th St., Zip 10025; tel. 212/870-6000), Amsterdam Ave. & 114th St., Zip 10025; tel. 212/870-6000; Gary Gambuti, pres. **A**1a 3 5 8 9 10 **F**1 2 3 4 5 6 7 8 9 10 11 12 13 14 15 16 20 21 23 24 26 27 28 29 30 32 33 34 35 36 37 38 40 41 43 44 45 46 47 48 49 51 52 53 54	23	10	S		1315	44496	1155	87.8	112	4477	279522	157284	6084
★□ ST. VINCENT'S HOSPITAL AND MEDICAL CENTER OF NEW YORK (Includes St. Vincent's Hospital and Medical Center of New York, Westchester Branch, Harrison), 153 W. 11th St., Zip 10011; tel. 212/790-7000; Sr. Margaret Sweeney, pres. & chief exec. off. **A**1a 2 3 5 6 8 9 10 **F**1 2 3 4 5 6 7 8 9 10 11 12 14 15 16 20 21 23 24 25 26 27 28 29 30 31 32 33 34 35 36 37 38 40 41 42 43 44 45 46 47 49 51 52 53 54; **S**5995	21	10	S		891	22127	771	86.5	25	2066	196384	91087	3165
★□ ST. VINCENT'S MEDICAL CENTER OF RICHMOND, 355 Bard Ave., Staten Island, Zip 10310; tel. 718/390-1234; Gary S. Horan, vice-pres. & dir. **A**1a 2 3 5 6 8 9 10 **F**1 2 3 5 6 10 12 14 15 16 20 21 23 24 26 27 28 29 30 31 32 33 34 35 36 37 38 40 41 42 43 44 45 46 47 49 50 51 52 53 54; **S**6095	21	10	S		447	16642	379	84.8	25	2151	77671	42167	1561
STATE UNIVERSITY HOSPITAL, DOWNSTATE MEDICAL CENTER, See University Hospital of Brooklyn-State University of New York Health Sciences Center at Brooklyn													
★□ STATEN ISLAND HOSPITAL, 475 Seaview Ave., Staten Island, Zip 10305; tel. 718/390-9000; Barry T. Zeman, pres. **A**1a 2 3 5 9 10 **F**1 2 3 5 6 7 8 9 10 11 12 14 15 16 20 23 24 25 26 27 28 32 33 34 35 36 37 38 40 42 44 45 46 47 48 49 50 51 52 53	23	10	S		462	16560	374	81.3	35	2672	81468	35839	1357
★□ UNION HOSPITAL OF THE BRONX, 260 E. 188th St., Bronx, Zip 10458; tel. 212/220-2020; Daniel S. Fruchter, vice-pres. & adm. **A**1a 9 10 **F**1 3 6 10 12 14 16 23 32 34 35 36 37 40 43 50	23	10	S		201	6308	99	49.3	18	771	16672	9028	412
UNIVERSITY HOSPITAL, See New York University Medical Center													
★□ UNIVERSITY HOSPITAL OF BROOKLYN-STATE UNIVERSITY OF NEW YORK HEALTH SCIENCES CENTER AT BROOKLYN (Formerly State University Hospital, Downstate Medical Center), 445 Lenox Rd., Brooklyn, Zip 11203; tel. 718/270-1000; Mary A. Piccione, exec. dir. **A**1a 3 5 8 10 **F**1 2 3 4 6 7 8 9 10 11 12 13 14 16 17 20 23 24 25 26 27 28 32 33 34 37 38 40 42 43 44 46 47 51 52 53 54	12	10	S		372	11498	307	82.5	30	1653	107436	52324	2030
★□ VETERANS ADMINISTRATION MEDICAL CENTER, First Ave. at E. 24th St., Zip 10010; tel. 212/686-7500; Sanford M. Garfunkel, dir. **A**1a 2 3 5 8 **F**1 2 3 4 6 10 12 14 15 16 19 20 23 24 25 26 27 28 30 32 33 34 41 42 43 44 46 47 48 49 53 54	45	10	S		851	14050	518	60.9	0	0	109228	63400	2712
★□ VETERANS ADMINISTRATION MEDICAL CENTER, 130 W. Kingsbridge Rd., Bronx, Zip 10468; tel. 212/584-9000; James S. Pooley, dir. (Total facility includes 120 beds in nursing home-type unit) **A**1a 2 3 5 8 **F**6 7 8 9 10 11 12 14 16 19 20 23 24 25 27 28 29 30 31 32 33 34 38 41 42 44 45 46 47 53	45	10	S	TF	776	12769	411	56.0	0	0	—	—	1976
				H	656	12665	—	—	0	0	—	—	—

Hospital, Address, Telephone, Administrator, Approval and Facility Codes, Multihospital System Code	Classification Codes				Inpatient Data				Newborn Data		Expense (thousands of dollars)		
★ American Hospital Association (AHA) membership ☐ Joint Commission on Accreditation of Hospitals (JCAH) accreditation + American Osteopathic Hospital Association (AOHA) membership ○ American Osteopathic Association (AOA) accreditation Δ Commission on Accreditation of Rehabilitation Facilities (CARF) accreditation Control codes 61, 63, 64, 71, 72 and 73 indicate hospitals listed by AOHA, but not registered by AHA. For definition of numerical codes, see page A2	Control	Service	Stay	Facilities	Beds	Admissions	Census	Occupancy (percent)	Bassinets	Births	Total	Payroll	Personnel
★☐ VETERANS ADMINISTRATION MEDICAL CENTER, 800 Poly Pl., Brooklyn, Zip 11209; tel. 718/836-6600; James J. Farsetta, dir. (Total facility includes 300 beds in nursing home-type unit) **A**1a 3 5 8 **F**1 2 3 4 6 7 8 10 11 12 14 15 16 19 20 23 24 25 26 27 28 29 30 32 33 34 35 38 41 42 43 44 45 46 47 48 49 50 53 54	45	10	S	TF	1208	10717	880	72.8	0	0	112006	68261	2451
				H	908	10631	591	—	0	0	98362	58944	2076
★☐ VICTORY MEMORIAL HOSPITAL, 9036 Seventh Ave., Brooklyn, Zip 11228; tel. 718/630-1234; Krishin Bhatia, adm. **A**1a 9 10 **F**1 3 6 7 12 14 15 16 23 35 40 41 42 44 45 46 47 53	23	10	S		254	10256	227	85.7	24	1191	33656	16416	698
☐ WESTCHESTER SQUARE MEDICAL CENTER, 2475 St. Raymond Ave., Bronx, Zip 10461; tel. 212/430-7300; Alan Kopman, pres. & chief exec. off. **A**1a 9 10 **F**1 3 6 9 10 12 14 15 16 23 35 45 46 47 50	33	10	S		205	6996	175	85.4	0	0	30181	14886	595
WOMAN'S HOSPITAL, See St. Luke's-Roosevelt Hospital Center													
☐ WOODHULL MEDICAL AND MENTAL HEALTH CENTER, 760 Broadway, Brooklyn, Zip 11206; tel. 718/963-8000; Carlos A. Loran, exec. dir. **A**1a 3 5 9 10 **F**1 3 5 6 10 15 16 20 23 24 26 27 28 29 30 33 34 35 37 40 44 45 46 47 48 49 50 52 53; **S**3075	14	10	S		489	19603	420	85.7	68	3267	161254	83433	1556
☐ WYCKOFF HEIGHTS HOSPITAL, 374 Stockholm St., Brooklyn, Zip 11237; tel. 718/963-7102; Andrew R. Razzore, pres. **A**1a 2 5 9 10 **F**3 6 10 11 12 20 42 45 46 47 52	23	10	S		312	11018	255	81.7	0	0	47611	27824	1059
NEWARK—Wayne County													
★☐ NEWARK-WAYNE COMMUNITY HOSPITAL, Driving Park Ave., P O Box 111, Zip 14513; tel. 315/332-2022; L. J. Danehy, pres. (Total facility includes 44 beds in nursing home-type unit) **A**1a 9 10 **F**1 3 6 9 10 11 12 14 15 16 19 23 24 26 30 35 36 37 40 42 43 44 45 46 47 50 52 53	23	10	S	TF	204	4848	145	71.1	22	395	15563	8067	485
				H	160	4822	101	—	22	395	15050	7573	453
NEWBURGH—Orange County													
★☐ ST. LUKE'S HOSPITAL, 70 Dubois St., P O Box 631, Zip 12550; tel. 914/561-4400; Robert L. Via, exec. dir. **A**1a 9 10 **F**1 2 3 6 10 12 14 15 16 20 23 34 35 36 38 40 45 46 47 52 53; **S**1755	23	10	S		242	9316	186	76.9	30	1117	26650	12553	670
NEWFANE—Niagara County													
★☐ INTER-COMMUNITY MEMORIAL HOSPITAL, 2600 William St., Zip 14108; tel. 716/778-5111; Leslie A. Hawkins, adm. **A**1a 9 10 **F**1 3 12 14 15 16 23 33 34 35 37 40 45 46 50 52	23	10	S		75	3127	55	73.3	13	304	5978	3094	186
NIAGARA FALLS—Niagara County													
★☐ NIAGARA FALLS MEMORIAL MEDICAL CENTER, 621 Tenth St., Zip 14302; tel. 716/278-4000; Don A. Corey, pres. **A**1a 3 9 10 **F**1 3 6 7 8 9 10 11 12 14 15 16 23 24 26 27 28 29 30 32 33 34 35 36 40 42 43 44 45 46 47 49 52 53	23	10	S		338	10406	237	67.3	44	788	35364	18544	1058
NORTH TARRYTOWN—Westchester County													
★☐ PHELPS MEMORIAL HOSPITAL CENTER, N. Broadway, Zip 10591; tel. 914/631-5100; Alton W. Noyes, pres. **A**1a 9 10 **F**1 2 3 5 6 10 12 14 15 16 21 23 24 25 26 27 28 29 30 32 33 34 35 40 42 43 44 45 46 47 49 50 52 53	23	10	S		225	7221	170	75.6	15	799	35167	17974	761
NORTH TONAWANDA—Niagara County													
☐ DE GRAFF MEMORIAL HOSPITAL, 445 Tremont St., Zip 14120; tel. 716/694-4500; Mark E. Celmer, dir. & chief exec. off. (Total facility includes 44 beds in nursing home-type unit) **A**1a 9 10 **F**1 3 5 6 10 12 14 15 16 19 23 24 26 34 35 36 37 40 41 42 44 45 46 47 50 52	23	10	S	TF	194	6332	168	86.6	23	602	20167	10515	655
				H	150	6300	124	—	23	602	18993	9993	618
NORTHPORT—Suffolk County													
★☐ VETERANS ADMINISTRATION MEDICAL CENTER, Middleville Rd., Zip 11768; tel. 516/261-4400; William H. Manley, dir. (Total facility includes 282 beds in nursing home-type unit) **A**1a 3 5 8 **F**1 2 3 6 10 11 12 14 15 16 19 20 21 23 24 25 26 27 28 29 30 31 32 33 34 35 41 42 43 44 46 47 48 49 50 53 54	45	10	S	TF	744	13156	608	78.5	0	0	83844	49073	1878
				H	462	15021	358	—	0	0	—	—	—
NORWICH—Chenango County													
★☐ CHENANGO MEMORIAL HOSPITAL, 179 N. Broad St., Zip 13815; tel. 607/335-4111; Richard E. Riley, chief exec. off. (Total facility includes 54 beds in nursing home-type unit) **A**1a 10 **F**1 3 6 10 12 14 16 19 23 24 34 35 36 41 43 44 45 46 47 52 53	23	10	S	TF	145	3838	106	73.1	10	361	10772	5287	340
				H	91	3810	52	—	10	361	10010	4741	303
NYACK—Rockland County													
★☐ NYACK HOSPITAL, N. Midland Ave., Zip 10960; tel. 914/358-6200; James M. Dawson, pres. **A**1a 9 10 **F**1 3 5 6 10 12 14 15 16 21 23 24 26 32 35 36 37 40 41 42 44 45 46 52 53	23	10	S		375	17890	295	78.7	27	1651	63729	28422	1284
OCEANSIDE—Nassau County													
★☐ SOUTH NASSAU COMMUNITIES HOSPITAL, 2445 Oceanside Rd., Zip 11572; tel. 516/763-2030; Michael Rodzenko, exec. dir. **A**1a 2 3 5 9 10 **F**1 2 3 6 8 9 10 11 12 14 15 16 20 23 24 26 27 28 30 32 33 34 35 36 37 38 40 42 44 45 46 50 52 53	23	10	S		429	15533	355	82.8	47	1551	50295	24237	1197
OGDENSBURG—St. Lawrence County													
★☐ A. BARTON HEPBURN HOSPITAL, 214 King St., Zip 13669; tel. 315/393-3600; Donald C. Lewis, exec. vice-pres. & adm. (Total facility includes 29 beds in nursing home-type unit) **A**1a 10 **F**1 3 6 12 14 15 16 19 20 23 24 30 35 36 42 45 46 47 50 52 53	23	10	S	TF	128	4350	100	78.1	20	517	13912	7115	394
				H	99	4328	71	—	20	517	13521	6806	—
★☐ ST. LAWRENCE PSYCHIATRIC CENTER, Sta. A, Zip 13669; tel. 315/393-3000; Lee D. Hanes MD, dir. **A**1b 10 **F**12 15 23 24 28 29 30 31 32 33 34 42 43 44 46 47 50	12	22	L		630	902	580	92.1	0	0	27857	24993	1005
OLEAN—Cattaraugus County													
★☐ OLEAN GENERAL HOSPITAL, 515 Main St., Zip 14760; tel. 716/373-2600; Theodore W. Gundlah, adm. **A**1a 9 10 **F**1 3 6 10 12 14 15 16 23 30 35 36 37 40 44 45 46 47 52 53	23	10	S		153	5848	87	56.9	16	463	13504	7205	419
★☐ ST. FRANCIS HOSPITAL, 2221 W. State St., Zip 14760; tel. 716/372-5300; Sr. Mary Croghan, adm. **A**1a 9 10 **F**1 3 6 10 12 14 16 23 27 30 32 35 40 42 44 45 46 47 52; **S**1385	21	10	S		111	4490	68	61.3	10	568	10025	5108	300
ONEIDA—Madison County													
★☐ ONEIDA CITY HOSPITAL, 321 Genesee St., Zip 13421; tel. 315/363-6000; Richard G. Smith, adm. (Total facility includes 108 beds in nursing home-type unit) **A**1a 9 10 **F**3 6 10 12 19 23 24 35 40 42 45 46 52 53	14	10	S	TF	209	4040	181	84.6	18	395	14168	7273	341
				H	101	3988	75	—	18	395	—	—	—
ONEONTA—Otsego County													
☐ AURELIA OSBORN FOX MEMORIAL HOSPITAL, 1 Norton Ave., Zip 13820; tel. 607/432-2000; Lorraine B. Kabot, pres. & chief exec. off. (Total facility includes 130 beds in nursing home-type unit) **A**1a 10 **F**1 2 3 6 10 12 14 15 16 17 19 23 35 36 40 44 45 46 52 53	23	10	S	TF	265	5734	225	84.0	7	559	26085	11461	514
				H	135	5662	96	—	7	559	23993	10008	445
ORANGEBURG—Rockland County													
☐ ROCKLAND CHILDREN'S PSYCHIATRIC CENTER, Convent Rd., Zip 10962; tel. 914/359-7400; Oleh Riznyk, dep. dir. adm. (Nonreporting) **A**1b	12	52	L		80	—	—	—	—	—	—	—	—
★☐ ROCKLAND PSYCHIATRIC CENTER, Zip 10962; tel. 914/359-1000; William F. Morris, actg. exec. dir. **A**1b 10 **F**3 12 15 18 23 24 28 29 30 31 32 33 42 43 44 45 46 47 50	12	22	L		1491	1166	1491	100.0	0	0	64397	40959	1929
OSSINING—Westchester County													
OSSINING CORRECTIONAL FACILITIES HOSPITAL, 354 Hunter St., Zip 10562; tel. 914/941-0108; Benjamin I. Dyett MD, dir. (Nonreporting)	12	11	S		25	—	—	—	—	—	—	—	—

Hospital, Address, Telephone, Administrator, Approval and Facility Codes, Multihospital System Code	Classification Codes				Inpatient Data				Newborn Data		Expense (thousands of dollars)		
★ American Hospital Association (AHA) membership □ Joint Commission on Accreditation of Hospitals (JCAH) accreditation + American Osteopathic Hospital Association (AOHA) membership ○ American Osteopathic Association (AOA) accreditation Δ Commission on Accreditation of Rehabilitation Facilities (CARF) accreditation Control codes 61, 63, 64, 71, 72 and 73 indicate hospitals listed by AOHA, but not registered by AHA. For definition of numerical codes, see page A2	Control	Service	Stay	Facilities	Beds	Admissions	Census	Occupancy (percent)	Bassinets	Births	Total	Payroll	Personnel
★□ STONY LODGE HOSPITAL, Croton Dam Rd., Zip 10562; Mailing Address Box 1250, Briarcliff Manor, Zip 10510; tel. 914/941-7400; M. Lourdes Winberry, adm. (Nonreporting) **A**1b	33	22	L		61	—	—	—	—	—	—	—	—
OSWEGO—Oswego County													
★□ OSWEGO HOSPITAL, 110 W. Sixth St., Zip 13126; tel. 315/349-5511; Corte J. Spencer, adm. (Total facility includes 38 beds in nursing home-type unit) **A**1a 9 10 **F**1 3 6 12 14 15 16 19 23 26 27 28 29 30 33 34 35 36 37 40 41 42 44 45 46 47 49 52 53	23	10	S	TF	202	5757	141	69.8	25	1002	19155	9952	519
				H	164	5731	104	—	25	1002	17752	9469	490
PATCHOGUE—Suffolk County													
★□ BROOKHAVEN MEMORIAL HOSPITAL MEDICAL CENTER, 101 Hospital Rd., Zip 11772; tel. 516/654-7100; Francis G. Fosmire, exec. vice-pres. **A**1a 2 3 5 9 10 **F**1 2 3 6 9 10 12 14 15 16 20 23 33 34 35 36 40 41 42 44 45 46 47 49 52 53	23	10	S		338	13093	275	81.4	24	1143	45620	24824	1145
PEEKSKILL—Westchester County													
★□ PEEKSKILL HOSPITAL, 1980 Crompond Rd., Zip 10566; tel. 914/737-9000; Charles F. Harrienger, adm. **A**1a 9 10 **F**1 3 6 10 12 14 15 16 21 23 35 36 40 45 46 47 49 53	23	10	S		114	4906	90	78.9	24	467	16165	8375	425
PENN YAN—Yates County													
★□ SOLDIERS AND SAILORS MEMORIAL HOSPITAL OF YATES COUNTY, 418 N. Main St., Zip 14527; tel. 315/536-4431; John D. Kelly, adm. (Total facility includes 80 beds in nursing home-type unit) **A**1a 9 10 **F**1 3 6 12 15 16 19 23 24 34 35 42 44 45 46 47	23	10	S	TF	142	1444	114	80.3	0	0	7276	3554	226
				H	62	1407	35	—	0	0	6200	2949	186
PLAINVIEW—Nassau County													
★□ CENTRAL GENERAL HOSPITAL, 888 Old Country Rd., Zip 11803; tel. 516/681-8900; Robert J. Bornstein, adm. (Nonreporting) **A**1a 2 9 10	33	10	S		300	—	—	—	—	—	—	—	—
PLATTSBURGH—Clinton County													
★□ CHAMPLAIN VALLEY PHYSICIANS HOSPITAL MEDICAL CENTER, 100 Beekman St., Zip 12901; tel. 518/561-2000; Kevin J. Carroll, pres. (Total facility includes 54 beds in nursing home-type unit) **A**1a 9 10 **F**1 2 3 5 6 7 8 9 10 11 12 14 15 16 19 20 23 24 26 27 30 35 36 37 38 40 42 44 45 46 47 50 52 53	23	10	S	TF	410	11139	299	72.0	25	2298	37083	20572	1058
				H	356	11134	245	—	25	2298	36409	20002	1026
U. S. AIR FORCE HOSPITAL, See Plattsburgh Air Force Base													
PLATTSBURGH AIR FORCE BASE—Clinton County													
U. S. AIR FORCE HOSPITAL, Zip 12903; tel. 518/565-7414; Maj. Steven C. Mirick, adm. (Nonreporting)	41	10	S		20	—	—	—	—	—	—	—	—
POMONA—Rockland County													
□ DOCTOR ROBERT L. YEAGER HEALTH CENTER (Formerly Rockland County Health Center) (Includes Summit Park Hospital-Rockland County Infirmary), Sanatorium Rd., Zip 10970; tel. 914/354-0200; Peter J. Muniz, adm. (Nonreporting) **A**1a 9	13	48	L		108	—	—	—	—	—	—	—	—
PORT CHESTER—Westchester County													
★□ HIGH POINT HOSPITAL, Upper King St., Zip 10573; tel. 914/939-4420; A. Gralnick MD, dir. **A**1b 10 **F**15 24 42	31	22	L		45	75	38	84.4	0	0	5088	—	67
★□ UNITED HOSPITAL, 406 Boston Post Rd., Zip 10573; tel. 914/939-7000; Kenneth F. Adamec, pres. (Total facility includes 40 beds in nursing home-type unit) **A**1a 9 10 **F**1 3 5 6 10 11 12 14 15 16 19 21 23 24 26 27 28 30 32 33 34 35 36 37 38 40 41 42 45 46 47 48 49 50 52 53	23	10	S	TF	281	8629	247	84.0	17	711	48437	22109	1027
				H	241	8611	207	—	17	711	47854	21526	1000
PORT JEFFERSON—Suffolk County													
★□ JOHN T. MATHER MEMORIAL HOSPITAL OF PORT JEFFERSON, N. Country Rd., Zip 11777; tel. 516/473-1320; Kenneth D. Roberts, pres. **A**1a 2 9 10 **F**1 3 5 6 9 10 12 14 15 16 20 23 24 26 27 30 32 33 35 37 42 44 45 46 47 48 50 52 53	23	10	S		238	7801	184	80.3	0	0	34417	16813	716
★□ ST. CHARLES HOSPITAL AND REHABILITATION CENTER, 200 Belle Terre Rd., Zip 11777; tel. 516/473-2800; Arthur E. Santilli, exec. vice-pres. **A**1a 2 3 5 9 10 **F**1 6 10 12 14 16 23 24 26 33 34 35 36 38 43 44 45 46 47 53 54	21	10	S		271	9543	212	78.2	41	1706	—	—	956
PORT JERVIS—Orange County													
★□ MERCY COMMUNITY HOSPITAL, 160 E. Main St., P O Box 1014, Zip 12771; tel. 914/856-5351; George H. St. George, adm. & chief exec. off. **A**1a 2 9 10 **F**3 6 10 12 14 16 23 35 36 40 45 46 47 52; **S**5165	21	10	S		97	4490	83	85.6	6	283	15509	6283	289
POTSDAM—St. Lawrence County													
★□ CANTON-POTSDAM HOSPITAL, 50 Leroy St., Zip 13676; tel. 315/265-3300; William J. Connors, pres. (Nonreporting) **A**1a 9 10	23	10	S		94	—	—	—	—	—	—	—	—
POUGHKEEPSIE—Dutchess County													
★□ HUDSON RIVER PSYCHIATRIC CENTER, Branch B, Zip 12601; tel. 914/452-8000; John H. Dominguez, exec. dir. **A**1b 10 **F**3 12 15 16 23 24 28 29 31 32 33 42 44 46 47 50	12	22	L		990	814	954	96.4	0	0	49493	32999	1371
★□ Δ SAINT FRANCIS HOSPITAL (Includes St. Francis Hospital-Beacon, Delavan Ave., Beacon, Zip 12508; tel. 914/831-3500; Richard H. Perkins, adm.; St. Francis Hospital, North Rd., Zip 12601; tel. 914/471-2000; Sr. M. Ann Elizabeth, pres.; Donald F. Murphy, exec. vice-pres.), N. Rd., Zip 12601; tel. 914/431-8116; Donald F. Murphy, exec. vice-pres. **A**1a 7 9 10 **F**1 3 6 10 12 14 15 16 20 23 24 26 27 28 30 32 33 34 35 36 40 41 44 48 52 53; **S**5925	21	10	S		396	11826	273	71.1	12	194	60056	25563	1221
★□ VASSAR BROTHERS HOSPITAL, Reade Pl., Zip 12601; tel. 914/454-8500; Ronald T. Mullahey, pres. **A**1a 2 9 10 **F**1 2 3 5 6 7 8 9 10 11 12 14 15 16 23 26 34 35 36 37 38 40 43 44 45 46 47 50 52 53	23	10	S		328	12892	244	74.2	36	2411	45637	20379	884
RHINEBECK—Dutchess County													
★□ NORTHERN DUTCHESS HOSPITAL, Springbrook Ave., Zip 12572; tel. 914/876-3001; Michael C. Mazzarella, chief exec. off. (Total facility includes 50 beds in nursing home-type unit) **A**1a 9 10 **F**1 3 6 9 10 12 14 15 16 19 21 23 24 35 36 37 40 41 42 44 45 46 47 53	23	10	S	TF	115	3429	102	88.7	10	781	11009	4783	275
				H	65	3397	54	—	10	781	9268	4309	244
RIVERHEAD—Suffolk County													
★□ CENTRAL SUFFOLK HOSPITAL, 1300 Roanoke Ave., Zip 11901; tel. 516/548-6000; Robert F. Ecroyd, exec. vice-pres. **A**1a 9 10 **F**1 3 6 9 10 12 14 15 16 19 20 23 24 26 34 35 36 37 40 42 44 45 46 47 52	23	10	S		150	5276	126	84.0	12	295	21846	9030	400
ROCHESTER—Monroe County													
★□ GENESEE HOSPITAL, 224 Alexander St., Zip 14607; tel. 716/263-6000; Paul W. Hanson, pres. (Total facility includes 40 beds in nursing home-type unit) **A**1a 2 3 5 8 9 10 **F**1 2 3 6 7 8 9 10 11 12 14 16 19 20 23 27 28 29 30 32 33 34 35 36 40 42 43 45 46 47 49 52 54	23	10	S	TF	421	15315	372	88.4	52	2915	78729	42319	1884
				H	381	15280	332	—	52	2915	78077	41766	1853
★□ HIGHLAND HOSPITAL OF ROCHESTER, 1000 S. Ave., Zip 14620; tel. 716/473-2200; Michael J. Weidner, pres. **A**1a 2 3 5 8 9 **F**1 3 6 7 8 9 10 11 12 14 15 16 23 24 34 35 36 37 40 45 46 47 50 53	23	10	S		272	10799	196	72.1	44	3503	41082	23441	1044
□ MONROE COMMUNITY HOSPITAL, 435 E. Henrietta Rd., Zip 14620; tel. 716/473-4080; J. Raymond Diehl Jr., exec. health adm. (Total facility includes 566 beds in nursing home-type unit) **A**1a 3 5 9 10 **F**1 16 19 23 24 25 26 28 32 34 42 44 45 46 47 50	13	49	S	TF	626	981	584	93.3	0	0	27582	13422	533
				H	60	536	35	—	0	0	4965	2416	243

★ American Hospital Association (AHA) membership
□ Joint Commission on Accreditation of Hospitals (JCAH) accreditation
+ American Osteopathic Hospital Association (AOHA) membership
○ American Osteopathic Association (AOA) accreditation
Δ Commission on Accreditation of Rehabilitation Facilities (CARF) accreditation
Control codes 61, 63, 64, 71, 72 and 73 indicate hospitals listed by AOHA, but not registered by AHA.
For definition of numerical codes, see page A2

Hospital, Address, Telephone, Administrator, Approval and Facility Codes, Multihospital System Code	Classification Codes				Inpatient Data				Newborn Data		Expense (thousands of dollars)		
	Control	Service	Stay	Facilities	Beds	Admissions	Census	Occupancy (percent)	Bassinets	Births	Total	Payroll	Personnel
★□ PARK RIDGE HOSPITAL, 1555 Long Pond Rd., Zip 14626; tel. 716/225-7150; Timothy R. McCormick, pres. **A**1a 2 9 10 **F**1 3 6 10 12 14 15 16 19 23 24 30 34 35 44 49 50 54	23	10	S		234	7621	206	88.0	0	0	—	—	704
★□ ROCHESTER GENERAL HOSPITAL, 1425 Portland Ave., Zip 14621; tel. 716/338-4000; Arthur E. Liebert, pres. **A**1a 2 3 5 8 10 **F**1 2 3 4 5 6 7 8 9 10 11 12 14 16 20 23 24 27 28 29 30 33 34 35 36 40 42 43 44 45 46 47 51 52 53 54	23	10	S		534	20083	450	84.3	45	2252	93492	44643	2217
★□ ROCHESTER PSYCHIATRIC CENTER, 1600 South Ave., Zip 14620; tel. 716/473-3230; Martin H. Von Holden, exec. dir. (Nonreporting) **A**1b 3 5 10	12	22	L		1025	—	—	—	—	—	—	—	—
★□ ROCHESTER ST. MARY'S HOSPITAL OF THE SISTERS OF CHARITY, 89 Genesee St., Zip 14611; tel. 716/464-3000; Sr. Mary Alice Roach, pres. **A**1a 2 3 5 8 9 10 **F**1 2 3 6 10 12 14 15 16 20 23 28 30 34 35 36 40 42 43 44 45 46 50 53; **S**1885	21	10	S		206	7471	180	87.4	26	1175	42917	18697	800
★□ STRONG MEMORIAL HOSPITAL OF THE UNIVERSITY OF ROCHESTER, 601 Elmwood Ave., Zip 14642; tel. 716/275-2644; Paul F. Griner MD, gen. dir. (Total facility includes 20 beds in nursing home-type unit) **A**1a 2 3 5 8 9 10 **F**1 3 4 5 6 7 8 9 10 11 12 13 14 15 16 17 19 20 22 23 24 26 27 28 29 30 32 33 34 35 36 37 38 39 40 42 43 44 45 46 47 49 51 52 53 54	23	10	S	TF	742	24264	639	86.1	40	3218	138815	64159	3188
				H	722	24145	621	—	40	3218	137182	63575	3164
ROCKVILLE CENTRE—Nassau County													
★□ MERCY HOSPITAL, 1000 N. Village Ave., Zip 11570; tel. 516/255-0111; Richard C. Herrmann, exec. vice-pres. **A**1a 2 3 5 9 10 **F**1 2 3 5 6 7 8 9 10 11 12 13 14 15 16 20 21 23 24 26 27 28 29 30 32 33 34 35 40 42 44 45 46 49 51 52 53	21	10	S		398	16018	342	85.9	30	2155	58342	32122	1334
ROME—Oneida County													
ROME DEVELOPMENTAL CENTER, Lower S. James St., Box 550, Zip 13440; tel. 315/336-2300; Philip F. Catchpole, dir. (Nonreporting)	12	62	L		660	—	—	—	—	—	—	—	—
★□ ROME HOSPITAL AND MURPHY MEMORIAL HOSPITAL, 1500 N. James St., Zip 13440; tel. 315/338-7000; John A. Gorman, adm. (Total facility includes 40 beds in nursing home-type unit) **A**1a 9 10 **F**1 3 6 10 12 15 16 19 21 23 34 35 37 40 41 42 45 46 50 52 53; **S**1755	14	10	S	TF	230	6815	191	83.0	22	575	19108	9361	594
				H	190	6781	152	—	22	575	18498	8967	567
U. S. AIR FORCE HOSPITAL, See Griffiss Air Force Base													
ROSLYN—Nassau County													
★□ ST. FRANCIS HOSPITAL (Cardiovascular Specialty), 100 Port Washington Blvd., Zip 11576; tel. 516/627-6200; Robert F. Vizza PhD, pres. & chief exec. off. **A**1a 5 9 10 **F**1 2 3 4 6 10 11 12 14 15 16 23 24 26 27 30 32 33 34 35 42 45 46 47 50 52 53 54	21	49	S		227	8507	215	94.7	0	0	54137	27135	943
RYE—Westchester County													
★□ RYE PSYCHIATRIC HOSPITAL CENTER, 754 Boston Post Rd., Zip 10580; tel. 914/967-4567; Jack C. Schoenholtz MD, med. dir. **A**1a 10 **F**24 29 32 33 42 43 46 47 50	33	22	L		31	216	22	71.0	0	0	—	—	—
SALAMANCA—Cattaraugus County													
★□ SALAMANCA DISTRICT HOSPITAL, 150 Parkway Dr., Zip 14779; tel. 716/945-1900; Jay Scott Parisella, adm. **A**1a 9 10 **F**1 25 35 45 46 50	16	10	S		60	1512	32	53.3	0	0	3589	1600	104
SARANAC LAKE—Franklin County													
★□ GENERAL HOSPITAL OF SARANAC LAKE, Lake Colby Dr., Zip 12983; tel. 518/891-4141; John J. Murphy, adm. **A**1a 9 10 **F**1 2 3 6 9 10 12 14 16 23 29 30 33 35 37 38 40 44 45 46 52 53	23	10	S		91	4231	79	86.8	8	288	9452	4847	317
SARATOGA SPRINGS—Saratoga County													
★□ SARATOGA HOSPITAL, 211 Church St., Zip 12866; tel. 518/584-6000; Wilfred J. Addison, adm. (Total facility includes 76 beds in nursing home-type unit) **A**1a 2 9 10 **F**1 3 6 10 12 14 16 19 23 26 27 30 33 34 35 36 40 45 46 47 52 53	23	10	S	TF	246	6477	199	80.9	26	894	24735	11966	700
				H	170	6430	127	—	26	894	23674	11129	649
SCHENECTADY—Schenectady County													
★□ BELLEVUE MATERNITY HOSPITAL, 2210 Troy Rd., Zip 12309; Mailing Address Box 1030, Zip 12301; tel. 518/346-9400; Michael A. Mangini, adm. (Nonreporting) **A**1a 9 10	33	44	S		40	—	—	—	—	—	—	—	—
★□ ELLIS HOSPITAL, 1101 Nott St., Zip 12308; tel. 518/382-4124; William E. Schirmer, pres. & chief exec. off. **A**1a 2 3 5 6 9 10 **F**1 3 6 7 8 9 10 11 12 14 15 16 20 23 26 27 28 30 32 33 34 35 36 37 40 43 46 47 49 50 52 53 54; **S**1755	23	10	S		413	11806	324	78.5	33	640	58504	30532	1568
★□ ST. CLARE'S HOSPITAL OF SCHENECTADY, 600 McClellan St., Zip 12304; tel. 518/382-2000; Jerome G. Stewart, pres. **A**1a 3 5 9 10 **F**1 3 6 10 12 14 15 16 23 34 35 36 40 44 45 46 47 52 53; **S**1485	21	10	S		271	9898	210	76.6	24	854	36630	15237	997
★□ Δ SUNNYVIEW HOSPITAL AND REHABILITATION CENTER, 1270 Belmont Ave., Zip 12308; tel. 518/382-4500; Bradford M. Goodwin, pres. & chief exec. off. **A**1a 3 5 7 9 10 **F**10 23 24 26 33 34 42 43 44 45	23	49	S		101	1062	87	86.1	0	0	10566	6764	302
SCOTIA—Schenectady County													
□ CONIFER PARK, Glenridge Rd., Zip 12302; tel. 518/399-6446; Garrett McGrath, adm. (Nonreporting) **A**1b 9	33	82	S		195	—	—	—	—	—	—	—	—
SEAFORD—Nassau County													
○ + MASSAPEQUA GENERAL HOSPITAL, 750 Hicksville Rd., Box 20, Zip 11783; tel. 516/454-3498; Alan E. Kelsky, chief exec. off. **A**9 10 11 12 **F**1 3 6 10 12 14 15 16 23 34 35 37 44 45 46 47	33	10	S		122	4314	82	67.2	0	0	16926	6187	358
SIDNEY—Delaware County													
★□ THE HOSPITAL, Pearl St., Zip 13838; tel. 607/563-3512; Leo G. Friel, chief exec. off. (Total facility includes 30 beds in nursing home-type unit) **A**1a 9 10 **F**1 3 6 12 14 15 16 19 23 34 35 36 40 44 45 46; **S**1905	14	10	S	TF	91	2802	65	71.4	5	346	—	—	195
				H	61	3297	35	—	5	346	—	—	164
SMITHTOWN—Suffolk County													
□ COMMUNITY HOSPITAL OF WESTERN SUFFOLK (Formerly Smithtown General Hospital), Smithtown By-Pass & Rte. 111, Zip 11787; tel. 516/979-9800; Martin Rosenblum, adm. **A**1a 10 **F**1 2 3 6 10 12 14 16 20 23 27 29 30 32 33 34 35 36 40 43 45 46 47 52 53; **S**3015	32	10	S		271	10688	210	77.5	32	868	33921	16930	747
SMITHTOWN GENERAL HOSPITAL, See Community Hospital of Western Suffolk													
★□ ST. JOHN'S EPISCOPAL HOSPITAL-SMITHTOWN, Rte. 25-A, Zip 11787; tel. 516/360-2000; George D. Pozgar, adm. **A**1a 9 **F**1 2 3 6 7 8 9 10 11 12 14 15 16 20 23 26 27 30 32 33 35 36 37 40 42 44 45 46 47 50 52 53 54; **S**0735	21	10	S		300	11934	244	81.3	24	1346	47171	23480	889
SODUS—Wayne County													
★□ MYERS COMMUNITY HOSPITAL, Middle Rd., Box 310, Zip 14551; tel. 315/483-9161; Terrance M. Bedient, adm. & chief exec. off. **A**1a 9 10 **F**1 3 14 15 16 23 26 34 35 40 43 45 46	23	10	S		54	2074	38	70.4	14	280	5199	2628	126
SOUTHAMPTON—Suffolk County													
★□ SOUTHAMPTON HOSPITAL, 240 Meeting House Lane, Zip 11968; tel. 516/283-2600; John Pfister Jr., exec. vice-pres. & adm. **A**1a 9 10 **F**1 2 3 6 7 8 9 10 11 12 14 15 16 23 30 32 35 36 37 38 40 45 46 50 52 53	23	10	S		194	5937	131	67.5	10	600	23486	12627	473
SPRINGVILLE—Erie County													
□ BERTRAND CHAFFEE HOSPITAL, 224 E. Main St., Zip 14141; tel. 716/592-2871; Roger A. Ford, adm. (Nonreporting) **A**1a 9 10	23	10	S		69	—	—	—	—	—	—	—	—

★ American Hospital Association (AHA) membership
☐ Joint Commission on Accreditation of Hospitals (JCAH) accreditation
+ American Osteopathic Hospital Association (AOHA) membership
○ American Osteopathic Association (AOA) accreditation
Δ Commission on Accreditation of Rehabilitation Facilities (CARF) accreditation
Control codes 61, 63, 64, 71, 72 and 73 indicate hospitals listed by AOHA, but not registered by AHA.
For definition of numerical codes, see page A2

Hospital, Address, Telephone, Administrator, Approval and Facility Codes, Multihospital System Code	Classi-fication Codes			Facilities	Inpatient Data				Newborn Data		Expense (thousands of dollars)		
	Control	Service	Stay		Beds	Admissions	Census	Occupancy (percent)	Bassinets	Births	Total	Payroll	Personnel
STAMFORD—Delaware County													
★☐ COMMUNITY HOSPITAL, Harper St., Zip 12167; tel. 607/652-7521; Roger A. Masse, adm. (Nonreporting) **A**1a 9 10	23	10	S		72	—	—	—	—	—	—	—	—
STAR LAKE—St. Lawrence County													
★ CLIFTON-FINE HOSPITAL, Oswegatchie Trail, Box 10, Zip 13690; tel. 315/848-3351; Harvey M. Radey Jr., adm. **A**9 10 **F**35 45	16	10	S		20	639	10	50.0	0	0	1393	711	47
STATEN ISLAND—Richmond County See New York City													
STONY BROOK—Suffolk County													
★☐ UNIVERSITY HOSPITAL, State University of New York, Zip 11794; tel. 516/689-8333; William T. Newell Jr., exec. dir. **A**1a 3 5 8 9 10 **F**1 2 3 4 6 7 8 9 10 11 12 13 14 15 16 20 22 23 24 27 28 29 30 32 33 34 35 36 37 38 40 42 43 44 45 46 47 51 52 53 54	12	10	S		453	13214	317	72.2	32	2073	127452	45677	3942
SUFFERN—Rockland County													
★☐ GOOD SAMARITAN HOSPITAL, Rte. 59, Zip 10901; tel. 914/357-3300; Sr. Joan Regan, pres. **A**1a 2 9 10 **F**1 2 3 5 6 7 8 9 10 11 12 14 15 16 20 21 23 24 26 27 28 30 32 33 34 35 36 40 41 42 44 45 46 47 49 50 52 53 54; **S**5815	21	10	S		370	15080	270	73.0	50	1708	61315	24223	1052
SYOSSET—Nassau County													
★☐ SYOSSET COMMUNITY HOSPITAL, 221 Jericho Turnpike, Zip 11791; tel. 516/496-6400; S. Marvin Freeman, pres. **A**1a 9 **F**3 6 10 12 14 15 16 20 23 24 27 30 33 35 36 37 40 42 44 45 46 47 53	23	10	S		174	7678	126	72.4	21	1180	32710	13104	469
SYRACUSE—Onondaga County													
☐ BENJAMIN RUSH CENTER, 672 S. Salina St., Zip 13202; tel. 315/476-2161; Alexandra Curtis, adm.; Francis J. McCarthy, pres. (Nonreporting) **A**1a b 9 10	31	22	L		100	—	—	—	—	—	—	—	—
★☐ COMMUNITY GENERAL HOSPITAL OF GREATER SYRACUSE, Broad Rd., Zip 13215; tel. 315/492-5011; Jerry L. Harris, pres. (Total facility includes 50 beds in nursing home-type unit) **A**1a 3 5 9 **F**1 3 6 12 14 15 16 19 23 24 27 28 30 32 35 36 40 45 46 52 53	23	10	S	TF H	357 307	13413 11521	273 233	76.5 —	40 40	1910 1910	45549 —	23943 —	1180 —
★☐ CROUSE-IRVING MEMORIAL HOSPITAL, 736 Irving Ave., Zip 13210; tel. 315/470-7111; James W. Maher, pres. **A**1a 3 5 6 9 10 **F**1 2 3 6 9 12 14 15 16 20 23 26 28 30 32 33 34 35 36 40 45 46 47 48 49 52 53 54	23	10	S		490	22126	454	92.7	46	4246	97870	45462	2095
★☐ RICHARD H. HUTCHINGS PSYCHIATRIC CENTER, 620 Madison St., Box 27, University Sta., Zip 13210; tel. 315/473-4980; John Scott, exec. dir. **A**1b 3 5 10 **F**15 24 28 29 30 32 33 42 43 46 50	12	22	L		176	1638	176	100.0	0	0	30929	20020	776
★☐ ST. JOSEPH'S HOSPITAL HEALTH CENTER, 301 Prospect Ave., Zip 13203; tel. 315/424-5111; James H. Abbott, adm. **A**1a 2 3 5 6 9 10 **F**1 2 3 4 6 9 10 11 12 14 15 16 20 23 27 28 29 30 32 33 34 35 36 40 42 45 46 51 52 54; **S**5955	21	10	S		457	17789	389	85.1	32	2706	68926	34490	1863
★☐ SUNY HEALTH SCIENCE CENTER AT SYRACUSE-UNIVERSITY HOSPITAL (Formerly University Hospital of Upstate Medical Center), 750 E. Adams St., Zip 13210; tel. 315/473-4513; John Bernard Henry MD, pres. **A**1a 2 3 5 8 9 **F**1 2 3 6 7 8 9 10 11 12 13 14 16 17 19 20 22 23 24 25 26 27 28 30 32 33 34 35 42 44 45 46 47 52 53 54	12	10	S		358	10210	271	75.7	0	0	93198	—	1812
UNIVERSITY HOSPITAL OF UPSTATE MEDICAL CENTER, See Suny Health Science Center at Syracuse-University Hospital													
★☐ VETERANS ADMINISTRATION MEDICAL CENTER, Irving Ave. & University Pl., Zip 13210; tel. 315/476-7461; Clyde H. Corsaro, dir. (Total facility includes 50 beds in nursing home-type unit) **A**1a 3 5 8 **F**1 2 3 6 10 11 12 13 15 16 19 20 23 24 26 27 28 30 32 33 34 42 44 46 47 50 53 54	45	10	S	TF H	323 273	6022 5919	245 203	72.5 —	0 0	0 0	42661 —	21703 —	772 747
TICONDEROGA—Essex County													
★☐ MOSES LUDINGTON HOSPITAL, Montcalm & Wicker Sts., Zip 12883; tel. 518/585-2831; Margaret Warden, adm. **A**1a 9 10 **F**1 3 6 14 15 16 23 35 36 40 45 46 49	23	10	S		44	1501	22	50.0	4	118	5168	2177	130
TROY—Rensselaer County													
★☐ LEONARD HOSPITAL, 74 New Turnpike Rd., Zip 12182; tel. 518/235-0310; John T. Murphy, pres. (Data for 273 days) **A**1a 9 10 **F**1 3 6 10 12 14 15 16 21 23 26 33 35 37 41 42 45 46 48 49 53	23	10	S		143	2565	102	71.3	0	0	10327	5283	409
★☐ SAMARITAN HOSPITAL, 2215 Burdett Ave., Zip 12180; tel. 518/271-3300; David A. Kadish, exec. vice-pres. **A**1a 2 6 9 10 **F**1 2 3 6 7 8 9 10 11 12 14 15 16 20 21 23 24 27 28 29 30 32 33 34 35 36 40 41 42 43 44 45 46 47 48 50 52 53	23	10	S		292	9332	229	78.4	50	1249	32513	—	1039
★☐ ST. MARY'S HOSPITAL OF TROY, 1300 Massachusetts Ave., Zip 12180; tel. 518/272-5000 **A**1a 10 **F**1 2 3 5 6 10 12 14 15 16 17 23 24 26 34 35 43 44 45 46 52 53; **S**1885	21	10	S		201	5885	171	85.1	0	0	22989	10900	644
UPTON—Suffolk County													
☐ CLINICAL RESEARCH CENTER, BROOKHAVEN NATIONAL LABORATORY (Medical Research), Zip 11973; tel. 516/282-3564; Kenneth P. Mohring, adm. (Nonreporting) **A**1a	23	49	S		11	—	—	—	—	—	—	—	—
UTICA—Oneida County													
★☐ CHILDRENS HOSPITAL AND REHABILITATION CENTER, 1675 Bennett St., Zip 13502; tel. 315/724-5101; Keith A. Fenstemacher, adm. **A**1a 9 10 **F**23 24 25 26 34 42 44 52	23	47	S		66	1841	37	56.1	0	0	6636	2271	127
★☐ FAXTON HOSPITAL, 1676 Sunset Ave., Zip 13502; tel. 315/732-3101; Keith A. Fenstemacher, adm. **A**1a 9 10 **F**1 3 6 7 8 9 10 11 12 14 16 21 34 35 46 48 53	23	10	S		122	5273	102	83.6	0	0	21248	9634	552
★☐ MOHAWK VALLEY PSYCHIATRIC CENTER (Formerly Utica-Marcy Psychiatric Center), 1213 Court St., Zip 13502; tel. 315/797-6800; Richard M. Heath, exec. dir. **A**1b 10 **F**15 19 23 24 25 28 29 30 31 32 33 34 41 42 44 45 46 47 48	12	22	L		1330	1447	1340	100.0	0	0	70759	47796	1896
★☐ ST. ELIZABETH HOSPITAL, 2209 Genesee St., Zip 13501; tel. 315/798-8100; Sr. Rose Vincent, exec. adm. **A**1a 3 5 6 9 10 **F**1 3 5 6 10 12 14 15 16 23 24 26 27 30 32 33 34 35 36 40 42 44 45 46 47 52 53 54; **S**5955	21	10	S		269	9158	178	64.5	30	1136	34419	17263	960
ST. LUKE'S MEMORIAL HOSPITAL CENTER, See New Hartford													
UTICA-MARCY PSYCHIATRIC CENTER, See Mohawk Valley Psychiatric Center													
VALHALLA—Westchester County													
★☐ BLYTHEDALE CHILDREN'S HOSPITAL, Bradhurst Ave., Zip 10595; tel. 914/592-7555; Robert Stone, exec. dir. **A**1a 3 **F**16 23 24 26 28 32 33 34 42 43 44 46	23	56	L		92	294	85	92.4	0	0	9899	6082	284
★☐ WESTCHESTER COUNTY MEDICAL CENTER, Valhalla Campus, Zip 10595; tel. 914/285-7000; Bernard M. Weinstein, comr. **A**1a b 2 3 5 8 9 10 **F**1 2 3 4 5 6 7 8 9 10 11 12 14 16 17 20 22 23 24 25 26 27 28 30 32 33 34 35 38 40 42 44 45 46 47 48 49 51 52 53 54	13	10	S		633	18225	559	89.9	6	780	158559	62491	2092
VALLEY STREAM—Nassau County													
★☐ FRANKLIN GENERAL HOSPITAL, 900 Franklin Ave., Zip 11580; tel. 516/825-8800; Albert Dicker, exec. dir. **A**1a 2 9 10 **F**1 3 5 6 7 8 9 10 12 14 15 16 20 23 24 25 26 27 30 32 33 35 36 38 40 41 42 44 45 46 47 52 53	23	10	S		305	11110	257	84.3	16	980	40131	20278	945
WALTON—Delaware County													
★☐ DELAWARE VALLEY HOSPITAL, 1 Titus Pl., Zip 13856; tel. 607/865-4101; Brian R. Mitteer, pres. **A**1a 2 9 10 **F**1 3 6 10 12 14 15 16 23 34 35 40 45 46 47	23	10	S		42	1823	26	61.9	6	145	4937	2277	155

Hospital, Address, Telephone, Administrator, Approval and Facility Codes, Multihospital System Code

- ★ American Hospital Association (AHA) membership
- □ Joint Commission on Accreditation of Hospitals (JCAH) accreditation
- + American Osteopathic Hospital Association (AOHA) membership
- ○ American Osteopathic Association (AOA) accreditation
- Δ Commission on Accreditation of Rehabilitation Facilities (CARF) accreditation

Control codes 61, 63, 64, 71, 72 and 73 indicate hospitals listed by AOHA, but not registered by AHA. For definition of numerical codes, see page A2

Hospital	Classification Codes: Control	Service	Stay	Facilities	Inpatient Data: Beds	Admissions	Census	Occupancy (percent)	Newborn Data: Bassinets	Births	Expense (thousands of dollars): Total	Payroll	Personnel
WARSAW—Wyoming County													
★□ WYOMING COUNTY COMMUNITY HOSPITAL, 400 N. Main St., Zip 14569; tel. 716/786-2233; Thomas J. Wheatley, adm. (Total facility includes 72 beds in nursing home-type unit) **A**1a 9 10 **F**1 3 6 10 12 14 15 16 19 23 24 35 36 40 42 44 45 46 47 50 52 53	13	10	S	TF	174	3953	144	82.3	20	500	13628	6314	389
				H	102	3867	73	—	20	500	12692	5435	304
WARWICK—Orange County													
★□ ST. ANTHONY COMMUNITY HOSPITAL, 15-19 Maple Ave., Zip 10990; tel. 914/986-2276; Dennis Harrington, pres. **A**1a 9 10 **F**1 6 10 12 14 15 16 19 23 35 40 45 46 47 52; **S**1485	21	10	S		73	3529	65	89.0	9	332	9112	4292	232
WATERLOO—Seneca County													
□ TAYLOR-BROWN MEMORIAL HOSPITAL, E. Main St., Zip 13165; tel. 315/539-9204; James J. Dooley, pres. & chief exec. off. (Total facility includes 33 beds in nursing home-type unit) **A**1a 9 10 **F**1 3 14 15 16 19 23 24 26 32 33 34 35 42 44 45 46 47 48 50	23	10	S	TF	89	1001	59	66.3	0	0	4513	2303	153
				H	56	996	26	—	0	0	4085	2004	123
WATERTOWN—Jefferson County													
□ HOUSE OF THE GOOD SAMARITAN, 830 Washington St., Zip 13601; tel. 315/785-4000; Robert J. Kayser, pres. & chief exec. off. (Nonreporting) **A**1a 9 10	23	10	S		262	—	—	—	—	—	—	—	—
★□ MERCY HOSPITAL OF WATERTOWN (Includes Madonna Home, McAuley Hall Health Related Facilities, Community Mental Health Center and Ambulatory Care Facility), 218 Stone St., Zip 13601; tel. 315/782-7400; Sr. Mary Pierre Seguin, pres. (Total facility includes 204 beds in nursing home-type unit) **A**1a 9 10 **F**1 3 6 10 11 12 14 15 16 19 20 23 24 26 27 28 29 30 32 33 34 35 36 40 41 42 43 44 45 46 47 48 49 50 52 53; **S**3595	21	10	S	TF	426	5789	315	73.9	24	358	24837	13708	875
				H	222	5645	115	—	24	358	19925	10997	712
WAVERLY—Tioga County													
★ TIOGA GENERAL HOSPITAL, 37 N. Chemung St., Zip 14892; tel. 607/565-2861; Frederick A. Kauffman, adm. (Nonreporting) **A**9 10; **S**0675	23	10	S		198	—	—	—	—	—	—	—	—
WELLSVILLE—Allegany County													
★□ MEMORIAL HOSPITAL OF WILLIAM F. AND GERTRUDE F. JONES, 191 N. Main St., Zip 14895; tel. 716/593-1100; William M. Diberardino, adm. & chief exec. off. **A**1a 9 10 **F**1 3 6 10 12 14 16 23 34 35 36 37 40 45 46 50 52	14	10	S		88	4116	68	67.3	14	410	8856	4328	244
WEST BRENTWOOD—Suffolk County													
★□ PILGRIM PSYCHIATRIC CENTER, Box A, Zip 11717; tel. 516/434-7500; Peggy O'Neill, exec. dir. **A**1b 10 **F**12 15 23 24 26 28 29 30 31 32 33 34 35 41 42 43 44 45 46 47 50	12	22	L		2944	961	2938	99.8	0	0	86761	80000	3441
WEST HAVERSTRAW—Rockland County													
★□ Δ HELEN HAYES HOSPITAL, Rte. 9w, Zip 10993; tel. 914/947-3000; Bernard Rose, dir. **A**1a 3 5 7 9 10 **F**15 16 23 24 26 28 32 33 34 38 42 44 45 46 47	12	46	L		155	930	123	79.4	0	0	30647	14701	600
WEST ISLIP—Suffolk County													
★□ GOOD SAMARITAN HOSPITAL, 1000 Montauk Hwy., Zip 11795; tel. 516/957-4000; Daniel P. Walsh, pres. (Total facility includes 100 beds in nursing home-type unit) **A**1a 9 10 **F**1 3 6 9 10 11 12 14 15 16 19 20 21 23 24 34 35 40 44 45 46 52 53 54	21	10	S	TF	515	18685	485	94.2	44	2695	65271	32882	1318
				H	415	18626	386	—	44	2695	61975	30909	1238
WEST POINT—Orange County													
★□ KELLER ARMY COMMUNITY HOSPITAL, U. S. Military Academy, Zip 10996; tel. 914/938-3305; Col. Barry W. Wolcott MC, cmdr. **A**1a **F**3 6 12 15 16 23 26 28 30 32 33 34 35 36 40 41 45 46 47	42	10	S		65	3830	34	52.3	9	215	18205	14417	491
WEST SENECA—Erie County													
□ WESTERN NEW YORK CHILDREN'S PSYCHIATRIC CENTER, 1010 E. & W. Rd., Zip 14224; tel. 716/674-9730; Cecile A. Davis, exec. dir. (Nonreporting) **A**1b	12	52	L		54	—	—	—	—	—	—	—	—
WESTFIELD—Chautauqua County													
★ WESTFIELD MEMORIAL HOSPITAL, 189 E. Main St., Zip 14787; tel. 716/326-4921; Morton Flexer, adm. (Nonreporting) **A**10	23	10	S		32	—	—	—	—	—	—	—	—
WHITE PLAINS—Westchester County													
★□ BURKE REHABILITATION CENTER, 785 Mamaroneck Ave., Zip 10605; tel. 914/948-0050; Fletcher H. McDowell MD, exec. dir. **A**1a 9 10 **F**16 23 24 26 32 42 44 45 46 47 50	23	46	L		150	1231	127	84.7	0	0	22187	12561	575
NEW YORK HOSPITAL, WESTCHESTER DIVISION, See Society of the New York Hospital, New York City													
★□ ST. AGNES HOSPITAL (Includes Children's Rehabilitation Center), 305 North St., Zip 10605; tel. 914/681-4500; Robert J. Trefry, exec. vice-pres. & chief exec. off. **A**1a 9 10 **F**1 3 5 6 10 12 14 15 16 23 24 26 31 34 35 40 41 44 45 46 47 52; **S**5925	21	10	S		191	5687	133	69.6	12	575	28562	14941	638
★□ WHITE PLAINS HOSPITAL MEDICAL CENTER, Davis Ave. at East Post Rd., Zip 10601; tel. 914/681-1200; Jon B. Schandler, pres. & chief exec. off. **A**1a 9 10 **F**1 2 3 5 6 14 15 16 21 23 24 26 27 28 29 30 32 33 34 35 36 40 41 42 43 44 45 46 47 50 52 53	23	10	S		301	11627	249	82.7	18	1358	53530	26260	1104
WILLARD—Seneca County													
★□ WILLARD PSYCHIATRIC CENTER, Zip 14588; tel. 607/869-3111; Anthony N. Mustille MD, dir. **A**1b 9 10 **F**12 15 23 24 26 28 30 31 32 33 34 42 44 46 48 50	12	22	L		676	741	634	91.8	0	0	32446	21334	942
WINGDALE—Dutchess County													
★□ HARLEM VALLEY PSYCHIATRIC CENTER, Zip 12594; tel. 914/832-6611; Wendy P. Acrish, exec. dir. **A**1b 10 **F**12 15 23 24 26 28 29 30 31 32 33 34 37 42 43 45 46 47 49 50	12	22	L		698	505	685	99.9	0	0	45277	28760	1287
YONKERS—Westchester County													
★□ ST. JOHN'S RIVERSIDE HOSPITAL, 967 N. Broadway, Zip 10701; tel. 914/964-4444; Louis F. Parker, exec. dir. **A**1a 9 10 **F**1 3 6 9 10 12 14 15 16 23 26 30 34 35 40 44 45 46 52 53	23	10	S		273	10576	200	73.3	28	1699	41746	21609	920
★□ ST. JOSEPH'S MEDICAL CENTER, 127 S. Broadway, Zip 10701; tel. 914/965-6700; Sr. Mary Linehan, pres. **A**1a 3 5 9 10 **F**1 3 5 6 10 12 14 15 16 20 23 24 26 27 28 29 30 32 33 34 35 42 44 45 46 49 50 52 53; **S**5995	23	10	S		194	5818	144	73.1	0	0	33464	16608	893
★□ YONKERS GENERAL HOSPITAL, Two Park Ave., Zip 10703; tel. 914/964-7300; Bertram J. Oppenheimer MD, adm. **A**1a 9 10 **F**1 3 6 10 11 12 14 15 16 23 24 26 30 34 35 37 44 48 53	23	10	S		190	6235	149	78.4	0	0	26021	14499	598

Hospital, Address, Telephone, Administrator, Approval and Facility Codes, Multihospital System Code	Classification Codes				Inpatient Data				Newborn Data		Expense (thousands of dollars)		
★ American Hospital Association (AHA) membership □ Joint Commission on Accreditation of Hospitals (JCAH) accreditation + American Osteopathic Hospital Association (AOHA) membership ○ American Osteopathic Association (AOA) accreditation Δ Commission on Accreditation of Rehabilitation Facilities (CARF) accreditation Control codes 61, 63, 64, 71, 72 and 73 indicate hospitals listed by AOHA, but not registered by AHA. For definition of numerical codes, see page A2	Control	Service	Stay	Facilities	Beds	Admissions	Census	Occupancy (percent)	Bassinets	Births	Total	Payroll	Personnel

North Carolina

AHOSKIE—Hertford County													
□ ROANOKE-CHOWAN HOSPITAL, Academy St., Box 1385, Zip 27910; tel. 919/332-8121; Peter N. Geilich, pres. **A**1a 9 10 **F**1 3 5 6 10 15 16 23 35 40 44 45 46 52	23	10	S		100	4416	74	74.0	14	443	11139	5484	349
ALBEMARLE—Stanly County													
⊞ STANLY MEMORIAL HOSPITAL, 301 Yadkin St., Zip 28001; Mailing Address Box 1489, Zip 28002; tel. 704/983-5111; Kenneth A. Shull, pres. **A**1a 9 10 **F**1 3 6 10 14 15 16 23 30 35 40 45 46	23	10	S		95	3380	53	47.3	15	461	9313	4125	442
ANDREWS—Cherokee County													
★ MOUNTAIN PARK MEDICAL CENTER, Murphy Hwy., Box E, Zip 28901; tel. 704/321-4231; Joseph R. Tucker, adm. **A**9 10 **F**2 6 10 14 15 16 35 46; **S**0025	23	10	S		61	1163	15	24.6	6	54	2671	1184	85
APEX—Wake County													
WESTERN WAKE HOSPITAL, 763 Hunter St., Zip 27502; tel. 919/362-8321; Diane Long RN, dir. **A**9 **F**1 3 6 10 16 35 47; **S**6705	23	10	S		20	222	5	25.0	0	0	1222	698	33
ASHEBORO—Randolph County													
⊞ RANDOLPH HOSPITAL, 373 N. Fayetteville St., Box 1048, Zip 27203; tel. 919/625-5151; John W. Ellis, adm. **A**1a 9 10 **F**1 2 3 6 9 10 14 15 16 23 30 34 35 40 45 46 47 52	23	10	S		145	4512	70	48.3	23	478	12623	6264	409
ASHEVILLE—Buncombe County													
APPALACHIAN HALL, Caledonia Rd., Box 5534, Zip 28813; tel. 704/253-3681; Jerry W. Tarrents, adm. & chief exec. off. **A**9 10 **F**10 15 24 28 30 32 33 34 46 47 48 49	33	22	L		100	708	65	65.0	0	0	6179	2952	157
□ HIGHLAND HOSPITAL, 49 Zillicoa St., Zip 28801; Mailing Address Box 1101, Zip 28802; tel. 704/254-3201; Jack W. Bonner III MD, chief exec. off. **A**1b 9 10 **F**24 28 29 30 32 33 34 49; **S**0825	33	22	L		98	246	69	62.2	0	0	7790	3475	206
⊞ MEMORIAL MISSION HOSPITAL, 509 Biltmore Ave., Zip 28801; tel. 704/255-4000; Robert F. Burgin, pres. **A**1a 2 3 5 9 10 **F**1 2 3 4 5 6 7 8 9 10 11 14 15 16 20 21 23 24 26 30 32 33 34 35 36 37 40 44 45 46 47 51 52 53 54	23	10	S		371	17655	302	79.3	32	2820	61491	26911	1467
⊞ ST. JOSEPH'S HOSPITAL, 428 Biltmore Ave., Zip 28801; tel. 704/255-3100; Sr. Mary Veronica Schumacher, pres. & chief exec. off. **A**1a 10 **F**1 2 3 6 10 15 16 20 23 27 33 34 35 45 53; **S**5985	23	10	S		283	13140	245	86.6	0	0	37491	15920	690
★ Δ THOMS REHABILITATION HOSPITAL, One Rotary Dr., Zip 28803; Mailing Address P O Box 15025, Zip 28813; tel. 704/274-2400; Charles D. Norvell, exec. dir. **A**7 9 10 **F**10 16 23 24 26 32 33 43 44 45 46; **S**0025	23	46	S		70	505	38	50.7	0	0	5811	3597	193
⊞ VETERANS ADMINISTRATION MEDICAL CENTER, Riceville & Tunnel Rds., Zip 28805; tel. 704/298-7911; Robert Dawson, dir. (Total facility includes 82 beds in nursing home-type unit) **A**1a 3 5 **F**2 3 4 6 10 12 14 15 16 19 23 24 26 27 28 30 31 33 34 35 42 44 45 46 47 49 53 54	45	10	S	TF	540	7575	442	79.4	0	0	44212	26726	1046
				H	458	7538	361	—	0	0	41427	24844	1003
BANNER ELK—Avery County													
⊞ CHARLES A. CANNON JR. MEMORIAL HOSPITAL, P O Box 8, Zip 28604; tel. 704/898-5111; J. Patrick Thompson, adm. **A**1a 9 10 **F**1 3 5 6 10 14 16 23 27 30 33 35 36 37 40 45 46	23	10	S		79	1870	35	44.3	20	45	4481	2123	136
BELHAVEN—Beaufort County													
PUNGO DISTRICT HOSPITAL, Front St., Zip 27810; tel. 919/943-2111; Dan C. White, adm. **A**9 10 **F**3 5 10 14 16 35 45 46; **S**0585	23	10	S		32	729	8	16.7	10	17	1913	823	61
BLACK MOUNTAIN—Buncombe County													
□ ALCOHOLIC REHABILITATION CENTER, Box 1441, Zip 28711; tel. 704/669-3402; Arthur D. Friedman, dir. **A**1b 9 10 **F**42	12	82	S		101	1299	82	81.2	0	0	3398	1971	98
BLOWING ROCK—Watauga County													
⊞ BLOWING ROCK HOSPITAL (Includes Dr. Charles Davant Rehabilitation and Extended Care Center), Chestnut St., Box 148, Zip 28605; tel. 704/295-3136; James P. White, adm. & chief exec. off. (Total facility includes 72 beds in nursing home-type unit) **A**1a 9 10 **F**1 6 10 14 15 16 19 23 35 45 46 47 50	23	10	S	TF	100	438	75	75.0	4	5	2764	1395	115
				H	28	383	6	—	4	5	—	—	—
BOILING SPRINGS—Cleveland County													
CRAWLEY MEMORIAL HOSPITAL, Box 996, Zip 28017; tel. 704/434-9466; John Washburn Jr., adm. **A**9 10 **F**1 14 23 34 45	23	10	S		51	2111	43	84.3	0	0	—	—	60
BOONE—Watauga County													
⊞ WATAUGA COUNTY HOSPITAL, Deerfield Rd., Zip 28607; tel. 704/264-2431; Virginia A. Groce, adm. **A**1a 9 10 **F**1 2 3 6 10 14 15 16 23 34 35 36 40 45 46 47	13	10	S		104	4726	71	58.2	12	668	10172	4899	313
BREVARD—Transylvania County													
⊞ TRANSYLVANIA COMMUNITY HOSPITAL, Medical Park Dr., Box 1116, Zip 28712; tel. 704/884-9111; Robert W. Purcell Sr., adm. **A**1a b 9 10 **F**1 2 3 6 10 15 16 23 24 31 35 36 40 41 44 45 46 47 48	23	10	S		96	2232	44	44.0	12	275	6619	3234	185
BRYSON CITY—Swain County													
⊞ SWAIN COUNTY HOSPITAL, 965 Plateau St., Zip 28713; tel. 704/488-2155; James Earl Douthit, adm. **A**1a 9 10 **F**1 6 10 12 14 16 23 35 36 45 46 47 50	23	10	S		48	1459	20	41.7	8	42	2834	1572	98
BURGAW—Pender County													
⊞ PENDER MEMORIAL HOSPITAL, 507 Freemont St., Box 835, Zip 28425; tel. 919/259-5451; Cameron Highsmith, adm. (Total facility includes 23 beds in nursing home-type unit) **A**1a 9 10 **F**1 5 6 10 14 15 16 23 34 35 43 45 50	13	10	S	TF	66	1409	41	74.5	0	0	3995	1815	139
				H	43	1317	26	—	0	0	—	—	—
BURLINGTON—Alamance County													
⊞ ALAMANCE COUNTY HOSPITAL, 327 N. Graham Hopedale Rd., Box 3157, Zip 27215; tel. 919/228-1371; Richard Maxwell, vice-pres. oper. **A**1a 9 10 **F**1 2 3 6 10 14 15 16 23 24 30 34 35 36 38 40 41 44 45 46 48 53; **S**0025	23	10	S		133	3865	72	51.4	15	400	—	—	409
⊞ ALAMANCE MEMORIAL HOSPITAL (Formerly Memorial Hospital of Alamance County), 730 Hermitage Rd., Box 4008, Zip 27215; tel. 919/229-2600; John G. Currin Jr., vice-pres. oper. (Total facility includes 81 beds in nursing home-type unit) **A**1a 9 10 **F**1 3 5 6 10 12 14 15 16 19 21 23 24 26 27 30 32 33 35 36 37 40 44 45 46 47 50 52 53; **S**0025	23	10	S	TF	220	3949	155	70.1	20	708	14280	5997	423
				H	139	3839	75	—	20	708	—	—	—
MEMORIAL HOSPITAL OF ALAMANCE COUNTY, See Alamance Memorial Hospital													
BUTNER—Granville County													
□ JOHN UMSTEAD HOSPITAL, 12th St., Zip 27509; tel. 919/575-7211; M. F. Hall Jr., dir. (Total facility includes 32 beds in nursing home-type unit) **A**1b 3 5 9 10 **F**10 15 19 23 24 28 29 30 32 33 43 44 45 46 47 50	12	22	L	TF	758	2200	688	90.8	0	0	34067	22019	1208
				H	726	2182	657	—	0	0	—	—	—

Hospital, Address, Telephone, Administrator, Approval and Facility Codes, Multihospital System Code	Classification Codes			Facilities	Inpatient Data				Newborn Data		Expense (thousands of dollars)		Personnel
	Control	Service	Stay		Beds	Admissions	Census	Occupancy (percent)	Bassinets	Births	Total	Payroll	
CAMP LEJEUNE—Onslow County													
★□ NAVAL HOSPITAL, Zip 28542; tel. 919/451-4007; Capt. R. A. Margulies MC USN, CO **A**1a 2 **F**1 3 6 10 12 14 15 16 23 26 27 28 30 32 33 34 35 37 40 47 48 49 52	43	10	S		145	7819	102	53.4	32	913	15837	5402	530
CHAPEL HILL—Orange County													
★□ NORTH CAROLINA MEMORIAL HOSPITAL, Manning Dr., Zip 27514; tel. 919/966-4131; Eric B. Munson, exec. dir. **A**1a 2 3 5 8 9 10 **F**1 2 3 4 5 6 8 9 10 11 14 15 16 20 22 23 24 25 26 27 28 29 30 32 33 34 35 37 38 40 43 44 45 46 47 50 51 52 53 54	12	10	S		576	19155	439	76.2	15	1723	142826	64756	3132
CHARLOTTE—Mecklenburg County													
CHARLOTTE EYE, EAR AND THROAT HOSPITAL, See Humana Specialty Hospital-Charlotte													
★□ CHARLOTTE MEMORIAL HOSPITAL AND MEDICAL CENTER, 1000 Blythe Blvd., Zip 28203; Mailing Address P O Box 32861, Zip 28232; tel. 704/338-2000; Harry A. Nurkin PhD, pres. **A**1a 3 5 8 9 10 **F**1 2 3 4 5 6 8 9 10 11 13 14 15 16 17 20 23 27 28 30 32 33 34 35 36 37 38 40 45 46 47 50 51 52 53 54; **S**0705	16	10	S		843	25736	603	77.1	48	3771	129227	58497	3217
★□ Δ CHARLOTTE REHABILITATION HOSPITAL, 1100 Blythe Blvd., Zip 28203; tel. 704/338-4300; A. Charles Collier, adm. **A**1a 7 9 10 **F**10 16 23 24 26 33 34 44 46; **S**0705	23	46	L		88	808	74	84.1	0	0	8074	4760	228
★□ CHARLOTTE TREATMENT CENTER, Box 240197, Zip 28224; tel. 704/554-8373; James F. Emmert, exec. dir. **A**1b **F**15 49	23	82	L		64	628	52	81.3	0	0	2973	1488	73
★□ HUMANA SPECIALTY HOSPITAL-CHARLOTTE (Formerly Charlotte Eye, Ear and Throat Hospital), 1600 E. Third St., Zip 28204; Mailing Address P O Box 36939, Zip 28236; tel. 704/371-3105; William E. Sheron, exec. dir. **A**1a 9 10 **F**1 5 10 14 15 47; **S**1235	33	45	S		68	1287	7	10.3	0	0	4411	1376	71
★□ MERCY HOSPITAL, 2001 Vail Ave., Zip 28207; tel. 704/379-5000; Sr. Mary Jerome Spradley, pres.; V. Gregg Watters, exec. vice-pres. **A**1a 6 9 10 **F**1 2 3 4 6 10 14 15 16 23 24 26 32 35 41 43 45 46 47 53 54; **S**5985	21	10	S		243	8840	164	53.2	0	0	37304	16653	798
★□ ORTHOPAEDIC HOSPITAL OF CHARLOTTE, 1901 Randolph Rd., Zip 28207; tel. 704/375-6792; William E. Collins, adm. **A**1a 3 9 10 **F**1 12 14 15 16 23 26 32 34 35 41; **S**1755	33	47	S		166	3319	62	37.3	0	0	20700	8500	340
★□ PRESBYTERIAN HOSPITAL, 200 Hawthorne Lane, Zip 28204; Mailing Address Box 33549, Zip 28233; tel. 704/371-4000; Byron L. Bullard, pres. **A**1a 6 9 10 **F**1 2 3 5 6 7 8 9 10 11 15 16 23 27 32 33 35 36 37 40 41 44 45 46 47 51 52 53	23	10	S		566	26169	433	79.4	64	5485	83292	40571	2255
UNIVERSITY MEMORIAL HOSPITAL, P O Box 26015, Zip 28221; tel. 704/547-9200; Charles D. Herring, adm. **A**9 10 **F**1 6 10 12 14 15 16 23 26 32 36 46 50; **S**0705	16	10	S		48	983	16	33.3	13	106	9240	2877	161
CHEROKEE—Swain County													
★□ U. S. PUBLIC HEALTH SERVICE INDIAN HOSPITAL, Zip 28719; tel. 704/497-9163; James E. Mills, actg. adm. **A**1a 10 **F**6 12 14 15 23 28 33 34 35 37 40 41 52	47	10	S		32	1187	12	37.5	4	42	6650	3253	130
CHERRY POINT—Craven County													
★□ NAVAL HOSPITAL, Zip 28533; tel. 919/466-3620; Capt. H. B. Price MSC USN, CO **A**1a **F**1 6 14 15 16 23 33 34 35 36 37 40 45 47 49 52	43	10	S		40	2163	17	42.5	10	645	12610	9459	316
CLINTON—Sampson County													
★□ SAMPSON COUNTY MEMORIAL HOSPITAL, 607 Beaman St., Drawer 258, Zip 28328; tel. 919/592-8511; Lee Pridgen, adm. **A**1a 9 10 **F**1 3 6 10 14 16 23 35 36 40 45 46 52 53	23	10	S		146	3789	66	45.2	23	521	11874	5762	337
CLYDE—Haywood County													
★□ HAYWOOD COUNTY HOSPITAL, 90 Hospital Dr., Zip 28721; tel. 704/456-7311; Grady H. Stokes, adm. **A**1a 9 10 **F**1 3 6 10 15 16 23 34 35 36 40 41 43 44 45 46 47 52 53	13	10	S		152	5876	91	51.1	15	376	16187	7542	463
COLUMBUS—Polk County													
★□ ST. LUKE'S HOSPITAL, 220 Hospital Dr., Zip 28722; tel. 704/894-3311; Thomas M. Kelly, pres. **A**1a 9 10 **F**1 3 6 10 15 16 23 30 33 35 36 37 40 45 46 47 50; **S**0025	23	10	S		52	1264	33	51.6	0	0	4669	2364	147
CONCORD—Cabarrus County													
★□ CABARRUS MEMORIAL HOSPITAL, 920 Church St. N., Zip 28025; tel. 704/786-2111; Robert L. Wall, pres. **A**1a 6 9 10 **F**1 3 6 10 15 16 23 30 34 35 36 40 43 45 46 53	23	10	S		362	13131	238	58.2	30	1338	37253	20413	943
CROSSNORE—Avery County													
★□ SLOOP MEMORIAL HOSPITAL, Box 220, Zip 28616; tel. 704/733-9231; F. L. Blair, adm. **A**1a 10 **F**1 3 6 7 10 11 15 16 23 24 35 36 40 43 45 46 47 49 50	23	10	S		38	1567	21	55.3	8	142	3800	1679	120
DANBURY—Stokes County													
★□ STOKES-REYNOLDS MEMORIAL HOSPITAL, Box 10, Zip 27016; tel. 919/593-2831; Sandra D. Priddy, adm. (Total facility includes 40 beds in nursing home-type unit) **A**1a 9 10 **F**1 3 6 10 15 16 19 23 32 34 35 36 40 46 47 50	13	10	S	TF	94	1425	62	66.0	6	62	4778	2224	165
				H	54	1317	26	—	6	62	4309	1972	—
DUNN—Harnett County													
★□ BETSY JOHNSON MEMORIAL HOSPITAL, 800 Tilghman Dr., Box 1706, Zip 28334; tel. 919/892-7161; Shannon D. Brown, adm. **A**1a 9 10 **F**1 2 3 6 10 14 16 23 34 35 45 46 47 53	23	10	S		91	3496	53	46.1	17	276	8183	5400	236
DURHAM—Durham County													
★□ DUKE UNIVERSITY HOSPITAL, Box 3708, Zip 27710; tel. 919/684-8111; William J. Donelan, dir. & chief oper. off. **A**1a 2 3 5 8 9 10 **F**1 2 3 4 5 6 7 8 9 10 11 13 14 16 20 22 23 24 25 26 27 28 30 31 32 33 34 35 37 38 40 43 44 45 46 47 50 51 52 53 54	23	10	S		968	35652	833	86.7	24	1972	247767	100186	5157
★□ DURHAM COUNTY GENERAL HOSPITAL, 3643 N. Roxboro St., Zip 27704; tel. 919/470-4000; Richard L. Myers, pres. **A**1a 3 5 6 9 10 **F**1 2 3 6 10 14 15 16 23 27 32 35 40 45 46 47 49 50 52 53	23	10	S		405	15581	271	60.2	43	2168	59155	31136	1607
★ LENOX BAKER CHILDREN'S HOSPITAL, 3000 Erwin Rd., Zip 27705; tel. 919/683-6890; J. Robert Gray, dir. **A**9 10 **F**10 15 23 24 26 29 33 34 36 43 44 46 47	12	46	S		40	342	14	35.0	0	0	2318	1552	92
★□ MCPHERSON HOSPITAL, 1110 W. Main St., Zip 27701; tel. 919/682-9341; Thomas G. Peyton, adm. **A**1a 3 5 9 10 **F**1 9 10 34 43 47	33	45	S		24	1086	5	25.0	0	0	5300	1800	131
★□ VETERANS ADMINISTRATION MEDICAL CENTER, 508 Fulton St., Zip 27705; tel. 919/286-0411; Alvis B. Carr Jr., dir. **A**1a 3 5 8 **F**1 2 3 4 6 7 8 9 10 11 12 13 14 15 16 20 23 24 26 27 28 30 32 33 34 35 38 41 42 44 45 46 47 49 50 53 54	45	10	S		444	10256	344	77.5	0	0	65495	35556	1156
EDEN—Rockingham County													
★□ MOREHEAD MEMORIAL HOSPITAL, 117 E. King's Hwy., Zip 27288; tel. 919/623-9711; Robert W. Mellbye, pres. (Total facility includes 24 beds in nursing home-type unit) **A**1a 9 10 **F**1 3 6 9 10 11 14 15 16 23 26 35 36 40 43 44 45 46 47 52; **S**2495	23	10	S	TF	109	3610	65	59.6	16	501	9142	4246	290
				H	85	3577	56	—	16	501	—	—	—
EDENTON—Chowan County													
★□ CHOWAN HOSPITAL, Virginia Rd., Box 629, Zip 27932; tel. 919/482-8451; Marvin A. Bryan, dir. (Total facility includes 56 beds in nursing home-type unit) **A**1a 9 10 **F**1 3 6 10 14 15 16 19 23 35 36 37 40 43 45 46 52; **S**0025	23	10	S	TF	126	2185	88	69.8	8	413	7103	3113	209
				H	70	2119	35	—	8	413	5921	2583	180
ELIZABETH CITY—Pasquotank County													
★□ ALBEMARLE HOSPITAL, Hwy. 17 N., Box 1587, Zip 27909; tel. 919/335-0531; Robert G. Jeffries, adm. **A**1a 9 10 **F**1 2 3 6 10 14 15 16 20 23 35 36 40 45 46 52 53	13	10	S		173	5470	110	58.2	28	968	15593	6766	501
ELIZABETHTOWN—Bladen County													
★ BLADEN COUNTY HOSPITAL, Clarkton Rd., Box 398, Zip 28337; tel. 919/862-4043; Mervin F. Strine, exec. dir. **A**9 10 **F**1 6 10 14 15 16 23 35 40 45 46 47	13	10	S		62	2274	33	53.2	6	186	5581	2844	199

★ American Hospital Association (AHA) membership
□ Joint Commission on Accreditation of Hospitals (JCAH) accreditation
+ American Osteopathic Hospital Association (AOHA) membership
○ American Osteopathic Association (AOA) accreditation
Δ Commission on Accreditation of Rehabilitation Facilities (CARF) accreditation
Control codes 61, 63, 64, 71, 72 and 73 indicate hospitals listed by AOHA, but not registered by AHA.
For definition of numerical codes, see page A2

Hospital, Address, Telephone, Administrator, Approval and Facility Codes, Multihospital System Code

★ American Hospital Association (AHA) membership
□ Joint Commission on Accreditation of Hospitals (JCAH) accreditation
+ American Osteopathic Hospital Association (AOHA) membership
○ American Osteopathic Association (AOA) accreditation
Δ Commission on Accreditation of Rehabilitation Facilities (CARF) accreditation
Control codes 61, 63, 64, 71, 72 and 73 indicate hospitals listed by AOHA, but not registered by AHA.
For definition of numerical codes, see page A2

Hospital	Classification Codes: Control	Service	Stay	Facilities	Inpatient Data: Beds	Admissions	Census	Occupancy (percent)	Newborn Data: Bassinets	Births	Expense (thousands of dollars): Total	Payroll	Personnel
ELKIN—Surry County													
★□ HUGH CHATHAM MEMORIAL HOSPITAL, Parkwood Dr., Zip 28621; tel. 919/835-3722; William S. Clark, adm. (Total facility includes 64 beds in nursing home-type unit) **A**1a 9 10 **F**1 3 6 10 14 15 16 19 23 35 40 44 45; **S**2495	23	10	S	TF	122	2896	103	73.0	6	199	6519	3088	226
				H	58	2854	40	—	6	199	5548	2423	—
ERWIN—Harnett County													
□ GOOD HOPE HOSPITAL, Denim Dr., Box 668, Zip 28339; tel. 919/897-6151; Philip S. Lakernick, adm. **A**1a 9 10 **F**1 3 6 10 14 15 16 23 26 28 30 32 35 45 46 47 49 52 53	23	10	S		67	2336	46	66.7	0	0	6719	3241	202
FAYETTEVILLE—Cumberland County													
★□ Δ CAPE FEAR VALLEY MEDICAL CENTER, Owen Dr., Box 2000, Zip 28302; tel. 919/323-6151; John T. Carlisle, dir. **A**1a 3 5 7 9 10 **F**1 2 3 5 6 7 8 9 10 11 14 15 16 20 23 24 25 26 27 33 34 35 36 37 40 41 44 45 46 47 50 52 53; **S**0025	23	10	S		342	15558	289	69.3	68	3943	47155	22273	1280
★□ HIGHSMITH-RAINEY MEMORIAL HOSPITAL, 150 Robeson St., Zip 28301; tel. 919/483-7400; G. Michael Girone, adm. **A**1a 9 10 **F**1 2 3 6 10 12 14 16 23 34 35 53; **S**1755	33	10	S		150	6597	109	72.7	0	0	21208	7045	407
★□ VETERANS ADMINISTRATION MEDICAL CENTER, 2300 Ramsey St., Zip 28301; tel. 919/488-2120; B. E. Phillips, dir. (Total facility includes 77 beds in nursing home-type unit) **A**1a 8 **F**1 3 6 10 11 12 14 16 19 20 21 23 24 26 27 28 30 33 34 35 42 44 45 46	45	10	S	TF	349	5937	264	75.6	0	0	26321	15850	641
				H	272	5906	197	—	0	0	23964	14757	619
FLETCHER—Henderson County													
★□ PARK RIDGE HOSPITAL (Formerly Fletcher Hospital), Naples Rd., P O Box 1569, Zip 28732; tel. 704/684-8501; Robert Burchard, pres. **A**1a 10 **F**1 3 6 10 15 16 23 29 30 32 35 36 37 40 45 46; **S**4165	23	10	S		62	2090	37	45.1	10	151	8795	3179	185
FORT BRAGG—Cumberland County													
★□ WOMACK ARMY COMMUNITY HOSPITAL, Zip 28307; tel. 919/396-2906; Col. Livio F. Pardi, cmdr. **A**1a 3 5 **F**1 3 6 10 12 14 15 16 19 20 23 24 26 27 28 30 32 33 34 35 37 39 40 41 42 44 45 47 49 52 53	42	10	S		288	15073	181	76.1	31	1939	76976	51247	1356
FRANKLIN—Macon County													
★□ ANGEL COMMUNITY HOSPITAL, Riverview & White Oak Sts., Box 1209, Zip 28734; tel. 704/524-8411 **A**1a 9 10 **F**1 3 6 10 14 16 23 26 27 30 32 33 34 35 41 45 46 47; **S**1755	23	10	S		81	2349	35	43.2	6	165	5972	2572	168
FUQUAY-VARINA—Wake County													
SOUTHERN WAKE HOSPITAL, 400 W. Ranson St., Zip 27526; tel. 919/552-2206; W. J. Mountford Jr., dir. **A**9 **F**1 3 6 10 16 23 35 46 47; **S**6705	23	10	S		28	379	7	25.0	0	0	1541	778	33
GASTONIA—Gaston County													
★□ GASTON MEMORIAL HOSPITAL, 2525 Court Dr., Box 1747, Zip 28053; tel. 704/866-2000; Wayne F. Shovelin, pres. **A**1a 9 10 **F**1 2 3 6 7 9 10 11 14 16 23 27 30 33 34 35 36 40 44 45 46 47 52 53	23	10	S		340	16627	271	79.7	40	2011	36920	18306	1053
GOLDSBORO—Wayne County													
□ CHERRY HOSPITAL, Caller Box 8000, Zip 27530; tel. 919/731-3202; J. Field Montgomery Jr., dir. (Total facility includes 66 beds in nursing home-type unit) **A**1a 3 5 9 10 **F**3 10 14 15 19 23 24 30 32 33 44 46 47 50	12	22	L	TF	737	2395	717	95.3	0	0	33492	21881	1115
				H	671	2393	654	—	0	0	—	—	—
U. S. AIR FORCE HOSPITAL SEYMOUR JOHNSON, See Seymour Johnson Air Force Base													
★□ WAYNE MEMORIAL HOSPITAL (Formerly Wayne County Memorial Hospital), 2700 Wayne Memorial Dr., Zip 27530; tel. 919/736-1110; James W. Hubbell, pres. & chief exec. off. **A**1a 9 10 **F**1 3 6 9 10 14 16 23 27 30 35 40 44 45 47 52 53	23	10	S		260	9655	156	52.7	40	1290	25450	12069	682
GREENSBORO—Guilford County													
★□ CHARTER HILLS HOSPITAL, 700 Walter Reed Dr., Zip 27403; tel. 919/852-4821; Ms Billie Martin Pierce, adm. (Nonreporting) **A**1b 10; **S**0695	33	22	S		100	—	—	—	—	—	—	—	—
★□ FELLOWSHIP HALL, Hicone Rd., Box 6929, Zip 27415; tel. 919/621-3381; Ed F. Ward, exec. dir. **A**1b 9	23	82	S		48	534	42	87.5	0	0	—	—	48
★□ HUMANA HOSPITAL -GREENSBORO, 801 Green Valley Rd., Zip 27408; Mailing Address P O Box 29526, Zip 27429; tel. 919/373-8555; E. William Jochim, exec. dir. **A**1a 9 10 **F**1 3 6 10 14 15 16 23 33 35 37 45 46 47 53; **S**1235	33	10	S		109	2765	45	42.5	0	0	—	—	216
★□ L. RICHARDSON MEMORIAL HOSPITAL, 2401 Southside Blvd., Drawer 16167, Zip 27406; tel. 919/275-9741; Henry A. Swicegood, pres. **A**1a 9 10 **F**1 3 6 10 14 15 16 23 32 34 35 45 46 47; **S**1755	23	10	S		68	1631	38	55.9	0	0	6610	2760	151
★□ MOSES H. CONE MEMORIAL HOSPITAL, 1200 N. Elm St., Zip 27401; tel. 919/379-3900; Dennis R. Barry, pres. **A**1a 3 5 8 9 10 **F**1 2 3 4 5 6 7 9 10 11 14 15 16 20 23 24 25 26 27 30 33 34 35 36 37 38 40 43 44 45 46 51 52 53 54	23	10	S		486	20108	417	85.8	40	3211	81387	39308	1965
★□ WESLEY LONG COMMUNITY HOSPITAL, 501 N. Elam Ave., Drawer X-3, Zip 27402; tel. 919/854-6100; John A. Schrull, dir. **A**1a 9 10 **F**1 3 6 10 14 15 16 23 24 26 30 31 34 35 36 37 40 44 45 46 47 50 52 53	23	10	S		254	9095	168	56.6	32	1005	33693	16493	949
GREENVILLE—Pitt County													
★□ Δ PITT COUNTY MEMORIAL HOSPITAL, 200 Statonsburg Rd., Box 6028, Zip 27834; tel. 919/757-4100; Jack W. Richardson, pres. **A**1a 3 5 7 8 9 10 **F**1 2 3 4 5 6 9 10 14 15 16 20 21 23 24 25 26 27 29 30 32 33 34 35 36 37 38 40 44 45 46 47 51 52 53 54	23	10	S		560	19065	415	74.1	42	2371	89260	41984	2567
□ WALTER B. JONES ALCOHOLIC REHABILITATION CENTER, Rte. 1, Box 20-A, Zip 27834; tel. 919/758-3151; Thomas L. Reece, dir. **A**1b 9 10 **F**10 24 32 33	12	82	S		76	1092	66	86.8	0	0	2600	1750	88
HAMLET—Richmond County													
★□ HAMLET HOSPITAL, Rice & Vance Sts., Box 1109, Zip 28345; tel. 919/582-3611; Bill Young, adm. **A**1a 9 10 **F**1 6 10 14 15 16 21 23 27 30 32 33 34 35 45 46 47 50 52	23	10	S		33	1577	24	54.5	0	0	2800	1350	81
HENDERSON—Vance County													
★□ MARIA PARHAM HOSPITAL, Drawer 59, Zip 27536; tel. 919/438-4143; Samuel T. Waddell, adm. **A**1a 9 10 **F**1 10 14 16 23 35 37 40 45 46	23	10	S		80	3469	48	53.3	20	580	7106	2868	247
HENDERSONVILLE—Henderson County													
★□ MARGARET R. PARDEE MEMORIAL HOSPITAL, 715 Fleming St., Zip 28739; tel. 704/693-6522; Frank J. Aaron, adm. (Total facility includes 40 beds in nursing home-type unit) **A**1a 9 10 **F**1 3 6 10 12 14 15 16 19 23 30 33 35 36 40 44 45 46 47 50 52 53	13	10	S	TF	273	7267	154	56.4	26	539	15908	—	501
				H	233	6983	115	—	26	539	—	—	—
HICKORY—Catawba County													
★□ AMI FRYE REGIONAL MEDICAL CENTER (Formerly Glenn R. Frye Memorial Hospital), 420 N. Center St., Zip 28601; tel. 704/322-6070 **A**1a 9 10 **F**1 2 3 5 6 10 14 15 16 23 24 25 26 27 30 31 32 33 34 35 36 40 41 43 44 45 46 47 51 52 53 54; **S**0125	33	10	S		275	8191	145	54.1	19	939	30246	11290	670
★□ CATAWBA MEMORIAL HOSPITAL, 810 Fairgrove Church Rd. S.E., Zip 28602; tel. 704/322-0450; David O. Rice Sr., pres. **A**1a 9 10 **F**1 2 3 6 7 8 9 10 11 14 15 16 23 27 30 32 34 35 36 37 40 45 46 47 51 52 53	13	10	S		199	6926	119	52.0	32	1031	22797	11675	630
GLENN R. FRYE MEMORIAL HOSPITAL, See AMI Frye Regional Medical Center													
□ HICKORY MEMORIAL HOSPITAL, 219 N. Center St., Zip 28601; Mailing Address P O Box 369, Zip 28603; tel. 704/328-2226; Leland R. Blessum, exec. dir. **A**1b 9 10 **F**24 30 32 33; **S**9605	33	22	S		64	323	20	31.3	0	0	1924	1101	95

Hospital, Address, Telephone, Administrator, Approval and Facility Codes, Multihospital System Code	Classification Codes				Inpatient Data				Newborn Data		Expense (thousands of dollars)		
★ American Hospital Association (AHA) membership □ Joint Commission on Accreditation of Hospitals (JCAH) accreditation + American Osteopathic Hospital Association (AOHA) membership ○ American Osteopathic Association (AOA) accreditation Δ Commission on Accreditation of Rehabilitation Facilities (CARF) accreditation Control codes 61, 63, 64, 71, 72 and 73 indicate hospitals listed by AOHA, but not registered by AHA. For definition of numerical codes, see page A2	Control	Service	Stay	Facilities	Beds	Admissions	Census	Occupancy (percent)	Bassinets	Births	Total	Payroll	Personnel
HIGH POINT—Guilford County													
★□ HIGH POINT REGIONAL HOSPITAL (Formerly High Point Memorial Hospital), 601 N. Elm St., P O Box HP-5, Zip 27261; tel. 919/884-8400; J. Daniel Butler, pres. **A**1a 9 10 **F**1 2 3 5 6 10 14 15 16 23 29 30 33 35 36 40 44 45 46 47 50 52 53 54	23	10	S		259	12175	199	69.1	28	1552	34604	14368	—
HIGHLANDS—Macon County													
★□ HIGHLANDS-CASHIERS HOSPITAL, Fifth St., Box 190, Zip 28741; tel. 704/526-2151; Jack Calloway, pres. **A**1a 9 10 **F**10 14 15 16 23 35 37 45 46	23	10	S		27	283	6	22.2	0	0	1162	568	32
JACKSONVILLE—Onslow County													
★□ ONSLOW MEMORIAL HOSPITAL, 317 Western Blvd., Box 1358, Zip 28540; tel. 919/577-2345; W. Dennis Combs, adm. **A**1a 9 10 **F**1 2 3 5 6 10 14 15 16 23 30 32 34 35 36 40 43 45 46 47 52 53	23	10	S		150	8005	97	64.7	22	2267	16899	7968	489
JEFFERSON—Ashe County													
★□ ASHE MEMORIAL HOSPITAL, P O Box 8, Zip 28640; tel. 919/246-7101; Gary Bishop, adm. **A**1a 9 10 **F**1 6 10 16 23 34 35 36 40 45 46 47 53; **S**1755	23	10	S		34	1643	25	45.5	10	89	4331	1760	114
KENANSVILLE—Duplin County													
★□ DUPLIN GENERAL HOSPITAL, Zip 28349; tel. 919/296-0941; Richard E. Harrell, adm. (Total facility includes 20 beds in nursing home-type unit) **A**1a 9 10 **F**1 3 6 10 16 23 27 30 33 34 35 40 45 46	23	10	S	TF H	80 60	1967 1953	32 30	40.0 —	6 6	333 333	5110 5047	— —	172 —
KINGS MOUNTAIN—Cleveland County													
★□ KINGS MOUNTAIN HOSPITAL, 706 W. King St., Zip 28086; tel. 704/739-3601; M. Huitt Reep, adm. **A**1a 9 10 **F**6 12 14 16 23 35 45 46 53	23	10	S		102	2236	41	40.2	12	136	8800	4400	164
KINSTON—Lenoir County													
CASWELL CENTER, 2415 W. Vernon Ave., Zip 28501; tel. 919/522-1261; Ronald G. Curran EdD, adm. (Nonreporting) **A**9	12	62	L		1000	—	—	—	—	—	—	—	—
★□ LENOIR MEMORIAL HOSPITAL, 100 Airport Rd., P O Box 1678, Zip 28501; tel. 919/522-7171; L. Daniel Duval Jr., pres. **A**1a 6 9 10 **F**1 2 3 6 9 10 14 15 16 23 26 30 35 36 40 45 46 47 52 53	23	10	S		247	10493	150	60.7	22	820	26735	11668	658
LAURINBURG—Scotland County													
★□ SCOTLAND MEMORIAL HOSPITAL, 500 Lauchwood Dr., Zip 28352; tel. 919/276-2121; Robert R. Martin, adm. (Total facility includes 40 beds in nursing home-type unit) **A**1a 9 10 **F**1 3 6 10 14 15 16 19 23 34 35 40 45 46 47 52	23	10	S	TF H	125 85	4643 4590	100 61	80.0 —	25 25	846 846	12942 11909	5410 4808	326 —
LENOIR—Caldwell County													
★ BLACKWELDER MEMORIAL HOSPITAL, 111 Boundary St. S.W., Box 1470, Zip 28645; tel. 704/754-3451; Cecil Hayes, asst. adm. **A**9 10 **F**1 6 10 12 14 15 16 30 35 47	23	10	S		31	573	8	25.8	0	0	1800	830	36
★□ CALDWELL MEMORIAL HOSPITAL, 321 Mulberry St. S.W., P O Box 1890, Zip 28645; tel. 704/754-8421; Frederick L. Soule, pres. & chief exec. off. **A**1a 9 10 **F**1 2 6 10 14 15 16 23 35 36 40 45 46 47 52	23	10	S		107	4618	65	60.7	17	438	12149	5204	337
LEXINGTON—Davidson County													
★□ LEXINGTON MEMORIAL HOSPITAL, Old Salisbury Rd., Box 1817, Zip 27293; tel. 704/246-5161; Stuart H. Fine, pres. **A**1a 9 10 **F**1 3 5 6 10 14 15 16 23 30 35 36 37 40 43 45 46 47	23	10	S		94	3895	53	56.4	20	612	10396	4721	315
LINCOLNTON—Lincoln County													
□ LINCOLN COUNTY HOSPITAL, Box 677, Zip 28092; tel. 704/735-3071; Kenneth C. Wehunt, adm. **A**1a 9 10 **F**1 3 6 10 15 16 23 35 40 45 46 50	23	10	S		70	3169	39	35.5	16	432	9400	4350	229
LOUISBURG—Franklin County													
★ FRANKLIN MEMORIAL HOSPITAL, 100 Hospital Dr., Box 609, Zip 27549; tel. 919/496-5131; Robert L. W. Miller, adm. **A**9 10 **F**15 36 45 49 53; **S**1755	23	10	S		69	1794	35	48.6	4	35	4739	2981	149
LUMBERTON—Robeson County													
★□ SOUTHEASTERN GENERAL HOSPITAL, W. 27th St., Box 1408, Zip 28359; tel. 919/738-6444; Donald C. Hiscott, pres. (Total facility includes 80 beds in nursing home-type unit) **A**1a 9 10 **F**1 3 6 10 14 15 16 19 23 27 30 32 34 35 36 40 45 46 47 48 51 52 53	23	10	S	TF H	376 296	10375 10245	276 197	73.2 —	45 45	1416 1416	29950 28250	13710 12610	870 —
MARION—McDowell County													
★□ MCDOWELL HOSPITAL, 100 Rankin Dr., Zip 28752; tel. 704/652-2125; Les A. Donahue, adm. **A**1a 9 10 **F**1 6 12 14 15 16 23 30 33 34 35 36 43 45 46 53	23	10	S		65	3447	46	70.8	8	193	8098	2968	180
MCCAIN—Hoke County													
MCCAIN HOSPITAL, Zip 28361; tel. 919/944-2351; Nancy C. Lowe, supt. **A**9 **F**15 16 23 32 33 35 50	12	11	S		81	645	51	52.0	0	0	7000	4300	213
MOCKSVILLE—Davie County													
★□ DAVIE COUNTY HOSPITAL, Foster & Hospital Sts., Box 908, Zip 27028; tel. 704/634-8100; Christopher Dux, adm. **A**1a 9 10 **F**1 2 3 6 10 12 14 15 16 23 35 36 40 45 50	13	10	S		64	1810	30	46.2	8	51	5183	2606	143
MONROE—Union County													
★□ UNION MEMORIAL HOSPITAL, 600 Hospital Dr., P O Box 5003, Zip 28110; tel. 704/283-2111; J. Larry Bishop, pres. (Total facility includes 66 beds in nursing home-type unit) **A**1a 9 10 **F**1 2 3 6 10 14 15 16 19 23 35 36 40 44 45 46 50 52 53	23	10	S	TF H	226 160	4800 4753	132 67	58.4 —	17 17	716 716	17041 15361	7952 7334	466 —
MOORESVILLE—Iredell County													
□ LOWRANCE HOSPITAL, 610 E. Center Ave., Box 360, Zip 28115; tel. 704/663-1113; Richard P. Blackburn, exec. dir. **A**1a 9 10 **F**1 3 6 10 14 16 23 34 35 40 45 46 47; **S**1775	23	10	S		107	1739	29	22.7	11	0	5987	2642	153
MOREHEAD CITY—Carteret County													
★□ CARTERET GENERAL HOSPITAL, 3500 Arendell St., Zip 28557; tel. 919/247-1500; Fred A. Odell III, pres. **A**1a 9 10 **F**1 3 6 10 14 15 16 23 29 32 34 35 40 43 45 46 47	23	10	S		117	5044	84	71.8	13	663	14042	5728	334
MORGANTON—Burke County													
□ BROUGHTON HOSPITAL, 1000 S. Sterling St., Zip 28655; tel. 704/433-2111; Arthur J. Robarge PhD, dir. (Total facility includes 30 beds in nursing home-type unit) **A**1b 9 10 **F**3 6 10 11 14 15 16 19 23 24 30 32 33 44 46 47 50	12	22	L	TF H	909 879	2249 2217	804 777	88.4 —	0 0	0 0	39388 —	8716 —	1511 —
★□ GRACE HOSPITAL, 2201 S. Sterling St., Zip 28655; tel. 704/438-2000; John A. Taft Jr., adm. **A**1a 9 10 **F**1 3 6 10 14 15 16 23 34 35 36 40 45 46 47 52	23	10	S		161	6105	95	59.0	24	705	18992	7682	427
MOUNT AIRY—Surry County													
★□ NORTHERN HOSPITAL OF SURRY COUNTY, 830 Rockford St., Box 1101, Zip 27030; tel. 919/789-9541; John K. Lockhart, adm. **A**1a 9 10 **F**1 2 6 10 14 15 16 23 35 36 37 40 44 45 46 53	16	10	S		108	4969	66	61.1	10	389	13149	5625	330
MURPHY—Cherokee County													
MURPHY MEDICAL CENTER, 2002 Us Hwy. 64 E., Box 479, Zip 28906; tel. 704/837-8161; Richard F. Helmbold, adm. (Newly Registered) (Total facility includes 120 beds in nursing home-type unit) **A**9 10 **F**1 3 6 9 10 15 16 19 23 29 35 36 45 46 47 50	23	10	S	TF H	170 50	1600 1446	137 20	80.6 —	9 9	140 140	5861 4025	730 409	126 —
NEW BERN—Craven County													
★□ CRAVEN COUNTY HOSPITAL, 2000 Neuse Blvd., Box 2157, Zip 28561; tel. 919/633-8121; Donald B. Logan, pres. **A**1a 9 10 **F**1 2 3 6 7 8 9 10 11 14 15 16 23 27 34 35 40 41 44 45 46 47 50 52 53	23	10	S		246	10466	187	77.3	17	1149	29614	14987	850

Hospital, Address, Telephone, Administrator, Approval and Facility Codes, Multihospital System Code	Classification Codes				Inpatient Data				Newborn Data		Expense (thousands of dollars)		
★ American Hospital Association (AHA) membership □ Joint Commission on Accreditation of Hospitals (JCAH) accreditation + American Osteopathic Hospital Association (AOHA) membership ○ American Osteopathic Association (AOA) accreditation Δ Commission on Accreditation of Rehabilitation Facilities (CARF) accreditation Control codes 61, 63, 64, 71, 72 and 73 indicate hospitals listed by AOHA, but not registered by AHA. For definition of numerical codes, see page A2	Control	Service	Stay	Facilities	Beds	Admissions	Census	Occupancy (percent)	Bassinets	Births	Total	Payroll	Personnel
NORTH WILKESBORO—Wilkes County													
⊞ WILKES GENERAL HOSPITAL, W. D St., Box 609, Zip 28659; tel. 919/651-8100; John W. Bryan Jr., adm. **A**1a 9 10 **F**1 2 3 5 6 10 15 16 21 23 30 34 35 40 45 46 47 52	14	10	S		133	6036	93	69.9	20	596	12741	6218	355
OXFORD—Granville County													
⊞ GRANVILLE MEDICAL CENTER (Formerly Granville Hospital), College St., Box 947, Zip 27565; tel. 919/693-5115 **A**1a 9 10 **F**1 3 6 10 14 15 16 23 30 33 35 40 45 46 52; **S**0025	13	10	S		66	1735	26	39.4	6	198	—	2392	130
PINEHURST—Moore County													
⊞ MOORE REGIONAL HOSPITAL (Formerly Moore Memorial Hospital), Page Rd., Box 3000, Zip 28374; tel. 919/295-1000; James Crenshaw Thompson, pres. **A**1a 9 10 **F**1 3 5 6 8 10 14 15 16 23 27 30 32 34 35 36 37 40 44 45 46 47 48 51 52 53	23	10	S		310	12339	238	77.8	14	1042	37112	17520	983
PINEVILLE—Mecklenburg County													
□ CPC CEDAR SPRING HOSPITAL, 9600 Pineville-Matthews Rd., P O Box 39, Zip 28134; tel. 704/541-6676; Ervin M. Funderburk Jr., adm. **A**1b 9 10 **F**15 23 24 28 30 32 33 42 44 47 49	33	22	L		50	205	31	51.7	0	0	—	—	67
PLYMOUTH—Washington County													
⊞ WASHINGTON COUNTY HOSPITAL, Hwy. 64 E., Zip 27962; tel. 919/793-4135; Lowell M. Rhodes, adm. **A**1a 9 10 **F**1 3 10 14 15 16 23 35 40 45 46	23	10	S		49	1234	17	34.7	8	130	—	—	104
RALEIGH—Wake County													
CENTRAL PRISON HOSPITAL, 1300 Western Blvd., Zip 27606; tel. 919/834-0130; Robert J. Newton, adm. (Nonreporting)	12	11	S		241	—	—	—	—	—	—	—	—
□ DOROTHEA DIX HOSPITAL, 820 S. Boylan Ave., Zip 27611; tel. 919/733-5324; A. G. Tolley MD, dir. **A**1a 3 5 9 10 **F**3 10 14 15 16 23 24 28 30 32 33 34 44 45 46 47 50	12	22	L		682	3510	623	91.3	0	0	38941	25079	1251
⊞ HOLLY HILL HOSPITAL, 3019 Falstaff Rd., Zip 27610; tel. 919/755-1840; Lawrence H. Pomeroy, exec. dir. **A**1b 10 **F**10 15 23 24 30 33 43; **S**1755	33	22	S		106	1190	85	79.4	0	0	—	—	151
⊞ RALEIGH COMMUNITY HOSPITAL, 3400 Old Wake Forest Rd., Zip 27609; Mailing Address P O Box 28280, Zip 27611; tel. 919/872-4800; Harrison T. Ferris, adm. **A**1a 9 10 **F**1 3 6 10 12 14 15 16 23 26 34 35 45 46 47 53; **S**1755	33	10	S		140	5750	77	55.0	0	0	—	—	380
⊞ REX HOSPITAL, 4420 Lake Boone Trail, Zip 27607; tel. 919/783-3100; John R. Willis, pres. **A**1a 9 10 **F**1 2 3 6 7 8 9 10 11 14 15 16 23 24 26 34 35 36 37 40 44 45 46 52 53	23	10	S		394	20117	296	75.1	35	2703	60585	28976	1370
★ WAKE COUNTY ALCOHOLISM TREATMENT CENTER, 3000 Falstaff Rd., Zip 27610; tel. 919/821-7650; Margaret Houseworth, exec. dir. **A**9 10 **F**10 28 30 32 33 34 35 46 49	13	82	S		34	1042	24	70.6	0	0	2372	1394	89
⊞ WAKE MEDICAL CENTER, 3000 New Bern Ave., Zip 27610; tel. 919/755-8000; Raymond L. Champ, pres. **A**1a 3 5 8 9 10 **F**1 2 3 4 5 6 9 10 14 15 16 20 23 24 34 35 36 37 40 45 46 47 51 52 53 54; **S**6705	23	10	S		513	19735	408	79.5	24	3310	86992	41337	2007
REIDSVILLE—Rockingham County													
⊞ ANNIE PENN MEMORIAL HOSPITAL, 618 S. Main St., Zip 27320; tel. 919/349-8461; James P. Knight, adm. (Total facility includes 31 beds in nursing home-type unit) **A**1a 9 10 **F**1 3 6 10 14 15 16 23 24 28 34 35 36 37 40 41 44 45 46	23	10	S	TF	152	3330	67	44.1	16	265	10664	4380	993
				H	121	3315	63	—	16	265	10579	4320	—
ROANOKE RAPIDS—Halifax County													
⊞ HALIFAX MEMORIAL HOSPITAL, 250 Smith Church Rd., P O Box 1089, Zip 27870; tel. 919/535-8011; M. E. Gilstrap, chief exec. off. **A**1a 9 10 **F**1 2 6 10 12 14 15 16 23 27 29 30 33 34 35 40 45 46 52 53	23	10	S		190	7262	127	66.8	18	751	15094	7328	423
ROBERSONVILLE—Martin County													
ROBERSONVILLE COMMUNITY HOSPITAL, N. Main St., Box 1210, Zip 27871; tel. 919/795-3126; Mamie R. Smith, adm. **A**9 10 **F**10 16 21 23 35 45	23	10	S		12	183	3	25.0	0	0	440	237	13
ROCKINGHAM—Richmond County													
⊞ RICHMOND MEMORIAL HOSPITAL, Aldrin & Long Drives, Box 1928, Zip 28379; tel. 919/997-2561; James M. Iseman, exec. dir. **A**1a 9 10 **F**1 3 6 10 15 16 23 34 35 36 40 41 45 46 47 53	23	10	S		76	3356	47	61.8	18	388	5969	3941	275
ROCKY MOUNT—Nash County													
⊞ COMMUNITY HOSPITAL OF ROCKY MOUNT, 1031 Noell Lane, Zip 27804; tel. 919/443-9101; G. Michael Bass, chief exec. off. **A**1a 9 10 **F**1 3 10 16 23 35 45 46	33	10	S		50	1185	21	42.0	0	0	—	—	100
⊞ NASH GENERAL HOSPITAL, Curtis Ellis Dr., Zip 27804; tel. 919/443-8000; Bryant T. Aldridge, pres. **A**1a 9 10 **F**1 2 3 6 10 14 15 16 20 23 24 27 30 33 35 36 37 40 43 44 45 46 47 50 52 53	23	10	S		282	11459	219	77.7	39	1362	29885	15713	854
ROXBORO—Person County													
⊞ PERSON COUNTY MEMORIAL HOSPITAL (Includes Reginald L. Harris Annex), 615 Ridge Rd., Zip 27573; tel. 919/599-2121; S. Grant Boone Jr., adm. (Total facility includes 23 beds in nursing home-type unit) **A**1a 9 10 **F**1 3 5 6 10 15 16 19 23 34 35 36 40 45 46 47; **S**1755	23	10	S	TF	77	1248	43	55.8	10	108	4746	2460	151
				H	54	1216	—	—	10	108	4120	2085	—
RUTHERFORDTON—Rutherford County													
⊞ RUTHERFORD HOSPITAL, 308 S. Ridgecrest Ave., Zip 28139; tel. 704/287-7371; Thomas E. Cecconi, pres. **A**1a 9 10 **F**1 3 6 10 14 15 16 23 26 29 30 33 34 35 36 40 45 46 47 53; **S**2495	23	10	S		165	4489	89	53.9	20	620	12841	5919	375
SALISBURY—Rowan County													
⊞ ROWAN MEMORIAL HOSPITAL, 612 Mocksville Ave., Zip 28144; tel. 704/638-1000; M. Earl Bullard, dir. **A**1a 10 **F**1 2 3 6 10 14 15 16 23 35 40 45 46 47 52 53	23	10	S		263	9838	177	60.8	36	1051	24891	12314	761
⊞ VETERANS ADMINISTRATION HOSPITAL, 1601 Brenner Ave., Zip 28144; tel. 704/636-2351; Thomas L. Ayres, dir. (Total facility includes 93 beds in nursing home-type unit) **A**1a **F**1 3 6 10 12 14 15 16 19 23 24 25 26 28 31 33 42 44 46 47 48 50	45	22	L	TF	894	5819	787	88.0	0	0	54175	30328	1300
				H	801	5741	696	—	0	0	50649	28562	1222
SANFORD—Lee County													
⊞ AMI CENTRAL CAROLINA HOSPITAL (Formerly Central Carolina Hospital), 1135 Carthage St., Zip 27330; tel. 919/774-4100; Phil Shaw, exec. dir. **A**1a 10 **F**1 3 6 10 14 15 16 23 34 35 36 37 40 45 46 47; **S**0125	33	10	S		142	4553	62	43.7	18	660	13615	4353	218
SCOTLAND NECK—Halifax County													
★ OUR COMMUNITY HOSPITAL, 708 House Ave., Box 405, Zip 27874; tel. 919/826-4144; John K. Parks, adm. **A**9 10 **F**10 14 35	23	10	S		20	137	7	35.0	0	0	686	381	28
SEA LEVEL—Carteret County													
★ SEA LEVEL HOSPITAL, DIVISION OF DUKE UNIVERSITY MEDICAL CENTER, U. S. Hwy. 70, Zip 28577; tel. 919/225-4611; Bea Vaughan, adm. (Total facility includes 60 beds in nursing home-type unit) **A**9 10 **F**1 10 14 16 19 23 35 45 46	21	10	S	TF	76	528	52	68.4	0	0	3248	1353	91
				H	16	442	8	—	0	0	2950	1126	—
SEYMOUR JOHNSON AIR FORCE BASE—Wayne County													
U. S. AIR FORCE HOSPITAL SEYMOUR JOHNSON, Zip 27531; tel. 919/736-5276 (Nonreporting)	41	10	S		40	—	—	—	—	—	—	—	—
SHELBY—Cleveland County													
⊞ CLEVELAND MEMORIAL HOSPITAL, 201 Grover St., Zip 28150; tel. 704/487-3000; C. Curtis Copenhaver, pres. **A**1a 2 9 10 **F**1 2 3 6 7 8 9 10 11 14 15 16 23 34 35 36 40 45 46 52 53	23	10	S		300	8011	143	47.7	36	1135	23700	12155	732

Hospital, Address, Telephone, Administrator, Approval and Facility Codes, Multihospital System Code	Classification Codes			Facilities	Inpatient Data				Newborn Data		Expense (thousands of dollars)		
★ American Hospital Association (AHA) membership ☐ Joint Commission on Accreditation of Hospitals (JCAH) accreditation + American Osteopathic Hospital Association (AOHA) membership ○ American Osteopathic Association (AOA) accreditation Δ Commission on Accreditation of Rehabilitation Facilities (CARF) accreditation Control codes 61, 63, 64, 71, 72 and 73 indicate hospitals listed by AOHA, but not registered by AHA. For definition of numerical codes, see page A2	Control	Service	Stay	Facilities	Beds	Admissions	Census	Occupancy (percent)	Bassinets	Births	Total	Payroll	Personnel
SILER CITY—Chatham County													
☐★ CHATHAM HOSPITAL, W. Third & Ivy Sts., Box 649, Zip 27344; tel. 919/663-2113; Frank Beirne, adm. **A**1a 9 10 **F**1 6 10 14 15 16 23 34 35 36 40 45 46; **S**0025	23	10	S		68	1561	30	44.1	0	215	4912	2161	116
SMITHFIELD—Johnston County													
☐★ JOHNSTON MEMORIAL HOSPITAL, Hwy. 301 N., Box 1376, Zip 27577; tel. 919/934-8171; Herman L. Mullins, pres. **A**1a 9 10 **F**1 3 5 6 10 14 15 16 23 27 30 32 33 34 35 36 40 45 46 52; **S**1755	13	10	S		97	4630	66	47.8	22	458	11392	4494	319
SOUTHPORT—Brunswick County													
★ J. ARTHUR DOSHER MEMORIAL HOSPITAL, 924 Howe St., Zip 28461; tel. 919/457-5271; C. Arthur Pittman, adm. **A**9 10 **F**1 3 6 10 14 15 16 23 26 33 34 35 44 45 46	15	10	S		40	1352	15	37.5	0	0	3769	1694	113
SPARTA—Alleghany County													
☐ ALLEGHANY COUNTY MEMORIAL HOSPITAL, Box 9, Zip 28675; tel. 919/372-5511; Margaret E. Cox, adm. **A**1a 9 10 **F**1 6 10 35 40	23	10	S		46	1149	27	58.7	9	65	2064	1092	79
SPRUCE PINE—Mitchell County													
☐★ BLUE RIDGE HOSPITAL SYSTEMS, SPRUCE PINE COMMUNITY HOSPITAL DIVISION, 125 Hospital Dr., Zip 28777; tel. 704/765-4201; David W. Spangler, adm. **A**1a 9 10 **F**1 2 10 14 16 23 34 35 36 40 45 46 47; **S**1755	23	10	S		92	2527	35	38.0	6	207	6225	2660	177
STATESVILLE—Iredell County													
☐★ DAVIS COMMUNITY HOSPITAL, Old Mocksville Rd., P O Box 1800, Zip 28677; tel. 704/873-0281; Steven L. Blaine, adm. **A**1a 9 10 **F**1 2 3 6 10 12 14 15 16 23 35 40 45 47 52 53; **S**1755	33	10	S		128	4337	68	49.3	18	465	13161	5373	285
☐★ IREDELL MEMORIAL HOSPITAL, Brookdale Dr. & Hartness Rd., Box 1400, Zip 28677; tel. 704/873-5661; Arnold Nunnery, chief exec. off. **A**1a 9 10 **F**1 2 3 6 10 14 15 16 23 30 32 35 36 40 45 46 47 53	23	10	S		217	7333	126	63.0	12	740	20362	9564	540
SUPPLY—Brunswick County													
★ BRUNSWICK HOSPITAL, U. S. Hwy. 17 S., P O Box 139, Zip 28462; tel. 919/754-8121; Rodney R. Pulley, adm. **A**9 10 **F**1 6 10 14 15 16 23 32 33 34 35 37 40 45 46 47 50; **S**1755	16	10	S		30	1247	15	33.3	6	116	3801	1685	133
SYLVA—Jackson County													
☐★ C. J. HARRIS COMMUNITY HOSPITAL, 59 Hospital Rd., Zip 28779; tel. 704/586-7000; Donald C. Morgan, pres. (Nonreporting) **A**1a 9 10	23	10	S		80	—	—	—	—	—	—	—	—
TARBORO—Edgecombe County													
☐★ HCA HERITAGE HOSPITAL, 111 Hospital Dr., Zip 27886; tel. 919/641-7700; J. Lewis Ridgeway, exec. dir. **A**1a 9 10 **F**1 3 6 10 12 14 15 16 23 29 32 34 35 40 46 47 50 52; **S**1755	33	10	S		89	3418	58	53.7	15	361	—	—	265
TAYLORSVILLE—Alexander County													
☐★ ALEXANDER COUNTY HOSPITAL, 326 Third St. S.W., Zip 28681; tel. 704/632-4282; L. Ridgeway, adm. **A**1a 9 10 **F**1 2 6 10 16 23 35 40 43 45 46 52	23	10	S		51	1501	26	51.0	7	17	3927	1687	113
THOMASVILLE—Davidson County													
☐★ COMMUNITY GENERAL HOSPITAL OF THOMASVILLE, 207 Old Lexington Rd., Box 789, Zip 27360; tel. 919/472-2000; Perry T. Jones, pres. **A**1a 9 10 **F**1 3 5 6 10 14 15 16 23 27 35 36 40 43 45 46 47 52 53	23	10	S		128	4154	75	58.6	15	460	12211	5511	358
TROY—Montgomery County													
★ MONTGOMERY MEMORIAL HOSPITAL, 520 Allen St., Box 486, Zip 27371; tel. 919/572-1301; James L. Muse, adm. **A**9 10 **F**1 3 6 9 10 14 16 23 34 35 40	23	10	S		57	1887	30	52.6	14	223	4838	2320	134
VALDESE—Burke County													
☐★ VALDESE GENERAL HOSPITAL, Box 700, Zip 28690; tel. 704/874-2251; Robert H. Luse, pres. **A**1a 2 9 10 **F**1 3 6 7 8 9 10 14 15 16 23 35 36 40 45 52	23	10	S		82	2623	44	40.0	12	274	10065	4981	280
WADESBORO—Anson County													
☐★ ANSON COUNTY HOSPITAL AND SKILLED NURSING FACILITY, 500 Morven Rd., Zip 28170; tel. 704/694-5131; Thomas W. Northrop, adm. (Total facility includes 45 beds in nursing home-type unit) **A**1a 9 10 **F**1 10 14 15 16 19 23 35 45 50; **S**0025	23	10	S	TF	97	26263	5	5.2	10	226	6579	2984	203
				H	52	10116	5	—	10	226	—	—	—
WAKE FOREST—Wake County													
NORTHERN WAKE HOSPITAL, Allen Rd., P O Box 152, Zip 27587; tel. 919/556-5151; Diane Long, interim dir. **A**9 **F**1 10 16 23 35 47; **S**6705	23	10	S		20	380	6	30.0	0	0	1168	650	32
WASHINGTON—Beaufort County													
☐★ BEAUFORT COUNTY HOSPITAL, 628 E. 12th St., Zip 27889; tel. 919/946-1911; Kenneth E. Ragland, adm. **A**1a 9 10 **F**1 3 6 10 14 15 16 23 30 32 33 35 40 45 46 47 50 53; **S**0025	23	10	S		151	3774	56	37.1	15	386	11059	5408	355
WHITEVILLE—Columbus County													
★ COLUMBUS COUNTY HOSPITAL, 500 Jefferson St., Zip 28472; tel. 919/642-8011; Ralph L. Rogers, adm. **A**9 10 **F**1 2 3 6 9 10 14 15 16 23 34 35 36 40 52	23	10	S		135	6540	101	66.4	20	631	13407	6231	437
WILLIAMSTON—Martin County													
☐★ MARTIN GENERAL HOSPITAL, 310 S. McCaskey Rd., P O Box 1128, Zip 27892; tel. 919/792-2186; George H. Brandt Jr., adm. **A**1a 9 10 **F**1 3 10 14 15 16 23 35 40 45; **S**0025	13	10	S		49	1379	18	36.7	6	203	4189	1707	134
WILMINGTON—New Hanover County													
☐★ CAPE FEAR MEMORIAL HOSPITAL, 5301 Wrightsville Ave., Zip 28403; tel. 919/395-8100; Joseph L. Soto, exec. dir. **A**1a 9 10 **F**1 3 6 10 12 15 16 23 33 35 37 40 44 45 46 47 50	23	10	S		77	3379	52	48.6	11	415	12871	5550	331
☐★ NEW HANOVER MEMORIAL HOSPITAL, 2131 S. 17th St., Zip 28401; Mailing Address Box 9000, Zip 28402; tel. 919/343-7000; William F. Morrison, chief exec. off. **A**1a 3 5 9 10 **F**1 2 3 5 6 7 8 9 10 12 14 15 16 20 23 24 26 27 30 32 33 34 35 36 37 40 44 45 46 47 51 52 53	23	10	S		429	18143	340	80.0	26	2227	54427	27715	1524
WILSON—Wilson County													
☐★ WILSON MEMORIAL HOSPITAL, 1705 S. Tarboro St., Zip 27893; tel. 919/399-8040; Charles D. Setliffe, adm. **A**1a 9 10 **F**1 2 3 6 9 10 16 20 23 27 28 30 33 35 40 45 48 52 53	23	10	S		277	11650	205	74.0	15	1052	30408	15451	811
WINDSOR—Bertie County													
☐★ BERTIE MEMORIAL HOSPITAL (Formerly Bertie County Memorial Hospital), 401 Sterlingworth St., Zip 27983; tel. 919/794-3141; Gary A. Dolack, chief exec. off. **A**1a 9 10 **F**1 10 14 15 16 23 35 45 46 47 50; **S**9795	13	10	S		49	301	5	10.2	8	0	2774	—	43
WINSTON-SALEM—Forsyth County													
AMOS COTTAGE REHABILITATION HOSPITAL, 3325 Silas Creek Pkwy., Zip 27103; Douglas M. Cody, adm. **A**9 **F**10 15 23 24 26 32 33 34 38 44 45 46 47	23	46	L		41	74	23	56.1	0	0	1859	1207	92
CHARTER MANDALA CENTER HOSPITAL, See Charter Mandala Hospital													
☐★ CHARTER MANDALA HOSPITAL (Formerly Charter Mandala Center Hospital), 3637 Old Vineyard Rd., Zip 27104; tel. 919/768-7710; Billie Martin Pierce, exec. dir. **A**1b 9 10 **F**15 24 32 33 47; **S**0695	33	22	S		99	1056	66	75.9	0	0	—	—	134

★ American Hospital Association (AHA) membership
□ Joint Commission on Accreditation of Hospitals (JCAH) accreditation
\+ American Osteopathic Hospital Association (AOHA) membership
○ American Osteopathic Association (AOA) accreditation
Δ Commission on Accreditation of Rehabilitation Facilities (CARF) accreditation
Control codes 61, 63, 64, 71, 72 and 73 indicate hospitals listed by AOHA, but not registered by AHA.
For definition of numerical codes, see page A2

Hospital, Address, Telephone, Administrator, Approval and Facility Codes, Multihospital System Code	Classification Codes				Inpatient Data				Newborn Data		Expense (thousands of dollars)		
	Control	Service	Stay	Facilities	Beds	Admissions	Census	Occupancy (percent)	Bassinets	Births	Total	Payroll	Personnel
★□ Δ FORSYTH MEMORIAL HOSPITAL, 3333 Silas Creek Pkwy., Zip 27103; tel. 919/773-3000; Paul M. Wiles, pres. & chief exec. off. **A**1a 3 5 7 9 10 **F**1 2 3 6 9 10 11 14 15 16 20 23 24 25 26 27 30 33 34 35 36 37 40 44 45 46 47 51 52 53 54	23	10	S		719	34275	603	85.3	57	4789	84112	41325	2147
★□ MEDICAL PARK HOSPITAL, 1950 S. Hawthorne Rd., Zip 27103; tel. 919/768-7680; Earl H. Tyndall Jr., exec. dir. **A**1a 9 10 **F**1 3 10 14 15 16 23 34 43 47; **S**1755	32	10	S		136	5751	72	52.9	0	0	12850	5441	282
★□ NORTH CAROLINA BAPTIST HOSPITAL, 300 S. Hawthorne Rd., Zip 27103; tel. 919/748-2011; John E. Lynch, pres. **A**1a 2 3 5 8 9 10 **F**1 2 3 4 5 6 7 8 9 10 11 13 14 16 17 20 22 23 24 26 27 28 30 33 34 35 38 39 44 45 46 47 51 52 53 54	23	10	S		642	23198	518	80.7	0	0	116439	55917	3213
YADKINVILLE—Yadkin County													
★□ HOOTS MEMORIAL HOSPITAL, 625 W. Main St., P O Box 68, Zip 27055; tel. 919/679-2041; George Repa, adm. **A**1a 9 10 **F**1 3 6 10 15 16 23 34 35 36 37 40 45 46 52	13	10	S		34	1191	19	35.2	8	77	3797	1548	123
ZEBULON—Wake County													
EASTERN WAKE HOSPITAL, 320 Hospital Rd., P O Box 275, Zip 27597; tel. 919/269-7406; William J. Mountford Jr., adm. **A**9 **F**1 6 10 16 23 35 47; **S**6705	23	10	S		20	224	4	20.0	0	0	1284	693	32

Hospital, Address, Telephone, Administrator, Approval and Facility Codes, Multihospital System Code	Classification Codes				Inpatient Data				Newborn Data		Expense (thousands of dollars)		
★ American Hospital Association (AHA) membership □ Joint Commission on Accreditation of Hospitals (JCAH) accreditation + American Osteopathic Hospital Association (AOHA) membership ○ American Osteopathic Association (AOA) accreditation Δ Commission on Accreditation of Rehabilitation Facilities (CARF) accreditation Control codes 61, 63, 64, 71, 72 and 73 indicate hospitals listed by AOHA, but not registered by AHA. For definition of numerical codes, see page A2	Control	Service	Stay	Facilities	Beds	Admissions	Census	Occupancy (percent)	Bassinets	Births	Total	Payroll	Personnel

North Dakota

Hospital	Control	Service	Stay	Facilities	Beds	Admissions	Census	Occupancy (percent)	Bassinets	Births	Total	Payroll	Personnel
ASHLEY—McIntosh County													
★ ASHLEY MEDICAL CENTER (Formerly McIntosh County Memorial Hospital), 612 N. Center Ave., Zip 58413; tel. 701/288-3433; Leo Geiger, adm. (Total facility includes 30 beds in nursing home-type unit) **A**9 10 **F**1 3 14 15 19 34 35 36 40 41 42 43 45 46 47 50	23	10	S	TF	56	373	45	80.4	6	20	1663	789	66
				H	26	362	15	—	6	20	1208	536	45
BELCOURT—Rolette County													
⊞ U. S. PUBLIC HEALTH SERVICE INDIAN HOSPITAL, Zip 58316; tel. 701/477-6111; Clarence Frederick, dir. **A**1a 10 **F**1 6 10 12 14 15 28 29 30 32 33 34 35 37 40 48 49 52	47	10	S		46	1618	16	34.8	8	125	3798	2413	108
BISMARCK—Burleigh County													
⊞ Δ MEDCENTER ONE, 300 N. Seventh St., Zip 58501; Mailing Address Box 640, Zip 58502; tel. 701/224-6000; Terrance G. Brosseau, pres. **A**1a 2 3 5 6 7 9 10 **F**1 3 4 5 6 7 8 9 10 11 12 14 15 16 20 23 24 25 26 30 32 33 35 36 40 42 44 45 46 47 51 52 54	23	10	S		268	8377	148	55.2	12	565	39858	14908	630
⊞ ST. ALEXIUS MEDICAL CENTER, 900 E. Broadway, Zip 58501; Mailing Address Box 1658, Zip 58502; tel. 701/224-7000; Richard Tschider, adm. **A**1a 2 3 5 9 10 **F**1 3 4 5 6 9 10 11 12 15 16 20 23 24 26 27 28 29 30 32 33 34 35 36 40 41 42 43 45 46 47 50 51 52 53 54; **S**0545	21	10	S		278	10383	177	63.7	20	1316	44779	18719	899
BOTTINEAU—Bottineau County													
★ ST. ANDREW'S HOSPITAL, 316 Ohmer St., Zip 58318; tel. 701/228-2255; Keith Korman, pres. (Total facility includes 26 beds in nursing home-type unit) **A**9 10 **F**1 6 12 14 15 16 19 23 34 35 36 40 41 42 44 45 46 47 49 50 52; **S**5805	23	10	S	TF	67	874	38	56.7	4	58	2484	1160	75
				H	41	834	13	—	4	58	2293	973	58
BOWMAN—Bowman County													
⊞ ST. LUKE'S TRI-STATE HOSPITAL, Drawer C, Zip 58623; tel. 701/523-5265; Norris Sabe, adm. **A**1a 9 10 **F**1 3 6 12 14 15 16 23 34 35 37 40 43 45 50 52	23	10	S		39	726	11	28.2	8	31	1516	885	53
CANDO—Towner County													
⊞ TOWNER COUNTY MEMORIAL HOSPITAL, Zip 58324; tel. 701/968-4411; Sr. M. Arnoldine Nieberler, adm. **A**1a 9 10 **F**1 6 16 23 26 34 35 36 40 41 43 45 52 53; **S**5975	21	10	S		34	483	5	14.7	4	46	1127	616	41
CARRINGTON—Foster County													
⊞ CARRINGTON HEALTH CENTER (Formerly Carrington Hospital), 800 N. Fourth St., Zip 58421; tel. 701/652-3141; Duane D. Jerde, chief exec. off. (Total facility includes 38 beds in nursing home-type unit) **A**1a 9 10 **F**1 5 6 10 15 16 19 23 35 36 40 41 45 50 52; **S**5175	21	10	S	TF	66	1198	50	75.8	8	83	3138	1454	83
				H	28	1178	13	—	8	83	2330	931	62
CAVALIER—Pembina County													
★ PEMBINA COUNTY MEMORIAL HOSPITAL, 205 E. Third Ave., Zip 58220; tel. 701/265-8461; Jim Manlin, adm. **A**9 10 **F**1 3 6 14 15 16 23 26 34 35 40 41 43 45 46 50 53; **S**2235	23	10	S		53	366	6	11.3	5	140	2864	1508	86
COOPERSTOWN—Griggs County													
GRIGGS COUNTY HOSPITAL AND NURSING HOME, Box 728, Zip 58425; tel. 701/797-2221; Joan Bachman, adm. (Total facility includes 50 beds in nursing home-type unit) **A**9 10 **F**1 15 16 19 30 35 36 37 40 45 50	23	10	S	TF	74	465	61	82.4	6	18	1620	903	67
				H	24	456	11	—	6	18	831	393	30
CROSBY—Divide County													
ST. LUKE'S HOSPITAL, 702 First St. Southwest, Zip 58730; tel. 701/965-6384; Kenneth Unhjem, adm. **A**9 10 **F**1 2 6 15 16 23 34 35 40 45 52	23	10	S		25	454	7	28.0	4	23	961	515	34
DEVILS LAKE—Ramsey County													
⊞ MERCY HOSPITAL, E. Seventh St., Zip 58301; tel. 701/662-2131; Marlene Krein, pres. **A**1a 9 10 **F**1 2 3 6 10 14 15 16 23 34 35 36 40 41 45 52 53; **S**5175	21	10	S		110	2607	39	35.5	13	351	6913	3802	188
DICKINSON—Stark County													
⊞ ST. JOSEPH'S HOSPITAL AND HEALTH CENTER, Seventh St. W., Zip 58601; tel. 701/225-7200; John S. Studsrud, adm. **A**1a 9 10 **F**1 3 6 10 12 14 15 16 20 21 23 24 27 28 29 30 32 33 34 35 36 40 41 42 43 44 45 46 47 48 49 52 53; **S**5855	21	10	S		101	3964	55	54.5	20	610	13510	5833	305
ELGIN—Grant County													
JACOBSON MEMORIAL HOSPITAL CARE CENTER, 601 East St. N., Zip 58533; tel. 701/584-2792; Jacqueline Seibel, adm. (Nonreporting) **A**9 10	23	10	S		50	—	—	—	—	—	—	—	—
ELLENDALE—Dickey County													
★ DICKEY COUNTY MEMORIAL HOSPITAL, 241 Main St., Box 220, Zip 58436; tel. 701/349-3611; Gordon Smith, adm. **A**9 10 **F**6 23 35 36 40 45 46; **S**5255	23	10	S		21	372	5	23.8	2	22	1022	464	32
FARGO—Cass County													
⊞ DAKOTA HOSPITAL, 1720 S. University Dr., P O Box 6014, Zip 58108; tel. 701/280-4100; D. D. Wightman, pres. **A**1a 2 3 5 9 10 **F**1 2 3 4 5 6 10 12 14 15 16 20 21 23 24 25 26 28 29 30 32 33 34 35 36 37 38 40 41 42 43 44 45 46 50 52 53 54	23	10	S		184	7974	147	79.9	19	655	34803	13717	711
NEUROSCIENCE HOSPITAL-MERITCARE, See St. Luke's Hospitals													
⊞ ST. JOHN'S HOSPITAL, 510 Fourth St. S., Zip 58103; tel. 701/232-3331; Mel Euetener, adm. **A**1a 2 9 10 **F**1 3 6 7 9 10 11 12 13 15 16 23 24 35 36 40 45 47 48 49 52 53; **S**1395	21	10	S		159	4331	95	53.1	22	579	13360	6975	327
⊞ ST. LUKE'S HOSPITALS (Includes Neuroscience Hospital-Meritcare; St. Luke's General Hospital-Meritcare, Children's Hospital-Meritcare), Fifth St. N. & Mills Ave., Zip 58122; tel.701/280-5000; Lloyd V. Smith, pres. **A**1a 2 3 5 6 9 10 **F**1 2 3 4 5 6 7 8 9 10 11 12 14 15 16 17 20 23 24 25 26 27 29 30 32 33 35 36 40 41 42 44 45 46 50 51 52 53 54	23	10	S		458	13965	288	62.9	16	1178	68189	31571	1382
⊞ VETERANS ADMINISTRATION CENTER, Elm St. & 21st Ave. N., Zip 58102; tel. 701/232-3241; David C. Engstrom MD, dir. (Total facility includes 50 beds in nursing home-type unit) **A**1a 2 3 5 **F**1 3 6 10 12 14 15 16 19 20 23 24 26 28 29 30 32 33 34 35 42 44 46 47 49 50 53	45	10	S	TF	217	4767	179	82.5	0	0	30004	13940	566
				H	167	4554	134	—	0	0	28043	12528	539
FORT YATES—Sioux County													
★ U. S. PUBLIC HEALTH SERVICE INDIAN HOSPITAL, Zip 58538; tel. 701/854-3831; James Cournoyer, serv. unit dir. **A**10 **F**12 14 15 16 28 34 35 37 40 41 49 52	47	10	S		32	993	9	28.1	7	80	2144	1261	80
GARRISON—McLean County													
★ GARRISON MEMORIAL HOSPITAL, Zip 58540; tel. 701/463-2275; Sr. Madonna Wagendorf, adm. (Total facility includes 24 beds in nursing home-type unit) **A**9 10 **F**1 6 10 16 19 23 35 40 45 46 52 53; **S**0545	21	10	S	TF	56	559	30	53.6	2	10	1420	847	67
				H	32	535	7	—	2	10	1232	681	56
GRAFTON—Walsh County													
⊞ UNITY HOSPITAL, 164 W. 13th St., Zip 58237; tel. 701/352-1620; Dan E. Will, adm. **A**1a 9 10 **F**1 3 6 15 16 21 23 35 36 40 41 45 53	23	10	S		27	860	13	48.1	5	148	2259	1138	58

★ American Hospital Association (AHA) membership
□ Joint Commission on Accreditation of Hospitals (JCAH) accreditation
+ American Osteopathic Hospital Association (AOHA) membership
○ American Osteopathic Association (AOA) accreditation
Δ Commission on Accreditation of Rehabilitation Facilities (CARF) accreditation
Control codes 61, 63, 64, 71, 72 and 73 indicate hospitals listed by AOHA, but not registered by AHA.
For definition of numerical codes, see page A2

Hospital, Address, Telephone, Administrator, Approval and Facility Codes, Multihospital System Code	Classification Codes				Inpatient Data				Newborn Data		Expense (thousands of dollars)		
	Control	Service	Stay	Facilities	Beds	Admissions	Census	Occupancy (percent)	Bassinets	Births	Total	Payroll	Personnel
GRAND FORKS—Grand Forks County													
★ Δ MEDICAL CENTER REHABILITATION HOSPITAL, 1300 S. Columbia Rd., Zip 58201; Mailing Address P O Box 8202, University Sta., Zip 58202; tel. 701/780-2311; Kenneth L. Koch, adm. **A**7 9 10 **F**15 16 23 24 26 33 42 44 45 46	12	46	S		88	838	43	48.9	0	0	9052	5362	314
⊞ UNITED HOSPITAL, 1200 S. Columbia Rd., Zip 58201; tel. 701/780-5000; Robert M. Jacobson, pres. **A**1a 2 3 5 9 10 **F**1 3 5 6 7 8 9 10 11 12 14 15 16 20 21 23 24 27 29 30 32 33 34 35 36 40 41 42 44 45 46 47 48 49 52 53 54; **S**9905	23	10	S		279	10138	175	62.5	24	1458	50248	23141	1012
★ UNITED RECOVERY CENTER, Medical Park, Zip 58206; Mailing Address Zip 58201; tel. 701/780-5900; Russ Warner, chief exec. off. (Nonreporting); **S**9905	23	82	S		38	—	—	—	—	—	—	—	—
GRAND FORKS AIR FORCE BASE—Grand Forks County													
U. S. AIR FORCE HOSPITAL, Grand Forks Sac, Zip 58205; tel. 701/594-6723; Gary J. Seitz, adm. **F**1 6 15 23 28 29 30 33 34 35 37 40 46 47	41	10	S		35	3053	24	68.6	13	465	—	—	266
HANKINSON—Richland County													
★ ST. GERARD'S COMMUNITY HOSPITAL, 613 First Ave. S.W., Zip 58041; tel. 701/242-7891; Gene Hoefs, adm. (Total facility includes 23 beds in nursing home-type unit) **A**9 10 **F**1 6 14 15 19 34 35 36 40 41 43 45 47 52; **S**5975	21	10	S	TF	54	257	28	51.9	4	12	1140	673	52
				H	31	247	5	—	4	12	695	428	38
HARVEY—Wells County													
★ ST. ALOISIUS MEDICAL CENTER (Formerly St. Aloisius Hospital), 325 E. Brewster St., Zip 58341; tel. 701/324-4651; Michael Pfeifer, pres. (Total facility includes 116 beds in nursing home-type unit) **A**9 10 **F**1 6 15 16 17 19 23 26 28 33 34 35 36 40 41 42 44 45 46 47 49 50 53 54; **S**5805	21	10	S	TF	165	969	135	81.8	6	78	4620	2323	159
				H	49	932	19	—	6	78	2735	1542	103
HAZEN—Mercer County													
★ HAZEN MEMORIAL HOSPITAL, P O Box 428, Zip 58545; tel. 701/748-2225; Clarence A. Lee, adm. **A**9 10 **F**1 3 6 15 16 23 34 35 36 37 40 43 45 46 50 52 53	23	10	S		37	979	13	35.1	6	46	2162	952	60
HETTINGER—Adams County													
⊞ COMMUNITY MEMORIAL HOSPITAL, Rte. 2, Box 124, Zip 58639; tel. 701/567-4561; James R. Hubbard, adm. **A**1a 9 10 **F**1 3 6 10 14 15 16 23 34 35 40 44 45 47 49 52 53	23	10	S		46	1913	24	52.2	6	252	4914	1836	113
HILLSBORO—Traill County													
★ COMMUNITY HOSPITAL, Zip 58045; tel. 701/436-4501; Bruce D. Bowersox, adm. **A**9 10 **F**21 34 35 45	23	10	S		24	261	8	33.3	5	18	586	342	23
JAMESTOWN—Stutsman County													
⊞ JAMESTOWN HOSPITAL, 419 Fifth St. N.E., Zip 58401; tel. 701/252-1050; Richard W. Hall, pres. **A**1a 9 10 **F**1 3 6 10 12 15 16 21 23 24 26 33 35 36 40 41 53	23	10	S		60	2413	28	33.7	12	415	6742	3592	166
⊞ NORTH DAKOTA STATE HOSPITAL, Box 476, Zip 58401; tel. 701/252-7733; Timothy Hunt, adm. **A**1b 3 9 10 **F**3 15 19 23 24 29 30 31 32 33 35 42 43 45 46 47 48 49 50	12	22	L		680	2805	509	74.4	0	0	21915	13719	755
KENMARE—Ward County													
★ KENMARE COMMUNITY HOSPITAL, 317 First Ave. N.W., P O Box 337, Zip 58746; tel. 701/385-4296; Daniel O. Olson, adm. (Total facility includes 12 beds in nursing home-type unit) **A**9 10 **F**1 6 19 23 35 36 40 45 52; **S**5395	21	10	S	TF	36	487	27	75.0	6	15	1170	598	39
				H	24	475	16	—	6	15	819	418	—
LANGDON—Cavalier County													
★ CAVALIER COUNTY MEMORIAL HOSPITAL, 909 Second St., Zip 58249; tel. 701/256-2731; Daryl J. Wilkens, adm. **A**9 10 **F**1 3 6 15 16 23 34 35 40 41 45 46 53	23	10	S		28	785	11	39.3	6	78	1416	738	45
LINTON—Emmons County													
★ LINTON HOSPITAL, 518 N. Broadway, Rural Rte. 1, Box 161-A, Zip 58552; tel. 701/254-4511; Larry E. Ellingson, adm. **A**9 10 **F**1 2 14 23 35 36 37 40 43 45 46 52	23	10	S		25	467	5	20.0	5	64	982	414	36
LISBON—Ransom County													
⊞ COMMUNITY MEMORIAL HOSPITAL, 905 Main St., Zip 58054; tel. 701/683-5241; Wendell Rawlings, adm. (Total facility includes 45 beds in nursing home-type unit) **A**1a 9 10 **F**1 3 6 14 15 16 19 23 34 35 37 40 41 42 44 45 46 53; **S**2235	23	10	S	TF	70	1212	60	85.7	7	46	3218	1518	101
				H	25	1175	16	—	7	46	2260	939	66
MANDAN—Morton County													
⊞ MANDAN HOSPITAL, 1000 18th St. N.W., Zip 58554; tel. 701/663-6471; David L. Brown, adm. **A**1a 2 9 10 **F**1 3 6 10 12 14 15 16 23 24 35 36 40 44 45 46 52 53; **S**6235	23	10	S		54	851	10	18.5	10	74	2940	1403	73
MAYVILLE—Traill County													
★ UNION HOSPITAL, 42 Sixth Ave. S.E., Zip 58257; tel. 701/786-3800; John Salness, adm. **A**9 10 **F**1 2 6 10 14 15 16 21 23 24 26 30 35 36 40 45 46 49 52 53	23	10	S		48	761	11	22.9	4	62	1869	1128	53
MCVILLE—Nelson County													
★ COMMUNITY HOSPITAL IN NELSON COUNTY, Zip 58254; tel. 701/322-4328; C. Gary Kopp, adm. **A**9 10 **F**14 15 35 41 45	23	10	S		19	408	8	42.1	0	0	811	358	29
MINOT—Ward County													
⊞ ST. JOSEPH'S HOSPITAL, Third St. & Burdick Expwy. S.E., Zip 58701; tel. 701/857-2000; Walter A. Strauch, pres. **A**1a 2 3 5 9 10 **F**1 3 6 7 8 9 10 12 14 15 16 21 23 24 27 30 32 33 34 35 36 40 42 44 45 46 47 48 49 52 53 54; **S**5395	21	10	S		177	5041	104	58.8	20	433	18945	8756	405
⊞ TRINITY MEDICAL CENTER, Burdick Expwy. at Main St., Zip 58701; tel. 701/857-5000; Terry G. Hoff, pres. (Total facility includes 373 beds in nursing home-type unit) **A**1a 3 5 6 9 10 **F**1 3 4 5 6 7 9 10 11 12 14 15 16 19 20 23 24 26 33 34 35 36 40 41 44 45 46 51 52 53 54	23	10	S	TF	565	6499	417	73.8	12	768	32949	15152	766
				H	192	6202	100	—	12	768	26415	11192	559
MINOT AIR FORCE BASE—Ward County													
□ U. S. AIR FORCE REGIONAL HOSPITAL, 12th St. & Ninth Ave. N.W., Zip 58701; tel. 701/857-4213; Maj. Robert D. Silver, adm. **A**1a **F**3 6 14 15 16 23 26 28 30 32 33 34 35 36 37 40 45 46 47	41	10	S		40	2815	29	72.5	17	533	5380	—	356
MOHALL—Renville County													
★ RENVILLE BOTTINEAU MEMORIAL HOSPITAL, Zip 58761; tel. 701/756-6312; Paul K. Longden, adm. **A**9 10 **F**1 6 14 15 23 24 35 40 45	23	10	S		26	264	5	19.2	8	11	610	360	30
NEW ROCKFORD—Eddy County													
⊞ CITY HOSPITAL, 214 Second Ave. S., Zip 58356; tel. 701/947-2411; Thomas J. O'Halloran, pres. & chief exec. off. (Nonreporting) **A**1a 9 10; **S**5175	21	10	S		26	—	—	—	—	—	—	—	—
NORTHWOOD—Grand Forks County													
★ NORTHWOOD DEACONESS HOSPITAL AND HOME ASSOCIATION, Zip 58267; tel. 701/587-6060; Larry E. Feickert, chief adm. off. (Total facility includes 128 beds in nursing home-type unit) **A**9 10 **F**1 2 14 15 16 19 23 24 26 34 35 36 41 42 45 50	21	10	S	TF	154	455	120	77.9	6	35	2954	1673	124
				H	26	401	13	—	6	35	1038	571	30
OAKES—Dickey County													
⊞ OAKES COMMUNITY HOSPITAL, 314 S. Eighth St., Zip 58474; tel. 701/742-3291; Sr. Mary Jane Reiber, adm. **A**1a 9 10 **F**1 6 14 16 23 26 36 41 45 52 53; **S**5975	21	10	S		32	888	14	43.8	4	31	1523	797	55
PARK RIVER—Walsh County													
★ ST. ANSGAR'S HOSPITAL, 715 Vivian St., Zip 58270; tel. 701/284-7233 (Nonreporting) **A**3 9 10; **S**5175	21	10	S		25	—	—	—	—	—	—	—	—
RICHARDTON—Stark County													
RICHARDTON COMMUNITY HOSPITAL, P O Box H, Zip 58652; tel. 701/974-3304; Anthony J. Kleinjan, adm. **A**9 10 **F**1 6 35 36 40 45 50 52	33	10	S		25	371	5	20.0	4	1	615	352	25

Hospital, Address, Telephone, Administrator, Approval and Facility Codes, Multihospital System Code	Classification Codes				Inpatient Data				Newborn Data		Expense (thousands of dollars)		
★ American Hospital Association (AHA) membership □ Joint Commission on Accreditation of Hospitals (JCAH) accreditation + American Osteopathic Hospital Association (AOHA) membership ○ American Osteopathic Association (AOA) accreditation Δ Commission on Accreditation of Rehabilitation Facilities (CARF) accreditation Control codes 61, 63, 64, 71, 72 and 73 indicate hospitals listed by AOHA, but not registered by AHA. For definition of numerical codes, see page A2	Control	Service	Stay	Facilities	Beds	Admissions	Census	Occupancy (percent)	Bassinets	Births	Total	Payroll	Personnel
ROLETTE—Rolette County													
★ ROLETTE COMMUNITY HOSPITAL, Box 218, Zip 58366; tel. 701/246-3391; Terry L. Goehring, adm. (Nonreporting) **A**9 10	23	10	S		49	—	—	—	—	—	—	—	—
ROLLA—Rolette County													
★□ ROLLA COMMUNITY HOSPITAL, 213 Third St. N.E., P O Box 759, Zip 58367; tel. 701/477-3161; Michael A. Baumgartner, pres. & chief exec. off. (Total facility includes 37 beds in nursing home-type unit) **A**1a 9 10 **F**1 6 14 15 16 17 19 23 34 35 36 40 41 45 50 52 53; **S**5805	21	10	S	TF	96	1245	53	55.2	6	127	3813	1924	128
				H	59	1229	16	—	6	127	—	—	104
RUGBY—Pierce County													
★□ GOOD SAMARITAN HOSPITAL ASSOCIATION, Rugby Hts., Zip 58368; tel. 701/776-5261; Charles K. Schulz, exec. dir. (Total facility includes 184 beds in nursing home-type unit) **A**1a 2 9 10 **F**1 3 6 10 15 16 19 23 24 26 34 35 36 37 41 42 43 44 45 46 47 49 50 53	23	10	S	TF	233	1410	213	91.4	8	121	6598	3465	225
				H	49	1289	33	—	8	121	—	—	203
STANLEY—Mountrail County													
★ STANLEY COMMUNITY HOSPITAL, 502 Third St. S.E., Box 399, Zip 58784; tel. 701/628-2424; Charles Kramer, adm. **A**9 10 **F**1 3 14 15 23 35 36 40 41 52	23	10	S		28	839	10	35.7	6	92	998	549	40
TIOGA—Williams County													
★ TIOGA COMMUNITY HOSPITAL, 810 N. Welo St., Box 597, Zip 58852; tel. 701/664-3306; Lowell D. Herfindahl, adm. **A**9 10 **F**1 3 6 14 15 16 23 35 37 40 41 43 45 46 47 52	23	10	S		29	954	10	34.5	5	23	1603	908	61
TURTLE LAKE—McLean County													
COMMUNITY MEMORIAL HOSPITAL, Zip 58575; tel. 701/448-2331; Michael G. Didier, adm. **A**9 10 **F**1 6 10 15 16 23 34 35 45 50 52	23	10	S		35	270	6	17.1	6	0	776	375	16
VALLEY CITY—Barnes County													
★□ MERCY HOSPITAL, 570 Chautauqua Blvd., Zip 58072; tel. 701/845-0440; Ray Weisgarber, pres. & chief exec. off. **A**1a 9 10 **F**1 3 6 10 12 14 15 16 23 26 33 34 35 36 40 41 44 45 46 50 53; **S**5175	21	10	S		40	1707	21	52.5	15	187	3823	2176	111
WATFORD CITY—McKenzie County													
★ MCKENZIE COUNTY MEMORIAL HOSPITAL, 508 N. Main St., Zip 58854; tel. 701/842-2361; Larry Sievers, adm. **A**9 10 **F**1 14 17 35 40 45	23	10	S		26	743	9	34.6	7	79	1210	529	33
WILLISTON—Williams County													
★□ MERCY MEDICAL CENTER AND HOSPITAL (Formerly Mercy Hospital), 1301 15th Ave. W., Zip 58801; tel. 701/774-7400; Robert A. Fale, actg. pres. **A**1a 2 9 10 **F**1 2 6 10 12 14 15 16 23 24 26 30 32 34 35 36 40 41 43 44 45 46 48 49 50 52 53; **S**5175	21	10	S		84	4354	56	57.7	20	669	15650	6646	256
WISHEK—McIntosh County													
★ WISHEK COMMUNITY HOSPITAL, 315 Tenth St. S., P O Box 647, Zip 58495; tel. 701/452-2326; Roger L. Salisbury, adm. **A**9 10 **F**1 2 6 15 17 34 35 40 45 46 53; **S**2235	23	10	S		31	934	10	32.3	6	22	1548	728	47

Hospital, Address, Telephone, Administrator, Approval and Facility Codes, Multihospital System Code	Classification Codes: Control	Service	Stay	Facilities	Inpatient Data: Beds	Admissions	Census	Occupancy (percent)	Newborn Data: Bassinets	Births	Expense (thousands of dollars): Total	Payroll	Personnel
★ American Hospital Association (AHA) membership ☐ Joint Commission on Accreditation of Hospitals (JCAH) accreditation + American Osteopathic Hospital Association (AOHA) membership ○ American Osteopathic Association (AOA) accreditation Δ Commission on Accreditation of Rehabilitation Facilities (CARF) accreditation Control codes 61, 63, 64, 71, 72 and 73 indicate hospitals listed by AOHA, but not registered by AHA. For definition of numerical codes, see page A2													

Ohio

Hospital	Control	Service	Stay	Facilities	Beds	Admissions	Census	Occupancy (percent)	Bassinets	Births	Total	Payroll	Personnel
AKRON—Summit County													
★☐ AKRON CITY HOSPITAL, 525 E. Market St., Zip 44309; tel. 216/375-3000; Albert F. Gilbert PhD, pres. **A**1a 2 3 5 6 8 9 10 **F**1 2 3 4 5 6 7 8 9 10 11 12 13 14 15 16 20 23 24 25 27 34 35 36 37 40 42 44 45 46 53 54	23	10	S		513	23516	417	83.1	50	3503	118910	45259	2293
★☐ AKRON GENERAL MEDICAL CENTER, 400 Wabash Ave., Zip 44307; tel. 216/384-6000; Michael A. West, pres. **A**1a 2 3 5 8 9 10 **F**1 2 3 4 5 6 7 8 9 10 11 12 14 15 16 23 24 26 27 28 30 32 33 34 35 36 37 38 40 42 44 45 46 47 50 52 53 54	23	10	S		394	16588	312	77.2	30	1910	83635	37551	1550
★☐ CHILDREN'S HOSPITAL MEDICAL CENTER OF AKRON, 281 Locust St., Zip 44308; tel. 216/379-8200; William H. Considine, pres. **A**1a 3 5 8 9 10 **F**1 5 6 10 12 13 14 15 16 20 22 23 24 26 27 28 30 32 33 34 35 38 41 42 44 45 46 47 51 53 54	23	50	S		253	9563	166	65.6	0	0	52907	27764	1237
★☐ Δ EDWIN SHAW HOSPITAL, 1621 Flickinger Rd., Zip 44312; tel. 216/784-1271; Daniel K. Church, exec. dir. (Total facility includes 38 beds in nursing home-type unit) **A**1a 7 9 10 **F**15 19 23 24 26 33 34 42 44 45 46 48 49 50	13	46	S	TF	154	1752	114	74.0	0	0	11781	6340	363
				H	116	1661	78	—	0	0	9602	5167	328
★☐ SAINT THOMAS MEDICAL CENTER (Formerly St. Thomas Hospital Medical Center), 444 N. Main St., Zip 44310; tel. 216/379-1111; Margaret Anne Brosnan, pres. **A**1a 2 3 5 6 8 9 10 **F**1 2 3 5 6 9 10 11 12 14 15 16 20 23 24 26 27 28 30 32 33 34 35 36 40 41 44 45 46 47 48 49 50 53 54	23	10	S		388	11662	233	61.8	33	1207	45884	20098	1135
ALLIANCE—Stark County													
☐ ALLIANCE COMMUNITY HOSPITAL (Formerly Alliance City Hospital), 264 E. Rice St., Zip 44601; tel. 216/821-1000; Melvin P. Pucci, adm. & chief exec. off. **A**1a 9 10 **F**1 3 6 9 10 12 14 15 16 23 24 30 33 35 40 44 45 46 52	23	10	S		178	6912	94	52.8	18	723	19355	9861	546
AMHERST—Lorain County													
★☐ AMHERST HOSPITAL, 254 Cleveland Ave., Zip 44001; tel. 216/988-2831; J. A. Lewandowski, exec. dir. **A**1a 9 10 **F**1 3 6 12 14 15 16 35 36 40 44 45 46; **S**2495	23	10	S		70	1965	25	35.7	13	252	7408	3463	186
ASHLAND—Ashland County													
★☐ SAMARITAN HOSPITAL, 1025 Center St., Zip 44805; tel. 419/289-0491; William C. Kelley Jr., pres. **A**1a 9 10 **F**1 3 5 6 10 12 14 15 16 17 23 34 35 36 40 41 45 46 52 53	23	10	S		96	3630	41	41.4	13	562	10867	4634	246
ASHTABULA—Ashtabula County													
★☐ ASHTABULA COUNTY MEDICAL CENTER, 2420 Lake Ave., Zip 44004; tel. 216/998-3111; Floyd E. Farley, pres. & chief exec. off. **A**1a 9 10 **F**1 3 6 10 12 14 15 16 20 23 26 27 28 30 32 33 34 35 36 40 44 45 46 47 52 53	23	10	S		246	7470	106	44.0	20	638	20028	11061	520
ATHENS—Athens County													
ATHENS MENTAL HEALTH CENTER, Zip 45701; tel. 614/592-3031; Francine Middelman, med. dir. (Nonreporting) **A**9 10	12	22	L		241	—	—	—	—	—	—	—	—
★☐ ○ O'BLENESS MEMORIAL HOSPITAL, Hospital Dr., Zip 45701; tel. 614/593-5551; Richard F. Castrop, exec. dir. **A**1a 9 10 11 **F**1 3 6 10 12 14 15 16 23 33 34 35 36 40 45 46 53	23	10	S		101	4102	54	53.5	18	744	10586	5295	289
BARBERTON—Summit County													
★☐ BARBERTON CITIZENS HOSPITAL, 155 Fifth St. N.E., Tuscora Park, Zip 44203; tel. 216/745-1611; Mike Bernatovicz, pres. (Total facility includes 46 beds in nursing home-type unit) **A**1a 2 3 5 9 10 **F**1 2 3 5 6 9 10 11 12 14 15 16 19 23 24 25 26 27 30 32 33 34 35 36 40 42 44 45 46 52 53	23	10	S	TF	373	10689	183	54.3	31	840	39285	21431	940
				H	327	10635	180	—	31	840	39194	21357	917
BARNESVILLE—Belmont County													
★ BARNESVILLE HOSPITAL ASSOCIATION, 639 W. Main St., Zip 43713; tel. 614/425-3941; Albert R. Hanna, interim adm. (Nonreporting) **A**9 10; **S**8865	23	10	S		99	—	—	—	—	—	—	—	—
BATAVIA—Clermont County													
★☐ CLERMONT MERCY HOSPITAL, 3000 Hospital Dr., Zip 45103; tel. 513/732-8200; Sr. Mary George RN, pres. **A**1a 9 10 **F**1 3 6 8 10 12 14 15 16 23 24 26 27 30 32 33 34 35 42 44 45 46 47 52 53; **S**5155	21	10	S		133	5486	102	76.7	0	0	23513	10067	431
BEDFORD—Cuyahoga County													
★☐ COMMUNITY HOSPITAL OF BEDFORD, 44 Blaine St., Zip 44146; tel. 216/439-2000; William E. Polack, exec. dir. **A**1a 10 **F**1 3 6 10 12 14 16 23 24 30 33 34 35 36 37 40 44 45 46 47 48 49	23	10	S		110	3967	62	56.4	12	434	16321	7045	330
BELLAIRE—Belmont County													
★☐ CITY HOSPITAL, 4697 Harrison St., Box A, Zip 43906; tel. 614/671-1200; Lawrence R. England, dir. **A**1a 9 10 **F**1 3 6 12 14 15 16 23 27 30 32 33 34 35 36 40 45 46 47 50 53	23	10	S		83	2948	45	54.2	14	265	10154	4856	251
BELLEFONTAINE—Logan County													
★☐ MARY RUTAN HOSPITAL, 205 Palmer Ave., Zip 43311; tel. 513/592-4015; Ewing H. Crawfis, pres. **A**1a 9 10 **F**1 3 6 10 12 14 15 16 23 26 34 35 36 37 40 41 44 45 46 47 52 53	23	10	S		105	3797	48	45.7	15	533	12712	4744	308
BELLEVUE—Sandusky County													
☐ BELLEVUE HOSPITAL, 811 Northwest St., Box 309, Zip 44811; tel. 419/483-4040; Martin F. Goetze, pres. (Nonreporting) **A**1a 9 10	23	10	S		47	—	—	—	—	—	—	—	—
BLUFFTON—Allen County													
★ BLUFFTON COMMUNITY HOSPITAL, 139 Garau St., Zip 45817; tel. 419/358-9010; Clifford K. Harmon, adm. **A**9 10 **F**1 3 6 14 16 23 35 40 45 46 47	23	10	S		42	1336	16	38.1	14	335	3172	1693	94
BOWLING GREEN—Wood County													
★☐ WOOD COUNTY HOSPITAL, 950 W. Wooster St., Zip 43402; tel. 419/352-6571; William E. Culbertson, adm. **A**1a 9 10 **F**1 3 6 10 12 14 16 23 33 34 35 36 40 44 45 46 52 53	23	10	S		125	6160	82	62.1	19	689	13694	6743	323
BRYAN—Williams County													
BRYAN COMMUNITY HOSPITAL, See Community Hospitals of Williams County													
☐ COMMUNITY HOSPITAL OF WILLIAMS COUNTY (Includes Bryan Community Hospital, 433 W. High St., Zip 43506; tel. 419/636-1131; Williams County General Hospital, Snyder & Lincoln Ave., Montpelier, Zip 43543; tel. 419/485-3154), 433 W. High St., Zip 43506; tel. 419/485-3154; Rusty O. Brunicardi, pres. (Data not available) **A**1a 9 10 **F**1 3 6 10 12 14 15 16 23 24 26 30 33 35 36 49 50 52 53	23	10	S		115	—	—	—	—	—	—	—	—
BUCYRUS—Crawford County													
★☐ BUCYRUS COMMUNITY HOSPITAL, 629 N. Sandusky St., Box 627, Zip 44820; tel. 419/562-4677; Robert A. Bowers, adm. **A**1a 9 10 **F**1 3 6 10 14 16 23 34 35 36 40 44 45 46 53	23	10	S		72	1846	22	30.6	12	239	5581	2723	149
CADIZ—Harrison County													
★☐ HARRISON COMMUNITY HOSPITAL, 951 E. Market St., Zip 43907; tel. 614/942-4631; Gary D. Tipton, chief exec. off. (Nonreporting) **A**1a 9 10	23	10	S		48	—	—	—	—	—	—	—	—

★ American Hospital Association (AHA) membership
□ Joint Commission on Accreditation of Hospitals (JCAH) accreditation
+ American Osteopathic Hospital Association (AOHA) membership
○ American Osteopathic Association (AOA) accreditation
Δ Commission on Accreditation of Rehabilitation Facilities (CARF) accreditation
Control codes 61, 63, 64, 71, 72 and 73 indicate hospitals listed by AOHA, but not registered by AHA.
For definition of numerical codes, see page A2

Hospital, Address, Telephone, Administrator, Approval and Facility Codes, Multihospital System Code	Classification Codes				Inpatient Data				Newborn Data		Expense (thousands of dollars)		
	Control	Service	Stay	Facilities	Beds	Admissions	Census	Occupancy (percent)	Bassinets	Births	Total	Payroll	Personnel
CAMBRIDGE—Guernsey County													
□ CAMBRIDGE MENTAL HEALTH AND DEVELOPMENTAL CENTER, County Rd. 35 N., Zip 43725; tel. 614/439-1371; Prabha R. Tripathi MD, med. dir. **A**1b 9 10 **F**23 24 30 32 33 42 44 45 46 47	12	22	L		410	711	353	86.1	0	0	17823	14822	557
★□ GUERNSEY MEMORIAL HOSPITAL, 1341 N. Clark St., P O Box 610, Zip 43725; tel. 614/439-3561; H. Dale Gotschall, pres. & chief exec. off. **A**1a 9 10 **F**1 3 6 10 12 14 15 16 23 34 35 36 40 45 46 53	23	10	S		202	6866	122	60.4	19	583	20356	8762	461
CANTON—Stark County													
★□ AULTMAN HOSPITAL, 2600 Sixth St. S.W., Zip 44710; tel. 216/452-9911; Richard J. Pryce, pres. **A**1a 3 5 6 8 9 10 **F**1 2 3 4 5 6 7 8 9 10 11 12 14 15 16 20 21 23 24 26 27 28 30 32 33 34 35 36 37 38 40 41 44 45 46 47 51 52 53 54	23	10	S		604	24850	473	78.3	68	2861	94857	40030	2186
★□ TIMKEN MERCY MEDICAL CENTER, 1320 Timken Mercy Dr. N.W., Zip 44708; tel. 216/489-1000; Mark A. Nadel, pres. & chief exec. off. **A**1a 2 3 5 9 10 **F**1 2 3 5 6 7 8 9 10 11 12 14 15 16 20 21 23 24 25 26 27 30 32 33 34 35 36 40 41 42 44 45 46 47 51 52 53 54; **S**5125	21	10	S		555	17378	348	62.7	39	1445	69137	36014	1821
CHAGRIN FALLS—Cuyahoga County													
★ WINDSOR HOSPITAL, 115 E. Summit St., Zip 44022; tel. 216/247-5300; Edward A. Graves, adm. (Nonreporting) **A** 9 10	23	22	S		71	—	—	—	—	—	—	—	—
CHARDON—Geauga County													
★□ GEAUGA HOSPITAL (Formerly Geauga Community Hospital), 13207 Ravenna Rd., Box 249, Zip 44024; tel. 216/286-6131; Paul C. Jacobs, pres. **A**1a 2 9 10 **F**1 3 6 10 12 14 15 16 23 24 34 35 36 40 44 45 46 47 48 53	23	10	S		108	4739	72	66.7	20	526	19630	8950	401
CHILLICOTHE—Ross County													
★□ MEDICAL CENTER HOSPITAL, 272 Hospital Rd., Zip 45601; tel. 614/772-7500; Miles L. Waggoner, pres. **A**1a 9 10 **F**1 3 6 8 10 12 14 15 16 21 23 27 30 33 35 36 40 41 44 46 52 53	23	10	S		245	8084	125	51.0	35	1057	26033	12259	593
★□ VETERANS ADMINISTRATION MEDICAL CENTER, 17273 State Rte. 104, Zip 45601; tel. 614/773-1141; Troy E. Page, dir. (Total facility includes 90 beds in nursing home-type unit) **A**1a **F**1 3 6 12 14 15 16 19 20 23 24 26 28 30 31 33 34 35 42 44 46 47 48 49 50	45	22	L	TF	927	6054	646	68.9	0	0	49207	31742	1361
				H	837	5927	568	—	0	0	45639	29177	1243
CINCINNATI—Hamilton County													
★ BETHESDA NORTH HOSPITAL, 10500 Montgomery Rd., Zip 45242; tel. 513/745-1111 **A**9 **F**1 3 6 9 10 11 12 14 15 16 20 21 23 24 26 34 35 43 44 45 46 47 53; **S**0415	21	10	S		287	13397	233	81.2	0	0	52655	23830	914
★□ Δ BETHESDA OAK HOSPITAL, 619 Oak St., Zip 45206; tel. 513/569-6111; Larry W. Collins, group vice-pres. **A**1a 2 3 5 6 7 9 10 **F**1 3 6 7 8 9 10 11 12 14 15 16 20 21 23 24 25 26 27 28 31 32 33 34 35 36 37 38 39 40 41 42 43 44 45 46 47 48 49 53 54; **S**0415	21	10	S		519	17971	317	61.1	76	4738	69826	33263	1900
□ CAREUNIT HOSPITAL OF CINCINNATI, 3156 Glenmore Ave., Zip 45211; tel. 513/481-8822; Larry J. Burge, adm. (Nonreporting) **A**1b ; **S**0275	32	82	S		84	—	—	—	—	—	—	—	—
CHILDREN'S HOSPITAL AND CONVALESCENT HOSPITAL FOR CHILDREN, See Children's Hospital Medical Center													
★□ CHILDREN'S HOSPITAL MEDICAL CENTER (Includes Adolescent Clinic, Children Dental Care Foundation, Children's Hospital Research Foundation, Cincinnati Center for Developmental Disorders, United Cerebral Palsy Childrens Division) (Includes Children's Hospital and Convalescent Hospital for Children, Elland & Bethesda Aves., Zip 45229; tel. 513/559-4200), Elland & Bethesda Aves., Zip 45229; tel. 513/559-4200; William K. Schubert, pres. **A**1a 2 3 5 8 9 10 **F**1 4 6 10 11 12 13 15 16 19 20 23 24 26 27 28 30 32 33 34 35 38 42 44 45 46 47 51 53 54	23	50	S		330	14292	230	69.7	0	0	84933	—	1547
★□ CHRIST HOSPITAL, 2139 Auburn Ave., Zip 45219; tel. 513/369-2000; Jack M. Cook, pres. **A**1a 2 3 5 6 8 9 10 **F**1 3 4 6 7 8 9 10 11 12 13 14 16 20 23 24 27 30 34 35 36 40 42 44 45 46 47 48 53 54	23	10	S		660	24152	485	73.5	66	4682	108300	52664	2338
CHRISTIAN R. HOLMES DIVISION, See University of Cincinnati Hospital													
★□ Δ DANIEL DRAKE MEMORIAL HOSPITAL, 151 W. Galbraith Rd., Zip 45216; tel. 513/761-3440; J. C. Taylor, chief exec. off. (Total facility includes 244 beds in nursing home-type unit) **A**1a 7 9 10 **F**12 16 19 23 24 26 32 33 34 42 44 45 46	13	46	L	TF	347	529	337	94.7	0	0	25713	15651	747
				H	103	208	104	—	0	0	7945	4836	241
★□ DEACONESS HOSPITAL, 311 Straight St., Zip 45219; tel. 513/559-2100; E. Anthony Woods, pres. **A**1a 6 9 10 **F**1 2 3 4 6 9 10 12 15 16 20 23 24 26 34 35 41 44 45 46 50 53 54	23	10	S		276	8817	163	59.1	0	0	42926	18727	846
★□ EMERSON A. NORTH HOSPITAL, 5642 Hamilton Ave., Zip 45224; tel. 513/541-0135; Stephen R. Halley, asst. adm. (Nonreporting) **A**1b 10; **S**6525	33	82	S		112	—	—	—	—	—	—	—	—
★□ GOOD SAMARITAN HOSPITAL, 3217 Clifton Ave., Zip 45220; tel. 513/872-1400; Roger W. Weseli, pres. (Total facility includes 132 beds in nursing home-type unit) **A**1a 2 3 5 6 8 9 10 **F**1 2 3 4 5 6 7 8 9 10 11 12 14 15 16 19 20 23 24 25 26 27 30 32 34 35 36 40 41 42 44 45 46 47 51 52 53 54; **S**5115	21	10	S	TF	719	23957	572	76.9	72	4991	126736	54599	2409
				H	587	23834	456	—	72	4991	123739	53001	2296
★□ JEWISH HOSPITAL OF CINCINNATI, 3200 Burnet Ave., Zip 45229; tel. 513/569-2000; Warren C. Falberg, pres. **A**1a 2 3 5 6 9 10 **F**1 2 3 4 6 7 8 9 10 11 12 14 15 16 20 23 24 25 26 27 28 29 30 32 33 34 35 36 37 40 42 43 44 45 46 50 53 54	23	10	S		607	18205	367	60.5	60	1273	95295	41372	1779
★ ○ + OTTO C. EPP MEMORIAL HOSPITAL, 8000 Kenwood Rd., Zip 45236; tel. 513/745-2200; James H. Moss, pres. (Nonreporting) **A**9 10 11	23	10	S		80	—	—	—	—	—	—	—	—
★□ OUR LADY OF MERCY HOSPITAL, Rowan Hills Dr., Zip 45227; tel. 513/527-5500; Sr. Marjorie Bosse, pres. **A**1a 9 10 **F**1 3 6 9 10 12 14 15 16 23 24 34 35 36 40 44 45 46 47 53; **S**5155	21	10	S		198	9124	138	69.7	33	1284	39944	17553	806
□ PAULINE WARFIELD LEWIS CENTER, 1101 Summit Rd., Zip 45237; tel. 513/948-3600; Raymond T. Gonzalez, supt. **A**1b 10 **F**15 16 23 24 32 33 42 44 45 46 47 50	12	22	L		401	289	370	92.3	0	0	—	—	524
□ PROVIDENCE HOSPITAL, 2446 Kipling Ave., Zip 45239; tel. 513/853-5000; Earl R. Gilreath, pres. **A**1a 3 5 9 10 **F**1 2 3 6 9 10 11 12 14 15 16 23 24 25 26 34 35 41 44 45 46 47 53; **S**1485	21	10	S		372	11884	215	57.8	0	0	51640	24771	1125
□ ROLLMAN PSYCHIATRIC INSTITUTE, 3009 Burnet Ave., Zip 45219; tel. 513/559-3357; Paul A. Guggenheim, supt. **A**1b 10 **F**15 24 32 33 42 45 46 47	12	22	S		146	2031	143	97.9	0	0	6715	6314	215
★□ SHRINERS BURNS INSTITUTE (Formerly Shriners Hospital for Crippled Children, Shriners Burns Institute, Cincinnati Unit), 202 Goodman St., Zip 45219; tel. 513/751-3900; Ronald R. Hitzler, adm. **A**1a **F**13 16 22 23 24 34 42 46; **S**4125	23	59	S		30	716	18	60.0	0	0	—	—	230
★□ ST. FRANCIS-ST. GEORGE HOSPITAL, 3131 Queen City Ave., Zip 45238; tel. 513/389-5000; William M. Copeland, pres. **A**1a 2 9 10 **F**1 3 6 9 10 11 12 14 15 16 23 24 26 34 35 44 45 46 47 53; **S**1485	21	10	S		290	10831	216	74.5	0	0	51867	22476	982
UNIVERSITY HOSPITAL, See University of Cincinnati Hospital													
★□ UNIVERSITY OF CINCINNATI HOSPITAL (Includes Christian R. Holmes Division, Eden & Bethesda Aves., Zip 45219; tel. 513/872-7611; University Hospital, 234 Goodman St., Zip 45267; tel. 513/872-3100), Carl H. Iseman, adm. **A**1a 2 3 5 8 9 10 **F**1 3 4 5 6 7 8 9 10 11 12 13 14 15 16 17 20 22 23 24 26 27 28 30 32 33 34 35 36 37 38 40 42 44 45 46 47 49 50 51 53 54	12	10	S		659	24632	511	77.5	45	3121	171965	—	3104

Hospital, Address, Telephone, Administrator, Approval and Facility Codes, Multihospital System Code	Classification Codes: Control	Service	Stay	Facilities	Inpatient Data: Beds	Admissions	Census	Occupancy (percent)	Newborn Data: Bassinets	Births	Expense (thousands of dollars): Total	Payroll	Personnel
★ American Hospital Association (AHA) membership □ Joint Commission on Accreditation of Hospitals (JCAH) accreditation + American Osteopathic Hospital Association (AOHA) membership ○ American Osteopathic Association (AOA) accreditation Δ Commission on Accreditation of Rehabilitation Facilities (CARF) accreditation Control codes 61, 63, 64, 71, 72 and 73 indicate hospitals listed by AOHA, but not registered by AHA. For definition of numerical codes, see page A2													
⊞ VETERANS ADMINISTRATION MEDICAL CENTER, 3200 Vine St., Zip 45220; tel. 513/861-3100; Donald L. Ziegenhorn, dir. (Total facility includes 206 beds in nursing home-type unit) **A**1a 3 5 8 **F**1 3 6 9 10 12 14 15 16 17 19 20 23 24 26 27 28 30 32 33 34 35 42 44 46 47 48 49 53 54	45	10	S	TF	560	11207	424	75.7	0	0	63187	36361	1193
				H	354	11064	237	—	0	0	52800	28398	1039
CIRCLEVILLE—Pickaway County													
□ BERGER HOSPITAL, 600 N. Pickaway St., Zip 43113; tel. 614/474-2126; Charles D. Rideout, adm. (Nonreporting) **A**1a 9 10	15	10	S		73	—	—	—	—	—	—	—	—
CLEVELAND—Cuyahoga County													
BOLWELL HEALTH CENTER, See University Hospitals of Cleveland													
⊞ CLEVELAND CLINIC HOSPITAL, 9500 Euclid Ave., Zip 44106; tel. 216/444-2320; James E. Lees, dir. oper. **A**1a 2 3 5 8 9 10 **F**1 2 3 4 6 7 8 9 10 11 12 13 14 15 16 17 20 23 24 26 27 28 29 32 33 34 35 37 38 42 44 48 49 50 52 53 54	23	10	S		1031	32291	757	73.4	0	0	—	—	4964
□ CLEVELAND PSYCHIATRIC INSTITUTE, 1708 Aiken Ave., Zip 44109; tel. 216/661-6200; Ella Thomas, supt. **A**1b 3 9 10 **F**24 32 33 42 45 46 47	12	22	S		226	3354	241	100.0	0	0	12700	7722	404
⊞ Δ CUYAHOGA COUNTY HOSPITALS (Includes Cleveland Metropolitan General Hospital; Highland View Hospital), 3395 Scranton Rd., Zip 44109; tel. 216/398-6000; Henry E. Manning, pres. (Total facility includes 320 beds in nursing home-type unit) **A**1a 3 5 6 7 8 9 10 **F**1 2 3 4 5 6 7 8 9 10 11 12 14 15 16 19 20 22 23 24 25 26 27 28 30 32 33 34 35 36 37 38 40 42 44 45 46 47 49 50 51 52 53 54	13	10	S	TF	1041	20426	825	79.3	48	3537	184729	111320	4726
				H	721	20041	513	—	48	3537	166753	100191	4186
⊞ DEACONESS HOSPITAL OF CLEVELAND, 4229 Pearl Rd., Zip 44109; tel. 216/459-6300; W. Allen Intihar, pres. **A**1a 2 9 10 **F**1 2 3 6 10 12 14 15 16 20 23 24 27 32 33 35 36 40 41 42 44 45 46 47 54	23	10	S		316	9759	221	69.9	27	929	44711	20949	958
⊞ FAIRVIEW GENERAL HOSPITAL, 18101 Lorain Ave., Zip 44111; tel. 216/476-7000; Thomas Lamotte, pres. **A**1a 3 5 6 9 10 **F**1 2 3 4 6 10 12 14 15 16 20 23 24 25 26 27 28 30 34 35 36 37 40 41 42 44 45 46 47 50 51 52 53 54	23	10	S		475	18708	329	69.3	66	3225	72478	37502	1790
⊞ GLENBEIGH HOSPITAL-CLEVELAND, 18120 Puritas Ave., Zip 44135; tel. 216/476-0222; Theodore R. Sucher III, exec. dir. **A**1b **F**15 32 33 34 42 43 46 47 49; **S**0645	33	82	S		100	815	57	57.0	0	0	—	—	170
⊞ GRACE HOSPITAL, 2307 W. 14th St., Zip 44113; tel. 216/687-1500; Ed Baginski, adm. **A**1a 9 10 **F**1 3 6 10 12 14 16 23 35 41 44 45 46 47 52	23	10	S		87	1800	29	33.3	0	0	7883	4106	189
HANNA HOUSE, See University Hospitals of Cleveland													
HANNA PAVILION, See University Hospitals of Cleveland													
⊞ HEALTH HILL HOSPITAL FOR CHILDREN, 2801 Martin Luther King Jr Dr., Zip 44104; tel. 216/721-5400; Thomas A. Rathbone, exec. dir. (Nonreporting) **A**1a 9 10	23	56	L		52	—	—	—	—	—	—	—	—
HUMPHREY BUILDING, See University Hospitals of Cleveland													
⊞ HURON ROAD HOSPITAL, 13951 Terrace Rd., Zip 44112; tel. 216/761-3300; Sandra H. Austin, sr. vice-pres. & chief oper. off. **A**1a 2 3 5 6 10 **F**1 2 3 4 6 10 12 14 15 16 20 23 24 26 27 28 29 30 32 33 34 35 41 42 44 45 46 47 48 49 50 53 54; **S**8835	23	10	S		387	8889	212	54.8	0	0	47931	23739	1195
LAKESIDE HOSPITAL, See University Hospitals of Cleveland													
⊞ LUTHERAN MEDICAL CENTER, 2609 Franklin Blvd., Zip 44113; tel. 216/696-4300; Robert A. Wiltsie MD, pres. **A**1a 2 3 5 9 10 **F**1 2 3 6 7 8 9 10 11 12 14 15 16 17 19 20 21 23 24 26 27 28 32 33 34 35 37 42 43 44 45 46 53 54	21	10	S		202	4936	114	56.4	0	0	36123	15386	614
MACDONALD HOSITAL FOR WOMEN, See University Hospitals of Cleveland													
⊞ MT. SINAI MEDICAL CENTER, One Mtx Sinai Dr., Zip 44106; tel. 216/421-4000; Robert J. Shakno, pres. & chief exec. off. **A**1a 3 5 8 9 10 **F**1 2 3 4 5 6 7 8 9 10 11 12 14 15 16 17 20 23 24 26 27 28 32 33 34 35 36 37 38 40 41 44 45 46 47 50 52 53 54	23	10	S		450	15944	307	68.2	32	1506	106955	47222	1785
RAINBOW BABIES AND CHILDREN'S HOSPITAL, See University Hospitals of Cleveland													
★ ○ RICHMOND HEIGHTS GENERAL HOSPITAL, 27100 Chardon Rd., Zip 44143; tel. 216/585-6500; Nicholas W. Zinni, pres. & chief exec. off. **A**10 11 12 13 **F**1 2 3 6 10 12 14 15 16 23 30 32 33 34 35 44 45 46 47 50 52 53	23	10	S		138	4492	84	60.9	0	0	24818	9776	500
⊞ SAINT LUKE'S HOSPITAL, 11311 Shaker Blvd., Zip 44104; tel. 216/368-7000; P. David Youngdahl, pres. (Nonreporting) **A**1a 3 5 8 9 10	23	10	S		375	—	—	—	—	—	—	—	—
⊞ SALVATION ARMY BOOTH MEMORIAL HOSPITAL, 1881 Torbenson Dr., Zip 44112; tel. 216/692-3500; Maj. Carol A. Bryant, adm. **A**1a 10 **F**1 6 12 14 16 23 34 36 37 40 45 46 47	21	10	S		62	1512	15	24.2	32	876	6626	2794	161
⊞ ST. ALEXIS HOSPITAL, 5163 Broadway, Zip 44127; tel. 216/429-8000; Larry K. Lehner, pres. & chief exec. off. (Total facility includes 20 beds in nursing home-type unit) **A**1a 2 9 10 **F**1 2 3 5 6 10 11 12 14 16 19 20 23 24 28 32 34 35 36 40 44 45 46 53; **S**5345	21	10	S	TF	201	6922	133	66.2	18	434	31028	16064	788
				H	181	6851	127	—	18	434	30841	15899	765
⊞ ST. JOHN HOSPITAL, 7911 Detroit Ave., Zip 44102; tel. 216/651-7000; Sr. Judith Ann Karam, pres. **A**1a 3 9 10 **F**1 2 3 6 8 10 11 12 15 16 20 23 24 26 27 28 30 32 33 34 35 41 42 44 45 46 50 52 53; **S**5125	21	10	S		225	4855	134	59.6	0	0	31732	14603	641
⊞ ST. VINCENT CHARITY HOSPITAL AND HEALTH CENTER, 2351 E. 22nd St., Zip 44115; tel. 216/861-6200; David D'Eramo PhD, pres. & chief exec. off. **A**1a 2 3 5 6 9 10 **F**1 2 3 4 5 6 7 8 9 10 11 12 13 14 15 16 20 23 24 26 27 28 30 32 33 34 35 41 42 44 45 46 47 48 49 52 53 54; **S**5125	21	10	S		414	12183	297	65.6	0	0	75288	36875	1604
⊞ UNIVERSITY HOSPITALS OF CLEVELAND (Includes Bolwell Health Center; Hanna House; Hanna Pavilion; Humphrey Building; Lakeside Hospital; MacDonald Hosital for Women; Rainbow Babies and Children's Hospital), 2074 Abington Rd., Zip 44106; tel. 216/844-1000; James A. Block MD, pres. & chief exec. off. **A**1a 2 3 5 8 9 10 **F**1 2 3 4 5 6 7 8 9 10 11 12 13 14 15 16 17 20 23 24 26 27 28 30 32 33 34 35 36 37 38 39 40 41 42 43 44 45 46 47 49 50 51 52 53 54	23	10	S		771	29564	649	84.2	73	3106	220204	105483	4800
⊞ VETERANS ADMINISTRATION MEDICAL CENTER (Includes Brecksville Unit, 10000 Brecksville Rd., Zip 44141; tel. 216/526-3030), 10701 East Blvd., Zip 44106; tel. 216/791-3800; P. Stajduhar MD, dir. (Total facility includes 195 beds in nursing home-type unit) **A**1a 3 5 8 **F**1 2 3 4 6 7 8 9 10 11 12 14 15 16 19 20 23 24 25 26 27 28 30 31 32 33 34 35 38 41 42 44 46 47 48 49 50 53 54	45	10	S	TF	1398	18104	847	60.6	0	0	130093	71221	2871
				H	1203	17885	699	—	0	0	123221	66099	—
COLDWATER—Mercer County													
⊞ MERCER COUNTY JOINT TOWNSHIP COMMUNITY HOSPITAL, 800 W. Main St., Zip 45828; tel. 419/678-2341; Lysle E. Schmidt, adm. **A**1a 9 10 **F**1 3 6 10 12 15 23 34 35 36 40 44 45 46 47 53	16	10	S		93	4195	55	59.1	15	585	12216	5076	289
COLUMBUS—Franklin County													
□ CENTRAL OHIO PSYCHIATRIC HOSPITAL, 1960 W. Broad St., Zip 43223; tel. 614/274-7231; C. Dan Miller, supt. **A**1b 9 10 **F**3 12 15 19 23 24 32 33 42 46 47 50	12	22	L		485	1523	438	86.6	0	0	29182	17755	652
⊞ CHILDREN'S HOSPITAL, 700 Children's Dr., Zip 43205; tel. 614/461-2000; Stuart W. Williams, exec. dir. **A**1a 2 3 5 8 9 10 **F**1 4 5 6 10 12 13 14 15 16 20 22 23 24 26 28 30 31 32 33 34 35 38 42 44 45 46 51 53 54	23	50	S		286	12939	218	75.4	0	0	75816	37515	1704
★ ○ + DOCTORS HOSPITAL (Includes Doctors Hospital West, 5100 W. Broad St., Zip 43228; tel. 614/297-5000; Richard L. Sims, pres.), 1087 Dennison Ave., Zip 43201; tel. 614/297-4000; Richard A. Vincent, exec. vice-pres. oper. **A**9 10 11 12 13 **F**1 3 4 5 6 7 8 9 10 11 12 14 15 16 17 20 21 23 24 26 28 30 33 34 35 36 37 40 41 42 44 45 46 50 51 52 53 54; **S**1045	23	10	S		404	17824	288	67.6	23	1456	67918	29624	1630

Hospital, Address, Telephone, Administrator, Approval and Facility Codes, Multihospital System Code	Classification Codes: Control	Service	Stay	Facilities	Inpatient Data: Beds	Admissions	Census	Occupancy (percent)	Newborn Data: Bassinets	Births	Expense (thousands of dollars): Total	Payroll	Personnel
★□ GRANT MEDICAL CENTER (Formerly Grant Hospital), 111 S. Grant Ave., Zip 43215; tel. 614/461-3232; William Hendrickson, pres. **A**1a 2 3 5 8 9 10 **F**1 2 4 5 6 7 8 9 10 11 12 14 15 16 20 23 24 26 27 30 32 33 34 35 36 37 45 46 47 51 53 54; **S**8865	23	10	S		473	19027	323	66.5	41	3273	98577	37696	1642
★□ MERCY HOSPITAL, 1430 S. High St., Zip 43207; tel. 614/445-5000; David B. Moses, chief exec. off. **A**1a 9 10 **F**1 2 3 6 10 14 15 16 23 26 34 35 41 46 47 48 49 53	23	10	S		187	5307	112	59.9	0	0	16301	7412	434
MOUNT CARMEL EAST HOSPITAL, See Mount Carmel Health													
★□ MOUNT CARMEL HEALTH (Includes Mount Carmel East Hospital, 6001 E. Broad St., Zip 43213; tel. 614/868-6000; Coyla C. Anderson, exec. vice-pres.; Mount Carmel Medical Center, 793 W. State St., Zip 43222; tel. 614/225-5000; Gail Leonard, exec. vice-pres.), 793 W. State St., Zip 43222; tel. 614/225-5000; Sr. Gladys Marie, pres. & chief exec. off. **A**1a 2 3 5 6 9 10 **F**1 2 3 4 5 6 7 8 9 10 11 12 14 15 16 20 21 23 24 26 27 28 32 33 34 35 36 40 41 42 44 45 46 47 49 50 53 54; **S**5585	21	10	S		815	29346	510	62.6	55	3121	128270	—	2424
MOUNT CARMEL MEDICAL CENTER, See Mount Carmel Health													
★□ Δ OHIO STATE UNIVERSITY HOSPITALS, 410 W. Tenth Ave., Zip 43210; tel. 614/293-8000; Michael H. Covert, exec. dir. & asst. vice-pres. health serv. **A**1a 2 3 5 7 8 9 10 **F**1 2 3 4 5 6 7 8 9 10 11 12 13 14 15 16 17 20 22 23 24 25 26 27 28 29 30 32 33 34 35 36 37 38 40 42 43 44 45 46 50 51 53 54	12	10	S		791	26048	621	79.4	35	3293	178282	78958	3380
★□ RIVERSIDE METHODIST HOSPITALS, 3535 Olentangy River Rd., Zip 43214; tel. 614/261-5000; Erie Chapman III, pres. & chief exec. off. (Total facility includes 48 beds in nursing home-type unit) **A**1a 2 3 5 8 9 10 **F**1 2 3 4 5 6 7 8 9 10 11 12 15 16 19 20 21 23 24 26 27 28 29 30 32 33 34 35 36 37 40 41 42 44 45 46 47 48 49 50 51 52 53 54; **S**9095	21	10	S	TF	858	35366	697	83.0	50	4015	145339	68572	3563
				H	810	34572	663	—	50	4015	143559	—	—
★□ ST. ANTHONY MEDICAL CENTER, 1492 E. Broad St., Zip 43205; tel. 614/251-3000; Charles E. Housley, pres. **A**1a 3 5 9 10 **F**1 3 5 6 10 12 14 15 16 20 21 23 24 26 34 35 37 42 44 46 48 49 53; **S**1485	21	10	S		404	11867	263	65.1	0	0	57548	23988	1220
CONNEAUT—Ashtabula County													
★□ BROWN MEMORIAL HOSPITAL, 158 W. Main Rd., P O Box 648, Zip 44030; tel. 216/593-1131; George M. Whitney, adm. **A**1a 9 10 **F**1 3 6 15 16 23 35 36 40 45 47 50	23	10	S		70	2784	32	45.7	8	254	7634	3879	208
COSHOCTON—Coshocton County													
★□ COSHOCTON COUNTY MEMORIAL HOSPITAL, 1460 Orange St., Zip 43812; tel. 614/622-6411; A. F. Cacchillo, adm. (Total facility includes 61 beds in nursing home-type unit) **A**1a 9 10 **F**1 3 6 10 14 15 16 19 21 23 26 34 35 36 37 40 45 46 50 52 53	23	10	S	TF	160	3190	104	63.8	14	428	9726	5028	276
				H	99	3061	49	—	14	428	8690	4470	241
CRESTLINE—Crawford County													
□ CRESTLINE MEMORIAL HOSPITAL, 291 Heiser Ct., Zip 44827; tel. 419/683-1212; Joseph A. D'Ettorre, adm. **A**1a 9 10 **F**1 6 10 12 14 15 16 23 24 26 30 35 42 45 46 47 48 49 53	23	10	S		55	877	18	32.7	0	0	—	—	95
CUYAHOGA FALLS—Summit County													
○ + CUYAHOGA FALLS GENERAL HOSPITAL, 1900 23rd St., Zip 44223; tel. 216/929-2911; Richard Royer, pres. **A**10 11 12 13 **F**1 3 6 10 11 12 14 15 16 23 24 26 27 30 32 33 34 35 36 40 42 44 45 46 52 53	23	10	S		181	5259	105	55.9	13	283	23220	11217	535
□ FALLSVIEW PSYCHIATRIC HOSPITAL, 330 Broadway E., Zip 44221; tel. 216/929-8301; Hae Wohn Johng MD, med. dir. **A**1b 3 5 9 10 **F**24 30 32 33 45 46 47	12	22	S		131	1865	114	87.0	0	0	7206	5059	226
DAYTON—Montgomery County													
★□ CHILDREN'S MEDICAL CENTER, One Children's Plaza, Zip 45404; tel. 513/226-8300; Laurence P. Harkness, pres. & chief exec. off. **A**1a 3 5 9 10 **F**1 3 5 6 10 12 14 15 16 22 23 24 26 28 32 33 34 35 38 41 42 43 44 45 46 47 51 53 54	23	50	S		139	5645	96	69.1	0	0	36926	17639	828
□ DARTMOUTH HOSPITAL, 1038 Salem Ave., Zip 45406; tel. 513/278-7917; George Chopivsky, chief exec. off.; Judy Wortham, assoc. adm. **A**1a b 10 **F**24 28 32 33 34 42 47 49	33	22	S		38	494	28	73.7	0	0	4902	1900	95
DAYTON MENTAL HEALTH CENTER, 2611 Wayne Ave., Zip 45420; tel. 513/258-0440; Patricia A. Torvik PhD, supt. **A** 9 10 **F**19 24 32 33 42 45 46 47 50	12	22	L		405	1148	360	88.9	0	0	20961	13727	597
★□ GOOD SAMARITAN HOSPITAL AND HEALTH CENTER, 2222 Philadelphia Dr., Zip 45406; tel. 513/278-2612; James P. Fitzgerald, pres. **A**1a 2 3 5 8 9 10 **F**1 2 3 4 5 6 8 9 10 11 12 14 15 16 20 23 24 26 27 28 29 30 32 33 34 35 36 40 41 42 44 45 46 47 48 49 51 53 54; **S**5115	21	10	S		576	21272	417	72.4	32	1708	103980	48788	2299
★ ○ + GRANDVIEW HOSPITAL AND MEDICAL CENTER (Includes Southview Hospital and Family Health Center, 1997 Miamisburg-Centerville Rd., Zip 45459; tel. 513/439-6000; Michael J. Setty, vice-pres. & adm.), 405 Grand Ave., Zip 45405; tel. 513/226-3200; Richard J. Minor, pres. & chief exec. off. **A**9 10 11 12 13 **F**1 2 3 4 5 6 10 11 12 14 15 16 20 23 24 26 27 28 29 30 32 33 34 35 36 37 40 42 45 46 47 50 52 53 54; **S**1495	23	10	S		362	12891	250	69.1	35	751	75946	30211	1414
★□ Δ MIAMI VALLEY HOSPITAL, One Wyoming St., Zip 45409; tel. 513/223-6192; Karl R. Tague, pres. & chief exec. off. **A**1a 2 3 5 7 8 9 10 **F**1 2 3 4 5 6 7 8 9 10 11 12 13 14 15 16 20 22 23 24 25 26 27 29 30 32 33 34 35 36 37 38 40 41 42 43 44 46 47 48 49 50 51 53 54	23	10	S		731	23842	487	66.6	44	3047	134415	54839	2374
SOUTHVIEW HOSPITAL AND FAMILY HEALTH CENTER, See Grandview Hospital and Medical Center													
★□ Δ ST. ELIZABETH MEDICAL CENTER, 601 Edwin C Moses Blvd., Zip 45408; tel. 513/229-6000; Thomas A. Beckett, pres. **A**1a 2 3 5 7 8 9 10 **F**1 2 3 4 5 6 7 8 9 10 11 12 14 15 16 20 21 23 24 25 26 27 30 31 32 33 34 35 36 38 40 41 42 44 46 51 52 53 54; **S**1485	21	10	S		564	19734	437	77.5	35	2305	87228	46425	2090
DAYTON—Montgomery County													
U. S. AIR FORCE MEDICAL CENTER WRIGHT-PATTERSON, See Wright-Patterson Air Force Base													
★□ VETERANS ADMINISTRATION MEDICAL CENTER, 4100 W. Third St., Zip 45428; tel. 513/268-6511; Alan G. Harper, dir. (Total facility includes 959 beds in nursing home-type unit) **A**1a b 3 5 8 **F**1 2 3 6 10 11 12 14 15 16 19 20 21 23 24 25 26 27 28 30 32 33 34 42 44 46 47 48 49 50 54	45	10	S	TF	1499	10683	1247	83.2	0	0	65898	43363	1673
				H	540	10155	415	—	0	0	46415	29947	1544
DEFIANCE—Defiance County													
★□ DEFIANCE HOSPITAL, 1206 E. Second St., Zip 43512; tel. 419/782-6955; Clifford J. Bauer, adm. **A**1a 9 10 **F**1 3 6 10 12 14 15 16 23 27 30 32 33 34 35 36 40 41 43 45 46 47 52 53; **S**1755	23	10	S		107	4350	59	48.8	18	515	13167	5546	275
DELAWARE—Delaware County													
★□ GRADY MEMORIAL HOSPITAL, 561 W. Central Ave., Zip 43015; tel. 614/369-8711; Everett P. Weber Jr., exec. dir. (Nonreporting) **A**1a 9 10	23	10	S		117	—	—	—	—	—	—	—	—
DENNISON—Tuscarawas County													
★□ TWIN CITY HOSPITAL, N. First & Fuhr Sts., Zip 44621; tel. 614/922-2800; Edward A. Roberto, chief exec. off. **A**1a 9 10 **F**1 3 6 14 15 16 23 34 35 36 40 41 44 45 46 53	23	10	S		55	1678	23	40.4	9	129	5659	2629	157

★ American Hospital Association (AHA) membership
□ Joint Commission on Accreditation of Hospitals (JCAH) accreditation
\+ American Osteopathic Hospital Association (AOHA) membership
○ American Osteopathic Association (AOA) accreditation
Δ Commission on Accreditation of Rehabilitation Facilities (CARF) accreditation
Control codes 61, 63, 64, 71, 72 and 73 indicate hospitals listed by AOHA, but not registered by AHA.
For definition of numerical codes, see page A2

Hospital, Address, Telephone, Administrator, Approval and Facility Codes, Multihospital System Code

- ★ American Hospital Association (AHA) membership
- □ Joint Commission on Accreditation of Hospitals (JCAH) accreditation
- + American Osteopathic Hospital Association (AOHA) membership
- ○ American Osteopathic Association (AOA) accreditation
- Δ Commission on Accreditation of Rehabilitation Facilities (CARF) accreditation

Control codes 61, 63, 64, 71, 72 and 73 indicate hospitals listed by AOHA, but not registered by AHA. For definition of numerical codes, see page A2

Hospital	Classification Codes				Inpatient Data				Newborn Data		Expense (thousands of dollars)		
	Control	Service	Stay	Facilities	Beds	Admissions	Census	Occupancy (percent)	Bassinets	Births	Total	Payroll	Personnel
DOVER—Tuscarawas County													
★□ UNION HOSPITAL, 659 Boulevard, Zip 44622; tel. 216/343-3311; William W. Harding, pres. **A**1a 2 9 10 **F**1 3 6 10 12 14 15 16 23 27 30 35 40 44 45 46 47 52 53	23	10	S		220	6016	105	47.7	22	734	17664	9588	480
EAST LIVERPOOL—Columbiana County													
★□ EAST LIVERPOOL CITY HOSPITAL, 425 W. Fifth St., Zip 43920; tel. 216/385-7200; Bruce Nielsen, pres. **A**1a 9 10 **F**1 3 6 10 12 14 15 16 23 24 26 27 30 32 33 34 35 40 42 44 45 52 53	23	10	S		249	6473	88	35.3	26	620	20197	9708	456
★□ POTTERS MEDICAL CENTER, 401 W. Sixth St., Zip 43920; tel. 216/386-5003; Rodney Cadle, adm. **A**1a 10 **F**1 3 6 12 16 28 32 33 35 43	33	10	S		43	983	23	53.5	0	0	6080	2413	121
ELYRIA—Lorain County													
★□ ELYRIA MEMORIAL HOSPITAL, 630 E. River St., Zip 44035; tel. 216/323-3221; Donald R. Taylor, adm. **A**1a 2 6 9 10 **F**1 2 3 4 5 6 10 12 14 15 16 20 23 24 26 27 30 33 34 35 36 37 40 44 45 46 52 53 54	23	10	S		363	11624	165	45.7	37	1259	40247	19134	914
EUCLID—Cuyahoga County													
★□ Δ EUCLID GENERAL HOSPITAL, 18901 Lake Shore Blvd., Zip 44119; tel. 216/531-9000; Emil E. Hornack Jr., sr. vice-pres. & chief oper. off. **A**1a 7 9 10 **F**1 3 6 9 10 11 12 14 15 16 20 23 24 25 26 32 33 35 36 40 42 44 45 46 47 52 53 54; **S**8835	23	10	S		345	10241	230	66.7	32	1372	43687	22237	1062
FAIRFIELD—Butler County													
MERCY HOSPITAL OF FAIRFIELD, See Mercy Hospital, Hamilton													
FINDLAY—Hancock County													
★□ BLANCHARD VALLEY HOSPITAL, 145 W. Wallace St., Zip 45840; tel. 419/423-4500; William E. Ruse, pres. **A**1a 9 10 **F**1 2 3 5 6 10 11 12 14 15 16 23 24 26 27 30 33 35 36 37 40 44 45 52 53	23	10	S		239	9296	129	54.0	22	1136	23095	11647	597
FOSTORIA—Seneca County													
★□ FOSTORIA CITY HOSPITAL, 501 Van Buren St., Zip 44830; tel. 419/435-7734; Wayne Moore, adm. **A**1a 9 10 **F**1 3 6 10 11 14 15 16 23 35 36 40 41 45 52 53; **S**2495	23	10	S		80	2539	32	40.0	12	176	7636	3221	177
FREMONT—Sandusky County													
★□ MEMORIAL HOSPITAL, 715 S. Taft Ave., Zip 43420; tel. 419/332-7321; Jack M. Bryan, pres. **A**1a 9 10 **F**1 3 6 10 12 14 15 16 21 23 24 26 27 29 30 32 33 34 35 36 40 41 44 45 46 47 52 53	23	10	S		186	6056	80	43.0	18	820	20266	8543	459
GALION—Crawford County													
★□ GALION COMMUNITY HOSPITAL, Portland Way S., Zip 44833; tel. 419/468-4841; John C. Imhoff, pres. **A**1a 9 10 **F**1 3 6 10 12 14 16 23 35 36 37 40 44 45 46 52 53	23	10	S		129	3966	56	43.4	12	288	11488	5585	312
GALLIPOLIS—Gallia County													
★□ HOLZER MEDICAL CENTER, 385 Jackson Pike, Zip 45631; tel. 614/446-5000; Charles I. Adkins Jr., pres. **A**1a 2 9 10 **F**1 2 3 6 7 8 9 10 11 12 14 15 16 23 34 35 40 41 46 52 53	23	10	S		269	9480	141	52.4	30	888	26918	11924	652
GARFIELD HEIGHTS—Cuyahoga County													
★□ MARYMOUNT HOSPITAL, 12300 McCracken Rd., Zip 44125; tel. 216/581-0500; Thomas J. Trudell, pres. & chief exec. off. **A**1a 9 10 **F**1 3 5 6 9 10 11 12 14 15 16 20 23 24 26 28 29 30 32 33 34 35 36 40 42 43 44 45 46 48 49 53; **S**5445	21	10	S		279	9588	197	70.6	18	1059	44167	26465	1005
GENEVA—Ashtabula County													
★□ MEMORIAL HOSPITAL OF GENEVA, 870 W. Main St., Zip 44041; tel. 216/466-1141; Jack D. Holt, adm. **A**1a 9 10 **F**1 3 6 14 16 17 23 35 36 40 44 45	23	10	S		54	2484	33	61.1	9	297	6266	3278	160
GEORGETOWN—Brown County													
□ BROWN COUNTY GENERAL HOSPITAL, 425 Home St., Zip 45121; tel. 513/378-6121; David A. Ferrell, adm. **A**1a 9 10 **F**1 3 6 10 15 16 23 34 35 37 40 41 44 45 46 47 48 49 50 52 53	13	10	S		62	2705	38	52.1	9	405	7936	3913	206
GRANVILLE—Licking County													
WHISLER MEMORIAL HOSPITAL, DENISON UNIVERSITY, Zip 43023; tel. 614/587-6200; A. P. Jonas MD, adm. (Nonreporting)	23	11	S		16	—	—	—	—	—	—	—	—
GREEN SPRINGS—Sandusky County													
★□ Δ ST. FRANCIS REHABILITATION HOSPITAL AND NURSING HOME, 401 N. Broadway, Zip 44836; tel. 419/639-2626; Sr. Michael Marie Wiesen, adm. (Total facility includes 147 beds in nursing home-type unit) **A**1a 7 10 **F**16 19 23 24 32 34 42 44 45 46	21	46	L	TF	183	468	159	86.9	0	0	7257	4004	201
				H	36	255	28	—	0	0	—	—	102
GREENFIELD—Highland County													
★□ GREENFIELD AREA MEDICAL CENTER, 545 South St., Zip 45123; tel. 513/981-2116; Thomas E. Daugherty, adm. **A**1a 9 10 **F**1 10 14 15 16 23 24 25 26 34 35 41 44 45 46 47 49; **S**1755	23	10	S		44	932	18	40.9	0	0	3012	1400	87
GREENVILLE—Darke County													
□ WAYNE HOSPITAL, 835 Sweitzer St., Zip 45331; tel. 513/548-1141; Raymond E. Laughlin, adm. **A**1a 9 10 **F**1 3 6 10 12 16 23 35 36 40 44 45 46 52 53	23	10	S		92	3581	49	52.7	14	521	10195	4846	272
HAMILTON—Butler County													
★□ FORT HAMILTON-HUGHES MEMORIAL HOSPITAL AND HEALTHCARE CORPORATION, 630 Eaton Ave., Zip 45013; tel. 513/867-2000; James A. Kingsbury, pres. & chief exec. off. **A**1a 9 10 **F**1 3 6 7 8 9 10 11 12 15 16 23 24 26 27 30 33 34 35 36 37 40 42 44 45 46 47 48 49 52 53	23	10	S		271	10473	189	66.8	36	1722	39032	16581	828
★□ MERCY HOSPITAL (Includes Mercy Hospital of Fairfield, 3000 Mack Rd., Zip 45014; Mailing Address P O Box 418, Zip 45012; tel. 513/867-7400; Mercy Hospital of Hamilton, 100 Riverfront Plaza, Zip 45011; Mailing Address P O Box 418, Zip 45012; tel 513/867-6400), 100 Riverfront Plaza, Zip 45011; Mailing Address Box 418, Zip 45012; tel. 513/867-6400; Sr. Mary Rene Mullen, pres. **A**1a 9 10 **F**1 3 6 9 10 11 12 14 15 16 19 23 24 26 34 35 44 45 46 47 52 53; **S**5155	21	10	S		317	11003	185	58.4	0	0	48849	20825	1024
HICKSVILLE—Defiance County													
★ COMMUNITY MEMORIAL HOSPITAL, 208 N. Columbus St., Zip 43526; tel. 419/542-7573; W. R. Plassman, adm. (Nonreporting) **A**9 10	16	10	S		30	—	—	—	—	—	—	—	—
HILLSBORO—Highland County													
★ HIGHLAND DISTRICT HOSPITAL, 1275 N. High St., Zip 45133; tel. 513/393-6100; Eloise Yochum, adm. **A**9 10 **F**1 6 10 15 16 23 34 35 36 40 45 46 53	16	10	S		53	1499	18	34.0	12	244	5179	2309	148
IRONTON—Lawrence County													
★□ LAWRENCE COUNTY GENERAL HOSPITAL, 2228 S. Ninth St., Zip 45638; tel. 614/532-3231; Norman Greene, exec. dir. (Nonreporting) **A**1a 9 10; **S**2495	13	10	S		117	—	—	—	—	—	—	—	—
KENTON—Hardin County													
★□ HARDIN MEMORIAL HOSPITAL, 921 E. Franklin St., Zip 43326; tel. 419/673-0761; Lamar L. Wyse, pres. **A**1a 9 10 **F**1 3 6 10 12 14 15 16 23 34 35 37 40 45 46 47 53; **S**9095	23	10	S		86	2062	27	31.4	13	258	6478	2673	155

★ American Hospital Association (AHA) membership
☐ Joint Commission on Accreditation of Hospitals (JCAH) accreditation
+ American Osteopathic Hospital Association (AOHA) membership
○ American Osteopathic Association (AOA) accreditation
Δ Commission on Accreditation of Rehabilitation Facilities (CARF) accreditation
Control codes 61, 63, 64, 71, 72 and 73 indicate hospitals listed by AOHA, but not registered by AHA.
For definition of numerical codes, see page A2

Hospital, Address, Telephone, Administrator, Approval and Facility Codes, Multihospital System Code	Classification Codes				Inpatient Data				Newborn Data		Expense (thousands of dollars)		
	Control	Service	Stay	Facilities	Beds	Admissions	Census	Occupancy (percent)	Bassinets	Births	Total	Payroll	Personnel
KETTERING—Montgomery County													
C. F. KETTERING MEMORIAL HOSPITAL, See Kettering Medical Center													
⊞ KETTERING MEDICAL CENTER (Includes C. F. Kettering Memorial Hospital, 3535 Southern Blvd., Zip 45429; tel. 513/298-4331; Robert Lee Willett, pres.; Sycamore Hospital, 2150 Leiter Rd., Miamisburg, Zip 45342; tel. 513/866-0551; Elliott Fortner, adm.), 3535 Southern Blvd., Zip 45429; tel. 513/298-4331; Robert Lee Willett, pres. **A**1a 2 3 5 8 9 10 **F**1 2 3 4 5 6 7 8 9 10 11 12 15 16 17 19 20 23 24 26 27 28 29 30 32 33 34 35 36 37 39 40 41 43 44 45 46 47 49 51 52 53 54; **S**9355	21	10	S		608	19822	415	68.3	34	1925	128168	55085	2697
LAKEWOOD—Cuyahoga County													
⊞ LAKEWOOD HOSPITAL, 14519 Detroit Ave., Zip 44107; tel. 216/521-4200; Jules W. Bouthillet, chief exec. off. **A**1a 9 10 **F**1 2 3 4 6 9 10 11 12 14 15 16 20 21 23 24 26 27 30 31 32 33 34 35 41 42 44 45 46 47 49 50 52 53 54	14	10	S		295	9519	218	73.9	0	0	47259	20770	950
LANCASTER—Fairfield County													
⊞ LANCASTER-FAIRFIELD COMMUNITY HOSPITAL, 401 N. Ewing St., Zip 43130; tel. 614/687-8000; Joseph D. McKelvey, pres. **A**1a 9 10 **F**1 2 3 6 10 12 14 15 16 23 24 34 35 36 40 44 45 46 47 52 53	23	10	S		179	7736	108	60.3	20	1063	23083	9389	536
LIMA—Allen County													
⊞ LIMA MEMORIAL HOSPITAL, 1001 Bellefontaine Ave., Zip 45804; tel. 419/228-3335; Gregory W. Turner, pres. **A**1a 9 10 **F**1 3 6 7 8 9 10 11 12 14 15 16 17 20 23 24 26 34 35 36 40 41 42 44 45 46 47 52 53 54	23	10	S		300	11271	195	65.0	24	910	41756	19002	982
OAKWOOD FORENSIC CENTER, 3200 N. West St., Zip 45801; tel. 419/225-8052; Alaric W. Sawyer, supt. **F**3 16 30 32 33 46 47	12	22	L		153	223	96	63.2	0	0	11380	7786	314
⊞ ST. RITA'S MEDICAL CENTER, 730 W. Market St., Zip 45801; tel. 419/227-3361; Sr. Rita Mary Wasserman, pres. **A**1a 9 10 **F**1 2 3 6 7 8 9 10 11 12 14 15 16 21 23 24 26 27 30 32 34 35 36 38 40 41 42 44 45 46 47 48 52 53; **S**5155	21	10	S		376	13725	249	66.2	40	1797	51432	25854	1276
LODI—Medina County													
⊞ LODI COMMUNITY HOSPITAL, 225 Elyria St., Zip 44254; tel. 216/948-1222; Thomas L. Lockard, adm. **A**1a 9 10 **F**1 6 14 15 16 23 35 45 46 47	23	10	S		30	949	13	43.3	0	0	2702	1319	75
LOGAN—Hocking County													
☐ HOCKING VALLEY COMMUNITY HOSPITAL, Rte. 2, State Rte. 664, Box 966, Zip 43138; tel. 614/385-5631; Larry Willard, adm. (Total facility includes 30 beds in nursing home-type unit) **A**1a 9 10 **F**1 3 6 12 14 15 16 19 23 24 30 34 35 40 44 45 46 50 53	13	10	S	TF	93	2091	49	52.7	12	200	6109	2693	165
				H	63	2021	29	—	12	200	—	—	150
LONDON—Madison County													
⊞ MADISON COUNTY HOSPITAL, 210 N. Main St., Zip 43140; tel. 614/852-1372; Gary J. Lehman, pres. & chief exec. off. **A**1a 9 10 **F**1 3 6 9 10 12 14 15 16 23 24 26 27 28 29 30 31 32 33 34 35 36 40 42 43 44 45 46 48 49 53 54	23	10	S		109	2309	40	36.7	12	263	9441	4207	234
LORAIN—Lorain County													
⊞ Δ LORAIN COMMUNITY HOSPITAL, 3700 Kolbe Rd., Zip 44053; tel. 216/282-9121; Paul C. Balcom, exec. dir. **A**1a 7 9 10 **F**1 3 6 9 10 12 14 15 16 20 23 24 26 27 30 32 33 34 35 37 41 42 44 45 46 47 48 49 52 53	23	10	S		286	7746	180	62.9	0	0	43088	18996	887
⊞ ST. JOSEPH HOSPITAL AND HEALTH CENTER (Formerly St. Joseph Hospital), 205 W. 20th St., Zip 44052; tel. 216/245-6851; Ronald M. Streem, exec. dir. **A**1a 2 9 10 **F**1 2 3 6 7 8 9 10 11 12 14 15 16 21 23 24 26 27 28 30 32 33 34 35 37 40 41 42 44 45 46 47 49 50 52 53; **S**5645	21	10	S		272	9799	148	54.4	26	1014	38016	19515	946
LOUDONVILLE—Ashland County													
★ KETTERING HOSPITAL, 546 N. Union St., Zip 44842; tel. 419/994-4121; Jim Schweitzer, adm. (Nonreporting) **A**9 10	23	10	S		23	—	—	—	—	—	—	—	—
LOUISVILLE—Stark County													
⊞ MOLLY STARK HOSPITAL (Long-Term Skilled Nursing, Mental Retardation, Rehabilitation, Alcoholism and Chemical Dependency), 7900 Columbus Rd. N.E., Zip 44641; tel. 216/875-5531; Steven K. Hegedeos, adm. (Total facility includes 115 beds in nursing home-type unit) **A**1a 9 10 **F**12 16 19 23 24 33 34 42 44 46 47 48 49	13	49	L	TF	157	483	102	65.0	0	0	6422	3525	323
				H	42	441	20	—	0	0	—	—	254
MADISON—Lake County													
○ + NORTHEASTERN OHIO GENERAL HOSPITAL, 2041 Hubbard Rd., Zip 44057; tel. 216/428-2121; Neil H. Gilman, adm. **A**9 10 11 **F**1 3 6 10 12 14 15 16 23 34 35 37 40 45 46	23	10	S		76	1777	26	34.2	7	59	6191	2850	155
MANSFIELD—Richland County													
⊞ MANSFIELD GENERAL HOSPITAL, 335 Glessner Ave., Zip 44903; tel. 419/526-8000; James E. Meyer, pres. **A**1a 6 9 10 **F**1 2 3 5 6 7 8 9 10 11 12 14 15 16 21 23 24 26 27 28 29 30 32 33 34 35 36 37 40 41 42 45 46 47 52 53	23	10	S		396	12620	215	54.3	32	1421	37381	20446	1076
★ PEOPLE'S HOSPITAL, 597 Park Ave. E., Zip 44905; tel. 419/524-9411; Joseph Damoff, adm. (Nonreporting) **A**9 10	23	10	S		111	—	—	—	—	—	—	—	—
⊞ RICHLAND HOSPITAL, 1451 Lucas Rd., Box 637, Zip 44901; tel. 419/589-5511; S. J. Cocuzza, adm. **A**1b 9 10 **F**23 24 27 28 30 32 33 34 42 45 46 47 48 49	23	22	S		92	906	64	89.7	0	0	5867	2787	150
MARIETTA—Washington County													
⊞ MARIETTA MEMORIAL HOSPITAL, 401 Mathews St., Zip 45750; tel. 614/374-1400; Larry J. Unroe, pres. **A**1a 9 10 **F**1 3 6 10 12 14 15 16 23 24 28 30 32 33 34 35 36 37 40 43 45 46 47 48 52 53	23	10	S		213	6250	100	46.9	22	696	20249	9513	480
○ + SELBY GENERAL HOSPITAL, 1106 Colgate Dr., Zip 45750; tel. 614/373-0582; John M. O'Shea, pres. & adm. (Nonreporting) **A**9 10 11 12; **S**2495	23	10	S		74	—	—	—	—	—	—	—	—
MARION—Marion County													
COMMUNITY MEDCENTER HOSPITAL, See Medcenter Hospital													
⊞ MARION GENERAL HOSPITAL, McKinley Park Dr., Zip 43302; tel. 614/383-8400; P. Donald Muhlenthaler, pres. **A**1a b 2 9 10 **F**1 3 6 7 10 11 12 14 15 16 21 23 24 27 30 32 33 34 35 36 40 41 45 46 47 52 53; **S**9095	23	10	S		257	7232	104	40.5	21	1275	26407	12109	624
⊞ MEDCENTER HOSPITAL (Formerly Community Medcenter Hospital), 1050 Delaware Ave., Zip 43302; tel. 614/387-8604; Robert R. Tracht, adm. **A**1a 9 10 **F**1 3 4 5 6 7 8 10 11 12 14 15 16 23 24 25 26 28 32 33 35 37 42 44 45 48 49 50 52 53 54	23	10	S		162	4504	86	53.1	0	0	17930	5834	331
MARTINS FERRY—Belmont County													
⊞ EAST OHIO REGIONAL HOSPITAL, 90 N. Fourth St., Zip 43935; tel. 614/633-1100; Brent A. Marsteller, adm. (Nonreporting) **A**1a 9 10; **S**3315	23	10	S		236	—	—	—	—	—	—	—	—
MARYSVILLE—Union County													
⊞ MEMORIAL HOSPITAL, 500 London Ave., Zip 43040; tel. 513/644-6115; Danny L. Boggs, adm. **A**1a 9 10 **F**1 3 6 10 12 14 15 16 23 24 34 35 36 40 41 44 45 46 47 53	13	10	S		97	2377	30	30.9	11	277	10668	4775	251
MASSILLON—Stark County													
○ + DOCTORS HOSPITAL OF STARK COUNTY, 400 Austin Ave. N.W., Zip 44646; tel. 216/837-7200; David R. Hirsh, pres. **A**9 10 11 12 13 **F**1 6 10 12 14 15 16 23 24 26 34 35 36 41 44 45 46 52 53 54	23	10	S		232	7373	117	51.8	12	520	27905	12607	659
⊞ MASSILLON COMMUNITY HOSPITAL, 875 Eighth St. N.E., Zip 44646; Mailing Address P O Box 805, Zip 44648; tel. 216/832-8761; Jack W. Topoleski, pres. **A**1a 9 10 **F**1 2 3 6 10 12 14 15 16 23 35 36 40 41 45 46 47 48 52 53	23	10	S		205	7126	126	61.5	20	282	25762	11562	639

★ American Hospital Association (AHA) membership
□ Joint Commission on Accreditation of Hospitals (JCAH) accreditation
\+ American Osteopathic Hospital Association (AOHA) membership
○ American Osteopathic Association (AOA) accreditation
Δ Commission on Accreditation of Rehabilitation Facilities (CARF) accreditation
Control codes 61, 63, 64, 71, 72 and 73 indicate hospitals listed by AOHA, but not registered by AHA.
For definition of numerical codes, see page A2

Hospital, Address, Telephone, Administrator, Approval and Facility Codes, Multihospital System Code	Classification Codes				Inpatient Data				Newborn Data		Expense (thousands of dollars)		
	Control	Service	Stay	Facilities	Beds	Admissions	Census	Occupancy (percent)	Bassinets	Births	Total	Payroll	Personnel
□ MASSILLON STATE HOSPITAL, 3000 Erie St. S.W., Box 540, Zip 44648; tel. 216/833-3135; Terry A. Veney, actg. supt. **A**1b 10 **F**15 23 24 30 32 33 42 46 47 50	12	22	L		381	367	342	89.8	0	0	19842	12198	463
MAUMEE—Lucas County													
⧆ ST. LUKE'S HOSPITAL, 5901 Monclova Rd., Zip 43537; tel. 419/893-5911; Frank J. Bartell III, pres. **A**1a 10 **F**1 2 3 5 6 10 12 14 15 16 23 24 26 34 35 44 45 46 52 53	23	10	S		246	8875	159	64.6	0	0	35475	16957	699
MAYFIELD HEIGHTS—Cuyahoga County													
⧆ HILLCREST HOSPITAL, 6780 Mayfield Rd., Zip 44124; tel. 216/449-4500; David H. Plate, pres. & chief oper. off. **A**1a 2 9 10 **F**1 2 3 6 10 12 14 15 16 21 23 24 26 34 35 36 37 40 41 43 44 45 46 47 51 53; **S**8835	23	10	S		305	13752	232	76.1	9	2734	58780	27897	1104
MEDINA—Medina County													
⧆ MEDINA COMMUNITY HOSPITAL, 990 E. Washington St., P O Box 427, Zip 44258; tel. 216/723-3231; Edward A. Hall, pres. **A**1a 2 9 10 **F**1 3 6 10 12 15 16 23 34 35 36 39 40 44 45 46 47 52 53	23	10	S		118	5093	71	60.2	21	792	15909	7489	406
MIAMISBURG—Montgomery County													
SYCAMORE HOSPITAL, See Kettering Medical Center, Kettering													
MIDDLEBURG HEIGHTS—Cuyahoga County													
⧆ SOUTHWEST COMMUNITY HEALTH SYSTEM AND HOSPITAL, 18697 E. Bagley Rd., Zip 44130; tel. 216/826-8000; L. Jon Schurmeier, pres. **A**1a 2 10 **F**1 2 3 6 10 12 14 15 16 17 20 23 24 27 29 32 33 34 35 36 40 41 42 44 45 46 47 48 52 53	23	10	S		296	14347	262	88.5	30	1372	52132	25465	1216
MIDDLETOWN—Butler County													
⧆ MIDDLETOWN REGIONAL HOSPITAL, 105 McKnight Dr., Zip 45044; tel. 513/424-2111; James R. Flynn, pres. **A**1a 9 10 **F**1 2 3 5 6 9 10 11 12 15 16 23 24 25 26 27 28 30 32 33 34 35 36 37 40 42 44 45 46 47 49 52 53	23	10	S		342	12185	201	57.9	30	1111	44231	21359	1100
MILLERSBURG—Holmes County													
⧆ JOEL POMERENE MEMORIAL HOSPITAL, 500 Wooster Rd., Zip 44654; tel. 216/674-1015; Rex A. Wheeler, chief exec. off. **A**1a 9 10 **F**1 3 6 14 15 16 23 34 35 36 37 40 44 45 50	13	10	S		53	2015	21	39.6	14	609	4119	2060	112
MONTPELIER—Williams County													
WILLIAMS COUNTY GENERAL HOSPITAL, See Community Hospitals of Williams County, Bryan													
MOUNT GILEAD—Morrow County													
⧆ MORROW COUNTY HOSPITAL, 651 W. Marion Rd., Zip 43338; tel. 419/946-5015; Randal M. Arnett, adm. (Total facility includes 10 beds in nursing home-type unit) **A**1a 9 10 **F**1 3 6 12 14 15 16 19 23 34 35 37 40 44 45 46 50; **S**9095	13	10	S	TF	61	1124	15	24.6	10	140	3489	1298	84
				H	51	1089	13	—	10	140	3382	1222	80
MOUNT VERNON—Knox County													
⧆ KNOX COMMUNITY HOSPITAL, 1330 Coshocton Rd., Zip 43050; tel. 614/393-9000; Richard H. Finley, adm. **A**1a 9 10 **F**1 3 6 10 14 15 23 24 35 36 40 45 46 47 52 53; **S**1755	23	10	S		153	4339	60	39.2	15	435	16771	5015	271
NAPOLEON—Henry County													
★ HENRY COUNTY HOSPITAL, 11-600 State Rd. 424, Zip 43545; tel. 419/592-4015; Carey W. Plummer, chief exec. off. **A**10 **F**1 3 6 12 14 15 16 23 35 36 40 43 45 46 53	23	10	S		50	1427	16	32.0	8	228	4729	1680	107
NELSONVILLE—Athens County													
○ + DOCTORS HOSPITAL OF NELSONVILLE, W. Franklin St., Zip 45764; tel. 614/753-1931; Mark R. Seckinger, adm. **A**9 10 11 12 **F**1 3 6 9 10 14 16 23 24 33 34 35 45 46 52 53; **S**1045	23	10	S		83	1290	20	24.1	0	0	—	—	115
NEWARK—Licking County													
⧆ LICKING MEMORIAL HOSPITAL, 1320 W. Main St., Zip 43055; tel. 614/344-0331; William J. Andrews, pres. **A**1a 9 10 **F**1 2 3 6 7 8 9 10 11 12 14 15 16 23 27 29 30 33 34 35 36 40 44 45 46 47 52 53	23	10	S		214	9534	132	61.1	30	1360	25570	12996	730
NORTHFIELD—Summit County													
□ SAGAMORE HILLS CHILDREN'S PSYCHIATRIC HOSPITAL, 11910 Dunham Rd., Zip 44067; tel. 216/467-7955; D. W. Thernes Jr., supt. **A**1b 9 **F**24 30 32 33 42 44 46 47	12	52	L		64	178	45	70.3	0	0	4630	3996	148
WESTERN RESERVE PSYCHIATRIC HABILITATION CENTER, Box 305, Zip 44067; tel. 216/467-7131; Richard J. Wingard, supt. (Nonreporting) **A** 9 10	12	22	L		599	—	—	—	—	—	—	—	—
NORWALK—Huron County													
⧆ FISHER-TITUS MEDICAL CENTER (Formerly Fisher-Titus Memorial Hospital), 272 Benedict Ave., Zip 44857; tel. 419/668-8101; Richard C. Westhofen, pres. (Total facility includes 50 beds in nursing home-type unit) **A**1a 9 10 **F**1 3 6 10 12 14 15 16 19 23 24 26 34 35 36 40 41 44 45 46 47 52 53	23	10	S	TF	162	3806	97	59.9	11	474	14599	6218	295
				H	112	3761	49	—	11	474	13724	5832	271
OAK HILL—Jackson County													
⧆ OAK HILL COMMUNITY MEDICAL CENTER, 350 Charlotte Ave., Zip 45656; tel. 614/682-7717; D. H. Diener, adm. (Total facility includes 24 beds in nursing home-type unit) **A**1a 9 10 **F**1 3 14 16 19 23 35 41 45	23	10	S	TF	68	1199	39	57.4	0	0	—	—	116
				H	44	1176	17	—	0	0	—	—	99
OBERLIN—Lorain County													
□ ALLEN MEMORIAL HOSPITAL, 200 W. Lorain St., Zip 44074; tel. 216/775-1211; Duane E. Horning, exec. dir. **A**1a 9 10 **F**1 3 9 10 12 14 15 16 23 26 27 32 33 35 36 40 43 45 46 47 49 52	23	10	S		97	2557	32	33.0	16	509	8781	4470	212
OREGON—Lucas County													
⧆ ST. CHARLES HOSPITAL, 2600 Navarre Ave., Zip 43616; tel. 419/698-7200; Sr. Phyllis Ann Gerold, exec. dir. **A**1a 2 10 **F**1 2 3 5 6 7 8 9 10 11 12 14 15 16 20 23 24 26 27 30 32 33 35 36 40 42 44 45 46 47 49 52 53; **S**5155	21	10	S		342	12400	255	74.6	20	807	56144	27843	1364
ORRVILLE—Wayne County													
⧆ DUNLAP MEMORIAL HOSPITAL, 832 S. Main St., Zip 44667; tel. 216/682-3010; Harvey Norris, adm. (Nonreporting) **A**1a 9 10	23	10	S		62	—	—	—	—	—	—	—	—
OXFORD—Butler County													
⧆ MCCULLOUGH-HYDE MEMORIAL HOSPITAL, 110 N. Poplar St., Zip 45056; tel. 513/523-2111; Richard A. Daniels, adm. **A**1a 9 10 **F**1 3 6 10 14 15 16 23 24 33 34 35 36 40 44 45 46 52 53	23	10	S		80	3687	40	50.0	11	608	9832	5074	231
PAINESVILLE—Lake County													
⧆ LAKE HOSPITAL SYSTEM (Includes Lakewest Hospital, 36000 Euclid Ave., Willoughby, Zip 44094; tel. 216/953-9600), Washington at Liberty, Zip 44077; tel. 216/354-2400; Frank L. Muddle, pres. **A**1a 9 10 **F**1 3 6 10 12 14 15 16 23 24 32 34 35 36 38 40 41 44 45 46 47 50 53 54	23	10	S		359	11630	168	46.8	44	1328	46887	21800	1093
PARMA—Cuyahoga County													
⧆ KAISER FOUNDATION HOSPITAL-PARMA, 12301 Snow Rd., Zip 44130; tel. 216/362-2000; A. Linwood, adm. **A**1a 9 10 **F**1 3 6 9 12 14 15 16 23 26 32 33 35 37 44 46 47 52; **S**2105	23	10	S		61	3604	53	86.9	0	0	—	—	411
⧆ PARMA COMMUNITY GENERAL HOSPITAL, 7007 Powers Blvd., Zip 44129; tel. 216/888-1800; Bernard J. Schlueter, adm. & chief exec. off. **A**1a 2 9 10 **F**1 2 3 6 10 12 14 15 16 20 21 23 24 33 35 36 40 41 44 45 46 47 52 53	23	10	S		315	11970	235	74.6	37	1209	53942	26519	1293

Hospital, Address, Telephone, Administrator, Approval and Facility Codes, Multihospital System Code	Classification Codes				Inpatient Data				Newborn Data		Expense (thousands of dollars)		
★ American Hospital Association (AHA) membership ☐ Joint Commission on Accreditation of Hospitals (JCAH) accreditation + American Osteopathic Hospital Association (AOHA) membership ○ American Osteopathic Association (AOA) accreditation Δ Commission on Accreditation of Rehabilitation Facilities (CARF) accreditation Control codes 61, 63, 64, 71, 72 and 73 indicate hospitals listed by AOHA, but not registered by AHA. For definition of numerical codes, see page A2	Control	Service	Stay	Facilities	Beds	Admissions	Census	Occupancy (percent)	Bassinets	Births	Total	Payroll	Personnel
PAULDING—Paulding County													
★ PAULDING COUNTY HOSPITAL, Rural Rte. 2, Box 1240, Zip 45879; tel. 419/399-4080; John D. Sluss, adm. **A**9 10 **F**1 6 10 16 21 23 34 35 40 41 44 45 46 52 53	13	10	S		47	1406	17	36.2	9	136	4619	2100	114
PIQUA—Miami County													
⊞ PIQUA MEMORIAL MEDICAL CENTER, 624 Park Ave., Zip 45356; tel. 513/778-4600; Rose Marie Derks, adm. **A**1a 9 10 **F**1 3 5 6 9 10 12 14 15 16 23 24 34 35 36 37 40 41 43 44 45 46 52 53	23	10	S		149	4853	75	50.3	18	371	15364	5688	363
POMEROY—Meigs County													
⊞ VETERANS MEMORIAL HOSPITAL OF MEIGS COUNTY, 115 E. Memorial Dr., Zip 45769; tel. 614/992-2104; Walter S. Lucas, adm. (Nonreporting) **A**1a 9 10	23	10	S		70	—	—	—	—	—	—	—	—
PORT CLINTON—Ottawa County													
⊞ H. B. MAGRUDER MEMORIAL HOSPITAL, 615 Fulton St., Zip 43452; tel. 419/734-3131; Robert Dumminger, adm. **A**1a 9 10 **F**1 3 5 6 10 11 14 15 16 23 32 33 35 36 40 45 46 47 52 53	23	10	S		71	3428	43	60.6	3	162	8174	3928	214
PORTSMOUTH—Scioto County													
⊞ MERCY HOSPITAL, 1248 Kinneys Lane, Zip 45662; tel. 614/353-2131; James P. Weems, vice-pres. & chief exec. off. **A**1a 9 10 **F**1 3 6 10 11 12 14 15 16 20 23 34 35 41 45 46 47 52 53; **S**9095	23	10	S		177	6850	130	73.4	0	0	23567	10441	634
⊞ SCIOTO MEMORIAL HOSPITAL, 1805 27th St., Zip 45662; tel. 614/354-7581; Earl McLane, pres. & chief exec. off. **A**1a 9 10 **F**1 3 6 7 8 9 10 11 12 14 16 23 24 34 35 36 37 38 40 41 44 45 46 52 53; **S**9095	23	10	S		225	8746	141	62.7	32	1484	25150	11341	731
⊞ SOUTHERN HILLS HOSPITAL, 727 Eighth St., Box 1528, Zip 45662; tel. 614/354-8651; Earl L. McLane, pres. & chief exec. off. **A**1a b 9 10 **F**1 6 12 14 16 23 24 27 28 30 32 33 34 42 48 49; **S**9095	23	10	S		126	2284	63	50.0	0	0	6688	2690	157
RAVENNA—Portage County													
⊞ ROBINSON MEMORIAL HOSPITAL, 6847 N. Chestnut St., Zip 44266; tel. 216/297-0811; Richard E. Clapp, pres. **A**1a 2 3 5 9 10 **F**1 2 3 6 9 10 11 12 14 15 16 23 24 26 33 34 35 36 40 41 42 44 45 46 47 52 53 54	13	10	S		325	12167	159	48.9	30	1066	43081	22241	1162
ROCK CREEK—Ashtabula County													
GLENBEIGH ADULT HOSPITAL, See Glenbeigh Hospital of Rock Creek													
☐ GLENBEIGH HOSPITAL OF ROCK CREEK (Formerly Glenbeigh Adult Hospital), Rte. 45, P O Box 298, Zip 44084; tel. 216/953-0177; Allen Drum, exec. dir. **A**1b **F**32 33 42; **S**0645	33	82	S		80	640	51	63.8	0	0	4287	1389	91
SALEM—Columbiana County													
⊞ SALEM COMMUNITY HOSPITAL, 1995 E. State St., Zip 44460; tel. 216/332-1551; Robert F. Rice, adm. **A**1a 9 10 **F**1 3 6 7 8 9 10 11 12 16 17 23 34 35 36 40 45 46 48 52 53 54	23	10	S		237	7919	108	45.6	17	840	21379	11232	575
SANDUSKY—Erie County													
DECATUR STREET FACILITY, See Firelands Community Hospital													
★ ○ + FIRELANDS COMMUNITY HOSPITAL (Includes Decatur Street Facility, 1101 Decatur St., Zip 44870, tel. 419/626-7400; Hayes Avenue Facility, 2020 Hayes Ave., Zip 44870; tel. 419/627-5000), 1101 Decatur St., P O Caller 5005, Zip 44870; tel. 419/626-7400; Nelson Alward, pres. **A**2 9 10 11 12 13 **F**1 3 6 7 8 9 10 11 12 14 15 16 23 24 27 28 29 30 31 33 34 35 36 44 45 46 47 53	23	10	S		273	7868	115	42.1	28	1203	34372	13816	593
HAYES AVENUE FACILITY, See Firelands Community Hospital													
⊞ PROVIDENCE HOSPITAL, 1912 Hayes Ave., Zip 44870; tel. 419/625-8450; Sr. Nancy Linenkugel, pres. (Total facility includes 46 beds in nursing home-type unit) **A**1a 2 6 9 10 **F**1 2 3 6 7 8 9 10 11 12 14 15 16 19 20 23 24 26 34 35 41 42 44 46 52 53; **S**5375	21	10	S	TF H	215 169	6679 6420	123 105	57.2 —	0 0	0 0	24267 23371	11148 10571	566 547
SHELBY—Richland County													
⊞ SHELBY MEMORIAL HOSPITAL, Morris Rd., Box 608, Zip 44875; tel. 419/342-5015; Timothy C. Dutton, pres. (Nonreporting) **A**1a 9 10	23	10	S		55	—	—	—	—	—	—	—	—
SIDNEY—Shelby County													
⊞ WILSON MEMORIAL HOSPITAL, 915 W. Michigan St., Zip 45365; tel. 513/498-2311; Michael Ehler, exec. dir. **A**1a 9 10 **F**1 3 6 10 12 14 16 23 35 37 40 41 45 52 53	23	10	S		112	3668	49	43.8	16	455	10408	4806	271
SPRINGFIELD—Clark County													
⊞ COMMUNITY HOSPITAL OF SPRINGFIELD AND CLARK COUNTY, 2615 E. High St., Box 1228, Zip 45501; tel. 513/325-0531; Neal E. Kresheck, pres. & chief exec. off. **A**1a 2 3 5 6 9 10 **F**1 2 3 6 9 10 12 14 15 16 20 21 23 24 26 30 34 35 36 37 40 41 45 46 47 48 49 50 53 54	23	10	S		313	11969	190	60.7	54	2200	44541	20322	1082
⊞ MERCY MEDICAL CENTER, 1343 N. Fountain Blvd., Zip 45501; tel. 513/390-5000; Jerrold A. Maki, exec. vice-pres. & chief oper. off. **A**1a 2 3 5 9 10 **F**1 2 3 5 6 7 8 9 10 11 12 14 15 16 20 21 23 24 25 28 29 30 31 32 33 34 35 42 43 44 45 46 47 52 53 54; **S**5155	21	10	S		337	10239	181	53.7	0	0	41564	18182	947
ST. MARYS—Auglaize County													
⊞ JOINT TOWNSHIP DISTRICT MEMORIAL HOSPITAL, 200 St. Clair St., Zip 45885; tel. 419/394-3335; James R. Chick, chief exec. off. **A**1a 9 10 **F**1 3 6 10 12 15 16 23 34 35 36 40 45 46 47 52 53	16	10	S		100	4355	59	53.6	15	538	13676	5912	307
STEUBENVILLE—Jefferson County													
☐ OHIO VALLEY HOSPITAL, One Ross Park, Zip 43952; tel. 614/283-7000; Fred B. Brower, pres. **A**1a 2 6 9 10 **F**1 2 3 6 7 9 10 11 12 14 15 16 23 34 35 36 40 45 46 47 52 53	23	10	S		386	7903	130	33.7	28	859	28166	14458	715
⊞ ST. JOHN MEDICAL CENTER, St. John Hts., Zip 43952; tel. 614/264-8000; Sr. Alice Warrick, pres. **A**1a 9 10 **F**1 2 3 6 7 8 9 10 11 12 14 15 16 20 23 27 28 29 30 32 33 34 35 41 42 44 45 46 47 48 49 52 53 54; **S**5375	21	10	S		201	6971	121	61.7	0	0	26218	12308	574
SYLVANIA—Lucas County													
⊞ FLOWER MEMORIAL HOSPITAL, 5200 Harroun Rd., Zip 43560; tel. 419/885-1444; Dale D. Stoll, pres. (Total facility includes 202 beds in nursing home-type unit) **A**1a b 2 3 5 9 10 **F**1 2 3 5 6 7 8 9 10 11 12 14 15 16 17 19 21 23 24 25 34 35 36 40 41 42 44 45 46 47 48 49 52 53	23	10	S	TF H	509 307	10047 9271	334 194	65.6 —	30 30	769 769	48106 41996	24026 20423	1029 824
TIFFIN—Seneca County													
⊞ MERCY HOSPITAL, 485 W. Market St., Box 727, Zip 44883; tel. 419/447-3130; Sr. Marie Catherine Wise, pres. **A**1a 9 10 **F**1 3 6 10 12 14 15 16 23 30 35 36 40 45 46; **S**5155	23	10	S		95	4179	56	58.9	13	553	12958	5568	306
TOLEDO—Lucas County													
⊞ Δ MEDICAL COLLEGE OF OHIO HOSPITAL, 3000 Arlington Ave., C S. 10008, Zip 43699; tel. 419/381-4172; David J. Kolasky, exec. dir. **A**1a b 2 3 5 7 8 9 10 **F**1 3 4 6 7 8 9 10 11 12 13 14 15 16 17 20 23 24 25 26 27 28 29 30 32 33 34 35 37 38 42 44 46 50 52 53 54	12	10	S		274	7548	236	86.1	0	0	64161	26346	1042
⊞ MERCY HOSPITAL, 2200 Jefferson Ave., Zip 43624; tel. 419/259-1500; Sr. Phyllis Ann Gerold, pres. (Nonreporting) **A**1a 3 5 6 9 10; **S**5155	21	10	S		350	—	—	—	—	—	—	—	—

Hospital, Address, Telephone, Administrator, Approval and Facility Codes, Multihospital System Code

- ★ American Hospital Association (AHA) membership
- □ Joint Commission on Accreditation of Hospitals (JCAH) accreditation
- + American Osteopathic Hospital Association (AOHA) membership
- ○ American Osteopathic Association (AOA) accreditation
- Δ Commission on Accreditation of Rehabilitation Facilities (CARF) accreditation

Control codes 61, 63, 64, 71, 72 and 73 indicate hospitals listed by AOHA, but not registered by AHA. For definition of numerical codes, see page A2

Hospital	Classification Codes				Inpatient Data				Newborn Data		Expense (thousands of dollars)		
	Control	Service	Stay	Facilities	Beds	Admissions	Census	Occupancy (percent)	Bassinets	Births	Total	Payroll	Personnel
○ + PARKVIEW HOSPITAL, 1920 Parkwood Ave., Zip 43624; tel. 419/242-8471; Bernhardt A. Zeiher, pres. & chief exec. off. **A**9 10 11 12 13 **F**1 3 6 10 12 14 15 16 23 33 34 35 36 37 40 44 45 46 49 50 52 53	23	10	S		130	5171	77	59.2	10	542	21611	9243	403
★□ RIVERSIDE HOSPITAL, 1600 Superior St., Zip 43604; tel. 419/729-6000; Carroll L. Ashley, pres. **A**1a 9 10 **F**1 2 3 5 6 10 12 14 15 16 20 21 23 24 26 27 30 32 33 34 35 36 37 40 41 42 44 45 46 47 50 51 52 53	23	10	S		254	11468	169	66.5	24	1118	46043	19189	918
★□ ST. VINCENT MEDICAL CENTER, 2213 Cherry St., Zip 43608; tel. 419/321-3232; Lawrence O. Leaman, pres. **A**1a 2 3 5 6 9 10 **F**1 2 3 4 5 6 7 8 9 10 11 12 14 15 16 20 21 22 23 24 25 26 27 30 32 33 34 35 36 39 40 42 43 44 45 46 47 48 49 50 51 52 53 54; **S**5885	21	10	S		731	19653	449	61.4	36	1568	—	—	2555
★□ TOLEDO HOSPITAL, 2142 N. Cove Blvd., Zip 43606; tel. 419/471-4218; Bryan A. Rogers, pres. **A**1a b 2 3 5 6 8 9 10 **F**1 2 3 4 6 7 8 9 10 11 12 13 14 15 16 20 23 24 26 27 29 30 32 33 34 35 36 37 40 41 42 44 45 46 47 48 49 51 52 53 54	23	10	S		720	29214	556	77.2	44	4375	151866	77091	3462
□ TOLEDO MENTAL HEALTH CENTER, 930 S. Detroit Ave., Caller 10002, Zip 43699; tel. 419/381-1881; George P. Gintoli, supt. **A**1b 3 5 9 10 **F**15 19 23 24 30 32 33 42 44 45 46 50	12	22	L		431	1260	414	96.1	0	0	16816	14514	576
TROY—Miami County													
★□ DETTMER HOSPITAL (Includes Koester Unit), 3130 N. Dixie Hwy., Zip 45373; tel. 513/335-5624; Rebecca Neubauer-Rice, adm. (Total facility includes 39 beds in nursing home-type unit) **A**1a b 9 10 **F**1 3 6 10 11 12 14 15 16 19 23 24 25 26 27 28 29 30 31 32 33 34 35 36 40 42 44 45 46 47 48 49 52 53	23	10	S	TF H	196 157	3690 3602	113 77	57.7 —	14 14	328 328	15242 14635	7179 6741	436 397
★□ STOUDER MEMORIAL HOSPITAL, 920 Summit Ave., Zip 45373; tel. 513/335-0011; James O. Detwiler, adm. **A**1a 9 10 **F**1 3 6 7 8 10 11 12 14 15 16 23 24 30 34 35 36 40 44 45 46 47 52	23	10	S		126	4689	67	53.2	10	442	16349	6361	364
UPPER SANDUSKY—Wyandot County													
WYANDOT MEMORIAL HOSPITAL, 885 N. Sandusky Ave., Zip 43351; tel. 419/294-4991; John D. Harbaugh, adm. **A**9 10 **F**1 2 6 14 15 21 34 35 40 45	16	10	S		42	1423	18	42.9	8	174	4335	1842	109
URBANA—Champaign County													
★□ MERCY MEMORIAL HOSPITAL, 904 Scioto St., Zip 43078; tel. 513/653-5231; Robert E. Morrison, pres. **A**1a 2 9 10 **F**1 2 6 9 10 14 16 21 23 34 35 41 45 46 47 49 53; **S**5155	21	10	S		73	560	9	12.3	0	0	9584	4224	236
VAN WERT—Van Wert County													
★□ VAN WERT COUNTY HOSPITAL, 1250 S. Washington St., Zip 45891; tel. 419/238-2390; Jon M. See, pres. **A**1a 9 10 **F**1 3 9 10 12 15 16 17 20 21 23 28 30 35 36 40 44 45 46 52 53	23	10	S		100	2644	38	38.0	21	320	9153	4798	234
WADSWORTH—Medina County													
★□ WADSWORTH-RITTMAN HOSPITAL, 195 Wadsworth Rd., Zip 44281; tel. 216/334-1504; James W. Brumlow Jr., pres. **A**1a 9 10 **F**1 3 6 10 12 14 16 23 34 35 36 40 45 46 47 53	23	10	S		87	2620	35	39.3	10	374	9357	4342	236
WARREN—Trumbull County													
★□ Δ HILLSIDE HOSPITAL (General Medical and Rehabilitation), 8747 Squires Lane N.E., Zip 44484; tel. 216/841-3700; William P. Filarey, exec. dir. **A**1a 7 9 10 **F**15 16 23 24 25 26 33 34 42 43 44 45 46 47 48 49	13	49	S		109	960	56	51.4	0	0	8218	4717	253
★□ ST. JOSEPH RIVERSIDE HOSPITAL, 1400 Tod Ave. N.W., Zip 44485; tel. 216/841-4000; Sr. Mildred Ely, exec. dir. **A**1a 9 10 **F**1 3 5 6 7 8 9 10 11 12 13 14 15 16 23 24 27 29 30 32 33 34 35 36 40 42 43 45 46 47 48 49 52 53; **S**5645	21	10	S		209	8506	126	60.3	23	796	30851	14156	693
★□ TRUMBULL MEMORIAL HOSPITAL, 1350 E. Market St., Zip 44482; tel. 216/841-9011; Charles A. Johns, exec. dir. **A**1a 2 6 9 10 **F**1 2 3 5 6 7 8 9 10 11 12 14 15 16 23 24 26 27 30 33 34 35 36 40 41 42 44 45 46 52 53	23	10	S		464	15822	265	57.1	60	1383	60180	28993	1404
★ ○ WARREN GENERAL HOSPITAL, 667 Eastland Ave. S.E., Box 2128, Zip 44484; tel. 216/373-9000; Roy D. Pilasky, exec. dir. **A**9 10 11 12 13 **F**1 3 6 10 12 14 16 23 35 40 44 45 46 52 53	23	10	S		166	8209	137	68.2	16	388	30477	14107	662
WARRENSVILLE HEIGHTS—Cuyahoga County													
○ + BRENTWOOD HOSPITAL, 4110 Warrensville Center Rd., Zip 44122; tel. 216/283-2900; Theodore F. Classen DO, adm. **A**10 11 12 13 **F**1 3 6 10 12 14 16 23 24 26 32 33 35 36 40 44 45 46 47 52 53	23	10	S		195	5657	107	54.9	25	275	29296	12139	528
★□ SUBURBAN COMMUNITY HOSPITAL, 4180 Warrensville Center Rd., Zip 44122; tel. 216/491-6000; Matthew C. Gresko, sr. vice-pres. & chief oper. off. **A**1a 9 10 **F**1 3 6 10 12 14 15 16 20 23 24 30 33 34 35 44 45 46 50 53; **S**8835	23	10	S		180	4841	101	56.1	0	0	23637	11666	486
WASHINGTON COURT HOUSE—Fayette County													
★□ FAYETTE COUNTY MEMORIAL HOSPITAL, 1430 Columbus Ave., Zip 43160; tel. 614/335-1210; H. James Graham, adm. **A**1a 9 10 **F**1 3 6 12 14 15 16 23 26 34 35 36 40 41 45 47 53	13	10	S		63	3184	42	66.7	10	494	7947	4055	172
WAUSEON—Fulton County													
★□ FULTON COUNTY HEALTH CENTER, 725 S. Shoop Ave., Zip 43567; tel. 419/335-2015; E. Dean Beck, adm. **A**1a 9 10 **F**1 3 6 10 12 14 15 16 23 24 27 34 35 40 42 45 46 53	23	10	S		86	3327	54	62.8	12	385	10631	4749	240
WAVERLY—Pike County													
★□ PIKE COMMUNITY HOSPITAL, 100 Dawn Lane, Zip 45690; tel. 614/947-2186; Don J. Sabol, adm. (Nonreporting) **A**1a 9 10; **S**8865	23	10	S		56	—	—	—	—	—	—	—	—
WELLINGTON—Lorain County													
★ WELLINGTON COMMUNITY HOSPITAL, 510 Dickson St., Zip 44090; tel. 216/647-2345; David W. W. Snyder, adm. **A**9 10 **F**1 6 15 16 23 35 45	23	10	S		23	532	7	29.2	0	0	1734	764	52
WEST UNION—Adams County													
★□ ADAMS COUNTY HOSPITAL, 210 N. Wilson Dr., Zip 45693; tel. 513/544-5571; Gregory Nowak, adm. **A**1a 9 10 **F**1 6 10 12 14 16 23 34 35 40 44 45 46 53	13	10	S		68	1860	24	35.3	6	161	5904	2572	169
WESTERVILLE—Franklin County													
★□ ST. ANN'S HOSPITAL OF COLUMBUS, 500 S. Cleveland Ave., Zip 43081; tel. 614/898-4000; John B. Sandman, pres. & chief exec. off. **A**1a 3 5 9 10 **F**1 3 5 6 10 12 14 15 16 23 24 26 34 35 36 40 41 44 45 46 47 53	21	10	S		151	8151	96	63.6	32	3063	32198	12149	638
WESTLAKE—Cuyahoga County													
★□ ○ + ST. JOHN AND WEST SHORE HOSPITAL, 29000 Center Ridge Rd., Zip 44145; tel. 216/835-8000; John A. Rowland, pres. **A**1a 10 11 **F**1 2 3 6 9 10 12 15 16 23 24 26 34 35 36 40 41 44 45 46 48 49 53; **S**5125	23	10	S		200	8415	147	73.5	30	914	37088	17518	750
WILLARD—Huron County													
★□ WILLARD AREA HOSPITAL, 110 E. Howard St., Zip 44890; tel. 419/933-2931; Frederick M. Welfel, adm. **A**1a 9 10 **F**1 2 3 6 15 16 23 35 40 46 52 53; **S**2495	23	10	S		64	1687	19	29.7	10	167	4916	2325	129
WILLOUGHBY—Lake County													
LAKEWEST HOSPITAL, See Lake Hospital System, Painesville													
★□ RIDGECLIFF HOSPITAL, 35900 Euclid Ave., Zip 44094; tel. 216/951-1177; Irene A. Keal PhD, exec. dir. **A**1b 10 **F**3 24 26 28 29 30 32 33 34 42 46 47 48 49	23	22	S		160	1702	95	59.4	0	0	10299	5386	252

Hospital, Address, Telephone, Administrator, Approval and Facility Codes, Multihospital System Code	Classification Codes				Inpatient Data				Newborn Data		Expense (thousands of dollars)		
★ American Hospital Association (AHA) membership □ Joint Commission on Accreditation of Hospitals (JCAH) accreditation + American Osteopathic Hospital Association (AOHA) membership ○ American Osteopathic Association (AOA) accreditation Δ Commission on Accreditation of Rehabilitation Facilities (CARF) accreditation Control codes 61, 63, 64, 71, 72 and 73 indicate hospitals listed by AOHA, but not registered by AHA. For definition of numerical codes, see page A2	Control	Service	Stay	Facilities	Beds	Admissions	Census	Occupancy (percent)	Bassinets	Births	Total	Payroll	Personnel
WILMINGTON—Clinton County													
★□ CLINTON MEMORIAL HOSPITAL, 610 W. Main St., Zip 45177; tel. 513/382-6611; Thomas F. Kurtz, pres. **A**1a 9 10 **F**1 3 6 8 10 12 14 15 16 21 23 24 26 28 35 36 40 41 43 44 45 46 47 52 53	13	10	S		116	4857	74	63.8	17	542	14951	7594	357
WOOSTER—Wayne County													
★□ WOOSTER COMMUNITY HOSPITAL, 1761 Beall Ave., Zip 44691; tel. 216/263-8100; Richard G. Bajus, adm. **A**1a 9 10 **F**1 2 3 5 6 10 12 14 15 16 23 24 26 29 35 36 40 44 46 52 53	14	10	S		123	4989	66	53.7	24	836	14958	7924	404
WORTHINGTON—Franklin County													
★□ HARDING HOSPITAL, 445 E. Granville Rd., Zip 43085; tel. 614/885-5381; Thomas D. Pittman, adm. **A**1a 3 5 9 10 **F**24 28 29 30 32 33 34 42 43 46 49	23	22	L		120	348	76	63.3	0	0	12573	7796	371
WRIGHT-PATTERSON AIR FORCE BASE—Greene County													
★□ U. S. AIR FORCE MEDICAL CENTER WRIGHT-PATTERSON, Zip 45433; tel. 513/257-9133; Col. Bruce D. Wilhelm MSC USAF, adm. (Nonreporting) **A**1a 2 3 5	41	10	S		314	—	—	—	—	—	—	—	—
XENIA—Greene County													
★□ GREENE MEMORIAL HOSPITAL, 1141 N. Monroe Dr., Zip 45385; tel. 513/372-8011; Herman N. Menapace, pres. **A**1a 2 3 5 8 9 10 **F**1 3 6 10 12 14 15 16 23 24 26 27 28 29 30 31 32 33 34 35 36 40 41 44 45 46 47 48 49 53	23	10	S		216	5970	124	57.4	21	699	21364	9771	528
YOUNGSTOWN—Mahoning County													
★□ ST. ELIZABETH HOSPITAL MEDICAL CENTER, 1044 Belmont Ave., Box 1790, Zip 44501; tel. 216/746-7211; Sr. Susan Schorsten, exec. dir. **A**1a 2 3 5 6 8 9 10 **F**1 2 3 4 5 6 7 8 9 10 11 12 14 15 16 20 23 24 26 27 28 30 34 35 36 37 40 44 45 46 50 51 52 53 54; **S**5645	21	10	S		773	24921	547	70.8	46	2572	116070	59635	2673
★□ TOD CHILDREN'S HOSPITAL, 500 Gypsy Lane, Zip 44501; tel. 216/747-6700; Patricia A. Hrinko, dir. **A**1a 3 5 10 **F**1 6 10 12 14 15 16 20 23 27 30 32 33 34 35 46 47 51 53; **S**7005	23	50	S		97	2224	46	47.4	0	0	—	—	150
★□ WESTERN RESERVE CARE SYSTEMS-NORTHSIDE MEDICAL CENTER, 500 Gypsy Lane, Zip 44501; tel. 216/747-1444; Roland R. Carlson, vice-pres. oper. **A**1a 3 9 10 **F**1 3 4 6 10 12 14 15 16 20 23 24 27 32 33 34 35 36 37 38 40 41 42 46 47 53 54; **S**7005	23	10	S		304	11677	230	63.2	21	1445	—	—	1289
★□ WESTERN RESERVE CARE SYSTEMS-SOUTHSIDE MEDICAL CENTER, 345 Oak Hill Ave., Zip 44501; tel. 216/747-0777; Roland R. Carlson, vice-pres. oper. **A**1a 2 3 5 9 **F**1 3 6 7 8 9 10 11 12 14 15 16 23 24 25 34 35 44 46 47 53; **S**7005	23	10	S		217	8787	230	96.6	0	0	—	—	1044
□ WOODSIDE RECEIVING HOSPITAL, 800 E. Indianola Ave., Zip 44502; tel. 216/788-8712; Frank D. Fleischer, supt.; Muhammad I. Khan MD, med. dir. (Nonreporting) **A**1b 9 10	12	22	L		138	—	—	—	—	—	—	—	—
○ + YOUNGSTOWN OSTEOPATHIC HOSPITAL, 1319 Florencedale Ave., Zip 44501; Mailing Address Box 1258, Zip 44505; tel. 216/744-9200; Mark C. Barabas, adm. & chief exec. off. (Nonreporting) **A**9 10 11 12 13	23	10	S		175	—	—	—	—	—	—	—	—
ZANESVILLE—Muskingum County													
★□ BETHESDA HOSPITAL, 2951 N. Maple Ave., Zip 43701; tel. 614/454-4000; William R. VanGieson, pres. & chief exec. off. **A**1a 9 10 **F**1 2 3 6 9 10 11 12 14 15 16 20 23 24 27 29 30 32 33 34 35 36 37 40 42 43 45 46 47 52 53 54	23	10	S		260	9934	162	62.3	30	1189	31793	15342	728
★□ Δ GOOD SAMARITAN MEDICAL CENTER AND REHABILITATION CENTER, 800 Forest Ave., Zip 43701; tel. 614/454-5000; Daniel J. Rissing, pres. (Total facility includes 18 beds in nursing home-type unit) **A**1a 7 9 10 **F**1 2 3 6 8 10 11 12 14 15 16 19 21 23 24 25 26 32 33 34 35 36 37 40 41 44 45 46 47 48 49 52 53; **S**1455	21	10	S	TF	284	8869	190	66.9	20	698	38038	16576	831
				H	266	8728	178	—	20	698	37710	16291	—

Hospital, Address, Telephone, Administrator, Approval and Facility Codes, Multihospital System Code	Classification Codes				Inpatient Data				Newborn Data		Expense (thousands of dollars)		
★ American Hospital Association (AHA) membership □ Joint Commission on Accreditation of Hospitals (JCAH) accreditation + American Osteopathic Hospital Association (AOHA) membership ○ American Osteopathic Association (AOA) accreditation Δ Commission on Accreditation of Rehabilitation Facilities (CARF) accreditation Control codes 61, 63, 64, 71, 72 and 73 indicate hospitals listed by AOHA, but not registered by AHA. For definition of numerical codes, see page A2	Control	Service	Stay	Facilities	Beds	Admissions	Census	Occupancy (percent)	Bassinets	Births	Total	Payroll	Personnel

Oklahoma

Hospital	Control	Service	Stay	Facilities	Beds	Admissions	Census	Occupancy (percent)	Bassinets	Births	Total	Payroll	Personnel
ADA—Pontotoc County													
★□ CARL ALBERT INDIAN HEALTH FACILITY, 1001 N. Country Club Rd., Zip 74820; tel. 405/436-3980; Edward L. Kruger, serv. unit dir. **A**1a 10 **F**1 3 6 12 15 16 28 33 34 35 36 37 40 43 47 52	47	10	S		53	2278	26	49.1	13	788	7851	4806	146
★□ VALLEY VIEW REGIONAL HOSPITAL (Formerly Valley View Hospital), 430 N. Monta Vista, Zip 74820; tel. 405/332-2323; Philip Fisher, pres. **A**1a 2 9 10 **F**1 2 3 5 6 15 16 17 23 35 40 41 44 45 46 47 51 53 54	23	10	S		149	5636	97	65.1	15	503	17377	8231	500
AFTON—Ottawa County													
○ AFTON MEMORIAL HOSPITAL, 134 S. Main St., Drawer L, Zip 74331; tel. 918/257-8322 (Nonreporting) **A**9 10 11	33	10	S		26	—	—	—	—	—	—	—	—
ALTUS—Jackson County													
★□ JACKSON COUNTY MEMORIAL HOSPITAL, 1200 E. Pecan St., Box 8190, Zip 73523; tel. 405/482-4781; William G. Wilson, chief exec. off. **A**1a 9 10 **F**1 3 6 10 12 16 19 23 35 40 41 42 44 45 46 47	16	10	S		130	5028	87	66.9	10	400	16117	5642	362
U. S. AIR FORCE HOSPITAL ALTUS, See Altus Air Force Base													
ALTUS AIR FORCE BASE—Jackson County													
U. S. AIR FORCE HOSPITAL ALTUS, Zip 73523; tel. 405/481-5205; Maj. Garry Hayes, adm. (Nonreporting)	41	10	S		28	—	—	—	—	—	—	—	—
ALVA—Woods County													
SHARE MEDICAL CENTER, 800 Share Dr., Zip 73717; tel. 405/327-2800; Al Allee, adm. (Total facility includes 80 beds in nursing home-type unit) **A**9 10 **F**1 6 14 19 23 34 35 45 46; **S**1865	16	10	S	TF	120	732	80	66.7	4	76	2646	1295	92
				H	40	679	8	—	4	76	1739	741	48
ANADARKO—Caddo County													
★□ ANADARKO MUNICIPAL HOSPITAL, 1002 Central Blvd. E., Zip 73005; tel. 405/247-2551; Jack Martin, adm. **A**1a 9 10 **F**1 6 14 16 23 35 37 40 44 45 47 52 53 54	14	10	S		49	992	12	24.5	10	46	2127	978	61
ANTLERS—Pushmataha County													
PUSHMATAHA COUNTY-TOWN OF ANTLERS HOSPITAL AUTHORITY, 510 E. Main St., Box G, Zip 74523; tel. 405/298-3344 **A**9 10 **F**1 3 6 16 23 34 35 40 41 45	15	10	S		50	1440	19	38.0	6	161	2807	1273	84
ARDMORE—Carter County													
★□ ARDMORE ADVENTIST HOSPITAL, 1012 14th St. N.W., Zip 73401; tel. 405/223-4050; Sam C. Loewen, adm. **A**1a 9 10 **F**6 14 15 16 21 23 34 35 36 41 45 46 47 53; **S**4165	21	10	S		72	2176	29	40.3	6	330	5510	2169	134
★□ MEMORIAL HOSPITAL OF SOUTHERN OKLAHOMA, 1011 14th Ave., Zip 73401; tel. 405/223-5400; Howard A. Walker Jr., adm. **A**1a 9 10 **F**1 3 6 8 9 10 12 15 16 23 34 35 40 41 45 53	16	10	S		145	5290	80	55.2	25	567	13973	6502	337
ATOKA—Atoka County													
ATOKA MEMORIAL HOSPITAL, 1501 S. Virginia, Zip 74525; tel. 405/889-3333; Andy Freeman, adm. **A**9 10 **F**1 16 23 35 45; **S**1865	13	10	S		37	769	11	29.7	8	19	1576	777	47
BARTLESVILLE—Washington County													
★□ JANE PHILLIPS EPISCOPAL-MEMORIAL MEDICAL CENTER (Includes Jane Phillips Episcopal Hospital Division, 3500 E. Frank Phillips Blvd., Zip 74003; Memorial Hospital of Washington County, 3500 E. Frank Phillips Blvd., Zip 74003), 3500 E. Frank Phillips Blvd., Zip 74003; tel. 918/333-7200; Randall J. Fale, adm. (Total facility includes 68 beds in nursing home-type unit) **A**1a 2 3 5 9 10 **F**1 2 3 5 6 9 10 11 12 14 15 16 19 21 23 24 25 27 30 32 33 35 36 40 44 45 46 47 48 49 52 53	21	10	S	TF	312	8241	201	64.4	16	1076	28905	11723	569
				H	244	8185	140	—	16	1076	27641	11060	528
MEMORIAL HOSPITAL OF WASHINGTON COUNTY, See Jane Phillips Episcopal-Memorial Medical Center													
BEAVER—Beaver County													
★□ BEAVER COUNTY MEMORIAL HOSPITAL, 212 E. Eighth St., Box 640, Zip 73932; tel. 405/625-4551; Lavern Melton, adm. **A**1a 9 10 **F**1 16 35	13	10	S		27	603	8	27.6	6	82	1348	574	46
BETHANY—Oklahoma County													
□ BETHANY GENERAL HOSPITAL, 7600 N.W. 23rd St., Zip 73008; tel. 405/787-3450; Ron J. Sloan, adm. **A**1a 9 10 **F**1 3 6 10 15 16 23 24 27 29 30 32 33 35 41 42 44 45 46 53	14	10	S		68	2016	33	48.5	0	0	6756	3193	193
BLACKWELL—Kay County													
★□ BLACKWELL REGIONAL HOSPITAL, 13th St. & Ferguson Ave., Zip 74631; tel. 405/363-2311; Roland D. Gee, adm. (Data for 181 days) **A**1a 9 10 **F**1 14 16 23 35 45 46; **S**0305	21	10	S		53	983	33	62.3	8	19	1794	888	109
BOISE CITY—Cimarron County													
CIMARRON MEMORIAL HOSPITAL, 100 S. Ellis, Zip 73933; tel. 405/544-2501 (Nonreporting) **A**9 10	13	10	S		64	—	—	—	—	—	—	—	—
BRISTOW—Creek County													
★□ BRISTOW MEMORIAL HOSPITAL, Seventh & Spruce Sts., Box 780, Zip 74010; tel. 918/367-2215; W. Michael Shawn, adm. **A**1a 9 10 **F**1 2 14 16 35 37 40; **S**0305	23	10	S		38	719	9	23.7	5	10	1618	848	61
BROKEN ARROW—Tulsa County													
□ BROKEN ARROW MEDICAL CENTER, 3000 S. Elm Pl., Zip 74012; tel. 918/455-3535; Bruce Switzer, adm. **A**1a 9 10 **F**1 3 6 10 11 14 15 16 23 35 36 40 45 46	23	10	S		67	1467	20	29.9	9	80	7006	2751	152
BUFFALO—Harper County													
HARPER COUNTY COMMUNITY HOSPITAL, Box 60, Zip 73834; tel. 405/735-2555; Dennis Immell, chief exec. off. **A**9 10 **F**1 35 41	13	10	S		25	503	6	24.0	4	32	804	470	—
CARNEGIE—Caddo County													
CARNEGIE TRI-COUNTY MUNICIPAL HOSPITAL, 102 N. Broadway, Box 97, Zip 73015; tel. 405/654-1050; Patti Davis, adm. **A**9 10 **F**12 15 16 34 35 43	14	10	S		34	796	10	29.4	4	58	1331	669	62
CHEROKEE—Alfalfa County													
□ ALFALFA COUNTY HOSPITAL, Fifth & Oklahoma Sts., Zip 73728; tel. 405/596-3501; Larry Perkins, adm. **A**1a 9 10 **F**1 3 14 16 23 35 45 46	13	10	S		20	420	7	35.0	4	32	1247	529	35
CHICKASHA—Grady County													
★□ GRADY MEMORIAL HOSPITAL, 2220 Iowa, Zip 73018; tel. 405/224-2300; Roger R. Boid, adm. **A**1a 2 9 10 **F**1 3 6 10 12 15 16 23 35 40 41 45 46 53	16	10	S		156	4748	67	42.9	20	684	11102	5984	335
CLAREMORE—Rogers County													
★□ AMI CLAREMORE REGIONAL MEDICAL CENTER, 1202 N. Muskogee St., Zip 74017; tel. 918/341-2556; Betty W. Walker, exec. dir. **A**1a 9 10 **F**1 3 6 10 16 23 34 35 40 41 45 46; **S**0125	33	10	S		74	2543	32	43.2	8	260	8177	2517	140

Hospital, Address, Telephone, Administrator, Approval and Facility Codes, Multihospital System Code	Classification Codes				Inpatient Data				Newborn Data		Expense (thousands of dollars)		
★ American Hospital Association (AHA) membership □ Joint Commission on Accreditation of Hospitals (JCAH) accreditation + American Osteopathic Hospital Association (AOHA) membership ○ American Osteopathic Association (AOA) accreditation Δ Commission on Accreditation of Rehabilitation Facilities (CARF) accreditation Control codes 61, 63, 64, 71, 72 and 73 indicate hospitals listed by AOHA, but not registered by AHA. For definition of numerical codes, see page A2	Control	Service	Stay	Facilities	Beds	Admissions	Census	Occupancy (percent)	Bassinets	Births	Total	Payroll	Personnel
★□ U. S. PUBLIC HEALTH SERVICE COMPREHENSIVE INDIAN HEALTH FACILITY, 101 S. Moore Ave., Zip 74017; tel. 918/341-8430; Thomas B. Talamini, serv. unit dir.; Lindel V. Adair, adm. off. **A**1a 10 **F**1 3 6 15 16 34 35 36 37 40 45 46 52	47	10	S		50	3006	32	64.0	13	973	8848	6081	262
CLEVELAND—Pawnee County													
CLEVELAND AREA HOSPITAL, 1401 W. Pawnee St., Zip 74020; tel. 918/358-2501; Bob H. Cox, adm. **A**9 10 **F**1 14 16 35 41 45	16	10	S		25	500	7	28.0	4	0	1646	778	48
CLINTON—Custer County													
★□ CLINTON REGIONAL HOSPITAL, 100 N. 30th St., Box 1569, Zip 73601; tel. 405/323-2363; Ronald Dorris, adm. **A**1a 9 10 **F**1 6 10 12 15 16 20 23 34 35 45 46 47 53; **S**2495	14	10	S		75	2554	29	38.7	15	425	5831	2972	150
★□ U. S. PUBLIC HEALTH SERVICE INDIAN HOSPITAL, Rte. 4, Box 213, Zip 73601; tel. 405/323-2884; Joseph Bennett, dir.; Thedis Mitchell, adm. off. **A**1a 10 **F**6 14 15 28 34 35 37 47 49 50	47	10	S		14	750	8	57.1	0	0	1751	1138	58
COALGATE—Coal County													
MARY HURLEY HOSPITAL, 22 N. Covington St., Zip 74538; tel. 405/927-2327; Larry C. Key EdD, chief exec. off. **A**9 10 **F**1 2 14 16 35 37 40	23	10	S		20	598	7	35.0	4	15	1241	633	42
CORDELL—Washita County													
★□ CORDELL MEMORIAL HOSPITAL, 1220 N. Church St., Zip 73632; tel. 405/832-3338; Scott Copeland, actg. adm. **A**1a 9 10 **F**1 3 6 14 15 16 23 35 40 42 52; **S**0305	23	10	S		28	590	7	25.0	10	29	1606	774	38
CUSHING—Payne County													
★□ CUSHING REGIONAL HOSPITAL, 1027 E. Cherry, Box 1409, Zip 74023; tel. 918/225-2915; Ron Cackler, adm. (Total facility includes 17 beds in nursing home-type unit) **A**1a 9 10 **F**1 3 6 10 14 16 19 23 24 34 35 36 40 41 44 45 46 47 52 53	23	10	S	TF	92	1861	27	29.7	6	144	4798	2259	144
				H	75	1714	22	—	6	144	4614	2113	132
DRUMRIGHT—Creek County													
★ DRUMRIGHT MEMORIAL HOSPITAL, 501 Lou S. Allard Dr., Zip 74030; tel. 918/352-2525; Gary F. Henderson, adm. **A**9 10 **F**1 3 6 14 16 34 35 45 46 53	23	10	S		39	1555	21	53.8	4	49	4232	1791	105
DUNCAN—Stephens County													
★□ DUNCAN REGIONAL HOSPITAL, 1407 Whisenant Dr., P O Box 2000, Zip 73533; tel. 405/252-5300; David Robertson, adm. (Total facility includes 12 beds in nursing home-type unit) **A**1a 9 10 **F**1 3 6 10 12 14 15 16 19 20 23 24 35 40 41 44 45 46 47 53	23	10	S	TF	108	4174	56	51.9	14	497	12165	4974	287
				H	96	4110	54	—	14	497	12098	4920	—
DURANT—Bryan County													
★□ MEDICAL CENTER OF SOUTHEASTERN OKLAHOMA (Formerly Bryan Memorial Hospital), 1800 University, Zip 74701; Mailing Address P O Box 1207, Zip 74702; tel. 405/924-3080; Harry D. Provost Jr., adm. **A**1a 9 10 **F**1 3 5 6 10 15 16 23 34 35 36 41 45 46; **S**6525	33	10	S		80	3652	44	55.0	10	368	8657	3423	191
EDMOND—Oklahoma County													
★□ EDMOND MEMORIAL HOSPITAL, 1 S. Bryant St., Zip 73034; tel. 405/341-6100; Joel A. Hart, adm. **A**1a 9 10 **F**1 3 10 12 13 15 16 17 23 32 34 35 36 40 44 45 48 49 53; **S**1755	33	10	S		85	3639	51	60.0	12	658	—	—	202
EL RENO—Canadian County													
FEDERAL CORRECTIONAL INSTITUTION HOSPITAL, Box 1000, Zip 73036; tel. 405/262-4875; D. M. Mifflin, adm. **F**1 5 15 20 28 29 30 32 33 34 35 43	48	11	S		25	639	10	40.0	0	0	1210	651	20
★ PARK VIEW HOSPITAL, 2115 Parkview Dr., P O Box 129, Zip 73036; tel. 405/262-2640; Lex Smith, adm. **A**9 10 **F**1 3 6 14 16 23 24 26 34 35 36 40 41 42 44 45 46	14	10	S		54	1528	19	35.2	10	156	3692	1998	127
ELK CITY—Beckham County													
★□ COMMUNITY HOSPITAL, 1705 W. Second St., Zip 73644; Mailing Address P O Box 2339, Zip 73648; tel. 405/225-2511; Talton L. Francis, adm. **A**1a 9 10 **F**1 3 5 6 10 14 15 16 23 24 26 35 36 45 46 49 53	23	10	S		78	2453	32	41.0	6	314	5624	2687	207
ENID—Garfield County													
★□ BASS MEMORIAL BAPTIST HOSPITAL, 600 S. Monroe, Box 3168, Zip 73702; tel. 405/233-2300; W. Eugene Baxter Drph, adm. (Total facility includes 11 beds in nursing home-type unit) **A**1a 3 5 9 10 **F**1 6 7 8 9 10 11 12 14 15 16 19 23 33 34 35 36 37 41 43 44 45 46 47 53; **S**0305	21	10	S	TF	96	3943	58	60.4	8	351	10307	4832	266
				H	85	3781	53	—	8	351	—	—	—
○ + ENID MEMORIAL HOSPITAL, Fourth & Park Sts., Box 3467, Zip 73701; tel. 405/234-3371; Steve Hendley, adm. **A**9 10 11 12 **F**1 3 6 12 15 16 23 34 35 36 40 41 45 46 47 48 50 53	23	10	S		104	3876	60	57.7	6	330	13864	6429	280
★□ ST. MARY'S HOSPITAL, 305 S. Fifth St., Box 232, Zip 73701; tel. 405/233-6100; Mary T. Brasseaux, adm. (Total facility includes 14 beds in nursing home-type unit) **A**1a 3 5 9 10 **F**1 2 3 5 6 10 11 12 15 16 19 20 23 24 27 28 30 31 32 34 35 36 40 41 44 46 47 50 51 52 53 54; **S**1755	21	10	S	TF	221	9074	160	72.4	10	772	—	—	545
				H	207	8942	153	—	10	772	—	—	—
EUFAULA—McIntosh County													
COMMUNITY HOSPITAL-LAKEVIEW (Formerly Eufaula Community Hospital), P O Box 629, Zip 74432; tel. 918/689-2535; Jim Robertson Jr., adm. **A**9 10 **F**1 2 6 12 14 15 34 35 45 47 53	33	10	S		33	913	12	36.4	0	0	1926	752	61
FAIRFAX—Osage County													
★ FAIRFAX MEMORIAL HOSPITAL, Taft Ave. & Hwy. 18, Box 219, Zip 74637; tel. 918/642-3291; Robert C. Bray, adm. **A**9 10 **F**1 6 16 35 45	14	10	S		19	883	12	63.2	0	0	1416	6304	44
FAIRVIEW—Major County													
★ FAIRVIEW HOSPITAL, 523 E. State Rd., Zip 73737; tel. 405/227-3721; Mark Hart, adm. **A**9 10 **F**1 3 16 35 45 46	14	10	S		31	771	8	25.8	5	45	1376	747	53
FORT SILL—Comanche County													
★□ REYNOLDS ARMY COMMUNITY HOSPITAL, 4700 Hartell Blvd., Zip 73503; tel. 405/351-6354; Jack E. Bradford, dep. comr. & chief exec. off. **A**1a **F**3 6 10 11 12 14 15 16 21 23 26 28 30 32 33 34 35 36 37 40 45 46 47 52 53	42	10	S		187	8848	103	55.1	27	1274	36216	24497	937
FORT SUPPLY—Woodward County													
★□ WESTERN STATE HOSPITAL, Box 1, Zip 73841; tel. 405/766-2311; David Statton, dep. supt. adm. (Nonreporting) **A**1b 10	12	22	L		477	—	—	—	—	—	—	—	—
FREDERICK—Tillman County													
★□ MEMORIAL HOSPITAL, 319 E. Josephine, Zip 73542; tel. 405/335-7565; Ralph Paulding, chief exec. off. **A**1a 9 10 **F**1 3 6 12 14 15 16 23 26 34 35 41 44 45 46	16	10	S		48	1127	22	45.8	8	44	3241	1733	110
GROVE—Delaware County													
★□ GROVE GENERAL HOSPITAL, 1310 S. Main St., Box 1348, Zip 74344; tel. 918/786-2243; Henry C. Lamb, adm. **A**1a 9 10 **F**1 2 6 14 16 23 35 45; **S**0305	23	10	S		59	2161	27	60.0	4	117	4890	2073	152
GUTHRIE—Logan County													
★□ LOGAN COUNTY HEALTH CENTER, Hwy. 33 W. at Academy Rd., Box 1017, Zip 73044; tel. 405/282-6700; Michael R. Morris, adm. **A**1a 9 10 **F**1 3 6 10 14 15 16 23 26 34 35 45 46 47	16	10	S		50	1746	25	50.0	6	51	5171	2109	136
GUYMON—Texas County													
MEMORIAL HOSPITAL, 520 Medical Dr., Zip 73942; tel. 405/338-6515; Floyd N. Price, adm. **A**9 10 **F**1 3 6 10 12 14 15 16 23 35 36 40 41 45 46 47	13	10	S		47	2164	23	52.3	6	253	4384	2003	129

Hospital, Address, Telephone, Administrator, Approval and Facility Codes, Multihospital System Code	Classification Codes				Inpatient Data				Newborn Data		Expense (thousands of dollars)		
★ American Hospital Association (AHA) membership □ Joint Commission on Accreditation of Hospitals (JCAH) accreditation + American Osteopathic Hospital Association (AOHA) membership ○ American Osteopathic Association (AOA) accreditation Δ Commission on Accreditation of Rehabilitation Facilities (CARF) accreditation Control codes 61, 63, 64, 71, 72 and 73 indicate hospitals listed by AOHA, but not registered by AHA. For definition of numerical codes, see page A2	Control	Service	Stay	Facilities	Beds	Admissions	Census	Occupancy (percent)	Bassinets	Births	Total	Payroll	Personnel
HEALDTON—Carter County													
HEALDTON MUNICIPAL HOSPITAL, 918 S.W. Eighth St., Box 928, Zip 73438; tel. 405/229-0701; Zeb Wright, adm. **A**9 10 **F**1 2 6 14 16 35 40 45; **S**1865	14	10	S		28	655	8	28.6	4	55	1110	522	37
HENRYETTA—Okmulgee County													
□ HENRYETTA MEDICAL CENTER, P O Box 1269, Zip 74437; tel. 918/652-4463; James P. Bailey, adm. (Nonreporting) **A**1a 10	16	10	S		52	—	—	—	—	—	—	—	—
HOBART—Kiowa County													
★ ELKVIEW GENERAL HOSPITAL, 429 W. Elm St., Box 633, Zip 73651; tel. 405/726-3324; J. W. Finch, adm. **A**9 10 **F**1 3 6 10 16 23 30 35 45	16	10	S		50	1771	25	50.0	8	117	2480	1223	75
HOLDENVILLE—Hughes County													
□ HOLDENVILLE GENERAL HOSPITAL, 100 Crestview Dr., Zip 74848; tel. 405/379-6631; Gary M. Moore, adm. **A**1a 9 10 **F**1 3 6 10 14 15 16 23 34 35 43 45 52 53	14	10	S		49	1221	18	36.7	8	43	2728	1173	78
HOLLIS—Harmon County													
□ HARMON MEMORIAL HOSPITAL, 400 E. Chestnut St., P O Box 791, Zip 73550; tel. 405/688-3363; Frank D. Loveless, adm. (Nonreporting) **A**1a 9 10	13	10	S		32	—	—	—	—	—	—	—	—
HOMINY—Osage County													
HOMINY CITY HOSPITAL, N. Hwy. 99, Box 460, Zip 74035; tel. 918/885-2154; Howard Peterson, actg. adm. **A**9 10 **F**1 6 16 23 34 35 45	16	10	S		26	344	5	19.2	0	0	1093	492	40
HUGO—Choctaw County													
⊞ CHOCTAW MEMORIAL HOSPITAL, 1405 E. Kirk Rd., Zip 74743; tel. 405/326-6414; Lynn Breen, actg. adm. **A**1a 10 **F**1 3 6 14 16 23 35 40 45 46 47; **S**0305	16	10	S		63	1093	15	23.8	5	46	2959	1073	96
IDABEL—McCurtain County													
⊞ MCCURTAIN MEMORIAL HOSPITAL, Jumper Memorial Bypass, Box 1019, Zip 74745; tel. 405/286-7623; Alfred S. Loveday, adm. **A**1a 9 10 **F**1 3 6 10 12 15 16 23 34 35 45 53	16	10	S		119	2523	35	29.4	8	299	5139	2239	154
JAY—Delaware County													
⊞ JAY MEMORIAL HOSPITAL, Osage & Washbourne Sts., Box 1140, Zip 74346; tel. 918/253-4284; Fred P. Summary, adm. (Nonreporting) **A**1a 9 10; **S**9795	33	10	S		28	—	—	—	—	—	—	—	—
KINGFISHER—Kingfisher County													
★ COMMUNITY HOSPITAL, 500 S. Ninth St., Box 59, Zip 73750; tel. 405/375-3141; Max Armstrong, adm. (Nonreporting) **A**9 10	23	10	S		35	—	—	—	—	—	—	—	—
LAWTON—Comanche County													
⊞ AMI SOUTHWESTERN MEDICAL CENTER (Formerly AMI Southwestern Hospital), 5602 S.W. Lee Blvd., Zip 73505; Mailing Address P O Box 7290, Zip 73506; tel. 405/355-2700; Thomas L. Rine, exec. dir. **A**1a 9 **F**1 3 6 7 8 9 10 16 19 23 24 34 35 36 40 41 44 45 46 52; **S**0125	33	10	S		109	2644	47	43.1	6	81	—	—	240
⊞ COMANCHE COUNTY MEMORIAL HOSPITAL, 3401 Gore Blvd., Zip 73505; Mailing Address Box 129, Zip 73502; tel. 405/355-8620; Randy Curry, pres. **A**1a 9 10 **F**1 2 3 5 6 12 15 16 23 24 25 26 33 34 35 36 37 40 41 42 44 46 47 48 52 53 54	16	10	S		283	7800	117	41.3	34	1255	26399	9702	598
⊞ U. S. PUBLIC HEALTH SERVICE INDIAN HOSPITAL, Zip 73507; tel. 405/353-0350; Bryce Poolaw MD, chief exec. off. **A**1a 10 **F**1 14 15 16 28 32 33 34 35 37 38 40 43 50 52	47	10	S		52	1860	24	46.2	12	379	6635	3539	168
LINDSAY—Garvin County													
LINDSAY MUNICIPAL HOSPITAL, Hwy. 19 W., Box 888, Zip 73052; tel. 405/756-4321; Billy M. Lee, adm. **A**9 10 **F**1 16 35 40	14	10	S		25	1126	16	64.0	5	44	2280	1163	75
MADILL—Marshall County													
★ MARSHALL MEMORIAL HOSPITAL, 1 Hospital Dr., P O Box 827, Zip 73446; tel. 405/795-3384; Curtis R. Pryor, adm. **A**9 10 **F**16 35 46	13	10	S		50	1293	19	38.0	5	61	2359	1180	84
MANGUM—Greer County													
★ MANGUM CITY HOSPITAL, 2100 N. Louis Tittle St., Box 280, Zip 73554; tel. 405/782-3353; Jim Ivey, adm. **A**9 10 **F**14 16 23 35 45 48 53	14	10	S		40	986	18	45.0	6	50	2087	978	118
MARIETTA—Love County													
★ LOVE COUNTY HEALTH CENTER, 300 Wanda, Box 70, Zip 73448; tel. 405/276-3347; Jerry Cole, adm. (Nonreporting) **A**9 10	13	10	S		30	—	—	—	—	—	—	—	—
MCALESTER—Pittsburg County													
⊞ MCALESTER REGIONAL HOSPITAL, One Clark Bass Blvd., Zip 74501; Mailing Address P O Box 1228, Zip 74502; tel. 918/426-1800; Ed Majors, adm. (Total facility includes 24 beds in nursing home-type unit) **A**1a 9 10 **F**1 3 6 10 12 14 15 16 17 19 20 23 33 34 35 36 41 44 45 46 47 53	16	10	S	TF	200	6838	102	51.0	16	675	15736	7511	442
				H	176	6525	93	—	16	675	—	—	429
MIAMI—Ottawa County													
⊞ BAPTIST REGIONAL HEALTH CENTER, 200 Second St. S.W., Zip 74354; Mailing Address Box 1207, Zip 74355; tel. 918/542-6611; Bob Phillips, adm. **A**1a 9 10 **F**1 3 6 10 14 15 16 23 35 36 40 41 45 46 47 52 53; **S**0305	23	10	S		134	4457	70	52.2	15	368	11750	5163	320
□ WILLOW CREST HOSPITAL, 130 A St. S.W., Zip 74354; tel. 918/542-1836; John Gohman II, adm. (Nonreporting) **A**1a 10; **S**1055	33	22	S		42	—	—	—	—	—	—	—	—
MIDWEST CITY—Oklahoma County													
⊞ MIDWEST CITY MEMORIAL HOSPITAL, 2825 Parklawn Dr., Zip 73110; tel. 405/737-4411; William D. Mulinix, pres. **A**1a 9 10 **F**1 3 4 5 6 10 12 14 15 16 20 23 24 26 34 35 36 37 40 44 45 46 53	14	10	S		142	7386	104	73.2	24	889	23796	10875	553
MOORE—Cleveland County													
⊞ MOORE MUNICIPAL HOSPITAL, 1500 S.E. Fourth St., Box 6949, Zip 73160; tel. 405/794-7721; James McAlister, adm. **A**1a 9 10 **F**1 3 6 12 14 16 23 34 35 36 40 45	16	10	S		55	1938	20	36.4	10	257	5626	2198	114
MUSKOGEE—Muskogee County													
⊞ MUSKOGEE REGIONAL MEDICAL CENTER, 300 Edna M Rockefeller Dr., Zip 74401; tel. 918/682-5501; Douglas V. Johnson, adm. **A**1a 2 9 10 **F**1 3 6 7 8 10 11 12 13 15 16 20 23 24 25 27 30 32 33 34 35 37 40 41 42 44 45 46 47 52 53	16	10	S		326	9654	178	54.6	25	1014	36029	17641	936
⊞ VETERANS ADMINISTRATION MEDICAL CENTER, Honor Heights Dr., Zip 74401; tel. 918/683-3261; Fred F. Salas, dir. **A**1a 3 5 **F**1 3 6 10 12 14 15 16 21 23 24 26 28 29 30 32 33 34 35 44 45 46 47 48 49 50	45	10	S		193	4719	141	70.1	0	0	36363	19415	638
NORMAN—Cleveland County													
□ CENTRAL STATE GRIFFIN MEMORIAL HOSPITAL, Box 151, Zip 73070; tel. 405/321-4880; James K. O'Toole MD, supt. **A**1b 3 5 10 **F**12 14 15 16 23 24 32 33 34 42 46 47 50	12	22	L		446	3356	411	72.7	0	0	26973	15920	788
★ CHARLES B. GODDARD HOSPITAL, UNIVERSITY OF OKLAHOMA, 620 Elm Ave., Zip 73069; tel. 405/325-4611; Carl S. Whittle, adm. **A**9 **F**23 28 30 32 33 34 37 52	12	11	S		54	131	1	1.9	0	0	2849	1953	84
⊞ NORMAN REGIONAL HOSPITAL, 901 N. Porter St., Box 1308, Zip 73070; tel. 405/321-1700; Craig W. Jones, adm. **A**1a 9 10 **F**1 2 3 6 8 9 10 12 14 15 16 23 24 27 30 32 35 36 40 41 42 44 45 46 47 48 52 53	15	10	S		268	10238	151	59.7	26	1339	29094	14673	740
NOWATA—Nowata County													
★ NOWATA GENERAL HOSPITAL, 237 S. Locust St., Box 426, Zip 74048; tel. 918/273-3102; Frank Hufford, adm. **A**9 10 **F**1 2 10 16 35 40 46	23	10	S		42	709	8	19.0	10	44	1230	675	50

Hospital, Address, Telephone, Administrator, Approval and Facility Codes, Multihospital System Code

★ American Hospital Association (AHA) membership
□ Joint Commission on Accreditation of Hospitals (JCAH) accreditation
+ American Osteopathic Hospital Association (AOHA) membership
○ American Osteopathic Association (AOA) accreditation
Δ Commission on Accreditation of Rehabilitation Facilities (CARF) accreditation
Control codes 61, 63, 64, 71, 72 and 73 indicate hospitals listed by AOHA, but not registered by AHA.
For definition of numerical codes, see page A2

Hospital	Classification Codes: Control	Service	Stay	Facilities	Inpatient Data: Beds	Admissions	Census	Occupancy (percent)	Newborn Data: Bassinets	Births	Expense (thousands of dollars): Total	Payroll	Personnel
OKARCHE—Kingfisher County													
★□ OKARCHE MEMORIAL HOSPITAL, 300 Memorial Dr., P O Box 218, Zip 73762; tel. 405/263-4811; Jim M. Robertson, adm. **A**1a 9 10 **F**1 16 35 45 47; **S**0305	23	10	S		25	670	7	28.0	6	97	1304	711	51
OKEENE—Blaine County													
□ OKEENE MUNICIPAL HOSPITAL, 400 East St., P O Box 489, Zip 73763; tel. 405/822-4417; Delbert L. Robison, adm. (Nonreporting) **A**1a 9 10	14	10	S		80	—	—	—	—	—	—	—	—
OKLAHOMA CITY—Oklahoma County													
AMI DOCTORS GENERAL HOSPITAL, See Doctors General Hospital													
★□ BAPTIST MEDICAL CENTER OF OKLAHOMA, 3300 N.W. Expwy., Zip 73112; tel. 405/949-3011; Stanley Hupfeld, chief exec. off. **A**1a 2 3 5 9 10 **F**1 2 3 4 6 7 8 9 10 11 12 13 14 15 16 20 22 23 24 25 26 27 28 29 30 33 34 35 36 37 44 45 46 47 51 53 54	23	10	S		504	20002	388	77.0	35	1762	78811	36012	1910
★□ BONE AND JOINT HOSPITAL, 1111 N. Dewey Ave., Zip 73103; tel. 405/272-9671; James A. Hyde, adm. **A**1a 3 5 9 10 **F**15 23 34 35	23	47	S		102	2619	49	48.0	0	0	13591	5800	376
★□ DEACONESS HOSPITAL, 5501 N. Portland Ave., Zip 73112; tel. 405/946-5581; Melvin J. Spencer, adm. **A**1a 9 10 **F**1 3 6 10 11 12 14 16 23 35 36 40 41 44 46 53 54	21	10	S		197	8303	124	62.9	40	1407	24270	12443	656
★ DOCTORS GENERAL HOSPITAL (Formerly AMI Doctors General Hospital), 1407 N. Robinson Ave., Zip 73103; tel. 405/236-3011; Donald G. Carney, exec. dir. **A**9 10 **F**1 3 6 16 23 24 27 33 34 40 42 44 45 46	33	10	S		106	1632	29	27.4	4	43	7518	2494	153
○ + HILLCREST HEALTH CENTER (Formerly Hillcrest Osteopathic Hospital), 2129 S.W. 59th St., Zip 73119; tel. 405/685-6671; James M. MacCallum, exec. vice-pres. **A**9 10 11 12 13 **F**1 3 5 6 10 12 14 15 16 19 23 24 27 28 30 32 33 35 36 40 41 43 44 46 47 48 49 52 53	23	10	S		174	5683	101	58.4	10	468	18274	8397	334
★□ MERCY HEALTH CENTER, 4300 W. Memorial Rd., Zip 73120; tel. 405/755-1515; Gary J. Blan, pres. & chief exec. off. **A**1a 2 9 10 **F**1 3 4 6 7 8 9 10 11 12 14 15 16 17 20 23 24 26 33 34 35 36 40 41 45 46 49 50 51 53 54; **S**5185	21	10	S		292	12785	215	73.6	32	1978	49639	23627	992
O'DONOGHUE REHABILITATION INSTITUTE, See Oklahoma Teaching Hospitals													
OKLAHOMA CHILDREN'S MEMORIAL HOSPITAL, See Oklahoma Teaching Hospitals													
★□ Δ OKLAHOMA TEACHING HOSPITALS (Includes O'Donoghue Rehabilitation Institute, 1122 N.E. 13th St., Zip 73104; tel. 405/271-6955; Pamela F. Troup, adm.; Oklahoma Children's Memorial Hospital, 940 N.E. 13th St., Zip 73104; tel. 405/271-6165; Edward Finley, adm.), P O Box 26307, Zip 73126; tel. 405/271-5911; Antonio A. Padilla, chief exec. off. **A**1a 2 3 5 7 8 9 10 **F**1 2 3 4 6 7 8 9 10 11 12 13 14 15 16 20 22 23 24 25 26 27 28 29 30 32 33 34 35 37 40 42 44 45 46 47 51 52 53 54	12	10	S		598	20014	427	62.2	44	3653	151038	67726	2955
★□ PRESBYTERIAN HOSPITAL, N.E. 13th St. at Lincoln Blvd., Zip 73104; tel. 405/271-5100; Dennis C. Millirons, adm. **A**1a 2 3 5 9 10 **F**1 3 4 5 6 7 8 9 10 11 12 13 14 15 16 20 23 24 26 33 34 35 36 37 38 40 41 42 43 45 46 47 49 51 52 53 54; **S**1755	33	10	S		316	13149	227	71.8	25	1403	75397	26468	1246
★□ SOUTH COMMUNITY HOSPITAL, 1001 S.W. 44th St., Zip 73109; tel. 405/636-7000; Dan E. Tipton, pres. **A**1a 2 9 10 **F**1 3 4 5 6 7 8 9 10 11 12 14 15 16 20 23 24 25 26 33 34 35 36 40 44 45 46 52 53 54	23	10	S		280	11391	213	76.1	22	805	49216	20736	1091
★□ ST. ANTHONY HOSPITAL, 1000 N. Lee St., Box 205, Zip 73101; tel. 405/272-7000; Richard J. Mooney, pres. **A**1a 2 3 5 9 10 **F**1 2 3 4 6 7 8 9 10 11 12 13 14 15 16 20 23 24 26 27 30 32 33 34 35 40 42 43 44 45 46 47 48 49 50 52 53 54	21	10	S		532	16526	386	70.8	20	736	76777	39578	1755
★□ VETERANS ADMINISTRATION MEDICAL CENTER, 921 N.E. 13th St., Zip 73104; tel. 405/272-9876; Steven J. Gentling, dir. **A**1a b 3 5 8 **F**1 4 6 7 9 10 11 12 14 15 16 19 20 21 23 24 25 26 28 29 30 32 33 34 42 43 44 45 46 47 49 53 54	45	10	S		399	13234	308	77.2	0	0	65185	33456	1299
OKMULGEE—Okmulgee County													
★□ OKMULGEE MEMORIAL HOSPITAL AUTHORITY, 1401 Morris Dr., Box 1038, Zip 74447; tel. 918/756-4233; Jerry D. Johnson, adm. **A**1a 2 9 10 **F**1 3 6 10 12 14 16 19 23 35 36 41 45 46 47	23	10	S		79	2580	32	40.5	10	440	7683	3727	168
PAULS VALLEY—Garvin County													
□ PAULS VALLEY GENERAL HOSPITAL, 100 Valley Dr., Box 639, Zip 73075; tel. 405/238-5501; William L. Legate, adm. **A**1a 9 10 **F**1 6 14 15 16 23 34 35 45 51	14	10	S		70	2611	33	47.1	10	202	5082	2646	160
PAWHUSKA—Osage County													
★□ PAWHUSKA HOSPITAL, 1101 E. 15th St., Zip 74056; tel. 918/287-3232; Daniel Hampton, adm. **A**1a 9 10 **F**1 10 12 16 20 23 34 35 36 40 43 45 46	23	10	S		33	715	9	27.3	5	62	1272	686	56
PAWNEE—Pawnee County													
★□ PAWNEE MUNICIPAL HOSPITAL, 1212 Fourth St., Box 467, Zip 74058; tel. 918/762-2577; Jerry L. James, adm. **A**1a 9 10 12 **F**1 2 16 23 35 40 41 44 50	14	10	S		40	1292	15	37.5	4	108	2791	1272	79
PERRY—Noble County													
★□ PERRY MEMORIAL HOSPITAL, 501 14th St., Zip 73077; tel. 405/336-3541; W. C. Wingfield, adm. **A**1a 9 10 **F**1 16 23 35 41 45 46	16	10	S		28	547	10	35.7	8	43	1678	834	53
PONCA CITY—Kay County													
★□ ST. JOSEPH REGIONAL MEDICAL CENTER OF NORTHERN OKLAHOMA (Formerly St. Joseph Regional Medical Center), 14th St. & Hartford Ave., Box 1270, Zip 74602; tel. 405/765-3321; Sr. Maureen Dougherty, pres. **A**1a 9 10 **F**1 3 6 7 8 10 11 12 15 16 20 23 24 26 27 33 35 36 40 41 44 45 46 48 52 53; **S**5435	21	10	S		167	5894	90	53.9	13	686	16931	8117	—
POTEAU—Le Flore County													
★□ EASTERN OKLAHOMA MEDICAL CENTER (Formerly LeFlore County Memorial Hospital), 105 Wall St., Zip 74953; tel. 918/647-8161; Bobby Cox, adm. **A**1a 9 10 **F**1 3 5 6 10 16 19 20 23 34 35 36 40 41 45 46 53	16	10	S		84	2311	30	35.7	9	278	4924	2006	162
PRYOR—Mayes County													
★□ GRAND VALLEY HOSPITAL, 1111 E. Center St., Box 278, Zip 74362; tel. 918/825-1600; Kenneth J. Fields, adm. **A**1a 9 10 **F**1 3 6 10 15 16 23 24 35 37 40 41 44 45 46 47; **S**0305	23	10	S		55	2107	25	45.5	8	89	5567	2778	160
+ MOOTS OSTEOPATHIC HOSPITAL, 8 N. Rowe St., Box 188, Zip 74361; tel. 918/825-2155; Jimee Moots, adm. (Nonreporting) **A**9 10	33	10	S		23	—	—	—	—	—	—	—	—
PURCELL—McClain County													
□ PURCELL MUNICIPAL HOSPITAL, 1500 N. Green Ave., Zip 73080; tel. 405/527-6524; Warren K. Spellman, adm. (Nonreporting) **A**1a 9 10; **S**1865	16	10	S		42	—	—	—	—	—	—	—	—
SALLISAW—Sequoyah County													
SEQUOYAH MEMORIAL HOSPITAL, 213 E. Redwood St., Box 505, Zip 74955; tel. 918/775-4483; Carrie Lee McClure, adm. **A**9 10 **F**1 3 6 16 34 35 40 45	15	10	S		50	1686	20	40.0	5	190	2796	1200	79
SAND SPRINGS—Tulsa County													
HISSOM MEMORIAL CENTER, Rte. 4, Box 14, Zip 74063; tel. 918/245-5911; Julia L. Teska PhD, supt. (Nonreporting)	12	52	L		529	—	—	—	—	—	—	—	—
SAPULPA—Creek County													
□ BARTLETT MEMORIAL MEDICAL CENTER, 519 S. Division St., Box 1368, Zip 74066; tel. 918/224-4280; W. D. Robinson, adm. **A**1a 9 10 **F**1 3 6 10 16 23 24 25 28 33 34 35 40 44 45 46 47	23	10	S		113	2884	44	38.9	8	141	9988	3939	266

Hospital, Address, Telephone, Administrator, Approval and Facility Codes, Multihospital System Code	Classification Codes			Facilities	Inpatient Data				Newborn Data		Expense (thousands of dollars)		
	Control	Service	Stay	Facilities	Beds	Admissions	Census	Occupancy (percent)	Bassinets	Births	Total	Payroll	Personnel
SAYRE—Beckham County													
★□ SAYRE MEMORIAL HOSPITAL, 501 E. Washington St., Box 680, Zip 73662; tel. 405/928-5541; Larry Anderson, adm. **A**1a 9 10 **F**1 6 14 16 20 23 26 34 35 36 43 45 46 50	23	10	S		46	831	12	26.1	5	88	1922	1018	79
SEMINOLE—Seminole County													
□ SEMINOLE MUNICIPAL HOSPITAL, 606 W. Evans St., P O Box 2130, Zip 74868; tel. 405/382-0600; Jerrell J. Horton, chief exec. off. (Nonreporting) **A**1a 9 10	14	10	S		63	—	—	—	—	—	—	—	—
SHATTUCK—Ellis County													
★□ NEWMAN MEMORIAL HOSPITAL, 905 S. Main St., Zip 73858; tel. 405/938-2551; Walter Shain, adm. (Total facility includes 24 beds in nursing home-type unit) **A**1a 2 9 10 **F**1 3 5 6 10 12 14 15 16 19 23 34 35 40 41 43 45 46 47 53; **S**2495	16	10	S	TF	114	1810	25	21.9	5	162	5497	2604	167
				H	90	1703	22	—	5	162	5374	2517	159
SHAWNEE—Pottawatomie County													
□ GREENLEAF CENTER -SHAWNEE, 1601 Gordon Cooper Dr., Zip 74801; tel. 405/275-9610; Joel Montgomery, adm. (Newly Registered) **A**1b 9 10; **S**1155	33	49	S		50	—	—	—	—	—	—	—	—
★□ MISSION HILL MEMORIAL HOSPITAL, 1900 Gordon Cooper Dr., Zip 74801; tel. 405/273-2240; Pat Thomason, adm. **A**1a 9 10 **F**1 3 6 12 14 15 16 23 26 30 34 35 36 40 45 46 50	16	10	S		53	1890	22	41.5	14	325	4079	2010	119
★□ SHAWNEE MEDICAL CENTER HOSPITAL, 1102 W. MacArthur, Box 909, Zip 74801; tel. 405/273-2270; Leon Noss, adm. (Nonreporting) **A**1a 2 9 10	16	10	S		104	—	—	—	—	—	—	—	—
SPENCER—Oklahoma County													
★□ WILLOW VIEW HOSPITAL, 2601 Spencer Rd., Zip 73084; Mailing Address P O Box 11137, Oklahoma City, Zip 73136; tel. 405/427-2441; Gary Watson, adm. **A**1b 10 **F**16 24 28 33 34 42; **S**2495	23	22	S		93	625	69	74.2	0	0	5188	3059	161
STIGLER—Haskell County													
HASKELL COUNTY MEMORIAL HOSPITAL, 401 N.W. H St., Zip 74462; tel. 918/967-4683; Faye Marquier, adm. **A**9 10 **F**1 3 16 35	13	10	S		45	446	5	11.1	6	21	774	422	33
STILLWATER—Payne County													
OKLAHOMA STATE UNIVERSITY HOSPITAL AND CLINIC, 1202 Farm Rd., Zip 74078; tel. 405/624-7030; Donald Cooper MD, med. dir. **A**9 **F**1 28 30 33 34 35 37 43	12	11	S		19	254	1	5.3	0	0	—	—	53
★□ STILLWATER MEDICAL CENTER, 1323 W. Sixth Ave., Box 2408, Zip 74076; tel. 405/372-1480; Robert E. Park, adm. **A**1a 9 10 **F**1 3 6 10 12 15 16 20 23 24 26 27 29 33 34 35 36 37 40 42 46 47 50 52 53	14	10	S		132	6082	78	59.1	17	993	14567	6397	346
STROUD—Lincoln County													
★□ STROUD MUNICIPAL HOSPITAL, Hwy. 66 W., P O Box 530, Zip 74079; tel. 918/968-3571; W. M. Shawn, adm. (Nonreporting) **A**1a 9 10; **S**0305	23	10	S		30	—	—	—	—	—	—	—	—
SULPHUR—Murray County													
ARBUCKLE MEMORIAL HOSPITAL, Hwy. 7 W., Box 411, Zip 73086; tel. 405/622-2161; Marvin R. Hyde, adm. (Nonreporting) **A**9 10	13	10	S		58	—	—	—	—	—	—	—	—
OKLAHOMA VETERANS CENTER, Box 200, Zip 73086; tel. 405/622-2144; Jerry J. Stewart, adm. **F**16 19 20 23 42 46 47	12	48	L		176	158	161	91.5	0	0	4300	2656	157
TAHLEQUAH—Cherokee County													
★□ TAHLEQUAH CITY HOSPITAL, 1400 E. Downing St., Box 1008, Zip 74465; tel. 918/456-0641; Don L. Coffman, adm. (Nonreporting) **A**1a 9 10; **S**1755	16	10	S		51	—	—	—	—	—	—	—	—
★□ WILLIAM W. HASTINGS INDIAN HOSPITAL, 100 S. Bliss Ave., Zip 74464; tel. 918/458-3317; Danny B. Whitekiller, adm. (Nonreporting) **A**1a 10	47	10	S		60	—	—	—	—	—	—	—	—
TALIHINA—Le Flore County													
★□ CHOCTAW NATION INDIAN HOSPITAL, Rte. 2, Box 1725, Zip 74571; tel. 918/567-2211; Gabe Payton EdD, adm. **A**1a 10 **F**1 15 34 35 37 40 41 49 52	47	10	S		52	1365	17	32.7	12	249	6302	2773	235
THOMAS—Custer County													
★ THOMAS MEMORIAL HOSPITAL, 610 E. Broadway, P O Box 348, Zip 73669; tel. 405/661-3561; Jerry Jones, adm. (Nonreporting) **A**9 10	23	10	S		93	—	—	—	—	—	—	—	—
TINKER AIR FORCE BASE—Oklahoma County													
□ U. S. AIR FORCE HOSPITAL TINKER, Zip 73145; tel. 405/734-8211; Col. Stanley L. Betts, cmdr. (Nonreporting) **A**1a	41	10	S		50	—	—	—	—	—	—	—	—
TISHOMINGO—Johnston County													
★ JOHNSTON MEMORIAL HOSPITAL, 1101 S. Byrd St., Zip 73460; tel. 405/371-2327; Donald W. Jackson, adm. **A**9 10 **F**1 14 15 16 23 35 41 45	13	10	S		42	1056	17	40.5	6	91	2036	1004	76
TULSA—Tulsa County													
★□ AMI DOCTORS HOSPITAL (Formerly Doctors Medical Center), 2323 S. Harvard Ave., Zip 74114; tel. 918/744-4000; Harvey M. Shapiro, exec. dir. & chief exec. off. **A**1a 9 10 **F**1 3 6 10 14 15 16 19 23 24 34 35 36 40 41 42 44 45 46 49 52 53; **S**0125	33	10	S		122	3975	68	55.7	14	215	20186	5744	334
□ BROOKHAVEN HOSPITAL, 201 S. Garnett Rd., Zip 74128; tel. 918/438-4257; Harvey W. Glasser MD, (Newly Registered) **A**1a 9 10	33	82	S		42	—	—	—	—	—	—	—	—
★□ CHILDREN'S MEDICAL CENTER, 5300 E. Skelly Dr., Zip 74135; Mailing Address Box 35648, Zip 74153; tel. 918/664-6600; James Stansbarger, adm. **A**1b 3 5 9 10 **F**12 15 23 24 26 28 30 31 32 33 34 38 42 44 45 46 49 52	23	52	L		101	497	79	78.2	0	0	10688	6802	301
★□ CITY OF FAITH HOSPITAL, 8181 S. Lewis, Zip 74137; tel. 918/493-1000; B. Joe Gunn, adm. **A**1a 3 5 8 9 10 **F**1 3 4 6 7 8 9 10 11 12 14 15 16 17 19 20 23 24 27 30 32 35 36 37 40 41 44 45 46 47 48 49 50 52 53 54	23	10	S		140	5463	119	85.0	30	755	33218	10115	446
DOCTORS MEDICAL CENTER, See AMI Doctors Hospital													
★□ Δ HILLCREST MEDICAL CENTER, 12th & Utica, Zip 74104; tel. 918/584-1351; John C. Goldthorpe, pres. **A**1a 2 3 5 7 9 10 **F**1 2 3 4 5 6 7 8 9 10 11 12 13 14 15 16 19 20 22 23 24 25 26 27 28 30 32 33 34 35 36 37 40 41 42 44 45 46 47 48 52 53 54	23	10	S		487	15675	310	63.7	50	2793	75838	33130	1606
★ ○ + OKLAHOMA OSTEOPATHIC HOSPITAL, Ninth & Jackson Sts., Zip 74127; tel. 918/587-2561; Otto M. Janke, pres. & chief exec. off. **A**9 10 11 12 13 **F**1 3 4 5 6 9 10 11 12 13 14 15 16 17 19 20 23 24 26 27 28 29 30 32 33 34 35 36 40 41 43 44 45 46 47 48 49 51 52 53 54	23	10	S		392	11946	244	62.2	29	1104	53611	23465	1194
PARKSIDE CENTER (Formerly Tulsa Psychiatric Center), 1620 E. 12th St., Zip 74120; tel. 918/582-2131; William T. Duncan, chief exec. off. **A**3 5 10 **F**24 28 30 32 33 35 45 48 49	23	22	S		40	378	11	47.8	0	0	4670	2318	117
★□ SAINT FRANCIS HOSPITAL, 6161 S. Yale Ave., Zip 74136; tel. 918/494-2200; Sr. Mary Blandine Fleming, adm. (Total facility includes 30 beds in nursing home-type unit) **A**1a 2 3 5 8 9 10 **F**1 2 3 4 5 6 7 8 9 10 11 12 14 15 16 17 19 20 21 23 24 27 30 32 33 34 35 36 40 41 42 44 45 46 47 51 52 53 54; **S**0605	21	10	S	TF	726	29708	532	75.4	30	3324	119295	56299	2736
				H	696	29161	509	—	30	3324	118720	55760	2714
★□ SHADOW MOUNTAIN INSTITUTE, 6262 S. Sheridan, Zip 74133; tel. 918/492-8200; Donald E. Carlson, adm. **A**1b **F**15 24 28 29 30 32 33 42 43 44 48 49; **S**0665	33	52	L		100	326	78	77.2	0	0	5915	2805	208
★□ ST. JOHN MEDICAL CENTER, 1923 S. Utica Ave., Zip 74104; tel. 918/744-2345; Sr. M. Therese Gottschalk, chief exec. off. (Nonreporting) **A**1a 2 3 5 9 10; **S**5875	21	10	S		648	—	—	—	—	—	—	—	—
TULSA PSYCHIATRIC CENTER, See Parkside Center													
VINITA—Craig County													
★□ CRAIG GENERAL HOSPITAL, 735 N. Foreman St., Box 326, Zip 74301; tel. 918/256-7551; A. T. Shackelford, adm. **A**1a 9 10 **F**1 2 3 14 15 16 23 35 40 45 52	13	10	S		50	1096	12	24.0	7	87	2175	1076	64

★ American Hospital Association (AHA) membership
□ Joint Commission on Accreditation of Hospitals (JCAH) accreditation
\+ American Osteopathic Hospital Association (AOHA) membership
○ American Osteopathic Association (AOA) accreditation
Δ Commission on Accreditation of Rehabilitation Facilities (CARF) accreditation
Control codes 61, 63, 64, 71, 72 and 73 indicate hospitals listed by AOHA, but not registered by AHA.
For definition of numerical codes, see page A2

Hospital, Address, Telephone, Administrator, Approval and Facility Codes, Multihospital System Code	Classification Codes				Inpatient Data				Newborn Data		Expense (thousands of dollars)		
★ American Hospital Association (AHA) membership □ Joint Commission on Accreditation of Hospitals (JCAH) accreditation + American Osteopathic Hospital Association (AOHA) membership ○ American Osteopathic Association (AOA) accreditation Δ Commission on Accreditation of Rehabilitation Facilities (CARF) accreditation Control codes 61, 63, 64, 71, 72 and 73 indicate hospitals listed by AOHA, but not registered by AHA. For definition of numerical codes, see page A2	Control	Service	Stay	Facilities	Beds	Admissions	Census	Occupancy (percent)	Bassinets	Births	Total	Payroll	Personnel
□ EASTERN STATE HOSPITAL, P O Box 69, Zip 74301; tel. 918/256-7841; Charles Buckholtz, supt. (Nonreporting) **A**1a 10	12	22	L		364	—	—	—	—	—	—	—	—
WAGONER—Wagoner County													
★□ WAGONER COMMUNITY HOSPITAL, 1200 W. Cherokee, Box 407, Zip 74467; tel. 918/485-5514; Tim Francis, adm. **A**1a 9 10 **F**1 3 6 10 16 17 23 34 35 45 46 47 53; **S**1755	33	10	S		100	1825	36	36.0	6	119	8466	2832	135
WATONGA—Blaine County													
★ WATONGA MUNICIPAL HOSPITAL, 500 N. Nash Blvd., Box 370, Zip 73772; tel. 405/623-7211; John C. Neal, adm. **A**9 10 **F**1 2 14 15 16 21 23 34 35 37 40 41 45	14	10	S		35	608	8	22.9	4	34	1476	806	54
WAURIKA—Jefferson County													
★ JEFFERSON COUNTY HOSPITAL, Box 90, Zip 73573; tel. 405/228-2344; Don Phelps, adm. **A**9 10 **F**1 6 16 23 35 40 41 45	13	10	S		36	675	10	27.8	3	33	1193	644	44
WAYNOKA—Woods County													
E. P. CLAPPER MEMORIAL MEDICAL CENTER, 500 S. Nickerson St., Box 157, Zip 73860; tel. 405/824-2411; John Parker, adm. **A**9 10 **F**1 12 14 16 23 29 30 35 45	23	10	S		24	359	4	16.7	5	6	785	369	41
WEATHERFORD—Custer County													
★ SOUTHWESTERN MEMORIAL HOSPITAL (Formerly Weatherford Hospital Authority), 215 N. Kansas St., Zip 73096; tel. 405/772-5551; Ronnie D. Walker, pres. **A**9 10 **F**1 2 6 12 14 15 16 35 40 45 52 53	16	10	S		60	1210	12	20.0	6	273	2204	1152	49
WETUMKA—Hughes County													
WETUMKA GENERAL HOSPITAL, 325 S. Washita, Zip 74883; tel. 405/452-3276; Keith E. Calvert, interim adm. **A**9 10 **F**3 35 45 52; **S**1865	16	10	S		34	419	6	17.6	0	0	1092	429	25
WEWOKA—Seminole County													
WEWOKA MEMORIAL HOSPITAL, 300 E. 14th St., Box 1536, Zip 74884; tel. 405/257-3311; Marla Peixotto RN, adm. **A**9 10 **F**1 2 6 10 11 15 16 23 30 34 35 36 43 45 46 47	14	10	S		28	1299	14	50.0	7	95	1732	738	75
WILBURTON—Latimer County													
LATIMER COUNTY GENERAL HOSPITAL, Hwy. 2 N., Zip 74578; tel. 918/465-2391; Gerald Downing, adm. **A**9 10 **F**1 3 16 34 35 40 45	13	10	S		33	554	9	27.3	4	21	1121	650	53
WOODWARD—Woodward County													
★ WOODWARD HOSPITAL AND HEALTH CENTER, 900 17th St., Box 489, Zip 73802; tel. 405/256-5511; John H. Welsh, adm. **A**9 10 **F**1 2 6 10 15 16 23 35 36 40 45; **S**1865	23	10	S		60	1742	21	35.0	10	236	5921	2338	129

Hospital, Address, Telephone, Administrator, Approval and Facility Codes, Multihospital System Code

- ★ American Hospital Association (AHA) membership
- ☐ Joint Commission on Accreditation of Hospitals (JCAH) accreditation
- + American Osteopathic Hospital Association (AOHA) membership
- ○ American Osteopathic Association (AOA) accreditation
- Δ Commission on Accreditation of Rehabilitation Facilities (CARF) accreditation

Control codes 61, 63, 64, 71, 72 and 73 indicate hospitals listed by AOHA, but not registered by AHA. For definition of numerical codes, see page A2

Oregon

Hospital, Address, Telephone, Administrator, Approval and Facility Codes, Multihospital System Code	Classification Codes: Control	Service	Stay	Facilities	Inpatient Data: Beds	Admissions	Census	Occupancy (percent)	Newborn Data: Bassinets	Births	Expense (thousands of dollars): Total	Payroll	Personnel
ALBANY—Linn County													
★☐ ALBANY GENERAL HOSPITAL, 1046 W. Sixth Ave., Zip 97321; tel. 503/926-2244; Richard Delano, pres. **A**1a 2 9 10 **F**1 3 6 10 12 14 15 16 23 24 26 30 34 35 36 40 41 44 45 46 47 52	23	10	S		106	4123	45	42.5	15	543	13363	5996	301
ASHLAND—Jackson County													
★☐ ASHLAND COMMUNITY HOSPITAL, 280 Maple St., Box 98, Zip 97520; tel. 503/482-2441; Thomas M. Mack, chief exec. off. **A**1a 9 10 **F**1 3 6 14 15 16 21 23 30 35 36 37 40 41 45 47	14	10	S		58	2004	17	29.3	6	351	5153	2591	112
ASTORIA—Clatsop County													
★☐ COLUMBIA MEMORIAL HOSPITAL, 2111 Exchange St., Zip 97103; tel. 503/325-4321; A. D. Cobbin, exec. dir. **A**1a 9 10 **F**1 3 6 10 12 14 15 16 21 23 24 26 34 35 36 40 43 45 47 48 53	23	10	S		46	2297	24	43.6	6	396	7949	3954	192
BAKER—Baker County													
★☐ ST. ELIZABETH HOSPITAL AND HEALTH CARE CENTER (Formerly St. Elizabeth Community Hospital), 3325 Pocahontas Rd., Zip 97814; tel. 503/523-6461; Walter S. Busch, pres. & adm. **A**1a 9 10 **F**1 3 6 15 16 21 23 35 36 40 41 44 45 52; **S**5325	21	10	S		40	1004	12	30.0	6	115	4657	2251	107
BANDON—Coos County													
★ SOUTHERN COOS GENERAL HOSPITAL, 640 W. Fourth, Zip 97411; tel. 503/347-2426; Robert S. Smith, adm. **A**9 10 **F**1 15 16 35 45 46	16	10	S		24	399	4	16.7	0	0	1022	603	33
BEND—Deschutes County													
★☐ ST. CHARLES MEDICAL CENTER, 2500 N.E. Neff Rd., Zip 97701; tel. 503/382-4321; Sr. Kathryn Hellmann, pres. & chief exec. off. **A**1a 9 10 **F**1 2 3 6 7 8 9 10 11 12 14 15 16 20 23 24 27 30 34 35 36 40 44 45 46 47 52 53 54	23	10	S		164	7927	98	59.8	13	949	26227	12941	591
BURNS—Harney County													
HARNEY COUNTY HOSPITAL, 557 W. Washington St., Zip 97720; tel. 503/573-7281; Judge Dale White, actg. adm. **A**9 10 **F**1 3 16 23 37 45 52	13	10	S		44	669	7	15.9	8	75	2011	915	47
CANYONVILLE—Douglas County													
+ FOREST GLEN HOSPITAL, 495 S.W. First St., P O Box 198, Zip 97417; tel. 503/839-4211; David L. Harman, pres. **A**9 10 **F**1 6 12 14 15 16 23 35 40 45 47 52; **S**5175	33	10	S		23	537	5	21.7	2	54	1307	—	36
CENTRAL POINT—Jackson County													
★☐ CASCADE COMMUNITY HOSPITAL, 600 S. Second St., Zip 97502; tel. 503/664-1205; Dahl Gardner, adm. **A**1a 9 10 **F**1 3 6 15 16 23 30 35 45	23	10	S		28	595	6	21.4	0	0	2218	1075	76
CLACKAMAS—Clackamas County													
★☐ KAISER SUNNYSIDE MEDICAL CENTER, 10200 S.E. Sunnyside Rd., Zip 97015; tel. 503/652-2880; Kay Schweickart, area adm. **A**1a 10 **F**1 2 3 6 9 10 11 14 15 16 20 23 24 28 30 34 35 37 40 44 45 46 47 52 53 54; **S**2105	23	10	S		155	10194	133	85.8	24	1498	—	—	1001
COOS BAY—Coos County													
★☐ BAY AREA HOSPITAL, 1775 Thompson Rd., Zip 97420; tel. 503/269-8111; G. Kent Ballantyne, adm. **A**1a 9 10 **F**1 3 6 10 12 15 16 23 26 29 30 35 36 40 41 42 43 44 45 52	16	10	S		156	6850	87	55.8	18	606	20726	10007	426
COQUILLE—Coos County													
COQUILLE VALLEY HOSPITAL, 940 E. Fifth St., Zip 97423; tel. 503/396-3101; Edna J. Cotner, adm. **A**9 10 **F**15 16 35 36 40 41 43	16	10	S		30	819	7	23.3	4	122	1925	857	56
CORVALLIS—Benton County													
★☐ GOOD SAMARITAN HOSPITAL, 3600 N.W. Samaritan Dr., Box 1068, Zip 97339; tel. 503/757-5111 **A**1a 2 9 10 **F**1 3 5 6 7 8 9 10 11 12 14 15 16 23 24 26 28 30 32 33 34 35 36 40 41 44 45 46 52 53	21	10	S		143	6715	83	58.0	22	1194	22838	10856	472
COTTAGE GROVE—Lane County													
★☐ COTTAGE GROVE HOSPITAL, 1340 Birch Ave., Zip 97424; tel. 503/942-0511; John L. Hoopes, adm. (Total facility includes 30 beds in nursing home-type unit) **A**1a 9 10 **F**1 3 6 14 15 16 19 21 23 26 35 36 40 41 42 44 45 46 47 49 50; **S**0585	23	10	S	TF H	65 35	1479 1385	42 13	64.6 —	8 8	224 224	4852 4466	2506 2292	110 99
DALLAS—Polk County													
☐ VALLEY COMMUNITY HOSPITAL, 550 S.E. Clay St., Zip 97338; tel. 503/623-8301; Ed Zintgraff, exec. dir. **A**1a 10 **F**1 3 6 12 14 15 16 23 24 34 35 36 40 41 44 53; **S**1805	33	10	S		44	1926	20	45.5	8	241	8853	3347	182
ENTERPRISE—Wallowa County													
★ WALLOWA MEMORIAL HOSPITAL, 401 E. First St., Box 460, Zip 97828; tel. 503/426-3111; Chris Cronberg, adm. (Total facility includes 32 beds in nursing home-type unit) **A**9 10 **F**1 6 14 16 19 21 23 34 35 36 40 41 52	13	10	S	TF H	76 44	776 768	39 8	51.3 —	4 4	53 53	2725 2024	1370 966	98 62
EUGENE—Lane County													
☐ EUGENE HOSPITAL (Formerly Eugene Clinic), 1162 Willamette St., Zip 97401; tel. 503/687-6000; Hugh Prichard, exec. dir. (Nonreporting) **A**1a 9 10; **S**0585	33	10	S		57	—	—	—	—	—	—	—	—
★☐ Δ SACRED HEART GENERAL HOSPITAL, 1255 Hilyard St., Box 10905, Zip 97440; tel. 503/686-7300; Sr. Monica Heeran, adm. **A**1a 2 7 9 10 **F**1 3 4 5 6 7 8 9 10 11 14 15 16 20 21 23 24 25 26 27 28 29 30 32 33 34 35 36 40 41 42 43 45 46 47 48 49 51 53 54; **S**5415	21	10	S		399	18741	290	73.2	22	2354	73421	35197	1379
FLORENCE—Lane County													
★ WESTERN LANE HOSPITAL, 1525 12th St., Box 580, Zip 97439; tel. 503/997-8412; Reed G. Condie, adm. **A**9 10 **F**6 14 16 23 35 36 40 41 45; **S**5415	16	10	S		24	1024	10	41.7	4	115	3502	1766	89
FOREST GROVE—Washington County													
★☐ FOREST GROVE COMMUNITY HOSPITAL, 1809 Maple St., Zip 97116; tel. 503/357-2173; William E. Winter, adm. **A**1a 9 10 **F**1 3 6 12 14 15 16 23 34 35 36 40 45 46 47 48	23	10	S		58	1447	27	46.6	6	283	5543	2009	94
GOLD BEACH—Curry County													
★ CURRY GENERAL HOSPITAL, 220 E. Fourth St., Zip 97444; tel. 503/247-6621; Gordon Ensley, adm. **A**9 10 **F**1 3 6 15 16 34 35 37 40	33	10	S		24	678	6	25.0	5	71	4482	1492	73
GRANTS PASS—Josephine County													
★☐ JOSEPHINE MEMORIAL HOSPITAL, 715 N.W. Dimmick St., Zip 97526; tel. 503/476-6831; Clint Lea, adm. **A**1a 2 9 10 **F**1 3 6 10 12 16 23 24 30 35 36 40 41 44 45 47 53; **S**1755	23	10	S		81	3316	37	45.7	22	689	11525	5649	249
☐ SOUTHERN OREGON MEDICAL CENTER, 1505 N.W. Washington Blvd., Zip 97526; tel. 503/479-7531; Stephen R. Hixon, adm. **A**1a 9 10 **F**1 3 6 10 12 14 15 16 23 24 30 35 44 45 47	33	10	S		63	2411	29	46.0	0	0	9521	4682	252

Hospital, Address, Telephone, Administrator, Approval and Facility Codes, Multihospital System Code	Classification Codes			Facilities	Inpatient Data				Newborn Data		Expense (thousands of dollars)		
★ American Hospital Association (AHA) membership □ Joint Commission on Accreditation of Hospitals (JCAH) accreditation + American Osteopathic Hospital Association (AOHA) membership ○ American Osteopathic Association (AOA) accreditation Δ Commission on Accreditation of Rehabilitation Facilities (CARF) accreditation Control codes 61, 63, 64, 71, 72 and 73 indicate hospitals listed by AOHA, but not registered by AHA. For definition of numerical codes, see page A2	Control	Service	Stay	Facilities	Beds	Admissions	Census	Occupancy (percent)	Bassinets	Births	Total	Payroll	Personnel
GRESHAM—Multnomah County													
★□ MOUNT HOOD MEDICAL CENTER, 24800 S.E. Stark, P O Box 718, Zip 97030; tel. 503/667-1122; Joseph J. Henery, adm. **A**1a b 10 **F**1 3 6 10 14 15 16 20 23 24 26 34 35 43 44 46 48 49 50 53; **S**2755	23	10	S		108	3233	57	52.8	0	1	18630	6171	294
HEPPNER—Morrow County													
PIONEER MEMORIAL HOSPITAL, 564 E. Pioneer Dr., P O Box 9, Zip 97836; tel. 503/676-9133; John Hempel, adm. & chief exec. off. (Total facility includes 32 beds in nursing home-type unit) **A**9 10 **F**3 14 16 19 35 45 46 50; **S**5325	13	10	S	TF	44	316	28	63.6	0	24	1234	727	59
				H	12	251	2	—	0	24	977	488	—
HERMISTON—Umatilla County													
★□ GOOD SHEPHERD COMMUNITY HOSPITAL, 610 N.W. 11th Ave., Zip 97838; tel. 503/567-6483; Roy Baker, chief exec. off. **A**1a 9 10 **F**1 3 6 10 12 14 16 23 34 35 36 37 40 43 45 46 52	23	10	S		74	2381	30	45.5	8	456	7264	2966	150
HILLSBORO—Washington County													
□ TUALITY COMMUNITY HOSPITAL, 335 S.E. Eighth, P O Box 309, Zip 97123; tel. 503/681-1163; William E. Winter, adm. **A**1a 9 10 **F**1 3 6 10 12 14 15 16 23 24 34 35 40 45 46 47 53 54	23	10	S		137	8049	76	55.5	12	732	25496	7715	378
HOOD RIVER—Hood River County													
★ HOOD RIVER MEMORIAL HOSPITAL, 13th & May Sts., P O Box 149, Zip 97031; tel. 503/386-3911; Donald F. Kelter, adm. **A**9 10 **F**1 3 6 16 23 35 36 40 41 52	23	10	S		45	1375	12	26.7	9	173	3380	1659	111
JOHN DAY—Grant County													
★ BLUE MOUNTAIN HOSPITAL, 170 Ford Rd., Zip 97845; tel. 503/575-1311; Donna M. Krausse, adm. **A**9 10 **F**1 3 6 14 16 23 34 35 36 37 40 41 43 45 47	16	10	S		39	659	6	15.4	8	111	1975	1083	63
KLAMATH FALLS—Klamath County													
★□ MERLE WEST MEDICAL CENTER, 2865 Daggett St., Zip 97601; tel. 503/882-6311; David R. Arnold, chief exec. off. **A**1a 2 10 **F**1 3 5 6 10 12 14 15 16 23 24 26 27 28 29 30 32 33 34 35 36 40 41 44 45 46 47 52 53	23	10	S		194	6636	84	43.3	20	888	20835	10536	517
LA GRANDE—Union County													
★□ GRANDE RONDE HOSPITAL, 900 Sunset Dr., Box 3290, Zip 97850; tel. 503/963-8421; James A. Mattes, adm. **A**1a 9 10 **F**1 3 6 10 12 15 16 23 30 34 35 36 40 45 46 50 52 53	23	10	S		84	2461	29	34.5	10	396	9666	4475	206
LAKEVIEW—Lake County													
LAKE DISTRICT HOSPITAL, 700 S. J St., Zip 97630; tel. 503/947-2114; Clark Graebel, adm. (Total facility includes 47 beds in nursing home-type unit) **A**9 10 **F**1 16 19 23 35 40 42 45 52	16	10	S	TF	68	850	41	60.3	4	129	2654	1436	81
				H	21	775	6	—	4	129	2214	1215	61
LEBANON—Linn County													
★□ LEBANON COMMUNITY HOSPITAL, 525 N. Santiam Hwy., P O Box 739, Zip 97355; tel. 503/258-2101; Gene Kanagy, adm. **A**1a 9 10 **F**1 3 6 15 16 21 23 26 34 35 36 40 43 44 45 46 47 52 53	21	10	S		67	3301	29	34.1	12	373	7833	4388	220
LINCOLN CITY—Lincoln County													
★□ NORTH LINCOLN HOSPITAL, 3043 N. Park Dr., Box 767, Zip 97367; tel. 503/994-3661; Eric Buckland, adm. **A**1a 9 10 **F**1 2 3 6 10 12 14 15 16 23 35 36 40 41 43 45 46	16	10	S		50	1614	17	34.0	3	122	5642	2718	133
MADRAS—Jefferson County													
MOUNTAIN VIEW DISTRICT HOSPITAL, 1270 A St., Zip 97741; tel. 503/475-3882; Ronald W. Barnes, adm. (Total facility includes 68 beds in nursing home-type unit) **A**9 10 **F**1 3 6 14 15 16 19 23 24 26 27 33 34 35 40 41 43 45 46 50 52; **S**0585	16	10	S	TF	102	1325	70	68.6	6	192	3756	1893	113
				H	34	1231	10	—	6	192	2745	1278	81
MCMINNVILLE—Yamhill County													
★□ MCMINNVILLE COMMUNITY HOSPITAL, 603 S. Baker St., Zip 97128; tel. 503/472-6131; Stephen J. Aragon, adm. **A**1a 9 10 **F**1 6 12 14 15 16 23 34 35 36 43 44 45 46 47 49 53; **S**1755	33	10	S		80	2461	31	38.8	6	496	—	—	—
MEDFORD—Jackson County													
★□ Δ PROVIDENCE HOSPITAL, 1111 Crater Lake Ave., Zip 97504; tel. 503/773-6611; Bernard J. Stormberg, adm. **A**1a 2 7 9 10 **F**1 3 5 6 10 12 14 15 16 20 23 24 25 26 29 30 34 35 41 42 44 45 46 47 50 53; **S**5275	21	10	S		168	5768	94	56.0	0	0	21719	10361	491
★□ ROGUE VALLEY MEDICAL CENTER, 2825 Barnett Rd., Zip 97504; tel. 503/773-6281; Gary A. McCormack, adm. **A**1a 2 9 10 **F**1 3 4 6 7 8 9 10 11 12 14 15 16 20 21 23 24 26 27 28 29 32 34 35 36 40 44 45 46 47 48 49 51 52 53 54	23	10	S		305	12402	182	59.7	22	1722	44467	22730	1078
MILWAUKIE—Clackamas County													
DWYER COMMUNITY HOSPITAL, See Providence Milwaukie Hospital													
★□ PROVIDENCE MILWAUKIE HOSPITAL (Formerly Dwyer Community Hospital), 10150 S.E. 32nd Ave., Zip 97222; tel. 503/659-6111; Robert W. Vial, pres. **A**1a 9 10 **F**1 3 6 10 12 14 15 16 23 34 35 36 40 43 45 46 49 53; **S**5275	23	10	S		56	2710	30	53.6	9	338	11063	4975	251
NEWBERG—Yamhill County													
★□ NEWBERG COMMUNITY HOSPITAL, 501 Villa Rd., Zip 97132; tel. 503/538-1372; Mark W. Meinert, adm. **A**1a 9 10 **F**1 3 6 12 14 15 16 23 24 34 35 36 37 40 41 43 45 46 50 52 53; **S**5275	14	10	S		44	1894	18	40.9	6	189	6151	3036	144
NEWPORT—Lincoln County													
□ PACIFIC COMMUNITIES HOSPITAL, 721 S.W. Ninth St., Zip 97365; tel. 503/265-2244; James R. Watson, adm. **A**1a 9 10 **F**1 3 6 10 12 14 16 23 24 35 36 40 41 44 45 53	16	10	S		48	1476	17	35.4	4	130	6186	2963	161
NYSSA—Malheur County													
MALHEUR MEMORIAL HOSPITAL DISTRICT, 1109 Park Ave., Zip 97913; tel. 503/372-2211; Richard W. Jones, adm. (Total facility includes 46 beds in nursing home-type unit) **A**9 10 **F**1 3 6 14 15 16 19 23 34 35 36 37 40 43 45	16	10	S	TF	72	377	45	62.5	8	70	2007	1302	80
				H	26	305	3	—	8	70	1079	664	—
ONTARIO—Malheur County													
★□ HOLY ROSARY HOSPITAL, 351 S.W. Ninth St., Zip 97914; tel. 503/889-5331; David J. Goode, adm. **A**1a 9 10 **F**1 3 6 10 12 14 15 16 23 35 36 40 45 52 53; **S**5175	23	10	S		77	4059	46	59.7	8	600	11058	4883	292
OREGON CITY—Clackamas County													
★□ WILLAMETTE FALLS HOSPITAL, 1500 Division St., Zip 97045; tel. 503/656-1631; Robert Steed, adm. **A**1a 2 9 10 **F**1 3 6 10 12 14 15 16 20 23 26 34 35 36 40 43 45 46 47 52 53	23	10	S		112	5246	61	54.5	16	721	18525	8951	332
PENDLETON—Umatilla County													
EASTERN OREGON PSYCHIATRIC CENTER, 2575 Westgate, Zip 97801; tel. 503/276-0810; Steven Feinstein, adm. (Nonreporting) **A**10	12	22	L		150	—	—	—	—	—	—	—	—
★□ ST. ANTHONY HOSPITAL, 1601 S.E. Court Ave., Zip 97801; tel. 503/276-5121; Sr. Helen Ann Gaidos, pres. & chief exec. off. **A**1a 2 9 10 **F**1 3 6 10 11 12 14 15 16 21 23 26 27 30 32 33 35 36 40 41 42 43 44 45 46 47 48 49 53; **S**5325	23	10	S		104	2783	48	46.2	4	40	12595	4908	288
PORTLAND—Multnomah and Washington Counties													
★□ BESS KAISER MEDICAL CENTER, 5055 N. Greeley Ave., Zip 97217; tel. 503/285-9321; Ken Myers, area adm. **A**1a 2 10 **F**1 3 5 6 9 10 14 15 16 21 23 24 28 30 34 35 36 37 40 41 42 44 45 46 47 50 52 53 54; **S**2105	23	10	S		202	12630	167	83.5	49	2174	—	—	969

Hospital, Address, Telephone, Administrator, Approval and Facility Codes, Multihospital System Code

★ American Hospital Association (AHA) membership
□ Joint Commission on Accreditation of Hospitals (JCAH) accreditation
+ American Osteopathic Hospital Association (AOHA) membership
○ American Osteopathic Association (AOA) accreditation
Δ Commission on Accreditation of Rehabilitation Facilities (CARF) accreditation
Control codes 61, 63, 64, 71, 72 and 73 indicate hospitals listed by AOHA, but not registered by AHA.
For definition of numerical codes, see page A2

Hospital	Classification Codes				Inpatient Data				Newborn Data		Expense (thousands of dollars)		
	Control	Service	Stay	Facilities	Beds	Admissions	Census	Occupancy (percent)	Bassinets	Births	Total	Payroll	Personnel
★ □ CAREUNIT HOSPITAL OF PORTLAND, 1927 N.W. Lovejoy St., Zip 97209; tel. 503/224-6500; Joann Beardslee, adm. (Data for 153 days) **A**1a 9 10 **F**1 15 32 33 34 42 43 46 47 49; **S**0275	32	82	S		92	399	49	53.3	0	0	1990	775	106
□ CPC CEDAR HILLS HOSPITAL, 10300 S.W. Eastridge St., Zip 97225; tel. 503/297-2252; Christopher J. Krenk, adm. **A**1b 9 10 **F**24 28 29 30 32 33 42 49; **S**0785	33	22	S		64	566	39	60.9	0	0	—	—	88
DOERNBECHER MEMORIAL HOSPITAL FOR CHILDREN, See Oregon Health Sciences University Hospital													
○ + EASTMORELAND HOSPITAL (Formerly Eastmoreland General Hospital), 2900 S.E. Steele St., Zip 97202; tel. 503/234-0411; John D. Cochran, adm. (Nonreporting) **A**9 10 11 12; **S**1375	23	10	S		100	—	—	—	—	—	—	—	—
★ □ Δ EMANUEL HOSPITAL AND HEALTH CENTER (Formerly Emanuel Hospital), 2801 N. Gantenbein Ave., Zip 97227; tel. 503/280-3200; Fred R. Eaton, adm. **A**1a 2 3 5 7 8 9 10 **F**1 2 3 4 5 6 7 8 9 10 11 12 14 15 16 20 22 23 24 25 26 34 35 36 37 38 40 42 43 44 45 46 47 50 51 52 53 54; **S**2755	23	10	S		344	13296	225	65.4	18	1866	77835	36599	1576
GENERAL OUT-PATIENT CLINIC, See Oregon Health Sciences University Hospital													
★ □ Δ GOOD SAMARITAN HOSPITAL AND MEDICAL CENTER (Includes Good Samaritan Hospital and Medical Center; Rehabilitation Institute of Oregon), 1015 N.W. 22nd Ave., Zip 97210; tel. 503/229-7711; Chester L. Stocks, exec. vice-pres. **A**1a 2 3 5 7 9 10 **F**1 2 3 4 6 7 8 9 10 11 12 14 15 16 17 20 23 24 25 26 28 30 32 33 34 35 36 37 40 41 42 43 44 45 46 47 50 53 54	21	10	S		345	16123	246	71.5	30	2349	101799	47024	1922
★ HOLLADAY PARK MEDICAL CENTER (Formerly Holladay Park Hospital), 1225 N.E. Second Ave., Zip 97232; tel. 503/233-4567; Jane Cummins, adm. **A**9 10 **F**1 3 6 10 12 14 15 16 23 24 27 29 30 32 34 35 45 46 47 48 53 54; **S**2755	23	10	S		165	4248	73	44.2	0	0	20526	8234	310
★ HORIZON RECOVERY CENTER, 6050 S.W. Old Scholls Ferry Rd., Zip 97223; tel. 503/292-6671; Michael J. Millenheft, adm. **A**10 **F**33 34 49; **S**6525	33	82	S		30	236	6	20.0	0	0	1645	—	23
□ MEDICAL CENTER HOSPITALS, 511 S.W. Tenth Ave., Zip 97205; tel. 503/295-2977; William Holdner, actg. adm. (Nonreporting) **A**1a 9 10	33	10	S		41	—	—	—	—	—	—	—	—
□ OREGON HEALTH SCIENCES UNIVERSITY HOSPITAL (Includes Doernbecher Memorial Hospital for Children; General Out-Patient Clinic; University Hospital), 3181 S.W. Sam Jackson Park Rd., Zip 97201; tel. 503/225-8311; David M. Witter Jr., dir. **A**1a 2 3 5 8 9 10 **F**1 2 3 4 5 6 7 8 9 10 11 12 13 14 15 16 20 23 24 26 27 28 29 30 32 33 34 35 36 37 38 40 42 43 44 45 46 47 49 51 52 53 54	12	10	S		327	14047	227	69.4	28	2247	107886	46629	2048
★ □ PORTLAND ADVENTIST MEDICAL CENTER, 10123 S.E. Market, Zip 97216; tel. 503/257-2500; Larry D. Dodds, pres. **A**1a 2 10 **F**1 2 3 5 6 7 8 10 11 12 14 15 16 20 23 24 25 26 27 28 29 30 32 33 34 35 36 37 40 42 43 44 45 46 47 49 52 53 54; **S**0235	21	10	S		302	11497	146	48.3	34	2062	48894	21692	1056
★ □ PROVIDENCE MEDICAL CENTER, 4805 N.E. Glisan St., Zip 97213; tel. 503/230-1111; John P. Lee, adm. **A**1a 2 3 5 8 9 10 **F**1 2 3 4 5 6 7 8 9 10 11 12 14 15 16 17 18 20 21 23 24 25 26 27 28 30 32 33 34 35 36 37 41 42 43 44 46 48 49 50 53 54; **S**5275	21	10	S		437	14675	264	60.4	12	759	75374	36841	1378
REHABILITATION INSTITUTE OF OREGON, See Good Samaritan Hospital and Medical Center													
★ □ RIVERSIDE PSYCHIATRIC HOSPITAL (Formerly Riverside Hospital), 1400 S.E. Umatilla St., Zip 97202; tel. 503/234-5353; Jon M. Orr, adm. (Nonreporting) **A**1b 10; **S**6525	33	82	S		66	—	—	—	—	—	—	—	—
★ □ SHRINERS HOSPITAL FOR CRIPPLED CHILDREN, 3101 S.W. Sam Jackson Park Rd., Zip 97201; tel. 503/241-5090; Gary L. Morel, adm. **A**1a 3 5 **F**23 24 26 34 42 44; **S**4125	23	57	S		40	774	18	45.0	0	0	—	—	156
★ □ ST. VINCENT HOSPITAL AND MEDICAL CENTER, 9205 S.W. Barnes Rd., Zip 97225; tel. 503/297-4411; Greg Van Pelt, adm. **A**1a 2 3 5 9 10 **F**1 2 3 4 5 6 7 8 9 10 11 12 14 15 16 17 20 21 23 24 26 27 28 29 30 32 33 34 35 36 37 40 41 42 43 44 45 46 49 53 54; **S**5275	21	10	S		451	18092	280	62.1	24	2264	94328	42987	1687
UNIVERSITY HOSPITAL, See Oregon Health Sciences University Hospital													
★ □ VETERANS ADMINISTRATION MEDICAL CENTER, 3710 U. S. Veterans Hospital Rd., Box 1034, Zip 97207; tel. 503/222-9221; Barry L. Bell, dir. (Total facility includes 120 beds in nursing home-type unit) **A**1a 2 3 5 8 **F**1 2 3 4 6 9 10 12 14 15 16 17 19 20 21 23 24 25 26 27 28 29 30 31 32 33 34 41 42 43 44 45 46 48 49 50 53 54	45	10	S	TF	687	14888	480	68.4	0	0	104213	50653	2015
				H	567	14642	370	—	0	0	—	—	1908
□ WOODLAND PARK HOSPITAL, 10300 N.E. Hancock, Zip 97220; tel. 503/257-5500; Richard Sanderson, adm. **A**1a 9 10 **F**1 3 6 10 12 14 16 21 23 27 33 34 35 36 40 45 50 53; **S**1375	33	10	S		156	3987	48	30.8	15	638	18347	5970	294
PRINEVILLE—Crook County													
PIONEER MEMORIAL HOSPITAL (Includes Crook County Nursing Home), 1201 N. Elm St., Zip 97754; tel. 503/447-6254; Joe Gorbea, adm. **A**9 10 **F**1 3 6 14 16 23 35 36 40 43 52; **S**0235	23	10	S		33	1015	9	27.3	5	99	3007	1520	72
REDMOND—Deschutes County													
□ CENTRAL OREGON DISTRICT HOSPITAL, 1253 N. Canal Blvd., Zip 97756; tel. 503/548-8131; Robert C. Lippard, adm. **A**1a 9 10 **F**1 3 6 10 12 14 15 16 23 26 35 36 37 40 41 44 45 46 47 48 49	16	10	S		67	2118	25	37.3	10	238	6318	3130	170
REEDSPORT—Douglas County													
LOWER UMPQUA HOSPITAL DISTRICT, 600 Ranch Rd., Zip 97467; tel. 503/271-2171; Richard R. Bell, exec. dir. (Total facility includes 22 beds in nursing home-type unit) **A**9 10 **F**1 3 6 12 14 15 16 19 23 34 35 36 41 43 44 45 50 53; **S**0585	16	10	S	TF	40	658	24	60.0	5	104	2923	1593	91
				H	18	586	5	—	5	104	2685	1364	71
ROSEBURG—Douglas County													
★ □ DOUGLAS COMMUNITY HOSPITAL, 738 W. Harvard Blvd., Zip 97470; tel. 503/673-6641; Greg Stock, adm. **A**1a 9 10 **F**1 3 5 6 9 10 11 12 14 15 16 21 23 24 26 33 35 36 37 40 41 43 44 45 46 47 48 49 50 52 53; **S**1755	33	10	S		118	3817	58	49.2	13	599	15868	7258	298
★ □ MERCY MEDICAL CENTER, 2700 Stewart Pkwy., Zip 97470; tel. 503/673-0611; Sr. Jacquetta Taylor, pres. & chief exec. off. **A**1a 9 10 **F**1 3 6 9 10 11 12 14 15 16 20 21 23 24 27 29 30 33 34 35 40 41 44 45 46 47 52 53 54; **S**5175	21	10	S		111	5521	68	61.3	12	434	18722	8427	433
★ □ VETERANS ADMINISTRATION MEDICAL CENTER, Zip 97470; tel. 503/440-1000; Perry C. Norman, dir. (Total facility includes 75 beds in nursing home-type unit) **A**1a b **F**1 3 6 10 12 14 15 16 19 23 24 26 27 28 29 30 31 32 33 34 42 44 46 47 48 49 53	45	10	S	TF	417	4380	265	63.5	0	0	26355	15790	618
				H	342	4336	191	—	0	0	—	—	573
SALEM—Marion County													
□ OREGON STATE HOSPITAL, 2600 Center St. N.E., Zip 97310; tel. 503/378-2348; Robert J. Benning, supt. **A**1b 3 5 10 **F**16 23 24 32 33 42 46 47 50	12	22	L		529	1669	511	81.8	0	0	27079	16137	783

★ American Hospital Association (AHA) membership
□ Joint Commission on Accreditation of Hospitals (JCAH) accreditation
+ American Osteopathic Hospital Association (AOHA) membership
○ American Osteopathic Association (AOA) accreditation
Δ Commission on Accreditation of Rehabilitation Facilities (CARF) accreditation
Control codes 61, 63, 64, 71, 72 and 73 indicate hospitals listed by AOHA, but not registered by AHA.
For definition of numerical codes, see page A2

Hospital, Address, Telephone, Administrator, Approval and Facility Codes, Multihospital System Code	Classification Codes				Inpatient Data				Newborn Data		Expense (thousands of dollars)		
	Control	Service	Stay	Facilities	Beds	Admissions	Census	Occupancy (percent)	Bassinets	Births	Total	Payroll	Personnel
⊞ SALEM HOSPITAL (Includes General Unit, 2561 Center St. N.E., Zip 97301; Memorial Unit, 665 Winter St. S.E., Zip 97301), Box 14001, Zip 97309; tel. 503/370-5200; Evan S. Lewis, pres. **A**1a 2 9 10 **F**1 2 3 6 7 8 9 10 11 12 14 16 20 23 24 25 26 30 35 36 40 44 45 46 49 51 52 53 54	23	10	S		434	19873	290	66.8	20	2792	62945	33546	1410
SEASIDE—Clatsop County													
★ SEASIDE GENERAL HOSPITAL, 725 S. Wahanna Rd., Box 740, Zip 97138; tel. 503/738-8463; Gerald Baker, adm. **A**9 10 **F**1 3 6 10 12 15 16 21 23 28 34 35 36 40 41 45 46 47 50 52 53; **S**5275	21	10	S		34	1011	10	29.4	4	84	3481	1503	73
SILVERTON—Marion County													
⊞ SILVERTON HOSPITAL, 342 Fairview St., Zip 97381; tel. 503/873-6336; James Edmark, adm. **A**1a 9 10 **F**1 3 6 12 14 16 23 35 36 40 45 52	23	10	S		38	1672	14	36.8	6	342	3539	1945	74
SPRINGFIELD—Lane County													
⊞ MCKENZIE-WILLAMETTE HOSPITAL, 1460 G St., Zip 97477; tel. 503/726-4400; W. Stewart Tittle, pres. **A**1a 9 10 **F**1 3 6 9 10 11 12 14 15 16 21 23 24 26 35 36 37 40 41 43 44 45 46 50 52 53	23	10	S		114	4796	57	50.0	14	699	20406	7903	331
ST. HELENS—Columbia County													
★ ST. HELEN'S HOSPITAL AND HEALTH CENTER, 500 N. Columbia River Hwy., Zip 97051; tel. 503/397-1188; Charles R. Laird, adm. **A**9 10 **F**1 3 5 6 12 14 15 16 23 35 36 37 40 41 43 44 45 50; **S**5415	21	10	S		44	1230	11	25.0	8	94	6585	2594	112
STAYTON—Marion County													
⊞ SANTIAM MEMORIAL HOSPITAL, 1401 N. Tenth St., Zip 97383; tel. 503/769-2175; Peter L. Rochetto, adm. **A**1a 9 10 **F**1 14 15 16 23 34 35 40 45 52	23	10	S		40	742	7	17.5	5	36	2159	989	54
THE DALLES—Wasco County													
⊞ MID-COLUMBIA MEDICAL CENTER, 19th & Nevada St., Zip 97058; tel. 503/296-1111; Mark D. Scott, pres. **A**1a 9 10 **F**1 3 5 6 10 12 14 15 16 23 34 35 36 37 40 41 43 44 45 46 47 52 53	23	10	S		125	3350	41	32.8	14	395	12066	5245	239
TILLAMOOK—Tillamook County													
□ TILLAMOOK COUNTY GENERAL HOSPITAL, 1000 Third St., Zip 97141; tel. 503/842-4444; Wendell Hesseltine, pres. **A**1a 9 10 **F**1 3 6 10 14 16 23 27 35 36 40 43 45 46 47 53; **S**0235	21	10	S		40	1568	15	37.5	7	168	5732	2460	100
TUALATIN—Clackamas County													
⊞ MERIDIAN PARK HOSPITAL, 19300 S.W. 65th St., Zip 97062; tel. 503/692-1212; Carleton G. Lindgren, adm. **A**1a 2 9 10 **F**1 3 6 10 12 14 15 16 21 23 24 30 34 35 43 44 45 46 50 53; **S**2755	23	10	S		150	5255	66	44.0	0	0	22340	8908	357
WHEELER—Tillamook County													
★ HARVEY E. RINEHART MEMORIAL HOSPITAL, Box 16, Zip 97147; tel. 503/368-5119; Tom Gillespie, adm. (Total facility includes 50 beds in nursing home-type unit) **A**9 10 **F**1 3 6 14 16 17 19 23 34 35 43 45 46 53	16	10	S	TF	72	416	54	75.0	0	0	2114	1159	74
				H	22	386	4	—	0	0	1824	878	—
WILSONVILLE—Clackamas County													
□ DAMMASCH STATE HOSPITAL, 28801 S.W. 110th St., Box 38, Zip 97070; tel. 503/682-3111; Victor M. Holm MD, supt. **A**1a 10 **F**23 24 30 32 33 42 45 46 47	12	22	L		375	2527	340	90.7	0	0	13628	8026	410

Hospital, Address, Telephone, Administrator, Approval and Facility Codes, Multihospital System Code	Classification Codes: Control	Service	Stay	Facilities	Inpatient Data: Beds	Admissions	Census	Occupancy (percent)	Newborn Data: Bassinets	Births	Expense (thousands of dollars): Total	Payroll	Personnel
★ American Hospital Association (AHA) membership □ Joint Commission on Accreditation of Hospitals (JCAH) accreditation + American Osteopathic Hospital Association (AOHA) membership ○ American Osteopathic Association (AOA) accreditation Δ Commission on Accreditation of Rehabilitation Facilities (CARF) accreditation Control codes 61, 63, 64, 71, 72 and 73 indicate hospitals listed by AOHA, but not registered by AHA. For definition of numerical codes, see page A2													

Pennsylvania

Hospital	Control	Service	Stay	Facilities	Beds	Admissions	Census	Occupancy (percent)	Bassinets	Births	Total	Payroll	Personnel
ABINGTON—Montgomery County													
★□ ABINGTON MEMORIAL HOSPITAL, 1200 York Rd., Zip 19001; tel. 215/576-2000; Felix Pilla, pres. & chief exec. off. **A**1a 3 5 6 9 10 **F**1 2 3 5 6 7 8 9 10 11 12 14 15 16 20 23 24 26 27 28 30 32 33 34 35 36 37 38 40 41 44 45 46 47 49 51 52 53	23	10	S		476	18280	334	70.2	42	2973	83777	40946	1707
ALIQUIPPA—Beaver County													
★□ ALIQUIPPA HOSPITAL, 2500 Hospital Dr., Zip 15001; tel. 412/857-1212; Howard W. Vanscoy Jr., pres. & chief exec. off. **A**1a 9 10 **F**1 2 3 5 6 10 12 14 15 16 20 21 23 26 30 34 35 41 45 48 53	23	10	S		175	5945	116	66.3	0	0	23209	10019	470
ALLENTOWN—Lehigh County													
★□ ALLENTOWN HOSPITAL, 17th & Chew Sts., Zip 18102; tel. 215/778-2300; Darryl R. Lippman, pres. **A**1a 2 3 5 6 9 10 **F**1 2 3 6 7 8 9 10 11 12 14 15 16 20 21 23 24 26 27 28 30 31 32 33 34 35 36 37 38 40 41 42 44 45 46 47 51 52 53; **S**1695	23	10	S		305	12462	249	81.6	35	2902	55705	25923	1271
○ + ALLENTOWN OSTEOPATHIC MEDICAL CENTER, 1736 Hamilton St., Zip 18104; tel. 215/770-8300; Marvin C. Miles, pres. **A**9 10 11 12 13 **F**1 3 6 10 12 14 15 16 23 34 35 40 44 45 46 47 48 50 52 53	23	10	S		150	6177	101	67.3	10	610	21410	10289	495
□ ALLENTOWN STATE HOSPITAL, 1600 Hanover Ave., Zip 18103; tel. 215/821-6211; Dale E. Newhart, supt. (Nonreporting) **A**1b 10	12	22	L		628	—	—	—	—	—	—	—	—
Δ GOOD SHEPHERD REHABILITATION HOSPITAL, Sixth & St. John Sts., Zip 18103; tel. 215/776-3111; Rev. Dale Sandstrom, pres. **A**7 9 10 **F**15 23 24 26 32 33 34 42 44 46	23	46	S		60	827	54	90.0	0	0	10081	7001	278
★□ LEHIGH VALLEY HOSPITAL CENTER, 1200 S. Cedar Crest Blvd., P O Box 689, Zip 18105; tel. 215/776-8000; Samuel R. Huston, pres. & chief exec. off. **A**1a 2 3 5 8 9 10 **F**1 2 3 4 5 6 10 11 12 14 15 16 20 22 23 24 30 32 34 35 44 45 46 47 53 54; **S**1695	23	10	S		460	17420	386	83.9	0	0	94307	42771	1838
★□ SACRED HEART HOSPITAL, 421 Chew St., Zip 18102; tel. 215/776-4500; Orlando Pozzuoli, pres. **A**1a 2 3 5 9 10 **F**1 2 3 6 7 8 9 10 11 12 13 15 16 21 23 26 30 32 33 34 35 37 40 44 45 46 50 52 53	23	10	S		232	8154	157	67.7	20	835	35786	15130	748
ALTOONA—Blair County													
ALTOONA CENTER, 1515 Fourth St., Zip 16601; tel. 814/946-6900; John C. Williams, dir. **F**15 23 24 33 42 44 47	12	62	L		138	10	133	96.4	0	0	6008	3437	179
★□ ALTOONA HOSPITAL, Howard Ave. & Seventh St., Zip 16603; tel. 814/946-2011; Albert C. Knauss, pres. & chief exec. off. **A**1a 2 3 5 6 9 10 **F**1 2 3 6 7 9 10 11 12 14 15 16 20 21 23 24 26 27 28 29 30 31 32 33 34 35 36 37 38 40 42 44 45 46 47 49 50 51 52 53 54	23	10	S		310	13250	227	69.6	32	1394	51818	26024	1119
★□ MERCY HOSPITAL, 2500 Seventh Ave., Zip 16603; tel. 814/944-1681; Sr. Anne M. Trzeciak, exec. dir. **A**1a 2 6 9 10 **F**1 2 3 5 6 7 8 9 10 11 12 14 15 16 17 21 23 24 25 26 33 34 35 36 40 41 42 44 45 46 47 52	23	10	S		183	6432	133	72.7	8	427	25119	11739	599
Δ REHABILITATION HOSPITAL OF ALTOONA, 2005 Valley View Blvd., Zip 16602; tel. 814/944-3535; Anthony F. Misitano, adm. (Nonreporting) **A**7 10	33	46	S		60	—	—	—	—	—	—	—	—
★□ VETERANS ADMINISTRATION MEDICAL CENTER, Pleasant Valley Blvd. & 27th St., Zip 16603; tel. 814/943-8164; John J. Ruff, dir. (Total facility includes 33 beds in nursing home-type unit) **A**1a **F**1 3 6 12 14 15 16 19 23 24 28 42 44 46	45	10	S	TF H	139 106	2708 2674	114 83	76.0 —	0 0	0 0	20012 —	9511 —	351 335
AMBLER—Montgomery County													
□ HORSHAM CLINIC, Welsh Rd. & Butler Pike, Zip 19002; tel. 215/643-7800; Levon D. Tashjian MD, med. dir. **A**1b 9 10 **F**30 32 33 42 46 47; **S**0295	33	22	L		118	736	104	95.4	0	0	13810	5972	239
ASHLAND—Schuylkill County													
□ ASHLAND STATE GENERAL HOSPITAL, Rte. 61, Zip 17921; tel. 717/875-2000; John David Francis, adm. (Total facility includes 18 beds in nursing home-type unit) **A**1a 9 10 **F**1 3 6 10 12 14 15 16 19 23 35 40 44 45 50 52 53; **S**3825	12	10	S	TF H	161 143	4491 4411	97 80	60.2 —	8 8	202 202	14844 14421	6732 6438	330 314
BEAVER—Beaver County													
★□ THE MEDICAL CENTER (Formerly Medical Center of Beaver County), 1000 Dutch Ridge Rd., Zip 15009; tel. 412/728-7000; Robert N. Gibson, pres. **A**1a 3 5 9 10 **F**1 2 3 5 6 8 10 11 12 15 16 21 23 24 30 34 35 36 37 40 41 43 44 45 46 47 52 53	23	10	S		491	16304	289	58.5	48	1533	68332	32905	1542
BELLEFONTE—Centre County													
□ Δ REHAB HOSPITAL FOR SPECIAL SERVICES, R D 5, Box 451-A, Zip 16823; tel. 814/359-3421; Dennis C. Falck, adm. (Nonreporting) **A**1a 7 10; **S**0825	33	46	L		65	—	—	—	—	—	—	—	—
BENSALEM—Bucks County													
□ LIVENGRIN FOUNDATION, 4833 Hulmeville Rd., Zip 19020; tel. 215/639-2300; Harriet Browne, adm. **A**1b **F**49	23	82	S		73	997	56	76.7	0	0	2884	1507	85
BENSALEM—Philadelphia County													
□ OXFORD HEALTH SERVICES (Formerly Oxford Hospital), P O Box 1270, Zip 19020; tel. 215/757-0130; J. C. Amos Jr., adm. (Nonreporting) **A**1a 9	23	10	S		58	—	—	—	—	—	—	—	—
BERWICK—Columbia County													
★□ BERWICK HOSPITAL CENTER (Formerly Berwick Hospital), 701 E. 16th St., Zip 18603; tel. 717/759-5000; Terance P. John, pres. & chief exec. off. (Total facility includes 120 beds in nursing home-type unit) **A**1a 9 10 **F**1 3 6 10 12 14 15 16 19 23 24 35 36 40 41 42 44 45 46 47 50 52 53	23	10	S	TF H	299 179	5819 5735	196 80	65.6 —	10 10	418 418	17430 14936	8575 7379	539 447
BERWYN—Chester County													
★□ DEVEREUX FOUNDATION-BOND DIVISION, 826 Maple Ave., Zip 19312; tel. 215/296-6868 (Nonreporting) **A**1b 9; **S**0845	23	52	L		329	—	—	—	—	—	—	—	—
BETHLEHEM—Lehigh and Northampton Counties													
★□ MUHLENBERG HOSPITAL CENTER (Formerly Muhlenberg Medical Center), Schoenersville Rd., Zip 18017; tel. 215/861-2200; William R. Mason, pres. **A**1a 9 10 **F**1 3 6 10 12 14 15 16 23 24 27 28 30 33 34 35 45 46 47; **S**1025	23	10	S		148	5106	107	72.3	0	0	18867	8592	422
★□ ST. LUKE'S HOSPITAL, 801 Ostrum St., Zip 18015; tel. 215/691-4141; Richard A. Anderson, pres. **A**1a 2 3 5 6 9 10 **F**1 3 4 6 7 8 9 10 11 12 14 15 16 20 23 24 26 27 28 30 33 34 35 36 37 38 40 44 45 46 52 53 54; **S**1025	23	10	S		419	13925	258	61.6	23	1817	59039	28891	1394
BLOOMSBURG—Columbia County													
★□ BLOOMSBURG HOSPITAL, 549 E. Fair St., Zip 17815; tel. 717/387-2100; Robert Spinelli, adm. **A**1a 9 10 **F**1 3 6 10 14 16 23 26 34 35 36 40 43 45 46 47 48 52 53; **S**3825	23	10	S		133	3843	54	40.6	18	451	11598	5761	345
BRADDOCK—Allegheny County													
★□ BRADDOCK GENERAL HOSPITAL, 400 Holland Ave., Zip 15104; tel. 412/636-5000; Frederick A. Hough, exec. dir. **A**1a 9 10 **F**1 2 3 6 10 12 14 15 16 23 27 30 33 35 43 46 47 52 53	23	10	S		195	6303	154	73.3	0	0	25773	12930	597

★ American Hospital Association (AHA) membership
☐ Joint Commission on Accreditation of Hospitals (JCAH) accreditation
+ American Osteopathic Hospital Association (AOHA) membership
○ American Osteopathic Association (AOA) accreditation
Δ Commission on Accreditation of Rehabilitation Facilities (CARF) accreditation
Control codes 61, 63, 64, 71, 72 and 73 indicate hospitals listed by AOHA, but not registered by AHA. For definition of numerical codes, see page A2

Hospital, Address, Telephone, Administrator, Approval and Facility Codes, Multihospital System Code	Classification Codes				Inpatient Data				Newborn Data		Expense (thousands of dollars)		
	Control	Service	Stay	Facilities	Beds	Admissions	Census	Occupancy (percent)	Bassinets	Births	Total	Payroll	Personnel
BRADFORD—McKean County													
⊞ BRADFORD HOSPITAL (Includes Bradford Nursing Pavilion), 116-156 Interstate Pkwy., Zip 16701; tel. 814/368-4143; Michael G. Guley, pres. & chief exec. off. (Total facility includes 95 beds in nursing home-type unit) **A**1a 9 10 **F**1 3 6 10 12 14 15 16 19 20 23 27 30 32 35 36 37 40 45 46 52 53	23	10	S	TF	255	5092	177	69.4	12	338	14774	8138	478
				H	160	5042	85	—	12	338	12943	6943	421
BRIDGEVILLE—Allegheny County													
☐ MAYVIEW STATE HOSPITAL, 1601 Mayview Rd., Zip 15017; tel. 412/257-6200 **A**1a 10 **F**19 23 24 32 33 42 46 47 50	12	22	L		909	848	722	79.4	0	0	52396	29009	1250
BRISTOL—Bucks County													
DELAWARE VALLEY MEDICAL CENTER, See Langhorne													
⊞ LOWER BUCKS HOSPITAL, Bath Rd. & Orchard Ave., Zip 19007; tel. 215/785-9200; Carroll J. Thomas, adm. **A**1a 3 5 9 10 **F**1 2 3 6 12 14 15 16 20 23 24 26 27 30 32 33 34 35 36 40 41 42 45 46 52 53	23	10	S		316	10564	213	67.4	36	1330	36926	19031	846
BROOKVILLE—Jefferson County													
⊞ BROOKVILLE HOSPITAL, 100 Hospital Rd., Zip 15825; tel. 814/849-2312; Warren J. Bassett, pres. **A**1a 9 10 **F**1 3 6 10 12 15 16 23 33 35 36 40 41 45 53	23	10	S		73	2818	42	60.0	6	195	10351	4733	263
BROWNSVILLE—Fayette County													
⊞ BROWNSVILLE GENERAL HOSPITAL, 125 Simpson Rd., Zip 15417; tel. 412/785-7200; Charles Lonchar, chief exec. off. **A**1a 9 10 **F**1 3 6 10 12 15 16 23 26 30 34 35 37 44 45 46 53; **S**1755	23	10	S		102	3499	64	62.7	0	0	10499	4958	253
BRYN MAWR—Montgomery County													
BRYN MAWR COLLEGE INFIRMARY, Bryn Mawr College Campus, Zip 19010; tel. 215/645-6223; Kay Kerr MD, adm. (Nonreporting)	23	11	S		10	—	—	—	—	—	—	—	—
⊞ BRYN MAWR HOSPITAL, Bryn Mawr Ave., Zip 19010; tel. 215/896-3000; Carl I. Bergkvist, pres. **A**1a 2 3 5 6 8 9 10 **F**1 2 3 4 6 7 8 9 10 11 12 14 15 16 20 21 23 24 26 28 30 32 33 34 35 36 37 40 41 42 44 45 46 47 48 49 51 52 53 54; **S**7775	23	10	S		349	13872	272	73.7	20	1918	79917	36806	1800
BUTLER—Butler County													
⊞ BUTLER MEMORIAL HOSPITAL, 911 E. Brady St., Zip 16001; tel. 412/283-6666; Scott A. Becker, pres.; Carol A. Dietrich, chief oper. off. **A**1a 9 10 **F**1 2 3 6 10 12 14 15 16 23 26 27 28 29 30 33 34 35 36 40 45 47 48 49 53	23	10	S		270	10380	220	83.7	24	894	37992	18552	833
⊞ VETERANS ADMINISTRATION MEDICAL CENTER, Zip 16001; tel. 412/287-4781; Reginald L. Mosior, dir. (Total facility includes 147 beds in nursing home-type unit) **A**1a **F**1 3 6 12 14 15 16 19 23 24 25 26 28 32 33 34 35 41 42 44 45 46 47 48 49 50	45	10	L	TF	367	2333	324	84.8	0	0	22461	14734	660
				H	220	2227	205	—	0	0	15917	11142	597
CALN TOWNSHIP—Chester County													
⊞ BRANDYWINE HOSPITAL (Formerly Listed Under Coatesville), 201 Reeceville Rd., Zip 19320; tel. 215/383-8000; Norman A. Ledwin, pres. **A**1a 6 9 10 **F**1 3 5 6 10 12 14 15 16 20 23 24 26 27 30 32 33 34 35 36 37 40 42 43 44 45 46 47 48 52 53	23	10	S		208	8275	145	69.7	12	708	33834	13986	720
CAMP HILL—Cumberland County													
⊞ HOLY SPIRIT HOSPITAL, N. 21st St., Zip 17011; tel. 717/763-2100; Sr. Ursula Frei, pres. **A**1a 9 10 **F**1 3 6 10 12 13 14 15 16 23 27 28 29 30 32 33 34 35 36 40 42 43 44 45 46 48 49 52 53	21	10	S		345	12926	249	72.2	24	652	42388	21354	1080
STATE CORRECTIONAL INSTITUTION AT CAMP HILL, Box 200, Zip 17011; tel. 717/737-4531; R. J. Langland, adm. health serv. (Nonreporting)	12	11	S		34	—	—	—	—	—	—	—	—
CANONSBURG—Washington County													
⊞ CANONSBURG GENERAL HOSPITAL, R D 1, Box 147, Rte. 519, Zip 15317; tel. 412/745-6100; Gary L. Perecko, pres.; Barbara A. Bensaia, exec. vice-pres. & chief oper. off. (Total facility includes 32 beds in nursing home-type unit) **A**1a 9 10 **F**1 3 6 10 12 15 16 19 20 23 24 26 30 32 33 34 35 42 44 45 53	23	10	S	TF	120	4296	103	85.8	0	0	18917	8570	388
				H	88	3989	77	—	0	0	—	—	369
CARBONDALE—Lackawanna County													
⊞ CARBONDALE GENERAL HOSPITAL, 185 Fallbrook St., Zip 18407; tel. 717/282-1330; Joseph C. Kogelman, adm. & chief exec. off. **A**1a 9 10 **F**3 6 12 14 15 16 23 35 45 47 52	23	10	S		67	1369	28	41.8	0	0	4922	2244	127
⊞ ST. JOSEPH'S HOSPITAL, 100 Lincoln Ave., Zip 18407; tel. 717/282-2100; Sr. Jean Coughlin, exec. dir. **A**1a 9 10 **F**1 6 14 15 16 23 27 32 34 35 40 42 45 46 52 53	21	10	S		93	3590	63	67.7	10	439	11998	4680	287
CARLISLE—Cumberland County													
⊞ CARLISLE HOSPITAL, 246 Parker St., Box 310, Zip 17013; tel. 717/249-1212; James E. Wood, pres. **A**1a 9 10 **F**3 5 7 8 9 10 12 14 15 17 20 21 23 26 27 30 34 36 40 41 42 44 45 46 52 54	23	10	S		234	6285	105	44.9	32	829	23787	11641	594
CARNEGIE—Allegheny County													
WOODVILLE STATE HOSPITAL, Zip 15106; tel. 412/645-6400; Suzanne B. Kreinbrook MD, supt. (Total facility includes 182 beds in nursing home-type unit) **A**10 **F**19 23 24 32 33 42 44 46 47	12	22	L	TF	615	562	539	89.5	0	0	33180	18952	895
				H	433	534	379	—	0	0	—	—	778
CHAMBERSBURG—Franklin County													
⊞ CHAMBERSBURG HOSPITAL, 112 N. Seventh St., P O Box 187, Zip 17201; tel. 717/264-5171; Stephen H. Franklin, pres. **A**1a 9 10 **F**1 2 3 6 10 12 14 15 16 23 24 26 27 28 30 31 32 33 34 35 36 37 40 42 44 45 46 47 52 53	23	10	S		226	8744	134	59.3	22	931	26977	12645	675
CHESTER—Delaware County													
⊞ CROZER-CHESTER MEDICAL CENTER, 15th St. & Upland Ave., Zip 19013; tel. 215/447-2000; John C. McMeekin, pres. & chief exec. off. **A**1a 2 3 5 8 10 **F**1 2 3 6 7 8 9 10 11 12 14 15 16 20 22 23 24 25 26 27 28 29 30 32 33 34 35 36 37 38 40 41 42 43 44 45 46 47 48 49 50 51 52 53 54	23	10	S		413	14173	289	70.0	30	2226	82889	45827	1973
⊞ SACRED HEART MEDICAL CENTER, Ninth & Wilson Sts., Zip 19013; tel. 215/494-0700; Sr. Mary Margaret, pres. **A**1a 9 10 **F**1 2 3 6 10 12 14 15 16 21 23 24 27 28 30 32 33 34 35 36 40 44 45 46 52 53; **S**0285	21	10	S		236	8372	188	79.7	10	714	29207	14669	742
CLARION—Clarion County													
★ ○ + CLARION OSTEOPATHIC COMMUNITY HOSPITAL, One Hospital Dr., Zip 16214; tel. 814/226-9500; Roy W. Wright, adm. **A**9 10 11 12 **F**1 3 6 12 14 16 17 23 34 35 36 40 44 45 46 53; **S**1755	23	10	S		94	3516	57	60.6	10	304	11224	3960	224
CLARKS SUMMIT—Lackawanna County													
☐ CLARKS SUMMIT STATE HOSPITAL, Rte. 3, Box 15, Zip 18411; tel. 717/586-2011; Kathleen D. Reese, supt. (Total facility includes 167 beds in nursing home-type unit) **A**1b 10 **F**15 16 19 23 24 32 33 42 44 46 47 50	12	22	L	TF	512	507	473	81.6	0	0	24832	14542	800
				H	345	455	297	—	0	0	—	—	702
CLEARFIELD—Clearfield County													
⊞ CLEARFIELD HOSPITAL, 809 Turnpike Ave., Box 992, Zip 16830; tel. 814/765-5341; Christopher B. Cook, pres. **A**1a 9 10 **F**1 3 6 10 12 14 15 16 23 24 30 34 35 36 40 41 43 44 45 46 47 52 53	23	10	S		133	5347	80	52.6	23	437	16705	8355	416
COALDALE—Schuylkill County													
☐ COALDALE STATE GENERAL HOSPITAL, Seventh St., Zip 18218; tel. 717/645-2131; Frank J. Parano, adm. (Nonreporting) **A**1a 9 10; **S**0745	12	10	S		162	—	—	—	—	—	—	—	—
COATESVILLE—Chester County													
BRANDYWINE HOSPITAL, See Caln Township													

Hospital, Address, Telephone, Administrator, Approval and Facility Codes, Multihospital System Code	Classification Codes				Inpatient Data				Newborn Data		Expense (thousands of dollars)		
★ American Hospital Association (AHA) membership ☐ Joint Commission on Accreditation of Hospitals (JCAH) accreditation + American Osteopathic Hospital Association (AOHA) membership ○ American Osteopathic Association (AOA) accreditation Δ Commission on Accreditation of Rehabilitation Facilities (CARF) accreditation Control codes 61, 63, 64, 71, 72 and 73 indicate hospitals listed by AOHA, but not registered by AHA. For definition of numerical codes, see page A2	Control	Service	Stay	Facilities	Beds	Admissions	Census	Occupancy (percent)	Bassinets	Births	Total	Payroll	Personnel
⊞ VETERANS ADMINISTRATION MEDICAL CENTER, Zip 19320; tel. 215/383-0218; R. C. Meiler, dir. (Total facility includes 120 beds in nursing home-type unit) **A**1a b **F**1 3 6 10 12 15 16 19 23 24 26 28 29 33 34 35 42 43 44 46 48 49 50	45	22	L	TF H	1097 977	4401 4240	940 827	85.7 —	0 0	0 0	64700 —	38351 —	1599 —
COLUMBIA—Lancaster County													
⊞ COLUMBIA HOSPITAL, 631 Poplar St., Zip 17512; tel. 717/684-2841; Robert F. Katana, pres. & chief exec. off. **A**1a 10 **F**1 6 9 12 14 15 16 21 23 34 35 36 40 45 46 47 48 52	23	10	S		76	1793	36	47.4	5	130	5097	2802	143
CONNELLSVILLE—Fayette County													
⊞ HIGHLANDS HOSPITAL AND HEALTH CENTER (Formerly Connellsville State General Hospital), Cottage & Murphy Aves., Zip 15425; tel. 412/628-1500; Michael J. Evans, exec. dir. **A**1a 9 10 **F**1 6 12 14 15 16 23 26 27 32 33 34 35 42 44 45 46 52; **S**1355	23	10	S		69	1974	28	40.6	0	0	7314	3153	170
CORRY—Erie County													
☐ CORRY MEMORIAL HOSPITAL, 612 W. Smith St., Zip 16407; tel. 814/664-4641; Raymond A. Graeca, pres. (Nonreporting) **A**1a 9 10	23	10	S		86	—	—	—	—	—	—	—	—
COUDERSPORT—Potter County													
⊞ CHARLES COLE MEMORIAL HOSPITAL, Rural Delivery 3, U. S. Rte. 6, Zip 16915; tel. 814/274-9300; Benjamin L. Stimaker, exec. dir. (Total facility includes 48 beds in nursing home-type unit) **A**1a 9 10 **F**1 3 6 10 12 15 16 19 23 26 28 30 32 33 35 40 42 44 45 46 52 53	23	10	S	TF H	133 85	3717 3643	90 47	65.2 —	12 12	403 403	11489 —	4985 —	317 —
CRESSON—Cambria County													
ALTOONA CENTER, See Altoona													
DANVILLE—Montour County													
☐ DANVILLE STATE HOSPITAL, Zip 17821; tel. 717/275-7011; Ford S. Thompson, actg. supt. (Total facility includes 174 beds in nursing home-type unit) **A**1b 10 **F**15 19 23 24 33 42 46	12	22	L	TF H	614 440	361 361	568 386	92.5 —	0 0	0 0	30474 —	25766 —	841 —
⊞ GEISINGER MEDICAL CENTER, N. Academy Ave., Zip 17822; tel. 717/271-6211; F. Kenneth Ackerman Jr., sr. vice-pres. & adm. dir. **A**1a 2 3 5 6 8 9 10 **F**1 2 3 4 5 6 7 8 9 10 11 12 13 14 15 16 17 20 23 24 25 26 27 28 29 30 32 33 34 35 36 37 38 39 40 42 43 44 45 46 47 49 51 52 53 54; **S**5570	23	10	S		566	19265	409	72.3	20	1074	127340	52125	2816
DARBY—Philadelphia County													
MERCY CATHOLIC MEDICAL CENTER, See Philadelphia													
DEVON—Chester County													
⊞ Δ DEVEREUX FOUNDATION-FRENCH DIVISION, 119 Old Lancaster Rd., Box 400, Zip 19333; tel. 215/964-3000; Gery Sasko, adm. (Nonreporting) **A**1b 7; **S**0845	23	52	L		231	—	—	—	—	—	—	—	—
DOWNINGTOWN—Chester County													
VILLA ST. JOHN VIANNEY HOSPITAL, Lincoln Hwy. & Woodbine Rd., Box 219, Zip 19335; tel. 215/269-2600; Sr. Joan Dreisbach, adm. **F**15 24 30 31 33 42 46	21	22	L		54	46	29	53.7	0	0	1047	552	49
DOYLESTOWN—Bucks County													
★ DELAWARE VALLEY MENTAL HEALTH FOUNDATION, 833 E. Butler Ave., Zip 18901; tel. 215/345-0444; Herbert S. Haigh, exec. vice-pres. (Nonreporting) **A**10	23	22	S		41	—	—	—	—	—	—	—	—
⊞ Δ DOYLESTOWN HOSPITAL, 595 W. State St., Zip 18901; tel. 215/345-2200; Jaromir Marik, pres. & chief exec. off. **A**1a 7 9 10 **F**1 3 5 6 7 10 12 14 15 16 20 21 23 24 25 26 27 30 33 34 35 36 40 41 42 44 46 47 53	23	10	S		213	8856	174	81.7	18	872	34011	17239	915
DREXEL HILL—Delaware County													
⊞ DELAWARE COUNTY MEMORIAL HOSPITAL, 501 N. Lansdowne Ave., Zip 19026; tel. 215/284-8100; Richard D. Thomas, pres. **A**1a 2 3 5 9 10 **F**1 2 3 6 10 12 14 15 16 20 21 23 24 25 26 32 33 34 35 36 37 40 41 42 44 45 46 47 48 49 50 53	23	10	S		303	10910	240	79.2	20	1263	44484	21568	990
DUBOIS—Clearfield County													
⊞ DUBOIS REGIONAL MEDICAL CENTER, 100 Hospital Ave., P O Box 447, Zip 15801; tel. 814/371-2200; Peter W. Monge, chief exec. off. **A**1a c 9 10 **F**1 3 6 10 12 14 15 16 20 21 23 24 27 30 32 34 35 36 40 41 43 44 45 46 48 49 51 52	23	10	S		214	9646	153	70.5	18	784	29035	14126	799
EAGLEVILLE—Montgomery County													
⊞ EAGLEVILLE HOSPITAL, 100 Eagleville Rd., Zip 19408; tel. 215/539-6000; Frederick M. Carey, chief exec. off. **A**1b 9 10 **F**15 24 29 30 32 33 42 46	23	82	S		139	2074	128	92.1	0	0	10976	6654	288
EAST STROUDSBURG—Monroe County													
⊞ POCONO HOSPITAL, 206 E. Brown St., Zip 18301; tel. 717/421-4000; Patrick Mutch, interim adm. **A**1a 10 **F**1 3 6 10 11 12 14 15 16 23 24 26 27 28 30 32 33 34 35 36 37 40 44 45 46 47 52 53; **S**1755	23	10	S		223	8734	169	75.8	30	843	32109	16249	693
EASTON—Northampton County													
⊞ EASTON HOSPITAL, 21st & Lehigh Sts., Zip 18042; tel. 215/250-4000; Charles L. Keim, pres. **A**1a 2 3 5 9 10 **F**1 3 6 9 10 11 12 15 16 19 21 23 24 25 26 27 29 30 33 34 35 36 37 40 44 45 46 47 50 52 53 54	23	10	S		369	12528	257	67.8	22	914	45817	23780	1074
ELIZABETHTOWN—Lancaster County													
PENNSYLVANIA UNIVERSITY-ELIZABETHTOWN HOSPITAL AND REHABILITATION CENTER, See Pennsylvania State University Hospital													
ELKINS PARK—Montgomery County													
☐ ROLLING HILL HOSPITAL, 60 E. Township Line, Zip 19117; tel. 215/663-6000; Frederick L. Hollander, exec. dir. **A**1a 3 5 9 10 **F**1 3 6 11 12 14 15 16 20 23 24 25 26 33 35 36 38 40 41 42 43 44 45 46 53; **S**6345	23	10	S		259	9070	172	66.4	24	1548	44607	18494	857
ELLWOOD CITY—Lawrence County													
⊞ ELLWOOD CITY HOSPITAL (Includes Mary Evans Extended Care Center), 724 Pershing St., Zip 16117; tel. 412/752-0081; Herbert S. Skuba, pres. (Total facility includes 19 beds in nursing home-type unit) **A**1a 9 10 **F**1 3 6 10 12 14 16 19 23 26 34 35 40 41 45 52 53	23	10	S	TF H	125 106	3916 3774	70 61	56.0 —	12 12	206 206	11479 11284	5595 5500	293 287
EPHRATA—Lancaster County													
⊞ EPHRATA COMMUNITY HOSPITAL, Martin Ave., Zip 17522; tel. 717/733-0311; John M. Porter Jr., pres. **A**1a 9 10 **F**1 3 6 10 12 14 15 16 21 23 24 27 30 32 33 34 35 36 40 44 45 46 47 52 53	23	10	S		134	5086	82	55.4	16	596	15205	9161	406
ERIE—Erie County													
⊞ HAMOT MEDICAL CENTER, 201 State St., Zip 16550; tel. 814/870-6000; Dana R. Lundquist, pres. **A**1a 2 3 5 8 9 10 **F**1 3 4 5 6 7 8 9 10 11 12 14 15 16 20 22 23 24 26 27 28 29 30 32 33 34 35 36 37 38 40 42 43 44 45 46 47 48 50 51 52 53 54	23	10	S		510	17830	354	69.4	22	1866	81813	36451	1619
☐ Δ LAKE ERIE INSTITUTE OF REHABILITATION, 137 W. Second St., Zip 16507; tel. 814/453-5602; Urban J. Lariccia, pres. (Nonreporting) **A**1a 7 10; **S**0825	33	49	L		90	—	—	—	—	—	—	—	—
★ ○ + METROX HEALTH CENTER, 252 W. 11th St., Zip 16501; tel. 814/455-3961; Luis A Hernandez, adm. **A**9 10 11 12 13 **F**1 2 3 6 10 11 12 14 16 23 34 35 40 45 46 47 52 53; **S**1755	23	10	S		150	3422	57	38.0	10	42	12566	5124	254

Hospital, Address, Telephone, Administrator, Approval and Facility Codes, Multihospital System Code	Classification Codes: Control	Service	Stay	Facilities	Inpatient Data: Beds	Admissions	Census	Occupancy (percent)	Newborn Data: Bassinets	Births	Expense (thousands of dollars): Total	Payroll	Personnel
○ + MILLCREEK COMMUNITY HOSPITAL, 5515 Peach St., Zip 16509; tel. 814/864-4031; James A. Schaffner, pres. **A**10 11 12 13 **F**1 3 6 10 12 15 16 23 26 32 35 36 40 44 45 46 47 50 52 53	23	10	S		101	3926	62	61.4	7	292	10599	5056	252
★□ Δ SAINT VINCENT HEALTH CENTER, 232 W. 25th St., Zip 16544; tel. 814/452-5000; Sr. Margaret Ann Hardner, pres. **A**1a 3 5 6 7 8 9 10 **F**1 2 3 4 5 6 10 12 14 15 16 17 20 23 24 25 26 27 28 29 30 32 33 34 35 36 40 41 42 44 45 46 47 48 49 50 51 52 53 54	21	10	S		580	20267	391	67.4	25	1796	83692	38999	1891
★□ SHRINERS HOSPITALS FOR CRIPPLED CHILDREN, 1645 W. Eighth St., Zip 16505; tel. 814/452-4164; Richard W. Brzuz, adm. **A**1a 3 5 **F**23 34 42 46; **S**4125	23	57	S		30	667	14	46.7	0	0	—	—	65
★□ VETERANS ADMINISTRATION MEDICAL CENTER, 135 E. 38th St., Zip 16504; tel. 814/868-8661; Jack D. Graham, dir. (Total facility includes 40 beds in nursing home-type unit) **A**1a **F**1 3 12 14 15 16 19 23 24 26 28 32 33 34 35 42 44 45 46	45	10	S	TF	178	2949	146	82.0	0	0	16263	10917	382
				H	138	2905	107	—	0	0	—	—	369
EVERETT—Bedford County													
★□ MEMORIAL HOSPITAL OF BEDFORD COUNTY, Rural Delivery 1, Box 80, Zip 15537; tel. 814/623-6161; James C. Vreeland, dir. **A**1a 9 10 **F**1 3 6 10 12 14 15 16 21 23 26 30 34 35 36 37 40 44 45 46 50 52 53	23	10	S		105	3787	55	52.4	12	341	10494	4513	261
FARRELL—Mercer County													
○ + SHENANGO VALLEY MEDICAL CENTER (Formerly Shenango Valley Osteopathic Hospital), 2200 Memorial Dr. Ext., Zip 16121; tel. 412/981-3500; J. Larry Heinike, pres. **A**9 10 11 12 13 **F**1 3 6 12 14 15 16 21 23 35 41 45 46 52 53	23	10	S		104	4512	74	71.2	0	0	15447	7021	348
FORT WASHINGTON—Montgomery County													
□ NORTHWESTERN INSTITUTE OF PSYCHIATRY, 450 Bethlehem Pike, Zip 19034; tel. 215/641-5300; Marc Lazarus, exec. dir. (Nonreporting) **A**1b 3 9 10; **S**0455	23	22	S		146	—	—	—	—	—	—	—	—
FRANKLIN—Venango County													
★□ FRANKLIN REGIONAL MEDICAL CENTER, 1 Spruce St., Zip 16323; tel. 814/437-7000; James P. Reber, pres. **A**1a 2 3 5 9 10 **F**1 3 6 7 8 9 10 11 12 14 15 16 17 20 23 24 25 26 28 30 32 33 34 35 36 37 40 43 44 45 46 50 52	23	10	S		228	9910	157	68.9	12	517	33457	15898	755
GETTYSBURG—Adams County													
★□ GETTYSBURG HOSPITAL, 147 Gettys St., Zip 17325; tel. 717/334-2121; John E. Barrett Jr., pres. **A**1a 9 10 **F**1 3 6 10 12 14 15 16 23 26 33 34 35 36 40 45 46 47 52 53	23	10	S		102	4468	70	68.6	20	585	17060	8165	360
GREENSBURG—Westmoreland County													
★□ WESTMORELAND HOSPITAL, 532 W. Pittsburgh St., Zip 15601; tel. 412/832-4000; Walter Van Dyke, exec. dir. **A**1a 2 9 10 **F**1 2 3 6 7 8 9 10 11 12 14 15 16 20 23 24 27 28 29 30 32 33 34 35 36 40 45 46 48 52 53; **S**2395	23	10	S		355	14392	272	76.6	25	770	50871	25326	1199
GREENVILLE—Mercer County													
GREENVILLE HOSPITAL, See Greenville Regional Hospital													
★□ GREENVILLE REGIONAL HOSPITAL (Formerly Greenville Hospital), 110 N. Main St., Zip 16125; tel. 412/588-2100; J. William Eddy, pres. & chief exec. off. **A**1a 2 9 10 **F**1 3 6 10 11 12 14 15 16 21 23 28 30 32 33 34 35 36 41 44 45 47 49 52 53	23	10	S		226	9709	161	71.2	22	737	33544	14419	715
GROVE CITY—Mercer County													
★□ ○ + UNITED COMMUNITY HOSPITAL, Cranberry Rd., R D 5, Box 5005, Zip 16127; tel. 412/458-5442; James R. Kelly Jr., adm. **A**1a 9 10 11 **F**1 3 6 10 12 15 16 23 26 35 36 40 41 44 45 46 49 52 53; **S**1755	23	10	S		128	4276	67	52.3	8	392	14768	5859	299
HANOVER—York County													
★□ HANOVER GENERAL HOSPITAL, 300 Highland Ave., Zip 17331; tel. 717/637-3711; Philip W. Pennington, pres. (Total facility includes 41 beds in nursing home-type unit) **A**1a 9 10 **F**1 3 6 10 12 16 19 23 27 35 36 40 42 45 46 51 52 53	23	10	S	TF	195	6486	132	67.7	14	828	18195	8091	425
				H	154	6267	102	—	14	828	17134	7705	405
HARRISBURG—Dauphin County													
○ + COMMUNITY GENERAL OSTEOPATHIC HOSPITAL, 4300 Londonderry Rd., P O Box 3000, Zip 17105; tel. 717/652-3000; George R. Strohl Jr., pres. **A**9 10 11 12 13 **F**1 3 6 10 12 14 15 16 23 24 30 32 33 34 35 36 40 44 45 46 53	23	10	S		157	5929	113	72.0	17	348	23076	11022	531
★□ HARRISBURG HOSPITAL, S. Front St., Zip 17101; tel. 717/782-3131; Milton H. Appleyard, pres. & chief exec. off. **A**1a 3 5 8 9 10 **F**1 2 3 4 6 10 12 14 16 23 24 27 34 35 36 40 41 44 45 46 47 51 53 54	23	10	S		431	16743	325	75.4	34	3262	76872	32081	1755
□ HARRISBURG STATE HOSPITAL, Cameron & Maclay Sts., Pouch A, Zip 17105; tel. 717/257-7600; Ford S. Thompson Jr., adm. **A**1b 10 **F**1 15 24 42 46 47 50	12	22	L		487	304	449	92.2	0	0	23895	14832	672
★□ POLYCLINIC MEDICAL CENTER OF HARRISBURG, 2601 N. Third St., Zip 17110; tel. 717/782-4141; Douglas J. Spurlock, pres. & chief exec. off. (Total facility includes 80 beds in nursing home-type unit) **A**1a 3 5 9 10 **F**1 2 3 4 6 7 8 9 10 11 12 14 15 16 19 20 23 24 25 26 27 29 30 33 34 35 36 38 40 42 44 45 46 47 50 51 52 53 54	23	10	S	TF	560	14516	385	68.8	36	1623	63517	32202	1683
				H	480	14285	309	—	36	1623	62172	31394	1636
HAVERFORD—Delaware County													
□ HAVERFORD STATE HOSPITAL, 3500 Darby Rd., Zip 19041; tel. 215/525-9620; John K. Fong DO, dir. (Total facility includes 76 beds in nursing home-type unit) **A**1b 3 5 9 10 **F**19 23 24 30 32 33 42 46 47	12	22	L	TF	407	565	404	99.3	0	0	24872	12852	591
				H	331	556	333	—	0	0	20734	11930	537
HAVERTOWN—Delaware County													
★□ HAVERFORD COMMUNITY HOSPITAL, 2000 Old West Chester Pike, Zip 19083; tel. 215/645-3600; Cornelius Serle, adm. **A**1a 10 **F**1 3 6 12 15 16 23 24 26 33 35 44 45 46 48 53; **S**1755	23	10	S		103	3472	57	55.3	0	0	14750	6305	348
HAZLETON—Luzerne County													
★□ HAZLETON GENERAL HOSPITAL (Formerly Hazleton State General Hospital), 700 E. Broad St., Zip 18201; tel. 717/454-4357; E. Richard Moore, exec. vice-pres. (Nonreporting) **A**1a 10	23	10	S		184	—	—	—	—	—	—	—	—
★□ HAZLETON-ST. JOSEPH MEDICAL CENTER, 687 N. Church St., Zip 18201; tel. 717/459-4444; Sr. M. Edwinalda RN, pres. **A**1a 9 10 **F**1 3 6 10 12 14 15 16 23 35 36 40 41 45 46 52 53; **S**0285	21	10	S		190	6117	119	62.6	15	659	19728	8299	548
HERSHEY—Dauphin County													
★□ Δ PENNSYLVANIA STATE UNIVERSITY HOSPITAL (Includes Pennsylvania University-Elizabethtown Hospital and Rehabilitation Center, Elizabethtown, Zip 17022; tel. 717/367-1161; Thomas Hemming, adm.), 500 University Dr., Zip 17033; tel. 717/531-8521; Howard J. Peterson, dir. & assoc. vice-pres. health adm. **A**1a 2 3 5 7 8 9 10 **F**1 3 4 6 7 8 9 10 11 12 13 14 15 16 17 20 23 24 25 26 27 28 30 32 33 34 35 37 38 40 42 44 45 46 47 51 52 53 54	23	10	S		381	12393	293	76.9	16	833	82465	40113	1858
HOMESTEAD—Allegheny County													
HOMESTEAD CENTER, See South Hills Health Systems, Pittsburgh													
HONESDALE—Wayne County													
★□ WAYNE COUNTY MEMORIAL HOSPITAL, Park & West Sts., Zip 18431; tel. 717/253-1300; John M. Sherwood, exec. dir. (Total facility includes 28 beds in nursing home-type unit) **A**1a 9 10 **F**1 3 6 10 12 14 15 16 19 23 24 35 36 40 41 42 44 45 46 48 52 53	23	10	S	TF	119	3413	80	58.0	15	300	13842	6150	331
				H	91	3224	54	—	15	300	—	—	312

★ American Hospital Association (AHA) membership
□ Joint Commission on Accreditation of Hospitals (JCAH) accreditation
+ American Osteopathic Hospital Association (AOHA) membership
○ American Osteopathic Association (AOA) accreditation
Δ Commission on Accreditation of Rehabilitation Facilities (CARF) accreditation
Control codes 61, 63, 64, 71, 72 and 73 indicate hospitals listed by AOHA, but not registered by AHA.
For definition of numerical codes, see page A2

Hospital, Address, Telephone, Administrator, Approval and Facility Codes, Multihospital System Code	Classification Codes				Inpatient Data				Newborn Data		Expense (thousands of dollars)		
★ American Hospital Association (AHA) membership ☐ Joint Commission on Accreditation of Hospitals (JCAH) accreditation + American Osteopathic Hospital Association (AOHA) membership ○ American Osteopathic Association (AOA) accreditation Δ Commission on Accreditation of Rehabilitation Facilities (CARF) accreditation Control codes 61, 63, 64, 71, 72 and 73 indicate hospitals listed by AOHA, but not registered by AHA. For definition of numerical codes, see page A2	Control	Service	Stay	Facilities	Beds	Admissions	Census	Occupancy (percent)	Bassinets	Births	Total	Payroll	Personnel
HUNTINGDON—Huntingdon County													
⊞ J. C. BLAIR MEMORIAL HOSPITAL, Warm Springs Ave., Zip 16652; tel. 814/643-2290; Robert R. Stanley, adm. **A**1a 9 10 **F**1 3 6 10 12 14 15 16 21 23 24 26 27 28 30 32 34 35 36 40 42 44 45 46 47 52 53; **S**1755	23	10	S		104	3747	55	52.9	14	397	12780	5153	294
INDIANA—Indiana County													
⊞ INDIANA HOSPITAL, P O Box 788, Zip 15701; tel. 412/357-7000; Donald D. Sandoval, adm. **A**1a 9 10 **F**1 3 6 9 10 12 16 23 24 35 36 40 45 46 52 53	23	10	S		168	7962	117	69.2	18	695	24982	11959	624
JEANNETTE—Westmoreland County													
⊞ JEANNETTE DISTRICT MEMORIAL HOSPITAL, 600 Jefferson Ave., Zip 15644; tel. 412/527-3551; Dorothy M. Sarsfield, actg. exec. dir. **A**1a 9 10 **F**1 2 3 6 10 12 14 15 16 23 24 25 26 35 36 40 44 45 46 47 52 53	23	10	S		166	6546	121	72.9	6	342	27073	13731	614
⊞ MONSOUR MEDICAL CENTER, 70 Lincoln Hwy. E., Zip 15644; tel. 412/527-1511; Michael J. Hurd, adm. **A**1a 3 9 10 **F**1 3 5 6 10 12 15 16 23 32 34 35 36 37 38 40 45 46 48 52 53 54; **S**0985	23	10	S		233	6058	114	48.9	10	342	20060	8125	512
JERSEY SHORE—Lycoming County													
☐ JERSEY SHORE HOSPITAL, Thompson St., Zip 17740; tel. 717/398-0100; Thomas S. Lawton Jr., exec. dir. (Nonreporting) **A**1a 10	23	10	S		73	—	—	—	—	—	—	—	—
JOHNSTOWN—Cambria County													
⊞ CONEMAUGH VALLEY MEMORIAL HOSPITAL, 1086 Franklin St., Zip 15905; tel. 814/533-9000; Howard R. Jones, pres. & chief exec. off. **A**1a 2 3 5 6 8 9 10 **F**1 2 3 6 8 9 10 11 12 15 16 23 24 26 27 28 29 30 31 32 33 34 35 36 37 40 41 42 44 45 46 50 51 52 53	23	10	S		402	12955	260	64.7	20	1041	58758	28260	1465
⊞ LEE HOSPITAL, 320 Main St., Zip 15901; tel. 814/533-0123; John W. Ungar, pres. & chief exec. off. **A**1a 9 10 **F**1 2 3 6 7 8 9 10 11 12 14 15 16 23 24 26 30 33 34 35 36 37 40 41 42 44 45 46 47 50 52 53 54	23	10	S		321	8760	168	52.3	16	461	38816	19034	987
⊞ MERCY HOSPITAL OF JOHNSTOWN, 1020 Franklin St., Zip 15905; tel. 814/533-1000; T. R. Baranik, pres. (Total facility includes 75 beds in nursing home-type unit) **A**1a 9 10 **F**1 3 6 10 12 14 15 16 19 20 23 24 26 27 31 32 33 34 35 36 37 40 41 42 43 44 45 46 47 48 49 50 53; **S**5195	21	10	S	TF	218	6108	164	75.2	12	413	26860	12786	666
				H	143	5887	—	—	12	413	—	—	—
KANE—McKean County													
⊞ COMMUNITY HOSPITAL, N. Fraley St., Zip 16735; tel. 814/837-8585; Charles Ehredt, chief exec. off. **A**1a 9 10 **F**1 3 6 12 14 15 16 23 35 36 40 41 44 45 46 47 52 53	23	10	S		51	1740	22	41.5	6	118	4644	2311	138
KINGSTON—Luzerne County													
⊞ NESBITT MEMORIAL HOSPITAL, 562 Wyoming Ave., Zip 18704; tel. 717/288-1411; Ron Stern, adm. **A**1a 3 5 9 10 **F**1 3 6 9 10 11 12 14 15 16 20 23 26 35 36 37 40 44 45 46 47 50 52 53; **S**3825	23	10	S		215	12306	175	81.4	19	2054	33576	15372	801
KITTANNING—Armstrong County													
⊞ ARMSTRONG COUNTY MEMORIAL HOSPITAL, Rural Delivery 8, Box 50, Zip 16201; tel. 412/543-8500; Robert L. Engel, pres. **A**1a 9 10 **F**1 3 6 7 8 9 10 11 12 14 15 16 23 24 27 30 33 35 36 40 41 42 44 45 46 53	23	10	S		164	8392	159	97.0	20	682	22902	11607	570
LAFAYETTE HILL—Montgomery County													
☐ EUGENIA HOSPITAL, 660 Thomas Rd., Zip 19444; tel. 215/836-1380; Eugene Wayne, pres. & chief exec. off.; Jeffrey Dekret MD, med. dir. **A**1b 10 **F**15 23 24 32 33 42 44 47 50	33	22	S		126	1232	97	77.0	0	0	—	—	216
LANCASTER—Lancaster County													
★ ○ + COMMUNITY HOSPITAL OF LANCASTER, 1100 E. Orange St., Box 3002, Zip 17604; tel. 717/397-3711; Joanne J. Kiser, pres. **A**9 10 11 12 13 **F**1 3 5 6 10 12 14 15 16 20 21 23 24 25 26 27 28 31 33 34 35 36 37 40 44 45 46 51 52 53	23	10	S		206	7140	122	58.7	12	956	24109	11083	600
⊞ LANCASTER GENERAL HOSPITAL, 555 N. Duke St., Box 3555, Zip 17603; tel. 717/299-5511; Harvey M. Yorke, sr. vice-pres. **A**1a 2 3 5 6 10 **F**1 3 4 5 6 7 8 9 10 11 12 14 15 16 20 21 23 24 25 26 27 30 32 33 34 35 36 37 40 44 45 46 51 52 53 54	23	10	S		582	21004	383	65.9	40	2448	81934	39552	1890
⊞ Δ ST. JOSEPH HOSPITAL, 250 College Ave., Box 3509, Zip 17604; tel. 717/291-8211; Sr. Margaret Aloysius McGrail, pres. **A**1a 2 6 7 10 **F**1 3 5 6 10 12 14 15 16 20 21 23 24 25 26 27 28 29 30 32 33 34 35 36 37 40 42 43 44 45 46 47 48 49 52 53 54; **S**5325	21	10	S		309	12320	220	71.2	20	1283	43062	21457	1036
LANGHORNE—Bucks County													
○ + DELAWARE VALLEY MEDICAL CENTER (Formerly Listed Under Bristol), 200 Oxford Valley Rd., Zip 19047; tel. 215/750-3000; Rocco Mastricolo, chief oper. off. **A**10 11 12 13 **F**1 2 3 5 6 10 12 14 15 16 20 23 24 27 30 33 34 35 41 44 45 46 47 48 52 53	23	10	S		173	5815	110	63.6	0	0	32920	12569	704
⊞ SAINT MARY HOSPITAL, Langhorne-Newtown Rd., Zip 19047; tel. 215/750-2000; Sr. Clare Carty, pres. & chief exec. off. **A**1a 9 10 **F**1 3 5 6 10 12 14 15 16 20 23 24 25 26 34 35 36 40 41 42 44 45 46 47 53; **S**5325	21	10	S		251	9131	172	68.5	20	1263	39632	17968	805
LANSDALE—Montgomery County													
⊞ NORTH PENN HOSPITAL, 100 Medical Campus Dr., Zip 19446; tel. 215/368-2100; Robert H. McKay, pres. **A**1a 2 9 10 **F**1 3 6 10 12 14 15 16 21 23 24 26 35 36 40 44 45 46 47 52 53	23	10	S		150	5661	87	58.0	15	699	21303	9877	529
LATROBE—Westmoreland County													
⊞ LATROBE AREA HOSPITAL, W. Second Ave., Zip 15650; tel. 412/537-1000; Douglas A. Clark, exec. dir. (Total facility includes 18 beds in nursing home-type unit) **A**1a 2 3 5 8 9 10 **F**1 2 3 6 10 12 14 16 19 20 21 23 24 27 28 29 30 32 33 34 35 36 37 40 41 44 45 46 50 52 53	23	10	S	TF	281	12010	213	75.8	22	1046	44992	25746	1068
				H	263	11712	198	—	22	1046	44533	25374	1054
LEBANON—Lebanon County													
⊞ GOOD SAMARITAN HOSPITAL, Fourth & Walnut Sts., Zip 17042; tel. 717/272-7611; David L. Broderic, pres. & chief exec. off. **A**1a 9 10 **F**1 3 6 10 11 12 14 15 16 21 23 24 26 34 35 41 43 44 45 46 47 52 53	23	10	S		151	6188	118	69.4	0	0	25198	12278	661
☐ LEBANON VALLEY GENERAL HOSPITAL, 30 N. Fourth St., Zip 17042; tel. 717/273-8521; Maureen Gallo, adm. **A**1a 9 10 **F**1 3 6 9 10 12 14 15 16 23 24 34 35 36 40 44 45 46 47; **S**1775	33	10	S		92	2652	35	38.0	21	948	7257	2779	143
⊞ VETERANS ADMINISTRATION MEDICAL CENTER, Zip 17042; tel. 717/272-6621; Leonard Washington Jr., dir. (Total facility includes 120 beds in nursing home-type unit) **A**1a **F**1 3 6 12 14 15 16 19 21 23 24 27 28 29 30 31 32 33 34 35 41 42 43 44 46 48 49 50	45	10	L	TF	945	3641	664	70.3	0	0	46928	28576	1177
				H	825	3422	553	—	0	0	—	—	1125
LEHIGHTON—Carbon County													
⊞ GNADEN HUETTEN MEMORIAL HOSPITAL, 11th & Hamilton Sts., Zip 18235; tel. 215/377-1300; Dereck Marshall, pres. (Total facility includes 83 beds in nursing home-type unit) **A**1a 9 10 **F**1 3 6 10 12 14 15 16 19 21 23 24 27 28 29 30 32 33 35 36 37 40 41 42 43 44 45 46 47 49 50 52; **S**1695	23	10	S	TF	200	4028	146	71.6	7	245	14677	6442	415
				H	117	3967	64	—	7	245	12880	5742	362
LEWISBURG—Union County													
☐ EVANGELICAL COMMUNITY HOSPITAL, One Hospital Dr., Zip 17837; tel. 717/523-2500; Michael Daniloff, pres. **A**1a 9 10 **F**1 2 3 6 10 11 12 14 15 16 23 24 26 30 32 33 35 36 40 41 43 44 45 46 52 53	23	10	S		155	6668	94	60.6	22	1075	15571	7244	469

Hospital, Address, Telephone, Administrator, Approval and Facility Codes, Multihospital System Code

- ★ American Hospital Association (AHA) membership
- □ Joint Commission on Accreditation of Hospitals (JCAH) accreditation
- + American Osteopathic Hospital Association (AOHA) membership
- ○ American Osteopathic Association (AOA) accreditation
- Δ Commission on Accreditation of Rehabilitation Facilities (CARF) accreditation

Control codes 61, 63, 64, 71, 72 and 73 indicate hospitals listed by AOHA, but not registered by AHA. For definition of numerical codes, see page A2

Hospital	Classification Codes				Inpatient Data				Newborn Data		Expense (thousands of dollars)		
	Control	Service	Stay	Facilities	Beds	Admissions	Census	Occupancy (percent)	Bassinets	Births	Total	Payroll	Personnel
U. S. PENITENTIARY HOSPITAL, Rte. 3, Zip 17837; tel. 717/523-1251; Ronald D. Hillwig, adm. (Nonreporting)	48	11	S		17	—	—	—	—	—	—	—	—
LEWISTOWN—Mifflin County													
★□ LEWISTOWN HOSPITAL, Fourth & Highland Ave., Zip 17044; tel. 717/248-5411; William H. Dewire, pres. & chief exec. off. **A**1a 2 9 10 **F**1 2 3 5 6 7 8 10 12 13 14 15 16 20 21 23 24 26 27 28 30 32 33 34 35 36 37 40 41 42 44 45 46 49 52 53	23	10	S		185	8757	153	82.7	16	755	27975	13849	718
LIGONIER—Westmoreland County													
★ WESTMORELAND MCGINNIS HOSPITAL, 221 W. Main St., Zip 15658; tel. 412/238-9573; Joseph J. Peluso, exec. dir. (Nonreporting) **A**9 10; **S**2395	31	10	S		17	—	—	—	—	—	—	—	—
LOCK HAVEN—Clinton County													
★□ LOCK HAVEN HOSPITAL AND EXTENDED CARE UNIT, 24 Cree Dr., Zip 17745; tel. 717/893-5000; Albert W. Speth, pres. (Total facility includes 120 beds in nursing home-type unit) **A**1a 9 10 **F**1 3 6 10 12 14 15 16 19 23 24 34 35 36 40 42 44 45 46 52 53	23	10	S	TF	271	4711	167	61.6	10	360	13807	6126	447
				H	151	4261	57	—	10	360	11412	4937	341
MALVERN—Chester County													
★□ Δ BRYN MAWR REHABILITATION HOSPITAL, 414 Paoli Pike, Zip 19355; tel. 215/251-5400; Thomas M. Nojunas, exec. vice-pres. **A**1a 7 9 10 **F**16 23 24 26 28 33 42 44 45 46; **S**7775	23	46	S		92	1174	80	87.0	0	0	11954	6929	315
★□ MALVERN INSTITUTE, 940 King Rd., Zip 19355; tel. 215/647-0330; Joseph J. Driscoll, adm. (Data for 304 days) **A**1b **F**15 32 33 34 42 46 49; **S**0455	33	82	S		36	263	21	58.3	0	0	1231	408	35
MCCONNELLSBURG—Fulton County													
★ FULTON COUNTY MEDICAL CENTER, 216 S. First St., Zip 17233; tel. 717/485-3155; Thomas Fite, adm. (Total facility includes 57 beds in nursing home-type unit) **A**9 10 **F**1 3 6 12 14 15 16 19 23 34 35 40 43 44 45 46 50 52; **S**2495	23	10	S	TF	100	1587	73	73.0	6	251	4086	1917	141
				H	43	1552	17	—	6	251	—	—	109
MCKEES ROCKS—Allegheny County													
★□ OHIO VALLEY GENERAL HOSPITAL, Heckel Rd., Zip 15136; tel. 412/777-6161; William F. Provenzano, pres. **A**1a 6 10 **F**1 3 6 10 12 14 15 16 20 22 23 24 26 34 35 36 40 44 45 46 47 53; **S**1755	23	10	S		137	5005	100	73.0	10	443	22598	8670	454
MCKEESPORT—Allegheny County													
★□ MCKEESPORT HOSPITAL, 1500 Fifth Ave., Zip 15132; tel. 412/664-2000; Thomas H. Prickett, exec. dir. **A**1a 3 9 10 **F**1 2 3 6 7 8 9 10 11 12 14 15 16 20 23 24 26 27 30 34 35 36 37 40 44 45 46 47 51 52 53	23	10	S		438	12739	287	65.5	13	746	59203	31184	1384
MEADOWBROOK—Montgomery County													
★□ HOLY REDEEMER HOSPITAL AND MEDICAL CENTER, 1648 Huntingdon Pike, Zip 19046; tel. 215/947-3000; John F. Dunleavy, pres. **A**1a 9 10 **F**1 3 6 10 12 14 15 16 20 21 23 24 26 30 32 33 34 35 36 40 41 44 45 46 50 52 53	21	10	S		278	11780	212	77.4	30	1705	47286	23116	1225
MEADVILLE—Crawford County													
GROVE STREET FACILITY, See Meadville Medical Center													
LIBERTY STREET FACILITY, See Meadville Medical Center													
★□ MEADVILLE MEDICAL CENTER (Includes Liberty Street Facility, 751 Liberty St., Zip 16335; tel. 814/336-3121; Grove Street Facility, 1034 Grove St., Zip 16335; tel. 814/336-4777; Sr. Anastasia Valimont, adm.), P O Box 1167, Zip 16335; tel. 814/333-5000; Anthony J. Defail, chief exec. off. **A**1a 9 10 **F**1 3 6 10 12 14 16 23 24 26 27 28 29 30 32 33 34 35 36 40 41 42 44 45 46 48 49 50 52 53	23	10	S		320	9717	178	54.8	12	738	33489	15382	774
MECHANICSBURG—Cumberland County													
★□ Δ REHAB HOSPITAL IN MECHANICSBURG (Formerly Rehab Hospital for Special Services), 175 Lancaster Blvd., P O Box 2016, Zip 17055; tel. 717/691-3700; Kurt A. Meyer, adm. & chief exec. off. **A**1a 7 10 **F**15 16 23 24 26 33 34 42 44 46; **S**0825	33	46	S		92	1171	79	85.9	0	0	8626	3960	226
★□ SEIDLE MEMORIAL HOSPITAL, 120 S. Filbert St., Zip 17055; tel. 717/766-7691; David S. Zimmerman, adm. (Nonreporting) **A**1a 9 10	23	10	S		58	—	—	—	—	—	—	—	—
MEDIA—Delaware County													
★□ RIDDLE MEMORIAL HOSPITAL, Baltimore Pike, Hwy. 1, Zip 19063; tel. 215/566-9400; Donald L. Laughlin, pres. **A**1a 9 10 **F**1 3 6 10 12 14 15 16 18 23 34 35 36 40 41 44 45 46 47 53	23	10	S		233	8049	153	65.7	29	1067	30088	14710	678
MEYERSDALE—Somerset County													
★□ MEYERSDALE COMMUNITY HOSPITAL, 200 Hospital Dr., Zip 15552; tel. 814/634-5911; Mary A. Thomas, adm. **A**1a 9 10 **F**1 3 6 15 16 23 26 35 40 44 45 46	23	10	S		43	1199	17	39.5	10	213	3007	1564	106
MONONGAHELA—Washington County													
★□ MONONGAHELA VALLEY HOSPITAL, Country Club Rd., Zip 15063; tel. 412/258-2000; Anthony M. Lombardi Jr., pres. **A**1a 9 10 **F**1 2 3 6 7 8 9 10 11 12 14 15 16 20 23 26 27 30 33 34 35 37 40 42 44 45 46 47 48 52 53	23	10	S		304	11345	231	76.0	18	606	45936	19928	989
MONROEVILLE—Allegheny County													
EAST SUBURBAN HEALTH CENTER, See Forbes Regional Health Center													
★ FORBES REGIONAL HEALTH CENTER (Formerly East Suburban Health Center), 2570 Haymaker Rd., Zip 15146; tel. 412/273-2424; Dana W. Ramish, exec. dir. **A**3 5 10 **F**1 3 6 9 10 11 12 14 15 16 20 23 24 26 27 30 32 33 34 35 36 37 40 42 44 45 46 47 50 52 53 54; **S**1355	23	10	S		348	15032	265	76.1	24	1368	54651	19939	847
MONTROSE—Susquehanna County													
★□ MONTROSE GENERAL HOSPITAL, 3 Grow Ave., Zip 18801; tel. 717/278-3801; Eudora S. Bennett RN, exec. dir. **A**1a 9 10 **F**1 3 6 12 14 15 16 23 33 34 35 37 40 44	33	10	S		39	1329	17	43.6	8	92	4228	1756	122
MOUNT GRETNA—Lebanon County													
★□ PHILHAVEN HOSPITAL, 283 S. Butler Rd., P O Box 550, Zip 17064; tel. 717/273-8871; Rowland Shank PhD, exec. dir. **A**1b 10 **F**24 28 29 30 31 32 33 42 50	21	22	S		96	990	66	82.5	0	0	8961	5677	346
MOUNT PLEASANT—Westmoreland County													
★□ FRICK COMMUNITY HEALTH CENTER (Formerly Henry Clay Frick Community Hospital), S. Church St., Zip 15666; tel. 412/547-1500; Joseph A. O'Leary, exec. dir. **A**1a 9 10 **F**1 2 3 6 10 12 14 15 16 23 24 26 30 32 33 34 35 37 40 45 46 47 52 53	23	10	S		210	8782	142	67.6	21	792	26147	14362	643
MUNCY—Lycoming County													
★□ MUNCY VALLEY HOSPITAL, 215 E. Water St., Zip 17756; tel. 717/546-8282; George J. Geib, actg. chief exec. off. (Total facility includes 59 beds in nursing home-type unit) **A**1a 9 10 **F**1 3 6 10 12 15 16 19 21 23 34 35 36 40 42 45 46 47 49 50 52	23	10	S	TF	136	2405	91	66.9	7	161	8575	4094	232
				H	77	2327	34	—	7	161	7352	3567	196
NANTICOKE—Luzerne County													
□ NANTICOKE STATE GENERAL HOSPITAL, W. Washington St., Zip 18634; tel. 717/735-5000; Thomas J. Graham, adm. **A**1a 9 10 **F**1 3 6 10 12 14 15 16 23 27 30 34 35 45 46 52 53; **S**5195	12	10	S		82	2051	49	59.8	0	0	8014	3256	155
NATRONA HEIGHTS—Allegheny County													
★□ ALLEGHENY VALLEY HOSPITAL, 1301 Carlisle St., Zip 15065; tel. 412/224-5100; John R. England, adm. **A**1a 2 9 10 **F**1 3 6 7 8 9 10 11 12 14 15 16 23 24 27 33 34 35 36 40 41 44 45 46 52 53 54	23	10	S		277	10847	220	79.4	30	789	39642	18641	873

Hospital, Address, Telephone, Administrator, Approval and Facility Codes, Multihospital System Code	Classification Codes: Control	Service	Stay	Facilities	Inpatient Data: Beds	Admissions	Census	Occupancy (percent)	Newborn Data: Bassinets	Births	Expense (thousands of dollars): Total	Payroll	Personnel
★ American Hospital Association (AHA) membership □ Joint Commission on Accreditation of Hospitals (JCAH) accreditation + American Osteopathic Hospital Association (AOHA) membership ○ American Osteopathic Association (AOA) accreditation Δ Commission on Accreditation of Rehabilitation Facilities (CARF) accreditation Control codes 61, 63, 64, 71, 72 and 73 indicate hospitals listed by AOHA, but not registered by AHA. For definition of numerical codes, see page A2													
NEW CASTLE—Lawrence County													
★□ JAMESON MEMORIAL HOSPITAL, 1211 Wilmington Ave., Zip 16105; tel. 412/658-9001; Thomas White, pres. **A**1a 2 6 9 10 **F**1 2 3 6 7 8 9 10 11 12 14 15 16 20 23 34 35 36 40 41 44 45 46 47 52 53	23	10	S		230	8415	156	67.8	25	917	30440	13893	743
★□ ST. FRANCIS HOSPITAL OF NEW CASTLE, S. Mercer at Phillips St., Zip 16101; tel. 412/658-3511; Joseph S. Noviello, pres., chm. & chief exec. off. **A**1a 6 9 10 **F**1 3 6 7 8 10 11 12 14 15 16 21 23 24 25 26 27 28 30 32 35 39 41 42 44 45 46 53	21	10	S		144	5232	121	84.0	0	0	17728	9646	463
NEW KENSINGTON—Westmoreland County													
★□ CITIZENS GENERAL HOSPITAL, 651 Fourth Ave., Zip 15068; tel. 412/337-3541; Robert E. Marino, exec. dir. **A**1a 6 9 10 **F**1 3 6 10 12 14 16 23 30 35 37 40 45 46 52 53	23	10	S		231	7723	137	67.8	24	474	31145	13789	612
NORRISTOWN—Montgomery County													
□ MONTGOMERY COUNTY EMERGENCY SERVICE, Stanbridge & Sterigere Sts., Zip 19401; Mailing Address Caller Box 3005, Zip 19404; tel. 215/279-6100; Naomi R. Dank PhD, exec. dir. **A**1b 9 10 **F**15 24 27 28 30 32 33 42 46 47 49 50	23	49	S		36	1651	31	86.1	0	0	3197	2328	136
★□ MONTGOMERY HOSPITAL, Fornance & Powell Sts., Zip 19401; tel. 215/270-2000; Harry W. Gehman, pres. **A**1a 2 3 5 9 10 **F**1 2 3 6 7 8 9 10 11 12 14 15 16 23 24 26 27 32 33 34 35 36 40 41 42 43 44 45 46 47 52 53	23	10	S		254	8396	163	68.5	23	846	40597	20430	941
□ NORRISTOWN STATE HOSPITAL, Stanbridge & Sterigere Sts., Zip 19401; tel. 215/270-1015; Dorothy M. Cleaver MD, supt. (Total facility includes 229 beds in nursing home-type unit) **A**1a 3 5 9 10 **F**16 19 23 24 42 44 46	12	22	L	TF	1123	824	955	85.0	0	0	54277	29575	1351
				H	894	789	781	—	0	0	—	—	—
★□ Δ SACRED HEART HOSPITAL, 1430 DeKalb St., Zip 19401; tel. 215/278-8200; Arthur C. Godin, pres. **A**1a 2 7 9 10 **F**1 2 3 6 10 12 14 15 16 23 24 25 26 32 34 35 36 40 42 44 45 46 47 52 53	23	10	S		260	8459	174	66.9	13	616	37694	18004	838
○ + SUBURBAN GENERAL HOSPITAL, 2701 De Kalb Pike, Zip 19401; tel. 215/278-2000; Edward R. Solvibile, pres. **A**9 10 11 12 13 **F**1 3 6 12 14 15 16 23 24 34 35 36 40 41 44 45 46 47 53	23	10	S		127	4995	86	67.7	12	399	22456	9584	464
□ VALLEY FORGE MEDICAL CENTER AND HOSPITAL, 1033 W. Germantown Pike, Zip 19403; tel. 215/539-8500; Alice K. Hand, adm. **A**1a b 9 10 **F**23 32 35 48	33	10	S		67	2663	57	85.1	0	0	7622	3950	119
OIL CITY—Venango County													
□ OIL CITY AREA HEALTH CENTER, 174 E. Bissell Ave., Box 1068, Zip 16301; tel. 814/677-1711; Neil E. Todhunter, pres. (Nonreporting) **A**1a 9 10	23	10	S		177	—	—	—	—	—	—	—	—
PALMERTON—Carbon County													
□ PALMERTON HOSPITAL, 135 Lafayette Ave., Zip 18071; tel. 215/826-3141; Barbara Spadt, adm. (Nonreporting) **A**1a 9 10	23	10	S		70	—	—	—	—	—	—	—	—
PAOLI—Chester County													
★□ PAOLI MEMORIAL HOSPITAL, Lancaster Pike, Zip 19301; tel. 215/648-1000; William Michael Tomlinson, pres. **A**1a 2 9 10 **F**1 3 6 10 12 14 15 16 17 21 23 24 26 27 30 31 32 33 34 35 41 42 43 44 45 46 47 48 49 52 53; **S**7775	23	10	S		188	7407	130	69.1	0	0	32295	14797	660
PECKVILLE—Lackawanna County													
★□ MID-VALLEY HOSPITAL, 1400 Main St., Zip 18452; tel. 717/489-7546; Harold Pinkus, adm. **A**1a 9 10 **F**1 3 6 12 14 15 16 23 30 32 35 41 44 45 53	23	10	S		66	1685	29	43.9	0	0	6104	2977	193
PHILADELPHIA—Philadelphia County													
★□ ALBERT EINSTEIN MEDICAL CENTER (Includes Mount Sinai-Daroff Division, Fifth & Reed Sts., Zip 19147; tel. 215/339-3456; Adelaide Hinton, actg. gen. dir.; Northern Division, York & Tabor Rds., Zip 19141; tel. 215/456-7890; A. Susan Bernini, vice-pres. & gen. dir.), York & Tabor Rds., Zip 19141; tel. 215/456-7890; Martin Goldsmith, pres. (Total facility includes 52 beds in nursing home-type unit) **A**1a 2 3 5 6 8 9 10 **F**1 2 3 4 5 6 7 8 9 10 11 12 13 14 15 16 17 19 20 21 23 24 26 27 28 29 30 32 33 34 35 36 37 38 40 41 42 44 45 46 47 48 51 52 53 54	23	10	S	TF	699	22445	594	80.6	34	1279	193448	94205	3179
				H	647	21637	544	—	34	1279	189515	—	3098
ALL SAINTS' REHABILITATION HOSPITAL, See Wyndmoor													
★□ AMERICAN ONCOLOGIC HOSPITAL-HOSPITAL OF THE FOX CHASE CANCER CENTER, Central & Shelmire Aves., Zip 19111; tel. 215/728-6900; James F. Lynch, adm. **A**1a 2 3 5 9 10 **F**1 3 7 8 9 10 11 17 21 23 24 26 34 44 45 46 53	23	49	S		100	2298	50	50.0	0	0	22422	8265	439
BROAD STREET HOSPITAL AND MEDICAL CENTER, See University Medical Center													
★□ CHESTNUT HILL HOSPITAL, 8835 Germantown Ave., Zip 19118; tel. 215/248-8200; Cary F. Leptuck, pres. & chief exec. off.; Ralph T. Starr, bd. chm. **A**1a 3 5 6 9 10 **F**1 2 3 6 10 12 15 16 20 23 24 26 34 35 36 37 40 45 46 47 53	23	10	S		210	8019	146	71.2	21	1408	32841	16410	752
★□ CHILDREN'S HOSPITAL OF PHILADELPHIA, 34th St. & Civic Center Blvd., Zip 19104; tel. 215/596-9100; Edmond F. Notebaert, pres. **A**1a 2 3 5 9 10 **F**1 4 5 6 10 12 14 15 18 19 34 35 37 38 43 45 46 47 51 53 54	23	50	S		254	12697	205	80.7	0	0	87543	39433	1946
★□ CHILDREN'S REHABILITATION HOSPITAL (Formerly Children's Heart Hospital), 3955 Conshohocken Ave., Zip 19131; tel. 215/877-7708; David E. Bohner, adm.; Steven Bachrach MD, med. dir. **A**1a 9 **F**15 16 23 24 26 34 42 44 45 46	23	56	L		65	283	43	66.2	0	0	5376	3078	148
EASTERN PENNSYLVANIA PSYCHIATRIC INSTITUTE, See Hospital of the Medical College of Pennsylvania													
★□ EPISCOPAL HOSPITAL (Includes George L. Harrison Memorial House), Front St. & Lehigh Ave., Zip 19125; tel. 215/427-7000; Stanley W. Elwell, pres. (Total facility includes 35 beds in nursing home-type unit) **A**1a 2 3 5 6 8 9 10 **F**1 3 4 5 6 10 11 12 14 15 16 19 20 23 24 26 33 34 35 37 38 40 41 42 44 45 46 51 53 54	23	10	S	TF	320	9414	209	65.3	16	1398	49664	23420	1008
				H	285	9276	175	—	16	1398	48832	22981	976
□ FAIRMOUNT INSTITUTE, 561 Fairthorne Ave., Zip 19128; tel. 215/487-4000; C. W. Brett PhD, chief exec. off. (Nonreporting) **A**1b 9 10	33	22	S		152	—	—	—	—	—	—	—	—
★□ FRANKFORD HOSPITAL OF THE CITY OF PHILADELPHIA (Includes Frankford Campus, Frankford Ave. & Wakeling St., Zip 19124; tel. 215/831-2000; Torresdale Campus, Knights & Red Lion Rds., Zip 19114; tel. 215/934-4000), Knights & Red Lion Rds., Zip 19114; tel. 215/934-4000; John B. Neff, pres. **A**1a 3 5 6 8 9 10 **F**1 3 5 6 10 11 12 14 15 16 23 34 35 36 37 40 44 45 46 47 48 49 52 53	23	10	S		320	14578	279	87.2	30	2142	65407	32424	1308
★□ FRIEDMAN HOSPITAL OF THE HOME FOR THE JEWISH AGED (Geriatric), 5301 Old York Rd., Zip 19141; tel. 215/456-2900; Bernard Liebowitz, exec. vice-pres. (Nonreporting) **A**1a 10	23	49	S		574	—	—	—	—	—	—	—	—
★□ FRIENDS HOSPITAL, Roosevelt Blvd. & Adams Ave., Zip 19124; tel. 215/831-4600; James M. Delaplane MD, dir. (Total facility includes 13 beds in nursing home-type unit) **A**1b 3 5 9 10 **F**24 28 29 32 33 34 42 43 45 46 50	23	22	L	TF	205	2126	185	90.2	0	0	20634	11843	472
				H	192	2125	173	—	0	0	20383	11672	464
★□ GERMANTOWN HOSPITAL AND MEDICAL CENTER, One Penn Blvd., Zip 19144; tel. 215/951-8000; Joseph F. Farrell, pres. & chief exec. off.; Hugh J. Maher, exec. vice-pres. & adm. **A**1a 3 5 6 8 9 10 **F**1 2 3 6 7 8 9 10 11 12 14 15 16 20 23 24 26 32 34 35 36 37 38 40 41 42 44 45 46 47 49 53	23	10	S		282	8198	197	69.9	21	683	44551	21136	885
★□ GRADUATE HOSPITAL, One Graduate Plaza, Zip 19146; tel. 215/893-2000; James P. Duffy, pres. **A**1a 2 3 5 8 9 10 **F**1 2 3 4 5 6 10 12 14 15 16 20 23 24 25 26 28 30 32 33 34 35 43 44 45 46 47 53 54	23	10	S		320	10799	245	76.6	0	0	78925	27772	1443

★ American Hospital Association (AHA) membership
□ Joint Commission on Accreditation of Hospitals (JCAH) accreditation
+ American Osteopathic Hospital Association (AOHA) membership
○ American Osteopathic Association (AOA) accreditation
Δ Commission on Accreditation of Rehabilitation Facilities (CARF) accreditation
Control codes 61, 63, 64, 71, 72 and 73 indicate hospitals listed by AOHA, but not registered by AHA.
For definition of numerical codes, see page A2

Hospital, Address, Telephone, Administrator, Approval and Facility Codes, Multihospital System Code	Classification Codes				Inpatient Data				Newborn Data		Expense (thousands of dollars)		
	Control	Service	Stay	Facilities	Beds	Admissions	Census	Occupancy (percent)	Bassinets	Births	Total	Payroll	Personnel
★□ HAHNEMANN UNIVERSITY HOSPITAL, Broad & Vine Sts., Zip 19102; tel. 215/448-7143; Howard J. Goldstein, vice-pres. health affairs & exec. dir. **A**1a 2 3 5 8 9 10 **F**1 2 3 4 5 6 7 8 9 10 11 12 13 14 15 16 20 23 24 25 26 27 28 30 32 33 34 35 36 37 38 40 41 42 44 45 46 47 51 52 53 54	23	10	S		552	16487	420	76.1	18	1438	128640	51181	1684
○ + HOSPITAL OF PHILADELPHIA COLLEGE OF OSTEOPATHIC MEDICINE, 4150 City Ave., Zip 19131; tel. 215/581-6000; Walter R. Brand, exec. dir. **A**10 11 12 13 **F**1 2 3 6 7 8 9 10 11 12 14 15 16 20 21 23 24 26 27 28 33 34 35 37 40 41 42 44 45 46 47 50 51 52 53	23	10	S		250	6022	118	47.2	10	637	40401	19665	646
★□ HOSPITAL OF THE MEDICAL COLLEGE OF PENNSYLVANIA (Includes Eastern Pennsylvania Psychiatric Institute, Henry Ave. & Abbottsford Rd., Zip 19129; tel. 215/842-4000), 3300 Henry Ave., Zip 19129; tel. 215/842-6000; Leland I. White, exec. dir. **A**1a 3 5 8 9 10 **F**1 2 3 4 6 7 8 9 10 11 12 14 15 16 17 20 23 24 26 27 28 29 30 32 33 34 35 36 37 38 40 42 44 49 50 51 52 53 54	23	10	S		393	13130	305	77.6	34	1770	78903	35164	2305
★□ Δ HOSPITAL OF THE UNIVERSITY OF PENNSYLVANIA, 3400 Spruce St., Zip 19104; tel. 215/662-4000; C. Edward Schwartz, exec. dir. & vice-pres. health serv. **A**1a 2 3 5 7 8 9 10 **F**1 3 4 6 7 8 9 10 11 12 13 14 15 16 17 20 21 23 24 25 26 27 28 30 32 33 34 35 36 37 38 39 40 42 43 44 45 46 47 50 51 53 54	23	10	S		714	26157	590	82.6	47	3280	214084	85399	3972
□ INSTITUTE OF PENNSYLVANIA HOSPITAL, 111 N. 49th St., Zip 19139; tel. 215/471-2000; H. Robert Cathcart, pres. **A**1a 3 5 10 **F**15 23 24 28 32 33 42 45; **S**3455	23	22	L		224	1131	185	82.6	0	0	23025	14182	607
★□ JAMES C. GIUFFRE MEDICAL CENTER, Girard Ave. at Eighth St., Zip 19122; tel. 215/787-2000; G. Francis Craven, adm. **A**1a 10 **F**1 3 6 10 12 14 16 17 23 28 33 34 35 47 48 49 53	23	10	S		228	7851	159	69.7	0	0	31205	15567	638
★□ JEANES HOSPITAL (Includes Friends Hall at Fox Chase), 7600 Central Ave., Zip 19111; tel. 215/728-2000; Edward J. Armstrong, pres. **A**1a 2 9 10 **F**1 3 6 12 14 16 23 24 34 35 36 40 41 44 45 46 47 51 52	23	10	S		198	8255	162	81.8	15	849	35553	—	924
□ JOHN F. KENNEDY MEMORIAL HOSPITAL, Langdon & Cheltenham Aves., Zip 19124; tel. 215/831-7000; Earl Stout, exec. dir. **A**1a 9 10 **F**1 3 6 10 11 12 14 15 16 20 23 28 30 32 33 34 35 45 46 47 52 53	23	10	S		206	4478	101	49.0	0	0	28081	14470	676
□ KENSINGTON HOSPITAL, 136 W. Diamond St., Zip 19122; tel. 215/426-8100; William Delamar, chief exec. off. **A**1a 10 **F**1 6 12 14 28 32 34 37 48	23	10	S		45	2764	36	80.0	0	0	6435	2930	168
★□ LANKENAU HOSPITAL, Lancaster Ave. W. of City Line, Zip 19151; tel. 215/645-2000; Ralph F. Moriarty, pres. **A**1a 3 5 6 8 9 10 **F**1 3 4 6 7 8 9 10 11 12 14 15 16 20 21 23 24 26 27 32 33 34 35 36 37 40 43 44 45 46 47 53 54; **S**7775	23	10	S		403	15959	346	85.9	34	1926	81210	39109	1649
★□ LAWNDALE COMMUNITY HOSPITAL, 6129 Palmetto St., Zip 19111; tel. 215/728-5500; Morton H. Rappaport, chief exec. off. **A**1a 9 10 **F**1 3 6 15 16 23 24 26 32 33 35 44 46 47; **S**6345	23	10	S		63	2694	46	73.0	0	0	9528	3445	205
★□ Δ MAGEE REHABILITATION HOSPITAL, Six Franklin Plaza, Zip 19102; tel. 215/587-3000; William E. Staas Jr. MD, pres. & med. dir.; Francis R. Coyne, vice-pres. **A**1a 7 9 10 **F**15 23 24 26 33 34 42 43 44 45 46	23	46	L		96	914	88	91.7	0	0	18051	8348	391
MATERNITY HOSPITAL, See Pennsylvania Hospital													
MEMORIAL HOSPITAL, ROXBOROUGH, See Roxborough Memorial Hospital													
★□ MERCY CATHOLIC MEDICAL CENTER (Includes Fitzgerald Mercy Division, Lansdowne Ave. & Baily Rd., Darby, Zip 19023; tel. 215/237-4000; Misericordia Division, 54th St. & Cedar Ave., Zip 19143; tel. 215/748-9000), Lansdowne Ave. & Baily Rd., Zip 19023; tel. 215/237-4000; Plato A. Marinakos, exec. vice-pres. **A**1a 2 3 5 8 9 10 **F**1 2 3 6 7 8 9 10 11 12 14 15 16 20 21 23 24 25 26 27 30 32 33 34 35 36 39 40 41 42 44 45 46 47 48 50 51 52 53; **S**3595	21	10	S		625	20493	514	82.2	25	1626	113995	60370	2480
★□ METHODIST HOSPITAL, 2301 S. Broad St., Zip 19148; tel. 215/952-9000; Joseph I. Ierardi, pres. & chief exec. off. **A**1a 3 5 6 9 10 **F**1 2 3 5 6 10 12 14 15 16 20 23 26 34 35 36 37 40 41 45 46 47 49 53	23	10	S		251	9469	208	82.9	22	1492	46654	20574	859
○ + METROPOLITAN HOSPITAL-CENTRAL DIVISION, 201 N. Eighth St., Zip 19106; tel. 215/238-2000; Robert V. Giardinelli, exec. dir. (Nonreporting) **A**9 10 11 12 13; **S**7995	23	10	S		184	—	—	—	—	—	—	—	—
○ + METROPOLITAN HOSPITAL-PARKVIEW DIVISION, 1331 E. Wyoming Ave., Zip 19124; tel. 215/537-7400; Irvin Berland, exec. dir. **A**9 10 11 12 13 **F**1 3 6 10 11 12 14 15 16 20 23 24 26 27 28 30 32 33 35 40 42 44 46 47 50 52 53; **S**7995	23	10	S		231	7795	170	73.6	12	563	41200	17813	693
★□ Δ MOSS REHABILITATION HOSPITAL, 12th St. & Tabor Rd., Zip 19141; tel. 215/329-5715; Sy Schlossman, pres. **A**1a 3 5 7 9 10 **F**15 16 23 24 26 32 33 34 42 43 44 45 46 47	23	46	S		142	1682	128	90.1	0	0	17980	11061	478
★□ NAVAL HOSPITAL, Zip 19145; tel. 215/897-8234; Capt. L. Carey Hodges MC USN, CO **A**1a **F**1 3 6 10 12 14 15 16 23 27 28 30 32 33 34 35 37 43 47 48 49 52	43	10	S		78	3217	52	51.5	0	279	—	—	794
★□ NAZARETH HOSPITAL, 2601 Holme Ave., Zip 19152; tel. 215/335-6000; Sr. M. Therese, pres. & chief exec. off. **A**1a 9 10 **F**1 2 3 6 7 8 9 10 11 12 14 15 16 23 24 27 33 35 40 44 46 52	21	10	S		365	11604	291	78.9	25	540	46677	28132	1293
★□ NORTHEASTERN HOSPITAL OF PHILADELPHIA, 2301 E. Allegheny Ave., Zip 19134; tel. 215/291-3000; Helen J. Zawisza, adm. **A**1a 2 3 5 6 9 10 **F**1 2 3 6 10 12 14 16 23 34 35 37 40 43 44 45 46 47 52 53	23	10	S		231	7126	153	66.2	20	693	37103	17534	850
★□ PENNSYLVANIA HOSPITAL (Includes Maternity Hospital; Philadelphia Dispensary for the Medical Relief of the Poor; Philadelphia Lying-in Charity Hospital; Preston Maternity Hospital; Southern Dispensary), Eighth & Spruce Sts., Zip 19107; tel. 215/829-3000; H. Robert Cathcart, pres. **A**1a 2 3 5 8 9 10 **F**1 2 3 6 7 8 9 10 11 12 14 15 16 20 21 23 24 26 27 28 29 30 32 33 34 35 36 37 38 40 41 42 43 44 45 47 49 50 51 53; **S**3455	23	10	S		450	17532	349	77.6	50	3963	111092	47346	1929
PHILADELPHIA DISPENSARY FOR THE MEDICAL RELIEF OF THE POOR, See Pennsylvania Hospital													
PHILADELPHIA LYING-IN CHARITY HOSPITAL, See Pennsylvania Hospital													
★□ PHILADELPHIA PSYCHIATRIC CENTER, Ford Rd. & Monument Ave., Zip 19131; tel. 215/877-2000; Alfred A. Meltzer, vice-pres. & gen. dir. **A**1b 3 5 9 10 **F**15 23 24 28 32 33 34 42 45 46 47 49	23	22	S		137	1849	124	90.5	0	0	15613	9025	336
□ PHILADELPHIA STATE HOSPITAL, 14000 Roosevelt Blvd., Zip 19114; tel. 215/671-4101; C. Charles Erb, supt. (Total facility includes 80 beds in nursing home-type unit) **A**1b 3 5 9 **F**15 19 23 24 33 42 44 45 46 47 50	12	22	L	TF	590	398	566	83.7	0	0	36631	21290	896
				H	510	390	476	—	0	0	32282	19242	839
★□ PRESBYTERIAN-UNIVERSITY OF PENNSYLVANIA MEDICAL CENTER, 39th & Market Sts., Zip 19104; tel. 215/662-8000; I. Donald Snook Jr., pres. **A**1a 3 5 6 8 9 10 **F**1 2 3 4 6 10 12 14 15 16 21 23 35 41 44 45 46 47 53 54	23	10	S		308	10376	227	73.7	0	0	81053	33534	1362
PRESTON MATERNITY HOSPITAL, See Pennsylvania Hospital													
★□ ROXBOROUGH MEMORIAL HOSPITAL (Formerly Memorial Hospital, Roxborough), 5800 Ridge Ave., Zip 19128; tel. 215/483-9900; Marvin Mashner, pres. **A**1a 6 9 10 **F**1 3 6 10 12 15 16 23 35 36 40 41 45 46 47 53	23	10	S		162	5403	115	71.0	11	407	26961	13580	689
□ SALVATION ARMY BOOTH MATERNITY CENTER, 6051 Overbrook Ave., Zip 19131; tel. 215/878-7800; Maj. Dorothy Bair, adm. (Nonreporting) **A**1a	21	44	S		18	—	—	—	—	—	—	—	—
★□ SHRINERS HOSPITALS FOR CRIPPLED CHILDREN, 8400 Roosevelt Blvd., Zip 19152; tel. 215/332-4500; James F. Casey, adm. **A**1a 3 5 **F**1 19 23 24 26 34 42 44 46; **S**4125	23	57	S		80	671	42	52.5	0	0	—	—	167
SOUTHERN DISPENSARY, See Pennsylvania Hospital													

Hospital, Address, Telephone, Administrator, Approval and Facility Codes, Multihospital System Code	Classification Codes				Inpatient Data				Newborn Data		Expense (thousands of dollars)		
★ American Hospital Association (AHA) membership ☐ Joint Commission on Accreditation of Hospitals (JCAH) accreditation + American Osteopathic Hospital Association (AOHA) membership ○ American Osteopathic Association (AOA) accreditation Δ Commission on Accreditation of Rehabilitation Facilities (CARF) accreditation Control codes 61, 63, 64, 71, 72 and 73 indicate hospitals listed by AOHA, but not registered by AHA. For definition of numerical codes, see page A2	Control	Service	Stay	Facilities	Beds	Admissions	Census	Occupancy (percent)	Bassinets	Births	Total	Payroll	Personnel
⊞ ST. AGNES MEDICAL CENTER, 1900 S. Broad St., Zip 19145; tel. 215/339-4100; Sr. M. Clarence, pres. & chief exec. off. **A**1a 3 5 6 9 10 **F**1 2 3 6 10 12 13 14 15 16 20 22 23 24 25 26 30 32 34 35 41 42 44 45 46 47 53; **S**5325	21	10	S		230	6066	167	72.6	0	0	44732	18127	755
⊞ ST. CHRISTOPHER'S HOSPITAL FOR CHILDREN, Fifth St. & Lehigh Ave., Zip 19133; tel. 215/427-5000; Calvin Bland, exec. dir.; Ralph W. Brenner, bd. chm. **A**1a 3 5 8 9 10 **F**1 2 3 4 5 6 10 12 13 14 15 16 20 22 23 24 26 28 30 32 33 34 35 37 38 42 44 45 46 47 51 53 54; **S**6345	23	50	S		146	6979	111	76.0	0	0	45964	20101	896
⊞ ST. JOSEPH'S HOSPITAL, 16th St. & Girard Ave., Zip 19130; tel. 215/787-9000; Sr. Mary Anita, adm. **A**1a 9 10 **F**1 3 5 6 10 12 14 15 16 20 23 34 35 41 44 45 46 47 49 53; **S**1345	23	10	S		178	5144	148	83.1	0	1	34099	15091	589
⊞ ST. MARY HOSPITAL, Frankford Ave. & Palmer St., Zip 19125; tel. 215/291-2000; Edmond L. Plummer Jr., pres. & chief exec. off. **A**1a 9 10 **F**1 3 6 9 10 12 14 15 16 23 24 27 30 32 33 34 35 36 40 43 44 45 46 48 52 53; **S**5325	21	10	S		160	5756	109	68.1	19	803	20989	10825	531
⊞ TEMPLE UNIVERSITY HOSPITAL, Broad & Ontario Sts., Zip 19140; tel. 215/221-2000; Michael K. Jhin, exec. dir. & chief exec. off. **A**1a 2 3 5 8 9 10 **F**1 2 3 4 5 6 7 8 9 10 11 12 13 14 15 16 17 20 23 24 26 27 30 32 33 35 36 37 38 40 42 44 45 46 47 50 51 53 54	23	10	S		504	14731	327	64.9	24	1944	101536	43265	—
⊞ Δ THOMAS JEFFERSON UNIVERSITY HOSPITAL, 11th & Walnut Sts., Zip 19107; tel. 215/928-6000; Michael J. Bradley, exec. dir. **A**1a 2 3 5 7 8 9 10 **F**1 2 3 4 5 6 7 8 9 10 11 12 13 14 15 16 20 23 24 25 26 27 28 29 30 32 33 34 35 36 37 38 40 41 42 43 44 45 46 47 49 50 51 52 53 54	23	10	S		687	21866	543	79.0	46	2634	190309	80309	2941
☐ UNIVERSITY MEDICAL CENTER (Formerly Broad Street Hospital and Medical Center), 739 S. Broad St., Zip 19147; tel. 215/545-7770; Francis J. Martin, adm. (Nonreporting) **A**1a 9 10	32	10	S		97	—	—	—	—	—	—	—	—
⊞ VETERANS ADMINISTRATION MEDICAL CENTER, University & Woodland Aves., Zip 19104; tel. 215/382-2400; R. T. Williams, dir. **A**1a 3 5 8 **F**1 3 6 8 9 10 11 12 14 15 16 20 23 24 25 26 27 28 29 30 32 33 34 35 41 42 43 44 46 47 48 49 50 53 54	45	10	S		380	10087	314	78.1	0	0	76963	43450	1453
⊞ WEST PARK HOSPITAL, Ford Rd. & Fairmount Park, Zip 19131; tel. 215/578-3400; Martin Radowill, exec. dir. **A**1a 3 5 9 10 **F**1 3 6 10 11 12 14 15 16 23 34 35 37 45 46 47 48 49 50 53	23	10	S		103	3146	66	64.1	0	0	19830	8066	337
⊞ WILLS EYE HOSPITAL, Ninth & Walnut Sts., Zip 19107; tel. 215/928-3000; D. McWilliams Kessler, exec. dir. **A**1a 3 5 9 10 **F**1 6 9 12 13 15 17 34 35 45 46 47 53	23	49	S		120	5370	44	36.7	0	0	28770	11430	487
PHILIPSBURG—Centre County													
☐ PHILIPSBURG STATE GENERAL HOSPITAL, Zip 16866; tel. 814/342-3320; John J. Razem, adm. **A**1a 9 10 **F**1 3 6 10 12 14 16 23 35 36 40 44 45 46 52	12	10	S		130	3820	59	45.4	12	256	12208	5092	225
PHOENIXVILLE—Chester County													
⊞ PHOENIXVILLE HOSPITAL, 140 Nutt Rd., Zip 19460; tel. 215/933-9281; Thomas J. Donnelly, pres. **A**1a 9 10 **F**1 3 6 10 12 14 15 16 23 26 30 32 33 35 36 37 40 45 46 50 53	23	10	S		140	7165	117	72.2	20	1141	24258	10337	516
PITTSBURGH—Allegheny County													
⊞ ALLEGHENY GENERAL HOSPITAL, 320 E. North Ave., Zip 15212; tel. 412/359-3131; Sherif S. Abdelhak, pres. & chief exec. off. (Nonreporting) **A**1a 2 3 5 8 9 10	23	10	S		678	—	—	—	—	—	—	—	—
☐ CENTRAL MEDICAL CENTER AND HOSPITAL, 1200 Centre Ave., Zip 15219; tel. 412/562-3000; Thomas M. Gallagher, pres. **A**1a 3 10 **F**1 3 4 6 10 12 14 15 16 20 23 24 25 30 32 34 35 37 42 44 45 46 47 48 53 54	23	10	S		141	4546	78	55.3	0	0	34261	10876	512
★ CHILDREN'S HOME OF PITTSBURGH (Infant Acute), 5618 Kentucky Ave., Zip 15232; tel. 412/441-4884; B. Marlene West, exec. dir. (Nonreporting) **A**9 10	23	59	S		6	—	—	—	—	—	—	—	—
⊞ CHILDREN'S HOSPITAL OF PITTSBURGH, 3705 Fifth Ave., Zip 15213; tel. 412/647-5325; Edwin K. Zechman Jr., pres. **A**1a 2 3 5 8 9 10 **F**1 3 4 5 12 13 15 16 23 24 26 28 30 32 33 34 35 38 41 44 46 47 51 52 53 54	23	10	S		207	9049	148	67.0	0	0	66204	25973	1433
⊞ DIVINE PROVIDENCE HOSPITAL OF PITTSBURGH, 1004 Arch St., Zip 15212; tel. 412/323-5600; Ronald H. Mangold, adm. **A**1a 9 10 **F**1 3 6 10 12 14 16 20 23 35 44 45 46 53	21	10	S		167	5392	135	80.8	0	0	20981	9398	527
⊞ EYE AND EAR HOSPITAL OF PITTSBURGH, 230 Lothrop St., Zip 15213; tel. 412/647-2010; George A. Huber, adm. **A**1a 2 3 5 8 9 10 **F**1 3 13 15 34 35 44 46	23	45	S		77	4775	44	57.1	0	0	24994	8465	445
⊞ FORBES METROPOLITAN HEALTH CENTER, 225 Penn Ave., Zip 15221; tel. 412/247-2424; Richard T. Merk, exec. dir. **A**1a 9 10 **F**1 3 6 9 10 12 14 15 16 20 23 24 26 30 33 34 35 41 44 45 46 53; **S**1355	23	10	S		144	5536	115	79.9	0	0	30571	9608	471
⊞ HARMARVILLE REHABILITATION CENTER, Box 11460, Guys Run Rd., Zip 15238; tel. 412/781-5700; Robert E. Henger, sr. vice-pres. & chief oper. off. **A**1a 3 9 10 **F**15 23 24 26 33 34 42 43 44 46	23	46	L		200	1793	171	85.5	0	0	25857	14724	664
JEFFERSON CENTER, See South Hills Health System													
⊞ MAGEE-WOMENS HOSPITAL (Gynecology, Obstetrics and Neonatology), Forbes Ave. & Halket St., Zip 15213; tel. 412/647-1000; Geoffrey J. Suszkowski, pres. (Nonreporting) **A**1a 2 3 5 8 9 10	23	49	S		330	—	—	—	—	—	—	—	—
⊞ MERCY HOSPITAL OF PITTSBURGH, 1400 Locust St., Zip 15219; tel. 412/232-8111; Sr. Joanne Marie Andiorio, pres. **A**1a 2 3 5 6 8 9 10 **F**1 2 3 4 5 6 7 8 9 10 11 12 14 15 16 20 22 23 24 25 26 27 28 30 32 33 34 35 36 37 40 42 44 45 46 47 51 52 53 54; **S**3595	23	10	S		486	17001	397	81.7	16	614	104221	44160	2221
⊞ MONTEFIORE HOSPITAL, 3459 Fifth Ave., Zip 15213; tel. 412/648-6000; Irwin Goldberg, pres. (Data not available) **A**1a 3 5 8 9 10 **F**1 2 4 6 7 8 9 10 11 12 13 14 15 16 20 24 25 26 30 32 34 35 37 39 41 42 44 45 46 47 50 53 54	23	10	S		406	—	—	—	—	—	—	—	—
⊞ NORTH HILLS PASSAVANT HOSPITAL, 9100 Babcock Blvd., Zip 15237; tel. 412/367-6700; Alexander McAliley, pres. **A**1a 9 10 **F**1 3 6 10 12 15 16 20 23 24 26 30 33 34 35 36 37 40 41 44 45 46 47 52	23	10	S		292	12412	218	74.7	24	1305	41569	19919	1029
★ PODIATRY HOSPITAL OF PITTSBURGH, 215 S. Negley Ave., Zip 15206; tel. 412/661-0814; Joan Abaray, chief exec. off. **A**9 10 **F**1 10 16 20 23 34 43 45	23	49	S		27	1388	5	18.5	0	0	3202	1520	93
⊞ PRESBYTERIAN-UNIVERSITY HOSPITAL, DeSoto at O'Hara Sts., Zip 15213; tel. 412/647-2345; Patricia Shehorn, interim chief oper. off. **A**1a 2 3 5 8 9 10 **F**1 3 4 5 6 10 11 12 13 15 16 20 23 24 34 35 45 46 50 53 54	23	10	S		568	17949	439	77.3	0	0	139675	51875	2244
⊞ Δ REHABILITATION INSTITUTE OF PITTSBURGH, 6301 Northumberland St., Zip 15217; tel. 412/521-9000; John A. Wilson, pres. **A**1a 7 **F**23 24 26 28 32 33 34 42 43 44 46 47	23	46	L		124	222	56	45.2	0	0	14104	8156	392
⊞ SHADYSIDE HOSPITAL, 5230 Centre Ave., Zip 15232; tel. 412/622-2121; Henry A. Mordoh, pres. **A**1a 3 5 6 8 9 10 **F**1 2 3 4 6 8 10 11 12 14 16 23 24 30 32 33 35 40 43 45 46 50 53 54	23	10	S		474	15503	346	73.0	8	533	82619	35352	1601
⊞ SOUTH HILLS HEALTH SYSTEM (Includes Homestead Center, Homestead; Jefferson Center), Coal Valley Rd., Zip 15025; Mailing Address Box 18119, Zip 15236; tel. 412/469-5000; George H. Yeckel, pres. (Total facility includes 74 beds in nursing home-type unit) **A**1a 9 10 **F**1 3 6 10 12 14 15 16 19 20 21 23 24 25 26 27 28 30 32 33 34 35 41 42 44 45 46 47 49 50 52 53	23	10	S	TF H	464 390	15619 15125	406 338	87.5 —	0 0	0 0	75754 —	34293 —	1892 1846
⊞ SOUTH SIDE HOSPITAL OF PITTSBURGH, 2000 Mary St., Zip 15203; tel. 412/488-5550; Randall J. Stasik, pres. & chief exec. off. **A**1a 9 10 **F**1 3 6 10 12 14 15 16 19 20 23 24 25 26 30 33 34 35 41 44 45 46 47 53	23	10	S		215	7161	178	85.6	0	0	35609	15082	769
⊞ ST. CLAIR MEMORIAL HOSPITAL, 1000 Bower Hill Rd., Zip 15243; tel. 412/561-4900; Benjamin E. Snead, pres. **A**1a 9 10 **F**1 2 3 6 10 12 14 15 16 20 21 23 24 26 27 30 33 34 35 36 37 40 41 44 45 46 52 53	23	10	S		371	14078	265	71.4	30	1592	52376	26587	1213

★ American Hospital Association (AHA) membership
☐ Joint Commission on Accreditation of Hospitals (JCAH) accreditation
\+ American Osteopathic Hospital Association (AOHA) membership
○ American Osteopathic Association (AOA) accreditation
Δ Commission on Accreditation of Rehabilitation Facilities (CARF) accreditation
Control codes 61, 63, 64, 71, 72 and 73 indicate hospitals listed by AOHA, but not registered by AHA.
For definition of numerical codes, see page A2

Hospital, Address, Telephone, Administrator, Approval and Facility Codes, Multihospital System Code	Classification Codes				Inpatient Data				Newborn Data		Expense (thousands of dollars)		
	Control	Service	Stay	Facilities	Beds	Admissions	Census	Occupancy (percent)	Bassinets	Births	Total	Payroll	Personnel
▣ Δ ST. FRANCIS MEDICAL CENTER, 45th St. off Penn Ave., Zip 15201; tel. 412/622-4343; Sr. M. Rosita Wellinger, exec. vice-pres. & chief exec. off. **A**1a 2 3 5 6 7 8 9 10 **F**1 2 3 4 6 7 8 9 10 11 12 14 15 16 17 19 22 23 24 26 27 28 29 30 32 34 35 36 40 41 42 43 44 45 46 47 48 49 50 51 52 53 54	23	10	S		697	16502	509	73.0	15	640	98469	44348	2208
▣ ST. JOHN'S HEALTH AND HOSPITAL CENTER, 3339 McClure Ave., Zip 15212; tel. 412/766-8300; Harold D. Sanders, pres. (Total facility includes 69 beds in nursing home-type unit) **A**1a 9 10 **F**1 3 6 10 12 15 16 19 23 24 26 27 28 29 30 31 32 33 34 35 41 42 45 46 48 49 50 53	23	10	S	TF	247	5084	189	75.6	0	0	18174	9063	535
				H	178	5028	122	—	0	0	16753	8285	476
▣ ST. MARGARET MEMORIAL HOSPITAL, 815 Freeport Rd., Zip 15215; tel. 412/784-4000; Stanley J. Kevish, pres. **A**1a 3 5 6 9 10 **F**1 2 3 5 6 10 12 14 15 16 20 23 24 25 26 30 34 35 37 42 43 44 45 46 47 50 53	23	10	S		267	8608	200	74.9	0	0	45654	18491	900
STATE CORRECTIONAL INSTITUTION HOSPITAL, Doerr St., Box 99901, Zip 15233; tel. 412/761-1955; Joseph Morrash, adm. (Nonreporting)	12	11	S		29	—	—	—	—	—	—	—	—
▣ SUBURBAN GENERAL HOSPITAL, S. Jackson Ave., Zip 15202; tel. 412/734-1800; Thomas D. McConnell, pres. **A**1a 9 10 **F**1 2 3 6 10 12 14 15 16 20 23 24 25 26 32 33 34 35 41 42 44 45 46 50 52 53	23	10	S		214	5584	128	59.8	0	0	22854	10844	564
▣ UNIVERSITY OF PITTSBURGH WESTERN PSYCHIATRIC INSTITUTE AND CLINIC, 3811 O'Hara St., Zip 15213; tel. 412/624-3528; Thomas Detre MD, dir.; George A. Huber, adm. **A**1a 3 5 8 9 10 **F**15 24 28 29 30 32 33 34 35 42 43 44 46 47 49 50	23	22	S		213	2801	206	98.6	0	0	62743	32984	1303
▣ VETERANS ADMINISTRATION MEDICAL CENTER, University Dr. C, Zip 15240; tel. 412/683-3000; Thomas A. Gigliotti, dir. (Total facility includes 228 beds in nursing home-type unit) **A**1a 3 5 8 **F**1 2 3 4 6 10 12 14 15 16 19 20 21 23 24 25 26 30 32 33 34 35 37 41 42 44 45 46 47 53 54	45	10	S	TF	858	13118	659	76.8	0	0	78118	43053	1545
				H	630	12971	447	—	0	0	71420	37908	1469
▣ VETERANS ADMINISTRATION MEDICAL CENTER, Highland Dr., Zip 15206; tel. 412/363-4900; Reedes Hurt, dir. **A**1a **F**12 15 16 19 21 23 24 26 28 29 30 31 32 33 34 35 37 41 42 43 44 46 48 49 50	45	22	L		707	3400	542	76.7	0	0	39814	24665	1034
▣ WESTERN PENNSYLVANIA HOSPITAL, 4800 Friendship Ave., Zip 15224; tel. 412/578-5000; Steven A. Caywood, pres. & chief exec. off. **A**1a 3 5 6 8 9 10 **F**1 2 3 4 7 8 9 10 11 12 14 15 16 20 21 22 23 24 26 27 28 30 32 33 34 35 36 37 38 40 41 42 44 45 46 47 50 51 52 53 54	23	10	S		538	17350	386	69.4	30	1710	106872	44371	2269
POTTSTOWN—Montgomery County													
▣ POTTSTOWN MEMORIAL MEDICAL CENTER, 1600 E. High St., Zip 19464; tel. 215/327-7000; Larry A. Crowell, pres. & chief exec. off. **A**1a 9 10 **F**1 2 3 6 10 11 12 14 15 16 23 24 28 29 30 34 35 36 37 39 40 42 43 44 45 46 47 49 53	23	10	S		239	10348	169	71.3	25	836	35967	16566	834
POTTSVILLE—Schuylkill County													
▣ GOOD SAMARITAN HOSPITAL OF POTTSVILLE, PENNSYLVANIA, E. Norwegian & Tremont Sts., Zip 17901; tel. 717/621-4000; Frederick Siembieda, pres. **A**1a 9 10 **F**1 2 6 10 12 14 15 16 20 21 23 30 34 35 36 40 44 45 46 47 49 51 52 53; **S**1885	21	10	S		175	7401	143	74.1	20	605	23072	10082	576
▣ POTTSVILLE HOSPITAL AND WARNE CLINIC, 420 S. Jackson St., Zip 17901; tel. 717/622-6120; Thomas J. Lonergan, adm. **A**1a 2 6 9 10 **F**1 2 3 6 10 12 14 15 16 21 23 24 27 30 32 33 34 35 36 40 41 42 44 45 46 47 52 53; **S**0745	23	10	S		179	6479	133	77.8	15	416	21042	10478	577
PUNXSUTAWNEY—Jefferson County													
☐ PUNXSUTAWNEY AREA HOSPITAL, R D 5, Rte. 36 N., Zip 15767; tel. 814/938-4500; Daniel D. Blough Jr., adm. **A**1a 9 10 **F**1 3 6 10 12 14 15 16 23 35 40 41 44 45 46 47 52 53	23	10	S		75	2299	31	40.3	10	224	7242	3134	202
QUAKERTOWN—Bucks County													
▣ QUAKERTOWN COMMUNITY HOSPITAL, 11th & Park Ave., Zip 18951; tel. 215/536-2400; Roger B. Hiser, chief exec. off. & adm. **A**1a 2 9 10 **F**1 3 6 10 12 14 15 16 20 21 23 24 27 32 33 34 35 37 41 42 44 45 46 47 50 53	23	10	S		89	3113	63	70.8	0	0	14785	6021	313
READING—Berks County													
▣ COMMUNITY GENERAL HOSPITAL, 145 N. Sixth St., Zip 19601; Mailing Address P O Box 1728, Zip 19603; tel. 215/376-4881; Lawrence Scanlan Jr., pres. **A**1a 2 9 10 **F**1 3 6 10 12 14 15 16 21 23 34 35 36 37 40 44 45 46 47 49 50 52 53; **S**0745	23	10	S		173	5948	102	64.2	26	779	25002	11318	547
▣ READING HOSPITAL AND MEDICAL CENTER, Sixth Ave. & Spruce St., Zip 19603; tel. 215/378-6257; James B. Gronseth, vice chm. **A**1a 2 3 5 6 9 10 **F**1 2 3 4 5 6 7 8 9 10 11 12 14 15 16 20 21 23 24 26 27 28 29 30 32 33 34 35 36 37 38 40 42 44 45 46 47 49 50 51 52 53 54; **S**0745	23	10	S		573	23768	468	81.7	38	2331	84181	42737	2164
▣ READING REHABILITATION HOSPITAL, Rte. 1, Box 250, Zip 19607; tel. 215/777-7615; Landon Kite, pres. **A**1a 10 **F**15 23 24 26 33 34 42 44 46; **S**9355	21	46	L		88	919	79	89.8	0	0	9267	5700	300
▣ SAINT JOSEPH HOSPITAL, 215 N. 12th St., Box 316, Zip 19603; tel. 215/378-2000; Sr. Francis Anne Harper, pres. & chief exec. off. **A**1a 2 3 5 6 9 10 **F**1 2 3 6 7 8 9 10 11 12 14 15 16 20 23 24 26 27 30 32 33 34 35 36 40 42 44 45 46 47 49 52 53 54; **S**5325	21	10	S		315	10176	179	56.8	16	827	39045	19214	980
RENOVO—Clinton County													
★ BUCKTAIL MEDICAL CENTER, 1001 Pine St., Zip 17764; tel. 717/923-1000; Susan M. Cannon, adm. (Total facility includes 37 beds in nursing home-type unit) **A**9 10 **F**1 14 19 23 34 35 45 46 52	23	10	S	TF	50	512	39	78.0	0	0	1700	666	63
				H	13	458	5	—	0	0	1098	451	32
RIDGWAY—Elk County													
★ ELK COUNTY GENERAL HOSPITAL, 94 Hospital St., P O Box M, Zip 15853; tel. 814/776-6111; Charles E. Rice, adm. **A**9 10 **F**1 3 6 12 14 16 23 27 30 32 33 35 36 40 45 47 53	23	10	S		83	2318	40	48.2	6	206	6451	2981	186
RIDLEY PARK—Delaware County													
▣ TAYLOR HOSPITAL, E. Chester Pike, Zip 19078; tel. 215/595-6000; W. Scott Murray, pres. **A**1a 3 5 9 10 **F**1 3 6 10 12 14 15 16 21 23 24 25 26 32 33 35 37 41 42 44 45 46 47 53	23	10	S		203	6193	145	71.4	0	0	25697	13015	582
ROARING SPRING—Blair County													
▣ NASON HOSPITAL, Nason Dr., Zip 16673; tel. 814/224-2141; John P. Kinney, pres. **A**1a 9 10 **F**1 3 6 10 12 14 15 16 23 24 34 35 40 41 44 45 52 53	23	10	S		84	2507	39	46.4	8	152	8962	4065	222
ROCHESTER—Beaver County													
▣ COMMUNITY MENTAL HEALTH CENTER OF BEAVER COUNTY, 176 Virginia Ave., Zip 15074; tel. 412/775-5208; John D. Sipes, exec. dir. **A**1b 10 **F**24 28 29 30 32 33 34 35 43 46	21	22	S		34	527	32	94.1	0	0	4397	2996	136
SAYRE—Bradford County													
▣ ROBERT PACKER HOSPITAL, Guthrie Square, Zip 18840; tel. 717/888-6666; Gary B. Morrison, pres. (Data for 303 days) **A**1a 2 3 5 6 9 10 **F**1 3 4 5 6 7 8 9 10 11 12 14 15 16 20 23 24 25 27 30 32 33 34 35 36 37 39 40 45 46 52 53 54; **S**0675	23	10	S		366	13606	302	82.5	16	1023	55449	21938	1209
SCRANTON—Lackawanna County													
▣ Δ ALLIED SERVICES FOR THE HANDICAPPED, 475 Morgan Hwy., Zip 18508; Mailing Address Box 1103, Zip 18501; tel. 717/348-1300; James Brady, pres. **A**1a 7 9 **F**15 16 23 24 26 33 34 42 44 45 46 47	23	46	L		90	737	80	88.9	0	0	10731	3986	285
CLARKS SUMMIT STATE HOSPITAL, See Clarks Summit													

Hospital, Address, Telephone, Administrator, Approval and Facility Codes, Multihospital System Code	Classification Codes				Inpatient Data				Newborn Data		Expense (thousands of dollars)		
★ American Hospital Association (AHA) membership □ Joint Commission on Accreditation of Hospitals (JCAH) accreditation + American Osteopathic Hospital Association (AOHA) membership ○ American Osteopathic Association (AOA) accreditation Δ Commission on Accreditation of Rehabilitation Facilities (CARF) accreditation Control codes 61, 63, 64, 71, 72 and 73 indicate hospitals listed by AOHA, but not registered by AHA. For definition of numerical codes, see page A2	Control	Service	Stay	Facilities	Beds	Admissions	Census	Occupancy (percent)	Bassinets	Births	Total	Payroll	Personnel
★□ COMMUNITY MEDICAL CENTER, 1822 Mulberry St., P O Box 1123, Zip 18510; tel. 717/969-8000; Adrian A. Samojlowicz PhD, pres. **A**1a 3 5 6 9 10 **F**1 3 5 6 10 11 12 14 15 16 19 20 23 24 26 27 30 32 33 35 36 38 40 44 45 46 47 51 52 53	23	10	S		327	13744	231	73.6	28	1785	49276	23739	1022
★□ MERCY HOSPITAL OF SCRANTON (Formerly Mercy Hospital), 746 Jefferson Ave., Zip 18501; tel. 717/348-7100; Sr. William Joseph, pres. **A**1a 2 3 5 6 9 10 **F**1 3 4 6 7 8 9 10 11 12 14 15 16 23 26 32 33 34 35 36 40 45 46 47 52 53 54; **S**5195	21	10	S		365	12529	253	69.3	33	1060	61216	27055	1314
★□ MOSES TAYLOR HOSPITAL, 700 Quincy Ave., Zip 18510; tel. 717/963-2100; James L. Kinney, pres. (Total facility includes 32 beds in nursing home-type unit) **A**1a 2 3 5 9 10 **F**1 3 6 10 11 12 14 15 16 19 20 23 26 30 34 35 37 44 45 46 47 50 52 53	23	10	S	TF	262	6465	176	67.2	0	0	38113	15699	794
				H	230	6237	146	—	0	0	36190	15161	773
□ SCRANTON STATE GENERAL HOSPITAL, 205 Mulberry St., Zip 18501; tel. 717/963-4211; Susan E. Bruce, adm. (Nonreporting) **A**1a 9 10; **S**3825	12	10	S		176	—	—	—	—	—	—	—	—
SELLERSVILLE—Bucks County													
★□ GRAND VIEW HOSPITAL, Lawn Ave., Zip 18960; tel. 215/257-3611; Philip J. Byrne, exec. vice-pres. (Total facility includes 20 beds in nursing home-type unit) **A**1a 2 9 10 **F**1 3 6 7 8 9 10 11 12 14 15 16 19 21 23 24 27 29 30 35 36 40 41 44 45 46 47 48 52 53	23	10	S	TF	250	8730	170	69.1	20	1296	35772	18766	941
				H	230	8449	155	—	20	1296	35195	18217	921
SEWICKLEY—Allegheny County													
★□ Δ D. T. WATSON REHABILITATION HOSPITAL, Camp Meeting Rd., Zip 15143; tel. 412/741-9500; Steven J. Mozolak, pres. **A**1a 7 10 **F**23 24 26 42 44 45 46	23	46	S		37	324	19	51.4	0	0	5955	3115	182
★□ SEWICKLEY VALLEY HOSPITAL, Blackburn Rd., Zip 15143; tel. 412/741-6600; Donald W. Spalding, pres. **A**1a 6 9 10 **F**1 3 6 10 12 13 14 15 16 20 21 23 24 25 27 28 29 30 32 33 34 35 36 40 41 42 44 45 46 52 53	23	10	S		207	9689	163	78.7	23	994	41740	19819	1039
SHAMOKIN—Northumberland County													
□ SHAMOKIN STATE GENERAL HOSPITAL, Rte. 2, Zip 17872; tel. 717/644-0321; Robert D. Greco, adm. (Nonreporting) **A**1a 9 10	12	10	S		72	—	—	—	—	—	—	—	—
SHARON—Mercer County													
★□ SHARON GENERAL HOSPITAL, 740 E. State St., Zip 16146; tel. 412/983-3911; Eugene J. O'Meara, pres. **A**1a 6 9 10 **F**1 3 6 8 10 11 12 15 16 21 23 27 30 35 40 41 45 46 47 49 50 52 53	23	10	S		212	7817	142	67.0	24	707	27884	13282	700
SHICKSHINNY—Luzerne County													
CLEAR BROOK LODGE (Residential Treatment Center for Adolescent Alcoholism and Other Chemical Dependencies), Rural Delivery 2, Box 146a, Zip 18655; tel. 717/864-3116; Dave Lombard, pres. & chief exec. off. (Nonreporting)	23	82	L		65	—	—	—	—	—	—	—	—
SOMERSET—Somerset County													
★□ SOMERSET COMMUNITY HOSPITAL, 225 S. Center Ave., Zip 15501; tel. 814/443-2626; Michael J. Farrell, adm. (Total facility includes 18 beds in nursing home-type unit) **A**1a 9 10 **F**1 3 5 6 12 14 15 16 19 21 23 24 26 27 28 29 30 32 33 34 35 36 40 42 43 44 45 46 47 52 53	23	10	S	TF	166	6170	95	57.2	12	352	16053	8031	477
				H	148	6043	89	—	12	352	15801	7823	—
□ SOMERSET STATE HOSPITAL, Rte. 5, Box 631, Zip 15501; tel. 814/445-6501; William H. Cummings, supt. **A**1a 10 **F**23 24 28 30 32 33 42 46 47	12	22	L		316	271	284	89.9	0	0	13941	8203	381
SOUTH MOUNTAIN—Franklin County													
SOUTH MOUNTAIN RESTORATION CENTER (Geriatric), Zip 17261; tel. 717/749-3121; Bruce Darney, adm. **F**1 19 23 24 33 42 44 46 50	12	49	L		748	134	689	91.7	0	0	21418	13128	672
SPANGLER—Cambria County													
★□ MINERS HOSPITAL NORTHERN CAMBRIA, Crawford Ave. & First St., Zip 15775; tel. 814/948-7171; LeRoy D. Miller, adm. **A**1a 9 10 **F**1 3 6 12 14 15 16 23 34 35 40 44 45 52	23	10	S		75	3003	33	44.0	14	210	9391	4282	186
SPRINGFIELD—Delaware County													
○ + METROPOLITAN HOSPITAL-SPRINGFIELD DIVISION, 190 W. Sproul Rd., Zip 19064; tel. 215/328-8700; Gerald E. Pierson, exec. dir. (Nonreporting) **A**9 10 11 12 13; **S**7995	23	10	S		122	—	—	—	—	—	—	—	—
ST. MARYS—Elk County													
★□ ANDREW KAUL MEMORIAL HOSPITAL, Johnsonburg Rd., Zip 15857; tel. 814/781-7500; Guido J. Berasi, adm. (Total facility includes 138 beds in nursing home-type unit) **A**1a 9 10 **F**1 3 6 10 16 19 23 34 40 42 45 46 52	23	10	S	TF	236	3835	175	74.2	18	295	12869	6818	397
				H	98	3595	44	—	18	295	10161	5135	281
STATE COLLEGE—Centre County													
★□ CENTRE COMMUNITY HOSPITAL, 1800 E. Park Ave., Zip 16803; tel. 814/238-4351; Jack E. Branigan, exec. dir. **A**1a 2 6 9 10 **F**1 3 6 8 10 11 12 14 15 16 20 21 23 24 27 30 33 34 35 36 37 40 42 45 46 47 52 53	23	10	S		200	8056	131	65.5	24	1241	27973	14924	618
SUNBURY—Northumberland County													
★□ SUNBURY COMMUNITY HOSPITAL, 350 N. 11th St., P O Box 737, Zip 17801; tel. 717/286-3333; Nicholas A. Prisco, chief exec. off. (Nonreporting) **A**1a 9 10	23	10	S		167	—	—	—	—	—	—	—	—
SUSQUEHANNA—Susquehanna County													
★□ BARNES-KASSON COUNTY HOSPITAL, 400 Turnpike St., Zip 18847; tel. 717/853-3135; Sara C. Iveson, exec. dir. (Total facility includes 49 beds in nursing home-type unit) **A**1a 9 10 **F**1 3 6 12 15 16 19 23 34 35 40 41 42 44 45 46	23	10	S	TF	96	2163	81	83.5	8	143	5560	2930	191
				H	47	2106	33	—	8	143	4930	2567	165
TITUSVILLE—Crawford County													
★□ TITUSVILLE HOSPITAL, 406 W. Oak St., Zip 16354; tel. 814/827-1851; William A. Likar, pres. (Nonreporting) **A**1a 9 10	23	10	S		100	—	—	—	—	—	—	—	—
TORRANCE—Westmoreland County													
TORRANCE STATE HOSPITAL, Zip 15779; tel. 412/459-8000; Ray E. Bullard Jr. MD, supt. (Total facility includes 134 beds in nursing home-type unit) **A**10 **F**12 15 19 23 24 32 33 42 44 46	12	22	L	TF	552	295	485	80.0	0	0	28750	17822	715
				H	418	262	315	—	0	0	—	—	632
TOWANDA—Bradford County													
★□ MEMORIAL HOSPITAL, One Hospital Dr., Zip 18848; tel. 717/265-2191; J. Michael Crandall, pres. (Total facility includes 44 beds in nursing home-type unit) **A**1a 9 10 **F**1 3 6 10 12 14 15 16 19 20 23 34 35 36 40 41 42 44 45 46 47 50 52	23	10	S	TF	99	2837	75	74.3	12	281	8461	3995	203
				H	55	2660	36	—	12	281	—	—	180
TREVOSE—Bucks County													
□ EASTERN STATE SCHOOL AND HOSPITAL, 3740 Lincoln Hwy., Zip 19047; tel. 215/671-3141; Robert E. Switzer MD, supt. **A**1b 9 10 **F**24 32 33 42 43 44 46 47	12	52	L		184	204	148	80.4	0	0	15021	7468	410
TROY—Bradford County													
★ ○ TROY COMMUNITY HOSPITAL, 100 John St., Zip 16947; tel. 717/297-2121; Mark A. Webster, pres. **A**9 10 11 **F**1 3 6 10 14 15 16 23 26 35 37 40 45 52; **S**0675	23	10	S		65	792	12	18.5	10	8	2379	1050	75
TUNKHANNOCK—Wyoming County													
★□ TYLER MEMORIAL HOSPITAL, Rural Delivery 1, Zip 18657; tel. 717/836-2161; John A. Ireland, pres. **A**1a 2 9 10 **F**1 3 6 10 12 14 16 23 32 33 35 36 40 45 46 52 53	23	10	S		89	4200	57	64.0	8	320	10377	4535	225
TYRONE—Blair County													
★□ TYRONE HOSPITAL, Clay Ave. Ext., Zip 16686; tel. 814/684-1255; Thomas D. Robinson, chief exec. off. **A**1a 9 10 **F**1 3 6 12 14 15 16 19 23 34 35 37 44 45 47 49; **S**1755	23	10	S		59	1865	25	42.4	11	93	5375	2398	144

Hospital, Address, Telephone, Administrator, Approval and Facility Codes, Multihospital System Code

★ American Hospital Association (AHA) membership
☐ Joint Commission on Accreditation of Hospitals (JCAH) accreditation
+ American Osteopathic Hospital Association (AOHA) membership
○ American Osteopathic Association (AOA) accreditation
Δ Commission on Accreditation of Rehabilitation Facilities (CARF) accreditation
Control codes 61, 63, 64, 71, 72 and 73 indicate hospitals listed by AOHA, but not registered by AHA.
For definition of numerical codes, see page A2

Hospital, Address, Telephone, Administrator, Approval and Facility Codes, Multihospital System Code	Classification Codes				Inpatient Data				Newborn Data		Expense (thousands of dollars)		
	Control	Service	Stay	Facilities	Beds	Admissions	Census	Occupancy (percent)	Bassinets	Births	Total	Payroll	Personnel
UNION CITY—Erie County													
⊞ UNION CITY MEMORIAL HOSPITAL, 130 N. Main St., Zip 16438; tel. 814/438-3817; N. Alexander Bowler, exec. dir. **A**1a 9 10 **F**1 3 6 14 15 16 23 30 34 35 37 40 43 45 46 47 52 53	23	10	S		35	1457	19	54.3	8	69	2772	1522	100
UNIONTOWN—Fayette County													
⊞ UNIONTOWN HOSPITAL, 500 W. Berkeley St., Zip 15401; tel. 412/430-5000; William J. Grego Jr., pres. **A**1a 6 9 10 **F**1 3 6 10 12 14 15 16 23 24 26 32 34 35 40 44 45 46 47 52 53	23	10	S		230	9874	156	63.2	41	874	33412	18533	843
UNIVERSITY PARK—Centre County													
RITENOUR HEALTH CENTER, Shortlidge & Pollock Rds., Penn State University, Zip 16802; tel. 814/865-6555; Harry M. McDermott MD, dir. **F**1 15 23 27 28 29 30 32 33 34 35 37 43 46 49	12	11	S		13	687	1	7.7	0	0	2597	1920	100
WARMINSTER—Bucks County													
☐ WARMINSTER GENERAL HOSPITAL, 225 Newtown Rd., Zip 18974; tel. 215/441-6600; Vail P. Garvin, exec. dir. **A**1a 9 10 **F**1 3 5 6 10 12 14 15 16 20 23 24 26 27 30 32 33 34 35 42 44 45 46 47 48 49 50 52 53; **S**6345	23	10	S		180	5731	122	67.8	0	0	27625	10900	557
WARREN—Warren County													
★ WARREN DENTAL ARTS HOSPITAL (Dental), 128 Pennsylvania Ave. E., Zip 16365; tel. 814/723-4488; Robert A. Probst DDS, adm. **F**1 15 34 35	33	49	S		6	157	1	16.7	0	0	—	—	32
⊞ WARREN GENERAL HOSPITAL, 2 Crescent Park W., Zip 16365; tel. 814/723-3300; Rodney E. Betts, pres. **A**1a 9 10 **F**1 3 6 7 8 9 10 11 12 13 14 15 16 23 24 26 27 30 32 35 36 40 45 46 48 52 53	23	10	S		134	4995	91	60.7	11	501	16502	8023	421
☐ WARREN STATE HOSPITAL, Box 249, Zip 16365; tel. 814/723-5500; Beryl R. Johnson PhD, supt. (Total facility includes 24 beds in nursing home-type unit) **A**1a 10 **F**12 19 24 33 42 44 46 47	12	22	L	TF	620	380	495	79.8	0	0	31140	17968	807
				H	596	336	475	—	0	0	—	—	—
WASHINGTON—Washington County													
⊞ WASHINGTON HOSPITAL, 155 Wilson Ave., Zip 15301; tel. 412/225-7000; E. L. Strosser, pres. **A**1a 3 6 9 10 **F**1 2 3 6 10 11 12 14 15 16 23 24 26 27 30 33 34 35 36 37 40 42 44 45 46 52 53	23	10	S		296	12930	224	75.7	30	1060	53969	30122	1254
WAYMART—Wayne County													
FARVIEW STATE HOSPITAL, Box 128, Zip 18472; tel. 717/488-6111; Irene L. Vauter, actg. supt. **F**24 33 42	12	22	L		250	373	206	82.4	0	0	22341	13601	535
WAYNESBORO—Franklin County													
⊞ WAYNESBORO HOSPITAL, 501 E. Main St., Zip 17268; tel. 717/762-8171; William G. George, pres. **A**1a 9 10 **F**1 3 6 10 12 14 15 16 23 24 30 32 33 35 36 37 40 44 45 48 50 53	23	10	S		88	3267	46	52.3	10	551	9434	4735	261
WAYNESBURG—Greene County													
⊞ GREENE COUNTY MEMORIAL HOSPITAL, Seventh St. & Bonar Ave., Zip 15370; tel. 412/627-3101; Michael Flinn, adm. **A**1a 9 10 **F**1 3 10 12 15 16 17 20 23 34 35 40 41 45 46 47 52 53	23	10	S		70	3086	50	57.5	11	275	12965	6477	288
WELLSBORO—Tioga County													
⊞ SOLDIERS AND SAILORS MEMORIAL HOSPITAL, 32-36 Central Ave., Zip 16901; tel. 717/724-1631; Robert H. Morris, exec. dir. **A**1a 9 10 **F**1 3 6 10 12 14 15 16 23 27 30 32 33 34 35 40 45 46 47 50 52 53	23	10	S		127	4379	72	55.4	15	399	11635	5345	329
WERNERSVILLE—Berks County													
⊞ CARON FOUNDATION (Includes Chit Chat Farms, Chit Chat West, Caron Hospital, Chit Chat Westfield, Chit Chat Winchester and Caron Counseling Services), Rd. 3, Galen Hall Rd., Box A, Zip 19565; tel. 215/678-2332; Richard W. Esterly, chief exec. off. **A**1b 9 10 **F**15 45 46 49	23	82	S		151	1660	127	87.0	0	0	6551	1794	198
☐ WERNERSVILLE STATE HOSPITAL, Zip 19565; tel. 215/678-3411; Thomas V. Sellars, supt. (Total facility includes 193 beds in nursing home-type unit) **A**1b 10 **F**15 19 23 24 30 33 41 42 46 50	12	22	L	TF	575	644	486	80.6	0	0	24460	14823	634
				H	382	600	337	—	0	0	—	—	550
WEST CHESTER—Chester County													
⊞ HOSPITALS OF CHESTER COUNTY (Formerly Chester County Hospital), 701 E. Marshall St., Zip 19380; tel. 215/431-5000; H. L. Perry Pepper, pres. **A**1a 2 6 9 10 **F**1 2 3 6 7 8 9 10 11 12 14 15 16 23 30 34 35 36 38 40 44 45 46 47 52 53	23	10	S		251	11157	167	66.5	40	1638	38668	19500	896
WEST GROVE—Chester County													
⊞ SOUTHERN CHESTER COUNTY MEDICAL CENTER, 1015 W. Baltimore Pike, Zip 19390; tel. 215/869-1000; Larry K. Spaid, pres. **A**1a 9 10 **F**1 3 6 10 14 15 16 23 33 34 35 41 44 45 46 47 49	23	10	S		77	2929	43	55.8	0	0	12283	5159	242
WILKES-BARRE—Luzerne County													
☐ CLEAR BROOK MANOR, Rd. 10 E. Northampton St., Zip 18702; tel. 717/823-1171; Donald Noll, dir. (Nonreporting) **A**1b	23	82	L		50	—	—	—	—	—	—	—	—
⊞ GEISINGER WYOMING VALLEY MEDICAL CENTER (Formerly NPW Medical Center), 1000 E. Mountain Dr., Zip 18711; tel. 717/826-7300; Conrad W. Schintz, sr. vice-pres. **A**1a 6 9 10 **F**1 2 3 6 10 12 14 15 16 23 24 25 26 30 32 33 34 35 36 37 44 45 46 52 53; **S**5570	23	10	S		230	7441	155	67.4	20	395	33806	13485	679
⊞ MERCY HOSPITAL OF WILKES-BARRE (Formerly Mercy Hospital), 25 Church St., Box 658, Zip 18765; tel. 717/826-3100; Henry J. Morris, interim pres. & chief exec. off. **A**1a 9 10 **F**1 2 6 10 11 12 14 15 16 23 24 27 34 35 36 37 40 45 46 52 53; **S**5195	23	10	S		235	8566	182	77.4	24	93	36172	17401	854
NPW MEDICAL CENTER, See Geisinger Wyoming Valley Medical Center													
⊞ VETERANS ADMINISTRATION MEDICAL CENTER, 1111 East End Blvd., Zip 18711; tel. 717/824-3521; Michael A. Parrell, dir. (Total facility includes 120 beds in nursing home-type unit) **A**1a 2 3 5 **F**1 3 6 10 12 14 15 16 19 21 23 24 26 27 28 32 33 34 42 44 45 46 47	45	10	S	TF	560	7013	556	99.3	0	0	52785	31652	1048
				H	440	6976	440	—	0	0	46811	28023	985
⊞ WILKES-BARRE GENERAL HOSPITAL, N. River & Auburn Sts., Zip 18764; tel. 717/829-8111; Allan E. Atzrott, pres. **A**1a 3 5 9 10 **F**1 2 3 5 6 7 8 9 10 11 12 15 16 20 23 27 30 32 33 34 35 36 37 40 44 45 46 47 50 52 53 54	23	10	S		444	17230	345	77.9	22	645	55724	24784	1434
WILLIAMSBURG—Blair County													
⊞ NEW BEGINNINGS AT COVE FORGE (Formerly Cove Forge Treatment Center), Rte. 1, Box 79, P O Box B, Zip 16693; tel. 814/832-2121; George E. Obermeier, exec. dir. (Nonreporting) **A**1b ; **S**1315	33	82	L		69	—	—	—	—	—	—	—	—
WILLIAMSPORT—Lycoming County													
⊞ DIVINE PROVIDENCE HOSPITAL, 1100 Grampian Blvd., Zip 17701; tel. 717/326-8181; Sr. Jean Mohl, pres. **A**1a 2 9 10 **F**1 3 6 7 8 9 10 11 12 14 15 16 20 23 24 25 26 27 28 29 30 32 33 34 35 36 40 44 45 46 49 52 53 54	23	10	S		235	6922	128	55.2	20	466	32523	15523	856
⊞ Δ WILLIAMSPORT HOSPITAL AND MEDICAL CENTER (Formerly Williamsport Hospital), 777 Rural Ave., Zip 17701; tel. 717/321-1000; Donald R. Creamer, pres. & chief exec. off. **A**1a 2 3 5 6 7 9 10 **F**1 2 3 6 9 10 11 12 14 15 16 23 24 25 26 27 33 34 35 36 37 40 42 44 45 46 47 48 52 53 54	23	10	S		310	12054	207	66.8	26	990	46106	23919	1222

Hospital, Address, Telephone, Administrator, Approval and Facility Codes, Multihospital System Code	Classification Codes			Facilities	Inpatient Data				Newborn Data		Expense (thousands of dollars)		Personnel
	Control	Service	Stay		Beds	Admissions	Census	Occupancy (percent)	Bassinets	Births	Total	Payroll	
WILLOW GROVE—Montgomery County													
□ HUNTINGTON HOSPITAL, 200 Fitzwatertown Rd., Zip 19090; tel. 215/657-4010; Eugene C. Wayne, adm. (Nonreporting) **A**1b 9 10	33	22	S		29	—	—	—	—	—	—	—	—
WINDBER—Somerset County													
[★] WINDBER HOSPITAL AND WHEELING CLINIC, 600 Somerset Ave., Zip 15963; tel. 814/467-6611; Robert A. Chrzan, pres. **A**1a 9 10 **F**1 3 6 10 12 14 16 21 23 35 40 41 45 52 53	23	10	S		108	3296	50	46.3	6	249	10185	4828	268
WYNDMOOR—Montgomery County													
[★] Δ ALL SAINTS' REHABILITATION HOSPITAL (Formerly Listed Under Philadelphia), 8601 Stenton Ave., Zip 19118; tel. 215/233-6200; Leslie I. Gilman, dir. (Total facility includes 31 beds in nursing home-type unit) **A**1a 7 10 **F**15 19 23 24 26 32 33 34 42 44 45 46 47 49	21	46	S	TF	83	625	69	83.1	0	0	6188	3068	222
				H	52	610	39	—	0	0	4744	2398	—
YORK—York County													
○ + MEMORIAL HOSPITAL, 325 S. Belmont St., Zip 17403; Mailing Address P O Box M-118, Zip 17405; tel. 717/843-8623; Dennis P. Heinle, pres. **A**9 10 11 12 13 **F**1 3 6 10 12 14 15 16 23 24 30 34 35 37 40 45 46 47 50 52 53	23	10	S		162	6998	112	69.1	16	555	22892	10492	604
□ Δ REHAB HOSPITAL FOR SPECIAL SERVICES OF YORK, 1850 Normandie Dr., Zip 17404; tel. 717/767-6941; Marie P. Cloney, adm. **A**1a 7 10 **F**15 16 23 24 26 28 33 34 42 44 46 50; **S**0825	33	46	S		88	963	59	67.0	0	0	6548	3254	217
[★] YORK HOSPITAL, 1001 S. George St., Zip 17405; tel. 717/771-2345; Paul H. Keiser, pres. **A**1a 2 3 5 8 9 10 **F**1 3 4 5 6 7 8 9 10 11 12 14 15 16 20 21 23 24 26 27 30 32 33 34 35 36 37 38 40 41 42 44 45 46 47 49 50 51 52 53 54	23	10	S		563	20994	392	69.6	25	2646	81590	42546	2168

★ American Hospital Association (AHA) membership
□ Joint Commission on Accreditation of Hospitals (JCAH) accreditation
+ American Osteopathic Hospital Association (AOHA) membership
○ American Osteopathic Association (AOA) accreditation
Δ Commission on Accreditation of Rehabilitation Facilities (CARF) accreditation
Control codes 61, 63, 64, 71, 72 and 73 indicate hospitals listed by AOHA, but not registered by AHA.
For definition of numerical codes, see page A2

Hospital, Address, Telephone, Administrator, Approval and Facility Codes, Multihospital System Code

- ★ American Hospital Association (AHA) membership
- □ Joint Commission on Accreditation of Hospitals (JCAH) accreditation
- \+ American Osteopathic Hospital Association (AOHA) membership
- ○ American Osteopathic Association (AOA) accreditation
- Δ Commission on Accreditation of Rehabilitation Facilities (CARF) accreditation

Control codes 61, 63, 64, 71, 72 and 73 indicate hospitals listed by AOHA, but not registered by AHA. For definition of numerical codes, see page A2

Rhode Island

Hospital, Address, Telephone, Administrator, Approval and Facility Codes, Multihospital System Code	Classification Codes				Inpatient Data				Newborn Data		Expense (thousands of dollars)		
	Control	Service	Stay	Facilities	Beds	Admissions	Census	Occupancy (percent)	Bassinets	Births	Total	Payroll	Personnel
CENTRAL FALLS—Providence County													
★□ NOTRE DAME HOSPITAL, 1000 Broad St., Zip 02863; tel. 401/726-1800; Peter A. Hofstetter, adm. **A**1a 9 10 **F**1 6 12 14 15 16 23 34 44 45 46 47; **S**1755	23	10	S		41	1126	20	48.8	0	0	4597	1998	104
CRANSTON—Providence County													
○ + CRANSTON GENERAL HOSPITAL OSTEOPATHIC, 1763 Broad St., Zip 02905; tel. 401/781-9200; Elliot E. Benadon, adm. **A**9 10 11 12 13 **F**1 3 6 10 12 14 16 23 35 45 46 47 52 53	23	10	S		79	2477	48	60.8	0	0	10609	4670	264
★□ CENTER GENERAL HOSPITAL, Box 8269, Zip 02920; tel. 401/464-3666; Peter Megrdichian, adm. **A**1a 10 **F**6 12 14 15 16 19 23 24 25 29 33 42 44 45 46 47 50	12	48	L		505	533	479	87.6	0	0	39933	19372	919
□ INSTITUTE OF MENTAL HEALTH-RHODE ISLAND MEDICAL CENTER, Box 8281, Zip 02920; tel. 401/464-2495; David Askew PhD, clin. adm. off. **A**1b 10 **F**19 24 30 32 33 42 46 47	12	22	L		385	857	286	73.9	0	0	27075	13356	584
NEWPORT—Newport County													
★□ NAVAL HOSPITAL, Zip 02841; tel. 401/841-3771; Capt. F. G. Sanford MC USN, CO **A**1a 2 **F**1 3 6 10 11 12 14 15 16 23 26 27 28 29 30 32 33 34 35 37 40 43 45 46 47 48 49 52	43	10	S		106	3142	50	42.4	0	326	24626	18526	542
★□ Δ NEWPORT HOSPITAL, Friendship St., Zip 02840; tel. 401/846-6400; Robert J. Healey, pres. **A**1a 6 7 9 10 **F**1 2 3 6 10 12 14 15 16 23 24 25 26 27 30 33 35 36 37 40 42 44 45 46 52 53	23	10	S		217	6502	136	62.7	12	601	28014	14710	688
NORTH PROVIDENCE—Providence County													
OUR LADY OF FATIMA UNIT, See St. Joseph Hospital, Providence													
NORTH SMITHFIELD—Providence County													
★□ JOHN E. FOGARTY MEMORIAL HOSPITAL, Eddie Dowling Hwy., Mailing Address Woonsocket, Zip 02895; tel. 401/769-2200; John C. McAvinn, adm. **A**1a 9 10 **F**1 3 6 10 12 14 16 23 30 34 35 45 46	23	10	S		116	3366	70	60.3	0	0	14177	7641	380
PAWTUCKET—Providence County													
★□ MEMORIAL HOSPITAL, Prospect St., Zip 02860; tel. 401/722-6000; Francis R. Dietz, pres. **A**1a 3 5 8 9 10 **F**1 3 6 10 12 14 15 16 20 23 24 25 26 32 33 34 35 40 41 44 45 46 52 53	23	10	S		294	10580	235	79.9	30	693	46627	23634	1229
PROVIDENCE—Providence County													
★□ BUTLER HOSPITAL, 345 Blackstone Blvd., Zip 02906; tel. 401/456-3700; Frank A. Delmonico, dir. adm. **A**1a b 3 5 9 10 **F**24 28 29 30 32 33 42 43 46 49	23	22	S		108	2646	104	96.3	0	0	13243	7402	316
★□ MIRIAM HOSPITAL, 164 Summit Ave., Zip 02906; tel. 401/274-3700; Daniel A. Kane, pres. **A**1a 3 5 8 9 10 **F**1 3 4 6 10 11 12 14 15 16 20 23 26 32 33 34 35 41 45 46 50 53 54	23	10	S		247	9232	205	83.0	0	0	51091	24128	1130
OUR LADY OF PROVIDENCE UNIT, See St. Joseph Hospital													
★□ RHODE ISLAND HOSPITAL, 593 Eddy St., Zip 02903; tel. 401/277-4000; Delanson Y. Hopkins, pres. **A**1a 2 3 5 8 9 10 **F**1 2 3 4 5 6 7 8 9 10 11 12 15 16 19 20 23 24 26 27 28 30 32 33 34 35 38 41 42 43 44 45 46 47 49 52 53 54	23	10	S		719	25275	604	84.0	0	0	174002	—	3749
★□ ROGER WILLIAMS GENERAL HOSPITAL, 825 Chalkstone Ave., Zip 02908; tel. 401/456-2000; Vito F. Rallo, pres. **A**1a 3 5 8 9 10 **F**1 3 6 9 10 12 14 15 16 20 23 28 34 35 41 43 45 46 49 50 52 53 54	23	10	S		238	7887	173	72.7	0	0	45182	20235	1052
★□ ST. JOSEPH HOSPITAL (Includes Our Lady of Fatima Unit, 200 High Service Ave., North Providence, Zip 02904; tel. 401/456-3000; Mark T. Hough, sr. vice-pres.; Our Lady of Providence Unit, 21 Peace St., Zip 02907; tel. 401/456-3000; R. Michael Smith, sr. vice-pres.), Mailing Address 200 High Service Ave., North Providence, Zip 02904; tel. 401/456-3000; A. Edward Azevedo, pres. **A**1a 6 9 10 **F**1 2 3 6 9 10 12 14 15 16 20 23 24 32 33 34 35 36 40 44 45 46 47 52 53	21	10	S		447	13771	322	72.0	12	477	65411	35766	1634
★□ VETERANS ADMINISTRATION MEDICAL CENTER, Davis Park, Zip 02908; tel. 401/273-7100; Edward H. Seiler, dir. **A**1a 3 5 8 **F**1 2 3 6 10 12 14 15 16 19 20 23 24 25 26 27 28 29 31 32 33 34 42 43 44 46 48 49 50	45	10	S		311	9307	222	79.0	0	0	—	22660	803
★□ WOMEN AND INFANTS HOSPITAL OF RHODE ISLAND (Perinatal Medicine and Gynecology), 101 Dudley St., Zip 02905; tel. 401/274-1100; Thomas G. Parris Jr., pres. **A**1a 3 5 8 9 10 **F**1 6 12 14 15 16 28 32 34 35 36 37 38 40 45 46 47 51	23	49	S		178	11253	156	79.2	79	8091	40008	19618	861
RIVERSIDE—Providence County													
★□ EMMA PENDLETON BRADLEY HOSPITAL, 1011 Veterans Memorial Pkwy., Zip 02915; tel. 401/434-3400; Thomas F. Anders MD, exec. dir. **A**1b 3 5 10 **F**19 24 28 29 30 32 33 34 42 43 44 46	23	52	L		56	239	52	92.9	0	0	11579	6114	308
WAKEFIELD—Washington County													
★□ SOUTH COUNTY HOSPITAL, 95 Kenyon Ave., Zip 02879; tel. 401/783-3361; Donald J. Mazzarelli, pres. **A**1a 9 10 **F**1 3 6 10 12 14 15 16 23 24 26 30 32 34 35 36 40 42 43 44 45 46 52 53	23	10	S		100	3937	66	66.0	5	376	16071	6991	388
WALLUM LAKE—Providence County													
★□ DR. U. E. ZAMBARANO MEMORIAL HOSPITAL, Zip 02884; tel. 401/568-2551; James P. Benedict, adm. **A**1a 10 **F**6 16 23 24 33 42 44 46 47 50	12	49	L		313	113	266	85.0	0	0	15099	8497	428
WARWICK—Kent County													
★□ KENT COUNTY MEMORIAL HOSPITAL, 455 Tollgate Rd., Zip 02886; tel. 401/737-7000; John Hynes, adm. **A**1a 2 9 10 **F**1 3 6 10 11 12 14 16 23 27 29 32 33 35 36 40 41 44 45 46 52 53	23	10	S		359	14904	317	88.3	42	1846	55015	27258	1398
WESTERLY—Washington County													
★□ WESTERLY HOSPITAL, Wells St., Zip 02891; tel. 401/596-6000; S. Jeffrey Bastable, exec. vice-pres. & chief exec. off. **A**1a 9 10 **F**1 3 6 10 12 14 15 16 20 23 26 34 35 36 40 44 45 46 52	23	10	S		141	5097	79	56.0	18	640	16350	8343	415
WOONSOCKET—Providence County													
★□ WOONSOCKET HOSPITAL, 115 Cass Ave., Zip 02895; tel. 401/767-3211; Robert D. Walker, pres. & chief exec. off. **A**1a 9 10 **F**1 2 3 6 10 12 14 16 23 24 26 27 30 32 33 35 36 40 44 45 46 47 52 53	23	10	S		245	7557	137	55.9	40	797	26613	14996	706

★ American Hospital Association (AHA) membership
☐ Joint Commission on Accreditation of Hospitals (JCAH) accreditation
+ American Osteopathic Hospital Association (AOHA) membership
○ American Osteopathic Association (AOA) accreditation
Δ Commission on Accreditation of Rehabilitation Facilities (CARF) accreditation
Control codes 61, 63, 64, 71, 72 and 73 indicate hospitals listed by AOHA, but not registered by AHA.
For definition of numerical codes, see page A2

South Carolina

Hospital, Address, Telephone, Administrator, Approval and Facility Codes, Multihospital System Code	Classification Codes				Inpatient Data				Newborn Data		Expense (thousands of dollars)		
	Control	Service	Stay	Facilities	Beds	Admissions	Census	Occupancy (percent)	Bassinets	Births	Total	Payroll	Personnel
ABBEVILLE—Abbeville County													
★ ABBEVILLE COUNTY MEMORIAL HOSPITAL, Hwy. 72, P O Box 887, Zip 29620; tel. 803/459-5011; Brad D. Ingram, adm. **A**9 10 **F**1 3 6 12 16 23 26 30 35 37 40 44 45 47	13	10	S		73	1502	21	28.8	6	193	3699	1642	112
AIKEN—Aiken County													
★☐ HCA AIKEN REGIONAL MEDICAL CENTER (Formerly Aiken Community Hospital), 202 University Pkwy., Zip 29801; Mailing Address Drawer 1117, Zip 29802; tel. 803/642-0800; John E. Strickland, adm. **A**1a 2 9 10 **F**1 3 6 10 12 14 15 16 20 23 30 35 36 37 40 45 46 47 52 53; **S**1755	33	10	S		190	7523	120	63.3	23	495	22976	8303	471
ANDERSON—Anderson County													
★☐ ANDERSON MEMORIAL HOSPITAL, 800 N. Fant St., Zip 29621; tel. 803/261-1000; D. K. Oglesby Jr., pres. **A**1a 2 3 5 9 10 **F**1 2 3 6 7 8 9 10 11 12 14 15 16 23 24 26 27 28 30 32 33 34 35 37 40 41 42 45 46 47 52 53	23	10	S		438	18223	327	76.0	30	1831	52075	23976	1520
BAMBERG—Bamberg County													
★☐ BAMBERG COUNTY MEMORIAL HOSPITAL, North & McGee Sts., Zip 29003; tel. 803/245-4321; Charles V. Morgan, adm. (Total facility includes 22 beds in nursing home-type unit) **A**1a 9 10 **F**1 3 6 16 23 35 45 46; **S**0025	13	10	S	TF	81	2456	62	76.5	12	157	5560	2389	195
				H	59	2430	40	—	12	157	5094	2165	175
BARNWELL—Barnwell County													
BARNWELL COUNTY HOSPITAL, Reynolds & Wren Sts., Box 588, Zip 29812; tel. 803/259-3571; John R. Eckert, exec. dir. (Total facility includes 40 beds in nursing home-type unit) **A**9 10 **F**1 6 19 23 35 40; **S**5895	13	10	S	TF	93	1242	63	67.7	12	129	4154	1901	166
				H	53	1218	23	—	12	129	3308	1413	126
BEAUFORT—Beaufort County													
★☐ BEAUFORT MEMORIAL HOSPITAL (Formerly Beaufort County Memorial Hospital), Ribaut Rd., Drawer 1068, Zip 29901; tel. 803/524-3311; P. Jack Austin Jr., pres. **A**1a 9 10 **F**1 3 6 10 12 14 15 16 20 23 30 34 35 40 45 46 47; **S**2495	13	10	S		99	4787	57	57.6	15	1014	9479	4424	265
★☐ NAVAL HOSPITAL, Zip 29902; tel. 803/525-5301; Capt. Jeffery W. Baldwin MSC USN, CO **A**1a **F**1 3 6 14 23 28 32 33 34 35 36 40 45 46 47 48 49	43	10	S		59	3332	36	61.0	23	449	—	—	568
BENNETTSVILLE—Marlboro County													
★☐ MARLBORO PARK HOSPITAL, Box 738, Zip 29512; tel. 803/479-2881; Norman G. Rentz, adm. **A**1a 9 10 **F**1 2 3 6 10 14 15 16 23 26 30 35 40 44 45 46 47 52; **S**1755	33	10	S		111	2427	43	38.7	10	222	—	—	179
BISHOPVILLE—Lee County													
★☐ LEE COUNTY MEMORIAL HOSPITAL, 800 W. Church St., Box 528, Zip 29010; tel. 803/484-5313; A. Terry Dixon, dir. **A**1a 9 10 **F**1 3 6 14 15 19 35 37	13	10	S		51	1022	12	23.5	4	117	1928	871	61
CAMDEN—Kershaw County													
★☐ KERSHAW COUNTY MEMORIAL HOSPITAL, 1315 Roberts St., Zip 29020; tel. 803/432-4311; L. H. Young, adm. (Total facility includes 88 beds in nursing home-type unit) **A**1a 9 10 **F**3 6 10 12 15 16 19 23 33 35 40 44 45 46 52	13	10	S	TF	180	4545	149	82.8	16	413	11329	5674	430
				H	92	4504	62	—	16	413	9984	5051	368
CHARLESTON—Charleston County													
★☐ CHARLESTON MEMORIAL HOSPITAL, 326 Calhoun St., Zip 29401; tel. 803/577-0600; Lynn W. Beasley, adm.; Agnes E. Arnold, assoc. adm. **A**1a 3 5 9 10 **F**1 3 6 12 14 15 16 19 23 27 30 35 37 43 45 46 47	13	10	S		141	3689	91	64.5	0	0	13672	6158	397
★☐ MUSC MEDICAL CENTER OF MEDICAL UNIVERSITY OF SOUTH CAROLINA (Formerly Medical University Hospital of the Medical University of South Carolina), 171 Ashley Ave., Zip 29425; tel. 803/792-3131; William A. McLees PhD, exec. dir. **A**1a 2 3 5 8 9 10 **F**1 4 5 6 7 8 9 10 11 12 13 14 15 16 19 20 23 24 26 27 28 30 32 33 34 37 38 42 44 46 47 49 51 53 54	12	10	S		434	17384	340	78.3	30	3312	93519	43577	2216
★☐ NAVAL HOSPITAL, Zip 29408; tel. 803/743-5670; Capt. W. F. Miner MC USN, CO **A**1a 3 5 **F**1 2 3 6 10 11 12 14 15 16 23 24 26 27 28 29 30 32 33 34 35 37 40 47 48 49 52	43	10	S		232	9160	119	51.3	32	1456	46602	33858	1055
★☐ ROPER HOSPITAL, 316 Calhoun St., Zip 29401; tel. 803/724-2000; Austin Letson Jr., pres. & chief exec. off. **A**1a 3 5 9 10 **F**1 2 3 4 5 6 7 8 9 10 11 12 14 15 16 19 20 23 24 26 35 40 45 46 47 52 53 54	23	10	S		381	14167	292	76.6	24	1427	53058	26654	1415
☐ SOUTHERN PINES PSYCHIATRIC HOSPITAL, 2777 Speissegger, Zip 29406; tel. 803/747-5830; Daniel K. Morrisey, adm. **A**1b 10 **F**1 20 24 27 28 29 30 32 33 34 42 43; **S**0395	33	22	S		108	953	68	63.3	0	0	—	—	174
★☐ ST. FRANCIS XAVIER HOSPITAL, 135 Rutledge Ave., Zip 29401; tel. 803/577-1000; Douglas L. Fairfax, pres. **A**1a 9 10 **F**1 3 6 10 11 12 14 15 16 23 24 34 35 39 44 46 47 52 53; **S**5745	21	10	S		283	10421	224	74.2	26	1416	36360	16315	825
★☐ TRIDENT REGIONAL MEDICAL CENTER, 9330 Medical Plaza Dr., Zip 29418; tel. 803/797-7000; Frank J. DeMarco III, adm. **A**1a 9 10 **F**1 3 4 6 7 8 9 10 11 12 14 15 16 20 23 24 26 27 34 35 37 40 42 46 47 52 53 54; **S**1755	33	10	S		266	12304	221	83.1	20	1300	—	—	860
★☐ VETERANS ADMINISTRATION MEDICAL CENTER, 109 Bee St., Zip 29403; tel. 803/577-5011; Michael M. Linder, dir. **A**1a b 3 5 8 **F**1 2 3 4 6 10 12 14 15 16 19 20 23 24 26 27 28 33 34 35 42 44 46 47 49 54	45	10	S		280	6997	237	84.6	0	0	39148	24947	929
CHERAW—Chesterfield County													
★☐ CHESTERFIELD GENERAL HOSPITAL, Hwy. 9, Box 151, Zip 29520; tel. 803/537-7881; Jim Madory, adm. **A**1a 9 10 **F**1 3 6 10 14 15 16 19 23 26 27 29 30 35 37 40 45 46 47 50 52 53; **S**1755	33	10	S		72	2320	26	36.1	9	337	7556	2433	142
CHESTER—Chester County													
★☐ CHESTER COUNTY HOSPITAL, Great Falls Rd., Zip 29706; tel. 803/377-3151; Ron V. Hunter, adm. (Total facility includes 62 beds in nursing home-type unit) **A**1a 9 10 **F**1 3 6 10 12 14 15 16 19 23 35 45 46 47	23	10	S	TF	141	3194	111	78.7	16	375	8905	4137	366
				H	79	3157	49	—	16	375	8205	3644	314
CLINTON—Laurens County													
★☐ BAILEY MEMORIAL HOSPITAL, P O Box 976, Zip 29325; tel. 803/833-2550; Clem P. Ham, adm. (Total facility includes 43 beds in nursing home-type unit) **A**1a 10 **F**3 12 14 15 16 19 23 35 44 45 47 50	16	10	S	TF	111	1707	67	60.4	12	106	4799	2046	204
				H	68	1688	25	—	12	106	3977	1746	176
WHITTEN CENTER HOSPITAL, Whitten Center, Drawer 239, Zip 29325; tel. 803/833-2733; George Dellaportas, adm. **A**10 **F**15 20 23 24 30 33 42 44	12	12	S		26	373	16	59.9	0	0	2142	1568	64
COLUMBIA—Richland County													
★☐ BAPTIST MEDICAL CENTER, Taylor at Marion St., Zip 29220; tel. 803/771-5010; Charles D. Beaman Jr., pres. **A**1a 2 10 **F**1 2 3 6 7 8 9 10 11 12 14 15 16 19 21 23 24 27 28 29 30 32 33 34 35 39 40 42 45 46 47 51 52 53; **S**4155	21	10	S		475	18904	366	77.1	40	2484	63307	29686	1628

Hospital, Address, Telephone, Administrator, Approval and Facility Codes, Multihospital System Code	Classification Codes				Inpatient Data				Newborn Data		Expense (thousands of dollars)		
★ American Hospital Association (AHA) membership □ Joint Commission on Accreditation of Hospitals (JCAH) accreditation + American Osteopathic Hospital Association (AOHA) membership ○ American Osteopathic Association (AOA) accreditation Δ Commission on Accreditation of Rehabilitation Facilities (CARF) accreditation Control codes 61, 63, 64, 71, 72 and 73 indicate hospitals listed by AOHA, but not registered by AHA. For definition of numerical codes, see page A2	Control	Service	Stay	Facilities	Beds	Admissions	Census	Occupancy (percent)	Bassinets	Births	Total	Payroll	Personnel
CRAFTS-FARROW STATE HOSPITAL, 7901 Farrow Rd., Zip 29203; tel. 803/737-7171; L. Gregory Pearce Jr., dir. (Nonreporting) **A**9 10	12	22	L		875	—	—	—	—	—	—	—	—
MIDLANDS CENTER, 8301 Farrow Rd., Zip 29203; tel. 803/758-4677; H. R. Gudmundson MD, dir. **A**10 **F**1 16 23 24 26 29 33 34 35 38 42 43 44 46 47	12	12	S		34	316	14	41.2	0	0	1061	313	58
★□ PROVIDENCE HOSPITAL, 2435 Forest Dr., Zip 29204; tel. 803/256-5300; Sr. Mary Jacob, pres. **A**1a 9 10 **F**1 2 3 4 6 10 12 13 14 15 16 19 23 26 35 45 46 54; **S**5125	21	10	S		212	8412	166	78.3	0	0	40745	16128	735
★□ RICHLAND MEMORIAL HOSPITAL, Five Richland Medical Park, Zip 29203; tel. 803/765-7000; William L. Ivey, pres. **A**1a 2 3 5 9 10 **F**1 2 3 4 5 6 7 8 9 10 11 12 13 14 15 16 17 19 20 21 23 24 26 27 30 32 33 34 35 37 38 40 41 42 43 44 45 46 47 51 52 53 54	13	10	S		533	19434	450	84.4	40	2466	95046	45978	2200
□ SOUTH CAROLINA STATE HOSPITAL, 2100 Bull St., Box 119, Zip 29202; tel. 803/734-6520; Jaime E. Condom MD, dir. **A**1b 9 10 **F**15 24 30 32 33 42 44 45 46 47	12	22	L		967	3903	960	99.3	0	0	—	—	976
★□ WILLIAM JENNINGS BRYAN DORN VETERANS HOSPITAL, Zip 29201; tel. 803/776-4000; Joan S. Kershner, dir. (Total facility includes 120 beds in nursing home-type unit) **A**1a 2 3 5 **F**1 2 3 6 10 11 12 14 16 19 20 23 24 26 27 28 30 31 32 33 34 35 42 44 45 46 47 48 49 50 53	45	10	S	TF	580	10056	471	81.2	0	0	—	—	1266
				H	460	9884	359	—	0	0	—	—	1182
★□ WILLIAM S. HALL PSYCHIATRIC INSTITUTE, 1800 Colonial Dr., Box 202, Zip 29202; tel. 803/734-7111; Deborah A. Martin, adm. (Nonreporting) **A**1a 3 5 9 10	12	22	L		106	—	—	—	—	—	—	—	—
CONWAY—Horry County													
★□ CONWAY HOSPITAL, 300 Singleton Ridge Rd., Box 829, Zip 29526; tel. 803/347-7111; James S. Zoller, pres. & chief exec. off. **A**1a 9 10 **F**1 3 6 10 12 14 15 35 40 45 47 52 53	23	10	S		142	6348	90	66.2	17	788	17037	6631	400
DARLINGTON—Darlington County													
HUMANA HOSPITAL DARLINGTON, See Southland Medical Center													
★□ SOUTHLAND MEDICAL CENTER (Formerly Humana Hospital Darlington), 115 Medford Dr., Box 506, Zip 29532; tel. 803/393-4007; James B. Wood, adm. **A**1a 9 10 **F**1 3 6 10 11 14 15 16 35 45 46 47; **S**1375	33	10	S		76	1503	22	28.9	10	376	4462	1838	111
★□ WILSON CLINIC AND HOSPITAL, Hwy. 34 E., Box 510, Zip 29532; tel. 803/395-1100; Joseph P. Zager, adm. **A**1a 9 10 **F**1 6 14 15 16 35 37 40 47 53; **S**1755	33	10	S		72	2036	35	48.6	10	136	—	—	155
DILLON—Dillon County													
★□ ST. EUGENE COMMUNITY HOSPITAL, 301 E. Jackson St., Zip 29536; tel. 803/774-4111; Leo F. Childers Jr., exec. dir. **A**1a 9 10 **F**1 3 6 10 14 15 16 19 23 35 40 43 45 46 47 52 53; **S**5455	21	10	S		70	4445	58	82.9	11	279	8633	3905	251
EASLEY—Pickens County													
★□ BAPTIST MEDICAL CENTER EASLEY (Formerly Easley Baptist Hospital), Fleetwood Dr., Box 687, Zip 29641; tel. 803/859-6365; P. Sherman Hendricks, exec. vice-pres. **A**1a 9 10 **F**1 3 6 10 12 14 15 16 23 24 34 35 37 40 44 45 46 47 50 52 53; **S**4155	21	10	S		109	5098	64	58.7	12	568	13759	5676	280
EDGEFIELD—Edgefield County													
★□ EDGEFIELD COUNTY HOSPITAL, Bausket St., Box 590, Zip 29824; tel. 803/637-3174; Richard H. Satcher, adm. **A**1a 9 10 **F**1 6 14 15 16 23 26 35 37 40 45 46 50	13	10	S		59	891	17	28.8	6	58	2147	967	69
FAIRFAX—Allendale County													
★ ALLENDALE COUNTY HOSPITAL, Hwy. 278 W., Box 218, Zip 29827; tel. 803/632-3311; M. K. Hiatt, adm. (Total facility includes 44 beds in nursing home-type unit) **A**9 10 **F**19 35	13	10	S	TF	84	1313	58	69.0	6	104	—	—	141
				H	40	1281	15	—	6	104	—	—	103
FLORENCE—Florence County													
★□ BRUCE HOSPITAL SYSTEM (Formerly Bruce Hospital), 121 E. Cedar St., Zip 29501; tel. 803/664-3000; John W. McGinnis, pres. **A**1a 9 10 **F**1 2 3 6 10 12 14 15 16 34 35 41 43 46 47 48 53	23	10	S		153	6716	121	79.1	0	0	18371	8177	423
□ FLORENCE GENERAL HOSPITAL, 512 S. Irby St., Zip 29501; tel. 803/667-3200; Fred Schilling, pres. **A**1a 9 10 **F**1 3 5 6 10 12 14 15 16 19 20 30 34 35 40 43 46 47 52 53	23	10	S		187	4568	81	43.3	8	23	12890	5678	309
★□ MCLEOD REGIONAL MEDICAL CENTER, 555 E. Cheves St., Zip 29501; tel. 803/667-2000; J. Bruce Barragan, pres. & chief exec. off. **A**1a 2 3 5 9 10 **F**1 2 3 4 5 6 7 8 9 10 11 12 13 14 15 20 21 23 24 26 27 30 33 34 35 36 40 42 43 45 46 47 51 52 53 54	23	10	S		290	15256	229	75.2	20	2488	52759	21114	1288
FORT JACKSON—Richland County													
★□ MONCRIEF ARMY COMMUNITY HOSPITAL, P O Box 499, Zip 29207; tel. 803/751-2116; Col. James C. Connolly MC, CO; Col. William R. Hill MSC, deputy cmdr. admin **A**1a 2 **F**1 3 6 10 12 14 15 16 23 24 26 27 28 30 32 33 34 35 37 40 46 47 49 52	42	10	S		158	9533	122	77.2	7	433	41491	31323	880
GAFFNEY—Cherokee County													
□ CHEROKEE MEMORIAL HOSPITAL, 1420 N. Limestone St., Zip 29340; tel. 803/487-4271; Tim Moran, adm. **A**1a 9 10 **F**1 3 6 12 14 15 16 23 34 35 40 45 46 47 50 52; **S**3015	33	10	S		143	4560	66	46.2	15	323	11341	4349	245
GEORGETOWN—Georgetown County													
★□ GEORGETOWN MEMORIAL HOSPITAL, 606 Black River Rd., Drawer 1718, Zip 29442; tel. 803/527-1341; Paul D. Gatens, adm. **A**1a 9 10 **F**1 3 6 10 12 14 15 16 20 21 23 24 35 40 45 46 47 50 52 53; **S**1755	23	10	S		132	6135	102	77.3	12	708	16480	7863	369
GREENVILLE—Greenville County													
★□ GREENVILLE GENERAL HOSPITAL, 100 Mallard St., Zip 29601; Mailing Address 701 Grove Rd., Zip 29605; tel. 803/242-8689; Thomas E. Hassett III, vice-pres. **A**1a 9 10 **F**15 21 23 26 41 46; **S**1555	23	46	S		89	254	12	13.5	0	0	4225	2920	63
★□ Δ GREENVILLE MEMORIAL HOSPITAL (Includes Roger C. Peace Rehabilitation Hospital, 701 Grove Rd., Zip 29605; tel. 803/242-7700; John E. Pettett Jr., adm.), 701 Grove Rd., Zip 29605; tel. 803/242-7000; Frank D. Pinckney, adm. **A**1a 7 10 **F**1 2 3 4 5 6 7 8 9 10 11 12 14 15 16 20 23 24 25 26 28 29 30 32 33 34 35 36 37 40 42 43 45 46 51 52 53 54; **S**1555	23	10	S		712	30035	511	71.8	76	4711	112014	51200	2573
★□ MARSHALL I. PICKENS HOSPITAL, 701 Grove Rd., Zip 29605; tel. 803/242-7836; John E. Pettett Jr., adm. **A**1a 9 **F**15 24 28 29 30 32 33 34 42 43 45 46; **S**1555	23	22	S		90	1156	51	59.5	0	0	5788	3146	173
★□ SHRINERS HOSPITALS FOR CRIPPLED CHILDREN, 2100 N. Pleasantburg Dr., Zip 29609; tel. 803/244-4530; John R. Hetrick, adm. **A**1a 3 5 **F**15 23 24 26 34 42 45 46 47; **S**4125	23	57	S		62	937	41	66.1	0	0	—	—	152
★□ ST. FRANCIS HOSPITAL (Formerly St. Francis Community Hospital), One St. Francis Dr., Zip 29601; tel. 803/255-1000; Richard C. Neugent, pres. **A**1a 9 10 **F**1 2 3 6 10 12 14 15 16 19 20 23 24 26 34 35 42 45 46 53 54; **S**1485	23	10	S		214	10032	176	82.2	0	0	37799	15244	849
W. J. BARGE MEMORIAL HOSPITAL, Wade Hampton Blvd., Zip 29614; tel. 803/242-5100; William Brown, adm. **A**9 **F**1 15 16 23 34 35 43	23	11	S		79	2487	16	20.0	6	122	1105	362	32
GREENWOOD—Greenwood County													
★□ SELF MEMORIAL HOSPITAL, 1325 Spring St., Zip 29646; tel. 803/227-4111; J. L. Dozier Jr., pres. **A**1a 2 3 5 9 10 **F**1 2 3 6 7 8 9 10 11 12 14 15 16 19 20 21 23 24 27 29 30 34 35 40 41 42 44 45 46 47 51 52 53	23	10	S		315	12884	261	82.9	32	1764	37500	18814	1015

Hospital, Address, Telephone, Administrator, Approval and Facility Codes, Multihospital System Code	Classification Codes				Inpatient Data				Newborn Data		Expense (thousands of dollars)		
★ American Hospital Association (AHA) membership □ Joint Commission on Accreditation of Hospitals (JCAH) accreditation + American Osteopathic Hospital Association (AOHA) membership ○ American Osteopathic Association (AOA) accreditation Δ Commission on Accreditation of Rehabilitation Facilities (CARF) accreditation Control codes 61, 63, 64, 71, 72 and 73 indicate hospitals listed by AOHA, but not registered by AHA. For definition of numerical codes, see page A2	Control	Service	Stay	Facilities	Beds	Admissions	Census	Occupancy (percent)	Bassinets	Births	Total	Payroll	Personnel
GREER—Greenville County													
⊞ ALLEN BENNETT MEMORIAL HOSPITAL (Includes Roger Huntington Nursing Center), Box 1149, Zip 29652; tel. 803/879-0200; Michael W. Massey, adm. (Total facility includes 88 beds in nursing home-type unit) **A**1a 9 10 **F**1 6 14 15 16 23 35 37 45 46 47; **S**1555	23	10	S	TF H	174 86	3207 1593	122 41	70.1 —	13 13	288 288	9835 8169	4958 3823	276 198
□ BRIERWOOD HOSPITAL, 2700 E. Phillips Rd., Zip 29651; tel. 803/879-3402; Tommy R. Harris, adm. (Newly Registered) **A**1a 9 10	33	22	S		60	—	—	—	—	—	—	—	—
HARTSVILLE—Darlington County													
⊞ BYERLY HOSPITAL, 413 E. Carolina Ave., Zip 29550; tel. 803/332-6511; L. E. Dunman Jr., adm. **A**1a 9 10 **F**1 3 6 10 12 14 16 23 35 40 45 52; **S**1755	23	10	S		104	4265	62	59.6	10	222	9019	3835	245
HILTON HEAD ISLAND—Beaufort County													
⊞ HILTON HEAD HOSPITAL, P O Box 1117, Zip 29925; tel. 803/681-6122; Creighton E. Likes Jr., adm. **A**1a 9 10 **F**1 3 6 10 12 15 16 23 24 26 35 40 44 45 46 53; **S**1755	23	10	S		64	2972	35	54.7	6	220	10876	4135	208
JOHNS ISLAND—Charleston County													
⊞ NEW BEGINNINGS AT FENWICK HALL (Formerly Fenwick Hall Hospital), 1709 River Rd., Box 688, Zip 29455; tel. 803/559-2461; John H. Magill, exec. dir. **A**1b 9 **F**15 24 28 32 33 42 48; **S**1315	33	82	S		40	107	7	18.5	0	0	3723	1030	50
KINGSTREE—Williamsburg County													
□ WILLIAMSBURG COUNTY MEMORIAL HOSPITAL, 500 Nelson Blvd., Box 568, Zip 29556; tel. 803/354-9661; Francis G. Albarano Jr., adm. **A**1a 9 10 **F**1 6 10 12 14 15 16 23 26 34 35 37 40 45 47; **S**1755	13	10	S		60	2521	36	60.0	11	323	7354	3538	149
LADSON—Charleston County													
COASTAL CENTER, Jamison Rd., Zip 29456; tel. 803/873-5750; Erbert F. Cicenia, supt. (Nonreporting)	12	12	S		11	—	—	—	—	—	—	—	—
LAKE CITY—Florence County													
LOWER FLORENCE COUNTY HOSPITAL, U. S. Hwy. 52 N., Box 1035, Zip 29560; tel. 803/394-2036; Joseph N. James Jr., interim adm. **A**9 10 **F**1 6 14 16 34 35 43; **S**0025	16	10	S		72	1682	28	38.9	0	0	3593	1542	113
LANCASTER—Lancaster County													
⊞ ELLIOTT WHITE SPRINGS MEMORIAL HOSPITAL, 800 W. Meeting St., Zip 29720; tel. 803/286-1214; Dace W. Jones Jr., pres. (Total facility includes 111 beds in nursing home-type unit) **A**1a 9 10 **F**1 3 6 10 12 14 15 16 19 21 23 24 26 34 35 40 41 42 44 45 46 52 53	23	10	S	TF H	235 124	5160 5070	204 96	86.8 —	28 28	562 562	15532 13227	7294 5910	552 491
LAURENS—Laurens County													
⊞ LAURENS DISTRICT HOSPITAL, 420 Farley Ave., Zip 29360; tel. 803/984-4511; Clem P. Ham, adm. **A**1a 9 10 **F**1 6 14 15 16 19 23 33 34 35 41 43 44 45 47 53	16	10	S		47	1538	30	63.8	11	0	3622	1612	131
LOCKHART—Union County													
★ HOPE HOSPITAL, 20 N. Third St., Box 280, Zip 29364; tel. 803/545-6500; Mildred W. Purvis, adm. **F**15 19	13	10	S		16	203	6	37.5	0	0	445	205	11
LORIS—Horry County													
⊞ LORIS COMMUNITY HOSPITAL, 3212 Casey St., Zip 29569; tel. 803/756-4011; Frank M. Watts, adm. (Total facility includes 40 beds in nursing home-type unit) **A**1a 9 10 **F**1 3 6 10 12 14 16 17 19 23 35 40 45 47 52 53	16	10	S	TF H	145 105	3605 3566	92 53	63.4 —	10 10	304 304	9850 9067	3845 3391	274 —
MANNING—Clarendon County													
⊞ CLARENDON MEMORIAL HOSPITAL, 510 S. Mill St., Box 550, Zip 29102; tel. 803/435-8463; Charlie M. Horton, adm. **A**1a 9 10 **F**1 3 6 14 15 16 29 35 40 43 45; **S**0025	16	10	S		56	2145	35	62.5	16	283	5090	2455	175
MARION—Marion County													
□ ENGLISH PARK MEDICAL CENTER, 1305 N. Main St., Zip 29571; tel. 803/423-7945; Joyce Dudley, actg. exec. dir. (Nonreporting) **A**1a 10 **F**1 3 4 6 12 14 15 34 35 42; **S**9605	33	10	S		50	1313	21	41.0	8	188	—	—	94
⊞ MARION MEMORIAL HOSPITAL (Formerly Marion County Memorial Hospital), 1108 N. Main St., Box 1150, Zip 29571; tel. 803/423-3210; Bobby T. Phillips, adm. **A**1a 9 10 **F**1 3 6 14 15 16 19 23 35 46 47 53	16	10	S		63	3173	43	68.3	16	428	7770	3183	227
MOUNT PLEASANT—Charleston County													
★ AMI EAST COOPER COMMUNITY HOSPITAL (Formerly East Cooper Community Hospital), 1200 Hwy. 17 N., P O Box 128, Zip 29464; tel. 802/881-0100; Ronald J. Baker, pres. (Data for 234 days) **A**10 **F**1 3 6 15 16 23 30 34 35 37 50 53; **S**0125	33	10	S		70	1168	44	62.9	6	160	8715	2117	157
EAST COOPER COMMUNITY HOSPITAL, See AMI East Cooper Community Hospital													
MULLINS—Marion County													
⊞ MULLINS HOSPITAL, 518 S. Main St., Drawer 849, Zip 29574; tel. 803/464-8211; Margie Webster, adm. **A**1a 9 10 **F**1 3 6 10 12 14 16 19 23 35 46	16	10	S		80	3746	52	65.0	6	101	7083	2700	213
MYRTLE BEACH—Horry County													
⊞ HCA GRAND STRAND GENERAL HOSPITAL (Formerly Grand Strand General Hospital), 809 82nd Pkwy., Zip 29577; tel. 803/449-4411; Frank Ceruzzi, adm. **A**1a 9 10 **F**1 3 6 10 12 14 15 16 20 23 35 40 45 53; **S**1755	33	10	S		133	6750	92	69.2	19	1035	—	—	389
U. S. AIR FORCE HOSPITAL, See Myrtle Beach Air Force Base													
MYRTLE BEACH AIR FORCE BASE—Horry County													
U. S. AIR FORCE HOSPITAL, Zip 29577; tel. 803/238-7234; Maj. Gary W. Szwast, adm. (Nonreporting)	41	10	S		27	—	—	—	—	—	—	—	—
NEWBERRY—Newberry County													
⊞ NEWBERRY COUNTY MEMORIAL HOSPITAL, 2669 Kinard St., P O Box 497, Zip 29108; tel. 803/276-7570; Donnie J. Weeks, adm. **A**1a 9 10 **F**1 3 6 10 14 15 16 19 23 35 40 45 46 47; **S**1755	13	10	S		102	2908	46	45.1	9	370	7139	3007	195
NORTH CHARLESTON—Charleston County													
★ BAKER HOSPITAL, 2750 Speissegger Dr., Zip 29405; tel. 803/744-2110; Richard E. Hudson, adm. **A**10 **F**1 3 6 10 14 15 16 23 32 33 35 45 46 47 48 49 53; **S**0025	23	10	S		104	2234	57	54.8	0	0	10167	3301	192
ORANGEBURG—Orangeburg County													
⊞ ORANGEBURG-CALHOUN REGIONAL HOSPITAL (Formerly Orangeburg Regional Hospital), 3000 Saint Matthews Rd., Zip 29115; tel. 803/533-2200; H. Filmore Mabry, adm. **A**1a 2 6 9 10 **F**1 2 3 6 10 11 12 14 15 16 19 23 24 26 27 29 30 33 35 37 40 45 46 52 53 54	13	10	S		286	11297	207	72.4	19	1536	31813	13858	961
PICKENS—Pickens County													
⊞ CANNON MEMORIAL HOSPITAL, 515 Pendleton St., Box 188, Zip 29671; tel. 803/878-4791; James A. Uzzell, adm. **A**1a 9 10 **F**1 3 6 15 16 23 35 45	23	10	S		83	1632	27	32.5	0	0	5020	1872	127
RIDGELAND—Jasper County													
LIVE OAKS HOSPITAL, Hwy. 278, Drawer 400, Zip 29936; tel. 803/726-8111; William B. Sowell Jr., adm. **A**9 10 **F**6 7 10 14 15 16 24 34 42 45 46 50; **S**1935	33	10	S		46	952	21	45.7	0	0	2407	607	65
ROCK HILL—York County													
⊞ AMI PIEDMONT MEDICAL CENTER (Formerly Piedmont Medical Center), 222 S. Herlong Ave., Zip 29730; tel. 803/329-1234; Paul A. Walker, exec. dir. **A**1a 9 10 **F**1 2 3 6 10 12 14 15 16 19 23 27 30 32 33 35 40 45 46 52 53; **S**0125	33	10	S		273	10368	152	55.7	25	1680	30832	8976	600

★ American Hospital Association (AHA) membership
□ Joint Commission on Accreditation of Hospitals (JCAH) accreditation
+ American Osteopathic Hospital Association (AOHA) membership
○ American Osteopathic Association (AOA) accreditation
Δ Commission on Accreditation of Rehabilitation Facilities (CARF) accreditation
Control codes 61, 63, 64, 71, 72 and 73 indicate hospitals listed by AOHA, but not registered by AHA.
For definition of numerical codes, see page A2

Hospital, Address, Telephone, Administrator, Approval and Facility Codes, Multihospital System Code	Classification Codes				Inpatient Data				Newborn Data		Expense (thousands of dollars)		
	Control	Service	Stay	Facilities	Beds	Admissions	Census	Occupancy (percent)	Bassinets	Births	Total	Payroll	Personnel
SENECA—Oconee County													
★□ OCONEE MEMORIAL HOSPITAL (Includes Lila Doyle Nursing Care Facility), Hwy. 123, P O Box 858, Zip 29679; tel. 803/882-3351; W. H. Hudson, pres. **A**1a 9 10 **F**1 2 6 10 12 14 15 16 19 23 35 45 46 53	23	10	S		111	4586	83	74.8	20	521	13962	6700	421
SHAW AIR FORCE BASE—Sumter County													
□ U. S. AIR FORCE HOSPITAL SHAW, Zip 29152; tel. 803/668-2639; Lt. Col. Robert E. Shields MSC USAF, adm. **A**1a **F**1 3 6 12 14 15 33 34 35 37 40 46 47 52	41	10	S		40	2500	28	63.6	16	419	—	—	391
SIMPSONVILLE—Greenville County													
★□ HILLCREST HOSPITAL, Box 279, Zip 29681; tel. 803/967-6100; Jack A. Macauley, adm. **A**1a 9 10 **F**1 2 3 6 12 14 15 16 23 35 37 40 45 46 52; **S**1555	23	10	S		56	1650	26	46.4	10	197	5473	2773	137
SPARTANBURG—Spartanburg County													
★□ AMI DOCTORS MEMORIAL HOSPITAL (Formerly Doctors Memorial Hospital), 389 Serpentine Dr., Zip 29303; tel. 803/585-8781; Rodney L. Helms, exec. dir. **A**1a 10 **F**1 3 6 12 14 15 16 23 26 50 53; **S**0125	33	10	S		104	2689	38	36.5	0	0	7732	2639	193
DOCTORS MEMORIAL HOSPITAL, See AMI Doctors Memorial Hospital													
★□ MARY BLACK MEMORIAL HOSPITAL, 1700 Skylyn Dr., Zip 29303; Mailing Address Box 3217, Zip 29304; tel. 803/573-3000; Gerald W. Landis, pres. **A**1a 9 10 **F**1 3 6 10 12 14 15 16 23 35 40 45 46 47 53; **S**1755	23	10	S		165	7510	118	71.5	23	949	20294	8153	467
SPARTANBURG GENERAL HOSPITAL, See Spartanburg Regional Medical Center													
★□ SPARTANBURG REGIONAL MEDICAL CENTER (Formerly Spartanburg General Hospital), 101 E. Wood St., Zip 29303; tel. 803/591-6000; Charles C. Boone, pres. **A**1a 2 3 5 9 10 **F**1 2 3 4 5 6 7 8 9 10 11 12 13 14 15 16 19 21 23 24 27 30 32 33 34 35 37 40 41 42 44 45 46 47 51 52 53 54; **S**4195	13	10	S		526	20389	432	82.1	36	2180	75713	35655	2112
SUMTER—Sumter County													
★□ TUOMEY HOSPITAL, 129 N. Washington St., Zip 29150; tel. 803/775-1171; Louis H. Bremer Jr., adm. **A**1a 9 10 **F**1 3 6 10 12 14 16 20 23 24 27 30 32 33 34 35 40 44 46 47 52 53; **S**1755	23	10	S		206	9028	185	89.8	26	1486	26288	10469	668
TRAVELERS REST—Greenville County													
★□ NORTH GREENVILLE HOSPITAL, 807 N. Main St., Zip 29690; tel. 803/834-5131; John Smith, adm. **A**1a 9 10 **F**15 45 46 49; **S**1555	23	82	S		53	527	37	77.1	0	0	2975	1239	85
UNION—Union County													
★□ WALLACE THOMSON HOSPITAL, 322 W. South St., Box 789, Zip 29379; tel. 803/427-0351; Elwood R. Eason, adm. **A**1a 9 10 **F**1 3 6 14 16 23 24 35 45 46 47 53	16	10	S		92	2813	56	59.6	14	267	8430	3359	263
VARNVILLE—Hampton County													
★ HAMPTON GENERAL HOSPITAL, 503 Carolina Ave. W., P O Box 338, Zip 29944; tel. 803/943-2771; Athalene B. Mole, adm. (Total facility includes 44 beds in nursing home-type unit) **A**9 10 **F**14 16 35 50	13	10	S	TF	112	1603	62	55.8	14	179	3067	1399	115
				H	68	1593	19	—	14	179	2447	1094	88
WALTERBORO—Colleton County													
★□ COLLETON REGIONAL HOSPITAL, 501 Robertson Blvd., Zip 29488; tel. 803/549-6371; Donald H. Caldwell, adm. **A**1a 9 10 **F**1 2 3 6 10 12 14 15 16 35 40 46 47 52; **S**1755	33	10	S		145	3352	56	38.6	12	365	11386	3954	262
WEST COLUMBIA—Lexington County													
★□ CHARTER RIVERS HOSPITAL, 2900 Sunset Blvd., P O Box 4116, Zip 29169; tel. 803/796-9911; John R. Reedy, exec. dir. (Nonreporting) **A**1a 10; **S**0695	33	22	S		80	—	—	—	—	—	—	—	—
★□ LEXINGTON COUNTY HOSPITAL, 2720 Sunset Blvd., Zip 29169; tel. 803/791-2000; George I. Rentz, pres. **A**1a 9 10 **F**1 2 3 6 10 12 14 15 16 19 23 35 37 40 43 45 46 47 52 53	13	10	S		258	14137	233	84.1	41	2059	46182	20627	999
WINNSBORO—Fairfield County													
★□ FAIRFIELD MEMORIAL HOSPITAL, 321 By-Pass, Box 620, Zip 29180; tel. 803/635-5548; Charles B. Chapman, adm. **A**1a 9 10 **F**1 6 14 16 35 45 46 47	13	10	S		33	901	13	37.1	10	33	3290	1678	110
WOODRUFF—Spartanburg County													
★ B. J. WORKMAN MEMORIAL HOSPITAL, 751 E. Georgia St., P O Box 699, Zip 29388; tel. 803/476-8122; C. Milton Snipes, adm. **A**9 10 **F**1 12 14 23 35 45; **S**4195	13	10	S		54	908	18	33.3	0	0	2599	1159	63
YORK—York County													
★□ DIVINE SAVIOUR HOSPITAL, 111 S. Congress St., Box 629, Zip 29745; tel. 803/684-4231; John W. Bailey, adm. (Total facility includes 51 beds in nursing home-type unit) **A**1a 9 10 **F**1 6 14 15 19 35 42 45 47; **S**5745	21	10	S	TF	102	1103	67	65.7	6	6	3820	1520	154
				H	51	1057	17	—	6	6	2650	1022	114

Hospital, Address, Telephone, Administrator, Approval and Facility Codes, Multihospital System Code	Classification Codes: Control	Service	Stay	Facilities	Inpatient Data: Beds	Admissions	Census	Occupancy (percent)	Newborn Data: Bassinets	Births	Expense (thousands of dollars): Total	Payroll	Personnel
★ American Hospital Association (AHA) membership □ Joint Commission on Accreditation of Hospitals (JCAH) accreditation + American Osteopathic Hospital Association (AOHA) membership ○ American Osteopathic Association (AOA) accreditation Δ Commission on Accreditation of Rehabilitation Facilities (CARF) accreditation Control codes 61, 63, 64, 71, 72 and 73 indicate hospitals listed by AOHA, but not registered by AHA. For definition of numerical codes, see page A2													

South Dakota

Hospital	Control	Service	Stay	Facilities	Beds	Admissions	Census	Occupancy (percent)	Bassinets	Births	Total	Payroll	Personnel
ABERDEEN—Brown County													
★□ DAKOTA MIDLAND HOSPITAL, 1400 15th Ave. N.W., Zip 57401; tel. 605/622-3300; Philo Hall, exec. vice-pres. **A**1a 9 10 **F**1 3 5 6 7 8 10 11 12 14 15 16 21 23 27 28 30 32 33 34 35 36 40 41 44 45 46 48 49 51 52 53; **S**6235	23	10	S		132	3418	54	40.9	9	218	11946	4983	256
★□ ST. LUKE'S HOSPITAL, 305 S. State St., Zip 57401; tel. 605/229-3230; Dale J. Stein, exec. dir. **A**1a 2 9 10 **F**1 3 5 6 10 12 14 15 16 20 23 24 26 27 28 30 32 33 34 35 36 37 39 40 41 42 43 44 45 46 52 53; **S**5255	21	10	S		160	6364	93	58.1	20	563	20415	9909	525
ARMOUR—Douglas County													
★ DOUGLAS COUNTY MEMORIAL HOSPITAL, Box 160, Zip 57313; tel. 605/724-2159; Judy McCarthy, adm. **A**9 10 **F**1 34 35 36 42 45 52	13	10	S		16	241	5	31.3	4	36	554	297	23
BELLE FOURCHE—Butte County													
BELLE FOURCHE HEALTH CARE CENTER, 2200 13th Ave., Zip 57717; tel. 605/892-3331; Larry Potter, adm. (Total facility includes 100 beds in nursing home-type unit) **A**9 10 **F**1 3 5 6 10 15 16 19 23 33 35 37 40 41 43 45 46; **S**3165	23	10	S	TF	130	1032	100	76.9	4	98	3743	1866	133
				H	30	910	8	—	4	98	2066	1013	57
BOWDLE—Edmunds County													
★ BOWDLE HOSPITAL, P O Box 556, Zip 57428; tel. 605/285-6146; Edward G. Leake, adm. **A**9 10 **F**1 6 14 34 35 45	33	10	S		20	169	2	10.0	4	2	782	237	20
BRITTON—Marshall County													
□ MARSHALL COUNTY MEMORIAL HOSPITAL, 413 Ninth St., Box 230, Zip 57430; tel. 605/448-2253; Gerald Huss, adm. **A**1a 9 10 **F**6 14 35 40; **S**5255	13	10	S		38	531	7	18.4	9	35	1006	442	34
BROOKINGS—Brookings County													
★□ BROOKINGS HOSPITAL, 300 22nd Ave., Zip 57006; tel. 605/692-6351; David B. Johnson, adm. (Total facility includes 79 beds in nursing home-type unit) **A**1a 9 10 **F**1 3 6 10 12 14 16 19 23 24 26 33 35 36 40 41 45 47	14	10	S	TF	140	2112	105	75.0	11	321	6066	3546	182
				H	61	2082	27	—	11	321	4700	2654	138
BURKE—Gregory County													
COMMUNITY MEMORIAL HOSPITAL, Box 319, Zip 57523; tel. 605/775-2621; Michael G. Peterson, adm. **A**9 10 **F**14 35 40 45 52	23	10	S		25	442	11	44.0	6	45	555	312	21
CANTON—Lincoln County													
★ CANTON-INWOOD MEMORIAL HOSPITAL, Hiawatha Dr., Drawer 39, Zip 57013; tel. 605/987-2621; John Devick, adm. **A**9 10 **F**1 2 3 16 23 34 35 36 45 46	23	10	S		28	579	12	42.9	5	27	1083	531	42
CHAMBERLAIN—Brule County													
★ MID DAKOTA HOSPITAL, S. Byron Blvd., Box 307, Zip 57325; tel. 605/734-5511; Donald B. Naiberk, chief exec. off. **A**9 10 **F**1 3 6 14 15 16 34 35 36 45 52	23	10	S		54	1750	18	33.3	6	135	3613	1575	95
CLEAR LAKE—Deuel County													
★ DEUEL COUNTY MEMORIAL HOSPITAL, 701 Third Ave. S., Zip 57226; tel. 605/874-2141; Bruce L. Davidson, adm. **A**9 10 **F**1 15 16 34 35 36 41 43 45 47 50; **S**2235	23	10	S		20	303	4	20.0	4	22	806	436	28
CUSTER—Custer County													
CUSTER COMMUNITY HOSPITAL, 1039 Montgomery St., Zip 57730; tel. 605/673-2229; Stephen G. Amundson, exec. dir. **A**9 10 **F**1 6 10 14 15 23 34 35 36 37 42 45 46 47 50	33	10	S		16	607	9	56.3	4	50	3429	1055	51
DE SMET—Kingsbury County													
DE SMET MEMORIAL HOSPITAL, 306 Prairie Ave. S.W., Zip 57231; tel. 605/854-3329; Dennis J. Muser, adm. **A**9 10 **F**1 6 14 16 35 40 43 45 53	14	10	S		17	445	5	29.4	6	35	644	363	29
DEADWOOD—Lawrence County													
★ NORTHERN HILLS GENERAL HOSPITAL, 61 Charles St., Zip 57732; tel. 605/578-2313; Donald E. Thrall, pres. **A**9 10 **F**1 6 12 15 16 23 35 36 43 45 46 50	23	10	S		39	1372	16	41.0	6	151	3471	1570	100
DELL RAPIDS—Minnehaha County													
DELL RAPIDS COMMUNITY HOSPITAL, 909 N. Iowa St., Zip 57022; tel. 605/428-5431; Jeff Dahl, adm. **A**9 10 **F**1 3 6 15 16 23 24 34 35 44 45 46	23	10	S		29	854	12	41.4	4	82	1512	779	55
EAGLE BUTTE—Dewey County													
★ U. S. PUBLIC HEALTH SERVICE INDIAN HOSPITAL, Zip 57625; tel. 605/964-2811; Arlene M. Marshall, adm. **A**10 **F**6 14 15 34 35 36 37 40 52	47	10	S		26	881	6	23.1	5	112	1935	1161	49
ELLSWORTH AIR FORCE BASE—Meade County													
U. S. AIR FORCE HOSPITAL, Zip 57706; tel. 605/399-3201; Lt. Col. Roland J. Carroll Jr., adm. (Nonreporting)	41	10	S		35	—	—	—	—	—	—	—	—
EUREKA—McPherson County													
EUREKA COMMUNITY HOSPITAL, East Ave. & Ninth St., Zip 57437; tel. 605/284-2661; Walter R. Dohn, adm. **A**9 10 **F**2 10 14 16 30 34 35 40 45 50 52	23	10	S		25	649	8	32.0	3	34	798	376	30
FAULKTON—Faulk County													
FAULK COUNTY MEMORIAL HOSPITAL, P O Box 100, Zip 57438; tel. 605/598-6262; Gerald Huss, adm. **A**9 10 **F**1 6 16 35 40 45 52; **S**5255	13	10	S		32	359	4	11.8	6	17	816	390	28
FLANDREAU—Moody County													
FLANDREAU MUNICIPAL HOSPITAL, 214 N. Prairie Ave., Zip 57028; tel. 605/997-2433; Orlo Bjerk, adm. **A**9 10 **F**1 6 14 15 16 23 29 34 35 36 37 40 43 45 50 52	14	10	S		20	398	4	20.0	5	37	727	378	27
FORT MEADE—Meade County													
★□ VETERANS ADMINISTRATION MEDICAL CENTER, Zip 57741; tel. 605/347-2511; Carl J. Gerber MD, dir. **A**1a **F**1 3 6 15 16 19 23 24 26 27 28 30 31 32 33 34 42 44 46 47 48 49 50	45	10	L		349	3290	279	88.0	0	0	23535	14121	553
FREEMAN—Hutchinson County													
★ FREEMAN COMMUNITY HOSPITAL, 510 E. Eighth St., P O Box 370, Zip 57029; tel. 605/925-4231; Larry Ravenberg, adm. (Total facility includes 59 beds in nursing home-type unit) **A**9 10 **F**1 3 14 16 19 23 34 35 36 37 40 41 44 45 46	23	10	S	TF	83	568	65	77.4	8	41	1753	985	75
				H	24	522	8	—	8	41	827	413	32
GETTYSBURG—Potter County													
★ GETTYSBURG MEMORIAL HOSPITAL, 606 E. Garfield, Zip 57442; tel. 605/765-2488; Arthur C. Quance, adm. **A**9 10 **F**1 6 16 35 40 41 45 52; **S**5175	21	10	S		28	609	9	32.1	4	35	1337	695	41
GREGORY—Gregory County													
★ GREGORY COMMUNITY HOSPITAL, 400 Park St., Box 408, Zip 57533; tel. 605/835-8394; Terry E. Davis, adm. (Total facility includes 58 beds in nursing home-type unit) **A**9 10 **F**1 2 15 19 23 35 41 45; **S**2235	23	10	S	TF	90	790	67	74.4	7	58	2709	1306	91
				H	32	783	10	—	7	58	1767	750	45

Hospital, Address, Telephone, Administrator, Approval and Facility Codes, Multihospital System Code	Classification Codes				Inpatient Data				Newborn Data		Expense (thousands of dollars)		
★ American Hospital Association (AHA) membership ☐ Joint Commission on Accreditation of Hospitals (JCAH) accreditation + American Osteopathic Hospital Association (AOHA) membership ○ American Osteopathic Association (AOA) accreditation Δ Commission on Accreditation of Rehabilitation Facilities (CARF) accreditation Control codes 61, 63, 64, 71, 72 and 73 indicate hospitals listed by AOHA, but not registered by AHA. For definition of numerical codes, see page A2	Control	Service	Stay	Facilities	Beds	Admissions	Census	Occupancy (percent)	Bassinets	Births	Total	Payroll	Personnel
HOT SPRINGS—Fall River County													
★ SOUTHERN HILLS GENERAL HOSPITAL (Includes Lutheran Nursing Home), 209 N. 16th St., Zip 57747; tel. 605/745-3159; Ronald J. Cork, adm. (Total facility includes 48 beds in nursing home-type unit) **A**9 10 **F**1 3 6 14 16 19 23 35 36 40 43 44 45; **S**2235	23	10	S	TF	74	859	49	66.2	6	82	2335	1133	66
				H	26	817	8	—	6	82	1720	778	49
⊞ VETERANS ADMINISTRATION MEDICAL CENTER, Zip 57747; tel. 605/745-4101; James S. Exparza, dir. **A**1a b **F**1 3 6 10 12 14 15 16 19 20 23 24 26 27 28 29 30 32 33 34 35 42 44 45 46 47 48 49 50	45	10	S		232	3527	145	62.5	0	0	22071	12545	494
HOVEN—Potter County													
★ HOLY INFANT HOSPITAL, Main St., Zip 57450; tel. 605/948-2262; Thomas Earl Brown, adm. **A**9 10 **F**1 14 15 16 30 34 35 37 40 43 45 52; **S**5255	23	10	S		30	199	3	10.0	4	15	864	380	30
HURON—Beadle County													
⊞ HURON REGIONAL MEDICAL CENTER, Fourth & Iowa Sts. S.E., Zip 57350; tel. 605/352-6431; Richard C. Sommer, adm. **A**1a 9 10 **F**1 3 6 10 12 14 15 16 20 21 23 24 26 30 34 35 36 37 40 41 43 44 45 46 47 52 53; **S**1755	23	10	S		118	3385	48	40.7	10	365	8522	3777	207
IPSWICH—Edmunds County													
★ IPSWICH COMMUNITY HOSPITAL, 507 Bloemendaal Dr., Box 326, Zip 57451; tel. 605/426-6011; Ken Trammell, adm. **A**9 10 **F**35 45; **S**6235	23	10	S		21	637	11	52.4	4	48	1095	477	25
LAKE PRESTON—Kingsbury County													
KINGSBURY COUNTY MEMORIAL HOSPITAL, Fourth & Manor Ave., Zip 57249; tel. 605/847-4451; Robert Houser, adm. (Total facility includes 65 beds in nursing home-type unit) **A**9 10 **F**1 3 6 14 15 16 19 23 34 35 36 37 41 43 44 45 50; **S**3165	23	10	S	TF	86	586	62	72.1	4	29	2209	1071	87
				H	21	527	6	—	4	29	1361	581	44
LEMMON—Perkins County													
⊞ FIVE COUNTIES HOSPITAL, 401 Sixth Ave. W., Box 479, Zip 57638; tel. 605/374-3871; James Hubbard, adm. (Total facility includes 32 beds in nursing home-type unit) **A**1a 9 10 **F**19 23 35 43 45	23	10	S	TF	58	248	43	74.1	0	0	1137	596	54
				H	26	241	11	—	0	0	614	382	36
MADISON—Lake County													
⊞ MADISON COMMUNITY HOSPITAL, 917 N. Washington Ave., Zip 57042; tel. 605/256-6551; Robert D. Kroese, adm. & chief exec. off. **A**1a 9 10 **F**1 3 6 15 16 23 35 36 37 40 41 44 45	23	10	S		49	1244	17	34.7	8	142	2347	1354	82
MARTIN—Bennett County													
BENNETT COUNTY COMMUNITY HOSPITAL, Merriman Star Rte., P O Box 70, Zip 57551; tel. 605/685-6622; Tom E. Bland, adm. (Total facility includes 50 beds in nursing home-type unit) **A**9 10 **F**14 19 23 35 40 45 46 52	13	10	S	TF	70	465	45	64.3	4	29	1523	772	75
				H	20	426	5	—	4	29	834	416	42
MILBANK—Grant County													
⊞ ST. BERNARD'S PROVIDENCE HOSPITAL (Includes St. William Home for the Aged), 901 E. Virgil Ave., Box 432, Zip 57252; tel. 605/432-4538; Sr. Margaret Mary Vogel, adm. (Total facility includes 80 beds in nursing home-type unit) **A**1a 9 10 **F**1 12 15 16 19 23 34 35 40 45 50 52	23	10	S	TF	115	677	83	72.2	5	72	2643	1209	111
				H	35	666	8	—	5	72	1400	717	54
MILLER—Hand County													
HAND COUNTY MEMORIAL HOSPITAL, 423 W. Second Ave., Box 22, Zip 57362; tel. 605/853-2421; Jon Clegg, actg. adm. **A**9 10 **F**1 3 6 12 14 16 23 34 35 36 40 45 46 50	23	10	S		30	668	8	26.7	6	42	1073	572	47
MITCHELL—Davison County													
⊞ METHODIST HOSPITAL, 909 S. Miller St., Zip 57301; tel. 605/996-5627; Willis Bultje, adm. **A**1a 9 10 **F**1 3 6 10 12 13 14 15 16 23 26 29 30 32 33 34 35 36 37 40 41 43 44 45 52; **S**1755	21	10	S		80	1666	25	31.3	6	130	5830	2431	132
⊞ ST. JOSEPH HOSPITAL, Fifth & Foster, Zip 57301; tel. 605/996-6531; Fred Slunecka, exec. dir. **A**1a 9 10 **F**1 3 6 12 14 15 16 21 23 34 35 36 40 41 45 46 47 52 53; **S**5255	21	10	S		120	2715	41	34.2	16	300	8474	3990	189
MOBRIDGE—Walworth County													
⊞ MOBRIDGE REGIONAL HOSPITAL (Formerly Mobridge Community Hospital), P O Box 580, Zip 57601; tel. 605/845-3693; Howard Bergman, adm. **A**1a 9 10 **F**1 3 6 10 15 16 23 35 40 41 45 52	23	10	S		46	1688	21	45.7	7	140	2783	1561	84
PARKSTON—Hutchinson County													
★ ST. BENEDICT HOSPITAL, Glynn Dr., P O Box B, Zip 57366; tel. 605/928-3311; Gale Walker, adm. **A**9 10 **F**1 3 10 12 16 23 26 35 40 52; **S**1635	21	10	S		30	629	10	33.3	8	91	1160	546	39
PHILIP—Haakon County													
HANS P. PETERSON MEMORIAL HOSPITAL, 603 W. Pine, P O Box 790, Zip 57567; tel. 605/859-2511; Gerald E. Carl, chief exec. off.; E. Jeanne Hunt, asst. adm. (Total facility includes 30 beds in nursing home-type unit) **A**9 10 **F**1 14 19 23 35 45	23	10	S	TF	50	354	35	70.0	5	25	1293	587	42
				H	20	338	6	—	5	25	938	435	23
PIERRE—Hughes County													
⊞ ST. MARY'S HOSPITAL, 800 E. Dakota Ave., Zip 57501; tel. 605/224-3100; James D. M. Russell, adm. **A**1a 9 10 **F**1 3 6 10 14 15 16 20 23 35 36 40 41 45 47 52 53; **S**5175	23	10	S		86	3487	41	47.7	20	436	8645	4258	231
PINE RIDGE—Shannon County													
⊞ U. S. PUBLIC HEALTH SERVICE INDIAN HOSPITAL, Zip 57770; tel. 605/867-5131; W. J. Gobert, serv. unit dir. **A**1a 10 **F**1 6 14 15 28 32 34 35 36 37 40 41 47 49 52	47	10	S		58	3106	29	50.0	13	421	5777	3123	208
PLATTE—Charles Mix County													
★ PLATTE COMMUNITY MEMORIAL HOSPITAL, 609 E. Seventh, P O Box 891, Zip 57369; tel. 605/337-3364; Patricia Biddle RN, adm. (Total facility includes 48 beds in nursing home-type unit) **A**9 10 **F**1 2 6 14 15 16 19 23 34 35 43 45 46 50	23	10	S	TF	69	322	58	81.7	6	57	1112	632	46
				H	21	310	11	—	6	57	—	316	23
RAPID CITY—Pennington County													
Δ BLACK HILLS REHABILITATION HOSPITAL, 2908 Fifth St., Zip 57701; tel. 605/343-8500; Melvin J. Platt, sr. vice-pres. & chief oper. off. (Total facility includes 47 beds in nursing home-type unit) **A**7 10 **F**15 16 19 23 24 26 34 42 44 46; **S**8495	23	46	S	TF	98	805	46	46.9	0	0	3998	1852	97
				H	51	784	37	—	0	0	3639	1751	—
⊞ RAPID CITY REGIONAL HOSPITAL (Includes Rapid City Regional Hospital-Main, 353 Fairmont Blvd., Zip 57701; Rapid City Regional Hospital-West, 915 Mountain View Rd., Zip 57701), Mailing Address P O Box 6000, Zip 57709; tel. 605/341-1000; Adil Ameer, sr. exec. vice-pres. **A**1a 2 6 9 10 **F**1 3 6 7 9 10 11 12 14 15 16 20 21 23 24 27 30 31 34 35 36 40 41 45 46 47 49 51 52 53; **S**8495	23	10	S		299	13260	189	63.2	28	1518	39230	15789	774
★ U. S. PUBLIC HEALTH SERVICE INDIAN HOSPITAL, 3200 Canyon Lake Dr., Zip 57702; tel. 605/348-1900 **A**10 **F**8 15 27 28 29 30 32 34 35 37 43 46 50 52	47	10	S		40	1043	21	52.5	0	0	4161	2745	124
REDFIELD—Spink County													
★ COMMUNITY MEMORIAL HOSPITAL, 110 W. Tenth Ave., Zip 57469; tel. 605/472-1111; Laurel E. Winjum, adm. **A**9 10 **F**1 3 8 16 17 34 35 43 45 46 50 52	14	10	S		44	788	16	36.4	6	20	1581	570	55
ROSEBUD—Todd County													
★ U. S. PUBLIC HEALTH SERVICE INDIAN HOSPITAL, Zip 57570; tel. 605/747-2231; W. J. Gobert, health syst adm.; Marilyn Hogan, adm. off. **A**10 **F**6 12 14 15 34 35 36 37 40 41 52	47	10	S		29	1959	15	51.7	8	185	3472	2036	103

★ American Hospital Association (AHA) membership
□ Joint Commission on Accreditation of Hospitals (JCAH) accreditation
+ American Osteopathic Hospital Association (AOHA) membership
○ American Osteopathic Association (AOA) accreditation
Δ Commission on Accreditation of Rehabilitation Facilities (CARF) accreditation
Control codes 61, 63, 64, 71, 72 and 73 indicate hospitals listed by AOHA, but not registered by AHA.
For definition of numerical codes, see page A2

Hospital, Address, Telephone, Administrator, Approval and Facility Codes, Multihospital System Code	Classification Codes				Inpatient Data				Newborn Data		Expense (thousands of dollars)		
	Control	Service	Stay	Facilities	Beds	Admissions	Census	Occupancy (percent)	Bassinets	Births	Total	Payroll	Personnel
SCOTLAND—Bon Homme County													
★ LANDMANN-JUNGMAN MEMORIAL HOSPITAL, 600 Billars St., P O Box 307, Zip 57059; tel. 605/583-2226; Michael B. Peterson, adm. **A**9 10 **F**1 14 15 23 35 37 44	23	10	S		23	652	10	43.5	3	17	1265	717	41
SIOUX FALLS—Minnehaha County													
CRIPPLED CHILDRENS HOSPITAL AND SCHOOL, 2501 W. 26th St., Zip 57105; tel. 605/336-1840; Gaylen Holmes, pres. **F**15 23 24 26 41 44 45 46	23	56	L		96	23	96	99.0	0	0	3292	1776	158
⊞ MCKENNAN HOSPITAL, 800 E. 21st St., Zip 57101; tel. 605/339-8000; Roger C. Paavola, exec. dir. **A**1a 3 5 9 10 **F**1 2 3 5 6 9 10 11 12 14 15 16 20 21 22 23 24 25 26 27 28 29 30 32 33 34 35 36 40 41 42 43 44 45 46 47 50 52 53; **S**5255	21	10	S		401	11874	247	61.6	25	867	49203	20806	1043
⊞ ROYAL C. JOHNSON VETERANS MEMORIAL HOSPITAL, 2501 W. 22nd St., P O Box 5046, Zip 57117; tel. 605/333-6847; Dexter D. Dix, dir. (Total facility includes 75 beds in nursing home-type unit) **A**1a 3 5 **F**1 3 6 10 12 15 16 19 20 23 24 26 27 28 30 31 33 34 35 42 44 46 47 49	45	10	S	TF	321	4469	217	67.6	0	0	30379	14467	597
				H	246	4255	146	—	0	0	—	—	569
⊞ SIOUX VALLEY HOSPITAL, 1100 S. Euclid Ave., P O Box 5039, Zip 57117; tel. 605/333-1000; Lyle E. Schroeder, pres. **A**1a 2 3 5 9 10 **F**1 2 3 4 5 6 9 10 12 13 14 15 16 20 23 24 26 30 33 34 35 36 37 38 40 43 44 45 46 47 52 53 54	23	10	S		456	17921	336	73.7	36	1916	70775	35079	1857
SISSETON—Roberts County													
★ COTEAU DES PRAIRIES HOSPITAL, 205 Orchard Dr., Zip 57262; tel. 605/698-7647; Delano Christianson, adm. **A**9 10 **F**1 3 14 15 16 34 35 37 45	23	10	S		31	710	8	25.8	6	81	1119	578	39
★ U. S. PUBLIC HEALTH SERVICE INDIAN HOSPITAL, Chestnut St., Zip 57262; tel. 605/698-7606; Daryl D. Russell, adm. **A**10 **F**6 12 14 15 34 35 37 40 52	47	10	S		20	590	6	30.0	5	47	1687	1068	54
SPEARFISH—Lawrence County													
★ LOOKOUT MEMORIAL HOSPITAL, 1440 N. Main St., Zip 57783; tel. 605/642-2617; Glenn Bryant, adm. **A**9 10 **F**1 2 6 15 16 23 35 36 40 45 49 52; **S**2235	23	10	S		35	1317	14	40.0	6	220	2950	1313	82
STURGIS—Meade County													
★ COMMUNITY MEMORIAL HOSPITAL, 2100 Davenport St., P O Box 279, Zip 57785; tel. 605/347-2536; Michael M. Penticoff, adm. (Total facility includes 84 beds in nursing home-type unit) **A**9 10 **F**1 3 6 11 14 16 19 23 26 35 41 44 45; **S**3165	23	10	S	TF	121	1368	98	81.0	9	96	3726	2002	141
				H	37	1312	15	—	9	96	2219	1151	67
TYNDALL—Bon Homme County													
★ ST. MICHAEL'S HOSPITAL, Third St. & Broadway, Box 27, Zip 57066; tel. 605/589-3341; Gale N. Walker, chief exec. off. (Total facility includes 9 beds in nursing home-type unit) **A**9 10 **F**2 16 19 35 40 45; **S**1635	21	10	S	TF	34	559	17	50.0	6	33	1036	543	30
				H	25	519	9	—	6	33	819	467	20
VERMILLION—Clay County													
★ DAKOTA HOSPITAL, 801 E. Main St., P O Box 316, Zip 57069; tel. 605/624-2611; Bill D. Wilson, chief exec. off. **A**9 10 **F**1 2 6 14 15 16 23 34 35 36 37 40 41 44 45 50 52; **S**6235	23	10	S		47	1012	12	25.5	8	84	2328	1299	77
VIBORG—Turner County													
★ PIONEER MEMORIAL HOSPITAL, Washington St., P O Box 368, Zip 57070; tel. 605/326-5161; Warren G. Kuhler, adm. (Total facility includes 52 beds in nursing home-type unit) **A**9 10 **F**1 3 10 15 19 23 34 35 40 41 45 52	23	10	S	TF	85	585	63	74.1	5	38	1353	694	58
				H	33	568	12	—	5	38	818	443	37
WAGNER—Charles Mix County													
★ U. S. PUBLIC HEALTH SERVICE INDIAN HOSPITAL, Box 490, Zip 57380; tel. 605/384-3621; George E. Howell, serv. unit dir. **A**10 **F**14 15 34 35 37 40 52	47	10	S		26	587	6	23.1	5	23	1666	1027	103
★ WAGNER COMMUNITY MEMORIAL HOSPITAL (Formerly Listed Under Wagner Heights), Third St., P O Box 280, Zip 57380; tel. 605/384-3611; Mary Ann Jorgensen, adm. **A**9 10 **F**1 2 3 14 15 16 23 34 35 36 37 43 45	23	10	S		20	927	9	45.0	5	68	1322	561	35
WAGNER HEIGHTS—Charles Mix County													
WAGNER COMMUNITY MEMORIAL HOSPITAL, See Wagner													
WATERTOWN—Codington County													
PRAIRIE LAKES HOSPITAL EAST, See Prairie Lakes Hospital													
PRAIRIE LAKES HOSPITAL WEST, See Prairie Lakes Hospital													
⊞ PRAIRIE LAKES HOSPITAL (Includes Prairie Lakes Hospital East, 420 N. Fourth St. N.E., Zip 57201; tel. 605/886-8431; Prairie Lakes Hospital West, 400 Tenth Ave. N.W., Zip 57201; tel. 605/886-8491), 400 Tenth Ave. N.W., Zip 57201; tel. 605/886-8491; Edmond L. Weiland, adm. (Total facility includes 51 beds in nursing home-type unit) **A**1a 2 9 10 **F**1 3 6 12 15 16 17 19 20 23 24 26 34 35 36 37 40 41 45 46 47 51 52; **S**6235	23	10	S	TF	205	3409	89	43.4	14	611	11243	5416	343
				H	154	3369	44	—	14	611	—	5086	312
WEBSTER—Day County													
⊞ LAKE AREA HOSPITAL, N. First St., P O Box 489, Zip 57274; tel. 605/345-3336; Gilbert Despiegler, adm. **A**1a 9 10 **F**1 3 14 15 16 17 23 35 45 47	23	10	S		34	704	11	31.4	8	28	1795	984	59
WESSINGTON SPRINGS—Jerauld County													
★ WESKOTA MEMORIAL MEDICAL CENTER, 609 First St. N.E., Zip 57382; tel. 605/539-1201; Thomas V. Richter, adm. **A**9 10 **F**15 23 34 35 40 41 44 45 52	23	10	S		28	500	8	28.6	5	29	960	479	33
WINNER—Tripp County													
★ BAPTIST HOSPITAL, 745 E. Eighth St., Box 745, Zip 57580; tel. 605/842-2110; Dean Vaughn, adm. **A**9 10 **F**1 12 14 15 16 21 23 26 34 35 40 41 45 46 47 52	21	10	S		40	1354	20	50.0	6	110	2900	1523	87
YANKTON—Yankton County													
⊞ SACRED HEART HOSPITAL, 501 Summit, Zip 57078; tel. 605/665-9371; Dennis A. Sokol, pres. & chief exec. off. (Total facility includes 113 beds in nursing home-type unit) **A**1a 2 3 5 9 10 **F**1 3 6 12 14 15 16 19 20 23 24 25 26 32 33 34 35 36 40 41 44 45 46 47 50 52 53; **S**1635	21	10	S	TF	257	5277	181	70.4	16	766	16550	6951	436
				H	144	5209	77	—	16	766	14647	6387	386

Hospital, Address, Telephone, Administrator, Approval and Facility Codes, Multihospital System Code	Classification Codes				Inpatient Data				Newborn Data		Expense (thousands of dollars)		
★ American Hospital Association (AHA) membership □ Joint Commission on Accreditation of Hospitals (JCAH) accreditation + American Osteopathic Hospital Association (AOHA) membership ○ American Osteopathic Association (AOA) accreditation Δ Commission on Accreditation of Rehabilitation Facilities (CARF) accreditation Control codes 61, 63, 64, 71, 72 and 73 indicate hospitals listed by AOHA, but not registered by AHA. For definition of numerical codes, see page A2	Control	Service	Stay	Facilities	Beds	Admissions	Census	Occupancy (percent)	Bassinets	Births	Total	Payroll	Personnel

Tennessee

Hospital	Control	Service	Stay	Facilities	Beds	Admissions	Census	Occupancy (percent)	Bassinets	Births	Total	Payroll	Personnel
ATHENS—McMinn County													
⊞ ATHENS COMMUNITY HOSPITAL, 1114 W. Madison Ave., Box 250, Zip 37303; tel. 615/745-1411 **A**1a 9 10 **F**1 3 6 10 12 14 15 16 23 34 35 36 37 43 44 46 47 53; **S**1755	33	10	S		109	3790	49	45.0	12	369	—	—	204
BOLIVAR—Hardeman County													
⊞ COMMUNITY HOSPITAL OF BOLIVAR, 650 Nuckolls Rd., P O Box C, Zip 38008; tel. 901/658-3100; Terry Lambert, adm. **A**1a 9 10 **F**1 3 6 10 14 16 23 24 30 35 41 44 46 47	23	10	S		56	1781	28	50.0	6	126	3941	1864	147
BRISTOL—Sullivan County													
⊞ BRISTOL MEMORIAL HOSPITAL, 209 Memorial Dr., Zip 37620; tel. 615/968-1121; Phillip G. Sansam, exec. vice-pres.; Michelle Piatek, adm. **A**1a 2 3 5 9 10 **F**1 2 3 6 7 8 9 10 11 12 14 15 16 17 20 21 23 24 27 28 32 33 34 35 36 37 40 41 43 45 46 47 49 52 53 54; **S**1755	23	10	S		356	13450	251	70.5	36	1007	39793	18124	1043
BROWNSVILLE—Haywood County													
⊞ HAYWOOD PARK GENERAL HOSPITAL, 2545 N. Washington Ave., Zip 38012; tel. 901/772-4110; Stephen Shepherd, adm. **A**1a 9 10 **F**1 6 10 12 14 15 16 20 23 35 37 45 47 53; **S**1755	33	10	S		62	2734	36	58.1	8	233	4225	1660	95
CAMDEN—Benton County													
★ BENTON COMMUNITY HOSPITAL (Formerly Benton County General Hospital), Hospital St., Zip 38320; tel. 901/584-6135; Robert D. Wimberley, adm. **A**9 10 **F**6 14 16 23 35 47; **S**1755	33	10	S		93	3034	43	46.2	0	0	—	—	153
CARTHAGE—Smith County													
★ CARTHAGE GENERAL HOSPITAL, Hwy. 70 N., P O Box 319, Zip 37030; tel. 615/735-9815; Dorothy C. Rutherford, adm. **A**9 10 **F**1 6 35 37 41 43 53	33	10	S		29	737	9	31.0	0	0	1177	614	53
⊞ SMITH COUNTY MEMORIAL HOSPITAL, N. Main St., Zip 37030; tel. 615/735-1560; Michael W. Garfield, adm. **A**1a 9 10 **F**1 3 15 16 23 35 40 46 47 53; **S**1755	33	10	S		66	1713	22	33.3	7	120	3213	1296	76
CENTERVILLE—Hickman County													
⊞ HICKMAN COUNTY HEALTH SERVICES (Formerly Hickman County Hospital and Nursing Home), 135 E. Swan St., Zip 37033; tel. 615/729-4271; John Boone, adm. (Total facility includes 40 beds in nursing home-type unit) **A**1a 9 10 **F**1 6 14 15 16 19 23 26 35 41	13	10	S	TF	64	862	53	82.8	0	0	3072	1463	110
				H	24	845	13	—	0	0	2591	1167	86
CHATTANOOGA—Hamilton County													
BARONESS ERLANGER HOSPITAL, See Erlanger Medical Center													
⊞ DIAGNOSTIC CENTER HOSPITAL (Internal Medicine), 2412 McCallie Ave., Zip 37404; tel. 615/698-0221; David L. Dunlap, adm. (Nonreporting) **A**1a 9 10; **S**1755	33	49	S		80	—	—	—	—	—	—	—	—
⊞ DOWNTOWN GENERAL HOSPITAL, 709 Walnut St., Zip 37402; tel. 615/266-7721; Edward L. Lynsky, adm. **A**1a 9 10 **F**1 3 6 15 16 23 34 35 46 53; **S**1755	23	10	S		65	1325	24	36.9	0	0	4674	1709	102
⊞ ERLANGER MEDICAL CENTER (Includes Baroness Erlanger Hospital, 975 E. Third St., Zip 37403; tel. 615/778-7000; T. C. Thompson Children's Hospital Medical Center, 910 Blackford St., Zip 37403; tel. 615/778-6011; Willie D. Miller Eye Center, 975 E. Third St., Zip 37403; tel. 615/778-6011), 975 E. Third St., Zip 37403; tel. 615/778-7000; Thomas C. Winston, pres. **A**1a 2 3 5 6 8 9 10 **F**1 2 3 4 5 6 7 8 9 10 11 12 14 16 19 20 21 23 24 30 33 34 35 36 37 38 40 41 42 44 45 46 47 48 51 52 53 54	16	10	S		611	26210	431	70.5	70	3447	115329	49087	2702
⊞ HUMANA HOSPITAL -EAST RIDGE, 941 Spring Creek Rd., Zip 37412; tel. 615/894-7870; Peter T. Petruzzi, exec. dir. (Nonreporting) **A**1a 9 10; **S**1235	33	10	S		128	—	—	—	—	—	—	—	—
⊞ MEMORIAL HOSPITAL, 2500 Citico Ave., Zip 37404; tel. 615/629-8100; Sr. Thomas De Sales Bailey, pres. (Total facility includes 15 beds in nursing home-type unit) **A**1a 9 10 **F**1 3 4 6 9 10 11 12 14 15 16 19 20 23 32 34 35 41 42 45 46 53 54; **S**3045	21	10	S	TF	365	11442	218	59.7	0	0	45384	19663	999
				H	350	11320	210	—	0	0	45193	19507	984
□ METROPOLITAN HOSPITAL, 511 McCallie Ave., Zip 37402; tel. 615/265-3303; Gary Jones, chief exec. off. **A**1a 9 10 **F**1 6 14 15 16 35 43 47; **S**0905	33	10	S		64	1123	11	17.2	0	0	—	—	74
□ MOCCASIN BEND MENTAL HEALTH INSTITUTE, Moccasin Bend Rd., Zip 37405; tel. 615/265-2271; William A. White Jr., adm.; William C. Greer MD, supt. (Total facility includes 84 beds in nursing home-type unit) **A**1b 10 **F**3 15 24 29 30 32 33 42 46 47 50	12	22	L	TF	251	1305	232	92.4	0	0	12152	7684	599
				H	167	1298	145	—	0	0	10701	6697	503
⊞ NORTH PARK HOSPITAL, 2051 Hamill Rd., Zip 37343; tel. 615/870-1300; William A. Adams, adm. **A**1a 10 **F**1 3 5 6 10 12 15 16 23 24 34 35 37 44 46 47 53; **S**1755	33	10	S		83	3418	52	62.7	0	0	12710	4121	217
⊞ PARKRIDGE MEDICAL CENTER (Formerly Parkridge Hospital), 2333 McCallie Ave., Zip 37404; tel. 615/698-6061; David L. Dunlap, adm. **A**1a 9 10 **F**1 2 3 6 9 10 11 12 14 15 16 20 23 26 34 35 46 47 53 54; **S**1755	33	10	S		296	8204	144	48.6	0	0	30608	10067	565
RED BANK COMMUNITY HOSPITAL, See Riverchase Hospital													
⊞ RIVERCHASE HOSPITAL (Formerly Red Bank Community Hospital), 632 Morrison Springs Rd., Zip 37415; tel. 615/870-2211; Niles V. Floyd, adm. (Nonreporting) **A**1a 10	33	10	S		57	—	—	—	—	—	—	—	—
T. C. THOMPSON CHILDREN'S HOSPITAL MEDICAL CENTER, See Erlanger Medical Center													
⊞ VALLEY HOSPITAL (Formerly Valley Psychiatric Hospital), Shallowford Rd., P O Box 21887, Zip 37421; tel. 615/894-4220; James C. Kestner, adm. **A**1b 10 **F**15 24 32 33 42 44; **S**1755	33	22	L		100	956	88	88.0	0	0	6424	1523	171
WILLIE D. MILLER EYE CENTER, See Erlanger Medical Center													
CLARKSVILLE—Montgomery County													
⊞ MEMORIAL HOSPITAL, Madison St., Box 3160, Zip 37040; tel. 615/552-6622; Carney Willis Wright, adm. **A**1a 9 10 **F**1 3 6 10 11 12 14 15 16 21 23 27 30 32 33 35 40 41 45 46 52 53	16	10	S		194	8307	119	61.3	28	857	19192	8880	530
CLEVELAND—Bradley County													
⊞ BRADLEY COUNTY MEMORIAL HOSPITAL, N. Chambliss Ave., Box 3060, Zip 37311; tel. 615/479-0111; William E. Torrence, adm. **A**1a 9 10 **F**1 3 5 6 10 12 14 15 16 20 21 23 26 30 35 36 37 40 41 42 44 45 46 48 49 52 53	13	10	S		221	8313	112	50.7	28	1154	21453	9693	572
□ CLEVELAND COMMUNITY HOSPITAL, 2800 W. Side Dr. N.W., Zip 37311; tel. 615/479-4131; Gerald H. Frost, adm. **A**1a 9 10 **F**1 3 6 10 12 14 15 16 23 24 27 30 32 33 34 35 41 46 53; **S**5895	33	10	S		100	2211	35	35.0	0	0	3820	1222	119

★ American Hospital Association (AHA) membership
□ Joint Commission on Accreditation of Hospitals (JCAH) accreditation
+ American Osteopathic Hospital Association (AOHA) membership
○ American Osteopathic Association (AOA) accreditation
Δ Commission on Accreditation of Rehabilitation Facilities (CARF) accreditation
Control codes 61, 63, 64, 71, 72 and 73 indicate hospitals listed by AOHA, but not registered by AHA.
For definition of numerical codes, see page A2

Hospital, Address, Telephone, Administrator, Approval and Facility Codes, Multihospital System Code	Classification Codes				Inpatient Data				Newborn Data		Expense (thousands of dollars)		
	Control	Service	Stay	Facilities	Beds	Admissions	Census	Occupancy (percent)	Bassinets	Births	Total	Payroll	Personnel
COLUMBIA—Maury County													
★□ MAURY COUNTY HOSPITAL, 1224 Trotwood Ave., Zip 38401; tel. 615/381-1111; William R. Walter, adm. **A**1a 9 10 **F**1 2 3 5 6 7 8 9 10 11 12 14 15 16 23 26 29 30 35 36 40 41 44 45 46 52 53	13	10	S		235	10690	136	57.9	18	1157	24372	11437	616
COOKEVILLE—Putnam County													
★□ COOKEVILLE GENERAL HOSPITAL, 142 W. Fifth St., Box 340, Zip 38501; tel. 615/528-2541; Walter S. Fitzpatrick Jr., adm. **A**1a 9 10 **F**1 3 6 10 12 15 16 20 23 26 33 34 35 36 39 40 45 46 47 52 53	14	10	S		155	6890	95	61.7	21	1013	18192	7659	460
COPPERHILL—Polk County													
★□ COPPER BASIN MEDICAL CENTER, State Hwy. 68, Drawer X, Zip 37317; tel. 615/496-5511; George A. McGee, adm. **A**1a 9 10 **F**3 6 10 16 23 35 36 46; **S**0885	16	10	S		44	1999	28	63.6	11	9	3312	1762	97
COVINGTON—Tipton County													
★□ BAPTIST MEMORIAL HOSPITAL-TIPTON, 1995 Hwy. 51 S., Box 737, Zip 38019; tel. 901/476-2621; William T. Moorer, adm. **A**1a 9 10 **F**1 3 6 10 16 23 35 41 47 53; **S**1625	21	10	S		99	2865	42	46.7	10	37	9592	3644	181
CROSSVILLE—Cumberland County													
★□ CUMBERLAND MEDICAL CENTER, 811 S. Main St., P O Box 667, Zip 38555; tel. 615/484-9511; Robert C. Couch, pres. **A**1a 9 10 **F**1 3 6 12 14 15 16 23 34 35 40 41 43 45 46 47 53	23	10	S		172	7560	109	63.4	16	682	14759	6737	500
DAYTON—Rhea County													
★ RHEA COUNTY MEDICAL CENTER, Hwy. 27 N., Box 629, Zip 37321; tel. 615/775-1121; Barbara J. Heath, adm. (Total facility includes 107 beds in nursing home-type unit) **A**9 10 **F**1 3 6 10 12 15 16 19 20 23 35 40 45 47	13	10	S	TF	164	2141	124	75.6	8	163	5631	2583	199
				H	57	2117	22	—	8	163	4255	1901	142
DICKSON—Dickson County													
★□ GOODLARK MEDICAL CENTER, 111 Hwy. 70 E., Zip 37055; tel. 615/446-0446; Daniel S. Jones, adm. & chief exec. off. **A**1a 9 10 **F**1 3 6 10 12 14 16 17 23 34 35 36 37 40 46 52 53 54	23	10	S		144	6300	97	67.4	10	461	9742	4677	382
DUNLAP—Sequatchie County													
□ SEQUATCHIE GENERAL HOSPITAL, Cedar St., Box 787, Zip 37327; tel. 615/949-3611; Danny Mankin, adm. **A**1a 9 10 **F**10 12 16 23 35 47; **S**0075	33	10	S		49	991	11	22.4	0	0	2098	990	49
DYERSBURG—Dyer County													
★□ METHODIST HOSPITAL OF DYERSBURG (Formerly Parkview Methodist Medical Center), 400 Tickle St., Zip 38024; tel. 901/285-2410; Randall Hoover, adm. (Total facility includes 113 beds in nursing home-type unit) **A**1a 9 10 **F**3 6 7 8 9 10 11 12 14 16 19 23 34 35 40 41 46 52 53; **S**9345	23	10	S	TF	225	5249	188	75.2	20	732	17443	6483	370
				H	112	5189	75	—	20	732	16029	5803	314
ELIZABETHTON—Carter County													
★□ HCA SYCAMORE SHOALS HOSPITAL (Formerly Carter County Memorial Hospital), 1501 W. Elk Ave., Zip 37643; tel. 615/542-1300; Will O. Landers, adm. **A**1a 9 10 **F**1 3 6 12 14 15 16 23 35 36 40 43 44 45 46 47 52; **S**1755	33	10	S		128	3278	46	35.9	12	332	—	—	208
ERIN—Houston County													
★□ TRINITY HOSPITAL, Main St., Box 489, Zip 37061; tel. 615/289-4211; Terrell Sellers, adm. **A**1a 9 10 **F**1 6 14 15 16 34 35 43; **S**1755	33	10	S		40	1345	19	47.5	6	77	2576	1010	64
ERWIN—Unicoi County													
★□ UNICOI COUNTY MEMORIAL HOSPITAL, Greenway Circle, Zip 37650; tel. 615/743-3141; James L. McMackin, adm. (Total facility includes 46 beds in nursing home-type unit) **A**1a 9 10 **F**1 14 16 19 23 35 44 45 47 53	15	10	S	TF	94	1336	63	67.0	0	0	3631	1877	146
				H	48	1280	18	—	0	0	2597	1256	109
ETOWAH—McMinn County													
★□ WOODS MEMORIAL HOSPITAL, Hwy. 411 N., Box 410, Zip 37331; tel. 615/263-5521; Daniel G. Miller, adm. (Total facility includes 44 beds in nursing home-type unit) **A**1a 9 10 **F**1 6 10 14 15 16 19 21 23 30 35 44 45 47 53	16	10	S	TF	116	3186	81	69.8	0	0	4966	2184	149
				H	72	3173	38	—	0	0	4416	1920	126
FAYETTEVILLE—Lincoln County													
★□ LINCOLN REGIONAL HOSPITAL, 700 W. Maple Ave., Zip 37334; tel. 615/433-1561; Edward A. Perdue, adm. **A**1a 9 10 **F**1 3 6 10 14 15 16 23 24 32 34 35 40 43 45 46 47 52 53; **S**1755	13	10	S		110	2998	45	40.9	9	150	6418	2553	191
FRANKLIN—Williamson County													
□ WILLIAMSON MEDICAL CENTER (Formerly Williamson County Hospital), 2021 Carothers Rd., P O Box 1600, Zip 37065; tel. 615/791-0500; Ronald G. Joyner, exec. vice-pres. **A**1a 9 10 **F**1 3 6 10 12 15 16 23 24 32 33 35 40 43 44 45 46 52 53	23	10	S		140	4630	74	52.9	10	388	15661	7855	449
GAINESBORO—Jackson County													
★□ JACKSON COUNTY HOSPITAL, S. Murray St., Box 36, Zip 38562; tel. 615/268-0211; Gary Chaffin, adm. (Nonreporting) **A**1a 9 10	33	10	S		41	—	—	—	—	—	—	—	—
GALLATIN—Sumner County													
★□ SUMNER MEMORIAL HOSPITAL, Hartsville Pike, P O Box 1558, Zip 37066; tel. 615/452-4210; James L. Decker, adm. **A**1a 9 10 **F**1 3 6 10 12 14 15 16 23 26 29 30 33 34 35 36 37 40 41 42 45 46 52 53	13	10	S		120	5193	97	80.8	12	520	14785	7177	389
GREENEVILLE—Greene County													
★□ LAUGHLIN MEMORIAL HOSPITAL, 215 N. College St., Zip 37743; tel. 615/639-6161; Jack G. Wilson, adm. **A**1a 9 10 **F**1 3 6 8 9 10 11 12 15 16 23 35 36 40 41 46 50 51 52 53	23	10	S		177	6474	83	46.9	18	423	10888	4764	351
★□ TAKOMA ADVENTIST HOSPITAL, 401 Takoma Ave., Box 1300, Zip 37743; tel. 615/639-3151; Gladys V. Duran, pres. **A**1a 9 10 **F**1 3 6 9 10 11 12 15 16 23 34 35 36 40 41 46 48 49 53; **S**4165	21	10	S		108	3414	50	46.3	12	259	9374	3586	240
HARRIMAN—Roane County													
★□ HARRIMAN CITY HOSPITAL, 412 Devonia St., Box 489, Zip 37748; tel. 615/882-1323; Harry Wade, adm. **A**1a 9 10 **F**1 6 15 16 23 35 40 45 47 53	14	10	S		83	3507	42	48.8	8	261	6287	3065	215
HARTSVILLE—Trousdale County													
HARTSVILLE GENERAL HOSPITAL, Church St., Zip 37074; tel. 615/374-2221; John C. Hester, adm. (Nonreporting) **A**9 10	33	10	S		34	—	—	—	—	—	—	—	—
HENDERSONVILLE—Sumner County													
★□ HCA HENDERSONVILLE HOSPITAL (Formerly Hendersonville Hospital), 355 New Shackle Island Rd., Zip 37075; tel. 615/822-4911; Donald R. Sailer, adm. **A**1a 9 10 **F**1 3 6 10 12 14 15 16 23 30 32 33 35 36 40 42 46 47 53; **S**1755	33	10	S		75	2797	35	46.7	12	469	—	—	207
HOHENWALD—Lewis County													
□ LEWIS COUNTY HOSPITAL, Linden Hwy., P O Box 38, Zip 38462; tel. 615/796-4901; Michael Edwards, adm. (Nonreporting) **A**1a 9 10; **S**0075	33	10	S		52	—	—	—	—	—	—	—	—
HUMBOLDT—Gibson County													
★□ HUMBOLDT CEDAR CREST HOSPITAL, 3525 Chere Carol Rd., Zip 38343; tel. 901/784-2321; Rodney R. Smith, adm. **A**1a 9 10 **F**1 2 3 10 16 23 35 37 40 46 52; **S**1755	33	10	S		62	1246	20	32.3	8	37	3577	1376	80
HUNTINGDON—Carroll County													
□ BAPTIST MEMORIAL HOSPITAL-HUNTINGDON, 631 R B Wilson Dr., Zip 38344; tel. 901/986-4461; Stephen L. Mansfield, adm. **A**1a 9 10 **F**1 3 6 10 14 16 23 26 34 35 36 41 43 45 46 53; **S**1625	23	10	S		72	2331	47	65.3	0	0	5354	2016	154

★ American Hospital Association (AHA) membership
☐ Joint Commission on Accreditation of Hospitals (JCAH) accreditation
+ American Osteopathic Hospital Association (AOHA) membership
○ American Osteopathic Association (AOA) accreditation
Δ Commission on Accreditation of Rehabilitation Facilities (CARF) accreditation
Control codes 61, 63, 64, 71, 72 and 73 indicate hospitals listed by AOHA, but not registered by AHA.
For definition of numerical codes, see page A2

Hospital, Address, Telephone, Administrator, Approval and Facility Codes, Multihospital System Code	Classification Codes				Inpatient Data				Newborn Data		Expense (thousands of dollars)		
	Control	Service	Stay	Facilities	Beds	Admissions	Census	Occupancy (percent)	Bassinets	Births	Total	Payroll	Personnel
JACKSON—Madison County													
★☐ HCA REGIONAL HOSPITAL OF JACKSON (Formerly Regional Hospital of Jackson), 49 Old Hickory Blvd., Zip 38305; tel. 901/668-2100; Donald H. Wilkerson, adm. **A**1a b 9 10 **F**1 3 6 10 12 15 16 20 23 24 27 33 34 35 42 46 47 48 49 53; **S**1755	33	10	S		166	4903	93	56.0	0	0	15283	5127	303
JACKSON COUNSELING CENTER AND PSYCHIATRIC HOSPITAL, 238 Summar Dr., Zip 38301; tel. 901/424-8751; Andrew R. Eickhoff PhD, exec. dir. **A**10 **F**24 28 29 30 32 33 42	23	22	S		24	431	18	75.0	0	0	3193	1610	106
★☐ JACKSON-MADISON COUNTY GENERAL HOSPITAL, 708 W. Forest Ave., Zip 38301; tel. 901/425-5000; James T. Moss, pres. **A**1a 3 5 9 10 **F**1 2 3 4 5 6 7 8 9 10 11 12 14 15 16 20 21 23 24 34 35 36 40 41 44 45 46 47 51 52 53 54	16	10	S		659	23821	393	59.6	32	2786	67852	32941	1863
REGIONAL HOSPITAL OF JACKSON, See HCA Regional Hospital of Jackson													
JAMESTOWN—Fentress County													
FENTRESS COUNTY GENERAL HOSPITAL, Hwy. 52-W, Drawer N, Zip 38556; tel. 615/879-8171; Donald E. Downey, adm. **A**9 10 **F**3 6 14 16 23 34 35 45 46; **S**5765	33	10	S		72	3125	46	63.9	4	62	5930	2320	154
JEFFERSON CITY—Jefferson County													
★☐ JEFFERSON MEMORIAL HOSPITAL, Bishop St., Zip 37760; tel. 615/475-2091; Robert H. Foster, adm. **A**1a 9 10 **F**1 2 6 14 15 16 23 34 35 40 45 46	15	10	S		91	2837	43	47.3	10	111	5715	2951	211
JELLICO—Campbell County													
★☐ JELLICO COMMUNITY HOSPITAL, Rte. 1, Box 197, Zip 37762; tel. 615/784-7252; Keith L. Hausman, pres. **A**1a 9 10 **F**6 10 12 16 23 26 34 35 41 52; **S**4165	21	10	S		50	3480	39	78.0	12	416	5455	2912	147
JOHNSON CITY—Washington County													
★☐ JOHNSON CITY EYE AND EAR HOSPITAL, 203 E. Watauga Ave., Zip 37601; tel. 615/926-1111; J. Lori Caudell, adm. **A**1a 9 10 **F**1 13 15 34 47; **S**1755	33	45	S		39	981	5	12.8	0	0	2479	797	46
★☐ JOHNSON CITY MEDICAL CENTER HOSPITAL, 400 State of Franklin Rd., Zip 37601; tel. 615/461-6111; D. Gene Clark, adm. **A**1a 2 3 5 9 10 **F**1 3 6 7 8 9 10 11 12 14 15 16 20 23 24 26 30 32 34 35 36 37 38 41 44 45 46 47 51 53 54	23	10	S		365	14939	221	60.5	24	1751	49538	22341	1281
★ NORTH SIDE HOSPITAL, 401 Princeton Rd., Zip 37601; tel. 615/282-4111; David Glover, adm. **A**9 10 **F**1 3 6 10 12 14 15 16 23 24 26 27 28 30 32 33 34 35 42 44 48 53; **S**1755	33	10	S		154	3544	64	41.6	0	0	12921	4353	237
VETERANS ADMINISTRATION MEDICAL CENTER, See Mountain Home													
WOODRIDGE HOSPITAL, 403 State of Franklin Rd., Zip 37601; tel. 615/928-7111; Gary D. Varner, adm. **A**3 10 **F**3 24 32 33 34 42 46 47 48	23	22	S		75	1046	54	72.0	0	0	4968	2841	150
KINGSPORT—Sullivan County													
★☐ HOLSTON VALLEY HOSPITAL AND MEDICAL CENTER, W. Ravine St., Box 238, Zip 37662; tel. 615/246-3322; John A. Dodson, exec. dir. **A**1a 2 3 5 9 10 **F**1 2 3 4 6 7 8 9 10 11 12 14 15 16 20 21 23 24 26 27 30 32 34 35 36 37 40 41 42 45 46 50 52 53 54	23	10	S		417	14940	298	73.0	60	1195	60147	28673	1483
★☐ INDIAN PATH HOSPITAL, 2000 Brookside Rd., Zip 37660; tel. 615/246-4311; Joe Fisher, adm. **A**1a 9 10 **F**1 3 6 10 12 14 15 16 20 23 24 26 30 34 35 36 40 42 43 46 47 53; **S**1755	33	10	S		295	7356	146	49.5	5	303	27917	9786	566
★☐ INDIAN PATH PAVILION, 2300 Pavilion Dr., Zip 37660; tel. 615/229-7874; Janet M. Creager, adm. (Nonreporting) **A**1a b 10; **S**1755	33	22	S		46	—	—	—	—	—	—	—	—
KNOXVILLE—Knox County													
★☐ EAST TENNESSEE BAPTIST HOSPITAL, 137 Blount Ave. S.E., Zip 37920; Mailing Address Box 1788, Zip 37901; tel. 615/632-5011; Robert C. Chandler, pres. & chief exec. off. **A**1a 2 6 9 10 **F**1 3 4 5 6 7 8 9 10 11 12 14 15 16 17 20 21 23 32 33 34 35 37 41 43 45 46 47 50 53 54	21	10	S		285	17582	260	91.2	0	0	52110	21652	1135
★☐ EAST TENNESSEE CHILDREN'S HOSPITAL, 2018 Clinch Ave., Zip 37916; Mailing Address P O Box 15010, Zip 37901; tel. 615/546-7711; Robert F. Koppel, adm. **A**1a 9 10 **F**1 5 6 14 15 16 23 24 26 27 28 29 30 32 33 34 35 41 42 44 45 46 47 51	23	50	S		109	5116	71	68.9	0	0	15450	7472	446
★☐ Δ FORT SANDERS REGIONAL MEDICAL CENTER, 1901 Clinch Ave. S.W., Zip 37916; tel. 615/546-2811; Alan C. Guy, pres. **A**1a 2 6 7 9 10 **F**1 3 6 7 8 9 10 11 12 14 15 16 17 21 23 24 25 26 33 35 36 40 41 42 44 45 46 47 53 54	21	10	S		575	16931	333	57.9	40	2092	61626	26964	1490
★☐ HCA PARK WEST MEDICAL CENTERS (Formerly Park West Hospital), 9352 Park West Blvd., P O Box 22993, Zip 37933; tel. 615/693-5151; Wayne Heatherly, adm. & chief exec. off. **A**1a 9 10 **F**1 3 6 10 11 12 14 15 16 17 20 23 24 27 30 32 33 34 35 39 43 44 46 47 50 53 54; **S**1755	33	10	S		325	11699	193	59.4	0	0	39432	12420	680
☐ LAKESHORE MENTAL HEALTH INSTITUTE, 5908 Lyons View Dr., Zip 37919; tel. 615/584-1561; James L. Cox PhD, supt. (Nonreporting) **A**1b 10	12	22	L		662	—	—	—	—	—	—	—	—
★ + NORTHWEST GENERAL HOSPITAL, 5310 Western Ave., Zip 37921; tel. 615/584-9191; Stephen W. Larcen PhD, adm. (Nonreporting) **A**9 10; **S**0075	33	10	S		23	—	—	—	—	—	—	—	—
PARK WEST HOSPITAL, See HCA Park West Medical Centers													
★☐ ST. MARY'S MEDICAL CENTER, Oak Hill Ave., Zip 37917; tel. 615/971-7836; L. Lynn Nipper, pres. **A**1a 6 9 10 **F**1 2 3 5 6 7 8 9 10 11 12 14 15 16 17 20 21 23 24 26 27 30 32 33 34 35 36 41 42 43 44 45 46 47 48 49 50 52 53 54; **S**5155	21	10	S		510	20822	401	78.6	20	1893	—	—	1681
★☐ UNIVERSITY OF TENNESSEE MEMORIAL HOSPITAL, 1924 Alcoa Hwy., Zip 37920; tel. 615/544-9000; Gene Hall, adm. **A**1a 2 3 5 9 10 **F**1 2 3 4 5 6 7 8 9 10 11 12 13 14 15 16 18 20 23 24 27 30 32 34 35 36 37 40 43 44 45 46 47 51 52 53 54	12	10	S		505	17107	370	73.3	30	2392	90466	38150	2033
LA FOLLETTE—Campbell County													
★☐ LA FOLLETTE MEDICAL CENTER, E. Central Ave., Box 1301, Zip 37766; tel. 615/562-2211; J. B. Wright, adm. (Total facility includes 98 beds in nursing home-type unit) **A**1a 9 10 **F**1 3 6 12 15 16 19 23 26 35 41 44 45 46 50 52 53	14	10	S	TF	165	3121	136	82.4	0	0	7430	3562	297
				H	67	2944	43	—	0	0	5618	2732	199
LAFAYETTE—Macon County													
★☐ MACON COUNTY GENERAL HOSPITAL, 204 Medical Dr., Zip 37083; tel. 615/666-2147; Dennis Wolford, adm. **A**1a 9 10 **F**1 3 6 12 14 15 16 23 35 44; **S**1755	23	10	S		43	1555	19	44.2	0	0	2700	1019	77
LAKE CITY—Anderson County													
★ ST. MARY'S NORTH HOSPITAL, 901 S. Main St., Zip 37769; tel. 615/426-7455; Anne Loggans, adm. (Nonreporting) **A**9 10; **S**5155	21	10	S		20	—	—	—	—	—	—	—	—
LAWRENCEBURG—Lawrence County													
CROCKETT GENERAL HOSPITAL, See HCA Crockett Hospital													
★☐ HCA CROCKETT HOSPITAL (Formerly Crockett General Hospital), U. S. Hwy. 43 S., Box 726, Zip 38464; tel. 615/762-6571; John B. Crysel, adm. **A**1a 9 10 **F**1 3 6 10 12 14 15 16 23 34 35 40 41 43 44 46 53; **S**1755	33	10	S		106	2817	33	31.1	11	203	5309	2263	127
★☐ SCOTT MEMORIAL HOSPITAL, Box 747, Zip 38464; tel. 615/762-7501; P. B. Mitchell, pres. **A**1a 10 **F**1 3 6 12 14 15 16 23 27 29 34 35 40 41 44 45 46 47 48 53; **S**4165	21	10	S		64	2302	24	37.5	6	244	4770	1923	127
LEBANON—Wilson County													
★☐ HUMANA HOSPITAL -MCFARLAND, 500 Park Ave., Zip 37087; tel. 615/449-0500; Larry Keller, exec. dir. **A**1a 9 10 **F**3 12 14 16 23 33 34 35 40 44 45 46 47 53; **S**1235	33	10	S		159	6043	99	62.3	10	272	13124	4985	296
☐ UNIVERSITY MEDICAL CENTER, 1411 Baddour Pkwy., Zip 37087; tel. 615/444-8262; Claude W. Harbarger, adm. **A**1a 9 10 **F**1 3 6 10 12 14 15 16 23 27 30 32 33 34 35 36 40 44 46 48 53; **S**3015	33	10	S		125	3860	72	57.6	9	321	—	—	224

Hospital, Address, Telephone, Administrator, Approval and Facility Codes, Multihospital System Code	Classification Codes				Inpatient Data				Newborn Data		Expense (thousands of dollars)		
★ American Hospital Association (AHA) membership □ Joint Commission on Accreditation of Hospitals (JCAH) accreditation + American Osteopathic Hospital Association (AOHA) membership ○ American Osteopathic Association (AOA) accreditation Δ Commission on Accreditation of Rehabilitation Facilities (CARF) accreditation Control codes 61, 63, 64, 71, 72 and 73 indicate hospitals listed by AOHA, but not registered by AHA. For definition of numerical codes, see page A2	Control	Service	Stay	Facilities	Beds	Admissions	Census	Occupancy (percent)	Bassinets	Births	Total	Payroll	Personnel
LEWISBURG—Marshall County													
★□ LEWISBURG COMMUNITY HOSPITAL, Ellington Pkwy., P O Box 380, Zip 37091; tel. 615/359-6241; Hugh Kroell, adm. (Nonreporting) **A**1a 9 10; **S**6525	33	10	S		119	—	—	—	—	—	—	—	—
LEXINGTON—Henderson County													
★□ METHODIST HOSPITAL OF LEXINGTON, Church St., Box 160, Zip 38351; tel. 901/968-3646; Dick Heflin, adm. **A**1a 9 10 **F**1 2 6 10 14 15 16 23 26 35 41 45 46 47; **S**9345	21	10	S		42	2073	23	54.8	6	104	3846	1503	94
LINDEN—Perry County													
PERRY MEMORIAL HOSPITAL, Hwy. 13 S., Box 86, Zip 37096; tel. 615/589-2121; Jerry K. Crowell, adm. **A**9 10 **F**3 6 10 14 16 35 41 45 46 47; **S**0075	33	10	S		53	1645	25	47.2	5	51	3998	1719	95
LIVINGSTON—Overton County													
★□ HCA REGIONAL HOSPITAL-LIVINGSTON (Formerly Livingston Community Hospital), 315 Oak St., Zip 38570; tel. 615/823-5611; Martin A. Schoenbachler Jr., adm. **A**1a 9 10 **F**1 3 6 10 14 15 16 23 35 36 40 46 52 53; **S**1755	33	10	S		106	4090	60	56.6	10	251	7689	2854	175
LIVINGSTON COMMUNITY HOSPITAL, See HCA Regional Hospital-Livingston													
LOUDON—Loudon County													
★□ LOUDON COUNTY MEMORIAL HOSPITAL, Vonore Rd., Box 217, Zip 37774; tel. 615/458-4691; James L. Jarrett, adm. **A**1a 9 10 **F**1 3 6 10 14 15 16 23 35 44 46 53; **S**1755	13	10	S		50	2201	23	46.0	12	161	4382	1742	114
LOUISVILLE—Blount County													
★□ PENINSULA HOSPITAL (Formerly Peninsula Psychiatric Hospital), Zip 37777; tel. 615/970-9800; J. Joe Maples, adm.; William C. Greer, chief exec. off. **A**1b **F**24 28 29 30 31 32 33 34 42 43 48 49	33	22	L		137	906	89	88.1	0	0	7529	3046	202
MADISON—Davidson County													
MADISON HOSPITAL, See Tennessee Christian Medical Center													
★□ NASHVILLE MEMORIAL HOSPITAL, 612 W. Due West Ave., Zip 37115; tel. 615/865-3511; J. D. Elliott, pres. **A**1a 9 10 **F**1 2 3 5 6 9 10 11 12 14 15 16 23 24 26 30 34 35 36 40 44 45 46 47 52 53 54	23	10	S		314	11636	210	66.9	18	449	37514	16019	885
★□ TENNESSEE CHRISTIAN MEDICAL CENTER (Formerly Madison Hospital), 500 Hospital Dr., Zip 37115; tel. 615/865-2373; Dennis Kiley, actg. pres. **A**1a 9 10 **F**1 3 6 10 12 14 15 16 20 23 24 25 26 27 32 33 34 35 36 37 40 42 44 45 46 47 48 52 53; **S**4165	21	10	S		253	5415	148	58.5	18	264	27060	11456	548
MANCHESTER—Coffee County													
★ COFFEE MEDICAL CENTER, 1001 McArthur Dr., Zip 37355; tel. 615/728-3586; Carl B. Allen, adm. (Total facility includes 66 beds in nursing home-type unit) **A**9 10 **F**6 16 19 23 35 36 40 43 44 45 46; **S**0885	13	10	S	TF	126	1496	85	67.5	15	38	4019	—	127
				H	60	1455	21	—	15	38	3199	—	84
MARTIN—Weakley County													
★□ VOLUNTEER GENERAL HOSPITAL, Mount Pelia Rd., Box 967, Zip 38237; tel. 901/587-4261; Joe D. Depew, adm. **A**1a 9 10 **F**1 3 6 10 12 14 15 16 23 26 35 36 40 43 45 46 53; **S**1755	33	10	S		100	3013	52	52.0	9	226	8034	2835	181
MARYVILLE—Blount County													
★□ BLOUNT MEMORIAL HOSPITAL, 907 E. Lamar Alexander Pkwy., Zip 37801; tel. 615/983-7211; Joseph M. Dawson, adm. **A**1a 9 10 **F**1 2 3 6 10 12 14 15 16 21 23 30 32 33 34 35 36 40 41 42 44 45 46 47 48 52 53	13	10	S		221	9082	163	73.8	30	793	29568	11942	692
MCKENZIE—Carroll County													
★□ METHODIST HOSPITAL OF MCKENZIE, 945 N. Highland, Zip 38201; tel. 901/352-5344; G. L. Miles, adm. **A**1a 10 **F**1 3 6 14 16 23 34 35 41 42 45 47 53; **S**9345	23	10	S		54	1841	25	46.3	5	230	4085	1465	103
MCMINNVILLE—Warren County													
★□ RIVER PARK HOSPITAL, Sparta Rd., Zip 37110; tel. 615/473-8411; William A. Summers, adm. **A**1a 9 10 **F**1 3 6 10 12 14 15 16 20 23 26 34 35 43 45 47 50 53; **S**1755	33	10	S		89	2861	46	51.7	0	0	8077	2810	181
WARREN REGIONAL HOSPITAL (Formerly Warren County General Hospital), 1509 Sparta Rd., Zip 37110; tel. 615/473-3151; Douglas Rivers, adm. **A**9 10 **F**3 6 10 14 16 23 35 36 45	33	10	S		63	2261	25	39.7	12	152	5071	2009	85
MEMPHIS—Shelby County													
★□ Δ BAPTIST MEMORIAL HOSPITAL (Includes Baptist Memorial Hospital East, 6019 Walnut Grove Rd., Zip 38119; Regional Rehabilitation Center, 1025 E. H Crump Blvd., Zip 38104), 899 Madison Ave., Zip 38146; tel. 901/522-5252; Joseph H. Powell, pres. (Total facility includes 44 beds in nursing home-type unit) **A**1a 2 3 5 6 7 8 9 10 **F**1 2 3 4 6 7 8 9 10 11 12 13 14 15 16 17 19 20 23 24 25 26 27 30 33 34 35 36 40 42 44 45 47 50 51 52 53 54; **S**1625	21	10	S	TF	1669	49915	1156	69.3	60	5465	208728	105965	5523
				H	1625	49812	1149	—	60	5465	—	—	5494
BAPTIST MEMORIAL HOSPITAL EAST, See Baptist Memorial Hospital													
★ BAPTIST SPECIALTY HOSPITAL (Formerly Humana Specialty Hospital-Memphis) (Eye, Ear, Nose and Throat), 1060 Madison Ave., Zip 38104; Mailing Address P O Box 40029, Zip 38174; tel. 901/523-2121; James E. Ramer, actg. adm. **A**9 10 **F**1 34; **S**1625	21	49	S		50	175	1	2.0	0	0	1615	434	39
★□ CHARTER LAKESIDE HOSPITAL, 2911 Brunswick Rd., Mailing Address P O Box 341308, Bartlett, Zip 38134; tel. 901/377-4700; Sherry Thornton, adm. **A**1b 3 9 10 **F**15 23 24 30 32 33 42 46 48 49; **S**0695	33	22	L		150	1286	126	84.0	0	0	—	—	221
★□ EASTWOOD HOSPITAL, 3000 Getwell Rd., Zip 38118; tel. 901/369-8500; John F. Davis, exec. dir. **A**1a 9 10 **F**3 6 10 12 14 16 23 27 29 30 34 35 45 46 47 48 53; **S**0395	33	10	S		243	5254	99	32.8	0	0	21670	—	364
HUMANA SPECIALTY HOSPITAL-MEMPHIS, See Baptist Specialty Hospital													
★□ LE BONHEUR CHILDREN'S MEDICAL CENTER, One Children's Plaza, Zip 38103; tel. 901/522-3000; Eugene K. Cashman Jr., pres. & chief exec. off. **A**1a 3 5 9 10 **F**1 3 4 6 10 12 13 14 15 16 19 20 23 26 28 30 32 33 34 35 38 42 43 44 45 46 47 53 54	23	50	S		173	13663	136	78.6	0	0	37071	15674	856
□ MEMPHIS MENTAL HEALTH INSTITUTE, 865 Poplar Ave., P O Box 40966, Zip 38174; tel. 901/524-1200; Robert D. Fink MD, supt. **A**1b 3 5 9 10 **F**15 19 25 30 33 42 45 46 47 48 49	12	22	S		211	1866	189	91.3	0	0	11481	5943	403
★□ METHODIST HOSPITAL NORTH-JESSE HARRIS MEMORIAL HOSPITAL (Formerly Jesse Harris Memorial Methodist Hospital), 3960 New Covington Pike, Zip 38128; tel. 901/372-5200; Thomas H. Gee, vice-pres. **A**1a **F**1 3 5 6 9 10 11 12 14 15 16 23 24 30 35 37 44 45 46 47 53; **S**9345	21	10	S		162	6053	113	66.5	0	0	—	—	383
★□ METHODIST HOSPITAL SOUTH-JOHN R. FLIPPIN MEMORIAL HOSPITAL, 1300 Wesley Dr., Zip 38116; tel. 901/346-3700; James B. Hunter, vice-pres. **A**1a **F**1 3 5 6 9 10 11 12 14 15 16 23 24 30 35 37 45 46 47 53; **S**9345	21	10	S		164	6062	117	71.3	0	0	—	—	373
★□ METHODIST HOSPITAL-CENTRAL UNIT, 1265 Union Ave., Zip 38104; tel. 901/726-7000; Judge T. Calton, pres. **A**1a 2 3 5 6 8 9 10 **F**1 2 3 4 5 6 7 8 9 10 11 12 13 14 15 16 17 19 20 21 23 24 25 26 27 30 32 33 34 35 36 37 40 41 42 44 45 46 47 51 53 54; **S**9345	21	10	S		833	27611	683	82.0	40	1765	—	—	2889
□ MID-SOUTH HOSPITAL (Ophthalmology and Adolescent Psychiatry and Adult Psychiatry), 135 N. Pauline St., Zip 38105; tel. 901/527-5211; James E. Hughes, adm. (Nonreporting) **A**1a b 9; **S**0825	33	49	S		190	—	—	—	—	—	—	—	—

Hospital, Address, Telephone, Administrator, Approval and Facility Codes, Multihospital System Code	Classification Codes				Inpatient Data				Newborn Data		Expense (thousands of dollars)		
★ American Hospital Association (AHA) membership ☐ Joint Commission on Accreditation of Hospitals (JCAH) accreditation + American Osteopathic Hospital Association (AOHA) membership ○ American Osteopathic Association (AOA) accreditation Δ Commission on Accreditation of Rehabilitation Facilities (CARF) accreditation Control codes 61, 63, 64, 71, 72 and 73 indicate hospitals listed by AOHA, but not registered by AHA. For definition of numerical codes, see page A2	Control	Service	Stay	Facilities	Beds	Admissions	Census	Occupancy (percent)	Bassinets	Births	Total	Payroll	Personnel
⊞ REGIONAL MEDICAL CENTER AT MEMPHIS, 877 Jefferson Ave., Zip 38103; tel. 901/575-7928; Gary S. Shorb, pres. **A**1a 2 3 5 8 9 10 **F**3 5 6 7 8 9 10 11 14 16 22 23 24 26 30 32 34 35 36 40 44 45 46 47 51 53	16	10	S		449	21573	374	83.0	75	7779	102738	52130	2391
REGIONAL REHABILITATION CENTER, See Baptist Memorial Hospital													
⊞ ST. FRANCIS HOSPITAL, 5959 Park Ave., Zip 38119; Mailing Address P O Box 171808, Zip 38187; tel. 901/765-1000; M. Rita Schroeder, pres. (Total facility includes 186 beds in nursing home-type unit) **A**1a 2 3 5 9 10 **F**1 3 4 5 6 7 8 9 10 11 12 14 15 16 19 20 21 23 24 25 26 27 28 30 32 33 34 35 36 40 41 42 43 44 45 46 47 48 49 52 53 54	21	10	S	TF	879	20959	627	71.3	31	1006	84697	37478	1721
				H	693	20640	450	—	31	1006	81797	36220	1633
⊞ Δ ST. JOSEPH HOSPITAL, 220 Overton Ave., Box 178, Zip 38101; tel. 901/577-2700; Sr. M. Annette Crone, chief exec. off. **A**1a 6 7 9 10 **F**2 3 6 7 9 10 11 12 14 16 20 23 24 25 26 27 28 32 33 34 35 36 40 41 42 44 45 46 48 49 52 53; **S**5345	21	10	S		440	9570	326	74.1	18	1810	51880	22259	1144
⊞ ST. JUDE CHILDREN'S RESEARCH HOSPITAL (Pediatric Cancer Research), 332 N. Lauderdale St., Box 318, Zip 38101; tel. 901/522-0300; Frederick F. Nowak, chief oper. off. **A**1a 2 3 5 9 10 **F**6 7 8 9 10 11 12 14 16 23 33 34 45 46 52	23	59	S		48	1584	25	52.1	0	0	43401	21165	804
☐ UNIVERSITY OF TENNESSEE MEDICAL CENTER (Includes Van Vleet Memorial Cancer Center, 3 N. Dunlap St., Zip 38103; William F. Bowld Hospital, 951 Court Ave., Zip 38103), 951 Court Ave., Zip 38103; tel. 901/577-4000; Charles W. Mercer MD, dir. **A**1a 2 3 5 9 10 **F**1 3 4 12 13 15 16 20 23 33 34 35 39 43 44 46 54	12	10	S		126	3935	82	65.1	0	0	19439	8270	396
VAN VLEET MEMORIAL CANCER CENTER, See University of Tennessee Medical Center													
⊞ VETERANS ADMINISTRATION MEDICAL CENTER, 1030 Jefferson Ave., Zip 38104; tel. 901/523-8990; K. L. Mulholland Jr., dir. (Total facility includes 120 beds in nursing home-type unit) **A**1a 3 5 8 **F**3 4 6 7 8 9 10 11 12 14 15 16 19 20 21 23 24 26 27 28 29 30 31 32 33 34 35 41 42 43 44 45 46 47 48 49 50 53 54	45	10	S	TF	1006	19311	720	71.6	0	0	83966	56956	2142
				H	886	18869	610	—	0	0	78712	53154	2057
WILLIAM F. BOWLD HOSPITAL, See University of Tennessee Medical Center													
MILAN—Gibson County													
⊞ CITY OF MILAN HOSPITAL, 710 S. Liberty St., P O Box 719, Zip 38358; tel. 901/686-1591; Donald Chaffin, adm. **A**1a 9 10 **F**1 3 6 10 15 16 23 35 40 45 46 53; **S**1755	14	10	S		72	1972	24	33.3	10	103	4467	1756	107
MILLINGTON—Shelby County													
⊞ NAVAL HOSPITAL, Zip 38054; tel. 901/872-5804; Capt. W. E. Clayton MC USN, CO (Nonreporting) **A**1a 2	43	10	S		77	—	—	—	—	—	—	—	—
MORRISTOWN—Hamblen County													
⊞ HUMANA HOSPITAL -MORRISTOWN, 726 McFarland St., Zip 37814; tel. 615/586-2302; Stephen L. Taylor, exec. dir. **A**1a 9 10 **F**1 3 6 10 15 16 23 24 27 35 46 53; **S**1235	33	10	S		135	3335	66	48.9	0	0	8613	3253	197
⊞ MORRISTOWN-HAMBLEN HOSPITAL, 908 W. Fourth North St., Zip 37814; tel. 615/586-4231; Rudolph McKinley Jr., adm. **A**1a 9 10 **F**1 3 6 10 12 14 15 16 23 33 34 35 40 45 46 47 52 53	23	10	S		127	5846	85	55.6	16	814	12357	5621	361
MOUNTAIN CITY—Washington County													
⊞ JOHNSON COUNTY MEMORIAL HOSPITAL, Box 49, Zip 37683; tel. 615/727-7731; G. Gay Hamilton, adm. **A**1a 9 10 **F**14 16 23 35 45 46 47; **S**1755	23	10	S		66	1114	15	22.7	10	51	—	—	104
MOUNTAIN HOME—Washington County													
⊞ VETERANS ADMINISTRATION MEDICAL CENTER, Zip 37684; tel. 615/926-1171; Jonathan F. Fitts, dir. (Total facility includes 58 beds in nursing home-type unit) **A**1a 2 3 5 8 **F**1 2 3 6 10 12 14 15 16 19 23 24 26 27 28 30 31 32 33 34 35 42 44 45 46 47 48 49 50	45	10	S	TF	504	7323	405	79.6	0	0	51645	32037	1189
				H	446	7287	348	—	0	0	—	—	—
MURFREESBORO—Rutherford County													
⊞ ALVIN C. YORK VETERANS ADMINISTRATION MEDICAL CENTER (Formerly Veterans Administration Medical Center), 3400 Lebanon Rd., Zip 37130; tel. 615/893-1360; Ronald L. Nelson, dir. (Total facility includes 48 beds in nursing home-type unit) **A**1a 3 5 **F**1 3 6 10 12 14 15 16 19 23 24 26 27 28 30 31 32 33 34 35 42 44 46 48 49	45	10	L	TF	667	3970	519	77.8	0	0	43173	29184	1207
				H	619	3946	473	—	0	0	40790	27410	1179
⊞ MIDDLE TENNESSEE MEDICAL CENTER, N. University St., P O Box 1178, Zip 37130; tel. 615/893-8240; Arthur W. Hastings, pres. & chief exec. off. **A**1a 9 **F**1 2 3 6 9 10 11 12 14 15 16 20 23 35 40 41 44 45 46 47 52 53	23	10	S		191	9108	128	66.3	22	1369	21969	10830	598
VETERANS ADMINISTRATION MEDICAL CENTER, See Alvin C. York Veterans Administration Medical Center													
NASHVILLE—Davidson County													
⊞ BAPTIST HOSPITAL, 2000 Church St., Zip 37236; tel. 615/329-5555; C. David Stringfield, pres. **A**1a 3 5 9 10 **F**1 4 6 7 8 9 10 11 12 14 15 16 17 20 23 24 34 35 36 39 42 44 45 46 47 53 54	21	10	S		651	30149	481	73.9	64	4205	—	—	—
DONELSON HOSPITAL, See HCA Donelson Hospital													
EDGEFIELD HOSPITAL, See HCA Edgefield Hospital													
⊞ GEORGE W. HUBBARD HOSPITAL OF MEHARRY MEDICAL COLLEGE, 1005 D B Todd Blvd., Zip 37208; tel. 615/327-5851; Andre L. Lee Dpa, exec. dir. **A**1a 2 3 5 8 9 10 **F**6 7 8 9 10 11 12 14 16 20 23 24 27 30 32 33 34 35 36 40 43 44 45 46 47 52 53	23	10	S		230	4735	100	43.5	0	0	20907	10631	482
⊞ HCA DONELSON HOSPITAL (Formerly Donelson Hospital), 3055 Lebanon Rd., Zip 37214; tel. 615/871-3000; Neil Serle', adm. **A**1a 10 **F**1 2 3 6 10 11 12 14 15 16 23 29 30 33 34 35 36 40 46 47 53; **S**1755	33	10	S		218	6957	123	56.4	25	460	24565	8931	471
⊞ HCA EDGEFIELD HOSPITAL (Formerly Edgefield Hospital), 610 Gallatin Rd., Zip 37206; tel. 615/226-4330; Jack P. Nyiri, adm. **A**1a 9 10 **F**1 3 6 10 12 14 15 16 23 27 35 44 46 47 53; **S**1755	33	10	S		97	2948	37	38.1	0	0	9591	3647	201
⊞ HCA PARK VIEW MEDICAL CENTER (Formerly Park View Medical Center), 230 25th Ave. N., P O Box 1225, Zip 37202; tel. 615/340-1000; Ernest Bacon, adm. **A**1a b 9 10 **F**1 2 3 4 6 7 8 9 10 11 12 14 16 17 20 23 24 26 29 34 35 42 53 54; **S**1755	33	10	S		441	12073	314	71.0	0	0	—	—	979
★ HCA PARTHENON PAVILION (Formerly Parthenon Pavilion), 2401 Murphy Ave., Zip 37203; tel. 615/327-2237; James W. Weiss, chief exec. off. & adm. **F**24 28 30 32 33 42 47 50; **S**1755	33	22	S		158	1758	113	71.5	0	0	8204	3708	205
⊞ HCA SOUTHERN HILLS MEDICAL CENTER (Formerly Southern Hills Medical Center), 391 Wallace Rd., Zip 37211; tel. 615/781-4100; John L. Fitzgerald, adm. **A**1a 9 10 **F**1 3 6 10 12 14 15 16 20 23 35 36 37 40 46 50 53; **S**1755	33	10	S		136	6721	95	69.9	12	627	—	—	482
⊞ HCA WEST SIDE HOSPITAL (Formerly West Side Hospital), 2221 Murphy Ave., Zip 37203; tel. 615/329-6000; Samuel G. Feazell, adm. **A**1a 9 10 **F**1 3 6 9 10 12 14 15 16 20 23 26 35 36 40 45 53 54; **S**1755	33	10	S		182	7825	99	54.4	20	1209	25520	9292	520
⊞ METROPOLITAN NASHVILLE GENERAL HOSPITAL, 72 Hermitage Ave., Zip 37210; tel. 615/259-5775; John M. Stone, dir. & adm. **A**1a 2 3 5 9 10 **F**1 2 3 5 6 9 10 12 14 15 16 23 28 33 34 35 37 40 45 46 47 51 52 53	15	10	S		178	7959	126	70.4	31	1648	31470	14504	700
☐ MIDDLE TENNESSEE MENTAL HEALTH INSTITUTE, 1501 Murfreesboro Rd., Zip 37217; tel. 615/366-7616; Leon S. Joyner, supt. (Total facility includes 75 beds in nursing home-type unit) **A**1b 3 5 10 **F**3 12 19 24 32 33 42 46 47 50	12	22	L	TF	489	1683	429	86.7	0	0	23064	13527	970
				H	414	1673	351	—	0	0	21623	13183	905
★ NASHVILLE METROPOLITAN BORDEAUX HOSPITAL (Chronic Disease and Skilled Nursing), County Hospital Rd., Zip 37218; tel. 615/259-7000; Wayne I. Hayes, adm. (Total facility includes 526 beds in nursing home-type unit) **A**10 **F**16 19 23 42 44 46 50	15	49	L	TF	541	189	511	94.5	0	0	13954	8216	513
				H	15	7	5	—	0	0	—	—	176

★ American Hospital Association (AHA) membership
□ Joint Commission on Accreditation of Hospitals (JCAH) accreditation
\+ American Osteopathic Hospital Association (AOHA) membership
○ American Osteopathic Association (AOA) accreditation
Δ Commission on Accreditation of Rehabilitation Facilities (CARF) accreditation
Control codes 61, 63, 64, 71, 72 and 73 indicate hospitals listed by AOHA, but not registered by AHA.
For definition of numerical codes, see page A2

Hospital, Address, Telephone, Administrator, Approval and Facility Codes, Multihospital System Code	Classification Codes				Inpatient Data				Newborn Data		Expense (thousands of dollars)		
	Control	Service	Stay	Facilities	Beds	Admissions	Census	Occupancy (percent)	Bassinets	Births	Total	Payroll	Personnel
PARK VIEW MEDICAL CENTER, See HCA Park View Medical Center													
PARTHENON PAVILION, See HCA Parthenon Pavilion													
SOUTHERN HILLS MEDICAL CENTER, See HCA Southern Hills Medical Center													
★□ ST. THOMAS HOSPITAL, 4220 Harding Rd., Zip 37205; Mailing Address Box 380, Zip 37202; tel. 615/386-2111; Sr. Juliana Beuerlein, pres. **A**1a 3 5 9 10 **F**1 3 4 5 6 7 8 9 10 11 12 13 14 15 16 20 23 24 26 27 32 33 34 35 41 42 45 46 47 53 54; **S**1885	21	10	S		571	21126	465	81.4	0	0	109845	47929	2535
TENNESSEE STATE PENITENTIARY HOSPITAL, Sta. A West, Zip 37219; tel. 615/741-4611; Lyall Craft, adm. (Nonreporting)	12	11	S		102	—	—	—	—	—	—	—	—
★□ VANDERBILT UNIVERSITY HOSPITAL, 1161 21st Ave. S., Zip 37232; tel. 615/322-5000; Norman B. Urmy, dir. **A**1a 2 3 5 8 9 10 **F**1 3 4 5 6 7 8 9 10 11 12 13 14 15 16 17 19 20 22 23 24 25 26 27 28 29 30 31 32 33 34 35 36 37 38 40 41 42 44 45 46 47 48 49 50 51 52 53 54	23	10	S		626	19964	481	76.0	20	1148	139681	57705	3194
★□ VETERANS ADMINISTRATION MEDICAL CENTER, 1310 24th Ave. S., Zip 37203; tel. 615/327-4751; Larry E. Deters, dir. **A**1a 3 5 8 **F**1 2 3 4 6 10 11 12 13 14 15 16 19 20 21 23 24 26 27 28 30 32 33 34 38 44 45 46 47 48 49 53 54	45	10	S		429	12507	326	73.3	0	0	67884	30627	1231
WEST SIDE HOSPITAL, See HCA West Side Hospital													
NEWPORT—Cocke County													
COCKE COUNTY BAPTIST HOSPITAL, 702-710 Second St., Zip 37821; tel. 615/625-2200; Wayne Buckner, adm. (Nonreporting) **A**9 10	21	10	S		130	—	—	—	—	—	—	—	—
OAK RIDGE—Anderson County													
★□ METHODIST MEDICAL CENTER OF OAK RIDGE, 990 Oak Ridge Turnpike, P O Box 529, Zip 37831; tel. 615/481-1000; Marshall Whisnant, pres.; George Mathews, adm. (Nonreporting) **A**1a 9 10	21	10	S		265	—	—	—	—	—	—	—	—
□ RIDGEVIEW PSYCHIATRIC HOSPITAL AND CENTER, 240 W. Tyrone Rd., Zip 37830; tel. 615/482-1076; Ben Bursten MD, chief exec. off. (Nonreporting) **A**1b 10	23	22	S		43	—	—	—	—	—	—	—	—
ONEIDA—Scott County													
□ SCOTT COUNTY HOSPITAL, U. S. Hwy. 27, Box 308, Zip 37841; tel. 615/569-8521; J. Clifton Quinn, adm. & chief exec. off. (Total facility includes 52 beds in nursing home-type unit) **A**1a 9 10 **F**1 3 6 14 16 19 23 35 53	13	10	S	TF	147	3649	102	69.4	0	0	7967	3562	285
				H	95	3617	50	—	0	0	7114	3144	244
PARIS—Henry County													
★□ HENRY COUNTY MEDICAL CENTER (Formerly Henry County General Hospital), Tyson Ave., Box 1030, Zip 38242; tel. 901/642-1220; Dwayne French, adm. **A**1a 9 10 **F**1 2 3 6 10 12 14 16 23 29 30 34 35 37 40 41 45 47 50 52 53	13	10	S		140	4611	70	50.0	15	163	8448	3816	262
PARSONS—Decatur County													
DECATUR COUNTY GENERAL HOSPITAL, 1200 Tennessee Ave. S., Box 249, Zip 38363; tel. 901/847-3031; Larry N. Lindsey, adm. **A**9 10 **F**1 3 6 16 23 34 35 46 47 53	13	10	S		40	1675	29	72.5	5	0	2953	1405	96
PIKEVILLE—Bledsoe County													
BLEDSOE COUNTY HOSPITAL, Box 428, Zip 37367; tel. 615/447-2112; Donald E. Downey, adm. **A**9 10 **F**1 6 12 14 16 23 35; **S**5765	33	10	S		32	1520	18	56.3	0	0	2991	1020	75
PORTLAND—Sumner County													
★□ HIGHLAND HOSPITAL, 500 Redbud Dr., Zip 37148; tel. 615/325-7301; Jerry F. Medanich, pres. **A**1a 9 10 **F**1 3 6 10 15 16 23 33 35 36 40 45 46; **S**4165	21	10	S		48	1878	23	47.9	3	104	5468	1902	121
PULASKI—Giles County													
□ HILLSIDE HOSPITAL, 1265 E. College St., Zip 38478; tel. 615/363-7531; Thomas E. Smith, adm. **A**1a 9 10 **F**1 3 6 10 12 15 16 17 23 34 35 37 40 43 45 46 52 53 54; **S**0875	33	10	S		95	5526	83	87.4	8	166	—	—	191
RIPLEY—Lauderdale County													
★□ BAPTIST MEMORIAL HOSPITAL-LAUDERDALE, 326 Asbury Rd., Zip 38063; tel. 901/635-1331; William E. Torrence Jr., adm. **A**1a 9 10 **F**1 3 6 10 14 16 23 26 35 41 44 45 46 47; **S**1625	21	10	S		70	1720	31	44.3	0	0	5070	1957	111
ROCKWOOD—Roane County													
★□ CHAMBERLAIN MEMORIAL HOSPITAL, 241 S. Chamberlain Ave., Box 388, Zip 37854; tel. 615/354-1121; John B. Couch, adm. **A**1a 9 10 **F**1 3 6 14 15 16 23 34 35 40 52 53	23	10	S		97	2831	41	42.3	5	172	6612	2834	206
ROGERSVILLE—Hawkins County													
★□ HAWKINS COUNTY MEMORIAL HOSPITAL, Locust St., Zip 37857; tel. 615/272-2671; R. Frank Testerman, adm. **A**1a 9 10 **F**1 6 10 14 15 16 23 30 34 35 36 37 40 45 46 47 50 52 53	13	10	S		55	2519	35	63.6	13	150	5005	1801	133
SAVANNAH—Hardin County													
HARDIN COUNTY GENERAL HOSPITAL, 2006 Wayne Rd., Zip 38372; tel. 901/925-4954; Tommye O'Neal, adm. (Total facility includes 48 beds in nursing home-type unit) **A**9 10 **F**1 6 10 14 15 16 19 21 23 34 41 45 46 53	13	10	S	TF	131	2304	87	66.4	0	0	4956	2468	216
				H	83	2279	39	—	0	0	—	—	185
SELMER—McNairy County													
★□ MCNAIRY COUNTY GENERAL HOSPITAL, 705 E. Poplar Ave., Zip 38375; tel. 901/645-3221; Robert P. Hanna, adm. **A**1a 9 10 **F**1 6 10 14 15 16 23 35 40 45 47 52 53	13	10	S		86	2263	28	32.6	18	190	4947	2008	141
SEVIERVILLE—Sevier County													
★□ FT SANDERS-SEVIER MEDICAL CENTER, 709 Middle Creek Rd., Zip 37862; tel. 615/453-7111; James N. Kulpan, adm. (Total facility includes 54 beds in nursing home-type unit) **A**1a 9 10 **F**1 3 6 10 14 15 16 19 23 24 32 34 35 36 40 44 45 46 53	23	10	S	TF	133	2266	82	61.7	6	187	6602	3040	235
				H	79	2244	29	—	6	187	5995	2658	204
SEWANEE—Franklin County													
★□ EMERALD-HODGSON HOSPITAL, University Ave., Zip 37375; tel. 615/598-5691; John Stanfield, adm. (Nonreporting) **A**1a 9 10; **S**0885	23	10	S		34	—	—	—	—	—	—	—	—
SHELBYVILLE—Bedford County													
□ BEDFORD COUNTY GENERAL HOSPITAL, 845 Union St., Zip 37160; tel. 615/684-3211; Richard L. Graham, adm. (Total facility includes 97 beds in nursing home-type unit) **A**1a 9 10 **F**1 3 6 14 15 16 19 23 34 35 40 44 45 46 47 52	13	10	S	TF	176	3157	138	69.3	16	251	7158	3927	269
				H	79	3056	40	—	16	251	6008	3155	214
SMITHVILLE—De Kalb County													
★□ DEKALB GENERAL HOSPITAL, W. Main St., Box 640, Zip 37166; tel. 615/597-7171; Bob Haley, adm. **A**1a 9 10 **F**3 6 14 15 16 17 23 34 35 47 53; **S**1755	33	10	S		54	1392	25	46.3	6	126	4296	1452	90
SMYRNA—Rutherford County													
★□ HCA SMYRNA HOSPITAL, Hwy. 41 S., Box 306, Zip 37167; tel. 615/459-5671; Kenneth L. Atchley, adm. **A**1a 9 10 **F**1 3 6 12 16 35 45 47 53; **S**1755	33	10	S		33	1185	15	45.5	0	0	3113	1135	60
SNEEDVILLE—Hancock County													
HANCOCK COUNTY HOSPITAL, Main St., Zip 37869; tel. 615/733-2266; Truett H. Pierce MD, adm. (Nonreporting) **A**9 10	13	10	S		31	—	—	—	—	—	—	—	—
SOMERVILLE—Fayette County													
★□ METHODIST HOSPITAL OF SOMERVILLE, 214 Lakeview Rd., Box 98, Zip 38068; tel. 901/465-3594; Carlos Smith, adm. **A**1a 10 **F**1 3 6 10 12 14 16 23 26 35 36 40 41 45; **S**9345	21	10	S		39	1593	18	46.2	6	132	3956	1574	113

Hospital, Address, Telephone, Administrator, Approval and Facility Codes, Multihospital System Code	Classification Codes				Inpatient Data				Newborn Data		Expense (thousands of dollars)		
★ American Hospital Association (AHA) membership □ Joint Commission on Accreditation of Hospitals (JCAH) accreditation + American Osteopathic Hospital Association (AOHA) membership ○ American Osteopathic Association (AOA) accreditation Δ Commission on Accreditation of Rehabilitation Facilities (CARF) accreditation Control codes 61, 63, 64, 71, 72 and 73 indicate hospitals listed by AOHA, but not registered by AHA. For definition of numerical codes, see page A2	Control	Service	Stay	Facilities	Beds	Admissions	Census	Occupancy (percent)	Bassinets	Births	Total	Payroll	Personnel
SOUTH PITTSBURG—Marion County													
★□ SOUTH PITTSBURG MUNICIPAL HOSPITAL, 210 W. 12th St., Zip 37380; tel. 615/837-6781; Melville P. Mottet, adm. **A**1a 9 10 **F**1 3 5 6 10 15 16 23 35 40 45 47; **S**1755	33	10	S		60	2171	28	46.7	6	112	4143	1713	105
SPARTA—White County													
★□ WHITE COUNTY COMMUNITY HOSPITAL, 401 Sewell Rd., Zip 38583; tel. 615/738-9211; Michael R. Brown, adm. (Nonreporting) **A**1a 9 10	33	10	S		55	—	—	—	—	—	—	—	—
SPRINGFIELD—Robertson County													
★□ JESSE HOLMAN JONES HOSPITAL, Brown St., Zip 37172; tel. 615/384-2411; Norma Calhoun, adm. **A**1a 9 10 **F**1 3 14 15 16 20 21 23 34 35 36 40 41 45 46 47 52	13	10	S		101	4675	66	65.3	15	414	11262	5284	311
SWEETWATER—Monroe County													
★ SWEETWATER HOSPITAL, 304 Wright St., Zip 37874; tel. 615/337-6171; Scott Bowman, adm. (Nonreporting) **A**9 10	23	10	S		59	—	—	—	—	—	—	—	—
TAZEWELL—Claiborne County													
★□ CLAIBORNE COUNTY HOSPITAL, 1000 Old Knoxville Rd., Box 219, Zip 37879; tel. 615/626-4211; Patricia Gray, adm. (Nonreporting) **A**1a 9 10	13	10	S		135	—	—	—	—	—	—	—	—
TRENTON—Gibson County													
FORUM HOSPITAL TRENTON (Formerly Memorial Hospital), 2036 Hwy. 45 By-Pass, Zip 38382; tel. 901/855-4500; Ray Holmes, adm. (Nonreporting) **A**9; **S**0905	33	10	S		90	—	—	—	—	—	—	—	—
□ GIBSON GENERAL HOSPITAL, Hospital Dr., Box 488, Zip 38382; tel. 901/855-2551; Walter J. Stephenson, adm. **A**1a 9 10 **F**1 2 3 6 15 16 23 34 35 41 42 44 45 46 47 50 52 53; **S**1375	33	10	S		101	1701	25	24.8	6	126	5754	1943	130
MEMORIAL HOSPITAL, See Forum Hospital Trenton													
TULLAHOMA—Coffee County													
□ JOHN W. HARTON REGIONAL MEDICAL CENTER, New Shelbyville Hwy., Box 460, Zip 37388; tel. 615/455-0601; Tom Anderson, adm. (Nonreporting) **A**1a 9 10; **S**3015	33	10	S		137	—	—	—	—	—	—	—	—
UNION CITY—Obion County													
★□ BAPTIST MEMORIAL HOSPITAL-UNION CITY, Russell & Bishop Sts., Box 310, Zip 38261; tel. 901/885-2410; David C. Hogan, adm. **A**1a 9 10 **F**1 3 6 7 8 9 10 11 12 14 15 16 23 26 27 30 32 33 34 35 36 40 45 47 48 52 53; **S**1625	21	10	S		120	4864	76	57.1	20	565	12277	4680	292
WAVERLY—Humphreys County													
□ THREE RIVERS COMMUNITY HOSPITAL (Formerly Nautilus Memorial Hospital), S. Church St., Zip 37185; tel. 615/296-4203; L. Joe Austin, adm. (Nonreporting) **A**1a 9 10; **S**1375	33	10	S		52	—	—	—	—	—	—	—	—
WAYNESBORO—Wayne County													
□ WAYNE COUNTY GENERAL HOSPITAL, Hwy. 64 E., P O Box 580, Zip 38485; tel. 615/722-5411; B. Richard Moseley, adm. **A**1a 9 10 **F**1 3 6 14 16 23 35 40 45 47; **S**5895	33	10	S		70	1278	16	22.9	6	3	—	—	78
WESTERN INSTITUTE—Hardeman County													
□ WESTERN MENTAL HEALTH INSTITUTE, Hwy. 64 W., Zip 38074; tel. 901/658-5141; Evelyn C. Robertson Jr., supt. (Total facility includes 48 beds in nursing home-type unit) **A**1b 10 **F**3 12 23 24 25 30 32 33 42 44 45 46 47 52	12	22	L	TF	353	1000	266	75.4	0	0	17000	—	711
				H	305	940	258	—	0	0	—	—	—
WINCHESTER—Franklin County													
★□ METHODIST HOSPITAL OF MIDDLE TENNESSEE, Cowan Rd., Zip 37398; tel. 615/967-8200; Thomas L. Harper, adm. (Total facility includes 36 beds in nursing home-type unit) **A**1a 9 10 **F**1 3 6 10 12 14 15 16 19 23 35 36 37 40 41 45 50; **S**9345	21	10	S	TF	116	3693	84	68.9	9	558	10791	3548	250
				H	80	3678	49	—	9	558	—	—	229
WOODBURY—Cannon County													
★□ HCA STONES RIVER HOSPITAL (Formerly Stones River Hospital), Doolittle Rd., P O Box 458, Zip 37190; tel. 615/563-4001; Ken Parker, adm. **A**1a 9 10 **F**1 3 6 10 16 23 34 35 36 45 47 48 49 53; **S**1755	33	10	S		85	1393	25	29.4	12	44	4515	1769	113

★ American Hospital Association (AHA) membership
□ Joint Commission on Accreditation of Hospitals (JCAH) accreditation
+ American Osteopathic Hospital Association (AOHA) membership
○ American Osteopathic Association (AOA) accreditation
Δ Commission on Accreditation of Rehabilitation Facilities (CARF) accreditation
Control codes 61, 63, 64, 71, 72 and 73 indicate hospitals listed by AOHA, but not registered by AHA.
For definition of numerical codes, see page A2

Texas

Hospital, Address, Telephone, Administrator, Approval and Facility Codes, Multihospital System Code	Classification Codes				Inpatient Data				Newborn Data		Expense (thousands of dollars)		
	Control	Service	Stay	Facilities	Beds	Admissions	Census	Occupancy (percent)	Bassinets	Births	Total	Payroll	Personnel
ABILENE—Taylor County													
⊞ HENDRICK MEDICAL CENTER, 1242 N. 19th Sts., Zip 79601; tel. 915/670-2000; Michael C. Waters, pres. (Nonreporting) **A**1a 3 5 9 10; **S**3535	21	10	S		452	—	—	—	—	—	—	—	—
⊞ HUMANA HOSPITAL -ABILENE, 6250 Hwy. 83-84 at Antilley Rd., Zip 79606; tel. 915/695-9900; David M. Collins, exec. dir. **A**1a 9 10 **F**1 2 3 4 6 10 12 15 16 23 30 34 35 36 37 40 45 46 52 53 54; **S**1235	33	10	S		160	5957	107	66.9	22	244	—	—	491
U. S. AIR FORCE HOSPITAL, See Dyess Air Force Base													
⊞ WOODS PSYCHIATRIC INSTITUTE, 1115 Industrial, P O Box 5749, Zip 79608; tel. 915/698-2320; Everett E. Woods, chief exec. off. **A**1b 10 **F**28 32 33 42 48 49	33	22	L		96	181	77	80.2	0	0	—	—	173
ALBANY—Shackelford County													
★ SHACKELFORD COUNTY HOSPITAL DISTRICT, 600 Greer St., Box 876, Zip 76430; tel. 817/762-3313; Nick Shankles, adm. **A**9 10 **F**35	16	10	S		24	152	3	12.5	3	12	—	—	21
ALICE—Jim Wells County													
⊞ AMI PHYSICIANS AND SURGEONS HOSPITAL (Formerly Physicians and Surgeons Hospital), 300 E. Third St., Zip 78332; tel. 512/664-4376; John C. Woodson, exec. dir. (Nonreporting) **A**1a 9 10; **S**0125	33	10	S		90	—	—	—	—	—	—	—	—
ALPINE—Brewster County													
□ BREWSTER MEMORIAL HOSPITAL (Formerly Big Bend Memorial Hospital), 801 E. Brown St., Box 180, Zip 79831; tel. 915/837-3447; Don Karl, interim adm. **A**1a 9 10 **F**1 3 5 6 12 14 15 16 23 26 34 35 40 41 43 44 45 47; **S**0725	16	10	S		34	1066	12	35.3	7	216	3173	1540	83
ALVIN—Brazoria County													
⊞ AMI ALVIN COMMUNITY HOSPITAL (Formerly Alvin Community Hospital), 301 Medic Lane, Zip 77511; tel. 713/331-6141; Terry Kirk, chief oper. off. **A**1a 9 10 **F**1 3 6 10 16 17 23 34 35 40 46 47 48 53; **S**0125	33	10	S		76	2080	41	54.2	2	26	—	—	149
AMARILLO—Potter County													
⊞ AMARILLO HOSPITAL DISTRICT (Includes Northwest Texas Hospital, 1501 Coulter, Zip 79106; Mailing Address Box 1110, Zip 79175; Psychiatric Pavilion, 7201 Evans, Zip 79106), Box 1110, Zip 79175; tel. 806/358-9031; Joel T. Allison, exec. dir. (Nonreporting) **A**1a 2 3 5 9 10	16	10	S		392	—	—	—	—	—	—	—	—
○ + FAMILY HOSPITAL CENTER (Formerly Southwest Osteopathic Hospital), 2828 S.W. 27th St., Box 7408, Zip 79109; tel. 806/358-3131; Rod Bailey, exec. vice-pres. **A**9 10 11 **F**1 3 6 14 15 16 34 35 40 43 45 50	23	10	S		50	1037	16	32.0	7	85	3836	2015	114
⊞ HIGH PLAINS BAPTIST HOSPITAL, 1600 Wallace Blvd., Zip 79106; tel. 806/358-3151; T. H. Holloway Jr., pres. **A**1a 2 3 5 9 10 **F**1 2 3 4 6 9 10 12 13 15 16 23 24 26 33 34 36 37 40 42 44 45 46 47 53 54	21	10	S		308	9709	185	60.1	33	858	37296	17444	912
NORTHWEST TEXAS HOSPITAL, See Amarillo Hospital District													
PSYCHIATRIC PAVILION, See Amarillo Hospital District													
SOUTHWEST OSTEOPATHIC HOSPITAL, See Family Hospital Center													
⊞ ST. ANTHONY'S HOSPITAL, 200 N.W. Seventh, Zip 79107; Mailing Address Box 950, Zip 79176; tel. 806/376-4411; William D. Myers, pres. (Total facility includes 30 beds in nursing home-type unit) **A**1a 2 3 5 9 10 **F**1 2 3 4 6 7 8 9 10 11 12 14 15 16 19 20 21 23 24 26 34 35 43 44 45 46 48 50 52 53 54; **S**5565	21	10	S	TF	314	11299	219	69.7	0	0	47173	18515	1065
				H	284	10788	200	—	0	0	46707	18080	—
⊞ VETERANS ADMINISTRATION MEDICAL CENTER, 6010 Amarillo Blvd. W., Zip 79106; tel. 806/355-9703; R. Michael Harwell, dir. **A**1a 2 3 5 **F**1 3 6 10 12 15 16 23 26 28 34 44 46	45	10	S		132	4038	101	76.5	0	0	23429	—	421
AMHERST—Lamb County													
SOUTH PLAINS HOSPITAL CLINIC, 1400 Main St., Box 487, Zip 79312; tel. 806/246-3536; Louise S. Landers, adm. (Nonreporting) **A**9 10	23	10	S		35	—	—	—	—	—	—	—	—
ANAHUAC—Chambers County													
★ BAYSIDE COMMUNITY HOSPITAL (Formerly Chambers Memorial Hospital), 200 S. Front St., Box 398, Zip 77514; tel. 713/267-3143; Billy Don York, adm. **A**9 10 **F**1 6 12 14 15 23 34 35 36 37 41 42 45 47 53	16	10	S		17	515	5	23.7	3	45	1605	713	46
ANDREWS—Andrews County													
⊞ PERMIAN GENERAL HOSPITAL, N.E. By-Pass, Box 2108, Zip 79714; tel. 915/523-2200; Glen D. Bunn, chief exec. off. **A**1a 9 10 **F**1 3 6 12 14 16 23 27 29 30 32 33 34 35 36 40 41 43 44 45 47 52 53	13	10	S		104	3183	39	37.5	8	495	9507	4709	243
ANGLETON—Brazoria County													
⊞ ANGLETON-DANBURY GENERAL HOSPITAL, 132 Hospital Dr., Zip 77515; tel. 409/849-7721; James R. Perry, adm. **A**1a 9 10 **F**1 3 5 6 10 16 20 23 35 40 43 45 52; **S**0725	16	10	S		61	1963	25	41.0	6	131	5754	3569	133
ANSON—Jones County													
⊞ ANSON GENERAL HOSPITAL, 100 First St., Zip 79501; tel. 915/823-3231; Dudley R. White, adm. **A**1a 9 10 **F**1 3 16 23 35 40 43	15	10	S		45	964	19	42.2	8	5	1692	775	62
ARANSAS PASS—San Patricio County													
★ AMI COASTAL BEND HOSPITAL, 1711 W. Wheeler St., Zip 78336; tel. 512/758-8585; Ken Noteboom, exec. dir. **A**9 10 **F**1 3 5 6 10 12 15 16 34 35 36 37 43 45 46 50; **S**0125	33	10	S		75	2456	35	46.7	6	320	10709	3132	156
ARCHER CITY—Archer County													
★ ARCHER COUNTY HOSPITAL, 410 E. Chestnut St., Box 368, Zip 76351; tel. 817/574-4586; Daniel D. Powell, adm. **A**9 10 **F**1 5 15 30 35 43 45 50; **S**6005	13	10	S		26	181	2	7.7	6	27	728	362	24
ARLINGTON—Tarrant County													
ARLINGTON COMMUNITY HOSPITAL, See HCA South Arlington Medical Center													
⊞ ARLINGTON MEMORIAL HOSPITAL, 800 W. Randol Mill Rd., Zip 76012; tel. 817/274-5581; Rex C. McRae, adm. **A**1a 9 10 **F**1 2 3 4 5 6 9 10 12 15 16 20 23 24 35 36 40 44 45 46 50 51 53 54	23	10	S		361	15752	246	68.1	44	3013	46250	21061	1150
⊞ CPC MILLWOOD HOSPITAL, 1011 N. Cooper St., Zip 76011; tel. 817/261-3121; Harry G. Harrier, adm. **A**1b 10 **F**24 27 28 29 30 32 33 42 44 48; **S**0785	33	22	L		155	974	85	59.6	0	0	—	—	147
⊞ HCA SOUTH ARLINGTON MEDICAL CENTER (Formerly Arlington Community Hospital), 3301 Matlock Rd., Zip 76015; tel. 817/465-3241; James J. Cliborne Jr., adm. **A**1a 9 **F**1 3 6 12 14 15 16 17 19 23 24 26 29 30 34 35 36 37 38 40 42 43 44 45 46 47 50 52 53; **S**1755	33	10	S		185	6389	93	50.3	24	1116	—	—	385
⊞ WILLOW CREEK ADOLESCENT CENTER, 7000 Hwy. 287 S., P O Box 171208, Zip 76003; tel. 817/572-3355; Ralph B. Shelton, bd. chm. (Newly Registered) **A**1a b 9	33	22	L		55	—	—	—	—	—	—	—	—

★ American Hospital Association (AHA) membership
□ Joint Commission on Accreditation of Hospitals (JCAH) accreditation
\+ American Osteopathic Hospital Association (AOHA) membership
○ American Osteopathic Association (AOA) accreditation
Δ Commission on Accreditation of Rehabilitation Facilities (CARF) accreditation
Control codes 61, 63, 64, 71, 72 and 73 indicate hospitals listed by AOHA, but not registered by AHA.
For definition of numerical codes, see page A2

Hospital, Address, Telephone, Administrator, Approval and Facility Codes, Multihospital System Code	Classification Codes				Inpatient Data				Newborn Data		Expense (thousands of dollars)		
	Control	Service	Stay	Facilities	Beds	Admissions	Census	Occupancy (percent)	Bassinets	Births	Total	Payroll	Personnel
ASPERMONT—Stonewall County													
★ STONEWALL MEMORIAL HOSPITAL, U. S. Hwy. 380 & 83 N., Drawer C, U. S. Hwy., Zip 79502; tel. 817/989-3551; Sharon Riggs, adm. (Nonreporting) **A**9 10	16	10	S		25	—	—	—	—	—	—	—	—
ATHENS—Henderson County													
★□ LAKELAND MEDICAL CENTER, 2000 S. Palestine, Zip 75751; tel. 214/675-2216; Gene McIntyre, adm. **A**1a 9 10 **F**1 3 6 15 16 23 35 36 40 43 45 46 47; **S**1895	23	10	S		103	3593	48	60.8	8	372	—	—	175
ATLANTA—Cass County													
ATLANTA MEMORIAL HOSPITAL, 903 S. Williams St., Box 1049, Zip 75551; tel. 214/796-4151; Thomas Nance, adm. **A**9 10 **F**1 3 6 10 14 16 23 35 36 41 45 46	16	10	S		53	1351	17	32.1	8	205	2358	1157	76
★ BROOKS HOSPITAL, Louise St., P O Box 1069, Zip 75551; tel. 214/796-2873; Jesse Brooks MD, adm. **A**9 **F**1 3 12 14 16 23 24 30 34 35 36 37 40 50 52	33	10	S		43	2221	32	74.4	5	2	1512	926	63
AUSTIN—Travis County													
□ AUSTIN STATE HOSPITAL, 4110 Guadalupe St., Zip 78751; tel. 512/452-0381; Kenny Dudley, supt. **A**1b 3 5 10 **F**12 14 15 19 23 24 26 28 30 32 33 34 42 43 44 45 46 47 48 49 50	12	22	L		603	3476	628	85.6	0	0	—	—	1226
AUSTIN STATE SCHOOL, 2203 W. 35th St., Box 1269, Zip 78767; tel. 512/454-4731; Paul Schedler, med. dir. **A**9 **F**46 47	12	62	L		692	1	692	100.0	0	0	23843	17098	1141
□ BRACKENRIDGE HOSPITAL, 601 E. 15th St., Zip 78701; tel. 512/476-6461; Thomas N. Young, adm. **A**1a 3 5 9 10 **F**1 2 3 4 5 6 12 13 14 15 16 20 23 24 25 26 30 34 35 36 37 40 42 44 45 46 51 52 53 54	14	10	S		387	16513	271	70.0	24	3258	68794	36231	1345
BROWN SCHOOLS HEALTHCARE REHABILITATION CENTER (Formerly The Brown Schools-Ranch Treatment Center), P O Box 43148, Zip 78745; tel. 512/444-4835; Tony Merka, dir. (Nonreporting); **S**0395	33	22	L		151	—	—	—	—	—	—	—	—
★□ CHARTER LANE HOSPITAL, 8402 Cross Park Dr., Zip 78761; tel. 512/837-1800; Donald P. Weber, adm. (Nonreporting) **A**1a 9 10; **S**0695	33	22	S		72	—	—	—	—	—	—	—	—
★□ HCA SHOAL CREEK HOSPITAL (Formerly Shoal Creek Hospital), 3501 Mills Ave., Zip 78731; tel. 512/452-0361; Richard D. Jones Jr., adm. **A**1b 9 10 **F**12 15 16 23 24 28 30 32 33 34 42 44 46 47 48 49 50; **S**1755	33	22	S		230	2234	116	50.4	0	0	—	—	214
★□ HCA SOUTH AUSTIN MEDICAL CENTER (Formerly South Austin Community Hospital), 901 W. Ben White Blvd., Zip 78704; tel. 512/447-2211; Michael S. Spurlock, chief exec. off. **A**1a 9 10 **F**1 3 6 9 10 12 14 15 16 23 24 30 34 35 36 37 39 40 44 45 46 50 53; **S**1755	33	10	S		134	4813	61	59.8	14	744	—	—	270
★□ HOLY CROSS HOSPITAL, 2600 E. Martin Luther King Jr Blvd., Zip 78702; tel. 512/477-9811; Pierre M. Dossman Jr., adm. (Total facility includes 26 beds in nursing home-type unit) **A**1a 9 10 **F**1 3 6 9 10 11 12 14 15 16 19 23 29 32 33 34 38 41 45 46 50; **S**1885	21	10	S	TF	70	1259	27	41.5	0	0	7994	3704	173
				H	44	1245	27	—	0	0	7966	3690	157
★□ OAKS TREATMENT CENTER-BROWN SCHOOLS, 1407 W. Stassney Lane, Zip 78745; tel. 512/444-9561; James A. Eberwine, dir. **A**1a b **F**14 30 31 33 42 44; **S**0395	33	22	L		120	92	113	94.2	0	0	—	—	253
★□ SETON MEDICAL CENTER, 1201 W. 38th St., Zip 78705; tel. 512/459-2121; Judith P. Smith, pres. **A**1a 9 10 **F**1 2 3 4 5 6 9 11 12 13 15 16 20 23 24 34 35 36 40 45 46 47 51 53 54; **S**1885	23	10	S		491	25844	383	78.0	38	4935	75767	36867	1740
SHOAL CREEK HOSPITAL, See HCA Shoal Creek Hospital													
SOUTH AUSTIN COMMUNITY HOSPITAL, See HCA South Austin Medical Center													
★□ ST. DAVID'S COMMUNITY HOSPITAL, 919 E. 32nd St., Zip 78705; Mailing Address Box 4039, Zip 78765; tel. 512/476-7111; Jack L. Campbell, pres. **A**1a 9 10 **F**1 3 4 6 7 9 10 11 12 14 15 16 17 23 24 25 26 34 35 36 37 40 41 42 44 45 46 47 51 53 54	23	10	S		325	14410	217	66.8	54	2973	48599	22390	894
STUDENT HEALTH CENTER, UNIVERSITY OF TEXAS AT AUSTIN, See University of Texas Student Health Center													
THE BROWN SCHOOLS-RANCH TREATMENT CENTER, See Brown Schools Healthcare Rehabilitation Center													
U. S. AIR FORCE HOSPITAL, See Bergstrom Air Force Base													
□ UNIVERSITY OF TEXAS STUDENT HEALTH CENTER (Formerly Student Health Center, University of Texas at Austin), 105 W. 26th St., Zip 78713; tel. 512/471-4955; Paul V. Thomas, assoc. dir. **A**1a **F**1 12 15 23 28 30 32 33 34 37 43 46 47 49	12	11	S		8	313	2	6.3	0	0	3920	2539	132
AZLE—Tarrant County													
★□ HARRIS METHODIST NORTHWEST (Formerly Harris Hospital-Eagle Mountain Area Suburban Hospital), 108 Denver Trail, Zip 76020; tel. 817/444-2575; N. Richard Belanger, adm. & vice-pres **A**1a 9 10 **F**1 3 16 23 34 35 36 40 45 46 50; **S**2345	23	10	S		36	964	12	35.3	6	150	3496	1397	79
BALLINGER—Runnels County													
BALLINGER MEMORIAL HOSPITAL, Bronte Hwy. & Ave. B, Zip 76821; tel. 915/365-2531; Gwen McLarty, adm. **A**9 10 **F**1 6 10 15 16 23 34 35 43 45	23	10	S		30	736	12	40.0	7	80	1665	863	58
BASTROP—Bastrop County													
□ BASTROP COMMUNITY HOSPITAL (Formerly Bastrop Memorial Hospital), 104 Loop 150 West, Zip 78602; tel. 512/321-3921; Jim Koch, exec. dir. **A**1a 9 10 **F**1 10 14 16 17 23 34 35 41 45; **S**1365	33	10	S		25	917	11	44.0	6	134	—	—	49
BAY CITY—Matagorda County													
★□ MATAGORDA GENERAL HOSPITAL, 1115 Ave. G, Zip 77414; tel. 409/245-6383; Shannon C. Flynn, chief exec. off. **A**1a 9 10 **F**1 3 6 10 12 14 15 16 20 21 23 30 35 36 40 41 43 45 46 53; **S**2645	16	10	S		90	3208	42	46.7	14	579	9811	3962	239
BAYTOWN—Harris County													
★□ GULF COAST HOSPITAL, 2800 Garth Rd., Zip 77521; tel. 713/425-9100; Larry Hough, adm. **A**1a 9 10 **F**1 3 6 15 16 23 28 29 30 32 33 34 35 36 40 43 45 46 47 52; **S**1755	33	10	S		139	3927	58	41.7	12	540	14756	5005	280
★□ HUMANA HOSPITAL -BAYTOWN, 1700 Bowie School Dr., Box 1451, Zip 77520; tel. 713/420-6100; William K. Atkinson, exec. dir. **A**1a 9 10 **F**1 2 3 6 12 14 15 16 23 24 27 28 29 30 32 34 35 36 37 40 42 43 45 46 47 48 49 53; **S**1235	33	10	S		191	3947	110	57.6	8	172	—	—	329
★□ SAN JACINTO METHODIST HOSPITAL, 1101 Decker Dr., Zip 77520; tel. 713/420-8600; Russ Schneider, adm. **A**1a 3 5 9 10 **F**1 3 6 10 12 14 15 16 23 26 27 29 30 32 33 34 35 36 37 40 41 43 46 49 53; **S**7235	21	10	S		138	3620	57	37.0	22	661	13142	5773	281
BEAUMONT—Jefferson County													
★□ BAPTIST HOSPITAL OF SOUTHEAST TEXAS, College & 11th Sts., Drawer 1591, Zip 77704; tel. 409/835-3781; Selman Clark, pres. **A**1a 9 10 **F**1 2 3 4 5 6 7 10 11 12 14 15 16 20 22 23 24 26 30 32 33 34 35 37 38 41 42 43 44 45 46 48 49 52 53 54	21	10	S		332	7134	166	50.0	0	0	32824	14501	734
★□ BEAUMONT MEDICAL SURGICAL HOSPITAL, 3080 College, Box 5817, Zip 77701; tel. 409/833-1411; Gary R. Grover, exec. dir. **A**1a 9 10 **F**1 3 6 10 12 14 15 16 23 29 30 34 35 37 43 46 53; **S**1235	33	10	S		250	5531	95	38.0	0	0	—	—	398
★□ BEAUMONT NEUROLOGICAL HOSPITAL, 3250 Fannin St., Zip 77701; tel. 409/835-4921; Neal Cury, adm. **A**1b 9 10 **F**15 24 30 32 33 42 48; **S**1755	33	22	S		111	1198	68	61.2	0	0	6179	2830	154
★□ ST. ELIZABETH HOSPITAL, 2830 Calder Ave., Zip 77702; Mailing Address Box 5405, Zip 77706; tel. 409/892-7171; Sr. M. Carmelita Brett, adm. **A**1a 2 9 10 **F**1 3 4 5 6 7 8 9 10 11 12 13 14 15 16 20 23 24 26 34 35 36 40 43 46 47 51 52 53 54; **S**0605	23	10	S		489	19536	334	68.3	40	2761	72663	31659	1531

Hospital, Address, Telephone, Administrator, Approval and Facility Codes, Multihospital System Code

- ★ American Hospital Association (AHA) membership
- □ Joint Commission on Accreditation of Hospitals (JCAH) accreditation
- \+ American Osteopathic Hospital Association (AOHA) membership
- ○ American Osteopathic Association (AOA) accreditation
- Δ Commission on Accreditation of Rehabilitation Facilities (CARF) accreditation

Control codes 61, 63, 64, 71, 72 and 73 indicate hospitals listed by AOHA, but not registered by AHA. For definition of numerical codes, see page A2

Hospital	Classification Codes				Inpatient Data				Newborn Data		Expense (thousands of dollars)		
	Control	Service	Stay	Facilities	Beds	Admissions	Census	Occupancy (percent)	Bassinets	Births	Total	Payroll	Personnel
BEDFORD—Tarrant County													
★□ HARRIS METHODIST-HURST-EULESS-BEDFORD (Formerly Harris Hospital-Hurst-Euless-Bedford) (Includes Harris Methodist-HEB North, 1600 Hospital Pkwy., Box 669, Zip 76022; tel. 817/283-1561; Harris Methodist-HEB South, 2219 W. Euless Blvd., Euless, Zip 76039; tel. 817/283-1561), R. William Whitman, Jr., sr. vice-pres. **A**1a 9 10 **F**1 3 5 6 9 10 12 14 15 16 17 20 23 24 25 26 27 28 30 32 33 34 35 36 37 40 42 44 45 46 47 48 49 53; **S**2345	21	10	S		251	7963	145	57.3	22	1347	32787	13166	614
★ ○ + HCA NORTHEAST COMMUNITY HOSPITAL (Formerly Northeast Community Hospital), 1301 Airport Freeway, Zip 76021; tel. 817/282-9211; Robert Martin, chief exec. off. (Nonreporting) **A**9 10 11 12 13; **S**1755	33	10	S		200	—	—	—	—	—	—	—	—
NORTHEAST COMMUNITY HOSPITAL, See HCA Northeast Community Hospital													
BEEVILLE—Bee County													
★□ BEEVILLE MEMORIAL HOSPITAL (Formerly Memorial Hospital), 1500 E. Houston St., Zip 78102; tel. 512/358-5431; Donald C. Rocke, adm. **A**1a 9 10 **F**1 3 6 12 14 15 16 23 35 37 45	23	10	S		59	2325	31	52.5	0	474	6409	3413	167
BELLVILLE—Austin County													
★□ BELLVILLE GENERAL HOSPITAL, 44 N. Cummings, Box 148, Zip 77418; tel. 409/865-3141; Charles W. Guidry, adm. **A**1a 9 10 **F**1 6 14 16 23 45 53	16	10	S		32	1389	16	50.0	6	169	2526	1012	50
BERGSTROM AIR FORCE BASE—Travis County													
U. S. AIR FORCE HOSPITAL, Zip 78743; tel. 512/479-2903; Maj. Herman Greenberg, adm. **F**1 6 15 23 33 34 35 40 46	41	10	S		46	2210	25	54.3	12	399	—	—	323
BIG LAKE—Reagan County													
REAGAN MEMORIAL HOSPITAL, 805 N. Main St., Zip 76932; tel. 915/884-2561; Ron Galloway, adm. **A**9 10 **F**1 34 35 40 52	16	10	S		27	436	3	11.1	6	100	898	480	31
BIG SPRING—Howard County													
□ BIG SPRING STATE HOSPITAL, Lamesa Hwy., P O Box 231, Zip 79721; tel. 915/267-8216; Robert Von Rosenberg, actg. supt. **A**1b 9 10 **F**23 24 28 29 30 31 32 33 34 42 43 46 47 48 49 50	12	22	L		351	1632	329	93.7	0	0	15819	12672	767
□ HALL-BENNETT MEMORIAL HOSPITAL, 411 E. Ninth St., Box 2071, Zip 79720; tel. 915/267-7411; Charles A. Weeg, adm. **A**1a 9 10 **F**1 5 16 34 35 36 43 50	23	10	S		48	994	17	35.4	3	39	3451	2092	102
MALONE-HOGAN HOSPITAL, See Scenic Mountain Medical Center													
★□ SCENIC MOUNTAIN MEDICAL CENTER (Formerly Malone-Hogan Hospital), 1601 W. 11th Pl., Zip 79720; tel. 915/263-1211; Keith King, actg. adm. (Nonreporting) **A**1a 9 10; **S**5895	33	10	S		116	—	—	—	—	—	—	—	—
★□ VETERANS ADMINISTRATION MEDICAL CENTER, 2400 S. Gregg St., Zip 79720; tel. 915/263-7361; Conrad Alexander, dir. (Total facility includes 40 beds in nursing home-type unit) **A**1a 2 3 5 **F**1 3 6 10 12 14 15 16 23 24 26 27 28 29 30 31 32 33 34 35 42 44 46 48 49 50	45	10	S	TF	249	3384	161	64.7	0	0	—	—	370
				H	209	3308	119	—	0	0	—	—	350
BONHAM—Fannin County													
FANNIN COUNTY HOSPITAL, 504 Lipscomb Blvd., Zip 75418; tel. 214/583-8585; Michael Moseley, adm. (Nonreporting) **A**9 10	16	10	S		65	—	—	—	—	—	—	—	—
★□ SAM RAYBURN MEMORIAL VETERANS CENTER, E. Ninth St. & Lipscomb Dr., Zip 75418; tel. 214/583-2111; Alfonso Estrada Jr., dir. (Total facility includes 325 beds in nursing home-type unit) **A**1a **F**3 14 16 19 23 24 26 27 28 30 33 34 42 44 46 47 49	45	10	S	TF	403	2644	345	85.6	0	0	—	—	349
				H	78	2682	68	—	0	0	—	—	306
BORGER—Hutchinson County													
★□ GOLDEN PLAINS COMMUNITY HOSPITAL, 200 S. McGee St., Zip 79007; tel. 806/273-2851; Wayne Cheek, actg. adm. **A**1a 9 10 **F**1 3 6 12 14 15 16 23 34 35 36 40 41 43 46 47	33	10	S		99	1784	18	18.6	14	375	—	—	115
BOWIE—Montague County													
★ BOWIE MEMORIAL HOSPITAL, Lamb & Greenwood Sts., Box 1128, Zip 76230; tel. 817/872-1126; C. Lynn Heller, adm. **A**9 10 **F**1 3 6 10 12 16 23 35 41 43 44 45 46 53	16	10	S		54	1744	27	50.9	6	130	2862	1350	99
BRADY—McCulloch County													
HEART OF TEXAS MEMORIAL HOSPITAL, Nine Rd., P O Box 1150, Zip 76825; tel. 915/597-2901; Charles Van Tine, exec. dir. **A**9 10 **F**1 3 6 16 23 35 40 41 44 45 47; **S**0725	16	10	S		50	1296	15	30.0	6	110	2269	1036	58
BRECKENRIDGE—Stephens County													
STEPHENS MEMORIAL HOSPITAL, 200 S. Geneva St., Zip 76024; tel. 817/559-2241; Charles Ballew, adm. **A**9 10 **F**3 16 23 35 40 41 45 50	13	10	S		54	726	8	14.8	4	63	2249	946	51
BRENHAM—Washington County													
□ BOHNE MEMORIAL HOSPITAL, 700 Medical Pkwy., Zip 77833; tel. 409/836-6173; John Simms, adm. **A**1a 9 10 **F**1 3 6 9 14 15 16 23 26 34 35 36 40 45 47	23	10	S		53	1590	19	34.5	12	308	4737	1825	89
★ ST. JUDE HOSPITAL, 1306 N. Park St., Box 1089, Zip 77833; tel. 409/836-6101; Ben Tobias, adm. **A**9 10 **F**1 3 6 9 10 12 15 16 23 35 36 40 45 52 53; **S**5375	21	10	S		52	1642	19	36.5	6	289	5558	2440	148
BRIDGEPORT—Wise County													
★ BRIDGEPORT HOSPITAL, 1301 Halsell St., Zip 76026; tel. 817/683-2228; Robert E. Webster, adm. **A**9 10 **F**6 10 14 16 23 40 47	33	10	S		39	1353	15	38.5	5	87	—	—	74
BROWNFIELD—Terry County													
★□ BROWNFIELD REGIONAL MEDICAL CENTER, 705 E. Felt, Zip 79316; tel. 806/637-3551; Pat McMillan, adm. **A**1a 9 10 **F**1 3 6 15 16 23 35 36 40 43 45 47 53	16	10	S		65	1175	20	30.8	8	39	3759	1848	115
BROWNSVILLE—Cameron County													
★□ AMI BROWNSVILLE MEDICAL CENTER (Formerly Brownsville Medical Center), 1040 W. Jefferson St., Box 3590, Zip 78520; tel. 512/544-1400; G. Tucker Grau, exec. dir. **A**1a 9 10 **F**1 3 6 9 10 12 15 16 20 23 35 36 40 41 43 45 46 47 52 53; **S**0125	33	10	S		148	6268	86	58.1	20	960	19102	5675	294
BROWNSVILLE MEDICAL CENTER, See AMI Brownsville Medical Center													
★□ HCA VALLEY REGIONAL MEDICAL CENTER (Formerly Valley Community Hospital), 1 Ted Hunt Blvd., Box 3710, Zip 78520; tel. 512/831-9611; Leon J. Belila, adm. (Data for 266 days) **A**1a 9 10 **F**1 3 5 6 10 11 12 14 15 16 34 35 36 40 45 46 47 48 49 52; **S**1755	33	10	S		158	2677	47	29.7	14	462	—	—	254
VALLEY COMMUNITY HOSPITAL, See HCA Valley Regional Medical Center													
BROWNWOOD—Brown County													
★□ BROWNWOOD REGIONAL HOSPITAL, Burnet & Streckert Sts., Box 760, Zip 76804; tel. 915/646-8541; James W. Saylor, adm. **A**1a 9 10 **F**1 3 6 7 9 10 11 12 15 16 23 35 37 40 45 46 47 52 53; **S**1755	33	10	S		158	5753	90	57.0	10	613	—	—	360
BRYAN—Brazos County													
★ GREENLEAF PSYCHIATRIC HOSPITAL (Formerly Greenleaf Hospital), 405 W. 28th St., Zip 77803; tel. 409/822-7326; Steve Koran, adm. **A** 9 10 **F**15 24 30 32 33 42 48 49; **S**1755	33	22	S		70	503	32	43.8	0	0	—	—	69
HUMANA HOSPITAL-BRAZOS VALLEY, See College Station													
★□ ST. JOSEPH HOSPITAL AND HEALTH CENTER (Formerly St. Joseph Hospital), 2801 Franciscan Dr., Zip 77801; tel. 409/776-3777; Sr. Gretchen Kunz, pres. **A**1a 9 10 **F**1 3 5 6 9 10 11 12 15 16 23 30 34 35 36 40 45 51 52 53; **S**5375	21	10	S		167	7726	97	58.1	30	2165	21410	9543	486

Hospital, Address, Telephone, Administrator, Approval and Facility Codes, Multihospital System Code	Classification Codes				Inpatient Data				Newborn Data		Expense (thousands of dollars)		
★ American Hospital Association (AHA) membership ☐ Joint Commission on Accreditation of Hospitals (JCAH) accreditation + American Osteopathic Hospital Association (AOHA) membership ○ American Osteopathic Association (AOA) accreditation Δ Commission on Accreditation of Rehabilitation Facilities (CARF) accreditation Control codes 61, 63, 64, 71, 72 and 73 indicate hospitals listed by AOHA, but not registered by AHA. For definition of numerical codes, see page A2	Control	Service	Stay	Facilities	Beds	Admissions	Census	Occupancy (percent)	Bassinets	Births	Total	Payroll	Personnel
BUFFALO—Leon County													
LEON MEMORIAL HOSPITAL (Formerly Leon County Memorial Hospital), Hospital Dr., Box 159, Zip 75831; tel. 214/322-4231; Glenn W. Ross Jr., adm. **A**9 10 **F**1 6 14 15 16 23 35 37 45 46; **S**1375	33	10	S		36	427	5	13.9	5	39	2013	660	45
BUNA—Jasper County													
☐ BUNA MEDICAL CENTER HOSPITAL, N. Hwy. 96, Box H, Zip 77612; tel. 713/994-3576; Wayne D. Butchee, adm. (Total facility includes 60 beds in nursing home-type unit) **A**1a 9 10 **F**1 10 12 16 19 23 35 50	33	10	S	TF	93	472	58	62.4	0	0	1747	856	85
				H	33	450	7	—	0	0	1160	503	56
BURNET—Burnet County													
☐ SHEPPERD MEMORIAL HOSPITAL, 501 Buchanan Dr., Zip 78611; tel. 512/756-2141; John J. Hayes, adm. **A**1a 9 10 **F**1 3 6 10 12 14 16 23 34 35 43 45 47	16	10	S		50	1754	17	34.0	6	209	2819	1255	95
CALDWELL—Burleson County													
BURLESON COUNTY HOSPITAL, 1101 Woodson Dr., Zip 77836; tel. 409/567-3245; Beverly Mahlmann, adm. (Nonreporting) **A**9 10	16	10	S		37	—	—	—	—	—	—	—	—
CAMERON—Milam County													
CAMERON COMMUNITY HOSPITAL, 512 N. Jefferson St., Zip 76520; tel. 817/697-6553; Edith Barron, adm. **A**10 **F**1 16 35 45	33	10	S		48	309	4	8.3	3	6	1302	500	49
⧆ ST. EDWARD HOSPITAL OF CAMERON, 806 N. Crockett St., P O Box 969, Zip 76520; tel. 817/697-6664; Robert M. Spille, adm. **A**1a 9 10 **F**1 6 10 12 14 15 16 23 34 35 40 45; **S**0605	21	10	S		46	652	8	17.4	9	59	1754	822	61
CANADIAN—Hemphill County													
HEMPHILL COUNTY HOSPITAL, 1020 S. Fourth St., Zip 79014; tel. 806/323-6422; Richard D. Arnold, adm. **A**9 10 **F**1 3 6 12 14 16 34 35 40 43 45 46	16	10	S		25	590	6	24.0	6	27	1878	837	55
CANYON—Randall County													
⧆ PALO DURO HOSPITAL, 2 Hospital Dr., Zip 79015; tel. 806/655-7751; Bob L. Bybee, adm. **A**1a 9 10 **F**3 6 15 16 23 35 40 41 42 44 45 48 50 52	16	10	S		49	1718	21	42.9	8	198	4113	1958	103
CARRIZO SPRINGS—Dimmit County													
DIMMIT COUNTY MEMORIAL HOSPITAL, 704 Hospital Dr., Zip 78834; tel. 512/876-2424; Ernest Flores Jr., adm. **A**9 10 **F**1 6 10 11 14 15 16 17 23 34 35 41 43 47	13	10	S		49	1503	15	30.6	5	247	2754	1330	99
CARROLLTON—Denton County													
TRINITY MEDICAL CENTER, 4343 N. Josey Lane, Zip 75010; tel. 214/492-1010; Robert L. Smith, adm. **A**10 **F**1 3 6 10 12 14 15 16 20 23 35 36 37 40 44 45 46 53; **S**3015	33	10	S		133	3692	37	27.8	35	1087	—	—	258
CARSWELL AIR FORCE BASE—Tarrant County													
☐ U. S. AIR FORCE REGIONAL HOSPITAL CARSWELL, Zip 76127; tel. 817/782-4895; Col. F. R. Stephen, adm. **A**1a 2 3 **F**1 3 5 6 12 14 15 16 23 28 30 32 33 34 35 37 40 45 46 47 49 52	41	10	S		110	5913	78	70.9	25	707	—	—	731
CARTHAGE—Panola County													
☐ PANOLA GENERAL HOSPITAL, 409 Cottage Rd., Box 549, Zip 75633; tel. 214/693-3841; Rex Thomas Simmons, chief exec. off. **A**1a 9 10 **F**1 3 6 10 15 16 23 34 35 40 41 43 45 52	13	10	S		60	1675	21	35.5	8	151	4453	2259	133
CENTER—Shelby County													
☐ MEMORIAL HOSPITAL, 602 Hurst St., Box 32, Zip 75935; tel. 409/598-2781; Jo Ann Brashear, adm. **A**1a 9 10 **F**1 3 14 15 16 34 35 37 41 43 47	33	10	S		44	1533	20	45.5	7	124	3390	1458	81
☐ SHELBY GENERAL HOSPITAL, 114 Hurst St., Box 1168, Zip 75935; tel. 409/598-5611; Karen Baxter, adm. **A**1a 9 10 **F**1 6 14 16 35	13	10	S		39	414	7	17.9	0	0	1217	605	39
CENTER POINT—Kerr County													
⧆ STARLITE VILLAGE HOSPITAL, Elm Pass Rd., Box 317, Zip 78010; tel. 512/634-2213; Annabelle Lindner, adm. **A**1b 9 10 **F**10 15 16 17 20 24 27 29 30 33 34 35 42 49	33	10	S		37	456	37	100.0	0	0	3110	904	51
CHANNELVIEW—Harris County													
⧆ SUN BELT REGIONAL MEDICAL CENTER EAST, 15101 E. Freeway, Zip 77530; tel. 713/452-1511; James P. Donovan III, adm. **A**1a 9 10 **F**1 3 6 10 14 16 17 23 28 32 35 36 40 43 45 46 47; **S**1755	33	10	S		96	2451	33	34.3	16	524	8457	2861	150
CHILDRESS—Childress County													
☐ CHILDRESS GENERAL HOSPITAL, Hwy. 83 N., Box 1030, Zip 79201; tel. 817/937-6371; Pat L. Horn, adm. (Nonreporting) **A**1a 9 10; **S**1765	16	10	S		75	—	—	—	—	—	—	—	—
CHILLICOTHE—Hardeman County													
★ CHILLICOTHE HOSPITAL DISTRICT, 303 Ave. I, Box 370, Zip 79225; tel. 817/852-5131; Bill Johnson, adm. **A**9 10 **F**15 34 35 45 50	16	10	S		34	345	6	17.6	0	0	1019	438	35
CISCO—Eastland County													
☐ E. L. GRAHAM MEMORIAL HOSPITAL, W. Hwy. 80, Box 321, Zip 76437; tel. 817/442-3951; Helen Orr, adm. **A**1a 9 10 **F**1 6 10 15 16 35 40 45; **S**3535	23	10	S		30	343	5	16.7	7	15	922	522	37
CLARKSVILLE—Red River County													
⧆ RED RIVER GENERAL HOSPITAL, Hwy. 82 W., Box 1270, Zip 75426; tel. 214/427-3851; James D. Luft, exec. dir. **A**1a 9 10 **F**3 6 14 15 16 23 34 35 41 45 47	16	10	S		66	1704	19	28.8	0	0	3482	1521	101
CLEBURNE—Johnson County													
⧆ WALLS REGIONAL HOSPITAL (Formerly Memorial Hospital), 201 Walls Dr., Zip 76031; tel. 817/641-2551; Nick H. Kupferle III, adm. **A**1a 9 **F**1 3 6 10 12 14 15 16 23 27 30 35 36 40 45 46; **S**2345	21	10	S		110	4784	57	59.5	16	767	13173	5445	299
CLEVELAND—Liberty County													
⧆ CHARTER COMMUNITY HOSPITAL OF CLEVELAND, 300 E. Crockett St., Box 1688, Zip 77327; tel. 713/593-1811; Timothy W. McGill, adm. (Nonreporting) **A**1a 9 10; **S**0695	33	10	S		73	—	—	—	—	—	—	—	—
CLIFTON—Bosque County													
⧆ GOODALL-WITCHER HOSPITAL, 101 S. Ave. T, Box 549, Zip 76634; tel. 817/675-8322; Jim B. Smith, adm. (Total facility includes 13 beds in nursing home-type unit) **A**1a 9 10 **F**1 3 6 10 12 16 19 23 26 34 35 40 41 43 45 53	23	10	S	TF	72	1868	25	34.7	5	245	3478	1853	117
				H	59	1852	24	—	5	245	3470	1844	—
COLEMAN—Coleman County													
OVERALL-MORRIS MEMORIAL HOSPITAL, 310 S. Pecos St., Zip 76834; tel. 915/625-2135; Terry Frazier, adm. **A**9 10 **F**3 6 14 16 23 35 45	21	10	S		46	840	11	23.9	5	62	1004	718	47
COLLEGE STATION—Brazos County													
⧆ HUMANA HOSPITAL-BRAZOS VALLEY (Formerly Humana Hospital-Bryan College Station, Bryan), 1604 Rock Prairie Rd., Zip 77840; tel. 409/764-5100; Pat Cornelison, exec. dir. **A**1a 9 10 **F**1 2 3 5 6 10 12 13 14 15 16 23 32 34 35 37 43 45 46 47 50; **S**1235	33	10	S		65	2635	40	61.5	0	0	—	—	180
COLORADO CITY—Mitchell County													
MITCHELL COUNTY HOSPITAL (Formerly Root Memorial Hospital), 1543 Chestnut St., Zip 79512; tel. 915/728-3431; Ray Mason, dm **A**9 10 **F**1 6 10 16 23 35 41 45	16	10	S		39	763	11	28.2	6	72	2869	1570	106
COLUMBUS—Colorado County													
☐ COLUMBUS COMMUNITY HOSPITAL, 110 Shult Dr., Box 865, Zip 78934; tel. 409/732-2371; Michael T. Portacci, exec. dir. **A**1a 9 10 **F**1 3 6 15 16 23 35 41 45; **S**0725	23	10	S		40	613	7	17.5	4	51	2886	1086	65

Hospital, Address, Telephone, Administrator, Approval and Facility Codes, Multihospital System Code	Classification Codes			Facilities	Inpatient Data				Newborn Data		Expense (thousands of dollars)		Personnel
★ American Hospital Association (AHA) membership □ Joint Commission on Accreditation of Hospitals (JCAH) accreditation + American Osteopathic Hospital Association (AOHA) membership ○ American Osteopathic Association (AOA) accreditation Δ Commission on Accreditation of Rehabilitation Facilities (CARF) accreditation Control codes 61, 63, 64, 71, 72 and 73 indicate hospitals listed by AOHA, but not registered by AHA. For definition of numerical codes, see page A2	Control	Service	Stay		Beds	Admissions	Census	Occupancy (percent)	Bassinets	Births	Total	Payroll	
COMANCHE—Comanche County													
COMANCHE COMMUNITY HOSPITAL, 211 S. Austin St., Box 443, Zip 76442; tel. 915/356-2012; Charley C. Latham, adm. **A**9 10 **F**1 6 15 16 23 34 35 45; **S**3535	23	10	S		20	766	11	50.0	4	114	1573	721	43
COMFORT—Kendall County													
COMFORT COMMUNITY HOSPITAL, 700 Faltin St., Box 338, Zip 78013; tel. 512/995-2330; Paul M. Calmes, adm. (Nonreporting) **A**9 10	33	10	S		82	—	—	—	—	—	—	—	—
CONROE—Montgomery County													
DOCTORS HOSPITAL, See HCA Doctors Hospital													
⊞ HCA DOCTORS HOSPITAL (Formerly Doctors Hospital), 3205 W. Davis, Zip 77304; Mailing Address Box 1349, Zip 77301; tel. 409/756-0631; Duane K. Rossmann, adm. **A**1a 9 10 **F**1 3 6 9 12 14 15 35 36 40 50 52; **S**1755	33	10	S		85	3089	41	45.3	8	435	—	—	198
⊞ MEDICAL CENTER HOSPITAL, 504 Medical Center Blvd., Box 1538, Zip 77305; tel. 713/539-1111; John Single, adm. **A**1a 3 9 10 **F**1 3 5 6 7 9 10 11 12 14 15 16 20 23 26 34 35 36 37 40 43 45 46 47 50 52 54; **S**7235	16	10	S		152	7382	107	70.4	32	1384	—	—	594
CORPUS CHRISTI—Nueces County													
ADA WILSON HOSPITAL OF PHYSICAL MEDICINE AND REHABILITATION, 3511 S. Alameda St., Zip 78411; tel. 512/853-9977; David W. Anderson, adm. **A**9 **F**23 24 25 26 32 33 34 42 44 45 46	23	56	L		80	11	72	90.0	0	0	—	—	116
⊞ AMI RIVERSIDE HOSPITAL (Formerly Riverside Hospital), 13725 Farm Rd. 624, Zip 78410; tel. 512/387-1541; Jean F. Adams, exec. dir. **A**1a 10 **F**1 3 6 10 12 14 15 16 23 34 35 36 40 41 45; **S**0125	33	10	S		89	2897	40	44.9	10	423	—	—	166
CHARTER HOSPITAL OF CORPUS CHRISTI, 3126 Rodd Field Rd., Zip 78414; tel. 512/993-8893; Michael A. Zieman, adm. **A**9 10 **F**15 23 24 27 28 29 30 32 33 42 43 44 48 49	33	22	S		80	79	5	6.7	0	0	—	—	71
○ + CORPUS CHRISTI OSTEOPATHIC HOSPITAL, 1502 Tarlton St., Box 7807, Zip 78415; tel. 512/886-2300; Robert R. Tamez, adm. **A**9 10 11 12 **F**1 3 6 10 11 16 23 33 34 36 37 40 47 48 49 50 53	23	10	S		100	2080	38	38.0	10	411	6950	3047	168
⊞ DRISCOLL FOUNDATION CHILDREN'S HOSPITAL, 3533 S. Alameda St., Drawer 6530, Zip 78411; tel. 512/850-5000; Gordon W. Epperson, pres. **A**1a 3 5 9 10 **F**1 4 6 12 14 16 29 30 33 34 35 42 45 46 47 51 52 53 54	23	50	S		123	4781	88	71.5	0	0	22199	10948	686
⊞ HUMANA HOSPITAL CORPUS CHRISTI, 3315 S. Alameda, Box 3828, Zip 78404; tel. 512/857-1400; LeRoy A. Hagens, exec. dir. **A**1a 10 **F**1 3 6 10 12 14 15 16 20 23 34 35 36 40 43 46 47 53; **S**1235	33	10	S		193	8324	122	63.2	20	1648	—	—	441
⊞ MEMORIAL MEDICAL CENTER, 2606 Hospital Blvd., Box 5280, Zip 78405; tel. 512/881-4100; Wheeler Lipes, pres. **A**1a 2 3 5 9 10 **F**1 2 3 4 5 6 7 8 9 10 11 12 14 15 16 17 20 22 23 24 27 28 30 32 34 35 36 40 41 45 46 52 53 54	16	10	S		360	13801	253	70.3	36	1949	—	—	1236
⊞ NAVAL HOSPITAL, Zip 78419; tel. 512/939-2685; Capt. C. R. Loar MSC USN, CO **A**1a 2 **F**1 6 10 14 16 23 28 30 32 33 34 35 46 47 48	43	10	S		40	1259	27	58.7	0	0	20263	—	424
PHYSICIANS AND SURGEONS GENERAL HOSPITAL, See Southside Community Hospital													
RIVERSIDE HOSPITAL, See AMI Riverside Hospital													
□ SOUTHSIDE COMMUNITY HOSPITAL (Formerly Physicians and Surgeons General Hospital), 4626 Weber Rd., Zip 78411; tel. 512/854-2031; J. H. O'Dell, adm. **A**1a 9 10 **F**1 3 6 10 12 14 15 16 23 24 27 28 29 30 32 33 35 42 45 48 49 53; **S**3015	33	10	S		164	3595	78	47.6	0	0	—	—	216
⊞ SPOHN HOSPITAL, 600 Elizabeth St., Zip 78404; tel. 512/881-3000; Sr. Kathleen Coughlin, pres. **A**1a 2 9 10 **F**1 2 3 4 6 7 8 9 10 11 12 14 16 17 20 21 23 24 26 35 36 40 41 43 45 46 47 52 53 54; **S**5565	21	10	S		419	19127	342	75.8	50	2328	70638	26287	1449
CORSICANA—Navarro County													
⊞ NAVARRO REGIONAL HOSPITAL, 3201 W. Hwy. 22, Zip 75110; tel. 214/872-4861; Harvey L. Fishero, adm. **A**1a 9 10 **F**1 3 6 12 15 16 20 23 27 30 32 33 34 35 36 40 45 46 47 52 53; **S**1755	33	10	S		129	5688	86	66.7	13	723	—	—	305
CRANE—Crane County													
CRANE MEMORIAL HOSPITAL, 1310 S. Alford, Zip 79731; tel. 915/558-3555; Charles N. Butts, adm. **A**9 10 **F**1 16 35 37 40	13	10	S		28	349	4	14.3	6	70	—	—	38
CROCKETT—Houston County													
⊞ HOUSTON COUNTY HOSPITAL, Loop 304 E., Box 1129, Zip 75835; tel. 409/544-2002; Jonathan F. Godfrey, adm. **A**1a 9 10 **F**1 3 6 10 15 16 23 34 35 40 41 45 46 47 50; **S**1755	16	10	S		72	1731	26	36.1	10	176	4045	1774	99
CROSBYTON—Crosby County													
★ CROSBYTON CLINIC HOSPITAL, 710 W. Main St., Zip 79322; tel. 806/675-2382; Jean Lemley, adm. **A**9 10 **F**6 23 34 35 41 45	23	10	S		46	809	16	34.8	0	0	2226	1065	82
CROWELL—Foard County													
★ FOARD COUNTY HOSPITAL, 118 N. First St., Box 355, Zip 79227; tel. 817/684-1861; Dorothy Autry, adm. **A**9 10 **F**35 40	16	10	S		24	255	6	25.0	2	0	670	404	30
CUERO—De Witt County													
⊞ CUERO COMMUNITY HOSPITAL, N. Esplanade, P O Box 807, Zip 77954; tel. 512/275-6191; Larry Krupala, adm. **A**1a 9 10 **F**1 3 6 10 12 16 23 35 40 41 45 46 53	16	10	S		67	1851	28	41.8	6	232	4409	2212	125
DALHART—Dallam County													
★ COON MEMORIAL HOSPITAL AND HOME, 1411 Denver Ave., P O Box 1500, Zip 79022; tel. 806/249-4571; Earl N. Sheehy, pres. (Total facility includes 88 beds in nursing home-type unit) **A**9 10 **F**1 6 16 19 21 35 40 45; **S**5565	21	10	S	TF H	108 20	636 600	64 8	59.3 —	4 4	21 21	3399 2056	1528 758	121 51
DALLAS—Dallas County													
★ AMI MEDICAL ARTS HOSPITAL (Formerly Medical Arts Hospital), 6161 Harry Hines Blvd., Zip 75235; Mailing Address P O Box 45188, Zip 75245; tel. 214/688-1111; Phillip L. Coppage, chief exec. off. **A**9 10 **F**1 6 10 15 23 26 34 53; **S**0125	33	10	S		71	1966	30	42.3	0	0	—	—	126
★ Δ BAYLOR INSTITUTE FOR REHABILITATION, 3504 Swiss Ave., Zip 75204; tel. 214/826-7030; F. Dana Ellerbe, exec. dir. **A**3 7 9 10 **F**16 23 24 26 33 34 42 44; **S**0095	23	46	L		74	503	69	93.2	0	0	10500	5294	268
⊞ BAYLOR UNIVERSITY MEDICAL CENTER (Includes Carr P. Collins Hospital; Erik and Margaret Jonsson Hospital; George W. Truett Memorial Hospital; Karl and Esther Hoblitzelle Memorial Hospital; A. Webb Roberts Hospital, Zip 75246), 3500 Gaston Ave., Zip 75246; tel. 214/820-0111; Boone Powell Jr., pres. (Nonreporting) **A**1a b 2 3 5 8 9 10; **S**0095	21	10	S		1455	—	—	—	—	—	—	—	—
CARR P. COLLINS HOSPITAL, See Baylor University Medical Center													
⊞ CHARLTON METHODIST HOSPITAL, 3500 Wheatland Rd., Box 225357, Zip 75265; tel. 214/296-2511; Kim Holland, exec. dir. & vice-pres. **A**1a 9 10 **F**1 3 6 10 11 12 15 16 23 24 34 35 36 40 44 45 46 48 49; **S**2735	23	10	S		143	5062	81	65.3	12	572	—	—	341
⊞ CHILDREN'S MEDICAL CENTER OF DALLAS, 1935 Motor St., Zip 75235; tel. 214/920-2000; George D. Farr, pres. & chief exec. off.; Michael D. Williams, exec. vice-pres. & chief oper. off. **A**1a 3 5 9 10 **F**1 4 6 12 13 15 16 20 23 24 27 28 32 33 34 38 41 43 44 45 46 52 53 54	23	50	S		168	7262	127	76.0	0	0	46896	22086	994

Hospital, Address, Telephone, Administrator, Approval and Facility Codes, Multihospital System Code	Classification Codes				Inpatient Data				Newborn Data		Expense (thousands of dollars)		
★ American Hospital Association (AHA) membership □ Joint Commission on Accreditation of Hospitals (JCAH) accreditation + American Osteopathic Hospital Association (AOHA) membership ○ American Osteopathic Association (AOA) accreditation Δ Commission on Accreditation of Rehabilitation Facilities (CARF) accreditation Control codes 61, 63, 64, 71, 72 and 73 indicate hospitals listed by AOHA, but not registered by AHA. For definition of numerical codes, see page A2	Control	Service	Stay	Facilities	Beds	Admissions	Census	Occupancy (percent)	Bassinets	Births	Total	Payroll	Personnel
⊞ DALLAS COUNTY HOSPITAL DISTRICT-PARKLAND MEMORIAL HOSPITAL, 5201 Harry Hines Blvd., Zip 75235; tel. 214/637-8000; Ron J. Anderson MD, chief exec. off. **A**1a 2 3 5 8 9 10 **F**1 3 4 5 6 7 8 9 10 11 12 13 14 16 20 22 23 24 25 26 27 28 30 32 33 34 35 36 37 38 40 44 45 46 47 50 51 52 53 54	16	10	S		819	34235	684	83.5	102	14065	160732	80822	4229
○ + DALLAS FAMILY HOSPITAL, 2929 S. Hampton Rd., Zip 75224; tel. 214/330-4611; John B. Isbell, chief exec. off.; Christopher P. O'Connor, mng. dir. **A**9 10 11 12 13 **F**1 3 6 10 12 14 15 16 21 23 34 35 43 44 53; **S**9555	33	10	S		72	2940	47	58.0	0	0	13022	4233	211
⊞ DALLAS MEDICAL AND SURGICAL CLINIC-HOSPITAL, 4105 Live Oak St., Zip 75204; Mailing Address Box 28, Zip 75221; tel. 214/823-4151; Alan Kennon, adm. (Nonreporting) **A**1a 10	33	10	S		43	—	—	—	—	—	—	—	—
○ DALLAS MEMORIAL HOSPITAL, 5003 Ross Ave., Zip 75206; tel. 214/824-3071; James J. Fitzgerald, adm. **A**9 10 11 12 13 **F**1 3 6 10 12 14 15 16 23 34 40 45 48 49 53	23	10	S		78	1765	28	43.1	6	287	6393	2796	154
□ Δ DALLAS REHABILITATION INSTITUTE, 9713 Harry Hines Blvd., Zip 75220; tel. 214/358-6000; Malcolm Berry, exec. dir. **A**1a 7 10 **F**1 10 12 15 16 23 24 26 32 33 34 41 42 44 53	33	46	L		120	414	53	64.6	0	0	—	—	395
□ DOCTORS HOSPITAL OF DALLAS, 9440 Poppy Dr., Zip 75218; tel. 214/324-6100; Chris Dicicco, chief exec. off.; C. Eugene Ward, adm. (Nonreporting) **A**1a 9 10; **S**3015	33	10	S		220	—	—	—	—	—	—	—	—
ERIK AND MARGARET JONSSON HOSPITAL, See Baylor University Medical Center													
⊞ GASTON EPISCOPAL HOSPITAL, 3505 Gaston Ave., Zip 75246; tel. 214/823-8101; Charles M. Cooper III, adm. **A**1a 9 10 **F**1 3 6 12 16 21 23 33 43 45 46	23	10	S		104	2776	49	47.1	0	0	12902	5210	297
⊞ GENERAL HOSPITAL OF LAKEWOOD, 1600 Abrams Rd., Zip 75214; tel. 214/824-4541; Steven D. Porter, adm. **A**1a 10 **F**1 3 17 19 23 35; **S**6525	33	10	S		71	888	19	26.8	0	0	—	—	79
GEORGE W. TRUETT MEMORIAL HOSPITAL, See Baylor University Medical Center													
⊞ GRANVILLE C. MORTON HOSPITAL AT WADLEY INSTITUTES (Hematology and Oncology), 9000 Harry Hines Blvd., Zip 75235; tel. 214/351-8340; James E. Robertson, adm. **A**1a 3 9 10 **F**1 6 7 8 9 10 11 12 14 15 16 20 23 34 43 45 46 47 53	23	49	S		38	1211	27	49.1	0	0	—	—	177
□ GREEN OAKS PSYCHIATRIC HOSPITAL, 7808 Clodus Fields Dr., Zip 75251; tel. 214/991-9504; Liam J. Mulvaney, adm. **A**1a 10 **F**15 24 28 30 32 33 42 44; **S**0395	33	22	L		106	448	86	90.5	0	0	—	—	182
⊞ HORIZON HOSPITAL (Formerly Raleigh Hills Hospital), 2345 Reagan St., Zip 75219; tel. 214/521-7541; Lynda Hoffman, adm. (Nonreporting) **A**1b 9; **S**6525	33	82	S		26	—	—	—	—	—	—	—	—
⊞ HUMANA HOSPITAL -MEDICAL CITY DALLAS, 7777 Forest Lane, Zip 75230; tel. 214/661-7000; Ira B. Korman PhD, exec. dir. **A**1a 9 10 **F**1 2 3 4 6 7 8 9 10 11 12 15 16 17 20 23 24 33 34 35 36 37 39 40 44 45 46 47 51 52 53 54; **S**1235	33	10	S		420	20263	281	66.3	56	4365	—	—	1221
KARL AND ESTHER HOBLITZELLE MEMORIAL HOSPITAL, See Baylor University Medical Center													
LAKE CLIFF HOSPITAL, 201 E. Colorado, Zip 75203; tel. 214/942-8711; Judith McDermott, adm. (Newly Registered) **A**9 10 **F**1 6 10 16 23 34 43 53	32	10	S		31	1223	21	67.7	0	0	3882	821	40
★ MARY SHIELS HOSPITAL, 3515 Howell St., Zip 75204; tel. 214/528-9061; Rob Shiels, adm. **A**9 10 **F**43	33	10	S		10	222	1	10.0	0	0	3060	1096	41
MEDICAL ARTS HOSPITAL, See AMI Medical Arts Hospital													
⊞ METHODIST MEDICAL CENTER, 301 W. Colorado Blvd., Zip 75208; Mailing Address Box 225999, Zip 75265; tel. 214/944-8181; John W. Carver, exec. dir. & sr. vice-pres. **A**1a 2 8 9 10 **F**1 2 3 4 5 6 7 8 9 10 11 12 13 14 15 16 20 23 24 30 32 33 34 35 36 37 40 42 44 45 46 47 51 52 53 54; **S**2735	23	10	S		404	15441	281	69.6	36	3152	—	—	1371
★ ○ + METROPOLITAN HOSPITAL, 7525 Scyene Rd., Zip 75227; tel. 214/381-7171; Steve Peterson, adm. **A**9 10 11 **F**1 3 6 12 16 23 27 32 33 34 35 36 40 42 45 46 47 48 52; **S**1755	23	10	S		100	1806	37	32.3	10	172	6492	2783	186
⊞ OAK CLIFF MEDICAL AND SURGICAL HOSPITAL, 233 W. Tenth St., Box 4446, Zip 75208; tel. 214/946-5191; Donn C. Baker, adm. **A**1a 9 10 **F**1 3 6 12 16 24 27 33 34 35 42 43 45 46 47 50; **S**9555	33	10	S		71	2037	34	47.3	0	0	7498	3417	140
⊞ PRESBYTERIAN HOSPITAL, 8200 Walnut Hill Lane, Zip 75231; tel. 214/369-4111; Doug Hawthorne, pres. & chief exec. off.; R. Reed Fraley, exec. dir. (Nonreporting) **A**1a 2 3 5 8 9 10; **S**1130	23	10	S		720	—	—	—	—	—	—	—	—
RALEIGH HILLS HOSPITAL, See Horizon Hospital													
□ RHD MEMORIAL MEDICAL CENTER, Seven Medical Pkwy., Zip 75234; Mailing Address P O Box 819094, Zip 75381; tel. 214/247-1000; James R. Shafer, exec. dir.; Jeff Webster, adm. (Total facility includes 102 beds in nursing home-type unit) **A**1a 9 10 **F**1 3 4 5 6 9 10 11 12 15 16 17 19 20 23 24 34 35 42 43 44 45 46 47 53 54; **S**3015	33	10	S	TF H	258 156	5587 5334	147 86	48.2 —	0 0	0 0	33265 32494	8283 7775	433 —
⊞ SOUTHEASTERN METHODIST HOSPITAL, 9202 Elam Rd., Zip 75217; tel. 214/372-7600; Gene R. Barron, exec. dir. & vice-pres. **A**1a 9 10 **F**1 3 6 10 12 15 16 23 24 34 35 40 42 44 45 46 48 49; **S**2735	23	10	S		101	2642	50	49.5	6	114	—	—	189
⊞ ST. PAUL MEDICAL CENTER, 5909 Harry Hines Blvd., Zip 75235; tel. 214/879-1000; Anthony L. Bunker, pres. **A**1a 2 3 5 8 9 10 **F**1 3 4 6 7 8 9 10 11 12 14 15 16 17 20 23 24 26 27 29 30 32 33 34 35 36 40 43 44 45 46 47 48 51 52 53 54; **S**1885	21	10	S		417	18918	318	63.1	44	4313	77551	35605	1543
⊞ TEXAS SCOTTISH RITE HOSPITAL FOR CRIPPLED CHILDREN, 2222 Welborn St., Box 190567, Zip 75219; tel. 214/521-3168; J. C. Montgomery Jr., exec. vice-pres.; Robert Walker, adm. **A**1a 3 5 9 **F**1 6 15 23 24 33 34 38 42 44 45 46	23	57	S		64	1710	37	57.8	0	0	20000	—	386
⊞ TIMBERLAWN PSYCHIATRIC HOSPITAL, 4600 Samuell Blvd., Zip 75227; Mailing Address Box 11288, Zip 75223; tel. 214/381-7181; Wayne Hallford, adm. **A**1b 3 9 **F**24 28 29 32 33 42 43	33	22	L		218	398	194	93.7	0	0	21290	11488	466
⊞ VETERANS ADMINISTRATION MEDICAL CENTER, 4500 S. Lancaster Rd., Zip 75216; tel. 214/376-5451; C. Wayne Hawkins, dir. (Total facility includes 120 beds in nursing home-type unit) **A**1a 3 5 8 **F**1 3 4 6 7 8 9 10 11 12 14 15 16 19 20 21 23 24 25 26 27 28 29 30 32 33 34 35 38 41 42 43 44 46 47 48 49 50 53 54	45	10	S	TF H	800 680	19586 19347	629 521	78.6 —	0 0	0 0	— —	— —	1842 1770
DE LEON—Comanche County													
⊞ DE LEON HOSPITAL, 407 S. Texas Ave., Box 319, Zip 76444; tel. 817/893-2011; Michael K. Hare, adm. **A**1a 9 10 **F**1 3 6 10 14 15 16 23 30 35 37 40 41 45	16	10	S		40	995	18	45.0	5	72	2756	1077	66
DECATUR—Wise County													
⊞ DECATUR COMMUNITY HOSPITAL, 2100 S. Fm 51, Zip 76234; tel. 817/627-5921; Joseph F. Sloan, adm. **A**1a 10 **F**1 3 6 10 15 16 17 23 35 40 41 45 46 53; **S**2345	16	10	S		50	1543	18	36.0	5	201	3467	1600	92
DEER PARK—Harris County													
★ HCA DEER PARK HOSPITAL (Formerly Deer Park Hospital), 4525 Glenwood, Zip 77536; tel. 713/479-0955; Manuel Ramos Jr., adm. & chief exec. off. **A**9 **F**15 23 24 28 29 32 33 34 42 43 47 48 49; **S**1755	33	22	L		116	372	41	34.7	0	0	—	—	127
DEL RIO—Val Verde County													
U. S. AIR FORCE HOSPITAL, See Laughlin Air Force Base													
⊞ VAL VERDE MEMORIAL HOSPITAL, 801 Bedell Ave., P O Box 1527, Zip 78840; tel. 512/775-8566; Larry Dorsey, adm. **A**1a 9 10 **F**1 3 6 10 12 15 16 23 30 35 40 44 45 53; **S**0725	16	10	S		84	3151	41	48.8	12	612	9233	3730	246

Hospital, Address, Telephone, Administrator, Approval and Facility Codes, Multihospital System Code	Classification Codes			Facilities	Inpatient Data				Newborn Data		Expense (thousands of dollars)		
★ American Hospital Association (AHA) membership □ Joint Commission on Accreditation of Hospitals (JCAH) accreditation + American Osteopathic Hospital Association (AOHA) membership ○ American Osteopathic Association (AOA) accreditation Δ Commission on Accreditation of Rehabilitation Facilities (CARF) accreditation Control codes 61, 63, 64, 71, 72 and 73 indicate hospitals listed by AOHA, but not registered by AHA. For definition of numerical codes, see page A2	Control	Service	Stay	Facilities	Beds	Admissions	Census	Occupancy (percent)	Bassinets	Births	Total	Payroll	Personnel
DENISON—Grayson County													
★□ TEXOMA MEDICAL CENTER (Includes Texoma Medical Center East, 401 E. Hull St., Zip 75020; tel. 214/465-3432), 1000 Memorial Dr., Box 890, Zip 75020; tel. 214/465-2313; Mike Mayes, pres. **A**1a 9 10 **F**1 3 5 6 7 8 9 11 12 16 20 23 24 26 27 34 36 40 44 45 47 48 52 53 54	16	10	S		235	8514	138	58.7	18	863	29106	12779	648
TEXOMA MEDICAL CENTER EAST, See Texoma Medical Center													
DENTON—Denton County													
★□ AMI DENTON REGIONAL MEDICAL CENTER (Formerly Westgate Medical Center), 4405 N. Interstate 35, Zip 76201; tel. 817/566-4000; Donald S. Ciulla, exec. dir. **A**1a 9 10 **F**1 2 3 5 6 9 10 12 14 15 16 20 23 24 26 34 35 41 43 44 45 46 47 52 53 54; **S**0125	33	10	S		195	4852	76	39.0	0	0	18793	6138	357
★□ FLOW MEMORIAL HOSPITAL, 1310 Scripture St., Zip 76201; tel. 817/387-5861; Charles B. Linton, chief exec. off. **A**1a 9 10 **F**1 3 6 12 14 15 16 23 24 27 30 32 33 34 35 36 40 41 42 43 45 46 50 53; **S**2495	15	10	S		129	5124	66	47.8	15	1482	15166	6499	274
WESTGATE MEDICAL CENTER, See AMI Denton Regional Medical Center													
DENVER CITY—Yoakum County													
★ YOAKUM COUNTY HOSPITAL, 612 W. Fourth St., Drawer 1130, Zip 79323; tel. 806/592-5484; Ed Rodgers, adm. **A**9 10 **F**2 6 35 37 40 45	13	10	S		43	741	8	18.6	9	92	2611	969	54
DILLEY—Frio County													
WINTER GARDEN MEDICAL CENTER, Hwy. 85 W., Box 29, Zip 78017; tel. 512/965-1551; Sam Hotchkiss, adm. (Nonreporting) **A**9 10	33	10	S		37	—	—	—	—	—	—	—	—
DIMMITT—Castro County													
★ PLAINS MEMORIAL HOSPITAL, 310 W. Halsell St., Box 278, Zip 79027; tel. 806/647-2191; Garry Allan, adm. **A**9 10 **F**1 3 6 16 35 37 40 41 45 53	16	10	S		46	767	7	15.8	5	117	1554	833	49
DUBLIN—Erath County													
★ HARRIS METHODIST -DUBLIN (Formerly Dublin Medical Center), 205 N. Patrick St., Box O, Zip 76446; tel. 817/445-3322; John Hodges, adm. **A**9 10 **F**1 14 15 16 23 24 35 40; **S**2345	21	10	S		36	1047	13	36.1	6	112	2349	863	52
DUMAS—Moore County													
□ MEMORIAL HOSPITAL, 224 E. Second St., Zip 79029; tel. 806/935-7171; James R. Wurts, adm. **A**1a 9 10 **F**1 3 6 10 16 23 34 35 40 45 52	16	10	S		80	1839	18	22.5	10	280	2955	1328	86
DYESS AIR FORCE BASE—Taylor County													
U. S. AIR FORCE HOSPITAL, Zip 79607; tel. 915/696-2345; Lt. Col. Harold H. Hunter Jr. MSC USAF, adm. **F**1 3 6 14 15 16 23 33 34 35 37 40 45 46 47 52	41	10	S		35	2272	23	65.7	19	433	—	—	319
EAGLE LAKE—Colorado County													
★□ EAGLE LAKE COMMUNITY HOSPITAL, 600 S. Austin Rd., Zip 77434; tel. 409/234-5571; Jack M. Harrell, adm. **A**1a 9 10 **F**1 6 16 23 35 45	23	10	S		46	1436	18	39.1	4	98	2783	1374	70
EAGLE PASS—Maverick County													
★ MAVERICK COUNTY HOSPITAL DISTRICT, 350 S. Adams St., Zip 78852; tel. 512/773-5321; Robert F. Valliant, adm. **A**9 10 **F**6 12 16 23 34 35 40 45 46 52; **S**1755	16	10	S		77	3644	49	63.6	13	762	7185	3211	216
EASTLAND—Eastland County													
EASTLAND MEMORIAL HOSPITAL, 304 S. Daugherty St., Box 897, Zip 76448; tel. 817/629-2603; Marcia Carr, adm. **A**9 10 **F**1 3 16 34 35 40	23	10	S		46	1231	16	34.8	4	96	2385	1365	79
EDEN—Concho County													
CONCHO COUNTY HOSPITAL, Eaker & Burleson Sts., Box L, Zip 76837; tel. 915/869-5911; Albert M. Everett Jr., adm. **A**9 10 12 **F**35 41 43 50	16	10	S		20	393	7	34.7	0	0	859	466	21
EDINBURG—Hidalgo County													
★□ EDINBURG GENERAL HOSPITAL, 333 W. Freddy Gonzalez Dr., Zip 78539; tel. 512/383-6211; Dora Valverde, interim chief exec. off. (Nonreporting) **A**1a 9 10	14	10	S		98	—	—	—	—	—	—	—	—
EDNA—Jackson County													
★□ EDNA HOSPITAL, 1013 S. Wells St., P O Box 670, Zip 77957; tel. 512/782-5241; Kenneth W. Randall, adm. **A**1a 9 10 **F**1 6 10 12 14 16 23 34 35 45 46 47; **S**0725	16	10	S		35	771	7	20.0	5	14	1800	894	56
EL CAMPO—Wharton County													
★□ MEMORIAL HOSPITAL -EL CAMPO (Formerly El Campo Memorial Hospital), 303 Sandy Corner Rd., Box 1568, Zip 77437; tel. 409/543-6251; Wendell Porth, chief exec. off. (Data for 306 days) **A**1a 9 10 **F**1 3 6 9 10 15 16 23 24 26 34 35 36 37 40 42 44 45 50 52 53; **S**2645	23	10	S		41	1303	21	51.2	9	147	3748	1525	110
EL PASO—El Paso County													
★□ HCA SUN TOWERS HOSPITAL (Formerly Sun Towers Hospital), 1801 N. Oregon St., Zip 79902; tel. 915/532-6281; William W. Webster, adm. **A**1a 9 10 **F**1 3 4 6 10 12 14 15 16 19 21 22 23 24 34 35 39 44 45 53 54; **S**1755	33	10	S		145	4559	82	56.4	0	0	—	—	404
★□ HCA VISTA HILLS MEDICAL CENTER (Formerly Vista Hills Medical Center), 10301 Gateway W., Zip 79925; tel. 915/595-9000; Jack F. Houghton, adm. **A**1a 9 10 **F**1 3 4 5 6 10 11 12 14 15 16 23 26 34 35 36 40 44 46 47 53 54; **S**1755	33	10	S		182	6111	97	53.3	12	557	—	—	429
★□ HOTEL DIEU MEDICAL CENTER, 1014 N. Stanton St., Zip 79902; Mailing Address Box 5411, Zip 79954; tel. 915/545-3111; Beth O'Brien, pres. **A**1a 3 5 9 **F**1 3 4 6 9 10 11 12 15 16 20 23 26 34 35 44 46 48 49 52 54; **S**1885	23	10	S		207	5598	104	50.2	0	0	—	—	613
NORTHPARK HOSPITAL (Formerly Northpark Community Hospital), 9005 Marks St., Zip 79904; tel. 915/757-0356; Dennis M. Fargie, adm. **A**9 10 **F**1 15 16 23 26 34 35 43 46 50	33	10	S		27	690	10	37.0	0	0	1965	962	72
★□ PROVIDENCE MEMORIAL HOSPITAL, 2001 N. Oregon St., Zip 79902; tel. 915/542-6011; Robert I. Richardson, exec. vice-pres. **A**1a 2 3 5 9 10 **F**1 2 3 4 6 7 8 9 10 11 12 14 15 16 23 24 25 26 27 28 29 30 32 33 34 35 36 40 42 44 45 46 47 51 52 53 54	23	10	S		426	17538	307	72.0	35	2642	—	—	1360
□ R. E. THOMASON GENERAL HOSPITAL, 4815 Alameda Ave., Zip 79905; Mailing Address Box 20009, Zip 79998; tel. 915/544-1200; Bill Kennedy, exec. dir. **A**1a 2 3 5 9 10 **F**1 2 3 5 15 23 24 26 34 35 37 40 44 46 49 51 52	16	10	S		300	12043	164	56.4	44	3839	35101	13877	898
□ SIERRA MEDICAL CENTER, 1625 Medical Center Dr., Zip 79902; tel. 915/532-4000; L. Marcus Fry Jr., chief exec. off.; Sonja Hagel, assoc. adm. **A**1a 9 10 **F**1 2 3 4 6 10 12 14 15 16 20 23 34 35 36 40 43 44 45 46 47 50 51 52 53 54; **S**3015	33	10	S		266	10270	146	54.9	27	2041	—	—	646
★□ SOUTHWESTERN GENERAL HOSPITAL, 2001 Murchison, Zip 79912; tel. 915/533-9361; William Grinwis, adm. (Nonreporting) **A**1a 9 10	33	10	S		89	—	—	—	—	—	—	—	—
SUN TOWERS HOSPITAL, See HCA Sun Towers Hospital													
★□ SUN VALLEY REGIONAL HOSPITAL, 1155 Idaho St., Zip 79902; tel. 915/544-4000; Robert E. Thackston, adm. (Nonreporting) **A**1b 9 10; **S**1755	33	22	S		125	—	—	—	—	—	—	—	—
○ TIGUA GENERAL HOSPITAL, 7722 N. Loop Rd., Zip 79915; tel. 915/779-2424; Frank M. Braden, adm. **A**9 10 11 **F**1 3 6 10 16 23 35 40 52	33	10	S		50	1842	25	50.0	6	158	4944	1458	112
VISTA HILLS MEDICAL CENTER, See HCA Vista Hills Medical Center													
★□ WILLIAM BEAUMONT ARMY MEDICAL CENTER, Piedras St., Zip 79920; tel. 915/569-2203; Col. Gerald C. Owver MSC, chief of staff **A**1a 2 3 5 **F**2 3 5 6 7 10 11 12 14 15 16 20 23 24 26 27 28 29 30 32 33 34 35 36 37 38 40 42 44 45 46 47 48 49 51 52 53 54	42	10	S		479	17141	335	69.9	17	1704	99170	78096	2126

★ American Hospital Association (AHA) membership
□ Joint Commission on Accreditation of Hospitals (JCAH) accreditation
+ American Osteopathic Hospital Association (AOHA) membership
○ American Osteopathic Association (AOA) accreditation
Δ Commission on Accreditation of Rehabilitation Facilities (CARF) accreditation
Control codes 61, 63, 64, 71, 72 and 73 indicate hospitals listed by AOHA, but not registered by AHA. For definition of numerical codes, see page A2

Hospital, Address, Telephone, Administrator, Approval and Facility Codes, Multihospital System Code	Classification Codes				Inpatient Data				Newborn Data		Expense (thousands of dollars)		
	Control	Service	Stay	Facilities	Beds	Admissions	Census	Occupancy (percent)	Bassinets	Births	Total	Payroll	Personnel
YSLETA GENERAL HOSPITAL, 118 N. Harris St., Zip 79907; Mailing Address Box 17689, Zip 79917; tel. 915/859-7901; Pedro A. Ortega MD, adm. & pres. **A**9 **F**1 12 40 52	33	10	S		19	91	3	17.3	6	9	—	—	28
ELDORADO—Schleicher County													
SCHLEICHER COUNTY MEDICAL CENTER, 305 Mertzon Hwy., Box V, Zip 76936; tel. 915/853-2507; Jack H. Black, adm. (Total facility includes 34 beds in nursing home-type unit) **A**9 10 **F**1 16 19 23 35 40 41 45 46	16	10	S	TF	50	314	35	70.0	2	7	1346	790	56
				H	16	271	3	—	2	7	855	494	29
ELECTRA—Wichita County													
ELECTRA MEMORIAL HOSPITAL, Hwy. 25 S., Box 1227, Zip 76360; tel. 817/495-3981; Bobby R. Morgan, adm. **A**9 10 **F**1 3 14 16 35 45; **S**1775	33	10	S		25	353	5	20.0	1	3	—	—	29
ENNIS—Ellis County													
□ BAYLOR MEDICAL CENTER AT ENNIS (Formerly Ennis Community Hospital), 803 W. Lampasas St., Zip 75119; tel. 214/875-3837; Ronald Hudspeth, pres. **A**1a 9 10 **F**1 3 6 10 16 23 34 35 40 41 45; **S**0095	23	10	S		43	1692	19	44.2	10	239	5288	2240	106
FAIRFIELD—Freestone County													
FAIRFIELD MEMORIAL HOSPITAL, 125 Newman St., Zip 75840; tel. 214/389-2121; J. T. Taylor, adm. **A**9 10 **F**1 3 6 12 14 16 35 45	16	10	S		47	1434	21	44.7	6	145	2872	1370	92
FALFURRIAS—Brooks County													
BROOKS COUNTY HOSPITAL, 1400 S. St. Mary's St., Zip 78355; tel. 512/325-2511; Frankie Rogers, adm. **A**9 10 **F**1 3 6 15 16 34 35 43 45 50	13	10	S		31	1069	8	25.8	13	257	2211	1079	78
FLORESVILLE—Wilson County													
★□ WILSON MEMORIAL HOSPITAL, 1301 Hospital Blvd., Zip 78114; tel. 512/393-3122; Pete Delgado, adm. **A**1a 9 10 **F**1 2 6 16 23 24 30 35 40 41 43 45 46 47 50; **S**0725	16	10	S		44	1062	13	29.5	7	114	2983	1283	89
FLOYDADA—Floyd County													
CAPROCK HOSPITAL DISTRICT (Formerly Caprock Hospital Medical Services), 901 W. Crockett St., Box 540, Zip 79235; tel. 806/983-2875; Guy Hazlett, adm. (Nonreporting) **A**9 10	16	10	S		40	—	—	—	—	—	—	—	—
FORT HOOD—Bell County													
★□ DARNALL ARMY COMMUNITY HOSPITAL, Zip 76544; tel. 817/288-8001; Col. Reginald G. Moore III MC, cmdr. **A**1a 3 5 **F**1 2 3 6 10 11 12 14 16 23 24 26 27 28 29 30 32 33 34 35 37 38 40 42 44 46 47 49 51 52 53	42	10	S		218	12290	139	63.8	46	2184	75733	—	1432
FORT SAM HOUSTON—Bexar County													
★□ BROOKE ARMY MEDICAL CENTER, Zip 78234; tel. 512/221-3225; Col. Bobby K. Helton, chief of staff; Brig. Gen. Girard Seitter III, cmdr. **A**1a 2 3 5 **F**1 2 3 4 5 6 7 8 9 10 11 12 14 15 16 18 19 20 22 23 24 26 27 28 29 30 32 33 34 35 36 37 38 40 42 43 44 49 50 51 52 53 54	42	10	S		694	19940	483	69.6	15	925	—	—	2661
FORT STOCKTON—Pecos County													
★□ PECOS COUNTY MEMORIAL HOSPITAL, Sanderson Hwy., Box 1648, Zip 79735; tel. 915/336-2241; William H. Maloy, adm. **A**1a 9 10 **F**1 6 16 23 35 40 41 45 46; **S**1755	13	10	S		37	1377	15	40.5	8	276	3333	1604	78
FORT WORTH—Tarrant County													
★□ ALL SAINTS EPISCOPAL HOSPITAL OF FORT WORTH, 1400 Eighth Ave., Zip 76104; Mailing Address P O Box 31, Zip 76101; tel. 817/926-2544; Stanley F. Hupfeld, pres. **A**1a 9 10 **F**1 2 3 6 9 10 11 12 14 15 16 20 23 24 25 26 27 28 30 31 32 34 35 36 40 41 42 43 45 46 47 53 54	23	10	S		417	16787	282	65.5	30	1800	53645	27531	1342
CAREUNIT HOSPITAL OF DALLAS-FORT WORTH, 1066 W. Magnolia Ave., Zip 76104; tel. 817/336-2828; Dorothy Grasty, adm.; B. Ahmed MD, med. dir. **A**9 10 **F**15 27 29 32 33 42 46; **S**0275	33	82	S		83	1223	65	78.3	0	0	—	—	125
□ CONTINENTAL HOSPITAL NORTH (Formerly Northwest Hospital), 2100 Hwy. 183 N.W., Zip 76106; tel. 817/626-5481; Joel V. Bailey, exec. dir. **A**1a 9 10 **F**1 3 10 12 14 15 16 23 35; **S**0245	33	10	S		49	764	11	22.4	0	0	3958	1472	68
□ CONTINENTAL HOSPITAL SUBURBAN, 701 S. Cherry Lane, Box 5128, Zip 76108; tel. 817/246-2491; James C. Karsch, exec. dir. **A**1a 9 10 **F**1 3 6 10 15 16 23 35 40 52 53; **S**0245	33	10	S		48	803	12	25.0	0	27	—	—	73
COOK CHILDREN'S HOSPITAL, See Cook-Fort Worth Children's Medical Center													
□ COOK-FORT WORTH CHILDREN'S MEDICAL CENTER (Includes Cook Children's Hospital, 1212 W. Lancaster St., Zip 76102; tel. 817/885-4000; Fort Worth Children's Hospital, 1400 Cooper St., Zip 76104; tel. 817/885-4000), 1400 Cooper St., Zip 76104; tel. 817/885-4000; Russell K. Tolman, pres. **A**1a 3 9 10 **F**1 6 12 14 15 16 23 34 35 42 45 46 47 51	23	50	S		155	6521	96	61.9	0	0	30405	14850	709
★ DUNCAN MEMORIAL HOSPITAL, 2308 Hemphill St., Zip 76110; tel. 817/926-3304; Janice Everett, adm. **A** 9 10 **F**15 33 37 40	23	44	S		19	473	5	26.3	25	253	1660	767	37
FORT WORTH CHILDREN'S HOSPITAL, See Cook-Fort Worth Children's Medical Center													
○ + FORT WORTH OSTEOPATHIC MEDICAL CENTER, 1000 Montgomery St., Zip 76107; tel. 817/731-4311; John P. Hawkins, exec. vice-pres. **A**9 10 11 12 13 **F**1 3 5 15 16 20 23 24 26 29 34 35 39 40 44 45 46 47 51 52 53 54	23	10	S		200	6853	135	67.5	15	624	30033	12288	696
★□ Δ HARRIS METHODIST -FORT WORTH (Formerly Harris Hospital-Methodist), 1301 Pennsylvania Ave., Zip 76104; tel. 817/882-2000; Chuck Brosseau, sr. vice-pres. & adm. (Nonreporting) **A**1a 3 7 9 10; **S**2345	21	10	S		547	—	—	—	—	—	—	—	—
★□ HUGULEY MEMORIAL HOSPITAL, 11801 S. Freeway, Box 6337, Zip 76115; tel. 817/293-9110; John D. Koobs, pres. **A**1a 9 10 **F**1 3 12 14 15 16 19 21 23 24 25 26 27 35 41 43 44 45 46 47 52 53; **S**4165	21	10	S		120	5737	86	71.0	8	718	9352	24790	460
JOHN PETER SMITH HOSPITAL, See Tarrant County Hospital District													
★□ MEDICAL PLAZA HOSPITAL, 1612 W. Humbolt St., Zip 76104; tel. 817/336-2100; Robert B. Evans, adm. **A**1a 9 10 **F**1 2 3 4 6 9 10 12 14 15 16 17 20 23 24 32 33 34 35 37 42 44 45 46 53 54; **S**1755	33	10	S		250	6662	114	45.6	0	0	—	—	507
NORTH HILLS MEDICAL CENTER, See North Richland Hills													
NORTHWEST HOSPITAL, See Continental Hospital North													
□ PSYCHIATRIC INSTITUTE OF FORT WORTH, 815 Eighth Ave., Zip 76104; tel. 817/335-4040; Peter J. Alexis, adm. **A**1b 9 10 **F**24 28 29 30 32 33 42 43 49 50; **S**0825	33	22	L		118	701	83	43.0	0	0	—	—	224
★□ Δ SAINT JOSEPH HOSPITAL, 1401 S. Main St., Zip 76104; tel. 817/336-9371; Kevin R. Andrews, pres. & chief exec. off. **A**1a 7 9 10 **F**1 3 6 10 12 14 15 16 20 21 23 24 25 26 27 28 30 32 33 34 35 41 42 44 45 46 47 53; **S**5565	21	10	S		379	11767	246	64.9	0	0	44956	20107	1060
★□ SCHICK SHADEL HOSPITAL, 4101 Frawley Dr., Zip 76118; tel. 817/284-9217; Rolfe Floyd, adm. **A**1a 9 10 **F**15 33 47 49; **S**0575	33	82	S		50	1836	31	62.0	0	0	6254	1734	100
★□ TARRANT COUNTY HOSPITAL DISTRICT (Includes John Peter Smith Hospital), 1500 S. Main St., Zip 76104; tel. 817/921-3431; M. Tim Philpot, adm. **A**1a 3 5 9 **F**1 3 5 6 9 12 14 15 16 20 23 24 26 27 30 34 35 37 40 42 44 45 46 47 51 52 53	16	10	S		380	17381	297	78.2	36	5854	57143	24016	1371
TWIN OAKS MEDICAL CENTER, 2919 Markum Dr., Zip 76117; tel. 817/831-0311; Chris Dicicco, adm. **A**9 10 **F**6 10 16 23 35 43 53; **S**3015	33	10	S		31	486	6	19.4	0	0	—	—	52
U. S. AIR FORCE REGIONAL HOSPITAL CARSWELL, See Carswell Air Force Base													

Hospital, Address, Telephone, Administrator, Approval and Facility Codes, Multihospital System Code	Classification Codes				Inpatient Data				Newborn Data		Expense (thousands of dollars)		
★ American Hospital Association (AHA) membership ☐ Joint Commission on Accreditation of Hospitals (JCAH) accreditation + American Osteopathic Hospital Association (AOHA) membership ○ American Osteopathic Association (AOA) accreditation △ Commission on Accreditation of Rehabilitation Facilities (CARF) accreditation Control codes 61, 63, 64, 71, 72 and 73 indicate hospitals listed by AOHA, but not registered by AHA. For definition of numerical codes, see page A2	Control	Service	Stay	Facilities	Beds	Admissions	Census	Occupancy (percent)	Bassinets	Births	Total	Payroll	Personnel
FREDERICKSBURG—Gillespie County													
⊞ HILL COUNTRY MEMORIAL HOSPITAL, 1020 Kerrville Rd., Box 835, Zip 78624; tel. 512/997-4353; Jerry L. Durr, adm. **A**1a 9 10 **F**1 3 6 15 16 34 35 40 41 45 47 53	23	10	S		61	2345	28	45.9	4	328	4743	2032	154
FRIONA—Parmer County													
★ PARMER COUNTY COMMUNITY HOSPITAL, 1307 Cleveland St., Zip 79035; tel. 806/247-2754; Elda E. Hart, adm. **A**9 10 **F**3 14 35 45	23	10	S		34	354	4	11.8	6	0	—	—	39
GAINESVILLE—Cooke County													
GAINESVILLE MEMORIAL HOSPITAL, 1016 Ritchey St., Zip 76240; tel. 817/665-1751; Gerald Culwell, adm. (Total facility includes 22 beds in nursing home-type unit) **A**9 10 **F**3 6 10 12 14 15 16 19 23 35 40 41 44 45 52 53	16	10	S	TF H	72 50	2660 2541	36 31	50.0 —	8 8	282 282	7523 7398	3420 3318	220 212
GALENA PARK—Harris County													
⊞ DEATON HOSPITAL, 208 N. Main St., Zip 77547; tel. 713/672-6311; Don D. Nichols, dir. **A**1a 9 10 **F**6 15 24 42	33	10	S		25	371	7	28.0	0	0	1581	749	47
GALVESTON—Galveston County													
⊞ SHRINERS HOSPITALS FOR CRIPPLED CHILDREN-BURNS INSTITUTE-GALVESTON UNIT, 610 Texas Ave., Zip 77550; tel. 409/761-2516; C. Nick Wilson PhD, adm. **A**1a 3 **F**1 12 13 15 16 22 23 24 26 33 34 42 44; **S**4125	23	59	S		30	805	20	66.7	0	0	—	—	231
⊞ ST. MARY'S HOSPITAL, 404 St. Mary's Blvd., Zip 77550; tel. 409/766-4300; Keith B. Reed Jr., adm. **A**1a 9 10 **F**1 3 6 10 12 14 15 16 19 23 27 32 33 34 35 36 40 42 44 45 46 47 53; **S**0605	23	10	S	TF H	282 257	5411 5301	169 162	59.7 —	20 20	448 448	26712 —	12094 —	626 —
☐ UNIVERSITY OF TEXAS MEDICAL BRANCH HOSPITALS, Eighth & Mechanic Sts., Zip 77550; tel. 409/761-1881; Alvin L. Leblanc MD, vice-pres. **A**1a 2 3 5 8 9 10 **F**1 2 3 4 6 7 8 9 10 11 12 13 14 15 16 17 18 22 23 24 25 26 27 28 29 30 32 33 34 35 36 37 38 40 41 42 43 44 45 46 47 48 49 50 51 52 53 54	12	10	S		880	29537	653	73.5	50	4531	189456	93986	3448
GANADO—Jackson County													
★ MAURITZ MEMORIAL HOSPITAL, 206 Sutherland St., Drawer C, Zip 77962; tel. 512/782-5241; Kenneth W. Randall, adm. **A**9 10 **F**6 10 12 14 16 23 34 35 45 46 47; **S**0725	16	10	S		50	425	5	10.0	10	49	1223	634	32
GARLAND—Dallas County													
⊞ GARLAND COMMUNITY HOSPITAL, 122 S. Intl. Rd., Zip 75042; tel. 214/276-7116; Kevin J. Hicks, adm. **A**1a 9 10 **F**1 3 6 10 16 34 35 41 43 48 49; **S**6525	33	10	S		128	2508	37	28.7	0	0	—	—	203
⊞ MEMORIAL HOSPITAL OF GARLAND, 2300 Marie Curie Blvd., Zip 75042; Mailing Address Box 469009, Zip 75046; tel. 214/276-9511; Gary D. Brock, adm. **A**1a 9 10 **F**1 3 6 10 12 14 15 16 20 23 24 27 32 33 35 36 40 42 45 46 48 50 53	23	10	S		182	7707	117	63.9	35	1396	23938	11984	563
GATESVILLE—Coryell County													
⊞ CORYELL MEMORIAL HOSPITAL, 1507 W. Main St., P O Box 659, Zip 76528; tel. 817/865-8251; Thomas R. Sweeden, adm. **A**1a 9 10 **F**1 3 6 10 12 14 15 16 23 35 41 45 46 47; **S**1755	16	10	S		55	1188	18	32.7	7	169	3793	1522	97
GEORGETOWN—Williamson County													
⊞ GEORGETOWN HOSPITAL, 2000 Scenic Dr., Zip 78626; tel. 512/863-6531; Kenneth W. Poteete, adm. **A**1a 9 10 **F**3 6 10 12 14 15 16 23 34 35 40 41 43 44 45 47 49 53	16	10	S		66	2372	27	40.7	6	480	5654	2815	148
GIDDINGS—Lee County													
LEE MEMORIAL HOSPITAL, P O Box 819, Zip 78942; tel. 409/542-3141; Steven L. Smith, adm. (Nonreporting) **A**9 10	23	10	S		32	—	—	—	—	—	—	—	—
GILMER—Upshur County													
☐ BAYLOR MEDICAL CENTER AT GILMER (Formerly Ford Memorial Hospital), 712 N. Wood St., Zip 75644; tel. 214/843-5611; James A. Summersett III, exec. dir. **A**1a 9 10 **F**1 3 5 6 10 12 14 16 23 34 35 37 43 45 46 50 53; **S**0095	21	10	S		46	1239	20	43.5	0	1	—	—	113
GLADEWATER—Gregg County													
⊞ GLADEWATER MUNICIPAL HOSPITAL, 300 W. Upshur Ave., Zip 75647; tel. 214/845-2281; Joy D. Evans, actg. adm. **A**1a 9 10 **F**1 3 6 10 12 16 23 35 37 40 41 43 45 46 47 53	16	10	S		54	1189	16	29.6	3	94	3021	1321	81
★ HART CLINIC HOSPITAL, 801 N. Main St., Zip 75647; tel. 214/845-2515; Walter F. Hart MD, adm. (Nonreporting) **A**9	31	10	S		18	—	—	—	—	—	—	—	—
GLEN ROSE—Somervell County													
★ MARKS-ENGLISH HOSPITAL, 1307-09 Holden St., Box 997, Zip 76043; tel. 817/897-2215; Gary A. Marks, adm. **A**9 10 **F**15 16 23 35; **S**2345	21	10	S		26	573	7	26.9	0	0	1666	646	34
GOLDTHWAITE—Mills County													
CHILDRESS GENERAL HOSPITAL, 1219 Parker St., Box 289, Zip 76844; tel. 915/648-2212; James Reese, adm. **A**9 10 **F**1 35	33	10	S		25	513	5	20.0	2	51	875	395	38
GOLIAD—Goliad County													
GOLIAD COUNTY HOSPITAL, 303 W. Franklin St., Box 938, Zip 77963; tel. 512/645-8221; Doug Eaves, adm. **A**9 10 **F**1 14 16	13	10	S		26	562	8	28.6	4	49	1445	682	50
GONZALES—Gonzales County													
MEMORIAL HOSPITAL, Hwy. 90 A By Pass, Box 587, Zip 78629; tel. 512/672-7581; Dudley Staton, interim adm. **A**10 **F**1 3 6 10 16 34 35 40 41 45 47 53	16	10	S		42	948	14	33.3	5	172	2919	1455	101
⊞ WARM SPRINGS REHABILITATION HOSPITAL, Box 58, Zip 78629; tel. 512/672-6592; David Gumper, adm. **A**1a 9 10 **F**1 12 16 23 24 26 33 42 44 46	23	46	S		68	498	39	57.4	0	0	5550	2747	198
GRAHAM—Young County													
GRAHAM GENERAL HOSPITAL, 1301 Montgomery Rd., Box 1390, Zip 76046; tel. 817/549-3400; Patrick L. Wallace, adm. **A**9 10 **F**1 3 6 16 23 35 40 45	14	10	S		43	1883	18	41.9	4	226	3116	1432	89
GRANBURY—Hood County													
★ HOOD GENERAL HOSPITAL, 1310 Paluxy Rd., Zip 76048; tel. 817/573-2683; Joe S. Langford, adm. **A**9 10 **F**1 3 6 12 14 15 16 23 26 34 35 36 40 44 45 47; **S**1755	16	10	S		63	1736	25	39.7	6	173	6006	2549	152
GRAND PRAIRIE—Dallas County													
⊞ ○ + DALLAS-FORT WORTH MEDICAL CENTER, 2709 Hospital Blvd., Zip 75051; tel. 214/641-5000; Dan Nielsen, pres. **A**1a 10 11 12 13 **F**1 3 6 9 10 11 12 14 15 16 20 23 24 33 35 36 40 42 43 45 46 48 49 53 54; **S**1755	23	10	S		197	6436	117	59.4	16	770	28075	9902	462
WHITCOMB MEMORIAL HOSPITAL, 1005 S.W. Third St., Box 451, Zip 75051; tel. 214/264-1676; Dale Whitcomb MD, adm. **A**9 **F**1 34 35 36 43	31	10	S		9	234	2	22.2	5	23	—	—	26
GRAND SALINE—Van Zandt County													
COZBY-GERMANY HOSPITAL, 707 N. Waldrip St., Zip 75140; tel. 214/962-4242; Windell M. McCord, adm. **A**9 10 **F**1 5 6 16 17 23 34 35 41; **S**1895	23	10	S		40	979	12	30.0	6	57	1870	929	51
GRAPEVINE—Tarrant County													
⊞ BAYLOR MEDICAL CENTER AT GRAPEVINE (Formerly Grapevine Medical Center), 1650 W. College St., Zip 76051; tel. 817/488-7546; Arthur L. Hohenberger, exec. dir. **A**1a 9 10 **F**1 3 6 14 16 23 24 34 35 36 41 43 44 46 53; **S**0095	23	10	S		45	2053	26	55.3	5	197	6564	2850	121
GREENVILLE—Hunt County													
CITIZENS GENERAL HOSPITAL, See Citizens Hospital of Commerce, Commerce													
⊞ HUNT MEMORIAL HOSPITAL DISTRICT (Includes Citizens General Hospital, 4215 Joe Ramsey Blvd., Drawer 1059, Zip 75401; tel. 214/454-2120; Rod Mizell, adm.), P O Drawer 1059, Zip 75401; tel. 214/886-3161; Homer Horton Jr., adm. **A**1a 9 **F**1 3 6 10 12 14 15 16 23 34 35 36 40 42 44 45 46 47 53	16	10	S		126	5576	75	59.5	15	694	11881	7873	340

Hospital, Address, Telephone, Administrator, Approval and Facility Codes, Multihospital System Code	Classification Codes				Inpatient Data				Newborn Data		Expense (thousands of dollars)		
★ American Hospital Association (AHA) membership □ Joint Commission on Accreditation of Hospitals (JCAH) accreditation + American Osteopathic Hospital Association (AOHA) membership ○ American Osteopathic Association (AOA) accreditation Δ Commission on Accreditation of Rehabilitation Facilities (CARF) accreditation Control codes 61, 63, 64, 71, 72 and 73 indicate hospitals listed by AOHA, but not registered by AHA. For definition of numerical codes, see page A2	Control	Service	Stay	Facilities	Beds	Admissions	Census	Occupancy (percent)	Bassinets	Births	Total	Payroll	Personnel
GROESBECK—Limestone County													
SOUTH LIMESTONE HOSPITAL, 900 N. Ellis St., Box 438, Zip 76642; tel. 817/729-3281; Larry F. Parsons, adm. **A**9 10 **F**1 6 10 14 16 23 35 43 45	16	10	S		36	1056	14	38.9	4	61	1973	960	64
GROVES—Jefferson County													
○ + DOCTORS HOSPITAL, 5500 39th St., Zip 77619; tel. 713/962-5733; Eric Hasemeier, exec. dir. **A**9 10 11 12 **F**1 3 10 12 15 16 17 23 30 33 34 35 36 43 45 46 47; **S**1805	33	10	S		106	2550	38	35.8	6	91	13198	3463	246
HALE CENTER—Hale County													
★□ HI-PLAINS HOSPITAL, 203 W. Fourth St., Zip 79041; tel. 806/839-2471; Gordon H. Russell, adm. (Nonreporting) **A**1a 9 10	23	10	S		84	—	—	—	—	—	—	—	—
HALLETTSVILLE—Lavaca County													
LAVACA MEDICAL CENTER, 1400 N. Texana St., Zip 77964; tel. 512/798-3671; Bob Lively, adm. (Nonreporting) **A**9 10	16	10	S		30	—	—	—	—	—	—	—	—
HAMILTON—Hamilton County													
★ HARRIS METHODIST -HAMILTON (Formerly Hamilton General Hospital), 400 N. Brown Ave., Zip 76531; tel. 817/386-3151; Paul C. Roberts, vice-pres. & adm. (Nonreporting) **A**9 10; **S**2345	21	10	S		39	—	—	—	—	—	—	—	—
HAMLIN—Jones County													
★ HAMLIN MEMORIAL HOSPITAL, 632 N.W. Second St., P O Box 387, Zip 79520; tel. 915/576-3646; Steve Grappe, adm. **A**9 10 **F**1 2 6 10 16 23 34 35 45	16	10	S		25	483	9	36.0	5	39	1327	621	45
HARLINGEN—Cameron County													
RIO GRANDE STATE CENTER, Box 2668, Zip 78551; tel. 512/423-5077; Blas Cantu Jr., supt. (Nonreporting) **A**9	12	49	L		190	—	—	—	—	—	—	—	—
★□ SOUTH TEXAS HOSPITAL, 1301 Rangerville Rd., Zip 78550; Mailing Address P O Box 592, Zip 78551; tel. 512/423-3420; Albert L. Gore MD, dir. **A**1a 9 10 **F**6 14 15 16 34 45 46 52	12	33	S		125	1079	68	54.4	0	0	7661	4245	219
★□ VALLEY BAPTIST MEDICAL CENTER, 2101 Pease St., Zip 78550; Mailing Address Box 2588, Zip 78551; tel. 512/421-1100; Ben M. McKibbens, pres. **A**1a 2 9 10 **F**1 2 3 4 5 6 7 8 9 10 11 12 14 16 20 21 23 24 26 27 30 33 35 36 40 41 42 44 45 46 47 51 52 53 54	21	10	S		300	12505	208	69.3	28	1725	—	—	1125
HASKELL—Haskell County													
HASKELL MEMORIAL HOSPITAL, 1 N. Ave. N, Zip 79521; tel. 817/864-2621; Bud Comedy, adm. (Nonreporting) **A**9 10	16	10	S		30	—	—	—	—	—	—	—	—
HEARNE—Robertson County													
CENTRAL TEXAS MEDICAL CENTER (Formerly Robertson County Community Hospital), 704 Wheelock St., Box 393, Zip 77859; tel. 409/279-3434; Frank E. Rogers, adm. (Nonreporting) **A**9 10; **S**1365	23	10	S		33	—	—	—	—	—	—	—	—
HEMPHILL—Sabine County													
★ SABINE COUNTY HOSPITAL, Hwy. 83 W., Drawer W., Zip 75948; tel. 409/787-3300; J. D. Miller Jr., adm. **A**9 10 **F**1 6 14 16 23 35 37 40 42 45 50 52 53	16	10	S		36	837	11	31.6	6	79	1737	646	50
HENDERSON—Rusk County													
★□ HENDERSON MEMORIAL HOSPITAL, 300 Wilson St., Zip 75652; tel. 214/657-7541; Ronald J. Clifford, chief exec. off. (Total facility includes 16 beds in nursing home-type unit) **A**1a 10 **F**1 3 6 10 16 19 23 34 35 40 41 43 44 45 46 50 53; **S**7235	23	10	S	TF	86	3440	43	50.0	13	455	7509	2802	247
				H	70	3397	42	—	13	455	7475	2770	232
HENRIETTA—Clay County													
★ CLAY COUNTY MEMORIAL HOSPITAL, 310 W. South St., Box 270, Zip 76365; tel. 817/538-5621; Johnny Richardson, adm. **A**9 10 **F**1 16 34 35 40 45 47; **S**6005	13	10	S		42	627	9	21.4	4	58	1691	637	44
HEREFORD—Deaf Smith County													
★□ DEAF SMITH GENERAL HOSPITAL, 800 E. Third St., Box 1858, Zip 79045; tel. 806/364-2141; James E. Bullard, adm. (Nonreporting) **A**1a 2 9 10	16	10	S		66	—	—	—	—	—	—	—	—
HICO—Hamilton County													
HICO CITY HOSPITAL, First St. & Hwy. 281, Box 68, Zip 76457; tel. 817/796-4268; Marvin Walters, adm. **A**9 10 **F**35	14	10	S		26	626	8	30.8	0	0	924	460	32
HILLSBORO—Hill County													
★□ HILL REGIONAL HOSPITAL (Formerly Grant-Buie Hospital), 101 Circle Dr., Zip 76645; tel. 817/582-8425; Jack Reamy, adm. **A**1a 9 10 **F**1 2 3 6 10 12 14 15 16 23 35 37 40 43 45 46 47 52 53; **S**5895	33	10	S		92	1406	20	21.7	6	105	—	—	80
HONDO—Medina County													
MEDINA COMMUNITY HOSPITAL (Formerly Medina Memorial Hospital), Hwy. 462, Zip 78861; tel. 512/426-5363; Ernest Parisi, adm. **A**9 10 **F**1 6 10 12 14 15 16 23 24 34 35 36 37 40 41 42 43 44 47 53; **S**0725	15	10	S		29	1054	11	38.4	10	235	2373	1236	80
HOUSTON—Harris County													
★□ AMI BELLAIRE HOSPITAL (Formerly Bellaire General Hospital), 5314 Dashwood St., Zip 77081; tel. 713/669-4000; Laurence R. Gore, chief exec. off. **A**1a 9 10 **F**1 3 5 6 10 12 14 15 16 24 28 29 30 32 33 34 35 42 44 46 50; **S**0125	33	10	S		119	2737	65	42.8	0	0	17899	4931	281
AMI CITIZENS GENERAL HOSPITAL, See Institute for Immunological Disorders													
★□ AMI EASTWAY GENERAL HOSPITAL (Formerly Eastway General Hospital), 9339 North Loop E., Zip 77029; Mailing Address Box 24216, Zip 77229; tel. 713/675-3241; Lanny Chopin, exec. dir. **A**1a 9 10 **F**1 3 16 23 43 50; **S**0125	33	10	S		150	150	40	26.5	0	0	—	—	148
★□ AMI HEIGHTS HOSPITAL (Formerly Heights Hospital), 1917 Ashland St., Zip 77008; Mailing Address Box 7497, Zip 77248; tel. 713/861-6161; Brian S. Barbe, exec. dir. **A**1a 9 10 **F**1 2 3 6 10 12 14 15 16 23 35 36 40 41 46 52 53; **S**0125	33	10	S		213	4814	84	39.4	19	298	—	—	309
★□ AMI PARK PLAZA HOSPITAL (Formerly Park Plaza Hospital), 1313 Hermann Dr., Box 8347, Zip 77004; tel. 713/527-5000; Carl W. Fitch Sr., pres. & chief exec. off. **A**1a 2 9 10 **F**1 3 6 7 8 9 10 11 12 14 15 16 17 20 23 32 33 34 35 36 40 43 46 47 53 54; **S**0125	33	10	S		269	10826	193	71.7	30	1308	57329	17587	752
★□ AMI PARKWAY HOSPITAL (Formerly Parkway Hospital), 233 W. Parker Rd., Zip 77076; tel. 713/697-2831; Phillip Hurley, exec. dir. **A**1a 9 10 **F**1 14 15 16 33 34 35 36 37 41 43 45 46 47 50 52; **S**0125	33	10	S		180	5381	80	44.3	12	663	17921	4928	321
★□ AMI TWELVE OAKS HOSPITAL (Formerly Twelve Oaks Hospital), 4200 Portsmouth St., Zip 77027; tel. 713/623-2500; Walter J. Ornsteen, exec. dir. (Total facility includes 40 beds in nursing home-type unit) **A**1a 9 10 **F**1 3 6 10 12 14 16 19 20 23 24 25 26 30 34 35 41 42 44 45 46 47 53; **S**0125	33	10	S	TF	336	4063	97	28.9	0	0	—	—	339
				H	296	3868	85	—	0	0	—	—	—
★□ AMI WESTBURY HOSPITAL (Formerly Westbury Hospital), 5556 Gasmer Rd., Zip 77035; tel. 713/729-1111; Mel Bishop, exec. dir. **A**1a 9 10 **F**1 3 6 12 15 16 23 26 34 35 46 53; **S**0125	33	10	S		123	1825	31	25.2	0	0	11246	3570	174
BELLAIRE GENERAL HOSPITAL, See AMI Bellaire Hospital													
★□ BELLE PARK HOSPITAL, 4427 Belle Park Dr., Zip 77072; tel. 713/933-6000; Arthur M. Ginsberg, adm. **A**1a 9 10 **F**3 15 24 28 29 30 32 42 48 49; **S**1755	33	22	L		152	547	114	75.0	0	0	—	—	232
BEN TAUB GENERAL HOSPITAL, See Harris County Hospital District													
★□ CYPRESS FAIRBANKS MEDICAL CENTER, 10655 Steepletop Dr., Zip 77065; tel. 713/890-4285; Bill Klier, adm. (Nonreporting) **A**1a 9 10	32	10	S		90	—	—	—	—	—	—	—	—

Hospital, Address, Telephone, Administrator, Approval and Facility Codes, Multihospital System Code	Classification Codes				Inpatient Data				Newborn Data		Expense (thousands of dollars)		
★ American Hospital Association (AHA) membership ☐ Joint Commission on Accreditation of Hospitals (JCAH) accreditation + American Osteopathic Hospital Association (AOHA) membership ○ American Osteopathic Association (AOA) accreditation Δ Commission on Accreditation of Rehabilitation Facilities (CARF) accreditation Control codes 61, 63, 64, 71, 72 and 73 indicate hospitals listed by AOHA, but not registered by AHA. For definition of numerical codes, see page A2	Control	Service	Stay	Facilities	Beds	Admissions	Census	Occupancy (percent)	Bassinets	Births	Total	Payroll	Personnel
⊞ DIAGNOSTIC CENTER HOSPITAL, 6447 Main St., Zip 77030; tel. 713/790-0790; William A. Gregory, adm. **A**1a 9 10 **F**1 2 3 15 16 20 23 24 34 41 42 43 44 46 54; **S**1755	33	10	S		183	5631	104	56.8	0	0	—	—	483
⊞ DOCTORS' HOSPITAL, 5815 Airline Dr., Zip 77076; tel. 713/695-6041; Ronald Colichia, adm. **A**1a 9 **F**1 3 6 10 12 16 17 23 34 35 40 43 53	32	10	S		114	4774	77	67.5	6	615	—	—	309
EASTWAY GENERAL HOSPITAL, See AMI Eastway General Hospital													
⊞ HARRIS COUNTY HOSPITAL DISTRICT (Includes Ben Taub General Hospital, 1502 Taub Loop, Zip 77030; tel. 713/791-7000; Michael R. Bullard, adm.; Jefferson Davis Hospital, 1801 Allen Pkwy., Zip 77019; tel. 713/751-8000; Lois Jean Moore, adm.; Quintin Mease Hospital, 3601 N. Macgregor, Zip 77004; tel. 713/528-1499; Michael R. Bullard, adm.), 726 Gillette, Zip 77019; Mailing Address Box 66769, Zip 77266; tel. 713/652-1200; Richard L. Durbin, chief adm. (Nonreporting) **A**1a 2 3 5 8 9 10	16	10	S		854	—	—	—	—	—	—	—	—
☐ HARRIS COUNTY PSYCHIATRIC CENTER, P O Box 20249, Zip 77225; tel. 713/741-7800; Martin E. Tullis, adm. (Newly Registered) **A**1a 9 10	12	22	S		125	—	—	—	—	—	—	—	—
HCA GULF PINES HOSPITAL, 205 Hollow Tree Lane, Zip 77090; tel. 713/537-0700; Linda Jubinsky, adm. (Newly Registered) **A**9 10; **S**1755	33	22	S		140	—	—	—	—	—	—	—	—
HEIGHTS HOSPITAL, See AMI Heights Hospital													
⊞ HERMANN HOSPITAL, 6411 Fannin, Zip 77030; tel. 713/797-4011; Jeptha W. Dalston PhD, chief exec. off. **A**1a 3 5 8 9 10 **F**1 2 3 4 5 6 9 10 11 12 13 14 15 16 20 22 23 24 27 30 32 33 34 35 36 37 40 42 44 46 48 49 51 52 53 54	23	10	S		766	27815	606	78.7	35	5070	159506	72303	3187
⊞ HORIZON HOSPITAL, 6160 South Loop E., Zip 77087; tel. 713/644-7047; Edwin Frank Jr., adm. (Nonreporting) **A**1b 9; **S**6525	33	82	S		70	—	—	—	—	—	—	—	—
★ HOUSTON INTERNATIONAL HOSPITAL, 6441 Main St., Zip 77030; tel. 713/795-5921; Ann Joyce Bossett, adm. **A**9 10 **F**15 24 30 31 42 43 48 53; **S**1755	33	22	S		135	1450	111	73.0	0	0	—	—	208
⊞ HOUSTON NORTHWEST MEDICAL CENTER, 710 Fm 1960 W., Box 90730, Zip 77090; tel. 713/440-1000; J. Barry Shevchuk, adm. **A**1a 9 10 **F**1 3 4 5 6 9 10 11 12 15 16 20 23 27 30 32 33 35 36 37 40 42 43 45 46 47 50 52 53 54; **S**6525	33	10	S		377	16925	251	67.5	34	2322	62354	20873	952
★ INSTITUTE FOR IMMUNOLOGICAL DISORDERS (Formerly AMI Citizens General Hospital), 7407 N. Freeway, Zip 77076; tel. 713/691-3531; Jean Settlemyre, chief exec. off. (Nonreporting) **A**9 10; **S**0125	33	10	S		107	—	—	—	—	—	—	—	—
⊞ Δ INSTITUTE FOR REHABILITATION AND RESEARCH, 1333 Moursund Ave., Zip 77030; Mailing Address Box 20095, Zip 77225; tel. 713/799-5000; William A. Spencer MD, pres. **A**1a 3 5 7 8 9 **F**3 16 23 24 26 34 42	23	46	L		91	689	62	68.0	0	0	18640	10014	375
JEFFERSON DAVIS HOSPITAL, See Harris County Hospital District													
⊞ Δ MEDICAL CENTER DEL ORO HOSPITAL, 8081 Greenbriar, Zip 77054; tel. 713/790-8100; Anne W. Brown, exec. dir. **A**1a 7 9 10 **F**1 3 4 6 9 10 11 12 14 15 16 23 24 25 26 28 29 32 33 34 37 42 43 44 47 53 54; **S**1755	33	10	S		258	3998	119	46.1	0	0	—	—	473
⊞ MEMORIAL CITY MEDICAL CENTER (Formerly Memorial City General Hospital), 920 Frostwood Dr., Box 19173, Zip 77024; tel. 713/932-3000; Robert M. Bryant, adm. **A**1a 9 10 **F**1 3 4 5 6 7 8 9 10 11 12 15 16 17 20 23 30 32 33 34 35 36 40 41 45 46 47 52 53 54	33	10	S		471	15506	231	49.0	35	2733	51381	17386	995
⊞ MEMORIAL HOSPITAL SYSTEM (Includes Memorial Care System, 7777 Southwest Freeway, Zip 77074; tel. 713/776-6992; Dan S. Wilford, pres.; Memorial Northwest Hospital, 1635 North Loop W., Zip 77008; tel. 713/869-6601; Edward Myers, vice-pres.; Southeast Unit, 1180 Astoria, Zip 77017; tel. 713/929-6100; Steve Sanders, vice-pres.; Memorial Southwest Hospital, 7600 Beechnut, Zip 77074; tel. 713/776-5000; Michael Waters, vice-pres.), Donald B. Wagner, vice-pres. & adm. **A**1a 3 5 9 10 **F**1 2 3 4 6 7 8 9 10 11 12 14 15 16 17 20 23 24 25 26 27 28 29 30 32 33 34 35 36 37 40 41 42 43 44 45 46 47 48 50 53 54; **S**2645	23	10	S		975	30406	600	60.9	69	3470	151523	69510	2974
☐ OMNI HOSPITAL AND MEDICAL CENTER, 8214 Homestead Rd., Zip 77028; tel. 713/631-1550; Dennis Shaw, adm. (Nonreporting) **A**1a 9 10	33	10	S		84	—	—	—	—	—	—	—	—
PARK PLAZA HOSPITAL, See AMI Park Plaza Hospital													
PARKWAY HOSPITAL, See AMI Parkway Hospital													
☐ RIVERSIDE GENERAL HOSPITAL, 3204 Ennis, Zip 77004; tel. 713/526-2441; Earnest Gibson III, adm. (Nonreporting) **A**1a 9 10	23	10	S		86	—	—	—	—	—	—	—	—
⊞ ROSEWOOD MEDICAL CENTER, 9200 Westheimer Rd., Zip 77063; tel. 713/780-7900; Rod Seidel, adm. **A**1a 9 10 **F**1 3 5 6 7 8 9 10 11 12 14 15 16 23 24 25 26 27 28 29 30 32 33 34 35 36 40 41 42 43 44 45 46 47 53; **S**2195	33	10	S		184	6721	111	53.4	22	895	21791	—	436
⊞ SAM HOUSTON MEMORIAL HOSPITAL, 1615 Hillendahl, Zip 77055; tel. 713/468-4311; A. C. Buchahan, adm. **A**1a 9 10 **F**1 3 6 10 12 14 16 20 23 34 35 37 41 42 43 46 47 52 53; **S**2195	33	10	S		208	3858	72	34.6	0	0	—	—	323
☐ SHARPSTOWN GENERAL HOSPITAL, 6700 Bellaire at Tarnef, Zip 77074; Mailing Address P O Box 740389, Zip 77274; tel. 713/774-7611; Dan Hill, adm. **A**1a 9 10 **F**1 3 6 9 10 12 14 15 16 20 23 24 26 30 34 35 36 37 40 43; **S**1375	33	10	S		206	4809	92	44.0	25	883	24294	6983	317
⊞ SHRINERS HOSPITALS FOR CRIPPLED CHILDREN, 1402 Outer Belt Dr., Zip 77030; tel. 713/797-1616; Eleanor R. Jackson, adm. **A**1a 3 5 **F**15 23 24 26 34 38 46; **S**4125	23	57	S		40	548	31	77.5	0	0	—	—	92
⊞ SPRING BRANCH MEMORIAL HOSPITAL, 8850 Long Point Rd., Box 55227, Zip 77055; tel. 713/467-6555; Eddie A. George, adm. **A**1a 9 10 **F**1 2 3 4 5 6 9 12 14 15 16 20 23 28 29 32 33 34 35 36 40 43 45 46 47 51 52 53 54; **S**1755	33	10	S		282	8466	138	48.9	36	1302	—	—	633
⊞ SPRING SHADOWS GLEN, 2801 Gessner, Zip 77080; tel. 713/462-4000; G. Jerry Mueck, adm. **A**1b **F**3 15 24 28 29 30 32 33 42 43 44 46 48 49	33	22	L		176	1043	126	73.7	0	0	11418	5342	289
★ ST. ANTHONY CENTER, 6301 Almeda Rd., Zip 77021; tel. 713/748-5021; Sr. Mary Alma Murphy, exec. dir.; Jerry Allen Lerman, adm. (Total facility includes 325 beds in nursing home-type unit) **A**10 **F**16 19 23 24 33 42 44 45 46 47; **S**0605	23	46	L	TF	372	1024	297	79.8	0	0	10835	6118	471
				H	47	143	14	—	0	0	—	—	249
⊞ ST. ELIZABETH HOSPITAL, 4514 Lyons Ave., Zip 77020; tel. 713/675-1711; Sr. Mary Damian Murphy, adm. **A**1a 9 10 **F**1 3 6 12 14 15 16 23 26 32 34 35 40 43 50; **S**0605	21	10	S		35	1312	20	30.3	8	224	4545	2127	103
⊞ ST. JOSEPH HOSPITAL, 1919 LaBranch St., Zip 77002; tel. 713/757-1000; Sr. M. Anastasia Enright, adm. **A**1a 2 3 5 9 10 **F**1 2 3 4 5 6 7 8 9 10 11 12 14 16 20 23 24 26 28 29 30 32 33 34 35 36 39 42 43 45 46 47 49 51 52 53 54; **S**0605	21	10	S		667	20083	447	64.3	28	2861	104116	49687	2069
⊞ ST. LUKE'S EPISCOPAL HOSPITAL, 6720 Bertner Ave., Zip 77030; Mailing Address Box 20269, Zip 77225; tel. 713/791-2011; John A. Burdine MD, pres. & chief exec. off. (Nonreporting) **A**1a 3 5 9 10	23	10	S		825	—	—	—	—	—	—	—	—
⊞ SUN BELT REGIONAL MEDICAL CENTER, 13111 E. Freeway, Zip 77015; tel. 713/455-6911; Don H. McBride, adm. **A**1a 9 10 **F**1 3 6 10 12 14 15 16 23 34 35 43 44 45 46 47 53; **S**1755	33	10	S		129	3297	51	39.5	0	0	—	—	226
⊞ TEXAS CHILDREN'S HOSPITAL, 6621 Fannin St., Zip 77030; Mailing Address Box 20269, Zip 77225; tel. 713/791-2831; Alexander R. White Jr., exec. dir. **A**1a 3 5 8 9 10 **F**1 4 6 10 12 13 15 16 17 20 22 23 24 28 32 34 35 38 41 42 44 45 46 47 53 54	23	50	S		288	11812	229	79.5	0	0	73804	33256	1441
⊞ THE METHODIST HOSPITAL, 6565 Fannin, Zip 77030; tel. 713/790-3311; Larry L. Mathis, pres. & chief exec. off. **A**1a 3 5 8 9 10 **F**1 2 3 4 6 7 8 9 10 11 12 13 14 15 16 17 20 23 24 26 27 29 30 32 33 34 35 38 39 40 41 42 43 44 46 47 50 53 54; **S**7235	23	10	S		1172	37174	825	70.4	27	2015	236869	110494	5150
TWELVE OAKS HOSPITAL, See AMI Twelve Oaks Hospital													

Hospital, Address, Telephone, Administrator, Approval and Facility Codes, Multihospital System Code	Classification Codes				Inpatient Data				Newborn Data		Expense (thousands of dollars)		
★ American Hospital Association (AHA) membership □ Joint Commission on Accreditation of Hospitals (JCAH) accreditation + American Osteopathic Hospital Association (AOHA) membership ○ American Osteopathic Association (AOA) accreditation Δ Commission on Accreditation of Rehabilitation Facilities (CARF) accreditation Control codes 61, 63, 64, 71, 72 and 73 indicate hospitals listed by AOHA, but not registered by AHA. For definition of numerical codes, see page A2	Control	Service	Stay	Facilities	Beds	Admissions	Census	Occupancy (percent)	Bassinets	Births	Total	Payroll	Personnel
★□ UNIVERSITY OF TEXAS M. D. ANDERSON HOSPITAL AND TUMOR INSTITUTE AT HOUSTON (Cancer and Related Neoplastic Diseases), 1515 Holcombe Blvd., Zip 77030; tel. 713/792-6000; Charles A. Lemaistre MD, pres. **A**1a 2 3 5 8 **F**1 3 6 7 8 9 10 11 12 14 15 16 17 23 33 34 38 44 46 47 52 53	12	49	S		514	15267	385	74.9	0	0	—	—	5608
★□ VETERANS ADMINISTRATION MEDICAL CENTER, 2002 Holcombe Blvd., Zip 77030; tel. 713/795-4411; John V. Sheehan, dir. (Total facility includes 103 beds in nursing home-type unit) **A**1a 3 5 8 **F**1 2 3 4 5 6 7 8 9 10 11 12 14 15 16 19 20 23 24 25 26 27 28 29 30 31 32 33 34 35 37 38 41 42 43 44 45 46 47 48 49 50 53 54	45	10	S	TF	1058	20239	863	79.8	0	0	—	—	2611
				H	955	20016	778	—	0	0	—	—	2579
★□ WEST HOUSTON MEDICAL CENTER, 12141 Richmond Ave., Zip 77082; tel. 713/558-3444; A. W. Layne, adm. **A**1a 10 **F**1 3 4 5 6 10 12 16 20 23 24 35 36 40 46 47 53 54; **S**1755	33	10	S		141	4756	63	44.7	30	831	26027	7506	379
□ WEST OAKS-PSYCHIATRIC INSTITUTE OF HOUSTON, 6500 Hornwood, Zip 77074; Mailing Address Box 741389, Zip 77274; tel. 713/995-0909; Kay Swint, adm. (Nonreporting) **A**1b 9 10; **S**0395	32	22	L		184	—	—	—	—	—	—	—	—
WESTBURY HOSPITAL, See AMI Westbury Hospital													
★□ WOMAN'S HOSPITAL OF TEXAS, 7600 Fannin St., Zip 77054; tel. 713/790-1234; Judy Novak, chief exec. off. **A**1a 9 10 **F**1 3 6 9 14 15 16 23 24 34 36 37 40 46 47 48 51; **S**1755	33	10	S		160	7289	100	62.5	56	3883	—	—	371
★□ YALE CLINIC AND HOSPITAL, 510 W. Tidwell Rd., Zip 77091; tel. 713/691-1111; A. W. Vila DO, adm. (Nonreporting) **A**1a 9	33	10	S		80	—	—	—	—	—	—	—	—
YORK PLAZA HOSPITAL AND MEDICAL CENTER, 2807 Little York Rd., Zip 77093; tel. 713/697-2961; John H. Nienhuser, adm. **A**9 10 **F**1 3 6 10 16 23 34 35	33	10	S		83	2433	37	45.7	0	0	9098	2557	—
HUBBARD—Hill County													
HUBBARD HOSPITAL, 701 N. Fifth St., Box 308, Zip 76648; tel. 817/576-2551; Milton Meadows, adm. **A**9 **F**1 6 14 15 16 23 35 40 45 47 50 52	33	10	S		30	370	4	11.6	2	10	1767	650	33
HUMBLE—Harris County													
★□ HEALTHSOUTH (Formerly Humble Rehabilitation Hospital), 18903 Memorial S. Blvd., Zip 77338; tel. 713/446-6148; Carl A. Risley Jr., adm. (Nonreporting) **A**1a 10	33	46	L		90	—	—	—	—	—	—	—	—
HUMBLE REHABILITATION HOSPITAL, See Healthsouth													
★□ NORTHEAST MEDICAL CENTER HOSPITAL, 18951 Memorial N., Zip 77338; tel. 713/540-7801; Monty E. McLaurin, adm. **A**1a 9 10 **F**1 2 3 4 6 10 12 14 15 16 23 24 27 32 33 34 35 36 40 42 45 46 47 53 54; **S**2645	16	10	S		195	8605	132	67.7	36	1131	33558	12715	590
HUNT—Kerr County													
★□ LA HACIENDA TREATMENT CENTER, Fm 1340, Box 1, Zip 78024; tel. 512/238-4222; John Lacy, adm. **A**1b 9 **F**32 33; **S**6525	33	82	S		50	640	44	88.0	0	0	—	—	67
HUNTSVILLE—Walker County													
★□ HUNTSVILLE MEMORIAL HOSPITAL, 3000 I-45, Zip 77340; tel. 409/291-3411; Ralph E. Beaty, adm. **A**1a 9 10 **F**1 3 6 10 12 15 16 23 33 34 35 40 44 45 46 47 50 52 53; **S**1755	23	10	S		121	5331	78	70.3	20	795	14950	5935	336
IRAAN—Pecos County													
□ GENERAL HOSPITAL, Box 665, Zip 79744; tel. 915/639-2871; Paul Harper, adm. **A**1a 9 10 **F**1 6 34 35 40	13	10	S		14	161	2	14.3	2	45	768	388	25
IRVING—Dallas County													
AMI PIONEER PARK MEDICAL CENTER, See Pioneer Park Hospital													
★□ IRVING COMMUNITY HOSPITAL, 1901 MacArthur Blvd., Zip 75061; tel. 214/579-8100; Morris H. Parrish, chief exec. off. **A**1a 9 10 **F**1 3 4 6 10 12 14 15 16 17 20 23 24 25 26 30 35 36 37 40 41 42 44 45 46 47 52 53 54	16	10	S		238	9664	142	59.9	26	1648	31591	14219	755
★□ PIONEER PARK HOSPITAL (Formerly AMI Pioneer Park Medical Center), 1745 W. Irving Blvd., Zip 75061; tel. 214/254-8186; Diane D. King, adm. (Data for 130 days) **A**1a 9 10 **F**1 3 6 10 14 15 16 23 35 50 53	33	10	S		50	828	44	88.0	0	0	—	—	86
JACKSBORO—Jack County													
JACK COUNTY HOSPITAL, 717 Magnolia St., Zip 76056; tel. 817/567-2655; Hershel J. Earp, adm. **A**9 10 **F**1 14 16 35 41 45 52	13	10	S		20	624	8	40.0	2	9	1283	625	47
JACKSONVILLE—Cherokee County													
★□ NAN TRAVIS MEMORIAL HOSPITAL, 501 S. Ragsdale St., Zip 75766; tel. 214/586-9881; Thomas M. Kish, pres. **A**1a 9 10 **F**1 3 6 9 10 11 12 15 16 23 34 35 36 40 41 43 45 46 47 49 53; **S**7235	23	10	S		130	5286	92	70.8	12	321	13917	6184	363
JASPER—Jasper County													
□ JASPER MEMORIAL HOSPITAL, 1275 S. Second St., Zip 75951; tel. 409/384-5461; Haskell G. Silkwood, adm. **A**1a 9 10 **F**1 3 6 10 12 14 15 16 23 33 34 35 36 37 40 41 43 44 45 53	16	10	S		56	1496	18	32.1	8	171	4334	1888	113
★□ MARY E. DICKERSON MEMORIAL HOSPITAL, 1001 Dickerson Dr., Zip 75951; tel. 409/384-2575; Jerry Bucher, chief exec. off. (Data for 316 days) **A**1a 9 10 **F**1 6 16 23 34 35 36 45 53; **S**0905	33	10	S		49	2000	15	30.6	5	170	2768	962	62
JEFFERSON—Marion County													
★□ MARION COUNTY HOSPITAL, 1115 N. Walcott St., Zip 75657; tel. 214/665-2561; Douglas Langley, pres. **A**1a 9 10 **F**1 6 12 14 16 23 30 34 35 40 45	21	10	S		37	593	7	18.9	4	52	235	108	39
JOURDANTON—Atascosa County													
★□ TRI-CITY COMMUNITY HOSPITAL (Formerly Mercy Hospital), Hwy. 97 E., Box 189, Zip 78026; tel. 512/769-3515; Dean P. Lemmers, adm. **A**1a 9 10 **F**1 8 14 16 17 35 40 45	23	10	S		30	1912	18	56.3	2	171	3092	1597	100
JUNCTION—Kimble County													
KIMBLE HOSPITAL, 2101 Main St., Zip 76849; tel. 915/446-3321; Sandra A. Woolen, adm. **A**9 10 **F**1 3 6 14 16 35 37	16	10	S		18	381	4	22.2	3	45	906	505	37
KATY—Fort Bend County													
★□ AMI KATY COMMUNITY HOSPITAL (Formerly Katy Community Hospital), 5602 Medical Center Dr., Box 656, Zip 77450; tel. 713/392-1111; Warren Wilkey, exec. dir. **A**1a 9 10 **F**1 3 6 10 12 14 16 23 34 35 36 40 43 45 46 52 53; **S**0125	33	10	S		100	3070	39	39.0	10	476	13607	4513	235
KAUFMAN—Kaufman County													
★□ PRESBYTERIAN HOSPITAL OF KAUFMAN, Hwy. 243 W. at Hwy. 175, Box 310, Zip 75142; tel. 214/932-2183; Patty Pettigrew, exec. dir. **A**1a 9 10 **F**1 3 6 12 16 23 35 37 40 45 46; **S**1130	23	10	S		60	2753	38	64.4	6	243	8211	3219	204
KENEDY—Karnes County													
OTTO KAISER MEMORIAL HOSPITAL, Hwy. 181 N., Rte. 1, Box 450, Zip 78119; tel. 512/583-3401; Harold L. Boening, adm. **A**9 10 **F**1 2 3 6 16 23 35 41 45 53	16	10	S		46	798	9	20.0	3	49	1901	848	64
KERMIT—Winkler County													
★□ MEMORIAL HOSPITAL, 821 Jeffee Dr., Zip 79745; tel. 915/586-5864; Charles P. Clark III, adm. **A**1a 9 10 **F**1 3 6 12 14 15 16 23 35 40 41 43 45	13	10	S		47	1205	16	34.0	8	120	3424	1541	90
KERRVILLE—Kerr County													
□ KERRVILLE STATE HOSPITAL, 721 Thompson Dr., Box 1468, Zip 78029; tel. 512/896-2211; Luther W. Ross MD, supt. **A**1b 9 10 **F**23 24 28 30 32 33 42 44 46 47 48 49	12	22	L		710	817	512	72.1	0	0	—	—	877

★ American Hospital Association (AHA) membership
□ Joint Commission on Accreditation of Hospitals (JCAH) accreditation
+ American Osteopathic Hospital Association (AOHA) membership
○ American Osteopathic Association (AOA) accreditation
Δ Commission on Accreditation of Rehabilitation Facilities (CARF) accreditation
Control codes 61, 63, 64, 71, 72 and 73 indicate hospitals listed by AOHA, but not registered by AHA.
For definition of numerical codes, see page A2

Hospital, Address, Telephone, Administrator, Approval and Facility Codes, Multihospital System Code	Classification Codes				Inpatient Data				Newborn Data		Expense (thousands of dollars)		
	Control	Service	Stay	Facilities	Beds	Admissions	Census	Occupancy (percent)	Bassinets	Births	Total	Payroll	Personnel
★□ SID PETERSON MEMORIAL HOSPITAL, 710 Water St., Zip 78028; tel. 512/896-4200; F. W. Hall Jr., adm. **A**1a 9 10 **F**1 3 6 10 15 16 20 23 34 35 36 37 40 41 43 45 47 53	23	10	S		123	5291	77	63.6	10	593	—	—	368
★□ VETERANS ADMINISTRATION MEDICAL CENTER, 3600 Memorial Blvd., Zip 78028; tel. 512/896-2020; Arnold E. Mouish, dir. (Total facility includes 120 beds in nursing home-type unit) **A**1a **F**1 3 6 12 14 15 16 19 23 24 26 28 29 30 32 33 34 35 41 42 44 46 47 49 50	45	10	S	TF	378	6071	307	79.9	0	0	22815	15390	689
				H	258	5969	195	—	0	0	—	—	616
KILGORE—Gregg County													
★□ ROY H. LAIRD MEMORIAL HOSPITAL, 1612 S. Henderson Blvd., Zip 75662; tel. 214/984-3505; Roderick Lagrone, adm. **A**1a 9 10 **F**1 3 6 10 12 14 16 23 35 36 40 41 43 45 50	14	10	S		47	1851	20	33.9	5	142	3719	1855	124
KILLEEN—Bell County													
★□ METROPLEX HOSPITAL, 2201 S. Clear Creek Rd., Zip 76542; tel. 817/526-7523; Norman L. McBride, pres. **A**1a 9 10 **F**1 3 6 10 12 15 16 23 35 36 40 41 45 46 47 51; **S**4165	21	10	S		79	3556	46	58.2	20	1087	10959	4245	224
KINGSVILLE—Kleberg County													
★□ SPOHN KLEBERG MEMORIAL HOSPITAL (Formerly Kleberg Memorial Hospital), 1300 General Cavazos Blvd., P O Box 1197, Zip 78363; tel. 512/595-1661; Allan C. Sonduck, pres. & chief exec. off. **A**1a 9 10 **F**1 3 6 12 14 15 16 23 26 30 34 35 36 40 41 42 43 44 45 52 53; **S**5565	21	10	S		68	3317	44	64.7	3	683	10665	3901	216
KIRBYVILLE—Jasper County													
KIRBYVILLE COMMUNITY HOSPITAL (Formerly Max Mixson Memorial Hospital), 201 E. Lavielle St., P O Box 580, Zip 75956; tel. 409/423-2218; George Rountree, adm.; D. J. Cone, asst. adm. **A**9 **F**16 35 46	31	10	S		24	570	8	35.9	0	0	—	—	47
LA GRANGE—Fayette County													
★ FAYETTE MEMORIAL HOSPITAL, 543 N. Jackson St., Zip 78945; tel. 409/968-3166; Herbert A. Cope, adm. **A**9 10 **F**1 6 10 12 14 16 23 34 35 36 40 43 45 50 53	23	10	S		43	1390	20	46.5	5	216	3079	1297	89
LACKLAND AIR FORCE BASE—Bexar County													
★□ WILFORD HALL U. S. AIR FORCE MEDICAL CENTER, Zip 78236; tel. 512/670-7353; Maj. Gen. Vernon Chong MC USAF, cmdr.; Col. Robert M. Young MSC USAF, adm. **A**1a 2 3 5 **F**1 2 3 4 5 6 7 8 9 10 11 12 13 14 15 16 18 20 23 24 26 27 28 30 32 33 34 35 37 38 40 41 44 46 47 48 49 51 52 53 54	41	10	S		879	22338	710	83.8	20	1578	—	—	3594
LAKE JACKSON—Brazoria County													
★ BRAZOSPORT MEMORIAL HOSPITAL, 100 Medical Dr., Zip 77566; tel. 409/297-4411; Troy A. Dean, adm. **A**10 **F**1 3 5 6 10 12 15 16 23 24 27 30 35 36 40 45 46 47 48 52 53; **S**1755	23	10	S		165	6451	100	60.6	22	864	20685	8363	452
LAMESA—Dawson County													
MEDICAL ARTS HOSPITAL, 1600 N. Bryan Ave., Zip 79331; tel. 806/872-2183; Ron Rives, adm. (Nonreporting) **A**9 10	13	10	S		50	—	—	—	—	—	—	—	—
LAMPASAS—Lampasas County													
★□ ROLLINS-BROOK HOSPITAL, 608 N. Key Ave., Box 589, Zip 76550; tel. 512/556-3682; Michael L. Littell, adm. **A**1a 9 10 **F**1 6 15 16 21 23 24 35 36 40 41 43 44 45; **S**1365	33	10	S		23	1014	10	43.5	4	143	2118	822	56
LANCASTER—Chambers County													
★□ HCA MIDWAY PARK MEDICAL CENTER (Formerly Midway Park General Hospital), 2600 W. Pleasant Run Rd., Zip 75146; tel. 214/223-9600; Jim White, adm. (Nonreporting) **A**1a 9 10; **S**1755	33	10	S		104	—	—	—	—	—	—	—	—
LAREDO—Webb County													
★□ AMI DOCTORS HOSPITAL OF LAREDO (Formerly Doctors Hospital of Laredo), 500 E. Mann Rd., Zip 78041; tel. 512/723-1131; Ernie Domenech, exec. dir. (Nonreporting) **A**1a 9 10; **S**0125	33	10	S		78	—	—	—	—	—	—	—	—
DOCTORS HOSPITAL OF LAREDO, See AMI Doctors Hospital of Laredo													
★□ MERCY REGIONAL MEDICAL CENTER, 1515 Logan Ave., Drawer 2068, Zip 78044; tel. 512/727-6222; Ernesto M. Flores Jr., pres. **A**1a 9 10 **F**1 3 6 10 12 14 15 16 20 23 35 36 40 41 43 45 47 50 51 52 53; **S**5185	21	10	S		288	13207	196	68.1	30	2331	27507	13202	943
LAUGHLIN AIR FORCE BASE—Val Verde County													
U. S. AIR FORCE HOSPITAL, Zip 78843; tel. 512/298-2311; Capt. Larry F. Wittgan, adm. **F**1 3 6 15 23 32 33 34 35 36 40 46 47 52	41	10	S		20	1276	12	60.0	8	238	—	—	214
LEVELLAND—Hockley County													
□ COOK MEMORIAL HOSPITAL, 1900 S. College Ave., Zip 79336; tel. 806/894-4963; Larry G. Todd, exec. dir. (Nonreporting) **A**1a 9 10; **S**3025	33	10	S		74	—	—	—	—	—	—	—	—
LEWISVILLE—Denton County													
□ LEWISVILLE MEMORIAL HOSPITAL, 500 W. Main, Zip 75067; tel. 214/420-1000; David G. Purifoy, pres. **A**1a 9 10 **F**1 3 6 10 12 14 15 16 23 24 26 30 33 35 36 42 43 44 46 51 53	33	10	S		148	5936	63	42.6	14	802	16796	7006	437
LIBERTY—Liberty County													
□ YETTIE KERSTING MEMORIAL HOSPITAL, 1353 N. Travis St., Zip 77575; tel. 409/336-7316; Billy Pettit, adm. (Nonreporting) **A**1a 9 10	16	10	S		49	—	—	—	—	—	—	—	—
LINDEN—Cass County													
★□ LINDEN MUNICIPAL HOSPITAL, N. Kaufman St., Box 32, Zip 75563; tel. 214/756-5561; Harold Jerry Trammell, adm. **A**1a 9 10 **F**1 3 6 16 23 26 35 40 41 45	16	10	S		53	1224	20	37.7	7	109	2423	1211	87
LITTLEFIELD—Lamb County													
LITTLEFIELD MEDICAL CENTER, 1500 S. Sunset, Zip 79339; tel. 806/385-6411; Gary Moore, adm. (Total facility includes 6 beds in nursing home-type unit) **A**9 10 **F**1 3 14 16 19 23 35 45; **S**1375	33	10	S	TF	75	980	11	14.7	5	96	—	—	57
				H	69	960	—	—	5	96	—	—	—
LIVERPOOL—Brazoria County													
★□ PARKSIDE LODGE-CHOCOLATE BAYON (Formerly Brookwood Recovery Center), 638 Harbor Rd., P O Box 168, Zip 77577; tel. 713/393-2023; Don LeRoy Devens, exec. dir. **A**1b **F**15 42	33	82	L		42	170	16	38.1	0	0	2220	747	38
LIVINGSTON—Polk County													
LAKE LIVINGSTON MEDICAL CENTER (Formerly Livingston Memorial Hospital), 602 E. Church St., P O Box 1257, Zip 77351; tel. 713/327-4381; Thomas Gilbert, adm. (Nonreporting) **A**9 10	16	10	S		41	—	—	—	—	—	—	—	—
LLANO—Llano County													
LLANO MEMORIAL HOSPITAL, 200 W. Ollie St., Zip 78643; tel. 915/247-5040; James L. Alexander, adm. **A**9 10 **F**1 6 16 23 35 40 43 45	13	10	S		30	938	11	36.7	6	58	1445	785	56
LOCKHART—Caldwell County													
LOCKHART HOSPITAL, 901 Bois D'Arc St., Zip 78644; tel. 512/398-3433; Robert T. Martel, adm. **A**9 10 **F**1 6 14 16 23 35 37 45 53; **S**0985	33	10	S		24	834	12	50.0	0	27	2494	—	57
LOCKNEY—Floyd County													
LOCKNEY GENERAL HOSPITAL, 320 N. Main St., Box 37, Zip 79241; tel. 806/652-3373; Jerry Burleson, adm. **A**9 10 **F**1 16 34 35 37 40 43 52	16	10	S		20	557	6	30.0	5	181	1212	633	46

Hospital, Address, Telephone, Administrator, Approval and Facility Codes, Multihospital System Code	Classification Codes			Facilities	Inpatient Data				Newborn Data		Expense (thousands of dollars)		
★ American Hospital Association (AHA) membership □ Joint Commission on Accreditation of Hospitals (JCAH) accreditation + American Osteopathic Hospital Association (AOHA) membership ○ American Osteopathic Association (AOA) accreditation Δ Commission on Accreditation of Rehabilitation Facilities (CARF) accreditation Control codes 61, 63, 64, 71, 72 and 73 indicate hospitals listed by AOHA, but not registered by AHA. For definition of numerical codes, see page A2	Control	Service	Stay	Facilities	Beds	Admissions	Census	Occupancy (percent)	Bassinets	Births	Total	Payroll	Personnel
LONE STAR—Morris County													
★ HOSPITAL IN THE PINES, Hwy. 259 N., Box 357, Zip 75668; tel. 214/656-2561; Lewis E. Robertson, adm. (Nonreporting) **A**9 10; **S**1895	23	10	S		39	—	—	—	—	—	—	—	—
LONGVIEW—Gregg County													
⊞ GOOD SHEPHERD MEDICAL CENTER, 621 N. Fifth St., Zip 75601; tel. 214/236-2000; Jerry D. Adair, pres. & chief exec. off. **A**1a 3 9 10 **F**1 3 5 6 10 12 15 16 20 23 24 27 30 35 36 40 41 43 44 45 46 47 52 53 54	23	10	S		240	10951	148	62.7	45	2378	34839	14181	819
⊞ HCA LONGVIEW REGIONAL HOSPITAL (Formerly Longview Regional Hospital), 2901 N. Fourth St., Zip 75601; tel. 214/758-1818; Alan McMillin, adm. **A**1a 9 10 **F**1 3 6 10 12 15 16 17 23 35 36 40 45 46 47 51 52 53; **S**1755	33	10	S		83	3700	52	62.7	15	123	—	—	268
LUBBOCK—Lubbock County													
⊞ CHARTER PLAINS HOSPITAL, 801 N. Quaker, P O Box 10560, Zip 79408; tel. 806/744-5505; Don S. McLendon, adm. **A**1a 9 10 **F**15 16 28 32 33 34 42 48 49; **S**0695	33	22	S		80	375	33	41.3	0	0	—	—	90
□ ○ + COMMUNITY HOSPITAL OF LUBBOCK, 5301 University Ave., Zip 79413; tel. 806/795-9301; Ken E. Worley, exec. dir. **A**1a 10 11 **F**1 3 6 10 12 14 15 16 23 32 34 35 36 37 40 43 45 47 50; **S**3025	33	10	S		76	1825	22	28.9	8	365	6041	2324	137
□ HIGHLAND HOSPITAL, 2412 50th St., Zip 79412; tel. 806/795-8251; Tim L. Stroud, adm. **A**1a 2 9 10 **F**1 3 6 10 16 23 34 35 45 47 53; **S**0875	33	10	S		123	2788	55	44.7	0	0	—	—	181
⊞ LUBBOCK COUNTY HOSPITAL DISTRICT-LUBBOCK GENERAL HOSPITAL, 602 Indiana Ave., Box 5980, Zip 79417; tel. 806/743-3111; Jim Courtney, chief exec. off. **A**1a 2 3 5 9 10 **F**1 2 3 4 5 6 10 12 13 14 15 16 20 22 23 24 28 30 32 33 34 35 36 37 38 40 44 45 46 47 50 51 52 53 54	16	10	S		276	11191	184	66.7	30	2533	43956	19362	910
⊞ METHODIST HOSPITAL, 3615 19th St., Zip 79410; Mailing Address Box 1201, Zip 79408; tel. 806/792-1011; William D. Poteet III, pres. **A**1a 2 6 9 10 **F**1 2 3 4 5 6 7 8 9 10 11 12 15 16 17 20 23 24 26 27 30 32 33 34 35 36 37 40 42 45 46 52 53 54	21	10	S		549	20222	357	65.0	30	2116	68381	37165	1757
□ SOUTH PARK MEDICAL CENTER, 6610 S. Quaker Ave., Zip 79413; tel. 806/792-7112; Lowell S. Benton, exec. dir. **A**1a 10 **F**1 3 6 10 11 14 15 16 20 23 34 35 36 40 45 46 47 53; **S**3025	33	10	S		99	3229	62	62.6	9	240	10140	3573	248
⊞ ST. MARY OF THE PLAINS HOSPITAL, 4000 24th St., Zip 79410; tel. 806/796-6000; Jake Henry Jr., pres. & chief exec. off. **A**1a 3 5 9 10 **F**1 3 4 6 10 12 14 16 20 23 24 25 27 30 32 33 34 35 36 42 44 45 46 47 48 53 54; **S**5425	21	10	S		290	8586	202	71.7	0	0	35064	14148	796
U. S. AIR FORCE HOSPITAL, See Reese Air Force Base													
⊞ WEST TEXAS HOSPITAL, 1401 Ninth St., Zip 79401; Mailing Address Box 10537, Zip 79408; tel. 806/765-9381; Frank Grubbs, adm. (Nonreporting) **A**1a 9 10	33	10	S		155	—	—	—	—	—	—	—	—
LUFKIN—Angelina County													
⊞ HCA WOODLAND HEIGHTS MEDICAL CENTER (Formerly Woodland Heights General Hospital), 500 Gaslight Blvd., Zip 75901; tel. 409/634-8311; M. L. Lagarde III, adm. **A**1a 9 **F**1 3 5 6 10 11 12 14 15 16 17 23 34 35 36 41 46 47 48 53; **S**1755	33	10	S		117	4703	64	54.7	12	751	12408	4729	255
⊞ MEMORIAL MEDICAL CENTER OF EAST TEXAS (Formerly Memorial Hospital), Frank & Franklin Sts., Box 1447, Zip 75901; tel. 713/634-8111; Walter Gary Deer, exec. vice-pres. & adm. (Nonreporting) **A**1a 9 10	23	10	S		254	—	—	—	—	—	—	—	—
LULING—Caldwell County													
EDGAR B. DAVIS MEMORIAL HOSPITAL, 130 Hays St., Zip 78648; tel. 512/875-5643; Gloria C. Zahnow, adm. **A**9 10 **F**1 6 12 14 16 23 35 42 43 45 53	14	10	S		30	783	9	30.0	4	74	1277	595	42
MADISONVILLE—Madison County													
□ MADISON COUNTY MEDICAL CENTER, 100 W. Cross St., Box 698, Zip 77864; tel. 409/348-2631; Ricky D. Wallace, adm. **A**1a 9 10 **F**1 3 6 12 14 16 20 23 34 35 36 40 41 45 47 50 52; **S**1755	13	10	S		52	1213	20	38.5	5	83	4328	1839	102
MANSFIELD—Tarrant County													
⊞ HCA MANSFIELD HOSPITAL (Formerly Mansfield Community Hospital), 1802 Hwy. 157 N., Zip 76063; tel. 817/473-6101; Jim Cliborne, adm. (Nonreporting) **A**1a 9 10; **S**1755	33	10	S		55	—	—	—	—	—	—	—	—
MARLIN—Falls County													
⊞ TORBETT, HUTCHINGS, SMITH MEMORIAL HOSPITAL, 322 Coleman St., Box 60, Zip 76661; tel. 817/883-3561; G. B. Erwin Sr., adm. **A**1a 9 10 **F**1 3 6 19 23 34 35 40 41 45	23	10	S		69	590	14	20.3	6	16	3582	162	92
⊞ VETERANS ADMINISTRATION MEDICAL CENTER, 1016 Ward St., Zip 76661; tel. 817/883-3511; John E. Barnett MD, actg. dir. **A**1a **F**3 12 14 15 16 19 23 24 26 34 35 42 46 50	45	10	L		202	2351	170	84.2	0	0	11829	8646	323
MARSHALL—Harrison County													
⊞ MEMORIAL HOSPITAL, 811 S. Washington, Box 1599, Zip 75670; tel. 214/935-9311; James E. Pears, adm. & pres. **A**1a 9 10 **F**1 3 6 10 12 14 15 16 23 26 29 30 32 35 40 45 46 47	23	10	S		106	4495	49	46.2	12	450	8651	4077	246
MCALLEN—Hidalgo County													
⊞ CHARTER PALMS HOSPITAL, 1421 E. Jackson Ave., P O Box 5239, Zip 78501; tel. 512/631-5421; Jon C. O'Shaughnessy, adm. **A**1b 9 10 **F**28 29 32 42 48 49; **S**0695	33	22	S		80	597	37	46.3	0	0	—	—	78
⊞ MCALLEN MEDICAL CENTER (Formerly McAllen Methodist Hospital), 301 W. Expwy. 83, Zip 78503; tel. 512/632-4000; John L. Mims, adm. **A**1a 2 3 5 9 10 **F**1 3 4 6 9 10 11 12 14 15 16 17 20 23 24 26 27 30 33 34 35 36 37 40 42 44 45 47 51 52 53 54; **S**9555	33	10	S		293	13189	203	65.3	20	3161	40190	15341	784
⊞ RIO GRANDE REGIONAL HOSPITAL, 101 E. Ridge Rd., Zip 78503; tel. 512/631-9111; William A. Burns, adm. (Nonreporting) **A**1a 9 10; **S**1755	33	10	S		165	—	—	—	—	—	—	—	—
MCCAMEY—Upton County													
MCCAMEY HOSPITAL, Box 1200, Zip 79752; tel. 915/652-8626; James R. Queen Jr., adm. (Total facility includes 30 beds in nursing home-type unit) **A**9 10 **F**1 15 16 19 34 35	16	10	S	TF H	46 16	291 277	31 3	67.4 —	7 7	13 13	2132 1496	930 562	66 45
MCKINNEY—Collin County													
⊞ AMI NORTH TEXAS MEDICAL CENTER, 1800 N. Graves St., Box 370, Zip 75069; tel. 214/548-3000; Steven Woerner, exec. dir. **A**1a 9 10 **F**1 3 6 7 10 14 15 16 20 23 24 34 35 36 40 41 42 44 45 46 52 53; **S**0125	33	10	S		134	3799	51	37.9	16	630	15181	4715	234
⊞ HCA WYSONG MEDICAL CENTER (Formerly Wysong Memorial Hospital), 130 S. Central Expwy., Zip 75069; tel. 214/542-9382; Tod Lambert, chief exec. off. **A**1a 9 10 **F**1 5 6 10 12 14 15 16 23 24 26 33 34 35 37 42 43 44 48; **S**1755	33	10	S		99	1835	42	42.4	0	23	7524	2714	160
MEMPHIS—Hall County													
HALL COUNTY HOSPITAL, 1800 N. Boykin Dr., Zip 79245; tel. 806/259-3504; Jerry Weatherly, adm. **A**9 10 **F**1 35 40 41 43	13	10	S		28	584	7	24.2	8	58	1210	652	51
MENARD—Menard County													
MENARD HOSPITAL, Gay & San Saba Sts., Box 608, Zip 76859; tel. 915/396-4515; Edward Zachary, adm. (Total facility includes 40 beds in nursing home-type unit) **A**9 10 **F**19 23 35 41 45	16	10	S	TF H	70 30	254 234	38 2	54.3 —	3 3	0 0	1444 1001	745 554	71 50

★ American Hospital Association (AHA) membership
☐ Joint Commission on Accreditation of Hospitals (JCAH) accreditation
+ American Osteopathic Hospital Association (AOHA) membership
○ American Osteopathic Association (AOA) accreditation
Δ Commission on Accreditation of Rehabilitation Facilities (CARF) accreditation
Control codes 61, 63, 64, 71, 72 and 73 indicate hospitals listed by AOHA, but not registered by AHA.
For definition of numerical codes, see page A2

Hospital, Address, Telephone, Administrator, Approval and Facility Codes, Multihospital System Code	Classification Codes				Inpatient Data				Newborn Data		Expense (thousands of dollars)		
	Control	Service	Stay	Facilities	Beds	Admissions	Census	Occupancy (percent)	Bassinets	Births	Total	Payroll	Personnel
MERIDIAN—Bosque County													
★ MERIDIAN HOSPITAL, 1114 N. Main St., Box 677, Zip 76665; tel. 817/435-2308; Gary Marks, vice-pres. (Nonreporting) **A**9 10; **S**2345	23	10	S		123	—	—	—	—	—	—	—	—
MESQUITE—Dallas County													
★☐ CHARTER SUBURBAN HOSPITAL MESQUITE (Formerly Charter Suburban Hospital), 1011 N. Galloway Ave., Zip 75149; tel. 214/320-7000; Barrett L. Brown, adm. **A**1a 9 10 **F**1 3 4 6 12 13 14 15 16 23 26 34 35 43 53 54; **S**0695	33	10	S		152	4355	51	33.8	0	0	—	—	302
★☐ MESQUITE COMMUNITY HOSPITAL, 3500 Hwy. 67 E., Zip 75150; tel. 214/270-3300; Raymond P. Deblasi, adm. **A**1a 9 10 **F**1 3 6 10 12 14 15 16 23 24 32 35 36 40 43 46 48 49 53	33	10	S		141	4605	73	51.8	12	857	14211	5856	327
★☐ + MESQUITE PHYSICIANS HOSPITAL, 1527 N. Galloway, Zip 75149; tel. 214/285-6391; Steven D. Porter, adm. **A**1a 9 10 **F**1 3 6 7 10 14 16 23 27 28 30 33 35 36 40 53; **S**6525	33	10	S		127	1407	27	21.3	6	81	—	—	154
MEXIA—Limestone County													
★☐ HARRIS METHODIST -MEXIA (Formerly General Mexia Memorial Hospital), 312 E. Glendale St., Zip 76667; tel. 817/562-5332; Roger Jenkins, adm. **A**1a 9 10 **F**1 15 16 23 35 40 45; **S**2345	23	10	S		47	1075	13	28.9	6	128	2594	1069	56
MIDLAND—Midland County													
★☐ CLEARVIEW HOSPITAL, P O Box 4757, Zip 79704; tel. 915/697-5200; Philip H. Lundberg, adm. (Data for 267 days) **A**1b 9 10 **F**15 24 32 34 42 46 49; **S**9855	23	82	S		49	201	15	30.6	0	0	2769	912	55
★☐ MIDLAND MEMORIAL HOSPITAL, 2200 W. Illinois Ave., Zip 79701; tel. 915/685-1111; Ray M. Branson, pres. **A**1a 2 9 10 **F**1 3 5 6 7 8 9 10 11 12 14 16 23 24 26 30 33 35 36 40 44 45 46 52 53 54	16	10	S		204	10890	140	69.0	85	2350	41406	16773	743
PARKVIEW HOSPITAL, See Physicians and Surgeons Hospital													
PHYSICIANS AND SURGEONS HOSPITAL (Formerly Parkview Hospital), 3201 Sage St., Zip 79705; tel. 915/683-2273; Richard C. Liley, adm. (Data for 193 days) **A**9 10 **F**1 3 4 6 10 14 15 16 17 23 33 34 35 37 43 45 54; **S**0195	33	10	S		44	824	16	36.4	0	0	2615	991	120
MINERAL WELLS—Palo Pinto County													
★☐ PALO PINTO GENERAL HOSPITAL, 400 S.W. 25th Ave., Zip 76067; tel. 817/325-7891; Patrick Murray, adm. **A**1a 9 10 **F**1 3 6 10 12 15 16 23 35 40 41 45 46	16	10	S		85	3065	42	49.4	10	339	8773	3689	201
MISSION—Hidalgo County													
★ MISSION HOSPITAL, 900 S. Bryan Rd., Zip 78572; tel. 512/580-9101; Thomas B. Symonds, adm. (Nonreporting) **A**9 10; **S**1755	23	10	S		58	—	—	—	—	—	—	—	—
MISSOURI CITY—Fort Bend County													
★☐ AMI FORT BEND COMMUNITY HOSPITAL (Formerly Fort Bend Community Hospital), 3803 Fm 1092 at Hwy. 6, Zip 77459; tel. 713/499-4800; Frederick R. Grates, exec. dir. **A**1a 9 10 **F**1 3 6 10 12 14 15 16 23 24 34 35 36 40 43 44 45 46 53; **S**0125	33	10	S		80	2257	24	30.0	6	337	10275	3288	170
MONAHANS—Ward County													
★☐ WARD MEMORIAL HOSPITAL, 406 S. Gary St., Zip 79756; tel. 915/943-2511; Gary F. Shreve, adm. **A**1a 9 10 **F**1 3 6 15 16 23 24 35 41 42 45	13	10	S		49	1337	13	26.5	7	228	—	—	97
MORTON—Cochran County													
★ COCHRAN MEMORIAL HOSPITAL, 201 E. Grant St., Zip 79346; tel. 806/266-5565; Truman Swinney, adm. **A**9 10 **F**1 6 10 34 35 40	16	10	S		30	547	6	20.0	5	55	1208	691	38
MOUNT PLEASANT—Titus County													
★☐ TITUS COUNTY MEMORIAL HOSPITAL, 2001 N. Jefferson, Zip 75455; tel. 214/572-8573; B. R. Marxsen, adm. **A**1a 9 10 **F**1 3 6 10 12 14 16 23 34 35 40 45 47 53	16	10	S		131	5608	82	62.6	15	740	13640	6062	407
MOUNT VERNON—Franklin County													
★ FRANKLIN COUNTY HOSPITAL, Hwy. 37 S., Box 477, Zip 75457; tel. 214/537-4552; Dianne Lett, actg. adm. **A**9 10 **F**1 3 6 10 14 15 16 23 26 29 30 34 35 40 43 45 50 53; **S**1895	13	10	S		39	720	13	33.3	4	27	2466	1108	80
MUENSTER—Cooke County													
MUENSTER HOSPITAL DISTRICT, 605 N. Maple St., Box 370, Zip 76252; tel. 817/759-2271; Herman W. Carroll, adm. **A**9 10 **F**1 6 15 35 45	16	10	S		32	655	8	25.0	5	59	1118	722	40
NACOGDOCHES—Nacogdoches County													
★☐ AMI NACOGDOCHES MEDICAL CENTER HOSPITAL (Formerly Nacogdoches Medical Center Hospital), 4920 N.E. Stallings, Box 1604, Zip 75963; tel. 409/569-9481; Bryant H. Krenek Jr., exec. dir. **A**1a 9 10 **F**1 3 6 10 12 14 15 16 23 33 34 35 36 37 40 41 43 44 46 50 52; **S**0125	33	10	S		150	4969	60	40.8	15	695	13835	4626	200
★☐ MEMORIAL HOSPITAL, 1204 Mound St., Zip 75961; tel. 409/564-4611; Don Crow, adm. **A**1a 9 10 **F**1 3 5 6 10 12 14 16 17 20 23 34 35 36 40 41 45 46 47 48 53; **S**7235	16	10	S		204	5371	93	45.6	12	277	17534	7010	453
NACOGDOCHES MEDICAL CENTER HOSPITAL, See AMI Nacogdoches Medical Center Hospital													
NAPLES—Morris County													
DAVID GRANBERRY MEMORIAL HOSPITAL, Craig & Willis Sts., Box 38, Zip 75568; tel. 214/897-5643; Jerry C. Varnado, adm. **A**9 10 **F**1 3 6 16 23 35 45; **S**1895	23	10	S		36	644	8	22.2	4	44	1771	782	46
NASSAU BAY—Harris County													
★☐ ST. JOHN HOSPITAL, 2050 Space Park Dr., Zip 77058; tel. 713/333-5503; Gary Stremel, adm. **A**1a 9 10 **F**1 3 6 9 10 11 12 14 15 16 23 24 30 32 33 34 35 36 37 40 42 44 46 47 49 52 53; **S**0605	21	10	S		130	5647	85	65.4	8	200	—	—	485
NAVASOTA—Grimes County													
NAVASOTA REGIONAL HOSPITAL (Formerly Grimes Memorial Hospital), 210 S. Judson St., Zip 77868; tel. 409/825-6585; William W. Fox, exec. dir. **A**9 10 **F**1 3 6 23 35 40 43 45 46; **S**1365	23	10	S		57	1757	24	42.1	12	119	4726	2421	124
NEDERLAND—Jefferson County													
★☐ AMI MID-JEFFERSON COUNTY HOSPITAL (Formerly Mid-Jefferson County Hospital), Hwy. 365 & 27th St., P O Box 1917, Zip 77627; tel. 409/727-2321; John Grossmeier, exec. dir. **A**1a 9 10 **F**1 3 6 10 14 15 16 23 26 30 33 34 35 36 40 43 45 46 47 50 52; **S**0125	33	10	S		104	3274	43	41.3	15	526	9814	3854	181
NEW BOSTON—Bowie County													
☐ NEW BOSTON GENERAL HOSPITAL, 520 Hospital Dr., Box 7, Zip 75570; tel. 214/628-5531; John Stevens, exec. dir. **A**1a 9 10 **F**1 3 6 14 16 23 34 35 36 45 47 48 49; **S**9795	33	10	S		63	801	14	22.2	6	151	3409	1219	76
NEW BRAUNFELS—Comal County													
★☐ MCKENNA MEMORIAL HOSPITAL, 143 E. Garza St., Zip 78130; tel. 512/625-9111; Marion P. Johnson, adm. **A**1a 9 10 **F**1 3 6 10 12 16 23 26 35 36 40 46 47 50	23	10	S		88	4514	51	58.0	16	677	11107	4439	270
NEWTON—Newton County													
NEWTON COUNTY MEMORIAL HOSPITAL, Hwy. 87 S.W., Drawer A, Zip 75966; tel. 409/379-2651; John H. Templain, adm. **A**9 10 **F**1 14 15 16 37	13	10	S		49	818	8	15.7	4	71	1127	532	37
NOCONA—Montague County													
★ NOCONA GENERAL HOSPITAL, 100 Park St., Box 570, Zip 76255; tel. 817/825-3235; Wanda Billings, adm. **A**9 10 **F**1 6 10 12 14 34 35 36 45	16	10	S		40	419	5	12.5	4	1	924	498	40

★ American Hospital Association (AHA) membership
□ Joint Commission on Accreditation of Hospitals (JCAH) accreditation
+ American Osteopathic Hospital Association (AOHA) membership
○ American Osteopathic Association (AOA) accreditation
Δ Commission on Accreditation of Rehabilitation Facilities (CARF) accreditation
Control codes 61, 63, 64, 71, 72 and 73 indicate hospitals listed by AOHA, but not registered by AHA. For definition of numerical codes, see page A2

Hospital, Address, Telephone, Administrator, Approval and Facility Codes, Multihospital System Code	Classification Codes				Inpatient Data				Newborn Data		Expense (thousands of dollars)		
	Control	Service	Stay	Facilities	Beds	Admissions	Census	Occupancy (percent)	Bassinets	Births	Total	Payroll	Personnel
NORTH RICHLAND HILLS—Tarrant County													
★□ NORTH HILLS MEDICAL CENTER (Formerly Listed Under Fort Worth), 4401 Booth Calloway Rd., Zip 76180; tel. 817/284-1431; William M. Gracey, adm. **A**1a 10 **F**1 3 5 6 10 14 15 16 23 29 30 34 35 36 37 45 46 47 53; **S**1755	33	10	S		160	5692	75	46.9	10	794	—	—	325
ODESSA—Ector County													
★□ AMI ODESSA WOMEN'S AND CHILDREN'S HOSPITAL (Formerly Odessa Women's and Children's Hospital) (Ob, Gynecological and Pediatrics), 520 E. Sixth St., Box 4859, Zip 79760; tel. 915/334-8200; Bill Simpson, actg. dir. (Nonreporting) **A**1a 9 10; **S**0125	32	49	S		114	—	—	—	—	—	—	—	—
★□ MEDICAL CENTER HOSPITAL, Drawer 7239, Zip 79760; tel. 915/333-7111; W. Sam Glenney, adm. **A**1a 2 3 5 9 10 **F**1 2 3 4 6 7 8 9 10 11 12 13 14 16 20 23 35 36 37 40 45 47 51 52 53 54; **S**1755	13	10	S		362	13965	228	63.2	18	1303	44331	23284	861
ODESSA WOMEN'S AND CHILDREN'S HOSPITAL, See AMI Odessa Women's-Children Hospital													
OLNEY—Young County													
★ HAMILTON HOSPITAL, 903 W. Hamilton St., Box 158, Zip 76374; tel. 817/564-5521; Freddie Joe Dunagan, adm. **A**9 10 **F**1 3 14 16 23 35 36 40 45	16	10	S		44	787	12	27.3	10	49	2417	1310	75
ORANGE—Orange County													
□ ORANGE MEMORIAL HOSPITAL, 608 Strickland, Zip 77630; tel. 713/883-9361; James Berry, adm. **A**1a 9 10 **F**1 3 6 10 12 14 15 16 23 26 35 36 40 45 46 48 52 53; **S**2195	33	10	S		172	4087	56	32.6	29	453	15767	5946	309
OZONA—Crockett County													
CROCKETT COUNTY HOSPITAL, Ave. H & First St., Box 640, Zip 76943; tel. 915/392-2671; Bill Boswell, adm. **A**9 10 **F**1 3 34 35 43 45 46 52	13	10	S		20	81	1	5.0	1	1	672	342	23
PALACIOS—Matagorda County													
★□ WAGNER GENERAL HOSPITAL, 310 Green St., Box 859, Zip 77465; tel. 512/972-2511; Donald G. Hyett, adm. **A**1a 9 10 **F**1 14 16 23 34 35 45 46 47; **S**2645	16	10	S		35	681	11	31.4	6	75	1868	911	54
PALESTINE—Anderson County													
★□ ANDERSON COUNTY MEMORIAL HOSPITAL (Formerly Memorial Hospital), 900 S. Sycamore St., Box 740, Zip 75801; tel. 214/729-6981; William K. Brown, adm. & chief exec. off. **A**1a 9 10 **F**1 3 6 12 14 16 23 34 35 39 40	13	10	S		99	4915	61	61.6	16	609	10491	5294	291
PAMPA—Gray County													
CORONADO COMMUNITY HOSPITAL, See HCA Coronado Hospital													
★□ HCA CORONADO HOSPITAL (Formerly Coronado Community Hospital), One Medical Plaza, Box 5000, Zip 79065; tel. 806/665-3721; Norman L. Knox, adm. **A**1a 9 10 **F**1 3 6 12 15 16 23 34 35 40 43 45 46 47 53; **S**1755	33	10	S		126	3861	65	51.6	12	378	12956	4511	245
PARIS—Lamar County													
★□ MCCUISTION REGIONAL MEDICAL CENTER, 865 Deshong Dr., Box 160, Zip 75460; tel. 214/737-1111; Anthony A. Daigle, adm. (Total facility includes 30 beds in nursing home-type unit) **A**1a 9 10 **F**1 3 6 10 12 14 15 16 17 19 23 24 26 33 35 36 37 40 41 43 45 49 50 52 53	23	10	S	TF	178	6489	111	62.4	18	944	17131	8064	462
				H	148	6205	101	—	18	944	16917	7857	448
★□ ST. JOSEPH'S HOSPITAL AND HEALTH CENTER (Formerly St. Joseph's Hospital), 820 Clarksville St., Box 70, Zip 75460; tel. 214/785-4521; Sr. Mary Eustace Farrell, pres. **A**1a 9 10 **F**1 3 5 6 9 12 14 15 16 19 20 21 23 24 25 26 27 29 30 32 33 35 41 42 44 45 46 47 52; **S**5565	21	10	S		175	5354	103	61.3	0	0	17404	7032	464
PASADENA—Harris County													
★□ BELTWAY COMMUNITY HOSPITAL, 4040 Red Bluff Rd., Zip 77503; tel. 713/473-3311; Kenneth Randall, adm. **A**1a 9 10 **F**1 3 6 16 23 35 36 40 47; **S**0695	33	10	S		99	2451	30	30.3	11	202	—	—	122
★□ HCA PASADENA BAYSHORE MEDICAL CENTER (Formerly Pasadena Bayshore Medical Center), 4000 Spencer Hwy., Zip 77504; tel. 713/944-6666; Donald L. Francis, adm. **A**1a 2 9 10 **F**1 2 3 4 5 6 10 12 14 15 16 23 24 26 27 30 32 33 34 35 36 40 43 46 47 48 52 53 54; **S**1755	33	10	S		301	7732	142	36.2	22	710	—	—	648
★□ HUMANA HOSPITAL -SOUTHMORE, 906 E. Southmore St., Box 1879, Zip 77502; tel. 713/477-0411; Nadine Cook, exec. dir. (Nonreporting) **A**1a 9 10; **S**1235	33	10	S		208	—	—	—	—	—	—	—	—
PASADENA BAYSHORE MEDICAL CENTER, See HCA Pasadena Bayshore Medical Center													
□ PASADENA GENERAL HOSPITAL, 1004 Seymour St., Zip 77506; tel. 713/473-1771; Rand Wortman, adm. **A**1a 9 10 **F**1 3 6 10 12 14 15 16 23 26 34 35 45 46 48; **S**1375	33	10	S		72	1708	31	39.7	0	0	—	—	157
PEARSALL—Frio County													
FRIO HOSPITAL, 320 Berry Ranch Rd., Zip 78061; tel. 512/334-3617; Frank T. Williams Jr., adm. **A**9 10 **F**1 35 41 42; **S**0725	23	10	S		22	1140	9	40.9	6	162	1805	646	45
PECOS—Reeves County													
★ REEVES COUNTY HOSPITAL, 2323 Texas St., Drawer 2058, Zip 79772; tel. 915/447-3551; C. W. Hesseltine, pres. **A**10 **F**1 3 6 10 15 16 23 34 35 40 41 45 46 47 52; **S**4165	23	10	S		62	1052	11	17.7	8	266	4145	1376	75
PERRYTON—Ochiltree County													
OCHILTREE GENERAL HOSPITAL, 31st & Garrett Dr., Zip 79070; tel. 806/435-3606; Jerry Weatherly, adm. (Nonreporting) **A**9 10	16	10	S		65	—	—	—	—	—	—	—	—
PITTSBURG—Camp County													
★□ PITTSBURG MEDICAL CENTER, 414 Quitman St., Zip 75686; tel. 214/856-6663; Lewis E. Robertson Jr., adm. **A**1a 9 10 **F**1 3 6 12 14 15 16 23 26 34 35 40 41 45 52; **S**1895	23	10	S		49	1219	16	32.7	8	179	3362	1633	101
PLAINVIEW—Hale County													
□ CENTRAL PLAINS REGIONAL HOSPITAL, 2601 Dimmitt Rd., Zip 79072; tel. 806/296-5531; Donald J. Cosper, exec. dir. **A**1a 2 9 10 **F**1 3 5 6 10 11 12 14 16 21 23 27 34 35 40 43 45 53; **S**0875	33	10	S		151	3459	45	29.8	6	403	—	—	200
PLANO—Collin County													
★□ HCA MEDICAL CENTER OF PLANO (Formerly Plano General Hospital), 3901 W. 15th St., Zip 75075; tel. 214/596-6800; Allyn Harris, adm. **A**1a 9 10 **F**1 3 4 6 10 12 15 16 17 20 23 24 26 27 30 32 33 34 35 36 37 40 42 44 46 47 52 53 54; **S**1755	33	10	S		233	10537	139	59.7	36	2005	—	—	616
PORT ARTHUR—Jefferson County													
★□ AMI PARK PLACE HOSPITAL (Formerly Park Place Hospital), 3050 39th St., Zip 77642; Mailing Address Box 1648, Zip 77640; tel. 409/983-4951; Luis G. Silva, exec. dir. **A**1a 9 10 **F**1 3 5 6 7 9 10 11 12 14 15 16 23 27 29 34 35 36 40 41 43 45 46 47 48 49 52 53; **S**0125	33	10	S		223	5066	99	44.4	12	543	—	—	338
PARK PLACE HOSPITAL, See AMI Park Place Hospital													
★□ ST. MARY HOSPITAL, 3600 Gates Blvd., Zip 77642; Mailing Address Box 3696, Zip 77643; tel. 409/985-7431; Sr. Edith Judge, adm. **A**1a 3 5 9 10 **F**1 2 3 4 6 10 12 14 15 16 20 23 24 26 30 34 35 36 40 45 46 47 52 53 54; **S**0605	21	10	S		278	8234	142	51.1	22	814	36964	14934	759
PORT LAVACA—Calhoun County													
□ MEMORIAL MEDICAL CENTER (Formerly Champ Traylor Memorial Hospital), 810 N. Ann St., Box 25, Zip 77979; tel. 512/552-6713; Mike Munnerlyn, adm. **A**1a 9 10 **F**1 3 5 6 14 15 16 23 24 34 35 40 41 42 43 45 46 47 50 52; **S**0725	13	10	S		53	1954	21	39.6	14	233	4205	1954	158
POST—Garza County													
★ GARZA MEMORIAL HOSPITAL, 608 W. Sixth St., Zip 79356; tel. 806/495-2828; Maritta Reed, adm. **A**9 10 **F**6 19 35 40	16	10	S		19	255	2	10.5	7	33	—	—	31

★ American Hospital Association (AHA) membership
□ Joint Commission on Accreditation of Hospitals (JCAH) accreditation
+ American Osteopathic Hospital Association (AOHA) membership
○ American Osteopathic Association (AOA) accreditation
Δ Commission on Accreditation of Rehabilitation Facilities (CARF) accreditation
Control codes 61, 63, 64, 71, 72 and 73 indicate hospitals listed by AOHA, but not registered by AHA.
For definition of numerical codes, see page A2

Hospital, Address, Telephone, Administrator, Approval and Facility Codes, Multihospital System Code	Classification Codes				Inpatient Data				Newborn Data		Expense (thousands of dollars)		
	Control	Service	Stay	Facilities	Beds	Admissions	Census	Occupancy (percent)	Bassinets	Births	Total	Payroll	Personnel
QUANAH—Hardeman County													
★ QUANAH MEDICAL CENTER (Formerly Hardeman County Memorial Hospital), 402 Mercer St., Box 210, Zip 79252; tel. 817/663-2795; Vickie Smith, adm. **A**9 10 **F**1 16 34 35 53; **S**1765	33	10	S		20	1800	4	20.0	0	0	—	—	72
QUITMAN—Wood County													
★ WOOD COUNTY CENTRAL HOSPITAL DISTRICT, 117 Winnsboro St., P O Box 1000, Zip 75783; tel. 214/763-4505; Marion Stanberry, adm. **A**9 10 **F**1 6 10 15 23 35 44 53; **S**1895	16	10	S		28	1010	11	39.3	3	63	1907	839	58
RANGER—Eastland County													
RANGER GENERAL HOSPITAL, Hwy. 80 W., Zip 76470; tel. 817/647-1156; Lena Fonville, adm. **A**9 10 **F**1 3 5 6 14 15 16 17 30 34 35 37 40 41 45 50 53	16	10	S		36	574	9	25.0	6	17	—	—	47
RANKIN—Upton County													
RANKIN HOSPITAL DISTRICT, 1105 Elizabeth St., Box 327, Zip 79778; tel. 915/693-2443; Leon H. Feuge, adm. **A**9 10 **F**35	16	10	S		20	246	2	10.0	6	57	1135	635	30
REESE AIR FORCE BASE—Lubbock County													
U. S. AIR FORCE HOSPITAL, Zip 79489; tel. 806/885-3542; Maj. Michael V. Neese USAF MSC, adm. **A**3 5 **F**1 14 15 21 23 28 33 34 35 37 40 45 46 47	41	10	S		26	596	8	30.8	8	200	2885	666	214
REFUGIO—Refugio County													
⊞ REFUGIO COUNTY MEMORIAL HOSPITAL (Formerly Memorial Hospital), 107 Swift St., Zip 78377; tel. 512/526-2321; Bruce Giessel, adm. **A**1a 9 10 **F**6 14 15 16 23 35 41 45; **S**0725	16	10	S		49	510	8	16.3	0	0	3297	1455	81
RICHARDSON—Dallas County													
⊞ RICHARDSON MEDICAL CENTER, 401 W. Campbell Rd., Zip 75080; tel. 214/231-1441; H. Kenneth May, pres. & chief exec. off. (Nonreporting) **A**1a 9 10	23	10	S		242	—	—	—	—	—	—	—	—
RICHMOND—Fort Bend County													
⊞ POLLY RYON MEMORIAL HOSPITAL, 1705 Jackson St., Zip 77469; tel. 713/342-2811; Harold F. Taylor, adm. **A**1a 9 10 **F**1 3 6 15 16 20 23 26 34 35 36 40 44 45 46 53; **S**2645	23	10	S		109	3956	60	62.5	26	730	12494	5101	297
RIO GRANDE CITY—Starr County													
★ STARR COUNTY MEMORIAL HOSPITAL, P O Box 78, Zip 78582; tel. 512/487-5561; Thalia H. Munoz, adm. **A**9 10 **F**1 3 6 10 14 15 30 35 36 40 43 45 50 52	16	10	S		44	2629	23	52.3	8	587	3507	1635	113
ROCKDALE—Milam County													
★ RICHARDS MEMORIAL HOSPITAL, 1700 Brazos St., Drawer 1010, Zip 76567; tel. 512/446-2513 (Nonreporting) **A**9 10; **S**0725	16	10	S		47	—	—	—	—	—	—	—	—
ROSEBUD—Falls County													
⊞ ROSEBUD COMMUNITY HOSPITAL, 420 East Ave. E., Zip 76510; Mailing Address Drawer 618, Zip 76570; tel. 817/583-7983; Larry D. Luedke, adm. **A**1a 9 10 **F**1 6 10 16 23 34 35 36 41 45 47; **S**8985	23	10	S		38	874	13	34.2	4	70	2394	840	88
ROSENBERG—Fort Bend County													
⊞ ORCHARD CREEK HOSPITAL (Formerly Orchard Creek Family Recovery Center), 4910 Airport Ave., Zip 77471; tel. 713/342-0010; Jerry C. Wilson, adm. **A**1b 9 **F**15 17 24 31 32 33 42 44 48	33	22	L		82	295	32	65.3	0	0	4040	1445	101
ROTAN—Fisher County													
★ FISHER COUNTY HOSPITAL DISTRICT, Roby Hwy., Drawer F, Zip 79546; tel. 915/735-2256; Gary McGee, actg. adm. **A**9 10 **F**1 6 14 16 23 35 40 45	16	10	S		30	678	8	26.7	6	42	1699	761	48
ROUND ROCK—Williamson County													
⊞ AMI ROUND ROCK COMMUNITY HOSPITAL (Formerly Round Rock Community Hospital), 2400 Round Rock Ave., P O Box 125, Zip 78681; tel. 512/255-6066; Scott D. Evans, exec. dir. **A**1a 9 10 **F**1 3 6 9 10 12 14 15 16 23 24 26 30 32 33 34 35 36 40 41 43 44 46 47 52 53; **S**0125	33	10	S		63	2880	32	50.8	10	614	—	—	176
RUSK—Cherokee County													
□ CHEROKEE MEDICAL CENTER (Formerly Rusk Memorial Hospital), Copeland & Bonner Sts., Box 317, Zip 75785; tel. 214/683-2273; Duane Sherbondy, adm. **A**1a 9 10 **F**1 6 10 12 14 16 23 34 35 45 46; **S**1895	33	10	S		49	877	11	22.4	6	66	1879	945	61
RUSK MEMORIAL HOSPITAL, See Cherokee Medical Center													
□ RUSK STATE HOSPITAL, Jacksonville Hwy. N., Box 318, Zip 75785; tel. 214/683-3421; John V. White MD, supt. **A**1b 10 **F**16 23 24 28 30 32 33 34 42 44 46 47 48 49 50	12	22	L		995	2155	564	53.6	0	0	29833	23882	1344
SAN ANGELO—Tom Green County													
⊞ ANGELO COMMUNITY HOSPITAL, 3501 Knickerbocker Rd., Zip 76904; tel. 915/949-9511; Robert E. Butler, pres. **A**1a 2 9 10 **F**1 3 5 6 10 12 14 15 16 20 23 26 34 35 36 38 40 43 45 46 47 49 50 53 54	23	10	S		142	5927	86	60.6	30	1129	—	—	311
★ BAPTIST MEMORIALS GERIATRIC CENTER, 902 N. Main St., Zip 76901; Mailing Address Box 5661, Zip 76902; tel. 915/655-7391; W. D. McDonald, adm. (Total facility includes 208 beds in nursing home-type unit) **A**9 10 **F**19 23 42 45 46	21	49	L	TF	326	570	283	86.8	0	0	6339	3401	333
				H	118	118	94	—	0	0	2063	1082	92
⊞ SHANNON WEST TEXAS MEMORIAL HOSPITAL, 120 E. Harris St., Box 1879, Zip 76902; tel. 915/653-6741; Thomas G. Alexander, pres. & chief exec. off.; Jim Fillpot, exec. vice-pres. & chief oper. off. (Total facility includes 10 beds in nursing home-type unit) **A**1a 9 10 **F**1 3 5 6 7 8 9 10 11 12 15 16 17 19 20 23 30 35 36 40 41 43 45 46 47 52 53 54	23	10	S	TF	212	9236	135	63.7	17	1098	27127	12182	669
				H	202	9214	134	—	17	1098	27082	12150	659
⊞ ST. JOHN'S HOSPITAL AND HEALTH CENTER, 2018 Pulliam St., P O Drawer 5741, Zip 76902; tel. 915/655-3181; P. Denny Oreb, pres. & chief exec. off. (Nonreporting) **A**1a 9 10; **S**5565	23	10	S		137	—	—	—	—	—	—	—	—
SAN ANTONIO—Bexar County													
⊞ AUDIE L. MURPHY MEMORIAL VETERANS HOSPITAL, 7400 Merton Minter Blvd., Zip 78284; tel. 512/696-9660; Jose R. Coronado, dir. **A**1a 2 3 5 8 **F**1 2 3 4 6 10 12 15 16 20 21 23 24 25 26 27 28 29 30 31 32 33 34 35 41 42 43 44 45 46 48 49 50 53 54	45	10	S		674	20318	510	75.7	0	0	86795	45811	1816
⊞ BAPTIST MEDICAL CENTER, 111 Dallas St., Zip 78286; tel. 512/222-8431; David A. Garrett, pres. **A**1a 3 5 6 9 10 **F**1 2 3 4 5 6 7 8 9 10 11 12 13 14 15 16 20 23 27 30 32 33 34 35 36 37 39 40 42 46 47 52 53 54; **S**0265	21	10	S		568	20985	393	54.4	100	2175	—	—	2126
⊞ BEXAR COUNTY HOSPITAL DISTRICT (Includes Brady-Green Community Health Center, tel. 512/270-3400; Frank T. Escueta, adm.; Medical Center Hospital, tel. 512/694-3030; Jeff Turner, adm.), Mailing Address 4502 Medical Dr., Zip 78284; John A. Guest, exec. dir. **A**1a 2 3 5 8 9 **F**1 2 3 4 5 6 9 10 11 12 13 14 15 16 20 23 24 26 27 28 29 30 32 33 34 35 36 37 38 40 44 45 46 47 51 52 53 54	16	10	S		549	27181	394	72.3	52	7008	94525	52335	2069
BRADY-GREEN COMMUNITY HEALTH CENTER, See Bexar County Hospital District													
BROOKE ARMY MEDICAL CENTER, See Fort Sam Houston													
⊞ CHARTER REAL (Formerly Charter Real Hospital), 8550 Huebner Rd., Zip 78240; tel. 512/699-8585; Jerry W. Echols, adm. (Nonreporting) **A**10; **S**0695	33	82	S		80	—	—	—	—	—	—	—	—
COLONIAL HILLS HOSPITAL (Formerly Park North General Hospital) (Psychiatric), 4330 Vance Jackson Rd., Zip 78230; tel. 512/341-5131; James M. Hunt, adm. **A**1b 9 10 **F**24 30 32 33 42 48; **S**0825	33	22	S		75	814	35	46.7	0	0	—	—	132

★ American Hospital Association (AHA) membership
□ Joint Commission on Accreditation of Hospitals (JCAH) accreditation
+ American Osteopathic Hospital Association (AOHA) membership
○ American Osteopathic Association (AOA) accreditation
Δ Commission on Accreditation of Rehabilitation Facilities (CARF) accreditation
Control codes 61, 63, 64, 71, 72 and 73 indicate hospitals listed by AOHA, but not registered by AHA.
For definition of numerical codes, see page A2

Hospital, Address, Telephone, Administrator, Approval and Facility Codes, Multihospital System Code	Classification Codes				Inpatient Data				Newborn Data		Expense (thousands of dollars)		
	Control	Service	Stay	Facilities	Beds	Admissions	Census	Occupancy (percent)	Bassinets	Births	Total	Payroll	Personnel
★□ + HORIZON HOSPITAL (Formerly Raleigh Hills Hospital), 210 W. Ashby Pl., Zip 78212; tel. 512/736-2211; Joe Ruley, adm. **A**1b 9 10 **F**24 32 33 42 44 49 52; **S**6525	33	22	L		45	175	19	65.5	0	0	4873	1139	36
★□ HUMANA HOSPITAL -METROPOLITAN, 1310 McCullough Ave., Zip 78212; tel. 512/271-2200; Earl H. Denning III, exec. dir. **A**1a 9 10 **F**1 3 4 6 9 10 11 12 14 15 16 17 20 23 24 26 27 28 29 30 32 34 35 36 40 42 43 46 47 53 54; **S**1235	33	10	S		233	8026	126	54.1	8	1773	—	—	576
★□ HUMANA HOSPITAL -SAN ANTONIO, 8026 Floyd Curl Dr., Zip 78229; tel. 512/692-8107; Timothy L. Austin, exec. dir. **A**1a 3 9 10 **F**1 2 3 4 6 10 12 13 14 16 17 20 23 24 30 32 33 34 35 39 41 43 46 53 54; **S**1235	33	10	S		329	10525	195	59.3	0	0	—	—	673
★□ HUMANA WOMEN'S HOSPITAL-SOUTH TEXAS, 8109 Fredericksburg Rd., Zip 78229; tel. 512/699-8000; Thomas E. Casaday, exec. dir. **A**1a 9 10 **F**1 3 6 12 14 15 16 36 37 40 46 51; **S**1235	33	44	S		121	5484	54	44.6	73	3838	—	—	332
Δ KING WILLIAM HEALTH CARE CENTER (Formerly St. Benedict Health Care Center), 323 E. Johnson St., Zip 78204; tel. 512/222-0171; Stephen B. Hill, exec. dir. (Total facility includes 181 beds in nursing home-type unit) **A**7 9 10 **F**1 15 16 18 19 21 23 24 26 32 33 34 35 41 42 43 44 46 47 50	33	10	L	TF	235	869	184	79.7	0	0	—	—	258
				H	54	459	43	—	0	0	—	—	152
★□ LUTHERAN GENERAL HOSPITAL, 701 S. Zarzamora, Zip 78285; tel. 512/434-5252; T. F. Jackson Jr., adm. **A**1a 9 10 **F**1 3 6 10 14 15 16 20 26 33 34 35 41 45 46 47 52 53	21	10	S		109	3396	64	58.7	0	0	16366	6523	388
MEDICAL CENTER HOSPITAL, See Bexar County Hospital District													
★□ NIX MEDICAL CENTER, 414 Navarro St., Zip 78205; tel. 512/271-1800; John F. Strieby, pres. & chief exec. off. **A**1a 9 10 **F**1 3 4 6 7 8 9 10 11 12 14 15 16 17 20 23 26 34 36 37 40 43 53 54	32	10	S		121	4876	73	60.3	10	190	—	—	331
□ NORTHEAST BAPTIST HOSPITAL, 8811 Village Dr., Zip 78286; tel. 512/653-2330; Ray M. Harris, adm. **A**1a 9 **F**1 2 3 5 6 9 10 11 12 13 14 15 16 20 23 30 34 35 36 37 40 46 47 52 53; **S**0265	21	10	S		227	9280	139	51.5	50	1389	—	—	625
PARK NORTH GENERAL HOSPITAL, See Colonial Hills Hospital													
RALEIGH HILLS HOSPITAL, See Horizon Hospital													
□ SAN ANTONIO CHILDREN'S CENTER, 2939 W. Woodlawn, Zip 78228; tel. 512/736-4273; Carl M. Pfeifer MD, pres. **A**1b 3 5 9 **F**15 24 28 30 32 33 34 42 44 46	23	52	L		84	248	65	81.3	0	0	5502	2726	166
★□ SAN ANTONIO STATE CHEST HOSPITAL, 2303 S.E. Military Dr., Box 23340, Zip 78223; tel. 512/534-8857; Robert E. Neimes MD, dir. **A**1a 9 10 **F**1 3 6 10 12 14 15 16 19 23 24 34 46 47 52	12	33	S		150	2009	93	62.0	0	0	11833	6488	323
SAN ANTONIO STATE HOSPITAL, Box 23310 Highland Hills Sta., Zip 78223; tel. 512/532-8811; Robert M. Inglis MD, supt. **A** 9 10 **F**3 12 15 19 23 24 28 30 31 32 33 34 35 42 44 46 47 48 49	12	22	L		847	3525	653	76.2	0	0	26901	22350	1330
★□ SANTA ROSA MEDICAL CENTER, 519 W. Houston St., Zip 78207; Mailing Address Box 7330, Sta. A, Zip 78285; tel. 512/228-2011; Sr. Angela Clare Moran, pres. & chief exec. off. **A**1a 2 3 5 9 10 **F**1 3 4 5 6 7 8 9 10 11 12 13 15 16 20 21 23 24 25 26 27 30 32 33 34 35 36 38 40 41 42 43 44 45 46 48 49 51 52 53 54; **S**5565	21	10	S		793	22315	530	66.8	30	2304	—	—	2823
□ SOUTHEAST BAPTIST HOSPITAL, 4214 E. Southcross, Zip 78222; tel. 512/337-6900; Harry E. Smith, adm. **A**1a 9 **F**1 2 3 5 6 9 10 11 12 13 14 15 16 20 23 30 34 35 36 37 40 46 47 52 53; **S**0265	21	10	S		143	6010	100	54.3	30	588	—	—	440
★□ SOUTHWEST GENERAL HOSPITAL, 7400 Barlite Blvd., Zip 78224; tel. 512/921-2000; Louis Garcia, adm. (Nonreporting) **A**1a 9 10; **S**1755	33	10	S		191	—	—	—	—	—	—	—	—
★□ SOUTHWEST TEXAS METHODIST HOSPITAL, 7700 Floyd Curl Dr., Zip 78229; tel. 512/692-4000; John E. Hombeak, adm. **A**1a 2 9 10 **F**1 2 3 4 6 9 10 12 14 15 16 17 20 23 30 35 36 37 40 45 46 51 52 53 54	23	10	S		502	21983	377	75.1	48	2477	83066	40176	1925
ST. BENEDICT HEALTH CARE CENTER, See King William Health Care Center													
★□ ST. LUKE'S LUTHERAN HOSPITAL, 7930 Floyd Curl Dr., Box 29100, Zip 78229; tel. 512/690-8600; William T. Dunn, adm. **A**1a 9 10 **F**1 2 3 4 5 6 10 12 14 16 20 23 30 33 34 35 45 46 54; **S**1375	21	10	S		251	6876	126	52.5	0	0	26004	10509	444
★ VILLAGE OAKS REGIONAL HOSPITAL, 12412 Judson Rd., Zip 78233; tel. 512/650-4949; William Blanchard, adm. (Nonreporting) **A**9 10; **S**1755	33	10	S		66	—	—	—	—	—	—	—	—
SAN AUGUSTINE—San Augustine County													
SAN AUGUSTINE MEMORIAL HOSPITAL, 511 Hospital St., Box 658, Zip 75972; tel. 409/275-3446; Norman K. Reynolds, adm. **A**9 10 **F**6 35 41	33	10	S		30	369	8	26.3	6	10	—	—	38
SAN BENITO—Cameron County													
★□ DOLLY VINSANT MEMORIAL HOSPITAL, E. Hwy. 77, Box 42, Zip 78586; tel. 512/399-1313; Paul McCord, adm. **A**1a 9 10 **F**1 6 15 16 23 35 37 40 45 52	23	10	S		63	2779	34	54.0	18	550	5190	2354	151
SAN MARCOS—Hays County													
★□ HAYS MEMORIAL HOSPITAL, 1301 Wonder World Dr., Box 767, Zip 78667; tel. 512/353-8979; Ray Carney, adm. **A**1a 9 10 **F**1 3 6 10 12 14 16 23 34 35 36 43 45 49 53; **S**4165	23	10	S		109	3940	48	44.3	18	791	13959	4517	258
SAN MARCOS—Travis County													
□ THE BROWN SCHOOLS-SAN MARCOS TREATMENT CENTER, Box 768, Zip 78666; tel. 512/392-7111; Dick Hardin, dir. (Nonreporting) **A**1b ; **S**0395	33	22	L		225	—	—	—	—	—	—	—	—
SAN SABA—San Saba County													
SAN SABA HOSPITAL (Formerly San Saba Memorial Hospital), 2005 W. Wallace St., Zip 76877; tel. 915/372-5171; Wendell Alford, adm. (Nonreporting) **A**9 10; **S**1365	13	10	S		34	—	—	—	—	—	—	—	—
SEALY—Austin County													
★ BRAZOS VALLEY HOSPITAL, 526 Ward St., Zip 77474; tel. 409/885-4181; Terry J. Fontenot, adm. (Nonreporting) **A**9 10; **S**9795	33	10	S		25	—	—	—	—	—	—	—	—
SEGUIN—Guadalupe County													
★□ GUADALUPE VALLEY HOSPITAL, 1215 E. Court St., Zip 78155; tel. 512/379-2411; Don L. Richey, adm. **A**1a 9 10 **F**1 3 6 9 10 12 16 23 34 35 36 40 41 45 53	15	10	S		75	3984	46	61.3	12	764	7825	4022	271
SEMINOLE—Gaines County													
★ MEMORIAL HOSPITAL, 209 N.W. Eighth St., Zip 79360; tel. 915/758-5811; George Cristy, adm. **A**9 10 **F**1 3 5 10 14 16 23 35 40 45	16	10	S		49	898	9	18.4	8	109	3424	1476	77
SEYMOUR—Baylor County													
SEYMOUR HOSPITAL AUTHORITY, Stadium Dr., Box 351, Zip 76380; tel. 817/888-5572; Larry Suit, adm. **A**9 10 **F**1 3 15 16 23 35 45; **S**3535	16	10	S		49	1102	21	42.9	5	53	2307	1031	80
SHAMROCK—Wheeler County													
SHAMROCK GENERAL HOSPITAL, 1000 S. Main St., Zip 79079; tel. 806/256-2114; Joe Duerr, adm. **A**9 10 **F**1 6 10 16 35 37 40 45	16	10	S		43	898	10	23.3	6	72	1628	812	57
SHEPPARD AIR FORCE BASE—Wichita County													
★□ U. S. AIR FORCE REGIONAL HOSPITAL, Zip 76311; tel. 817/851-2004; Col. Richard C. Yeomans, adm.; Col. William F. Belk, cmdr. **A**1a **F**1 3 6 10 12 14 15 16 23 24 27 28 30 32 33 34 35 37 40 42 45 46 47 48 49 53	41	10	S		150	4794	114	76.0	7	395	—	—	718
SHERMAN—Grayson County													
★□ AMI MEDICAL PLAZA HOSPITAL (Formerly Medical Plaza Hospital), 1111 Gallagher Dr., Zip 75090; tel. 214/870-7000; Bill Rowton, actg. exec. dir. (Total facility includes 12 beds in nursing home-type unit) **A**1a 9 10 **F**1 2 3 6 10 12 15 16 19 23 27 33 34 35 37 41 43 45 47 50 53; **S**0125	33	10	S	TF	176	3509	71	40.3	0	0	15344	2169	57
				H	164	3468	70	—	0	0	—	—	—

Hospital, Address, Telephone, Administrator, Approval and Facility Codes, Multihospital System Code	Classification Codes			Facilities	Inpatient Data				Newborn Data		Expense (thousands of dollars)		
★ American Hospital Association (AHA) membership □ Joint Commission on Accreditation of Hospitals (JCAH) accreditation + American Osteopathic Hospital Association (AOHA) membership ○ American Osteopathic Association (AOA) accreditation Δ Commission on Accreditation of Rehabilitation Facilities (CARF) accreditation Control codes 61, 63, 64, 71, 72 and 73 indicate hospitals listed by AOHA, but not registered by AHA. For definition of numerical codes, see page A2	Control	Service	Stay	Facilities	Beds	Admissions	Census	Occupancy (percent)	Bassinets	Births	Total	Payroll	Personnel
MEDICAL PLAZA HOSPITAL, See AMI Medical Plaza Hospital													
★□ WILSON N. JONES MEMORIAL HOSPITAL, 500 N. Highland Ave., Box 1258, Zip 75090; tel. 214/893-4611; Harry F. Barnes, adm. **A**1a 9 10 **F**1 3 5 6 10 12 14 15 16 23 24 26 34 35 36 37 40 41 44 45 46 47 53	23	10	S		227	6733	108	49.3	18	1020	23841	11546	616
SHINER—Lavaca County													
SHINER HOSPITAL, 118 N. Ave. D, P O Box 85, Zip 77984; tel. 512/594-3325; Wayne Jalufka, adm. **A**9 10 **F**1 6 16 23 34 35 45	23	10	S		30	677	10	33.3	5	14	—	—	49
SILSBEE—Hardin County													
SILSBEE DOCTORS HOSPITAL, Hwy. 418, Box 1208, Zip 77656; tel. 409/385-5531; Gene T. Jordan, adm. **A**9 10 **F**1 6 16 23 35 36; **S**2195	33	10	S		69	2182	27	39.1	8	243	5041	1785	115
SMITHVILLE—Bastrop County													
SMITHVILLE HOSPITAL (Includes Towers Nursing Home), Ninth & Mills Sts., Box 89, Zip 78957; tel. 512/237-3214; James Langford, adm. **A**9 10 **F**1 6 14 16 34 35 40 41 43 45 50 52 53	16	10	S		35	473	7	20.0	2	8	—	—	43
SNYDER—Scurry County													
★□ D. M. COGDELL MEMORIAL HOSPITAL, Cogdell Center, Zip 79549; tel. 915/573-6374; Cyrus B. Miller Jr., adm. **A**1a 9 10 **F**1 3 5 6 12 16 23 35 36 40 41 43 44 45 53	13	10	S		89	1832	29	32.6	10	216	5067	2461	144
SONORA—Sutton County													
LILLIAN M. HUDSPETH MEMORIAL HOSPITAL, 308 Hudspeth Ave., Box 455, Zip 76950; tel. 915/387-2521; M. Scott Gilmore, adm. (Total facility includes 39 beds in nursing home-type unit) **A**9 10 **F**10 12 14 15 19 34 35 36 43 45 46 50	23	10	S	TF	60	233	36	60.0	6	29	1276	643	55
				H	21	209	2	—	6	29	746	396	25
SPEARMAN—Hansford County													
HANSFORD HOSPITAL, 707 S. Roland St., Zip 79081; tel. 806/659-2535; Dennis Robertson, adm. (Total facility includes 39 beds in nursing home-type unit) **A**9 10 **F**1 16 19 35 36 40 45	16	10	S	TF	67	667	44	65.7	4	16	2293	1023	74
				H	28	653	6	—	4	16	1471	604	44
STAMFORD—Jones County													
STAMFORD MEMORIAL HOSPITAL, Hwy. 6 E., Box 911, Zip 79553; tel. 915/773-2725; Donald B. Hopkins, adm. **A**9 10 **F**1 6 10 14 16 23 34 35 36 40 43 45	16	10	S		35	1186	19	42.1	8	112	—	—	70
STANTON—Martin County													
MARTIN COUNTY HOSPITAL DISTRICT, 610 N. St. Peter St., Box 640, Zip 79782; tel. 915/756-3345; Larry Elliott, adm. **A**9 10 **F**1 6 16 34 35 37	16	10	S		26	714	7	26.9	2	87	1327	659	39
STEPHENVILLE—Erath County													
★□ HARRIS METHODIST -STEPHENVILLE (Formerly Stephenville General Hospital), 411 N. Belknap St., Box 1399, Zip 76401; tel. 817/965-3115; Ray Reynolds, adm. (Nonreporting) **A**1a 9 10; **S**2345	23	10	S		86	—	—	—	—	—	—	—	—
STERLING CITY—Sterling County													
★ STERLING COUNTY HOSPITAL, Ennis & Waxahachie Sts., Box 3, Zip 76951; tel. 915/378-3201; Mildred S. Emery, adm. (Total facility includes 29 beds in nursing home-type unit) **A**9 10 **F**15 19 35 40 52	13	10	S	TF	45	65	20	44.4	4	0	1044	608	49
				H	16	54	1	—	4	0	843	435	24
SULPHUR SPRINGS—Hopkins County													
★□ HOPKINS COUNTY MEMORIAL HOSPITAL, 115 Airport Rd., Box 275, Zip 75482; tel. 214/885-7671; Donald R. Magee, adm. **A**1a 9 10 **F**1 3 6 16 23 35 40 45 53	16	10	S		100	4095	53	53.0	13	679	8136	4134	261
SWEENY—Brazoria County													
□ SWEENY COMMUNITY HOSPITAL, 305 N. McKinney St., Box 1000, Zip 77480; tel. 409/548-3311; Michael A. Kozar, chief exec. off. **A**1a 9 10 **F**1 3 6 12 15 16 23 35 43 45 47; **S**0725	16	10	S		38	1010	11	28.9	5	43	3375	1633	87
SWEETWATER—Nolan County													
★□ ROLLING PLAINS MEMORIAL HOSPITAL, 200 E. Arizona St., P O Box 510, Zip 79556; tel. 915/235-1701; Ralph K. Neff, adm. **A**1a 9 10 **F**1 3 6 12 14 15 16 21 23 30 35 40 41 43 44 45 46 47 50; **S**1755	15	10	S		61	2465	32	52.5	6	294	5325	2059	154
TAFT—San Patricio County													
★□ TAFT HOSPITAL DISTRICT, 1220 Gregory St., Zip 78390; tel. 512/528-2545; Douglas Langley, adm. (Total facility includes 30 beds in nursing home-type unit) **A**1a 9 10 **F**1 6 16 19 23 35 41 45 53; **S**0725	16	10	S	TF	94	1356	40	43.0	10	254	3674	1564	158
				H	64	1345	14	—	10	254	3481	1381	137
TAHOKA—Lynn County													
LYNN COUNTY HOSPITAL DISTRICT, Box 1310, Zip 79373; tel. 806/998-4533; John Brooks, adm. **A**9 10 **F**1 6 10 15 16 35 37 41 45	16	10	S		24	563	6	25.0	6	84	1337	678	52
TAYLOR—Williamson County													
□ JOHNS COMMUNITY HOSPITAL, 305 Mallard Lane, Zip 76574; tel. 512/352-7611; Ernest Balla, adm. **A**1a 9 10 **F**1 3 6 10 15 16 23 34 35 36 40 41 43 44 45 53	23	10	S		65	1623	25	38.5	10	243	—	—	95
TEAGUE—Freestone County													
TEAGUE GENERAL HOSPITAL, Hwy. 84 at Eighth Ave., Box 599, Zip 75860; tel. 817/739-2536; Randy Powell, adm. **A**9 10 **F**1 6 10 12 14 15 16 17 23 26 34 35 37 41 43 45 46 50; **S**1765	16	10	S		28	1015	12	42.9	7	41	1637	800	53
TEMPLE—Bell County													
★□ KING'S DAUGHTERS HOSPITAL, 1901 S.W. H K Dodgen Loop, Zip 76502; tel. 817/771-8600; Richard L. Epperson, adm. **A**1a 2 9 10 **F**1 3 5 6 10 11 12 14 15 16 23 26 34 35 36 37 40 43 45 46 52	23	10	S		134	5176	84	62.2	12	648	12749	6115	357
★□ OLIN E. TEAGUE VETERANS' CENTER, 1901 S. First St., Zip 76501; tel. 817/778-4811; E. A. Borrell, dir. (Total facility includes 120 beds in nursing home-type unit) **A**1a b 2 3 5 **F**1 3 6 12 14 15 16 19 21 23 24 25 26 27 28 29 30 31 32 33 34 35 38 41 42 44 46 48 49 50 53	45	10	S	TF	643	10743	489	75.7	0	0	62482	34490	1431
				H	523	10249	376	—	0	0	—	—	1376
★□ SCOTT AND WHITE MEMORIAL HOSPITAL, 2401 S. 31st St., Zip 76508; tel. 817/774-2111; Joe M. Dickson, adm. (Total facility includes 28 beds in nursing home-type unit) **A**1a 2 3 5 8 9 10 **F**1 2 3 4 6 7 8 9 10 11 12 14 15 16 17 19 20 23 24 25 26 27 28 32 33 35 36 37 38 40 41 42 44 45 46 47 48 49 51 52 53 54	23	10	S	TF	418	16831	277	64.7	32	2124	56298	33971	3081
				H	390	15974	254	—	32	2124	54858	—	—
TERRELL—Kaufman County													
★□ AMI TERRELL COMMUNITY HOSPITAL (Formerly Terrell Community Hospital), 1551 S. Virginia, Zip 75160; tel. 214/563-7611; Larry Graham, exec. dir. **A**1a 9 **F**1 2 5 6 10 15 16 23 24 26 34 35 37 40 43 45 53; **S**0125	33	10	S		73	2019	26	35.6	6	241	8171	2563	126
COLONIAL HOSPITAL, 502 W. College St., Zip 75160; tel. 214/563-2671; Thomas R. Legacy, adm. **A**9 10 **F**1 3 6 16 34 35 40 42 43 45 46; **S**0875	33	10	S		37	1496	21	56.8	0	78	—	—	94
TERRELL COMMUNITY HOSPITAL, See AMI Terrell Community Hospital													
□ TERRELL STATE HOSPITAL, Brin St., Box 70, Zip 75160; tel. 214/563-6452; Don A. Gilbert, supt. **A**1b 9 10 **F**16 19 23 24 26 28 29 30 32 33 34 35 42 44 45 46 47 48 49 50	12	22	L		825	2426	644	76.6	0	0	—	—	1287
TEXARKANA—Bowie County													
★□ AMI TEXARKANA COMMUNITY HOSPITAL (Formerly Texarkana Community Hospital), 2501 College Dr., Zip 75501; tel. 214/798-5100; Jerry Kincade, exec. dir. **A**1a 9 10 **F**1 3 6 10 12 14 16 23 34 35 41 46 48 49 53; **S**0125	33	10	S		110	3099	46	41.8	0	0	—	—	208
FEDERAL CORRECTIONAL INSTITUTION HOSPITAL, FCI Rd., Zip 75501; tel. 214/838-4587; David M. Mifflin, adm. (Nonreporting) **F**1 34 35	46	10	S		15	—	—	—	—	—	—	—	—

★ American Hospital Association (AHA) membership
☐ Joint Commission on Accreditation of Hospitals (JCAH) accreditation
+ American Osteopathic Hospital Association (AOHA) membership
○ American Osteopathic Association (AOA) accreditation
Δ Commission on Accreditation of Rehabilitation Facilities (CARF) accreditation
Control codes 61, 63, 64, 71, 72 and 73 indicate hospitals listed by AOHA, but not registered by AHA. For definition of numerical codes, see page A2

Hospital, Address, Telephone, Administrator, Approval and Facility Codes, Multihospital System Code	**Classification Codes**				**Inpatient Data**				**Newborn Data**		**Expense (thousands of dollars)**		
	Control	Service	Stay	Facilities	Beds	Admissions	Census	Occupancy (percent)	Bassinets	Births	Total	Payroll	Personnel
TEXARKANA COMMUNITY HOSPITAL, See AMI Texarkana Community Hospital													
★☐ WADLEY REGIONAL MEDICAL CENTER, 1000 Pine St., Zip 75501; Mailing Address Box 1878, Zip 75504; tel. 214/793-4511; Jroyston Brown MD, pres. & chief exec. off. **A**1a 9 10 **F**1 3 4 5 6 7 9 10 11 12 15 16 17 19 20 23 27 30 32 33 35 36 39 40 45 46 48 52 53 54	23	10	S		376	12911	216	57.4	33	1999	38228	16351	946
TEXAS CITY—Galveston County													
★☐ AMI DANFORTH HOSPITAL (Formerly Danforth Hospital), 519 Ninth Ave. N., Zip 77590; tel. 409/948-8411; Carl Abdalian, exec. dir. **A**1a 9 10 **F**1 3 6 10 14 16 23 24 25 26 34 35 41 44 45 46 53; **S**0125	33	10	S		113	1967	44	38.9	0	0	10332	3865	181
DANFORTH HOSPITAL, See AMI Danforth Hospital													
★☐ MAINLAND CENTER HOSPITAL, 6601 Fm 1764, Box 2756, Zip 77592; tel. 409/938-5000; Edward J. Smith, pres. **A**1a 10 **F**1 2 3 5 6 12 14 15 16 23 24 26 27 28 30 33 34 35 40 41 42 44 45 48 49 52 53 54; **S**7235	13	10	S		310	6118	151	48.7	25	677	—	—	695
THE WOODLANDS—Montgomery County													
☐ LAURELWOOD HOSPITAL, Zip 77380; Mailing Address P O Box 7695, Zip 77387; tel. 713/367-4422; Michael Haley, chief exec. off. **A**1a 9 10 **F**12 27 29 32 33 42 48; **S**0825	33	22	L		156	616	80	80.0	0	0	—	—	201
THROCKMORTON—Throckmorton County													
THROCKMORTON COUNTY MEMORIAL HOSPITAL, Seymour Hwy., Box 729, Zip 76083; tel. 817/849-2151; Gerald Moore, adm. **A**9 10	13	10	S		25	305	5	20.0	0	0	—	—	33
TOMBALL—Harris County													
★☐ TOMBALL REGIONAL HOSPITAL (Formerly Tomball Community Hospital), 605 Holderrieth St., Box 889, Zip 77375; tel. 713/351-1623; Robert F. Schaper, adm. **A**1a 10 **F**1 3 6 10 15 16 23 26 35 36 43 45 46 47; **S**7235	16	10	S		140	5087	80	57.1	8	440	16157	7169	344
TRINITY—Trinity County													
TRINITY MEMORIAL HOSPITAL, Box 471, Zip 75862; tel. 409/594-3541; Dean Leiser, adm. **A**9 10 **F**1 16 34 35 37 40 41 43 45 46; **S**0725	33	10	S		30	464	6	20.0	4	46	—	—	42
TULIA—Swisher County													
SWISHER MEMORIAL HOSPITAL DISTRICT, 539 S.E. Second, Zip 79088; tel. 806/995-3581; Max Garrett, adm. (Nonreporting) **A**9 10	16	10	S		30	—	—	—	—	—	—	—	—
TYLER—Smith County													
★☐ COMMUNITY HOSPITAL OF TYLER, 929 N. Glenwood Blvd., Zip 75702; Mailing Address Box 4250, Zip 75712; tel. 214/597-3381; Robert L. Kidd, adm. **A**1a 10 **F**1 3 6 10 15 16 29 34 35 36 37 43 45 46 47 50	33	10	S		66	1263	16	24.2	4	156	5175	1641	95
+ DOCTORS' MEMORIAL HOSPITAL, 1400 W. South West Loop 323, Zip 75701; tel. 214/561-3771; Olie E. Clem, adm. (Nonreporting) **A**9 10	23	10	S		52	—	—	—	—	—	—	—	—
★☐ MEDICAL CENTER HOSPITAL, 1000 S. Beckham St., Drawer 6400, Zip 75711; tel. 214/597-0351; Elmer G. Ellis, pres. (Nonreporting) **A**1a 3 9 10; **S**1895	23	10	S		278	—	—	—	—	—	—	—	—
★☐ MOTHER FRANCES HOSPITAL REGIONAL HEALTH CARE CENTER (Formerly Mother Frances Hospital), 800 E. Dawson, Zip 75701; tel. 214/593-8441; J. Lindsey Bradley Jr., pres. **A**1a 9 10 **F**1 3 4 5 6 9 10 11 15 16 23 24 26 28 30 32 34 35 36 40 41 45 46 47 51 52 53 54; **S**6005	23	10	S		248	13394	180	72.3	37	2814	43878	15919	886
★☐ UNIVERSITY OF TEXAS HEALTH CENTER AT TYLER (Pulmonary and Heart Disease), Gladewater Hwy., Box 2003, Zip 75710; tel. 214/877-3451; George A. Hurst MD, dir.; David S. Turman, assoc. dir. **A**1a 9 10 **F**1 3 4 7 10 12 13 14 15 17 21 24 42 44 46 47 53	12	49	S		244	4520	137	56.1	0	0	31998	19720	927
★☐ UNIVERSITY PARK HOSPITAL (Adult and Adolescent Psychiatric, Alcohol and Chemical Dependency), 4101 University Blvd., Zip 75701; tel. 214/566-8666; Gary L. Stokes, adm. **A**1b 10 **F**15 24 28 29 30 32 33 34 42 45 48 49 50; **S**1895	23	22	S		80	817	40	50.0	0	0	4361	1874	85
UVALDE—Uvalde County													
UVALDE COUNTY HOSPITAL AUTHORITY, Garner Field Rd., Zip 78801; tel. 512/278-6251; B. M. Durr, adm. **A**9 10 **F**1 3 6 10 12 14 16 23 35 40 45 46 47 53	16	10	S		59	2138	25	42.4	8	289	4008	1872	116
VAN HORN—Culberson County													
CULBERSON COUNTY HOSPITAL, See Culberson County Hospital District													
★ CULBERSON COUNTY HOSPITAL DISTRICT (Formerly Culberson County Hospital), Eisenhower Rd. & Farm Market Rd. 2185, Box 609, Zip 79855; tel. 915/283-2760; R. Edwin Norris, adm. **A**9 **F**10 35 40 45	16	10	S		25	238	2	8.0	5	44	660	390	24
VERNON—Wilbarger County													
★☐ WILBARGER GENERAL HOSPITAL, 920 Hillcrest Dr., Zip 76384; tel. 817/552-9351; Sadie Schoolar, adm. **A**1a 9 10 **F**1 6 12 14 16 23 34 35 36 40 45 46 47 52 53	16	10	S		100	2035	29	29.0	14	265	4384	2168	127
VICTORIA—Victoria County													
★☐ CITIZENS MEDICAL CENTER (Formerly Citizens Memorial Hospital), 2701 Hospital Dr., Zip 77901; tel. 512/573-9181; David P. Brown, adm. **A**1a 9 10 **F**1 3 4 5 6 7 8 9 10 11 15 16 20 23 26 27 28 30 32 33 34 35 40 42 43 45 46 47 48 49 53 54; **S**7235	13	10	S		235	7759	138	63.3	15	562	24168	10084	559
★☐ DETAR HOSPITAL, 506 E. San Antonio St., Box 2089, Zip 77902; tel. 512/575-7441; Charles Sexton, adm. **A**1a 9 10 **F**1 3 6 9 10 11 12 14 15 16 23 26 34 35 36 40 43 46 47 52 53; **S**1755	33	10	S		214	8332	118	55.1	28	1620	—	—	496
★☐ DEVEREUX FOUNDATION-TEXAS BRANCH, Box 2666, Zip 77902; tel. 512/575-8271; John F. Strahm, adm. (Nonreporting) **A**1b ; **S**0845	23	52	L		78	—	—	—	—	—	—	—	—
☐ VICTORIA REGIONAL MEDICAL CENTER, 101 Medical Dr., Zip 77904; tel. 512/573-6100; Ashton J. Hecker Jr., adm. (Newly Registered) **A**1a 9 10 **F**1 3 6 10 12 14 15 16 20 23 26 28 30 32 33 34 35 46 47 50 53	33	10	S		84	2866	48	57.1	0	0	—	—	162
WACO—McLennan County													
BRAZOS CENTER FOR PSYCHIATRY, See Brazos Psychiatric Hospital													
★☐ BRAZOS PSYCHIATRIC HOSPITAL (Formerly Brazos Center for Psychiatry), 301 Londonderry Dr., P O Box 21446, Zip 76702; tel. 817/772-3500; Charles H. Caperton, adm. **A**1b 9 10 **F**15 24 28 30 32 33 34 42 48 49 50; **S**1755	33	22	S		80	579	37	46.3	0	0	5518	1435	71
★☐ HILLCREST BAPTIST MEDICAL CENTER, 3000 Herring Ave., Box 5100, Zip 76708; tel. 817/756-8011; Alton Pearson, pres. **A**1a 2 3 9 10 **F**1 2 3 5 6 7 8 9 10 11 12 15 16 20 21 23 24 26 30 35 40 41 43 44 45 46 52 53	21	10	S		295	15818	209	70.8	48	3354	41791	18182	1044
☐ METHODIST HOME CHILDREN'S GUIDANCE CENTER, 1111 Herring Ave., Zip 76708; tel. 817/753-0181; Suzanne Conway, adm. **A**1b **F**28 29 30 31 32 33	21	52	L		22	62	17	77.3	0	0	—	—	42
★☐ PROVIDENCE HOSPITAL, 1700 Providence Dr., Zip 76703; Mailing Address Box 2589, Zip 76702; tel. 817/753-4551; Kent Keahey, adm. **A**1a 2 3 9 10 **F**1 2 3 4 6 10 12 14 15 16 20 23 24 26 27 28 29 30 32 33 34 35 41 42 44 45 46 49 53 54; **S**1885	21	10	S		213	6623	126	59.2	0	0	22706	9251	503
★☐ VETERANS ADMINISTRATION MEDICAL CENTER, 4800 Memorial Dr., Zip 76711; tel. 817/752-6581; M. E. Baker, actg. dir. (Total facility includes 84 beds in nursing home-type unit) **A**1b **F**6 12 14 15 16 19 23 24 26 28 29 30 31 32 33 34 35 42 44 45 46 47 48 49 50	45	22	L	TF	1070	4057	761	71.1	0	0	49215	32757	1372
				H	986	4015	679	—	0	0	—	—	1339
WAXAHACHIE—Ellis County													
★☐ BAYLOR MEDICAL CENTER AT WAXAHACHIE (Formerly Tenery Community Hospital), 1405 W. Jefferson St., Zip 75165; tel. 214/937-5910; James M. Person, exec. dir. **A**1a 9 10 **F**1 3 6 12 16 23 30 35 36 40 41 45 46 47; **S**0095	23	10	S		48	2176	27	56.3	8	248	5953	2552	137

★ American Hospital Association (AHA) membership
□ Joint Commission on Accreditation of Hospitals (JCAH) accreditation
+ American Osteopathic Hospital Association (AOHA) membership
○ American Osteopathic Association (AOA) accreditation
Δ Commission on Accreditation of Rehabilitation Facilities (CARF) accreditation
Control codes 61, 63, 64, 71, 72 and 73 indicate hospitals listed by AOHA, but not registered by AHA.
For definition of numerical codes, see page A2

Hospital, Address, Telephone, Administrator, Approval and Facility Codes, Multihospital System Code	Classification Codes				Inpatient Data				Newborn Data		Expense (thousands of dollars)		
	Control	Service	Stay	Facilities	Beds	Admissions	Census	Occupancy (percent)	Bassinets	Births	Total	Payroll	Personnel
WEATHERFORD—Parker County													
□ CAMPBELL MEMORIAL HOSPITAL, 713 E. Anderson St., Zip 76086; tel. 817/594-8751; Charles Meisner, adm. **A**1a 9 10 **F**1 3 6 15 16 23 27 29 35 40 45 52	16	10	S		97	2879	29	29.9	12	495	6876	3183	209
WEBSTER—Harris County													
□ BAYWOOD HOSPITAL, 709 Medical Center Blvd., Zip 77598; tel. 713/332-9550; Ronald Cronen, adm. **A**1a 10 **F**3 15 17 24 29 30 32 33 42 48; **S**0825	33	22	L		100	541	50	50.0	0	0	6512	2327	167
★□ HUMANA HOSPITAL -CLEAR LAKE, 500 Medical Center Blvd., Zip 77598; tel. 713/332-2511; William J. Gresco, exec. dir. **A**1a 9 10 **F**1 2 3 4 6 7 8 9 10 12 14 15 16 23 24 30 34 35 36 40 46 52 53 54; **S**1235	33	10	S		467	11904	176	37.7	28	1817	—	—	703
WEIMAR—Colorado County													
★□ COLORADO-FAYETTE MEDICAL CENTER (Formerly Youens Memorial Hospital), 400 Youens Dr., Zip 78962; tel. 409/725-9531; Jane Rouse, adm. **A**1a 9 10 **F**1 3 6 14 16 23 35 41 45	23	10	S		38	1066	15	40.5	5	97	3258	1616	93
WELLINGTON—Collingsworth County													
COLLINGSWORTH GENERAL HOSPITAL, 1014 15th St., Zip 79095; tel. 806/447-2521; Perry Foster, adm. (Nonreporting) **A**9 10	16	10	S		25	—	—	—	—	—	—	—	—
WESLACO—Hidalgo County													
★□ KNAPP MEDICAL CENTER (Formerly Knapp Memorial Methodist Hospital), 1330 E. Sixth St., Box 1110, Zip 78596; tel. 512/968-8567; Robert W. VanderVeer, adm. **A**1a 9 10 **F**1 3 6 10 12 14 15 16 23 26 34 35 40 41 43 45 46 47 52 53	21	10	S		180	6737	77	42.8	20	1664	14721	7019	443
WEST—McLennan County													
□ WEST COMMUNITY HOSPITAL, 501 Meadow Dr., Box 478, Zip 76691; tel. 817/826-5381; Daniel W. Martin, adm. **A**1a 9 10 **F**1 3 6 10 15 16 23 32 34 40 43 45 46 53; **S**0725	16	10	S		49	1107	16	32.7	4	31	2839	1020	68
WHARTON—Wharton County													
★□ GULF COAST MEDICAL CENTER, 1400 Hwy. 59 Bypass, P O Box 3004, Zip 77488; tel. 409/532-2500; L. Gene Matthews, adm. **A**1a 2 9 10 **F**1 3 6 7 8 9 10 11 12 15 16 20 23 35 36 40 41 45 47 52 53; **S**1755	33	10	S		117	3685	51	43.6	20	647	—	—	267
WHEELER—Wheeler County													
PARKVIEW HOSPITAL, 1000 Sweetwater St., Box 1030, Zip 79096; tel. 806/826-5581; B. W. Robertson, adm. (Nonreporting) **A**9 10	16	10	S		40	—	—	—	—	—	—	—	—
WHITNEY—Hill County													
★ LAKE WHITNEY MEMORIAL HOSPITAL (Formerly Whitney Hospital), 201 N. San Jacinto St., Box 458, Zip 76692; tel. 817/694-3165; Billy J. Neely, adm. **A**9 10 **F**1 3 16 23 35 40 43 45 46	16	10	S		56	941	13	23.2	6	34	1973	905	56
WICHITA FALLS—Wichita County													
★□ BETHANIA REGIONAL HEALTH CARE CENTER, 1600 11th St., Zip 76301; tel. 817/723-4111; Sr. M. Electa, adm. **A**1a 3 5 9 10 **F**1 2 3 4 6 10 11 12 14 16 20 23 24 25 34 35 41 42 44 45 53 54; **S**6005	21	10	S		190	8137	142	70.6	0	0	30723	13591	690
★□ HCA RED RIVER HOSPITAL (Formerly Red River Hospital), 1505 Eighth St., Zip 76301; tel. 817/322-3171; Thomas L. Ryba, adm. **A**1b 9 10 **F**15 24 30 32 33 42 48 49 50; **S**1755	33	22	S		62	521	34	54.8	0	0	3631	1379	79
RED RIVER HOSPITAL, See HCA Red River Hospital													
□ WICHITA FALLS STATE HOSPITAL, Lake Rd., Box 300, Zip 76307; tel. 817/692-1220; Richard M. Bruner, supt. **A**1b 9 10 **F**1 15 23 24 28 30 32 33 34 35 42 44 46 47 48 49 50	12	22	L		606	1763	488	80.3	0	0	18988	15850	980
★□ WICHITA GENERAL HOSPITAL, 1600 Eighth St., Zip 76301; tel. 817/723-1461; William Clay Ellis, chief exec. off. **A**1a 3 5 9 10 **F**1 2 3 5 6 7 8 9 10 11 12 14 16 20 23 27 30 35 36 40 45 46 47 52 53	23	10	S		239	11203	158	66.1	30	2232	27912	13042	767
WILMER—Dallas County													
□ PARKSIDE LODGE-DALLAS FT WORTH (Formerly Brookwood Recovery Center-Dallas), 200 Green Rd., P O Box 98, Zip 75172; tel. 214/988-1503; Tommy Tolleson, exec. dir. (Nonreporting) **A**1b	33	82	L		66	—	—	—	—	—	—	—	—
WINNIE—Chambers County													
□ BAPTIST HOSPITAL-WINNIE (Formerly Medical Center of Winnie), Broadway at Campbell Rd., Box 208, Zip 77665; tel. 409/296-2131; Carol Carrell RN, exec. dir. (Nonreporting) **A**1a 9 10	21	10	S		76	—	—	—	—	—	—	—	—
WINNSBORO—Wood County													
★ PRESBYTERIAN HOSPITAL OF WINNSBORO, 504 E. Coke Rd., Box 106, Zip 75494; tel. 214/342-5227; Jerry Hopper, exec. dir. **A**9 10 **F**1 3 6 15 35 43 45 53; **S**1130	33	10	S		50	833	13	28.3	6	15	3917	1222	115
WINTERS—Runnels County													
NORTH RUNNELS HOSPITAL, E. Hwy. 53, Box 185, Zip 79567; tel. 915/754-4553; Rita Williams, adm. **A**9 10 **F**1 6 10 15 16 17 30 34 35 40 41 43 50	16	10	S		25	464	6	24.0	5	18	1074	544	45
WOODVILLE—Tyler County													
TYLER COUNTY HOSPITAL, 1100 W. Bluff St., Zip 75979; tel. 409/283-2521; James A. Molsbee, adm. **A**9 10 **F**1 6 15 16 23 24 35 40 44 45	16	10	S		48	1394	20	41.7	6	128	2711	1274	90
WORTHAM—Freestone County													
★ WORTHAM HOSPITAL, S. Hwy. 14, Box 428, Zip 76693; tel. 817/765-3363; Robert Peralta, exec. dir. **A**10 **F**12 14 16 35 48 49; **S**9795	33	10	S		27	368	7	25.9	0	0	3237	914	39
WYLIE—Collin County													
WYLIE COMMUNITY HOSPITAL, 801 W. Hwy. 78, Box 1500, Zip 75098; tel. 214/442-5414; Spencer Guimarin, adm. **A**9 10 **F**1 3 6 14 15 16 23 29 32 33 34 35 36 43 45 46 47 50; **S**1375	33	10	S		37	1032	9	24.3	6	313	—	—	50
YOAKUM—Lavaca County													
★□ YOAKUM CATHOLIC HOSPITAL, 303 Hubbard St., Box 753, Zip 77995; tel. 512/293-2321; Elwood E. Currier Jr., chief exec. off. **A**1a 9 10 **F**1 6 16 23 24 34 35 40 44 45 46 53; **S**5565	21	10	S		18	1020	15	71.4	6	172	2763	1181	83

Hospital, Address, Telephone, Administrator, Approval and Facility Codes, Multihospital System Code	Classification Codes				Inpatient Data				Newborn Data		Expense (thousands of dollars)		
★ American Hospital Association (AHA) membership □ Joint Commission on Accreditation of Hospitals (JCAH) accreditation + American Osteopathic Hospital Association (AOHA) membership ○ American Osteopathic Association (AOA) accreditation Δ Commission on Accreditation of Rehabilitation Facilities (CARF) accreditation Control codes 61, 63, 64, 71, 72 and 73 indicate hospitals listed by AOHA, but not registered by AHA For definition of numerical codes, see page A2	Control	Service	Stay	Facilities	Beds	Admissions	Census	Occupancy (percent)	Bassinets	Births	Total	Payroll	Personnel

Utah

Hospital	Control	Service	Stay	Facilities	Beds	Admissions	Census	Occupancy (percent)	Bassinets	Births	Total	Payroll	Personnel
AMERICAN FORK—Utah County													
★□ AMERICAN FORK HOSPITAL, 1100 East 170 North, Zip 84003; tel. 801/756-6001; Craig M. Smedley, adm. **A**1a 9 10 **F**1 3 5 6 14 15 16 23 27 32 33 35 36 40 45 46 52 53; **S**1815	23	10	S		72	3905	41	56.9	14	1044	12381	5128	290
BEAVER—Beaver County													
BEAVER VALLEY HOSPITAL, 85 N. 400 East, Box 820, Zip 84713; tel. 801/438-2416; Lee Strong, adm. (Nonreporting) **A**9 10	14	10	S		10	—	—	—	—	—	—	—	—
BOUNTIFUL—Davis County													
★□ LAKEVIEW HOSPITAL, 630 E. Medical Dr., Zip 84010; tel. 801/292-6231; Lindel L. Carriger, adm. **A**1a 9 10 **F**1 3 6 10 12 14 16 20 23 27 30 31 32 34 35 36 40 42 45 48 49 52 53; **S**1755	33	10	S		128	4498	55	42.8	38	1108	13398	6041	313
BRIGHAM CITY—Box Elder County													
★□ BRIGHAM CITY COMMUNITY HOSPITAL, 950 S. 500 W., Zip 84302; tel. 801/734-9471; Stephen L. Walston, adm. **A**1a 9 10 **F**1 3 6 11 14 15 16 21 23 24 27 30 32 33 34 35 36 41 44 45 46 47; **S**1755	33	10	S		50	1862	19	38.0	14	461	4964	2525	116
CEDAR CITY—Iron County													
★□ VALLEY VIEW MEDICAL CENTER, 595 South 75 East, Zip 84720; tel. 801/586-6587; Mark F. Dalley, adm. **A**1a 9 10 **F**1 3 6 12 14 15 16 23 30 34 35 36 40 45 46 50 53; **S**1815	23	10	S		48	1487	13	27.1	12	376	4768	1910	101
DELTA—Millard County													
★ DELTA COMMUNITY HOSPITAL (Formerly Delta Community Medical Center), 126 S. White Sage Ave., Zip 84624; tel. 801/864-5591; Roy Barraclough, adm. **A**9 10 **F**1 12 15 23 29 33 34 35 36 40 41 42 45 46 50; **S**1815	23	10	S		20	552	5	25.0	6	135	2178	801	64
FILLMORE—Millard County													
★ FILLMORE COMMUNITY MEDICAL CENTER, 674 S. Hwy. 99, P O Box 746, Zip 84631; tel. 801/743-5591; Roy E. Barraclough, adm. **A**9 10 **F**1 10 12 14 15 23 33 34 35 36 40 41 42 45 46 47 52; **S**1815	23	10	S		20	394	12	60.0	7	77	1652	591	40
GUNNISON—Sanpete County													
GUNNISON VALLEY HOSPITAL, Zip 84634; tel. 801/528-7246; Dale A. Rosenlund, adm. (Nonreporting) **A**9 10	14	10	S		21	—	—	—	—	—	—	—	—
HEBER CITY—Wasatch County													
★ WASATCH COUNTY HOSPITAL, 55 South Fifth East, Zip 84032; tel. 801/654-2500; Wayne T. Terry, adm. **A**9 10 **F**1 14 15 16 23 28 29 30 35 36 41 42 45 46 47 50; **S**1815	23	10	S		40	934	9	22.5	6	183	2929	1358	88
HILL AIR FORCE BASE—Davis County													
□ U. S. AIR FORCE HOSPITAL, Zip 84056; tel. 801/777-5457; Col. Stanley L. Betts, cmdr.; Lt. Col. Harry C. McLain, adm. (Nonreporting) **A**1a	41	10	S		30	—	—	—	—	—	—	—	—
KANAB—Kane County													
□ KANE COUNTY HOSPITAL, 220 W. 300 N., Box G, Zip 84741; tel. 801/644-5811; Mark P. Toohey, adm. (Nonreporting) **A**1a 9 10	23	10	S		33	—	—	—	—	—	—	—	—
LAYTON—Davis County													
★□ HUMANA HOSPITAL -DAVIS NORTH, 1600 W. Antelope Dr., Zip 84041; tel. 801/825-9561; Dean S. Holman, exec. dir. **A**1a 9 10 **F**1 3 6 10 12 14 15 16 23 35 36 40 46 52 53; **S**1235	33	33	S		110	3925	42	38.2	18	698	12006	4863	205
LOGAN—Cache County													
★□ LOGAN REGIONAL HOSPITAL, 1400 North 500 East, P O Box 3368, Zip 84321; tel. 801/752-2050; Douglas R. Fonnesbeck, adm. **A**1a 9 10 **F**1 3 6 10 12 14 15 16 20 23 24 26 27 28 30 32 33 34 35 36 37 38 39 40 41 44 45 46 47 48 49 50 51 52 53; **S**1815	23	10	S		148	6749	60	40.5	24	1740	18582	7986	423
MILFORD—Beaver County													
MILFORD VALLEY MEMORIAL HOSPITAL, N. Main St., Zip 84751; tel. 801/387-2411; Mary Wiseman, adm. (Total facility includes 24 beds in nursing home-type unit) **A**9 10 **F**1 15 16 19 21 23 34 35 37 40 41 42 45 50 52	13	10	S	TF	34	309	25	73.5	4	19	—	—	30
				H	10	278	3	—	4	19	—	—	—
MOAB—Grand County													
ALLEN MEMORIAL HOSPITAL, 719 W. Fourth North St., Box 998, Zip 84532; tel. 801/259-7191; Terrell Bloxham, adm. **A**9 10 **F**1 3 15 16 19 34 35 36 37 40 41 45 52	16	10	S		38	495	12	31.6	2	108	1531	726	39
MONTICELLO—San Juan County													
★□ SAN JUAN HOSPITAL, 384 W. First North, Box 308, Zip 84535; tel. 801/587-2116; John Fellmeth, adm. **A**1a 9 10 **F**1 6 15 16 35 40 52	13	10	S		24	727	5	20.8	8	131	1224	589	35
MONUMENT VALLEY—San Juan County													
MONUMENT VALLEY ADVENTIST HOSPITAL, Box 4, Zip 84536; tel. 801/727-3241; Stanley McCluskey, adm. **A**9 10 **F**1 6 14 34 35 37 40 50 52; **S**0235	21	10	S		23	522	6	26.1	5	99	1693	890	60
MOUNT PLEASANT—Sanpete County													
★ SANPETE VALLEY HOSPITAL, 1100 S. Medical Dr., Zip 84647; tel. 801/462-2441; George Winn, adm. **A**9 10 **F**1 6 15 23 29 30 33 35 36 41 42 45 46 49 50; **S**1815	23	10	S		20	514	8	40.0	8	119	1990	612	36
MURRAY—Salt Lake County													
★□ COTTONWOOD HOSPITAL MEDICAL CENTER, 5770 S. 300 East, Zip 84107; tel. 801/262-3461; Floyd J. McDermott, adm. **A**1a 2 9 10 **F**1 3 6 10 12 14 15 16 23 26 27 28 32 33 34 35 36 40 45 46 47 52 53 54; **S**1815	23	10	S		227	11084	126	55.5	30	2846	35258	16294	861
NEPHI—Juab County													
CENTRAL VALLEY MEDICAL CENTER (Formerly Juab County Hospital), 549 N. 400 East, Zip 84648; tel. 801/623-1242; Mark R. Stoddard, adm. & chief exec. off. **A**9 10 **F**1 6 16 21 23 28 30 34 35 36 37 41 42 45 46 50	23	10	S		22	595	5	22.7	6	70	2184	1115	57
OGDEN—Weber County													
★□ Δ MCKAY-DEE HOSPITAL CENTER, 3939 Harrison Blvd., Box 9370, Zip 84409; tel. 801/627-2800; Thomas Hanrahan, adm. **A**1a 3 5 7 9 10 **F**1 2 3 4 5 6 10 12 14 15 16 17 19 20 23 24 25 26 27 28 29 30 32 33 34 35 36 40 41 42 44 45 46 47 48 49 51 52 53 54; **S**1815	23	10	S		380	15653	244	64.2	40	3141	59472	28264	1294
★□ ST. BENEDICT'S HOSPITAL, 5475 South 500 East, Zip 84405; tel. 801/479-2111; Kimbal Wheatley, pres. & chief oper. off. **A**1a 9 10 **F**1 2 3 7 8 9 10 11 12 14 15 16 23 27 28 29 30 32 33 34 35 36 40 41 45 46 47 48 49 52 53 54; **S**5585	21	10	S		188	8218	121	64.4	19	1410	31320	11993	753
OREM—Utah County													
□ CHARTER CANYON HOSPITAL, 1350 E. 750 N., Zip 84057; tel. 801/225-2800; Larry W. Carter, adm. (Newly Registered) **A**1a 9 10	33	22	S		62	—	—	—	—	—	—	—	—

Hospital, Address, Telephone, Administrator, Approval and Facility Codes, Multihospital System Code	Classification Codes				Inpatient Data				Newborn Data		Expense (thousands of dollars)		
★ American Hospital Association (AHA) membership □ Joint Commission on Accreditation of Hospitals (JCAH) accreditation + American Osteopathic Hospital Association (AOHA) membership ○ American Osteopathic Association (AOA) accreditation Δ Commission on Accreditation of Rehabilitation Facilities (CARF) accreditation Control codes 61, 63, 64, 71, 72 and 73 indicate hospitals listed by AOHA, but not registered by AHA. For definition of numerical codes, see page A2	Control	Service	Stay	Facilities	Beds	Admissions	Census	Occupancy (percent)	Bassinets	Births	Total	Payroll	Personnel
★ OREM COMMUNITY HOSPITAL, 331 N. 400 W., Zip 84057; tel. 801/224-4080; Laurel D. Kay, adm. **A**9 10 **F**1 6 15 16 23 24 28 30 32 33 34 35 36 37 40 42 45 46; **S**1815	23	44	S		20	1178	7	35.0	10	765	3757	1326	43
PANGUITCH—Garfield County													
★□ GARFIELD MEMORIAL HOSPITAL AND CLINICS, 200 N. Fourth East, P O Box 389, Zip 84759; tel. 801/676-8811; Wayne R. Ross, adm. **A**1a 9 10 **F**1 6 15 16 23 34 35 41 42 45; **S**1815	23	10	S		20	773	14	70.0	5	95	2070	1055	48
PAYSON—Utah County													
★□ MOUNTAIN VIEW HOSPITAL, 1000 E. Hwy. 6, Zip 84651; tel. 801/465-9201; Michael A. Graham, adm. **A**1a 9 10 **F**1 3 6 10 12 14 15 16 23 27 30 32 33 34 35 36 37 40 45 46 47 49 52 53; **S**1755	33	10	S		118	3905	51	43.2	14	732	—	—	280
PRICE—Carbon County													
★□ CASTLEVIEW HOSPITAL, 300 N. Hospital Dr., R.F.D. 2, Box 46, Zip 84501; tel. 801/637-4800; Don Larsen, adm. **A**1a 9 10 **F**1 3 6 12 15 16 23 24 26 27 29 30 32 33 34 35 36 37 42 45 47 52; **S**1755	33	10	S		88	4194	44	50.0	20	591	—	—	262
PROVO—Utah County													
HSA RIVERWOOD HOSPITAL, 1067 N. 500 W., Zip 84604; tel. 801/377-4017; M. Thomas Mitchell, adm. (Newly Registered) **A**9 10	33	22	S		36	—	—	—	—	—	—	—	—
UTAH STATE HOSPITAL, 1300 E. Center St., Box 270, Zip 84603; tel. 801/373-4400; Paul I. Thorpe, supt. **A** 3 5 9 10 **F**15 23 24 33 42 46 47 50	12	22	L		318	370	304	95.6	0	0	15218	9057	530
★□ UTAH VALLEY REGIONAL MEDICAL CENTER, 1034 N. Fifth West, Zip 84603; tel. 801/373-7850; Mark J. Howard, exec. dir. **A**1a 9 10 **F**1 2 3 4 5 6 7 8 9 10 11 12 14 15 16 23 26 27 28 30 32 33 34 35 36 37 40 41 42 44 45 46 48 49 51 52 53 54; **S**1815	23	10	S		326	16399	232	71.2	57	3775	60813	29075	1223
RICHFIELD—Sevier County													
★□ SEVIER VALLEY HOSPITAL, 1100 N. Main St., Zip 84701; tel. 801/896-8271; Carlos F. Madsen, adm. **A**1a 9 10 **F**1 6 12 16 21 26 34 36 45 49; **S**1815	23	10	S		42	1300	12	29.1	10	272	4290	1361	92
ROOSEVELT—Duchesne County													
★ DUCHESNE COUNTY HOSPITAL, 250 W. 300 North, 75-2, Zip 84066; tel. 801/722-4691; Chad Evans, adm. (Nonreporting) **A**9 10	13	10	S		32	—	—	—	—	—	—	—	—
SALT LAKE CITY—Salt Lake County													
★ DOXEY-HATCH MEDICAL CENTER, 1255 E. 3900 S., Zip 84124; tel. 801/262-3401; Scott W. Robertson, adm. (Newly Registered) **A**9 10	32	48	L		180	—	—	—	—	—	—	—	—
★□ Δ HOLY CROSS HOSPITAL, 1045 E. First South St., Zip 84102; tel. 801/350-4111; Kenneth Rock, interim pres. **A**1a 2 3 5 7 9 10 **F**1 3 4 5 6 10 12 14 15 16 20 21 23 24 25 26 27 30 32 33 34 35 36 38 40 41 42 43 44 45 46 47 53 54; **S**5585	21	10	S		293	14367	184	62.8	40	3117	44305	18064	1063
★□ LDS HOSPITAL, Eighth Ave. & C. St., Zip 84143; tel. 801/321-1100; Gary William Farnes, adm. **A**1a 2 3 5 9 10 **F**1 2 3 4 5 6 7 8 9 10 11 12 13 14 15 16 17 20 23 24 27 28 29 30 32 33 34 35 36 37 38 39 40 41 42 44 45 46 47 48 49 53 54; **S**1815	23	10	S		475	22527	330	70.2	95	4476	110423	44422	2121
★□ PRIMARY CHILDREN'S MEDICAL CENTER, 320 12th Ave., Zip 84103; tel. 801/521-1221; Donald R. Poulter, adm. **A**1a 3 5 9 **F**1 4 5 6 9 10 12 14 15 16 23 24 25 26 27 28 29 30 32 33 34 35 38 41 42 44 45 46 47 51 53 54; **S**1815	23	50	S		188	5770	149	81.0	0	0	44670	21743	1094
★□ SHRINERS HOSPITALS FOR CRIPPLED CHILDREN, Fairfax Ave. & Virginia St., Zip 84103; tel. 801/532-5307; Marie N. Holm, adm. **A**1a 3 5 **F**23 34 42 46; **S**4125	23	57	S		45	484	23	51.1	0	0	—	—	84
★□ ST. MARK'S HOSPITAL, 1200 East 3900 South, Zip 84124; tel. 801/268-7111; T. J. Hartford Jr., pres. **A**1a 2 9 10 **F**1 2 3 4 5 6 10 11 12 14 15 16 20 23 27 30 33 35 36 40 43 45 46 52 53 54	21	10	S		306	12517	178	58.2	40	2026	39711	17639	767
★□ Δ UNIVERSITY OF UTAH HEALTH SCIENCES CENTER, 50 N. Medical Dr., Zip 84132; tel. 801/581-2378; George W. Belsey, adm. **A**1a 2 3 5 7 8 9 10 **F**1 3 4 5 6 7 8 9 10 11 12 13 14 16 17 20 22 23 24 25 26 27 28 29 30 31 32 33 34 35 36 38 40 41 42 44 45 46 47 51 52 53 54	12	10	S		370	11654	282	76.2	20	1423	85745	31810	1826
★□ VETERANS ADMINISTRATION MEDICAL CENTER, 500 Foothill Dr., Zip 84148; tel. 801/582-1565; William L. Hodson, adm. (Total facility includes 10 beds in nursing home-type unit) **A**1a 2 3 5 **F**3 4 6 10 12 13 14 15 16 19 20 23 24 25 26 27 28 29 30 31 32 33 34 35 41 42 43 44 46 47 48 49 50 53 54	45	10	S	TF H	392 382	10749 10708	283 276	72.2 —	0 0	0 0	68283 67995	34123 33854	1202 1196
□ WESTERN INSTITUTE OF NEUROPSYCHIATRY, 501 Chipeta Way, Zip 84108; tel. 801/583-2500; H. Don Moyer, adm. (Newly Registered) **A**1a 9	33	22	S		90	—	—	—	—	—	—	—	—
SANDY—Salt Lake County													
★ ALTA VIEW HOSPITAL, 9660 S. 1300 E., Zip 84070; tel. 801/572-2600; Jay Southwick, adm. **A**9 10 **F**1 6 12 14 15 16 23 30 34 35 36 40 45 46 47 50 53; **S**1815	23	10	S		50	3650	32	64.0	20	1024	—	—	235
ST. GEORGE—Washington County													
★□ DIXIE MEDICAL CENTER, 544 S. 400 East St., Zip 84770; tel. 801/673-9681; L. Steven Wilson, adm. **A**1a 9 10 **F**1 3 5 6 7 8 10 11 12 14 15 16 21 23 24 27 28 30 32 33 34 35 36 37 39 40 41 42 43 44 46 49 50 53; **S**1815	23	10	S		104	6088	68	65.4	16	1037	17319	6801	371
TOOELE—Tooele County													
□ TOOELE VALLEY REGIONAL MEDICAL CENTER (Formerly Tooele Valley Hospital), 211 S. 100 East, Box 88, Zip 84074; tel. 801/882-1697; Scott F. Blakley, adm. (Nonreporting) **A**1a 9 10; **S**9795	13	10	S		33	—	—	—	—	—	—	—	—
TREMONTON—Box Elder County													
★□ BEAR RIVER VALLEY HOSPITAL, 440 W. 600 N., Zip 84337; tel. 801/257-7441; Robert F. Jex, adm. **A**1a 9 10 **F**1 6 15 23 35 36 44 45 46; **S**1815	23	10	S		20	622	6	30.0	4	124	1656	621	25
VERNAL—Uintah County													
★ ASHLEY VALLEY MEDICAL CENTER, 151 W. 200 North, Zip 84078; tel. 801/789-3342; Ron Perry, adm. (Nonreporting) **A**9 10; **S**1755	33	10	S		36	—	—	—	—	—	—	—	—
WEST JORDAN—Salt Lake County													
□ RIVENDELL CHILDREN AND YOUTH CENTER, 5899 W. Rivendell Dr., P O Box 459, Zip 84084; tel. 801/561-3377; Jared U. Balmer, exec. dir. (Newly Registered) **A**1a 9	33	22	L		78	—	—	—	—	—	—	—	—
WEST VALLEY CITY—Salt Lake County													
★□ PIONEER VALLEY HOSPITAL, 3460 S. Pioneer Pkwy., Zip 84120; tel. 801/968-9061; Kay Matsumura, adm. **A**1a 2 9 10 **F**1 3 6 10 12 14 15 16 20 23 24 27 30 32 33 34 35 36 40 42 45 46 49 52 53; **S**1755	33	10	S		139	5019	58	41.7	20	630	15207	5951	354

Hospital, Address, Telephone, Administrator, Approval and Facility Codes, Multihospital System Code

- ★ American Hospital Association (AHA) membership
- □ Joint Commission on Accreditation of Hospitals (JCAH) accreditation
- + American Osteopathic Hospital Association (AOHA) membership
- ○ American Osteopathic Association (AOA) accreditation
- Δ Commission on Accreditation of Rehabilitation Facilities (CARF) accreditation

Control codes 61, 63, 64, 71, 72 and 73 indicate hospitals listed by AOHA, but not registered by AHA. For definition of numerical codes, see page A2

Vermont

Hospital	Classification Codes: Control	Service	Stay	Facilities	Inpatient Data: Beds	Admissions	Census	Occupancy (percent)	Newborn Data: Bassinets	Births	Expense (thousands of dollars): Total	Payroll	Personnel
BARRE—Washington County													
CENTRAL VERMONT HOSPITAL, See Central Vermont Medical Center, Berlin													
MCFARLAND HOUSE, See Central Vermont Medical Center, Berlin													
BELLOWS FALLS—Windham County													
⊠ ROCKINGHAM MEMORIAL HOSPITAL, Hospital Ct., Zip 05101; tel. 802/463-3903; Gilbert Theriault, adm.; John D. Enright, asst. adm. (Nonreporting) **A**1a 9 10	23	10	S		30	—	—	—	—	—	—	—	—
BENNINGTON—Bennington County													
⊠ SOUTHWESTERN VERMONT MEDICAL CENTER, 100 Hospital Dr. E., Zip 05201; tel. 802/442-6361; Robert D. Stout, pres. (Total facility includes 100 beds in nursing home-type unit) **A**1a 2 9 10 **F**1 3 6 10 12 14 15 16 19 21 23 24 26 27 29 30 32 35 37 40 44 45 46 47 52 53	23	10	S	TF	260	5697	175	73.8	20	608	19300	10071	587
				H	160	5554	126	—	20	608	17922	9351	517
BERLIN—Washington County													
⊠ CENTRAL VERMONT MEDICAL CENTER (Includes Central Vermont Hospital, Mailing Address Box 547, Barre, Zip 05641; tel. 802/229-9121; Heaton House, Heaton St., Montpelier, Zip 05602; McFarland House, 71 Washington St., Barre, Zip 05641), Mailing Address Box 547, Barre, Zip 05641; tel. 802/229-9121; Joel H. Walker, pres. (Total facility includes 145 beds in nursing home-type unit) **A**1a 9 10 **F**1 3 6 10 12 14 15 16 19 23 24 26 27 29 30 32 33 35 36 37 40 44 45 46 47 52 53	23	10	S	TF	325	5949	233	71.7	16	718	20170	10157	579
				H	180	5843	89	—	16	718	17027	8319	450
BRATTLEBORO—Windham County													
⊠ BRATTLEBORO MEMORIAL HOSPITAL, 9 Belmont Ave., Zip 05301; tel. 802/257-0341; William M. Milligan Jr., exec. vice-pres. **A**1a 9 10 **F**1 3 6 10 12 14 15 16 23 35 36 40 44 45 46 47 52 53	23	10	S		84	2723	37	44.0	10	510	9655	4750	234
⊠ BRATTLEBORO RETREAT, 75 Linden St., Zip 05301; tel. 802/257-7785; William B. Beach Jr. MD, chief exec. off. (Total facility includes 117 beds in nursing home-type unit) **A**1a b 3 10 **F**15 19 24 28 32 33 34 42 46 47 48 49	23	22	L	TF	260	1049	220	85.9	0	0	—	—	524
				H	143	1007	109	—	0	0	—	—	436
BURLINGTON—Chittenden County													
⊠ MEDICAL CENTER HOSPITAL OF VERMONT, Colchester Ave., Zip 05401; tel. 802/656-2345; James H. Taylor, pres. (Total facility includes 42 beds in nursing home-type unit) **A**1a 2 3 5 8 9 10 **F**1 2 3 4 5 6 7 8 9 10 11 12 13 14 15 16 18 19 20 23 24 25 26 27 28 29 30 32 33 34 35 36 37 38 40 42 44 45 46 47 49 50 51 52 53 54	23	10	S	TF	501	17779	404	81.8	38	2558	91380	39415	2026
				H	459	17730	364	—	38	2558	90762	38848	1996
MIDDLEBURY—Addison County													
⊠ PORTER MEDICAL CENTER, South St., Zip 05753; tel. 802/388-7901; James L. Daily, pres. (Total facility includes 50 beds in nursing home-type unit) **A**1a 9 10 **F**1 3 6 7 10 12 14 15 16 19 23 24 26 34 35 36 40 44 45 46	23	10	S	TF	95	1961	75	78.9	10	465	8105	4595	267
				H	45	1911	25	—	10	465	6785	3710	214
MONTPELIER—Washington County													
HEATON HOUSE, See Central Vermont Medical Center, Berlin													
MORRISVILLE—Lamoille County													
⊠ COPLEY HOSPITAL, Washington Hwy., Zip 05661; tel. 802/888-4231; Carolyn C. Roberts, pres. **A**1a 9 10 **F**1 3 6 10 12 14 15 16 23 24 26 30 34 35 36 40 45 46 47	23	10	S		54	1782	26	48.1	8	270	6524	3213	181
NEWPORT—Orleans County													
⊠ NORTH COUNTRY HOSPITAL AND HEALTH CENTER, Prouty Dr., Zip 05855; tel. 802/334-7331; James E. Cassidy, pres. **A**1a 9 10 **F**1 3 6 10 12 14 15 16 23 26 30 32 35 36 37 40 45 46 47 52	23	10	S		80	2570	38	47.5	16	321	7842	4048	227
RANDOLPH—Orange County													
⊠ GIFFORD MEMORIAL HOSPITAL, 44 S. Main St., Box 2000, Zip 05060; tel. 802/728-4441; Philip D. Levesque, adm. **A**1a 2 9 10 **F**1 3 6 10 12 14 15 16 23 34 35 36 40 41 44 45 46 47	23	10	S		53	1596	23	43.4	10	383	5153	2601	145
RUTLAND—Rutland County													
⊠ RUTLAND REGIONAL MEDICAL CENTER, 160 Allen St., Zip 05701; tel. 802/775-7111; Richard T. Schmidt, pres. **A**1a 2 9 10 **F**1 3 5 6 9 10 12 14 15 16 23 24 26 27 29 34 35 36 40 44 45 46 47 52 53	23	10	S		217	8490	156	69.6	21	839	26899	13702	676
SPRINGFIELD—Windsor County													
⊠ SPRINGFIELD HOSPITAL, 25 Ridgewood Rd., P O Box 853, Zip 05156; tel. 802/885-2151; David J. Pagniucci, adm. **A**1a 9 10 **F**1 3 6 10 12 14 15 16 21 23 24 26 34 35 36 40 44 45 46 50 53 54	23	10	S		66	2579	37	56.1	8	316	8608	4089	209
ST. ALBANS—Franklin County													
⊠ NORTHWESTERN MEDICAL CENTER, Box 1370, Zip 05478; tel. 802/524-5911; Wesley W. Oswald, exec. dir. **A**1a 9 10 **F**1 3 6 12 14 15 16 23 30 33 34 35 36 40 44 45 46 52 53; **S**1755	23	10	S		77	2727	43	55.8	21	354	8714	4330	227
ST. JOHNSBURY—Caledonia County													
⊠ NORTHEASTERN VERMONT REGIONAL HOSPITAL, Hospital Dr., Zip 05819; tel. 802/748-8141; Paul R. Bengtson, chief exec. off. **A**1a 9 10 **F**1 3 6 10 12 14 15 16 21 23 26 30 32 35 36 40 44 45 46 47 48 52 53; **S**2495	23	10	S		100	2699	36	36.0	10	328	8602	3823	213
TOWNSHEND—Windham County													
★ GRACE COTTAGE HOSPITAL (Includes Stratton House Nursing Home), Rte. 35, P O Box 216, Zip 05353; tel. 802/365-7676; Carlos G. Otis MD, adm. (Total facility includes 18 beds in nursing home-type unit) **A**9 10 **F**1 19 24 35 36 37 40 45	23	10	S	TF	37	323	25	67.6	4	28	1315	733	50
				H	19	314	7	—	4	28	936	481	37
WATERBURY—Washington County													
VERMONT STATE HOSPITAL, 103 S. Main St., Zip 05676; tel. 802/241-3100; Claudia P. Stone, exec. dir. **F**23 24 30 32 33 42 46 47	12	22	L		189	478	178	64.3	0	0	9729	5962	316
WHITE RIVER JUNCTION—Windsor County													
⊠ VETERANS ADMINISTRATION MEDICAL CENTER, N. Hartland Rd., Zip 05001; tel. 802/295-9363; Thomas F. Wheaton, dir. (Total facility includes 30 beds in nursing home-type unit) **A**1a 3 5 8 **F**1 3 6 10 12 14 15 16 19 23 24 26 27 28 30 32 33 34 41 42 44 46 48 49 50 53	45	10	S	TF	224	4657	153	68.3	0	0	23082	14756	573
				H	194	4458	132	—	0	0	—	—	556
WINDSOR—Windsor County													
⊠ MT. ASCUTNEY HOSPITAL AND HEALTH CENTER, Rural Rte. 1, Box 6, Zip 05089; tel. 802/674-6711; Richard Slusky, adm. (Total facility includes 40 beds in nursing home-type unit) **A**1a 9 10 **F**1 3 6 14 16 19 21 23 24 27 28 32 33 35 42 43 44 45 46	23	10	S	TF	70	949	49	70.0	0	0	4213	2182	135
				H	30	833	15	—	0	0	—	—	—
WINOOSKI—Chittenden County													
⊠ FANNY ALLEN HOSPITAL, 101 College Pkwy., Zip 05404; tel. 802/655-1234; Sr. Madeleine Bachand, adm. **A**1a 3 5 10 **F**1 3 6 12 14 15 16 23 30 32 33 34 35 45 46 47 49	21	10	S		94	3290	73	75.3	0	0	12286	5892	293

Hospital, Address, Telephone, Administrator, Approval and Facility Codes, Multihospital System Code	Classification Codes				Inpatient Data				Newborn Data		Expense (thousands of dollars)		
★ American Hospital Association (AHA) membership □ Joint Commission on Accreditation of Hospitals (JCAH) accreditation + American Osteopathic Hospital Association (AOHA) membership ○ American Osteopathic Association (AOA) accreditation Δ Commission on Accreditation of Rehabilitation Facilities (CARF) accreditation Control codes 61, 63, 64, 71, 72 and 73 indicate hospitals listed by AOHA, but not registered by AHA. For definition of numerical codes, see page A2	Control	Service	Stay	Facilities	Beds	Admissions	Census	Occupancy (percent)	Bassinets	Births	Total	Payroll	Personnel
Virginia													
ABINGDON—Washington County													
⊞ JOHNSTON MEMORIAL HOSPITAL, Court St., Zip 24210; tel. 703/628-3121; Robert L. Kay, adm. **A**1a 9 10 **F**1 2 3 6 10 12 14 16 23 34 35 36 40 45 46 51 52 53	23	10	S		154	5655	103	66.9	12	584	11905	5587	401
ALEXANDRIA—Independent City													
⊞ ALEXANDRIA HOSPITAL, 4320 Seminary Rd., Zip 22304; tel. 703/379-3000; J. Edward Sweet Jr., pres. **A**1a 2 6 9 10 **F**1 2 3 5 6 9 10 11 12 14 15 16 17 20 23 24 26 27 30 33 35 36 37 40 44 45 46 47 51 52 53 54	23	10	S		374	15650	277	74.1	32	3190	60773	30828	1316
CIRCLE TERRACE HOSPITAL, See Reston Hospital Center, Reston													
⊞ JEFFERSON MEMORIAL HOSPITAL, 4600 King St., Zip 22302; tel. 703/931-9700; Richard Levy Jr., adm. (Nonreporting) **A**1a 9 10; **S**1305	33	10	S		120	—	—	—	—	—	—	—	—
⊞ MOUNT VERNON HOSPITAL, 2501 Parker's Lane, Zip 22306; tel. 703/664-7000; Stephen C. Rupp, vice-pres. & adm. **A**1a 9 10 **F**1 3 6 10 11 12 14 15 16 20 23 24 25 26 27 30 33 35 42 43 44 45 46 47 53; **S**1305	23	10	S		167	6194	151	90.4	0	0	33842	15978	706
ARLINGTON—Arlington County													
⊞ ARLINGTON HOSPITAL, 1701 N. George Mason Dr., Zip 22205; tel. 703/558-5000; John P. Sverha, pres. **A**1a b 2 3 5 9 10 **F**1 2 3 5 6 7 8 9 10 11 12 14 15 16 20 23 24 26 27 29 34 35 36 40 42 44 45 46 47 48 49 52 53 54	23	10	S		355	15632	298	84.4	23	2567	56252	27882	1086
⊞ HCA NORTHERN VIRGINIA DOCTORS HOSPITAL (Formerly Northern Virginia Doctors Hospital), 601 S. Carlin Springs Rd., Zip 22204; tel. 703/671-1200; Ray L. Hemness, adm. **A**1a 2 9 10 **F**1 3 6 10 12 14 15 16 20 23 24 26 34 35 43 44 46 47 53; **S**1755	33	10	S		198	5431	110	55.6	0	0	23783	10023	502
⊞ HOSPICE OF NORTHERN VIRGINIA, 4715 N. 15th St., Zip 22205; tel. 703/525-7070; Mary L. Stone, adm. **A**1a 10 **F**21 23 24 41 46 47	23	49	S		15	339	13	86.7	0	0	3305	1797	91
⊞ NATIONAL HOSPITAL FOR ORTHOPAEDICS AND REHABILITATION, 2455 Army Navy Dr., Zip 22206; tel. 703/920-6700; Edward J. Jenkins, adm. **A**1a 9 10 **F**1 3 5 6 10 14 15 16 23 24 25 26 34 35 44 45 46 47	23	47	S		147	3829	94	63.9	0	0	23458	11688	601
NORTHERN VIRGINIA DOCTORS HOSPITAL, See HCA Northern Virginia Doctors Hospital													
BEDFORD—Bedford County													
⊞ BEDFORD COUNTY MEMORIAL HOSPITAL, Oakwood Ext., Box 688, Zip 24523; tel. 703/586-2441; John H. Fretz, adm. (Total facility includes 100 beds in nursing home-type unit) **A**1a 9 10 **F**1 3 6 14 15 16 19 23 34 35 36 37 40 41 42 44 45 46 47 50 53; **S**0070	23	10	S	TF H	169 69	2383 2224	122 25	72.2 —	9 9	309 309	7804 6032	3997 3353	356 282
BIG STONE GAP—Wise County													
⊞ LONESOME PINE HOSPITAL, Holton Ave., Drawer I, Zip 24219; tel. 703/523-3111; Stephen K. Givens, adm. **A**1a 2 9 10 **F**1 3 6 15 16 34 35 36 40 41 45 47 52; **S**0070	23	10	S		60	3289	43	71.7	10	452	8350	4022	213
BLACKSBURG—Montgomery County													
⊞ MONTGOMERY REGIONAL HOSPITAL (Formerly Montgomery County Hospital), Rte. 460 S., Zip 24060; tel. 703/951-1111; Robert D. Fraraccio, adm. **A**1a 9 10 **F**1 3 6 15 16 23 30 34 35 36 37 40 45 46 47 52 53; **S**1755	33	10	S		146	4546	72	49.3	12	559	—	—	350
BURKEVILLE—Nottoway County													
⊞ PIEDMONT GERIATRIC HOSPITAL (Gero-Psychiatric), Zip 23922; tel. 804/767-4401; Willard R. Pierce Jr., dir. **A**1b 9 10 **F**23 27 32 42 46 47 50	12	49	L		230	129	218	94.0	0	0	7721	5145	333
CATAWBA—Roanoke County													
□ CATAWBA HOSPITAL, Zip 24070; tel. 703/375-4200; R. Michael Marsh PhD, dir. **A**1b 9 10 **F**15 24 33 42 46 47 50	12	22	L		240	374	221	92.1	0	0	8320	5438	328
CHARLOTTESVILLE—Independent City													
BLUE RIDGE HOSPITAL, See University of Virginia Hospitals													
□ CHARTER HOSPITAL OF CHARLOTTESVILLE (Formerly David C. Wilson Hospital), 2101 Arlington Blvd., Zip 22903; tel. 804/977-1120; Jerome E. Johnson, adm. (Nonreporting) **A**1b 9 10	33	22	S		60	—	—	—	—	—	—	—	—
CHILDREN'S REHABILITATION CENTER UNIVERSITY OF VIRGINIA HOSPITAL, See University of Virginia Hospitals													
DAVID C. WILSON HOSPITAL, See Charter Hospital of Charlottesville													
⊞ MARTHA JEFFERSON HOSPITAL, 459 Locust Ave., Zip 22901; tel. 804/293-0111; John D. Holly III, pres. **A**1a 9 10 **F**1 2 3 6 10 12 14 15 16 23 24 34 35 36 37 40 41 44 45 47 52 53	23	10	S		176	9403	139	79.0	24	1265	22469	10154	585
⊞ UNIVERSITY OF VIRGINIA HOSPITALS (Includes Blue Ridge Hospital, Rte. 20 S., Zip 22901; tel. 804/924-9002; Marcus G. Kuhn, adm.; Melvina Hamilton, med. dir.; Children's Rehabilitation Center University of Virginia Hospital, 2270 Ivy Rd., Zip 22901; tel. 804/924-5500; Gene Carpenter, adm.), Jefferson Park Ave., Box 148, Medical Center, Zip 22908; tel. 804/924-0211; John T. Ashley MD, exec. dir. **A**1a 2 3 5 8 9 10 **F**1 2 3 4 5 6 7 8 9 10 11 12 13 14 15 16 17 20 22 23 24 25 26 27 28 30 32 33 34 35 36 37 38 39 40 42 44 45 46 47 48 49 50 51 52 53 54	12	10	S		796	26690	563	70.7	31	1576	177429	63499	3430
CHESAPEAKE—Independent City													
⊞ CHESAPEAKE GENERAL HOSPITAL, 736 Battlefield Blvd. N., P O Box 2028, Zip 23320; tel. 804/547-8121; Donald S. Buckley, pres. **A**1a 2 9 10 **F**1 3 6 10 12 14 15 16 23 30 34 35 36 40 41 44 45 46 52 53	16	10	S		210	8023	146	69.5	24	77	29385	14136	748
CULPEPER—Culpeper County													
⊞ CULPEPER MEMORIAL HOSPITAL, 501 Sunset Lane, Box 592, Zip 22701; tel. 703/829-4100; William A. Gravely Jr., pres. **A**1a 9 10 **F**1 3 6 10 12 14 15 16 23 27 29 30 32 33 34 35 36 40 41 43 44 45 46 47 52 53	23	10	S		84	3068	46	54.8	12	243	9748	4359	289
DANVILLE—Independent City													
⊞ MEMORIAL HOSPITAL, 142 S. Main St., Zip 24541; tel. 804/799-2100; Hunter A. Grumbles, adm. **A**1a 2 3 5 6 9 10 **F**2 3 6 7 8 10 12 14 15 16 20 23 24 27 29 35 36 40 41 42 45 46 47 48 52 53	23	10	S		377	13134	280	74.3	26	1211	—	—	1277
EMPORIA—Greensville County													
⊞ GREENSVILLE MEMORIAL HOSPITAL, 214 Weaver Ave., Zip 23847; tel. 804/348-2000; John A. Thurman, adm. **A**1a 9 10 **F**1 3 6 12 14 15 16 23 34 35 40 45 47 53	23	10	S		127	4227	72	56.7	13	215	9458	4688	307
FAIRFAX—Independent City													
⊞ COMMONWEALTH HOSPITAL, 4315 Chain Bridge Rd., Zip 22030; tel. 703/691-3600; Steven E. Brown, adm. (Nonreporting) **A**1a 2 9 10; **S**1305	23	10	S		160	—	—	—	—	—	—	—	—
FALLS CHURCH—Independent City													
★ DOMINION HOSPITAL, 2960 Sleepy Hollow Rd., Zip 22044; tel. 703/536-2000; Donald E. Annis, exec. dir. (Total facility includes 58 beds in nursing home-type unit) **A** 10 **F**15 19 24 30 42 48; **S**1755	33	22	S	TF H	158 100	1293 1264	128 70	81.0 —	0 0	0 0	10380 9624	4658 4081	208 151

Hospital, Address, Telephone, Administrator, Approval and Facility Codes, Multihospital System Code	Classification Codes				Inpatient Data				Newborn Data		Expense (thousands of dollars)		
★ American Hospital Association (AHA) membership □ Joint Commission on Accreditation of Hospitals (JCAH) accreditation + American Osteopathic Hospital Association (AOHA) membership ○ American Osteopathic Association (AOA) accreditation Δ Commission on Accreditation of Rehabilitation Facilities (CARF) accreditation Control codes 61, 63, 64, 71, 72 and 73 indicate hospitals listed by AOHA, but not registered by AHA. For definition of numerical codes, see page A2	Control	Service	Stay	Facilities	Beds	Admissions	Census	Occupancy (percent)	Bassinets	Births	Total	Payroll	Personnel
★□ FAIRFAX HOSPITAL, 3300 Gallows Rd., Zip 22046; tel. 703/698-1110; Everett M. Devaney, vice-pres. & adm. (Nonreporting) **A**1a 2 3 5 8 9 10; **S**1305	23	10	S		656	—	—	—	—	—	—	—	—
FARMVILLE—Prince Edward County													
★□ SOUTHSIDE COMMUNITY HOSPITAL, 800 Oak St., Zip 23901; tel. 804/392-8811; Thomas J. Rice, adm. **A**1a 9 10 **F**1 3 6 14 15 16 23 35 36 40 41 44 45 46 47 52 53; **S**0070	23	10	S		117	3720	54	46.2	14	285	9087	3853	263
FISHERSVILLE—Augusta County													
★□ Δ WOODROW WILSON REHABILITATION CENTER-HOSPITAL, Zip 22939; tel. 703/885-9711; Melinda J. Miller, adm. (Nonreporting) **A**1a 7 9 10	12	46	L		64	—	—	—	—	—	—	—	—
FORT BELVOIR—Fairfax County													
★□ DEWITT ARMY COMMUNITY HOSPITAL (Formerly DeWitt Army Hospital), Zip 22060; tel. 703/664-1471; Col. James L. Stewart Jr., cmdr. **A**1a 3 5 **F**2 3 6 12 14 15 16 23 28 30 32 33 34 35 37 40 45 46 47 49 50 52	42	10	S		149	7265	70	47.0	25	1229	33391	26452	790
FORT EUSTIS—Independent City													
★□ MCDONALD ARMY COMMUNITY HOSPITAL, Zip 23604; tel. 804/878-3204; Col. Edward K. Jeffer, cmdr. **A**1a **F**1 3 6 12 14 15 23 28 30 32 33 34 35 41 45 46 47 49 52	42	10	S		57	3937	37	64.9	0	0	16542	12588	588
FORT LEE—Prince George County													
★□ KENNER ARMY COMMUNITY HOSPITAL, Zip 23801; tel. 804/734-3443; Col. Seymour Levine MC, CO **A**1a **F**1 3 6 10 12 14 15 23 26 28 29 30 32 33 34 35 37 46 47 49	42	10	S		101	3981	55	54.5	0	0	20765	15232	479
FRANKLIN—Independent City													
★□ SOUTHAMPTON MEMORIAL HOSPITAL, 100 Fairview Dr., Drawer 817, Zip 23851; tel. 804/562-5161; Edward J. Patnesky, pres. & chief exec. off. (Total facility includes 131 beds in nursing home-type unit) **A**1a 9 10 **F**1 3 6 10 11 12 14 15 16 19 23 24 26 29 30 32 33 34 35 36 37 40 42 44 45 46 50 52 53	23	10	S	TF	221	3060	168	76.0	12	403	12530	5728	415
				H	90	3012	46	—	12	403	—	—	349
FREDERICKSBURG—Spotsylvania County													
★□ MARY WASHINGTON HOSPITAL, 2300 Fall Hill Ave., Zip 22401; tel. 703/899-1100; William F. Jacobs Jr., pres. **A**1a 2 9 10 **F**1 3 6 7 8 9 10 11 12 14 15 16 20 23 24 26 27 29 30 33 34 35 36 40 41 42 44 45 46 52 53	23	10	S		283	14083	242	85.5	40	1484	39334	18321	1023
FRONT ROYAL—Warren County													
★□ WARREN MEMORIAL HOSPITAL, 1000 Shenandoah Ave., Zip 22630; tel. 703/636-0300; C. Douglas Rosen, adm. (Total facility includes 40 beds in nursing home-type unit) **A**1a 9 10 **F**1 3 6 10 12 14 15 16 19 23 26 35 36 37 40 41 42 45 46 47 52 53	23	10	S	TF	151	2389	75	49.7	8	232	9092	4085	256
				H	111	2366	36	—	8	232	8820	3860	241
GALAX—Independent City													
★□ TWIN COUNTY COMMUNITY HOSPITAL, 200 Hospital Dr., Zip 24333; tel. 703/236-8181; Kenneth L. Waddell, pres. **A**1a 9 10 **F**1 3 6 10 12 14 15 16 21 23 34 35 36 40 41 44 45 46 47 53	23	10	S		149	5507	94	63.1	22	466	13267	6251	426
GLOUCESTER—Gloucester County													
□ WALTER REED MEMORIAL HOSPITAL, Rte. 17, Zip 23061; tel. 804/693-4400; William B. Downey, vice-pres. (Nonreporting) **A**1a 9 10; **S**4810	23	10	S		71	—	—	—	—	—	—	—	—
GRUNDY—Buchanan County													
★□ BUCHANAN GENERAL HOSPITAL, Zip 24614; Mailing Address Rte. 4, Box 335-E., Zip 26414; tel. 703/935-8831; John McClellan, adm. **A**1a 9 10 **F**1 3 6 12 14 16 23 35 40 41 45 46 47 52 53; **S**1755	23	10	S		194	9893	137	70.6	8	207	18938	7656	467
HAMPTON—Independent City													
★□ HAMPTON GENERAL HOSPITAL, 3120 Victoria Blvd., Zip 23661; Mailing Address Drawer 640, Zip 23669; tel. 804/727-7000; Roger M. Eitelman, adm. (Total facility includes 13 beds in nursing home-type unit) **A**1a 9 10 **F**1 2 3 5 6 9 10 11 12 14 15 16 19 20 23 24 25 32 33 34 35 36 37 40 41 44 45 46 47 52 53	23	10	S	TF	323	10865	216	66.9	37	1712	39441	16653	1054
				H	310	10831	213	—	37	1712	—	—	—
★□ PENINSULA HOSPITAL, 2244 Executive Dr., Zip 23666; tel. 804/827-1001; David Hoidal, adm. (Nonreporting) **A**1b 9; **S**1755	33	22	S		125	—	—	—	—	—	—	—	—
U. S. AIR FORCE REGIONAL HOSPITAL, See Langley Air Force Base													
★□ VETERANS ADMINISTRATION MEDICAL CENTER, Zip 23667; tel. 804/722-9961; Allan S. Goss, dir. (Total facility includes 120 beds in nursing home-type unit) **A**1a 2 3 5 8 **F**1 3 6 10 11 12 14 15 16 19 20 21 23 24 26 27 28 30 32 33 34 35 38 41 42 44 46 47 48 50 53	45	10	S	TF	531	7570	442	83.2	0	0	51300	35668	1251
				H	411	7271	328	—	0	0	46512	31991	1193
HARRISONBURG—Independent City													
★□ ROCKINGHAM MEMORIAL HOSPITAL, 235 Cantrell Ave., Zip 22801; tel. 703/433-4100; T. Carter Melton, pres. **A**1a 2 9 10 **F**1 2 3 6 8 9 10 11 12 14 15 16 20 21 23 24 27 29 35 36 40 45 52 53	23	10	S		277	10705	186	67.1	28	1294	28405	14697	867
HOPEWELL—Independent City													
★□ JOHN RANDOLPH HOSPITAL, 411 W. Randolph Rd., Box 971, Zip 23860; tel. 804/541-1600; Franklin D. Boyce, chief exec. off. **A**1a 9 10 **F**1 3 6 10 12 14 15 16 23 24 26 34 35 36 40 45 46 47 52 53	16	10	S		100	5550	81	81.0	10	349	18444	7319	413
HOT SPRINGS—Bath County													
★ BATH COUNTY COMMUNITY HOSPITAL, Drawer Z, Zip 24445; tel. 703/839-5333; Ripley P. Owen, adm. **A**9 10 **F**1 3 12 14 16 23 34 35 36 40 41	23	10	S		25	972	13	52.0	4	36	2673	1637	78
KILMARNOCK—Lancaster County													
★□ RAPPAHANNOCK GENERAL HOSPITAL, Box 1449, Zip 22482; tel. 804/435-8000; R. Frederick Baensch, adm. (Nonreporting) **A**1a 9 10; **S**1755	23	10	S		76	—	—	—	—	—	—	—	—
LANGLEY AIR FORCE BASE—Independent City													
□ U. S. AIR FORCE REGIONAL HOSPITAL, Zip 23665; tel. 804/764-6825; Col. Edward B. Degroot III MSC USAF, adm. **A**1a **F**1 3 12 14 15 16 23 24 26 28 30 33 34 35 36 37 40 42 43 46 49 50 52	41	10	S		99	4925	40	44.9	20	1046	—	—	598
LEBANON—Russell County													
□ RUSSELL COUNTY MEDICAL CENTER, Carroll & Tate Sts., Zip 24266; tel. 703/889-1224; Martin S. Rash, adm. **A**1a 9 10 **F**1 3 6 12 14 15 16 23 26 30 34 35 36 37 40 41 43 45 46 53; **S**0875	33	10	S		78	2798	40	51.3	7	205	—	—	182
LEESBURG—Loudoun County													
★□ GRAYDON MANOR, 301 Childrens Center Rd., Zip 22075; tel. 703/777-3485; Bernard Haberlein, exec. dir. **A**1b **F**28 29 32 33 42	23	52	L		61	46	56	91.8	0	0	3082	2037	105
★□ LOUDOUN MEMORIAL HOSPITAL, 224 Cornwall St. N.W., Zip 22075; tel. 703/777-3300; Kent Stevens, pres. (Total facility includes 100 beds in nursing home-type unit) **A**1a 2 9 10 **F**1 3 6 10 12 14 15 16 19 23 24 27 34 35 36 40 42 44 45 46 47 52 53	23	10	S	TF	219	4597	159	72.6	13	737	20512	10617	531
				H	119	4476	66	—	13	737	17802	9293	447
□ SPRINGWOOD PSYCHIATRIC INSTITUTE, Rte. 4, Box 50, Zip 22075; tel. 703/777-0800; C. Gibson Dunn MD, chief exec. off. (Nonreporting) **A**1b 10; **S**0825	33	22	L		30	—	—	—	—	—	—	—	—
LEXINGTON—Rockbridge County													
★□ STONEWALL JACKSON HOSPITAL, Spotswood Dr., Zip 24450; tel. 703/463-9141; L. E. Richardson, pres. (Total facility includes 50 beds in nursing home-type unit) **A**1a 9 10 **F**1 3 6 14 15 16 19 23 35 36 40 41 42 44 45 46 47 53	23	10	S	TF	130	2463	74	56.9	8	276	7730	2992	211
				H	80	2373	26	—	8	276	6568	2690	184
LOW MOOR—Alleghany County													
★□ ALLEGHANY REGIONAL HOSPITAL, Interstate 64 & State Rd. 696, Box 7, Zip 24457; tel. 703/862-6011; Walter R. Parmer, adm. (Nonreporting) **A**1a 9 10; **S**1755	23	10	S		214	—	—	—	—	—	—	—	—

★ American Hospital Association (AHA) membership
☐ Joint Commission on Accreditation of Hospitals (JCAH) accreditation
+ American Osteopathic Hospital Association (AOHA) membership
○ American Osteopathic Association (AOA) accreditation
Δ Commission on Accreditation of Rehabilitation Facilities (CARF) accreditation
Control codes 61, 63, 64, 71, 72 and 73 indicate hospitals listed by AOHA, but not registered by AHA.
For definition of numerical codes, see page A2

Hospital, Address, Telephone, Administrator, Approval and Facility Codes, Multihospital System Code	Classification Codes				Inpatient Data				Newborn Data		Expense (thousands of dollars)		
	Control	Service	Stay	Facilities	Beds	Admissions	Census	Occupancy (percent)	Bassinets	Births	Total	Payroll	Personnel
LURAY—Page County													
⊞ PAGE MEMORIAL HOSPITAL, 200 Memorial Dr., Zip 22835; tel. 703/743-4561; John S. Berry, adm. **A**1a 9 10 **F**1 6 14 15 16 21 23 35 41 44 45 46	23	10	S		34	1271	18	38.3	0	2	4059	1990	120
LYNCHBURG—Independent City													
⊞ LYNCHBURG GENERAL HOSPITAL (Formerly Lynchburg General-Marshall Lodge Hospitals) (Includes Guggenheimer Long Term Care Division), Tate Springs Rd., Zip 24506; tel. 804/528-2000; L. Darrell Powers, pres. (Total facility includes 110 beds in nursing home-type unit) **A**1a 2 3 5 6 9 10 **F**1 3 6 7 8 9 10 11 12 14 16 19 21 23 24 30 35 42 45 50 53	23	10	S	TF	380	10706	298	78.4	0	0	34648	18051	926
				H	270	10541	194	—	0	0	32589	17059	859
⊞ VIRGINIA BAPTIST HOSPITAL, 3300 Rivermont Ave., Zip 24503; tel. 804/522-4000; Thomas C. Jividen, pres. (Total facility includes 36 beds in nursing home-type unit) **A**1a 2 3 5 9 10 **F**1 2 3 6 10 12 14 16 19 20 23 24 25 27 32 34 36 40 41 42 44 45 46 48 51 52 53 54	23	10	S	TF	322	11696	214	67.7	39	2147	33117	16296	932
				H	286	11326	182	—	39	2147	—	—	898
MADISON HEIGHTS—Amherst County													
★ CENTRAL VIRGINIA TRAINING CENTER, Zip 24572; Mailing Address Box 1098, Lynchburg, Zip 24505; tel. 804/528-6326; B. R. Walker PhD, dir. **A**9 10 **F**3 12 14 16 19 23 24 32 34 38 39 42 43 44 46 47	12	62	L		1680	68	1546	92.0	0	0	58364	38895	2510
MANASSAS—Prince William County													
⊞ PRINCE WILLIAM HOSPITAL, 8700 Sudley Rd., Box 2610, Zip 22110; tel. 703/369-8000; Elwyn L. Derring, exec. vice-pres. **A**1a 2 9 10 **F**1 3 6 10 12 14 15 16 23 24 27 30 32 34 35 36 40 42 44 45 46 47 48 49 50 52 53	23	10	S		170	6833	114	67.1	16	1135	24132	12143	608
MARION—Smyth County													
⊞ SMYTH COUNTY COMMUNITY HOSPITAL, Park Blvd., P O Box 880, Zip 24354; tel. 703/783-3141; Deane E. Beamer, exec. dir. **A**1a 9 10 **F**1 3 6 12 14 16 23 35 40 44 45 52 53	23	10	S		165	4442	79	47.9	21	335	10418	4975	354
★ SOUTHWESTERN STATE HOSPITAL, 502 E. Main St., Zip 24354; tel. 703/783-6921; David A. Rosenquist, dir. (Nonreporting) **A**9 10	12	22	L		468	—	—	—	—	—	—	—	—
MARTINSVILLE—Independent City													
⊞ MEMORIAL HOSPITAL OF MARTINSVILLE AND HENRY COUNTY, 320 Hospital Dr., Zip 24112; Mailing Address Box 4788, Zip 24115; tel. 703/666-7200; Clyde L. Britt, exec. dir. **A**1a 2 10 **F**1 2 3 6 10 12 14 15 16 21 23 24 27 34 35 40 45 46 52 53; **S**1755	23	10	S		207	8475	161	77.8	40	910	22494	10976	663
NASSAWADOX—Northampton County													
⊞ NORTHAMPTON-ACCOMACK MEMORIAL HOSPITAL, Zip 23413; tel. 804/442-8000; Roy Layne, adm. (Total facility includes 13 beds in nursing home-type unit) **A**1a 9 10 **F**1 3 6 7 8 9 10 11 12 14 16 19 23 24 34 35 36 40 42 44 45 46 52 53	13	10	S	TF	158	4635	86	58.1	14	556	11856	5948	375
				H	145	4594	85	—	14	556	—	—	369
NEW KENT—New Kent County													
⊞ CUMBERLAND A. HOSPITAL FOR CHILDREN & ADOLESCENTS (Formerly Cumberland Hospital) (Rehabilitation and Behavioral), Rte. 637, P O Box 150, Zip 23124; tel. 804/737-7713; Stephen A. Rosenberg, adm. **A**1a 9 10 **F**15 16 19 23 24 29 32 33 42 44; **S**0395	33	59	L		72	130	41	56.9	0	0	—	—	195
NEWPORT NEWS—Independent City													
⊞ CHARTER COLONIAL INSTITUTE FOR CHILD AND ADOLESCENT PSYCHIATRY, 17579 Warwick Blvd., Zip 23603; tel. 804/887-2611; J. Shawn O'Connor, adm. **A**1b 9 **F**24 29 30 32 33 42 43; **S**0695	33	22	L		60	313	54	90.0	0	0	6943	1713	115
⊞ MARY IMMACULATE HOSPITAL, 800 Denbigh Blvd., Zip 23602; tel. 804/872-0100; Michael B. Cronin, chief exec. off. **A**1a 9 10 **F**1 3 5 6 10 12 14 15 16 20 21 23 24 26 30 33 34 35 36 40 41 44 45 46 47 50 53; **S**5085	23	10	S		110	4956	70	73.7	25	1206	15801	6478	425
MCDONALD ARMY COMMUNITY HOSPITAL, See Fort Eustis													
⊞ NEWPORT NEWS GENERAL HOSPITAL, 5100 Marshall Ave., Zip 23607; Mailing Address P O Box 5769, Zip 23605; tel. 804/247-7200; Frederick D. Hobby, adm. **A**1a 9 10 **F**1 3 6 10 12 14 15 16 23 34 35 37 41 45 46 52	23	10	S		94	2432	48	51.1	0	0	8717	2987	257
⊞ RIVERSIDE HOSPITAL (Includes Riverside Hospital Mental Health Center), 500 J Clyde Morris Blvd., Zip 23601; tel. 804/599-2000; Nelson L. St. Clair Jr., pres. **A**1a 2 3 5 6 9 10 **F**1 2 3 4 5 6 7 8 9 10 11 12 14 15 16 17 20 21 23 24 26 27 28 29 30 31 32 33 34 35 36 37 40 41 42 44 45 46 47 48 49 50 52 53 54; **S**4810	23	10	S		576	19411	413	66.1	43	2635	75823	30342	1450
NORFOLK—Independent City													
⊞ CHILDREN'S HOSPITAL OF THE KING'S DAUGHTERS, 800 W. Olney Rd., Zip 23507; tel. 804/628-7000; Lorraine Zippiroli, pres. **A**1a 3 5 9 **F**1 3 6 12 14 15 16 23 24 33 34 41 42 43 44 45 46 47 51	23	50	S		128	5407	100	78.1	0	0	32167	13967	721
☐ COMMUNITY MENTAL HEALTH CENTER AND PSYCHIATRIC INSTITUTE, 721 Fairfax Ave., Box 1980, Zip 23501; tel. 804/446-5000; Melvin N. Bass, exec. dir. (Nonreporting) **A**1b 3 5 9	23	22	L		80	—	—	—	—	—	—	—	—
⊞ DEPAUL HOSPITAL, 150 Kingsley Lane, Zip 23505; tel. 804/489-5000; Sr. Mary Carroll Eby, adm. (Total facility includes 12 beds in nursing home-type unit) **A**1a 2 3 5 6 9 10 **F**1 2 3 5 6 7 8 9 10 11 12 14 15 16 19 23 24 26 27 30 31 32 33 34 35 36 40 41 42 43 44 45 46 47 49 52 53 54; **S**1885	21	10	S	TF	369	14737	267	73.2	32	2986	53722	27143	1387
				H	357	14627	261	—	32	2986	53494	26945	1369
★ LAKE TAYLOR CITY HOSPITAL, 1309 Kempsville Rd., Zip 23502; tel. 804/461-5001; George P. Phillips, adm. (Nonreporting) **A**10; **S**4810	14	10	L		333	—	—	—	—	—	—	—	—
⊞ LEIGH MEMORIAL HOSPITAL, 830 Kempsville Rd., Zip 23502; tel. 804/466-6000; Richard A. Hanson, adm. **A**1a 3 5 9 10 **F**1 2 3 6 10 12 14 15 16 23 24 30 35 45 46 47 52 53; **S**2565	23	10	S		250	8905	169	67.6	0	0	32628	14646	756
⊞ NORFOLK COMMUNITY HOSPITAL, 2539 Corprew Ave., Zip 23504; tel. 804/628-1400; Phillip D. Brooks, adm. (Total facility includes 13 beds in nursing home-type unit) **A**1a 9 10 **F**1 3 6 12 14 15 16 17 19 23 34 35 36 37 40 42 44 45 46 47	23	10	S	TF	126	3504	76	59.4	26	360	13747	6565	388
				H	113	3405	71	—	26	360	13575	6495	—
⊞ NORFOLK GENERAL HOSPITAL, 600 Gresham Dr., Zip 23507; tel. 804/628-3000; Edward L. Berdick, adm. **A**1a 2 3 5 6 9 10 **F**1 2 3 4 5 6 7 8 9 10 11 12 13 14 15 16 17 20 21 22 23 24 25 27 30 34 35 36 37 39 40 41 42 45 46 47 53 54; **S**2565	23	10	S		644	23315	466	72.4	62	4238	108066	47276	2351
⊞ NORFOLK PSYCHIATRIC CENTER (Formerly Virginia Center for Psychiatry), 100 Kingsley Lane, Zip 23505; tel. 804/489-1072; Dorothy Z. Horowitz, adm. (Nonreporting) **A**1b 10; **S**0295	33	22	S		75	—	—	—	—	—	—	—	—
RHODES DENTAL HOSPITAL (Dental), 501 E. Brambleton Ave., Box 1282, Zip 23501; tel. 804/622-8734; L. Cecil Rhodes DDS, adm. (Nonreporting)	33	49	S		6	—	—	—	—	—	—	—	—
TIDEWATER PSYCHIATRIC INSTITUTE-NORFOLK, 860 Kempsville Rd., Zip 23502; tel. 804/461-4565; John D. Vick, adm. (Nonreporting) **A**9 10; **S**0825	33	22	S		65	—	—	—	—	—	—	—	—
VIRGINIA CENTER FOR PSYCHIATRY, See Norfolk Psychiatric Center													
NORTON—Independent City													
☐ NORTON COMMUNITY HOSPITAL, 100 15th St., Zip 24273; tel. 703/679-1221; David Bevins, adm. **A**1a 9 10 **F**1 2 6 12 14 15 16 21 23 34 35 41 47 52 53; **S**8985	23	10	S		129	4879	67	51.9	0	0	12958	4678	232
⊞ ST. MARY'S HOSPITAL, Third St. N.E., Zip 24273; tel. 703/679-1151; Robert J. Spera, adm. (Total facility includes 44 beds in nursing home-type unit) **A**1a 9 10 **F**1 3 6 16 19 23 27 28 29 32 33 34 35 36 40 41 45 46 47 48 49 52	23	10	S	TF	132	3136	86	65.2	12	451	8293	3674	289
				H	88	3081	43	—	12	451	7949	3374	261

Hospital, Address, Telephone, Administrator, Approval and Facility Codes, Multihospital System Code	Classification Codes: Control	Classification Codes: Service	Classification Codes: Stay	Facilities	Inpatient Data: Beds	Inpatient Data: Admissions	Inpatient Data: Census	Inpatient Data: Occupancy (percent)	Newborn Data: Bassinets	Newborn Data: Births	Expense (thousands of dollars): Total	Expense (thousands of dollars): Payroll	Personnel
★ American Hospital Association (AHA) membership □ Joint Commission on Accreditation of Hospitals (JCAH) accreditation + American Osteopathic Hospital Association (AOHA) membership ○ American Osteopathic Association (AOA) accreditation Δ Commission on Accreditation of Rehabilitation Facilities (CARF) accreditation Control codes 61, 63, 64, 71, 72 and 73 indicate hospitals listed by AOHA, but not registered by AHA. For definition of numerical codes, see page A2													
PEARISBURG—Giles County													
★□ GILES MEMORIAL HOSPITAL, 235 S. Buchanan St., Zip 24134; tel. 703/921-6000; David E. Deering, adm. (Nonreporting) **A**1a 9 10; **S**0070	23	10	S		52	—	—	—	—	—	—	—	—
PENNINGTON GAP—Lee County													
□ LEE COUNTY COMMUNITY HOSPITAL, W. Morgan Ave., P O Box 70, Zip 24277; tel. 703/546-1440; Ken Ragland, adm. (Nonreporting) **A**1a 9 10; **S**8985	23	10	S		80	—	—	—	—	—	—	—	—
PETERSBURG—Dinwiddie County													
CENTRAL STATE HOSPITAL, Box 4030, Zip 23803; tel. 804/861-7000 (Nonreporting) **A**9	12	22	L		670	—	—	—	—	—	—	—	—
PETERSBURG GENERAL HOSPITAL, See Southside Regional Medical Center													
★□ POPLAR SPRINGS HOSPITAL, 350 Wagner Rd., Zip 23805; tel. 804/733-6874; James L. Legge, adm. **A**1b 9 10 **F**24 29 30 32 33 42 43 48; **S**1755	33	22	S		100	1109	79	79.0	0	0	7978	2969	155
★□ SOUTHSIDE REGIONAL MEDICAL CENTER (Formerly Petersburg General Hospital), 801 S. Adams St., Zip 23803; tel. 804/862-5000; Kirby H. Smith Jr., exec. dir. **A**1a 6 9 10 **F**1 3 6 7 9 10 11 12 14 15 16 20 23 24 26 27 30 32 33 34 35 36 37 40 41 44 45 46 47 52 53	16	10	S		325	13454	249	68.0	30	1329	39533	18311	1121
PORTSMOUTH—Independent City													
★□ MARYVIEW HOSPITAL, 3636 High St., Zip 23707; tel. 804/398-2200; J. Bland Burkhardt Jr., chief exec. off. **A**1a 2 3 5 9 10 **F**1 2 3 6 7 9 10 11 12 14 15 16 20 21 23 24 26 27 29 30 32 33 34 35 36 40 41 42 44 45 46 47 52 53; **S**5085	21	10	S		288	10043	204	70.8	20	550	38618	18381	842
★□ NAVAL HOSPITAL, Zip 23708; tel. 804/398-5111; Capt. L. Carey Hodges MC USN, CO (Nonreporting) **A**1a 2 3 5	43	10	S		574	—	—	—	—	—	—	—	—
★□ Δ PORTSMOUTH GENERAL HOSPITAL, 850 Crawford Pkwy., Zip 23704; tel. 804/398-4000; J. B. Frith, adm. **A**1a 2 3 5 7 9 10 **F**1 2 3 6 10 12 13 14 15 16 20 23 24 25 26 32 34 35 36 37 40 41 44 45 46 47 53; **S**1755	23	10	S		173	6955	129	74.6	34	1595	25433	12539	679
★□ PORTSMOUTH PSYCHIATRIC CENTER (Formerly Virginia Center for Psychiatry), 301 Fort Lane, Zip 23704; tel. 804/393-0061; Jim Legge, adm. (Nonreporting) **A**1b 10; **S**0295	33	22	L		186	—	—	—	—	—	—	—	—
VIRGINIA CENTER FOR PSYCHIATRY, See Portsmouth Psychiatric Center													
PULASKI—Pulaski County													
★□ PULASKI COMMUNITY HOSPITAL, 2400 Lee Hwy., Box 759, Zip 24301; tel. 703/980-6822; Edgar L. Belcher, adm. **A**1a 9 10 **F**1 3 6 10 12 14 15 16 20 23 32 34 35 40 41 44 46 47 52 53; **S**1755	33	10	S		153	4375	91	59.5	6	235	—	—	308
RADFORD—Independent City													
★□ RADFORD COMMUNITY HOSPITAL, Eighth & Randolph Sts., Box 3527, Zip 24143; tel. 703/731-2000; Lester L. Lamb, pres. **A**1a 9 10 **F**1 3 6 9 10 12 14 15 16 20 23 35 36 37 40 44 45 46 47 52 53	23	10	S		175	5439	81	46.3	27	276	16231	7175	427
□ ST. ALBANS PSYCHIATRIC HOSPITAL, Rte. 11, Lee Hwy., Box 3608, Zip 24143; tel. 703/639-2481; Robert L. Terrell Jr., adm. **A**1a 9 10 **F**15 23 24 28 29 30 32 33 42 44 45 46 49	23	22	S		162	1744	129	79.6	0	0	12402	7383	418
RESTON—Arlington County													
★□ RESTON HOSPITAL CENTER (Formerly Circle Terrace Hospital, Alexandria), 1850 Town Center Pkwy., Zip 22090; tel. 703/689-9000; James L. Perkins, adm. (Nonreporting) **A**1a 9 10; **S**1755	33	10	S		105	—	—	—	—	—	—	—	—
RICHLANDS—Tazewell County													
★□ HUMANA HOSPITAL -CLINCH VALLEY, 2949 W. Front St., Zip 24641; tel. 703/963-0811; W. A. Gillespie, exec. dir. **A**1a 9 10 **F**1 3 6 10 12 14 15 16 23 26 34 35 36 40 44 45 46 49 52 53; **S**1235	33	10	S		135	7823	120	88.9	14	529	—	—	421
MATTIE WILLIAMS HOSPITAL, 200 Washington Square, Zip 24641; tel. 703/964-6711; James L. Davis, adm. (Nonreporting) **A**9 10	33	10	S		76	—	—	—	—	—	—	—	—
RICHMOND—Independent City													
★□ CHARTER WESTBROOK HOSPITAL, 1500 Westbrook Ave., Box 9127, Zip 23227; tel. 804/266-9671; Richard Woodard, adm. (Nonreporting) **A**1b 9 10; **S**0695	33	22	L		175	—	—	—	—	—	—	—	—
★□ CHILDREN'S HOSPITAL, 2924 Brook Rd., Zip 23220; tel. 804/321-7474; Ralph Ownby MD, med. dir. & chief oper. off. **A**1a 3 5 9 **F**1 6 15 23 24 26 33 34 38 42 44 45 46 47 52	23	57	S		36	654	13	36.1	0	0	6458	2647	170
★□ CHIPPENHAM HOSPITAL, 7101 Jahnke Rd., Zip 23225; tel. 804/320-3911; Robert L. Hancock, adm. **A**1a 3 5 9 10 **F**1 2 3 4 6 10 12 14 15 16 23 24 27 30 33 34 35 36 37 40 41 42 44 46 47 52 53 54; **S**1755	33	10	S		470	15043	312	66.4	35	2004	—	—	1134
★□ HENRICO DOCTOR'S HOSPITAL, 1602 Skipwith Rd., Zip 23229; tel. 804/289-4500; J. Stephen Lindsey, exec. dir. **A**1a 9 10 **F**1 2 3 4 6 10 12 14 15 16 23 26 34 35 36 37 40 41 44 46 47 53 54; **S**1755	33	10	S		312	13260	234	75.0	46	3260	—	—	863
★□ HUMANA HOSPITAL -ST. LUKES, 7700 Parham Rd., Zip 23229; tel. 804/747-5600; Nancy R. Hofheimer, exec. dir. **A**1a 9 10 **F**1 2 3 6 12 14 15 16 20 23 24 26 34 35 45 46 47 53 54; **S**1235	33	10	S		200	5133	97	48.5	0	0	22165	7256	351
★□ HUNTER HOLMES MCGUIRE VETERANS ADMINISTRATION MEDICAL CENTER, 1201 Broad Rock Blvd., Zip 23249; tel. 804/230-0001; James W. Holsinger Jr. MD, dir. (Total facility includes 120 beds in nursing home-type unit) **A**1a 3 5 8 **F**1 2 3 4 6 10 12 13 14 15 16 17 19 20 23 24 25 26 27 28 30 32 33 34 35 41 42 44 46 47 48 49 50 53 54	45	10	S	TF	814	16771	639	78.5	0	0	97656	—	2219
				H	694	16671	527	—	0	0	—	—	—
★□ JOHNSTON-WILLIS HOSPITAL, 1401 Johnston-Willis Dr., Zip 23235; tel. 804/320-2900; Wickliffe S. Lyne, adm. **A**1a 9 10 **F**1 2 3 6 7 8 9 10 11 12 14 15 16 17 21 23 24 25 26 34 35 43 44 46 53; **S**1755	33	10	S		232	6960	136	58.6	0	0	—	—	651
★□ MEDICAL COLLEGE OF VIRGINIA HOSPITALS, VIRGINIA COMMONWEALTH UNIVERSITY, 401 N. 12th St., Zip 23298; tel. 804/786-9000; Carl R. Fischer, exec. dir. **A**1a 2 3 5 8 9 10 **F**1 2 3 4 5 6 7 8 9 10 11 12 13 14 15 16 17 20 21 22 23 24 26 27 28 32 33 34 35 36 37 38 39 40 41 42 44 45 46 47 48 49 51 52 53 54	12	10	S		881	28910	709	80.5	50	4354	195776	78913	4018
★□ METROPOLITAN HOSPITAL (Formerly Richmond Metropolitan Hospital), 701 W. Grace St., Zip 23220; tel. 804/775-4100; Thomas G. Honaker III, chief exec. off. (Nonreporting) **A**1a 9 10; **S**0985	23	10	S		180	—	—	—	—	—	—	—	—
□ PSYCHIATRIC INSTITUTE OF RICHMOND, 3001 Fifth Ave., Zip 23222; tel. 804/329-3400; H. James Mathay, adm. **A**1b 9 **F**15 19 24 30 32 42 48; **S**0825	33	52	L		84	329	53	63.1	0	0	—	—	128
□ RETREAT HOSPITAL, 2621 Grove Ave., Zip 23220; tel. 804/254-5100; H. J. Van Brackle, adm. (Nonreporting) **A**1a 9 10	23	10	S		230	—	—	—	—	—	—	—	—
★□ RICHMOND COMMUNITY HOSPITAL, 1500 N. 28th St., Zip 23223; Mailing Address Box 27184, Zip 23261; tel. 804/225-1700; Phyllis A. Wingate, exec. dir. **A**1a 9 10 **F**1 3 6 12 14 15 16 20 23 24 27 33 34 37 42 46 47 53; **S**1755	23	10	S		102	2727	63	61.8	0	0	9913	4067	228
★□ RICHMOND EYE AND EAR HOSPITAL, 1001 E. Marshall St., Zip 23219; tel. 804/775-4500; Robert G. Notarianni, adm. **A**1a 9 10 **F**1 15 43 45 46; **S**1755	23	45	S		60	1539	8	13.3	0	0	5458	2008	115
★□ RICHMOND MEMORIAL HOSPITAL, 1300 Westwood Ave., Zip 23227; Mailing Address Box 26783, Zip 23261; tel. 804/254-6000; Samuel F. Lillard, pres. **A**1a 2 3 5 6 9 10 **F**1 3 6 10 12 14 15 16 20 24 27 34 35 36 40 45 46 47 50 52 53 54	23	10	S		351	11679	253	72.1	25	587	—	—	1465

Hospital, Address, Telephone, Administrator, Approval and Facility Codes, Multihospital System Code	Classification Codes				Inpatient Data				Newborn Data		Expense (thousands of dollars)		
★ American Hospital Association (AHA) membership □ Joint Commission on Accreditation of Hospitals (JCAH) accreditation + American Osteopathic Hospital Association (AOHA) membership ○ American Osteopathic Association (AOA) accreditation Δ Commission on Accreditation of Rehabilitation Facilities (CARF) accreditation Control codes 61, 63, 64, 71, 72 and 73 indicate hospitals listed by AOHA, but not registered by AHA. For definition of numerical codes, see page A2	Control	Service	Stay	Facilities	Beds	Admissions	Census	Occupancy (percent)	Bassinets	Births	Total	Payroll	Personnel
RICHMOND METROPOLITAN HOSPITAL, See Metropolitan Hospital													
★□ ST. JOHN'S HOSPITAL, Rte. 2, Box 389, Zip 23233; tel. 804/784-3501; Mark Hierholzer, exec. vice-pres. (Nonreporting) **A**1b 9; **S**5085	23	82	S		70	—	—	—	—	—	—	—	—
★□ ST. MARY'S HOSPITAL, 5801 Bremo Rd., Zip 23226; tel. 804/285-2011; Richard D. O'Hallaron, exec. vice-pres. **A**1a 2 9 10 **F**1 2 3 6 7 8 9 10 11 12 14 15 16 21 23 24 27 35 36 40 41 42 45 46 52 53 54; **S**5085	21	10	S		369	13981	250	67.8	42	1764	52556	23287	1019
★□ STUART CIRCLE HOSPITAL, 413-21 Stuart Circle, Zip 23220; tel. 804/358-7051; Donald S. Biskin, exec. dir. (Nonreporting) **A**1a 9 10; **S**0695	33	10	S		153	—	—	—	—	—	—	—	—
VIRGINIA STATE PENITENTIARY HOSPITAL, 500 Spring St., Zip 23219; Mailing Address P O Box 27264, Zip 23261; tel. 804/786-2101; L. Waggoner, adm. **F**1 15 23 24 27 28 29 30 32 33 34 35 42	12	11	S		40	836	11	27.5	0	0	—	—	46
ROANOKE—Independent City													
★□ COMMUNITY HOSPITAL OF ROANOKE VALLEY, 101 Elm Ave. S.E., Box 12946, Zip 24029; tel. 703/985-8000; William R. Reid, pres. **A**1a 2 3 5 9 10 **F**1 2 3 5 6 9 10 11 12 14 15 16 20 23 24 26 32 33 34 35 36 37 38 40 41 44 45 46 47 52 53	23	10	S		310	10709	199	64.2	27	1152	38130	19402	1050
★□ GILL MEMORIAL EYE, EAR, NOSE AND THROAT HOSPITAL, 711 S. Jefferson St., Zip 24011; Mailing Address P O Box 1560, Zip 24007; tel. 703/343-3368; Donald J. Love, vice-pres. **A**1a 9 10 **F**1 15 34 44; **S**0070	33	45	S		12	432	2	8.3	0	0	1859	853	47
★□ ROANOKE MEMORIAL HOSPITALS (Includes Roanoke Memorial Rehabilitation Center, P O Box 13367, Zip 24033), Belleview at Jefferson St., Box 13367, Zip 24033; tel. 703/981-7000; Thomas L. Robertson, pres. **A**1a 2 3 5 6 9 10 **F**1 2 3 4 5 6 7 8 9 10 11 12 14 15 16 20 21 23 24 25 26 27 28 30 31 32 33 34 35 36 37 38 40 41 42 44 46 47 49 51 52 53 54; **S**0070	23	10	S		683	21035	461	67.2	16	1702	88890	38987	2188
ROANOKE MEMORIAL REHABILITATION CENTER, See Roanoke Memorial Hospitals													
ROCKY MOUNT—Franklin County													
★□ FRANKLIN MEMORIAL HOSPITAL, 124 Floyd Ave. S.W., Zip 24151; tel. 703/483-5277; William C. Garrett Jr., adm. **A**1a 9 10 **F**1 3 6 14 16 23 34 35 40 41 45 46 47; **S**0070	23	10	S		62	1769	22	35.5	11	171	4395	2327	144
SALEM—Roanoke County													
★□ LEWIS-GALE HOSPITAL, 1900 Electric Rd., Zip 24153; tel. 703/989-4261; Karl N. Miller, adm. **A**1a 2 9 10 **F**1 2 3 5 6 9 10 11 12 14 15 16 17 19 23 24 25 26 34 35 36 40 42 44 46 48 52 53 54; **S**1755	33	10	S		380	12869	267	72.8	25	962	—	—	981
MOUNT REGIS CENTER, 405 Kimball Ave., Zip 24153; tel. 703/389-4761; John Burns, exec. dir. (Nonreporting)	33	82	S		25	—	—	—	—	—	—	—	—
★□ ROANOKE VALLEY PSYCHIATRIC CENTER, 1902 Braeburn Dr., Zip 24153; tel. 703/772-2800; William W. Semones, adm. **A**1b 10 **F**24 30 32 33 42 44; **S**1755	33	22	S		145	1628	106	73.1	0	0	11006	3935	226
★□ VETERANS ADMINISTRATION MEDICAL CENTER, 1970 Boulevard, Zip 24153; tel. 703/982-2463; H. E. Davis, dir. (Total facility includes 100 beds in nursing home-type unit) **A**1a 2 3 5 8 **F**1 2 3 6 12 14 15 16 19 20 21 23 24 26 27 28 29 30 31 32 33 34 35 41 42 44 45 46 47 48 49 50 53	45	10	L	TF	827	7720	690	83.4	0	0	61657	37187	1567
				H	727	7572	595	—	0	0	—	—	1525
SOUTH BOSTON—Independent City													
★□ HALIFAX-SOUTH BOSTON COMMUNITY HOSPITAL, 2204 Wilborn Ave., Zip 24592; tel. 804/575-7961 **A**1a 9 10 **F**1 3 6 10 11 12 14 15 16 23 24 35 36 40 41 44 45 46 47 52 53; **S**1755	23	10	S		192	5844	106	55.2	20	627	13576	6258	408
SOUTH HILL—Mecklenburg County													
★□ COMMUNITY MEMORIAL HOSPITAL, 125 Buena Vista Circle, Box 90, Zip 23970; tel. 804/447-3151; John M. Faulkner, pres. (Total facility includes 140 beds in nursing home-type unit) **A**1a 9 **F**1 3 6 10 11 14 15 16 19 23 34 35 40 41 42 44 45 50 53	23	10	S	TF	260	3486	198	76.2	16	160	10668	5017	416
				H	120	3365	63	—	16	160	8161	3931	295
STAUNTON—Independent City													
★□ DE JARNETTE CENTER, Richmond Rd., Box 2309, Zip 24401; tel. 703/332-8800; Andrea C. Newsome, dir. **A**1b 3 5 9 10 **F**30 32 33 42 44 46 47	12	52	L		60	129	48	80.0	0	0	3405	2255	139
★□ KING'S DAUGHTERS' HOSPITAL, 1410 N. Augusta St., Box 3000, Zip 24401; tel. 703/887-2000; Paul Flanagan, adm. **A**1a 9 10 **F**1 3 6 7 10 11 12 14 15 16 23 35 36 40 41 44 45 46 47 52 53	23	10	S		198	6679	126	63.6	23	472	16943	9411	533
★□ WESTERN STATE HOSPITAL, Box 2500, Zip 24401; tel. 703/885-9455; L. F. Harding, dir. (Total facility includes 254 beds in nursing home-type unit) **A**1b 9 10 **F**15 19 23 24 33 42 44 46 47 48 50	12	22	L	TF	762	1129	688	90.1	0	0	33992	20028	1243
				H	508	1127	455	—	0	0	—	—	—
STUART—Patrick County													
★□ R. J. REYNOLDS-PATRICK COUNTY MEMORIAL HOSPITAL, Rte. 2, Box 11, Zip 24171; tel. 703/694-3151; Felix Fraraccio, adm. **A**1a 9 10 **F**1 3 6 14 15 16 23 26 35 36 44 45 52	23	10	S		77	1697	22	28.6	10	118	4192	2154	135
SUFFOLK—Independent City													
★□ LOUISE OBICI MEMORIAL HOSPITAL, 1900 N. Main St., P O Box 1100, Zip 23434; tel. 804/934-4000; Robert R. Everett, pres. **A**1a 2 6 9 10 **F**1 3 6 10 12 14 15 16 23 30 35 36 40 44 45 46 52	23	10	S		202	7934	137	67.8	20	752	23125	12046	544
TAPPAHANNOCK—Essex County													
★□ TIDEWATER MEMORIAL HOSPITAL, Rte. 2, Box 256, Zip 22560; tel. 804/443-3311; Louise B. Osborn, pres. (Total facility includes 17 beds in nursing home-type unit) **A**1a 9 10 **F**1 3 6 10 14 15 16 19 23 35 41 45 46 47 48 49 52	23	10	S	TF	100	1762	38	38.0	0	6	6517	2953	188
				H	83	1652	26	—	0	6	—	—	175
TAZEWELL—Tazewell County													
★□ TAZEWELL COMMUNITY HOSPITAL, Box 607, Zip 24651; tel. 703/988-2506; Robert E. Huch, adm. **A**1a 10 **F**1 3 6 14 15 16 23 35 40 41 45 46 47 53; **S**0070	23	10	S		50	2049	29	58.0	8	68	5106	2396	168
VIRGINIA BEACH—Independent City													
★□ HUMANA HOSPITAL -BAYSIDE, 800 Independence Blvd., Zip 23455; tel. 804/460-8000; Jerry R. Sutphin, exec. dir. **A**1a 9 10 **F**1 3 6 10 11 12 14 15 16 23 26 29 34 35 41 45 46 47 48 49 50 52 53; **S**1235	33	10	S		250	6684	123	49.2	0	0	26171	8399	414
□ TIDEWATER PSYCHIATRIC INSTITUTE, 1701 Will-O-Wisp Dr., Zip 23454; tel. 804/481-1211; Stuart Ashman MD, chief exec. off. (Nonreporting) **A**1b 9 10; **S**0825	33	22	S		61	—	—	—	—	—	—	—	—
★□ VIRGINIA BEACH GENERAL HOSPITAL, 1060 First Colonial Rd., Zip 23454; tel. 804/481-8000; Rita B. Wood, chief oper. off. **A**1a 2 3 5 9 10 **F**2 3 6 7 8 9 10 11 12 14 15 16 23 24 30 34 35 36 41 44 45 46 47 52 53	23	10	S		235	13797	200	85.1	40	3090	44615	20371	1084
WARRENTON—Fauquier County													
★□ FAUQUIER HOSPITAL, 500 Hospital Dr., Zip 22186; tel. 703/347-2550; William H. Green Jr., adm. **A**1a 9 10 **F**1 3 6 10 12 14 15 16 23 26 34 35 36 41 45 46 52 53	23	10	S		121	4720	83	68.6	12	540	14061	5606	362
WAYNESBORO—Independent City													
★□ WAYNESBORO COMMUNITY HOSPITAL, 501 Oak Ave., Zip 22980; tel. 703/942-2273; Roger W. Cooper, chief exec. off. (Nonreporting) **A**1a 9 10	23	10	S		171	—	—	—	—	—	—	—	—
WILLIAMSBURG—Independent City													
★ EASTERN STATE HOSPITAL, Drawer A, Zip 23187; tel. 804/253-5161; David C. Pribble, dir. **A**5 9 10 **F**1 14 15 19 23 24 32 33 38 42 44 48 50	12	22	L		1008	3752	870	86.0	0	0	36679	23528	1456

Hospital, Address, Telephone, Administrator, Approval and Facility Codes, Multihospital System Code	Classification Codes: Control	Service	Stay	Facilities	Inpatient Data: Beds	Admissions	Census	Occupancy (percent)	Newborn Data: Bassinets	Births	Expense (thousands of dollars): Total	Payroll	Personnel
★ American Hospital Association (AHA) membership □ Joint Commission on Accreditation of Hospitals (JCAH) accreditation + American Osteopathic Hospital Association (AOHA) membership ○ American Osteopathic Association (AOA) accreditation Δ Commission on Accreditation of Rehabilitation Facilities (CARF) accreditation Control codes 61, 63, 64, 71, 72 and 73 indicate hospitals listed by AOHA, but not registered by AHA. For definition of numerical codes, see page A2													
★□ WILLIAMSBURG COMMUNITY HOSPITAL, 1238 Mount Vernon Ave., Zip 23185; tel. 804/253-6000; Kenneth H. Axtell, pres. **A**1a 9 10 **F**1 3 6 10 12 15 16 20 23 26 30 32 35 36 40 41 44 45 47 49 53	23	10	S		111	4997	75	67.6	20	710	16858	9105	447
WINCHESTER—Independent City													
★□ WINCHESTER MEDICAL CENTER, S. Stewart St., Box 3340, Zip 22601; tel. 703/662-4121; David W. Goff, pres. **A**1a 2 9 10 **F**1 2 3 4 6 7 8 9 10 11 12 14 16 20 23 24 27 30 33 35 36 40 41 42 45 46 52 53 54	23	10	S		343	15129	253	67.1	36	1507	37571	18543	1075
WISE—Wise County													
★□ WISE APPALACHIAN REGIONAL HOSPITAL, P O Box 3267, Zip 24293; tel. 703/328-2511; Ruby J. Salyers, adm. **A**1a 9 10 **F**1 2 3 6 15 16 23 35 36 37 40 41 45 47 52 53; **S**0145	23	10	S		67	3285	41	61.2	11	219	7400	3093	163
WOODBRIDGE—Prince William County													
★□ POTOMAC HOSPITAL, 2300 Opitz Blvd., Zip 22191; tel. 703/670-1313; William M. Moss, pres. **A**1a 9 10 **F**1 3 6 10 12 14 15 16 20 23 24 27 30 32 33 34 35 36 37 40 41 44 45 46 47 51 52 53	23	10	S		158	7073	104	65.8	11	1030	24697	11387	516
WOODSTOCK—Shenandoah County													
★□ SHENANDOAH COUNTY MEMORIAL HOSPITAL, Rte. 11, Box 508, Zip 22664; tel. 703/459-4021; Edwin E. Hurysz, adm. (Nonreporting) **A**1a 9 10	23	10	S		133	—	—	—	—	—	—	—	—
WYTHEVILLE—Wythe County													
□ WYTHE COUNTY COMMUNITY HOSPITAL, 600 W. Ridge Rd., Zip 24382; tel. 703/228-2181; Scott Adams, adm. **A**1a 9 10 **F**1 3 6 10 14 15 16 23 34 35 40 41 44 45 46 47 53; **S**0070	23	10	S		106	2738	57	53.8	14	213	7822	3499	237
★ WYTHEVILLE HOSPITAL, 2505 E. Main St., Zip 24382; tel. 703/228-3141; David G. Saliba, adm. **A**9 10 **F**1 3 14 16 23 34 35 45 52	23	10	S		54	691	13	24.1	0	0	2089	1098	78

Hospital, Address, Telephone, Administrator, Approval and Facility Codes, Multihospital System Code

★ American Hospital Association (AHA) membership
□ Joint Commission on Accreditation of Hospitals (JCAH) accreditation
+ American Osteopathic Hospital Association (AOHA) membership
○ American Osteopathic Association (AOA) accreditation
Δ Commission on Accreditation of Rehabilitation Facilities (CARF) accreditation
Control codes 61, 63, 64, 71, 72 and 73 indicate hospitals listed by AOHA, but not registered by AHA.
For definition of numerical codes, see page A2

Washington

Hospital, Address, Telephone, Administrator, Approval and Facility Codes, Multihospital System Code	Classification Codes: Control	Service	Stay	Facilities	Inpatient Data: Beds	Admissions	Census	Occupancy (percent)	Newborn Data: Bassinets	Births	Expense (thousands of dollars): Total	Payroll	Personnel
ABERDEEN—Grays Harbor County													
□ GRAYS HARBOR COMMUNITY HOSPITAL, 915 Anderson Dr., Zip 98520; tel. 206/532-8330; Dwight K. Ogburn, pres. & chief exec. off. **A**1a 2 9 10 **F**1 3 5 6 10 12 14 16 21 23 24 26 30 35 36 40 44 45 46 47 53	23	10	S		96	4991	50	52.1	16	784	12094	5411	251
★□ ST. JOSEPH HOSPITAL, 1006 N. H St., Zip 98520; tel. 206/533-0450; Sr. Charlotte Van Dyke, adm. (Total facility includes 34 beds in nursing home-type unit) **A**1a 2 9 10 **F**1 2 5 6 10 12 14 15 16 19 23 26 34 35 44 45 46 47 48 49 53; **S**5275	21	10	S	TF	95	1433	61	64.2	0	0	9935	4127	194
				H	61	1399	27	—	0	0	9644	3854	175
ANACORTES—Skagit County													
★□ ISLAND HOSPITAL, 24th St. & M Ave., Zip 98221; tel. 206/293-3181; C. Philip Sandifer, adm. (Nonreporting) **A**1a 2 9 10	16	10	S		39	—	—	—	—	—	—	—	—
ARLINGTON—Snohomish County													
★ SNOHOMISH COUNTY PUBLIC HOSPITAL DISTRICT THREE, CASCADE VALLEY HOSPITAL, 330 S. Stillaguamish St., Box 370, Zip 98223; tel. 206/435-2133; Joe Hopkins, adm. **A**9 10 **F**1 3 6 12 14 15 16 17 23 34 35 37 40 43 45 50 53	16	10	S		36	1369	14	38.9	5	185	5912	2536	120
AUBURN—King County													
□ AUBURN GENERAL HOSPITAL, 20 Second St. N.E., Zip 98002; tel. 206/833-7711; Michael M. Gherardini, adm. (Nonreporting) **A**1a 2 9 10; **S**9555	33	10	S		111	—	—	—	—	—	—	—	—
BELLEVUE—King County													
★□ OVERLAKE HOSPITAL MEDICAL CENTER, 1035 116th Ave. N.E., Zip 98004; tel. 206/462-5335; Sanderson J. Jeghers, pres. & chief exec. off. **A**1a 2 9 10 **F**1 2 3 5 6 10 12 15 16 23 24 25 26 27 30 32 33 34 35 36 37 40 42 43 44 45 46 52 53 54	23	10	S		218	12137	160	73.4	40	2335	41216	19915	717
BELLINGHAM—Whatcom County													
★□ ST. JOSEPH HOSPITAL, 2901 Squalicum Pkwy., Zip 98225; tel. 206/734-5400; Sr. Catherine McInnes, adm. **A**1a 2 9 10 **F**1 3 6 10 15 16 23 24 34 35 36 40 41 45 46 52 53 54; **S**5415	23	10	S		126	5570	58	49.6	24	1490	19671	8086	389
★□ ST. LUKE'S GENERAL HOSPITAL, 809 E. Chestnut St., Zip 98225; tel. 206/734-8300; William G. Gordon, exec. vice-pres. & chief exec. off. **A**1a 2 9 10 **F**1 2 3 5 6 10 12 15 16 23 24 25 26 27 30 32 35 42 44 45 46 53; **S**6905	23	10	S		117	3905	54	46.2	0	0	17572	7608	325
BREMERTON—Kitsap County													
★□ HARRISON MEMORIAL HOSPITAL, 2520 Cherry Ave., Zip 98310; tel. 206/377-3911; Robert W. Bradley, pres. **A**1a 2 9 10 **F**1 3 5 6 9 10 12 15 16 20 23 24 27 29 30 33 35 36 37 40 41 43 44 45 46 47 52 53 54	23	10	S		222	12203	151	68.0	28	1617	31444	14389	622
★□ NAVAL HOSPITAL, Boone Rd., Zip 98312; tel. 206/479-6600; Capt. J. W. Winebright MC USN, CO **A**1a 2 3 5 **F**1 3 6 10 11 12 14 16 23 26 27 28 30 32 33 34 35 36 37 40 41 43 45 46 47 48 49 52	43	10	S		155	4823	78	60.9	15	757	36959	20968	830
BREWSTER—Okanogan County													
★ OKANOGAN-DOUGLAS COUNTY HOSPITAL, Box 577, Zip 98812; tel. 509/689-2517; Howard M. Gamble, adm. **A**10 **F**1 3 6 16 23 34 36 40 43 47	16	10	S		48	1063	13	27.1	6	111	2729	1359	78
CENTRALIA—Lewis County													
□ CENTRALIA GENERAL HOSPITAL, 1820 Cooks Hill Rd., Zip 98531; tel. 206/736-2803; John R. Hanson, mng. dir. (Nonreporting) **A**1a 9 10; **S**9555	33	10	S		57	—	—	—	—	—	—	—	—
CHEHALIS—Lewis County													
★□ ST. HELEN HOSPITAL, 500 S.E. Washington Ave., P O Box 1507, Zip 98532; tel. 206/748-4444; John W. Holtermann, adm. (Total facility includes 41 beds in nursing home-type unit) **A**1a 9 10 **F**1 3 6 10 14 15 16 19 21 23 24 25 26 30 35 36 40 41 44 45 46 50 53; **S**5275	21	10	S	TF	104	2957	62	59.6	7	403	10488	4839	228
				H	63	2762	31	—	7	403	10214	4597	209
CHELAN—Chelan County													
★ LAKE CHELAN COMMUNITY HOSPITAL, 503 E. Highland Ave., Box 908, Zip 98816; tel. 509/682-2531; Edmon W. Myers, adm. (Nonreporting) **A**9 10	16	10	S		28	—	—	—	—	—	—	—	—
CHEWELAH—Stevens County													
★□ ST. JOSEPH'S HOSPITAL, 500 E. Webster Ave., P O Box 197, Zip 99109; tel. 509/935-8211; Eddie L. Grady, pres. **A**1a 9 10 **F**1 6 15 16 23 34 35 36 40 43 45 46 47 50 52; **S**5175	21	10	S		25	1223	10	40.0	6	49	2523	1088	66
CLARKSTON—Asotin County													
□ TRI-STATE MEMORIAL HOSPITAL, 1221 Highland Ave., P O Box 189, Zip 99403; tel. 509/758-5511; Dave Farlowe, adm. **A**1a 9 10 **F**1 3 15 16 23 30 34 35 43 44 45 46 50	23	10	S		58	1406	18	31.0	0	0	5110	2191	120
COLFAX—Whitman County													
★□ WHITMAN COMMUNITY HOSPITAL, Almota Rd., Box 32, Zip 99111; tel. 509/397-3435; W. Jeff Waller, adm. (Nonreporting) **A**1a 9 10	23	10	S		44	—	—	—	—	—	—	—	—
COLVILLE—Stevens County													
★□ MOUNT CARMEL HOSPITAL, 982 E. Columbia St., Box 351, Zip 99114; tel. 509/684-2561; Gloria Cooper, pres. **A**1a 9 10 **F**1 3 6 14 15 16 23 24 33 34 35 36 37 40 43 45 46 47 50 52; **S**5175	21	10	S		48	1224	12	25.0	9	225	3176	1687	89
COUPEVILLE—Island County													
★□ WHIDBEY GENERAL HOSPITAL, Main St., Box 400, Zip 98239; tel. 206/678-5151; Robert Zylstra, adm. **A**1a 2 9 10 **F**1 3 5 6 10 12 14 15 16 21 23 30 35 36 37 40 41 45 46 52 53	16	10	S		51	1815	24	47.1	6	205	7847	4077	178
DAVENPORT—Lincoln County													
★ LINCOLN COUNTY HOSPITAL DISTRICT THREE, 10 Nichols St., Box 68, Zip 99122; tel. 509/725-7101; Thomas J. Martin, adm. (Total facility includes 69 beds in nursing home-type unit) **A**9 10 **F**1 6 15 16 19 23 35 36 37 42 43 45 46	16	10	S	TF	93	651	78	83.9	6	56	2547	907	90
				H	24	602	10	—	6	56	1460	446	41
DAYTON—Columbia County													
★ DAYTON GENERAL HOSPITAL, 1012 S. Third St., Zip 99328; tel. 509/382-2531; Garvin Olson, adm. **A**9 10 **F**1 6 16 23 30 35 41 45 46	16	10	S		28	265	10	35.7	6	29	1563	744	45
EDMONDS—Snohomish County													
★□ STEVENS MEMORIAL HOSPITAL, 21600 76th Ave. W., Zip 98020; tel. 206/774-0555; Jon D. Smiley, adm. **A**1a 2 9 10 **F**1 3 5 6 10 12 14 15 16 17 21 23 24 25 27 30 34 35 36 37 40 45 46 53	16	10	S		183	9422	127	69.4	16	1545	32666	15680	653
ELLENSBURG—Kittitas County													
★□ KITTITAS VALLEY COMMUNITY HOSPITAL, 603 S. Chestnut St., Zip 98926; tel. 509/962-9841; J. D. Ingram, adm. **A**1a 9 10 **F**1 3 6 14 16 23 34 35 36 40 44 45 46 47	16	10	S		41	1395	13	31.7	7	260	4039	2050	106

Hospital, Address, Telephone, Administrator, Approval and Facility Codes, Multihospital System Code	Classification Codes				Inpatient Data				Newborn Data		Expense (thousands of dollars)		
★ American Hospital Association (AHA) membership □ Joint Commission on Accreditation of Hospitals (JCAH) accreditation + American Osteopathic Hospital Association (AOHA) membership ○ American Osteopathic Association (AOA) accreditation Δ Commission on Accreditation of Rehabilitation Facilities (CARF) accreditation Control codes 61, 63, 64, 71, 72 and 73 indicate hospitals listed by AOHA, but not registered by AHA. For definition of numerical codes, see page A2	Control	Service	Stay	Facilities	Beds	Admissions	Census	Occupancy (percent)	Bassinets	Births	Total	Payroll	Personnel
ENUMCLAW—King County													
COMMUNITY MEMORIAL HOSPITAL, 2125 C St., P O Box 216, Zip 98022; tel. 206/825-2505; Dennis A. Popp, adm. **A**9 10 **F**1 3 6 10 12 14 16 23 24 35 36 40 45 53	23	10	S		38	1570	15	39.5	8	313	4746	2136	79
EPHRATA—Grant County													
★ COLUMBIA BASIN HOSPITAL, 200 Southeast Blvd., Zip 98823; tel. 509/754-4631; Merlin Traylor, adm. (Nonreporting) **A**9 10	16	10	S		54	—	—	—	—	—	—	—	—
EVERETT—Snohomish County													
⊞ GENERAL HOSPITAL OF EVERETT, 14th & Colby Ave., P O Box 1147, Zip 98206; tel. 206/258-6300; Mark D. Judy, adm. **A**1a 2 9 10 **F**1 3 4 5 6 10 12 15 16 17 20 23 24 26 27 34 35 36 37 40 44 45 46 53 54	23	10	S		229	10466	129	58.9	31	2612	37125	16402	603
⊞ Δ PROVIDENCE HOSPITAL, Pacific & Nassau Sts., Zip 98201; Mailing Address Box 1067, Zip 98206; tel. 206/258-7123; Carl A. Munding, adm. **A**1a 2 7 9 10 **F**1 3 7 8 9 10 11 12 14 15 16 17 20 23 24 25 26 30 34 35 42 43 44 45 46 47 52 53 54; **S**5275	23	10	S		188	7690	122	64.9	0	0	39528	17475	709
FAIRCHILD AIR FORCE BASE—Spokane County													
□ U. S. AIR FORCE HOSPITAL, Zip 99011; tel. 509/247-5216; Col. Thomas C. Cock MC USAF, cmdr.; Col. Theodore W. Oatley MSC USAF, adm. **A**1a **F**3 6 12 15 16 23 28 30 33 34 35 37 40 46 47	41	10	S		45	3302	33	67.3	11	447	—	—	381
FORKS—Clallam County													
★ FORKS COMMUNITY HOSPITAL, Bogachiel Way, Rte. 3, Box 3575, Zip 98331; tel. 206/374-6271; Vernon D. McIvor, adm. (Nonreporting) **A**9 10	16	10	S		23	—	—	—	—	—	—	—	—
FORT STEILACOOM—Pierce County													
□ WESTERN STATE HOSPITAL, Zip 98494; tel. 206/756-2525; R. Darrell Hamilton MD, supt. (Nonreporting) **A**1b 9 10	12	22	L		1094	—	—	—	—	—	—	—	—
GOLDENDALE—Klickitat County													
⊞ KLICKITAT VALLEY HOSPITAL, Roosevelt & A Sts., Box 5, Zip 98620; tel. 509/773-4022; Dennis Blaine, adm. **A**1a 9 10 **F**1 2 6 14 15 16 23 27 30 33 34 35 36 37 40 49 52	16	10	S		38	638	6	15.8	8	78	1900	1000	49
GRAND COULEE—Grant County													
COULEE COMMUNITY HOSPITAL, 411 Fortuyn Rd., P O Box H, Zip 99133; tel. 509/633-1753; David A. Page, adm. (Nonreporting) **A**9 10; **S**0585	23	10	S		46	—	—	—	—	—	—	—	—
ILWACO—Pacific County													
★ OCEAN BEACH HOSPITAL, Box H, Zip 98624; tel. 206/642-3181; Donald W. Stubsten, adm. **A**9 10 **F**1 6 16 23 24 35 45	16	10	S		25	696	7	28.0	0	0	2754	1279	61
KENNEWICK—Benton County													
⊞ KENNEWICK GENERAL HOSPITAL, 900 S. Auburn St., Box 6128, Zip 99336; tel. 509/586-6111; Michael Fraser, chief exec. off. & adm. **A**1a 2 9 10 **F**1 3 6 12 14 15 16 23 34 35 36 40 41 43 45 46 47 52 53	16	10	S		65	3779	35	53.8	12	817	11635	5422	234
KIRKLAND—King County													
□ CAREUNIT HOSPITAL OF KIRKLAND, 10322 N.E. 132nd, Zip 98034; tel. 206/821-1122; Janice K. Chiles, adm. **A**1a 10 **F**15 16 24 33 42 46 49; **S**0275	33	82	S		83	932	66	79.5	0	0	5593	2166	78
□ CPC FAIRFAX HOSPITAL (Formerly Fairfax Hospital), 10200 N.E. 132nd St., Zip 98034; tel. 206/821-2000; Greg Fritz, adm. (Nonreporting) **A**1b 9 10; **S**0785	33	22	S		133	—	—	—	—	—	—	—	—
⊞ EVERGREEN HOSPITAL MEDICAL CENTER (Formerly Evergreen General Hospital), 12040 N.E. 128th St., Zip 98034; tel. 206/821-1111; Andrew Fallat, adm. **A**1a 2 9 10 **F**1 3 5 6 8 10 15 16 23 24 32 35 36 40 44 45 46 47 53 54	16	10	S		109	6989	83	72.8	16	1388	24998	10573	441
FAIRFAX HOSPITAL, See CPC Fairfax Hospital													
LONGVIEW—Cowlitz County													
⊞ MONTICELLO MEDICAL CENTER, 600 Broadway, P O Box 638, Zip 98632; tel. 206/423-5850; Joseph M. Horner, adm. **A**1a 2 9 10 **F**1 3 6 14 15 16 23 35 36 40 43 44 45 46 48 49 51 52 53; **S**5415	23	10	S		122	3577	40	32.8	20	1264	12317	5718	245
⊞ ST. JOHN'S HOSPITAL, 1614 E. Kessler Blvd., P O Box 3002, Zip 98632; tel. 206/423-1530; Sr. Anne Hayes, adm. **A**1a 2 9 10 **F**1 3 5 6 8 9 10 12 14 15 16 20 23 24 25 26 27 29 30 34 35 41 42 43 44 45 46 47 49 52 53; **S**5415	23	10	S		151	6354	82	54.3	0	0	24723	10426	554
MCCLEARY—Grays Harbor County													
MARK REED HOSPITAL, 322 S. Birch St., P O Box 28, Zip 98557; tel. 206/495-3244; Jean E. Roberts, adm. (Nonreporting) **A**9 10	16	10	S		20	—	—	—	—	—	—	—	—
MEDICAL LAKE—Spokane County													
□ EASTERN STATE HOSPITAL, Box A, Zip 99022; tel. 509/299-3121; Harold P. Robb MD, adm. **A**1b 9 10 **F**3 16 23 24 30 32 33 42 44 46 47	12	22	L		392	1741	393	100.0	0	0	21635	12946	603
METALINE FALLS—Pend Oreille County													
★ MOUNT LINTON HOSPITAL, 103 N. Grandview, Box 67, Zip 99153; tel. 509/446-4701; Doris M. Carroll, actg. adm. (Nonreporting) **A**9 10	16	10	S		19	—	—	—	—	—	—	—	—
MONROE—Snohomish County													
⊞ VALLEY GENERAL HOSPITAL, 14701 179th S.E., Zip 98272; tel. 206/794-7497; Lane A. Savitch, chief exec. off. (Nonreporting) **A**1a 9 10	16	10	S		72	—	—	—	—	—	—	—	—
MORTON—Lewis County													
MORTON GENERAL HOSPITAL, Fifth & Adams Sts., Drawer C, Zip 98356; tel. 206/496-5112; David B. Coffler, adm. **A**9 10 **F**1 6 14 15 16 23 24 30 34 35 36 40 43 44 46	16	10	S		20	573	5	25.0	6	66	2143	912	41
MOSES LAKE—Grant County													
★ SAMARITAN HOSPITAL, 801 E. Wheeler Rd., Zip 98837; tel. 509/765-5606; Michael J. Tuohy, adm. **A**9 10 **F**1 3 6 10 14 15 16 23 26 34 35 36 40 43 44 45 46	16	10	S		50	2904	27	54.0	10	640	7594	3708	186
MOUNT VERNON—Skagit County													
⊞ SKAGIT VALLEY HOSPITAL AND HEALTH CENTER (Formerly Skagit Valley Hospital), 1415 Kincaid St., P O Box 1376, Zip 98273; tel. 206/424-4111; L. V. Davidson, adm. **A**1a 2 9 10 **F**1 3 6 9 10 12 15 16 23 24 27 30 32 33 34 35 36 37 40 45 46 47 53	16	10	S		137	5183	71	51.8	12	670	19387	9395	393
NEWPORT—Pend Oreille County													
★ NEWPORT COMMUNITY HOSPITAL, Scott & Pine Sts., Box 669, Zip 99156; tel. 509/447-2441 **A**9 10 **F**1 6 14 15 16 23 34 35 36 37 43 45 50	16	10	S		24	296	2	8.3	5	40	1412	667	—
OAK HARBOR—Island County													
⊞ NAVAL HOSPITAL (Formerly Listed Under Whidbey Island), Zip 98278; tel. 206/679-5400; Capt. W. J. McDaniel MC USN, CO **A**1a **F**1 6 14 16 23 28 30 34 35 37 40 45 46 47 52	43	10	S		20	1733	13	65.0	12	500	—	—	224
ODESSA—Lincoln County													
★ MEMORIAL HOSPITAL, 502 E. Amende St., Box 368, Zip 99159; tel. 509/982-2611; Donald W. James, adm. (Total facility includes 23 beds in nursing home-type unit) **A**9 10 **F**19 35 40 45 52	16	10	S	TF H	44 21	69 56	26 3	59.1 —	5 5	2 2	904 446	553 277	42 27
OLYMPIA—Thurston County													
★ BLACK HILLS COMMUNITY HOSPITAL, 3900 Capital Mall Dr. S.W., Zip 98502; tel. 206/754-5858; Gary L. Worrell, adm. **A**9 10 **F**1 3 6 10 14 15 16 23 24 26 34 35 37 42 43 45 46 47 53; **S**1755	33	10	S		110	1479	16	14.5	0	0	—	—	157

★ American Hospital Association (AHA) membership
□ Joint Commission on Accreditation of Hospitals (JCAH) accreditation
\+ American Osteopathic Hospital Association (AOHA) membership
○ American Osteopathic Association (AOA) accreditation
Δ Commission on Accreditation of Rehabilitation Facilities (CARF) accreditation
Control codes 61, 63, 64, 71, 72 and 73 indicate hospitals listed by AOHA, but not registered by AHA.
For definition of numerical codes, see page A2

Hospital, Address, Telephone, Administrator, Approval and Facility Codes, Multihospital System Code	Classification Codes				Inpatient Data				Newborn Data		Expense (thousands of dollars)		
	Control	Service	Stay	Facilities	Beds	Admissions	Census	Occupancy (percent)	Bassinets	Births	Total	Payroll	Personnel
★□ ST. PETER HOSPITAL, 413 N. Lilly Rd., Zip 98506; tel. 206/491-9480; David L. Bjornson, adm. **A**1a 2 9 10 **F**1 2 3 5 6 9 12 15 16 20 23 24 27 30 32 33 35 36 40 42 44 45 46 48 52 53 54; **S**5275	21	10	S		340	15237	184	54.1	35	2108	50557	23037	1078
OMAK—Okanogan County													
★ MID-VALLEY HOSPITAL, 810 Valley Way, Box 551, Zip 98841; tel. 509/826-1760; Robert L. Whitbeck, adm. **A**9 10 **F**1 3 10 15 16 35 45	16	10	S		44	1237	11	25.0	6	277	3849	2042	106
OTHELLO—Adams County													
★ OTHELLO COMMUNITY HOSPITAL, 350 N. 14th St., Zip 99344; tel. 509/488-2636; Jerry Lane, adm. (Nonreporting) **A**9 10	16	10	S		38	—	—	—	—	—	—	—	—
PASCO—Franklin County													
★□ OUR LADY OF LOURDES HEALTH CENTER (Formerly Our Lady of Lourdes Hospital), 520 N. Fourth St., Zip 99301; Mailing Address Box 2568, Zip 99302; tel. 509/547-7704; Thomas Corley, adm. **A**1a 2 9 10 **F**1 3 6 10 12 15 16 21 23 35 36 40 44 45 46 48 49 52 53; **S**5945	23	10	S		95	3021	35	36.8	12	425	11754	4531	200
POMEROY—Garfield County													
GARFIELD COUNTY MEMORIAL HOSPITAL, 66 N. Sixth St., P O Box 880, Zip 99347; tel. 509/843-1591; George Ledgerwood, interim adm. (Nonreporting) **A**9 10	16	10	S		14	—	—	—	—	—	—	—	—
PORT ANGELES—Clallam County													
□ OLYMPIC MEMORIAL HOSPITAL, 939 Caroline St., Zip 98362; tel. 206/457-8513; Allen Remington, chief exec. off. **A**1a 9 10 **F**1 3 6 10 12 14 15 16 20 23 32 34 35 36 40 44 45 46 47 53	16	10	S		126	5338	55	43.7	15	647	15069	7871	341
PORT TOWNSEND—Jefferson County													
★ JEFFERSON GENERAL HOSPITAL, Ninth & Sheridan Aves., Zip 98368; tel. 206/385-2200; Victor Dirksen, adm. **A**9 10 **F**1 3 6 15 16 19 21 23 24 34 35 36 40 41 43 44 45 46 49 52	16	10	S		43	1285	14	32.6	0	143	4563	2453	95
PROSSER—Benton County													
★ PROSSER MEMORIAL HOSPITAL, 723 Memorial St., Zip 99350; tel. 509/786-2222; Gerard Fischer, adm. (Total facility includes 26 beds in nursing home-type unit) **A**9 10 **F**1 6 16 19 23 34 35 36 40 45 46 47 52	16	10	S	TF	49	1129	33	67.3	6	296	3046	1561	83
				H	23	1089	10	—	6	296	2742	1327	64
PULLMAN—Whitman County													
★□ PULLMAN MEMORIAL HOSPITAL (Formerly Memorial Hospital), Washington Ave., Zip 99163; tel. 509/332-2541; Johnny Kay Hawks, adm. **A**1a 9 10 **F**1 6 10 23 34 35 36 40 45 46	16	10	S		42	2495	16	38.1	8	418	4938	2331	115
PUYALLUP—Pierce County													
★□ Δ GOOD SAMARITAN COMMUNITY HEALTHCARE (Formerly Good Samaritan Hospital), 407 14th Ave. S.E., Box 1247, Zip 98372; tel. 206/848-6661; David K. Hamry, pres. **A**1a 2 7 9 10 **F**1 2 3 5 6 10 14 15 16 21 23 24 25 26 28 29 30 32 33 34 35 36 37 40 41 42 43 44 45 46 47 50 52 53	21	10	S		198	8518	124	62.6	14	1324	36012	20309	803
QUINCY—Grant County													
QUINCY VALLEY HOSPITAL, 908 Tenth Ave. S.W., Zip 98848; tel. 509/787-3531; Gordon Burch, adm. **A**9 10 **F**14 23 35 45	16	10	S		16	438	5	31.3	4	75	1183	525	34
REDMOND—King County													
★ GROUP HEALTH EASTSIDE HOSPITAL, 2700 152nd Ave. N.E., Zip 98052; tel. 206/883-5151; Richard Marks, reg. vice-pres. **F**1 3 6 10 12 15 16 23 24 28 30 32 33 34 35 36 37 40 42 45 46 47 52 53; **S**9995	23	10	S		142	12049	115	81.0	22	1523	—	—	740
RENTON—King County													
★□ VALLEY MEDICAL CENTER, 400 S. 43rd St., Zip 98055; tel. 206/228-3450; Richard D. Roodman, adm. **A**1a 3 5 9 10 **F**1 2 3 6 7 12 15 16 23 24 25 27 29 30 32 33 35 36 40 44 45 46 47 50 52 53 54	16	10	S		292	13315	176	56.2	23	2424	48364	22722	870
REPUBLIC—Ferry County													
FERRY COUNTY MEMORIAL HOSPITAL, Box 365, Zip 99166; tel. 509/775-3998; Louis D. Kraml, adm. (Nonreporting) **A**9 10	23	10	S		25	—	—	—	—	—	—	—	—
RICHLAND—Benton County													
★□ KADLEC MEDICAL CENTER, 888 Swift Blvd., Zip 99352; tel. 509/946-4611; Jon R. Davis, chief exec. off. **A**1a 9 10 **F**1 3 5 6 9 10 12 14 15 16 23 30 34 35 36 40 45 46 51 52 53 54	23	10	S		144	6256	72	50.0	19	1178	25450	10294	480
MID-COLUMBIA MENTAL HEALTH CENTER, 1175 Gribble Ave., Zip 99352; tel. 509/943-9104; Thomas Corley, exec. dir. **A**10 **F**28 29 30 32 33 34 35 46 49	23	22	S		32	784	20	62.5	0	0	3497	2022	73
RITZVILLE—Adams County													
RITZVILLE MEMORIAL HOSPITAL, 903 S. Adams St., Zip 99169; tel. 509/659-1200; Charlotte Hardt, adm. (Nonreporting) **A**9 10	16	10	S		20	—	—	—	—	—	—	—	—
SEATTLE—King County													
★□ BALLARD COMMUNITY HOSPITAL, N.W. Market & Barnes, Box C-70707, Zip 98107; tel. 206/782-2700; Patrick R. Mahoney, adm. **A**1a 9 10 **F**1 3 6 10 12 15 16 23 24 25 26 34 35 41 42 44 45 46 48 49 50 53	23	10	S		147	3866	89	60.5	0	0	22401	9294	473
★□ CHILDREN'S ORTHOPEDIC HOSPITAL AND MEDICAL CENTER, 4800 Sand Point Way N.E., Box C-5371, Zip 98105; tel. 206/526-2000; Treuman Katz, chief exec. off.; Patrick Shumaker, exec. dir. & chief oper. off. **A**1a 2 3 5 8 9 10 **F**1 4 6 10 12 13 15 16 20 23 24 25 26 27 28 29 30 32 33 34 35 38 42 43 44 45 46 51 53 54	23	50	S		200	7944	154	77.0	0	0	58215	28057	1158
○ + FIFTH AVENUE MEDICAL CENTER (Formerly Waldo General Hospital), 10560 Fifth Ave. N.E., Box 75977, Zip 98125; tel. 206/364-2050; Albert Yonck, dir. **A**9 10 11 12 **F**1 3 6 10 12 15 16 17 23 24 33 34 36 37 40 44 53	23	10	S		60	1069	13	21.7	0	10	6230	2586	121
★□ GROUP HEALTH COOPERATIVE CENTRAL HOSPITAL, 201 16th Ave. E., Zip 98112; tel. 206/326-3000; Cheryl M. Scott, reg. vice-pres. (Total facility includes 38 beds in nursing home-type unit) **A**1a 2 3 5 10 **F**1 3 6 7 8 9 10 11 12 15 16 19 20 21 23 24 26 28 30 33 34 35 36 37 39 40 41 42 43 44 45 46 47 49 52 53; **S**9995	23	10	S	TF	278	15429	265	87.2	20	1434	—	—	909
				H	240	15026	240	—	20	1434	—	—	893
★□ HARBORVIEW MEDICAL CENTER, 325 Ninth Ave., Zip 98104; tel. 206/223-3000; David W. Gitch, adm. **A**1a 3 5 8 9 10 **F**1 3 5 6 10 12 14 15 16 20 22 23 24 25 26 27 28 29 30 32 33 34 35 37 42 43 44 45 46 47 50 53; **S**6415	13	10	S		330	11414	286	86.7	0	0	85558	35401	1797
★□ HIGHLINE COMMUNITY HOSPITAL, 16251 Sylvester Rd. S.W., Zip 98166; tel. 206/244-9970; Paul Tucker, adm. (Nonreporting) **A**1a 2 9 10	23	10	S		107	—	—	—	—	—	—	—	—
MEDICAL DENTAL HOSPITAL, 509 Olive Way, Zip 98101; tel. 206/623-4755; Eleanor H. Rhees, exec. dir. (Nonreporting) **A**9 10	33	10	S		21	—	—	—	—	—	—	—	—
NORTHGATE GENERAL HOSPITAL, See Northwest General Hospital													
★□ NORTHWEST HOSPITAL (Includes Northgate General Hospital, 120 Northgate Plaza, Zip 98125; tel. 206/362-5000; C. W. Schneider, adm.), 1550 N. 115th St., Zip 98133; tel. 206/364-0500; James D. Hart, exec. dir. **A**1a 2 9 10 **F**1 2 3 6 7 9 10 12 14 15 16 21 23 24 25 26 30 33 34 35 36 37 40 44 45 46 50 53	23	10	S		246	10257	151	61.4	22	2361	47521	21291	933
□ PACIFIC MEDICAL CENTER, 1200 12th Ave. S., Zip 98144; tel. 206/326-4000; Richard K. Tompkins MD, pres. & chief exec. off. (Nonreporting) **A**1a 3 5 8 9 10	23	10	S		152	—	—	—	—	—	—	—	—
★□ PROVIDENCE MEDICAL CENTER, 500 17th Ave., Zip 98122; tel. 206/326-5555; Peter Bigelow, adm. **A**1a 2 3 5 9 10 **F**1 2 3 4 5 6 7 8 9 10 11 12 14 15 16 20 23 24 26 27 29 30 33 34 35 36 42 44 45 46 47 49 53 54; **S**5275	21	10	S		359	13433	232	64.6	12	1036	73428	32947	1536

★ American Hospital Association (AHA) membership
□ Joint Commission on Accreditation of Hospitals (JCAH) accreditation
\+ American Osteopathic Hospital Association (AOHA) membership
○ American Osteopathic Association (AOA) accreditation
Δ Commission on Accreditation of Rehabilitation Facilities (CARF) accreditation
Control codes 61, 63, 64, 71, 72 and 73 indicate hospitals listed by AOHA, but not registered by AHA. For definition of numerical codes, see page A2

Hospital, Address, Telephone, Administrator, Approval and Facility Codes, Multihospital System Code	Classification Codes				Inpatient Data				Newborn Data		Expense (thousands of dollars)		
	Control	Service	Stay	Facilities	Beds	Admissions	Census	Occupancy (percent)	Bassinets	Births	Total	Payroll	Personnel
□ RIVERTON HOSPITAL, 12844 Military Rd. S., Zip 98168; tel. 206/244-0180; Gerard Manse, mng. dir. **A**1a 9 10 **F**1 3 6 7 10 15 16 23 24 26 34 35 36 40 44 45 46 47 48 49 53; **S**9555	33	10	S		142	3708	64	45.1	12	563	14188	6397	282
★□ SAINT CABRINI HOSPITAL OF SEATTLE, Terry & Madison, Zip 98104; tel. 206/682-0500; Ronald C. M. Bergstrom, adm. **A**1a 9 10 **F**1 3 5 6 10 12 14 15 16 23 24 27 28 32 33 34 35 42 45 46 47 48 49 50 53	21	10	S		150	3847	93	62.0	0	0	18002	8398	366
★□ SCHICK SHADEL HOSPITAL, 12101 Ambaum Blvd. S.W., Zip 98146; Mailing Address Box 48149, Zip 98148; tel. 206/244-8100; Mary Ellen Stewart, adm. **A**1a 9 10 **F**15 32 33 47; **S**0575	33	82	S		63	2514	36	58.1	0	0	5698	2136	91
★ ○ + SHOREWOOD OSTEOPATHIC HOSPITAL, 12845 Ambaum Blvd. S.W., Zip 98146; tel. 206/243-1455; David J. Myers, adm. **A**9 10 11 **F**1 3 6 10 12 15 16 23 34 35 50; **S**1035	23	10	S		32	783	11	34.4	0	0	3767	1686	71
★□ SWEDISH HOSPITAL MEDICAL CENTER, 747 Summit Ave., Zip 98104; tel. 206/386-6000; Allan W. Lobb MD, exec. dir. **A**1a 2 3 5 9 10 **F**1 2 3 4 6 7 8 9 10 11 13 16 20 21 23 24 34 35 36 37 38 40 41 44 45 46 47 51 52 53 54	23	10	S		628	30283	458	72.9	40	3803	136482	58486	2546
★□ UNIVERSITY HOSPITAL, 1959 N.E. Pacific St., Zip 98195; tel. 206/548-3300; Irma E. Goertzen, adm. **A**1a 3 5 8 9 10 **F**1 3 4 6 7 8 9 10 11 12 13 15 16 17 20 23 24 25 26 27 28 30 32 33 34 35 37 38 40 42 43 44 45 46 47 50 51 53 54; **S**6415	12	10	S		355	12341	277	81.7	20	2053	106452	41045	1776
★□ VETERANS ADMINISTRATION MEDICAL CENTER, 1660 S. Columbian Way, Zip 98108; tel. 206/762-1010; James T. Krajeck, dir. (Total facility includes 60 beds in nursing home-type unit) **A**1a 3 5 8 **F**1 2 3 6 10 11 12 15 16 19 20 23 24 25 26 27 28 32 33 34 41 42 43 44 46 48 49 50 53 54	45	10	S	TF	488	10650	361	74.0	0	0	95396	46819	1633
				H	428	10354	313	—	0	0	93379	—	1592
★□ VIRGINIA MASON HOSPITAL, 925 Seneca St., Zip 98101; Mailing Address Box 1930, Zip 98111; tel. 206/624-1144; Donald R. Olson, adm. **A**1a 2 3 5 9 10 **F**1 3 4 13 15 16 20 25 33 34 35 36 39 40 43 45 46 47 50 54	23	10	S		336	13185	221	65.8	30	1142	66664	23885	1225
WALDO GENERAL HOSPITAL, See Fifth Avenue Medical Center													
★□ WEST SEATTLE COMMUNITY HOSPITAL, 2600 S.W. Holden St., Zip 98126; tel. 206/938-6000; Dwight E. Harshbarger, adm. **A**1a 9 10 **F**1 3 6 10 12 15 16 23 24 35 43 45 46 47; **S**6525	33	10	S		61	1443	21	34.4	0	0	9701	3777	161
SEDRO WOOLLEY—Skagit County													
★□ UNITED GENERAL HOSPITAL, 1971 Hwy. 20, Box 410, Zip 98284; tel. 206/856-6021; Geoffrey A. Norwood, chief exec. off. **A**1a 2 9 10 **F**1 3 6 7 8 9 10 11 15 16 23 24 26 33 34 35 36 37 40 43 44 45 46 47 50 53; **S**1755	16	10	S		97	3365	40	41.2	6	308	14308	5587	208
SHELTON—Mason County													
★□ MASON GENERAL HOSPITAL, 2100 Sherwood Lane, Zip 98584; tel. 206/426-1611; Steve Smith, adm. (Nonreporting) **A**1a 9 10	16	10	S		58	—	—	—	—	—	—	—	—
SNOQUALMIE—King County													
★ SNOQUALMIE VALLEY HOSPITAL, 1505 Meadowbrook Way S.E., Zip 98065; tel. 206/888-1438; John P. Holt, adm. (Nonreporting) **A**9 10; **S**5415	21	10	S		28	—	—	—	—	—	—	—	—
SOUTH BEND—Pacific County													
WILLAPA HARBOR HOSPITAL, Alder & Cedar Sts., Box 438, Zip 98586; tel. 206/875-5526; Steve Diamanti, adm. **A**9 10 **F**1 3 6 15 16 34 35 45	16	10	S		36	1077	8	22.2	5	136	2380	1164	69
SPOKANE—Spokane County													
★□ DEACONESS MEDICAL CENTER-SPOKANE, 800 W. Fifth Ave., Zip 99210; tel. 509/458-5800; Jon K. Mitchell, pres. **A**1a 2 3 5 9 10 **F**1 2 3 4 6 10 12 15 16 23 24 25 26 30 33 34 35 36 37 38 40 42 43 44 45 46 47 48 49 51 52 53 54; **S**0945	23	10	S		352	14227	224	63.6	26	2036	72261	34161	1405
★□ HOLY FAMILY HOSPITAL, 5633 N. Lidgerwood St., Zip 99207; tel. 509/482-0111; Michael D. Wilson, pres. **A**1a 9 10 **F**1 3 5 6 8 9 10 11 15 16 23 26 35 36 40 45 46 47 52 54; **S**5175	21	10	S		200	6827	94	47.0	6	656	26335	12850	448
★ MOUNTAINVIEW HOSPITAL OF SPOKANE (Formerly Raleigh Hills Hospital of Spokane), 628 S. Cowley, Zip 99202; Mailing Address Box 598, Zip 99210; tel. 509/624-3226; Arlene Ingwerson, adm. (Nonreporting) **A** 9 10; **S**6525	33	82	S		34	—	—	—	—	—	—	—	—
RALEIGH HILLS HOSPITAL OF SPOKANE, See Mountainview Hospital of Spokane													
★□ Δ SACRED HEART MEDICAL CENTER, W. 101 Eighth Ave., Zip 99220; tel. 509/455-3131; Sr. Peter Claver RN, pres. **A**1a 2 3 5 7 9 10 **F**1 2 3 4 5 6 7 8 9 10 11 12 13 15 16 20 23 24 25 26 27 30 32 33 34 35 36 39 40 42 43 44 45 46 47 51 52 53 54; **S**5265	21	10	S		631	21613	404	64.0	18	2320	104936	54745	2125
★□ SHRINERS HOSPITALS FOR CRIPPLED CHILDREN-SPOKANE UNIT, N. 820 Summit Blvd., Zip 99201; tel. 509/327-9521; Howard L. Parrett, adm. **A**1a 3 **F**15 23 24 26 34 38 42 47; **S**4125	23	57	S		30	612	21	70.0	0	0	—	—	75
★□ ST. LUKE'S MEMORIAL HOSPITAL, S. 711 Cowley, P O Box 288, Zip 99202; tel. 509/838-1447; Ernest R. McNeely Jr., pres. (Nonreporting) **A**1a 9 10; **S**0945	23	10	S		146	—	—	—	—	—	—	—	—
★□ VALLEY HOSPITAL AND MEDICAL CENTER, E. 12606 Mission Ave., Zip 99216; Mailing Address P O Box 288, Zip 99210; tel. 509/924-6650; Thomas M. White, pres. **A**1a 9 10 **F**1 3 6 10 12 15 16 21 23 34 35 36 40 43 44 45 52 53; **S**0945	23	10	S		123	4535	52	43.7	12	392	17916	7632	283
★□ VETERANS ADMINISTRATION MEDICAL CENTER, N. 4815 Assembly St., Zip 99205; tel. 509/328-4521; E. J. Mack, dir. (Total facility includes 60 beds in nursing home-type unit) **A**1a **F**1 3 6 10 12 15 16 19 23 24 26 28 31 32 33 34 42 45 46 49 50 54	45	10	S	TF	247	3917	196	80.3	0	0	19986	12336	467
				H	187	3835	140	—	0	0	—	—	408
SUNNYSIDE—Yakima County													
★ ○ + SUNNYSIDE COMMUNITY HOSPITAL (Formerly Sunnyside General Hospital) (Includes Valley Memorial Hospital, Tenth & Tacoma Aves., P O Box 540, Zip 98944; tel. 509/837-2101), Tenth & Tacoma Ave., P O Box 719, Zip 98944; tel. 509/837-2101; Robert L. Brendgard, adm. **A**9 10 11 12 **F**1 3 6 12 14 15 16 21 23 33 34 35 36 37 40 45 46 52; **S**0585	23	10	S		80	1971	16	20.0	12	266	6937	—	130
TACOMA—Pierce County													
DOCTORS HOSPITAL OF TACOMA, See Tacoma General Hospital													
★□ GHC INPATIENT CENTER TACOMA GENERAL, 315 S. K St., Zip 98405; tel. 206/383-6156; Bob Pfotenhauer, adm. (Newly Registered) **A**1a 9; **S**9995	23	10	S		36	—	—	—	—	—	—	—	—
★□ HUMANA HOSPITAL -TACOMA, S. 19th & Union Sts., Zip 98405; Mailing Address P O Box 11414, Zip 98411; tel. 206/572-2323; Sharon Armstrong, exec. dir. (Nonreporting) **A**1a 9 10; **S**1235	33	10	S		155	—	—	—	—	—	—	—	—
★□ LAKEWOOD HOSPITAL (Formerly Lakewood General Hospital), 5702 100th St. S.W., Zip 98499; tel. 206/588-1711; Richard Vanberg, adm. **A**1a 9 10 **F**1 3 6 10 12 14 15 16 23 34 35 36 40 43 44 45 46 48 53; **S**0585	23	10	S		87	3557	54	62.1	16	447	15766	6565	264
★□ MADIGAN ARMY MEDICAL CENTER, Zip 98431; tel. 206/967-7082; Col. T. M. Pittman, exec. off. **A**1a 2 3 5 **F**1 2 3 5 6 7 8 9 10 12 14 15 16 20 23 24 26 27 28 30 32 33 34 35 36 37 40 44 46 47 51 52 53 54	42	10	S		368	17549	263	71.5	30	2541	77545	52185	2743
★□ MARY BRIDGE CHILDREN'S HEALTH CENTER (Includes Mary Bridge Children's Hospital), 311 S. L St., Box 5299, Zip 98405; tel. 206/594-1400; Charles Hoffman, adm. **A**1a 3 5 9 10 **F**1 5 6 12 15 16 23 24 26 34 35 38 42 43 44 45 46 47; **S**6555	23	50	S		58	2488	28	48.3	0	0	12774	6171	256

Hospital, Address, Telephone, Administrator, Approval and Facility Codes, Multihospital System Code	Classification Codes				Inpatient Data				Newborn Data		Expense (thousands of dollars)		
★ American Hospital Association (AHA) membership □ Joint Commission on Accreditation of Hospitals (JCAH) accreditation + American Osteopathic Hospital Association (AOHA) membership ○ American Osteopathic Association (AOA) accreditation Δ Commission on Accreditation of Rehabilitation Facilities (CARF) accreditation Control codes 61, 63, 64, 71, 72 and 73 indicate hospitals listed by AOHA, but not registered by AHA For definition of numerical codes, see page A2	Control	Service	Stay	Facilities	Beds	Admissions	Census	Occupancy (percent)	Bassinets	Births	Total	Payroll	Personnel
★ PUGET SOUND HOSPITAL, 215 S. 36th St., Zip 98408; Mailing Address P O Box 11412, Zip 98411; tel. 206/474-0561; Bruce Brandler, adm. (Nonreporting) **A**1a 9 10; **S**1375	33	10	S		153	—	—	—	—	—	—	—	—
★ Δ ST. JOSEPH HOSPITAL AND HEALTH CARE CENTER, 1718 S. I St., Zip 98401; tel. 206/627-4101; John Long, pres. & chief exec. off. **A**1a 7 9 10 **F**1 2 3 4 6 10 12 14 15 16 20 21 22 23 24 25 27 30 32 33 34 35 36 40 42 43 44 46 47 53 54; **S**5325	21	10	S		340	14101	211	62.1	18	2299	65504	27823	1202
★ TACOMA GENERAL HOSPITAL (Includes Doctors Hospital of Tacoma, 737 Fawcett Ave., Zip 98402; tel. 206/627-8111; Charles Hoffman, adm.), 315 S. K St., P O Box 5299, Zip 98405; tel. 206/594-1000; Charles F. Hoffman, exec. vice-pres. & adm. **A**1a 2 3 5 9 10 **F**1 2 3 4 5 6 9 10 12 15 16 23 24 35 36 40 43 45 46 47 50 51 53 54; **S**6555	23	10	S		310	16204	206	66.5	27	3760	69698	29638	1370
★ VETERANS ADMINISTRATION MEDICAL CENTER, American Lake, Zip 98493; tel. 206/582-8440; Frank Taylor, dir. (Total facility includes 76 beds in nursing home-type unit) **A**1a b **F**1 3 7 10 15 16 19 23 24 25 26 27 28 31 32 33 34 42 43 44 46 47 48 49 50	45	10	L	TF	426	3817	324	76.1	0	0	33797	23715	808
				H	350	3787	253	—	0	0	32062	22197	765
TONASKET—Okanogan County													
NORTH VALLEY HOSPITAL, Second & Western, P O Box 488, Zip 98855; tel. 509/486-2151; Gordon McLean, chief exec. off. & adm. (Total facility includes 70 beds in nursing home-type unit) **A**9 10 **F**1 3 16 19 23 35 36 45 50	16	10	S	TF	97	677	58	72.5	6	90	—	—	101
				H	27	626	6	—	6	90	—	—	—
TOPPENISH—Yakima County													
★ PROVIDENCE CENTRAL MEMORIAL HOSPITAL (Formerly Central Memorial Hospital), 502 W. Fourth St., Box 672, Zip 98948; tel. 509/865-3105; Roy W. Holmes, adm. **A**1a 9 10 **F**1 3 6 14 15 16 21 23 34 35 36 40 41 45 47 52; **S**5275	23	10	S		63	1903	19	30.2	12	422	5062	2437	130
VANCOUVER—Clark County													
★ SOUTHWEST WASHINGTON HOSPITALS (Includes St. Joseph Community Hospital, 600 N.E. 92nd Ave., Zip 98664; tel. 206/256-2000; Vancouver Memorial Hospital, 3400 Main St., Zip 98663; tel. 206/696-5000), 600 N. 92nd Ave., Zip 98664; Mailing Address P O Box 1600, Zip 98668; tel. 206/256-2147; I. Douglas Streckert, adm. **A**1a 2 9 10 **F**1 3 6 7 8 9 10 11 12 14 16 20 21 23 24 27 30 32 33 35 36 37 40 41 43 44 45 46 47 48 49 52 53 54	23	10	S		338	14562	216	61.2	43	2181	51873	24237	1032
ST. JOSEPH COMMUNITY HOSPITAL, See Southwest Washington Hospitals													
VANCOUVER MEMORIAL HOSPITAL, See Southwest Washington Hospitals													
WALLA WALLA—Walla Walla County													
★ Δ ST. MARY MEDICAL CENTER, 401 W. Poplar St., Box 1477, Zip 99362; tel. 509/525-3320; John A. Isely, pres. **A**1a 2 7 9 10 **F**1 3 5 6 7 8 9 10 11 12 14 15 16 23 24 25 26 27 28 30 32 34 35 36 37 38 40 41 42 44 45 46 51 52 54; **S**5265	21	10	S		136	4403	62	45.6	15	598	18406	8734	368
STATE PENITENTIARY HOSPITAL, Box 520, Zip 99362; tel. 509/525-3610; K. Marsh, adm. (Nonreporting)	12	11	S		49	—	—	—	—	—	—	—	—
★ VETERANS ADMINISTRATION MEDICAL CENTER, 77 Wainwright Dr., Zip 99362; tel. 509/525-5200; Tom Trujillo, dir. **A**1a **F**1 3 6 12 14 16 19 23 24 25 26 27 28 32 33 34 42 44 46 47 48 49	45	10	S		119	2339	78	65.5	0	0	12980	7152	286
□ WALLA WALLA GENERAL HOSPITAL, 1025 S. Second Ave., Box 1398, Zip 99362; tel. 509/525-0480; Rodney T. Applegate, pres. **A**1a 2 9 10 **F**1 3 6 12 14 15 16 23 27 29 30 31 32 33 34 35 36 37 40 43 45 46 47 52 53; **S**0235	21	10	S		72	2466	30	41.7	5	306	10129	3964	173
WENATCHEE—Chelan County													
★ CENTRAL WASHINGTON HOSPITAL, 1300 Fuller St., Box 1887, Zip 98801; tel. 509/662-1511; Thomas J. Troy, adm. **A**1a 9 10 **F**1 2 3 5 6 9 12 14 15 16 20 21 23 24 35 36 37 40 41 44 45 46 52 54	23	10	S		176	8586	101	58.4	12	1129	23106	11090	404
WHIDBEY ISLAND—Island County													
NAVAL HOSPITAL, See Oak Harbor													
WHITE SALMON—Klickitat County													
SKYLINE HOSPITAL, Box 99, Zip 98672; tel. 509/493-1101; Geir T. Bakke, adm. **A**9 10 **F**1 3 5 6 12 14 15 16 23 34 35 36 40 42 45 47 52	16	10	S		27	810	8	29.6	6	133	2125	1114	59
YAKIMA—Yakima County													
+ NEW VALLEY OSTEOPATHIC HOSPITAL, 3003 Tieton Dr., Zip 98902; tel. 509/453-6561; Shane H. Roberts, adm. (Nonreporting) **A**9 10	23	10	S		30	—	—	—	—	—	—	—	—
★ ST. ELIZABETH MEDICAL CENTER, 110 S. Ninth Ave., Zip 98902; tel. 509/575-5000; Sr. Karin Dufault RN PhD, adm. (Nonreporting) **A**1a 2 9 10; **S**5275	21	10	S		189	—	—	—	—	—	—	—	—
★ YAKIMA VALLEY MEMORIAL HOSPITAL, 2811 Tieton Dr., Zip 98902; tel. 509/575-8000; Richard W. Linneweh Jr., adm. **A**1a 2 9 10 **F**1 2 3 5 6 7 8 9 10 11 12 14 15 16 21 23 24 26 27 28 30 32 34 35 36 37 38 40 45 46 51 52 53	23	10	S		224	10407	134	59.8	28	2458	30236	14555	695

★ American Hospital Association (AHA) membership
☐ Joint Commission on Accreditation of Hospitals (JCAH) accreditation
+ American Osteopathic Hospital Association (AOHA) membership
○ American Osteopathic Association (AOA) accreditation
Δ Commission on Accreditation of Rehabilitation Facilities (CARF) accreditation
Control codes 61, 63, 64, 71, 72 and 73 indicate hospitals listed by AOHA, but not registered by AHA.
For definition of numerical codes, see page A2

West Virginia

Hospital, Address, Telephone, Administrator, Approval and Facility Codes, Multihospital System Code	Classification Codes				Inpatient Data				Newborn Data		Expense (thousands of dollars)		
	Control	Service	Stay	Facilities	Beds	Admissions	Census	Occupancy (percent)	Bassinets	Births	Total	Payroll	Personnel
BECKLEY—Raleigh County													
APPALACHIAN REGIONAL HOSPITAL, See Beckley Appalachian Regional Hospital													
★☐ BECKLEY APPALACHIAN REGIONAL HOSPITAL (Formerly Appalachian Regional Hospital), 306 Stanaford Rd., Zip 25801; tel. 304/255-3000; Roger J. Wolz, adm. **A**1a 9 10 **F**1 2 3 6 10 12 14 15 16 23 30 32 33 35 36 37 45 46 49 52; **S**0145	23	10	S		202	4147	83	41.1	0	0	12666	5734	223
BECKLEY HOSPITAL, 1007 S. Oakwood Ave., Zip 25801; tel. 304/256-1200; Albert M. Tieche, adm. **A**9 10 **F**1 3 14 35 53	33	10	S		94	2872	54	57.4	0	0	9853	4259	288
★☐ RALEIGH GENERAL HOSPITAL, 1710 Harper Rd., Zip 25801; tel. 304/256-4100; Kenneth M. Holt, adm. **A**1a 9 10 **F**1 2 3 5 6 10 12 14 16 23 30 34 35 36 40 45 46 52 53; **S**1755	33	10	S		238	11636	167	70.2	38	1434	26379	9754	512
★☐ VETERANS ADMINISTRATION MEDICAL CENTER, 200 Veterans Ave., Zip 25801; tel. 304/255-2121; D. R. Pisegna, dir. (Total facility includes 42 beds in nursing home-type unit) **A**1a **F**1 3 6 10 12 14 15 16 19 20 23 26 28 34 35 41 42 44 45 46 47 50	45	10	S	TF	216	4532	172	79.6	0	0	15982	9764	376
				H	174	4526	131	—	0	0	—	—	—
BERKELEY SPRINGS—Morgan County													
★ MORGAN COUNTY WAR MEMORIAL HOSPITAL, 1124 Fairfax St., Zip 25411; tel. 304/258-1234; John Shepard, adm. (Nonreporting) **A**9 10; **S**1755	13	10	S		60	—	—	—	—	—	—	—	—
BLUEFIELD—Mercer County													
☐ BLUEFIELD COMMUNITY HOSPITAL, 500 Cherry St., Zip 24701; tel. 304/327-2511; Eugene P. Pawlowski, adm. **A**1a 9 10 **F**1 2 3 6 7 8 9 10 11 12 14 15 16 20 23 24 26 32 33 34 35 36 37 40 43 44 45 46 50 52 53	23	10	S		265	9623	151	57.0	30	1188	31335	13021	701
★☐ HUMANA HOSPITAL-ST. LUKE'S, 1333 Southview Dr., P O Box 1190, Zip 24701; tel. 304/327-8121; Bradly R. Anderson, exec. dir. **A**1a 9 10 **F**1 3 6 10 12 14 15 16 20 23 33 35 43 46 50; **S**1235	33	10	S		79	2821	41	51.9	0	0	11338	3080	196
BUCKHANNON—Upshur County													
★ ELIZABETH C. LEONARD MEMORIAL HOSPITAL, 78 W. Main St., Zip 26201; tel. 304/472-1336; Betty M. Rusmisell, adm. (Nonreporting) **A**9 10	23	10	S		48	—	—	—	—	—	—	—	—
★☐ ST. JOSEPH'S HOSPITAL, Amalia Dr., Zip 26201; tel. 304/472-2000; Sr. Mary Herbert, adm. (Total facility includes 16 beds in nursing home-type unit) **A**1a 9 10 **F**1 3 6 14 15 16 19 24 26 27 30 32 33 35 36 40 42 45 47 52; **S**5235	23	10	S	TF	95	2474	59	62.1	8	237	7874	3024	193
				H	79	2469	44	—	8	237	7531	2842	179
CHARLESTON—Kanawha County													
★☐ CHARLESTON AREA MEDICAL CENTER (Includes General Division, Brooks & Washington Sts., Box 1393, Zip 25325; tel. 304/348-6200; Memorial Division, 3200 MacCorkle Ave. S.E., Zip 25304; tel. 304/348-4321; Kanawha Valley Memorial Hospital, 800 Pennsylvania Ave., Zip 25302; Mailing Address P O Box 6669, Charleston, Zip 25362; tel. 304/347-9200; J. Darrel Richmond, pres. & chief exec. off.), Morris St., Box 1547, Zip 25326; tel. 304/348-7627; James C. Crews, pres. **A**1a 2 3 5 8 9 10 **F**1 2 3 4 5 6 9 10 11 12 14 15 16 17 19 23 24 26 27 28 29 30 32 33 34 35 38 39 40 42 44 45 46 47 49 50 51 52 53 54; **S**0955	23	10	S		934	33229	645	69.1	58	4020	145565	61511	3194
★☐ EYE AND EAR CLINIC OF CHARLESTON, 1306 Kanawha Blvd. E., Box 2271, Zip 25328; tel. 304/343-4371; Robert E. Lee, adm. **A**1a 9 10 **F**1 10 34 44	33	45	S		35	1379	6	17.1	0	0	3686	1377	72
GENERAL DIVISION, See Charleston Area Medical Center													
★☐ HIGHLAND HOSPITAL, 300 56th St. S.E., Zip 25304; tel. 304/925-4756; Edwin L. Johnson, adm. **A**1b 3 9 10 **F**15 24 32 33 42	23	22	S		80	1217	55	68.8	0	0	2984	1721	104
MEMORIAL DIVISION, See Charleston Area Medical Center													
★☐ ST. FRANCIS HOSPITAL, 333 Laidley St., Zip 25301; Mailing Address Box 471, Zip 25322; tel. 304/347-6500; Wilfred Wright, pres. **A**1a 9 10 **F**1 3 6 10 11 12 14 15 16 23 32 34 44 45 46 47 50 53	21	10	S		206	6793	132	64.1	0	0	34121	14180	670
CLARKSBURG—Harrison County													
★☐ LOUIS A. JOHNSON VETERANS ADMINISTRATION MEDICAL CENTER, Zip 26301; tel. 304/623-3461; W. G. Wright, dir. **A**1a b 2 **F**1 2 3 6 10 12 14 15 16 20 23 24 26 27 28 30 31 32 33 34 35 42 46 49	45	10	S		184	5825	146	71.2	0	0	22814	11223	402
★☐ UNITED HOSPITAL CENTER, U. S. Rte. 19 S., Box 1680, Zip 26301; tel. 304/624-2121; D. Max Francis, pres. (Total facility includes 35 beds in nursing home-type unit) **A**1a 3 5 9 10 **F**1 3 6 7 8 9 10 11 12 14 15 16 19 20 23 29 30 35 45 46 47 52 53 54	23	10	S	TF	330	14290	235	71.2	20	1114	42432	19826	962
				H	295	14204	222	—	20	1114	41935	19614	—
ELKINS—Randolph County													
★☐ DAVIS MEMORIAL HOSPITAL, Gorman Ave. & Reed St., Box 1484, Zip 26241; tel. 304/636-3300; Robert L. Hammer II, chief exec. off. **A**1a 9 10 **F**1 6 10 12 14 15 16 23 35 36 40 41 43 45 46 47 52 53	23	10	S		129	6165	78	63.4	8	515	15614	6773	432
FAIRMONT—Marion County													
★☐ FAIRMONT GENERAL HOSPITAL, 1325 Locust Ave., Zip 26554; tel. 304/367-7100; Robert M. Ptomey, adm. & chief exec. off. **A**1a 9 10 **F**1 2 3 6 10 12 14 15 16 23 26 27 28 30 32 35 40 44 45 47 48 52 53	23	10	S		224	8305	135	60.3	34	638	28373	14683	691
GASSAWAY—Braxton County													
★ BRAXTON COUNTY MEMORIAL HOSPITAL, 100 Hoylman Dr., Zip 26624; tel. 304/364-5156; Kenneth L. Wilson, adm. **A**10 **F**1 14 15 16 23 34 35 40 41 45 46 53; **S**0955	23	10	S		30	1184	13	43.3	6	10	3023	1212	98
GLEN DALE—Marshall County													
★☐ REYNOLDS MEMORIAL HOSPITAL, 800 Wheeling Ave., Zip 26038; tel. 304/845-3211; John Sicurella, exec. dir. **A**1a 9 10 **F**1 3 5 6 10 12 14 16 23 34 35 36 40 41 45 46 52 53	23	10	S		193	5994	98	50.8	10	212	21803	9259	521
GRAFTON—Taylor County													
★☐ GRAFTON CITY HOSPITAL, Rte. 50 & Market St., P O Box 279, Zip 26354; tel. 304/265-0400; Randy Smith, adm. (Total facility includes 68 beds in nursing home-type unit) **A**1a 9 10 **F**1 3 6 12 16 19 23 35 40 42 44 45 50 52; **S**1755	14	10	S	TF	127	1303	78	61.4	6	88	4461	2106	204
				H	59	1168	16	—	6	88	—	—	164
GRANTSVILLE—Calhoun County													
★☐ CALHOUN GENERAL HOSPITAL, Box 490, Zip 26147; tel. 304/354-6121; Jessie P. Sisk, actg. adm. **A**1a 9 10 **F**1 6 12 14 15 16 34 35 45 46 47; **S**0025	23	10	S		30	1047	15	50.0	8	97	2793	1095	72
HINTON—Summers County													
★☐ SUMMERS COUNTY HOSPITAL, Terrace St., Drawer 940, Zip 25951; tel. 304/466-1000; Frank Basile, adm. **A**1a 9 10 **F**1 3 6 10 12 14 16 23 35 36 45; **S**1755	13	10	S		95	2320	33	34.7	2	161	5613	2695	193
HOLDEN—Logan County													
★☐ HOLDEN HOSPITAL, Box K, Zip 25625; tel. 304/239-2331; Leonard Varacalli, adm. **A**1a 9 10 **F**15 16 23 24 32 34 35 45 52	33	10	S		36	830	10	27.8	0	0	2230	1064	53

Hospital, Address, Telephone, Administrator, Approval and Facility Codes, Multihospital System Code	Classification Codes				Inpatient Data				Newborn Data		Expense (thousands of dollars)		
★ American Hospital Association (AHA) membership ☐ Joint Commission on Accreditation of Hospitals (JCAH) accreditation + American Osteopathic Hospital Association (AOHA) membership ○ American Osteopathic Association (AOA) accreditation Δ Commission on Accreditation of Rehabilitation Facilities (CARF) accreditation Control codes 61, 63, 64, 71, 72 and 73 indicate hospitals listed by AOHA, but not registered by AHA. For definition of numerical codes, see page A2	Control	Service	Stay	Facilities	Beds	Admissions	Census	Occupancy (percent)	Bassinets	Births	Total	Payroll	Personnel
HUNTINGTON—Cabell County													
★☐ + CABELL HUNTINGTON HOSPITAL, 1340 Hal Greer Blvd., Zip 25701; tel. 304/526-2000; Donald H. Hutton, pres. **A**1a 3 5 8 9 10 **F**1 3 5 6 9 10 11 12 14 15 16 20 21 22 23 24 26 34 35 36 37 40 41 44 45 46 51 52 53	15	10	S		302	13320	209	69.2	46	1842	43570	21652	1021
★ GUTHRIE MEMORIAL HOSPITAL, 547 Sixth Ave., Zip 25701; tel. 304/697-5300; Gary L. Ripley MD, adm. (Nonreporting) **A**9 10	23	10	S		32	—	—	—	—	—	—	—	—
★☐ HCA HUNTINGTON HOSPITAL (Formerly Huntington Hospital), 1230 Sixth Ave., Box 1875, Zip 25719; tel. 304/526-9111; Richard Welch, adm. **A**1a 9 10 **F**1 3 6 7 12 14 16 23 24 27 30 32 33 34 35 40 42 44 46 52; **S**1755	33	10	S		90	2138	49	54.4	0	0	10407	4427	250
★☐ ST. MARY'S HOSPITAL, 2900 First Ave., Zip 25701; tel. 304/526-1234; Steve J. Soltis, exec. dir. **A**1a 2 3 5 6 9 10 **F**1 2 3 4 6 7 8 9 10 11 12 14 15 16 23 27 30 32 33 34 35 36 40 41 42 44 45 46 48 49 50 52 53 54; **S**5235	21	10	S		440	16052	289	65.7	21	831	50127	25067	1230
HUNTINGTON—Wayne County													
★☐ VETERANS ADMINISTRATION MEDICAL CENTER, 1540 Spring Valley Dr., Zip 25704; tel. 304/429-6741; Thomas W. Kiernan MD, actg. dir. **A**1a 2 3 5 8 **F**1 3 6 10 12 14 15 16 19 23 24 26 28 32 33 34 35 44 46 49	45	10	S		180	4124	130	72.2	0	0	28367	13018	498
HURRICANE—Putnam County													
★☐ PUTNAM GENERAL HOSPITAL, 1400 Hospital Dr., P O Box 507, Zip 25526; tel. 304/757-9800; Shirley A. Perry, adm. **A**1a 10 **F**1 3 6 10 12 14 15 16 23 26 34 35 41 46 50; **S**1755	33	10	S		68	2059	34	50.0	0	0	9576	3366	188
KEYSER—Mineral County													
★☐ POTOMAC VALLEY HOSPITAL, S. Mineral St., Zip 26726; tel. 304/788-3141; Robert L. Rush, adm. **A**1a 9 10 **F**1 3 6 12 14 16 23 34 35 45 47	33	10	S		42	1452	26	56.5	0	0	5340	1559	149
KINGWOOD—Preston County													
★☐ PRESTON MEMORIAL HOSPITAL, 300 S. Price St., Zip 26537; tel. 304/329-1400; Leonard Daugherty, adm. **A**1a 9 10 **F**1 3 6 10 12 14 15 16 21 23 34 35 36 37 40 43 44 45 46 48 49 52	23	10	S		57	1939	36	63.2	7	260	6043	2433	—
LOGAN—Logan County													
★ GUYAN VALLEY HOSPITAL, 396 Dingess St., Zip 25601; tel. 304/752-1210; Earl Lambert, adm. (Nonreporting) **A**9	23	10	S		24	—	—	—	—	—	—	—	—
★☐ LOGAN GENERAL HOSPITAL, 20 Hospital Dr., Zip 25601; tel. 304/752-1101; C. David Morrison, adm. (Nonreporting) **A**1a 9 10	23	10	S		116	—	—	—	—	—	—	—	—
MADISON—Boone County													
★☐ BOONE MEMORIAL HOSPITAL, 701 Madison Ave., Zip 25130; tel. 304/369-1230; Tommy H. Mullins, adm. **A**1a 9 10 **F**1 6 14 15 16 23 24 34 35 40 42 45	13	10	S		42	1081	16	38.1	7	9	3525	1523	88
MAN—Logan County													
★☐ MAN APPALACHIAN REGIONAL HOSPITAL, 700 E. McDonald, P O Box 485, Zip 25635; tel. 304/583-6511; Jason M. Riggins, adm. (Data for 251 days) **A**1a 9 10 **F**1 6 14 15 16 20 23 35 37 40 41 45 46 52; **S**0145	23	10	S		82	2817	41	50.0	12	252	5750	2576	79
MARLINTON—Pocahontas County													
★ POCAHONTAS MEMORIAL HOSPITAL, 103 Eighth St., Zip 24954; tel. 304/799-7400; L. H. Loftin, adm. **A**9 10 **F**1 12 14 15 16 30 34 35 41 45 47 49 50	13	10	S		40	801	13	32.5	4	0	1704	835	75
MARTINSBURG—Berkeley County													
★☐ CITY HOSPITAL, Dry Run Rd., P O Box 1418, Zip 25401; tel. 304/263-8971; J. Daniel Miller, adm. **A**1a 9 10 **F**1 3 6 10 12 14 15 16 21 23 24 27 32 34 35 36 40 41 42 44 45 46 47 52 53; **S**1755	23	10	S		226	7502	117	51.8	20	642	21350	8981	471
★☐ VETERANS ADMINISTRATION MEDICAL CENTER, Zip 25401; tel. 304/263-0811; I. V. Billes, dir. (Total facility includes 120 beds in nursing home-type unit) **A**1a **F**1 3 6 10 12 14 15 16 19 23 24 26 27 28 29 30 32 33 34 35 41 42 44 46 47 48 49 50	45	10	S	TF	497	6828	419	84.3	0	0	48146	33509	1251
				H	377	6420	302	—	0	0	—	—	1185
MONTGOMERY—Fayette County													
★☐ MONTGOMERY GENERAL HOSPITAL, Washington & Sixth Ave., Zip 25136; tel. 304/442-5151; Kenneth R. Fultz, pres. **A**1a 9 10 **F**1 3 6 14 15 16 23 35 36 40 41 44 45 46 47 52 53	23	10	S		110	4060	68	61.8	12	191	12728	4971	276
MORGANTOWN—Monongalia County													
★☐ MONONGALIA GENERAL HOSPITAL, 1200 J D Anderson Dr., Zip 26505; tel. 304/598-1212; Thomas J. Senker, pres. & chief exec. off. **A**1a 3 5 9 10 **F**1 3 6 10 11 12 14 15 16 23 26 30 32 33 34 35 36 37 40 43 45 46 47 50 52 53 54	23	10	S		220	9967	154	70.0	40	807	33014	14698	823
★☐ WEST VIRGINIA UNIVERSITY HOSPITAL, Medical Center Dr., Box 6401, Zip 26506; tel. 304/293-7075; Bernard G. Westfall, pres. (Nonreporting) **A**1a 2 3 5 8 9 10	12	10	S		452	—	—	—	—	—	—	—	—
MULLENS—Wyoming County													
★ WYOMING GENERAL HOSPITAL, 1238 Guyandotte Ave., Box 847, Zip 25882; tel. 304/294-4940; Alfred I. Lovitz, chief exec. off. (Nonreporting) **A**9 10	33	10	S		56	—	—	—	—	—	—	—	—
NEW MARTINSVILLE—Wetzel County													
★☐ WETZEL COUNTY HOSPITAL, 3 E. Benjamin Dr., Zip 26155; tel. 304/455-1212; Brian K. Felici, adm. **A**1a 9 10 **F**1 3 4 6 10 12 14 16 17 23 34 35 36 45 46 54	13	10	S		72	2372	34	47.2	6	185	6876	2669	146
OAK HILL—Fayette County													
★☐ PLATEAU MEDICAL CENTER, 430 Main St., Zip 25901; tel. 304/465-0551; Charles E. Kuebler, adm. (Nonreporting) **A**1a 10; **S**1375	33	10	S		91	—	—	—	—	—	—	—	—
PARKERSBURG—Wood County													
★☐ CAMDEN-CLARK MEMORIAL HOSPITAL, 800 Garfield Ave., P O Box 718, Zip 26102; tel. 304/424-2111; Leo D. Carsner, adm. **A**1a 2 9 10 **F**1 2 3 5 6 7 8 9 10 11 12 14 15 16 23 26 30 33 34 35 36 37 40 44 45 46 52 53	14	10	S		259	10626	183	70.7	28	561	32990	15911	911
★☐ ST. JOSEPH'S HOSPITAL, 19th St. & Murdoch Ave., Box 327, Zip 26101; tel. 304/424-4111; Arthur A. Maher, pres. & chief exec. off. **A**1a 9 10 **F**1 2 3 6 10 12 14 15 16 20 23 24 27 29 30 32 33 35 36 38 40 42 44 46 52 53	21	10	S		296	11871	223	75.3	20	1038	39688	18976	1014
PARSONS—Tucker County													
TUCKER COUNTY HOSPITAL, Box 280, Zip 26287; tel. 304/478-2511; James W. Michael, adm. **A**9 10 **F**1 3 12 15 16 34 35	33	10	S		23	481	7	17.1	0	8	1149	279	42
PETERSBURG—Grant County													
★ GRANT MEMORIAL HOSPITAL, Box 1019, Zip 26847; tel. 304/257-1026; Robert L. Harman, adm. (Total facility includes 10 beds in nursing home-type unit) **A**9 10 **F**1 3 6 10 14 15 16 19 23 35 36 37 40 45	13	10	S	TF	59	2247	39	66.1	6	187	5429	2533	178
				H	49	2131	29	—	6	187	4648	2168	—
PHILIPPI—Barbour County													
★☐ BROADDUS HOSPITAL, College Hill, Zip 26416; tel. 304/457-1760; Don D. Stoner, adm. **A**1a 9 10 **F**1 3 6 12 14 15 16 23 26 35 36 37 40 42 44 45 49 50 52; **S**0145	23	10	S		61	2439	38	53.5	6	144	5411	2734	171
POINT PLEASANT—Mason County													
★☐ PLEASANT VALLEY HOSPITAL, Valley Dr., Zip 25550; tel. 304/675-4340; Michael G. Sellards, exec. dir. (Total facility includes 100 beds in nursing home-type unit) **A**1a 9 10 **F**1 3 6 10 12 14 16 19 23 26 35 40 41 45 46 52	23	10	S	TF	228	4617	157	68.9	12	470	14137	6519	394
				H	128	4509	61	—	12	470	12113	5517	322

Hospital, Address, Telephone, Administrator, Approval and Facility Codes, Multihospital System Code	Classification Codes				Inpatient Data				Newborn Data		Expense (thousands of dollars)		
★ American Hospital Association (AHA) membership □ Joint Commission on Accreditation of Hospitals (JCAH) accreditation + American Osteopathic Hospital Association (AOHA) membership ○ American Osteopathic Association (AOA) accreditation Δ Commission on Accreditation of Rehabilitation Facilities (CARF) accreditation Control codes 61, 63, 64, 71, 72 and 73 indicate hospitals listed by AOHA, but not registered by AHA. For definition of numerical codes, see page A2	Control	Service	Stay	Facilities	Beds	Admissions	Census	Occupancy (percent)	Bassinets	Births	Total	Payroll	Personnel
PRINCETON—Mercer County													
★□ PRINCETON COMMUNITY HOSPITAL, 12th St., Zip 24740; tel. 304/487-7000; William L. Sheppard, adm. **A**1a 9 10 **F**1 2 3 6 10 12 14 15 16 20 23 26 27 29 30 32 33 34 35 36 37 40 43 44 46 47 49 50 52 53	14	10	S		215	10174	160	74.4	18	499	27328	13335	764
RANSON—Jefferson County													
★□ JEFFERSON MEMORIAL HOSPITAL, 300 S. Preston St., Zip 25438; tel. 304/725-3411; James O. Bryan, adm. **A**1a 9 10 **F**1 3 6 12 15 16 23 35 36 40 45 52 53	23	10	S		70	2996	39	55.7	10	390	6941	3380	192
RICHWOOD—Nicholas County													
★□ SACRED HEART HOSPITAL, Riverside Addition, Zip 26261; tel. 304/846-2573; David W. Forinash, adm. **A**1a 9 10 **F**1 6 14 15 16 23 34 35 40 41 45 50	21	10	S		34	802	11	32.4	6	33	3462	1084	87
RIPLEY—Jackson County													
★□ JACKSON GENERAL HOSPITAL, Pinnell St., Zip 25271; tel. 304/372-2731; William S. Chapman, exec. dir. **A**1a 9 10 **F**1 2 3 6 10 12 14 16 23 34 35 40 45 48 52 53	23	10	S		95	2292	32	33.7	8	76	6410	3189	203
ROMNEY—Hampshire County													
★ HAMPSHIRE MEMORIAL HOSPITAL, Zip 26757; tel. 304/822-4561; Harry E. Schweinsberg, chief exec. off. **A**9 10 **F**1 3 6 10 15 16 23 34 35 42 44 50	33	10	S		29	955	13	31.0	0	0	2301	918	88
RONCEVERTE—Greenbrier County													
★□ HUMANA HOSPITAL-GREENBRIER VALLEY, Davis-Stuart Rd., Box 497, Zip 24970; tel. 304/647-4411; D. Dale Landon, exec. dir. **A**1a 9 10 **F**1 2 3 6 10 12 14 15 16 34 35 36 40 45 46 52; **S**1235	33	10	S		122	4110	69	56.6	12	440	12529	4388	255
SISTERSVILLE—Tyler County													
SISTERSVILLE GENERAL HOSPITAL, 314 S. Wells St., Zip 26175; tel. 304/652-2611; Sue G. Roberts, actg. adm. **A**9 10 **F**1 6 14 15 16 34 35 40 45	14	10	S		28	719	9	31.0	6	69	1663	877	48
SOUTH CHARLESTON—Kanawha County													
○ + SOUTH CHARLESTON COMMUNITY HOSPITAL, 30 McCorkle Ave., Zip 25303; tel. 304/744-5311; Brock A. Slabach, adm. **A**9 10 11 12 **F**1 3 14 16 17 23 34 35 48	23	10	S		47	1027	22	46.8	0	0	5256	2007	130
★□ THOMAS MEMORIAL HOSPITAL (Formerly Herbert J. Thomas Memorial Hospital), 4605 MacCorkle Ave. S.W., Zip 25309; tel. 304/766-3600; Gary L. Park, pres. & chief exec. off. **A**1a 3 5 9 10 **F**1 3 5 6 9 10 11 12 14 15 16 20 23 26 33 34 35 36 40 41 42 44 45 46 47 48 49 52 53	23	10	S		259	9127	179	69.1	12	370	36184	17261	771
SPENCER—Roane County													
★ ROANE GENERAL HOSPITAL, 200 Hospital Dr., Zip 25276; tel. 304/927-4444; David G. Graham, adm. **A**9 10 **F**1 6 10 14 16 23 34 35 36 40 44 45 52	23	10	S		80	3014	39	48.8	6	207	—	3030	200
□ SPENCER HOSPITAL, Box 160, Zip 25276; tel. 304/927-2110; Barbara A. Martin, adm. **A**1a **F**23 42 46 47	12	62	L		142	94	142	100.0	0	0	4116	3052	238
SUMMERSVILLE—Nicholas County													
★ SUMMERSVILLE MEMORIAL HOSPITAL, 400 Fairview Hts. Rd., Zip 26651; tel. 304/872-2891; W. Don Smith II, adm. (Total facility includes 44 beds in nursing home-type unit) **A**9 10 **F**1 3 6 12 14 15 16 19 34 35 40 45 46 52 53	14	10	S	TF H	74 30	1504 1475	59 16	79.7 —	8 8	287 287	4411 3691	2082 1737	140 80
WEBSTER SPRINGS—Webster County													
★ WEBSTER COUNTY MEMORIAL HOSPITAL, 324 Miller Mountain Dr., Zip 26288; tel. 304/847-5682; Joe H. Clifton, adm. **A**9 10 **F**1 6 14 16 35 40 45 52	13	10	S		35	960	9	13.8	6	82	1467	787	61
WEIRTON—Brooke County													
★□ WEIRTON MEDICAL CENTER, 601 Colliers Way, Zip 26062; tel. 304/797-6000; Charles A. Okey, exec. dir. **A**1a 9 10 **F**1 3 6 7 9 10 11 12 14 15 16 23 29 30 34 35 37 40 45 46 48 52 53 54	23	10	S		265	8038	115	43.4	21	262	24581	10827	628
WEIRTON—Hancock County													
+ WEIRTON OSTEOPATHIC HOSPITAL, 3045 Pennsylvania Ave., Zip 26062; tel. 304/723-1200; Charles Graham, adm. **A**9 10 **F**1 5 6 16 19 34 45 46 52	23	10	S		16	655	8	50.0	0	0	1318	449	31
WELCH—McDowell County													
□ STEVENS CLINIC HOSPITAL, U. S. 52 E., Zip 24801; tel. 304/436-3161; Joseph E. Peery Jr., adm. **A**1a 9 10 **F**1 2 6 10 14 15 16 23 34 35 43 45 46 47 50 53	33	10	S		72	2531	29	30.2	0	0	8073	4086	167
WESTON—Lewis County													
★□ STONEWALL JACKSON MEMORIAL HOSPITAL, Rte. 4, Box 10, Zip 26452; tel. 304/269-3000; David D. Shaffer, chief exec. off. **A**1a 9 10 **F**1 3 6 10 14 15 16 23 26 34 35 36 37 40 45 46 47 53	23	10	S		70	2532	32	45.7	6	336	6179	3136	176
WESTON HOSPITAL, River Ave., Drawer 1127, Zip 26452; tel. 304/269-1210; Rein Valdov, adm. **F**15 23 30 32 33 42 46 47	12	22	L		460	996	362	78.7	0	0	12385	8482	602
WHEELING—Ohio County													
★□ OHIO VALLEY MEDICAL CENTER (Includes Peterson Hospital), 2000 Eoff St., Zip 26003; tel. 304/234-0123; George Brannen, chief oper. off. (Nonreporting) **A**1a 2 3 5 6 8 9 10; **S**3315	23	10	S		629	—	—	—	—	—	—	—	—
★□ WHEELING HOSPITAL, Medical Park, Zip 26003; tel. 304/243-3000; Samuel G. Nazzaro, adm. & chief exec. off. **A**1a 2 3 5 10 **F**1 2 3 5 6 7 8 9 10 11 12 14 15 16 23 24 26 30 32 33 34 35 36 40 41 44 45 46 52 53 54	23	10	S		281	11896	189	67.3	27	1289	39810	16983	933
WILLIAMSON—Mingo County													
APPALACHIAN REGIONAL HOSPITAL, See South Williamson, Ky.													
WILLIAMSON MEMORIAL HOSPITAL, P O Box 1980, Zip 25661; tel. 304/235-2500; Stephen L. Midkiff, adm. (Nonreporting) **A**9 10; **S**1775	33	10	S		72	—	—	—	—	—	—	—	—

Hospital, Address, Telephone, Administrator, Approval and Facility Codes, Multihospital System Code	Classification Codes				Inpatient Data				Newborn Data		Expense (thousands of dollars)		
★ American Hospital Association (AHA) membership □ Joint Commission on Accreditation of Hospitals (JCAH) accreditation + American Osteopathic Hospital Association (AOHA) membership ○ American Osteopathic Association (AOA) accreditation Δ Commission on Accreditation of Rehabilitation Facilities (CARF) accreditation Control codes 61, 63, 64, 71, 72 and 73 indicate hospitals listed by AOHA, but not registered by AHA. For definition of numerical codes, see page A2	Control	Service	Stay	Facilities	Beds	Admissions	Census	Occupancy (percent)	Bassinets	Births	Total	Payroll	Personnel

Wisconsin

	Control	Service	Stay	Facilities	Beds	Admissions	Census	Occupancy (percent)	Bassinets	Births	Total	Payroll	Personnel
ALGOMA—Kewaunee County													
□ ALGOMA MEMORIAL HOSPITAL (Includes Algoma Memorial Long Term Care Unit), 1510 Fremont St., Zip 54201; tel. 414/487-5511; Kenneth Secor, dir. (Total facility includes 51 beds in nursing home-type unit) **A**1a 9 10 **F**1 6 10 14 15 16 19 23 26 34 35 40 43 49 50	14	10	S	TF	77	603	52	67.5	10	42	2229	1239	76
				H	26	554	6	—	10	42	1518	816	57
AMERY—Polk County													
⊠ APPLE RIVER HOSPITAL (Formerly Apple River Valley Memorial Hospital), 221 Scholl St., Zip 54001; tel. 715/268-7151; J. Kenneth Jones, adm. **A**1a 9 10 **F**1 3 6 12 14 15 16 23 26 34 35 36 40 53; **S**1755	23	10	S		49	1167	14	28.6	5	129	3331	1446	76
ANTIGO—Langlade County													
□ LANGLADE MEMORIAL HOSPITAL, 112 E. Fifth Ave., Zip 54409; tel. 715/623-2331; Kevin J. Keighron, exec. dir. **A**1a 9 10 **F**1 3 6 12 15 16 23 24 26 34 35 36 40 44 50; **S**3615	21	10	S		80	2280	31	38.8	12	263	6207	2924	154
APPLETON—Outagamie County													
⊠ APPLETON MEDICAL CENTER, 1818 N. Meade St., Zip 54911; tel. 414/731-4101; C. William Freeby MD, pres. **A**1a 2 3 5 9 10 **F**1 3 4 6 10 12 14 15 16 21 23 24 26 32 34 35 36 40 50 52 53 54	23	10	S		156	5906	88	48.4	21	776	24862	11271	588
⊠ Δ ST. ELIZABETH HOSPITAL, 1506 S. Oneida St., Zip 54915; tel. 414/738-2000; Otto L. Cox, pres. **A**1a 2 3 5 7 9 10 **F**1 5 6 7 8 9 10 11 12 14 16 20 23 24 26 30 32 33 34 35 36 41 42 44 45 46 47 49 51 53 54; **S**6745	21	10	S		279	9144	169	60.6	32	1145	34880	17548	694
ARCADIA—Trempealeau County													
⊠ ST. JOSEPH'S HOSPITAL OF ARCADIA, 464 S. St. Joseph Ave., Zip 54612; tel. 608/323-3341; Bruce E. Roesler, adm. (Total facility includes 75 beds in nursing home-type unit) **A**1a 9 10 **F**1 3 14 15 16 19 23 34 35 36 40 42 52; **S**9650	23	10	S	TF	101	438	76	75.2	4	58	2128	1147	91
				H	26	401	5	—	4	58	1095	605	56
ASHLAND—Ashland County													
⊠ MEMORIAL MEDICAL CENTER, 1615 Maple Lane, Zip 54806; tel. 715/682-4563; Lowell J. Miller, pres. **A**1a 9 10 **F**1 2 3 6 7 10 12 14 15 16 23 24 26 27 28 30 32 33 34 35 36 40 48 49 52 53	23	10	S		161	4557	76	47.2	17	648	11092	5804	303
BALDWIN—St. Croix County													
★ BALDWIN COMMUNITY MEMORIAL HOSPITAL, Zip 54002; tel. 715/684-3311; Gordon Palmer, adm. **A**9 10 **F**1 5 6 14 15 16 23 26 30 34 35 36 40 50	23	10	S		33	979	13	39.4	5	64	2341	1161	60
BARABOO—Sauk County													
⊠ ST. CLARE HOSPITAL, 707 14th St., Zip 53913; tel. 608/356-5561; Ronald J. Levy, exec. dir. **A**1a 9 10 **F**1 3 6 10 11 14 15 16 23 24 26 33 34 35 36 40 50 52; **S**5455	23	10	S		100	2670	38	38.0	8	270	8144	3699	179
BARRON—Barron County													
⊠ BARRON MEMORIAL MEDICAL CENTER, 1222 Woodland Ave., Zip 54812; tel. 715/537-3186; Gerald Olson, adm. (Total facility includes 50 beds in nursing home-type unit) **A**1a 10 **F**1 3 14 16 19 23 24 26 29 30 34 35 36 40 52 53	23	10	S	TF	98	1455	67	68.4	6	135	4862	2343	136
				H	48	1393	19	—	6	135	3966	1798	97
BEAVER DAM—Dodge County													
⊠ BEAVER DAM COMMUNITY HOSPITALS (Includes Hillside Unit, 707 S. University Ave., Zip 53916; tel. 414/887-7181; Lakeview Unit, 208 La Crosse St., Zip 53916; tel. 414/887-7181), 707 S. University Ave., Zip 53916; tel. 414/887-7181; John R. Landdeck, exec. dir. (Total facility includes 123 beds in nursing home-type unit) **A**1a 9 10 **F**1 3 6 9 12 14 15 16 19 23 24 26 34 35 40 42 44 52 53	23	10	S	TF	213	3554	163	76.2	18	437	13540	6856	396
				H	90	3499	43	—	18	437	11012	5413	306
HILLSIDE UNIT, See Beaver Dam Community Hospitals													
LAKEVIEW UNIT, See Beaver Dam Community Hospitals													
BELOIT—Rock County													
⊠ BELOIT MEMORIAL HOSPITAL, 1969 W. Hart Rd., Zip 53511; tel. 608/364-5011; Michael E. Rindler, pres. **A**1a 10 **F**1 3 6 7 8 10 11 12 15 16 23 24 26 34 35 36 40 44 52 53	23	10	S		174	6993	102	58.6	20	846	18607	9076	458
BERLIN—Green Lake County													
⊠ BERLIN HOSPITAL ASSOCIATION (Includes Berlin Memorial Hospital and Julliette Manor Nursing Home), 225 Memorial Dr., Zip 54923; tel. 414/361-1313; Patrick E. Linton, pres. (Total facility includes 102 beds in nursing home-type unit) **A**1a 10 **F**1 3 6 14 16 19 23 26 34 35 36 40 44 49 50	23	10	S	TF	163	2714	132	81.0	11	266	10124	4587	243
				H	61	2654	34	—	11	266	8298	3425	171
BLACK RIVER FALLS—Jackson County													
⊠ BLACK RIVER MEMORIAL HOSPITAL, 711 W. Adams St., Zip 54615; tel. 715/284-5361; Roger W. Wiste, adm. **A**1a 9 10 **F**1 2 5 14 16 23 34 35 36 40	23	10	S		51	1568	19	37.3	6	213	3362	1620	92
BLOOMER—Chippewa County													
★ BLOOMER COMMUNITY MEMORIAL HOSPITAL AND SKILLED NURSING FACILITY, 1501 Thompson St., Zip 54724; tel. 715/568-2000; Edward Wittrock, chief exec. off. (Total facility includes 75 beds in nursing home-type unit) **A**9 10 **F**1 19 23 26 34 35 40 42	23	10	S	TF	112	903	71	63.4	5	97	2998	1638	101
				H	37	846	11	—	5	97	2413	1208	73
BOSCOBEL—Grant County													
★ MEMORIAL HOSPITAL OF BOSCOBEL, 205 Parker St., Zip 53805; tel. 608/375-4112; Gerhard O. Qualey, adm. (Total facility includes 104 beds in nursing home-type unit) **A**9 10 **F**1 3 10 12 14 16 19 23 24 27 34 35 40 42 52 53; **S**0825	23	10	S	TF	136	1241	107	82.3	4	102	3943	1831	127
				H	32	1158	13	—	4	102	2534	963	67
BROOKFIELD—Waukesha County													
⊠ ELMBROOK MEMORIAL HOSPITAL, 19333 W. North Ave., Zip 53005; tel. 414/785-2000; Stephen R. Young, pres. **A**1a 9 10 **F**1 3 6 9 10 12 15 16 21 23 24 25 26 33 34 35 36 40 43 44 48 49 50 53; **S**6745	21	10	S		136	5206	90	66.2	24	584	20850	9572	442
BURLINGTON—Racine County													
⊠ MEMORIAL HOSPITAL, 301 Randolph St., Zip 53105; tel. 414/763-2411 **A**1a 9 10 **F**1 3 5 6 10 12 14 15 16 23 24 26 28 30 32 33 34 35 36 40 44 50 52 53	23	10	S		90	4069	54	45.0	14	596	11725	5205	264
CHILTON—Calumet County													
★ CALUMET MEMORIAL HOSPITAL, 614 Memorial Dr., Zip 53014; tel. 414/849-2386; Joseph L. Schumacher, adm. **A**9 **F**1 3 6 10 12 14 15 16 23 24 30 34 35 36 40 41 43 50 52 53	23	10	S		53	1321	17	31.5	10	144	4118	1852	85
CHIPPEWA FALLS—Chippewa County													
⊠ ST. JOSEPH'S HOSPITAL, 2661 County Trunk I, Zip 54729; tel. 715/723-1811; David B. Fish, exec. vice-pres. & adm. **A**1a 9 10 **F**1 3 12 15 16 23 30 34 35 40 41 48 49 53; **S**5355	21	10	S		149	4407	85	57.0	12	430	12880	6437	298

Hospital, Address, Telephone, Administrator, Approval and Facility Codes, Multihospital System Code	Classification Codes				Inpatient Data				Newborn Data		Expense (thousands of dollars)		
★ American Hospital Association (AHA) membership ☐ Joint Commission on Accreditation of Hospitals (JCAH) accreditation + American Osteopathic Hospital Association (AOHA) membership ○ American Osteopathic Association (AOA) accreditation Δ Commission on Accreditation of Rehabilitation Facilities (CARF) accreditation Control codes 61, 63, 64, 71, 72 and 73 indicate hospitals listed by AOHA, but not registered by AHA. For definition of numerical codes, see page A2	Control	Service	Stay	Facilities	Beds	Admissions	Census	Occupancy (percent)	Bassinets	Births	Total	Payroll	Personnel
CLINTONVILLE—Waupaca County													
☐★ CLINTONVILLE COMMUNITY HOSPITAL, 35 N. Anne St., Zip 54929; tel. 715/823-3121; Andrew V. Lagatta, exec. vice-pres. **A**1a 9 10 **F**1 12 14 16 23 34 35 40 52	23	10	S		35	964	12	34.3	8	156	2468	1025	67
COLUMBUS—Columbia County													
☐★ COLUMBUS COMMUNITY HOSPITAL, 1515 Park Ave., Zip 53925; tel. 414/623-2200; Miles Meyer, adm. **A**1a 9 10 **F**1 3 6 12 14 15 16 23 24 26 33 34 35 36 40 43 44	23	10	S		53	1596	19	35.8	6	206	4335	2065	99
CUDAHY—Milwaukee County													
☐★ TRINITY MEMORIAL HOSPITAL, 5900 S. Lake Dr., Zip 53110; tel. 414/769-9000; Kenneth V. Schreiner, pres. & chief exec. off. **A**1a 2 9 10 **F**1 3 5 6 7 8 10 11 12 14 15 16 23 24 26 28 30 32 33 34 35 36 40 41 43 44 52 53 54; **S**1395	23	10	S		185	6224	115	62.2	23	314	26495	13540	600
CUMBERLAND—Barron County													
☐ CUMBERLAND MEMORIAL HOSPITAL, Box 37, Zip 54829; tel. 715/822-2741; Earl F. Strub, adm. (Total facility includes 49 beds in nursing home-type unit) **A**1a 9 10 **F**1 14 16 19 23 24 26 29 30 32 33 34 35 40 50	23	10	S	TF	89	1380	66	74.2	6	142	4001	2243	147
				H	40	1350	18	—	6	142	3106	1711	117
DARLINGTON—Lafayette County													
★ MEMORIAL HOSPITAL OF LAFAYETTE COUNTY, 800 Clay St., Zip 53530; tel. 608/776-4466; Craig W. C. Schmidt, adm. **A**9 10 **F**1 15 16 23 30 34 35 36 40 52 53	13	10	S		28	842	7	25.0	6	134	1756	851	57
DODGEVILLE—Iowa County													
☐ MEMORIAL HOSPITAL OF IOWA COUNTY, 825 S. Iowa St., Zip 53533; tel. 608/935-2711; Rosellen Crow, adm. (Total facility includes 44 beds in nursing home-type unit) **A**1a 9 10 **F**1 3 6 14 15 16 19 23 24 26 30 34 35 36 40 43 49 50 53	23	10	S	TF	84	1754	56	66.7	7	229	5243	2177	124
				H	40	1698	17	—	7	229	4832	1846	103
DURAND—Pepin County													
★ CHIPPEWA VALLEY HOSPITAL AND OAKVIEW CARE CENTER (Formerly Chippewa Valley Hospital and Nursing Home), 1620 Third Ave. W., Zip 54736; tel. 715/672-4211; Malcolm P. Cole, adm. (Total facility includes 60 beds in nursing home-type unit) **A**9 10 **F**1 14 15 16 19 23 26 34 35 36 40 42 43; **S**9355	21	10	S	TF	90	858	51	56.7	4	102	3375	1323	87
				H	30	788	9	—	4	102	2249	752	66
EAGLE RIVER—Vilas County													
★ EAGLE RIVER MEMORIAL HOSPITAL, P O Box 129, Zip 54521; tel. 715/479-7411; Jerome S. Burdick, chief exec. off. & adm. **A**9 10 **F**1 3 14 15 16 23 24 28 30 32 33 34 35 40 41 42 43 44 49 52	23	10	S		41	866	9	22.0	4	62	3180	1463	89
EAU CLAIRE—Eau Claire County													
☐★ LUTHER HOSPITAL, 1221 Whipple St., Zip 54702; tel. 715/839-3311; Douglas R. Trembath, pres. **A**1a 2 3 5 9 10 **F**1 2 3 5 6 7 8 9 10 11 12 14 15 16 20 21 23 24 26 27 28 29 30 32 33 34 35 36 40 41 42 43 44 48 49 50 51 52 53 54	23	10	S		228	7394	112	49.1	24	1205	25078	11876	650
☐★ Δ SACRED HEART HOSPITAL, 900 W. Clairemont Ave., Zip 54701; tel. 715/839-4121; Matthew W. Hubler, exec. vice-pres. **A**1a 2 3 5 7 9 10 **F**1 3 5 6 7 8 9 10 11 12 14 15 16 21 23 24 25 26 27 28 29 30 32 33 34 35 36 37 38 40 42 44 49 50 52 53; **S**5355	21	10	S		334	8912	160	47.9	22	503	31973	16611	766
EDGERTON—Rock County													
☐ MEMORIAL COMMUNITY HOSPITAL, 313 Stoughton Rd., Zip 53534; tel. 608/884-3441; Harlan J. Murphy, adm. (Total facility includes 61 beds in nursing home-type unit) **A**1a 9 10 **F**1 3 16 19 23 24 35 40 41 48 53	23	10	S	TF	115	1386	85	64.9	6	63	6343	3276	156
				H	54	1303	26	—	6	63	5465	2867	130
ELKHORN—Walworth County													
☐★ LAKELAND HOSPITAL, Hwy. NN, Box 1002, Zip 53121; tel. 414/741-2000; William H. Lange, adm. **A**1a 9 10 **F**1 3 6 10 12 15 16 21 23 26 30 34 35 36 40 50 52 53	13	10	S		119	4723	59	46.8	14	488	12404	5781	305
FOND DU LAC—Fond Du Lac County													
☐★ Δ ST. AGNES HOSPITAL, 430 E. Division St., Zip 54935; tel. 414/929-2300; James J. Sexton, pres. **A**1a 2 7 9 10 **F**1 3 6 7 8 9 10 11 16 21 23 24 26 27 32 33 34 35 36 39 40 41 44 48 49 50 52 53; **S**5695	21	10	S		233	8441	170	73.0	24	1341	29476	15195	668
FORT ATKINSON—Jefferson County													
☐★ FORT ATKINSON MEMORIAL HOSPITAL, 611 E. Sherman Ave., Zip 53538; tel. 414/563-2451; John C. Albaugh, pres. **A**1a 9 10 **F**1 3 5 6 10 14 15 16 23 24 26 28 30 34 35 36 40 41 50 53	23	10	S		113	3658	51	45.1	14	331	9973	4641	251
FREDERIC—Polk County													
FREDERIC MUNICIPAL HOSPITAL, United Way & Hwy. 35, Zip 54837; tel. 715/327-4201; Curtis M. Wassberg, adm. **A**9 10 **F**1 3 5 14 16 23 26 34 35 40 50	14	10	S		25	506	7	28.0	4	29	1290	511	37
FRIENDSHIP—Adams County													
☐ ADAMS COUNTY MEMORIAL HOSPITAL AND NURSING CARE UNIT, 402 W. Lake St., P O Box 40, Zip 53934; tel. 608/339-3331; Allen Teal, adm. (Total facility includes 18 beds in nursing home-type unit) **A**1a 9 10 **F**1 6 14 16 19 23 26 32 34 35 36 40 41 43 52	23	10	S	TF	67	1451	34	50.7	6	88	3973	2117	120
				H	49	1431	16	—	6	88	3568	1835	109
GRANTSBURG—Burnett County													
☐ BURNETT GENERAL HOSPITAL, St. George Ave. & Parkview Dr., P O Box 99, Zip 54840; tel. 715/463-5353; Stanley J. Gaynor, adm. (Total facility includes 53 beds in nursing home-type unit) **A**1a 9 10 **F**1 16 19 23 34 35 36 40 50	23	10	S	TF	84	686	61	72.6	5	90	2872	1623	100
				H	31	661	9	—	5	90	2393	1247	68
GREEN BAY—Brown County													
☐★ BELLIN MEMORIAL HOSPITAL, 744 S. Webster Ave., Zip 54301; Mailing Address Box 1700, Zip 54305; tel. 414/433-3500; Thomas D. Arndt, pres. **A**1a 9 10 **F**1 3 4 6 10 12 14 15 16 21 23 24 26 27 28 29 31 32 34 36 37 40 41 42 43 48 49 50 52 53 54	21	10	S		242	9806	172	71.1	30	1740	41190	19816	1022
☐ BROWN COUNTY MENTAL HEALTH CENTER, 2900 St. Anthony Dr., Zip 54301; tel. 414/468-1136; Robert J. Cole, exec. dir. (Total facility includes 190 beds in nursing home-type unit) **A**1a 10 **F**19 24 28 29 30 32 33 42 48 49	13	22	S	TF	278	1416	240	86.3	0	0	10528	6463	335
				H	88	1364	56	—	0	0	5218	3257	167
☐★ ST. MARY'S HOSPITAL MEDICAL CENTER, 1726 Shawano Ave., Zip 54303; tel. 414/498-4200; James G. Coller, exec. vice-pres. & adm. **A**1a 9 10 **F**1 3 6 9 10 12 14 16 23 26 30 33 34 35 36 40 52; **S**5355	21	10	S		158	6514	84	53.2	12	538	18723	8799	402
☐★ Δ ST. VINCENT HOSPITAL, 835 S. Van Buren St., P O Box 13508, Zip 54307; tel. 414/433-0111; Joseph J. Neidenbach, adm. **A**1a 2 7 9 10 **F**1 2 3 5 6 7 8 9 10 11 12 14 16 20 23 24 25 26 27 28 29 30 33 34 35 36 38 40 41 42 43 44 49 51 52 53; **S**5355	21	10	S		442	13187	262	59.3	25	1582	51829	27666	1296
HARTFORD—Washington County													
☐★ HARTFORD MEMORIAL HOSPITAL, 1032 E. Sumner St., Zip 53027; tel. 414/673-2300; Mark Schwartz, pres. **A**1a 9 10 **F**1 3 6 10 11 12 16 23 26 34 35 40 44 52 53	23	10	S		71	2255	35	49.3	13	264	7444	2760	178
HAYWARD—Sawyer County													
☐★ HAYWARD AREA MEMORIAL HOSPITAL, Rte. 3, Box 3999, Zip 54843; tel. 715/634-8911; Barbara A. Peickert, chief exec. off. (Total facility includes 76 beds in nursing home-type unit) **A**1a 9 10 **F**1 16 19 23 35 36 40 44	23	10	S	TF	117	1115	81	69.2	5	71	4001	1825	126
				H	41	1044	13	—	5	71	2828	1109	68
HILLSBORO—Vernon County													
☐★ ST. JOSEPH'S MEMORIAL HOSPITAL, 400 Water Ave., Zip 54634; tel. 608/489-2211; Rolin H. Johnson, chief exec. off. (Total facility includes 65 beds in nursing home-type unit) **A**1a 9 10 **F**1 3 16 19 21 23 34 35 36 40 52; **S**5705	21	10	S	TF	99	1111	72	72.7	6	120	3496	1721	116
				H	34	1059	12	—	6	120	2268	1053	81

Hospital, Address, Telephone, Administrator, Approval and Facility Codes, Multihospital System Code	Classification Codes				Inpatient Data				Newborn Data		Expense (thousands of dollars)		
★ American Hospital Association (AHA) membership □ Joint Commission on Accreditation of Hospitals (JCAH) accreditation + American Osteopathic Hospital Association (AOHA) membership ○ American Osteopathic Association (AOA) accreditation Δ Commission on Accreditation of Rehabilitation Facilities (CARF) accreditation Control codes 61, 63, 64, 71, 72 and 73 indicate hospitals listed by AOHA, but not registered by AHA. For definition of numerical codes, see page A2	Control	Service	Stay	Facilities	Beds	Admissions	Census	Occupancy (percent)	Bassinets	Births	Total	Payroll	Personnel
HUDSON—St. Croix County													
★□ HUDSON MEDICAL CENTER (Formerly Hudson Memorial Hospital), 400 Wisconsin St., Box 361, Zip 54016; tel. 715/386-9321; John Hartz, adm. **A**1a 9 10 **F**1 3 12 14 15 21 23 24 26 32 34 35 36 40 41 44 45 47	23	10	S		45	1340	17	37.8	8	208	5058	2376	124
JANESVILLE—Rock County													
ANDERSON ALCOHOLIC REHABILITATION HOSPITAL, See Parkside Lodge of Wisconsin													
★□ MERCY HOSPITAL OF JANESVILLE, 1000 Mineral Point Ave., Zip 53545; tel. 608/756-6000; Sr. M. Michael Berry, adm. **A**1a 2 9 10 **F**1 3 6 10 11 12 15 16 23 24 34 35 36 40 52 53	23	10	S		202	9340	130	59.6	24	1438	24019	12346	600
□ PARKSIDE LODGE OF WISCONSIN (Formerly Anderson Alcoholic Rehabilitation Hospital), 320 Lincoln St., Box 749, Zip 53545; tel. 608/754-2264; Ron Del Ciello, dir. **A**1b **F**33 42 49	33	82	S		19	218	13	68.4	0	0	2398	909	22
KAUKAUNA—Outagamie County													
★□ KAUKAUNA COMMUNITY HOSPITAL, 308 E. 14th St., Zip 54130; tel. 414/766-4211; Jeffrey K. Jenkins, pres. **A**1a 9 10 **F**1 2 12 14 16 17 23 34 35 36 40 45 46 47; **S**6745	23	10	S		52	1167	17	32.7	8	152	2918	1396	80
KENOSHA—Kenosha County													
★□ KENOSHA HOSPITAL AND MEDICAL CENTER (Formerly Kenosha Memorial Hospital), 6308 Eighth Ave., Zip 53140; tel. 414/656-2011; Richard O. Schmidt Jr., pres. & chief exec. off. **A**1a 9 10 **F**1 3 5 6 10 12 15 16 23 24 26 27 28 29 30 31 32 33 34 35 41 42 43 44 49 50 52 53 54	23	10	S		209	5401	89	42.6	0	0	24412	12126	505
★□ ST. CATHERINE'S HOSPITAL (Formerly St. Catherine's Hospital and Medical Center), 3556 Seventh Ave., Zip 53140; tel. 414/656-3011; Michael W. Muenzberg, pres. **A**1a b 3 5 9 10 **F**1 3 5 6 7 8 9 10 11 12 14 15 16 20 23 24 26 27 30 32 33 34 35 36 40 42 43 48 49 50 53	23	10	S		216	6637	112	51.9	44	1538	25077	12534	547
KEWAUNEE—Kewaunee County													
★□ ST. MARY'S KEWAUNEE AREA MEMORIAL HOSPITAL, First & Lincoln Sts., Zip 54216; tel. 414/388-2210; David R. Haupt, adm. **A**1a 9 10 **F**1 14 16 23 34 35 40	23	10	S		30	470	6	20.0	4	56	1362	588	31
LA CROSSE—La Crosse County													
LA CROSSE LUTHERAN HOSPITAL, See Lutheran Hospital-La Crosse													
★□ Δ LUTHERAN HOSPITAL-LA CROSSE (Formerly La Crosse Lutheran Hospital), 1910 South Ave., Zip 54601; tel. 608/785-0530; Jack Schwem, pres. **A**1a b 2 3 5 7 9 10 **F**1 2 3 4 5 6 7 8 9 10 11 12 14 15 16 20 21 23 24 25 26 27 28 29 30 32 33 34 35 36 40 41 42 44 49 50 51 52 53 54	23	10	S		369	15041	265	71.8	24	1496	58747	30069	1472
★□ ST. FRANCIS MEDICAL CENTER, 700 West Avenue S., Zip 54601; tel. 608/785-0940; Sr. Celesta Day, adm. **A**1a 2 3 5 9 10 **F**1 3 5 6 9 10 11 12 14 15 16 19 23 24 25 26 27 28 29 30 32 33 34 35 36 37 38 40 42 43 44 48 49 50 51 52 53; **S**9650	21	10	S		361	9273	179	49.6	20	1113	32425	16822	948
LADYSMITH—Rusk County													
★□ RUSK COUNTY MEMORIAL HOSPITAL AND NURSING HOME, 900 College Ave. W., Zip 54848; tel. 715/532-5561; J. Michael Shaw, adm. (Total facility includes 117 beds in nursing home-type unit) **A**1a 9 10 **F**1 3 16 19 23 35 36 40 50 52	13	10	S	TF	152	1395	128	84.2	6	210	5902	2894	150
				H	35	1347	14	—	6	210	3523	1663	78
LANCASTER—Grant County													
□ MEMORIAL HOSPITAL, 507 S. Monroe St., Zip 53813; tel. 608/723-2143; Ronald F. Bruni, adm. **A**1a 9 10 **F**1 3 6 7 10 16 23 34 35 40 53	14	10	S		32	1464	17	53.1	7	219	3140	1425	86
MADISON—Dane County													
CENTRAL WISCONSIN CENTER FOR DEVELOPMENTALLY DISABLED, 317 Knutson Dr., Zip 53704; tel. 608/249-2151; R. C. Scheerenberger PhD, dir. **F**16 23 24 26 32 33 38 42 44	12	12	S		44	256	12	27.3	0	0	—	—	—
MENDOTA MENTAL HEALTH INSTITUTE, 301 Troy Dr., Zip 53704; tel. 608/244-2411; Terence W. Schnapp, chief exec. off. **A** 3 5 10 **F**24 28 30 32 33 42 44 50	12	22	L		296	610	239	80.7	0	0	19664	13959	606
★□ Δ MERITER HOSPITAL (Includes Meriter-Madison General Hospital, 202 S. Park St., Zip 53715; tel. 608/267-6000; Meriter-Methodist Hospital, 309 W. Washington Ave., Zip 53703; tel. 608/251-2371), 202 S. Park St., Zip 53715; tel. 608/267-6000; Terri L. Potter, pres. (Total facility includes 120 beds in nursing home-type unit) **A**1a 2 3 5 7 8 9 10 **F**1 3 5 6 7 8 9 10 11 12 13 14 15 16 19 20 23 24 26 27 30 32 33 34 35 36 37 38 40 44 48 49 51 52 53 54	23	10	S	TF	763	27179	494	64.7	55	2973	88615	45061	1782
				H	643	27073	377	—	55	2973	85146	43118	1686
MERITER-MADISON GENERAL HOSPITAL, See Meriter Hospital													
MERITER-METHODIST HOSPITAL, See Meriter Hospital													
★□ ST. MARYS HOSPITAL MEDICAL CENTER, 707 S. Mills St., Zip 53715; tel. 608/251-6100; Gerald W. Lefert, exec. dir. **A**1a 3 5 9 10 **F**1 2 3 4 5 6 9 10 11 12 14 16 23 24 27 29 30 33 34 35 36 40 42 43 44 50 51 52 53 54; **S**5455	23	10	S		357	16129	239	66.9	30	2363	50983	24331	1097
★□ Δ UNIVERSITY OF WISCONSIN HOSPITAL AND CLINICS, 600 Highland Ave., Zip 53792; tel. 608/263-6400; Gordon M. Derzon, supt. **A**1a 3 5 7 8 9 10 **F**1 2 3 4 5 6 7 8 9 10 11 12 14 15 16 17 20 22 23 24 25 26 27 28 30 33 34 35 38 41 42 43 44 50 52 53 54	12	10	S		503	15618	350	69.6	0	0	121798	52381	2552
★□ WILLIAM S. MIDDLETON MEMORIAL VETERANS HOSPITAL, 2500 Overlook Terr., Zip 53705; tel. 608/256-1901; Nathan L. Geraths, dir. **A**1a 3 5 8 **F**2 3 4 6 9 10 11 12 14 15 16 19 20 23 24 26 27 28 30 32 33 34 41 44 49 50 53 54	45	10	S		306	8925	203	66.3	0	0	43979	26152	943
MANITOWOC—Manitowoc County													
★□ HOLY FAMILY MEDICAL CENTER (Formerly Holy Family Hospital), 2300 Western Ave., Zip 54220; tel. 414/684-2011; LeRoy F. Pesce, pres. **A**1a 9 10 **F**1 3 5 6 7 8 9 10 11 12 14 15 16 23 24 26 27 28 30 32 33 34 35 36 40 41 42 44 48 49 52 53; **S**1455	21	10	S		147	4926	78	53.1	26	671	18117	7999	422
□ MEMORIAL HOSPITAL, 333 Reed Ave., Zip 54220; tel. 414/682-7765; Ray Wimmer Jr., pres. **A**1a 9 10 **F**1 3 6 10 12 14 16 23 24 34 35 43 44 50 52 53	23	10	S		87	1933	31	35.6	0	0	6759	3082	168
MARINETTE—Marinette County													
★□ BAY AREA MEDICAL CENTER (Formerly Marinette General Hospital), 3100 Shore Dr., Zip 54143; tel. 715/735-6621; Thomas K. Prusak, chief exec. off. **A**1a 2 9 10 **F**1 3 5 6 12 14 15 16 20 23 26 30 34 35 40 44 53; **S**2495	23	10	S		99	3000	37	37.4	13	581	8059	3509	175
MARSHFIELD—Wood County													
□ NORWOOD HEALTH CENTER, 1600 N. Chestnut Ave., Zip 54449; tel. 715/384-2188; Kurt Baker, dep. dir. (Total facility includes 66 beds in nursing home-type unit) **A**1b 10 **F**19 24 32 33 42	13	22	S	TF	85	387	77	90.6	0	0	3452	2040	133
				H	19	375	12	—	0	0	1652	908	53
★□ Δ ST. JOSEPH'S HOSPITAL, 611 St. Joseph Ave., Zip 54449; tel. 715/387-1713; David R. Jaye, pres. **A**1a 2 3 5 6 7 9 10 **F**1 3 4 5 7 8 9 10 12 14 16 20 21 23 24 25 26 27 29 30 33 34 35 36 40 41 44 48 49 50 51 52 54; **S**5305	21	10	S		524	15353	342	65.3	22	1290	69319	30278	1259
MAUSTON—Juneau County													
□ HESS MEMORIAL HOSPITAL, 1050 Division St., Zip 53948; tel. 608/847-6161; Daniel N. Manders, adm. (Total facility includes 60 beds in nursing home-type unit) **A**1a 9 10 **F**1 10 16 19 23 24 26 33 34 35 36 40 43 50 53	23	10	S	TF	100	1634	78	78.0	4	167	5250	2621	145
				H	40	1561	20	—	4	167	3476	1695	96
MEDFORD—Taylor County													
★□ MEMORIAL HOSPITAL OF TAYLOR COUNTY (Includes Memorial Nursing Home), 135 S. Gibson St., Zip 54451; tel. 715/748-2600; Eugene W. Arnett, pres. (Total facility includes 104 beds in nursing home-type unit) **A**1a 9 10 **F**1 2 6 14 16 19 23 34 35 36 40 42 52	23	10	S	TF	164	1843	120	73.2	10	288	6165	3501	188
				H	60	1715	19	—	10	288	3751	2232	130

Hospital, Address, Telephone, Administrator, Approval and Facility Codes, Multihospital System Code	Classification Codes				Inpatient Data				Newborn Data		Expense (thousands of dollars)		
★ American Hospital Association (AHA) membership □ Joint Commission on Accreditation of Hospitals (JCAH) accreditation + American Osteopathic Hospital Association (AOHA) membership ○ American Osteopathic Association (AOA) accreditation Δ Commission on Accreditation of Rehabilitation Facilities (CARF) accreditation Control codes 61, 63, 64, 71, 72 and 73 indicate hospitals listed by AOHA, but not registered by AHA. For definition of numerical codes, see page A2	Control	Service	Stay	Facilities	Beds	Admissions	Census	Occupancy (percent)	Bassinets	Births	Total	Payroll	Personnel
MENOMONEE FALLS—Waukesha County													
★□ COMMUNITY MEMORIAL HOSPITAL, W180 N8085 Town Hall Rd., P O Box 408, Zip 53051; tel. 414/251-1000; Robert E. Drisner, pres. **A**1a 9 10 **F**1 3 5 6 10 12 14 16 23 24 26 30 32 33 34 35 36 40 41 44 52 53	23	10	S		150	7020	100	62.5	20	1120	23568	11907	582
MENOMONIE—Dunn County													
DUNN COUNTY HEALTH CARE CENTER, Rte. 2, Box 150, Zip 54751; tel. 715/232-2661; Gregory M. Roberts, adm. (Total facility includes 256 beds in nursing home-type unit) **F**19 30 32 33 42 50	13	22	S	TF	280	619	263	93.9	0	0	6911	4472	199
				H	24	478	13	—	0	0	961	567	46
★□ MYRTLE WERTH MEDICAL CENTER, 2321 Stout Rd., Zip 54751; tel. 715/235-5531; Thomas Miller III, chief exec. off. **A**1a 9 10 **F**1 3 7 12 14 15 16 23 26 34 35 36 40 50 53	23	10	S		63	2226	27	42.9	12	445	4928	2185	129
MERRILL—Lincoln County													
★□ HOLY CROSS HOSPITAL, 601 Center Ave. S., Zip 54452; tel. 715/536-5511; B. Joe Younker, adm. **A**1a 9 10 **F**1 3 6 14 15 16 23 24 34 35 36 40 46; **S**5855	21	10	S		53	1772	24	37.5	10	183	6233	2632	154
MILWAUKEE—Milwaukee County													
★□ CHILDREN'S HOSPITAL OF WISCONSIN (Formerly Milwaukee Children's Hospital), 1700 W. Wisconsin Ave., Box 1997, Zip 53201; tel. 414/931-1010; Jon E. Vice, pres. **A**1a 3 5 8 9 10 **F**1 3 4 5 6 12 13 15 16 21 23 24 26 28 33 34 35 38 42 44 51 53 54	23	50	S		170	11090	132	77.6	0	0	43807	18623	858
★□ COLUMBIA HOSPITAL, 2025 E. Newport Ave., Zip 53211; tel. 414/961-3300; John F. Schuler, pres. **A**1a 2 3 5 9 10 **F**1 2 3 5 6 7 8 9 10 11 12 14 16 23 24 25 26 27 28 30 32 33 34 35 36 40 42 44 50 53 54	23	10	S		394	11768	239	58.9	35	1017	64823	25767	1132
□ DE PAUL REHABILITATION HOSPITAL, 4143 S. 13th St., Zip 53221; tel. 414/281-4400; A. Bela Maroti, pres. (Total facility includes 95 beds in nursing home-type unit) **A**1b 9 10 **F**19 24 27 28 32 33 34 42 43 49	23	82	L	TF	219	2131	177	80.8	0	0	18505	9061	390
				H	124	1869	83	—	0	0	16378	7710	308
★□ FAMILY HOSPITAL (Formerly Family Hospital and Nursing Home), 2711 W. Wells St., Zip 53208; Mailing Address Box 11-0, Zip 53201; tel. 414/937-2100; Kimberlye Ramsey, adm. **A**1a 9 10 **F**1 3 6 9 15 16 19 21 23 24 26 27 28 29 30 32 34 35 36 37 38 40 41 42 43 44 50 53	23	10	S	TF	335	5064	231	69.0	15	1133	21654	10932	532
				H	162	4615	73	—	15	1133	17907	8744	422
★ FIRST HOSPITAL-MILWAUKEE (Formerly First Hospital), 3330 W. Wells St., Zip 53208; tel. 414/342-7262; Linda A. W. McCaskill, adm. & chief exec. off. **A**10 **F**1 23 24 27 30 32 49; **S**0295	33	10	S		14	108	5	35.7	0	0	1671	751	42
★□ FROEDTERT MEMORIAL LUTHERAN HOSPITAL, 9200 W. Wisconsin Ave., Zip 53226; tel. 414/259-3000; Dean K. Roe, pres. **A**1a 3 5 8 9 10 **F**1 3 6 10 16 20 23 24 44 53	23	10	S		236	7366	151	64.0	0	0	48069	14212	777
★□ GOOD SAMARITAN MEDICAL CENTER, John N. Schwartz, pres. & chief exec. off. **A**1a 2 3 5 6 9 10 **F**1 3 4 6 7 8 10 11 12 14 16 20 23 24 26 27 30 32 33 34 35 36 40 42 44 53 54	23	10	S		385	11998	245	56.5	44	1422	59696	25235	1380
★ IVANHOE TREATMENT CENTER, 2203 E. Ivanhoe Pl., Zip 53202; tel. 414/271-4030; M. Romberger, adm. **F**24 34 49	33	82	S		10	137	6	60.0	0	0	455	226	13
○ + LAKEVIEW HOSPITAL, 10010 W. Blue Mound Rd., Zip 53226; tel. 414/771-5200; J. E. Race, adm. **A**9 10 11 12 13 **F**1 3 6 10 12 14 16 23 32 33 34 40 44	23	10	S		118	2481	42	35.6	11	59	7814	3865	213
MILWAUKEE CHILDREN'S HOSPITAL, See Children's Hospital of Wisconsin													
★□ MILWAUKEE COUNTY MEDICAL COMPLEX (Includes Regional Eye Institute), 8700 W. Wisconsin Ave., Zip 53226; tel. 414/257-5936; William I. Jenkins, adm. **A**1a 2 3 5 6 8 10 **F**1 2 3 4 5 6 7 8 9 10 11 12 14 15 16 17 23 24 25 27 30 32 33 34 35 36 38 40 44 50 51 53 54; **S**3775	13	10	S		318	10136	219	70.6	16	612	97088	35384	1717
□ MILWAUKEE COUNTY MENTAL HEALTH COMPLEX (Formerly Listed Under Wauwatosa), 9455 Watertown Plank Rd., Zip 53226; tel. 414/257-7483; Robert D. Speer, adm. (Total facility includes 552 beds in nursing home-type unit) **A**1b 3 5 10 **F**19 26 28 30 32 33 34 42 43 49 50; **S**3775	13	22	S	TF	864	6347	806	93.3	0	0	60254	32361	1469
				H	312	6125	287	—	0	0	39079	21448	1054
★□ MILWAUKEE PSYCHIATRIC HOSPITAL (Formerly Listed Under Wauwatosa), 1220 Dewey Ave., Zip 53213; tel. 414/258-2600; Gerald E. Schley, pres. **A**1b 3 5 9 10 **F**24 26 28 29 32 33 34 42 48 49 50	23	22	L		119	929	102	85.7	0	0	10303	5247	254
★□ MOUNT SINAI MEDICAL CENTER, 950 N. 12th St., Zip 53233; Mailing Address Box 342, Zip 53201; tel. 414/289-8200; Sarah Dean, pres. **A**1a 2 3 5 8 9 10 **F**1 2 3 4 6 7 8 9 10 11 12 14 16 20 21 23 24 26 27 28 29 30 32 33 34 35 36 38 40 42 43 44 49 50 51 53 54	23	10	S		370	12358	211	57.0	33	2864	74011	31242	1557
○ + NORTHWEST GENERAL HOSPITAL, 5310 W. Capitol Dr., Zip 53216; tel. 414/447-8543; Robert G. Polahar, adm. **A**9 10 11 12 13 **F**1 3 6 10 12 16 23 24 26 34 35 36 40 52	23	10	S		130	3480	53	40.8	6	264	12577	5989	266
★□ Δ SACRED HEART REHABILITATION HOSPITAL, 1545 S. Layton Blvd., Zip 53215; tel. 414/383-4490; Ferdinand Leyva, pres. **A**1a 7 9 10 **F**23 24 26 33 34 42 44 50	21	46	L		96	926	84	87.5	0	0	11871	6400	331
★□ ST. ANTHONY HOSPITAL, 1004 N. Tenth St., Zip 53233; tel. 414/271-1965; James F. Zahradka, pres. **A**1a 9 10 **F**1 3 6 10 12 14 16 23 26 32 34 35 44 48 49; **S**1395	21	10	S		104	2853	52	50.0	0	0	8263	3872	225
★□ ST. FRANCIS HOSPITAL, 3237 S. 16th St., Zip 53215; tel. 414/647-5000; Karl Rajani, pres. & chief exec. off. **A**1a 2 9 10 **F**1 3 6 10 11 12 14 15 16 21 23 24 26 28 32 34 35 36 40 44 50 51 53; **S**1345	23	10	S		269	9800	168	62.5	31	1947	37849	19428	907
★□ ST. JOSEPH'S HOSPITAL, 5000 W. Chambers St., Zip 53210; tel. 414/447-2000; Thomas L. Feurig, pres. **A**1a 2 3 5 8 9 10 **F**1 3 4 6 7 8 9 10 11 12 14 15 16 21 23 24 25 26 30 33 34 35 36 37 40 42 44 50 51 52 53 54; **S**6745	21	10	S		486	17695	341	60.7	72	3507	80645	40865	1856
★□ Δ ST. LUKE'S HOSPITAL, 2900 W. Oklahoma Ave., Zip 53215; tel. 414/649-6000; G. Edwin Howe, pres. **A**1a 2 3 5 7 8 9 10 **F**1 2 3 4 5 6 7 8 9 10 11 12 14 16 20 23 24 25 26 27 30 32 33 35 42 44 50 52 53 54	23	10	S		490	16287	348	66.3	0	0	106387	45721	1930
★□ ST. MARY'S HOSPITAL, 2323 N. Lake Dr., Box 503, Zip 53201; tel. 414/225-8000; Sr. Julie Hanser, pres. **A**1a 2 3 5 9 10 **F**1 2 3 4 6 7 8 9 10 11 12 14 16 20 21 22 23 24 26 33 34 35 36 40 43 44 50 52 53 54; **S**1885	21	10	S		314	10545	184	58.6	30	2119	61158	23895	1077
★□ ST. MARY'S HOSPITAL (Formerly St. Mary's Hill Hospital), 2350 N. Lake Dr., Zip 53211; tel. 414/271-5555; Sr. Ellinda Leichtfeld, pres. & chief exec. off. **A**1b 8 9 10 **F**24 28 29 30 32 34 42 43 49	21	22	L		100	516	74	74.0	0	0	5423	3530	152
★□ ST. MICHAEL HOSPITAL, 2400 W. Villard Ave., Zip 53209; tel. 414/527-8000; John A. Comiskey, pres. **A**1a 2 3 5 9 10 **F**1 2 3 6 9 10 11 12 14 16 20 23 24 26 27 28 29 30 32 33 34 35 36 40 42 43 44 48 49 50 52 53 54; **S**6745	21	10	S		280	10183	218	77.9	33	1090	52856	25578	1170
★□ VETERANS ADMINISTRATION MEDICAL CENTER (Formerly Veterans Administration Hospital), 5000 W. National Ave., Zip 53295; tel. 414/384-2000; R. E. Struble, dir. (Total facility includes 200 beds in nursing home-type unit) **A**1a 2 3 5 8 **F**1 2 3 4 6 7 8 9 10 11 12 14 15 16 19 20 23 24 25 26 27 28 29 30 32 33 34 35 39 41 42 44 48 49 50 53 54	45	10	S	TF	849	14485	590	67.7	0	0	101300	59412	1778
				H	649	14053	425	—	0	0	—	—	1710
MONDOVI—Buffalo County													
BUFFALO MEDICAL CENTER (Formerly Buffalo Memorial Hospital), 200 Memorial Dr., Zip 54755; tel. 715/926-4201; Larry Welsh, adm. (Total facility includes 119 beds in nursing home-type unit) **A**9 10 **F**1 14 16 19 23 30 34 35 40 42 48 49 50 53	23	10	S	TF	148	688	106	71.6	5	27	3142	1532	96
				H	29	573	12	—	5	27	1563	676	36

★ American Hospital Association (AHA) membership
□ Joint Commission on Accreditation of Hospitals (JCAH) accreditation
+ American Osteopathic Hospital Association (AOHA) membership
○ American Osteopathic Association (AOA) accreditation
Δ Commission on Accreditation of Rehabilitation Facilities (CARF) accreditation
Control codes 61, 63, 64, 71, 72 and 73 indicate hospitals listed by AOHA, but not registered by AHA.
For definition of numerical codes, see page A2

Hospital, Address, Telephone, Administrator, Approval and Facility Codes, Multihospital System Code	Classification Codes				Inpatient Data				Newborn Data		Expense (thousands of dollars)		
	Control	Service	Stay	Facilities	Beds	Admissions	Census	Occupancy (percent)	Bassinets	Births	Total	Payroll	Personnel
MONROE—Green County													
★□ ST. CLARE HOSPITAL OF MONROE, 515 22nd Ave., Zip 53566; tel. 608/328-0100; James D. Beyers, pres. **A**1a 2 9 10 **F**1 3 6 10 12 16 23 24 26 27 30 32 33 34 35 36 40 41 50 52 53; **S**5695	21	10	S		174	6286	95	54.6	20	602	16281	8527	426
NEENAH—Winnebago County													
★□ Δ THEDA CLARK REGIONAL MEDICAL CENTER, 130 Second St., Zip 54956; tel. 414/729-3100; James C. Dickson, pres. & chief exec. off. **A**1a 7 9 10 **F**1 4 5 6 9 10 11 12 14 15 16 20 23 24 26 28 30 32 33 34 35 36 37 38 42 43 44 49 50 53 54	23	10	S		306	10881	214	69.9	24	1389	42617	20560	959
NEILLSVILLE—Clark County													
★□ MEMORIAL HOSPITAL (Includes Neillsville Memorial Home), 216 Sunset Pl., Zip 54456; tel. 715/743-3101; Glen E. Grady, adm. (Total facility includes 176 beds in nursing home-type unit) **A**1a 9 10 **F**1 6 14 16 17 19 23 24 26 30 34 35 40 41 42 44 50	23	10	S	TF	216	1413	179	82.9	6	91	5661	2974	212
				H	40	1239	15	—	6	91	3167	1478	115
NEW BERLIN—Waukesha County													
○ + NEW BERLIN MEMORIAL HOSPITAL, 13750 W. National Ave., Zip 53151; tel. 414/782-2700; James E. Lyons, pres. **A**10 11 12 **F**1 3 6 10 12 14 15 16 23 24 26 32 34 35 41 44 50 52	23	10	S		126	2262	36	28.6	0	0	9996	4676	182
NEW LONDON—Waupaca and Ontagamie Counties													
★□ NEW LONDON FAMILY MEDICAL CENTER (Formerly New London Community Hospital), 1405 Mill St., Zip 54961; tel. 414/982-5330; Michael P. Hanson, adm. **A**1a 9 10 **F**1 3 12 16 23 33 34 35 40 52 53	23	10	S		52	1836	21	40.4	4	170	4434	2186	124
NEW RICHMOND—St. Croix County													
HOLY FAMILY HOSPITAL, 535 Hospital Rd., Zip 54017; tel. 715/246-2101; Donald M. Michels, pres. (Nonreporting) **A**9 10; **S**5945	21	10	S		40	—	—	—	—	—	—	—	—
OCONOMOWOC—Waukesha County													
KETTLE MORAINE HOSPITAL, 4839 N. Hewitts Point Rd., Box C, Zip 53066; tel. 414/567-0201; Scott D. Martin, pres. **A** 9 10 **F**32 33 34 42 49	23	82	S		58	636	39	67.2	0	0	3680	1763	93
★□ MEMORIAL HOSPITAL AT OCONOMOWOC, 791 E. Summit Ave., Zip 53066; tel. 414/567-0371; Fred Spade, adm. **A**1a 9 10 **F**1 3 6 10 11 12 16 23 24 26 35 36 40 41 44 52	23	10	S		130	4146	55	42.3	8	618	15055	7119	323
★ ROGERS MEMORIAL HOSPITAL, 34810 Pabst Rd., Zip 53066; tel. 414/567-5535; Owen Otto MD, adm. **A**9 10 **F**30 32 42 50	23	22	L		90	381	48	53.3	0	0	2154	1284	91
OCONTO—Oconto County													
□ OCONTO MEMORIAL HOSPITAL, 405 First St., Zip 54153; tel. 414/834-5151; Anthony G. Markon, adm. **A**1a 9 10 **F**1 12 14 16 23 24 26 29 30 33 34 35 40 42 44	14	10	S		30	500	6	20.0	5	58	1690	905	49
OCONTO FALLS—Oconto County													
COMMUNITY MEMORIAL HOSPITAL, 855 S. Main St., Zip 54154; tel. 414/846-3444; Richard Cayer, adm. **A**9 10 **F**1 3 6 14 16 23 24 26 34 35 36 40 44 53	23	10	S		55	1380	16	29.1	6	120	4190	1922	109
OSCEOLA—Polk County													
★ LADD MEMORIAL HOSPITAL, 301 River St., Zip 54020; tel. 715/294-2111; Del Zempel, adm. **A**9 10 **F**1 10 23 26 34 35 36 40 43 50	23	10	S		38	758	9	23.7	4	78	1805	1175	72
OSHKOSH—Winnebago County													
★□ Δ MERCY MEDICAL CENTER, 631 Hazel St., Box 1100, Zip 54902; tel. 414/236-2000; Joseph P. Ross, pres. **A**1a 2 3 7 9 10 **F**1 3 5 6 9 10 11 12 14 15 16 21 23 24 25 26 27 28 29 30 32 34 35 36 40 41 42 44 49 50 52 53; **S**5305	21	10	S		217	8271	159	72.9	20	712	32522	17244	805
OSSEO—Trempealeau County													
★□ OSSEO AREA MUNICIPAL HOSPITAL AND NURSING HOME, 674 Eighth St., Zip 54758; tel. 715/597-3121; James G. Sokup, adm. (Total facility includes 90 beds in nursing home-type unit) **A**1a 9 10 **F**1 2 3 14 19 23 24 34 35 36 40 42 52 53	14	10	S	TF	128	624	75	58.6	4	43	2637	1460	105
				H	38	564	6	—	4	43	1487	773	57
PARK FALLS—Price County													
★□ FLAMBEAU MEDICAL CENTER, 98 Sherry Ave., Box 310, Zip 54552; tel. 715/762-2484; Harold S. Geller, adm. **A**1a 9 10 **F**1 3 16 23 34 35 36 40	23	10	S		42	1295	19	45.2	5	167	3483	1582	83
PHELPS—Vilas County													
★ NORTHWOODS HOSPITAL, Box 26, Zip 54554; tel. 715/545-2313; Theodore F. Kruse, adm. (Total facility includes 81 beds in nursing home-type unit) **A**9 10 **F**1 16 19 23 24 34 35 40 43 44 52	23	10	S	TF	99	375	84	84.8	6	15	2646	1334	88
				H	18	328	5	—	6	15	1408	603	34
PLATTEVILLE—Grant County													
★□ SOUTHWEST HEALTH CENTER, 1100 Fifth Ave., Zip 53818; tel. 608/348-2331; Kenneth W. Creswick, pres. (Total facility includes 94 beds in nursing home-type unit) **A**1a 9 10 **F**1 3 6 15 16 19 23 24 34 35 36 40 43 44 53	23	10	S	TF	136	1132	99	70.7	5	142	5583	2594	163
				H	42	1072	11	—	5	142	3904	1556	81
PLYMOUTH—Sheboygan County													
★□ VALLEY VIEW MEDICAL CENTER, 901 Reed St., Zip 53073; tel. 414/893-1771; Patrick Trotter, pres. (Total facility includes 60 beds in nursing home-type unit) **A**1a 9 10 **F**1 6 14 16 19 23 26 34 35 36 40 42	23	10	S	TF	108	1026	70	64.8	8	99	3963	1854	118
				H	48	985	11	—	8	99	2587	1283	92
PORT WASHINGTON—Ozaukee County													
★□ ST. MARY'S HOSPITAL-OZAUKEE, 743 N. Montgomery St., Zip 53074; tel. 414/284-5511; Charles C. Lobeck, sr. vice-pres. & chief oper. off. **A**1a 9 10 **F**1 3 6 16 23 24 26 34 35 36 40 45 49 53	21	10	S		94	2387	36	38.3	11	239	9615	4310	165
PORTAGE—Columbia County													
★□ DIVINE SAVIOR HOSPITAL AND NURSING HOME, 1015 W. Pleasant St., P O Box 387, Zip 53901; tel. 608/742-4131; Kenneth Van Bree, exec. dir. (Total facility includes 111 beds in nursing home-type unit) **A**1a 9 10 **F**1 3 6 10 16 19 23 24 30 33 34 35 36 38 40 44 48 52 53; **S**0585	21	10	S	TF	184	2490	136	73.9	10	271	8862	3990	243
				H	73	2408	28	—	10	271	6922	2860	169
PRAIRIE DU CHIEN—Crawford County													
★□ PRAIRIE DU CHIEN MEMORIAL HOSPITAL, 705 E. Taylor St., Zip 53821; tel. 608/326-2431; Harold W. Brown, adm. **A**1a 9 10 **F**1 3 14 15 21 23 34 35 36 40 41 44 53	23	10	S		49	1651	20	40.8	4	172	3747	1834	99
PRAIRIE DU SAC—Sauk County													
★□ SAUK PRAIRIE MEMORIAL HOSPITAL, 80 First St., Zip 53578; tel. 608/643-3311; Wilbur C. Beach, adm. **A**1a 9 10 **F**1 3 16 23 24 26 30 34 35 40 42 43 50 53	23	10	S		50	1648	24	48.0	6	169	4922	2098	132
PRESCOTT—Pierce County													
□ RIVERWOOD CENTER (Formerly St. Croixdale Hospital), 445 Court St. N., Zip 54021; tel. 715/262-3286; Ray G. Chapman, adm. **A**1b 9 10 **F**24 29 30 32 33 42 43; **S**0825	33	22	S		37	371	19	51.4	0	0	2473	936	69
RACINE—Racine County													
★□ A CENTER OF RACINE, 2000 Domanik Dr., Zip 53404; tel. 414/632-6141; Rev. E. W. Belter DD, pres. & exec. dir. **A**1b 9 10 **F**33 34 43 49; **S**6745	23	82	S		26	659	16	61.5	0	0	2539	1374	65
★□ ST. LUKE'S HOSPITAL, 1320 Wisconsin Ave., Zip 53403; tel. 414/636-2011; Ray L. Di Iulio, pres. **A**1a 9 10 **F**1 3 5 6 7 8 10 11 12 14 15 16 20 21 23 24 25 26 27 28 30 32 33 34 35 36 40 42 48 50 53	23	10	S		199	7566	135	67.8	38	2263	29764	12728	668

★ American Hospital Association (AHA) membership
□ Joint Commission on Accreditation of Hospitals (JCAH) accreditation
+ American Osteopathic Hospital Association (AOHA) membership
○ American Osteopathic Association (AOA) accreditation
Δ Commission on Accreditation of Rehabilitation Facilities (CARF) accreditation
Control codes 61, 63, 64, 71, 72 and 73 indicate hospitals listed by AOHA, but not registered by AHA.
For definition of numerical codes, see page A2

Hospital, Address, Telephone, Administrator, Approval and Facility Codes, Multihospital System Code	Classification Codes				Inpatient Data				Newborn Data		Expense (thousands of dollars)		
	Control	Service	Stay	Facilities	Beds	Admissions	Census	Occupancy (percent)	Bassinets	Births	Total	Payroll	Personnel
□★ ST. MARY'S MEDICAL CENTER, 3801 Spring St., Zip 53405; tel. 414/636-4011; Edward P. DeMeulenaere, pres. **A**1a 9 10 **F**1 3 5 6 9 10 11 12 14 16 23 24 26 30 32 34 35 44 50 52 53 54; **S**6745	21	10	S		216	8529	138	63.9	0	0	29743	12496	655
REEDSBURG—Sauk County													
□ REEDSBURG MEMORIAL HOSPITAL, 2000 N. Dewey St., Zip 53959; tel. 608/524-6487; George L. Johnson, adm. (Total facility includes 50 beds in nursing home-type unit) **A**1a 9 10 **F**1 3 12 16 19 23 24 26 34 35 36 40 53	23	10	S	TF	103	1667	73	70.9	10	183	5744	2556	151
				H	53	1660	23	—	10	183	4853	1982	111
RHINELANDER—Oneida County													
□★ SACRED HEART-ST. MARY'S HOSPITALS (Includes Sacred Heart Hospital, 216 N. Seventh St., Tomahawk, Zip 54487; tel. 715/453-2181; St. Mary's Hospital, 1044 Kabel Ave., Zip 54501; tel. 715/369-3311), Kevin O'Donnell, pres. **A**1a 9 **F**1 3 6 10 12 14 16 23 24 26 27 29 30 32 33 34 35 36 40 42 44 48 49 52 53; **S**5305	21	10	S		193	5173	88	45.6	16	587	15799	6856	355
ST. MARY'S HOSPITAL, See Sacred Heart-St. Mary's Hospital													
RICE LAKE—Barron County													
□★ LAKEVIEW MEDICAL CENTER, 1100 N. Main St., Zip 54868; tel. 715/234-1515; Paul F. Markgren, adm. **A**1a 10 **F**1 3 10 16 20 23 26 34 35 36 40 41 44 52	23	10	S		75	3037	38	50.7	10	411	8064	3886	201
RICHLAND CENTER—Richland County													
□ RICHLAND HOSPITAL, 431 N. Park St., Zip 53581; tel. 608/647-6321; Thomas J. Werner, adm. **A**1a 9 10 **F**1 3 6 12 14 15 16 21 23 24 26 34 35 36 40 43 52 53	23	10	S		55	1628	24	42.1	7	248	3944	2184	127
RIPON—Fond Du Lac County													
□★ RIPON MEMORIAL HOSPITAL, 933 Newbury St., P O Box 390, Zip 54971; tel. 414/748-3101; Peter Sensenbrenner, adm. **A**1a 9 10 **F**1 3 6 10 14 15 16 23 28 34 35 36 40 43 50	23	10	S		40	1225	15	37.5	6	103	3182	1473	84
RIVER FALLS—St. Croix County													
□★ RIVER FALLS AREA HOSPITAL, 550 N. Main St., Zip 54022; tel. 715/425-6155; Eric L. Pousard, adm. (Total facility includes 63 beds in nursing home-type unit) **A**1a 9 10 **F**1 3 16 19 23 24 26 30 34 35 36 40 44 53; **S**6235	23	10	S	TF	105	1337	73	69.5	8	250	4304	2128	100
				H	42	1280	12	—	8	250	2985	1530	68
SHAWANO—Shawano County													
□★ SHAWANO COMMUNITY HOSPITAL, 309 N. Bartlette St., Zip 54166; tel. 715/526-2111; Harry J. Wernecke, adm. **A**1a 9 10 **F**1 10 12 14 16 23 34 35 36 40 52	23	10	S		72	2281	27	37.5	16	377	5591	2518	148
SHEBOYGAN—Sheboygan County													
□★ SHEBOYGAN MEMORIAL MEDICAL CENTER (Formerly Sheboygan Memorial Hospital), 2629 N. Seventh St., Zip 53081; tel. 414/457-5033; Patrick J. Trotter, pres. **A**1a 9 10 **F**1 3 5 6 10 12 14 15 16 21 23 24 26 27 30 32 33 34 35 36 38 40 42 44 48 50 52 53	23	10	S		150	5421	82	54.7	16	660	17699	8401	343
□★ ST. NICHOLAS HOSPITAL, 1601 N. Taylor Dr., Zip 53081; tel. 414/459-8300; Michael E. Zilm, exec. vice-pres. **A**1a 9 10 **F**1 3 5 6 9 10 11 12 14 15 16 20 21 23 24 26 34 35 36 39 40 41 44 50 52 53; **S**5355	21	10	S		145	6136	85	58.6	16	751	19574	8978	416
SHELL LAKE—Washburn County													
□★ INDIANHEAD MEDICAL CENTER, 215 Fourth Ave. W., Zip 54871; tel. 715/468-7833; Lance F. Gillham, adm. **A**1a 9 10 **F**1 3 16 23 26 34 35 36 40 52; **S**1325	23	10	S		49	956	12	24.5	3	67	2505	1284	62
SPARTA—Monroe County													
□★ ST. MARY'S HOSPITAL, W. Main & K Sts., Zip 54656; tel. 608/269-2132; Sr. Julie Tydrich, adm. (Total facility includes 21 beds in nursing home-type unit) **A**1a 9 10 **F**3 5 6 14 15 16 19 23 24 34 35 36 40 44 53; **S**9650	21	10	S	TF	65	1092	32	49.2	10	139	2695	1342	92
				H	44	1081	11	—	10	139	2128	1011	83
SPOONER—Washburn County													
□ COMMUNITY MEMORIAL HOSPITAL AND NURSING HOME, 819 Ash St., Zip 54801; tel. 715/635-2111; Craig Barness, adm. (Total facility includes 90 beds in nursing home-type unit) **A**1a 9 10 **F**1 14 16 19 23 34 35 36 40 44 52	23	10	S	TF	136	1362	98	72.1	8	159	4669	2519	140
				H	46	1293	14	—	8	159	3080	1493	72
ST. CROIX FALLS—Polk County													
□★ ST. CROIX VALLEY MEMORIAL HOSPITAL, S. Adams St., Zip 54024; tel. 715/483-3261; James Bigogno, chief exec. off. **A**1a 9 10 **F**1 3 10 16 23 26 30 33 34 35 36 40 48 49; **S**6235	23	10	S		84	2261	36	42.9	9	263	5745	2636	126
STANLEY—Chippewa County													
□★ VICTORY MEMORIAL HOSPITAL, 230 E. Fourth Ave., Zip 54768; tel. 715/644-5571; Leland J. Olkowski, adm. (Total facility includes 86 beds in nursing home-type unit) **A**1a 9 10 **F**1 3 14 15 16 19 23 24 26 28 30 32 34 35 36 40 42 50 52 53	23	10	S	TF	127	895	91	71.7	5	121	4336	2534	177
				H	41	827	11	—	5	121	2822	1549	82
STEVENS POINT—Portage County													
□★ ST. MICHAEL'S HOSPITAL, 900 Illinois Ave., Zip 54481; tel. 715/346-5000; Richard R. Lansing, pres. **A**1a 9 10 **F**1 3 6 8 10 12 14 16 20 23 24 27 32 34 35 36 40 52 53; **S**5305	21	10	S		129	5311	75	58.1	23	904	21030	8784	423
STOUGHTON—Dane County													
□ STOUGHTON HOSPITAL ASSOCIATION, 900 Ridge St., Zip 53589; tel. 608/873-6611; Frank G. Fougerousse, pres. **A**1a 9 10 **F**1 3 5 6 12 14 15 16 23 24 26 28 29 30 32 33 34 35 36 40 41 43 44 48 49 50 52 53	23	10	S		69	1615	30	43.5	5	93	6029	2959	166
STURGEON BAY—Door County													
□★ DOOR COUNTY MEMORIAL HOSPITAL, 330 S. 16th Pl., Zip 54235; tel. 414/743-5566; David G. Triebes, pres. (Total facility includes 30 beds in nursing home-type unit) **A**1a 9 10 **F**1 3 6 12 16 23 24 30 32 34 35 36 40 41 44 52	23	10	S	TF	93	2230	59	63.4	12	272	7154	3902	192
				H	63	2173	30	—	12	272	6710	3573	—
SUPERIOR—Douglas County													
□★ SUPERIOR MEMORIAL HOSPITAL, 3500 Tower Ave., Zip 54880; tel. 715/392-8281; Keith J. Petersen, chief exec. off. **A**1a 9 10 **F**1 3 6 12 14 16 23 26 33 34 35 36 40 53; **S**2495	23	10	S		52	2671	35	67.3	5	228	8741	3904	181
TOMAH—Monroe County													
□ TOMAH MEMORIAL HOSPITAL, 321 Butts Ave., Box 548, Zip 54660; tel. 608/372-2181; Donald B. Smith, chief exec. off. **A**1a 9 10 **F**1 6 16 23 26 34 35 36 40 52 53	23	10	S		45	1425	18	40.0	7	181	3420	1588	89
□★ VETERANS ADMINISTRATION MEDICAL CENTER, Zip 54660; tel. 608/372-1777; Jon E. Crisman, dir. (Total facility includes 100 beds in nursing home-type unit) **A**1a b **F**1 3 6 12 14 15 16 19 23 24 26 28 29 30 31 32 33 34 35 41 42 43 44 48 49 50	45	22	L	TF	886	3455	587	72.6	0	0	32541	22131	991
				H	786	3346	488	—	0	0	29287	19918	938
TOMAHAWK—Lincoln County													
SACRED HEART HOSPITAL, See Sacred Heart-St. Mary's Hospitals, Rhinelander													
TWO RIVERS—Manitowoc County													
□ TWO RIVERS COMMUNITY HOSPITAL AND HAMILTON MEMORIAL HOME, 25th & Garfield Sts., Zip 54241; tel. 414/793-1178; Willard L. Sperry, pres. (Total facility includes 85 beds in nursing home-type unit) **A**1a 9 10 **F**1 3 9 14 16 19 23 24 34 35 36 40 52	23	10	S	TF	158	1912	106	67.1	12	378	6700	3380	165
				H	73	1867	22	—	12	378	5186	2401	117

Hospital, Address, Telephone, Administrator, Approval and Facility Codes, Multihospital System Code	Classification Codes				Inpatient Data				Newborn Data		Expense (thousands of dollars)		
★ American Hospital Association (AHA) membership □ Joint Commission on Accreditation of Hospitals (JCAH) accreditation + American Osteopathic Hospital Association (AOHA) membership ○ American Osteopathic Association (AOA) accreditation Δ Commission on Accreditation of Rehabilitation Facilities (CARF) accreditation Control codes 61, 63, 64, 71, 72 and 73 indicate hospitals listed by AOHA, but not registered by AHA. For definition of numerical codes, see page A2	Control	Service	Stay	Facilities	Beds	Admissions	Census	Occupancy (percent)	Bassinets	Births	Total	Payroll	Personnel
VIROQUA—Vernon County													
□ VERNON MEMORIAL HOSPITAL, 507 S. Main St., Zip 54665; tel. 608/637-2101; James H. Hudson, chief exec. off. **A**1a 9 10 **F**1 6 14 16 21 23 24 26 34 35 36 40 44 49 50 52	23	10	S		49	1890	23	46.9	12	259	4034	2300	141
WASHBURN—Bayfield County													
★ BAYFIELD COUNTY MEMORIAL HOSPITAL, 320 Superior Ave., Zip 54891; tel. 715/373-2621; John J. Blahnik, adm. (Total facility includes 86 beds in nursing home-type unit) **A**9 10 **F**1 16 19 23 36 40 44 50	23	23	S	TF	121	468	88	72.7	4	38	—	—	103
				H	35	421	5	—	4	38	—	—	46
WATERTOWN—Dodge County													
★□ WATERTOWN MEMORIAL HOSPITAL, 125 Hospital Dr., Zip 53094; tel. 414/261-4210; Leo C. Bargielski, pres. **A**1a 9 10 **F**1 3 6 10 15 16 23 24 32 33 34 35 36 40 41 43 44 49 50 52 53	23	10	S		103	3382	39	37.9	12	454	8931	4428	236
WAUKESHA—Waukesha County													
★□ Δ WAUKESHA MEMORIAL HOSPITAL, 725 American Ave., Zip 53188; tel. 414/544-2011; Rexford W. Titus III, pres. & chief exec. off. **A**1a 2 3 5 7 9 10 **F**1 2 3 5 6 7 8 10 11 12 14 15 16 23 24 25 26 27 29 30 32 33 34 35 36 40 41 42 44 48 50 52 53	23	10	S		400	11276	207	51.8	40	1544	41197	19020	795
WAUPACA—Waupaca County													
★□ RIVERSIDE COMMUNITY MEMORIAL HOSPITAL, 800 Riverside Dr., Zip 54981; te' 715/258-1000; David L. Stansberry, adm. **A**1a 9 10 **F**1 3 6 12 16 23 33 34 35 40 52 53; **S**1755	23	10	S		67	2086	28	41.8	8	196	5711	2784	142
WAUPUN—Dodge and Fond Du Lac Counties													
★□ WAUPUN MEMORIAL HOSPITAL, 620 W. Brown St., Zip 53963; tel. 414/324-5581; Steven H. Spencer, pres. **A**1a 9 10 **F**1 3 6 12 14 15 16 20 23 26 33 34 35 36 41 44 53; **S**9555	21	10	S		55	1762	21	38.2	6	189	6359	2590	186
WAUSAU—Marathon County													
NORTH CENTRAL HEALTH CARE FACILITIES, 1100 Lakeview Dr., Zip 54401; tel. 715/848-4600; Peter Desantis, pres. (Total facility includes 389 beds in nursing home-type unit) **F**15 19 23 24 26 28 29 30 31 32 33 34 42 43 44 48 49 50	13	22	S	TF	439	1609	422	96.1	0	0	16221	9455	534
				H	50	1409	39	—	0	0	8065	4701	251
★□ WAUSAU HOSPITAL CENTER, 333 Pine Ridge Blvd., Zip 54401; tel. 715/847-2121; Donald C. Sibery, pres. & chief exec. off. **A**1a 2 3 5 10 **F**1 3 4 5 6 7 8 9 10 11 12 16 21 23 24 26 27 28 29 30 32 34 35 36 40 42 44 52 53 54	23	10	S		300	10877	168	56.0	25	1492	38516	17162	887
WAUWATOSA—Milwaukee County													
MILWAUKEE COUNTY MENTAL HEALTH COMPLEX, See Milwaukee													
MILWAUKEE PSYCHIATRIC HOSPITAL, See Milwaukee													
WEST ALLIS—Milwaukee County													
★□ WEST ALLIS MEMORIAL HOSPITAL, 8901 W. Lincoln Ave., Zip 53227; tel. 414/546-6000; Ronald W. Labott, pres. **A**1a 2 9 10 **F**1 3 6 7 8 9 10 11 12 14 16 23 24 26 32 33 34 35 36 40 44 50 53	23	10	S		238	9564	159	57.0	26	1713	41342	20987	902
WEST BEND—Washington County													
★□ ST. JOSEPH'S COMMUNITY HOSPITAL, 551 Silverbrook Dr., Zip 53095; tel. 414/334-5533; Fred J. Bury, exec. dir. **A**1a 9 10 **F**1 3 6 10 12 14 16 23 34 35 40 50 52 53	23	10	S		109	4135	57	52.3	24	617	11840	6068	295
WHITEHALL—Trempealeau County													
TRI-COUNTY MEMORIAL HOSPITAL, 1801 Lincoln St., Zip 54773; tel. 715/538-4361; Ronald B. Fields, pres. (Total facility includes 68 beds in nursing home-type unit) **A**9 10 **F**1 3 6 15 16 19 21 23 26 30 35 40 41 42 52	23	10	S	TF	103	596	74	71.8	0	0	2939	1472	122
				H	35	530	8	—	0	0	1814	813	66
WILD ROSE—Waushara County													
★ WILD ROSE COMMUNITY MEMORIAL HOSPITAL, Box 243, Zip 54984; tel. 414/622-3257; Roy W. Grunwaldt, adm. **A**9 10 **F**1 15 16 23 30 34 35 40 53	23	10	S		32	748	10	31.3	4	80	1901	910	62
WINNEBAGO—Winnebago County													
WINNEBAGO MENTAL HEALTH INSTITUTE, Box 9, Zip 54985; tel. 414/235-4910; H. David Goers, dir. **A**3 10 **F**23 24 32 33 38 42 48	12	22	L		310	793	236	76.9	0	0	17310	11590	484
WISCONSIN RAPIDS—Wood County													
★□ RIVERVIEW HOSPITAL (Includes Riverview Manor), 410 Dewey St., Zip 54494; tel. 715/423-6060; Daniel J. Hymans, adm. (Total facility includes 118 beds in nursing home-type unit) **A**1a 9 10 **F**1 3 6 7 10 11 12 14 16 19 23 24 29 34 35 36 40 52 53	23	10	S	TF	199	3594	150	75.4	20	663	14631	7170	360
				H	81	3430	41	—	20	663	12216	6007	283
WOODRUFF—Oneida County													
★□ HOWARD YOUNG MEDICAL CENTER, 240 Maple, Box 470, Zip 54568; tel. 715/356-8000; George Anast MD, pres.; Paul A. Miller, exec. vice-pres. **A**1a 9 10 **F**1 3 6 10 12 14 16 20 21 30 35 36 40 41 45 50 52	23	10	S		109	3201	54	49.5	10	200	12685	5158	291

Hospital, Address, Telephone, Administrator, Approval and Facility Codes, Multihospital System Code

- ★ American Hospital Association (AHA) membership
- □ Joint Commission on Accreditation of Hospitals (JCAH) accreditation
- + American Osteopathic Hospital Association (AOHA) membership
- ○ American Osteopathic Association (AOA) accreditation
- Δ Commission on Accreditation of Rehabilitation Facilities (CARF) accreditation

Control codes 61, 63, 64, 71, 72 and 73 indicate hospitals listed by AOHA, but not registered by AHA. For definition of numerical codes, see page A2

Wyoming

Hospital, Address, Telephone, Administrator, Approval and Facility Codes, Multihospital System Code	Classification Codes				Inpatient Data				Newborn Data		Expense (thousands of dollars)		
	Control	Service	Stay	Facilities	Beds	Admissions	Census	Occupancy (percent)	Bassinets	Births	Total	Payroll	Personnel
AFTON—Lincoln County													
★ STAR VALLEY HOSPITAL, 110 Hospital Lane, P O Box 578, Zip 83110; tel. 307/886-3841; Jon D. Hoopes, adm. **A**9 10 **F**1 6 14 23 34 35 40 45 47; **S**1815	16	10	S		15	566	4	26.7	5	121	1390	600	34
BUFFALO—Johnson County													
★□ JOHNSON COUNTY MEMORIAL HOSPITAL, 497 W. Lott St., Zip 82834; tel. 307/684-5521; Jerry E. Jurena, adm. (Total facility includes 48 beds in nursing home-type unit) **A**1a 9 10 **F**1 3 6 14 15 16 19 23 35 40 41 43 44 45 46 47 50 52; **S**2235	23	10	S	TF	83	654	56	67.5	8	85	3357	1739	112
				H	35	630	14	—	8	85	2570	1273	76
CASPER—Natrona County													
★□ WYOMING MEDICAL CENTER (Formerly Memorial Hospital of Natrona County), 1233 E. Second St., Zip 82601; tel. 307/577-7201; J. Douglas Bird, pres. **A**1a 3 9 10 **F**1 2 3 4 5 6 7 8 9 10 11 12 14 15 16 20 21 23 24 25 26 29 30 32 33 34 35 36 37 40 42 43 44 45 46 52 53 54	13	10	S		282	8942	129	45.7	38	1364	29165	13828	800
CHEYENNE—Laramie County													
★□ DE PAUL HOSPITAL, 2600 E. 18th St., Zip 82001; tel. 307/632-6411; Sr. Mary Clarice Lousberg, pres. **A**1a 2 3 9 10 **F**1 3 5 6 10 12 15 16 21 23 24 34 35 41 44 45 46 47 48 49 50 52 53 54; **S**5095	21	10	S		121	3936	69	57.0	0	0	11996	5555	361
★□ MEMORIAL HOSPITAL OF LARAMIE COUNTY, 300 E. 23rd St., Zip 82001; tel. 307/634-2273; Jon M. Gates, adm. **A**1a 2 3 9 10 **F**1 3 6 8 9 10 11 15 16 20 23 30 33 35 36 40 44 45 47 53	13	10	S		152	4963	75	49.3	16	919	14591	7088	334
U. S. AIR FORCE HOSPITAL, See Francis E. Warren Air Force Base													
★□ VETERANS ADMINISTRATION CENTER, 2360 E. Pershing Blvd., Zip 82001; tel. 307/778-7550; George H. Andrios Jr., dir. (Total facility includes 47 beds in nursing home-type unit) **A**1a **F**1 3 6 10 12 15 16 19 23 27 28 30 32 34 35 42 44 46 49	45	10	S	TF	173	2273	114	65.9	0	0	14526	8025	306
				H	126	2239	68	—	0	0	12528	6533	281
CODY—Park County													
★□ WEST PARK HOSPITAL, 707 Sheridan Ave., Zip 82414; tel. 307/527-7501; Ruth McDaniel, adm. (Total facility includes 105 beds in nursing home-type unit) **A**1a 10 **F**1 3 10 12 15 16 17 19 23 24 28 34 35 36 40 44 45 46 47 49 50; **S**0585	16	10	S	TF	147	2336	108	73.5	8	279	9994	3998	249
				H	42	2247	23	—	8	279	8416	3147	198
DOUGLAS—Converse County													
★ CONVERSE COUNTY MEMORIAL HOSPITAL, 111 S. Fifth St., Zip 82633; tel. 307/358-2122; Paul Balerud, adm. **A**9 10 **F**1 3 6 10 14 15 16 23 30 34 35 36 40 43 45 50 52	13	10	S		44	927	12	27.3	6	132	3386	1576	90
EVANSTON—Uinta County													
★ IHC EVANSTON REGIONAL HOSPITAL (Formerly Uinta Medical Center), 190 Arrowhead Dr., Zip 82930; tel. 307/789-3636; Joseph B. May III, adm. **A**9 10 **F**1 3 6 12 14 15 16 23 26 35 36 40 45 46; **S**1815	23	10	S		42	1398	13	31.0	6	286	5268	1875	81
UINTA MEDICAL CENTER, See Ihc Evanston Regional Hospital													
★ WYOMING STATE HOSPITAL, Box 177, Zip 82930; tel. 307/789-3464; William N. Karn MD, supt. **A**9 10 **F**1 15 23 24 30 32 33 42 45 46 47 50 52	12	22	L		388	865	261	67.3	0	0	11916	7870	408
FRANCIS E WARREN AIR FORCE BASE—Laramie County													
U. S. AIR FORCE HOSPITAL, Zip 82005; tel. 307/775-2277; Lt. Col. Joseph E. Kelley, cmdr. **F**1 6 14 15 23 28 29 30 32 33 34 35 36 37 40 43 45 46 47 49	41	10	S		25	1976	19	65.5	8	325	—	—	252
GILLETTE—Campbell County													
★□ CAMPBELL COUNTY MEMORIAL HOSPITAL, 501 S. Burma Ave., Box 3011, Zip 82716; tel. 307/682-8811; Joseph Brown, adm. **A**1a 9 10 **F**1 3 6 10 12 14 15 16 23 27 28 29 30 32 33 34 35 36 40 42 45 46 49 52 53	16	10	S		92	4172	50	54.3	24	721	19070	8092	360
GREYBULL—Big Horn County													
★ SOUTH BIG HORN COUNTY HOSPITAL, River Rte., Zip 82426; tel. 307/568-3311; Donn S. Swartz, adm. (Total facility includes 29 beds in nursing home-type unit) **A**9 10 **F**1 3 6 16 19 23 34 35 36 40 43 45 46 50; **S**9355	16	10	S	TF	57	556	34	59.6	4	30	1871	880	51
				H	28	520	5	—	4	30	1254	539	—
JACKSON—Teton County													
★□ ST. JOHN'S HOSPITAL, Box 428, Zip 83001; tel. 307/733-3636; A. Dale Morgan, adm. (Total facility includes 12 beds in nursing home-type unit) **A**1a 9 10 **F**1 3 6 10 12 14 15 16 19 23 24 26 28 33 34 35 36 40 44 45 50; **S**1755	16	10	S	TF	55	2335	33	60.0	5	334	6377	2912	156
				H	43	2331	22	—	5	334	6209	2759	142
KEMMERER—Lincoln County													
★ SOUTH LINCOLN MEDICAL CENTER (Formerly South Lincoln Hospital District), Moose & Onyx Sts., Box 390, Zip 83101; tel. 307/877-4401; James MacKay Jr., chief exec. off. (Nonreporting) **A**9 10	16	10	S		20	—	—	—	—	—	—	—	—
LANDER—Fremont County													
□ LANDER VALLEY REGIONAL MEDICAL CENTER, 1320 Bishop Randall Dr., Zip 82520; tel. 307/332-4420; Hugh S. Simcoe III, mgn dir. (Nonreporting) **A**1a 9 10; **S**8985	33	10	S		107	—	—	—	—	—	—	—	—
PINERIDGE HOSPITAL, 150 Wyoming St., Zip 82520; tel. 307/332-5700; Hugh Simcoe, adm. (Nonreporting) **A**10; **S**8985	33	49	S		47	—	—	—	—	—	—	—	—
LARAMIE—Albany County													
★□ IVINSON MEMORIAL HOSPITAL, 255 N. 30th St., Zip 82070; tel. 307/742-2141; Thomas A. Nord, chief exec. off. **A**1a 9 10 **F**1 2 6 10 12 14 15 16 23 24 27 30 32 33 34 35 36 37 40 41 44 45 46 47 52 53	16	10	S		99	4335	48	48.5	16	546	11661	5560	286
LOVELL—Big Horn County													
★ NORTH BIG HORN HOSPITAL, 115 Lane 12, P O Box 518, Zip 82431; tel. 307/548-2771; Jeanie Hocking, chief exec. off. (Total facility includes 60 beds in nursing home-type unit) **A**9 10 **F**1 6 16 19 23 35 36 40 45 52	16	10	S	TF	90	708	46	51.1	8	86	3183	1573	95
				H	30	638	7	—	8	86	2244	1020	61
LUSK—Niobrara County													
★ NIOBRARA COUNTY MEMORIAL HOSPITAL, 939 Ballencee Ave., Box 780, Zip 82225; tel. 307/334-2711; Craig E. Aasved, adm. (Nonreporting) **A**9 10; **S**2235	23	10	S		51	—	—	—	—	—	—	—	—
NEWCASTLE—Weston County													
★ WESTON COUNTY MEMORIAL HOSPITAL, 1124 Washington St., Zip 82701; tel. 307/746-4491; Evonne Ulmer, chief exec. off. (Total facility includes 41 beds in nursing home-type unit) **A**9 10 **F**1 2 6 15 16 19 34 35 36 37 40 41 42 46 52	13	10	S	TF	69	648	46	64.8	6	129	2117	1200	78
				H	28	633	7	—	6	129	1384	724	53

★ American Hospital Association (AHA) membership
□ Joint Commission on Accreditation of Hospitals (JCAH) accreditation
+ American Osteopathic Hospital Association (AOHA) membership
○ American Osteopathic Association (AOA) accreditation
Δ Commission on Accreditation of Rehabilitation Facilities (CARF) accreditation
Control codes 61, 63, 64, 71, 72 and 73 indicate hospitals listed by AOHA, but not registered by AHA.
For definition of numerical codes, see page A2

Hospital, Address, Telephone, Administrator, Approval and Facility Codes, Multihospital System Code	Classification Codes				Inpatient Data				Newborn Data		Expense (thousands of dollars)		
	Control	Service	Stay	Facilities	Beds	Admissions	Census	Occupancy (percent)	Bassinets	Births	Total	Payroll	Personnel
POWELL—Park County													
★□ POWELL HOSPITAL, 777 Ave. H, Zip 82435; tel. 307/754-2267; R. D. Cozzens, adm. (Total facility includes 73 beds in nursing home-type unit) **A**1a 9 10 **F**1 3 6 10 12 15 16 19 21 23 24 34 35 36 40 42 43 44 45 46 47 50 52 53; **S**2235	23	10	S	TF H	113 40	1275 1204	88 13	77.9 —	6 6	149 149	6331 4807	2716 1777	145 92
RAWLINS—Carbon County													
★□ MEMORIAL HOSPITAL OF CARBON COUNTY, 2221 W. Elm, Zip 82301; tel. 307/324-2221; Richard H. Mills, exec. dir. **A**1a 9 10 **F**1 3 6 10 12 15 16 23 34 35 36 40 45 46 47 52 53	13	10	S		85	2525	29	34.1	11	187	7829	3955	178
RIVERTON—Fremont County													
★□ HCA RIVERTON HOSPITAL (Formerly Riverton Memorial Hospital), 2100 W. Sunset, Box 1280, Zip 82501; tel. 307/856-4161; Bruce K. Birchell, adm. **A**1a 9 10 **F**1 3 5 6 10 12 14 15 23 32 36 40 45 46 52 53; **S**1755	33	10	S		64	2817	29	47.5	11	270	7827	2769	136
ROCK SPRINGS—Sweetwater County													
★□ MEMORIAL HOSPITAL OF SWEETWATER COUNTY, 1200 College Dr., Box 1359, Zip 82901; tel. 307/362-3711; John M. Ferry, exec. dir. **A**1a 9 10 **F**1 3 6 10 12 14 15 16 17 23 29 30 34 35 36 40 45 46 52 53 54	13	10	S		100	4075	44	44.0	14	873	12737	6147	300
SHERIDAN—Sheridan County													
★□ MEMORIAL HOSPITAL OF SHERIDAN COUNTY, 1401 W. Fifth St., Zip 82801; tel. 307/674-4481; John Owen Yale, adm. **A**1a 9 10 **F**1 3 6 7 8 10 12 15 16 23 30 32 35 36 40 41 45 46 47 52	13	10	S		88	3123	38	43.2	18	513	8700	4640	239
★□ VETERANS ADMINISTRATION MEDICAL CENTER, Zip 82801; tel. 307/672-3473; Fred J. Smith, dir. (Total facility includes 100 beds in nursing home-type unit) **A**1a **F**1 3 6 15 16 19 20 23 24 26 28 31 33 34 41 42 44 45 46 48 49 50	45	22	L	TF H	339 239	1687 1645	264 183	77.9 —	0 0	0 0	19231 —	12092 —	473 —
SUNDANCE—Crook County													
CROOK COUNTY MEMORIAL HOSPITAL, 713 Oak St., Box 517, Zip 82729; tel. 307/283-3501; Ron Wolf, adm. (Nonreporting) **A**9 10	13	10	S		16	—	—	—	—	—	—	—	—
THERMOPOLIS—Hot Springs County													
★□ HOT SPRINGS COUNTY MEMORIAL HOSPITAL, Hot Springs State Park, Zip 82443; tel. 307/864-3121; Donald R. Carlson, adm. (Nonreporting) **A**1a 9 10	13	10	S		49	—	—	—	—	—	—	—	—
TORRINGTON—Goshen County													
★□ COMMUNITY HOSPITAL, 2000 Campbell Dr., Zip 82240; tel. 307/532-4181; Jim D. Lebrun, adm. **A**1a 9 10 **F**1 3 6 12 15 16 17 23 34 35 36 40 41 45 47; **S**2235	23	10	S		53	1621	25	47.2	7	152	4447	1783	100
WHEATLAND—Platte County													
★□ PLATTE COUNTY MEMORIAL HOSPITAL, 201 14th St., Zip 82201; tel. 307/322-3636; Duaine C. Kanwischer, adm. **A**1a 9 10 **F**1 3 6 16 23 34 35 36 40 44 45 46 52; **S**2235	23	10	S		43	1366	20	46.5	10	117	2766	1326	79
WORLAND—Washakie County													
★□ WASHAKIE MEMORIAL HOSPITAL, 400 S. 15th St., Box 700, Zip 82401; tel. 307/347-3221; Howard Megorden, adm. (Nonreporting) **A**1a 9 10; **S**2235	23	10	S		36	—	—	—	—	—	—	—	—

Hospitals in Areas Associated with the United States, by Area

Hospital, Address, Telephone, Administrator, Approval and Facility Codes, Multihospital System Code

- ★ American Hospital Association (AHA) membership
- □ Joint Commission on Accreditation of Hospitals (JCAH) accreditation
- + American Osteopathic Hospital Association (AOHA) membership
- ○ American Osteopathic Association (AOA) accreditation
- Δ Commission on Accreditation of Rehabilitation Facilities (CARF) accreditation

Control codes 61, 63, 64, 71, 72 and 73 indicate hospitals listed by AOHA, but not registered by AHA. For definition of numerical codes, see page A2

American Samoa

Hospital, Address, Telephone, Administrator, Approval and Facility Codes, Multihospital System Code	Classification Codes: Control	Service	Stay	Facilities	Inpatient Data: Beds	Admissions	Census	Occupancy (percent)	Newborn Data: Bassinets	Births	Expense (thousands of dollars): Total	Payroll	Personnel
PAGO PAGO													
LYNDON B. JOHNSON TROPICAL MEDICAL CENTER, Zip 96799; tel. 684/633-1222; Eliu F. Paopao, adm. (Nonreporting) **A**10	16	10	S		150	—	—	—	—	—	—	—	—

Marshall Islands

Hospital, Address, Telephone, Administrator, Approval and Facility Codes, Multihospital System Code	Classification Codes: Control	Service	Stay	Facilities	Inpatient Data: Beds	Admissions	Census	Occupancy (percent)	Newborn Data: Bassinets	Births	Expense (thousands of dollars): Total	Payroll	Personnel
KWAJALEIN ISLAND—Marshall Islands													
KWAJALEIN MISSILE RANGE HOSPITAL, Mailing Address Box 1702, APO San Francisco, CA, Zip 96555; tel. 805/238-7994; Ray West, adm. (Nonreporting)	42	10	S		25								

Guam

Hospital, Address, Telephone, Administrator, Approval and Facility Codes, Multihospital System Code	Classification Codes: Control	Service	Stay	Facilities	Inpatient Data: Beds	Admissions	Census	Occupancy (percent)	Newborn Data: Bassinets	Births	Expense (thousands of dollars): Total	Payroll	Personnel
AGANA													
□★ NAVAL HOSPITAL, Mailing Address FPO, Box 7607, San Francisco, Zip 96630; tel. 000/344-9234 **A**1a **F**1 3 6 10 12 14 15 16 23 28 30 33 34 35 36 37 40 43 46 47 48 50 52	43	10	S		61	3390	39	63.9	18	920	25431	15930	477
TAMUNING													
GUAM MEMORIAL HOSPITAL AUTHORITY, 850 Gov Carlos G Camacho Rd., tel. 671/646-6711; John C. Rosario, adm. **F**1 3 6 10 12 14 15 16 19 20 23 24 26 30 35 36 37 40 42 43 44 46 50 51 52 53	16	10	S		221	8812	166	75.1	22	2313	35667	12039	663

Puerto Rico

Hospital, Address, Telephone, Administrator, Approval and Facility Codes, Multihospital System Code	Classification Codes: Control	Service	Stay	Facilities	Inpatient Data: Beds	Admissions	Census	Occupancy (percent)	Newborn Data: Bassinets	Births	Expense (thousands of dollars): Total	Payroll	Personnel
AGUADILLA—Aguadilla District													
★ AGUADILLA GENERAL HOSPITAL, Carr Aguadilla San Juan, P O Box 3968, Zip 00605; tel. 809/891-3000; Luis Jaime Ramos, adm. **A**10 **F**12 14 23 34 35 36 40 43 45 52	16	10	S		221	8812	166	75.1	22	2313	35667	12039	663
AIBONITO—Ponce District													
★ MENNONITE GENERAL HOSPITAL, Box 1379, Zip 00609; tel. 809/735-8001; Domingo Torres Zayas, chief exec. off. (Nonreporting) **A**9 10	23	10	S		100	—	—	—	—	—	—	—	—
ARECIBO—Arecibo District													
ARECIBO HEALTH CENTER, Regimiento 65 St., Box 831, Zip 00612; tel. 809/878-1414; Luis Perez Rivera, adm. (Nonreporting)	12	10	S		128	—	—	—	—	—	—	—	—
★ ARECIBO REGIONAL HOSPITAL, San Luis Ave., Box 397, Zip 00612; tel. 809/878-7272; Teodoro Muniz, exec. dir. (Nonreporting) **A**9 10	12	10	S		183	—	—	—	—	—	—	—	—
HOSPITAL DR. SUSONI, 55 Nicomedes Rivera St., Zip 00612; Hector Barreto MD, med. dir. (Nonreporting) **A**10	33	10	S		73	—	—	—	—	—	—	—	—
HOSPITAL EL BUEN PASTOR, 52 De Diego, Box 413, Zip 00612; tel. 809/878-2730; Pascasio Laguillo, med. dir. (Nonreporting)	33	10	S		72	—	—	—	—	—	—	—	—
ARROYO—Guayama District													
★ LAFAYETTE HOSPITAL, 207 Central Lafayette St., Zip 00615; tel. 809/839-3232; Fran K. Santiago, adm. **A**9 10 **F**1 15 16 23 24 34 35 44	33	10	S		66	2050	21	31.8	6	16	2125	823	—
BARRANQUITAS—Guayama District													
BARRANQUITAS HEALTH CENTER, Calle Barcelo, Box 728, Zip 00618; Nereida Hernandez, adm. **A**10 **F**15 34 35 37 40 43 45 52	12	10	S		21	320	3	14.3	4	16	1908	997	173
BAYAMON—San Juan District See San Juan													
BAYAMON—Bayamon District													
□★ HOSPITAL HERMANOS MELENDEZ, Rte. 2, KM 11-8, P O Box 306, Zip 00619; tel. 809/785-9784; Domingo Velez, adm. (Nonreporting) **A**1a 9 10	33	10	S		203	—	—	—	—	—	—	—	—
★ HOSPITAL MATILDE BRENES, Ext. Hermanas Davila, Box 2957, Zip 00619; tel. 809/786-6315; Prudencio Laureano, adm. (Nonreporting) **A**9 10	33	10	S		106	—	—	—	—	—	—	—	—
□★ HOSPITAL REGIONAL DR. RAMON RUIZ ARNAU, Ave. Laurel Santa Juanita, Zip 00619; tel. 809/787-5151; Neffer E. Carrillo, adm. (Total facility includes 48 beds in nursing home-type unit) **A**1a 3 5 9 10 **F**1 3 6 12 14 15 16 19 20 23 24 34 35 36 37 40 42 44 52 54	12	10	S	TF	396	16975	280	70.7	85	5312	25249	10016	1130
				H	348	16834	259	—	85	5312	24941	9799	—
□★ HOSPITAL SAN PABLO, Calle San Cruz 70, Box 236, Zip 00621; tel. 809/786-7474; Roberto Hernandez, exec. adm. **A**1a 3 5 9 10 **F**1 3 6 10 12 16 23 32 34 35 36 37 40 43 45 46 47 50 52 53	33	10	S		330	17023	265	80.3	30	1539	27604	7880	762

Hospital, Address, Telephone, Administrator, Approval and Facility Codes, Multihospital System Code	Classification Codes				Inpatient Data				Newborn Data		Expense (thousands of dollars)		
★ American Hospital Association (AHA) membership □ Joint Commission on Accreditation of Hospitals (JCAH) accreditation + American Osteopathic Hospital Association (AOHA) membership ○ American Osteopathic Association (AOA) accreditation Δ Commission on Accreditation of Rehabilitation Facilities (CARF) accreditation Control codes 61, 63, 64, 71, 72 and 73 indicate hospitals listed by AOHA, but not registered by AHA. For definition of numerical codes, see page A2	Control	Service	Stay	Facilities	Beds	Admissions	Census	Occupancy (percent)	Bassinets	Births	Total	Payroll	Personnel
CAGUAS—Guayama District													
□ CAGUAS REGIONAL HOSPITAL, Carretera Caguas A Cayey, Box 5729, Zip 00626; tel. 809/744-3170; Rogelio Diaz Reyes, adm. (Nonreporting) **A**1a 3 5 9	12	10	S		288	—	—	—	—	—	—	—	—
HOSPITAL SAN RAFAEL, 1 Munoz Rivera St., Box 997, Zip 00626; tel. 809/743-1011; Maria Teresa Dominguez, adm. **A**9 10 **F**1 3 6 12 16 35 40 47 52	33	10	S		104	6166	80	76.9	8	604	8477	3499	302
CAPARRA—San Juan District See San Juan													
CASTANER—Arecibo District													
★ CASTANER GENERAL HOSPITAL, KM 64-2, Rte. 135, Box 23, Zip 00631; tel. 809/829-5010; Onan E. Perez, adm. **A**10 **F**12 14 15 34 35 36 43	23	10	S		33	1416	17	51.5	9	161	1395	889	93
CAYEY—Guayama District													
CLINICA FONT, 4 H Mendoza St., Box 967, Zip 00634; tel. 809/738-2181; Radames Muniz MD, med. dir. (Nonreporting) **A**9 10	33	10	S		65	—	—	—	—	—	—	—	—
HOSPITAL DE AREA DE CAYEY, Calle Luis Barreras, Box 1247, Zip 00633; tel. 809/738-3550; Sr. Maximiliano Fernandez, adm. (Nonreporting) **A**10	14	10	S		38	—	—	—	—	—	—	—	—
★ REHABILITATION AND WORK CENTER MENTAL HEALTH PROGRAM, Rd. Puerto Rico 14, Zip 00633; tel. 809/738-2141; Maxim Fernandez, adm. (Nonreporting)	12	22	L		200	—	—	—	—	—	—	—	—
FAJARDO—Humacao District													
★ DOCTORS GUBERN'S HOSPITAL, 110 Antonio R Barcelo, Box 846, Zip 00648; tel. 809/863-0924; Montserrat G. De Garcia, exec. dir. (Nonreporting) **A**10	33	10	S		51	—	—	—	—	—	—	—	—
DR. GUBERN'S HOSPITAL, General Valero Ave. 267, Box 846, Zip 00648; tel. 809/863-0669; Montserrat Garcia, exec. dir. (Nonreporting) **A**9	33	10	S		51	—	—	—	—	—	—	—	—
⊞ FAJARDO REGIONAL HOSPITAL, General Valero Ave., P O Box 1283, Zip 00648; tel. 809/863-0505; Luis Acevedo, adm. (Nonreporting) **A**1a 9 10	33	10	S		180	—	—	—	—	—	—	—	—
GUAYAMA—Guayama District													
★ HOSPITAL SANTA ROSA, Aveterans Ave., Box 988, Zip 00654; tel. 809/864-0101; Humberto M. Monserrate, adm. **A**10 **F**1 3 6 16 23 26 35 36 37; **S**0695	23	10	S		99	3787	49	49.5	8	106	3570	1425	158
HATO REY—San Juan District See San Juan													
HUMACAO—Humacao District													
⊞ FONT MARTELO HOSPITAL, 3 Font Martelo St., Box 639, Zip 00661; tel. 809/852-2424; Rene Rivera, adm. **A**1a 9 10 **F**1 6 15 16 23 35 36 37	33	10	S		105	4756	65	61.9	16	441	5091	2040	222
HOSPITAL DE AREA DR. VICTOR R. NUNEZ, Box 9009, Zip 00661; tel. 809/852-2727; Ahmed Alvarez Pabon, exec. dir. **A**10 **F**1 3 12 14 15 21 23 24 26 34 35 37 40 43 44 45 46 52	12	10	S		118	6189	78	66.1	23	1631	10484	4515	530
★ HOSPITAL DR. DOMINGUEZ, 300 Font Martelo St., Box 699, Zip 00661; tel. 809/852-0505; Alfredo Gotay Zorrilla, adm. (Nonreporting) **A**9 10	33	10	S		63	—	—	—	—	—	—	—	—
⊞ RYDER MEMORIAL HOSPITAL, Box 489, Zip 00661; tel. 809/852-0768; Saturnino Pena Flores, exec. dir. (Total facility includes 210 beds in nursing home-type unit) **A**1a 10 **F**1 3 6 10 12 15 16 18 19 23 24 26 28 33 34 35 36 37 40 41 42 44 46 50 52 53	23	10	S	TF	354	7647	119	33.6	17	531	13877	5026	593
				H	144	7051	90	—	17	531	13362	4761	564
LAS MARIAS—Mayaguez District													
CENTRO DE SALUD, B Maravilla Sur, Zip 00670; tel. 809/827-2230; Hilda Alers, adm. (Nonreporting)	12	10	S		10	—	—	—	—	—	—	—	—
MAYAGUEZ—Mayaguez District													
□ BELLA VISTA HOSPITAL, Box 1750, Zip 00709; tel. 809/834-2350; Nemuel O. Artiles, adm. **A**1a 9 10 **F**1 3 5 6 12 14 15 16 23 34 35 37 40 43 46 47 52	21	10	S		157	7585	108	68.8	14	715	10446	4457	481
★ CLINICA DOCTOR PEREA, 15 Dr. Basora St., Box 170, Zip 00709; tel. 809/834-0101; Augusto Perea, adm. (Nonreporting)	33	10	S		107	—	—	—	—	—	—	—	—
CLINICA ESPANOLA, Bo La Quinta, Zip 00708; tel. 809/832-0442; Emigdio Inigo-Agostini MD, bd. pres. (Nonreporting) **A**9 10	33	10	S		70	—	—	—	—	—	—	—	—
□ MAYAGUEZ MEDICAL CENTER, Zip 00708; tel. 809/832-8686; Miguel A. Sepulveda, adm. (Nonreporting) **A**1a 2 3 5 9 10	12	10	S		246	—	—	—	—	—	—	—	—
PONCE—Ponce District													
⊞ DR. PILA'S HOSPITAL, Avenida Las Americas, Mailing Address Box 1910, Zip 00733; tel. 809/848-6605; Rene Rivera, exec. dir. **A**1a 3 5 9 10 **F**1 12 14 16 24 26 30 34 35 41	23	10	S		109	5996	80	71.4	15	460	—	—	—
⊞ HOSPITAL DE DAMAS, Ponce By Pass, Zip 00731; tel. 809/840-8686; Tomas Martinez, adm. **A**1a 2 3 5 9 10 **F**3 6 10 12 14 16 20 23 34 35 36 40 41 45 46 52 53	23	10	S		356	14338	247	69.4	15	884	25145	9278	726
⊞ HOSPITAL ONCOLOGICO ANDRES GRILLASCA (Cancer), Centro Medico De Ponce, Box 1324, Zip 00733; tel. 809/848-0800; Raul A. Armstrong MD, exec. dir. **A**1a 2 3 5 9 10 **F**1 3 6 7 8 9 12 15 16 18 24 32 45 46 53	23	49	S		86	1424	35	40.7	0	0	2962	1210	129
⊞ HOSPITAL SAN LUCAS (Formerly St. Luke's Episcopal Hospital), Guadalupe St., Box 2027, Zip 00731; tel. 809/840-4545; Pedro Brull-Joy, exec. dir. **A**1a 3 5 9 10 **F**1 3 4 5 6 10 12 14 16 20 23 34 35 36 40 45 46 52 54; **S**0695	21	10	S		160	7753	124	77.5	25	885	13017	3849	353
⊞ PONCE REGIONAL HOSPITAL, Barrio Machuelo, Zip 00731; tel. 809/844-2080; Pedro A. Rosado MD, med. dir.; Nilda R. Camacho, adm. **A**1a 3 5 10 **F**1 2 3 4 5 7 10 11 12 14 15 16 17 20 21 29 34 35 38 40 43 45 46 50 52	16	10	S		466	16845	273	58.6	71	4954	20716	8918	1142
ST. LUKE'S EPISCOPAL HOSPITAL, See Hospital San Lucas													
RIO PIEDRAS—San Juan District See San Juan													
ROOSEVELT ROADS—San Juan District See San Juan													
SAN GERMAN—Mayaguez District													
⊞ HOSPITAL DE LA CONCEPCION, 41 Luna St., Box 285, Zip 00753; tel. 809/892-1860; Herson E. Morales, adm. (Nonreporting) **A**1a 2 3 5 9 10	21	10	S		167	—	—	—	—	—	—	—	—
SAN GERMAN AREA HOSPITAL, Javilla St., Zip 00753; tel. 809/892-1362; Miguel A. Sepulveda, adm. (Nonreporting) **A**10	12	10	S		42	—	—	—	—	—	—	—	—
SAN JUAN—San Juan District (Includes all hospitals in Caparra, Celba, Hato Rey, Rio Piedras, Roosevelt Roads and Santurce)													
⊞ ASHFORD PRESBYTERIAN COMMUNITY HOSPITAL, 1451 Ashford Ave. Condado, Zip 00907; Mailing Address Box 32, Zip 00902; tel. 809/721-2160; Ivan Millon, exec. dir. (Nonreporting) **A**1a 9 10	23	10	S		207	—	—	—	—	—	—	—	—
⊞ AUXILIO MUTUO HOSPITAL, Ponce De Leon Ave., Box 1227, Zip 00919; tel. 809/758-2000; Manuel Guzman, adm. **A**1a 10 **F**1 2 3 6 10 13 16 20 23 34 35 52	23	10	S		386	16400	302	78.2	28	1142	33226	14041	954
⊞ CLINICA DR. EUGENIO FERNANDEZ GARCIA, Avenida Munoz Rivera 358 Stop 30, Box 1269, Hato Rey, Zip 00919; tel. 809/753-8130; Eugenio Fernandez-Cerra MD, adm. (Nonreporting) **A**1b 10	33	22	L		188	—	—	—	—	—	—	—	—
⊞ DOCTORS HOSPITAL, 1395 San Rafael St., Box 11338, Santurce Sta., Zip 00910; tel. 809/723-2950; Jose Luis Suarez Fonseca, adm. **A**1a 9 10 **F**1 3 6 12 16 23 35 36 37 43 46 52	33	10	S		132	6845	90	63.8	24	928	8725	3097	291
HATO REY COMMUNITY HOSPITAL (Formerly Hospital Nuestra Senora De Guadalupe), 435 Ponce De Leon Ave., Hato Rey, Zip 00917; tel. 809/754-0909; Miguel A. Solivan, adm. (Nonreporting) **A**9; **S**1935	33	10	S		246	—	—	—	—	—	—	—	—
⊞ HATO REY PSYCHIATRIC HOSPITAL, Carretera Numero 2 K 2 8, Zip 00917; Mailing Address Call Box 60-89, Zip 00619; tel. 809/793-3030; Fernando J. Cabrera MD, exec. dir. (Nonreporting) **A**1b 10	33	22	L		475	—	—	—	—	—	—	—	—

★ American Hospital Association (AHA) membership
□ Joint Commission on Accreditation of Hospitals (JCAH) accreditation
+ American Osteopathic Hospital Association (AOHA) membership
○ American Osteopathic Association (AOA) accreditation
Δ Commission on Accreditation of Rehabilitation Facilities (CARF) accreditation
Control codes 61, 63, 64, 71, 72 and 73 indicate hospitals listed by AOHA, but not registered by AHA.
For definition of numerical codes, see page A2

Hospital, Address, Telephone, Administrator, Approval and Facility Codes, Multihospital System Code	Classification Codes				Inpatient Data				Newborn Data		Expense (thousands of dollars)		
	Control	Service	Stay	Facilities	Beds	Admissions	Census	Occupancy (percent)	Bassinets	Births	Total	Payroll	Personnel
HOSPITAL DE DIEGO, 310 De Diego Ave. Stop 22, Zip 00923; Mailing Address Box 41268, Santurce, Zip 00940; tel. 809/721-8181; Celia Molano Cardenas, adm. **A**9 **F**1 2 3 6 16 23 35 36 40 52	33	10	S		114	5123	61	53.5	13	475	6220	2099	238
★□ HOSPITAL DELAWARE MAESTRO, Domenech Ave., Box 4708, Zip 00936; tel. 809/758-8383; Filiberto Garcia, adm. (Nonreporting) **A**1a	23	10	S		335	—	—	—	—	—	—	—	—
HOSPITAL DRES HNOS RAMOS YORDAN, Ave. De Diego Esq 40 So, Rio Piedras, Zip 00922; tel. 808/792-6110; Luis Ernesto Ramos Yordan MD, exec. dir. (Nonreporting)	33	10	S		67	—	—	—	—	—	—	—	—
□ HOSPITAL MIMIYA, De Diego 303, Santurce Sta., Zip 00909; tel. 809/721-2590; Jose Rivera Escalona, adm. (Nonreporting) **A**1a 9 10	33	10	S		48	—	—	—	—	—	—	—	—
HOSPITAL NUESTRA SENORA DE GUADALUPE, See Hato Rey Community Hospital													
★□ HOSPITAL PAVIA, 1462 Asia St., Zip 00909; Mailing Address Box 11137, Santurce Sta., Zip 00910; tel. 809/727-6060; Alfredo E. Volckers, exec. dir. **A**1a 9 10 **F**1 2 3 6 15 16 40 47 50 52 54; **S**9605	33	10	S		172	9926	134	83.2	25	1477	—	—	352
HOSPITAL SAN MARTIN, Avenida De Diego 371, Rio Piedras, Zip 00923; tel. 809/751-2543; Joaquin Rodriguez MD, med. dir. (Nonreporting) **A**9 10	33	10	S		141	—	—	—	—	—	—	—	—
★□ I. GONZALEZ MARTINEZ ONCOLOGIC HOSPITAL (Cancer), Puerto Rico Medical Center, Box 1811, Hato Rey, Zip 00919; tel. 809/753-8433; Alfredo Gonzalez Gomez, adm. **A**1a 2 3 5 10 **F**1 3 6 7 8 9 10 11 12 14 16 34 46	23	49	S		130	2699	91	64.1	0	0	—	—	350
★ INDUSTRIAL HOSPITAL, Puerto Rico Medical Center, Box 5028, Zip 00936; tel. 809/754-2500; Cecilio Casanova Peraza, adm. **A**3 **F**1 3 15 22 23 24 25 26 34 35 42	12	10	S		133	2202	80	77.7	0	0	—	—	494
★ INSTITUTO OFTALMICO DE PUERTO RICO (Ophthalmology), Ponce De Leon 160, Zip 00901; Mailing Address Box 2206, Zip 00903; tel. 809/722-3163; Carmen Echandi, adm. (Nonreporting) **A**10	33	49	S		66	—	—	—	—	—	—	—	—
□ METROPOLITAN HOSPITAL, Box Eh, Caparra Hts., Zip 00922; tel. 809/783-6200; Rosita Esteras, adm.; Hiram Soler Favale MD, med. dir. (Nonreporting) **A**1a 10	33	10	S		180	—	—	—	—	—	—	—	—
★□ NAVAL HOSPITAL, Zip 00635; Mailing Address FPO, P O Box 3007, Miami, Zip 34051; tel. 809/865-2000; CDR J. E. Shepherd, exec. off. **A**1a **F**1 3 6 12 14 23 27 28 30 32 33 34 35 47 48	43	10	S		56	2220	28	50.0	12	317	—	—	280
SAN CARLOS GENERAL HOSPITAL, 1822 Ponce Deleon Ave., Stop 26, Santurce, Zip 00909; tel. 809/727-5858; Jose Alvarez Alvarez MD, med. dir. & adm. (Nonreporting) **A**9 10	33	10	S		106	—	—	—	—	—	—	—	—
★ SAN JORGE HOSPITAL, 258 San Jorge Ave., Zip 00912; tel. 809/727-8310; Victor R. Marrero, adm. (Nonreporting) **A**9 10	33	10	S		91	—	—	—	—	—	—	—	—
★□ SAN JUAN MUNICIPAL HOSPITAL, Apartado 21405, Rio Piedras, Zip 00928; tel. 809/765-6728; Jorge Luis Matta, adm. (Nonreporting) **A**1a 3 5 10	14	10	S		437	—	—	—	—	—	—	—	—
★ STATE PSYCHIATRIC HOSPITAL, Box 61, Zip 00936; tel. 809/765-8313; Luis M. Polo MD, med. dir. (Nonreporting)	12	22	L		425	—	—	—	—	—	—	—	—
★□ UNIVERSITY HOSPITAL, Puerto Rico Medical Center, Rio Piedras Sta., Zip 00935; tel. 809/765-4100; Rafael Burgos Calderon MD, chief exec. off. (Nonreporting) **A**1a 2 3 5 8 9 10	12	10	S		335	—	—	—	—	—	—	—	—
★□ UNIVERSITY PEDIATRIC HOSPITAL, GPO Box 5067, Zip 00936; tel. 809/754-1265; Ida Nilsa Guzman, adm. (Nonreporting) **A**1a 3 5	12	50	S		172	—	—	—	—	—	—	—	—
★□ VETERANS ADMINISTRATION MEDICAL CENTER, GPO Box 4867, Zip 00936; tel. 809/753-4665; Charles C. Freeman, dir. **A**1a 2 3 5 8 **F**1 2 3 4 6 7 8 9 10 11 12 14 15 16 20 23 24 25 26 27 28 30 31 32 33 34 35 41 42 44 46 47 49 50 53 54	45	10	S		692	10703	608	87.9	0	0	105132	46067	1778
UTUADO—Arecibo District													
HOSPITAL SAN MIGUEL, Colomer Sanchez St., Box 1450, Zip 00761; tel. 809/894-2708; Bethsa I. Hernandez, exec. dir. (Nonreporting) **A**9	33	10	S		53	—	—	—	—	—	—	—	—

Virgin Islands

Hospital	Control	Service	Stay	Facilities	Beds	Admissions	Census	Occupancy (percent)	Bassinets	Births	Total	Payroll	Personnel
CHARLOTTE AMALIE—St. Thomas County													
★ ST. THOMAS HOSPITAL AND COMMUNITY HEALTH SERVICE, Hospital Line, Box 8028, Zip 00801; tel. 809/774-1321 **A**10 **F**1 3 6 10 12 13 14 15 16 20 23 24 26 27 28 29 30 32 35 40 42 45 46 51 52 53	12	10	S		194	5797	112	57.7	26	1155	—	—	—
ST. CROIX—St. Croix County													

U.S. Government Hospitals Outside the United States, by Area

AZORES

Terceira Island: U.S. Air Force Hospital, Lajes Field

BELGIUM

Brussels: Shape Medical Center ★

CRETE

Iraklion: U.S. Air Force Hospital

CUBA

Guantanamo Bay: U.S. Naval Hospital ★

GERMANY

Augsburg: U.S. Army Hospital ★
Bad Cannstatt: U.S. Army Hospital ★
Berlin: U.S. Army Hospital ★
Bitburg: U.S. Air Force Hospital, Bitburg AB
Bremerhaven: U.S. Army Hospital ★
Frankfurt: U.S. Army Regional Medical Center ★
Hunern: U.S. Air Force Hospital, Hahn AB
Heidelberg: U.S. Army Hospital ★
Landstuhl: U.S. Army Regional Medical Center ★
Nuremburg: U.S. Army Hospital ★
Wiesbaden: U.S. Air Force Regional Medical Center
Wurzburg: U.S. Army Hospital ★

GREECE

Athens: U.S. Air Force Hospital, Hellinikon AB

ITALY

Naples: U.S. Naval Hospital ★
Vicenza: U.S. Army Hospital ★

★ Indicates membership in the American Hospital Association

JAPAN

Honshu: U.S. Air Force Hospital, MISAWA AB
U.S. Air Force Hospital, Yokota AB
Okinawa: U.S. Naval Hospital ★
Yokosuka: U.S. Naval Hospital ★

KOREA

Kunsan: U.S. Air Force Hospital
Osan-Ni: U.S. Air Force Hospital, Osan AB
Seoul: U.S. Army Community Hospital ★

PANAMA

Ancon: GORGAS Army Hospital ★

REPUBLIC OF THE PHILIPPINES

Luzon: U.S. Air Force Regional Medical Center, Clark AB
Subic Bay: U.S. Naval Hospital ★

SPAIN

Rota: U.S. Naval Hospital ★
Torrejon: U.S. Air Force Hospital, Torrejon AB

TURKEY

Incirlik: U.S. Air Force Hospital, Incirlik AB

UNITED KINGDOM (ENGLAND)

Lakenheath: U.S. Air Force Hospital, RAF Lakenheath
Upper Heyford: U.S. Air Force Hospital, RAF Upper Heyford

All U.S. Hospitals, Alphabetically

This list includes all U.S. hospitals by hospital name. Address, telephone number, administrator, individual hospital data, and approval, facility, multihospital system, and classification codes are provided in the Section "Hospitals in the United States, by State."

A

A CENTER OF RACINE, Racine, WI
A. BARTON HEPBURN HOSPITAL, Ogdensburg, NY
A. L. VADHEIM MEMORIAL HOSPITAL, Tyler, MN
A. LINDSAY AND OLIVE B. O'CONNOR HOSPITAL, Delhi, NY
ABBEVILLE COUNTY MEMORIAL HOSPITAL, Abbeville, SC
ABBEVILLE GENERAL HOSPITAL, Abbeville, LA
ABBOTT-NORTHWESTERN HOSPITAL, Minneapolis, MN
ABERDEEN-MONROE COUNTY HOSPITAL, Aberdeen, MS
ABERNETHY MEMORIAL HOSPITAL, Flomaton, AL
ABINGTON MEMORIAL HOSPITAL, Abington, PA
ABRAHAM JACOBI GENERAL CARE AND PSYCHIATRIC UNITS, Bronx, NY, See Bronx Municipal Hospital Center
ABRAHAM LINCOLN MEMORIAL HOSPITAL, Lincoln, IL
ABROM KAPLAN MEMORIAL HOSPITAL, Kaplan, LA
ACADIA-ST. LANDRY HOSPITAL, Church Point, LA
ACOMA-CANONCITO-LAGUNA HOSPITAL, San Fidel, NM
ADA MUNICIPAL HOSPITAL, Ada, MN
ADA WILSON HOSPITAL OF PHYSICAL MEDICINE AND REHABILITATION, Corpus Christi, TX
ADAIR COUNTY MEMORIAL HOSPITAL, Greenfield, IA
ADAMS COUNTY HOSPITAL, West Union, OH
ADAMS COUNTY MEMORIAL HOSPITAL, Decatur, IN
ADAMS COUNTY MEMORIAL HOSPITAL AND NURSING CARE UNIT, Friendship, WI
ADDISON COMMUNITY HOSPITAL AUTHORITY, Addison, MI
ADDISON GILBERT HOSPITAL, Gloucester, MA
ADIRONDACK REGIONAL HOSPITAL, Corinth, NY
ADOLF MEYER MENTAL HEALTH AND DEVELOPMENTAL CENTER, Decatur, IL
AFTON MEMORIAL HOSPITAL, Afton, OK
AGUADILLA GENERAL HOSPITAL, Aguadilla, P.R.
AITKIN COMMUNITY HOSPITAL, Aitkin, MN
AKRON CITY HOSPITAL, Akron, OH
AKRON GENERAL MEDICAL CENTER, Akron, OH
AKRON HOSPITAL, Akron, IA
ALACHUA GENERAL HOSPITAL, Gainesville, FL
ALAMANCE COUNTY HOSPITAL, Burlington, NC
ALAMANCE MEMORIAL HOSPITAL (Formerly Memorial Hospital of Alamance County), Burlington, NC
ALAMEDA HOSPITAL, Alameda, CA
ALAMOSA COMMUNITY HOSPITAL, Alamosa, CO
ALASKA PSYCHIATRIC INSTITUTE, Anchorage, AK
ALBANY AREA HOSPITAL (Formerly Albany Community Hospital), Albany, MN
ALBANY GENERAL HOSPITAL, Albany, OR
ALBANY MEDICAL CENTER HOSPITAL, Albany, NY
ALBEMARLE HOSPITAL, Elizabeth City, NC
ALBERT EINSTEIN MEDICAL CENTER, Philadelphia, PA
ALBERT LINDLEY LEE MEMORIAL HOSPITAL, Fulton, NY
ALBERT M. KELLER MEMORIAL HOSPITAL, Fayette, MO
ALBERT MERRITT BILLINGS HOSPITAL, Chicago, IL, See University of Chicago Hospitals and Clinics
ALBION COMMUNITY HOSPITAL, Albion, MI
ALCOHOLIC REHABILITATION CENTER, Black Mountain, NC
ALEXANDER COUNTY HOSPITAL, Taylorsville, NC
ALEXANDRIA HOSPITAL, Alexandria, VA
ALEXIAN BROTHERS HOSPITAL, St. Louis, MO
ALEXIAN BROTHERS HOSPITAL, Elizabeth, NJ
ALEXIAN BROTHERS HOSPITAL OF SAN JOSE, San Jose, CA
ALEXIAN BROTHERS MEDICAL CENTER, Elk Grove Village, IL
ALFALFA COUNTY HOSPITAL, Cherokee, OK
ALFRED I. DUPONT INSTITUTE, Wilmington, DE
ALGOMA MEMORIAL HOSPITAL, Algoma, WI
ALHAMBRA COMMUNITY HOSPITAL, Alhambra, CA
ALICE HYDE HOSPITAL ASSOCIATION, Malone, NY
ALICE PECK DAY MEMORIAL HOSPITAL, Lebanon, NH
ALIQUIPPA HOSPITAL, Aliquippa, PA
ALISAL COMMUNITY HOSPITAL, Salinas, CA, See Community Hospital of Salinas
ALL CHILDREN'S HOSPITAL, St. Petersburg, FL
ALL SAINTS EPISCOPAL HOSPITAL OF FORT WORTH, Fort Worth, TX
ALL SAINTS' REHABILITATION HOSPITAL (Formerly Listed Under Philadelphia), Wyndmoor, PA
ALLEGAN GENERAL HOSPITAL, Allegan, MI
ALLEGHANY COUNTY MEMORIAL HOSPITAL, Sparta, NC
ALLEGHANY REGIONAL HOSPITAL, Low Moor, VA
ALLEGHENY GENERAL HOSPITAL, Pittsburgh, PA
ALLEGHENY VALLEY HOSPITAL, Natrona Heights, PA
ALLEN BENNETT MEMORIAL HOSPITAL, Greer, SC
ALLEN COUNTY HOSPITAL, Iola, KS
ALLEN COUNTY WAR MEMORIAL HOSPITAL, Scottsville, KY
ALLEN MEMORIAL HOSPITAL, Waterloo, IA
ALLEN MEMORIAL HOSPITAL, Oberlin, OH
ALLEN MEMORIAL HOSPITAL, Moab, UT
ALLEN PARISH HOSPITAL, Kinder, LA
ALLENDALE COUNTY HOSPITAL, Fairfax, SC
ALLENTOWN HOSPITAL, Allentown, PA
ALLENTOWN OSTEOPATHIC MEDICAL CENTER, Allentown, PA
ALLENTOWN STATE HOSPITAL, Allentown, PA
ALLIANCE COMMUNITY HOSPITAL (Formerly Alliance City Hospital), Alliance, OH
ALLIED SERVICES FOR THE HANDICAPPED, Scranton, PA
ALPENA GENERAL HOSPITAL, Alpena, MI
ALTA BATES HOSPITAL, Berkeley, CA
ALTA DISTRICT HOSPITAL (Formerly Alta Hospital District), Dinuba, CA
ALTA VIEW HOSPITAL, Sandy, UT
ALTON MEMORIAL HOSPITAL, Alton, IL
ALTON MENTAL HEALTH CENTER, Alton, IL
ALTOONA CENTER, Altoona, PA
ALTOONA HOSPITAL, Altoona, PA
ALVARADO COMMUNITY HOSPITAL, San Diego, CA, See Alvarado Hospital Medical Center
ALVARADO HOSPITAL MEDICAL CENTER (Formerly Alvarado Community Hospital), San Diego, CA
ALVIN C. YORK VETERANS ADMINISTRATION MEDICAL CENTER (Formerly Veterans Administration Medical Center), Murfreesboro, TN
AMADOR HOSPITAL, Jackson, CA
AMARILLO HOSPITAL DISTRICT, Amarillo, TX
AMC CANCER RESEARCH CENTER, Lakewood, CO
AMELIA BROWN FRAZIER REHABILITATION CENTER, Louisville, KY, See Frazier Rehabilitation Center
AMERICAN FORK HOSPITAL, American Fork, UT
AMERICAN HOSPITAL OF MIAMI, Miami, FL, See AMI Kendall Regional Medical Center
AMERICAN INTERNATIONAL HOSPITAL, Zion, IL
AMERICAN LEGION HOSPITAL, Crowley, LA
AMERICAN ONCOLOGIC HOSPITAL-HOSPITAL OF THE FOX CHASE CANCER CENTER, Philadelphia, PA
AMERICAN RIVER HOSPITAL (Formerly Eskaton American River Hospital), Carmichael, CA
AMESBURY HOSPITAL, Amesbury, MA
AMHERST HOSPITAL, Amherst, OH
AMI ALVIN COMMUNITY HOSPITAL (Formerly Alvin Community Hospital), Alvin, TX
AMI ANCLOTE MANOR PSYCHIATRIC HOSPITAL (Formerly AMI Anclote Manor Hospital), Tarpon Springs, FL
AMI ARROYO GRANDE COMMUNITY HOSPITAL (Formerly Arroyo Grande Community Hospital), Arroyo Grande, CA
AMI BARROW MEDICAL CENTER (Formerly Barrow Medical Center), Winder, GA
AMI BELLAIRE HOSPITAL (Formerly Bellaire General Hospital), Houston, TX
AMI BROOKWOOD COMMUNITY HOSPITAL (Formerly Brookwood Community Hospital), Orlando, FL
AMI BROOKWOOD MEDICAL CENTER (Formerly Brookwood Medical Center), Birmingham, AL
AMI BROWNSVILLE MEDICAL CENTER (Formerly Brownsville Medical Center), Brownsville, TX
AMI CENTRAL ARKANSAS GENERAL HOSPITAL (Formerly Central Arkansas General Hospital), Searcy, AR
AMI CENTRAL CAROLINA HOSPITAL (Formerly Central Carolina Hospital), Sanford, NC
AMI CIRCLE CITY HOSPITAL (Formerly Circle City Hospital), Corona, CA
AMI CITIZENS GENERAL HOSPITAL, Houston, TX, See Institute for Immunological Disorders
AMI CLAIREMONT COMMUNITY HOSPITAL (Formerly Clairemont Community Hospital), San Diego, CA
AMI CLAREMORE REGIONAL MEDICAL CENTER, Claremore, OK
AMI CLEARWATER COMMUNITY HOSPITAL (Formerly Clearwater Community Hospital), Clearwater, FL
AMI COASTAL BEND HOSPITAL, Aransas Pass, TX
AMI COLUMBIA REGIONAL HOSPITAL (Formerly Columbia Regional Hospital), Columbia, MO
AMI COMMUNITY HOSPITAL OF SANTA CRUZ (Formerly Community Hospital of Santa Cruz), Santa Cruz, CA
AMI CULVER UNION HOSPITAL (Formerly Culver Union Hospital), Crawfordsville, IN
AMI DANFORTH HOSPITAL (Formerly Danforth Hospital), Texas City, TX
AMI DELAWARE AMO HOSPITAL (Formerly Delaware Amo Psychiatric Hospital), Torrance, CA
AMI DENTON REGIONAL MEDICAL CENTER (Formerly Westgate Medical Center), Denton, TX
AMI DOCTORS GENERAL HOSPITAL, Oklahoma City, OK, See Doctors General Hospital
AMI DOCTORS HOSPITAL (Formerly Doctors Medical Center), Tulsa, OK
AMI DOCTORS HOSPITAL OF LAREDO (Formerly Doctors Hospital of Laredo), Laredo, TX
AMI DOCTORS MEMORIAL HOSPITAL (Formerly Doctors Memorial Hospital), Spartanburg, SC
AMI DOCTORS' HOSPITAL (Formerly Doctors' Hospital of Prince George's County), Lanham, MD
AMI DOCTORS' HOSPITAL OF OPELOUSAS (Formerly Doctors' Hospital of Opelousas), Opelousas, LA
AMI EAST COOPER COMMUNITY HOSPITAL (Formerly East Cooper Community Hospital), Mount Pleasant, SC
AMI EASTWAY GENERAL HOSPITAL (Formerly Eastway General Hospital), Houston, TX
AMI FORT BEND COMMUNITY HOSPITAL (Formerly Fort Bend Community Hospital), Missouri City, TX
AMI FRYE REGIONAL MEDICAL CENTER (Formerly Glenn R. Frye Memorial Hospital), Hickory, NC
AMI GARDEN PARK COMMUNITY HOSPITAL (Formerly Garden Park Community Hospital), Gulfport, MS
AMI GLENDORA COMMUNITY HOSPITAL (Formerly Glendora Community Hospital), Glendora, CA
AMI GRIFFIN-SPALDING HOSPITAL (Formerly Griffin-Spalding County Hospital), Griffin, GA
AMI HEALDSBURG GENERAL HOSPITAL (Formerly Healdsburg General Hospital), Healdsburg, CA
AMI HEIGHTS HOSPITAL (Formerly Heights Hospital), Houston, TX
AMI HIGHLAND PARK HOSPITAL (Formerly Highland Park Hospital), Covington, LA
AMI KATY COMMUNITY HOSPITAL (Formerly Katy Community Hospital), Katy, TX
AMI KENDALL REGIONAL MEDICAL CENTER (Formerly American Hospital of Miami), Miami, FL
AMI LAKE CITY MEDICAL CENTER (Formerly Lake City Medical Center), Lake City, FL
AMI LUCY LEE HOSPITAL (Formerly Lucy Lee Hospital), Poplar Bluff, MO
AMI MEDICAL ARTS HOSPITAL (Formerly Medical Arts Hospital), Dallas, TX
AMI MEDICAL CENTER OF GARDEN GROVE (Formerly Medical Center of Garden Grove), Garden Grove, CA
AMI MEDICAL CENTER OF NORTH HOLLYWOOD, Los Angeles, CA
AMI MEDICAL PARK HOSPITAL (Formerly Medical Park Hospital), Hope, AR
AMI MEDICAL PLAZA HOSPITAL (Formerly Medical Plaza Hospital), Sherman, TX
AMI MEMORIAL HOSPITAL OF TAMPA (Formerly Memorial Hospital of Tampa), Tampa, FL
AMI MID-JEFFERSON COUNTY HOSPITAL (Formerly Mid-Jefferson County Hospital), Nederland, TX
AMI MISSION BAY HOSPITAL (Formerly Mission Bay Memorial Hospital), San Diego, CA

AMI NACOGDOCHES MEDICAL CENTER HOSPITAL (Formerly Nacogdoches Medical Center Hospital), Nacogdoches, TX
AMI NATIONAL PARK MEDICAL CENTER (Formerly National Park Medical Center), Hot Springs, AR
AMI NORTH FULTON MEDICAL CENTER (Formerly North Fulton Medical Center), Roswell, GA
AMI NORTH RIDGE GENERAL HOSPITAL, Fort Lauderdale, FL, See AMI North Ridge Medical Center
AMI NORTH RIDGE MEDICAL CENTER (Formerly AMI North Ridge General Hospital), Fort Lauderdale, FL
AMI NORTH TEXAS MEDICAL CENTER, McKinney, TX
AMI ODESSA WOMEN'S AND CHILDREN'S HOSPITAL (Formerly Odessa Women's and Children's Hospital), Odessa, TX
AMI PALM BEACH GARDENS MEDICAL CENTER (Formerly Palm Beach Gardens Medical Center), Palm Beach Gardens, FL
AMI PALMETTO GENERAL HOSPITAL (Formerly Palmetto General Hospital), Hialeah, FL
AMI PARK PLACE HOSPITAL (Formerly Park Place Hospital), Port Arthur, TX
AMI PARK PLAZA HOSPITAL (Formerly Park Plaza Hospital), Houston, TX
AMI PARKWAY HOSPITAL (Formerly Parkway Hospital), Houston, TX
AMI PARKWAY REGIONAL MEDICAL CENTER (Formerly Parkway Regional Medical Center), North Miami Beach, FL
AMI PEMBROKE HOSPITAL, Pembroke, MA
AMI PHYSICIANS AND SURGEONS HOSPITAL (Formerly Physicians and Surgeons Hospital), Alice, TX
AMI PIEDMONT MEDICAL CENTER (Formerly Piedmont Medical Center), Rock Hill, SC
AMI PIONEER PARK MEDICAL CENTER, Irving, TX, See Pioneer Park Hospital
AMI PRESBYTERIAN AURORA HOSPITAL, Aurora, CO
AMI PRESBYTERIAN-DENVER HOSPITAL, Denver, CO
AMI PRESBYTERIAN-ST. LUKE'S MEDICAL CENTER, Denver, CO
AMI RANCHO ENCINO HOSPITAL (Formerly Rancho Encino Hospital), Los Angeles, CA
AMI RIVERSIDE HOSPITAL (Formerly Riverside Hospital), Corpus Christi, TX
AMI ROUND ROCK COMMUNITY HOSPITAL (Formerly Round Rock Community Hospital), Round Rock, TX
AMI SAINT JOSEPH HOSPITAL (Formerly Saint Joseph Hospital), Omaha, NE
AMI SAN DIMAS COMMUNITY HOSPITAL (Formerly San Dimas Community Hospital), San Dimas, CA
AMI SIERRA VISTA HOSPITAL, San Luis Obispo, CA, See AMI Sierra Vista Regional Medical Center
AMI SIERRA VISTA REGIONAL MEDICAL CENTER (Formerly AMI Sierra Vista Hospital), San Luis Obispo, CA
AMI SOUTH BAY HOSPITAL (Formerly South Bay Hospital), Redondo Beach, CA
AMI SOUTHEASTERN MEDICAL CENTER (Formerly Southeastern Medical Center), North Miami Beach, FL
AMI SOUTHWESTERN MEDICAL CENTER (Formerly AMI Southwestern Hospital), Lawton, OK
AMI ST. JOSEPH CENTER FOR MENTAL HEALTH (Formerly St. Joseph Center for Mental Health), Omaha, NE
AMI ST. JUDE MEDICAL CENTER, Kenner, LA
AMI ST. MARY'S HOSPITAL (Formerly St. Mary's Hospital), Russellville, AR
AMI TARZANA REGIONAL MEDICAL CENTER (Formerly Medical Center of Tarzana Hospital), Los Angeles, CA
AMI TERRELL COMMUNITY HOSPITAL (Formerly Terrell Community Hospital), Terrell, TX
AMI TEXARKANA COMMUNITY HOSPITAL (Formerly Texarkana Community Hospital), Texarkana, TX
AMI TOWN AND COUNTRY MEDICAL CENTER (Formerly Town and Country Hospital), Tampa, FL
AMI TWELVE OAKS HOSPITAL (Formerly Twelve Oaks Hospital), Houston, TX
AMI VALLEY MEDICAL CENTER (Formerly El Cajon Valley Hospital), El Cajon, CA
AMI WEST ALABAMA HOSPITAL (Formerly AMI West Alabama General Hospital), Northport, AL
AMI WESTBURY HOSPITAL (Formerly Westbury Hospital), Houston, TX
AMI WESTPARK COMMUNITY HOSPITAL (Formerly Westpark Community Hospital), Hammond, LA
AMI WESTWOOD LODGE HOSPITAL (Formerly Westwood Lodge Hospital), Westwood, MA
AMOS COTTAGE REHABILITATION HOSPITAL, Winston-Salem, NC
AMSTERDAM MEMORIAL HOSPITAL, Amsterdam, NY
ANACAPA ADVENTIST HOSPITAL (Formerly Port Hueneme Adventist Hospital), Port Hueneme, CA
ANADARKO MUNICIPAL HOSPITAL, Anadarko, OK
ANAHEIM GENERAL HOSPITAL, Anaheim, CA
ANAHEIM MEMORIAL HOSPITAL, Anaheim, CA
ANAMOSA COMMUNITY HOSPITAL, Anamosa, IA
ANCHOR HOSPITAL, Atlanta, GA
ANCORA PSYCHIATRIC HOSPITAL, Hammonton, NJ
ANDERSON ALCOHOLIC REHABILITATION HOSPITAL, Janesville, WI, See Parkside Lodge of Wisconsin
ANDERSON COUNTY HOSPITAL, Garnett, KS
ANDERSON COUNTY MEMORIAL HOSPITAL (Formerly Memorial Hospital), Palestine, TX
ANDERSON HOSPITAL (Formerly Oliver C. Anderson Hospital), Maryville, IL
ANDERSON MEMORIAL HOSPITAL, Norway, MI, See Dickinson County Hospitals, Iron Mountain
ANDERSON MEMORIAL HOSPITAL, Anderson, SC
ANDREW KAUL MEMORIAL HOSPITAL, St. Marys, PA
ANDREW MCFARLAND MENTAL HEALTH CENTER, Springfield, IL
ANDROSCOGGIN VALLEY HOSPITAL, Berlin, NH
ANGEL COMMUNITY HOSPITAL, Franklin, NC
ANGELO COMMUNITY HOSPITAL, San Angelo, TX
ANGLETON-DANBURY GENERAL HOSPITAL, Angleton, TX
ANNA JAQUES HOSPITAL, Newburyport, MA
ANNA MENTAL HEALTH AND DEVELOPMENTAL CENTER, Anna, IL
ANNAPOLIS HOSPITAL, Wayne, MI
ANNE ARUNDEL GENERAL HOSPITAL, Annapolis, MD
ANNEEWAKEE HOSPITAL, Douglasville, GA
ANNIE JEFFREY MEMORIAL COUNTY HOSPITAL, Osceola, NE
ANNIE PENN MEMORIAL HOSPITAL, Reidsville, NC
ANOKA-METROPOLITAN REGIONAL TREATMENT CENTER (Formerly Anoka State Hospital), Anoka, MN
ANSON COUNTY HOSPITAL AND SKILLED NURSING FACILITY, Wadesboro, NC
ANSON GENERAL HOSPITAL, Anson, TX
ANTELOPE MEMORIAL HOSPITAL, Neligh, NE
ANTELOPE VALLEY HOSPITAL MEDICAL CENTER, Lancaster, CA
APPALACHIAN HALL, Asheville, NC
APPALACHIAN REGIONAL HOSPITAL, Beckley, WV, See Beckley Appalachian Regional Hospital
APPLE RIVER HOSPITAL (Formerly Apple River Valley Memorial Hospital), Amery, WI
APPLETON MEDICAL CENTER, Appleton, WI
APPLETON MUNICIPAL HOSPITAL AND NURSING HOME, Appleton, MN
APPLING GENERAL HOSPITAL, Baxley, GA
ARAB HOSPITAL, Arab, AL
ARBUCKLE MEMORIAL HOSPITAL, Sulphur, OK
ARCADIA VALLEY HOSPITAL, Pilot Knob, MO
ARCHBISHOP BERGAN MERCY HOSPITAL, Omaha, NE
ARCHBOLD HOSPITAL, Wallingford, CT
ARCHER COUNTY HOSPITAL, Archer City, TX
ARDEN HILL HOSPITAL, Goshen, NY
ARDMORE ACRES HOSPITAL, Livonia, MI
ARDMORE ADVENTIST HOSPITAL, Ardmore, OK
ARECIBO HEALTH CENTER, Arecibo, P.R.
ARECIBO REGIONAL HOSPITAL, Arecibo, P.R.
ARH REGIONAL MEDICAL CENTER (Formerly Hazard Appalachian Regional Hospital), Hazard, KY
ARIZONA STATE HOSPITAL, Phoenix, AZ
ARKANSAS CHILDREN'S HOSPITAL, Little Rock, AR
ARKANSAS CITY MEMORIAL HOSPITAL, Arkansas City, KS
ARKANSAS METHODIST HOSPITAL, Paragould, AR
ARKANSAS REHABILITATION INSTITUTE, Little Rock, AR
ARKANSAS STATE HOSPITAL, Little Rock, AR
ARKANSAS VALLEY REGIONAL MEDICAL CENTER (Formerly La Junta Medical Center), La Junta, CO
ARLINGTON COMMUNITY HOSPITAL, Arlington, TX, See HCA South Arlington Medical Center
ARLINGTON HOSPITAL, Arlington, VA
ARLINGTON MEMORIAL HOSPITAL, Arlington, TX
ARLINGTON MUNICIPAL HOSPITAL, Arlington, MN
ARMS ACRES, Carmel, NY
ARMSTRONG COUNTY MEMORIAL HOSPITAL, Kittanning, PA
ARNOLD GREGORY MEMORIAL HOSPITAL AND SKILLED NURSING FACILITIES, Albion, NY
ARNOLD MEMORIAL HOSPITAL, Adrian, MN
ARNOT-OGDEN MEMORIAL HOSPITAL, Elmira, NY
AROOSTOOK MEDICAL CENTER, Presque Isle, ME
ARTESIA GENERAL HOSPITAL, Artesia, NM
ASBURY HOSPITAL, Salina, KS
ASHE MEMORIAL HOSPITAL, Jefferson, NC
ASHFORD PRESBYTERIAN COMMUNITY HOSPITAL, San Juan, P.R.
ASHLAND COMMUNITY HOSPITAL, Ashland, OR
ASHLAND DISTRICT HOSPITAL, Ashland, KS
ASHLAND STATE GENERAL HOSPITAL, Ashland, PA
ASHLEY MEDICAL CENTER (Formerly McIntosh County Memorial Hospital), Ashley, ND
ASHLEY MEMORIAL HOSPITAL, Crossett, AR
ASHLEY VALLEY MEDICAL CENTER, Vernal, UT
ASHTABULA COUNTY MEDICAL CENTER, Ashtabula, OH
ASHTON MEMORIAL HOSPITAL, Ashton, ID
ASPEN VALLEY HOSPITAL DISTRICT, Aspen, CO
ASSUMPTION GENERAL HOSPITAL, Napoleonville, LA
ASTORIA GENERAL HOSPITAL, Long Island City, NY
ATASCADERO STATE HOSPITAL, Atascadero, CA
ATCHISON HOSPITAL, Atchison, KS
ATHENS COMMUNITY HOSPITAL, Athens, TN
ATHENS MENTAL HEALTH CENTER, Athens, OH
ATHENS REGIONAL MEDICAL CENTER (Formerly Athens General Hospital), Athens, GA
ATHENS-LIMESTONE HOSPITAL, Athens, AL
ATHOL MEMORIAL HOSPITAL, Athol, MA
ATLANTA HOSPITAL (Formerly Atlanta Community Hospital), Atlanta, GA
ATLANTA MEMORIAL HOSPITAL, Atlanta, TX
ATLANTIC CITY MEDICAL CENTER, Atlantic City, NJ
ATLANTICARE MEDICAL CENTER, Lynn, MA
ATOKA MEMORIAL HOSPITAL, Atoka, OK
ATTICA DISTRICT HOSPITAL ONE, Attica, KS
AUBURN FAITH COMMUNITY HOSPITAL, Auburn, CA
AUBURN GENERAL HOSPITAL, Auburn, WA
AUBURN MEMORIAL HOSPITAL, Auburn, NY
AUDIE L. MURPHY MEMORIAL VETERANS HOSPITAL, San Antonio, TX
AUDRAIN MEDICAL CENTER, Mexico, MO
AUDUBON COUNTY MEMORIAL HOSPITAL, Audubon, IA
AUGUSTA MEDICAL COMPLEX, Augusta, KS
AUGUSTA MENTAL HEALTH INSTITUTE, Augusta, ME
AUGUSTANA HOSPITAL AND HEALTH CARE CENTER, Chicago, IL
AULTMAN HOSPITAL, Canton, OH
AURELIA OSBORN FOX MEMORIAL HOSPITAL, Oneonta, NY
AURORA COMMUNITY HOSPITAL, Aurora, MO
AUSTEN RIGGS CENTER, Stockbridge, MA
AUSTIN STATE HOSPITAL, Austin, TX
AUSTIN STATE SCHOOL, Austin, TX
AUTAUGA MEDICAL CENTER, Prattville, AL
AUXILIO MUTUO HOSPITAL, San Juan, P.R.
AVALON MUNICIPAL HOSPITAL, Avalon, CA
AVENAL DISTRICT HOSPITAL, Avenal, CA
AXTELL CHRISTIAN HOSPITAL, Newton, KS

B

B. J. WORKMAN MEMORIAL HOSPITAL, Woodruff, SC
BACON COUNTY HOSPITAL, Alma, GA
BAILEY MEMORIAL HOSPITAL, Clinton, SC
BAKER HOSPITAL, North Charleston, SC
BAKERSFIELD COMMUNITY HOSPITAL, Bakersfield, CA
BAKERSFIELD MEMORIAL HOSPITAL (Formerly Greater Bakersfield Memorial Hospital), Bakersfield, CA
BALDPATE HOSPITAL, Georgetown, MA
BALDWIN COMMUNITY MEMORIAL HOSPITAL, Baldwin, WI
BALDWIN COUNTY HOSPITAL, Milledgeville, GA
BALL MEMORIAL HOSPITAL, Muncie, IN
BALLARD COMMUNITY HOSPITAL, Seattle, WA
BALLINGER MEMORIAL HOSPITAL, Ballinger, TX
BALTIMORE COUNTY GENERAL HOSPITAL, Randallstown, MD
BAMBERG COUNTY MEMORIAL HOSPITAL, Bamberg, SC
BANGOR MENTAL HEALTH INSTITUTE, Bangor, ME
BANKS-JACKSON-COMMERCE HOSPITAL, Commerce, GA
BANNOCK REGIONAL MEDICAL CENTER, Pocatello, ID
BAPTIST HOSPITAL, Pensacola, FL
BAPTIST HOSPITAL, Winner, SD
BAPTIST HOSPITAL, Nashville, TN
BAPTIST HOSPITAL EAST, Louisville, KY, See Louisville Baptist Hospitals
BAPTIST HOSPITAL FUND, St. Paul, MN
BAPTIST HOSPITAL HIGHLANDS, Louisville, KY, See Louisville Baptist Hospitals
BAPTIST HOSPITAL OF MIAMI, Miami, FL
BAPTIST HOSPITAL OF SOUTHEAST TEXAS, Beaumont, TX
BAPTIST HOSPITAL-WINNIE (Formerly Medical Center of Winnie), Winnie, TX
BAPTIST MEDICAL CENTER, Montgomery, AL
BAPTIST MEDICAL CENTER, Little Rock, AR
BAPTIST MEDICAL CENTER, Jacksonville, FL
BAPTIST MEDICAL CENTER, Kansas City, MO

BAPTIST MEDICAL CENTER, Columbia, SC
BAPTIST MEDICAL CENTER, San Antonio, TX
BAPTIST MEDICAL CENTER EASLEY (Formerly Easley Baptist Hospital), Easley, SC
BAPTIST MEDICAL CENTER OF NEW YORK, Brooklyn, NY
BAPTIST MEDICAL CENTER OF OKLAHOMA, Oklahoma City, OK
BAPTIST MEDICAL CENTER-CHEROKEE, Centre, AL
BAPTIST MEDICAL CENTER-DEKALB, Fort Payne, AL
BAPTIST MEDICAL CENTER-MONTCLAIR, Birmingham, AL
BAPTIST MEDICAL CENTER-PRINCETON, Birmingham, AL
BAPTIST MEMORIAL HOSPITAL, Gadsden, AL
BAPTIST MEMORIAL HOSPITAL, Memphis, TN
BAPTIST MEMORIAL HOSPITAL EAST, Memphis, TN, See Baptist Memorial Hospital
BAPTIST MEMORIAL HOSPITAL-BOONEVILLE, Booneville, MS
BAPTIST MEMORIAL HOSPITAL-EASTERN OZARKS, Hardy, AR
BAPTIST MEMORIAL HOSPITAL-FORREST CITY, Forrest City, AR
BAPTIST MEMORIAL HOSPITAL-HUNTINGDON, Huntingdon, TN
BAPTIST MEMORIAL HOSPITAL-LAUDERDALE, Ripley, TN
BAPTIST MEMORIAL HOSPITAL-TIPTON, Covington, TN
BAPTIST MEMORIAL HOSPITAL-UNION CITY, Union City, TN
BAPTIST MEMORIALS GERIATRIC CENTER, San Angelo, TX
BAPTIST REGIONAL HEALTH CENTER, Miami, OK
BAPTIST REGIONAL MEDICAL CENTER (Formerly Southeastern Kentucky Bapt Hospital), Corbin, KY
BAPTIST SPECIALTY HOSPITAL (Formerly Humana Specialty Hospital-Memphis), Memphis, TN
BARAGA COUNTY MEMORIAL HOSPITAL, L'Anse, MI
BARBERTON CITIZENS HOSPITAL, Barberton, OH
BARLOW HOSPITAL, Los Angeles, CA
BARNARD FREE SKIN AND CANCER HOSPITAL, St. Louis, MO, See Barnes Hospital
BARNERT MEMORIAL HOSPITAL CENTER, Paterson, NJ
BARNES HOSPITAL, St. Louis, MO
BARNES-KASSON COUNTY HOSPITAL, Susquehanna, PA
BARNESVILLE HOSPITAL ASSOCIATION, Barnesville, OH
BARNSTABLE COUNTY HOSPITAL, Pocasset, MA
BARNWELL COUNTY HOSPITAL, Barnwell, SC
BARONESS ERLANGER HOSPITAL, Chattanooga, TN, See Erlanger Medical Center
BARRANQUITAS HEALTH CENTER, Barranquitas, P.R.
BARRETT MEMORIAL HOSPITAL, Dillon, MT
BARRON MEMORIAL MEDICAL CENTER, Barron, WI
BARSTOW COMMUNITY HOSPITAL, Barstow, CA
BARTHOLOMEW COUNTY HOSPITAL, Columbus, IN
BARTLETT MEMORIAL HOSPITAL, Juneau, AK
BARTLETT MEMORIAL MEDICAL CENTER, Sapulpa, OK
BARTON COUNTY MEMORIAL HOSPITAL, Lamar, MO
BARTON MEMORIAL HOSPITAL, South Lake Tahoe, CA
BARTOW MEMORIAL HOSPITAL, Bartow, FL
BASCOM PALMER EYE INSTITUTE AND ANNE BATES LEACH EYE HOSPITAL, Miami, FL
BASS MEMORIAL BAPTIST HOSPITAL, Enid, OK
BASSETT ARMY COMMUNITY HOSPITAL, Fairbanks, AK
BASTROP COMMUNITY HOSPITAL (Formerly Bastrop Memorial Hospital), Bastrop, TX
BATES COUNTY MEMORIAL HOSPITAL, Butler, MO
BATES MEMORIAL HOSPITAL, Bentonville, AR
BATH COUNTY COMMUNITY HOSPITAL, Hot Springs, VA
BATH MEMORIAL HOSPITAL, Bath, ME
BATON ROUGE GENERAL MEDICAL CENTER, Baton Rouge, LA
BATTLE CREEK ADVENTIST HOSPITAL, Battle Creek, MI
BATTLE MOUNTAIN GENERAL HOSPITAL, Battle Mountain, NV
BAUM HARMON MEMORIAL HOSPITAL, Primghar, IA
BAXTER COUNTY REGIONAL HOSPITAL, Mountain Home, AR
BAXTER MEMORIAL HOSPITAL, Baxter Springs, KS
BAY AREA HOSPITAL, Coos Bay, OR
BAY AREA MEDICAL CENTER (Formerly Marinette General Hospital), Marinette, WI
BAY AREA MEDICAL CENTER-MENOMINEE (Formerly Menominee County Lloyd Hospital), Menominee, MI
BAY HARBOR HOSPITAL, Los Angeles, CA
BAY MEDICAL CENTER, Panama City, FL
BAY MEDICAL CENTER, Bay City, MI
BAY OSTEOPATHIC HOSPITAL, Bay City, MI
BAYFIELD COUNTY MEMORIAL HOSPITAL, Washburn, WI
BAYFRONT MEDICAL CENTER, St. Petersburg, FL
BAYLEY SETON HOSPITAL, Staten Island, NY
BAYLOR INSTITUTE FOR REHABILITATION, Dallas, TX
BAYLOR MEDICAL CENTER AT ENNIS (Formerly Ennis Community Hospital), Ennis, TX
BAYLOR MEDICAL CENTER AT GILMER (Formerly Ford Memorial Hospital), Gilmer, TX
BAYLOR MEDICAL CENTER AT GRAPEVINE (Formerly Grapevine Medical Center), Grapevine, TX
BAYLOR MEDICAL CENTER AT WAXAHACHIE (Formerly Tenery Community Hospital), Waxahachie, TX
BAYLOR UNIVERSITY MEDICAL CENTER, Dallas, TX
BAYNE-JONES ARMY COMMUNITY HOSPITAL, Fort Polk, LA
BAYONNE HOSPITAL, Bayonne, NJ
BAYSHORE COMMUNITY HOSPITAL, Holmdel, NJ
BAYSIDE COMMUNITY HOSPITAL (Formerly Chambers Memorial Hospital), Anahuac, TX
BAYSTATE MEDICAL CENTER, Springfield, MA
BAYWOOD HOSPITAL, Webster, TX
BEACH COMMUNITY HOSPITAL, Buena Park, CA, See Buena Park Doctors Hospital
BEACHAM MEMORIAL HOSPITAL, Magnolia, MS
BEACHES HOSPITAL, Jacksonville Beach, FL
BEAR LAKE MEMORIAL HOSPITAL, Montpelier, ID
BEAR RIVER VALLEY HOSPITAL, Tremonton, UT
BEAR VALLEY COMMUNITY HOSPITAL, Big Bear Lake, CA
BEATRICE COMMUNITY HOSPITAL AND HEALTH CENTER, Beatrice, NE
BEAUFORT COUNTY HOSPITAL, Washington, NC
BEAUFORT MEMORIAL HOSPITAL (Formerly Beaufort County Memorial Hospital), Beaufort, SC
BEAUMONT MEDICAL SURGICAL HOSPITAL, Beaumont, TX
BEAUMONT NEUROLOGICAL HOSPITAL, Beaumont, TX
BEAUREGARD MEMORIAL HOSPITAL, De Ridder, LA
BEAVER COUNTY MEMORIAL HOSPITAL, Beaver, OK
BEAVER DAM COMMUNITY HOSPITALS, Beaver Dam, WI
BEAVER VALLEY HOSPITAL, Beaver, UT
BECKLEY APPALACHIAN REGIONAL HOSPITAL (Formerly Appalachian Regional Hospital), Beckley, WV
BECKLEY HOSPITAL, Beckley, WV
BEDFORD COUNTY GENERAL HOSPITAL, Shelbyville, TN
BEDFORD COUNTY MEMORIAL HOSPITAL, Bedford, VA
BEDFORD MEDICAL CENTER, Bedford, IN
BEEBE HOSPITAL OF SUSSEX COUNTY, Lewes, DE
BEECH HILL HOSPITAL, Dublin, NH
BEEVILLE MEMORIAL HOSPITAL (Formerly Memorial Hospital), Beeville, TX
BELLA VISTA HOSPITAL, Mayaguez, P.R.
BELLAIRE GENERAL HOSPITAL, Houston, TX, See AMI Bellaire Hospital
BELLE FOURCHE HEALTH CARE CENTER, Belle Fourche, SD
BELLE PARK HOSPITAL, Houston, TX
BELLEVUE HOSPITAL, Bellevue, OH
BELLEVUE HOSPITAL CENTER, New York, NY
BELLEVUE MATERNITY HOSPITAL, Schenectady, NY
BELLFLOWER DOCTORS HOSPITAL, Bellflower, CA
BELLIN MEMORIAL HOSPITAL, Green Bay, WI
BELLVILLE GENERAL HOSPITAL, Bellville, TX
BELLWOOD GENERAL HOSPITAL, Bellflower, CA
BELMOND COMMUNITY HOSPITAL, Belmond, IA
BELMONT COMMUNITY HOSPITAL, Chicago, IL
BELOIT MEMORIAL HOSPITAL, Beloit, WI
BELTWAY COMMUNITY HOSPITAL, Pasadena, TX
BEN TAUB GENERAL HOSPITAL, Houston, TX, See Harris County Hospital District
BENEDICTINE HOSPITAL, Kingston, NY
BENEWAH COMMUNITY HOSPITAL, St. Maries, ID
BENJAMIN RUSH CENTER, Syracuse, NY
BENNETT COUNTY COMMUNITY HOSPITAL, Martin, SD
BENSON HOSPITAL, Benson, AZ
BENTON COMMUNITY HOSPITAL (Formerly Benton County General Hospital), Camden, TN
BEREA HOSPITAL, Berea, KY
BERGEN PINES COUNTY HOSPITAL, Paramus, NJ
BERGER HOSPITAL, Circleville, OH
BERKSHIRE MEDICAL CENTER, Pittsfield, MA
BERLIN HOSPITAL ASSOCIATION, Berlin, WI
BERRIEN COUNTY HOSPITAL, Nashville, GA
BERRIEN GENERAL HOSPITAL, Berrien Center, MI
BERTIE MEMORIAL HOSPITAL (Formerly Bertie County Memorial Hospital), Windsor, NC
BERTRAND CHAFFEE HOSPITAL, Springville, NY
BERWICK HOSPITAL CENTER (Formerly Berwick Hospital), Berwick, PA
BESS KAISER MEDICAL CENTER, Portland, OR
BESSEMER CARRAWAY MEDICAL CENTER, Bessemer, AL
BETH ISRAEL HOSPITAL, Denver, CO
BETH ISRAEL HOSPITAL, Boston, MA
BETH ISRAEL HOSPITAL, Passaic, NJ
BETH ISRAEL MEDICAL CENTER, New York, NY
BETHANIA REGIONAL HEALTH CARE CENTER, Wichita Falls, TX
BETHANY GENERAL HOSPITAL, Bethany, OK
BETHANY HOSPITAL, Chicago, IL
BETHANY HOSPITAL, Framingham, MA
BETHANY MEDICAL CENTER, Kansas City, KS
BETHANY METHODIST HOSPITAL, Chicago, IL, See Methodist Hospital of Chicago
BETHEL DEACONESS HOSPITAL, Newton, KS
BETHESDA GENERAL HOSPITAL, St. Louis, MO
BETHESDA HOSPITAL, Chicago, IL
BETHESDA HOSPITAL, Zanesville, OH
BETHESDA LUTHERAN MEDICAL CENTER, St. Paul, MN
BETHESDA MEMORIAL HOSPITAL, Boynton Beach, FL
BETHESDA NORTH HOSPITAL, Cincinnati, OH
BETHESDA OAK HOSPITAL, Cincinnati, OH
BETHESDA PSYCHEALTH SYSTEM (Formerly Bethesda Hospital and Community Mental Health Center), Denver, CO
BETSY JOHNSON MEMORIAL HOSPITAL, Dunn, NC
BETTY BACHARACH REHABILITATION HOSPITAL, Pomona, NJ
BEVERLY GLEN HOSPITAL, Los Angeles, CA
BEVERLY HILLS MEDICAL CENTER, Los Angeles, CA
BEVERLY HOSPITAL, Montebello, CA
BEVERLY HOSPITAL, Beverly, MA
BEXAR COUNTY HOSPITAL DISTRICT, San Antonio, TX
BEYER MEMORIAL HOSPITAL, Ypsilanti, MI
BI-COUNTY COMMUNITY HOSPITAL, Warren, MI
BIBB MEDICAL CENTER, Centreville, AL
BIENVILLE GENERAL HOSPITAL, Arcadia, LA
BIG HORN COUNTY MEMORIAL HOSPITAL, Hardin, MT
BIG SANDY MEDICAL CENTER, Big Sandy, MT
BIG SPRING STATE HOSPITAL, Big Spring, TX
BIGGS-GRIDLEY MEMORIAL HOSPITAL, Gridley, CA
BILLINGS DEACONESS HOSPITAL, Billings, MT, See Deaconess Medical Center
BILOXI REGIONAL MEDICAL CENTER, Biloxi, MS
BINGHAM MEMORIAL HOSPITAL, Blackfoot, ID
BINGHAMTON GENERAL HOSPITAL, Binghamton, NY, See United Health Services, Johnson City
BINGHAMTON PSYCHIATRIC CENTER, Binghamton, NY
BISHOP CLARKSON MEMORIAL HOSPITAL, Omaha, NE
BLACK HILLS COMMUNITY HOSPITAL, Olympia, WA
BLACK HILLS REHABILITATION HOSPITAL, Rapid City, SD
BLACK RIVER MEMORIAL HOSPITAL, Black River Falls, WI
BLACKFORD COUNTY HOSPITAL, Hartford City, IN
BLACKWELDER MEMORIAL HOSPITAL, Lenoir, NC
BLACKWELL REGIONAL HOSPITAL, Blackwell, OK
BLADEN COUNTY HOSPITAL, Elizabethtown, NC
BLAINE COUNTY MEDICAL CENTER, Hailey, ID
BLANCHARD VALLEY HOSPITAL, Findlay, OH
BLECKLEY MEMORIAL HOSPITAL, Cochran, GA
BLEDSOE COUNTY HOSPITAL, Pikeville, TN
BLESSING HOSPITAL, Quincy, IL
BLODGETT MEMORIAL MEDICAL CENTER, Grand Rapids, MI
BLOOMER COMMUNITY MEMORIAL HOSPITAL AND SKILLED NURSING FACILITY, Bloomer, WI
BLOOMINGTON HOSPITAL, Bloomington, IN
BLOOMSBURG HOSPITAL, Bloomsburg, PA
BLOSS MEMORIAL DISTRICT HOSPITAL, Atwater, CA
BLOUNT MEMORIAL HOSPITAL, Oneonta, AL
BLOUNT MEMORIAL HOSPITAL, Maryville, TN
BLOWING ROCK HOSPITAL, Blowing Rock, NC
BLUE HILL MEMORIAL HOSPITAL, Blue Hill, ME
BLUE MOUNTAIN HOSPITAL, John Day, OR
BLUE RIDGE HOSPITAL, Charlottesville, VA, See University of Virginia Hospitals
BLUE RIDGE HOSPITAL SYSTEMS, SPRUCE PINE COMMUNITY HOSPITAL DIVISION, Spruce Pine, NC
BLUEFIELD COMMUNITY HOSPITAL, Bluefield, WV
BLUFFTON COMMUNITY HOSPITAL, Bluffton, OH
BLYTHEDALE CHILDREN'S HOSPITAL, Valhalla, NY
BOAZ-ALBERTVILLE MEDICAL CENTER (Formerly Boaz-Albertville Hospital), Boaz, AL
BOB WILSON MEMORIAL GRANT COUNTY HOSPITAL, Ulysses, KS
BOBS ROBERTS MEMORIAL HOSPITAL FOR CHILDREN, Chicago, IL, See University of Chicago Hospitals and Clinics

BOCA RATON COMMUNITY HOSPITAL, Boca Raton, FL
BOGALUSA COMMUNITY MEDICAL CENTER, Bogalusa, LA
BOHNE MEMORIAL HOSPITAL, Brenham, TX
BOLIVAR COUNTY HOSPITAL, Cleveland, MS
BOLWELL HEALTH CENTER, Cleveland, OH, See University Hospitals of Cleveland
BON SECOURS HOSPITAL, North Miami, FL
BON SECOURS HOSPITAL, Baltimore, MD
BON SECOURS HOSPITAL, Grosse Pointe, MI
BON SECOURS HOSPITAL OF METHUEN, Methuen, MA
BONE AND JOINT HOSPITAL, Oklahoma City, OK
BONNE TERRE HOSPITAL, Bonne Terre, MO
BONNER GENERAL HOSPITAL, Sandpoint, ID
BOONE COUNTY COMMUNITY HOSPITAL, Albion, NE
BOONE COUNTY HOSPITAL, Boone, IA
BOONE HOSPITAL CENTER, Columbia, MO
BOONE MEMORIAL HOSPITAL, Madison, WV
BOONEVILLE CITY HOSPITAL, Booneville, AR
BOOTH MEMORIAL MEDICAL CENTER, Flushing, NY
BORGESS MEDICAL CENTER, Kalamazoo, MI
BOSSIER MEDICAL CENTER, Bossier City, LA
BOSTON CITY HOSPITAL, Boston, MA
BOSTON HOSPITAL FOR WOMEN, Boston, MA, See Brigham and Women's Hospital
BOTHWELL REGIONAL HEALTH CENTER, Sedalia, MO
BOTSFORD GENERAL HOSPITAL-OSTEOPATHIC, Farmington Hills, MI
BOULDER CITY HOSPITAL, Boulder City, NV
BOULDER COMMUNITY HOSPITAL, Boulder, CO
BOULDER MEMORIAL HOSPITAL, Boulder, CO
BOULDER PSYCHIATRIC INSTITUTE, Boulder, CO
BOULEVARD HOSPITAL, Long Island City, NY
BOURNEWOOD HOSPITAL, Brookline, MA
BOWDLE HOSPITAL, Bowdle, SD
BOWDON AREA HOSPITAL, Bowdon, GA
BOWIE MEMORIAL HOSPITAL, Bowie, TX
BOWLING GREEN INN, Mandeville, LA
BOX BUTTE GENERAL HOSPITAL, Alliance, NE
BOYS TOWN NATIONAL INSTITUTE FOR COMMUNICATION DISORDERS IN CHILDREN, Omaha, NE
BOZEMAN DEACONESS HOSPITAL, Bozeman, MT
BRACKENRIDGE HOSPITAL, Austin, TX
BRADDOCK GENERAL HOSPITAL, Braddock, PA
BRADFORD HOSPITAL, Starke, FL
BRADFORD HOSPITAL, Bradford, PA
BRADLEY CENTER, Columbus, GA
BRADLEY COUNTY MEMORIAL HOSPITAL, Warren, AR
BRADLEY COUNTY MEMORIAL HOSPITAL, Cleveland, TN
BRADLEY MEMORIAL HOSPITAL, Southington, CT
BRADY-GREEN COMMUNITY HEALTH CENTER, San Antonio, TX, See Bexar County Hospital District
BRAINERD REGIONAL HUMAN SERVICES CENTER (Formerly Brainerd State Hospital), Brainerd, MN
BRAINTREE HOSPITAL, Braintree, MA
BRANDYWINE HOSPITAL (Formerly Listed Under Coatesville), Caln Township, PA
BRATTLEBORO MEMORIAL HOSPITAL, Brattleboro, VT
BRATTLEBORO RETREAT, Brattleboro, VT
BRAWNER PSYCHIATRIC INSTITUTE, Smyrna, GA
BRAXTON COUNTY MEMORIAL HOSPITAL, Gassaway, WV
BRAZOS CENTER FOR PSYCHIATRY, Waco, TX, See Brazos Psychiatric Hospital
BRAZOS PSYCHIATRIC HOSPITAL (Formerly Brazos Center for Psychiatry), Waco, TX
BRAZOS VALLEY HOSPITAL, Sealy, TX
BRAZOSPORT MEMORIAL HOSPITAL, Lake Jackson, TX
BREA COMMUNITY HOSPITAL, Brea, CA
BREA HOSPITAL-NEUROPSYCHIATRIC CENTER, Brea, CA
BRECKINRIDGE MEMORIAL HOSPITAL, Hardinsburg, KY
BREECH MEDICAL CENTER, Lebanon, MO
BRENT GENERAL HOSPITAL, Detroit, MI
BRENTWOOD HOSPITAL, Warrensville Heights, OH
BRENTWOOD VETERANS ADMINISTRATION DIVISION, Los Angeles, CA, See Veterans Administration Medical Center-West Los Angeles
BREVARD MENTAL HEALTH CENTER, Melbourne, FL
BREWSTER MEMORIAL HOSPITAL (Formerly Big Bend Memorial Hospital), Alpine, TX
BRIDGEPORT HOSPITAL, Bridgeport, CT
BRIDGEPORT HOSPITAL, Bridgeport, TX
BRIDGETON HOSPITAL, Bridgeton, NJ
BRIDGEWATER STATE HOSPITAL, Bridgewater, MA
BRIDGEWAY, North Little Rock, AR
BRIERWOOD HOSPITAL, Greer, SC
BRIGHAM AND WOMEN'S HOSPITAL, Boston, MA
BRIGHAM CITY COMMUNITY HOSPITAL, Brigham City, UT
BRIGHTON HOSPITAL, Brighton, MI
BRISTOL HOSPITAL, Bristol, CT
BRISTOL MEMORIAL HOSPITAL, Bristol, TN
BRISTOW MEMORIAL HOSPITAL, Bristow, OK
BROAD STREET HOSPITAL AND MEDICAL CENTER, Philadelphia, PA, See University Medical Center
BROADDUS HOSPITAL, Philippi, WV
BROADLAWNS MEDICAL CENTER, Des Moines, IA
BROADWATER COMMUNITY HOSPITAL, Townsend, MT
BROCKTON HOSPITAL, Brockton, MA
BROCKTON-WEST ROXBURY VETERANS ADMINISTRATION MEDICAL CENTER, Brockton, MA
BRODSTONE MEMORIAL NUCKOLLS COUNTY HOSPITAL, Superior, NE
BROKAW HOSPITAL, Normal, IL
BROKEN ARROW MEDICAL CENTER, Broken Arrow, OK
BRONSON METHODIST HOSPITAL, Kalamazoo, MI
BRONSON VICKSBURG HOSPITAL (Formerly Franklin Community Hospital), Vicksburg, MI
BRONX CHILDREN'S PSYCHIATRIC CENTER, Bronx, NY
BRONX MUNICIPAL HOSPITAL CENTER, Bronx, NY
BRONX PSYCHIATRIC CENTER, Bronx, NY
BRONX-LEBANON HOSPITAL CENTER, Bronx, NY
BROOK LANE PSYCHIATRIC CENTER, Hagerstown, MD
BROOKDALE HOSPITAL MEDICAL CENTER, Brooklyn, NY
BROOKE ARMY MEDICAL CENTER, San Antonio, TX
BROOKHAVEN HOSPITAL, Tulsa, OK
BROOKHAVEN MEMORIAL HOSPITAL MEDICAL CENTER, Patchogue, NY
BROOKINGS HOSPITAL, Brookings, SD
BROOKLINE HOSPITAL, Brookline, MA
BROOKLYN HOSPITAL, Brooklyn, NY, See Brooklyn Hospital-Caledonian Hospital
BROOKLYN HOSPITAL-CALEDONIAN HOSPITAL, Brooklyn, NY
BROOKS COUNTY HOSPITAL, Falfurrias, TX
BROOKS HOSPITAL, Atlanta, TX
BROOKS MEMORIAL HOSPITAL, Dunkirk, NY
BROOKSIDE HOSPITAL, San Pablo, CA
BROOKVILLE HOSPITAL, Brookville, PA
BROOKWOOD COMMUNITY HOSPITAL, Orlando, FL, See AMI Brookwood Community Hospital
BROOKWOOD HOSPITAL, Santa Rosa, CA, See North Coast Rehabilitation Center
BROOKWOOD MEDICAL CENTER, Birmingham, AL, See AMI Brookwood Medical Center
BROTMAN MEDICAL CENTER, Culver City, CA, See HCA Brotman Medical Center
BROUGHTON HOSPITAL, Morganton, NC
BROWARD GENERAL MEDICAL CENTER, Fort Lauderdale, FL
BROWN COUNTY GENERAL HOSPITAL, Georgetown, OH
BROWN COUNTY HOSPITAL, Ainsworth, NE
BROWN COUNTY MENTAL HEALTH CENTER, Green Bay, WI
BROWN MEMORIAL HOSPITAL, Conneaut, OH
BROWN SCHOOLS HEALTHCARE REHABILITATION CENTER (Formerly The Brown Schools-Ranch Treatment Center), Austin, TX
BROWNFIELD REGIONAL MEDICAL CENTER, Brownfield, TX
BROWNSVILLE GENERAL HOSPITAL, Brownsville, PA
BROWNSVILLE MEDICAL CENTER, Brownsville, TX, See AMI Brownsville Medical Center
BROWNWOOD REGIONAL HOSPITAL, Brownwood, TX
BRUCE HOSPITAL SYSTEM (Formerly Bruce Hospital), Florence, SC
BRUNSWICK GENERAL HOSPITAL, Amityville, NY
BRUNSWICK HALL, Amityville, NY
BRUNSWICK HOSPITAL, Supply, NC
BRUNSWICK HOUSE ALCOHOLISM TREATMENT CENTER, Amityville, NY
BRUNSWICK PHYSICAL MEDICINE AND REHABILITATION HOSPITAL (Formerly Brunswick Rehabilitation Hospital), Amityville, NY
BRY-LIN HOSPITAL, Buffalo, NY
BRYAN COMMUNITY HOSPITAL, Bryan, OH, See Community Hospitals of Williams County
BRYAN MEMORIAL HOSPITAL, Lincoln, NE
BRYAN W. WHITFIELD MEMORIAL HOSPITAL, Demopolis, AL
BRYCE HOSPITAL, Tuscaloosa, AL
BRYN MAWR COLLEGE INFIRMARY, Bryn Mawr, PA
BRYN MAWR HOSPITAL, Bryn Mawr, PA
BRYN MAWR REHABILITATION HOSPITAL, Malvern, PA
BUCHANAN GENERAL HOSPITAL, Grundy, VA
BUCKTAIL MEDICAL CENTER, Renovo, PA
BUCYRUS COMMUNITY HOSPITAL, Bucyrus, OH
BUENA PARK COMMUNITY HOSPITAL, Buena Park, CA
BUENA PARK DOCTORS HOSPITAL (Formerly Beach Community Hospital), Buena Park, CA
BUENA VISTA COUNTY HOSPITAL, Storm Lake, IA
BUFFALO COLUMBUS HOSPITAL, Buffalo, NY
BUFFALO GENERAL HOSPITAL, Buffalo, NY
BUFFALO MEDICAL CENTER (Formerly Buffalo Memorial Hospital), Mondovi, WI
BUFFALO MEMORIAL HOSPITAL, Buffalo, MN, See Health Central of Buffalo
BUFFALO PSYCHIATRIC CENTER, Buffalo, NY
BUFORD HOSPITAL, Buford, GA, See Gwinnett Hospital Systems, Lawrenceville
BULL SHOALS COMMUNITY HOSPITAL AND CLINIC, Bull Shoals, AR
BULLHEAD COMMUNITY HOSPITAL, Bullhead City, AZ
BULLOCH MEMORIAL HOSPITAL, Statesboro, GA
BULLOCK COUNTY HOSPITAL, Union Springs, AL
BUNA MEDICAL CENTER HOSPITAL, Buna, TX
BUNKIE GENERAL HOSPITAL, Bunkie, LA
BURBANK COMMUNITY HOSPITAL, Burbank, CA
BURBANK HOSPITAL, Fitchburg, MA
BURDETTE TOMLIN MEMORIAL HOSPITAL, Cape May Court House, NJ
BURDICK-WEST MEMORIAL HOSPITAL, Haleyville, AL
BURGESS MEMORIAL HOSPITAL, Onawa, IA
BURKE COUNTY HOSPITAL, Waynesboro, GA
BURKE REHABILITATION CENTER, White Plains, NY
BURLESON COUNTY HOSPITAL, Caldwell, TX
BURLINGTON MEDICAL CENTER, Burlington, IA
BURNETT GENERAL HOSPITAL, Grantsburg, WI
BURNHAM HOSPITAL, Champaign, IL
BUTLER COUNTY HOSPITAL, David City, NE
BUTLER HOSPITAL, Providence, RI
BUTLER MEMORIAL HOSPITAL, Butler, PA
BUTTERWORTH HOSPITAL, Grand Rapids, MI
BUTTONWOOD HOSPITAL OF BURLINGTON COUNTY (Formerly Evergreen Park Psychiatric Hospital), New Lisbon, NJ
BYERLY HOSPITAL, Hartsville, SC
BYRD MEMORIAL HOSPITAL, Leesville, LA

C

C. F. KETTERING MEMORIAL HOSPITAL, Kettering, OH, See Kettering Medical Center
C. F. MENNINGER MEMORIAL HOSPITAL, Topeka, KS
C. J. HARRIS COMMUNITY HOSPITAL, Sylva, NC
CABARRUS MEMORIAL HOSPITAL, Concord, NC
CABELL HUNTINGTON HOSPITAL, Huntington, WV
CABRINI MEDICAL CENTER, New York, NY
CAGUAS REGIONAL HOSPITAL, Caguas, P.R.
CALAIS REGIONAL HOSPITAL, Calais, ME
CALDWELL COUNTY HOSPITAL, Princeton, KY
CALDWELL MEMORIAL HOSPITAL, Columbia, LA
CALDWELL MEMORIAL HOSPITAL, Lenoir, NC
CALEDONIA HEALTH CARE CENTER, Caledonia, MN
CALEDONIAN HOSPITAL, Brooklyn, NY, See Brooklyn Hospital-Caledonian Hospital
CALEXICO HOSPITAL, Calexico, CA
CALHOUN GENERAL HOSPITAL (Formerly Calhoun Hospital), Blountstown, FL
CALHOUN GENERAL HOSPITAL, Grantsville, WV
CALHOUN MEMORIAL HOSPITAL, Arlington, GA
CALIFORNIA HOSPITAL MEDICAL CENTER, Los Angeles, CA, See California Medical Center-Los Angeles
CALIFORNIA MEDICAL CENTER-LOS ANGELES (Formerly California Hospital Medical Center), Los Angeles, CA
CALIFORNIA MEDICAL FACILITY, Vacaville, CA
CALIFORNIA MENS COLONY HOSPITAL, San Luis Obispo, CA
CALIFORNIA PODIATRY HOSPITAL, San Francisco, CA, See Pacific Coast Hospital
CALIFORNIA SURGICAL CENTER HOSPITAL, WOMEN'S HOSPITAL OF OAKLAND, Oakland, CA
CALLAWAY COMMUNITY HOSPITAL, Fulton, MO
CALLAWAY HOSPITAL DISTRICT, Callaway, NE
CALUMET MEMORIAL HOSPITAL, Chilton, WI
CALUMET PUBLIC HOSPITAL, Laurium, MI
CALVARY HOSPITAL, Bronx, NY
CALVERT MEMORIAL HOSPITAL, Prince Frederick, MD
CAMARILLO STATE HOSPITAL AND DEVELOPMENT CENTER (Formerly Camarillo State Hospital), Camarillo, CA
CAMBRIDGE HOSPITAL, Cambridge, MA
CAMBRIDGE MEMORIAL HOSPITAL, Cambridge, NE
CAMBRIDGE MENTAL HEALTH AND DEVELOPMENTAL CENTER, Cambridge, OH
CAMDEN COUNTY HEALTH SERVICES CENTER (Formerly Listed Under Lakeland), Blackwood, NJ
CAMDEN-CLARK MEMORIAL HOSPITAL, Parkersburg, WV

CAMERON COMMUNITY HOSPITAL, Cameron, MO
CAMERON COMMUNITY HOSPITAL, Cameron, TX
CAMERON MEMORIAL COMMUNITY HOSPITAL, Angola, IN
CAMPBELL COUNTY MEMORIAL HOSPITAL, Gillette, WY
CAMPBELL MEMORIAL HOSPITAL, Weatherford, TX
CAMPBELLTON GRACEVILLE HOSPITAL, Graceville, FL
CANANDAIGUA VETERANS ADMINISTRATION MEDICAL CENTER, Canandaigua, NY
CANBY COMMUNITY HOSPITAL DISTRICT ONE, Canby, MN
CANDLER COUNTY HOSPITAL, Metter, GA
CANDLER GENERAL HOSPITAL, Savannah, GA
CANEY MUNICIPAL HOSPITAL, Caney, KS
CANNON MEMORIAL HOSPITAL, Pickens, SC
CANOGA PARK HOSPITAL, Los Angeles, CA
CANONSBURG GENERAL HOSPITAL, Canonsburg, PA
CANTON-INWOOD MEMORIAL HOSPITAL, Canton, SD
CANTON-POTSDAM HOSPITAL, Potsdam, NY
CAPE CANAVERAL HOSPITAL, Cocoa Beach, FL
CAPE COD HOSPITAL, Hyannis, MA
CAPE CORAL HOSPITAL, Cape Coral, FL
CAPE FEAR MEMORIAL HOSPITAL, Wilmington, NC
CAPE FEAR VALLEY MEDICAL CENTER, Fayetteville, NC
CAPISTRANO BY THE SEA HOSPITAL, Dana Point, CA
CAPITAL DISTRICT PSYCHIATRIC CENTER, Albany, NY
CAPITOL HILL HOSPITAL, Washington, DC
CAPROCK HOSPITAL DISTRICT (Formerly Caprock Hospital Medical Services), Floydada, TX
CARBON COUNTY MEMORIAL HOSPITAL, Red Lodge, MT
CARBONDALE GENERAL HOSPITAL, Carbondale, PA
CARDINAL CUSHING GENERAL HOSPITAL, Brockton, MA
CARDINAL GLENNON CHILDREN'S HOSPITAL, St. Louis, MO
CARDINAL HILL HOSPITAL, Lexington, KY
CAREUNIT BEHAVIORAL CENTER LOS ANGELES (Formerly Care Unit Hospital of Los Angeles), Los Angeles, CA
CAREUNIT HOSPITAL OF CINCINNATI, Cincinnati, OH
CAREUNIT HOSPITAL OF DALLAS-FORT WORTH, Fort Worth, TX
CAREUNIT HOSPITAL OF KIRKLAND, Kirkland, WA
CAREUNIT HOSPITAL OF ORANGE, Orange, CA
CAREUNIT HOSPITAL OF PORTLAND, Portland, OR
CAREUNIT HOSPITAL OF ST. LOUIS, St. Louis, MO
CAREUNIT OF JACKSONVILLE BEACH, Jacksonville, FL
CARIBOU MEMORIAL HOSPITAL AND NURSING HOME, Soda Springs, ID
CARL ALBERT INDIAN HEALTH FACILITY, Ada, OK
CARLE FOUNDATION HOSPITAL, Urbana, IL
CARLINVILLE AREA HOSPITAL, Carlinville, IL
CARLISLE HOSPITAL, Carlisle, PA
CARMI TOWNSHIP HOSPITAL, Carmi, IL
CARNEGIE TRI-COUNTY MUNICIPAL HOSPITAL, Carnegie, OK
CARNEY HOSPITAL, Boston, MA
CARO COMMUNITY HOSPITAL, Caro, MI
CARO REGIONAL MENTAL HEALTH CENTER, Caro, MI
CARON FOUNDATION, Wernersville, PA
CARONDELET COMMUNITY HOSPITALS, Minneapolis, MN
CARR P. COLLINS HOSPITAL, Dallas, TX, See Baylor University Medical Center
CARRAWAY METHODIST MEDICAL CENTER, Birmingham, AL
CARRIE TINGLEY HOSPITAL (Formerly Carrie Tingley Crippled Children's Hospital), Albuquerque, NM
CARRIER FOUNDATION, Belle Mead, NJ
CARRINGTON HEALTH CENTER (Formerly Carrington Hospital), Carrington, ND
CARROLL COUNTY GENERAL HOSPITAL, Westminster, MD
CARROLL COUNTY MEMORIAL HOSPITAL, Carrollton, KY
CARROLL COUNTY MEMORIAL HOSPITAL, Carrollton, MO
CARROLL GENERAL HOSPITAL, Berryville, AR
CARROLLWOOD COMMUNITY HOSPITAL, Tampa, FL
CARSON CITY HOSPITAL, Carson City, MI
CARSON TAHOE HOSPITAL, Carson City, NV
CARTERET GENERAL HOSPITAL, Morehead City, NC
CARTHAGE AREA HOSPITAL, Carthage, NY
CARTHAGE GENERAL HOSPITAL, Carthage, TN
CARY MEDICAL CENTER, Caribou, ME
CASA COLINA HOSPITAL FOR REHABILITATIVE MEDICINE, Pomona, CA
CASA GRANDE REGIONAL MEDICAL CENTER, Casa Grande, AZ
CASCADE COMMUNITY HOSPITAL, Central Point, OR
CASEY COUNTY WAR MEMORIAL HOSPITAL, Liberty, KY
CASS COUNTY MEMORIAL HOSPITAL, Atlantic, IA
CASS MEDICAL CENTER, Harrisonville, MO
CASSIA MEMORIAL HOSPITAL AND MEDICAL CENTER, Burley, ID
CASTANER GENERAL HOSPITAL, Castaner, P.R.
CASTINE COMMUNITY HOSPITAL, Castine, ME
CASTLE MEDICAL CENTER, Kailua, HI
CASTLEVIEW HOSPITAL, Price, UT
CASWELL CENTER, Kinston, NC
CATAHOULA MEMORIAL HOSPITAL (Formerly Catahoula Parish Hospital), Jonesville, LA
CATAWBA HOSPITAL, Catawba, VA
CATAWBA MEMORIAL HOSPITAL, Hickory, NC
CATHERINE MCAULEY HEALTH CENTER, Ann Arbor, MI
CATHOLIC MEDICAL CENTER, Manchester, NH
CATHOLIC MEDICAL CENTER OF BROOKLYN AND QUEENS, Jamaica, NY
CAVALIER COUNTY MEMORIAL HOSPITAL, Langdon, ND
CAVERNA MEMORIAL HOSPITAL, Horse Cave, KY
CAYLOR-NICKEL HOSPITAL, Bluffton, IN
CDU OF ACADIANA, Lafayette, LA
CECIL H. AND IDA M. GREEN HOSPITAL OF SCRIPPS CLINIC, La Jolla, CA, See Green Hospital of Scripps Clinic
CEDAR COUNTY MEMORIAL HOSPITAL, El Dorado Springs, MO
CEDAR SPRINGS PSYCHIATRIC HOSPITAL, Colorado Springs, CO
CEDAR VALE REGIONAL HOSPITAL, Cedar Vale, KS
CEDARCREST REGIONAL HOSPITAL, Newington, CT
CEDARS MEDICAL CENTER, Miami, FL
CEDARS-SINAI MEDICAL CENTER, Los Angeles, CA
CENTER GENERAL HOSPITAL, Cranston, RI
CENTINELA HOSPITAL MEDICAL CENTER, Inglewood, CA
CENTINELA MAMMOTH HOSPITAL, Mammoth Lakes, CA
CENTRAL ALABAMA COMMUNITY HOSPITAL (Formerly Bapt Medical Center-Chilton), Clanton, AL
CENTRAL ARKANSAS GENERAL HOSPITAL, Searcy, AR, See AMI Central Arkansas General Hospital
CENTRAL BAPTIST HOSPITAL, Lexington, KY
CENTRAL COMMUNITY HOSPITAL, Chicago, IL
CENTRAL COMMUNITY HOSPITAL, Clifton, IL
CENTRAL COMMUNITY HOSPITAL, Elkader, IA
CENTRAL DUPAGE HOSPITAL, Winfield, IL
CENTRAL FLORIDA REGIONAL HOSPITAL, Sanford, FL
CENTRAL GENERAL HOSPITAL, Plainview, NY
CENTRAL HOSPITAL, Somerville, MA
CENTRAL ISLIP PSYCHIATRIC CENTER, Central Islip, NY
CENTRAL KANSAS MEDICAL CENTER, Great Bend, KS
CENTRAL LOUISIANA STATE HOSPITAL, Pineville, LA
CENTRAL MAINE MEDICAL CENTER, Lewiston, ME
CENTRAL MEDICAL CENTER AND HOSPITAL, Pittsburgh, PA
CENTRAL MEDICAL CENTER HOSPITAL, St. Louis, MO
CENTRAL MICHIGAN COMMUNITY HOSPITAL, Mount Pleasant, MI
CENTRAL MONTANA HOSPITAL, Lewistown, MT
CENTRAL OHIO PSYCHIATRIC HOSPITAL, Columbus, OH
CENTRAL OREGON DISTRICT HOSPITAL, Redmond, OR
CENTRAL OZARKS MEDICAL CENTER, Yellville, AR
CENTRAL PENINSULA GENERAL HOSPITAL, Soldotna, AK
CENTRAL PLAINS REGIONAL HOSPITAL, Plainview, TX
CENTRAL PRISON HOSPITAL, Raleigh, NC
CENTRAL STATE GRIFFIN MEMORIAL HOSPITAL, Norman, OK
CENTRAL STATE HOSPITAL, Milledgeville, GA
CENTRAL STATE HOSPITAL, Indianapolis, IN
CENTRAL STATE HOSPITAL, Louisville, KY
CENTRAL STATE HOSPITAL, Petersburg, VA
CENTRAL SUFFOLK HOSPITAL, Riverhead, NY
CENTRAL TEXAS MEDICAL CENTER (Formerly Robertson County Community Hospital), Hearne, TX
CENTRAL VALLEY MEDICAL CENTER (Formerly Juab County Hospital), Nephi, UT
CENTRAL VERMONT HOSPITAL, Barre, VT, See Central Vermont Medical Center, Berlin
CENTRAL VERMONT MEDICAL CENTER, Berlin, VT
CENTRAL VIRGINIA TRAINING CENTER, Madison Heights, VA
CENTRAL WASHINGTON HOSPITAL, Wenatchee, WA
CENTRAL WISCONSIN CENTER FOR DEVELOPMENTALLY DISABLED, Madison, WI
CENTRALIA GENERAL HOSPITAL, Centralia, WA
CENTRE COMMUNITY HOSPITAL, State College, PA
CENTREVILLE TOWNSHIP HOSPITAL, Centreville, IL
CENTRO ASTURIANO HOSPITAL, Tampa, FL
CENTRO DE SALUD, Las Marias, P.R.
CENTRO ESPANOL MEMORIAL HOSPITAL, Tampa, FL
CENTURY CITY HOSPITAL, Los Angeles, CA
CENTURY COMMUNITY HOSPITAL, Los Angeles, CA
CHADRON COMMUNITY HOSPITAL, Chadron, NE
CHAFFEE GENERAL HOSPITAL, Chaffee, MO
CHALMETTE GENERAL HOSPITAL, Chalmette, LA
CHAMBERLAIN MEMORIAL HOSPITAL, Rockwood, TN
CHAMBERS COUNTY HOSPITAL, Lafayette, AL
CHAMBERSBURG HOSPITAL, Chambersburg, PA
CHAMPLAIN VALLEY PHYSICIANS HOSPITAL MEDICAL CENTER, Plattsburgh, NY
CHANDLER COMMUNITY HOSPITAL, Chandler, AZ
CHANNEL ISLANDS COMMUNITY HOSPITAL, Oxnard, CA
CHANNEL ISLANDS COMMUNITY HOSPITAL-CARE UNIT, Oxnard, CA
CHAPMAN GENERAL HOSPITAL, Orange, CA
CHARITY HOSPITAL AT NEW ORLEANS, New Orleans, LA
CHARLES A. CANNON JR. MEMORIAL HOSPITAL, Banner Elk, NC
CHARLES A. DEAN MEMORIAL HOSPITAL, Greenville, ME, See Mid-Maine Medical Center, Waterville
CHARLES B. GODDARD HOSPITAL, UNIVERSITY OF OKLAHOMA, Norman, OK
CHARLES COLE MEMORIAL HOSPITAL, Coudersport, PA
CHARLES E. STILL OSTEOPATHIC HOSPITAL, Jefferson City, MO
CHARLES GILMAN SMITH HOSPITAL, Chicago, IL, See University of Chicago Hospitals and Clinics
CHARLES L. NEUMILLER MEMORIAL HOSPITAL, San Quentin, CA
CHARLES RIVER HOSPITAL, Wellesley, MA
CHARLES S. WILSON MEMORIAL HOSPITAL, Johnson City, NY, See United Health Services
CHARLESTON AREA MEDICAL CENTER, Charleston, WV
CHARLESTON MEMORIAL HOSPITAL, Charleston, SC
CHARLEVOIX AREA HOSPITAL, Charlevoix, MI
CHARLOTTE EYE, EAR AND THROAT HOSPITAL, Charlotte, NC, See Humana Specialty Hospital-Charlotte
CHARLOTTE HUNGERFORD HOSPITAL, Torrington, CT
CHARLOTTE MEMORIAL HOSPITAL AND MEDICAL CENTER, Charlotte, NC
CHARLOTTE REHABILITATION HOSPITAL, Charlotte, NC
CHARLOTTE TREATMENT CENTER, Charlotte, NC
CHARLTON MEMORIAL HOSPITAL, Folkston, GA
CHARLTON MEMORIAL HOSPITAL, Fall River, MA
CHARLTON METHODIST HOSPITAL, Dallas, TX
CHARTER BARCLAY HOSPITAL, Chicago, IL
CHARTER BEACON (Formerly Charter Beacon Hospital), Fort Wayne, IN
CHARTER BROAD OAKS HOSPITAL, Savannah, GA
CHARTER BY-THE-SEA HOSPITAL, St. Simons Island, GA
CHARTER CANYON HOSPITAL, Orem, UT
CHARTER COLONIAL INSTITUTE FOR CHILD AND ADOLESCENT PSYCHIATRY, Newport News, VA
CHARTER COMMUNITY HOSPITAL, Hawaiian Gardens, CA
CHARTER COMMUNITY HOSPITAL OF CLEVELAND, Cleveland, TX
CHARTER COMMUNITY HOSPITAL OF DES MOINES (Formerly Charter Community Hospital), Des Moines, IA
CHARTER GLADE HOSPITAL, Fort Myers, FL
CHARTER GROVE HOSPITAL, Corona, CA
CHARTER HILLS HOSPITAL, Greensboro, NC
CHARTER HOSPITAL OF CHARLOTTESVILLE (Formerly David C. Wilson Hospital), Charlottesville, VA
CHARTER HOSPITAL OF CORPUS CHRISTI, Corpus Christi, TX
CHARTER HOSPITAL OF JACKSON (Formerly Riverside Hospital), Jackson, MS
CHARTER HOSPITAL OF LAS VEGAS, Las Vegas, NV
CHARTER HOSPITAL OF LONG BEACH (Formerly Charter Baywood Hospital), Long Beach, CA
CHARTER HOSPITAL OF TAMPA BAY (Formerly Tampa Heights Hospital), Tampa, FL
CHARTER LAKE HOSPITAL, Macon, GA
CHARTER LAKESIDE HOSPITAL, Memphis, TN
CHARTER LANE HOSPITAL, Austin, TX
CHARTER MANDALA CENTER HOSPITAL, Winston-Salem, NC, See Charter Mandala Hospital
CHARTER MANDALA HOSPITAL (Formerly Charter Mandala Center Hospital), Winston-Salem, NC
CHARTER NORTH HOSPITAL, Anchorage, AK
CHARTER NORTHSIDE HOSPITAL (Formerly Charter Northside Community Hospital), Macon, GA
CHARTER OAK HOSPITAL, Covina, CA
CHARTER PACIFIC HOSPITAL, Torrance, CA
CHARTER PALMS HOSPITAL, McAllen, TX
CHARTER PEACHFORD HOSPITAL, Atlanta, GA

CHARTER PLAINS HOSPITAL, Lubbock, TX
CHARTER REAL (Formerly Charter Real Hospital), San Antonio, TX
CHARTER RETREAT HOSPITAL AND RECOVERY CENTER, Decatur, AL
CHARTER RIDGE HOSPITAL, Lexington, KY
CHARTER RIVERS HOSPITAL, West Columbia, SC
CHARTER SOUTHLAND HOSPITAL, Mobile, AL
CHARTER SPRINGS HOSPITAL, Ocala, FL
CHARTER SUBURBAN HOSPITAL -PARAMOUNT (Formerly Charter Suburban Hospital), Paramount, CA
CHARTER SUBURBAN HOSPITAL MESQUITE (Formerly Charter Suburban Hospital), Mesquite, TX
CHARTER VISTA HOSPITAL, Fayetteville, AR
CHARTER WESTBROOK HOSPITAL, Richmond, VA
CHARTER WINDS HOSPITAL, Athens, GA
CHARTER WOODS HOSPITAL, Dothan, AL
CHARTERTON HOSPITAL, La Grange, KY
CHASE COUNTY COMMUNITY HOSPITAL, Imperial, NE
CHATHAM HOSPITAL, Siler City, NC
CHATTOOGA COUNTY HOSPITAL, Summerville, GA
CHELSEA COMMUNITY HOSPITAL, Chelsea, MI
CHEMICAL DEPENDENCY CENTER, Oakdale, IA, See University of Iowa Hospitals and Clinics, Iowa City
CHEMICAL DEPENDENCY INSTITUTE OF NORTHERN CALIFORNIA, Campbell, CA
CHENANGO MEMORIAL HOSPITAL, Norwich, NY
CHEROKEE MEDICAL CENTER (Formerly Rusk Memorial Hospital), Rusk, TX
CHEROKEE MEMORIAL HOSPITAL, Gaffney, SC
CHERRY COUNTY HOSPITAL, Valentine, NE
CHERRY HILL DIVISION, Cherry Hill, NJ, See Kennedy Memorial Hospitals-University Medical Center
CHERRY HOSPITAL, Goldsboro, NC
CHESAPEAKE GENERAL HOSPITAL, Chesapeake, VA
CHESHIRE MEDICAL CENTER, Keene, NH
CHESTER COUNTY HOSPITAL, Chester, SC
CHESTER MENTAL HEALTH CENTER, Chester, IL
CHESTERFIELD GENERAL HOSPITAL, Cheraw, SC
CHESTNUT HILL HOSPITAL, Philadelphia, PA
CHESTNUT LODGE HOSPITAL (Formerly Chestnut Lodge), Rockville, MD
CHEYENNE COUNTY HOSPITAL, St. Francis, KS
CHICAGO LAKESHORE HOSPITAL, Chicago, IL
CHICAGO LYING-IN HOSPITAL, Chicago, IL, See University of Chicago Hospitals and Clinics
CHICAGO OSTEOPATHIC MEDICAL CENTERS, Chicago, IL
CHICAGO WESLEY MEMORIAL HOSPITAL, Chicago, IL, See Northwestern Memorial Hospital
CHICAGO-READ MENTAL HEALTH CENTER, Chicago, IL
CHICO COMMUNITY HOSPITAL, Chico, CA
CHICOT MEMORIAL HOSPITAL, Lake Village, AR
CHILD'S HOSPITAL, Albany, NY
CHILDREN'S HOME OF PITTSBURGH, Pittsburgh, PA
CHILDREN'S HOSPITAL, Denver, CO
CHILDREN'S HOSPITAL, New Orleans, LA
CHILDREN'S HOSPITAL, Baltimore, MD
CHILDREN'S HOSPITAL, Boston, MA
CHILDREN'S HOSPITAL, St. Paul, MN
CHILDREN'S HOSPITAL, St. Louis, MO
CHILDREN'S HOSPITAL, Buffalo, NY
CHILDREN'S HOSPITAL, Columbus, OH
CHILDREN'S HOSPITAL, Richmond, VA
CHILDREN'S HOSPITAL AND CONVALESCENT HOSPITAL FOR CHILDREN, Cincinnati, OH, See Children's Hospital Medical Center
CHILDREN'S HOSPITAL AND HEALTH CENTER, San Diego, CA
CHILDREN'S HOSPITAL AT STANFORD, Palo Alto, CA
CHILDREN'S HOSPITAL MEDICAL CENTER, Cincinnati, OH
CHILDREN'S HOSPITAL MEDICAL CENTER OF AKRON, Akron, OH
CHILDREN'S HOSPITAL MEDICAL CENTER OF NORTHERN CALIFORNIA, Oakland, CA
CHILDREN'S HOSPITAL NATIONAL MEDICAL CENTER, Washington, DC
CHILDREN'S HOSPITAL OF ALABAMA, Birmingham, AL
CHILDREN'S HOSPITAL OF MICHIGAN, Detroit, MI
CHILDREN'S HOSPITAL OF NEW JERSEY, Newark, NJ, See United Hospitals Medical Center
CHILDREN'S HOSPITAL OF PHILADELPHIA, Philadelphia, PA
CHILDREN'S HOSPITAL OF PITTSBURGH, Pittsburgh, PA
CHILDREN'S HOSPITAL OF SAN FRANCISCO, San Francisco, CA
CHILDREN'S HOSPITAL OF THE KING'S DAUGHTERS, Norfolk, VA
CHILDREN'S HOSPITAL OF WISCONSIN (Formerly Milwaukee Children's Hospital), Milwaukee, WI
CHILDREN'S MEDICAL CENTER, Dayton, OH
CHILDREN'S MEDICAL CENTER, Tulsa, OK
CHILDREN'S MEDICAL CENTER OF DALLAS, Dallas, TX
CHILDREN'S MEMORIAL HOSPITAL, Chicago, IL
CHILDREN'S MERCY HOSPITAL, Kansas City, MO
CHILDREN'S ORTHOPEDIC HOSPITAL AND MEDICAL CENTER, Seattle, WA
CHILDREN'S PSYCHIATRIC HOSPITAL OF NORTHERN KENTUCKY, Covington, KY
CHILDREN'S REHABILITATION CENTER UNIVERSITY OF VIRGINIA HOSPITAL, Charlottesville, VA, See University of Virginia Hospitals
CHILDREN'S REHABILITATION HOSPITAL (Formerly Children's Heart Hospital), Philadelphia, PA
CHILDREN'S SEASHORE HOUSE, Atlantic City, NJ
CHILDREN'S SPECIALIZED HOSPITAL, Mountainside, NJ
CHILDRENS DIVISION OF MENNINGER FOUNDATION, Topeka, KS
CHILDRENS HOSPITAL AND REHABILITATION CENTER, Utica, NY
CHILDRENS HOSPITAL OF LOS ANGELES, Los Angeles, CA
CHILDRENS HOSPITAL OF ORANGE COUNTY, Orange, CA
CHILDRENS MEMORIAL HOSPITAL, Omaha, NE
CHILDRESS GENERAL HOSPITAL, Childress, TX
CHILDRESS GENERAL HOSPITAL, Goldthwaite, TX
CHILLICOTHE HOSPITAL DISTRICT, Chillicothe, TX
CHILTON MEMORIAL HOSPITAL, Pompton Plains, NJ
CHINESE HOSPITAL, San Francisco, CA
CHINLE COMPREHENSIVE HEALTH CARE FACILITY, Chinle, AZ
CHINO COMMUNITY HOSPITAL, Chino, CA
CHIPPENHAM HOSPITAL, Richmond, VA
CHIPPEWA COUNTY MONTEVIDEO HOSPITAL, Montevideo, MN
CHIPPEWA VALLEY HOSPITAL AND OAKVIEW CARE CENTER (Formerly Chippewa Valley Hospital and Nursing Home), Durand, WI
CHISAGO HEALTH SERVICES (Formerly Chisago Lakes Hospital and Skilled Nursing Unit), Chisago City, MN
CHOATE MEMORIAL HOSPITAL, Woburn, MA, See Choate-Symmes Hospitals
CHOATE-SYMMES HOSPITALS, Woburn, MA
CHOCTAW COUNTY HOSPITAL, Ackerman, MS
CHOCTAW HEALTH CENTER, Philadelphia, MS
CHOCTAW MEMORIAL HOSPITAL, Hugo, OK
CHOCTAW NATION INDIAN HOSPITAL, Talihina, OK
CHOUTEAU COUNTY DISTRICT HOSPITAL, Fort Benton, MT
CHOWAN HOSPITAL, Edenton, NC
CHOWCHILLA DISTRICT MEMORIAL HOSPITAL, Chowchilla, CA
CHRIST HOSPITAL, Jersey City, NJ
CHRIST HOSPITAL, Cincinnati, OH
CHRIST HOSPITAL AND MEDICAL CENTER (Formerly Christ Hospital), Oak Lawn, IL
CHRISTIAN HEALTH CARE CENTER, Wyckoff, NJ
CHRISTIAN HOSPITAL NORTHEAST, St. Louis, MO, See Christian Hospitals Northeast-Northwest
CHRISTIAN HOSPITAL NORTHWEST, Florissant, MO, See Christian Hospitals Northeast-Northwest, St. Louis
CHRISTIAN HOSPITALS NORTHEAST-NORTHWEST, St. Louis, MO
CHRISTIAN R. HOLMES DIVISION, Cincinnati, OH, See University of Cincinnati Hospital
CHRISTIANA HOSPITAL, Wilmington, DE, See Wilmington Medical Center
CHURCH HOSPITAL CORPORATION, Baltimore, MD
CHURCHILL REGIONAL MEDICAL CENTER, Fallon, NV
CIBOLA GENERAL HOSPITAL, Grants, NM
CIGNA HOSPITAL OF LOS ANGELES, Los Angeles, CA
CIMARRON MEMORIAL HOSPITAL, Boise City, OK
CIRCLE CITY HOSPITAL, Corona, CA, See AMI Circle City Hospital
CIRCLE TERRACE HOSPITAL, Alexandria, VA, See Reston Hospital Center, Reston
CITIZENS GENERAL HOSPITAL, New Kensington, PA
CITIZENS GENERAL HOSPITAL, Greenville, TX, See Citizens Hospital of Commerce, Commerce
CITIZENS HOSPITAL, Talladega, AL
CITIZENS MEDICAL CENTER, Colby, KS
CITIZENS MEDICAL CENTER (Formerly Citizens Memorial Hospital), Victoria, TX
CITIZENS MEMORIAL HOSPITAL, Bolivar, MO
CITRUS MEMORIAL HOSPITAL, Inverness, FL
CITY HOSPITAL, New Rockford, ND
CITY HOSPITAL, Bellaire, OH
CITY HOSPITAL, Martinsburg, WV
CITY HOSPITAL CENTER AT ELMHURST, , NY
CITY OF FAITH HOSPITAL, Tulsa, OK
CITY OF HOPE NATIONAL MEDICAL CENTER, Duarte, CA
CITY OF MILAN HOSPITAL, Milan, TN
CLAGETT MEMORIAL HOSPITAL, Rifle, CO
CLAIBORNE COUNTY HOSPITAL, Port Gibson, MS
CLAIBORNE COUNTY HOSPITAL, Tazewell, TN
CLAIREMONT COMMUNITY HOSPITAL, San Diego, CA, See AMI Clairemont Community Hospital
CLARA MAASS MEDICAL CENTER, Belleville, NJ
CLARE COMMUNITY HOSPITAL, Clare, MI
CLARENDON MEMORIAL HOSPITAL, Manning, SC
CLARINDA MUNICIPAL HOSPITAL, Clarinda, IA
CLARION OSTEOPATHIC COMMUNITY HOSPITAL, Clarion, PA
CLARISSA C. PECK PAVILION OF THE CHICAGO HOME FOR INCURABLES, Chicago, IL, See University of Chicago Hospitals and Clinics
CLARK COUNTY HOSPITAL, Winchester, KY
CLARK COUNTY MEMORIAL HOSPITAL, Jeffersonville, IN
CLARK FORK VALLEY HOSPITAL, Plains, MT
CLARKE COUNTY PUBLIC HOSPITAL, Osceola, IA
CLARKE HOSPITAL, Jackson, AL
CLARKS SUMMIT STATE HOSPITAL, Clarks Summit, PA
CLAY COUNTY HOSPITAL, Flora, IL
CLAY COUNTY HOSPITAL, Brazil, IN
CLAY COUNTY HOSPITAL, Clay Center, KS
CLAY COUNTY HOSPITAL AND NURSING HOME, Ashland, AL
CLAY COUNTY MEDICAL CENTER, West Point, MS
CLAY COUNTY MEMORIAL HOSPITAL, Henrietta, TX
CLAY MEMORIAL HOSPITAL, Green Cove Springs, FL
CLAYTON GENERAL HOSPITAL, Riverdale, GA
CLEAR BROOK LODGE, Shickshinny, PA
CLEAR BROOK MANOR, Wilkes-Barre, PA
CLEARFIELD HOSPITAL, Clearfield, PA
CLEARVIEW HOSPITAL, Midland, TX
CLEARWATER COMMUNITY HOSPITAL, Clearwater, FL, See AMI Clearwater Community Hospital
CLEARWATER COUNTY MEMORIAL HOSPITAL, Bagley, MN
CLEARWATER VALLEY HOSPITAL, Orofino, ID
CLEBURNE COMMUNITY MEDICAL CENTER AND NURSING HOME (Formerly Cleburne Hospital), Heflin, AL
CLEBURNE COUNTY HOSPITAL, Heber Springs, AR
CLEBURNE HOSPITAL, Heflin, AL, See Cleburne Community Medical Center and Nursing Home
CLEO WALLACE CENTER HOSPITAL, Broomfield, CO
CLERMONT MERCY HOSPITAL, Batavia, OH
CLEVELAND AREA HOSPITAL, Cleveland, OK
CLEVELAND CLINIC HOSPITAL, Cleveland, OH
CLEVELAND COMMUNITY HOSPITAL, Cleveland, TN
CLEVELAND MEMORIAL HOSPITAL, Shelby, NC
CLEVELAND PSYCHIATRIC INSTITUTE, Cleveland, OH
CLIFTON SPRINGS HOSPITAL AND CLINIC, Clifton Springs, NY
CLIFTON T. PERKINS HOSPITAL CENTER, Jessup, MD
CLIFTON-FINE HOSPITAL, Star Lake, NY
CLINCH MEMORIAL HOSPITAL, Homerville, GA
CLINICA DOCTOR PEREA, Mayaguez, P.R.
CLINICA DR. EUGENIO FERNANDEZ GARCIA, Hato Rey, P.R.
CLINICA ESPANOLA, Mayaguez, P.R.
CLINICA FONT, Cayey, P.R.
CLINICAL CENTER, NATIONAL INSTITUTES OF HEALTH, Bethesda, MD
CLINICAL RESEARCH CENTER, BROOKHAVEN NATIONAL LABORATORY, Upton, NY
CLINTON COMMUNITY HOSPITAL, Clinton, MD, See Parkwood Hospital
CLINTON COUNTY HOSPITAL, Frankfort, IN
CLINTON COUNTY WAR MEMORIAL HOSPITAL, Albany, KY
CLINTON HOSPITAL, Clinton, MA
CLINTON MEMORIAL HOSPITAL, St. Johns, MI
CLINTON MEMORIAL HOSPITAL, Wilmington, OH
CLINTON REGIONAL HOSPITAL, Clinton, OK
CLINTON VALLEY CENTER, Pontiac, MI
CLINTONVILLE COMMUNITY HOSPITAL, Clintonville, WI
CLOVIS COMMUNITY HOSPITAL, Clovis, CA
CLOVIS HIGH PLAINS HOSPITAL, Clovis, NM
COALDALE STATE GENERAL HOSPITAL, Coaldale, PA
COALINGA DISTRICT HOSPITAL, Coalinga, CA
COAST PLAZA MEDICAL CENTER, Norwalk, CA
COASTAL CENTER, Ladson, SC
COASTAL COMMUNITIES HOSPITAL (Formerly Mercy General Hospital), Santa Ana, CA
COASTAL COMMUNITIES HOSPITAL, Bunnell, FL
COBB GENERAL HOSPITAL, Austell, GA
COBB MEMORIAL HOSPITAL, Royston, GA
COCHRAN MEMORIAL HOSPITAL, Morton, TX
COCKE COUNTY BAPTIST HOSPITAL, Newport, TN
COFFEE MEDICAL CENTER, Manchester, TN
COFFEE REGIONAL HOSPITAL, Douglas, GA
COFFEY COUNTY HOSPITAL, Burlington, KS

COFFEYVILLE REGIONAL MEDICAL CENTER, Coffeyville, KS
COHOES MEMORIAL HOSPITAL, Cohoes, NY
COLDWATER CANYON HOSPITAL, Los Angeles, CA
COLE HOSPITAL, Champaign, IL
COLER MEMORIAL HOSPITAL, New York, NY
COLFAX GENERAL HOSPITAL, Springer, NM, See Colfax Health Care System, Raton
COLFAX HEALTH CARE SYSTEMS, Raton, NM, See Miners' Colfax Medical Center
COLISEUM MEDICAL CENTER, New Orleans, LA, See CPC Coliseum Medical Center
COLISEUM PSYCHIATRIC HOSPITAL, Macon, GA, See HCA Coliseum Psychiatric Hospital
COLLEGE HOSPITAL, Cerritos, CA
COLLETON REGIONAL HOSPITAL, Walterboro, SC
COLLINGSWORTH GENERAL HOSPITAL, Wellington, TX
COLMERY-O'NEIL VETERANS ADMINISTRATION MEDICAL CENTER, Topeka, KS
COLONEL FLORENCE A. BLANCHFIELD ARMY COMMUNITY HOSPITAL, Fort Campbell, KY
COLONIAL HILLS HOSPITAL (Formerly Park North General Hospital), San Antonio, TX
COLONIAL HOSPITAL, Terrell, TX
COLORADO STATE HOSPITAL, Pueblo, CO
COLORADO-FAYETTE MEDICAL CENTER (Formerly Youens Memorial Hospital), Weimar, TX
COLQUITT REGIONAL MEDICAL CENTER, Moultrie, GA
COLUMBIA BASIN HOSPITAL, Ephrata, WA
COLUMBIA HOSPITAL, Columbia, PA
COLUMBIA HOSPITAL, Milwaukee, WI
COLUMBIA HOSPITAL FOR WOMEN MEDICAL CENTER, Washington, DC
COLUMBIA MEMORIAL HOSPITAL, Hudson, NY
COLUMBIA MEMORIAL HOSPITAL, Astoria, OR
COLUMBIA REGIONAL HOSPITAL, Columbia, MO, See AMI Columbia Regional Hospital
COLUMBIA REGIONAL MEDICAL CENTER (Formerly Columbia General Hospital), Andalusia, AL
COLUMBUS COMMUNITY HOSPITAL, Columbus, NE
COLUMBUS COMMUNITY HOSPITAL, Columbus, TX
COLUMBUS COMMUNITY HOSPITAL, Columbus, WI
COLUMBUS COUNTY HOSPITAL, Whiteville, NC
COLUMBUS HOSPITAL, Chicago, IL
COLUMBUS HOSPITAL, Columbus, MS
COLUMBUS HOSPITAL, Great Falls, MT
COLUMBUS HOSPITAL, Newark, NJ
COLUSA COMMUNITY HOSPITAL, Colusa, CA
COMANCHE COMMUNITY HOSPITAL, Comanche, TX
COMANCHE COUNTY HOSPITAL, Coldwater, KS
COMANCHE COUNTY MEMORIAL HOSPITAL, Lawton, OK
COMFORT COMMUNITY HOSPITAL, Comfort, TX
COMFREY HOSPITAL, Comfrey, MN
COMMONWEALTH HOSPITAL, Fairfax, VA
COMMUNITY GENERAL HOSPITAL, Sterling, IL
COMMUNITY GENERAL HOSPITAL, Reading, PA
COMMUNITY GENERAL HOSPITAL OF GREATER SYRACUSE, Syracuse, NY
COMMUNITY GENERAL HOSPITAL OF SULLIVAN COUNTY, Harris, NY
COMMUNITY GENERAL HOSPITAL OF THOMASVILLE, Thomasville, NC
COMMUNITY GENERAL OSTEOPATHIC HOSPITAL, Harrisburg, PA
COMMUNITY HEALTH CENTER OF BRANCH COUNTY, Coldwater, MI
COMMUNITY HOSPITAL, Birmingham, AL, See Medical Park West
COMMUNITY HOSPITAL, Tallassee, AL
COMMUNITY HOSPITAL, Wickenburg, AZ
COMMUNITY HOSPITAL, Santa Rosa, CA
COMMUNITY HOSPITAL, Grand Junction, CO
COMMUNITY HOSPITAL, New Port Richey, FL, See HCA New Port Richey Hospital
COMMUNITY HOSPITAL, Bonners Ferry, ID
COMMUNITY HOSPITAL, Council, ID
COMMUNITY HOSPITAL, East St. Louis, IL, See Gateway Community Hospital
COMMUNITY HOSPITAL, Munster, IN
COMMUNITY HOSPITAL, Williamsport, IN
COMMUNITY HOSPITAL, Mayfield, KY
COMMUNITY HOSPITAL, Watervliet, MI
COMMUNITY HOSPITAL, Cannon Falls, MN
COMMUNITY HOSPITAL, Luverne, MN
COMMUNITY HOSPITAL, Fairfax, MO
COMMUNITY HOSPITAL, Poplar, MT
COMMUNITY HOSPITAL, Falls City, NE
COMMUNITY HOSPITAL, McCook, NE
COMMUNITY HOSPITAL, Stamford, NY
COMMUNITY HOSPITAL, Hillsboro, ND
COMMUNITY HOSPITAL, Elk City, OK
COMMUNITY HOSPITAL, Kingfisher, OK
COMMUNITY HOSPITAL, Kane, PA
COMMUNITY HOSPITAL, Torrington, WY
COMMUNITY HOSPITAL AND HEALTH CARE CENTER, St. Peter, MN
COMMUNITY HOSPITAL AND REHABILITATION CENTER OF LOS GATOS-SARATOGA, Los Gatos, CA
COMMUNITY HOSPITAL ASSOCIATION, Battle Creek, MI
COMMUNITY HOSPITAL AT GLEN COVE, Glen Cove, NY
COMMUNITY HOSPITAL IN NELSON COUNTY, McVille, ND
COMMUNITY HOSPITAL MEDICAL CENTER, Phoenix, AZ
COMMUNITY HOSPITAL OF ANACONDA, Anaconda, MT
COMMUNITY HOSPITAL OF ANDALUSIA, Andalusia, AL, See HCA Andalusia Hospital
COMMUNITY HOSPITAL OF ANDERSON AND MADISON COUNTY, Anderson, IN
COMMUNITY HOSPITAL OF BEDFORD, Bedford, OH
COMMUNITY HOSPITAL OF BOLIVAR, Bolivar, TN
COMMUNITY HOSPITAL OF BREMEN (Formerly Community Hospital of German Township), Bremen, IN
COMMUNITY HOSPITAL OF BROOKLYN, Brooklyn, NY
COMMUNITY HOSPITAL OF CHULA VISTA, Chula Vista, CA
COMMUNITY HOSPITAL OF DE QUEEN, De Queen, AR
COMMUNITY HOSPITAL OF GARDENA, Gardena, CA
COMMUNITY HOSPITAL OF HUNTINGTON PARK, Huntington Park, CA
COMMUNITY HOSPITAL OF LANCASTER, Lancaster, PA
COMMUNITY HOSPITAL OF LODI (Formerly Lodi Community Hospital), Lodi, CA
COMMUNITY HOSPITAL OF LUBBOCK, Lubbock, TX
COMMUNITY HOSPITAL OF NORTH LAS VEGAS, North Las Vegas, NV
COMMUNITY HOSPITAL OF OTTAWA, Ottawa, IL
COMMUNITY HOSPITAL OF ROANOKE VALLEY, Roanoke, VA
COMMUNITY HOSPITAL OF ROCKY MOUNT, Rocky Mount, NC
COMMUNITY HOSPITAL OF SACRAMENTO, Sacramento, CA
COMMUNITY HOSPITAL OF SALINAS (Formerly Alisal Community Hospital), Salinas, CA
COMMUNITY HOSPITAL OF SANTA CRUZ, Santa Cruz, CA, See AMI Community Hospital of Santa Cruz
COMMUNITY HOSPITAL OF SPRINGFIELD AND CLARK COUNTY, Springfield, OH
COMMUNITY HOSPITAL OF THE MONTEREY PENINSULA, Monterey, CA
COMMUNITY HOSPITAL OF TYLER, Tyler, TX
COMMUNITY HOSPITAL OF WESTERN SUFFOLK (Formerly Smithtown General Hospital), Smithtown, NY
COMMUNITY HOSPITAL OF WILLIAMS COUNTY, Bryan, OH
COMMUNITY HOSPITAL SCHOHARIE COUNTY, Cobleskill, NY
COMMUNITY HOSPITAL-LAKEVIEW (Formerly Eufaula Community Hospital), Eufaula, OK
COMMUNITY HOSPITAL-ONAGA (Formerly Community Hospital District Number One), Onaga, KS
COMMUNITY HOSPITALS OF INDIANA (Formerly Community Hospital of Indianapolis), Indianapolis, IN
COMMUNITY MEDCENTER HOSPITAL, Marion, OH, See Medcenter Hospital
COMMUNITY MEDICAL CENTER, Scranton, PA
COMMUNITY MEMORIAL HOSPITAL, Monmouth, IL
COMMUNITY MEMORIAL HOSPITAL, Staunton, IL
COMMUNITY MEMORIAL HOSPITAL, Clarion, IA
COMMUNITY MEMORIAL HOSPITAL, Hartley, IA
COMMUNITY MEMORIAL HOSPITAL, Missouri Valley, IA
COMMUNITY MEMORIAL HOSPITAL, Postville, IA
COMMUNITY MEMORIAL HOSPITAL, Sumner, IA
COMMUNITY MEMORIAL HOSPITAL, Marysville, KS
COMMUNITY MEMORIAL HOSPITAL, Cheboygan, MI
COMMUNITY MEMORIAL HOSPITAL, Sidney, MT
COMMUNITY MEMORIAL HOSPITAL, Burwell, NE
COMMUNITY MEMORIAL HOSPITAL, Crawford, NE
COMMUNITY MEMORIAL HOSPITAL, Humboldt, NE
COMMUNITY MEMORIAL HOSPITAL, Syracuse, NE
COMMUNITY MEMORIAL HOSPITAL, Toms River, NJ
COMMUNITY MEMORIAL HOSPITAL, Hamilton, NY
COMMUNITY MEMORIAL HOSPITAL, Hettinger, ND
COMMUNITY MEMORIAL HOSPITAL, Lisbon, ND
COMMUNITY MEMORIAL HOSPITAL, Turtle Lake, ND
COMMUNITY MEMORIAL HOSPITAL, Hicksville, OH
COMMUNITY MEMORIAL HOSPITAL, Burke, SD
COMMUNITY MEMORIAL HOSPITAL, Redfield, SD
COMMUNITY MEMORIAL HOSPITAL, Sturgis, SD
COMMUNITY MEMORIAL HOSPITAL, South Hill, VA
COMMUNITY MEMORIAL HOSPITAL, Enumclaw, WA
COMMUNITY MEMORIAL HOSPITAL, Menomonee Falls, WI
COMMUNITY MEMORIAL HOSPITAL, Oconto Falls, WI
COMMUNITY MEMORIAL HOSPITAL AND CONVALESCENT AND NURSING CARE SECTION, Cloquet, MN
COMMUNITY MEMORIAL HOSPITAL AND CONVALESCENT AND REHABILITATION UNIT, Winona, MN
COMMUNITY MEMORIAL HOSPITAL AND NURSING HOME, Spooner, WI
COMMUNITY MEMORIAL HOSPITAL AND NURSING HOME, Spring Valley, MN
COMMUNITY MEMORIAL HOSPITAL OF DEER RIVER, Deer River, MN
COMMUNITY MEMORIAL HOSPITAL OF SAN BUENAVENTURA, Ventura, CA
COMMUNITY MENTAL HEALTH CENTER AND PSYCHIATRIC INSTITUTE, Norfolk, VA
COMMUNITY MENTAL HEALTH CENTER OF BEAVER COUNTY, Rochester, PA
COMMUNITY METHODIST HOSPITAL, Henderson, KY
CONCHO COUNTY HOSPITAL, Eden, TX
CONCORD HOSPITAL, Concord, NH
CONCOURSE DIVISION, Bronx, NY, See Bronx-Lebanon Hospital Center
CONDELL MEMORIAL HOSPITAL, Libertyville, IL
CONEJOS COUNTY HOSPITAL, La Jara, CO
CONEMAUGH VALLEY MEMORIAL HOSPITAL, Johnstown, PA
CONEY ISLAND HOSPITAL, Brooklyn, NY
CONIFER PARK, Scotia, NY
CONNECTICUT DEPARTMENT OF CORRECTION'S HOSPITAL, Somers, CT
CONNECTICUT MENTAL HEALTH CENTER, New Haven, CT
CONNECTICUT VALLEY HOSPITAL, Middletown, CT
CONSTANCE BULTMAN WILSON CENTER FOR ADOLESCENT PSYCHIATRY, Faribault, MN, See Wilson Center for Adolescent Psychiatry
CONTINENTAL HOSPITAL NORTH (Formerly Northwest Hospital), Fort Worth, TX
CONTINENTAL HOSPITAL SUBURBAN, Fort Worth, TX
CONVERSE COUNTY MEMORIAL HOSPITAL, Douglas, WY
CONWAY HOSPITAL, Morrilton, AR
CONWAY HOSPITAL, Conway, SC
CONWAY REGIONAL HOSPITAL (Formerly Conway Memorial Hospital), Conway, AR
COOK CHILDREN'S HOSPITAL, Fort Worth, TX, See Cook-Fort Worth Children's Medical Center
COOK COMMUNITY HOSPITAL, Cook, MN
COOK COUNTY HOSPITAL, Chicago, IL
COOK COUNTY NORTH SHORE HOSPITAL, Grand Marais, MN
COOK MEMORIAL HOSPITAL, Levelland, TX
COOK-FORT WORTH CHILDREN'S MEDICAL CENTER, Fort Worth, TX
COOKEVILLE GENERAL HOSPITAL, Cookeville, TN
COOLEY DICKINSON HOSPITAL, Northampton, MA
COON MEMORIAL HOSPITAL AND HOME, Dalhart, TX
COOPER COUNTY MEMORIAL HOSPITAL, Boonville, MO
COOPER GREEN HOSPITAL, Birmingham, AL
COOPER HOSPITAL-UNIVERSITY MEDICAL CENTER, Camden, NJ
COPLEY HOSPITAL, Morrisville, VT
COPLEY MEMORIAL HOSPITAL, Aurora, IL
COPPER BASIN MEDICAL CENTER, Copperhill, TN
COPPER QUEEN COMMUNITY HOSPITAL, Bisbee, AZ
COQUILLE VALLEY HOSPITAL, Coquille, OR
CORAL GABLES HOSPITAL, Coral Gables, FL
CORAL REEF HOSPITAL, Miami, FL
CORAL RIDGE PSYCHIATRIC HOSPITAL, Fort Lauderdale, FL
CORCORAN DISTRICT HOSPITAL, Corcoran, CA
CORDELL MEMORIAL HOSPITAL, Cordell, OK
CORDOVA COMMUNITY HOSPITAL, Cordova, AK
CORNING COMMUNITY HOSPITAL, Corning, AR
CORNING HOSPITAL, Corning, NY
CORNING MEMORIAL HOSPITAL, Corning, CA
CORNWALL HOSPITAL, Cornwall, NY
CORONA COMMUNITY HOSPITAL, Corona, CA
CORONADO COMMUNITY HOSPITAL, Pampa, TX, See HCA Coronado Hospital
CORONADO HOSPITAL, Coronado, CA
CORPUS CHRISTI OSTEOPATHIC HOSPITAL, Corpus Christi, TX
CORRY MEMORIAL HOSPITAL, Corry, PA
CORTLAND MEMORIAL HOSPITAL, Cortland, NY
CORYELL MEMORIAL HOSPITAL, Gatesville, TX
COSHOCTON COUNTY MEMORIAL HOSPITAL, Coshocton, OH
COSTA MESA MEDICAL CENTER HOSPITAL, Costa Mesa, CA
COTEAU DES PRAIRIES HOSPITAL, Sisseton, SD
COTTAGE GROVE HOSPITAL, Cottage Grove, OR
COTTAGE HOSPITAL, Woodsville, NH

COTTAGE HOSPITAL OF GROSSE POINTE, Grosse Pointe Farms, MI
COTTONWOOD HOSPITAL MEDICAL CENTER, Murray, UT
COULEE COMMUNITY HOSPITAL, Grand Coulee, WA
COUNTRY HOME FOR CONVALESCENT CHILDREN, Chicago, IL, See University of Chicago Hospitals and Clinics
COUNTRY PLACE, Litchfield, CT
COVENANT MEDICAL CENTER, Waterloo, IA
COVINA VALLEY COMMUNITY HOSPITAL, West Covina, CA
COVINGTON COUNTY HOSPITAL, Collins, MS
COWELL HOSPITAL AND STUDENT HEALTH CENTER, Davis, CA
COZAD COMMUNITY HOSPITAL, Cozad, NE
COZBY-GERMANY HOSPITAL, Grand Saline, TX
CPC ALHAMBRA HOSPITAL, Rosemead, CA
CPC BELMONT HILLS HOSPITAL (Formerly Belmont Hills Psychiatric Center), Belmont, CA
CPC CEDAR HILLS HOSPITAL, Portland, OR
CPC CEDAR SPRING HOSPITAL, Pineville, NC
CPC COLISEUM MEDICAL CENTER (Formerly Coliseum Medical Center), New Orleans, LA
CPC EAST LAKE HOSPITAL, New Orleans, LA
CPC FAIRFAX HOSPITAL (Formerly Fairfax Hospital), Kirkland, WA
CPC FORT LAUDERDALE HOSPITAL (Formerly Fort Lauderdale Hospital), Fort Lauderdale, FL
CPC HORIZON HOSPITAL (Formerly Horizon Hospital), Pomona, CA
CPC INTERMOUNTAIN HOSPITAL OF BOISE, Boise, ID
CPC MEADOW WOOD HOSPITAL, Baton Rouge, LA
CPC MILLWOOD HOSPITAL, Arlington, TX
CPC OLD ORCHARD HOSPITAL, Skokie, IL
CPC PARKWOOD HOSPITAL (Formerly Peachtree-Parkwood Hospital), Atlanta, GA
CPC SAN LUIS REY HOSPITAL (Formerly San Luis Rey Hospital), Encinitas, CA
CPC SAND HILL HOSPITAL (Formerly Sand Hill Hospital), Gulfport, MS
CPC SANTA ANA PSYCHIATRIC HOSPITAL (Formerly Santa Ana Psychiatric Hospital), Santa Ana, CA
CPC ST. JOHNS RIVER HOSPITAL (Formerly St. Johns River Hospital), Jacksonville, FL
CPC VALLE VISTA HOSPITAL, Greenwood, IN
CPC VISTA DELAWARE MAR HOSPITAL, Ventura, CA
CPC WALNUT CREEK HOSPITAL (Formerly Walnut Creek Hospital), Walnut Creek, CA
CPC WELDON SPRING HOSPITAL (Formerly Weldon Spring Hospital), St. Charles, MO
CPC WESTWOOD HOSPITAL, Los Angeles, CA
CRAFTS-FARROW STATE HOSPITAL, Columbia, SC
CRAIG GENERAL HOSPITAL, Vinita, OK
CRAIG HOSPITAL, Englewood, CO
CRAIG HOUSE HOSPITAL, Beacon, NY
CRANE MEMORIAL HOSPITAL, Crane, TX
CRANSTON GENERAL HOSPITAL OSTEOPATHIC, Cranston, RI
CRAVEN COUNTY HOSPITAL, New Bern, NC
CRAWFORD COUNTY HOSPITAL DISTRICT ONE, Girard, KS
CRAWFORD COUNTY MEMORIAL HOSPITAL, Van Buren, AR
CRAWFORD COUNTY MEMORIAL HOSPITAL, Denison, IA
CRAWFORD LONG HOSPITAL OF EMORY UNIVERSITY (Formerly Crawford W. Long Memorial Hospital), Atlanta, GA
CRAWFORD MEMORIAL HOSPITAL, Robinson, IL
CRAWLEY MEMORIAL HOSPITAL, Boiling Springs, NC
CREEDMOOR PSYCHIATRIC CENTER, , NY
CRENSHAW CENTER HOSPITAL, Los Angeles, CA
CRENSHAW COUNTY HOSPITAL, Luverne, AL
CRESTLINE MEMORIAL HOSPITAL, Crestline, OH
CRESTWOOD HOSPITAL, Huntsville, AL
CRETE MUNICIPAL HOSPITAL, Crete, NE
CRIPPLED CHILDRENS HOSPITAL AND SCHOOL, Sioux Falls, SD
CRISP COUNTY HOSPITAL, Cordele, GA
CRITTENDEN COUNTY HOSPITAL, Marion, KY
CRITTENDEN MEMORIAL HOSPITAL, West Memphis, AR
CRITTENTON CENTER, Kansas City, MO
CRITTENTON HOSPITAL, Rochester, MI
CROCKETT COUNTY HOSPITAL, Ozona, TX
CROCKETT GENERAL HOSPITAL, Lawrenceburg, TN, See HCA Crockett Hospital
CROOK COUNTY MEMORIAL HOSPITAL, Sundance, WY
CROSBYTON CLINIC HOSPITAL, Crosbyton, TX
CROSS COUNTY HOSPITAL, Wynne, AR
CROSSROADS COMMUNITY HOSPITAL (Formerly Mount Vernon Hospital), Mount Vernon, IL
CROSSROADS HOSPITAL, Los Angeles, CA
CROTCHED MOUNTAIN REHABILITATION CENTER, Greenfield, NH
CROUSE-IRVING MEMORIAL HOSPITAL, Syracuse, NY
CROWNSVILLE HOSPITAL CENTER, Crownsville, MD
CROZER-CHESTER MEDICAL CENTER, Chester, PA
CRYSTAL FALLS COMMUNITY HOSPITAL, Crystal Falls, MI
CUBA HOSPITAL, Cuba, NM
CUBA MEMORIAL HOSPITAL, Cuba, NY
CUERO COMMUNITY HOSPITAL, Cuero, TX
CULBERSON COUNTY HOSPITAL, Van Horn, TX, See Culberson County Hospital District
CULBERSON COUNTY HOSPITAL DISTRICT (Formerly Culberson County Hospital), Van Horn, TX
CULLMAN MEDICAL CENTER, Cullman, AL
CULPEPER MEMORIAL HOSPITAL, Culpeper, VA
CUMBERLAND A. HOSPITAL FOR CHILDREN &ADOLESC ENTS (Formerly Cumberland Hospital), New Kent, VA
CUMBERLAND COUNTY HOSPITAL, Burkesville, KY
CUMBERLAND MEDICAL CENTER, Crossville, TN
CUMBERLAND MEMORIAL HOSPITAL, Cumberland, WI
CURRY GENERAL HOSPITAL, Gold Beach, OR
CUSHING HOSPITAL, Framingham, MA
CUSHING MEMORIAL HOSPITAL, Leavenworth, KS
CUSHING REGIONAL HOSPITAL, Cushing, OK
CUSTER COMMUNITY HOSPITAL, Custer, SD
CUTLER ARMY HOSPITAL (Formerly Cutler Army Community Hospital), Fort Devens, MA
CUYAHOGA COUNTY HOSPITALS, Cleveland, OH
CUYAHOGA FALLS GENERAL HOSPITAL, Cuyahoga Falls, OH
CUYUNA RANGE DISTRICT HOSPITAL, Crosby, MN
CYPRESS FAIRBANKS MEDICAL CENTER, Houston, TX
CYPRESS HOSPITAL, Lafayette, LA

D

D. M. COGDELL MEMORIAL HOSPITAL, Snyder, TX
D. T. WATSON REHABILITATION HOSPITAL, Sewickley, PA
D. W. MCMILLAN MEMORIAL HOSPITAL, Brewton, AL
DADE COUNTY MEMORIAL HOSPITAL, Lockwood, MO
DAHL MEMORIAL HOSPITAL, Ekalaka, MT
DAKOTA HOSPITAL, Fargo, ND
DAKOTA HOSPITAL, Vermillion, SD
DAKOTA MIDLAND HOSPITAL, Aberdeen, SD
DALE COUNTY HOSPITAL, Ozark, AL
DALLAS COUNTY HOSPITAL, Fordyce, AR
DALLAS COUNTY HOSPITAL, Perry, IA
DALLAS COUNTY HOSPITAL DISTRICT-PARKLAND MEMORIAL HOSPITAL, Dallas, TX
DALLAS FAMILY HOSPITAL, Dallas, TX
DALLAS MEDICAL AND SURGICAL CLINIC-HOSPITAL, Dallas, TX
DALLAS MEMORIAL HOSPITAL, Dallas, TX
DALLAS REHABILITATION INSTITUTE, Dallas, TX
DALLAS-FORT WORTH MEDICAL CENTER, Grand Prairie, TX
DAMERON HOSPITAL, Stockton, CA
DAMMASCH STATE HOSPITAL, Wilsonville, OR
DANA-FARBER CANCER INSTITUTE, Boston, MA
DANBURY HOSPITAL, Danbury, CT
DANFORTH HOSPITAL, Texas City, TX, See AMI Danforth Hospital
DANIEL DRAKE MEMORIAL HOSPITAL, Cincinnati, OH
DANIEL FREEMAN MARINA HOSPITAL, Los Angeles, CA
DANIEL FREEMAN MEMORIAL HOSPITAL, Inglewood, CA
DANIELS MEMORIAL HOSPITAL, Scobey, MT
DANVERS STATE HOSPITAL, Hathorne, MA
DANVILLE STATE HOSPITAL, Danville, PA
DARDANELLE HOSPITAL, Dardanelle, AR
DARNALL ARMY COMMUNITY HOSPITAL, Fort Hood, TX
DARTMOUTH HOSPITAL, Dayton, OH
DAUTERIVE HOSPITAL, New Iberia, LA
DAVENPORT MEDICAL CENTER, Davenport, IA
DAVID C. WILSON HOSPITAL, Charlottesville, VA, See Charter Hospital of Charlottesville
DAVID GRANBERRY MEMORIAL HOSPITAL, Naples, TX
DAVID GRANT U. S. AIR FORCE MEDICAL CENTER, Fairfield, CA
DAVIE COUNTY HOSPITAL, Mocksville, NC
DAVIESS COUNTY HOSPITAL, Washington, IN
DAVIS COMMUNITY HOSPITAL, Statesville, NC
DAVIS COUNTY HOSPITAL, Bloomfield, IA
DAVIS MEMORIAL HOSPITAL, Elkins, WV
DAY KIMBALL HOSPITAL, Putnam, CT
DAYTON GENERAL HOSPITAL, Dayton, WA
DAYTON MENTAL HEALTH CENTER, Dayton, OH
DCH REGIONAL MEDICAL CENTER (Formerly Druid City Hospital Regional Medical Center), Tuscaloosa, AL
DCH REHABILITATION PAVILION, Tuscaloosa, AL
DE GRAFF MEMORIAL HOSPITAL, North Tonawanda, NY
DE JARNETTE CENTER, Staunton, VA
DE LA RONDE HOSPITAL, Chalmette, LA
DE LEON HOSPITAL, De Leon, TX
DE PAUL HOSPITAL, New Orleans, LA
DE PAUL HOSPITAL, Cheyenne, WY
DE PAUL REHABILITATION HOSPITAL, Milwaukee, WI
DE POO MEMORIAL DOCTORS HOSPITAL, Key West, FL
DE SMET MEMORIAL HOSPITAL, De Smet, SD
DE SOTO GENERAL HOSPITAL, Mansfield, LA
DEACONESS HOSPITAL, Evansville, IN
DEACONESS HOSPITAL, St. Louis, MO
DEACONESS HOSPITAL, Cincinnati, OH
DEACONESS HOSPITAL, Oklahoma City, OK
DEACONESS HOSPITAL DIVISION, Buffalo, NY, See Buffalo General Hospital
DEACONESS HOSPITAL OF CLEVELAND, Cleveland, OH
DEACONESS MEDICAL CENTER (Formerly Billings Deaconess Hospital), Billings, MT
DEACONESS MEDICAL CENTER-SPOKANE, Spokane, WA
DEAF SMITH GENERAL HOSPITAL, Hereford, TX
DEARBORN COUNTY HOSPITAL, Lawrenceburg, IN
DEARBORN MEDICAL CENTRE HOSPITAL, Dearborn, MI, See Oakwood Springwells Health Center
DEATON HOSPITAL, Galena Park, TX
DEATON HOSPITAL AND MEDICAL CENTER OF CHRIST LUTHERAN CHURCH, Baltimore, MD
DEBORAH HEART AND LUNG CENTER, Browns Mills, NJ
DECATUR COMMUNITY HOSPITAL, Decatur, TX
DECATUR COUNTY GENERAL HOSPITAL, Parsons, TN
DECATUR COUNTY HOSPITAL, Leon, IA
DECATUR COUNTY HOSPITAL, Oberlin, KS
DECATUR COUNTY MEMORIAL HOSPITAL, Greensburg, IN
DECATUR GENERAL HOSPITAL, Decatur, AL
DECATUR HOSPITAL, Decatur, GA
DECATUR MEMORIAL HOSPITAL, Decatur, IL
DECATUR STREET FACILITY, Sandusky, OH, See Fistreet Facility
DECHAIRO HOSPITAL, Westmoreland, KS
DECKERVILLE COMMUNITY HOSPITAL, Deckerville, MI
DEEPDALE GENERAL HOSPITAL, Little Neck, NY
DEER'S HEAD CENTER, Salisbury, MD
DEFIANCE HOSPITAL, Defiance, OH
DEKALB GENERAL HOSPITAL, Decatur, GA
DEKALB GENERAL HOSPITAL, Smithville, TN
DEKALB MEMORIAL HOSPITAL, Auburn, IN
DELANO REGIONAL MEDICAL CENTER, Delano, CA
DELAWARE COUNTY MEMORIAL HOSPITAL, Manchester, IA
DELAWARE COUNTY MEMORIAL HOSPITAL, Drexel Hill, PA
DELAWARE HOSPITAL FOR THE CHRONICALLY ILL, Smyrna, DE
DELAWARE PUERTO HOSPITAL, Patterson, CA
DELAWARE STATE HOSPITAL, New Castle, DE
DELAWARE VALLEY HOSPITAL, Walton, NY
DELAWARE VALLEY MEDICAL CENTER (Formerly Listed Under Bristol), Langhorne, PA
DELAWARE VALLEY MENTAL HEALTH FOUNDATION, Doylestown, PA
DELL RAPIDS COMMUNITY HOSPITAL, Dell Rapids, SD
DELNOR COMMUNITY HOSPITAL, St. Charles, IL
DELRAY COMMUNITY HOSPITAL, Delray Beach, FL
DELTA COMMUNITY HOSPITAL (Formerly Delta Community Medical Center), Delta, UT
DELTA COUNTY MEMORIAL HOSPITAL, Delta, CO
DELTA MEDICAL CENTER, Brinkley, AR
DELTA MEDICAL CENTER, Greenville, MS
DELTA MEMORIAL HOSPITAL, Dumas, AR
DELTA MEMORIAL HOSPITAL, Antioch, CA
DENVER HEALTH AND HOSPITALS, Denver, CO
DEPAUL HEALTH CENTER, Bridgeton, MO
DEPAUL HOSPITAL, Norfolk, VA
DEPAUL NORTHSHORE HOSPITAL, Covington, LA
DEQUINCY MEMORIAL HOSPITAL, De Quincy, LA
DERMOTT-CHICOT MEMORIAL HOSPITAL, Dermott, AR
DES MOINES GENERAL HOSPITAL, Des Moines, IA
DESERT HOSPITAL, Palm Springs, CA
DESERT SAMARITAN HOSPITAL AND HEALTH CENTER, Mesa, AZ
DESERT SPRINGS HOSPITAL, Las Vegas, NV
DESOTO MEMORIAL HOSPITAL, Arcadia, FL
DETAR HOSPITAL, Victoria, TX

DETROIT OSTEOPATHIC HOSPITAL (Formerly Listed Under Detroit), Highland Park, MI
DETROIT RECEIVING HOSPITAL AND UNIVERSITY HEALTH CENTER, Detroit, MI
DETROIT-MACOMB HOSPITAL CORPORATION, Detroit, MI
DETTMER HOSPITAL, Troy, OH
DEUEL COUNTY MEMORIAL HOSPITAL, Clear Lake, SD
DEVEREUX CENTER-GEORGIA BRANCH, Kennesaw, GA
DEVEREUX FOUNDATION-BOND DIVISION, Berwyn, PA
DEVEREUX FOUNDATION-CALIFORNIA (Formerly Devereux Foundation-California Treadway Division, Goleta), Santa Barbara, CA
DEVEREUX FOUNDATION-FRENCH DIVISION, Devon, PA
DEVEREUX FOUNDATION-TEXAS BRANCH, Victoria, TX
DEWITT ARMY COMMUNITY HOSPITAL (Formerly DeWitt Army Hospital), Fort Belvoir, VA
DEWITT CITY HOSPITAL, De Witt, AR
DEWITT COMMUNITY HOSPITAL, De Witt, IA
DEXTER MEMORIAL HOSPITAL, Dexter, MO
DIAGNOSTIC CENTER HOSPITAL, Chattanooga, TN
DIAGNOSTIC CENTER HOSPITAL, Houston, TX
DICK HALL'S HOUSE, Hanover, NH
DICKEY COUNTY MEMORIAL HOSPITAL, Ellendale, ND
DICKINSON COUNTY HOSPITALS, Iron Mountain, MI
DICKINSON COUNTY MEMORIAL HOSPITAL, Spirit Lake, IA
DIMMIT COUNTY MEMORIAL HOSPITAL, Carrizo Springs, TX
DISTRICT MEMORIAL HOSPITAL, Forest Lake, MN
DISTRICT OF COLUMBIA GENERAL HOSPITAL, Washington, DC
DISTRICT TWO COMMUNITY HOSPITAL, Durant, MS
DIVINE PROVIDENCE HOSPITAL, Williamsport, PA
DIVINE PROVIDENCE HOSPITAL AND HOME, Ivanhoe, MN
DIVINE PROVIDENCE HOSPITAL OF PITTSBURGH, Pittsburgh, PA
DIVINE REDEEMER MEMORIAL HOSPITAL, South St. Paul, MN
DIVINE SAVIOR HOSPITAL AND NURSING HOME, Portage, WI
DIVINE SAVIOUR HOSPITAL, York, SC
DIXIE MEDICAL CENTER, St. George, UT
DIXON MEMORIAL HOSPITAL, Denham Springs, LA
DOBBS FERRY HOSPITAL, Dobbs Ferry, NY
DOCTOR ROBERT L. YEAGER HEALTH CENTER (Formerly Rockland County Health Center), Pomona, NY
DOCTORS GENERAL HOSPITAL, Plantation, FL
DOCTORS GENERAL HOSPITAL (Formerly AMI Doctors General Hospital), Oklahoma City, OK
DOCTORS GUBERN'S HOSPITAL, Fajardo, P.R.
DOCTORS HOSPITAL, Little Rock, AR
DOCTORS HOSPITAL, Sarasota, FL
DOCTORS HOSPITAL, Columbus, GA
DOCTORS HOSPITAL, Tucker, GA
DOCTORS HOSPITAL, Detroit, MI
DOCTORS HOSPITAL, Jackson, MS
DOCTORS HOSPITAL, New York, NY
DOCTORS HOSPITAL, Conroe, TX, See HCA Doctors Hospital
DOCTORS HOSPITAL, Groves, TX
DOCTORS HOSPITAL, San Juan, P.R.
DOCTORS HOSPITAL, Columbus, OH
DOCTORS HOSPITAL OF DALLAS, Dallas, TX
DOCTORS HOSPITAL OF HOLLYWOOD, Hollywood, FL
DOCTORS HOSPITAL OF JEFFERSON, Metairie, LA
DOCTORS HOSPITAL OF LAKE WORTH, Lake Worth, FL, See HCA Doctors Hospital
DOCTORS HOSPITAL OF LAKEWOOD-CLARK, Lakewood, CA
DOCTORS HOSPITAL OF LAKEWOOD-SOUTH STREET, Lakewood, CA
DOCTORS HOSPITAL OF LAREDO, Laredo, TX, See AMI Doctors Hospital of Laredo
DOCTORS HOSPITAL OF MANTECA (Formerly Manteca Hospital), Manteca, CA
DOCTORS HOSPITAL OF MOBILE, Mobile, AL
DOCTORS HOSPITAL OF NELSONVILLE, Nelsonville, OH
DOCTORS HOSPITAL OF PINOLE, Pinole, CA
DOCTORS HOSPITAL OF SANTA ANA, Santa Ana, CA
DOCTORS HOSPITAL OF STARK COUNTY, Massillon, OH
DOCTORS HOSPITAL OF TACOMA, Tacoma, WA, See Tacoma General Hospital
DOCTORS HOSPITAL OF WORCESTER, Worcester, MA
DOCTORS MEDICAL CENTER, Modesto, CA
DOCTORS MEDICAL CENTER, Tulsa, OK, See AMI Doctors Hospital
DOCTORS MEMORIAL HOSPITAL, Bonifay, FL
DOCTORS MEMORIAL HOSPITAL, Perry, FL
DOCTORS MEMORIAL HOSPITAL, Atlanta, GA
DOCTORS MEMORIAL HOSPITAL, Spartanburg, SC, See AMI Doctors Memorial Hospital
DOCTORS REGIONAL MEDICAL CENTER, Poplar Bluff, MO
DOCTORS' HOSPITAL, Coral Gables, FL
DOCTORS' HOSPITAL, Shreveport, LA
DOCTORS' HOSPITAL, Houston, TX
DOCTORS' HOSPITAL OF MONTCLAIR, Montclair, CA
DOCTORS' HOSPITAL OF OPELOUSAS, Opelousas, LA, See AMI Doctors' Hospital of Opelousas
DOCTORS' HOSPITAL OF STATEN ISLAND, Staten Island, NY
DOCTORS' MEMORIAL HOSPITAL, Tyler, TX
DODGE COUNTY HOSPITAL, Eastman, GA
DODGE HOSPITAL, Miami, FL, See Harbor View
DOERNBECHER MEMORIAL HOSPITAL FOR CHILDREN, Portland, OR, See Oregon Health Sciences University Hospital
DOLLY VINSANT MEMORIAL HOSPITAL, San Benito, TX
DOMINGUEZ MEDICAL CENTER (Formerly Dominguez Valley Hospital), Long Beach, CA
DOMINGUEZ VALLEY HOSPITAL, Long Beach, CA, See Dominguez Medical Center
DOMINICAN SANTA CRUZ HOSPITAL, Santa Cruz, CA
DOMINION HOSPITAL, Falls Church, VA
DONALSONVILLE HOSPITAL, Donalsonville, GA
DONELSON HOSPITAL, Nashville, TN, See HCA Donelson Hospital
DOOLY MEDICAL CENTER, Vienna, GA
DOOR COUNTY MEMORIAL HOSPITAL, Sturgeon Bay, WI
DORCHESTER GENERAL HOSPITAL, Cambridge, MD
DORCHESTER MENTAL HEALTH CENTER, Boston, MA
DORMINY MEDICAL CENTER (Formerly Dorminy Memorial Hospital), Fitzgerald, GA
DOROTHEA DIX HOSPITAL, Raleigh, NC
DOS PALOS MEMORIAL HOSPITAL, Dos Palos, CA
DOUGLAS COMMUNITY HOSPITAL, Roseburg, OR
DOUGLAS COUNTY HOSPITAL, Alexandria, MN
DOUGLAS COUNTY HOSPITAL, Omaha, NE
DOUGLAS COUNTY JARMAN MEMORIAL HOSPITAL, Tuscola, IL
DOUGLAS COUNTY MEMORIAL HOSPITAL, Armour, SD
DOUGLAS GENERAL HOSPITAL, Douglasville, GA
DOVER GENERAL HOSPITAL AND MEDICAL CENTER, Dover, NJ
DOWN EAST COMMUNITY HOSPITAL, Machias, ME
DOWNEY COMMUNITY HOSPITAL, Downey, CA
DOWNTOWN GENERAL HOSPITAL, Chattanooga, TN
DOXEY-HATCH MEDICAL CENTER, Salt Lake City, UT
DOYLESTOWN HOSPITAL, Doylestown, PA
DR. DAN C. TRIGG MEMORIAL HOSPITAL, Tucumcari, NM
DR. GUBERN'S HOSPITAL, Fajardo, P.R.
DR. HENRY SCHMIDT MEMORIAL HOSPITAL, Westbrook, MN
DR. J. ROBERT SHAUGHNESSY CHRONIC DISEASE-REHABILITATION HOSPITAL, Salem, MA
DR. JOHN M. MEADOWS MEMORIAL HOSPITAL, Vidalia, GA
DR. JOHN WARNER HOSPITAL, Clinton, IL
DR. PILA'S HOSPITAL, Ponce, P.R.
DR. U. E. ZAMBARANO MEMORIAL HOSPITAL, Wallum Lake, RI
DR. WALTER OLIN MOSS REGIONAL HOSPITAL, Lake Charles, LA
DREW MEMORIAL HOSPITAL, Monticello, AR
DRISCOLL FOUNDATION CHILDREN'S HOSPITAL, Corpus Christi, TX
DRUID CITY HOSPITAL REGIONAL MEDICAL CENTER, Tuscaloosa, AL, See Dch Regional Medical Center
DRUMRIGHT MEMORIAL HOSPITAL, Drumright, OK
DUBOIS REGIONAL MEDICAL CENTER, Dubois, PA
DUCHESNE COUNTY HOSPITAL, Roosevelt, UT
DUKE UNIVERSITY HOSPITAL, Durham, NC
DUKES MEMORIAL HOSPITAL, Peru, IN
DUNCAN MEMORIAL HOSPITAL, Fort Worth, TX
DUNCAN REGIONAL HOSPITAL, Duncan, OK
DUNDY COUNTY HOSPITAL, Benkelman, NE
DUNLAP MEMORIAL HOSPITAL, Orrville, OH
DUNN COUNTY HEALTH CARE CENTER, Menomonie, WI
DUNN MEMORIAL HOSPITAL, Bedford, IN
DUPLIN GENERAL HOSPITAL, Kenansville, NC
DURHAM COUNTY GENERAL HOSPITAL, Durham, NC
DWIGHT DAVID EISENHOWER ARMY MEDICAL CENTER, Fort Gordon, GA
DWYER COMMUNITY HOSPITAL, Milwaukie, OR, See Providence Milwaukie Hospital

E

E. A. CONWAY MEMORIAL HOSPITAL, Monroe, LA
E. J. NOBLE HOSPITAL OF ALEXANDRIA BAY, Alexandria Bay, NY
E. L. GRAHAM MEMORIAL HOSPITAL, Cisco, TX
E. P. CLAPPER MEMORIAL MEDICAL CENTER, Waynoka, OK
E. S. PIKE MEMORIAL HOSPITAL, Kentwood, LA
EAGLE LAKE COMMUNITY HOSPITAL, Eagle Lake, TX
EAGLE RIVER MEMORIAL HOSPITAL, Eagle River, WI
EAGLEVILLE HOSPITAL, Eagleville, PA
EARL K. LONG MEMORIAL HOSPITAL, Baton Rouge, LA
EARLY MEMORIAL HOSPITAL, Blakely, GA
EAST ALABAMA MEDICAL CENTER, Opelika, AL
EAST ASCENSION GENERAL HOSPITAL, Gonzales, LA
EAST COOPER COMMUNITY HOSPITAL, Mount Pleasant, SC, See AMI East Cooper Community Hospital
EAST JEFFERSON GENERAL HOSPITAL, Metairie, LA
EAST LIVERPOOL CITY HOSPITAL, East Liverpool, OH
EAST LOS ANGELES DOCTORS HOSPITAL, Los Angeles, CA
EAST LOUISIANA STATE HOSPITAL, Jackson, LA
EAST MISSISSIPPI STATE HOSPITAL, Meridian, MS
EAST MORGAN COUNTY HOSPITAL, Brush, CO
EAST OHIO REGIONAL HOSPITAL, Martins Ferry, OH
EAST ORANGE GENERAL HOSPITAL, East Orange, NJ
EAST PASCO MEDICAL CENTER, Zephyrhills, FL
EAST SHOSHONE HOSPITAL, Silverton, ID
EAST SUBURBAN HEALTH CENTER, Monroeville, PA, See Forbes Regional Health Center
EAST TENNESSEE BAPTIST HOSPITAL, Knoxville, TN
EAST TENNESSEE CHILDREN'S HOSPITAL, Knoxville, TN
EASTERN IDAHO REGIONAL MEDICAL CENTER, Idaho Falls, ID
EASTERN LONG ISLAND HOSPITAL, Greenport, NY
EASTERN MAINE MEDICAL CENTER, Bangor, ME
EASTERN NEW MEXICO MEDICAL CENTER, Roswell, NM
EASTERN OKLAHOMA MEDICAL CENTER (Formerly LeFlore County Memorial Hospital), Poteau, OK
EASTERN OREGON PSYCHIATRIC CENTER, Pendleton, OR
EASTERN PENNSYLVANIA PSYCHIATRIC INSTITUTE, Philadelphia, PA, See Hospital of the Medical College of Pennsylvania
EASTERN PLUMAS DISTRICT HOSPITAL, Portola, CA
EASTERN SHORE HOSPITAL CENTER, Cambridge, MD
EASTERN STATE HOSPITAL, Lexington, KY
EASTERN STATE HOSPITAL, Vinita, OK
EASTERN STATE HOSPITAL, Williamsburg, VA
EASTERN STATE HOSPITAL, Medical Lake, WA
EASTERN STATE SCHOOL AND HOSPITAL, Trevose, PA
EASTERN WAKE HOSPITAL, Zebulon, NC
EASTLAND MEMORIAL HOSPITAL, Eastland, TX
EASTMORELAND HOSPITAL (Formerly Eastmoreland General Hospital), Portland, OR
EASTON HOSPITAL, Easton, PA
EASTWAY GENERAL HOSPITAL, Houston, TX, See AMI Eastway General Hospital
EASTWOOD HOSPITAL, Memphis, TN
EATON RAPIDS COMMUNITY HOSPITAL, Eaton Rapids, MI
ED FRASER MEMORIAL HOSPITAL, Macclenny, FL
EDEN HOSPITAL MEDICAL CENTER (Formerly Eden Hospital), Castro Valley, CA
EDGAR B. DAVIS MEMORIAL HOSPITAL, Luling, TX
EDGE MEMORIAL HOSPITAL, Troy, AL
EDGEFIELD COUNTY HOSPITAL, Edgefield, SC
EDGEFIELD HOSPITAL, Nashville, TN, See HCA Edgefield Hospital
EDGEMONT HOSPITAL, Los Angeles, CA
EDGEWATER HOSPITAL, Chicago, IL
EDGEWOOD CHEMICAL DEPENDENCY UNIT, St. Louis, MO, See St. John's Mercy Medical Center
EDINBURG GENERAL HOSPITAL, Edinburg, TX
EDITH NOURSE ROGERS MEMORIAL VETERANS HOSPITAL, Bedford, MA
EDMOND MEMORIAL HOSPITAL, Edmond, OK
EDNA HOSPITAL, Edna, TX
EDWARD A. UTLAUT MEMORIAL HOSPITAL, Greenville, IL
EDWARD H. WHITE II MEMORIAL HOSPITAL, St. Petersburg, FL, See HCA Edward White Hospital
EDWARD HOSPITAL, Naperville, IL
EDWARD JOHN NOBLE HOSPITAL OF GOUVERNEUR, Gouverneur, NY
EDWARD W. MCCREADY MEMORIAL HOSPITAL, Crisfield, MD

EDWARD W. SPARROW HOSPITAL, Lansing, MI
EDWARDS COUNTY HOSPITAL, Kinsley, KS
EDWIN SHAW HOSPITAL, Akron, OH
EFFINGHAM COUNTY HOSPITAL AND EXTENDED CARE FACILITY, Springfield, GA
EHRLING BERGQUIST U. S. AIR FORCE REGIONAL HOSPITAL, Omaha, NE
EISENHOWER MEDICAL CENTER, Rancho Mirage, CA
EISENHOWER MEDICAL CENTER, Colorado Springs, CO
EL CAMINO HOSPITAL, Mountain View, CA
EL CENTRO REGIONAL MEDICAL CENTER (Formerly El Centro Community Hospital), El Centro, CA
EL DORADO HOSPITAL AND MEDICAL CENTER, Tucson, AZ
ELBA GENERAL HOSPITAL, Elba, AL
ELBERT MEMORIAL HOSPITAL (Formerly Elberton-Elbert County Hospital), Elberton, GA
ELDORA REGIONAL MEDICAL CENTER (Formerly Eldora Community Hospital), Eldora, IA
ELECTRA MEMORIAL HOSPITAL, Electra, TX
ELGIN MENTAL HEALTH CENTER, Elgin, IL
ELIZA COFFEE MEMORIAL HOSPITAL, Florence, AL
ELIZABETH C. LEONARD MEMORIAL HOSPITAL, Buckhannon, WV
ELIZABETH GENERAL MEDICAL CENTER, Elizabeth, NJ
ELIZABETHTOWN COMMUNITY HOSPITAL, Elizabethtown, NY
ELK COUNTY GENERAL HOSPITAL, Ridgway, PA
ELKHART GENERAL HOSPITAL, Elkhart, IN
ELKO GENERAL HOSPITAL, Elko, NV
ELKVIEW GENERAL HOSPITAL, Hobart, OK
ELLENVILLE COMMUNITY HOSPITAL, Ellenville, NY
ELLETT MEMORIAL HOSPITAL, Appleton City, MO
ELLINWOOD DISTRICT HOSPITAL, Ellinwood, KS
ELLIOT HOSPITAL, Manchester, NH
ELLIOTT WHITE SPRINGS MEMORIAL HOSPITAL, Lancaster, SC
ELLIS FISCHEL ST. CANCER CENTER, Columbia, MO
ELLIS HOSPITAL, Schenectady, NY
ELLISVILLE MUNICIPAL HOSPITAL, Ellisville, MS
ELLSWORTH COUNTY VETERANS MEMORIAL HOSPITAL, Ellsworth, KS
ELLSWORTH MUNICIPAL HOSPITAL, Iowa Falls, IA
ELLWOOD CITY HOSPITAL, Ellwood City, PA
ELMBROOK MEMORIAL HOSPITAL, Brookfield, WI
ELMCREST PSYCHIATRIC INSTITUTE, Portland, CT
ELMER COMMUNITY HOSPITAL, Elmer, NJ
ELMHURST MEMORIAL HOSPITAL, Elmhurst, IL
ELMIRA PSYCHIATRIC CENTER, Elmira, NY
ELMORE COUNTY HOSPITAL, Wetumpka, AL
ELMORE MEDICAL CENTER (Formerly Elmore Memorial Hospital), Mountain Home, ID
ELY-BLOOMENSON COMMUNITY HOSPITAL, Ely, MN
ELYRIA MEMORIAL HOSPITAL, Elyria, OH
EMANUEL COUNTY HOSPITAL, Swainsboro, GA
EMANUEL HOSPITAL AND HEALTH CENTER (Formerly Emanuel Hospital), Portland, OR
EMANUEL MEDICAL CENTER, Turlock, CA
EMERALD-HODGSON HOSPITAL, Sewanee, TN
EMERSON A. NORTH HOSPITAL, Cincinnati, OH
EMERSON HOSPITAL, Concord, MA
EMMA L. BIXBY HOSPITAL, Adrian, MI
EMMA LAING STEVENS HOSPITAL, Granville, NY
EMMA PENDLETON BRADLEY HOSPITAL, Riverside, RI
EMORY UNIVERSITY HOSPITAL, Atlanta, GA
ENCINO HOSPITAL, Los Angeles, CA
ENGLEWOOD HOSPITAL, Englewood, NJ
ENGLISH PARK MEDICAL CENTER, Marion, SC
ENID MEMORIAL HOSPITAL, Enid, OK
ENTERPRISE HOSPITAL, Enterprise, AL
EPHRAIM MCDOWELL REGIONAL MEDICAL CENTER (Formerly Ephraim McDowell Memorial Hospital), Danville, KY
EPHRATA COMMUNITY HOSPITAL, Ephrata, PA
EPISCOPAL HOSPITAL, Philadelphia, PA
ERIE COUNTY MEDICAL CENTER, Buffalo, NY
ERIK AND MARGARET JONSSON HOSPITAL, Dallas, TX, See Baylor University Medical Center
ERLANGER MEDICAL CENTER, Chattanooga, TN
ERNEST V. COWELL MEMORIAL HOSPITAL, Berkeley, CA
ESKATON AMERICAN RIVER HOSPITAL, Carmichael, CA, See American River Hospital
ESPANOLA HOSPITAL, Espanola, NM
ESSEX COUNTY HOSPITAL CENTER, Cedar Grove, NJ
ESTELLE DOHENY EYE HOSPITAL, Los Angeles, CA
ESTES PARK MEDICAL CENTER, Estes Park, CO
ESTUDILLO HOSPITAL, San Leandro, CA
EUCLID GENERAL HOSPITAL, Euclid, OH
EUGENE DUPONT MEMORIAL HOSPITAL, Wilmington, DE, See Wilmington Medical Center
EUGENE HOSPITAL (Formerly Eugene Clinic), Eugene, OR
EUGENIA HOSPITAL, Lafayette Hill, PA
EUREKA COMMUNITY HOSPITAL (Formerly Eureka Hospital), Eureka, IL
EUREKA COMMUNITY HOSPITAL, Eureka, SD
EUREKA SPRINGS HOSPITAL, Eureka Springs, AR
EVANGELICAL COMMUNITY HOSPITAL, Lewisburg, PA
EVANS MEMORIAL HOSPITAL, Claxton, GA
EVANSTON HOSPITAL, Evanston, IL
EVANSVILLE STATE HOSPITAL, Evansville, IN
EVELETH FITZGERALD COMMUNITY HOSPITAL, Eveleth, MN
EVERETT A. GLADMAN MEMORIAL HOSPITAL, Oakland, CA
EVERGLADES MEMORIAL HOSPITAL, Pahokee, FL
EVERGREEN HOSPITAL MEDICAL CENTER (Formerly Evergreen General Hospital), Kirkland, WA
EXCELSTOR SPRINGS CITY HOSPITAL AND CONVALESCENT CENTER, Excelsior Springs, MO
EXETER HOSPITAL, Exeter, NH
EYE AND EAR CLINIC OF CHARLESTON, Charleston, WV
EYE AND EAR HOSPITAL OF PITTSBURGH, Pittsburgh, PA
EYE FOUNDATION HOSPITAL, Birmingham, AL
EYE, EAR, NOSE AND THROAT HOSPITAL, New Orleans, LA

F

F. ALBERT KLEIN UNIT, Burlington, IA, See Burlington Medical Center
F. EDWARD HEBERT HOSPITAL, New Orleans, LA
F. G. RILEY MEMORIAL HOSPITAL, Meridian, MS, See Riley Memorial Hospital
FAIR OAKS HOSPITAL, Summit, NJ
FAIRBANKS HOSPITAL, Indianapolis, IN
FAIRBANKS MEMORIAL HOSPITAL, Fairbanks, AK
FAIRBURY HOSPITAL, Fairbury, IL
FAIRFAX HOSPITAL, Falls Church, VA
FAIRFAX HOSPITAL, Kirkland, WA, See CPC Fairfax Hospital
FAIRFAX MEMORIAL HOSPITAL, Fairfax, OK
FAIRFIELD HILLS HOSPITAL, Newtown, CT
FAIRFIELD MEMORIAL HOSPITAL, Fairfield, IL
FAIRFIELD MEMORIAL HOSPITAL, Winnsboro, SC
FAIRFIELD MEMORIAL HOSPITAL, Fairfield, TX
FAIRLAWN HOSPITAL, Worcester, MA
FAIRMONT COMMUNITY HOSPITAL, Fairmont, MN
FAIRMONT GENERAL HOSPITAL, Fairmont, WV
FAIRMONT HOSPITAL, San Leandro, CA
FAIRMOUNT INSTITUTE, Philadelphia, PA
FAIRVIEW DEACONESS CENTER (Formerly Fairview Deaconess Hospital), Minneapolis, MN
FAIRVIEW GENERAL HOSPITAL, Cleveland, OH
FAIRVIEW HOSPITAL, Bayou Vista, LA
FAIRVIEW HOSPITAL, Great Barrington, MA
FAIRVIEW HOSPITAL, Fairview, OK
FAIRVIEW PARK HOSPITAL, Dublin, GA
FAIRVIEW PRINCETON HOSPITAL, Princeton, MN
FAIRVIEW RIDGES HOSPITAL, Burnsville, MN
FAIRVIEW RIVERSIDE HOSPITAL (Formerly Fairview Hospital), Minneapolis, MN
FAIRVIEW SOUTHDALE HOSPITAL (Formerly Listed Under Edina), Minneapolis, MN
FAITH HOSPITAL, St. Louis, MO
FAJARDO REGIONAL HOSPITAL, Fajardo, P.R.
FALKIRK HOSPITAL, Central Valley, NY
FALLBROOK HOSPITAL DISTRICT, Fallbrook, CA
FALLON MEMORIAL HOSPITAL, Baker, MT
FALLSTON GENERAL HOSPITAL, Fallston, MD
FALLSVIEW PSYCHIATRIC HOSPITAL, Cuyahoga Falls, OH
FALMOUTH HOSPITAL, Falmouth, MA
FAMILY HEALTH WEST, Fruita, CO
FAMILY HOSPITAL (Formerly Family Hospital and Nursing Home), Milwaukee, WI
FAMILY HOSPITAL CENTER (Formerly Southwest Osteopathic Hospital), Amarillo, TX
FANNIN COUNTY HOSPITAL, Bonham, TX
FANNIN REGIONAL HOSPITAL, Blue Ridge, GA
FANNY ALLEN HOSPITAL, Winooski, VT
FARIBAULT REGIONAL CENTER (Formerly Faribault State Hospital), Faribault, MN
FARMINGTON COMMUNITY HOSPITAL, Farmington, MO
FARMINGTON STATE HOSPITAL, Farmington, MO
FARREN MEMORIAL HOSPITAL, Montague, MA
FARVIEW STATE HOSPITAL, Waymart, PA
FAULK COUNTY MEMORIAL HOSPITAL, Faulkton, SD
FAULKNER HOSPITAL, Boston, MA
FAUQUIER HOSPITAL, Warrenton, VA
FAWCETT MEMORIAL HOSPITAL, Port Charlotte, FL
FAXTON HOSPITAL, Utica, NY
FAYETTE COUNTY HOSPITAL, Fayette, AL
FAYETTE COUNTY HOSPITAL, Vandalia, IL
FAYETTE COUNTY MEMORIAL HOSPITAL, Washington Court House, OH
FAYETTE MEMORIAL HOSPITAL, Connersville, IN
FAYETTE MEMORIAL HOSPITAL, La Grange, TX
FAYETTEVILLE CITY HOSPITAL, Fayetteville, AR
FEATHER RIVER HOSPITAL, Paradise, CA
FEDERAL CORRECTIONAL INSTITUTE HOSPITAL, Ashland, KY
FEDERAL CORRECTIONAL INSTITUTION, Los Angeles, CA
FEDERAL CORRECTIONAL INSTITUTION HOSPITAL, El Reno, OK
FEDERAL CORRECTIONAL INSTITUTION HOSPITAL, Texarkana, TX
FELLOWSHIP HALL, Greensboro, NC
FENTRESS COUNTY GENERAL HOSPITAL, Jamestown, TN
FERGUS FALLS REGIONAL TREATMENT CENTER (Formerly Fergus Falls State Hospital), Fergus Falls, MN
FERGUSON HOSPITAL, Grand Rapids, MI
FERRELL HOSPITAL, Eldorado, IL
FERRY COUNTY MEMORIAL HOSPITAL, Republic, WA
FIELD MEMORIAL COMMUNITY HOSPITAL, Centreville, MS
FIFTH AVENUE MEDICAL CENTER (Formerly Waldo General Hospital), Seattle, WA
FILLMORE COMMUNITY MEDICAL CENTER, Fillmore, UT
FILLMORE COUNTY HOSPITAL, Geneva, NE
FINLEY HOSPITAL, Dubuque, IA
FIRELANDS COMMUNITY HOSPITAL, Sandusky, OH
FIRST HEALTH COURTLAND (Formerly Community Hospital of Courtland), Courtland, AL
FIRST HEALTH JACKSON (Formerly D. E. Jackson Memorial Hospital), Lester, AL
FIRST HEALTH JENKINS (Formerly Jenkins Community Hospital), Jenkins, KY
FIRST HOSPITAL-MILWAUKEE (Formerly First Hospital), Milwaukee, WI
FISH MEMORIAL HOSPITAL, New Smyrna Beach, FL
FISH MEMORIAL HOSPITAL AT DELAND, De Land, FL
FISHER COUNTY HOSPITAL DISTRICT, Rotan, TX
FISHER-TITUS MEDICAL CENTER (Formerly Fisher-Titus Memorial Hospital), Norwalk, OH
FISHERMEN'S HOSPITAL, Marathon, FL
FITZSIMONS ARMY MEDICAL CENTER, Aurora, CO
FIVE COUNTIES HOSPITAL, Lemmon, SD
FLAGET MEMORIAL HOSPITAL, Bardstown, KY
FLAGLER HOSPITAL, St. Augustine, FL
FLAGSTAFF MEDICAL CENTER, Flagstaff, AZ
FLAMBEAU MEDICAL CENTER, Park Falls, WI
FLANDREAU MUNICIPAL HOSPITAL, Flandreau, SD
FLEMING COUNTY HOSPITAL, Flemingsburg, KY
FLINT OSTEOPATHIC HOSPITAL, Flint, MI
FLORALA MEMORIAL HOSPITAL, Florala, AL
FLORENCE GENERAL HOSPITAL, Florence, SC
FLORIDA ALCOHOLISM TREATMENT CENTER, Avon Park, FL
FLORIDA CAMELOT (Formerly Camelot Care Center), Land'o'lakes, FL
FLORIDA COMMUNITY HOSPITAL (Formerly Washington County Hospital), Chipley, FL
FLORIDA HOSPITAL MEDICAL CENTER, Orlando, FL
FLORIDA HOSPITAL-ALTAMONTE, Altamonte Springs, FL, See Florida Hospital, Orlando
FLORIDA HOSPITAL-APOPKA, Apopka, FL, See Florida Hospital, Orlando
FLORIDA KEYS MEMORIAL HOSPITAL, Key West, FL
FLORIDA MEDICAL CENTER HOSPITAL, Fort Lauderdale, FL
FLORIDA STATE HOSPITAL, Chattahoochee, FL
FLOW MEMORIAL HOSPITAL, Denton, TX
FLOWER MEMORIAL HOSPITAL, Sylvania, OH
FLOWERS HOSPITAL, Dothan, AL
FLOYD COUNTY MEMORIAL HOSPITAL, Charles City, IA
FLOYD MEDICAL CENTER, Rome, GA
FLOYD MEMORIAL HOSPITAL (Formerly Memorial Hospital), New Albany, IN
FLOYD VALLEY HOSPITAL, Le Mars, IA
FLUSHING HOSPITAL AND MEDICAL CENTER, Flushing, NY
FOARD COUNTY HOSPITAL, Crowell, TX
FONT MARTELO HOSPITAL, Humacao, P.R.
FOOTHILL PRESBYTERIAN HOSPITAL-MORRIS L. JOHNSTON MEMORIAL, Glendora, CA
FORBES METROPOLITAN HEALTH CENTER, Pittsburgh, PA
FORBES REGIONAL HEALTH CENTER (Formerly East Suburban Health Center), Monroeville, PA
FOREST CITY COMMUNITY HOSPITAL, Forest City, IA
FOREST GLEN HOSPITAL, Canyonville, OR
FOREST GROVE COMMUNITY HOSPITAL, Forest Grove, OR
FOREST HOSPITAL, Des Plaines, IL

FOREST VIEW PSYCHIATRIC HOSPITAL, Grand Rapids, MI
FORKOSH MEMORIAL HOSPITAL, Chicago, IL, See Lincoln West Hospital
FORKS COMMUNITY HOSPITAL, Forks, WA
FORREST COUNTY GENERAL HOSPITAL, Hattiesburg, MS
FORSYTH MEMORIAL HOSPITAL, Winston-Salem, NC
FORT ATKINSON MEMORIAL HOSPITAL, Fort Atkinson, WI
FORT BAYARD MEDICAL CENTER, Fort Bayard, NM
FORT GAINES HOSPITAL, Fort Gaines, GA
FORT HAMILTON-HUGHES MEMORIAL HOSPITAL AND HEALTHCARE CORPORATION, Hamilton, OH
FORT LAUDERDALE HOSPITAL, Fort Lauderdale, FL, See CPC Fort Lauderdale Hospital
FORT LOGAN HOSPITAL, Stanford, KY
FORT LOGAN MENTAL HEALTH CENTER, Denver, CO
FORT MADISON COMMUNITY HOSPITAL, Fort Madison, IA
FORT MORGAN COMMUNITY HOSPITAL, Fort Morgan, CO
FORT MYERS COMMUNITY HOSPITAL, Fort Myers, FL, See Southwest Florida Regional Medical Center
FORT SANDERS REGIONAL MEDICAL CENTER, Knoxville, TN
FORT WAYNE STATE HOSPITAL AND TRAINING CENTER, Fort Wayne, IN
FORT WORTH CHILDREN'S HOSPITAL, Fort Worth, TX, See Cook-Fort Worth Children's Medical Center
FORT WORTH OSTEOPATHIC MEDICAL CENTER, Fort Worth, TX
FORTY-FIFTH STREET MENTAL HEALTH CENTER, West Palm Beach, FL
FORUM HOSPITAL (Formerly Horizon Hospital), Ellisville, MO
FORUM HOSPITAL TRENTON (Formerly Memorial Hospital), Trenton, TN
FOSSTON MUNICIPAL HOSPITAL, Fosston, MN
FOSTER G. MCGAW HOSPITAL, LOYOLA UNIVERSITY OF CHICAGO, Maywood, IL
FOSTORIA CITY HOSPITAL, Fostoria, OH
FOUNTAIN VALLEY REGIONAL HOSPITAL AND MEDICAL CENTER (Formerly Fountain Valley Community Hospital), Fountain Valley, CA
FOUR WINDS HOSPITAL, Katonah, NY
FOWLER MUNICIPAL HOSPITAL, Fowler, CA
FOX ARMY COMMUNITY HOSPITAL, Huntsville, AL
FRAMINGHAM UNION HOSPITAL, Framingham, MA
FRANCES MAHON DEACONESS HOSPITAL, Glasgow, MT
FRANCES P. MEMORIAL HOSPITAL, New Bedford, MA
FRANCIS A. BELL MEMORIAL HOSPITAL, Ishpeming, MI
FRANCIS SCOTT KEY MEDICAL CENTER, Baltimore, MD
FRANCISCAN MEDICAL CENTER, Rock Island, IL
FRANK CUNEO MEMORIAL HOSPITAL, Chicago, IL
FRANK R. HOWARD MEMORIAL HOSPITAL, Willits, CA
FRANKFORD HOSPITAL OF THE CITY OF PHILADELPHIA, Philadelphia, PA
FRANKLIN BOULEVARD COMMUNITY HOSPITAL, Chicago, IL
FRANKLIN COUNTY HOSPITAL, Mount Vernon, TX
FRANKLIN COUNTY MEDICAL CENTER, Preston, ID
FRANKLIN COUNTY MEMORIAL HOSPITAL, Meadville, MS
FRANKLIN COUNTY MEMORIAL HOSPITAL, Franklin, NE
FRANKLIN DELANO ROOSEVELT VETERANS ADMINISTRATION HOSPITAL, Montrose, NY
FRANKLIN FOUNDATION HOSPITAL, Franklin, LA
FRANKLIN GENERAL HOSPITAL, Hampton, IA
FRANKLIN GENERAL HOSPITAL, Valley Stream, NY
FRANKLIN HOSPITAL AND SKILLED NURSING CARE UNIT, Benton, IL
FRANKLIN MCLEAN MEMORIAL RESEARCH INSTITUTE, Chicago, IL, See University of Chicago Hospitals and Clinics
FRANKLIN MEDICAL CENTER, Greenfield, MA
FRANKLIN MEMORIAL HOSPITAL, Farmington, ME
FRANKLIN MEMORIAL HOSPITAL, Louisburg, NC
FRANKLIN MEMORIAL HOSPITAL, Rocky Mount, VA
FRANKLIN PARISH HOSPITAL, Winnsboro, LA
FRANKLIN REGIONAL HOSPITAL, Franklin, NH
FRANKLIN REGIONAL MEDICAL CENTER, Franklin, PA
FRANKLIN SQUARE HOSPITAL, Baltimore, MD
FRANKLIN-SIMPSON MEMORIAL HOSPITAL, Franklin, KY
FRAZIER REHABILITATION CENTER (Formerly Amelia Brown Frazier Rehabilitation Center), Louisville, KY
FREDERIC MUNICIPAL HOSPITAL, Frederic, WI
FREDERICK FERRIS THOMPSON HOSPITAL, Canandaigua, NY
FREDERICK MEMORIAL HOSPITAL, Frederick, MD
FREDONIA REGIONAL HOSPITAL, Fredonia, KS
FREEHOLD AREA HOSPITAL, Freehold, NJ
FREEMAN COMMUNITY HOSPITAL, Freeman, SD
FREEMAN HOSPITAL, Joplin, MO
FREEPORT HOSPITAL, Freeport, NY
FREEPORT MEMORIAL HOSPITAL, Freeport, IL
FREMONT MEDICAL CENTER, Yuba City, CA
FRENCH HOSPITAL, San Francisco, CA
FRENCH HOSPITAL MEDICAL CENTER (Formerly French Hospital), San Luis Obispo, CA
FRENCH HOSPITAL OF LOS ANGELES, Los Angeles, CA
FRESNO COMMUNITY HOSPITAL AND MEDICAL CENTER, Fresno, CA
FRESNO CONVALESCENT HOSPITAL, Fresno, CA, See Sierra Hospital
FRICK COMMUNITY HEALTH CENTER (Formerly Henry Clay Frick Community Hospital), Mount Pleasant, PA
FRIEDMAN HOSPITAL OF THE HOME FOR THE JEWISH AGED, Philadelphia, PA
FRIENDS HOSPITAL, Philadelphia, PA
FRIO HOSPITAL, Pearsall, TX
FRISBIE MEMORIAL HOSPITAL, Rochester, NH
FRITZER MEMORIAL HOSPITAL, Oxford, NE
FROEDTERT MEMORIAL LUTHERAN HOSPITAL, Milwaukee, WI
FROSTBURG COMMUNITY HOSPITAL, Frostburg, MD
FT SANDERS-SEVIER MEDICAL CENTER, Sevierville, TN
FULLER MEMORIAL HOSPITAL, South Attleboro, MA
FULLERTON MEMORIAL HOSPITAL, Fullerton, NE
FULTON COUNTY HEALTH CENTER, Wauseon, OH
FULTON COUNTY HOSPITAL, Salem, AR
FULTON COUNTY MEDICAL CENTER, McConnellsburg, PA
FULTON DIVISION, Bronx, NY, See Bronx-Lebanon Hospital Center
FULTON STATE HOSPITAL, Fulton, MO

G

G. N. WILCOX MEMORIAL HOSPITAL (Formerly G. N. Wilcox Memorial Hospital and Health Center), Lihue, HI
G. PIERCE WOOD MEMORIAL HOSPITAL, Arcadia, FL
GADSDEN MEMORIAL HOSPITAL, Quincy, FL
GAINESVILLE MEMORIAL HOSPITAL, Gainesville, TX
GALENA-STAUSS HOSPITAL, Galena, IL
GALESBURG COTTAGE HOSPITAL, Galesburg, IL
GALION COMMUNITY HOSPITAL, Galion, OH
GALLUP INDIAN MEDICAL CENTER, Gallup, NM
GARDEN CITY OSTEOPATHIC HOSPITAL, Garden City, MI
GARDEN COUNTY HOSPITAL, Oshkosh, NE
GARDEN PARK COMMUNITY HOSPITAL, Gulfport, MS, See AMI Garden Park Community Hospital
GARDEN STATE REHABILITATION HOSPITAL, Toms River, NJ
GARDEN-SULLIVAN HOSPITAL, San Francisco, CA, See Pacific Medical Center
GARFIELD COUNTY MEMORIAL HOSPITAL, Pomeroy, WA
GARFIELD MEDICAL CENTER, Monterey Park, CA
GARFIELD MEMORIAL HOSPITAL AND CLINICS, Panguitch, UT
GARLAND COMMUNITY HOSPITAL, Garland, TX
GARRARD COUNTY MEMORIAL HOSPITAL, Lancaster, KY
GARRETT COUNTY MEMORIAL HOSPITAL, Oakland, MD
GARRISON MEMORIAL HOSPITAL, Garrison, ND
GARY MEMORIAL HOSPITAL, Breaux Bridge, LA
GARZA MEMORIAL HOSPITAL, Post, TX
GASTON EPISCOPAL HOSPITAL, Dallas, TX
GASTON MEMORIAL HOSPITAL, Gastonia, NC
GATEWAY COMMUNITY HOSPITAL (Formerly Community Hospital), East St. Louis, IL
GATEWAYS HOSPITAL AND MENTAL HEALTH CENTER, Los Angeles, CA
GAYLORD COMMUNITY HOSPITAL, Gaylord, MN
GAYLORD HOSPITAL, Wallingford, CT
GEARY COMMUNITY HOSPITAL, Junction City, KS
GEAUGA HOSPITAL (Formerly Geauga Community Hospital), Chardon, OH
GEISINGER MEDICAL CENTER, Danville, PA
GEISINGER WYOMING VALLEY MEDICAL CENTER (Formerly NPW Medical Center), Wilkes-Barre, PA
GENERAL DIVISION, Charleston, WV, See Charleston Area Medical Center
GENERAL HOSPITAL, Eureka, CA
GENERAL HOSPITAL, Iraan, TX
GENERAL HOSPITAL CENTER AT PASSAIC (Formerly Passaic General Hospital), Passaic, NJ
GENERAL HOSPITAL OF EVERETT, Everett, WA
GENERAL HOSPITAL OF LAKEWOOD, Dallas, TX
GENERAL HOSPITAL OF SARANAC LAKE, Saranac Lake, NY
GENERAL JOHN J. PERSHING MEMORIAL HOSPITAL, Brookfield, MO
GENERAL LEONARD WOOD ARMY COMMUNITY HOSPITAL, Fort Leonard Wood, MO
GENERAL OUT-PATIENT CLINIC, Portland, OR, See Oregon Health Sciences University Hospital
GENESEE HOSPITAL, Rochester, NY
GENESEE MEMORIAL HOSPITAL, Flint, MI
GENESEE MEMORIAL HOSPITAL, Batavia, NY
GENEVA GENERAL HOSPITAL, Geneva, NY
GENOA COMMUNITY HOSPITAL, Genoa, NE
GENTRY COUNTY MEMORIAL HOSPITAL, Albany, MO
GEORGE A. ZELLER MENTAL HEALTH CENTER, Peoria, IL
GEORGE ADE MEMORIAL HOSPITAL, Brook, IN
GEORGE COUNTY-MOBILE INFIRMARY (Formerly George County Hospital), Lucedale, MS
GEORGE E. WEEMS MEMORIAL HOSPITAL, Apalachicola, FL
GEORGE H. LANIER MEMORIAL HOSPITAL AND NURSING HOME (Formerly Listed Under Langdale), Valley, AL
GEORGE L. MEE MEMORIAL HOSPITAL, King City, CA
GEORGE W. HUBBARD HOSPITAL OF MEHARRY MEDICAL COLLEGE, Nashville, TN
GEORGE W. TRUETT MEMORIAL HOSPITAL, Dallas, TX, See Baylor University Medical Center
GEORGE WASHINGTON UNIVERSITY HOSPITAL, Washington, DC
GEORGETOWN HOSPITAL, Georgetown, TX
GEORGETOWN MEMORIAL HOSPITAL, Georgetown, SC
GEORGETOWN UNIVERSITY MEDICAL CENTER, Washington, DC
GEORGIA BAPTIST MEDICAL CENTER, Atlanta, GA
GEORGIA MENTAL HEALTH INSTITUTE, Atlanta, GA
GEORGIA REGIONAL HOSPITAL AT ATLANTA, Decatur, GA
GEORGIA REGIONAL HOSPITAL AT AUGUSTA, Augusta, GA
GEORGIA REGIONAL HOSPITAL AT SAVANNAH, Savannah, GA
GEORGIANA COMMUNITY HOSPITAL, Georgiana, AL
GERALD CHAMPION MEMORIAL HOSPITAL, Alamogordo, NM
GERBER MEMORIAL HOSPITAL, Fremont, MI
GERMANTOWN HOSPITAL AND MEDICAL CENTER, Philadelphia, PA
GERTRUDE DUNN HICKS MEMORIAL HOSPITAL, Chicago, IL, See University of Chicago Hospitals and Clinics
GETTYSBURG HOSPITAL, Gettysburg, PA
GETTYSBURG MEMORIAL HOSPITAL, Gettysburg, SD
GHC INPATIENT CENTER TACOMA GENERAL (Formerly Inpatient Center at Tacoma General), Tacoma, WA
GIBSON COMMUNITY HOSPITAL, Gibson City, IL
GIBSON GENERAL HOSPITAL, Princeton, IN
GIBSON GENERAL HOSPITAL, Trenton, TN
GIFFORD MEMORIAL HOSPITAL, Randolph, VT
GILA COUNTY GENERAL HOSPITAL, Globe, AZ
GILA REGIONAL MEDICAL CENTER, Silver City, NM
GILES MEMORIAL HOSPITAL, Pearisburg, VA
GILL MEMORIAL EYE, EAR, NOSE AND THROAT HOSPITAL, Roanoke, VA
GILLETTE CHILDREN'S HOSPITAL, St. Paul, MN
GILLIS W. LONG HANSEN'S DISEASE CENTER (Formerly National Hansen's Disease Center), Carville, LA
GILMAN HOSPITAL, St. Marys, GA
GILMORE MEMORIAL HOSPITAL, Amory, MS
GLACIAL RIDGE HOSPITAL, Glenwood, MN
GLACIER COUNTY MEDICAL CENTER, Cut Bank, MT
GLADES GENERAL HOSPITAL, Belle Glade, FL
GLADEWATER MUNICIPAL HOSPITAL, Gladewater, TX
GLADWIN AREA HOSPITAL, Gladwin, MI
GLEN EDEN HOSPITAL, Warren, MI
GLENBEIGH ADULT HOSPITAL, Rock Creek, OH, See Glenbeigh Hospital of Rock Creek
GLENBEIGH HOSPITAL OF ROCK CREEK (Formerly Glenbeigh Adult Hospital), Rock Creek, OH
GLENBEIGH HOSPITAL-CLEVELAND, Cleveland, OH
GLENBROOK HOSPITAL, Glenview, IL, See Evanston Hospital, Evanston
GLENCOE AREA HEALTH CENTER, Glencoe, MN
GLENDALE ADVENTIST MEDICAL CENTER, Glendale, CA
GLENDALE HEIGHTS COMMUNITY HOSPITAL, Glendale Heights, IL
GLENDALE MEMORIAL HOSPITAL AND HEALTH CENTER (Formerly Memorial Hospital of Glendale), Glendale, CA
GLENDIVE COMMUNITY HOSPITAL, Glendive, MT

GLENDORA COMMUNITY HOSPITAL, Glendora, CA, See AMI Glendora Community Hospital
GLENN R. FRYE MEMORIAL HOSPITAL, Hickory, NC, See AMI Frye Regional Medical Center
GLENS FALLS HOSPITAL, Glens Falls, NY
GLENWOOD REGIONAL MEDICAL CENTER, West Monroe, LA
GLENWOOD STATE HOSPITAL SCHOOL, Glenwood, IA
GLOVER MEMORIAL HOSPITAL, Needham, MA
GLYNN-BRUNSWICK MEMORIAL HOSPITAL, Brunswick, GA
GNADEN HUETTEN MEMORIAL HOSPITAL, Lehighton, PA
GODDARD MEMORIAL HOSPITAL, Stoughton, MA
GOLDEN PLAINS COMMUNITY HOSPITAL, Borger, TX
GOLDEN TRIANGLE REGIONAL MEDICAL CENTER, Columbus, MS
GOLDEN VALLEY HEALTH CENTER, Golden Valley, MN, See Health Central, Minneapolis
GOLDEN VALLEY MEMORIAL HOSPITAL, Clinton, MO
GOLDWATER MEMORIAL HOSPITAL, New York, NY
GOLETA VALLEY COMMUNITY HOSPITAL, Santa Barbara, CA
GOLIAD COUNTY HOSPITAL, Goliad, TX
GOOD HOPE HOSPITAL, Erwin, NC
GOOD SAMARITAN COMMUNITY HEALTHCARE (Formerly Good Samaritan Hospital), Puyallup, WA
GOOD SAMARITAN HOSPITAL, West Palm Beach, FL
GOOD SAMARITAN HOSPITAL, Downers Grove, IL
GOOD SAMARITAN HOSPITAL, Mount Vernon, IL
GOOD SAMARITAN HOSPITAL, Vincennes, IN
GOOD SAMARITAN HOSPITAL, Lexington, KY
GOOD SAMARITAN HOSPITAL, Kearney, NE
GOOD SAMARITAN HOSPITAL, Suffern, NY
GOOD SAMARITAN HOSPITAL, West Islip, NY
GOOD SAMARITAN HOSPITAL, Cincinnati, OH
GOOD SAMARITAN HOSPITAL, Corvallis, OR
GOOD SAMARITAN HOSPITAL, Lebanon, PA
GOOD SAMARITAN HOSPITAL AND HEALTH CENTER, Dayton, OH
GOOD SAMARITAN HOSPITAL AND MEDICAL CENTER, Portland, OR
GOOD SAMARITAN HOSPITAL ASSOCIATION, Rugby, ND
GOOD SAMARITAN HOSPITAL OF MARYLAND, Baltimore, MD
GOOD SAMARITAN HOSPITAL OF POTTSVILLE, PENNSYLVANIA, Pottsville, PA
GOOD SAMARITAN HOSPITAL OF SANTA CLARA VALLEY, San Jose, CA
GOOD SAMARITAN MEDICAL CENTER, Phoenix, AZ
GOOD SAMARITAN MEDICAL CENTER, Milwaukee, WI
GOOD SAMARITAN MEDICAL CENTER AND REHABILITATION CENTER, Zanesville, OH
GOOD SHEPHERD COMMUNITY HOSPITAL, Hermiston, OR
GOOD SHEPHERD HOSPITAL, Barrington, IL
GOOD SHEPHERD MEDICAL CENTER, Longview, TX
GOOD SHEPHERD REHABILITATION HOSPITAL, Allentown, PA
GOODALL-WITCHER HOSPITAL, Clifton, TX
GOODING COUNTY MEMORIAL HOSPITAL, Gooding, ID
GOODLARK MEDICAL CENTER, Dickson, TN
GORDON HOSPITAL, Calhoun, GA
GORDON MEMORIAL HOSPITAL DISTRICT, Gordon, NE
GOSHEN GENERAL HOSPITAL, Goshen, IN
GOTHENBURG MEMORIAL HOSPITAL, Gothenburg, NE
GOTTLIEB MEMORIAL HOSPITAL, Melrose Park, IL
GOVE COUNTY HOSPITAL, Quinter, KS
GOWANDA PSYCHIATRIC CENTER, Helmuth, NY
GRACE COTTAGE HOSPITAL, Townshend, VT
GRACE HOSPITAL, Detroit, MI
GRACE HOSPITAL, Morganton, NC
GRACE HOSPITAL, Cleveland, OH
GRACEWOOD STATE SCHOOL AND HOSPITAL, Gracewood, GA
GRACIE SQUARE HOSPITAL, New York, NY
GRADUATE HOSPITAL, Philadelphia, PA
GRADY GENERAL HOSPITAL, Cairo, GA
GRADY MEMORIAL HOSPITAL, Atlanta, GA
GRADY MEMORIAL HOSPITAL, Delaware, OH
GRADY MEMORIAL HOSPITAL, Chickasha, OK
GRAFTON CITY HOSPITAL, Grafton, WV
GRAHAM COUNTY HOSPITAL, Hill City, KS
GRAHAM GENERAL HOSPITAL, Graham, TX
GRAHAM HOSPITAL, Canton, IL
GRANADA HILLS COMMUNITY HOSPITAL, Los Angeles, CA
GRAND VALLEY HOSPITAL, Pryor, OK
GRAND VIEW HOSPITAL, Ironwood, MI
GRAND VIEW HOSPITAL, Sellersville, PA
GRANDE RONDE HOSPITAL, La Grande, OR
GRANDVIEW HOSPITAL AND MEDICAL CENTER, Dayton, OH
GRANITE COUNTY MEMORIAL HOSPITAL AND NURSING HOME, Philipsburg, MT
GRANITE FALLS MUNICIPAL HOSPITAL AND MANOR, Granite Falls, MN
GRANT CENTER HOSPITAL, Miami, FL
GRANT COUNTY HOSPITAL, Williamstown, KY
GRANT COUNTY HOSPITAL, Elbow Lake, MN
GRANT HOSPITAL OF CHICAGO, Chicago, IL
GRANT MEDICAL CENTER (Formerly Grant Hospital), Columbus, OH
GRANT MEMORIAL HOSPITAL, Petersburg, WV
GRANVILLE C. MORTON HOSPITAL AT WADLEY INSTITUTES, Dallas, TX
GRANVILLE MEDICAL CENTER (Formerly Granville Hospital), Oxford, NC
GRAPE COMMUNITY HOSPITAL-SOUTHWEST IOWA MEDICAL CENTER (Formerly Grape Community Hospital), Hamburg, IA
GRATIOT COMMUNITY HOSPITAL, Alma, MI
GRAVETTE MEDICAL CENTER HOSPITAL, Gravette, AR
GRAY'S HOSPITAL, Batesville, AR
GRAYDON MANOR, Leesburg, VA
GRAYS HARBOR COMMUNITY HOSPITAL, Aberdeen, WA
GRAYSON COUNTY HOSPITAL, Leitchfield, KY
GREAT PLAINS REGIONAL MEDICAL CENTER, North Platte, NE
GREATER BAKERSFIELD MEMORIAL HOSPITAL, Bakersfield, CA, See Bakersfield Memorial Hospital
GREATER BALTIMORE MEDICAL CENTER, Baltimore, MD
GREATER BRIDGEPORT COMMUNITY MENTAL HEALTH CENTER, Bridgeport, CT
GREATER COMMUNITY HOSPITAL, Creston, IA
GREATER EL MONTE COMMUNITY HOSPITAL, South El Monte, CA
GREATER LAUREL BELTSVILLE HOSPITAL, Laurel, MD
GREATER SOUTHEAST COMMUNITY HOSPITAL, Washington, DC
GREELEY COUNTY HOSPITAL, Tribune, KS
GREEN HOSPITAL OF SCRIPPS CLINIC (Formerly Cecil H. and Ida M. Green Hospital of Scripps Clinic), La Jolla, CA
GREEN OAKS PSYCHIATRIC HOSPITAL, Dallas, TX
GREENBUSH COMMUNITY HOSPITAL AND CONVALESCENT AND NURSING CARE UNIT, Greenbush, MN
GREENE COUNTY GENERAL HOSPITAL, Linton, IN
GREENE COUNTY HOSPITAL, Eutaw, AL
GREENE COUNTY HOSPITAL AND EXTENDED CARE FACILITY, Leakesville, MS
GREENE COUNTY MEDICAL CENTER, Jefferson, IA
GREENE COUNTY MEMORIAL HOSPITAL, Waynesburg, PA
GREENE MEMORIAL HOSPITAL, Xenia, OH
GREENFIELD AREA MEDICAL CENTER, Greenfield, OH
GREENLAWN HOSPITAL, Atmore, AL
GREENLEAF CENTER, Fort Oglethorpe, GA
GREENLEAF CENTER (Formerly Valdosta Center), Valdosta, GA
GREENLEAF CENTER -SHAWNEE, Shawnee, OK
GREENLEAF PSYCHIATRIC HOSPITAL (Formerly Greenleaf Hospital), Bryan, TX
GREENSVILLE MEMORIAL HOSPITAL, Emporia, VA
GREENVIEW HOSPITAL, Bowling Green, KY, See HCA Greenview Hospital
GREENVILLE GENERAL HOSPITAL, Greenville, SC
GREENVILLE HOSPITAL, Jersey City, NJ
GREENVILLE HOSPITAL, Greenville, PA, See Greenville Regional Hospital
GREENVILLE MEMORIAL HOSPITAL, Greenville, SC
GREENVILLE REGIONAL HOSPITAL (Formerly Greenville Hospital), Greenville, PA
GREENWELL SPRINGS HOSPITAL, Greenwell Springs, LA
GREENWICH HOSPITAL, Greenwich, CT
GREENWOOD COUNTY HOSPITAL, Eureka, KS
GREENWOOD LEFLORE HOSPITAL, Greenwood, MS
GREGORY COMMUNITY HOSPITAL, Gregory, SD
GRENADA LAKE MEDICAL CENTER (Formerly Grenada County Hospital), Grenada, MS
GREYSTONE PARK PSYCHIATRIC HOSPITAL, Greystone Park, NJ
GRIFFIN HOSPITAL, Derby, CT
GRIGGS COUNTY HOSPITAL AND NURSING HOME, Cooperstown, ND
GRIM-SMITH HOSPITAL AND CLINIC, Kirksville, MO
GRINNELL GENERAL HOSPITAL, Grinnell, IA
GRISELL MEMORIAL HOSPITAL DISTRICT ONE, Ransom, KS
GRITMAN MEMORIAL HOSPITAL, Moscow, ID
GROSSMONT DISTRICT HOSPITAL, La Mesa, CA
GROUP HEALTH COOPERATIVE CENTRAL HOSPITAL, Seattle, WA
GROUP HEALTH EASTSIDE HOSPITAL, Redmond, WA
GROVE GENERAL HOSPITAL, Grove, OK
GROVE HILL MEMORIAL HOSPITAL, Grove Hill, AL
GROVE STREET FACILITY, Meadville, PA, See Meadville Medical Center
GROVER MANOR HOSPITAL, Revere, MA
GRUNDY COUNTY MEMORIAL HOSPITAL, Grundy Center, IA
GUADALUPE MEDICAL CENTER, Carlsbad, NM
GUADALUPE VALLEY HOSPITAL, Seguin, TX
GUAM MEMORIAL HOSPITAL AUTHORITY, Tamuning, Guam
GUERNSEY MEMORIAL HOSPITAL, Cambridge, OH
GUEYDAN MEMORIAL HOSPITAL, Gueydan, LA
GULF BREEZE HOSPITAL, Gulf Breeze, FL
GULF COAST COMMUNITY HOSPITAL, Panama City, FL, See HCA Gulf Coast Hospital
GULF COAST COMMUNITY HOSPITAL, Biloxi, MS
GULF COAST HOSPITAL, Baytown, TX
GULF COAST MEDICAL CENTER, Wharton, TX
GULF OAKS HOSPITAL AND CLINIC, Biloxi, MS, See Gulf Coast Community Hospital
GULF PINES HOSPITAL, Port St. Joe, FL
GUNDRY HOSPITAL, Baltimore, MD
GUNNISON VALLEY HOSPITAL (Formerly Gunnison County Public Hospital), Gunnison, CO
GUNNISON VALLEY HOSPITAL, Gunnison, UT
GUNTERSVILLE HOSPITAL, Guntersville, AL
GURDON MUNICIPAL HOSPITAL, Gurdon, AR
GUTHRIE COUNTY HOSPITAL, Guthrie Center, IA
GUTHRIE MEMORIAL HOSPITAL, Huntington, WV
GUTTENBERG MUNICIPAL HOSPITAL, Guttenberg, IA
GUYAN VALLEY HOSPITAL, Logan, WV
GWINNETT HOSPITAL SYSTEM, Lawrenceville, GA
GWINNETT MEDICAL CENTER, Lawrenceville, GA, See Gwinnett Hospital Systems

H

H. B. MAGRUDER MEMORIAL HOSPITAL, Port Clinton, OH
H. C. SOLOMON MENTAL HEALTH CENTER, Lowell, MA
H. C. WATKINS MEMORIAL HOSPITAL, Quitman, MS
H. DOUGLAS SINGER MENTAL HEALTH AND DEVELOPMENTAL CENTER, Rockford, IL
HABERSHAM COUNTY MEDICAL CENTER, Demorest, GA
HACKENSACK MEDICAL CENTER, Hackensack, NJ
HACKETTSTOWN COMMUNITY HOSPITAL, Hackettstown, NJ
HACKLEY HOSPITAL, Muskegon, MI
HADLEY MEMORIAL HOSPITAL, Washington, DC
HADLEY REGIONAL MEDICAL CENTER, Hays, KS
HAHNEMANN HOSPITAL, Boston, MA
HAHNEMANN UNIVERSITY HOSPITAL, Philadelphia, PA
HALE COUNTY HOSPITAL, Greensboro, AL
HALIFAX HOSPITAL MEDICAL CENTER, Daytona Beach, FL
HALIFAX MEMORIAL HOSPITAL, Roanoke Rapids, NC
HALIFAX-SOUTH BOSTON COMMUNITY HOSPITAL, South Boston, VA
HALL COUNTY HOSPITAL, Memphis, TX
HALL-BENNETT MEMORIAL HOSPITAL, Big Spring, TX
HALL-BROOKE HOSPITAL, A DIVISION OF HALL-BROOKE FOUNDATION, Westport, CT
HALSTEAD HOSPITAL, Halstead, KS
HAMILTON AVENUE HOSPITAL, Monticello, NY
HAMILTON CENTER, Terre Haute, IN
HAMILTON COUNTY HOSPITAL, Syracuse, KS
HAMILTON COUNTY MEMORIAL HOSPITAL, Jasper, FL
HAMILTON COUNTY PUBLIC HOSPITAL, Webster City, IA
HAMILTON HOSPITAL, Hamilton, NJ
HAMILTON HOSPITAL, Olney, TX
HAMILTON MEDICAL CENTER, Dalton, GA
HAMILTON MEDICAL CENTER HOSPITAL, Lafayette, LA
HAMILTON MEMORIAL HOSPITAL, McLeansboro, IL
HAMLET HOSPITAL, Hamlet, NC
HAMLIN MEMORIAL HOSPITAL, Hamlin, TX
HAMMOND-HENRY HOSPITAL, Geneseo, IL
HAMOT MEDICAL CENTER, Erie, PA
HAMPSHIRE COUNTY LONG TERM CARE FACILITY, Leeds, MA
HAMPSHIRE MEMORIAL HOSPITAL, Romney, WV
HAMPTON GENERAL HOSPITAL, Varnville, SC
HAMPTON GENERAL HOSPITAL, Hampton, VA
HANA MEDICAL CENTER, Hana, HI, See Maui Memorial Hospital, Wailuku
HANCOCK COUNTY HOSPITAL, Sneedville, TN
HANCOCK COUNTY MEMORIAL HOSPITAL, Britt, IA
HANCOCK MEDICAL CENTER (Formerly Hancock General Hospital), Bay St. Louis, MS

HANCOCK MEMORIAL HOSPITAL, Sparta, GA
HANCOCK MEMORIAL HOSPITAL, Greenfield, IN
HAND COUNTY MEMORIAL HOSPITAL, Miller, SD
HANFORD COMMUNITY HOSPITAL, Hanford, CA
HANNA HOUSE, Cleveland, OH, See University Hospitals of Cleveland
HANNA PAVILION, Cleveland, OH, See University Hospitals of Cleveland
HANOVER GENERAL HOSPITAL, Hanover, PA
HANS P. PETERSON MEMORIAL HOSPITAL, Philip, SD
HANSFORD HOSPITAL, Spearman, TX
HARBOR BEACH COMMUNITY HOSPITAL, Harbor Beach, MI
HARBOR VIEW (Formerly Dodge Hospital), Miami, FL
HARBOR VIEW MEDICAL CENTER, San Diego, CA
HARBOR VIEW MERCY HOSPITAL, Fort Smith, AR
HARBORSIDE HOSPITAL, St. Petersburg, FL
HARBORVIEW MEDICAL CENTER, Seattle, WA
HARBOUR SHORES HOSPITAL OF LAWNWOOD, Fort Pierce, FL
HARDEE MEMORIAL HOSPITAL, Wauchula, FL
HARDIN COUNTY GENERAL HOSPITAL, Rosiclare, IL
HARDIN COUNTY GENERAL HOSPITAL, Savannah, TN
HARDIN MEMORIAL HOSPITAL, Elizabethtown, KY
HARDIN MEMORIAL HOSPITAL, Kenton, OH
HARDING HOSPITAL, Worthington, OH
HARDTNER MEDICAL CENTER, Olla, LA
HARDY WILSON MEMORIAL HOSPITAL, Hazelhurst, MS
HARFORD MEMORIAL HOSPITAL, Havre De Grace, MD
HARLAN APPALACHIAN REGIONAL HOSPITAL, Harlan, KY
HARLAN COUNTY HOSPITAL, Alma, NE
HARLEM HOSPITAL CENTER, New York, NY
HARLEM VALLEY PSYCHIATRIC CENTER, Wingdale, NY
HARMARVILLE REHABILITATION CENTER, Pittsburgh, PA
HARMON MEMORIAL HOSPITAL, Hollis, OK
HARMONY COMMUNITY HOSPITAL, Harmony, MN
HARMS MEMORIAL HOSPITAL, American Falls, ID
HARNEY COUNTY HOSPITAL, Burns, OR
HAROLD D. CHOPE COMMUNITY HOSPITAL, San Mateo, CA
HARPER COUNTY COMMUNITY HOSPITAL, Buffalo, OK
HARPER HOSPITAL, Detroit, MI
HARRIMAN CITY HOSPITAL, Harriman, TN
HARRINGTON MEMORIAL HOSPITAL, Southbridge, MA
HARRIS COUNTY HOSPITAL DISTRICT, Houston, TX
HARRIS COUNTY PSYCHIATRIC CENTER, Houston, TX
HARRIS HOSPITAL (Formerly Harris Hospital and Clinic), Newport, AR
HARRIS HOSPITAL AND CLINIC, Newport, AR, See Harris Hospital
HARRIS METHODIST -DUBLIN (Formerly Dublin Medical Center), Dublin, TX
HARRIS METHODIST -FORT WORTH (Formerly Harris Hospital-Methodist), Fort Worth, TX
HARRIS METHODIST -HAMILTON (Formerly Hamilton General Hospital), Hamilton, TX
HARRIS METHODIST -MEXIA (Formerly General Mexia Memorial Hospital), Mexia, TX
HARRIS METHODIST -STEPHENVILLE (Formerly Stephenville General Hospital), Stephenville, TX
HARRIS METHODIST NORTHWEST (Formerly Harris Hospital-Eagle Mountain Area Suburban Hospital), Azle, TX
HARRIS METHODIST-HURST-EULESS-BEDFORD (Formerly Harris Hospital-Hurst-Euless-Bedford), Bedford, TX
HARRISBURG HOSPITAL, Harrisburg, PA
HARRISBURG MEDICAL CENTER, Harrisburg, IL
HARRISBURG STATE HOSPITAL, Harrisburg, PA
HARRISON COMMUNITY HOSPITAL, Mount Clemens, MI
HARRISON COMMUNITY HOSPITAL, Cadiz, OH
HARRISON COUNTY HOSPITAL, Corydon, IN
HARRISON MEMORIAL HOSPITAL, Cynthiana, KY
HARRISON MEMORIAL HOSPITAL, Bremerton, WA
HARRY S. TRUMAN MEMORIAL VETERANS HOSPITAL, Columbia, MO
HART CLINIC HOSPITAL, Gladewater, TX
HART COUNTY HOSPITAL, Hartwell, GA
HARTFORD HOSPITAL, Hartford, CT
HARTFORD MEMORIAL HOSPITAL, Hartford, WI
HARTGROVE HOSPITAL, Chicago, IL
HARTSELLE MEDICAL CENTER, Hartselle, AL
HARTSVILLE GENERAL HOSPITAL, Hartsville, TN
HARVARD COMMUNITY MEMORIAL HOSPITAL, Harvard, IL
HARVEY E. RINEHART MEMORIAL HOSPITAL, Wheeler, OR
HASKELL COUNTY MEMORIAL HOSPITAL, Stigler, OK
HASKELL MEMORIAL HOSPITAL, Haskell, TX
HASTINGS REGIONAL CENTER, Hastings, NE
HATO REY COMMUNITY HOSPITAL (Formerly Hospital Nuestra Senora De Guadalupe), San Juan, P.R.
HATO REY PSYCHIATRIC HOSPITAL, Bayamon, P.R.
HAVASU REGIONAL HOSPITAL, Lake Havasu City, AZ
HAVERFORD COMMUNITY HOSPITAL, Havertown, PA
HAVERFORD STATE HOSPITAL, Haverford, PA
HAVERHILL MUNICIPAL-HALE HOSPITAL, Haverhill, MA
HAWAII STATE HOSPITAL, Kaneohe, HI
HAWARDEN COMMUNITY HOSPITAL, Hawarden, IA
HAWKINS COUNTY MEMORIAL HOSPITAL, Rogersville, TN
HAWLEY U. S. ARMY COMMUNITY HOSPITAL, Indianapolis, IN
HAWTHORN CENTER, Northville, MI
HAWTHORNE HOSPITAL (Formerly Memorial Hospital of Hawthorne), Hawthorne, CA
HAXTUN HOSPITAL DISTRICT, Haxtun, CO
HAYES AVENUE FACILITY, Sandusky, OH, See Firelands Community Hospital
HAYES-GREEN-BEACH MEMORIAL HOSPITAL, Charlotte, MI
HAYS MEMORIAL HOSPITAL, San Marcos, TX
HAYWARD AREA MEMORIAL HOSPITAL, Hayward, WI
HAYWARD HOSPITAL (Formerly Hayward Vesper Hospital), Hayward, CA
HAYWARD VESPER HOSPITAL, Hayward, CA, See Hayward Hospital
HAYWOOD COUNTY HOSPITAL, Clyde, NC
HAYWOOD PARK GENERAL HOSPITAL, Brownsville, TN
HAZEL HAWKINS CONVALESCENT HOSPITAL, Hollister, CA, See San Benito Hospital District
HAZEL HAWKINS MEMORIAL HOSPITAL, Hollister, CA, See San Benito Hospital District
HAZEN MEMORIAL HOSPITAL, Hazen, ND
HAZLETON GENERAL HOSPITAL (Formerly Hazleton State General Hospital), Hazleton, PA
HAZLETON-ST. JOSEPH MEDICAL CENTER, Hazleton, PA
HCA AIKEN REGIONAL MEDICAL CENTER (Formerly Aiken Community Hospital), Aiken, SC
HCA ANDALUSIA HOSPITAL (Formerly Community Hospital of Andalusia), Andalusia, AL
HCA BAYONET POINT-HUDSON REGIONAL MEDICAL CENTER (Formerly Bayonet Point-Hudson Regional Medical Center), Hudson, FL
HCA BOURBON GENERAL HOSPITAL (Formerly Bourbon General Hospital), Paris, KY
HCA BROTMAN MEDICAL CENTER (Formerly Brotman Medical Center), Culver City, CA
HCA COLISEUM MEDICAL CENTERS (Formerly Coliseum Park Hospital), Macon, GA
HCA COLISEUM PSYCHIATRIC HOSPITAL (Formerly Coliseum Psychiatric Hospital), Macon, GA
HCA CORONADO HOSPITAL (Formerly Coronado Community Hospital), Pampa, TX
HCA CROCKETT HOSPITAL (Formerly Crockett General Hospital), Lawrenceburg, TN
HCA DEER PARK HOSPITAL (Formerly Deer Park Hospital), Deer Park, TX
HCA DOCTORS HOSPITAL (Formerly Doctors Hospital of Lake Worth), Lake Worth, FL
HCA DOCTORS HOSPITAL (Formerly Doctors Hospital), Conroe, TX
HCA DONELSON HOSPITAL (Formerly Donelson Hospital), Nashville, TN
HCA EAST POINTE HOSPITAL (Formerly East Pointe Hospital), Lehigh Acres, FL
HCA EDGEFIELD HOSPITAL (Formerly Edgefield Hospital), Nashville, TN
HCA EDWARD WHITE HOSPITAL (Formerly Edward H. White Ii Memorial Hospital), St. Petersburg, FL
HCA GRAND STRAND GENERAL HOSPITAL (Formerly Grand Strand General Hospital), Myrtle Beach, SC
HCA GRANT CENTER HOSPITAL OF NORTH FLORIDA (Formerly Grant Center Hospital -Ocala), Citra, FL
HCA GREENVIEW HOSPITAL (Formerly Greenview Hospital), Bowling Green, KY
HCA GULF COAST HOSPITAL (Formerly Gulf Coast Community Hospital), Panama City, FL
HCA GULF PINES HOSPITAL, Houston, TX
HCA HENDERSONVILLE HOSPITAL (Formerly Hendersonville Hospital), Hendersonville, TN
HCA HERITAGE HOSPITAL, Tarboro, NC
HCA HUNTINGTON HOSPITAL (Formerly Huntington Hospital), Huntington, WV
HCA LARGO MEDICAL CENTER HOSPITAL (Formerly Largo Medical Center Hospital), Largo, FL
HCA LOGAN MEMORIAL HOSPITAL (Formerly Logan County Hospital), Russellville, KY
HCA LONGVIEW REGIONAL HOSPITAL (Formerly Longview Regional Hospital), Longview, TX
HCA MANSFIELD HOSPITAL (Formerly Mansfield Community Hospital), Mansfield, TX
HCA MEDICAL CENTER OF PLANO (Formerly Plano General Hospital), Plano, TX
HCA MEDICAL CENTER OF PORT ST. LUCIE (Formerly Port St. Lucie Hospital), Port St. Lucie, FL
HCA MIDWAY PARK MEDICAL CENTER (Formerly Midway Park General Hospital), Lancaster, TX
HCA NEW PORT RICHEY HOSPITAL (Formerly Community Hospital), New Port Richey, FL
HCA NORTH BEACH HOSPITAL (Formerly North Beach Community Hospital), Fort Lauderdale, FL
HCA NORTH CLARK COMMUNITY HOSPITAL (Formerly North Clark Community Hospital), Charlestown, IN
HCA NORTH FLORIDA REGIONAL MEDICAL CENTER (Formerly North Florida Regional Hospital), Gainesville, FL
HCA NORTH OKALOOSA MEDICAL CENTER (Formerly Crestview Community Hospital), Crestview, FL
HCA NORTHEAST COMMUNITY HOSPITAL (Formerly Northeast Community Hospital), Bedford, TX
HCA NORTHERN VIRGINIA DOCTORS HOSPITAL (Formerly Northern Virginia Doctors Hospital), Arlington, VA
HCA NORTHWEST REGIONAL HOSPITAL (Formerly Northwest Regional Hospital), Margate, FL
HCA OAK HILL HOSPITAL (Formerly Oak Hill Community Hospital), Spring Hill, FL
HCA PALMYRA MEDICAL CENTERS (Formerly Palmyra Medical Centers), Albany, GA
HCA PARK VIEW MEDICAL CENTER (Formerly Park View Medical Center), Nashville, TN
HCA PARK WEST MEDICAL CENTERS (Formerly Park West Hospital), Knoxville, TN
HCA PARKWAY MEDICAL CENTER (Formerly Parkway Regional Hospital), Lithia Springs, GA
HCA PARTHENON PAVILION (Formerly Parthenon Pavilion), Nashville, TN
HCA PASADENA BAYSHORE MEDICAL CENTER (Formerly Pasadena Bayshore Medical Center), Pasadena, TX
HCA RAULERSON HOSPITAL (Formerly H. H. Raulerson Jr. Memorial Hospital), Okeechobee, FL
HCA RED RIVER HOSPITAL (Formerly Red River Hospital), Wichita Falls, TX
HCA REGIONAL HOSPITAL OF JACKSON (Formerly Regional Hospital of Jackson), Jackson, TN
HCA REGIONAL HOSPITAL-LIVINGSTON (Formerly Livingston Community Hospital), Livingston, TN
HCA RIVEREDGE HOSPITAL (Formerly Riveredge Hospital), Forest Park, IL
HCA RIVERTON HOSPITAL (Formerly Riverton Memorial Hospital), Riverton, WY
HCA SANTA ROSA MEDICAL CENTER (Formerly Santa Rosa Hospital), Milton, FL
HCA SHOAL CREEK HOSPITAL (Formerly Shoal Creek Hospital), Austin, TX
HCA SMYRNA HOSPITAL, Smyrna, TN
HCA SOUTH ARLINGTON MEDICAL CENTER (Formerly Arlington Community Hospital), Arlington, TX
HCA SOUTH AUSTIN MEDICAL CENTER (Formerly South Austin Community Hospital), Austin, TX
HCA SOUTHERN HILLS MEDICAL CENTER (Formerly Southern Hills Medical Center), Nashville, TN
HCA SPRING VIEW HOSPITAL (Formerly Spring View Hospital), Lebanon, KY
HCA STONES RIVER HOSPITAL (Formerly Stones River Hospital), Woodbury, TN
HCA SUN CITY HOSPITAL (Formerly Sun City Regional Medical Center), Sun City Center, FL
HCA SUN TOWERS HOSPITAL (Formerly Sun Towers Hospital), El Paso, TX
HCA SYCAMORE SHOALS HOSPITAL (Formerly Carter County Memorial Hospital), Elizabethton, TN
HCA VALLEY REGIONAL MEDICAL CENTER (Formerly Valley Community Hospital), Brownsville, TX
HCA VISTA HILLS MEDICAL CENTER (Formerly Vista Hills Medical Center), El Paso, TX
HCA WEST PACES FERRY HOSPITAL (Formerly West Paces Ferry Hospital), Atlanta, GA
HCA WEST SIDE HOSPITAL (Formerly West Side Hospital), Nashville, TN
HCA WOODLAND HEIGHTS MEDICAL CENTER (Formerly Woodland Heights General Hospital), Lufkin, TX
HCA WYSONG MEDICAL CENTER (Formerly Wysong Memorial Hospital), McKinney, TX
HEALDTON MUNICIPAL HOSPITAL, Healdton, OK
HEALTH CENTRAL METROPOLITAN HOSPITALS, Minneapolis, MN
HEALTH CENTRAL OF BUFFALO (Formerly Buffalo Memorial Hospital), Buffalo, MN
HEALTH CENTRAL OF OWATONNA (Formerly Owatonna City Hospital), Owatonna, MN
HEALTH HILL HOSPITAL FOR CHILDREN, Cleveland, OH
HEALTHCARE MEDICAL CENTER OF TUSTIN, Tustin, CA

HEALTHSOUTH (Formerly Humble Rehabilitation Hospital), Humble, TX
HEALTHWIN HOSPITAL, South Bend, IN
HEART OF FLORIDA HOSPITAL, Haines City, FL
HEART OF TEXAS MEMORIAL HOSPITAL, Brady, TX
HEARTLAND HOSPITAL EAST (Formerly St. Joseph Hospital), St. Joseph, MO
HEARTLAND HOSPITAL WEST (Formerly Methodist Medical Center), St. Joseph, MO
HEATON HOUSE, Montpelier, VT, See Central Vermont Medical Center, Berlin
HEBREW HOME AND HOSPITAL, Hartford, CT
HEBREW HOSPITAL FOR CHRONIC SICK, Bronx, NY
HEBREW REHABILITATION CENTER FOR AGED, Boston, MA
HEDRICK MEDICAL CENTER, Chillicothe, MO
HEGG MEMORIAL HEALTH CENTER (Formerly Hegg Memorial Hospital), Rock Valley, IA
HEIGHTS GENERAL HOSPITAL, Albuquerque, NM
HEIGHTS HOSPITAL, Houston, TX, See AMI Heights Hospital
HEIGHTS PSYCHIATRIC HOSPITAL, Albuquerque, NM
HELEN HAYES HOSPITAL, West Haverstraw, NY
HELEN KELLER MEMORIAL HOSPITAL, Sheffield, AL
HELEN NEWBERRY JOY HOSPITAL, Newberry, MI
HELEN POWELL CONVALESCENT CENTER, Des Moines, IA, See Iowa Methodist Medical Center
HELENA HOSPITAL, Helena, AR
HELENE FULD MEDICAL CENTER, Trenton, NJ
HEMET VALLEY HOSPITAL DISTRICT, Hemet, CA
HEMPHILL COUNTY HOSPITAL, Canadian, TX
HEMPSTEAD GENERAL HOSPITAL MEDICAL CENTER, Hempstead, NY
HENDERSON COMMUNITY HOSPITAL, Henderson, NE
HENDERSON MEMORIAL HOSPITAL, Henderson, TX
HENDRICK MEDICAL CENTER, Abilene, TX
HENDRICKS COMMUNITY HOSPITAL, Hendricks, MN
HENDRICKS COUNTY HOSPITAL, Danville, IN
HENDRY GENERAL HOSPITAL, Clewiston, FL
HENNEPIN COUNTY MEDICAL CENTER, Minneapolis, MN
HENRICO DOCTOR'S HOSPITAL, Richmond, VA
HENRIETTA D. GOODALL HOSPITAL, Sanford, ME
HENRIETTA EGLESTON HOSPITAL FOR CHILDREN, Atlanta, GA
HENRY AND LUCY MOSES DIVISION AND LOEB CENTER SKILLED NURSING FACILITY, Bronx, NY, See Montefiore Medical Center
HENRY COUNTY HEALTH CENTER, Mount Pleasant, IA
HENRY COUNTY HOSPITAL, Napoleon, OH
HENRY COUNTY HOSPITAL AND NURSING HOME, Abbeville, AL
HENRY COUNTY MEDICAL CENTER (Formerly Henry County General Hospital), Paris, TN
HENRY COUNTY MEMORIAL HOSPITAL, New Castle, IN
HENRY D. ALTOBELLO CHILDREN AND YOUTH CENTER, Meriden, CT
HENRY FORD HOSPITAL, Detroit, MI
HENRY GENERAL HOSPITAL, Stockbridge, GA
HENRY HEYWOOD MEMORIAL HOSPITAL, Gardner, MA
HENRY MAYO NEWHALL MEMORIAL HOSPITAL, Valencia, CA
HENRYETTA MEDICAL CENTER, Henryetta, OK
HERINGTON MUNICIPAL HOSPITAL, Herington, KS
HERITAGE HOSPITAL, Muskegon Heights, MI
HERITAGE HOSPITAL, Taylor, MI
HERMANN AREA DISTRICT HOSPITAL, Hermann, MO
HERMANN HOSPITAL, Houston, TX
HERON LAKE MUNICIPAL HOSPITAL, Heron Lake, MN
HERRICK HOSPITAL AND HEALTH CENTER, Berkeley, CA
HERRICK MEMORIAL HOSPITAL, Tecumseh, MI
HERRIN HOSPITAL, Herrin, IL
HESS MEMORIAL HOSPITAL, Mauston, WI
HI-DESERT MEDICAL CENTER, Joshua Tree, CA
HI-PLAINS HEALTH CENTER (Formerly Kit Carson County Memorial Hospital), Burlington, CO
HI-PLAINS HOSPITAL, Hale Center, TX
HIALEAH HOSPITAL, Hialeah, FL
HIAWATHA COMMUNITY HOSPITAL, Hiawatha, KS
HICKMAN COUNTY HEALTH SERVICES (Formerly Hickman County Hospital and Nursing Home), Centerville, TN
HICKORY MEMORIAL HOSPITAL, Hickory, NC
HICO CITY HOSPITAL, Hico, TX
HIGGINS GENERAL HOSPITAL, Bremen, GA
HIGH PLAINS BAPTIST HOSPITAL, Amarillo, TX
HIGH POINT HOSPITAL, Port Chester, NY
HIGH POINT REGIONAL HOSPITAL (Formerly High Point Memorial Hospital), High Point, NC
HIGHLAND CENTER HOSPITAL, Denver, CO
HIGHLAND DISTRICT HOSPITAL, Hillsboro, OH
HIGHLAND GENERAL HOSPITAL, Oakland, CA
HIGHLAND HOSPITAL, Belvidere, IL
HIGHLAND HOSPITAL, Shreveport, LA
HIGHLAND HOSPITAL, Asheville, NC
HIGHLAND HOSPITAL, Portland, TN
HIGHLAND HOSPITAL, Lubbock, TX
HIGHLAND HOSPITAL, Charleston, WV
HIGHLAND HOSPITAL OF ROCHESTER, Rochester, NY
HIGHLAND PARK HOSPITAL (Formerly Highland Park General Hospital), Miami, FL
HIGHLAND PARK HOSPITAL, Highland Park, IL
HIGHLAND PARK HOSPITAL, Covington, LA, See AMI Highland Park Hospital
HIGHLANDS HOSPITAL AND HEALTH CENTER (Formerly Connellsville State General Hospital), Connellsville, PA
HIGHLANDS REGIONAL MEDICAL CENTER (Formerly Highlands General Hospital), Sebring, FL
HIGHLANDS REGIONAL MEDICAL CENTER, Prestonsburg, KY
HIGHLANDS-CASHIERS HOSPITAL, Highlands, NC
HIGHLINE COMMUNITY HOSPITAL, Seattle, WA
HIGHSMITH-RAINEY MEMORIAL HOSPITAL, Fayetteville, NC
HILL COUNTRY MEMORIAL HOSPITAL, Fredericksburg, TX
HILL CREST HOSPITAL, Birmingham, AL, See HSA Hill Crest Sunrise Hospital
HILL REGIONAL HOSPITAL (Formerly Grant-Buie Hospital), Hillsboro, TX
HILLCREST BAPTIST MEDICAL CENTER, Waco, TX
HILLCREST HEALTH CENTER (Formerly Hillcrest Osteopathic Hospital), Oklahoma City, OK
HILLCREST HOSPITAL, Pittsfield, MA
HILLCREST HOSPITAL, Calhoun City, MS
HILLCREST HOSPITAL, Mayfield Heights, OH
HILLCREST HOSPITAL, Simpsonville, SC
HILLCREST MEDICAL CENTER, Tulsa, OK
HILLS AND DALES GENERAL HOSPITAL, Cass City, MI
HILLSBORO HOSPITAL, Hillsboro, IL
HILLSBOROUGH COUNTY HOSPITAL, Tampa, FL
HILLSDALE COMMUNITY HEALTH CENTER, Hillsdale, MI
HILLSIDE DIVISION, Glen Oaks, NY, See Long Island Jewish-Hillside Medical Center
HILLSIDE HOSPITAL, San Diego, CA
HILLSIDE HOSPITAL, Warren, OH
HILLSIDE HOSPITAL, Pulaski, TN
HILLSIDE UNIT, Beaver Dam, WI, See Beaver Dam Community Hospitals
HILO HOSPITAL, Hilo, HI
HILTON HEAD HOSPITAL, Hilton Head Island, SC
HINDS GENERAL HOSPITAL, Jackson, MS
HINSDALE HOSPITAL, Hinsdale, IL
HISSOM MEMORIAL CENTER, Sand Springs, OK
HOAG MEMORIAL HOSPITAL PRESBYTERIAN, Newport Beach, CA
HOCKING VALLEY COMMUNITY HOSPITAL, Logan, OH
HODGEMAN COUNTY HEALTH CENTER, Jetmore, KS
HOISINGTON LUTHERAN HOSPITAL, Hoisington, KS
HOLDEN HOSPITAL, Holden, MA
HOLDEN HOSPITAL, Holden, WV
HOLDENVILLE GENERAL HOSPITAL, Holdenville, OK
HOLIDAY DIVISION, Orlando, FL, See Orlando Regional Medical Center
HOLLADAY PARK MEDICAL CENTER (Formerly Holladay Park Hospital), Portland, OR
HOLLAND COMMUNITY HOSPITAL, Holland, MI
HOLLY HILL HOSPITAL, Raleigh, NC
HOLLYWOOD COMMUNITY HOSPITAL, Los Angeles, CA
HOLLYWOOD MEDICAL CENTER, Hollywood, FL
HOLLYWOOD PAVILION, Hollywood, FL
HOLLYWOOD PRESBYTERIAN MEDICAL CENTER, Los Angeles, CA
HOLMES REGIONAL MEDICAL CENTER, Melbourne, FL
HOLSTON VALLEY HOSPITAL AND MEDICAL CENTER, Kingsport, TN
HOLTON CITY HOSPITAL, Holton, KS
HOLY CROSS HOSPITAL, Los Angeles, CA
HOLY CROSS HOSPITAL, Fort Lauderdale, FL
HOLY CROSS HOSPITAL, Chicago, IL
HOLY CROSS HOSPITAL, Detroit, MI
HOLY CROSS HOSPITAL, Taos, NM
HOLY CROSS HOSPITAL, Austin, TX
HOLY CROSS HOSPITAL, Salt Lake City, UT
HOLY CROSS HOSPITAL, Merrill, WI
HOLY CROSS HOSPITAL AND HEALTH CENTER, Nogales, AZ
HOLY CROSS HOSPITAL OF SILVER SPRING, Silver Spring, MD
HOLY CROSS PARKVIEW HOSPITAL, Plymouth, IN
HOLY FAMILY HOSPITAL, Des Plaines, IL
HOLY FAMILY HOSPITAL, Estherville, IA
HOLY FAMILY HOSPITAL, Spokane, WA
HOLY FAMILY HOSPITAL, New Richmond, WI
HOLY FAMILY MEDICAL CENTER (Formerly Holy Family Hospital), Manitowoc, WI
HOLY INFANT HOSPITAL, Hoven, SD
HOLY NAME HOSPITAL, Teaneck, NJ
HOLY NAME OF JESUS MEDICAL CENTER (Formerly Holy Name of Jesus Hospital), Gadsden, AL
HOLY REDEEMER HOSPITAL AND MEDICAL CENTER, Meadowbrook, PA
HOLY ROSARY HOSPITAL, Miles City, MT
HOLY ROSARY HOSPITAL, Ontario, OR
HOLY SPIRIT HOSPITAL, Camp Hill, PA
HOLY TRINITY HOSPITAL, Graceville, MN
HOLYOKE HOSPITAL, Holyoke, MA
HOLZER MEDICAL CENTER, Gallipolis, OH
HOME FOR DESTITUTE CRIPPLED CHILDREN, Chicago, IL, See University of Chicago Hospitals and Clinics
HOMER D. COBB MEMORIAL HOSPITAL, Phenix City, AL
HOMER MEMORIAL HOSPITAL, Homer, LA
HOMESTEAD CENTER, Homestead, PA, See South Hills Health Systems, Pittsburgh
HOMINY CITY HOSPITAL, Hominy, OK
HONOKAA HOSPITAL, Honokaa, HI
HOOD GENERAL HOSPITAL, Granbury, TX
HOOD MEMORIAL HOSPITAL, Amite, LA
HOOD RIVER MEMORIAL HOSPITAL, Hood River, OR
HOOPESTON REGIONAL HOSPITAL (Formerly Hoopeston Community Memorial Hospital), Hoopeston, IL
HOOTS MEMORIAL HOSPITAL, Yadkinville, NC
HOPE HOSPITAL, Lockhart, SC
HOPEDALE HOSPITAL, Hopedale, IL
HOPKINS COUNTY MEMORIAL HOSPITAL, Sulphur Springs, TX
HORIZON HOSPITAL, Pomona, CA, See CPC Horizon Hospital
HORIZON HOSPITAL (Formerly Horizon Recovery Hospital), Denver, CO
HORIZON HOSPITAL, Clearwater, FL
HORIZON HOSPITAL (Formerly Raleigh Hills Hospital), Dallas, TX
HORIZON HOSPITAL, Houston, TX
HORIZON HOSPITAL (Formerly Raleigh Hills Hospital), San Antonio, TX
HORIZON RECOVERY CENTER, Anchorage, AK
HORIZON RECOVERY CENTER, Portland, OR
HORN MEMORIAL HOSPITAL, Ida Grove, IA
HORSHAM CLINIC, Ambler, PA
HORTON COMMUNITY HOSPITAL, Horton, KS
HORTON MEMORIAL HOSPITAL, Middletown, NY
HOSPICE OF NORTHERN VIRGINIA, Arlington, VA
HOSPITAL CENTER AT ORANGE, Orange, NJ
HOSPITAL DE AREA DE CAYEY, Cayey, P.R.
HOSPITAL DE AREA DR. VICTOR R. NUNEZ, Humacao, P.R.
HOSPITAL DE DAMAS, Ponce, P.R.
HOSPITAL DE DIEGO, San Juan, P.R.
HOSPITAL DE LA CONCEPCION, San German, P.R.
HOSPITAL DELAWARE MAESTRO, San Juan, P.R.
HOSPITAL DELAWARE PUEBLO, Los Angeles, CA
HOSPITAL DISTRICT NUMBER FIVE OF HARPER COUNTY, Harper, KS
HOSPITAL DISTRICT NUMBER ONE OF RICE COUNTY, Lyons, KS
HOSPITAL DISTRICT NUMBER SIX OF HARPER COUNTY (Formerly Anthony Hospital and Clinic), Anthony, KS
HOSPITAL DISTRICT ONE OF SUMNER COUNTY, Caldwell, KS
HOSPITAL DR. DOMINGUEZ, Humacao, P.R.
HOSPITAL DR. SUSONI, Arecibo, P.R.
HOSPITAL DRES HNOS RAMOS YORDAN, Rio Piedras, P.R.
HOSPITAL EL BUEN PASTOR, Arecibo, P.R.
HOSPITAL FOR JOINT DISEASES ORTHOPAEDIC INSTITUTE, New York, NY
HOSPITAL FOR SICK CHILDREN, Washington, DC
HOSPITAL FOR SPECIAL SURGERY, New York, NY
HOSPITAL HERMANOS MELENDEZ, Bayamon, P.R.
HOSPITAL IN THE PINES, Lone Star, TX
HOSPITAL MATILDE BRENES, Bayamon, P.R.
HOSPITAL MIMIYA, San Juan, P.R.
HOSPITAL NUESTRA SENORA DE GUADALUPE, San Juan, P.R., See Hato Rey Community Hospital
HOSPITAL OF ENGLEWOOD, Chicago, IL
HOSPITAL OF PHILADELPHIA COLLEGE OF OSTEOPATHIC MEDICINE, Philadelphia, PA
HOSPITAL OF SAINT RAPHAEL, New Haven, CT
HOSPITAL OF THE CALIFORNIA INSTITUTION FOR MEN, Chino, CA
HOSPITAL OF THE GOOD SAMARITAN, Los Angeles, CA
HOSPITAL OF THE MEDICAL COLLEGE OF PENNSYLVANIA, Philadelphia, PA
HOSPITAL OF THE UNIVERSITY OF PENNSYLVANIA, Philadelphia, PA
HOSPITAL ONCOLOGICO ANDRES GRILLASCA, Ponce, P.R.

HOSPITAL PAVIA, San Juan, P.R.
HOSPITAL REGIONAL DR. RAMON RUIZ ARNAU, Bayamon, P.R.
HOSPITAL SAN LUCAS (Formerly St. Luke's Episcopal Hospital), Ponce, P.R.
HOSPITAL SAN MARTIN, Rio Piedras, P.R.
HOSPITAL SAN MIGUEL, Utuado, P.R.
HOSPITAL SAN PABLO, Bayamon, P.R.
HOSPITAL SAN RAFAEL, Caguas, P.R.
HOSPITAL SANTA ROSA, Guayama, P.R.
HOSPITALS OF CHESTER COUNTY (Formerly Chester County Hospital), West Chester, PA
HOT SPRING COUNTY MEMORIAL HOSPITAL, Malvern, AR
HOT SPRINGS COUNTY MEMORIAL HOSPITAL, Thermopolis, WY
HOTEL DIEU HOSPITAL, New Orleans, LA
HOTEL DIEU MEDICAL CENTER, El Paso, TX
HOULTON REGIONAL HOSPITAL, Houlton, ME
HOUSATONIC ADOLESCENT HOSPITAL, Newtown, CT
HOUSE OF THE GOOD SAMARITAN, Watertown, NY
HOUSTON COMMUNITY HOSPITAL, Houston, MS
HOUSTON COUNTY HOSPITAL, Crockett, TX
HOUSTON INTERNATIONAL HOSPITAL, Houston, TX
HOUSTON MEDICAL CENTER (Formerly Medical Center of Houston County), Warner Robins, GA
HOUSTON NORTHWEST MEDICAL CENTER, Houston, TX
HOWARD COMMUNITY HOSPITAL, Kokomo, IN
HOWARD COUNTY COMMUNITY HOSPITAL, St. Paul, NE
HOWARD COUNTY GENERAL HOSPITAL, Columbia, MD
HOWARD COUNTY HOSPITAL, Cresco, IA
HOWARD MEMORIAL HOSPITAL (Formerly Howard County Memorial Hospital), Nashville, AR
HOWARD UNIVERSITY HOSPITAL, Washington, DC
HOWARD YOUNG MEDICAL CENTER, Woodruff, WI
HSA BAYOU OAKS HOSPITAL, Houma, LA
HSA GREENBRIER HOSPITAL, Covington, LA
HSA HEARTLAND HOSPITAL, Nevada, MO
HSA HILL CREST SUNRISE HOSPITAL (Formerly Hill Crest Hospital), Birmingham, AL
HSA RIVERWOOD HOSPITAL, Provo, UT
HUBBARD HOSPITAL, Hubbard, TX
HUBBARD REGIONAL HOSPITAL, Webster, MA
HUDSON COUNTY MEADOWVIEW HOSPITAL, Secaucus, NJ
HUDSON MEDICAL CENTER (Formerly Hudson Memorial Hospital), Hudson, WI
HUDSON RIVER PSYCHIATRIC CENTER, Poughkeepsie, NY
HUERFANO MEMORIAL HOSPITAL, Walsenburg, CO
HUEY P. LONG MEMORIAL HOSPITAL, Pineville, LA
HUGGINS HOSPITAL, Wolfeboro, NH
HUGH CHATHAM MEMORIAL HOSPITAL, Elkin, NC
HUGHES SPALDING MEDICAL CENTER, Atlanta, GA
HUGHSTON SPORTS MEDICINE HOSPITAL, Columbus, GA
HUGULEY MEMORIAL HOSPITAL, Fort Worth, TX
HUMAN RESOURCE INSTITUTE, Brookline, MA
HUMANA HOSPITAL -ABILENE, Abilene, TX
HUMANA HOSPITAL -ALASKA, Anchorage, AK
HUMANA HOSPITAL -AUDUBON, Louisville, KY
HUMANA HOSPITAL -AUGUSTA, Augusta, GA
HUMANA HOSPITAL -AURORA, Aurora, CO
HUMANA HOSPITAL -BAYSIDE, Virginia Beach, VA
HUMANA HOSPITAL -BAYTOWN, Baytown, TX
HUMANA HOSPITAL -BENNETT, Plantation, FL
HUMANA HOSPITAL -BISCAYNE, Miami, FL
HUMANA HOSPITAL -BRANDON, Brandon, FL
HUMANA HOSPITAL -BRENTWOOD, Shreveport, LA
HUMANA HOSPITAL -CLEAR LAKE, Webster, TX
HUMANA HOSPITAL -CLINCH VALLEY, Richlands, VA
HUMANA HOSPITAL -CYPRESS, Pompano Beach, FL
HUMANA HOSPITAL -DAVIS NORTH, Layton, UT
HUMANA HOSPITAL -DAYTONA BEACH, Daytona Beach, FL
HUMANA HOSPITAL -DESERT VALLEY, Phoenix, AZ
HUMANA HOSPITAL -DODGE CITY, Dodge City, KS
HUMANA HOSPITAL -EAST MONTGOMERY, Montgomery, AL
HUMANA HOSPITAL -EAST RIDGE, Chattanooga, TN
HUMANA HOSPITAL -ENTERPRISE, Enterprise, AL
HUMANA HOSPITAL -FLORENCE, Florence, AL
HUMANA HOSPITAL -GREENSBORO, Greensboro, NC
HUMANA HOSPITAL -GWINNETT, Snellville, GA
HUMANA HOSPITAL -HOFFMAN ESTATES, Hoffman Estates, IL
HUMANA HOSPITAL -HUNTINGTON BEACH, Huntington Beach, CA
HUMANA HOSPITAL -KISSIMMEE, Kissimmee, FL
HUMANA HOSPITAL -LAKE CHARLES, Lake Charles, LA
HUMANA HOSPITAL -LAKE CUMBERLAND, Somerset, KY
HUMANA HOSPITAL -LEXINGTON, Lexington, KY
HUMANA HOSPITAL -LOUISA, Louisa, KY
HUMANA HOSPITAL -LUCERNE, Orlando, FL
HUMANA HOSPITAL -MARKSVILLE, Marksville, LA
HUMANA HOSPITAL -MCFARLAND, Lebanon, TN
HUMANA HOSPITAL -MEDICAL CITY DALLAS, Dallas, TX
HUMANA HOSPITAL -METROPOLITAN, San Antonio, TX
HUMANA HOSPITAL -MORRISTOWN, Morristown, TN
HUMANA HOSPITAL -NATCHEZ, Natchez, MS
HUMANA HOSPITAL -NEW ORLEANS (Formerly Humana Women's Hospital-East Orleans), New Orleans, LA
HUMANA HOSPITAL -NEWNAN, Newnan, GA
HUMANA HOSPITAL -OAKDALE, Oakdale, LA
HUMANA HOSPITAL -ORANGE PARK, Orange Park, FL
HUMANA HOSPITAL -OVERLAND PARK, Overland Park, KS
HUMANA HOSPITAL -PALM BEACHES, West Palm Beach, FL
HUMANA HOSPITAL -PASCO, Dade City, FL
HUMANA HOSPITAL -PHOENIX, Phoenix, AZ
HUMANA HOSPITAL -RUSSELLVILLE, Russellville, AL
HUMANA HOSPITAL -SAN ANTONIO, San Antonio, TX
HUMANA HOSPITAL -SAN LEANDRO, San Leandro, CA
HUMANA HOSPITAL -SEBASTIAN, Sebastian, FL
HUMANA HOSPITAL -SHOALS (Formerly Listed Under Sheffield), Muscle Shoals, AL
HUMANA HOSPITAL -SOUTH BROWARD, Hollywood, FL
HUMANA HOSPITAL -SOUTHMORE, Pasadena, TX
HUMANA HOSPITAL -SOUTHWEST, Louisville, KY
HUMANA HOSPITAL -SPRINGFIELD, Springfield, IL
HUMANA HOSPITAL -SPRINGHILL, Springhill, LA
HUMANA HOSPITAL -ST. LUKES, Richmond, VA
HUMANA HOSPITAL -ST. PETERSBURG, St. Petersburg, FL
HUMANA HOSPITAL -SUBURBAN, Louisville, KY
HUMANA HOSPITAL -SUN BAY, St. Petersburg, FL
HUMANA HOSPITAL -SUNRISE, Las Vegas, NV
HUMANA HOSPITAL -TACOMA, Tacoma, WA
HUMANA HOSPITAL -UNIVERSITY, Louisville, KY
HUMANA HOSPITAL -VILLE PLATTE, Ville Platte, LA
HUMANA HOSPITAL -WEST ANAHEIM, Anaheim, CA
HUMANA HOSPITAL -WEST HILLS, Los Angeles, CA
HUMANA HOSPITAL -WESTMINSTER, Westminster, CA
HUMANA HOSPITAL -WINN PARISH, Winnfield, LA
HUMANA HOSPITAL CORPUS CHRISTI, Corpus Christi, TX
HUMANA HOSPITAL DARLINGTON, Darlington, SC, See Southland Medical Center
HUMANA HOSPITAL-BRAZOS VALLEY (Formerly Humana Hospital-Bryan College Station, Bryan), College Station, TX
HUMANA HOSPITAL-CARTERSVILLE (Formerly Sam Howell Memorial Hospital), Cartersville, GA
HUMANA HOSPITAL-FORT WALTON BEACH, Fort Walton Beach, FL
HUMANA HOSPITAL-GREENBRIER VALLEY, Ronceverte, WV
HUMANA HOSPITAL-HUNTSVILLE, Huntsville, AL
HUMANA HOSPITAL-MOUNTAIN VIEW (Formerly Valley View Hospital and Medical Center, Denver), Thornton, CO
HUMANA HOSPITAL-NORTHSIDE, St. Petersburg, FL
HUMANA HOSPITAL-ST. LUKE'S, Bluefield, WV
HUMANA SPECIALTY HOSPITAL-CHARLOTTE (Formerly Charlotte Eye, Ear and Throat Hospital), Charlotte, NC
HUMANA SPECIALTY HOSPITAL-MEMPHIS, Memphis, TN, See Baptist Specialty Hospital
HUMANA WOMEN'S HOSPITAL -TAMPA, Tampa, FL
HUMANA WOMEN'S HOSPITAL-INDIANAPOLIS, Indianapolis, IN
HUMANA WOMEN'S HOSPITAL-SOUTH TEXAS, San Antonio, TX
HUMBLE REHABILITATION HOSPITAL, Humble, TX, See Healthsouth
HUMBOLDT CEDAR CREST HOSPITAL, Humboldt, TN
HUMBOLDT COUNTY MEMORIAL HOSPITAL, Humboldt, IA
HUMBOLDT GENERAL HOSPITAL, Winnemucca, NV
HUMPHREY BUILDING, Cleveland, OH, See University Hospitals of Cleveland
HUMPHREYS COUNTY MEMORIAL HOSPITAL, Belzoni, MS
HUNT MEMORIAL HOSPITAL, Danvers, MA
HUNT MEMORIAL HOSPITAL DISTRICT, Greenville, TX
HUNTER HOLMES MCGUIRE VETERANS ADMINISTRATION MEDICAL CENTER, Richmond, VA
HUNTERDON MEDICAL CENTER, Flemington, NJ
HUNTINGTON HOSPITAL, Huntington, NY
HUNTINGTON HOSPITAL, Willow Grove, PA
HUNTINGTON MEMORIAL HOSPITAL, Pasadena, CA
HUNTINGTON MEMORIAL HOSPITAL, Huntington, IN
HUNTSVILLE HOSPITAL, Huntsville, AL
HUNTSVILLE MEMORIAL HOSPITAL, Huntsville, AR
HUNTSVILLE MEMORIAL HOSPITAL, Huntsville, TX
HURLEY MEDICAL CENTER, Flint, MI
HURON MEMORIAL HOSPITAL, Bad Axe, MI
HURON REGIONAL MEDICAL CENTER, Huron, SD
HURON ROAD HOSPITAL, Cleveland, OH
HURTADO HEALTH CENTER, New Brunswick, NJ
HUTCHESON MEDICAL CENTER, Fort Oglethorpe, GA
HUTCHINSON COMMUNITY HOSPITAL, Hutchinson, MN
HUTCHINSON HOSPITAL CORPORATION, Hutchinson, KS
HUTZEL HOSPITAL, Detroit, MI
HYDE PARK HOSPITAL (Formerly Hyde Park Community Hospital), Chicago, IL

I

I. GONZALEZ MARTINEZ ONCOLOGIC HOSPITAL, Hato Rey, P.R.
IBERIA GENERAL HOSPITAL AND MEDICAL CENTER, New Iberia, LA
IDAHO ELKS REHABILITATION HOSPITAL, Boise, ID
IDAHO STATE SCHOOL AND HOSPITAL, Nampa, ID
IHC EVANSTON REGIONAL HOSPITAL (Formerly Uinta Medical Center), Evanston, WY
ILLINI COMMUNITY HOSPITAL, Pittsfield, IL
ILLINI HOSPITAL, Silvis, IL
ILLINOIS MASONIC MEDICAL CENTER, Chicago, IL
ILLINOIS STATE PSYCHIATRIC INSTITUTE, Chicago, IL
ILLINOIS VALLEY COMMUNITY HOSPITAL, Peru, IL
IMMANUEL MEDICAL CENTER, Omaha, NE
IMMANUEL-ST. JOSEPH'S HOSPITAL, Mankato, MN
IMPERIAL POINT MEDICAL CENTER, Fort Lauderdale, FL
INCARNATE WORD HOSPITAL, St. Louis, MO
INDEPENDENCE REGIONAL HEALTH CENTER (Formerly Independence Sanitarium and Hospital), Independence, MO
INDIAN PATH HOSPITAL, Kingsport, TN
INDIAN PATH PAVILION, Kingsport, TN
INDIAN RIVER COMMUNITY MENTAL HEALTH CENTER, Fort Pierce, FL
INDIAN RIVER MEMORIAL HOSPITAL, Vero Beach, FL
INDIAN VALLEY HOSPITAL DISTRICT, Greenville, CA
INDIANA HOSPITAL, Indiana, PA
INDIANA UNIVERSITY HOSPITALS, Indianapolis, IN
INDIANHEAD MEDICAL CENTER, Shell Lake, WI
INDUSTRIAL HOSPITAL, San Juan, P.R.
INGALLS MEMORIAL HOSPITAL, Harvey, IL
INGHAM MEDICAL CENTER, Lansing, MI
INGLESIDE HOSPITAL, Rosemead, CA
INGLEWOOD GENERAL HOSPITAL, Inglewood, CA
INLAND VALLEY REGIONAL MEDICAL CENTER (Formerly Mission Valley Medical Center, Lake Elsinore), Wildomar, CA
INPATIENT CENTER AT TACOMA GENERAL, Tacoma, WA, See Ghc Inpatient Center Tacoma General
INSIGHT HOSPITAL, Lafayette, LA
INSTITUTE FOR IMMUNOLOGICAL DISORDERS (Formerly AMI Citizens General Hospital), Houston, TX
INSTITUTE FOR REHABILITATION AND RESEARCH, Houston, TX
INSTITUTE OF LIVING, Hartford, CT
INSTITUTE OF MENTAL HEALTH-RHODE ISLAND MEDICAL CENTER, Cranston, RI
INSTITUTE OF PENNSYLVANIA HOSPITAL, Philadelphia, PA
INSTITUTE OF PSYCHIATRY, Chicago, IL, See Northwestern Memorial Hospital
INSTITUTO OFTALMICO DE PUERTO RICO, San Juan, P.R.
INTER-COMMUNITY MEDICAL CENTER, Covina, CA
INTER-COMMUNITY MEMORIAL HOSPITAL, Newfane, NY
INTERFAITH MEDICAL CENTER, Brooklyn, NY
INTERFAITH MEDICAL CENTER-BROOKLYN JEWISH DIVISION, Brooklyn, NY, See Interfaith Medical Center
INTERNATIONAL FALLS MEMORIAL HOSPITAL, International Falls, MN
IONIA COUNTY MEMORIAL HOSPITAL, Ionia, MI
IOWA LUTHERAN HOSPITAL, Des Moines, IA
IOWA MEDICAL AND CLASSIFICATION CENTER (Formerly Iowa Security and Medical Facility), Oakdale, IA
IOWA METHODIST MEDICAL CENTER, Des Moines, IA
IPSWICH COMMUNITY HOSPITAL, Ipswich, SD
IRA DAVENPORT MEMORIAL HOSPITAL, Bath, NY
IREDELL MEMORIAL HOSPITAL, Statesville, NC

IRON COUNTY GENERAL HOSPITAL, Iron River, MI
IROQUOIS MEMORIAL HOSPITAL AND RESIDENT HOME, Watseka, IL
IRVING COMMUNITY HOSPITAL, Irving, TX
IRVINGTON GENERAL HOSPITAL, Irvington, NJ
IRWIN ARMY COMMUNITY HOSPITAL, Fort Riley, KS
IRWIN COUNTY HOSPITAL, Ocilla, GA
ISHAM INFIRMARY, Andover, MA
ISLAND HOSPITAL, Anacortes, WA
ITASCA MEMORIAL HOSPITAL, Grand Rapids, MN
ITAWAMBA COUNTY HOSPITAL, Fulton, MS
IVANHOE TREATMENT CENTER, Milwaukee, WI
IVINSON MEMORIAL HOSPITAL, Laramie, WY

J

J. ARTHUR DOSHER MEMORIAL HOSPITAL, Southport, NC
J. C. BLAIR MEMORIAL HOSPITAL, Huntingdon, PA
J. PAUL JONES HOSPITAL, Camden, AL
JACK COUNTY HOSPITAL, Jacksboro, TX
JACK D. WEILER HOSPITAL OF EINSTEIN COLLEGE OF MEDICINE, Bronx, NY, See Montefiore Medical Center
JACKMAN REGION HEALTH CENTER, Jackman, ME, See Mid-Maine Medical Center, Waterville
JACKSON BROOK INSTITUTE, South Portland, ME
JACKSON COUNSELING CENTER AND PSYCHIATRIC HOSPITAL, Jackson, TN
JACKSON COUNTY HOSPITAL, Scottsboro, AL
JACKSON COUNTY HOSPITAL, Gainesboro, TN
JACKSON COUNTY MEMORIAL HOSPITAL, Altus, OK
JACKSON COUNTY PUBLIC HOSPITAL, Maquoketa, IA
JACKSON COUNTY SCHNECK MEMORIAL HOSPITAL, Seymour, IN
JACKSON GENERAL HOSPITAL, Ripley, WV
JACKSON HOSPITAL, Marianna, FL
JACKSON HOSPITAL AND CLINIC, Montgomery, AL
JACKSON MUNICIPAL HOSPITAL AND NURSING HOME, Jackson, MN
JACKSON OSTEOPATHIC HOSPITAL, Jackson, MI
JACKSON PARISH HOSPITAL, Jonesboro, LA
JACKSON PARK HOSPITAL, Chicago, IL
JACKSON-MADISON COUNTY GENERAL HOSPITAL, Jackson, TN
JACKSONVILLE HOSPITAL, Jacksonville, AL
JACKSONVILLE MEDICAL CENTER, Jacksonville, FL
JACOBSON MEMORIAL HOSPITAL CARE CENTER, Elgin, ND
JAMAICA HOSPITAL, Jamaica, NY
JAMES A. HALEY VETERANS HOSPITAL, Tampa, FL
JAMES ARCHER SMITH HOSPITAL, Homestead, FL
JAMES B. HAGGIN MEMORIAL HOSPITAL, Harrodsburg, KY
JAMES C. GIUFFRE MEDICAL CENTER, Philadelphia, PA
JAMES LAWRENCE KERNAN HOSPITAL, Baltimore, MD
JAMES M. JACKSON MEMORIAL HOSPITAL, Miami, FL
JAMES WHITCOMB RILEY HOSPITAL, Indianapolis, IN, See Indiana University Hospitals
JAMESON MEMORIAL HOSPITAL, New Castle, PA
JAMESTOWN GENERAL HOSPITAL, Jamestown, NY
JAMESTOWN HOSPITAL, Jamestown, ND
JANE LAMB HEALTH CENTER, Clinton, IA
JANE PHILLIPS EPISCOPAL-MEMORIAL MEDICAL CENTER, Bartlesville, OK
JANE TODD CRAWFORD MEMORIAL HOSPITAL, Greensburg, KY
JASPER COUNTY HOSPITAL, Rensselaer, IN
JASPER GENERAL HOSPITAL, Bay Springs, MS
JASPER MEMORIAL HOSPITAL, Monticello, GA
JASPER MEMORIAL HOSPITAL, Jasper, TX
JAY COUNTY HOSPITAL, Portland, IN
JAY HOSPITAL, Jay, FL
JAY MEMORIAL HOSPITAL, Jay, OK
JEANES HOSPITAL, Philadelphia, PA
JEANNETTE DISTRICT MEMORIAL HOSPITAL, Jeannette, PA
JEFF ANDERSON REGIONAL MEDICAL CENTER, Meridian, MS
JEFF DAVIS HOSPITAL, Hazlehurst, GA
JEFFERSON CENTER, Pittsburgh, PA, See South Hills Health System
JEFFERSON COUNTY HOSPITAL, Fairfield, IA
JEFFERSON COUNTY HOSPITAL, Fayette, MS
JEFFERSON COUNTY HOSPITAL, Waurika, OK
JEFFERSON COUNTY MEMORIAL HOSPITAL, Winchester, KS
JEFFERSON COUNTY MEMORIAL HOSPITAL, Fairbury, NE
JEFFERSON DAVIS COUNTY HOSPITAL, Prentiss, MS
JEFFERSON DAVIS HOSPITAL, Houston, TX, See Harris County Hospital District
JEFFERSON DAVIS MEMORIAL HOSPITAL, Natchez, MS
JEFFERSON GENERAL HOSPITAL, Port Townsend, WA
JEFFERSON HOSPITAL, Louisville, GA
JEFFERSON MEMORIAL HOSPITAL, Crystal City, MO
JEFFERSON MEMORIAL HOSPITAL, Jefferson City, TN
JEFFERSON MEMORIAL HOSPITAL, Alexandria, VA
JEFFERSON MEMORIAL HOSPITAL, Ranson, WV
JEFFERSON REGIONAL MEDICAL CENTER, Pine Bluff, AR
JELLICO COMMUNITY HOSPITAL, Jellico, TN
JENKINS COUNTY HOSPITAL, Millen, GA
JENNIE EDMUNDSON MEMORIAL HOSPITAL, Council Bluffs, IA
JENNIE M. MELHAM MEMORIAL MEDICAL CENTER, Broken Bow, NE
JENNIE STUART MEDICAL CENTER, Hopkinsville, KY
JENNINGS AMERICAN LEGION HOSPITAL, Jennings, LA
JENNINGS COMMUNITY HOSPITAL, North Vernon, IN
JERRY L. PETTIS MEMORIAL VETERANS HOSPITAL, Loma Linda, CA
JERSEY CITY MEDICAL CENTER, Jersey City, NJ
JERSEY COMMUNITY HOSPITAL, Jerseyville, IL
JERSEY SHORE HOSPITAL, Jersey Shore, PA
JERSEY SHORE MEDICAL CENTER, Neptune, NJ
JESS PARRISH MEMORIAL HOSPITAL, Titusville, FL
JESSE HOLMAN JONES HOSPITAL, Springfield, TN
JESSE PARKER WILLIAMS HOSPITAL, Atlanta, GA
JEWELL COUNTY HOSPITAL, Mankato, KS
JEWISH HOSPITAL, Louisville, KY
JEWISH HOSPITAL AND REHABILITATION CENTER OF NEW JERSEY, Jersey City, NJ
JEWISH HOSPITAL OF CINCINNATI, Cincinnati, OH
JEWISH HOSPITAL OF ST. LOUIS, St. Louis, MO
JEWISH MEMORIAL HOSPITAL, Boston, MA
JO ELLEN SMITH MEDICAL CENTER, New Orleans, LA
JOAN GLANCY MEMORIAL HOSPITAL, Duluth, GA, See Gwinnett Hospital Systems, Lawrenceville
JOEL POMERENE MEMORIAL HOSPITAL, Millersburg, OH
JOHN A. ANDREW COMMUNITY HOSPITAL, Tuskegee Institute, AL
JOHN AND MARY KIRBY HOSPITAL, Monticello, IL
JOHN C. FREMONT HOSPITAL, Mariposa, CA
JOHN C. LINCOLN HOSPITAL AND HEALTH CENTER, Phoenix, AZ
JOHN D. ARCHBOLD MEMORIAL HOSPITAL, Thomasville, GA
JOHN E. FOGARTY MEMORIAL HOSPITAL, North Smithfield, RI
JOHN E. RUNNELLS HOSPITAL OF UNION COUNTY, Berkeley Heights, NJ
JOHN F. KENNEDY COMMUNITY HOSPITAL, Edison, NJ, See John F. Kennedy Medical Center
JOHN F. KENNEDY MEDICAL CENTER (Formerly Northwest Hospital), Chicago, IL
JOHN F. KENNEDY MEDICAL CENTER (Formerly John F. Kennedy Community Hospital), Edison, NJ
JOHN F. KENNEDY MEMORIAL HOSPITAL, Indio, CA
JOHN F. KENNEDY MEMORIAL HOSPITAL, Atlantis, FL
JOHN F. KENNEDY MEMORIAL HOSPITAL, Philadelphia, PA
JOHN FITZGIBBON MEMORIAL HOSPITAL, Marshall, MO
JOHN J. MADDEN MENTAL HEALTH CENTER, Hines, IL
JOHN L. MCCLELLAN MEMORIAL VETERANS HOSPITAL, Little Rock, AR
JOHN MCDONALD HOSPITAL, Monticello, IA
JOHN MUIR MEMORIAL HOSPITAL, Walnut Creek, CA
JOHN PETER SMITH HOSPITAL, Fort Worth, TX, See Tarrant County Hospital District
JOHN RANDOLPH HOSPITAL, Hopewell, VA
JOHN T. MATHER MEMORIAL HOSPITAL OF PORT JEFFERSON, Port Jefferson, NY
JOHN UMSTEAD HOSPITAL, Butner, NC
JOHN W. HARTON REGIONAL MEDICAL CENTER, Tullahoma, TN
JOHNS COMMUNITY HOSPITAL, Taylor, TX
JOHNS HOPKINS HOSPITAL, Baltimore, MD
JOHNSON CITY EYE AND EAR HOSPITAL, Johnson City, TN
JOHNSON CITY MEDICAL CENTER HOSPITAL, Johnson City, TN
JOHNSON COUNTY HOSPITAL, Tecumseh, NE
JOHNSON COUNTY MEMORIAL HOSPITAL, Franklin, IN
JOHNSON COUNTY MEMORIAL HOSPITAL, Mountain City, TN
JOHNSON COUNTY MEMORIAL HOSPITAL, Buffalo, WY
JOHNSON COUNTY REGIONAL HOSPITAL, Clarksville, AR
JOHNSON MEMORIAL HOSPITAL, Stafford Springs, CT
JOHNSON MEMORIAL HOSPITAL AND HOME, Dawson, MN
JOHNSTON MEMORIAL HOSPITAL, Smithfield, NC
JOHNSTON MEMORIAL HOSPITAL, Tishomingo, OK
JOHNSTON MEMORIAL HOSPITAL, Abingdon, VA
JOHNSTON R. BOWMAN HEALTH CENTER, Chicago, IL, See Rush-Presbyterian-St. Luke's Medical Center
JOHNSTON-WILLIS HOSPITAL, Richmond, VA
JOHNSTOWN HOSPITAL, Johnstown, NY
JOINT DISEASES NORTH GENERAL HOSPITAL, New York, NY
JOINT TOWNSHIP DISTRICT MEMORIAL HOSPITAL, St. Marys, OH
JONES COUNTY COMMUNITY HOSPITAL, Laurel, MS
JORDAN HOSPITAL, Plymouth, MA
JOSEPH B. WHITEHEAD MEMORIAL INFIRMARY, GEORGIA INSTITUTE OF TECHNOLOGY, Atlanta, GA
JOSEPH P. KENNEDY JR. MEMORIAL HOSPITAL, Boston, MA
JOSEPHINE MEMORIAL HOSPITAL, Grants Pass, OR
JOSIAH B. THOMAS HOSPITAL, Peabody, MA
JULIA L. BUTTERFIELD MEMORIAL HOSPITAL, Cold Spring, NY
JUPITER HOSPITAL, Jupiter, FL

K

KADLEC MEDICAL CENTER, Richland, WA
KAHUKU HOSPITAL, Kahuku, HI
KAISER FOUNDATION HOSPITAL, Anaheim, CA
KAISER FOUNDATION HOSPITAL, El Cajon, CA, See Kaiser Foundation Hospital, San Diego
KAISER FOUNDATION HOSPITAL, Fontana, CA
KAISER FOUNDATION HOSPITAL, Hayward, CA
KAISER FOUNDATION HOSPITAL, Los Angeles, CA
KAISER FOUNDATION HOSPITAL, Los Angeles, CA
KAISER FOUNDATION HOSPITAL, Martinez, CA
KAISER FOUNDATION HOSPITAL, Norwalk, CA, See Kaiser Foundation Hospital, Bellflower
KAISER FOUNDATION HOSPITAL, Oakland, CA
KAISER FOUNDATION HOSPITAL, Redwood City, CA
KAISER FOUNDATION HOSPITAL, Richmond, CA
KAISER FOUNDATION HOSPITAL, Sacramento, CA
KAISER FOUNDATION HOSPITAL, San Francisco, CA
KAISER FOUNDATION HOSPITAL, Santa Clara, CA
KAISER FOUNDATION HOSPITAL, South San Francisco, CA
KAISER FOUNDATION HOSPITAL, Walnut Creek, CA
KAISER FOUNDATION HOSPITAL, Honolulu, HI
KAISER FOUNDATION HOSPITAL, Bellflower, CA
KAISER FOUNDATION HOSPITAL, San Diego, CA
KAISER FOUNDATION HOSPITAL AND REHABILITATION CENTER, Vallejo, CA
KAISER FOUNDATION HOSPITAL-PARMA, Parma, OH
KAISER FOUNDATION HOSPITAL-SAN RAFAEL (Formerly Listed Under Terra Linda), San Rafael, CA
KAISER FOUNDATION HOSPITAL-SUNSET, Los Angeles, CA
KAISER FOUNDATION HOSPITAL-WEST LOS ANGELES, Los Angeles, CA
KAISER FOUNDATION MENTAL HEALTH CENTER, Los Angeles, CA
KAISER SUNNYSIDE MEDICAL CENTER, Clackamas, OR
KALAMAZOO REGIONAL PSYCHIATRIC HOSPITAL, Kalamazoo, MI
KALISPELL REGIONAL HOSPITAL, Kalispell, MT
KALKASKA MEMORIAL HOSPITAL, Kalkaska, MI
KANABEC HOSPITAL, Mora, MN
KANAKANAK HOSPITAL, Dillingham, AK
KANE COUNTY HOSPITAL, Kanab, UT
KANSAS INSTITUTE, Olathe, KS
KANSAS NEUROLOGICAL INSTITUTE, Topeka, KS
KAPIOLANI MEDICAL CENTER FOR WOMEN AND CHILDREN (Formerly Kapiolani Women's and Children's Medical Center), Honolulu, HI
KARL AND ESTHER HOBLITZELLE MEMORIAL HOSPITAL, Dallas, TX, See Baylor University Medical Center
KARLSTAD MEMORIAL HOSPITAL, Karlstad, MN
KASEMAN PRESBYTERIAN HOSPITAL, Albuquerque, NM
KATHERINE SHAW BETHEA HOSPITAL, Dixon, IL
KAU HOSPITAL, Pahala, HI
KAUAI VETERANS MEMORIAL HOSPITAL, Waimea, HI
KAUKAUNA COMMUNITY HOSPITAL, Kaukauna, WI
KAWEAH DELTA DISTRICT HOSPITAL, Visalia, CA
KEARNEY COUNTY COMMUNITY HOSPITAL, Minden, NE

KEARNY COUNTY HOSPITAL, Lakin, KS
KELLER ARMY COMMUNITY HOSPITAL, West Point, NY
KELLING HOSPITAL, Waverly, MO
KELSEY MEMORIAL HOSPITAL, Lakeview, MI
KENDRICK MEMORIAL HOSPITAL, Mooresville, IN
KENMARE COMMUNITY HOSPITAL, Kenmare, ND
KENMORE MERCY HOSPITAL, Kenmore, NY
KENNEBEC VALLEY MEDICAL CENTER, Augusta, ME
KENNECOTT SAMARITAN HOSPITAL, Kearny, AZ
KENNEDY INSTITUTE FOR HANDICAPPED CHILDREN, Baltimore, MD
KENNEDY MEMORIAL HOSPITALS AT SADDLE BROOK (Formerly Saddle Brook General Hospital), Saddle Brook, NJ
KENNEDY MEMORIAL HOSPITALS UNIVERSITY MEDICAL CENTER, Stratford, NJ
KENNER ARMY COMMUNITY HOSPITAL, Fort Lee, VA
KENNESTONE HOSPITAL, Marietta, GA
KENNESTONE HOSPITAL AT WINDY HILL, Marietta, GA
KENNEWICK GENERAL HOSPITAL, Kennewick, WA
KENOSHA HOSPITAL AND MEDICAL CENTER (Formerly Kenosha Memorial Hospital), Kenosha, WI
KENSINGTON HOSPITAL, Philadelphia, PA
KENT AND QUEEN ANNE'S HOSPITAL, Chestertown, MD
KENT COMMUNITY HOSPITAL COMPLEX, Grand Rapids, MI
KENT COUNTY MEMORIAL HOSPITAL, Warwick, RI
KENT GENERAL HOSPITAL, Dover, DE
KENTFIELD MEDICAL HOSPITAL, Kentfield, CA
KEOKUK AREA HOSPITAL, Keokuk, IA
KEOKUK COUNTY HEALTH CENTER (Formerly Keokuk County Hospital), Sigourney, IA
KERN MEDICAL CENTER, Bakersfield, CA
KERN VALLEY HOSPITAL, Lake Isabella, CA
KERN VIEW HOSPITAL (Formerly Kern View Community Mental Health Center and Hospital), Bakersfield, CA
KERRVILLE STATE HOSPITAL, Kerrville, TX
KERSHAW COUNTY MEMORIAL HOSPITAL, Camden, SC
KESSLER INSTITUTE FOR REHABILITATION, West Orange, NJ
KESWICK-HOME FOR INCURABLES OF BALTIMORE CITY, Baltimore, MD
KETCHIKAN GENERAL HOSPITAL, Ketchikan, AK
KETTERING HOSPITAL, Loudonville, OH
KETTERING MEDICAL CENTER, Kettering, OH
KETTLE MORAINE HOSPITAL, Oconomowoc, WI
KEWANEE PUBLIC HOSPITAL, Kewanee, IL
KILMICHAEL HOSPITAL, Kilmichael, MS
KIMBALL COUNTY HOSPITAL, Kimball, NE
KIMBALL MEDICAL CENTER, Lakewood, NJ
KIMBLE HOSPITAL, Junction, TX
KIMBROUGH ARMY COMMUNITY HOSPITAL, Fort George G. Meade, MD
KING WILLIAM HEALTH CARE CENTER (Formerly St. Benedict Health Care Center), San Antonio, TX
KING'S DAUGHTERS HOSPITAL, Shelbyville, KY, See United Medical Center Shelbyville
KING'S DAUGHTERS HOSPITAL, Brookhaven, MS
KING'S DAUGHTERS HOSPITAL, Greenville, MS
KING'S DAUGHTERS HOSPITAL, Yazoo City, MS
KING'S DAUGHTERS HOSPITAL, Temple, TX
KING'S DAUGHTERS MEMORIAL HOSPITAL, Frankfort, KY
KING'S DAUGHTERS' HOSPITAL, Madison, IN
KING'S DAUGHTERS' HOSPITAL, Staunton, VA
KING'S DAUGHTERS' MEDICAL CENTER, Ashland, KY
KINGMAN COMMUNITY HOSPITAL, Kingman, KS
KINGMAN REGIONAL HOSPITAL, Kingman, AZ
KINGS COUNTY HOSPITAL CENTER, Brooklyn, NY
KINGS HIGHWAY HOSPITAL CENTER, Brooklyn, NY
KINGS MOUNTAIN HOSPITAL, Kings Mountain, NC
KINGS PARK PSYCHIATRIC CENTER, Kings Park, NY
KINGS VIEW HOSPITAL, Reedley, CA
KINGSBORO PSYCHIATRIC CENTER, Brooklyn, NY
KINGSBROOK JEWISH MEDICAL CENTER, Brooklyn, NY
KINGSBURG GENERAL HOSPITAL, Kingsburg, CA
KINGSBURY COUNTY MEMORIAL HOSPITAL, Lake Preston, SD
KINGSTON HOSPITAL, Kingston, NY
KINGSWOOD HOSPITAL, Ferndale, MI
KINGWOOD HOSPITAL (Formerly Walters Hospital Foundation), Michigan City, IN
KINO COMMUNITY HOSPITAL, Tucson, AZ
KIOWA COUNTY MEMORIAL HOSPITAL, Greensburg, KS
KIOWA DISTRICT HOSPITAL, Kiowa, KS
KIRBYVILLE COMMUNITY HOSPITAL (Formerly Max Mixson Memorial Hospital), Kirbyville, TX
KIRKSVILLE OSTEOPATHIC MEDICAL CENTER, Kirksville, MO
KISHWAUKEE COMMUNITY HOSPITAL, De Kalb, IL
KISSIMMEE MEMORIAL HOSPITAL, Kissimmee, FL
KITTITAS VALLEY COMMUNITY HOSPITAL, Ellensburg, WA
KITTSON MEMORIAL HOSPITAL, Hallock, MN
KLAMATH-TRINITY COMMUNITY HOSPITAL, Hoopa, CA
KLICKITAT VALLEY HOSPITAL, Goldendale, WA
KMI MEDICAL CENTER, Louisville, KY
KNAPP MEDICAL CENTER (Formerly Knapp Memorial Methodist Hospital), Weslaco, TX
KNOLLWOOD PARK HOSPITAL, Mobile, AL
KNOX COMMUNITY HOSPITAL, Mount Vernon, OH
KNOX COUNTY GENERAL HOSPITAL, Barbourville, KY
KNOXVILLE AREA COMMUNITY HOSPITAL, Knoxville, IA
KOALA CENTER, Bushnell, FL
KOALA CENTER, Columbus, IN
KODIAK ISLAND HOSPITAL, Kodiak, AK
KOHALA HOSPITAL, Kohala, HI
KONA HOSPITAL, Kealakekua, HI
KOOTENAI MEDICAL CENTER, Coeur D'Alene, ID
KOSAIR-CHILDREN HOSPITAL, Louisville, KY
KOSCIUSKO COMMUNITY HOSPITAL, Warsaw, IN
KOSSUTH COUNTY HOSPITAL, Algona, IA
KREMMLING MEMORIAL HOSPITAL, Kremmling, CO
KUAKINI MEDICAL CENTER, Honolulu, HI
KUHN MEMORIAL STATE HOSPITAL, Vicksburg, MS
KULA GENERAL HOSPITAL, Kula, HI, See Kula Hospital
KULA HOSPITAL, Kula, HI
KWAJALEIN MISSILE RANGE HOSPITAL (Formerly Kwajalein Missile Range Army Hospital), Kwajalein Island, Marshall Islands

L

L. RICHARDSON MEMORIAL HOSPITAL, Greensboro, NC
L. S. HUCKABAY MD MEMORIAL HOSPITAL, Coushatta, LA
L. V. STABLER MEMORIAL HOSPITAL OF GREENVILLE, Greenville, AL
L. W. BLAKE MEMORIAL HOSPITAL, Bradenton, FL
LA CROSSE LUTHERAN HOSPITAL, La Crosse, WI, See Lutheran Hospital-Los Angeles Crosse
LA FOLLETTE MEDICAL CENTER, La Follette, TN
LA GRANGE MEMORIAL HOSPITAL (Formerly Community Memorial General Hospital), La Grange, IL
LA HABRA COMMUNITY HOSPITAL, La Habra, CA
LA HACIENDA TREATMENT CENTER, Hunt, TX
LA HARPE HOSPITAL, La Harpe, IL
LA JUNTA MEDICAL CENTER, La Junta, CO, See Arkansas Valley Regional Medical Center
LA PALMA INTERCOMMUNITY HOSPITAL, La Palma, CA
LA PLATA COMMUNITY HOSPITAL, Durango, CO
LA RABIDA CHILDREN'S HOSPITAL AND RESEARCH CENTER, Chicago, IL
LA SALLE GENERAL HOSPITAL, Jena, LA
LABETTE COUNTY MEDICAL CENTER, Parsons, KS
LAC COUNTY-KING-DREW MEDICAL CENTER, Los Angeles, CA
LAC-HARBOR-UNIVERSITY OF CALIFORNIA AT LOS ANGELES MEDICAL CENTER, Torrance, CA
LAC-HIGH DESERT HOSPITAL, Lancaster, CA
LAC-RANCHO LOS AMIGOS MEDICAL CENTER (Formerly Rancho Los Amigos Medical Center), Downey, CA
LAC-UNIVERSITY OF SOUTHERN CALIFORNIA MEDICAL CENTER, Los Angeles, CA
LACROIX HOSPITAL, White Pine, MI
LADD MEMORIAL HOSPITAL, Osceola, WI
LADY OF THE SEA GENERAL HOSPITAL, Galliano, LA
LAFAYETTE CLINIC, Detroit, MI
LAFAYETTE COUNTY MEMORIAL HOSPITAL, Lewisville, AR
LAFAYETTE GENERAL MEDICAL CENTER (Formerly Lafayette General Hospital), Lafayette, LA
LAFAYETTE HOME HOSPITAL, Lafayette, IN
LAFAYETTE HOSPITAL, Arroyo, P.R.
LAFAYETTE REGIONAL HEALTH CENTER, Lexington, MO
LAFENE STUDENT HEALTH CENTER AND UNIVERSITY HOSPITAL, Manhattan, KS
LAGRANGE HOSPITAL, Lagrange, IN
LAGUARDIA HOSPITAL, , NY
LAGUNA HONDA HOSPITAL AND REHABILITATION CENTER, San Francisco, CA
LAHEY CLINIC HOSPITAL, Burlington, MA
LAIRD HOSPITAL, Union, MS
LAKE AREA HOSPITAL, Webster, SD
LAKE CHARLES MEMORIAL HOSPITAL, Lake Charles, LA
LAKE CHELAN COMMUNITY HOSPITAL, Chelan, WA
LAKE CITY HOSPITAL, Lake City, MN
LAKE CITY MEDICAL CENTER, Lake City, FL, See AMI Lake City Medical Center
LAKE CLIFF HOSPITAL, Dallas, TX
LAKE DISTRICT HOSPITAL, Lakeview, OR
LAKE ERIE INSTITUTE OF REHABILITATION, Erie, PA
LAKE FOREST HOSPITAL, Lake Forest, IL
LAKE HOSPITAL OF THE PALM BEACHES, Lake Worth, FL
LAKE HOSPITAL SYSTEM, Painesville, OH
LAKE LIVINGSTON MEDICAL CENTER (Formerly Livingston Memorial Hospital), Livingston, TX
LAKE MEDICAL CENTER (Formerly Lake Community Hospital), Leesburg, FL
LAKE OF THE OZARKS GENERAL HOSPITAL, Osage Beach, MO
LAKE REGION HOSPITAL AND NURSING HOME, Fergus Falls, MN
LAKE SEMINOLE HOSPITAL, Seminole, FL
LAKE SHORE HOSPITAL, Lake City, FL
LAKE SHORE HOSPITAL, Manchester, NH
LAKE SHORE HOSPITAL, Irving, NY
LAKE TAYLOR CITY HOSPITAL, Norfolk, VA
LAKE VIEW COMMUNITY HOSPITAL, Paw Paw, MI
LAKE VIEW MEMORIAL HOSPITAL, Two Harbors, MN
LAKE WALES HOSPITAL, Lake Wales, FL
LAKE WHITNEY MEMORIAL HOSPITAL (Formerly Whitney Hospital), Whitney, TX
LAKEFIELD MUNICIPAL HOSPITAL, Lakefield, MN
LAKELAND HOSPITAL, Elkhorn, WI
LAKELAND MEDICAL CENTER, Athens, TX
LAKELAND REGIONAL MEDICAL CENTER, Lakeland, FL
LAKES REGION GENERAL HOSPITAL, Laconia, NH
LAKESHORE COMMUNITY HOSPITAL, Dadeville, AL
LAKESHORE COMMUNITY HOSPITAL, Shelby, MI
LAKESHORE HOSPITAL, Birmingham, AL
LAKESHORE HOSPITAL, Detroit, MI, See Michigan Osteopathic Medical Center
LAKESHORE MENTAL HEALTH INSTITUTE, Knoxville, TN
LAKESIDE COMMUNITY HOSPITAL, Lakeport, CA
LAKESIDE COMMUNITY HOSPITAL (Formerly Forsyth County Hospital), Cumming, GA
LAKESIDE COMMUNITY HOSPITAL, Chicago, IL
LAKESIDE COMMUNITY HOSPITAL, Incline Village, NV
LAKESIDE HOSPITAL, Metairie, LA
LAKESIDE HOSPITAL, Kansas City, MO
LAKESIDE HOSPITAL, Cleveland, OH, See University Hospitals of Cleveland
LAKESIDE MEMORIAL HOSPITAL, Brockport, NY
LAKEVIEW COMMUNITY HOSPITAL, Eufaula, AL
LAKEVIEW HOSPITAL, Bountiful, UT
LAKEVIEW HOSPITAL, Milwaukee, WI
LAKEVIEW MEDICAL CENTER, Danville, IL
LAKEVIEW MEDICAL CENTER, Rice Lake, WI
LAKEVIEW MEMORIAL HOSPITAL, Stillwater, MN
LAKEVIEW UNIT, Beaver Dam, WI, See Beaver Dam Community Hospitals
LAKEVILLE HOSPITAL, Lakeville, MA
LAKEWEST HOSPITAL, Willoughby, OH, See Lake Hospital System, Painesville
LAKEWOOD HOSPITAL, Morgan City, LA
LAKEWOOD HOSPITAL, Lakewood, OH
LAKEWOOD HOSPITAL (Formerly Lakewood General Hospital), Tacoma, WA
LALLIE KEMP CHARITY HOSPITAL, Independence, LA
LAMAR REGIONAL HOSPITAL (Formerly LaMar Carraway Medical Center), Vernon, AL
LAMONT INFIRMARY, Exeter, NH
LANAI COMMUNITY HOSPITAL, Lanai City, HI
LANCASTER COMMUNITY HOSPITAL, Lancaster, CA
LANCASTER GENERAL HOSPITAL, Lancaster, PA
LANCASTER-FAIRFIELD COMMUNITY HOSPITAL, Lancaster, OH
LANDER VALLEY REGIONAL MEDICAL CENTER, Lander, WY
LANDMANN-JUNGMAN MEMORIAL HOSPITAL, Scotland, SD
LANE COUNTY HOSPITAL, Dighton, KS
LANE MEMORIAL HOSPITAL, Zachary, LA
LANGLADE MEMORIAL HOSPITAL, Antigo, WI
LANGLEY PORTER PSYCHIATRIC INSTITUTE-HOSPITALS AND CLINICS, San Francisco, CA
LANIER PARK HOSPITAL, Gainesville, GA
LANKENAU HOSPITAL, Philadelphia, PA
LANSING GENERAL HOSPITAL, Lansing, MI
LANTERMAN DEVELOPMENTAL CENTER (Formerly Lanterman State Hospital and Developmental Center), Pomona, CA

LAPEER GENERAL HOSPITAL (Formerly Lapeer County General Hospital), Lapeer, MI
LAPORTE HOSPITAL, Laporte, IN
LARGO MEDICAL CENTER HOSPITAL, Largo, FL, See HCA Largo Medical Center Hospital
LARKIN GENERAL HOSPITAL, South Miami, FL
LARNED STATE HOSPITAL, Larned, KS
LARUE D. CARTER MEMORIAL HOSPITAL, Indianapolis, IN
LAS ENCINAS HOSPITAL, Pasadena, CA
LAS OLAS COMMUNITY HOSPITAL, Fort Lauderdale, FL
LAS VEGAS MEDICAL CENTER, Las Vegas, NM
LASSEN COMMUNITY HOSPITAL, Susanville, CA
LATIMER COUNTY GENERAL HOSPITAL, Wilburton, OK
LATROBE AREA HOSPITAL, Latrobe, PA
LAUGHLIN MEMORIAL HOSPITAL, Greeneville, TN
LAUGHLIN PAVILION, Kirksville, MO, See Kirksville Osteopathic Health Center
LAUREL GROVE HOSPITAL, Castro Valley, CA
LAURELWOOD HOSPITAL, The Woodlands, TX
LAURENS DISTRICT HOSPITAL, Laurens, SC
LAVACA MEDICAL CENTER, Hallettsville, TX
LAWNDALE COMMUNITY HOSPITAL, Philadelphia, PA
LAWNWOOD REGIONAL MEDICAL CENTER, Fort Pierce, FL
LAWRENCE AND MEMORIAL HOSPITAL, New London, CT
LAWRENCE COUNTY GENERAL HOSPITAL, Ironton, OH
LAWRENCE COUNTY HOSPITAL, Moulton, AL
LAWRENCE COUNTY HOSPITAL, Monticello, MS
LAWRENCE COUNTY MEMORIAL HOSPITAL, Lawrenceville, IL
LAWRENCE F. QUIGLEY MEMORIAL HOSPITAL, Chelsea, MA
LAWRENCE GENERAL HOSPITAL, Lawrence, MA
LAWRENCE HOSPITAL, Bronxville, NY
LAWRENCE MEMORIAL HOSPITAL, Walnut Ridge, AR
LAWRENCE MEMORIAL HOSPITAL, Lawrence, KS
LAWRENCE MEMORIAL HOSPITAL OF MEDFORD, Medford, MA
LDS HOSPITAL, Salt Lake City, UT
LE BONHEUR CHILDREN'S MEDICAL CENTER, Memphis, TN
LEA REGIONAL HOSPITAL, Hobbs, NM
LEAHI HOSPITAL, Honolulu, HI
LEAKE COUNTY MEMORIAL HOSPITAL, Carthage, MS
LEBANON COMMUNITY HOSPITAL, Lebanon, OR
LEBANON VALLEY GENERAL HOSPITAL, Lebanon, PA
LEE COUNTY COMMUNITY HOSPITAL, Pennington Gap, VA
LEE COUNTY MEMORIAL HOSPITAL, Bishopville, SC
LEE HOSPITAL, Johnstown, PA
LEE MEMORIAL HOSPITAL, Marianna, AR
LEE MEMORIAL HOSPITAL, Fort Myers, FL
LEE MEMORIAL HOSPITAL, Dowagiac, MI
LEE MEMORIAL HOSPITAL, Giddings, TX
LEE'S SUMMIT COMMUNITY HOSPITAL, Lees Summit, MO
LEELANAU MEMORIAL HOSPITAL, Northport, MI
LEESBURG REGIONAL MEDICAL CENTER, Leesburg, FL
LEESVILLE GENERAL HOSPITAL, Leesville, LA
LEHIGH VALLEY HOSPITAL CENTER, Allentown, PA
LEIGH MEMORIAL HOSPITAL, Norfolk, VA
LEILA HOSPITAL AND HEALTH CENTER, Battle Creek, MI
LELAND MEMORIAL HOSPITAL, Riverdale, MD
LEMUEL SHATTUCK HOSPITAL, Boston, MA
LENOIR MEMORIAL HOSPITAL, Kinston, NC
LENOX BAKER CHILDREN'S HOSPITAL, Durham, NC
LENOX HILL HOSPITAL, New York, NY
LEO N. LEVI NATIONAL ARTHRITIS HOSPITAL, Hot Springs National Park, AR, See Levi Arthritis Hospital
LEOMINSTER HOSPITAL, Leominster, MA
LEON MEMORIAL HOSPITAL (Formerly Leon County Memorial Hospital), Buffalo, TX
LEONARD HOSPITAL, Troy, NY
LEONARD MORSE HOSPITAL, Natick, MA
LESTER E. COX MEDICAL CENTERS, Springfield, MO
LETTERMAN ARMY MEDICAL CENTER, San Francisco, CA
LEVERING HOSPITAL, Hannibal, MO
LEVI ARTHRITIS HOSPITAL (Formerly Leo N. Levi National Arthritis Hospital), Hot Springs National Park, AR
LEVINDALE HEBREW GERIATRIC CENTER AND HOSPITAL, Baltimore, MD
LEWIS COUNTY GENERAL HOSPITAL, Lowville, NY
LEWIS COUNTY HOSPITAL, Hohenwald, TN
LEWIS R. PYLE MEMORIAL HOSPITAL, Payson, AZ
LEWIS-GALE HOSPITAL, Salem, VA
LEWISBURG COMMUNITY HOSPITAL, Lewisburg, TN
LEWISTOWN HOSPITAL, Lewistown, PA
LEWISVILLE MEMORIAL HOSPITAL, Lewisville, TX
LEXINGTON COUNTY HOSPITAL, West Columbia, SC
LEXINGTON MEMORIAL HOSPITAL, Lexington, NC
LIBERTY COUNTY HOSPITAL AND NURSING HOME, Chester, MT
LIBERTY HOSPITAL, Liberty, MO
LIBERTY MEDICAL CENTER, Baltimore, MD
LIBERTY MEMORIAL HOSPITAL, Hinesville, GA
LIBERTY STREET FACILITY, Meadville, PA, See Meadville Medical Center
LICKING MEMORIAL HOSPITAL, Newark, OH
LIFESPRING MENTAL HEALTH SERVICES (Formerly Southern Indiana Mental Health and Guidance Center), Jeffersonville, IN
LILLIAN M. HUDSPETH MEMORIAL HOSPITAL, Sonora, TX
LIMA MEMORIAL HOSPITAL, Lima, OH
LINCOLN COMMUNITY HOSPITAL AND NURSING HOME, Hugo, CO
LINCOLN COUNTY HOSPITAL, Lincoln, KS
LINCOLN COUNTY HOSPITAL, Lincolnton, NC
LINCOLN COUNTY HOSPITAL DISTRICT THREE, Davenport, WA
LINCOLN COUNTY MEDICAL CENTER (Formerly Ruidoso Hondo Valley Hospital), Ruidoso, NM
LINCOLN COUNTY MEMORIAL HOSPITAL, Troy, MO
LINCOLN DEVELOPMENTAL CENTER, Lincoln, IL
LINCOLN GENERAL HOSPITAL, Ruston, LA
LINCOLN GENERAL HOSPITAL, Lincoln, NE
LINCOLN HOSPITAL MEDICAL CENTER, Los Angeles, CA
LINCOLN MEDICAL AND MENTAL HEALTH CENTER, Bronx, NY
LINCOLN REGIONAL CENTER, Lincoln, NE
LINCOLN REGIONAL HOSPITAL, Fayetteville, TN
LINCOLN WEST HOSPITAL (Formerly Forkosh Memorial Hospital), Chicago, IL
LINDA VISTA COMMUNITY HOSPITAL (Formerly Santa Fe Community Hospital), Los Angeles, CA
LINDELL HOSPITAL, St. Louis, MO
LINDEN MUNICIPAL HOSPITAL, Linden, TX
LINDSAY HOSPITAL MEDICAL CENTER, Lindsay, CA
LINDSAY MUNICIPAL HOSPITAL, Lindsay, OK
LINDSBORG COMMUNITY HOSPITAL, Lindsborg, KS
LINTON HOSPITAL, Linton, ND
LITTLE COMPANY OF MARY HOSPITAL, Torrance, CA
LITTLE COMPANY OF MARY HOSPITAL, Evergreen Park, IL
LITTLE FALLS HOSPITAL, Little Falls, NY
LITTLE RIVER MEMORIAL HOSPITAL, Ashdown, AR
LITTLE ROCK DIVISION, Little Rock, AR, See John L. McClellan Memorial Veterans Hospital
LITTLE TRAVERSE DIVISION, Petoskey, MI, See Northern Michigan Hospitals
LITTLEFIELD MEDICAL CENTER, Littlefield, TX
LITTLETON HOSPITAL, Littleton, NH
LITZENBERG MEMORIAL COUNTY HOSPITAL, Central City, NE
LIVE OAKS HOSPITAL, Ridgeland, SC
LIVENGRIN FOUNDATION, Bensalem, PA
LIVINGSTON COMMUNITY HOSPITAL, Livingston, TN, See HCA Regional Hospital-Livingston
LIVINGSTON COUNTY HOSPITAL, Salem, KY
LIVINGSTON MEMORIAL HOSPITAL, Livingston, MT
LIVINGSTON-TOMBIGBEE REGIONAL MEDICAL CENTER, Livingston, AL
LLANO MEMORIAL HOSPITAL, Llano, TX
LLOYD NOLAND HOSPITAL AND HEALTH CENTERS (Formerly Listed Under Fairfield), Birmingham, AL
LOCK HAVEN HOSPITAL AND EXTENDED CARE UNIT, Lock Haven, PA
LOCKHART HOSPITAL, Lockhart, TX
LOCKNEY GENERAL HOSPITAL, Lockney, TX
LOCKPORT MEMORIAL HOSPITAL, Lockport, NY
LOCKWOOD-MACDONALD DIVISION, Petoskey, MI, See Northern Michigan Hospitals
LODI COMMUNITY HOSPITAL, Lodi, CA, See Community Hospital of Lodi
LODI COMMUNITY HOSPITAL, Lodi, OH
LODI MEMORIAL HOSPITAL, Lodi, CA
LOGAN COUNTY HEALTH CENTER, Guthrie, OK
LOGAN COUNTY HOSPITAL, Sterling, CO
LOGAN COUNTY HOSPITAL, Oakley, KS
LOGAN GENERAL HOSPITAL, Logan, WV
LOGAN REGIONAL HOSPITAL, Logan, UT
LOGANSPORT STATE HOSPITAL, Logansport, IN
LOMA LINDA COMMUNITY HOSPITAL, Loma Linda, CA
LOMA LINDA UNIVERSITY MEDICAL CENTER, Loma Linda, CA
LOMPOC DISTRICT HOSPITAL, Lompoc, CA
LONESOME PINE HOSPITAL, Big Stone Gap, VA
LONG BEACH COMMUNITY HOSPITAL, Long Beach, CA
LONG BEACH HOSPITAL, Long Beach, CA
LONG BEACH MEMORIAL HOSPITAL, Long Beach, NY
LONG ISLAND COLLEGE HOSPITAL, Brooklyn, NY
LONG ISLAND HOSPITAL (Formerly Listed Under Quincy), Boston, MA
LONG ISLAND JEWISH MEDICAL CENTER (Formerly Long Island Jewish-Hillside Medical Center), New York, NY
LONG PRAIRIE MEMORIAL HOSPITAL, Long Prairie, MN
LONGMONT UNITED HOSPITAL, Longmont, CO
LONGVIEW GENERAL HOSPITAL, Graysville, AL
LOOKOUT MEMORIAL HOSPITAL, Spearfish, SD
LORAIN COMMUNITY HOSPITAL, Lorain, OH
LORETTO HOSPITAL, Chicago, IL
LORING HOSPITAL, Sac City, IA
LORIS COMMUNITY HOSPITAL, Loris, SC
LOS ALAMITOS MEDICAL CENTER, Los Alamitos, CA
LOS ALAMOS MEDICAL CENTER, Los Alamos, NM
LOS ALTOS HOSPITAL AND MENTAL HEALTH CENTER (Formerly Los Altos Hospital), Long Beach, CA
LOS ANGELES COMMUNITY HOSPITAL, Los Angeles, CA
LOS ANGELES COUNTY CENTRAL JAIL HOSPITAL, Los Angeles, CA
LOS ANGELES COUNTY-OLIVE VIEW MEDICAL CENTER, Sylmar, CA
LOS BANOS COMMUNITY HOSPITAL, Los Banos, CA
LOS LUNAS HOSPITAL AND TRAINING SCHOOL, Los Lunas, NM
LOS MEDANOS COMMUNITY HOSPITAL (Formerly Los Medanos Community Hospital District), Pittsburg, CA
LOS ROBLES REGIONAL MEDICAL CENTER, Thousand Oaks, CA
LOST RIVERS DISTRICT HOSPITAL (Formerly Lost Rivers Hospital), Arco, ID
LOUDON COUNTY MEMORIAL HOSPITAL, Loudon, TN
LOUDOUN MEMORIAL HOSPITAL, Leesburg, VA
LOUIS A. JOHNSON VETERANS ADMINISTRATION MEDICAL CENTER, Clarksburg, WV
LOUIS A. WEISS MEMORIAL HOSPITAL, Chicago, IL
LOUIS SMITH MEMORIAL HOSPITAL, Lakeland, GA
LOUISE OBICI MEMORIAL HOSPITAL, Suffolk, VA
LOUISIANA STATE UNIVERSITY HOSPITAL, Shreveport, LA
LOUISVILLE BAPTIST HOSPITALS, Louisville, KY
LOURDES HOSPITAL, Paducah, KY
LOVE COUNTY HEALTH CENTER, Marietta, OK
LOVELACE MEDICAL CENTER, Albuquerque, NM
LOWELL GENERAL HOSPITAL, Lowell, MA
LOWER BUCKS HOSPITAL, Bristol, PA
LOWER FLORENCE COUNTY HOSPITAL, Lake City, SC
LOWER UMPQUA HOSPITAL DISTRICT, Reedsport, OR
LOWRANCE HOSPITAL, Mooresville, NC
LUBBOCK COUNTY HOSPITAL DISTRICT-LUBBOCK GENERAL HOSPITAL, Lubbock, TX
LUCAS COUNTY HEALTH CENTER (Formerly Lucas County Memorial Hospital), Chariton, IA
LUCIUS OLEN CROSBY MEMORIAL HOSPITAL, Picayune, MS
LUCY LEE HOSPITAL, Poplar Bluff, MO, See AMI Lucy Lee Hospital
LUDLOW HOSPITAL, Ludlow, MA
LUMBERTON CITIZENS HOSPITAL, Lumberton, MS
LUNDBERG MEMORIAL HOSPITAL, Creighton, NE
LUTHER HOSPITAL, Eau Claire, WI
LUTHERAN CENTER-SUBSTANCE ABUSE, Park Ridge, IL, See Parkside Lutheran Hospital
LUTHERAN COMMUNITY HOSPITAL, Norfolk, NE
LUTHERAN GENERAL HOSPITAL, Park Ridge, IL
LUTHERAN GENERAL HOSPITAL, Omaha, NE, See Lutheran Medical Center
LUTHERAN GENERAL HOSPITAL, San Antonio, TX
LUTHERAN HOSPITAL, Moline, IL
LUTHERAN HOSPITAL OF FORT WAYNE, Fort Wayne, IN
LUTHERAN HOSPITAL-LOS ANGELES CROSSE (Formerly La Crosse Lutheran Hospital), La Crosse, WI
LUTHERAN MEDICAL CENTER, Wheat Ridge, CO
LUTHERAN MEDICAL CENTER, St. Louis, MO
LUTHERAN MEDICAL CENTER, Brooklyn, NY
LUTHERAN MEDICAL CENTER, Cleveland, OH
LUTHERAN MEDICAL CENTER, Omaha, NE
LYKES MEMORIAL HOSPITAL, Brooksville, FL
LYNCHBURG GENERAL HOSPITAL (Formerly Lynchburg General-Marshall Lodge Hospitals), Lynchburg, VA
LYNDON B. JOHNSON TROPICAL MEDICAL CENTER, Pago Pago, American Samoa
LYNN COUNTY HOSPITAL DISTRICT, Tahoka, TX
LYNN HOSPITAL, Lynn, MA, See Atlanticare Medical Center
LYNN HOSPITAL, Lincoln Park, MI, See Oakwood Downriver Medical Center

M

M. I. T. MEDICAL DEPARTMENT, Cambridge, MA
MACDONALD HOSITAL FOR WOMEN, Cleveland, OH, See University Hospitals of Cleveland
MACKINAC STRAITS HOSPITAL AND HEALTH CENTER, St. Ignace, MI
MACNEAL HOSPITAL, Berwyn, IL
MACON COUNTY GENERAL HOSPITAL, Lafayette, TN
MACON COUNTY MEDICAL CENTER, Montezuma, GA
MAD RIVER COMMUNITY HOSPITAL, Arcata, CA
MADELIA COMMUNITY HOSPITAL, Madelia, MN
MADERA COMMUNITY HOSPITAL, Madera, CA
MADIGAN ARMY MEDICAL CENTER, Tacoma, WA
MADISON COMMUNITY HOSPITAL, Madison Heights, MI
MADISON COMMUNITY HOSPITAL, Madison, SD
MADISON COUNTY HOSPITAL, London, OH
MADISON COUNTY MEDICAL CENTER, Madisonville, TX
MADISON COUNTY MEMORIAL HOSPITAL, Madison, FL
MADISON COUNTY MEMORIAL HOSPITAL, Winterset, IA
MADISON GENERAL HOSPITAL, Canton, MS
MADISON HOSPITAL, Madison, MN
MADISON HOSPITAL, Madison, TN, See Tennessee Christian Medical Center
MADISON MEMORIAL HOSPITAL, Rexburg, ID
MADISON MEMORIAL HOSPITAL, Fredericktown, MO
MADISON PARISH HOSPITAL, Tallulah, LA
MADISON STATE HOSPITAL, Madison, IN
MADISON VALLEY HOSPITAL, Ennis, MT
MADONNA CENTERS, Lincoln, NE
MAGEE GENERAL HOSPITAL, Magee, MS
MAGEE REHABILITATION HOSPITAL, Philadelphia, PA
MAGEE-WOMENS HOSPITAL, Pittsburgh, PA
MAGIC VALLEY REGIONAL MEDICAL CENTER, Twin Falls, ID
MAGNOLIA HOSPITAL, Magnolia, AR
MAGNOLIA HOSPITAL, Corinth, MS
MAHASKA COUNTY HOSPITAL, Oskaloosa, IA
MAHNOMEN COUNTY AND VILLAGE HOSPITAL AND NURSING CENTER, Mahnomen, MN
MAIMONIDES MEDICAL CENTER, Brooklyn, NY
MAINE COAST MEMORIAL HOSPITAL, Ellsworth, ME
MAINE MEDICAL CENTER, Portland, ME
MAINLAND CENTER HOSPITAL, Texas City, TX
MAJOR HOSPITAL, Shelbyville, IN
MALCOLM BLISS MENTAL HEALTH CENTER, St. Louis, MO
MALCOLM GROW U. S. AIR FORCE MEDICAL CENTER, Camp Springs, MD
MALDEN HOSPITAL, Malden, MA
MALHEUR MEMORIAL HOSPITAL DISTRICT, Nyssa, OR
MALONE-HOGAN HOSPITAL, Big Spring, TX, See Scenic Mountain Medical Center
MALVERN INSTITUTE, Malvern, PA
MAN APPALACHIAN REGIONAL HOSPITAL, Man, WV
MANATEE MEMORIAL HOSPITAL, Bradenton, FL
MANCHESTER MEMORIAL HOSPITAL, Manchester, CT
MANDAN HOSPITAL, Mandan, ND
MANGUM CITY HOSPITAL, Mangum, OK
MANHATTAN EYE, EAR AND THROAT HOSPITAL, New York, NY
MANHATTAN PSYCHIATRIC CENTER-WARD'S ISLAND, New York, NY
MANNING GENERAL HOSPITAL, Manning, IA
MANSFIELD GENERAL HOSPITAL, Mansfield, OH
MANY HOSPITAL, Many, LA
MARCUM AND WALLACE MEMORIAL HOSPITAL, Irvine, KY
MARCUS DALY MEMORIAL HOSPITAL, Hamilton, MT
MARCUS J. LAWRENCE MEMORIAL HOSPITAL, Cottonwood, AZ
MARENGO MEMORIAL HOSPITAL, Marengo, IA
MARGARET MARY COMMUNITY HOSPITAL, Batesville, IN
MARGARET R. PARDEE MEMORIAL HOSPITAL, Hendersonville, NC
MARGARETVILLE MEMORIAL HOSPITAL, Margaretville, NY
MARIA PARHAM HOSPITAL, Henderson, NC
MARIAN HEALTH CENTER, Sioux City, IA
MARIAN MANOR MEDICAL CENTER, Riverview, MI
MARIAN MEDICAL CENTER, Santa Maria, CA
MARIANJOY REHABILITATION CENTER, Wheaton, IL
MARICOPA MEDICAL CENTER, Phoenix, AZ
MARIETTA MEMORIAL HOSPITAL, Marietta, OH
MARIN GENERAL HOSPITAL, San Rafael, CA
MARINERS HOSPITAL, Tavernier, FL
MARION COMMUNITY HOSPITAL, Ocala, FL
MARION COUNTY GENERAL HOSPITAL, Hamilton, AL
MARION COUNTY GENERAL HOSPITAL, Columbia, MS
MARION COUNTY HOSPITAL, Jefferson, TX
MARION GENERAL HOSPITAL, Marion, IN
MARION GENERAL HOSPITAL, Marion, OH
MARION MEMORIAL HOSPITAL, Buena Vista, GA
MARION MEMORIAL HOSPITAL, Marion, IL
MARION MEMORIAL HOSPITAL (Formerly Marion County Memorial Hospital), Marion, SC
MARK REED HOSPITAL, McCleary, WA
MARKS-ENGLISH HOSPITAL, Glen Rose, TX
MARLBORO PARK HOSPITAL, Bennettsville, SC
MARLBORO PSYCHIATRIC HOSPITAL, Marlboro, NJ
MARLBOROUGH HOSPITAL, Marlborough, MA
MARLETTE COMMUNITY HOSPITAL, Marlette, MI
MARQUETTE GENERAL HOSPITAL, Marquette, MI
MARSH VALLEY HOSPITAL, Downey, ID
MARSHAL HALE MEMORIAL HOSPITAL, San Francisco, CA
MARSHALL BROWNING HOSPITAL, Du Quoin, IL
MARSHALL COUNTY HOSPITAL, Benton, KY
MARSHALL COUNTY HOSPITAL, Holly Springs, MS
MARSHALL COUNTY MEMORIAL HOSPITAL, Britton, SD
MARSHALL HABILITATION CENTER, Marshall, MO
MARSHALL HOSPITAL, Placerville, CA
MARSHALL I. PICKENS HOSPITAL, Greenville, SC
MARSHALL MEMORIAL HOSPITAL, Madill, OK
MARSHALLTOWN MEDICAL AND SURGICAL CENTER, Marshalltown, IA
MARTHA JEFFERSON HOSPITAL, Charlottesville, VA
MARTHA WASHINGTON HOSPITAL, Chicago, IL
MARTHA'S VINEYARD HOSPITAL, Oak Bluffs, MA
MARTIN ARMY COMMUNITY HOSPITAL, Fort Benning, GA
MARTIN COUNTY HOSPITAL DISTRICT, Stanton, TX
MARTIN GENERAL HOSPITAL, Williamston, NC
MARTIN LUTHER HOSPITAL MEDICAL CENTER, Anaheim, CA
MARTIN MEMORIAL HOSPITAL, Stuart, FL
MARY BLACK MEMORIAL HOSPITAL, Spartanburg, SC
MARY BRECKINRIDGE HOSPITAL (Formerly Mary Breckinridge Hospital-Frontier Nursing Service), Hyden, KY
MARY BRIDGE CHILDREN'S HEALTH CENTER, Tacoma, WA
MARY CHILES HOSPITAL, Mount Sterling, KY
MARY E. DICKERSON MEMORIAL HOSPITAL, Jasper, TX
MARY FREE BED HOSPITAL AND REHABILITATION CENTER, Grand Rapids, MI
MARY GREELEY MEDICAL CENTER, Ames, IA
MARY HITCHCOCK MEMORIAL HOSPITAL, Hanover, NH
MARY HURLEY HOSPITAL, Coalgate, OK
MARY IMMACULATE HOSPITAL, Newport News, VA
MARY IMOGENE BASSETT HOSPITAL AND CLINICS, Cooperstown, NY
MARY LANE HOSPITAL, Ware, MA
MARY LANNING MEMORIAL HOSPITAL, Hastings, NE
MARY MCCLELLAN HOSPITAL, Cambridge, NY
MARY RUTAN HOSPITAL, Bellefontaine, OH
MARY SHERMAN HOSPITAL, Sullivan, IN
MARY SHIELS HOSPITAL, Dallas, TX
MARY THOMPSON HOSPITAL, Chicago, IL
MARY WASHINGTON HOSPITAL, Fredericksburg, VA
MARYLAND GENERAL HOSPITAL, Baltimore, MD
MARYMOUNT HOSPITAL, London, KY
MARYMOUNT HOSPITAL, Garfield Heights, OH
MARYVALE SAMARITAN HOSPITAL, Phoenix, AZ
MARYVIEW HOSPITAL, Portsmouth, VA
MASON DISTRICT HOSPITAL, Havana, IL
MASON GENERAL HOSPITAL, Shelton, WA
MASONIC HOME AND HOSPITAL (Formerly Masonic Hospital), Wallingford, CT
MASSAC MEMORIAL HOSPITAL, Metropolis, IL
MASSACHUSETTS EYE AND EAR INFIRMARY, Boston, MA
MASSACHUSETTS GENERAL HOSPITAL, Boston, MA
MASSACHUSETTS HOSPITAL SCHOOL, Canton, MA
MASSACHUSETTS MENTAL HEALTH CENTER, Boston, MA
MASSACHUSETTS OSTEOPATHIC HOSPITAL AND MEDICAL CENTER, Boston, MA
MASSAPEQUA GENERAL HOSPITAL, Seaford, NY
MASSENA MEMORIAL HOSPITAL, Massena, NY
MASSILLON COMMUNITY HOSPITAL, Massillon, OH
MASSILLON STATE HOSPITAL, Massillon, OH
MATAGORDA GENERAL HOSPITAL, Bay City, TX
MATERNITY HOSPITAL, Philadelphia, PA, See Pennsylvania Hospital
MATHENY SCHOOL, Peapack, NJ
MATTAPAN HOSPITAL, Boston, MA
MATTIE WILLIAMS HOSPITAL, Richlands, VA
MATTY HERSEE HOSPITAL, Meridian, MS
MAUDE NORTON MEMORIAL CITY HOSPITAL, Columbus, KS
MAUI MEMORIAL HOSPITAL, Wailuku, HI, See Maui Community Hospital
MAUI MEMORIAL HOSPITAL, Wailuku, HI
MAURITZ MEMORIAL HOSPITAL, Ganado, TX
MAURY COUNTY HOSPITAL, Columbia, TN
MAVERICK COUNTY HOSPITAL DISTRICT, Eagle Pass, TX
MAXICARE MEDICAL CENTER, Los Angeles, CA
MAYAGUEZ MEDICAL CENTER, Mayaguez, P.R.
MAYERS MEMORIAL HOSPITAL, Fall River Mills, CA
MAYO REGIONAL HOSPITAL, Dover-Foxcroft, ME
MAYVIEW STATE HOSPITAL, Bridgeville, PA
MCALESTER REGIONAL HOSPITAL, McAlester, OK
MCALLEN MEDICAL CENTER (Formerly McAllen Methodist Hospital), McAllen, TX
MCCAIN HOSPITAL, McCain, NC
MCCALL MEMORIAL HOSPITAL, McCall, ID
MCCAMEY HOSPITAL, McCamey, TX
MCCONE COUNTY HOSPITAL, Circle, MT
MCCRAY MEMORIAL HOSPITAL, Kendallville, IN
MCCUISTION REGIONAL MEDICAL CENTER, Paris, TX
MCCULLOUGH-HYDE MEMORIAL HOSPITAL, Oxford, OH
MCCUNE-BROOKS HOSPITAL, Carthage, MO
MCCURTAIN MEMORIAL HOSPITAL, Idabel, OK
MCDONALD ARMY COMMUNITY HOSPITAL, Newport News, VA
MCDONOUGH DISTRICT HOSPITAL, Macomb, IL
MCDOWELL APPALACHIAN REGIONAL HEALTH CARE (Formerly McDowell Appalachian Regional Hospital), McDowell, KY
MCDOWELL HOSPITAL, Marion, NC
MCDUFFIE COUNTY HOSPITAL, Thomson, GA
MCFARLAND HOUSE, Barre, VT, See Central Vermont Medical Center, Berlin
MCGEHEE-DESHA COUNTY HOSPITAL, McGehee, AR
MCKAY-DEE HOSPITAL CENTER, Ogden, UT
MCKEE MEDICAL CENTER, Loveland, CO
MCKEESPORT HOSPITAL, McKeesport, PA
MCKENNA MEMORIAL HOSPITAL, New Braunfels, TX
MCKENNAN HOSPITAL, Sioux Falls, SD
MCKENZIE COUNTY MEMORIAL HOSPITAL, Watford City, ND
MCKENZIE MEMORIAL HOSPITAL, Sandusky, MI
MCKENZIE-WILLAMETTE HOSPITAL, Springfield, OR
MCKINLEY MEMORIAL HOSPITAL, Urbana, IL
MCLAREN GENERAL HOSPITAL, Flint, MI
MCLEAN COUNTY GENERAL HOSPITAL, Calhoun, KY
MCLEAN HOSPITAL, Belmont, MA
MCLEOD REGIONAL MEDICAL CENTER, Florence, SC
MCMINNVILLE COMMUNITY HOSPITAL, McMinnville, OR
MCNAIRY COUNTY GENERAL HOSPITAL, Selmer, TN
MCPHERSON COMMUNITY HEALTH CENTER, Howell, MI
MCPHERSON HOSPITAL, Durham, NC
MEADE DISTRICT HOSPITAL, Meade, KS
MEADOWBROOK HOSPITAL (Formerly Gardner Community Medical Center), Gardner, KS
MEADOWCREST HOSPITAL, Gretna, LA
MEADOWLANDS HOSPITAL MEDICAL CENTER (Formerly Riverside General Hospital), Secaucus, NJ
MEADOWVIEW REGIONAL HOSPITAL, Maysville, KY
MEADVILLE MEDICAL CENTER, Meadville, PA
MEASE HOSPITAL COUNTRYSIDE, Safety Harbor, FL
MEASE HOSPITAL DUNEDIN (Formerly Mease Health Care), Dunedin, FL
MECOSTA COUNTY GENERAL HOSPITAL, Big Rapids, MI
MEDCENTER HOSPITAL (Formerly Community Medcenter Hospital), Marion, OH
MEDCENTER ONE, Bismarck, ND
MEDFIELD CENTER, Largo, FL
MEDFIELD STATE HOSPITAL, Medfield, MA
MEDICAL ARTS CENTER HOSPITAL, New York, NY
MEDICAL ARTS HOSPITAL, Dallas, TX, See AMI Medical Arts Hospital
MEDICAL ARTS HOSPITAL, Lamesa, TX
MEDICAL CENTER, Columbus, GA
MEDICAL CENTER AT BOWLING GREEN, Bowling Green, KY
MEDICAL CENTER AT PRINCETON, Princeton, NJ
MEDICAL CENTER AT THE UNIVERSITY OF CALIFORNIA, San Francisco, CA, See University of California, San Francisco Medical Center
MEDICAL CENTER DEL ORO HOSPITAL, Houston, TX
MEDICAL CENTER EAST, Birmingham, AL
MEDICAL CENTER HOSPITAL, Punta Gorda, FL
MEDICAL CENTER HOSPITAL, Chillicothe, OH
MEDICAL CENTER HOSPITAL, Conroe, TX
MEDICAL CENTER HOSPITAL, Odessa, TX
MEDICAL CENTER HOSPITAL, San Antonio, TX, See Bexar County Hospital District

MEDICAL CENTER HOSPITAL, Tyler, TX
MEDICAL CENTER HOSPITAL OF VERMONT, Burlington, VT
MEDICAL CENTER HOSPITALS, Portland, OR
MEDICAL CENTER OF BATON ROUGE, Baton Rouge, LA
MEDICAL CENTER OF CALICO ROCK, Calico Rock, AR
MEDICAL CENTER OF CENTRAL GEORGIA, Macon, GA
MEDICAL CENTER OF DELAWARE, Wilmington, DE
MEDICAL CENTER OF INDEPENDENCE, Independence, MO
MEDICAL CENTER OF LA MIRADA (Formerly La Mirada Community Hospital), La Mirada, CA
MEDICAL CENTER OF SOUTHEASTERN OKLAHOMA (Formerly Bryan Memorial Hospital), Durant, OK
MEDICAL CENTER REHABILITATION HOSPITAL, Grand Forks, ND
MEDICAL COLLEGE OF GEORGIA HOSPITAL AND CLINICS, Augusta, GA
MEDICAL COLLEGE OF OHIO HOSPITAL, Toledo, OH
MEDICAL COLLEGE OF VIRGINIA HOSPITALS, VIRGINIA COMMONWEALTH UNIVERSITY, Richmond, VA
MEDICAL DENTAL HOSPITAL, Seattle, WA
MEDICAL PARK HOSPITAL, Winston-Salem, NC
MEDICAL PARK WEST (Formerly Community Hospital), Birmingham, AL
MEDICAL PLAZA HOSPITAL, Fort Worth, TX
MEDICAL PLAZA HOSPITAL, Sherman, TX, See AMI Medical Plaza Hospital
MEDICINE LODGE MEMORIAL HOSPITAL, Medicine Lodge, KS
MEDINA COMMUNITY HOSPITAL, Medina, OH
MEDINA COMMUNITY HOSPITAL (Formerly Medina Memorial Hospital), Hondo, TX
MEDINA MEMORIAL HOSPITAL, Medina, NY
MEEKER COUNTY MEMORIAL HOSPITAL, Litchfield, MN
MELISSA MEMORIAL HOSPITAL, Holyoke, CO
MELROSE HOSPITAL AND PINE VILLA CONVALESCENT AND NURSING CARE UNIT, Melrose, MN
MELROSE-WAKEFIELD HOSPITAL ASSOCIATION, Melrose, MA
MEMORIAL CITY MEDICAL CENTER (Formerly Memorial City General Hospital), Houston, TX
MEMORIAL COMMUNITY HOSPITAL, Jefferson City, MO
MEMORIAL COMMUNITY HOSPITAL, Blair, NE
MEMORIAL COMMUNITY HOSPITAL, Edgerton, WI
MEMORIAL DIVISION, Charleston, WV, See Charleston Area Medical Center
MEMORIAL GENERAL HOSPITAL, Las Cruces, NM
MEMORIAL HOSPITAL, North Little Rock, AR
MEMORIAL HOSPITAL, Siloam Springs, AR
MEMORIAL HOSPITAL, Colorado Springs, CO
MEMORIAL HOSPITAL, Craig, CO
MEMORIAL HOSPITAL, Greeley, CO
MEMORIAL HOSPITAL, Meriden, CT
MEMORIAL HOSPITAL, Hollywood, FL
MEMORIAL HOSPITAL, Ormond Beach, FL
MEMORIAL HOSPITAL, Sarasota, FL, See Sarasota Memorial Hospital
MEMORIAL HOSPITAL, Bainbridge, GA
MEMORIAL HOSPITAL, Waycross, GA
MEMORIAL HOSPITAL, Weiser, ID
MEMORIAL HOSPITAL, Belleville, IL
MEMORIAL HOSPITAL, Carbondale, IL
MEMORIAL HOSPITAL, Carthage, IL
MEMORIAL HOSPITAL, Chester, IL
MEMORIAL HOSPITAL, Logansport, IN
MEMORIAL HOSPITAL, Abilene, KS
MEMORIAL HOSPITAL, Manhattan, KS
MEMORIAL HOSPITAL, McPherson, KS
MEMORIAL HOSPITAL, Manchester, KY
MEMORIAL HOSPITAL, Cumberland, MD
MEMORIAL HOSPITAL, Owosso, MI
MEMORIAL HOSPITAL, St. Joseph, MI, See Southwestern Michigan Health Care Association
MEMORIAL HOSPITAL, Cambridge, MN
MEMORIAL HOSPITAL, Aurora, NE
MEMORIAL HOSPITAL, Schuyler, NE
MEMORIAL HOSPITAL, Seward, NE
MEMORIAL HOSPITAL, Nashua, NH, See Nashua Memorial Hospital
MEMORIAL HOSPITAL, North Conway, NH
MEMORIAL HOSPITAL, Albany, NY
MEMORIAL HOSPITAL, Fremont, OH
MEMORIAL HOSPITAL, Marysville, OH
MEMORIAL HOSPITAL, Frederick, OK
MEMORIAL HOSPITAL, Guymon, OK
MEMORIAL HOSPITAL, Towanda, PA
MEMORIAL HOSPITAL, York, PA
MEMORIAL HOSPITAL, Pawtucket, RI
MEMORIAL HOSPITAL, Chattanooga, TN
MEMORIAL HOSPITAL, Clarksville, TN
MEMORIAL HOSPITAL, Trenton, TN, See Forum Hospital Trenton
MEMORIAL HOSPITAL, Center, TX
MEMORIAL HOSPITAL, Dumas, TX
MEMORIAL HOSPITAL, Gonzales, TX
MEMORIAL HOSPITAL, Kermit, TX
MEMORIAL HOSPITAL, Marshall, TX
MEMORIAL HOSPITAL, Nacogdoches, TX
MEMORIAL HOSPITAL, Seminole, TX
MEMORIAL HOSPITAL, Danville, VA
MEMORIAL HOSPITAL, Odessa, WA
MEMORIAL HOSPITAL, Burlington, WI
MEMORIAL HOSPITAL, Lancaster, WI
MEMORIAL HOSPITAL, Manitowoc, WI
MEMORIAL HOSPITAL, Neillsville, WI
MEMORIAL HOSPITAL -EL CAMPO (Formerly El Campo Memorial Hospital), El Campo, TX
MEMORIAL HOSPITAL AND HEALTH CARE CENTER, Jasper, IN
MEMORIAL HOSPITAL AND HOME, Perham, MN
MEMORIAL HOSPITAL AND HOME, Sidney, NE
MEMORIAL HOSPITAL AND NURSING HOME OF GREENE COUNTY, Catskill, NY
MEMORIAL HOSPITAL AT EASTON MARYLAND, Easton, MD
MEMORIAL HOSPITAL AT EXETER, Exeter, CA
MEMORIAL HOSPITAL AT GULFPORT, Gulfport, MS
MEMORIAL HOSPITAL AT OCONOMOWOC, Oconomowoc, WI
MEMORIAL HOSPITAL CERES, , CA, See Memorial Hospital Association, Modesto
MEMORIAL HOSPITAL CORPORATION OF TOPEKA, Topeka, KS
MEMORIAL HOSPITAL FOR CANCER AND ALLIED DISEASES, New York, NY
MEMORIAL HOSPITAL FOR MCHENRY COUNTY, Woodstock, IL
MEMORIAL HOSPITAL MEDICAL CENTER, Modesto, CA, See Memorial Hospital Association
MEMORIAL HOSPITAL OF ADEL, Adel, GA
MEMORIAL HOSPITAL OF ALAMANCE COUNTY, Burlington, NC, See Alamance Memorial Hospital
MEMORIAL HOSPITAL OF BEDFORD COUNTY, Everett, PA
MEMORIAL HOSPITAL OF BOSCOBEL, Boscobel, WI
MEMORIAL HOSPITAL OF BURLINGTON COUNTY, Mount Holly, NJ
MEMORIAL HOSPITAL OF CARBON COUNTY, Rawlins, WY
MEMORIAL HOSPITAL OF DODGE COUNTY, Fremont, NE
MEMORIAL HOSPITAL OF GARDENA, Gardena, CA
MEMORIAL HOSPITAL OF GARLAND, Garland, TX
MEMORIAL HOSPITAL OF GENEVA, Geneva, OH
MEMORIAL HOSPITAL OF GLENDALE, Glendale, CA, See Glendale Memorial Hospital and Health Center
MEMORIAL HOSPITAL OF HAWTHORNE, Hawthorne, CA, See Hawthorne Hospital
MEMORIAL HOSPITAL OF IOWA COUNTY, Dodgeville, WI
MEMORIAL HOSPITAL OF LAFAYETTE COUNTY, Darlington, WI
MEMORIAL HOSPITAL OF LARAMIE COUNTY, Cheyenne, WY
MEMORIAL HOSPITAL OF MARTINSVILLE AND HENRY COUNTY, Martinsville, VA
MEMORIAL HOSPITAL OF MICHIGAN CITY, Michigan City, IN
MEMORIAL HOSPITAL OF SALEM COUNTY (Formerly Salem County Memorial Hospital), Salem, NJ
MEMORIAL HOSPITAL OF SAN GORGONIO PASS (Formerly San Gorgonio Pass Memorial Hospital), Banning, CA
MEMORIAL HOSPITAL OF SANTA BARBARA, Santa Barbara, CA, See Rehabilitation Institute of Santa Barbara
MEMORIAL HOSPITAL OF SHERIDAN COUNTY, Sheridan, WY
MEMORIAL HOSPITAL OF SOUTH BEND, South Bend, IN
MEMORIAL HOSPITAL OF SOUTHERN OKLAHOMA, Ardmore, OK
MEMORIAL HOSPITAL OF SWEETWATER COUNTY, Rock Springs, WY
MEMORIAL HOSPITAL OF TAMPA, Tampa, FL, See AMI Memorial Hospital of Tampa
MEMORIAL HOSPITAL OF TAYLOR COUNTY, Medford, WI
MEMORIAL HOSPITAL OF WASHINGTON COUNTY, Sandersville, GA
MEMORIAL HOSPITAL OF WASHINGTON COUNTY, Bartlesville, OK, See Jane Phillips Episcopal-Memorial Medical Center
MEMORIAL HOSPITAL OF WILLIAM F. AND GERTRUDE F. JONES, Wellsville, NY
MEMORIAL HOSPITAL SYSTEM, Houston, TX
MEMORIAL HOSPITAL-SAN LEANDRO, San Leandro, CA
MEMORIAL HOSPITAL, ROXBOROUGH, Philadelphia, PA, See Roxborough Memorial Hospital
MEMORIAL HOSPITALS ASSOCIATION, Modesto, CA
MEMORIAL MEDICAL CENTER, Long Beach, CA
MEMORIAL MEDICAL CENTER, Savannah, GA
MEMORIAL MEDICAL CENTER, Springfield, IL
MEMORIAL MEDICAL CENTER, Corpus Christi, TX
MEMORIAL MEDICAL CENTER (Formerly Champ Traylor Memorial Hospital), Port Lavaca, TX
MEMORIAL MEDICAL CENTER, Ashland, WI
MEMORIAL MEDICAL CENTER OF EAST TEXAS (Formerly Memorial Hospital), Lufkin, TX
MEMORIAL MEDICAL CENTER OF JACKSONVILLE, Jacksonville, FL
MEMORIAL MEDICAL CENTER OF WEST MICHIGAN, Ludington, MI
MEMORIAL MISSION HOSPITAL, Asheville, NC
MEMORIAL REGIONAL REHABILITATION CENTER, Jacksonville, FL
MEMPHIS MENTAL HEALTH INSTITUTE, Memphis, TN
MENARD HOSPITAL, Menard, TX
MENDOCINO COAST DISTRICT HOSPITAL, Fort Bragg, CA
MENDOCINO COMMUNITY HOSPITAL, Ukiah, CA
MENDOTA COMMUNITY HOSPITAL, Mendota, IL
MENDOTA MENTAL HEALTH INSTITUTE, Madison, WI
MENNONITE GENERAL HOSPITAL, Aibonito, P.R.
MENNONITE HOSPITAL, Bloomington, IL
MENORAH MEDICAL CENTER, Kansas City, MO
MENTAL HEALTH INSTITUTE, Cherokee, IA
MENTAL HEALTH INSTITUTE, Clarinda, IA
MENTAL HEALTH INSTITUTE, Independence, IA
MENTAL HEALTH INSTITUTE, Mount Pleasant, IA
MERCED COMMUNITY MEDICAL CENTER, Merced, CA
MERCER COUNTY HOSPITAL, Aledo, IL
MERCER COUNTY JOINT TOWNSHIP COMMUNITY HOSPITAL, Coldwater, OH
MERCER MEDICAL CENTER, Trenton, NJ
MERCY CATHOLIC MEDICAL CENTER, Philadelphia, PA
MERCY CENTER FOR HEALTH CARE SERVICES, Aurora, IL
MERCY COMMUNITY HOSPITAL, Port Jervis, NY
MERCY HEALTH CENTER, Oklahoma City, OK
MERCY HEALTH CENTER, Dubuque, IA
MERCY HOSPITAL, Bakersfield, CA
MERCY HOSPITAL, Merced, CA
MERCY HOSPITAL, Miami, FL
MERCY HOSPITAL, Urbana, IL
MERCY HOSPITAL, Elwood, IN
MERCY HOSPITAL, Cedar Rapids, IA
MERCY HOSPITAL (Formerly Rosary Hospital), Corning, IA
MERCY HOSPITAL, Council Bluffs, IA
MERCY HOSPITAL, Davenport, IA
MERCY HOSPITAL, Iowa City, IA
MERCY HOSPITAL, Moundridge, KS
MERCY HOSPITAL, Owensboro, KY
MERCY HOSPITAL, Portland, ME
MERCY HOSPITAL, Baltimore, MD
MERCY HOSPITAL, Springfield, MA
MERCY HOSPITAL, Benton Harbor, MI, See Southwestern Michigan Health Care Association, St. Joseph
MERCY HOSPITAL, Cadillac, MI
MERCY HOSPITAL, Grayling, MI
MERCY HOSPITAL, Muskegon, MI
MERCY HOSPITAL, Port Huron, MI
MERCY HOSPITAL, Moose Lake, MN
MERCY HOSPITAL (Formerly Mercy Hospital-Tri County), Mansfield, MO
MERCY HOSPITAL, Buffalo, NY
MERCY HOSPITAL, Rockville Centre, NY
MERCY HOSPITAL, Charlotte, NC
MERCY HOSPITAL, Devils Lake, ND
MERCY HOSPITAL, Valley City, ND
MERCY HOSPITAL, Columbus, OH
MERCY HOSPITAL, Portsmouth, OH
MERCY HOSPITAL, Tiffin, OH
MERCY HOSPITAL, Toledo, OH
MERCY HOSPITAL, Altoona, PA
MERCY HOSPITAL, Hamilton, OH
MERCY HOSPITAL AND MEDICAL CENTER, San Diego, CA
MERCY HOSPITAL AND MEDICAL CENTER, Chicago, IL
MERCY HOSPITAL AND PINEWOOD NURSING HOME, Waldron, AR
MERCY HOSPITAL MEDICAL CENTER, Des Moines, IA
MERCY HOSPITAL OF FAIRFIELD, , OH, See Mercy Hospital, Hamilton
MERCY HOSPITAL OF FOLSOM, Folsom, CA
MERCY HOSPITAL OF FRANCISCAN SISTERS, Oelwein, IA

MERCY HOSPITAL OF JANESVILLE, Janesville, WI
MERCY HOSPITAL OF JOHNSTOWN, Johnstown, PA
MERCY HOSPITAL OF NEW ORLEANS, New Orleans, LA
MERCY HOSPITAL OF PITTSBURGH, Pittsburgh, PA
MERCY HOSPITAL OF SACRAMENTO, Sacramento, CA
MERCY HOSPITAL OF SCRANTON (Formerly Mercy Hospital), Scranton, PA
MERCY HOSPITAL OF WATERTOWN, Watertown, NY
MERCY HOSPITAL OF WILKES-BARRE (Formerly Mercy Hospital), Wilkes-Barre, PA
MERCY HOSPITALS OF KANSAS, Fort Scott, KS
MERCY HOSPITALS OF KANSAS, Independence, KS
MERCY MEDICAL CENTER, Redding, CA
MERCY MEDICAL CENTER, Denver, CO
MERCY MEDICAL CENTER, Durango, CO
MERCY MEDICAL CENTER, Nampa, ID
MERCY MEDICAL CENTER, Coon Rapids, MN, See Health Central, Minneapolis
MERCY MEDICAL CENTER, Springfield, OH
MERCY MEDICAL CENTER, Roseburg, OR
MERCY MEDICAL CENTER, Oshkosh, WI
MERCY MEDICAL CENTER AND HOSPITAL (Formerly Mercy Hospital), Williston, ND
MERCY MEDICAL CENTER MOUNT SHASTA (Formerly Mount Shasta Community Hospital), Mount Shasta, CA
MERCY MEMORIAL HOSPITAL, Monroe, MI
MERCY MEMORIAL HOSPITAL, Urbana, OH
MERCY MEMORIAL MEDICAL CENTER, St. Joseph, MI
MERCY REGIONAL MEDICAL CENTER, Vicksburg, MS
MERCY REGIONAL MEDICAL CENTER, Laredo, TX
MERCY SAN JUAN HOSPITAL, Carmichael, CA
MERCY-MODOC MEDICAL CENTER, Alturas, CA, See Modoc Medical Center
MERIDEN-WALLINGFORD HOSPITAL, Meriden, CT
MERIDIAN HOSPITAL, Meridian, TX
MERIDIAN PARK HOSPITAL, Tualatin, OR
MERIDIAN REGIONAL HOSPITAL, Meridian, MS
MERITER HOSPITAL, Madison, WI
MERITER-MADISON GENERAL HOSPITAL, Madison, WI, See Meriter Hospital
MERITER-METHODIST HOSPITAL, Madison, WI, See Meriter Hospital
MERIWETHER MEMORIAL HOSPITAL, Warm Springs, GA
MERLE WEST MEDICAL CENTER, Klamath Falls, OR
MERRILL PIONEER COMMUNITY HOSPITAL, Rock Rapids, IA
MERRITHEW MEMORIAL HOSPITAL, Martinez, CA
MERRYVILLE GENERAL HOSPITAL, Merryville, LA
MESA GENERAL HOSPITAL MEDICAL CENTER, Mesa, AZ
MESA LUTHERAN HOSPITAL, Mesa, AZ
MESA MEMORIAL HOSPITAL, Grand Junction, CO, See St. Mary's Hospital and Medical Center
MESA VISTA HOSPITAL, San Diego, CA
MESABI REGIONAL MEDICAL CENTER, Hibbing, MN
MESQUITE COMMUNITY HOSPITAL, Mesquite, TX
MESQUITE PHYSICIANS HOSPITAL, Mesquite, TX
METHODIST EVANGELICAL HOSPITAL, Louisville, KY
METHODIST HOME CHILDREN'S GUIDANCE CENTER, Waco, TX
METHODIST HOSPITAL, Sacramento, CA
METHODIST HOSPITAL, Jacksonville, FL
METHODIST HOSPITAL (Formerly Listed Under Minneapolis), St. Louis Park, MN
METHODIST HOSPITAL, Omaha, NE
METHODIST HOSPITAL, Brooklyn, NY
METHODIST HOSPITAL, Philadelphia, PA
METHODIST HOSPITAL, Mitchell, SD
METHODIST HOSPITAL, Lubbock, TX
METHODIST HOSPITAL NORTH-JESSE HARRIS MEMORIAL HOSPITAL (Formerly Jesse Harris Memorial Methodist Hospital), Memphis, TN
METHODIST HOSPITAL OF CHICAGO (Formerly Bethany Methodist Hospital), Chicago, IL
METHODIST HOSPITAL OF DYERSBURG (Formerly Parkview Methodist Medical Center), Dyersburg, TN
METHODIST HOSPITAL OF HATTIESBURG (Formerly Methodist Hospital), Hattiesburg, MS
METHODIST HOSPITAL OF INDIANA, Indianapolis, IN
METHODIST HOSPITAL OF JONESBORO, Jonesboro, AR
METHODIST HOSPITAL OF KENTUCKY, Pikeville, KY
METHODIST HOSPITAL OF LEXINGTON, Lexington, TN
METHODIST HOSPITAL OF MCKENZIE, McKenzie, TN
METHODIST HOSPITAL OF MIDDLE MISSISSIPPI (Formerly Holmes County Hospital), Lexington, MS
METHODIST HOSPITAL OF MIDDLE TENNESSEE, Winchester, TN
METHODIST HOSPITAL OF SOMERVILLE, Somerville, TN
METHODIST HOSPITAL OF SOUTHERN CALIFORNIA, Arcadia, CA
METHODIST HOSPITAL OF STONE COUNTY (Formerly Stone County Hospital), Wiggins, MS
METHODIST HOSPITAL SOUTH-JOHN R. FLIPPIN MEMORIAL HOSPITAL, Memphis, TN
METHODIST HOSPITAL-CENTRAL UNIT, Memphis, TN
METHODIST HOSPITALS NORTHWEST IN, Gary, IN
METHODIST MEDICAL CENTER, St. Joseph, MO, See Heartland Hospital West
METHODIST MEDICAL CENTER, Dallas, TX
METHODIST MEDICAL CENTER OF ILLINOIS, Peoria, IL
METHODIST MEDICAL CENTER OF OAK RIDGE, Oak Ridge, TN
METROPLEX HOSPITAL, Killeen, TX
METROPOLITAN GENERAL HOSPITAL, Pinellas Park, FL
METROPOLITAN HOSPITAL, Los Angeles, CA
METROPOLITAN HOSPITAL, Atlanta, GA
METROPOLITAN HOSPITAL, Grand Rapids, MI
METROPOLITAN HOSPITAL, Chattanooga, TN
METROPOLITAN HOSPITAL, Dallas, TX
METROPOLITAN HOSPITAL (Formerly Richmond Metropolitan Hospital), Richmond, VA
METROPOLITAN HOSPITAL, Caparra, P.R.
METROPOLITAN HOSPITAL CENTER, New York, NY
METROPOLITAN HOSPITAL-CENTRAL DIVISION, Philadelphia, PA
METROPOLITAN HOSPITAL-PARKVIEW DIVISION, Philadelphia, PA
METROPOLITAN HOSPITAL-SPRINGFIELD DIVISION, Springfield, PA
METROPOLITAN MEDICAL CENTER, Minneapolis, MN
METROPOLITAN NASHVILLE GENERAL HOSPITAL, Nashville, TN
METROPOLITAN STATE HOSPITAL, Norwalk, CA
METROPOLITAN STATE HOSPITAL, Waltham, MA
METROX HEALTH CENTER, Erie, PA
MEYERSDALE COMMUNITY HOSPITAL, Meyersdale, PA
MIAMI CHILDREN'S HOSPITAL, Miami, FL
MIAMI COUNTY HOSPITAL, Paola, KS
MIAMI GENERAL HOSPITAL, Miami, FL
MIAMI HEART INSTITUTE, Miami Beach, FL
MIAMI INSPIRATION HOSPITAL, Miami, AZ
MIAMI VALLEY HOSPITAL, Dayton, OH
MICHAEL REESE HOSPITAL AND MEDICAL CENTER, Chicago, IL
MICHIANA COMMUNITY HOSPITAL (Formerly South Bend Osteopathic Hospital), South Bend, IN
MICHIGAN OSTEOPATHIC MEDICAL CENTER, Detroit, MI
MID DAKOTA HOSPITAL, Chamberlain, SD
MID MISSOURI MENTAL HEALTH CENTER, Columbia, MO
MID-COLUMBIA MEDICAL CENTER, The Dalles, OR
MID-COLUMBIA MENTAL HEALTH CENTER, Richland, WA
MID-ISLAND HOSPITAL, Bethpage, NY
MID-MAINE MEDICAL CENTER, Waterville, ME
MID-SOUTH HOSPITAL, Memphis, TN
MID-VALLEY HOSPITAL, Peckville, PA
MID-VALLEY HOSPITAL, Omak, WA
MIDDLE GEORGIA HOSPITAL, Macon, GA
MIDDLE TENNESSEE MEDICAL CENTER, Murfreesboro, TN
MIDDLE TENNESSEE MENTAL HEALTH INSTITUTE, Nashville, TN
MIDDLESBORO APPALACHIAN REGIONAL HOSPITAL, Middlesboro, KY
MIDDLESEX COUNTY HOSPITAL, Waltham, MA
MIDDLESEX GENERAL-UNIVERSITY HOSPITAL, New Brunswick, NJ, See Robert Wood Johnson University Hospital
MIDDLESEX MEMORIAL HOSPITAL, Middletown, CT
MIDDLETOWN PSYCHIATRIC CENTER, Middletown, NY
MIDDLETOWN REGIONAL HOSPITAL, Middletown, OH
MIDLAND HOSPITAL CENTER, Midland, MI
MIDLAND MEMORIAL HOSPITAL, Midland, TX
MIDLANDS CENTER, Columbia, SC
MIDLANDS COMMUNITY HOSPITAL, Papillion, NE
MIDTOWN HOSPITAL, Atlanta, GA
MIDWAY HOSPITAL, St. Paul, MN, See Baptist Hospital Fund
MIDWAY HOSPITAL MEDICAL CENTER, Los Angeles, CA
MIDWEST CITY MEMORIAL HOSPITAL, Midwest City, OK
MIDWOOD COMMUNITY HOSPITAL, Stanton, CA
MILACA FAIRVIEW HOSPITAL (Formerly Milaca Area District Hospital), Milaca, MN
MILES MEMORIAL HOSPITAL, Damariscotta, ME
MILFORD HOSPITAL, Milford, CT
MILFORD MEMORIAL HOSPITAL, Milford, DE
MILFORD VALLEY MEMORIAL HOSPITAL, Milford, UT
MILFORD-WHITINSVILLE REGIONAL HOSPITAL, Milford, MA
MILLARD FILLMORE HOSPITAL, Buffalo, NY
MILLCREEK COMMUNITY HOSPITAL, Erie, PA
MILLE LACS HOSPITAL (Formerly Community Mercy Hospital), Onamia, MN
MILLER COUNTY HOSPITAL, Colquitt, GA
MILLER-DWAN MEDICAL CENTER, Duluth, MN
MILLINOCKET REGIONAL HOSPITAL, Millinocket, ME
MILLS MEMORIAL HOSPITAL, San Mateo, CA
MILLVILLE HOSPITAL, Millville, NJ
MILTON COMMUNITY HOSPITAL, River Rouge, MI
MILTON MEDICAL CENTER, Milton, MA
MILWAUKEE CHILDREN'S HOSPITAL, Milwaukee, WI, See Children's Hospital of Wisconsin
MILWAUKEE COUNTY MEDICAL COMPLEX, Milwaukee, WI
MILWAUKEE COUNTY MENTAL HEALTH COMPLEX (Formerly Listed Under Wauwatosa), Milwaukee, WI
MILWAUKEE PSYCHIATRIC HOSPITAL (Formerly Listed Under Wauwatosa), Milwaukee, WI
MIMBRES MEMORIAL HOSPITAL, Deming, NM
MINDEN MEDICAL CENTER, Minden, LA
MINERAL AREA OSTEOPATHIC HOSPITAL, Farmington, MO
MINERAL COUNTY HOSPITAL, Superior, MT
MINERS HOSPITAL NORTHERN CAMBRIA, Spangler, PA
MINERS' COLFAX MEDICAL CENTER (Formerly Miners' Hospital of New Mexico), Raton, NM
MINERS' COLFAX MEDICAL CENTER (Formerly Colfax Health Care Systems), Raton, NM
MINIDOKA MEMORIAL HOSPITAL, Rupert, ID
MINNEAPOLIS CHILDREN'S MEDICAL CENTER, Minneapolis, MN
MINNEOLA DISTRICT HOSPITAL, Minneola, KS
MINNESOTA VALLEY MEMORIAL HOSPITAL, Le Sueur, MN
MINNEWASKA DISTRICT HOSPITAL, Starbuck, MN
MINNIE G. BOSWELL MEMORIAL HOSPITAL, Greensboro, GA
MIRIAM HOSPITAL, Providence, RI
MISSION BAY MEMORIAL HOSPITAL, San Diego, CA, See AMI Mission Bay Hospital
MISSION COMMUNITY HOSPITAL, Mission Viejo, CA
MISSION HILL MEMORIAL HOSPITAL, Shawnee, OK
MISSION HOSPITAL, Huntington Park, CA
MISSION HOSPITAL, Mission, TX
MISSION OAKS HOSPITAL (Formerly Valley West General Hospital), Los Gatos, CA
MISSION VALLEY HOSPITAL, St. Ignatius, MT
MISSISSIPPI BAPTIST MEDICAL CENTER, Jackson, MS
MISSISSIPPI COUNTY HOSPITALS-BLYTHEVILLE (Formerly Chickasawba Hospital), Blytheville, AR
MISSISSIPPI METHODIST HOSPITAL AND REHABILITATION CENTER, Jackson, MS
MISSISSIPPI STATE HOSPITAL, Whitfield, MS
MISSOULA COMMUNITY HOSPITAL, Missoula, MT
MISSOULA GENERAL HOSPITAL, Missoula, MT
MISSOURI BAPTIST HOSPITAL, St. Louis, MO
MISSOURI DELTA MEDICAL CENTER (Formerly Missouri Delta Community Hospital), Sikeston, MO
MISSOURI REHABILITATION CENTER (Formerly Missouri State Chest Hospital), Mount Vernon, MO
MISSOURI STATE PENITENTIARY HOSPITAL, Jefferson City, MO
MITCHELL COUNTY COMMUNITY HOSPITAL, Beloit, KS
MITCHELL COUNTY HOSPITAL, Camilla, GA
MITCHELL COUNTY HOSPITAL (Formerly Root Memorial Hospital), Colorado City, TX
MITCHELL COUNTY MEMORIAL HOSPITAL, Osage, IA
MIZELL MEMORIAL HOSPITAL, Opp, AL
MOBERLY REGIONAL MEDICAL CENTER, Moberly, MO
MOBILE INFIRMARY MEDICAL CENTER (Formerly Mobile Infirmary), Mobile, AL
MOBRIDGE REGIONAL HOSPITAL (Formerly Mobridge Community Hospital), Mobridge, SD
MOCCASIN BEND MENTAL HEALTH INSTITUTE, Chattanooga, TN
MODESTO CITY HOSPITAL, Modesto, CA
MODOC MEDICAL CENTER (Formerly Mercy-Modoc Medical Center), Alturas, CA
MOHAWK VALLEY GENERAL HOSPITAL, Ilion, NY
MOHAWK VALLEY PSYCHIATRIC CENTER (Formerly Utica-Marcy Psychiatric Center), Utica, NY
MOLINE PUBLIC HOSPITAL, Moline, IL
MOLLY STARK HOSPITAL, Louisville, OH
MOLOKAI GENERAL HOSPITAL, Kaunakakai, HI
MONADNOCK COMMUNITY HOSPITAL, Peterborough, NH

MONCRIEF ARMY COMMUNITY HOSPITAL, Fort Jackson, SC
MONMOUTH MEDICAL CENTER, Long Branch, NJ
MONO GENERAL HOSPITAL, Bridgeport, CA
MONONGAHELA VALLEY HOSPITAL, Monongahela, PA
MONONGALIA GENERAL HOSPITAL, Morgantown, WV
MONROE COMMUNITY HOSPITAL, Rochester, NY
MONROE COUNTY HOSPITAL, Monroeville, AL
MONROE COUNTY HOSPITAL, Forsyth, GA
MONROE COUNTY HOSPITAL, Albia, IA
MONROE COUNTY MEDICAL CENTER, Tompkinsville, KY
MONROVIA COMMUNITY HOSPITAL, Monrovia, CA
MONSIGNOR CLEMENT KERN HOSPITAL FOR SPECIAL SURGERY, Warren, MI
MONSOUR MEDICAL CENTER, Jeannette, PA
MONTANA DEACONESS MEDICAL CENTER, Great Falls, MT
MONTANA STATE HOSPITAL, Warm Spring, MT
MONTCLAIR COMMUNITY HOSPITAL, Montclair, NJ
MONTE VILLA HOSPITAL, Morgan Hill, CA
MONTE VISTA COMMUNITY HOSPITAL, Monte Vista, CO
MONTEBELLO REHABILITATION HOSPITAL (Formerly Montebello Hospital), Baltimore, MD
MONTEFIORE HOSPITAL, Pittsburgh, PA
MONTEFIORE MEDICAL CENTER, Bronx, NY
MONTELEPRE MEMORIAL HOSPITAL, New Orleans, LA
MONTEREY PARK HOSPITAL, Monterey Park, CA
MONTEVISTA CENTRE, Las Vegas, NV
MONTFORT JONES MEMORIAL HOSPITAL, Kosciusko, MS
MONTGOMERY COUNTY EMERGENCY SERVICE, Norristown, PA
MONTGOMERY COUNTY MEMORIAL HOSPITAL, Red Oak, IA
MONTGOMERY GENERAL HOSPITAL, Olney, MD
MONTGOMERY GENERAL HOSPITAL, Montgomery, WV
MONTGOMERY HOSPITAL, Norristown, PA
MONTGOMERY MEMORIAL HOSPITAL, Troy, NC
MONTGOMERY REGIONAL HOSPITAL (Formerly Montgomery County Hospital), Blacksburg, VA
MONTICELLO MEDICAL CENTER, Longview, WA
MONTICELLO-BIG LAKE COMMUNITY HOSPITAL, Monticello, MN
MONTROSE GENERAL HOSPITAL, Montrose, PA
MONTROSE MEMORIAL HOSPITAL, Montrose, CO
MONUMENT VALLEY ADVENTIST HOSPITAL, Monument Valley, UT
MOORE MUNICIPAL HOSPITAL, Moore, OK
MOORE REGIONAL HOSPITAL (Formerly Moore Memorial Hospital), Pinehurst, NC
MOOSA MEMORIAL HOSPITAL, Eunice, LA
MOOSE LAKE STATE HOSPITAL, Moose Lake, MN
MOOTS OSTEOPATHIC HOSPITAL, Pryor, OK
MOREHEAD MEMORIAL HOSPITAL, Eden, NC
MOREHOUSE GENERAL HOSPITAL, Bastrop, LA
MORENCI AREA HOSPITAL, Morenci, MI
MORENCI HOSPITAL, Morenci, AZ
MORGAN COUNTY APPALACHIAN REGIONAL HOSPITAL, West Liberty, KY
MORGAN COUNTY MEMORIAL HOSPITAL, Martinsville, IN
MORGAN COUNTY WAR MEMORIAL HOSPITAL, Berkeley Springs, WV
MORGAN MEMORIAL HOSPITAL, Madison, GA
MORITZ COMMUNITY HOSPITAL, Sun Valley, ID
MORRILL COUNTY COMMUNITY HOSPITAL, Bridgeport, NE
MORRIS COUNTY HOSPITAL, Council Grove, KS
MORRIS HOSPITAL, Morris, IL
MORRISON COMMUNITY HOSPITAL, Morrison, IL
MORRISTOWN MEMORIAL HOSPITAL, Morristown, NJ
MORRISTOWN-HAMBLEN HOSPITAL, Morristown, TN
MORROW COUNTY HOSPITAL, Mount Gilead, OH
MORROW MEMORIAL HOSPITAL, Auburndale, FL
MORTON COUNTY HOSPITAL, Elkhart, KS
MORTON F. PLANT HOSPITAL, Clearwater, FL
MORTON GENERAL HOSPITAL, Morton, WA
MORTON HOSPITAL AND MEDICAL CENTER (Formerly Morton Hospital), Taunton, MA
MOSES H. CONE MEMORIAL HOSPITAL, Greensboro, NC
MOSES LUDINGTON HOSPITAL, Ticonderoga, NY
MOSES TAYLOR HOSPITAL, Scranton, PA
MOSS REHABILITATION HOSPITAL, Philadelphia, PA
MOTHER FRANCES HOSPITAL REGIONAL HEALTH CARE CENTER (Formerly Mother Frances Hospital), Tyler, TX
MOTION PICTURE AND TELEVISION HOSPITAL, Los Angeles, CA
MOUNDS PARK HOSPITAL, St. Paul, MN, See Baptist Hospital Fund
MOUNT AIRY PSYCHIATRIC CENTER, Denver, CO
MOUNT AUBURN HOSPITAL, Cambridge, MA
MOUNT CARMEL EAST HOSPITAL, Columbus, OH, See Hawkes Hospital of Mount Carmel
MOUNT CARMEL HEALTH, Columbus, OH
MOUNT CARMEL HOSPITAL, Colville, WA
MOUNT CARMEL MEDICAL CENTER, Pittsburg, KS
MOUNT CARMEL MEDICAL CENTER, Columbus, OH, See Hawkes Hospital of Mount Carmel
MOUNT CARMEL MERCY HOSPITAL, Detroit, MI
MOUNT CLEMENS GENERAL HOSPITAL, Mount Clemens, MI
MOUNT DESERT ISLAND HOSPITAL, Bar Harbor, ME
MOUNT EDGECUMBE HOSPITAL (Formerly U. S. Public Health Service Alaska Native Hospital), Sitka, AK
MOUNT GRAHAM COMMUNITY HOSPITAL, Safford, AZ
MOUNT GRANT GENERAL HOSPITAL, Hawthorne, NV
MOUNT HOOD MEDICAL CENTER, Gresham, OR
MOUNT LINTON HOSPITAL, Metaline Falls, WA
MOUNT PLEASANT HOSPITAL, Lynn, MA
MOUNT REGIS CENTER, Salem, VA
MOUNT SAN RAFAEL HOSPITAL, Trinidad, CO
MOUNT SINAI HOSPITAL, Hartford, CT
MOUNT SINAI HOSPITAL, Minneapolis, MN
MOUNT SINAI HOSPITAL MEDICAL CENTER OF CHICAGO, Chicago, IL
MOUNT SINAI MEDICAL CENTER, Miami Beach, FL
MOUNT SINAI MEDICAL CENTER (Formerly Mount Sinai Hospital), New York, NY
MOUNT SINAI MEDICAL CENTER, Milwaukee, WI
MOUNT ST. MARY'S HOSPITAL OF NIAGARA FALLS, Lewiston, NY
MOUNT VERNON HOSPITAL, Mount Vernon, IL, See Crossroads Community Hospital
MOUNT VERNON HOSPITAL, Mount Vernon, NY
MOUNT VERNON HOSPITAL, Alexandria, VA
MOUNT WASHINGTON PEDIATRIC HOSPITAL, Baltimore, MD
MOUNT ZION HOSPITAL AND MEDICAL CENTER, San Francisco, CA
MOUNTAIN LAKE COMMUNITY HOSPITAL, Mountain Lake, MN
MOUNTAIN MANOR TREATMENT CENTER FOR ALCOHOLISM, Emmitsburg, MD
MOUNTAIN PARK MEDICAL CENTER, Andrews, NC
MOUNTAIN VIEW BAPTIST HOSPITAL, Gadsden, AL
MOUNTAIN VIEW DISTRICT HOSPITAL, Madras, OR
MOUNTAIN VIEW HOSPITAL, Payson, UT
MOUNTAIN VIEW MEDICAL CENTER (Formerly Simi Valley Community Hospital), Simi Valley, CA
MOUNTAINS COMMUNITY HOSPITAL, Lake Arrowhead, CA
MOUNTAINSIDE HOSPITAL, Montclair, NJ
MOUNTAINVIEW HOSPITAL OF SPOKANE (Formerly Raleigh Hills Hospital of Spokane), Spokane, WA
MOUNTAINVIEW MEMORIAL HOSPITAL, White Sulphur Springs, MT
MT. ASCUTNEY HOSPITAL AND HEALTH CENTER, Windsor, VT
MT. DIABLO HOSPITAL MEDICAL CENTER, Concord, CA
MT. SINAI MEDICAL CENTER, Cleveland, OH
MUENSTER HOSPITAL DISTRICT, Muenster, TX
MUHLENBERG COMMUNITY HOSPITAL, Greenville, KY
MUHLENBERG HOSPITAL CENTER (Formerly Muhlenberg Medical Center), Bethlehem, PA
MUHLENBERG REGIONAL MEDICAL CENTER (Formerly Muhlenberg Hospital), Plainfield, NJ
MULLINS HOSPITAL, Mullins, SC
MUNCY VALLEY HOSPITAL, Muncy, PA
MUNISING MEMORIAL HOSPITAL, Munising, MI
MUNROE REGIONAL MEDICAL CENTER, Ocala, FL
MUNSON ARMY COMMUNITY HOSPITAL, Fort Leavenworth, KS
MUNSON MEDICAL CENTER, Traverse City, MI
MURPHY MEDICAL CENTER, Murphy, NC
MURRAY COUNTY MEMORIAL HOSPITAL, Slayton, MN
MURRAY-CALLOWAY COUNTY HOSPITAL, Murray, KY
MUSC MEDICAL CENTER OF MEDICAL UNIVERSITY OF SOUTH CAROLINA (Formerly Medical University Hospital of the Medical University of South Carolina), Charleston, SC
MUSCATATUCK STATE DEVELOPMENTAL CENTER (Formerly Muscatatuck State Hospital and Training Center), Butlerville, IN
MUSCATINE GENERAL HOSPITAL, Muscatine, IA
MUSKEGON GENERAL HOSPITAL, Muskegon, MI
MUSKOGEE REGIONAL MEDICAL CENTER, Muskogee, OK
MYERS COMMUNITY HOSPITAL, Sodus, NY
MYRTLE WERTH MEDICAL CENTER, Menomonie, WI
MYRTUE MEMORIAL HOSPITAL (Formerly Shelby County Myrtue Memorial Hospital), Harlan, IA

N

N. T. ENLOE MEMORIAL HOSPITAL, Chico, CA
NACOGDOCHES MEDICAL CENTER HOSPITAL, Nacogdoches, TX, See AMI Nacogdoches Medical Center Hospital
NAEVE HOSPITAL, Albert Lea, MN
NAN TRAVIS MEMORIAL HOSPITAL, Jacksonville, TX
NANCY ADELE MCELWEE MEMORIAL HOSPITAL, Chicago, IL, See University of Chicago Hospitals and Clinics
NANTICOKE MEMORIAL HOSPITAL, Seaford, DE
NANTICOKE STATE GENERAL HOSPITAL, Nanticoke, PA
NANTUCKET COTTAGE HOSPITAL, Nantucket, MA
NAPA STATE HOSPITAL (Formerly Listed Under Imola), Napa, CA
NAPLES COMMUNITY HOSPITAL, Naples, FL
NAPLES RESEARCH AND COUNSELING CENTER, Naples, FL
NASH GENERAL HOSPITAL, Rocky Mount, NC
NASHOBA COMMUNITY HOSPITAL, Ayer, MA
NASHUA BROOKSIDE HOSPITAL, Nashua, NH
NASHUA MEMORIAL HOSPITAL (Formerly Memorial Hospital), Nashua, NH
NASHVILLE MEMORIAL HOSPITAL, Madison, TN
NASHVILLE METROPOLITAN BORDEAUX HOSPITAL, Nashville, TN
NASON HOSPITAL, Roaring Spring, PA
NASSAU COUNTY MEDICAL CENTER, East Meadow, NY
NASSAU GENERAL HOSPITAL, Fernandina Beach, FL
NATCHAUG HOSPITAL (Formerly Listed Under Mansfield), Mansfield Center, CT
NATCHITOCHES PARISH HOSPITAL, Natchitoches, LA
NATHAN B. VAN ETTEN GENERAL CARE HOSPITAL, Bronx, NY, See Bronx Municipal Hospital Center
NATHAN GOLDBLATT MEMORIAL HOSPITAL AND GOLDBLATT PAVILION, Chicago, IL, See University of Chicago Hospitals and Clinics
NATHAN LITTAUER HOSPITAL, Gloversville, NY
NATIONAL HOSPITAL FOR ORTHOPAEDICS AND REHABILITATION, Arlington, VA
NATIONAL JEWISH CENTER FOR IMMUNOLOGY AND RESPIRATORY MEDICINE (Formerly National Jewish Hospital and Research Center-National Asthma Center), Denver, CO
NATIVIDAD MEDICAL CENTER, Salinas, CA
NAUKEAG HOSPITAL, Ashburnham, MA
NAVAL HOSPITAL, Camp Pendleton, CA
NAVAL HOSPITAL, Lemoore, CA
NAVAL HOSPITAL, Oakland, CA
NAVAL HOSPITAL, San Diego, CA
NAVAL HOSPITAL, Groton, CT
NAVAL HOSPITAL, Jacksonville, FL
NAVAL HOSPITAL, Orlando, FL
NAVAL HOSPITAL, Pensacola, FL
NAVAL HOSPITAL, Great Lakes, IL
NAVAL HOSPITAL, Bethesda, MD
NAVAL HOSPITAL, Patuxent River, MD
NAVAL HOSPITAL, Camp Lejeune, NC
NAVAL HOSPITAL, Cherry Point, NC
NAVAL HOSPITAL, Philadelphia, PA
NAVAL HOSPITAL, Newport, RI
NAVAL HOSPITAL, Beaufort, SC
NAVAL HOSPITAL, Charleston, SC
NAVAL HOSPITAL, Millington, TN
NAVAL HOSPITAL, Corpus Christi, TX
NAVAL HOSPITAL, Portsmouth, VA
NAVAL HOSPITAL, Bremerton, WA
NAVAL HOSPITAL (Formerly Listed Under Whidbey Island), Oak Harbor, WA
NAVAL HOSPITAL, Agana, Guam
NAVAL HOSPITAL, Roosevelt Roads, P.R.
NAVAL HOSPITAL, Long Beach, CA
NAVAPACHE HOSPITAL, Show Low, AZ
NAVARRO REGIONAL HOSPITAL, Corsicana, TX
NAVASOTA REGIONAL HOSPITAL (Formerly Grimes Memorial Hospital), Navasota, TX
NAZARETH HOSPITAL, Philadelphia, PA
NEEDLES-DESERT COMMUNITIES HOSPITAL, Needles, CA
NEMAHA COUNTY HOSPITAL, Auburn, NE
NEMAHA VALLEY COMMUNITY HOSPITAL, Seneca, KS
NEOSHO MEMORIAL HOSPITAL, Chanute, KS
NESBITT MEMORIAL HOSPITAL, Kingston, PA
NESS COUNTY HOSPITAL DISTRICT NUMBER TWO, Ness City, KS
NEUROSCIENCE HOSPITAL-MERITCARE, Fargo, ND, See St. Luke's Hospitals
NEVADA CITY HOSPITAL, Nevada, MO

NEVADA MENTAL HEALTH INSTITUTE (Formerly Listed Under Reno), Sparks, NV
NEVADA STATE HOSPITAL, Nevada, MO
NEW BEGINNING AT HIDDEN BROOK, Bel Air, MD
NEW BEGINNINGS AT COVE FORGE (Formerly Cove Forge Treatment Center), Williamsburg, PA
NEW BEGINNINGS AT FENWICK HALL (Formerly Fenwick Hall Hospital), Johns Island, SC
NEW BEGINNINGS-WARWICK MANOR, East New Market, MD
NEW BERLIN MEMORIAL HOSPITAL, New Berlin, WI
NEW BOSTON GENERAL HOSPITAL, New Boston, TX
NEW BRITAIN GENERAL HOSPITAL, New Britain, CT
NEW BRITAIN MEMORIAL HOSPITAL, New Britain, CT
NEW CENTER HOSPITAL, Detroit, MI
NEW ENGLAND BAPTIST HOSPITAL, Boston, MA
NEW ENGLAND DEACONESS HOSPITAL, Boston, MA
NEW ENGLAND MEDICAL CENTER, Boston, MA
NEW ENGLAND MEMORIAL HOSPITAL, Stoneham, MA
NEW ENGLAND REHABILITATION HOSPITAL, Woburn, MA
NEW ENGLAND SINAI HOSPITAL, Stoughton, MA
NEW HAMPSHIRE HOSPITAL, Concord, NH
NEW HANOVER MEMORIAL HOSPITAL, Wilmington, NC
NEW JERSEY ORTHOPAEDIC HOSPITAL UNIT, Orange, NJ, See Hospital Center at Orange
NEW JERSEY STATE PRISON HOSPITAL, Trenton, NJ
NEW LONDON FAMILY MEDICAL CENTER (Formerly New London Community Hospital), New London, WI
NEW LONDON HOSPITAL, New London, NH
NEW MEXICO REHABILITATION CENTER, Roswell, NM
NEW MILFORD HOSPITAL, New Milford, CT
NEW ORLEANS GENERAL HOSPITAL, New Orleans, LA
NEW ROCHELLE HOSPITAL MEDICAL CENTER, New Rochelle, NY
NEW VALLEY OSTEOPATHIC HOSPITAL, Yakima, WA
NEW YORK EYE AND EAR INFIRMARY, New York, NY
NEW YORK HOSPITAL, New York, NY, See Society of the New York Hospital
NEW YORK HOSPITAL, WESTCHESTER DIVISION, White Plains, NY, See Society of the New York Hospital, New York City
NEW YORK INFIRMARY-BEEKMAN DOWNTOWN HOSPITAL, New York, NY
NEW YORK STATE PSYCHIATRIC INSTITUTE, New York, NY
NEW YORK UNIVERSITY MEDICAL CENTER, New York, NY
NEWARK BETH ISRAEL MEDICAL CENTER, Newark, NJ
NEWARK EYE AND EAR INFIRMARY, Newark, NJ, See United Hospitals Medical Center
NEWARK-WAYNE COMMUNITY HOSPITAL, Newark, NY
NEWBERG COMMUNITY HOSPITAL, Newberg, OR
NEWBERRY COUNTY MEMORIAL HOSPITAL, Newberry, SC
NEWBERRY REGIONAL MENTAL HEALTH CENTER, Newberry, MI
NEWCOMB MEDICAL CENTER, Vineland, NJ
NEWHALL COMMUNITY HOSPITAL, Newhall, CA
NEWINGTON CHILDREN'S HOSPITAL, Newington, CT
NEWMAN MEMORIAL COUNTY HOSPITAL, Emporia, KS
NEWMAN MEMORIAL HOSPITAL, Shattuck, OK
NEWNAN HOSPITAL, Newnan, GA
NEWPORT COMMUNITY HOSPITAL, Newport, WA
NEWPORT HARBOR PSYCHIATRIC INSTITUTE, Newport Beach, CA
NEWPORT HOSPITAL, Newport, NH
NEWPORT HOSPITAL, Newport, RI
NEWPORT HOSPITAL AND CLINIC, Newport, AR
NEWPORT NEWS GENERAL HOSPITAL, Newport News, VA
NEWTON COUNTY MEMORIAL HOSPITAL, Newton, TX
NEWTON GENERAL HOSPITAL, Covington, GA
NEWTON MEMORIAL HOSPITAL, Newton, NJ
NEWTON-WELLESLEY HOSPITAL (Formerly Listed Under Newton Lower Falls), Newton, MA
NIAGARA FALLS MEMORIAL MEDICAL CENTER, Niagara Falls, NY
NICHOLAS COUNTY HOSPITAL, Carlisle, KY
NICHOLAS H. NOYES MEMORIAL HOSPITAL, Dansville, NY
NIOBRARA COUNTY MEMORIAL HOSPITAL, Lusk, WY
NIOBRARA VALLEY HOSPITAL, Lynch, NE
NIX MEDICAL CENTER, San Antonio, TX
NKC HOSPITALS, Louisville, KY
NOBLE ARMY COMMUNITY HOSPITAL, Fort McClellan, AL
NOBLE HOSPITAL, Westfield, MA
NOCONA GENERAL HOSPITAL, Nocona, TX
NOLL MEMORIAL HOSPITAL, Bethany, MO
NOR-LEA GENERAL HOSPITAL, Lovington, NM
NORFOLK COMMUNITY HOSPITAL, Norfolk, VA
NORFOLK COUNTY HOSPITAL, Braintree, MA
NORFOLK GENERAL HOSPITAL, Norfolk, VA
NORFOLK PSYCHIATRIC CENTER (Formerly Virginia Center for Psychiatry), Norfolk, VA
NORFOLK REGIONAL CENTER, Norfolk, NE
NORMAN REGIONAL HOSPITAL, Norman, OK
NORMANDY OSTEOPATHIC HOSPITAL-NORTH, St. Louis, MO, See Normandy Osteopathic Medical Center
NORMANDY OSTEOPATHIC HOSPITAL-SOUTH, St. Louis, MO, See Normandy Osteopathic Medical Center
NORMANDY OSTEOPATHIC MEDICAL CENTER, St. Louis, MO
NORRISTOWN STATE HOSPITAL, Norristown, PA
NORTH ADAMS REGIONAL HOSPITAL, North Adams, MA
NORTH ARKANSAS MEDICAL CENTER (Formerly Boone County Hospital), Harrison, AR
NORTH ARUNDEL HOSPITAL, Glen Burnie, MD
NORTH BALDWIN HOSPITAL, Bay Minette, AL
NORTH BEACH COMMUNITY HOSPITAL, Fort Lauderdale, FL, See HCA North Beach Hospital
NORTH BIG HORN HOSPITAL, Lovell, WY
NORTH BROWARD MEDICAL CENTER, Pompano Beach, FL
NORTH CADDO MEMORIAL HOSPITAL, Vivian, LA
NORTH CAROLINA BAPTIST HOSPITAL, Winston-Salem, NC
NORTH CAROLINA MEMORIAL HOSPITAL, Chapel Hill, NC
NORTH CENTRAL BRONX HOSPITAL, Bronx, NY
NORTH CENTRAL HEALTH CARE FACILITIES, Wausau, WI
NORTH CHARLES HOSPITAL (Formerly North Charles General Hospital), Baltimore, MD
NORTH CLAIBORNE HOSPITAL, Haynesville, LA
NORTH COAST REHABILITATION CENTER (Formerly Brookwood Hospital), Santa Rosa, CA
NORTH COLORADO MEDICAL CENTER, Greeley, CO
NORTH COUNTRY HOSPITAL, Bemidji, MN
NORTH COUNTRY HOSPITAL AND HEALTH CENTER, Newport, VT
NORTH DAKOTA STATE HOSPITAL, Jamestown, ND
NORTH DETROIT GENERAL HOSPITAL, Detroit, MI
NORTH FLORIDA REGIONAL HOSPITAL, Gainesville, FL, See HCA North Florida Regional Medical Center
NORTH GABLES HOSPITAL, Coral Gables, FL
NORTH GEORGIA MEDICAL CENTER (Formerly Watkins Memorial Hospital), Ellijay, GA
NORTH GREENVILLE HOSPITAL, Travelers Rest, SC
NORTH HILLS MEDICAL CENTER (Formerly Listed Under Fort Worth), North Richland Hills, TX
NORTH HILLS PASSAVANT HOSPITAL, Pittsburgh, PA
NORTH IOWA MEDICAL CENTER, Mason City, IA
NORTH JACKSON HOSPITAL, Bridgeport, AL
NORTH KANSAS CITY HOSPITAL (Formerly North Kansas City Memorial Hospital), North Kansas City, MO
NORTH KERN HOSPITAL, Wasco, CA
NORTH LINCOLN HOSPITAL, Lincoln City, OR
NORTH LITTLE ROCK DIVISION, North Little Rock, AR, See John L. McCellan Memorial Veterans Hospital, Little Rock
NORTH MEMORIAL MEDICAL CENTER (Formerly Listed Under Minneapolis), Robbinsdale, MN
NORTH MIAMI MEDICAL CENTER (Formerly North Miami General Hospital), North Miami, FL
NORTH MISSISSIPPI MEDICAL CENTER, Tupelo, MS
NORTH MOBILE COMMUNITY HOSPITAL, Satsuma, AL
NORTH MONROE COMMUNITY HOSPITAL, Monroe, LA
NORTH OTTAWA COMMUNITY HOSPITAL, Grand Haven, MI
NORTH PANOLA REGIONAL HOSPITAL AND NURSING CENTER, Sardis, MS
NORTH PARK HOSPITAL, Chattanooga, TN
NORTH PENN HOSPITAL, Lansdale, PA
NORTH RUNNELS HOSPITAL, Winters, TX
NORTH SHORE CHILDREN'S HOSPITAL, Salem, MA
NORTH SHORE MEDICAL CENTER, Miami, FL
NORTH SHORE PSYCHIATRIC HOSPITAL, Slidell, LA
NORTH SHORE UNIVERSITY HOSPITAL, Manhasset, NY
NORTH SIDE HOSPITAL, Johnson City, TN
NORTH SUNFLOWER COUNTY HOSPITAL, Ruleville, MS
NORTH VALLEY HOSPITAL, Whitefish, MT
NORTH VALLEY HOSPITAL, Tonasket, WA
NORTHAMPTON STATE HOSPITAL, Northampton, MA
NORTHAMPTON-ACCOMACK MEMORIAL HOSPITAL, Nassawadox, VA
NORTHBAY MEDICAL CENTER (Formerly Intercommunity Hospital), Fairfield, CA
NORTHEAST ALABAMA REGIONAL MEDICAL CENTER, Anniston, AL
NORTHEAST BAPTIST HOSPITAL, San Antonio, TX
NORTHEAST COMMUNITY HOSPITAL, Bedford, TX, See HCA Northeast Community Hospital
NORTHEAST FLORIDA STATE HOSPITAL, Macclenny, FL
NORTHEAST GEORGIA MEDICAL CENTER, Gainesville, GA
NORTHEAST MEDICAL CENTER HOSPITAL, Humble, TX
NORTHEASTERN HOSPITAL OF PHILADELPHIA, Philadelphia, PA
NORTHEASTERN OHIO GENERAL HOSPITAL, Madison, OH
NORTHEASTERN REGIONAL HOSPITAL, Las Vegas, NM
NORTHEASTERN VERMONT REGIONAL HOSPITAL, St. Johnsbury, VT
NORTHERN COCHISE COMMUNITY HOSPITAL, Willcox, AZ
NORTHERN CUMBERLAND MEMORIAL HOSPITAL, Bridgton, ME
NORTHERN DUTCHESS HOSPITAL, Rhinebeck, NY
NORTHERN HILLS GENERAL HOSPITAL, Deadwood, SD
NORTHERN HOSPITAL OF SURRY COUNTY, Mount Airy, NC
NORTHERN ILLINOIS MEDICAL CENTER, McHenry, IL
NORTHERN INYO HOSPITAL, Bishop, CA
NORTHERN ITASCA DISTRICT HOSPITAL AND CONVALESCENT AND NURSING CARE UNIT, Bigfork, MN
NORTHERN MAINE MEDICAL CENTER, Fort Kent, ME
NORTHERN MICHIGAN HOSPITALS, Petoskey, MI
NORTHERN MONTANA HOSPITAL, Havre, MT
NORTHERN OCEAN HOSPITAL SYSTEM, Point Pleasant, NJ
NORTHERN VIRGINIA DOCTORS HOSPITAL, Arlington, VA, See HCA Northern Virginia Doctors Hospital
NORTHERN WAKE HOSPITAL, Wake Forest, NC
NORTHERN WESTCHESTER HOSPITAL CENTER, Mount Kisco, NY
NORTHFIELD HOSPITAL (Formerly Northfield City Hospital), Northfield, MN
NORTHGATE GENERAL HOSPITAL, Seattle, WA, See Northwest General Hospital
NORTHLAND MEDICAL CENTER, Holbrook, AZ
NORTHLAND MEDICAL CENTER (Formerly Mecosta Memorial Hospital), Stanwood, MI
NORTHPARK HOSPITAL (Formerly Northpark Community Hospital), El Paso, TX
NORTHRIDGE, HOSPITAL MEDICAL CENTER, Los Angeles, CA
NORTHSIDE HOSPITAL, Atlanta, GA
NORTHSIDE PRESBYTERIAN HOSPITAL, Albuquerque, NM
NORTHVILLE REGIONAL PSYCHIATRIC HOSPITAL, Northville, MI
NORTHWEST COMMUNITY HOSPITAL, Arlington Heights, IL
NORTHWEST GENERAL HOSPITAL, Detroit, MI
NORTHWEST GENERAL HOSPITAL, Knoxville, TN
NORTHWEST GENERAL HOSPITAL, Milwaukee, WI
NORTHWEST GEORGIA REGIONAL HOSPITAL, Rome, GA
NORTHWEST HOSPITAL, Tucson, AZ
NORTHWEST HOSPITAL, Chicago, IL, See John F. Kennedy Medical Center
NORTHWEST HOSPITAL, Fort Worth, TX, See Continental Hospital North
NORTHWEST HOSPITAL, Seattle, WA
NORTHWEST IOWA HEALTH CENTER (Formerly Community Memorial Hospital and Nursing Home), Sheldon, IA
NORTHWEST KANSAS REGIONAL MEDICAL CENTER, Goodland, KS
NORTHWEST MEDICAL CENTER (Formerly Northwestern Hospital Services), Thief River Falls, MN
NORTHWEST MISSISSIPPI REGIONAL MEDICAL CENTER, Clarksdale, MS
NORTHWEST TEXAS HOSPITAL, , TX, See Amarillo Hospital District
NORTHWESTERN INSTITUTE OF PSYCHIATRY, Fort Washington, PA
NORTHWESTERN MEDICAL CENTER, St. Albans, VT
NORTHWESTERN MEMORIAL HOSPITAL, Chicago, IL
NORTHWESTERN UNIVERSITY STUDENT HEALTH SERVICE HOSPITAL, Evanston, IL
NORTHWESTERN UNIVERSITY-MEDX REGIONAL MEDICAL CENTER-WEST VALLEY, Los Angeles, CA
NORTHWOOD DEACONESS HOSPITAL AND HOME ASSOCIATION, Northwood, ND
NORTHWOODS HOSPITAL, Phelps, WI
NORTON COMMUNITY HOSPITAL, Norton, VA
NORTON COUNTY HOSPITAL, Norton, KS

NORTON HOSPITAL, Louisville, KY, See NKC Hospitals
NORTON SOUND REGIONAL HOSPITAL, Nome, AK
NORTON STATE HOSPITAL, Norton, KS
NORWALK COMMUNITY HOSPITAL, Norwalk, CA
NORWALK HOSPITAL, Norwalk, CT
NORWEGIAN-AMERICAN HOSPITAL, Chicago, IL
NORWICH HOSPITAL, Norwich, CT
NORWOOD HEALTH CENTER, Marshfield, WI
NORWOOD HOSPITAL, Norwood, MA
NOTRE DAME HOSPITAL, Central Falls, RI
NOVATO COMMUNITY HOSPITAL, Novato, CA
NOWATA GENERAL HOSPITAL, Nowata, OK
NOXUBEE GENERAL HOSPITAL, Macon, MS
NPW MEDICAL CENTER, Wilkes-Barre, PA, See Geisinger Wyoming Valley Medical Center
NYACK HOSPITAL, Nyack, NY
NYE GENERAL HOSPITAL, Tonopah, NV

O

O'BLENESS MEMORIAL HOSPITAL, Athens, OH
O'CONNOR HOSPITAL, San Jose, CA
O'DONOGHUE REHABILITATION INSTITUTE, Oklahoma City, OK, See Oklahoma Teaching Hospitals
OAK CLIFF MEDICAL AND SURGICAL HOSPITAL, Dallas, TX
OAK FOREST HOSPITAL OF COOK COUNTY, Oak Forest, IL
OAK HILL COMMUNITY MEDICAL CENTER, Oak Hill, OH
OAK HILL HOSPITAL, Joplin, MO
OAK PARK HOSPITAL, Oak Park, IL
OAK VALLEY DISTRICT HOSPITAL, Oakdale, CA
OAKES COMMUNITY HOSPITAL, Oakes, ND
OAKLAND GENERAL HOSPITAL OSTEOPATHIC, Madison Heights, MI
OAKLAND HOSPITAL, Oakland, CA
OAKLAND MEMORIAL HOSPITAL, Oakland, NE
OAKLAWN HOSPITAL, Marshall, MI
OAKS TREATMENT CENTER-BROWN SCHOOLS, Austin, TX
OAKWOOD DOWNRIVER MEDICAL CENTER (Formerly Lynn Hospital), Lincoln Park, MI
OAKWOOD FORENSIC CENTER, Lima, OH
OAKWOOD HOSPITAL, Dearborn, MI
OAKWOOD SPRINGWELLS HEALTH CENTER (Formerly Dearborn Medical Centre Hospital), Dearborn, MI
OCEAN BEACH HOSPITAL, Ilwaco, WA
OCEANA HOSPITAL, Hart, MI
OCHILTREE GENERAL HOSPITAL, Perryton, TX
OCHSNER FOUNDATION HOSPITAL, New Orleans, LA
OCONEE MEMORIAL HOSPITAL, Seneca, SC
OCONTO MEMORIAL HOSPITAL, Oconto, WI
ODESSA WOMEN'S AND CHILDREN'S HOSPITAL, Odessa, TX, See AMI Odessa Women's-Children Hospital
OGALLALA COMMUNITY HOSPITAL, Ogallala, NE
OHIO COUNTY HOSPITAL, Hartford, KY
OHIO STATE UNIVERSITY HOSPITALS, Columbus, OH
OHIO VALLEY GENERAL HOSPITAL, McKees Rocks, PA
OHIO VALLEY HOSPITAL, Steubenville, OH
OHIO VALLEY MEDICAL CENTER, Wheeling, WV
OIL CITY AREA HEALTH CENTER, Oil City, PA
OJAI VALLEY COMMUNITY HOSPITAL, Ojai, CA
OKANOGAN-DOUGLAS COUNTY HOSPITAL, Brewster, WA
OKARCHE MEMORIAL HOSPITAL, Okarche, OK
OKEENE MUNICIPAL HOSPITAL, Okeene, OK
OKLAHOMA CHILDREN'S MEMORIAL HOSPITAL, Oklahoma City, OK, See Oklahoma Teaching Hospitals
OKLAHOMA OSTEOPATHIC HOSPITAL, Tulsa, OK
OKLAHOMA STATE UNIVERSITY HOSPITAL AND CLINIC, Stillwater, OK
OKLAHOMA TEACHING HOSPITALS, Oklahoma City, OK
OKLAHOMA VETERANS CENTER, Sulphur, OK
OKMULGEE MEMORIAL HOSPITAL AUTHORITY, Okmulgee, OK
OKOLONA COMMUNITY HOSPITAL, Okolona, MS
OKTIBBEHA COUNTY HOSPITAL, Starkville, MS
OLATHE MEDICAL CENTER (Formerly Olathe Community Hospital), Olathe, KS
OLD BRIDGE DIVISION, Perth Amboy, NJ, See Raritan Bay Medical Center
OLEAN GENERAL HOSPITAL, Olean, NY
OLIN E. TEAGUE VETERANS' CENTER, Temple, TX
OLMSTED COMMUNITY HOSPITAL, Rochester, MN
OLYMPIA FIELDS OSTEOPATHIC MEDICAL CENTER, Olympia Fields, IL
OLYMPIC MEMORIAL HOSPITAL, Port Angeles, WA
OMNI HOSPITAL AND MEDICAL CENTER, Houston, TX
ONEIDA CITY HOSPITAL, Oneida, NY
ONEIDA HOSPITAL, Malad City, ID
ONSLOW MEMORIAL HOSPITAL, Jacksonville, NC
ONTARIO COMMUNITY HOSPITAL, Ontario, CA
ONTONAGON MEMORIAL HOSPITAL, Ontonagon, MI
OPELOUSAS GENERAL HOSPITAL, Opelousas, LA
ORANGE CITY MUNICIPAL HOSPITAL, Orange City, IA
ORANGE COUNTY HOSPITAL, Paoli, IN
ORANGE MEMORIAL DIVISION, Orlando, FL, See Orlando Regional Medical Center
ORANGE MEMORIAL HOSPITAL, Orange, TX
ORANGE MEMORIAL HOSPITAL UNIT, Orange, NJ, See Hospital Center at Orange
ORANGEBURG-CALHOUN REGIONAL HOSPITAL (Formerly Orangeburg Regional Hospital), Orangeburg, SC
ORCHARD CREEK HOSPITAL (Formerly Orchard Creek Family Recovery Center), Rosenberg, TX
ORCHARD HILLS HOSPITAL (Formerly Belding Community Hospital), Belding, MI
OREGON HEALTH SCIENCES UNIVERSITY HOSPITAL, Portland, OR
OREGON STATE HOSPITAL, Salem, OR
OREM COMMUNITY HOSPITAL, Orem, UT
ORLANDO GENERAL HOSPITAL, Orlando, FL
ORLANDO REGIONAL MEDICAL CENTER, Orlando, FL
ORLANDO REGIONAL MEDICAL CENTER ST. CLOUD, St. Cloud, FL
OROVILLE HOSPITAL, Oroville, CA
ORTHOPAEDIC HOSPITAL, Los Angeles, CA
ORTHOPAEDIC HOSPITAL OF CHARLOTTE, Charlotte, NC
ORTHOPEDIC UNIT, Newark, NJ, See United Hospitals Medical Center
ORTONVILLE AREA HEALTH SERVICES, Ortonville, MN
OSAWATOMIE STATE HOSPITAL, Osawatomie, KS
OSBORNE COUNTY MEMORIAL HOSPITAL, Osborne, KS
OSCEOLA COMMUNITY HOSPITAL, Sibley, IA
OSCEOLA MEMORIAL HOSPITAL, Osceola, AR
OSMOND GENERAL HOSPITAL, Osmond, NE
OSSEO AREA MUNICIPAL HOSPITAL AND NURSING HOME, Osseo, WI
OSSINING CORRECTIONAL FACILITIES HOSPITAL, Ossining, NY
OSTEOPATHIC HOSPITAL OF MAINE, Portland, ME
OSWEGO CITY HOSPITAL, Oswego, KS
OSWEGO HOSPITAL, Oswego, NY
OTHELLO COMMUNITY HOSPITAL, Othello, WA
OTIS HOSPITAL, Cambridge, MA
OTSEGO MEMORIAL HOSPITAL, Gaylord, MI
OTTAWA COUNTY HOSPITAL, Minneapolis, KS
OTTO C. EPP MEMORIAL HOSPITAL, Cincinnati, OH
OTTO KAISER MEMORIAL HOSPITAL, Kenedy, TX
OTTUMWA REGIONAL HEALTH CENTER, Ottumwa, IA
OUACHITA HOSPITAL, Camden, AR
OUR COMMUNITY HOSPITAL, Scotland Neck, NC
OUR LADY OF BELLEFONTE HOSPITAL, Ashland, KY
OUR LADY OF FATIMA UNIT, North Providence, RI, See St. Joseph Hospital, Providence
OUR LADY OF LOURDES HEALTH CENTER (Formerly Our Lady of Lourdes Hospital), Pasco, WA
OUR LADY OF LOURDES HOSPITAL, Norfolk, NE
OUR LADY OF LOURDES MEDICAL CENTER, Camden, NJ
OUR LADY OF LOURDES MEMORIAL HOSPITAL, Binghamton, NY
OUR LADY OF LOURDES REGIONAL MEDICAL CENTER, Lafayette, LA
OUR LADY OF MERCY HOSPITAL, Dyer, IN
OUR LADY OF MERCY HOSPITAL, Cincinnati, OH
OUR LADY OF MERCY MEDICAL CENTER, Bronx, NY
OUR LADY OF PEACE HOSPITAL, Louisville, KY
OUR LADY OF PROVIDENCE UNIT, Providence, RI, See St. Joseph Hospital
OUR LADY OF THE LAKE REGIONAL MEDICAL CENTER, Baton Rouge, LA
OUR LADY OF THE WAY HOSPITAL, Martin, KY
OUR LADY OF VICTORY HOSPITAL, Lackawanna, NY
OUTER DRIVE HOSPITAL, Lincoln Park, MI
OVERALL-MORRIS MEMORIAL HOSPITAL, Coleman, TX
OVERLAKE HOSPITAL MEDICAL CENTER, Bellevue, WA
OVERLOOK HOSPITAL, Summit, NJ
OWEN COUNTY MEMORIAL HOSPITAL, Owenton, KY
OWENSBORO-DAVIESS COUNTY HOSPITAL, Owensboro, KY
OXFORD HEALTH SERVICES (Formerly Oxford Hospital), Bensalem, PA
OXFORD-LAFAYETTE MEDICAL CENTER (Formerly Oxford-Lafayette County Hospital), Oxford, MS
OZARKS MEDICAL CENTER, West Plains, MO

P

PACIFIC COAST HOSPITAL (Formerly California Podiatry Hospital), San Francisco, CA
PACIFIC COMMUNITIES HOSPITAL, Newport, OR
PACIFIC HOSPITAL OF LONG BEACH, Long Beach, CA
PACIFIC MEDICAL CENTER, Seattle, WA
PACIFIC PRESBYTERIAN HOSPITAL, San Francisco, CA, See Pacific Presbyterian Medical Center
PACIFIC PRESBYTERIAN MEDICAL CENTER (Formerly Pacific Medical Center), San Francisco, CA
PACIFICA COMMUNITY HOSPITAL, Huntington Beach, CA
PAGE HOSPITAL, Page, AZ
PAGE MEMORIAL HOSPITAL, Luray, VA
PALISADES GENERAL HOSPITAL, North Bergen, NJ
PALM DRIVE HOSPITAL, Sebastopol, CA
PALM SPRINGS GENERAL HOSPITAL, Hialeah, FL
PALMDALE HOSPITAL MEDICAL CENTER, Palmdale, CA
PALMER MEMORIAL HOSPITAL, West Union, IA
PALMERTON HOSPITAL, Palmerton, PA
PALMETTO GENERAL HOSPITAL, Hialeah, FL, See AMI Palmetto General Hospital
PALMS OF PASADENA HOSPITAL, St. Petersburg, FL
PALMVIEW HOSPITAL, Lakeland, FL
PALO ALTO COUNTY HOSPITAL, Emmetsburg, IA
PALO DURO HOSPITAL, Canyon, TX
PALO PINTO GENERAL HOSPITAL, Mineral Wells, TX
PALO VERDE HOSPITAL, Tucson, AZ
PALO VERDE HOSPITAL, Blythe, CA
PALOMAR MEMORIAL HOSPITAL, Escondido, CA
PALOS COMMUNITY HOSPITAL, Palos Heights, IL
PAN AMERICAN HOSPITAL, Miami, FL
PANA COMMUNITY HOSPITAL, Pana, IL
PANOLA GENERAL HOSPITAL, Carthage, TX
PANORAMA COMMUNITY HOSPITAL, Los Angeles, CA
PAOLI MEMORIAL HOSPITAL, Paoli, PA
PARADISE VALLEY HOSPITAL, National City, CA
PARIS COMMUNITY HOSPITAL, Paris, IL
PARK CITY HOSPITAL, Bridgeport, CT
PARK LANE MEDICAL CENTER, Kansas City, MO
PARK NORTH GENERAL HOSPITAL, San Antonio, TX, See Colonial Hills Hospital
PARK PLACE HOSPITAL, Port Arthur, TX, See AMI Park Place Hospital
PARK PLAZA HOSPITAL, Houston, TX, See AMI Park Plaza Hospital
PARK RIDGE HOSPITAL, Rochester, NY
PARK RIDGE HOSPITAL (Formerly Fletcher Hospital), Fletcher, NC
PARK VIEW HOSPITAL, El Reno, OK
PARK VIEW MEDICAL CENTER, Nashville, TN, See HCA Park View Medical Center
PARK WEST HOSPITAL, Knoxville, TN, See HCA Park West Medical Centers
PARKER COMMUNITY HOSPITAL, Parker, AZ
PARKERS PRAIRIE DISTRICT HOSPITAL, Parkers Prairie, MN
PARKLAND HOSPITAL, Baton Rouge, LA
PARKLAND MEDICAL CENTER, Derry, NH
PARKRIDGE MEDICAL CENTER (Formerly Parkridge Hospital), Chattanooga, TN
PARKSIDE CENTER (Formerly Tulsa Psychiatric Center), Tulsa, OK
PARKSIDE LODGE OF WISCONSIN (Formerly Anderson Alcoholic Rehabilitation Hospital), Janesville, WI
PARKSIDE LODGE-CHOCOLATE BAYON (Formerly Brookwood Recovery Center), Liverpool, TX
PARKSIDE LODGE-DALLAS FT WORTH (Formerly Brookwood Recovery Center-Dallas), Wilmer, TX
PARKSIDE LUTHERAN HOSPITAL (Formerly Lutheran Center-Substance Abuse), Park Ridge, IL
PARKVIEW COMMUNITY HOSPITAL, Riverside, CA
PARKVIEW EPISCOPAL MEDICAL CENTER, Pueblo, CO
PARKVIEW HOSPITAL, Toledo, OH
PARKVIEW HOSPITAL, Midland, TX, See Physicians and Surgeons Hospital
PARKVIEW HOSPITAL, Wheeler, TX
PARKVIEW MEMORIAL HOSPITAL, Fort Wayne, IN
PARKVIEW MEMORIAL HOSPITAL, Brunswick, ME
PARKWAY HOSPITAL, , NY
PARKWAY HOSPITAL, Houston, TX, See AMI Parkway Hospital
PARKWAY MEDICAL CENTER HOSPITAL, Decatur, AL
PARKWAY REGIONAL HOSPITAL (Formerly Fulton Hospital), Fulton, KY
PARKWAY REGIONAL MEDICAL CENTER, North Miami Beach, FL, See AMI Parkway Regional Medical Center
PARKWOOD HOSPITAL (Formerly Clinton Community Hospital), Clinton, MD

PARKWOOD HOSPITAL, New Bedford, MA
PARMA COMMUNITY GENERAL HOSPITAL, Parma, OH
PARMER COUNTY COMMUNITY HOSPITAL, Friona, TX
PARSONS HOSPITAL, Flushing, NY
PARSONS STATE HOSPITAL AND TRAINING CENTER, Parsons, KS
PARTHENON PAVILION, Nashville, TN, See HCA Parthenon Pavilion
PASADENA BAYSHORE MEDICAL CENTER, Pasadena, TX, See HCA Pasadena Bayshore Medical Center
PASADENA COMMUNITY HOSPITAL, Pasadena, CA
PASADENA GENERAL HOSPITAL, Pasadena, TX
PASCACK VALLEY HOSPITAL, Westwood, NJ
PASSAIC GENERAL HOSPITAL, Passaic, NJ, See General Hospital Center at Passaic
PASSAVANT AREA HOSPITAL, Jacksonville, IL
PASSAVANT MEMORIAL HOSPITAL, Chicago, IL, See Northwestern Memorial Hospital
PATTERSON ARMY COMMUNITY HOSPITAL (Formerly Patterson U. S. Army Community Hospital), Fort Monmouth, NJ
PATTERSON HOSPITAL, Cuthbert, GA
PATTIE A. CLAY HOSPITAL, Richmond, KY
PATTON STATE HOSPITAL, Patton, CA
PAUL B. HALL REGIONAL MEDICAL CENTER, Paintsville, KY
PAUL OLIVER MEMORIAL HOSPITAL, Frankfort, MI
PAULDING COUNTY HOSPITAL, Paulding, OH
PAULDING MEMORIAL MEDICAL CENTER (Formerly Paulding Memorial Hospital), Dallas, GA
PAULINE WARFIELD LEWIS CENTER, Cincinnati, OH
PAULS VALLEY GENERAL HOSPITAL, Pauls Valley, OK
PAWATING HOSPITAL, Niles, MI
PAWHUSKA HOSPITAL, Pawhuska, OK
PAWNEE COUNTY MEMORIAL HOSPITAL, Pawnee City, NE
PAWNEE MUNICIPAL HOSPITAL, Pawnee, OK
PAXTON COMMUNITY HOSPITAL, Paxton, IL
PAYNE WHITNEY PSYCHIATRIC CLINIC, New York, NY, See Society of the New York Hospital
PAYNESVILLE COMMUNITY HOSPITAL, Paynesville, MN
PEACH COUNTY HOSPITAL, Fort Valley, GA
PEACHTREE-PARKWOOD HOSPITAL, Atlanta, GA, See CPC Parkwood Hospital
PEARCE HOSPITAL, Eldorado, IL
PEARL RIVER COUNTY HOSPITAL, Poplarville, MS
PECOS COUNTY MEMORIAL HOSPITAL, Fort Stockton, TX
PEEKSKILL HOSPITAL, Peekskill, NY
PEKIN MEMORIAL HOSPITAL, Pekin, IL
PELHAM BAY GENERAL HOSPITAL, Bronx, NY
PELICAN VALLEY HEALTH CENTER, Pelican Rapids, MN
PELLA COMMUNITY HOSPITAL, Pella, IA
PEMBINA COUNTY MEMORIAL HOSPITAL, Cavalier, ND
PEMBROKE PINES GENERAL HOSPITAL, Pembroke Pines, FL
PEMISCOT COUNTY MEMORIAL HOSPITAL, Hayti, MO
PENDER COMMUNITY HOSPITAL, Pender, NE
PENDER MEMORIAL HOSPITAL, Burgaw, NC
PENDLETON MEMORIAL METHODIST HOSPITAL, New Orleans, LA
PENINSULA GENERAL HOSPITAL MEDICAL CENTER, Salisbury, MD
PENINSULA HOSPITAL (Formerly Peninsula Psychiatric Hospital), Louisville, TN
PENINSULA HOSPITAL, Hampton, VA
PENINSULA HOSPITAL AND MEDICAL CENTER, Burlingame, CA
PENINSULA HOSPITAL CENTER, Far Rockaway, NY
PENINSULA MEDICAL CENTER, Ormond Beach, FL
PENNOCK HOSPITAL, Hastings, MI
PENNSYLVANIA HOSPITAL, Philadelphia, PA
PENNSYLVANIA STATE UNIVERSITY HOSPITAL, Hershey, PA
PENNSYLVANIA UNIVERSITY-ELIZABETHTOWN HOSPITAL AND REHABILITATION CENTER, Elizabethtown, PA, See Pennsylvania State University Hospital
PENOBSCOT BAY MEDICAL CENTER, Rockport, ME
PENOBSCOT VALLEY HOSPITAL, Lincoln, ME
PENROSE CANCER HOSPITAL, Colorado Springs, CO, See Penrose Hospitals
PENROSE COMMUNITY HOSPITAL, Colorado Springs, CO, See Penrose Hospitals
PENROSE HOSPITALS, Colorado Springs, CO
PEOPLE'S HOSPITAL, Mansfield, OH
PEOPLE'S MEMORIAL HOSPITAL, Independence, IA
PERALTA HOSPITAL, Oakland, CA
PERKINS COUNTY COMMUNITY HOSPITAL, Grant, NE
PERMIAN GENERAL HOSPITAL, Andrews, TX
PERRY COMMUNITY HOSPITAL, Marion, AL
PERRY COUNTY GENERAL HOSPITAL, Richton, MS
PERRY COUNTY MEMORIAL HOSPITAL, Tell City, IN
PERRY COUNTY MEMORIAL HOSPITAL, Perryville, MO
PERRY HOSPITAL (Formerly Perry Houston County Hospital), Perry, GA
PERRY MEMORIAL HOSPITAL, Princeton, IL
PERRY MEMORIAL HOSPITAL, Perry, OK
PERRY MEMORIAL HOSPITAL, Linden, TN
PERSHING GENERAL HOSPITAL, Lovelock, NV
PERSON COUNTY MEMORIAL HOSPITAL, Roxboro, NC
PERTH AMBOY DIVISION, Perth Amboy, NJ, See Raritan Bay Medical Center
PETALUMA VALLEY HOSPITAL, Petaluma, CA
PETERSBURG GENERAL HOSPITAL, Petersburg, VA, See Southside Regional Medical Center
PETERSBURG GENERAL HOSPITAL AND LONG TERM CARE FACILITY, Petersburg, AK
PHELPS COUNTY REGIONAL MEDICAL CENTER, Rolla, MO
PHELPS MEMORIAL HEALTH CENTER, Holdrege, NE
PHELPS MEMORIAL HOSPITAL CENTER, North Tarrytown, NY
PHILADELPHIA DISPENSARY FOR THE MEDICAL RELIEF OF THE POOR, Philadelphia, PA, See Pennsylvania Hospital
PHILADELPHIA LYING-IN CHARITY HOSPITAL, Philadelphia, PA, See Pennsylvania Hospital
PHILADELPHIA PSYCHIATRIC CENTER, Philadelphia, PA
PHILADELPHIA STATE HOSPITAL, Philadelphia, PA
PHILHAVEN HOSPITAL, Mount Gretna, PA
PHILIP D. ARMOUR CLINICAL RESEARCH BUILDING, Chicago, IL, See University of Chicago Hospitals and Clinics
PHILIPSBURG STATE GENERAL HOSPITAL, Philipsburg, PA
PHILLIPS COUNTY HOSPITAL, Phillipsburg, KS
PHILLIPS COUNTY HOSPITAL, Malta, MT
PHOEBE PUTNEY MEMORIAL HOSPITAL, Albany, GA
PHOENIX BAPTIST HOSPITAL AND MEDICAL CENTER, Phoenix, AZ
PHOENIX CAMELBACK HOSPITAL, Phoenix, AZ
PHOENIX CHILDREN'S HOSPITAL, Phoenix, AZ
PHOENIX GENERAL HOSPITAL, Phoenix, AZ
PHOENIX INDIAN MEDICAL CENTER, Phoenix, AZ
PHOENIX MEMORIAL HOSPITAL, Phoenix, AZ
PHOENIXVILLE HOSPITAL, Phoenixville, PA
PHYSICIANS AND SURGEONS GENERAL HOSPITAL, Corpus Christi, TX, See Southside Community Hospital
PHYSICIANS AND SURGEONS HOSPITAL, Atlanta, GA
PHYSICIANS AND SURGEONS HOSPITAL, Shreveport, LA
PHYSICIANS AND SURGEONS HOSPITAL (Formerly Parkview Hospital), Midland, TX
PHYSICIANS HOSPITAL, New York, NY
PHYSICIANS MEMORIAL HOSPITAL, La Plata, MD
PICKENS COUNTY MEDICAL CENTER (Formerly Pickens County Hospital), Carrollton, AL
PICKENS GENERAL HOSPITAL, Jasper, GA
PICO RIVERA COMMUNITY HOSPITAL, Pico Rivera, CA
PIEDMONT GERIATRIC HOSPITAL, Burkeville, VA
PIEDMONT HOSPITAL, Atlanta, GA
PIEDMONT HOSPITAL AND NURSING HOME, Piedmont, AL
PIERCE COUNTY HOSPITAL, Blackshear, GA
PIGGOTT COMMUNITY HOSPITAL, Piggott, AR
PIKE COMMUNITY HOSPITAL, Waverly, OH
PIKE COUNTY MEMORIAL HOSPITAL, Louisiana, MO
PILGRIM PSYCHIATRIC CENTER, West Brentwood, NY
PINAL GENERAL HOSPITAL, Florence, AZ
PINCKNEYVILLE COMMUNITY HOSPITAL, Pinckneyville, IL
PINE FOREST SANITARIUM AND HOSPITAL, Chunky, MS
PINE REST CHRISTIAN HOSPITAL, Grand Rapids, MI
PINECREST HOSPITAL, Santa Barbara, CA
PINECREST REHABILITATION HOSPITAL AT DELRAY, Delray, FL
PINECREST STATE SCHOOL HOSPITAL, Pineville, LA
PINELAND CENTER (Formerly Listed Under New Gloucester), Pownal, ME
PINERIDGE HOSPITAL, Lander, WY
PINEVILLE COMMUNITY HOSPITAL, Pineville, KY
PIONEER HOSPITAL, Artesia, CA
PIONEER MEMORIAL HOSPITAL, Heppner, OR
PIONEER MEMORIAL HOSPITAL, Prineville, OR
PIONEER MEMORIAL HOSPITAL, Viborg, SD
PIONEER PARK HOSPITAL (Formerly AMI Pioneer Park Medical Center), Irving, TX
PIONEER VALLEY HOSPITAL, West Valley City, UT
PIONEERS HOSPITAL OF RIO BLANCO COUNTY, Meeker, CO
PIONEERS MEMORIAL HOSPITAL, Brawley, CA
PIPESTONE COUNTY MEDICAL CENTER, Pipestone, MN
PIPP COMMUNITY HOSPITAL, Plainwell, MI
PIQUA MEMORIAL MEDICAL CENTER, Piqua, OH
PITT COUNTY MEMORIAL HOSPITAL, Greenville, NC
PITTSBURG MEDICAL CENTER, Pittsburg, TX
PLACENTIA-LINDA COMMUNITY HOSPITAL, Placentia, CA
PLACID MEMORIAL HOSPITAL, Lake Placid, NY
PLAINS MEMORIAL HOSPITAL, Dimmitt, TX
PLAINVIEW PUBLIC HOSPITAL, Plainview, NE
PLAINVILLE RURAL HOSPITAL DISTRICT, Plainville, KS
PLANTATION GENERAL HOSPITAL, Plantation, FL
PLAQUEMINES PARISH GENERAL HOSPITAL, Port Sulphur, LA
PLATEAU MEDICAL CENTER, Oak Hill, WV
PLATTE COMMUNITY MEMORIAL HOSPITAL, Platte, SD
PLATTE COUNTY MEMORIAL HOSPITAL, Wheatland, WY
PLATTE VALLEY MEDICAL CENTER, Brighton, CO
PLEASANT HILL GENERAL HOSPITAL, Pleasant Hill, LA
PLEASANT VALLEY HOSPITAL, Camarillo, CA
PLEASANT VALLEY HOSPITAL, Point Pleasant, WV
PLUMAS DISTRICT HOSPITAL, Quincy, CA
PLYMOUTH COUNTY HOSPITAL, Hanson, MA
POCAHONTAS COMMUNITY HOSPITAL, Pocahontas, IA
POCAHONTAS MEMORIAL HOSPITAL, Marlinton, WV
POCATELLO REGIONAL MEDICAL CENTER, Pocatello, ID
POCONO HOSPITAL, East Stroudsburg, PA
PODIATRY HOSPITAL OF PITTSBURGH, Pittsburgh, PA
POINTE COUPEE GENERAL HOSPITAL, New Roads, LA
POLK GENERAL HOSPITAL, Bartow, FL
POLK GENERAL HOSPITAL, Cedartown, GA
POLLY RYON MEMORIAL HOSPITAL, Richmond, TX
POLYCLINIC MEDICAL CENTER OF HARRISBURG, Harrisburg, PA
POMERADO HOSPITAL, Poway, CA
POMONA VALLEY COMMUNITY HOSPITAL, Pomona, CA
PONCE REGIONAL HOSPITAL, Ponce, P.R.
PONDERA MEDICAL CENTER, Conrad, MT
PONTIAC CORRECTIONAL CENTER, Pontiac, IL
PONTIAC GENERAL HOSPITAL, Pontiac, MI
PONTIAC OSTEOPATHIC HOSPITAL, Pontiac, MI
PONTOTOC COMMUNITY HOSPITAL AND EXTENDED CARE FACILITY, Pontotoc, MS
POPLAR SPRINGS HOSPITAL, Petersburg, VA
PORT HURON HOSPITAL, Port Huron, MI
PORTAGE VIEW HOSPITAL, Hancock, MI
PORTER MEDICAL CENTER, Middlebury, VT
PORTER MEMORIAL HOSPITAL, Denver, CO
PORTER MEMORIAL HOSPITAL, Valparaiso, IN
PORTERVILLE DEVELOPMENTAL CENTER (Formerly Porterville State Hospital), Porterville, CA
PORTERVILLE STATE HOSPITAL, Porterville, CA, See Porterville Developmental Center
PORTLAND ADVENTIST MEDICAL CENTER, Portland, OR
PORTSMOUTH GENERAL HOSPITAL, Portsmouth, VA
PORTSMOUTH PSYCHIATRIC CENTER (Formerly Virginia Center for Psychiatric), Portsmouth, VA
PORTSMOUTH REGIONAL HOSPITAL (Formerly Portsmouth Hospital), Portsmouth, NH
POTOMAC HOSPITAL, Woodbridge, VA
POTOMAC VALLEY HOSPITAL, Keyser, WV
POTTERS MEDICAL CENTER, East Liverpool, OH
POTTSTOWN MEMORIAL MEDICAL CENTER, Pottstown, PA
POTTSVILLE HOSPITAL AND WARNE CLINIC, Pottsville, PA
POUDRE VALLEY HOSPITAL, Fort Collins, CO
POWELL COUNTY MEMORIAL HOSPITAL, Deer Lodge, MT
POWELL HOSPITAL, Powell, WY
PRAIRIE COMMUNITY HOSPITAL, Terry, MT
PRAIRIE DU CHIEN MEMORIAL HOSPITAL, Prairie Du Chien, WI
PRAIRIE LAKES HOSPITAL EAST, Watertown, SD, See Prairie Lakes Hospital
PRAIRIE LAKES HOSPITAL WEST, Watertown, SD, See Prairie Lakes Hospital
PRAIRIE LAKES HOSPTIAL, Watertown, SD
PRAIRIE VIEW MENTAL HEALTH CENTER, Newton, KS
PRATT REGIONAL MEDICAL CENTER, Pratt, KS
PRENTICE WOMEN'S HOSPITAL, Chicago, IL, See Northwestern Memorial Hospital
PRESBYTERIAN HOSPITAL, Albuquerque, NM
PRESBYTERIAN HOSPITAL, Charlotte, NC
PRESBYTERIAN HOSPITAL, Oklahoma City, OK
PRESBYTERIAN HOSPITAL, Dallas, TX
PRESBYTERIAN HOSPITAL IN THE CITY OF NEW YORK, New York, NY
PRESBYTERIAN HOSPITAL OF KAUFMAN, Kaufman, TX
PRESBYTERIAN HOSPITAL OF WINNSBORO, Winnsboro, TX
PRESBYTERIAN INTERCOMMUNITY HOSPITAL, Whittier, CA

PRESBYTERIAN UNIT, Newark, NJ, See United Hospitals Medical Center
PRESBYTERIAN-UNIVERSITY HOSPITAL, Pittsburgh, PA
PRESBYTERIAN-UNIVERSITY OF PENNSYLVANIA MEDICAL CENTER, Philadelphia, PA
PRESTON MATERNITY HOSPITAL, Philadelphia, PA, See Pennsylvania Hospital
PRESTON MEMORIAL HOSPITAL, Kingwood, WV
PREVOST MEMORIAL HOSPITAL, Donaldsonville, LA
PRIMARY CHILDREN'S MEDICAL CENTER, Salt Lake City, UT
PRINCE GEORGE'S HOSPITAL CENTER (Formerly Prince George's General Hospital and Medical Center), Cheverly, MD
PRINCE WILLIAM HOSPITAL, Manassas, VA
PRINCETON COMMUNITY HOSPITAL, Princeton, WV
PRINCETON UNIVERSITY HEALTH SERVICES, MCCOSH HEALTH CENTER, Princeton, NJ
PROCTOR COMMUNITY HOSPITAL, Peoria, IL
PROSSER MEMORIAL HOSPITAL, Prosser, WA
PROVIDENCE CENTRAL MEMORIAL HOSPITAL (Formerly Central Memorial Hospital), Toppenish, WA
PROVIDENCE HOSPITAL, Mobile, AL
PROVIDENCE HOSPITAL, Anchorage, AK
PROVIDENCE HOSPITAL, Oakland, CA
PROVIDENCE HOSPITAL, Washington, DC
PROVIDENCE HOSPITAL, Holyoke, MA
PROVIDENCE HOSPITAL, Southfield, MI
PROVIDENCE HOSPITAL, Cincinnati, OH
PROVIDENCE HOSPITAL, Sandusky, OH
PROVIDENCE HOSPITAL, Medford, OR
PROVIDENCE HOSPITAL, Columbia, SC
PROVIDENCE HOSPITAL, Waco, TX
PROVIDENCE HOSPITAL, Everett, WA
PROVIDENCE MEDICAL CENTER, Wayne, NE
PROVIDENCE MEDICAL CENTER, Portland, OR
PROVIDENCE MEDICAL CENTER, Seattle, WA
PROVIDENCE MEMORIAL HOSPITAL, El Paso, TX
PROVIDENCE MILWAUKIE HOSPITAL (Formerly Dwyer Community Hospital), Milwaukie, OR
PROVIDENCE-ST. MARGARET HEALTH CENTER, Kansas City, KS
PROVIDENT MEDICAL CENTER, Chicago, IL
PROWERS MEDICAL CENTER, Lamar, CO
PSYCHIATRIC CENTER OF MICHIGAN, New Baltimore, MI
PSYCHIATRIC HOSPITAL, Iowa City, IA, See University of Iowa Hospitals and Clinics
PSYCHIATRIC INSTITUTE OF ATLANTA, Atlanta, GA
PSYCHIATRIC INSTITUTE OF FORT WORTH, Fort Worth, TX
PSYCHIATRIC INSTITUTE OF MONTGOMERY COUNTY, Rockville, MD
PSYCHIATRIC INSTITUTE OF RICHMOND, Richmond, VA
PSYCHIATRIC INSTITUTE OF WASHINGTON, Washington, DC
PSYCHIATRIC PAVILION, Amarillo, TX, See Amarillo Hospital District
PUBLIC HOSPITAL OF THE TOWN OF SALEM, Salem, IL
PUGET SOUND HOSPITAL, Tacoma, WA
PULASKI COMMUNITY HOSPITAL, Pulaski, VA
PULASKI MEMORIAL HOSPITAL, Winamac, IN
PULLMAN MEMORIAL HOSPITAL (Formerly Memorial Hospital), Pullman, WA
PUNGO DISTRICT HOSPITAL, Belhaven, NC
PUNXSUTAWNEY AREA HOSPITAL, Punxsutawney, PA
PURCELL MUNICIPAL HOSPITAL, Purcell, OK
PURDUE UNIVERSITY STUDENT HOSPITAL (Formerly Listed Under Lafayette), West Lafayette, IN
PUSHMATAHA COUNTY-TOWN OF ANTLERS HOSPITAL AUTHORITY, Antlers, OK
PUTNAM COMMUNITY HOSPITAL, Palatka, FL
PUTNAM COUNTY HOSPITAL, Greencastle, IN
PUTNAM GENERAL HOSPITAL, Eatonton, GA
PUTNAM GENERAL HOSPITAL, Hurricane, WV
PUTNAM HOSPITAL CENTER, Carmel, NY

Q

QUAKERTOWN COMMUNITY HOSPITAL, Quakertown, PA
QUANAH MEDICAL CENTER (Formerly Hardeman County Memorial Hospital), Quanah, TX
QUEEN OF ANGELS MEDICAL CENTER, Los Angeles, CA
QUEEN OF PEACE HOSPITAL, New Prague, MN
QUEEN OF THE VALLEY HOSPITAL, Napa, CA
QUEEN OF THE VALLEY HOSPITAL, West Covina, CA
QUEEN'S MEDICAL CENTER, Honolulu, HI
QUEENS CHILDREN'S PSYCHIATRIC CENTER, Bellerose, NY
QUEENS HOSPITAL CENTER, Jamaica, NY
QUEENY TOWER, St. Louis, MO, See Barnes Hospital
QUINCY CITY HOSPITAL, Quincy, MA
QUINCY VALLEY HOSPITAL, Quincy, WA
QUITMAN COUNTY HOSPITAL, Marks, MS

R

R. E. THOMASON GENERAL HOSPITAL, El Paso, TX
R. J. REYNOLDS-PATRICK COUNTY MEMORIAL HOSPITAL, Stuart, VA
R. J. TAYLOR MEMORIAL HOSPITAL, Hawkinsville, GA
R. T. JONES MEMORIAL HOSPITAL, Canton, GA
RABUN COUNTY MEMORIAL HOSPITAL, Clayton, GA
RADFORD COMMUNITY HOSPITAL, Radford, VA
RAHWAY HOSPITAL, Rahway, NJ
RAINBOW BABIES AND CHILDREN'S HOSPITAL, Cleveland, OH, See University Hospitals of Cleveland
RALEIGH COMMUNITY HOSPITAL, Raleigh, NC
RALEIGH GENERAL HOSPITAL, Beckley, WV
RALEIGH HILLS HOSPITAL, Dallas, TX, See Horizon Hospital
RALEIGH HILLS HOSPITAL, San Antonio, TX, See Horizon Hospital
RALEIGH HILLS HOSPITAL OF SPOKANE, Spokane, WA, See Mountainview Hospital of Spokane
RALPH K. DAVIES MEDICAL CENTER-FRANKLIN HOSPITAL, San Francisco, CA
RANCHO PARK HOSPITAL, El Cajon, CA
RAND-JOHNSON, St. Louis, MO, See Barnes Hospital
RANDOLPH COUNTY HOSPITAL, Roanoke, AL
RANDOLPH COUNTY HOSPITAL, Winchester, IN
RANDOLPH COUNTY MEDICAL CENTER, Pocahontas, AR
RANDOLPH HOSPITAL, Asheboro, NC
RANGELY DISTRICT HOSPITAL, Rangely, CO
RANGER GENERAL HOSPITAL, Ranger, TX
RANKIN GENERAL HOSPITAL, Brandon, MS
RANKIN HOSPITAL DISTRICT, Rankin, TX
RANSOM MEMORIAL HOSPITAL, Ottawa, KS
RAPID CITY REGIONAL HOSPITAL, Rapid City, SD
RAPIDES GENERAL HOSPITAL, Alexandria, LA
RAPPAHANNOCK GENERAL HOSPITAL, Kilmarnock, VA
RARITAN BAY MEDICAL CENTER, Perth Amboy, NJ
RAVENSWOOD HOSPITAL MEDICAL CENTER, Chicago, IL
RAWLINS COUNTY HOSPITAL, Atwood, KS
RAY COUNTY MEMORIAL HOSPITAL, Richmond, MO
RAYMOND BLANK MEMORIAL HOSPITAL FOR CHILDREN, Des Moines, IA, See Iowa Methodist Medical Center
RAYMOND W. BLISS ARMY COMMUNITY HOSPITAL, Fort Huachuca, AZ
RAYNE-BRANCH HOSPITAL, Rayne, LA
READING HOSPITAL AND MEDICAL CENTER, Reading, PA
READING REHABILITATION HOSPITAL, Reading, PA
REAGAN MEMORIAL HOSPITAL, Big Lake, TX
REBSAMEN REGIONAL MEDICAL CENTER, Jacksonville, AR
RECEPTION AND MEDICAL CENTER HOSPITAL, Lake Butler, FL
RED BANK COMMUNITY HOSPITAL, Chattanooga, TN, See Riverchase Hospital
RED BAY HOSPITAL, Red Bay, AL
RED BIRD MOUNTAIN MEDICAL CENTER (Formerly Red Bird Hospital), Beverly, KY
RED RIVER GENERAL HOSPITAL, Clarksville, TX
RED RIVER HOSPITAL, Wichita Falls, TX, See HCA Red River Hospital
REDBUD COMMUNITY HOSPITAL, Clearlake, CA
REDDING MEDICAL CENTER, Redding, CA
REDFORD COMMUNITY HOSPITAL, Redford, MI
REDGATE MEMORIAL HOSPITAL, Long Beach, CA
REDINGTON-FAIRVIEW GENERAL HOSPITAL, Skowhegan, ME
REDLANDS COMMUNITY HOSPITAL, Redlands, CA
REDMOND PARK HOSPITAL, Rome, GA
REDWOOD FALLS MUNICIPAL HOSPITAL, Redwood Falls, MN
REDWOOD MEMORIAL HOSPITAL, Fortuna, CA
REED CITY HOSPITAL, Reed City, MI
REEDSBURG MEMORIAL HOSPITAL, Reedsburg, WI
REEVES COUNTY HOSPITAL, Pecos, TX
REFUGIO COUNTY MEMORIAL HOSPITAL (Formerly Memorial Hospital), Refugio, TX
REGENT HOSPITAL, New York, NY
REGENT HOSPITAL -ACADIANA (Formerly Regent Hospital), Erath, LA
REGENT HOSPITAL -EAST CARROLL (Formerly East Carroll Parish Hospital), Lake Providence, LA
REGENT HOSPITAL FELICIANA (Formerly Feliciana Medical Center), Clinton, LA
REGINA MEDICAL COMPLEX (Formerly Regina Memorial Hospital), Hastings, MN
REGIONAL HOSPITAL OF JACKSON, Jackson, TN, See HCA Regional Hospital of Jackson
REGIONAL MEDICAL CENTER, Madisonville, KY
REGIONAL MEDICAL CENTER AT MEMPHIS, Memphis, TN
REGIONAL MEMORIAL HOSPITAL, Brunswick, ME
REGIONAL REHABILITATION CENTER, Memphis, TN, See Baptist Memorial Hospital
REHABILITATION AND WORK CENTER MENTAL HEALTH PROGRAM, Cayey, P.R.
REHABILITATION HOSPITAL IN MECHANICSBURG (Formerly Rehabilitation Hospital for Special Services), Mechanicsburg, PA
REHABILITATION HOSPITAL OF ALTOONA, Altoona, PA
REHABILITATION HOSPITAL OF THE PACIFIC, Honolulu, HI
REHABILITATION INSTITUTE, Detroit, MI
REHABILITATION INSTITUTE, Kansas City, MO
REHABILITATION INSTITUTE OF CHICAGO, Chicago, IL
REHABILITATION INSTITUTE OF OREGON, Portland, OR, See Good Samaritan Hospital and Medical Center
REHABILITATION INSTITUTE OF PITTSBURGH, Pittsburgh, PA
REHABILITATION INSTITUTE OF SANTA BARBARA (Formerly Memorial Hospital of Santa Barbara), Santa Barbara, CA
REHABILITATION INSTITUTE OF WEST FLORIDA, Pensacola, FL, See West Florida Regional Medical Center
REHABX HOSPITAL FOR SPECIAL SERVICES OF YORK, York, PA
REHABX HOSPITAL FOR SPECIAL SERVICES, Bellefonte, PA
REHOBOTH MCKINLEY CHRISTIAN HOSPITAL, Gallup, NM
REID MEMORIAL HOSPITAL, Richmond, IN
RENVILLE BOTTINEAU MEMORIAL HOSPITAL, Mohall, ND
RENVILLE COUNTY HOSPITAL, Olivia, MN
REPUBLIC COUNTY HOSPITAL, Belleville, KS
RESEARCH BELTON HOSPITAL, Belton, MO
RESEARCH MEDICAL CENTER, Kansas City, MO
RESEARCH PSYCHIATRIC CENTER, Kansas City, MO
RESTON HOSPITAL CENTER (Formerly Circle Terrace Hospital, Alexandria), Reston, VA
RESURRECTION HOSPITAL, Chicago, IL
RETREAT HOSPITAL, Richmond, VA
REX HOSPITAL, Raleigh, NC
REYNOLDS ARMY COMMUNITY HOSPITAL, Fort Sill, OK
REYNOLDS COUNTY MEMORIAL HOSPITAL, Ellington, MO
REYNOLDS MEMORIAL HOSPITAL, Glen Dale, WV
RHD MEMORIAL MEDICAL CENTER, Dallas, TX
RHEA COUNTY MEDICAL CENTER, Dayton, TN
RHODE ISLAND HOSPITAL, Providence, RI
RHODES DENTAL HOSPITAL, Norfolk, VA
RICE COUNTY DISTRICT ONE HOSPITAL, Faribault, MN
RICE MEMORIAL HOSPITAL, Willmar, MN
RICHARD H. HUTCHINGS PSYCHIATRIC CENTER, Syracuse, NY
RICHARD H. YOUNG MEMORIAL HOSPITAL, Omaha, NE, See Lutheran Medical Center
RICHARD L. ROUDEBUSH VETERANS ADMINISTRATION MEDICAL CENTER, Indianapolis, IN
RICHARDS MEMORIAL HOSPITAL, Rockdale, TX
RICHARDSON MEDICAL CENTER, Richardson, TX
RICHARDTON COMMUNITY HOSPITAL, Richardton, ND
RICHLAND HOSPITAL, Mansfield, OH
RICHLAND HOSPITAL, Richland Center, WI
RICHLAND MEMORIAL HOSPITAL, Olney, IL
RICHLAND MEMORIAL HOSPITAL, Columbia, SC
RICHLAND PARISH HOSPITAL-DELHI, Delhi, LA
RICHLAND PARISH HOSPITAL-RAYVILLE, Rayville, LA
RICHMOND COMMUNITY HOSPITAL, Richmond, VA
RICHMOND EYE AND EAR HOSPITAL, Richmond, VA
RICHMOND HEIGHTS GENERAL HOSPITAL, Cleveland, OH
RICHMOND MEMORIAL HOSPITAL, Rockingham, NC
RICHMOND MEMORIAL HOSPITAL, Richmond, VA
RICHMOND MEMORIAL HOSPITAL AND HEALTH CENTER, Staten Island, NY
RICHMOND METROPOLITAN HOSPITAL, Richmond, VA, See Metropolitan Hospital

RICHMOND STATE HOSPITAL, Richmond, IN
RIDDLE MEMORIAL HOSPITAL, Media, PA
RIDEOUT MEMORIAL HOSPITAL, Marysville, CA
RIDGECLIFF HOSPITAL, Willoughby, OH
RIDGECREST COMMUNITY HOSPITAL, Ridgecrest, CA
RIDGECREST HOSPITAL, Clayton, GA
RIDGEVIEW INSTITUTE, Smyrna, GA
RIDGEVIEW PSYCHIATRIC HOSPITAL AND CENTER, Oak Ridge, TN
RILEY MEMORIAL HOSPITAL (Formerly F. G. Riley Memorial Hospital), Meridian, MS
RILEY-KEMPER COMMUNITY HOSPITAL (Formerly Kemper County Hospital), De Kalb, MS
RINGGOLD COUNTY HOSPITAL, Mount Ayr, IA
RIO GRANDE REGIONAL HOSPITAL, McAllen, TX
RIO GRANDE STATE CENTER, Harlingen, TX
RIO HONDO MEMORIAL HOSPITAL, Downey, CA
RIPLEY COUNTY MEMORIAL HOSPITAL, Doniphan, MO
RIPON MEMORIAL HOSPITAL, Ripon, WI
RITENOUR HEALTH CENTER, University Park, PA
RITZVILLE MEMORIAL HOSPITAL, Ritzville, WA
RIVENDELL CHILDREN AND YOUTH CENTER, West Jordan, UT
RIVER DISTRICT HOSPITAL, St. Clair, MI
RIVER FALLS AREA HOSPITAL, River Falls, WI
RIVER OAKS HOSPITAL (Formerly Listed Under New Orleans), Harahan, LA
RIVER OAKS HOSPITAL, Jackson, MS
RIVER PARISHES MEDICAL CENTER, Laplace, LA
RIVER PARK HOSPITAL, McMinnville, TN
RIVER WEST MEDICAL CENTER, Plaquemine, LA
RIVERCHASE HOSPITAL (Formerly Red Bank Community Hospital), Chattanooga, TN
RIVERLAND MEDICAL CENTER (Formerly Concordia Parish Hospital), Ferriday, LA
RIVERSIDE COMMUNITY HOSPITAL, Riverside, CA
RIVERSIDE COMMUNITY HOSPITAL, Bossier City, LA
RIVERSIDE COMMUNITY HOSPITAL-KNOLLWOOD CENTER, Riverside, CA
RIVERSIDE COMMUNITY MEMORIAL HOSPITAL, Waupaca, WI
RIVERSIDE GENERAL HOSPITAL, Secaucus, NJ, See Meadowlands Hospital Medical Center
RIVERSIDE GENERAL HOSPITAL, Houston, TX
RIVERSIDE GENERAL HOSPITAL-UNIVERSITY MEDICAL CENTER, Riverside, CA
RIVERSIDE HOSPITAL, Wilmington, DE
RIVERSIDE HOSPITAL, Jacksonville, FL
RIVERSIDE HOSPITAL, New Port Richey, FL
RIVERSIDE HOSPITAL, Wichita, KS
RIVERSIDE HOSPITAL, Jackson, MS, See Charter Hospital of Jackson
RIVERSIDE HOSPITAL, Boonton, NJ, See St. Clare's-Riverside Medical Center, Denville
RIVERSIDE HOSPITAL, Toledo, OH
RIVERSIDE HOSPITAL, Corpus Christi, TX, See AMI Riverside Hospital
RIVERSIDE HOSPITAL, Newport News, VA
RIVERSIDE MEDICAL CENTER, Kankakee, IL
RIVERSIDE MEDICAL CENTER, Franklinton, LA
RIVERSIDE METHODIST HOSPITALS, Columbus, OH
RIVERSIDE OSTEOPATHIC HOSPITAL, Trenton, MI
RIVERSIDE PSYCHIATRIC HOSPITAL (Formerly Riverside Hospital), Portland, OR
RIVERTON HOSPITAL, Seattle, WA
RIVERVIEW HOSPITAL, Little Rock, AR
RIVERVIEW HOSPITAL, Noblesville, IN
RIVERVIEW HOSPITAL, Wisconsin Rapids, WI
RIVERVIEW HOSPITAL ASSOCIATION, Crookston, MN
RIVERVIEW HOSPITAL FOR CHILDREN, Middletown, CT
RIVERVIEW MEDICAL CENTER, Red Bank, NJ
RIVERWOOD CENTER (Formerly St. Croixdale Hospital), Prescott, WI
ROANE GENERAL HOSPITAL, Spencer, WV
ROANOKE MEMORIAL HOSPITALS, Roanoke, VA
ROANOKE MEMORIAL REHABILITATION CENTER, Roanoke, VA, See Roanoke Memorial Hospitals
ROANOKE VALLEY PSYCHIATRIC CENTER, Salem, VA
ROANOKE-CHOWAN HOSPITAL, Ahoskie, NC
ROBERSONVILLE COMMUNITY HOSPITAL, Robersonville, NC
ROBERT F. KENNEDY MEDICAL CENTER, Hawthorne, CA
ROBERT PACKER HOSPITAL, Sayre, PA
ROBERT W. LONG HOSPITAL, Indianapolis, IN, See Indiana University Hospitals
ROBERT WOOD JOHNSON JR. REHABILITATION INSTITUTE, Edison, NJ
ROBERT WOOD JOHNSON UNIVERSITY HOSPITAL (Formerly Middlesex General-University Hospital), New Brunswick, NJ
ROBINSON MEMORIAL HOSPITAL, Ravenna, OH
ROCHELLE COMMUNITY HOSPITAL, Rochelle, IL
ROCHESTER GENERAL HOSPITAL, Rochester, NY
ROCHESTER METHODIST HOSPITAL, Rochester, MN
ROCHESTER PSYCHIATRIC CENTER, Rochester, NY
ROCHESTER ST. MARY'S HOSPITAL OF THE SISTERS OF CHARITY, Rochester, NY
ROCK COUNTY HOSPITAL, Bassett, NE
ROCKCASTLE HOSPITAL (Formerly Rockcastle County Hospital), Mount Vernon, KY
ROCKDALE HOSPITAL (Formerly Rockdale County Hospital), Conyers, GA
ROCKEFELLER UNIVERSITY HOSPITAL, New York, NY
ROCKFORD CENTER, Wilmington, DE
ROCKFORD MEMORIAL HOSPITAL, Rockford, IL
ROCKINGHAM MEMORIAL HOSPITAL, Bellows Falls, VT
ROCKINGHAM MEMORIAL HOSPITAL, Harrisonburg, VA
ROCKLAND CHILDREN'S PSYCHIATRIC CENTER, Orangeburg, NY
ROCKLAND PSYCHIATRIC CENTER, Orangeburg, NY
ROCKMART-ARAGON HOSPITAL, Rockmart, GA
ROCKVILLE GENERAL HOSPITAL, Rockville, CT
ROCKY MOUNTAIN HOSPITAL, Denver, CO
ROGER WILLIAMS GENERAL HOSPITAL, Providence, RI
ROGERS CITY HOSPITAL, Rogers City, MI
ROGERS MEMORIAL HOSPITAL, Oconomowoc, WI
ROGUE VALLEY MEDICAL CENTER, Medford, OR
ROLETTE COMMUNITY HOSPITAL, Rolette, ND
ROLLA COMMUNITY HOSPITAL, Rolla, ND
ROLLING HILL HOSPITAL, Elkins Park, PA
ROLLING PLAINS MEMORIAL HOSPITAL, Sweetwater, TX
ROLLINS-BROOK HOSPITAL, Lampasas, TX
ROLLMAN PSYCHIATRIC INSTITUTE, Cincinnati, OH
ROME DEVELOPMENTAL CENTER, Rome, NY
ROME HOSPITAL AND MURPHY MEMORIAL HOSPITAL, Rome, NY
ROOSEVELT GENERAL HOSPITAL, Portales, NM
ROOSEVELT HOSPITAL, Edison, NJ
ROOSEVELT HOSPITAL, New York, NY, See St. Luke's-Roosevelt Hospital Center
ROOSEVELT MEMORIAL HOSPITAL, Culbertson, MT
ROOSEVELT WARM SPRINGS INSTITUTE FOR REHABILITATION, Warm Springs, GA
ROPER HOSPITAL, Charleston, SC
ROSE MEDICAL CENTER, Denver, CO
ROSEAU AREA HOSPITAL, Roseau, MN
ROSEBUD COMMUNITY HOSPITAL, Forsyth, MT
ROSEBUD COMMUNITY HOSPITAL, Rosebud, TX
ROSELAND COMMUNITY HOSPITAL, Chicago, IL
ROSEVILLE COMMUNITY HOSPITAL, Roseville, CA
ROSEWOOD MEDICAL CENTER, Houston, TX
ROSS GENERAL HOSPITAL, Ross, CA
ROSWELL PARK MEMORIAL INSTITUTE, Buffalo, NY
ROTARY REHABILITATION HOSPITAL, Mobile, AL
ROUNDUP MEMORIAL HOSPITAL, Roundup, MT
ROUTT MEMORIAL HOSPITAL, Steamboat Springs, CO
ROWAN MEMORIAL HOSPITAL, Salisbury, NC
ROXBOROUGH MEMORIAL HOSPITAL (Formerly Memorial Hospital, Roxborough), Philadelphia, PA
ROY H. LAIRD MEMORIAL HOSPITAL, Kilgore, TX
ROYAL C. JOHNSON VETERANS MEMORIAL HOSPITAL, Sioux Falls, SD
RUBY VALLEY HOSPITAL, Sheridan, MT
RUMFORD COMMUNITY HOSPITAL, Rumford, ME
RUSH CITY HOSPITAL, Rush City, MN
RUSH COUNTY MEMORIAL HOSPITAL, La Crosse, KS
RUSH FOUNDATION HOSPITAL, Meridian, MS
RUSH HOSPITAL-BULTER, Butler, AL
RUSH HOSPITAL-NEWTON, Newton, MS
RUSH MEMORIAL HOSPITAL, Rushville, IN
RUSH-HILL HOSPITAL OF YORK, York, AL
RUSH-PRESBYTERIAN-ST. LUKE'S MEDICAL CENTER, Chicago, IL
RUSK COUNTY MEMORIAL HOSPITAL AND NURSING HOME, Ladysmith, WI
RUSK INSTITUTE, New York, NY, See New York University Medical Center
RUSK MEMORIAL HOSPITAL, Rusk, TX, See Cherokee Medical Center
RUSK STATE HOSPITAL, Rusk, TX
RUSSELL CITY HOSPITAL, Russell, KS
RUSSELL COUNTY HOSPITAL, Russell Springs, KY
RUSSELL COUNTY MEDICAL CENTER, Lebanon, VA
RUSSELL HOSPITAL, Alexander City, AL
RUSSELL MEMORIAL HOSPITAL, Onaway, MI
RUTHERFORD HOSPITAL, Rutherfordton, NC
RUTLAND HEIGHTS HOSPITAL, Rutland, MA
RUTLAND REGIONAL MEDICAL CENTER, Rutland, VT
RYDER MEMORIAL HOSPITAL, Humacao, P.R.
RYE PSYCHIATRIC HOSPITAL CENTER, Rye, NY

S

S. E. LACKEY MEMORIAL HOSPITAL, Forest, MS
SABETHA COMMUNITY HOSPITAL, Sabetha, KS
SABINE COUNTY HOSPITAL, Hemphill, TX
SABINE MEDICAL CENTER, Many, LA
SAC-OSAGE HOSPITAL, Osceola, MO
SACRED HEART GENERAL HOSPITAL, Eugene, OR
SACRED HEART HOSPITAL, Hanford, CA
SACRED HEART HOSPITAL, Cumberland, MD
SACRED HEART HOSPITAL, Allentown, PA
SACRED HEART HOSPITAL, Norristown, PA
SACRED HEART HOSPITAL, Yankton, SD
SACRED HEART HOSPITAL, Richwood, WV
SACRED HEART HOSPITAL, Eau Claire, WI
SACRED HEART HOSPITAL, Tomahawk, WI, See Sacred Heart-St. Mary's Hospitals, Rhinelander
SACRED HEART HOSPITAL OF PENSACOLA, Pensacola, FL
SACRED HEART MEDICAL CENTER, Chester, PA
SACRED HEART MEDICAL CENTER, Spokane, WA
SACRED HEART REHABILITATION HOSPITAL, Milwaukee, WI
SACRED HEART-ST. MARY'S HOSPITALS, Rhinelander, WI
SADDLEBACK COMMUNITY HOSPITAL, Laguna Hills, CA
SAGAMORE CHILDREN'S PSYCHIATRIC CENTER (Formerly Sagamore Children's Center), Melville, NY
SAGAMORE HILLS CHILDREN'S PSYCHIATRIC HOSPITAL, Northfield, OH
SAGE MEMORIAL HOSPITAL, Ganado, AZ
SAGINAW COMMUNITY HOSPITAL, Saginaw, MI
SAGINAW GENERAL HOSPITAL, Saginaw, MI
SAINT ALPHONSUS REGIONAL MEDICAL CENTER, Boise, ID
SAINT ANTHONY MEDICAL CENTER (Formerly St. Anthony Hospital-Medical Center), Rockford, IL
SAINT ANTHONY'S HOSPITAL, Alton, IL
SAINT CABRINI HOSPITAL OF SEATTLE, Seattle, WA
SAINT ELIZABETHS HOSPITAL, Washington, DC
SAINT FRANCIS HOSPITAL, Tulsa, OK
SAINT FRANCIS HOSPITAL, Poughkeepsie, NY
SAINT FRANCIS HOSPITAL AND MEDICAL CENTER, Hartford, CT
SAINT FRANCIS MEDICAL CENTER, Peoria, IL
SAINT FRANCIS MEDICAL CENTER, Grand Island, NE
SAINT JAMES HOSPITAL, Pontiac, IL
SAINT JAMES HOSPITAL OF NEWARK, Newark, NJ
SAINT JOHN'S HOSPITAL AND HEALTH CENTER, Santa Monica, CA
SAINT JOSEPH HEALTH CENTER OF KANSAS CITY (Formerly Saint Joseph Hospital of Kansas City), Kansas City, MO
SAINT JOSEPH HOSPITAL, Denver, CO
SAINT JOSEPH HOSPITAL, Elgin, IL
SAINT JOSEPH HOSPITAL, Mishawaka, IN
SAINT JOSEPH HOSPITAL, Omaha, NE, See AMI Saint Joseph Hospital
SAINT JOSEPH HOSPITAL, Reading, PA
SAINT JOSEPH HOSPITAL, Fort Worth, TX
SAINT JOSEPH HOSPITAL AND HEALTH CENTER (Formerly St. Joseph Memorial Hospital), Kokomo, IN
SAINT JOSEPH'S HOSPITAL, Atlanta, GA
SAINT JOSEPH'S HOSPITAL OF DAHLONEGA (Formerly Lumpkin County Hospital), Dahlonega, GA
SAINT JOSEPH'S MEDICAL CENTER OF STOCKTON (Formerly St. Joseph's Hospital of Stockton), Stockton, CA
SAINT LOUIS MEMORIAL HOSPITAL, St. Louis, MO
SAINT LUKE'S HOSPITAL, Cleveland, OH
SAINT MARY HOSPITAL, Langhorne, PA
SAINT MARY OF NAZARETH HOSPITAL CENTER, Chicago, IL
SAINT MICHAEL'S MEDICAL CENTER, Newark, NJ
SAINT THERESE MEDICAL CENTER, Waukegan, IL
SAINT THOMAS MEDICAL CENTER (Formerly St. Thomas Hospital Medical Center), Akron, OH
SAINT VINCENT HEALTH CENTER, Erie, PA
SAINT VINCENT HOSPITAL, Worcester, MA
SAINT VINCENT HOSPITAL AND HEALTH CENTER, Billings, MT
SAINTS MARY AND ELIZABETH HOSPITAL, Louisville, KY
SALAMANCA DISTRICT HOSPITAL, Salamanca, NY
SALE HOSPITAL (Formerly Sale Memorial Hospital), Neosho, MO
SALEM COMMUNITY HOSPITAL, Salem, OH
SALEM HOSPITAL, Hillsboro, KS
SALEM HOSPITAL, Salem, MA

SALEM HOSPITAL, Salem, OR
SALEM MEMORIAL DISTRICT HOSPITAL, Salem, MO
SALIDA HOSPITAL, Salida, CO
SALINAS VALLEY MEMORIAL HOSPITAL, Salinas, CA
SALINE COMMUNITY HOSPITAL, Saline, MI
SALINE MEMORIAL HOSPITAL, Benton, AR
SALVATION ARMY BOOTH MATERNITY CENTER, Philadelphia, PA
SALVATION ARMY BOOTH MEMORIAL HOSPITAL, Cleveland, OH
SALVATION ARMY WILLIAM BOOTH MEMORIAL HOSPITAL, Florence, KY
SAM HOUSTON MEMORIAL HOSPITAL, Houston, TX
SAM RAYBURN MEMORIAL VETERANS CENTER, Bonham, TX
SAMARITAN HEALTH CENTER, Bay City, MI, See Bay Medical Center
SAMARITAN HEALTH CENTER, Detroit, MI
SAMARITAN HOSPITAL, St. Paul, MN
SAMARITAN HOSPITAL, Troy, NY
SAMARITAN HOSPITAL, Ashland, OH
SAMARITAN HOSPITAL, Moses Lake, WA
SAMARITAN MEMORIAL HOSPITAL, Macon, MO
SAMPSON COUNTY MEMORIAL HOSPITAL, Clinton, NC
SAMS AND WHATLEY HOSPITAL, Reynolds, GA
SAMUEL MAHELONA MEMORIAL HOSPITAL, Kapaa, HI
SAMUEL MERRITT HOSPITAL, Oakland, CA
SAN ANTONIO CHILDREN'S CENTER, San Antonio, TX
SAN ANTONIO COMMUNITY HOSPITAL, Upland, CA
SAN ANTONIO STATE CHEST HOSPITAL, San Antonio, TX
SAN ANTONIO STATE HOSPITAL, San Antonio, TX
SAN AUGUSTINE MEMORIAL HOSPITAL, San Augustine, TX
SAN BENITO HOSPITAL DISTRICT, Hollister, CA
SAN BERNARDINO COMMUNITY HOSPITAL, San Bernardino, CA
SAN BERNARDINO COUNTY MEDICAL CENTER, San Bernardino, CA
SAN CARLOS GENERAL HOSPITAL, San Juan, P.R.
SAN CLEMENTE GENERAL HOSPITAL, San Clemente, CA
SAN DIEGO COUNTY HILLCREST MENTAL HEALTH FACILITY, San Diego, CA
SAN DIEGO COUNTY LOMA PORTAL MENTAL HEALTH FACILITY, San Diego, CA
SAN DIEGO PHYSICIANS AND SURGEONS HOSPITAL, San Diego, CA
SAN FERNANDO COMMUNITY HOSPITAL, San Fernando, CA
SAN FRANCISCO GENERAL HOSPITAL MEDICAL CENTER, San Francisco, CA
SAN GABRIEL VALLEY MEDICAL CENTER (Formerly Community Hospital of San Gabriel), San Gabriel, CA
SAN GERMAN AREA HOSPITAL, San German, P.R.
SAN JACINTO METHODIST HOSPITAL, Baytown, TX
SAN JOAQUIN COMMUNITY HOSPITAL, Bakersfield, CA
SAN JOAQUIN GENERAL HOSPITAL, Stockton, CA
SAN JORGE HOSPITAL, San Juan, P.R.
SAN JOSE HOSPITAL, San Jose, CA
SAN JUAN HOSPITAL, Monticello, UT
SAN JUAN MUNICIPAL HOSPITAL, San Juan, P.R.
SAN JUAN REGIONAL MEDICAL CENTER, Farmington, NM
SAN LUIS OBISPO GENERAL HOSPITAL, San Luis Obispo, CA
SAN LUIS REY HOSPITAL, Encinitas, CA, See CPC San Luis Rey Hospital
SAN MANUEL DIVISION HOSPITAL, MAGMA COPPER COMPANY, San Manuel, AZ
SAN PEDRO PENINSULA HOSPITAL, Los Angeles, CA
SAN SABA HOSPITAL (Formerly San Saba Memorial Hospital), San Saba, TX
SANCTA MARIA HOSPITAL, Cambridge, MA
SANDSTONE AREA HOSPITAL AND NURSING HOME, Sandstone, MN
SANDWICH COMMUNITY HOSPITAL, Sandwich, IL
SANFORD MEMORIAL HOSPITAL AND NURSING HOME, Farmington, MN
SANGER HOSPITAL, Sanger, CA
SANPETE VALLEY HOSPITAL, Mount Pleasant, UT
SANTA ANA HOSPITAL MEDICAL CENTER, Santa Ana, CA
SANTA ANA PSYCHIATRIC HOSPITAL, Santa Ana, CA, See CPC Santa Ana Psychiatric Hospital
SANTA BARBARA COTTAGE HOSPITAL, Santa Barbara, CA
SANTA CLARA VALLEY MEDICAL CENTER, San Jose, CA
SANTA FE COMMUNITY HOSPITAL, Los Angeles, CA, See Linda Vista Community Hospital
SANTA MARTA HOSPITAL, Los Angeles, CA
SANTA MONICA HOSPITAL MEDICAL CENTER, Santa Monica, CA
SANTA PAULA MEMORIAL HOSPITAL, Santa Paula, CA
SANTA ROSA MEDICAL CENTER, San Antonio, TX
SANTA ROSA MEMORIAL HOSPITAL, Santa Rosa, CA
SANTA TERESA COMMUNITY HOSPITAL, San Jose, CA
SANTA TERESITA HOSPITAL, Duarte, CA
SANTA YNEZ VALLEY HOSPITAL, Solvang, CA
SANTIAM MEMORIAL HOSPITAL, Stayton, OR
SARAH BUSH LINCOLN HEALTH CENTER, Mattoon, IL
SARAH D. CULBERTSON MEMORIAL HOSPITAL, Rushville, IL
SARASOTA MEMORIAL HOSPITAL (Formerly Memorial Hospital), Sarasota, FL
SARASOTA PALMS HOSPITAL, Sarasota, FL
SARATOGA COMMUNITY HOSPITAL, Detroit, MI
SARATOGA HOSPITAL, Saratoga Springs, NY
SARGENT DISTRICT HOSPITAL, Sargent, NE
SARTORI MEMORIAL HOSPITAL, Cedar Falls, IA
SATANTA DISTRICT HOSPITAL, Satanta, KS
SAUK PRAIRIE MEMORIAL HOSPITAL, Prairie Du Sac, WI
SAUNDERS COUNTY COMMUNITY HOSPITAL, Wahoo, NE
SAUNDERS HOSPITAL, Avon, IL
SAVANNA CITY HOSPITAL, Savanna, IL
SAVOY MEMORIAL HOSPITAL, Mamou, LA
SAYRE MEMORIAL HOSPITAL, Sayre, OK
SCENIC GENERAL HOSPITAL, Modesto, CA
SCENIC MOUNTAIN MEDICAL CENTER (Formerly Malone-Hogan Hospital), Big Spring, TX
SCHEURER HOSPITAL, Pigeon, MI
SCHICK SHADEL HOSPITAL, Santa Barbara, CA
SCHICK SHADEL HOSPITAL, Fort Worth, TX
SCHICK SHADEL HOSPITAL, Seattle, WA
SCHLEICHER COUNTY MEDICAL CENTER, Eldorado, TX
SCHOOLCRAFT MEMORIAL HOSPITAL, Manistique, MI
SCHUMPERT MEDICAL CENTER, Shreveport, LA
SCHUYLER HOSPITAL, Montour Falls, NY
SCHWAB REHABILITATION CENTER, Chicago, IL
SCIOTO MEMORIAL HOSPITAL, Portsmouth, OH
SCOTLAND COUNTY MEMORIAL HOSPITAL, Memphis, MO
SCOTLAND MEMORIAL HOSPITAL, Laurinburg, NC
SCOTT AND WHITE MEMORIAL HOSPITAL, Temple, TX
SCOTT COUNTY HOSPITAL, Scott City, KS
SCOTT COUNTY HOSPITAL, Oneida, TN
SCOTT COUNTY MEMORIAL HOSPITAL, Scottsburg, IN
SCOTT GENERAL HOSPITAL, Georgetown, KY
SCOTT MEMORIAL HOSPITAL, Lawrenceburg, TN
SCOTTISH RITE CHILDREN'S HOSPITAL, Atlanta, GA
SCOTTSDALE CAMELBACK HOSPITAL, Scottsdale, AZ
SCOTTSDALE COMMUNITY HOSPITAL, Scottsdale, AZ
SCOTTSDALE MEMORIAL HOSPITAL, Scottsdale, AZ
SCRANTON STATE GENERAL HOSPITAL, Scranton, PA
SCREVEN COUNTY HOSPITAL, Sylvania, GA
SCRIPPS MEMORIAL HOSPITAL-CHULA VISTA, Chula Vista, CA
SCRIPPS MEMORIAL HOSPITAL-ENCINITAS, Encinitas, CA
SCRIPPS MEMORIAL HOSPITAL-LA JOLLA, La Jolla, CA
SEA LEVEL HOSPITAL, DIVISION OF DUKE UNIVERSITY MEDICAL CENTER, Sea Level, NC
SEABORNE HOSPITAL, Dover, NH
SEARCY HOSPITAL, Mount Vernon, AL
SEASIDE GENERAL HOSPITAL, Seaside, OR
SEAWAY HOSPITAL, Trenton, MI
SEBASTICOOK VALLEY HOSPITAL, Pittsfield, ME
SEDAN CITY HOSPITAL, Sedan, KS
SEDGWICK COUNTY HOSPITAL, Julesburg, CO
SEIDLE MEMORIAL HOSPITAL, Mechanicsburg, PA
SELBY GENERAL HOSPITAL, Marietta, OH
SELF MEMORIAL HOSPITAL, Greenwood, SC
SELMA DISTRICT HOSPITAL, Selma, CA
SELMA MEDICAL CENTER, Selma, AL
SEMINOLE MUNICIPAL HOSPITAL, Seminole, OK
SEMINOLE POINT HOSPITAL (Formerly Seminole Point), Sunapee, NH
SENECA DISTRICT HOSPITAL, Chester, CA
SEQUATCHIE GENERAL HOSPITAL, Dunlap, TN
SEQUOIA HOSPITAL DISTRICT, Redwood City, CA
SEQUOYAH MEMORIAL HOSPITAL, Sallisaw, OK
SERRA MEMORIAL HEALTH CENTER, Los Angeles, CA
SETON MEDICAL CENTER, Daly City, CA
SETON MEDICAL CENTER, Austin, TX
SEVEN RIVERS COMMUNITY HOSPITAL, Crystal River, FL
SEVENTH WARD GENERAL HOSPITAL, Hammond, LA
SEVIER VALLEY HOSPITAL, Richfield, UT
SEWARD GENERAL HOSPITAL, Seward, AK
SEWICKLEY VALLEY HOSPITAL, Sewickley, PA
SEYMOUR HOSPITAL AUTHORITY, Seymour, TX
SHACKELFORD COUNTY HOSPITAL DISTRICT, Albany, TX
SHADOW MOUNTAIN INSTITUTE, Tulsa, OK
SHADY GROVE ADVENTIST HOSPITAL, Rockville, MD
SHADYSIDE HOSPITAL, Pittsburgh, PA
SHALLOWFORD HOSPITAL (Formerly Shallowford Community Hospital), Chamblee, GA
SHAMOKIN STATE GENERAL HOSPITAL, Shamokin, PA
SHAMROCK GENERAL HOSPITAL, Shamrock, TX
SHANDS HOSPITAL AT THE UNIVERSITY OF FLORIDA, Gainesville, FL
SHANNON WEST TEXAS MEMORIAL HOSPITAL, San Angelo, TX
SHARE MEDICAL CENTER, Alva, OK
SHARON GENERAL HOSPITAL, Sharon, PA
SHARON HOSPITAL, Sharon, CT
SHARP CABRILLO HOSPITAL, San Diego, CA
SHARP MEMORIAL HOSPITAL, San Diego, CA
SHARPSTOWN GENERAL HOSPITAL, Houston, TX
SHASTA GENERAL HOSPITAL, Redding, CA
SHAWANO COMMUNITY HOSPITAL, Shawano, WI
SHAWNEE MEDICAL CENTER HOSPITAL, Shawnee, OK
SHAWNEE MISSION MEDICAL CENTER, Shawnee Mission, KS
SHEBOYGAN MEMORIAL MEDICAL CENTER (Formerly Sheboygan Memorial Hospital), Sheboygan, WI
SHEEHAN MEMORIAL HOSPITAL (Formerly Sheehan Emergency Hospital), Buffalo, NY
SHELBY GENERAL HOSPITAL, Center, TX
SHELBY MEDICAL CENTER, Alabaster, AL
SHELBY MEMORIAL HOSPITAL, Shelbyville, IL
SHELBY MEMORIAL HOSPITAL, Shelby, OH
SHENANDOAH COUNTY MEMORIAL HOSPITAL, Woodstock, VA
SHENANDOAH MEMORIAL HOSPITAL, Shenandoah, IA
SHENANGO VALLEY MEDICAL CENTER (Formerly Shenango Valley Osteopathic Hospital), Farrell, PA
SHEPHERD SPINAL CENTER, Atlanta, GA
SHEPPARD AND ENOCH PRATT HOSPITAL (Formerly Listed Under Towson), Baltimore, MD
SHEPPERD MEMORIAL HOSPITAL, Burnet, TX
SHERIDAN COMMUNITY HOSPITAL, Sheridan, MI
SHERIDAN COUNTY HOSPITAL, Hoxie, KS
SHERIDAN MEMORIAL HOSPITAL, Plentywood, MT
SHERIDAN ROAD HOSPITAL, Chicago, IL, See Rush-Presbyterian-St. Luke's Medical Center
SHERMAN HOSPITAL, Elgin, IL
SHERMAN OAKS COMMUNITY HOSPITAL, Los Angeles, CA
SHINER HOSPITAL, Shiner, TX
SHOAL CREEK HOSPITAL, Austin, TX, See HCA Shoal Creek Hospital
SHODAIR CHILDREN'S HOSPITAL, Helena, MT
SHORE MEMORIAL HOSPITAL, Somers Point, NJ
SHOREWOOD OSTEOPATHIC HOSPITAL, Seattle, WA
SHOSHONE MEDICAL CENTER, Kellogg, ID
SHRINERS BURNS INSTITUTE, Boston, MA
SHRINERS BURNS INSTITUTE (Formerly Shriners Hospital for Crippled Children, Shriners Burns Institute, Cincinnati Unit), Cincinnati, OH
SHRINERS HOSPITAL FOR CRIPPLED CHILDREN, San Francisco, CA
SHRINERS HOSPITAL FOR CRIPPLED CHILDREN, Honolulu, HI
SHRINERS HOSPITAL FOR CRIPPLED CHILDREN, Portland, OR
SHRINERS HOSPITALS FOR CRIPPLED CHILDREN, Los Angeles, CA
SHRINERS HOSPITALS FOR CRIPPLED CHILDREN, Tampa, FL
SHRINERS HOSPITALS FOR CRIPPLED CHILDREN, Chicago, IL
SHRINERS HOSPITALS FOR CRIPPLED CHILDREN, Lexington, KY
SHRINERS HOSPITALS FOR CRIPPLED CHILDREN, Shreveport, LA
SHRINERS HOSPITALS FOR CRIPPLED CHILDREN, Springfield, MA
SHRINERS HOSPITALS FOR CRIPPLED CHILDREN, Minneapolis, MN
SHRINERS HOSPITALS FOR CRIPPLED CHILDREN, St. Louis, MO
SHRINERS HOSPITALS FOR CRIPPLED CHILDREN, Erie, PA
SHRINERS HOSPITALS FOR CRIPPLED CHILDREN, Philadelphia, PA
SHRINERS HOSPITALS FOR CRIPPLED CHILDREN, Greenville, SC
SHRINERS HOSPITALS FOR CRIPPLED CHILDREN-BURNS INSTITUTE-GALVESTON UNIT, Galveston, TX
SHRINERS HOSPITALS FOR CRIPPLED CHILDREN, Houston, TX
SHRINERS HOSPITALS FOR CRIPPLED CHILDREN, Salt Lake City, UT

SHRINERS HOSPITALS FOR CRIPPLED CHILDREN-SPOKANE UNIT, Spokane, WA
SIBLEY MEMORIAL HOSPITAL, Washington, DC
SID PETERSON MEMORIAL HOSPITAL, Kerrville, TX
SIERRA COMMUNITY HOSPITAL, Fresno, CA
SIERRA HOSPITAL, Sonora, CA, See Sonora Community Hospital
SIERRA MEDICAL CENTER, El Paso, TX
SIERRA NEVADA MEMORIAL HOSPITAL, Grass Valley, CA
SIERRA ROYALE HOSPITAL, Azusa, CA
SIERRA VALLEY COMMUNITY HOSPITAL (Formerly Sierra Valley District Hospital), Loyalton, CA
SIERRA VIEW DISTRICT HOSPITAL, Porterville, CA
SIERRA VISTA COMMUNITY HOSPITAL, Sierra Vista, AZ
SIERRA VISTA HOSPITAL, Truth Or Consequences, NM
SIERRA-KINGS DISTRICT HOSPITAL, Reedley, CA
SILAS B. HAYS ARMY COMMUNITY HOSPITAL, Fort Ord, CA
SILSBEE DOCTORS HOSPITAL, Silsbee, TX
SILVAIN AND ARMA WYLER CHILDREN'S HOSPITAL, Chicago, IL, See University of Chicago Hospitals and Clinics
SILVER CROSS HOSPITAL, Joliet, IL
SILVER HILL FOUNDATION HOSPITAL, New Canaan, CT
SILVERTON HOSPITAL, Silverton, OR
SIMI VALLEY ADVENTIST HOSPITAL, Simi Valley, CA
SIMI VALLEY COMMUNITY HOSPITAL, Simi Valley, CA, See Mountain View Medical Center
SIMPSON GENERAL HOSPITAL, Mendenhall, MS
SIMPSON INFIRMARY, WELLESLEY COLLEGE, Wellesley, MA
SINAI HOSPITAL OF BALTIMORE, Baltimore, MD
SINAI HOSPITAL OF DETROIT, Detroit, MI
SINGING RIVER HOSPITAL SYSTEM, Pascagoula, MS
SIOUX CENTER COMMUNITY HOSPITAL, Sioux Center, IA
SIOUX VALLEY HOSPITAL, New Ulm, MN
SIOUX VALLEY HOSPITAL, Sioux Falls, SD
SIOUX VALLEY MEMORIAL HOSPITAL, Cherokee, IA
SISKIYOU GENERAL HOSPITAL, Yreka, CA
SISTER KENNY INSTITUTE, Minneapolis, MN, See Abbott-Northwestern Hospital Corporation
SISTERS OF CHARITY HOSPITAL, Buffalo, NY
SISTERSVILLE GENERAL HOSPITAL, Sistersville, WV
SITKA COMMUNITY HOSPITAL, Sitka, AK
SKAGGS COMMUNITY HOSPITAL, Branson, MO
SKAGIT VALLEY HOSPITAL AND HEALTH CENTER (Formerly Skagit Valley Hospital), Mount Vernon, WA
SKIFF MEDICAL CENTER (Formerly Mary Frances Skiff Memorial Hospital), Newton, IA
SKOKIE VALLEY HOSPITAL, Skokie, IL
SKYLINE HOSPITAL, White Salmon, WA
SLEEPY EYE MUNICIPAL HOSPITAL, Sleepy Eye, MN
SLIDELL MEMORIAL HOSPITAL, Slidell, LA
SLOOP MEMORIAL HOSPITAL, Crossnore, NC
SMITH COUNTY MEMORIAL HOSPITAL, Smith Center, KS
SMITH COUNTY MEMORIAL HOSPITAL, Carthage, TN
SMITH HOSPITAL, Hahira, GA
SMITHTOWN GENERAL HOSPITAL, Smithtown, NY, See Community Hospital of Western Suffolk
SMITHVILLE HOSPITAL, Smithville, TX
SMYRNA HOSPITAL, Smyrna, GA
SMYTH COUNTY COMMUNITY HOSPITAL, Marion, VA
SNOHOMISH COUNTY PUBLIC HOSPITAL DISTRICT THREE, CASCADE VALLEY HOSPITAL, Arlington, WA
SNOQUALMIE VALLEY HOSPITAL, Snoqualmie, WA
SOCIETY OF THE NEW YORK HOSPITAL, New York, NY
SOCORRO GENERAL HOSPITAL, Socorro, NM
SOLDIERS AND SAILORS MEMORIAL HOSPITAL, Wellsboro, PA
SOLDIERS AND SAILORS MEMORIAL HOSPITAL OF YATES COUNTY, Penn Yan, NY
SOLDIERS' HOME IN HOLYOKE, Holyoke, MA
SOMERSET COMMUNITY HOSPITAL, Somerset, PA
SOMERSET MEDICAL CENTER, Somerville, NJ
SOMERSET STATE HOSPITAL, Somerset, PA
SOMERVILLE HOSPITAL, Somerville, MA
SONOMA DEVELOPMENTAL CENTER (Formerly Sonoma State Hospital), Eldridge, CA
SONOMA VALLEY HOSPITAL, Sonoma, CA
SONORA COMMUNITY HOSPITAL, Sonora, CA
SOUTH AMBOY MEMORIAL HOSPITAL AND COMMUNITY MENTAL HEALTH CENTER, South Amboy, NJ
SOUTH AUSTIN COMMUNITY HOSPITAL, Austin, TX, See HCA South Austin Medical Center
SOUTH BALDWIN HOSPITAL, Foley, AL
SOUTH BALTIMORE GENERAL HOSPITAL, Baltimore, MD
SOUTH BARRY COUNTY MEMORIAL HOSPITAL, Cassville, MO
SOUTH BEACH PSYCHIATRIC CENTER, Staten Island, NY
SOUTH BEND OSTEOPATHIC HOSPITAL, South Bend, IN, See Michiana Community Hospital
SOUTH BERGEN HOSPITAL, Hasbrouck Heights, NJ
SOUTH BIG HORN COUNTY HOSPITAL, Greybull, WY
SOUTH CAMERON MEMORIAL HOSPITAL, Cameron, LA
SOUTH CAROLINA STATE HOSPITAL, Columbia, SC
SOUTH CHARLESTON COMMUNITY HOSPITAL, South Charleston, WV
SOUTH CHICAGO COMMUNITY HOSPITAL, Chicago, IL
SOUTH COAST MEDICAL CENTER, South Laguna, CA
SOUTH COMMUNITY HOSPITAL, Oklahoma City, OK
SOUTH COUNTY HOSPITAL, Wakefield, RI
SOUTH FLORIDA BAPTIST HOSPITAL, Plant City, FL
SOUTH FLORIDA STATE HOSPITAL, West Hollywood, FL
SOUTH FULTON HOSPITAL, East Point, GA
SOUTH GEORGIA MEDICAL CENTER, Valdosta, GA
SOUTH HAVEN COMMUNITY HOSPITAL, South Haven, MI
SOUTH HIGHLANDS HOSPITAL, Birmingham, AL
SOUTH HILLS HEALTH SYSTEM, Pittsburgh, PA
SOUTH LAKE MEMORIAL HOSPITAL, Clermont, FL
SOUTH LIMESTONE HOSPITAL, Groesbeck, TX
SOUTH LINCOLN MEDICAL CENTER (Formerly South Lincoln Hospital District), Kemmerer, WY
SOUTH LYON COMMUNITY HOSPITAL (Formerly Lyon Health Center), Yerington, NV
SOUTH MACOMB HOSPITAL, Warren, MI, See Detroit-Macomb Hospital Corporation, Detroit
SOUTH MIAMI HOSPITAL, South Miami, FL
SOUTH MISSISSIPPI STATE HOSPITAL, Laurel, MS
SOUTH MOUNTAIN RESTORATION CENTER, South Mountain, PA
SOUTH NASSAU COMMUNITIES HOSPITAL, Oceanside, NY
SOUTH OAKS HOSPITAL, Amityville, NY
SOUTH PANOLA COMMUNITY HOSPITAL, Batesville, MS
SOUTH PARK MEDICAL CENTER, Lubbock, TX
SOUTH PENINSULA HOSPITAL, Homer, AK
SOUTH PITTSBURG MUNICIPAL HOSPITAL, South Pittsburg, TN
SOUTH PLAINS HOSPITAL CLINIC, Amherst, TX
SOUTH SHORE HOSPITAL, Chicago, IL
SOUTH SHORE HOSPITAL, South Weymouth, MA
SOUTH SHORE HOSPITAL AND MEDICAL CENTER, Miami Beach, FL
SOUTH SIDE HOSPITAL OF PITTSBURGH, Pittsburgh, PA
SOUTH SUBURBAN HOSPITAL, Hazel Crest, IL
SOUTH SUNFLOWER COUNTY HOSPITAL, Indianola, MS
SOUTH TEXAS HOSPITAL, Harlingen, TX
SOUTH WASHINGTON COUNTY HOSPITAL, Hollandale, MS
SOUTHAMPTON HOSPITAL, Southampton, NY
SOUTHAMPTON MEMORIAL HOSPITAL, Franklin, VA
SOUTHEAST ALABAMA MEDICAL CENTER, Dothan, AL
SOUTHEAST ARIZONA MEDICAL CENTER, Douglas, AZ
SOUTHEAST BAPTIST HOSPITAL, San Antonio, TX
SOUTHEAST COLORADO HOSPITAL, Springfield, CO
SOUTHEAST LOUISIANA HOSPITAL, Mandeville, LA
SOUTHEAST MISSOURI HOSPITAL, Cape Girardeau, MO
SOUTHEASTERN GENERAL HOSPITAL, Lumberton, NC
SOUTHEASTERN MEDICAL CENTER, North Miami Beach, FL, See AMI Southeastern Medical Center
SOUTHEASTERN METHODIST HOSPITAL, Dallas, TX
SOUTHERN BAPTIST HOSPITAL, New Orleans, LA
SOUTHERN CHESTER COUNTY MEDICAL CENTER, West Grove, PA
SOUTHERN COOS GENERAL HOSPITAL, Bandon, OR
SOUTHERN DISPENSARY, Philadelphia, PA, See Pennsylvania Hospital
SOUTHERN HILLS GENERAL HOSPITAL, Hot Springs, SD
SOUTHERN HILLS HOSPITAL, Portsmouth, OH
SOUTHERN HILLS MEDICAL CENTER, Nashville, TN, See HCA Southern Hills Medical Center
SOUTHERN HUMBOLDT COMMUNITY HOSPITAL DISTRICT, Garberville, CA
SOUTHERN INYO HOSPITAL, Lone Pine, CA
SOUTHERN MAINE MEDICAL CENTER (Formerly Webber Hospital Association), Biddeford, ME
SOUTHERN MARYLAND HOSPITAL, Clinton, MD
SOUTHERN NEVADA MEMORIAL HOSPITAL, Las Vegas, NV, See University Medical Center of Southern Nevada
SOUTHERN OCEAN COUNTY HOSPITAL, Manahawkin, NJ
SOUTHERN OREGON MEDICAL CENTER, Grants Pass, OR
SOUTHERN PINES PSYCHIATRIC HOSPITAL, Charleston, SC
SOUTHERN WAKE HOSPITAL, Fuquay-Varina, NC
SOUTHFIELD REHABILITATION HOSPITAL (Formerly Southfield Rehabilitation Center), Southfield, MI
SOUTHLAKE CAMPUS, Merrillville, IN, See Methodist Hospital of Gary, Gary
SOUTHLAND MEDICAL CENTER (Formerly Humana Hospital Darlington), Darlington, SC
SOUTHSIDE COMMUNITY HOSPITAL (Formerly Physicians and Surgeons General Hospital), Corpus Christi, TX
SOUTHSIDE COMMUNITY HOSPITAL, Farmville, VA
SOUTHSIDE HOSPITAL, Bay Shore, NY
SOUTHSIDE REGIONAL MEDICAL CENTER (Formerly Petersburg General Hospital), Petersburg, VA
SOUTHVIEW HOSPITAL AND FAMILY HEALTH CENTER, Dayton, OH, See Grandview Hospital and Medical Center
SOUTHWEST COMMUNITY HEALTH SYSTEM AND HOSPITAL, Middleburg Heights, OH
SOUTHWEST DETROIT HOSPITAL, Detroit, MI
SOUTHWEST FLORIDA REGIONAL MEDICAL CENTER (Formerly Fort Myers Community Hospital), Fort Myers, FL
SOUTHWEST GENERAL HOSPITAL, San Antonio, TX
SOUTHWEST HEALTH CENTER, Platteville, WI
SOUTHWEST HOSPITAL AND MEDICAL CENTER (Formerly Southwest Community Hospital), Atlanta, GA
SOUTHWEST MEDICAL CENTER, Prescott, AR
SOUTHWEST MEDICAL CENTER, Liberal, KS
SOUTHWEST MEMORIAL HOSPITAL, Cortez, CO
SOUTHWEST MISSISSIPPI REGIONAL MEDICAL CENTER, McComb, MS
SOUTHWEST OSTEOPATHIC HOSPITAL, Amarillo, TX, See Family Hospital Center
SOUTHWEST TEXAS METHODIST HOSPITAL, San Antonio, TX
SOUTHWEST WASHINGTON HOSPITALS, Vancouver, WA
SOUTHWESTERN GENERAL HOSPITAL, El Paso, TX
SOUTHWESTERN MEMORIAL HOSPITAL (Formerly Weatherford Hospital Authority), Weatherford, OK
SOUTHWESTERN MICHIGAN REHABILITATION HOSPITAL, Battle Creek, MI
SOUTHWESTERN STATE HOSPITAL, Marion, VA
SOUTHWESTERN VERMONT MEDICAL CENTER, Bennington, VT
SOUTHWOOD COMMUNITY HOSPITAL, Norfolk, MA
SOUTHWOOD PSYCHIATRIC HOSPITAL, Chula Vista, CA
SPALDING REHABILITATION HOSPITAL, Denver, CO
SPARKS REGIONAL MEDICAL CENTER, Fort Smith, AR
SPARTA COMMUNITY HOSPITAL, Sparta, IL
SPARTANBURG GENERAL HOSPITAL, Spartanburg, SC, See Spartanburg Regional Medical Center
SPARTANBURG REGIONAL MEDICAL CENTER (Formerly Spartanburg General Hospital), Spartanburg, SC
SPAULDING REHABILITATION HOSPITAL, Boston, MA
SPEARE MEMORIAL HOSPITAL (Formerly Sceva Speare Memorial Hospital), Plymouth, NH
SPEARVILLE DISTRICT HOSPITAL, Spearville, KS
SPELMAN MEMORIAL HOSPITAL, Smithville, MO
SPENCER HOSPITAL, Spencer, WV
SPENCER MUNICIPAL HOSPITAL, Spencer, IA
SPOFFORD HALL HOSPITAL (Formerly Spofford Hall), Spofford, NH
SPOHN HOSPITAL, Corpus Christi, TX
SPOHN KLEBERG MEMORIAL HOSPITAL (Formerly Kleberg Memorial Hospital), Kingsville, TX
SPRING BRANCH MEMORIAL HOSPITAL, Houston, TX
SPRING GROVE HOSPITAL CENTER (Formerly Listed Under Baltimore), Catonsville, MD
SPRING SHADOWS GLEN, Houston, TX
SPRINGDALE MEMORIAL HOSPITAL, Springdale, AR
SPRINGFIELD COMMUNITY HOSPITAL, Springfield, MN
SPRINGFIELD GENERAL HOSPITAL, Springfield, MO
SPRINGFIELD HOSPITAL, Springfield, MA, See Baystate Medical Center
SPRINGFIELD HOSPITAL, Springfield, VT
SPRINGFIELD HOSPITAL CENTER, Sykesville, MD
SPRINGFIELD MUNICIPAL HOSPITAL, Springfield, MA
SPRINGFIELD PARK CENTRAL HOSPITAL, Springfield, MO
SPRINGHILL MEMORIAL HOSPITAL, Mobile, AL
SPRINGWOOD PSYCHIATRIC INSTITUTE, Leesburg, VA
ST. AGNES HOSPITAL, White Plains, NY
ST. AGNES HOSPITAL, Fond Du Lac, WI
ST. AGNES HOSPITAL AND MEDICAL CENTER, Fresno, CA

ST. AGNES HOSPITAL OF THE CITY OF BALTIMORE, Baltimore, MD
ST. AGNES MEDICAL CENTER, Philadelphia, PA
ST. ALBANS PSYCHIATRIC HOSPITAL, Radford, VA
ST. ALEXIS HOSPITAL, Cleveland, OH
ST. ALEXIUS MEDICAL CENTER, Bismarck, ND
ST. ALOISIUS MEDICAL CENTER (Formerly St. Aloisius Hospital), Harvey, ND
ST. ANDREW'S HOSPITAL, Bottineau, ND
ST. ANDREWS HOSPITAL, Boothbay Harbor, ME
ST. ANN'S HOSPITAL OF COLUMBUS, Westerville, OH
ST. ANNE GENERAL HOSPITAL, Raceland, LA
ST. ANNE'S HOSPITAL, Chicago, IL
ST. ANNE'S HOSPITAL, Fall River, MA
ST. ANNE'S HOSPITAL-WEST, Northlake, IL
ST. ANSGAR HOSPITAL, Moorhead, MN
ST. ANSGAR'S HOSPITAL, Park River, ND
ST. ANTHONY CENTER, Houston, TX
ST. ANTHONY COMMUNITY HOSPITAL, Warwick, NY
ST. ANTHONY HOSPITAL, Chicago, IL
ST. ANTHONY HOSPITAL, Michigan City, IN
ST. ANTHONY HOSPITAL, Hays, KS
ST. ANTHONY HOSPITAL, Oklahoma City, OK
ST. ANTHONY HOSPITAL, Pendleton, OR
ST. ANTHONY HOSPITAL, Milwaukee, WI
ST. ANTHONY HOSPITAL CENTRAL, Denver, CO, See St. Anthony Hospital Systems
ST. ANTHONY HOSPITAL NORTH, Westminster, CO, See St. Anthony Hospital Systems, Denver
ST. ANTHONY HOSPITAL SYSTEMS, Denver, CO
ST. ANTHONY MEDICAL CENTER, Crown Point, IN
ST. ANTHONY MEDICAL CENTER (Formerly St. Anthony Hospital), Louisville, KY
ST. ANTHONY MEDICAL CENTER, Columbus, OH
ST. ANTHONY REGIONAL HOSPITAL, Carroll, IA
ST. ANTHONY'S HOSPITAL, St. Petersburg, FL
ST. ANTHONY'S HOSPITAL, O'Neill, NE
ST. ANTHONY'S HOSPITAL, Amarillo, TX
ST. ANTHONY'S MEDICAL CENTER, St. Louis, MO
ST. ANTHONY'S MEMORIAL HOSPITAL, Effingham, IL
ST. AUGUSTINE GENERAL HOSPITAL, St. Augustine, FL
ST. BARNABAS HOSPITAL, Bronx, NY
ST. BARNABAS MEDICAL CENTER, Livingston, NJ
ST. BENEDICT HEALTH CARE CENTER, San Antonio, TX, See King William Health Care Center
ST. BENEDICT HOSPITAL, Parkston, SD
ST. BENEDICT'S FAMILY MEDICAL CENTER (Formerly St. Benedict's Hospital), Jerome, ID
ST. BENEDICT'S HOSPITAL, Ogden, UT
ST. BERNARD HOSPITAL, Chicago, IL
ST. BERNARD'S PROVIDENCE HOSPITAL, Milbank, SD
ST. BERNARD'S REGIONAL MEDICAL CENTER, Jonesboro, AR
ST. BERNARDINE MEDICAL CENTER (Formerly St. Bernardine Hospital), San Bernardino, CA
ST. CATHERINE HOSPITAL, Garden City, KS
ST. CATHERINE HOSPITAL OF EAST CHICAGO, East Chicago, IN
ST. CATHERINE HOSPITAL ON HALF MOON BAY, Moss Beach, CA
ST. CATHERINE'S HOSPITAL (Formerly St. Catherine's Hospital and Medical Center), Kenosha, WI
ST. CHARLES GENERAL HOSPITAL, New Orleans, LA
ST. CHARLES HOSPITAL, Luling, LA
ST. CHARLES HOSPITAL, Oregon, OH
ST. CHARLES HOSPITAL AND REHABILITATION CENTER, Port Jefferson, NY
ST. CHARLES MEDICAL CENTER, Bend, OR
ST. CHRISTOPHER'S HOSPITAL FOR CHILDREN, Philadelphia, PA
ST. CLAIR MEMORIAL HOSPITAL, Pittsburgh, PA
ST. CLAIR REGIONAL HOSPITAL (Formerly St. Clair County Hospital), Pell City, AL
ST. CLAIRE MEDICAL CENTER, Morehead, KY
ST. CLARE HOSPITAL, Baraboo, WI
ST. CLARE HOSPITAL OF MONROE, Monroe, WI
ST. CLARE'S -RIVERSIDE MEDICAL CENTER, Denville, NJ
ST. CLARE'S HOSPITAL, Denville, NJ, See St. Clare's-Riverside Medical Center
ST. CLARE'S HOSPITAL AND HEALTH CENTER, New York, NY
ST. CLARE'S HOSPITAL OF SCHENECTADY, Schenectady, NY
ST. CLEMENT HOSPITAL, Red Bud, IL
ST. CLOUD HOSPITAL, St. Cloud, MN
ST. CROIX HOSPITAL AND COMMUNITY HEALTH CENTER, St. Croix, Virgin Islands
ST. CROIX VALLEY MEMORIAL HOSPITAL, St. Croix Falls, WI
ST. DAVID'S COMMUNITY HOSPITAL, Austin, TX
ST. DOMINIC-JACKSON MEMORIAL HOSPITAL, Jackson, MS
ST. EDWARD HOSPITAL OF CAMERON, Cameron, TX
ST. EDWARD MERCY MEDICAL CENTER, Fort Smith, AR
ST. ELIZABETH COMMUNITY HEALTH CENTER, Lincoln, NE
ST. ELIZABETH COMMUNITY HOSPITAL, Red Bluff, CA
ST. ELIZABETH HOSPITAL, Danville, IL
ST. ELIZABETH HOSPITAL, Wabasha, MN
ST. ELIZABETH HOSPITAL, Elizabeth, NJ
ST. ELIZABETH HOSPITAL, Utica, NY
ST. ELIZABETH HOSPITAL, Beaumont, TX
ST. ELIZABETH HOSPITAL, Houston, TX
ST. ELIZABETH HOSPITAL, Appleton, WI
ST. ELIZABETH HOSPITAL AND HEALTH CARE CENTER (Formerly St. Elizabeth Community Hospital), Baker, OR
ST. ELIZABETH HOSPITAL MEDICAL CENTER, Lafayette, IN
ST. ELIZABETH HOSPITAL MEDICAL CENTER, Youngstown, OH
ST. ELIZABETH MEDICAL CENTER, Granite City, IL
ST. ELIZABETH MEDICAL CENTER, Dayton, OH
ST. ELIZABETH MEDICAL CENTER, Yakima, WA
ST. ELIZABETH MEDICAL CENTER-NORTH, Covington, KY
ST. ELIZABETH MEDICAL CENTER-SOUTH, Edgewood, KY, See St. Elizabeth Medical Center-North, Covington
ST. ELIZABETH'S HOSPITAL, Belleville, IL
ST. ELIZABETH'S HOSPITAL, Chicago, IL
ST. ELIZABETH'S HOSPITAL, Hannibal, MO
ST. ELIZABETH'S HOSPITAL OF BOSTON, Boston, MA
ST. EUGENE COMMUNITY HOSPITAL, Dillon, SC
ST. FRANCES CABRINI HOSPITAL, Alexandria, LA
ST. FRANCES XAVIER CABRINI HOSPITAL, Chicago, IL
ST. FRANCIS AT ELLSWORTH, Ellsworth, KS
ST. FRANCIS AT SALINA, Salina, KS
ST. FRANCIS HOSPITAL, Wilmington, DE
ST. FRANCIS HOSPITAL, Miami Beach, FL
ST. FRANCIS HOSPITAL, Columbus, GA
ST. FRANCIS HOSPITAL, Blue Island, IL
ST. FRANCIS HOSPITAL, Evanston, IL
ST. FRANCIS HOSPITAL, Litchfield, IL
ST. FRANCIS HOSPITAL, Escanaba, MI
ST. FRANCIS HOSPITAL, Marceline, MO
ST. FRANCIS HOSPITAL, Maryville, MO
ST. FRANCIS HOSPITAL, Mountain View, MO
ST. FRANCIS HOSPITAL, Jersey City, NJ
ST. FRANCIS HOSPITAL, Olean, NY
ST. FRANCIS HOSPITAL, Roslyn, NY
ST. FRANCIS HOSPITAL (Formerly St. Francis Community Hospital), Greenville, SC
ST. FRANCIS HOSPITAL, Memphis, TN
ST. FRANCIS HOSPITAL, Charleston, WV
ST. FRANCIS HOSPITAL, Milwaukee, WI
ST. FRANCIS HOSPITAL AND MEDICAL CENTER, Topeka, KS
ST. FRANCIS HOSPITAL CENTER, Beech Grove, IN
ST. FRANCIS HOSPITAL OF BUFFALO, Buffalo, NY
ST. FRANCIS HOSPITAL OF NEW CASTLE, New Castle, PA
ST. FRANCIS HOSPITAL OF SANTA BARBARA, Santa Barbara, CA
ST. FRANCIS HOSPITAL SYSTEMS, Colorado Springs, CO
ST. FRANCIS MEDICAL CENTER, Lynwood, CA
ST. FRANCIS MEDICAL CENTER (Formerly St. Francis Hospital), Honolulu, HI
ST. FRANCIS MEDICAL CENTER, Monroe, LA
ST. FRANCIS MEDICAL CENTER, Breckenridge, MN
ST. FRANCIS MEDICAL CENTER, Cape Girardeau, MO
ST. FRANCIS MEDICAL CENTER, Trenton, NJ
ST. FRANCIS MEDICAL CENTER, Pittsburgh, PA
ST. FRANCIS MEDICAL CENTER, La Crosse, WI
ST. FRANCIS MEMORIAL HOSPITAL, San Francisco, CA
ST. FRANCIS MEMORIAL HOSPITAL, West Point, NE
ST. FRANCIS REGIONAL MEDICAL CENTER, Wichita, KS
ST. FRANCIS REGIONAL MEDICAL CENTER, Shakopee, MN
ST. FRANCIS REHABILITATION HOSPITAL AND NURSING HOME, Green Springs, OH
ST. FRANCIS XAVIER HOSPITAL, Charleston, SC
ST. FRANCIS-ST. GEORGE HOSPITAL, Cincinnati, OH
ST. GABRIEL'S HOSPITAL, Little Falls, MN
ST. GERARD'S COMMUNITY HOSPITAL, Hankinson, ND
ST. HELEN HOSPITAL, Chehalis, WA
ST. HELEN'S HOSPITAL AND HEALTH CENTER, St. Helens, OR
ST. HELENA HOSPITAL AND HEALTH CENTER, Deer Park, CA
ST. HELENA PARISH HOSPITAL, Greensburg, LA
ST. JAMES COMMUNITY HOSPITAL, Butte, MT
ST. JAMES HOSPITAL MEDICAL CENTER (Formerly St. James Hospital), Chicago Heights, IL
ST. JAMES MERCY HOSPITAL, Hornell, NY
ST. JAMES PARISH HOSPITAL, Lutcher, LA
ST. JEROME HOSPITAL, Batavia, NY
ST. JOHN AND WEST SHORE HOSPITAL, Westlake, OH
ST. JOHN DISTRICT HOSPITAL, St. John, KS
ST. JOHN HOSPITAL, Leavenworth, KS
ST. JOHN HOSPITAL, Detroit, MI
ST. JOHN HOSPITAL, Cleveland, OH
ST. JOHN HOSPITAL, Nassau Bay, TX
ST. JOHN MEDICAL CENTER, Steubenville, OH
ST. JOHN MEDICAL CENTER, Tulsa, OK
ST. JOHN OF GOD HOSPITAL, Boston, MA
ST. JOHN'S EASTSIDE HOSPITAL (Formerly St. John's Hospital), St. Paul, MN
ST. JOHN'S EPISCOPAL DIVISION, Brooklyn, NY, See Interfaith Medical Center
ST. JOHN'S EPISCOPAL HOSPITAL-SMITHTOWN, Smithtown, NY
ST. JOHN'S EPISCOPAL HOSPITAL-SOUTH SHORE, Far Rockaway, NY
ST. JOHN'S HEALTH AND HOSPITAL CENTER, Pittsburgh, PA
ST. JOHN'S HEALTHCARE CORPORATION (Formerly St. John's Medical Center), Anderson, IN
ST. JOHN'S HOSPITAL, Springfield, IL
ST. JOHN'S HOSPITAL, Salina, KS
ST. JOHN'S HOSPITAL, Lowell, MA
ST. JOHN'S HOSPITAL, Browerville, MN
ST. JOHN'S HOSPITAL, Red Wing, MN
ST. JOHN'S HOSPITAL, Fargo, ND
ST. JOHN'S HOSPITAL, Richmond, VA
ST. JOHN'S HOSPITAL, Longview, WA
ST. JOHN'S HOSPITAL, Jackson, WY
ST. JOHN'S HOSPITAL AND HEALTH CENTER, San Angelo, TX
ST. JOHN'S LUTHERAN HOSPITAL, Libby, MT
ST. JOHN'S MERCY HOSPITAL, Washington, MO, See St. John's Mercy Medical Center, St. Louis
ST. JOHN'S MERCY MEDICAL CENTER, St. Louis, MO
ST. JOHN'S REGIONAL HEALTH CENTER, Springfield, MO
ST. JOHN'S REGIONAL MEDICAL CENTER, Oxnard, CA
ST. JOHN'S REGIONAL MEDICAL CENTER, Joplin, MO
ST. JOHN'S RIVERSIDE HOSPITAL, Yonkers, NY
ST. JOHNS RIVER HOSPITAL, Jacksonville, FL, See CPC St. Johns River Hospital
ST. JOSEPH CENTER FOR MENTAL HEALTH, Omaha, NE, See AMI St. Joseph Center for Mental Health
ST. JOSEPH COMMUNITY HOSPITAL, New Hampton, IA
ST. JOSEPH COMMUNITY HOSPITAL, Vancouver, WA, See Southwest Washington Hospitals
ST. JOSEPH HEALTH AND REHABILITATION CENTER (Formerly St. Joseph Hospital), Ottumwa, IA
ST. JOSEPH HEALTH CARE CORPORATION (Formerly St. Joseph Hospital), Albuquerque, NM
ST. JOSEPH HEALTH CENTER, St. Charles, MO
ST. JOSEPH HOSPITAL, Eureka, CA
ST. JOSEPH HOSPITAL, Orange, CA
ST. JOSEPH HOSPITAL, Del Norte, CO
ST. JOSEPH HOSPITAL, Florence, CO
ST. JOSEPH HOSPITAL, Port Charlotte, FL
ST. JOSEPH HOSPITAL, Augusta, GA
ST. JOSEPH HOSPITAL, Ottumwa, IA, See St. Joseph Health and Rehabilitation Center
ST. JOSEPH HOSPITAL, Concordia, KS
ST. JOSEPH HOSPITAL, Lexington, KY
ST. JOSEPH HOSPITAL, Bangor, ME
ST. JOSEPH HOSPITAL (Formerly Listed Under Baltimore), Towson, MD
ST. JOSEPH HOSPITAL, Flint, MI
ST. JOSEPH HOSPITAL (Formerly Listed Under St. Louis), Kirkwood, MO
ST. JOSEPH HOSPITAL, St. Joseph, MO, See Heartland Hospital East
ST. JOSEPH HOSPITAL, Polson, MT
ST. JOSEPH HOSPITAL, Nashua, NH
ST. JOSEPH HOSPITAL, Lancaster, PA
ST. JOSEPH HOSPITAL, Mitchell, SD
ST. JOSEPH HOSPITAL, Memphis, TN
ST. JOSEPH HOSPITAL, Houston, TX
ST. JOSEPH HOSPITAL, Aberdeen, WA
ST. JOSEPH HOSPITAL, Bellingham, WA
ST. JOSEPH HOSPITAL, Providence, RI
ST. JOSEPH HOSPITAL AND HEALTH CARE CENTER (Formerly St. Joseph Hospital), Chicago, IL
ST. JOSEPH HOSPITAL AND HEALTH CARE CENTER, Tacoma, WA
ST. JOSEPH HOSPITAL AND HEALTH CENTER (Formerly St. Joseph Hospital), Lorain, OH
ST. JOSEPH HOSPITAL AND HEALTH CENTER (Formerly St. Joseph Hospital), Bryan, TX
ST. JOSEPH HOSPITAL OF THE PLAINS, Cheyenne Wells, CO
ST. JOSEPH INTERCOMMUNITY HOSPITAL, Cheektowaga, NY

ST. JOSEPH MEDICAL CENTER, Burbank, CA
ST. JOSEPH MEDICAL CENTER (Formerly St. Joseph Hospital), Stamford, CT
ST. JOSEPH MEDICAL CENTER, Joliet, IL
ST. JOSEPH MEDICAL CENTER, Wichita, KS
ST. JOSEPH MEMORIAL HOSPITAL, Murphysboro, IL
ST. JOSEPH MEMORIAL HOSPITAL, Kokomo, IN, See Saint Joseph Hospital and Health Center
ST. JOSEPH MEMORIAL HOSPITAL, Larned, KS
ST. JOSEPH MERCY HOSPITAL, Clinton, IA
ST. JOSEPH MERCY HOSPITAL, Mason City, IA
ST. JOSEPH MERCY HOSPITAL, Pontiac, MI
ST. JOSEPH REGIONAL MEDICAL CENTER (Formerly St. Joseph's Hospital), Lewiston, ID
ST. JOSEPH REGIONAL MEDICAL CENTER OF NORTHERN OKLAHOMA (Formerly St. Joseph Regional Medical Center), Ponca City, OK
ST. JOSEPH RIVERSIDE HOSPITAL, Warren, OH
ST. JOSEPH STATE HOSPITAL, St. Joseph, MO
ST. JOSEPH'S COMMUNITY HOSPITAL, West Bend, WI
ST. JOSEPH'S DIVISION, St. Paul, MN, See Carondelet Community Hospitals
ST. JOSEPH'S HOSPITAL, Tampa, FL
ST. JOSEPH'S HOSPITAL, Savannah, GA
ST. JOSEPH'S HOSPITAL, Alton, IL
ST. JOSEPH'S HOSPITAL, Belvidere, IL
ST. JOSEPH'S HOSPITAL, Breese, IL
ST. JOSEPH'S HOSPITAL, Highland, IL
ST. JOSEPH'S HOSPITAL, Huntingburg, IN
ST. JOSEPH'S HOSPITAL, Lowell, MA
ST. JOSEPH'S HOSPITAL, Park Rapids, MN
ST. JOSEPH'S HOSPITAL, Elmira, NY
ST. JOSEPH'S HOSPITAL, Asheville, NC
ST. JOSEPH'S HOSPITAL, Minot, ND
ST. JOSEPH'S HOSPITAL, Carbondale, PA
ST. JOSEPH'S HOSPITAL, Philadelphia, PA
ST. JOSEPH'S HOSPITAL, Chewelah, WA
ST. JOSEPH'S HOSPITAL, Buckhannon, WV
ST. JOSEPH'S HOSPITAL, Parkersburg, WV
ST. JOSEPH'S HOSPITAL, Chippewa Falls, WI
ST. JOSEPH'S HOSPITAL, Marshfield, WI
ST. JOSEPH'S HOSPITAL, Milwaukee, WI
ST. JOSEPH'S HOSPITAL AND HEALTH CENTER (Formerly St. Joseph's Hospital and Health Care Center), Tucson, AZ
ST. JOSEPH'S HOSPITAL AND HEALTH CENTER, Dickinson, ND
ST. JOSEPH'S HOSPITAL AND HEALTH CENTER (Formerly St. Joseph's Hospital), Paris, TX
ST. JOSEPH'S HOSPITAL AND MEDICAL CENTER, Phoenix, AZ
ST. JOSEPH'S HOSPITAL AND MEDICAL CENTER, Paterson, NJ
ST. JOSEPH'S HOSPITAL CENTER (Formerly St. Joseph Hospitals), Mount Clemens, MI
ST. JOSEPH'S HOSPITAL HEALTH CENTER, Syracuse, NY
ST. JOSEPH'S HOSPITAL MEDICAL CENTER, Bloomington, IL
ST. JOSEPH'S HOSPITAL OF ARCADIA, Arcadia, WI
ST. JOSEPH'S MEDICAL CENTER (Formerly St. Joseph's Hospital), Fort Wayne, IN
ST. JOSEPH'S MEDICAL CENTER, South Bend, IN
ST. JOSEPH'S MEDICAL CENTER, Brainerd, MN
ST. JOSEPH'S MEDICAL CENTER, Yonkers, NY
ST. JOSEPH'S MEMORIAL HOSPITAL, Hillsboro, WI
ST. JOSEPH'S MERCY HOSPITAL, Centerville, IA
ST. JOSEPH'S OAK PARK HOSPITAL, Stockton, CA
ST. JOSEPH'S REGIONAL HEALTH CENTER, Hot Springs National Park, AR
ST. JOSEPH'S-ALMONT COMMUNITY HOSPITAL, Almont, MI, See St. Joseph Hospitals
ST. JOSEPH'S-MARK TWAIN HOSPITAL (Formerly Mark Twain Hospital District), San Andreas, CA
ST. JUDE CHILDREN'S RESEARCH HOSPITAL, Memphis, TN
ST. JUDE HOSPITAL, Brenham, TX
ST. JUDE HOSPITAL YORBA LINDA, Yorba Linda, CA
ST. JUDE HOSPITAL-FULLERTON, Fullerton, CA
ST. LAWRENCE HOSPITAL, Lansing, MI
ST. LAWRENCE PSYCHIATRIC CENTER, Ogdensburg, NY
ST. LAWRENCE REHABILITATION CENTER, Lawrenceville, NJ
ST. LOUIS REGIONAL MEDICAL CENTER (Formerly St. Luke's Hospital), St. Louis, MO
ST. LOUIS STATE HOSPITAL COMPLEX, St. Louis, MO
ST. LUKE COMMUNITY HOSPITAL, Ronan, MT
ST. LUKE GENERAL HOSPITAL, Arnaudville, LA
ST. LUKE HOSPITAL, Marion, KS
ST. LUKE HOSPITAL, Fort Thomas, KY
ST. LUKE MEDICAL CENTER (Formerly St. Luke Hospital), Pasadena, CA
ST. LUKE'S BEHAVIORAL HEALTH CENTER, Phoenix, AZ
ST. LUKE'S EPISCOPAL HOSPITAL, Houston, TX
ST. LUKE'S EPISCOPAL HOSPITAL, Ponce, P.R., See Hospital San Lucas
ST. LUKE'S GENERAL HOSPITAL, Bellingham, WA
ST. LUKE'S HOSPITAL, San Francisco, CA
ST. LUKE'S HOSPITAL, Jacksonville, FL
ST. LUKE'S HOSPITAL, Davenport, IA
ST. LUKE'S HOSPITAL, Saginaw, MI
ST. LUKE'S HOSPITAL, Duluth, MN
ST. LUKE'S HOSPITAL, Chesterfield, MO
ST. LUKE'S HOSPITAL, Kansas City, MO
ST. LUKE'S HOSPITAL, Newburgh, NY
ST. LUKE'S HOSPITAL, Columbus, NC
ST. LUKE'S HOSPITAL, Crosby, ND
ST. LUKE'S HOSPITAL, Maumee, OH
ST. LUKE'S HOSPITAL, Bethlehem, PA
ST. LUKE'S HOSPITAL, Aberdeen, SD
ST. LUKE'S HOSPITAL, Milwaukee, WI
ST. LUKE'S HOSPITAL, Racine, WI
ST. LUKE'S HOSPITAL CENTER, New York, NY, See St. Luke's-Roosevelt Hospital Center
ST. LUKE'S HOSPITAL OF NEW BEDFORD, New Bedford, MA
ST. LUKE'S HOSPITALS, Fargo, ND
ST. LUKE'S LUTHERAN HOSPITAL, San Antonio, TX
ST. LUKE'S MEDICAL CENTER, Phoenix, AZ
ST. LUKE'S MEMORIAL HOSPITAL, Spokane, WA
ST. LUKE'S MEMORIAL HOSPITAL CENTER, New Hartford, NY
ST. LUKE'S METHODIST HOSPITAL, Cedar Rapids, IA
ST. LUKE'S REGIONAL MEDICAL CENTER, Boise, ID
ST. LUKE'S REGIONAL MEDICAL CENTER, Sioux City, IA
ST. LUKE'S TRI-STATE HOSPITAL, Bowman, ND
ST. LUKE'S-ROOSEVELT HOSPITAL CENTER, New York, NY
ST. LUKES HOSPITAL, Wellington, KS
ST. LUKES HOSPITAL OF MIDDLEBOROUGH, Middleboro, MA
ST. MARGARET HOSPITAL, Hammond, IN
ST. MARGARET MEMORIAL HOSPITAL, Pittsburgh, PA
ST. MARGARET'S HOSPITAL, Montgomery, AL
ST. MARGARET'S HOSPITAL, Spring Valley, IL
ST. MARGARET'S HOSPITAL FOR WOMEN, Boston, MA
ST. MARK'S HOSPITAL, Salt Lake City, UT
ST. MARY DESERT VALLEY HOSPITAL, Apple Valley, CA
ST. MARY HOSPITAL, Quincy, IL
ST. MARY HOSPITAL, Manhattan, KS
ST. MARY HOSPITAL, Livonia, MI
ST. MARY HOSPITAL, Hoboken, NJ
ST. MARY HOSPITAL, Philadelphia, PA
ST. MARY HOSPITAL, Port Arthur, TX
ST. MARY MEDICAL CENTER, Long Beach, CA
ST. MARY MEDICAL CENTER, Hobart, IN, See St. Mary Medical Center, Gary
ST. MARY MEDICAL CENTER, Walla Walla, WA
ST. MARY MEDICAL CENTER, Gary, IN
ST. MARY OF THE PLAINS HOSPITAL, Lubbock, TX
ST. MARY-CORWIN HOSPITAL REGIONAL MEDICAL AND HEALTH CENTER, Pueblo, CO
ST. MARY-ROGERS MEMORIAL HOSPITAL, Rogers, AR
ST. MARY'S DIVISION, Minneapolis, MN, See Carondelet Community Hospitals
ST. MARY'S GENERAL HOSPITAL, Lewiston, ME
ST. MARY'S HEALTH CENTER (Formerly St. Mary's Hospital), Emporia, KS
ST. MARY'S HEALTH CENTER, Jefferson City, MO
ST. MARY'S HEALTH CENTER, St. Louis, MO
ST. MARY'S HEALTH SERVICES (Formerly St. Mary's Hospital), Grand Rapids, MI
ST. MARY'S HOSPITAL, Waterbury, CT
ST. MARY'S HOSPITAL, West Palm Beach, FL
ST. MARY'S HOSPITAL, Athens, GA
ST. MARY'S HOSPITAL, Cottonwood, ID
ST. MARY'S HOSPITAL, Centralia, IL
ST. MARY'S HOSPITAL, Decatur, IL
ST. MARY'S HOSPITAL, East St. Louis, IL
ST. MARY'S HOSPITAL, Galesburg, IL
ST. MARY'S HOSPITAL, Streator, IL
ST. MARY'S HOSPITAL, Leonardtown, MD
ST. MARY'S HOSPITAL, Saginaw, MI
ST. MARY'S HOSPITAL, Kansas City, MO
ST. MARY'S HOSPITAL, Nebraska City, NE
ST. MARY'S HOSPITAL, Reno, NV
ST. MARY'S HOSPITAL, Orange, NJ
ST. MARY'S HOSPITAL, Passaic, NJ
ST. MARY'S HOSPITAL, Amsterdam, NY
ST. MARY'S HOSPITAL, Enid, OK
ST. MARY'S HOSPITAL, Pierre, SD
ST. MARY'S HOSPITAL, Galveston, TX
ST. MARY'S HOSPITAL, Norton, VA
ST. MARY'S HOSPITAL, Richmond, VA
ST. MARY'S HOSPITAL, Huntington, WV
ST. MARY'S HOSPITAL (Formerly St. Mary's Hill Hospital), Milwaukee, WI
ST. MARY'S HOSPITAL, Milwaukee, WI
ST. MARY'S HOSPITAL, Rhinelander, WI, See Sacred Heart-St. Mary's Hospital
ST. MARY'S HOSPITAL, Sparta, WI
ST. MARY'S HOSPITAL AND HEALTH CENTER, Tucson, AZ
ST. MARY'S HOSPITAL AND HOME, Winsted, MN
ST. MARY'S HOSPITAL AND MEDICAL CENTER, San Francisco, CA
ST. MARY'S HOSPITAL AND MEDICAL CENTER, Grand Junction, CO
ST. MARY'S HOSPITAL AND NURSING HOME, Detroit Lakes, MN
ST. MARY'S HOSPITAL MEDICAL CENTER, Green Bay, WI
ST. MARY'S HOSPITAL OF BLUE SPRINGS, Blue Springs, MO
ST. MARY'S HOSPITAL OF KANKAKEE, Kankakee, IL
ST. MARY'S HOSPITAL OF TROY, Troy, NY
ST. MARY'S HOSPITAL-OZAUKEE, Port Washington, WI
ST. MARY'S KEWAUNEE AREA MEMORIAL HOSPITAL, Kewaunee, WI
ST. MARY'S MEDICAL CENTER, Duluth, MN
ST. MARY'S MEDICAL CENTER, Knoxville, TN
ST. MARY'S MEDICAL CENTER, Racine, WI
ST. MARY'S MEDICAL CENTER OF EVANSVILLE, Evansville, IN
ST. MARY'S NORTH HOSPITAL, Lake City, TN
ST. MARY'S REGIONAL HEALTH CENTER (Formerly St. Mary's Hospital), Roswell, NM
ST. MARY'S UNIT, Dyersville, IA, See Mercy Health Center, Dubuque
ST. MARYS HOSPITAL MEDICAL CENTER, Madison, WI
ST. MARYS HOSPITAL OF ROCHESTER, Rochester, MN
ST. MICHAEL HOSPITAL, Texarkana, AR
ST. MICHAEL HOSPITAL, Milwaukee, WI
ST. MICHAEL'S HOSPITAL, Sauk Centre, MN
ST. MICHAEL'S HOSPITAL, Tyndall, SD
ST. MICHAEL'S HOSPITAL, Stevens Point, WI
ST. NICHOLAS HOSPITAL, Sheboygan, WI
ST. OLAF HOSPITAL, Austin, MN
ST. PATRICK HOSPITAL, Lake Charles, LA
ST. PATRICK HOSPITAL, Missoula, MT
ST. PAUL MEDICAL CENTER, Dallas, TX
ST. PAUL-RAMSEY MEDICAL CENTER, St. Paul, MN
ST. PETER HOSPITAL, Olympia, WA
ST. PETER REGIONAL TREATMENT CENTER, St. Peter, MN
ST. PETER'S COMMUNITY HOSPITAL, Helena, MT
ST. PETER'S HOSPITAL, Albany, NY
ST. PETER'S MEDICAL CENTER, New Brunswick, NJ
ST. PETERS COMMUNITY HOSPITAL, St. Peters, MO
ST. RITA'S MEDICAL CENTER, Lima, OH
ST. ROSE DE LIMA HOSPITAL, Henderson, NV
ST. ROSE HOSPITAL, Hayward, CA
ST. TAMMANY PARISH HOSPITAL, Covington, LA
ST. THOMAS HOSPITAL, Nashville, TN
ST. THOMAS HOSPITAL AND COMMUNITY HEALTH SERVICE, Charlotte Amalie, Virgin Islands
ST. THOMAS HOSPITAL MEDICAL CENTER, Akron, OH, See Saint Thomas Medical Center
ST. THOMAS MORE HOSPITAL AND PROGRESSIVE CARE CENTER, Canon City, CO
ST. VINCENT CHARITY HOSPITAL AND HEALTH CENTER, Cleveland, OH
ST. VINCENT GENERAL HOSPITAL, Leadville, CO
ST. VINCENT HOSPITAL, Santa Fe, NM
ST. VINCENT HOSPITAL, Green Bay, WI
ST. VINCENT HOSPITAL AND HEALTH CARE CENTER, Indianapolis, IN
ST. VINCENT HOSPITAL AND MEDICAL CENTER, Portland, OR
ST. VINCENT INFIRMARY, Little Rock, AR
ST. VINCENT MEDICAL CENTER, Los Angeles, CA
ST. VINCENT MEDICAL CENTER, Toledo, OH
ST. VINCENT MEMORIAL HOSPITAL, Taylorville, IL
ST. VINCENT PAVILION, San Jose, CA, See O'Connor Hospital
ST. VINCENT STRESS CENTER, Indianapolis, IN, See St. Vincent Hospital and Health Care Center
ST. VINCENT'S HOSPITAL, Birmingham, AL
ST. VINCENT'S HOSPITAL, Monett, MO
ST. VINCENT'S HOSPITAL AND MEDICAL CENTER OF NEW YORK, New York, NY
ST. VINCENT'S HOSPITAL AND MEDICAL CENTER OF NEW YORK, WESTCHESTER BRANCH, Harrison, NY, See St. Vincent's Hospital and Medical Center of New York, New York City
ST. VINCENT'S MEDICAL CENTER, Bridgeport, CT
ST. VINCENT'S MEDICAL CENTER, Jacksonville, FL
ST. VINCENT'S MEDICAL CENTER OF RICHMOND, Staten Island, NY
ST. VINCENT'S PSYCHIATRIC DIVISION, Bridgeton, MO, See DePaul Community Health Center

STAFFORD DISTRICT HOSPITAL NUMBER FOUR, Stafford, KS
STAMFORD HOSPITAL, Stamford, CT
STAMFORD MEMORIAL HOSPITAL, Stamford, TX
STANDISH COMMUNITY HOSPITAL, Standish, MI
STANFORD UNIVERSITY HOSPITAL, Stanford, CA
STANLEY COMMUNITY HOSPITAL, Stanley, ND
STANLY MEMORIAL HOSPITAL, Albemarle, NC
STANTON COUNTY HOSPITAL AND LONG TERM CARE UNIT, Johnson, KS
STAR LODGE HOSPITAL, Scotts Valley, CA
STAR VALLEY HOSPITAL, Afton, WY
STARKE MEMORIAL HOSPITAL, Knox, IN
STARLITE VILLAGE HOSPITAL, Center Point, TX
STARR COUNTY MEMORIAL HOSPITAL, Rio Grande City, TX
STATE CORRECTIONAL INSTITUTION AT CAMP HILL, Camp Hill, PA
STATE CORRECTIONAL INSTITUTION HOSPITAL, Pittsburgh, PA
STATE HOSPITAL NORTH, Orofino, ID
STATE HOSPITAL SOUTH, Blackfoot, ID
STATE PENITENTIARY HOSPITAL, Walla Walla, WA
STATE PSYCHIATRIC HOSPITAL, San Juan, P.R.
STATE UNIVERSITY HOSPITAL, DOWNSTATE MEDICAL CENTER, Brooklyn, NY, See University Hospital of Brooklyn-State University of New York Health Sciences Center at Brooklyn
STATEN ISLAND HOSPITAL, Staten Island, NY
STATEVILLE CORRECTIONAL CENTER HOSPITAL, Joliet, IL
STE GENEVIEVE COUNTY MEMORIAL HOSPITAL, Ste Genevieve, MO
STEELE MEMORIAL HOSPITAL, Salmon, ID
STEPHENS COUNTY HOSPITAL, Toccoa, GA
STEPHENS MEMORIAL HOSPITAL, Norway, ME
STEPHENS MEMORIAL HOSPITAL, Breckenridge, TX
STERLING COUNTY HOSPITAL, Sterling City, TX
STERLINGTON MEMORIAL HOSPITAL, Sterlington, LA
STEVENS CLINIC HOSPITAL, Welch, WV
STEVENS COMMUNITY MEMORIAL HOSPITAL, Morris, MN
STEVENS COUNTY HOSPITAL, Hugoton, KS
STEVENS MEMORIAL HOSPITAL, Edmonds, WA
STEWART MEMORIAL COMMUNITY HOSPITAL, Lake City, IA
STILLMAN INFIRMARY, HARVARD UNIVERSITY HEALTH SERVICES, Cambridge, MA
STILLWATER COMMUNITY HOSPITAL, Columbus, MT
STILLWATER MEDICAL CENTER, Stillwater, OK
STOKES-REYNOLDS MEMORIAL HOSPITAL, Danbury, NC
STONE COUNTY MEDICAL CENTER (Formerly Mountain View General Hospital), Mountain View, AR
STONEWALL JACKSON HOSPITAL, Lexington, VA
STONEWALL JACKSON MEMORIAL HOSPITAL, Weston, WV
STONEWALL MEMORIAL HOSPITAL, Aspermont, TX
STONY LODGE HOSPITAL, Ossining, NY
STORMONT-VAIL REGIONAL MEDICAL CENTER, Topeka, KS
STORY CITY MEMORIAL HOSPITAL, Story City, IA
STORY COUNTY HOSPITAL AND HEALTH CARE FACILITY, Nevada, IA
STOUDER MEMORIAL HOSPITAL, Troy, OH
STOUGHTON HOSPITAL ASSOCIATION, Stoughton, WI
STRAITH MEMORIAL HOSPITAL, Southfield, MI
STRAUB CLINIC AND HOSPITAL, Honolulu, HI
STRINGFELLOW MEMORIAL HOSPITAL, Anniston, AL
STRONG MEMORIAL HOSPITAL OF THE UNIVERSITY OF ROCHESTER, Rochester, NY
STROUD MUNICIPAL HOSPITAL, Stroud, OK
STUART CIRCLE HOSPITAL, Richmond, VA
STUDENT HEALTH CENTER, UNIVERSITY OF TEXAS AT AUSTIN, Austin, TX, See University of Texas Student Health Center
STURDY MEMORIAL HOSPITAL, Attleboro, MA
STURGIS HOSPITAL, Sturgis, MI
STUTTGART MEMORIAL HOSPITAL, Stuttgart, AR
SUBURBAN COMMUNITY HOSPITAL, Warrensville Heights, OH
SUBURBAN GENERAL HOSPITAL, Norristown, PA
SUBURBAN GENERAL HOSPITAL, Pittsburgh, PA
SUBURBAN HOSPITAL, Bethesda, MD
SUBURBAN HOSPITAL AND SANITARIUM OF COOK COUNTY, Hinsdale, IL
SULLIVAN COMMUNITY HOSPITAL, Sullivan, MO
SULLIVAN COUNTY MEMORIAL HOSPITAL, Milan, MO
SUMMERS COUNTY HOSPITAL, Hinton, WV
SUMMERSVILLE MEMORIAL HOSPITAL, Summersville, WV
SUMNER MEMORIAL HOSPITAL, Gallatin, TN
SUMTER REGIONAL HOSPITAL, Americus, GA
SUN BELT REGIONAL MEDICAL CENTER, Houston, TX
SUN BELT REGIONAL MEDICAL CENTER EAST, Channelview, TX
SUN COAST HOSPITAL, Largo, FL
SUN TOWERS HOSPITAL, El Paso, TX, See HCA Sun Towers Hospital
SUN VALLEY REGIONAL HOSPITAL, El Paso, TX
SUNBURY COMMUNITY HOSPITAL, Sunbury, PA
SUNNYSIDE COMMUNITY HOSPITAL (Formerly Sunnyside General Hospital), Sunnyside, WA
SUNNYVIEW HOSPITAL AND REHABILITATION CENTER, Schenectady, NY
SUNY HEALTH SCIENCE CENTER AT SYRACUSE-UNIVERSITY HOSPITAL (Formerly University Hospital of Upstate Medical Center), Syracuse, NY
SUPERIOR MEMORIAL HOSPITAL, Superior, WI
SUSAN B. ALLEN MEMORIAL HOSPITAL, El Dorado, KS
SUTTER COAST HOSPITAL (Formerly Seaside Hospital and Medical Clinic), Crescent City, CA
SUTTER COMMUNITY HOSPITALS, Sacramento, CA
SUTTER DAVIS HOSPITAL, Davis, CA
SUTTER GENERAL HOSPITAL, Sacramento, CA, See Sutter Community Hospitals
SUTTER MEMORIAL HOSPITAL, Sacramento, CA, See Sutter Community Hospitals
SUTTER SOLANO MEDICAL CENTER, Vallejo, CA
SUWANNEE HOSPITAL (Formerly Suwannee County Hospital), Live Oak, FL
SWAIN COUNTY HOSPITAL, Bryson City, NC
SWEDISH COVENANT HOSPITAL, Chicago, IL
SWEDISH HOSPITAL MEDICAL CENTER, Seattle, WA
SWEDISH MEDICAL CENTER, Englewood, CO
SWEDISHAMERICAN HOSPITAL, Rockford, IL
SWEENY COMMUNITY HOSPITAL, Sweeny, TX
SWEET GRASS COMMUNITY HOSPITAL, Big Timber, MT
SWEET SPRINGS COMMUNITY HOSPITAL, Sweet Springs, MO
SWEETWATER HOSPITAL, Sweetwater, TN
SWIFT COUNTY-BENSON HOSPITAL, Benson, MN
SWISHER MEMORIAL HOSPITAL DISTRICT, Tulia, TX
SWOPE RIDGE REHABILITATION HOSPITAL, Kansas City, MO
SYCAMORE HOSPITAL (Formerly Sycamore Municipal Hospital), Sycamore, IL
SYCAMORE HOSPITAL, Miamisburg, OH, See Kettering Medical Center, Kettering
SYLACAUGA HOSPITAL, Sylacauga, AL
SYLVAN GROVE HOSPITAL, Jackson, GA
SYMMES HOSPITAL, Arlington, MA, See Choate-Symmes Hospitals, Woburn
SYOSSET COMMUNITY HOSPITAL, Syosset, NY
SYRINGA GENERAL HOSPITAL, Grangeville, ID

T

T. C. THOMPSON CHILDREN'S HOSPITAL MEDICAL CENTER, Chattanooga, TN, See Erlanger Medical Center
T. J. SAMSON COMMUNITY HOSPITAL, Glasgow, KY
TACOMA GENERAL HOSPITAL, Tacoma, WA
TAFT HOSPITAL DISTRICT, Taft, TX
TAHLEQUAH CITY HOSPITAL, Tahlequah, OK
TAHOE FOREST HOSPITAL DISTRICT, Truckee, CA
TAKOMA ADVENTIST HOSPITAL, Greeneville, TN
TALLAHASSEE COMMUNITY HOSPITAL, Tallahassee, FL
TALLAHASSEE MEMORIAL REGIONAL MEDICAL CENTER, Tallahassee, FL
TALLAHATCHIE GENERAL HOSPITAL, Charleston, MS
TAMPA BAY COMMUNITY HOSPITAL, Tampa, FL
TAMPA GENERAL HOSPITAL, Tampa, FL
TAMPA HEIGHTS HOSPITAL, Tampa, FL, See Charter Hospital of Tampa Bay
TANNER MEDICAL CENTER, Carrollton, GA
TANNER MEDICAL CENTER-VILLA RICA (Formerly Villa Rica City Hospital), Villa Rica, GA
TARPON SPRINGS GENERAL HOSPITAL, Tarpon Springs, FL
TARRANT COUNTY HOSPITAL DISTRICT, Fort Worth, TX
TAUNTON STATE HOSPITAL, Taunton, MA
TAWAS ST. JOSEPH HOSPITAL, Tawas City, MI
TAYLOR COUNTY HOSPITAL, Campbellsville, KY
TAYLOR HOSPITAL (Formerly James A. Taylor Osteopathic Hospital), Bangor, ME
TAYLOR HOSPITAL, Ridley Park, PA
TAYLOR MANOR HOSPITAL, Ellicott City, MD
TAYLOR-BROWN MEMORIAL HOSPITAL, Waterloo, NY
TAZEWELL COMMUNITY HOSPITAL, Tazewell, VA
TEAGUE GENERAL HOSPITAL, Teague, TX
TEHACHAPI HOSPITAL, Tehachapi, CA
TEMPE ST. LUKE'S HOSPITAL, Tempe, AZ
TEMPLE COMMUNITY HOSPITAL, Los Angeles, CA
TEMPLE UNIVERSITY HOSPITAL, Philadelphia, PA
TEMPLETON COLONY, Baldwinville, MA, See Walter E. Fernald State School, Waltham
TENNESSEE CHRISTIAN MEDICAL CENTER (Formerly Madison Hospital), Madison, TN
TENNESSEE STATE PENITENTIARY HOSPITAL, Nashville, TN
TENSAS MEMORIAL HOSPITAL, Newellton, LA
TERRACE PLAZA MEDICAL CENTER, Baldwin Park, CA
TERRE HAUTE REGIONAL HOSPITAL, Terre Haute, IN
TERREBONNE GENERAL MEDICAL CENTER, Houma, LA
TERRELL COMMUNITY HOSPITAL, Terrell, TX, See AMI Terrell Community Hospital
TERRELL COUNTY HOSPITAL, Dawson, GA
TERRELL STATE HOSPITAL, Terrell, TX
TETON MEDICAL CENTER, Choteau, MT
TETON VALLEY HOSPITAL, Driggs, ID
TEWKSBURY HOSPITAL, Tewksbury, MA
TEXARKANA COMMUNITY HOSPITAL, Texarkana, TX, See AMI Texarkana Community Hospital
TEXAS CHILDREN'S HOSPITAL, Houston, TX
TEXAS COUNTY MEMORIAL HOSPITAL, Houston, MO
TEXAS SCOTTISH RITE HOSPITAL FOR CRIPPLED CHILDREN, Dallas, TX
TEXOMA MEDICAL CENTER, Denison, TX
TEXOMA MEDICAL CENTER EAST, Denison, TX, See Texoma Medical Center
THAGGARD HOSPITAL, Madden, MS
THAYER COUNTY MEMORIAL HOSPITAL, Hebron, NE
THE ARBOUR, Boston, MA
THE BROWN SCHOOLS-RANCH TREATMENT CENTER, Austin, TX, See Brown Schools Healthcare Rehabilitation Center
THE BROWN SCHOOLS-SAN MARCOS TREATMENT CENTER, San Marcos, TX
THE FRIARY, Gulf Breeze, FL
THE HOSPITAL, Sidney, NY
THE MEDICAL CENTER (Formerly Medical Center of Beaver County), Beaver, PA
THE METHODIST HOSPITAL, Houston, TX
THE PAVILION, Pensacola, FL, See West Florida Regional Medical Center
THE PAVILION, St. Louis, MO, See Barnes Hospital
THEDA CLARK REGIONAL MEDICAL CENTER, Neenah, WI
THIBODAUX GENERAL HOSPITAL, Thibodaux, LA
THOMAS B. FINAN CENTER, Cumberland, MD
THOMAS H. BOYD MEMORIAL HOSPITAL, Carrollton, IL
THOMAS HOSPITAL, Fairhope, AL
THOMAS JEFFERSON UNIVERSITY HOSPITAL, Philadelphia, PA
THOMAS MEMORIAL HOSPITAL, Thomas, OK
THOMAS MEMORIAL HOSPITAL (Formerly Herbert J. Thomas Memorial Hospital), South Charleston, WV
THOMASVILLE HOSPITAL, Thomasville, AL
THOMS REHABILITATION HOSPITAL, Asheville, NC
THOREK HOSPITAL AND MEDICAL CENTER, Chicago, IL
THORN HOSPITAL, Hudson, MI
THREE RIVERS AREA HOSPITAL, Three Rivers, MI
THREE RIVERS COMMUNITY HOSPITAL (Formerly Nautilus Memorial Hospital), Waverly, TN
THREE RIVERS HOSPITAL AND MEDICAL CENTER, McRae, GA
THROCKMORTON COUNTY MEMORIAL HOSPITAL, Throckmorton, TX
THUNDERBIRD SAMARITAN HOSPITAL AND HEALTH CENTER, Glendale, AZ
TIDEWATER MEMORIAL HOSPITAL, Tappahannock, VA
TIDEWATER PSYCHIATRIC INSTITUTE, Virginia Beach, VA
TIDEWATER PSYCHIATRIC INSTITUTE-NORFOLK, Norfolk, VA
TIFT GENERAL HOSPITAL, Tifton, GA
TIGUA GENERAL HOSPITAL, El Paso, TX
TILDEN COMMUNITY HOSPITAL, Tilden, NE
TILLAMOOK COUNTY GENERAL HOSPITAL, Tillamook, OR
TIMBERLAWN PSYCHIATRIC HOSPITAL, Dallas, TX
TIMKEN MERCY MEDICAL CENTER, Canton, OH
TINLEY PARK MENTAL HEALTH CENTER, Tinley Park, IL
TIOGA COMMUNITY HOSPITAL, Tioga, ND
TIOGA GENERAL HOSPITAL, Waverly, NY
TIPPAH COUNTY HOSPITAL, Ripley, MS
TIPTON COUNTY MEMORIAL HOSPITAL, Tipton, IN
TISHOMINGO HOSPITAL (Formerly Tishomingo County Hospital), Iuka, MS
TITUS COUNTY MEMORIAL HOSPITAL, Mount Pleasant, TX

TITUSVILLE HOSPITAL, Titusville, PA
TOBEY HOSPITAL, Wareham, MA
TOD CHILDREN'S HOSPITAL, Youngstown, OH
TOLEDO HOSPITAL, Toledo, OH
TOLEDO MENTAL HEALTH CENTER, Toledo, OH
TOLFREE MEMORIAL HOSPITAL, West Branch, MI
TOMAH MEMORIAL HOSPITAL, Tomah, WI
TOMBALL REGIONAL HOSPITAL (Formerly Tomball Community Hospital), Tomball, TX
TOMPKINS COMMUNITY HOSPITAL, Ithaca, NY
TOOELE VALLEY REGIONAL MEDICAL CENTER (Formerly Tooele Valley Hospital), Tooele, UT
TOOLE COUNTY HOSPITAL AND NURSING HOME, Shelby, MT
TOPEKA STATE HOSPITAL, Topeka, KS
TORBETT, HUTCHINGS, SMITH MEMORIAL HOSPITAL, Marlin, TX
TORRANCE MEMORIAL HOSPITAL MEDICAL CENTER, Torrance, CA
TORRANCE STATE HOSPITAL, Torrance, PA
TOURO INFIRMARY, New Orleans, LA
TOWN AND COUNTRY HOSPITAL, Tampa, FL, See AMI Town and Country Medical Center
TOWNER COUNTY MEMORIAL HOSPITAL, Cando, ND
TOWNS COUNTY HOSPITAL, Hiawassee, GA
TRACY COMMUNITY MEMORIAL HOSPITAL, Tracy, CA
TRACY MUNICIPAL HOSPITAL, Tracy, MN
TRANSYLVANIA COMMUNITY HOSPITAL, Brevard, NC
TRAVERSE CITY OSTEOPATHIC HOSPITAL, Traverse City, MI
TRAVERSE CITY REGIONAL PSYCHIATRIC HOSPITAL, Traverse City, MI
TREASURE COAST REHABILITATION HOSPITAL, Vero Beach, FL
TREGO COUNTY-LEMKE MEMORIAL HOSPITAL, Wakeeney, KS
TRENTON PSYCHIATRIC HOSPITAL, Trenton, NJ
TRI-CITY COMMUNITY HOSPITAL (Formerly Mercy Hospital), Jourdanton, TX
TRI-CITY MEDICAL CENTER (Formerly Tri-City Hospital), Oceanside, CA
TRI-COUNTY AREA HOSPITAL, Lexington, NE
TRI-COUNTY COMMUNITY HOSPITAL, Edmore, MI
TRI-COUNTY HOSPITAL, Wadena, MN
TRI-COUNTY MEMORIAL HOSPITAL, Gowanda, NY
TRI-COUNTY MEMORIAL HOSPITAL, Whitehall, WI
TRI-STATE MEMORIAL HOSPITAL, Clarkston, WA
TRI-WARD GENERAL HOSPITAL, Bernice, LA
TRIDENT REGIONAL MEDICAL CENTER, Charleston, SC
TRIGG COUNTY HOSPITAL, Cadiz, KY
TRIMONT COMMUNITY HOSPITAL, Trimont, MN
TRINITY GENERAL HOSPITAL, Weaverville, CA
TRINITY HOSPITAL, Baudette, MN
TRINITY HOSPITAL, Wolf Point, MT
TRINITY HOSPITAL, Erin, TN
TRINITY LUTHERAN HOSPITAL, Kansas City, MO
TRINITY MEDICAL CENTER, Minot, ND
TRINITY MEDICAL CENTER, Carrollton, TX
TRINITY MEMORIAL HOSPITAL, Trinity, TX
TRINITY MEMORIAL HOSPITAL, Cudahy, WI
TRINITY REGIONAL HOSPITAL, Fort Dodge, IA
TRIPLER ARMY MEDICAL CENTER, Honolulu, HI
TROY COMMUNITY HOSPITAL, Troy, PA
TRUCKEE MEADOWS HOSPITAL, Reno, NV
TRUMAN MEDICAL CENTER-EAST, Kansas City, MO
TRUMAN MEDICAL CENTER-WEST, Kansas City, MO
TRUMBULL MEMORIAL HOSPITAL, Warren, OH
TUALITY COMMUNITY HOSPITAL, Hillsboro, OR
TUCKER COUNTY HOSPITAL, Parsons, WV
TUCSON GENERAL HOSPITAL, Tucson, AZ
TUCSON MEDICAL CENTER, Tucson, AZ
TUCSON PSYCHIATRIC INSTITUTE, Tucson, AZ
TULANE UNIVERSITY HOSPITAL AND CLINICS, New Orleans, LA
TULARE DISTRICT HOSPITAL, Tulare, CA
TULSA PSYCHIATRIC CENTER, Tulsa, OK, See Parkside Center
TUNICA COUNTY HOSPITAL, Tunica, MS
TUOLUMNE GENERAL HOSPITAL, Sonora, CA
TUOMEY HOSPITAL, Sumter, SC
TURNER COUNTY HOSPITAL, Ashburn, GA
TURNER MEMORIAL HOSPITAL, Ozark, AR
TURNING POINT CARE CENTER, Moultrie, GA
TWEETEN-LUTHERAN HEALTH CARE CENTER (Formerly Tweeten Memorial Hospital and Convalescent Home), Spring Grove, MN
TWELVE OAKS HOSPITAL, Houston, TX, See AMI Twelve Oaks Hospital
TWIN CITIES COMMUNITY HOSPITAL, Templeton, CA
TWIN CITIES HOSPITAL, Niceville, FL
TWIN CITY HOSPITAL, Dennison, OH
TWIN COUNTY COMMUNITY HOSPITAL, Galax, VA
TWIN FALLS CLINIC HOSPITAL, Twin Falls, ID
TWIN OAKS MEDICAL CENTER, Fort Worth, TX
TWIN RIVERS MEDICAL CENTER, Arkadelphia, AR
TWIN RIVERS REGIONAL MEDICAL CENTER, Kennett, MO
TWO RIVERS COMMUNITY HOSPITAL AND HAMILTON MEMORIAL HOME, Two Rivers, WI
TYLER COUNTY HOSPITAL, Woodville, TX
TYLER HOLMES MEMORIAL HOSPITAL, Winona, MS
TYLER MEMORIAL HOSPITAL, Tunkhannock, PA
TYRONE HOSPITAL, Tyrone, PA

U

U. S. AIR FORCE ACADEMY HOSPITAL, Usaf Academy, CO
U. S. AIR FORCE HOSPITAL, Tucson, AZ
U. S. AIR FORCE HOSPITAL, Williams Air Force Base, AZ
U. S. AIR FORCE HOSPITAL, Blytheville, AR
U. S. AIR FORCE HOSPITAL, Jacksonville, AR
U. S. AIR FORCE HOSPITAL, Victorville, CA
U. S. AIR FORCE HOSPITAL, Mather Air Force Base, CA
U. S. AIR FORCE HOSPITAL, Lompoc, CA
U. S. AIR FORCE HOSPITAL, Homestead, FL
U. S. AIR FORCE HOSPITAL, Patrick Air Force Base, FL
U. S. AIR FORCE HOSPITAL, Panama City, FL
U. S. AIR FORCE HOSPITAL, Wichita, KS
U. S. AIR FORCE HOSPITAL, Shreveport, LA
U. S. AIR FORCE HOSPITAL, England Air Force Base, LA
U. S. AIR FORCE HOSPITAL, K I Sawyer Air Force Base, MI
U. S. AIR FORCE HOSPITAL, Oscoda, MI
U. S. AIR FORCE HOSPITAL, Columbus, MS
U. S. AIR FORCE HOSPITAL, Malmstrom Air Force Base, MT
U. S. AIR FORCE HOSPITAL, Las Vegas, NV
U. S. AIR FORCE HOSPITAL, Cannon Air Force Base, NM
U. S. AIR FORCE HOSPITAL, Holloman Air Force Base, NM
U. S. AIR FORCE HOSPITAL, Rome, NY
U. S. AIR FORCE HOSPITAL, Plattsburgh, NY
U. S. AIR FORCE HOSPITAL, Grand Forks Air Force Base, ND
U. S. AIR FORCE HOSPITAL, Myrtle Beach, SC
U. S. AIR FORCE HOSPITAL, Ellsworth Air Force Base, SD
U. S. AIR FORCE HOSPITAL, Austin, TX
U. S. AIR FORCE HOSPITAL, Abilene, TX
U. S. AIR FORCE HOSPITAL, Del Rio, TX
U. S. AIR FORCE HOSPITAL, Lubbock, TX
U. S. AIR FORCE HOSPITAL, Hill Air Force Base, UT
U. S. AIR FORCE HOSPITAL, Fairchild Air Force Base, WA
U. S. AIR FORCE HOSPITAL, Cheyenne, WY
U. S. AIR FORCE HOSPITAL -EDWARDS, Edwards Air Force Base, CA
U. S. AIR FORCE HOSPITAL ALTUS, Altus, OK
U. S. AIR FORCE HOSPITAL BEALE, Beale Air Force Base, CA
U. S. AIR FORCE HOSPITAL CHANUTE, Rantoul, IL
U. S. AIR FORCE HOSPITAL DOVER, Dover, DE
U. S. AIR FORCE HOSPITAL LUKE, Glendale, AZ
U. S. AIR FORCE HOSPITAL MOODY, Valdosta, GA
U. S. AIR FORCE HOSPITAL MOUNTAIN HOME, Mountain Home Air Force Base, ID
U. S. AIR FORCE HOSPITAL PEASE, Portsmouth, NH
U. S. AIR FORCE HOSPITAL ROBINS, Robins Air Force Base, GA
U. S. AIR FORCE HOSPITAL SEYMOUR JOHNSON, Goldsboro, NC
U. S. AIR FORCE HOSPITAL SHAW, Shaw Air Force Base, SC
U. S. AIR FORCE HOSPITAL TINKER, Tinker Air Force Base, OK
U. S. AIR FORCE HOSPITAL WHITEMAN, Whiteman Air Force Base, MO
U. S. AIR FORCE HOSPITAL-CASTLE, Castle Air Force Base, CA
U. S. AIR FORCE HOSPITAL-KIRTLAND, Kirtland Air Force Base, NM
U. S. AIR FORCE MEDICAL CENTER, Scott Air Force Base, IL
U. S. AIR FORCE MEDICAL CENTER KEESLER, Biloxi, MS
U. S. AIR FORCE MEDICAL CENTER WRIGHT-PATTERSON, Dayton, OH
U. S. AIR FORCE REGIONAL HOSPITAL, Riverside, CA
U. S. AIR FORCE REGIONAL HOSPITAL, Eglin Air Force Base, FL
U. S. AIR FORCE REGIONAL HOSPITAL, Minot Air Force Base, ND
U. S. AIR FORCE REGIONAL HOSPITAL, Sheppard Air Force Base, TX
U. S. AIR FORCE REGIONAL HOSPITAL, Hampton, VA
U. S. AIR FORCE REGIONAL HOSPITAL CARSWELL, Fort Worth, TX
U. S. AIR FORCE REGIONAL HOSPITAL ELMENDORF, Anchorage, AK
U. S. AIR FORCE REGIONAL HOSPITAL MACDILL, Tampa, FL
U. S. AIR FORCE REGIONAL HOSPITAL MAXWELL, Montgomery, AL
U. S. ARMY COMMUNITY HOSPITAL, Fort Carson, CO
U. S. IRELAND ARMY COMMUNITY HOSPITAL, Fort Knox, KY
U. S. LYSTER ARMY HOSPITAL, Fort Rucker, AL
U. S. MEDICAL CENTER FOR FEDERAL PRISONERS, Springfield, MO
U. S. PENITENTIARY HOSPITAL, Lompoc, CA
U. S. PENITENTIARY HOSPITAL, Atlanta, GA
U. S. PENITENTIARY HOSPITAL, Lewisburg, PA
U. S. PENITENTIARY, HOSPITAL UNIT, Leavenworth, KS
U. S. PUBLIC HEALTH SERVICE ALASKA NATIVE HOSPITAL, Barrow, AK
U. S. PUBLIC HEALTH SERVICE ALASKA NATIVE HOSPITAL, Kotzebue, AK
U. S. PUBLIC HEALTH SERVICE ALASKA NATIVE MEDICAL CENTER, Anchorage, AK
U. S. PUBLIC HEALTH SERVICE COMPREHENSIVE INDIAN HEALTH FACILITY, Claremore, OK
U. S. PUBLIC HEALTH SERVICE FORT YUMA INDIAN HOSPITAL, Winterhaven, CA
U. S. PUBLIC HEALTH SERVICE INDIAN HOSPITAL, Fort Defiance, AZ
U. S. PUBLIC HEALTH SERVICE INDIAN HOSPITAL, Parker, AZ
U. S. PUBLIC HEALTH SERVICE INDIAN HOSPITAL, Sacaton, AZ
U. S. PUBLIC HEALTH SERVICE INDIAN HOSPITAL, San Carlos, AZ
U. S. PUBLIC HEALTH SERVICE INDIAN HOSPITAL, Sells, AZ
U. S. PUBLIC HEALTH SERVICE INDIAN HOSPITAL, Tuba City, AZ
U. S. PUBLIC HEALTH SERVICE INDIAN HOSPITAL, Whiteriver, AZ
U. S. PUBLIC HEALTH SERVICE INDIAN HOSPITAL, Cass Lake, MN
U. S. PUBLIC HEALTH SERVICE INDIAN HOSPITAL, Redlake, MN
U. S. PUBLIC HEALTH SERVICE INDIAN HOSPITAL, Browning, MT
U. S. PUBLIC HEALTH SERVICE INDIAN HOSPITAL, Crow Agency, MT
U. S. PUBLIC HEALTH SERVICE INDIAN HOSPITAL, Harlem, MT
U. S. PUBLIC HEALTH SERVICE INDIAN HOSPITAL, Winnebago, NE
U. S. PUBLIC HEALTH SERVICE INDIAN HOSPITAL, Schurz, NV
U. S. PUBLIC HEALTH SERVICE INDIAN HOSPITAL, Albuquerque, NM
U. S. PUBLIC HEALTH SERVICE INDIAN HOSPITAL, Crownpoint, NM
U. S. PUBLIC HEALTH SERVICE INDIAN HOSPITAL, Mescalero, NM
U. S. PUBLIC HEALTH SERVICE INDIAN HOSPITAL, Santa Fe, NM
U. S. PUBLIC HEALTH SERVICE INDIAN HOSPITAL, Shiprock, NM
U. S. PUBLIC HEALTH SERVICE INDIAN HOSPITAL, Zuni, NM
U. S. PUBLIC HEALTH SERVICE INDIAN HOSPITAL, Cherokee, NC
U. S. PUBLIC HEALTH SERVICE INDIAN HOSPITAL, Belcourt, ND
U. S. PUBLIC HEALTH SERVICE INDIAN HOSPITAL, Fort Yates, ND
U. S. PUBLIC HEALTH SERVICE INDIAN HOSPITAL, Clinton, OK
U. S. PUBLIC HEALTH SERVICE INDIAN HOSPITAL, Lawton, OK
U. S. PUBLIC HEALTH SERVICE INDIAN HOSPITAL, Eagle Butte, SD
U. S. PUBLIC HEALTH SERVICE INDIAN HOSPITAL, Pine Ridge, SD
U. S. PUBLIC HEALTH SERVICE INDIAN HOSPITAL, Rapid City, SD
U. S. PUBLIC HEALTH SERVICE INDIAN HOSPITAL, Rosebud, SD
U. S. PUBLIC HEALTH SERVICE INDIAN HOSPITAL, Sisseton, SD
U. S. PUBLIC HEALTH SERVICE INDIAN HOSPITAL, Wagner, SD
U. S. PUBLIC HEALTH SERVICE OWYHEE COMMUNITY HEALTH FACILITY, Owyhee, NV

U. S. PUBLIC HEALTH SERVICE YUKON-KUSKOKWIM DELTA REGIONAL HOSPITAL, Bethel, AK
U. S. PUBLIC HEALTH SERVICE, KEAMS CANYON INDIAN HOSPITAL AND CLINICS, Keams Canyon, AZ
UINTA MEDICAL CENTER, Evanston, WY, See Ihc Evanston Regional Hospital
UKIAH ADVENTIST HOSPITAL, Ukiah, CA
UKIAH GENERAL HOSPITAL, Ukiah, CA
UNDERWOOD-MEMORIAL HOSPITAL, Woodbury, NJ
UNICOI COUNTY MEMORIAL HOSPITAL, Erwin, TN
UNION CITY MEMORIAL HOSPITAL, Union City, IN
UNION CITY MEMORIAL HOSPITAL, Union City, PA
UNION COUNTY GENERAL HOSPITAL, New Albany, MS
UNION COUNTY GENERAL HOSPITAL, Clayton, NM
UNION COUNTY HOSPITAL, Anna, IL
UNION GENERAL HOSPITAL, Blairsville, GA
UNION GENERAL HOSPITAL, Farmerville, LA
UNION HOSPITAL, Terre Haute, IN
UNION HOSPITAL, Lynn, MA, See Atlanticare Medical Center
UNION HOSPITAL (Formerly Memorial General Hospital), Union, NJ
UNION HOSPITAL, Mayville, ND
UNION HOSPITAL, Dover, OH
UNION HOSPITAL OF CECIL COUNTY, Elkton, MD
UNION HOSPITAL OF THE BRONX, Bronx, NY
UNION MEDICAL CENTER, El Dorado, AR
UNION MEMORIAL HOSPITAL, Baltimore, MD
UNION MEMORIAL HOSPITAL, Monroe, NC
UNION PRINTERS HOME, Colorado Springs, CO
UNIONTOWN HOSPITAL, Uniontown, PA
UNITED COMMUNITY HOSPITAL, Grove City, PA
UNITED DISTRICT HOSPITAL AND HOME, Staples, MN
UNITED GENERAL HOSPITAL, Sedro Woolley, WA
UNITED HEALTH SERVICES (Formerly Listed Under Johnson City), Binghamton, NY
UNITED HOSPITAL, St. Paul, MN
UNITED HOSPITAL, Port Chester, NY
UNITED HOSPITAL, Grand Forks, ND
UNITED HOSPITAL CENTER, Clarksburg, WV
UNITED HOSPITAL DISTRICT, Blue Earth, MN
UNITED HOSPITALS MEDICAL CENTER, Newark, NJ
UNITED MEDICAL CENTER NEW ORLEANS, New Orleans, LA
UNITED MEDICAL CENTER SHELBYVILLE (Formerly King's Daughters Hospital), Shelbyville, KY
UNITED MEMORIAL HOSPITAL, Greenville, MI
UNITED RECOVERY CENTER, Grand Forks, ND
UNITY HOSPITAL, Grafton, ND
UNITY MEDICAL CENTER, Fridley, MN, See Health Central, Minneapolis
UNIVERSITY COMMUNITY HOSPITAL, Tamarac, FL
UNIVERSITY COMMUNITY HOSPITAL, Tampa, FL
UNIVERSITY GENERAL HOSPITAL, Seminole, FL
UNIVERSITY HEALTH CENTER, UNIVERSITY OF NEBRASKA, Lincoln, NE
UNIVERSITY HEALTH SERVICE, UNIVERSITY OF GEORGIA, Athens, GA
UNIVERSITY HEALTH SERVICES, Amherst, MA
UNIVERSITY HEIGHTS HOSPITAL, Indianapolis, IN
UNIVERSITY HOSPITAL, Denver, CO
UNIVERSITY HOSPITAL (Formerly Daytona Beach General Hospital), Holly Hill, FL
UNIVERSITY HOSPITAL, Augusta, GA
UNIVERSITY HOSPITAL, Indianapolis, IN, See Indiana University Hospitals
UNIVERSITY HOSPITAL, Lexington, KY
UNIVERSITY HOSPITAL, Boston, MA
UNIVERSITY HOSPITAL, Jackson, MS
UNIVERSITY HOSPITAL, New York, NY, See New York University Medical Center
UNIVERSITY HOSPITAL, Stony Brook, NY
UNIVERSITY HOSPITAL, Cincinnati, OH, See University of Cincinnati Hospital
UNIVERSITY HOSPITAL, Portland, OR, See Oregon Health Sciences University Hospital
UNIVERSITY HOSPITAL, Seattle, WA
UNIVERSITY HOSPITAL, San Juan, P.R.
UNIVERSITY HOSPITAL -UNIVERSITY OF NEBRASKA, Omaha, NE
UNIVERSITY HOSPITAL AND CLINIC, Pensacola, FL
UNIVERSITY HOSPITAL OF ARKANSAS (Formerly University Hospital and Ambulatory Care Center), Little Rock, AR
UNIVERSITY HOSPITAL OF BROOKLYN-STATE UNIVERSITY OF NEW YORK HEALTH SCIENCES CENTER AT BROOKLYN (Formerly State University Hospital, Downstate Medical Center), Brooklyn, NY
UNIVERSITY HOSPITAL OF JACKSONVILLE, Jacksonville, FL
UNIVERSITY HOSPITAL OF UPSTATE MEDICAL CENTER, Syracuse, NY, See Suny Health Science Center at Syracuse-University Hospital
UNIVERSITY HOSPITAL SCHOOL, Iowa City, IA, See University of Iowa Hospitals and Clinics
UNIVERSITY HOSPITAL, ST. LOUIS UNIVERSITY MEDICAL CENTER (Formerly St. Louis University Hospitals), St. Louis, MO
UNIVERSITY HOSPITALS OF CLEVELAND, Cleveland, OH
UNIVERSITY MEDICAL CENTER, Tucson, AZ
UNIVERSITY MEDICAL CENTER, Lafayette, LA
UNIVERSITY MEDICAL CENTER (Formerly Broad Street Hospital and Medical Center), Philadelphia, PA
UNIVERSITY MEDICAL CENTER, Lebanon, TN
UNIVERSITY MEDICAL CENTER OF SOUTHERN NEVADA (Formerly Southern Nevada Memorial Hospital), Las Vegas, NV
UNIVERSITY MEMORIAL HOSPITAL, Charlotte, NC
UNIVERSITY OF ALABAMA HOSPITAL, Birmingham, AL
UNIVERSITY OF CALIFORNIA AT LOS ANGELES MEDICAL CENTER, Los Angeles, CA
UNIVERSITY OF CALIFORNIA AT LOS ANGELES NEUROPSYCHIATRIC HOSPITAL, Los Angeles, CA
UNIVERSITY OF CALIFORNIA DAVIS MEDICAL CENTER, Sacramento, CA
UNIVERSITY OF CALIFORNIA IRVINE MEDICAL CENTER, Orange, CA
UNIVERSITY OF CALIFORNIA SAN DIEGO MEDICAL CENTER, San Diego, CA
UNIVERSITY OF CALIFORNIA, SAN FRANCISCO MEDICAL CENTER (Formerly Medical Center at the University of California), San Francisco, CA
UNIVERSITY OF CHICAGO HOSPITALS (Formerly University of Chicago Hospitals and Clinics), Chicago, IL
UNIVERSITY OF CINCINNATI HOSPITAL, Cincinnati, OH
UNIVERSITY OF CONNECTICUT HEALTH CENTER, JOHN DEMPSEY HOSPITAL, Farmington, CT
UNIVERSITY OF CONNECTICUT HEALTH CENTER, UNCAS ON THAMES HOSPITAL, Norwich, CT
UNIVERSITY OF HEALTH SCIENCES, UNIVERSITY HOSPITAL, Kansas City, MO
UNIVERSITY OF ILLINOIS HOSPITAL, Chicago, IL
UNIVERSITY OF IOWA HOSPITALS AND CLINICS, Iowa City, IA
UNIVERSITY OF KANSAS HOSPITAL (Formerly University of Kansas College of Health Sciences and Bell Memorial Hospital), Kansas City, KS
UNIVERSITY OF MARYLAND MEDICAL SYSTEMS, Baltimore, MD
UNIVERSITY OF MASSACHUSETTS MEDICAL CENTER (Formerly University of Massachusetts Medical School and Teaching Hospital), Worcester, MA
UNIVERSITY OF MEDICINE AND DENTISTRY OF NEW JERSEY-UNIVERSITY HOSPITAL, Newark, NJ
UNIVERSITY OF MIAMI HOSPITAL AND CLINICS-NCCH, Miami, FL
UNIVERSITY OF MICHIGAN HOSPITALS, Ann Arbor, MI
UNIVERSITY OF MINNESOTA HOSPITAL AND CLINIC, Minneapolis, MN
UNIVERSITY OF MISSOURI-COLUMBIA HOSPITAL AND CLINICS, Columbia, MO
UNIVERSITY OF NEW MEXICO HOSPITAL-BERNALILLO COUNTY MEDICAL CENTER, Albuquerque, NM
UNIVERSITY OF NEW MEXICO MENTAL HEALTH CENTER, Albuquerque, NM
UNIVERSITY OF PITTSBURGH WESTERN PSYCHIATRIC INSTITUTE AND CLINIC, Pittsburgh, PA
UNIVERSITY OF SOUTH ALABAMA MEDICAL CENTER, Mobile, AL
UNIVERSITY OF SOUTHERN CALIFORNIA-KENNETH NORRIS JR. CANCER HOSPITAL, Los Angeles, CA
UNIVERSITY OF TENNESSEE MEDICAL CENTER, Memphis, TN
UNIVERSITY OF TENNESSEE MEMORIAL HOSPITAL, Knoxville, TN
UNIVERSITY OF TEXAS HEALTH CENTER AT TYLER, Tyler, TX
UNIVERSITY OF TEXAS M. D. ANDERSON HOSPITAL AND TUMOR INSTITUTE AT HOUSTON, Houston, TX
UNIVERSITY OF TEXAS MEDICAL BRANCH HOSPITALS, Galveston, TX
UNIVERSITY OF TEXAS STUDENT HEALTH CENTER (Formerly Student Health Center, University of Texas at Austin), Austin, TX
UNIVERSITY OF UTAH HEALTH SCIENCES CENTER, Salt Lake City, UT
UNIVERSITY OF VIRGINIA HOSPITALS, Charlottesville, VA
UNIVERSITY OF WISCONSIN HOSPITAL AND CLINICS, Madison, WI
UNIVERSITY PARK HOSPITAL, Tyler, TX
UNIVERSITY PEDIATRIC HOSPITAL, San Juan, P.R.
UNIVERSITY PSYCHIATRIC SERIVCES, Omaha, NE, See University Hospital-University of Nebraska
UPPER CONNECTICUT VALLEY HOSPITAL, Colebrook, NH
UPSON COUNTY HOSPITAL, Thomaston, GA
UTAH STATE HOSPITAL, Provo, UT
UTAH VALLEY REGIONAL MEDICAL CENTER, Provo, UT
UTICA-MARCY PSYCHIATRIC CENTER, Utica, NY, See Mohawk Valley Psychiatric Center
UVALDE COUNTY HOSPITAL AUTHORITY, Uvalde, TX

V

VAIL VALLEY MEDICAL CENTER, Vail, CO
VAL VERDE MEMORIAL HOSPITAL, Del Rio, TX
VALDESE GENERAL HOSPITAL, Valdese, NC
VALDEZ COMMUNITY HOSPITAL, Valdez, AK
VALDOSTA CENTER, Valdosta, GA, See Greenleaf Center
VALENCIA PRESBYTERIAN HOSPITAL, Belen, NM
VALLEY BAPTIST MEDICAL CENTER, Harlingen, TX
VALLEY CHILDREN'S HOSPITAL, Fresno, CA
VALLEY COMMUNITY HOSPITAL, Santa Maria, CA
VALLEY COMMUNITY HOSPITAL (Formerly Glenn General Hospital), Willows, CA
VALLEY COMMUNITY HOSPITAL, Dallas, OR
VALLEY COMMUNITY HOSPITAL, Brownsville, TX, See HCA Valley Regional Medical Center
VALLEY COUNTY HOSPITAL, Cascade, ID
VALLEY COUNTY HOSPITAL, Ord, NE
VALLEY FORGE MEDICAL CENTER AND HOSPITAL, Norristown, PA
VALLEY GENERAL HOSPITAL, Monroe, WA
VALLEY HOSPITAL, Palmer, AK
VALLEY HOSPITAL, Ridgewood, NJ
VALLEY HOSPITAL (Formerly Valley Psychiatric Hospital), Chattanooga, TN
VALLEY HOSPITAL AND MEDICAL CENTER, Spokane, WA
VALLEY HOSPITAL MEDICAL CENTER, Los Angeles, CA
VALLEY HOSPITAL MEDICAL CENTER, Las Vegas, NV
VALLEY INSTITUTE OF PSYCHIATRY, Owensboro, KY
VALLEY LUTHERAN HOSPITAL, Mesa, AZ
VALLEY MEDICAL CENTER, Renton, WA
VALLEY MEDICAL CENTER OF FRESNO, Fresno, CA
VALLEY MEMORIAL HOSPITAL, Livermore, CA
VALLEY PARK MEDICAL CENTER, Canoga Park, CA, See Northwestern University-Medx Regional Medical Center-West Valley
VALLEY PRESBYTERIAN HOSPITAL, Los Angeles, CA
VALLEY REGIONAL HOSPITAL, Claremont, NH
VALLEY SPRINGS COMMUNITY HOSPITAL, De Funiak Springs, FL
VALLEY VIEW COMMUNITY HOSPITAL, Youngtown, AZ
VALLEY VIEW HOSPITAL, Glenwood Springs, CO
VALLEY VIEW MEDICAL CENTER, Morganfield, KY
VALLEY VIEW MEDICAL CENTER, Cedar City, UT
VALLEY VIEW MEDICAL CENTER, Plymouth, WI
VALLEY VIEW REGIONAL HOSPITAL (Formerly Valley View Hospital), Ada, OK
VALLEY WEST GENERAL HOSPITAL, Los Gatos, CA, See Mission Oaks Hospital
VAN BUREN COMMUNITY HOSPITAL, Van Buren, ME
VAN BUREN COUNTY MEMORIAL HOSPITAL, Clinton, AR
VAN BUREN COUNTY MEMORIAL HOSPITAL, Keosauqua, IA
VAN NUYS COMMUNITY HOSPITAL, Los Angeles, CA
VAN NUYS HOSPITAL, Los Angeles, CA
VAN VLEET MEMORIAL CANCER CENTER, Memphis, TN, See University of Tennessee Medical Center
VAN WERT COUNTY HOSPITAL, Van Wert, OH
VANCOUVER MEMORIAL HOSPITAL, Vancouver, WA, See Southwest Washington Hospitals
VANDERBILT UNIVERSITY HOSPITAL, Nashville, TN
VASSAR BROTHERS HOSPITAL, Poughkeepsie, NY
VAUGHAN REGIONAL MEDICAL CENTER, Selma, AL
VENICE HOSPITAL, Venice, FL
VENTURA COUNTY MEDICAL CENTER, Ventura, CA
VERDUGO HILLS HOSPITAL, Glendale, CA
VERMILLION COUNTY HOSPITAL, Clinton, IN
VERMONT STATE HOSPITAL, Waterbury, VT
VERNON MEMORIAL HOSPITAL, Viroqua, WI
VETERANS ADMINISTRATION CENTER, Fargo, ND
VETERANS ADMINISTRATION CENTER, Cheyenne, WY
VETERANS ADMINISTRATION HOSPITAL, Hines, IL
VETERANS ADMINISTRATION HOSPITAL, Fort Harrison, MT
VETERANS ADMINISTRATION HOSPITAL, Salisbury, NC
VETERANS ADMINISTRATION LAKESIDE MEDICAL CENTER, Chicago, IL
VETERANS ADMINISTRATION MEDICAL CENTER, Birmingham, AL
VETERANS ADMINISTRATION MEDICAL CENTER, Montgomery, AL

VETERANS ADMINISTRATION MEDICAL CENTER, Tuscaloosa, AL
VETERANS ADMINISTRATION MEDICAL CENTER, Tuskegee, AL
VETERANS ADMINISTRATION MEDICAL CENTER, Phoenix, AZ
VETERANS ADMINISTRATION MEDICAL CENTER, Prescott, AZ
VETERANS ADMINISTRATION MEDICAL CENTER, Tucson, AZ
VETERANS ADMINISTRATION MEDICAL CENTER, Fayetteville, AR
VETERANS ADMINISTRATION MEDICAL CENTER, Fresno, CA
VETERANS ADMINISTRATION MEDICAL CENTER, Livermore, CA
VETERANS ADMINISTRATION MEDICAL CENTER, Long Beach, CA
VETERANS ADMINISTRATION MEDICAL CENTER, Los Angeles, CA
VETERANS ADMINISTRATION MEDICAL CENTER, Martinez, CA
VETERANS ADMINISTRATION MEDICAL CENTER, Palo Alto, CA
VETERANS ADMINISTRATION MEDICAL CENTER, San Diego, CA
VETERANS ADMINISTRATION MEDICAL CENTER, San Francisco, CA
VETERANS ADMINISTRATION MEDICAL CENTER, Denver, CO
VETERANS ADMINISTRATION MEDICAL CENTER, Fort Lyon, CO
VETERANS ADMINISTRATION MEDICAL CENTER, Grand Junction, CO
VETERANS ADMINISTRATION MEDICAL CENTER, Newington, CT
VETERANS ADMINISTRATION MEDICAL CENTER, West Haven, CT
VETERANS ADMINISTRATION MEDICAL CENTER, Wilmington, DE
VETERANS ADMINISTRATION MEDICAL CENTER, Washington, DC
VETERANS ADMINISTRATION MEDICAL CENTER, Bay Pines, FL
VETERANS ADMINISTRATION MEDICAL CENTER, Gainesville, FL
VETERANS ADMINISTRATION MEDICAL CENTER, Lake City, FL
VETERANS ADMINISTRATION MEDICAL CENTER, Miami, FL
VETERANS ADMINISTRATION MEDICAL CENTER, Augusta, GA
VETERANS ADMINISTRATION MEDICAL CENTER, Dublin, GA
VETERANS ADMINISTRATION MEDICAL CENTER, Boise, ID
VETERANS ADMINISTRATION MEDICAL CENTER, Danville, IL
VETERANS ADMINISTRATION MEDICAL CENTER, Marion, IL
VETERANS ADMINISTRATION MEDICAL CENTER, North Chicago, IL
VETERANS ADMINISTRATION MEDICAL CENTER, Fort Wayne, IN
VETERANS ADMINISTRATION MEDICAL CENTER, Marion, IN
VETERANS ADMINISTRATION MEDICAL CENTER, Des Moines, IA
VETERANS ADMINISTRATION MEDICAL CENTER, Iowa City, IA
VETERANS ADMINISTRATION MEDICAL CENTER, Knoxville, IA
VETERANS ADMINISTRATION MEDICAL CENTER, Leavenworth, KS
VETERANS ADMINISTRATION MEDICAL CENTER, Wichita, KS
VETERANS ADMINISTRATION MEDICAL CENTER, Lexington, KY
VETERANS ADMINISTRATION MEDICAL CENTER, Louisville, KY
VETERANS ADMINISTRATION MEDICAL CENTER, Alexandria, LA
VETERANS ADMINISTRATION MEDICAL CENTER, New Orleans, LA
VETERANS ADMINISTRATION MEDICAL CENTER, Shreveport, LA
VETERANS ADMINISTRATION MEDICAL CENTER, Togus, ME
VETERANS ADMINISTRATION MEDICAL CENTER, Baltimore, MD
VETERANS ADMINISTRATION MEDICAL CENTER, Fort Howard, MD
VETERANS ADMINISTRATION MEDICAL CENTER, Perry Point, MD
VETERANS ADMINISTRATION MEDICAL CENTER, Boston, MA
VETERANS ADMINISTRATION MEDICAL CENTER, Boston, MA, See Boockton-West Roxbury Veterans Administration Medical Center
VETERANS ADMINISTRATION MEDICAL CENTER, Brockton, MA, See Brockton-West Roxbury Veterans Administration Medical Center
VETERANS ADMINISTRATION MEDICAL CENTER, Northampton, MA
VETERANS ADMINISTRATION MEDICAL CENTER, Allen Park, MI
VETERANS ADMINISTRATION MEDICAL CENTER, Ann Arbor, MI
VETERANS ADMINISTRATION MEDICAL CENTER, Battle Creek, MI
VETERANS ADMINISTRATION MEDICAL CENTER, Iron Mountain, MI
VETERANS ADMINISTRATION MEDICAL CENTER, Saginaw, MI
VETERANS ADMINISTRATION MEDICAL CENTER, Minneapolis, MN
VETERANS ADMINISTRATION MEDICAL CENTER, St. Cloud, MN
VETERANS ADMINISTRATION MEDICAL CENTER, Biloxi, MS
VETERANS ADMINISTRATION MEDICAL CENTER, Jackson, MS
VETERANS ADMINISTRATION MEDICAL CENTER, Kansas City, MO
VETERANS ADMINISTRATION MEDICAL CENTER, Poplar Bluff, MO
VETERANS ADMINISTRATION MEDICAL CENTER, St. Louis, MO
VETERANS ADMINISTRATION MEDICAL CENTER, Miles City, MT
VETERANS ADMINISTRATION MEDICAL CENTER, Grand Island, NE
VETERANS ADMINISTRATION MEDICAL CENTER, Lincoln, NE
VETERANS ADMINISTRATION MEDICAL CENTER, Omaha, NE
VETERANS ADMINISTRATION MEDICAL CENTER, Reno, NV
VETERANS ADMINISTRATION MEDICAL CENTER, Manchester, NH
VETERANS ADMINISTRATION MEDICAL CENTER, East Orange, NJ
VETERANS ADMINISTRATION MEDICAL CENTER, Lyons, NJ
VETERANS ADMINISTRATION MEDICAL CENTER, Albuquerque, NM
VETERANS ADMINISTRATION MEDICAL CENTER, Albany, NY
VETERANS ADMINISTRATION MEDICAL CENTER, Batavia, NY
VETERANS ADMINISTRATION MEDICAL CENTER, Bath, NY
VETERANS ADMINISTRATION MEDICAL CENTER, Buffalo, NY
VETERANS ADMINISTRATION MEDICAL CENTER, Castle Point, NY
VETERANS ADMINISTRATION MEDICAL CENTER, Brooklyn, NY
VETERANS ADMINISTRATION MEDICAL CENTER, New York, NY
VETERANS ADMINISTRATION MEDICAL CENTER, Bronx, NY
VETERANS ADMINISTRATION MEDICAL CENTER, Northport, NY
VETERANS ADMINISTRATION MEDICAL CENTER, Syracuse, NY
VETERANS ADMINISTRATION MEDICAL CENTER, Asheville, NC
VETERANS ADMINISTRATION MEDICAL CENTER, Durham, NC
VETERANS ADMINISTRATION MEDICAL CENTER, Fayetteville, NC
VETERANS ADMINISTRATION MEDICAL CENTER, Chillicothe, OH
VETERANS ADMINISTRATION MEDICAL CENTER, Cincinnati, OH
VETERANS ADMINISTRATION MEDICAL CENTER, Dayton, OH
VETERANS ADMINISTRATION MEDICAL CENTER, Muskogee, OK
VETERANS ADMINISTRATION MEDICAL CENTER, Oklahoma City, OK
VETERANS ADMINISTRATION MEDICAL CENTER, Portland, OR
VETERANS ADMINISTRATION MEDICAL CENTER, Roseburg, OR
VETERANS ADMINISTRATION MEDICAL CENTER, Altoona, PA
VETERANS ADMINISTRATION MEDICAL CENTER, Butler, PA
VETERANS ADMINISTRATION MEDICAL CENTER, Coatesville, PA
VETERANS ADMINISTRATION MEDICAL CENTER, Erie, PA
VETERANS ADMINISTRATION MEDICAL CENTER, Lebanon, PA
VETERANS ADMINISTRATION MEDICAL CENTER, Philadelphia, PA
VETERANS ADMINISTRATION MEDICAL CENTER, Pittsburgh, PA
VETERANS ADMINISTRATION MEDICAL CENTER, Pittsburgh, PA
VETERANS ADMINISTRATION MEDICAL CENTER, Wilkes-Barre, PA
VETERANS ADMINISTRATION MEDICAL CENTER, Providence, RI
VETERANS ADMINISTRATION MEDICAL CENTER, Charleston, SC
VETERANS ADMINISTRATION MEDICAL CENTER, Fort Meade, SD
VETERANS ADMINISTRATION MEDICAL CENTER, Hot Springs, SD
VETERANS ADMINISTRATION MEDICAL CENTER, Memphis, TN
VETERANS ADMINISTRATION MEDICAL CENTER, Mountain Home, TN
VETERANS ADMINISTRATION MEDICAL CENTER, Murfreesboro, TN, See Alvin C. York Veterans Administration Medical Center
VETERANS ADMINISTRATION MEDICAL CENTER, Nashville, TN
VETERANS ADMINISTRATION MEDICAL CENTER, Amarillo, TX
VETERANS ADMINISTRATION MEDICAL CENTER, Big Spring, TX
VETERANS ADMINISTRATION MEDICAL CENTER, Dallas, TX
VETERANS ADMINISTRATION MEDICAL CENTER, Houston, TX
VETERANS ADMINISTRATION MEDICAL CENTER, Kerrville, TX
VETERANS ADMINISTRATION MEDICAL CENTER, Marlin, TX
VETERANS ADMINISTRATION MEDICAL CENTER, Waco, TX
VETERANS ADMINISTRATION MEDICAL CENTER, Salt Lake City, UT
VETERANS ADMINISTRATION MEDICAL CENTER, White River Junction, VT
VETERANS ADMINISTRATION MEDICAL CENTER, Hampton, VA
VETERANS ADMINISTRATION MEDICAL CENTER, Salem, VA
VETERANS ADMINISTRATION MEDICAL CENTER, Seattle, WA
VETERANS ADMINISTRATION MEDICAL CENTER, Spokane, WA
VETERANS ADMINISTRATION MEDICAL CENTER, Tacoma, WA
VETERANS ADMINISTRATION MEDICAL CENTER, Walla Walla, WA
VETERANS ADMINISTRATION MEDICAL CENTER, Beckley, WV
VETERANS ADMINISTRATION MEDICAL CENTER, Huntington, WV
VETERANS ADMINISTRATION MEDICAL CENTER, Martinsburg, WV
VETERANS ADMINISTRATION MEDICAL CENTER (Formerly Veterans Administration Hospital), Milwaukee, WI
VETERANS ADMINISTRATION MEDICAL CENTER, Tomah, WI
VETERANS ADMINISTRATION MEDICAL CENTER, Sheridan, WY
VETERANS ADMINISTRATION MEDICAL CENTER, San Juan, P.R.
VETERANS ADMINISTRATION MEDICAL CENTER, Cleveland, OH
VETERANS ADMINISTRATION MEDICAL CENTER ATLANTA, Decatur, GA
VETERANS ADMINISTRATION MEDICAL CENTER-WEST LOS ANGELES, Los Angeles, CA
VETERANS ADMINISTRATION WEST SIDE MEDICAL CENTER, Chicago, IL
VETERANS HOME AND HOSPITAL, Rocky Hill, CT
VETERANS HOME OF CALIFORNIA, Yountville, CA
VETERANS MEMORIAL HOSPITAL, Waukon, IA
VETERANS MEMORIAL HOSPITAL OF MEIGS COUNTY, Pomeroy, OH
VICKSBURG MEDICAL CENTER, Vicksburg, MS
VICTOR VALLEY COMMUNITY HOSPITAL, Victorville, CA
VICTORIA HOSPITAL, Miami, FL
VICTORIA REGIONAL MEDICAL CENTER, Victoria, TX
VICTORY MEMORIAL HOSPITAL, Waukegan, IL
VICTORY MEMORIAL HOSPITAL, Brooklyn, NY
VICTORY MEMORIAL HOSPITAL, Stanley, WI
VILLA FELICIANA GERIATRIC HOSPITAL, Jackson, LA

VILLA ST. JOHN VIANNEY HOSPITAL, Downingtown, PA
VILLAGE OAKS REGIONAL HOSPITAL, San Antonio, TX
VILLAVIEW COMMUNITY HOSPITAL, San Diego, CA
VINCENT MEMORIAL HOSPITAL, Boston, MA, See Massachusetts General Hospital
VINELAND DEVELOPMENT CENTER HOSPITAL, Vineland, NJ
VIRGINIA BAPTIST HOSPITAL, Lynchburg, VA
VIRGINIA BEACH GENERAL HOSPITAL, Virginia Beach, VA
VIRGINIA CENTER FOR PSYCHIATRIC, Portsmouth, VA, See Portsmouth Psychiatric Center
VIRGINIA CENTER FOR PSYCHIATRY, Norfolk, VA, See Norfolk Psychiatric Center
VIRGINIA GAY HOSPITAL, Vinton, IA
VIRGINIA MASON HOSPITAL, Seattle, WA
VIRGINIA REGIONAL MEDICAL CENTER, Virginia, MN
VIRGINIA STATE PENITENTIARY HOSPITAL, Richmond, VA
VISALIA COMMUNITY HOSPITAL, Visalia, CA
VISITORS HOSPITAL, Buchanan, MI
VISTA HILL HOSPITAL, Chula Vista, CA
VISTA HILLS MEDICAL CENTER, El Paso, TX, See HCA Vista Hills Medical Center
VISTA SANDIA HOSPITAL, Albuquerque, NM
VOLUNTEER GENERAL HOSPITAL, Martin, TN

W

W. A. FOOTE MEMORIAL HOSPITAL, Jackson, MI
W. J. BARGE MEMORIAL HOSPITAL, Greenville, SC
WABASH COUNTY HOSPITAL, Wabash, IN
WABASH GENERAL HOSPITAL DISTRICT, Mount Carmel, IL
WABASH VALLEY HOSPITAL (Formerly Wabash Valley Hospital Mental Health Center), West Lafayette, IN
WACONIA RIDGEVIEW HOSPITAL, Waconia, MN
WADLEY REGIONAL MEDICAL CENTER, Texarkana, TX
WADSWORTH VETERANS ADMINISTRATION DIVISION, Los Angeles, CA, See Veterans Administration Medical Center-West Los Angeles
WADSWORTH-RITTMAN HOSPITAL, Wadsworth, OH
WAGNER COMMUNITY MEMORIAL HOSPITAL (Formerly Listed Under Wagner Heights), Wagner, SD
WAGNER GENERAL HOSPITAL, Palacios, TX
WAGONER COMMUNITY HOSPITAL, Wagoner, OK
WAHIAWA GENERAL HOSPITAL, Wahiawa, HI
WAKE COUNTY ALCOHOLISM TREATMENT CENTER, Raleigh, NC
WAKE MEDICAL CENTER, Raleigh, NC
WAKEFIELD HEALTHCARE CENTER, Wakefield, NE
WALDO COUNTY GENERAL HOSPITAL, Belfast, ME
WALDO GENERAL HOSPITAL, Seattle, WA, See Fifth Avenue Medical Center
WALKER MEMORIAL HOSPITAL, Avon Park, FL
WALKER REGIONAL MEDICAL CENTER, Jasper, AL
WALLA WALLA GENERAL HOSPITAL, Walla Walla, WA
WALLACE THOMSON HOSPITAL, Union, SC
WALLKILL VALLEY GENERAL HOSPITAL, Sussex, NJ
WALLOWA MEMORIAL HOSPITAL, Enterprise, OR
WALLS REGIONAL HOSPITAL (Formerly Memorial Hospital), Cleburne, TX
WALNUT CREEK HOSPITAL, Walnut Creek, CA, See CPC Walnut Creek Hospital
WALSH DISTRICT HOSPITAL, Walsh, CO
WALSON ARMY COMMUNITY HOSPITAL, Fort Dix, NJ
WALTER B. JONES ALCOHOLIC REHABILITATION CENTER, Greenville, NC
WALTER E. FERNALD STATE SCHOOL, Waltham, MA
WALTER KNOX MEMORIAL HOSPITAL, Emmett, ID
WALTER O. BOSWELL MEMORIAL HOSPITAL, Sun City, AZ
WALTER P. REUTHER PSYCHIATRIC HOSPITAL (Formerly Listed Under Eloise), Westland, MI
WALTER REED ARMY MEDICAL CENTER, Washington, DC
WALTER REED MEMORIAL HOSPITAL, Gloucester, VA
WALTERS HOSPITAL FOUNDATION, Michigan City, IN, See Kingwood Hospital
WALTHALL COUNTY GENERAL HOSPITAL, Tylertown, MS
WALTHAMWESTON HOSPITAL AND MEDICAL CENTER, Waltham, MA
WALTON COUNTY HOSPITAL AND WALTON COUNTY HOSPITAL CONVALESCENT WING, Monroe, GA
WAMEGO CITY HOSPITAL, Wamego, KS
WAR MEMORIAL HOSPITAL, Sault Ste Marie, MI
WARD MEMORIAL HOSPITAL, Monahans, TX
WARDENBURG STUDENT HEALTH SERVICE, Boulder, CO
WARM SPRINGS REHABILITATION HOSPITAL, Gonzales, TX
WARMINSTER GENERAL HOSPITAL, Warminster, PA
WARNER BROWN HOSPITAL, El Dorado, AR
WARRACK MEDICAL CENTER HOSPITAL, Santa Rosa, CA
WARREN COMMUNITY HOSPITAL, Warren, MN
WARREN DENTAL ARTS HOSPITAL, Warren, PA
WARREN GENERAL HOSPITAL, Warren, OH
WARREN GENERAL HOSPITAL, Warren, PA
WARREN HOSPITAL, Phillipsburg, NJ
WARREN MEMORIAL HOSPITAL, Friend, NE
WARREN MEMORIAL HOSPITAL, Front Royal, VA
WARREN REGIONAL HOSPITAL (Formerly Warren County General Hospital), McMinnville, TN
WARREN STATE HOSPITAL, Warren, PA
WARRICK HOSPITAL, Boonville, IN
WASATCH COUNTY HOSPITAL, Heber City, UT
WASECA AREA MEMORIAL HOSPITAL, Waseca, MN
WASHAKIE MEMORIAL HOSPITAL, Worland, WY
WASHINGTON ADVENTIST HOSPITAL, Takoma Park, MD
WASHINGTON COUNTY HOSPITAL, Chatom, AL
WASHINGTON COUNTY HOSPITAL, Nashville, IL
WASHINGTON COUNTY HOSPITAL, Washington, IA
WASHINGTON COUNTY HOSPITAL, Washington, KS
WASHINGTON COUNTY HOSPITAL, Hagerstown, MD
WASHINGTON COUNTY HOSPITAL, Plymouth, NC
WASHINGTON COUNTY HOSPITAL, DISTRICT ONE, Hanover, KS
WASHINGTON COUNTY MEMORIAL HOSPITAL, Salem, IN
WASHINGTON COUNTY MEMORIAL HOSPITAL, Potosi, MO
WASHINGTON COUNTY PUBLIC HOSPITAL, Akron, CO
WASHINGTON HOSPITAL, Fremont, CA
WASHINGTON HOSPITAL, Washington, PA
WASHINGTON HOSPITAL CENTER, Washington, DC
WASHINGTON MEDICAL CENTER, Culver City, CA
WASHINGTON REGIONAL MEDICAL CENTER, Fayetteville, AR
WASHINGTON TOWNSHIP DIVISION, Turnersville, NJ, See Kennedy Memorial Hospitals-University Medical Center
WASHINGTON-ST. TAMMANY CHARITY HOSPITAL, Bogalusa, LA
WASHOE MEDICAL CENTER, Reno, NV
WATAUGA COUNTY HOSPITAL, Boone, NC
WATERBURY HOSPITAL, Waterbury, CT
WATERMAN MEDICAL CENTER, Eustis, FL
WATERTOWN MEMORIAL HOSPITAL, Watertown, WI
WATERVILLE OSTEOPATHIC HOSPITAL, Waterville, ME
WATKINS MEMORIAL HOSPITAL, Lawrence, KS
WATONGA MUNICIPAL HOSPITAL, Watonga, OK
WATONWAN MEMORIAL HOSPITAL, St. James, MN
WATSONVILLE COMMUNITY HOSPITAL, Watsonville, CA
WAUKESHA MEMORIAL HOSPITAL, Waukesha, WI
WAUPUN MEMORIAL HOSPITAL, Waupun, WI
WAUSAU HOSPITAL CENTER, Wausau, WI
WAVERLY MUNICIPAL HOSPITAL, Waverly, IA
WAYNE COUNTY GENERAL HOSPITAL, Waynesboro, TN
WAYNE COUNTY HOSPITAL, Corydon, IA
WAYNE COUNTY HOSPITAL, Monticello, KY
WAYNE COUNTY MEMORIAL HOSPITAL, Honesdale, PA
WAYNE GENERAL HOSPITAL, Waynesboro, MS
WAYNE GENERAL HOSPITAL, Wayne, NJ
WAYNE HOSPITAL, Greenville, OH
WAYNE MEMORIAL HOSPITAL, Jesup, GA
WAYNE MEMORIAL HOSPITAL (Formerly Wayne County Memorial Hospital), Goldsboro, NC
WAYNESBORO COMMUNITY HOSPITAL, Waynesboro, VA
WAYNESBORO HOSPITAL, Waynesboro, PA
WEBSTER COUNTY COMMUNITY HOSPITAL, Red Cloud, NE
WEBSTER COUNTY MEMORIAL HOSPITAL, Webster Springs, WV
WEBSTER GENERAL HOSPITAL, Eupora, MS
WEDOWEE HOSPITAL, Wedowee, AL
WEED ARMY COMMUNITY HOSPITAL, Fort Irwin, CA
WEEKS MEMORIAL HOSPITAL, Lancaster, NH
WEINER MEMORIAL MEDICAL CENTER, Marshall, MN
WEIRTON MEDICAL CENTER, Weirton, WV
WEIRTON OSTEOPATHIC HOSPITAL, Weirton, WV
WEISBROD MEMORIAL HOSPITAL, Eads, CO
WELBORN MEMORIAL BAPTIST HOSPITAL, Evansville, IN
WELKIND REHABILITATION HOSPITAL, Chester, NJ
WELLINGTON COMMUNITY HOSPITAL, Wellington, OH
WELLINGTON HOSPITAL AND CLINIC, Wellington, KS
WELLS COMMUNITY HOSPITAL, Bluffton, IN
WELLS HOSPITAL (Formerly Wells Municipal Hospital), Wells, MN
WELLSPRING FOUNDATION, Bethlehem, CT
WELSH GENERAL HOSPITAL, Welsh, LA
WENTWORTH-DOUGLASS HOSPITAL, Dover, NH
WERNERSVILLE STATE HOSPITAL, Wernersville, PA
WESKOTA MEMORIAL MEDICAL CENTER, Wessington Springs, SD
WESLEY LONG COMMUNITY HOSPITAL, Greensboro, NC
WESLEY MEDICAL CENTER, Wichita, KS
WESSON MEMORIAL HOSPITAL, Springfield, MA, See Baystate Medical Center
WESSON WOMEN'S HOSPITAL, Springfield, MA, See Baystate Medical Center
WEST ALLIS MEMORIAL HOSPITAL, West Allis, WI
WEST CALCASIEU-CAMERON HOSPITAL, Sulphur, LA
WEST CARROLL MEMORIAL HOSPITAL, Oak Grove, LA
WEST COMMUNITY HOSPITAL, West, TX
WEST COVINA HOSPITAL, West Covina, CA
WEST ESSEX GENERAL HOSPITAL, Livingston, NJ
WEST FELICIANA PARISH HOSPITAL, Saint Francisville, LA
WEST FLORIDA HOSPITAL, Pensacola, FL, See West Florida Regional Medical Center
WEST FLORIDA REGIONAL MEDICAL CENTER, Pensacola, FL
WEST FRANKFORT UNITED MINE WORKERS OF AMERICA UNION HOSPITAL, West Frankfort, IL
WEST GEORGIA MEDICAL CENTER, La Grange, GA
WEST HOLLYWOOD HOSPITAL, Los Angeles, CA
WEST HOLT MEMORIAL HOSPITAL, Atkinson, NE
WEST HOUSTON MEDICAL CENTER, Houston, TX
WEST HUDSON HOSPITAL, Kearny, NJ
WEST JEFFERSON MEDICAL CENTER (Formerly West Jefferson General Hospital), Marrero, LA
WEST JERSEY HOSPITAL GARDEN STATE DIVISION (Formerly West Jersey Health Systems, Garden State Community Hospital Division), Marlton, NJ
WEST JERSEY HOSPITAL SOUTHERN DIVISION, Berlin, NJ
WEST JERSEY HOSPITAL, EASTERN DIVISION, Voorhees, NJ
WEST JERSEY HOSPITAL, NORTHERN DIVISION, Camden, NJ
WEST LAKE HOSPITAL, Longwood, FL
WEST NEBRASKA GENERAL HOSPITAL, Scottsbluff, NE
WEST OAKS-PSYCHIATRIC INSTITUTE OF HOUSTON, Houston, TX
WEST ORANGE MEMORIAL HOSPITAL, Winter Garden, FL
WEST PACES FERRY HOSPITAL, Atlanta, GA, See HCA West Paces Ferry Hospital
WEST PARK HOSPITAL, Los Angeles, CA, See Northwestern University-MEDX Regional Medical Center-West Valley
WEST PARK HOSPITAL, Philadelphia, PA
WEST PARK HOSPITAL, Cody, WY
WEST SEATTLE COMMUNITY HOSPITAL, Seattle, WA
WEST SHORE HOSPITAL, Manistee, MI
WEST SIDE COMMUNITY HOSPITAL DISTRICT, Newman, CA
WEST SIDE DISTRICT HOSPITAL, Taft, CA
WEST SIDE HOSPITAL, Nashville, TN, See HCA West Side Hospital
WEST SUBURBAN HOSPITAL MEDICAL CENTER, Oak Park, IL
WEST TEXAS HOSPITAL, Lubbock, TX
WEST VALLEY CAMELBACK HOSPITAL, Glendale, AZ
WEST VALLEY MEDICAL CENTER (Formerly Caldwell Memorial Hospital), Caldwell, ID
WEST VIRGINIA UNIVERSITY HOSPITAL, Morgantown, WV
WEST VOLUSIA MEMORIAL HOSPITAL, De Land, FL
WESTBOROUGH STATE HOSPITAL, Westborough, MA
WESTBROOK COMMUNITY HOSPITAL, Westbrook, ME
WESTBURY HOSPITAL, Houston, TX, See AMI Westbury Hospital
WESTCHESTER COUNTY MEDICAL CENTER, Valhalla, NY
WESTCHESTER GENERAL HOSPITAL, Miami, FL
WESTCHESTER SQUARE MEDICAL CENTER, Bronx, NY
WESTERLY HOSPITAL, Westerly, RI
WESTERN BAPTIST HOSPITAL, Paducah, KY
WESTERN INSTITUTE OF NEUROPSYCHIATRY, Salt Lake City, UT
WESTERN LANE HOSPITAL, Florence, OR
WESTERN MARYLAND CENTER, Hagerstown, MD
WESTERN MASSACHUSETTS HOSPITAL, Westfield, MA
WESTERN MEDICAL CENTER, Santa Ana, CA
WESTERN MEDICAL CENTER ANAHEIM, Anaheim, CA
WESTERN MENTAL HEALTH INSTITUTE, Western Institute, TN

WESTERN MISSOURI MEDICAL CENTER (Formerly Johnson County Memorial Hospital), Warrensburg, MO
WESTERN MISSOURI MENTAL HEALTH CENTER, Kansas City, MO
WESTERN NEW YORK CHILDREN'S PSYCHIATRIC CENTER, West Seneca, NY
WESTERN PENNSYLVANIA HOSPITAL, Pittsburgh, PA
WESTERN RESERVE CARE SYSTEMS-NORTHSIDE MEDICAL CENTER, Youngstown, OH
WESTERN RESERVE CARE SYSTEMS-SOUTHSIDE MEDICAL CENTER, Youngstown, OH
WESTERN RESERVE PSYCHIATRIC HABILITATION CENTER, Northfield, OH
WESTERN STATE HOSPITAL, Hopkinsville, KY
WESTERN STATE HOSPITAL, Fort Supply, OK
WESTERN STATE HOSPITAL, Staunton, VA
WESTERN STATE HOSPITAL, Fort Steilacoom, WA
WESTERN WAKE HOSPITAL, Apex, NC
WESTFIELD MEMORIAL HOSPITAL, Westfield, NY
WESTGATE MEDICAL CENTER, Denton, TX, See AMI Denton Regional Medical Center
WESTLAKE COMMUNITY HOSPITAL, Westlake Village, CA
WESTLAKE COMMUNITY HOSPITAL, Melrose Park, IL
WESTLAKE CUMBERLAND HOSPITAL, Columbia, KY
WESTLAND MEDICAL CENTER, Westland, MI
WESTMORELAND HOSPITAL, Greensburg, PA
WESTMORELAND MCGINNIS HOSPITAL, Ligonier, PA
WESTON COUNTY MEMORIAL HOSPITAL, Newcastle, WY
WESTON HOSPITAL, Weston, WV
WESTPARK COMMUNITY HOSPITAL, Hammond, LA, See AMI Westpark Community Hospital
WESTSIDE HOSPITAL, Los Angeles, CA
WESTVIEW HOSPITAL, Indianapolis, IN
WETUMKA GENERAL HOSPITAL, Wetumka, OK
WETZEL COUNTY HOSPITAL, New Martinsville, WV
WEWOKA MEMORIAL HOSPITAL, Wewoka, OK
WHEATLAND MEMORIAL HOSPITAL, Harlowton, MT
WHEATON COMMUNITY HOSPITAL, Wheaton, MN
WHEELER COUNTY HOSPITAL, Glenwood, GA
WHEELER HOSPITAL, Gilroy, CA
WHEELING HOSPITAL, Wheeling, WV
WHEELOCK MEMORIAL HOSPITAL, Goodrich, MI
WHIDBEY GENERAL HOSPITAL, Coupeville, WA
WHIDDEN MEMORIAL HOSPITAL, Everett, MA
WHISLER MEMORIAL HOSPITAL, DENISON UNIVERSITY, Granville, OH
WHISPERING PINES HOSPITAL, Keene, NH
WHITCOMB MEMORIAL HOSPITAL, Grand Prairie, TX
WHITE COMMUNITY HOSPITAL, Aurora, MN
WHITE COUNTY COMMUNITY HOSPITAL, Sparta, TN
WHITE COUNTY MEMORIAL HOSPITAL, Searcy, AR
WHITE COUNTY MEMORIAL HOSPITAL, Monticello, IN
WHITE HALL HOSPITAL, White Hall, IL
WHITE MEMORIAL MEDICAL CENTER, Los Angeles, CA
WHITE MOUNTAIN COMMUNITIES HOSPITAL, Springerville, AZ
WHITE PLAINS HOSPITAL MEDICAL CENTER, White Plains, NY
WHITE RIVER MEDICAL CENTER, Batesville, AR
WHITESBURG APPALACHIAN REGIONAL HOSPITAL, Whitesburg, KY
WHITFIELD MEDICAL SURGICAL HOSPITAL, Whitfield, MS
WHITINSVILLE DIVISION, Whitinsville, MA, See Milford-Whitinsville Regional Hospital, Milford
WHITLEY COUNTY MEMORIAL HOSPITAL, Columbia City, IN
WHITMAN COMMUNITY HOSPITAL, Colfax, WA
WHITTEN CENTER HOSPITAL, Clinton, SC
WHITTIER HOSPITAL MEDICAL CENTER, Whittier, CA
WHITTIER REHABILITATION HOSPITAL, Haverhill, MA
WICHITA COUNTY HOSPITAL, Leoti, KS
WICHITA FALLS STATE HOSPITAL, Wichita Falls, TX
WICHITA GENERAL HOSPITAL, Wichita Falls, TX
WILBARGER GENERAL HOSPITAL, Vernon, TX
WILD ROSE COMMUNITY MEMORIAL HOSPITAL, Wild Rose, WI
WILFORD HALL U. S. AIR FORCE MEDICAL CENTER, Lackland Air Force Base, TX
WILHELMINA MEDICAL CENTER, Mena, AR
WILKES GENERAL HOSPITAL, North Wilkesboro, NC
WILKES-BARRE GENERAL HOSPITAL, Wilkes-Barre, PA
WILLAMETTE FALLS HOSPITAL, Oregon City, OR
WILLAPA HARBOR HOSPITAL, South Bend, WA
WILLARD AREA HOSPITAL, Willard, OH
WILLARD PSYCHIATRIC CENTER, Willard, NY
WILLIAM B. KESSLER MEMORIAL HOSPITAL, Hammonton, NJ
WILLIAM BEAUMONT ARMY MEDICAL CENTER, El Paso, TX
WILLIAM BEAUMONT HOSPITAL, Royal Oak, MI
WILLIAM BEAUMONT HOSPITAL-TROY, Troy, MI
WILLIAM BEE RIRIE HOSPITAL, Ely, NV
WILLIAM F. BOWLD HOSPITAL, Memphis, TN, See University of Tennessee Medical Center
WILLIAM JENNINGS BRYAN DORN VETERANS HOSPITAL, Columbia, SC
WILLIAM N. WISHARD MEMORIAL HOSPITAL, Indianapolis, IN
WILLIAM NEWTON MEMORIAL HOSPITAL, Winfield, KS
WILLIAM S. HALL PSYCHIATRIC INSTITUTE, Columbia, SC
WILLIAM S. MIDDLETON MEMORIAL VETERANS HOSPITAL, Madison, WI
WILLIAM W. BACKUS HOSPITAL, Norwich, CT
WILLIAM W. HASTINGS INDIAN HOSPITAL, Tahlequah, OK
WILLIAMS COUNTY GENERAL HOSPITAL, Montpelier, OH, See Community Hospitals of Williams County, Bryan
WILLIAMSBURG COMMUNITY HOSPITAL, Williamsburg, VA
WILLIAMSBURG COUNTY MEMORIAL HOSPITAL, Kingstree, SC
WILLIAMSON APPALACHIAN REGIONAL HOSPITAL, South Williamson, KY
WILLIAMSON MEDICAL CENTER (Formerly Williamson County Hospital), Franklin, TN
WILLIAMSON MEMORIAL HOSPITAL, Williamson, WV
WILLIAMSPORT HOSPITAL AND MEDICAL CENTER (Formerly Williamsport Hospital), Williamsport, PA
WILLIE D. MILLER EYE CENTER, Chattanooga, TN, See Erlanger Medical Center
WILLINGWAY HOSPITAL, Statesboro, GA
WILLIS-KNIGHTON MEDICAL CENTER, Shreveport, LA
WILLISTON MEMORIAL HOSPITAL, Williston, FL
WILLMAR REGIONAL TREATMENT CENTER (Formerly Willmar State Hospital), Willmar, MN
WILLOW CREEK ADOLESCENT CENTER, Arlington, TX
WILLOW CREST HOSPITAL, Miami, OK
WILLOW VIEW HOSPITAL, Spencer, OK
WILLS EYE HOSPITAL, Philadelphia, PA
WILLS MEMORIAL HOSPITAL, Washington, GA
WILMINGTON HOSPITAL, Wilmington, DE, See Wilmington Medical Center
WILSON CENTER FOR ADOLESCENT PSYCHIATRY (Formerly Constance Bultman Wilson Center for Adolescent Psychiatry), Faribault, MN
WILSON CLINIC AND HOSPITAL, Darlington, SC
WILSON COUNTY HOSPITAL, Neodesha, KS
WILSON MEMORIAL HOSPITAL, Wilson, NC
WILSON MEMORIAL HOSPITAL, Sidney, OH
WILSON MEMORIAL HOSPITAL, Floresville, TX
WILSON N. JONES MEMORIAL HOSPITAL, Sherman, TX
WINCHESTER HOSPITAL, Winchester, MA
WINCHESTER MEDICAL CENTER, Winchester, VA
WINDBER HOSPITAL AND WHEELING CLINIC, Windber, PA
WINDHAM COMMUNITY MEMORIAL HOSPITAL, Willimantic, CT
WINDOM AREA HOSPITAL, Windom, MN
WINDSOR HOSPITAL, Chagrin Falls, OH
WINFIELD CARRAWAY HOSPITAL, Winfield, AL
WINFIELD STATE HOSPITAL AND TRAINING CENTER, Winfield, KS
WING MEMORIAL HOSPITAL AND MEDICAL CENTERS (Formerly Wing Memorial Hospital), Palmer, MA
WINN ARMY COMMUNITY HOSPITAL, Fort Stewart, GA
WINNEBAGO MENTAL HEALTH INSTITUTE, Winnebago, WI
WINNESHIEK COUNTY MEMORIAL HOSPITAL, Decorah, IA
WINONA MEMORIAL HOSPITAL, Indianapolis, IN
WINSLOW MEMORIAL HOSPITAL, Winslow, AZ
WINSTED MEMORIAL HOSPITAL, Winsted, CT
WINSTON COUNTY COMMUNITY HOSPITAL AND NURSING HOME, Louisville, MS
WINTER GARDEN MEDICAL CENTER, Dilley, TX
WINTER HAVEN HOSPITAL, Winter Haven, FL
WINTER PARK MEMORIAL HOSPITAL, Winter Park, FL
WINTHROP HOSPITAL, Winthrop, MA
WINTHROP-UNIVERSITY HOSPITAL, Mineola, NY
WIREGRASS HOSPITAL, Geneva, AL
WIRTH OSTEOPATHIC HOSPITAL, Oakland City, IN
WISE APPALACHIAN REGIONAL HOSPITAL, Wise, VA
WISHEK COMMUNITY HOSPITAL, Wishek, ND
WITHAM MEMORIAL HOSPITAL, Lebanon, IN
WOHL-WASHINGTON UNIVERSITY CLINICS, St. Louis, MO, See Barnes Hospital
WOMACK ARMY COMMUNITY HOSPITAL, Fort Bragg, NC
WOMAN'S CHRISTIAN ASSOCIATION HOSPITAL, Jamestown, NY
WOMAN'S HOSPITAL, Baton Rouge, LA
WOMAN'S HOSPITAL, Jackson, MS
WOMAN'S HOSPITAL, New York, NY, See St. Luke's-Roosevelt Hospital Center
WOMAN'S HOSPITAL OF TEXAS, Houston, TX
WOMEN AND INFANTS HOSPITAL OF RHODE ISLAND, Providence, RI
WOMEN'S AND CHILDREN'S HOSPITAL (Formerly Woman's Hospital of Acadiana), Lafayette, LA
WOMENS HOSPITAL, Las Vegas, NV
WOOD COUNTY CENTRAL HOSPITAL DISTRICT, Quitman, TX
WOOD COUNTY HOSPITAL, Bowling Green, OH
WOOD RIVER TOWNSHIP HOSPITAL, Wood River, IL
WOODBINE DEVELOPMENTAL CENTER, Woodbine, NJ
WOODBRIDGE DEVELOPMENT CENTER, Woodbridge, NJ
WOODFORD MEMORIAL HOSPITAL, Versailles, KY
WOODHULL MEDICAL AND MENTAL HEALTH CENTER, Brooklyn, NY
WOODLAND COMMUNITY HOSPITAL, Cullman, AL
WOODLAND HILLS HOSPITAL, West Monroe, LA
WOODLAND MEMORIAL HOSPITAL, Woodland, CA
WOODLAND PARK HOSPITAL, Portland, OR
WOODLAWN HOSPITAL, Rochester, IN
WOODRIDGE HOSPITAL, Clayton, GA
WOODRIDGE HOSPITAL, Johnson City, TN
WOODROW WILSON REHABILITATION CENTER-HOSPITAL, Fishersville, VA
WOODRUFF COMMUNITY HOSPITAL, Long Beach, CA
WOODRUFF COUNTY HOSPITAL, McCrory, AR
WOODS MEMORIAL HOSPITAL, Etowah, TN
WOODS PSYCHIATRIC INSTITUTE, Abilene, TX
WOODSIDE MEDICAL, Pontiac, MI
WOODSIDE RECEIVING HOSPITAL, Youngstown, OH
WOODSIDE WOMEN'S HOSPITAL, Redwood City, CA
WOODSTOCK HOSPITAL (Formerly Cherokee Atomedic Hospital), Woodstock, GA
WOODVIEW REGIONAL HOSPITAL (Formerly Listed Under Tioga), Pineville, LA
WOODVIEW-CALABASAS HOSPITAL, Calabasas, CA
WOODVILLE STATE HOSPITAL, Carnegie, PA
WOODWARD HOSPITAL AND HEALTH CENTER, Woodward, OK
WOODWARD STATE HOSPITAL-SCHOOL, Woodward, IA
WOONSOCKET HOSPITAL, Woonsocket, RI
WOOSTER COMMUNITY HOSPITAL, Wooster, OH
WORCESTER CITY HOSPITAL, Worcester, MA
WORCESTER COUNTY HOSPITAL, Boylston, MA
WORCESTER HAHNEMANN HOSPITAL, Worcester, MA
WORCESTER MEMORIAL HOSPITAL, Worcester, MA
WORCESTER STATE HOSPITAL, Worcester, MA
WORTH COMMUNITY HOSPITAL, Sylvester, GA
WORTHAM HOSPITAL, Wortham, TX
WORTHINGTON REGIONAL HOSPITAL, Worthington, MN
WRANGELL GENERAL HOSPITAL AND LONG TERM CARE FACILITY, Wrangell, AK
WRAY COMMUNITY DISTRICT HOSPITAL, Wray, CO
WRIGHT MEMORIAL HOSPITAL, Trenton, MO
WUESTHOFF MEMORIAL HOSPITAL, Rockledge, FL
WYANDOT MEMORIAL HOSPITAL, Upper Sandusky, OH
WYANDOTTE GENERAL HOSPITAL, Wyandotte, MI
WYCKOFF HEIGHTS HOSPITAL, Brooklyn, NY
WYLIE COMMUNITY HOSPITAL, Wylie, TX
WYMAN PARK MEDICAL CENTER (Formerly Wyman Park Health Systems), Baltimore, MD
WYOMING COUNTY COMMUNITY HOSPITAL, Warsaw, NY
WYOMING GENERAL HOSPITAL, Mullens, WV
WYOMING MEDICAL CENTER (Formerly Memorial Hospital of Natrona County), Casper, WY
WYOMING STATE HOSPITAL, Evanston, WY
WYTHE COUNTY COMMUNITY HOSPITAL, Wytheville, VA
WYTHEVILLE HOSPITAL, Wytheville, VA

Y

YAKIMA VALLEY MEMORIAL HOSPITAL, Yakima, WA
YALE CLINIC AND HOSPITAL, Houston, TX
YALE COMMUNITY HOSPITAL, Yale, MI
YALE PSYCHIATRIC INSTITUTE, New Haven, CT
YALE UNIVERSITY HEALTH SERVICES (Formerly Yale University Health Services Center), New Haven, CT
YALE-NEW HAVEN HOSPITAL, New Haven, CT
YALOBUSHA GENERAL HOSPITAL, Water Valley, MS
YAVAPAI REGIONAL MEDICAL CENTER, Prescott, AZ
YELL COUNTY HOSPITAL, Danville, AR

YETTIE KERSTING MEMORIAL HOSPITAL, Liberty, TX
YOAKUM CATHOLIC HOSPITAL, Yoakum, TX
YOAKUM COUNTY HOSPITAL, Denver City, TX
YOLO GENERAL HOSPITAL, Woodland, CA
YONKERS GENERAL HOSPITAL, Yonkers, NY
YORK GENERAL HOSPITAL, York, NE
YORK HOSPITAL, York, ME
YORK HOSPITAL, York, PA
YORK PLAZA HOSPITAL AND MEDICAL CENTER, Houston, TX
YOUNGSTOWN OSTEOPATHIC HOSPITAL, Youngstown, OH
YOUNKER MEMORIAL REHABILITATION CENTER, Des Moines, IA, See Iowa Methodist Medical Center
YOUVILLE REHABILITATION AND CHRONIC DISEASE HOSPITAL, Cambridge, MA
YPSILANTI REGIONAL PSYCHIATRIC HOSPITAL, Ypsilanti, MI
YSLETA GENERAL HOSPITAL, El Paso, TX
YUMA DISTRICT HOSPITAL, Yuma, CO
YUMA REGIONAL MEDICAL CENTER, Yuma, AZ

Z

ZEELAND COMMUNITY HOSPITAL, Zeeland, MI
ZUMBROTA COMMUNITY HOSPITAL, Zumbrota, MN
ZURBRUGG MEMORIAL HOSPITAL-RIVERSIDE DIVISION, Riverside, NJ
ZURBRUGG MEMORIAL HOSPITAL, RANCOCAS VALLEY DIVISION, Willingboro, NJ

Accredited Long-Term Care Facilities

The long-term care facilities listed have been accredited as of March 11, 1987, by the Joint Commission on Accreditation of Hospitals by decision of the Accreditation Committee of the Board of Commissioners.

The facilities listed here have been found to be in substantial compliance with the Joint Commission standards for long-term care facilities, as found in the Accreditation Manual for Long-Term Care Facilities.

Those facilities designated by a star (★) are associate members of the American Hospital Association.

Alabama

ANNISTON
Golden Springs Health Care
CENTREVILLE
Bibb Medical Center Hospital
FAYETTE
Fayette County Hospital
FLORENCE
Eliza Coffee Memorial Hospital
GENEVA
Wiregrass Hospital and Nursing Home
HAMILTON
Marion County Nursing Home
MONTGOMERY
Veterans Administration Medical Center
MOULTON
Moulton Nursing Home
SCOTTSBORO
Jackson County Hospital
SYLACAUGA
Sylacauga Nursing Home
YORK
Sumpter Nursing Center

Arizona

DOUGLAS
Southeast Arizona Medical Center
FLORENCE
Pinal County Nursing Home
GLOBE
Gila County General Hospital
PHOENIX
Phoenix Memorial Hospital
Phoenix Mountain Nursing Center
Vantage Convalescent Center
Veterans Administration Medical Center
SCOTTSDALE
Scottsdale Convalescent Plaza
TUCSON
Santa Rosa Convalescent Center
Veterans Administration Medical Center
WICKENBURG
Community Hospital Association

Arkansas

CAMDEN
Quachita County Hospital
HOT SPRINGS
AMI/National Park Medical
LITTLE ROCK
Veterans Administration Medical Center
PINE BLUFF
Davis Skilled Nursing Facility
ROGERS
St. Mary-Rogers Memorial Hospital
WALNUT RIDGE
Lawrence Memorial Hospital

California

BAKERSFIELD
Mercy Hospital
BALDWIN PARK
Sierra View
BURBANK
Esther Parisean Pavilion
CARMICHAEL
★ Eskaton Manzanita Manor
Mount Olivette Care Center
DELANO
Delano Regional Medical Center
DOWNEY
Rancho Los Amigos Hospital
EL CAJON
El Cajon Valley Convalescent Center, Inc.
FRESNO
Neducak Medical Center
Veterans Administration
GARDEN GROVE
Orangegrove Rehabilitation Hospital
Palm Grove Convalescent Center
HIGHLAND PARK
Amberwood Convalescent Center
HOLLYWOOD
Brier Oak Terrace Convalescent Center
INGLEWOOD
Kaiser Foundation Hospital
JACKSON
Amador Hospital
LA JOLLA
Torrey Pines Convalescent Center
LA MESA
California Convalescent Hospital at La Mesa
LANCASTER
Los Angeles County High Desert Hospital
LINDSAY
Lindsay Hospital Medical
LOMA LINDA
Veterans Administration Medical Center—Jerry L. Pettis Memorial
LOMITA
Peninsula Rehabilitation Center
LONG BEACH
Alamitos-Belmont Rehabilitation Hospital
St. Mary Medical Center
Veterans Administration Medical Center
LOS ANGELES
Culver West Convalescent Hospital
Veterans Administration Medical Center—West Los Angeles
MENLO PARK
College Park Convalescence Hospital
MODESTO
Memorial Hospitals Association
MOSS BEACH
St. Catherine's Hospital
NATIONAL CITY
Friendship Manor Convalescent Center
ORINDA
Orinda Rehabilitation and Convalescent Hospital
PALO ALTO
Veterans Administration Medical Center
PASADENA
Kaiser Foundation Hospital
SACRAMENTO
Mercy Hospital of Sacramento
SAN DIEGO
Children's Convalescent Hospital
DBA/Knollwood West Convalescent Hospital
St. Paul's Health Care Center
SAN LEANDRO
St. Luke's Extended Care Hospital
SANTA ANA
Western Medical Center
SANTA BARBARA
Californian-Santa Barbara Convalescent Center
Pinecrest Hospital
SANTA MARIA
Villa Maria Convalescent Hospital
SANTEE
Edgemoor Geriatric Hospital
SEPULVEDA
Veterans Administration Medical Center
TORRANCE
Bay Harbor Rehabilitation Center
TUJUNGA
Oakview Convalescent Hospital
TUSTIN
Western Neuro Care Center
WALNUT CREEK
Walnut Creek Convalescent Hospital
WOODLAND HILLS
Motion Picture and TV Hospital
YOUNTVILLE
Veterans Home of California/Nelson M. Holderman Memorial Hospital

Colorado

CORTEZ
Vista Grande Nursing Home
DENVER
AMI Presbyterian-St. Luke's Medical Center
Beth Israel Hospital and Geriatric Center
Veterans Administration Medical Center
ESTES PARK
Prospect Park
NORTHGLENN
Castle Garden Nursing Home

★ *Refer to headnote above.*

RIFLE
Grand River Hospital District—E. Dene Moore Memorial Home
STEAMBOAT SPRINGS
Routt Memorial Hospital Extended Care

Connecticut

AVON
Avon Convalescent Home
BRANFORD
Branford Hills Health Care Center
CHESHIRE
New Lakeview Convalescent Home
DANBURY
Filosa Convalescent Home, Inc.
Glen Hill Convalescent Center
DARIEN
Darien Convalescent Center
EAST HAVEN
Talmadge Park Health Care Facility
FAIRFIELD
Jewish Home for the Elderly of Fairfield County
FORESTVILLE
Forestville Nursing Center
HAMDEN
Hamden Health Care Facility
MERIDEN
Meriden Nursing Home
MILFORD
Golden Hill Health Care Center
NEW BRITAIN
Andrew House Healthcare
NEW CANAAN
Waveny Care Center, Inc.
NEW HAVEN
New Fairview Hall Convalescent Home
Winthrop Continuing Care Center
NEW LONDON
Nutmeg Pavilion Healthcare
NEWINGTON
Jefferson House
NEWTOWN
Ashlar of Newtown
NORWICH
Hamilton Pavilion Health Center
ROCKVILLE
Rockville Memorial Nursing Home, Inc.
SHELTON
Flora and Mary Hewitt Memorial Hospital, Inc.
SIMSBURY
McLean Home
SOUTHBURY
River Glen Continuing Care Center
SOUTHINGTON
Woodmere Health Care Center
SOUTHPORT
Southport Manor Convalescent Center
TORRINGTON
Adams House Healthcare
WALLINGFORD
Brook Hollow Health Care Center
Masonic Home and Hospital
WATERBURY
Cedar Lane Rehabilitation and Health Care Center
Whitewood Rehabilitation Center
WEST HARTFORD
Brookview Health Care Facility
St. Mary Home, Inc.
WEST HAVEN
Sound View Specialized Care Center
Veterans Administration Medical Center
WINDSOR
Mountain View Health Care

Delaware

WILMINGTON
Veterans Administration Medical Center

District of Columbia

WASHINGTON
Benjamin King Health Center
Health Care Institute

Florida

APOPKA
Florida Living Nursing Center
BARTOW
Polk General Hospital/The
BOCA RATON
Boca Raton Convalescent Center
BRADENTON
Center at Manatee Springs
BROOKSVILLE
Brooksville Nursing Manor
CAPE CORAL
Cape Coral Nursing Pavilion
CLEARWATER
Morton F. Plant Hospital and Nursing Home
CRYSTAL RIVER
Cypress Cove Care Center
DADE CITY
Royal Oak Nursing Resort
HUDSON
Bear Creek Nursing Center
JACKSONVILLE
River Garden Hebrew Home for the Aged
JUPITER
Palm Beach Martin County
LAKE WALES
Lake Wales Convalescent Center
NEW PORT RICHEY
Heather Hill Nursing Home
Richey Manor Nursing Home
NORTH MIAMI
Villa Maria Nursing and Rehabilitation Center
NORTH MIAMI BEACH
Greynolds Park Manor, Inc.
PENSACOLA
Baptist Hospital Special Care
POMPANO BEACH
Colonial Palms Nursing Home, Inc.
SARASOTA
Beneva Nursing Pavilion
Sarasota Nursing Pavilion
SOUTH PASADENA
Deluxe Care Inn
TALLAHASSEE
Extended Care of Tallahassee
Long-Term Care Unit of Tallahassee Regional Medical Center
TAMPA
Medicenter of Tampa
University Park Convalescent Center, Inc.
Veterans Administration Medical Center
TRENTON
Medic-Ayers Nursing Center
VENICE
Venice Nursing Pavilion North
Venice Nursing Pavilion South
WEST PALM BEACH
Convalescent Center of the Palm Beaches

Georgia

ATLANTA
Christian City Convalescent Center
Piedmont Hospital
★ Wesley Woods Health Center
AUGUSTA
Georgia War Veterans Nursing Home
BLAKELY
Early Memorial Hospital
CAMILLA
Mitchell Convalescent Center
COLUMBUS
Muscogee Manor Nursing Home
Oak Manor, Inc.
Pine Manor, Inc.
DALLAS
Paulding Memorial Hospital
DECATUR
DeKalb General Hospital Nursing Home Unit
Veterans Administration Medical Center-Atlanta
DEMOREST
Habersham County Medical Center
DUBLIN
Veterans Administration Medical Center
EAST POINT
South Fulton Hospital Extended Care Unit
HIGH SHOALS
Family Life Enrichment Centers, Inc.
JESUP
Altamaha Convalescent Center
LA GRANGE
West Georgia Medical Center
MARIETTA
Hillhaven Rehabilitation and Convalescent Center
MILLEDGEVILLE
Central State Hospital
MONROE
Walton County Hospital Convalescent Unit
PELHAM
Pelham Parkway Nursing Home
ROSSVILLE
Rossville Convalescent Center, Inc.
ROYSTON
Brown Memorial Convalescent Center
SAVANNAH
Chatham Nursing Home
Hillhaven Convalescent Center
SPRINGFIELD
Effingham County Hospital and Extended Care Facility
SWAINSBORO
Emanuel County Hospital and Nursing Home

Hawaii

HILO
Hilo Hospital Extended Care Division
HONOLULU
Convalescent Center of Honolulu
Island Nursing Home
Kuakini Geriatric Care, Inc.
Nuuanu Hale Hospital
St. Francis Hospital
LIHUE
G. N. Wilcox Memorial Hospital and Health Center
WAHIAWA
Wahiawa General Hospital Skilled Nursing Facility and Intensive Care Facility

Idaho

IDAHO FALLS
Idaho Falls Hospital Nursing Home
LEWISTON
Lewiston Care Center

Illinois

ALTON
Eunice C. Smith Home/Long-Term Care of Alton Memorial Hospital
ANNA
Union County Skilled Nursing Home
BELLEVILLE
Four Fountains Inc.
BENSENVILLE
The Anchorage
BERWYN
Fairfax Health Care Center
CHICAGO
California Gardens Nursing
Chevy Chase Nursing Center
Halsted Terrace Nursing Center
Illinois Masonic Medical Center
Johnston R. Bowman Health Center for the Elderly at Rush-Presbyterian St. Luke's Medical Center
Lakeland Manor Nursing Center
Monroe Pavilion Health Care
Ora G. Morrow Nursing Center
Ravenswood Hospital Medical Center
Sherwin Manor Nursing Center
Wellington Plaza Nursing and Therapy Center, Inc.
Wentworth Nursing Center
CRESTWOOD
Crestwood Heights Nursing Centers
DANVILLE
Americana Healthcare Center
DECATUR
St. Mary's Hospital
DES PLAINES
Oakton Pavilion Healthcare
DIXON
Dixon Health Center
EAST PEORIA
Good Samaritan Nursing Home Corporation
EAST ST. LOUIS
Gateway Community Hospital
EVANSTON
St. Francis Extended Care Center
FAIRBURY
Helen Lewis Smith Pavilion
FRANKLIN PARK
Westlake Pavilion
GENESEO
Hammond-Henry District Hospital
GREENVILLE
Fair Oaks Nursing Home
HARVEY
Heather Manor Nursing Center
HILLSBORO
Hillsboro Hospital
HOMEWOOD
Mercy Health Care and Rehabilitation Center
HOOPESTON
Hoopeston Community Memorial Hospital and Nursing Home
INDIANHEAD PARK
White Oak Nursing Center
JOLIET
Deerbrook Nursing Center
LA GRANGE
Colonial Manor Living Center
LA GRANGE PARK
Fairview Health Care Center
LAKE BLUFF
Lake Bluff Health Care Center
MCLEANSBORO
Hamilton Memorial Nursing Center
MONTICELLO
Piatt County Nursing Home
MORTON GROVE
Bethany Terrace
MOUNT MORRIS
Pinecrest Manor
MOUNT VERNON
Jeffersonian, The
NAPERVILLE
Community Convalescent Center
Oxford Lane Nursing Center
NILES
Regency Nursing Centre
NORRIDGE
Norridge Nursing Centre
NORTH CHICAGO
Veterans Administration Medical Center
NORTHBROOK
Glen Oaks Nursing Home, Inc.
OAK FOREST
Oak Forest Hospital
OSWEGO
Tillers Nursing Home, Inc.
PARK RIDGE
Park Ridge Terrace Nursing Home
PEORIA
Lutheran Home of Greater Peoria
PEORIA HEIGHTS
Galena Park Home
RIVERWOODS
Brentwood North Nursing
ROCKFORD
★ Alma Nelson Manor
Amberwood Healthcare Centre
Briar Glen Healthcare Centre
Park Strathmoor
SKOKIE
Jacob and Marcelle Lieberman Geriatric Center
Old Orchard Manor
WATSEKA
Iroquois Memorial Hospital and Resident Home
WAUKEGAN
Bayside Terrace
Terrace Nursing Home
WHEATON
DuPage Convalescent Center
WILMETTE
Normandy House
ZION
Crown Manor

Indiana

BROWNSBURG
Golden Manor Health Care Center
CLINTON
Vermillion Convalescent Center
COVINGTON
Covington Manor Health Care Center
CROWN POINT
St. Anthony Home, Inc.
DYER
Regency Place of Dyer
EVANSVILLE
Holiday Care Center
Regina Continuing Care Center
HUNTINGTON
Miller's Merry Manor
INDIANAPOLIS
Indianapolis Jewish Home, Inc., Hooverwood
Northwest Manor Healthcare
LAFAYETTE
Lafayette Home Hospital, Inc.
LAWRENCEBURG
Terrace View Health Care Center
MADISON
Clifty Falls Convalescent Center
MARION
Veterans Administration Medical Center
MARTINSVILLE
The Heritage House Convalescent Center
MICHIGAN CITY
Woodview Rehabilitation Center
PLAINFIELD
Clarks Creek Health Care Center
PRINCETON
Forest Del Convalescent Center
Gibson General Hospital
RICHMOND
Reid Memorial Hospital-Jenkins Hall
SHELBYVILLE
Heritage House Children's Center, Inc.
SOUTH BEND
Regency Place
VALPARAISO
Willows Rehabilitation Center
VINCENNES
Crestview Convalescent Home
YORKTOWN
Yorktown Health Care Center

Iowa

ANAMOSA
Anamosa Care Center
BELLEVUE
Mill Valley Care Center
BETTENDORF
Bettendorf Health Care Center
BURLINGTON
St. Francis Continuation Care and Nursing Home Center
CARROLL
St. Anthony Nursing Home
CEDAR RAPIDS
Mercy Hospital, Hallmar Division
DANVILLE
Danville Care Center
EDGEWOOD
Edgewood Convalescent Home
ELKADER
Elkader Care Center
JEFFERSON
Greene County Medical Center
KNOXVILLE
Veterans Administration Medical Center Nursing Home

★ *Refer to headnote on page A357*

LONE TREE
Lone Tree Health Care Center
MARION
Willow Gardens Home and Nursing Home
MARSHALLTOWN
Iowa Veterans Home
McGREGOR
Great River Care Center
MONTEZUMA
Senior Home
MONTICELLO
Senior Home
NEW HAMPTON
Health Care Manor
NEW LONDON
New London Care Center
OTTUMWA
St. Joseph Hospital
PLEASANT VALLEY
Riverview Manor
STATE CENTER
State Center Manor
WHEATLAND
Wheatland Manor, Inc.

Kansas

ATCHISON
Atchison Hospital
HUTCHINSON
Hutchinson Hospital
LEAVENWORTH
Veterans Administration Medical Center
WICHITA
Veterans Administration Medical Center

Kentucky

BENTON
Marshall County Hospital and Long-Term Care Facility
BEREA
Berea Hospital, Inc.
DAWSON SPRINGS
Dawson Springs Health Care Center
GLASGOW
Homewood Health Care Center
HOPKINSVILLE
Pinecrest Manor
LEXINGTON
Veterans Administration Medical Center
LOUISVILLE
Nazareth Home
MADISONVILLE
Kentucky Rest Haven
MURRAY
Murray-Calloway County Hospital
PIKESVILLE
Mountain Manor—Pikesville
PRESTONBURG
Riverview Manor Nursing Home

Louisiana

ALEXANDRIA
Veterans Administration Medical Center
BATON ROUGE
Baton Rouge General Medical Center (The Guest House)
Baton Rouge General Medical Center
MONROE
St. Francis Medical Center
NATCHITOCHES
Natchitoches Parish Hospital Long-Term Care Unit
NEW ORLEANS
CPC Coliseum Medical Center
Jo Ellen Smith Medical Center
Lafon Nursing Home of Holy Family
ZACHARY
Lane Memorial Hospital

Maine

AUGUSTA
Augusta Mental Health Institute
DAMARISCOTTA
Miles Memorial Hospital
ROCKLAND
Knox Division—Penobscot Bay Medical Center—Intensive Care Facility
SANFORD
Hillcrest Manor Division

Maryland

BALTIMORE
Francis Scott Key Medical Center
Keswick Home for Incurables of Baltimore
Levindale Hebrew Geriatric Center
BETHESDA
Carriage Hill-Bethesda Inc.
FORT HOWARD
Veterans Administration Medical Center
PRINCE FREDERICK
Calvert House
SILVER SPRING
Carriage Hill Nursing Center

Massachusetts

ABINGTON
Colony House First Healthcare
ACTON
Suburban Manor Convalescent and Nursing Home, Inc.
ARLINGTON
Park Avenue Nursing Convalescent
BEDFORD
Edith Nourse Rogers Memorial
BEVERLY
Beverly Nursing Home
Blueberry Hill Healthcare
BOSTON
Resthaven Nursing Home
Sherrill House, Inc.
BRAINTREE
John Scott House Nursing Home, Inc.
BRIGHTON
Greenery Rehabilitation and Skilled Nursing Center
Oakwood Long Term Care Center
BROCKTON
Brockton-West Rosbury Veterans Administration Medical Center
Embassy House Healthcare
CONCORD
Rivercrest Long-Term Care Facility
DANVERS
Liberty Pavilion Nursing Home
EAST BOSTON
Columbus Nursing Home
EAST BRAINTREE
Elihu White Nursing and Rehabilitation Home
FALL RIVER
Kimwell Health Care Center
FRAMINGHAM
Cushing Hospital
GREAT BARRINGTON
Great Barrington Healthcare Nursing Home
Willowwood Nursing and Retirement Facility
HAVERHILL
Union Mission Nursing Home
HOLYOKE
Brookwood Court Nursing Home Skilled Nursing Facility
Buckley Nursing and Retirement Home
HYANNIS
Lewis Bay Convalescent Home
HYDE PARK
Parkwell Nursing Home
LANCASTER
River Terrace Healthcare
LEOMINSTER
Fairlawn Nursing Home, Inc.
LONGMEADOW
★ Jewish Nursing Home of Western Massachusetts
LOWELL
Christian Hill Convalescent Home
D'Youville Manor Nursing Home
LYNN
Lenox Hill Nursing and Rehabilitation Care Facility
MARBLEHEAD
Devereux Nursing Home
MIDDLEBORO
Forest Manor Long-Term Care Facility
MILFORD
Blaire House of Milford
MILTON
Milton Health Care Facility
NEW BEDFORD
Blaire House of New Bedford
Sacred Heart Nursing Home
NORTH ANDOVER
Stevens Hall Long-Term Care Facility
NORTH EASTON
Easton-Lincoln Nursing Home
NORWOOD
Charlwell House Nursing Home
Ellis Nursing Home
OAK BLUFFS
Martha's Vineyard Hospital
PALMER
Palmer House Healthcare
RANDOLPH
Hollywell Nursing Home, Inc.
ROSLINDALE
The Recuperative Center
RUTLAND
Rutland Heights Hospital
SALEM
Dr. J. Robert Shaughnessy Chronic Disease and Rehabilitation Hospital
SOUTH BOSTON
Marian Manor
SOUTH DARTMOUTH
Brandon Woods of Dartmouth
SPRINGFIELD
Baystate Medical Center
TEWKSBURY
Blaire House Long-Term Care Facility
WALTHAM
Reservoir Nursing Home, Inc.
WEBSTER
Webster Manor
WEYMOUTH
Colonial Nursing Home and Rehabilitation Center
WORCESTER
Blaire House Long-Term Care
Heywood Valley Nursing Home
West Side House

★ *Refer to headnote on page A357*

Michigan

ALLEN PARK
Allen Park Convalescent Home, Inc.
BATTLE CREEK
Calhoun County Medical Care Facility
BERRIEN CENTER
Berrien General Hospital
BLOOMFIELD HILLS
Georgian Bloomfield, Inc.
CHEBOYGAN
Community Memorial Hospital Long-Term Care Facility
DEARBORN HEIGHTS
Dearborn Heights Convalescent Center, Inc.
DETROIT
Americare Convalescent Center, Inc.
Jewish Home for the Aged No. 2
St. Clare Convalescent Center
ESSEXVILLE
Bay County Medical Care Facility
FARMINGTON
Oak Hill Nursing Home, Inc.
GRAND BLANC
Riverbend Nursing Home, Inc.
GRAND RAPIDS
Grand Valley Nursing Centre
Sherbrooke Nursing Home
GROSSE POINTE
Georgian East Nursing Center
HARBOR BEACH
Harbor Beach Community Hospital Long-Term Care Unit
HARPER WOODS
Cottage-Belmont Nursing Center
HOWELL
Greenbriar Convalescent Center
Livingston Care Center
LIVONIA
Dorvin Convalescent and Nursing Center, Inc.
Middlebelt Nursing Centre, Inc.
University Convalescent and Nursing Home
MARLETTE
Marlette Community Hospital
MONROE
Beach Nursing Home, Inc.
MOUNT CLEMENS
Martha T. Berry Memorial Medical Care Facility
MT. PLEASANT
Isabella County Medical Care
NORTHPORT
Leelanau Memorial Hospital Long-Term Care Unit
PLYMOUTH
Plymouth Court (Hendry)
PONTIAC
Grovecrest Convalescent Center, Inc.
Oakland County Medical Care Facility
REED CITY
Reed City Hospital Extended Care
RICHMOND
Medilodge of Richmond
ROGERS CITY
Presque Isle Extended Care Facility of Rogers City Hospital
ROSEVILLE
Cottage Rose Villa Nursing Center
SOUTHFIELD
Jewish Home for the Aged No. 1
WARREN
Abbey Convalescent and Nursing Home
WESTLAND
Walter P. Reuther Psychiatric Hospital
Westland Convalescent Center, Inc.

Minnesota

ANOKA
Anoka Maple Manor
ARDEN HILLS
Johanna Shores
BLOOMINGTON
Bloomington Maple Manor
CAMBRIDGE
Cambridge Health Care Center
CLOQUET
Community Memorial Hospital and Convalescent and Nursing Care Section
COLD SPRING
Assumption Nursing Home
COLUMBIA HEIGHTS
Crest View Lutheran Home Association
DETROIT LAKES
St. Mary's Nursing Home
FAIRMONT
Fairmont Community Hospital
FERGUS FALLS
Lake Regional Hospital and Nursing Home
GOLDEN VALLEY
Weldwood Health Care Center
GRAND RAPIDS
Itasca Memorial Hospital Convalescent and Nursing Care Unit
HASTINGS
Regina Memorial Hospital and Nursing Home
LONG PRAIRIE
Memorial Hospital and Nursing Home
MAPLEWOOD
Maplewood Maple Manor Care Center
MILACA
Elim Home

MINNEAPOLIS
Augustana Home of Minneapolis
Nicollet Health Care Center
St. Mary's Hospital and Rehabilitation Center
Walker Methodist Residence and Health Center, Inc.
MINNETONKA
Oak Terrace Nursing Home
NEW HOPE
Ambassador Health Care Center
NEW ULM
Sioux Valley Hospital, Inc.
PERHAM
Memorial Hospital and Homes
PINE CITY
Lakeside Nursing Home, Inc.
PRINCETON
Elim Home
ROBBINSDALE
Crystal Lake Health Care Center
ROSEAU
Roseau Area Hospital Convalescent and Nursing Care
ROSEVILLE
Golden Age Health Care Center, Inc.
Lake Ridge Health Care Center
SAUK CENTRE
St. Michael's Hospital and Nursing Home
ST. CLOUD
Veterans Administration Medical Center
ST. PAUL
Bethesda Lutheran Infirmary
Lyngblomsten Care Center
Sholom Home, Inc.
White House Health Care Center
STILLWATER
Stillwater Maple Manor Care
VIRGINIA
Virginia Municipal Hospital
WABASHA
St. Elizabeth Hospital and Convalescent and Nursing Care Unit
WACONIA
Waconia Health Care Center, Inc.
WASECA
Lake Shore Inn Nursing Home, Inc.
WAYZATA
Hillcrest Health Care and Retirement Center
WINONA
Community Memorial Hospital and Convalescent and Nursing Care Unit
WINSTED
St. Mary's Nursing Home
WOODBURY
Woodbury Health Care Center, Inc.

Mississippi

BAY SPRINGS
Jasper General Hospital and Nursing Home
BILOXI
Veterans Administration Medical Center
LOUISVILLE
Winston County Nursing Home
SARDIS
North Panola Regional Hospital and Nursing Center

Missouri

BRIDGETON
DePaul Community Health Center
CHESTERFIELD
Jewish Center for Aged
EUREKA
Price Memorial Skilled Nursing Facility
St. Joseph's Hill Infirmary
EXCELSIOR SPRINGS
Excelsior Springs City Convalescent Center
FREDERICKTOWN
Madison Memorial Hospital—Stockhoff Memorial Nursing Home
HAYTI
Pemiscot County Memorial Hospital
KANSAS CITY
Swope Ridge Rehabilitation
Trinity Lutheran Hospital
Truman Medical Center, East
MARCELINE
St. Francis Hospital
POPLAR BLUFF
Veterans Administration Medical Center
ST. LOUIS
Lutheran Charities Association Extended Care Facility
St. Anthony Medical Center

Montana

GLENDIVE
Glendive Community Hospital and Nursing Home
GREAT FALLS
Deaconess Skilled Nursing Center

Nebraska

AURORA
Memorial Hospital Long-Term Care Facility
BEATRICE
Beatrice Community Hospital and Health Center
FAIRBURY
Jefferson County Memorial Hospital, Inc.
FREMONT
Memorial Hospital of Dodge County Skilled Nursing Facility
GRAND ISLAND
Veterans Administration Medical Center
MACY
Carl T. Curtis Health Education Center
OMAHA
Douglas County Hospital and Annex
Immanuel-Fontanelle Home
Mercy Care Center

New Hampshire

CONCORD
New Hampshire Hospital
HANOVER
Hanover Terrace Healthcare Facility
NASHUA
Greenbriar Terrace Healthcare

New Jersey

BLACKWOOD
Camden County Health Services Center
CAMDEN
Plaza Medical Nursing Facility
CEDAR GROVE
Hartwyck West Nursing Home
Waterview Nursing Center
CLIFTON
Daughters of Miriam Center for the Aged
CRESSKILL
Dunroven Nursing Home
JERSEY CITY
Jewish Hospital and Rehabilitation Center
LAKEWOOD
Medicenter—Lakewood
LINWOOD
Linwood Convalescent Center
LYONS
Veterans Administration Medical Center
MEDFORD
Medford Convalescent and Nursing Center, Inc.
PLAINFIELD
Hartwych at Plainfield
WESTWOOD
Valley Nursing Home
WYCKOFF
Christian Health Care Center

New Mexico

ALBUQUERQUE
Pickard Presbyterian
LAS CRUCES
Mountain Shadows Health Care Center
PORTALES
Roosevelt General Hospital and Nursing Home
ROSWELL
Casa Maria Health Care Centre

New York

ALBANY
Veterans Administration Medical Center
AMITYVILLE
Broadlawn Manor Nursing Home
AMSTERDAM
Amsterdam Memorial Hospital and Skilled Nursing Facility
BATAVIA
Genesee County Nursing Home
Veterans Administration Medical Center
BATH
Veterans Administration Medical Center
BAYSIDE
Ozanam Hall of Queens Nursing Home, Inc.
★ St. Mary's Hospital for Children
BRONX
Bainbridge Nursing Home
★ Beth Abraham Hospital
★ Concourse Nursing Home
★ Daughters of Jacob Nursing Home Co.
Eastchester Park Nursing Home
Fieldston Lodge Nursing Home
Frances Schervier Home and Hospital
★ Hebrew Home for the Aged at Riverdale
Hebrew Hospital for the Chronically Sick
Kings Bridge Heights
Knightsbridge Heights Manor
Laconia Nursing Home
Montefiore Medical Center
Morningside House Nursing Home Co.
Morris Park Nursing Home
Pelham Parkway Nursing Home
Providence Rest Nursing Home
Split Rock Nursing Home
St. Patricks Home for the Aged
Wayne Skilled Nursing and Health Care Facility
Workmen's Circle Home and Infirmary for the Aged
BROOKLYN
Aishel Avraham Residential Health Facility
Baptist Medical Center of New York
Cobble Hill Nursing Home, Inc.
Menorah Home and Hospital

★ *Refer to headnote on page A357*

★ Metropolitan Jewish Geriatric Nursing Home Co., Inc.
Oxford Nursing Home
Palm Gardens Nursing Home
Rutland Nursing Home of Kingsbrook Jewish Medical Center
Samuel Schulman Institute
St. John's Episcopal Homes for the Aged and the Blind
Wartburg Nursing Home, Inc.
BUFFALO
Mercy Hospital of Buffalo
Nazareth Nursing Home and Health-Related Facility
Veterans Administration Medical Center
CAMBRIDGE
Mary McClellan Skilled Nursing Facility
CANANDAIGUA
Veterans Administration Medical Center
CASTLE POINT
Veterans Administration Medical Center
CATSKILL
Memorial Hospital and Nursing Home
CLIFTON SPRINGS
Clifton Springs Hospital and Clinic
COHOES
Mary and Alice Ford Nursing Home Company, Inc.
CORTLAND
Highgate Manor of Cortland
EDGEMERE
Rockaway Care Center
ELMIRA
Arnot-Ogden Memorial Hospital Skilled Nursing Facility
FAR ROCKAWAY
Bezalel Nursing Home
★ Haven Manor Health-Related Facility
Peninsula Hospital Center
FLUSHING
Flushing Manor Nursing and Care Center
Long Island Nursing Home
Waterview Nursing Care Center
FOREST HILLS
Fairview Nursing Home
GLEN COVE
Glengariff Corporation—Nursing Home
GOUVERNEUR
Kinney Nursing Home
GREAT NECK
Grace Plaza of Great Neck, Inc.
HAMILTON
Community Memorial Hospital Long-Term Care Facility
HYDE PARK
Victory Lake Nursing Center
ILION
Mohawk Valley Nursing Home, Inc.
IRVING
Lake Shore Hospital
JAMAICA
Margaret Tietz Center for Nursing Care, Inc.
JOHNSON CITY
Wilson Memorial Extended Care
LONG BEACH
Long Beach Memorial Nursing Home, Inc.
MALONE
The Alice Hyde Hospital Association
MASSAPEQUA
Park View Nursing Home, Inc.
MEDINA
Orchard Manor Nursing Home and Health-Related Facility, Inc.
MIDDLE VILLAGE
Dry Harbor Nursing Home and Health-Related Facility
MONSEY
Northern Metropolitan Rehabilitation Health Care Facility
MONTGOMERY
Montgomery Nursing Home
MOUNT VERNON
Shalom Nursing Home
NEW ROCHELLE
Howe Avenue Nursing Home
NEW YORK
American Nursing Home
Coler Memorial Hospital
De Witt Nursing Home
East Haven Health-Related Facility
Florence Nightingale Nursing Home
Goldwater Memorial Hospital Public Home Infirmary
★ Gouverneur Skilled Nursing Facility
NORTHPORT
Veterans Administration Medical Center
OGDENSBURG
St. Joseph's Home
ONEIDA
Oneida City Hospitals
ONEONTA
Aurelia Osborn Fox Memorial Hospital
PENN YAN
Soldiers and Sailors Memorial
PLATTSBURGH
Sacred Heart Home, Inc.
POMONA
Summit Park Hospital
PORT CHESTER
United Hospital—Long-Term Care
RHINEBECK
Ferncliff Nursing Home
ROCHESTER
Park Ridge Nursing Home
Wesley-on-East

ROCKAWAY PARK
Park Nursing Home
Promenade Nursing Home
ROME
Rome Hospital and Murphy Memorial Hospital
SARATOGA SPRINGS
Saratoga Hospital, The
Wesley Health Care Center, Inc.
SPRINGVILLE
Jennie B. Richard Chaffee Nursing Home
ST. ALBANS
Veterans Administration Medical Center
STAATSBURG
Hyde Park Nursing Home
STAMFORD
Community Hospital/Skilled
STATEN ISLAND
Clove Lake Nursing Home and Health-Related Facility
Eger Lutheran Home, Inc., and Eger Nursing Home
Golden Gate Health Care Center
★ Sea View Hospital and Home
Silver Lake Nursing Home
Verrazano Nursing Home
SYRACUSE
Loretto Geriatric Center
Veterans Administration Medical Center
TICONDEROGA
Moses-Ludington Nursing Home, Inc.
TROY
Highgate Manor of Rensselaer
James A. Eddy Memorial
UNIONDALE
A. Holly Patterson Home for Nassau County Aged and Infirm
VALHALLA
Ruth Taylor Institute Long-Term Care Facility
WARSAW
Wyoming County Community Hospital and Long-Term Care Facility
WATERTOWN
Samaritan-Keep Nursing Home, Inc.
WHITE PLAINS
★ Nathan Miller Center for Nursing Care, Inc.
WHITESTONE
Clearview Nursing Home

North Carolina

ASHEBORO
Brian Center of Asheboro
ASHEVILLE
Hillhaven Rehabilitation and Convalescent Center
Veterans Administration Medical Center
BLOWING ROCK
Blowing Rock Hospital and Long-Term Care, Inc.
BOONE
Watauga Nursing Care Center
BREVARD
Brian Center of Brevard, Inc.
BURLINGTON
Alamance Memorial Hospital
CANTON
Canton Health Care Center, Inc.
CHARLOTTE
Brian Center/Health
CLEMMONS
Blumenthal Jewish Home for the Aged
DANBURY
Stokes-Reynolds Memorial Hospital Skilled Nursing Facility
EDENTON
Chowan Hospital, Inc.
ELKIN
Hugh Chatham Memorial Hospital Nursing Center
GASTONIA
Brian Center Nursing Care-Gastonia
HUNTERSVILLE
Huntersville Hospital
JACKSONVILLE
Britthaven of Jacksonville
LENOIR
The Brian Center of Nursing Care-Lenoir
LUMBERTON
Southeastern General Hospital, Inc., Long-Term Care Facility
MONROE
Union Memorial Hospital
MOORESVILLE
The Brian Center of Nursing Care—Mooresville
RALEIGH
The Brian Center of Nursing Care—Raleigh
RUTHERFORDTON
Rutherford Nursing Center
SALISBURY
Rowan Manor Nursing Center
SILER CITY
Meadowbrook Manor
STATESVILLE
Brian Center of Nursing Care of Statesville
WADESBORO
Anson County Hospital
WILSON
North Carolina Special Care Center
WINSTON-SALEM
Silas Creek Manor
Winston-Salem Convalescent Center

North Dakota

FARGO
Elim Home
JAMESTOWN
Central Dakota Nursing Home
LISBON
Community Memorial Hospital
ROLLA
Rolla Community Hospital
VALLEY CITY
Sheyenne Care Center

Ohio

AKRON
Edwin Shaw Hospital
CINCINNATI
Drake Memorial Hospital
CLEVELAND
St. Augustine Manor
Sunny Acres Skilled Nursing Facility
CLEVELAND HEIGHTS
The Montefiore Home
COLUMBUS
Northland Terrace, Inc.
St. Luke Convalescent Center
Whetstone Convalescent Center
COSHOCTON
Coshocton County Memorial Hospital Extended Care Facility
DAYTON
King Tree Center, Inc.
Maria-Joseph Living Care Center
Veterans Administration Medical Center
FAIRFIELD
Community Multicare Center
GREEN SPRINGS
St. Francis Rehabilitation Hospital and Nursing Home
KIRTLAND
Western Reserve Convalescent Home
Western Reserve Extended Care, Inc.
LEBANON
Otterbein Home
MANSFIELD
Geriatric Center of Mansfield Memorial Homes
MARTINS FERRY
East Ohio Regional Hospital
MASSILLON
Hanover House, Inc.
Rose Lane Health Care Center
NAVARRE
Navarre Community Health Center
NEWARK
Newark Healthcare Centre
NORTH RANDALL
Suburban Pavilion, Inc.
NORWALK
Norwalk Memorial Home of Fisher-Titus Memorial Hospital
OAK HILL
Oak Hill Community Medical Center, Inc.
RIPLEY
Ohio Valley Manor Convalescent Center
SANDUSKY
Providence Hospital, Inc.
SEBRING
Crandall Medical Center
SYLVANIA
★ Lake Park Hospital and Nursing Care Center
TROY
Dettmer Hospital—Koester Unit
WADSWORTH
Wadsworth Health Care Center, Inc.
WESTERVILLE
Manor Care-Westerville Nursing Center
WESTLAKE
Lutheran Home, The

Oklahoma

ALTUS
Jackson County Memorial
ARDMORE
Oklahoma Veteran's Center
BARTLESVILLE
Jane Phillips Episcopal Memorial Medical Center, Geriatric Center
BEAVER
Beaver County Nursing Home
CLINTON
Oklahoma Veterans Center
NORMAN
Norman Veterans Center
OKLAHOMA CITY
Four Seasons Nursing Center of Northwest Oklahoma City
SULPHUR
Oklahoma Veteran's Center
TALIHINA
Oklahoma Veterans Administration Center—Talihina Division
TULSA
Hillcrest Medical Center

Oregon

COTTAGE GROVE
Cottage Grove Hospital
PORTLAND
Mount St. Joseph's Residence and Extended Care Center
Veterans Administration Medical Center
ROSEBURG
Rose Haven Nursing Center
Veterans Administration Medical Center

Pennsylvania

ALLENTOWN
Liberty Nursing Center
ALTOONA
Veterans Administration Medical Center
BRISTOL
Medicenter of America/Bristol
BUTLER
Veterans Administration Medical Center
CANONSBURG
Canonsburg General Hospital
CLARKS SUMMIT
Clarks Summit State Hospital
COALDALE
Coaldale State Geriatric Center
COATESVILLE
Veterans Administration Medical Center
COLUMBIA
Heatherbank Rehabilitation and Skilled Nursing Facility
CORNWALL
Cornwall Manor of the United Methodist Church
DANVILLE
Danville State Hospital
DOYLESTOWN
Medical Center for Aging
Neshaminy Manor Home
ERIE
Lake Erie Institute of Rehabilitation
HANOVER
Hanover General Hospital—Hillview House
HATBORO
The White Billet Nursing Home Corporation
HAVERFORD
Haverford State Hospital
HAZLETON
St. Luke Manor
St. Luke Pavilion
HOMESTEAD
Willis Nursing Center
LANCASTER
Lancashire Hall Nursing Home
LEBANON
Veterans Administration Medical Center
LITITZ
Moravian Manor
LOCK HAVEN
Lock Haven Hospital and Extended Care Facility
MEADVILLE
Wesbury United Methodist Home and Nursing Hospital
MECHANICSBURG
Seidle Memorial Hospital and Skilled Nursing Facility
MEDIA
Bishop Nursing Home, Inc.
Manchester House Nursing and Convalescent Center
MILFORD
Hillcrest Home
MUNCY
Muncy Valley Hospital Skilled Nursing Facility
NANTICOKE
St. Stanislaus Medical Care Center
OAKMONT
Oakmont Presbyterian Home
PHILADELPHIA
Ashton Hall Nursing Home
Episcopal Hospital
Friends Hall at Fox Chase
Philadelphia Nursing Home
Philadelphia State Hospital
PITTSBURGH
The Angelus Convalescent Center, Inc.
Wightman Health Center
QUINCY
Quincy United Methodist Home
SCRANTON
Allied Services Long-Term Care Facility
SEWICKLEY
Valley Care Nursing Home
VALENCIA
Valencia Woods Nursing Center
WARMINSTER
Centennial Springs Healthcare Center
WARRINGTON
Fox Nursing Home
WASHINGTON
Presbyterian Medical Center
WERNERSVILLE
Wernersville State Hospital
WEXFORD
Wexford House Nursing Center
WILKES BARRE
Veterans Administration Medical Center
YORK
Colonial Manor Nursing Home
Rest Haven—York

★ *Refer to headnote on page A357*

Rhode Island

CRANSTON
General Hospital at the Rhode Island Medical Center
PROVIDENCE
St. Elizabeth Home
WALLUM LAKE
Dr. U. E. Zambarano Memorial Hospital

South Carolina

AIKEN
Mattie C. Hall Health Care Center
ANDERSON
Anderson Health Care Center, Inc.
Latham Nursing Home
BEAUFORT
Bay View Nursing Center, Inc.
BENNETTSVILLE
Dundee Nursing Home
BISHOPVILLE
Lee County Memorial Hospital
CAMDEN
A. Sam Karesh Long-Term Care Center
CHESTER
Chester County Nursing Center
CLINTON
Bailey Nursing Home
COLUMBIA
Brian Center—Columbia
Brian Center of Nursing
Capitol Convalescent Center
C. M. Tucker Jr. Human Research Center
Veterans Administration Medical Center
CONWAY
Conway Nursing Center
GAFFNEY
Cherokee County Memorial
GREENVILLE
Greenville Hospital System
Oakmont West Nursing Center
GREENWOOD
Greenwood Nursing Home
LANCASTER
Marion Sims Nursing Center and Grace White Memorial Nursing Home
LAURENS
Laurens Nursing Center
LORIS
Loris Community Hospital Nursing Home
MOUNT PLEASANT
Charleston Nursing Center, Inc.
SENECA
Lila Doyle Nursing Care Facility
SUMTER
Cypress Nursing Facility Inc.
Hampton Nursing Center Inc.
Hopewell Intermediate Care Center
Williamsburg Nursing Center
YORK
Divine Saviour Hospital and Nursing Home

South Dakota

BROOKINGS
Brookings Hospital and Brook View Manor
FT. MEADE
Veterans Administration Medical Center
HOT SPRINGS
Veterans Administration Medical Center
LEMMON
Five Counties Hospital and Nursing Home
MILBANK
St. William's Home for the Aged
RAPID CITY
Rushmore National Health System

Tennessee

ATHENS
Athens Health Care Center, Inc.
CHATTANOOGA
Parkwood Health Care, Inc.
COLUMBIA
Columbia Health Care Center
Hillview Health Care Center
COOKEVILLE
Cookeville Health Care Center Inc.
DICKSON
Green Valley Health Care Center, Inc.
DUNLAP
Sequatchie Health Care Center, Inc.
DYERSBURG
Parkview Methodist Medical Center Convalescent Unit
ERWIN
Unicoi County Memorial Hospital Long-Term Care Unit
FAYETTEVILLE
Lincoln Health Care Facilities
FRANKLIN
Franklin Health Care Center
JOHNSON CITY
Colonial Hill Health Care Center
Veterans Administration Medical Center
KNOXVILLE
Knoxville Convalescent and Nursing Home, Inc.
Knoxville Health Care Center
LAWRENCEBURG
Lawrenceburg Health Care Center
LEWISBURG
Merihil Health Care Center
Oakwood Health Care Center
MCMINNVILLE
McMinnville Health Care Center
MEMPHIS
Allen Morgan Nursing Center
St. Francis Hospital
MILAN
Ridgewood Health Care Center, Inc.
MURFREESBORO
Murfreesboro Nursing Facility
Veterans Administration Medical Center
NASHVILLE
Middle Tennessee Mental Health Institute
Nashville Health Care Center
University Health Care Center
OAK RIDGE
Oak Ridge Health Care Center
ONEIDA
Scott County Hospital and Nursing Home
PULASKI
Pulaski Health Care Center
SEVIERVILLE
Fort Sanders Service Medical Center
SHELBYVILLE
Bedford County Nursing Home
SMITHVILLE
Sunny Point Health Care Center
SOMERVILLE
Somerville Health Care Center
SPARTA
Sparta Health Care Center
SPRINGFIELD
Springfield Health Care Center
TAZEWELL
Clairborne County Hospital and Nursing Home
WINCHESTER
Methodist Hospital of Middle Tennessee

Texas

AUSTIN
Holy Cross Hospital
BIG SPRINGS
Veterans Administration Medical Center
BUNA
Buna Nursing Home
CARTHAGE
Panola Nursing Home
DALLAS
Veterans Administration Medical Center
EL PASO
Four Seasons Nursing Home
GALVESTON
St. Mary's Hospital
HALE CENTER
High Plains Hospital and Nursing Home
MARLIN
Veterans Administration Medical Center
SAN ANGELO
Baptist Memorial Geriatric Center
TEMPLE
Veterans Administration Medical Center
WACO
Veterans Administration Medical Center

Utah

DRAPER
Lanore's Nursing Home
SALT LAKE CITY
Wasatch Villa Convalescent Center

Vermont

BRATTLEBORO
Brattleboro Retreat
BURLINGTON
Birchwood Terrace Healthcare
Medical Center Nursing Home
VERNON
Vernon Advent Christian Home
WHITE RIVER JUNCTION
Brookside Nursing Home, Inc.

Virginia

ALEXANDRIA
Goodwin House
Woodbine Nursing and Convalescent Center
ARLINGTON
Camelot Hall—Cherrydale
Crystal City Nursing Center
BRIDGEWATER
Bridgewater Home, Inc.
BRISTOL
Bristol Health Care Center, Inc.
CHARLOTTESVILLE
Martha Jefferson House
CHESAPEAKE
Camelot Hall Nursing Home
DANVILLE
Camelot Hall Nursing Home
FAIRFAX
Fairfax Nursing Center, Inc.
FRANKLIN
Southampton Memorial Hospital, East Pavilion
HAMPTON
Hampton Convalescent Center

★ *Refer to headnote on page A357*

HARRISONBURG
Camelot Hall Nursing Home
LEESBURG
Loudoun Memorial Hospital Long-Term Care Facility
LYNCHBURG
Camelot Hall Nursing Home
Guggenheimer Memorial Hospital
Virginia Baptist Hospital Skilled Nursing Facility
MARION
Francis Marion Manor
NEWPORT NEWS
James River Convalescent Center, Inc.
Patrick Henry Hospital for the Chronically Ill, Inc.
NORFOLK
Hillhaven Rehabilitation and Convalescent Center
PORTSMOUTH
Manning Convalescent Home
RICHMOND
Camelot Hall Nursing Home
University Park
Veterans Administration Medical Center
The Windsor
SALEM
Veterans Administration Medical Center
SOUTH HILL
Community Memorial Hospital—W. S. Hundley Annex
VINTON
Camelot Hall Nursing Home
VIRGINIA BEACH
Camelot Hall Nursing Home
Medicenter of America, Inc.—Virginia Beach
WINCHESTER
Hillcrest Manor Nursing Home, Inc.

Washington

CHEHALIS
St. Helen Hospital
KIRKLAND
Evergreen Vista Convalescent Center, Inc.
MERCER ISLAND
Mercer Island Villa
REDMOND
Cascade Vista Convalescent Center
RENTON
Valley Villa Care Center
SEATTLE
Arden Nursing Home
Moderncare—West Seattle, Inc.
Park Ridge Care Center
Park West Care Center, Inc.
SPOKANE
Veterans Administration Medical Center
TACOMA
Orchard Park Convalescent and Rehabilitation Center
Veterans Administration Medical Center
VANCOUVER
Hillhaven Convalescent Center

West Virginia

BECKLEY
Veterans Administration Center
ELKINS
Elkins Convalescent Hospital
GRAFTON
Wallace B. Murphy, M.D. Nursing Care Facility
MARTINSBURG
Veterans Administration Medical Center
PARKERSBURG
Parkview Health Care Center

Wisconsin

ALGOMA
Algoma Memorial Hospital and Long-Term Care Unit
APPLETON
Appleton Extended Care Center
Outagamie County Health Center
BARABOO
Jefferson Meadows Care Center
BELOIT
Caravilla
BERLIN
Juliett Manor
CUBA CITY
Southwest Health Center Nursing Home
CUMBERLAND
Cumberland Memorial Hospital and Extended Care Unit
DODGEVILLE
Memorial Hospital of Iowa
EAU CLAIRE
The Clairemont
EDGERTON
Memorial Community Hospital and Long-Term Care Unit
FOND DU LAC
St. Francis Home
GLENDALE
AMS Green Tree Health Care Center
GRANTSBURG
Burnett General Hospital
GREENFIELD
Clement Manor

JANESVILLE
Cedar Crest Health Center
Rock County Health Services Complex
JEFFERSON
Countryside Home
LA CROSSE
Hillview Nursing Home
St. Francis Nursing Home
LADYSMITH
Rusk County Memorial Hospital
MADISON
Attic Angel Nursing Home
Methodist Health Center
Oakwood Lutheran Homes Association, Inc.
MARSHFIELD
Norwood Health Center
MEDFORD
Memorial Nursing Home
MEQUON
Mequon Care Center
MILWAUKEE
DePaul Rehabilitation
Milwaukee County Nursing Home
Milwaukee Jewish Home
St. Mary's Nursing Home
Veterans Administration Medical Center
OCONOMOWOC
Lutheran Homes of Oconomowoc
OSHKOSH
Bethel Home Inc.
Evergreen Manor, Inc.
OSSEO
Osseo Area Municipal Hospital and Nursing Home
OWEN
Clark County Health Care Center
PARK FALLS
Park Manor, Ltd.
PLYMOUTH
Valley View Medical Center
REEDSBURG
Edward Snyder Nursing Home
Sauk County Health Care Center
RICHLAND CENTER
Pine Valley Manor
RIVER FALLS
River Falls Area Hospital—Kinnie Home Division
SHEBOYGAN
Meadow View Manor Nursing Home, Inc.
SOUTH MILWAUKEE
Franciscan Villa
STANLEY
Victory Memorial Hospital
TOMAH
Veterans Administration Medical Center
TWO RIVERS
Hamilton Memorial Home
WEST ALLIS
Methodist Manor Health Care, Inc.
Villa Clement, Inc.
WEST SALEM
Lakeview Health Center
WISCONSIN RAPIDS
Riverview Manor

Wyoming

BUFFALO
Johnson County Memorial Hospital—Amie Holt Nursing Home
CHEYENNE
Veterans Administration Medical Center
CODY
West Park Hospital
POWELL
Powell Hospital and Nursing Home
SHERIDAN
Veterans Administration Medical Center
WHEATLAND
Platte County Memorial Hospital

U.S. Associated Areas

Puerto Rico

HUMACAO
Ryder Memorial Hospital

★ *Refer to headnote on page A357*

Multihospital Systems, Multistate Alliances and Networks

Introduction

Multihospital Systems

The American Hospital Association first sought to identify multihospital systems in 1973 when it distributed an AHA Special Survey on Selected Hospital Topics to hospitals throughout the United States. The survey defined a multihospital system as an organization consisting of two or more hospitals for which at least one of the following conditions existed:

1. The hospitals are legally incorporated as one corporate institution with a common board of directors, legally responsible and accountable for all member institutions.
2. The hospitals are part of a chain of hospitals whose overall policy is determined by a board of directors which also provides centralized administrative service.
3. The hospitals have a major affiliation agreement, a management contract, or a lease with an organization responsible for major policy decisions.

In other words, multihospital systems were organizations which shared a corporate structure responsible for executive management and/or policy for two or more owned, leased or contract-managed hospitals.

The wording of these criteria has since been simplified by the AHA. A multihospital system is now simply defined as two or more hospitals owned, leased, sponsored, or contract managed by a central organization.

Multi-institutional arrangements are vertically integrated systems which combine different kinds of health care service units such as hospitals, clinics, ambulatory care institutions, long-term care facilities, nursing homes, and/or mental health facilities. These arrangements are often organized in such a way as to provide comprehensive health care services.

Multihospital systems, on the other hand, are horizontally organized, involving a combination of similar health care delivery units. They can be local or regional, for profit or not-for-profit. Nearly every hospital participates in some form of multi-institutional arrangement. These may include shared services, group purchasing, and teaching affiliations.

The AHA's definition used here is more specific. It stresses the formal structure of these multihospital systems. Systems are generally formalized in order to allow participation in the exchange of administrative services, medical technology, and other, including economic, resources.

Alliances and Networks

An alliance is a formal arrangement, for specific purposes, among several hospitals and/or hospital systems that functions under a set of by-laws or other written rules by which each member agrees to abide. (Alliances are further described at the beginning of Part 3.) A network is an interconnected or interrelated group of hospitals or multihospital systems.

Part 1

The first part of this section is an alphabetical list of multihospital systems. Each of the systems listed contains two or more hospitals, which are listed under the system by state. Data for this section were compiled from the 1986 Annual Survey and the membership information base as published in section A of the 1987 *AHA Guide*.

One of the following codes appears after the name of each system listed in Part 1 to indicate the type of organizational control reported by that system:

- CC = Catholic (Roman) church-related system, not-for-profit
- CO = Other church-related system, not-for-profit
- NP = Other not-for-profit system, including nonfederal, governmental systems
- IO = Investor-owned, for profit system

One of the following codes appears after the name of each hospital in Part 1 to indicate how that hospital is related to the system:

- O = Owned
- L = Leased
- S = Sponsored
- CM = Contract-managed

Part 2

Part 2 of this section lists multihospital systems in three ways: by system code, alphabetically, and geographically by state and city.

Part 3

Part 3 of this section is an alphabetical list of alliances and their individual members. This section was developed from research conducted by the AHA's Section for Multihospital Systems.

Every effort has been made to be as inclusive and accurate as possible. However, as in all efforts of this type, there may be omissions. For further information write to the Section for Multihospital Systems, American Hospital Association, 840 N. Lake Shore Drive, Chicago, IL 60611, or call 312/280-6392.

Multihospital Systems and Their Hospitals

ADVENTIST HEALTH SYSTEM (CO)
2301 East Lamar Blvd., Arlington, TX 76006; 817/649-8700; Donald W. Welch, pres.

***9355: ADVENTIST HEALTH SYSTEM-EASTERN AND MIDDLE AMERICA** (CO)
8800 W. 75th St., Shawnee Mission, KS 66204; 913/677-8000; J. Russell Shawver, pres.

Colorado: Boulder Memorial Hospital (O, 87 beds), 311 Mapleton Ave., Boulder 80302; tel. 303/443-0230; Warren M. Clark, pres.

Platte Valley Medical Center (O, 58 beds), 1850 Egbert St., P O Box 98, Brighton 80601; tel. 303/659-1531; Harold A. Buck, adm.

Porter Memorial Hospital (O, 347 beds), 2525 S. Downing St., Denver 80210; tel. 303/778-1955; Donald L. Hanson, pres.

Sedgwick County Hospital (CM, 52 beds), 900 Cedar St., Julesburg 80737; tel. 303/474-3323; Richard L. Scott, adm.

District of Columbia: Hadley Memorial Hospital (O, 76 beds), 4601 Martin Luther King Jr Ave. S.W., Washington 20032; tel. 202/574-5700; Albert Dudley, pres.

Illinois: Hyde Park Hospital (CM, 184 beds), 5800 S. Stony Island Ave., Chicago 60637; tel. 312/643-9200; Jon W. Gepford, pres.

Thorek Hospital and Medical Center (O, 218 beds), 850 W. Irving Park Rd., Chicago 60613; tel. 312/525-6780; Jon Gepford, pres.

Glendale Heights Community Hospital (O, 186 beds), 1505 Jill Ct., Glendale Heights 60139; tel. 312/858-9700; A. A. Chacon, pres.

Hinsdale Hospital (O, 468 beds), 120 N. Oak St., Hinsdale 60521; tel. 312/887-2400; Ken Bauer, pres.

Kansas: Northwest Kansas Regional Medical Center (O, 49 beds), First & Sherman Sts., Box 540, Goodland 67735; tel. 913/899-3625; Rick Ketchum, adm.

Shawnee Mission Medical Center (O, 383 beds), 9100 W. 74th St., Shawnee Mission 66201; tel. 913/676-2000; Cleo Johnson, pres.

Maine: Parkview Memorial Hospital (O, 55 beds), 329 Maine St., Brunswick 04011; tel. 207/729-1641; Kurt K. Ganter, pres.

Maryland: Leland Memorial Hospital (O, 120 beds), 4401 E.-W. Hwy., Riverdale 20737; tel. 301/699-2000; Charley O. Eldridge, pres.

Shady Grove Adventist Hospital (O, 224 beds), 9901 Medical Center Dr., Rockville 20850; tel. 301/279-6000; Bryan L. Breckenridge, pres.

Washington Adventist Hospital (O, 300 beds), 7600 Carroll Ave., Takoma Park 20912; tel. 301/891-7600; Ronald D. Marx, pres.

Massachusetts: Fuller Memorial Hospital (O, 82 beds), 231 Washington St., South Attleboro 02703; tel. 617/761-8500; Ronald C. Brown, pres.

New England Memorial Hospital (O, 301 beds), 5 Woodland Rd., Stoneham 02180; tel. 617/665-1740; Wolfgang Von Maack, pres.

Michigan: Battle Creek Adventist Hospital (O, 136 beds), 165 N. Washington Ave., Battle Creek 49016; tel. 616/964-7121; Teddric J. Mohr, pres.

Tri-County Community Hospital (O, 44 beds), 1131 E. Howard City & Edmore Rd., Edmore 48829; tel. 517/427-5116; Darwin Finkbeiner, pres.

Minnesota: Karlstad Memorial Hospital (CM, 19 beds), Third & Washington, Box I, Karlstad 56732; tel. 218/436-2141; Jerry D. Peak, adm.

Pipestone County Medical Center (CM, 87 beds), 911 Fifth Ave. S.W., P O Box 370, Pipestone 56164; tel. 507/825-5811; Allan J. Christensen, adm.

Missouri: Moberly Regional Medical Center (O, 115 beds), 1515 Union St., P O Box 3000, Moberly 65270; tel. 816/263-8400; James C. Culpepper, adm.

New Hampshire: Beech Hill Hospital (O, 140 beds), New Harrisville Rd., Box 254, Dublin 03444; tel. 603/563-8511; John H. Valentine, pres.

New Jersey: Hackettstown Community Hospital (O, 106 beds), 651 Willow Grove St., Hackettstown 07840; tel. 201/852-5100; Gene C. Milton, pres. & chief exec. off.

Ohio: Kettering Medical Center (O, 608 beds), 3535 Southern Blvd., Kettering 45429; tel. 513/298-4331; Robert Lee Willett, pres.

Pennsylvania: Reading Rehabilitation Hospital (O, 88 beds), Rte. 1, Box 250, Zip 19607; tel. 215/777-7615; Landon Kite, pres.

Wisconsin: Chippewa Valley Hospital and Oakview Care Center (O, 90 beds), 1620 Third Ave. W., Durand 54736; tel. 715/672-4211; Malcolm P. Cole, adm.

Wyoming: South Big Horn County Hospital (L, 57 beds), River Rte., Greybull 82426; tel. 307/568-3311; Donn S. Swartz, adm.

Owned, leased, sponsored:	24 hospitals	4338 beds
Contract-managed:	4 hospitals	342 beds
Totals:	28 hospitals	4680 beds

***4165: ADVENTIST HEALTH SYSTEM-SUNBELT HEALTH CARE CORPORATION** (CO)
2400 Bedford Rd., Orlando, FL 32803; 305/897-1919; Mardian J. Blair, pres.

Florida: Walker Memorial Hospital (O, 122 beds), U. S. Hwy. 27 N., P O Box 1200, Avon Park 33825; tel. 813/453-7511; William C. Sager, pres.

Florida Hospital Medical Center (O, 1071 beds), 601 E. Rollins St., Orlando 32803; tel. 305/896-6611; Thomas L. Werner, pres.

Medical Center Hospital (O, 208 beds), 809 E. Marion Ave., Punta Gorda 33950; tel. 813/639-3131; Valgene Devitt, pres.

East Pasco Medical Center (O, 85 beds), 2500 N. Hwy. 301, Zephyrhills 34248; tel. 813/788-0411; Bob Dodd, adm.

Georgia: Gordon Hospital (L, 65 beds), Red Bud Rd., P O Box 938, Calhoun 30701; tel. 404/629-2895; Robert E. Trimble, pres.

Louis Smith Memorial Hospital (L, 40 beds), 852 W. Thigpen Rd., Box 306, Lakeland 31635; tel. 912/482-3110; Paul Massengill, pres.

Smyrna Hospital (O, 100 beds), 3949 S. Cobb Dr., Smyrna 30080; tel. 404/434-0710; James McAlvin, pres.

Kentucky: Memorial Hospital (O, 63 beds), 401 Memorial Dr., Manchester 40962; tel. 606/598-5104; D. Thomas Amos, pres.

New Mexico: Sierra Vista Hospital (O, 34 beds), 800 E. Ninth Ave., Truth Or Consequences 87901; tel. 505/894-2111; Domenica Rush RN, pres.

For explanation of codes following names, see page B2.
*Indicates Type III membership in the American Hospital Association.

North Carolina: Park Ridge Hospital (CM, 62 beds), Naples Rd., P O Box 1569, Fletcher 28732; tel. 704/684-8501; Robert Burchard, pres.

Oklahoma: Ardmore Adventist Hospital (O, 72 beds), 1012 14th St. N.W., Ardmore 73401; tel. 405/223-4050; Sam C. Loewen, adm.

Tennessee: Takoma Adventist Hospital (O, 108 beds), 401 Takoma Ave., Box 1300, Greeneville 37743; tel. 615/639-3151; Gladys V. Duran, pres.

Jellico Community Hospital (L, 50 beds), Rte. 1, Box 197, Jellico 37762; tel. 615/784-7252; Keith L. Hausman, pres.

Scott Memorial Hospital (O, 64 beds), Box 747, Lawrenceburg 38464; tel. 615/762-7501; P. B. Mitchell, pres.

Tennessee Christian Medical Center (O, 253 beds), 500 Hospital Dr., Madison 37115; tel. 615/865-2373; Dennis Kiley, actg. pres.

Highland Hospital (O, 48 beds), 500 Redbud Dr., Portland 37148; tel. 615/325-7301; Jerry F. Medanich, pres.

Texas: Huguley Memorial Hospital (O, 150 beds), 11801 S. Freeway, Box 6337, Fort Worth 76115; tel. 817/293-9110; John D. Koobs, pres.

Metroplex Hospital (CM, 79 beds), 2201 S. Clear Creek Rd., Killeen 76542; tel. 817/526-7523; Norman L. McBride, pres.

Reeves County Hospital (L, 62 beds), 2323 Texas St., Drawer 2058, Pecos 79772; tel. 915/447-3551; C. W. Hesseltine, pres.

Hays Memorial Hospital (O, 109 beds), 1301 Wonder World Dr., Box 767, San Marcos 78667; tel. 512/353-8979; Ray Carney, adm.

Owned, leased, sponsored:	18 hospitals	2704 beds
Contract-managed:	2 hospitals	141 beds
Totals:	20 hospitals	2845 beds

0235: ADVENTIST HEALTH SYSTEM-WEST (CO)
P O Box 619002, Roseville, CA 95661; 916/781-2000; Frank F. Dupper, pres.

California: St. Helena Hospital and Health Center (O, 165 beds), P O Box 250, Deer Park 94576; tel. 707/963-3611; Leonard Yost, pres.

Glendale Adventist Medical Center (O, 604 beds), 1509 Wilson Terr., Glendale 91206; tel. 818/409-8000; Bob Scott, pres.

Hanford Community Hospital (O, 50 beds), 450 Greenfield Ave., Hanford 93230; Mailing Address Box 240, Hanford, Zip 93232; tel. 209/582-9000; Fred Manchur, pres.

White Memorial Medical Center (O, 247 beds), 1720 Brooklyn Ave., Los Angeles 90033; tel. 213/268-5000; Michael H. Jackson, pres.

Paradise Valley Hospital (O, 210 beds), 2400 E. Fourth St., National City 92050; tel. 619/267-9500; Fred M. Harder, adm.

Feather River Hospital (O, 125 beds), 5974 Pentz Rd., Paradise 95969; tel. 916/877-9361; George Pifer, pres.

Anacapa Adventist Hospital (O, 49 beds), 307 E. Clara St., Port Hueneme 93041; tel. 805/488-3661; Darwin Remboldt, pres.

Mountain View Medical Center (O, 70 beds), 1575 Erringer Rd., Simi Valley 93065; tel. 805/527-9383; James Pappas, exec. dir.

Simi Valley Adventist Hospital (O, 139 beds), 2975 N. Sycamore Dr., Box 819, Simi Valley 93062; tel. 805/527-2462; Darwin R. Remboldt, pres.

Sonora Community Hospital (O, 104 beds), 1 S. Forest Rd., Sonora 95370; tel. 209/532-3161; Stan B. Berry, pres.

Ukiah Adventist Hospital (O, 43 beds), 275 Hospital Dr., Box 859, Ukiah 95482; tel. 707/462-6631; Edwin L. Ermshar, pres.

Frank R. Howard Memorial Hospital (L, 38 beds), Madrone & Manzanita Sts., Box 1430, Willits 95490; tel. 707/459-6801; Robert J. Walker, adm.

Hawaii: Castle Medical Center (O, 156 beds), 640 Ulukahiki St., Kailua 96734; tel. 808/263-5500; Terry W. White, pres. & adm.

Oregon: Portland Adventist Medical Center (O, 302 beds), 10123 S.E. Market, Portland 97216; tel. 503/257-2500; Larry D. Dodds, pres.

Pioneer Memorial Hospital (CM, 33 beds), 1201 N. Elm St., Prineville 97754; tel. 503/447-6254; Joe Gorbea, adm.

Tillamook County General Hospital (L, 40 beds), 1000 Third St., Tillamook 97141; tel. 503/842-4444; Wendell Hesseltine, pres.

Utah: Monument Valley Adventist Hospital (CM, 23 beds), Box 4, Monument Valley 84536; tel. 801/727-3241; Stanley McCluskey, adm.

Washington: Walla Walla General Hospital (O, 72 beds), 1025 S. Second Ave., Box 1398, Walla Walla 99362; tel. 509/525-0480; Rodney T. Applegate, pres.

Owned, leased, sponsored:	16 hospitals	2414 beds
Contract-managed:	2 hospitals	56 beds
Totals:	18 hospitals	2470 beds

0225: ALAMEDA COUNTY HEALTH CARE SERVICES AGENCY (NP)
499 Fifth St., Oakland, CA 94607; 415/268-2722; David J. Kears, dir.

California: Highland General Hospital (O, 244 beds), 1411 E. 31st St., Oakland 94602; tel. 415/534-8055; Joyce Berger, dir.

Fairmont Hospital (O, 249 beds), 15400 Foothill Blvd., San Leandro 94578; tel. 415/667-7820; Neil R. Petersen, actg. adm.

Owned, leased, sponsored:	2 hospitals	493 beds
Contract-managed:	0 hospitals	0 beds
Totals:	2 hospitals	493 beds

***0065: ALEXIAN BROTHERS HEALTH SYSTEMS INC.** (CC)
600 Alexian Way, Elk Grove Village, IL 60007; 312/640-7550; Bruce Fisher, exec. vice-pres.

California: Alexian Brothers Hospital of San Jose (O, 204 beds), 225 N. Jackson Ave., San Jose 95116; tel. 408/259-5000; Dean Grant, pres. & chief exec. off.

Illinois: Alexian Brothers Medical Center (O, 370 beds), 800 W. Biesterfield Rd., Elk Grove Village 60007; tel. 312/437-5500; Brother Philip Kennedy, pres. & chief exec.off.

Missouri: Alexian Brothers Hospital (O, 181 beds), 3933 S. Broadway, St. Louis 63118; tel. 314/865-3333; Deno Fabbre, pres. & chief exec. off.

New Jersey: Alexian Brothers Hospital (O, 190 beds), 655 E. Jersey St., Elizabeth 07206; tel. 201/351-9000; Michael J. Schwartz, pres. & chief exec. off.

Owned, leased, sponsored:	4 hospitals	945 beds
Contract-managed:	0 hospitals	0 beds
Totals:	4 hospitals	945 beds

***1385: ALLEGANY HEALTH SYSTEM** (CC)
11300 Fourth St. N., Suite 220, St. Petersburg, FL 33702; 813/577-9363; James E. Grobmyer, pres.

Florida: St. Francis Hospital (S, 273 beds), 250 W. 63rd St., Miami Beach 33141; tel. 305/868-5000; Sr. Margaret McManus, pres. & chief exec. off.

St. Anthony's Hospital (S, 434 beds), 601 12th St. N., St. Petersburg 33705; tel. 813/825-1100; Daniel T. McMurray, pres.

St. Joseph's Hospital (S, 649 beds), 3001 W. Buffalo Ave., Tampa 33607; Mailing Address Box 4227, Tampa, Zip 33677; tel. 813/870-4000; Sr. Marie Celeste Sullivan,pres.

St. Mary's Hospital (S, 358 beds), 901 45th St., West Palm Beach 33407; tel. 305/844-6300; John E. Fidler, pres.

New Jersey: Our Lady of Lourdes Medical Center (S, 398 beds), 1600 Haddon Ave., Camden 08103; tel. 609/757-3500; Sr. Elizabeth Corry, pres. & chief exec. off.

New York: St. Francis Hospital (S, 111 beds), 2221 W. State St., Olean 14760; tel. 716/372-5300; Sr. Mary Croghan, adm.

Owned, leased, sponsored:	6 hospitals	2223 beds
Contract-managed:	0 hospitals	0 beds
Totals:	6 hospitals	2223 beds

***2565: ALLIANCE HEALTH SYSTEM** (NP)
18 Koger Executive Center, Suite 202, Norfolk, VA 23502; 804/466-6000; Glenn R. Mitchell, pres.

For explanation of codes following names, see page B2.
*Indicates Type III membership in the American Hospital Association.

Virginia: Leigh Memorial Hospital (O, 250 beds), 830 Kempsville Rd., Norfolk 23502; tel. 804/466-6000; Richard A. Hanson, adm.

Norfolk General Hospital (O, 644 beds), 600 Gresham Dr., Norfolk 23507; tel. 804/628-3000; Edward L. Berdick, adm.

Owned, leased, sponsored:	2 hospitals	894 beds
Contract-managed:	0 hospitals	0 beds
Totals:	2 hospitals	894 beds

0045: AMERICAN HEALTH GROUP INTERNATIONAL, INC. (IO)
401 Park Pl., Suite 500, Kirkland, WA 98033; 206/827-1195; Michael D. Drobot, pres.

California: Pacifica Community Hospital (O, 109 beds), 18792 Delaware St., Huntington Beach 92648; tel. 714/842-0611; Philip P. Gustafson, exec. dir.

Palmdale Hospital Medical Center (O, 123 beds), 1212 E. Ave. S, Palmdale 93550; tel. 805/273-2211; Reid Anderson, exec. dir.

Serra Memorial Health Center (O, 232 beds), 9449 San Fernando Rd., Sun Valley 91352; tel. 818/767-3310; Jerry Hawley, adm. & chief oper. off.

New Mexico: Roosevelt General Hospital (O, 99 beds), 1700 S. Ave. O, P O Box 60, Portales 88130; tel. 505/356-4411; George McGowan, exec. dir.

Owned, leased, sponsored:	4 hospitals	563 beds
Contract-managed:	0 hospitals	0 beds
Totals:	4 hospitals	563 beds

0075: AMERICAN HEALTHCARE CORPORATION (IO)
21 W. End Ave., Suite 1100, Nashville, TN 37203; 615/327-2200; Don R. Abercrombie, pres., chm. & chief exec. off.

Massachusetts: Central Hospital (CM, 99 beds), 26 Central St., Somerville 02143; tel. 617/625-8900; Marvin Stern, adm.

Mississippi: Thaggard Hospital (O, 22 beds), Box 157, Madden 39109; tel. 601/267-4562; Ronald Yarborogh, adm.

Tennessee: Sequatchie General Hospital (O, 49 beds), Cedar St., Box 787, Dunlap 37327; tel. 615/949-3611; Danny Mankin, adm.

Lewis County Hospital (O, 52 beds), Linden Hwy., P O Box 38, Hohenwald 38462; tel. 615/796-4901; Michael Edwards, adm.

Northwest General Hospital (O, 23 beds), 5310 Western Ave., Knoxville 37921; tel. 615/584-9191; Stephen W. Larcen PhD, adm.

Perry Memorial Hospital (O, 53 beds), Hwy. 13 S., Box 86, Linden 37096; tel. 615/589-2121; Jerry K. Crowell, adm.

Owned, leased, sponsored:	5 hospitals	199 beds
Contract-managed:	1 hospitals	99 beds
Totals:	6 hospitals	298 beds

1375: AMERICAN HEALTHCARE MANAGEMENT, INC. (IO)
14160 Dallas Pkwy., Suite 900, Dallas, TX 75240; 214/385-7000; John A. Bradley PhD, bd. chm. & chief exec. off.

California: Community Hospital of Huntington Park (L, 56 beds), 2623 E. Slauson Ave., Huntington Park 90255; tel. 213/583-1931; Peter J. S. Friedman, adm.

Mission Hospital (L, 127 beds), 3111 E. Florence Ave., Huntington Park 90255; tel. 213/582-8261; Robert P. Hutchins, adm.

Woodruff Community Hospital (O, 99 beds), 3800 Woodruff Ave., Long Beach 90808; tel. 213/421-8241; Maryann J. Greenwel¢o

Linda Vista Community Hospital (O, 150 beds), 610 S. St. Louis St., Los Angeles 90023; tel. 213/265-0789; Louis Rubino, adm.

Monterey Park Hospital (O, 96 beds), 900 S. Atlantic Blvd., Monterey Park 91754; tel. 818/570-9000; Reggie Panis, adm.

Chapman General Hospital (O, 99 beds), 2601 E. Chapman Ave., Orange 92669; tel. 714/633-0011; Daryl S. Crane Jr., adm.

San Clemente General Hospital (O, 116 beds), 654 Camino De Los Mares, San Clemente 92672; tel. 714/661-4402; Thomas W. McClintock, adm.

Greater El Monte Community Hospital (O, 115 beds), 1701 S. Santa Anita Ave., South El Monte 91733; tel. 818/579-7777; Kenneth R. Dillard, chief exec. off.

Florida: Riverside Hospital (O, 100 beds), 500 Indiana Ave., New Port Richey 33552; tel. 813/842-8468; Bradley Reid, adm.

Harborside Hospital (O, 143 beds), 401 15th St. N., St. Petersburg 33705; Mailing Address P O Box 11748, St. Petersburg, Zip 33733; tel. 813/821-2021; Lynn C.Orfgen, adm.

Illinois: St. Joseph's Hospital (L, 60 beds), 1005 Julien St., Belvidere 61008; tel. 815/544-3411; W. Daniel Cobbs, adm.

Kentucky: Marymount Hospital (L, 55 beds), E. Ninth St., London 40741; tel. 606/878-6520; Lowell Jones, adm.

Louisiana: Minden Medical Center (O, 108 beds), 1 Medical Plaza, Minden 71055; tel. 318/377-2321; George E. French III, adm.

Minnesota: St. John's Hospital (L, 32 beds), 540 Eighth St. W., Browerville 56438; tel. 612/594-2204; Debra M. Noble, adm.

St. Mary's Hospital and Nursing Home (L, 153 beds), 1014 Lincoln Ave., Detroit Lakes 56501; tel. 218/847-5611; Barry B. Fewson, adm.

Divine Redeemer Memorial Hospital (L, 82 beds), 724 19th Ave. N., South St. Paul 55075; tel. 612/450-4500; Drew Haynes, adm.

Samaritan Hospital (O, 98 beds), 1515 Charles Ave., St. Paul 55104; tel. 612/645-9111; Joel B. Warner, adm.

Mississippi: Doctors Hospital (O, 162 beds), 2969 University Dr., Box 4783, Jackson 39216; tel. 601/982-8321; Ronald T. Seal, adm.

Montana: Missoula General Hospital (O, 50 beds), 902 N. Orange St., Missoula 59802; tel. 406/542-2191; Karen Foster, adm.

Nevada: Community Hospital of North Las Vegas (O, 163 beds), 1409 E. Lake Mead Blvd., North Las Vegas 89030; tel. 702/649-7711; Victor Brewer, adm.

Oregon: Eastmoreland Hospital (O, 100 beds), 2900 S.E. Steele St., Portland 97202; tel. 503/234-0411; John D. Cochran, adm.

Woodland Park Hospital (L, 156 beds), 10300 N.E. Hancock, Portland 97220; tel. 503/257-5500; Richard Sanderson, adm.

South Carolina: Southland Medical Center (O, 76 beds), 115 Medford Dr., Box 506, Darlington 29532; tel. 803/393-4007; James B. Wood, adm.

Tennessee: Gibson General Hospital (O, 101 beds), Hospital Dr., Box 488, Trenton 38382; tel. 901/855-2551; Walter J. Stephenson, adm.

Three Rivers Community Hospital (O, 52 beds), S. Church St., Waverly 37185; tel. 615/296-4203; L. Joe Austin, adm.

Texas: Leon Memorial Hospital (O, 36 beds), Hospital Dr., Box 159, Buffalo 75831; tel. 214/322-4231; Glenn W. Ross Jr., adm.

Sharpstown General Hospital (O, 206 beds), 6700 Bellaire at Tarnef, Houston 77074; Mailing Address P O Box 740389, Houston, Zip 77274; tel. 713/774-7611; DanHill, adm.

Littlefield Medical Center (L, 75 beds), 1500 S. Sunset, Littlefield 79339; tel. 806/385-6411; Gary Moore, adm.

Pasadena General Hospital (L, 72 beds), 1004 Seymour St., Pasadena 77506; tel. 713/473-1771; Rand Wortman, adm.

St. Luke's Lutheran Hospital (CM, 251 beds), 7930 Floyd Curl Dr., Box 29100, San Antonio 78229; tel. 512/690-8600; William T. Dunn, adm.

Wylie Community Hospital (O, 37 beds), 801 W. Hwy. 78, Box 1500, Wylie 75098; tel. 214/442-5414; Spencer Guimarin, adm.

Washington: Puget Sound Hospital (O, 153 beds), 215 S. 36th St., Tacoma 98408; Mailing Address P O Box 11412, Tacoma, Zip 98411; tel. 206/474-0561; Bruce Brandler, adm.

West Virginia: Plateau Medical Center (O, 91 beds), 430 Main St., Oak Hill 25901; tel. 304/465-0551; Charles E. Kuebler, adm.

Owned, leased, sponsored:	32 hospitals	3219 beds
Contract-managed:	1 hospitals	251 beds
Totals:	33 hospitals	3470 beds

For explanation of codes following names, see page B2.
*Indicates Type III membership in the American Hospital Association.

0195: AMERICAN MEDICAL CENTERS (IO)
P O Box 2526, Norcross, GA 30071; 615/244-8410; Paul T. Agee, sr. vice-pres. & chief exec. off.

Georgia: Smith Hospital (O, 71 beds), 117 E. Main St., Hahira 31632; tel. 912/794-2502; Lucilla Acree, adm.

Texas: Physicians and Surgeons Hospital (O, 44 beds), 3201 Sage St., Midland 79705; tel. 915/683-2273; Richard C. Liley, adm.

Owned, leased, sponsored:	2 hospitals	115 beds
Contract-managed:	0 hospitals	0 beds
Totals:	2 hospitals	115 beds

***0125: AMERICAN MEDICAL INTERNATIONAL** (IO)
414 N. Camden Dr., Beverly Hills, CA 90210; 213/278-6200; Walter Weisman, pres. & chief exec. off.

Alabama: AMI Brookwood Medical Center (O, 586 beds), 2010 Brookwood Medical Center Dr., Birmingham 35259; tel. 205/877-1000; Gregory H. Burfitt, pres.

AMI West Alabama Hospital (O, 156 beds), 2700 11th Ave., Northport 35476; tel. 205/339-5100; Steve Scully, pres.

Arkansas: AMI Medical Park Hospital (O, 75 beds), 2001 S. Main St., Box 460, Hope 71801; tel. 501/777-2323; Donald G. Carney, exec. dir.

AMI National Park Medical Center (O, 155 beds), 3110 Malvern Rd., Box 1137, Hot Springs 71901; tel. 501/321-1000; Warner N. Kass, exec. dir.

AMI St. Mary's Hospital (O, 144 beds), 1808 W. Main St., Russellville 72801; tel. 501/968-2841; Jerry D. Mabry, exec. dir.

AMI Central Arkansas General Hospital (O, 113 beds), 1200 S. Main, Searcy 72143; tel. 501/268-7171; David C. Laffoon, chief exec. off.

California: AMI Arroyo Grande Community Hospital (O, 79 beds), 345 S. Halcyon Rd., Arroyo Grande 93420; tel. 805/489-4261; Richard N. Wooslayer, dir.

AMI Circle City Hospital (O, 99 beds), 730 Old Magnolia Ave., P O Box 310, Corona 91719; tel. 714/736-7252; Henry Gothelf, exec. dir.

AMI Valley Medical Center (O, 189 beds), 1688 E. Main St., El Cajon 92021; tel. 619/440-1122; Jerry Gillman, exec. dir.

AMI Rancho Encino Hospital (O, 102 beds), 5333 Balboa Blvd., Encino 91316; tel. 818/788-4400; Frank Montague, chief exec. off.

AMI Medical Center of Garden Grove (O, 175 beds), 12601 Garden Grove Blvd., Garden Grove 92643; tel. 714/537-5160; Mark Meyers, exec. dir.

AMI Glendora Community Hospital (O, 143 beds), 150 W. Alosta Ave., Glendora 91740; tel. 818/335-0231; Joe Gagliardi, exec. dir.

AMI Healdsburg General Hospital (O, 49 beds), 1375 University St., Box 696, Healdsburg 95448; tel. 707/433-4461; Duane M. Kenward, exec. dir.

AMI Medical Center of North Hollywood (O, 182 beds), 12629 Riverside Dr., North Hollywood 91607; tel. 818/984-1165; Michael Weinstein, pres. & chief exec. off.

AMI South Bay Hospital (L, 203 beds), 514 N. Prospect Ave., Redondo Beach 90277; tel. 213/376-9474; Lynn C. Orfgen, exec. dir.

AMI Clairemont Community Hospital (O, 136 beds), 5255 Mount Etna Dr., San Diego 92117; tel. 619/278-8100; Steve Hall, exec. dir.

AMI Mission Bay Hospital (O, 150 beds), 3030 Bunker Hill St., San Diego 92109; tel. 619/274-7721; Steve Hall, exec. dir.

AMI San Dimas Community Hospital (O, 99 beds), 1350 W. Covina Blvd., San Dimas 91773; tel. 714/599-6811; Ruben Fernandez, exec. dir.

AMI Sierra Vista Regional Medical Center (O, 175 beds), 1010 Murray Ave., San Luis Obispo 93401; Mailing Address Box 1367, San Luis Obispo, Zip 93406; tel.805/546-7600; Glenn D. Carlson, chief exec. off.

AMI Community Hospital of Santa Cruz (O, 180 beds), 610 Frederick St., Santa Cruz 95062; tel. 408/426-3282; Ann Klein, exec. dir.

AMI Tarzana Regional Medical Center (O, 212 beds), 18321 Clark St., Tarzana 91356; tel. 818/881-0800; Arnold N. Kimmel, exec. dir.

AMI Delaware Amo Hospital (O, 166 beds), 23700 Camino Del Sol, Torrance 90505; tel. 213/530-1151; William H. Bennett Jr., exec. dir.

Visalia Community Hospital (O, 52 beds), 1633 S. Court St., Box 911, Visalia 93277; tel. 209/733-1333; Larry C. Andrews, exec. dir.

Colorado: AMI Presbyterian Aurora Hospital (O, 106 beds), 700 Potomac St., Aurora 80011; tel. 303/363-7200; H. Phil Herre, exec. dir.

AMI Presbyterian-Denver Hospital (O, 223 beds), 1719 E. 19th Ave., Denver 80218; tel. 303/839-6100; Donald Lenz, exec. dir.

AMI Presbyterian-St. Luke's Medical Center (O, 366 beds), 601 E. 19th Ave., Denver 80203; tel. 303/839-1000; Donald W. Lenz, exec. dir.

Estes Park Medical Center (CM, 76 beds), 555 Prospect, Box 2740, Estes Park 80517; tel. 303/586-2317; Karen I. Spotts, chief exec. off.

Vail Valley Medical Center (CM, 19 beds), 181 W. Meadow Dr., Vail 81657; tel. 303/476-2451; Ray McMahan, adm.

Florida: AMI Clearwater Community Hospital (O, 120 beds), 1521 E. Druid Rd., Clearwater 33516; tel. 813/447-4571; Reynold Jennings, exec. dir.

AMI North Ridge Medical Center (O, 278 beds), 5757 N. Dixie Hwy., Fort Lauderdale 33334; tel. 305/776-6000; Don Steigman, exec. dir.

AMI Palmetto General Hospital (O, 360 beds), 2001 W. 68th St., Hialeah 33016; tel. 305/823-5000; Edward Tudanger, exec. dir.

AMI Lake City Medical Center (O, 75 beds), 1701 W. Duval St., Lake City 32055; tel. 904/752-2922; Steve Chapman, chief exec. off.

AMI Kendall Regional Medical Center (O, 314 beds), 11750 Bird Rd., Miami 33175; tel. 305/223-3000; Larry E. Hanan, exec. dir.

AMI Parkway Regional Medical Center (O, 412 beds), 160 N.W. 170th St., North Miami Beach 33169; tel. 305/651-1100; Jay S. Weinstein, assoc. exec. dir.

AMI Southeastern Medical Center (O, 224 beds), 1750 N.E. 167th St., North Miami Beach 33162; tel. 305/945-5400; Neil Natkow DO, exec. dir.

AMI Brookwood Community Hospital (O, 153 beds), 1800 Mercy Dr., P O Box 15400, Orlando 32808; tel. 305/295-5151; Gary L. Rowe, chief exec. off.

AMI Palm Beach Gardens Medical Center (O, 204 beds), 3360 Burns Rd., Palm Beach Gardens 33410; tel. 305/622-1411; Jack Barto, exec. dir.

AMI Memorial Hospital of Tampa (O, 158 beds), 2901 Swann Ave., Tampa 33609; Mailing Address Box 18054, Tampa, Zip 33679; tel. 813/877-0441; Keith Henthorne, chiefexec. off.; Vincent Nico, asst. adm.

AMI Town and Country Medical Center (L, 201 beds), 6001 Webb Rd., Tampa 33615; tel. 813/885-6666; Gerald McAteer, exec. dir.

AMI Anclote Manor Psychiatric Hospital (O, 100 beds), 1527 Riverside Dr., Tarpon Springs 33589; tel. 813/937-4211; Walter Wellborn MD, dir.

Georgia: AMI Griffin-Spalding Hospital (O, 173 beds), S. Eighth St., P O Drawer V, Griffin 30224; tel. 404/228-2721; Thomas A. Gordy, exec. dir.

AMI North Fulton Medical Center (O, 147 beds), 11585 Alpharetta St., Roswell 30076; tel. 404/475-5552; Frederick Bailey, dir.

AMI Barrow Medical Center (O, 60 beds), 1035 N. Broad St., Box 768, Winder 30680; tel. 404/867-3400; Gerald Trevisol, exec. dir.

Indiana: AMI Culver Union Hospital (O, 120 beds), 1710 Lafayette Rd., Crawfordsville 47933; tel. 317/362-2800; Michael L. Collins, exec. dir.

Louisiana: AMI Highland Park Hospital (O, 104 beds), One Park Pl., Drawer 1269, Covington 70433; tel. 504/892-5900; Gerald Peterman, exec. dir.

For explanation of codes following names, see page B2.
*Indicates Type III membership in the American Hospital Association.

AMI Westpark Community Hospital (O, 50 beds), 1900 S. Morrison Blvd., Hammond 70403; Mailing Address P O Box 2608, Hammond, Zip 70404; tel. 504/542-7777; SteveTurner, pres.

AMI St. Jude Medical Center (O, 149 beds), 180 W. Esplanade Ave., Kenner 70065; tel. 504/468-8600; John W. McDaniel, pres. & chief exec. off.

AMI Doctors' Hospital of Opelousas (O, 81 beds), 5101 Hwy. 167 S., Opelousas 70570; tel. 318/948-2100; Brian Riddle, chief exec. off.

Maryland: AMI Doctors' Hospital (O, 250 beds), 8118 Good Luck Rd., Lanham 20706; tel. 301/552-9400; Phil Down, exec. dir.

Massachusetts: AMI Pembroke Hospital (O, 100 beds), 199 Oak St., Pembroke 02359; tel. 617/826-8161; Sherwin Z. Goodblatt, Exec. Dir., dir.

AMI Westwood Lodge Hospital (O, 75 beds), 45 Clapboardtree St., Westwood 02090; tel. 617/762-7764; Sherwin Z. Goodblatt, exec. dir.

Mississippi: AMI Garden Park Community Hospital (O, 120 beds), 1520 Broad Ave., Gulfport 39501; tel. 601/864-4210; L. V. Johnston, exec. dir.

Missouri: AMI Columbia Regional Hospital (O, 286 beds), 404 Keene St., Columbia 65201; tel. 314/875-9000; Ed Clawson, chief exec. off.

AMI Lucy Lee Hospital (O, 168 beds), 2620 Westwood Blvd., Poplar Bluff 63901; tel. 314/785-7721; William L. Bradley, dir.

Nebraska: AMI Saint Joseph Hospital (O, 293 beds), 601 N. 30th St., Omaha 68131; tel. 402/449-4000; Kenneth G. Hermann, exec. dir.

AMI St. Joseph Center for Health (O, 131 beds), 819 Dorcas, Omaha 68108; tel. 402/449-4653; Johanna M. Anderson, exec. dir.

North Carolina: AMI Frye Regional Medical Center (O, 275 beds), 420 N. Center St., Hickory 28601; tel. 704/322-6070

AMI Central Carolina Hospital (O, 142 beds), 1135 Carthage St., Sanford 27330; tel. 919/774-4100; Phil Shaw, exec. dir.

Oklahoma: AMI Claremore Regional Medical Center (O, 74 beds), 1202 N. Muskogee St., Claremore 74017; tel. 918/341-2556; Betty W. Walker, exec. dir.

AMI Southwestern Medical Center (O, 109 beds), 5602 S.W. Lee Blvd., Lawton 73505; Mailing Address P O Box 7290, Lawton, Zip 73506; tel. 405/355-2700; Thomas L.Rine, exec. dir.

AMI Doctors Hospital (O, 122 beds), 2323 S. Harvard Ave., Tulsa 74114; tel. 918/744-4000; Harvey M. Shapiro, exec. dir. & chief exec. off.

South Carolina: AMI East Cooper Community Hospital (O, 70 beds), 1200 Hwy. 17 N., P O Box 128, Mount Pleasant 29464; tel. 802/881-0100; Ronald J. Baker, pres.

AMI Piedmont Medical Center (O, 273 beds), 222 S. Herlong Ave., Rock Hill 29730; tel. 803/329-1234; Paul A. Walker, exec. dir.

AMI Doctors Memorial Hospital (O, 104 beds), 389 Serpentine Dr., Spartanburg 29303; tel. 803/585-8781; Rodney L. Helms, exec. dir.

Texas: AMI Physicians and Surgeons Hospital (O, 90 beds), 300 E. Third St., Alice 78332; tel. 512/664-4376; John C. Woodson, exec. dir.

AMI Alvin Community Hospital (O, 76 beds), 301 Medic Lane, Alvin 77511; tel. 713/331-6141; Terry Kirk, chief oper. off.

AMI Coastal Bend Hospital (O, 75 beds), 1711 W. Wheeler St., Aransas Pass 78336; tel. 512/758-8585; Ken Noteboom, exec. dir.

AMI Brownsville Medical Center (O, 148 beds), 1040 W. Jefferson St., Box 3590, Brownsville 78520; tel. 512/544-1400; G. Tucker Grau, exec. dir.

AMI Riverside Hospital (O, 89 beds), 13725 Farm Rd. 624, Corpus Christi 78410; tel. 512/387-1541; Jean F. Adams, exec. dir.

AMI Medical Arts Hospital (L, 71 beds), 6161 Harry Hines Blvd., Dallas 75235; Mailing Address P O Box 45188, Dallas, Zip 75245; tel. 214/688-1111; Phillip L.Coppage, chief exec. off.

AMI Denton Regional Medical Center (L, 195 beds), 4405 N. Interstate 35, Denton 76201; tel. 817/566-4000; Donald S. Ciulla, exec. dir.

AMI Bellaire Hospital (L, 119 beds), 5314 Dashwood St., Houston 77081; tel. 713/669-4000; Laurence R. Gore, chief exec. off.

AMI Eastway General Hospital (O, 150 beds), 9339 North Loop E., Houston 77029; Mailing Address Box 24216, Houston, Zip 77229; tel. 713/675-3241; Lanny Chopin,exec. dir.

AMI Heights Hospital (O, 213 beds), 1917 Ashland St., Houston 77008; Mailing Address Box 7497, Houston, Zip 77248; tel. 713/861-6161; Brian S. Barbe, exec. dir.

AMI Park Plaza Hospital (O, 269 beds), 1313 Hermann Dr., Box 8347, Houston 77004; tel. 713/527-5000; Carl W. Fitch Sr., pres.

AMI Parkway Hospital (O, 180 beds), 233 W. Parker Rd., Houston 77076; tel. 713/697-2831; Phillip Hurley, exec. dir.

AMI Twelve Oaks Hospital (O, 336 beds), 4200 Portsmouth St., Houston 77027; tel. 713/623-2500; Walter J. Ornsteen, exec. dir.

AMI Westbury Hospital (O, 123 beds), 5556 Gasmer Rd., Houston 77035; tel. 713/729-1111; Mel Bishop, exec. dir.

Institute for Immunologic Disorders (O, 107 beds), 7407 N. Freeway, Houston 77076; tel. 713/691-3531; Jean Settlemyre, chief exec. off.

AMI Katy Community Hospital (O, 100 beds), 5602 Medical Center Dr., Box 656, Katy 77450; tel. 713/392-1111; Warren Wilkey, exec. dir.

AMI Doctors Hospital of Laredo (O, 78 beds), 500 E. Mann Rd., Laredo 78041; tel. 512/723-1131; Ernie Domenech, exec. dir.

AMI North Texas Medical Center (O, 138 beds), 1800 N. Graves St., Box 370, McKinney 75069; tel. 214/548-3000; Steven Woerner, exec. dir.

AMI Fort Bend Community Hospital (O, 80 beds), 3803 Fm 1092 at Hwy. 6, Missouri City 77459; tel. 713/499-4800; Frederick R. Grates, dir.

AMI Nacogdoches Medical Center Hospital (O, 150 beds), 4920 N.E. Stallings, Box 1604, Nacogdoches 75963; tel. 409/569-9481; Bryant H. Krenek Jr., dir.

AMI Mid-Jefferson County Hospital (O, 104 beds), Hwy. 365 & 27th St., P O Box 1917, Nederland 77627; tel. 409/727-2321; John Grossmeier, exec. dir.

AMI Odessa Women's-Children Hospital (O, 114 beds), 520 E. Sixth St., Box 4859, Odessa 79760; tel. 915/334-8200; Bill Simpson, actg. dir.

AMI Park Place Hospital (O, 223 beds), 3050 39th St., Port Arthur 77642; Mailing Address Box 1648, Port Arthur, Zip 77640; tel. 409/983-4951; Luis G. Silva, exec.dir.

AMI Round Rock Community Hospital (O, 63 beds), 2400 Round Rock Ave., P O Box 125, Round Rock 78681; tel. 512/255-6066; Scott D. Evans, exec. dir.

AMI Medical Plaza Hospital (O, 176 beds), 1111 Gallagher Dr., Sherman 75090; tel. 214/870-7000; Bill Rowton, actg. exec. dir.

AMI Terrell Community Hospital (L, 73 beds), 1551 S. Virginia, Terrell 75160; tel. 214/563-7611; Larry Graham, exec. dir.

AMI Texarkana Community Hospital (L, 110 beds), 2501 College Dr., Texarkana 75501; tel. 214/798-5100; Jerry Kincade, exec. dir.

AMI Danforth Hospital (O, 113 beds), 519 Ninth Ave. N., Texas City 77590; tel. 409/948-8411; Carl Abdalian, exec. dir.

Owned, leased, sponsored:	90 hospitals	4153 beds
Contract-managed:	2 hospitals	95 beds
Totals:	92 hospitals	4248 beds

0985: AMERIHEALTH, INC. (IO)
2849 Paces Ferry Rd., Suite 790, Atlanta, GA 30339; 404/435-1776; William G. White, pres.

Alabama: Autauga Medical Center (O, 62 beds), 124 S. Memorial Dr., Prattville 36067; tel. 205/365-0651; Willis S. Sanders, chief exec. off.

Florida: North Gables Hospital (CM, 53 beds), 5190 S.W. Eighth St., Coral Gables 33134; tel. 305/445-1364; William P. Rauschberg, adm.

Georgia: Ridgecrest Hospital (CM, 45 beds), Hwy. 76 W. Germany Rd., Box 376, Clayton 30525; tel. 404/782-4297; Richard J. Turner Jr., adm.

For explanation of codes following names, see page B2.
*Indicates Type III membership in the American Hospital Association.

Pennsylvania: Monsour Medical Center (CM, 233 beds), 70 Lincoln Hwy. E., Jeannette 15644; tel. 412/527-1511; Michael J. Hurd, adm.

Texas: Lockhart Hospital (O, 24 beds), 901 Bois D'Arc St., Lockhart 78644; tel. 512/398-3433; Robert T. Martel, adm.

Virginia: Metropolitan Hospital (O, 180 beds), 701 W. Grace St., Richmond 23220; tel. 804/775-4100; Thomas G. Honaker III, chief exec. off.

Owned, leased, sponsored:	3 hospitals	266 beds
Contract-managed:	3 hospitals	331 beds
Totals:	6 hospitals	597 beds

***0135: ANCILLA SYSTEMS, INC.** (CC)
1100 Elmhurst Rd., Elk Grove Village, IL 60007; 312/964-4210; Sr. Judian Brietentract, pres.

Illinois: St. Anne's Hospital (O, 239 beds), 4950 W. Thomas St., Chicago 60651; tel. 312/378-7100; Reginald P. Gibson, assoc. exec. dir.

St. Elizabeth's Hospital (O, 277 beds), 1431 N. Claremont Ave., Chicago 60622; tel. 312/278-2000; Bernard Dickens Sr., chief exec. off.

St. Mary's Hospital (O, 273 beds), 129 N. Eighth St., East St. Louis 62201; tel. 618/274-1900; Philip J. Karst PhD, exec. dir.

St. Anne's Hospital-West (O, 78 beds), 365 E. North Ave., Northlake 60164; tel. 312/345-8100; Bernard Dickens Sr., chief exec. off.

Indiana: Community Hospital of Bremen (CM, 28 beds), 411 S. Whitlock St., Bremen 46506; tel. 219/546-2211; Jerome J. Bozek, adm.

St. Catherine Hospital of East Chicago (O, 409 beds), 4321 Fir St., East Chicago 46312; tel. 219/392-1700; John R. Birdzell, chief exec. off.

St. Joseph's Medical Center (O, 327 beds), 700 Broadway, Fort Wayne 46802; tel. 219/425-3000; Stanley A. Abramowski, exec. dir.

St. Mary Medical Center (O, 349 beds), 540 Tyler St., Gary 46402; tel. 219/882-9411; John Birdzell, chief exec. off.

Saint Joseph Hospital (O, 117 beds), 215 W. Fourth St., Mishawaka 46544; tel. 219/259-2431; Allen V. Rupiper, exec. dir.

Owned, leased, sponsored:	8 hospitals	2069 beds
Contract-managed:	1 hospitals	28 beds
Totals:	9 hospitals	2097 beds

***0145: APPALACHIAN REGIONAL HEALTHCARE** (NP)
Box 8086, Zip 40533; 606/255-4431; Robert L. Johnson, pres.

Kentucky: Harlan Appalachian Regional Hospital (O, 110 beds), Martins Fork Rd., Harlan 40831; tel. 606/573-1400; Ray G. Roberts, adm.

Arh Regional Medical Center (O, 156 beds), P O Box 7000, Hazard 41701; tel. 606/439-1331; Russ D. Sword, adm.

McDowell Appalachian Regional Health Care (O, 60 beds), Rte. 122, Box 247, McDowell 41647; tel. 606/377-2411; Edward V. Collins, adm.

Middlesboro Appalachian Regional Hospital (O, 96 beds), 3600 W. Cumberland Ave., Box 340, Middlesboro 40965; tel. 606/248-3300; John I. Frederick, adm.

Williamson Appalachian Regional Hospital (O, 143 beds), 2000 Central Ave., South Williamson 41503; tel. 606/237-1010; W. D. Crosley, adm.

Morgan County Appalachian Regional Hospital (L, 45 beds), Wells Hill Rd., Box 579, West Liberty 41472; tel. 606/743-3186; Raymond Rowlett, adm.

Whitesburg Appalachian Regional Hospital (O, 71 beds), 550 Jenkins Rd., Whitesburg 41858; tel. 606/633-2211; Paul V. Miles, adm.

Virginia: Wise Appalachian Regional Hospital (O, 67 beds), P O Box 3267, Wise 24293; tel. 703/328-2511; Ruby J. Salyers, adm.

West Virginia: Beckley Appalachian Regional Hospital (O, 202 beds), 306 Stanaford Rd., Beckley 25801; tel. 304/255-3000; Roger J. Wolz, adm.

Man Appalachian Regional Hospital (O, 82 beds), 700 E. McDonald, P O Box 485, Man 25635; tel. 304/583-6511; Jason M. Riggins, adm.

Broaddus Hospital (CM, 61 beds), College Hill, Philippi 26416; tel. 304/457-1760; Don D. Stoner, adm.

Owned, leased, sponsored:	10 hospitals	1032 beds
Contract-managed:	1 hospitals	61 beds
Totals:	11 hospitals	1093 beds

***0205: ASC HEALTH SYSTEM** (CC)
3 Eagle Center, Suite 1, P O Box 568, O'Fallon, IL 62269; 618/632-1284; Joseph B. Ahlschier, pres.

Illinois: St. Joseph Memorial Hospital (O, 62 beds), 800 N. Second St., P O Box 588, Murphysboro 62966; tel. 618/684-3156; John D. Groves, pres. & chief exec. off.

St. Clement Hospital (O, 105 beds), 325 Spring St., Red Bud 62278; tel. 618/282-3831; Harlow J. Herman, pres.

St. Vincent Memorial Hospital (O, 167 beds), 201 E. Pleasant St., Taylorville 62568; tel. 217/824-3331; Robert B. Cooper, pres.

Owned, leased, sponsored:	3 hospitals	334 beds
Contract-managed:	0 hospitals	0 beds
Totals:	3 hospitals	334 beds

***0865: ATLANTIC HEALTH SYSTEMS, INC.** (NP)
466 Southern Blvd., Chatham, NJ 07928; 201/514-1993; Thomas J. Foley, pres. & chief exec. off.

New Jersey: Morristown Memorial Hospital (CM, 606 beds), 100 Madison Ave., Morristown 07960; tel. 201/540-5000; Donald A. Bradley, pres.

Overlook Hospital (CM, 564 beds), 99 Beauvoir Ave. at Sylvan Rd., Summit 07901; tel. 201/522-2000; Thomas J. Foley, pres. & chief exec. off.

Owned, leased, sponsored:	0 hospitals	0 beds
Contract-managed:	2 hospitals	1170 beds
Totals:	2 hospitals	1170 beds

1625: BAPTIST MEMORIAL HEALTHCARE DEVELOPMENT CORPORATION (NP)
899 Madison Ave., Memphis, TN 38146; Bobby Hancock, sr. vice-pres. asst.

Arkansas: Baptist Memorial Hospital-Forrest City (O, 112 beds), I-40 at State Rd. 284, Box 667, Forrest City 72335; tel. 501/633-2020; Thomas F. Kennedy, adm.

Baptist Memorial Hospital-Eastern Ozarks (O, 25 beds), S. Allegheny Dr., Hardy 72543; tel. 501/257-4101; Ted Spurlock, adm.

Mississippi: Baptist Memorial Hospital-Booneville (O, 78 beds), Washington & Second Sts., Booneville 38829; tel. 601/728-5331; John Tompkins, adm.

Tennessee: Baptist Memorial Hospital-Tipton (O, 99 beds), 1995 Hwy. 51 S., Box 737, Covington 38019; tel. 901/476-2621; William T. Moorer, adm.

Baptist Memorial Hospital-Huntingdon (O, 72 beds), 631 R B Wilson Dr., Huntingdon 38344; tel. 901/986-4461; Stephen L. Mansfield, adm.

Baptist Memorial Hospital (O, 1669 beds), 899 Madison Ave., Memphis 38146; tel. 901/522-5252; Joseph H. Powell, pres.

Baptist Specialty Hospital (O, 50 beds), 1060 Madison Ave., Memphis 38104; Mailing Address P O Box 40029, Memphis, Zip 38174; tel. 901/523-2121; James E. Ramer,actg. adm.

Baptist Memorial Hospital-Lauderdale (O, 70 beds), 326 Asbury Rd., Ripley 38063; tel. 901/635-1331; William E. Torrence Jr., adm.

Baptist Memorial Hospital-Union City (O, 120 beds), Russell & Bishop Sts., Box 310, Union City 38261; tel. 901/885-2410; David C. Hogan, adm.

Owned, leased, sponsored:	9 hospitals	2295 beds
Contract-managed:	0 hospitals	0 beds
Totals:	9 hospitals	2295 beds

For explanation of codes following names, see page B2.
*Indicates Type III membership in the American Hospital Association.

***0305: BAPTIST HEALTH CARE CORPORATION** (NP)
7428 Nicholson Dr., Oklahoma City, OK 73132; 405/721-6504; Joe L. Ingram MD, pres.

Oklahoma: Blackwell Regional Hospital (L, 53 beds), 13th St. & Ferguson Ave., Blackwell 74631; tel. 405/363-2311; Roland D. Gee, adm.

Bristow Memorial Hospital (L, 38 beds), Seventh & Spruce Sts., Box 780, Bristow 74010; tel. 918/367-2215; W. Michael Shawn, adm.

Cordell Memorial Hospital (L, 28 beds), 1220 N. Church St., Cordell 73632; tel. 405/832-3338; Scott Copeland, actg. adm.

Bass Memorial Baptist Hospital (O, 96 beds), 600 S. Monroe, Box 3168, Enid 73702; tel. 405/233-2300; W. Eugene Baxter Drph, adm.

Grove General Hospital (O, 59 beds), 1310 S. Main St., Box 1348, Grove 74344; tel. 918/786-2243; Henry C. Lamb, adm.

Choctaw Memorial Hospital (CM, 63 beds), 1405 E. Kirk Rd., Hugo 74743; tel. 405/326-6414; Lynn Breen, actg. adm.

Baptist Regional Health Center (O, 134 beds), 200 Second St. S.W., Miami 74354; Mailing Address Box 1207, Miami, Zip 74355; tel. 918/542-6611; Bob Phillips, adm.

Okarche Memorial Hospital (L, 25 beds), 300 Memorial Dr., P O Box 218, Okarche 73762; tel. 405/263-4811; Jim M. Robertson, adm.

Grand Valley Hospital (L, 55 beds), 1111 E. Center St., Box 278, Pryor 74362; tel. 918/825-1600; Kenneth J. Fields, adm.

Stroud Municipal Hospital (L, 30 beds), Hwy. 66 W., P O Box 530, Stroud 74079; tel. 918/968-3571; W. M. Shawn, adm.

Owned, leased, sponsored:	9 hospitals	518 beds
Contract-managed:	1 hospitals	63 beds
Totals:	10 hospitals	581 beds

***0315: BAPTIST HEALTHCARE, INC.** (CO)
4007 Kresgee Way, Louisville, KY 40207; 502/561-3277; Ben R. Brewer, pres.

Kentucky: Baptist Regional Medical Center (O, 210 beds), 1 Trillium Way, Corbin 40701; tel. 606/528-1212; Kerry G. Gillihan, adm.

Central Baptist Hospital (O, 338 beds), 1740 S. Limestone St., Lexington 40503; tel. 606/278-3411; Dan H. Akin, pres.

Louisville Baptist Hospitals (O, 545 beds), Tommy J. Smith, pres.

Western Baptist Hospital (O, 344 beds), 2501 Kentucky Ave., Paducah 42001; tel. 502/575-2100; H. Earl Feezor, pres.

Owned, leased, sponsored:	4 hospitals	1437 beds
Contract-managed:	0 hospitals	0 beds
Totals:	4 hospitals	1437 beds

***8810: BAPTIST HOSPITAL AND HEALTH SYSTEMS** (NP)
2224 W. Northern Ave., Suite D-300, Phoenix, AZ 85021; 602/864-1184; J. Barry Johnson, pres.

Arizona: Bullhead Community Hospital (O, 36 beds), 2735 Silver Creek Rd., Bullhead City 86442; tel. 602/763-2273; Joseph P. Harrington, vice-pres. & adm.

Phoenix Baptist Hospital and Medical Center (O, 241 beds), 6025 N. 20th Ave., Phoenix 85015; tel. 602/249-0212; James E. Bagley, sr. exec. vice-pres.

Valley View Community Hospital (L, 104 beds), 12207 N. 113th Ave., Youngtown 85363; tel. 602/933-0155; Larry A. Mullins, exec. vice-pres.

California: Villaview Community Hospital (O, 100 beds), 5550 University Ave., P O Box 5587, San Diego 92105; tel. 619/582-3516; T. N. Pendleton, pres.

Florida: Manatee Memorial Hospital (O, 512 beds), 206 Second St. E., Bradenton 33508; tel. 813/746-5111; Gerald L. Wissink, chief exec. off.

Owned, leased, sponsored:	5 hospitals	993 beds
Contract-managed:	0 hospitals	0 beds
Totals:	5 hospitals	993 beds

***0345: BAPTIST MEDICAL CENTERS** (CO)
2700 U. S. Hwy. 280, P O Box 30040, Birmingham, AL 35222; 205/322-9319; Emmett Johnson, pres.

Alabama: Baptist Medical Center-Montclair (O, 591 beds), 800 Montclair Rd., Birmingham 35213; tel. 205/592-1000; Dennis A. Hall, pres.

Baptist Medical Center-Princeton (O, 443 beds), 701 Princeton Ave. S.W., Birmingham 35211; tel. 205/783-3000; Byron Harrell, pres.

Baptist Medical Center-Cherokee (O, 60 beds), 400 Northwood Dr., Box 150, Centre 35960; tel. 205/927-5531; Barry S. Cochran, exec. dir.

Cullman Medical Center (CM, 169 beds), 401 Arnold St. N.E., P O Box 1108, Cullman 35056; tel. 205/734-1210; Larry W. Throneberry, adm.

Baptist Medical Center-DeKalb (O, 116 beds), 200 Medical Center Dr., P O Box 778, Fort Payne 35967; tel. 205/845-3150; William Hynson, adm.

Owned, leased, sponsored:	4 hospitals	1210 beds
Contract-managed:	1 hospitals	169 beds
Totals:	5 hospitals	1379 beds

***0355: BAPTIST MEDICAL SYSTEM** (NP)
9601 Interstate 630, Exit 7, Little Rock, AR 72205; 501/227-2000; Russell D. Harrington Jr., pres.

Arkansas: Twin Rivers Medical Center (L, 57 beds), 3050 Twin Rivers Dr., Box 98, Arkadelphia 71923; tel. 501/246-9801; Dan Gathright, sr. vice-pres.

White River Medical Center (CM, 97 beds), 1710 Harrison St., Batesville 72501; Mailing Address P O Box 2197, Batesville, Zip 72503; tel. 501/793-1200; Steven B.Lampkin, adm.

Arkansas Rehabilitation Institute (O, 110 beds), 9601 Interstate 630, Exit 7, Little Rock 72205; tel. 501/223-7578; Robin H. Hagaman, sr. vice-pres. & adm.

Baptist Medical Center (O, 617 beds), 9601 Interstate 630, Exit 7, Little Rock 72205; tel. 501/227-2000; Dale Collins, sr. vice-pres.

Memorial Hospital (L, 186 beds), One Pershing Circle, North Little Rock 72114; tel. 501/771-3000; Harrison M. Dean, sr. vice-pres. & adm.

Owned, leased, sponsored:	4 hospitals	970 beds
Contract-managed:	1 hospitals	97 beds
Totals:	5 hospitals	1067 beds

0265: BAPTIST MEMORIAL HOSPITAL SYSTEM (CO)
111 Dallas St., San Antonio, TX 78286; 512/222-8431; David Garrett, pres. & chief exec. off.

Texas: Baptist Medical Center (O, 568 beds), 111 Dallas St., San Antonio 78286; tel. 512/222-8431; David A. Garrett, pres.

Northeast Baptist Hospital (O, 227 beds), 8811 Village Dr., San Antonio 78286; tel. 512/653-2330; Ray M. Harris, adm.

Southeast Baptist Hospital (O, 143 beds), 4214 E. Southcross, San Antonio 78222; tel. 512/337-6900; Harry E. Smith, adm.

Owned, leased, sponsored:	3 hospitals	938 beds
Contract-managed:	0 hospitals	0 beds
Totals:	3 hospitals	938 beds

***0185: BAPTIST REGIONAL HEALTH SERVICES, INC.** (NP)
P O Box 17500, Pensacola, FL 32522; 904/434-4805; James F. Vickery, pres.

Alabama: Mizell Memorial Hospital (O, 99 beds), 702 Main St., Box 429, Opp 36467; tel. 205/493-3541; Don Nelson, adm.

Florida: Gulf Breeze Hospital (O, 29 beds), 1110 Gulf Breeze Pkwy., P O Box 159, Gulf Breeze 32561; tel. 904/934-2000; Richard C. Fulford, adm.

Jay Hospital (L, 52 beds), 221 S. Alabama St., Jay 32565; tel. 904/675-4532; Grady D. Ivey, adm.

For explanation of codes following names, see page B2.
*Indicates Type III membership in the American Hospital Association.

Baptist Hospital (O, 520 beds), Box 17500, Pensacola 32522; tel. 904/434-4011; John N. Robbins, adm.

Owned, leased, sponsored:	4 hospitals	700 beds
Contract-managed:	0 hospitals	0 beds
Totals:	4 hospitals	700 beds

1935: BASIC AMERICAN MEDICAL, INC. (IO)
4000 E. Southport Rd., Indianapolis, IN 46237; 317/783-5461; Brady R. Justice Jr., pres.

Alabama: Henry County Hospital and Nursing Home (L, 108 beds), 212 Dothan Rd., P O Box 639, Abbeville 36310; tel. 205/585-2241; Ann S. Medley, adm.

Georgiana Community Hospital (L, 22 beds), Jones & Miranda Sts., Box 548, Georgiana 36033; tel. 205/376-2205; John Atchison, adm.

Cleburne Community Medical Center and Nursing Home (L, 70 beds), 411 Ross St. S., Box 398, Heflin 36264; tel. 205/463-2121; William B. Ross, adm.

Perry Community Hospital (L, 67 beds), E. Lafayette St., P O Box 149, Marion 36756; tel. 205/683-6111; Marshall L. Nero, adm.

Piedmont Hospital and Nursing Home (L, 78 beds), Calhoun St., Box 330, Piedmont 36272; tel. 205/447-6041; James M. Jumper, adm.

Thomasville Hospital (O, 43 beds), Hwy. 43 N., Drawer 429, Thomasville 36784; tel. 205/636-4431; Benny Ray Stephens, adm.

Wedowee Hospital (L, 34 beds), 301 N. Main St., Box 307, Wedowee 36278; tel. 205/357-2111; Kerlene Mitchell, adm.

Florida: George E. Weems Memorial Hospital (L, 29 beds), Washington Square, Apalachicola 32320; tel. 904/653-8853; Henry D. Shiver, adm.

Southwest Florida Regional Medical Center (O, 400 beds), 3785 Evans Ave., Box 7146, Fort Myers 33901; tel. 813/939-1147; Herbert F. Dorsett, pres.

Campbellton Graceville Hospital (L, 50 beds), 1305 College Dr., Graceville 32440; tel. 904/263-4431; Douglas J. Hammond, adm.

Kissimmee Memorial Hospital (O, 120 beds), 200 Hilda St., Kissimmee 32741; Mailing Address P O Box 2108, Kissimmee, Zip 32742; tel. 305/846-4343; Denny W. Powell,pres.

Fawcett Memorial Hospital (O, 254 beds), 21298 Olean Blvd., Port Charlotte 33952; tel. 813/629-1181; R. Wayne Cole, pres.

Gulf Pines Hospital (O, 45 beds), 102 20th St., P O Box 40, Port St. Joe 32456; tel. 904/227-1121; David Odum, adm.

Georgia: Marion Memorial Hospital (L, 80 beds), Hwy. 41, Box 197, Buena Vista 31803; tel. 912/649-2331; L. E. Peace III, adm.

Terrell County Hospital (O, 34 beds), Cinderella Lane, Box 150, Dawson 31742; tel. 912/995-2121; Kenneth W. Hamilton, adm.

Fort Gaines Hospital (O, 84 beds), Clay County, Box 160, Fort Gaines 31751; tel. 912/768-2521; William B. Ross, adm.

Wheeler County Hospital (O, 40 beds), Third St., Box 398, Glenwood 30428; tel. 912/523-5113; David P. Crowson, adm.

Three Rivers Hospital and Medical Center (O, 48 beds), U. S. 341 S., Rte. 1, Box 5, McRae 31055; tel. 912/868-5621; Gary D. Ballard, adm.

New Jersey: Englewood Hospital (O, 547 beds), 350 Engle St., Englewood 07631; tel. 201/894-3000; Ronald C. Dematteo, pres.

Puerto Rico: Hato Rey Community Hospital (O, 246 beds), 435 Ponce De Leon Ave., Hato Rey, San Juan 00917; tel. 809/754-0909; Miguel A. Solivan, adm.

South Carolina: Live Oaks Hospital (L, 46 beds), Hwy. 278, Drawer 400, Ridgeland 29936; tel. 803/726-8111; William B. Sowell Jr., adm.

Owned, leased, sponsored:	21 hospitals	2445 beds
Contract-managed:	0 hospitals	0 beds
Totals:	21 hospitals	2445 beds

0095: BAYLOR HEALTH CARE SYSTEM (NP)
3201 Worth St., P O Box 26265, Dallas, TX 75226; 214/820-2891; Boone Powell Jr., pres.

Texas: Baylor Institute for Rehabilitation (O, 74 beds), 3504 Swiss Ave., Dallas 75204; tel. 214/826-7030; F. Dana Ellerbe, exec. dir.

Baylor University Medical Center (O, 1455 beds), 3500 Gaston Ave., Dallas 75246; tel. 214/820-0111; Boone Powell Jr., pres.

Baylor Medical Center at Ennis (O, 43 beds), 803 W. Lampasas St., Ennis 75119; tel. 214/875-3837; Ronald Hudspeth, pres.

Baylor Medical Center at Gilmer (O, 46 beds), 712 N. Wood St., Gilmer 75644; tel. 214/843-5611; James A. Summersett III, exec. dir.

Baylor Medical Center at Grapevine (O, 45 beds), 1650 W. College St., Grapevine 76051; tel. 817/488-7546; Arthur L. Hohenberger, exec. dir.

Baylor Medical Center at Waxahachie (O, 48 beds), 1405 W. Jefferson St., Waxahachie 75165; tel. 214/937-5910; James M. Person, exec. dir.

Owned, leased, sponsored:	6 hospitals	1711 beds
Contract-managed:	0 hospitals	0 beds
Totals:	6 hospitals	1711 beds

***1095: BAYSTATE HEALTH SYSTEMS, INC.** (NP)
759 Chestnut St., Springfield, MA 01199; 413/787-3345; Michael J. Daly, pres. & chief exec. off.

Massachusetts: Franklin Medical Center (O, 142 beds), 164 High St., Greenfield 01301; tel. 413/772-0211; Richard Harris, pres.

Baystate Medical Center (O, 741 beds), 759 Chestnut St., Springfield 01199; tel. 413/787-2500; Michael J. Daly, pres.

Owned, leased, sponsored:	2 hospitals	883 beds
Contract-managed:	0 hospitals	0 beds
Totals:	2 hospitals	883 beds

0515: BENEDICTINE HEALTH SYSTEM (CC)
1028 E. Eighth St., Duluth, MN 55805; 218/722-4799; Sr. Rebecca Wright, pres.

Minnesota: St. Joseph's Medical Center (O, 162 beds), 523 N. Third St., Brainerd 56401; tel. 218/829-2861; James E. Koerper, pres.

St. Mary's Medical Center (O, 303 beds), 407 E. Third St., Duluth 55805; tel. 218/726-4000; Sr. Kathleen Hofer, pres.

Owned, leased, sponsored:	2 hospitals	465 beds
Contract-managed:	0 hospitals	0 beds
Totals:	2 hospitals	465 beds

1635: BENEDICTINE HEALTH SYSTEM (CC)
1005 W. Eighth St., Yankton, SD 57078; 605/668-1511; Sr. Rosaria Kranz, pres.

Colorado: St. Thomas More Hospital and Progressive Care Center (O, 201 beds), 1019 Sheridan St., Canon City 81212; tel. 303/275-3381; Sr. Judith Kuhn, adm.

South Dakota: St. Benedict Hospital (O, 30 beds), Glynn Dr., P O Box B, Parkston 57366; tel. 605/928-3311; Gale Walker, adm.

St. Michael's Hospital (O, 34 beds), Third St. & Broadway, Box 27, Tyndall 57066; tel. 605/589-3341; Gale N. Walker, chief exec. off.

Sacred Heart Hospital (O, 257 beds), 501 Summit, Yankton 57078; tel. 605/665-9371; Dennis A. Sokol, pres. & chief exec. off.

Owned, leased, sponsored:	4 hospitals	522 beds
Contract-managed:	0 hospitals	0 beds
Totals:	4 hospitals	522 beds

For explanation of codes following names, see page B2.
*Indicates Type III membership in the American Hospital Association

0505: BENEDICTINE SISTERS (CC)
Priory of St. Gertrude, Box 107, Cottonwood, ID 83522; 208/962-3224; Sr. Mary Matthew Geis,

Idaho: St. Mary's Hospital (O, 28 beds), Lewiston & North Sts., P O Box 137, Cottonwood 83522; tel. 208/962-3251; John R. Hull, adm.

St. Benedict's Family Medical Center (O, 80 beds), 709 N. Lincoln Ave., Box 586, Jerome 83338; tel. 208/324-4301; Robert D. Campbell, chief exec. off.

Owned, leased, sponsored:	2 hospitals	108 beds
Contract-managed:	0 hospitals	0 beds
Totals:	2 hospitals	108 beds

0535: BENEDICTINE SISTERS (CC)
St. Benedicts Convent, St. Joseph, MN 56374; 612/362-5100; Sr. Katherine Howard,

Minnesota: Queen of Peace Hospital (S, 56 beds), 301 Second St. N.E., New Prague 56071; tel. 612/758-4431; Sr. Jean Juenemann, chief exec. off.

St. Cloud Hospital (S, 360 beds), 1406 Sixth Ave. N., St. Cloud 56301; tel. 612/251-2700; John R. Frobenius, exec. vice-pres.

Owned, leased, sponsored:	2 hospitals	416 beds
Contract-managed:	0 hospitals	0 beds
Totals:	2 hospitals	416 beds

0545: BENEDICTINE SISTERS OF THE ANNUNCIATION (CC)
7520 University Dr., Bismarck, ND 58501; 701/255-1520; Sr. Susan Lardy, prioress

North Dakota: St. Alexius Medical Center (O, 278 beds), 900 E. Broadway, Bismarck 58501; Mailing Address Box 1658, Bismarck, Zip 58502; tel. 701/224-7000; Richard Tschider,adm.

Garrison Memorial Hospital (O, 56 beds), Garrison 58540; tel. 701/463-2275; Sr. Madonna Wagendorf, adm.

Owned, leased, sponsored:	2 hospitals	334 beds
Contract-managed:	0 hospitals	0 beds
Totals:	2 hospitals	334 beds

***0745: BERKSHIRE HEALTH SYSTEMS** (NP)
Sixth & Spruce, West Reading, PA 19603; 215/378-6257; James B. Gronseth, chief exec. off.

Pennsylvania: Coaldale State General Hospital (CM, 162 beds), Seventh St., Coaldale 18218; tel. 717/645-2131; Frank J. Parano, adm.

Pottsville Hospital and Warne Clinic (CM, 179 beds), 420 S. Jackson St., Pottsville 17901; tel. 717/622-6120; Thomas J. Lonergan, adm.

Community General Hospital (O, 173 beds), 145 N. Sixth St., Reading 19601; Mailing Address P O Box 1728, Reading, Zip 19603; tel. 215/376-4881; Lawrence ScanlanJr., pres.

Reading Hospital and Medical Center (O, 573 beds), Sixth Ave. & Spruce St., Reading 19603; tel. 215/378-6257; James B. Gronseth, vice chm.

Owned, leased, sponsored:	2 hospitals	746 beds
Contract-managed:	2 hospitals	341 beds
Totals:	4 hospitals	1087 beds

0285: BERNARDINE SISTERS OF THE 3RD ORDER OF ST. FRANCIS (CC)
647 Springmill Rd.-Maryview, Villanova, PA 19085; 215/525-2686; Sr. M. Gerald, supr. gen.

Pennsylvania: Sacred Heart Medical Center (S, 236 beds), Ninth & Wilson Sts., Chester 19013; tel. 215/494-0700; Sr. Mary Margaret, pres.

Hazleton-St. Joseph Medical Center (S, 190 beds), 687 N. Church St., Hazleton 18201; tel. 717/459-4444; Sr. M. Edwinalda RN, pres.

Owned, leased, sponsored:	2 hospitals	426 beds
Contract-managed:	0 hospitals	0 beds
Totals:	2 hospitals	426 beds

***0415: BETHESDA HOSPITAL, INC.** (NP)
619 Oak St., Cincinnati, OH 45206; 513/569-6111; L. Thomas Wilburn Jr., chm. & chief exec. off.

Ohio: Bethesda North Hospital (O, 287 beds), 10500 Montgomery Rd., Cincinnati 45242; tel. 513/745-1111

Bethesda Oak Hospital (O, 519 beds), 619 Oak St., Cincinnati 45206; tel. 513/569-6111; Larry W. Collins, group vice-pres.

Owned, leased, sponsored:	2 hospitals	806 beds
Contract-managed:	0 hospitals	0 beds
Totals:	2 hospitals	806 beds

***5085: BON SECOURS HEALTH SYSTEM, INC.** (CC)
5457 Twin Knolls Rd., Suite 300, Columbia, MD 21045; 301/992-7330; John P. Brozovich, pres. & chief exec. off. oper.

Florida: Bon Secours Hospital (O, 272 beds), 1050 N.E. 125th St., North Miami 33161; tel. 305/891-8850; Warren R. Slavin, exec. vice-pres.

Maryland: Bon Secours Hospital (O, 202 beds), 2000 W. Baltimore St., Baltimore 21223; tel. 301/362-3000; Victor A. Broccolino, chief exec. off. & exec. vice-pres.

Michigan: Bon Secours Hospital (O, 311 beds), 468 Cadieux Rd., Grosse Pointe 48230; tel. 313/343-1000; Christopher M. Carney, exec. dir. & chief exec. off.

Virginia: Mary Immaculate Hospital (CM, 110 beds), 800 Denbigh Blvd., Newport News 23602; tel. 804/872-0100; Michael B. Cronin, chief exec. off.

Maryview Hospital (O, 288 beds), 3636 High St., Portsmouth 23707; tel. 804/398-2200; J. Bland Burkhardt Jr., chief exec. off.

St. John's Hospital (O, 70 beds), Rte. 2, Box 389, Richmond 23233; tel. 804/784-3501; Mark Hierholzer, exec. vice-pres.

St. Mary's Hospital (O, 369 beds), 5801 Bremo Rd., Richmond 23226; tel. 804/285-2011; Richard D. O'Hallaron, exec. vice-pres.

Owned, leased, sponsored:	6 hospitals	1512 beds
Contract-managed:	1 hospitals	110 beds
Totals:	7 hospitals	1622 beds

0585: BRIM AND ASSOCIATES, INC. (IO)
177 N. E. 102nd Ave., Portland, OR 97220; 503/256-2070; A. E. Brim, pres.

Arizona: Navapache Hospital (CM, 29 beds), 2200 Show Low Lake Rd., Show Low 85901; tel. 602/537-4375; Jim Marovich, adm.

California: Pioneers Memorial Hospital (CM, 78 beds), 207 W. Legion Rd., Brawley 92227; tel. 619/344-2120; Willis D. Cox, adm.

Redbud Community Hospital (CM, 40 beds), Box 6720, Clearlake 95422; tel. 707/994-6486; Rusty Shelton, exec. dir.

General Hospital (CM, 84 beds), 2200 Harrison Ave., Eureka 95501; tel. 707/445-5111; Vern Reed, chief exec. off.

George L. Mee Memorial Hospital (CM, 42 beds), 300 Canal St., King City 93930; tel. 408/385-5491; Arthur Marcello, adm.

John C. Fremont Hospital (CM, 34 beds), 5189 Hospital Rd., Box 216, Mariposa 95338; tel. 209/966-3631; David W. Goger, chief exec. off.

Merced Community Medical Center (CM, 158 beds), 301 E. 13th St., Box 231, Merced 95340; tel. 209/385-7000; Kenneth E. Monfore Jr., chief exec. off.

Community Hospital of Salinas (CM, 42 beds), 970 Circle Dr., Salinas 93905; tel. 408/424-0381; James R. Schlaak, adm.

Natividad Medical Center (CM, 173 beds), 1330 Natividad Rd., Salinas 93902; Mailing Address Box 81611, Salinas, Zip 93912; tel. 408/757-0200; James H. Youree,adm.

Community Hospital (CM, 145 beds), 3325 Chanate Rd., Santa Rosa 95404; tel. 707/544-3340; Larry E. Hood, adm.

North Coast Rehabilitation Center (CM, 61 beds), 151 Sotoyome St., Santa Rosa 95405; tel. 707/542-2771; Pamela Killian, adm.

For explanation of codes following names, see page B2.
*Indicates Type III membership in the American Hospital Association.

Tuolumne General Hospital (CM, 64 beds), 101 E. Hospital Rd., Sonora 95370; tel. 209/532-3401; Lawrence C. Long, adm.

Victor Valley Community Hospital (CM, 91 beds), 15248 11th St., Victorville 92392; tel. 619/245-8691

Covina Valley Community Hospital (CM, 76 beds), 845 N. Lark Ellen Ave., West Covina 91791; tel. 818/339-5451; David L. Hendry, adm.

Colorado: Weisbrod Memorial Hospital (CM, 42 beds), 1208 Luther St., P O Box 817, Eads 81036; tel. 303/438-5401; Andrew Wills, adm.

Fort Morgan Community Hospital (CM, 40 beds), 1000 Lincoln St., Fort Morgan 80701; tel. 303/867-5671; Gary J. Guidetti, chief exec. off.

Yuma District Hospital (CM, 18 beds), 910 S. Main St., Yuma 80759; tel. 303/848-5405; James Naeve, adm.

Georgia: Glynn-Brunswick Memorial Hospital (CM, 340 beds), 3100 Kemble Ave., Brunswick 31520; Mailing Address Box 1518, Brunswick, Zip 31521; tel. 912/264-6960; DavidDunham, adm.

Idaho: Memorial Hospital (CM, 27 beds), 645 E. Fifth St., Box 550, Weiser 83672; tel. 208/549-0370; Byron Quinton, exec. dir.

Illinois: Norwegian-American Hospital (CM, 230 beds), 1044 N. Francisco Ave., Chicago 60622; tel. 312/278-8800; William Leyhe, adm.

American International Hospital (CM, 95 beds), Emmaus & Shiloh Blvd., Zion 60099; tel. 312/872-4561; Kenneth F. Sample, adm.

Missouri: St. Louis Regional Medical Center (CM, 231 beds), 5535 Delmar Blvd., St. Louis 63112; tel. 314/361-1212; Robert B. Johnson, chief exec. off.

Montana: Barrett Memorial Hospital (CM, 31 beds), 1260 S. Atlantic St., Dillon 59725; tel. 406/683-2324; Myron Mortier, exec. dir.

Rosebud Community Hospital (CM, 75 beds), 383 N. 17th Ave., Forsyth 59327; tel. 406/356-2161; Joyce Asay, adm.

Big Horn County Memorial Hospital (CM, 50 beds), 17 N. Miles St., Hardin 59034; tel. 406/665-2310; Mike N. Sinclair, exec. dir.

St. John's Lutheran Hospital (CM, 29 beds), 350 Louisiana Ave., Libby 59923; tel. 406/293-7761; Raymond Bergroos, adm.

Missoula Community Hospital (CM, 125 beds), 2827 Fort Missoula Rd., Missoula 59801; tel. 406/728-4100; Grant M. Winn, exec. dir.

Clark Fork Valley Hospital (CM, 44 beds), Box 768, Plains 59859; tel. 406/826-3601; Michael Billing, chief exec. off.

Roundup Memorial Hospital (CM, 33 beds), 1202 Third St. W., P O Box 627, Roundup 59072; tel. 406/323-2302; Fern E. Mikkelson, exec. dir.

Mineral County Hospital (CM, 30 beds), Roosevelt & Brooklyn, Box 66, Superior 59872; tel. 406/822-4841; Madelyn Faller, exec. dir.

North Valley Hospital (CM, 100 beds), 6575 Hwy. 93 S., Whitefish 59937; tel. 406/862-2501; Dale Jessup, adm.

Trinity Hospital (CM, 42 beds), 315 K St., Wolf Point 59201; tel. 406/653-2100

New Jersey: Bergen Pines County Hospital (CM, 1045 beds), E. Ridgewood Ave., Paramus 07652; tel. 201/967-4000; Frank Kopczynski, interim chief exec. off.

New Mexico: Northeastern Regional Hospital (CM, 62 beds), 1235 Eighth St., Box 238, Las Vegas 87701; tel. 505/425-6751; Larry Thompson, adm.

Holy Cross Hospital (CM, 33 beds), Santa Fe Rd., Box Dd, Taos 87571; tel. 505/758-8883; Leigh Cox, adm.

North Carolina: Pungo District Hospital (CM, 32 beds), Front St., Belhaven 27810; tel. 919/943-2111; Dan C. White, adm.

Oregon: Cottage Grove Hospital (CM, 65 beds), 1340 Birch Ave., Cottage Grove 97424; tel. 503/942-0511; John L. Hoopes, adm.

Eugene Hospital (CM, 57 beds), 1162 Willamette St., Eugene 97401; tel. 503/687-6000; Hugh Prichard, exec. dir.

Mountain View District Hospital (CM, 102 beds), 1270 A St., Madras 97741; tel. 503/475-3882; Ronald W. Barnes, adm.

Lower Umpqua Hospital District (CM, 40 beds), 600 Ranch Rd., Reedsport 97467; tel. 503/271-2171; Richard R. Bell, exec. dir.

Washington: Coulee Community Hospital (CM, 46 beds), 411 Fortuyn Rd., P O Box H, Grand Coulee 99133; tel. 509/633-1753; David A. Page, adm.

Sunnyside Community Hospital (CM, 80 beds), Tenth & Tacoma Ave., P O Box 719, Sunnyside 98944; tel. 509/837-2101; Robert L. Brendgard, adm.

Lakewood Hospital (CM, 87 beds), 5702 100th St. S.W., Tacoma 98499; tel. 206/588-1711; Richard Vanberg, adm.

Wisconsin: Divine Savior Hospital and Nursing Home (CM, 184 beds), 1015 W. Pleasant St., P O Box 387, Portage 53901; tel. 608/742-4131; Kenneth Van Bree, exec. dir.

Wyoming: West Park Hospital (CM, 147 beds), 707 Sheridan Ave., Cody 82414; tel. 307/527-7501; Ruth McDaniel, adm.

Owned, leased, sponsored:	0 hospitals	0 beds
Contract-managed:	45 hospitals	4679 beds
Totals:	45 hospitals	4679 beds

9305: BROMENN HEALTHCARE (CO)
807 N. Main St., Bloomington, IL 61702; 309/827-4321; Jeffrey B. Schaub, pres.

Illinois: Mennonite Hospital (O, 221 beds), 807 N. Main St., Bloomington 61702; tel. 309/827-4321; David A. Schertz, chief oper. off.

Eureka Community Hospital (O, 35 beds), 101 S. Major St., Eureka 61530; tel. 309/467-2371; Kay Schraith, adm.

Brokaw Hospital (O, 213 beds), Virginia & Franklin Sts., Normal 61761; tel. 309/454-1400

Owned, leased, sponsored:	3 hospitals	469 beds
Contract-managed:	0 hospitals	0 beds
Totals:	3 hospitals	469 beds

***0595: BRONSON HEALTHCARE GROUP, INC.** (NP)
One Healthcare Plaza, Kalamazoo, MI 49007; 616/344-5222; Russell P. Kneen, chm. & chief exec. off.

Michigan: Bronson Methodist Hospital (O, 456 beds), 252 E. Lovell St., Kalamazoo 49007; tel. 616/383-7654; Peter W. Froyd, pres.

Bronson Vicksburg Hospital (O, 41 beds), 13326 N. Boulevard, Vicksburg 49097; tel. 616/649-2321; Edward Spartz, pres.

Owned, leased, sponsored:	2 hospitals	497 beds
Contract-managed:	0 hospitals	0 beds
Totals:	2 hospitals	497 beds

6665: BRUNSWICK HOSPITAL CENTER (IO)
366 Broadway, Amityville, NY 11701; 516/789-7000; Benjamin M. Stein MD, pres.

New York: Brunswick General Hospital (O, 255 beds), 366 Broadway, Amityville 11701; tel. 516/789-7000; Benjamin M. Stein MD, pres.

Brunswick Hall (O, 122 beds), 80 Louden Ave., Amityville 11701; tel. 516/789-7100; Benjamin M. Stein MD, pres.; Harold Lasker MD, med. dir.

Brunswick House Alcoholism Treatment Center (O, 76 beds), 81 Louden Ave., Amityville 11701; tel. 516/789-7361; Barbara L. McGinley, exec. dir.; Joseph D. BeasleyMD, med. dir.

Brunswick Physical Medicine and Rehabilitation Hospital (O, 64 beds), 366 Broadway, Amityville 11701; tel. 516/789-7000; Benjamin M. Stein MD, pres.; EduardoRodriguez MD, med. dir.

Owned, leased, sponsored:	4 hospitals	517 beds
Contract-managed:	0 hospitals	0 beds
Totals:	4 hospitals	517 beds

For explanation of codes following names, see page B2.
*Indicates Type III membership in the American Hospital Association.

***0955: CAMCARE, INC.** (NP)
Box 1547, Charleston, WV 25326; 304/348-7627; James C. Crews, pres.

West Virginia: Charleston Area Medical Center (O, 934 beds), Morris St., Box 1547, Charleston 25326; tel. 304/348-7627; James C. Crews, pres.

Braxton County Memorial Hospital (CM, 30 beds), 100 Hoylman Dr., Gassaway 26624; tel. 304/364-5156; Kenneth L. Wilson, adm.

Owned, leased, sponsored:	1 hospitals	934 beds
Contract-managed:	1 hospitals	30 beds
Totals:	2 hospitals	964 beds

***9855: CAMELBACK HOSPITALS, INC.** (NP)
7447 E. Earll Dr., Scottsdale, AZ 85251; 602/941-7660; Daniel W. Capps, pres. & chief exec. off.

Arizona: West Valley Camelback Hospital (O, 84 beds), 5625 W. Thunderbird Rd., Glendale 85306; tel. 602/588-4700; Dale Rinard, chief exec. off.

Phoenix Camelback Hospital (O, 89 beds), 5055 N. 34th St., Phoenix 85018; tel. 602/955-6200; Beryl Janick, vice-pres. & chief exec. off.

Scottsdale Camelback Hospital (O, 98 beds), 7575 E. Earll Dr., Scottsdale 85251; tel. 602/941-7500; Frank Adame Jr., chief exec. off.

Texas: Clearview Hospital (O, 49 beds), P O Box 4757, Midland 79704; tel. 915/697-5200; Philip H. Lundberg, adm.

Owned, leased, sponsored:	4 hospitals	320 beds
Contract-managed:	0 hospitals	0 beds
Totals:	4 hospitals	320 beds

***5175: CATHOLIC HEALTH CORPORATION** (CC)
920 S. 107th Ave., Omaha, NE 68114; 402/393-7661; Diane Moeller, pres.

California: Sacred Heart Hospital (CM, 88 beds), 1025 N. Douty St., Box 480, Hanford 93232; tel. 209/582-2551; Matt Luebbers, interim adm.

Mercy Hospital (CM, 93 beds), 2740 M St., Merced 95340; tel. 209/384-6444; Louis J. Carlentine, chief exec. off.

St. Elizabeth Community Hospital (CM, 76 beds), 2550 Sister Mary Columba Dr., Red Bluff 96080; tel. 916/527-2112; R. Michael Barry, pres. & chief exec. off.

Colorado: Mercy Medical Center (CM, 386 beds), 1650 Fillmore St., Denver 80206; tel. 303/393-3000; Daniel Aten, pres.

Mercy Medical Center (CM, 101 beds), 375 E. Park Ave., Durango 81301; tel. 303/247-4311; Michael J. Lawler, pres.

Idaho: Mercy Medical Center (CM, 85 beds), 1512 12th Avenue Rd., Nampa 83651; tel. 208/467-1171; C. Kregg Hanson, pres. & chief exec. off.

Iowa: St. Joseph's Mercy Hospital (CM, 55 beds), Rte. 3, Centerville 52544; tel. 515/437-4111; Kenneth L. Smithmier, chief exec. off.

Mercy Hospital (CM, 35 beds), Rosary Dr., Box 368, Corning 50841; tel. 515/322-3121; James C. Ruppert, adm.

Mercy Hospital (CM, 284 beds), 800 Mercy Dr., Box 1c, Council Bluffs 51502; tel. 712/328-5000; Mervin M. Riepe, pres.

Mercy Hospital Medical Center (CM, 500 beds), Sixth & University Ave., Des Moines 50314; tel. 515/247-3121; Sr. Patricia Clare Sullivan, pres.

St. Joseph Health and Rehabilitation Center (CM, 90 beds), 312 E. Alta Vista Ave., Ottumwa 52501; tel. 515/684-4651; Sr. Pauline Tursi, pres.

Kansas: St. Catherine Hospital (CM, 112 beds), 608 N. Fifth St., Garden City 67846; tel. 316/275-6111; Steven D. Wilkinson, pres. & chief exec. off.

Central Kansas Medical Center (CM, 135 beds), 3515 Broadway St., Great Bend 67530; tel. 316/792-2511; Sr. Philomena Hrencher, pres.

St. Joseph Memorial Hospital (CM, 68 beds), 923 Carroll Ave., Larned 67550; tel. 316/285-3161; Garrett E. Colquette, chief oper. off.

Minnesota: Divine Providence Hospital and Home (CM, 79 beds), Ivanhoe 56142; tel. 507/694-1414; Sr. Mariette Ketterer, adm.

Missouri: St. John's Regional Medical Center (CM, 345 beds), 2727 McClelland Blvd., Joplin 64804; tel. 417/781-2727; Robert J. Fanning, pres. & chief exec. off.

Nebraska: Archbishop Bergan Mercy Hospital (CM, 619 beds), 7500 Mercy Rd., Omaha 68124; tel. 402/398-6060; Larry C. Rennecker, pres.

North Dakota: Carrington Health Center (CM, 66 beds), 800 N. Fourth St., Carrington 58421; tel. 701/652-3141; Duane D. Jerde, chief exec. off.

Mercy Hospital (CM, 110 beds), E. Seventh St., Devils Lake 58301; tel. 701/662-2131; Marlene Krein, pres.

City Hospital (CM, 26 beds), 214 Second Ave. S., New Rockford 58356; tel. 701/947-2411; Thomas J. O'Halloran, pres. & chief exec. off.

St. Ansgar's Hospital (CM, 25 beds), 715 Vivian St., Park River 58270; tel. 701/284-7233

Mercy Hospital (CM, 40 beds), 570 Chautauqua Blvd., Valley City 58072; tel. 701/845-0440; Ray Weisgarber, pres. & chief exec. off.

Mercy Medical Center and Hospital (CM, 84 beds), 1301 15th Ave. W., Williston 58801; tel. 701/774-7400; Robert A. Fale, actg. pres.

Oregon: Forest Glen Hospital (CM, 23 beds), 495 S.W. First St., P O Box 198, Canyonville 97417; tel. 503/839-4211; David L. Harman, pres.

Holy Rosary Hospital (CM, 77 beds), 351 S.W. Ninth St., Ontario 97914; tel. 503/889-5331; David J. Goode, adm.

Mercy Medical Center (CM, 111 beds), 2700 Stewart Pkwy., Roseburg 97470; tel. 503/673-0611; Sr. Jacquetta Taylor, pres. & chief exec. off.

South Dakota: Gettysburg Memorial Hospital (CM, 28 beds), 606 E. Garfield, Gettysburg 57442; tel. 605/765-2488; Arthur C. Quance, adm.

St. Mary's Hospital (CM, 86 beds), 800 E. Dakota Ave., Pierre 57501; tel. 605/224-3100; James D. M. Russell, adm.

Washington: St. Joseph's Hospital (CM, 25 beds), 500 E. Webster Ave., P O Box 197, Chewelah 99109; tel. 509/935-8211; Eddie L. Grady, pres.

Mount Carmel Hospital (CM, 48 beds), 982 E. Columbia St., Box 351, Colville 99114; tel. 509/684-2561; Gloria Cooper, pres.

Holy Family Hospital (CM, 200 beds), 5633 N. Lidgerwood St., Spokane 99207; tel. 509/482-0111; Michael D. Wilson, pres.

Owned, leased, sponsored:	0 hospitals	0 beds
Contract-managed:	31 hospitals	4100 beds
Totals:	31 hospitals	4100 beds

***5205: CATHOLIC HEALTHCARE WEST** (CC)
2300 Adeline Dr., Burlingame, CA 94010; 415/340-7470; Robert C. Densmore, pres.

Arizona: St. Joseph's Hospital and Medical Center (S, 656 beds), 350 W. Thomas Rd., Phoenix 85013; Mailing Address Box 2071, Phoenix, Zip 85001; tel. 602/285-3000; JohnJ. Buckley Jr., pres.

California: Mercy Hospital (S, 276 beds), 2215 Truxtun Ave., Bakersfield 93301; Mailing Address Box 119, Bakersfield, Zip 93302; tel. 805/327-3371; Sr. Phyllis Hughes,pres.

Mercy San Juan Hospital (O, 211 beds), 6501 Coyle Ave., P O Box 479, Carmichael 95608; tel. 916/537-5000; Gregg R. Schnepple, pres.

Mercy Hospital of Folsom (O, 34 beds), 223 Fargo Way, Folsom 95630; tel. 916/985-4441; J. R. Eason, adm.

Mercy Medical Center Mount Shasta (O, 33 beds), 914 Pine St., P O Box 239, Mount Shasta 96067; tel. 916/926-6111; James R. Hoss, adm.

For explanation of codes following names, see page B2.
*Indicates Type III membership in the American Hospital Association.

St. John's Regional Medical Center (S, 260 beds), 333 N. F St., Oxnard 93030; tel. 805/988-2500; Daniel R. Herlinger, pres.

Mercy Medical Center (O, 188 beds), Clairmont Hts., Redding 96001; Mailing Address Box 6009, Redding, Zip 96099; tel. 916/243-2121; George A. Govier, chief exec.off.

Mercy Hospital of Sacramento (O, 385 beds), 4001 J St., Sacramento 95819; tel. 916/453-4545; Sr. Bridget McCarthy, pres. & chief exec. off.

Mercy Hospital and Medical Center (S, 416 beds), 4077 Fifth Ave., San Diego 92103; tel. 619/294-8111; Richard L. Keyser, pres. & chief exec. off.

St. Mary's Hospital and Medical Center (S, 489 beds), 450 Stanyan St., San Francisco 94117; tel. 415/668-1000; James E. Metcalfe, pres.

Owned, leased, sponsored:	10 hospitals	2948 beds
Contract-managed:	0 hospitals	0 beds
Totals:	10 hospitals	2948 beds

***5805: CENTRAL MANAGEMENT CORPORATION** (CC)
112-114 Roberts St., Suite 208, Fargo, ND 58102; 701/237-9290; James Dunne, pres.

Illinois: St. Margaret's Hospital (O, 100 beds), 600 E. First St., Spring Valley 61362; tel. 815/664-5311; Kelby K. Krabbenhoft, pres.

Iowa: Guttenberg Municipal Hospital (CM, 37 beds), Second & Main St., Box A, Guttenberg 52052; tel. 319/252-1121

Van Buren County Memorial Hospital (CM, 40 beds), Rural Rte. 1, Box 70, Keosauqua 52565; tel. 319/293-3171; Ronald J. Volk, adm.

North Dakota: St. Andrew's Hospital (O, 67 beds), 316 Ohmer St., Bottineau 58318; tel. 701/228-2255; Keith Korman, pres.

St. Aloisius Medical Center (O, 165 beds), 325 E. Brewster St., Harvey 58341; tel. 701/324-4651; Michael Pfeifer, pres.

Rolla Community Hospital (O, 96 beds), 213 Third St. N.E., P O Box 759, Rolla 58367; tel. 701/477-3161; Michael A. Baumgartner, pres. & chief exec. off.

Owned, leased, sponsored:	4 hospitals	428 beds
Contract-managed:	2 hospitals	77 beds
Totals:	6 hospitals	505 beds

0665: CENTURY HEALTHCARE CORPORATION (IO)
7615 E. 63rd Pl., Suite 200, Tulsa, OK 74133; 918/250-9651; Jerry D. Dillon, pres. & chief exec. off.

California: Newport Harbor Psychiatric Institute (O, 34 beds), 1501 E. 16th St., Newport Beach 92663; tel. 714/642-9310; Tom Heitman, adm.

Oklahoma: Shadow Mountain Institute (O, 100 beds), 6262 S. Sheridan, Tulsa 74133; tel. 918/492-8200; Donald E. Carlson, adm.

Owned, leased, sponsored:	2 hospitals	134 beds
Contract-managed:	0 hospitals	0 beds
Totals:	2 hospitals	134 beds

0705: CHARLOTTE-MECKLENBURG HOSPITAL AUTHORITY (NP)
Box 32861, Charlotte, NC 28232; 704/338-2145; Harry A. Nurkin PhD, pres.

North Carolina: Charlotte Memorial Hospital and Medical Center (O, 843 beds), 1000 Blythe Blvd., Charlotte 28203; Mailing Address P O Box 32861, Charlotte, Zip 28232; tel.704/338-2000; Harry A. Nurkin PhD, pres.

Charlotte Rehabilitation Hospital (O, 88 beds), 1100 Blythe Blvd., Charlotte 28203; tel. 704/338-4300; A. Charles Collier, adm.

University Memorial Hospital (O, 48 beds), P O Box 26015, Charlotte 28221; tel. 704/547-9200; Charles D. Herring, adm.

Owned, leased, sponsored:	3 hospitals	979 beds
Contract-managed:	0 hospitals	0 beds
Totals:	3 hospitals	979 beds

***0695: CHARTER MEDICAL CORPORATION** (IO)
577 Mulberry St., Macon, GA 31202; Mailing Address P O Box 209, Macon, Zip 31298; 912/742-1161; William A. Fickling Jr., chm. & chief exec. off.

Alabama: Charter Retreat Hospital and Recovery Center (O, 104 beds), 2205 Beltline Rd. S.W., P O Box 1230, Decatur 35602; tel. 205/350-1450; Pamela W. McCullough, adm.

Charter Woods Hospital (O, 75 beds), 700 Cottonwood Rd., P O Box 6138, Dothan 36301; tel. 205/793-6660; Allen W. Moon, adm.

Charter Southland Hospital (O, 84 beds), 5800 Southland Dr., P O Box 9699, Mobile 36609; tel. 205/666-7900; James F. Button, adm.

Alaska: Charter North Hospital (O, 80 beds), 2530 Debarr Rd., Anchorage 99508; tel. 907/258-7575; Steven D. Berkshire, adm.

Arkansas: Charter Vista Hospital (O, 65 beds), 4253 Crossover Rd., Fayetteville 72702; tel. 501/521-5731; Dan Johnson, group adm.

California: Charter Grove Hospital (O, 82 beds), 2005 Kellogg Ave., Corona 91719; tel. 714/735-2910; James P. Fridlington, adm.

Charter Oak Hospital (O, 83 beds), 1161 E. Covina Blvd., Covina 91724; tel. 818/966-1632; Barbara Cech Noblet, adm.

Charter Community Hospital (O, 150 beds), 21530 S. Pioneer Blvd., Hawaiian Gardens 90716; tel. 213/860-0401; Wendy Bardet, adm.

Charter Hospital of Long Beach (O, 187 beds), 6060 Paramount Blvd., Long Beach 90805; tel. 213/634-9102; James Sholes, chief exec. off.

Charter Suburban Hospital -Paramount (O, 184 beds), 16453 S. Colorado Ave., Paramount 90723; tel. 213/531-3110; Gary W. Turner, adm.

Charter Pacific Hospital (O, 63 beds), 4025 W. 226th St., Torrance 90505; tel. 213/373-7733; Steven Hirsch, adm.

Florida: Charter Glade Hospital (O, 104 beds), 3550 Colonial Blvd., P O Box 06120, Fort Myers 33906; tel. 813/939-0403; Stanley G. Hilliard, adm.

Charter Springs Hospital (O, 68 beds), 3130 S.W. 27th Ave., P O Box 3338, Ocala 32678; tel. 904/237-7293; Gregory A. Williams, adm.

Charter Hospital of Tampa Bay (O, 133 beds), 4004 N. Riverside Dr., Tampa 33603; tel. 813/238-8671; James P. Hackett Jr., adm.

Georgia: Charter Winds Hospital (O, 65 beds), 240 Mitchell Bridge Rd., P O Box 6297, Athens 30604; tel. 404/546-7277; Elbert T. McQueen, adm.

Charter Peachford Hospital (O, 214 beds), 2151 Peachford Rd., Atlanta 30338; tel. 404/455-3200; James W. Eyler, adm.

Metropolitan Hospital (O, 64 beds), 3223 Howell Mill Rd. N.W., Atlanta 30327; tel. 404/351-0500; Richard F. Jensen, adm.

Shallowford Hospital (O, 157 beds), 4575 N. Shallowford Rd., Box 80846, Chamblee 30338; tel. 404/455-6000; Erich J. Wolters, adm.

Charter Lake Hospital (O, 80 beds), 3500 Riverside Dr., P O Box 7067, Macon 31209; tel. 912/474-6200; Olivia E. Cunningham, adm.

Charter Northside Hospital (O, 103 beds), 400 Charter Blvd., P O Box 4627, Macon 31210; tel. 912/477-9520; Darrell Lumpkin, adm.

Middle Georgia Hospital (O, 119 beds), 888 Pine St., Box 6278, Macon 31297; tel. 912/743-1551; Paul D. Vogen, adm.

Charter Broad Oaks Hospital (O, 88 beds), 5002 Waters Ave., Savannah 31406; Mailing Address P O Box 13604, Savannah, Zip 31416; tel. 912/354-3911; John M.Stribling, exec. dir.

Charter by-the-Sea Hospital (O, 60 beds), 2927 Demere Rd., St. Simons Island 31522; tel. 912/638-1999; James R. Thomas, adm.

Illinois: Charter Barclay Hospital (O, 118 beds), 4700 N. Clarendon Ave., Chicago 60640; tel. 312/728-7100; Edward M. Goldberg, adm.

Indiana: Charter Beacon (O, 65 beds), 1720 Beacon St., Fort Wayne 46805; tel. 219/423-3651; Gerald H. Wallman, adm.

Iowa: Charter Community Hospital-Des Moines (O, 118 beds), 1818 48th St., Des Moines 50310; tel. 515/271-6000; Dennis Janssen, adm.

For explanation of codes following names, see page B2.
*Indicates Type III membership in the American Hospital Association.

Kentucky: Charterton Hospital (O, 66 beds), 507 Yager Ave., P O Box 400, La Grange 40031; tel. 502/222-7148; Ralph E. Suratt, adm.

Charter Ridge Hospital (O, 80 beds), 3050 Rio Dosa Dr., Lexington 40509; tel. 606/269-2325; Stuart Dinney, adm.

Louisiana: Insight Hospital (O, 34 beds), 310 Youngsville Hwy., Lafayette 70508; tel. 318/837-8787; Kenneth O'Rourke, adm.

Nevada: Charter Hospital of Las Vegas (O, 80 beds), 7000 W. Spring Mountain Rd., Las Vegas 89180; tel. 702/876-4357; David Richardson, adm.

Desert Springs Hospital (O, 225 beds), 2075 E. Flamingo Rd., Las Vegas 89119; Mailing Address P O Box 19204, Las Vegas, Zip 89132; tel. 702/733-8800; Thomas L.Koenig, adm.

North Carolina: Charter Hills Hospital (O, 100 beds), 700 Walter Reed Dr., Greensboro 27403; tel. 919/852-4821; Ms Billie Martin Pierce, adm.

Charter Mandala Hospital (O, 99 beds), 3637 Old Vineyard Rd., Winston-Salem 27104; tel. 919/768-7710; Billie Martin Pierce, exec. dir.

Puerto Rico: Hospital Santa Rosa (CM, 99 beds), Aveterans Ave., Box 988, Guayama 00654; tel. 809/864-0101; Humberto M. Monserrate, adm.

Hospital San Lucas (CM, 160 beds), Guadalupe St., Box 2027, Ponce 00731; tel. 809/840-4545; Pedro Brull-Joy, exec. dir.

South Carolina: Charter Rivers Hospital (O, 80 beds), 2900 Sunset Blvd., P O Box 4116, West Columbia 29169; tel. 803/796-9911; John R. Reedy, exec. dir.

Tennessee: Charter Lakeside Hospital (O, 150 beds), 2911 Brunswick Rd., Memphis 38134, Mailing Address P O Box 341308, Bartlett, Zip 38134; tel. 901/377-4700; SherryThornton, adm.

Texas: Charter Lane Hospital (O, 72 beds), 8402 Cross Park Dr., Austin 78761; tel. 512/837-1800; Donald P. Weber, adm.

Charter Community Hospital of Cleveland (O, 73 beds), 300 E. Crockett St., Box 1688, Cleveland 77327; tel. 713/593-1811; Timothy W. McGill, adm.

Charter Plains Hospital (O, 80 beds), 801 N. Quaker, P O Box 10560, Lubbock 79408; tel. 806/744-5505; Don S. McLendon, adm.

Charter Palms Hospital (O, 80 beds), 1421 E. Jackson Ave., P O Box 5239, McAllen 78501; tel. 512/631-5421; Jon C. O'Shaughnessy, adm.

Charter Suburban Hospital Mesquite (O, 142 beds), 1011 N. Galloway Ave., Mesquite 75149; tel. 214/320-7000; Barrett L. Brown, adm.

Beltway Community Hospital (O, 99 beds), 4040 Red Bluff Rd., Pasadena 77503; tel. 713/473-3311; Kenneth Randall, adm.

Charter Real (O, 80 beds), 8550 Huebner Rd., San Antonio 78240; tel. 512/699-8585; Jerry W. Echols, adm.

Virginia: Charter Colonial Institute for Child and Adolescent Psychiatry (O, 60 beds), 17579 Warwick Blvd., Newport News 23603; tel. 804/887-2611; J. Shawn O'Connor, adm.

Charter Westbrook Hospital (O, 175 beds), 1500 Westbrook Ave., Box 9127, Richmond 23227; tel. 804/266-9671; Richard Woodard, adm.

Stuart Circle Hospital (O, 153 beds), 413-21 Stuart Circle, Richmond 23220; tel. 804/358-7051; Donald S. Biskin, exec. dir.

Owned, leased, sponsored:	45 hospitals	4641 beds
Contract-managed:	2 hospitals	259 beds
Totals:	47 hospitals	4900 beds

***0565: CHRISTIAN HEALTH SERVICES DEVELOPMENT CORPORATION** (NP)
11155 Dunn Rd., St. Louis, MO 63136; 314/355-0095; Fred L. Brown, pres. & chief exec. off.

Illinois: Clay County Hospital (CM, 40 beds), 700 N. Mill St., Flora 62839; tel. 618/662-2131; John E. Monnahan, adm.

Public Hospital of the Town of Salem (CM, 64 beds), Bryan Memorial Park, Salem 62881; tel. 618/548-3194; Charles D. Roberts, adm.

Missouri: Bonne Terre Hospital (L, 56 beds), 10 Lake Dr., Bonne Terre 63628; tel. 314/358-2211; Daniel L. Gantz, adm.

Hedrick Medical Center (L, 62 beds), 100 Central St., Chillicothe 64601; tel. 816/646-1480; Mark E. Marley, adm.

Pike County Memorial Hospital (CM, 54 beds), 2305 W. Georgia St., Louisiana 63353; tel. 314/754-5531; Richard L. Conklin, adm.

Christian Hospitals Northeast-Northwest (O, 646 beds), 11133 Dunn Rd., St. Louis 63136; tel. 314/355-2300; Fred L. Brown, pres. & chief exec. off.

Owned, leased, sponsored:	3 hospitals	764 beds
Contract-managed:	3 hospitals	158 beds
Totals:	6 hospitals	922 beds

***0735: CHURCH-CHARITY FOUNDATION OF LONG ISLAND** (CO)
393 Front St., Hempstead, NY 11550; 516/560-6460; William E. McCauley, exec. vice-pres.

New York: St. John's Episcopal Hospital-South Shore (O, 300 beds), 327 Beach 19th St., Far Rockaway 11691; tel. 212/917-3000; Keith F. Safian, adm.

St. John's Episcopal Hospital-Smithtown (O, 300 beds), Rte. 25-A, Smithtown 11787; tel. 516/360-2000; George D. Pozgar, adm.

Owned, leased, sponsored:	2 hospitals	600 beds
Contract-managed:	0 hospitals	0 beds
Totals:	2 hospitals	600 beds

***8805: COLUMBUS-CUNEO-CABRINI MEDICAL CENTER** (CC)
676 N. St. Clair, Suite 1900, Chicago, IL 60611; 312/943-1333; James P. Hamill, chief exec. off.

Illinois: Columbus Hospital (O, 330 beds), 2520 N. Lakeview Ave., Chicago 60614; tel. 312/883-7300; William R. Blanchard, chief oper. off.

Frank Cuneo Memorial Hospital (O, 100 beds), 750 W. Montrose Ave., Chicago 60613; tel. 312/883-8300; Barbara Runyen, chief oper. off.

St. Frances Xavier Cabrini Hospital (O, 201 beds), 811 S. Lytle St., Chicago 60607; tel. 312/883-4343; Lawrence A. Biro EdD, chief oper. off.

Owned, leased, sponsored:	3 hospitals	631 beds
Contract-managed:	0 hospitals	0 beds
Totals:	3 hospitals	631 beds

0215: COMMUNITY CARE SYSTEMS, INC. (IO)
210 Lincoln St., Boston, MA 02111; 617/451-0300; Frederick J. Thacher, pres.

Massachusetts: Hahnemann Hospital (CM, 65 beds), 1515 Commonwealth Ave., Brighton, Boston 02135; tel. 617/254-1100; Joanna B. Kennedy, chief exec. off.

Charles River Hospital (O, 58 beds), 203 Grove St., Wellesley 02181; tel. 617/235-8400; Joel Rosenhaus, pres. & chief exec. off.

New Hampshire: Lake Shore Hospital (O, 90 beds), 200 Zachary Rd., Manchester 03103; tel. 603/645-6700; Ronald C. Andrews, pres.

Owned, leased, sponsored:	2 hospitals	148 beds
Contract-managed:	1 hospitals	65 beds
Totals:	3 hospitals	213 beds

0875: COMMUNITY HEALTH SYSTEMS, INC. (IO)
14550 Torrey Chase Blvd., 450, Houston, TX 77014; E. Thomas Chaney, pres.

Florida: Lake Seminole Hospital (O, 99 beds), 9675 Seminole Blvd., P O Box 4001, Seminole 33542; tel. 813/393-4646; Dan F. Ausman, adm.

University General Hospital (O, 140 beds), 10200 Seminole Blvd., Seminole 33544; tel. 813/397-5511; Frank W. Harris, adm.

Georgia: Fannin Regional Hospital (O, 51 beds), Hwy. 5 N., Box 1549, Blue Ridge 30513; tel. 404/632-3711; Emil Miller, adm.

For explanation of codes following names, see page B2.
*Indicates Type III membership in the American Hospital Association.

Tennessee: Hillside Hospital (O, 95 beds), 1265 E. College St., Pulaski 38478; tel. 615/363-7531; Thomas E. Smith, adm.

Texas: Highland Hospital (O, 123 beds), 2412 50th St., Lubbock 79412; tel. 806/795-8251; Tim L. Stroud, adm.

Central Plains Regional Hospital (L, 151 beds), 2601 Dimmitt Rd., Plainview 79072; tel. 806/296-5531; Donald J. Cosper, exec. dir.

Colonial Hospital (O, 37 beds), 502 W. College St., Terrell 75160; tel. 214/563-2671; Thomas R. Legacy, adm.

Virginia: Russell County Medical Center (O, 78 beds), Carroll & Tate Sts., Lebanon 24266; tel. 703/889-1224; Martin S. Rash, adm.

Owned, leased, sponsored:	8 hospitals	774 beds
Contract-managed:	0 hospitals	0 beds
Totals:	8 hospitals	774 beds

1085: COMMUNITY HOSPITALS OF CENTRAL CALIFORNIA (NP)
Fresno & R Sts., P O Box 1232, Fresno, CA 93715; 209/442-6000; James D. Helzer, pres. & chief exec. off.

California: Clovis Community Hospital (O, 63 beds), 88 N. Dewitt Ave., Clovis 93612; tel. 209/298-8041; James D. Helzer, pres. & chief exec. off.; Norm Andrews, vice-pres.& chief oper. off.

Fresno Community Hospital and Medical Center (O, 458 beds), Fresno & R Sts., Box 1232, Fresno 93715; tel. 209/442-6000; James D. Helzer, pres. & chief exec. off.;Bryan Ballard, vice-pres. & chief oper. off.

Sierra Community Hospital (O, 77 beds), 2025 E. Dakota Ave., Fresno 93726; tel. 209/221-5600; John W. Frye Jr., vice-pres. & chief oper. off.

Sierra-Kings District Hospital (CM, 36 beds), 372 W. Cypress Ave., Reedley 93654; tel. 209/638-8155; Jerry Sullivan, adm.

Owned, leased, sponsored:	3 hospitals	598 beds
Contract-managed:	1 hospitals	36 beds
Totals:	4 hospitals	634 beds

0785: COMMUNITY PSYCHIATRIC CENTERS (IO)
2204 E. Fourth St., Santa Ana, CA 92705; 714/835-4535; James W. Conte, Pres. & Chief Exec. off., pres.

California: CPC Belmont Hills Hospital (O, 54 beds), 1301 Ralston Ave., Belmont 94002; tel. 415/593-2143; Patrick D. Cecil, adm.

CPC San Luis Rey Hospital (O, 83 beds), 1015 Devonshire Dr., Encinitas 92024; tel. 619/753-1245; William T. Sparrow, adm.

CPC Westwood Hospital (O, 94 beds), 2112 S. Barrington Ave., Los Angeles 90025; tel. 213/479-4281; Sue L. Blackburn, adm.

CPC Horizon Hospital (O, 79 beds), 566 N. Gordon St., Pomona 91768; tel. 714/629-4011; Marnell R. Davis, sr. adm.

CPC Alhambra Hospital (O, 98 beds), 4619 N. Rosemead Blvd., P O Box 369, Rosemead 91770; tel. 818/286-1191; Margaret Minnick, adm.

CPC Santa Ana Psychiatric Hospital (O, 32 beds), 2212 E. Fourth St., Santa Ana 92705; tel. 714/543-8481; Al Smith, adm.

CPC Walnut Creek Hospital (O, 108 beds), 175 La Casa Via, Walnut Creek 94598; tel. 415/933-7990; Kenneth W. Pearce, adm.

Florida: CPC Fort Lauderdale Hospital (O, 100 beds), 1601 E. Las Olas Blvd., Fort Lauderdale 33301; tel. 305/463-4321; Robert Heyman, adm.

CPC St. Johns River Hospital (O, 99 beds), 6300 Beach Blvd., Jacksonville 32216; tel. 904/724-9202; Patrick G. Kelly, adm.

Georgia: CPC Parkwood Hospital (O, 130 beds), 1999 Cliff Valley Way N.E., Atlanta 30329; tel. 404/633-8431; Ronald E. Yates, adm.

Idaho: CPC Intermountain Hospital of Boise (O, 75 beds), 303 N. Allumbaugh St., Boise 83704; tel. 208/377-8400; Paul Logan, adm.

Illinois: CPC Old Orchard Hospital (O, 99 beds), 9700 Kenton St., Skokie 60076; tel. 312/676-7600; Phil Donahue, adm.

Louisiana: CPC Coliseum Medical Center (O, 164 beds), 3601 Coliseum St., New Orleans 70115; tel. 504/897-9700; John R. Wastak, adm.

CPC East Lake Hospital (O, 60 beds), 5650 Read Blvd., New Orleans 70127; tel. 504/241-0888; Stuart Podolnick, adm.

Mississippi: CPC Sand Hill Hospital (O, 60 beds), 12222 Hwy. 49 N., Gulfport 39503; tel. 601/831-1700; Phillip W. Langston, adm.

Missouri: CPC Weldon Spring Hospital (O, 104 beds), 5931 Hwy. 94 S., St. Charles 63303; tel. 314/441-7300; Ina Watts, adm.

Oregon: CPC Cedar Hills Hospital (O, 64 beds), 10300 S.W. Eastridge St., Portland 97225; tel. 503/297-2252; Christopher J. Krenk, adm.

Texas: CPC Millwood Hospital (O, 130 beds), 1011 N. Cooper St., Arlington 76011; tel. 817/261-3121; Harry G. Harrier, adm.

Washington: CPC Fairfax Hospital (O, 133 beds), 10200 N.E. 132nd St., Kirkland 98034; tel. 206/821-2000; Greg Fritz, adm.

Owned, leased, sponsored:	19 hospitals	1766 beds
Contract-managed:	0 hospitals	0 beds
Totals:	19 hospitals	1766 beds

0275: COMPREHENSIVE CARE CORPORATION (IO)
18551 Von Karman Ave., Irvine, CA 92715; 714/851-2273; Richard Santoni PhD, pres.

California: Brea Hospital-Neuropsychiatric Center (O, 142 beds), 875 N. Brea Blvd., Brea 92621; tel. 714/529-4963; David J. Delmastro, vice-pres. & exec. dir.

Careunit Behavioral Center Los Angeles (O, 104 beds), 5035 Coliseum St., Los Angeles 90016; tel. 213/295-6441; Gregory L. McAllester, adm.

Careunit Hospital of Orange (O, 103 beds), 401 S. Tustin Ave., Orange 92666; tel. 714/633-9582; Richard Tradewell, adm.

Crossroads Hospital (O, 43 beds), 6323 Woodman Ave., Van Nuys 91401; tel. 818/782-2470; Rebecca Highman, adm.

Florida: Careunit of Jacksonville Beach (O, 84 beds), 1320 Roberts Dr., Jacksonville 32250; tel. 904/241-5133; Joe H. McWaters, adm.

Missouri: Careunit Hospital of St. Louis (O, 144 beds), 1755 S. Grand Blvd., St. Louis 63104; tel. 314/771-0500; Vincent B. Sullivan, adm.

Ohio: Careunit Hospital of Cincinnati (O, 84 beds), 3156 Glenmore Ave., Cincinnati 45211; tel. 513/481-8822; Larry J. Burge, adm.

Oregon: Careunit Hospital of Portland (O, 92 beds), 1927 N.W. Lovejoy St., Portland 97209; tel. 503/224-6500; Joann Beardslee, adm.

Texas: Careunit Hospital of Dallas-Fort Worth (O, 83 beds), 1066 W. Magnolia Ave., Fort Worth 76104; tel. 817/336-2828; Dorothy Grasty, adm.; B. Ahmed MD, med. dir.

Washington: Careunit Hospital of Kirkland (O, 83 beds), 10322 N.E. 132nd, Kirkland 98034; tel. 206/821-1122; Janice K. Chiles, adm.

Owned, leased, sponsored:	10 hospitals	962 beds
Contract-managed:	0 hospitals	0 beds
Totals:	10 hospitals	962 beds

5695: CONGREGATION OF ST. AGNES (CC)
475 Gillett St., Fond Du Lac, WI 54935; 414/923-2121; Sr. Mary Mollison, corp dir.

Kansas: St. Anthony Hospital (S, 120 beds), 2220 Canterbury Rd., Hays 67601; tel. 913/625-7301; Oren M. Windholz, pres.

Wisconsin: St. Agnes Hospital (S, 233 beds), 430 E. Division St., Fond Du Lac 54935; tel. 414/929-2300; James J. Sexton, pres.

St. Clare Hospital of Monroe (S, 174 beds), 515 22nd Ave., Monroe 53566; tel. 608/328-0100; James D. Beyers, pres.

Owned, leased, sponsored:	3 hospitals	527 beds
Contract-managed:	0 hospitals	0 beds
Totals:	3 hospitals	527 beds

For explanation of codes following names, see page B2.
*Indicates Type III membership in the American Hospital Association.

0245: CONTINENTAL MEDICAL, INC. (IO)
880 Johnson Ferry Rd. N.E., 260, Atlanta, GA 30342; 404/255-8220; Richard V. Urquhart, pres.

Texas: Continental Hospital North (O, 49 beds), 2100 Hwy. 183 N.W., Fort Worth 76106; tel. 817/626-5481; Joel V. Bailey, exec. dir.

Continental Hospital Suburban (O, 48 beds), 701 S. Cherry Lane, Box 5128, Fort Worth 76108; tel. 817/246-2491; James C. Karsch, exec. dir.

Owned, leased, sponsored:	2 hospitals	97 beds
Contract-managed:	0 hospitals	0 beds
Totals:	2 hospitals	97 beds

***5885: COVENANT HEALTH SYSTEMS, INC.** (CC)
10 Pelham Rd., Lexington, MA 02173; 617/862-1634; Sr. Dorothy Cooper, pres.

Massachusetts: Youville Rehabilitation and Chronic Disease Hospital (O, 305 beds), 1575 Cambridge St., Cambridge 02138; tel. 617/876-4344; Sr. Annette Caron, pres. & chiefexec. off.

New Hampshire: St. Joseph Hospital (O, 218 beds), 172 Kinsley St., Caller Service 2013, Nashua 03061; tel. 603/889-6681; Peter B. Davis, pres.

Ohio: St. Vincent Medical Center (O, 731 beds), 2213 Cherry St., Toledo 43608; tel. 419/321-3232; Lawrence O. Leaman, pres.

Owned, leased, sponsored:	3 hospitals	1254 beds
Contract-managed:	0 hospitals	0 beds
Totals:	3 hospitals	1254 beds

***5435: CSJ HEALTH SYSTEM OF WICHITA** (CC)
3720 E. Bayley, Wichita, KS 67218; 316/686-7171; Sr. Antoinette Yelek, pres.

California: St. Rose Hospital (O, 175 beds), 27200 Calaroga Ave., Hayward 94545; tel. 415/782-6200; Dean Van Metre, pres. & chief exec. off.

Colorado: St. Joseph Hospital (O, 73 beds), 1280 Grande Ave., Box 248, Del Norte 81132; tel. 303/657-3311; Edwin L. Medford, pres. & chief exec. off.

Kansas: St. Joseph Hospital (O, 53 beds), 1100 Highland Dr., Concordia 66901; tel. 913/243-1234; Sr. Elizabeth Stover, pres.

St. Mary's Health Center (O, 44 beds), 15th Ave. & State St., Emporia 66801; tel. 316/342-2450; Mark I. Barnett, chief exec. off.

Halstead Hospital (O, 190 beds), 328 Poplar St., Halstead 67056; tel. 316/835-2651; Richard L. Nierman, pres.

St. Mary Hospital (O, 100 beds), 1823 College Ave., Box 1047, Manhattan 66502; tel. 913/776-3322; Daniel P. Broyles, pres. & adm.

Mount Carmel Medical Center (O, 163 beds), Centennial & Rouse Sts., Pittsburg 66762; tel. 316/231-6100; Dan Lingor, pres. & chief exec. off.

Pratt Regional Medical Center (CM, 84 beds), 200 Commodore St., Pratt 67124; tel. 316/672-6476; Roland G. Walsh, pres. & chief exec. off.

St. John's Hospital (O, 204 beds), 139 N. Penn St., Salina 67401; Mailing Address P O Box 5201, Salina, Zip 67402; tel. 913/827-5591; Roy E. White, adm.

St. Joseph Medical Center (O, 473 beds), 3600 E. Harry St., Wichita 67218; tel. 316/685-1111; Gerald S. Cambron, pres. & chief exec. off.; Sr. Mary Alice Girrens,exec. vice-pres. & chief oper. off.

Oklahoma: St. Joseph Regional Medical Center of Northern Oklahoma (O, 167 beds), 14th St. & Hartford Ave., Box 1270, Ponca City 74602; tel. 405/765-3321; Sr. MaureenDougherty, pres.

Owned, leased, sponsored:	10 hospitals	1642 beds
Contract-managed:	1 hospitals	84 beds
Totals:	11 hospitals	1726 beds

1885: DAUGHTERS OF CHARITY NATIONAL HEALTH SYSTEM (CC)
7806 National Bridge Rd., P.O. Drawer 5730, St. Louis, MO 63121; 314/389-8900; Sr. Irene Kraus, pres.

Alabama: St. Vincent's Hospital (O, 325 beds), 2701 Ninth Court S., Birmingham 35205; Mailing Address P O Box 915, Birmingham, Zip 35201; tel. 205/939-7000; Sr. AlmedaGolson, pres.

Providence Hospital (O, 349 beds), 1504 Springhill Ave., Mobile 36604; Mailing Address Box 3201, Mobile, Zip 36652; tel. 205/438-7611; Sr. Elise Boudreaux, pres.

St. Margaret's Hospital (O, 230 beds), 301 S. Ripley, Box 311, Montgomery 36101; tel. 205/269-8000; Matthias D. Maguire, pres.

California: Seton Medical Center (S, 295 beds), 1900 Sullivan Ave., Daly City 94015; tel. 415/992-4000; Frank C. Hudson, pres. & chief exec. off.

Queen of Angels Medical Center (S, 226 beds), 2301 Bellevue Ave., Los Angeles 90026; tel. 213/413-3000; Richard F. Smith, pres. & chief exec. off.

St. Vincent Medical Center (S, 313 beds), 2131 W. Third St., P O Box 57992, Los Angeles 90057; tel. 213/484-7111; Vincent F. Guinan, pres.

St. Francis Medical Center (S, 426 beds), 3630 E. Imperial Hwy., Lynwood 90262; tel. 213/603-6000; Sr. Elizabeth Joseph Keaveney, pres. & chief exec. off.

O'Connor Hospital (S, 285 beds), 2105 Forest Ave., San Jose 95128; tel. 408/947-2500; William C. Finlayson, pres. & chief exec. off.

Connecticut: St. Vincent's Medical Center (O, 362 beds), 2800 Main St., Bridgeport 06606; tel. 203/576-6000; William J. Riordan, pres. & chief exec. off.

District of Columbia: Providence Hospital (O, 342 beds), 1150 Varnum St. N.E., Washington 20017; tel. 202/269-7000; Sr. Catherine Norton, pres.

Florida: St. Vincent's Medical Center (O, 528 beds), 1800 Barrs St., Box 2982, Jacksonville 32203; tel. 904/387-7300; Sr. Mary Clare Hughes, pres.

Sacred Heart Hospital of Pensacola (O, 380 beds), 5151 N. Ninth Ave., Pensacola 32513; tel. 904/474-7000; Sr. Virginia Cotter, pres.

Illinois: St. Joseph Hospital and Health Care Center (O, 312 beds), 2900 N. Lake Shore Dr., Chicago 60657; tel. 312/975-3000; Michael Connelly, pres.

Indiana: Warrick Hospital (CM, 48 beds), 1116 Millis Ave., Box 629, Boonville 47601; tel. 812/897-4800; Sr. Renee Rose, adm. & chief exec. off.

St. Mary's Medical Center of Evansville (O, 526 beds), 3700 Washington Ave., Evansville 47750; tel. 812/479-4000; Sr. Xavier Ballance, pres.

Louisiana: Hotel Dieu Hospital (S, 283 beds), 2021 Perdido St., New Orleans 70112; Mailing Address Box 61262, New Orleans, Zip 70161; tel. 504/588-3000; Sr. MarieBreitling, pres.

Maryland: St. Agnes Hospital of the City of Baltimore (O, 480 beds), 900 Caton Ave., Baltimore 21229; tel. 301/368-6000; Sr. Mary Louise, pres.

Sacred Heart Hospital (O, 240 beds), 900 Seton Dr., Cumberland 21502; tel. 301/759-4200; Sr. Cecilia Rose, pres.

Massachusetts: Carney Hospital (O, 416 beds), 2100 Dorchester Ave., Dorchester, Boston 02124; tel. 617/296-4000; John W. Logue, pres.

Michigan: St. Mary's Hospital (O, 238 beds), 830 S. Jefferson Ave., Saginaw 48601; tel. 517/776-8000; Edward Cook, pres. & chief exec. off.

For explanation of codes following names, see page B2.
*Indicates Type III membership in the American Hospital Association.

Providence Hospital (O, 457 beds), 16001 W. Nine Mile Rd., Southfield 48075; Mailing Address Box 2043, Southfield, Zip 48037; tel. 313/424-3000; Brian M.Connolly, pres.

Missouri: DePaul Health Center (S, 563 beds), 12303 Depaul Dr., Bridgeton 63044; tel. 314/344-6000; Frank A. Petrich, pres.

New York: Our Lady of Lourdes Memorial Hospital (O, 267 beds), 169 Riverside Dr., Binghamton 13905; tel. 607/798-5111; Sr. Margaret Tuley, pres. & chief exec. off.

Sisters of Charity Hospital (O, 530 beds), 2157 Main St., Buffalo 14214; tel. 716/862-2000; Sr. Angela Bontempo, pres.

Rochester St. Mary's Hospital of the Sisters of Charity (O, 206 beds), 89 Genesee St., Rochester 14611; tel. 716/464-3000; Sr. Mary Alice Roach, pres.

St. Mary's Hospital of Troy (O, 201 beds), 1300 Massachusetts Ave., Troy 12180; tel. 518/272-5000

Pennsylvania: Good Samaritan Hospital of Pottsville, Pennsylvania (O, 175 beds), E. Norwegian & Tremont Sts., Pottsville 17901; tel. 717/621-4000; Frederick Siembieda, pres.

Tennessee: St. Thomas Hospital (O, 571 beds), 4220 Harding Rd., Nashville 37205; Mailing Address Box 380, Nashville, Zip 37202; tel. 615/386-2111; Sr. Juliana Beuerlein,pres.

Texas: Holy Cross Hospital (S, 70 beds), 2600 E. Martin Luther King Jr Blvd., Austin 78702; tel. 512/477-9811; Pierre M. Dossman Jr., adm.

Seton Medical Center (S, 491 beds), 1201 W. 38th St., Austin 78705; tel. 512/459-2121; Judith P. Smith, pres.

St. Paul Medical Center (S, 417 beds), 5909 Harry Hines Blvd., Dallas 75235; tel. 214/879-1000; Anthony L. Bunker, pres.

Hotel Dieu Medical Center (S, 207 beds), 1014 N. Stanton St., El Paso 79902; Mailing Address Box 5411, El Paso, Zip 79954; tel. 915/545-3111; Beth O'Brien, pres.

Providence Hospital (S, 213 beds), 1700 Providence Dr., Waco 76703; Mailing Address Box 2589, Waco, Zip 76702; tel. 817/753-4551; Kent Keahey, adm.

Virginia: DePaul Hospital (O, 369 beds), 150 Kingsley Lane, Norfolk 23505; tel. 804/489-5000; Sr. Mary Carroll Eby, adm.

Wisconsin: St. Mary's Hospital (O, 314 beds), 2323 N. Lake Dr., Box 503, Milwaukee 53201; tel. 414/225-8000; Sr. Julie Hanser, pres.

Owned, leased, sponsored:	34 hospitals	11607 beds
Contract-managed:	1 hospitals	48 beds
Totals:	35 hospitals	11655 beds

6995: DEPARTMENT OF HEALTH AND HOSPITALS, HOSPITAL SERVICES DIVISION (NP)
818 Harrison Ave., Boston, MA 02118; 617/424-5365; Lewis Pollack, comr.

Massachusetts: Boston City Hospital (O, 391 beds), 818 Harrison Ave., Boston 02118; tel. 617/424-5000; Lewis W. Pollack, comr.

Long Island Hospital (O, 193 beds), Boston Harbor, Boston 02169; tel. 617/328-1371; Meribah Stanton, dir.

Mattapan Hospital (O, 165 beds), 249 River St., Boston 02126; tel. 617/298-7900; Katherine K. Domoto MD, med. dir.

Owned, leased, sponsored:	3 hospitals	749 beds
Contract-managed:	0 hospitals	0 beds
Totals:	3 hospitals	749 beds

3775: MILWAUKEE COUNTY DEPARTMENT OF HEALTH AND HUMAN SERVICES (NP)
8731 Watertown Plank Rd., Milwaukee, WI 53226; 414/257-6489; James W. Wahner, dir.

Wisconsin: Milwaukee County Medical Complex (O, 318 beds), 8700 W. Wisconsin Ave., Milwaukee 53226; tel. 414/257-5936; William I. Jenkins, adm.

Milwaukee County Mental Health Complex (O, 864 beds), 9455 Watertown Plank Rd., Milwaukee 53226; tel. 414/257-7483; Robert D. Speer, adm.

Owned, leased, sponsored:	2 hospitals	1182 beds
Contract-managed:	0 hospitals	0 beds
Totals:	2 hospitals	1182 beds

***0845: DEVEREUX FOUNDATION** (NP)
19 S. Waterloo Rd., Devon, PA 19333; 215/964-3050; Ronald P. Burd, pres.

California: Devereux Foundation-California (O, 56 beds), Box 1079, Santa Barbara 93102; tel. 805/968-2525; Thomas P. McCool, dir.

Georgia: Devereux Center-Georgia Branch (O, 82 beds), 1980 Stanley Rd., Kennesaw 30144; tel. 404/427-0147; Ralph L. Comerford, adm.

Pennsylvania: Devereux Foundation-Bond Division (O, 329 beds), 826 Maple Ave., Berwyn 19312; tel. 215/296-6868

Devereux Foundation-French Division (O, 231 beds), 119 Old Lancaster Rd., Box 400, Devon 19333; tel. 215/964-3000; Gery Sasko, adm.

Texas: Devereux Foundation-Texas Branch (O, 78 beds), Box 2666, Victoria 77902; tel. 512/575-8271; John F. Strahm, adm.

Owned, leased, sponsored:	5 hospitals	776 beds
Contract-managed:	0 hospitals	0 beds
Totals:	5 hospitals	776 beds

1435: DOCTOR JOHN MCDONALD HEALTH SYSTEMS (IO)
5000 University Dr., P O Box 141739, Coral Gables, FL 33114; 305/666-2111; William H. Comte, pres.

Florida: Doctors' Hospital (O, 260 beds), 5000 University Dr., P O Box 14-1739, Coral Gables 33114; tel. 305/666-2111; William H. Comte, pres.

Larkin General Hospital (O, 112 beds), 7031 S.W. 62nd Ave., South Miami 33243; tel. 305/666-6500; William H. Comte, pres.

Owned, leased, sponsored:	2 hospitals	372 beds
Contract-managed:	0 hospitals	0 beds
Totals:	2 hospitals	372 beds

1045: DOCTORS HOSPITAL (NP)
1087 Dennison Ave., Columbus, OH 43215; 614/297-4000; Richard L. Sims, pres.

Ohio: Doctors Hospital (O, 404 beds), 1087 Dennison Ave., Columbus 43201; tel. 614/297-4000; Richard A. Vincent, vice-pres.

Doctors Hospital of Nelsonville (O, 83 beds), W. Franklin St., Nelsonville 45764; tel. 614/753-1931; Mark R. Seckinger, adm.

Owned, leased, sponsored:	2 hospitals	487 beds
Contract-managed:	0 hospitals	0 beds
Totals:	2 hospitals	487 beds

For explanation of codes following names, see page B2.
*Indicates Type III membership in the American Hospital Association.

1195: DOMINICAN SISTERS CONGREGATION OF THE MOST HOLY NAME (CC)
Dominican Convent-San Rafael, San Rafael, CA 94901; 415/454-9221; Sr. Jeremy,

California: Saint Joseph's Medical Center (O, 311 beds), 1800 N. California St., Stockton 95204; tel. 209/943-2000; Sr. Mary Gabriel, pres.; Edward G. Schroeder, chiefexec. off.

St. Joseph's Oak Park Hospital (O, 43 beds), 2510 N. California St., Stockton 95204; tel. 209/948-2100; Gary L. Spaugh, adm.; Kathryn Konklin Yarbrough, asst.adm.

Nevada: Churchill Regional Medical Center (L, 40 beds), 155 N. Taylor St., Box 1240, Fallon 89406; tel. 702/423-3151; Thomas F. Grimes, adm.

St. Mary's Hospital (O, 370 beds), 235 W. Sixth St., Reno 89520; tel. 702/323-2041; W. J. Van Ry, chief exec. off.

Owned, leased, sponsored:	4 hospitals	764 beds
Contract-managed:	0 hospitals	0 beds
Totals:	4 hospitals	764 beds

1295: DOMINICAN SISTERS CONGREGATION OF OUR LADY OF THE SACRED HEART (CC)
1237 W. Monroe St., Springfield, IL 62704; 217/787-0481; Sr. M. Dominica Brennan,

Arkansas: St. Mary-Rogers Memorial Hospital (O, 146 beds), 1200 W. Walnut St., Rogers 72756; tel. 501/636-0200; Sr. Rosanne Timmerman, adm.

Mississippi: St. Dominic-Jackson Memorial Hospital (O, 358 beds), 969 Lakeland Dr., Jackson 39216; tel. 601/364-6848; Sr. John Vianney, pres.

Owned, leased, sponsored:	2 hospitals	504 beds
Contract-managed:	0 hospitals	0 beds
Totals:	2 hospitals	504 beds

1895: EAST TEXAS HOSPITAL FOUNDATION (NP)
P O Drawer 6400, Tyler, TX 75711; 214/597-0351; Elmer G. Ellis, pres.

Texas: Lakeland Medical Center (L, 103 beds), 2000 S. Palestine, Athens 75751; tel. 214/675-2216; Gene McIntyre, adm.

Cozby-Germany Hospital (L, 40 beds), 707 N. Waldrip St., Grand Saline 75140; tel. 214/962-4242; Windell M. McCord, adm.

Hospital in the Pines (CM, 39 beds), Hwy. 259 N., Box 357, Lone Star 75668; tel. 214/656-2561; Lewis E. Robertson, adm.

Pittsburg Medical Center (L, 49 beds), 414 Quitman St., Pittsburg 75686; tel. 214/856-6663; Lewis E. Robertson Jr., adm.

Medical Center Hospital (O, 278 beds), 1000 S. Beckham St., Drawer 6400, Tyler 75711; tel. 214/597-0351; Elmer G. Ellis, pres.

University Park Hospital (O, 80 beds), 4101 University Blvd., Tyler 75701; tel. 214/566-8666; Gary L. Stokes, adm.

Owned, leased, sponsored:	5 hospitals	550 beds
Contract-managed:	1 hospitals	39 beds
Totals:	6 hospitals	589 beds

***3595: EASTERN MERCY HEALTH SYSTEM** (CC)
Scott Plaza Two, Suite 403, Philadelphia, PA 19113; 215/521-4500; Daniel F. Russell, pres. & chief exec. off.

Florida: Holy Cross Hospital (S, 360 beds), 4725 N. Federal Hwy., Fort Lauderdale 33308; Mailing Address Box 23460, Fort Lauderdale, Zip 33307; tel. 305/771-8000; Sr. M.Mercy McGrady, exec. vice-pres.

Georgia: Saint Joseph's Hospital (S, 295 beds), 5665 Peachtree Dunwoody Rd. N.E., Atlanta 30342; tel. 404/851-7001; Kenneth E. Wheeler, pres.

Saint Joseph's Hospital of Dahlonega (S, 46 beds), 1111 Mountain Dr., Dahlonega 30533; tel. 404/864-6136; Tommy G. Reddin, sr. vice-pres. & chief oper. off.

Maine: Mercy Hospital (S, 200 beds), 144 State St., Portland 04101; tel. 207/879-3000; Howard R. Buckley, pres.

New York: St. Peter's Hospital (S, 437 beds), 315 S. Manning Blvd., Albany 12208; tel. 518/454-1550; Sr. Ellen Lawlor, pres.

St. James Mercy Hospital (S, 169 beds), 411 Canisteo St., Hornell 14843; tel. 607/324-3900; Sr. Mary Rene McNiff, adm.

Mercy Hospital of Watertown (S, 426 beds), 218 Stone St., Watertown 13601; tel. 315/782-7400; Sr. Mary P. Seguin, pres.

Pennsylvania: Mercy Catholic Medical Center (S, 625 beds), Lansdowne Ave. & Baily Rd., Philadelphia 19023; tel. 215/237-4000; Plato A. Marinakos, exec. vice-pres.

Mercy Hospital of Pittsburgh (S, 486 beds), 1400 Locust St., Pittsburgh 15219; tel. 412/232-8111; Sr. Joanne Marie Andiorio, pres.

Owned, leased, sponsored:	9 hospitals	3044 beds
Contract-managed:	0 hospitals	0 beds
Totals:	9 hospitals	3044 beds

***0945: EMPIRE HEALTH SERVICES** (NP)
S. 400 Jefferson St., Suite 333, Spokane, WA 99204; 509/458-7965; Jon K. Mitchell, pres. & chief exec. off.

Washington: Deaconess Medical Center-Spokane (O, 352 beds), 800 W. Fifth Ave., Spokane 99210; tel. 509/458-5800; Jon K. Mitchell, pres.

St. Luke's Memorial Hospital (O, 146 beds), S. 711 Cowley, P O Box 288, Spokane 99202; tel. 509/838-1447; Ernest R. McNeely Jr., pres.

Valley Hospital and Medical Center (O, 123 beds), E. 12606 Mission Ave., Spokane 99216; Mailing Address P O Box 288, Spokane, Zip 99210; tel. 509/924-6650; ThomasM. White, pres.

Owned, leased, sponsored:	3 hospitals	621 beds
Contract-managed:	0 hospitals	0 beds
Totals:	3 hospitals	621 beds

0885: ERLANGER HEALTH SERVICES (IO)
6400 Lee Hwy., Suite 106, Chattanooga, TN 37421; Ron Williams, pres.

Alabama: Medical Park West (L, 83 beds), 1915 19th St., Ensley, Birmingham 35218; tel. 205/783-1000; Lewis Mashburn, adm.

John A. Andrew Community Hospital (L, 59 beds), Tuskegee Institute 36088; tel. 205/727-9375; R. Roland Bradford, adm.

Tennessee: Copper Basin Medical Center (L, 44 beds), State Hwy. 68, Drawer X, Copperhill 37317; tel. 615/496-5511; George A. McGee, adm.

Coffee Medical Center (CM, 126 beds), 1001 McArthur Dr., Manchester 37355; tel. 615/728-3586; Carl B. Allen, adm.

Emerald-Hodgson Hospital (L, 34 beds), University Ave., Sewanee 37375; tel. 615/598-5691; John Stanfield, adm.

Owned, leased, sponsored:	4 hospitals	220 beds
Contract-managed:	1 hospitals	126 beds
Totals:	5 hospitals	346 beds

For explanation of codes following names, see page B2.
*Indicates Type III membership in the American Hospital Association.

1255: ESCAMBIA COUNTY HEALTH CARE AUTHORITY (NP)
Brewton, AL 36426; 205/867-8061; B. J. Griffin, adm.

Alabama: Greenlawn Hospital (O, 51 beds), 401 S. Eighth Ave., P O Drawer 1147, Atmore 36504; tel. 205/368-2500; Joseph W. Henry Sr., adm.

D. W. McMillan Memorial Hospital (O, 91 beds), 1301 Belleville Ave., Brewton 36426; Mailing Address Drawer 908, Brewton, Zip 36427; tel. 205/867-8061; Billy J.Griffin, adm.

Abernethy Memorial Hospital (O, 30 beds), Drawer A, Flomaton 36441; tel. 205/296-2427; Donny P. Myers, adm.

Owned, leased, sponsored:	3 hospitals	172 beds
Contract-managed:	0 hospitals	0 beds
Totals:	3 hospitals	172 beds

1215: ESKATON (NP)
5105 Manzanita Ave., Carmichael, CA 95608; 916/334-0810; Jack Billingsley, pres.

California: American River Hospital (O, 221 beds), 4747 Engle Rd., Carmichael 95608; tel. 916/486-3211; Merle E. Wolf, pres.

Lassen Community Hospital (O, 59 beds), 560 Hospital Lane, Susanville 96130; tel. 916/257-5325; John H. Loftus, chief exec. off.

Owned, leased, sponsored:	2 hospitals	280 beds
Contract-managed:	0 hospitals	0 beds
Totals:	2 hospitals	280 beds

***1225: EVANGELICAL HEALTH SYSTEMS** (CO)
2025 Windsor Dr., Oak Brook, IL 60521; 312/572-9393; John G. King, pres. & chief exec. off.

Illinois: Good Shepherd Hospital (O, 166 beds), 450 W. Hwy. 22, Barrington 60010; tel. 312/381-9600; Russell Feurer, vice-pres.

Bethany Hospital (O, 194 beds), 3435 W. Van Buren, Chicago 60624; tel. 312/265-7700; A. Kenneth Peterson, chief exec. off.

Good Samaritan Hospital (O, 287 beds), 3815 Highland Ave., Downers Grove 60515; tel. 312/963-5900; David M. McConkey, vice-pres. & chief exec.

Christ Hospital and Medical Center (O, 873 beds), 4440 W. 95th St., Oak Lawn 60453; tel. 312/425-8000; Joseph W. Beard, vice-pres.

Owned, leased, sponsored:	4 hospitals	1520 beds
Contract-managed:	0 hospitals	0 beds
Totals:	4 hospitals	1520 beds

1305: FAIRFAX HOSPITAL ASSOCIATION (NP)
8001 Braddock Rd., Springfield, VA 22151; 703/321-4213; J. Knox Singleton, pres.

Virginia: Jefferson Memorial Hospital (O, 120 beds), 4600 King St., Alexandria 22302; tel. 703/931-9700; Richard Levy Jr., adm.

Mount Vernon Hospital (O, 167 beds), 2501 Parker's Lane, Alexandria 22306; tel. 703/664-7000; Stephen C. Rupp, vice-pres. & adm.

Commonwealth Hospital (O, 160 beds), 4315 Chain Bridge Rd., Fairfax 22030; tel. 703/691-3600; Steven E. Brown, adm.

Fairfax Hospital (O, 656 beds), 3300 Gallows Rd., Falls Church 22046; tel. 703/698-1110; Everett M. Devaney, vice-pres. & adm.

Owned, leased, sponsored:	4 hospitals	1103 beds
Contract-managed:	0 hospitals	0 beds
Totals:	4 hospitals	1103 beds

***1325: FAIRVIEW HOSPITAL AND HEALTHCARE SERVICE** (NP)
2312 S. Sixth St., Minneapolis, MN 55454; 612/371-6300; Carl N. Platou, pres.

Iowa: Iowa Lutheran Hospital (O, 365 beds), University at Penn, Des Moines 50316; tel. 515/263-5612; Marlin J. Stirm, adm.

Minnesota: Fairview Ridges Hospital (O, 97 beds), 201 E. Nicollet Blvd., Burnsville 55337; tel. 612/892-2100; Mark M. Enger, vice-pres. adm.

Milaca Fairview Hospital (O, 41 beds), 150 N.W. Tenth St., Milaca 56353; tel. 612/983-3131; Eleanor Starr, adm.

Fairview Deaconess Center (O, 128 beds), 1400 E. 24th St., Minneapolis 55404; tel. 612/721-9100; Daniel K. Anderson, vice-pres. & adm.

Fairview Riverside Hospital (O, 492 beds), 2312 S. Sixth St., Minneapolis 55454; tel. 612/371-6300; Pamela L. Tibbetts, vice-pres. adm.

Fairview Southdale Hospital (O, 390 beds), 6401 France Ave. S., Minneapolis 55435; tel. 612/924-5000; Douglas N. Robinson, vice-pres.

Fairview Princeton Hospital (O, 35 beds), 704 First St., Princeton 55371; tel. 612/389-1313; Glenn G. Erickson, reg. adm.

Waseca Area Memorial Hospital (L, 19 beds), 100 Fifth Ave. N.W., Waseca 56093; tel. 507/835-1210; Dennis C. Miley, adm.

Wisconsin: Indianhead Medical Center (O, 49 beds), 215 Fourth Ave. W., Shell Lake 54871; tel. 715/468-7833; Lance F. Gillham, adm.

Owned, leased, sponsored:	9 hospitals	1616 beds
Contract-managed:	0 hospitals	0 beds
Totals:	9 hospitals	1616 beds

***1345: FELICIAN HEALTHCARE SYSTEMS, INC.** (CC)
1325 Enfield St., Enfield, CT 06082; 203/745-2542; M. Augustine Kloza, pres.

Florida: St. Joseph Hospital (O, 212 beds), 2500 Harbor Blvd., Port Charlotte 33952; tel. 813/625-4122; Col. Russel L. Bryant, actg. adm.

Illinois: St. Mary's Hospital (O, 256 beds), 400 N. Pleasant Ave., Centralia 62801; tel. 618/532-6731; Sr. Mary Stryzewski, pres.

Maine: St. Joseph Hospital (O, 130 beds), 297 Center St., Bangor 04401; tel. 207/947-8311; Sr. Mary Norberta, pres.

Michigan: St. Mary Hospital (O, 304 beds), 36475 Five Mile Rd., Livonia 48154; tel. 313/464-4800; Sr. Mary Modesta, pres. & chief exec. off.

Pennsylvania: St. Joseph's Hospital (O, 178 beds), 16th St. & Girard Ave., Philadelphia 19130; tel. 215/787-9000; Sr. Mary Anita, adm.

Wisconsin: St. Francis Hospital (O, 269 beds), 3237 S. 16th St., Milwaukee 53215; tel. 414/647-5000; Karl Rajani, pres. & chief exec. off.

Owned, leased, sponsored:	6 hospitals	1349 beds
Contract-managed:	0 hospitals	0 beds
Totals:	6 hospitals	1349 beds

1275: FIRST HEALTH, INC. (NP)
107 Public Square, Batesville, MS 38606; 601/563-7676; David A. Vance, pres.

Alabama: First Health Courtland (O, 35 beds), 101 Madison St., Box 466, Courtland 35618; tel. 205/637-2721; Carl J. Velte, adm.

First Health Jackson (O, 38 beds), Ivy Point Rd., Drawer A, Lester 35647; tel. 205/232-7511; Joe Gregory, adm.

Kentucky: First Health Jenkins (O, 60 beds), Main St., Drawer 472, Jenkins 41537; tel. 606/832-2171; Glenn R. Sago, adm.

Owned, leased, sponsored:	3 hospitals	133 beds
Contract-managed:	0 hospitals	0 beds
Totals:	3 hospitals	133 beds

0295: FIRST HOSPITAL CORPORATION (IO)
World Trade Ctr, Suite 870, Norfolk, VA 23510; 804/622-3034; Ronald I. Dozoretz MD, chm.

California: Southwood Psychiatric Hospital (O, 40 beds), 950 Third Ave., Chula Vista 92011; tel. 619/426-6310; Allan Kydd, adm.

For explanation of codes following names, see page B2.
*Indicates Type III membership in the American Hospital Association.

Pennsylvania: Horsham Clinic (O, 118 beds), Welsh Rd. & Butler Pike, Ambler 19002; tel. 215/643-7800; Levon D. Tashjian MD, med. dir.

Virginia: Norfolk Psychiatric Center (O, 75 beds), 100 Kingsley Lane, Norfolk 23505; tel. 804/489-1072; Dorothy Z. Horowitz, adm.

Portsmouth Psychiatric Center (O, 186 beds), 301 Fort Lane, Portsmouth 23704; tel. 804/393-0061; Jim Legge, adm.

Wisconsin: First Hospital-Milwaukee (CM, 14 beds), 3330 W. Wells St., Milwaukee 53208; tel. 414/342-7262; Linda A. W. McCaskill, adm.

Owned, leased, sponsored:	4 hospitals	419 beds
Contract-managed:	1 hospitals	14 beds
Totals:	5 hospitals	433 beds

***1355: FORBES HEALTHMARK** (NP)
500 Finley St., Pittsburgh, PA 15206; 412/665-3565; George H. Schmitt, chm.

Pennsylvania: Highlands Hospital and Health Center (O, 69 beds), Cottage & Murphy Aves., Connellsville 15425; tel. 412/628-1500; Michael J. Evans, exec. dir.

Forbes Regional Health Center (O, 348 beds), 2570 Haymaker Rd., Monroeville 15146; tel. 412/273-2424; Dana W. Ramish, exec. dir.

Forbes Metropolitan Health Center (O, 144 beds), 225 Penn Ave., Pittsburgh 15221; tel. 412/247-2424; Richard T. Merk, exec. dir.

Owned, leased, sponsored:	3 hospitals	561 beds
Contract-managed:	0 hospitals	0 beds
Totals:	3 hospitals	561 beds

0655: FOREST HEALTH SYSTEMS, INC. (IO)
555 Wilson Lane, Des Plains, IL 60016; 312/635-4100; Morris B. Squire, pres.

Illinois: Forest Hospital (O, 160 beds), 555 Wilson Lane, Des Plaines 60016; tel. 312/635-4100; Mary Jane Such, adm.

Missouri: Springfield Park Central Hospital (O, 149 beds), 440 S. Market Ave., Springfield 65806; Mailing Address P O Box 1715, Sss, Springfield, Zip 65805; tel.417/865-5581; Beverly J. Lawlor, adm.

Owned, leased, sponsored:	2 hospitals	309 beds
Contract-managed:	0 hospitals	0 beds
Totals:	2 hospitals	309 beds

0905: FORUM HEALTH INVESTORS, INC. (IO)
401 W. Peachtree N.W., 1600, Atlanta, GA 30308; 404/688-9019; J. Dennis Meaders, chief exec. off.

Illinois: Lincoln West Hospital (O, 201 beds), 2544 W. Montrose Ave., Chicago 60618; tel. 312/267-2200; Stephen M. Weinstein, chief exec. off.

Tennessee: Metropolitan Hospital (O, 64 beds), 511 McCallie Ave., Chattanooga 37402; tel. 615/265-3303; Gary Jones, chief exec. off.

Forum Hospital Trenton (O, 90 beds), 2036 Hwy. 45 By-Pass, Trenton 38382; tel. 901/855-4500; Ray Holmes, adm.

Texas: Mary E. Dickerson Memorial Hospital (O, 49 beds), 1001 Dickerson Dr., Jasper 75951; tel. 409/384-2575; Jerry Bucher, chief exec. off.

Owned, leased, sponsored:	4 hospitals	404 beds
Contract-managed:	0 hospitals	0 beds
Totals:	4 hospitals	404 beds

***1455: FRANCISCAN HEALTH ADVISORY SERVICES, INC.** (CC)
2409 S. Alverno Rd., Manitowoc, WI 54220; 414/684-7071; Sr. Laura Wolf, pres.

Nebraska: St. Francis Memorial Hospital (O, 49 beds), 430 N. Monitor St., West Point 68788; tel. 402/372-2404; Sr. Emy Beth Furrer, pres.

Ohio: Good Samaritan Medical Center and Rehabilitation Center (O, 284 beds), 800 Forest Ave., Zanesville 43701; tel. 614/454-5000; Daniel J. Rissing, pres.

Wisconsin: Holy Family Medical Center (O, 147 beds), 2300 Western Ave., Manitowoc 54220; tel. 414/684-2011; LeRoy F. Pesce, pres.

Owned, leased, sponsored:	3 hospitals	480 beds
Contract-managed:	0 hospitals	0 beds
Totals:	3 hospitals	480 beds

***5325: FRANCISCAN HEALTH SYSTEM** (CC)
Brandywine 1 Bldg., Suite 301, Rtes. 1 & 202, Chadds Ford, PA 19317; 215/358-3950; Ronald R. Aldrich, pres.

Delaware: St. Francis Hospital (O, 331 beds), Seventh & Clayton Sts., Wilmington 19805; tel. 302/421-4100; Paul C. King Jr., pres. & chief exec. off.

Maryland: St. Joseph Hospital (O, 349 beds), 7620 York Rd., Towson 21204; tel. 301/337-1000; Sr. Marie Cecilia Irwin, pres. & chief exec. off.

New Jersey: St. Lawrence Rehabilitation Center (CM, 142 beds), 2381 Lawrenceville Rd., Lawrenceville 08648; tel. 609/896-9500; S. Janet Henry, adm.

St. Francis Medical Center (O, 409 beds), 601 Hamilton Ave., Trenton 08629; tel. 609/599-5000; Patrick F. Roche, pres.

Oregon: St. Elizabeth Hospital and Health Center (O, 40 beds), 3325 Pocahontas Rd., Baker 97814; tel. 503/523-6461; Walter S. Busch, pres. & adm.

Pioneer Memorial Hospital (CM, 44 beds), 564 E. Pioneer Dr., P O Box 9, Heppner 97836; tel. 503/676-9133; John Hempel, adm. & chief exec. off.

St. Anthony Hospital (O, 104 beds), 1601 S.E. Court Ave., Pendleton 97801; tel. 503/276-5121; Sr. Helen Ann Gaidos, pres. & chief exec. off.

Pennsylvania: St. Joseph Hospital (O, 309 beds), 250 College Ave., Box 3509, Lancaster 17604; tel. 717/291-8211; Sr. Margaret Aloysius McGrail, pres.

Saint Mary Hospital (O, 251 beds), Langhorne-Newtown Rd., Langhorne 19047; tel. 215/750-2000; Sr. Clare Carty, pres. & chief exec. off.

St. Agnes Medical Center (O, 230 beds), 1900 S. Broad St., Philadelphia 19145; tel. 215/339-4100; Sr. M. Clarence, pres. & chief exec. off.

St. Mary Hospital (O, 160 beds), Frankford Ave. & Palmer St., Philadelphia 19125; tel. 215/291-2000; Edmond L. Plummer Jr., pres. & chief exec. off.

Saint Joseph Hospital (O, 315 beds), 215 N. 12th St., Box 316, Reading 19603; tel. 215/378-2000; Sr. Francis Anne Harper, pres. & chief exec. off.

Washington: St. Joseph Hospital and Health Care Center (O, 340 beds), 1718 S. I St., Tacoma 98401; tel. 206/627-4101; John Long, pres. & chief exec. off.

Owned, leased, sponsored:	11 hospitals	2838 beds
Contract-managed:	2 hospitals	186 beds
Totals:	13 hospitals	3024 beds

***9650: FRANCISCAN HEALTH SYSTEM, INC.** (CC)
615 S. Tenth St., La Crosse, WI 54601; 608/785-0940; Stewart W. Laird, pres.

Minnesota: Caledonia Health Care Center (O, 92 beds), 425 N. Badger, Caledonia 55921; tel. 507/724-3351; Sr. Elizabeth Amman, adm.

Wisconsin: St. Joseph's Hospital of Arcadia (O, 101 beds), 464 S. St. Joseph Ave., Arcadia 54612; tel. 608/323-3341; Bruce E. Roesler, adm.

St. Francis Medical Center (O, 361 beds), 700 West Avenue S., La Crosse 54601; tel. 608/785-0940; Sr. Celesta Day, adm.

St. Mary's Hospital (O, 65 beds), W. Main & K Sts., Sparta 54656; tel. 608/269-2132; Sr. Julie Tydrich, adm.

Owned, leased, sponsored:	4 hospitals	619 beds
Contract-managed:	0 hospitals	0 beds
Totals:	4 hospitals	619 beds

For explanation of codes following names, see page B2.
*Indicates Type III membership in the American Hospital Association.

1475: FRANCISCAN MISSIONARIES OF OUR LADY PROVINCIAL HOUSE (CC)
4200 Essen Lane, Baton Rouge, LA 70809; 504/927-7481; Sr. Brendan M. Ronayne,

Louisiana: Our Lady of the Lake Regional Medical Center (O, 683 beds), 5000 Hennessy Blvd., Baton Rouge 70809; tel. 504/765-6565; Robert C. Davidge, exec. dir.

Our Lady of Lourdes Regional Medical Center (O, 315 beds), 611 St. Landry St., Lafayette 70506; Mailing Address Box 4027c, Lafayette, Zip 70502; tel.318/234-7381; Dudley Romero, chief exec. off.

St. Francis Medical Center (O, 449 beds), 309 Jackson St., Monroe 71201; Mailing Address Box 1901, Monroe, Zip 71210; tel. 318/362-4000; Sr. Anne Marie Twohig,chief exec. off.

Owned, leased, sponsored:	3 hospitals	1447 beds
Contract-managed:	0 hospitals	0 beds
Totals:	3 hospitals	1447 beds

***5375: FRANCISCAN SERVICES CORPORATION** (CC)
6832 Convent Blvd., Sylvania, OH 43560; 419/882-8373; John W. O'Connell, pres.

Michigan: Holy Cross Hospital (S, 365 beds), 4777 E. Outer Dr., Detroit 48234; tel. 313/369-9100; Gerald E. Moore, pres.

Ohio: Providence Hospital (S, 215 beds), 1912 Hayes Ave., Sandusky 44870; tel. 419/625-8450; Sr. Nancy Linenkugel, pres.

St. John Medical Center (S, 201 beds), St. John Hts., Steubenville 43952; tel. 614/264-8000; Sr. Alice Warrick, pres.

Texas: St. Jude Hospital (S, 52 beds), 1306 N. Park St., Box 1089, Brenham 77833; tel. 409/836-6101; Ben Tobias, adm.

St. Joseph Hospital and Health Center (S, 167 beds), 2801 Franciscan Dr., Bryan 77801; tel. 409/776-3777; Sr. Gretchen Kunz, pres.

Owned, leased, sponsored:	5 hospitals	1000 beds
Contract-managed:	0 hospitals	0 beds
Totals:	5 hospitals	1000 beds

***1395: FRANCISCAN SISTERS HEALTH CARE** (CC)
116 S.E. Eighth Ave., Little Falls, MN 56345; 612/632-3601

Minnesota: Trinity Hospital (O, 34 beds), Main Ave. & Fifth St., Box E., Baudette 56623; tel. 218/634-2120; David A. Nelson, pres. & chief exec. off.

St. Francis Medical Center (O, 60 beds), 415 Oak St., Breckenridge 56520; tel. 218/643-3000; Mark C. McNelly, pres.

St. Gabriel's Hospital (O, 255 beds), 815 Second St. S.E., Little Falls 56345; tel. 612/632-5441; Gerald K. Spinner, pres.

St. Ansgar Hospital (O, 69 beds), 715 N. 11th St., Moorhead 56560; tel. 218/299-2200

Mille Lacs Hospital (CM, 108 beds), Onamia 56359; tel. 612/532-3154; Gene M. Helle, adm.

St. Joseph's Hospital (O, 50 beds), 600 Pleasant Ave., Park Rapids 56470; tel. 218/732-3311; David R. Hove, pres. & chief exec. off.

North Dakota: St. John's Hospital (O, 159 beds), 510 Fourth St. S., Fargo 58103; tel. 701/232-3331; Mel Euetener, adm.

Wisconsin: Trinity Memorial Hospital (O, 185 beds), 5900 S. Lake Dr., Cudahy 53110; tel. 414/769-9000; Kenneth V. Schreiner, pres. & chief exec. off.

St. Anthony Hospital (O, 104 beds), 1004 N. Tenth St., Milwaukee 53233; tel. 414/271-1965; James F. Zahradka, pres.

Owned, leased, sponsored:	8 hospitals	916 beds
Contract-managed:	1 hospitals	108 beds
Totals:	9 hospitals	1024 beds

***1415: FRANCISCAN SISTERS HEALTH CARE CORPORATION** (CC)
St. Francis Woods, Rte. 4, Mokena, IL 60448; 815/469-4888; Sr. Dismas Janssen, bd. chm. & pres.

California: St. Francis Hospital of Santa Barbara (S, 110 beds), 601 E. Micheltorena St., Santa Barbara 93103; tel. 805/962-7661; James A. Keens, adm.

Illinois: St. Anthony Hospital (O, 183 beds), 2875 W. 19th St., Chicago 60623; tel. 312/521-1710; Timothy P. Selz, pres.

St. Elizabeth Hospital (O, 236 beds), 600 Sager Ave., Danville 61832; tel. 217/442-6300; David T. Ochs, pres.

Saint Joseph Hospital (O, 280 beds), 77 N. Airlite St., Elgin 60123; tel. 312/695-3200; Robert J. Mohalski, pres.

St. Joseph Medical Center (O, 531 beds), 333 N. Madison St., Joliet 60435; tel. 815/725-7133; Edward J. Schlicksup Jr., pres.

Owned, leased, sponsored:	5 hospitals	1340 beds
Contract-managed:	0 hospitals	0 beds
Totals:	5 hospitals	1340 beds

1485: FRANCISCAN SISTERS OF THE POOR HEALTH SYSTEMS, INC. (CC)
186 Joralemon St., Brooklyn, NY 11201; 718/625-6530; Sr. Joanne Schuster, pres.

Illinois: St. Mary Hospital (S, 222 beds), 1415 Vermont St., Quincy 62301; tel. 217/223-1200; Roland D. Olen, pres.

Kentucky: Our Lady of Bellefonte Hospital (S, 127 beds), St. Christopher Dr., P O Box 789, Ashland 41101; tel. 606/836-0231; W. Leon Hisle, pres. & chief exec. off.; Sr.Mary Lawrence VanderBurg, exec. vice-pres.

New Jersey: St. Mary Hospital (S, 330 beds), 308 Willow Ave., Hoboken 07030; tel. 201/792-8000; Bruce Smith, adm.

St. Francis Hospital (S, 254 beds), 25 McWilliams Pl., Jersey City 07302; tel. 201/795-7000; Thomas A. Schember, pres.; Thomas F. Zenty, sr. vice-pres.

New York: St. Clare's Hospital of Schenectady (S, 271 beds), 600 McClellan St., Schenectady 12304; tel. 518/382-2000; Jerome G. Stewart, pres.

St. Anthony Community Hospital (S, 73 beds), 15-19 Maple Ave., Warwick 10990; tel. 914/986-2276; Dennis Harrington, pres.

Ohio: Providence Hospital (S, 372 beds), 2446 Kipling Ave., Cincinnati 45239; tel. 513/853-5000; Earl R. Gilreath, pres.

St. Francis-St. George Hospital (S, 290 beds), 3131 Queen City Ave., Cincinnati 45238; tel. 513/389-5000; William M. Copeland, pres.

St. Anthony Medical Center (S, 404 beds), 1492 E. Broad St., Columbus 43205; tel. 614/251-3000; Charles E. Housley, pres.

St. Elizabeth Medical Center (S, 564 beds), 601 Edwin C Moses Blvd., Dayton 45408; tel. 513/229-6000; Thomas A. Beckett, pres.

South Carolina: St. Francis Hospital (S, 214 beds), One St. Francis Dr., Greenville 29601; tel. 803/255-1000; Richard C. Neugent, pres.

Owned, leased, sponsored:	11 hospitals	3121 beds
Contract-managed:	0 hospitals	0 beds
Totals:	11 hospitals	3121 beds

5705: FRANCISCAN SISTERS OF PERPETUAL ADORATION (CC)
912 Market St., La Crosse, WI 54601; 608/782-5610; Sr. Patricia Alden, pres.

Iowa: St. Anthony Regional Hospital (S, 132 beds), S. Clark St., Carroll 51401; tel. 712/792-3581; Robert D. Blincow, adm.

Wisconsin: St. Joseph's Memorial Hospital (S, 99 beds), 400 Water Ave., Hillsboro 54634; tel. 608/489-2211; Rolin H. Johnson, chief exec. off.

Owned, leased, sponsored:	2 hospitals	231 beds
Contract-managed:	0 hospitals	0 beds
Totals:	2 hospitals	231 beds

For explanation of codes following names, see page B2.
*Indicates Type III membership in the American Hospital Association.

1425: FULTON-DE KALB HOSPITAL AUTHORITY (NP)
80 Butler St. S.E., Atlanta, GA 30335; 404/589-4307; J. W. Pinkston, exec. dir.

Georgia: Grady Memorial Hospital (O, 918 beds), 80 Butler St. S.E., Atlanta 30335; tel. 404/589-4252; J. W. Pinkston Jr., exec. dir.

Hughes Spalding Medical Center (O, 66 beds), 35 Butler St. S.E., Atlanta 30335; tel. 404/222-2200; T. L. Collier, actg. adm.

Owned, leased, sponsored:	2 hospitals	984 beds
Contract-managed:	0 hospitals	0 beds
Totals:	2 hospitals	984 beds

0495: GATEWAY MEDICAL SYSTEMS (IO)
2351 Bolton Rd. N.W., Third Fl, Atlanta, GA 30318; 404/351-9611; James R. Cheek, bd. chm.

Georgia: Physicians and Surgeons Hospital (O, 181 beds), 2355 Bolton Rd. N.W., Atlanta 30381; tel. 404/352-1200; Nolan Simmons, adm.

Illinois: Gateway Community Hospital (O, 217 beds), 1509 Martin Luther King Dr., East St. Louis 62201; tel. 618/874-7076; Christian C. Kolom, adm.

Louisiana: New Orleans General Hospital (O, 109 beds), 625 Jackson Ave., New Orleans 70130; tel. 504/587-0100; Patricia A. Beggs, adm.

Owned, leased, sponsored:	3 hospitals	507 beds
Contract-managed:	0 hospitals	0 beds
Totals:	3 hospitals	507 beds

5570: GEISINGER SYSTEM SERVICES (NP)
N. Academy Ave., Danville, PA 17822; 717/271-6631; Frank J. Trembulak, pres.

Pennsylvania: Geisinger Medical Center (O, 566 beds), N. Academy Ave., Danville 17822; tel. 717/271-6211; F. Kenneth Ackerman Jr., sr. vice-pres. & adm. dir.

Geisinger Wyoming Valley Medical Center (O, 230 beds), 1000 E. Mountain Dr., Wilkes-Barre 18711; tel. 717/826-7300; Conrad W. Schintz, sr. vice-pres.

Owned, leased, sponsored:	2 hospitals	796 beds
Contract-managed:	0 hospitals	0 beds
Totals:	2 hospitals	796 beds

0775: GENERAL HEALTH, INC. (NP)
5757 Corporate Blvd., Suite 202, Baton Rouge, LA 70808; 504/924-4324; Thomas H. Sawyer, pres.

Louisiana: Baton Rouge General Medical Center (O, 420 beds), 3600 Florida St., P O Box 2511, Baton Rouge 70821; tel. 504/387-7767; Edgar H. Silvey, chief exec. off.

Dixon Memorial Hospital (L, 52 beds), 10123 Florida Blvd., Denham Springs 70726; tel. 504/665-8211; Lonnie C. Graeber, adm.

St. Helena Parish Hospital (CM, 35 beds), Box 337, Greensburg 70441; tel. 504/222-6111; John M. Nolan, adm.

Owned, leased, sponsored:	2 hospitals	472 beds
Contract-managed:	1 hospitals	35 beds
Totals:	3 hospitals	507 beds

0645: GLENBEIGH, INC. (IO)
1001 N. U. S. Hwy., Suite 8, Jupiter, FL 33458; 305/747-6565; G. Norman McCann, pres.

Ohio: Glenbeigh Hospital-Cleveland (O, 100 beds), 18120 Puritas Ave., Cleveland 44135; tel. 216/476-0222; Theodore R. Sucher III, exec. dir.

Glenbeigh Hospital of Rock Creek (O, 80 beds), Rte. 45, P O Box 298, Rock Creek 44084; tel. 216/953-0177; Allen Drum, exec. dir.

Owned, leased, sponsored:	2 hospitals	180 beds
Contract-managed:	0 hospitals	0 beds
Totals:	2 hospitals	180 beds

1495: GRANDCOR (NP)
405 Grand Ave., Dayton, OH 45405; 513/222-7990; Richard J. Minor, pres. & chief exec. off.

Colorado: Memorial Hospital (O, 34 beds), 928 12th St., Greeley 80631; tel. 303/352-3123; W. Dale Ferguson, chief exec. off.

Ohio: Grandview Hospital and Medical Center (O, 362 beds), 405 Grand Ave., Dayton 45405; tel. 513/226-3200; Richard J. Minor, pres. & chief exec. off.

Owned, leased, sponsored:	2 hospitals	396 beds
Contract-managed:	0 hospitals	0 beds
Totals:	2 hospitals	396 beds

1535: GREAT PLAINS HEALTH ALLIANCE, INC. (NP)
Box 366, Phillipsburg, KS 67661; 913/543-2111; Curtis Erickson, pres. & chief exec. off.

Kansas: Rawlins County Hospital (CM, 27 beds), 707 Grant St., Box 47, Atwood 67730; tel. 913/626-3211; Pamela Thomas, adm.

Republic County Hospital (L, 86 beds), Belleville 66935; tel. 913/527-2255; Bonnie Elliott, adm.

Mitchell County Community Hospital (L, 89 beds), Eighth & Lincoln Aves., Beloit 67420; tel. 913/738-2266; Jeffrey S. Tarrant, adm.

Lane County Hospital (CM, 31 beds), 243 S. Second, Box 969, Dighton 67839; tel. 316/397-5321; Donna McGowan RN, adm.

Ellinwood District Hospital (L, 24 beds), 605 N. Main St., Ellinwood 67526; tel. 316/564-2548; Gordon L. Ensley, area dir.

Greenwood County Hospital (L, 46 beds), 100 W. 16th St., Eureka 67045; tel. 316/583-7451; Nancy McKenzie, adm.

Anderson County Hospital (CM, 71 beds), 421 S. Maple, Box 309, Garnett 66032; tel. 913/448-3131; Orlin E. Cunningham, adm.

Stanton County Hospital and Long Term Care Unit (CM, 46 beds), 404 N. Chestnut St., Box E, Johnson 67855; tel. 316/492-6250; David A. James, adm.

Wichita County Hospital (CM, 13 beds), 211 E. Earl, Leoti 67861; tel. 316/375-2233; Roger Pearson, adm.

Lincoln County Hospital (CM, 34 beds), 624 N. Second St., P O Box 406, Lincoln 67455; tel. 913/524-4403; Jolene Yager, adm.

Lindsborg Community Hospital (CM, 39 beds), 605 W. Lincoln St., Lindsborg 67456; tel. 913/227-3308; Bob Jones, adm.

Medicine Lodge Memorial Hospital (CM, 28 beds), 710 N. Walnut St., P O Drawer C, Medicine Lodge 67104; tel. 316/886-3771; Kevin White, adm.

Ottawa County Hospital (L, 39 beds), Box 209, Minneapolis 67467; tel. 913/392-2122; Joy Reed RN, adm.

Minneola District Hospital (CM, 15 beds), 212 Main St., Minneola 67865; tel. 316/885-4264; Blaine K. Miller, adm.

Phillips County Hospital (L, 62 beds), 1150 State St., Box 607, Phillipsburg 67661; tel. 913/543-5226; Joanne Johnson RN, adm.

Grisell Memorial Hospital District One (CM, 51 beds), P O Box 268, Ransom 67572; tel. 913/731-2231; Fern Mishler, adm.

Sabetha Community Hospital (L, 27 beds), 14th & Oregon Sts., P O Box 229, Sabetha 66534; tel. 913/284-2121; Rita Becker, adm.

Satanta District Hospital (CM, 38 beds), Box 159, Satanta 67870; tel. 316/649-2761; T. G. Lee, adm.

Scott County Hospital (L, 27 beds), 310 E. Third St., Scott City 67871; tel. 316/872-5811; Jackie John, adm.

Smith County Memorial Hospital (L, 52 beds), S. Main St., P O Box 349, Smith Center 66967; tel. 913/282-6661; J. H. Seitz, area dir.

Cheyenne County Hospital (L, 23 beds), 210 W. First St., P O Box 547, St. Francis 67756; tel. 913/332-2104; Shirley Billiar Adams RN, adm.

Greeley County Hospital (L, 18 beds), 506 Third St., Box 338, Tribune 67879; tel. 316/376-4221; Irene Pierce RN, adm.

Bob Wilson Memorial Grant County Hospital (CM, 42 beds), 415 N. Main St., Ulysses 67880; tel. 316/356-1266; Wally Boyd, adm.

For explanation of codes following names, see page B2.
*Indicates Type III membership in the American Hospital Association.

Trego County-Lemke Memorial Hospital (L, 64 beds), 320 13th St., Wakeeney 67672; tel. 913/743-2182; James Wahlmeier, adm.

Nebraska: Harlan County Hospital (CM, 25 beds), Alma 68920; tel. 308/928-2151; Ladonna Robison RN, adm.

Community Hospital (CM, 49 beds), 2307 Barada St., Falls City 68355; tel. 402/245-2428; Victor Lee, adm.

Owned, leased, sponsored:	12 hospitals	557 beds
Contract-managed:	14 hospitals	509 beds
Totals:	26 hospitals	1066 beds

1155: GREENLEAF HEALTH SYSTEMS, INC. (NP)
Two Northgate Park, Chattanooga, TN 37415; 615/870-5110; Dan B. Page, pres.

Georgia: Greenleaf Center (O, 60 beds), 500 Greenleaf Circle, Fort Oglethorpe 30742; tel. 404/861-4357; Jimmie W. Harden, adm.

Greenleaf Center (O, 70 beds), 2209 Pineview Dr., Valdosta 31602; tel. 912/247-4357; Allen R. Vessels, adm.

Oklahoma: Greenleaf Center -Shawnee (O, 50 beds), 1601 Gordon Cooper Dr., Shawnee 74801; tel. 405/275-9610; Joel Montgomery, adm.

Owned, leased, sponsored:	3 hospitals	180 beds
Contract-managed:	0 hospitals	0 beds
Totals:	3 hospitals	180 beds

***1555: GREENVILLE HOSPITAL SYSTEM** (NP)
701 Grove Rd., Greenville, SC 29605; 803/242-7000; Jack A. Skarupa, pres.

South Carolina: Greenville General Hospital (O, 89 beds), 100 Mallard St., Greenville 29601; Mailing Address 701 Grove Rd., Greenville, Zip 29605; tel. 803/242-8689; Thomas E.Hassett III, vice-pres.

Greenville Memorial Hospital (O, 712 beds), 701 Grove Rd., Greenville 29605; tel. 803/242-7000; Frank D. Pinckney, adm.

Marshall I. Pickens Hospital (O, 90 beds), 701 Grove Rd., Greenville 29605; tel. 803/242-7836; John E. Pettett Jr., adm.

Roger C. Peace Rehabilitation Hospital (O, 50 beds), 701 Grove Rd., Greenville 29605; tel. 803/242-7700; John E. Pettett Jr., adm.

Allen Bennett Memorial Hospital (O, 174 beds), Box 1149, Greer 29652; tel. 803/879-0200; Michael W. Massey, adm.

Hillcrest Hospital (O, 56 beds), Box 279, Simpsonville 29681; tel. 803/967-6100; Jack A. Macauley, adm.

North Greenville Hospital (O, 53 beds), 807 N. Main St., Travelers Rest 29690; tel. 803/834-5131; John Smith, adm.

Owned, leased, sponsored:	7 hospitals	1224 beds
Contract-managed:	0 hospitals	0 beds
Totals:	7 hospitals	1224 beds

***9995: GROUP HEALTH COOPERATIVE OF PUGET SOUND** (NP)
300 Elliott Ave. W., Seattle, WA 98119; 206/326-6844; Mr. Gail L. Warden, pres. & chief exec. off.

Washington: Group Health Eastside Hospital (O, 142 beds), 2700 152nd Ave. N.E., Redmond 98052; tel. 206/883-5151; Richard Marks, reg. vice-pres.

Group Health Cooperative Central Hospital (O, 278 beds), 201 16th Ave. E., Seattle 98112; tel. 206/326-3000; Cheryl M. Scott, reg. vice-pres.

Ghc Inpatient Center Tacoma General (L, 36 beds), 315 S. K St., Tacoma 98405; tel. 206/383-6156; Bob Pfotenhauer, adm.

Owned, leased, sponsored:	3 hospitals	456 beds
Contract-managed:	0 hospitals	0 beds
Totals:	3 hospitals	456 beds

0675: GUTHRIE MEDICAL CENTER (NP)
Guthrie Square, Sayre, PA 18840; 717/888-6666; Ralph H. Meyer, pres.

New York: Tioga General Hospital (O, 198 beds), 37 N. Chemung St., Waverly 14892; tel. 607/565-2861; Frederick A. Kauffman, adm.

Pennsylvania: Robert Packer Hospital (O, 366 beds), Guthrie Square, Sayre 18840; tel. 717/888-6666; Gary B. Morrison, pres.

Troy Community Hospital (O, 65 beds), 100 John St., Troy 16947; tel. 717/297-2121; Mark A. Webster, pres.

Owned, leased, sponsored:	3 hospitals	629 beds
Contract-managed:	0 hospitals	0 beds
Totals:	3 hospitals	629 beds

***1655: HARPER-GRACE HOSPITALS** (NP)
3990 John R St., Detroit, MI 48201; 313/745-9375; Michael H. Fritz, pres. & chief exec. off.

Michigan: Grace Hospital (O, 303 beds), 18700 Meyers Rd., Detroit 48235; tel. 313/966-3111; George P. Caralis, adm.

Harper Hospital (O, 709 beds), 3990 John R St., Detroit 48201; tel. 313/745-8111; Albert L. Greene, adm.

Owned, leased, sponsored:	2 hospitals	1012 beds
Contract-managed:	0 hospitals	0 beds
Totals:	2 hospitals	1012 beds

***2345: HARRIS METHODIST HEALTH SYSTEM** (CO)
1325 Pennsylvania Ave., Eighth Fl, Fort Worth, TX 76104; 817/878-5973; Ronald L. Smith, pres.

Texas: Harris Methodist Northwest (O, 36 beds), 108 Denver Trail, Azle 76020; tel. 817/444-2575; N. Richard Belanger, adm.

Harris Methodist -HEB (O, 251 beds), R. William Whitman, sr. vice-pres.

Walls Regional Hospital (O, 81 beds), 201 Walls Dr., Cleburne 76031; tel. 817/641-2551; Nick H. Kupferle III, adm.

Decatur Community Hospital (CM, 50 beds), 2100 S. Fm 51, Decatur 76234; tel. 817/627-5921; Joseph F. Sloan, adm.

Harris Methodist -Dublin (O, 36 beds), 205 N. Patrick St., Box O, Dublin 76446; tel. 817/445-3322; John Hodges, adm.

Harris Methodist -Fort Worth (O, 547 beds), 1301 Pennsylvania Ave., Fort Worth 76104; tel. 817/882-2000; Chuck Brosseau, sr. vice-pres. & adm.

Marks-English Hospital (O, 26 beds), 1307-09 Holden St., Box 997, Glen Rose 76043; tel. 817/897-2215; Gary A. Marks, adm.

Harris Methodist -Hamilton (O, 39 beds), 400 N. Brown Ave., Hamilton 76531; tel. 817/386-3151; Paul C. Roberts, vice-pres. & adm.

Meridian Hospital (O, 123 beds), 1114 N. Main St., Box 677, Meridian 76665; tel. 817/435-2308; Gary Marks, vice-pres.

Harris Methodist -Mexia (O, 47 beds), 312 E. Glendale St., Mexia 76667; tel. 817/562-5332; Roger Jenkins, adm.

Harris Methodist -Stephenville (O, 86 beds), 411 N. Belknap St., Box 1399, Stephenville 76401; tel. 817/965-3115; Ray Reynolds, adm.

Owned, leased, sponsored:	10 hospitals	1272 beds
Contract-managed:	1 hospitals	50 beds
Totals:	11 hospitals	1322 beds

1865: HCA OKLAHOMA HEALTH NETWORK (IO)
1601 N.W. Expwy., Suite 2200, Oklahoma City, OK 73118; 405/840-2284; Bruce Perry, pres.

Oklahoma: Share Medical Center (CM, 120 beds), 800 Share Dr., Alva 73717; tel. 405/327-2800; Al Allee, adm.

Atoka Memorial Hospital (CM, 37 beds), 1501 S. Virginia, Atoka 74525; tel. 405/889-3333; Andy Freeman, adm.

Healdton Municipal Hospital (CM, 28 beds), 918 S.W. Eighth St., Box 928, Healdton 73438; tel. 405/229-0701; Zeb Wright, adm.

Purcell Municipal Hospital (CM, 42 beds), 1500 N. Green Ave., Purcell 73080; tel. 405/527-6524; Warren K. Spellman, adm.

Wetumka General Hospital (CM, 34 beds), 325 S. Washita, Wetumka 74883; tel. 405/452-3276; Keith E. Calvert, interim adm.

For explanation of codes following names, see page B2.
*Indicates Type III membership in the American Hospital Association.

Woodward Hospital and Health Center (CM, 60 beds), 900 17th St., Box 489, Woodward 73802; tel. 405/256-5511; John H. Welsh, adm.

Owned, leased, sponsored:	0 hospitals	0 beds
Contract-managed:	6 hospitals	321 beds
Totals:	6 hospitals	321 beds

***5415: HEALTH AND HOSPITAL SERVICES** (CC)
1715 114th Ave. S.E., Suite 110, Bellevue, WA 98004; 206/454-8068; Sr. Joan M. McInnes, pres.

Alaska: Ketchikan General Hospital (L, 83 beds), 3100 Tongass Ave., Ketchikan 99901; tel. 907/225-5171; Sr. Barbara Haase, adm.

Oregon: Sacred Heart General Hospital (O, 399 beds), 1255 Hilyard St., Box 10905, Zip 97440; tel. 503/686-7300; Sr. Monica Heeran, adm.

Western Lane Hospital (CM, 24 beds), 1525 12th St., Box 580, Florence 97439; tel. 503/997-8412; Reed G. Condie, adm.

St. Helen's Hospital and Health Center (O, 44 beds), 500 N. Columbia River Hwy., St. Helens 97051; tel. 503/397-1188; Charles R. Laird, adm.

Washington: St. Joseph Hospital (O, 126 beds), 2901 Squalicum Pkwy., Bellingham 98225; tel. 206/734-5400; Sr. Catherine McInnes, adm.

Monticello Medical Center (O, 122 beds), 600 Broadway, P O Box 638, Longview 98632; tel. 206/423-5850; Joseph M. Horner, adm.

St. John's Hospital (O, 151 beds), 1614 E. Kessler Blvd., P O Box 3002, Longview 98632; tel. 206/423-1530; Sr. Anne Hayes, adm.

Snoqualmie Valley Hospital (L, 28 beds), 1505 Meadowbrook Way S.E., Snoqualmie 98065; tel. 206/888-1438; John P. Holt, adm.

Owned, leased, sponsored:	7 hospitals	953 beds
Contract-managed:	1 hospitals	24 beds
Totals:	8 hospitals	977 beds

***5945: HEALTH CARE CORPORATION OF THE SISTERS OF ST. JOSEPH OF CARONDELET** (CC)
77 W. Port Plaza, Suite 222, St. Louis, MO 63146; 314/576-5662; Sr. Mary K. Ford, pres.

Arizona: Holy Cross Hospital and Health Center (O, 80 beds), 1230 Target Range Rd., Nogales 85621; tel. 602/287-2771; Walt Connolly, adm.

St. Joseph's Hospital and Health Center (O, 305 beds), 350 N. Wilmot Rd., Tucson 85711; Mailing Address Box 12069, Tucson, Zip 85732; tel. 602/296-3211; Sr. St.Joan Willert, pres.

St. Mary's Hospital and Health Center (O, 332 beds), 1601 W. St. Mary's Rd., Tucson 85745; Mailing Address Box 5386, Tucson, Zip 85703; tel. 602/622-5833; Sr. St.Joan Willert, pres. & chief exec. off.

California: Daniel Freeman Memorial Hospital (O, 395 beds), 333 N. Prairie Ave., Inglewood 90301; Mailing Address Box 100, Inglewood, Zip 90306; tel. 213/674-7050; Sr.Regina Clare Salazar, pres.

Daniel Freeman Marina Hospital (O, 203 beds), 4650 Lincoln Blvd., Marina Del Rey 90291; tel. 213/823-8911; Stephen L. Packwood, adm.

Georgia: St. Joseph Hospital (O, 235 beds), 2260 Wrightsboro Rd., Augusta 30910; tel. 404/737-7400; William Sherwood Atkinson, pres.; Vincent Caponi, adm.

Idaho: St. Joseph Regional Medical Center (O, 139 beds), 415 Sixth St., Box 816, Lewiston 83501; tel. 208/743-2511; Howard A. Hayes, adm.

Minnesota: Carondelet Community Hospitals (O, 645 beds), Mailing Address 2414 S. Seventh St., Minneapolis 55454; John R. McIntire, pres.

Missouri: Saint Joseph Health Center Kansas (O, 279 beds), 1000 Carondelet Dr., Kansas City 64114; tel. 816/942-4400; Richard M. Abell, pres.

St. Joseph Hospital (O, 332 beds), 525 Couch Ave., Kirkwood, Kirkwood 63122; tel. 314/966-1500; Sr. Catherine Durr, pres.

New York: St. Mary's Hospital (O, 148 beds), 427 Guy Park Ave., Amsterdam 12010; tel. 518/842-1900; Peter E. Capobianco, adm.

Washington: Our Lady of Lourdes Health Center (O, 95 beds), 520 N. Fourth St., Pasco 99301; Mailing Address Box 2568, Pasco, Zip 99302; tel. 509/547-7704; Thomas Corley,adm.

Wisconsin: Holy Family Hospital (O, 40 beds), 535 Hospital Rd., New Richmond 54017; tel. 715/246-2101; Donald M. Michels, pres.

Owned, leased, sponsored:	13 hospitals	3228 beds
Contract-managed:	0 hospitals	0 beds
Totals:	13 hospitals	3228 beds

***6545: HEALTH CORPORATION OF THE ARCHDIOCESE OF NEWARK** (CC)
41 Centre St., Newark, NJ 07102; 201/596-3900; Margaret J. Straney, pres.

New Jersey: Saint James Hospital of Newark (O, 206 beds), 155 Jefferson St., Newark 07105; tel. 201/465-2707; Charles L. Brennan, pres.

Saint Michael's Medical Center (O, 411 beds), 268 Dr. Martin Luther King Jr Blvd., Newark 07102; tel. 201/877-5000; William J. Cornetta Jr., actg. pres.

St. Mary's Hospital (O, 228 beds), 135 S. Center St., Orange 07050; tel. 201/266-3000; Sr. Mary Fidelise, pres.

Owned, leased, sponsored:	3 hospitals	845 beds
Contract-managed:	0 hospitals	0 beds
Totals:	3 hospitals	845 beds

***0965: HEALTH DIMENSIONS, INC.** (NP)
2005 Hamilton Ave., Suite 300, San Jose, CA 95125; 408/599-2701; Robert K. Kirk, pres.

California: Wheeler Hospital (O, 56 beds), 651 Sixth St., Gilroy 95020; tel. 408/842-5621; Mort G. Walser, adm.

Good Samaritan Hospital of Santa Clara Valley (O, 388 beds), 2425 Samaritan Dr., San Jose 95124; tel. 408/559-2011; Richard E. Herington, adm.

San Jose Hospital (O, 289 beds), 675 E. Santa Clara St., San Jose 95112; tel. 408/998-3212; John C. Aird, pres.; Robert G. Brueckner, exec. vice-pres.

Owned, leased, sponsored:	3 hospitals	733 beds
Contract-managed:	0 hospitals	0 beds
Totals:	3 hospitals	733 beds

1905: HEALTH MANAGEMENT SERVICES (IO)
5793 Widewaters Pkwy., Syracuse, NY 13214; 315/445-2082; James W. Krembs, pres.

New York: Carthage Area Hospital (CM, 78 beds), W. Street Rd., Carthage 13619; tel. 315/493-1000; Jeffrey Drop, chief exec. off.

Edward John Noble Hospital of Gouverneur (CM, 47 beds), 77 W. Barney St., Gouverneur 13642; tel. 315/287-1000; Michael Delarm, adm.

Lewis County General Hospital (CM, 174 beds), N. State St., Lowville 13367; tel. 315/376-5200; Edward Sieber Jr., adm.

The Hospital (CM, 91 beds), Pearl St., Sidney 13838; tel. 607/563-3512; Leo G. Friel, chief exec. off.

Owned, leased, sponsored:	0 hospitals	0 beds
Contract-managed:	4 hospitals	390 beds
Totals:	4 hospitals	390 beds

8865: HEALTH MANAGEMENT SERVICES, INC. (IO)
340 E. Town St., Suite 7-800, Columbus, OH 43215; 614/461-3401; Ned Boatright, pres.

Ohio: Barnesville Hospital Association (CM, 99 beds), 639 W. Main St., Barnesville 43713; tel. 614/425-3941; Albert R. Hanna, interim adm.

Grant Medical Center (CM, 473 beds), 111 S. Grant Ave., Columbus 43215; tel. 614/461-3232; William Hendrickson, pres.

For explanation of codes following names, see page B2.
*Indicates Type III membership in the American Hospital Association.

Pike Community Hospital (CM, 56 beds), 100 Dawn Lane, Waverly 45690; tel. 614/947-2186; Don J. Sabol, adm.

Owned, leased, sponsored:	0 hospitals	0 beds
Contract-managed:	3 hospitals	628 beds
Totals:	3 hospitals	628 beds

0395: HEALTHCARE INTERNATIONAL, INC. (IO)
9737 Great Hills Trail, P O Box 4008, Austin, TX 78759; 512/346-4300; James L. Fariss, bd. chm.

California: Healthcare Medical Center of Tustin (O, 150 beds), 14662 Newport Ave., Tustin 92680; tel. 714/838-9600; Douglas Wilson Jr., exec. dir.

Colorado: Cedar Springs Psychiatric Hospital (O, 100 beds), 2135 Southgate Rd., Colorado Springs 80906; Mailing Address Box 640, Colorado Springs, Zip 80901; tel.303/633-4114; Richard A. Bangert, chief exec. off.

South Carolina: Southern Pines Psychiatric Hospital (O, 108 beds), 2777 Speissegger, Charleston 29406; tel. 803/747-5830; Daniel K. Morrisey, adm.

Tennessee: Eastwood Hospital (O, 243 beds), 3000 Getwell Rd., Memphis 38118; tel. 901/369-8500; John F. Davis, exec. dir.

Texas: Brown Schools Healthcare Rehabilitation Center (O, 151 beds), P O Box 43148, Austin 78745; tel. 512/444-4835; Tony Merka, dir.

Oaks Treatment Center-Brown Schools (O, 120 beds), 1407 W. Stassney Lane, Austin 78745; tel. 512/444-9561; James A. Eberwine, dir.

Green Oaks Psychiatric Hospital (O, 106 beds), 7808 Clodus Fields Dr., Dallas 75251; tel. 214/991-9504; Liam J. Mulvaney, adm.

West Oaks-Psychiatric Institute of Houston (O, 184 beds), 6500 Hornwood, Houston 77074; Mailing Address Box 741389, Houston, Zip 77274; tel. 713/995-0909; KaySwint, adm.

The Brown Schools-San Marcos Treatment Center (O, 225 beds), Box 768, San Marcos 78666; tel. 512/392-7111; Dick Hardin, dir.

Virginia: Cumberland A. Hospital for Children (O, 72 beds), Rte. 637, P O Box 150, New Kent 23124; tel. 804/737-7713; Stephen A. Rosenberg, adm.

Owned, leased, sponsored:	10 hospitals	1459 beds
Contract-managed:	0 hospitals	0 beds
Totals:	10 hospitals	1459 beds

1585: HEALTHCARE MANAGEMENT GROUP, INC. (IO)
146 Sylvan Dr., Jackson, GA 30233; 205/979-0805; Earl Bonds Jr., chief exec. off.

Alabama: J. Paul Jones Hospital (L, 30 beds), McWilliams Ave., Drawer B, Camden 36726; tel. 205/682-4131; James O. Graham, adm.

Georgia: Sylvan Grove Hospital (L, 28 beds), 1050 McDonough Rd., Jackson 30233; tel. 404/775-7861; Jack F. Frayer, pres.

Morgan Memorial Hospital (L, 26 beds), Canterbury Park, Box 860, Madison 30650; tel. 404/342-1666; Bob Baldwin, adm.

Louisiana: DeQuincy Memorial Hospital (CM, 49 beds), 110 W. Fourth St., Box 1166, De Quincy 70633; tel. 318/786-1200; Luther J. Lewis, adm.

Merryville General Hospital (CM, 74 beds), Bryan St., Drawer C, Merryville 70653; tel. 318/825-6181; D. W. Nichols, adm.

Owned, leased, sponsored:	3 hospitals	84 beds
Contract-managed:	2 hospitals	123 beds
Totals:	5 hospitals	207 beds

0405: HEALTHCARE SERVICES OF AMERICA (IO)
2000 Southbridge Pkwy., Suite 200, Birmingham, AL 35209; 205/879-8970; Charles A. Speir, bd. chm. & chief exec. off.

Alabama: HSA Hill Crest Sunrise Hospital (O, 119 beds), 6869 Fifth Ave. S., Box 2896, Birmingham 35212; tel. 205/833-9000; Isaac W. Ferniany PhD, adm.

Louisiana: HSA Greenbrier Hospital (O, 56 beds), Greenbrier Blvd., P O Box 1836, Covington 70434; tel. 504/893-2970; Dominic R. Catalano, adm.

Missouri: HSA Heartland Hospital (O, 66 beds), Ashland & Prewitt St., Nevada 64772; tel. 417/667-2666; James E. Ferguson, chief exec. off.

Owned, leased, sponsored:	3 hospitals	241 beds
Contract-managed:	0 hospitals	0 beds
Totals:	3 hospitals	241 beds

***1695: HEALTHEAST, INC.** (NP)
337 N. West St., Allentown, PA 18102; 215/778-2950; David P. Buchmueller, pres. & chief exec. off.

Pennsylvania: Allentown Hospital (O, 305 beds), 17th & Chew Sts., Allentown 18102; tel. 215/778-2300; Darryl R. Lippman, pres.

Lehigh Valley Hospital Center (O, 460 beds), 1200 S. Cedar Crest Blvd., P O Box 689, Allentown 18105; tel. 215/776-8000; Samuel R. Huston, pres. & chief exec.off.

Gnaden Huetten Memorial Hospital (O, 200 beds), 11th & Hamilton Sts., Lehighton 18235; tel. 215/377-1300; Dereck Marshall, pres.

Owned, leased, sponsored:	3 hospitals	965 beds
Contract-managed:	0 hospitals	0 beds
Totals:	3 hospitals	965 beds

***2755: HEALTHLINK** (NP)
500 N.E. Multnomah St., Portland, OR 97232; 503/234-4500; G. Rodney Wolford, pres.

Oregon: Mount Hood Medical Center (O, 108 beds), 24800 S.E. Stark, P O Box 718, Gresham 97030; tel. 503/667-1122; Joseph J. Henery, adm.

Emanuel Hospital and Health Center (O, 344 beds), 2801 N. Gantenbein Ave., Portland 97227; tel. 503/280-3200; Fred R. Eaton, adm.

Holladay Park Medical Center (O, 165 beds), 1225 N.E. Second Ave., Portland 97232; tel. 503/233-4567; Jane Cummins, adm.

Meridian Park Hospital (O, 150 beds), 19300 S.W. 65th St., Tualatin 97062; tel. 503/692-1212; Carleton G. Lindgren, adm.

Owned, leased, sponsored:	4 hospitals	767 beds
Contract-managed:	0 hospitals	0 beds
Totals:	4 hospitals	767 beds

***6235: HEALTHONE CORPORATION** (NP)
2810 57th Ave. N., Minneapolis, MN 55430; 612/333-1711; Richard S. Blair, interim pres. & chief exec. off.

Iowa: North Iowa Medical Center (CM, 64 beds), 910 N. Eisenhower Ave., Mason City 50401; tel. 515/424-0440; Ronald O. Ebersole, exec. dir.

Kansas: Memorial Hospital (CM, 74 beds), Sunset Ave. & Claflin Rd., Box 1208, Manhattan 66502; tel. 913/776-3300; E. Michael Nunamaker, chief exec. off.

Michigan: Central Michigan Community Hospital (CM, 123 beds), 1221 South Dr., Mount Pleasant 48858; tel. 517/772-6700; Paul K. Halverson, pres. & chief exec. off.

Minnesota: Health Central of Buffalo (O, 30 beds), 303 Catlin St., Buffalo 55313; tel. 612/682-1212; Steven P. Bresnahan, chief exec. off.

Granite Falls Municipal Hospital and Manor (CM, 94 beds), 345 Tenth Ave., Granite Falls 56241; tel. 612/564-3111; George Gerlach, adm.

Mesabi Regional Medical Center (CM, 175 beds), 750 E. 34th St., Hibbing 55746; tel. 218/262-4881; David M. Beach, chief exec. off.

Long Prairie Memorial Hospital (O, 157 beds), 20 Ninth St. S.E., Long Prairie 56347; tel. 612/732-2141; Kevin J. Smith, exec. vice-pres.

For explanation of codes following names, see page B2.
*Indicates Type III membership in the American Hospital Association.

Health Central Metropolitan Hospitals (O, 834 beds), 2810 57th Ave. N., Minneapolis 55430; tel. 612/574-7800; William Kreykes, pres.

Metropolitan Medical Center (O, 506 beds), 900 S. Eighth St., Minneapolis 55404; tel. 612/347-4444; Frank J. Larkin, pres. & chief exec. off.

Monticello-Big Lake Community Hospital (CM, 130 beds), 1013 Hart Blvd., Box 480, Monticello 55362; tel. 612/295-2945; Barbara Schwientek, exec. dir.

Sioux Valley Hospital (O, 85 beds), 1324 Fifth North St., Box 577, New Ulm 56073; tel. 507/354-2111; Robert Stevens, adm.

Health Central of Owatonna (O, 77 beds), 903 S. Oak, Owatonna 55060; tel. 507/451-3850; Richard G. Slieter, chief exec. off.

Children's Hospital (CM, 105 beds), 345 N. Smith Ave., St. Paul 55102; tel. 612/298-8666; Brock D. Nelson, adm.

United Hospital (O, 326 beds), 333 N. Smith Ave., St. Paul 55102; tel. 612/298-8888; Thomas H. Rockers, pres.

Northwest Medical Center (CM, 189 beds), 120 LaBree Ave. S., Thief River Falls 56701; tel. 218/681-4240; Richard A. Spyhalski, pres.

St. Mary's Hospital and Home (O, 120 beds), 551 Fourth St. N., P O Box 750, Winsted 55395; tel. 612/485-2151; Jeanne Johnson, chief exec. off.

North Dakota: Mandan Hospital (CM, 54 beds), 1000 18th St. N.W., Mandan 58554; tel. 701/663-6471; David L. Brown, adm.

South Dakota: Dakota Midland Hospital (O, 132 beds), 1400 15th Ave. N.W., Aberdeen 57401; tel. 605/622-3300; Philo Hall, exec. vice-pres.

Ipswich Community Hospital (CM, 21 beds), 507 Bloemendaal Dr., Box 326, Ipswich 57451; tel. 605/426-6011; Ken Trammell, adm.

Dakota Hospital (CM, 47 beds), 801 E. Main St., P O Box 316, Vermillion 57069; tel. 605/624-2611; Bill D. Wilson, chief exec. off.

Prairie Lakes Hosptial (CM, 205 beds), 400 Tenth Ave. N.W., Watertown 57201; tel. 605/886-8491; Edmond L. Weiland, adm.

Wisconsin: River Falls Area Hospital (O, 105 beds), 550 N. Main St., River Falls 54022; tel. 715/425-6155; Eric L. Pousard, adm.

St. Croix Valley Memorial Hospital (CM, 84 beds), S. Adams St., St. Croix Falls 54024; tel. 715/483-3261; James Bigogno, chief exec. off.

Owned, leased, sponsored:	10 hospitals	2372 beds
Contract-managed:	13 hospitals	1365 beds
Totals:	23 hospitals	3737 beds

2595: HEALTHSHARE, INC. (NP)
501 W. Mitchell St., Suite 300, Petoskey, MI 49770; 616/348-4567; John Rasmussen, pres.

Michigan: Northern Michigan Hospitals (O, 260 beds), 416 Connable St., Petoskey 49770; tel. 616/348-4000; James E. Raney, pres.

Mackinac Straits Hospital and Health Center (CM, 15 beds), 220 Burdette St., St. Ignace 49781; tel. 906/643-8585; John Taylor, actg. adm.

Owned, leased, sponsored:	1 hospitals	260 beds
Contract-managed:	1 hospitals	15 beds
Totals:	2 hospitals	275 beds

1365: HEALTHSTAR CORPORATION (IO)
3555 Timmons Lane, Suite 700, Houston, TX 77027; 713/627-2145; Hugh M. Morrison, bd. chm. & pres.

Texas: Bastrop Community Hospital (L, 25 beds), 104 Loop 150 West, Bastrop 78602; tel. 512/321-3921; Jim Koch, exec. dir.

Central Texas Medical Center (L, 33 beds), 704 Wheelock St., Box 393, Hearne 77859; tel. 409/279-3434; Frank E. Rogers, adm.

Rollins-Brook Hospital (O, 23 beds), 608 N. Key Ave., Box 589, Lampasas 76550; tel. 512/556-3682; Michael L. Littell, adm.

Navasota Regional Hospital (L, 57 beds), 210 S. Judson St., Navasota 77868; tel. 409/825-6585; William W. Fox, exec. dir.

San Saba Hospital (L, 34 beds), 2005 W. Wallace St., San Saba 76877; tel. 915/372-5171; Wendell Alford, adm.

Owned, leased, sponsored:	5 hospitals	172 beds
Contract-managed:	0 hospitals	0 beds
Totals:	5 hospitals	172 beds

***6905: HEALTHWEST MEDICAL CENTERS** (NP)
21800 Oxnard St., Suite 550, Woodland Hills, CA 91367; 818/716-2777; Roger H. Drue, pres.

California: La Palma Intercommunity Hospital (O, 136 beds), 7901 Walker St., La Palma 90623; Mailing Address P O Box 5850, Buena Park, Zip 90622; tel. 714/670-7400; John R.Cochran III, chief exec. off. & adm.

Lindsay Hospital Medical Center (O, 97 beds), 740 N. Sequoia Ave., Box 1297, Lindsay 93247; tel. 209/562-4955; Frank F. Guyton, adm.

Long Beach Community Hospital (O, 284 beds), 1720 Termino Ave., Long Beach 90804; Mailing Address Box 2587, Long Beach, Zip 90801; tel. 213/498-1000; Paul S.Viviano, exec. vice-pres. & chief exec. off.

Coldwater Canyon Hospital (O, 70 beds), 6421 Coldwater Canyon, North Hollywood 91606; tel. 818/769-1000; John M. Wilson, adm.

Northridge Hospital Medical Center (O, 345 beds), 18300 Roscoe Blvd., Northridge 91328; tel. 818/885-8500; Daniel F. Adams, exec. vice-pres. & chief exec. off.

Pasadena Community Hospital (O, 66 beds), 1845 N. Fair Oaks Ave., Pasadena 91103; tel. 818/798-7811; Kimberly Rocha, actg. adm.

Valley Hospital Medical Center (O, 198 beds), 14500 Sherman Circle, Van Nuys 91405; tel. 213/997-0101; David Gustafson, exec. vice-pres. & chief exec. off.

New Jersey: Meadowlands Hospital Medical Center (O, 200 beds), Meadowland Pkwy., Secaucus 07094; tel. 201/392-3100; Paul V. Cavalli MD, pres. & chief exec. off.

Washington: St. Luke's General Hospital (O, 117 beds), 809 E. Chestnut St., Bellingham 98225; tel. 206/734-8300; William G. Gordon, exec. vice-pres. & chief exec. off.

Owned, leased, sponsored:	9 hospitals	1513 beds
Contract-managed:	0 hospitals	0 beds
Totals:	9 hospitals	1513 beds

2195: HEI CORPORATION (IO)
7676 Woodway, Suite 112, Houston, TX 77063; 713/780-7802; George G. Alexander MD, chm. & chief exec. off.

Missouri: Sullivan Community Hospital (O, 73 beds), 751 Sappington Bridge Rd., Sullivan 63080; tel. 314/468-4186; Dave Rose, chief exec. off.

Texas: Rosewood Medical Center (O, 184 beds), 9200 Westheimer Rd., Houston 77063; tel. 713/780-7900; Rod Seidel, adm.

Sam Houston Memorial Hospital (O, 208 beds), 1615 Hillendahl, Houston 77055; tel. 713/468-4311; A. C. Buchahan, adm.

Orange Memorial Hospital (L, 172 beds), 608 Strickland, Orange 77630; tel. 713/883-9361; James Berry, adm.

Silsbee Doctors Hospital (O, 69 beds), Hwy. 418, Box 1208, Silsbee 77656; tel. 409/385-5531; Gene T. Jordan, adm.

Owned, leased, sponsored:	5 hospitals	706 beds
Contract-managed:	0 hospitals	0 beds
Totals:	5 hospitals	706 beds

3535: HENDRICK MEDICAL DEVELOPMENT CORPORATION (NP)
19th & Hickory St., Abilene, TX 79601; 915/677-3551; Michael C. Waters, pres.

Texas: Hendrick Medical Center (O, 452 beds), 1242 N. 19th Sts., Abilene 79601; tel. 915/670-2000; Michael C. Waters, pres.

E. L. Graham Memorial Hospital (L, 30 beds), W. Hwy. 80, Box 321, Cisco 76437; tel. 817/442-3951; Helen Orr, adm.

For explanation of codes following names, see page B2.
*Indicates Type III membership in the American Hospital Association.

Comanche Community Hospital (L, 20 beds), 211 S. Austin St., Box 443, Comanche 76442; tel. 915/356-2012; Charley C. Latham, adm.

Seymour Hospital Authority (CM, 49 beds), Stadium Dr., Box 351, Seymour 76380; tel. 817/888-5572; Larry Suit, adm.

Owned, leased, sponsored:	3 hospitals	502 beds
Contract-managed:	1 hospitals	49 beds
Totals:	4 hospitals	551 beds

0725: HERMANN AFFILIATED HOSPITAL SYSTEMS (NP)
1020 Holcombe, Suite 900, Houston, TX 77030; 713/796-0891; William E. Young, Jr., chief exec. off.

Texas: Brewster Memorial Hospital (CM, 34 beds), 801 E. Brown St., Box 180, Alpine 79831; tel. 915/837-3447; Don Karl, interim adm.

Angleton-Danbury General Hospital (CM, 61 beds), 132 Hospital Dr., Angleton 77515; tel. 409/849-7721; James R. Perry, adm.

Heart of Texas Memorial Hospital (CM, 50 beds), Nine Rd., P O Box 1150, Brady 76825; tel. 915/597-2901; Charles Van Tine, exec. dir.

Columbus Community Hospital (CM, 40 beds), 110 Shult Dr., Box 865, Columbus 78934; tel. 409/732-2371; Michael T. Portacci, exec. dir.

Val Verde Memorial Hospital (CM, 84 beds), 801 Bedell Ave., P O Box 1527, Del Rio 78840; tel. 512/775-8566; Larry Dorsey, adm.

Edna Hospital (CM, 35 beds), 1013 S. Wells St., P O Box 670, Edna 77957; tel. 512/782-5241; Kenneth W. Randall, adm.

Wilson Memorial Hospital (CM, 44 beds), 1301 Hospital Blvd., Floresville 78114; tel. 512/393-3122; Pete Delgado, adm.

Mauritz Memorial Hospital (CM, 50 beds), 206 Sutherland St., Drawer C, Ganado 77962; tel. 512/782-5241; Kenneth W. Randall, adm.

Medina Community Hospital (CM, 34 beds), Hwy. 462, Hondo 78861; tel. 512/426-5363; Ernest Parisi, adm.

Frio Hospital (CM, 22 beds), 320 Berry Ranch Rd., Pearsall 78061; tel. 512/334-3617; Frank T. Williams Jr., adm.

Memorial Medical Center (CM, 53 beds), 810 N. Ann St., Box 25, Port Lavaca 77979; tel. 512/552-6713; Mike Munnerlyn, adm.

Refugio County Memorial Hospital (CM, 49 beds), 107 Swift St., Refugio 78377; tel. 512/526-2321; Bruce Giessel, adm.

Richards Memorial Hospital (CM, 47 beds), 1700 Brazos St., Drawer 1010, Rockdale 76567; tel. 512/446-2513

Sweeny Community Hospital (CM, 38 beds), 305 N. McKinney St., Box 1000, Sweeny 77480; tel. 409/548-3311; Michael A. Kozar, chief exec. off.

Taft Hospital District (CM, 94 beds), 1220 Gregory St., Taft 78390; tel. 512/528-2545; Douglas Langley, adm.

Trinity Memorial Hospital (CM, 30 beds), Box 471, Trinity 75862; tel. 409/594-3541; Dean Leiser, adm.

West Community Hospital (CM, 49 beds), 501 Meadow Dr., Box 478, West 76691; tel. 817/826-5381; Daniel W. Martin, adm.

Owned, leased, sponsored:	0 hospitals	0 beds
Contract-managed:	17 hospitals	814 beds
Totals:	17 hospitals	814 beds

1525: HILLSBOROUGH COUNTY HOSPITAL AUTHORITY (NP)
Davis Island, Administrative Bldg., Tampa, FL 33607; 813/251-7383; Newell E. France, mng. dir.

Florida: Hillsborough County Hospital (O, 137 beds), 5906 N. 30th St., P O Box 11912, Tampa 33680; tel. 813/239-1186; Lanny W. Erickson, adm.

Tampa General Hospital (O, 596 beds), Davis Islands, Tampa 33606; Mailing Address P O Box 1289, Tampa, Zip 33601; tel. 813/253-0711; Newell E. France, pres.

Owned, leased, sponsored:	2 hospitals	733 beds
Contract-managed:	0 hospitals	0 beds
Totals:	2 hospitals	733 beds

***3395: HITCHCOCK ALLIANCE** (NP)
P O Box 1001, Hanover, NH 03755; 603/646-8150; William E. Welton, pres.

New Hampshire: Mary Hitchcock Memorial Hospital (O, 378 beds), 2 Maynard St., Hanover 03756; tel. 603/646-5000; James W. Varnum, pres.

Alice Peck Day Memorial Hospital (O, 78 beds), 125 Mascoma St., Lebanon 03766; tel. 603/448-3121

Owned, leased, sponsored:	2 hospitals	456 beds
Contract-managed:	0 hospitals	0 beds
Totals:	2 hospitals	456 beds

***5585: HOLY CROSS HEALTH SYSTEM CORPORATION** (CC)
3606 E. Jefferson Blvd., South Bend, IN 46615; 219/233-8558; William A. Himmelsbach Jr., pres. & chief exec. off.

California: Bloss Memorial District Hospital (CM, 23 beds), 1691 Third St., Atwater 95301; tel. 209/358-8201; Joseph N. Wierzba, adm.

Avenal District Hospital (CM, 28 beds), 317 Alpine St., Avenal 93204; tel. 209/386-5278; Sherman J. Hansen, adm.

St. Agnes Hospital and Medical Center (O, 320 beds), 1303 E. Herndon, Fresno 93710; tel. 209/449-3000; Sr. Ruth Marie Nickerson, pres. & chief exec. off.

Holy Cross Hospital (O, 311 beds), 15031 Rinaldi St., Mission Hills 91345; tel. 818/365-8051; Sr. M. Carolita, pres. & chief exec. off.

Idaho: Saint Alphonsus Regional Medical Center (O, 246 beds), 1055 N. Curtis Rd., Boise 83706; tel. 208/378-2121; Sr. Patricia Vandenberg, pres.

Valley County Hospital (CM, 10 beds), Cascade 83611; tel. 208/382-4242; Gerald L. Hart, adm.

Blaine County Medical Center (CM, 40 beds), Box 927, Hailey 83333; tel. 208/788-2222; David D. Farnes, pres.

McCall Memorial Hospital (CM, 21 beds), Forest & State Sts., Box 906, McCall 83638; tel. 208/634-2221; Karen Kellie, adm.

Elmore Medical Center (CM, 83 beds), 895 N. Sixth East St., Drawer H, Mountain Home 83647; tel. 208/587-8401; Jan G. Cox, adm.

Indiana: St. John's Healthcare Corporation (O, 371 beds), 2015 Jackson St., Anderson 46014; tel. 317/649-2511; James H. Stephens, pres.

Holy Cross Parkview Hospital (O, 58 beds), 1915 Lake Ave., P O Box 670, Plymouth 46563; tel. 219/936-3181; David Baytos, pres. & chief oper. off.

St. Joseph's Medical Center (O, 339 beds), 811 E. Madison St., Box 1935, South Bend 46634; tel. 219/237-7111; Don Larimore, pres.

Maryland: Holy Cross Hospital of Silver Spring (O, 460 beds), 1500 Forest Glen Rd., Silver Spring 20910; tel. 301/565-0100; Sr. Jean Louise, pres.

Ohio: Mount Carmel Health (O, 815 beds), 793 W. State St., Columbus 43222; tel. 614/225-5000; Sr. Gladys Marie, pres. & chief exec. off.; Russell W. Gardner, sr.vice-pres.

Utah: St. Benedict's Hospital (O, 188 beds), 5475 South 500 East, Ogden 84405; tel. 801/479-2111; Kimbal Wheatley, pres. & chief oper. off.

Holy Cross Hospital (O, 293 beds), 1045 E. First South St., Salt Lake City 84102; tel. 801/350-4111; Kenneth Rock, interim pres.

Owned, leased, sponsored:	10 hospitals	3401 beds
Contract-managed:	6 hospitals	205 beds
Totals:	16 hospitals	3606 beds

***5855: HOLY CROSS LIFE CARE SYSTEMS, INC.** (CC)
1500 O'Day St., Merrill, WI 54452; 715/536-5101; Robert E. Wulff, chief exec. off.

North Dakota: St. Joseph's Hospital and Health Center (S, 101 beds), Seventh St. W., Dickinson 58601; tel. 701/225-7200; John S. Studsrud, adm.

For explanation of codes following names, see page B2.
*Indicates Type III membership in the American Hospital Association.

Wisconsin: Holy Cross Hospital (S, 53 beds), 601 Center Ave. S., Merrill 54452; tel. 715/536-5511; B. Joe Younker, adm.

Owned, leased, sponsored:	2 hospitals	154 beds
Contract-managed:	0 hospitals	0 beds
Totals:	2 hospitals	154 beds

***6005: HOLY FAMILY OF NAZARETH SYSTEMS** (CC)
1814 Egyptian Way, Grand Prairie, TX 75051; Mailing Address Box 530959, Grand Prairie, Zip 75053; 214/641-4496; Sr. M. Beata, pres.

Texas: Archer County Hospital (CM, 26 beds), 410 E. Chestnut St., Box 368, Archer City 76351; tel. 817/574-4586; Daniel D. Powell, adm.

Clay County Memorial Hospital (CM, 42 beds), 310 W. South St., Box 270, Henrietta 76365; tel. 817/538-5621; Johnny Richardson, adm.

Mother Frances Hospital Regional Health Care Center (S, 248 beds), 800 E. Dawson, Tyler 75701; tel. 214/593-8441; J. Lindsey Bradley Jr., pres.

Bethania Regional Health Care Center (S, 190 beds), 1600 11th St., Wichita Falls 76301; tel. 817/723-4111; Sr. M. Electa, adm.

Owned, leased, sponsored:	2 hospitals	438 beds
Contract-managed:	2 hospitals	68 beds
Totals:	4 hospitals	506 beds

***1025: HORIZON HEALTH SYSTEM, INC.** (NP)
60 W. Broad St., Suite 201, Bethlehem, PA 18018; 215/865-9988; William P. Koughan, pres.

Pennsylvania: Muhlenberg Hospital Center (O, 148 beds), Schoenersville Rd., Bethlehem 18017; tel. 215/861-2200; William R. Mason, pres.

St. Luke's Hospital (O, 419 beds), 801 Ostrum St., Bethlehem 18015; tel. 215/691-4141; Richard A. Anderson, pres.

Owned, leased, sponsored:	2 hospitals	567 beds
Contract-managed:	0 hospitals	0 beds
Totals:	2 hospitals	567 beds

1035: HORIZON HEALTH SYSTEMS (NP)
21700 Greenfield Rd., Oak Park, MI 48237; 313/968-2800; James L. Rieder, pres. & chief exec. off.

Michigan: Detroit Osteopathic Hospital (O, 203 beds), 12523 Third Ave., Highland Park 48203; tel. 313/252-4556; Chris Allen, vice-pres.

Riverside Osteopathic Hospital (O, 188 beds), 150 Truax St., Trenton 48183; tel. 313/676-4200; Patrick L. Muldoon, vice-pres. & adm.

Bi-County Community Hospital (O, 247 beds), 13355 E. Ten Mile Rd., Warren 48089; tel. 313/759-7300; Gary W. Popiel, vice-pres. & adm.

Washington: Shorewood Osteopathic Hospital (O, 32 beds), 12845 Ambaum Blvd. S.W., Seattle 98146; tel. 206/243-1455; David J. Myers, adm.

Owned, leased, sponsored:	4 hospitals	670 beds
Contract-managed:	0 hospitals	0 beds
Totals:	4 hospitals	670 beds

***1755: HOSPITAL CORPORATION OF AMERICA** (IO)
One Park Plaza, Box 550, Nashville, TN 37202; 615/327-9551; Thomas F. Frist Jr. MD, chm.

Alabama: HCA Andalusia Hospital (O, 77 beds), S. Three Notch St., Box 760, Andalusia 36420; tel. 205/222-8466; Alease H. Daniel, adm.

South Highlands Hospital (CM, 179 beds), 1127 S. 12th St., Birmingham 35205; tel. 205/930-7000; Dennis H. Descher, chief exec. off.

Flowers Hospital (CM, 200 beds), 3228 W. Main St., Dothan 36301; Mailing Address Box 6907, Dothan, Zip 36302; tel. 205/793-5000; L. Keith Granger, adm.

Enterprise Hospital (CM, 197 beds), Dothan Hwy., Enterprise 36330; Mailing Address Box 1220, Enterprise, Zip 36331; tel. 205/347-9541; J. Alan Kent, adm.

Wiregrass Hospital (CM, 169 beds), 1200 W. Maple Ave., Geneva 36340; tel. 205/684-3655; Roger H. Mayers, adm.

Crestwood Hospital (O, 120 beds), One Hospital Dr., Huntsville 35801; tel. 205/882-3100; N. A. Thompson, adm.

Doctors Hospital of Mobile (O, 159 beds), 1700 Center St., Mobile 36604; Mailing Address Box 1708, Mobile, Zip 36633; tel. 205/438-4551; Stephen C. Loescher, adm.

Knollwood Park Hospital (O, 100 beds), 5600 Girby Rd., Mobile 36609; Mailing Address P O Box 9753, Mobile, Zip 36691; tel. 205/661-5020; Stephen C. Loescher, adm.

Monroe County Hospital (CM, 94 beds), Hwy. 21, Box 886, Monroeville 36461; tel. 205/575-3111; Michael S. Potter, adm.

Selma Medical Center (O, 180 beds), 1015 Medical Center Pkwy., Selma 36701; tel. 205/872-8461; Robert F. Letson, adm.

Arizona: El Dorado Hospital and Medical Center (O, 146 beds), 1400 N. Wilmot, Tucson 85712; Mailing Address Box 13070, Tucson, Zip 85732; tel. 602/886-6361; Roger L.Snapp, adm.

Kino Community Hospital (CM, 93 beds), 2800 E. Ajo Way, Tucson 85713; tel. 602/294-4471; Arthur A. Gonzalez, adm.

Northwest Hospital (O, 63 beds), 6200 N. La Cholla Blvd., Tucson 85741; tel. 602/742-9000; R. John Harris, chief exec. off.

Arkansas: Ouachita Hospital (CM, 150 beds), 638 California St., Box 797, Camden 71701; tel. 501/836-1000; C. C. McAllister, adm.

Ashley Memorial Hospital (CM, 61 beds), 400 Main St., Box 400, Crossett 71635; tel. 501/364-4111; Steve Reeder, adm.

Community Hospital of De Queen (O, 122 beds), Hwy. 70 W., Box 346, De Queen 71832; tel. 501/584-4111; Jim Pearce, adm.

Helena Hospital (CM, 155 beds), Newman Dr., Box 788, Helena 72342; tel. 501/338-6411; Raymond L. Board, adm.

Rebsamen Regional Medical Center (CM, 93 beds), 1400 Braden St., Box 159, Jacksonville 72076; tel. 501/982-9515; Robert L. Green, adm.

Chicot Memorial Hospital (CM, 62 beds), Hwys. 65 & 82, Box 512, Lake Village 71653; tel. 501/265-5351; Daniel R. Smigelski, adm.

Doctors Hospital (O, 310 beds), 6101 W. Capitol, Little Rock 72205; tel. 501/661-4000; W. Perry Kinder, adm.

Lee Memorial Hospital (CM, 25 beds), 528 W. Chestnut St., Drawer 567, Marianna 72360; tel. 501/295-2524; Carl Brown, adm.

Wilhelmina Medical Center (CM, 57 beds), N. Morrow St., Mena 71953; tel. 501/394-6100; Michael Lee, adm.

Howard Memorial Hospital (CM, 63 beds), Box 381, Zip 71852; tel. 501/845-4400; Lewis T. Peeples, adm.

Newport Hospital and Clinic (CM, 86 beds), 2000 McLain, Newport 72112; tel. 501/523-6721; Eugene Zuber, adm.

Memorial Hospital (CM, 73 beds), 205 E. Jefferson St., Siloam Springs 72761; tel. 501/524-4141; Larry N. Winder, adm.

California: Barstow Community Hospital (CM, 56 beds), 555 S. Seventh St., Barstow 92311; tel. 619/256-1761; Patricia Carey, adm.

Woodview-Calabasas Hospital (CM, 102 beds), 25100 Calabasas Rd., Calabasas 91302; tel. 818/888-7500; Robert Trostler, adm.

Chino Community Hospital (O, 118 beds), 5451 Walnut Ave., Chino 91710; tel. 714/627-6111; Dennis Bruns, adm.

HCA Brotman Medical Center (O, 327 beds), 3828 Delmas Terr., Box 2459, Culver City 90231; tel. 213/836-7000; Donald Bernstein DDS, adm.

Encino Hospital (O, 189 beds), 16237 Ventura Blvd., Encino 91436; tel. 818/995-5003; Stephen Bernstein, adm.

Memorial Hospital at Exeter (CM, 74 beds), 215 Crespi Ave., Exeter 93221; tel. 209/592-2151; Melba Jeffress, interim adm.

Community Hospital of Gardena (O, 55 beds), 1246 W. 155th St., Box 2106, Gardena 90247; tel. 213/323-5330; James Sato, adm.

For explanation of codes following names, see page B2.
*Indicates Type III membership in the American Hospital Association.

La Habra Community Hospital (O, 299 beds), 1251 W. Lambert Rd., La Habra 90631; tel. 213/694-3838; Raymond C. Webb Jr., adm.

Green Hospital of Scripps Clinic (O, 158 beds), 10666 N. Torrey Pines Rd., La Jolla 92037; tel. 714/455-9100; Richard M. Bracken, dir.

Estelle Doheny Eye Hospital (CM, 35 beds), 1537 Norfolk St., Los Angeles 90033; tel. 213/224-5000; Paul J. Hensler, adm.

Scenic General Hospital (CM, 117 beds), 830 Scenic Dr., Box 3271, Modesto 95353; tel. 209/571-6296; Phillipp K. Wessels, adm.

Las Encinas Hospital (O, 140 beds), 2900 E. Del Mar Blvd., Pasadena 91107; tel. 818/795-9901; Rachel S. Crenwelge, exec. dir.

Shasta General Hospital (CM, 73 beds), 2630 Hospital Lane, P O Box 6050, Redding 96099; tel. 916/241-3232; Jo-Ann Castrina-Hanula, adm.

Palm Drive Hospital (O, 56 beds), 501 Petaluma Ave., Sebastopol 95472; tel. 707/823-8511; Vance Fager, adm.

Los Robles Regional Medical Center (O, 212 beds), 215 W. Janss Rd., Thousand Oaks 91360; tel. 805/497-2727; Robert Quist, adm.

Ukiah General Hospital (O, 45 beds), 1120 S. Dora St., Box 3900, Ukiah 95482; tel. 707/462-3866; Kelly C. Morgan, adm.

Colorado: Southwest Memorial Hospital (CM, 137 beds), 1311 N. Mildred Rd., Cortez 81321; tel. 303/565-6666; Tyler A. Erickson, adm.

Rocky Mountain Hospital (CM, 109 beds), 4701 E. Ninth Ave., Denver 80220; tel. 303/393-5700; Keith Baldwin, adm.

Rose Medical Center (CM, 318 beds), 4567 E. Ninth Ave., Denver 80220; tel. 303/320-2121; Jeffrey A. Dorsey, exec. vice-pres.

Valley View Hospital (CM, 57 beds), 1906 Blake Ave., Box 1970, Glenwood Springs 81602; tel. 303/945-6535; John Johnson, adm.

Monte Vista Community Hospital (CM, 39 beds), 95 W. First Ave., Monte Vista 81144; tel. 303/852-3541; Dennis R. Turney, adm.

Parkview Episcopal Medical Center (CM, 239 beds), 400 W. 16th St., Pueblo 81003; tel. 303/584-4000; Michael D. Pugh, pres. & chief exec. off.

Delaware: Rockford Center (O, 58 beds), 1605 N. Broom St., Wilmington 19806; tel. 302/652-3892; Joseph F. Barszczewski, adm.

Florida: L. W. Blake Memorial Hospital (O, 383 beds), 2020 59th St. W., Bradenton 33529; Mailing Address P O Box 25004, Bradenton, Zip 33506; tel. 813/792-6611; LindellW. Orr, adm.

HCA Grant Center Hospital North Florida (O, 120 beds), U. S. Hwy. 301, P O Box 100, Citra 32627; tel. 904/595-3500; James Laws, adm.

South Lake Memorial Hospital (CM, 68 beds), 847 Eighth St., Clermont 32711; tel. 904/394-4071; Steven A. Grimm, adm. & chief exec. off.

HCA North Okaloosa Medical Center (O, 110 beds), 151 Redstone Ave. S.E., Crestview 32536; tel. 904/682-9731; James E. Rogers, adm.

Fish Memorial Hospital at DeLand (CM, 71 beds), 245 E. New York Ave., De Land 32724; Mailing Address P O Box 167, De Land, Zip 32721; tel. 904/734-2323; Thomas C.Dandridge, adm.

Nassau General Hospital (CM, 54 beds), 1700 E. Lime St., Fernandina Beach 32034; tel. 904/261-3627; Hugh R. White, adm.

HCA North Beach Hospital (O, 153 beds), 2835 N. Ocean Blvd., Fort Lauderdale 33308; tel. 305/565-3381; Lenore D. Robins, adm.

Harbour Shores Hospital of Lawnwood (O, 60 beds), 1860 N. Lawnwood Circle, P O Box 1540, Fort Pierce 33454; tel. 305/466-1500; Frederick L. Stevens Jr. PhD, adm.

Lawnwood Regional Medical Center (O, 225 beds), 1700 S. 23rd St., Fort Pierce 33450; Mailing Address Box 188, Fort Pierce, Zip 33454; tel. 305/461-4000; NicholasT. Carbone, adm.

HCA North Florida Regional Medical Center (O, 247 beds), State Rd. 26 at I-75, Box Nfr, Gainesville 32602; tel. 904/377-8511; Eugene C. Fleming, adm.

HCA Bayonet Point-Hudson Center (O, 200 beds), 14000 Fivay Rd., Hudson 33567; tel. 813/863-2411; Dan Chambers Jr., adm.

Beaches Hospital (CM, 82 beds), 1430 16th Ave. S., Jacksonville Beach 32250; tel. 904/246-6731; Bart A. Hove, adm.

Jupiter Hospital (CM, 156 beds), 1210 S. Old Dixie Hwy., Jupiter 33458; tel. 305/747-2234; Dino P. Cagni, exec. dir.

Florida Keys Memorial Hospital (CM, 120 beds), 5900 Junior College Rd., Key West 33040; tel. 305/294-5531; George Avery, adm.

HCA Doctors Hospital (O, 200 beds), 2829 Tenth Ave. N., Box 1649, Zip 33460; tel. 305/967-7800; Rodney F. Dorsette, adm.

HCA Largo Medical Center Hospital (O, 256 beds), 201 14th St. S.W., Largo 33540; Mailing Address P O Box 2905, Largo, Zip 34294; tel. 813/586-1411; WinstonRushing, adm.

Leesburg Regional Medical Center (CM, 132 beds), 600 E. Dixie Ave., Leesburg 32748; tel. 904/787-7222; Frederick D. Woodrell, pres.; Lynn Burnseo, exec.vice-pres.

HCA East Pointe Hospital (O, 88 beds), 1500 Lee Blvd., Lehigh Acres 33936; tel. 813/369-2101; Richard W. Klusmann, adm.

West Lake Hospital (O, 80 beds), 589 W. State Rd. 434, Longwood 32750; tel. 305/260-1900; Dennis Menard, adm.

HCA Northwest Regional Hospital (O, 150 beds), 5801 Colonial Dr., P O Box 639002, Margate 33063; tel. 305/974-0400; Joseph Feith, adm.

Jackson Hospital (CM, 107 beds), 800 Hospital Dr., P O Box 1608, Marianna 32446; tel. 904/526-2200; Chuck Ellis, adm.

Bascom Palmer Eye Institute and Anne Bates Leach Eye Hospital (CM, 100 beds), 900 N.W. 17th St., Miami 33136; tel. 305/326-6000; William F. Nowak, adm.

Grant Center Hospital (O, 140 beds), 20601 S.W. 157th Ave., Miami 33187; Mailing Address Box 1159, Miami, Zip 33197; tel. 305/251-0710; Walter Grono, adm.

Highland Park Hospital (O, 106 beds), 1660 N.W. Seventh Ct., Miami 33136; tel. 305/324-8111; Alan Markowitz PhD, adm.

HCA Santa Rosa Medical Center (L, 74 beds), 1450 Berryhill Rd., Milton 32570; Mailing Address P O Box 648, Milton, Zip 32572; tel. 904/623-9741; Jon C. Trezona,adm.

HCA New Port Richey Hospital (O, 414 beds), 205 High St., Box 996, New Port Richey 33552; tel. 813/848-1733; Andrew Oravec Jr., adm.

Twin Cities Hospital (O, 75 beds), Hwy. 85 N. & College Blvd., Niceville 32578; tel. 904/678-4131; Glen Jones, adm.

Marion Community Hospital (O, 190 beds), 1431 S.W. First Ave., Box 2200, Ocala 32670; tel. 904/732-2700; Terry Upton, adm.

HCA Raulerson Hospital (O, 93 beds), 1796 Hwy. 441 N., Box 1307, Okeechobee 33472; tel. 813/763-2151; Roy C. Vinson, adm.

Putnam Community Hospital (O, 120 beds), Hwy. 20 W., Palatka 32077; Mailing Address P O Drawer 778, Palatka, Zip 32078; tel. 904/328-5711; Michael S. Boggs, adm.

HCA Gulf Coast Hospital (O, 176 beds), 449 W. 23rd St., Panama City 32405; tel. 904/769-8341; Donald E. Butts, adm.

West Florida Regional Medical Center (O, 547 beds), 8383 N. David Hwy., P O Box 18900, Pensacola 32523; tel. 904/478-4460; John Kausch, adm.; Jeffrey A. Feeney,sr. asst. adm.

Plantation General Hospital (O, 264 beds), 401 N.W. 42nd Ave., Plantation 33317; tel. 305/587-5010; James Sample, adm.

HCA Medical Center of Port St. Lucie (O, 150 beds), 1800 S.E. Tiffany Ave., Port St. Lucie 33452; tel. 305/335-4000; C. Robert Benson, adm.

Central Florida Regional Hospital (O, 226 beds), 1401 W. Seminole Blvd., Sanford 32771; tel. 305/321-4500; James D. Tesar, adm.

Doctors Hospital (O, 168 beds), 2750 Bahia Vista St., Sarasota 33579; tel. 813/366-1411; H. Allen Williams, adm.

HCA Oak Hill Hospital (O, 96 beds), 11375 Cortez Blvd., P O Box 5300, Spring Hill 33526; tel. 904/596-6632; Dennis Taylor, adm.

For explanation of codes following names, see page B2.
*Indicates Type III membership in the American Hospital Association.

St. Augustine General Hospital (O, 115 beds), U. S. 1 S., St. Augustine 32084; Mailing Address Drawer 2208, St. Augustine, Zip 32085; tel. 904/824-8431; RaymondM. Johnson, adm.

HCA Edward White Hospital (O, 167 beds), 2323 Ninth Ave. N., St. Petersburg 33713; Mailing Address P O Box 12018, St. Petersburg, Zip 33733; tel. 813/323-1111;Bruce A. Klockars, adm.

HCA Sun City Hospital (O, 73 beds), 4016 State Rd. 674, Sun City Center 33570; tel. 813/634-3301; W. Harold O'Neal, adm.

Tallahassee Community Hospital (O, 180 beds), 2626 Capital Medical Blvd., Tallahassee 32308; tel. 904/656-5000; Kenneth J. Newell, adm.

University Community Hospital (O, 236 beds), 7201 N. University Dr., Tamarac 33321; tel. 305/721-2200; Lawrence L. Pieretti, adm.

Georgia: HCA Palmyra Medical Centers (O, 172 beds), 2000 Palmyra Rd., Box 1908, Albany 31703; tel. 912/888-3800; Douglas M. Parker, adm.

HCA West Paces Ferry Hospital (O, 294 beds), 3200 Howell Mill Rd. N.W., Atlanta 30327; tel. 404/351-0351; Chip Caldwell, adm.

Higgins General Hospital (CM, 59 beds), 200 Allen Memorial Dr., Box 745, Bremen 30110; tel. 404/537-2315; Robin Smith, adm.

Tanner Medical Center (CM, 222 beds), 705 Dixie St., Carrollton 30117; tel. 404/836-9666; James R. Giffin, adm.

Doctors Hospital (O, 252 beds), 616 19th St., Columbus 31993; Mailing Address P O Box 2188, Columbus, Zip 31902; tel. 404/571-4262; Ronald A. Schwartz, adm.

Hughston Sports Medicine Hospital (O, 100 beds), 6260 Hamilton Rd., Columbus 31905; Mailing Address P O Box 2319, Columbus, Zip 31902; tel. 404/576-2100; CharlesKeaton, adm.

Habersham County Medical Center (CM, 143 beds), Hwy. 441, Box 37, Demorest 30535; tel. 404/754-2161; Michael R. Blackburn, adm.

Fairview Park Hospital (O, 190 beds), 200 Industrial Blvd., Box 1408, Dublin 31021; tel. 912/275-2000; Dominic Ingrando, adm.

Charlton Memorial Hospital (CM, 46 beds), 1203 Third St., Box 188, Folkston 31537; tel. 912/496-2531; Charles Mitchener, adm.

Peach County Hospital (CM, 75 beds), 601 N. Camellia Blvd., Fort Valley 31030; tel. 912/825-8691

Lanier Park Hospital (O, 124 beds), 675 White Sulphur Rd., Gainesville 30501; Mailing Address P O Box 1354, Gainesville, Zip 30503; tel. 404/531-2301; T. MarvinGoldman, adm.

Wayne Memorial Hospital (CM, 123 beds), 865 S. First St., Box 408, Jesup 31545; tel. 912/427-6811; Charles R. Morgan II, adm.

HCA Parkway Medical Center (O, 226 beds), 1000 Thornton Rd., P O Box 570, Lithia Springs 30057; tel. 404/944-4141; Sonny Boggus Jr., adm.

HCA Coliseum Medical Centers (O, 250 beds), 350 Hospital Dr., Macon 31213; tel. 912/745-9461; Charles T. Neal, adm.

HCA Coliseum Psychiatric Hospital (O, 76 beds), 340 Hospital Dr., Macon 31201; Mailing Address Box 4366, Macon, Zip 31208; tel. 912/741-1355; Barbara D. Simpson,adm.

Redmond Park Hospital (O, 201 beds), 501 Redmond Rd., Box 4077, Rome 30161; tel. 404/291-0291; William Paul Rutledge, adm.

Memorial Medical Center (CM, 487 beds), 4700 Waters Ave., Savannah 31404; Mailing Address Box 23089, Savannah, Zip 31403; tel. 912/356-8000; Kenneth W. Wood,pres. & chief exec. off.

Emanuel County Hospital (CM, 118 beds), Kite Rd., Box 7, Swainsboro 30401; tel. 912/237-9911; Leland E. Farnell, adm.

Worth Community Hospital (O, 50 beds), Camilla Hwy., Box 545, Sylvester 31791; tel. 912/776-6961; John Smithhisler, adm.

Upson County Hospital (CM, 119 beds), 801 W. Gordon St., Box 1059, Thomaston 30286; tel. 404/647-8111; Ernest H. Borders, adm.

Doctors Hospital (O, 143 beds), 2160 Idlewood Rd., Tucker 30084; tel. 404/496-6740; Frank B. Murphy, adm.

Tanner Medical Center-Villa Rica (CM, 54 beds), 601 Dallas Rd., Box 638, Villa Rica 30180; tel. 404/459-3681; J. M. McCollum, adm.

Idaho: West Valley Medical Center (O, 133 beds), 1717 Arlington, Caldwell 83605; tel. 208/459-4641; Robert G. Conrad, adm.

Eastern Idaho Regional Medical Center (O, 334 beds), 3100 Channing Way, P O Box 2077, Idaho Falls 83403; tel. 208/529-6111; Max Lauderdale, adm.

Gritman Memorial Hospital (CM, 48 beds), 715 S. Washington St., Moscow 83843; tel. 208/882-4511; Robert A. Colvin, adm.

Magic Valley Regional Medical Center (CM, 152 beds), 650 Addison Ave. W., Twin Falls 83301; Mailing Address Box 409, Twin Falls, Zip 83303; tel. 208/737-2000;John Bingham, adm.

Illinois: Chicago Lakeshore Hospital (O, 104 beds), 4840 N. Marine Dr., Chicago 60640; tel. 312/878-9700; Jerome R. Kearney, adm.

HCA Riveredge Hospital (O, 204 beds), 8311 W. Roosevelt Rd., Forest Park 60130; tel. 312/771-7000; Joyce W. Washington, exec. dir.

Wabash General Hospital District (CM, 64 beds), 1418 College Dr., Mount Carmel 62863; tel. 618/262-8621; Bill Vokonas, adm.

Pana Community Hospital (CM, 60 beds), S. Locust St., Pana 62557; tel. 217/562-2131; John Mauldin, adm.

Illini Community Hospital (CM, 59 beds), 640 W. Washington St., Pittsfield 62363; tel. 217/285-2113; Kathleen Wegener, adm.

Crawford Memorial Hospital (CM, 105 beds), 1000 N. Allen St., Robinson 62454; tel. 618/544-3131; Merle Hansen, adm.

Fayette County Hospital (CM, 182 beds), Seventh & Taylor Sts., Vandalia 62471; tel. 618/283-1231; M. Jean Chambless, adm.

Memorial Hospital for McHenry County (CM, 123 beds), 527 W. South St., Woodstock 60098; tel. 815/338-2500; Philip G. Dionne, chief exec. off.

Indiana: HCA North Clark Community Hospital (O, 96 beds), 2200 Market St., Charlestown 47111; tel. 812/256-3301; Aaron R. Hazzard, adm.

McCray Memorial Hospital (CM, 66 beds), Hospital Dr., Box 249, Kendallville 46755; tel. 219/347-1100; Jennifer L. Smith, adm.

Terre Haute Regional Hospital (O, 284 beds), 601 Hospital Lane, Terre Haute 47802; tel. 812/232-0021; William C. Giermak, adm.

Iowa: Fort Madison Community Hospital (CM, 95 beds), 2210 Ave. H, Fort Madison 52627; tel. 319/372-6530; Stephen R. Schoaps, chief exec. off.

Knoxville Area Community Hospital (CM, 59 beds), 1002 S. Lincoln St., Knoxville 50138; tel. 515/842-2151; David Christiansen, adm.

Kansas: Coffeyville Regional Medical Center (CM, 83 beds), 1400 W. Fourth, Coffeyville 67337; tel. 316/251-1200; Raymond M. Dunning Jr., adm.

Newman Memorial County Hospital (CM, 178 beds), 12th & Chestnut Sts., Emporia 66801; tel. 316/343-6800; Thomas McCall, adm.

Fredonia Regional Hospital (CM, 32 beds), 1527 Madison St., Box 579, Fredonia 66736; tel. 316/378-2121; Richard Carter, chief oper. off.

Wesley Medical Center (O, 601 beds), 550 N. Hillside Ave., Wichita 67214; tel. 316/688-2468; A. B. Davis Jr., chm. & chief exec. off.; Donald M. Stewart, pres. &chief oper. off.

Kentucky: HCA Greenview Hospital (O, 211 beds), 1801 Ashley Circle, Box 370, Bowling Green 42101; tel. 502/781-4330; James C. Barnett, adm.

Hardin Memorial Hospital (CM, 235 beds), N. Dixie Hwy. 31 W., Elizabethtown 42701; tel. 502/737-1212; Warner Butters, adm.

Fleming County Hospital (CM, 52 beds), 920 Elizaville Ave., Box 388, Flemingsburg 41041; tel. 606/849-2351; Lee Ben Clarke, adm.

King's Daughters Memorial Hospital (O, 125 beds), King's Daughters Dr., Frankfort 40601; tel. 502/875-5240; Ronald T. Tyrer, adm.

Franklin-Simpson Memorial Hospital (CM, 50 beds), Brookhaven Rd., Franklin 42134; tel. 502/586-3253; Rita J. Wilder, adm.

For explanation of codes following names, see page B2.
*Indicates Type III membership in the American Hospital Association.

Scott General Hospital (O, 75 beds), 1140 Lexington Rd., Georgetown 40324; tel. 502/863-2141; Larry Kloess, adm.

Muhlenberg Community Hospital (CM, 135 beds), 440 Hopkinsville St., P O Box 387, Greenville 42345; tel. 502/338-4211; Charles J. Perry, adm.

Ohio County Hospital (CM, 68 beds), 1211 Main St., Hartford 42347; tel. 502/298-7411; Blaine Pieper, adm.

HCA Spring View Hospital (O, 113 beds), St. Mary Rd., Lebanon 40033; tel. 502/692-3161; Robert E. Garrison, adm.

Community Hospital (O, 89 beds), 206 W. South St., Mayfield 42066; tel. 502/247-5211; John Sullivan, adm.

Meadowview Regional Hospital (O, 111 beds), 989 W. Hwy. 10, Maysville 41056; tel. 606/759-5311; Gary J. Herbek, adm.

HCA Bourbon General Hospital (O, 60 beds), 9 Linville Dr., Paris 40361; tel. 606/987-3600; Gerald Fornoff, adm.

HCA Logan Memorial Hospital (O, 100 beds), 1625 S. Nashville Rd., P O Box 10, Russellville 42276; tel. 502/726-4011; Michael L. Graue, adm.

Monroe County Medical Center (CM, 49 beds), Cap Harlan Rd., Tompkinsville 42167; tel. 502/487-9231; Lance C. Labine, adm.

Louisiana: Medical Center of Baton Rouge (CM, 78 beds), 17000 Medical Center Dr., Baton Rouge 70816; tel. 504/922-4800; Jerry G. Moeller, adm.

Parkland Hospital (O, 174 beds), 2414 Bunker Hill Dr., Baton Rouge 70808; tel. 504/927-9050; Ralph J. Waite III, adm.

DePaul Northshore Hospital (O, 64 beds), Depaul Northshore Dr., P O Box 2439, Covington 70434; tel. 504/893-9200; Patrick J. Canal, adm.

Franklin Foundation Hospital (CM, 48 beds), 1501 Hospital Ave., Box 577, Franklin 70538; tel. 318/828-0760; Kyle J. Viator, adm.

Cypress Hospital (O, 94 beds), 302 Dulles Dr., Lafayette 70506; tel. 318/233-9024; Robert Leven, adm.

Hamilton Medical Center Hospital (O, 67 beds), 2810 Ambassador Caffery Pkwy., Lafayette 70506; tel. 318/981-2949; Thomas M. Weiss, adm.

Women's and Children's Hospital (O, 89 beds), 4600 Ambassador Caffery Pkwy., Lafayette 70508; tel. 318/981-9100; Karen Poole, adm.

Doctors Hospital of Jefferson (CM, 77 beds), 4320 Houma Blvd., Metairie 70006; tel. 504/456-5657; Robert L. Kinneberg Jr., Adm., adm.

Lakeside Hospital (O, 209 beds), 4700 I-10 Service Rd., Metairie 70001; tel. 504/885-3333; Gerald L. Parton, adm.

North Monroe Community Hospital (O, 110 beds), 3421 Medical Park Dr., Monroe 71203; tel. 318/388-1946; Arlen Reynolds, adm.

Dauterive Hospital (O, 116 beds), 600 N. Lewis St., P O Box 430, New Iberia 70560; tel. 318/365-7311; Clay Hurley, adm.

De Paul Hospital (O, 314 beds), 1040 Calhoun St., New Orleans 70118; tel. 504/899-8282; Sal A. Barbera, exec. dir.

Pointe Coupee General Hospital (CM, 27 beds), 2202 False River Dr., P O Box 578, New Roads 70760; tel. 504/638-6331; Jerry Marquette, adm.

Plaquemines Parish General Hospital (CM, 39 beds), Civic Dr., Rte. 2, Box 105, Port Sulphur 70083; tel. 504/564-3346; Judi Guthrie, adm.

Highland Hospital (O, 130 beds), 1006 Highland Ave., Shreveport 71101; tel. 318/227-2221; Ronald J. Elder, adm.

Maine: Cary Medical Center (CM, 65 beds), Mra Van Buren Rd., Box 37, Caribou 04736; tel. 207/498-3111; John J. McCormack, exec. dir.

Mayo Regional Hospital (CM, 52 beds), 75 W. Main St., Dover-Foxcroft 04426; tel. 207/564-8401; Robert McReavy, adm.

Houlton Regional Hospital (CM, 89 beds), 20 Hartford St., Houlton 04730; tel. 207/532-9471; Bradley C. Bean, adm.

Penobscot Valley Hospital (CM, 44 beds), Transalpine Rd., Lincoln 04457; tel. 207/794-3321; Ronald D. Victory, adm.

Sebasticook Valley Hospital (CM, 30 beds), Grove Hill, Pittsfield 04967; tel. 207/487-5141; Ann Morrison RN, pres.

Maryland: Children's Hospital (CM, 106 beds), 3825 Greenspring Ave., Baltimore 21211; tel. 301/462-6800; Stephen C. Loescher, chief exec. off.

Prince George's Hospital Center (CM, 558 beds), One Hospital Dr., Cheverly 20785; tel. 301/341-3300; Richard Graham, chief exec. off.

Greater Laurel Beltsville Hospital (CM, 180 beds), 7100 Contee Rd., Laurel 20707; tel. 301/725-4300; Gary M. Stein, adm.

Massachusetts: Athol Memorial Hospital (CM, 81 beds), 2033 Main St., Athol 01331; tel. 617/249-3511; William Difederico, pres.

Norfolk County Hospital (CM, 98 beds), 2001 Washington St., Braintree 02184; tel. 617/843-0690; John A. Barmack, adm.

Hunt Memorial Hospital (CM, 142 beds), Lindall St., Danvers 01923; tel. 617/774-4400; Edward F. Kittredge, adm.

Whittier Rehabilitation Hospital (CM, 112 beds), 76 Summer St., Haverhill 01830; tel. 617/372-8000; X. L. Papaioanou MD, adm.

Milford-Whitinsville Regional Hospital (CM, 183 beds), 14 Prospect St., Milford 01757; tel. 617/473-1190; Kenneth Luke, adm.

Jordan Hospital (CM, 147 beds), 275 Sandwich St., Plymouth 02360; tel. 617/746-2000; Peter A. Chapman, pres.

Quincy City Hospital (CM, 303 beds), 114 Whitwell St., Quincy 02169; tel. 617/773-6100; Mark J. Mundy, dir.

Hubbard Regional Hospital (CM, 82 beds), 340 Thompson Rd., Webster 01570; tel. 617/943-2600; Richard L. Cunningham, adm.

Worcester City Hospital (CM, 300 beds), 26 Queen St., Worcester 01610; tel. 617/799-8000; Thomas E. Cummings, adm.

Michigan: Orchard Hills Hospital (CM, 56 beds), 1534 W. State St., Belding 48809; tel. 616/794-0400; Robert F. Jernigan Jr., adm.

Iron County General Hospital (CM, 36 beds), 1400 W. Ice Lake Rd., Iron River 49935; tel. 906/265-6121; Jerry Miller, adm.

Rogers City Hospital (CM, 94 beds), 555 N. Bradley Hwy., Rogers City 49779; tel. 517/734-2151; Samuel S. Gregory, adm.

War Memorial Hospital (CM, 138 beds), 500 Osborn Blvd., Sault Ste Marie 49783; tel. 906/635-4350; Ronald L. Bodary, adm.

Three Rivers Area Hospital (CM, 72 beds), 214 Spring St., Three Rivers 49093; tel. 616/278-1145; James P. Perricone, pres.

Community Hospital (CM, 70 beds), Medical Park, Box 158, Watervliet 49098; tel. 616/463-3111; Robert I. Schmelter, adm.

Minnesota: International Falls Memorial Hospital (CM, 64 beds), 1800 Third St., International Falls 56649; tel. 218/283-4481; Randall M. Olson, adm.

Mount Sinai Hospital (CM, 173 beds), 2215 Park Ave., Minneapolis 55404; tel. 612/871-3700; Warren A. Green, adm.

Mississippi: Hancock Medical Center (CM, 56 beds), 149 Drinkwater Blvd., Bay St. Louis 39520; tel. 601/467-9081; Phillip R. Wolfe, adm.

Marion County General Hospital (CM, 90 beds), 1560 Sumrall Rd., Box 630, Columbia 39429; tel. 601/736-6303; John W. Reynolds, adm.

University Hospital (CM, 501 beds), 2500 N. State St., Jackson 39216; tel. 601/984-4100; David E. Bussone, dir.

Vicksburg Medical Center (O, 144 beds), 3311 Frontage Rd., Vicksburg 39180; tel. 601/636-2611; Wendell H. Baker Jr., adm.

Missouri: Community Hospital (CM, 51 beds), Hwy. 59, Fairfax 64446; tel. 816/686-2211; Lewis I. Alley, adm.

Medical Center of Independence (CM, 185 beds), 17203 E. 23rd St., Independence 64057; tel. 816/373-2300; Harold H. Kaseff, adm.

Research Psychiatric Center (O, 100 beds), 2323 E. 63rd St., Kansas City 64130; tel. 816/444-8161; Gail M. Oberta, adm.

Lee's Summit Community Hospital (CM, 92 beds), 530 N. Murray, P O Box 767, Lees Summit 64063; tel. 816/525-2950; David J. Maschger, chief exec. off.

For explanation of codes following names, see page B2.
*Indicates Type III membership in the American Hospital Association.

St. Peters Community Hospital (O, 102 beds), 10 Hospital Dr., St. Peters 63376; tel. 314/447-6600; Fred Woody, adm.

Nebraska: Great Plains Regional Medical Center (CM, 130 beds), 601 W. Leota St., Box 1167, North Platte 69101; tel. 308/534-9310; Cindy Bradley, adm.

Midlands Community Hospital (CM, 155 beds), 11111 S. 84th St., Papillion 68046; tel. 402/593-3000; Don M. Chase, adm.

Nevada: Montevista Centre (O, 80 beds), 5900 W. Rochelle Ave., P O Box 26874, Las Vegas 89126; tel. 702/364-1111; James T. Harper, adm.

University Medical Center Southern Nevada (CM, 436 beds), 1800 W. Charleston Blvd., Las Vegas 89102; tel. 702/383-2000; Richard J. Coughlin, adm.

Truckee Meadows Hospital (O, 95 beds), 1240 E. Ninth St., Reno 89512; Mailing Address P O Box 30012, Reno, Zip 89520; tel. 702/323-0478; Laura Thomas, adm.

New Hampshire: Parkland Medical Center (O, 58 beds), One Parkland Dr., Derry 03038; tel. 603/432-1500; Steven R. Gordon, adm.

Littleton Hospital (O, 54 beds), 107 Cottage St., Littleton 03561; tel. 603/444-7731; LeRoy Deabler, pres.

Portsmouth Regional Hospital (O, 106 beds), 333 Borthwick Ave., Portsmouth 03801; tel. 603/436-5110; William J. Schuler, adm.

New Jersey: University of Medicine and Dentistry of New Jersey-University Hospital (CM, 501 beds), 150 Bergen St., Newark 07103; tel. 201/456-4300; Marc H. Lory, chiefexec. off. & vice-pres.

Palisades General Hospital (CM, 202 beds), 7600 River Rd., North Bergen 07047; tel. 201/854-5000; Harry Berkowitz, pres.

New Mexico: Gerald Champion Memorial Hospital (CM, 59 beds), 1209 Ninth St., Box 597, Alamogordo 88310; tel. 505/437-3770; Carl W. Mantey, adm.

Heights General Hospital (CM, 80 beds), 4701 Montgomery N.E., Albuquerque 87109; tel. 505/888-7800; Polly Pine, adm.

Heights Psychiatric Hospital (O, 80 beds), 103 Hospital Loop N.E., Albuquerque 87109; tel. 505/883-8777; Andrea Brightwell, adm.

Lovelace Medical Center (O, 177 beds), 5400 Gibson Blvd. S.E., Albuquerque 87108; tel. 505/262-7000; Richard E. Gillock, vice-pres. & adm.

Guadalupe Medical Center (O, 144 beds), 2430 W. Pierce St., Carlsbad 88220; tel. 505/887-6633; Donald E. Barton, adm.

Cibola General Hospital (CM, 39 beds), 1212 Bonita Ave., Grants 87020; tel. 505/287-4446; Donald L. Caughron, adm.

Lea Regional Hospital (O, 216 beds), Lovington Hwy. 18, Box 3000, Hobbs 88240; tel. 505/392-6581; R. Gordon Taylor, adm.

Gila Regional Medical Center (CM, 68 beds), 1313 E. 32nd St., Silver City 88061; tel. 505/388-1591; Ronald L. McArthur, adm.

New York: Clifton Springs Hospital and Clinic (CM, 178 beds), 2 Coulter Rd., Clifton Springs 14432; tel. 315/462-9561; Robert Mincemoyer, exec. dir.

Brooks Memorial Hospital (CM, 133 beds), 529 Central Ave., Dunkirk 14048; tel. 716/366-1111; Richard H. Ketcham, exec. dir.

Mohawk Valley General Hospital (CM, 83 beds), 295 W. Main St., Ilion 13357; tel. 315/895-7474; Nicholas B. Munhofen II, adm.

Johnstown Hospital (CM, 39 beds), 201 S. Melcher St., Johnstown 12095; tel. 518/762-3161; Robert C. Winfrey, chief exec. off.

Massena Memorial Hospital (CM, 60 beds), One Hospital Dr., Massena 13662; tel. 315/764-1711; William S. Abbott, adm.

St. Luke's Hospital (CM, 242 beds), 70 Dubois St., P O Box 631, Newburgh 12550; tel. 914/561-4400; Robert L. Via, exec. dir.

Rome Hospital and Murphy Memorial Hospital (CM, 230 beds), 1500 N. James St., Rome 13440; tel. 315/338-7000; John A. Gorman, adm.

Ellis Hospital (CM, 413 beds), 1101 Nott St., Schenectady 12308; tel. 518/382-4124; William E. Schirmer, pres. & chief exec. off.

North Carolina: Orthopaedic Hospital of Charlotte (O, 166 beds), 1901 Randolph Rd., Charlotte 28207; tel. 704/375-6792; William E. Collins, adm.

Highsmith-Rainey Memorial Hospital (O, 150 beds), 150 Robeson St., Fayetteville 28301; tel. 919/483-7400; G. Michael Girone, adm.

Angel Community Hospital (CM, 81 beds), Riverview & White Oak Sts., Box 1209, Franklin 28734; tel. 704/524-8411

L. Richardson Memorial Hospital (CM, 68 beds), 2401 Southside Blvd., Drawer 16167, Greensboro 27406; tel. 919/275-9741; Henry A. Swicegood, pres.

Ashe Memorial Hospital (CM, 34 beds), P O Box 8, Jefferson 28640; tel. 919/246-7101; Gary Bishop, adm.

Franklin Memorial Hospital (O, 69 beds), 100 Hospital Dr., Box 609, Louisburg 27549; tel. 919/496-5131; Robert L. W. Miller, adm.

Holly Hill Hospital (O, 106 beds), 3019 Falstaff Rd., Raleigh 27610; tel. 919/755-1840; Lawrence H. Pomeroy, exec. dir.

Raleigh Community Hospital (O, 140 beds), 3400 Old Wake Forest Rd., Raleigh 27609; Mailing Address P O Box 28280, Raleigh, Zip 27611; tel. 919/872-4800; HarrisonT. Ferris, adm.

Person County Memorial Hospital (CM, 77 beds), 615 Ridge Rd., Roxboro 27573; tel. 919/599-2121; S. Grant Boone Jr., adm.

Johnston Memorial Hospital (CM, 97 beds), Hwy. 301 N., Box 1376, Smithfield 27577; tel. 919/934-8171; Herman L. Mullins, pres.

Blue Ridge Hospital Systems, Spruce Pine Community Hospital Division (CM, 92 beds), 125 Hospital Dr., Spruce Pine 28777; tel. 704/765-4201; David W. Spangler,adm.

Davis Community Hospital (O, 128 beds), Old Mocksville Rd., P O Box 1800, Statesville 28677; tel. 704/873-0281; Steven L. Blaine, adm.

Brunswick Hospital (O, 30 beds), U. S. Hwy. 17 S., P O Box 139, Supply 28462; tel. 919/754-8121; Rodney R. Pulley, adm.

HCA Heritage Hospital (O, 89 beds), 111 Hospital Dr., Tarboro 27886; tel. 919/641-7700; J. Lewis Ridgeway, exec. dir.

Medical Park Hospital (CM, 136 beds), 1950 S. Hawthorne Rd., Winston-Salem 27103; tel. 919/768-7680; Earl H. Tyndall Jr., exec. dir.

Ohio: Defiance Hospital (CM, 107 beds), 1206 E. Second St., Defiance 43512; tel. 419/782-6955; Clifford J. Bauer, adm.

Greenfield Area Medical Center (CM, 44 beds), 545 South St., Greenfield 45123; tel. 513/981-2116; Thomas E. Daugherty, adm.

Knox Community Hospital (CM, 153 beds), 1330 Coshocton Rd., Mount Vernon 43050; tel. 614/393-9000; Richard H. Finley, adm.

Oklahoma: Edmond Memorial Hospital (O, 85 beds), 1 S. Bryant St., Edmond 73034; tel. 405/341-6100; Joel A. Hart, adm.

St. Mary's Hospital (O, 221 beds), 305 S. Fifth St., Box 232, Enid 73701; tel. 405/233-6100; Mary T. Brasseaux, adm.

Presbyterian Hospital (O, 316 beds), N.E. 13th St. at Lincoln Blvd., Oklahoma City 73104; tel. 405/271-5100; Dennis C. Millirons, adm.

Tahlequah City Hospital (CM, 51 beds), 1400 E. Downing St., Box 1008, Tahlequah 74465; tel. 918/456-0641; Don L. Coffman, adm.

Wagoner Community Hospital (O, 100 beds), 1200 W. Cherokee, Box 407, Wagoner 74467; tel. 918/485-5514; Tim Francis, adm.

Oregon: Josephine Memorial Hospital (CM, 81 beds), 715 N.W. Dimmick St., Grants Pass 97526; tel. 503/476-6831; Clint Lea, adm.

McMinnville Community Hospital (O, 80 beds), 603 S. Baker St., McMinnville 97128; tel. 503/472-6131; Stephen J. Aragon, adm.

Douglas Community Hospital (O, 118 beds), 738 W. Harvard Blvd., Roseburg 97470; tel. 503/673-6641; Greg Stock, adm.

Pennsylvania: Brownsville General Hospital (CM, 102 beds), 125 Simpson Rd., Brownsville 15417; tel. 412/785-7200; Charles Lonchar, chief exec. off.

Clarion Osteopathic Community Hospital (CM, 94 beds), One Hospital Dr., Clarion 16214; tel. 814/226-9500; Roy W. Wright, adm.

For explanation of codes following names, see page B2.
*Indicates Type III membership in the American Hospital Association.

Pocono Hospital (CM, 223 beds), 206 E. Brown St., East Stroudsburg 18301; tel. 717/421-4000; Patrick Mutch, interim adm.

Metrox Health Center (CM, 150 beds), 252 W. 11th St., Erie 16501; tel. 814/455-3961; Luis A. Hernandez, adm.

United Community Hospital (CM, 128 beds), Cranberry Rd., R D 5, Box 5005, Grove City 16127; tel. 412/458-5442; James R. Kelly Jr., adm.

Haverford Community Hospital (CM, 103 beds), 2000 Old West Chester Pike, Havertown 19083; tel. 215/645-3600; Cornelius Serle, adm.

J. C. Blair Memorial Hospital (CM, 104 beds), Warm Springs Ave., Huntingdon 16652; tel. 814/643-2290; Robert R. Stanley, adm.

Ohio Valley General Hospital (CM, 137 beds), Heckel Rd., McKees Rocks 15136; tel. 412/777-6161; William F. Provenzano, pres.

Tyrone Hospital (CM, 59 beds), Clay Ave. Ext., Tyrone 16686; tel. 814/684-1255; Thomas D. Robinson, chief exec. off.

Rhode Island: Notre Dame Hospital (CM, 41 beds), 1000 Broad St., Central Falls 02863; tel. 401/726-1800; Peter A. Hofstetter, adm.

South Carolina: HCA Aiken Regional Medical Center (O, 190 beds), 202 University Pkwy., Aiken 29801; Mailing Address Drawer 1117, Aiken, Zip 29802; tel. 803/642-0800; John E.Strickland, adm.

Marlboro Park Hospital (O, 111 beds), Box 738, Zip 29512; tel. 803/479-2881; Norman G. Rentz, adm.

Trident Regional Medical Center (O, 266 beds), 9330 Medical Plaza Dr., Charleston 29418; tel. 803/797-7000; Frank J. DeMarco III, adm.

Chesterfield General Hospital (O, 72 beds), Hwy. 9, Box 151, Cheraw 29520; tel. 803/537-7881; Jim Madory, adm.

Wilson Clinic and Hospital (CM, 72 beds), Hwy. 34 E., Box 510, Darlington 29532; tel. 803/395-1100; Joseph P. Zager, adm.

Georgetown Memorial Hospital (CM, 132 beds), 606 Black River Rd., Drawer 1718, Georgetown 29442; tel. 803/527-1341; Paul D. Gatens, adm.

Byerly Hospital (CM, 104 beds), 413 E. Carolina Ave., Hartsville 29550; tel. 803/332-6511; L. E. Dunman Jr., adm.

Hilton Head Hospital (CM, 64 beds), P O Box 1117, Hilton Head Island 29925; tel. 803/681-6122; Creighton E. Likes Jr., adm.

Williamsburg County Memorial Hospital (CM, 60 beds), 500 Nelson Blvd., Box 568, Kingstree 29556; tel. 803/354-9661; Francis G. Albarano Jr., adm.

HCA Grand Strand General Hospital (O, 133 beds), 809 82nd Pkwy., Myrtle Beach 29577; tel. 803/449-4411; Frank Ceruzzi, adm.

Newberry County Memorial Hospital (CM, 102 beds), 2669 Kinard St., P O Box 497, Newberry 29108; tel. 803/276-7570; Donnie J. Weeks, adm.

Mary Black Memorial Hospital (CM, 165 beds), 1700 Skylyn Dr., Spartanburg 29303; Mailing Address Box 3217, Spartanburg, Zip 29304; tel. 803/573-3000; Gerald W.Landis, pres.

Tuomey Hospital (CM, 206 beds), 129 N. Washington St., Sumter 29150; tel. 803/775-1171; Louis H. Bremer Jr., adm.

Colleton Regional Hospital (O, 145 beds), 501 Robertson Blvd., Walterboro 29488; tel. 803/549-6371; Donald H. Caldwell, adm.

South Dakota: Huron Regional Medical Center (CM, 118 beds), Fourth & Iowa Sts. S.E., Huron 57350; tel. 605/352-6431; Richard C. Sommer, adm.

Methodist Hospital (CM, 80 beds), 909 S. Miller St., Mitchell 57301; tel. 605/996-5627; Willis Bultje, adm.

Tennessee: Athens Community Hospital (O, 109 beds), 1114 W. Madison Ave., Box 250, Athens 37303; tel. 615/745-1411

Bristol Memorial Hospital (CM, 356 beds), 209 Memorial Dr., Bristol 37620; tel. 615/968-1121; Phillip G. Sansam, exec. vice-pres.; Michelle Piatek, adm.

Haywood Park General Hospital (O, 62 beds), 2545 N. Washington Ave., Brownsville 38012; tel. 901/772-4110; Stephen Shepherd, adm.

Benton Community Hospital (O, 93 beds), Hospital St., Camden 38320; tel. 901/584-6135; Robert D. Wimberley, adm.

Smith County Memorial Hospital (O, 66 beds), N. Main St., Carthage 37030; tel. 615/735-1560; Michael W. Garfield, adm.

Diagnostic Center Hospital (O, 80 beds), 2412 McCallie Ave., Chattanooga 37404; tel. 615/698-0221; David L. Dunlap, adm.

Downtown General Hospital (CM, 65 beds), 709 Walnut St., Chattanooga 37402; tel. 615/266-7721; Edward L. Lynsky, adm.

North Park Hospital (O, 83 beds), 2051 Hamill Rd., Chattanooga 37343; tel. 615/870-1300; William A. Adams, adm.

Parkridge Medical Center (O, 296 beds), 2333 McCallie Ave., Chattanooga 37404; tel. 615/698-6061; David L. Dunlap, adm.

Valley Hospital (O, 100 beds), Shallowford Rd., P O Box 21887, Chattanooga 37421; tel. 615/894-4220; James C. Kestner, adm.

HCA Sycamore Shoals Hospital (O, 128 beds), 1501 W. Elk Ave., Elizabethton 37643; tel. 615/542-1300; Will O. Landers, adm.

Trinity Hospital (O, 40 beds), Main St., Box 489, Erin 37061; tel. 615/289-4211; Terrell Sellers, adm.

Lincoln Regional Hospital (CM, 110 beds), 700 W. Maple Ave., Fayetteville 37334; tel. 615/433-1561; Edward A. Perdue, adm.

HCA Hendersonville Hospital (O, 75 beds), 355 New Shackle Island Rd., Hendersonville 37075; tel. 615/822-4911; Donald R. Sailer, adm.

Humboldt Cedar Crest Hospital (O, 62 beds), 3525 Chere Carol Rd., Humboldt 38343; tel. 901/784-2321; Rodney R. Smith, adm.

HCA Regional Hospital of Jackson (O, 166 beds), 49 Old Hickory Blvd., Jackson 38305; tel. 901/668-2100; Donald H. Wilkerson, adm.

Johnson City Eye and Ear Hospital (O, 39 beds), 203 E. Watauga Ave., Johnson City 37601; tel. 615/926-1111; J. Lori Caudell, adm.

North Side Hospital (O, 154 beds), 401 Princeton Rd., Johnson City 37601; tel. 615/282-4111; David Glover, adm.

Indian Path Hospital (O, 295 beds), 2000 Brookside Rd., Kingsport 37660; tel. 615/246-4311; Joe Fisher, adm.

Indian Path Pavilion (O, 46 beds), 2300 Pavilion Dr., Kingsport 37660; tel. 615/229-7874; Janet M. Creager, adm.

HCA Park West Medical Centers (O, 325 beds), 9352 Park West Blvd., P O Box 22993, Knoxville 37933; tel. 615/693-5151; Wayne Heatherly, adm. & chief exec. off.

Macon County General Hospital (CM, 43 beds), 204 Medical Dr., Lafayette 37083; tel. 615/666-2147; Dennis Wolford, adm.

HCA Crockett Hospital (O, 106 beds), U. S. Hwy. 43 S., Box 726, Lawrenceburg 38464; tel. 615/762-6571; John B. Crysel, adm.

HCA Regional Hospital-Livingston (O, 106 beds), 315 Oak St., Livingston 38570; tel. 615/823-5611; Martin Schoenbachler, adm.

Loudon County Memorial Hospital (CM, 50 beds), Vonore Rd., Box 217, Loudon 37774; tel. 615/458-4691; James L. Jarrett, adm.

Volunteer General Hospital (O, 100 beds), Mount Pelia Rd., Box 967, Martin 38237; tel. 901/587-4261; Joe D. Depew, adm.

River Park Hospital (O, 89 beds), Sparta Rd., McMinnville 37110; tel. 615/473-8411; William A. Summers, adm.

City of Milan Hospital (CM, 72 beds), 710 S. Liberty St., P O Box 719, Milan 38358; tel. 901/686-1591; Donald Chaffin, adm.

Johnson County Memorial Hospital (CM, 66 beds), Box 49, Mountain City 37683; tel. 615/727-7731; G. Gay Hamilton, adm.

HCA Donelson Hospital (O, 218 beds), 3055 Lebanon Rd., Nashville 37214; tel. 615/871-3000; Neil Serle', adm.

HCA Edgefield Hospital (O, 97 beds), 610 Gallatin Rd., Nashville 37206; tel. 615/226-4330; Jack P. Nyiri, adm.

HCA Park View Medical Center (O, 441 beds), 230 25th Ave. N., P O Box 1225, Nashville 37202; tel. 615/340-1000; Ernest Bacon, adm.

HCA Parthenon Pavilion (O, 158 beds), 2401 Murphy Ave., Nashville 37203; tel. 615/327-2237; James W. Weiss, chief exec. off.

For explanation of codes following names, see page B2.
*Indicates Type III membership in the American Hospital Association.

HCA Southern Hills Medical Center (O, 136 beds), 391 Wallace Rd., Nashville 37211; tel. 615/781-4100; John L. Fitzgerald, adm.

HCA West Side Hospital (O, 182 beds), 2221 Murphy Ave., Nashville 37203; tel. 615/329-6000; Samuel G. Feazell, adm.

DeKalb General Hospital (O, 54 beds), W. Main St., Box 640, Smithville 37166; tel. 615/597-7171; Bob Haley, adm.

HCA Smyrna Hospital (O, 33 beds), Hwy. 41 S., Box 306, Smyrna 37167; tel. 615/459-5671; Kenneth L. Atchley, adm.

South Pittsburg Municipal Hospital (O, 60 beds), 210 W. 12th St., South Pittsburg 37380; tel. 615/837-6781; Melville P. Mottet, adm.

HCA Stones River Hospital (O, 85 beds), Doolittle Rd., P O Box 458, Woodbury 37190; tel. 615/563-4001; Ken Parker, adm.

Texas: HCA South Arlington Medical Center (O, 185 beds), 3301 Matlock Rd., Arlington 76015; tel. 817/465-3241; James J. Cliborne Jr., adm.

HCA Shoal Creek Hospital (O, 230 beds), 3501 Mills Ave., Austin 78731; tel. 512/452-0361; Richard D. Jones Jr., adm.

HCA South Austin Medical Center (O, 134 beds), 901 W. Ben White Blvd., Austin 78704; tel. 512/447-2211; Michael S. Spurlock, chief exec. off.

Gulf Coast Hospital (O, 139 beds), 2800 Garth Rd., Baytown 77521; tel. 713/425-9100; Larry Hough, adm.

Beaumont Neurological Hospital (O, 111 beds), 3250 Fannin St., Beaumont 77701; tel. 409/835-4921; Neal Cury, adm.

HCA Northeast Community Hospital (O, 200 beds), 1301 Airport Freeway, Bedford 76021; tel. 817/282-9211; Robert Martin, chief exec. off.

HCA Valley Regional Medical Center (O, 158 beds), 1 Ted Hunt Blvd., Box 3710, Brownsville 78520; tel. 512/831-9611; Leon J. Belila, adm.

Brownwood Regional Hospital (O, 158 beds), Burnet & Streckert Sts., Box 760, Brownwood 76804; tel. 915/646-8541; James W. Saylor, adm.

Greenleaf Psychiatric Hospital (O, 70 beds), 405 W. 28th St., Bryan 77803; tel. 409/822-7326; Steve Koran, adm.

Sun Belt Regional Medical Center East (O, 96 beds), 15101 E. Freeway, Channelview 77530; tel. 713/452-1511; James P. Donovan III, adm.

HCA Doctors Hospital (O, 95 beds), 3205 W. Davis, Conroe 77304; Mailing Address Box 1349, Conroe, Zip 77301; tel. 409/756-0631; Duane K. Rossmann, adm.

Navarro Regional Hospital (O, 129 beds), 3201 W. Hwy. 22, Corsicana 75110; tel. 214/872-4861; Harvey L. Fishero, adm.

Houston County Hospital (CM, 72 beds), Loop 304 E., Box 1129, Crockett 75835; tel. 409/544-2002; Jonathan F. Godfrey, adm.

Metropolitan Hospital (CM, 126 beds), 7525 Scyene Rd., Dallas 75227; tel. 214/381-7171; Steve Peterson, adm.

HCA Deer Park Hospital (O, 116 beds), 4525 Glenwood, Deer Park 77536; tel. 713/479-0955; Manuel Ramos Jr., adm. & chief exec. off.

Maverick County Hospital District (CM, 77 beds), 350 S. Adams St., Eagle Pass 78852; tel. 512/773-5321; Robert F. Valliant, adm.

HCA Sun Towers Hospital (O, 145 beds), 1801 N. Oregon St., El Paso 79902; tel. 915/532-6281; William W. Webster, adm.

HCA Vista Hills Medical Center (O, 182 beds), 10301 Gateway W., El Paso 79925; tel. 915/595-9000; Jack F. Houghton, adm.

Sun Valley Regional Hospital (O, 125 beds), 1155 Idaho St., El Paso 79902; tel. 915/544-4000; Robert E. Thackston, adm.

Pecos County Memorial Hospital (CM, 37 beds), Sanderson Hwy., Box 1648, Fort Stockton 79735; tel. 915/336-2241; Willia¢o/

Medical Plaza Hospital (O, 250 beds), 1612 W. Humbolt St., Fort Worth 76104; tel. 817/336-2100; Robert B. Evans, adm.

Coryell Memorial Hospital (CM, 55 beds), 1507 W. Main St., P O Box 659, Gatesville 76528; tel. 817/865-8251; Thomas R. Sweeden, adm.

Hood General Hospital (CM, 63 beds), 1310 Paluxy Rd., Granbury 76048; tel. 817/573-2683; Joe S. Langford, adm.

Dallas-Fort Worth Medical Center (CM, 197 beds), 2709 Hospital Blvd., Grand Prairie 75051; tel. 214/641-5000; Dan Nielsen, pres.

Belle Park Hospital (O, 152 beds), 4427 Belle Park Dr., Houston 77072; tel. 713/933-6000; Arthur M. Ginsberg, adm.

Diagnostic Center Hospital (O, 183 beds), 6447 Main St., Houston 77030; tel. 713/790-0790; William A. Gregory, adm.

HCA Gulf Pines Hospital (O, 140 beds), 205 Hollow Tree Lane, Houston 77090; tel. 713/537-0700; Linda Jubinsky, adm.

Houston International Hospital (O, 135 beds), 6441 Main St., Houston 77030; tel. 713/795-5921; Ann Joyce Bossett, adm.

Medical Center Del Oro Hospital (O, 258 beds), 8081 Greenbriar, Houston 77054; tel. 713/790-8100; Anne W. Brown, exec. dir.

Spring Branch Memorial Hospital (O, 282 beds), 8850 Long Point Rd., Box 55227, Houston 77055; tel. 713/467-6555; Eddie A. George, adm.

Sun Belt Regional Medical Center (O, 129 beds), 13111 E. Freeway, Houston 77015; tel. 713/455-6911; Don H. McBride, adC

West Houston Medical Center (O, 141 beds), 12141 Richmond Ave., Houston 77082; tel. 713/558-3444; A. W. Layne, adm.

Woman's Hospital of Texas (O, 160 beds), 7600 Fannin St., Houston 77054; tel. 713/790-1234; Judy Novak, chief exec. off.

Huntsville Memorial Hospital (CM, 121 beds), 3000 I-45, Huntsville 77340; tel. 409/291-3411; Ralph E. Beaty, adm.

Brazosport Memorial Hospital (CM, 165 beds), 100 Medical Dr., Lake Jackson 77566; tel. 409/297-4411; Troy A. Dean, adm.

HCA Midway Park Medical Center (O, 104 beds), 2600 W. Pleasant Run Rd., Lancaster 75146; tel. 214/223-9600; Jim White, adm.

HCA Longview Regional Hospital (O, 83 beds), 2901 N. Fourth St., Longview 75601; tel. 214/758-1818; Alan McMillin, adm.

HCA Woodland Heights Medical Center (O, 117 beds), 500 Gaslight Blvd., Lufkin 75901; tel. 409/634-8311; M. L. Lagarde III, adm.

Madison County Medical Center (CM, 52 beds), 100 W. Cross St., Box 698, Madisonville 77864; tel. 409/348-2631; Ricky D. Wallace, adm.

HCA Mansfield Hospital (O, 55 beds), 1802 Hwy. 157 N., Mansfield 76063; tel. 817/473-6101; Jim Cliborne, adm.

Rio Grande Regional Hospital (O, 165 beds), 101 E. Ridge Rd., McAllen 78503; tel. 512/631-9111; William A. Burns, adm.

HCA Wysong Medical Center (O, 99 beds), 130 S. Central Expwy., McKinney 75069; tel. 214/542-9382; Tod Lambert, chief exec. off.

Mission Hospital (CM, 58 beds), 900 S. Bryan Rd., Mission 78572; tel. 512/580-9101; Thomas B. Symonds, adm.

North Hills Medical Center (O, 160 beds), 4401 Booth Calloway Rd., North Richland Hills 76180; tel. 817/284-1431; William M. Gracey, adm.

Medical Center Hospital (CM, 362 beds), Drawer 7239, Zip 79760; tel. 915/333-7111; W. Sam Glenney, adm.

HCA Coronado Hospital (O, 126 beds), One Medical Plaza, Box 5000, Pampa 79065; tel. 806/665-3721; Norman L. Knox, adm.

HCA Pasadena Bayshore Medical Center (O, 301 beds), 4000 Spencer Hwy., Pasadena 77504; tel. 713/944-6666; Donald L. Francis, adm.

HCA Medical Center of Plano (O, 233 beds), 3901 W. 15th St., Plano 75075; tel. 214/596-6800; Allyn Harris, adm.

Southwest General Hospital (CM, 191 beds), 7400 Barlite Blvd., San Antonio 78224; tel. 512/921-2000; Louis Garcia, adm.

Village Oaks Regional Hospital (O, 66 beds), 12412 Judson Rd., San Antonio 78233; tel. 512/650-4949; William Blanchard, adm.

Rolling Plains Memorial Hospital (CM, 61 beds), 200 E. Arizona St., P O Box 510, Sweetwater 79556; tel. 915/235-1701; Ralph K. Neff, adm.

Detar Hospital (O, 214 beds), 506 E. San Antonio St., Box 2089, Victoria 77902; tel. 512/575-7441; Charles Sexton, adm.

For explanation of codes following names, see page B2.
*Indicates Type III membership in the American Hospital Association.

Brazos Psychiatric Hospital (O, 80 beds), 301 Londonderry Dr., P O Box 21446, Waco 76702; tel. 817/772-3500; Charles H. Caperton, adm.

Gulf Coast Medical Center (O, 117 beds), 1400 Hwy. 59 Bypass, P O Box 3004, Wharton 77488; tel. 409/532-2500; L. Gene Matthews, adm.

HCA Red River Hospital (O, 62 beds), 1505 Eighth St., Wichita Falls 76301; tel. 817/322-3171; Thomas L. Ryba, adm.

Utah: Lakeview Hospital (O, 128 beds), 630 E. Medical Dr., Bountiful 84010; tel. 801/292-6231; Lindel L. Carriger, adm.

Brigham City Community Hospital (O, 50 beds), 950 S. 500 W., Brigham City 84302; tel. 801/734-9471; Stephen L. Walston, adm.

Mountain View Hospital (O, 118 beds), 1000 E. Hwy. 6, Payson 84651; tel. 801/465-9201; Michael A. Graham, adm.

Castleview Hospital (O, 88 beds), 300 N. Hospital Dr., R.F.D. 2, Box 46, Price 84501; tel. 801/637-4800; Don Larsen, adm.

Ashley Valley Medical Center (O, 36 beds), 151 W. 200 North, Vernal 84078; tel. 801/789-3342; Ron Perry, adm.

Pioneer Valley Hospital (O, 139 beds), 3460 S. Pioneer Pkwy., West Valley City 84120; tel. 801/968-9061; Kay Matsumura, adm.

Vermont: Northwestern Medical Center (CM, 77 beds), Box 1370, St. Albans 05478; tel. 802/524-5911; Wesley W. Oswald, exec. dir.

Virginia: HCA Northern Virginia Doctors Hospital (O, 198 beds), 601 S. Carlin Springs Rd., Arlington 22204; tel. 703/671-1200; Ray L. Hemness, adm.

Montgomery Regional Hospital (O, 146 beds), Rte. 460 S., Blacksburg 24060; tel. 703/951-1111; Robert D. Fraraccio, adm.

Dominion Hospital (O, 158 beds), 2960 Sleepy Hollow Rd., Falls Church 22044; tel. 703/536-2000; Donald E. Annis, exec. dir.

Buchanan General Hospital (CM, 194 beds), Grundy 24614; Mailing Address Rte. 4, Box 335-E., Grundy, Zip 26414; tel. 703/935-8831; John McClellan, adm.

Peninsula Hospital (O, 125 beds), 2244 Executive Dr., Hampton 23666; tel. 804/827-1001; David Hoidal, adm.

Rappahannock General Hospital (CM, 76 beds), Box 1449, Kilmarnock 22482; tel. 804/435-8000; R. Frederick Baensch, adm.

Alleghany Regional Hospital (CM, 214 beds), Interstate 64 & State Rd. 696, Box 7, Low Moor 24457; tel. 703/862-6011; Walter R. Parmer, adm.

Memorial Hospital of Martinsville and Henry County (CM, 207 beds), 320 Hospital Dr., Martinsville 24112; Mailing Address Box 4788, Martinsville, Zip 24115; tel.703/666-7200; Clyde L. Britt, exec. dir.

Poplar Springs Hospital (O, 100 beds), 350 Wagner Rd., Petersburg 23805; tel. 804/733-6874; James L. Legge, adm.

Portsmouth General Hospital (CM, 173 beds), 850 Crawford Pkwy., Portsmouth 23704; tel. 804/398-4000; J. B. Frith, adm.

Pulaski Community Hospital (O, 153 beds), 2400 Lee Hwy., Box 759, Pulaski 24301; tel. 703/980-6822; Edgar L. Belcher, adm.

Reston Hospital Center (O, 105 beds), 1850 Town Center Pkwy., Reston 22090; tel. 703/689-9000; James L. Perkins, adm.

Chippenham Hospital (O, 470 beds), 7101 Jahnke Rd., Richmond 23225; tel. 804/320-3911; Robert L. Hancock, adm.

Henrico Doctor's Hospital (O, 312 beds), 1602 Skipwith Rd., Richmond 23229; tel. 804/289-4500; J. Stephen Lindsey, exec. dir.

Johnston-Willis Hospital (O, 232 beds), 1401 Johnston-Willis Dr., Richmond 23235; tel. 804/320-2900; Wickliffe S. Lyne, adm.

Richmond Community Hospital (CM, 102 beds), 1500 N. 28th St., Richmond 23223; Mailing Address Box 27184, Richmond, ZipCWingate, exec. dir.

Richmond Eye and Ear Hospital (CM, 60 beds), 1001 E. Marshall St., Richmond 23219; tel. 804/775-4500; Robert G. Notarianni, adm.

Lewis-Gale Hospital (O, 380 beds), 1900 Electric Rd., Salem 24153; tel. 703/989-4261; Karl N. Miller, adm.

Roanoke Valley Psychiatric Center (O, 145 beds), 1902 Braeburn Dr., Salem 24153; tel. 703/772-2800; William W. Semones, adm.

Halifax-South Boston Community Hospital (CM, 192 beds), 2204 Wilborn Ave., South Boston 24592; tel. 804/575-7961

Washington: Black Hills Community Hospital (O, 110 beds), 3900 Capital Mall Dr. S.W., Olympia 98502; tel. 206/754-5858; Gary L. Worrell, adm.

United General Hospital (CM, 97 beds), 1971 Hwy. 20, Box 410, Sedro Woolley 98284; tel. 206/856-6021; Geoffrey A. Norwood, chief exec. off.

West Virginia: Raleigh General Hospital (O, 238 beds), 1710 Harper Rd., Beckley 25801; tel. 304/256-4100; Kenneth M. Holt, adm.

Morgan County War Memorial Hospital (CM, 60 beds), 1124 Fairfax St., Berkeley Springs 25411; tel. 304/258-1234; John Shepard, adm.

Grafton City Hospital (CM, 127 beds), Rte. 50 & Market St., P O Box 279, Grafton 26354; tel. 304/265-0400; Randy Smith, adm.

Summers County Hospital (CM, 95 beds), Terrace St., Drawer 940, Hinton 25951; tel. 304/466-1000; Frank Basile, adm.

HCA Huntington Hospital (O, 90 beds), 1230 Sixth Ave., Box 1875, Huntington 25719; tel. 304/526-9111; Richard Welch, adm.

Putnam General Hospital (O, 68 beds), 1400 Hospital Dr., P O Box 507, Hurricane 25526; tel. 304/757-9800; Shirley A. Perry, adm.

City Hospital (CM, 226 beds), Dry Run Rd., P O Box 1418, Martinsburg 25401; tel. 304/263-8971; J. Daniel Miller, adm.

Wisconsin: Apple River Hospital (CM, 49 beds), 221 Scholl St., Amery 54001; tel. 715/268-7151; J. Kenneth Jones, adm.

Riverside Community Memorial Hospital (CM, 67 beds), 800 Riverside Dr., Waupaca 54981; tel. 715/258-1000; David L. Stansberry, adm.

Wyoming: St. John's Hospital (CM, 55 beds), Box 428, Jackson 83001; tel. 307/733-3636; A. Dale Morgan, adm.

HCA Riverton Hospital (O, 64 beds), 2100 W. Sunset, Box 1280, Riverton 82501; tel. 307/856-4161; Bruce K. Birchell, adm.

Owned, leased, sponsored:	218 hospitals	2794 beds
Contract-managed:	190 hospitals	2646 beds
Totals:	408 hospitals	5440 beds

1775: HOSPITAL MANAGEMENT ASSOCIATES (IO)
800 Laurel Oak Dr., Naples, FL 33963; 813/598-3104; William J. Schoen, bd. chm., pres. & chief exec. off.

Florida: Hendry General Hospital (CM, 66 beds), 524 W. Sagamore St., Clewiston 33440; tel. 813/983-9121; Joseph C. Greene Jr., adm.

Palmview Hospital (O, 66 beds), 2510 N. Florida Ave., Lakeland 33805; tel. 813/682-6105; Ryan Beaty, interim adm.

Fishermen's Hospital (L, 58 beds), 3301 Overseas Hwy., Marathon 33050; tel. 305/743-5533; Ray G. Musselman, adm.

Highlands Regional Medical Center (L, 99 beds), 3600 S. Highlands Ave., Drawer 2066, Sebring 33870; tel. 813/385-6101; Joe D. Pinion, exec. dir.

Kentucky: Paul B. Hall Regional Medical Center (O, 72 beds), 104 James S. Trimble Blvd., P O Box 1487, Paintsville 41240; tel. 606/789-3511; Samuel P. Fowler, adm.

Mississippi: Biloxi Regional Medical Center (CM, 188 beds), 300 Reynoir St., Box 128, Biloxi 39533; tel. 601/432-1571; James D. Baker, exec. dir.

North Carolina: Lowrance Hospital (O, 107 beds), 610 E. Center Ave., Box 360, Mooresville 28115; tel. 704/663-1113; Richard P. Blackburn, exec. dir.

Pennsylvania: Lebanon Valley General Hospital (O, 92 beds), 30 N. Fourth St., Lebanon 17042; tel. 717/273-8521; Maureen Gallo, adm.

Texas: Electra Memorial Hospital (L, 25 beds), Hwy. 25 S., Box 1227, Electra 76360; tel. 817/495-3981; Bobby R. Morgan, adm.

For explanation of codes following names, see page B2.
*Indicates Type III membership in the American Hospital Association.

West Virginia: Williamson Memorial Hospital (O, 72 beds), P O Box 1980, Williamson 25661; tel. 304/235-2500; Stephen L. Midkiff, adm.

Owned, leased, sponsored:	8 hospitals	591 beds
Contract-managed:	2 hospitals	254 beds
Totals:	10 hospitals	845 beds

*2495: HOSPITAL MANAGEMENT PROFESSIONALS, INC. (IO)

5200 Maryland Way, Suite 103, Brentwood, TN 37027; 615/373-8830; Michael W. Barton, pres.

Arkansas: Saline Memorial Hospital (CM, 113 beds), N. East at McNeil Sts., Benton 72015; tel. 501/776-0611; Lonnie Busby, adm.

Johnson County Regional Hospital (O, 68 beds), 1100 Poplar St., P O Box 738, Clarksville 72830; tel. 501/754-2060; Jerry Campbell, exec. dir.

Colorado: Salida Hospital (CM, 38 beds), First & B Sts., Box 429, Salida 81201; tel. 303/539-6661; Tim Crowley, chief exec. off.

Georgia: Dodge County Hospital (CM, 87 beds), 715 Griffin St., Box 706, Eastman 31023; tel. 912/374-3491; Richard D. Osmus, adm.

Dr. John M. Meadows Memorial Hospital (CM, 81 beds), 1703 Meadows Lane, Box 1048, Vidalia 30474; tel. 912/537-8921; Weston Bergman Jr., adm. & chief exec. off.

Illinois: Gibson Community Hospital (CM, 81 beds), 1120 N. Melvin St., P O Box 429, Gibson City 60936; tel. 217/784-4251; Terry Thompson, adm.

Kewanee Public Hospital (CM, 111 beds), 719 Elliott St., Kewanee 61443; tel. 309/853-3361; Glenn A. Doyle, adm.

Edward Hospital (CM, 163 beds), 801 S. Washington St., Naperville 60566; tel. 312/355-0450; John R. Whitcomb, pres.

Paris Community Hospital (CM, 98 beds), E. Court St., Paris 61944; tel. 217/465-4141; Lawrence Wills, adm.

Indiana: Starke Memorial Hospital (CM, 55 beds), 102 E. Culver Rd., Knox 46534; tel. 219/772-6231; Spencer L. Grover, exec. dir.

White County Memorial Hospital (CM, 59 beds), 1101 O'Connor Blvd., Monticello 47960; tel. 219/583-7111; Ed Pfeiffer, adm.

Kansas: Arkansas City Memorial Hospital (CM, 69 beds), 216 W. Birch Ave., Arkansas City 67005; tel. 316/442-2500; Robert J. King, adm.

Kentucky: Marshall County Hospital (CM, 80 beds), 503 George McClain Dr., Benton 42025; tel. 502/527-1336; Andrew J. Hetrick, adm.

Louisiana: Seventh Ward General Hospital (CM, 196 beds), Hwy. 51 S., Box 2668, Hammond 70404; tel. 504/345-2700; James E. Cathey Jr., adm.

Opelousas General Hospital (CM, 183 beds), 520 Prudhomme Lane, Box 1208, Opelousas 70571; tel. 318/948-3011; J. Michael Douthitt, adm.

Lincoln General Hospital (CM, 130 beds), White St., P O Drawer 1368, Ruston 71273; tel. 318/255-5780; Ronald K. Rooney, adm.

Lane Memorial Hospital (CM, 135 beds), 6300 Main St., Zachary 70791; tel. 504/654-4511; Charlie L. Massey, adm.

Michigan: Albion Community Hospital (CM, 55 beds), 809 W. Erie St., Albion 49224; tel. 517/629-2191; Richard C. Hoeth, pres.

Portage View Hospital (CM, 85 beds), 200 Michigan St., Hancock 49930; tel. 906/482-1122; Dave Woodland, adm.

Marlette Community Hospital (CM, 91 beds), 2770 Main St., Marlette 48453; tel. 517/635-7491; Darwin Root, adm.

Bay Area Medical Center-Menominee (CM, 78 beds), 1110 Tenth Ave., Menominee 49858; tel. 906/863-5571; Thomas K. Prusak, chief exec. off.

Lake View Community Hospital (CM, 159 beds), 408 Hazen St., Box 209, Paw Paw 49079; tel. 616/657-3141; James R. Phillippe, adm.

Minnesota: Virginia Regional Medical Center (CM, 295 beds), 901 Ninth St. N., Virginia 55792; tel. 218/741-3340; John A. Tucker, adm.

Missouri: Madison Memorial Hospital (CM, 163 beds), W. College Ave., Box 431, Fredericktown 63645; tel. 314/783-3341; O. Douglas Taylor, adm.

Phelps County Regional Medical Center (O, 200 beds), 1000 W. Tenth St., Rolla 65401; tel. 314/364-3100; Glen Marshall, adm.

North Carolina: Morehead Memorial Hospital (CM, 109 beds), 117 E. King's Hwy., Eden 27288; tel. 919/623-9711; Robert W. Mellbye, pres.

Hugh Chatham Memorial Hospital (CM, 122 beds), Parkwood Dr., Elkin 28621; tel. 919/835-3722; William S. Clark, adm.

Rutherford Hospital (CM, 165 beds), 308 S. Ridgecrest Ave., Rutherfordton 28139; tel. 704/287-7371; Thomas E. Cecconi, pres.

Ohio: Amherst Hospital (CM, 70 beds), 254 Cleveland Ave., Amherst 44001; tel. 216/988-2831; J. A. Lewandowski, exec. dir.

Fostoria City Hospital (CM, 80 beds), 501 Van Buren St., Fostoria 44830; tel. 419/435-7734; Wayne Moore, adm.

Lawrence County General Hospital (CM, 117 beds), 2228 S. Ninth St., Ironton 45638; tel. 614/532-3231; Norman Greene, exec. dir.

Selby General Hospital (CM, 74 beds), 1106 Colgate Dr., Marietta 45750; tel. 614/373-0582; John M. O'Shea, pres. & adm.

Willard Area Hospital (CM, 64 beds), 110 E. Howard St., Willard 44890; tel. 419/933-2931; Frederick M. Welfel, adm.

Oklahoma: Clinton Regional Hospital (CM, 75 beds), 100 N. 30th St., Box 1569, Clinton 73601; tel. 405/323-2363; Ronald Dorris, adm.

Newman Memorial Hospital (CM, 114 beds), 905 S. Main St., Shattuck 73858; tel. 405/938-2551; Walter Shain, adm.

Willow View Hospital (CM, 93 beds), 2601 Spencer Rd., Spencer 73084; Mailing Address P O Box 11137, Oklahoma City, Zip 73136; tel. 405/427-2441; Gary Watson, adm.

Pennsylvania: Fulton County Medical Center (CM, 100 beds), 216 S. First St., McConnellsburg 17233; tel. 717/485-3155; Thomas Fite, adm.

South Carolina: Beaufort Memorial Hospital (CM, 99 beds), Ribaut Rd., Drawer 1068, Beaufort 29901; tel. 803/524-3311; P. Jack Austin Jr., pres.

Texas: Flow Memorial Hospital (CM, 129 beds), 1310 Scripture St., Denton 76201; tel. 817/387-5861; Charles B. Linton, chief exec. off.

Vermont: Northeastern Vermont Regional Hospital (CM, 100 beds), Hospital Dr., St. Johnsbury 05819; tel. 802/748-8141; Paul R. Bengtson, chief exec. off.

Wisconsin: Bay Area Medical Center (CM, 99 beds), 3100 Shore Dr., Marinette 54143; tel. 715/735-6621; Thomas K. Prusak, chief exec. off.

Superior Memorial Hospital (CM, 52 beds), 3500 Tower Ave., Superior 54880; tel. 715/392-8281; Keith J. Petersen, chief exec. off.

Owned, leased, sponsored:	2 hospitals	268 beds
Contract-managed:	40 hospitals	4267 beds
Totals:	42 hospitals	4535 beds

*5355: HOSPITAL SISTERS HEALTH SYSTEM-HOSPITAL SISTERS OF THE THIRD ORDER OF ST. FRANCIS-AMERICAN PROVINCE (CC)

Sangamon Ave. Rd., Box 19431, Springfield, IL 62794; 217/522-6969; Sr. Marianna Kosior, pres.

Illinois: St. Elizabeth's Hospital (O, 447 beds), 211 S. Third St., Belleville 62222; tel. 618/234-2120; Gerald M. Harman, exec. vice-pres.

St. Joseph's Hospital (O, 93 beds), Jamestown Rd., Breese 62230; tel. 618/526-4511; Sr. Mary Anthony Menting, exec. vice-pres.

St. Mary's Hospital (O, 377 beds), 1800 E. Lake Shore Dr., Decatur 62525; tel. 217/429-2966; Terence J. Schuessler, exec. vice-pres. & chief exec. off.

St. Anthony's Memorial Hospital (O, 146 beds), 503 Maple St., Effingham 62401; tel. 217/342-2121; Gregory A. Voss, adm.

St. Joseph's Hospital (O, 106 beds), 1515 Main St., Highland 62249; tel. 618/654-7421; Mark W. Reifsteck, exec. vice-pres.

St. Francis Hospital (O, 138 beds), 1215 E. Union Ave., Litchfield 62056; tel. 217/324-2191; Sr. Mary Ann Laxen, exec. vice-pres.

For explanation of codes following names, see page B2.
*Indicates Type III membership in the American Hospital Association.

St. John's Hospital (O, 744 beds), 800 E. Carpenter St., Springfield 62769; tel. 217/544-6464; Sr. Ann Pitsenberger, exec. vice-pres.

St. Mary's Hospital (O, 164 beds), 111 E. Spring St., Streator 61364; tel. 815/673-2311; Jim Lansford, actg. adm.

Wisconsin: St. Joseph's Hospital (O, 149 beds), 2661 County Trunk I, Chippewa Falls 54729; tel. 715/723-1811; David B. Fish, exec. vice-pres. & adm.

Sacred Heart Hospital (O, 334 beds), 900 W. Clairemont Ave., Eau Claire 54701; tel. 715/839-4121; Matthew W. Hubler, exec. vice-pres.

St. Mary's Hospital Medical Center (O, 158 beds), 1726 Shawano Ave., Green Bay 54303; tel. 414/498-4200; James G. Coller, exec. vice-pres. & adm.

St. Vincent Hospital (O, 442 beds), 835 S. Van Buren St., P O Box 13508, Green Bay 54307; tel. 414/433-0111; Joseph J. Neidenbach, adm.

St. Nicholas Hospital (O, 145 beds), 1601 N. Taylor Dr., Sheboygan 53081; tel. 414/459-8300; Michael E. Zilm, exec. vice-pres.

Owned, leased, sponsored:	13 hospitals	3443 beds
Contract-managed:	0 hospitals	0 beds
Totals:	13 hospitals	3443 beds

***1235: HUMANA INC.** (IO)
500 W. Main St., Humana Bldg., Box 1438, Louisville, KY 40201; 502/580-1000; David A. Jones, bd. chm. & chief exec. off.; H. Wendell Cherry, pres. & chief oper. of

Alabama: Humana Hospital -Enterprise (O, 120 beds), 400 N. Edwards St., Enterprise 36330; tel. 205/347-0584; Wendell W. Briggs, exec. dir.

Humana Hospital -Florence (L, 155 beds), 2111 Cloyd Blvd., Box 2010, Florence 35631; tel. 205/767-8700; William M. Donohoo, exec. dir.

Humana Hospital-Huntsville (L, 323 beds), 911 Big Cove Rd. S.E., Huntsville 35801; tel. 205/532-5712; Patricia A. Davis, exec. dir.

Humana Hospital -East Montgomery (O, 150 beds), Taylor Rd., Box 17720, Montgomery 36193; tel. 205/277-8330; John W. Melton, exec. dir.

Humana Hospital -Shoals (O, 128 beds), 201 Avalon Ave., P O Box 3359, Muscle Shoals 35661; tel. 205/386-1600; Charles P. Stokes, dir.

Humana Hospital -Russellville (L, 100 beds), Hwy. 43 By-Pass, Box 1089, Russellville 35653; tel. 205/332-1611; Bradley K. Grover Sr., exec. dir.

Alaska: Humana Hospital -Alaska (O, 238 beds), 2801 Debarr Rd., Anchorage 99508; Mailing Address P O Box 143889, Anchorage, Zip 99514; tel. 907/276-1131; Mary D.Willis, exec. dir.

Arizona: Humana Hospital -Desert Valley (O, 117 beds), 3929 E. Bell Rd., Phoenix 85032; tel. 602/867-5600; Kenneth A. Levin, exec. dir.

Humana Hospital -Phoenix (O, 314 beds), 1947 E. Thomas Rd., Phoenix 85016; tel. 602/241-7600; Raymond A. Rouleau Jr., exec. dir.

California: Humana Hospital -West Anaheim (O, 243 beds), 3033 W. Orange Ave., Box 2097, Anaheim 92804; tel. 714/827-3000; John W. Hanshaw, exec. dir.

Humana Hospital -West Hills (O, 236 beds), 7300 Medical Center Dr., Canoga Park 91307; tel. 818/712-4110; Michael B. McCallister, exec. dir.

Humana Hospital -Huntington Beach (O, 141 beds), 17772 Beach Blvd., Huntington Beach 92647; tel. 714/842-1473; Mark Aanonson, exec. dir.

Humana Hospital -San Leandro (O, 136 beds), 13855 E. 14th St., San Leandro 94578; tel. 415/357-6500; Doris I. Porth, exec. dir.

Humana Hospital -Westminster (O, 182 beds), 200 Hospital Circle, Westminster 92683; tel. 714/896-9239; Debra Gray Mathias, exec. dir.

Colorado: Humana Hospital -Aurora (O, 200 beds), 1501 S. Potomac, Aurora 80012; tel. 303/695-2600; Timothy L. Austin, exec. dir.

Humana Hospital-Mountain View (O, 172 beds), 9191 Grant St., Thornton 80229; tel. 303/451-7800; Jack Shapiro, exec. dir.

Florida: Humana Hospital -Brandon (O, 220 beds), 119 Oakfield Dr., Brandon 33511; tel. 813/681-5551; William R. Heburn, exec. dir.

Humana Hospital -Pasco (O, 120 beds), 1550 Fort King Hwy., Dade City 33525; tel. 904/567-6726; Sandra J. Jones, exec. dir.

Humana Hospital -Daytona Beach (O, 214 beds), 400 N. Clyde Morris Blvd., Box 9000, Daytona Beach 32020; tel. 904/239-5000; William W. Ward, exec. dir.

Humana Hospital-Fort Walton Beach (O, 236 beds), 1000 Mar-Walt Dr., Fort Walton Beach 32548; tel. 904/862-1111; J. Michael Mastej, exec. dir.

Humana Hospital -South Broward (O, 256 beds), 5100 W. Hallandale Beach Blvd., Hollywood 33023; tel. 305/966-8100; Stephen L. Sutherlin, exec. dir.

Humana Hospital -Kissimmee (O, 169 beds), 700 W. Oak St., Kissimmee 32741; Mailing Address P O Box 2589, Kissimmee, Zip 32742; tel. 305/933-3601; James A. Shanks,exec. dir.

Humana Hospital -Biscayne (O, 458 beds), 20900 Biscayne Blvd., Miami 33180; tel. 305/932-0250; Robert M. Krieger, exec. dir.

Humana Hospital -Orange Park (O, 196 beds), 2001 Kingsley Ave., P O Box 2000, Orange Park 32067; tel. 904/272-8500; Lee R. Ledbetter, exec. dir.

Humana Hospital -Lucerne (O, 267 beds), 818 S. Main Lane, Orlando 32801; tel. 305/237-6111; Jeffrey E. Green, exec. dir.

Humana Hospital -Bennett (L, 204 beds), 8201 W. Broward Blvd., Plantation 33324; tel. 305/476-3915; H. Rex Etheredge, exec. dir.

Humana Hospital -Cypress (O, 273 beds), 600 S.W. Third St., Pompano Beach 33060; tel. 305/786-5030; Stephen P. Dexter, exec. dir.

Humana Hospital -Sebastian (O, 133 beds), 13695 N. U. S. Hwy. 1, Box 838, Sebastian 32958; tel. 305/589-3186; Mitchell B. Smith, exec. dir.

Humana Hospital -St. Petersburg (O, 219 beds), 6500 38th Ave. N., St. Petersburg 33710; Mailing Address Box 13096, St. Petersburg, Zip 33733; tel. 813/384-1414;David K. Donin, exec. dir.

Humana Hospital -Sun Bay (O, 200 beds), 3030 Sixth St. S., St. Petersburg 33705; tel. 813/823-1122; John B. Wheatley Jr., exec. dir.

Humana Hospital-Northside (O, 188 beds), 6000 49th St. N., St. Petersburg 33709; tel. 813/521-5000; Donald A. Shaffett, exec. dir.

Humana Women's Hospital -Tampa (L, 219 beds), 3030 W. Buffalo Ave., Tampa 33607; tel. 813/879-4730; William A. Marek, exec. dir.

Humana Hospital -Palm Beaches (O, 250 beds), 2201 45th St., West Palm Beach 33407; tel. 305/863-3801; Niels P. Vernegaard, exec. dir.

Georgia: Humana Hospital -Augusta (O, 374 beds), 3651 Wheeler Rd., Augusta 30910; tel. 404/863-3232; G. Wayne Peloquin, exec.C

Humana Hospital-Cartersville (O, 80 beds), Rte. 7, Hwy. 41 N., Box 1008, Cartersville 30120; tel. 404/382-1530; Keith Sandlin, exec. dir.

Humana Hospital -Newnan (O, 144 beds), 60 Hospital Rd., Newnan 30263; Mailing Address Box 2228, Newnan, Zip 30264; tel. 404/253-1912; Jack D. Davis PhD, exec.dir.

Humana Hospital -Gwinnett (O, 120 beds), 2160 Fountain Dr., Box 587, Snellville 30278; tel. 404/979-0200; David L. Harris, exec. dir.

Illinois: Humana Hospital -Hoffman Estates (O, 216 beds), 1555 N. Barrington Rd., Hoffman Estates 60194; tel. 312/843-2000; Donald L. Maloney II, exec. dir.

Humana Hospital -Springfield (O, 100 beds), 5230 S. Sixth St., Frontage Rd., Springfield 62703; tel. 217/529-7151; Austin D. Edwards, exec. dir.

For explanation of codes following names, see page B2.
*Indicates Type III membership in the American Hospital Association.

Indiana: Humana Women's Hospital-Indianapolis (O, 108 beds), 8111 Township Line Rd., Indianapolis 46260; tel. 317/872-1803; Jay W. Williams, exec. dir.

Kansas: Humana Hospital -Dodge City (O, 110 beds), 3001 Ave. A, Box 1478, Dodge City 67801; tel. 316/225-9050; I. Lynn Jeane, exec. dir.

Humana Hospital -Overland Park (O, 400 beds), 10500 Quivira Rd., P O Box 15959, Overland Park 66215; tel. 913/541-5000; Prosser Lee Ashbury Jr., exec. dir.

Kentucky: Humana Hospital -Lexington (O, 162 beds), 150 N. Eagle Creek Dr., P O Box 23260, Lexington 40523; tel. 606/268-4800; David L. Miller, exec. dir.

Humana Hospital -Louisa (L, 90 beds), Hwy. 644, Box 769, Louisa 41230; tel. 606/638-9451; James Ellison, exec. dir.

Humana Hospital -Audubon (O, 484 beds), One Audubon Plaza Dr., Box 17555, Louisville 40217; tel. 502/636-7111; Bruce W. MacLeod, exec. dir.

Humana Hospital -Southwest (O, 150 beds), 9820 Third St. Rd., Louisville 40272; tel. 502/933-2110; Max K. Harder, exec. dir.

Humana Hospital -Suburban (O, 380 beds), 4001 Dutchmans Lane, Louisville 40207; tel. 502/893-1000; Jeff Holland, chief exec. off.

Humana Hospital -University (L, 404 beds), 530 S. Jackson St., Louisville 40202; tel. 502/562-4000; David G. Laird, exec. dir.; Sam Holtzman, adm.

Humana Hospital -Lake Cumberland (O, 183 beds), 305 Langdon St., Box 620, Somerset 42501; tel. 606/679-7441; Derek W. Cimala, exec. dir.

Louisiana: Humana Hospital -Lake Charles (O, 90 beds), 4200 Nelson Rd., Lake Charles 70605; tel. 318/474-6370; Davis Walton, exec. dir.

Humana Hospital -Marksville (O, 55 beds), Box 255, Marksville 71351; tel. 318/253-8611; Lloyd C. Dupuy, exec. dir.

Humana Hospital -New Orleans (O, 150 beds), 6000 Bullard Rd., New Orleans 70128; Mailing Address P O Box 29504, New Orleans, Zip 70189; tel. 504/245-4851; JamesLe Doux, exec. dir.

Humana Hospital -Oakdale (O, 61 beds), 130 N. Hospital Dr., Box 629, Oakdale 71463; tel. 318/335-3700; Louis J. Deumite, exec. dir.

Humana Hospital -Brentwood (O, 174 beds), 1800 Irving Pl., Shreveport 71101; tel. 318/424-6761; Raymond Bane, exec. dir.

Humana Hospital -Springhill (O, 86 beds), 1001 Humana Dr., Box 917, Springhill 71075; tel. 318/539-9161; Ronald P. O'Neal, exec. dir.

Humana Hospital -Ville Platte (O, 124 beds), 800 E. Main St., Box 349, Ville Platte 70586; tel. 318/363-5684; James C. Colligan, exec. dir.

Humana Hospital -Winn Parish (O, 98 beds), 301 W. Boundary St., Box 152, Winnfield 71483; tel. 318/628-2721; Donald L. Kannady, exec. dir.

Mississippi: Humana Hospital -Natchez (O, 101 beds), 129 Jefferson Davis Blvd., Box 1203, Natchez 39120; tel. 601/446-7711; Thomas E. Casaday, exec. dir.

Nevada: Humana Hospital -Sunrise (O, 679 beds), 3186 Maryland Pkwy., Las Vegas 89109; Mailing Address Box 14157, Las Vegas, Zip 89114; tel. 702/731-8000; Donald L.Stewart, exec. dir.; Dan Brothman, adm.

North Carolina: Humana Spec Hospital-Charlotte (O, 68 beds), 1600 E. Third St., Charlotte 28204; Mailing Address P O Box 36939, Charlotte, Zip 28236; tel. 704/371-3105; WilliamSheron, exec. dir.

Humana Hospital -Greensboro (O, 109 beds), 801 Green Valley Rd., Greensboro 27408; Mailing Address P O Box 29526, Greensboro, Zip 27429; tel. 919/373-8555; E.William Jochim, exec. dir.

Tennessee: Humana Hospital -East Ridge (L, 128 beds), 941 Spring Creek Rd., Chattanooga 37412; tel. 615/894-7870; Peter T. Petruzzi, exec. dir.

Humana Hospital -McFarland (L, 159 beds), 500 Park Ave., Lebanon 37087; tel. 615/449-0500; Larry Keller, exec. dir.

Humana Hospital -Morristown (L, 135 beds), 726 McFarland St., Morristown 37814; tel. 615/586-2302; Stephen L. Taylor, exec. dir.

Texas: Humana Hospital -Abilene (O, 160 beds), 6250 Hwy. 83-84 at Antilley Rd., Abilene 79606; tel. 915/695-9900; David M. Collins, exec. dir.

Humana Hospital -Baytown (O, 191 beds), 1700 Bowie School Dr., Box 1451, Baytown 77520; tel. 713/420-6100; William K. Atkinson, exec. dir.

Beaumont Medical Surgical Hospital (L, 250 beds), 3080 College, Box 5817, Beaumont 77701; tel. 409/833-1411; Gary R. Grover, exec. dir.

Humana Hospital-Brazos Valley (O, 65 beds), 1604 Rock Prairie Rd., College Station 77840; tel. 409/764-5100; Pat Cornelison, exec. dir.

Humana Hospital Corpus Christi (O, 193 beds), 3315 S. Alameda, Box 3828, Corpus Christi 78404; tel. 512/857-1400; LeRoy A. Hagens, exec. dir.

Humana Hospital -Medical City Dallas (L, 420 beds), 7777 Forest Lane, Dallas 75230; tel. 214/661-7000; Ira B. Korman PhD, exec. dir.

Humana Hospital -Southmore (O, 208 beds), 906 E. Southmore St., Box 1879, Pasadena 77502; tel. 713/477-0411; Nadine Cook, exec. dir.

Humana Hospital -Metropolitan (O, 233 beds), 1310 McCullough Ave., San Antonio 78212; tel. 512/271-2200; Earl H. Denning III, exec. dir.

Humana Hospital -San Antonio (O, 329 beds), 8026 Floyd Curl Dr., San Antonio 78229; tel. 512/692-8107; Timothy L. Austin, exec. dir.

Humana Women's Hospital-South Texas (O, 121 beds), 8109 Fredericksburg Rd., San Antonio 78229; tel. 512/699-8000; Thomas E. Casaday, exec. dir.

Humana Hospital -Clear Lake (O, 467 beds), 500 Medical Center Blvd., Webster 77598; tel. 713/332-2511; William J. Gresco, exec. dir.

Utah: Humana Hospital -Davis North (O, 110 beds), 1600 W. Antelope Dr., Layton 84041; tel. 801/825-9561; Dean S. Holman, exec. dir.

Virginia: Humana Hospital -Clinch Valley (O, 135 beds), 2949 W. Front St., Richlands 24641; tel. 703/963-0811; W. A. Gillespie, exec. dir.

Humana Hospital -St. Lukes (O, 200 beds), 7700 Parham Rd., Richmond 23229; tel. 804/747-5600; Nancy R. Hofheimer, exec. dir.

Humana Hospital -Bayside (O, 250 beds), 800 Independence Blvd., Virginia Beach 23455; tel. 804/460-8000; Jerry R. Sutphin, exec. dir.

Washington: Humana Hospital -Tacoma (O, 155 beds), S. 19th & Union Sts., Tacoma 98405; Mailing Address P O Box 11414, Tacoma, Zip 98411; tel. 206/572-2323; SharonArmstrong, exec. dir.

West Virginia: Humana Hospital-St. Luke's (O, 79 beds), 1333 Southview Dr., P O Box 1190, Bluefield 24701; tel. 304/327-8121; Bradly R. Anderson, exec. dir.

Humana Hospital-Greenbrier Valley (L, 122 beds), Davis-Stuart Rd., Box 497, Ronceverte 24970; tel. 304/647-4411; D. Dale Landon, exec. dir.

Owned, leased, sponsored:	82 hospitals	6187 beds
Contract-managed:	0 hospitals	0 beds
Totals:	82 hospitals	6187 beds

***5645: HUMILITY OF MARY HEALTH CARE** (CC)
P O Box 841, Lorain, OH 44052; 216/871-0971; Sr. Frances Flanigan, chief exec. off.

Ohio: St. Joseph Hospital and Health Center (S, 272 beds), 205 W. 20th St., Lorain 44052; tel. 216/245-6851; Ronald M. Streem, exec. dir.

St. Joseph Riverside Hospital (S, 209 beds), 1400 Tod Ave. N.W., Warren 44485; tel. 216/841-4000; Sr. Mildred Ely, exec. dir.

For explanation of codes following names, see page B2.
*Indicates Type III membership in the American Hospital Association.

St. Elizabeth Hospital Medical Center (S, 773 beds), 1044 Belmont Ave., Box 1790, Youngstown 44501; tel. 216/746-7211; Sr. Susan Schorsten, exec. dir.

Owned, leased, sponsored:	3 hospitals	1254 beds
Contract-managed:	0 hospitals	0 beds
Totals:	3 hospitals	1254 beds

***5565: INCARNATE WORD HEALTH SERVICES** (CC)
303 W. Sunset Rd., San Antonio, TX 78209; 512/828-1733; Sr. Nora Marie Walsh, pres.

Missouri: Incarnate Word Hospital (O, 236 beds), 3545 Lafayette Ave., St. Louis 63104; tel. 314/664-6500; James R. Kaskie, pres. & chief exec. off.

Texas: St. Anthony's Hospital (O, 314 beds), 200 N.W. Seventh, Amarillo 79107; Mailing Address Box 950, Amarillo, Zip 79176; tel. 806/376-4411; William D. Myers, pres.

Spohn Hospital (O, 419 beds), 600 Elizabeth St., Corpus Christi 78404; tel. 512/881-3000; Sr. Kathleen Coughlin, pres.

Coon Memorial Hospital and Home (O, 108 beds), 1411 Denver Ave., P O Box 1500, Dalhart 79022; tel. 806/249-4571; Earl N. Sheehy, pres.

Saint Joseph Hospital (O, 379 beds), 1401 S. Main St., Fort Worth 76104; tel. 817/336-9371; Kevin R. Andrews, pres. & chief exec. off.

Spohn Kleberg Memorial Hospital (O, 68 beds), 1300 General Cavazos Blvd., P O Box 1197, Kingsville 78363; tel. 512/595-1661; Allan C. Sonduck, pres.

St. Joseph's Hospital and Health Center (O, 175 beds), 820 Clarksville St., Box 70, Paris 75460; tel. 214/785-4521; Sr. Mary Eustace Farrell, pres.

St. John's Hospital and Health Center (O, 137 beds), 2018 Pulliam St., P O Drawer 5741, San Angelo 76902; tel. 915/655-3181; P. Denny Oreb, pres. & chief exec.off.

Santa Rosa Medical Center (O, 825 beds), 519 W. Houston St., San Antonio 78207; Mailing Address Box 7330, Sta. A, San Antonio, Zip 78285; tel. 512/228-2011; Sr.Angela Clare Moran, pres. & chief exec. off.

Yoakum Catholic Hospital (O, 18 beds), 303 Hubbard St., Box 753, Yoakum 77995; tel. 512/293-2321; Elwood E. Currier Jr., chief exec. off.

Owned, leased, sponsored:	10 hospitals	2679 beds
Contract-managed:	0 hospitals	0 beds
Totals:	10 hospitals	2679 beds

***8855: INTERCARE HEALTH SYSTEMS** (NP)
98 James St., Mediplex Suite 400, Edison, NJ 08820; 201/632-1500; Michael T. Kornett, pres. & chief exec. off.

New Jersey: John F. Kennedy Medical Center (O, 380 beds), 59 James St., Edison 08818; tel. 201/321-7000

Robert Wood Johnson Jr. Rehabilitation Institute (O, 74 beds), James St., Edison 08818; tel. 201/321-7050; Scott Gephard, adm.

Owned, leased, sponsored:	2 hospitals	454 beds
Contract-managed:	0 hospitals	0 beds
Totals:	2 hospitals	454 beds

***1815: INTERMOUNTAIN HEALTH CARE, INC.** (NP)
36 S. State, 22nd Floor, Salt Lake City, UT 84111; 801/533-8282; Scott S. Parker, pres.

Idaho: Cassia Memorial Hospital and Medical Center (L, 87 beds), 2303 Park Ave., Box 489, Burley 83318; tel. 208/678-4444; Richard Packer, adm.

Pocatello Regional Medical Center (O, 110 beds), 777 Hospital Way, Pocatello 83201; tel. 208/234-0777; Richard M. Cagen, adm.

Utah: American Fork Hospital (O, 72 beds), 1100 East 170 North, American Fork 84003; tel. 801/756-6001; Craig M. Smedley, adm.

Valley View Medical Center (O, 48 beds), 595 South 75 East, Cedar City 84720; tel. 801/586-6587; Mark F. Dalley, adm.

Delta Community Hospital (O, 20 beds), 126 S. White Sage Ave., Delta 84624; tel. 801/864-5591; Roy Barraclough, adm.

Fillmore Community Medical Center (O, 20 beds), 674 S. Hwy. 99, P O Box 746, Fillmore 84631; tel. 801/743-5591; Roy E. Barraclough, adm.

Wasatch County Hospital (L, 40 beds), 55 South Fifth East, Heber City 84032; tel. 801/654-2500; Wayne T. Terry, adm.

Logan Regional Hospital (O, 148 beds), 1400 North 500 East, P O Box 3368, Logan 84321; tel. 801/752-2050; Douglas R. Fonnesbeck, adm.

Sanpete Valley Hospital (O, 20 beds), 1100 S. Medical Dr., Mount Pleasant 84647; tel. 801/462-2441; George Winn, adm.

Cottonwood Hospital Medical Center (O, 227 beds), 5770 S. 300 East, Murray 84107; tel. 801/262-3461; Floyd J. McDermott, adm.

McKay-Dee Hospital Center (O, 380 beds), 3939 Harrison Blvd., Box 9370, Ogden 84409; tel. 801/627-2800; Thomas Hanrahan, adm.

Orem Community Hospital (O, 20 beds), 331 N. 400 W., Orem 84057; tel. 801/224-4080; Laurel D. Kay, adm.

Garfield Memorial Hospital and Clinics (O, 20 beds), 200 N. Fourth East, P O Box 389, Panguitch 84759; tel. 801/676-8811; Wayne R. Ross, adm.

Utah Valley Regional Medical Center (O, 326 beds), 1034 N. Fifth West, Provo 84603; tel. 801/373-7850; Mark J. Howard, exec. dir.

Sevier Valley Hospital (O, 42 beds), 1100 N. Main St., Richfield 84701; tel. 801/896-8271; Carlos F. Madsen, adm.

LDS Hospital (O, 475 beds), Eighth Ave. & C. St., Salt Lake City 84143; tel. 801/321-1100; Gary William Farnes, adm.

Primary Children's Medical Center (O, 188 beds), 320 12th Ave., Salt Lake City 84103; tel. 801/521-1221; Donald R. Poulter, adm.

Alta View Hospital (O, 50 beds), 9660 S. 1300 E., Sandy 84070; tel. 801/572-2600; Jay Southwick, adm.

Dixie Medical Center (O, 104 beds), 544 S. 400 East St., St. George 84770; tel. 801/673-9681; L. Steven Wilson, adm.

Bear River Valley Hospital (O, 20 beds), 440 W. 600 N., Tremonton 84337; tel. 801/257-7441; Robert F. Jex, adm.

Wyoming: Star Valley Hospital (CM, 15 beds), 110 Hospital Lane, P O Box 578, Afton 83110; tel. 307/886-3841; Jon D. Hoopes, adm.

Ihc Evanston Regional Hospital (O, 42 beds), 190 Arrowhead Dr., Evanston 82930; tel. 307/789-3636; Joseph B. May III, adm.

Owned, leased, sponsored:	21 hospitals	2459 beds
Contract-managed:	1 hospitals	15 beds
Totals:	22 hospitals	2474 beds

***1595: IOWA METHODIST HEALTH SYSTEM** (NP)
1200 Pleasant St., Des Moines, IA 50308; 515/283-6201; David S. Ramsey, pres.

Iowa: Iowa Methodist Medical Center (O, 680 beds), 1200 Pleasant St., Des Moines 50308; tel. 515/283-6212; David S. Ramsey, pres.

Humboldt County Memorial Hospital (CM, 49 beds), 1000 N. 15th St., Box 587, Humboldt 50548; tel. 515/332-4200; Richard L. Abrahamson, adm.

Clarke County Public Hospital (CM, 48 beds), 800 S. Fillmore St., Osceola 50213; tel. 515/342-2184; Timothy F. Weyers, adm.

Mahaska County Hospital (CM, 53 beds), 1229 C Ave. E., Oskaloosa 52577; tel. 515/673-3431; David E. Rutter, adm.

Dallas County Hospital (CM, 53 beds), Tenth & Iowa Sts., Perry 50220; tel. 515/465-3547; William M. Deets, adm.

Owned, leased, sponsored:	1 hospitals	680 beds
Contract-managed:	4 hospitals	203 beds
Totals:	5 hospitals	883 beds

For explanation of codes following names, see page B2.
*Indicates Type III membership in the American Hospital Association.

***1015: JOHNS HOPKINS HEALTH SYSTEM** (NP)
600 N. Wolfe St., Baltimore, MD 21205; 301/955-1488;
Robert M. Heyssel MD, pres.

Maryland: Francis Scott Key Medical Center (O, 602 beds), 4940 Eastern Ave., Baltimore 21224; tel. 301/955-0120; Ronald R. Peterson, pres.

Johns Hopkins Hospital (L, 940 beds), 600 N. Wolfe St., Baltimore 21205; tel. 301/955-5000; Albert H. Owens Jr. MD, pres.

North Charles Hospital (O, 182 beds), 2724 N. Charles St., Baltimore 21218; tel. 301/338-2000; Irwin P. Bloom, pres.

Wyman Park Medical Center (O, 135 beds), 3100 Wyman Park Dr., Baltimore 21211; tel. 301/338-3000; Patrick H. Mattingly MD, pres.

Owned, leased, sponsored:	4 hospitals	1859 beds
Contract-managed:	0 hospitals	0 beds
Totals:	4 hospitals	1859 beds

0435: JUPITER HOSPITAL CORPORATION (IO)
249 E. Ocean Blvd., Long Beach, CA 90802;
213/437-7717; Bernard Broermann, chm.

California: Anaheim General Hospital (O, 99 beds), 3350 W. Ball Rd., Anaheim 92804; tel. 714/827-6700; Brad H. Jeffrey, exec. dir.

Bellflower Doctors Hospital (O, 163 beds), 9542 E. Artesia Blvd., Bellflower 90706; tel. 213/925-8355; Dennis Cheshire, adm.

Buena Park Doctors Hospital (O, 58 beds), 5742 Beach Blvd., Buena Park 90621; tel. 714/521-4770; David A. Robinson, adm.

Hawthorne Hospital (O, 73 beds), 13300 S. Hawthorne Blvd., Hawthorne 90250; tel. 213/679-3321; R. Kupferstein, adm.

Florida: Las Olas Community Hospital (O, 64 beds), 1516 E. Las Olas Blvd., Fort Lauderdale 33301; Mailing Address Box 030400, Fort Lauderdale, Zip 33303; tel.305/764-8900; Robert D. Kerley, adm.

Georgia: Atlanta Hospital (O, 72 beds), 705 Juniper St. N.E., Atlanta 30365; tel. 404/873-2871; Lewis A. Ransdell, adm.

Owned, leased, sponsored:	6 hospitals	529 beds
Contract-managed:	0 hospitals	0 beds
Totals:	6 hospitals	529 beds

***2105: KAISER FOUNDATION HOSPITALS** (NP)
One Kaiser Plaza, Oakland, CA 94612; 415/271-5910;
James A. Vohs, chm. & pres.

California: Kaiser Foundation Hospital (O, 178 beds), 441 N. Lakeview Ave., Anaheim 92807; tel. 714/978-4000; Patricia B. Siegel, adm.

Kaiser Foundation Hospital (O, 364 beds), 9400 E. Rosecrans Ave., Bellflower 90706; tel. 213/920-4321; Charles W. Washington Jr., adm.

Kaiser Foundation Hospital (O, 436 beds), 9961 Sierra Ave., Fontana 92335; tel. 714/829-5000; Susan E. Garrison, adm.

Kaiser Foundation Hospital (O, 231 beds), 25825 S. Vermont Ave., Harbor City 90710; tel. 213/325-5111; James C. Heidenreich, adm.

Kaiser Foundation Hospital (O, 230 beds), 27400 Hesperian Blvd., Hayward 94545; tel. 415/784-4000; Ivan Fawley, adm.

Kaiser Foundation Hospital-West Los Angeles (O, 220 beds), 6041 Cadillac Ave., Los Angeles 90034; tel. 213/857-2201; Ophelia Long RN, adm.

Kaiser Foundation Hospital-Sunset (O, 613 beds), 4867 Sunset Blvd., Los Angeles 90027; tel. 213/667-4011; Joseph William Hummel, adm.

Kaiser Foundation Mental Health Center (O, 55 beds), 765 W. College St., Los Angeles 90012; tel. 213/250-8500; Jose A. Samartin, adm.

Kaiser Foundation Hospital (O, 113 beds), 200 Muir Rd., Martinez 94553; tel. 415/372-1000; Donald D. Nesbit, adm.

Kaiser Foundation Hospital (O, 245 beds), 280 W. MacArthur Blvd., Oakland 94611; tel. 415/428-5000; Thomas DeMartino, adm.

Kaiser Foundation Hospital (O, 331 beds), 13652 Cantara St., Panorama City 91402; tel. 818/908-2000; Nancy A. Nightingale, adm.

Kaiser Foundation Hospital (O, 150 beds), 1150 Veterans Blvd., Redwood City 94063; tel. 415/780-2000; Carolyn Kever, adm.

Kaiser Foundation Hospital (O, 40 beds), 1330 Cutting Blvd., Richmond 94804; tel. 415/231-4600; John Rawls, adm.

Kaiser Foundation Hospital (O, 336 beds), 2025 Morse Ave., Sacramento 95825; tel. 916/973-5000; Jerry Newman, adm.

Kaiser Foundation Hospital (O, 281 beds), 4647 Zion Ave., San Diego 92120; tel. 619/584-5000; Kenneth F. Colling, adm.

Kaiser Foundation Hospital (O, 273 beds), 2425 Geary Blvd., San Francisco 94115; tel. 415/929-4000; Frank D. Alvarez, adm.

Santa Teresa Community Hospital (O, 222 beds), 250 Hospital Pkwy., San Jose 95119; tel. 408/972-7000; John H. Chappell, adm.

Kaiser Foundation Hospital-San Rafael (O, 119 beds), 99 Montecillo Rd., San Rafael 94903; tel. 415/499-2000; Patrice Dowd, adm.

Kaiser Foundation Hospital (O, 320 beds), 900 Kiely Blvd., Santa Clara 95051; tel. 408/985-4000; Thomas R. Seifert, adm.

Kaiser Foundation Hospital (O, 120 beds), 1200 El Camino Real, South San Francisco 94080; tel. 415/742-2547; Joseph L. Meresman, adm.

Kaiser Foundation Hospital and Rehabilitation Center (O, 231 beds), 975 Sereno Dr., Vallejo 94589; tel. 707/648-6000; Steve Williams, adm.

Kaiser Foundation Hospital (O, 179 beds), 1425 S. Main St., Walnut Creek 94596; tel. 415/943-2000; Kenneth P. Kentch, adm.

Hawaii: Kaiser Foundation Hospital (O, 158 beds), 3288 Moanalua Rd., Honolulu 96819; tel. 808/834-5333; Ronald J. Mikolajczyk, adm.

Ohio: Kaiser Foundation Hospital-Parma (O, 61 beds), 12301 Snow Rd., Parma 44130; tel. 216/362-2000; A. Linwood, adm.

Oregon: Kaiser Sunnyside Medical Center (O, 155 beds), 10200 S.E. Sunnyside Rd., Clackamas 97015; tel. 503/652-2880; Kay Schweickart, area adm.

Bess Kaiser Medical Center (O, 202 beds), 5055 N. Greeley Ave., Portland 97217; tel. 503/285-9321; Ken Myers, area adm.

Owned, leased, sponsored:	26 hospitals	5863 beds
Contract-managed:	0 hospitals	0 beds
Totals:	26 hospitals	5863 beds

***0995: KENNESTONE REGIONAL HEALTH CARE SYSTEMS** (NP)
677 Church St., Marietta, GA 30060; 404/428-2000;
Bernard L. Brown Jr., exec. dir.

Georgia: Kennestone Hospital (O, 517 beds), 677 Church St., Marietta 30060; tel. 404/428-2000; Bernard L. Brown Jr., adm.

Kennestone Hospital at Windy Hill (O, 85 beds), 2540 Windy Hill Rd., Marietta 30067; tel. 404/951-3100; John Richards, adm.

Owned, leased, sponsored:	2 hospitals	602 beds
Contract-managed:	0 hospitals	0 beds
Totals:	2 hospitals	602 beds

***2245: LHS CORPORATION** (NP)
1423 S. Grand Ave., Los Angeles, CA 90015;
213/748-0191; Samuel J. Tibbitts, pres.

California: Martin Luther Hospital Medical Center (O, 200 beds), 1830 W. Romneya Dr., Anaheim 92801; Mailing Address Box 3304, Anaheim, Zip 92803; tel. 714/491-5200; GeorgeH. Mack, pres. & exec. dir.

Lakeside Community Hospital (CM, 35 beds), 5176 Hill Rd. E., P O Box 729, Lakeport 95453; tel. 707/263-5651; Will Sellers, adm.

California Medical Center-Los Angeles (O, 278 beds), 1414 S. Hope St., Los Angeles 90015; tel. 213/748-2411; William F. Haug, pres.

University of Southern California-Kenneth Norris Jr. Cancer Hospital (CM, 45 beds), 1441 Eastlake Ave., P O Box 33804, Los Angeles 90033; tel. 213/224-6600; G.Peter Shostak, adm.

Redlands Community Hospital (CM, 195 beds), 350 Terracina Blvd., Box 3391, Redlands 92373; tel. 714/793-3101; George A. DeLange, pres.

For explanation of codes following names, see page B2.
*Indicates Type III membership in the American Hospital Association.

Ralph K. Davies Medical Center-Franklin Hospital (CM, 161 beds), Castro & Duboce Sts., San Francisco 94114; tel. 415/565-6779; George D. Monardo, pres.

Santa Monica Hospital Medical Center (O, 285 beds), 1225 15th St., Santa Monica 90404; tel. 213/319-4000; Leonard Labella Jr., pres. & exec. dir.

Henry Mayo Newhall Memorial Hospital (CM, 133 beds), 23845 W. McBean Pkwy., Valencia 91355; tel. 805/253-8000; Duffy Watson, pres.

Owned, leased, sponsored:	3 hospitals	763 beds
Contract-managed:	5 hospitals	569 beds
Totals:	8 hospitals	1332 beds

***2295: LITTLE COMPANY OF MARY SISTERS HEALTHCARE SYSTEMS** (CC)
9350 S. California Ave., Evergreen Park, IL 60642; 312/422-6200; Sr. Sharon Ann Walsh, prov. supr.

California: Little Company of Mary Hospital (O, 239 beds), 4101 Torrance Blvd., Torrance 90503; tel. 213/540-7676; James C. Lester, pres.

Illinois: Little Company of Mary Hospital (O, 386 beds), 2800 W. 95th St., Evergreen Park 60642; tel. 312/422-6200; Paul R. Wozniak, pres.

Indiana: Memorial Hospital and Health Care Center (O, 131 beds), 800 W. Ninth St., Jasper 47546; tel. 812/482-2345; Herman Kohlman, pres.

Owned, leased, sponsored:	3 hospitals	756 beds
Contract-managed:	0 hospitals	0 beds
Totals:	3 hospitals	756 beds

5755: LOS ANGELES COUNTY-DEPARTMENT OF HEALTH SERVICES (NP)
313 N. Figueroa St., Room 936, Los Angeles, CA 90012; 213/974-8101; Robert C. Gates, dir. health

California: Lac-Rancho Los Amigos Medical Center (O, 435 beds), 7601 E. Imperial Hwy., Downey 90242; tel. 213/940-7022; Armando Lopez Jr., exec. dir.

Lac-High Desert Hospital (O, 135 beds), 44900 N. 60th St. W., Lancaster 93536; tel. 805/945-8461; A. R. Fleischman, adm.

Lac County-King-Drew Medical Center (O, 396 beds), 12021 S. Wilmington Ave., Los Angeles 90059; tel. 213/603-5201; William A. Delgardo, adm.

Lac-University of Southern California Medical Center (O, 1454 beds), 1200 N. State St., Los Angeles 90033; tel. 213/226-2345; J. L. Buckingham, exec. dir.

Los Angeles County-Olive View Medical Center (O, 126 beds), 14445 Olive View Dr., Sylmar 91342; tel. 818/364-1555; Douglas D. Bagley, adm.

Lac-Harbor-University of California at Los Angeles Medical Center (O, 502 beds), 1000 W. Carson St., Torrance 90509; tel. 213/533-2101; Edward J. Foley, adm.

Owned, leased, sponsored:	6 hospitals	3048 beds
Contract-managed:	0 hospitals	0 beds
Totals:	6 hospitals	3048 beds

***6295: LUTHERAN GENERAL HEALTH CARE SYSTEMS** (CO)
1775 Dempster St., Park Ridge, IL 60068; 312/696-5600; George B. Caldwell, pres.

Illinois: Augustana Hospital and Health Care Center (O, 330 beds), 2035 N. Lincoln Ave., Chicago 60614; tel. 312/975-5000; David Jensen, pres.

Lutheran General Hospital (O, 587 beds), 1775 Dempster St., Park Ridge 60068; tel. 312/696-2210; Roger S. Hunt, pres. & chief exec. off.

Parkside Lutheran Hospital (O, 88 beds), 1700 Luther Lane, Park Ridge 60068; tel. 312/696-6050; Rev. John E. Keller, exec. dir.

Owned, leased, sponsored:	3 hospitals	1005 beds
Contract-managed:	0 hospitals	0 beds
Totals:	3 hospitals	1005 beds

***2235: LUTHERAN HOSPITALS AND HOMES SOCIETY OF AMERICA** (NP)
1202 Westrac Dr., Box 2087, Fargo, ND 58107; 701/293-9053; Michael O. Bice, pres. & chief exec. off.

Alaska: Fairbanks Memorial Hospital (L, 156 beds), 1650 Cowles St., Fairbanks 99701; tel. 907/452-8181; Philip Koon, adm.

Kodiak Island Hospital (CM, 44 beds), 1915 E. Rezanoff Dr., Kodiak 99615; tel. 907/486-3281; James H. Gingerich, adm.

Central Peninsula General Hospital (CM, 46 beds), 250 Hospital Pl., Soldotna 99669; tel. 907/262-4404; Michael J. Lockwood, adm.

Valdez Community Hospital (CM, 15 beds), 911 Meals Ave., Box 550, Valdez 99686; tel. 907/835-2249; Cathy Ringstad Winfree, adm.

Arizona: Mesa Lutheran Hospital (O, 375 beds), 525 W. Brown Rd., Mesa 85201; tel. 602/834-1211; Richard Probst, chief exec. off.

Valley Lutheran Hospital (O, 120 beds), 6644 Baywood Ave., Mesa 85206; tel. 602/981-2000; Charles R. Brackney, adm.

Colorado: Washington County Public Hospital (L, 19 beds), 465 Main St., Akron 80720; tel. 303/345-2211; Terry Hoffart, adm.

East Morgan County Hospital (L, 29 beds), 2400 Edison St., Box 565, Brush 80723; tel. 303/842-5151; Keith Mesmer, adm.

McKee Medical Center (O, 105 beds), 2000 Boise Ave., Loveland 80537; tel. 303/669-4640; Craig J. Broman, adm.

Logan County Hospital (L, 98 beds), 615 Fairhurst St., Box 3500, Sterling 80751; tel. 303/522-0122; Brian C. Larson, adm.

Kansas: St. Luke Hospital (L, 25 beds), 1014 E. Melvin St., Marion 66861; tel. 316/382-2179; Craig J. Hanson, adm.

Decatur County Hospital (L, 62 beds), 810 W. Columbia St., Oberlin 67749; tel. 913/475-2208; Charles P. Myers, adm.

Minnesota: Pelican Valley Health Center (CM, 59 beds), 211 E. Mill St., Pelican Rapids 56572; tel. 218/863-3111; Charles F. Harms, adm.

Montana: Teton Medical Center (L, 46 beds), 915 Fourth St. N.W., Box 820, Choteau 59422; tel. 406/466-5763; Richard P. Spilovoy, adm.

Pondera Medical Center (CM, 112 beds), 805 Sunset Blvd., Box 757, Conrad 59425; tel. 406/278-3211; Norman R. Campeau, adm.

Powell County Memorial Hospital (L, 35 beds), 1101 Texas Ave., Deer Lodge 59722; tel. 406/846-2212; Jon Frantsvog, adm.

Wheatland Memorial Hospital (CM, 56 beds), 530 Third St. N.W., Box 287, Harlowton 59036; tel. 406/632-4351; John H. Johnson, adm.

Carbon County Memorial Hospital (O, 52 beds), 600 W. 20th St., Box 580, Red Lodge 59068; tel. 406/446-2345; Mark Teckmeyer, adm.

Prairie Community Hospital (CM, 20 beds), 312 S. Adams Ave., Box 156, Terry 59349; tel. 406/637-5511; Earl K. Paulson, adm.

Mountainview Memorial Hospital (CM, 37 beds), 16 W. Main St., Box Q, White Sulphur Springs 59645; tel. 406/547-3321; M. E. Bedsaul, adm.

Nebraska: Cambridge Memorial Hospital (L, 67 beds), W. Hwy. 6 & 34, Cambridge 69022; tel. 308/697-3329; Don Harpst, adm.

Lundberg Memorial Hospital (L, 38 beds), Box 167, Creighton 68729; tel. 402/358-3322; Linda J. Neese, adm.

Thayer County Memorial Hospital (L, 18 beds), 120 Park Ave., P O Box 49, Hebron 68370; tel. 402/768-6041; Marilyn N. Cooper, adm.

Oakland Memorial Hospital (L, 23 beds), 601 E. Second St., Oakland 68045; tel. 402/685-5601; Craig Hanson, adm.

Pender Community Hospital (L, 39 beds), 603 Earl St., Box 100, Pender 68047; tel. 402/385-3083; Kenneth D. Olsson, adm.

For explanation of codes following names, see page B2.
*Indicates Type III membership in the American Hospital Association.

New Mexico: Union County General Hospital (L, 30 beds), 301 Harding St., Box 489, Clayton 88415; tel. 505/374-2585; Doris B. Turgeon, adm.

Los Alamos Medical Center (O, 80 beds), 3917 West Rd., Los Alamos 87544; tel. 505/662-4201; Paul J. Wilson, adm.

North Dakota: Pembina County Memorial Hospital (L, 53 beds), 205 E. Third Ave., Cavalier 58220; tel. 701/265-8461; Jim Manlin, adm.

Community Memorial Hospital (O, 70 beds), 905 Main St., Lisbon 58054; tel. 701/683-5241; Wendell Rawlings, adm.

Wishek Community Hospital (CM, 31 beds), 315 Tenth St. S., P O Box 647, Wishek 58495; tel. 701/452-2326; Roger L. Salisbury, adm.

South Dakota: Deuel County Memorial Hospital (L, 20 beds), 701 Third Ave. S., Clear Lake 57226; tel. 605/874-2141; Bruce L. Davidson, adm.

Gregory Community Hospital (O, 90 beds), 400 Park St., Box 408, Gregory 57533; tel. 605/835-8394; Terry E. Davis, adm.

Southern Hills General Hospital (O, 74 beds), 209 N. 16th St., Hot Springs 57747; tel. 605/745-3159; Ronald J. Cork, adm.

Lookout Memorial Hospital (O, 35 beds), 1440 N. Main St., Spearfish 57783; tel. 605/642-2617; Glenn Bryant, adm.

Wyoming: Johnson County Memorial Hospital (L, 83 beds), 497 W. Lott St., Buffalo 82834; tel. 307/684-5521; Jerry E. Jurena, adm.

Niobrara County Memorial Hospital (L, 51 beds), 939 Ballencee Ave., Box 780, Lusk 82225; tel. 307/334-2711; Craig E. Aasved, adm.

Powell Hospital (L, 113 beds), 777 Ave. H, Powell 82435; tel. 307/754-2267; R. D. Cozzens, adm.

Community Hospital (O, 53 beds), 2000 Campbell Dr., Torrington 82240; tel. 307/532-4181; Jim D. Lebrun, adm.

Platte County Memorial Hospital (L, 43 beds), 201 14th St., Wheatland 82201; tel. 307/322-3636; Duaine C. Kanwischer, adm.

Washakie Memorial Hospital (L, 36 beds), 400 S. 15th St., Box 700, Worland 82401; tel. 307/347-3221; Howard Megorden, adm.

Owned, leased, sponsored:	31 hospitals	2138 beds
Contract-managed:	9 hospitals	420 beds
Totals:	40 hospitals	2558 beds

---

*7775: MAIN LINE HEALTH, INC. (NP)
259 Radnor-Chester Rd., Suite 290, Radnor, PA 19087; 215/254-8840; Ralph F. Moriarty, pres.

Pennsylvania: Bryn Mawr Hospital (O, 349 beds), Bryn Mawr Ave., Bryn Mawr 19010; tel. 215/896-3000; Carl I. Bergkvist, pres.

Bryn Mawr Rehabilitation Hospital (O, 92 beds), 414 Paoli Pike, Malvern 19355; tel. 215/251-5400; Thomas M. Nojunas, exec. vice-pres.

Paoli Memorial Hospital (O, 188 beds), Lancaster Pike, Paoli 19301; tel. 215/648-1000; William Michael Tomlinson, pres.

Lankenau Hospital (O, 403 beds), Lancaster Ave. W. of City Line, Philadelphia 19151; tel. 215/645-2000; Ralph F. Moriarty, pres.

Owned, leased, sponsored:	4 hospitals	1032 beds
Contract-managed:	0 hospitals	0 beds
Totals:	4 hospitals	1032 beds

1335: MEASE HEALTH CARE (NP)
833 Milwaukee Ave., P O Box 760, Dunedin, FL 33528; 813/733-1111; Donald M. Schroder, pres. & chief exec. off.

Florida: Mease Hospital Dunedin (O, 199 beds), 833 Milwaukee Ave., Dunedin 33528; Mailing Address P O Box 760, Dunedin, Zip 34296; tel. 813/733-1111; Charles T. Frock,vice-pres. & adm.

Mease Hospital Countryside (O, 70 beds), 3231 McMullen-Booth Rd., Safety Harbor 33572; tel. 813/725-6222; Richard H. Katzeff, vice-pres.

Owned, leased, sponsored:	2 hospitals	269 beds
Contract-managed:	0 hospitals	0 beds
Totals:	2 hospitals	269 beds

3825: MEDIQ, INC. (IO)
One Mediq Plaza, Pennsauken, NJ 08110; 609/665-9300; Bernard Korman, pres.

Pennsylvania: Ashland State General Hospital (CM, 161 beds), Rte. 61, Ashland 17921; tel. 717/875-2000; John David Francis, adm.

Bloomsburg Hospital (CM, 133 beds), 549 E. Fair St., Bloomsburg 17815; tel. 717/387-2100; Robert Spinelli, adm.

Nesbitt Memorial Hospital (CM, 215 beds), 562 Wyoming Ave., Kingston 18704; tel. 717/288-1411; Ron Stern, adm.

Scranton State General Hospital (CM, 176 beds), 205 Mulberry St., Scranton 18501; tel. 717/963-4211; Susan E. Bruce, adm.

Owned, leased, sponsored:	0 hospitals	0 beds
Contract-managed:	4 hospitals	685 beds
Totals:	4 hospitals	685 beds

---

*6615: MEDLANTIC HEALTHCARE GROUP (NP)
100 Irving St. N.W., Washington, DC 20010; 202/541-6006; John P. McDaniel, pres.

District of Columbia: Capitol Hill Hospital (O, 250 beds), 700 Constitution Ave. N.E., Washington 20002; tel. 202/269-8000; William J. Haire, pres. & chief exec. off.

Columbia Hospital for Women Medical Center (O, 189 beds), 2425 L St. N.W., Washington 20037; tel. 202/293-6500; G. Patrick Kane, pres.

Washington Hospital Center (O, 784 beds), 110 Irving St. N.W., Washington 20010; tel. 202/541-0500; Dunlop Ecker, pres.

Owned, leased, sponsored:	3 hospitals	1223 beds
Contract-managed:	0 hospitals	0 beds
Totals:	3 hospitals	1223 beds

2645: MEMORIAL CARE SYSTEMS (NP)
7777 Southwest Fwy, Suite 100, Houston, TX 77074; 713/776-6992; Dan S. Wilford, pres.

Texas: Matagorda General Hospital (CM, 90 beds), 1115 Ave. G, Bay City 77414; tel. 409/245-6383; Shannon C. Flynn, chief exec. off.

Memorial Hospital -El Campo (L, 41 beds), 303 Sandy Corner Rd., Box 1568, El Campo 77437; tel. 409/543-6251; Wendell Porth, chief exec. off.

Memorial Hospital System (O, 975 beds), Donald B. Wagner, vice-pres. & adm.

Northeast Medical Center Hospital (S, 195 beds), 18951 Memorial N., Humble 77338; tel. 713/540-7801; Monty E. McLaurin, adm.

Wagner General Hospital (CM, 35 beds), 310 Green St., Box 859, Palacios 77465; tel. 512/972-2511; Donald G. Hyett, adm.

Polly Ryon Memorial Hospital (CM, 109 beds), 1705 Jackson St., Richmond 77469; tel. 713/342-2811; Harold F. Taylor, adm.

Owned, leased, sponsored:	3 hospitals	1211 beds
Contract-managed:	3 hospitals	234 beds
Totals:	6 hospitals	1445 beds

---

*5155: MERCY HEALTH CARE SYSTEM (CC)
2303 Grandview Ave., Cincinnati, OH 45206; 513/221-2736; Sr. M. Michaeleen, pres. & chief exec. off.

Kentucky: Marcum and Wallace Memorial Hospital (S, 26 beds), 201 Richmond Rd., Irvine 40336; tel. 606/723-2115; Daniel F. Sheehan, adm.

Mercy Hospital (S, 125 beds), 1006 Ford Ave., Owensboro 42301; Mailing Address P O Box 2839, Owensboro, Zip 42302; tel. 502/685-5181; Gerald J. Lagesse, pres.

For explanation of codes following names, see page B2.
*Indicates Type III membership in the American Hospital Association.

Ohio: Clermont Mercy Hospital (S, 133 beds), 3000 Hospital Dr., Batavia 45103; tel. 513/732-8200; Sr. Mary George RN, pres.

Our Lady of Mercy Hospital (S, 198 beds), Rowan Hills Dr., Cincinnati 45227; tel. 513/527-5500; Sr. Marjorie Bosse, pres.

Mercy Hospital (S, 317 beds), 100 Riverfront Plaza, Hamilton 45011; Mailing Address Box 418, Hamilton, Zip 45012; tel. 513/867-6400; Sr. Mary Rene Mullen, pres.

St. Rita's Medical Center (S, 376 beds), 730 W. Market St., Lima 45801; tel. 419/227-3361; Sr. Rita Mary Wasserman, pres.

St. Charles Hospital (S, 342 beds), 2600 Navarre Ave., Oregon 43616; tel. 419/698-7200; Sr. Phyllis Ann Gerold, exec. dir.

Mercy Medical Center (S, 337 beds), 1343 N. Fountain Blvd., Springfield 45501; tel. 513/390-5000; Jerrold A. Maki, exec. vice-pres. & chief oper. off.

Mercy Hospital (S, 95 beds), 485 W. Market St., Box 727, Tiffin 44883; tel. 419/447-3130; Sr. Marie Catherine Wise, pres.

Mercy Hospital (S, 350 beds), 2200 Jefferson Ave., Toledo 43624; tel. 419/259-1500; Sr. Phyllis Ann Gerold, pres.

Mercy Memorial Hospital (S, 73 beds), 904 Scioto St., Urbana 43078; tel. 513/653-5231; Robert E. Morrison, pres.

Tennessee: St. Mary's Medical Center (S, 510 beds), Oak Hill Ave., Knoxville 37917; tel. 615/971-7836; L. Lynn Nipper, pres.

St. Mary's North Hospital (S, 20 beds), 901 S. Main St., Lake City 37769; tel. 615/426-7455; Anne Loggans, adm.

Owned, leased, sponsored:	13 hospitals	2902 beds
Contract-managed:	0 hospitals	0 beds
Totals:	13 hospitals	2902 beds

***5195: MERCY HEALTH CARE SYSTEM** (CC)
Mercy Center, Lake St., Box 370, Dallas, PA 18612; 717/675-3535; William D. McGuire, pres. & chief exec. off.

Pennsylvania: Mercy Hospital of Johnstown (O, 218 beds), 1020 Franklin St., Johnstown 15905; tel. 814/533-1000; T. R. Baranik, pres.

Nanticoke State General Hospital (CM, 82 beds), W. Washington St., Nanticoke 18634; tel. 717/735-5000; Thomas J. Graham, adm.

Mercy Hospital of Scranton (O, 365 beds), 746 Jefferson Ave., Scranton 18501; tel. 717/348-7100; Sr. William Joseph, pres.

Mercy Hospital of Wilkes-Barre (O, 235 beds), 25 Church St., Box 658, Wilkes-Barre 18765; tel. 717/826-3100; Henry J. Morris, interim pres. & chief exec. off.

Owned, leased, sponsored:	3 hospitals	818 beds
Contract-managed:	1 hospitals	82 beds
Totals:	4 hospitals	900 beds

5545: MERCY HEALTH SYSTEMS WESTERN NEW YORK (CC)
565 Abbott Rd., Buffalo, NY 14220; 716/827-2375; Sr. Mary Annunciate, pres.

New York: St. Jerome Hospital (O, 106 beds), 16 Bank St., Batavia 14020; tel. 716/343-3131; Sr. Margaret Mary, adm.

Mercy Hospital (O, 453 beds), 565 Abbott Rd., Buffalo 14220; tel. 716/826-7000; Sr. Sheila Marie, adm.

Kenmore Mercy Hospital (O, 324 beds), 2950 Elmwood Ave., Kenmore 14217; tel. 716/879-6100; Sr. Mary Joel, adm.

Owned, leased, sponsored:	3 hospitals	883 beds
Contract-managed:	0 hospitals	0 beds
Totals:	3 hospitals	883 beds

5215: MERCY-CHICAGO PROVINCE HEALTHCARE SYSTEMS (CC)
1s450 Summit Ave., Oakbrook Terrance, IL 60181; 312/953-2970; Catherine C. Gallagher, exec. dir.

Illinois: Mercy Center for Health Care Services (O, 334 beds), 1325 N. Highland Ave., Aurora 60506; tel. 312/859-2222; Sr. Rita Meagher, pres.

Mercy Hospital and Medical Center (O, 502 beds), Stevenson Expwy. at King Dr., Chicago 60616; tel. 312/567-2000; Sr. Sheila Lyne, pres.

Iowa: Mercy Hospital (O, 265 beds), W. Central Park at Marquette, Box 4110, Davenport 52804; tel. 319/383-1000; H. Gerald Smith, pres. & chief exec. off.

Mercy Hospital (O, 240 beds), 500 Market St., Iowa City 52240; tel. 319/337-0500; Sr. Mary Venarda, chief exec. off.

Owned, leased, sponsored:	4 hospitals	1341 beds
Contract-managed:	0 hospitals	0 beds
Totals:	4 hospitals	1341 beds

***8835: MERIDIA HEALTH SYSTEM** (NP)
767 Beta Dr., Suite E., Mayfield Village, OH 44143; 216/449-7710; Robert Moss, pres.

Ohio: Huron Road Hospital (O, 387 beds), 13951 Terrace Rd., Cleveland 44112; tel. 216/761-3300; Sandra H. Austin, sr. vice-pres. & chief oper. off.

Euclid General Hospital (O, 345 beds), 18901 Lake Shore Blvd., Euclid 44119; tel. 216/531-9000; Emil E. Hornack Jr., sr. vice-pres. & chief oper. off.

Hillcrest Hospital (O, 305 beds), 6780 Mayfield Rd., Mayfield Heights 44124; tel. 216/449-4500; David H. Plate, pres. & chief oper. off.

Suburban Community Hospital (O, 180 beds), 4180 Warrensville Center Rd., Warrensville Heights 44122; tel. 216/491-6000; Matthew C. Gresko, sr. vice-pres. & chiefoper. off.

Owned, leased, sponsored:	4 hospitals	1217 beds
Contract-managed:	0 hospitals	0 beds
Totals:	4 hospitals	1217 beds

0685: MERRITT PERALTA MEDICAL CENTER (NP)
Hawthorne Ave. & Webster St., Oakland, CA 94609; 415/451-4900; Richard J. McCann, pres. & chief exec. off.

California: Delta Memorial Hospital (O, 53 beds), 3901 Lone Tree Way, P O Box 1469, Antioch 94509; tel. 415/757-1700; Lee Domanico, pres. & chief exec. off.

Peralta Hospital (O, 86 beds), 450 30th St., Oakland 94609; Mailing Address P O Box 23010, Oakland, Zip 94623; tel. 415/451-4900; Ronald A. Pavellas, adm.

Samuel Merritt Hospital (O, 256 beds), Hawthorne Ave. & Webster St., Oakland 94609; tel. 415/655-4000; Ronald A. Pavellas, adm.

Owned, leased, sponsored:	3 hospitals	395 beds
Contract-managed:	0 hospitals	0 beds
Totals:	3 hospitals	395 beds

***7235: METHODIST HEALTH CARE NETWORK** (CO)
5615 Kirby Dr., Suite 800, Houston, TX 77005; 713/831-2900; Michael Williamson, pres. & chief oper. off.; Larry L. Mathis, bd. chm. & chief exec. off.

Louisiana: Lafayette General Medical Center (CM, 214 beds), 1214 Coolidge Ave., Box 52009 OCS, Lafayette 70505; tel. 318/261-7991; John J. Burdin Jr., exec. vice-pres.

Texas: San Jacinto Methodist Hospital (O, 138 beds), 1101 Decker Dr., Baytown 77520; tel. 713/420-8600; Russ Schneider, adm.

Medical Center Hospital (CM, 152 beds), 504 Medical Center Blvd., Box 1538, Conroe 77305; tel. 713/539-1111; John Single, adm.

Henderson Memorial Hospital (CM, 86 beds), 300 Wilson St., Henderson 75652; tel. 214/657-7541; Ronald J. Clifford, chief exec. off.

The Methodist Hospital (O, 1172 beds), 6565 Fannin, Houston 77030; tel. 713/790-3311; Larry L. Mathis, pres. & chief exec. off.

Nan Travis Memorial Hospital (O, 130 beds), 501 S. Ragsdale St., Jacksonville 75766; tel. 214/586-9881; Thomas M. Kish, pres.

Memorial Hospital (CM, 204 beds), 1204 Mound St., Nacogdoches 75961; tel. 409/564-4611; Don Crow, adm.

For explanation of codes following names, see page B2.
*Indicates Type III membership in the American Hospital Association.

Mainland Center Hospital (CM, 310 beds), 6601 Fm 1764, Box 2756, Texas City 77592; tel. 409/938-5000; Edward J. Smith, pres.

Tomball Regional Hospital (CM, 140 beds), 605 Holderrieth St., Box 889, Tomball 77375; tel. 713/351-1623; Robert F. Schaper, adm.

Citizens Medical Center (CM, 235 beds), 2701 Hospital Dr., Victoria 77901; tel. 512/573-9181; David P. Brown, adm.

Owned, leased, sponsored:	3 hospitals	1440 beds
Contract-managed:	7 hospitals	1341 beds
Totals:	10 hospitals	2781 beds

***8875: METHODIST HEALTH SERVICES CORPORATION** (NP)
221 N.E. Glen Oak Ave., Peoria, IL 61636; 309/672-4826; James K. Knoble, pres.; Daniel P. Chonowski, exec. vice-pres.

Illinois: Fairbury Hospital (CM, 117 beds), 519 S. Fifth St., Fairbury 61739; tel. 815/692-2346; John L. Tummons PhD, adm.

Community Memorial Hospital (CM, 86 beds), 1000 W. Harlem Ave., Monmouth 61462; tel. 309/734-3141; David M. Coates PhD, pres.

Methodist Medical Center of Illinois (O, 479 beds), 221 N.E. Glen Oak Ave., Peoria 61636; tel. 309/672-5522; James K. Knoble, pres.

Illinois Valley Community Hospital (CM, 108 beds), 925 West St., Peru 61354; tèl. 815/223-3300; Ralph B. Berkley, adm.

Owned, leased, sponsored:	1 hospitals	479 beds
Contract-managed:	3 hospitals	311 beds
Totals:	4 hospitals	790 beds

2715: METHODIST HEALTH SYSTEM (CO)
580 W. Eighth St., Jacksonville, FL 32209; 904/798-8000; Marcus Drewa, pres.

Florida: Clay Memorial Hospital (CM, 60 beds), Oak & Green Sts., Box 808, Green Cove Springs 32043; tel. 904/284-3072; Thomas¢

Methodist Hospital (O, 244 beds), 580 W. Eighth St., Jacksonville 32209; tel. 904/798-8000; Marcus E. Drewa, pres.

Owned, leased, sponsored:	1 hospitals	244 beds
Contract-managed:	1 hospitals	60 beds
Totals:	2 hospitals	304 beds

***9345: METHODIST HEALTH SYSTEMS, INC.** (CO)
1211 Union Ave., Suite 700, Memphis, TN 38104; 901/726-2300; John T. Casey, pres.

Arkansas: Methodist Hospital of Jonesboro (O, 98 beds), 3024 Stadium Blvd., Jonesboro 72401; tel. 501/972-7000; Philip H. Walkley Jr., adm.

Mississippi: Methodist Hospital of Middle Mississippi (L, 84 beds), Box 641, Zip 39095; tel. 601/834-1321; Frank Jones, adm.

Tennessee: Methodist Hospital of Dyersburg (O, 225 beds), 400 Tickle St., Dyersburg 38024; tel. 901/285-2410; Randall Hoover, adm.

Methodist Hospital of Lexington (O, 42 beds), Church St., Box 160, Lexington 38351; tel. 901/968-3646; Dick Heflin, adm.

Methodist Hospital of McKenzie (O, 54 beds), 945 N. Highland, McKenzie 38201; tel. 901/352-5344; G. L. Miles, adm.

Methodist Hospital North-Jesse Harris Memorial Hospital (O, 162 beds), 3960 New Covington Pike, Memphis 38128; tel. 901/372-5200; Thomas H. Gee, vice-pres.

Methodist Hospital South-John R. Flippin Memorial Hospital (O, 164 beds), 1300 Wesley Dr., Memphis 38116; tel. 901/346-3700; James B. Hunter, vice-pres.

Methodist Hospital-Central Unit (O, 833 beds), 1265 Union Ave., Memphis 38104; tel. 901/726-7000; Judge T. Calton, pres.

Methodist Hospital of Somerville (O, 39 beds), 214 Lakeview Rd., Box 98, Somerville 38068; tel. 901/465-3594; Carlos Smith, adm.

Methodist Hospital of Middle Tennessee (O, 116 beds), Cowan Rd., Winchester 37398; tel. 615/967-8200; Thomas L. Harper, adm.

Owned, leased, sponsored:	10 hospitals	1817 beds
Contract-managed:	0 hospitals	0 beds
Totals:	10 hospitals	1817 beds

9335: METHODIST HOSPITAL OF INDIANA (CO)
1701 N. Senate Blvd., Indianapolis, IN 46202; 317/929-8510; Frank P. Lloyd MD, pres.

Indiana: Putnam County Hospital (CM, 85 beds), 1542 Bloomington St., Greencastle 46135; tel. 317/653-5121; John D. Fajt, exec. dir.

Methodist Hospital of Indiana (O, 1130 beds), 1701 N. Senate Blvd., P O Box 1367, Indianapolis 46206; tel. 317/924-6411; Frank Lloyd MD, pres. & chief exec. off.

Owned, leased, sponsored:	1 hospitals	1130 beds
Contract-managed:	1 hospitals	85 beds
Totals:	2 hospitals	1215 beds

***2735: METHODIST HOSPITALS OF DALLAS** (NP)
301 W. Colorado Blvd., Dallas, TX 75208; Mailing Address P O Box 655999, Dallas, Zip 75265; 214/944-8137; David H. Hitt, pres. & chief exec. off.

Texas: Charlton Methodist Hospital (O, 143 beds), 3500 Wheatland Rd., Box 225357, Dallas 75265; tel. 214/296-2511; Kim Holland, exec. dir. & vice-pres.

Methodist Medical Center (O, 404 beds), 301 W. Colorado Blvd., Dallas 75208; Mailing Address Box 225999, Dallas, Zip 75265; tel. 214/944-8181; John W. Carver,exec. dir. & sr. vice-pres.

Southeastern Methodist Hospital (O, 101 beds), 9202 Elam Rd., Dallas 75217; tel. 214/372-7600; Gene R. Barron, exec. dir. & vice-pres.

Owned, leased, sponsored:	3 hospitals	648 beds
Contract-managed:	0 hospitals	0 beds
Totals:	3 hospitals	648 beds

7995: METROPOLITAN HOSPITAL (NP)
801 Arch St., Fifth Floor, Philadelphia, PA 19107; 215/238-6700; Jack R. Dyson, actg. chief oper. off.

Pennsylvania: Metropolitan Hospital-Central Division (O, 184 beds), 201 N. Eighth St., Philadelphia 19106; tel. 215/238-2000; Robert V. Giardinelli, exec. dir.

Metropolitan Hospital-Parkview Division (O, 231 beds), 1331 E. Wyoming Ave., Philadelphia 19124; tel. 215/537-7400; Irvin Berland, exec. dir.

Metropolitan Hospital-Springfield Division (O, 122 beds), 190 W. Sproul Rd., Springfield 19064; tel. 215/328-8700; Gerald E. Pierson, exec. dir.

Owned, leased, sponsored:	3 hospitals	537 beds
Contract-managed:	0 hospitals	0 beds
Totals:	3 hospitals	537 beds

1615: MID FLORIDA MEDICAL SERVICES (IO)
200 Ave. F N.E., Winter Haven, FL 33880; 813/293-8226; Lance W. Annstasio, pres. & chief exec. off.

Florida: Morrow Memorial Hospital (CM, 40 beds), 105 Ariana Blvd., Box 277, Auburndale 33823; tel. 813/967-8511; Laurie McCraney, adm.

Heart of Florida Hospital (CM, 51 beds), Tenth St. & Wood Ave., Box 67, Haines City 33844; tel. 813/422-4971; Mary T. Erde, adm.

Winter Haven Hospital (O, 392 beds), 200 Ave. F N.E., Winter Haven 33881; tel. 813/293-1121; Lance W. Anastasio, adm.

Owned, leased, sponsored:	1 hospitals	392 beds
Contract-managed:	2 hospitals	91 beds
Totals:	3 hospitals	483 beds

6975: MILLS-PENINSULA HOSPITALS (NP)
50 S. San Mateo Dr., San Mateo, CA 94401; 415/579-2190; Charles H. Mason Jr., pres. & chief exec. off.

California: Peninsula Hospital and Medical Center (L, 310 beds), 1783 El Camino Real, Burlingame 94010; tel. 415/872-5400; Charles H. Mason Jr., pres. & chief exec. off.

For explanation of codes following names, see page B2.
*Indicates Type III membership in the American Hospital Association.

Mills Memorial Hospital (O, 344 beds), 100 S. San Mateo Dr., San Mateo 94401; tel. 415/579-2000; Charles H. Mason Jr., pres.

Owned, leased, sponsored:	2 hospitals	654 beds
Contract-managed:	0 hospitals	0 beds
Totals:	2 hospitals	654 beds

2855: MISSIONARY BENEDICTINE SISTERS AMERICAN PROVINCE (CC)
300 N. 18th St., Norfolk, NE 68701; 402/371-3438; Sr. Matilda Handl,

Minnesota: Holy Trinity Hospital (O, 40 beds), 115 W. Second St., Graceville 56240; tel. 612/748-7223; Sr. M. Paula Leick, adm.

Nebraska: Our Lady of Lourdes Hospital (O, 83 beds), 1500 Koenigstein Ave., Norfolk 68701; tel. 402/371-3402; Carl I. Maltas, adm.

Providence Medical Center (O, 31 beds), 1200 Providence Rd., Wayne 68787; tel. 402/375-3800; Marcile Thomas, adm.

Owned, leased, sponsored:	3 hospitals	154 beds
Contract-managed:	0 hospitals	0 beds
Totals:	3 hospitals	154 beds

2475: MISSISSIPPI COUNTY HOSPITAL SYSTEM (NP)
Box 108, Blytheville, AR 72315; 501/762-3300; William E. Peaks, adm.

Arkansas: Mississippi County Hospitals (O, 168 beds), Division & Highland Sts., Box 108, Blytheville 72315; tel. 501/762-3300; William Peaks, adm.

Osceola Memorial Hospital (O, 82 beds), 611 W. Lee Ave., Box 607, Osceola 72370; tel. 501/563-7000; Tommy L. Hatcher, vice-pres. & chief oper. off.

Owned, leased, sponsored:	2 hospitals	250 beds
Contract-managed:	0 hospitals	0 beds
Totals:	2 hospitals	250 beds

***6555: MULTICARE MEDICAL CENTER** (NP)
409 S. J St., P O Box 5277, Tacoma, WA 98405; 206/594-1251; W. Barry Connoley, pres.

Washington: Mary Bridge Children's Health Center (O, 58 beds), 311 S. L St., Box 5299, Tacoma 98405; tel. 206/594-1400; Charles Hoffman, adm.

Tacoma General Hospital (O, 310 beds), 315 S. K St., P O Box 5299, Tacoma 98405; tel. 206/594-1000; Charles F. Hoffman, exec. vice-pres. & adm.

Owned, leased, sponsored:	2 hospitals	368 beds
Contract-managed:	0 hospitals	0 beds
Totals:	2 hospitals	368 beds

5895: NATIONAL HEALTHCARE, INC. (IO)
444 N. Oates St., P O Box 1649, Dothan, AL 36302; 205/793-2399; Steve L. Phelps, pres. & chief exec. off.

Alabama: Central Alabama Community Hospital (O, 60 beds), 1010 Lay Dam Rd., Clanton 35045; tel. 205/755-2500; Michael C. Marshman, adm.

Lakeshore Community Hospital (L, 46 beds), Rte. 4, Box 8, Dadeville 36853; tel. 205/825-7821; Nancy Klinger, adm.

Southeast Alabama Medical Center (CM, 400 beds), Hwy. 84 E., P O Drawer 6987, Dothan 36302; tel. 205/793-8111; James R. Blackmon, adm.

Elba General Hospital (L, 122 beds), 987 Drayton St., P O Drawer G, Elba 36323; tel. 205/897-2257; Donna Etheridge, chief financial off.

Lakeview Community Hospital (O, 74 beds), 820 W. Washington St., Eufaula 36027; tel. 205/687-5761; Ron Dyer, adm.

Marion County General Hospital (O, 126 beds), 1315 Military St. S., Hamilton 35570; tel. 205/921-7861; W. Douglas Arnold, adm.

East Alabama Medical Center (CM, 311 beds), 2000 Pepperell Pkwy., Opelika 36802; tel. 205/749-3411; Terry A. Andrus, adm.

LaMar Regional Hospital (CM, 70 beds), 507 Fifth St. S.W., Box 308, Vernon 35592; tel. 205/695-7111; Donald B. Hatcher, adm.

Arkansas: Dallas County Hospital (L, 79 beds), 201 Clifton St., Fordyce 71742; tel. 501/352-3155; Curt Moberg, exec. dir.

Harris Hospital (O, 89 beds), 1205 McLain St., Newport 72112; tel. 501/523-8911; Jim Seward, exec. dir.

Randolph County Medical Center (L, 50 beds), 2801 Medical Center Dr., Pocahontas 72455; tel. 501/892-4511; Hank Fender, exec. dir.

Florida: Doctors Memorial Hospital (L, 34 beds), 401 E. Byrd Ave., Box 188, Bonifay 32425; tel. 904/547-4271; Robert R. Reddish, adm.

Florida Community Hospital (O, 45 beds), Hwy. 77 & 280, Box K, Chipley 32428; tel. 904/638-1610; J. Glenn Brown Jr., adm.

Georgia: Berrien County Hospital (O, 60 beds), 1221 E. McPherson St., P O Box 665, Nashville 31639; tel. 912/686-7471; Dale C. Armstrong, adm.

Dooly Medical Center (L, 43 beds), Pitts Rd., Box 278, Vienna 31092; tel. 912/268-4141; Mark Phillips, adm.

Illinois: Crossroads Community Hospital (O, 55 beds), 8 Doctors Park, Mount Vernon 62864; tel. 618/244-5500; Ron Wolff, adm.

Louisiana: Woodview Regional Hospital (O, 53 beds), 5505 Shreveport Hwy., Pineville 71360; tel. 318/640-0222; Robert R. Bash, adm.

Mississippi: Hillcrest Hospital (CM, 30 beds), Box 770, Calhoun City 38916; tel. 601/628-6611; Gene Wayne Schuler, adm.

Houston Community Hospital (O, 150 beds), Hwy. 8 E., Houston 38851; tel. 601/456-3701; David A. Wiley, adm.

Missouri: Doctors Regional Medical Center (O, 194 beds), 621 Pine Blvd., Poplar Bluff 63901; tel. 314/686-4111; Harold Boyer, adm.

South Carolina: Barnwell County Hospital (O, 93 beds), Reynolds & Wren Sts., Box 588, Barnwell 29812; tel. 803/259-3571; John R. Eckert, exec. dir.

Tennessee: Cleveland Community Hospital (O, 100 beds), 2800 W. Side Dr. N.W., Cleveland 37311; tel. 615/479-4131; Gerald H. Frost, adm.

Wayne County General Hospital (L, 70 beds), Hwy. 64 E., P O Box 580, Waynesboro 38485; tel. 615/722-5411; B. Richard Moseley, adm.

Texas: Scenic Mountain Medical Center (O, 116 beds), 1601 W. 11th Pl., Big Spring 79720; tel. 915/263-1211; Keith King, actg. adm.

Hill Regional Hospital (O, 92 beds), 101 Circle Dr., Hillsboro 76645; tel. 817/582-8425; Jack Reamy, adm.

Owned, leased, sponsored:	21 hospitals	1751 beds
Contract-managed:	4 hospitals	811 beds
Totals:	25 hospitals	2562 beds

3015: NATIONAL MEDICAL ENTERPRISES (IO)
11620 Wilshire Blvd., P O Box 25980, Los Angeles, CA 90025; 213/479-5526; Richard K. Eamer, chm. & chief exec. off.; Leonard Cohen, pres. & chief oper. off.

California: Calexico Hospital (CM, 34 beds), 450 Birch St., Calexico 92231; tel. 619/357-1191; Arthur Simmons, adm.

John F. Kennedy Memorial Hospital (O, 131 beds), 47-111 Monroe St., Indio 92201; Mailing Address P O Drawer LIII, Indio, Zip 92202; tel. 619/347-6191; Fredrick W.Hodges, chief exec. off.

Doctors Hospital of Lakewood-South Street (O, 162 beds), 3700 E. South St., Lakewood 90712; tel. 213/531-2550; Michael Kerr, chief exec. off. & exec. dir.

Dominguez Medical Center (O, 250 beds), 171 W. Bort St., P O Box 5806, Long Beach 90805; tel. 213/639-5151; Lorraine P. Auerbach, chief exec. off.

Los Alamitos Medical Center (O, 173 beds), 3751 Katella Ave., Los Alamitos 90720; tel. 213/598-1311; Nicholas V. McClure, exec. dir.

Century City Hospital (L, 195 beds), 2070 Century Park E., Los Angeles 90067; tel. 213/201-6610; Joel Bergenfeld, exec. dir.

For explanation of codes following names, see page B2.
*Indicates Type III membership in the American Hospital Association.

Century Community Hospital (CM, 50 beds), 9500 S. Broadway, Los Angeles 90003; tel. 213/777-7663; Robert Bourseau, adm.

Community Hospital and Rehabilitation Center of Los Gatos-Saratoga (L, 208 beds), 815 Pollard Rd., Los Gatos 95030; tel. 408/378-6131

Doctors Hospital of Manteca (O, 49 beds), 1205 E. North St., Box 191, Manteca 95336; tel. 209/823-3111; Woody Laughnan Jr., adm.

Doctors Medical Center (O, 298 beds), 1441 Florida Ave., Box 4138, Modesto 95352; tel. 209/578-1211; J. Douglas Dent, exec. dir.

Modesto City Hospital (O, 121 beds), 730 17th St., Modesto 95354; Mailing Address P O Box 700, Modesto, Zip 95353; tel. 209/577-2100; Hal Chilton, adm.

Doctors' Hospital of Montclair (O, 99 beds), 5000 San Bernardino St., Montclair 91763; tel. 714/625-5411; Richard Forrester, adm.

Garfield Medical Center (O, 229 beds), 525 N. Garfield Ave., Monterey Park 91754; tel. 818/573-2222; Roger W. Wessels, exec. dir.

Ontario Community Hospital (O, 99 beds), 550 N. Monterey, Ontario 91764; tel. 714/984-2201; John W. Packard, adm.

Doctors Hospital of Pinole (L, 137 beds), 2151 Appian Way, Pinole 94564; tel. 415/724-5000; Danny N. Mar, adm.

Placentia-Linda Community Hospital (O, 114 beds), 1301 Rose Dr., Placentia 92670; tel. 714/993-2000; Gary Fybel, adm.

Redding Medical Center (O, 132 beds), 1100 Butte St., Redding 96001; Mailing Address Box 2458, Redding, Zip 96099; tel. 916/244-5400; Gerald E. Knepp, adm.

Alvarado Hospital Medical Center (O, 214 beds), 6655 Alvarado Rd., San Diego 92120; tel. 619/287-3270; Daniel P. McLean, exec. dir.

San Diego Physicians and Surgeons Hospital (L, 156 beds), 446 26th St., San Diego 92102; tel. 619/234-4341; Scott Rhine, chief exec. off.

Twin Cities Community Hospital (O, 84 beds), 1100 Las Tablas Rd., Templeton 93465; tel. 805/434-2813; Floyd H. Anderson, adm.

Florida: Seven Rivers Community Hospital (O, 90 beds), 6201 N. Suncoast Blvd., Crystal River 32629; tel. 904/795-6560; Michael Heindel, adm.

Delray Community Hospital (O, 211 beds), 5352 Linton Blvd., Delray Beach 33445; tel. 305/498-4440; John D. Bartlett, exec. dir.

University Hospital (CM, 97 beds), 1340 Ridgewood Ave., Holly Hill 32017; tel. 904/677-5100; Robert Helms, pres.

Hollywood Medical Center (O, 334 beds), 3600 Washington St., Hollywood 33021; tel. 305/966-4500; Calvin K. Knight, exec. dir.

Palms of Pasadena Hospital (O, 310 beds), 1501 Pasadena Ave. S., St. Petersburg 33707; Mailing Address Box 6158, St. Petersburg, Zip 33736; tel. 813/381-1000;Erwin E. Abrams, adm.

Louisiana: Meadowcrest Hospital (O, 169 beds), 2500 Belle Chasse Hwy., Gretna 70056; tel. 504/392-3131; Mark F. Keiser, exec. dir.

Jo Ellen Smith Medical Center (O, 164 beds), 4444 General Meyer Ave., New Orleans 70114; tel. 504/363-7011; Ronald J. Ensor, adm.

St. Charles General Hospital (O, 161 beds), 3700 St. Charles Ave., New Orleans 70115; tel. 504/899-7441; Richard Freeman, adm.

Massachusetts: Leonard Morse Hospital (CM, 259 beds), 67 Union St., Natick 01760; tel. 617/653-3400; Janice B. Wyatt, pres. & chief exec. off.

Missouri: Kirksville Osteopathic Medical Center (L, 228 beds), 800 W. Jefferson, Kirksville 63501; tel. 816/626-2121; Edward R. Balotsky, exec. dir.

Lutheran Medical Center (L, 278 beds), 2639 Miami St., St. Louis 63118; tel. 314/772-1456; Harry J. Carr, exec. dir.

New York: Community Hospital of Western Suffolk (CM, 271 beds), Smithtown By-Pass & Rte. 111, Smithtown 11787; tel. 516/979-9800; Martin Rosenblum, adm.

South Carolina: Cherokee Memorial Hospital (L, 143 beds), 1420 N. Limestone St., Gaffney 29340; tel. 803/487-4271; Tim Moran, adm.

Tennessee: University Medical Center (O, 125 beds), 1411 Baddour Pkwy., Lebanon 37087; tel. 615/444-8262; Claude W. Harbarger, adm.

John W. Harton Regional Medical Center (O, 137 beds), New Shelbyville Hwy., Box 460, Tullahoma 37388; tel. 615/455-0601; Tom Anderson, adm.

Texas: Trinity Medical Center (L, 133 beds), 4343 N. Josey Lane, Carrollton 75010; tel. 214/492-1010; Robert L. Smith, adm.

Southside Community Hospital (O, 164 beds), 4626 Weber Rd., Corpus Christi 78411; tel. 512/854-2031; J. H. O'Dell, adm.

Doctors Hospital of Dallas (O, 220 beds), 9440 Poppy Dr., Dallas 75218; tel. 214/324-6100; Chris Dicicco, chief exec. off.; C. Eugene Ward, adm.

Rhd Memorial Medical Center (L, 258 beds), Seven Medical Pkwy., Dallas 75234; Mailing Address P O Box 819094, Dallas, Zip 75381; tel. 214/247-1000; James R.Shafer, exec. dir.; Jeff Webster, adm.

Sierra Medical Center (O, 266 beds), 1625 Medical Center Dr., El Paso 79902; tel. 915/532-4000; L. Marcus Fry Jr., chief exec. off.; Sonja Hagel, assoc. adm.

Twin Oaks Medical Center (L, 31 beds), 2919 Markum Dr., Fort Worth 76117; tel. 817/831-0311; Chris Dicicco, adm.

Owned, leased, sponsored:	36 hospitals	6273 beds
Contract-managed:	5 hospitals	711 beds
Totals:	41 hospitals	6984 beds

3175: NEPONSET VALLEY HEALTH SYSTEM (NP)
800 Washington St., Norwood, MA 02062; 617/769-4000; Frank S. Crane III, pres.

Massachusetts: Southwood Community Hospital (O, 183 beds), 111 Dedham St., tel. 617/668-0385; John D. Dalton, adm.

Norwood Hospital (O, 302 beds), 800 Washington St., Norwood 02062; tel. 617/769-4000; Frank S. Crane III, chief exec. off.

Owned, leased, sponsored:	2 hospitals	485 beds
Contract-managed:	0 hospitals	0 beds
Totals:	2 hospitals	485 beds

3075: NEW YORK CITY HEALTH AND HOSPITAL CORPORATION (NP)
125 Worth St., New York, NY 10013; 212/566-8038; Jo Ivey Boufford MD, actg. pres.

New York: Bronx Municipal Hospital Center (O, 811 beds), Pelham Pkwy. S. & Eastchester Rd., Bronx 10461; tel. 212/430-8141; Harold A. Levine, actg. exec. dir.

Lincoln Medical and Mental Health Center (O, 571 beds), 234 E. 149th St., Bronx 10451; tel. 212/579-5000; Angel Quinones, exec. dir.

North Central Bronx Hospital (O, 353 beds), 3424 Kossuth Ave., Bronx 10467; tel. 212/920-7171; A. Richard Plaatsman, exec. dir.

Coney Island Hospital (O, 445 beds), 2601 Ocean Pkwy., Brooklyn 11235; tel. 718/615-4000; Howard C. Cohen, exec. dir.

Kings County Hospital Center (O, 1221 beds), 451 Clarkson Ave., Brooklyn 11203; tel. 718/735-3131; Ira C. Clark, chief exec. off. & reg. adm.

Woodhull Medical and Mental Health Center (O, 489 beds), 760 Broadway, Brooklyn 11206; tel. 718/963-8000; Carlos A. Loran, exec. dir.

City Hospital Center at Elmhurst (O, 761 beds), 79-01 Broadway, Elmhurst Sta., Zip 11373; tel. 718/830-1515; Alan H. Channing, exec. dir.

Queens Hospital Center (O, 551 beds), 82-68 164th St., Jamaica 11432; tel. 718/990-3377; Lorraine Tregde, exec. dir.

Bellevue Hospital Center (O, 1197 beds), First Ave. & 27th St., New York 10016; tel. 212/561-4141; Harriet Dronska, exec. dir.

Coler Memorial Hospital (O, 1045 beds), Franklin D Roosevelt Island, New York 10044; tel. 212/688-9400; Mark J. Kator, exec. dir.

For explanation of codes following names, see page B2.
*Indicates Type III membership in the American Hospital Association.

Goldwater Memorial Hospital (O, 912 beds), Franklin D Roosevelt Island, New York 10044; tel. 212/750-6800; I. Bernard Hirsch, exec. dir.

Harlem Hospital Center (O, 725 beds), 506 Lenox Ave., New York 10037; tel. 212/491-1234; Charles E. Windsor, dir.

Metropolitan Hospital Center (O, 598 beds), 1901 First Ave., New York 10029; tel. 212/360-6262; Stephen N. Lenhardt, dir.

Owned, leased, sponsored:	13 hospitals	9679 beds
Contract-managed:	0 hospitals	0 beds
Totals:	13 hospitals	9679 beds

***0465: NEXUS HEALTHCARE CORPORATION** (NP)
Madison Ave., Summey Bldg., Suite 201, Mount Holly, NJ 08060; 609/261-7011; Chester B. Kaletkowski, pres.

New Jersey: Southern Ocean County Hospital (CM, 100 beds), 1140 W. Bay Ave., Manahawkin 08050; tel. 609/597-6011; David P. Laskowski, adm.

Memorial Hospital of Burlington County (CM, 322 beds), 175 Madison Ave., Mount Holly 08060; tel. 609/267-0700; Geoffrey Stone, adm.

Owned, leased, sponsored:	0 hospitals	0 beds
Contract-managed:	2 hospitals	422 beds
Totals:	2 hospitals	422 beds

3115: NORTH BROWARD HOSPITAL DISTRICT (NP)
1625 S.E. Third Ave., Fort Lauderdale, FL 33316; 305/355-4400; Robert L. Kennedy, exec. dir.

Florida: Broward General Medical Center (O, 681 beds), 1600 S. Andrews Ave., Fort Lauderdale 33316; tel. 305/355-4400; Richard J. Stull II, adm.

Imperial Point Medical Center (O, 204 beds), 6401 N. Federal Hwy., Fort Lauderdale 33308; tel. 305/776-8500; Thomas J. Corder, adm.

North Broward Medical Center (O, 347 beds), 201 Sample Rd., Pompano Beach 33064; tel. 305/941-8300; Thomas J. Corder, adm.

Owned, leased, sponsored:	3 hospitals	1232 beds
Contract-managed:	0 hospitals	0 beds
Totals:	3 hospitals	1232 beds

3165: NORTH CENTRAL HEALTH SERVICES (NP)
930 Tenth Ave., Spearfish, SD 57783; 605/642-2744; Larry Marshall, vice-pres.

South Dakota: Belle Fourche Health Care Center (O, 130 beds), 2200 13th Ave., Belle Fourche 57717; tel. 605/892-3331; Larry Potter, adm.

Kingsbury County Memorial Hospital (O, 86 beds), Fourth & Manor Ave., Lake Preston 57249; tel. 605/847-4451; Robert Houser, adm.

Community Memorial Hospital (O, 121 beds), 2100 Davenport St., P O Box 279, Sturgis 57785; tel. 605/347-2536; Michael M. Penticoff, adm.

Owned, leased, sponsored:	3 hospitals	337 beds
Contract-managed:	0 hospitals	0 beds
Totals:	3 hospitals	337 beds

1805: NUMED HOSPITALS, INC. (IO)
16633 Ventura Blvd., 13th Floor, Encino, CA 91436; 818/990-2000; Stephen Bowles, pres.

California: Terrace Plaza Medical Center (O, 95 beds), 14148 Francisquito Ave., Baldwin Park 91706; tel. 213/338-1101; Rolland E. Wick, exec. dir.

Northwestern University-Medical Regional Medical Center West Valley (O, 81 beds), 7011 Shoup Ave., Canoga Park 91307; tel. 818/348-0500; Claudia Haynes-Streaty,adm.

Northwestern University-Medical Regional Medical Center West Valley-North Campus (O, 139 beds), 22141 Roscoe Blvd., Canoga Park 91304; tel. 213/340-0580; GeorgeRooth, chief exec. off.

Medical Center of La Mirada (O, 141 beds), 14900 E. Imperial Hwy., La Mirada 90637; tel. 213/941-2251; Noel Hecht, exec. dir.

Merrithew Memorial Hospital (CM, 190 beds), 2500 Alhambra Ave., Martinez 94553; tel. 415/372-4200; Frank J. Puglisi Jr., exec. dir.

Coast Plaza Medical Center (O, 62 beds), 13100 Studebaker Rd., Norwalk 90650; tel. 213/868-3751; Arthur Gerrick, exec. dir.

Selma District Hospital (CM, 65 beds), 1141 Rose Ave., Selma 93662; tel. 209/891-1000; Jack Waller, chief exec. off.

Sherman Oaks Community Hospital (O, 156 beds), 4929 Van Nuys Blvd., Sherman Oaks 91403; tel. 818/981-7111; M. Marc Goldberg, chief exec. off.

Florida: Lake Medical Center (O, 162 beds), 200 N. Blvd. E., Leesburg 32748; Mailing Address Box 750, Leesburg, Zip 32749; tel. 904/787-6881; Joseph P. Lyons, exec. dir.

Pembroke Pines General Hospital (O, 301 beds), 2301 University Dr., Pembroke Pines 33024; tel. 305/962-9650; Edward Maas, exec. dir.

Oregon: Valley Community Hospital (O, 44 beds), 550 S.E. Clay St., Dallas 97338; tel. 503/623-8301; Ed Zintgraff, exec. dir.

Texas: Doctors Hospital (O, 106 beds), 5500 39th St., Groves 77619; tel. 713/962-5733; Eric Hasemeier, exec. dir.

Owned, leased, sponsored:	10 hospitals	1287 beds
Contract-managed:	2 hospitals	255 beds
Totals:	12 hospitals	1542 beds

0455: NUMED PSYCHIATRIC, INC. (IO)
1265 Drummers Lane, Suite 107, P O Box 754, Valley Forge, PA 19482; 215/687-5151; Edmund Bujalski, pres.

Illinois: Hartgrove Hospital (O, 99 beds), 520 N. Ridgeway Ave., Chicago 60624; tel. 312/722-3113; Katherine B. Wade, adm.

Pennsylvania: Northwestern Institute of Psychiatry (O, 146 beds), 450 Bethlehem Pike, Fort Washington 19034; tel. 215/641-5300; Marc Lazarus, exec. dir.

Malvern Institute (O, 36 beds), 940 King Rd., Malvern 19355; tel. 215/647-0330; Joseph J. Driscoll, adm.

Owned, leased, sponsored:	3 hospitals	281 beds
Contract-managed:	0 hospitals	0 beds
Totals:	3 hospitals	281 beds

0715: OFFICE OF HOSPITALS (NP)
P O Box 44215, Baton Rouge, LA 70804; 504/342-2595; Jack Edwards, dep. asst.

Louisiana: Earl K. Long Memorial Hospital (O, 174 beds), 5825 Airline Hwy., P O Box 52999, Baton Rouge 70805; tel. 504/356-3361; William C. Bankston, dir.

Washington-St. Tammany Charity Hospital (O, 68 beds), 400 Memphis St., Box 40, Bogalusa 70427; tel. 504/735-1322; Bill Mohon, adm.

Lallie Kemp Charity Hospital (O, 74 beds), P O Box 70, Zip 70443; tel. 504/878-9421; Thomas W. Landry, adm.

Villa Feliciana Geriatric Hospital (O, 490 beds), Box 438, Jackson 70748; tel. 504/634-7793; John A. London, adm.

University Medical Center (O, 168 beds), 2390 W. Congress St., P O Box 4016-C, Lafayette 70502; tel. 318/261-6000; Gerry Morris, adm.

For explanation of codes following names, see page B2.
*Indicates Type III membership in the American Hospital Association.

Dr. Walter Olin Moss Regional Hospital (O, 108 beds), 1000 Walters St., Lake Charles 70605; tel. 318/477-3350; Edward G. Poor, dir.

E. A. Conway Memorial Hospital (O, 181 beds), 4801 S. Grand St., Box 1881, Monroe 71201; tel. 318/387-8460; Roy D. Bostick, dir.

Huey P. Long Memorial Hospital (O, 137 beds), Hospital Blvd., Pineville 71360; Mailing Address Box 5352, Pineville, Zip 71361; tel. 318/448-0811; James E. Morgan,adm.

Owned, leased, sponsored:	8 hospitals	1400 beds
Contract-managed:	0 hospitals	0 beds
Totals:	8 hospitals	1400 beds

***3315: OHIO VALLEY HEALTH SERVICES AND EDUCATION CORPORATION** (NP)
90 N. Fourth St., Martins Ferry, OH 43935; 304/234-8765; David J. Campbell, vice chm. & chief exec. off.

Ohio: East Ohio Regional Hospital (O, 236 beds), 90 N. Fourth St., Martins Ferry 43935; tel. 614/633-1100; Brent A. Marsteller, adm.

West Virginia: Ohio Valley Medical Center (O, 629 beds), 2000 Eoff St., Wheeling 26003; tel. 304/234-0123; George Brannen, coo

Owned, leased, sponsored:	2 hospitals	865 beds
Contract-managed:	0 hospitals	0 beds
Totals:	2 hospitals	865 beds

3355: ORLANDO REGIONAL MEDICAL CENTER (NP)
1414 S. Kuhl Ave., Orlando, FL 32806; 305/841-5111; J. Gary Strack, pres.

Florida: Orlando Regional Medical Center (O, 781 beds), 1414 S. Kuhl Ave., Orlando 32806; tel. 305/841-5111; J. Gary Strack, pres. & chief exec. off.

Orlando Regional Medical Center St. Cloud (O, 68 beds), 2906 17th St., St. Cloud 32769; tel. 305/892-2135; Jim Norris, adm.

Owned, leased, sponsored:	2 hospitals	849 beds
Contract-managed:	0 hospitals	0 beds
Totals:	2 hospitals	849 beds

7555: PALOMAR POMERADO HOSPITAL DISTRICT (NP)
215 S. Hickory St., Suite 310, Escondido, CA 92025; 619/489-4860; Robert M. Edwards, chief exec. off.

California: Palomar Memorial Hospital (O, 267 beds), 555 E. Valley Pkwy., Escondido 92025; tel. 714/489-4864; Robert M. Edwards, pres. & chief exec. off.; Robert J.Harenski, exec. vice-pres. & adm.

Pomerado Hospital (O, 130 beds), 15615 Pomerado Rd., Poway 92064; tel. 619/485-6511; Robert M. Edwards, pres. & chief exec. off.; Victoria Penland, exec.vice-pres. & adm.

Owned, leased, sponsored:	2 hospitals	397 beds
Contract-managed:	0 hospitals	0 beds
Totals:	2 hospitals	397 beds

5765: PARACELSUS HEALTHCARE (IO)
155 N. Lake Ave., Suite 1100, Pasadena, CA 91101; 818/792-8600; R. J. Messenger, pres. & chief oper. off.

California: Bellwood General Hospital (O, 85 beds), 10250 E. Artesia Blvd., Bellflower 90706; tel. 213/866-9028; Joseph B. Courtney, reg. vice-pres.

Buena Park Community Hospital (O, 66 beds), 6850 Lincoln Ave., Buena Park 90620; tel. 714/827-1161; Paul R. Schmidt, adm.

Chico Community Hospital (O, 135 beds), 560 Cohasset Rd., Chico 95926; tel. 916/896-5000; Daniel Chesanow, chief exec. off.

Hollywood Community Hospital (O, 99 beds), 6245 De Longpre Ave., Hollywood 90028; tel. 213/462-2271; Rodger L. Morrison, adm.

West Hollywood Hospital (O, 44 beds), 1233 N. La Brea Ave., Hollywood 90038; tel. 213/874-6111; Jerry L. Dollison, adm.

Lancaster Community Hospital (O, 132 beds), 43830 N. Tenth St. W., Lancaster 93534; tel. 805/948-4781; Steven C. Schmidt, adm.

Community Hospital of Lodi (O, 93 beds), 800 S. Lower Sacramento Rd., Lodi 95242; tel. 209/333-0211; James T. Lassiter, adm.

Los Angeles Community Hospital (O, 142 beds), 4081 E. Olympic Blvd., Los Angeles 90023; tel. 213/267-0477; Kenneth H. Madfes, adm.

Monrovia Community Hospital (O, 49 beds), 323 S. Heliotrope Ave., Box 707, Monrovia 91016; tel. 818/359-8341; Dennis Cheshire, adm.

Norwalk Community Hospital (O, 50 beds), 13222 Bloomfield Ave., Norwalk 90650; tel. 213/863-4763; Paul Strom, adm.

Oakland Hospital (O, 90 beds), 2648 E. 14th St., Oakland 94601; tel. 415/532-3300; Walter J. Filkowski, adm.

Van Nuys Community Hospital (O, 63 beds), 14433 Emelita St., P O Box 2698, Van Nuys 91401; tel. 818/787-1511; Joseph Sharp, adm.

West Covina Hospital (O, 60 beds), 725 S. Orange Ave., West Covina 91790; tel. 818/338-8481; John Hogue, adm.

Florida: Peninsula Medical Center (O, 119 beds), 264 S. Atlantic Ave., Ormond Beach 32074; tel. 904/672-4161; Terry Hilker, adm.

Georgia: Macon County Medical Center (O, 50 beds), 509 Sumter St., Box 574, Montezuma 31063; tel. 912/472-2311; George L. Long, adm.

Mississippi: Woman's Hospital (O, 111 beds), P O Box 4546, Zip 39216; tel. 601/932-1000; Thomas E. Fitz Jr., exec. dir.

Nevada: Womens Hospital (L, 61 beds), 2025 E. Sahara Ave., Box 43417, Las Vegas 89116; tel. 702/735-7106; Ed Martinez, adm.

Tennessee: Fentress County General Hospital (O, 72 beds), Hwy. 52-W, Drawer N, Jamestown 38556; tel. 615/879-8171; Donald E. Downey, adm.

Bledsoe County Hospital (O, 32 beds), Box 428, Pikeville 37367; tel. 615/447-2112; Donald E. Downey, adm.

Owned, leased, sponsored:	19 hospitals	1553 beds
Contract-managed:	0 hospitals	0 beds
Totals:	19 hospitals	1553 beds

3455: PENNSYLVANIA HOSPITAL (NP)
Eighth & Spruce Sts., Philadelphia, PA 19107; 215/829-3312; H. Robert Cathcart, pres.

Pennsylvania: Institute of Pennsylvania Hospital (O, 224 beds), 111 N. 49th St., Philadelphia 19139; tel. 215/471-2000; H. Robert Cathcart, pres.

Pennsylvania Hospital (O, 450 beds), Eighth & Spruce Sts., Philadelphia 19107; tel. 215/829-3000; H. Robert Cathcart, pres.

Owned, leased, sponsored:	2 hospitals	674 beds
Contract-managed:	0 hospitals	0 beds
Totals:	2 hospitals	674 beds

***3465: PEOPLES COMMUNITY HOSPITAL AUTHORITY** (NP)
33000 Annapolis Ave., Wayne, MI 48184; 313/467-4600; Fred E. Blair, chief exec. off.

Michigan: Outer Drive Hospital (O, 253 beds), 26400 W. Outer Dr., Lincoln Park 48146; tel. 313/594-6000; Oliver G. Crump, adm.

Heritage Hospital (O, 281 beds), 24775 Haig Ave., Taylor 48180; tel. 313/295-5000; H. Arthur Sugarman, adm.

Seaway Hospital (O, 206 beds), 5450 Fort St., Trenton 48183; tel. 313/671-3800; Edward V. Slingerland, adm.

Annapolis Hospital (O, 276 beds), 33155 Annapolis Rd., Wayne 48184; tel. 313/467-4000; Wade C. Adams, adm.

Beyer Memorial Hospital (O, 169 beds), 135 S. Prospect St., Ypsilanti 48198; tel. 313/484-2200; Jane G. McCormick, adm.

Owned, leased, sponsored:	5 hospitals	1185 beds
Contract-managed:	0 hospitals	0 beds
Totals:	5 hospitals	1185 beds

For explanation of codes following names, see page B2.
*Indicates Type III membership in the American Hospital Association.

***1130: PRESBYTERIAN HEALTHCARE SYSTEMS** (NP)
8220 Walnut Hill Lane, Suite 700, Dallas, TX 75231; 214/696-8500; Douglas D. Hawthorne, pres.

Texas: Presbyterian Hospital (O, 720 beds), 8200 Walnut Hill Lane, Dallas 75231; tel. 214/369-4111; Doug Hawthorne, pres. & chief exec. off.; R. Reed Fraley, exec.dir.

Presbyterian Hospital of Kaufman (O, 60 beds), Hwy. 243 W. at Hwy. 175, Box 310, Kaufman 75142; tel. 214/932-2183; Patty Pettigrew, exec. dir.

Presbyterian Hospital of Winnsboro (O, 50 beds), 504 E. Coke Rd., Box 106, Winnsboro 75494; tel. 214/342-5227; Jerry Hopper, exec. dir.

Owned, leased, sponsored:	3 hospitals	830 beds
Contract-managed:	0 hospitals	0 beds
Totals:	3 hospitals	830 beds

***5255: PRESENTATION HEALTH SYSTEM** (CC)
1301 S. Ninth Ave., Suite 102, Aberdeen, SD 57105, Mailing Address , Sioux Falls, Zip 57105; 605/331-4999; Sr. Colman Coakley, pres.

Minnesota: A. L. Vadheim Memorial Hospital (CM, 67 beds), 240 Willow St., Tyler 56178; tel. 507/247-5521; Pamela J. Gilchrist, adm.

Montana: Holy Rosary Hospital (O, 109 beds), 2101 Clark St., Miles City 59301; tel. 406/232-2540; Michael R. Piper, exec. dir.

St. Joseph Hospital (O, 40 beds), Skyline Dr., Box 1010, Polson 59860; tel. 406/883-5377; E. R. Testerman, adm.

North Dakota: Dickey County Memorial Hospital (L, 21 beds), 241 Main St., Box 220, Ellendale 58436; tel. 701/349-3611; Gordon Smith, adm.

South Dakota: St. Luke's Hospital (O, 160 beds), 305 S. State St., Aberdeen 57401; tel. 605/229-3230; Dale J. Stein, exec. dir.

Marshall County Memorial Hospital (L, 38 beds), 413 Ninth St., Box 230, Britton 57430; tel. 605/448-2253; Gerald Huss, adm.

Faulk County Memorial Hospital (L, 32 beds), P O Box 100, Faulkton 57438; tel. 605/598-6262; Gerald Huss, adm.

Holy Infant Hospital (L, 30 beds), Main St., Hoven 57450; tel. 605/948-2262; Thomas Earl Brown, adm.

St. Joseph Hospital (O, 120 beds), Fifth & Foster, Mitchell 57301; tel. 605/996-6531; Fred Slunecka, exec. dir.

McKennan Hospital (O, 401 beds), 800 E. 21st St., Sioux Falls 57101; tel. 605/339-8000; Roger C. Paavola, exec. dir.

Owned, leased, sponsored:	9 hospitals	951 beds
Contract-managed:	1 hospitals	67 beds
Totals:	10 hospitals	1018 beds

1315: RECOVERY CENTERS OF AMERICA (IO)
1010 Wisconsin Ave., Washington, DC 20007; 202/298-3230; Thomas J. Doherty, exec. vice-pres.

Maryland: New Beginning at Hidden Brook (O, 52 beds), 522 Thomas Run Rd., Bel Air 21014; tel. 301/836-7490; Michael A. Barbieri, exec. dir.

New Beginnings-Warwick Manor (O, 39 beds), Rte. 1, Box 178, Zip 21631; tel. 301/943-8108; Breck Stringer, exec. dir.

Pennsylvania: New Beginnings at Cove Forge (O, 69 beds), Rte. 1, Box 79, P O Box B, Williamsburg 16693; tel. 814/832-2121; George E. Obermeier, dir.

South Carolina: New Beginnings at Fenwick Hall (O, 40 beds), 1709 River Rd., Box 688, Johns Island 29455; tel. 803/559-2461; John H. Magill, exec. dir.

Owned, leased, sponsored:	4 hospitals	200 beds
Contract-managed:	0 hospitals	0 beds
Totals:	4 hospitals	200 beds

1065: REGENT HEALTH SYSTEMS, INC. (NP)
Liberty St., P O Box 8754, Clinton, LA 70722; 504/683-3319; Charles J. Mueller, pres.

Louisiana: Regent Hospital Feliciana (O, 36 beds), Liberty St., Box 927, Clinton 70722; tel. 504/683-5109; Charles J. Mueller, chief exec. off.

Regent Hospital -Acadiana (O, 63 beds), 504 N. Broadway St., Erath 70533; tel. 318/937-5851; James L. Wentz, vice-pres.

Regent Hospital -East Carroll (O, 29 beds), 226 N. Hood St., Lake Providence 71254; tel. 318/559-2441; Shirley M. Sikes, adm.

Leesville General Hospital (O, 28 beds), Kurthwood Rd., Leesville 71446; tel. 318/239-3801; William W. Speaker, adm.

Owned, leased, sponsored:	4 hospitals	156 beds
Contract-managed:	0 hospitals	0 beds
Totals:	4 hospitals	156 beds

3615: RELIGIOUS HOSPITALLERS OF ST. JOSEPH, PROVINCE OF ST. JOSEPH (CC)
16 Manitou Crescent E., Mailing Address Kingston K7n 1b2, 613/389-0275

Illinois: St. Bernard Hospital (S, 217 beds), 64th & Dan Ryan Expwy., Chicago 60621; tel. 312/962-3900; David Kannankeril, pres. & chief exec. off.

Wisconsin: Langlade Memorial Hospital (S, 80 beds), 112 E. Fifth Ave., Antigo 54409; tel. 715/623-2331; Kevin J. Keighron, exec. dir.

Owned, leased, sponsored:	2 hospitals	297 beds
Contract-managed:	0 hospitals	0 beds
Totals:	2 hospitals	297 beds

***6525: REPUBLIC HEALTH CORPORATION** (IO)
15303 Dallas Pkwy., Suite 1400, Dallas, TX 75248; 214/851-3100; James E. Buncher, pres. & chief exec. off.

Alaska: Horizon Recovery Center (O, 34 beds), 1650 S. Bragaw, Anchorage 99508; tel. 907/277-1522; Gloria Heatherington, adm.

Arkansas: Crawford County Memorial Hospital (O, 70 beds), E. Main & S. 20th Sts., Box 409, Van Buren 72956; tel. 501/474-3401; Jeanne Bouxsein Parham, adm.

California: Bakersfield Community Hospital (CM, 64 beds), 901 Olive Dr., Bakersfield 93308; Mailing Address P O Box 5900, Bakersfield, Zip 93388; tel. 805/399-4461; Roy D.Friedlos, adm.

Rio Hondo Memorial Hospital (O, 146 beds), 8300 E. Telegraph Rd., Downey 90240; Mailing Address Caller 7020, Downey, Zip 90241; tel. 213/806-1821; Patrick A.Petre, adm.

Memorial Hospital of Gardena (O, 131 beds), 1145 W. Redondo Beach Blvd., Gardena 90247; tel. 213/532-4200; Seth Ellis, adm.

Hayward Hospital (O, 166 beds), 22455 Maple Ct., Hayward 94541; tel. 415/886-9500; Ken Breaux, adm.

Beverly Hills Medical Center (O, 241 beds), 1177 S. Beverly Dr., Los Angeles 90035; tel. 213/553-5155; Jeffrey P. Winter, adm.

Channel Islands Community Hospital (L, 85 beds), 540 Hobson Way, Oxnard 93030; Mailing Address Box 1148, Oxnard, Zip 93032; tel. 805/487-7941; Emma Mayer Orr,adm.

Ross General Hospital (O, 147 beds), 1150 Sir Francis Drake Blvd., P O Box Cs 6001, Ross 94957; tel. 415/453-7800; Roger W. Moore, adm.

Community Hospital of Sacramento (O, 100 beds), 2251 Hawthorne St., Sacramento 95815; tel. 916/929-2333; Howard J. Wooling, adm.

Harbor View Medical Center (L, 176 beds), 120 Elm St., San Diego 92101; tel. 619/232-4331; Margareta Norton, adm.

Memorial Hospital-San Leandro (O, 142 beds), 2800 Benedict Dr., San Leandro 94577; tel. 415/357-8300; Phillip J. Mazzuca, exec. dir.

Coastal Communities Hospital (O, 215 beds), 2701 S. Bristol, Santa Ana 92704; tel. 714/754-5454; Elizabeth J. Stark, adm.

For explanation of codes following names, see page B2.
*Indicates Type III membership in the American Hospital Association.

Colorado: Horizon Hospital (L, 53 beds), 1920 High St., Denver 80218; tel. 303/388-2491; Bruce B. McBogg, adm.

Florida: John F. Kennedy Memorial Hospital (CM, 369 beds), 4800 S. Congress Ave., Atlantis 33462; Mailing Address Box 1489, Lake Worth, Zip 33460; tel. 305/965-7300;James K. Johnson, adm.

Coral Gables Hospital (L, 226 beds), 3100 Douglas Rd., Coral Gables 33134; tel. 305/445-8461; Anthony M. Degina Jr., adm.

De Poo Memorial Doctors Hospital (CM, 34 beds), 1200 Kennedy Dr., Box 690, Key West 33040; tel. 305/294-4692; Larry Melby, adm.

North Miami Medical Center (O, 278 beds), 1701 N.E. 127th St., North Miami 33261; tel. 305/891-3550; Ed Goffinett, adm.

Georgia: Decatur Hospital (L, 120 beds), 450 N. Candler St., Decatur 30030; Mailing Address Box 40, Decatur, Zip 30031; tel. 404/377-0221; Dewey A. Greene, adm.

Indiana: Winona Memorial Hospital (O, 237 beds), 3232 N. Meridian St., Indianapolis 46208; tel. 317/924-3392; Howard W. Watts, adm.

Louisiana: Eye, Ear, Nose and Throat Hospital (CM, 47 beds), 145 Elk Pl., New Orleans 70112; tel. 504/595-6100; Donald E. Patterson, chief exec. off.

Woodland Hills Hospital (O, 90 beds), 6100 Cypress St., P O Box 1436, West Monroe 71294; tel. 318/396-5900; Betty Abanto, adm.

Mississippi: Meridian Regional Hospital (O, 154 beds), Hwy. 39 N., Meridian 39301; tel. 601/483-6211; Wallace H. Cooper Jr., adm.

Missouri: Saint Louis Memorial Hospital (CM, 40 beds), 1027 Bellevue Ave., St. Louis 63117; tel. 314/781-9997; Don M. Chase, adm.

Ohio: Emerson A. North Hospital (O, 112 beds), 5642 Hamilton Ave., Cincinnati 45224; tel. 513/541-0135; Stephen R. Halley, asst. adm.

Oklahoma: Medical Center of Southeastern Oklahoma (L, 80 beds), 1800 University, Durant 74701; Mailing Address P O Box 1207, Durant, Zip 74702; tel. 405/924-3080; HarryD. Provost Jr., adm.

Oregon: Horizon Recovery Center (O, 30 beds), 6050 S.W. Old Scholls Ferry Rd., Portland 97223; tel. 503/292-6671; Michael J. Millenheft, adm.

Riverside Psychiatric Hospital (O, 66 beds), 1400 S.E. Umatilla St., Portland 97202; tel. 503/234-5353; Jon M. Orr, adm.

Tennessee: Lewisburg Community Hospital (L, 119 beds), Ellington Pkwy., P O Box 380, Lewisburg 37091; tel. 615/359-6241; Hugh Kroell, adm.

Texas: General Hospital of Lakewood (O, 71 beds), 1600 Abrams Rd., Dallas 75214; tel. 214/824-4541; Steven D. Porter, adm.

Horizon Hospital (O, 26 beds), 2345 Reagan St., Dallas 75219; tel. 214/521-7541; Lynda Hoffman, adm.

Garland Community Hospital (O, 128 beds), 122 S. Intl. Rd., Garland 75042; tel. 214/276-7116; Kevin J. Hicks, adm.

Horizon Hospital (O, 70 beds), 6160 South Loop E., Houston 77087; tel. 713/644-7047; Edwin Frank Jr., adm.

Houston Northwest Medical Center (O, 377 beds), 710 Fm 1960 W., Box 90730, Houston 77090; tel. 713/440-1000; J. Barry Shevchuk, adm.

La Hacienda Treatment Center (O, 50 beds), Fm 1340, Box 1, Hunt 78024; tel. 512/238-4222; John Lacy, adm.

Mesquite Physicians Hospital (O, 127 beds), 1527 N. Galloway, Mesquite 75149; tel. 214/285-6391; Steven D. Porter, adm.

Horizon Hospital (O, 45 beds), 210 W. Ashby Pl., San Antonio 78212; tel. 512/736-2211; Joe Ruley, adm.

Washington: West Seattle Community Hospital (O, 61 beds), 2600 S.W. Holden St., Seattle 98126; tel. 206/938-6000; Dwight E. Harshbarger, adm.

Mountainview Hospital of Spokane (L, 34 beds), 628 S. Cowley, Spokane 99202; Mailing Address Box 598, Spokane, Zip 99210; tel. 509/624-3226; Arlene Ingwerson,adm.

Owned, leased, sponsored:	34 hospitals	4207 beds
Contract-managed:	5 hospitals	554 beds
Totals:	39 hospitals	4761 beds

***8815: RESEARCH HEALTH SERVICES** (NP)
6400 Prospect Ave., Kansas City, MO 64132; 816/276-9167; E. Wynn Presson, pres.

Kansas: Allen County Hospital (L, 45 beds), 101 S. First St., Box 540, Iola 66749; tel. 316/365-3131; Bill May, chief exec. off.

Missouri: Research Belton Hospital (O, 40 beds), 17065 S. 71 Hwy., Belton 64012; tel. 816/348-1200; Daryl W. Thornton, adm.

Cass Medical Center (CM, 50 beds), 1800 E. Mechanic St., Harrisonville 64701; tel. 816/884-3291; David G. Couser, chief exec. off.

Research Medical Center (O, 477 beds), 2316 E. Meyer Blvd., Kansas City 64132; tel. 816/276-4000; Richard W. Brown, pres.

Lafayette Regional Health Center (L, 38 beds), 15th & State St., Lexington 64067; tel. 816/259-2203; Frank I. Luddington, adm.

Owned, leased, sponsored:	4 hospitals	600 beds
Contract-managed:	1 hospitals	50 beds
Totals:	5 hospitals	650 beds

4810: RIVERSIDE HEALTHCARE ASSOCIATION, INC. (NP)
606 Denbigh Blvd., Suite 601, Newport News, VA 23602; 804/875-7500; Nelson L. St. Clair, pres.

Virginia: Walter Reed Memorial Hospital (O, 71 beds), Rte. 17, Gloucester 23061; tel. 804/693-4400; William B. Downey, vice-pres.

Riverside Hospital (O, 576 beds), 500 J Clyde Morris Blvd., Newport News 23601; tel. 804/599-2000; Nelson St. Clair, pres.

Lake Taylor City Hospital (CM, 333 beds), 1309 Kempsville Rd., Norfolk 23502; tel. 804/461-5001; George P. Phillips, adm.

Owned, leased, sponsored:	2 hospitals	647 beds
Contract-managed:	1 hospitals	333 beds
Totals:	3 hospitals	980 beds

0070: ROANOKE HOSPITAL ASSOCIATION (NP)
Box 13367, Roanoke, VA 24033; 703/981-7347; Thomas L. Robertson, pres.

Virginia: Bedford County Memorial Hospital (O, 169 beds), Oakwood Ext., Box 688, Bedford 24523; tel. 703/586-2441; John H. Fretz, adm.

Lonesome Pine Hospital (CM, 60 beds), Holton Ave., Drawer I, Big Stone Gap 24219; tel. 703/523-3111; Stephen K. Givens, adm.

Southside Community Hospital (CM, 117 beds), 800 Oak St., Farmville 23901; tel. 804/392-8811; Thomas J. Rice, adm.

Giles Memorial Hospital (CM, 52 beds), 235 S. Buchanan St., Pearisburg 24134; tel. 703/921-6000; David E. Deering, adm.

Gill Memorial Eye, Ear, Nose and Throat Hospital (O, 12 beds), 711 S. Jefferson St., Roanoke 24011; Mailing Address P O Box 1560, Roanoke, Zip 24007; tel.703/343-3368; Donald J. Love, vice-pres.

Roanoke Memorial Hospitals (O, 683 beds), Belleview at Jefferson St., Box 13367, Roanoke 24033; tel. 703/981-7000; Thomas L. Robertson, pres.

Franklin Memorial Hospital (CM, 62 beds), 124 Floyd Ave. S.W., Rocky Mount 24151; tel. 703/483-5277; William C. Garrett Jr., adm.

Tazewell Community Hospital (CM, 50 beds), Box 607, Tazewell 24651; tel. 703/988-2506; Robert E. Huch, adm.

Wythe County Community Hospital (CM, 106 beds), 600 W. Ridge Rd., Wytheville 24382; tel. 703/228-2181; Scott Adams, adm.

Owned, leased, sponsored:	3 hospitals	864 beds
Contract-managed:	6 hospitals	447 beds
Totals:	9 hospitals	1311 beds

8495: RUSHMORE NATIONAL HEALTH SYSTEMS (NP)
P O Box 2720, Rapid City, SD 57709; 605/341-8100; Gary Riedmann, pres.

South Dakota: Black Hills Rehabilitation Hospital (O, 98 beds), 2908 Fifth St., Rapid City 57701; tel. 605/343-8500; Melvin J. Platt, sr. vice-pres. & chief oper. off.

For explanation of codes following names, see page B2.
*Indicates Type III membership in the American Hospital Association.

Rapid City Regional Hospital (O, 299 beds), Mailing Address P O Box 6000, Zip 57709; tel. 605/341-1000; Adil Ameer, sr. exec. vice-pres.

Owned, leased, sponsored:	2 hospitals	397 beds
Contract-managed:	0 hospitals	0 beds
Totals:	2 hospitals	397 beds

***5395: SACRED HEART CORPORATION** (CC)
2861 W. 52nd Ave., Denver, CO 80221; 303/458-8611; Sr. Christina Oleske, pres.

Nebraska: St. Anthony's Hospital (O, 44 beds), Second & Adams Sts., O'Neill 68763; tel. 402/336-2611; Larry W. Veitz, adm.

North Dakota: Kenmare Community Hospital (O, 36 beds), 317 First Ave. N.W., P O Box 337, Kenmare 58746; tel. 701/385-4296; Daniel O. Olson, adm.

St. Joseph's Hospital (O, 177 beds), Third St. & Burdick Expwy. S.E., Minot 58701; tel. 701/857-2000; Walter A. Strauch, pres.

Owned, leased, sponsored:	3 hospitals	257 beds
Contract-managed:	0 hospitals	0 beds
Totals:	3 hospitals	257 beds

8985: SAFECARE COMPANY, INC/SAFECARE HEALTH SERVICE, INC. (IO)
900 Fourth Ave., Suite 800, P O Box 21485, Seattle, WA 98111; 206/223-4560; Stephen R. Jepson, sr. vice-pres. & pres.

Arizona: Southeast Arizona Medical Center (CM, 75 beds), Rural Rte. 1, Box 30, Douglas 85607; tel. 602/364-7931; Steve Jackson, adm.

Arkansas: Riverview Hospital (CM, 60 beds), 1310 Cantrell Rd., Little Rock 72201; tel. 501/375-5381; Lavon Henley, adm.

California: Chemical Dependency Institute of Northern California (O, 40 beds), 3333 S. Bascom Ave., Campbell 95008; tel. 408/559-2000; Roy R. Shelden, adm. & chief exec.off.

Colusa Community Hospital (CM, 56 beds), 199 E. Webster St., P O Box 331, Colusa 95932; tel. 916/458-5821; Ken Smith, adm.

Mission Oaks Hospital (O, 54 beds), 15891 Los Gatos-Almaden Rd., Los Gatos 95030; tel. 408/356-4111; Lee McLendon, adm.

Valley Community Hospital (CM, 62 beds), 1133 W. Sycamore St., P O Box 948, Willows 95988; tel. 916/934-3351; Andrew Radoszewski, adm.

Louisiana: Riverside Medical Center (CM, 48 beds), Enon Hwy., Box 528, Franklinton 70438; tel. 504/839-4431; James Branon, adm.

River Oaks Hospital (O, 126 beds), 1525 River Oaks Rd. W., Harahan 70123; tel. 504/734-1740; Gregory P. Roth, adm.

Missouri: Callaway Community Hospital (CM, 46 beds), 10 S. Hospital Dr., Fulton 65251; tel. 314/642-3376; G. S. Curtis Jr., adm.

Twin Rivers Regional Medical Center (O, 116 beds), 1301 First St., P O Box 787, Kennett 63857; tel. 314/888-4522; Warren N. Kerber, adm.

Texas: Rosebud Community Hospital (CM, 38 beds), 420 East Ave. E., Rosebud 76510; Mailing Address Drawer 618, Rosebud, Zip 76570; tel. 817/583-7983; Larry D. Luedke,adm.

Virginia: Norton Community Hospital (CM, 129 beds), 100 15th St., Norton 24273; tel. 703/679-1221; David Bevins, adm.

Lee County Community Hospital (CM, 80 beds), W. Morgan Ave., P O Box 70, Pennington Gap 24277; tel. 703/546-1440; Ken Ragland, adm.

Wyoming: Lander Valley Regional Medical Center (O, 107 beds), 1320 Bishop Randall Dr., Lander 82520; tel. 307/332-4420; Hugh S. Simcoe III, mgn dir.

Pineridge Hospital (O, 47 beds), 150 Wyoming St., Lander 82520; tel. 307/332-5700; Hugh Simcoe, adm.

Owned, leased, sponsored:	6 hospitals	490 beds
Contract-managed:	9 hospitals	594 beds
Totals:	15 hospitals	1084 beds

***4045: SAMARITAN HEALTH SERVICE** (NP)
1410 N. Third St., Phoenix, AZ 85004; 602/239-4106; David Reed, pres.

Arizona: Thunderbird Samaritan Hospital and Health Center (O, 210 beds), 5555 W. Thunderbird Rd., Glendale 85306; tel. 602/588-5555; Charles H. Welliver, chief exec.off.

Kennecott Samaritan Hospital (O, 20 beds), 100 Tilbury Dr., P O Box 368, Kearny 85237; tel. 602/363-5573; Glenda K. Hatfield, adm.

Havasu Regional Hospital (O, 88 beds), 101 Civic Center Lane, Lake Havasu City 86403; tel. 602/855-8185; Dennis G. Zielinski, adm.

Desert Samaritan Hospital and Health Center (O, 343 beds), 1400 S. Dobson Rd., Mesa 85202; tel. 602/835-3000; George A. Zara, chief exec. off.

Page Hospital (CM, 25 beds), N. Navajo Dr. & Vista Ave., Box 1447, Page 86040; tel. 602/645-2424; Kevin Poorten, adm.

Good Samaritan Medical Center (O, 640 beds), 1111 E. McDowell Rd., Phoenix 85006; Mailing Address Box 2989, Phoenix, Zip 85062; tel. 602/239-2000; Richard B.Uhrich MD, chief exec. off.

Maryvale Samaritan Hospital (O, 238 beds), 5102 W. Campbell Ave., Phoenix 85031; tel. 602/848-5000; Melvin E. Cunningham, vice-pres. & chief exec. off.

White Mountain Communities Hospital (CM, 25 beds), Box 471, Springerville 85938; tel. 602/333-4368; Dennis Silva, exec. dir.

Owned, leased, sponsored:	6 hospitals	1539 beds
Contract-managed:	2 hospitals	50 beds
Totals:	8 hospitals	1589 beds

1055: SAMISSA HEALTH CARE CORPORATION (NP)
3340 Ocean Park Blvd., Suite 3060, Santa Monica, CA 90405; 213/450-3637; Barry Fireman MD, pres.

California: Woodside Women's Hospital (O, 24 beds), 1600 Gordon St., Redwood City 94061; tel. 415/368-4134; Jacquelyn Thompson Aker, adm.

Oklahoma: Willow Crest Hospital (O, 42 beds), 130 A St. S.W., Miami 74354; tel. 918/542-1836; John Gohman II, adm.

Owned, leased, sponsored:	2 hospitals	66 beds
Contract-managed:	0 hospitals	0 beds
Totals:	2 hospitals	66 beds

***7895: SANTA FE HEALTHCARE** (NP)
720 S.W. Second Ave., P O Box 749, Gainesville, FL 32602; 904/375-4321; Edward C. Peddie, pres.

Florida: Alachua General Hospital (O, 415 beds), 801 S.W. Second Ave., P O Box Agh, Gainesville 32602; tel. 904/372-4321; Wassie Griffin, chief oper. off.

Suwannee Hospital (O, 50 beds), Fifth St., P O Drawer 1149, Live Oak 32060; tel. 904/362-1413; C. Elwin O'Steen, coo

Bradford Hospital (O, 30 beds), 922 E. Call St., P O Box 1210, Starke 32091; tel. 904/964-6000; Tim Rearick, chief oper. off.

Williston Memorial Hospital (L, 40 beds), 125 S.W. Seventh St., P O Drawer 550, Williston 32696; tel. 904/528-2801; John T. Myles, chief oper. off.

Owned, leased, sponsored:	4 hospitals	535 beds
Contract-managed:	0 hospitals	0 beds
Totals:	4 hospitals	535 beds

***0605: SCH HEALTH CARE SYSTEM** (CC)
6400 Lawndale Ave., Houston, TX 77023; 713/928-2931; Sr. Carmella O'Donoghue, pres.

Arkansas: St. Michael Hospital (O, 254 beds), Sixth & Hazel Sts., Texarkana 75502; tel. 501/774-2121; Thomas G. Byrne, adm.

California: St. Mary Medical Center (O, 431 beds), 1050 Linden Ave., Box 887, Long Beach 90801; tel. 213/491-9000; Sr. Mary Lucille Desmond, adm.

St. Bernardine Medical Center (O, 311 beds), 2101 N. Waterman Ave., San Bernardino 92404; tel. 714/883-8711; Sr. M. Nora Dwan, adm.

For explanation of codes following names, see page B2.
*Indicates Type III membership in the American Hospital Association.

Louisiana: St. Frances Cabrini Hospital (O, 232 beds), 3330 Masonic Dr., Alexandria 71301; tel. 318/487-1122; Jon C. Hilsabeck, adm.

St. Patrick Hospital (O, 273 beds), 524 S. Ryan St., Lake Charles 70601; tel. 318/436-2511; Sr. Mary Fatima McCarthy, adm.

Schumpert Medical Center (O, 625 beds), 915 Margaret Pl., Box 21976, Shreveport 71120; tel. 318/227-4500; Sr. M. Agnesita Brosnan, adm.

Oklahoma: Saint Francis Hospital (CM, 726 beds), 6161 S. Yale Ave., Tulsa 74136; tel. 918/494-2200; Sr. Mary Blandine Fleming, adm.

Texas: St. Elizabeth Hospital (O, 489 beds), 2830 Calder Ave., Beaumont 77702; Mailing Address Box 5405, Beaumont, Zip 77706; tel. 409/892-7171; Sr. M. CarmelitaBrett, adm.

St. Edward Hospital of Cameron (O, 46 beds), 806 N. Crockett St., P O Box 969, Cameron 76520; tel. 817/697-6664; Robert M. Spille, adm.

St. Mary's Hospital (O, 287 beds), 404 St. Mary's Blvd., Galveston 77550; tel. 409/766-4300; Keith B. Reed Jr., adm.

St. Anthony Center (O, 372 beds), 6301 Almeda Rd., Houston 77021; tel. 713/748-5021; Sr. Mary Alma Murphy, exec. dir.; Jerry Allen Lerman, adm.

St. Elizabeth Hospital (O, 35 beds), 4514 Lyons Ave., Houston 77020; tel. 713/675-1711; Sr. Mary Damian Murphy, adm.

St. Joseph Hospital (O, 722 beds), 1919 LaBranch St., Houston 77002; tel. 713/757-1000; Sr. M. Anastasia Enright, adm.

St. John Hospital (O, 130 beds), 2050 Space Park Dr., Nassau Bay 77058; tel. 713/333-5503; Gary Stremel, adm.

St. Mary Hospital (O, 278 beds), 3600 Gates Blvd., Port Arthur 77642; Mailing Address Box 3696, Port Arthur, Zip 77643; tel. 409/985-7431; Sr. Edith Judge, adm.

Owned, leased, sponsored:	14 hospitals	4485 beds
Contract-managed:	1 hospitals	726 beds
Totals:	15 hospitals	5211 beds

0575: SCHICK LABORATORIES, INC. (IO)

1901 Ave. of the States, Los Angeles, CA 90067; 213/553-3366; Patrick J. Frawley Jr., chm.

California: Schick Shadel Hospital (O, 30 beds), 45 E. Alamar, Santa Barbara 93105; tel. 805/687-2411; Richard J. Callanan, adm.

Texas: Schick Shadel Hospital (O, 50 beds), 4101 Frawley Dr., Fort Worth 76118; tel. 817/284-9217; Rolfe Floyd, adm.

Washington: Schick Shadel Hospital (O, 63 beds), 12101 Ambaum Blvd. S.W., Seattle 98146; Mailing Address Box 48149, Seattle, Zip 98148; tel. 206/244-8100; Mary EllenStewart, adm.

Owned, leased, sponsored:	3 hospitals	143 beds
Contract-managed:	0 hospitals	0 beds
Totals:	3 hospitals	143 beds

*1505: SCRIPPS MEMORIAL HOSPITALS (NP)

9888 Genesee Ave., La Jolla, CA 92038; 619/457-4123; Ames S. Early, pres.

California: Scripps Memorial Hospital-Chula Vista (O, 159 beds), 435 H St., Chula Vista 92012; Mailing Address Box 1537, Chula Vista, Zip 92010; tel. 619/691-7000; Jeff K.Bills, vice-pres. & adm.

Scripps Memorial Hospital-Encinitas (O, 93 beds), 354 Santa Fe Dr., P O Box 817, Encinitas 92024; tel. 619/753-6501; Steven J. Goe, vice-pres. & adm.

Scripps Memorial Hospital-La Jolla (O, 375 beds), 9888 Genesee Ave., La Jolla 92037; Mailing Address Box 28, La Jolla, Zip 92038; tel. 619/457-4123; Martin Buser,sr. vice-pres. & adm.

Owned, leased, sponsored:	3 hospitals	627 beds
Contract-managed:	0 hospitals	0 beds
Totals:	3 hospitals	627 beds

*4025: SERVANTCOR (CC)

175 S. Wall St., Kankakee, IL 60901; 815/937-2034; Joseph S. Feth, pres.

Illinois: Central Community Hospital (CM, 32 beds), 335 E. Fifth Ave., Box 68, Clifton 60927; tel. 815/694-2392; Dianne Soucie, adm.

St. Mary's Hospital of Kankakee (O, 250 beds), 500 W. Court St., Kankakee 60901; tel. 815/937-2490; Michael K. Winthrop, pres.

Mercy Hospital (O, 222 beds), 1400 W. Park Ave., Urbana 61801; tel. 217/337-2233; William Casey, pres. & chief exec. off.

Owned, leased, sponsored:	2 hospitals	472 beds
Contract-managed:	1 hospitals	32 beds
Totals:	3 hospitals	504 beds

*4125: SHRINERS HOSPITALS FOR CHILDREN (NP)

Box 25356, Tampa, FL 33622; 813/885-2575; Jack D. Hoard, exec. adm.

California: Shriners Hospitals for Crippled Children (O, 60 beds), 3160 Geneva St., Los Angeles 90020; tel. 213/388-3151; Paul D. Hargis, adm.

Shriners Hospital for Crippled Children (O, 48 beds), 1701 19th Ave., San Francisco 94122; tel. 415/665-1100; Ronald J. Castagno, adm.

Florida: Shriners Hospitals for Crippled Children (O, 60 beds), 12502 N. Pine Dr., Tampa 33612; tel. 813/972-2250; Gene Yeazell, adm.

Hawaii: Shriners Hospital for Crippled Children (O, 40 beds), 1310 Punahou St., Honolulu 96826; tel. 808/941-4466; Allan D. Robb, adm.

Illinois: Shriners Hospitals for Crippled Children (O, 60 beds), 2211 N. Oak Park Ave., Chicago 60635; tel. 312/622-5400; Vernon C. Showalter, adm.

Kentucky: Shriners Hospitals for Crippled Children (O, 36 beds), 1900 Richmond Rd., Lexington 40502; tel. 606/266-2101; Bobbie P. Spradlin RN, adm.

Louisiana: Shriners Hospitals for Crippled Children (O, 45 beds), 3100 Samford Ave., Shreveport 71103; tel. 318/222-5704; Gwendolyn McRae RN, adm.

Massachusetts: Shriners Burns Institute (O, 30 beds), 51 Blossom St., Boston 02114; tel. 617/722-3000; Salvatore P. Russo PhD, adm.

Shriners Hospitals for Crippled Children (O, 60 beds), 516 Carew St., Springfield 01104; tel. 413/781-6750; Edwin C. Thorn, adm.

Minnesota: Shriners Hospitals for Crippled Children (O, 40 beds), 2025 E. River Rd., Minneapolis 55414; tel. 612/339-6711; Roberta Antoine Dressen, adm.

Missouri: Shriners Hospitals for Crippled Children (O, 80 beds), 2001 S. Lindbergh Blvd., St. Louis 63131; tel. 314/432-3600; A. Duane Seabury Jr., adm.

Ohio: Shriners Burns Institute (O, 30 beds), 202 Goodman St., Cincinnati 45219; tel. 513/751-3900; Ronald R. Hitzler, adm.

Oregon: Shriners Hospital for Crippled Children (O, 40 beds), 3101 S.W. Sam Jackson Park Rd., Portland 97201; tel. 503/241-5090; Gary L. Morel, adm.

Pennsylvania: Shriners Hospitals for Crippled Children (O, 30 beds), 1645 W. Eighth St., Erie 16505; tel. 814/452-4164; Richard W. Brzuz, adm.

Shriners Hospitals for Crippled Children (O, 80 beds), 8400 Roosevelt Blvd., Philadelphia 19152; tel. 215/332-4500; James F. Casey, adm.

South Carolina: Shriners Hospitals for Crippled Children (O, 62 beds), 2100 N. Pleasantburg Dr., Greenville 29609; tel. 803/244-4530; John R. Hetrick, adm.

Texas: Shriners Hospitals for Crippled Children-Burns Institute-Galveston Unit (O, 30 beds), 610 Texas Ave., Galveston 77550; tel. 409/761-2516; C. Nick Wilson PhD,adm.

Shriners Hospitals for Crippled Children (O, 40 beds), 1402 Outer Belt Dr., Houston 77030; tel. 713/797-1616; Eleanor R. Jackson, adm.

For explanation of codes following names, see page B2.
*Indicates Type III membership in the American Hospital Association.

Utah: Shriners Hospitals for Crippled Children (O, 45 beds), Fairfax Ave. & Virginia St., Salt Lake City 84103; tel. 801/532-5307; Marie N. Holm, adm.

Washington: Shriners Hospitals for Crippled Children-Spokane Unit (O, 30 beds), N. 820 Summit Blvd., Spokane 99201; tel. 509/327-9521; Howard L. Parrett, adm.

Owned, leased, sponsored:	20 hospitals	946 beds
Contract-managed:	0 hospitals	0 beds
Totals:	20 hospitals	946 beds

5745: SISTERS OF CHARITY OF OUR LADY OF MERCY (CC)
Box 12410, Charleston, SC 29412; 803/795-6083; Sr. Anne Francis Campbell,

South Carolina: St. Francis Xavier Hospital (O, 283 beds), 135 Rutledge Ave., Charleston 29401; tel. 803/577-1000; Douglas L. Fairfax, pres.

Divine Saviour Hospital (O, 102 beds), 111 S. Congress St., Box 629, York 29745; tel. 803/684-4231; John W. Bailey, adm.

Owned, leased, sponsored:	2 hospitals	385 beds
Contract-managed:	0 hospitals	0 beds
Totals:	2 hospitals	385 beds

5995: SISTERS OF CHARITY CENTER (CC)
Mount St. Vincent On Hudson, Bronx, NY 10471; 212/549-9200; Sr. Agnes Connolly, pres.

New York: St. Vincent's Hospital and Medical Center of New York (S, 891 beds), 153 W. 11th St., New York 10011; tel. 212/790-7000; Sr. Margaret Sweeney, pres. & chiefexec. off.

St. Joseph's Medical Center (S, 194 beds), 127 S. Broadway, Yonkers 10701; tel. 914/965-6700; Sr. Mary Linehan, pres.

Owned, leased, sponsored:	2 hospitals	1085 beds
Contract-managed:	0 hospitals	0 beds
Totals:	2 hospitals	1085 beds

***5115: SISTERS OF CHARITY HEALTH CARE SYSTEMS, INC.** (CC)
345 Neeb Rd., Cincinnati, OH 45238; 513/922-9775; Sr. Celestia Koebel, pres.

Colorado: Penrose Hospitals (S, 460 beds), 2215 N. Cascade Ave., P O Box 7021, Colorado Springs 80933; tel. 303/630-5111; Sr. Myra James, pres.

St. Francis Hospital Systems (S, 204 beds), E. Pikes Peak at Prospect, Colorado Springs 80903; tel. 303/636-8800; Al Farr, pres. & chief exec. off.

St. Anthony Hospital Systems (S, 557 beds), 4231 W. 16th Ave., Denver 80204; tel. 303/629-3511; Douglas R. Cook, pres.

St. Joseph Hospital (S, 77 beds), 600 W. Third St., Florence 81226; tel. 303/784-4891; Thomas W. Laux, exec. vice-pres. & adm.

St. Mary-Corwin Hospital Regional Medical and Health Center (S, 307 beds), 1008 Minnequa Ave., Pueblo 81004; tel. 303/560-4000; Edmond T. Doyle, pres. & chiefexec. off.

Kentucky: Our Lady of the Way Hospital (S, 39 beds), Rte. 1428, Box 910, Martin 41649; tel. 606/285-5181; Sr. Monica Justinger, adm.

Michigan: St. Joseph's Hospital Center (S, 535 beds), Mailing Address 15855 19 Mile Rd., Mount Clemens 48044; tel. 313/263-2300; Mark L. Penkhus, pres. & chief exec. off.

Nebraska: Saint Francis Medical Center (S, 131 beds), 2620 W. Faidley Ave., Box 2118, Grand Island 68802; tel. 308/384-4600; Cale E. Neal, pres.

Good Samaritan Hospital (S, 185 beds), 31st St. & Central Ave., Kearney 68847; tel. 308/236-8511; LeRoy E. Rheault, pres.

St. Elizabeth Community Health Center (S, 218 beds), 555 S. 70th St., Lincoln 68510; tel. 402/489-7181; Robert J. Lanik, pres.

New Mexico: St. Joseph Health Care Corporation (S, 377 beds), 400 Walter St. N.E., Albuquerque 87102; tel. 505/848-8000; John M. Kirk, pres.

Ohio: Good Samaritan Hospital (S, 719 beds), 3217 Clifton Ave., Cincinnati 45220; tel. 513/872-1400; Roger W. Weseli, pres.

Good Samaritan Hospital and Health Center (S, 576 beds), 2222 Philadelphia Dr., Dayton 45406; tel. 513/278-2612; James P. Fitzgerald, pres.

Owned, leased, sponsored:	13 hospitals	4385 beds
Contract-managed:	0 hospitals	0 beds
Totals:	13 hospitals	4385 beds

***6095: SISTERS OF CHARITY HEALTH CARE SYSTEMS CORPORATION** (CC)
355 Bard Ave., Staten Island, NY 10310; 212/390-1650; John J. Depierro, pres. & chief exec. off.

New York: Bayley Seton Hospital (S, 204 beds), Bay St. & Vanderbilt Ave., Staten Island 10304; tel. 718/390-6000; Andrew J. Passeri, vice-pres. & dir.

St. Vincent's Medical Center of Richmond (S, 447 beds), 355 Bard Ave., Staten Island 10310; tel. 718/390-1234; Gary S. Horan, vice-pres. & dir.

Owned, leased, sponsored:	2 hospitals	651 beds
Contract-managed:	0 hospitals	0 beds
Totals:	2 hospitals	651 beds

***5095: SISTERS OF CHARITY OF LEAVENWORTH HEALTH SERVICES CORPORATION** (CC)
4200 S. Fourth St., Leavenworth, KS 66048; 913/682-1338; Sr. Macrina Ryan, pres.

California: Saint John's Hospital and Health Center (O, 551 beds), 1328 22nd St., Santa Monica 90404; tel. 213/829-5511; Sr. Marie Madeleine, pres.

Colorado: Saint Joseph Hospital (O, 565 beds), 1835 Franklin St., Denver 80218; tel. 303/837-7111; Sr. Mary Andrew, pres.

St. Mary's Hospital and Medical Center (O, 190 beds), Seventh St. & Patterson Rd., P O Box 1628, Grand Junction 81501; tel. 303/244-2273; Sr. Marianna Bauder,pres.

Kansas: St. John Hospital (O, 76 beds), 3500 S. Fourth St., Leavenworth 66048; tel. 913/682-3721; Sr. Mary Aloys Powell, exec. dir.

St. Francis Hospital and Medical Center (O, 311 beds), 1700 W. Seventh St., Topeka 66606; tel. 913/295-8000; Sr. Ann Marita Loosen, pres.

Montana: Saint Vincent Hospital and Health Center (O, 313 beds), P O Box 35200, Zip 59107; tel. 406/657-7101; William M. Murray, pres.

St. James Community Hospital (O, 274 beds), 400 S. Clark St., Butte 59701; tel. 406/782-8361; Sr. Loretto Marie Colwell, pres.

Wyoming: De Paul Hospital (O, 121 beds), 2600 E. 18th St., Cheyenne 82001; tel. 307/632-6411; Sr. Mary Clarice Lousberg, pres.

Owned, leased, sponsored:	8 hospitals	2401 beds
Contract-managed:	0 hospitals	0 beds
Totals:	8 hospitals	2401 beds

***3045: SISTERS OF CHARITY OF NAZARETH HEALTH CORPORATION** (CC)
9300 Shelbyville Rd., Suite 501, Louisville, KY 40222; 502/429-5055; Sr. Jane Frances Kennedy, pres.

Arkansas: St. Vincent Infirmary (O, 591 beds), Two St. Vincent Circle, Little Rock 72205; tel. 501/660-3000; Sr. Margaret Vincent Blandford, chief exec. off.; A. JackReynolds, pres.

Kentucky: Flaget Memorial Hospital (O, 52 beds), 201 Cathedral Manor, Bardstown 40004; tel. 502/348-3923; Michael McAndrew, pres.

St. Joseph Hospital (O, 468 beds), One St. Joseph Dr., Lexington 40504; tel. 606/278-3436; Sr. Michael Leo Mullaney, pres.

Saints Mary and Elizabeth Hospital (O, 331 beds), 4400 Churchman Ave., Louisville 40215; tel. 502/361-6011; A. Jack Reynolds, interim pres.

For explanation of codes following names, see page B2.
*Indicates Type III membership in the American Hospital Association.

Tennessee: Memorial Hospital (O, 365 beds), 2500 Citico Ave., Chattanooga 37404; tel. 615/629-8100; Sr. Thomas De Sales Bailey, pres.

Owned, leased, sponsored:	5 hospitals	1807 beds
Contract-managed:	0 hospitals	0 beds
Totals:	5 hospitals	1807 beds

***5125: SISTERS OF CHARITY OF ST. AUGUSTINE HEALTH AND HUMAN SERVICES** (CC)
5232 Broadview Rd., Richfield, OH 44286; 216/659-9283; Sr. Mary Patricia Barrett, pres.

Ohio: Timken Mercy Medical Center (S, 555 beds), 1320 Timken Mercy Dr. N.W., Canton 44708; tel. 216/489-1000; Mark A. Nadel, pres. & chief exec. off.

St. John Hospital (S, 225 beds), 7911 Detroit Ave., Cleveland 44102; tel. 216/651-7000; Sr. Judith Ann Karam, pres.

St. Vincent Charity Hospital and Health Center (S, 414 beds), 2351 E. 22nd St., Cleveland 44115; tel. 216/861-6200; David D'Eramo PhD, pres. & chief exec. off.

St. John and West Shore Hospital (O, 200 beds), 29000 Center Ridge Rd., Westlake 44145; tel. 216/835-8000; John A. Rowland, pres.

South Carolina: Providence Hospital (S, 212 beds), 2435 Forest Dr., Columbia 29204; tel. 803/256-5300; Sr. Mary Jacob, pres.

Owned, leased, sponsored:	5 hospitals	1606 beds
Contract-managed:	0 hospitals	0 beds
Totals:	5 hospitals	1606 beds

***5815: SISTERS OF CHARITY OF ST. ELIZABETH** (CC)
49 Demarest Rd., Paramus, NJ 07652; 201/539-1600; Sr. Ellen L. Joyce, gen. superior

Connecticut: Hospital of Saint Raphael (O, 441 beds), 1450 Chapel St., New Haven 06511; tel. 203/789-3000; Robert T. Beeman, pres.

New Jersey: St. Elizabeth Hospital (O, 328 beds), 225 Williamson St., Elizabeth 07207; tel. 201/527-5000; Sr. Elizabeth Ann Maloney, exec. dir.

St. Mary's Hospital (O, 222 beds), 211 Pennington Ave., Passaic 07055; tel. 201/470-3000; Hugh Quigley, adm.

St. Joseph's Hospital and Medical Center (O, 701 beds), 703 Main St., Paterson 07503; tel. 201/977-2000; Sr. Jane Frances Brady, pres.

New York: Good Samaritan Hospital (O, 370 beds), Rte. 59, Suffern 10901; tel. 914/357-3300; Sr. Joan Regan, pres.

Owned, leased, sponsored:	5 hospitals	2062 beds
Contract-managed:	0 hospitals	0 beds
Totals:	5 hospitals	2062 beds

5985: SISTERS OF MERCY (CC)
Sacred Heart Convent, Belmont, NC 28012; 704/825-2011; Sr. Jeanne Margaret McNally, supr. gen.

North Carolina: St. Joseph's Hospital (O, 283 beds), 428 Biltmore Ave., Asheville 28801; tel. 704/255-3100; Sr. Mary Veronica Schumacher, pres. & chief exec. off.

Mercy Hospital (O, 243 beds), 2001 Vail Ave., Charlotte 28207; tel. 704/379-5000; Sr. Mary Jerome Spradley, pres.; V. Gregg Watters, exec. vice-pres.

Owned, leased, sponsored:	2 hospitals	526 beds
Contract-managed:	0 hospitals	0 beds
Totals:	2 hospitals	526 beds

***5165: SISTERS OF MERCY HEALTH CORPORATION** (CC)
28550 Eleven Mile Rd., Farmington Hills, MI 48018; 313/478-9900; Ed Connors, pres.

Illinois: Savanna City Hospital (CM, 34 beds), 1125 N. Fifth St., Savanna 61074; tel. 815/273-7751; Richard D. Phillips, adm.

Indiana: Our Lady of Mercy Hospital (O, 264 beds), U. S. Hwy. 30, Dyer 46311; tel. 219/865-2141; J. Donald Manchak, pres.

Iowa: Kossuth County Hospital (CM, 40 beds), Hwy. 169 S., Algona 50511; tel. 515/295-2451; David Schultz, adm.

Belmond Community Hospital (CM, 22 beds), 403 First St. S.E., P O Box 326, Belmond 50421; tel. 515/444-3223; James R. Hovelson, adm.

Hancock County Memorial Hospital (CM, 30 beds), 531 Second St. N.W., Box 68, Britt 50423; tel. 515/843-3801; Lawrence N. Crail, adm.

St. Joseph Mercy Hospital (O, 141 beds), 1410 N. Fourth St., Clinton 52732; tel. 319/243-5900; Sr. Mary Margaret Westrick, pres. & chief exec. off.

Howard County Hospital (CM, 42 beds), 235 Eighth Ave. W., Cresco 52136; tel. 319/547-2101; Steven B. Reiter, adm.

Mercy Health Center (O, 400 beds), Mercy Dr., Dubuque 52001; Sr. Helen Huewe, pres.

Eldora Regional Medical Center (CM, 24 beds), 2413 Edgington Ave., Eldora 50627; tel. 515/858-5416; Jonathan Goble, adm.

Forest City Community Hospital (CM, 45 beds), Hwy. 9 E., Box 470, Forest City 50436; tel. 515/582-3113; Gregory E. Patten, adm.

Franklin General Hospital (CM, 92 beds), 1720 Central Ave. E., Hampton 50441; tel. 515/456-4721; Gary Busack, adm.

Ellsworth Municipal Hospital (CM, 42 beds), 110 Rocksylvania Ave., Iowa Falls 50126; tel. 515/648-4631; Daniel T. Meyer, adm.

St. Joseph Mercy Hospital (O, 318 beds), 84 Beaumont Dr., Mason City 50401; tel. 515/424-7211; David H. Vellinga, pres. & chief exec. off.

Hegg Memorial Health Center (CM, 122 beds), 1200 21st Ave., Rock Valley 51247; tel. 712/476-5305; Justin E. Cassel, adm.

Marian Health Center (O, 484 beds), 801 Fifth St., Sioux City 51101; Mailing Address Box 3168, Sioux City, Zip 51102; tel. 712/279-2010; Sr. Elizabeth Mary Burns,pres. & chief exec. off.

Michigan: Catherine McAuley Health Center (O, 614 beds), Robert E. Laverty, pres.; Garry C. Faja, vice-pres. & adm.

Leila Hospital and Health Center (O, 209 beds), 300 North Ave., Battle Creek 49016; tel. 616/966-8002; Donald F. Ryan, pres. & chief exec. off.

Mercy Hospital (O, 174 beds), 400 Hobart St., Cadillac 49601; tel. 616/779-7200; Robert Maher, pres.

Mount Carmel Mercy Hospital (O, 347 beds), 6071 W. Outer Dr., Detroit 48235; tel. 313/927-7000; LeRoy D. Fahle, pres.

Samaritan Health Center (O, 375 beds), 5555 Conner Ave., Detroit 48213; tel. 313/579-4000; Robert Peoples, pres.

St. Mary's Health Services (O, 370 beds), 200 Jefferson St. S.E., Grand Rapids 49503; tel. 616/774-6090; Stephen A. Robbins, actg. pres. & chief exec. off.

Mercy Hospital (O, 104 beds), 1100 Michigan Ave., Grayling 49738; tel. 517/384-5461; Robert J. Maher, pres. & chief exec. off.

St. Lawrence Hospital (O, 451 beds), 1210 W. Saginaw St., Lansing 48915; tel. 517/372-3610; Arthur Knueppel, pres.

Mercy Hospital (O, 228 beds), 1500 E. Sherman Blvd., P O Box 358, Muskegon 49443; tel. 616/739-9341; Alan J. Reberg, pres. & chief exec. off.

St. Joseph Mercy Hospital (O, 531 beds), 900 Woodward Ave., Pontiac 48053; tel. 313/858-3000; John P. Cullen, pres. & chief exec. off.

Mercy Hospital (O, 119 beds), 2601 Electric Ave., Port Huron 48061; tel. 313/985-1500; Robert Beyer, pres.

New York: Mercy Community Hospital (CM, 97 beds), 160 E. Main St., P O Box 1014, Port Jervis 12771; tel. 914/856-5351; George H. St. George, adm. & chief exec. off.

Owned, leased, sponsored:	16 hospitals	5129 beds
Contract-managed:	11 hospitals	590 beds
Totals:	27 hospitals	5719 beds

For explanation of codes following names, see page B2.
*Indicates Type III membership in the American Hospital Association.

***5185: SISTERS OF MERCY HEALTH SYSTEM** (CC)
2039 N. Geyer Rd., St. Louis, MO 63131; 314/965-6100; Sr. Mary R. Rocklage, chief exec. off.

Arkansas: St. Edward Mercy Medical Center (O, 343 beds), 7301 Rogers Ave., Fort Smith 72903; Mailing Address P O Box 2405, Fort Smith, Zip 72902; tel. 501/484-6000; Sr.Judith Marie Keith, chief exec. off.

St. Joseph's Regional Health Center (O, 267 beds), 100 Whittington Ave., Hot Springs National Park 71901; tel. 501/624-5451; Sr. Mary Werner, pres.

Mercy Hospital and Pinewood Nursing Home (O, 26 beds), Highways 71 & 80, Box Q, Waldron 72958; tel. 501/637-4135; Sr. Donald Mary, adm.

Kansas: Mercy Hospitals of Kansas (O, 162 beds), 821 Burke St., Fort Scott 66701; tel. 316/223-2200; Andrew B. Lorimer, chief exec. off.

Mercy Hospitals of Kansas (O, 93 beds), 800 W. Myrtle St., Box 388, Independence 67301; tel. 316/331-2200; Jerry Stevenson, vice-pres. & chief oper. off.

Louisiana: Mercy Hospital of New Orleans (O, 248 beds), 301 N. Jefferson Davis Pkwy., New Orleans 70119; tel. 504/486-7361; Sr. Barbara Grant, chief oper. off.

Mississippi: Mercy Regional Medical Center (O, 225 beds), 100 McAuley Dr., Box 271, Vicksburg 39180; tel. 601/631-2131; James S. Kaigler, adm. & chief oper. off.

Missouri: Mercy Hospital (O, 51 beds), Hwy. 60 & 5 N., Box 528, Mansfield 65704; tel. 417/924-3281; Mark E. Cross, adm.

St. John's Regional Health Center (O, 880 beds), 1235 E. Cherokee St., Springfield 65804; tel. 417/885-2000; James W. Swift, pres.

St. John's Mercy Medical Center (O, 911 beds), John T. Farrell, pres. & chief exec. off.

Oklahoma: Mercy Health Center (O, 292 beds), 4300 W. Memorial Rd., Oklahoma City 73120; tel. 405/755-1515; Gary J. Blan, pres. & chief exec. off.

Texas: Mercy Regional Medical Center (O, 288 beds), 1515 Logan Ave., Drawer 2068, Laredo 78044; tel. 512/727-6222; Ernesto M. Flores Jr., pres.

Owned, leased, sponsored:	12 hospitals	3786 beds
Contract-managed:	0 hospitals	0 beds
Totals:	12 hospitals	3786 beds

6015: SISTERS OF MERCY OF THE UNION-PROVINCE OF BALTIMORE (CC)
P O Box 11448, Baltimore, MD 21239; 301/435-4400; Sr. Angela Marie Ebberwein

Georgia: St. Joseph's Hospital (O, 311 beds), 11705 Mercy Blvd., Savannah 31419; tel. 912/925-4100; Sr. M. Faith McKean, pres.

Maryland: Mercy Hospital (O, 290 beds), 301 St. Paul Pl., Baltimore 21202; tel. 301/332-9000; Sr. Mary Thomas, pres.

Owned, leased, sponsored:	2 hospitals	601 beds
Contract-managed:	0 hospitals	0 beds
Totals:	2 hospitals	601 beds

***5235: SISTERS OF THE PALLOTTINE MISSIONARY SOCIETY** (CC)
2900 First Ave., Huntington, WV 25702; 304/696-2550; James Spencer, dir. finance

West Virginia: St. Joseph's Hospital (O, 95 beds), Amalia Dr., Buckhannon 26201; tel. 304/472-2000; Sr. Mary Herbert, adm.

St. Mary's Hospital (O, 440 beds), 2900 First Ave., Huntington 25701; tel. 304/526-1234; Steve J. Soltis, exec. dir.

Owned, leased, sponsored:	2 hospitals	535 beds
Contract-managed:	0 hospitals	0 beds
Totals:	2 hospitals	535 beds

5265: SISTERS OF PROVIDENCE-PROVINCE OF ST. IGNATIUS (CC)
9 E. Ninth Ave., Spokane, WA 99202; 509/455-4879; Sr. Barbara Ann Brenner, chief exec. off.

Montana: Columbus Hospital (O, 198 beds), 500 15th Ave. S., Box 5013, Great Falls 59403; tel. 406/727-3333; William J. Downer Jr., pres.

St. Patrick Hospital (O, 213 beds), 500 W. Broadway, Box 4587, Missoula 59806; tel. 406/543-7271; Lawrence L. White Jr., pres.

Washington: Sacred Heart Medical Center (O, 631 beds), W. 101 Eighth Ave., Spokane 99220; tel. 509/455-3131; Sr. Peter Claver RN, pres.

St. Mary Medical Center (O, 136 beds), 401 W. Poplar St., Box 1477, Walla Walla 99362; tel. 509/525-3320; John A. Isely, pres.

Owned, leased, sponsored:	4 hospitals	1178 beds
Contract-managed:	0 hospitals	0 beds
Totals:	4 hospitals	1178 beds

5275: SISTERS OF PROVIDENCE (CC)
520 Pike St., P O Box C11038, Seattle, WA 98111; 206/464-3355; Donald A. Brennan, pres.

Alaska: Providence Hospital (O, 324 beds), 3200 Providence Dr., Anchorage 99508; Mailing Address P O Box 196604, Anchorage, Zip 99519; tel. 907/562-2211; Al M. Camosso,chief exec. off.

California: St. Joseph Medical Center (O, 586 beds), Buena Vista & Alameda Sts., Burbank 91505; tel. 818/843-5111; James E. Sauer Jr., adm.

Providence Hospital (O, 230 beds), 3100 Summit St., Oakland 94609; Mailing Address Box 23020, Oakland, Zip 94623; tel. 415/835-4500; Sr. Dona Taylor, adm.

Oregon: Providence Hospital (O, 168 beds), 1111 Crater Lake Ave., Medford 97504; tel. 503/773-6611; Bernard J. Stormberg, adm.

Providence Milwaukie Hospital (O, 56 beds), 10150 S.E. 32nd Ave., Milwaukie 97222; tel. 503/659-6111; Robert W. Vial, pres.

Newberg Community Hospital (CM, 44 beds), 501 Villa Rd., Newberg 97132; tel. 503/538-1372; Mark W. Meinert, adm.

Providence Medical Center (O, 437 beds), 4805 N.E. Glisan St., Portland 97213; tel. 503/230-1111; John P. Lee, adm.

St. Vincent Hospital and Medical Center (O, 451 beds), 9205 S.W. Barnes Rd., Portland 97225; tel. 503/297-4411; Greg Van Pelt, adm.

Seaside General Hospital (L, 34 beds), 725 S. Wahanna Rd., Box 740, Seaside 97138; tel. 503/738-8463; Gerald Baker, adm.

Washington: St. Joseph Hospital (O, 95 beds), 1006 N. H St., Aberdeen 98520; tel. 206/533-0450; Sr. Charlotte Van Dyke, adm.

St. Helen Hospital (O, 104 beds), 500 S.E. Washington Ave., P O Box 1507, Chehalis 98532; tel. 206/748-4444; John W. Holtermann, adm.

Providence Hospital (O, 188 beds), Pacific & Nassau Sts., Everett 98201; Mailing Address Box 1067, Everett, Zip 98206; tel. 206/258-7123; Carl A. Munding, adm.

St. Peter Hospital (O, 340 beds), 413 N. Lilly Rd., Olympia 98506; tel. 206/491-9480; David L. Bjornson, adm.

Providence Medical Center (O, 359 beds), 500 17th Ave., Seattle 98122; tel. 206/326-5555; Peter Bigelow, adm.

Providence Central Memorial Hospital (O, 63 beds), 502 W. Fourth St., Box 672, Toppenish 98948; tel. 509/865-3105; Roy W. Holmes, adm.

St. Elizabeth Medical Center (O, 189 beds), 110 S. Ninth Ave., Yakima 98902; tel. 509/575-5000; Sr. Karin Dufault RN PhD, adm.

Owned, leased, sponsored:	15 hospitals	3624 beds
Contract-managed:	1 hospitals	44 beds
Totals:	16 hospitals	3668 beds

For explanation of codes following names, see page B2.
*Indicates Type III membership in the American Hospital Association.

***5285: SISTERS OF PROVIDENCE HEALTH AND HUMAN SERVICE** (CC)
209 Carew St., Springfield, MA 01104; 413/536-7511; Sr. Catherine Laboure, pres.

Massachusetts: Providence Hospital (O, 247 beds), 1233 Main St., Holyoke 01040; tel. 413/536-5111; William J. Laffey, pres.

Farren Memorial Hospital (O, 72 beds), 56 Main St., Montague 01376, Mailing Address Turners Falls, Zip 01376; tel. 413/774-3111; Alan J. Labonte, adm.

Mercy Hospital (O, 322 beds), 271 Carew St., Springfield 01101; Mailing Address Box 9012, Springfield, Zip 01102; tel. 413/781-9100; Sr. Mary Caritas, pres.

Owned, leased, sponsored:	3 hospitals	641 beds
Contract-managed:	0 hospitals	0 beds
Totals:	3 hospitals	641 beds

5685: SISTERS OF ST. CASIMIR (CC)
2601 W. Marquette Rd., Chicago, IL 60629; 312/434-6700; Sr. M. Joanella Fayert, pres.

Illinois: Holy Cross Hospital (O, 365 beds), 2701 W. 68th St., Chicago 60629; tel. 312/471-8000; Sr. Teresa Mary Clarkson, pres.

Loretto Hospital (O, 212 beds), 645 S. Central Ave., Chicago 60644; tel. 312/626-4300; Sr. Marion, pres. & chief exec. off.

Owned, leased, sponsored:	2 hospitals	577 beds
Contract-managed:	0 hospitals	0 beds
Totals:	2 hospitals	577 beds

5365: SISTERS OF ST. FRANCIS OF THE PROVINCE OF GOD (CC)
Grove & McRoberts Rds., Pittsburgh, PA 15234; 412/882-9911; Sr. Marietta Zvirblis, coor.

Illinois: St. Joseph's Hospital (O, 165 beds), 915 E. Fifth St., Alton 62002; tel. 618/463-5151; Sr. Barbara Jean Donovan, pres.

Good Samaritan Hospital (O, 188 beds), 605 N. 12th St., Mount Vernon 62864; tel. 618/242-4600; Herbert H. Bell, pres.

Owned, leased, sponsored:	2 hospitals	353 beds
Contract-managed:	0 hospitals	0 beds
Totals:	2 hospitals	353 beds

5925: SISTERS OF ST. FRANCIS OF THE MISSION OF THE IMMACULATE VIRGIN (CC)
Immaculate Conception Motherhouse, Hastings On Hudson, NY 10706; 914/478-3910; Sr. Mary Paul, supr. gen.

New York: Saint Francis Hospital (O, 396 beds), N. Rd., Poughkeepsie 12601; tel. 914/431-8116; Donald F. Murphy, exec. vice-pres.

St. Agnes Hospital (O, 191 beds), 305 N. St., White Plains 10605; tel. 914/681-4500; Robert J. Trefry, exec. vice-pres.

Owned, leased, sponsored:	2 hospitals	587 beds
Contract-managed:	0 hospitals	0 beds
Totals:	2 hospitals	587 beds

5975: SISTERS OF ST. FRANCIS-IMMACULATE HEART OF MARY-PROVINCE OF HANKINSON (CC)
St. Francis Convent, Hankinson, ND 58041; 701/242-7197; Sr. Mary Louise Jundt, dir.

North Dakota: Towner County Memorial Hospital (O, 34 beds), Cando 58324; tel. 701/968-4411; Sr. M. Arnoldine Nieberler, adm.

St. Gerard's Community Hospital (O, 54 beds), 613 First Ave. S.W., Hankinson 58041; tel. 701/242-7891; Gene Hoefs, adm.

Oakes Community Hospital (O, 32 beds), 314 S. Eighth St., Oakes 58474; tel. 701/742-3291; Sr. Mary Jane Reiber, adm.

Owned, leased, sponsored:	3 hospitals	120 beds
Contract-managed:	0 hospitals	0 beds
Totals:	3 hospitals	120 beds

5345: SISTERS OF ST. FRANCIS HEALTH SERVICES, INC. (CC)
1515 Dragoon Trail, P O Box 1290, Mishawaka, IN 46544; 219/259-3935; Sr. M. Theresa Solbach, pres.

Illinois: St. James Hospital Medical Center (O, 365 beds), Chicago Rd. at Lincoln Hwy., Chicago Heights 60411; tel. 312/756-1000; Sr. Antoinette Marie Van Der Werf, pres.

St. Francis Hospital (O, 469 beds), 355 Ridge Ave., Evanston 60202; tel. 312/492-4000; Sr. M. Alfreda Bracht, pres.

Indiana: St. Francis Hospital Center (O, 470 beds), 1600 Albany St., Beech Grove 46107; tel. 317/787-3311; Paul J. Stitzel, pres. & chief exec. off.

St. Margaret Hospital (O, 487 beds), 5454 Hohman Ave., Hammond 46320; tel. 219/932-2300; Sr. Jane Marie Klein, pres.

St. Elizabeth Hospital Medical Center (O, 257 beds), 1501 Hartford St., Lafayette 47904; Mailing Address Box 7501, Lafayette, Zip 47903; tel. 317/423-6011; PaulE. Hess, pres.

St. Anthony Hospital (O, 190 beds), 301 W. Homer St., Michigan City 46360; tel. 219/879-8511; Kevin D. Leahy, pres.

Kentucky: St. Anthony Medical Center (O, 237 beds), 1313 St. Anthony Pl., Louisville 40204; tel. 502/587-1161; Michael Budnick, adm.

Ohio: St. Alexis Hospital (O, 201 beds), 5163 Broadway, Cleveland 44127; tel. 216/429-8000; Larry K. Lehner, pres. & chief exec. off.

Tennessee: St. Joseph Hospital (O, 440 beds), 220 Overton Ave., Box 178, Memphis 38101; tel. 901/577-2700; Sr. M. Annette Crone, chief exec. off.

Owned, leased, sponsored:	9 hospitals	3116 beds
Contract-managed:	0 hospitals	0 beds
Totals:	9 hospitals	3116 beds

***5715: SISTERS OF ST. FRANCIS-3RD ORDER REGULAR OF BUFFALO** (CC)
400 Mill St., Williamsville, NY 14221; 716/632-2155; Sr. Maureen Ann, gen. minister

New York: St. Francis Hospital of Buffalo (O, 75 beds), 2787 Main St., Buffalo 14214; tel. 716/837-4200; Sr. Jeanne Weisbeck, adm.

Mount St. Mary's Hospital of Niagara Falls (O, 204 beds), 5300 Military Rd., Lewiston 14092; tel. 716/297-4800; Richard B. Russell, adm.

Owned, leased, sponsored:	2 hospitals	279 beds
Contract-managed:	0 hospitals	0 beds
Totals:	2 hospitals	279 beds

5445: SISTERS OF ST. JOSEPH-3RD ORDER OF ST. FRANCIS (CC)
105 E. Jefferson, P O Box 688, South Bend, IN 46624; 219/233-1166; Sr. Adalbert Stal, central treas.; Sr. Joanne Skalski, dir. inst spon hip bd.

Colorado: St. Joseph Hospital of the Plains (O, 32 beds), 602 N. Sixth St. W., P O Box 578, Cheyenne Wells 80810; tel. 303/767-5661; James L. Giedd, chief exec. off.

Ohio: Marymount Hospital (O, 279 beds), 12300 McCracken Rd., Garfield Heights 44125; tel. 216/581-0500; Thomas J. Trudell, pres. & chief exec. off.

Owned, leased, sponsored:	2 hospitals	311 beds
Contract-managed:	0 hospitals	0 beds
Totals:	2 hospitals	311 beds

5935: SISTERS OF ST. JOSEPH (CC)
Rural Rte. 3, Box 291a, Tipton, IN 46072; 317/456-5300; Sr. Veronica Baumgartner, pres.

Indiana: Mercy Hospital (O, 49 beds), 1331 S. A St., Elwood 46036; tel. 317/552-3336; James E. Baer, adm.

For explanation of codes following names, see page B2.
*Indicates Type III membership in the American Hospital Association.

Saint Joseph Hospital and Health Center (O, 152 beds), 1907 W. Sycamore St., Kokomo 46901; tel. 317/452-5611; Sr. M. Martin McEntee, pres.

Owned, leased, sponsored:	2 hospitals	201 beds
Contract-managed:	0 hospitals	0 beds
Totals:	2 hospitals	201 beds

5555: SISTERS OF ST. JOSEPH HEALTH SYSTEM (CC)
3427 Gull Rd., Nazareth, MI 49074; 616/381-2500; Sr. Irene Waldmann, pres.

Michigan: St. John Hospital (O, 568 beds), 22101 Moross Rd., Detroit 48236; tel. 313/343-4000; Glenn A. Wesselmann, pres. & chief exec. off.

Lee Memorial Hospital (O, 74 beds), 420 W. High St., Dowagiac 49047; tel. 616/782-8681; Roman I. Borszcz, adm.

St. Joseph Hospital (O, 423 beds), 302 Kensington Ave., Flint 48502; tel. 313/762-8000; Young S. Suh, pres.

Wheelock Memorial Hospital (O, 31 beds), 7280 State Rd., Goodrich 48438; tel. 313/636-2221; Norma J. Murphy, chief exec. off.

Borgess Medical Center (O, 462 beds), 1521 Gull Rd., Kalamazoo 49001; tel. 616/383-7000; R. Timothy Stack, pres.

Harrison Community Hospital (O, 96 beds), 26755 Ballard Rd., Mount Clemens 48045; tel. 313/465-5501; David Sessions, adm.

River District Hospital (CM, 68 beds), 4100 S. River Rd., St. Clair 48079; tel. 313/329-7111; William B. Leaver, adm.

Tawas St. Joseph Hospital (O, 65 beds), 200 Hemlock, P O Box 659, Tawas City 48764; tel. 517/362-3411; Michael Jones, pres.

Owned, leased, sponsored:	7 hospitals	1719 beds
Contract-managed:	1 hospitals	68 beds
Totals:	8 hospitals	1787 beds

5615: SISTERS OF ST. JOSEPH OF CHAMBERY-NORTH AMERICAN PROVINCE (CC)
27 Park Rd., West Hartford, CT 06119; 203/233-5126; Sr. Jean Sauntry, supr.

Connecticut: Saint Francis Hospital and Medical Center (CM, 569 beds), 114 Woodland St., Hartford 06105; tel. 203/548-4000; Sr. Francis Marie Garvey, pres. & treas.

St. Joseph Medical Center (CM, 200 beds), 128 Strawberry Hill Ave., Box 1222, Stamford 06904; tel. 203/327-3500; Sr. Daniel Marie McCabe, pres. & chief exec. off.

St. Mary's Hospital (CM, 301 beds), 56 Franklin St., Waterbury 06702; tel. 203/574-6000; Sr. Marquerite Waite, exec. dir.

Owned, leased, sponsored:	0 hospitals	0 beds
Contract-managed:	3 hospitals	1070 beds
Totals:	3 hospitals	1070 beds

5575: SISTERS OF THE HOLY FAMILY OF NAZARETH-SACRED HEART PROVINCE (CC)
353 N. River Rd., Des Plaines, IL 60016; 312/298-6760; Sr. M. Loretta Markiewicz, prov. supr.

Illinois: Saint Mary of Nazareth Hospital Center (O, 490 beds), 2233 W. Division St., Chicago 60622; tel. 312/770-2000; Sr. Stella Louise, pres.

Holy Family Hospital (O, 246 beds), 100 N. River Rd., Des Plaines 60016; tel. 312/297-1800; Sr. Patricia Ann, pres.

Owned, leased, sponsored:	2 hospitals	736 beds
Contract-managed:	0 hospitals	0 beds
Totals:	2 hospitals	736 beds

5305: SISTERS OF THE SORROWFUL MOTHER-MINISTRY CORPORATION (CC)
6618 N. Teutonia Ave., Milwaukee, WI 53209; 414/352-4056; Sr. M. Lois Bush, pres. & chief exec. off.

Iowa: Holy Family Hospital (O, 58 beds), 826 N. Eighth St., Estherville 51334; tel. 712/362-2631; Donald M. Schmaus, pres.

Kansas: St. Francis Regional Medical Center (O, 570 beds), 929 N. St. Francis Ave., Wichita 67214; tel. 316/268-5000; Sr. M. Sylvia Egan, pres. & chief exec. off.

Minnesota: St. Elizabeth Hospital (O, 97 beds), 1200 Fifth Grant Blvd. W., Wabasha 55981; tel. 612/565-4531; Thomas Crowley, adm.

Wisconsin: St. Joseph's Hospital (O, 524 beds), 611 St. Joseph Ave., Marshfield 54449; tel. 715/387-1713; David R. Jaye, pres.

Mercy Medical Center (O, 217 beds), 631 Hazel St., Box 1100, Oshkosh 54902; tel. 414/236-2000; Joseph P. Ross, pres.

Sacred Heart-St. Mary's Hospitals (O, 193 beds), Kevin O'Donnell, pres.

St. Michael's Hospital (O, 129 beds), 900 Illinois Ave., Stevens Point 54481; tel. 715/346-5000; Richard R. Lansing, pres.

Owned, leased, sponsored:	7 hospitals	1788 beds
Contract-managed:	0 hospitals	0 beds
Totals:	7 hospitals	1788 beds

5875: SISTERS OF THE SORROWFUL MOTHER-TULSA PROVINCIALATE (CC)
17600 E. 51st St. S., Broken Arrow, OK 74012; 918/355-5595; Sr. M. Julietta Mendoza, prov.

New Mexico: St. Mary's Regional Health Center (O, 238 beds), S. Main & Chisum Sts., Box 1938, Roswell 88201; tel. 505/622-1110; George S. Macko, chief exec. off.

Oklahoma: St. John Medical Center (O, 648 beds), 1923 S. Utica Ave., Tulsa 74104; tel. 918/744-2345; Sr. M. Therese Gottschalk, chief exec. off.

Owned, leased, sponsored:	2 hospitals	886 beds
Contract-managed:	0 hospitals	0 beds
Totals:	2 hospitals	886 beds

5955: SISTERS OF THE 3RD FRANCISCAN ORDER-MINOR CONVENTUALS (CC)
100 Michaels Ave., Syracuse, NY 13208; 315/425-0115; Sr. M. Aileen Griffin, supr. gen.

Hawaii: St. Francis Medical Center (O, 233 beds), 2230 Liliha St., Honolulu 96817; tel. 808/547-6011; Sr. Maureen Keleher, chief exec. off.

New York: St. Joseph's Hospital Health Center (O, 457 beds), 301 Prospect Ave., Syracuse 13203; tel. 315/424-5111; James H. Abbott, adm.

St. Elizabeth Hospital (O, 269 beds), 2209 Genesee St., Utica 13501; tel. 315/798-8100; Sr. Rose Vincent, exec. adm.

Owned, leased, sponsored:	3 hospitals	959 beds
Contract-managed:	0 hospitals	0 beds
Totals:	3 hospitals	959 beds

***5335: SISTERS OF THE 3RD ORDER OF ST. FRANCIS** (CC)
1124 N. Berkley Ave., Peoria, IL 61603; 309/655-2850; Sr. Frances Marie, exec. vice-pres.

Illinois: St. Joseph's Hospital Medical Center (O, 149 beds), 2200 E. Washington St., Box 1287, Bloomington 61701; tel. 309/662-3311; Kenneth J. Natzke, adm.

St. Mary's Hospital (O, 159 beds), 3333 N. Seminary St., Galesburg 61401; tel. 309/344-3161; Richard S. Kowalski, adm.

Saint Francis Medical Center (O, 855 beds), 530 N.E. Glen Oak Ave., Peoria 61637; tel. 309/655-2000; Sr. M. Canisia, adm.

Saint James Hospital (O, 91 beds), 610 E. Water St., Pontiac 61764; tel. 815/842-2828; Steve L. Urosevich, adm.

For explanation of codes following names, see page B2.
*Indicates Type III membership in the American Hospital Association.

Saint Anthony Medical Center (O, 258 beds), 5666 E. State St., Rockford 61101; tel. 815/226-2000; Kevin D. Schoeplein, adm.

Michigan: St. Francis Hospital (O, 110 beds), 3401 Ludington St., Escanaba 49829; tel. 906/786-3311; Robert Clark, adm.

Owned, leased, sponsored:	6 hospitals	1622 beds
Contract-managed:	0 hospitals	0 beds
Totals:	6 hospitals	1622 beds

***4155: SOUTH CAROLINA BAPTIST HOSPITALS** (CO)
1333 Taylor St., Columbia, SC 29201; 803/771-5046; William A. Boyce, pres.

South Carolina: Baptist Medical Center (O, 475 beds), Taylor at Marion St., Columbia 29220; tel. 803/771-5010; Charles D. Beaman Jr., pres.

Baptist Medical Center Easley (O, 109 beds), Fleetwood Dr., Box 687, Easley 29641; tel. 803/859-6365; P. Sherman Hendricks, exec. vice-pres.

Owned, leased, sponsored:	2 hospitals	584 beds
Contract-managed:	0 hospitals	0 beds
Totals:	2 hospitals	584 beds

1605: SOUTHEAST COMMUNITY HEALTH SERVICES (IO)
1433 Miccosukee Rd., Tallahassee, FL 32308; 904/681-5675; Keith Gilles, chief oper. off.

Florida: Doctors Memorial Hospital (L, 48 beds), 407 E. Ash St., P O Box 1090, Perry 32347; tel. 904/584-0800; William H. Anderson, adm.

Gadsden Memorial Hospital (L, 51 beds), Hwy. 90 E., Box 819, Quincy 32351; tel. 904/875-1100; Steven D. Patonai, adm.

Owned, leased, sponsored:	2 hospitals	99 beds
Contract-managed:	0 hospitals	0 beds
Totals:	2 hospitals	99 beds

***4175: SOUTHERN ILLINOIS HOSPITAL SERVICES** (NP)
608 E. College St., P O Box 522, Carbondale, IL 62903; 618/457-7833; Jerry A. Hickam, pres.

Illinois: Memorial Hospital (O, 151 beds), 404 W. Main St., Box 481, Carbondale 62901; tel. 618/549-0721; George Maroney, adm.

Herrin Hospital (O, 98 beds), 201 S. 14th St., Herrin 62948; tel. 618/942-2171; Larry Feil, adm.

Owned, leased, sponsored:	2 hospitals	249 beds
Contract-managed:	0 hospitals	0 beds
Totals:	2 hospitals	249 beds

***3505: SOUTHWEST COMMUNITY HEALTH SERVICES** (CO)
6100 Pan American Freeway N.E., Albuquerque, NM 87109; Mailing Address P O Box 26666, Albuquerque, Zip 87125; 505/823-8313; Richard Barr, pres.

Colorado: Delta County Memorial Hospital (CM, 52 beds), 100 Stafford Lane, Delta 81416; tel. 303/874-7681; Ken Moore, adm.

New Mexico: Kaseman Presbyterian Hospital (O, 192 beds), 8300 Constitution Ave. N.E., Albuquerque 87110; tel. 505/291-2000; Phillip J. Todd, adm.

Northside Presbyterian Hospital (O, 57 beds), 5901 Harper Dr. N.E., Albuquerque 87109; tel. 505/823-8500; Gordon R. Aird, adm.

Presbyterian Hospital (O, 413 beds), P O Box 26666, Albuquerque 87125; tel. 505/841-1443; Robert Luther, adm.

Artesia General Hospital (CM, 36 beds), 702 N. 13th St., Artesia 88210; tel. 505/748-3333; Joe Abrutz, adm.

Valencia Presbyterian Hospital (O, 25 beds), 609 S. Christopher Rd., Belen 87002; tel. 505/864-2221; John Zondlo, adm.

Clovis High Plains Hospital (O, 106 beds), 2100 N. Thomas St., Box 1688, Clovis 88101; tel. 505/769-2141; Phillip J. Todd, adm.

Espanola Hospital (O, 80 beds), 1010 Spruce St., Espanola 87532; tel. 505/753-7111; Grant H. Nelson, adm.

Nor-Lea General Hospital (CM, 28 beds), 1600 N. Main, Lovington 88260; tel. 505/396-6611; Nancy McIlwaine, adm.

Miners' Colfax Medical Center (CM, 60 beds), Hospital Dr., Raton 87740; tel. 505/445-3661; John E. Saint, adm.

Lincoln County Medical Center (L, 39 beds), 211 Sudderth Dr., P O Drawer 3c/d, Hollywood Sta., Ruidoso 88345; tel. 505/257-7381; Steve Keller, adm.

Socorro General Hospital (O, 32 beds), U. S. Hwy. 60 W., Box 1009, Socorro 87801; tel. 505/835-1140; Jeffrey M. Dye, adm.

Dr. Dan C. Trigg Memorial Hospital (L, 42 beds), 301 E. Miel De Luna Ave., P O Box 608, Tucumcari 88401; tel. 505/461-0141; Gary Little, adm.

Owned, leased, sponsored:	9 hospitals	986 beds
Contract-managed:	4 hospitals	176 beds
Totals:	13 hospitals	1162 beds

***2395: SOUTHWEST HEALTH SYSTEM** (NP)
133 Donohoe Rd., Greensburg, PA 15601; 412/836-6820; Joseph J. Peluso, pres. & chief exec. off.

Pennsylvania: Westmoreland Hospital (O, 355 beds), 532 W. Pittsburgh St., Greensburg 15601; tel. 412/832-4000; Walter Van Dyke, exec. dir.

Westmoreland McGinnis Hospital (O, 17 beds), 221 W. Main St., Ligonier 15658; tel. 412/238-9573; Joseph J. Peluso, exec. dir.

Owned, leased, sponsored:	2 hospitals	372 beds
Contract-managed:	0 hospitals	0 beds
Totals:	2 hospitals	372 beds

***4195: SPARTANBURG HOSPITAL SYSTEM** (NP)
101 E. Wood St., Spartanburg, SC 29303; 803/591-6107; Charles C. Boone, pres.

South Carolina: Spartanburg Regional Medical Center (O, 526 beds), 101 E. Wood St., Spartanburg 29303; tel. 803/591-6000; Charles C. Boone, pres.

B. J. Workman Memorial Hospital (O, 54 beds), 751 E. Georgia St., P O Box 699, Woodruff 29388; tel. 803/476-8122; C. Milton Snipes, adm.

Owned, leased, sponsored:	2 hospitals	580 beds
Contract-managed:	0 hospitals	0 beds
Totals:	2 hospitals	580 beds

0825: SPECIALTY HOSPITAL DIVISION OF NME (IO)
1010 Wisconsin Ave. N.W., Suite 900, Washington, DC 20007; 202/337-5600; Norman A. Zober, pres.

Arizona: Tucson Psychiatric Institute (O, 38 beds), 355 N. Wilmot Rd., Tucson 85711; tel. 602/745-5100; Tommie Duncan, adm.

California: Sierra Royale Hospital (O, 50 beds), 125 W. Sierra Madre Ave., Azusa 91702; tel. 818/334-0351; Diana Goulet, adm.

Doctors Hospital of Lakewood-Clark (O, 90 beds), 5300 Clark Ave., Lakewood 90712; tel. 213/866-9711; Michael Kerr, chief exec. off. & exec. dir.

Los Altos Hospital and Mental Health Center (O, 97 beds), 3340 Los Coyotes Diagonal, Box 8000, Long Beach 90808; tel. 213/421-9311; Thomas R. Mesa, adm.

Colorado: Boulder Psychiatric Institute (L, 64 beds), 4390 Baseline Rd., 777 29th St., Boulder 80303; tel. 303/447-2900; Andrew L. Braun, adm.

Connecticut: Elmcrest Psychiatric Institute (O, 105 beds), 25 Marlborough St., Portland 06480; tel. 203/342-0480

District of Columbia: Psychiatric Institute of Washington (L, 201 beds), 4460 McArthur Blvd. N.W., Washington 20007; tel. 202/944-3400; Howard Hoffman MD, chief exec. off.

For explanation of codes following names, see page B2.
*Indicates Type III membership in the American Hospital Association.

Florida: Lake Hospital of the Palm Beaches (O, 72 beds), 1710 Fourth Ave. N., Box 1668, Lake Worth 33460; tel. 305/588-7341; Mark E. Schneider, chief exec. off.; IrlExtein MD, med. dir.

Medfield Center (O, 32 beds), 12891 Seminole Blvd., Largo 33544; tel. 813/581-8757; Sherrie Klein, adm.

Sarasota Palms Hospital (O, 90 beds), 1650 S. Osprey Ave., Sarasota 33579; tel. 813/366-6070; Robert J. Constantine PhD, adm.

Georgia: Psychiatric Institute of Atlanta (O, 33 beds), 811 Juniper St. N.E., Atlanta 30308; tel. 404/881-5800; Mark A. Gould MD, chief exec. off.

Brawner Psychiatric Institute (O, 89 beds), 3180 Atlanta St. S.E., Smyrna 30080; tel. 404/436-0081; Brent J. Bryson, adm.

Indiana: Kingwood Hospital (O, 89 beds), 3714 S. Franklin St., Michigan City 46360; tel. 219/872-0531; Mary Lou Saxon, adm.

Maryland: Psychiatric Institute of Montgomery County (O, 75 beds), 14901 Broschart Rd., Rockville 20850; tel. 301/251-4500; John Meeks MD, chief exec. off.

Michigan: Psychiatric Center of Michigan (O, 48 beds), 35031 23 Mile Rd., New Baltimore 48047; tel. 313/725-5777; Raymond Buck MD, chief exec. off.

New Jersey: Fair Oaks Hospital (O, 144 beds), 19 Prospect St., Summit 07901; tel. 201/522-7000; William A. Howe, adm.

Garden State Rehabilitation Hospital (O, 146 beds), 14 Hospital Dr., Toms River 08753; tel. 201/244-3100; H. P. Thesingh, chief exec. off. & adm.

New York: Regent Hospital (O, 29 beds), 425 E. 61st St., New York 10021; tel. 212/935-3400; Ben Farbman, adm.; A. Carter Pottash MD, med. dir.

North Carolina: Highland Hospital (O, 98 beds), 49 Zillicoa St., Asheville 28801; Mailing Address Box 1101, Asheville, Zip 28802; tel. 704/254-3201; Jack W. Bonner III MD,chief exec. off.

Pennsylvania: Rehabx Hospital for Special Services (O, 65 beds), R D 5, Box 451-A, Bellefonte 16823; tel. 814/359-3421; Dennis C. Falck, adm.

Lake Erie Institute of Rehabilitation (O, 90 beds), 137 W. Second St., Erie 16507; tel. 814/453-5602; Urban J. Lariccia, pres.

Rehabilitation Hospital in Mechanicsburg (O, 92 beds), 175 Lancaster Blvd., P O Box 2016, Mechanicsburg 17055; tel. 717/691-3700; Kurt A. Meyer, chief exec. off.

Rehabx Hospital for Special Services of York (O, 88 beds), 1850 Normandie Dr., York 17404; tel. 717/767-6941; Marie P. Cloney, adm.

Tennessee: Mid-South Hospital (O, 190 beds), 135 N. Pauline St., Memphis 38105; tel. 901/527-5211; James E. Hughes, adm.

Texas: Psychiatric Institute of Fort Worth (O, 118 beds), 815 Eighth Ave., Fort Worth 76104; tel. 817/335-4040; Peter J. Alexis, adm.

Colonial Hills Hospital (O, 75 beds), 4330 Vance Jackson Rd., San Antonio 78230; tel. 512/341-5131; James M. Hunt, adm.

Laurelwood Hospital (O, 100 beds), The Woodlands 77380; Mailing Address P O Box 7695, The Woodlands, Zip 77387; tel. 713/367-4422; Michael Haley, chief exec. off.

Baywood Hospital (O, 100 beds), 709 Medical Center Blvd., Webster 77598; tel. 713/332-9550; Ronald Cronen, adm.

Virginia: Springwood Psychiatric Institute (L, 30 beds), Rte. 4, Box 50, Leesburg 22075; tel. 703/777-0800; C. Gibson Dunn MD, chief exec. off.

Tidewater Psychiatric Institute-Norfolk (O, 65 beds), 860 Kempsville Rd., Norfolk 23502; tel. 804/461-4565; John D. Vick, adm.

Psychiatric Institute of Richmond (O, 84 beds), 3001 Fifth Ave., Richmond 23222; tel. 804/329-3400; H. James Mathay, adm.

Tidewater Psychiatric Institute (O, 61 beds), 1701 Will-O-Wisp Dr., Virginia Beach 23454; tel. 804/481-1211; Stuart Ashman MD, chief exec. off.

Wisconsin: Memorial Hospital of Boscobel (O, 136 beds), 205 Parker St., Boscobel 53805; tel. 608/375-4112; Gerhard O. Qualey, adm.

Riverwood Center (O, 37 beds), 445 Court St. N., Prescott 54021; tel. 715/262-3286; Ray G. Chapman, adm.

Owned, leased, sponsored:	34 hospitals	2921 beds
Contract-managed:	0 hospitals	0 beds
Totals:	34 hospitals	2921 beds

0365: SPRINGHILL HEALTH SERVICES (IO)

3715 Dauphin St., Mobile, AL 36608; 205/342-3300; Bill A. Mason, pres.

Alabama: Springhill Memorial Hospital (O, 252 beds), 3719 Dauphin St., Box 8246, Mobile 36608; tel. 205/344-9630; Donald O. Bedsole MD, bd. chm.

Florida: Coral Reef Hospital (O, 190 beds), 9333 S.W. 152nd St., Miami 33157; tel. 305/251-2500; C. William Nordwall, chief exec. off.

Owned, leased, sponsored:	2 hospitals	442 beds
Contract-managed:	0 hospitals	0 beds
Totals:	2 hospitals	442 beds

*5455: SSM HEALTH CARE SYSTEM (CC)

1031 Bellevue Ave., St. Louis, MO 63117; 314/768-1600; Sr. Mary Jean Ryan, pres. & chief exec. off.

Illinois: St. Francis Hospital (O, 401 beds), 12935 S. Gregory St., Blue Island 60406; tel. 312/597-2000; Bryant R. Hanson, exec. dir.

Missouri: St. Mary's Hospital of Blue Springs (O, 72 beds), 201 W. R D Mize Rd., Blue Springs 64015; tel. 816/228-5900; N. Gary Wages, exec. dir.

St. Elizabeth's Hospital (S, 99 beds), 109 Virginia St., Box 551, Hannibal 63401; tel. 314/221-0414; Edson E. Swift, exec. dir.

St. Mary's Health Center (O, 130 beds), 610 W. Elm St., Jefferson City 65101; tel. 314/635-7642; Charles M. Harris, exec. dir.

St. Mary's Hospital (O, 264 beds), 2800 Main St., Kansas City 64108; tel. 816/753-5700; William P. Thompson, exec. dir.

St. Francis Hospital (S, 95 beds), 225 W. Hayden St., Marceline 64658; tel. 816/376-3521; Terry L. Watson, exec. dir.

Arcadia Valley Hospital (O, 50 beds), Hwy. 21, Pilot Knob 63663; tel. 314/546-3924; Kerry Noble, exec. dir.

St. Joseph Health Center (O, 402 beds), 300 First Capitol Dr., St. Charles 63301; tel. 314/947-5000; Martin J. Strussion, exec. dir.

Cardinal Glennon Children's Hospital (L, 190 beds), 1465 S. Grand Blvd., St. Louis 63104; tel. 314/577-5600; Douglas A. Ries, exec. dir.

St. Mary's Health Center (O, 482 beds), 6420 Clayton Rd., St. Louis 63117; tel. 314/768-8000; Sr. Betty Brucker, exec. dir.

South Carolina: St. Eugene Community Hospital (O, 70 beds), 301 E. Jackson St., Dillon 29536; tel. 803/774-4111; Leo F. Childers Jr., exec. dir.

Wisconsin: St. Clare Hospital (O, 100 beds), 707 14th St., Baraboo 53913; tel. 608/356-5561; Ronald J. Levy, exec. dir.

St. Marys Hospital Medical Center (O, 357 beds), 707 S. Mills St., Madison 53715; tel. 608/251-6100; Gerald W. Lefert, exec. dir.

Owned, leased, sponsored:	13 hospitals	2712 beds
Contract-managed:	0 hospitals	0 beds
Totals:	13 hospitals	2712 beds

*5425: ST. JOSEPH HEALTH SYSTEM (CC)

440 S. Batavia St., Orange, CA 92668; 714/997-7690; Robert W. O'Leary, pres.

California: St. Joseph Hospital (O, 69 beds), 2700 Dolbeer St., Eureka 95501; tel. 707/443-8051; Peter W. Kriger, pres. & chief exec. off.

Redwood Memorial Hospital (O, 47 beds), 3300 Renner Dr., Fortuna 95540; tel. 707/725-3361; Willard G. Foote, pres. & chief exec. off.

St. Jude Hospital-Fullerton (O, 301 beds), 101 E. Valencia Mesa Dr., Fullerton 92635; Mailing Address Box 4138, Fullerton, Zip 92634; tel. 714/871-3280; Sr. JaneFrances, pres.

For explanation of codes following names, see page B2.
*Indicates Type III membership in the American Hospital Association.

Queen of the Valley Hospital (O, 180 beds), 1000 Trancas St., Box 2340, Napa 94558; tel. 707/252-4411; Sr. Ann McGuinn, pres. & chief exec. off.

St. Joseph Hospital (O, 409 beds), 1100 W. Stewart Dr., Orange 92668; tel. 714/633-9111; Walter W. Noce Jr., pres. & chief exec. off.

Santa Rosa Memorial Hospital (O, 240 beds), 1165 Montgomery Dr., Santa Rosa 95405; Mailing Address Box 522, Santa Rosa, Zip 95402; tel. 707/546-3210; George L.Heidkamp, pres. & chief exec. off.

St. Jude Hospital Yorba Linda (O, 106 beds), 16850 E. Bastanchury Rd., Box 69, Yorba Linda 92686; tel. 714/993-3000; Gayle N. Bullock, pres. & chief exec. off.

Texas: St. Mary of the Plains Hospital (O, 358 beds), 4000 24th St., Lubbock 79410; tel. 806/796-6000; Jake Henry Jr., pres. & chief exec. off.

Owned, leased, sponsored:	8 hospitals	1710 beds
Contract-managed:	0 hospitals	0 beds
Totals:	8 hospitals	1710 beds

*** 7675: ST. LUKE'S HEALTH SYSTEM** (NP)
5025 E. Washington, Suite 200, Phoenix, AZ 85034; 602/231-0017; Brian C. Lockwood, pres.

Arizona: Parker Community Hospital (CM, 39 beds), Mohave Rd., Box 1149, Parker 85344; tel. 602/669-9201; William G. Coe, adm.

St. Luke's Behavioral Health Center (O, 150 beds), 1800 E. Van Buren, Phoenix 85006; tel. 602/251-8100; Robert A. Rundio, pres.

St. Luke's Medical Center (O, 241 beds), 1800 E. Van Buren St., Phoenix 85006; tel. 602/251-8100; Brian C. Lockwood, pres.

Tempe St. Luke's Hospital (O, 77 beds), 1500 S. Mill Ave., Tempe 85281; tel. 602/968-9411; Earl J. Motzer PhD, pres. & chief exec. off.

Owned, leased, sponsored:	3 hospitals	468 beds
Contract-managed:	1 hospitals	39 beds
Totals:	4 hospitals	507 beds

5845: ST. LUKE'S REGIONAL MEDICAL CENTER (NP)
2720 Stone Park Blvd., Sioux City, IA 51104; 712/279-3500; David O. Biorn, pres. & chief exec. off.

Iowa: Floyd Valley Hospital (CM, 44 beds), Hwy. 3 E., P O Box 10, Le Mars 51031; tel. 712/546-7871; J. Dwight Gray, adm.

Orange City Municipal Hospital (CM, 43 beds), 115 Fourth St. N.W., Orange City 51041; tel. 712/737-4984; J. Dwight Gray, adm.

St. Luke's Regional Medical Center (O, 371 beds), 2720 Stone Park Blvd., Sioux City 51104; tel. 712/279-3500; David O. Biorn, pres.

Owned, leased, sponsored:	1 hospitals	371 beds
Contract-managed:	2 hospitals	87 beds
Totals:	3 hospitals	458 beds

3555: STATE OF HAWAII, DEPARTMENT OF HEALTH (NP)
P O Box 3378, Honolulu, HI 96801; 808/548-7402; Jerry Walker, dep. dir.

Hawaii: Hilo Hospital (O, 274 beds), 1190 Waianuenue Ave., Hilo 96720; tel. 808/969-4111; Jerry E. Merrill, adm.

Honokaa Hospital (O, 30 beds), Box 237, Honokaa 96727; tel. 808/775-7211; Yoshito Iwamoto, adm.

Leahi Hospital (O, 166 beds), 3675 Kilauea Ave., Honolulu 96816; tel. 808/734-0221; Abraham L. Choy, adm.

Samuel Mahelona Memorial Hospital (O, 76 beds), 4800 Kawaihau Rd., Kapaa 96746; tel. 808/822-4961; John M. English, adm.

Kona Hospital (O, 59 beds), Box 69, Kealakekua 96750; tel. 808/322-9311; Jennie Wung, adm.

Kohala Hospital (O, 26 beds), Mailing Address Box 10, Kapaau, Zip 96755; tel. 808/889-6211; Jack O. Halstead, adm.

Kula Hospital (O, 105 beds), 204 Kula Hwy., Kula 96790; tel. 808/878-1221; Romel Dela Cruz, adm.

Lanai Community Hospital (O, 14 beds), 628 Seventh St., Box 797, Lanai City 96763; tel. 808/565-6411; Monica L. Borges, adm.

Kau Hospital (O, 15 beds), Box 40, Pahala 96777; tel. 808/928-8331; Kenji Nagao, adm.

Maui Memorial Hospital (O, 145 beds), 221 Mahalani St., Wailuku 96793; tel. 808/244-9056; Frederick M. Burkle Jr. MD, adm.

Kauai Veterans Memorial Hospital (O, 50 beds), Waimea Canyon Rd., Box 337, Waimea 96796; tel. 808/338-9431; Janet Kawamura, actg. adm.

Owned, leased, sponsored:	11 hospitals	960 beds
Contract-managed:	0 hospitals	0 beds
Totals:	11 hospitals	960 beds

0805: STORMONT-VAIL HEALTH SERVICES CORPORATION (NP)
1500 Southwest Tenth St., Topeka, KS 66604; 913/354-6112; Howard M. Chase, chief exec. off.

Kansas: Hiawatha Community Hospital (CM, 32 beds), 300 Utah St., Hiawatha 66434; tel. 913/742-2131; J. Michael Frost, adm.

Stormont-Vail Regional Medical Center (O, 338 beds), 1500 W. Tenth St., Topeka 66604; tel. 913/354-6000; Howard M. Chase, pres. & chief exec. off.

Wamego City Hospital (CM, 26 beds), 711 Genn Dr., Wamego 66547; tel. 913/456-2295; Lannie Zweimiller, adm.

Dechairo Hospital (O, 20 beds), Westmoreland 66549; tel. 913/457-3311; Donn Demaree, adm.

Owned, leased, sponsored:	2 hospitals	358 beds
Contract-managed:	2 hospitals	58 beds
Totals:	4 hospitals	416 beds

3025: SUMMIT HEALTH, LTD. (IO)
1800 Ave. of the Stars, Los Angeles, CA 90067; 213/201-4000; William L. Pierpoint, pres. & chief exec. off.

Arizona: Mesa General Hospital Medical Center (O, 115 beds), 515 N. Mesa Dr., Mesa 85201; tel. 602/969-9111; Mark Werber, exec. dir.

Community Hospital Medical Center (O, 75 beds), 6501 N. 19th Ave., Phoenix 85015; tel. 602/249-3434; Robert Cannon, exec. dir.

Tucson General Hospital (O, 157 beds), 3838 N. Campbell Ave., Tucson 85719; tel. 602/327-5431; Ken Seidel, exec. dir.

California: Midway Hospital Medical Center (O, 230 beds), 5925 San Vicente Blvd., Los Angeles 90019; Mailing Address Box 35909, Los Angeles, Zip 90035; tel. 213/938-3161;Philip A. Cohen, reg. vice-pres.

St. Luke Medical Center (O, 107 beds), 2632 E. Washington Blvd., Bin 7021, Pasadena 91109; tel. 818/797-1141; Harry F. Adams, exec. dir.

French Hospital Medical Center (O, 125 beds), 1911 Johnson Ave., San Luis Obispo 93401; tel. 805/543-5353; Jim Gstettenbauer, exec. dir.

For explanation of codes following names, see page B2.
*Indicates Type III membership in the American Hospital Association.

Doctors Hospital of Santa Ana (O, 54 beds), 1901 N. College Ave., Santa Ana 92706; tel. 714/547-2565; Robert J. Trautman, exec. dir.

Santa Ana Hospital Medical Center (O, 83 beds), 1901 N. Fairview St., Santa Ana 92706; tel. 714/554-1653; Thomas A. Salerno, exec. dir.

Valley Community Hospital (O, 48 beds), 505 E. Plaza Dr., Santa Maria 93454; tel. 805/925-0935; Bryan D. Burklow, exec. dir.

Whittier Hospital Medical Center (O, 179 beds), 15151 Janine Dr., Whittier 90605; tel. 213/945-3561; David A. Bianchi, exec. dir.

Colorado: Eisenhower Medical Center (O, 122 beds), 33 Barnes Ave., Colorado Springs 80909; tel. 303/475-2111; Joe O'Neill, exec. dir.

Iowa: Davenport Medical Center (O, 150 beds), 1111 W. Kimberly Rd., Davenport 52806; tel. 319/391-2020; Jeff Burres, exec. dir.

Texas: Cook Memorial Hospital (O, 74 beds), 1900 S. College Ave., Levelland 79336; tel. 806/894-4963; Larry G. Todd, exec. dir.

Community Hospital of Lubbock (O, 76 beds), 5301 University Ave., Lubbock 79413; tel. 806/795-9301; Ken E. Worley, exec. dir.

South Park Medical Center (O, 99 beds), 6610 S. Quaker Ave., Lubbock 79413; tel. 806/792-7112; Lowell S. Benton, exec. dir.

Owned, leased, sponsored:	15 hospitals	1694 beds
Contract-managed:	0 hospitals	0 beds
Totals:	15 hospitals	1694 beds

***0025: SUNHEALTH CORPORATION** (NP)
4501 Charlotte Park Dr., Box 668800, Charlotte, NC 28266; 704/529-3300; Ben W. Latimer, pres.

Alabama: Dale County Hospital (CM, 89 beds), 510 James St., Box 1149, Ozark 36360; tel. 205/774-2601; Robert J. Humphrey, adm.

Florida: Indian River Memorial Hospital (CM, 293 beds), 1000 36th St., Vero Beach 32960; tel. 305/567-4311; Michael J. O'Grady, pres.

Georgia: Minnie G. Boswell Memorial Hospital (CM, 29 beds), Siloam Rd., P O Box 329, Greensboro 30642; tel. 404/453-7331; Richard M. Yaun, adm.

Burke County Hospital (CM, 40 beds), 351 Liberty St., Waynesboro 30830; tel. 404/554-4435; James R. Emery, adm.

Louisiana: Terrebonne General Medical Center (CM, 219 beds), 936 E. Main St., Box 6037, Houma 70361; tel. 504/873-4141; Alex B. Smith, adm.

North Carolina: Mountain Park Medical Center (CM, 61 beds), Murphy Hwy., Box E, Andrews 28901; tel. 704/321-4231; Joseph R. Tucker, adm.

Thoms Rehabilitation Hospital (CM, 70 beds), One Rotary Dr., Asheville 28803; Mailing Address P O Box 15025, Asheville, Zip 28813; tel. 704/274-2400; Charles D.Norvell, exec. dir.

Alamance County Hospital (CM, 133 beds), 327 N. Graham Hopedale Rd., Box 3157, Burlington 27215; tel. 919/228-1371; Richard Maxwell, vice-pres. oper.

Alamance Memorial Hospital (CM, 220 beds), 730 Hermitage Rd., Box 4008, Burlington 27215; tel. 919/229-2600; John G. Currin Jr., vice-pres. oper.

St. Luke's Hospital (CM, 52 beds), 220 Hospital Dr., Columbus 28722; tel. 704/894-3311; Thomas M. Kelly, pres.

Chowan Hospital (CM, 126 beds), Virginia Rd., Box 629, Edenton 27932; tel. 919/482-8451; Marvin A. Bryan, dir.

Cape Fear Valley Medical Center (CM, 342 beds), Owen Dr., Box 2000, Fayetteville 28302; tel. 919/323-6151; John T. Carlisle, dir.

Granville Medical Center (CM, 66 beds), College St., Box 947, Oxford 27565; tel. 919/693-5115

Chatham Hospital (CM, 68 beds), W. Third & Ivy Sts., Box 649, Siler City 27344; tel. 919/663-2113; Frank Beirne, adm.

Anson County Hospital and Skilled Nursing Facility (CM, 97 beds), 500 Morven Rd., Wadesboro 28170; tel. 704/694-5131; Thomas W. Northrop, adm.

Beaufort County Hospital (CM, 151 beds), 628 E. 12th St., Washington 27889; tel. 919/946-1911; Kenneth E. Ragland, adm.

Martin General Hospital (CM, 49 beds), 310 S. McCaskey Rd., P O Box 1128, Williamston 27892; tel. 919/792-2186; George H. Brandt Jr., adm.

South Carolina: Bamberg County Memorial Hospital (CM, 81 beds), North & McGee Sts., Bamberg 29003; tel. 803/245-4321; Charles V. Morgan, adm.

Lower Florence County Hospital (CM, 72 beds), U. S. Hwy. 52 N., Box 1035, Lake City 29560; tel. 803/394-2036; Joseph N. James Jr., interim adm.

Clarendon Memorial Hospital (CM, 56 beds), 510 S. Mill St., Box 550, Manning 29102; tel. 803/435-8463; Charlie M. Horton, adm.

Baker Hospital (CM, 104 beds), 2750 Speissegger Dr., North Charleston 29405; tel. 803/744-2110; Richard E. Hudson, adm.

West Virginia: Calhoun General Hospital (CM, 30 beds), Box 490, Grantsville 26147; tel. 304/354-6121; Jessie P. Sisk, actg. adm.

Owned, leased, sponsored:	0 hospitals	0 beds
Contract-managed:	22 hospitals	2448 beds
Totals:	22 hospitals	2448 beds

8795: SUTTER HEALTH SYSTEM (NP)
1111 Howe Ave., Suite 600, Sacramento, CA 95825; 916/927-5211; Patrick G. Hays, pres. & chief exec. off.

California: Sutter Coast Hospital (L, 56 beds), 100 A St., Crescent City 95531; tel. 707/464-8511; John E. Menaugh, adm.

Sutter Davis Hospital (O, 48 beds), Rd. 99 at Covell Blvd., Davis 95616; Mailing Address P O Box 1617, Davis, Zip 95617; tel. 916/756-6440; Patrick R. Brady, adm.

Los Banos Community Hospital (CM, 48 beds), 520 W. I St., Los Banos 93635; tel. 209/826-0591; Lee Ashjian, adm.

Novato Community Hospital (O, 52 beds), 1625 Hill Rd., P O Box 1108, Novato 94947; tel. 415/897-3111; Joel Grey, adm.

Sutter Community Hospitals (O, 723 beds), 1111 Howe Ave., Suite 600, Zip 95825; tel. 916/927-5211; Patrick G. Hays, pres. & chief exec. off.

Sutter Solano Medical Center (O, 97 beds), 300 Hospital Dr., Vallejo 94589; Mailing Address P O Box 3189, Vallejo, Zip 94590; tel. 707/554-4444; Joseph A.Stewart, adm.

Owned, leased, sponsored:	5 hospitals	976 beds
Contract-managed:	1 hospitals	48 beds
Totals:	6 hospitals	1024 beds

***9255: TRUMAN MEDICAL CENTER** (NP)
2301 Holmes, Kansas City, MO 64108; 816/556-3153; James J. Mongan MD, exec. dir.

Missouri: Truman Medical Center-East (CM, 300 beds), 7900 Lee's Summit Rd., Kansas City 64139; tel. 816/373-4415; Clifford Browne Jr., adm.

Truman Medical Center-West (CM, 271 beds), 2301 Holmes St., Kansas City 64108; tel. 816/556-3000; Daniel M. Couch, adm. & dep. exec. dir.

Owned, leased, sponsored:	0 hospitals	0 beds
Contract-managed:	2 hospitals	571 beds
Totals:	2 hospitals	571 beds

For explanation of codes following names, see page B2.
*Indicates Type III membership in the American Hospital Association.

***9095: U. S. HEALTH CORPORATION** (NP)
3555 Olentangy River Rd., Suite 4000, Columbus, OH 43214; 614/261-5902; Erie Chapman III, pres. & chief exec. off.

Ohio: Riverside Methodist Hospitals (O, 858 beds), 3535 Olentangy River Rd., Columbus 43214; tel. 614/261-5000; Erie Chapman III, pres. & chief exec. off.

Hardin Memorial Hospital (CM, 86 beds), 921 E. Franklin St., Kenton 43326; tel. 419/673-0761; Lamar L. Wyse, pres.

Marion General Hospital (O, 257 beds), McKinley Park Dr., Marion 43302; tel. 614/383-8400; P. Donald Muhlenthaler, pres.

Morrow County Hospital (CM, 61 beds), 651 W. Marion Rd., Mount Gilead 43338; tel. 419/946-5015; Randal M. Arnett, adm.

Mercy Hospital (O, 177 beds), 1248 Kinneys Lane, Portsmouth 45662; tel. 614/353-2131; James P. Weems, vice-pres. & chief exec. off.

Scioto Memorial Hospital (O, 225 beds), 1805 27th St., Portsmouth 45662; tel. 614/354-7581; Earl McLane, pres. & chief exec. off.

Southern Hills Hospital (O, 126 beds), 727 Eighth St., Box 1528, Portsmouth 45662; tel. 614/354-8651; Earl L. McLane, pres. & chief exec. off.

Owned, leased, sponsored:	5 hospitals	1643 beds
Contract-managed:	2 hospitals	147 beds
Totals:	7 hospitals	1790 beds

***9905: UNITED HEALTH SERVICES, INC.** (NP)
1200 S. Columbia Rd., P O Box 6002, Grand Forks, ND 58201; 701/780-5200; Robert M. Jacobson, pres.

North Dakota: United Hospital (O, 279 beds), 1200 S. Columbia Rd., Grand Forks 58201; tel. 701/780-5000; Robert M. Jacobson, pres.

United Recovery Center (O, 38 beds), Medical Park, Grand Forks 58206; Mailing Address Grand Forks, Zip 58201; tel. 701/780-5900; Russ Warner, chief exec. off.

Owned, leased, sponsored:	2 hospitals	317 beds
Contract-managed:	0 hospitals	0 beds
Totals:	2 hospitals	317 beds

0335: UNITED HEALTHCARE, INC. (IO)
4015 Travis Dr., Nashville, TN 37211; 615/833-1077; Jerry E. Gilliland, pres. & chief exec. off.

Arkansas: Corning Community Hospital (O, 40 beds), Hospital Dr., Box 158, Corning 72422; tel. 501/857-6961; Donald F. Henry, adm.

Florida: Coastal Communities Hospital (O, 81 beds), Star Rte. 1, Box 2, Bunnell 32010; tel. 904/437-2211; Douglas W. Parker, adm.

Kentucky: Parkway Regional Hospital (O, 70 beds), 2000 Holiday Lane, Fulton 42041; tel. 502/472-2522; Michael J. McLaren, adm.

Owned, leased, sponsored:	3 hospitals	191 beds
Contract-managed:	0 hospitals	0 beds
Totals:	3 hospitals	191 beds

6345: UNITED HOSPITALS, INC. (NP)
100 W. Laurel Ave., Cheltenham, PA 19012; 215/663-5400; Myles G. Turtz MD, chm. & chief exec. off.

Pennsylvania: Rolling Hill Hospital (O, 259 beds), 60 E. Township Line, Elkins Park 19117; tel. 215/663-6000; Frederick L. Hollander, exec. dir.

Lawndale Community Hospital (O, 63 beds), 6129 Palmetto St., Philadelphia 19111; tel. 215/728-5500; Morton H. Rappaport, chief exec. off.

St. Christopher's Hospital for Children (O, 146 beds), Fifth St. & Lehigh Ave., Philadelphia 19133; tel. 215/427-5000; Calvin Bland, exec. dir.; Ralph W. Brenner,bd. chm.

Warminster General Hospital (O, 180 beds), 225 Newtown Rd., Warminster 18974; tel. 215/441-6600; Vail P. Garvin, exec. dir.

Owned, leased, sponsored:	4 hospitals	648 beds
Contract-managed:	0 hospitals	0 beds
Totals:	4 hospitals	648 beds

9605: UNITED MEDICAL CORPORATION (IO)
20 N. Orange Ave., Suite 1600, Orlando, FL 32801; 305/423-2200; Donald R. Dizney, chm.; James E. English, pres.

Florida: Tampa Bay Community Hospital (O, 73 beds), 4555 S. Manhattan Ave., Tampa 33611; tel. 813/839-6341; Stephen H. Noble, exec. dir.

Kentucky: Kmi Medical Center (O, 69 beds), 8521 Old Lagrange Rd., Louisville 40223; tel. 502/426-6380; Steve Miller, exec. dir.

United Medical Center Shelbyville (O, 76 beds), 727 Hospital Dr., P O Box 849, Shelbyville 40065; tel. 502/633-2345; Steve Corso, adm.

Louisiana: United Medical Center New Orleans (O, 136 beds), 3419 St. Claude Ave., New Orleans 70117; tel. 504/948-8200; Mark A. Meyers, exec. dir.

North Carolina: Hickory Memorial Hospital (O, 64 beds), 219 N. Center St., Hickory 28601; Mailing Address P O Box 369, Hickory, Zip 28603; tel. 704/328-2226; Leland R. Blessum,exec. dir.

Puerto Rico: Hospital Pavia (O, 172 beds), 1462 Asia St., San Juan 00909; Mailing Address Box 11137, Santurce Sta., San Juan, Zip 00910; tel. 809/727-6060; Alfredo E.Volckers, exec. dir.

South Carolina: English Park Medical Center (O, 50 beds), 1305 N. Main St., Marion 29571; tel. 803/423-7945; Joyce Dudley, actg. exec. dir.

Owned, leased, sponsored:	7 hospitals	640 beds
Contract-managed:	0 hospitals	0 beds
Totals:	7 hospitals	640 beds

9555: UNIVERSAL HEALTH SERVICES, INC. (IO)
367 S. Gulph Rd., King of Prussia, PA 19406; 215/768-3300; Alan B. Miller, pres.

California: Panorama Community Hospital (O, 96 beds), 14850 Roscoe Blvd., Panorama City 91402; tel. 818/787-2222; Charlotte McGuire, mng. dir.

Westlake Community Hospital (O, 98 beds), 4415 S. Lakeview Canyon Rd., Westlake Village 91361; tel. 818/706-8000; Douglass D. Dailey, dir.

Inland Valley Regional Medical Center (O, 62 beds), 36485 Inland Valley Dr., Wildomar 92395; tel. 714/677-8671; Dan C. McLaughlin, mng. dir.

Florida: Doctors Hospital of Hollywood (O, 124 beds), 1859 Van Buren St., Box 1220, Hollywood 33022; tel. 305/920-9000; Alex Spinos, adm.; Kenneth Berg, exec. dir.

University Hospital and Clinic (CM, 130 beds), 1200 W. Leonard St., Pensacola 32501; tel. 904/436-9011; Gib Newsome, adm.

Doctors General Hospital (O, 159 beds), 6701 W. Sunrise Blvd., Plantation 33313; tel. 305/581-7800; William C. Gompers, chief exec. off.

Illinois: Cole Hospital (CM, 65 beds), 809 W. Church St., P O Box 598, Champaign 61820; tel. 217/351-7200; Gary Callahan, adm.

Belmont Community Hospital (O, 134 beds), 4058 W. Melrose St., Chicago 60641; tel. 312/736-7000; John W. McCracken, exec. dir.

Bethesda Hospital (O, 129 beds), 2451 W. Howard St., Chicago 60645; tel. 312/761-6000; Richard A. Snow, mng. dir.

Louisiana: Chalmette General Hospital (O, 108 beds), 801 Virtu St., Chalmette 70043; tel. 504/277-7711; William E. Price, mng. dir.

De La Ronde Hospital (O, 118 beds), 9001 Patricia St., Chalmette 70043; tel. 504/277-8011; William E. Price, mng. dir.

River Parishes Medical Center (O, 102 beds), 500 Rue De Sante, Laplace 70068; tel. 504/652-7000; George J. Foss, mng. dir.

For explanation of codes following names, see page B2.
*Indicates Type III membership in the American Hospital Association.

Doctors' Hospital (L, 157 beds), 1130 Louisiana Ave., Box 1526, Shreveport 71165; tel. 318/227-1211; Charles E. Boyd, adm.

Massachusetts: The Arbour (O, 118 beds), 49 Robinwood Ave., Jamaica Plain, Boston 02130; tel. 617/522-4400; Roy A. Ettlinger, chief exec. off.

Human Resource Institute (O, 68 beds), 227 Babcock St., Brookline 02146; tel. 617/731-3200; Joseph W. Nolan, mng. dir.

Michigan: Forest View Psychiatric Hospital (O, 62 beds), 1055 Medical Park Dr. S.E., Grand Rapids 49506; tel. 616/942-9610; Stan A. Mills, mng. dir.

Mississippi: Gulf Coast Community Hospital (O, 185 beds), 4642 W. Beach Blvd., Biloxi 39535; Mailing Address Box 4518, Biloxi, Zip 39531; tel. 601/388-6711; Albert A. BrustIll, exec. dir.

Nevada: Valley Hospital Medical Center (O, 310 beds), 620 Shadow Lane, Las Vegas 89106; tel. 702/388-4000; Claus Eggers, adm.

Texas: Dallas Family Hospital (O, 72 beds), 2929 S. Hampton Rd., Dallas 75224; tel. 214/330-4611; John B. Isbell, chief exec. off.; Christopher P. O'Connor, mng. dir.

Oak Cliff Medical and Surgical Hospital (O, 88 beds), 233 W. Tenth St., Box 4446, Dallas 75208; tel. 214/946-5191; Donn C. Baker, adm.

McAllen Medical Center (O, 293 beds), 301 W. Expwy. 83, McAllen 78503; tel. 512/632-4000; John L. Mims, adm.

Washington: Auburn General Hospital (O, 111 beds), 20 Second St. N.E., Auburn 98002; tel. 206/833-7711; Michael M. Gherardini, adm.

Centralia General Hospital (O, 57 beds), 1820 Cooks Hill Rd., Centralia 98531; tel. 206/736-2803; John R. Hanson, mng. dir.

Riverton Hospital (O, 142 beds), 12844 Military Rd. S., Seattle 98168; tel. 206/244-0180; Gerard Manse, mng. dir.

Wisconsin: Waupun Memorial Hospital (CM, 55 beds), 620 W. Brown St., Waupun 53963; tel. 414/324-5581; Steven H. Spencer, pres.

Owned, leased, sponsored:	22 hospitals	2793 beds
Contract-managed:	3 hospitals	250 beds
Totals:	25 hospitals	3043 beds

*9105: UNIVERSITY OF ALABAMA HOSPITALS (NP)

619 S. 19th St., Birmingham, AL 35233; 205/934-4011; James E. Moon, adm.

Alabama: University of Alabama Hospital (O, 774 beds), 619 S. 19th St., Birmingham 35233; tel. 205/934-4011; James E. Moon, adm.

St. Clair Regional Hospital (CM, 72 beds), 2805 Hospital Dr., Pell City 35125; tel. 205/338-3301; C. M. Jones, adm.

George H. Lanier Memorial Hospital and Nursing Home (CM, 192 beds), 4800 48th St., Valley 36854; tel. 205/756-3111; Howard D. Clem Sr., adm.

Owned, leased, sponsored:	1 hospitals	774 beds
Contract-managed:	2 hospitals	264 beds
Totals:	3 hospitals	1038 beds

6405: UNIVERSITY OF CALIFORNIA-SYSTEMWIDE ADMINISTRATION (NP)

764 University Hall, Berkeley, CA 94720; 415/642-5192; C. L. Hopper MD, vice-pres. health affairs

California: Ernest V. Cowell Memorial Hospital (O, 20 beds), University of California, Berkeley 94720; tel. 415/642-6621; James R. Brown MD, dir.

Cowell Hospital and Student Health Center (O, 10 beds), University of California-Davis, Davis 95616; tel. 916/752-2300; William C. Waid, adm.; William E. BittnerMD, actg. med. staff dir.

University of California at Los Angeles Medical Center (O, 652 beds), 10833 Le Conte Ave., Los Angeles 90024; tel. 213/825-9111; Raymond G. Schultze MD, dir.

University of California at Los Angeles Neuropsychiatric Hospital (O, 161 beds), 760 Westwood Plaza, Los Angeles 90024; tel. 213/825-9548; Don A. Rockwell MD,dir.

University of California Irvine Medical Center (O, 382 beds), 101 the City Dr., Orange 92668; tel. 714/634-5678; Leon M. Schwartz, dir.

University of California Davis Medical Center (O, 439 beds), 2315 Stockton Blvd., Sacramento 95817; tel. 916/453-3096; Frank J. Loge, dir.

University of California San Diego Medical Center (O, 406 beds), 225 Dickinson St., San Diego 92103; tel. 619/294-6222; Michael R. Stringer, dir.

Langley Porter Psychiatric Institute-Hospitals and Clinics (O, 70 beds), 401 Parnassus Ave., San Francisco 94143; tel. 415/476-7000; Fariborz Amini MD, adm.

University of California, San Francisco Medical Center (O, 560 beds), San Francisco 94143; tel. 415/476-1401; William B. Kerr, dir.

Owned, leased, sponsored:	9 hospitals	2700 beds
Contract-managed:	0 hospitals	0 beds
Totals:	9 hospitals	2700 beds

*6415: UNIVERSITY OF WASHINGTON HOSPITALS (NP)

Sc-61 University of Washington, Seattle, WA 98195; 206/548-6364; Robert Muilenburg, exec. dir.

Washington: Harborview Medical Center (CM, 330 beds), 325 Ninth Ave., Seattle 98104; tel. 206/223-3000; David W. Gitch, adm.

University Hospital (O, 355 beds), 1959 N.E. Pacific St., Seattle 98195; tel. 206/548-3300; Irma E. Goertzen, adm.

Owned, leased, sponsored:	1 hospitals	355 beds
Contract-managed:	1 hospitals	330 beds
Totals:	2 hospitals	685 beds

*8895: VISTA HILL FOUNDATION (NP)

3420 Camino Del Rio N., Suite 100, San Diego, CA 92108; 619/563-1770; Ronald E. Fickle, pres. & chief exec. off.

California: Vista Hill Hospital (O, 58 beds), 730 Medical Center Ct., Chula Vista 92010; tel. 619/421-6900; Ruth Dundon, adm.

Mesa Vista Hospital (O, 150 beds), 7850 Vista Hill Ave., San Diego 92123; tel. 619/694-8300; Donald K. Allen, adm. & chief exec. off.

New Mexico: Vista Sandia Hospital (O, 92 beds), 501 Alameda Blvd. N.E., Albuquerque 87113; tel. 505/823-2000; Audrey M. Worrell MD, chief exec. off. & med. dir.

Owned, leased, sponsored:	3 hospitals	300 beds
Contract-managed:	0 hospitals	0 beds
Totals:	3 hospitals	300 beds

6705: WAKE MEDICAL CENTER (NP)

3000 New Bern Ave., Raleigh, NC 27610; 919/755-8112; Raymond L. Champ, pres.

North Carolina: Western Wake Hospital (O, 20 beds), 763 Hunter St., Apex 27502; tel. 919/362-8321; Diane Long RN, dir.

Southern Wake Hospital (O, 28 beds), 400 W. Ranson St., Fuquay-Varina 27526; tel. 919/552-2206; W. J. Mountford Jr., dir.

Wake Medical Center (O, 513 beds), 3000 New Bern Ave., Raleigh 27610; tel. 919/755-8000; Raymond L. Champ, pres.

Northern Wake Hospital (O, 20 beds), Allen Rd., P O Box 152, Wake Forest 27587; tel. 919/556-5151; Diane Long, interim dir.

Eastern Wake Hospital (O, 20 beds), 320 Hospital Rd., P O Box 275, Zebulon 27597; tel. 919/269-7406; William J. Mountford Jr., adm.

Owned, leased, sponsored:	5 hospitals	601 beds
Contract-managed:	0 hospitals	0 beds
Totals:	5 hospitals	601 beds

For explanation of codes following names, see page B2.
*Indicates Type III membership in the American Hospital Association.

***6725: WEST JERSEY HEALTH SYSTEM** (NP)
Mount Ephraim & Atlantic Aves., Camden, NJ 08104; 609/342-4600; Barry D. Brown, pres.; William Michael Tomlinson, exec. vice-pres.

New Jersey: West Jersey Hospital Southern Division (O, 95 beds), Townsend Ave. & White Horse Pike, Berlin 08009; tel. 609/768-6000; R. Ronald Lawson, exec. dir.

West Jersey Hospital, Northern Division (O, 224 beds), Mount Ephraim & Atlantic Aves., Camden 08104; tel. 609/342-4000; Michael P. Dennis, exec. dir.

West Jersey Hospital Garden State (O, 204 beds), Rte. 73 & Brick Rd., Marlton 08053; tel. 609/596-3500; Kevin M. Manley, exec. dir.

West Jersey Hospital, Eastern Division (O, 246 beds), Evesham Rd., Voorhees 08043; tel. 609/772-5000; Thomas H. Litz, exec. dir.

Owned, leased, sponsored:	4 hospitals	769 beds
Contract-managed:	0 hospitals	0 beds
Totals:	4 hospitals	769 beds

0615: WESTERN HOSPITAL CORPORATION (IO)
1124 Ballena Blvd., Alameda, CA 94501; 415/521-4110; Harvey W. Glasser MD, pres.

California: Amador Hospital (CM, 87 beds), 810 Court St., Jackson 95642; tel. 209/223-6600; Cliff D. Richards, adm.

Kentfield Medical Hospital (O, 48 beds), 1125-B Sir Francis Drake Blvd., Kentfield 94904; tel. 415/456-9680; James R. Belding, adm.

Crenshaw Center Hospital (O, 48 beds), 3831 Stocker St., Los Angeles 90008; tel. 213/292-0221; Robert Shell, adm.

Owned, leased, sponsored:	2 hospitals	96 beds
Contract-managed:	1 hospitals	87 beds
Totals:	3 hospitals	183 beds

***7005: WESTERN RESERVE CARE SYSTEM** (NP)
345 Oak Hill Ave., Youngstown, OH 44501; 216/747-9727; James E. Michels, pres.

Ohio: Tod Children's Hospital (O, 97 beds), 500 Gypsy Lane, Youngstown 44501; tel. 216/747-6700; Patricia A. Hrinko, dir.

Western Reserve Care Systems-Northside Medical Center (O, 304 beds), 500 Gypsy Lane, Youngstown 44501; tel. 216/747-1444; Roland R. Carlson, vice-pres. oper.

Western Reserve Care Systems-Southside Medical Center (O, 217 beds), 345 Oak Hill Ave., Youngstown 44501; tel. 216/747-0777; Roland R. Carlson, vice-pres. oper.

Owned, leased, sponsored:	3 hospitals	618 beds
Contract-managed:	0 hospitals	0 beds
Totals:	3 hospitals	618 beds

9795: WESTWORLD COMMUNITY HEALTHCARE, INC. (IO)
23832 Rockfield Rd., Lake Forest, CA 92630; 714/768-2981; Stephen F. Arterburn, pres. & chief exec. off.

Alabama: Livingston-Tombigbee Regional Medical Center (L, 72 beds), Hwy. 11 N., P O Drawer AA, Livingston 35470; tel. 205/652-9511; Paul E. Majors Jr., adm.

Arkansas: Delta Medical Center (L, 40 beds), 505 S. New York St., Brinkley 72021; tel. 501/734-4141; Alan C. Spears, adm.

Gurdon Municipal Hospital (L, 28 beds), Third & Walnut Sts., Gurdon 71743; tel. 501/353-4401; Jeffrey O'Brien, adm.

California: Bear Valley Community Hospital (L, 28 beds), 41870 Garstin Rd., Box 1732, Big Bear Lake 92315; tel. 714/866-6501; L. Wayne Sasser, exec. dir.

Kingsburg General Hospital (L, 38 beds), 1200 Smith St., Kingsburg 93631; tel. 209/897-5841; Owen Shafner, interim adm.

Mountains Community Hospital (L, 28 beds), Box 70, Lake Arrowhead 92352; tel. 714/336-3651; Joel Hile, adm.

Needles-Desert Communities Hospital (L, 39 beds), 1401 Bailey Ave., Needles 92363; tel. 619/326-4531; Hank N. Fishman, adm.

North Kern Hospital (O, 25 beds), 2101 Seventh St., Wasco 93280; tel. 805/758-5123; Scott Griffith, chief exec. off.

Illinois: Hoopeston Regional Hospital (O, 94 beds), 701 E. Orange St., Hoopeston 60942; tel. 217/283-5531; Daniel G. Van Wieringen, adm.

Paxton Community Hospital (L, 29 beds), 651 E. Pells St., P O Box 22, Paxton 60957; tel. 217/379-4811; Edward T. McGrath, exec. dir.

North Carolina: Bertie Memorial Hospital (L, 49 beds), 401 Sterlingworth St., Windsor 27983; tel. 919/794-3141; Gary A. Dolack, chief exec. off.

Oklahoma: Jay Memorial Hospital (O, 28 beds), Osage & Washbourne Sts., Box 1140, Jay 74346; tel. 918/253-4284; Fred P. Summary, adm.

Texas: New Boston General Hospital (O, 63 beds), 520 Hospital Dr., Box 7, New Boston 75570; tel. 214/628-5531; John Stevens, exec. dir.

Brazos Valley Hospital (O, 25 beds), 526 Ward St., Sealy 77474; tel. 409/885-4181; Terry J. Fontenot, adm.

Wortham Hospital (O, 27 beds), S. Hwy. 14, Box 428, Wortham 76693; tel. 817/765-3363; Robert Peralta, exec. dir.

Utah: Tooele Valley Regional Medical Center (L, 33 beds), 211 S. 100 East, Box 88, Tooele 84074; tel. 801/882-1697; Scott F. Blakley, adm.

Owned, leased, sponsored:	16 hospitals	646 beds
Contract-managed:	0 hospitals	0 beds
Totals:	16 hospitals	646 beds

*** 6745: WHEATON FRANCISCAN SERVICES, INC.** (CC)
26w171 Roosevelt Rd., P O Box 667, Wheaton, IL 60189; 312/462-9271; Wilfred Loebig, chief exec. off.

Illinois: Oak Park Hospital (S, 305 beds), 520 S. Maple Ave., Oak Park 60304; tel. 312/383-9300; Jacolyn Schlautman, actg. pres.

Marianjoy Rehabilitation Center (O, 91 beds), 26 W. 171 Roosevelt Rd., P O Box 795, Wheaton 60189; tel. 312/462-4000; Bruce A. Schurman, pres.

Iowa: Mercy Hospital of Franciscan Sisters (O, 49 beds), 201 Eighth Ave. S.E., Oelwein 50662; tel. 319/283-2314; Andrew J. Huff, pres.

Covenant Medical Center (O, 410 beds), 3421 W. Ninth St., Waterloo 50702; tel. 319/236-4111; Raymond F. Burfeind, pres. & chief exec. off.

Missouri: St. Francis Medical Center (S, 264 beds), 211 St. Francis Dr., Cape Girardeau 63701; tel. 314/335-1251; John J. Keusenkothen, pres.

Wisconsin: St. Elizabeth Hospital (O, 279 beds), 1506 S. Oneida St., Appleton 54915; tel. 414/738-2000; Otto L. Cox, pres.

Elmbrook Memorial Hospital (O, 136 beds), 19333 W. North Ave., Brookfield 53005; tel. 414/785-2000; Stephen R. Young, pres.

Kaukauna Community Hospital (O, 52 beds), 308 E. 14th St., Kaukauna 54130; tel. 414/766-4211; Jeffrey K. Jenkins, pres.

St. Joseph's Hospital (O, 486 beds), 5000 W. Chambers St., Milwaukee 53210; tel. 414/447-2000; Thomas L. Feurig, pres.

St. Michael Hospital (O, 280 beds), 2400 W. Villard Ave., Milwaukee 53209; tel. 414/527-8000; John A. Comiskey, pres.

A Center of Racine (O, 26 beds), 2000 Domanik Dr., Racine 53404; tel. 414/632-6141; Rev. E. W. Belter DD, pres. & exec. dir.

St. Mary's Medical Center (O, 216 beds), 3801 Spring St., Racine 53405; tel. 414/636-4011; Edward P. DeMeulenaere, pres.

Owned, leased, sponsored:	12 hospitals	2594 beds
Contract-managed:	0 hospitals	0 beds
Totals:	12 hospitals	2594 beds

For explanation of codes following names, see page B2.
*Indicates Type III membership in the American Hospital Association.

***9575: WILLIAM BEAUMONT HOSPITAL CORPORATION** (NP)
3601 W. Thirteen Mile Rd., Royal Oak, MI 48072; 313/288-8000; Kenneth E. Myers, pres.; Ted D. Wasson, exec. vice-pres.

Michigan: William Beaumont Hospital (O, 929 beds), 3601 W. Thirteen Mile Rd., Royal Oak 48072; tel. 313/288-8000; Kenneth J. Matzick, dir.

William Beaumont Hospital-Troy (O, 189 beds), 44201 Dequindre Rd., Troy 48098; tel. 313/828-5100; John D. Labriola, vice-pres. & dir.

Owned, leased, sponsored:	2 hospitals	1118 beds
Contract-managed:	0 hospitals	0 beds
Totals:	2 hospitals	1118 beds

***0015: ZURBRUGG MEMORIAL HOSPITAL** (NP)
Hospital Plaza, Riverside, NJ 08075; 609/461-6700; George D. Hartnett, pres.

New Jersey: Zurbrugg Memorial Hospital-Riverside Division (O, 173 beds), Hospital Plaza, Riverside 08075; tel. 609/461-6700; John Tegley, sr. vice-pres.

Zurbrugg Memorial Hospital, Rancocas Valley Division (O, 318 beds), Sunset Rd., Willingboro 08046; tel. 609/835-2900; George Hartnett, pres.

Owned, leased, sponsored:	2 hospitals	491 beds
Contract-managed:	0 hospitals	0 beds
Totals:	2 hospitals	491 beds

Headquarters of Multihospital Systems

Alphabetically

9355 Adventist Health System-Eastern and Middle America
4165 Adventist Health System-Sunbelt Health Care Corporation
0235 Adventist Health System-West
0225 Alameda County Health Care Services Agency
0065 Alexian Brothers Health Systems Inc.
1385 Allegany Health System
2565 Alliance Health System
0045 American Health Group International, Inc.
0075 American Healthcare Corporation
1375 American Healthcare Management, Inc.
0195 American Medical Centers
0125 American Medical International
0985 Amerihealth, Inc.
0135 Ancilla Systems, Inc.
0145 Appalachian Regional Healthcare
0205 Asc Health System
0865 Atlantic Health Systems, Inc.
0305 Baptist Health Care Corporation
0315 Baptist Healthcare, Inc.
8810 Baptist Hospital and Health Systems
0345 Baptist Medical Centers
0355 Baptist Medical System
1625 Baptist Memorial Healthcare Development Corporation
0265 Baptist Memorial Hospital System
0185 Baptist Regional Health Services, Inc.
1935 Basic American Medical, Inc.
0095 Baylor Health Care System
1095 Baystate Health Systems, Inc.
0515 Benedictine Health System
1635 Benedictine Health System
0505 Benedictine Sisters
0535 Benedictine Sisters
0545 Benedictine Sisters of the Annunciation
0745 Berkshire Health Systems
0285 Bernardine Sisters of the 3rd Order of St. Francis
0415 Bethesda Hospital, Inc.
5085 Bon Secours Health System, Inc.
0585 Brim and Associates, Inc.
9305 Bromenn Healthcare
0595 Bronson Healthcare Group, Inc.
6665 Brunswick Hospital Center
0955 Camcare, Inc.
9855 Camelback Hospitals, Inc.
5175 Catholic Health Corporation
5205 Catholic Healthcare West
5805 Central Management Corporation
0665 Century Healthcare Corporation
0705 Charlotte-Mecklenburg Hospital Authority
0695 Charter Medical Corporation
0565 Christian Health Services Development Corporation
0735 Church-Charity Foundation of Long Island
8805 Columbus-Cuneo-Cabrini Medical Center
0215 Community Care Systems, Inc.
0875 Community Health Systems, Inc.
1085 Community Hospitals of Central California
0785 Community Psychiatric Centers
0275 Comprehensive Care Corporation
5695 Congregation of St. Agnes
0245 Continental Medical, Inc.
5885 Covenant Health Systems, Inc.
5435 CSJ Health System of Wichita
1885 Daughters of Charity Health Systems-West
1885 Daughters of Charity Health Systems-East Central, Inc.
1885 Daughters of Charity Health Systems East
1885 Daughters of Charity National Health Systems-West Central
1885 Daughters of Charity National Health System
6995 Department of Health and Hospitals, Hospital Services Division
0845 Devereux Foundation
1435 Doctor John McDonald Health Systems
1045 Doctors Hospital
1195 Dominican Sisters Congregation of the Most Holy Name
1295 Dominican Sisters Congregation of Our Lady of the Sacred Heart
1895 East Texas Hospital Foundation
3595 Eastern Mercy Health System
0945 Empire Health Services
0885 Erlanger Health Services
1255 Escambia County Health Care Authority
1215 Eskaton
1225 Evangelical Health Systems
1305 Fairfax Hospital Association
1325 Fairview Hospital and Healthcare Services
1345 Felician Healthcare Systems, Inc.
1275 First Health, Inc.
0295 First Hospital Corporation
1355 Forbes Healthmark
0655 Forest Health Systems, Inc.
0905 Forum Health Investors, Inc.
1455 Franciscan Health Advisory Services, Inc.
5325 Franciscan Health System
9650 Franciscan Health System, Inc.
1475 Franciscan Missionaries of Our Lady Provincial House
5375 Franciscan Services Corporation
1395 Franciscan Sisters Health Care
1415 Franciscan Sisters Health Care Corporation
5705 Franciscan Sisters of Perpetual Adoration
1485 Franciscan Sisters of the Poor Health Systems, Inc.
1425 Fulton-De Kalb Hospital Authority
0495 Gateway Medical Systems
5570 Geisinger System Services
0775 General Health, Inc.
0645 Glenbeigh, Inc.
1495 Grandcor
1535 Great Plains Health Alliance, Inc.
1155 Greenleaf Health Systems, Inc.
1555 Greenville Hospital System
5885 Grey Nuns Health Systems, Inc.
9995 Group Health Cooperative of Puget Sound
0675 Guthrie Medical Center
1655 Harper-Grace Hospitals
2345 Harris Methodist Health System
1865 HCA Oklahoma Health Network
5415 Health and Hospital Services
5945 Health Care Corporation of the Sisters of St. Joseph of Carondelet
6545 Health Corporation of the Archdiocese of Newark
0965 Health Dimensions, Inc.
1905 Health Management Services
8865 Health Management Services, Inc.
0395 Healthcare International, Inc.
1585 Healthcare Management Group, Inc.
0405 Healthcare Services of America
1695 Healtheast, Inc.
2755 Healthlink
0955 Healthnet, Inc.
6235 HealthOne Corporation
2595 Healthshare, Inc.
1365 Healthstar Corporation
6905 Healthwest Foundation
6905 Healthwest Medical Centers
2195 Hei Corporation
3535 Hendrick Medical Development Corporation
0725 Hermann Affiliated Hospital Systems
1525 Hillsborough County Hospital Authority
3395 Hitchcock Alliance
5585 Holy Cross Health System Corporation
5855 Holy Cross Life Care Systems, Inc.
6005 Holy Family of Nazareth Health System
1025 Horizon Health System, Inc.
1035 Horizon Health Systems
1755 Hospital Corporation of America
1775 Hospital Management Associates
2495 Hospital Management Professionals, Inc.
5355 Hospital Sisters Health System-Hospital Sisters of the Third Order of St. Francis-American Province
1235 Humana Inc.
5645 Humility of Mary Health Care Corporation
5565 Incarnate Word Health Services
8855 Intercare Health Systems
1815 Intermountain Health Care, Inc.
1595 Iowa Methodist Health System
1015 Johns Hopkins Health System
0435 Jupiter Hospital Corporation
2105 Kaiser Foundation Hospitals
0995 Kennestone Regional Health Care Systems
2245 LHS Corporation
2295 Little Company of Mary Sisters Healthcare Systems
5755 Los Angeles County-Department of Health Services
6295 Lutheran General Health Care Systems
2245 Lutheran Hospital Society of Southern California
2235 Lutheran Hospitals and Homes Society of America
7775 Main Line Health, Inc.
1335 Mease Health Care
1135 Mediplex Group, Inc.
3825 Mediq, Inc.
6615 Medlantic Healthcare Group
2645 Memorial Care Systems
5155 Mercy Health Care System
5195 Mercy Health Care System
5545 Mercy Health System of Western New York
5215 Mercy-Chicago Province Healthcare Systems
0685 Merritt Peralta Medical Center
7235 Methodist Health Care Network
8875 Methodist Health Services Corporation
2715 Methodist Health System
9345 Methodist Health Systems, Inc.
9335 Methodist Hospital of Indiana
2735 Methodist Hospitals of Dallas
7995 Metropolitan Hospital
2755 Metropolitan Hospitals, Inc.
1615 Mid Florida Medical Services
6975 Mills-Peninsula Hospitals
3775 Milwaukee County Department of Health and Human Services
2855 Missionary Benedictine Sisters American Province
2475 Mississippi County Hospital System
6555 Multicare Medical Center
5895 National Healthcare, Inc.
3015 National Medical Enterprises
9265 Nebraska Methodist Health System, Inc.
3175 Neponset Valley Health System
3075 New York City Health and Hospital Corporation
0465 Nexus Healthcare Corporation
3115 North Broward Hospital District
3165 North Central Health Services
7555 Northern San Diego County Hospital District
1805 Numed Hospitals, Inc.
0455 Numed Psychiatric, Inc.
0715 Office of Hospitals
3315 Ohio Valley Health Services and Education Corporation
3355 Orlando Regional Medical Center
7555 Palomar Pomerado Hospital District
5765 Paracelsus Healthcare
3455 Pennsylvania Hospital
3465 Peoples Community Hospital Authority
1130 Presbyterian Healthcare Systems
5255 Presentation Health System
1315 Recovery Centers of America
1065 Regent Health Systems, Inc.
3615 Religious Hospitallers of St. Joseph, Province of St. Joseph
6525 Republic Health Corporation
8815 Research Health Services
4810 Riverside Healthcare Association, Inc.
0070 Roanoke Hospital Association
8495 Rushmore National Health Systems
5395 Sacred Heart Corporation
8985 Safecare Company, Inc/Safecare Health Service, Inc.
4045 Samaritan Health Service
1055 Samissa Health Care Corporation
7895 Santa Fe Healthcare
0605 SCH Health Care System
0575 Schick Laboratories, Inc.
1505 Scripps Memorial Hospitals
4025 Servantcor
4125 Shriners Hospitals for Crippled Children
5995 Sisters of Charity Center
5115 Sisters of Charity Health Care Systems, Inc.
6095 Sisters of Charity Health Care Systems Corporation
5095 Sisters of Charity of Leavenworth Health Services Corporation
3045 Sisters of Charity of Nazareth Health Corporation
5745 Sisters of Charity of Our Lady of Mercy
5125 Sisters of Charity of St. Augustine Health and Human Services
5815 Sisters of Charity of St. Elizabeth
5985 Sisters of Mercy
5165 Sisters of Mercy Health Corporation
5185 Sisters of Mercy Health Systems-St. Louis
6015 Sisters of Mercy of the Union-Province of Baltimore
5275 Sisters of Providence
5285 Sisters of Providence Health and Human Service
5265 Sisters of Providence-Province of St. Ignatius
5685 Sisters of St. Casimir
5345 Sisters of St. Francis Health Services, Inc.
5925 Sisters of St. Francis of the Mission of the Immaculate Virgin
5365 Sisters of St. Francis of the Province of God
5975 Sisters of St. Francis-Immaculate Heart of Mary-Province of Hankinson
5715 Sisters of St. Francis-3rd Order Regular of Buffalo
5935 Sisters of St. Joseph
5555 Sisters of St. Joseph Health System

★Indicates Type III membership in the American Hospital Association.

By System Code

0015 ★ZURBRUGG MEMORIAL HOSPITAL, Hospital Plaza, Riverside, NJ 08075; tel. 609/461-6700; George D. Hartnett, pres.

0025 ★SUNHEALTH CORPORATION, 4501 Charlotte Park Dr., Box 668800, Charlotte, NC 28266; tel. 704/529-3300; Ben W. Latimer, pres.

0045 AMERICAN HEALTH GROUP INTERNATIONAL, INC., 401 Park Pl., Suite 500, Kirkland, WA 98033; tel. 206/827-1195; Michael D. Drobot, pres.

0065 ★ALEXIAN BROTHERS HEALTH SYSTEMS INC. (Formerly Alexian Brothers of America, Inc.), 600 Alexian Way, Elk Grove Village, IL 60007; tel. 312/640-7550; Bruce Fisher, exec. vice-pres.

0070 ROANOKE HOSPITAL ASSOCIATION, Box 13367, Roanoke, VA 24033; tel. 703/981-7347; Thomas L. Robertson, pres.

0075 AMERICAN HEALTHCARE CORPORATION, 21 W. End Ave., Suite 1100, Nashville, TN 37203; tel. 615/327-2200; Don R. Abercrombie, pres., chm. & chief exec. off.

0095 BAYLOR HEALTH CARE SYSTEM, 3201 Worth St., P O Box 26265, Dallas, TX 75226; tel. 214/820-2891; Boone Powell Jr., pres.

0125 ★AMERICAN MEDICAL INTERNATIONAL, 414 N. Camden Dr., Beverly Hills, CA 90210; tel. 213/278-6200; Walter Weisman, pres. & chief exec. off.

0135 ANCILLA SYSTEMS, INC. (Formerly Ancilla Domini Health Services, Inc.), 1100 Elmhurst Rd., Elk Grove Village, IL 60007; tel. 312/694-4210; Edwin W. Murphy, pres.

0145 ★APPALACHIAN REGIONAL HEALTHCARE, Box 8086, Lexington, KY 40533; tel. 606/255-4431; Robert L. Johnson, pres.

0185 ★BAPTIST REGIONAL HEALTH SERVICES, INC., P O Box 17500, Pensacola, FL 32522; tel. 904/434-4805; James F. Vickery, pres.

0195 AMERICAN MEDICAL CENTERS (Formerly Listed Under Nashville), P O Box 2526, Norcross, GA 30071; tel. 615/244-8410; Paul T. Agee, sr. vice-pres. & chief exec. off.

0205 ★ASC HEALTH SYSTEM, 3 Eagle Center, Suite 1, P O Box 568, O'Fallon, IL 62269; tel. 618/632-1284; Joseph B. Ahlschier, pres.

0215 COMMUNITY CARE SYSTEMS, INC., 210 Lincoln St., Boston, MA 02111; tel. 617/451-0300; Frederick J. Thacher, pres.

0225 ALAMEDA COUNTY HEALTH CARE SERVICES AGENCY, 499 Fifth St., Oakland, CA 94607; tel. 415/268-2722; David J. Kears, dir.

0235 ADVENTIST HEALTH SYSTEM-WEST, P O Box 619002, Roseville, CA 95661; tel. 916/781-2000; Frank F. Dupper, pres.

0245 CONTINENTAL MEDICAL, INC., 880 Johnson Ferry Rd. N.E., 260, Atlanta, GA 30342; tel. 404/255-8220; Richard V. Urquhart, pres.

0265 BAPTIST MEMORIAL HOSPITAL SYSTEM, 111 Dallas St., San Antonio, TX 78286; tel. 512/222-8431; David Garrett, pres. & chief exec. off.

0275 COMPREHENSIVE CARE CORPORATION, 18551 Von Karman Ave., Irvine, CA 92715; tel. 714/851-2273; Richard Santoni PhD, pres.

0285 BERNARDINE SISTERS OF THE 3RD ORDER OF ST. FRANCIS, 647 Springmill Rd.-Maryview, Villanova, PA 19085; tel. 215/525-2686; Sr. M. Gerald, supr. gen.

0295 FIRST HOSPITAL CORPORATION, World Trade Ctr, Suite 870, Norfolk, VA 23510; tel. 804/622-3034; Ronald I. Dozoretz MD, chm.

0305 ★BAPTIST HEALTH CARE CORPORATION, 7428 Nicholson Dr., Oklahoma City, OK 73132; tel. 405/721-6504; Joe L. Ingram MD, pres.

0315 ★BAPTIST HEALTHCARE, INC. (Formerly Baptist Hospitals, Inc.), 4007 Kresgee Way, Louisville, KY 40207; tel. 502/561-3277; Ben R. Brewer, pres.

0335 UNITED HEALTHCARE, INC., 4015 Travis Dr., Nashville, TN 37211; tel. 615/833-1077; Jerry E. Gilliland, pres. & chief exec. off.

0345 ★BAPTIST MEDICAL CENTERS, 2700 U. S. Hwy. 280, P O Box 30040, Birmingham, AL 35222; tel. 205/322-9319; Emmett Johnson, pres.

0355 ★BAPTIST MEDICAL SYSTEM, 9601 Interstate 630, Exit 7, Little Rock, AR 72205; tel. 501/227-2000; Russell D. Harrington Jr., pres.

0365 SPRINGHILL HEALTH SERVICES, 3715 Dauphin St., Mobile, AL 36608; tel. 205/342-3300; Bill A. Mason, pres.0395HEALTHCARE INTERNATIONAL, INC., 9737 Great Hills Trail, P O Box 4008, Austin, TX 78759; tel. 512/346-4300; James L. Fariss, bd. chm.

0405 HEALTHCARE SERVICES OF AMERICA, 2000 Southbridge Pkwy., Suite 200, Birmingham, AL 35209; tel. 205/879-8970; Charles A. Speir, bd. chm. & chief exec. off.

0415 ★BETHESDA HOSPITAL, INC., 619 Oak St., Cincinnati, OH 45206; tel. 513/569-6111; L. Thomas Wilburn Jr., chm. & chief exec. off.

0435 JUPITER HOSPITAL CORPORATION, 249 E. Ocean Blvd., Long Beach, CA 90802; tel. 213/437-7717; Bernard Broermann, chm.

0455 NUMED PSYCHIATRIC, INC. (Formerly Maxim Healthcare Corporation), 1265 Drummers Lane, Suite 107, P O Box 754, Valley Forge, PA 19482; tel. 215/687-5151; Edmund Bujalski, pres. & chief exec. off.

0465 ★NEXUS HEALTHCARE CORPORATION, Madison Ave., Summey Bldg., Suite 201, Mount Holly, NJ 08060; tel. 609/261-7011; Chester B. Kaletkowski, pres.

0495 GATEWAY MEDICAL SYSTEMS (Formerly Listed Under St. Louis, Missouri), 2351 Bolton Rd. N.W., Third Fl, Atlanta, GA 30318; tel. 404/351-9611; James R. Cheek, bd. chm.

0505 BENEDICTINE SISTERS, Priory of St. Gertrude, Box 107, Cottonwood, ID 83522; tel. 208/962-3224; Sr. Mary Matthew Geis

0515 BENEDICTINE HEALTH SYSTEM (Formerly Benedictine Sisters), 1028 E. Eighth St., Duluth, MN 55805; tel. 218/722-4799; Sr. Rebecca Wright, pres.

0535 BENEDICTINE SISTERS, St. Benedicts Convent, St. Joseph, MN 56374; tel. 612/362-5100; Sr. Katherine Howard

0545 BENEDICTINE SISTERS OF THE ANNUNCIATION, 7520 University Dr., Bismarck, ND 58501; tel. 701/255-1520; Sr. Susan Lardy, prioress

0565 ★CHRISTIAN HEALTH SERVICES DEVELOPMENT CORPORATION, 11155 Dunn Rd., St. Louis, MO 63136; tel. 314/355-0095; Fred L. Brown, pres. & chief exec. off.

0575 SCHICK LABORATORIES, INC., 1901 Ave. of the Stars, Los Angeles, CA 90067; tel. 213/553-3366; Patrick J. Frawley Jr., chm.

0585 BRIM AND ASSOCIATES, INC., 177 N. E. 102nd Ave., Portland, OR 97220; tel. 503/256-2070; A. E. Brim, pres.

0595 ★BRONSON HEALTHCARE GROUP, INC., One Healthcare Plaza, Kalamazoo, MI 49007; tel. 616/344-5222; Russell P. Kneen, chm. & chief exec. off.

0605 ★SCH HEALTH CARE SYSTEM, 6400 Lawndale Ave., Houston, TX 77023; tel. 713/928-2931; Sr. Carmella O'Donoghue, pres.

0615 WESTERN HOSPITAL CORPORATION, 1124 Ballena Blvd., Alameda, CA 94501; tel. 415/521-4110; Harvey W. Glasser MD, pres.

0645 GLENBEIGH, INC., 1001 N. U. S. Hwy., Suite 8, Jupiter, FL 33458; tel. 305/747-6565; G. Norman McCann, pres.

0655 FOREST HEALTH SYSTEMS, INC., 555 Wilson Lane, Des Plains, IL 60016; tel. 312/635-4100; Morris B. Squire, pres.

0665 CENTURY HEALTHCARE CORPORATION, 7615 E. 63rd Pl., Suite 200, Tulsa, OK 74133; tel. 918/250-9651; Jerry D. Dillon, pres. & chief exec. off.

0675 GUTHRIE MEDICAL CENTER, Guthrie Square, Sayre, PA 18840; tel. 717/888-6666; Ralph H. Meyer, pres.

0685 MERRITT PERALTA MEDICAL CENTER, Hawthorne Ave. & Webster St., Oakland, CA 94609; tel. 415/451-4900; Richard J. McCann, pres. & chief exec. off.

0695 ★CHARTER MEDICAL CORPORATION, 577 Mulberry St., 31202; Mailing Address P O Box 209, Macon, GA Zip 31298; tel. 912/742-1161; William A. Fickling Jr., chm. & chief exec. off.

0705 CHARLOTTE-MECKLENBURG HOSPITAL AUTHORITY, Box 32861, Charlotte, NC 28232; tel. 704/338-2145; Harry A. Nurkin PhD, pres.

0715 OFFICE OF HOSPITALS, P O Box 44215, Baton Rouge, LA 70804; tel. 504/342-2595; Jack Edwards, dep. asst.

0725 HERMANN AFFILIATED HOSPITAL SYSTEMS, 1020 Holcombe, Suite 900, Houston, TX 77030; tel. 713/796-0891; William E. Young Jr., chief exec. off.

0735 ★CHURCH-CHARITY FOUNDATION OF LONG ISLAND, 393 Front St., Hempstead, NY 11550; tel. 516/560-6460; Alexander H. Williams III, exec. vice-pres.

0745 ★BERKSHIRE HEALTH SYSTEMS, Sixth & Spruce, West Reading, PA 19603; tel. 215/378-6257; James B. Gronseth, chief exec. off.

0775 GENERAL HEALTH, INC., 5757 Corporate Blvd., Suite 202, Baton Rouge, LA 70808; tel. 504/924-4324; Thomas H. Sawyer, pres.

0785 COMMUNITY PSYCHIATRIC CENTERS, 2204 E. Fourth St., Santa Ana, CA 92705; tel. 714/835-4535; James W. Conte, pres. & chief exec. off.

0805 STORMONT-VAIL HEALTH SERVICES CORPORATION, 1500 Southwest Tenth St., Topeka, KS 66604; tel. 913/354-6112; Howard M. Chase, chief exec. off.

0825 SPECIALTY HOSPITAL DIVISION OF NME, 1010 Wisconsin Ave. N.W., Suite 900, Washington, DC 20007; tel. 202/337-5600; Norman A. Zober, pres.

0845 ★DEVEREUX FOUNDATION, 19 S. Waterloo Rd., Devon, PA 19333; tel. 215/964-3050; Ronald P. Burd, pres.

0865 ★ATLANTIC HEALTH SYSTEMS, INC., 466 Southern Blvd., Chatham, NJ 07928; tel. 201/514-1993; Thomas J. Foley, pres. & chief exec. off.

0875 COMMUNITY HEALTH SYSTEMS, INC., 14550 Torrey Chase Blvd., 450, Houston, TX 77014; E. Thomas Chaney, pres.

0885 ERLANGER HEALTH SERVICES, 6400 Lee Hwy., Suite 106, Chattanooga, TN 37421; Ron Williams, pres.
0905 FORUM HEALTH INVESTORS, INC., 401 W. Peachtree N.W., 1600, Atlanta, GA 30308; tel. 404/688-9019; J. Dennis Meaders, chief exec. off.
0945 ★EMPIRE HEALTH SERVICES, S. 400 Jefferson St., Suite 333, Spokane, WA 99204; tel. 509/458-7965; Jon K. Mitchell, pres. & chief exec. off.
0955 ★CAMCARE, INC. (Formerly Healthnet, Inc.), Box 1547, Charleston, WV 25326; tel. 304/348-7627; James C. Crews, pres. & chief exec. off.
0965 ★HEALTH DIMENSIONS, INC., 2005 Hamilton Ave., Suite 300, San Jose, CA 95125; tel. 408/599-2701; Robert K. Kirk, pres.
0985 AMERIHEALTH, INC., 2849 Paces Ferry Rd., Suite 790, Atlanta, GA 30339; tel. 404/435-1776; William G. White, pres.
0995 ★KENNESTONE REGIONAL HEALTH CARE SYSTEMS, 677 Church St., Marietta, GA 30060; tel. 404/428-2000; Bernard L. Brown Jr., exec. dir.
1015 ★JOHNS HOPKINS HEALTH SYSTEM, 600 N. Wolfe St., Baltimore, MD 21205; tel. 301/955-1488; Robert M. Heyssel MD, pres.
1025 ★HORIZON HEALTH SYSTEM, INC., 60 W. Broad St., Suite 201, Bethlehem, PA 18018; tel. 215/865-9988; William P. Koughan, pres.
1035 ★HORIZON HEALTH SYSTEMS, 21700 Greenfield Rd., Oak Park, MI 48237; tel. 313/968-2800; James L. Rieder, pres. & chief exec. off.
1045 DOCTORS HOSPITAL, 1087 Dennison Ave., Columbus, OH 43215; tel. 614/297-4000; Richard L. Sims, pres.
1055 SAMISSA HEALTH CARE CORPORATION, 3340 Ocean Park Blvd., Suite 3060, Santa Monica, CA 90405; tel. 213/450-3637; Barry Fireman MD, pres.
1065 REGENT HEALTH SYSTEMS, INC., Liberty St., P O Box 8754, Clinton, LA 70722; tel. 504/683-3319; Charles J. Mueller, pres.
1085 COMMUNITY HOSPITALS OF CENTRAL CALIFORNIA, Fresno & R Sts., P O Box 1232, Fresno, CA 93715; tel. 209/442-6000; James D. Helzer, pres. & chief exec. off.
1095 ★BAYSTATE HEALTH SYSTEMS, INC., 759 Chestnut St., Springfield, MA 01199; tel. 413/787-3345; Michael J. Daly, pres. & chief exec. off.
1130 ★PRESBYTERIAN HEALTHCARE SYSTEMS (Formerly Presbyterian Medical Center), 8220 Walnut Hill Lane, Suite 700, Dallas, TX 75231; tel. 214/696-8500; Douglas D. Hawthorne, pres.
1135 MEDIPLEX GROUP, INC., 15 Walnut St., Wellesley, MA 02181; tel. 617/446-6900; Joseph N. Cassese, pres.
1155 GREENLEAF HEALTH SYSTEMS, INC., Two Northgate Park, Chattanooga, TN 37415; tel. 615/870-5110; Dan B. Page, pres.
1195 DOMINICAN SISTERS CONGREGATION OF THE MOST HOLY NAME, Dominican Convent-San Rafael, San Rafael, CA 94901; tel. 415/454-9221; Sr. Jeremy
1215 ESKATON, 5105 Manzanita Ave., Carmichael, CA 95608; tel. 916/334-0810; Jack Billingsley, pres.
1225 ★EVANGELICAL HEALTH SYSTEMS, 2025 Windsor Dr., Oak Brook, IL 60521; tel. 312/572-9393; John G. King, pres. & chief exec. off.
1235 ★HUMANA INC., 500 W. Main St., Humana Bldg., Box 1438, Louisville, KY 40201; tel. 502/580-1000; David A. Jones, bd. chm. & chief exec. off.; H. Wendell Cherry, pres. & chief oper. off.
1255 ESCAMBIA COUNTY HEALTH CARE AUTHORITY (Formerly Escambia County Hospital Board), Brewton, AL 36426; tel. 205/867-8061; B. J. Griffin, adm.
1275 FIRST HEALTH, INC., 107 Public Square, Batesville, MS 38606; tel. 601/563-7676; David A. Vance, pres.
1295 DOMINICAN SISTERS CONGREGATION OF OUR LADY OF THE SACRED HEART, 1237 W. Monroe St., Springfield, IL 62704; tel. 217/787-0481; Sr. M. Dominica Brennan
1305 ★FAIRFAX HOSPITAL ASSOCIATION, 8001 Braddock Rd., Springfield, VA 22151; tel. 703/321-4213; J. Knox Singleton, pres.
1315 RECOVERY CENTERS OF AMERICA, 1010 Wisconsin Ave., Washington, DC 20007; tel. 202/298-3230; Thomas J. Doherty, exec. vice-pres.
1325 ★FAIRVIEW HOSPITAL AND HEALTHCARE SERVICES (Formerly Fairview Community Hospitals), 2312 S. Sixth St., Minneapolis, MN 55454; tel. 612/371-6300; Carl N. Platou, pres.
1335 MEASE HEALTH CARE, 833 Milwaukee Ave., P O Box 760, Dunedin, FL 33528; tel. 813/733-1111; Donald M. Schroder, pres. & chief exec. off.
1345 ★FELICIAN HEALTHCARE SYSTEMS, INC., 1325 Enfield St., Enfield, CT 06082; tel. 203/745-2542; M. Augustine Kloza, pres.
1355 ★FORBES HEALTHMARK, 500 Finley St., Pittsburgh, PA 15206; tel. 412/665-3565; George H. Schmitt, chm.
1365 HEALTHSTAR CORPORATION, 3555 Timmons Lane, Suite 700, Houston, TX 77027; tel. 713/627-2145; Hugh M. Morrison, bd. chm. & pres.
1375 AMERICAN HEALTHCARE MANAGEMENT, INC., 14160 Dallas Pkwy., Suite 900, Dallas, TX 75240; tel. 214/385-7000; John A. Bradley PhD, bd. chm. & chief exec. off.
1385 ★ALLEGANY HEALTH SYSTEM, 11300 Fourth St. N., Suite 220, St. Petersburg, FL 33702; tel. 813/577-9363; James E. Grobmyer, pres.
1395 ★FRANCISCAN SISTERS HEALTH CARE, 116 S.E. Eighth Ave., Little Falls, MN 56345; tel. 612/632-3601; Sr. Felix Mushel, pres.
1415 ★FRANCISCAN SISTERS HEALTH CARE CORPORATION, St. Francis Woods, Rte. 4, Mokena, IL 60448; tel. 815/469-4888; Sr. Dismas Janssen, bd. chm. & pres.
1425 FULTON-DE KALB HOSPITAL AUTHORITY, 80 Butler St. S.E., Atlanta, GA 30335; tel. 404/589-4307; J. W. Pinkston, exec. dir.
1435 DOCTOR JOHN MCDONALD HEALTH SYSTEMS, 5000 University Dr., P O Box 141739, Coral Gables, FL 33114; tel. 305/666-2111; William H. Comte, pres.
1455 ★FRANCISCAN HEALTH ADVISORY SERVICES, INC., 2409 S. Alverno Rd., Manitowoc, WI 54220; tel. 414/684-7071; Sr. Laura Wolf, pres.
1475 FRANCISCAN MISSIONARIES OF OUR LADY PROVINCIAL HOUSE, 4200 Essen Lane, Baton Rouge, LA 70809; tel. 504/927-7481; Sr. Brendan M. Ronayne
1485 FRANCISCAN SISTERS OF THE POOR HEALTH SYSTEMS, INC., 186 Joralemon St., Brooklyn, NY 11201; tel. 718/625-6530; Sr. Joanne Schuster, pres.
1495 GRANDCOR, 405 Grand Ave., Dayton, OH 45405; tel. 513/222-7990; Richard J. Minor, pres. & chief exec. off.
1505 ★SCRIPPS MEMORIAL HOSPITALS, 9888 Genesee Ave., La Jolla, CA 92038; tel. 619/457-4123; Ames S. Early, pres.
1525 HILLSBOROUGH COUNTY HOSPITAL AUTHORITY, Davis Island, Administrative Bldg., Tampa, FL 33607; tel. 813/251-7383; Newell E. France, mng. dir.
1535 GREAT PLAINS HEALTH ALLIANCE, INC. (Formerly Great Plains Lutheran Hospitals), Box 366, Phillipsburg, KS 67661; tel. 913/543-2111; Curtis Erickson, pres. & chief exec. off.
1555 ★GREENVILLE HOSPITAL SYSTEM, 701 Grove Rd., Greenville, SC 29605; tel. 803/242-7000; Jack A. Skarupa, pres.
1585 HEALTHCARE MANAGEMENT GROUP, INC., 146 Sylvan Dr., Jackson, GA 30233; tel. 205/979-0805; Earl Bonds Jr., chief exec. off.
1595 ★IOWA METHODIST HEALTH SYSTEM, 1200 Pleasant St., Des Moines, IA 50308; tel. 515/283-6201; David S. Ramsey, pres.
1605 SOUTHEAST COMMUNITY HEALTH SERVICES, 1433 Miccosukee Rd., Tallahassee, FL 32308; tel. 904/681-5675; Keith Gilles, chief oper. off.
1615 MID FLORIDA MEDICAL SERVICES, 200 Ave. F N.E., Winter Haven, FL 33880; tel. 813/293-8226; Lance W. Annstasio, pres. & chief exec. off.
1625 BAPTIST MEMORIAL HEALTHCARE DEVELOPMENT CORPORATION, 899 Madison Ave., Memphis, TN 38146; Bobby Hancock, sr. vice-pres. asst.
1635 BENEDICTINE HEALTH SYSTEM, 1005 W. Eighth St., Yankton, SD 57078; tel. 605/668-1511; Sr. Rosaria Kranz, pres.
1655 ★HARPER-GRACE HOSPITALS, 3990 John R St., Detroit, MI 48201; tel. 313/745-9375; Michael H. Fritz, pres. & chief exec. off.
1695 ★HEALTHEAST, INC., 337 N. West St., Allentown, PA 18102; tel. 215/778-2950; David P. Buchmueller, pres. & chief exec. off.
1755 ★HOSPITAL CORPORATION OF AMERICA, One Park Plaza, Box 550, Nashville, TN 37202; tel. 615/327-9551; Thomas F. Frist Jr. MD, chm.
1775 HOSPITAL MANAGEMENT ASSOCIATES, 800 Laurel Oak Dr., Naples, FL 33963; tel. 813/598-3104; William J. Schoen, bd. chm., pres. & chief exec. off.
1805 NUMED HOSPITALS, INC. (Formerly Numed, Inc.), 16633 Ventura Blvd., 13th Floor, Encino, CA 91436; tel. 818/990-2000; Stephen Bowles, pres. & chief exec. off.
1815 ★INTERMOUNTAIN HEALTH CARE, INC., 36 S. State, 22nd Floor, Salt Lake City, UT 84111; tel. 801/533-8282; Scott S. Parker, pres.
1865 HCA OKLAHOMA HEALTH NETWORK, 1601 N.W. Expwy., Suite 2200, Oklahoma City, OK 73118; tel. 405/840-2284; Bruce Perry, pres.
1885 DAUGHTERS OF CHARITY NATIONAL HEALTH SYSTEM, 7806 National Bridge Rd., P.O. Drawer 5730, St. Louis, MO 63121; 314/389-8900; Sr. Irene Kraus, pres.
1895 EAST TEXAS HOSPITAL FOUNDATION, P O Drawer 6400, Tyler, TX 75711; tel. 214/597-0351; Elmer G. Ellis, pres.
1905 HEALTH MANAGEMENT SERVICES, 5793 Widewaters Pkwy., Syracuse, NY 13214; tel. 315/445-2082; James W. Krembs, pres.
1935 BASIC AMERICAN MEDICAL, INC., 4000 E. Southport Rd., Indianapolis, IN 46237; tel. 317/783-5461; Brady R. Justice Jr., pres.
2105 ★KAISER FOUNDATION HOSPITALS, One Kaiser Plaza, Oakland, CA 94612; tel. 415/271-5910; James A. Vohs, chm. & pres.
2195 HEI CORPORATION, 7676 Woodway, Suite 112, Houston, TX 77063; tel. 713/780-7802; George G. Alexander MD, chm. & chief exec. off.
2235 ★LUTHERAN HOSPITALS AND HOMES SOCIETY OF AMERICA, 1202 Westrac Dr., Box 2087, Fargo, ND 58107; tel. 701/293-9053; Michael O. Bice, pres. & chief exec. off.
2245 ★LHS CORPORATION (Formerly Lutheran Hospital Society of Southern California), 1423 S. Grand Ave., Los Angeles, CA 90015; tel. 213/748-0191; Samuel J. Tibbitts, pres.
2295 ★LITTLE COMPANY OF MARY SISTERS HEALTHCARE SYSTEMS, 9350 S. California Ave., Evergreen Park, IL 60642; tel. 312/422-6200; Sr. Sharon Ann Walsh, prov. supr.
2345 ★HARRIS METHODIST HEALTH SYSTEM, 1325 Pennsylvania Ave., Eighth Fl, Fort Worth, TX 76104; tel. 817/878-5973; Ronald L. Smith, pres.
2395 ★SOUTHWEST HEALTH SYSTEM, 133 Donohoe Rd., Greensburg, PA 15601; tel. 412/836-6820; Joseph J. Peluso, pres. & chief exec. off.
2475 MISSISSIPPI COUNTY HOSPITAL SYSTEM, Box 108, Blytheville, AR 72315; tel. 501/762-3300; William E. Peaks, adm.
2495 ★HOSPITAL MANAGEMENT PROFESSIONALS, INC., 5200 Maryland Way, Suite 103, Brentwood, TN 37027; tel. 615/373-8830; Michael W. Barton, pres.
2565 ★ALLIANCE HEALTH SYSTEM, 18 Koger Executive Center, Suite 202, Norfolk, VA 23502; tel. 804/466-6000; Glenn R. Mitchell, pres.
2595 HEALTHSHARE, INC., 501 W. Mitchell St., Suite 300, Petoskey, MI 49770; tel. 616/348-4567; John Rasmussen, pres.
2645 MEMORIAL CARE SYSTEMS, 7777 Southwest Fwy, Suite 100, Houston, TX 77074; tel. 713/776-6992; Dan S. Wilford, pres.
2715 METHODIST HEALTH SYSTEM (Formerly Methodist Hospital, Inc.), 580 W. Eighth St., Jacksonville, FL 32209; tel. 904/798-8000; Marcus Drewa, pres.
2735 ★METHODIST HOSPITALS OF DALLAS, 301 W. Colorado Blvd., 75208; Mailing Address P O Box 655999, Dallas, TX Zip 75265; tel. 214/944-8137; David H. Hitt, pres. & chief exec. off.
2755 ★HEALTHLINK (Formerly Metropolitan Hospitals, Inc.), 500 N.E. Multnomah St., Portland, OR 97232; tel. 503/234-4500; G. Rodney Wolford, pres.
2855 MISSIONARY BENEDICTINE SISTERS AMERICAN PROVINCE, 300 N. 18th St., Norfolk, NE 68701; tel. 402/371-3438; Sr. Matilda Handl
3015 NATIONAL MEDICAL ENTERPRISES, 11620 Wilshire Blvd., P O Box 25980, Los Angeles, CA 90025; tel. 213/479-5526; Richard K. Eamer, chm. & chief exec. off.; Leonard Cohen, pres. & chief oper. off.
3025 SUMMIT HEALTH, LTD., 1800 Ave. of the Stars, Los Angeles, CA 90067; tel. 213/201-4000; William L. Pierpoint, pres. & chief exec. off.
3045 ★SISTERS OF CHARITY OF NAZARETH HEALTH CORPORATION, 9300 Shelbyville Rd., Suite 501, Louisville, KY 40222; tel. 502/429-5055; Sr. Jane Frances Kennedy, pres.
3075 NEW YORK CITY HEALTH AND HOSPITAL CORPORATION, 125 Worth St., New York, NY 10013; tel. 212/566-8038; Jo Ivey Boufford MD, actg. pres.
3115 NORTH BROWARD HOSPITAL DISTRICT, 1625 S.E. Third Ave., Fort Lauderdale, FL 33316; tel. 305/355-4400; Robert L. Kennedy, exec. dir.
3165 NORTH CENTRAL HEALTH SERVICES, 930 Tenth Ave., Spearfish, SD 57783; tel. 605/642-2744; Larry Marshall, vice-pres.

3175 NEPONSET VALLEY HEALTH SYSTEM, 800 Washington St., Norwood, MA 02062; tel. 617/769-4000; Frank S. Crane III, pres.

3315 ★OHIO VALLEY HEALTH SERVICES AND EDUCATION CORPORATION, 90 N. Fourth St., Martins Ferry, OH 43935; tel. 304/234-8765; David J. Campbell, vice chm. & chief exec. off.

3355 ORLANDO REGIONAL MEDICAL CENTER, 1414 S. Kuhl Ave., Orlando, FL 32806; tel. 305/841-5111; J. Gary Strack, pres.

3395 ★HITCHCOCK ALLIANCE, P O Box 1001, Hanover, NH 03755; tel. 603/646-8150; James W. Varnum, pres.

3455 PENNSYLVANIA HOSPITAL (Formerly Pennsylvania Hospital Corporation), Eighth & Spruce Sts., Philadelphia, PA 19107; tel. 215/829-3312; H. Robert Cathcart, pres.

3465 ★PEOPLES COMMUNITY HOSPITAL AUTHORITY, 33000 Annapolis Ave., Wayne, MI 48184; tel. 313/467-4600; Fred E. Blair, chief exec. off.

3505 ★SOUTHWEST COMMUNITY HEALTH SERVICES, 6100 Pan American Freeway N.E., 87109; Mailing Address P O Box 26666, Albuquerque, NM Zip 87125; tel. 505/823-8313; Richard Barr, pres.

3535 HENDRICK MEDICAL DEVELOPMENT CORPORATION (Formerly Hendrick Medical Center), 19th & Hickory St., Abilene, TX 79601; tel. 915/677-3551; Michael C. Waters, pres.

3555 STATE OF HAWAII, DEPARTMENT OF HEALTH, P O Box 3378, Honolulu, HI 96801; tel. 808/548-7402; Jerry Walker, dep. dir.

3595 ★EASTERN MERCY HEALTH SYSTEM, Scott Plaza Two, Suite 403, Philadelphia, PA 19113; tel. 215/521-4500; Daniel F. Russell, pres. & chief exec. off.

3615 RELIGIOUS HOSPITALLERS OF ST. JOSEPH, PROVINCE OF ST. JOSEPH, 16 Manitou Crescent E., Kingston, Ont., Canada; tel. 613/389-0275

3775 MILWAUKEE COUNTY DEPARTMENT OF HEALTH AND HUMAN SERVICES (Formerly Milwaukee County Institute and Departments), 8731 Watertown Plank Rd., Milwaukee, WI 53226; tel. 414/257-6489; James W. Wahner, dir.

3825 MEDIQ, INC., One Mediq Plaza, Pennsauken, NJ 08110; tel. 609/665-9300; Bernard Korman, pres.

4025 ★SERVANTCOR, 175 S. Wall St., Kankakee, IL 60901; tel. 815/937-2034; Joseph S. Feth, pres.

4045 ★SAMARITAN HEALTH SERVICE, 1410 N. Third St., Phoenix, AZ 85004; tel. 602/239-4106; David Reed, pres.

4125 ★SHRINERS HOSPITALS FOR CRIPPLED CHILDREN (Formerly Shriner's Childrens Hospitals), Box 25356, Tampa, FL 33622; tel. 813/885-2575; Jack D. Hoard, exec. adm.

4155 ★SOUTH CAROLINA BAPTIST HOSPITALS, 1333 Taylor St., Columbia, SC 29201; tel. 803/771-5046; William A. Boyce, pres.

4165 ★ADVENTIST HEALTH SYSTEM-SUNBELT HEALTH CARE CORPORATION, 2400 Bedford Rd., Orlando, FL 32803; tel. 305/897-1919; Mardian J. Blair, pres.

4175 ★SOUTHERN ILLINOIS HOSPITAL SERVICES, 608 E. College St., P O Box 522, Carbondale, IL 62903; tel. 618/457-7833; Jerry A. Hickam, pres.

4195 ★SPARTANBURG HOSPITAL SYSTEM, 101 E. Wood St., Spartanburg, SC 29303; tel. 803/591-6107; Charles C. Boone, pres.

4810 RIVERSIDE HEALTHCARE ASSOCIATION, INC. (Formerly Riverside Hospital), 606 Denbigh Blvd., Suite 601, Newport News, VA 23602; tel. 804/875-7500; Nelson L. St. Clair, pres.

5085 ★BON SECOURS HEALTH SYSTEM, INC., 5457 Twin Knolls Rd., Suite 300, Columbia, MD 21045; tel. 301/992-7330; John P. Brozovich, pres. & chief exec. off. oper.

5095 ★SISTERS OF CHARITY OF LEAVENWORTH HEALTH SERVICES CORPORATION, 4200 S. Fourth St., Leavenworth, KS 66048; tel. 913/682-1338; Sr. Macrina Ryan, pres.

5115 ★SISTERS OF CHARITY HEALTH CARE SYSTEMS, INC., 345 Neeb Rd., Cincinnati, OH 45238; tel. 513/922-9775; Sr. Celestia Koebel, pres.

5125 ★SISTERS OF CHARITY OF ST. AUGUSTINE HEALTH AND HUMAN SERVICES, 5232 Broadview Rd., Richfield, OH 44286; tel. 216/659-9283; Sr. Mary Patricia Barrett, pres.

5155 ★MERCY HEALTH CARE SYSTEM, 2303 Grandview Ave., Cincinnati, OH 45206; tel. 513/221-2736; Sr. M. Michaeleen, pres. & chief exec. off.

5165 ★SISTERS OF MERCY HEALTH CORPORATION, 28550 Eleven Mile Rd., Farmington Hills, MI 48018; tel. 313/478-9900; Sr. Mary Corita Heid, pres.

5175 ★CATHOLIC HEALTH CORPORATION, 920 S. 107th Ave., Omaha, NE 68114; tel. 402/393-7661; Diane Moeller, pres.

5185 ★SISTERS OF MERCY HEALTH SYSTEMS-ST. LOUIS (Formerly Sisters of Mercy of the Union-Province of St. Louis), 2039 N. Geyer Rd., St. Louis, MO 63131; tel. 314/965-6100; Sr. Mary R. Rocklage, chief exec. off. & chairperson

5195 ★MERCY HEALTH CARE SYSTEM, Mercy Center, Lake St., Box 370, Dallas, PA 18612; tel. 717/675-3535; William D. McGuire, pres. & chief exec. off.

5205 ★CATHOLIC HEALTHCARE WEST (Formerly Mercy Health Systems), 2300 Adeline Dr., Burlingame, CA 94010; tel. 415/340-7470; Robert C. Densmore, pres.

5215 MERCY-CHICAGO PROVINCE HEALTHCARE SYSTEMS (Formerly Listed Under Chicago), 1s450 Summit Ave., Oakbrook Terrace, IL 60181; tel. 312/953-2970; Catherine C. Gallagher, exec. dir.

5235 ★SISTERS OF THE PALLOTTINE MISSIONARY SOCIETY, 2900 First Ave., Huntington, WV 25702; tel. 304/696-2550; James Spencer, dir. finance

5255 ★PRESENTATION HEALTH SYSTEM (Formerly Sisters of the Presentation of the Blessed Virgin Mary), 1301 S. Ninth Ave., Suite 102, Mailing Address , Sioux Falls, SD Zip 57105; tel. 605/331-4999; Sr. Colman Coakley, pres.

5265 ★SISTERS OF PROVIDENCE-PROVINCE OF ST. IGNATIUS, 9 E. Ninth Ave., Spokane, WA 99202; tel. 509/455-4879; Sr. Barbara Ann Brenner, chief exec. off.

5275 ★SISTERS OF PROVIDENCE (Formerly Sisters of Providence Health Care Corporations), 520 Pike St., P O Box C11038, Seattle, WA 98111; tel. 206/464-3355; Donald A. Brennan, pres.

5285 ★SISTERS OF PROVIDENCE HEALTH AND HUMAN SERVICE (Formerly Listed Under Holyoke), 209 Carew St., Springfield, MA 01104; tel. 413/536-7511; Sr Catherine Laboure, pres.

5305 ★SISTERS OF THE SORROWFUL MOTHER-MINISTRY CORPORATION, 6618 N. Teutonia Ave., Milwaukee, WI 53209; tel. 414/352-4056; Sr. M. Lois Bush, pres. & chief exec. off.

5325 ★FRANCISCAN HEALTH SYSTEM, Brandywine 1 Bldg., Suite 301, Rtes. 1 & 202, Chadds Ford, PA 19317; tel. 215/358-3950; Ronald R. Aldrich, pres.

5335 ★SISTERS OF THE 3RD ORDER OF ST. FRANCIS, 1124 N. Berkley Ave., Peoria, IL 61603; tel. 309/655-2850; Sr. Frances Marie, exec. vice-pres.

5345 ★SISTERS OF ST. FRANCIS HEALTH SERVICES, INC., 1515 Dragoon Trail, P O Box 1290, Mishawaka, IN 46544; tel. 219/256-3935; Sr. M. Theresa Solbach, pres.

5355 ★HOSPITAL SISTERS HEALTH SYSTEM-HOSPITAL SISTERS OF THE THIRD ORDER OF ST. FRANCIS-AMERICAN PROVINCE, Sangamon Ave. Rd., Box 19431, Springfield, IL 62794; tel. 217/522-6969; Sr. Marianna Kosior, pres.

5365 SISTERS OF ST. FRANCIS OF THE PROVINCE OF GOD, Grove & McRoberts Rds., Pittsburgh, PA 15234; tel. 412/882-9911; Sr. Marietta Zvirblis, coor.

5375 ★FRANCISCAN SERVICES CORPORATION, 6832 Convent Blvd., Sylvania, OH 43560; tel. 419/882-8373; John W. O'Connell, pres.

5395 ★SACRED HEART CORPORATION (Formerly Sisters of St. Francis of Penance and Christian Charity-Sacred Heart Province), 2861 W. 52nd Ave., Denver, CO 80221; tel. 303/458-8611; Sr. Christina Oleske, pres.

5415 ★HEALTH AND HOSPITAL SERVICES, 1715 114th Ave. S.E., Suite 110, Bellevue, WA 98004; tel. 206/454-8068; Sr. Joan M. McInnes, pres.

5425 ★ST. JOSEPH HEALTH SYSTEM, 440 S. Batavia St., Orange, CA 92668; tel. 714/997-7690; Robert W. O'Leary, pres.

5435 ★CSJ HEALTH SYSTEM OF WICHITA (Formerly Sisters of St. Joseph Health Systems of Wichita), 3720 E. Bayley, Wichita, KS 67218; tel. 316/686-7171; Sr. Antoinette Yelek, pres.; Gregory G. Guntly, chief exec. off.

5445 SISTERS OF ST. JOSEPH-3RD ORDER OF ST. FRANCIS, 105 E. Jefferson, P O Box 688, South Bend, IN 46624; tel. 219/233-1166; Sr. Adalbert Stal, central treas.; Sr. Joanne Skalski, dir. inst sponsorship bd.

5455 ★SSM HEALTH CARE SYSTEM (Formerly Sisters of St. Mary), 1031 Bellevue Ave., St. Louis, MO 63117; tel. 314/768-1600; Sr. Mary Jean Ryan, pres. & chief exec. off.

5545 MERCY HEALTH SYSTEM OF WESTERN NEW YORK (Formerly Sisters of Mercy), 565 Abbott Rd., Buffalo, NY 14220; tel. 716/827-2375; Sr. Mary Annunciate Kelleher, pres.

5555 ★SISTERS OF ST. JOSEPH HEALTH SYSTEM, 3427 Gull Rd., Nazareth, MI 49074; tel. 616/381-2500; Sr. Irene Waldmann, pres.

5565 ★INCARNATE WORD HEALTH SERVICES, 303 W. Sunset Rd., San Antonio, TX 78209; tel. 512/828-1733; Sr. Nora Marie Walsh, pres.

5570 GEISINGER SYSTEM SERVICES, N. Academy Ave., Danville, PA 17822; tel. 717/271-6631; Frank J. Trembulak, pres.

5575 SISTERS OF THE HOLY FAMILY OF NAZARETH-SACRED HEART PROVINCE, 353 N. River Rd., Des Plaines, IL 60016; tel. 312/298-6760; Sr. M. Loretta Markiewicz, prov. supr.

5585 ★HOLY CROSS HEALTH SYSTEM CORPORATION, 3606 E. Jefferson Blvd., South Bend, IN 46615; tel. 219/233-8558; William A. Himmelsbach Jr., pres. & chief exec. off.

5615 SISTERS OF ST. JOSEPH OF CHAMBERY-NORTH AMERICAN PROVINCE, 27 Park Rd., West Hartford, CT 06119; tel. 203/233-5126; Sr. Jean Sauntry, supr.

5645 ★HUMILITY OF MARY HEALTH CARE CORPORATION (Formerly Sisters of the Humility of Mary), P O Box 841, Lorain, OH 44052; tel. 216/871-0971; Sr. Frances Flanigan, chief exec. off.

5685 SISTERS OF ST. CASIMIR, 2601 W. Marquette Rd., Chicago, IL 60629; tel. 312/434-6700; Sr. M. Joanella Fayert, pres.

5695 ★CONGREGATION OF ST. AGNES, 475 Gillett St., Fond Du Lac, WI 54935; tel. 414/923-2121; Sr. Mary Mollison, corp dir.

5705 FRANCISCAN SISTERS OF PERPETUAL ADORATION, 912 Market St., La Crosse, WI 54601; tel. 608/782-5610; Sr. Patricia Alden, pres.

5715 ★SISTERS OF ST. FRANCIS-3RD ORDER REGULAR OF BUFFALO, 400 Mill St., Williamsville, NY 14221; tel. 716/632-2155; Sr. Maureen Ann, gen. minister

5745 SISTERS OF CHARITY OF OUR LADY OF MERCY, Box 12410, Charleston, SC 29412; tel. 803/795-6083; Sr. Anne Francis Campbell

5755 LOS ANGELES COUNTY-DEPARTMENT OF HEALTH SERVICES (Formerly County of Los Angeles-Department of Health Services), 313 N. Figueroa St., Room 936, Los Angeles, CA 90012; tel. 213/974-8101; Robert C. Gates, dir. health

5765 PARACELSUS HEALTHCARE (Formerly Paracelsus Hospital Corporation), 155 N. Lake Ave., Suite 1100, Pasadena, CA 91101; tel. 818/792-8600; R. J. Messenger, pres. & chief oper. off.

5805 ★CENTRAL MANAGEMENT CORPORATION, 112-114 Roberts St., Suite 208, Fargo, ND 58102; tel. 701/237-9290; James Dunne, pres.

5815 ★SISTERS OF CHARITY OF ST. ELIZABETH (Formerly Listed Under Jersey City), 49 Demarest Rd., Paramus, NJ 07652; tel. 201/539-1600; Sr. Ellen L. Joyce, gen. superior

5845 ST. LUKE'S REGIONAL MEDICAL CENTER, 2720 Stone Park Blvd., Sioux City, IA 51104; tel. 712/279-3500; David O. Biorn, pres. & chief exec. off.

5855 ★HOLY CROSS LIFE CARE SYSTEMS, INC. (Formerly Sisters of Mercy of the Holy Cross-Province of the U. S.), 1500 O'Day St., Merrill, WI 54452; tel. 715/536-5101; Robert E. Wulff, adm. & chief exec. off.

5875 SISTERS OF THE SORROWFUL MOTHER-TULSA PROVINCIALATE, 17600 E. 51st St. S., Broken Arrow, OK 74012; tel. 918/355-5595; Sr. M. Julietta Mendoza, prov.

5885 ★COVENANT HEALTH SYSTEMS, INC. (Formerly Grey Nuns Health Systems, Inc.), 10 Pelham Rd., Lexington, MA 02173; tel. 617/862-1634; Sr. Dorothy Cooper, pres. & chief exec. off.

5895 NATIONAL HEALTHCARE, INC., 444 N. Oates St., P O Box 1649, Dothan, AL 36302; tel. 205/793-2399; Steve L. Phelps, pres. & chief exec. off.

5925 SISTERS OF ST. FRANCIS OF THE MISSION OF THE IMMACULATE VIRGIN, Immaculate Conception Motherhouse, Hastings On Hudson, NY 10706; tel. 914/478-3910; Sr. Mary Paul, supr. gen.

5935 SISTERS OF ST. JOSEPH, Rural Rte. 3, Box 291a, Tipton, IN 46072; tel. 317/456-5300; Sr. Veronica Baumgartner, pres.

5945 ★HEALTH CARE CORPORATION OF THE SISTERS OF ST. JOSEPH OF CARONDELET, 77 W. Port Plaza, Suite 222, St. Louis, MO 63146; tel. 314/576-5662; Sr. Mary K. Ford, pres.

5955 SISTERS OF THE 3RD FRANCISCAN ORDER-MINOR CONVENTUALS, 100 Michaels Ave., Syracuse, NY 13208; tel. 315/425-0115; Sr. M. Aileen Griffin, supr. gen.

5975 SISTERS OF ST. FRANCIS-IMMACULATE HEART OF MARY-PROVINCE OF HANKINSON, St. Francis Convent, Hankinson, ND 58041; tel. 701/242-7197; Sr. Mary Louise Jundt, dir.

5985 SISTERS OF MERCY, Sacred Heart Convent, Belmont, NC 28012; tel. 704/825-2011; Sr. Jeanne Margaret McNally, supr. gen.

5995 SISTERS OF CHARITY CENTER, Mount St. Vincent On Hudson, Bronx, NY 10471; tel. 212/549-9200; Sr. Agnes Connolly, pres.

6005 ★HOLY FAMILY OF NAZARETH HEALTH SYSTEM (Formerly Sisters of the Holy Family of Nazareth-Vice Provincialate), 1814 Egyptian Way, 75051; Mailing Address Box 530959, Grand Prairie, TX Zip 75053; tel. 214/641-4496; Sr. M. Beata, pres.

6015 SISTERS OF MERCY OF THE UNION-PROVINCE OF BALTIMORE, P O Box 11448, Baltimore, MD 21239; tel. 301/435-4400; Sr. Angela Marie Ebberwein

6095 ★SISTERS OF CHARITY HEALTH CARE SYSTEMS CORPORATION, 355 Bard Ave., Staten Island, NY 10310; tel. 212/390-1650; John J. Depierro, pres. & chief exec. off.

6235 ★HEALTHONE CORPORATION, 2810 57th Ave. N., Minneapolis, MN 55430; tel. 612/333-1711; Richard S. Blair, interim pres. & chief exec. off.

6295 ★LUTHERAN GENERAL HEALTH CARE SYSTEMS (Formerly Lutheran Institute of Human Ecology), 1775 Dempster St., Park Ridge, IL 60068; tel. 312/696-5600; George B. Caldwell, pres.

6345 UNITED HOSPITALS, INC., 100 W. Laurel Ave., Cheltenham, PA 19012; tel. 215/663-5400; Myles G. Turtz MD, chm. & chief exec. off.

6405 UNIVERSITY OF CALIFORNIA-SYSTEMWIDE ADMINISTRATION, 764 University Hall, Berkeley, CA 94720; tel. 415/642-5192; C. L. Hopper MD, vice-pres. health affairs

6415 ★UNIVERSITY OF WASHINGTON HOSPITALS, Sc-61 University of Washington, Seattle, WA 98195; tel. 206/548-6364; Robert Muilenburg, exec. dir.

6525 ★REPUBLIC HEALTH CORPORATION, 15303 Dallas Pkwy., Suite 1400, Dallas, TX 75248; tel. 214/851-3100; James E. Buncher, pres. & chief exec. off.

6545 ★HEALTH CORPORATION OF THE ARCHDIOCESE OF NEWARK, 41 Centre St., Newark, NJ 07102; tel. 201/596-3900; Margaret J. Straney, pres.

6555 ★MULTICARE MEDICAL CENTER (Formerly Consolidated Hospitals), 409 S. J St., P O Box 5277, Tacoma, WA 98405; tel. 206/594-1251; W. Barry Connoley, pres. & chief exec. off.

6615 ★MEDLANTIC HEALTHCARE GROUP (Formerly Washington Healthcare Corporation), 100 Irving St. N.W., Washington, DC 20010; tel. 202/541-6006; John P. McDaniel, pres.

6665 BRUNSWICK HOSPITAL CENTER, 366 Broadway, Amityville, NY 11701; tel. 516/789-7000; Benjamin M. Stein MD, pres.

6705 WAKE MEDICAL CENTER (Formerly Wake County Hospital Systems), 3000 New Bern Ave., Raleigh, NC 27610; tel. 919/755-8112; Raymond L. Champ, pres.

6725 ★WEST JERSEY HEALTH SYSTEM, Mount Ephraim & Atlantic Aves., Camden, NJ 08104; tel. 609/342-4600; Barry D. Brown, pres.; William Michael Tomlinson, exec. vice-pres.

6745 ★WHEATON FRANCISCAN SERVICES, INC., 26w171 Roosevelt Rd., P O Box 667, Wheaton, IL 60189; tel. 312/462-9271; Willis F. Fry, pres. & chief exec. off.

6905 ★HEALTHWEST MEDICAL CENTERS (Formerly Healthwest Foundation), 21800 Oxnard St., Suite 550, Woodland Hills, CA 91367; tel. 818/716-2777; Roger H. Drue, pres.

6975 MILLS-PENINSULA HOSPITALS, 50 S. San Mateo Dr., San Mateo, CA 94401; tel. 415/579-2190; Charles H. Mason Jr., pres. & chief exec. off.

6995 DEPARTMENT OF HEALTH AND HOSPITALS, HOSPITAL SERVICES DIVISION, 818 Harrison Ave., Boston, MA 02118; tel. 617/424-5365; Lewis Pollack, comr.

7005 ★WESTERN RESERVE CARE SYSTEM, 345 Oak Hill Ave., Youngstown, OH 44501; tel. 216/747-9727; James E. Michels, pres.

7235 ★METHODIST HEALTH CARE NETWORK, 5615 Kirby Dr., Suite 800, Houston, TX 77005; tel. 713/831-2900; Michael Williamson, pres. & chief oper. off.; Larry L. Mathis, bd. chm. & chief exec. off.

7555 PALOMAR POMERADO HOSPITAL DISTRICT (Formerly Northern San Diego County Hospital District), 215 S. Hickory St., Suite 310, Escondido, CA 92025; tel. 619/489-4860; Robert M. Edwards, pres. & chief exec. off.

7675 ★ST. LUKE'S HEALTH SYSTEM, 5025 E. Washington, Suite 200, Phoenix, AZ 85034; tel. 602/231-0017; Brian C. Lockwood, pres.

7775 ★MAIN LINE HEALTH, INC. (Formerly Listed Under Philadelphia), 259 Radnor-Chester Rd., Suite 290, Radnor, PA 19087; tel. 215/254-8840; Ralph F. Moriarty, pres.

7895 ★SANTA FE HEALTHCARE (Formerly Santa Fe Healthcare System, Inc.), 720 S.W. Second Ave., P O Box 749, Gainesville, FL 32602; tel. 904/375-4321; Edward C. Peddie, pres.

7995 METROPOLITAN HOSPITAL, 801 Arch St., Fifth Floor, Philadelphia, PA 19107; tel. 215/238-6700; Jack R. Dyson, actg. chief oper. off.

8495 RUSHMORE NATIONAL HEALTH SYSTEMS, P O Box 2720, Rapid City, SD 57709; tel. 605/341-8100; Gary Riedmann, pres.

8795 SUTTER HEALTH SYSTEM (Formerly Sutter Community Hospitals), 1111 Howe Ave., Suite 600, Sacramento, CA 95825; tel. 916/927-5211; Patrick G. Hays, pres. & chief exec. off.

8805 ★COLUMBUS-CUNEO-CABRINI MEDICAL CENTER, 676 N. St. Clair, Suite 1900, Chicago, IL 60611; tel. 312/943-1333; James P. Hamill, chief exec. off.

8810 ★BAPTIST HOSPITAL AND HEALTH SYSTEMS, 2224 W. Northern Ave., Suite D-300, Phoenix, AZ 85021; tel. 602/864-1184; J. Barry Johnson, pres.

8815 ★RESEARCH HEALTH SERVICES, 6400 Prospect Ave., Kansas City, MO 64132; tel. 816/276-9167; E. Wynn Presson, pres.

8835 ★STRATEGIC HEALTH SYSTEMS, 767 Beta Dr., Suite E., Mayfield Village, OH 44143; tel. 216/449-7710; Robert Moss, pres.

8855 ★INTERCARE HEALTH SYSTEMS, 98 James St., Mediplex Suite 400, Edison, NJ 08820; tel. 201/632-1500; Michael T. Kornett, pres. & chief exec. off.

8865 HEALTH MANAGEMENT SERVICES, INC., 340 E. Town St., Suite 7-800, Columbus, OH 43215; tel. 614/461-3401; Ned Boatright, pres.

8875 ★METHODIST HEALTH SERVICES CORPORATION, 221 N.E. Glen Oak Ave., Peoria, IL 61636; tel. 309/672-4826; James K. Knoble, pres.; Daniel P. Chonowski, exec. vice-pres.

8895 ★VISTA HILL FOUNDATION, 3420 Camino Del Rio N., Suite 100, San Diego, CA 92108; tel. 619/563-1770; Ronald E. Fickle, pres. & chief exec. off.

8985 SAFECARE COMPANY, INC/SAFECARE HEALTH SERVICE, INC., 900 Fourth Ave., Suite 800, P O Box 21485, Seattle, WA 98111; tel. 206/223-4560; Stephen R. Jepson, sr. vice-pres. & pres.

9095 ★U. S. HEALTH CORPORATION, 3555 Olentangy River Rd., Suite 4000, Columbus, OH 43214; tel. 614/261-5902; Erie Chapman III, pres. & chief exec. off.

9105 ★UNIVERSITY OF ALABAMA HOSPITALS, 619 S. 19th St., Birmingham, AL 35233; tel. 205/934-4011; James E. Moon, adm.

9255 ★TRUMAN MEDICAL CENTER, 2301 Holmes, Kansas City, MO 64108; tel. 816/556-3153; James J. Mongan MD, exec. dir.

9265 NEBRASKA METHODIST HEALTH SYSTEM, INC., 8303 Dodge St., Omaha, NE 68114; tel. 402/390-4844; John W. Estabrook, pres. & chief exec. off.

9305 BROMENN HEALTHCARE, 807 N. Main St., Bloomington, IL 61702; tel. 309/827-4321; Jeffrey B. Schaub, pres.

9335 METHODIST HOSPITAL OF INDIANA, 1701 N. Senate Blvd., Indianapolis, IN 46202; tel. 317/929-8510; Frank P. Lloyd MD, pres.

9345 ★METHODIST HEALTH SYSTEMS, INC., 1211 Union Ave., Suite 700, Memphis, TN 38104; tel. 901/726-2300; John T. Casey, pres.

9355 ★ADVENTIST HEALTH SYSTEM-EASTERN AND MIDDLE AMERICA, 8800 W. 75th St., Shawnee Mission, KS 66204; tel. 913/677-8000; J. Russell Shawver, pres.

9555 UNIVERSAL HEALTH SERVICES, INC., 367 S. Gulph Rd., King of Prussia, PA 19406; tel. 215/768-3300; Alan B. Miller, pres.

9575 ★WILLIAM BEAUMONT HOSPITAL CORPORATION, 3601 W. Thirteen Mile Rd., Royal Oak, MI 48072; tel. 313/288-8000; Kenneth E. Myers, pres.; Ted D. Wasson, exec. vice-pres.

9605 UNITED MEDICAL CORPORATION, 20 N. Orange Ave., Suite 1600, Orlando, FL 32801; tel. 305/423-2200; Donald R. Dizney, chm.; James E. English, pres.

9650 ★FRANCISCAN HEALTH SYSTEM, INC. (Formerly St. Francis Health Corporation), 615 S. Tenth St., La Crosse, WI 54601; tel. 608/785-0940; Stewart W. Laird, pres.

9795 WESTWORLD COMMUNITY HEALTHCARE, INC., 23832 Rockfield Rd., Lake Forest, CA 92630; tel. 714/768-2981; Stephen F. Arterburn, pres. & chief exec. off.

9855 ★CAMELBACK HOSPITALS, INC., 7447 E. Earll Dr., Scottsdale, AZ 85251; tel. 602/941-7660; Daniel W. Capps, pres. & chief exec. off.

9905 ★UNITED HEALTH SERVICES, INC., 1200 S. Columbia Rd., P O Box 6002, Grand Forks, ND 58201; tel. 701/780-5200; Robert M. Jacobson, pres.

9995 ★GROUP HEALTH COOPERATIVE OF PUGET SOUND, 300 Elliott Ave. W., Seattle, WA 98119; tel. 206/326-6844; Mr. Gail L. Warden, pres. & chief exec. off.

Geographically

ALABAMA

Birmingham: 0345 ★BAPTIST MEDICAL CENTERS, 2700 U.S. Hwy. 280, P O Box 30040, 35222; tel. 205/322-9319; Emmett Johnson, pres.

0405 HEALTHCARE SERVICES OF AMERICA, 2000 Southbridge Pkwy., Suite 200, 35209; tel. 205/879-8970; Charles A. Speir, bd. chm. & chief exec. off.

9105 ★UNIVERSITY OF ALABAMA HOSPITALS, 619 S. 19th St., 35233; tel. 205/934-4011; James E. Moon, adm.

Brewton: 1255 ESCAMBIA COUNTY HEALTH CARE AUTHORITY (Formerly Escambia County Hospital Board), 36426; tel. 205/867-8061; B.J. Griffin, adm.

Dothan: 5895 NATIONAL HEALTHCARE, INC., 444 N. Oates St., P O Box 1649, 36302; tel. 205/793-2399; Steve L. Phelps, pres. & chief exec. off.

Mobile: 0365 SPRINGHILL HEALTH SERVICES, 3715 Dauphin St., 36608; tel. 205/342-3300; Bill A. Mason, pres.

ARIZONA

Phoenix: 8810 ★BAPTIST HOSPITAL AND HEALTH SYSTEMS, 2224 W. Northern Ave., Suite D-300, 85021; tel. 602/864-1184; J. Barry Johnson, pres.

4045 ★SAMARITAN HEALTH SERVICE, 1410 N. Third St., 85004; tel. 602/239-4106; David Reed, pres.

7675 ★ST. LUKE'S HEALTH SYSTEM, 5025 E. Washington, Suite 200, 85034; tel. 602/231-0017; Brian C. Lockwood, pres.

Scottsdale: 9855 ★CAMELBACK HOSPITALS, INC., 7447 E. Earll Dr., 85251; tel. 602/941-7660; Daniel W. Capps, pres. & chief exec. off.

ARKANSAS

Blytheville: 2475 MISSISSIPPI COUNTY HOSPITAL SYSTEM, Box 108, 72315; tel. 501/762-3300; William E. Peaks, adm.

Little Rock: 0355 ★BAPTIST MEDICAL SYSTEM, 9601 Interstate 630, Exit 7, 72205; tel. 501/227-2000; Russell D. Harrington Jr., pres.

CALIFORNIA

Alameda: 0615 WESTERN HOSPITAL CORPORATION, 1124 Ballena Blvd., 94501; tel. 415/521-4110; Harvey W. Glasser MD, pres.

Berkeley: 6405 UNIVERSITY OF CALIFORNIA-SYSTEMWIDE ADMINISTRATION, 764 University Hall, 94720; tel. 415/642-5192; C. L. Hopper MD, vice-pres. health affairs

Beverly Hills: 0125 ★AMERICAN MEDICAL INTERNATIONAL, 414 N. Camden Dr., 90210; tel. 213/278-6200; Walter Weisman, pres. & chief exec. off.

Burlingame: 5205 ★CATHOLIC HEALTHCARE WEST (Formerly Mercy Health Systems), 2300 Adeline Dr., 94010; tel. 415/340-7470; Robert C. Densmore, pres.

Carmichael: 1215 ESKATON, 5105 Manzanita Ave., 95608; tel. 916/334-0810; Jack Billingsley, pres.

Encino: 1805 NUMED HOSPITALS, INC. (formerly Numed, Inc.) 16633 Ventura Blvd., 13th Floor, 91436; tel. 818/990-2000; Stephen Bowles, pres. & chief exec. off.

Escondido: 7555 PALOMAR POMERADO HOSPITAL DISTRICT (Formerly Northern San Diego County Hospital District), 215 S. Hickory St., Suite 310, 92025; tel. 619/489-4860; Robert M. Edwards, pres. & chief exec. off.

Fresno: 1085 COMMUNITY HOSPITALS OF CENTRAL CALIFORNIA, Fresno & R Sts., P O Box 1232, 93715; tel. 209/442-6000; James D. Helzer, pres. & chief exec. off.

Irvine: 0275 COMPREHENSIVE CARE CORPORATION, 18551 Von Karman Ave., 92715; tel. 714/851-2273; Richard Santoni PhD, pres.

La Jolla: 1505 ★SCRIPPS MEMORIAL HOSPITALS, 9888 Genesee Ave., 92038; tel. 619/457-4123; Ames S. Early, pres.

Lake Forest: 9795 WESTWORLD COMMUNITY HEALTHCARE, INC., 23832 Rockfield Rd., 92630; tel. 714/768-2981; Stephen F. Arterburn, pres. & chief exec. off.

Long Beach: 0435 JUPITER HOSPITAL CORPORATION, 249 E. Ocean Blvd., 90802; tel. 213/437-7717; Bernard Broermann, chm.

Los Angeles: 5755 LOS ANGELES COUNTY-DEPARTMENT OF HEALTH SERVICES (Formerly County of Los Angeles-Department of Health Services), 313 N. Figueroa St., Room 936, 90012; tel. 213/974-8101; Robert C. Gates, dir. health

2245 ★LHS CORPORATION (Formerly Lutheran Hospital Society of Southern California), 1423 S. Grand Ave., 90015; tel. 213/748-0191; Samuel J. Tibbitts, pres.

3015 NATIONAL MEDICAL ENTERPRISES, 11620 Wilshire Blvd., P O Box 25980, 90025; tel. 213/479-5526; Richard K. Eamer, chm. & chief exec. off.; Leonard Cohen, pres. & chief oper. off.

0575 SCHICK LABORATORIES, INC., 1901 Ave. of the Stars, 90067; tel. 213/553-3366; Patrick J. Frawley Jr., chm.

3025 SUMMIT HEALTH, LTD., 1800 Ave. of the Stars, 90067; tel. 213/201-4000; William L. Pierpoint, pres. & chief exec. off.

Oakland: 0225 ALAMEDA COUNTY HEALTH CARE SERVICES AGENCY, 499 Fifth St., 94607; tel. 415/268-2722; David J. Kears, dir.

2105 ★KAISER FOUNDATION HOSPITALS, One Kaiser Plaza, 94612; tel. 415/271-5910; James A. Vohs, chm. & pres.

0685 MERRITT PERALTA MEDICAL CENTER, Hawthorne Ave. & Webster St. 94609; tel. 415/451-4900; Richard J. McCann, pres. & chief exec. off.

Orange: 5425 ★ST. JOSEPH HEALTH SYSTEM, 440 S. Batavia St., 92668; tel. 714/997-7690; Robert W. O'Leary, pres.

Pasadena: 5765 PARACELSUS HEALTHCARE (Formerly Paracelsus Hospital Corporation), 155 N. Lake Ave., Suite 1100, 91101; tel. 818/792-8600; R. J. Messenger, pres & chief oper. off.

Roseville: 0235 ADVENTIST HEALTH SYSTEM-WEST, P O Box 619002, 95661; tel. 916/781-2000; Frank F. Dupper, pres.

Sacramento: 8795 SUTTER HEALTH SYSTEM (Formerly Sutter Community Hospitals), 1111 Howe Ave., Suite 600, 95825; tel 916/927-5211; Patrick G. Hays, pres. & chief exec. off.

San Diego: 8895 ★VISTA HILL FOUNDATION, 3420 Camino Del Rio N., Suite 100, 92108; tel. 619/563-1770; Ronald E. Fickle, pres. & chief exec. off.

San Jose: 0965 ★HEALTH DIMENSIONS, INC., 2005 Hamilton Ave., Suite 300, 95125; tel. 408/599-2701; Robert K. Kirk, pres.

San Mateo: 6975 MILLS-PENINSULA HOSPITALS, 50 S. San Mateo Dr. 94401; tel. 415/579-2190; Charles H. Mason Jr., pres. & chief exec. off.

San Rafael: 1195 DOMINICAN SISTERS CONGREGATION OF THE MOST HOLY NAME, Dominican Convent-San Rafael, 94901; tel. 415/454-9221; Sr. Jeremy

Santa Ana: 0785 COMMUNITY PSYCHIATRIC CENTERS, 2204 E. Fourth St., 92705; tel. 714/835-4535; James W. Conte, pres. & chief exec. off.

Santa Monica: 1055 SAMISSA HEALTHCARE CORPORATION, 3340 Ocean Park Blvd., Suite 3060, 90405; tel. 213/450-3637; Barry Fireman, MD, pres.

Woodland Hills: 6905 ★HEALTHWEST MEDICAL CENTERS, (Formerly Healthwest Foundation), 21800 Oxnard St., Suite 550, 91367; tel. 818/716-2777; Roger H. Drue, pres.

COLORADO

Denver: 5395 ★SACRED HEART CORPORATION (Formerly Sisters of St. Francis of Penance and Christian Charity-Sacred Heart Province), 2861 W. 52nd Ave., 80221; tel. 303/458-8611; Sr. Christina Oleske, pres.

★Indicates Type III membership in the American Hospital Association.

CONNECTICUT

Enfield: 1345 ★FELICIAN HEALTHCARE SYSTEMS, INC., 1325 Enfield St., 06082; tel. 203/745-2542; M. Augustine Kloza, pres.

West Hartford: 5615 SISTERS OF ST. JOSEPH OF CHAMBERY-NORTH AMERICAN PROVINCE, 27 Park Rd., 06119; tel. 203/233-5126; Sr. Jean Sauntry, supr.

DISTRICT OF COLUMBIA

Washington: 6615 ★MEDLANTIC HEALTHCARE GROUP (Formerly Washington Healthcare Corp.), 100 Irving St. N.W., 20010; tel. 202/541-6006; John P. McDaniel, pres.

1315 RECOVERY CENTERS OF AMERICA, 1010 Wisconsin Ave. 20007; tel. 202/298-3230; Thomas J. Doherty, exec. v.p.

0825 SPECIALTY HOSPITAL DIVISION OF NME, 1010 Wisconsin Ave. N.W., Suite 900, 20007; tel. 202/337-5600; Norman A. Zober, pres.

FLORIDA

Coral Gables: 1435 DOCTOR JOHN MCDONALD HEALTH SYSTEMS, 5000 University Dr., P O Box 141739, 33114; tel. 305/666-2111; William H. Comte, pres.

Dunedin: 1335 MEASE HEALTH CARE, 833 Milwaukee Ave., PO Box 760, 33528; tel. 813/733-1111; Donald M. Schroder, pres. & chief exec. off.

Fort Lauderdale: 3115 NORTH BROWARD HOSPITAL DISTRICT, 1625 S.E. Third Ave., 33316; tel. 305/355-4400; Robert L. Kennedy, exec. dir.

Gainesville: 7895 ★SANTA FE HEALTHCARE (Formerly Santa Fe Healthcare System, Inc.,) 720 S.W. Second Ave., P O Box 749, 32602; tel. 904/375-4321; Edward C. Peddie, pres.

Jacksonville: 2715 METHODIST HEALTH SYSTEM (Formerly Methodist Hospital, Inc.,) 580 W. Eighth St., 32209; tel. 904/798-8000; Marcus Drewa, pres.

Jupiter: 0645 GLENBEIGH, INC., 1001 N. U.S. Hwy., Suite 8, 33458; tel. 305/747-6565; G. Norman McCann, pres.

Naples: 1775 HOSPITAL MANAGEMENT ASSOCIATES, 800 Laurel Oak Dr., 33963; tel. 813/598-3104; William J. Schoen, bd. chm., pres., & chief exec. off.

Orlando: 4165 ★ADVENTIST HEALTH SYSTEM-SUNBELT HEALTH CARE CORPORATION, 2400 Bedford Rd., 32803; tel. 305/897-1919; Mardian J. Blair, pres.

3355 ORLANDO REGIONAL MEDICAL CENTER, 1414 S. Kuhl Ave., 32806; tel. 305/841-5111; J. Gary Strack, pres.

9605 UNITED MEDICAL CORPORATION, 20 N. Orange Ave., Suite 1600, 32801; tel. 305/423-2200; Donald R. Dizney, chm,; James E. English, pres.

Pensacola: 0185 ★BAPTIST REGIONAL HEALTH SERVICES, INC., P O Box 17500, 32522; tel. 904/434-4805; James F. Vickery, pres.

St. Petersburg: 1385 ★ALLEGANY HEALTH SYSTEM, 11300 Fourth St. N., Suite 220, 33702; tel. 813/577-9363; James E. Grobmyer, pres.

Tampa: 1525 HILLSBOROUGH COUNTY HOSPITAL AUTHORITY, Davis Island, Administrative Bldg., 33607; tel. 813/251-7383; Newell E. France, mng. dir.

1615 MID FLORIDA MEDICAL SERVICES, 200 Ave. F N.E., Winter Haven, 33880; tel. 813/293-8226; Lance W. Annstasio, pres. & chief exec. off.

4125 ★SHRINERS HOSPITALS FOR CRIPPLED CHILDREN (Formerly Shriner's Children's Hospitals), Box 25356, 33622; tel. 813/885-2575; Jack D. Hoard, exec. adm.

1605 SOUTHEAST COMMUNITY HEALTH SERVICES, 1433 Miccosukee Rd., Tallahassee, 32308; tel. 904/681-5675; Keith Gilles, chief oper. off.

GEORGIA

Atlanta: 1425 FULTON-DE KALB HOSPITAL AUTHORITY, 80 Butler St. S.E., 30335; tel. 404/589-4307; J.W. Pinkston, exec. dir.

0495 GATEWAY MEDICAL SYSTEMS, (Formerly Listed Under St. Louis, Missouri), 2351 Bolton Rd. N.W., Third Fl., 30318; tel. 404/351-9611; James R. Cheek, bd. chm.

0985 AMERIHEALTH, INC., 2849 Paces Ferry Rd., Suite 790, 30339; tel. 404/435-1776; William G. White, pres.

0245 CONTINENTAL MEDICAL, INC., 880 Johnson Ferry Rd. N.E., 260, 30342; tel. 404/255-8220; Richard V. Urquhart, pres.

0905 FORUM HEALTH INVESTORS, INC., 401 W. Peachtree N.W., 1600, 30308; tel. 404/688-9019; J. Dennis Meaders, chief exec. off.

Jackson: 1585 HEALTHCARE MANAGEMENT GROUP, INC., 146 Sylvan Dr., 30233; tel. 205/979-0805; Earl Bonds Jr., chief exec. off.

Macon: 0695 ★CHARTER MEDICAL CORPORATION, 577 Mulberry St., 31202; Mailing Address P O Box 209, Zip 31298; tel. 912/742-1161; William A. Fickling Jr., chm. & chief exec. off.

Marietta: 0995 ★KENNESTONE REGIONAL HEALTH CARE SYSTEMS, 677 Church St., 30060; tel. 404/428-2000; Bernard L. Brown Jr., exec. dir.

Norcross: 0195 AMERICAN MEDICAL CENTERS (Formerly listed under Nashville), P O Box 2526, 30071; tel. 615/244-8410; Paul T. Agee, sr. vice-pres. & chief exec. off.

HAWAII

Honolulu: 3555 STATE OF HAWAII, DEPARTMENT OF HEALTH, P O Box 3378, 96801; tel. 808/548-7402; Jerry Walker, dep. dir.

IDAHO

Cottonwood: 0505 BENEDICTINE SISTERS, Priory of St. Gertrude, Box 107, 83522; tel. 208/962-3224; Sr. Mary Matthew Geis

ILLINOIS

Bloomington: 9305 BROMENN HEALTHCARE, 807 N. Main St., 61702; tel. 309/827-4321; Jeffrey B. Schaub, pres.

Carbondale: 4175 ★SOUTHERN ILLINOIS HOSPITAL SERVICES, 608 E. College St., P O Box 522, 62903; tel. 618/457-7833; Jerry A. Hickam, pres.

Chicago: 8805 ★COLUMBUS-CUNEO-CABRINI MEDICAL CENTER, 676 N. St. Clair, Suite 1900, 60611; tel. 312/943-1333; James P. Hamill, chief exec. off.

5685 SISTERS OF ST. CASIMIR, 2601 W. Marquette Rd., 60629; tel. 312/434-6700; Sr. M. Joanella Fayert, pres.

Des Plaines: 0655 FOREST HEALTH SYSTEMS, INC., 555 Wilson Lane, 60016; tel. 312/635-4100; Morris B. Squire, pres.

5575 SISTERS OF THE HOLY FAMILY OF NAZARETH-SACRED HEART PROVINCE, 353 N. River Rd., 60016; tel. 312/298-6760; Sr. M. Loretta Markiewicz, prov. supr.

Elk Grove Village: 0065 ★ALEXIAN BROTHERS HEALTH SYSTEMS, INC. (Formerly Alexian Brothers of America, Inc.), 600 Alexian Way, 60007; tel. 312/640-7550; Bruce Fisher, exec. vice-pres.

0135 ANCILLA SYSTEMS, INC. (Formerly Ancilla Domini Health Services, Inc.), 1100 Elmhurst Rd., 60007; tel. 312/694-4210; Edwin W. Murphy, pres.

Evergreen Park: 2295 ★LITTLE COMPANY OF MARY SISTERS HEALTHCARE SYSTEMS, 9350 S. California Ave., 60642; tel. 312/422-6200; Sr. Sharon Ann Walsh, prov. supr.

Kankakee: 4025 ★SERVANTCOR, 175 S. Wall St., 60901; tel. 815/937-2034; Joseph S. Feth, pres.

Mokena: 1415 ★FRANCISCAN SISTERS HEALTH CARE CORPORATION, St. Francis Woods, Rte. 4, 60448; tel. 815/469-4888; Sr. Dismas Janssen, bd. chm. & pres.

Oak Brook: 1225 ★EVANGELICAL HEALTH SYSTEMS, 2025 Windsor Dr., 60521; tel. 312/572-9393; John G. King, pres. & chief exec. off.

Oak Brook Terrace: 5215 MERCY-CHICAGO PROVINCE HEALTHCARE SYSTEMS (Formerly listed under Chicago), Is450 Summit Ave., 60181; tel. 312/953-2970; Catherine C. Gallagher, exec. dir.

O'Fallon: 0205 ★ASC HEALTH SYSTEM, 3 Eagle Center, Suite I, PO Box 568, 62269; tel. 618/632-1284; Joseph B. Ahlschier, pres.

Park Ridge: 6295 ★LUTHERAN GENERAL HEALTH CARE SYSTEMS (Formerly Lutheran Institute of Human Ecology), 1775 Dempster St., 60068; tel. 312/696-5600; George B. Caldwell, pres.

Peoria: 8875 ★METHODIST HEALTH SERVICES CORPORATION, 221 N.E. Glen Oak Ave., 61636; tel. 309/672-4826; James K. Knoble, pres,; Daniel P. Chonowski, exec. vice-pres.

5335 ★SISTERS OF THE 3RD ORDER OF ST. FRANCIS, 1124 N. Berkley Ave., 61603; tel. 309/655-2850; Sr. Frances Marie, exec. vice-pres.

★Indicates Type III membership in the American Hospital Association.

Springfield: 1295 DOMINICAN SISTERS CONGREGATION OF OUR LADY OF THE SACRED HEART, 1237 W. Monroe St., 62704; tel. 217/787-0481; Sr. M. Dominica Brennan

5355 ★HOSPITAL SISTERS HEALTH SYSTEM-HOSPITAL SISTERS OF THE THIRD ORDER OF ST. FRANCIS-AMERICAN PROVINCE, Sangamon Ave. Rd., Box 19431, 62794; tel. 217/522-6969; Sr. Marianna Kosior, pres.

Wheaton: 6745 ★WHEATON FRANCISCAN SERVICES, INC., 26w171 Roosevelt Rd., P O Box 667, 60189; tel. 312/462-9271; Willis F. Fry, pres. & chief exec. off.

INDIANA

Indianapolis: 1935 BASIC AMERICAN MEDICAL, INC., 4000 E. Southport Rd., 46237; tel. 317/783-5461; Brady R. Justice Jr., pres.

9335 METHODIST HOSPITAL OF INDIANA, 1701 N. Senate Blvd., 46202; tel. 317/929-8510; Frank P. Lloyd MD, pres.

Mishawaka: 5345 ★SISTERS OF ST. FRANCIS HEALTH SERVICES, INC., 1515 Dragoon Trail, P O Box 1290, Zip 46544; tel. 219/256-3935; Sr. M. Theresa Solbach, pres.

South Bend: 5585 ★HOLY CROSS HEALTH SYSTEM CORPORATION, 3606 E. Jefferson Blvd., 46615; tel. 219/233-8558; William A. Himmelsbach Jr., pres. & chief exec. off.

5445 SISTERS OF ST. JOSEPH-3RD ORDER OF ST. FRANCIS, I05 E. Jefferson, P O Box 688, 46624; tel. 219/233-1166; Sr. Adalbert Stal, central treas.; Sr. Joanne Skalski, dir. inst. sponsorship bd.

Tipton: 5935 SISTERS OF ST. JOSEPH, Rural Rte. 3, Box 291A, 46072; tel. 317/456-5300; Sr. Veronica Baumgartner, pres.

IOWA

Des Moines: 1595 ★IOWA METHODIST HEALTH SYSTEM, 1200 Pleasant St., 50308; tel. 515/283-6201; David S. Ramsey, pres.

Sioux City: 5845 ST. LUKE'S REGIONAL MEDICAL CENTER, 2720 Stone Park Blvd., 51104; tel. 712/279-3500; David O. Biorn, pres. & chief exec. off.

KANSAS

Leavenworth: 5095 ★SISTERS OF CHARITY OF LEAVENWORTH HEALTH SERVICES CORPORATION, 4200 S. Fourth St., 66048; tel. 913/682-1338; Sr. Macrina Ryan, pres.

Phillipsburg: 1535 GREAT PLAINS HEALTH ALLIANCE, INC. (Formerly Great Plains Lutheran Hospitals), Box 366, 67661; tel. 913/543-2111; Curtis Erickson, pres. & chief exec. off.

Shawnee Mission: 9355 ★ADVENTIST HEALTH SYSTEM-EASTERN AND MIDDLE AMERICA, 8800 W. 75th St., 66204; tel. 913/677-8000; J. Russell Shawver, pres.

Topeka: 0805 STORMONT-VAIL HEALTH SERVICES CORPORATION, I500 Southwest Tenth St., 66604; tel. 913/354-6112; Howard M. Chase, chief exec. off.

Wichita: 5435 ★CSJ HEALTH SYSTEM OF WICHITA (Formerly Sisters of St. Joseph Health Systems of Wichita), 3720 E. Bayley, 67218; tel. 316/686-7171; Sr. Antoinette Yelek, pres., Gregory G. Guntly, chief exec. off.

KENTUCKY

Lexington: 0145 ★APPALACHIAN REGIONAL HEALTHCARE, Box 8086, 40533; tel. 606/255-4431; Robert L. Johnson, pres.

Louisville: 0315 ★BAPTIST HEALTHCARE, INC., (Formerly Baptist Hospitals, Inc.), 4007 Kresgee Way, 40207; tel. 502/561-3277; Ben R. Brewer, pres.

1235 ★HUMANA INC., 500 W. Main St., Humana Bldg., Box 1438, 40201; tel. 502/580-1000; David A. Jones, bd. chm. & chief exec. off.; H. Wendell Cherry, pres. & chief oper. off.

3045 ★SISTERS OF CHARITY OF NAZARETH HEALTH CORPORATION, 9300 Shelbyville Rd., Suite 501, 40222; tel. 502/429-5055; Sr. Jane Frances Kennedy, pres.

LOUISIANA

Baton Rouge: 1475 FRANCISCAN MISSIONARIES OF OUR LADY PROVINCIAL HOUSE, 4200 Essen Lane, 70809; tel.504/927-7481; Sr. Brendan M. Ronayne

0775 GENERAL HEALTH, INC., 5757 Corporate Blvd., Suite 202, 70808; tel. 504/924-4324; Thomas H. Sawyer, pres.

0715 OFFICE OF HOSPITALS, P O Box 44215, 70804; tel. 504/342-2595; Jack Edwards, dep. asst.

Clinton: 1065 REGENT HEALTH SYSTEMS, INC., Liberty St., P O Box 8754, 70722; tel. 504/683-3319; Charles J. Mueller, pres.

MARYLAND

Baltimore: I0I5 ★JOHNS HOPKINS HEALTH SYSTEMS, 600 N. Wolfe St., 21205; tel. 301/955-1488; Robert M. Heyssel, MD, pres.

6015 SISTERS OF MERCY OF THE UNION-PROVINCE OF BALTIMORE, P O Box 11448, 21239; tel. 301/435-4400; Sr. Angela Marie Ebberwein

Columbia: 5085 ★BON SECOURS HEALTH SYSTEM, INC., 5457 Twin Knolls Rd., Suite 300, 21045; tel. 301/992-7330; John P. Brozovich, pres. & chief exec. off.

MASSACHUSETTS

Boston: 0215 COMMUNITY CARE SYSTEMS, INC., 210 Lincoln St., 02111; tel. 617/451-0300; Frederick J. Thacher, pres.

6995 DEPARTMENT OF HEALTH AND HOSPITALS, HOSPITAL SERVICES DIVISION, 818 Harrison Ave., 02118; tel. 617/424-5365; Lewis Pollack, comr.

Lexington: 5885 ★COVENANT HEALTH SYSTEMS, INC. (Formerly Grey Nuns Health Systems, Inc.), 10 Pelham Rd., 02173; tel. 617/862-1634; Sr. Dorothy Cooper, pres. & chief exec. off.

Norwood: 3175 NEPONSET VALLEY HEALTH SYSTEM, 800 Washington St., 02062; tel. 617/769-4000; Frank S. Crane III, pres.

Springfield: 1095 ★BAYSTATE HEALTH SYSTEMS, INC., 759 Chestnut St., 01199; tel. 413/787-3345; Michael J. Daly, pres. & chief exec. off.

5285 ★SISTERS OF PROVIDENCE HEALTH AND HUMAN SERVICE (Formerly Listed Under Holyoke), 209 Carew St., 01104; tel. 413/536-7511; Sr. Catherine Laboure, pres.

Wollesley: II35 MEDIPLEX GROUP, INC., I5 Walnut St., 02181; tel. 617/446-6900; Joseph N. Cassese, pres.

MICHIGAN

Detroit: 1655 ★HARPER-GRACE HOSPITALS, 3990 John R St., 48201; tel. 313/745-9375; Michael H. Fritz, pres. & chief exec. off.

Farmington Hills: 5165 ★SISTERS OF MERCY HEALTH CORPORATION, 28550 Eleven Mile Rd., 48018; tel. 313/478-9900; Sr. Mary Corita Heid, pres.

Kalamazoo: 0595 ★BRONSON HEALTHCARE GROUP, INC., One Healthcare Plaza, 49007; tel. 616/344-5222; Russell P. Kneen, chm. & chief exec. off.

Nazareth: 5555 ★SISTERS OF ST. JOSEPH HEALTH SYSTEM, 3427 Gull Rd., 49074; tel. 616/381-2500; Sr. Irene Waldmann, pres.

Oak Park: 1035 ★HORIZON HEALTH SYSTEMS, 21700 Greenfield Rd., 48237; tel. 313/968-2800; James L. Rieder, pres. & chief exec. off.

Petoskey: 2595 HEALTHSHARE, INC., 501 W. Mitchell St., Suite 300, 49770; tel. 616/348-4567; John Rasmussen, pres.

Royal Oak: 9575 ★WILLIAM BEAUMONT HOSPITAL CORPORATION, 3601 W. Thirteen Mile Rd., 48072; tel. 313/288-8000; Kenneth E. Myers, pres.; Ted D. Wasson, exec. vice-pres.

Wayne: 3465 ★PEOPLES COMMUNITY HOSPITAL AUTHORITY, 33000 Annapolis Ave., 48184; tel. 313/467-4600; Fred E. Blair, chief exec. off.

MINNESOTA

Duluth: 0515 BENEDICTINE HEALTH SYSTEM (Formerly BENEDICTINE SISTERS), 1028 E. Eighth St., 55805; tel. 218/722-4799; Sr. Rebecca Wright, pres.

Little Falls: 1395 ★FRANCISCAN SISTERS HEALTH CARE, 116 S.E. Eighth Ave., 56345; tel. 612/632-3601; Sr. Felix Mushel, pres.

Minneapolis: 1325 ★FAIRVIEW HOSPITAL AND HEALTHCARE SERVICES (Formerly Fairview Community Hospitals), 2312 S. Sixth St., 55454; tel. 612/371-6300; Carl N. Platou, pres.

6235 ★HEALTHONE CORPORATION, 2810 57th Ave. No., 55430; tel. 612/333-1711; Richard S. Blair, interim pres. & chief exec. off.

★Indicates Type III membership in the American Hospital Association.

St. Joseph: 0535 BENEDICTINE SISTERS, St. Benedict's Convent, 56374; tel. 612/362-5100; Sr. Katherine Howard

MISSISSIPPI

Batesville: 1275 FIRST HEALTH, INC., 107 Public Square, 38606; tel. 601/563-7676; David A. Vance, pres.

MISSOURI

Kansas City: 8815 ★RESEARCH HEALTH SERVICES, 6400 Prospect Ave., 64132; tel. 816/276-9167; E. Wynn Presson, pres.

9255 ★TRUMAN MEDICAL CENTER, 2301 Holmes, 64108; tel. 816/556-3153; James J. Mongan MD, exec. dir.

St. Louis: 0565 ★CHRISTIAN HEALTH SERVICES DEVELOPMENT CORPORATION, 11155 Dunn Rd., 63136; tel. 314/355-0095; Fred L. Brown, pres. & chief exec. off.

1885 DAUGHTERS OF CHARITY NATIONAL HEALTH SYSTEM, 7806 National Bridge Rd., P O Drawer 5730, 63121; tel. 314/389-8900; Sr. Irene Kraus, pres.

5945 ★HEALTH CARE CORPORATION OF THE SISTERS OF ST. JOSEPH OF CARONDELET, 77 W. Port Plaza, Suite 222, 63146; tel. 314/576-5662; Sr. Mary K. Ford, pres.

5185 ★SISTERS OF MERCY HEALTH SYSTEMS-ST. LOUIS (Formerly Sisters of Mercy of the Union- Province of St. Louis), 2039 N. Geyer Rd., 63131; tel. 314/965-6100; Sr. Mary R. Rocklage, chief exec. off. & chair person

5455 ★SSM HEALTH CARE SYSTEM (Formerly Sisters of St. Mary), 1031 Bellevue Ave., 63117; tel. 314/768-1600; Sr. Mary Jean Ryan, pres. & chief exec. off.

NEBRASKA

Norfolk: 2855 MISSIONARY BENEDICTINE SISTERS AMERICAN PROVINCE, 300 N. 18th St., 68701; tel. 402/371-3438; Sr. Matilda Handl

Omaha: 5175 ★CATHOLIC HEALTH CORPORATION, 920 S. 107th Ave., 68114; tel. 402/393-7661; Diane Moeller, pres.

9265 NEBRASKA METHODIST HEALTH SYSTEM, INC., 8303 Dodge St., 68114; tel. 402/390-4844; John W. Estabrook, pres. & chief exec. off.

NEW HAMPSHIRE

Hanover: 3395 ★HITCHCOCK ALLIANCE, P O Box 1001, 03755; tel. 603/646-8150; James W. Varnum, pres.

NEW JERSEY

Camden: 6725 ★WEST JERSEY HEALTH SYSTEM, Mount Ephraim & Atlantic Aves., 08104; tel. 609/342-4600; Barry D. Brown, pres.; William Michael Tomlinson, exec. vice-pres.

Chatham: 0865 ★ATLANTIC HEALTH SYSTEMS, INC., 466 Southern Blvd., 07928; tel. 201/514-1993; Thomas J. Foley, pres. & chief exec. off.

Edison: 8855 ★INTERCARE HEALTH SYSTEMS, 98 James St., Mediplex Suite 400, 08820; tel. 201/632-1500; Michael T. Kornett, pres. & chief exec. off.

Mount Holly: 0465 ★NEXUS HEALTHCARE CORPORATION, Madison Ave., Summey Bldg., Suite 201, 08060; tel. 609/261-7011; Chester B. Kaletkowski, pres.

Newark: 6545 ★HEALTH CORPORATION of the ARCHDIOCESE OF NEWARK, 41 Centre St., 07102; tel. 201/596-3900; Margaret J. Straney, pres.

Paramus: 5815 ★SISTERS OF CHARITY OF ST. ELIZABETH (Formerly listed under Jersey City), 49 Demarest Rd., 07652; tel. 201/539-1600; Sr. Ellen L. Joyce, gen. superior

Pennsauken: 3825 MEDIQ, INC. One Mediq Plaza, 08110; tel. 609/665-9300; Bernard Korman, pres.

Riverside: 0015 ★ZURBRUGG MEMORIAL HOSPITAL, Hospital Plaza, 08075; tel. 609/461-6700; George D. Hartnett, pres.

NEW MEXICO

Albuquerque: 3505 ★SOUTHWEST COMMUNITY HEALTH SERVICES, 6100 Pan American Freeway N.E., 87109; Mailing Address P O Box 26666, Zip 87125; tel. 505/823-8313; Richard Barr, pres.

NEW YORK

Amityville: 6665 BRUNSWICK HOSPITAL CENTER, 366 Broadway, 11701; tel. 516/789-7000; Benjamin M. Stein MD. pres.

Bronx: 5995 SISTERS OF CHARITY CENTER, Mount St. Vincent On Hudson, 10471; tel. 212/549-9200; Sr. Agnes Connolly, pres.

Brooklyn: 1485 FRANCISCAN SISTERS OF THE POOR HEALTH SYSTEMS, INC., 186 Joralemon St., 11201; tel. 718/625-6530; Sr. Joanne Schuster, pres.

Buffalo: 5545 MERCY HEALTH SYSTEM OF WESTERN NEW YORK (Formerly Sisters of Mercy), 565 Abbott Rd., 14220; tel. 716/827-2375; Sr. Mary Annunciate Kelleher, pres.

Hastings On Hudson: 5925 SISTERS OF ST. FRANCIS OF THE MISSION OF THE IMMACULATE VIRGIN, Immaculate Conception Motherhouse, 10706; tel. 914/478-3910; Sr. Mary Paul, supr. gen.

Hempstead: 0735 ★CHURCH-CHARITY FOUNDATION OF LONG ISLAND, 393 Front St., 11550; tel. 516/560-6460; Alexander H. Williams III, exec. vice-pres.

New York: 3075 NEW YORK CITY HEALTH AND HOSPITAL CORPORATION, 125 Worth St., 10013; tel. 212/566-8038; Jo Ivey Boufford MD, actg. pres.

Staten Island: 6095 ★SISTERS OF CHARITY HEALTH CARE SYSTEMS CORPORATION, 355 Bard Ave., 10310; tel. 212/390-1650; John J. Depierro, pres. & chief exec. off.

Syracuse: 1905 HEALTH MANAGEMENT SERVICES, 5793 Widewaters Pkwy., 13214; tel. 315/445-2082; James W. Krembs, pres.

5955 SISTERS OF THE 3RD FRANCISCAN ORDER-MINOR CONVENTUALS, 100 Michaels Ave., 13208; tel. 315/425-0115; Sr. M. Aileen Griffin, supr. gen.

Williamsville: 5715 ★SISTERS OF ST. FRANCIS-3RD ORDER REGULAR OF BUFFALO, 400 Mill St., 14221; tel. 716/632-2155; Sr. Maureen Ann, gen. minister

NORTH CAROLINA

Belmont: 5985 SISTERS OF MERCY, Sacred Heart Convent, 28012; tel. 704/825-2011; Sr. Jeanne Margaret McNally, supr. gen.

Charlotte: 0705 CHARLOTTE-MECKLENBURG HOSPITAL AUTHORITY, Box 32861, 28232; tel. 704/338-2145; Harry A. Nurkin PhD., pres.

0025 ★SUNHEALTH CORPORATION, 4501 Charlotte Park Dr., Box 668800, 28266; tel. 704/529-3300; Ben W. Latimer, pres.

Raleigh: 6705 WAKE MEDICAL CENTER (Formerly Wake County Hospital System), 3000 New Bern Ave., 27610; tel. 919/755-8112; Raymond L. Champ, pres.

NORTH DAKOTA

Bismarck: 0545 BENEDICTINE SISTERS OF THE ANNUNCIATION, 7520 University Dr., 58501; tel. 701/255-1520; Sr. Susan Lardy, prioress

Fargo: 5805 ★CENTRAL MANAGEMENT CORPORATION, 112-114 Roberts St., Suite 208, 58102; tel. 701/237-9290; James Dunne, pres.

2235 ★LUTHERAN HOSPITALS AND HOMES SOCIETY OF AMERICA, 1202 Westrac Dr., Box 2087, 58107; tel. 701/293-9053; Michael O. Bice, pres. & chief exec. off.

Grand Forks: 9905 ★UNITED HEALTH SERVICES, INC., 1200 S. Columbia Rd., P O Box 6002, 58201; tel. 701/780-5200; Robert M. Jacobson, pres.

Hankinson: 5975 SISTERS OF ST. FRANCIS-IMMACULATE HEART OF MARY-PROVINCE OF HANKINSON, St. Francis Convent, 58041; tel. 701/242-7197; Sr. Mary Louise Jundt, dir.

OHIO

Cincinnati: 0415 ★BETHESDA HOSPITAL, INC., 619 Oak St., 45206; tel. 513/569-6111; L. Thomas Wilburn Jr., chairman & chief exec. off.

★Indicates Type III membership in the American Hospital Association.

5155 ★MERCY HEALTH CARE SYSTEM, 2303 Grandview Ave., 45206; tel. 513/221-2736; Sr. M. Michaeleen, pres. & chief exec. off.

5115 ★SISTERS OF CHARITY HEALTH CARE SYSTEMS, INC., 345 Neeb Rd., 45238; tel. 513/922-9775; Sr. Celestia Koebel, pres.

Columbus: I045 DOCTORS HOSPITAL, I087 Dennison Ave., 43215; tel. 614/297-4000; Richard L. Sims, pres.

8865 HEALTH MANAGEMENT SERVICES, INC., 340 E. Town St., Suite 7-800, 43215; tel. 614/461-3401; Ned Boatright, pres.

9095 ★U.S. HEALTH CORPORATION, 3555 Olentangy River Rd., Suite 4000, 43214; tel. 614/261-5902; Erie Chapman III, pres. & chief exec. off.

Dayton: 1495 GRANDCOR, 405 Grand Ave., 45405; tel. 513/222-7990; Richard J. Minor, pres. & chief exec. off.

Lorain: 5645 ★HUMILITY OF MARY HEALTH CARE CORPORATION (Formerly Sisters of the Humility of Mary), P O Box 841, 44052; tel. 216/871-0971; Sr. Frances Flanigan, chief exec. off.

Martins Ferry: 3315 ★OHIO VALLEY HEALTH SERVICES AND EDUCATION CORPORATION, 90 N. Fourth St., 43935; tel. 304/234-8765; David J. Campbell, vice chairman & chief exec. off.

Mayfield Village: 8835 ★STRATEGIC HEALTH SYSTEMS, 767 Beta Dr., Suite E, 44143; tel. 216/449-7710; Robert Moss, pres.

Richfield: 5125 ★SISTERS OF CHARITY OF ST. AUGUSTINE HEALTH AND HUMAN SERVICES, 5232 Broadview Rd., 44286; tel. 216/659-9283; Sr. Mary Patricia Barrett, pres.

Sylvania: 5375 ★FRANCISCAN SERVICES CORPORATION, 6832 Convent Blvd., 43560; tel. 419/882-8373; John W. O'Connell, pres.

Youngstown: 7005 ★WESTERN RESERVE CARE SYSTEM, 345 Oak Hill Ave., 44501; tel. 216/747-9727; James E. Michels, pres.

OKLAHOMA

Broken Arrow: 5875 SISTERS OF THE SORROWFUL MOTHER-TULSA PROVINCIALATE, 17600 E. 51st St. S., 74012; tel. 918/355-5595; Sr. M. Julietta Mendoza, prov.

Oklahoma City: 0305 ★BAPTIST HEALTH CARE CORPORATION, 7428 Nicholson Dr., 73132; tel. 405/721-6504; Joe L. Ingram, MD, pres.

1865 HCA OKLAHOMA HEALTH NETWORK, I601 N.W. Expressway, Suite 2200, 73118; tel. 405/840-2284; Bruce Perry, pres.

Tulsa: 0665 CENTURY HEALTHCARE CORPORATION, 7615 E. 63rd Pl., Suite 200, 74133; tel. 918/250-9651; Jerry D. Dillon, pres. & chief exec. off.

OREGON

Portland: 0585 BRIM AND ASSOCIATES, INC., 177 N.E. 102nd Ave., 97220; tel. 503/256-2070; A. E. Brim, pres.

2755 ★HEALTHLINK (Formerly Metropolitan Hospitals, Inc.), 500 N.E. Multnomah St., 97232; tel. 503/234-4500; G. Rodney Wolford, pres.

PENNSYLVANIA

Allentown: 1695 ★HEALTHEAST, INC., 337 N. West St., 18102; tel. 215/778-2950; David P. Buchmueller, pres. & chief exec. off.

Bethlehem: 1025 ★HORIZON HEALTH SYSTEM, INC., 60 W. Broad St., Suite 201, 18018; tel. 215/865-9988; William P. Koughan, pres.

Chadds Ford: 5325 ★FRANCISCAN HEALTH SYSTEM, Brandywine 1 Bldg., Suite 301, Rtes. I & 202, 19317; tel. 215/358-3950; Ronald R. Aldrich, pres.

Cheltenham: 6345 UNITED HOSPITALS, INC., 100 W. Laurel Ave., 19012; tel. 215/663-5400; Myles G. Turtz MD, chm. & chief exec. off.

Dallas: 5195 ★MERCY HEALTH CARE SYSTEM, Mercy Center, Lake St., Box 370, 18612; tel. 717/675-3535; William D. McGuire, pres. & chief exec. off.

Danville: 5570 GEISINGER SYSTEM SERVICES, N. Academy Ave., 17822; tel. 717/271-6631; Frank J. Trembulak, pres.

Devon: 0845 ★DEVEREUX FOUNDATION, 19 S. Waterloo Rd., 19333; tel. 215/964-3050; Ronald P. Burd, pres.

Greensburg: 2395 ★SOUTHWEST HEALTH SYSTEM, 133 Donohoe Rd., 15601; tel. 412/836-6820; Joseph J. Peluso, pres. & chief exec. off.

King of Prussia: 9555 UNIVERSAL HEALTH SERVICES, INC., 367 S. Gulph Rd., 19406; tel. 215/768-3300; Alan B. Miller, pres.

Philadelphia: 3595 ★EASTERN MERCY HEALTH SYSTEM, Scott Plaza Two, Suite 403, 19113; tel. 215/521-4500; Daniel F. Russell, pres & chief exec. off.

7995 METROPOLITAN HOSPITAL, 801 Arch St., Fifth Floor, 19107; tel. 215/238-6700; Jack R. Dyson, actg. chief oper. off.

3455 PENNSYLVANIA HOSPITAL (Formerly Pennsylvania Hospital Corp.), Eighth & Spruce Sts., 19107; tel. 215/829-3312; H. Robert Cathcart, pres.

Pittsburgh: 1355 ★FORBES HEALTHMARK, 500 Finley St., 15206; tel. 412/665-3565; George H. Schmitt, chm.

5365 SISTERS OF ST. FRANCIS OF THE PROVINCE OF GOD, Grove & McRoberts Rds., 15234; tel. 412/882-9911; Sr. Marietta Zvirblis, coor.

Radnor: 7775 ★MAIN LINE HEALTH, INC. (Formerly Listed Under Philadelphia), 259 Radnor-Chester Rd., Suite 290, 19087; tel. 215/254-8840; Ralph F. Moriarty, pres.

Sayre: 0675 GUTHRIE MEDICAL CENTER, Guthrie Square, 18840; tel. 717/888-6666; Ralph H. Meyer, pres.

Valley Forge: 0455 NUMED PSYCHIATRIC, INC. (Formerly Maxim Healthcare Corporation), I265 Drummers Lane, Suite I07, PO Box 754, I9482; tel. 215/687-5151; Edmund Bujalski, pres. & chief exec. off.

Villanova: 0285 BERNARDINE SISTERS OF THE 3RD ORDER OF ST. FRANCIS, 647 Springmill Rd.-Maryview, 19085; tel. 215/525-2686; Sr. M. Gerald, supr. gen.

West Reading: 0745 ★BERKSHIRE HEALTH SYSTEMS, Sixth & Spruce, 19603; tel. 215/378-6257; James B. Gronseth, chief exec. off.

SOUTH CAROLINA

Charleston: 5745 SISTERS OF CHARITY OF OUR LADY OF MERCY, Box 12410, 29412; tel. 803/795-6083; Sr. Anne Francis Campbell

Columbia: 4155 ★SOUTH CAROLINA BAPTIST HOSPITALS, 1333 Taylor St., 29201; tel. 803/771-5046; William A. Boyce, pres.

Greenville: 1555 ★GREENVILLE HOSPITAL SYSTEM, 701 Grove Rd., 29605; tel. 803/242-7000; Jack A. Skarupa, pres.

Spartanburg: 4195 ★SPARTANBURG HOSPITAL SYSTEM, 101 E. Wood St., 29303; tel. 803/591-6107; Charles C. Boone, pres.

SOUTH DAKOTA

Rapid City: 8495 RUSHMORE NATIONAL HEALTH SYSTEMS, P O Box 2720, 57709; tel. 605/341-8100; Gary Riedmann, pres.

Sioux Falls: 5255 ★PRESENTATION HEALTH SYSTEM (Formerly Sisters of the Presentation of the Blessed Virgin Mary), I301 South 9th Ave., Suite I02, Mailing Address, Zip 57105; tel. 605/331-4999; Sr. Colman Coakley, pres.

Spearfish: 3165 NORTH CENTRAL HEALTH SERVICES, 930 Tenth Ave., 57783; tel. 605/642-2744; Larry Marshall, vice-pres.

Yankton: I635 BENEDICTINE HEALTH SYSTEM, I005 West 8th St., 57078; tel. 605/668-1511; Sr. Rosaria Kranz, pres.

TENNESSEE

Brentwood: 2495 ★HOSPITAL MANAGEMENT PROFESSIONALS, INC., 5200 Maryland Way, Suite 103, 37027; tel. 615/373-8830; Michael W. Barton, pres.

Chattanooga: 0885 ERLANGER HEALTH SERVICES, 6400 Lee Hwy., Suite I06, 37421; Ron Williams, pres.

II55 GREENLEAF HEALTH SYSTEMS, INC., Two Northgate Park, 37415; tel. 615/870-5110; Dan B. Page, pres.

Memphis: I625 BAPTIST MEMORIAL HEALTHCARE DEVELOPMENT CORPORATION, 899 Madison Ave., 38146; Bobby Hancock, sr. vice-pres. asst.

9345 ★METHODIST HEALTH SYSTEMS, INC., 1211 Union Ave., Suite 700, 38104; tel. 901/726-2300; John T. Casey, pres.

Nashville: 0075 AMERICAN HEALTHCARE CORPORATION, 21 W. End Ave., Suite 1100, 37203; tel. 615/327-2200; Don R. Abercrombie, pres., chm. & chief exec. off.

★Indicates Type III membership in the American Hospital Association.

1755 ★HOSPITAL CORPORATION OF AMERICA, One Park Plaza, Box 550, 37202; tel. 615/327-9551; Thomas F. Frist Jr. MD, chm.

0335 UNITED HEALTHCARE, INC., 4015 Travis Dr., 37211; tel. 615/833-1077; Jerry E. Gilliland, pres. & chief exec. off.

TEXAS

Abilene: 3535 HENDRICK MEDICAL DEVELOPMENT CORPORATION (Formerly Hendrick Medical Center), 19th & Hickory St., 79601; tel. 915/677-3551; Michael C. Waters, pres.

Austin: 0395 HEALTHCARE INTERNATIONAL, INC., 9737 Great Hills Trail, P O Box 4008, 78759; tel. 512/346-4300; James L. Fariss Bd., chairman

Dallas: 1375 AMERICAN HEALTHCARE MANAGEMENT, INC., 14160 Dallas Pkwy., Suite 900, 75240; tel. 214/385-7000; John A. Bradley PhD, bd. chm. & chief exec. off.

0095 BAYLOR HEALTH CARE SYSTEM, 3201 Worth St., P O Box 26265, 75226; tel. 214/820-2891; Boone Powell Jr., pres.

2735 ★METHODIST HOSPITALS OF DALLAS, 301 W. Colorado Blvd., 75208; Mailing Address P O Box 655999; Zip 75265; tel. 214/944-8137; David H. Hitt, pres. & chief exec. off.

1130 ★PRESBYTERIAN HEALTHCARE SYSTEMS (Formerly Presbyterian Medical Center), 8220 Walnut Hill Lane, Suite 700, 75231; tel. 214/696-8500; Douglas D. Hawthorne, pres.

6525 ★REPUBLIC HEALTH CORPORATION, 15303 Dallas Pkwy., Suite 1400, 75248; tel. 214/851-3100; James E. Buncher, pres. & chief exec. off.

Fort Worth: 2345 ★HARRIS METHODIST HEALTH SYSTEM, 1325 Pennsylvania Ave., Eighth Fl., 76104; tel. 817/878-5973; Ronald L. Smith, pres.

Grand Prairie: 6005 ★HOLY FAMILY OF NAZARETH HEALTH SYSTEM (Formerly Sisters of the Holy Family of Nazareth-Vice Provincialate), 1814 Egyptian Way, 75051; Mailing Address Box 530959, Zip 75053; tel. 214/641-4496; Sr. M. Beata, pres.

Houston: 0875 COMMUNITY HEALTH SYSTEMS, INC., 14550 Torrey Chase Blvd., 450, 77014; E. Thomas Chaney, pres.

1365 HEALTHSTAR CORPORATION, 3555 Timmons Lane, Suite 700, 77027; tel. 713/627-2145; Hugh M. Morrison, bd. chm. & pres.

2195 HEI CORPORATION, 7676 Woodway, Suite 112, 77063; tel. 713/780-7802; George G. Alexander MD, chm & chief exec. off.

0725 HERMANN AFFILIATED HOSPITALS SYSTEMS, 1020 Holcombe, Suite 900, 77030; tel. 713/796-0891; William E. Young Jr., chief exec. off.

2645 MEMORIAL CARE SYSTEMS, 7777 Southwest Freeway, Suite 100, 77074; tel. 713/776-6992; Dan S. Wilford, pres.

7235 ★METHODIST HEALTH CARE NETWORK, 5615 Kirby Dr., Suite 800, 77005; tel. 713/831-2900; Michael Williamson, pres. & chief oper. off.; Larry L. Mathis, bd. chm. & chief exec. off.

0605 ★SCH HEALTH CARE SYSTEM, 6400 Lawndale Ave., 77023; tel. 713/928-2931; Sr. Carmella O'Donoghue, pres.

San Antonio: 0265 BAPTIST MEMORIAL HOSPITAL SYSTEM, 111 Dallas St., 78286; tel. 512/222-8431; David Garrett, pres. & chief exec. off.

5565 ★INCARNATE WORD HEALTH SERVICES, 303 W. Sunset Rd., 78209; tel. 512/828-1733; Sr. Nora Marie Walsh, pres.

Tyler: 1895 EAST TEXAS HOSPITAL FOUNDATION, P O Drawer 6400, 75711; tel. 214/597-0351; Elmer G. Ellis, pres.

UTAH

Salt Lake City: 1815 ★INTERMOUNTAIN HEALTH CARE, INC., 36 S. State, 22nd Floor, 84111; tel. 801/533-8282; Scott S. Parker, pres.

VIRGINIA

Newport News: 4810 RIVERSIDE HEALTHCARE ASSOCIATION, INC. (Formerly Riverside Hospital), 606 Denbigh Blvd., Suite 601, 23602; tel. 804/875-7500; Nelson L. St. Clair, pres.

Norfolk: 2565 ★ALLIANCE HEALTH SYSTEM, 18 Koger Executive Center, Suite 202, 23502; tel. 804/466-6000; Glenn R. Mitchell, pres.

0295 FIRST HOSPITAL CORPORATION, World Trade Ctr., Suite 870, 23510; tel. 804/622-3034; Ronald I. Dozoretz MD, chm.

Roanoke: 0070 ROANOKE HOSPITAL ASSOCIATION, Box 13367, 24033; tel. 703/981-7347; Thomas L. Robertson, pres.

Springfield: 1305 ★FAIRFAX HOSPITAL ASSOCIATION, 8001 Braddock Rd., 22151; tel. 703/321-4213; J. Knox Singleton, pres.

WASHINGTON

Bellevue: 5415 ★HEALTH AND HOSPITAL SERVICES, 1715 114th Ave. S.E., Suite 110, 98004; tel. 206/454-8068; Sr. Joan M. McInnes, pres.

Kirkland: 0045 AMERICAN HEALTH GROUP INTERNATIONAL, INC., 401 Park Pl., Suite 500, 98033; tel. 206/827-1195; Michael D. Drobot, pres.

Seattle: 9995 ★GROUP HEALTH COOPERATIVE OF PUGET SOUND, 300 Elliott Ave. W., 98119; tel. 206/326-6844; Mr. Gail L. Warden, pres. & chief exec. off.

8985 SAFECARE COMPANY, INC/SAFECARE HEALTH SERVICE, INC., 900 Fourth Ave., Suite 800, P O Box 21485, 98111; tel. 206/223-4560; Stephen R. Jepson, sr. vice-pres. & pres.

5275 ★SISTERS OF PROVIDENCE (Formerly Sisters of Providence Health Care Corporations), 520 Pike St., P O Box C11038, 98111; tel. 206/464-3355; Donald A. Brennan, pres.

6415 ★UNIVERSITY OF WASHINGTON HOSPITALS, Sc-61 University of Washington, 98195; tel. 206/548-6364; Robert Muilenburg, exec. dir.

Spokane: 0945 ★EMPIRE HEALTH SERVICES, S. 400 Jefferson St., Ste. 333, 99204; tel. 509/458-7965; Jon K. Mitchell, pres. & chief exec. off.

5265 ★SISTERS OF PROVIDENCE-PROVINCE OF ST. IGNATIUS, 9 E. Ninth Ave., 99202; tel. 509/455-4879; Sr. Barbara Ann Brenner, chief exec. off.

Tacoma: 6555 ★MULTICARE MEDICAL CENTER (Formerly Consolidated Hospitals), 409 S. J St., P O Box 5277, 98405; tel. 206/594-125l; W. Barry Connoley, pres. & chief exec. off.

WEST VIRGINIA

Charleston: 0955 ★CAMCARE, INC., (Formerly Healthnet Inc.), Box 1547, 25326; tel. 304/348-7627; James C. Crews, pres. & chief exec. off.

Huntington: 5235 ★SISTERS OF THE PALLOTTINE MISSIONARY SOCIETY, 2900 First Ave., 25702; tel. 304/696-2550; James Spencer, dir. finance

WISCONSIN

Fond Du Lac: 5695 ★CONGREGATION OF ST. AGNES, 475 Gillett St., 54935; tel. 414/923-2121; Sr. Mary Mollison, corp. dir.

La Crosse: 9650 ★FRANCISCAN HEALTH SYSTEM, INC. (Formerly St. Francis Health Corporation), 615 S. Tenth St., 54601; tel. 608/785-0940; Stewart W. Laird, pres.

5705 FRANCISCAN SISTERS OF PERPETUAL ADORATION, 912 Market St., 54601; tel. 608/782-5610; Sr. Patricia Alden, pres.

Manitowoc: 1455 ★FRANCISCAN HEALTH ADVISORY SERVICES, INC., 2409 S. Alverno Rd., 54220; tel. 414/684-7071; Sr. Laura Wolf, pres.

Merrill: 5855 ★HOLY CROSS LIFE CARE SYSTEMS, INC. (Formerly Sisters of Mercy of the Holy Cross-Province of the U.S.), 1500 O'Day St., 54452; tel. 715/536-5101; Robert E. Wulff, adm. & chief exec. off.

Milwaukee: 3775 MILWAUKEE COUNTY DEPARTMENT OF HEALTH AND HUMAN SERVICES (Formerly Milwaukee County Institute and Departments), 8731 Watertown Plank Rd., 53226; tel. 414/257-6489; James W. Wahner, dir.

5305 ★SISTERS OF THE SORROWFUL MOTHER-MINISTRY CORPORATION, 6618 N. Teutonia Ave., 53209; tel. 414/352-4056; Sr. M. Lois Bush, pres. & chief exec. off.

CANADA

Kingston, Ontario: 3615 RELIGIOUS HOSPITALLERS OF ST. JOSEPH, PROVINCE OF ST. JOSEPH, 16 Manitou Crescent E., Kingston, Ont., Canada; tel. 613/389-0275

★Indicates Type III membership in the American Hospital Association.

Alliances and Networks

The following is an alphabetical list of alliances and their members. A hospital alliance is a formally organized group of hospitals or hospital systems that have come together for specific purposes and have specific membership criteria. An alliance is controlled by independent and autonomous member institutions. This is a key difference between alliances and multihospital systems. Multihospital systems are generally controlled through a corporate office, an alliance is controlled and/or owned by the member institutions. For more information call 312/280-6392.

ALLIANCE HEALTH NETWORK

303 West Sunset Road, Suite 202, San Antonio, TX 78209; 512/289-1103; Charles L. Kight, exec. vice-pres.

Texas: St. Anthony's Hospital (284 beds), 200 N.W. Seventh Street, Amarillo 79176-0001; 806/376-4411; Bill Myers, pres.

Archer County Hospital (26 beds), 410 East Chestnut St., Archer City 76351; 817/574-4586; Daniel D. Powell, admin.

Holy Cross Hospital (44 beds), 2600 E. Martin Luther King Jr., Blvd., Austin 78702; 512/477-9811; Pierre M. Dossman, Jr., admin.

Seton Medical Center (491 beds), 1201 W. 38th St., Austin 78705; 512/459-2121; Judith P. Smith, pres.

St. Elizabeth Hospital (489 beds), 2830 Calder Ave., Beaumont 77702; 713/892-7171; Sister Carmella Brett, admin.

St. Jude Hospital (52 beds), 1306 North Park, Brenham 77833; 409/836-6161; Ben Tobias, admin.

St. Joseph Hospital (167 beds), 2801 Fraciscan Dr., Bryan 77802-2544; 409/776-3777; Sister Gretchen Kunz, pres.

St. Edward Hospital of Cameron (46 beds), 806 N. Crockett, Cameron 76250; 817/697-6664; Robert Spille, admin.

Spohn Hospital (419 beds), 600 Elizabeth, P.O. Box 3666, Corpus Christi 78404; 512/881-3000; Sister Kathleen Coughlin, pres.

Coon Memorial Hospital (20 beds), 1411 Denver, Dalhart 79022; 806/249-4571; Earl Sheehy, ceo

St. Paul Medical Center (417 beds),* 5909 Harry Hines Blvd., Dallas 75235; 214/879-1000; Anthony L. Bunker, pres.

Hotel Dieu Medical Center (207 beds),* 1014 N. Stanton St., El Paso 79902; 915/545-3111; Allen F. Weikel, pres.

St. Joseph Hospital (379 beds), 1401 South Main St., Fort Worth 76104; 817/336-9371; Diane Stimson, Acting CEO

St. Mary's Hospital (287 beds), 404 Eighth Street, Galveston 77550; 409/763-5301; Keith Reed, admin.

Clay County Memorial Hospital (42 beds), 310 W. South St., Box 270, Henrietta 76365; 817/538-5621; Johnny Richardson, admin.

St. Joseph Hospital (722 beds), 1919 LaBranch, Houston 77002; 713/757-1000; Sister M. Anastasia Enright, admin.

Spohn Kleberg Memorial Hospital (68 beds), 1300 General Cavazos Boulevard, P.O. Box 1197, Kingsville 78363; 512/595-1661; Allan C. Sonduck, pres.

St. Mary of the Plains Hospital (358 beds), 4000 24th St., Lubbock 79410; 806/792-6812; Jake Henry, Jr., pres.

St. John's Hospital (130 beds), 2050 Space Park Drive, Nassau Bay 77058; 713/333-5503; Raymond Khoury, admin.

St. Joseph's Hospital (175 beds), 820 Clarksville St., Paris 75460; 214/785-4521; Sister Mary Eustace Farrell, pres.

St. Mary Hospital (278 beds), P.O. Box 3696, Port Arthur 77643; 409/985-7431; Sister Edith, admin.

St. John's Hospital (137 beds) 2018 Pulliam St., San Angelo 76905; 915/655-3181; Denny Oreb, pres.

Santa Rosa Medical Center (825 beds), P.O. Box 7330, Station A, San Antonio 78285; 512/228-2011; Sister Angela Clare, pres.

Providence Hospital (213 beds), 1700 Providence Dr., Waco 76703; 817/753-4551; Kent Keahey, admin.

Bethania Regional Health Care Center (I90 beds), 1600 11th St., Wichita Falls; 817/723-4111; Sister M. Reginella, admin.

Yoakum Catholic Hospital (18 beds), 303 Hubbard St., Box 753, Yoakum 77995; 512/293-2321; Elwood E. Currier, Jr., ceo

Totals: 26 hospitals
6,484 beds

AMERICAN HEALTHCARE SYSTEM

1205 Prospect, Suite 520, San Diego, CA 92037; 619/456-2811; Monroe E. Trout M.D., J.D., pres. & chief exec. off.

Arizona: Samaritan Health Service (NP, 8 hosps., 1589 beds),* 1410 N. Third St., Phoenix 85004; 602/239-4106; David A. Reed, pres.

California: HealthWest Foundation (NP, 9 hosps., 1513 beds),* 21800 Oxnard, Suite 550, Woodland Hills 91367; 818/716-2777; Paul A. Teslow, pres.

LHS Corp (NP, 8 hosps., 1332 beds),* 1423 S. Grand Ave., Los Angeles 90015; 213/742-6301; Samuel J. Tibbitts, pres.

Merritt Peralta Medical Center, (NP, 3 hosps., 395 beds),* 450 30th St., Oakland 94609; 415/451-4900; Richard J. McCann, pres. & chief exec. off.

Illinois: Evangelical Health Systems (CO, 4 hosps., 1520 beds),* 2025 Windsor Dr., Oak Brook 60521; 312/57209393; John G. King, pres.

Methodist Health Services Corp (CO, 4 hosps., 790 beds),* 221 N.E. Glen Oak Ave., Peoria 61636; 309/672-4826; James K. Knoble, pres.

Iowa: Iowa Methodist Health System (NP, 5 hosps., 883 beds),* 1200 Pleasant St., Des Moines 50308; 515/283-6347; David S. Ramsey, pres.

Maryland: Bon Secours Health System, Inc. (CC, 7 hosps., 1622 beds),* 5457 Twin Knolls Road, Suite 300, Columbia 21045; 301/992-7330; John P. Brozovich, chief exec. off.

Massachusetts: Baystate Health Systems, Inc. (NP, 2 hosps, 883 beds),* 759 Chestnut St., Springfield 01199; 413/787-3345; Michael J. Daly, pres.

Yankee Alliance (NP 12 hosps., 4062 beds)* 725 North St., Pittsfield 01201; 413/442-9568; John C. Johnson, chairman

Michigan: Detroit Medical Center (NP 6 hosps., 2079 beds)* 4201 Antoine, Detroit 48201; 313/745-5059; Richard L. Sejnost, exec. vice pres.

Mercy Health Services (CC, 27 hosps., 5719 beds),* 28700 Eleven Mile Rd., Farmington Hills 48018; 313/478-6313; Edward J. Connors, pres.

Minnesota: Fairview (NP 9 hosps., 1616 beds)* 2312 S. Sixth St. Minneapolis 55454; 612/371-6618; Carl N. Platou, pres.

Health One Corporation (NP, 23 hosps., 3737 beds),* 2810 57th Ave. N. Minneapolis 55430; 612/574-7800; Donald C. Wegmiller, pres.

Asterisk (*) = multihospital systems

Missouri: Christian Health Services Development Corporation (NP, 6 hosps., 922 beds),* 11133 Dunn Rd., St. Louis 63136; 314/355-2300; Fred L. Brown, pres. & chief exec. off.

Research Health Services (NP, 5 hosps., 650 beds),* 6400 Prospect #112, Kansas City 64132; 816/276-9167; E. Wynn Presson, pres.

New Mexico: Southwest Community Health Services (CO, 13 hosps., 1162 beds),* P.O. Box 26666, Albuquerque 87125; 505/823-8333; Richard R. Barr, pres.

North Carolina: SunHealth Corp (NP, 152 hosps., 40,468 beds),* P.O. Box 668800, Charlotte 28266; 704/529-3300; Ben W. Latimer, pres.

Ohio: Bethesda, Inc. (NP, 2 hosps., 806 beds),* 619 Oak St., Cincinnati 45206; 513/569-6141; L. Thomas Wilburn Jr., pres.

Oregon: HealthLink (NP, 4 hosps., 767 beds),* 5320 S.W. Macadam Ave., Portland 97201; 503/227-7288; G. Rodney Wolford, pres.

Pennsylvania: Forbes Healthmark Corporation (NP 3 hosps., 561 beds)* 500 Finley St., Pittsburgh 15206; 412/665-3565; George H. Schmitt, pres.

South Carolina: Greenville Hospital System (NP, 7 hosps., 1224 beds),* 701 Grove Rd., Greenville 29605; 803/242-7978; Jack Skarupa, pres.

South Dakota: Rushmore National Health System (NP, 2 hosps., 389 beds),* 353 Fairmont Blvd., Rapid City 57709; 605/341-8109; Gary P. Riedmann, pres. & chief exec. off.

Tennessee: Methodist Health Systems (CO, 10 hosps, 1817 beds),* 1211 Union Ave., #700, Memphis 38104; 901/726-2300; John T. Casey, pres. & chief exec. off.

Texas: Adventist Health System/United States (CO, 58 hosps., 9,995 beds),* 2221 East Lamar Blvd., Arlington 76006; 817/649-8700; Donald W. Welch, pres.

Harris Methodist Health System (CO, 11 hosps., 1322 beds),* 1325 W. Pennsylvania Ave., Eighth Floor, Fort Worth 76104; 817/878-5973; Ronald L. Smith, pres.

Hendrick Medical Center (NP, 4 hosps., 551 beds),* 1242 N. 19th St., Abilene 79601; 915/677-3551; Michael C. Waters, pres.

Methodist Healthcare Network, The (CO, 10 hosps., 2781 beds),* 6565 Fannin St., Houston 77030; 713/790-3366; Larry L. Mathis, pres. & chief exec. off.

Presbyterian Healthcare System (CO, 3 hosps., 830 beds),* 8220 Walnut Hill Lane, #700, Dallas 75231; 214/696-8500; Douglas D. Hawthorne, pres.

Virginia: Fairfax Hospital Association (NP, 4 hosps., 1103 beds),* 8001 Braddock Rd., Springfield 22151; 703/321-4213, J. Knox Singleton, pres.

Washington: Group Health Cooperative of Puget Sound (NP, 3 hosps., 456 beds),* 300 Elliot Ave. W., Seattle 98119; 206/326-6137; Mr. Gail L. Warden, chief exec. off.

Totals: 32 institutional shareholders
424 hospitals
93,544 beds

CHILD HEALTH CORPORATION OF AMERICA

c/o Children's Hospital and Medical Center, 4800 Sand Point Way N.E., Box C-5371, Seattle, WA 98105; 206/526-2000; Treuman Katz, bd. chm.

California: Valley Children's Hospital (127 beds), 3151 N. Millbrook, Fresno 93703; 209/225-3000; James D. Northway M.D., pres. & chief exec. off.

Children's Hospital of Los Angeles (331 beds), 4650 Sunset Blvd., Box 54700, Los Angeles 90054; 213/660-2450; Jane Hurd, chief exec. off.

Children's Hospital Medical Center of Northern California (149 beds), 747 52nd St., Oakland 94609; 415/428-3000; Antonie H. Paap, pres. & chief exec. off.

Children's Hospital of Orange County (155 beds), 455 S. Main St., Orange 92668; Mailing Address: P.O. Box 5700, zip 92613; 714/997-3000; Harold H. Wade, exec. dir.

Children's Hospital at Stanford (60 beds), 520 Sand Hill Rd., Palo Alto 94304; 415/327-4800; John R. Williams, exec. dir.

Children's Hospital and Health Center (107 beds), 8001 Frost St., San Diego 92123; 619/576-1700; Blair L. Sadler, pres.

Colorado: Denver Children's Hospital (182 beds), 1056 E. 19th Ave., Denver 80218; 303/861-8888; Lua R. Blankenship Jr., pres.

District of Columbia: Children's Hospital National Medical Center (279 beds), 111 Michigan Ave. N.W., zip 20010; 202/745-5000; Bruce M. Perry, pres. & chief exec. off.

New York: Children's Hospital of Buffalo (313 beds), 219 Bryant St., Buffalo 14222; 716/878-7000; J. Edward Stibbards, pres.

Ohio: Children's Hospital and Medical Center of Akron (253 beds), 281 Locust St., Akron 44308; 216/379-8200; William H. Considine, pres.

Children's Hospital (286 beds), 700 Children's Dr., Columbus 43205; 614/461-2000; Stuart W. Williams, exec. dir.

The Children's Medical Center (139 beds), One Children's Plaza, Dayton 45404; 513/226-8300; Laurence P. Harkness, pres. & chief exec. off.

Tennessee: LeBonheur Children's Medical Center (173 beds), One Children's Plaza, Memphis 38103; 901/522-3000; Eugene K. Cashman Jr., pres.

Virginia: Children's Hospital of the King's Daughters (128 beds), 800 W. Olney Rd., Norfolk 23507; 804/628-7000; Stephen S. Perry Jr., pres.

Washington: Children's Hospital and Medical Center (200 beds), 4800 Sand Point Way N.E., Box C-5371, Seattle 98105; 206/526-2000; Treuman Katz, pres. & chief exec. off., Patrick Shumaker, exec. dir. & chief oper. off.

Wisconsin: Children's Hospital of Wisconsin (170 beds), 1700 W. Wisconsin Ave., Box 1997, Milwaukee 53201; 414/931-1010; Jon E. Vice, pres.

Totals: 16 hospitals
3052 beds

CONSOLIDATED CATHOLIC HEALTH CARE

One Westbrook Corporate Center, Suite 400, Westchester, IL 60153; 312/531-8201; Michael F. Doody, pres.

Illinois: Missionary Sisters of the Sacred Heart/Western Province/ Columbus-Cuneo-Cabrini Medical Center (CC, 3 hosps., 631 beds),* 676 N. St. Clair, Suite 1900, Chicago 60611; 312/943-1333; James E. Hamill, chief exec. off.

Ancilla Systems, Inc. (CC, 9 hosps., 2097 beds),* 1100 Elmhurst Rd., Elk Grove Village 60007; 312/694-4210; Sr. M. Judian Breitenbach, chairman of the board

ServantCor (CC, 3 hosps., 504 beds),* 175 S. Wall St., Kankakee 60901; 815/937-2034; Joseph S. Feth, pres.

Franciscan Sisters Health Care Corporation (CC, 5 hosps., 1340 beds),* St. Francis Woods, Rte. 4, Mokena 60448; 815/469-4888; Sr. Dismas Janssen, bd. chm. & pres.

Sisters of the Third Order of St. Francis (CC, 6 hosps., 1622 beds),* 1124 N. Berkley Ave., Peoria 61603; 309/655-2850; Sr. Frances Marie Masching, exec. vice-pres.

Hospital Sisters Health System (CC, 13 hosps., 3443 beds),* Sangamon Ave. Rd., Box 42, Springfield 62705; 217/522-6969; Sr. Marianna Kosior, pres.

Wheaton Franciscan Services, Inc. (CC, 12 hosps., 2594 beds),* 26W171 Roosevelt Rd., P.O. Box 667, Wheaton 60189; 312/462-9271; Wilfred F. Loebig, Jr., chief exec. off.

Indiana: Holy Cross Health System Corporation (CC, 16 hosps., 3606 beds),* 3606 E. Jefferson Blvd., South Bend 46615; 219/233-8558; William A. Himmelsbach, Jr., pres. & chief exec. off.

Sisters of St. Francis Health Services, Inc. (CC, 9 hosps., 3116 beds),* 1515 Dragoon Trail, P.O. Box 1290, Mishawaka 46544; 219/259-3935; Sr. Mary Theresa Solbach, pres.

Asterisk (*) = multihospital systems

Maryland: Bon Secours Health System, Inc. (CC, 7 hosps., 1622 beds),* 5457 Twin Knolls Rd.; Suite 300, Columbia 21045; 301/992-7330; Sr. Regina Clifton, pres. & chief exec. off.

Massachusetts: Covenant Health Systems, Inc. (CC, 3 hosps., 1254 beds),* 10 Pelham Rd., Lexington 02173; 617/862-1634; Sr. Dorothy Cooper, SGM, pres.

Sisters of Providence Health and Human Services (CC, 3 hosps., 641 beds),* 209 Carew St., Springfield 01104; 413/536-7511; Sr. M. Catherine Laboure, pres.

Michigan: Mercy Health Services (CC, 27 hosps., 5719 beds),* 28550 Eleven Mile Rd., Farmington Hills 48018; 313/478-9900; Edward J. Connors, pres.

Ohio: Mercy Health Care System (CC, 13 hosps., 2902 beds),* 2303 Grandview Ave., Cincinnati 45206; 513/221-1800; Sr. M. Michaeleen Frieders, pres.

Sisters of Charity Health Care Systems, Inc. (CC, 13 hosps., 4385 beds),* 345 Neeb Rd., Cincinnati 45238; 513/922-9775; Sr. Celestia Koebel, pres.

Humility of Mary Health Care (CC, 3 hosps., 1254 beds),* P.O. Box 841, Lorain 44052; 216/871-0971; Sr. Frances Flanigan, chief exec. off.

Pennsylvania: Franciscan Health System (CC, 13 hosps., 3024 beds),* Brandywine 1 Bldg., Suite 301, Chadds Fords 19317; 215/358-3950; Ronald Aldrich, pres.

Texas: SC Health Care Systems (CC, 15 hosps., 5211 beds),* 6400 Lawndale Ave., Houston 77023; 713/928-2931; Sr. Carmella O'Donoghue, pres.

Incarnate Word Health Services (CC, 10 hosps., 3294 beds),* 310 W. Sunset Rd., San Antonio 78209; 512/828-1733; Sr. Nora Marie Walsh, CCVI, pres.

Washington: Sisters of Providence (CC, 16 hosps., 3668 beds),* 520 Pike St., P.O. Box C11038, Seattle 98111; 206/464-3355; Donald A. Brennan, pres.

Totals: 20 members
199 hospitals
51,927 beds

FIRST HOSPITALS, INC.
340 E. Town St., Ste. 7-800,. Columbus, OH 43215; 614/461-3237; Walter J. Furlong, pres.

California: Mills-Peninsula Corporation (654 beds), 50 S. San Mateo Dr., Suite 380, San Mateo, 94401; 415/579-2190; Charles H. Mason Jr., pres.

Kentucky: Methodist Evangelical Hospital (363 beds), 315 E. Broadway, Louisville 40202; 502/585-2241; E. Dean Grout, pres. & chief exec. off.

New Hampshire: Elliot Hospital (273 beds), 955 Auburn St., Manchester 03103; 603/669-5300; Francis J. Cronin, pres.

Ohio: Grant Medical Center (473 beds), 111 S. Grant Ave., Columbus, 43215; 614/461-3232; William Hendrickson, pres.

Pennsylvania: Central Medical Center & Hospital (141 beds), 1200 Centre Ave., Pittsburgh 15219; 412/562-3000; Thomas M. Gallagher, pres.

Lancaster General Hospital (572 beds), 555 N. Duke St., Lancaster, 17603; 771/299-5511; Harvey G. York, senior vice pres.

West Virginia: United Hospital Center (330 beds), U.S. Rt. 19, P.O. Box 1680, Clarksburg 26301; 304/624-2121; D. Max Francis, pres.

Totals: 7 hospitals
2806 beds

HEALTH NETWORK OF AMERICA, INC.
c/o Samaritan Health Service; 1410 North Third St., Phoenix, AZ 85004; 602/239-4100; David A. Reed, pres.

Arizona: SamCor/Samaritan Health Service (NP, 8 hosps., 1589 beds),* 1410 N. Third St., Phoenix 85004; 602/239-4106; David A. Reed, pres.

California: LHS Corporation (NP, 8 hosps., 1332 beds),* 1423 S. Grand Ave., Los Angeles 90015; 213/748-0191; Samuel J. Tibbitts, pres.

Oregon: HealthLink (NP, 4 hosps., 767 beds),* 5320 S.W. Macadam Ave., Portland 97201; 503/227-7288; G. Rodney Wolford, pres.

Totals: 20 hospitals
3688 beds

HEALTHFIRST NETWORK, INC.
122 W. 22nd St., Suite 332, Oak Brook, IL 60521; 312/954-1232; David E. Kolb, pres.

Illinois: Copley Memorial Hospital (212 beds), Lincoln & Weston Ave., Aurora 60505; 312/844-1000; Gregory W. Lintjer, pres.

Good Shepherd Hospital (166 beds), 450 W. Highway 22, Barrington 60010; 312/381-9600; Russell Feurer, vice-pres.

Augustana Hospital and Health Care Center (330 beds), 2035 N. Lincoln Ave., Chicago 60614; 312/975-5000; David Jensen, chief oper. off.

Bethany Hospital (194 beds), 3435 W. Van Buren, Chicago 60624; 312/265-7700; A. Nicholas Straub, vice-pres. & chief exec. off.

Mercy Hospital and Medical Center (502 beds), Stevenson Expwy. at King Dr., Chicago 60616; 312/567-2000; Sr. Sheila Lyne, pres.

South Chicago Community Hospital (440 beds), 2320 E. 93rd St., Chicago 60617; 312/978-2000; Harlan H. Newkirk, pres. & chief exec. off.

St. Anthony Hospital (183 beds), 2875 W. 19th St., Chicago 60623; 312/521-1710; Timothy P. Selz, pres.

Holy Family Hospital (246 beds), 100 N. River Rd., Des Plaines 60016; 312/297-1800; Sr. Patricia Ann, pres.

Good Samaritan Hospital (287 beds), 3815 Highland Ave., Downers Grove 60515; 312/963-5900; David M. McConkey, vice-pres. & chief exec. off.

St. Joseph Hospital and Healthcare Center (312 beds), 2900 N. Lake Shore Dr., Chicago 60657; 312/975-3000; Michael Connelly, pres.

Alexian Brothers Medical Center (370 beds), 800 W. Biesterfield Rd., Elk Grove Village 60007; 312/437-5500; Brother Philip Kennedy, pres. & chief exec. off.

St. Francis Hospital (469 beds), 355 Ridge Ave., Evanston 60202; 312/492-4000; Sr. M. Alfreda, pres.

South Suburban Hospital (217 beds), 178th St. & Kedzie Ave., Hazel Crest 60429; 312/799-8000; Robert Rutkowski, exec. vice-pres.

Highland Park Hospital (280 beds), 718 Glenview Ave., Highland Park 60035; 312/432-8000; Ronald G. Spaeth, pres. & chief exec. off.

St. Joseph Medical Center (531 beds), 333 N. Madison St., Joliet 60435; 815/725-7133; Edward J. Schlicksup Jr., pres.

LaGrange Memorial Hospital (247 beds), 5101 Willow Springs Rd., La Grange 60525; 312/352-1200; Joseph P. Calandra, pres.

Westlake Community Hospital (261 beds,), 1225 Superior St., Melrose Park 60160; 312/681-3000; Leonard J. Muller, pres.

Christ Hospital and Medical Center (873 beds), 4440 W. 95th St., Oak Lawn 60453; 312/425-8000; Joseph W. Beard, Vice Pres. & CEO

Lutheran General Hospital (587 beds), 1775 Dempster St., Park Ridge 60068; 312/696-2210; Roger S. Hunt, pres. & chief exec. off.

Victory Memorial Hospital (315 beds), 1324 N. Sherian Rd., Waukegan 60085; 312/360-3000; Donald Wasson, pres.

Swedish Covenant (247 beds), 5145 N. California Ave., Chicago, IL 60625; 312/878-8249; James B. McCormick, M.D., Pres. and CEO

Totals: 21 hospitals
7269 beds

Asterisk (*) = multihospital systems

HOSPITAL NETWORK, INC.
One Healthcare Plaza, Kalamazoo, MI 49007; 616/344-5587; Richard Fluke, pres. & ceo

Michigan: Allegan General Hospital (75 beds), 555 Linn St., Allegan 49010; 616/673-8424; Jack L. Denton, ceo

Bronson Healthcare Group, Inc. (2 hospitals, 497 beds),* One Healthcare Plaza, Kalamazoo 49007; 616/344-5222; Patric E. Ludwig, pres.

Bronson Methodist Hospital (456 beds), 252 E. Lovell Str., Kalamazoo 49007; 616/383-7654; Peter W. Froyd, pres.

Bronson Vicksburg Hospital (41 beds), 13326 North Blvd., Vicksburg 49097; 616/649-2321; Edward Spartz, pres.

Oaklawn Hospital (77 beds), 200 N. Madison St., Marshall 49068; 616/781-4271; Rob Covert, ceo

Pennock Hospital (92 beds), 1009 W. Green St., Hastings 49058; 616/945-3451; Daniel Hamilton, pres.

Sturgis Hospital (94 beds), 916 Myrtle, Sturgis 49091; 616/651-7824; Patrick A. Hite, ceo

Totals: 8 hospitals
1332 beds

INTERHEALTH
2550 University Ave. W., Suite 233N, St. Paul, MN 55114; 612/646-5574; Nancy Conlee Hart, exec. vice-pres.

Colorado: Lutheran Medical Center (380 beds), 8300 W. 38th Ave. Ct., Wheat Ridge 80033; 303/425-4500; James D. Willard , pres. & ceo

Illinois: Quad-Cities Health Care Resources (288 beds), 501 Tenth Ave., Moline 61265; 309/757-2611;Kenneth D. Moburg, pres. & ceo

Lutheran General Health Care System (CO, 3 hosps., 1,005 beds), *1775 Dempster St., Park Ridge 60068; 312/696-5110; George B. Caldwell, pres. & ceo

Indiana: The Lutheran Hospital of Ft. Wayne, Ind. (403 beds), 3024 Fairfield Ave., Ft. Wayne 46807; 219/458-2001; Frederick H. Kerr, pres. & ceo

Iowa: Allen Memorial Hospital (196 beds), 1825 Logan Ave., Waterloo 50703; 319/235-3987; Larry W. Pugh, pres. & ceo

Minnesota: Fairview Hospital and Healthcare Service (9 hosps., 1,616 beds),* 2312 S. Sixth St., Minneapolis 55454; 612/371-6300; Carl N. Platou, pres.

North Dakota: Lutheran Health Systems (NP, 40 hosps., 2,558 beds),* 1202 Westrac, Box 2087, Fargo 58107; 701/293-9053; Michael O. Bice, pres. & chief exec. off.

Texas: Lutheran General Hospital (109 beds), 701 S. Zarzamora, San Antonio 78207; 512/436-5252; Thames F. Jackson, pres. & ceo

Wisconsin: Sheboygan Memorial Medical Center (150 beds), 2629 N. Seventh St., Sheboygan 53081; 414/457-5033; Patrick J. Trotter, pres. & ceo

Totals: 9 shareholders
6075 beds

MAJOR CATHOLIC HOSPITAL ALLIANCE
1415 Elbridge Payne Rd., Suite 120, Chesterfield, MO; 314/532-2445; Charles H. Steib, pres.

Illinois: St. Elizabeth Medical Center (389 beds), 2100 Madison Ave., Granite City 62040; 618/798-3000; Ted Eilerman, pres.

Foster G. McGaw Hospital, Loyola University of Chicago (512 beds), 2160 S. First Ave., Maywood 60153; 312/531-3000; Robert S. Condry, dir.

Indiana: St. Vincent Hospital and Health Care Center (840 beds), 2001 W. 86th , Box 46240, Indianapolis 46260; 317/871-234ŧ ɔain J. Farris, pres.

Michigan: St. Joseph's Hospital Center (487 beds), 15855 19 Mile Rd., Mount Clemens 48044; 313/798-8551; Mark L. Penkhus, pres. & chief exec. off.

Ohio: Timken Mercy Medical Center (555 beds), 1320 Timken Mercy Dr. N.W., Canton 44708; 216/489-1000; Mark A. Nadel, pres. & chief exec. off.

Good Samaritan Hospital (719 hosp. beds,), 3217 Clifton Ave., Cincinnati 45220; 513/872-1400; Roger N. Weseli, pres.

St. Vincent Charity Hospital and Health Center (414 beds), 2351 E. 22nd St., Cleveland 44115; 216/861-6200; David D. Eramo, Ph.D., pres. & chief exec. off.

Mt. Carmel Health-Mt. Carmel Medical Center (815 beds), 793 W. State St., Columbus 43222; 614/225-5000; Sr. Gladys Marie Martin, pres. & chief exec. off.

Good Samaritan Hospital and Health Center (576 beds), 2222 Philadelphia Dr., Dayton 45406; 513/278-2612; James P. Fitzgerald, pres.

St. Vincent Medical Center (731 beds), 2213 Cherry St., Toledo 43608; 419/321-3232; Lawrence O. Leaman, exec. vice-pres.

St. Elizabeth Hospital Medical Center (773 beds), 1044 Belmont Ave., Box 1790, Youngstown 44501; 216/746-7211; Sr. Susan Schorsten, exec. dir.

Pennsylvania: St. Vincent Health Center (580 beds), 232 W. 25th St., Erie 16544; 814/452-5000; Sr. Margaret Ann Hardner, pres.

St. Francis Medical Center (697 beds), 45th St. off Penn Ave., Pittsburgh 15201; 412/622-4343; Sr. M. Rosita Wellinger, Exec. Vice President & Chief Executive Off.

Tennessee: St. Francis Hospital, Inc. (879 hosp. beds) 5959 Park Ave., Memphis 38119; Mailing address: P.O. Box 171808, zip 38187; 901/765-1000; M. Rita Schroeder, pres.

Wisconsin: St. Francis Health Corporation, Inc.-St. Francis Medical Center (361 beds), 700 West Ave. S., La Crosse 54601; 608/785-0940; Stewart W. Laird, pres.

St. Joseph's Hospital (524 beds), 611 St. Joseph Ave., Marshfield 54449; 715/387-1713; David R. Jaye, pres.

Totals: 16 hospitals
9,852 beds

PREMIER HOSPITALS ALLIANCE, INC.
One Westbrook Corporate Center, Westchester, IL 60153; 312/531-8220; Alan Weinstein, pres.

California: Mount Zion Hospital and Medical Center (298 beds), 1600 Divisadero St., San Francisco 94115; Mailing address: Box 7921, zip 94120; 415/567-6600; Martin J. Diamond, pres.

Connecticut: Mount Sinai Hospital (306 beds), 500 Blue Hills Ave., Hartford 06112; 203/242-4431; Robert B. Bruner, pres. & exec. dir.

Florida: Memorial Medical Center of Jacksonville (353 beds), 3625 University Blvd. S., Box 16325, Jacksonville 32216; 904/399-6111; E. K. Prentice, pres., Mark A. Mrozek, adm.

Mount Sinai Medical Center (699 beds), 4300 Alton Rd., Miami Beach 33140; 305/674-2121; Fred D. Hitt, pres. & chief exec. off.

Georgia: Georgia Baptist Medical Center (483 beds), 300 Boulevard N.E., Atlanta 30312; 404/653-4200; William C. Brown, adm. & chief exec. off.

Illinois: Michael Reese Hospital and Medical Center (689 beds), Lake Shore Drive at 31st St., Chicago 60616; 312/791-2000; Marvin B. Klein, pres.

Mount Sinai Hospital Medical Center of Chicago (379 beds), California Ave. & 15th St. Chicago 60608; 312/542-2000; Ruth M. Rothstein, pres.

Indiana: Methodist Hospital of Indiana (1130 beds), 1604 N. Capitol Ave., P.O. Box 1367, Indianapolis 46206; 317/924-6411; Frank Lloyd M.D., pres.

Kentucky: Jewish Hospital (442 beds), 217 E. Chestnut St., Louisville 40202; 502/587-4011; Henry C. Wagner, pres.

Louisiana: Touro Infirmary (405 beds), 1401 Foucher St., New Orleans 70115; 504/897-7011; Barth A. Weinberg, exec. dir.

Maryland: Sinai Hospital of Baltimore (569 beds), Belvedere Ave. at Greenspring, Baltimore 21215; 301/578-5678; B. Stanley Cohen, M.D., pres.

Asterisk (*) = multihospital systems

Massachusetts: Beth Israel Hospital (472 beds), 330 Brookline Ave., Boston 02215; 617/735-2000; Mitchell T. Rabkin, M.D., pres.

Michigan: Sinai Hospital of Detroit (545 beds), 6767 W. Outer Dr., Detroit 48235; 313/493-6824; Irving A. Shapiro, exec. vice-pres.

Borgess Medical Center (462 beds), 1521 Gull Rd., Kalamazoo 49001; 616/383-7000; R. Timothy Stack, pres.

Edward W. Sparrow Hospital (522 beds), 1215 E. Michigan Ave., P.O. Box 30480, Lansing 48909; 517/483-2501; F. K. Neumann, pres. & chief exec. off.

Missouri: Menorah Medical Center (298 beds), 4949 Rockhill Rd., Kansas City 64110; 816/276-8000; Sol Schaengold, pres.

The Jewish Hospital of St. Louis (550 beds), 216 S. Kingshighway Blvd., St. Louis 63110; Mailing address: Box 14109, zip 63178; 314/454-7000; David A. Gee, pres.

Nebraska: Bishop Clarkson Memorial Hospital (371 beds), Dewey Ave. & 44th St., Omaha 68105; 402/559-2000; Max Francis, pres.

New Jersey: Newark Beth Israel Medical Center (545 beds), 201 Lyons Ave., Newark 07112; 201/926-7000; Lester M. Bornstein, pres.

Barnert Memorial Hospital Center (212 beds), 680 Broadway, Paterson 07514; 201/977-6600; Bruce M. Topolosky, pres. & chief exec. off.

New York: Long Island College Hospital (567 beds), Brooklyn 11201; 212/780-1000; Harold L. Light, pres. & chief exec. off.

Long Island Jewish Medical Center (870 beds), New Hyde Park 11042; 718/470-7621; Robert K. Match, M.D., pres.

Beth Israel Medical Center (908 beds), First Ave. & 16th St., New York 10003; 212/420-2000; Robert G. Newman, M.D., pres.

Montefiore Medical Center (1242 beds), 111 E. 210 St., New York 10467; 212/920-6701; Spencer Foreman, M.D., pres.

Millard Fillmore Hospital (629 beds,), 3 Gates Circle, Buffalo 14209; 716/887-4600; Jan Jennings, pres.

Mount Sinai Medical Center (1112 beds), One Gustave L. Levy Pl., New York 10029; 212/650-6500; James F. Glenn M.D., pres., Barry Freedman, exec. vice-pres. & dir.

Staten Island Hospital (462 beds), 475 Seaview Ave., Staten Island 10305; 718/390-9000; Barry T. Zeman, exec. dir.

Ohio: Akron City Hospital (513 beds), 525 E. Market St., Akron 44309; 216/375-3000; Albert F. Gilbert Ph.D., pres.

Jewish Hospital of Cincinnati (607 beds), 3200 Burnet Ave., Cincinnati 45229; 513/569-2000; Warren C. Falberg, pres.

Mount Sinai Medical Center (450 beds), One Mt. Sinai Dr., Cleveland 44106; 216/421-4000; Robert J. Shakno, pres. and CEO

Pennsylvania: Albert Einstein Medical Center (699 hosp. beds,) York & Tabor Rds., Philadelphia 19141; 215/456-7890; Mark S. Levitan, pres.

Horizon Health System (567 beds), 60 W. Broad St., Suite 201, Bethlehem 18018; 215/865-9988; William P. Koughan, pres.

Montefiore Hospital Association of W. PA (406 beds), 3459 Fifth Ave., Pittsburgh 15213; 412/648-6000; Irwin Goldberg, pres.

Rhode Island: Miriam Hospital (247 beds), 164 Summit Ave., Providence 02906; 401/274-3700; Daniel A. Kane, pres.

Washington: Northwest Hospital (246 beds), 1550 N. 115th St., Seattle 98133; 206/364-0500; James D. Hart, exec. dir.

Wisconsin: Mount Sinai Medical Center (370 beds), 950 N. 12th St., Milwaukee 53233; Mailing address: Box 342, zip 53201; 414/289-8200; Sarah Dean, pres.

Totals: 37 owners
19,625 beds

THE SUNHEALTH NETWORK

SunHealth Corporation, 4501 Charlotte Park Dr., P.O. Box 668800, Charlotte, NC 28266-8800; 704/529-3300; Ben W. Latimer, pres.

Arkansas: Jefferson Regional Medical Center (400 beds), (affiliate: Dermott-Chicot Memorial Hospital, 700 W. Gaines St., Dermott 71638 - 39 beds), 1515 West 42nd Avenue, Pine Bluff 71603; 501/541-7100; Larry Barton, administrator

Delaware: Kent General Hospital (174 beds), 640 South State St., Dover 19901; 302/734-4701; Dennis E. Klima, pres.

Florida: Baptist Hospital of Miami, Inc. (371 beds), 8900 N. Kendall Dr., Miami 33176; 305/596-6503; Brian E. Keeley, Jr., executive director

Baptist Medical Center (531 beds), 800 Prudential Dr., Jacksonville 32207; 904/393-2000; William C. Mason III, pres.

Cape Coral Hospital (174 beds), 636 Del Prado Blvd., Cape Coral 33904; 813/574-2323; J. Michael Ward, pres.

Flagler Hospital (131 beds), 159 Marine Street, P.O. Box 100, St. Augustine 32084; 904/829-1311; James D. Conzemius, pres.

John F. Kennedy Memorial Hospital (369 beds), 4800 S. Congress Ave., Atlantis 33462; Mailing address: Box 1489, Lake Worth 33460; 305/965-7300; James K. Johnson, adm.

Morton Plant Hospital (614 beds. 126 long-term care beds), 323 Jeffords St., Clearwater 33516; Mailing address: P.O. Box 210, 33517; 813/462-7000; Duane T. Houtz, pres.

Naples Community Hospital (391 beds), 350 Seventh St. N., Naples 33940; Mailing address: P.O. Box 2507, zip 33939; 813/263-5111; William G. Crone, pres.

North Broward Hospital District (3 hosps., 1,232 beds),* 1625 S.E. Third Ave., Fort Lauderdale 33316; 305/355-5100; Robert L. Kennedy, executive dir.

Riverside Hospital (183 beds), 2033 Riverside Ave., Jacksonville 32204; 904/387-7018; R.D. O'Connor Ph.D., pres.

Sarasota Memorial Hospital (642 beds), 1700 S. Tamiami Trail, Sarasota 33579; 813/955-1266; Philip K. Beauchamp, pres.

Wuesthoff Memorial Hospital (264 beds), 110 Longwood Avenue, P.O. Box 6, Rockledge 23955; 305/636-2211; Robert Carman, pres.

Georgia: Crawford Long Memorial Hospital of Emory University (478 beds), 550 Peachtree St., NE, Atlanta 30365; 404/892-4411; John D. Henry, admin.

Emory University Hospital (555 beds), 1364 Clifton Rd. N.E.,. Atlanta 30322; 404/727-4881; Paul B. Hofmann, exec. dir.

Henrietta Egleston Hospital for Children (165 beds), 1405 Clifton Road, NE, Atlanta 30322; 404/325-6000; Selena D. Dunn, admin.

Hutcheson Medical Center (222 beds, 25 long-term care), 100 Gross Crescent Circle, Fort Oglethorpe 30742; 404/866-2121; W. Leonard Fant, pres.

Northside Hospital (375 beds), 1000 Johnson Ferry Rd. N.E., Atlanta 30042; 404/851-8700; W. Christopher Clark, pres. & chief exec. off.

St. Mary's Hospital of Athens, Inc. (204 beds), 1230 Baxter St., Athens 30613; 404/352-3033; Edward J. Fechtel Jr., Admin.

St. Francis Hospital (264 beds), Expwy. & Woodruff Rd., Box 7000, Columbus 31995; 404/322-8281; Sr. Patricia Garrigan, admin.

St. Joseph Center for Life, Inc. (235 beds), 2260 Wrightsboro Rd., Augusta 30910; 404/737-7401; William S. Atkinson, pres. and ceo

St. Joseph's Hospital, Inc. (311 beds), 11705 Mercy Blvd., Savannah 31420; 912/925-4100; Sr. Mary Faith McKean, pres.

University Hospital (708 beds,), 1350 Walton Way, Augusta 30910; 404/722-9011; Edward M. Gillespie, exec. dir.

Asterisk (*) = multihospital systems

Kentucky: Baptist Healthcare, Inc. (4 hosps., 1,437 beds),* 768 Barrett Avenue, Louisville 40204; 502/561-3277; Ben R. Brewer, pres.

Commonwealth Health Corporation - The Medical Center at Bowling Green (312 beds), 250 Park St., Box 56, Bowling Green 42102-0056; 502/781-2150; John C. Desmarais, pres. & chief exec. off.

The Methodist Hospital of Kentucky, Inc. (183 beds), 911 S. Bypass, Pikeville 41501; 606/437-9621; Lee D. Keene, adm.

T. J. Samson Community Hospital (174 beds), N. Race St., Box 257, Glasgow 42141; 502/651-6171; H. Glenn Joiner, adm.

Louisiana: General Health, Inc., (3 hosps., 507 beds)* P.O. Box 55482, Baton Rouge 70896-6482; 504/924-4324; Thomas H. Sawyer, pres.

Glenwood Regional Medical Center (185 beds), McMillan & Thomas Roads, West Monroe 71291; Mailing address: P.O. Box 35805, 71291; 318/329-4200; Larry D. Rentfro, ceo

Southern Baptist Hospital (463 beds,), 2700 Napoleon Ave., New Orleans 70115; 504/899-9311; Nelson Toebbe, ceo

Woman's Hospital (205 beds), P.O. Box 15379, Baton Rouge 70895; 504/927-1300; Thomas R. Hightower, adm.

Maryland: Carroll County General Hospital (159 beds), 200 Memorial Ave., Westminster 21157; 301/848-3000; Charles R. Graf, exec. vice-pres.

Church Hospital (196 beds), 100 N. Broadway, Baltimore 21231; 301/522-8000; Thomas G, Whedbee, Jr., pres.

Frederick Memorial Hospital (187 beds), West Seventh St., Frederick 21701; 301/694-3300; James K. Kluttz, pres.

The Memorial Hospital and Medical Center of Cumberland (247 beds), 600 Memorial Ave, Cumberland 21502; 301/777-4000; Donald C. McAneny, pres.

Peninsula General Hospital Medical Center (368 beds), 100 E. Carroll St., Salisbury 21801; 301/546-6400; John B. Stevens Jr., pres.

South Baltimore General Hospital (324 beds), 3001 S. Hanover St., Baltimore 21230; 301/347-3200; L. Barney Johnson, pres. & chief exec. off.

Suburban Hospital (360 beds), 8600 Old Georgegown Road, Bethesda 20814; 301/530-3100; Joan Finnerty, admin.

The Union Memorial Hospital (383 beds), 201 E. University Pkwy., Baltimore 21218; 301/554-2000; Charles D. Jenkins, pres.

Mississippi: Grenada Lake Medical Center (86 beds), 960 Avent Dr., Grenada 38901; 601/226-8111; Paul Wood, chief exec. off.

Hinds General Hospital (290 beds), 1850 Chadwick Dr., Jackson 39204; 601/376-1000; Robert G. Wilson, adm.

Wesley Health System, Inc. - Methodist Hospital of Hattiesburg (201 beds); (affiliate: Methodist Hospital of Stone County, Route 1, P.O. Box 5, Wiggins 39577 - 49 beds); 5001 W. Hardy St., Box 15355, Hattiesburg 39401; 601/268-8000; William K. Ray, pres. & chief exec. off.

North Carolina: C. J. Harris Community Hospital (80 beds), 59 Hospital Rd., Sylva 28779; 704/586-7000; Donald C. Morgan, pres.

Cabarrus Memorial Hospital (362 beds), 920 Church St., N., Concord 28025; 704/786-2111; Robert L. Wall, dir.

Caldwell Memorial Hospital (107 beds), 321 Mulberry St., SW, Lenoir 28645; 704/754-8421; Frederick L. Soule, pres.

Catawba Memorial Hospital (199 beds), 810 Fairgrove Church Road, SE, Hickory 28601; 704/322-0450; David O. Rice, pres.

Cleveland Memorial Hospital (300 beds), 201 Grover St., Shelby 28150; 704/487-3000; C. Curtis Copenhaver, pres.

Craven County Hospital (246 beds), 2000 Neuse Blvd., New Bern 28561; 919/633-8111; Donald P. Logan, pres.

Durham County Hospital Corporation-Durham County General Hospital (405 beds), 3643 N. Roxboro St., Durham 27704; 919/471-3411; Richard L. Myers, pres.

Gaston Memorial Hospital (340 beds), P.O. Box 1747, Gastonia 28053-1747; 704/866-2121; Wayne F. Shovelin, pres.

Grace Hospital (161 beds), 2201 S. Sterling St., Morganton 28655; 704/437-4511; John A. Taft, Jr., admin.

Halifax Memorial Hospital (190 beds), 250 Smith Church Rd., Roanoke Rapids 27870; 919/535-8011; M.E. Gilstrap, adm.

Haywood County Hospital (152 beds), 90 Hospital Dr., Clyde 28721; 704/456-7311; Grady H. Stokes, adm.

High Point Regional Hospital (259 beds), 601 N. Elm St., Box Hyde Park-5, High Point 27261; 919/884-8400; J. Daniel Butler, pres.

Lenoir Memorial Hospital (247 beds), 100 Airport Rd., Kinston 28501; 919/522-7171; L. Daniel DuVal Jr., pres.

Margaret Pardee Memorial Hospital (233 beds), 715 Fleming St., Hendersonville 28739; 704/693-6522; Frank J. Aaron, admin.

Memorial Mission Medical Center (371 beds), 509 Biltmore Ave., Asheville 28801; 704/255-4000; Robert F. Burgin, pres.

Moore Regional Hospital (310 beds), Page Rd., Box 3000, Pinehurst 28374; 919/295-7955; J. Crenshaw Thompson, pres.

Moses H. Cone Memorial Hospital (486 beds), 1200 N. Elm St., Greensboro 27401; 919/379-3900; Dennis R. Barry, pres.

New Hanover Memorial Hospital (429 beds), 2131 S. 17th St., Wilmington 28401; Mailing address: P.O. Box 9000, zip 28402; 919/343-7040; William F. Morrison, director

North Carolina Baptist Hospitals, Inc. (642 beds), 300 S. Hawthorne Rd., Winston-Salem 27103, 919/748-4750; Dr. John E. Lynch, pres.

Presbyterian Hospital (566 beds), 200 Hawthorne Ln., Charlotte 28204; Mailing address: P.O. Box 33549, zip 28233; 704/371-4000; Byron L. Bullard, pres.

Rex Hospital (394 beds), 4420 Lake Boone Trail, Raleigh 27607; 919/755-3100; John R. Willis, exec. dir.

Rowan Memorial Hospital, Inc. (263 beds), 612 Mocksvill Ave., Salisbury 28144; 704/638-1000; M. Earl Bullard, director

Southeastern General Hospital (296 beds, 19 long-term care beds), P.O. Box 1408, Lumberton 28359; 919/738-6441; Donald C. Hiscott, pres.

Stanly Memorial Hospital (95 beds), 301 Yadkin St., Albemarle 28001; 704/983-5111; Kenneth A. Shull, pres.

Wayne Memorial Hospital (260 beds), 2700 Wayne Memorial Dr., Goldsboro 27530; 919/736-1110; Joseph H. Hubbell, admin.

Wilson Memorial Hospital (277 beds), 1705 S. Tarboro St., Wilson 27893; 919/399-8040; Charles D. Setliffe, adm.

South Carolina: Anderson Memorial Hospital (438 beds), 800 N. Fant St., Anderson 29621; 803/261-1109; D. Kirk Oglesby Jr., pres.

Conway Hospital (142 beds), 300 Singleton Ridge Rd., Conway 29526; Mailing address: P.O. Box 829 29526; 803/347-7111; James S. Zoller, pres.

Lexington County Hospital (258 beds), 2720 Sunset Blvd., West Columbia 29169; 803/791-2000; George I. Rentz, pres.

McLeod Regional Medical Center (290 beds), 555 E. Cheves St., Florence 29501; 803/667-2000; J. Bruce Barragan, pres.

Orangeburg-Calhoun Regional Hospital (286 beds), 3000 Saint Matthews Rd., Orangeburg 29114; 803/533-2200; H. Filmore Mabry, adm.

Richland Memorial Hospital (533 beds), (affiliate: Lee County Memorial Hospital (35 beds); P.O. Box 528, Bishopville 29010); 3301 Harden Street, Columbia 29203; 803/765-6512; William L. Ivey, pres.

Self Memorial Hospital (315 beds), (affiliate: Edgefield County Hospital, (59 beds) P.O. Box 590 Edgefield 29824); 1325 Spring Street, Greenwood 29646; 803/227-4111; J. L. Dozier, Jr., pres.

Asterisk (*) = multihospital systems

Spartanburg General Hospital (526 beds), (affiliate: B. J. Workman Hospital, P.O. Box 699, Woodruff 29388 - 43 beds), 101 E. Wood St., Spartanburg 29303; 803/573-6107; Charles C. Boone, pres.

St. Francis Xavier Hospital (283 beds), 135 Rutledge Ave., Charleston 29401; 803/577-1002; Douglas L. Fairfax, pres.

Tennessee: The Baptist Health System of East Tennessee, Inc. (East Tennessee Baptist Hospital - 285 beds), (affiliate: Cocke County Baptist Hospital, 702 Second Str., Newport, 37821 - 130 beds), 137 Blount Ave., S.E., Knoxville 37901; Mailing address: P.O. Box 1788 37901; 615/632-5342; Robert C. Chandler, ceo

Blount Memorial Hospital, Inc. (221 beds), 907 Smoky Mountain Hwy., Maryville 37801-5193; 615/983-7211; Joseph M. Dawson, adm.

Bradley Memorial Hospital (221 beds), N. Chambliss Ave., Box 3060, Cleveland 37320-3060; 615/479-0180; William E. Torrence, adm.

Erlanger Medical Center (611 beds), (includes Boroness Erlanger Hospital, T.C. Thompson Children's Hospital Medical Center) 975 East Third Street, Chattanooga, 37403; 615/778-7000; Thomas C. Winston, pres.

Jackson-Madison County General Hospital (634 beds), 708 W. Forest Ave., Jackson 38301; 901/425-5000; James T. Moss, pres.

Methodist Health System (10 hosps., 1,817 beds)*, 1211 Union Ave., Suite 701, Memphis 28104; 901/726-2300; John T. Casey, President

Nashville Memorial Hospital (314 beds), 612 W. Due West Ave., Madison 37115; 615/865-3511; J.D. Elliott, pres.

Vanderbilt University Medical Center (626 beds), 1161 21st Ave. S., Nashville 37232; 615/322-2415; Norman B. Urmy, dir.

Texas: Knapp Memorial Methodist Hospital (180 beds), 133 E. Sixth St., Box 1110, Welasco 78596; 512/968-8567; Robert W. Vanderveer, adm.

McCuistion Regional Medial Center (148 beds), 875 DeShong Dr., Box 160, Paris 75460; 214/737-1111; Anthony A. Daigle, chief exec. off.

Methodist Hospitals of Dallas (3 hosps., 648 beds)*, 209 W. Oakenwald, P.O. Box 225999, Dallas s75265; 214/944-8137; David H. Hitt, pres.

Texoma Medical Center (235 beds), (includes Texoma Medical Center East), 1000 Memorial Drive, P.O. Box 890, Denison 75020; 214/465-2313; Mike Mayes, exec. director

Virginia: Bon Secours-St. Mary's Health Corporation (St. Mary's Hospital), (369 beds), 5801 Bremo Rd., Richmond 23226; 804/281-8316; Richard D. O'Halloran, exec vice-pres.

Chesapeake General Hospital (210 beds), 736 Battlefield Blvd., P.O. Box 2028, Chesapeake 23320; 804/547-8121; Donald S. Buckley, pres.

DePaul Hospital (357 beds), 150 Kingsley Ln., Norfolk 23505; 804/489-5000; Sr. Mary Carroll, EBY adm.

Fairfax Hospital Association (4 hosps., 1,103 beds)*, 8001 Braddock Road, Springfield 22151; 703/321-4213; J. Knox Singleton, pres.

Health Corporation of Virginia (Richmond Memorial Hospital, Samuel F. Lillard, President), (351 beds), 1300 Westwood Ave., Richmond 23227; 804/254-6100; John N. Simpson, pres.

John Randolph Hospital (100 beds), 411 W. Randolph Rd., Box 971, Hopewell 23860; 804/541-1600; Franklin D. Boyce, chief exec. off.

Johnston Memorial Hospital (154 beds), Court St., Abingdon 24210; 703/628-3121; Robert Lee Kay, admin.

Louise Obici Memorial Hospital (202 beds), 1900 N. Main St., P.O. Box 1100, Suffolk 23434; 804/934-4000; Robert R. Everett, pres.

Mayview Hospital (288 beds) 3636 High St., Portsmouth 23707; 804/398-2121; J. Bland Burkhardt, Jr., exec. vice-pres., ceo

The Memorial Hospital (377 beds), 142 S. Main St., Danville 24541; 804/799-2100; Hunter A. Grumbles, admin.

Potomac Hospital (158 beds), 2300 Opitz Blvd., Woodbridge 22191; 703/670-1313; William M. Moss, pres.

Retreat Hospital (230 beds) 2621 Grove Avenue, Richmond 23220; 804/254-5100; H. J. Van Brackle, admin.

Riverside Healthcare Association, Inc. (3 hosps., 980 beds)*, 606 Denbigh Blvd., Suite 601, Newport News 23602; 804/875-7500; Nelson L. St. Clair Jr., pres.

Roanoke Hospital Association (9 hosps., 1,311 beds)*, P.O. Box 13367, Roanoke 24033; 703/981-7000; Thomas L. Robertson, pres.

Smyth County Community Hospital (165 beds), P.O. Box 880, Marion 24354; 703/783-3141; Deane E. Beamer, exec. dir.

Southside Medical Systems, Inc. (Greensville Memorial Hospital) (127 beds), 214 Weaver Ave., Emporia 23847; 804/348-2000; John A. Thurman, adm.

Twin County Community Hospital (149 beds), 200 Hospital Dr., Galax 24333; 703/236-8181; Kenneth L. Waddell, pres.

Virginia Baptist Hospital (286 beds), 3300 Rivermont Ave., Lynchburg 24503; 804/552-4000; George W. Dawson, exec. dir.

Winchester Regional Health Systems, Inc. (Winchester Medical Center, Inc.) (343 beds), S. Stewart St., P.O. Box 3340, Winchester 22601; 703/662-4121; David Goff, pres.

West Virginia: Bluefield Community Hospital (265 beds), 500 Cherry St., Bluefield 24701; 304/327-2511; Eugene P. Pawlowski, adm.

Monongalia Health System (220 beds), 1200 J.D. Anderson Dr., Morgantown 26505; 304/598-1888; Thomas J. Senker, pres. & chief exec. off.

Pleasant Valley Hospital (228 beds), Valley Dr., Point Pleasant 25550; 304/675-4340; Michael G. Sellards, exec. dir.

Thomas Memorial Hospital (259 beds), 4605 MacCorkle Ave., S.W., South Charleston 25309; 304/783-3961; Gary Park, pres. & chief exec. off.

United Hospital Center (295 beds), U.S. Route 19 S., Box 1680, Clarksburg 26301; 304/624-2121; D. Max Francis, pres.

Totals: 114 partner organizations comprising
152 hospitals
41,104 beds

UNIVERSITY HOSPITAL CONSORTIUM
One MidAmerica Plaza, Suite 624, Oakbrook Terrace, IL 60181; 312/954-4707; Robert J. Baker, pres.

Alabama: University of Alabama Hospitals (774 beds), 619 S. 19th St., Birmingham 35233; 205/934-5314; James E. Moon, adm.

Arkansas: University of Arkansas for Medical Sciences-University Hospital, (327 beds), 4301 W. Markham St., Little Rock, AR 72205; 501/661-5662; Richard A. Pierson, exec. dir.

Arizona: University Medical Center Corporation-University Medical Center (241 beds), 1501 N. Campbell Ave., Tucson 85724; 602/626-0111; Alethea O. Caldwell, chief exec. off.

California: University of California, Los Angeles Medical Center (652 beds), 10833 Le Conte Ave., Los Angeles 90024; 213/825-5041; Raymond G. Schultz M.D., dir.

University of California, Irvine Medical Center (382 beds), 101 The City Dr., Orange, CA 92668; 714/634-5678; Leon M. Schwartz, vice chancellor, dir.

University of California, Davis Medical Center (439 beds), 2315 Stockton Blvd., Sacramento, CA 95817; 916/453-2011; Frank J. Loge, dir.

University of California, San Diego Medical Center (406 beds), 225 Dickinson-H-910, San Diego 92103; 619/543-6654; Michael R. Stringer, dir.

University of California, San Francisco Medical Center (560 beds), M-181, 505 Parnaussus St., San Francisco 94143-0208; 415/476-1401; William B. Kerr, dir.

Stanford University Hospital (597 beds), Room C204, Stanford 94305; 415/723-5222; Sheldon S. King, pres.

Asterisk (*) = multihospital systems

Colorado: University of Colorado Hospital (322 beds), 4200 East 9th St., Denver 80262; 303/394-8446; Robert M. Dickler, dir.

Connecticut: University of Connecticut Health Center-John Dempsey Hospital (232 beds), 263 Farmington Ave., Farmington 06032-9984; 203/674-2233; Helen L. Smits, M.D., assoc. vice-pres.

Florida: Shands Teaching Hospital and Clinics, Inc. (464 beds), 1600 Archer Rd., Gainesville 32610; 904/395-0040; John E. Ives, exec. vice-pres.

Georgia: Medical College of Georgia Hospital and Clinics (516 beds), 1120 15th St., Augusta 30912; 404/828-3925; R. Edward Howell, exec. dir.

Illinois: University of Chicago Hospitals (515 beds), 5841 S. Maryland Ave., Box 417, Chicago, IL 60637; 312/962-6500; Ralph O. Muller, pres.

University of Illinois Hospital at Chicago (530 beds), 1740 W. Taylor, Chicago 60612; 312/996-3896; James M. Malloy, dir.

Indiana: Indiana University Hospitals (573 beds), 1100 W. Michigan St., Indianapolis 46223; 317/274-4391; David J. Handel, dir.

William N. Wishard Memorial Hospital (415 beds), 1001 W. 10th St., Indianapolis, IN 46202; 317/630-6797; William T. Paynter, M.D., med. dir.

Kentucky: University Hospital, University of Kentucky Medical Center (433 beds), 800 Rose St., H-114, Lexington 40536; 606/233-5767; Frank A. Butler, exec. dir.

Massachusetts: University of Massachusetts-c/o University of Massachusetts Medical Center (348 beds), 55 Lake Ave. N., Worcester 01605; 617/856-4296; Keith J. Waterbrook, vice-chancellor & dir.

Minnesota: University of Minnesota Hospitals and Clinics (614 beds), Harvard St. at E. River Rd., Minneapolis 55455; 612/626-3000; Gregory Hart, Interim dir.

Missouri: University of Missouri, Columbia Hospital and Clinics (431 beds), One Hospital Dr., Room 1W-17, Columbia 65212; 314/882-3984; Robert B. Smith, dir.

University Hospital, (294 beds), 1325 S. Grand Blvd., St. Louis 63104; 314/577-8003; Herbert B. Schneiderman, exec. dir. & chief oper. off.

Nebraska: University of Nebraska Hospital (356 beds), 42nd St. and Dewey Ave., Omaha 68105; 402/559-7400; Brent Stevenson, interim dir.

New York: State University of New York-Health Science Center at Brooklyn (372 beds), 445 Lenox Rd., Box 23, Brooklyn 11203; 718/270-2401; Mary A. Piccione, exec. dir.

New York University Medical Center (878 beds), 550 First Ave., New York 10016; 212/340-5993; James J. Quinn, M.D. Vice Pres. Oper.

Suny Health Science Center at Syracuse (358 beds), 750 E. Adams St., Syracuse, NY 13210; 315/473-4513; John Bernard Henry, M.D. pres.

University Hospital-Health Science Center-State University of New York at Stony Brook (453 beds), Stony Brook 11794; 516/444-2701; William T. Newell Jr., exec. dir.

North Carolina: The North Carolina Memorial Hospital (439 beds), Manning Dr., Chapel Hill 27514; 919/966-5111; Eric B. Munson, exec. dir.

Ohio: Ohio State University Hospital (791 beds), 410 W. Tenth Ave., S-101 Rhodes Hall, Columbus 43210; 614/293-5555; Michael H. Covert, asst. vice-pres. & exec. dir.

Medical College Hospitals (274 beds), 3000 Arlington Ave., Box C.S. 10008, Toledo 43699; 419/381-3411; David J. Kolasky, exec. dir.

University Hospital (659 beds), 234 Goodman St., Cincinnati, OH 45267; 513/872-3100; Carl H. Iseman, admin.

Oklahoma: Oklahoma Teaching Hospitals (598 beds), P.O. Box 26307, 800 N.E. 13th St., Oklahoma City 73126; 405/271-5911; Antonio A. Padilla, chief exec. off.

Pennsylvania: Pennsylvania State University (381 beds), 500 University Dr., Hershey 17033; 717/531-8521; Howard J. Peterson, dir. & assoc. vice-pres., hlth adm.

Hahnemann University Hospital (552 beds), Broad and Vine Sts., Philadelphia 19102; 215/448-8450; Howard O. Goldstein, chief exec. off.

Thomas Jefferson University Hospital (687 beds), 111 S. 11th St., Philadelphia 19107; 215/928-8383; Michael J. Bradley, vice-pres.

Presbyterian-University Hospital of Pittsburgh (564 beds), DeSoto at O'Hara Sts., Pittsburgh 15213; 412/647-2345; Patricia O. Sheborn, interim chief oper. off.

Texas: Hermann Hospital and Trust (766 beds), 6411 Fannin, Houston 77030-1501; 713/797-4272; Jeptha W. Dalston, Ph.D., chief exec. off.

Utah: University of Utah Hospital (370 beds), 50 N. Medical Dr., Rm. 2743, Salt Lake City 84132; 801/581-2378; George W. Beasley, adm.

Virginia: University of Virginia Hospitals (796 beds), Box 148, Jefferson Park Ave., Charlotteville 22908; 804/924-2258; John T. Ashley, M.D., exec. dir.

Medical College of Virginia Hospitals (881 beds), 401 N. 12th St., Box 510, Richmond 23298; 804/786-0939; Carl R. Fischer, exec. dir.

Washington: Georgetown University Hospital, (539 beds), 3800 Reservoir Road, N.W., Washington, DC 20007; 202/625-7001; Charles M. O'Brien, Jr., hosp. admin.

Wisconsin: University of Wisconsin Hospital and Clinics (503 beds), 600 Highland Ave., Madison 53792; 608/263-8000; Gordon M. Derzon, supt.

Totals: 42 hospitals
21,282 beds

VOLUNTARY HOSPITALS OF AMERICA

5215 N. O'Connor Blvd., Williams Square, 12th Floor, P.O. Box 160909; Irving, TX 75016; 214/830-0000; Don L. Arnwine, chm., David P. Hunter, pres. & chief oper. off.

Alabama: Baptist Medical Centers (5 hosps., 1379 beds), 3201 Fourth Ave., S., Birmingham, AL 35222; 205/322-9300; Emmett R. Johnson, pres.

Related: Baptist Medical Ctr., Birmingham, AL
Baptist Med. Ctrs.-Cherokee, Centre, AL
Baptist Med. Ctrs.-Dekalb, Fort Payne, AL
Baptist Med. Ctrs.-Montclair, Birmingham, AL
Baptist Med. Ctrs.-Princeton, Birmingham, AL
Lakeshore Hospital, Birmingham, AL

Gulf Health, Inc. (671 beds), P.O. Box 2226-1 Mobile Infirmary Circle 36607, Mobile, AL 36652; 205/431-5500; E. Chandler Bramlett, pres.

Related: Mobile Infirmary, Mobile, AL

Baptist Health Services (434 beds), 2105 E. South Blvd., Montgomery 36116-2409; 205/288-2100; W. Taylor Morrow, pres.

Arizona: Lincoln Health Resources Corp. (282 beds), 9211 N. Second St., Phoenix 85020; 602/943-2381; Raymond W. Leitner, pres.

Tucson Medical Center, TM Care (562 beds), 5301 E. Grant Rd., Box 42195, Tucson 85733; 602/327-5461; Donald G. Shropshire, pres.

Related: Tucson Med. Ctr., Tucson, AZ
Copper Queen Community Hosp., Bisbee, AZ
Mt. Graham Comm. Hosp., Inc., Safford, AZ

Arkansas: Baptist Medical System (5 hosps., 1067 beds),* 9601 Interstate 630, Exit 7, Little Rock 72205; 501/227-2000; Russell D. Harrington Jr., pres.

Related: Baptist Medical Ctr., Little Rock, AR
Arkansas Rehab. Instit., Little Rock, AR
Baxter Cty Regional Hospital, Mountain Home, AR
Conway Memorial Hosp., Conway, AR

Asterisk (*) = multihospital systems

Mem. Hosp. of N. Little Rock, Little Rock, AR
St. Bernard's Reg. Med. Ctr., Jonesboro, AR
Stuttgart Memorial Hospital, Little Rock, AR
Twin Rivers Med. Ctr., Arkadelphia, AR
Warner Brown Hosp., El Dorado, AR
Washington Reg. Med. Ctr., Fayette, AR
White River Med. Ctr., Inc., Batesville, AR

Sparks Regional Medical Center (466 beds), 1311 S. "I" St., Fort Smith 72901; 501/441-4000; Charles R. Shuffield, pres.

California: Alta Bates Corporation (256 beds), 2855 Telegraph Ave., Suite 610, Berkeley, CA 94705; 415/540-0337; Kenneth W. Sargent, pres.

Related: Alta Bates Hospital, Berkeley, CA
Alta Bates Corporation, Albany, CA
Herrick Hosp. & Health Ctr., Berkeley, CA

Cedars-Sinai Medical Center (1013 beds), 8700 Beverly Blvd., Box 48750, Los Angeles 90048; 213/855-5711; Stuart J. Marylander, pres.

Community Hospitals of Central California (4 hosps., 634 beds), Fresno and R Streets, P.O. Box 1232, Fresno, CA 93715; 209/442-6000; James D. Helzer, pres.

Related: Fresno Comm. Hosp. & Med Ctr., Fresno, CA
Clovis Comm. Hospital, Clovis, CA
Sierra Hosp. Foundation, Fresno, CA
Sierra Kings District Hosp., Reedley, CA

Hoag Memorial Hospital Presbyterian (375 beds), 301 Newport Blvd., Box Y, Newport Beach 92658; 714/645-8600; Michael D. Stephens, pres. & chief exec. off.

Memorial Medical Center of Long Beach, Inc. (848 beds), 2801 Atlantic Ave., Long Beach 90801; 213/595-2311; George Koppel, acting chief exec. off.

Related: Memorial Med. Ctr. of Long Beach, Long Beach, CA
Saddleback Comm. Hosp., Laguna Hills, CA

Pacific Presbyterian Medical Center (391 beds), P.O. Box 7999, San Francisco 94120; 415/563-4321; B. E. Spivey, M.D., pres.

Related: Pacific Presbyterian Med. Ctr., San Francisco, CA
Garden Sullivan Hospital, San Francisco, CA
St. Luke's Hospital, San Francisco, CA

San Jose Health Center (289 beds), 675 East Santa Clara St., San Jose 95112; 408/998-3212; John C. Aird, pres.

Related: San Jose Hospital, San Jose, CA
The Good Samaritan Hosp. of Santa Clara Valley, San Jose, CA
Wheeler Hospital Assoc., Gilray, CA

Scripps Memorial Hospitals (3 hosps., 627 beds), 9888 Genesee Ave., La Jolla 92037; Mailing Address: Box 28, zip 92038; 619/457-4123; Ames S. Early, pres.

Related: Scripps Memorial Hosp., La Jolla, CA
Scripps Memorial Hosp., Chula Vista, CA

Sutter Health System (NP, 6 hosps., 1024 beds),* 1111 Howe Ave., Suite 600, Sacramento 95825; 916/454-2222; Patrick G. Hayes, pres. & chief exec. off.

Related: Sutter General Hosp., Sacramento, CA
Monticello Medical Ctr., Longview, WA
Novato Community Hospital, Novato, CA
Sutter Solano Med. Center, Vallejo, CA
Sutter Davis Hospital, Inc., Davis, CA

Valley Presbyterian Hospital (363 beds), 15107 Vanowen St., Van Nuys 91405; 818/782-6600; Robert C. Bills, pres.

Colorado: Swedish Medical Center (305 beds), 501 E. Hampden Ave., Englewood 80110; 303/788-6789; Lowell E. Palmquist, pres.

Related: Swedish Medical Ctr., Englewood, CO
Alamosa Community Hosp., Alamosa, CO

Connecticut: Hartford Hospital (903 hosp. beds, 90 nurs. home beds), 80 Seymore St., Hartford 06115; 203/524-2196; John K. Springer, pres.

Yale-New Haven Health Services Corp. (829 beds), 789 Howard Ave., New Haven, CT 06504; 203/785-5861; C. Thomas Smith, pres.

Related: Yale-New Haven Hosp., Inc., New Haven, CT
World War II Veterans Memorial Hosp., Meriden, CT

Florida: Baptist Regional Health Services, Inc. (NP, 4 hosps., 700 beds),* P.O. Box 17500, Pensacola 32522; 904/434-4011; James F. Vickery, pres.

Related: Baptist Hospital, Pensacola, FL
Abernethy Memorial Hospital, Flomaton, AL
D. W. McMillian Mem. Hosp., Brewton, AL
Greenlawn Hospital, Atmore, AL
Gulf Breeze, Gulf Breeze
Jay Hospital, Jay, FL
Mizell Memorial Hospital, Opp, AL
North Baldwin Hospital, Bay Minette, AL
South Baldwin, Foley, AL
Thomas Hospital, Fairhope, AL
Valley Springs, Comm. Hosp., Defuniak Springs, FL

Holmes Regional Healthcare Systems, Inc. (447 beds), 1350 S. Hickory St., Melbourne 32901; 305/727-7000; Ned B. Wilford, pres.

Related: James E. Holmes Reg. Med. Ctr., Melbourne, FL
Cape Canaveral Hospital, Cocoa Beach, FL

Lakeland Regional Medical Center (637 beds), Lakeland Hills Blvd., Drawer 448, Lakeland 33802; 813/687-1100; Jack T. Stephens, Jr., chief exec. off.

Orlando Regional Medical Center (849 beds), 1414 S. Kuhl Ave., Orlando 32806; 305/841-5111; J. Gary Strack, pres.

Related: Orlando Reg. Med. Ctr., Orlando, FL
Sand Lake Hosp., Orlando, FL
St. Cloud Hosp., St. Cloud, FL

Santa Fe Healthcare System, Inc. (NP, 4 hosps., 535 beds),* P.O. Box 749, Gainesville 32602; 904/375-4321; Edwin C. Peddie, pres. & chief exec. off.

Related: Santa Fe Healthcare Sys. Inc., Gainesville, FL
Alachua General Hosp., Gainesville, FL

Tallahassee Memorial Regional Medical Center (658 hosp. beds, 113 nurs. home beds), Magnolia Dr., & Miccousukee Rd., Tallahassee 32308; 904/681-1155; Middleton T. Mustian, pres. & chief exec. off.

Related: Tallahassee Mem. Regional Med. Ctr., Tallahassee, FL
Doctor's Memorial Hosp., Perry, FL
Gadsden Memorial Hosp., Quincy, FL

Georgia: Piedmont Hospital (490 hosp. beds,), 1968 Peachtree Rd., N.W., Atlanta 30309; 404/350-2222; Hulett D. Sumlin, adm.

Related: Piedmont Hospital, Atlanta, GA
Colquitt Regional Med. Ctr., Moultrie, GA
Sumter Regional Hosp., Americus

Hawaii: Queen's Medical Center (437 beds), 1301 Punchbowl St., Honolulu 96813; 808/538-9011; Fred A. Pritchard, pres.

Related: The Queen's Med. Ctr., Honolulu, HI
Wahiawa General Hosp., Wahiawa, HI

Idaho: St. Luke's Regional Medical Center (252 beds), 190 E. Bannock St., Boise 83712; 208/386-2222; Elbert E. Gilbertson, pres.

Related: St. Luke's Reg. Med. Ctr. Ltd., Boise, ID

Illinois: Decatur Memorial Hospital (316 hosp. beds, 54 nurs. home beds), 2300 N. Edward St., Decatur 62526; 217/877-8121; Donald Gent, pres.

Related: Decatur Memorial Hosp., Decatur, IL
The John & Mary E. Kirby Hosp., Monticello, IL

The Northwestern Memorial Group, (735 beds) 750 N. Lake Shore Dr., Chicago, IL 60611; 312/908-2000; David L. Everhart, pres. & chief exec. off.

Related: Northwestern Memorial Hospital, Chicago, IL

Evanston Hospital Corporation (543 beds), 2650 Ridge Ave., Evanston 60201; 312/492-2000; Bernard J. Lachner, pres. & chief exec. off.

Related: Evanston Hospital Corp., Evanston, IL
Children's Mem. Hosp., Chicago, IL
Glenbrook Hospital, Glenview, IL
Lakeland Health Svcs., Inc., Highland Park, IL

Asterisk (*) = multihospital systems

Ingalls Memorial Hospital (554 beds), One Ingalls Dr., Harvey 60426; 312/333-2300; Robert L. Harris, pres.

Memorial Medical Center System (566 beds), 800 N. Rutledge, Springfield 60426; 217/788-3000; Robert T. Clark, pres.

Indiana: Ball Memorial Hospital (532 beds), 2006 West Jackson St., Muncie 47303; 317/286-3456; Roy F. Erickson, Jr., pres.

Community Hospital of Indiana (565 beds), 1500 N. Ritter Ave., Indianapolis 46219; 317/353-1411; William E. Corley, pres.

Related: Comm. Hosp. of Indiana, Indianapolis, IN
Comm. Hospital North, Indianapolis, IN
Clinton County Hospital, Frankfort, IN
Fayette Memorial Hosp., Connersville, IN
Hancock Memorial Hosp., Greenfield, IN
Hendricks County Hosp., Danville, IN
Henry County Memorial Hosp., New Castle, IN
Johnson County Memorial Hosp., Franklin, IN
Major Hospital, Shelbyville, IN
Margaret Mary Comm. Hosp., Batesville, IN
Mary Sherman Hosp., Sullivan
Memorial Hosp. and Hlth. Care Ctr., Jasper, IN
Morgan County Memorial Hosp., Martinsville, IN
Reid Memorial Hosp., Richmond, IN
Riverview Hospital, Noblesville, IN
Union Hospital, Terre Haute, IN
Vermillion County Hospital, Clinton, IN
Westview Hospital, Indianapolis, IN

Deaconess Development Corp. (596 beds), 600 Mary St., Evansville 47747; 812/426-3000; James W. Vogel, chairman

Related: Deaconess Hospital, Inc., Evansville, IN
Carmi Township Hosp., Carmi, IL

Memorial Health System Inc. (475 beds), 205 W. Jefferson Blvd., Ste. 600, South Bend 46601; 219/284-7115; Stephen L. Ummel, pres.

Related: Memorial Health System, South Bend, IN
Healthwin Hosp., South Bend, IN
Mem. Hosp. of Michigan City, Michigan City, IN

Iowa: St. Luke's Methodist Hospital (455 beds), 1026 A Ave. N.E., Cedar Rapids 52402; 319/369-7211; Samuel T. Wallace, pres.

Related: St. Luke's Methodist Hosp., Cedar Rapids, IA
Anamosa Community Hosp., Anamosa, IA

Kansas: Stormont-Vail Regional Medical Center (338 beds),* 1500 Southwest 10th Str., Topeka 66608; 913/354-6000; Howard M. Chase, pres.

Related: Stormont Vail Reg. Med. Ctr., Topeka, KS
Dechairo Hospital, Westmoreland, KS
Hiawatha Hospital Assoc., Inc., Hiawatha, KS
Holton City Hospital, Holton, KS
Wamego City Hospital, Holton, KS

Kentucky: NKC Inc. (518 beds), 200 E. Chestnut St., P.O. Box 35070, Louisville 40232; 502/562-8000; Wade Mountz, vice-pres.

Related: NKC, Inc.: Kosairs-Children's Hosp. and Norton Hosp., Louisville, KY
Caldwell County Hospital, Princeton, KY
Carroll County Memo. Hosp., Carrollton, KY
Harrison County Hosp., Corydon, IN

Louisiana: Oschner Foundation Hospital (511 beds), 1516 Jefferson Hwy., New Orleans 70121; 504/838-3000; David R. Page, exec. vice-pres.

Our Lady of the Lake Regional Medical Center (651 beds), 5000 Hennessy Blvd., Baton Rouge 70809; 504/769-3100; Robert C. Davidge, exec. dir.

Willis-Knighton Medical Center (426 beds), 2600 Greenwood Rd., Shreveport 71103; 318/632-4600; James K. Elrod, pres.

Related: Willis-Knighton Med. Ctr., Shreveport, LA
Bunkie General Hospital, Bunkie, LA
Desota General, Hosp., Mansfield, LA
North Caddo Hosp. Svc. Dist., Vivian, LA
South Park Hosp., Shreveport, LA

Maine: Maine Medical Center (591 beds), 22 Bramhall St., Portland 04102; 207/871-0111; Edward C. Andrews Jr. M.D., pres.

Related: Maine Medical Ctr., Portland, ME
Main Coast Memorial Hosp., Ellsworth, ME
St. Joseph Hosp., Bangor, ME

Maryland: Johns Hopkins Health System (I859 beds),* 600 N. Wolfe St., Baltimore 21205; 301/955-5000; Robert M. Heyssel M.D., pres.

Massachusetts: The General Hospital Corp.-Massachusetts General Hospital (1082 beds), 32 Fruit St., Boston 02114; 617/726-2100; J. Robert Buchanan M.D., gen. dir.

Related: Massachusetts General Hosp., Boston, MA

Michigan: Butterworth Hospital (529 beds), 100 Michigan St. N.E., Grand Rapids 49503; 616/774-1774; William G. Gonzalez, pres.

Related: Memorial Medical Center, Ludington, MI
United Memorial, Greenville, MI

Henry Ford Health Care System (944 beds),* 2799 West Grand Blvd., Detroit 48202; 313/876-2600; Douglas S. Peters, pres.

Related: Henry Ford Hospital, Detroit, MI
Cottage Hospital of Grosse Point, Grosse Point Farms, MI

William Beaumont Hospital (III8 beds),* 3601 W. 13 Mile Rd., Royal Oak, MI 48072; 312/288-8000; Kenneth E. Myers, pres.

Minnesota: Lifespan, Inc.-Abott Northwestern Hospital (734 beds), 800 E. 28th St. at Chicago Ave., Minneapolis 55407; 612/874-4000; Gordon M. Sprenger, pres.

Related: Abbott-Northwestern Hosp., Minneapolis, MN
CHildren's Health Center, Minneapolis, MN

Mississippi: North Mississippi Health Services Inc. (585 beds), 830 S. Gloster St., Tupelo 38801; 601/841-3000; John D. Hicks, pres. & chief exec. off.

Related: North Miss. Medical Ctr., Tupelo, MS
Aberdeen-Monroe County Hosp., Aberdeen, MS
Clay County Medical Ctr., West Point, MS
Gilmore Memorial Hosp., Inc., Amory, MS
Golden Triangle Reg. Med. Ctr., Columbus, MS
Itawamba County Hosp., Fulton, MS
Magnolia Hospital, Corinth, MS
Marshall County Hosp., Holly Springs, MS
Noxubee General Hosp., Macon, MS
Okolona Comm. Hosp., Okolona, MS
Oxford-Lafayette County Hosp., Oxford, MS
Pontotoc Comm. Hosp. & Extended Care Facility, Pontotoc, MS
The Baldwyn Unit, Baldwyn, MS
Tippah County Hospital, Ripley, MS
Union City General Hosp., New Albany
Webster General Hosp., Eupora, MS

Missouri: Barnes Hospital (1054 beds), 4949 Barnes Hospital Plaza, St. Louis 63110; 314/362-5000; Max Poll, pres.

Lester E. Cox Medical Center (749 beds), 1423 N. Jefferson Ave., Springfield 65802; 417/836-3001; Charles M. Edwards, exec. admin.

St. Luke's Hospital of Kansas City (604 beds), Wornall Road at 44th St., Kansas City 64111; 816/932-2000; Charles C. Lindstrom, exec. vice-pres.

Nebraska: Methodist Hospital (667 beds), 8303 Dodge St., Omaha 68114; 402/390-4000; Stephen D. Long, pres.

New Hampshire: Mary Hitchcock Hospital (378 beds), 2 Maynard St., Hanover 03756; 603/646-7422; James W. Varnum, pres.

Related: Mary Hitchcock Memorial Hosp., Hanover, NH
Alice Peck Day Memorial, Lebanon, NH
Gifford Memorial Hosp., Randolph, VT
Mt. Ascutney Hosp. & Hlth. Ctr., Windsor

New Jersey: Memorial Hospital of Burlington County (322 beds), 175 Madison Ave., Mount Holly 08060; 609/267-0700; Geoffrey Stone, adm.

Related: Mem. Hosp. of Burlington Cty, Mt. Holly, NJ
Mount Holly Center, Mt. Holly, NJ
Southern Ocean Couunty Hosp., Manahawkin, NJ

New York: The Presbyterian Hospital in the City of New York (1291 beds), 622 W. 168th St., New York 10038; 212/305-2500; Thomas Q. Morris, M.D., pres.

Asterisk (*) = multihospital systems

The Society of the New York Hospital (1418 beds), 525 E. Sixty Eight St., New York, NY 10021; 212/472-5330; David D. Thompson, M.D., dir.

United Health Services, Inc. (526 hosp. beds, 100 nurs. home beds), Mitchell Avenue, Binghamton 13903; 607/771-2263; Gennaro J. Vasile, PhD, pres. & chief exec. off.

North Carolina: Carolina Medicorp, Inc. - Forsyth Memorial Hospital (695 beds), 3333 Silas Creek Pkwy., Winston-Salem 27103; 919/773-3000; Paul M. Wiles, pres.

Related: Forsyth County Hospital Authority Inc., Winston-Salem, NC
Hawthorne Surgical Center, Winston-Salem, NC

Charlotte Memorial Hospital and Medical Center, Inc. (843 beds), 1000 Blythe Blvd., (P.O. Box 32861, Charlotte, NC 28232) Charlotte 28203; 704/338-2000; Harry Nurkin, Ph.D., pres.

North Dakota: St. Luke's Hospitals of Fargo, Inc. (458 beds), Fifth Street No. & Mills Ave., Fargo 58122; 701/280-5100; Lloyd V. Smith, pres.

Ohio: Akron General Medical Center (394 beds), 400 Wabash Ave., Akron 44307; 216/384-6000; Michael A. West, pres.

Christ Hospital, Inc. (660 beds), 2139 Auburn Ave., Cincinnati 45219; 513/369-2000; Jack M. Cook, pres. & exec. dir.

Related: The Christ Hosp., Cincinnati, OH
Brown County General Hosp., Georgetown, OH

MedAmerica Health Systems Corporation (731 beds), One Wyoming St., Dayton 45409; 513/223-6192; L. R. Jordan, pres. & chief exec. off.

Related: Miami Valley Hosp., Dayton, OH

Toledo Hospital (720 beds), 2142 N. Core Blvd., Toledo 43606; 419/471-4218; Bryan A. Rogers, pres.

U. S. Health Corporation-Riverside Methodist Hospital (1790 beds), 3535 Olentangy River Rd., Columbus 43214; 614/261-5000; Erie Chapman, III, J.D., pres. & chief exec. off.

Related: Riverside Methodist Hosp., Columbus, OH
Hardin Memorial Hosp., Kenton, OH
Mercy Hospital, Portsmouth, OH
Morrow County Hosp., Mt. Gilead, OH
Southern Hills Hosp., Portsmouth, OH

Oklahoma: Hillcrest Medical Center (487 hosp. beds, 22 nurs. home beds), 1120 S. Utica, Tulsa 74104; 918/584-1351; John C. Goldthorpe, pres.

Oklahoma Health Care Corporation (504 beds), 3300 N.W. Expwy., Oklahoma City 73112; 405/949-3011; Stanley F. Hupfeld, pres.

Related: Baptist Med. Ctr. of Oklahoma, Oklahoma City, OK

Oregon: Good Samaritan Hospital and Medical Center (345 beds), 1015 N.W. 22nd Ave., Portland 97210; 503/229-7711; Chester L. Stocks, exec. vice-pres.

Related: Good Samaritan Hospital & Medical Ctr., Portland, OR
Forest Grove Community Hosp., Forest Grove, OR
St. Charles Medical Ctr., Bend, OR
Tuality Community Hosp. Inc., Hillsboro, OR
Williamette Falls Hosp., Oregon City, OR

Pennsylvania: Allegheny Health Services, Inc. (678 beds), 320 E. North Ave., Pittsburgh 15212; 412/359-3131; Sherif S. Abdelhak, pres.

Related: Allegheny General Hosp., Pittsburgh, PA

Pennsylvania Hospital Corporation (NP, 2 hosps., 674 beds),* Eighth and Spruce Sts., Philadelphia 19107; 215/829-3000; H. Robert Cathcart, pres.

Related: Pennsylvania Hospital, Philadelphia, PA
Institute of Pennsylvania Hospital, Philadelphia, PA

Guthrie Medical Center (NP, 3 hosps., 629 beds),* Guthrie Square, Sayre 18840; 717/888-6666; Ralph H. Meyer, pres.

Related: Guthrie Medical Ctr., Sayre, PA
Robert Packer Hosp., Sayre, PA
Tioga General Hosp., Waverly, NY
Troy Community Hosp., Troy, PA

Healtheast, Inc. (NP, 3 hosps., 965 beds),* 337 N. West St., Allentown 18102; 215/778-2950; David P. Buchmueller, pres.

Related: HealthEast, Inc., Allentown, PA
Gnaden Huetten, Lehighton, PA
Lehigh Valley Hosp. Ctr., Allentown, PA
The ALlentown Hosp., Allentown, PA

Rhode Island: Rhode Island Hospital (719 beds),* 593 Eddy St., Providence 02903; 401/277-4000; DeLanson Y. Hopkins, pres.

South Carolina: South Carolina Baptist Hospitals, Inc. (584 beds), 1333 Taylor St., Columbia 29201; 803/771-5042; William A. Boyce, pres.

Related: Baptist Med. Ctr. at Columbia, Columbia, SC
Easley Baptist Hosp., Easley, SC

South Dakota: Sioux Valley Hospital (456 beds), 1100 S. Euclid Ave., P.O. Box 5039; Sioux Falls 57117-5039; 605/333-1000; Lyle E. Schroeder, pres.

Related: Sioux Valley Hosp., Sioux Falls, SD
Arnold Memorial Hosp., Adrian, MN
Madison Hospital, Madison, WI

Tennessee: Baptist Hospital, Inc. (651 beds), 2000 Church St., Nashville, 37203; 615/329-5555, C. David Stringfield, pres.

Related: Baptist Hospital, Inc., Nashville, TN
Cookeville General Hosp., Cookeville, TN
Cumberland Medical Center, Crossville, TN
Goodlark Med. Ctr., Inc., Dickson, TN
Hickman County Hospital & Nursing Home, Centerville, TN
Jennie Stuart Med. Ctr., Hopkinsville, KY
Jesse Holman Jones Hosp., Springfield, TN
Maury County Hosp., Columbia, TN
Memorial Hospital, Clarksville, TN
Middle Tennessee Med. Ctr. Inc., Murfreesboro, TN
Williamson County Hosp., Franklin, TN

Baptist Memorial Hospital (1669 beds), 899 Madison Ave., Memphis 38146; 901/522-5252; Joseph H. Powell, pres.

Related: Baptist Memorial Hosp., Memphis, TN
Baptist Mem. Hosp.-Booneville, Booneville, MS
Baptist Mem. Hosp.-Huntington, Huntingdon, TN
Baptist Mem. Hosp.-E. Ozarks, Hardy, AR
Bapt. Mem. Hosp.-Forrest City, Forrest City, AR
Baptist Mem. Hosp.-Lauderdale, Ripley, TN
Baptist Mem. Hosp.-Tipton, Covington, TN
Baptist Mem. Hosp.-Union City, Union City, TN
Greenwood LeFlore Hosp., Greenwood, MS
Hardin County General Hosp., Savannah, TN
Mississippi County Hosp. Sys., Blytheville, AR

Fort Sanders Alliance (575 beds), 1901 Clinch Ave., S.W., Knoxville 37916; 615/522-2149; E. B. Copeland, pres.

Related: Fort Sanders Reg. Med. Ctr., Knoxville, TN
Harriman City Hosp., Harriman, TN
Holston Val. Hosp Med Ctr, Inc, Kingsport, TN
Johnson City Med. Ctr. Hosp., Johnson City, TN
Oak Ridge Medical Ctr., Oak Ridge, TN
Sevier Medical Ctr., Sevierville, TN

Texas: All Saints Espiscopal Hospital of Fort Worth (446 beds), 1400 Eighth Ave., Fort Worth 76104; Mailing Address: P.O. Box 31, zip 76101; 817/926-2544; Robert Ford, acting chief exec. off.

Baylor Health Care System (NP, 6 hosps., 1711 beds),* 3500 Gaston Ave., Dallas 75246; 214/820-0111; Boone Powell Jr., pres.

Related: Baylor University Medical Ctr., Dallas, TX
American British Cowdray, Mexico City, MX
Baylor Inst. for Rehab., Dallas, TX
Baylor Medical Ctr. at Ennis, Ennis, TX
Baylor Med. Ctr. at Grapevine, Grapevine, TX
Baylor Med. Ctr. at Waxahachie, Waxahachie, TX
Baylor Medical Ctr. at Gilmer, Gilmer, TX
Children's Med. Ctr. of Dallas, Dallas, TX
Gaston Episcopal Hosp., Dallas, TX
King Edward VII Mem. Hosp., Paget, BM
Memorial Hospital, Marshall, TX
Memorial Hospital of Gardland, Garland, TX
St. Brendan's Psych. Hosp., Devonshire, BM

Asterisk (*) = multihospital systems

Memorial Hospital System (1445 beds), 7777 Southwest Freeway, Suite 252, Houston 77074; 713/776-5100; Dan S. Wilford, pres.

Related: Memorial Southwest, Houston, TX
Memorial Northwest, Houston, TX
Memorial Southeast, Houston, TX
El Campo Memorial Hosp., El Campo, TX
Matagorda General Hosp. Dist., Bay City, TX
Northeast Medical Ctr. Hosp., Humble, TX
Polly Ryon Memorial Hosp., Richmond, TX

Methodist Hospital (549 beds), 3615 19th St., Lubbock 79410; Mailing Address: P.O. Box 1201; zip 79408; 806/792-1011; William D. Poteet III, pres.

Utah: St. Mark's Hospital (306 beds), 1200 East 3900 South, Salt Lake City 84124; 801/268-7077; T.J. Hartford Jr., admin.

Vermont: Medical Center Hospital of Vermont (459 hosp. beds, 42 nurs. home beds), 111 Colchester Ave., Burlington 05401; 802/656-2345; James H. Taylor, pres.

Virginia: Alliance Health System (NP, 2 hosps., 894 beds),* 18 Koger Exec. Ctr., Suite 202, Norfolk, 23502; 804/628-3000; Glen R. Mitchell, pres.

Related: Medical Center Hosp., Norfolk, VA
Leigh Memorial Hosp.
Norfolk General Hosp.

Washington: Medlantic Healthcare Group (NP, 3 hosps., 1223 beds),* 100 Irving St., N.W., Washington 20010; 202/541-6006; John P. McDaniel, pres.

Related: Washington Hospital Ctr., Washington, DC
Capitol Hill Hosp., Washington, DC
Melwood Farm, Olney, MD
National Rehab. Hosp., Washington, DC

Empire Health Services (621 beds),* West 800 Fifth Ave., Spokane 99204; 509/458-7965; Jon K. Mitchell, pres. & chief exec. off.

Related: Empire Health Services, Spokane, WA
Deaconess Medical Ctr., Spokane, WA
St. Luke's Memorial Hosp., Spokane, WA
Valley Hospital & Memorial Ctr., Spokane, WA

Multicare Medical Center-Tacoma General Hospital (368 beds),* 409 South J St., P.O. Box 5277, Tacoma 98405; 206/594-1250; Barry Connoley, chief exec. off.

Related: Tecoma General Hosp., Tecoma, WA

West Virginia: Camcare, Inc. (934 beds),* Brooks & Washington Steets, P.O. Box 1547, Charleston 25326; 304/348-6200; James C. Crews, pres.

Related: Healthnet (Charleston Area Med. Ctr.), Charleston, WV
Braxton County Mem. Hosp., Gassaway, WV
Kanawha Valley Division, Charleston, WV
West Virginia Univ. Hosp., Morgantown, WV

Wisconsin: General Health Services, Inc. (643 beds), 202 South Park St., Madison 53715; 608/255-9811; Gordon N. Johnsen, pres.

St. Luke's Samaritan Health Care, Inc. (557 beds), 3000 W. Mountana Ave., Milwaukee 53215-3628; 414/645-3000; G. Edwin Howe, pres.

Related: St. Luke's Hospital, Milwaukee, WI
Good Samaritan Hosp., Milwaukee, WI

VHA REGIONAL HEALTH CARE SYSTEMS

VHA Alabama

Shareholder Sponsors: Baptist Health Svcs. Corp.
Baptist Medical Center
Gulf Health, Inc.

Alabama

Baptist Health Services, Gadsden
Cullman Medical Center, Cullman
DCH Healthcare Authority, Tuscaloosa
Decatur General Hospital, Decatur
Eliza Coffee Memorial Hosp., Florence
Homer D. Cobb Memorial Hosp., Phenix City
Huntsville Hospital, Huntsville
Jackson County Hosp. Board, Scottsboro
Marshall County Healthcare Authority, Arab
Regional Health Services, Inc., Anniston

VHA Carolinas

Shareholder Sponsors: Carolina Medicorp, Inc.
Charlotte Memorial Hospital and Medical Centers, Inc.
South Carolina Baptist Hospital, Inc.
Fort Sanders Alliance

North Carolina/South Carolina

Nash General Hospital, Rocky Mount, NC
Roper Hospital, Charleston, SC
Wake County Hospital Sys., Inc., Raleigh, NC
Wesley Long Comm. Hosp., Inc., Greensboro, NC

VHA Central

Shareholder Sponsors: Akron General Hospital
Medamerica Health Sys. Corp.
The Christ Hospital
The Toledo Hospital
U.S. Health Corporation

Ohio

Ashtabula County Med. Ctr., Ashtabula
Aultman Hospital, Canton
Bethesda Hospital, Zanesville
Blanchard Valley Hospital, Findlay
Community Hosp. of Springfield and Clark County, Springfield
Elyria Memorial Hospital, Elyria
Fairview General Hospital, Cleveland
Ft. Hamilton-Hughes Mem. Hosp. Ctr., Hamilton
Greene Memorial Hospital, Xenia
Guernsey Memorial Hospital, Cambridge
Lake Hospital Systems, Inc., Willoughby
Lima Memorial Hospital, Lima
Mansfield General Hospital, Mansfield
Marymount Hospital, Garfield Heights
Memorial Hospital, Fremont
Middletown Regional Hospital, Middletown
Ohio Valley Regional, Steubenville
Sciota Memorial Hospital, Portsmouth
St. Luke Hospital, Ft. Thomas
St. Luke's Hospital, Maumee
Trumbull Memorial Hospital, Warren
Union Hospital, Dover
University Hosp. of Cleveland, Cleveland
Western Reserve Care System, Youngstown

VHA East

Shareholder Sponsors: Healtheast, Inc.
Pennsylvania Hospital

Pennsylvania

Berkshire Health System, W. Reading
Chester County Hospital, West Chester
Chestnut Hill Hospital, Philadelphia
Crozer-Chester Medical Ctr., Chester
Episcopal Hospital, Philadelphia
Frankford Health Care Sys., Inc., Philadelphia
Jeanes Hospital, Philadelphia
Montgomery Hospital, Norristown

VHA Florida

Shareholder Sponsors: Baptist Reg. Health Serv.
Holmes Regional Healthcare Systems, Inc.
Lakeland Regional Med. Ctr.
Orlando Reg. Med. Ctr.
Santa Fe Healthcare System, Inc.
Tallahassee Memorial
Regional Medical Ctr.

Florida

All Children's Hospital, Inc., St. Petersburg
Bay Medical Center, Panama City
Bayfront Med. Ctr., Inc., St. Petersburg
Bethesda Mem. Hosp., Inc., Boynton Beach
Boca Raton Comm. Hosp., Inc., Boca Raton
Citrus Memorial Hospital, Inverness
Good Samaritan Hospital, W. Palm Beach
Halifax Hospital Med. Ctr., Daytona Beach
Lake County Health Care Sys., Eustis

Asterisk (*) = multihospital systems

Lee Memorial Hospital, Ft. Myers
Martin Mem. Hosp. Assoc., Inc., Stuart
Mease Health Care, Safety Harbor
Memorial Hospital, Hollywood
Methodist Hospital, Jacksonville
Miami Heart Institute, Inc., Miami Beach
Munroe Regional Med. Ctr., Ocala
North Brevard Cty. Hosp. Dist., Titusville
North Shore Medical Ctr., Inc., Miami
South Miami Hospital, South Miami
St. Luke's Hospital, Jacksonville
Venice Hospital, Venice

VHA Georgia
Shareholder Sponsor: Piedmont Hospital

Georgia
Hospital Auth. of Clark County, Athens
Candler Health Services, Inc., Savannah
Cobb General Hospital, Austell
Dalton Whitfield County Hospital, Dalton
Dekalb General Hospital, Decatur
Floyd Medical Center, Rome
Gwinnett Hospital System, Lawrenceville
John D. Archbold Mem. Hosp., Thomasville
Kennestone Regional Healthcare, Marietta
Macon-Bibb County Hosp. Authority, Macon
*Murphy Medical Center, Murphy
Northeast Georgia Med. Ctr., Gainesville
Phoebe Putney Memorial Hosp., Albany
South Fulton Hospital, East Point
South Georgia Medical Ctr., Valdosta
The Medical Ctr. Hospital Authority, Columbus
*Towns Cty. Hosp. and Nursing Home, Hiawassee

VHA Gulf States
Shareholder Sponsors: North Miss. Medical Ctr.
Ochsner Foundation Hospital
Our Lady of the Lake Regional Medical Center
Willis-Knighton Med. Ctr.

Louisiana/Mississippi
*Beauregard Memorial Hospital, DeRidder, LA
*Catahoula Memorial Hospital, Jonesville, LA
Forrest County Gen. Hospital, Hattiesburg, MS
Jeff Anderson Reg. Med. Ctr., Meridian, MS
Lake Charles Memorial Hosp., Lake Charles, LA

Memorial Hospital of Gulfport, Gulfport, MS
Our Lady of the Lourdes Reg. Med. Ctr., Inc., Lafayette, LA
Acadia- St. Landry Hosp., Church Point, LA
Pendleton Mem. Method. Hosp., New Orleans, LA
Rapides General Hospital, Alexandria, LA
Singing River Hospital System, Pascagoula, MS
Southwest Reg. Med. Ctr., McComb, MS
St. Dominic-Jackson Mem. Hosp., Jackson, MS
St. Francis Med. Ctr., Inc., Monroe, LA

VHA Illinois
Shareholder Sponsors: Decatur Memorial Hospital
Memorial medical Center

Illinois
Alton Memorial Hospital, Alton
Bromenn Healthcare, Normal
Blessing Hospital, Quincy
Burnham Hospital, Champaign
Lakeview Medical Center, Danville
Lutheran Hospital, Moline
McDonough County Dist. Hosp., Macomb
Memorial Hospital, Belleville
Passavant Area Hospital, Jacksonville
Pekin Memorial Hospital, Pekin
Southern Illinois Hosp. Serv., Carbondale

VHA Iowa
Shareholder Sponsor: St. Luke's Methodist Hospital

Iowa
Burlington Medical Center, Burlington
Covenant Medical Center, Inc., Waterloo
Delaware County Mem. Hospital, Manchester
Floyd County Memorial Hospital, Charles City
Grinnell General Hospital, Grinnell
Henry County Health Center, Mt. Pleasant
Jackson County Public Hosp., Maquoketa
Jane Lamb Health Center, Clinton
Jefferson County Hospital, Fairfield
Ottumwa Reg. Health Center, Ottumwa
Sartori Memorial Hospital, Cedar Falls
St. Luke's Hospital, Davenport
The Finley Hospital, Dubuque
Trinity Reg. Hospital, Fort Dodge

VHA Massachusetts
Shareholder Sponsor: The General Hospital Corp.

Massachusetts
Beverly Hospital, Beverly
Burbank Hospital, Fitchburg
Cape Cod Hospital, Inc., Hyannis
Emerson Hospital, Concord
Lawrence General Hospital, Lawrence
Lawrence Mem. Hosp. of Medford, Inc., Medford
Lowell General Hospital, Lowell
Neponset Valley Health Sys., Norwood
Newton-Wellesley Hospital, Newton
South Shore Hosp., Inc., South Weymouth
St. Anne's Hospital Corporation, Fall River
St. Vincent Healthcare Sys., Inc., Worchester

VHA Metro New York
Shareholder Sponsors: The Society of the New York Hospitals
The Presbyterian Hospital in the City of New York

New York
Bronx-Lebanon, Bronx
Catholic Medical Center of Brooklyn & Queens, Inc., Brooklyn
Mercy Hospital, Rockville Center
New Rochelle Hospital, New Rochelle
Northern Westchester Hospital, Mount Kisco
Southampton Hospital, Bayshore
St. Barnabas Hospital, Bronx
The Brooklyn Hosp.-Caledonian Hosp., Brooklyn
The Church Charity Foundation of Long Island, Brooklyn
White Plains Hospital Med. Ctr., White Plains

VHA Michigan
Shareholder Sponsors: Butterworth Hospital
Henry Ford Hospital
William Beaumont Hospital

Michigan
Bay Medical Center, Bay City
Bronson Healthcare Group, Inc., Kalamazoo
Community Assoc., Battle Creek
Emma L. Bixby, Adrian
Holland Community Hospital, Holland
Ingham Medical Center, Lansing
McPherson Hospital, Howell
Mercy Memorial Health Corp., Benton Harbor
Northern Michigan Hospital, Petoskey
Oakwood Hospital, Dearborn
Port Huron Hospital, Port Huron
Saginaw General Hospital, Saginaw
St. Clair Health Corporation, Detroit
St. Joseph Health Sys., Inc., Flint
*Traverse City Osteopathic Hosp., Traverse City

VHA Mid America
Shareholder Sponsors: Barnes Hospital
St. Luke's Hosp. of Kansas City
Stormont-Vail Reg. Medical Center
Lester E. Cox Medical Ctr.

Kansas/Missouri/Iowa
Bethany Medical Center, Kansas City, KS
Farmington Community Hospital, Farmington, MO
Boone Hospital Center, Columbia, MO
Cameron Community Hospital, Cameron, MO
Freeman Hospital, Joplin, MO
Independence Reg. Hlth. Ctr., Independence, MO
Keokuk Area Hospital, Keokuk, IA
McCune-Brooks Hospital, Carthage, MO
Spelman Memorial Hospital, Smithville, MO
St. Francis Medical Center, Cape Girardeau, MO

*Regional Health Care System Affiliate

VHA Mid-Atlantic
Shareholder Sponsors: Alliance Health System
HealthNet, Inc.

West Virginia/Virginia/Maryland/N. Carolina/Delaware
Cabell Huntington Hospital, Huntington, WV
Children's Hospital of the King's Daughters, Inc., Norfolk, VA
Comm. Hosp. of Roanoke Valley, Roanoke, VA
Hartford Memorial Hospital, Havre de Grace, MO
Lynchburg Gen. Marshall Lodge Hospitals, Inc. Lynchburg, VA
Martha Jefferson Hospital, Charlottesville, VA
Mary Washington Hospital, Fredericksburg, VA
Milford Memorial Hosp., Inc., Milford, DE
Montgomery General Health Care Services, Montgomery, WV
Prince William Hospital Corp., Manassas, VA
Princeton Community Hospital, Princeton, WV
Radford Comm. Hospital, Inc., Radford, VA
Roanoke-Chowan Hospital, Inc., Ahoski, NC
Rockingham Memorial Hospital, Harrisburg, VA
Southhampton Memorial Hospital, Franklin, VA
St. Joseph's Hospital, Parkersburg, WV
The Alexandria Hospital, Alexandria, VA
The Fauquier Hospital, Inc., Warrenton, VA
The Memorial Hospital at Easton Maryland, Inc., Easton, MD
The Sheppard and Enoch Pratt Hospital, Baltimore, MD

VHA Midlands
Shareholder Sponsor: Nebraska Methodist Hosp.

Iowa/Nebraska
Beatrice Community Hospital, Beatrice, NE
Bryan Memorial Hospital, Lincoln, NE
Cass County Memorial Hospital, Altantic, IA
Children's Memorial Hospital, Omaha, NE
Jennie Edmundson Mem. Hosp., Council Bluffs, IA
Lutheran Community Hospital, Norfolk, NE
Mary Lanning Memorial Hosp., Hastings, NE
St. Luke's Reg. Med. Ctr., Sioux City, IA

VHA Mid-West
Shareholder Sponsors: Evanston Hospital Corp.
Ingalls Memorial Hospital
St. Luke's Samaritan Health Care, Inc.
Northwestern Memorial Group

Illinois/Wisconsin
Columbia Hospital, Milwaukee, WI
Com. Mem. Hosp. of Menomonee Falls, Inc., Menomonee Falls, WI
Elmhurst Memorial Hospital, Elmhurst, IL
Freeport Memorial Hospital, Freeport, IL
Katherine Shaw Bethea Hospital, Dixon, IL
Kenosha Memorial Hosp., Inc., Kenosha, WI
Kishwaukee Community Hospital, Dekalb, IL
Lake Forest Hospital, Lake Forest, IL
Macneal Hospital, Berwyn, IL
Ravenswood Hospital Med. Ctr., Chicago, IL
Riverside Medical Center, Kankakee, IL
Rockford Memorial Hospital, Rockford, IL
Rush-Presbyterian St. Luke's Medical Center, Chicago, IL
Sherman Hospital, Elgin, IL
Silver Cross Hospital Corp., Joliet, IL
St. Luke's Mem. Hosp., Inc., Racine, IL
Waukesha Hospital Sys., Inc., Waukesha, WI

VHA Mountain States
Shareholder Sponsors: St. Mark's Hospital
St. Luke's Hospital
Swedish Medical Center

Colorado/Idaho/Nebraska/Montana/Wyoming/New Mexico
Aspen Valley Hospital, Aspen, CO
Arkansas Valley Reg. Med. Ctr., La Junta, CO
Bannock Reg. Med. Ctr., Pocatello, ID
Bethesda Hospital Assn., Denver, CO
Bonner General Hospital, Sandpoint, ID
Boulder Community Hospital, Boulder, CO
*Cheyenne County Hospital Assoc., Sidney, NE
Community Hospital, Grand Junction, CO
Craig Hospital, Englewood, CO
Deaconess Medical Ctr. of Billings, Inc., Billings, MT
Hot Springs Memorial Hosp., Thermopolis, WY
Idaho Elks Rehab. Hosp., Boise, ID
Ivinson Memorial Hospital, Laramie, WY
Kootenai Medical Center, Coeur D'Alene, ID
Longmont United Hospital, Longmont, CO
Memorial Hospital, Colorado Springs, CO
Memorial Hosp. of Laramie Co., Cheyenne, WY
Memorial Hosp. of Sheridan Cty., Sheridan, WY
Montana Deaconess Med. Ctr., Great Falls, MT
Montrose Memorial Hospital, Montrose, CO
Moritz Community Hospital, Sun Valley, ID
Poudre Valley Hospital, Ft. Collins, CO
Routt Memorial Hospital, Steamboat Springs, CO
San Juan Regional Med. Ctr., Farmington, NM
Spalding Rehabilitation Hospital, Denver, CO
St. Benedict's Family Med. Ctr., Jerome, ID
West Nebraska General Hosp., Scottsbluff, NE
Wyoming Medical Center, Casper, WY

VHA New England
Shareholder Sponsors: Maine Medical Center
Mary Hitchcock Mem. Hosp.
Med. Ctr. Hospital of Vermont

Maine/Vermont
Central Vermont Medical Ctr., Berlin, VT
Central Maine Medical Center, Lewiston, ME
Concord Hospital, Corcord, NH
Elliott Hospital, Manchester, NH
Frisbie Memorial Hospital, Rochester, NH
Kennebec Valley Medical Ctr., Augusta, ME
Mid-Maine Medical Center, Waterville, ME
Nashua Memorial Hospital, Nashua, NH
Rutland Regional Medical Ctr., Rutland, VT
Southwestern Med. Ctr. of VT, Bennington, VT
The Aroostook Medical Ctr., Presque Isle, ME

VHA New Jersey
Shareholder Sponsor: Memorial Hospital of Burlington County

New Jersey
Atlantic City Medical Center, Atlantic City
Bridgeton Hospital, Bridgeton
Chilton Memorial Hospital, Pompton Plains
Christ Hospital, Jersey City
Clara Maass Medical Center, Belleville
Community Memorial Hospital, Toms River
Dover General Hosp. & Med. Ctr., Dover
Elizabeth General Med. Ctr., Elizabeth
Jersey Shore Medical Center, Neptune
*Millville Hospital, Millville
Muhlenberg Hospital, Plainfield
St. Peter's Medical Center, New Brunswick
Underwood-Memorial Hospital, Woodbury
Warren Hospital, Phillipsburg

VHA North Central
Shareholder Sponsors: Lifespan, Inc.
Sioux Valley Hospital
St. Luke's Hospitals of Fargo

Minnesota/North Dakota
*Arlington Municipal Hospital, Arlington, MN
*Comfrey Hospital, Comfrey, MN
Immanuel-St. Joseph Hospital, Mankato, MN
Jamestown Hospital, Jamestown, ND
Lake Region Hosp. & Nursing Home, Fergus Falls, MN
*Lakefield Municipal Hospital, Lakefield, MN
*Madelia Community Hospital, Madelia, MN
Medcenter One, Inc., Bismark, ND
*Mountain Lake Comm. Hospital, Mt. Lake, MN
North Country Hospital, Bemidji, MN
*Paynesville Community Hosp., Paynesville, MN
*Redwood Falls Municipal Hosp., Red Falls, MN
Rice Memorial Hospital, Willmare, MN
St. Cloud Hospital, St. Cloud, MN
St. Luke's Hospital of Duluth, Duluth, MN
*St. Peter Community Hospital, St. Peter, MN
*Stevens Comm. Mem. Hosp., Inc., Morris, MN
*Springfield Community Hosp., Springfield, MN
Trinity Medical Center, Minot, ND
United Health Services, Grand Forks, ND
Waconia Ridgeview Hospital, Waconia, MN
*Watonman Memorial Hospital, St. James, MN
*Weiner Memorial Medical Ctr., Marshall, MN
*Windom Area Hospital, Windom, MN

*Regional Health Care System Affiliate

VHA Northern California
Shareholder Sponsors: Alta Bates Corporation
Pacific Presbyterian
San Jose Health Center
Sutter Health System

California
John Muir Memorial Hospital, Walnut Creek, CA
Marin General Hospital, Greenbrae, CA
Mills-Peninsula Hospitals
St. Joseph's Hosp. of Stockton, Stockton, CA

VHA Oklahoma
Shareholder Sponsors: Hillcrest Medical Center
Oklahoma Helth Care Gorp.
(Baptist Medical Center)

Oklahoma
Baptist Regional Health Ctr., Miami, OK
Bass Memorial Baptist Hosp., Enid, OK
Deaconess Hospital, Oklahoma City, OK
Duncan Regional Hospital, Inc., Duncan, OK
Jackson County Memorial Hosp., Altus, OK
Jane Phillips Episcopal Hosp, Bartlesville, OK
LeFlore County Memo. Hosp. Auth., Poteau, OK
McAlester Reg. Hospital, McAlester, OK
Memorial Hosp. of Southern OK, Ardmore, OK
Midwest City Memorial Hosp., Midwest City, OK
Muskogee Regional Med Ctr., Muskogee, OK
Norman Regional Hospital, Norman, OK
Valley View Regional Hospital, Ada, OK

VHA Pennsylvania
Shareholder Sponsors: Allegheny Health Services, Inc.
Guthrie Medical Center

Pennsylvania/West Virginia
Allegheny Valley Hospital, Natrona Heights, PA
Altoona Hospital, Altoona, PA
Butler Area Health, Resources Development Corporaton, Butler, PA
Community Medical Center, Scranton, PA
Conemaugh Valley Memorial Hosp., Johnstown, PA
D. T. Watson Rehab. Hospital, Sewickley, PA
Hamot Health Systems, Inc., Erie, PA
Harrisburg Hospital, Harrisburg, PA
Lancaster General Hospital, Lancaster, PA
Latrobe Area Hospital, Latrobe, PA
Sewickley Valley Hospital, Sewickley, PA
Shadyside Hospital, Pittsburgh, PA
South Hills Health System, Pittsburgh, PA
St. Clair Memorial Hospital, Pittsburgh, PA
St. Margaret Memorial Hospital, Pittsburgh, PA
The Uniontown Hospital, Uniontown, PA
The Washington Hospital, Washington, PA
The Williamsport Hospital, Williamsport, PA
Wheeling Hospital, Wheeling, WV
Wilkes-Barre General Hosp., Wilkes-Barre, PA

VHA Southern New England
Shareholder Sponsors: Hartford Hospital
Yale-New Haven Health Service Corporation

Connecticut
Bridgeport Hospital, Bridgeport
Day Kimball Hospital, Putnam
Lawrence & Memorial Hospital, New London
Manchester Memorial Hospital, Manchester
Middlesex Memorial Hospital, Middletown
New Britain General Hospital, New Britain
Norwalk Hospital, Norwalk
Stamford Hospital, Stamford
The Charlotte Hungerford Hosp., Torrington
The Danbury Hospital, Danbury
The Gaylord Hospital, Willingford
The Greenwich General Hospital, Greenwich
The Institute of Living, Hartford
The Meriden-Wallingford Hosp., Meriden
The Waterbury Hospital, Waterbury

VHA Southwest
Shareholder Sponsors: All Saints Episcopal Hosp.
Baylor Health Care System
Memorial Hospital System
Methodist Hospital

Texas
Arlington Memorial Hospital, Arlington
Baptist Memorial Hosp. Sys., San Antonio
High Plains Baptist Hospital, Amarillo
Hillcrest Baptist Medical Ctr., Waco
Irving Community Hospital, Irving
King's Daughters Hospital, Temple
Midland Memorial Hospital, Midland
Mother Frances Hospital, Tyler
Providence Memorial Hospital, El Paso
Richardson Medical Center, Inc., Richardson
Shannon West Texas Memorial Hosp., San Angelo
St. David's Community Hosp., Austin
The Baptist Hospital, Beaumont
Valley Baptist Medical Center, Harlingen
Wadley Regional Medical Center, Texarkana
Wilson N. Jones Memorial Hosp., Sherman

VHA Tri-State
Shareholder Sponsors: Ball Memorial Hospital
Community Hosp. of IN
Deaconess Hosp., Inc.
Memorial Health System
NKC, Inc.

Indiana/Kentucky
Bartholomew County Hosp., Columbus, IN
Bloomington Hospital, Bloomington, IN
Comm. Hosp. of Anderson-Madison County, Inc., Anderson, IN
Comm. Methodist Hospital, Henderson, KY
Elkhart General Hospital, Elkhart, IN
Floyd Memorial Hospital, New Albany, IN
Lafayette Home Hospital, Lafayette, IN
La Porte Hospital, Inc., La Porte, IN
Marion General Hospital, Marion, IN
Parkview Memorial Hospital, Fort Wayne, IN
Porter Memorial Hospital, Valparaiso, IN
The Regional Medical Center of Hopkins County, Madisonville, KY

VHA Upstate New York
Shareholder Sponsors: Guthrie Medical Center
United Health Services

New York
Crouse Irving Memorial Hosp., Syracuse
DeGraff Memorial Hospital, No. Tonawanda
Geneva General Hospital, Geneva
Highland Hosp. of Rochester, Rochester
Mary Imogene Bassett Hospital, Cooperstown
Park Ridge Hospital, Rochester
Samaritan Hospital, Troy
The House of the Good Samaritan, Watertown
The Woman's Christian Assoc. of Jamestown, Jamestown
Tompkins Community Hospital, Ithaca
United Hospital, Port Chester
Vassar Brothers Hospital, Poughkeepsie

VHA West
Shareholder Sponsors: Cedars-Sinai Medical Ctr.
Community Hosp. of Central CA
Hoag Mem. Hosp. Presbyterian
Memorial Med. Ctr. Long Beach
Scripps Memorial Hospital
Valley Presbyterian Hospital

California
Anaheim Memorial Hospital, Anaheim
Antelope Valley Hosp. Med. Ctr., Lancaster
Emanuel Medical Center, Inc., Turlock
Greater Bakersfield Mem. Hosp., Bakersfield
Grossmont District Hospital, La Mesa
Memorial Hospital Association, Modesto
Pasadena Hospital Assoc., Ltd., Pasadena
Pomona Valley Community Hospital, Pomona
Presbyterian Inter-Comm. Hosp., Whittier
Queen of the Valley Hospital, West Covina
Riverside Community Hospital, Riverside
San Pedro Peninsula Hospital, San Pedro
Torrance Memorial Hospital Med. Ctr., Torrance

VHA Wisconsin
Shareholder Sponsor: Madison General Hospital

Wisconsin/Minnesota

Beaver Dam Community Hosp., Beaver Dam, WI
Calumet Memorial Hospital, Chilton, WI
LaCrosse Lutheran Hospital, LaCrosse, WI
Lakeview Medical Center, Inc. of Rice Lake, Rice Lake, WI
Memorial Hosp. of Taylor Co., Medford, WI
New London Family Med. Ctr., New London, WI
Shawano Community Hospital, Shawano, WI
St. Joseph's Hospital, West Bend, WI
Watertown Memorial Hospital, Watertown, WI

Totals: 95 shareholders
29 regional partnerships
686 total hospitals
160,572 total beds

YANKEE ALLIANCE

16 Haverhill St., Andover, MA 01810; 617/470-2000; R. Paul O'Neill, pres.

Connecticut: Hospital of St. Raphael (441 beds), 1450 Chapel St., New Haven 06511; 203/789-3000; Robert T. Beeman, pres.

Maine: Eastern Maine Medical Center (409 beds), 489 State St., Bangor 04401; 207/947-3711; Robert Brandow, pres.

Massachusetts: New England Deaconess Hospital (489 beds), 185 Pilgrim Rd., Boston 02215; 617/732-7000; Laurens McClure, pres.

Charlton Memorial Hospital Foundation (383 beds), 363 Highland Ave., Fall River 02720; 617/679-3131; Frederic C. Dreyer, Jr., pres.

Farmington Union Hospital (311 beds), 225 Turnpike Rd., Framingham 01772; 617/879-7111; James W. Walckner, exec. vice pres.

Intercare Health System-Leominster (118 beds), Hospital Rd., Leominster 01453; 617/537-4811; Carl Wathne, pres.

Intercare Health System-Worcester (315 beds), 10 Oak Ave., Worchester 01605; 617/793-6611; David A. Barrett, pres.

St. John's Hospital (254 beds), Hospital Dr., Lowell 01853; 617/458-1411; Sr. Maria Loyola, pres.

Berkshire Health Systems (369 beds), 725 North St., Pittsfield 01210; 413/499-4161; John C. Johnson, pres.

Salem Hospital (342 beds), 81 Highland Ave., Salem 01970; 617/I741-1200; Michael J. Geaney, Jr., pres.

Winchester Hospital (223 beds), 41 Highland Ave., Winchester 01890; 617/729-9000; Eugene E. Loubier, pres.

New York: Glens Falls Hospital (408 beds), 100 Park St., Glens Falls 12801; 518/792-3151; William E. Philion, pres.

Totals: 12 hospitals
4062 beds

Maps

Introduction

Section C of the 1987 *AHA Guide* presents a series of maps depicting the distribution of cities with hospitals in the United States.

The first 51 maps in this section show the location of cities with one or more hospitals in each of the 50 states and Puerto Rico. The number of hospitals in each city is indicated by the number in the dark circle beside each city name. The listing of hospitals in section A serves as a legend for these maps. Please refer to section A for more complete hospital data including mailing addresses. (In case of inconsistency between the maps and section A, the information in section A should be taken as correct.)

20 metropolitan area maps begin on page C57. These maps follow the same format as the state maps. Only those cities in the metropolitan area with one or more hospitals are shown. As with the state maps, please refer to section A for more information on the hospitals within these metropolitan areas.

Map Index

Alabama

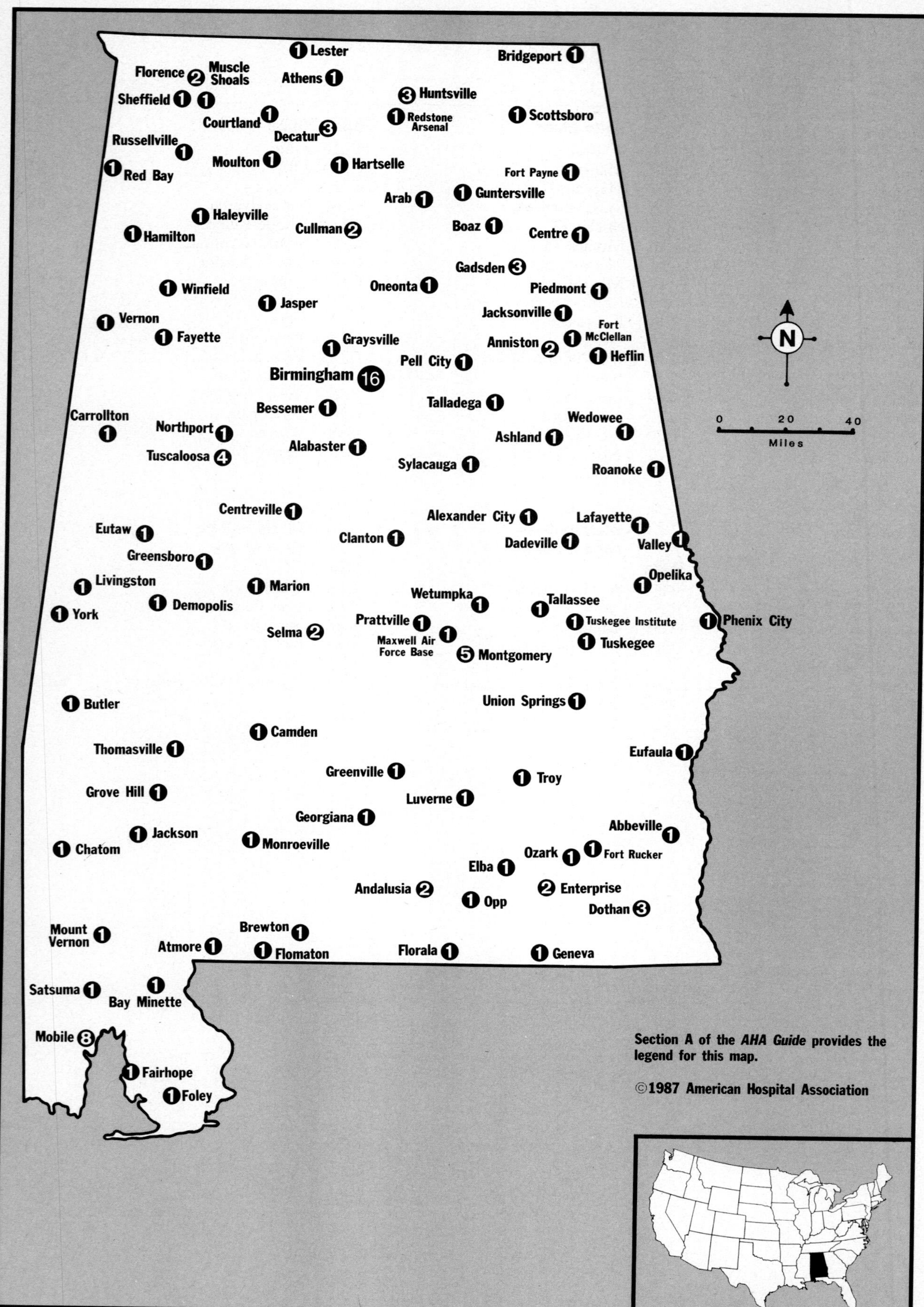

Section A of the *AHA Guide* provides the legend for this map.

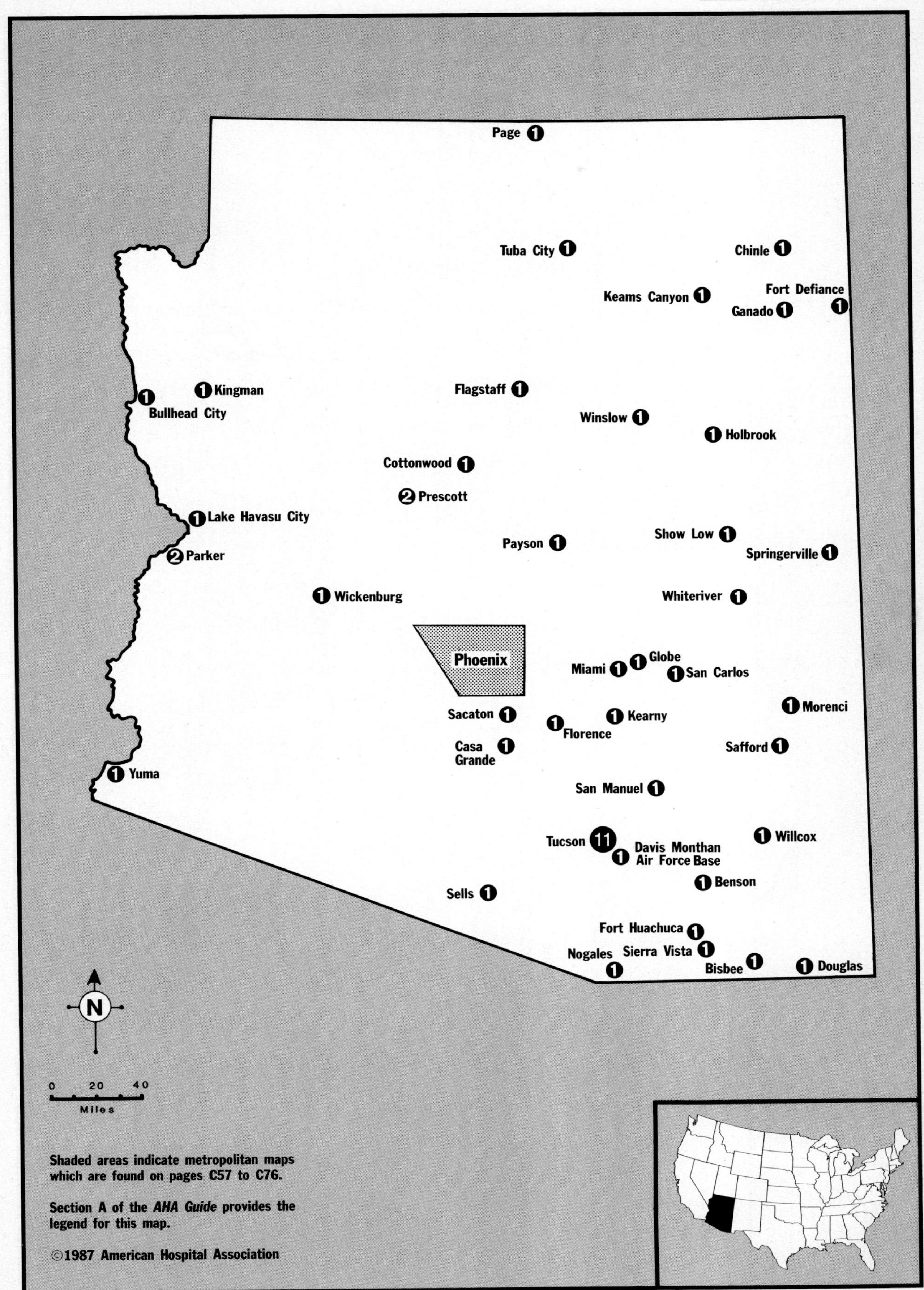

Shaded areas indicate metropolitan maps which are found on pages C57 to C76.

Section A of the *AHA Guide* provides the legend for this map.

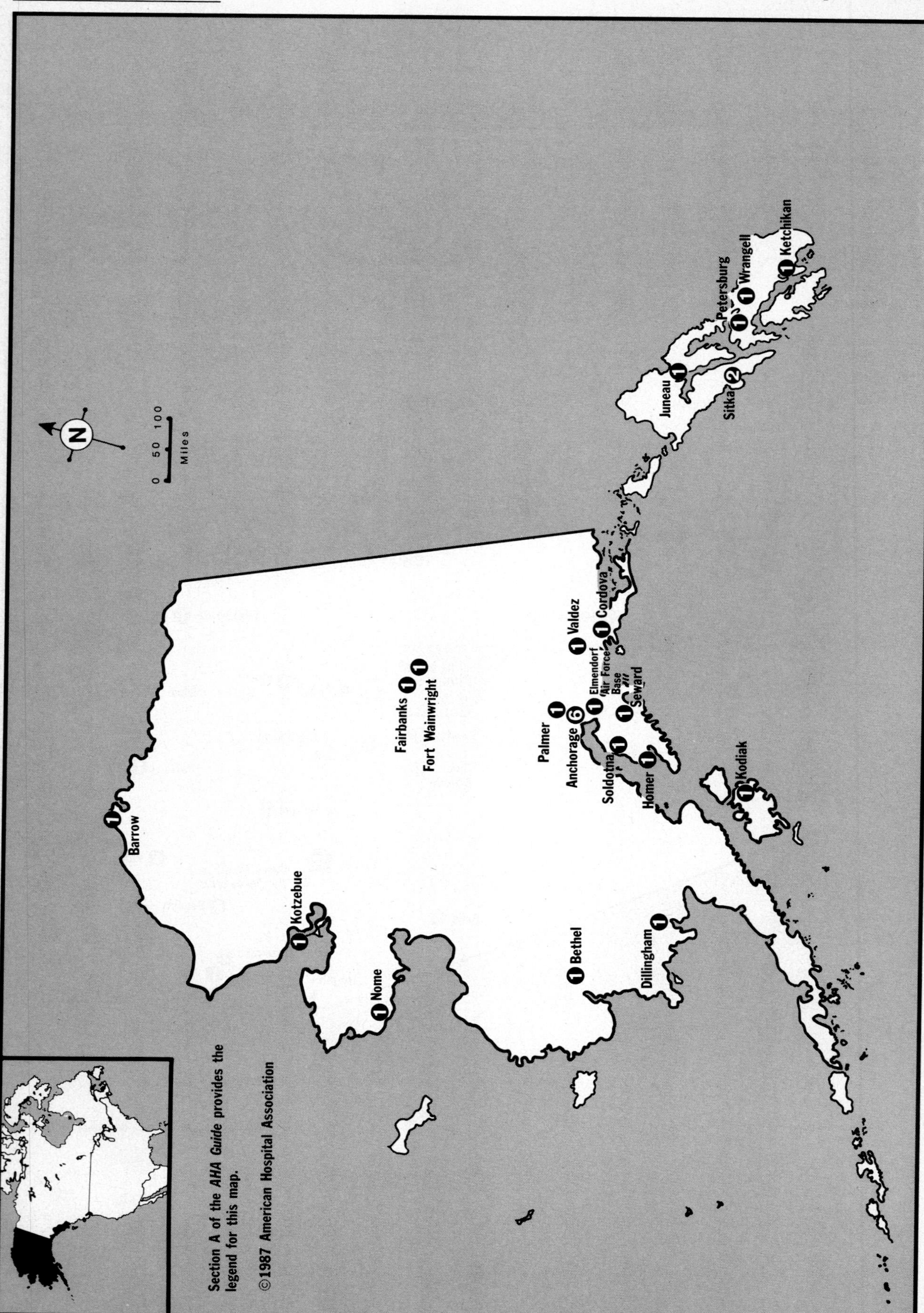
Barrow 1
Kotzebue 1
Nome 1
Fairbanks 1
Fort Wainwright 1
Bethel 1
Dillingham 1
Palmer 1
Anchorage 6
Soldotna 1
Homer 1
Elmendorf Air Force Base 1
Seward 1
Valdez 1
Cordova 1
Kodiak 1
Juneau 1
Sitka 2
Petersburg 1
Wrangell 1
Ketchikan 1
N
0 50 100
Miles
Section A of the AHA Guide provides the legend for this map.
©1987 American Hospital Association

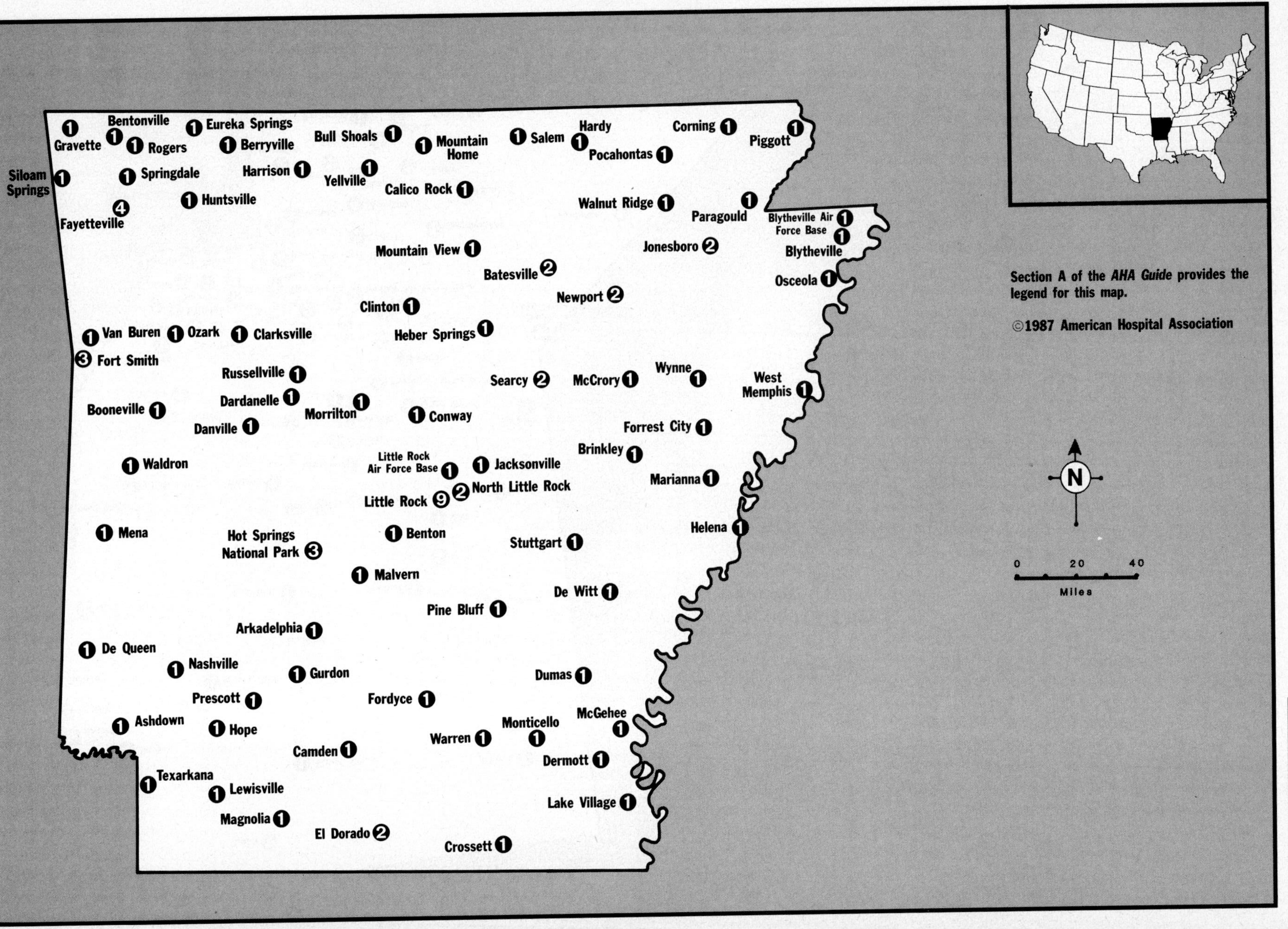
Section A of the *AHA Guide* provides the legend for this map.
©1987 American Hospital Association
N
0 20 40
Miles
Gravette 1
Bentonville 1
Rogers 1
Eureka Springs 1
Berryville 1
Bull Shoals 1
Mountain Home 1
Salem 1
Hardy 1
Pocahontas 1
Corning 1
Piggott 1
Siloam Springs 1
Springdale 1
Harrison 1
Yellville 1
Calico Rock 1
Fayetteville 4
Huntsville 1
Walnut Ridge 1
Paragould 1
Blytheville Air Force Base 1
Blytheville 1
Jonesboro 2
Mountain View 1
Batesville 2
Osceola 1
Newport 2
Clinton 1
Van Buren 1
Ozark 1
Clarksville 1
Heber Springs 1
Fort Smith 3
Russellville 1
Searcy 2
McCrory 1
Wynne 1
West Memphis 1
Dardanelle 1
Morrilton 1
Booneville 1
Conway 1
Danville 1
Forrest City 1
Brinkley 1
Little Rock Air Force Base 1
Jacksonville 1
Waldron 1
Marianna 1
North Little Rock 2
Little Rock 9
Helena 1
Mena 1
Hot Springs National Park 3
Benton 1
Stuttgart 1
Malvern 1
De Witt 1
Pine Bluff 1
Arkadelphia 1
De Queen 1
Nashville 1
Gurdon 1
Dumas 1
Prescott 1
Fordyce 1
Ashdown 1
Hope 1
Monticello 1
McGehee 1
Warren 1
Camden 1
Dermott 1
Texarkana 1
Lewisville 1
Lake Village 1
Magnolia 1
El Dorado 2
Crossett 1

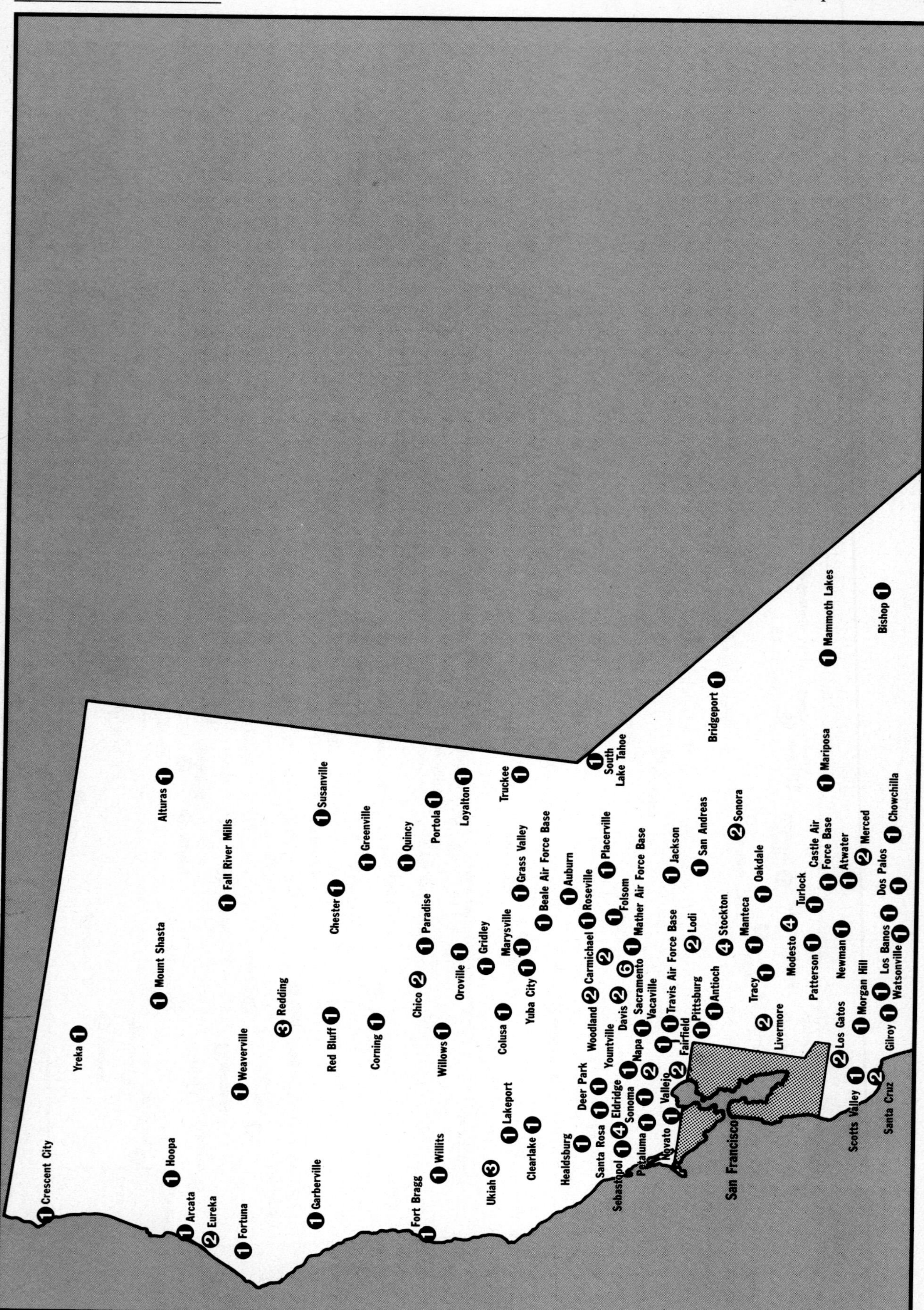
Crescent City
Yreka
Alturas
Mount Shasta
Hoopa
Arcata
Eureka
Fortuna
Garberville
Weaverville
Fall River Mills
Redding
Susanville
Red Bluff
Chester
Corning
Greenville
Quincy
Willows
Chico
Paradise
Oroville
Portola
Loyalton
Fort Bragg
Willits
Ukiah
Lakeport
Clearlake
Colusa
Gridley
Marysville
Yuba City
Truckee
Grass Valley
Beale Air Force Base
Auburn
Roseville
Placerville
South Lake Tahoe
Healdsburg
Santa Rosa
Sebastopol
Deer Park
Eldridge
Sonoma
Petaluma
Novato
Yountville
Napa
Vallejo
Woodland
Carmichael
Davis
Sacramento
Folsom
Mather Air Force Base
Vacaville
Fairfield
Travis Air Force Base
Jackson
San Andreas
Pittsburg
Antioch
Lodi
Stockton
Sonora
Manteca
Tracy
Oakdale
Livermore
Modesto
Turlock
Patterson
Newman
Castle Air Force Base
Atwater
Merced
Mariposa
San Francisco
Los Gatos
Morgan Hill
Gilroy
Los Banos
Dos Palos
Watsonville
Chowchilla
Scotts Valley
Santa Cruz
Bridgeport
Mammoth Lakes
Bishop

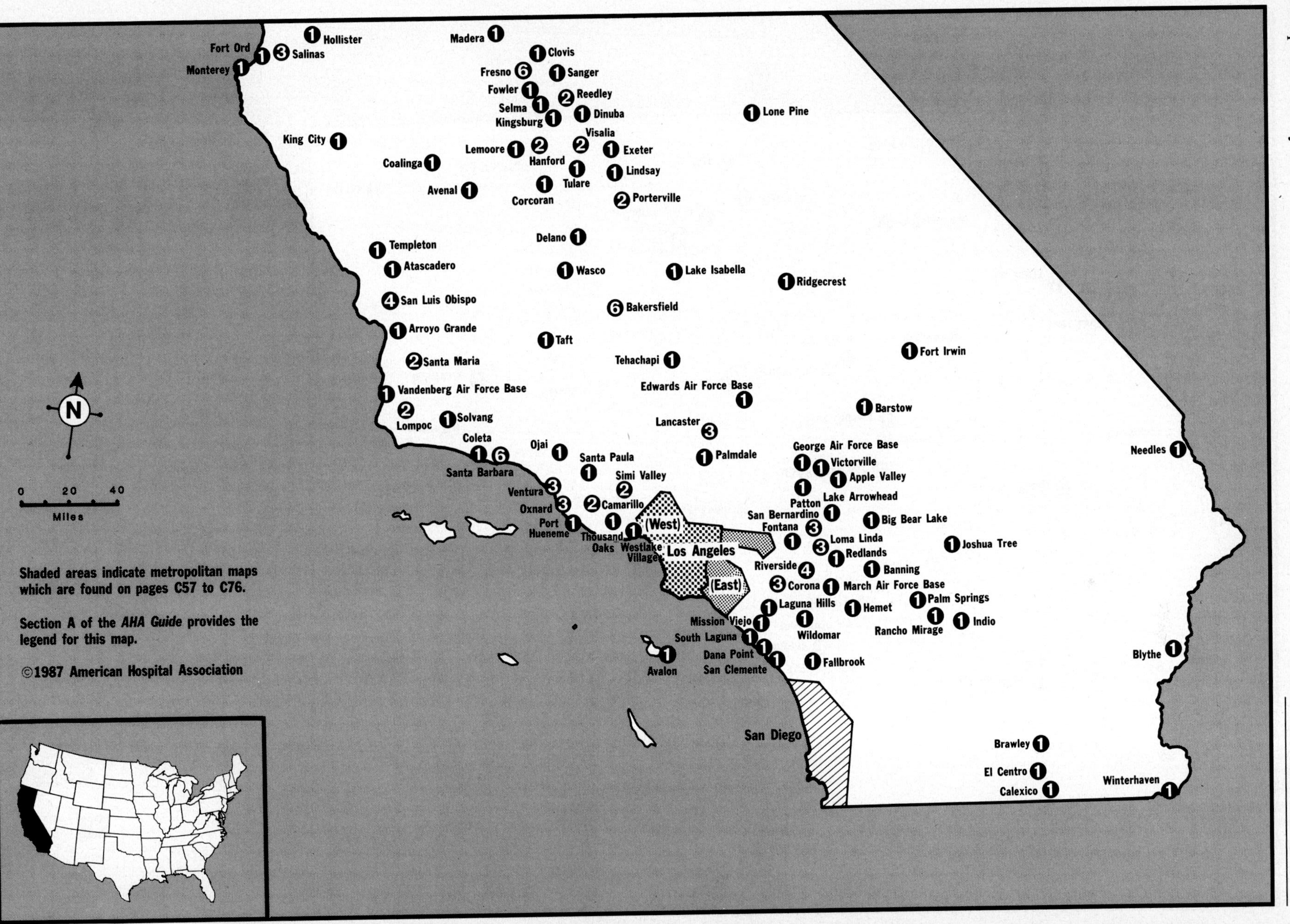
Hollister 1
Fort Ord 1
Salinas 3
Monterey 1
Madera 1
Clovis 1
Fresno 6
Sanger 1
Fowler 1
Reedley 2
Selma 1
Kingsburg 1
Dinuba 1
Lone Pine 1
King City 1
Visalia 2
Lemoore 1
Hanford 2
Exeter 1
Coalinga 1
Tulare 1
Lindsay 1
Avenal 1
Corcoran 1
Porterville 2
Delano 1
Templeton 1
Atascadero 1
Wasco 1
Lake Isabella 1
Ridgecrest 1
San Luis Obispo 4
Bakersfield 6
Arroyo Grande 1
Taft 1
Fort Irwin 1
Santa Maria 2
Tehachapi 1
Vandenberg Air Force Base 1
Edwards Air Force Base 1
Barstow 1
Lompoc 2
Solvang 1
Lancaster 3
Coleta 1
Santa Barbara 6
Ojai 1
Santa Paula 1
Palmdale 1
George Air Force Base 1
Victorville 1
Apple Valley 1
Needles 1
Simi Valley 2
Ventura 3
Oxnard 3
Camarillo 2
Patton 1
Lake Arrowhead 1
San Bernardino 3
Fontana 1
Big Bear Lake 1
Port Hueneme 1
Thousand Oaks 1
Westlake Village 1
(West)
Los Angeles
(East)
Loma Linda 3
Redlands 1
Joshua Tree 1
Riverside 4
Banning 1
Corona 3
March Air Force Base 1
Laguna Hills 1
Palm Springs 1
Hemet 1
Wildomar 1
Rancho Mirage 1
Indio 1
Mission Viejo 1
South Laguna 1
Dana Point 1
San Clemente 1
Avalon 1
Fallbrook 1
Blythe 1
San Diego
Brawley 1
El Centro 1
Calexico 1
Winterhaven 1
N
0 20 40
Miles
Shaded areas indicate metropolitan maps which are found on pages C57 to C76.
Section A of the *AHA Guide* provides the legend for this map.
©1987 American Hospital Association

Colorado

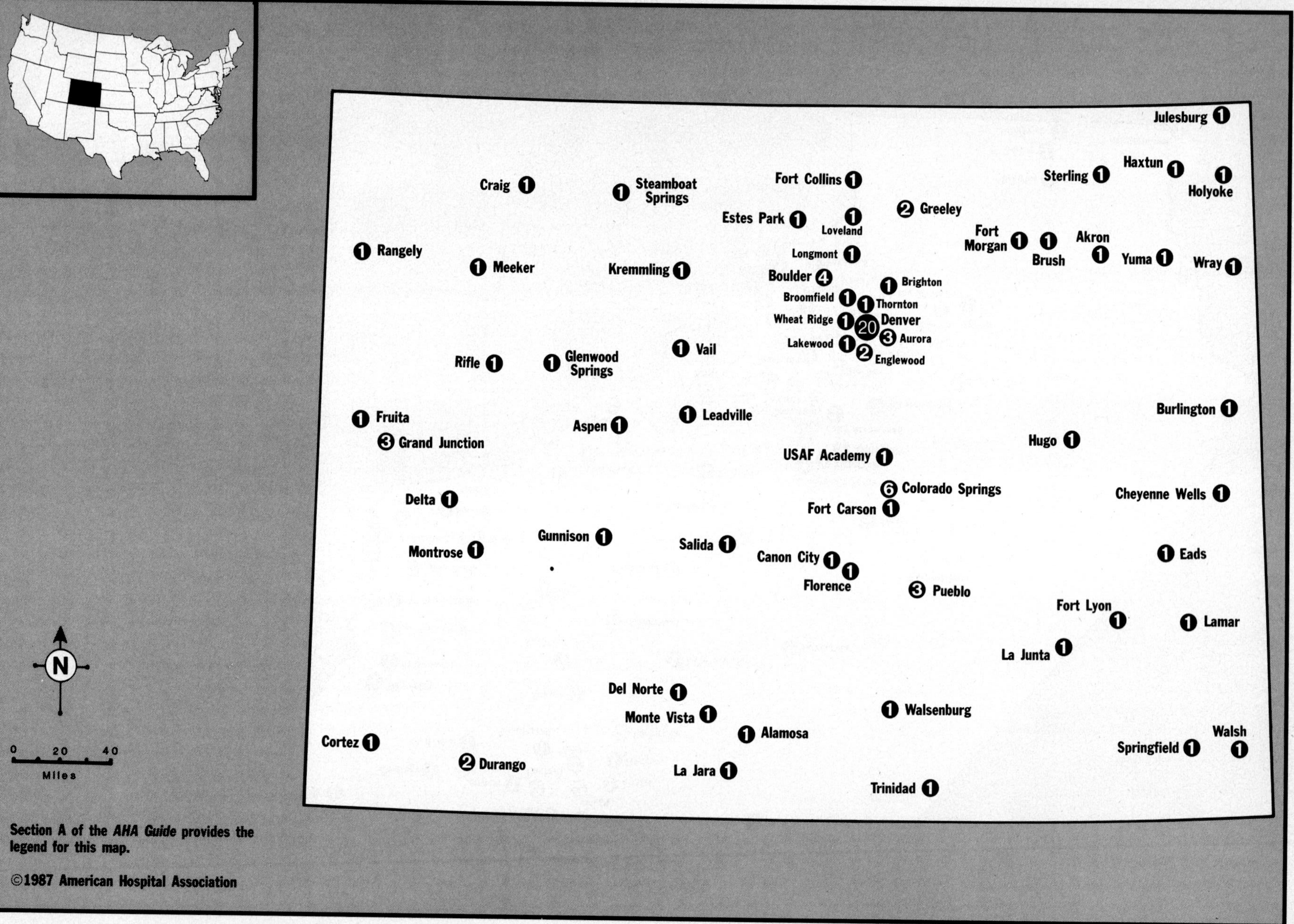
Julesburg 1
Haxtun 1
Holyoke 1
Sterling 1
Craig 1
Steamboat Springs 1
Fort Collins 1
Greeley 2
Estes Park 1
Loveland 1
Fort Morgan 1
Brush 1
Akron 1
Yuma 1
Wray 1
Rangely 1
Meeker 1
Kremmling 1
Longmont 1
Boulder 4
Brighton 1
Broomfield 1
Thornton 1
Wheat Ridge 1
Denver 20
Aurora 3
Lakewood 1
Englewood 2
Rifle 1
Glenwood Springs 1
Vail 1
Burlington 1
Fruita 1
Grand Junction 3
Aspen 1
Leadville 1
Hugo 1
USAF Academy 1
Colorado Springs 6
Fort Carson 1
Cheyenne Wells 1
Delta 1
Gunnison 1
Salida 1
Montrose 1
Canon City 1
Florence 1
Eads 1
Pueblo 3
Fort Lyon 1
Lamar 1
La Junta 1
Del Norte 1
Monte Vista 1
Walsenburg 1
Alamosa 1
Walsh 1
Cortez 1
Springfield 1
Durango 2
La Jara 1
Trinidad 1
N
0 20 40
Miles
Section A of the *AHA Guide* provides the legend for this map.
©1987 American Hospital Association

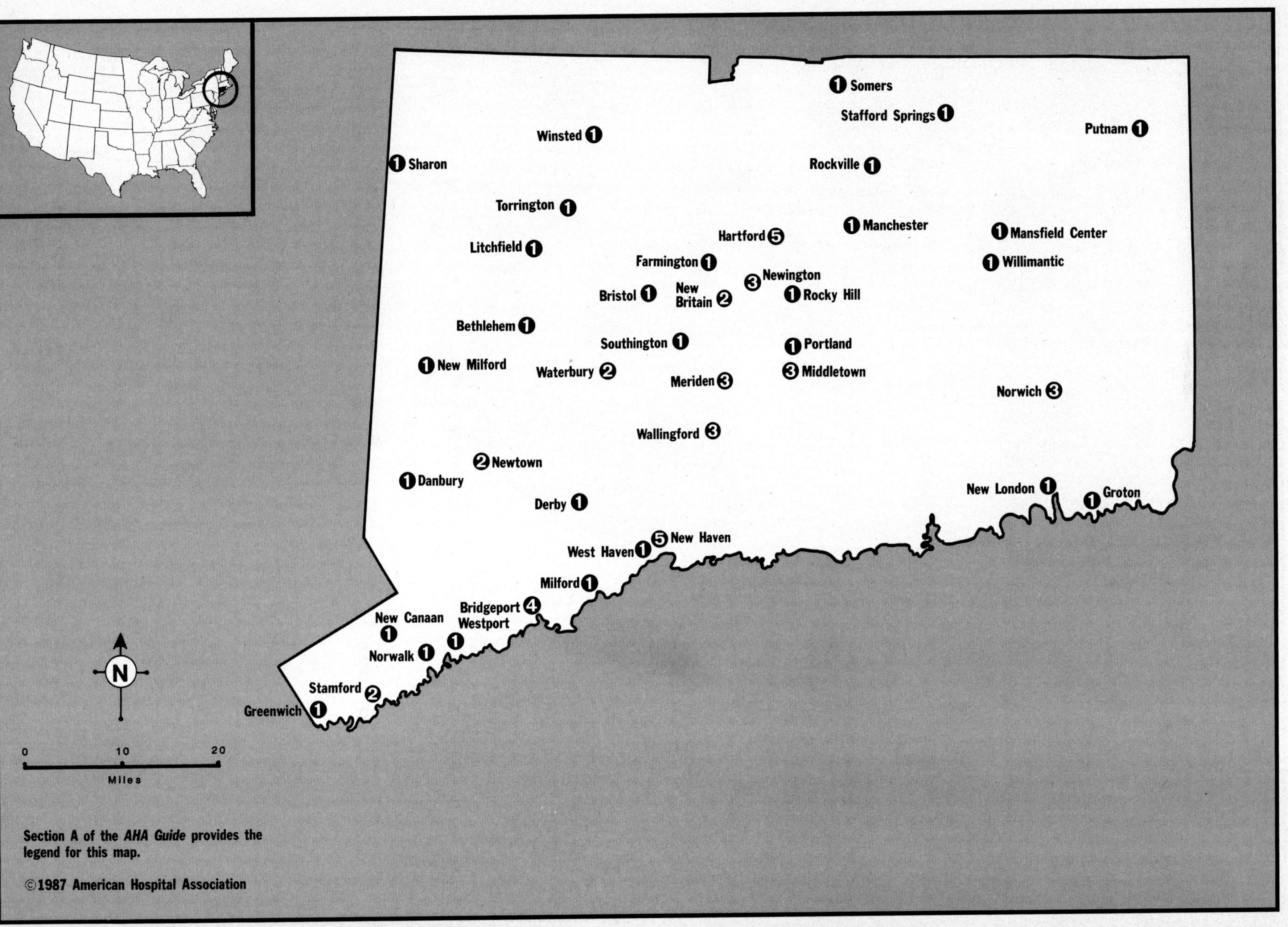
Somers 1
Stafford Springs 1
Putnam 1
Winsted 1
Sharon 1
Rockville 1
Torrington 1
Manchester 1
Mansfield Center 1
Hartford 5
Litchfield 1
Farmington 1
Willimantic 1
Newington 3
Bristol 1
New Britain 2
Rocky Hill 1
Bethlehem 1
Southington 1
Portland 1
New Milford 1
Waterbury 2
Middletown 3
Meriden 3
Norwich 3
Wallingford 3
Newtown 2
Danbury 1
New London 1
Groton 1
Derby 1
New Haven 5
West Haven 1
Milford 1
Bridgeport 4
Westport 1
New Canaan 1
Norwalk 1
Stamford 2
Greenwich 1
N
0
10
20
Miles
Section A of the *AHA Guide* provides the legend for this map.

Delaware

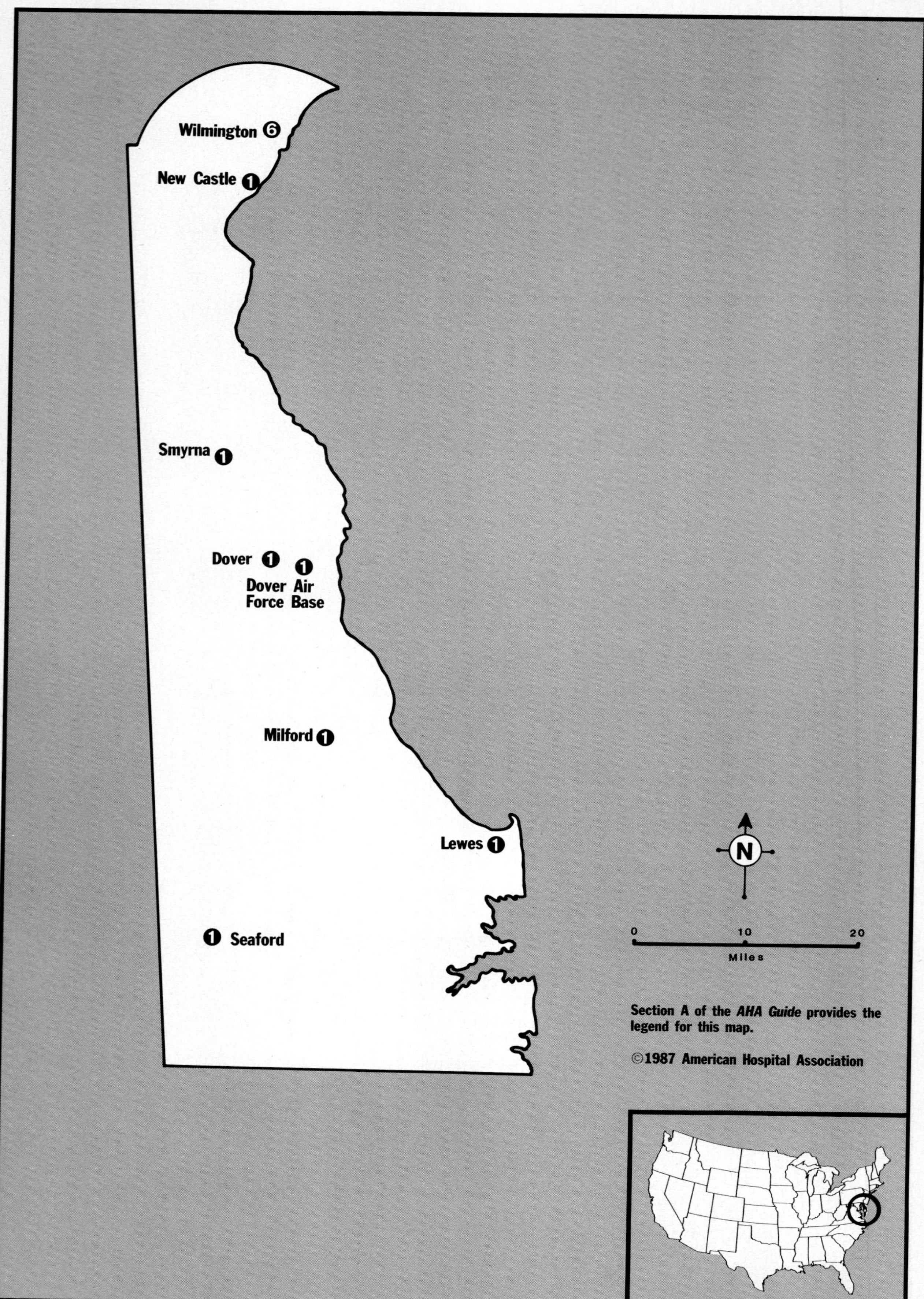
Wilmington 6
New Castle 1
Smyrna 1
Dover 1
1
Dover Air Force Base
Milford 1
Lewes 1
1 Seaford
N
0
10
20
Miles
Section A of the *AHA Guide* provides the legend for this map.
©1987 American Hospital Association

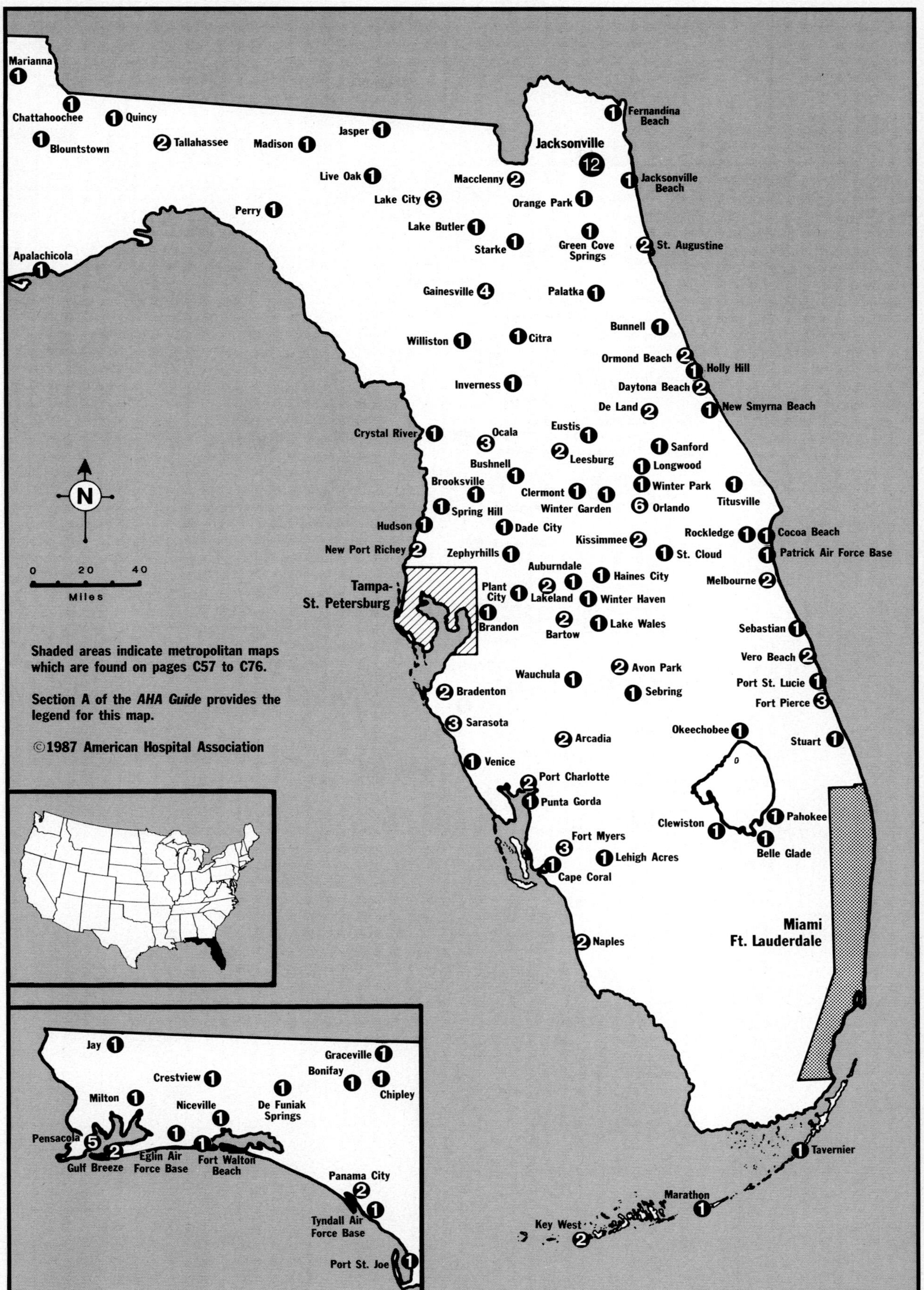
Marianna 1
Chattahoochee 1
Quincy 1
Blountstown 1
Tallahassee 2
Madison 1
Jasper 1
Live Oak 1
Lake City 3
Perry 1
Apalachicola 1
Macclenny 2
Jacksonville 12
Fernandina Beach 1
Jacksonville Beach 1
Orange Park 1
Lake Butler 1
Starke 1
Green Cove Springs 1
St. Augustine 2
Gainesville 4
Palatka 1
Bunnell 1
Williston 1
Citra 1
Ormond Beach 2
Holly Hill 1
Inverness 1
Daytona Beach 2
De Land 2
New Smyrna Beach 1
Crystal River 1
Ocala 3
Eustis 1
Leesburg 2
Sanford 1
Longwood 1
Bushnell 1
Brooksville 1
Clermont 1
Winter Garden 1
Winter Park 1
Titusville 1
Orlando 6
Spring Hill 1
Hudson 1
Dade City 1
Kissimmee 2
Rockledge 1
Cocoa Beach 1
New Port Richey 2
Zephyrhills 1
St. Cloud 1
Patrick Air Force Base 1
Auburndale 1
Haines City 1
Melbourne 2
Tampa-St. Petersburg
Plant City 1
Lakeland 2
Winter Haven 1
Brandon 1
Bartow 2
Lake Wales 1
Sebastian 1
Vero Beach 2
Wauchula 1
Avon Park 2
Port St. Lucie 1
Bradenton 2
Sebring 1
Fort Pierce 3
Sarasota 3
Arcadia 2
Okeechobee 1
Stuart 1
Venice 1
Port Charlotte 2
Punta Gorda 1
Clewiston 1
Pahokee 1
Belle Glade 1
Fort Myers 3
Lehigh Acres 1
Cape Coral 1
Naples 2
Miami
Ft. Lauderdale
Tavernier 1
Marathon 1
Key West 2
N
0 20 40
Miles
Shaded areas indicate metropolitan maps which are found on pages C57 to C76.
Section A of the *AHA Guide* provides the legend for this map.
©1987 American Hospital Association
Jay 1
Graceville 1
Bonifay 1
Chipley 1
Crestview 1
Milton 1
Niceville 1
De Funiak Springs 1
Pensacola 5
Gulf Breeze 2
Eglin Air Force Base 1
Fort Walton Beach 1
Panama City 2
Tyndall Air Force Base 1
Port St. Joe 1

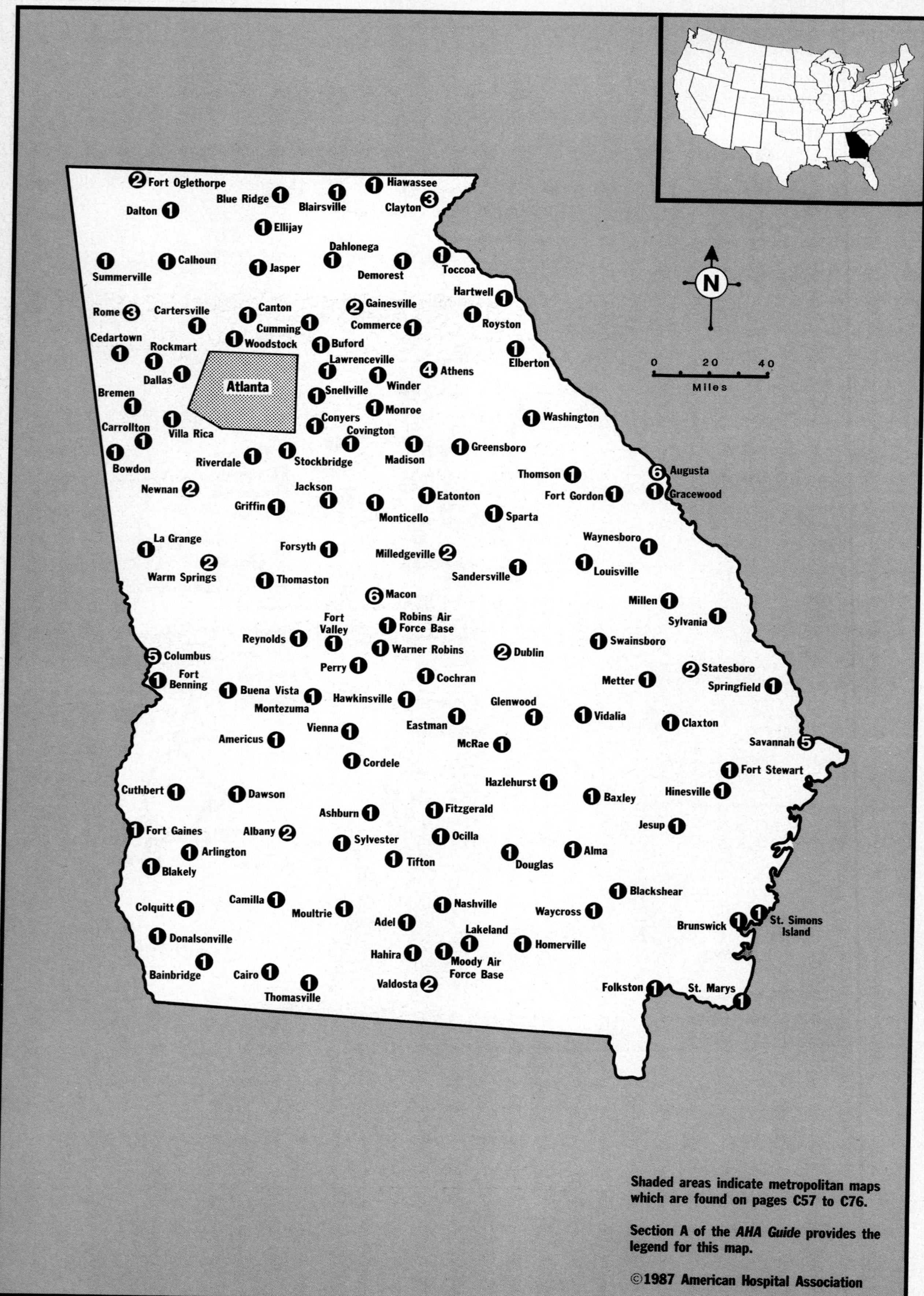

2 Fort Oglethorpe
Blue Ridge 1
1 Blairsville
1 Hiawassee
Clayton 3
Dalton 1
1 Ellijay
Dahlonega 1
1 Demorest
1 Toccoa
1 Summerville
1 Calhoun
1 Jasper
Hartwell 1
Rome 3
Cartersville 1
1 Canton
Cumming 1
2 Gainesville
Commerce 1
1 Royston
Cedartown 1
Rockmart 1
1 Woodstock
1 Buford
1 Elberton
Dallas 1
Atlanta
1 Lawrenceville
1 Winder
4 Athens
Bremen 1
1 Snellville
1 Monroe
Carrollton 1
1 Villa Rica
Conyers 1
Covington 1
1 Madison
1 Washington
1 Greensboro
1 Bowdon
Riverdale 1
1 Stockbridge
Thomson 1
6 Augusta
Newnan 2
Jackson 1
1 Eatonton
Fort Gordon 1
1 Gracewood
Griffin 1
1 Monticello
1 Sparta
1 La Grange
Forsyth 1
Milledgeville 2
Waynesboro 1
2 Warm Springs
1 Thomaston
Sandersville 1
1 Louisville
6 Macon
Millen 1
Fort Valley 1
1 Robins Air Force Base
Sylvania 1
Reynolds 1
1 Warner Robins
2 Dublin
1 Swainsboro
5 Columbus
1 Fort Benning
Perry 1
1 Cochran
2 Statesboro
Metter 1
Springfield 1
1 Buena Vista
Montezuma 1
Hawkinsville 1
Glenwood 1
1 Vidalia
1 Claxton
Eastman 1
Vienna 1
Americus 1
McRae 1
Savannah 5
1 Cordele
1 Fort Stewart
Hazlehurst 1
Cuthbert 1
1 Dawson
1 Baxley
Hinesville 1
Ashburn 1
1 Fitzgerald
1 Fort Gaines
Albany 2
Jesup 1
1 Sylvester
1 Ocilla
1 Arlington
1 Alma
1 Tifton
1 Douglas
1 Blakely
1 Blackshear
Camilla 1
Colquitt 1
Moultrie 1
1 Nashville
Waycross 1
Adel 1
Brunswick 1
1 St. Simons Island
Lakeland 1
1 Donalsonville
1 Homerville
Hahira 1
1 Moody Air Force Base
Bainbridge 1
Cairo 1
1 Thomasville
Valdosta 2
Folkston 1
St. Marys 1
N
0 20 40
Miles
Shaded areas indicate metropolitan maps which are found on pages C57 to C76.
Section A of the *AHA Guide* provides the legend for this map.
©1987 American Hospital Association

Idaho

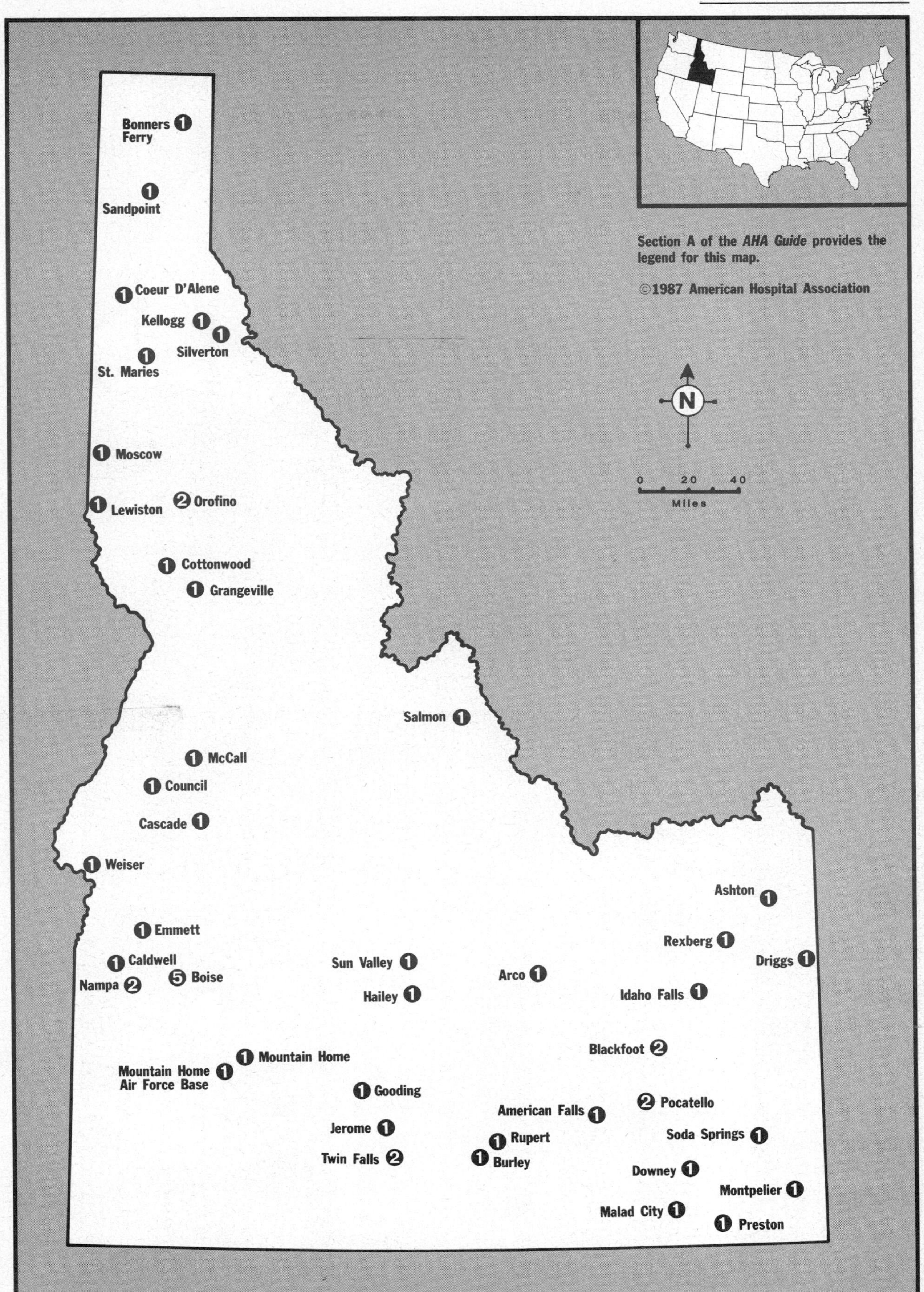

Section A of the *AHA Guide* provides the legend for this map.

Hawaii

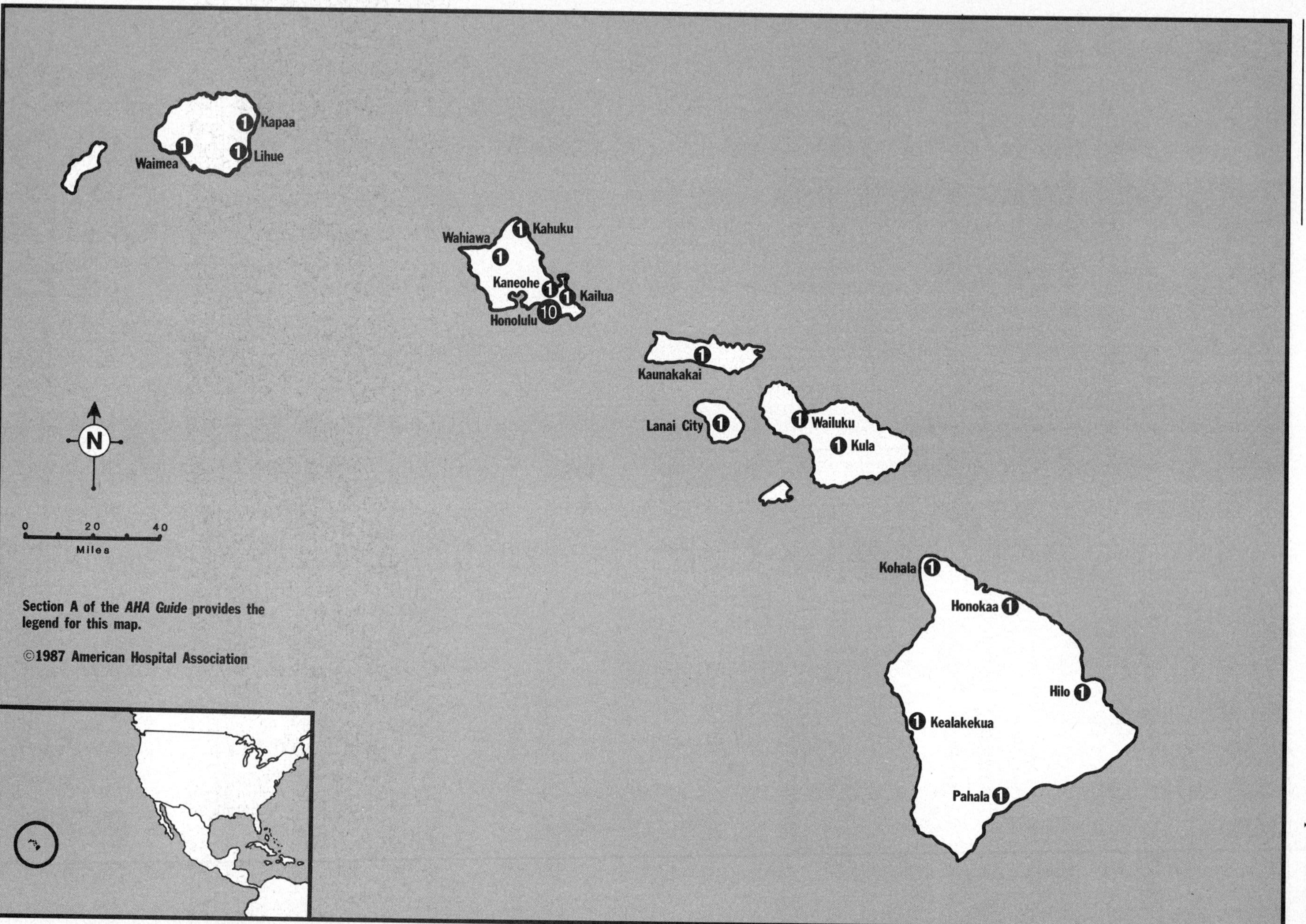
Kapaa
Waimea
Lihue
Wahiawa
Kahuku
Kaneohe
Kailua
Honolulu
10
Kaunakakai
Lanai City
Wailuku
Kula
Kohala
Honokaa
Hilo
Kealakekua
Pahala
N
0 20 40
Miles
Section A of the *AHA Guide* provides the legend for this map.
©1987 American Hospital Association

Iowa

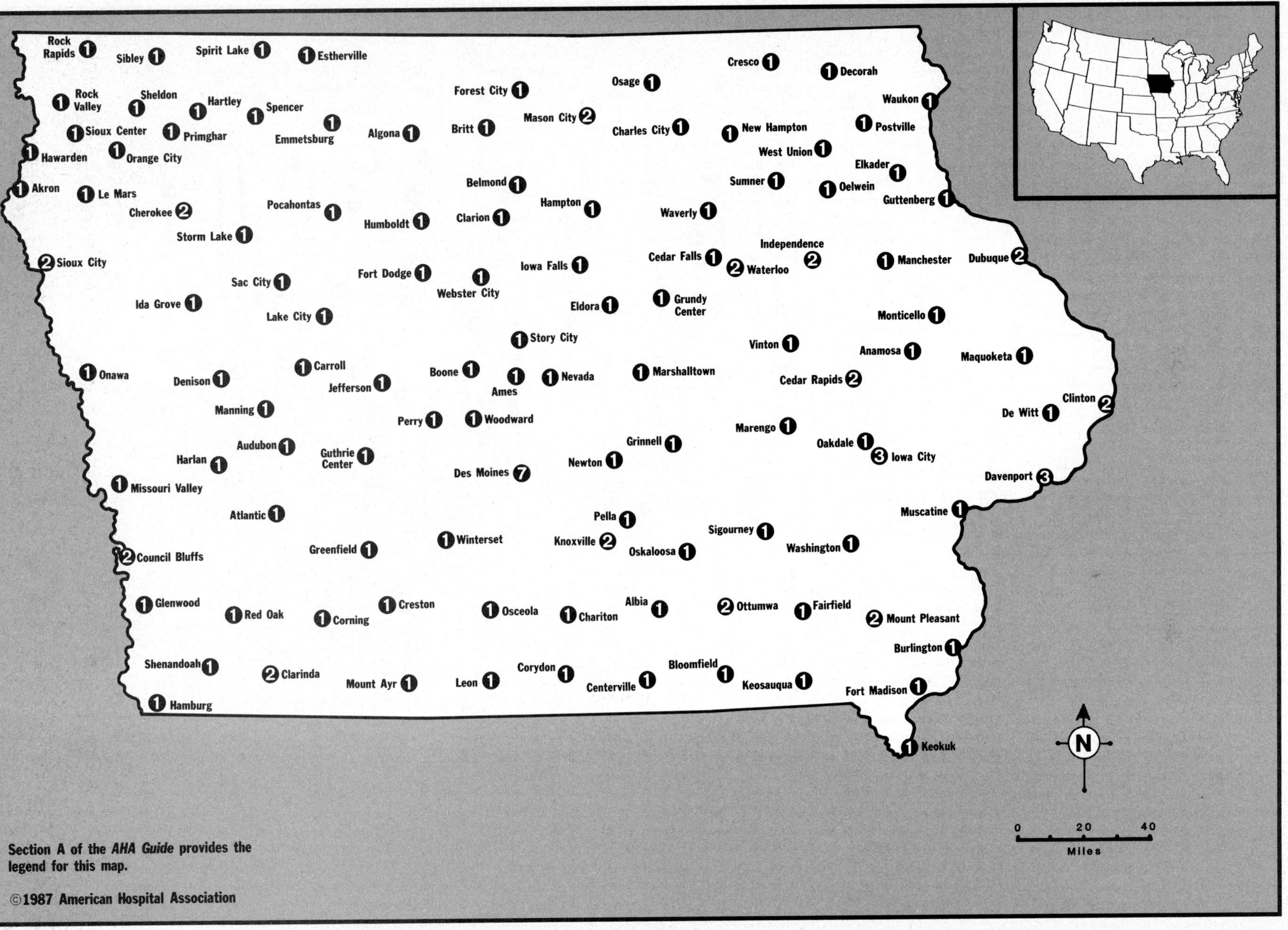
Rock Rapids 1
Sibley 1
Spirit Lake 1
Estherville 1
Rock Valley 1
Sheldon 1
Hartley 1
Spencer 1
Emmetsburg 1
Sioux Center 1
Primghar 1
Hawarden 1
Orange City 1
Akron 1
Le Mars 1
Cherokee 2
Storm Lake 1
Pocahontas 1
Sioux City 2
Ida Grove 1
Sac City 1
Lake City 1
Onawa 1
Denison 1
Carroll 1
Jefferson 1
Manning 1
Audubon 1
Harlan 1
Guthrie Center 1
Missouri Valley 1
Atlantic 1
Council Bluffs 2
Greenfield 1
Glenwood 1
Red Oak 1
Corning 1
Creston 1
Shenandoah 1
Clarinda 2
Mount Ayr 1
Hamburg 1
Algona 1
Humboldt 1
Fort Dodge 1
Webster City 1
Forest City 1
Britt 1
Belmond 1
Clarion 1
Mason City 2
Hampton 1
Iowa Falls 1
Eldora 1
Story City 1
Boone 1
Ames 1
Nevada 1
Perry 1
Woodward 1
Des Moines 7
Winterset 1
Osceola 1
Leon 1
Corydon 1
Osage 1
Charles City 1
Waverly 1
Cedar Falls 1
Waterloo 2
Grundy Center 1
Marshalltown 1
Newton 1
Grinnell 1
Pella 1
Knoxville 2
Oskaloosa 1
Chariton 1
Albia 1
Centerville 1
Bloomfield 1
Cresco 1
Decorah 1
New Hampton 1
West Union 1
Sumner 1
Oelwein 1
Elkader 1
Waukon 1
Postville 1
Guttenberg 1
Independence 2
Manchester 1
Dubuque 2
Monticello 1
Vinton 1
Anamosa 1
Maquoketa 1
Cedar Rapids 2
Marengo 1
Oakdale 1
Iowa City 3
De Witt 1
Clinton 2
Davenport 3
Muscatine 1
Sigourney 1
Washington 1
Ottumwa 2
Fairfield 1
Mount Pleasant 2
Burlington 1
Keosauqua 1
Fort Madison 1
Keokuk 1
N
0
20
40
Miles
Section A of the *AHA Guide* provides the legend for this map.

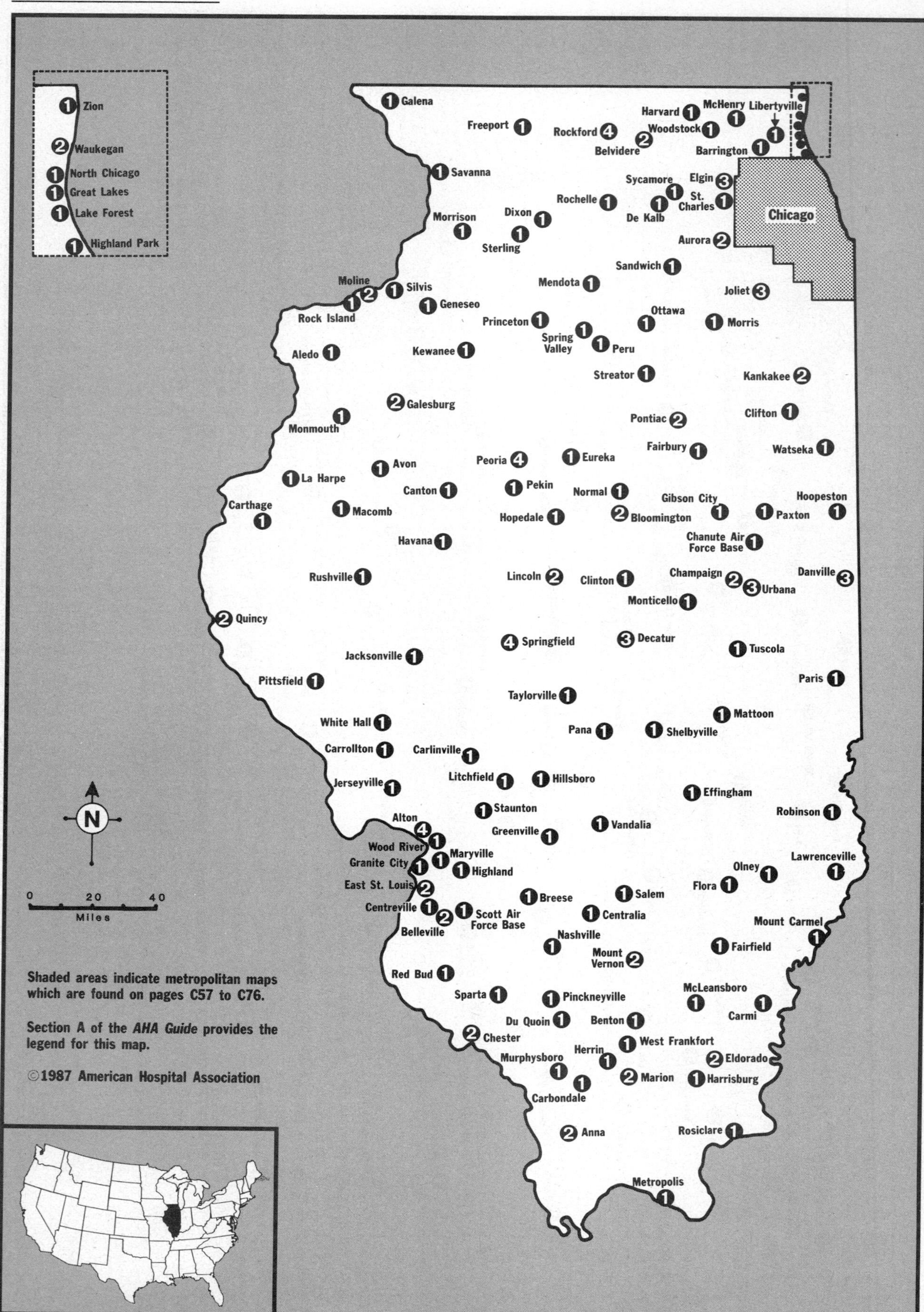
1 Zion
2 Waukegan
1 North Chicago
1 Great Lakes
1 Lake Forest
1 Highland Park
1 Galena
Freeport 1
Rockford 4
2 Belvidere
Harvard 1
McHenry 1
Libertyville 1
Woodstock 1
Barrington 1
1 Savanna
Sycamore 1
Elgin 3
St. Charles 1
Rochelle 1
1 De Kalb
Chicago
Morrison 1
Dixon 1
1 Sterling
Aurora 2
Sandwich 1
Mendota 1
Joliet 3
Moline 2
1 Silvis
1 Rock Island
1 Geneseo
Princeton 1
Ottawa 1
1 Morris
Spring Valley 1
1 Peru
Aledo 1
Kewanee 1
Streator 1
Kankakee 2
2 Galesburg
1 Monmouth
Pontiac 2
Clifton 1
Fairbury 1
Watseka 1
Peoria 4
1 Eureka
1 Avon
1 La Harpe
Canton 1
1 Pekin
Normal 1
Gibson City 1
Hoopeston 1
Carthage 1
1 Macomb
Hopedale 1
2 Bloomington
1 Paxton
Havana 1
Chanute Air Force Base 1
Rushville 1
Lincoln 2
Clinton 1
Champaign 2
3 Urbana
Danville 3
Monticello 1
2 Quincy
4 Springfield
3 Decatur
1 Tuscola
Jacksonville 1
Pittsfield 1
Paris 1
Taylorville 1
1 Mattoon
White Hall 1
Pana 1
1 Shelbyville
Carrollton 1
Carlinville 1
Litchfield 1
1 Hillsboro
Jerseyville 1
1 Effingham
1 Staunton
Robinson 1
Alton 4
Greenville 1
1 Vandalia
Wood River 1
1 Maryville
Granite City 1
1 Highland
Olney 1
Lawrenceville 1
East St. Louis 2
1 Breese
1 Salem
Flora 1
Centreville 1
2 Belleville
1 Scott Air Force Base
1 Centralia
Mount Carmel 1
Nashville 1
Mount Vernon 2
1 Fairfield
Red Bud 1
Sparta 1
1 Pinckneyville
McLeansboro 1
Carmi 1
Du Quoin 1
Benton 1
2 Chester
1 West Frankfort
Herrin 1
Murphysboro 1
2 Eldorado
1 Carbondale
2 Marion
1 Harrisburg
2 Anna
Rosiclare 1
Metropolis 1
N
0 20 40
Miles
Shaded areas indicate metropolitan maps which are found on pages C57 to C76.
Section A of the *AHA Guide* provides the legend for this map.
©1987 American Hospital Association

Indiana

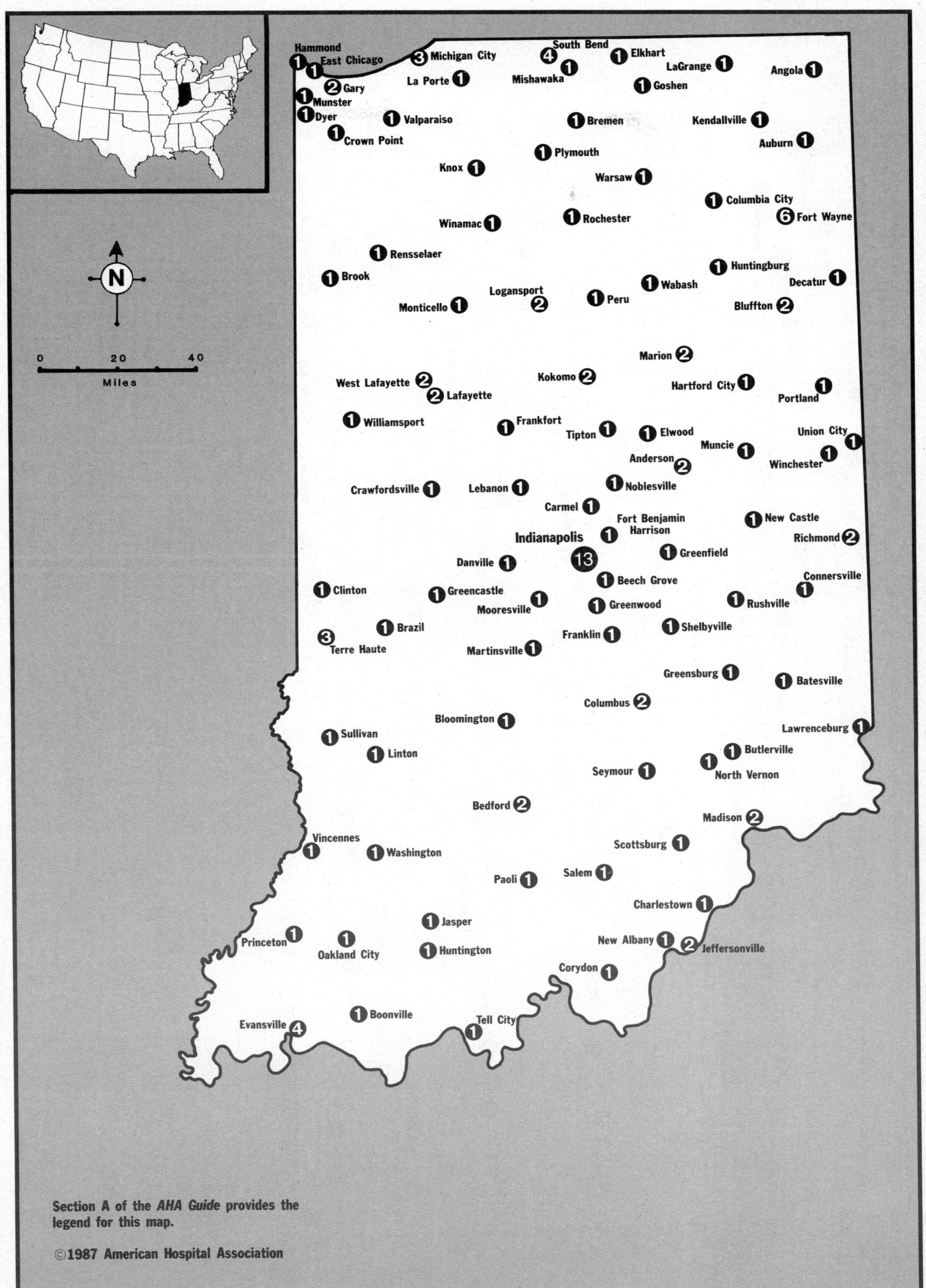
Hammond
East Chicago
Michigan City
South Bend
Elkhart
LaGrange
Angola
Gary
La Porte
Mishawaka
Goshen
Munster
Dyer
Valparaiso
Bremen
Kendallville
Crown Point
Auburn
Plymouth
Knox
Warsaw
Columbia City
Fort Wayne
Winamac
Rochester
Rensselaer
Huntingburg
Brook
Wabash
Decatur
Logansport
Peru
Monticello
Bluffton
N
0
20
40
Miles
Marion
West Lafayette
Kokomo
Hartford City
Lafayette
Portland
Williamsport
Frankfort
Tipton
Elwood
Union City
Muncie
Anderson
Winchester
Crawfordsville
Lebanon
Noblesville
Carmel
Fort Benjamin Harrison
New Castle
Indianapolis
Richmond
Greenfield
Danville
Connersville
Beech Grove
Clinton
Greencastle
Mooresville
Greenwood
Rushville
Brazil
Shelbyville
Terre Haute
Franklin
Martinsville
Greensburg
Batesville
Columbus
Bloomington
Lawrenceburg
Sullivan
Butlerville
Linton
Seymour
North Vernon
Bedford
Madison
Vincennes
Scottsburg
Washington
Paoli
Salem
Charlestown
Jasper
Princeton
New Albany
Jeffersonville
Oakland City
Huntington
Corydon
Boonville
Evansville
Tell City
Section A of the *AHA Guide* provides the legend for this map.
©1987 American Hospital Association

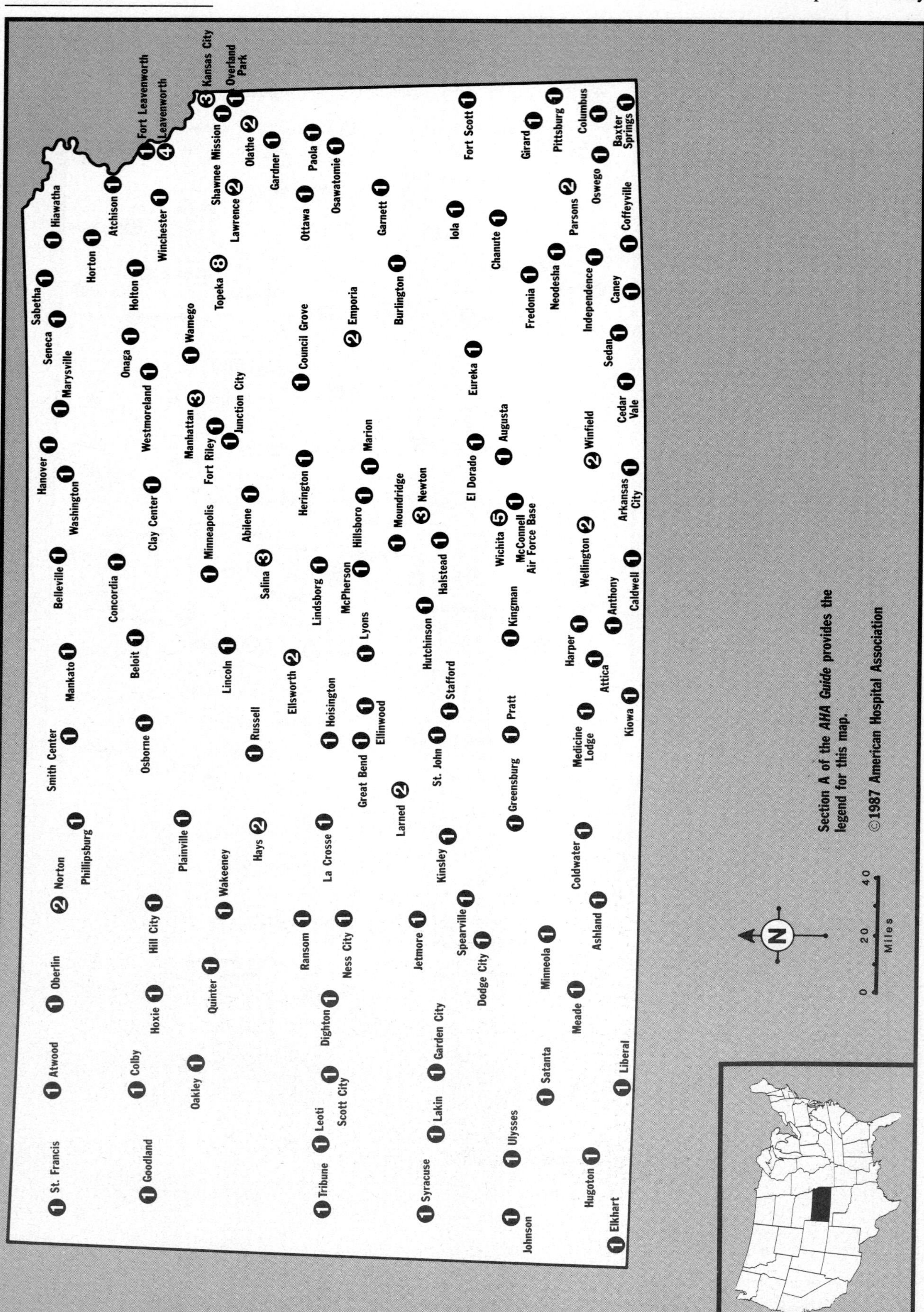

St. Francis 1
Atwood 1
Oberlin 1
Norton 2
Phillipsburg 1
Smith Center 1
Mankato 1
Belleville 1
Washington 1
Hanover 1
Marysville 1
Seneca 1
Sabetha 1
Hiawatha 1
Horton 1
Atchison 1
Fort Leavenworth 1
Leavenworth 4
Kansas City 3
Overland Park 1
Shawnee Mission 1
Olathe 2
Gardner 1
Paola 1
Osawatomie 1
Fort Scott 1
Pittsburg 1
Girard 1
Columbus 1
Baxter Springs 1
Oswego 1
Parsons 2
Coffeyville 1
Independence 1
Caney 1
Neodesha 1
Chanute 1
Iola 1
Garnett 1
Ottawa 1
Lawrence 2
Winchester 1
Holton 1
Topeka 8
Wamego 1
Onaga 1
Westmoreland 1
Manhattan 3
Junction City 1
Fort Riley 1
Clay Center 1
Concordia 1
Beloit 1
Osborne 1
Goodland 1
Colby 1
Hoxie 1
Hill City 1
Plainville 1
Oakley 1
Quinter 1
Wakeeney 1
Hays 2
Russell 1
Lincoln 1
Minneapolis 1
Abilene 1
Salina 3
Ellsworth 2
Council Grove 1
Emporia 2
Burlington 1
Fredonia 1
Eureka 1
Sedan 1
Cedar Vale 1
Winfield 2
Arkansas City 1
Augusta 1
El Dorado 1
Marion 1
Herington 1
Hillsboro 1
Moundridge 1
Newton 3
Lindsborg 1
McPherson 1
Lyons 1
Hoisington 1
Ellinwood 1
Great Bend 1
Halstead 1
Hutchinson 1
Wichita 5
McConnell Air Force Base 1
Wellington 2
Caldwell 1
Anthony 1
Kingman 1
Harper 1
Attica 1
Kiowa 1
Medicine Lodge 1
Pratt 1
Stafford 1
St. John 1
Greensburg 1
Larned 2
La Crosse 1
Ransom 1
Ness City 1
Dighton 1
Scott City 1
Leoti 1
Tribune 1
Syracuse 1
Lakin 1
Garden City 1
Jetmore 1
Kinsley 1
Spearville 1
Dodge City 1
Minneola 1
Ashland 1
Coldwater 1
Meade 1
Satanta 1
Ulysses 1
Johnson 1
Hugoton 1
Elkhart 1
Liberal 1
N
0 20 40
Miles
Section A of the *AHA Guide* provides the legend for this map.
©1987 American Hospital Association

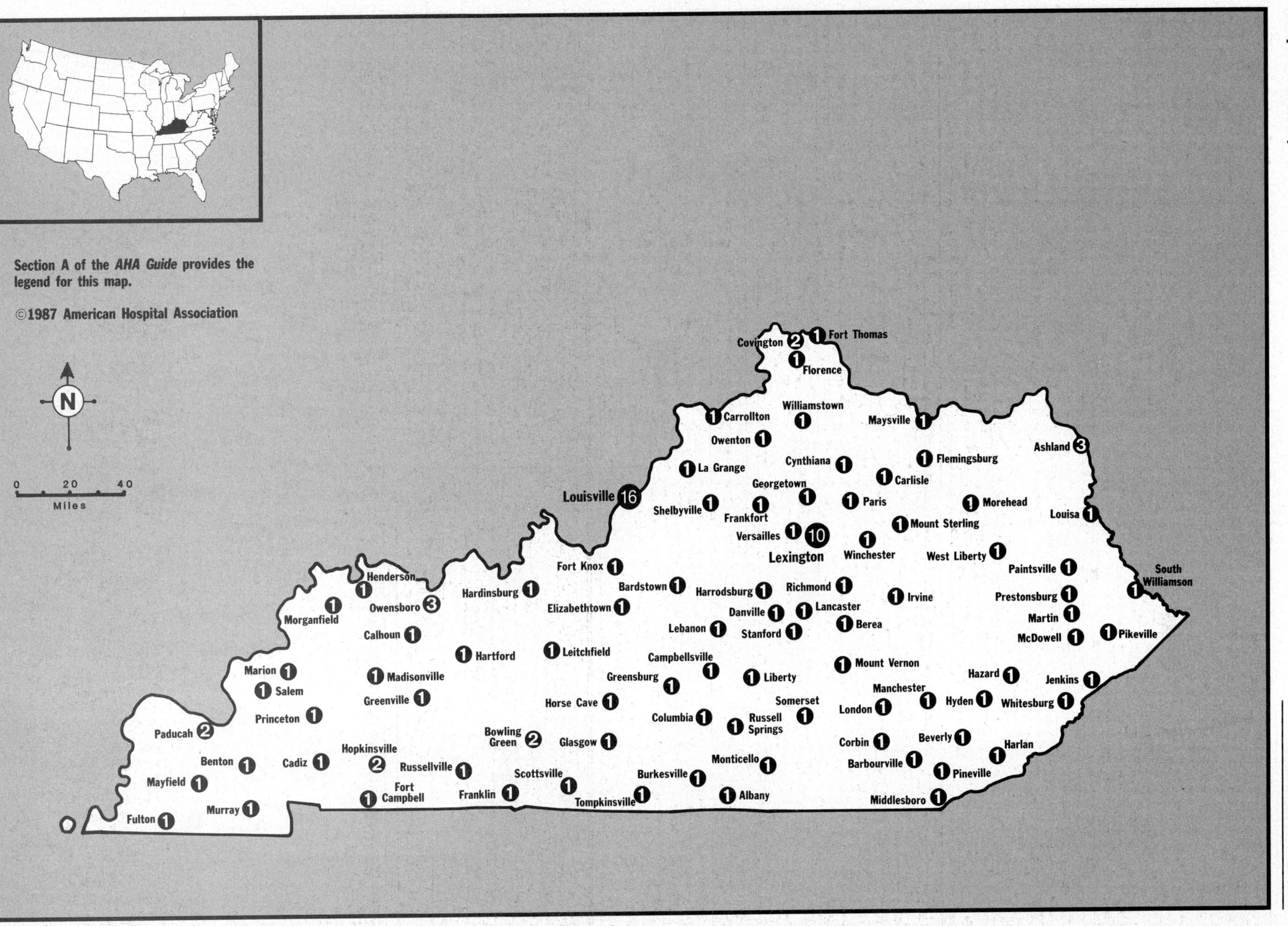
Section A of the *AHA Guide* provides the legend for this map.
©1987 American Hospital Association
N
0 20 40
Miles
Covington 2
Fort Thomas 1
Florence 1
Carrollton 1
Williamstown 1
Maysville 1
Owenton 1
Ashland 3
Flemingsburg 1
La Grange 1
Cynthiana 1
Carlisle 1
Georgetown 1
Louisville 16
Paris 1
Morehead 1
Shelbyville 1
Frankfort 1
Louisa 1
Mount Sterling 1
Versailles 1
Lexington 10
Winchester 1
West Liberty 1
Fort Knox 1
Paintsville 1
Henderson 1
South Williamson 1
Bardstown 1
Harrodsburg 1
Richmond 1
Hardinsburg 1
Irvine 1
Prestonsburg 1
Morganfield 1
Owensboro 3
Elizabethtown 1
Danville 1
Lancaster 1
Martin 1
Lebanon 1
Berea 1
Stanford 1
Calhoun 1
McDowell 1
Pikeville 1
Hartford 1
Leitchfield 1
Campbellsville 1
Marion 1
Mount Vernon 1
Madisonville 1
Greensburg 1
Liberty 1
Hazard 1
Jenkins 1
Salem 1
Manchester 1
Greenville 1
Somerset 1
Horse Cave 1
Hyden 1
Whitesburg 1
London 1
Princeton 1
Columbia 1
Russell Springs 1
Paducah 2
Bowling Green 2
Glasgow 1
Corbin 1
Beverly 1
Harlan 1
Hopkinsville 2
Benton 1
Cadiz 1
Monticello 1
Barbourville 1
Russellville 1
Scottsville 1
Burkesville 1
Pineville 1
Mayfield 1
Fort Campbell 1
Franklin 1
Murray 1
Albany 1
Middlesboro 1
Tompkinsville 1
Fulton 1

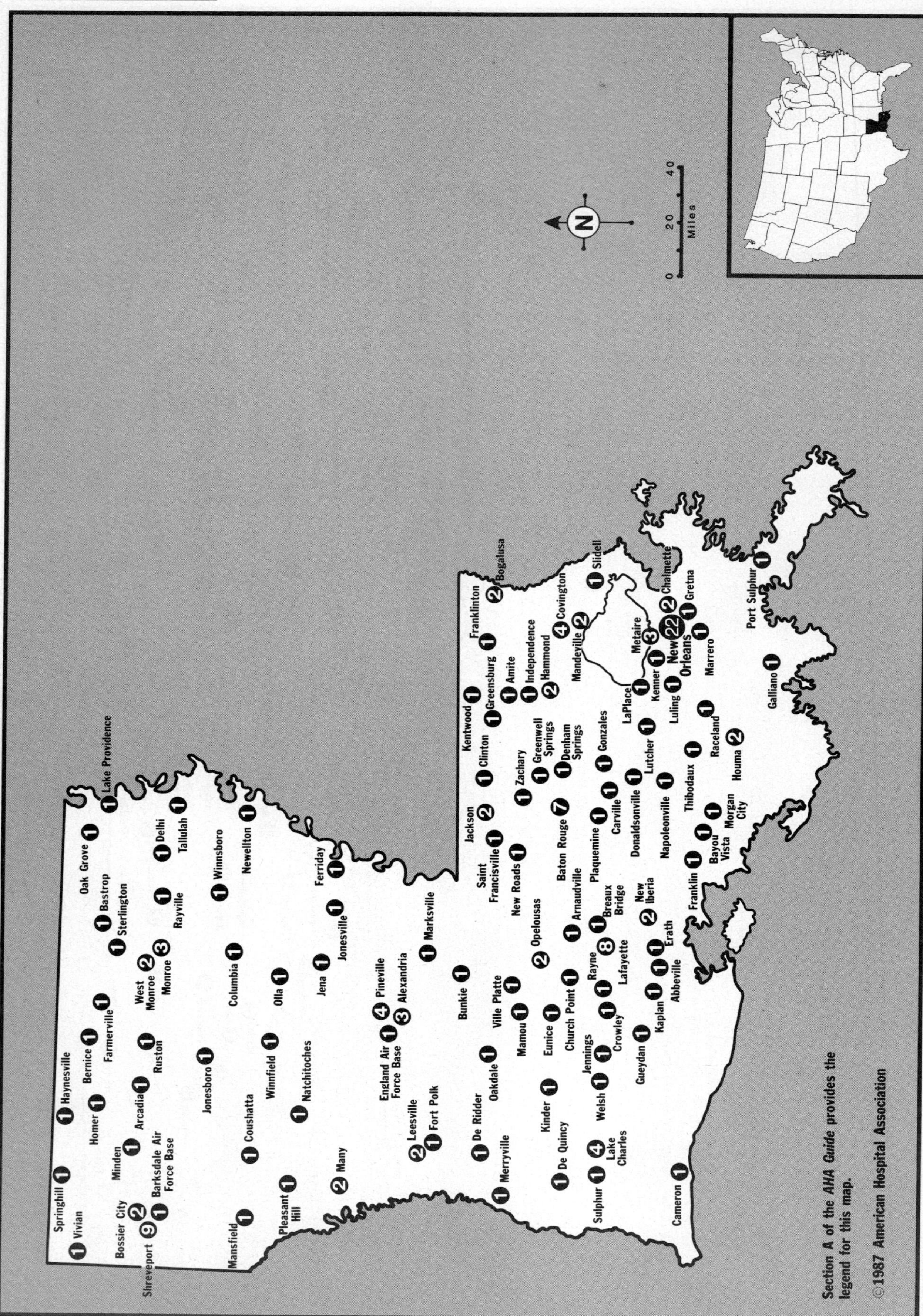
N
0
20
40
Miles
Vivian 1
Springhill 1
Haynesville 1
Homer 1
Minden 1
Bossier City 2
Shreveport 9
Barksdale Air Force Base 1
Arcadia 1
Bernice 1
Farmerville 1
Ruston 1
West Monroe 2
Monroe 3
Sterlington 1
Bastrop 1
Oak Grove 1
Lake Providence 1
Delhi 1
Rayville 1
Tallulah 1
Winnsboro 1
Newellton 1
Mansfield 1
Coushatta 1
Jonesboro 1
Columbia 1
Winnfield 1
Olla 1
Natchitoches 1
Pleasant Hill 1
Many 2
Jena 1
Jonesville 1
Ferriday 1
Leesville 2
Fort Polk 1
England Air Force Base 1
Pineville 4
Alexandria 3
Marksville 1
Bunkie 1
De Ridder 1
Merryville 1
Oakdale 1
Ville Platte 1
Mamou 1
Eunice 1
Opelousas 2
New Roads 1
Saint Francisville 1
Jackson 2
Clinton 1
Kentwood 1
Greensburg 1
Amite 1
Franklinton 1
Bogalusa 2
Independence 1
Hammond 2
Covington 4
Mandeville 2
Slidell 1
Zachary 1
Greenwell Springs 1
Denham Springs 1
Baton Rouge 7
Gonzales 1
Plaquemine 1
Carville 1
Donaldsonville 1
Lutcher 1
LaPlace 1
Kenner 1
Metairie 3
New Orleans 22
Chalmette 2
Gretna 1
Marrero 1
Luling 1
Raceland 1
Houma 2
Thibodaux 1
Napoleonville 1
Galliano 1
Port Sulphur 1
Morgan City 1
Bayou Vista 1
Franklin 1
New Iberia 2
Breaux Bridge 1
Arnaudville 1
Lafayette 8
Rayne 1
Erath 1
Abbeville 1
Kaplan 1
Crowley 1
Church Point 1
Gueydan 1
Jennings 1
Welsh 1
Kinder 1
De Quincy 1
Lake Charles 4
Sulphur 1
Cameron 1
Section A of the *AHA Guide* provides the legend for this map.
©1987 American Hospital Association

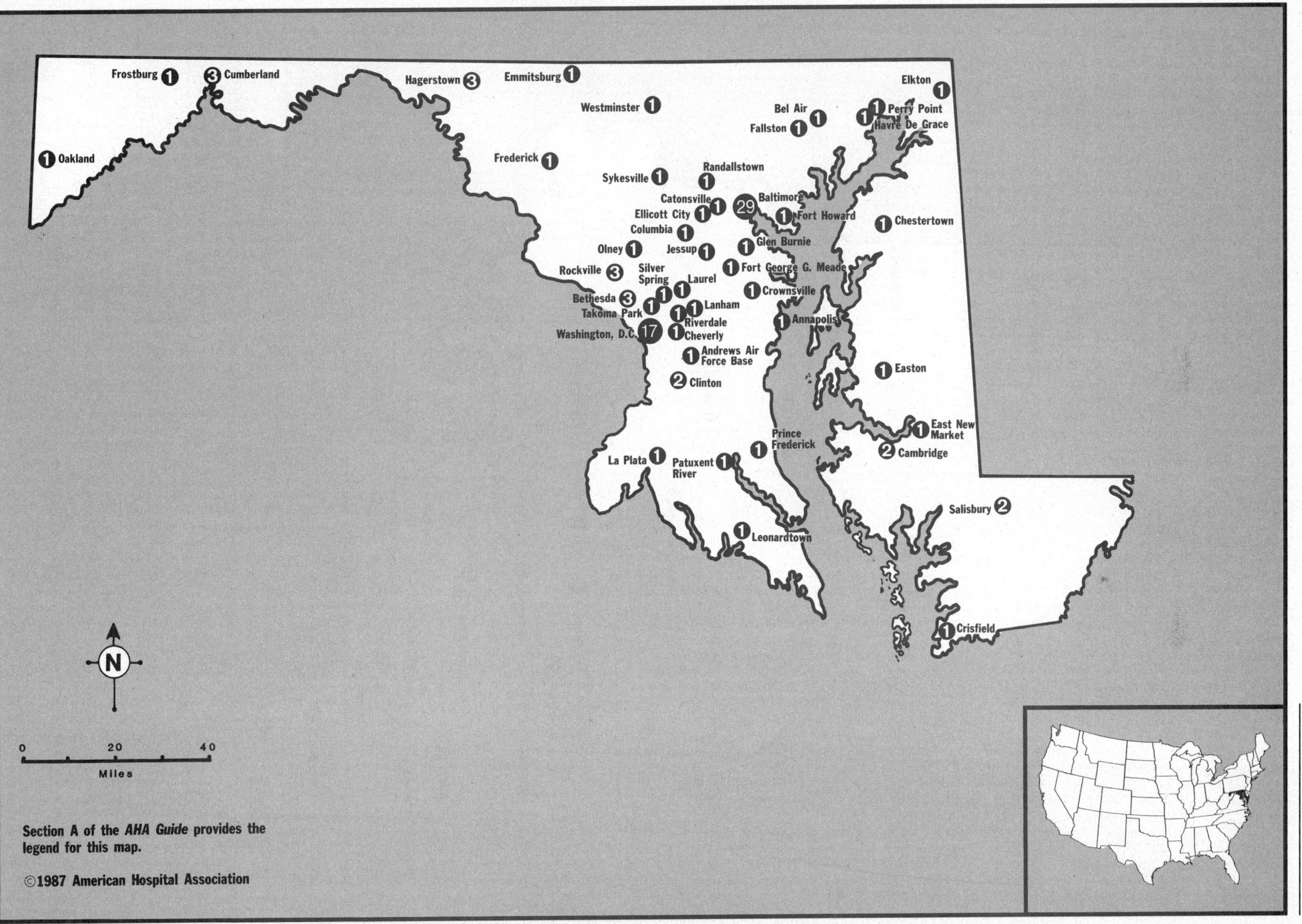

Section A of the *AHA Guide* provides the legend for this map.

Maine

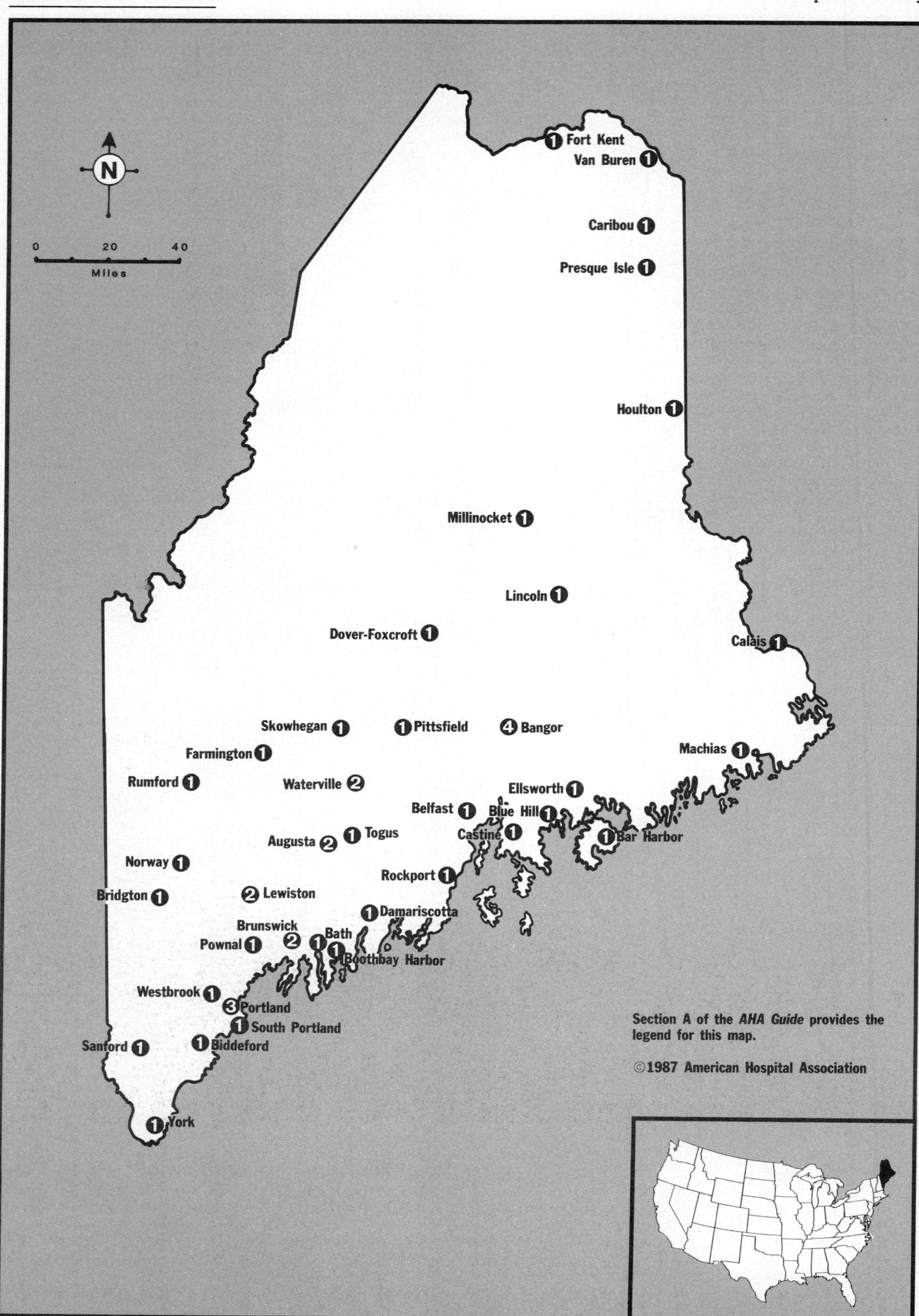
N
0 20 40
Miles
1 Fort Kent
Van Buren 1
Caribou 1
Presque Isle 1
Houlton 1
Millinocket 1
Lincoln 1
Dover-Foxcroft 1
Calais 1
Skowhegan 1
1 Pittsfield
4 Bangor
Farmington 1
Machias 1
Rumford 1
Waterville 2
Ellsworth 1
Belfast 1
Blue Hill 1
Castine 1
1 Bar Harbor
Augusta 2
1 Togus
Norway 1
Rockport 1
Bridgton 1
2 Lewiston
1 Damariscotta
Brunswick
Bath
Pownal 1
2
1
1
Boothbay Harbor
Westbrook 1
3 Portland
1 South Portland
Sanford 1
1 Biddeford
1 York
Section A of the AHA Guide provides the legend for this map.
©1987 American Hospital Association

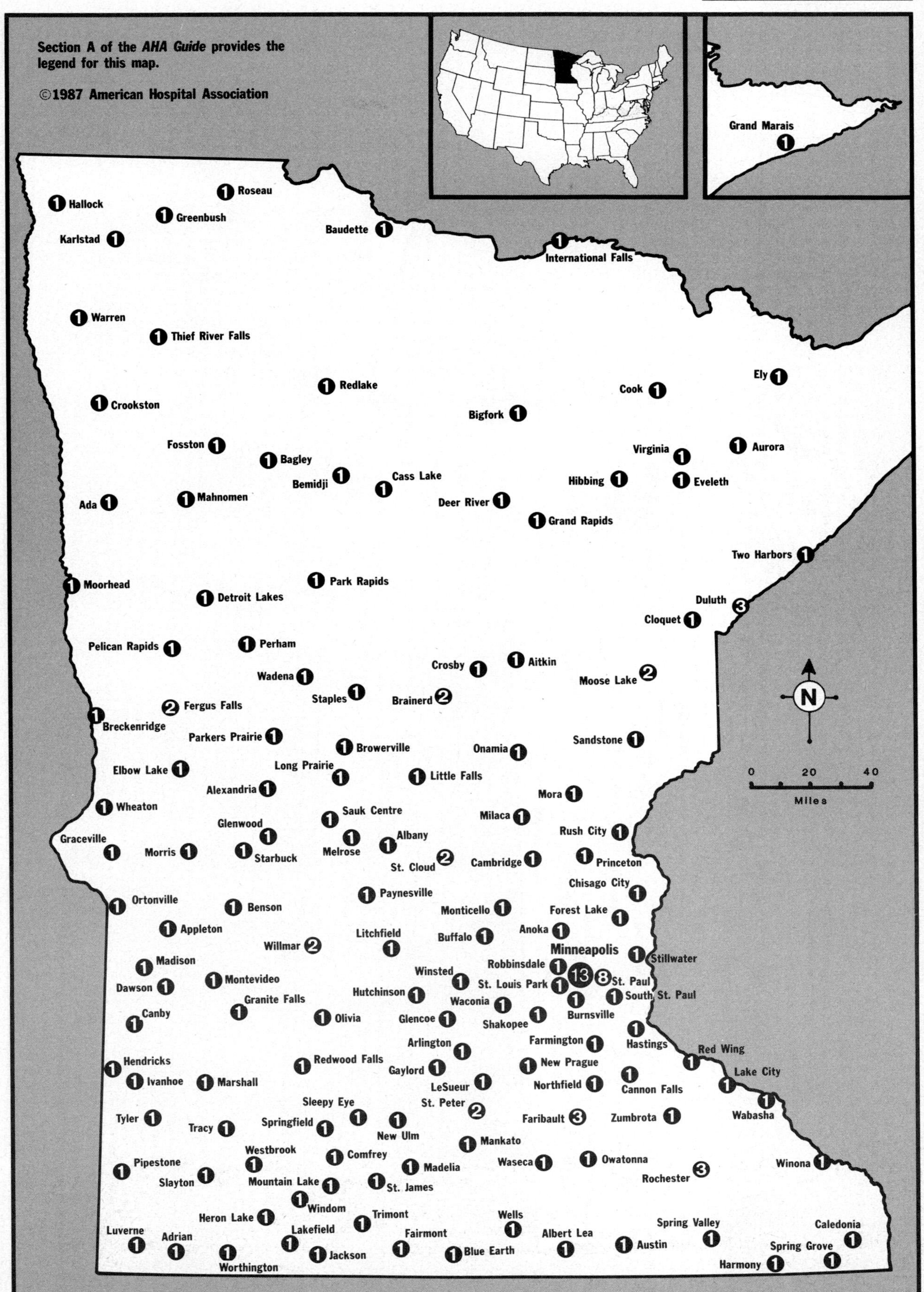
Section A of the *AHA Guide* provides the legend for this map.
©1987 American Hospital Association
Grand Marais 1
Hallock 1
Roseau 1
Greenbush 1
Karlstad 1
Baudette 1
International Falls 1
Warren 1
Thief River Falls 1
Redlake 1
Crookston 1
Ely 1
Cook 1
Bigfork 1
Fosston 1
Bagley 1
Bemidji 1
Cass Lake 1
Virginia 1
Aurora 1
Hibbing 1
Eveleth 1
Ada 1
Mahnomen 1
Deer River 1
Grand Rapids 1
Two Harbors 1
Moorhead 1
Park Rapids 1
Detroit Lakes 1
Duluth 3
Cloquet 1
Pelican Rapids 1
Perham 1
Crosby 1
Aitkin 1
Wadena 1
Moose Lake 2
Staples 1
Brainerd 2
Fergus Falls 2
Breckenridge 1
Parkers Prairie 1
Browerville 1
Onamia 1
Sandstone 1
Elbow Lake 1
Long Prairie 1
Little Falls 1
Alexandria 1
Mora 1
Wheaton 1
Sauk Centre 1
Milaca 1
Glenwood 1
Albany 1
Rush City 1
Graceville 1
Morris 1
Starbuck 1
Melrose 1
St. Cloud 2
Cambridge 1
Princeton 1
Chisago City 1
Ortonville 1
Paynesville 1
Monticello 1
Forest Lake 1
Benson 1
Appleton 1
Litchfield 1
Buffalo 1
Anoka 1
Willmar 2
Minneapolis 13
Stillwater 1
Madison 1
Robbinsdale 1
Winsted 1
St. Louis Park 1
St. Paul 8
Dawson 1
Montevideo 1
Hutchinson 1
Waconia 1
South St. Paul 1
Granite Falls 1
Canby 1
Olivia 1
Glencoe 1
Shakopee 1
Burnsville 1
Arlington 1
Farmington 1
Hastings 1
Red Wing 1
Hendricks 1
Redwood Falls 1
Gaylord 1
New Prague 1
Lake City 1
Ivanhoe 1
Marshall 1
LeSueur 1
Northfield 1
Cannon Falls 1
Sleepy Eye 1
St. Peter 2
Wabasha 1
Tyler 1
Tracy 1
Springfield 1
New Ulm 1
Faribault 3
Zumbrota 1
Mankato 1
Westbrook 1
Comfrey 1
Pipestone 1
Madelia 1
Waseca 1
Owatonna 1
Winona 1
Slayton 1
Mountain Lake 1
St. James 1
Rochester 3
Windom 1
Trimont 1
Wells 1
Heron Lake 1
Lakefield 1
Fairmont 1
Albert Lea 1
Spring Valley 1
Caledonia 1
Luverne 1
Adrian 1
Worthington 1
Jackson 1
Blue Earth 1
Austin 1
Spring Grove 1
Harmony 1
N
0 20 40
Miles

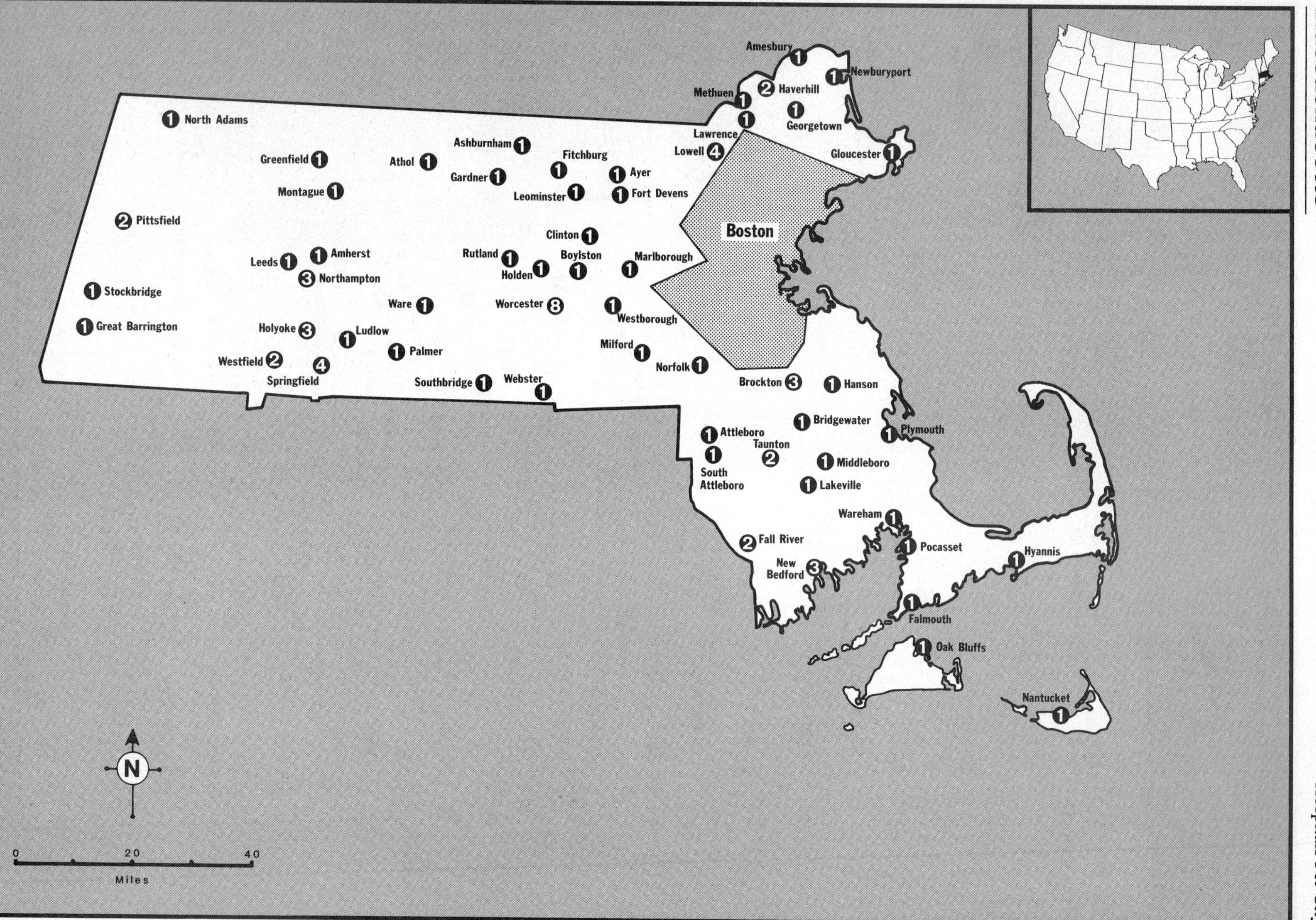

Amesbury 1
Newburyport 1
Methuen 1
Haverhill 2
Georgetown 1
Lawrence 1
Lowell 4
Gloucester 1
North Adams 1
Ashburnham 1
Greenfield 1
Athol 1
Fitchburg 1
Ayer 1
Gardner 1
Montague 1
Leominster 1
Fort Devens 1
Pittsfield 2
Boston
Clinton 1
Rutland 1
Boylston 1
Marlborough 1
Leeds 1
Amherst 1
Holden 1
Northampton 3
Stockbridge 1
Ware 1
Worcester 8
Westborough 1
Great Barrington 1
Holyoke 3
Ludlow 1
Milford 1
Palmer 1
Norfolk 1
Westfield 2
Springfield 4
Southbridge 1
Webster 1
Brockton 3
Hanson 1
Bridgewater 1
Attleboro 1
Plymouth 1
Taunton 2
South Attleboro 1
Middleboro 1
Lakeville 1
Wareham 1
Fall River 2
Pocasset 1
Hyannis 1
New Bedford 3
Falmouth 1
Oak Bluffs 1
Nantucket 1
N
0
20
40
Miles

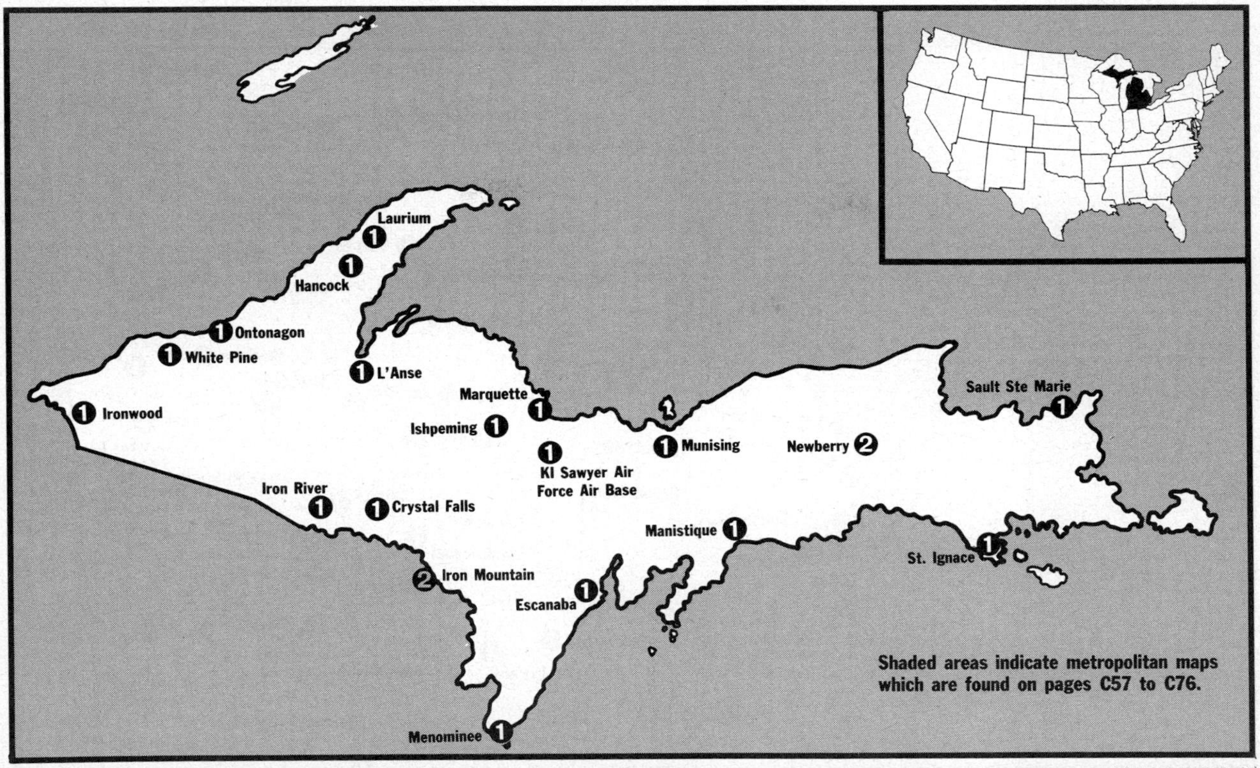

Laurium 1
Hancock 1
Ontonagon 1
White Pine 1
L'Anse 1
Ironwood 1
Marquette 1
Ishpeming 1
KI Sawyer Air Force Air Base 1
Munising 1
Newberry 2
Sault Ste Marie 1
Iron River 1
Crystal Falls 1
Manistique 1
St. Ignace 1
Iron Mountain 2
Escanaba 1
Menominee 1
Shaded areas indicate metropolitan maps which are found on pages C57 to C76.
Cheboygan 1 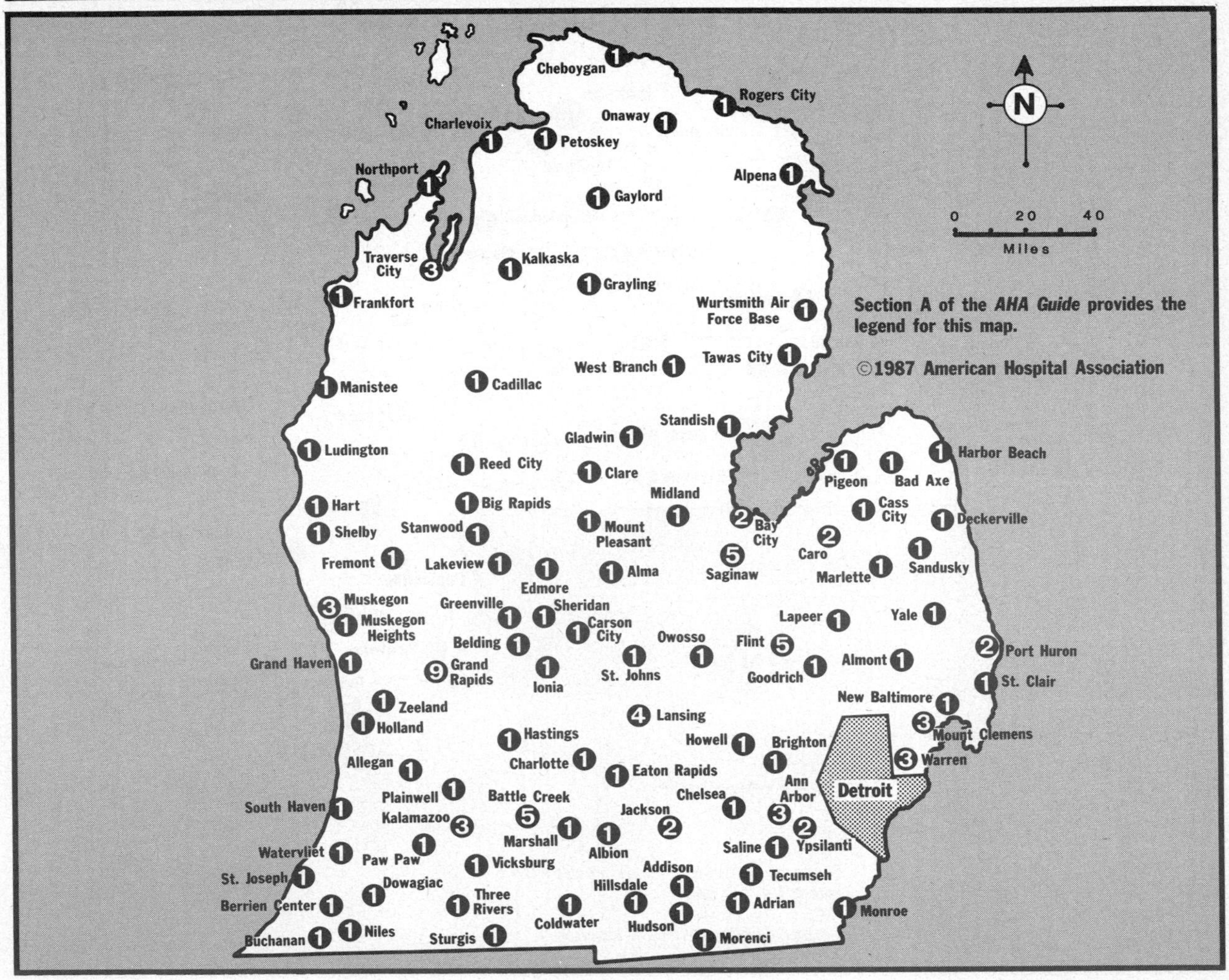
Rogers City 1
Onaway 1
Charlevoix 1
Petoskey 1
Northport 1
Alpena 1
Gaylord 1
N
0 20 40
Miles
Traverse City 3
Kalkaska 1
Grayling 1
Frankfort 1
Wurtsmith Air Force Base 1
Section A of the *AHA Guide* provides the legend for this map.
©1987 American Hospital Association
West Branch 1
Tawas City 1
Manistee 1
Cadillac 1
Standish 1
Gladwin 1
Ludington 1
Reed City 1
Clare 1
Harbor Beach 1
Pigeon 1
Bad Axe 1
Midland 1
Hart 1
Big Rapids 1
Cass City 1
Deckerville 1
Shelby 1
Stanwood 1
Mount Pleasant 1
Bay City 2
Caro 2
Fremont 1
Lakeview 1
Edmore 1
Alma 1
Saginaw 5
Marlette 1
Sandusky 1
Muskegon 3
Muskegon Heights 1
Greenville 1
Sheridan 1
Carson City 1
Lapeer 1
Yale 1
Belding 1
Owosso 1
Flint 5
Grand Haven 1
Grand Rapids 9
Ionia 1
St. Johns 1
Goodrich 1
Almont 1
Port Huron 2
St. Clair 1
New Baltimore 1
Zeeland 1
Holland 1
Lansing 4
Mount Clemens 3
Hastings 1
Howell 1
Brighton 1
Warren 3
Allegan 1
Charlotte 1
Eaton Rapids 1
Ann Arbor 3
Detroit
South Haven 1
Plainwell 1
Battle Creek 5
Chelsea 1
Kalamazoo 3
Jackson 2
Ypsilanti 2
Watervliet 1
Paw Paw 1
Marshall 1
Albion 1
Saline 1
Vicksburg 1
Addison 1
St. Joseph 1
Dowagiac 1
Three Rivers 1
Hillsdale 1
Tecumseh 1
Berrien Center 1
Coldwater 1
Adrian 1
Monroe 1
Buchanan 1
Niles 1
Sturgis 1
Hudson 1
Morenci 1

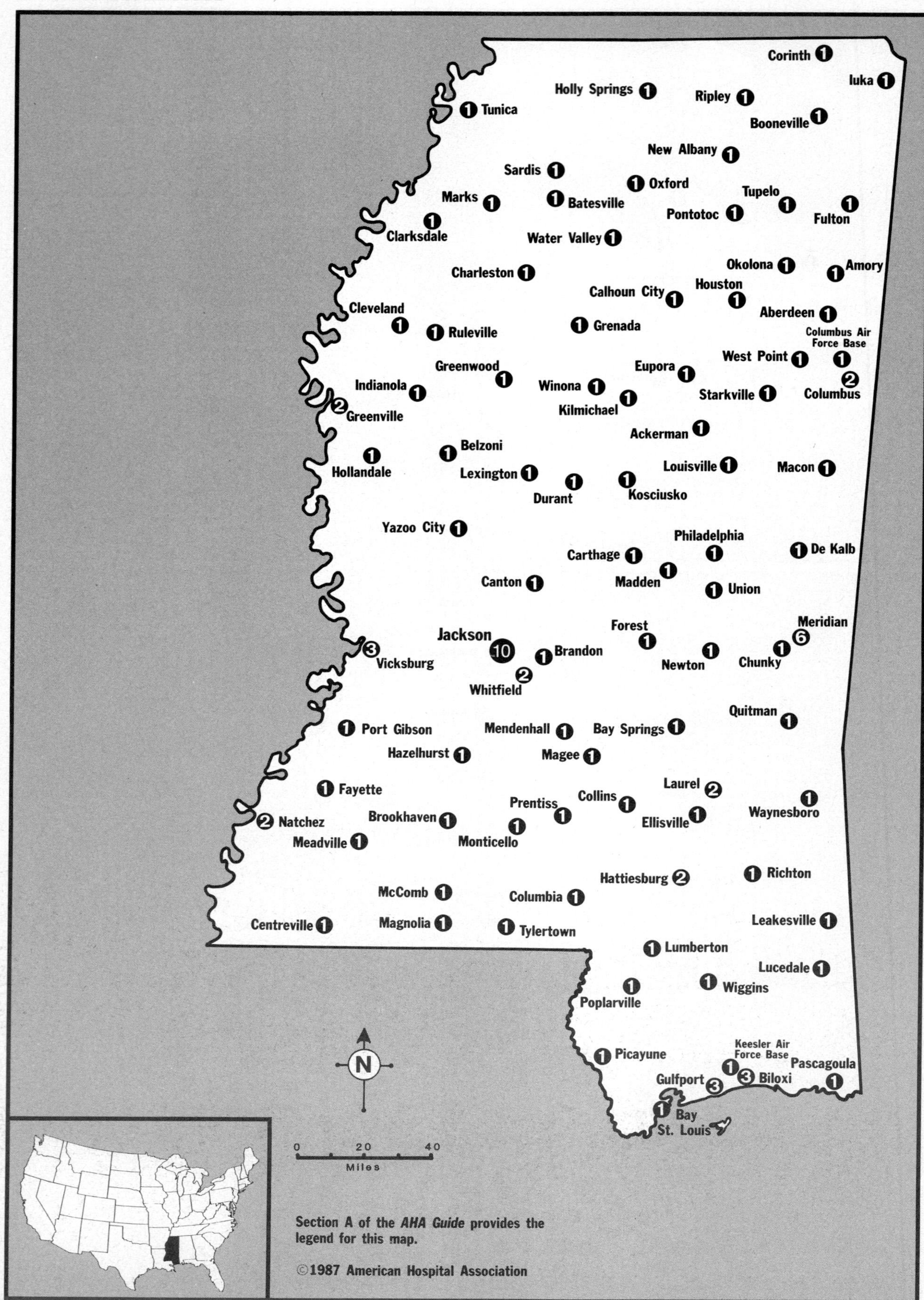
Corinth 1
Iuka 1
Holly Springs 1
Ripley 1
Tunica 1
Booneville 1
New Albany 1
Sardis 1
Oxford 1
Marks 1
Batesville 1
Tupelo 1
Pontotoc 1
Fulton 1
Clarksdale 1
Water Valley 1
Okolona 1
Amory 1
Charleston 1
Calhoun City 1
Houston 1
Cleveland 1
Ruleville 1
Grenada 1
Aberdeen 1
Columbus Air Force Base 1
West Point 1
Greenwood 1
Eupora 1
Indianola 1
Winona 1
Starkville 1
Columbus 2
Greenville 2
Kilmichael 1
Ackerman 1
Belzoni 1
Hollandale 1
Lexington 1
Louisville 1
Macon 1
Durant 1
Kosciusko 1
Yazoo City 1
Philadelphia 1
Carthage 1
De Kalb 1
Madden 1
Canton 1
Union 1
Forest 1
Meridian 6
Jackson 10
Brandon 1
Vicksburg 3
Newton 1
Chunky 1
Whitfield 2
Quitman 1
Port Gibson 1
Mendenhall 1
Bay Springs 1
Hazelhurst 1
Magee 1
Laurel 2
Fayette 1
Prentiss 1
Collins 1
Waynesboro 1
Natchez 2
Brookhaven 1
Ellisville 1
Meadville 1
Monticello 1
Hattiesburg 2
Richton 1
McComb 1
Columbia 1
Leakesville 1
Centreville 1
Magnolia 1
Tylertown 1
Lumberton 1
Lucedale 1
Wiggins 1
Poplarville 1
Picayune 1
Keesler Air Force Base 1
Pascagoula 1
Gulfport 3
Biloxi 3
Bay St. Louis 1
N
0 20 40
Miles
Section A of the *AHA Guide* provides the legend for this map.
©1987 American Hospital Association

Nevada

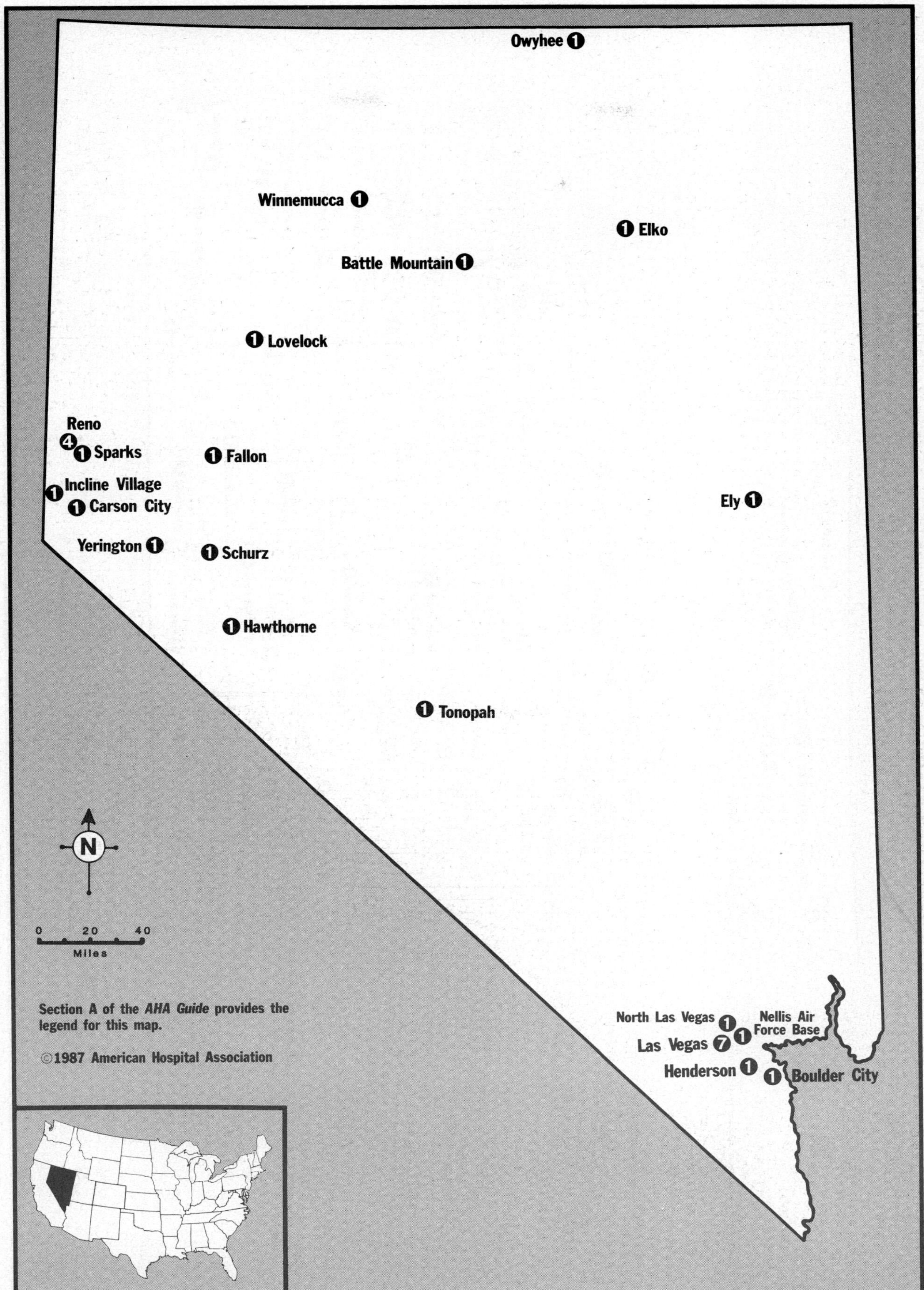
Owyhee 1
Winnemucca 1
Elko 1
Battle Mountain 1
Lovelock 1
Reno
4
Sparks 1
Fallon 1
Incline Village 1
Carson City 1
Ely 1
Yerington 1
Schurz 1
Hawthorne 1
Tonopah 1
N
0 20 40
Miles
Section A of the AHA Guide provides the legend for this map.
©1987 American Hospital Association
North Las Vegas 1
Nellis Air Force Base 1
Las Vegas 7
Henderson 1
Boulder City 1

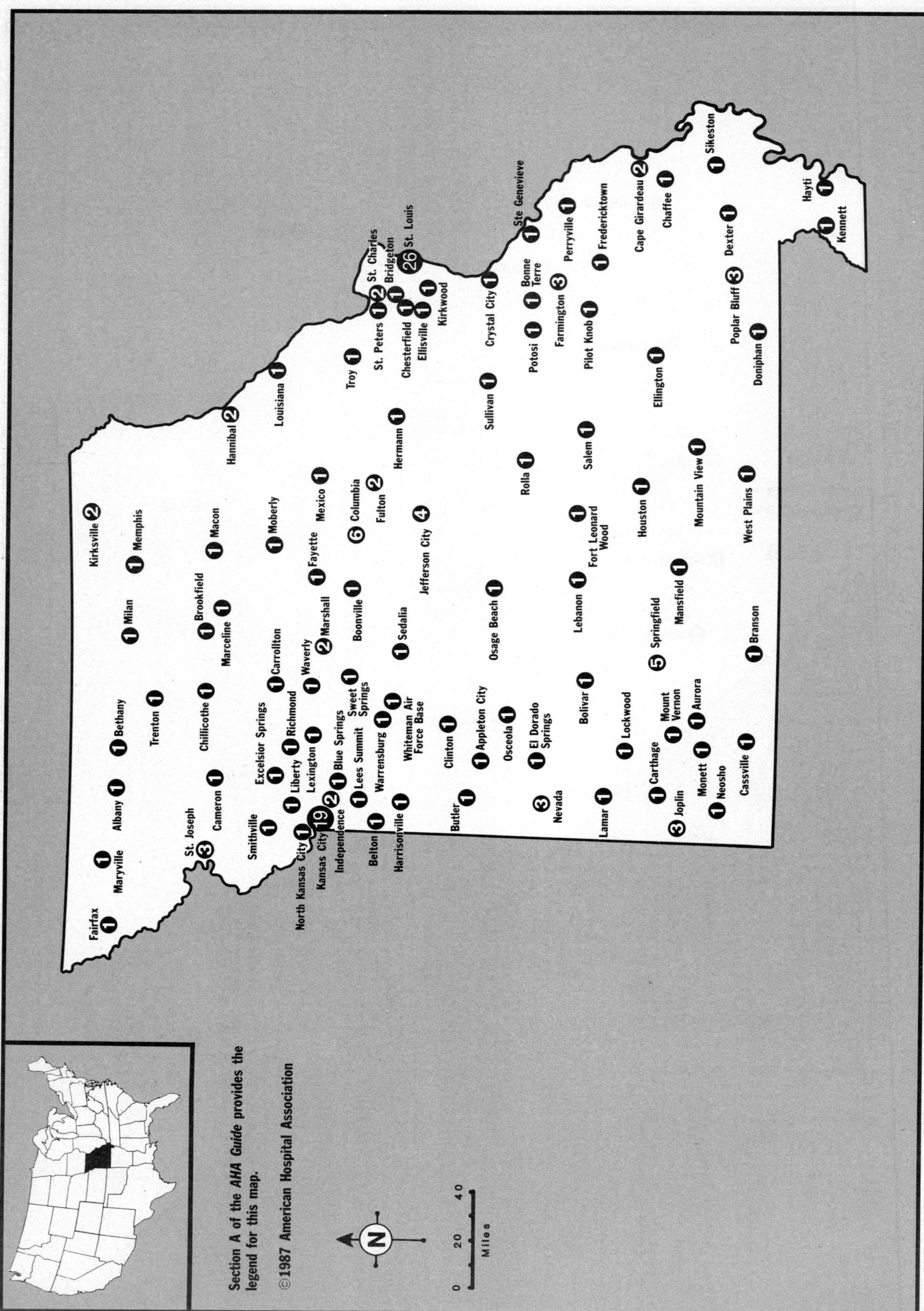
Fairfax 1
Maryville 1
St. Joseph 3
Albany 1
Bethany 1
Trenton 1
Milan 1
Kirksville 2
Memphis 1
Cameron 1
Chillicothe 1
Brookfield 1
Marceline 1
Macon 1
Smithville 1
Excelsior Springs 1
Liberty 1
Richmond 1
Carrollton 1
Moberly 1
North Kansas City 1
Kansas City 19
Independence 2
Blue Springs 1
Lexington 1
Waverly 1
Marshall 2
Fayette 1
Mexico 1
Columbia 6
Fulton 2
Hannibal 2
Louisiana 1
Troy 1
Lees Summit 1
Sweet Springs 1
Boonville 1
Jefferson City 4
Belton 1
Warrensburg 1
Harrisonville 1
Whiteman Air Force Base 1
Sedalia 1
Hermann 1
St. Peters 1
St. Charles 2
Bridgeton 1
St. Louis 26
Chesterfield 1
Ellisville 1
Kirkwood 1
Crystal City 1
Ste Genevieve 1
Butler 1
Clinton 1
Appleton City 1
Osceola 1
Osage Beach 1
Sullivan 1
Rolla 1
Potosi 1
Bonne Terre 1
Farmington 3
Perryville 1
Fredericktown 1
Pilot Knob 1
Salem 1
Nevada 3
El Dorado Springs 1
Bolivar 1
Lebanon 1
Fort Leonard Wood 1
Houston 1
Ellington 1
Cape Girardeau 2
Chaffee 1
Sikeston 1
Lamar 1
Lockwood 1
Springfield 5
Mansfield 1
Mountain View 1
West Plains 1
Doniphan 1
Poplar Bluff 3
Dexter 1
Hayti 1
Kennett 1
Carthage 1
Joplin 3
Mount Vernon 1
Aurora 1
Monett 1
Neosho 1
Cassville 1
Branson 1
Section A of the *AHA Guide* provides the legend for this map.
©1987 American Hospital Association
N
0 20 40
Miles

Montana

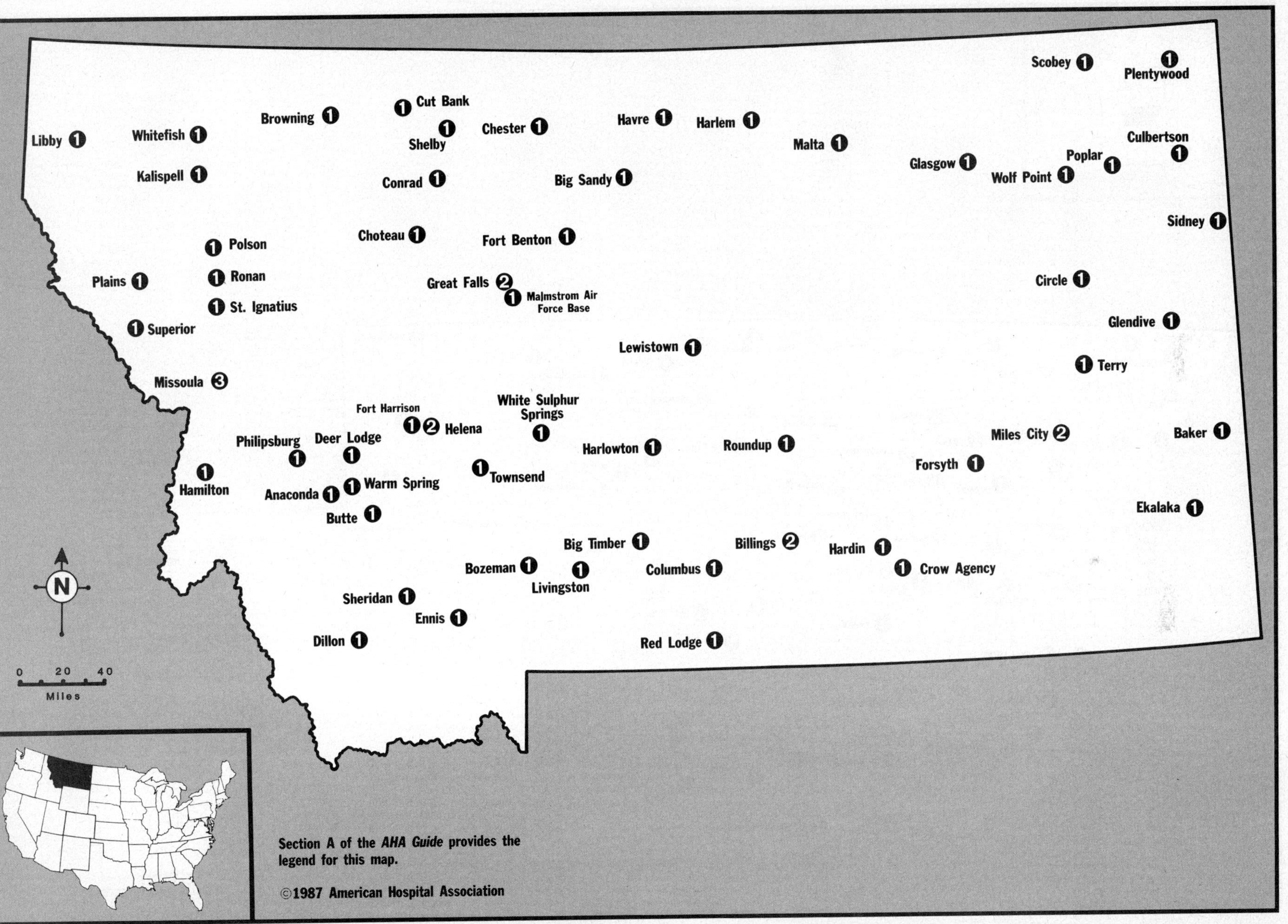
Scobey 1
Plentywood 1
Libby 1
Whitefish 1
Browning 1
Cut Bank 1
Shelby 1
Chester 1
Havre 1
Harlem 1
Culbertson 1
Malta 1
Poplar 1
Glasgow 1
Wolf Point 1
Kalispell 1
Conrad 1
Big Sandy 1
Sidney 1
Choteau 1
Fort Benton 1
Polson 1
Ronan 1
Plains 1
Great Falls 2
Malmstrom Air Force Base 1
Circle 1
St. Ignatius 1
Superior 1
Glendive 1
Lewistown 1
Terry 1
Missoula 3
Fort Harrison 1
Helena 2
White Sulphur Springs 1
Philipsburg 1
Deer Lodge 1
Miles City 2
Baker 1
Harlowton 1
Roundup 1
Townsend 1
Forsyth 1
Hamilton 1
Warm Spring 1
Anaconda 1
Butte 1
Ekalaka 1
Big Timber 1
Billings 2
Hardin 1
Bozeman 1
Livingston 1
Columbus 1
Crow Agency 1
Sheridan 1
Ennis 1
Dillon 1
Red Lodge 1
N
0 20 40
Miles
Section A of the *AHA Guide* provides the legend for this map.
©1987 American Hospital Association

Nebraska

Hospitals Per City

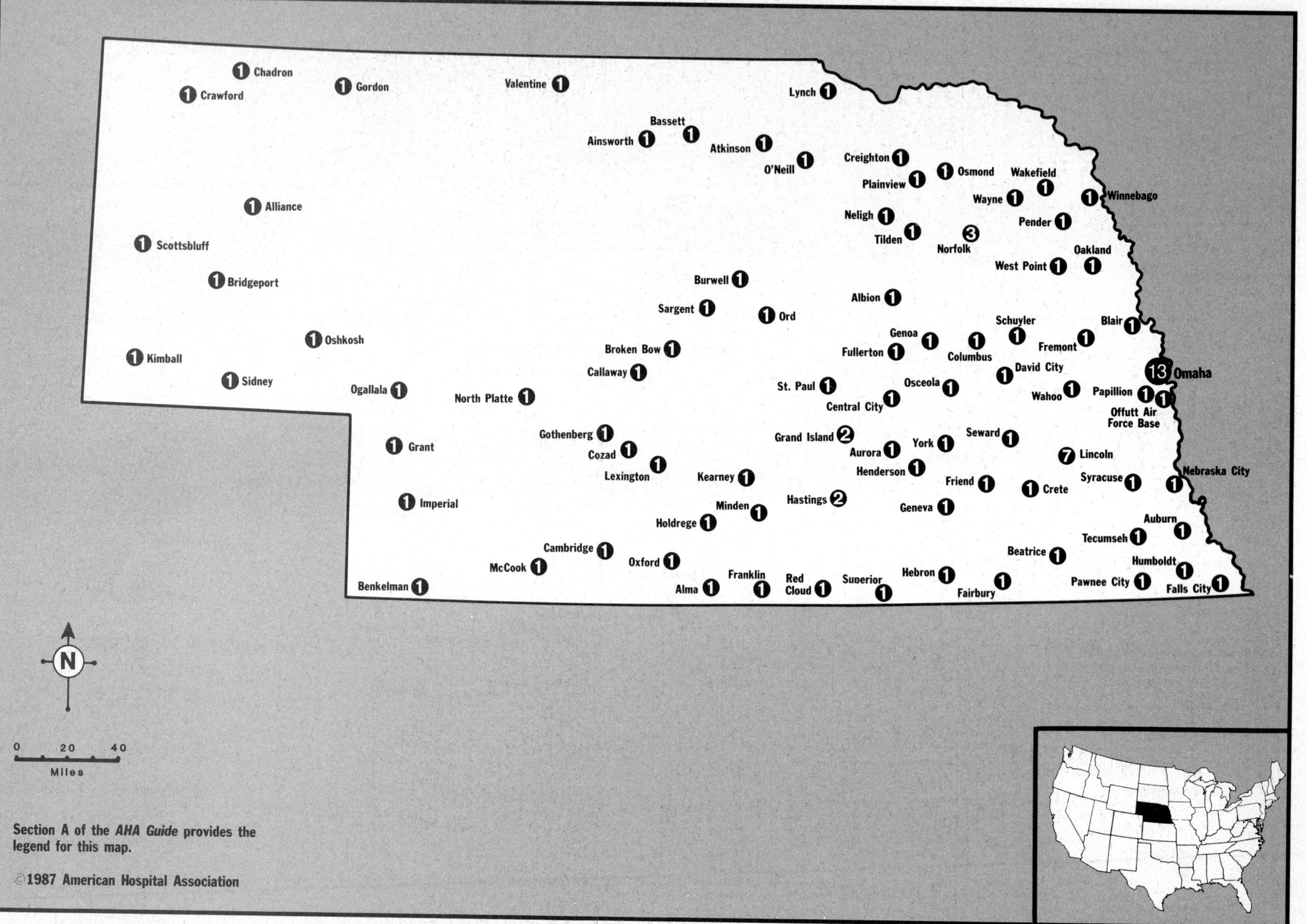

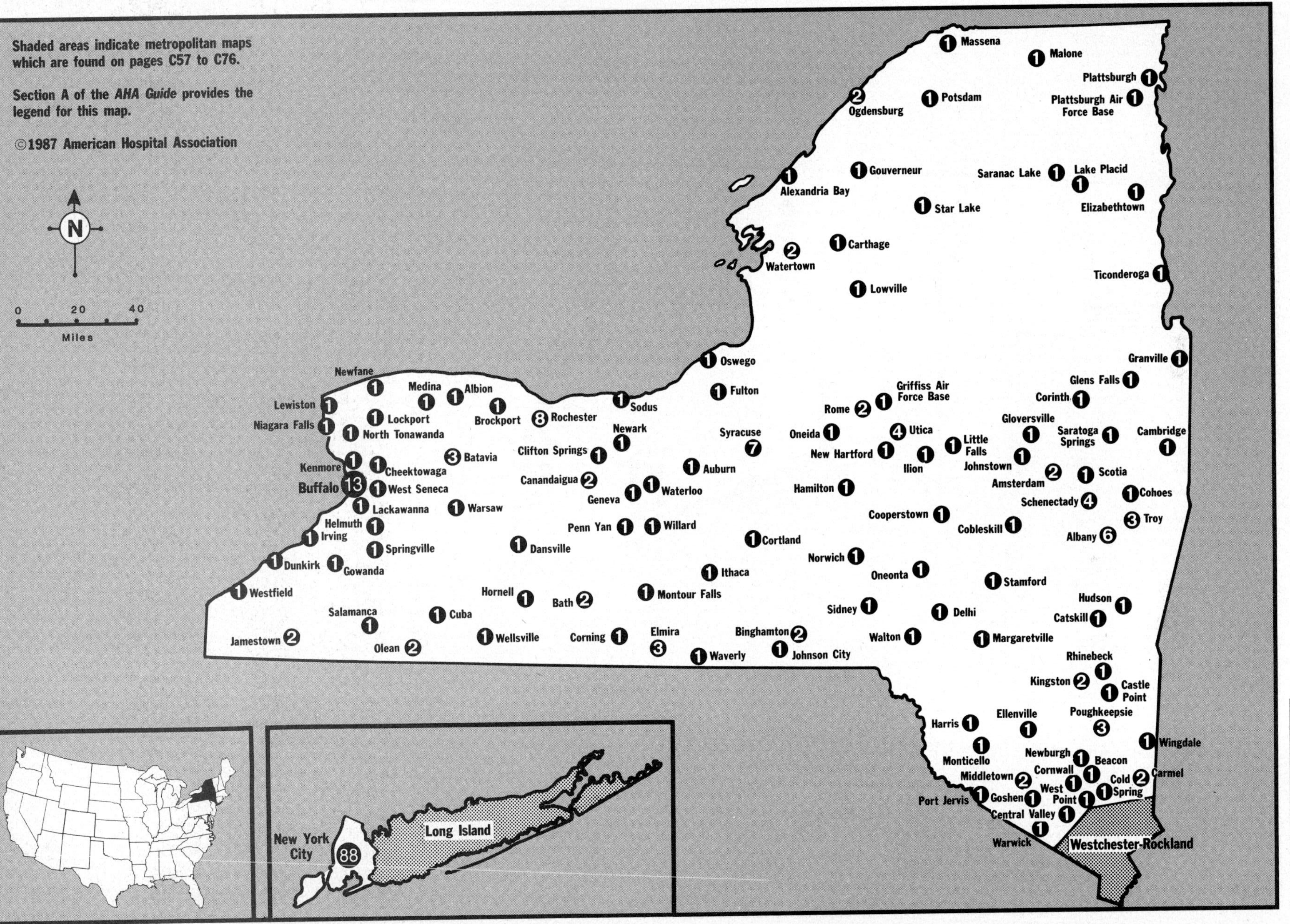
Shaded areas indicate metropolitan maps which are found on pages C57 to C76.
Section A of the *AHA Guide* provides the legend for this map.
©1987 American Hospital Association
N
0 20 40
Miles
Massena 1
Malone 1
Plattsburgh 1
Plattsburgh Air Force Base 1
Ogdensburg 2
Potsdam 1
Alexandria Bay 1
Gouverneur 1
Saranac Lake 1
Lake Placid 1
Elizabethtown 1
Star Lake 1
Watertown 2
Carthage 1
Lowville 1
Ticonderoga 1
Oswego 1
Fulton 1
Granville 1
Glens Falls 1
Corinth 1
Griffiss Air Force Base 1
Rome 2
Gloversville 1
Saratoga Springs 1
Cambridge 1
Oneida 1
Utica 4
Little Falls 1
New Hartford 1
Ilion 1
Johnstown 1
Amsterdam 2
Scotia 1
Schenectady 4
Cohoes 1
Troy 3
Albany 6
Hamilton 1
Cooperstown 1
Cobleskill 1
Syracuse 7
Auburn 1
Cortland 1
Norwich 1
Oneonta 1
Stamford 1
Hudson 1
Catskill 1
Sidney 1
Delhi 1
Walton 1
Margaretville 1
Binghamton 2
Johnson City 1
Ithaca 1
Montour Falls 1
Elmira 3
Waverly 1
Newfane 1
Lewiston 1
Niagara Falls 1
Medina 1
Albion 1
Lockport 1
North Tonawanda 1
Brockport 1
Rochester 8
Sodus 1
Newark 1
Clifton Springs 1
Canandaigua 2
Geneva 1
Waterloo 1
Penn Yan 1
Willard 1
Kenmore 1
Buffalo 13
Cheektowaga 1
West Seneca 1
Lackawanna 1
Batavia 3
Warsaw 1
Helmuth 1
Irving 1
Springville 1
Dansville 1
Dunkirk 1
Gowanda 1
Westfield 1
Salamanca 1
Cuba 1
Hornell 1
Bath 2
Wellsville 1
Corning 1
Jamestown 2
Olean 2
Rhinebeck 1
Kingston 2
Castle Point 1
Ellenville 1
Poughkeepsie 3
Harris 1
Monticello 1
Wingdale 1
Newburgh 1
Beacon 1
Cornwall 1
Cold Spring 1
Carmel 2
Middletown 2
West Point 1
Port Jervis 1
Goshen 1
Central Valley 1
Warwick 1
Westchester-Rockland
New York City 88
Long Island

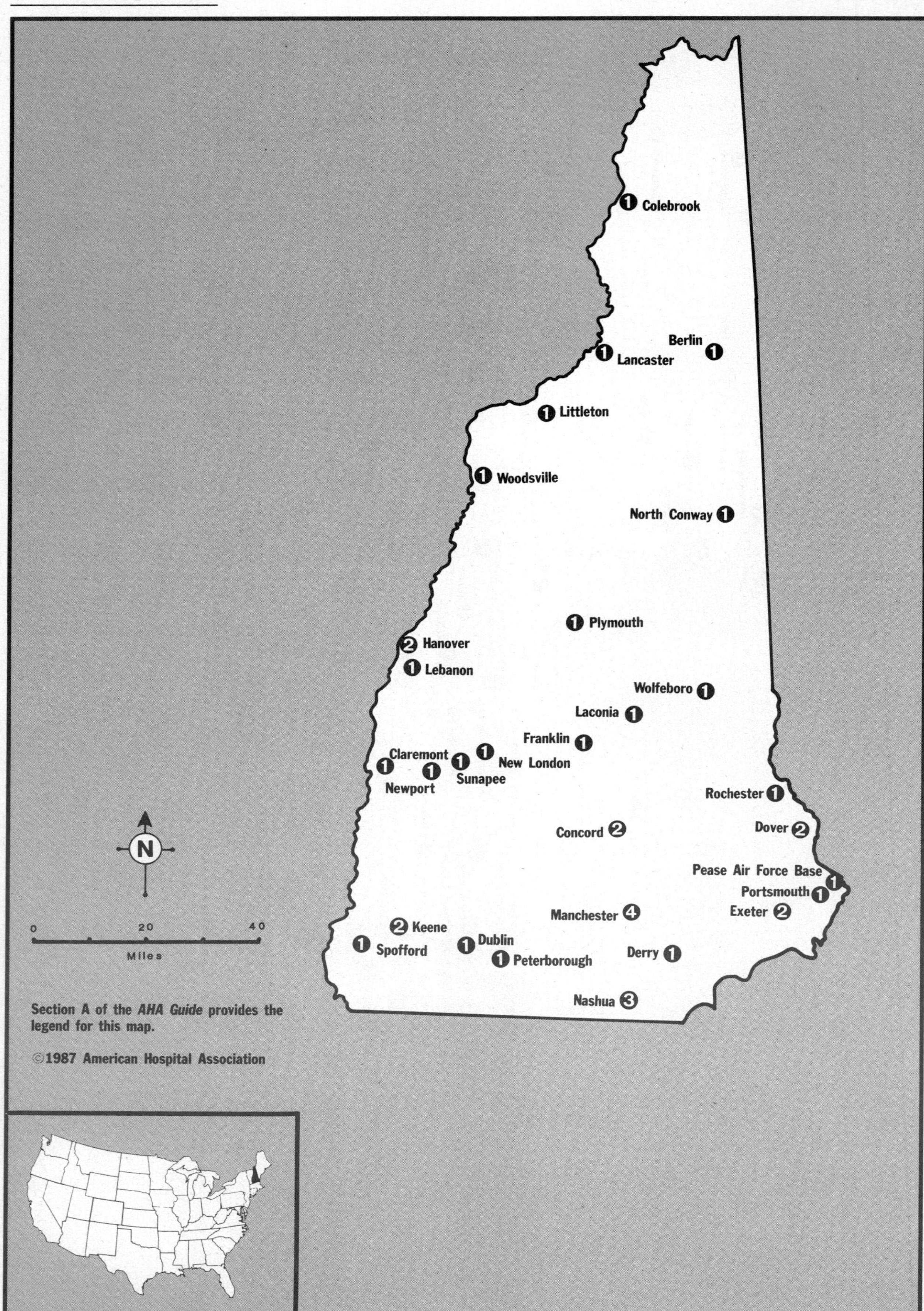

Section A of the *AHA Guide* provides the legend for this map.

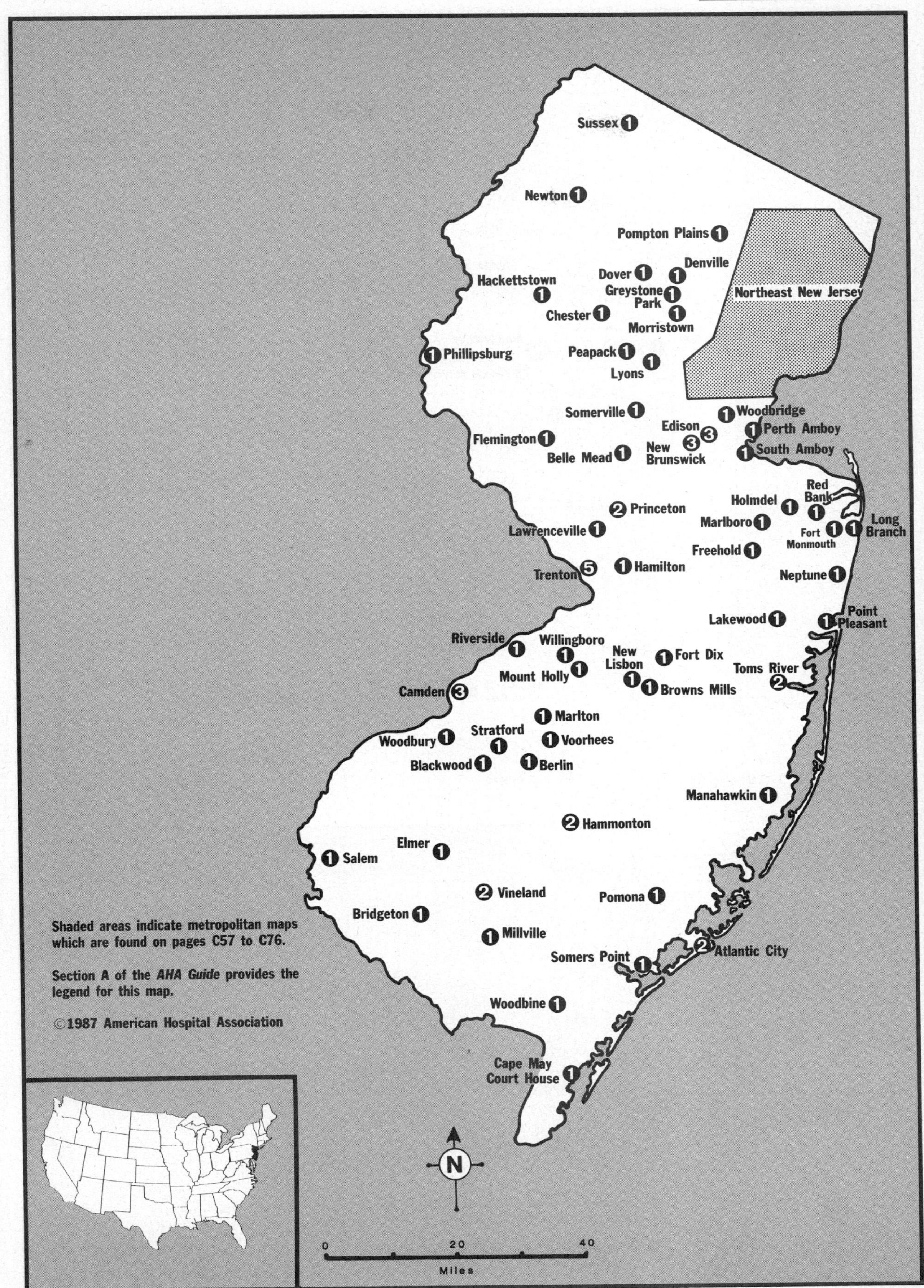
Sussex 1
Newton 1
Pompton Plains 1
Denville
Dover 1
1
Hackettstown
1
Greystone Park 1
Northeast New Jersey
Chester 1
1
Morristown
1 Phillipsburg
Peapack 1
1
Lyons
Somerville 1
1 Woodbridge
Edison
3
1 Perth Amboy
Flemington 1
New Brunswick 3
Belle Mead 1
1 South Amboy
Red Bank
Holmdel 1
1
2 Princeton
Marlboro 1
Long Branch
Fort Monmouth 1 1
Lawrenceville 1
Freehold 1
Trenton 5
1 Hamilton
Neptune 1
Lakewood 1
1 Point Pleasant
Riverside
1
Willingboro
1
New Lisbon
1 Fort Dix
Toms River
2
Mount Holly 1
1 1 Browns Mills
Camden 3
1 Marlton
Woodbury 1
Stratford
1
1 Voorhees
Blackwood 1
1 Berlin
Manahawkin 1
2 Hammonton
Elmer 1
1 Salem
2 Vineland
Pomona 1
Bridgeton 1
1 Millville
Shaded areas indicate metropolitan maps which are found on pages C57 to C76.
Section A of the AHA Guide provides the legend for this map.
©1987 American Hospital Association
Somers Point
1
2 Atlantic City
Woodbine 1
Cape May Court House 1
N
0
20
40
Miles

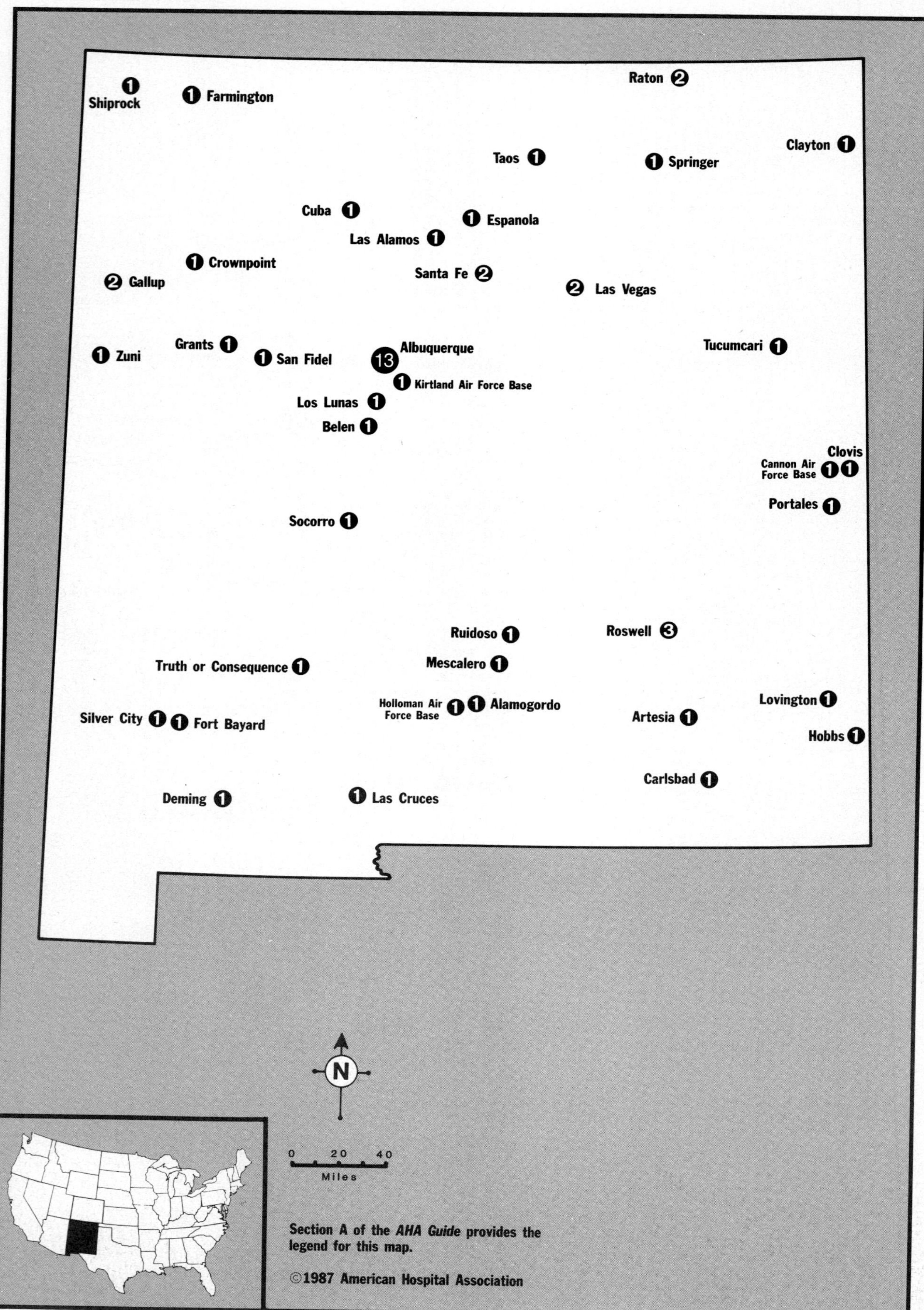
Shiprock 1
1 Farmington
Raton 2
Taos 1
1 Springer
Clayton 1
Cuba 1
1 Espanola
Las Alamos 1
1 Crownpoint
2 Gallup
Santa Fe 2
2 Las Vegas
1 Zuni
Grants 1
1 San Fidel
13 Albuquerque
1 Kirtland Air Force Base
Tucumcari 1
Los Lunas 1
Belen 1
Clovis
Cannon Air Force Base 1 1
Portales 1
Socorro 1
Ruidoso 1
Roswell 3
Truth or Consequence 1
Mescalero 1
Holloman Air Force Base 1 1 Alamogordo
Silver City 1 1 Fort Bayard
Artesia 1
Lovington 1
Hobbs 1
Carlsbad 1
Deming 1
1 Las Cruces
N
0 20 40
Miles
Section A of the AHA Guide provides the legend for this map.
©1987 American Hospital Association

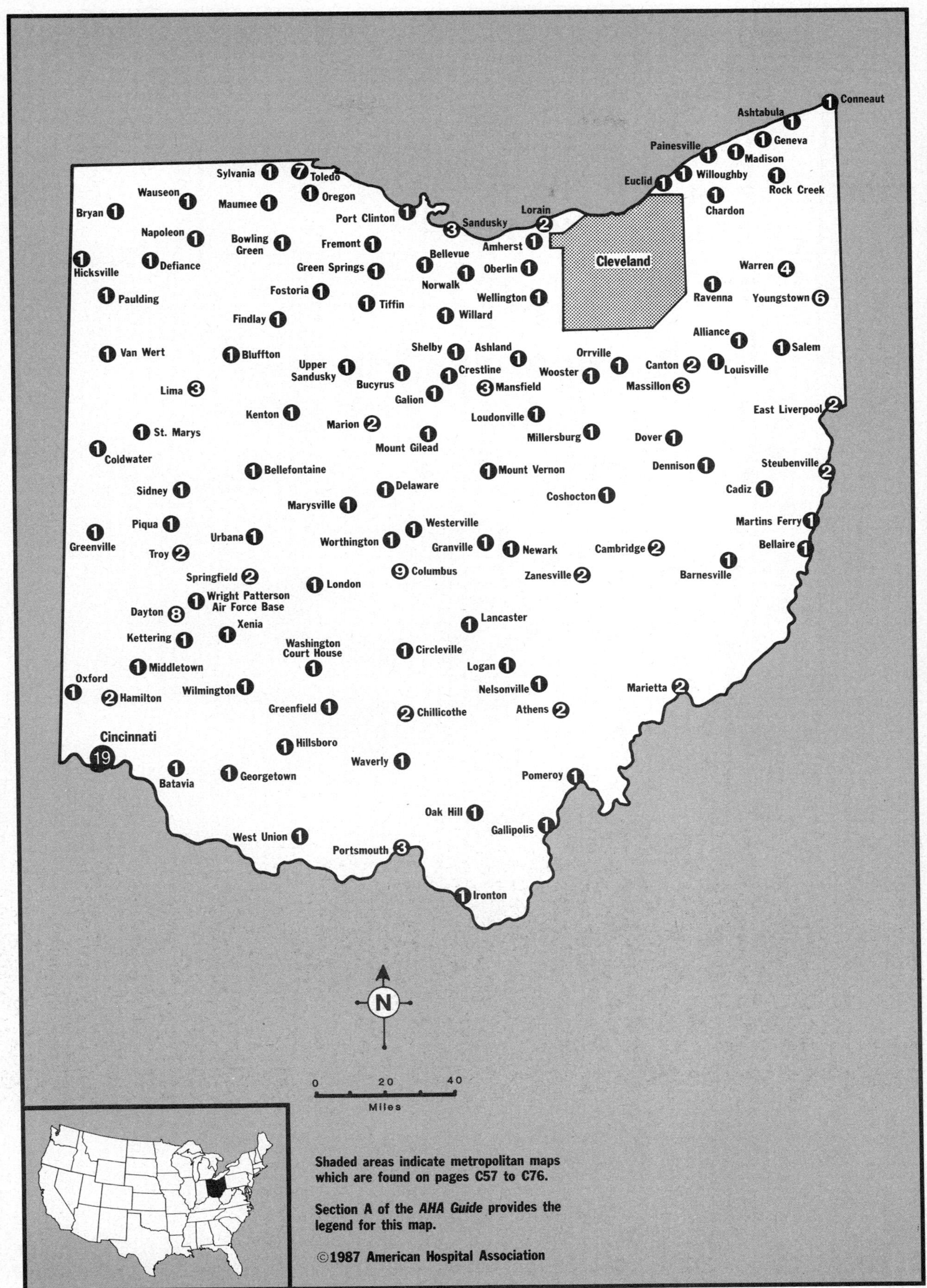
Conneaut 1
Ashtabula 1
Geneva 1
Painesville 1
Madison 1
Euclid 1
Willoughby 1
Rock Creek 1
Chardon 1
Sylvania 1
Toledo 7
Wauseon 1
Oregon 1
Maumee 1
Bryan 1
Port Clinton 1
Lorain
Sandusky 3
2
Napoleon 1
Bowling Green 1
Fremont 1
Amherst 1
Hicksville 1
Defiance 1
Bellevue 1
Cleveland
Green Springs 1
Norwalk 1
Oberlin 1
Warren 4
Fostoria 1
Paulding 1
Wellington 1
Ravenna 1
Youngstown 6
Tiffin 1
Willard 1
Findlay 1
Alliance 1
Van Wert 1
Bluffton 1
Shelby 1
Ashland 1
Orrville 1
Salem 1
Upper Sandusky 1
Crestline 1
Wooster 1
Canton 2
Louisville 1
Bucyrus 1
Lima 3
Galion 1
Mansfield 3
Massillon 3
Kenton 1
Loudonville 1
East Liverpool 2
Marion 2
St. Marys 1
Mount Gilead 1
Millersburg 1
Dover 1
Coldwater 1
Bellefontaine 1
Mount Vernon 1
Dennison 1
Steubenville 2
Delaware 1
Sidney 1
Coshocton 1
Cadiz 1
Marysville 1
Piqua 1
Westerville 1
Martins Ferry 1
Greenville 1
Urbana 1
Worthington 1
Granville 1
Newark 1
Cambridge 2
Bellaire 1
Troy 2
Columbus 9
Zanesville 2
Barnesville 1
Springfield 2
London 1
Wright Patterson Air Force Base 1
Dayton 8
Lancaster 1
Xenia 1
Kettering 1
Washington Court House 1
Circleville 1
Middletown 1
Logan 1
Oxford 1
Wilmington 1
Nelsonville 1
Marietta 2
Hamilton 2
Greenfield 1
Chillicothe 2
Athens 2
Cincinnati 19
Hillsboro 1
Batavia 1
Georgetown 1
Waverly 1
Pomeroy 1
Oak Hill 1
Gallipolis 1
West Union 1
Portsmouth 3
Ironton 1
N
0 20 40
Miles
Shaded areas indicate metropolitan maps which are found on pages C57 to C76.
Section A of the *AHA Guide* provides the legend for this map.
©1987 American Hospital Association

North Carolina

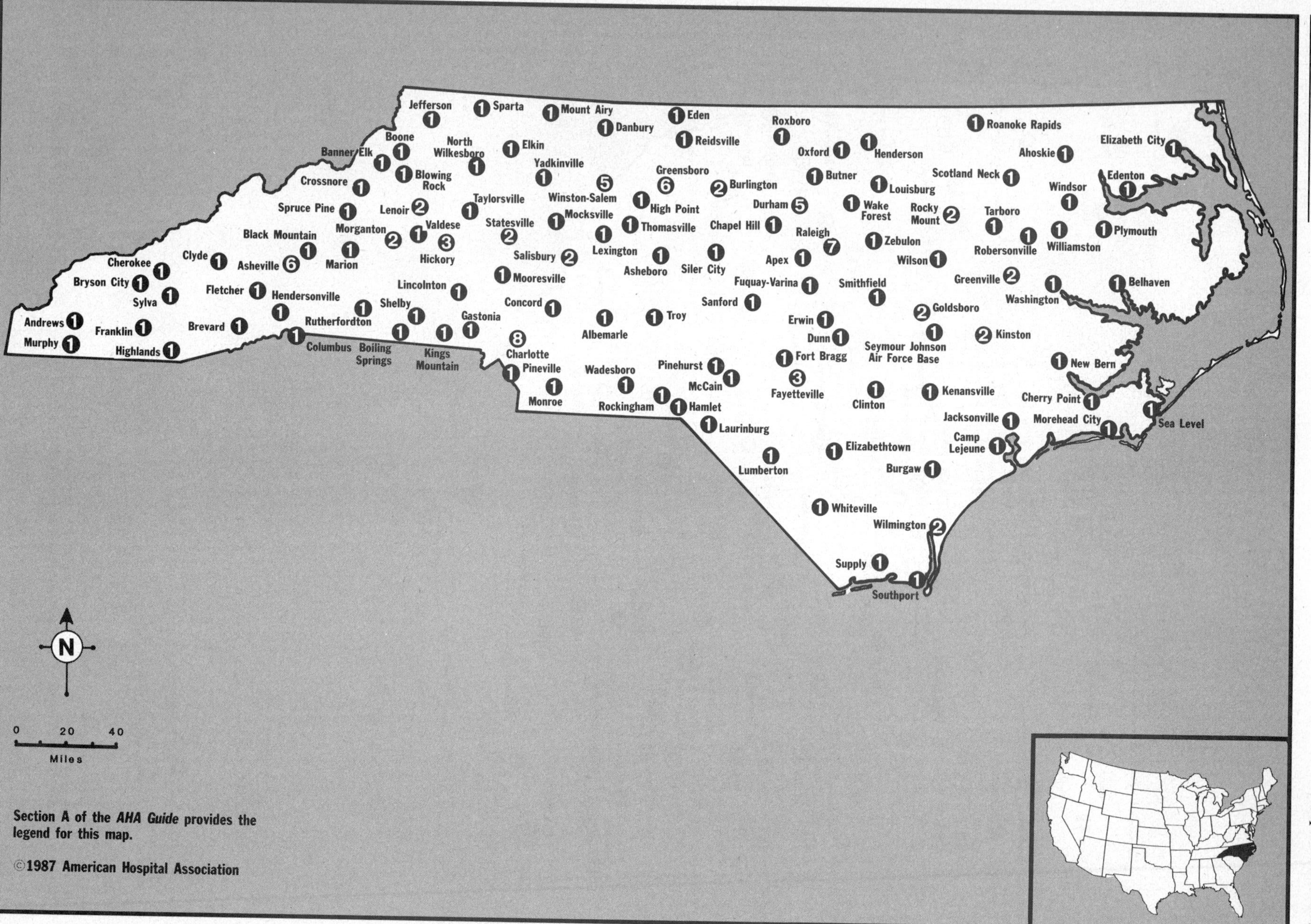

Section A of the *AHA Guide* provides the legend for this map.

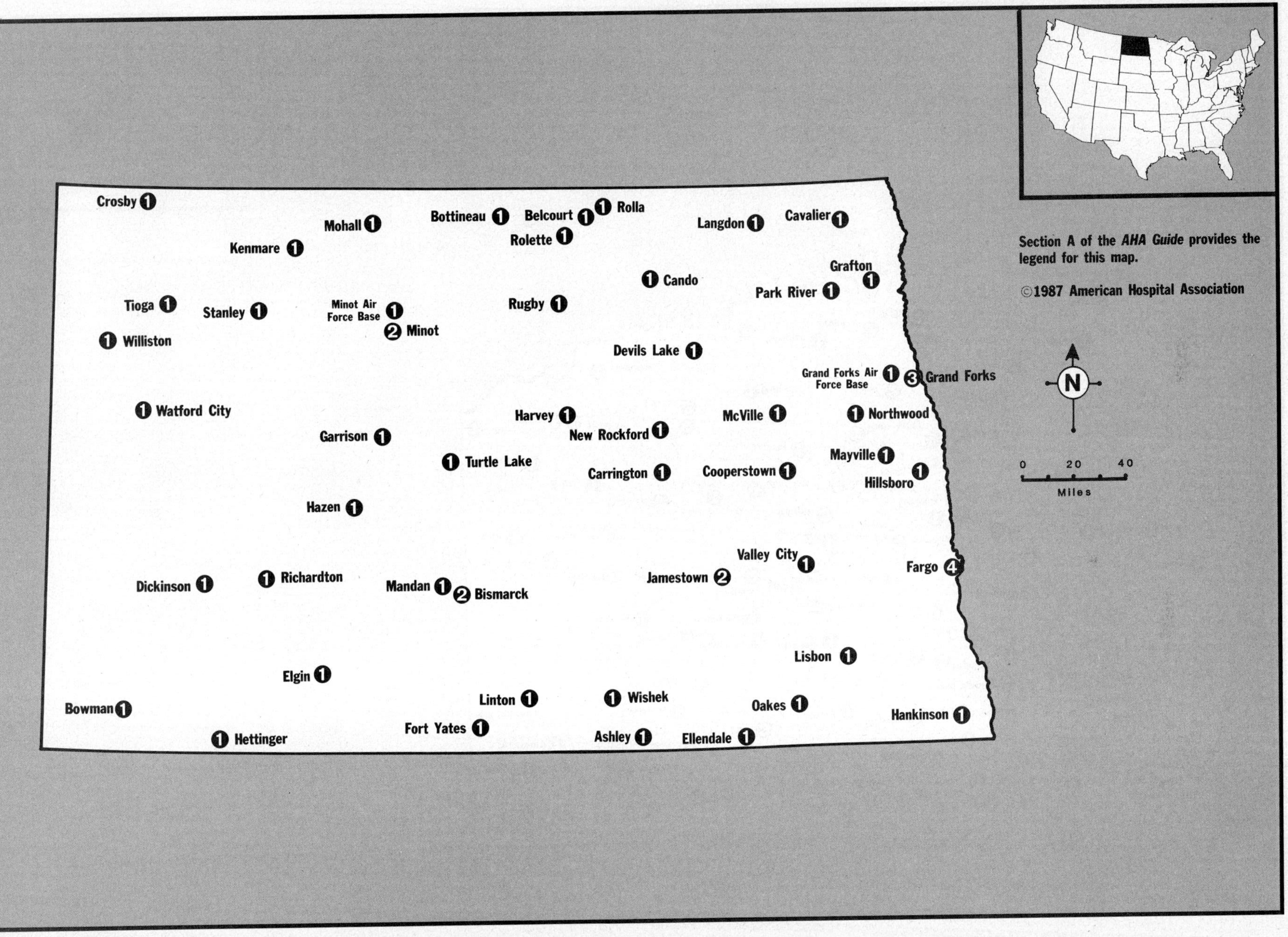
Section A of the *AHA Guide* provides the legend for this map.
©1987 American Hospital Association
N
0 20 40
Miles
Crosby 1
Mohall 1
Bottineau 1
Belcourt 1
Rolla 1
Rolette 1
Kenmare 1
Langdon 1
Cavalier 1
Grafton 1
Cando 1
Park River 1
Tioga 1
Stanley 1
Minot Air Force Base 1
Minot 2
Rugby 1
Williston 1
Devils Lake 1
Grand Forks Air Force Base 1
Grand Forks 3
Watford City 1
Harvey 1
McVille 1
Northwood 1
New Rockford 1
Garrison 1
Turtle Lake 1
Carrington 1
Cooperstown 1
Mayville 1
Hillsboro 1
Hazen 1
Valley City 1
Fargo 4
Dickinson 1
Richardton 1
Mandan 1
Bismarck 2
Jamestown 2
Lisbon 1
Elgin 1
Linton 1
Wishek 1
Oakes 1
Hankinson 1
Bowman 1
Fort Yates 1
Hettinger 1
Ashley 1
Ellendale 1

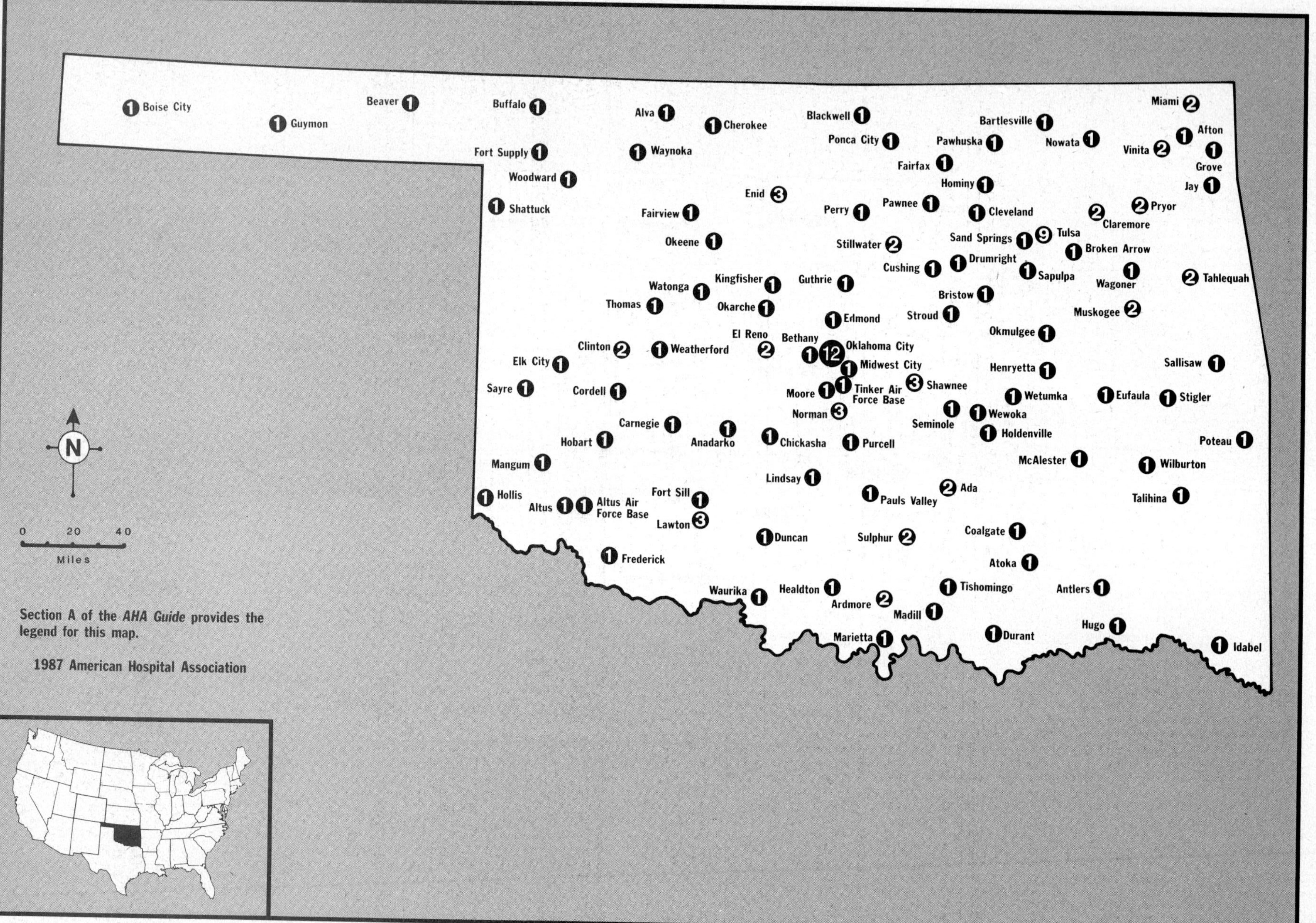

Boise City 1
Guymon 1
Beaver 1
Buffalo 1
Fort Supply 1
Woodward 1
Shattuck 1
Alva 1
Waynoka 1
Cherokee 1
Fairview 1
Okeene 1
Enid 3
Blackwell 1
Ponca City 1
Perry 1
Fairfax 1
Pawnee 1
Pawhuska 1
Hominy 1
Bartlesville 1
Cleveland 1
Nowata 1
Miami 2
Afton 1
Grove 1
Jay 1
Vinita 2
Pryor 2
Claremore 2
Tulsa 9
Sand Springs 1
Broken Arrow 1
Wagoner 1
Tahlequah 2
Muskogee 2
Sapulpa 1
Drumright 1
Cushing 1
Stillwater 2
Bristow 1
Stroud 1
Okmulgee 1
Henryetta 1
Sallisaw 1
Stigler 1
Eufaula 1
Poteau 1
Wilburton 1
Talihina 1
Idabel 1
Hugo 1
Antlers 1
McAlester 1
Wetumka 1
Wewoka 1
Holdenville 1
Seminole 1
Shawnee 3
Tinker Air Force Base 1
Midwest City 1
Oklahoma City 12
Bethany 1
Edmond 1
Guthrie 1
Moore 1
Norman 3
Purcell 1
Ada 2
Coalgate 1
Atoka 1
Tishomingo 1
Durant 1
Madill 1
Marietta 1
Ardmore 2
Sulphur 2
Pauls Valley 1
Chickasha 1
Lindsay 1
Duncan 1
Healdton 1
Waurika 1
Kingfisher 1
Okarche 1
El Reno 2
Watonga 1
Weatherford 1
Anadarko 1
Fort Sill 1
Lawton 3
Frederick 1
Carnegie 1
Thomas 1
Clinton 2
Cordell 1
Hobart 1
Altus 1 1 Altus Air Force Base
Mangum 1
Hollis 1
Elk City 1
Sayre 1
N
0 20 40
Miles
Section A of the *AHA Guide* provides the legend for this map.
1987 American Hospital Association

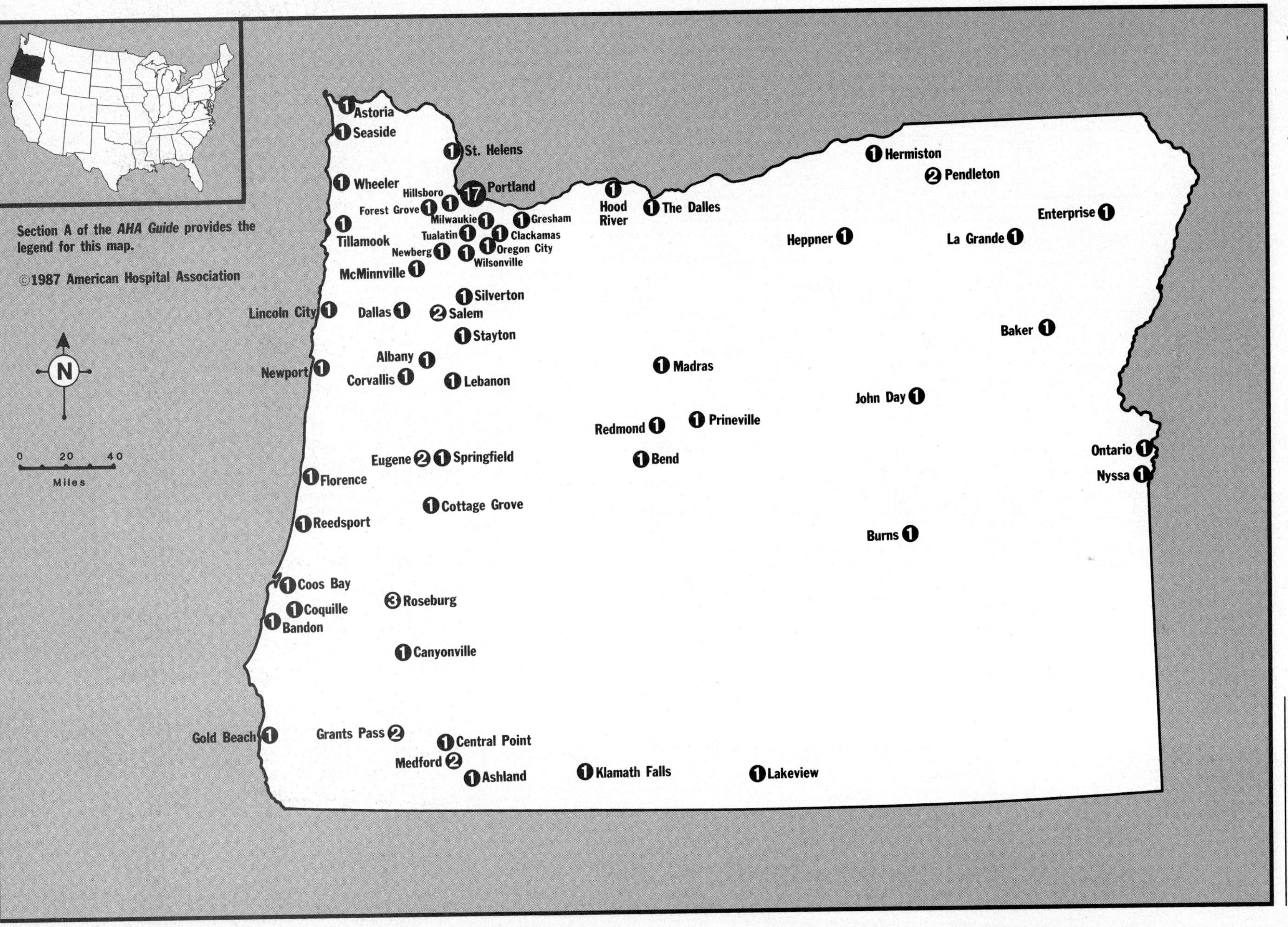
Astoria 1
Seaside 1
St. Helens 1
Wheeler 1
Hillsboro 1
Portland 17
Forest Grove 1
Milwaukie 1
Gresham 1
Tillamook 1
Tualatin 1
Clackamas 1
Newberg 1
Oregon City 1
Wilsonville 1
McMinnville 1
Hood River 1
The Dalles 1
Hermiston 1
Pendleton 2
Enterprise 1
Heppner 1
La Grande 1
Silverton 1
Lincoln City 1
Dallas 1
Salem 2
Stayton 1
Baker 1
Albany 1
Newport 1
Corvallis 1
Lebanon 1
Madras 1
John Day 1
Redmond 1
Prineville 1
Eugene 2
Springfield 1
Bend 1
Ontario 1
Nyssa 1
Florence 1
Cottage Grove 1
Reedsport 1
Burns 1
Coos Bay 1
Roseburg 3
Coquille 1
Bandon 1
Canyonville 1
Gold Beach 1
Grants Pass 2
Central Point 1
Medford 2
Ashland 1
Klamath Falls 1
Lakeview 1
Section A of the *AHA Guide* provides the legend for this map.
©1987 American Hospital Association
N
0 20 40
Miles

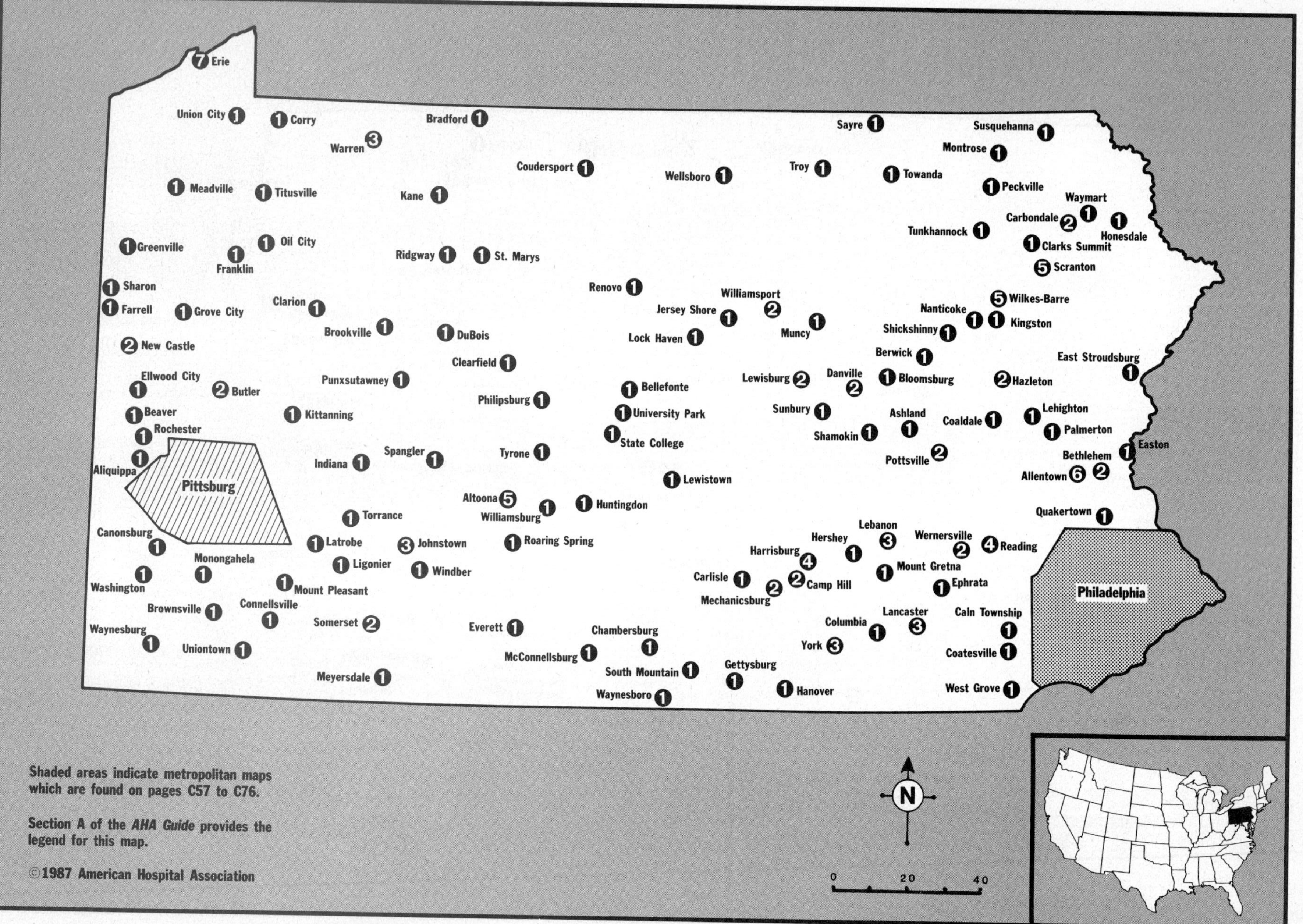
Erie 7
Union City 1
Corry 1
Bradford 1
Warren 3
Coudersport 1
Wellsboro 1
Sayre 1
Troy 1
Towanda 1
Susquehanna 1
Montrose 1
Peckville 1
Waymart 1
Carbondale 2
Honesdale 1
Tunkhannock 1
Clarks Summit 1
Scranton 5
Meadville 1
Titusville 1
Kane 1
Greenville 1
Oil City 1
Franklin 1
Ridgway 1
St. Marys 1
Sharon 1
Farrell 1
Grove City 1
Clarion 1
Renovo 1
Williamsport 2
Jersey Shore 1
Muncy 1
Wilkes-Barre 5
Nanticoke 1
Kingston 1
Shickshinny 1
Lock Haven 1
Brookville 1
DuBois 1
New Castle 2
Berwick 1
East Stroudsburg 1
Clearfield 1
Ellwood City 1
Butler 2
Punxsutawney 1
Bellefonte 1
Lewisburg 2
Danville 2
Bloomsburg 1
Hazleton 2
Philipsburg 1
Beaver 1
Rochester 1
Kittanning 1
University Park 1
Sunbury 1
Ashland 1
Coaldale 1
Lehighton 1
Palmerton 1
State College 1
Shamokin 1
Aliquippa 1
Pittsburg
Spangler 1
Indiana 1
Tyrone 1
Pottsville 2
Easton 1
Bethlehem 2
Allentown 6
Lewistown 1
Altoona 5
Williamsburg 1
Huntingdon 1
Torrance 1
Quakertown 1
Canonsburg 1
Latrobe 1
Johnstown 3
Roaring Spring 1
Lebanon 3
Hershey 1
Wernersville 2
Reading 4
Harrisburg 4
Monongahela 1
Ligonier 1
Windber 1
Mount Gretna 1
Washington 1
Mount Pleasant 1
Carlisle 1
Camp Hill 2
Ephrata 1
Mechanicsburg 2
Philadelphia
Brownsville 1
Connellsville 1
Lancaster 3
Caln Township 1
Somerset 2
Columbia 1
Waynesburg 1
Everett 1
Chambersburg 1
York 3
Uniontown 1
McConnellsburg 1
Coatesville 1
South Mountain 1
Gettysburg 1
Meyersdale 1
Hanover 1
West Grove 1
Waynesboro 1
Shaded areas indicate metropolitan maps which are found on pages C57 to C76.
Section A of the AHA Guide provides the legend for this map.
©1987 American Hospital Association
N
0 20 40

South Carolina

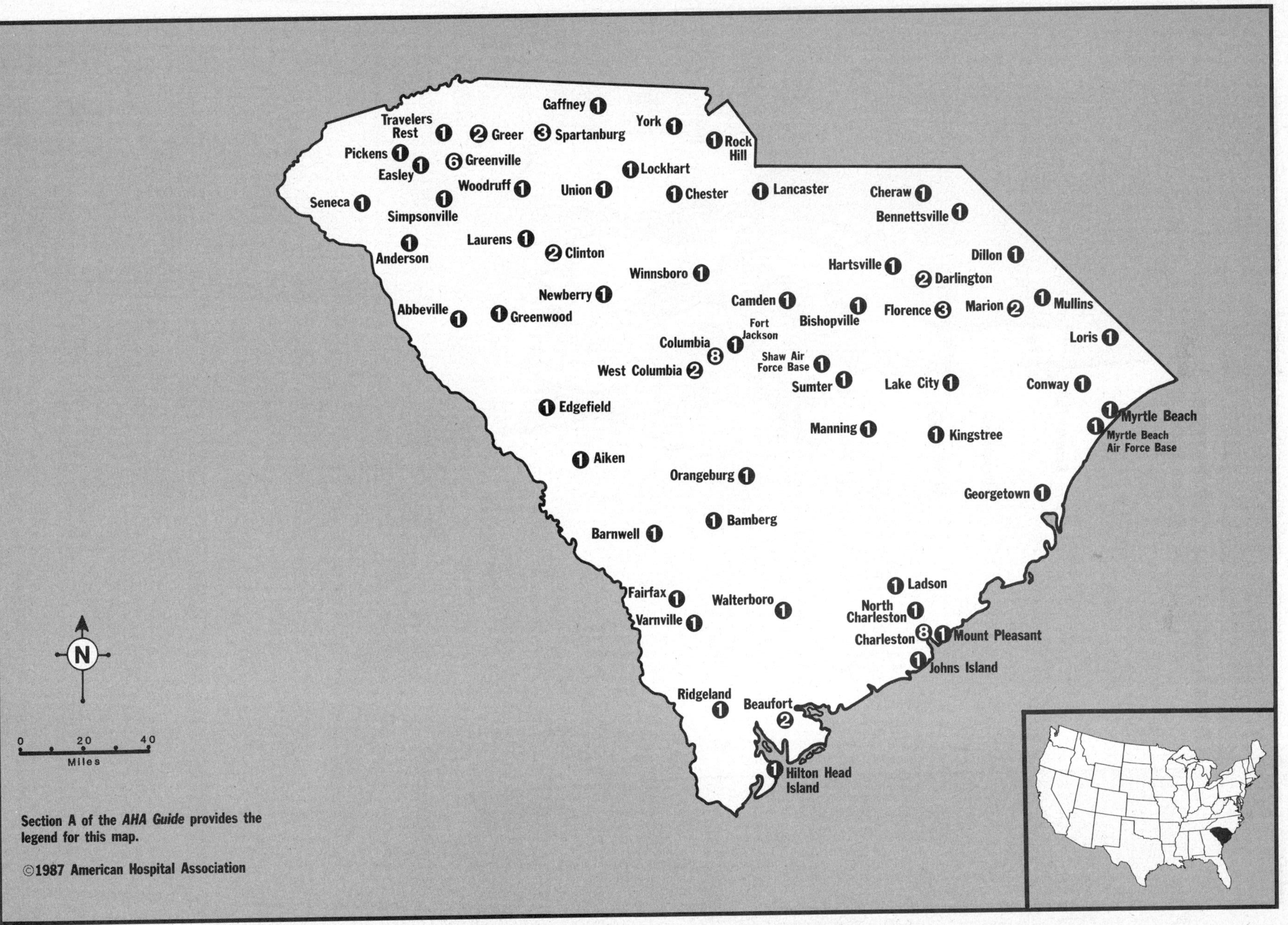

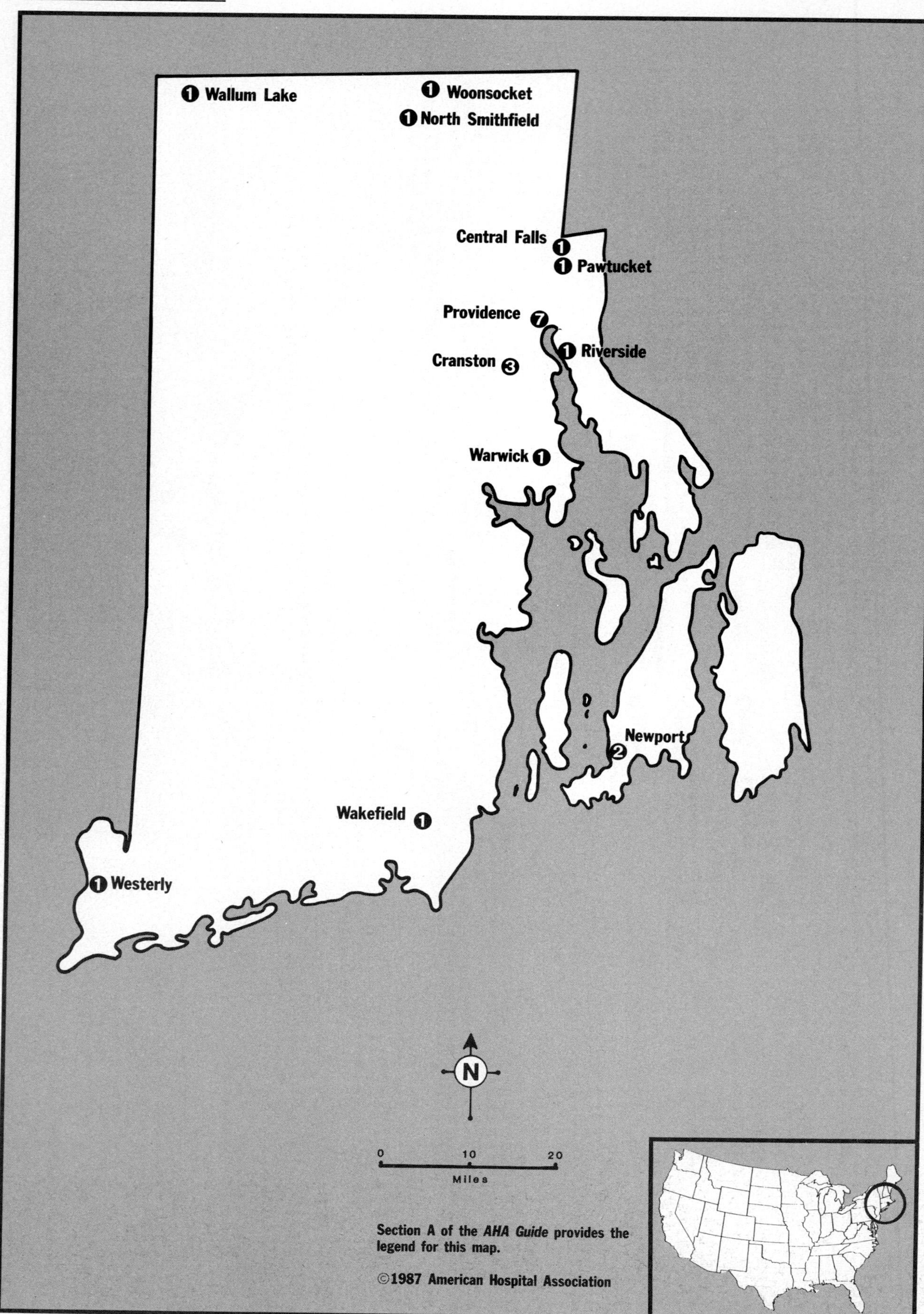

Section A of the *AHA Guide* provides the legend for this map.

Utah

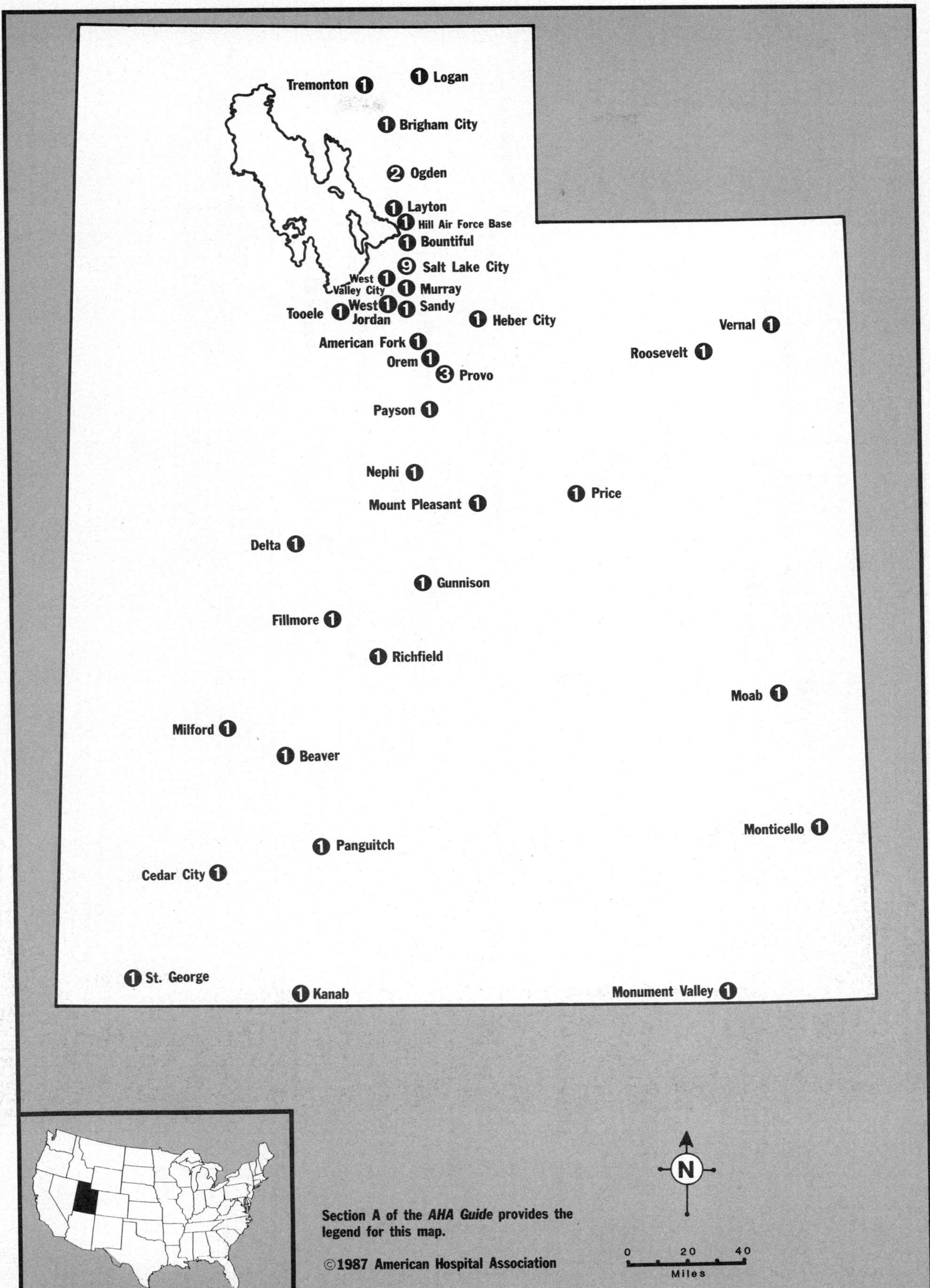

Section A of the *AHA Guide* provides the legend for this map.

South Dakota

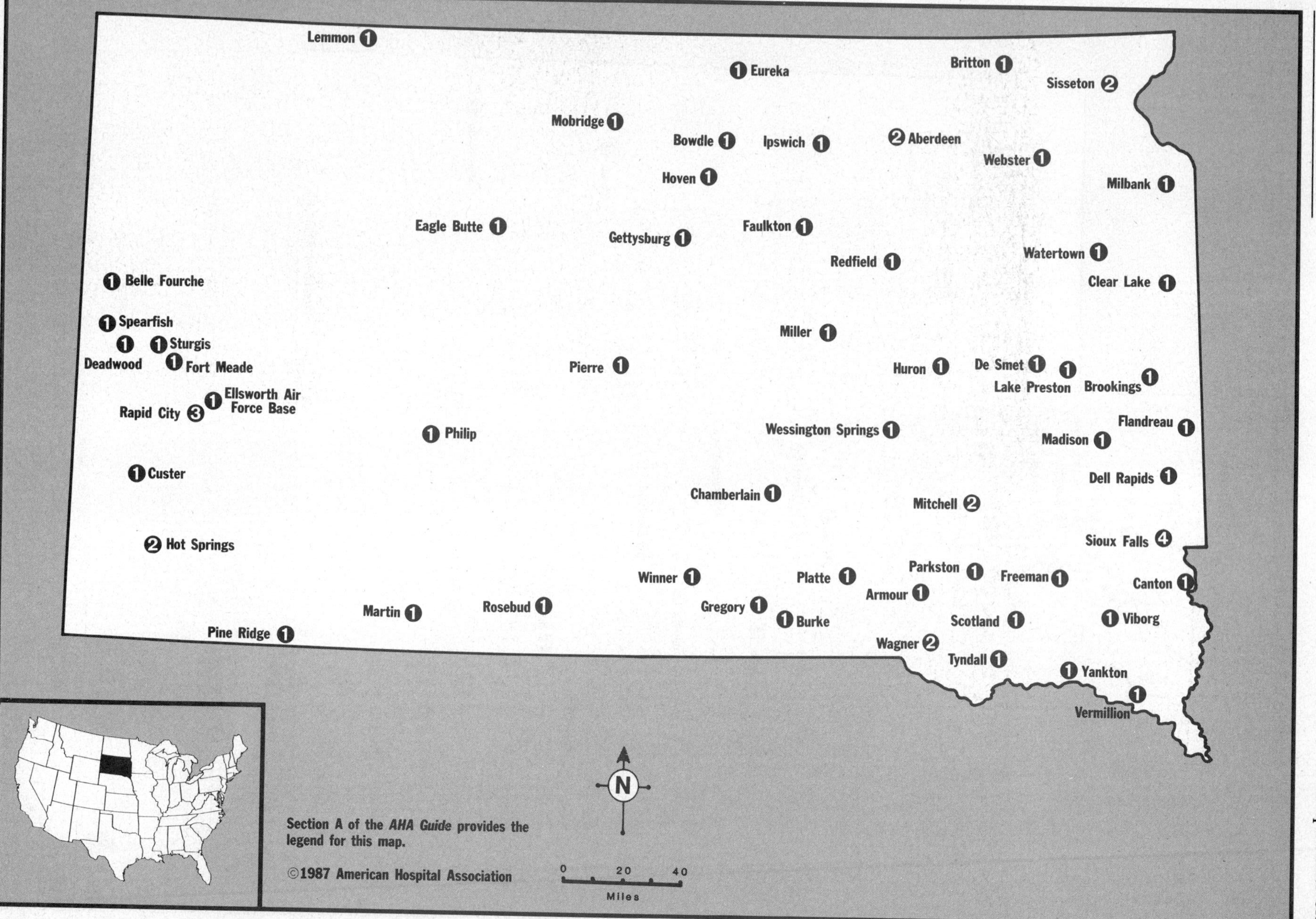

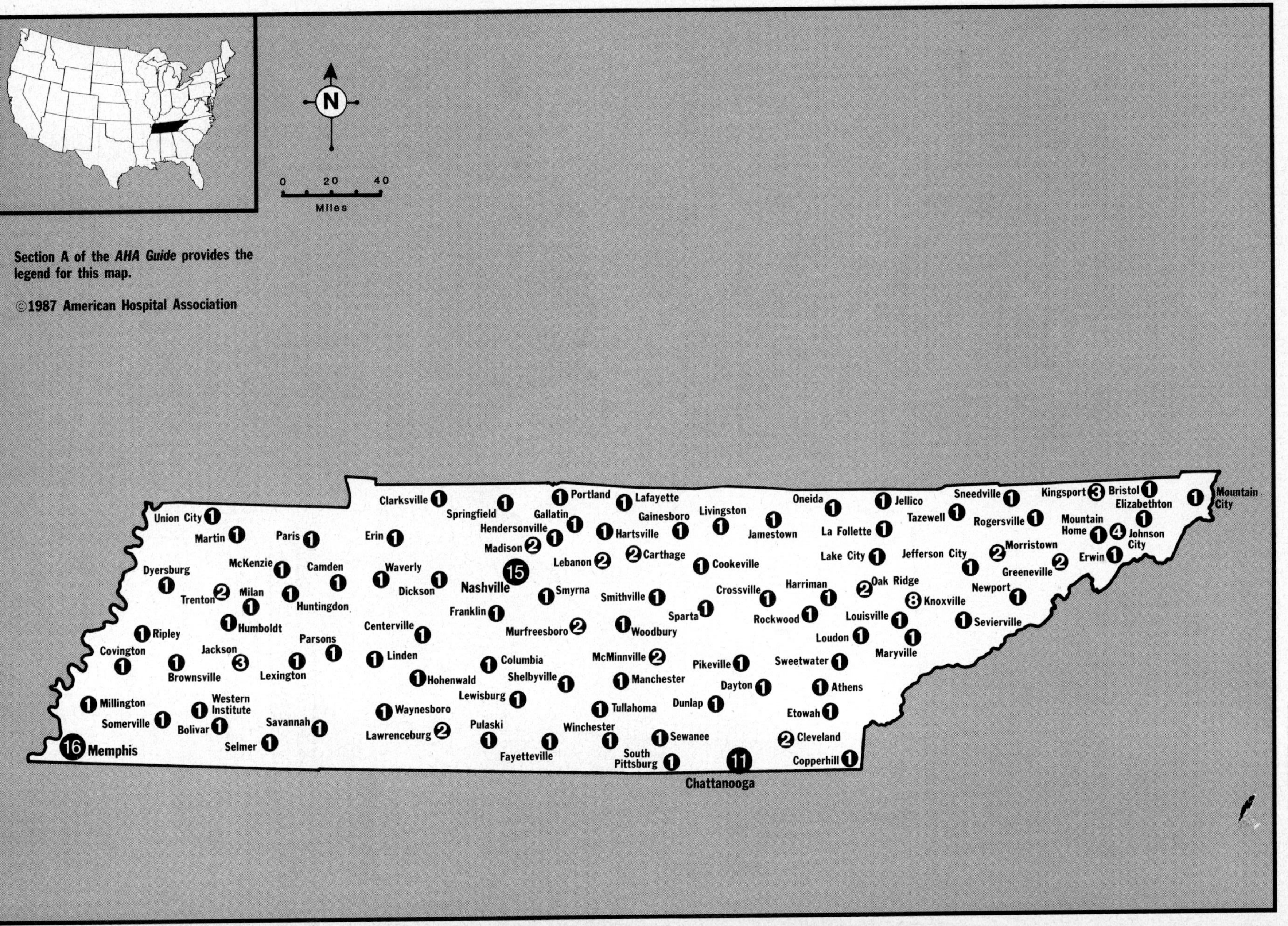
N
0 20 40
Miles
Section A of the AHA Guide provides the legend for this map.
©1987 American Hospital Association
Union City 1
Martin 1
Dyersburg 1
Trenton 2
Ripley 1
Covington 1
Millington 1
Somerville 1
Memphis 16
McKenzie 1
Milan 1
Humboldt 1
Jackson 3
Brownsville 1
Western Institute 1
Bolivar 1
Selmer 1
Paris 1
Camden 1
Huntingdon 1
Parsons 1
Lexington 1
Savannah 1
Clarksville 1
Erin 1
Waverly 1
Dickson 1
Centerville 1
Linden 1
Hohenwald 1
Waynesboro 1
Lawrenceburg 2
Springfield 1
Hendersonville 1
Madison 2
Nashville 15
Franklin 1
Columbia 1
Lewisburg 1
Pulaski 1
Portland 1
Gallatin 1
Lebanon 2
Smyrna 1
Murfreesboro 2
Shelbyville 1
Fayetteville 1
Lafayette 1
Gainesboro 1
Hartsville 1
Carthage 2
Smithville 1
Woodbury 1
McMinnville 2
Manchester 1
Tullahoma 1
Winchester 1
Sewanee 1
South Pittsburg 1
Livingston 1
Cookeville 1
Sparta 1
Jamestown 1
Crossville 1
Pikeville 1
Dunlap 1
Dayton 1
Chattanooga 11
Oneida 1
La Follette 1
Lake City 1
Harriman 1
Rockwood 1
Oak Ridge 2
Louisville 1
Loudon 1
Sweetwater 1
Athens 1
Etowah 1
Cleveland 2
Copperhill 1
Jellico 1
Tazewell 1
Jefferson City 1
Knoxville 8
Maryville 1
Sneedville 1
Rogersville 1
Morristown 2
Greeneville 2
Newport 1
Sevierville 1
Kingsport 3
Bristol 1
Elizabethton 1
Mountain Home 1
Johnson City 4
Erwin 1
Mountain City 1

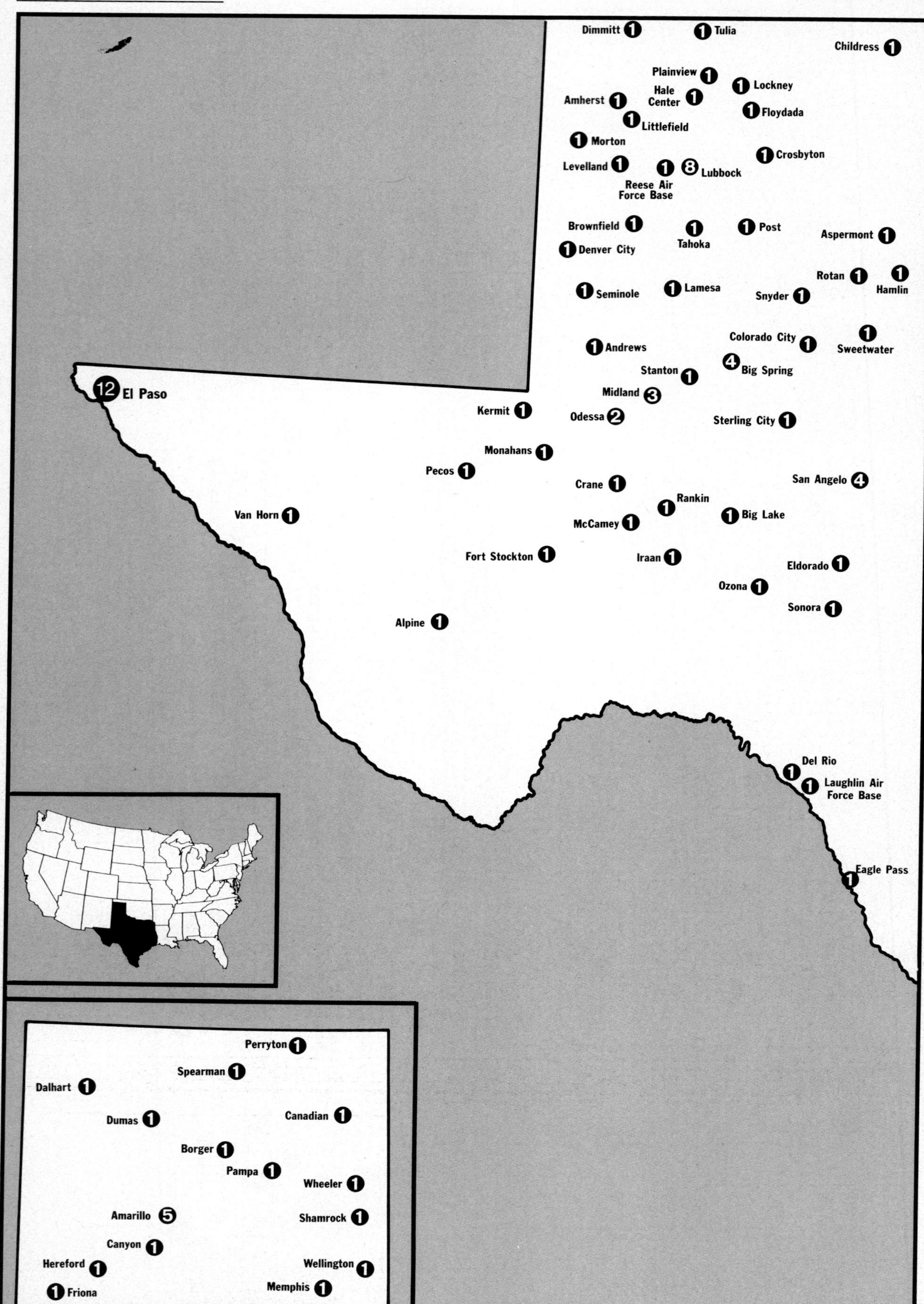
Dimmitt 1
1 Tulia
Childress 1
Plainview 1
1 Lockney
Hale Center 1
Amherst 1
1 Floydada
1 Littlefield
1 Morton
1 Crosbyton
Levelland 1
1 8 Lubbock
Reese Air Force Base
Brownfield 1
1 Tahoka
1 Post
Aspermont 1
1 Denver City
Rotan 1
1 Hamlin
1 Seminole
1 Lamesa
Snyder 1
Colorado City 1
1 Sweetwater
1 Andrews
4 Big Spring
Stanton 1
12 El Paso
Midland 3
Kermit 1
Odessa 2
Sterling City 1
Monahans 1
Pecos 1
Crane 1
San Angelo 4
Rankin 1
Van Horn 1
1 Big Lake
McCamey 1
Fort Stockton 1
Iraan 1
Eldorado 1
Ozona 1
Sonora 1
Alpine 1
Del Rio 1
1 Laughlin Air Force Base
Eagle Pass 1
Perryton 1
Spearman 1
Dalhart 1
Dumas 1
Canadian 1
Borger 1
Pampa 1
Wheeler 1
Amarillo 5
Shamrock 1
Canyon 1
Hereford 1
Wellington 1
1 Friona
Memphis 1

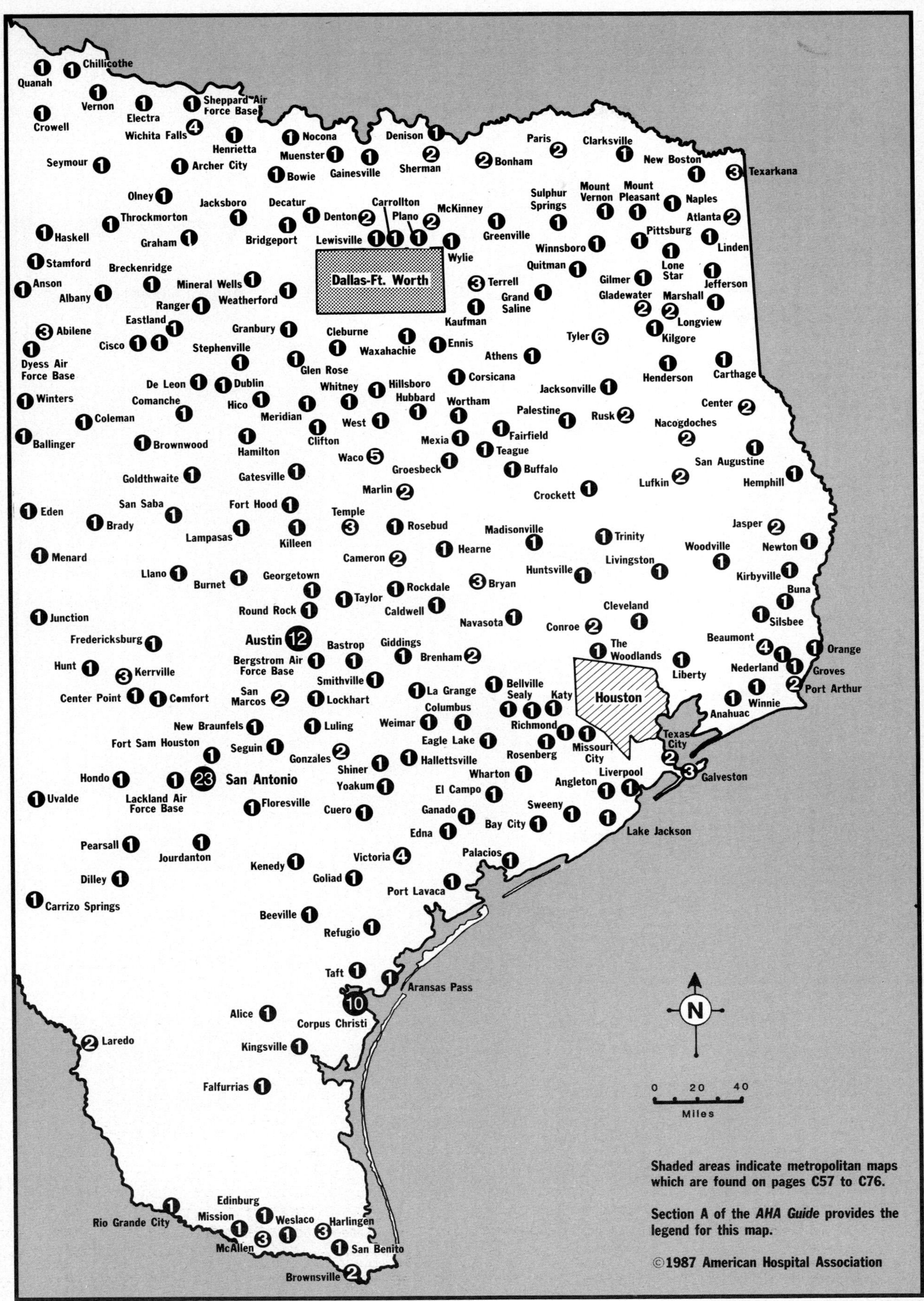
1 Quanah
1 Chillicothe
1 Vernon
1 Crowell
1 Electra
1 Sheppard Air Force Base
4 Wichita Falls
1 Henrietta
1 Nocona
1 Denison
1 Muenster
1 Gainesville
2 Sherman
1 Bowie
1 Archer City
1 Seymour
2 Bonham
2 Paris
1 Clarksville
1 New Boston
3 Texarkana
1 Olney
1 Throckmorton
1 Jacksboro
1 Decatur
1 Bridgeport
1 Haskell
1 Graham
2 Denton
Carrollton
Plano
2 McKinney
Lewisville
1 Wylie
1 Greenville
Sulphur Springs 1
Mount Vernon 1
Mount Pleasant 1
1 Naples
2 Atlanta
1 Pittsburg
1 Linden
1 Winnsboro
1 Stamford
Breckenridge 1
1 Anson
1 Albany
1 Mineral Wells
1 Weatherford
1 Ranger
Dallas-Ft. Worth
3 Terrell
1 Grand Saline
1 Quitman
1 Lone Star
1 Jefferson
1 Gilmer
2 Gladewater
2 Marshall
1 Longview
1 Kaufman
3 Abilene
1 Eastland
1 1 Cisco
1 Granbury
1 Cleburne
1 Waxahachie
1 Ennis
6 Tyler
1 Kilgore
1 Dyess Air Force Base
1 Stephenville
1 Glen Rose
1 Athens
1 Henderson
1 Carthage
1 De Leon
1 Dublin
1 Whitney
1 Hillsboro
1 Hubbard
1 Corsicana
1 Jacksonville
1 Winters
1 Comanche
1 Hico
1 Meridian
1 Wortham
1 Palestine
2 Rusk
2 Center
1 Coleman
1 Clifton
1 West
1 Mexia
1 Fairfield
2 Nacogdoches
1 Ballinger
1 Brownwood
1 Hamilton
5 Waco
1 Groesbeck
1 Teague
1 Buffalo
1 San Augustine
1 Goldthwaite
1 Gatesville
2 Marlin
1 Crockett
2 Lufkin
1 Hemphill
1 Eden
1 San Saba
1 Fort Hood
3 Temple
1 Rosebud
1 Madisonville
1 Trinity
2 Jasper
1 Brady
1 Lampasas
1 Killeen
1 Hearne
1 Woodville
1 Newton
1 Menard
2 Cameron
1 Livingston
1 Kirbyville
1 Huntsville
1 Llano
1 Burnet
1 Georgetown
1 Rockdale
3 Bryan
1 Buna
1 Taylor
1 Caldwell
1 Cleveland
1 Junction
1 Round Rock
1 Navasota
2 Conroe
1 Silsbee
1 Fredericksburg
12 Austin
1 Bastrop
1 Giddings
2 Brenham
1 The Woodlands
Beaumont 4
1 Orange
1 Liberty
1 Nederland
1 Groves
1 Hunt
3 Kerrville
1 Bergstrom Air Force Base
1 Smithville
1 La Grange
1 Bellville
1 Sealy
Katy
Houston
2 Port Arthur
1 Winnie
1 Center Point
1 Comfort
2 San Marcos
1 Lockhart
Columbus
1 1 1
1 Anahuac
1 New Braunfels
1 Luling
1 Weimar
1
1 Richmond
1 1
Texas City
1 Fort Sam Houston
1 Seguin
2 Gonzales
1 Eagle Lake
1 Rosenberg
Missouri City
2
1 Shiner
1 Hallettsville
1 Wharton
Liverpool
3 Galveston
1 Hondo
1
23 San Antonio
1 Yoakum
1 El Campo
1 Angleton
1 1
1 Uvalde
Lackland Air Force Base
1 Floresville
1 Cuero
1 Ganado
1 Sweeny
1 Bay City
1
1 Edna
Lake Jackson
1 Pearsall
1 Jourdanton
1 Kenedy
4 Victoria
1 Palacios
1 Goliad
1 Dilley
1 Port Lavaca
1 Carrizo Springs
1 Beeville
1 Refugio
1 Taft
1 Aransas Pass
10
1 Alice
Corpus Christi
2 Laredo
1 Kingsville
1 Falfurrias
N
0 20 40
Miles
1 Rio Grande City
Edinburg
1 Mission
1 Weslaco
3 Harlingen
3
1
McAllen
1 San Benito
2 Brownsville
Shaded areas indicate metropolitan maps which are found on pages C57 to C76.
Section A of the *AHA Guide* provides the legend for this map.
©1987 American Hospital Association

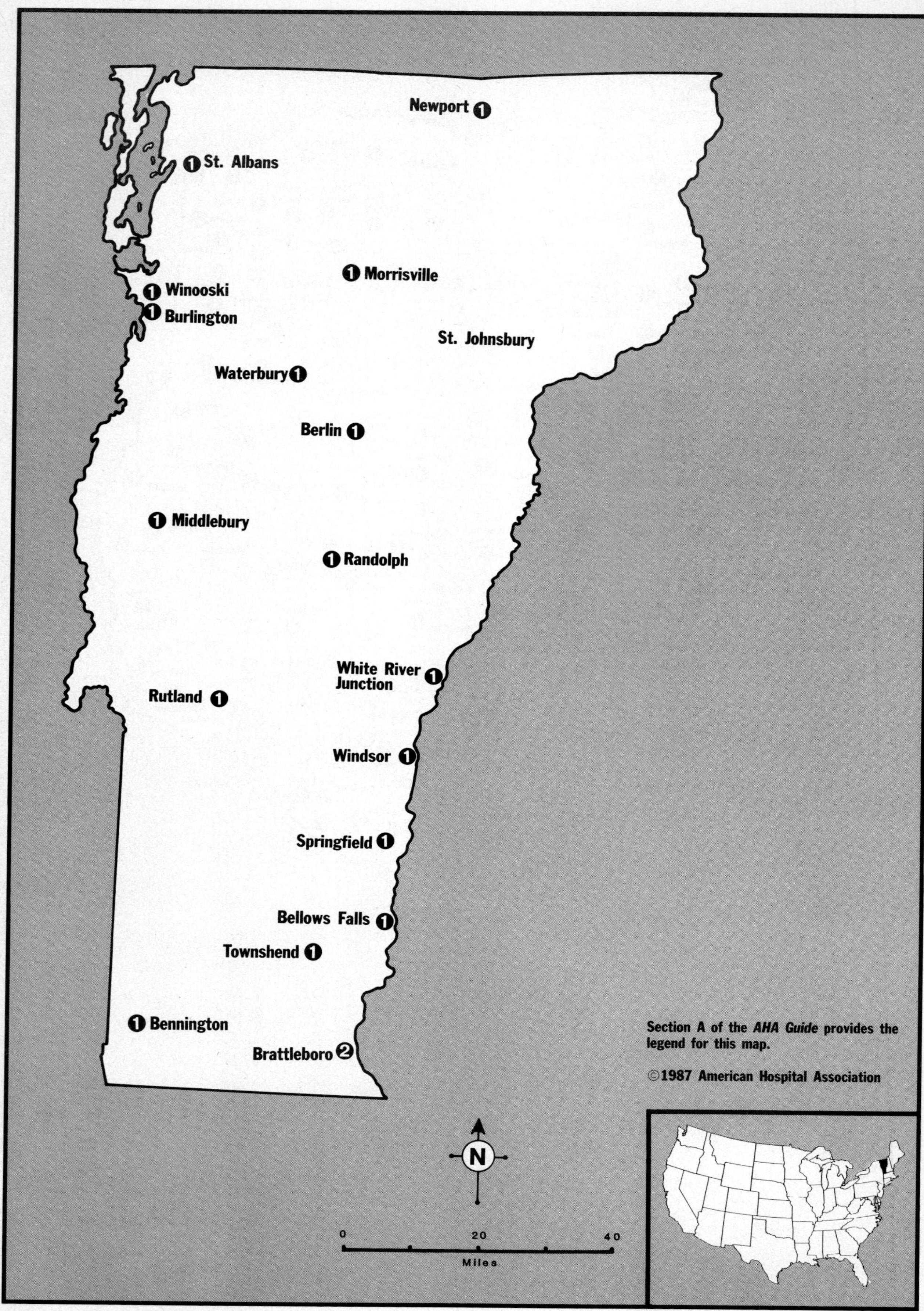
Newport 1
1 St. Albans
1 Morrisville
1 Winooski
1 Burlington
St. Johnsbury
Waterbury 1
Berlin 1
1 Middlebury
1 Randolph
White River Junction 1
Rutland 1
Windsor 1
Springfield 1
Bellows Falls 1
Townshend 1
1 Bennington
Brattleboro 2
Section A of the AHA Guide provides the legend for this map.
©1987 American Hospital Association
N
0
20
40
Miles

Wisconsin

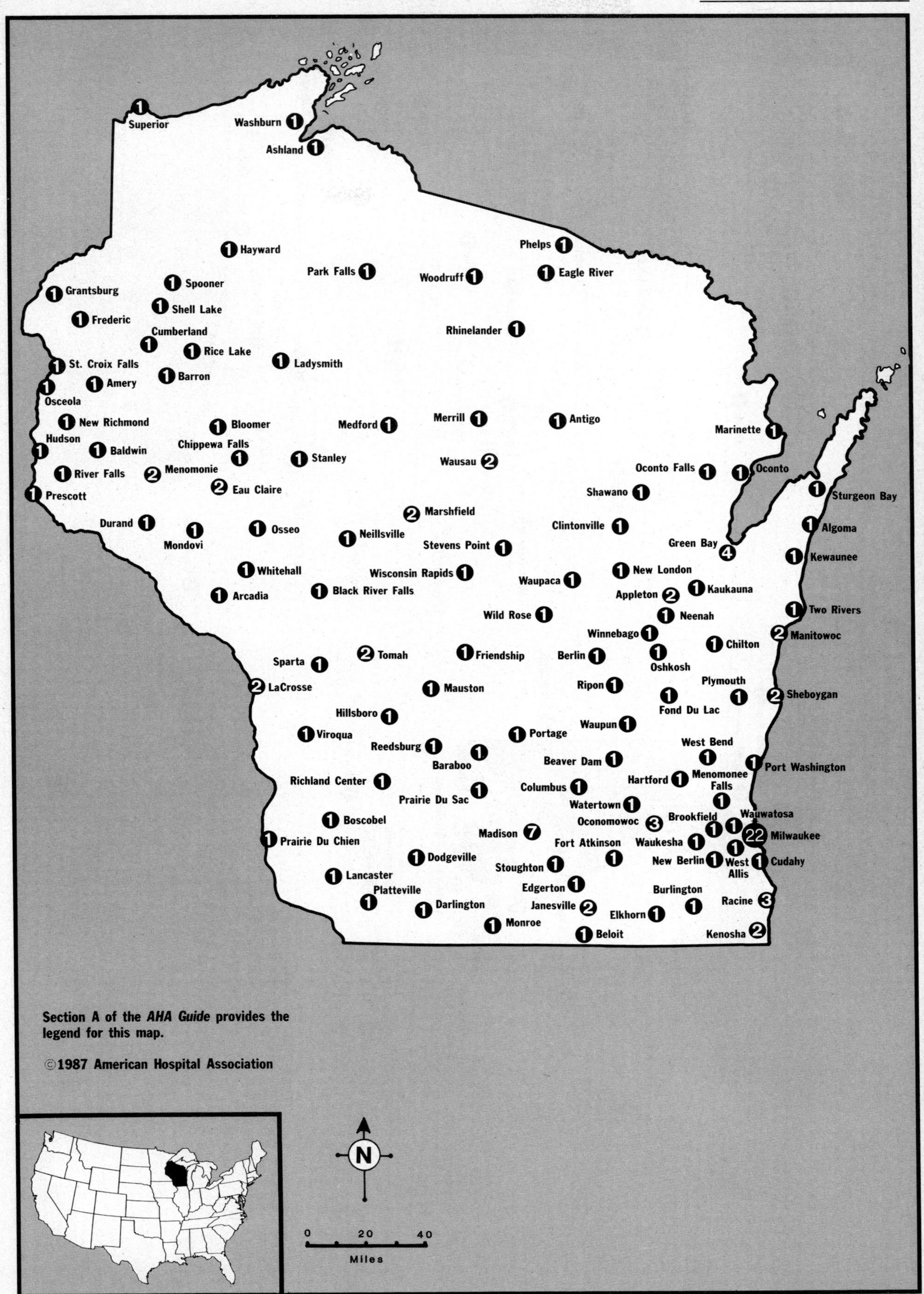
Superior 1
Washburn 1
Ashland 1
Hayward 1
Phelps 1
Park Falls 1
Woodruff 1
Eagle River 1
Grantsburg 1
Spooner 1
Shell Lake 1
Frederic 1
Cumberland 1
Rhinelander 1
Rice Lake 1
Ladysmith 1
St. Croix Falls 1
Barron 1
Amery 1
Osceola 1
New Richmond 1
Bloomer 1
Medford 1
Merrill 1
Antigo 1
Marinette 1
Hudson 1
Baldwin 1
Chippewa Falls 1
Stanley 1
Wausau 2
River Falls 1
Menomonie 2
Oconto Falls 1
Oconto 1
Eau Claire 2
Prescott 1
Shawano 1
Sturgeon Bay 1
Marshfield 2
Durand 1
Mondovi 1
Osseo 1
Neillsville 1
Clintonville 1
Algoma 1
Stevens Point 1
Green Bay 4
Kewaunee 1
Whitehall 1
Wisconsin Rapids 1
New London 1
Waupaca 1
Arcadia 1
Black River Falls 1
Appleton 2
Kaukauna 1
Two Rivers 1
Wild Rose 1
Neenah 1
Winnebago 1
Manitowoc 2
Chilton 1
Sparta 1
Tomah 2
Friendship 1
Berlin 1
Oshkosh 1
Plymouth 1
LaCrosse 2
Mauston 1
Ripon 1
Sheboygan 2
Fond Du Lac 1
Hillsboro 1
Waupun 1
Viroqua 1
Portage 1
West Bend 1
Reedsburg 1
Baraboo 1
Beaver Dam 1
Port Washington 1
Richland Center 1
Hartford 1
Menomonee Falls 1
Prairie Du Sac 1
Columbus 1
Watertown 1
Wauwatosa 1
Oconomowoc 3
Brookfield 1
Boscobel 1
Madison 7
Milwaukee 22
Prairie Du Chien 1
Fort Atkinson 1
Waukesha 1
Dodgeville 1
New Berlin 1
West Allis 1
Cudahy 1
Stoughton 1
Lancaster 1
Platteville 1
Edgerton 1
Burlington 1
Darlington 1
Janesville 2
Racine 3
Elkhorn 1
Monroe 1
Beloit 1
Kenosha 2
Section A of the *AHA Guide* provides the legend for this map.
©1987 American Hospital Association
N
0 20 40
Miles

Washington

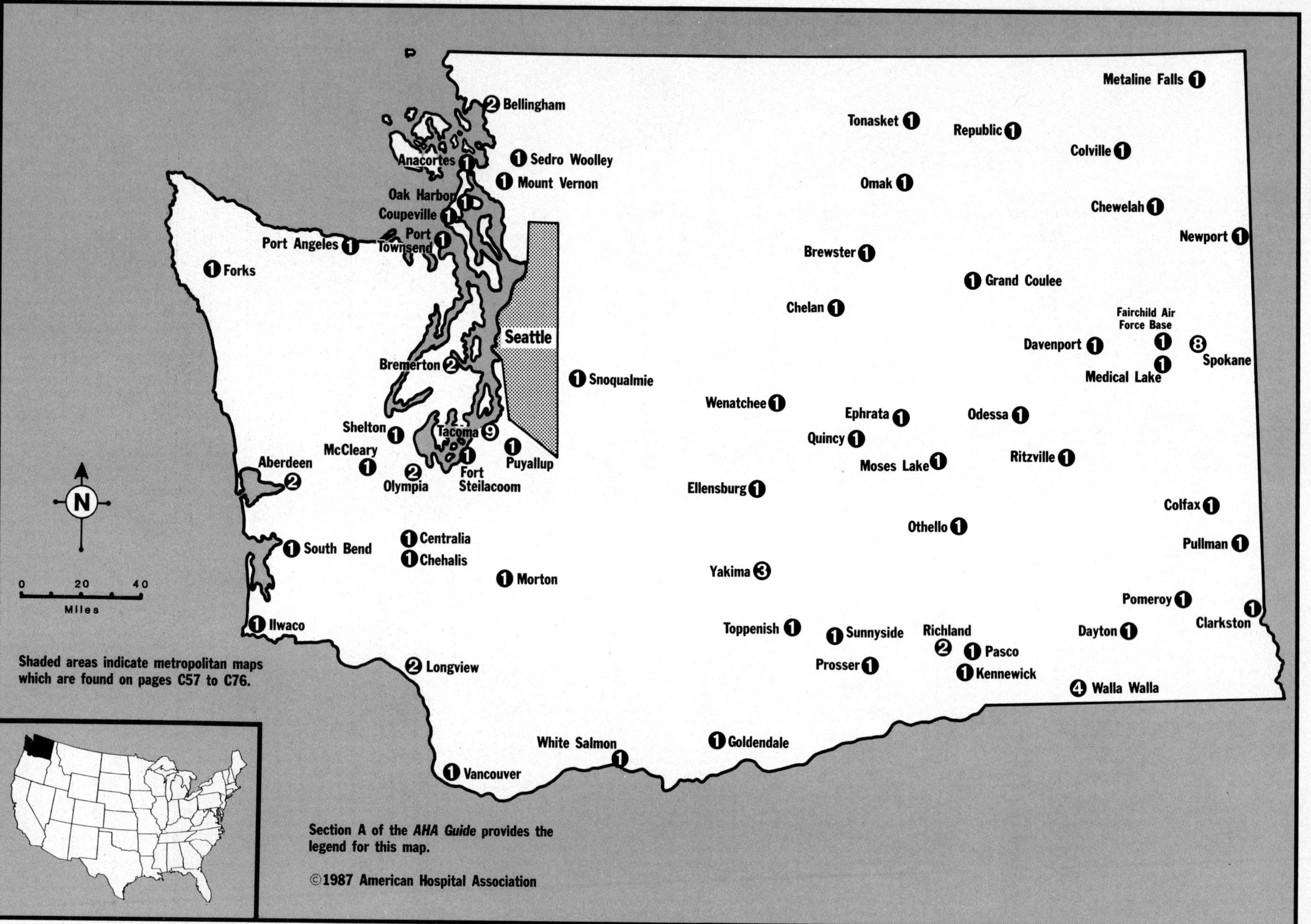

Metaline Falls 1
Bellingham 2
Tonasket 1
Republic 1
Colville 1
Anacortes 1
Sedro Woolley 1
Mount Vernon 1
Omak 1
Chewelah 1
Oak Harbor 1
Coupeville 1
Port Townsend 1
Port Angeles 1
Newport 1
Brewster 1
Forks 1
Grand Coulee 1
Chelan 1
Seattle
Fairchild Air Force Base 1
Davenport 1
Spokane 8
Bremerton 2
Medical Lake 1
Snoqualmie 1
Wenatchee 1
Ephrata 1
Odessa 1
Shelton 1
Tacoma 9
Quincy 1
McCleary 1
Puyallup 1
Moses Lake 1
Ritzville 1
Aberdeen 2
Olympia 2
Fort Steilacoom 1
Ellensburg 1
N
Colfax 1
Othello 1
Centralia 1
South Bend 1
Pullman 1
Chehalis 1
Yakima 3
Morton 1
0 20 40
Miles
Pomeroy 1
Clarkston 1
Ilwaco 1
Toppenish 1
Sunnyside 1
Richland 2
Dayton 1
Pasco 1
Prosser 1
Kennewick 1
Longview 2
Walla Walla 4
Shaded areas indicate metropolitan maps which are found on pages C57 to C76.
White Salmon 1
Goldendale 1
Vancouver 1
Section A of the AHA Guide provides the legend for this map.
©1987 American Hospital Association

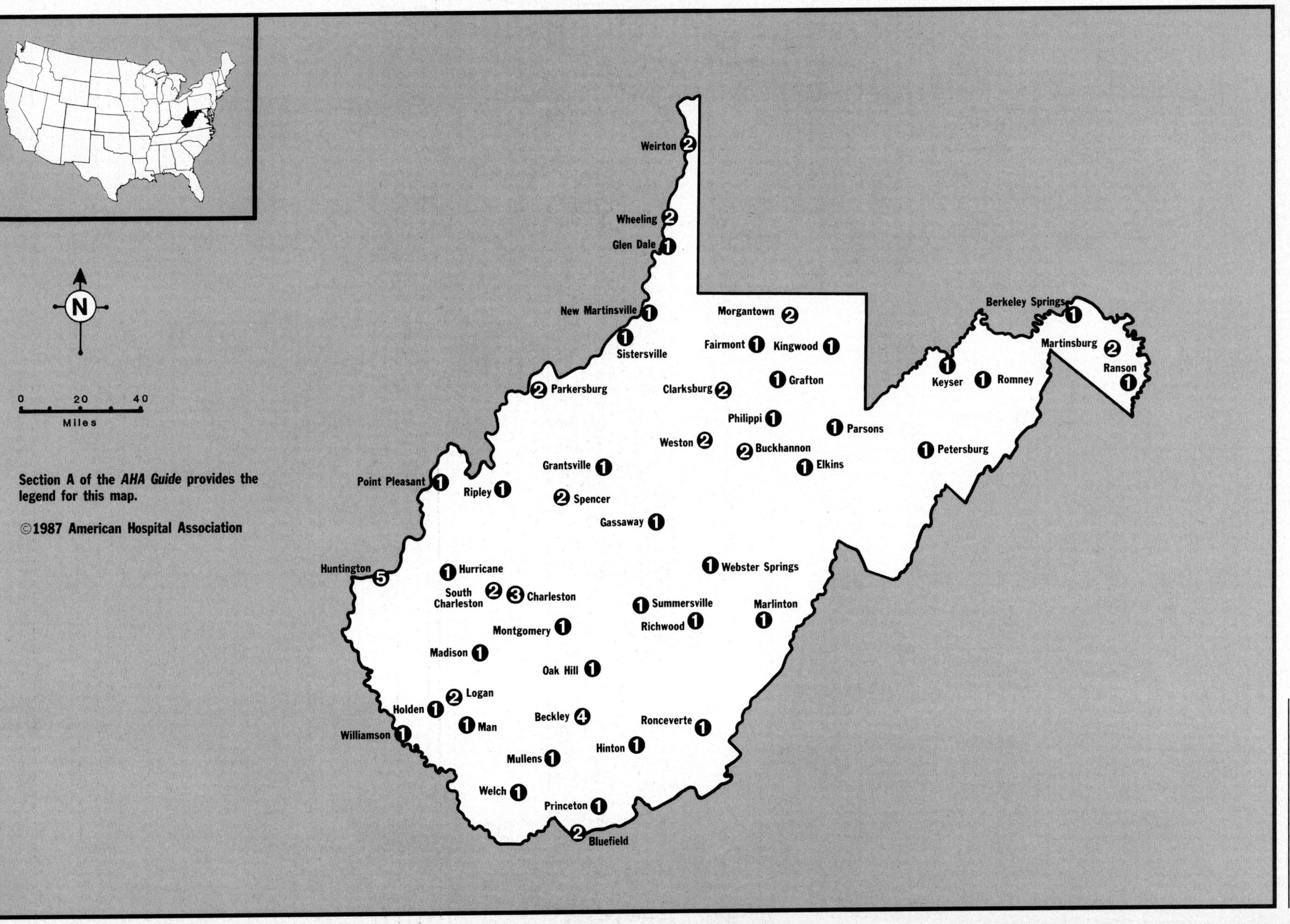
Weirton 2
Wheeling 2
Glen Dale 1
New Martinsville 1
Sistersville 1
Parkersburg 2
Morgantown 2
Fairmont 1
Kingwood 1
Grafton 1
Clarksburg 2
Philippi 1
Parsons 1
Weston 2
Buckhannon 2
Elkins 1
Berkeley Springs 1
Martinsburg 2
Ranson 1
Keyser 1
Romney 1
Petersburg 1
Point Pleasant 1
Ripley 1
Grantsville 1
Spencer 2
Gassaway 1
Huntington 5
Hurricane 1
South Charleston 2
Charleston 3
Webster Springs 1
Summersville 1
Richwood 1
Marlinton 1
Montgomery 1
Madison 1
Oak Hill 1
Logan 2
Holden 1
Man 1
Beckley 4
Ronceverte 1
Williamson 1
Hinton 1
Mullens 1
Welch 1
Princeton 1
Bluefield 2
N
0
20
40
Miles
Section A of the AHA Guide provides the legend for this map.
©1987 American Hospital Association

Wyoming

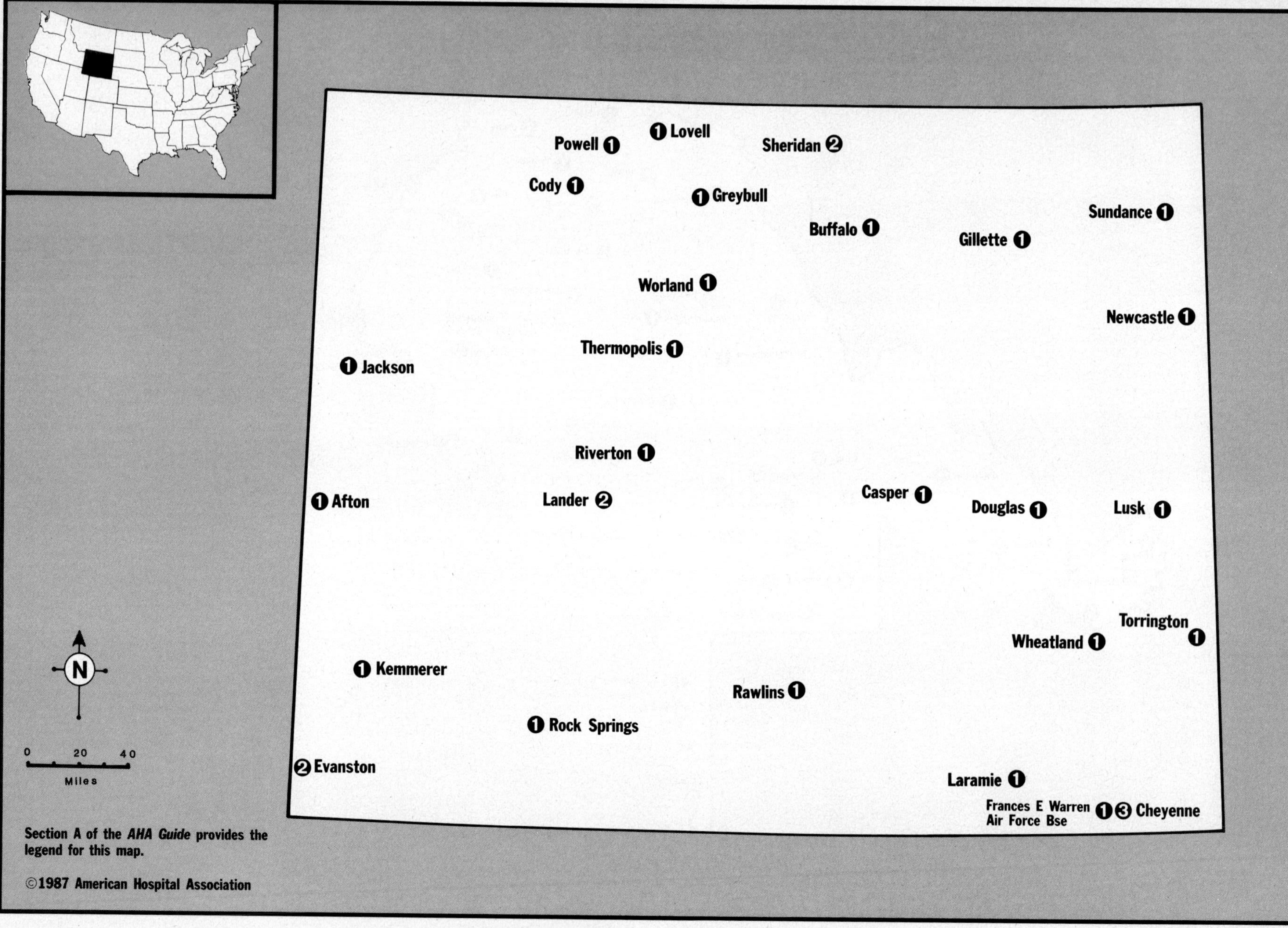
1 Lovell
Powell 1
Sheridan 2
Cody 1
1 Greybull
Sundance 1
Buffalo 1
Gillette 1
Worland 1
Newcastle 1
Thermopolis 1
1 Jackson
Riverton 1
1 Afton
Lander 2
Casper 1
Douglas 1
Lusk 1
Torrington 1
Wheatland 1
1 Kemmerer
Rawlins 1
1 Rock Springs
2 Evanston
Laramie 1
Frances E Warren Air Force Bse 1
3 Cheyenne
N
0 20 40
Miles
Section A of the *AHA Guide* provides the legend for this map.
©1987 American Hospital Association

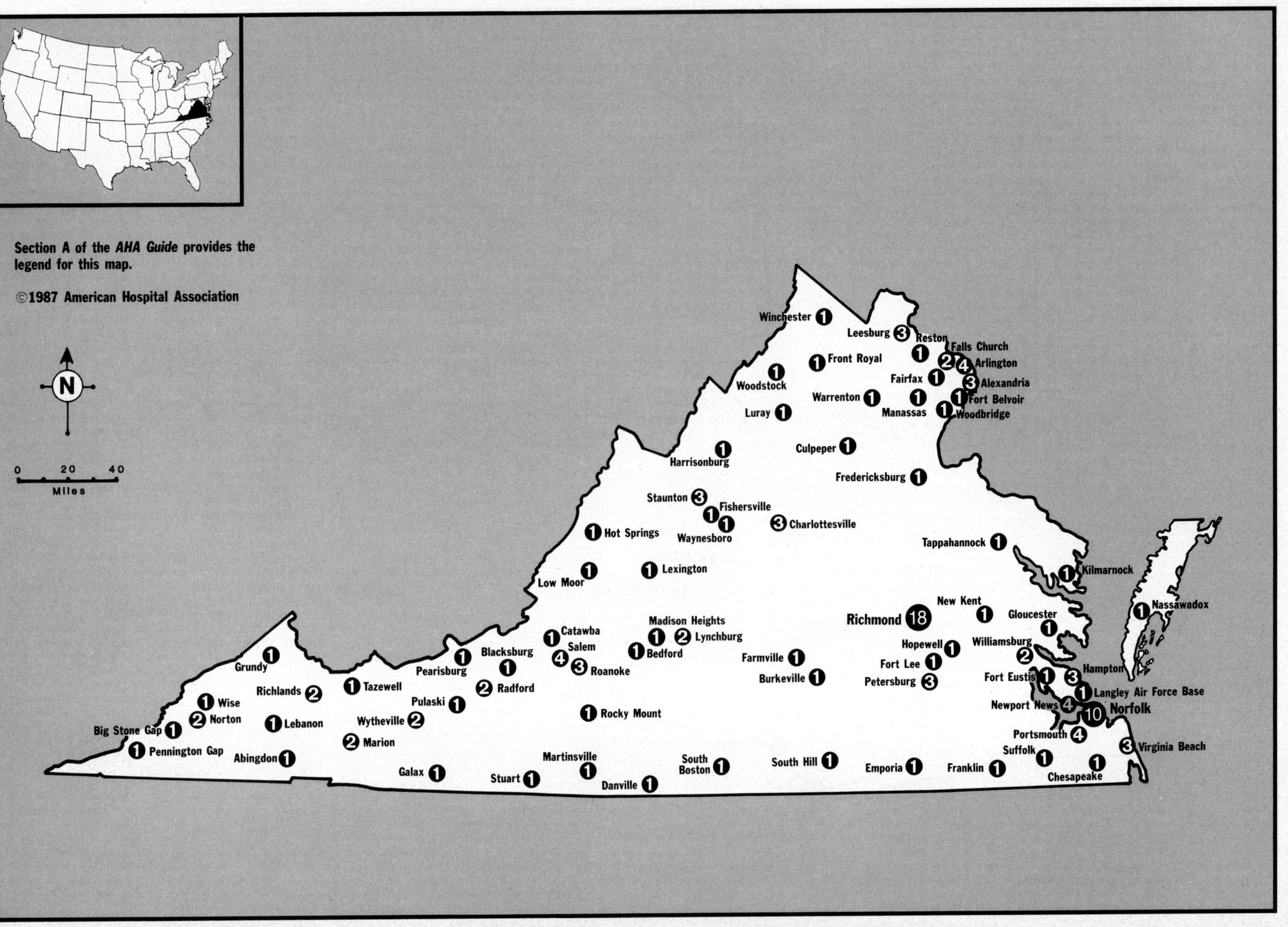

Section A of the *AHA Guide* provides the legend for this map.
©1987 American Hospital Association
N
0
20
40
Miles
Winchester 1
Leesburg 3
Reston 1
Falls Church 2
Arlington 4
Alexandria 3
Fort Belvoir 1
Woodbridge 1
Front Royal 1
Fairfax 1
Woodstock 1
Warrenton 1
Manassas 1
Luray 1
Harrisonburg 1
Culpeper 1
Fredericksburg 1
Staunton 3
Fishersville 1
Waynesboro 1
Charlottesville 3
Hot Springs 1
Tappahannock 1
Low Moor 1
Lexington 1
Kilmarnock 1
Nassawadox 1
New Kent 1
Richmond 18
Gloucester 1
Madison Heights 1
Lynchburg 2
Catawba 1
Salem 4
Roanoke 3
Bedford 1
Hopewell 1
Williamsburg 2
Grundy 1
Pearisburg 1
Blacksburg 1
Farmville 1
Fort Lee 1
Hampton 3
Fort Eustis 1
Burkeville 1
Petersburg 3
Langley Air Force Base 1
Richlands 2
Tazewell 1
Radford 2
Pulaski 1
Newport News 4
Norfolk 10
Wise 1
Norton 2
Rocky Mount 1
Big Stone Gap 1
Lebanon 1
Wytheville 2
Portsmouth 4
Marion 2
Virginia Beach 3
Pennington Gap 1
Abingdon 1
Martinsville 1
South Boston 1
South Hill 1
Suffolk 1
Galax 1
Stuart 1
Emporia 1
Franklin 1
Chesapeake 1
Danville 1

Puerto Rico

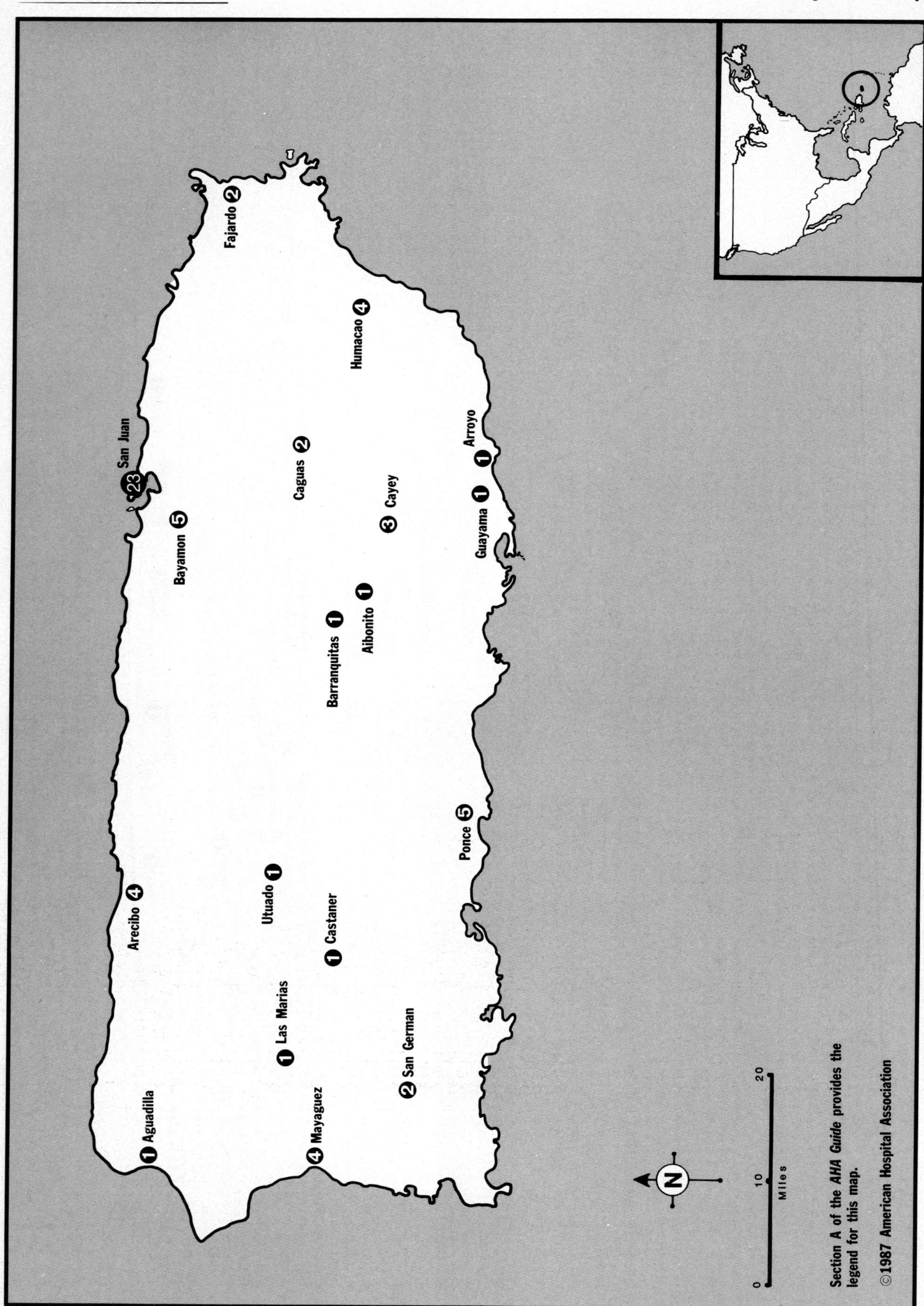
Fajardo 2
Humacao 4
San Juan 23
Caguas 2
Arroyo 1
Cayey 3
Guayama 1
Bayamon 5
Aibonito 1
Barranquitas 1
Ponce 5
Arecibo 4
Utuado 1
Castaner 1
Las Marias 1
San German 2
Aguadilla 1
Mayaguez 4
N
0
10
20
Miles
Section A of the *AHA Guide* provides the legend for this map.
©1987 American Hospital Association

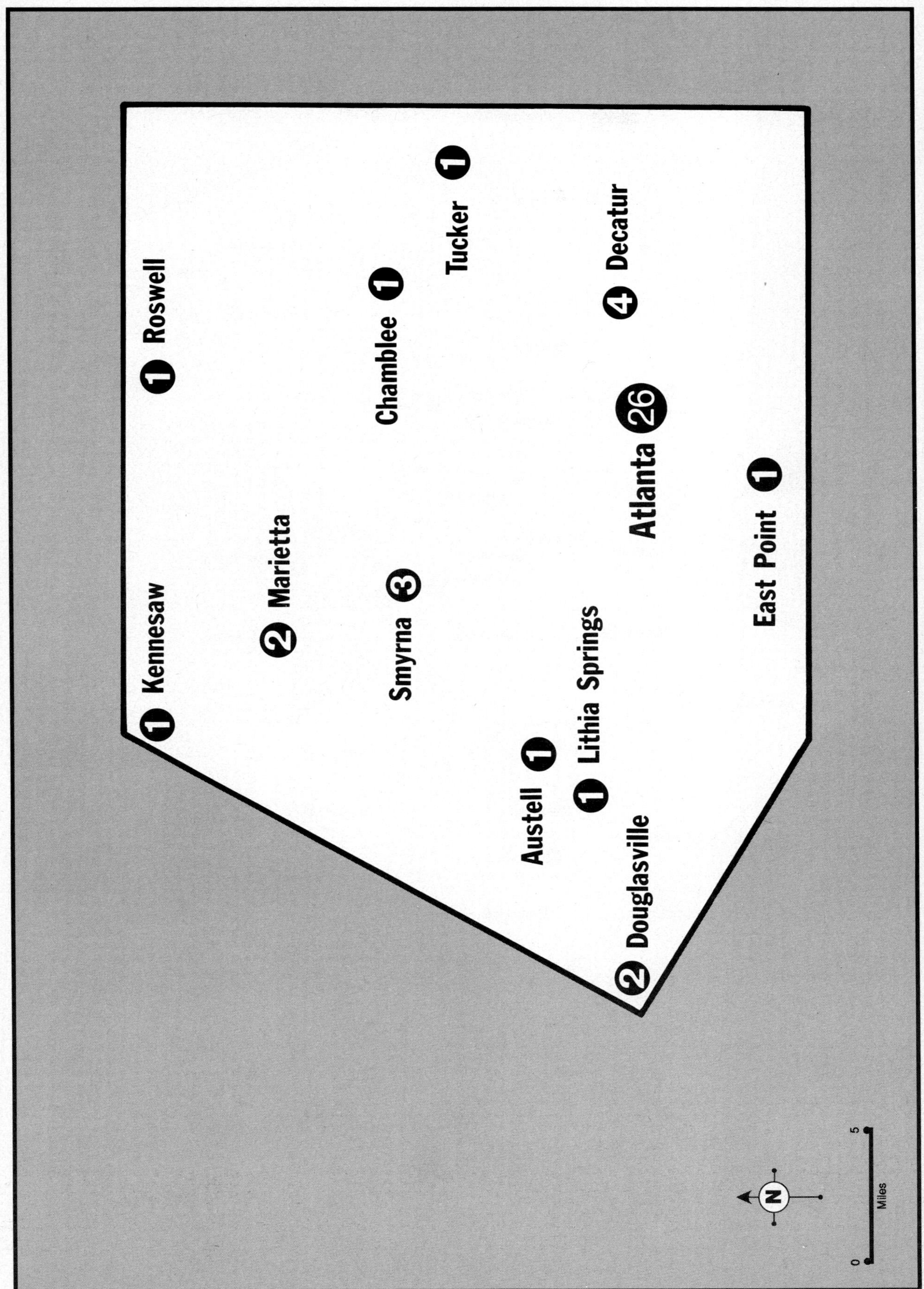
1 Kennesaw
1 Roswell
2 Marietta
Smyrna 3
Chamblee 1
Tucker 1
1 Lithia Springs
Austell 1
Atlanta 26
4 Decatur
2 Douglasville
East Point 1
N
0
5
Miles

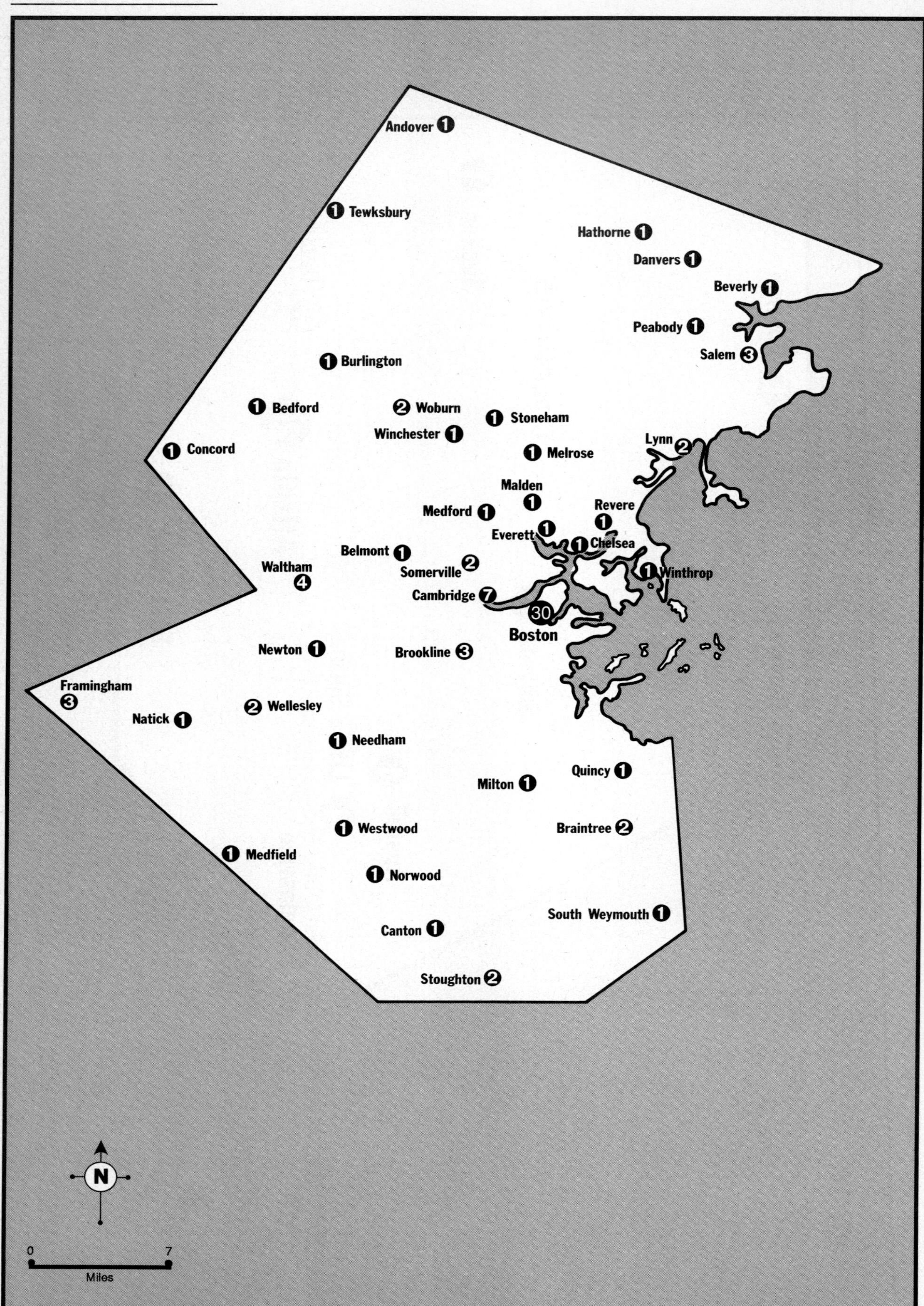
Andover 1
Tewksbury 1
Hathorne 1
Danvers 1
Beverly 1
Peabody 1
Salem 3
Burlington 1
Bedford 1
Woburn 2
Stoneham 1
Winchester 1
Concord 1
Lynn 2
Melrose 1
Malden 1
Medford 1
Revere 1
Everett 1
Chelsea 1
Belmont 1
Somerville 2
Winthrop 1
Waltham 4
Cambridge 7
30
Boston
Newton 1
Brookline 3
Framingham 3
Natick 1
Wellesley 2
Needham 1
Quincy 1
Milton 1
Westwood 1
Braintree 2
Medfield 1
Norwood 1
South Weymouth 1
Canton 1
Stoughton 2
N
0
7
Miles

Chicago

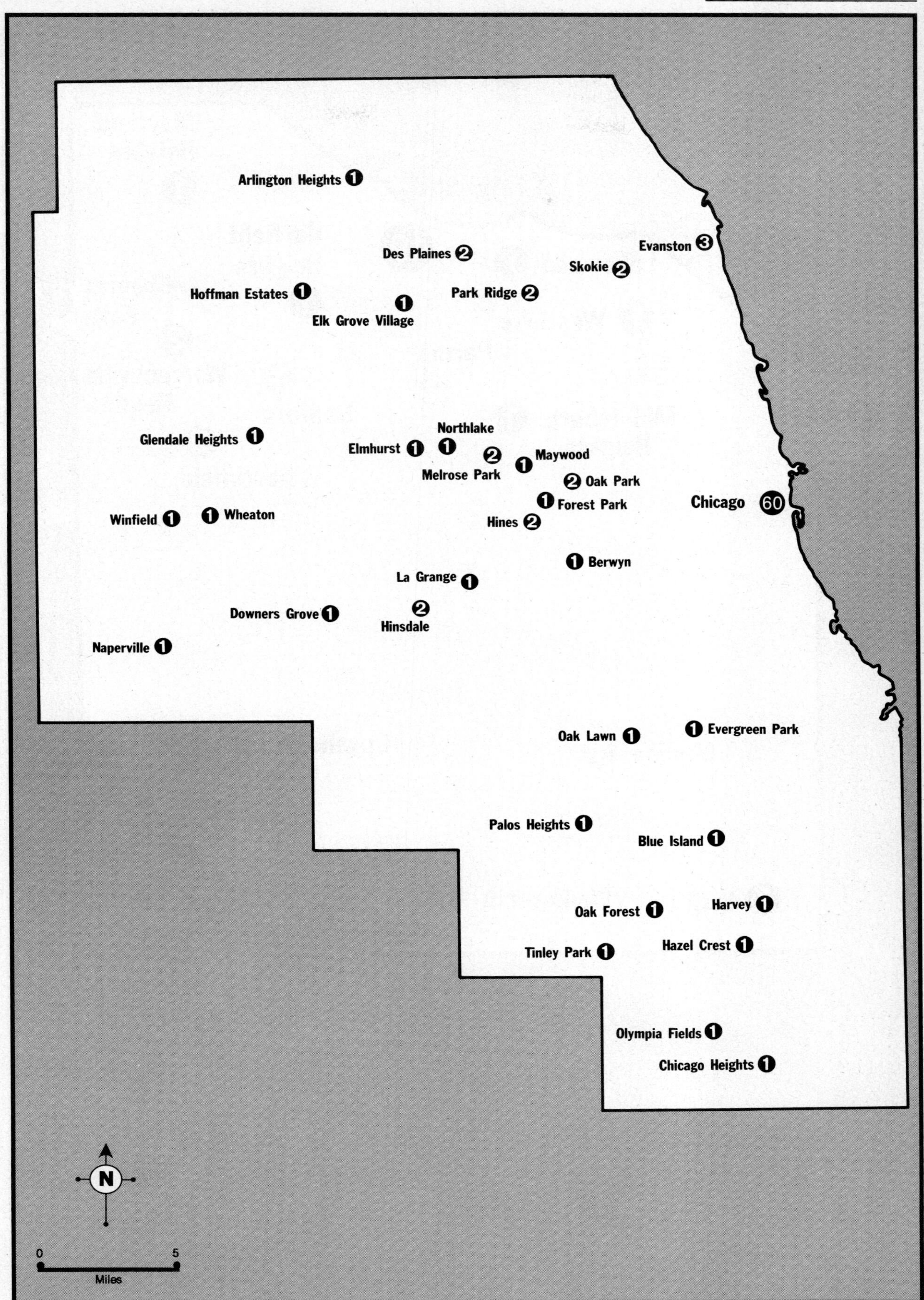
Arlington Heights 1
Des Plaines 2
Evanston 3
Skokie 2
Hoffman Estates 1
Park Ridge 2
Elk Grove Village 1
Northlake 1
Glendale Heights 1
Elmhurst 1
Melrose Park 2
Maywood 1
Oak Park 2
Forest Park 1
Chicago 60
Winfield 1
Wheaton 1
Hines 2
Berwyn 1
La Grange 1
Downers Grove 1
Hinsdale 2
Naperville 1
Oak Lawn 1
Evergreen Park 1
Palos Heights 1
Blue Island 1
Oak Forest 1
Harvey 1
Tinley Park 1
Hazel Crest 1
Olympia Fields 1
Chicago Heights 1
N
0
5
Miles

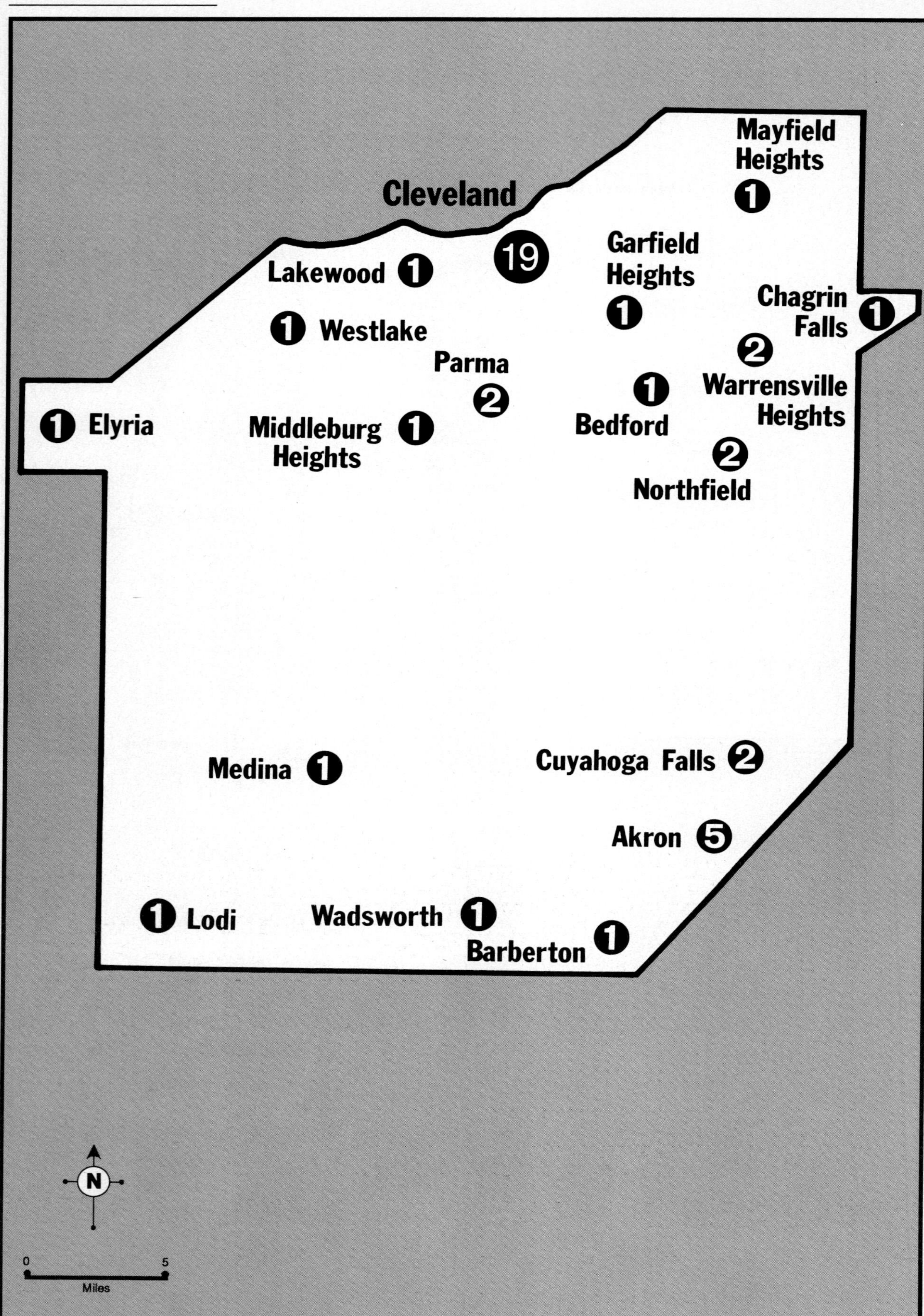
Mayfield Heights 1
Cleveland 19
Garfield Heights 1
Lakewood 1
Chagrin Falls 1
Westlake 1
2
Parma 2
1
Warrensville Heights
Elyria 1
Middleburg Heights 1
Bedford
2
Northfield
Medina 1
Cuyahoga Falls 2
Akron 5
Lodi 1
Wadsworth 1
Barberton 1
N
0
5
Miles

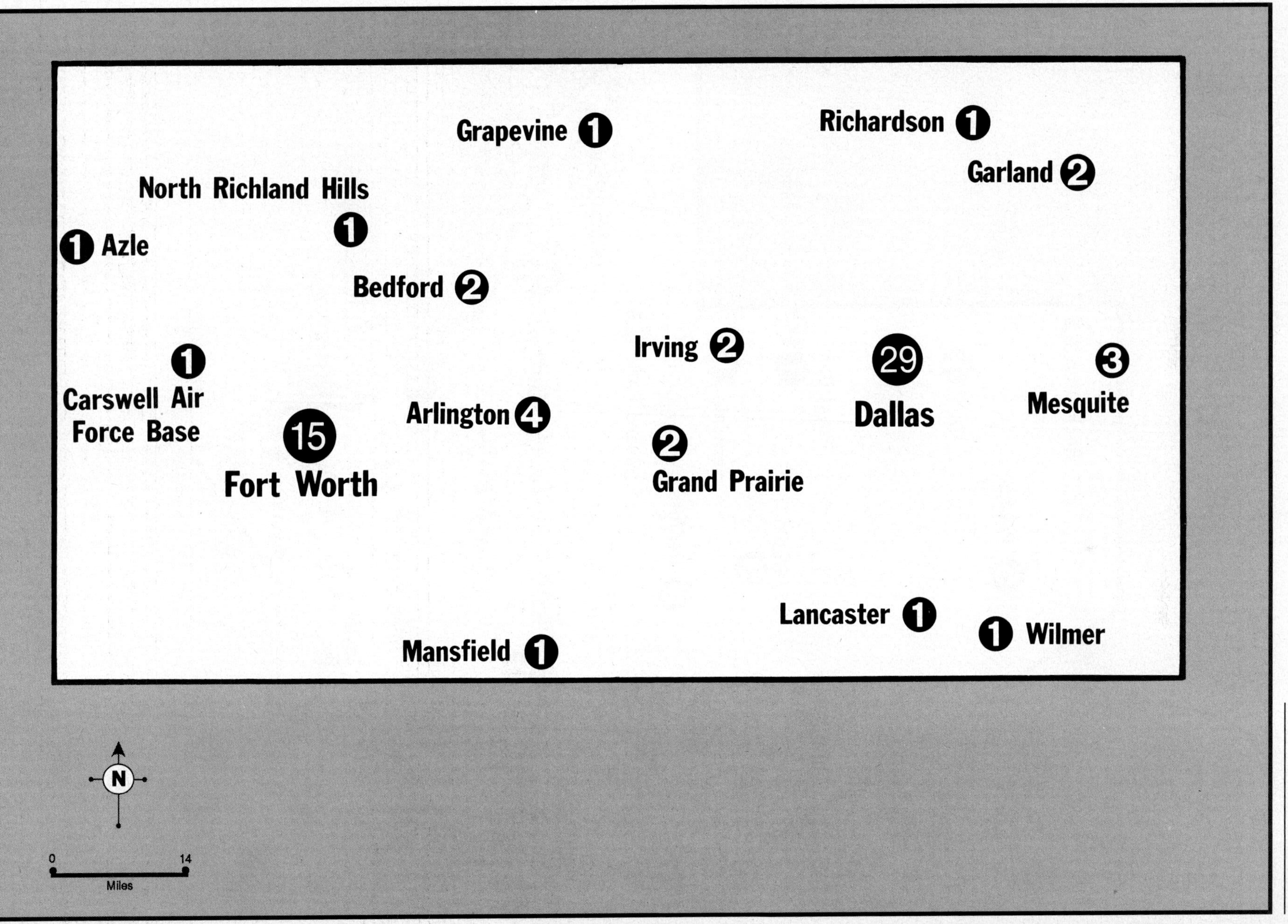
Grapevine 1
Richardson 1
Garland 2
North Richland Hills 1
Azle 1
Bedford 2
Irving 2
Dallas 29
Mesquite 3
Carswell Air Force Base 1
Arlington 4
Fort Worth 15
Grand Prairie 2
Lancaster 1
Wilmer 1
Mansfield 1
N
0
14
Miles

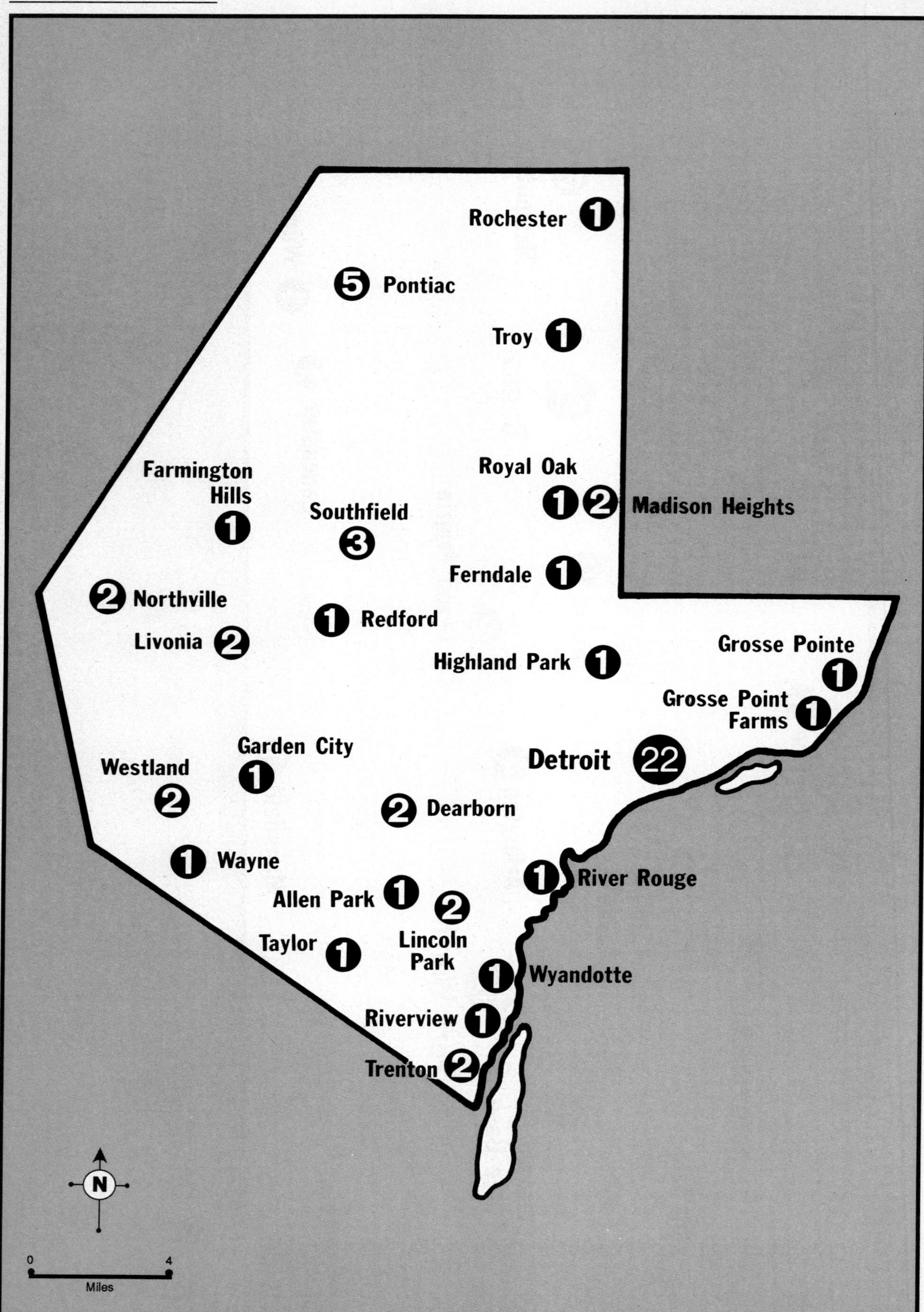
Rochester 1
5 Pontiac
Troy 1
Royal Oak
1 2 Madison Heights
Farmington Hills
1
Southfield
3
Ferndale 1
2 Northville
1 Redford
Livonia 2
Highland Park 1
Grosse Pointe
1
Grosse Point Farms 1
Detroit 22
Garden City
1
Westland
2
2 Dearborn
1 Wayne
1 River Rouge
Allen Park 1
2
Lincoln Park
Taylor 1
1 Wyandotte
Riverview 1
Trenton 2
N
0
4
Miles

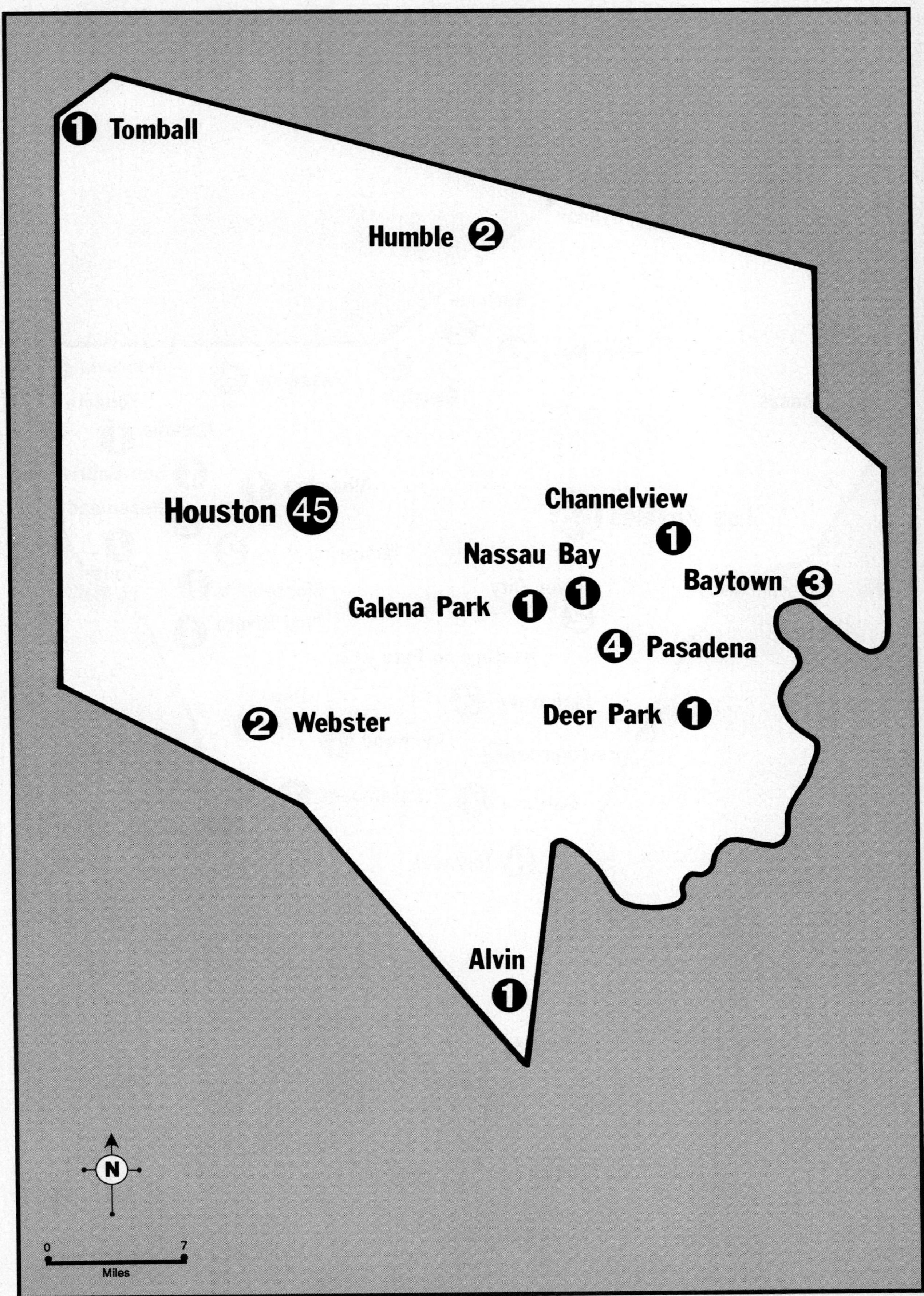
1 Tomball
Humble 2
Houston 45
Channelview
1
Nassau Bay
1
Baytown 3
Galena Park 1
4 Pasadena
Deer Park 1
2 Webster
Alvin
1
N
0
7
Miles

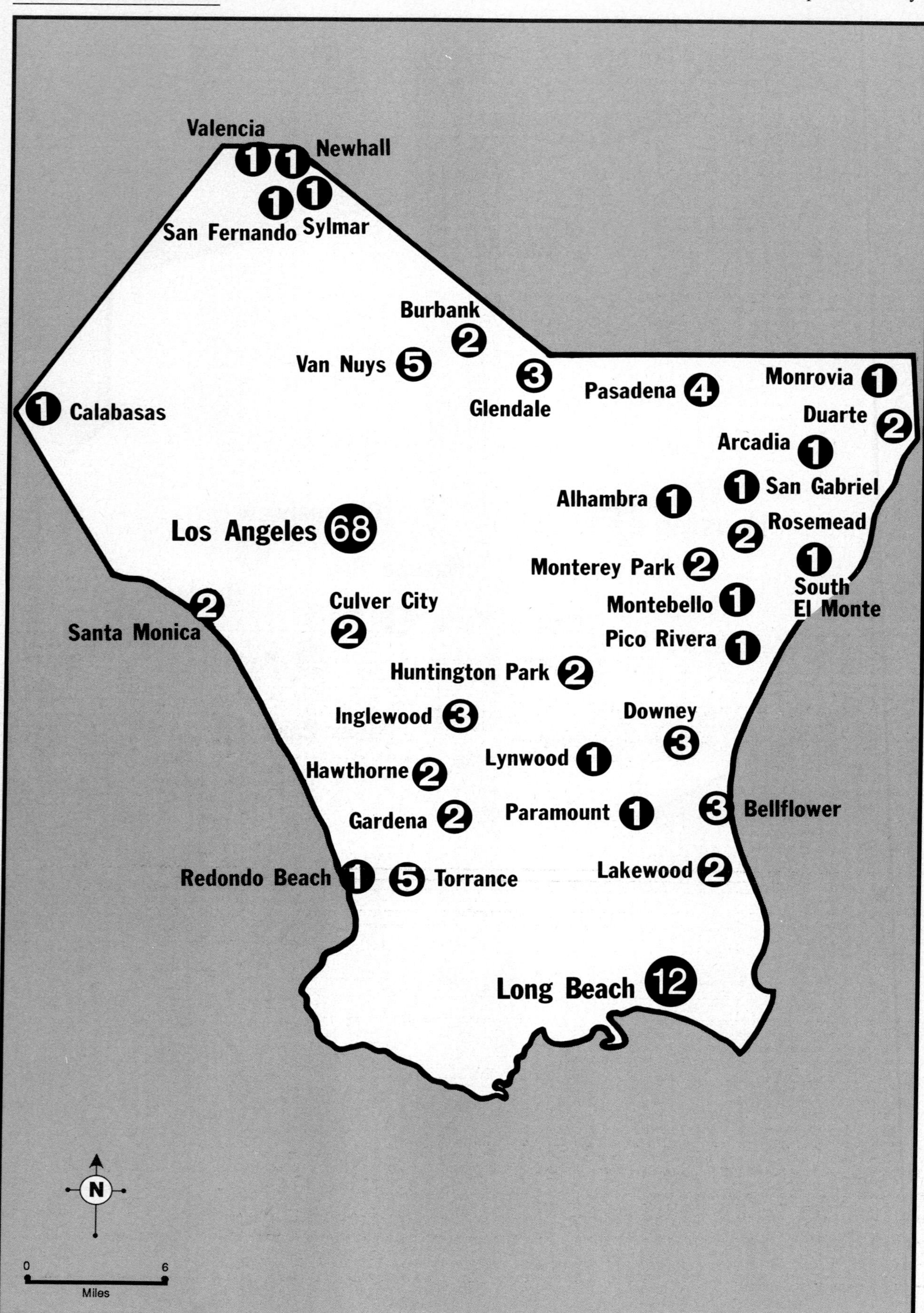
Valencia 1
Newhall 1
Sylmar 1
San Fernando 1
Burbank 2
Van Nuys 5
Glendale 3
Pasadena 4
Monrovia 1
Duarte 2
Arcadia 1
Calabasas 1
San Gabriel 1
Alhambra 1
Rosemead 2
Los Angeles 68
Monterey Park 2
South El Monte 1
Montebello 1
Culver City 2
Santa Monica 2
Pico Rivera 1
Huntington Park 2
Inglewood 3
Downey 3
Lynwood 1
Hawthorne 2
Paramount 1
Bellflower 3
Gardena 2
Lakewood 2
Redondo Beach 1
Torrance 5
Long Beach 12
N
0
6
Miles

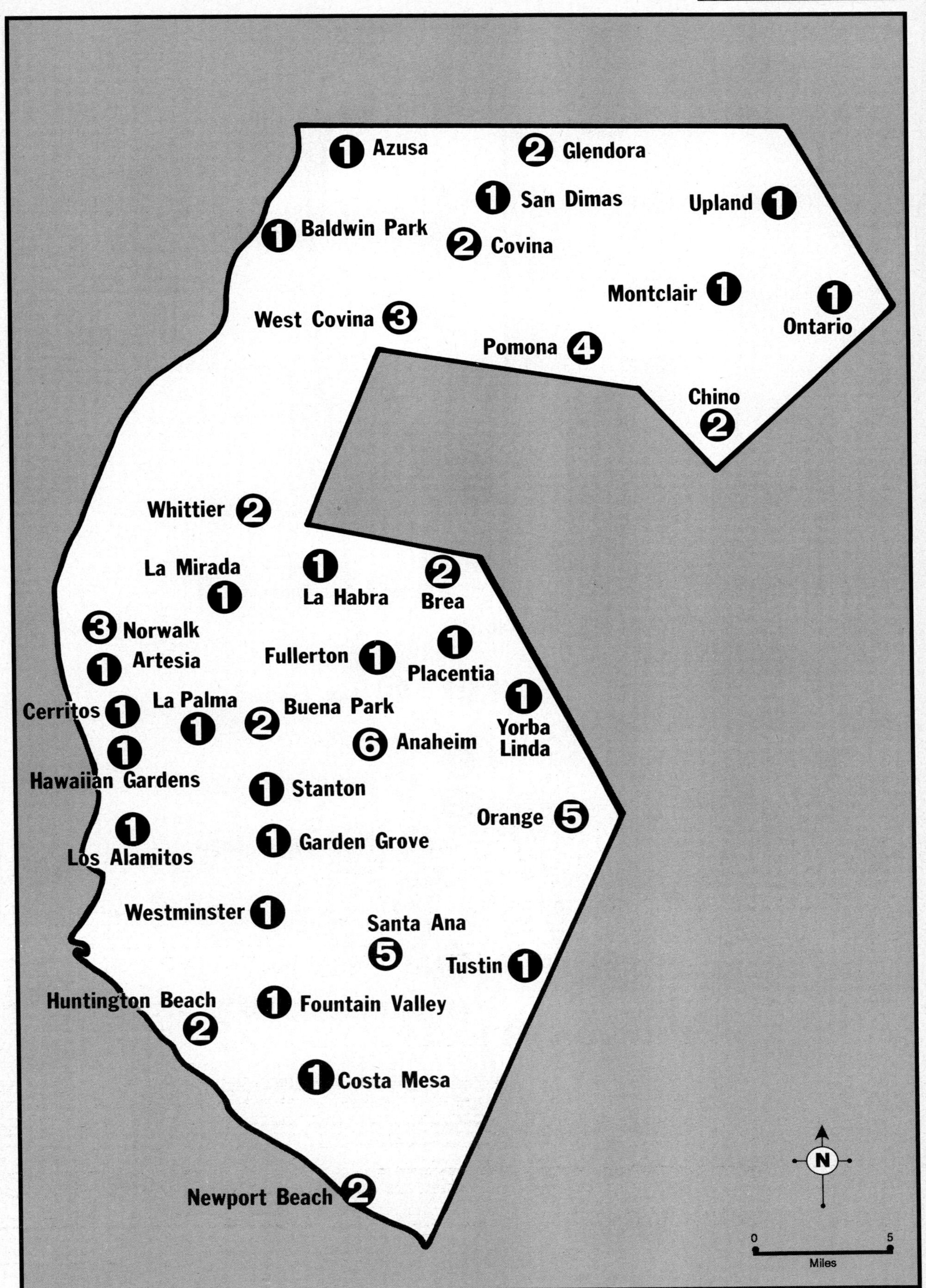
1 Azusa
2 Glendora
1 San Dimas
Upland 1
1 Baldwin Park
2 Covina
Montclair 1
1
Ontario
West Covina 3
Pomona 4
Chino
2
Whittier 2
La Mirada
1
1
La Habra
2
Brea
3 Norwalk
1 Artesia
Fullerton 1
1
Placentia
Cerritos 1
La Palma
1
2
Buena Park
1
Yorba
Linda
6 Anaheim
1
Hawaiian Gardens
1 Stanton
Orange 5
1
Los Alamitos
1 Garden Grove
Westminster 1
Santa Ana
5
Tustin 1
Huntington Beach
2
1 Fountain Valley
1 Costa Mesa
N
0
5
Miles
Newport Beach 2

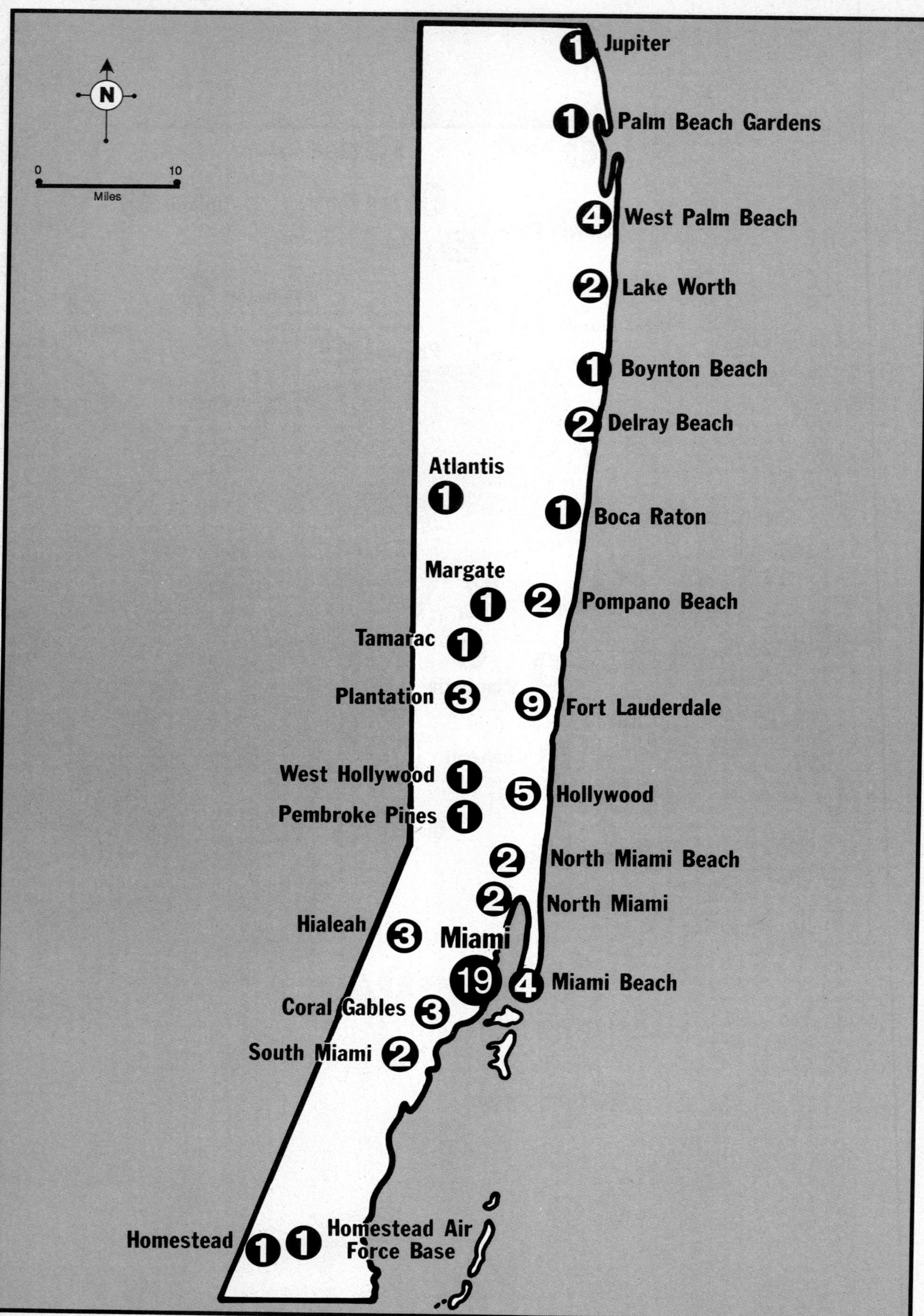
N
0
10
Miles
1 Jupiter
1 Palm Beach Gardens
4 West Palm Beach
2 Lake Worth
1 Boynton Beach
2 Delray Beach
Atlantis
1
1 Boca Raton
Margate
1
2 Pompano Beach
Tamarac 1
Plantation 3
9 Fort Lauderdale
West Hollywood 1
5 Hollywood
Pembroke Pines 1
2 North Miami Beach
2 North Miami
Hialeah 3
Miami
19
4 Miami Beach
Coral Gables 3
South Miami 2
Homestead 1
1 Homestead Air Force Base

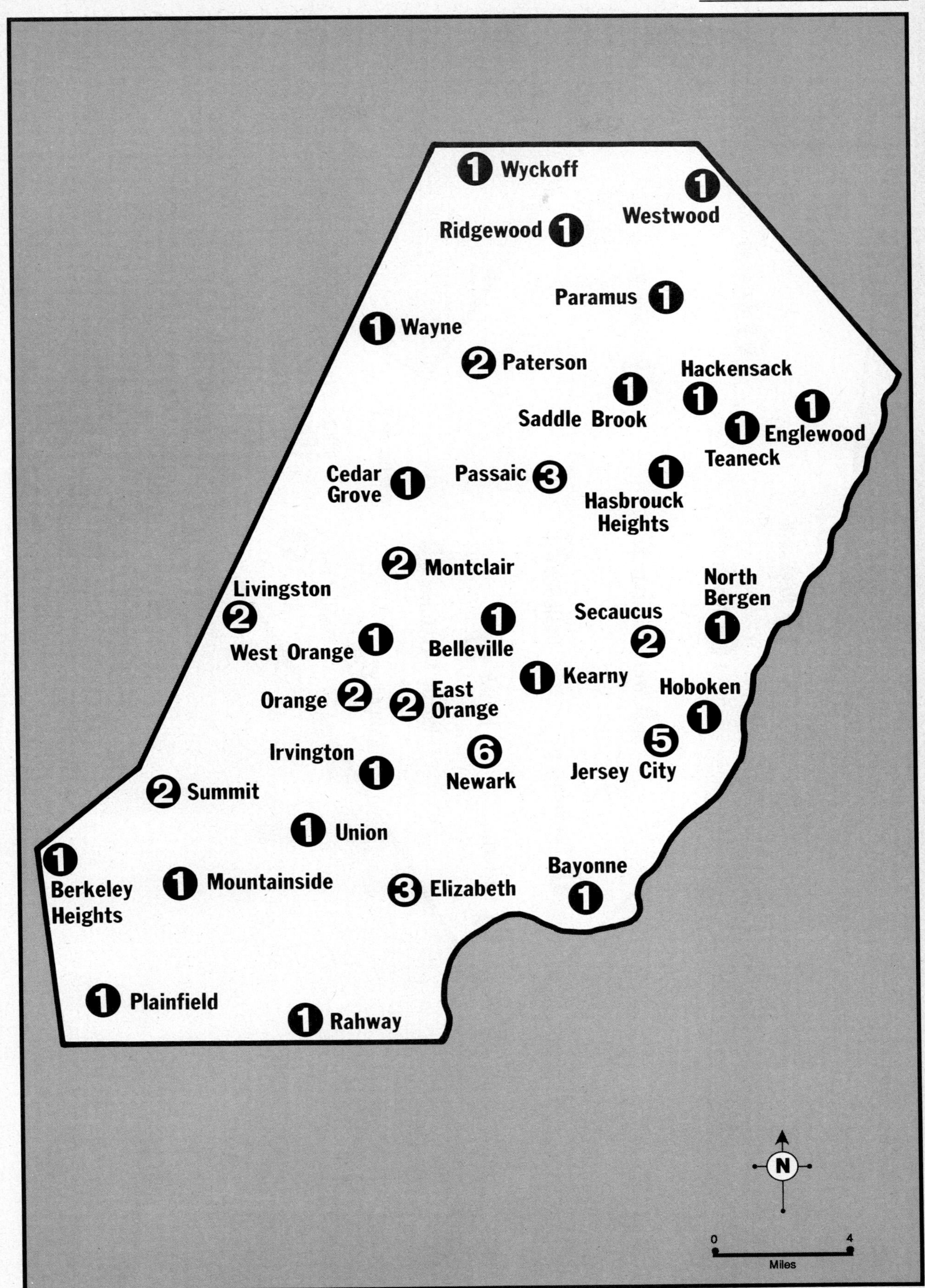
1 Wyckoff
1 Westwood
Ridgewood 1
Paramus 1
1 Wayne
2 Paterson
Hackensack
1
1
Saddle Brook
1 Englewood
1
Teaneck
Cedar Grove 1
Passaic 3
1
Hasbrouck Heights
2 Montclair
North Bergen
Livingston
2
1
Secaucus
2
1
West Orange 1
Belleville
1 Kearny
Hoboken
Orange 2
2 East Orange
1
Irvington
1
6
Newark
5
Jersey City
2 Summit
1 Union
1
Berkeley Heights
1 Mountainside
3 Elizabeth
Bayonne
1
1 Plainfield
1 Rahway
N
0
4
Miles

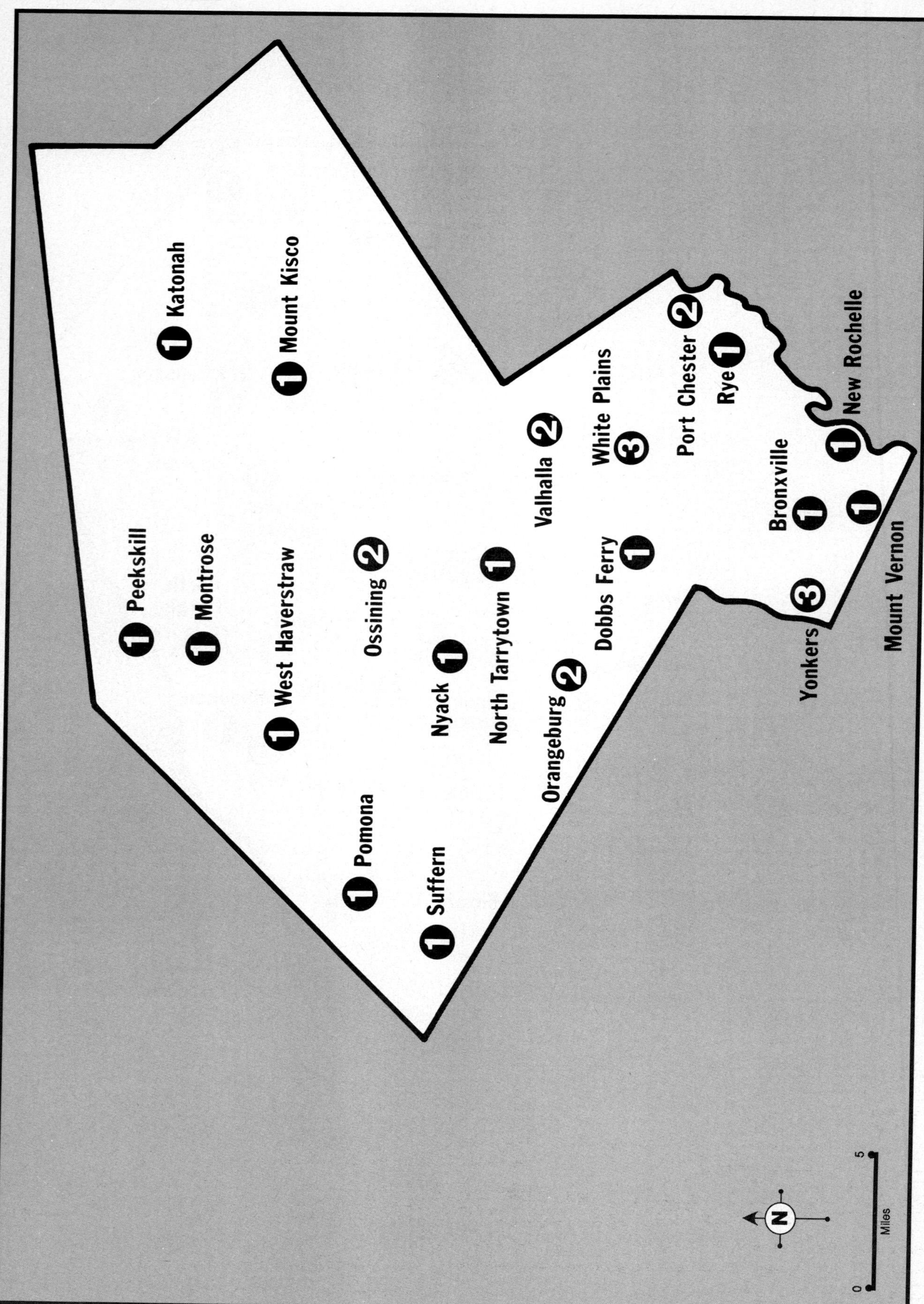
1 Katonah
1 Mount Kisco
1 Peekskill
1 Montrose
1 West Haverstraw
Ossining 2
Nyack 1
North Tarrytown 1
Valhalla 2
White Plains 3
Dobbs Ferry 1
Orangeburg 2
Port Chester 2
Rye 1
Bronxville 1
1 New Rochelle
1
Mount Vernon
3
Yonkers
1 Pomona
1 Suffern
N
0
5
Miles

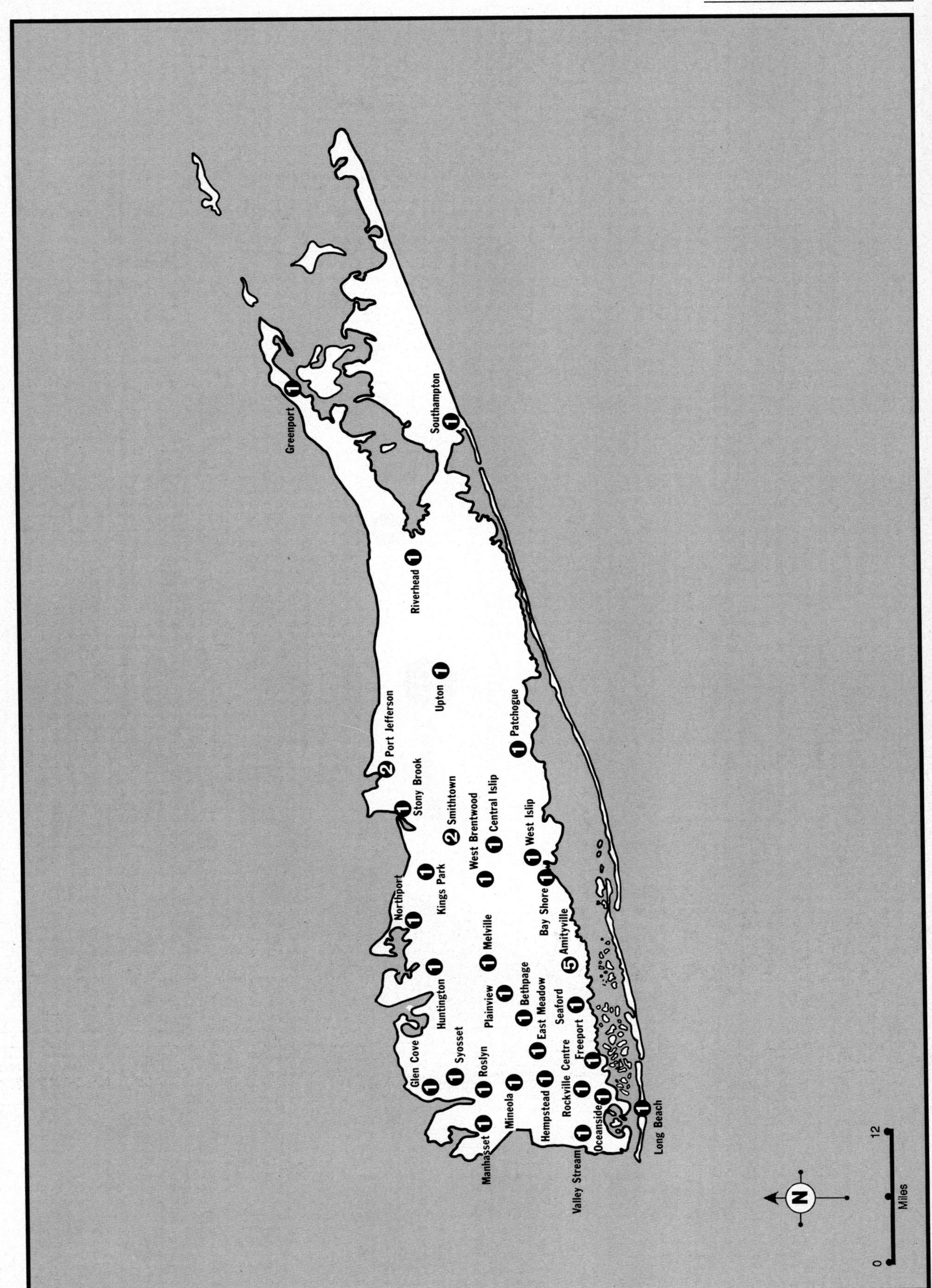
Greenport 1
Southampton 1
Riverhead 1
Upton 1
Port Jefferson 2
Patchogue 1
Stony Brook 1
Smithtown 2
Central Islip 1
West Brentwood 1
West Islip 1
Kings Park 1
Northport 1
Bay Shore 1
Melville 1
Amityville 5
Huntington 1
Plainview 1
Bethpage 1
Seaford 1
East Meadow 1
Syosset 1
Glen Cove 1
Roslyn 1
Freeport 1
Hempstead 1
Rockville Centre 1
Mineola 1
Manhasset 1
Oceanside 1
Long Beach 1
Valley Stream 1
N
0
12
Miles

Phoenix

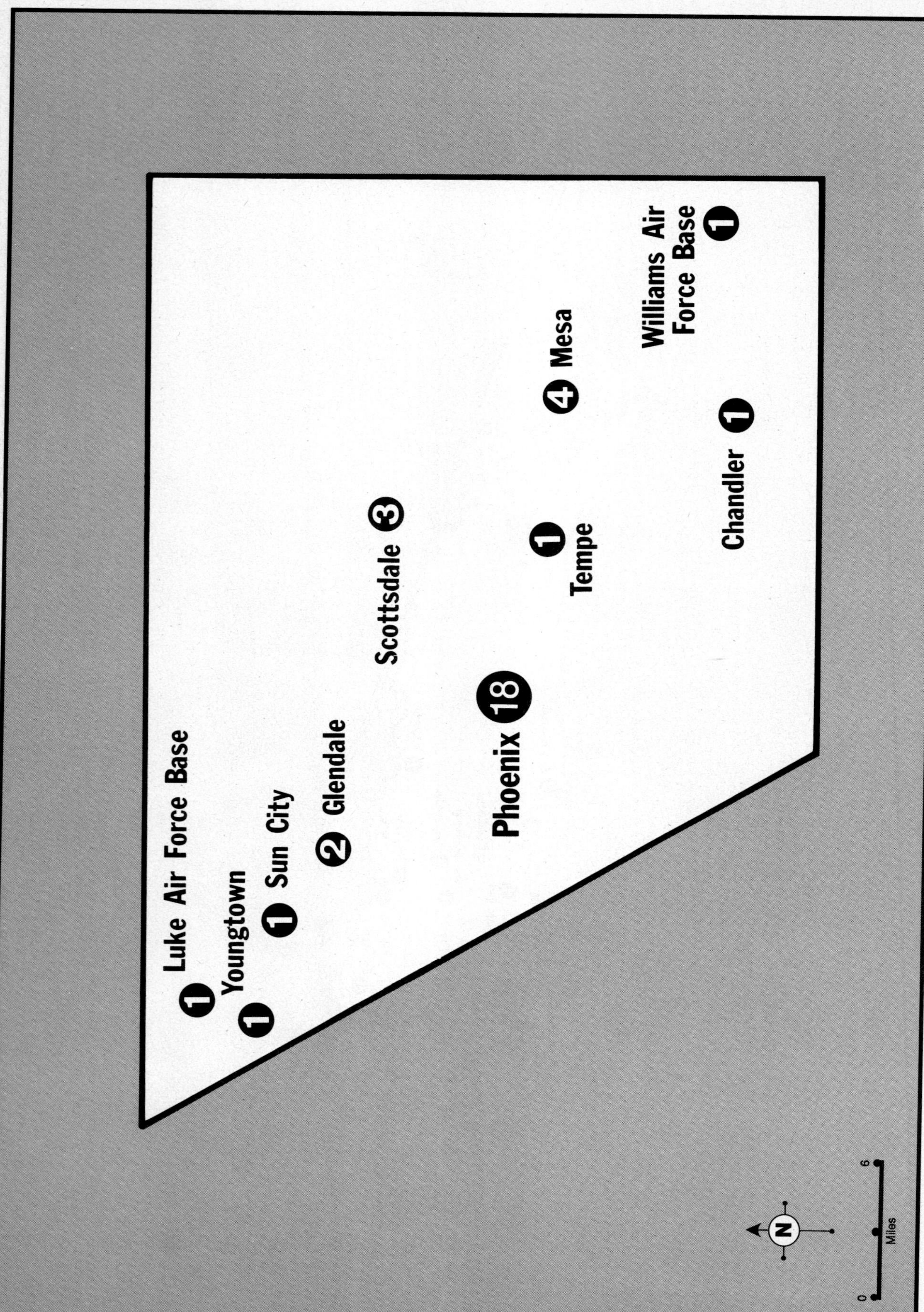
Luke Air Force Base 1
Youngtown 1
Sun City 1
Glendale 2
Phoenix 18
Scottsdale 3
Tempe 1
Mesa 4
Chandler 1
Williams Air Force Base 1
N
Miles
0
6

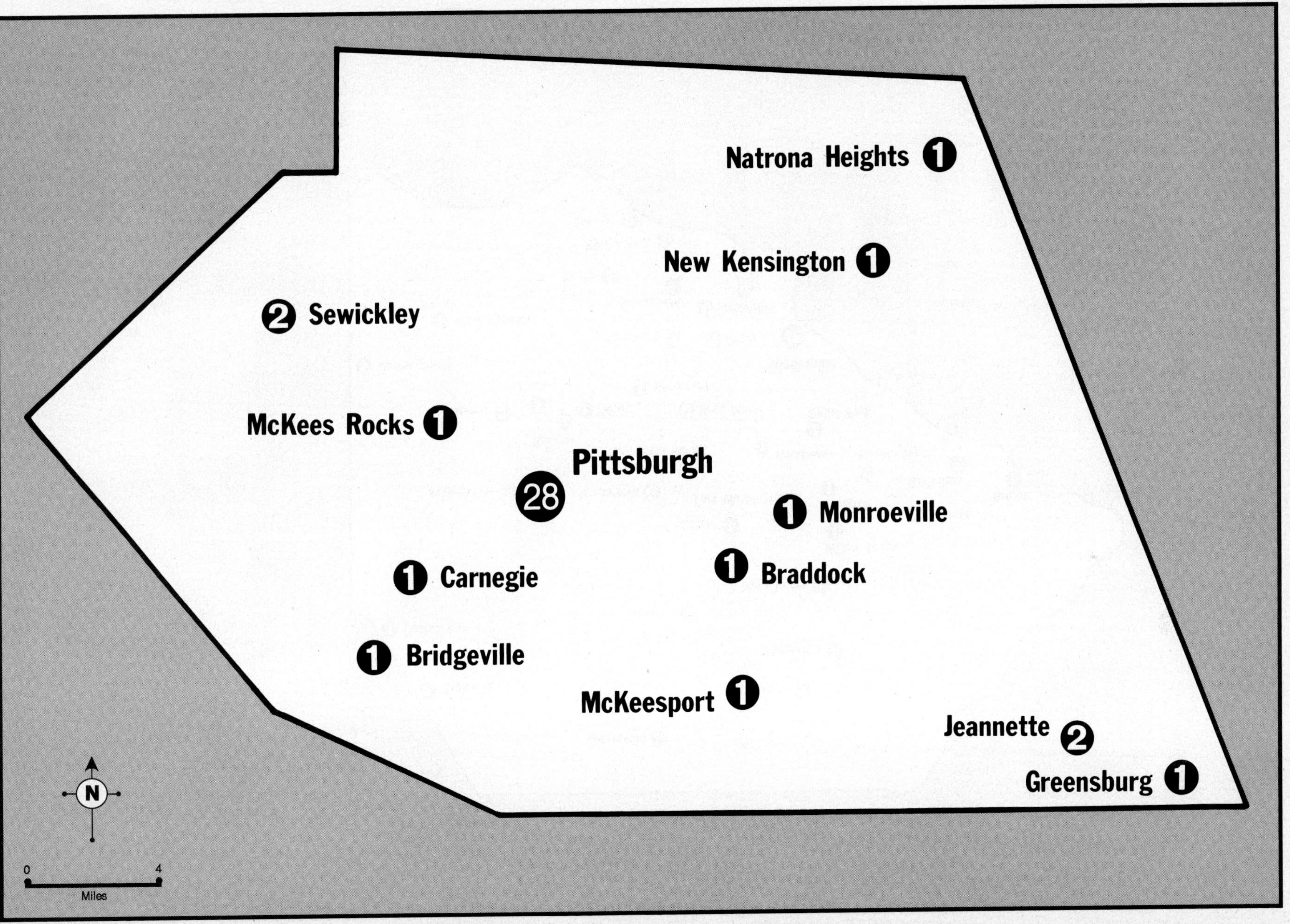
Natrona Heights 1
New Kensington 1
2 Sewickley
McKees Rocks 1
Pittsburgh
28
1 Monroeville
1 Carnegie
1 Braddock
1 Bridgeville
McKeesport 1
Jeannette 2
Greensburg 1
N
0
4
Miles

Philadelphia

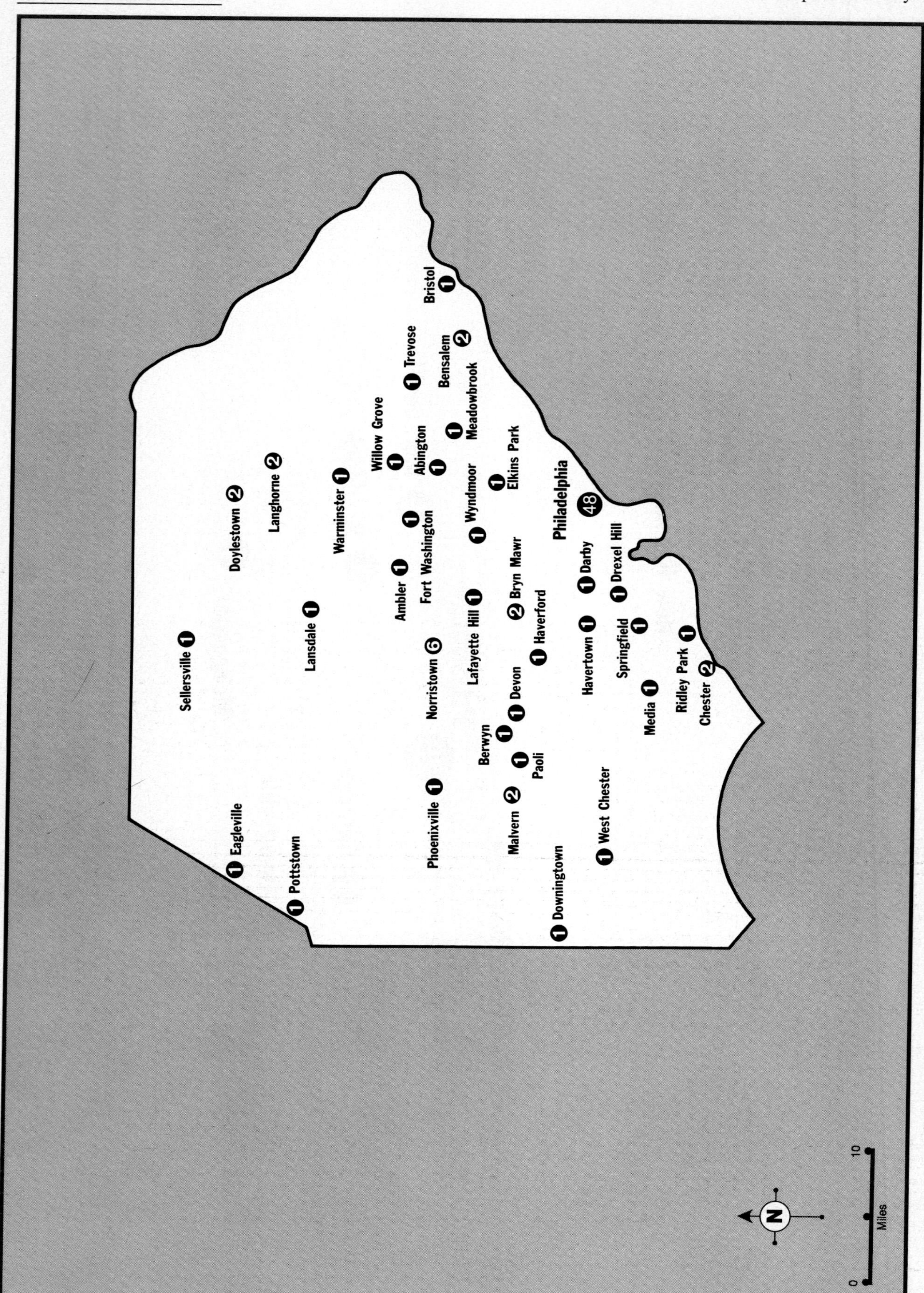

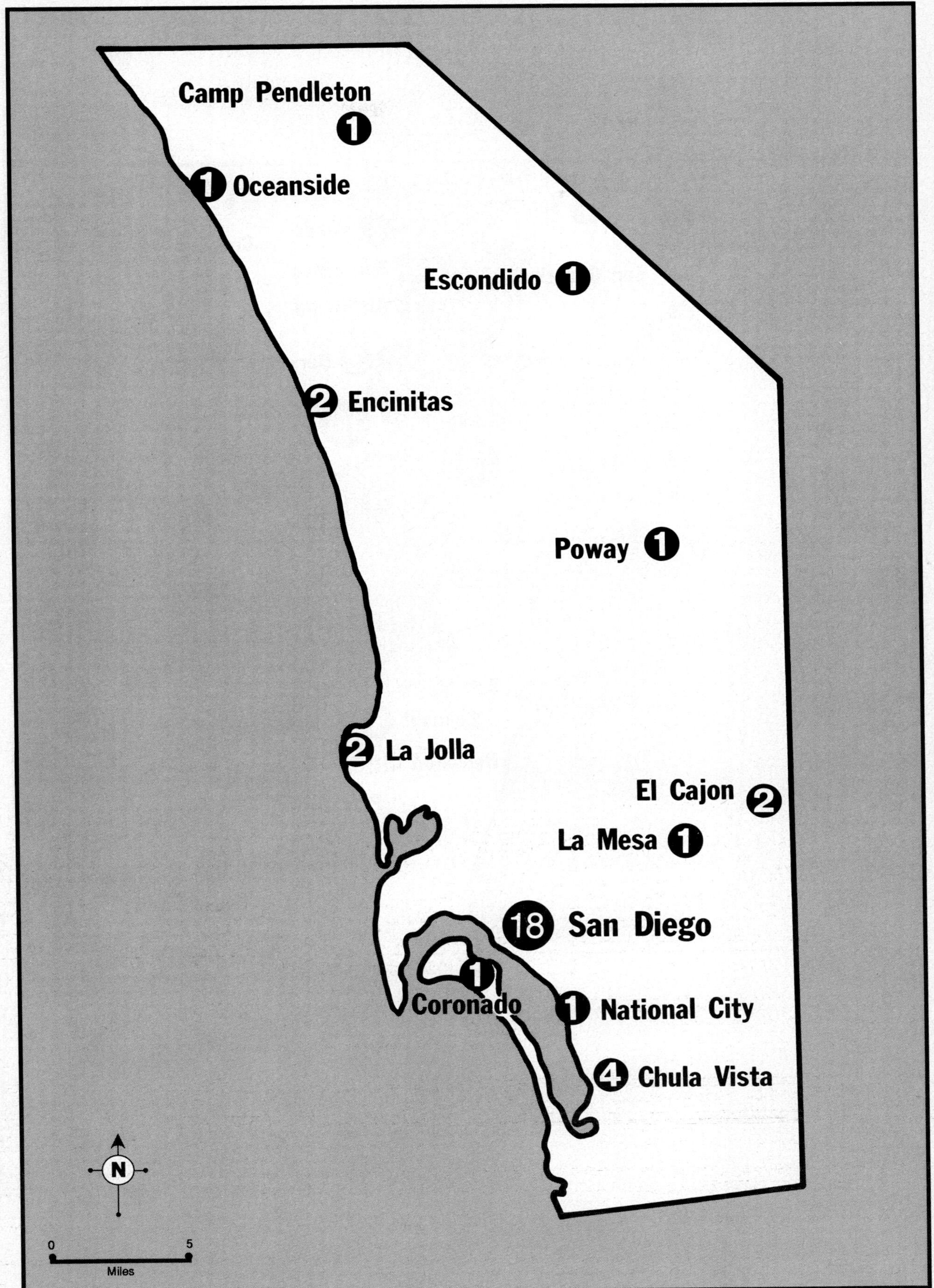
Camp Pendleton
1
1 Oceanside
Escondido 1
2 Encinitas
Poway 1
2 La Jolla
El Cajon 2
La Mesa 1
18 San Diego
1
Coronado
1 National City
4 Chula Vista
N
0
5
Miles

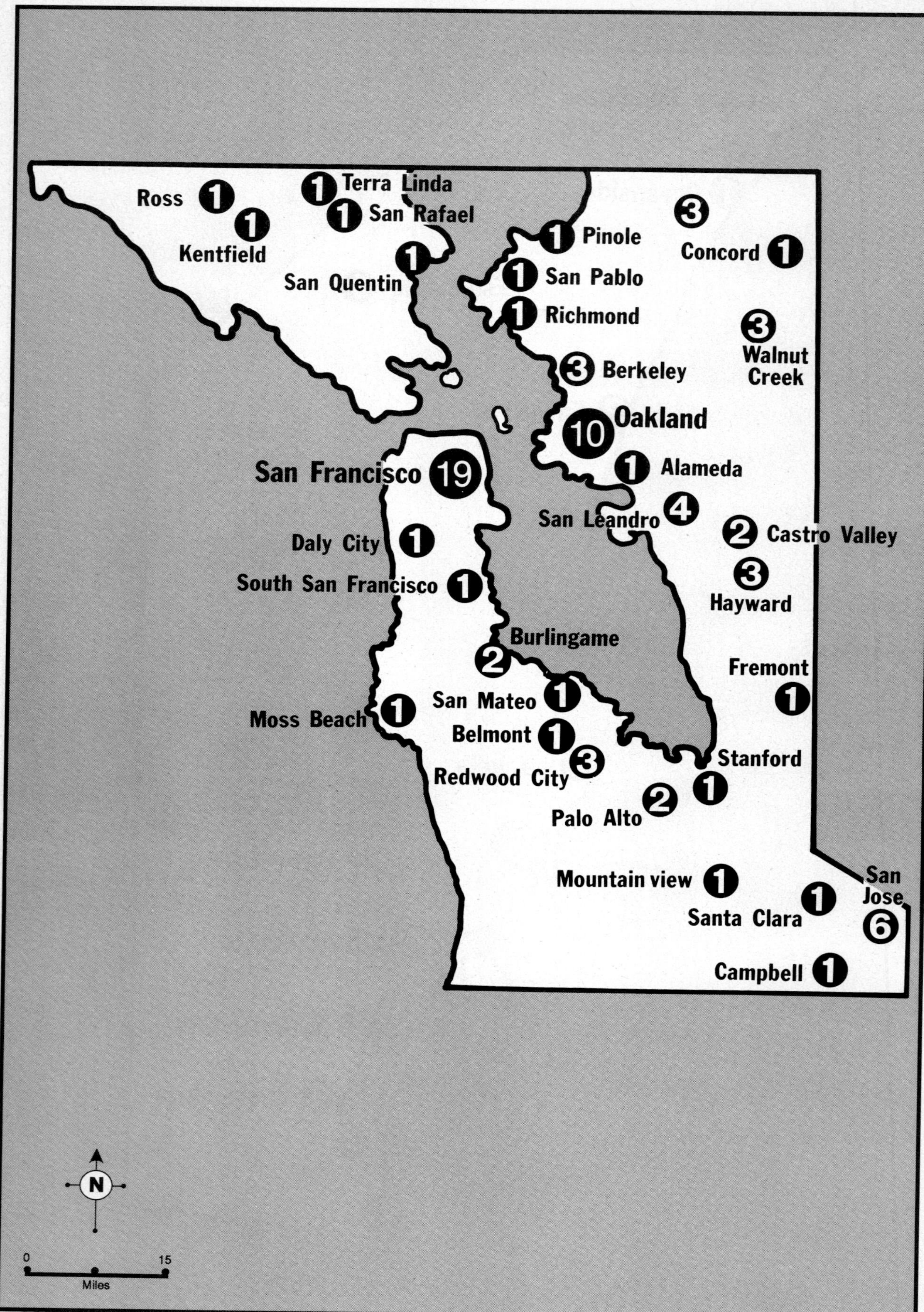

Ross 1
Kentfield 1
1 Terra Linda
1 San Rafael
San Quentin 1
1 Pinole
1 San Pablo
1 Richmond
3
Concord 1
3
Walnut Creek
3 Berkeley
10 Oakland
San Francisco 19
1 Alameda
San Leandro 4
2 Castro Valley
Daly City 1
South San Francisco 1
3
Hayward
Burlingame
2
Fremont
1
San Mateo 1
Moss Beach 1
Belmont 1
3
Redwood City
Stanford
1
2
Palo Alto
Mountain view 1
San Jose
6
1
Santa Clara
Campbell 1
N
0
15
Miles

Seattle

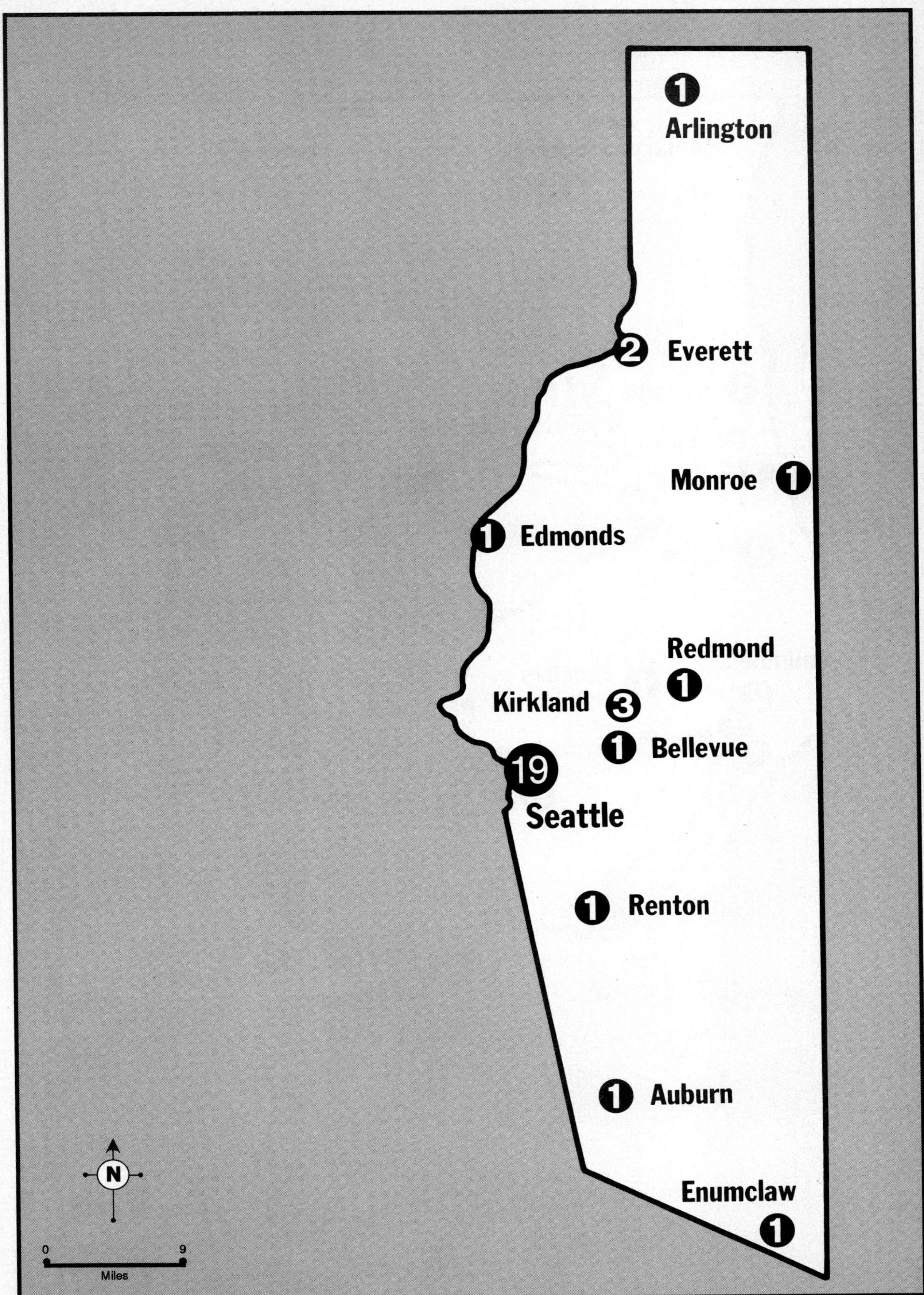
1
Arlington
2
Everett
Monroe
1
1
Edmonds
Redmond
1
Kirkland
3
1
Bellevue
19
Seattle
1
Renton
1
Auburn
Enumclaw
1
N
0
9
Miles

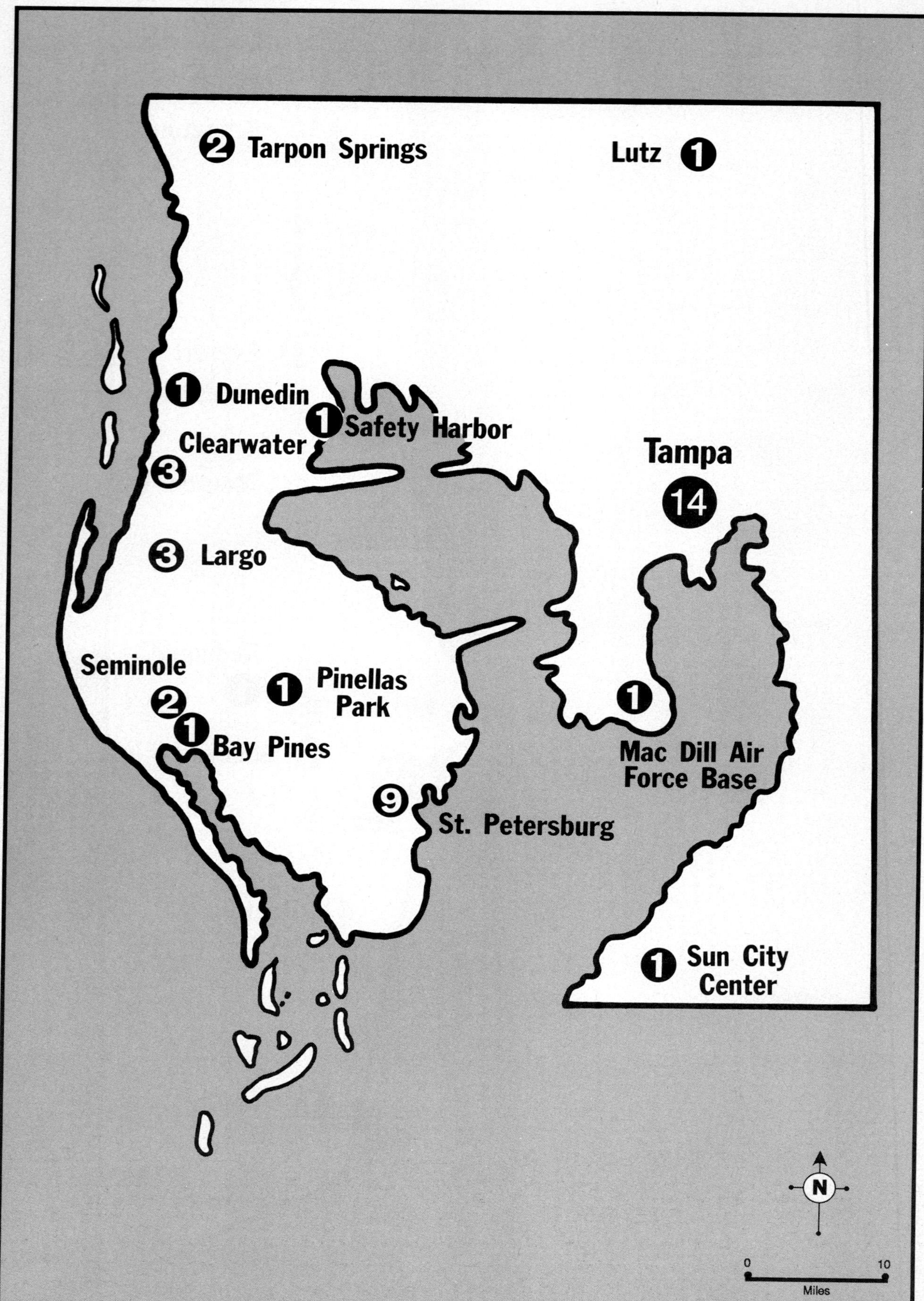
2 Tarpon Springs
Lutz 1
1 Dunedin
1 Safety Harbor
Clearwater
3
Tampa
14
3 Largo
Seminole
2
1 Bay Pines
1 Pinellas Park
1
Mac Dill Air Force Base
9
St. Petersburg
1 Sun City Center
N
0
10
Miles

AHA Members

For more information on membership requirements or to apply for institutional or personal membership, contact:
Manager, Department of Membership
American Hospital Association
840 N. Lake Shore Drive
Chicago, Illinois 60611.

Membership Categories

The American Hospital Association is primarily an organization of organizations—of hospitals and related institutions. Its object, according to its bylaws, is "to promote the welfare of the public through its leadership and its assistance to its members in the provision of better health care and services for all the people."

At present, AHA membership includes more than 5,300 hospitals in the United States and Canada, 149 multihospital systems, 200 hospital schools of nursing, 370 other organizations and agencies, and more than 41,000 personal members.

The major source of income for the AHA is its membership dues, which are established by the membership through the House of Delegates. The types of membership and the basis for dues for each type are described in the following paragraphs.

Institutional Members

Type I-A and II-A, Hospitals

General and special hospitals that care primarily for patients with conditions that usually require a comparatively short stay.

Types I-B and II-B, Hospitals

Hospitals that qualify for type I-A or type II-A membership and are owned, leased, sponsored, or contract-managed units of a type III member.

Type III, Multihospital Systems

Religious, investor-owned, or other organizations that own, lease, sponsor, or contract-manage two or more hospitals that qualify for type I-A or type II-A membership.

Membership dues are computed individually for each hospital and are based on total reported operating expenses for the most recent 12-month period. Type III members pay no dues other than those dues paid by their type B member units.

Provisional Members

Hospitals that are in the planning or construction stage and that, on completion, will be eligible for institutional membership type I or type II. Provisional membership may also be granted to applicant institutions that cannot, at present, meet the requirements of type I or type II membership.

Government Institution Group Members

Groups of government hospitals operated by the same unit of government may obtain institutional membership under a group plan. Membership dues are based on a special schedule set forth in the bylaws of the AHA.

Assembly for Hospital Schools of Nursing

State-approved hospital schools of nursing that are owned, operated, or controlled by an AHA institutional member. Membership dues are a fixed annual sum.

Contracting Hospitals

The AHA also provides membership services to certain hospitals that are prevented from holding membership because of legal or other restrictions.

Contracting hospitals pay dues on the same basis as if they were classified as type I or II members.

Associate Members

Associate members are organizations interested in the objectives of the AHA but not eligible for institutional membership. Membership dues are a fixed annual sum, depending on the location (inside or outside the United States and Canada) of the organization. The following list describes some of the groups included in the associate category.

Other Inpatient Care Institutions

Inpatient care institutions other than hospitals, such as extended care, nursing care, personal care, and sheltered care institutions.

Ambulatory Centers and Home Care Agencies

Organizations that provide diagnostic and treatment services, but do not provide inpatient care. Eligible members include ambulatory care centers, home care agencies, dispensaries, and clinics.

Blue Cross Plans

Not-for-profit hospital service organizations that are formally approved by the AHA Board of Trustees.

Health Maintenance Organizations and Health Care Corporations

Organizations that offer a prepaid health care plan program to the general public.

Shared Services Organizations

Shared services organizations or programs that are either freestanding or operated by allied hospital associations.

Health Planning Agencies

Metropolitan, state, and federal health planning agencies.

Associate Members (continued)

Associated University Programs in Health Administration

Schools of health administration.

Other Associate Members

Associate members of the AHA that do not fit into the previous groups, including insurance companies, architectural and consulting firms, government health agencies, voluntary health organizations, foundations, and hospitals located outside the United States and Canada.

Personal Members

Type A At-Large Members

Persons associated with institutional members or contracting hospitals; full-time students in hospital administration and such other health-related disciplines as may be designated from time to time by the AHA Board of Trustees; persons associated with associate members, government health agencies, or hospitals not located in a U.S. state; any person associated with a not-for-profit organization in the health field, provided such organization does not provide health care services; and such others as are designated from time to time by the AHA Board of Trustees. Membership dues are a fixed annual sum.

Type B At-Large Members

Persons associated with organizations eligible for but not holding institutional or associate membership and other persons interested in the objectives of the AHA. Membership dues are a fixed annual sum.

Type C Personal Members

Persons who qualify for type A at-large membership but hold membership in an affiliated society, academy, or other organized personal membership group of the AHA. Membership dues are a fixed annual sum recommended by the governing body of the group.

Type D Personal Members

Persons who qualify for type B at-large membership who hold membership in an affiliated society, academy, or other organized personal membership group of the AHA. Membership dues are a fixed annual sum recommended by the governing body of the group.

Life Members

Chairmen of the AHA Board of Trustees who have completed their terms of office, persons receiving an AHA award (including the Distinguished Service Award, the Award of Honor, the Justin Ford Kimball Award, and the Trustees Award), and persons who have paid annual dues applicable to a period of 30 years. Life members pay no dues.

Honorary Members

Persons so designated by the AHA Board of Trustees. Honorary members pay no dues.

Offices, Officers, and Historical Data

Headquarters: 840 N. Lake Shore Dr., Chicago 60611; tel. 312/280-6000
Region 1: 5 New England Executive Park, Burlington, MA 01803-5006; tel. 617/272-0787
Region 2: 760 Alexander Rd., CN-1, Center for Health Affairs, Princeton, NJ 08543-0001; tel. 609/452-9270
Region 3: Capitol Pl. III, 50 F St. N.W., Suite 1100, Washington, DC 20001; tel. 202/638-7368
Region 4: 15 Dunwoody Park, Suite 128, Atlanta, GA 30338; tel. 404/394-9510
Region 5: 840 N. Lake Shore Dr., Chicago, IL 60611; tel. 312/280-6661
Region 6: 1 Ward Pkwy., Suite 105, Kansas City, MO 64112; tel. 816/561-0501
Region 7: 1431 Greenway Dr., Suite 325, Irving, TX 75038; tel. 214/550-1520
Region 8: 2140 S. Holly St., Denver, CO 80222; tel. 303/758-2161
Region 9: 1023 12th St., Sacramento, CA 95814; tel. 916/447-7262
Washington Office: Capitol Pl. III, 50 F St. N.W., Washington, DC 20001; tel. 202/638-1100

Speaker of the House of Delegates: Scott S. Parker, Intermountain Health Care, Salt Lake City, UT 84111
Chairman of the Board of Trustees: Donald C. Wegmiller, Health Central Corp., Minneapolis, MN 55430
Chairman-Elect of the Board of Trustees: Eugene W. Arnett, Memorial Hospital of Taylor County, Medford, WI 54451
President: Carol M. McCarthy, Ph.D., J.D., 840 N. Lake Shore Dr., Chicago 60611
Secretary-Treasurer: David F. Drake, Ph.D., 840 N. Lake Shore Dr., Chicago 60611

Past Presidents/Chairmen†

1899 ★James S. Knowles
1900 ★James S. Knowles
1901 ★Charles S. Howell
1902 ★J. T. Duryea
1903 ★John Fehrenbatch
1904 ★Daniel D. Test
1905 ★George H. M. Rowe, M.D.
1906 ★George P. Ludham
1907 ★Renwick R. Ross, M.D.
1908 ★Sigismund S. Goldwater, M.D.
1909 ★John M. Peters, M.D.
1910 ★H. B. Howard, M.D.
1911 ★W. L. Babcock, M.D.
1912 ★Henry M. Hurd, M.D.
1913 ★F. A. Washburn, M.D.
1914 ★Thomas Howell, M.D.
1915 ★William O. Mann, M.D.
1916 ★Winford H. Smith, M.D.
1917 ★Robert J. Wilson, M.D.
1918 ★A. B. Ancker, M.D.
1919 ★A. R. Warner, M.D.
1920 ★Joseph B. Howland, M.D.
1921 ★Louis B. Baldwin, M.D.
1922 ★George O'Hanlon, M.D.
1923 ★Asa S. Bacon
1924 ★Malcolm T. MacEachern, M.D.
1925 ★E. S. Gilmore
1926 ★Arthur C. Bachmeyer, M.D.
1927 ★R. G. Brodrick, M.D.
1928 ★Joseph C. Doane, M.D.
1929 ★Louis H. Burlingham, M.D.
1930 ★Christopher G. Parnall, M.D.
1931 ★Lewis A. Sexton, M.D.
1932 ★Paul H. Fesler
1933 ★George F. Stephens, M.D.
1934 ★Nathaniel W. Faxon, M.D.
1935 ★Robert Jolly
1936 Robin C. Buerki, M.D.
1937 ★Claude W. Munger, M.D.
1938 ★Robert E. Neff
1939 ★G. Harvey Agnew, M.D.
1940 ★Fred G. Carter, M.D.
1941 ★B. W. Black, M.D.
1942 ★Basil C. MacLean, M.D.
1943 ★James A. Hamilton
1944 ★Frank J. Walter
1945 ★Donald C. Smelzer, M.D.
1946 ★Peter D. Ward, M.D.
1947 ★John H. Hayes
1948 ★Graham L. Davis
1949 ★Joseph G. Norby
1950 ★John H. Hatfield
1951 ★Charles F. Wilinsky, M.D.
1952 ★Anthony J. J. Rourke, M.D.
1953 ★Edwin L. Crosby, M.D.
1954 ★Ritz E. Heerman
1955 Frank R. Bradley
1956 ★Ray E. Brown
1957 Albert W. Snoke, M.D.
1958 ★Tol Terrell
1959 ★Ray Amberg
1960 Russell A. Nelson, M.D.
1961 Frank S. Groner
1962 ★Jack Masur, M.D.
1963 T. Stewart Hamilton, M.D.
1964 Stanley A. Ferguson
1965 Clarence E. Wonnacott
1966 Philip D. Bonnet, M.D.
1967 George E. Cartmill
1968 David B. Wilson, M.D.
1969 George Wm. Graham, M.D.
1970 ★Mark Berke
1971 Jack A. L. Hahn
1972 Stephen M. Morris
1973 ★John W. Kauffman
1974 Horace M. Cardwell
1975 Wade Mountz
1976 H. Robert Cathcart
1977 John M. Stagl
1978 Samuel J. Tibbitts
1979 W. Daniel Barker
1980 Sr. Irene Kraus
1981 Bernard J. Lachner
1982 Stanley R. Nelson
1983 Elbert E. Gilbertson
1984 Thomas R. Matherlee
1985 Jack A. Skarupa
1986 Scott S. Parker

Chief Executive Officers

1917-18 ★William H. Walsh, M.D.
1919-24 ★Andrew Robert Warner, M.D.
1925-27 ★William H. Walsh, M.D.
1928-42 ★Bert W. Caldwell, M.D.
1943-54 George Bugbee
1954-72 ★Edwin L. Crosby, M.D.
1972 Madison B. Brown, M.D. (acting)
1972-86 J. Alexander McMahon
1986- Carol M. McCarthy, Ph.D., J.D.

Distinguished Service Award

1934 ★Matthew O. Foley
1939 ★Malcolm T. MacEachern, M.D.
1940 ★Sigismund S. Goldwater, M.D.
1941 ★Frederic A. Washburn, M.D.
1942 ★Winford H. Smith, M.D.
1943 ★Arthur C. Bachmeyer, M.D.
1944 ★Rt. Rev. Msgr. Maurice F. Griffin, LL.D.
1945 ★Asa S. Bacon
1946 ★George F. Stephens, M.D.
1947 Robin C. Buerki, M.D.
1948 ★James A. Hamilton
1949 ★Claude W. Munger, M.D.
1950 ★Nathaniel W. Faxon, M.D.
1951 ★Bert W. Caldwell, M.D.
1952 ★Fred G. Carter, M.D.
1953 ★Basil C. MacLean, M.D.
1954 George Bugbee
1955 ★Joseph G. Norby
1956 ★Charles F. Wilinsky, M.D.
1957 ★John H. Hayes
1958 ★John N. Hatfield
1959 ★Edwin L. Crosby, M.D.
1960 ★Oliver G. Pratt
1961 ★E. M. Bluestone, M.D.
1962 Mother Loretto Bernard, S.C., R.N.
1963 ★Ray E. Brown
1964 Russell A. Nelson, M.D.
1965 Albert W. Snoke, M.D.
1966 Frank S. Groner
1967 ★Rev. John J. Flanagan, S.J.
1968 Stanley W. Martin
1969 T. Stewart Hamilton, M.D.
1970 ★Charles Patteson Cardwell Jr.
1971 ★Mark Berke
1972 Stanley A. Ferguson
1973 Jack A. L. Hahn
1974 George Wm. Graham, M.D.
1975 George E. Cartmill
1976 D. O. McClusky Jr.
1977 Boone Powell
1978 ★Richard J. Stull
1979 Horace M. Cardwell
1980 Donald W. Cordes
1981 Sr. Mary Brigh Cassidy
1982 R. Zach Thomas Jr.
1983 H. Robert Cathcart
1984 Matthew F. McNulty Jr., Sc.D.
1985 J. Alexander McMahon
1986 Sister Irene Kraus

★Deceased
† On June 3, 1972, the House of Delegates changed the title of the chief elected officer to chairman of the Board of Trustees, and the title of president was conferred on the chief executive officer of the Association.

Award of Honor

1966	★Senator Lister Hill
1967	★Emory W. Morris, D.D.S.
1971	Special Committee on Provision of Health Services (staff also)
1982	Walter J. McNerney

Justin Ford Kimball Award

1958	★E. A. van Steenwyk
1959	George A. Newbury
1960	C. Rufus Rorem, Ph.D.
1961	★James E. Stuart
1962	Frank Van Dyk
1963	William S. McNary
1964	Frank S. Groner
1965	★J. Douglas Colman
1967	Walter J. McNerney
1968	John W. Paynter
1970	★Edwin L. Crosby, M.D.
1971	H. Charles Abbott
1972	John R. Mannix
1973	Herman M. Somers
1974	William H. Ford, Ph.D.
1975	Earl H. Kammer
1976	J. Ed McConnell
1978	Edwin R. Werner
1979	Robert M. Cunningham Jr.
1981	★Maurice J. Norby
1982	Robert E. Rinehimer
1983	John B. Morgan Jr.
1984	Joseph F. Duplinsky
1985	David W. Stewart

Trustees Award

1959	★Joseph V. Friel
	★John H. Hayes
1960	Duncan D. Sutphen Jr.
1963	Eleanor C. Lambertsen, R.N., Ed.D.
1964	John R. Mannix
1965	★Albert G. Hahn
	★Maurice J. Norby
1966	Madison B. Brown, M.D.
	Kenneth Williamson
1967	★Alanson W. Wilcox
1968	E. Dwight Barnett, M.D.
1969	★Vane M. Hoge, M.D.
	Joseph H. McNinch, M.D.
1972	David F. Drake, Ph.D.
	Paul W. Earle
	Michael Lesparre
	Andrew Pattullo
1973	Tilden Cummings
	Edmond J. Lanigan
1974	James E. Hague
	Sister Marybelle
1975	Helen T. Yast
1976	Boynton P. Livingston
	James Ludlam
	Helen McGuire
1979	Newton J. Jacobson
	Edward W. Weimer
1980	Robert B. Hunter, M.D.
	Samuel J. Tibbitts
1981	Vernon A. Knutson
	John E. Sullivan
1982	John Bigelow
	Robert W. O'Leary
	Jack W. Owen
1984	Howard J. Berman
	O. Ray Hurst
	James R. Neely
1985	James E. Ferguson
	Cleveland Rodgers
1986	Rex N. Olsen
1987	Michael Lesparre

Citation for Meritorious Service

1968	★F. R. Knautz
	Sr. Conrad Mary, R.N.
1971	Hospital Council of Southern California
1972	College of Misericordia, Dallas, PA
1973	Madison B. Brown, M.D.
	Samuel J. Tibbitts
1975	Kenneth B. Babcock, M.D.
	Sr. Mary Maurita Sengelaube
1976	Chaiker Abbis
	Susan Jenkins
	Gordon McLachlan
1977	Theodore Cooper, M.D.
1979	Norman D. Burkett
	John L. Quigley
	★William M. Whelan
1980	★Sr. Grace Marie Hiltz
	Leo J. Gehrig, M.D.
1981	Richard Davi
	Pearl S. Fryar
1982	Jorge Brull Nater
1983	David M. Kinzer
1984	Donald L. Custis, M.D.
1985	John A. D. Cooper, M.D.
	Imperial Council of the Ancient Arabic Order of the Nobles of the Mystic Shrine for North America
1986	Howard F. Cook

Conventions

No.	Year	Location and Dates
1	1899	Cleveland, September 12-13
2	1900	Pittsburgh, August 21-23
3	1901	New York, September 10-12
4	1902	Philadelphia, October 14-16
5	1903	Cincinnati, October 20-22
6	1904	Atlantic City, September 21-23
7	1905	Boston, September 26-29
8	1906	Buffalo, September 18-21
9	1907	Chicago, September 17-20
10	1908	Toronto, September 29-October 2
11	1909	Washington, September 21-24
12	1910	St. Louis, September 20-23
13	1911	New York, September 19-22
14	1912	Detroit, September 24-27
15	1913	Boston, August 26-29
16	1914	St. Paul, August 25-28
17	1915	San Francisco, June 22-25
18	1916	Philadelphia, September 26-30
19	1917	Cleveland, September 10-15
20	1918	Atlantic City, September 24-28
21	1919	Cincinnati, September 8-12
22	1920	Montreal, October 4-8
23	1921	West Baden, Ind., September 12-16
24	1922	Atlantic City, September 25-28
25	1923	Milwaukee, October 27-November 3
26	1924	Buffalo, October 6-10
27	1925	Louisville, October 19-23
28	1926	Atlantic City, September 27-October 1
29	1927	Minneapolis, October 10-14
30	1928	San Francisco, August 6-10
31	1929	Atlantic City, June 17-21
32	1930	New Orleans, October 20-24
33	1931	Toronto, September 28-October 2
34	1932	Detroit, September 12-16
35	1933	Milwaukee, September 11-15
36	1934	Philadelphia, September 24-28
37	1935	St. Louis, September 30-October 4
38	1936	Cleveland, September 28-October 2
39	1937	Atlantic City, September 13-17
40	1938	Dallas, September 26-30
41	1939	Toronto, September 25-29
42	1940	Boston, September 16-20
43	1941	Atlantic City, September 15-19
44	1942	St. Louis, October 12-16
45	1943	Buffalo, September 13-17
46	1944	Cleveland, October 2-6
47	1945	Chicago, November 6-7 (House only)
48	1946	Philadelphia, September 30-October 3
49	1947	St. Louis, September 22-25
50	1948	Atlantic City, September 20-23
51	1949	Cleveland, September 26-29
52	1950	Atlantic City, September 18-21
53	1951	St. Louis, September 17-20
54	1952	Philadelphia, September 15-18
55	1953	San Francisco, August 31-September 3
56	1954	Chicago, September 13-16
57	1955	Atlantic City, September 19-22
58	1956	Chicago, September 17-20
59	1957	Atlantic City, September 30-October 2
60	1958	Chicago, August 18-21
61	1959	New York, August 24-27
62	1960	San Francisco, August 29-September 1
63	1961	Atlantic City, September 25-28
64	1962	Chicago, September 17-20
65	1963	New York, August 26-29
66	1964	Chicago, August 24-27
67	1965	San Francisco, August 30-September 2
68	1966	Chicago, August 29-September 1
69	1967	Chicago, August 21-24
70	1968	Atlantic City, September 16-19
71	1969	Chicago, August 18-21
72	1970	Houston, September 14-17
73	1971	Chicago, August 23-26
	1972	Chicago, August 7-10 (American Health Congress)
	1973	Chicago, August 20-23 (American Health Congress)
	1974	Chicago, August 12-15 (American Health Congress)
74	1975	Chicago, August 18-21
75	1976	Dallas, September 20-23
76	1977	Atlanta, August 29-September 1
77	1978	Anaheim, CA, September 11-14
78	1979	Chicago, August 27-30
79	1980	Montreal, July 28-31
80	1981	Philadelphia, August 31-September 3
81	1982	Atlanta, August 30-September 1
82	1983	Houston, August 1-3
83	1984	Denver, August 13-15
84	1985	Chicago, July 29-31
85	1986	Toronto, August 4-6
86	1987	Atlanta, July 27-29

★Deceased

Institutional Members

Types I and II

Hospitals

U.S. hospitals and hospitals in areas associated with the U.S. that are type I (short-term) or type II (long-term) members of the American Hospital Association are included in the list of hospitals in the first section of this guide. Membership is indicated by a star preceding the name of the hospital. Canadian types I and II members of the American Hospital Association are listed below.

Canada

Alberta

Edmonton: MISERICORDIA HOSPITAL, 16940 87th Ave.; G. M. Lane, pres.
ROYAL ALEXANDRA HOSPITAL, 10240 Kingsway Ave.; E. L. Casey, pres.
UNIVERSITY OF ALBERTA HOSPITAL, 8440 112th St., Zip T6G 2B7; Donald A. Cramp, pres.
Lamont: ARCHER MEMORIAL HOSPITAL, Harold James, adm.
St. Albert: STURGEON GENERAL HOSPITAL, 78 McKenney Ave.; Robert G. Sockett, dir.

British Columbia

Vancouver: CHILDREN'S HOSPITAL, 4480 Oak St., Zip V6H 3V4; J. Tegenfeldt, exec. dir.
VANCOUVER GENERAL HOSPITAL, 855 W. 12th Ave.; James B. Flett, pres.
Victoria: VICTORIA GENERAL HOSPITAL, 35 Helmcken Rd., Zip V8V 3B6

Manitoba

Portage La Prarie: PORTAGE DISTRICT GENERAL HOSPITAL, 524 Fifth St. S.E.; Garry C. Mattin, exec. dir.
Winnipeg: GRACE GENERAL HOSPITAL, 300 Booth Dr.; Maj. Irene Stickland, dir.
VICTORIA GENERAL HOSPITAL, 2340 Pembina Hwy.; Dieter Kuntz, exec. dir.
WINNIPEG MUNICIPAL HOSPITAL, 1 Morley Ave. E., Zip R3L 2P4; R. D. Cavey, adm.

New Brunswick

Edmundston: EDMUNDSTON REGIONAL HOSPITAL, 54 21st Ave.; Gilbert St.-Onge, exec. dir.
Saint John: CENTRACARE SAINT JOHN, 281 Lancaster Ave., Sta. B, Dwr. 3220; G. Buchanan, exec. dir.

Nova Scotia

Antigonish: ST. MARTHA'S HOSPITAL, 25 Bay St.; G. Shirley Young, adm.
Dartmouth: NOVA SCOTIA HOSPITAL, Box 1004; V. F. Simpson, adm.
Glace Bay: GLACE BAY COMMUNITY HOSPITAL, 197 Main St.; David Marchand, adm.
GLACE BAY GENERAL HOSPITAL, Brookside St.; Mrs. J. Hemsworth, adm.
North Sydney: NORTHSIDE HARBOR VIEW HOSPITAL, Purves St., Zip B2A 3M4; A. J. LeBlanc, exec. dir.
Sydney: ST. RITA HOSPITAL, 409 Kings Rd.; J. B. Beaton, adm.

Ontario

Brantford: ST. JOSEPH'S HOSPITAL, 63 Park Rd. N.; Ken Tremblay, exec. dir.
Brockville: ST VINCENT DE PAUL HOSPITAL, 42 Garden St.; Thomas P. Harrington, adm.
Chatham: PUBLIC GENERAL HOSPITAL, 106 Emma St.; Zip N7L 1A8; J. H. Shillington, exec. dir.
ST. JOSEPH'S HOSPITAL, 519 King St. W.; W. F. Hall, exec. dir.
Downsview: YORK-FINCH GENERAL HOSPITAL, 2111 Finch Ave. W.; Zip M3N 1N1; Michael J. O'Keefe, pres.
Guelph: HOMEWOOD SANITARIUM, 150 Delhi St., Zip N1E 6K9; M. O. Vincent, M.D., exec. dir.
London: ST. MARY'S HOSPITAL, 35 Grosvenor St., Zip N6A 1Y6; Sr. Cecilia, exec. dir.
Meaford: MEAFORD GENERAL HOSPITAL, 229 Nelson St., Box 340; Stephen M. Legate, adm.
Niagara-on-the-Lake: NIAGARA HOSPITAL, 176 Wellington St., Box 1270; Milton Alley, exec. dir.
Parry Sound: PARRY SOUND GENERAL HOSPITAL, 10 James St., Zip P2A 1T3; Norman Maciver, chf. exec. off.
Sarnia: SARNIA GENERAL HOSPITAL, 220 N. Mitton St., E. E. Redden, exec. dir.
ST. JOSEPH'S HOSPITAL, 290 N. Russell St., Zip N7T 6S3; F. N. Bagatto, exec. dir.
Strathroy: STRATHROY MIDDLESEX GENERAL HOSPITAL, 395 Carrie St., Zip N7G 3C9; Thomas Enright, exec. dir.
Sudbury: SUDBURY MEMORIAL HOSPITAL, 865 Regent St. S.; Esko J. Vainio, exec. dir.
Thornhill: SHOULDICE HOSPITAL, 7750 Bayview Ave., Box 370, Zip L3T 4A3; Alan O'Dell, adm.
Toronto: BAYCREST CENTRE - GERIATRIC CARE, 3560 Bathurst St.; Stephen E. Rudin, exec. dir.
CENTRAL HOSPITAL, 333 Sherbourne St.; Paul Rekai, M.D., adm.
DOCTORS HOSPITAL, 45 Brunswick Ave.; R. J. Brian McFarlane, dir.
MOUNT SINAI HOSPITAL, 600 University Ave.; Zip M5G 1X5; Gerald P. Turner, pres.
QUEEN ELIZABETH HOSPITAL, 550 University Ave.; Zip M5G 2A2; Clifford A. Nordal, pres.
ST. JOSEPH'S HEALTH CENTRE, 30 The Queensway, Zip M6R 1B5; Sr. Margaret Myatt, dir.
ST. MICHAEL'S HOSPITAL, 30 Bond St.; Sr. Christine Gaudet, dir.
Willowdale: NORTH YORK BRANSON HOSPITAL, 555 Finch Ave. W.; J. A. Bruce, adm.
Windsor: GRACE HOSPITAL, 339 Crawford Ave.; Maj. Douglas Kerr, dir.
HOTEL DIEU OF ST. JOSEPH, 1030 Quellette Ave.; Roman E. Mann, exec. dir.
WINDSOR WESTERN HOSPITAL CENTRE, 1453 Prince Rd., Zip N9C 3Z4; James J. Broderick, dir.

Quebec

Laval: JEWISH REHABILITATION HOSPITAL, 3205 Alton Goldbloom St., Zip H7V 1R2; Jacques Hendlisz, dir. gen.
Montreal: JEWISH GENERAL HOSPITAL, 3755 Cote St.-Catherine Rd.; Archie S. Deskin, exec. dir.
JEWISH HOSPITAL OF HOPE, 7745 Sherbrooke St. E.; Melvin J. Simak, gen. mgr.
MONTREAL CHILDREN'S HOSPITAL, 2300 Tupper St.; John S. Charters, dir.
MONTREAL GENERAL HOSPITAL, 1650 Cedar Ave., Zip H3G 1A4; Harvey Barkun, M.D., dir.
NOTRE DAME HOSPITAL, 1560 E. Sherbrooke; Marcel H. Labbe, dir. gen.
REDDY MEMORIAL HOSPITAL, 4039 Tupper St.; Rejean Plante, gen. mgr.
ROYAL VICTORIA HOSPITAL, 687 Pine Ave.; Zip H3A 1A1; Stephen W. Herbert, pres.
SHRINERS HOSPITAL FOR CRIPPLED CHILDREN, 1529 Cedar Ave.; Lise Chaput Clarke, adm.
Quebec: JEFFERY HALE'S HOSPITAL, 1250 Ste.-Foy Rd.; M. Roger Bertin, exec. dir.
Sherbrooke: SHERBROOKE HOSPITAL, 375 Argyle St., Zip J1J 3H5; D. A. MacKenzie, dir. gen.
Ste.-Agath Des Monts: MOUNT SINAI HOSPITAL CENTER, Box 1000; Joseph Rothbart, exec. dir.

Saskatchewan

Saskatoon: UNIVERSITY HOSPITAL, Zip S7N 0X0; A. Tony Dagnone, pres.

Type III

Multihospital Systems

Multihospital systems that are type III members of the American Hospital Association are included in the alphabetic and numeric lists of headquarters of multihospital systems in section A of this guide. Membership is indicated in the numeric list by a star (★) preceding the name of the system.

Provisional

This listing includes organizations that, as of June 1, 1987, were in the planning or construction stage and that, on completion, will be eligible for institutional membership of type I or II. Some hospitals are granted provisional membership for reasons related to other Association requirements. Hospitals classified as provisional members for reasons other than being under construction are indicated by a bullet (●).

California

Fountain Valley: ● FHP HOSPITAL -FOUNTAIN VALLEY, 9920 Talbert Ave., Zip 92728; tel. 714/962-4677; Steven J. Smith, chief exec. off. & adm.
Sacramento: KAISER FOUNDATION HOSPITAL, 6600 Bruceville Rd., Zip 95823; tel. 916/686-2000; Larry Brown, chief exec. off.
Woodland Hills: KAISER FOUNDATION HOSPITAL, 20940 Burbank Ave., Zip 91367; tel. 818/719-3800; James L. Breeden, adm.

District of Columbia

Washington: ● NATIONAL REHABILITATION HOSPITAL, 106 Irving St. N.W., Suite 101, Zip 20010; tel. 202/877-1000; Edward A. Eckenhoff, pres.

Florida

Coral Springs: CORAL SPRINGS MEDICAL CENTER, 3000 Coral Hills Dr., Zip 33065; tel. 305/344-3000; Jason H. Moore, adm.
Destin: ● HUMANA HOSPITAL -DESTIN, P. O. Box 996, Zip 32541; tel. 904/654-7600; James R. Wilson, exec. dir.
Gainesville: ● UPREACH PAVILION, 8900 N.W. 39th Ave., Zip 32606; Janet L. Christie, chief oper. off.
● VISTA PAVILION, 8900 N.E. 39th Ave., Zip 32606; Jose Llinas MD, adm. & med. dir.
Longwood: SOUTH SEMINOLE COMMUNITY HOSPITAL, 555 W. Sanlando Springs Dr., Box 1607, Zip 32750; tel. 305/834-1200; James W. Poucher, adm.

Loxahatchee: PALMS WEST HOSPITAL, 13001 Southern Blvd., Zip 33470; tel. 305/798-3300; Paul M. Pugh, adm.
Tampa: H. LEE MOFFITT CANCER CENTER, 12901 N. 30th St., Zip 33612; tel. 813/972-1350; William D. Fuchs, exec. dir.

Georgia

Atlanta: • CHARTER BROOK HOSPITAL, 3913 N. Peachtree Rd., Zip 30341; tel. 404/457-8315; Sherry Kollmeyer, adm.
Augusta: WALTON REHABILITATION HOSPITAL, 2603 Commons Blvd., Suite C, Zip 30909; tel. 404/737-2847; Dennis B. Skelley, pres. & chief exec. off.

Kansas

Lenexa: • CPC COLLEGE MEADOWS HOSPITAL, 14425 College Blvd., Zip 66215; tel. 913/469-1100; Sharon Kurz MD, adm.

Kentucky

Radcliff: LINCOLN TRAIL HOSPITAL, 3909 S. Wilson Rd., Zip 40160; tel. 502/351-9444; Bob Beare, adm.

Louisiana

Slidell: NORTHSHORE REGIONAL MEDICAL CENTER, 100 Medical Center Dr., Zip 70461; tel. 504/641-6997; Kirk R. Wascom, exec. dir.

Michigan

Milford: HURON VALLEY HOSPITAL, 1601 E. Commerce, P. O. Box 160, Zip 48042; tel. 313/363-1367; Glenn E. Lowery, pres. & chief exec. off.

Missouri

Springfield: • AMI SPRINGFIELD COMMUNITY HOSPITAL, 3535 S. Natl. Ave., Zip 65807; Robert P. Goodwin, exec. dir.

New Mexico

Santa Teresa: CHARTER HOSPITAL OF SANTA TERESA, 100 Charter Lane, Zip 88008; tel. 505/589-0033; Ted McLindon, adm.

Oregon

Eugene: • HORIZON RECOVERY CENTER, 2222 Coburg Rd., Zip 97401; tel. 503/345-9505; Dennis D. Jack, adm.
Gresham: • RIVERSIDE EAST, 4101 N.E. Division, Zip 97030; tel. 503/661-0775; Niel J. Neumann, adm.
Portland: • HOLBROOK CENTER, 17645 N.W. St. Helens Rd., Zip 97231; tel. 503/621-3201; Christopher Eskeli, adm.

Tennessee

Chattanooga: • CROSSROADS TREATMENT CENTER, 7525 Min Tom Rd., P. O. Box 21867, Zip 37421; James Kestner, adm.

Texas

Dallas: UNIVERSITY MEDICAL CENTER, 5323 Harry Hines, B10-100, Zip 75235; tel. 214/688-6854; Bruce G. Satzger, pres. & chief exec. off.
Kingwood: CHARTER HOSPITAL OF KINGWOOD, 2001 Ladbrook Dr., Zip 77339; tel. 713/358-2273; David M. Rumford, adm.
Laredo: CHARTER RIO GRANDE HOSPITAL, 6020 Springfield Ave., Zip 78040; tel. 512/722-0908; Ramiro Sandoval, adm.

Washington

Federal Way: ST. FRANCIS COMMUNITY HOSPITAL OF FEDERAL WAY, 34515 North Ave. S., Zip 98003

U.S. Associated Area

Puerto Rico

Rio Piedras: • CUPEY HOSPITAL AND NURSING HOME, Rfd 7, Zip 00928; tel. 809/761-8383; Ramon L. Rosario, exec. dir.

Assembly for Hospital Schools of Nursing

Alabama

Birmingham: ST. VINCENT'S HOSPITAL School of Nursing
Sylacauga: SYLACAUGA HOSPITAL School of Nursing

Arkansas

Little Rock: BAPTIST SYSTEM School of Nursing
Pine Bluff: JEFFERSON REGIONAL MEDICAL CENTER School of Nursing

California

Los Angeles: LOS ANGELES COUNTY-UNIVERSITY OF SOUTHERN CALIFORNIA MEDICAL CENTER School of Nursing

Colorado

Colorado Springs: MEMORIAL HOSPITAL Beth-El School of Nursing

Connecticut

Bridgeport: BRIDGEPORT HOSPITAL School of Nursing
ST. VINCENT'S MEDICAL CENTER School of Nursing
Hartford: SAINT FRANCIS HOSPITAL AND MEDICAL CENTER School of Nursing
Middletown: MIDDLESEX MEMORIAL HOSPITAL Ona M. Wilcox School of Nursing
Waterbury: ST. MARY'S HOSPITAL School of Nursing

Delaware

Lewes: BEEBE HOSPITAL OF SUSSEX COUNTY School of Nursing

Florida

Miami: JAMES M. JACKSON MEMORIAL HOSPITAL School of Nursing

Georgia

Atlanta: CRAWFORD LONG HOSPITAL EMORY UNIVERSITY School of Nursing
GEORGIA BAPTIST MEDICAL CENTER School of Nursing

Illinois

Canton: GRAHAM HOSPITAL School of Nursing
Chicago: AUGUSTANA HOSPITAL AND HEALTH CARE CENTER School of Nursing
ILLINOIS MASONIC MEDICAL CENTER School of Nursing
RAVENSWOOD HOSPITAL MEDICAL CENTER School of Nursing
ST. ANNE'S HOSPITAL School of Nursing
ST. MARY OF NAZARETH HOSPITAL CENTER School of Nursing
Danville: LAKEVIEW MEDICAL CENTER School of Nursing
Evanston: ST. FRANCIS HOSPITAL School of Nursing
Joliet: ST. JOSEPH MEDICAL CENTER School of Nursing
Moline: MOLINE PUBLIC HOSPITAL School of Nursing
Oak Lawn: CHRIST HOSPITAL Evangelical School of Nursing
Park Ridge: LUTHERAN GENERAL HOSPITAL School of Nursing
Peoria: METHODIST HOSPITAL OF CENTRAL ILLINOIS School of Nursing
SAINT FRANCIS MEDICAL CENTER School of Nursing
Quincy: BLESSING HOSPITAL School of Nursing
Rockford: ROCKFORD MEMORIAL HOSPITAL School of Nursing
SAINT ANTHONY MEDICAL CENTER School of Nursing

Indiana

Evansville: DEACONESS HOSPITAL School of Nursing
Fort Wayne: LUTHERAN HOSPITAL OF FORT WAYNE School of Nursing
PARKVIEW MEMORIAL HOSPITAL School of Nursing
ST. JOSEPH'S MEDICAL CENTER School of Nursing
Lafayette: ST. ELIZABETH HOSPITAL MEDICAL CENTER School of Nursing
South Bend: MEMORIAL HOSPITAL School of Nursing

Iowa

Cedar Rapids: ST. LUKE'S METHODIST HOSPITAL School of Nursing
Council Bluffs: JENNIE EDMUNDSON MEMORIAL HOSPITAL School of Nursing
Des Moines: IOWA METHODIST HOSPITAL School of Nursing
MERCY HOSPITAL MEDICAL CENTER School of Nursing
Sioux City: ST. LUKE'S REGIONAL MEDICAL CENTER School of Nursing

Kansas

Emporia: NEWMAN MEMORIAL COUNTY HOSPITAL School of Nursing
Topeka: STORMONT-VAIL REGIONAL MEDICAL CENTER School of Nursing

Louisiana

Baton Rouge: BATON ROUGE GENERAL MEDICAL CENTER School of Nursing
OUR LADY OF LAKE REGIONAL MEDICAL CENTER School of Nursing
New Orleans: CHARITY HOSPITAL OF LOUISIANA School of Nursing
TOURO INFIRMARY School of Nursing

Maine

Lewiston: CENTRAL MAINE MEDICAL CENTER School of Nursing

Maryland

Baltimore: UNION MEMORIAL HOSPITAL School of Nursing
Easton: MEMORIAL HOSPITAL AT EASTON MARYLAND School of Nursing

Massachusetts

Boston: NEW ENGLAND BAPTIST HOSPITAL School of Nursing
NEW ENGLAND DEACONESS HOSPITAL School of Nursing
Brockton: BROCKTON HOSPITAL School of Nursing
Framingham: FRAMINGHAM UNION HOSPITAL School of Nursing
Leominster: LEOMINSTER HOSPITAL School of Nursing
Malden: MALDEN HOSPITAL School of Nursing
Medford: LAWRENCE MEMORIAL HOSPITAL OF MEDFORD School of Nursing
Somerville: SOMERVILLE HOSPITAL School of Nursing
Springfield: BAYSTATE MEDICAL CENTER School of Nursing
Worcester: SAINT VINCENT HOSPITAL School of Nursing
WORCESTER CITY HOSPITAL School of Nursing
WORCESTER HAHNEMANN HOSPITAL School of Nursing

Michigan

Detroit: HENRY FORD HOSPITAL School of Nursing
Flint: HURLEY MEDICAL CENTER School of Nursing
Kalamazoo: BRONSON METHODIST HOSPITAL School of Nursing

Missouri

Kansas City: RESEARCH MEDICAL CENTER School of Nursing
ST. LUKE'S HOSPITAL School of Nursing
Springfield: LESTER E. COX MEDICAL CENTERS School of Nursing
ST. JOHN'S REGIONAL HEALTH CENTER School of Nursing
St. Joseph: HEARTLAND HOSPITAL WEST School of Nursing
St. Louis: BARNES HOSPITAL School of Nursing
DEACONESS HOSPITAL School of Nursing
JEWISH HOSPITAL OF ST. LOUIS School of Nursing
LUTHERAN MEDICAL CENTER School of Nursing
MISSOURI BAPTIST HOSPITAL School of Nursing
ST. LUKE'S HOSPITAL School of Nursing

Nebraska

Hastings: MARY LANNING MEMORIAL HOSPITAL School of Nursing
Lincoln: BRYAN MEMORIAL HOSPITAL School of Nursing
Omaha: BISHOP CLARKSON MEMORIAL HOSPITAL College of Nursing
METHODIST HOSPITAL School of Nursing

New Hampshire

Concord: CONCORD HOSPITAL School of Nursing

New Jersey

Belleville: CLARA MAASS MEDICAL CENTER School of Nursing
Camden: OUR LADY OF LOURDES MEDICAL CENTER School of Nursing
WEST JERSEY HOSPITAL, NORTHERN DIVISION Helene Fuld School of Nursing
Elizabeth: ELIZABETH GENERAL MEDICAL CENTER School of Nursing
Englewood: ENGLEWOOD HOSPITAL School of Nursing
Jersey City: CHRIST HOSPITAL School of Nursing
Montclair: MOUNTAINSIDE HOSPITAL School of Nursing
Orange: HOSPITAL CENTER AT ORANGE Winifred B. Baldwin School of Nursing
Plainfield: MUHLENBERG REGIONAL MEDICAL CENTER School of Nursing
Teaneck: HOLY NAME HOSPITAL School of Nursing
Trenton: HELENE FULD MEDICAL CENTER School of Nursing
MERCER MEDICAL CENTER School of Nursing
ST. FRANCIS MEDICAL CENTER School of Nursing

New York

Albany: ALBANY MEDICAL CENTER HOSPITAL School of Nursing
MEMORIAL HOSPITAL School of Nursing
Buffalo: MILLARD FILLMORE HOSPITAL School of Nursing
SISTERS OF CHARITY HOSPITAL School of Nursing
Elmira: ARNOT-OGDEN MEMORIAL HOSPITAL School of Nursing
Flushing: FLUSHING HOSPITAL AND MEDICAL CENTER School of Nursing
Hornell: ST. JAMES MERCY HOSPITAL School of Nursing
Jamaica: CATHOLIC MEDICAL CENTER OF BROOKLYN AND QUEENS School of Nursing
Mount Vernon: MOUNT VERNON HOSPITAL School of Nursing
New York: BETH ISRAEL MEDICAL CENTER School of Nursing
PRESBYTERIAN HOSPITAL IN NEW YORK Edna McConnell Clark School of Nursing
ST. VINCENT'S HOSPITAL AND MEDICAL CENTER OF NEW YORK School of Nursing
Schenectady: ELLIS HOSPITAL School of Nursing
Staten Island: ST. VINCENT'S MEDICAL CENTER School of Nursing
Syracuse: CROUSE-IRVING MEMORIAL HOSPITAL School of Nursing
ST. JOSEPH'S HOSPITAL HEALTH CENTER School of Nursing-Marian Hall
Troy: SAMARITAN HOSPITAL School of Nursing
Utica: ST. ELIZABETH HOSPITAL School of Nursing
Yonkers: ST. JOHN'S RIVERSIDE HOSPITAL Cochran School of Nursing

North Carolina

Charlotte: MERCY HOSPITAL School of Nursing
PRESBYTERIAN HOSPITAL School of Nursing
Concord: CABARRUS MEMORIAL HOSPITAL School of Nursing
Durham: DURHAM COUNTY GENERAL HOSPITAL Watts School of Nursing

North Dakota

Bismarck: MEDCENTER ONE School of Nursing
Minot: TRINITY MEDICAL CENTER School of Nursing

Ohio

Akron: AKRON CITY HOSPITAL Idabelle Firestone School of Nursing
SAINT THOMAS MEDICAL CENTER School of Nursing
Canton: AULTMAN HOSPITAL School of Nursing
Cincinnati: BETHESDA HOSPITAL School of Nursing
CHRIST HOSPITAL School of Nursing
DEACONESS HOSPITAL School of Nursing
GOOD SAMARITAN HOSPITAL School of Nursing
Cleveland: CLEVELAND METROPOLITAN GENERAL HOSPITAL School of Nursing
FAIRVIEW GENERAL HOSPITAL School of Nursing
ST. ALEXIS HOSPITAL School of Nursing
ST. VINCENT CHARITY HOSPITAL AND HEALTH School of Nursing
Columbus: MOUNT CARMEL MEDICAL CENTER School of Nursing
Mansfield: MANSFIELD GENERAL HOSPITAL School of Nursing
Sandusky: PROVIDENCE HOSPITAL School of Nursing
Springfield: COMMUNITY HOSPITAL OF SPRINGFIELD AND CLARK COUNTY School of Nursing
Toledo: MERCY HOSPITAL School of Nursing
ST. VINCENT MEDICAL CENTER School of Nursing
TOLEDO HOSPITAL School of Nursing
Warren: TRUMBULL MEMORIAL HOSPITAL School of Nursing
Youngstown: ST. ELIZABETH HOSPITAL MEDICAL CENTER School of Nursing

Pennsylvania

Abington: ABINGTON MEMORIAL HOSPITAL School of Nursing
Altoona: ALTOONA HOSPITAL School of Nursing
Bethlehem: ST. LUKE'S HOSPITAL School of Nursing
Bryn Mawr: BRYN MAWR HOSPITAL School of Nursing
Caln Township: BRANDYWINE HOSPITAL School of Nursing
Erie: SAINT VINCENT HEALTH CENTER School of Nursing
Johnstown: CONEMAUGH VALLEY MEMORIAL HOSPITAL School of Nursing
Lancaster: LANCASTER GENERAL HOSPITAL School of Nursing
McKees Rocks: OHIO VALLEY GENERAL HOSPITAL School of Nursing
New Castle: ST. FRANCIS HOSPITAL OF NEW CASTLE School of Nursing
New Kensington: CITIZENS GENERAL HOSPITAL School of Nursing
Philadelphia: EPISCOPAL HOSPITAL School of Nursing
FRANKFORD HOSPITAL School of Nursing
GERMANTOWN HOSPITAL AND MEDICAL CENTER School of Nursing
LANKENAU HOSPITAL School of Nursing
METHODIST HOSPITAL School of Nursing
ROXBOROUGH MEMORIAL HOSPITAL School of Nursing
ST. AGNES MEDICAL CENTER School of Nursing
Philipsburg: CENTRAL PENNSYLVANIA SCHOOL OF NURSING
Pittsburgh: MERCY HOSPITAL OF PITTSBURGH School of Nursing
SHADYSIDE HOSPITAL School of Nursing
ST. FRANCIS MEDICAL CENTER School of Nursing
ST. MARGARET MEMORIAL HOSPITAL Louise Suydam McClintic School of Nursing
WESTERN PENNSYLVANIA HOSPITAL School of Nursing
Pottsville: POTTSVILLE HOSPITAL AND WARNE CLINIC School of Nursing
Reading: READING HOSPITAL AND MEDICAL CENTER School of Nursing
Sayre: ROBERT PACKER HOSPITAL School of Nursing
Scranton: COMMUNITY MEDICAL CENTER School of Nursing
Sewickley: SEWICKLEY VALLEY HOSPITAL School of Nursing
Sharon: SHARON GENERAL HOSPITAL School of Nursing
Washington: WASHINGTON HOSPITAL School of Nursing
West Chester: CHESTER COUNTY HOSPITAL School of Nursing
Wilkes-Barre: GEISINGER-WYOMING VALLEY MEDICAL CENTER School of Nursing
Williamsport: WILLIAMSPORT HOSPITAL AND MEDICAL CENTER School of Nursing

Rhode Island

Newport: NEWPORT HOSPITAL School of Nursing
Providence: ST. JOSEPH HOSPITAL School of Nursing

South Dakota

Rapid City: RAPID CITY REGIONAL HOSPITAL School of Nursing

Tennessee

Knoxville: EAST TENNESSEE BAPTIST HOSPITAL School of Nursing
FORT SANDERS REGIONAL MEDICAL CENTER School of Nursing
Memphis: BAPTIST MEMORIAL HOSPITAL School of Nursing
METHODIST HOSPITAL-CENTRAL UNIT School of Nursing
ST. JOSEPH HOSPITAL School of Nursing

Texas

Lubbock: METHODIST HOSPITAL School of Nursing
San Antonio: BAPTIST MEDICAL CENTER School of Nursing

Virginia

Danville: MEMORIAL HOSPITAL School of Nursing
Lynchburg: LYNCHBURG GENERAL-MARSHALL LODGE HOSPITAL School of Nursing
Newport News: RIVERSIDE HOSPITAL School of Nursing
Norfolk: DEPAUL HOSPITAL School of Nursing
NORFOLK GENERAL HOSPITAL School of Nursing
Petersburg: SOUTHSIDE REGIONAL MEDICAL CENTER School of Nursing
Portsmouth: PORTSMOUTH GENERAL HOSPITAL School of Nursing
Richmond: RICHMOND MEMORIAL HOSPITAL School of Nursing
Roanoke: ROANOKE MEMORIAL HOSPITALS School of Nursing
Suffolk: LOUISE OBICI MEMORIAL HOSPITAL School of Nursing

West Virginia

Huntington: ST. MARY'S HOSPITAL School of Nursing
Wheeling: OHIO VALLEY MEDICAL CENTER School of Nursing

Wisconsin

Green Bay: BELLIN MEMORIAL HOSPITAL College of Nursing
Marshfield: ST. JOSEPH'S HOSPITAL School of Nursing
Milwaukee: COLUMBIA HOSPITAL College of Nursing

Associate Members

Other Inpatient Care Institutions

California

Carmichael: ESKATON MANZANITA MANOR, 5318 Manzanita Ave., Zip 95608; tel. 916/331-8513; Louis H. Koff, adm.

Florida

Miami: DOUGLAS GARDENS-MIAMI HOME AND HOSPITAL FOR THE AGED, 151 N.E. 52nd St., Zip 33137; tel. 305/751-8626; Marc Lichtman, exec. dir.

Georgia

Atlanta: WESLEY WOODS CENTER, 1841 Clifton Rd. N.E., Zip 30029; tel. 404/633-2521; Joan M. Carlson, exec. dir.

Illinois

Evanston: PRESBYTERIAN HOME, 3200 Grant St., Zip 60201; tel. 312/492-4800; Peter S. Mulvey, exec. dir.
Rockford: ALMA NELSON MANOR, 550 S. Mulford Rd., Zip 61108; tel. 815/399-4914; Barbara Peterson, adm.

Maryland

Suitland: SAINT LUKE INSTITUTE, 2420 Brooks Dr., Zip 20746; tel. 301/967-3700; Rev. Michael R. Peterson MD, pres. & med. dir.

Massachusetts

Longmeadow: JEWISH HOME FOR THE AGED, 770 Converse St., Zip 01106; tel. 413/567-6211; H. L. Braverman, exec. vice-pres.

Minnesota

Center City: HAZELDEN FOUNDATION, Box 11, Zip 55012; tel. 612/257-4010; D. C. Ollman, mgr. fiscal serv.

New Jersey

West Orange: THERESA GROTTA CENTER, 20 Summit St., Zip 07052; tel. 201/736-2000; Robert Meyers, exec. dir.

New York

Amityville: BRUNSWICK NURSING HOME, 366 Broadway, Zip 11701; tel. 516/264-5000; John T. Digilio Jr., pres.
Bayside: ST. MARY'S HOSPITAL FOR CHILDREN, 29-01 216th St., Zip 11360; tel. 718/990-8800; Stuart C. Kaplan, adm.
Bronx: BETH ABRAHAM HOSPITAL, 612 Allerton Ave., Zip 10467; tel. 212/881-2000; William H. Frohlich, actg. exec. dir.
CONCOURSE NURSING HOME, 1072 Grand Concourse, Zip 10456; tel. 212/681-4000; Helen Neiman, adm.
DAUGHTERS OF JACOB GERIATRIC, 1160 Teller Ave., Zip 10456; tel. 212/293-1500; Steven J. Bernstein, exec. dir.
HEBREW HOME FOR THE AGED AT RIVERDALE, 5901 Palisade Ave., Zip 10471; tel. 212/549-8700; Jacob Reingold, exec. vice-pres.
Brooklyn: M. J. G. NURSING HOME, 4915 Tenth Ave., Zip 11219; tel. 212/853-2800; Eli S. Feldman, exec. dir.
Far Rockaway: HAVEN MANOR HEALTH RELATED FACILITIES, 1441 Greenport Rd., Zip 11691; tel. 212/471-1500; Aron Cytryn, adm.
Hawthorne: ROSARY HILL HOME, 600 Linda Ave., Zip 10532; tel. 914/769-0114; Sr. M. Dominic, adm.
New York: GOUVERNEUR HOSPITAL, 227 Madison St., Zip 10002; tel. 212/374-4200; Alan Rosenblut, exec. dir.
JEWISH HOME AND HOSPITAL FOR AGED, 120 W. 106th St., Zip 10025; tel. 212/870-5000; Mitchell M. Waife, exec. vice-pres.
Staten Island: SEA VIEW HOSPITAL AND HOME, 460 Brielle Ave., Zip 10314; tel. 212/390-8181; Jane M. Lyons, exec. dir.
White Plains: NATHAN MILLER CENTER FOR NURSING CARE, 37 Dekalb Ave., Zip 10605; tel. 914/946-1440; Dulcy B. Miller, adm. dir.

North Carolina

Southern Pines: ST. JOSEPH OF THE PINES HOSPITAL, 590 Central Dr., Zip 28387; tel. 919/692-2212; George Kecatos, adm.

Ohio

Akron: LORANTFFY CARE CENTER, 2631 Copley Rd., Zip 44321; tel. 216/666-1313; Very Rev. Tibor Domotor, adm.
Hamilton: SCHRODER MANOR, 1302 Millville Ave., Zip 45013; tel. 513/894-3311; Sr. M. Pascaline Colling, pres. & chief exec. off.
Sylvania: LAKE PARK HOSPITAL AND NURSING CENTER, 5100 Harroun Rd., Zip 43560; tel. 419/885-1488; Georgia A. Poplar Rn, adm. dir.

Oregon

White City: VETERANS ADMINISTRATION DOMICILIARY, Zip 97503; tel. 503/826-2111; Bruce W. Glover, dir.

Pennsylvania

Philadelphia: INGLIS HOUSE (PHILADELPHIA HOME FOR INCURABLES), 2600 Belmont Ave., Zip 19131; tel. 215/878-5600; Frank E. Gable, pres.

Virginia

Falls Church: NORTHERN VIRGINIA MENTAL HEALTH INSTITUTE, 3302 Gallows Rd., Zip 22042; tel. 703/560-7700; Robert E. Strange MD, dir.
Stafford: POTOMAC POINT HEALTH CENTER, One Potomac Creek on U.S. 1, P.O. Box 820, Zip 22554; tel. 703/659-4000; C. C. Adams PhD, pres. & dir.

Ambulatory Centers and Home Care Agencies

California

Los Angeles: VETERANS ADMINISTRATION OUTPATIENT CLINIC, 425 S. Hill St., Zip 90013
Port Hueneme: NAVAL REGIONAL MEDICAL CLINIC, Zip 93043; tel. 805/982-4501
San Diego: NAVAL MEDICAL CLINIC, Zip 92136

District of Columbia

Washington: NAVAL MEDICAL CLINIC, Washington Naval Yard, Bldg. 183, Zip 20374; tel. 202/433-3492

Florida

Jacksonville: NEMOURS CHILDREN'S HOSPITAL, 5720 Atlantic Blvd., Zip 32207; tel. 904/721-4200; Barry P. Sales, adm.
Key West: NAVAL REGIONAL MEDICAL CLINIC, Roosevelt Blvd., Zip 33040; tel. 305/296-2461; W. A. Nacrelli, comdg. off.

Hawaii

Pearl Harbor: NAVAL REGIONAL MEDICAL CLINIC, Box 121, Zip 96860; tel. 808/471-3025; Capt D. E. Shuler Msc Usn, cmdg. off.

Illinois

Chicago: KOMED HEALTH CENTER, 501 E. 43rd St., Zip 60653; tel. 312/842-4850; John Farmer MD, med. dir.
MILE SQUARE HEALTH CENTER, 2045 W. Washington Blvd., Zip 60612; tel. 312/942-3700; F. Daniel Cantrell, pres.

Louisiana

New Orleans: NAVAL MEDICAL CLINIC, Zip 70142; tel. 504/361-2400

Maine

Portland: MARTIN'S POINT HEALTH CARE CENTER, 331 Veranda St., Zip 04103; tel. 207/774-5801; Johan Brouwer MD, adm. & dir.

Maryland

Annapolis: NAVAL MEDICAL CLINIC, Zip 21402; tel. 301/267-2501; Cmdr. Paul W. Johnson MSC USN, cmdg. off.

Massachusetts

Boston: VETERANS ADMINISTRATION OUTPATIENT CLINIC, 17 Court St., Zip 02108; Michael J. Kane, dir.

Michigan

Detroit: ST. CLAIR AMBULATORY CARE CORPORATION, 22151 Moross Rd., Zip 48236; tel. 313/343-3325; John F. Staub, pres.

Minnesota

Duluth: POLINSKY REHABILITATION CENTER, 530 E. Second St., Zip 55805; tel. 218/727-5083; David Jordahl, exec. dir.

Missouri

Kansas City: VISITING NURSE ASSOCIATION OF GREATER KANSAS CITY, 527 W. 39th St., Zip 64111; tel. 816/531-1200; Richard Roberson, exec. dir.

Nevada

Las Vegas: VETERANS ADMINISTRATION-OUTPATIENT CLINIC, 1703 W. Charleston Blvd., Zip 89102; tel. 702/389-3700; Paul G. Grogan, dir.

New Hampshire

Portsmouth: NAVAL MEDICAL CLINIC, Bldg. H-1, Zip 03801; tel. 207/439-1000; Capt F. M. Richardson, cmdg. off.

New York

Brooklyn: VETERANS ADMINISTRATION OUTPATIENT CLINIC, 35 Ryerson St., Zip 11205

Buffalo: VISITING NURSING ASSOCIATION GROUP, INC., 111 Great Arrow Ave., Zip 14216; tel. 716/874-5400; Alexine L. Janiszewski, pres.

New York: INTERNATIONAL CENTER FOR THE DISABLED, 340 E. 24th St., Zip 10010; tel. 212/679-0100; John B. Wingate, dir.

U. S. COAST GUARD OUTPATIENT CLINIC, U. S. Coast Guard Support Center, Bldg. 515, Zip 10004; tel. 212/668-7489; W. N. Vail, cmdg. off.

Ohio

Columbus: VETERANS ADMINISTRATION OUTPATIENT CLINIC, 2090 Kenny Rd., Zip 43221; tel. 614/469-5663; Troy E. Page, dir.

Pennsylvania

Hazleton: HAZLETON SPECIALTY SURGICAL HOSPITAL, 1701 E. Broad St., Zip 18201; tel. 717/455-5889; Eugene M. Koval DDS, adm.

Philadelphia: NORTHEAST COMMUNITY CENTER FOR MENTAL HEALTH AND MENTAL RETARDATION, Roosevelt Blvd. & Adams Ave., Zip 19124; tel. 215/743-1600; Howard J. Kaufman, exec. dir.

Pittsburgh: CRAIG HOUSE-TECHNOMA, 751 N. Negley Ave., Zip 15206; tel. 412/361-2801; Richard L. Kerchnner, adm.

Texas

Austin: BAILEY SQUARE SURGICAL CENTER, 1111 W. 34th St., Zip 78705; tel. 512/454-6753; Norma White Rn, adm.

El Paso: VETERANS ADMINISTRATION OUTPATIENT CLINIC, 5919 Brook Hollow Dr., Zip 79925; tel. 915/541-7876; Bruce W. Glover, dir.

Randolph AFB: U. S. AIR FORCE CLINIC RANDOLPH, Zip 78150; tel. 512/652-5701; Col. Corydon G. Himelberger MC USAF, cmdr.

San Antonio: CANCER THERAPY AND RESEARCH FOUNDATION OF SOUTH TEXAS, 4450 Medical Dr., Zip 78229; tel. 512/690-1111; Diane Roberts, assoc. dir.

Virginia

Norfolk: NAVAL MEDICAL CLINIC, Zip 23508

Quantico: NAVAL REGIONAL MEDICAL CLINIC, Zip 22134; tel. 703/640-2236; Cdr R. A. Payton, cmdg. off.

Washington

Seattle: NAVAL REGIONAL MEDICAL CLINIC, 7500 Sand Point Way, Zip 98105; tel. 206/527-3827; Robert A. Jeffs, cmdg. off.

Wisconsin

Milwaukee: CURATIVE REHABILITATION CENTER, 1000 N. 92nd St., Zip 53226; tel. 414/259-1414; Eugene M. Cox, pres.

Racine: CURATIVE WORKSHOP OF RACINE, 2335 Northwestern Ave., Zip 53404; tel. 414/637-4441; Lyle E. Zielke, exec. dir.

Blue Cross Plans

Arizona

BLUE CROSS AND BLUE SHIELD OF ARIZONA, 2444 W. Las Palmaritas Dr., Box 13466, Phoenix 85002; tel. 602/864-4400; Robert Bulla, pres.

California

BLUE CROSS OF CALIFORNIA, 21155 Oxnard St., Box 70000, Woodland Hills 91470; tel. 213/666-3100; L. Schaeffer, pres.

Connecticut

BLUE CROSS AND BLUE SHIELD OF CONNECTICUT, 370 Bassett Rd., North Haven 06473; tel. 203/239-4911; John E. Donnelly MD, med. dir.

Florida

BLUE CROSS AND BLUE SHIELD OF FLORIDA, INC., 8657 Baypine Rd., Suite 204, Jacksonville 32202; tel. 904/791-6111; William E. Flaherty, pres.

Georgia

BLUE CROSS AND BLUE SHIELD OF GEORGIA-ATLANTA, 3348 Peachtree Rd. N.E., Box 4445, Atlanta 30302; tel. 404/262-8200; F. R. Higginbotham, pres.

Illinois

BLUE CROSS-BLUE SHIELD, 233 N. Michigan Ave., Chicago 60601; tel. 312/661-2500; S. Martin Hickman, pres.

Iowa

BLUE CROSS OF IOWA, 636 Grand Ave., Des Moines 50307; tel. 515/244-8961; D. Eugene Sibery, pres.

Kansas

BLUE CROSS AND BLUE SHIELD OF KANSAS, 1133 Topeka Ave., Box 239, Topeka 66629; tel. 913/234-9592; Marlon Dauner, vice-pres.

Kentucky

BLUE CROSS AND BLUE SHIELD OF KENTUCKY, 9901 Linn Sta. Rd., Louisville 40223; tel. 502/452-1511; G. Douglas Sutherland, pres.

Missouri

BLUE CROSS HOSPITAL SERVICE, INC., OF MISSOURI, 4444 Forest Park Blvd., St. Louis 63108; tel. 314/241-1800; Robert E. Shelton, pres.

Montana

BLUE CROSS AND BLUE SHIELD OF MONTANA, 3360 Tenth Ave. S., Box 5004, Great Falls 59403; tel. 406/761-7310; Terry R. Screnar, pres.

New York

EMPIRE BLUE CROSS AND BLUE SHIELD, 1251 New Scotland Rd., Box 8650, Albany 12208; tel. 518/439-7451; Chester E. Burrell, pres.

BLUE CROSS OF WESTERN NEW YORK, INC., 298 Main St., Buffalo 14202; tel. 716/849-6900; Charles E. Rath, pres.

BLUE CROSS AND BLUE SHIELD OF THE ROCHESTER AREA, 150 E. Main St., Rochester 14647; tel. 716/454-1700; David W. Stewart, chm. & chf. exec. off.

BLUE CROSS AND BLUE SHIELD OF CENTRAL NEW YORK, 344 S. Warren St., Box 4809, Syracuse 13221; tel. 315/424-3801; Albert F. Antonini, pres. & chief exec. off.

Ohio

COMMUNITY MUTUAL INSURANCE CO, 1351 William Howard Taft Rd., Cincinnati 45206; tel. 513/872-8100; Dwane R. Houser, pres.

BLUE CROSS AND BLUE SHIELD OF NORTHERN OHIO, 2066 E. Ninth St., Cleveland 44115; tel. 216/687-7000; John Burry Jr., pres.

BLUE CROSS OF CENTRAL OHIO, 255 E. Main St., Box 16526, Columbus 43216; tel. 614/228-2651; John B. Reinhardt Jr., pres.

Oklahoma

BLUE CROSS AND BLUE SHIELD OF OKLAHOMA, 1215 S. Boulder Ave., Box 3283, Tulsa 74102; tel. 918/583-0861; Brian Sowers, Sr. vice-pres.

Pennsylvania

CAPITAL BLUE CROSS, 100 Pine St., Harrisburg 17101; tel. 717/234-5031; Richard D. Rife, pres.

BLUE CROSS OF WESTERN PENNSYLVANIA, 1 Smithfield St., Pittsburgh 15222; tel. 412/391-0500; Eugene J. Barone, pres.

BLUE CROSS OF NORTHEASTERN PENNSYLVANIA, 70 N. Main St., Wilkes-Barre 18711; tel. 717/824-5741; Gilbert D. Tough, pres.

Tennessee

BLUE CROSS-BLUE SHIELD OF TENNESSEE, 801 Pine St., Chattanooga 37402; tel. 615/755-5600; J. Robert McGuff, pres.

BLUE CROSS AND BLUE SHIELD OF MEMPHIS, 85 N. Danny Thomas Blvd., P. O. Box 98, Memphis 38101; tel. 901/529-3111; Arthur P. Waymire, pres.

Texas

BLUE CROSS AND BLUE SHIELD OF TEXAS, INC., Main at N. Central Expwy., Box 225924, Dallas 75265; tel. 214/741-3761; John D. Melton, pres.

Virginia

BLUE CROSS AND BLUE SHIELD OF VIRGINIA, 2015 Staples Mill Rd., Box 27401, Richmond 23279; tel. 804/359-7000; S. William Carroll, vice-pres. prov. serv.

Canada

Alberta

ALBERTA BLUE CROSS PLAN, 10025 108th St., Edmonton; tel. 403/429-5221; F. D. Huntington, exec. dir.

New Brunswick

MARITIME HOSPITAL SERVICE ASSOCIATION, 110 Macbeath Ave., Drawer 220, Moncton; tel. 506/854-1811; L. R. Furlong, pres.

Ontario

ONTARIO BLUE CROSS, 150 Ferrand Dr., Don Mills; tel. 416/429-2661; H. Dunbar Russel, pres.

Foreign

Jamaica

BLUE CROSS OF JAMAICA, 85 Hope Rd., Kingston; tel. 7-9821; Hylton O. McIntosh, mgr.

Health Maintenance Organizations/Health Care Corporations

Hawaii

KAISER FOUNDATION HEALTH PLAN, INC., 677 Ala Moana Blvd., Honolulu 96813; Ronald W. B. Wyatt, vice-pres.

Ohio

KAISER FOUNDATION-CLEVELAND, 2475 Martin L. King Jr. Dr., Cleveland 44120; tel. 216/795-8000; Jay Nisenfeld, adm.

Shared Services Organizations

California

Los Angeles: COUNCIL SHARED SERVICES, 6255 Sunset Blvd., Suite 817, Zip 90028; tel. 213/469-7311; Robert A. Schapper, exec. dir.

Colorado

Denver: HOSPITAL SHARED SERVICES OF COLORADO, INC., 1395 S. Platte River Dr., Zip 80223; tel. 303/722-5566; George R. Schiel, pres.

Georgia

Marietta: SHARED SERVICES FOR SOUTHERN HOSPITALS, INC., 1675 Terrell Mill Rd., Suite 180, Zip 30067; John D. McQueary, pres.

Illinois

Westchester: PREMIER HOSPITALS ALLIANCE, INC., 1 Westbrook Corporate Center, Suite 700, Zip 60153; tel. 312/531-8220; Alan Weinstein, pres.

Indiana

Notre Dame: HOLY CROSS SHARED SERVICES, INC., Saint Mary's-Bertrand Hall, Zip 46556; tel. 219/284-4615; John A. O'Connell, exec. dir.

Iowa

Des Moines: MIDWEST METHODIST HOSPITAL NETWORK, 1221 Center St., Suite 13, Zip 50309; tel. 515/283-6361; Donald W. Cordes, exec. dir.

Kentucky

Louisville: HEALTH DATA NETWORK, 840 Barret Ave., Box 4478, Zip 40204; tel. 502/585-1391; B. W. Mathis, pres.

Madisonville: WESTERN KENTUCKY HOSPITAL SERVICES, U. S. Hwy. 41 N., P. O. Box 1127, Zip 42431; Richard V. Harris, exec. vice-pres.

Maryland

Baltimore: DAUGHTERS OF CHARITY HEALTH SYSTEM EAST, 1001 Pine Hts. Ave., Suite 303, Zip 21229; tel. 301/644-3568; James E. Small, pres. & chief exec. off.

Massachusetts

Boston: MEDICAL AREA SERVICE CORPORATION, 59 Binney St., Zip 02115; tel. 617/732-2310; Steven M. Tritman, pres.

Michigan

Lansing: MICHIGAN HOSPITAL ASSOCIATION SERVICE CORPORATION, 6215 W. St. Joseph Hwy., Zip 48917; tel. 517/323-3443; Fritz Kellermann, Sr. vice-pres.

Minnesota

Eden Prairie: AFFILIATED HOSPITAL SERVICE, INC., 9905 Hamilton Rd., Zip 55344; tel. 612/941-9770; Gerald W. Schilling, dir.

Missouri

Springfield: MID-CONTINENT HOSPITAL SERVICES, INC., 1902 E. Meadowmere, Zip 65804; tel. 417/864-6488; Jerry W. Holden, pres.

Ohio

Cleveland: GREATER CLEVELAND HOSPITAL ASSOCIATION, 1226 Huron Rd., Zip 44115; tel. 216/696-6900; C. Wayne Rice, pres.

Oklahoma

Dewey: MEDSOURCE CORPORATION, 2100 Patridge Rd., Zip 74029; Roger H. Box, pres.

Pennsylvania

Allentown: HOSPITAL CENTRAL SERVICE, INC., 2171 28th St. S.W., Zip 18103; tel. 215/791-2222; J. Michael Lee, pres.

Rhode Island

Providence: HARICOMP, INC., Box 9427, Zip 02940; Gerald G. McClure, pres.

South Dakota

Sioux Falls: PRESENTATION SHARED HEALTH SERVICES, INC., 3009 E. Tenth St., Zip 57103; tel. 605/339-1703; E. Jeff Baron, exec. dir.

Texas

Austin: TEXAS HOSPITAL ASSOCIATION, 6225 U. S. Hwy. 290 E., Box 15587, Zip 78723; tel. 512/453-7204; O. Ray Hurst, pres.

Utah

Salt Lake City: IHC HOSPITALS, INC., 36 S. State St., Zip 84111; tel. 801/533-8282; Theron J. Godfrey, vice-pres.

Health Systems Agencies

Michigan

Detroit: GREATER DETROIT HEALTH HOSPITAL COUNCIL, INC., 1900 Book Bldg., Zip 48226; tel. 313/963-4990; Symond R. Gottlieb, exec. dir.
Grand Rapids: WEST MICHIGAN HEALTH SYSTEMS AGENCY, 72 Monroe Center N.W., Suite 200, Zip 49503; tel. 616/459-1323; Phillip E. Van Heest, exec. dir.

Canada

British Columbia

Burnaby: GREATER VANCOUVER REGIONAL HOSPITAL DISTRICT, 4330 Kingsway St., Zip ; tel. 604/731-1155; Greg Stump, dir.

Associated University Programs in Health Administration

Alabama

Birmingham: UNIVERSITY OF ALABAMA AT BIRMINGHAM, SCHOOL OF COMMUNITY AND ALLIED HEALTH, Zip 35294; tel. 205/934-5661; Keith D. Blayney Phd, dean

Arizona

Tempe: CENTER FOR HEALTH SERVICES ADMINISTRATION, COLLEGE OF BUSINESS, ARIZONA STATE UNIVERSITY, Zip 85287; tel. 602/965-7778; Eugene S. Schneller, prof. & dir.

California

Los Angeles: UCLA, SCHOOL OF PUBLIC HEALTH, PROGRAM IN HEALTH SERVICES MANAGEMENT, University of California, Zip 90024; Beverlee Myers, actg. dir.
San Francisco: GOLDEN GATE UNIVERSITY, 536 Mission St., Zip 94105; tel. 415/442-0777; Mary Woempner, asst. lib.

District of Columbia

Washington: DEPARTMENT OF HEALTH SERVICES ADMINISTRATION, GEORGE WASHINGTON UNIVERSITY, Zip 20052; tel. 202/676-6220; Richard F. Southby Phd, prof. & chm.

Georgia

Atlanta: GEORGIA STATE UNIVERSITY, INSTITUTE OF HEALTH ADMINISTRATION, University Plaza, Zip 30303; tel. 404/658-2000; Everett A. Johnson, dir.

Illinois

Carbondale: SOUTHERN ILLINOIS UNIVERSITY, SCHOOL OF TECHNICAL CAREERS, Zip 62901; tel. 618/536-6682; Elaine M. Vitello Phd
Chicago: UNIVERSITY OF CHICAGO, GRADUATE SCHOOL OF BUSINESS, GRADUATE PROGRAM IN HEALTH ADMINISTRATION, 1101 E. 58th St., Zip 60637; tel. 312/753-4191; Ronald Andersen Phd, dir.
Evanston: PROGRAM IN HOSPITAL AND HEALTH SERVICE MANAGEMENT, KELLOGG GRADUATE SCHOOL OF MANAGEMENT, NORTHWESTERN UNIVERSITY, Leverone Hall, Zip 60201; tel. 312/492-5540; Hilmon S. Sorey, prog. dir.
Park Forest South: PROGRAM IN HEALTH SERVICE ADMINISTRATION, SCHOOL OF HEALTH PROFESSIONS, GOVERNORS STATE UNIVERSITY, Zip 60466; tel. 312/534-5000; D. L. Gellatly, actg. chm.

Iowa

Iowa City: GRADUATE PROGRAM IN HOSPITAL AND HEALTH ADMINISTRATION, UNIVERSITY OF IOWA, 1700 Steindler Bldg., Zip 52242; tel. 319/356-2593; Samuel Levey

Maryland

Baltimore: THE JOHNS HOPKINS UNIVERSITY, CENTER FOR HOSPITAL FINANCE AND MANAGEMENT, 624 N. Broadway, Suite 301, Zip 21205; tel. 301/955-2300; Leslie E. Hutchinson, budget coor.
Bethesda: NAVAL SCHOOL OF HEALTH SCIENCES, National Naval Medical Center, Zip 20014; tel. 202/545-6700

Massachusetts

Boston: BOSTON UNIVERSITY HEALTH MANAGEMENT PROGRAMS, 685 Commonwealth Ave., Room 334, Zip 02215; tel. 617/353-2730; S. M. Davidson, dir.

Michigan

Ann Arbor: PROGRAM AND BUREAU OF HOSPITAL ADMINISTRATION, UNIVERSITY OF MICHIGAN, 1420 Washington Hts., Zip 48109; tel. 313/764-1382; Howard S. Zuckerman Phd, dir.

Missouri

Columbia: UNIVERSITY OF MISSOURI, GRADUATE STUDIES IN HEALTH SERVICES MANAGEMENT, 324 Clark Hall, Zip 65211; tel. 314/882-6178; Gordon D. Brown Phd, prof. & dir.
St. Louis: PROGRAM IN HOSPITAL AND HEALTH CARE ADMINISTRATION, ST. LOUIS UNIVERSITY, 3525 Caroline St., Zip 63104; tel. 314/773-0646; Thomas C. Dolan Phd, dir.
PROGRAM IN HEALTH ADMINISTRATION AND PLANNING, WASHINGTON UNIVERSITY SCHOOL OF MEDICINE, 4547 Clayton Ave., Zip 63110; tel. 314/454-3277; James O. Hepner Phd, dir.

New York

Schenectady: UNION UNIVERSITY, HEALTH STUDIES CENTER, Bailey Hall, Zip 12308; tel. 518/370-6253; James Lambrinos, dir.
Valhalla: NEW YORK MEDICAL COLLEGE, Zip 10595; tel. 914/347-5044; John J. Connolly, pres.

North Carolina

Durham: DUKE UNIVERSITY, DEPARTMENT OF HEALTH ADMINISTRATION, Box 3018, Zip 27710; J. Alexander McMahon, chm.

Ohio

Columbus: GRADUATE PROGRAM IN HOSPITAL AND HEALTH SERVICES ADMINISTRATION, OHIO STATE UNIVERSITY, 246 Samp, 1583 Perry St., Zip 43210; tel. 614/422-9708; Stephen F. Loebs Phd, chm. & assoc. prof.

Pennsylvania

Philadelphia: TEMPLE UNIVERSITY, DEPARTMENT OF HEALTH ADMINISTRATION, SCHOOL OF BUSINESS ADMINISTRATION, Zip 19121; tel. 215/787-8082; David Barton Smith, chm.
University Park: GRADUATE STUDIES IN HEALTH PLANNING AND ADMINISTRATION, PENNSYLVANIA STATE UNIVERSITY, 115 Human Development Bldg., Zip 16802; tel. 814/863-2859; Stanley P. Mayers Jr., prog. head

Texas

Fort Sam Houston: ARMY-BAYLOR UNIVERSITY PROGRAM IN HEALTH CARE ADMINISTRATION, Medical Field Service School, Zip 78234; tel. 512/221-5009
Galveston: UNIVERSITY OF TEXAS, SCHOOL OF ALLIED HEALTH SCIENCES, DEPARTMENT OF HEALTH RELATED STUDIES, Zip 77550; tel. 713/763-3521; John G. Bruhn, dean

Washington

Seattle: GRADUATE PROGRAM IN HEALTH SERVICE ADMINISTRATION AND PLANNING, UNIVERSITY OF WASHINGTON, Zip 98195; tel. 206/543-8778; Thomas W. Bice, dir.

Other Associate Members

Associate member organizations are designated as follows:

(01) *Architecture and Construction*
(02) *Associations*
(03) *Certified Public Accountants*
(04) *Communication Systems*
(05) *Consultants*
(05A) *Full Service*
(05B) *Employee Benefits*
(05C) *Strategic Planning/Competitive Strategies*
(05D) *Communications*
(05E) *Information Systems*
(05F) *Management*
(05G) *Accounting*
(05H) *Financial*
(05I) *Procurement and Turn-Key Implementation*
(06) *Facilities Management*
(07) *Food Service Management*
(08) *Information Systems*
(09) *Insurance Brokers*
(10) *Investment Bankers*
(11) *Manufacturers and Suppliers*
(12) *Services*
(12A) *Educational Programs*
(12B) *Management*
(12C) *Recruiters*
(12D) *Other*
(13) *Other*
(14) *Equipment Maintenance*

United States

A. T. & T. COMMUNICATIONS, 295 N. Maple Ave., Room 5319A3, Basking Ridge, NJ, Zip 07920; Helen L. Davis, mgr. health **(05D)**
ACUTE CARE AFFILIATES, 2855 Telegraph Ave., Suite 210, Berkeley, CA, Zip 94705; tel. 415/540-1800; David A. Seeley, pres. **(13)**
AFFILIATED HEALTHCARE SYSTEMS, 489 State St., Bangor, ME, Zip 04401, tel. 207/945-7070; Francis J. Hannon, exec. vice-pres. **(13)**
ALADDIN SYNERGETICS, INC., P. O. Box 100255, Nashville, TN, Zip 37210; tel. 615/748-3000 **(13)**
AMERICAN ASSOCIATION OF HEALTHCARE CONSULTANTS, 1235 Jefferson Davis Hwy., 602, Arlington, VA, Zip 22202; tel. 703/979-3180; Vaughan A. Smith, pres. **(02)**
AMERICAN ASSOCIATION OF NURSE ANESTHETISTS, 216 Higgins Rd., Park Ridge, IL, Zip 60068; tel. 312/692-7050; John F. Garde, exec. dir. **(02)**
AMERICAN EXPRESS TRAVEL RELATED SERVICES, World Financial Center, 35th Floor, New York, NY, Zip 10285; tel. 212/640-5179; Ruth K.Tolles, dir. health industry **(12D)**
AMERICAN MEDICAL INTERNATIONAL-PROFESSIONAL HOSPITAL SERVICES, 12960 Coral Tree Pl., Los Angeles, CA, Zip 90066; tel. 213/821-2323;Wayne Owens, vice-pres. **(13)**
AMERICAN PHYSICAL THERAPY ASSOCIATION, 1111 N. Fairfax St., Alexandria, VA, Zip 22314; tel. 703/684-2782; Royce Noland, interim exec. dir. **(02)**
AMERICAN SOCIETY FOR MEDICAL TECHNOLOGY, 3 Metro Center, Suite 750, Bethesda, MD, Zip 20814; tel. 301/961-1931; Lynn Podell, exec. dir. **(02)**
AMERICAN SOCIETY OF HOSPITAL PHARMACISTS, 4630 Montgomery Ave., Bethesda, MD, Zip 20814; tel. 301/657-3000; Joseph A. Oddis, exec.dir. **(02)**
AMERIHEALTH, INC., 2849 Paces Ferry Rd., Suite 790, Atlanta, GA, Zip 30339; tel. 404/435-1776; William G. White, pres. **(13)**
AMERITECH SERVICES, INC., 1900 E. Golf Rd., Schaumburg, IL, Zip 60195; tel. 312/310-2000; Mary Lynn Ziemer, mgr. **(05D)**
APPLIED MANAGEMENT SYSTEMS, INC., 5 New England Executive Park, Burlington, MA, Zip 01803; tel. 617/272-8001; Alan J. Goldberg, pres. **(05F)**
ARA SERVICES, INC.-HOSPITAL FOOD MANAGEMENT, Independence Square W., Philadelphia, PA, Zip 19106; tel. 215/923-7700; R. William Edmundson, pres. **(07)**
ARMED FORCES INSTITUTE OF PATHOLOGY, Washington, DC, Zip 20306; tel. 202/576-2900; Col. William R. Tuten III, exec. off. **(13)**
ARTHUR ANDERSEN AND COMPANY, 911 Wilshire Blvd., Los Angeles, CA, Zip 90017; tel. 213/614-6424; James L. Johnson, partner **(03)**
ARTHUR ANDERSEN AND COMPANY, 33 W. Monroe St., Chicago, IL, Zip 60603; tel. 312/580-0033 **(03)**
ASSOCIATION OF UNIVERSITY PROGRAMS IN HEALTH ADMINISTRATION, 1911 N. Fort Myer Dr., Suite 503, Arlington, VA, Zip 22209; tel. 703/524-0511; Gary L. Filerman, pres. **(02)**
BBC HEALTH CARE FACILITIES, 1144 Hampton Ave., St. Louis, MO, Zip 63139; tel. 314/428-0321; Frank A. Bottini, dir. mktg. **(01)**
BARTON-MALOW COMPANY, 13155 Cloverdale, P. O. Box 5200, Detroit, MI, Zip 48235; tel. 313/548-2000; Donald Shalibo, vice-pres. **(01)**
BAXTER TRAVENOL LABORATORIES, INC., One Baxter Pkwy., Deerfield, IL, Zip 60015; tel. 312/940-6511; Linda Mengelt, dir. **(11)**
BECKMAN INSTRUMENTS, INC., 250 S. Kraemer Blvd., Brea, CA, Zip 92621; tel. 714/993-8596; Larry Cohen, mktg. mgr. **(11)**
BLUE CROSS AND BLUE SHIELD ASSOCIATION, 676 N. St. Clair, Chicago, IL, Zip 60611; tel. 312/440-6000; Bernard Tresnowski, pres. **(02)**
BLUNT ELLIS AND LOEWI, INC., 333 W. Wacker Dr., Suite 300, Chicago, IL, Zip 60606; tel. 312/630-8500; James L. Harvitt, vice-pres. **(10)**
ALEX BROWN AND SONS, INC., 1 Boston Pl., 31st Floor, Boston, MA, Zip 02108; tel. 617/723-7300; Jonathan Osgood, vice-pres. **(10)**
CALMAQUIP ENGINEERING CORPORATION, 7240 N.W. 12th St., Miami, FL, Zip 33126; tel. 305/592-4510; Manuel J. Hidalgo, health care consult. **(05I)**
CANNON MILLS COMPANY, 1271 Avenue of the Americas, New York, NY, Zip 10020; tel. 212/957-2590; Robert S. Loughlin, vice-pres. & national sales mgr. **(11)**
CAREER CONSULTANTS, 736 Thimble Shoals Blvd., Newport News, VA, Zip 23606; tel. 804/873-8462; David R. Bender, pres. **(12C)**
CHI SYSTEMS, INC., 130 S. First St., Ann Arbor, MI, Zip 48104; tel. 313/761-3912; Karl G. Bartscht, chief exec. off. **(05A)**
CIBA CORNING DIAGNOSTICS CORPORATION, 63 North St., Medfield, MA, Zip 02052; tel. 617/359-7711; Joann Jasinski, mgr. mktg. oper. **(11)**
CITIBANK, 55 Water St., 47th Floor, New York, NY, Zip 10043; tel. 212/668-3783; Robert N. Bruce, vice-pres. **(10)**
CONCORDIA MANAGEMENT CORPORATION, 10920 Ambassador Dr., Suite 415, Kansas City, MO, Zip 64153; tel. 816/891-7701; Grant E. Ackerman, vice-pres. U. S. oper. **(01)**
CONNECTICUT HOSPITAL ASSOCIATION, 10 Alexander Dr., Box 90, Wallingford, CT, Zip 06492; tel. 203/265-7611; Dennis P. May, pres. **(02)**
CONTINENTAL ILLINOIS NATIONAL BANK AND TRUST COMPANY OF CHICAGO, 231 S. La Salle St., Chicago, IL, Zip 60697; tel. 312/828-7830; Cathryne L. Spittell, banking off. **(12D)**
CONTROL DATA, P. O. Box 0-HQA03I, Minneapolis, MN, Zip 55440; tel. 612/853-8810; Phillip G. Martin, vice-pres. healthcare serv. **(05E)**
COOPERS AND LYBRAND, 1251 Avenue. of the Americas, New York, NY, Zip 10020; tel. 212/536-2000; Gregory Moses, partner **(05G)**
COPELAND COMPANIES, 399 Thornall St., Edison, NJ, Zip 08837; tel. 201/494-2902; Mark M. Skinner, sr. vice-pres. sales **(09)**
DANICO, INC., 812 Lancaster Ave., Villanova, PA, Zip 19085; tel. 215/527-8615; Daniel J. Keating III, pres. **(12D)**
DAY HOSPITAL AND PHYSICAL REHABILITATION CENTERS, 17435 N. Seventh St., Suite 1079, Phoenix, AR, Zip 85022; tel. 602/867-1410; Lester H. Rubin, pres. **(13)**
DELOITTE HASKINS AND SELLS, 250 E. Fifth St., P. O. Box 85340, Cincinnati, OH, Zip 45201; tel. 513/784-7100; Thomas A. Gilman, natl. dir. hlth. care serv. **(03)**
DEPARTMENT OF AIR FORCE MEDICAL SERVICE, Bldg. 5681, Bolling AFB, DC, Zip 20332; tel. 202/545-6700 **(13)**
DEPARTMENT OF THE ARMY, OFFICE OF THE SURGEON GENERAL, Washington, DC, Zip 20310; tel. 202/545-6700 **(13)**
DEPARTMENT OF HEALTH AND HUMAN SERVICES, PUBLIC HEALTH SERVICE, DIVISION OF INDIAN HEALTH, HEALTH CARE ADMINISTRATION BRANCH, 5600 Fisher Lane, Room 6-22, Rockville, MD, Zip 20857; tel. 301/443-1085; Robert L. Thurmon, chief **(13)**
DEPARTMENT OF THE NAVY, BUREAU OF MEDICINE AND SURGERY, 2300 E St. N.W., Washington, DC, Zip 20372; tel. 202/545-6700; VADM J. William Cox, surg. gen. **(13)**
DETROIT MEDICAL CENTER CORPORATION, 4201 St. Antoine Blvd., Detroit, MI, Zip 48201; tel. 313/494-5191; Joseph L. Hudson, pres. & chief exec. off. **(13)**
DISC VILLAGE TREATMENT CENTER, 1/3 Miles Natural Bridge Rd., P. O. Box 568, Woodville, FL, Zip 32362; tel. 904/421-4115; Thomas K. Olk, exec. dir. **(13)**
DOCTORS CLINIC, P. O. Box 617, Alton, IL, Zip 62002; tel. 618/474-7850; T. Bruce Vest MD, adm. **(13)**
DONALDSON, LUFKIN AND JENRETTE SECURITIES CORPORATION, 140 Broadway, New York, NY, Zip 10005; tel. 212/504-3006; William J. Brock, sr. vice-pres. & mgr. health care finance **(09)**
DUKE ENDOWMENT, 200 S. Tryon St., Suite 1100, Charlotte, NC, Zip 28202; tel. 704/376-0291; Billy G. McCall, exec. dir. hosp. & child care sect. **(13)**
ECONOMICS LABORATORY, INC., 4 Corporate Park Dr., White Plains, NY, Zip 10604; tel. 914/694-8626; D. W. Kallgren, mgr. support functions **(12D)**
ELLERBE ASSOCIATES, INC., One Appletree Square, Minneapolis, MN, Zip 55420; tel. 612/853-2537; John C. Gaunt, exec. vice-pres. **(01)**
ERNST AND WHINNEY, 2000 National City Center, Cleveland, OH, Zip 44114; tel. 216/861-5000 **(05H)**
FARRIS AND ASSOCIATES, INC., 16216 Baxter Rd., Suite 200, St. Louis MO, Zip 63108; tel. 314/532-4880; James Bowey, vice-pres. **(05A)**
FEDERATION OF AMERICAN CLINICS, 400 Hamilton Ave., Suite 200, Palo Alto, CA, Zip 94301; tel. 415/321-8333; Frederick S. Fink, pres. & chief exec. off. **(12B)**
FITZGERALD HEALTH MANAGEMENT SERVICES, 4400 W. 109th, Suite 200, Overland Park, KS, Zip 66211; tel. 913/345-8700; Joanne B. Plummer, vice-pres. **(05F)**
GARRETT ASSOCIATES, INC., 950 E. Paces Ferry Rd., Suite 1455, Atlanta, GA, Zip 30326; tel. 404/364-0001; Donald Garrett, pres. **(05F)**
GTE, One Stamford Forum, Stamford, CT, Zip 06904; tel. 203/965-2973; John B. Walker, mgr. market segmentation **(12D)**
HAWAII STATE DEPARTMENT OF HEALTH, 1250 Punchbowl St., Box 3378, Honolulu, HI, Zip 96813; tel. 808/961-4255; Abelina Shaw, dep. dir. **(13)**
HBE CORPORATION, 11330 Olive Blvd., P. O. Box 27339, St. Louis, MO, Zip 63141; tel. 314/567-9000; Michael Carlson, exec. vice-pres. & dir. mktg. **(01)**
HEALTH PARTNERS INTERNATIONAL, 18425 N.W. Second Ave., Suite 100-S, Miami, FL, Zip 33169; tel. 305/651-5441; Caroline J. Wesenberg, chief oper. off. **(12D)**

HEALTH TECH, INC., 1401 Walnut St., Suite 1000, Philadelphia, PA, Zip 19102; tel. 215/568-5711; Gretchen Sennott, mgr. **(05A)**
HEALTHCARE TELEVISION, 21 B St., Burlington, MA, Zip 01803; 617/270-0074; Richard M. Porter, mgr. **(05D)**
HEALTHSOUTH REHABILITATION CORPORATION, Two Perimeter Park S., Birmingham, AL, Zip 35243; tel. 205/967-7116; Anthony J. Tanner, sr. vice-pres. **(13)**
HENNINGSON, DURHAM AND RICHARDSON, 8404 Indian Hills Dr., Omaha, NE, Zip 68114; tel. 402/391-0123; Lawrence Hawthorne, group vice-pres. **(01)**
HERMAN MILLER, INC. HEALTH SCIENCE DIVISION, 8500 Byron Rd., Zeeland, MI, Zip 49464; tel. 616/530-4194; Lee Kimbrough, dir. mktg. **(11)**
HERMAN SMITH ASSOCIATES, 120 E. Ogden, Hinsdale, IL, Zip 60521; tel. 312/323-3510; Jeffrey J. Frommelt, pres. **(05A)**
HONEYWELL INFORMATION SYSTEMS, INC.-APPLICATION SYSTEMS DIVISION, 6465 Wayzata Blvd., Suite 800, St. Louis Park, MN, Zip 55426; tel. 612/541-4403; Cynthia L. Bottrell, mgr. sales comm. **(05E)**
HOSPITAL BILLING AND COLLECTION SERVICE, LTD, Two Penn's Way, Suite 300, New Castle, DE, Zip 19720; tel. 302/323-7000; Robert B. Burleigh, vice-pres. **(12D)**
HOSPITAL COUNCIL OF SOUTHERN CALIFORNIA, 6255 Sunset Blvd., Suite 817, Los Angeles, CA, Zip 90028; tel. 213/469-7311; Stephen W. Gamble, pres. **(02)**
HOSPITAL MARKETING RESOURCE, 20245 W. Twelve Mile Rd., 1810, Southfield, MI, Zip 48076; tel. 313/358-1811; Alan Sussman, pres. **(05A)**
HOSPITAL SATELLITE NETWORK, 1901 Avenue of the Stars, Los Angeles, CA, Zip 90067; tel. 213/277-6710; Thomas A. Rasmussen, vice-pres. oper. **(12A)**
HOSPITAL UNDERWRITERS MUTUAL COMPANY, 24 Computer Dr. W., Albany, NY, Zip 12205; tel. 518/458-7985; Thomas L. Hawkins Jr. MD, pres. **(09)**
HUNTCOR, INC., 426 N. 44th St., Phoenix, AR, Zip 85008; tel. 602/225-9500; James A. Wood, dir. preconstruction & dev.**(01)**
INFORMATION STRATEGIES, INC., 236 Boston Post Rd., Orange, CT, Zip 06477; tel. 203/795-6016; Henry Friedman, coor. comm. **(05E)**
INSTITUTE OF PHYSICAL MEDICINE AND REHABILITATION, 6501 N. Sheridan Rd., Peoria, IL, Zip 61614; tel. 309/692-8110; James W. Roodhouse, adm. **(13)**
INTERMEDICS, INC., 240 Tarpon Inn Village, Freeport, TX, Zip 77541; tel. 409/233-8611; Jacques P. Schwartz, exec. vice-pres. **(11)**
INTERNATIONAL ASSOCIATION FOR HOSPITAL SECURITY, P. O. Box 637, Lombard, IL, Zip 60148; tel. 312/953-0990; Nancy Felesena, sec. **(02)**
JACKSON AND COKER, INC., 400 Perimeter Center Terr., Suite 760, Atlanta, GA, Zip 30346; tel. 404/393-1210; Jackson C. Coker, exec.vice-pres. **(12C)**
JAROS, BAUM AND BOLLES, 345 Park Ave., New York, NY, Zip 10154; tel. 212/758-9000; Richard T. Baum, partner **(05A)**
JOHNSON AND JOHNSON, 501 George St., P. O. Box 4000; New Brunswick, NJ, Zip 08903; tel. 201/524-9293; Philip E. Doyle, vice-pres. **(11)**
KABIVITRUM, INC., 1311 Harbor Bay Pkwy., Alameda, CA, Zip 94501;tel. 415/769-4656; Ron Devore, vice-pres. & gen. mgr. **(11)**
KAREN LANE ASSOCIATES, INC., 312 Broad Ave., Englewood, NJ, Zip 07631; tel. 201/947-4402; Karen Lane, pres. **(05F)**
KURT SALMON ASSOCIATES, INC., 400 Colony Square, Atlanta, GA, Zip 30361; tel. 404/892-0321; W. Barry Moore, national dir. **(05F)**
LAVENTHOL AND HORWATH, 300 S. Riverside Plaza, Chicago, IL, Zip 60606; tel. 312/648-0555; Harold Koloms, partner **(05G)**
LEO A. DALY COMPANY, 900 Circle 75 Pkwy., Suite 200, Atlanta, GA, Zip 30339; Lloyd A. Meyer, assoc. **(01)**
M. D. BUYLINE, INC., 5910 N. Central Expwy., Dallas, TX, Zip 75206, tel. 214/368-1881; Sharon McFarland, exec. vice-pres. **(12D)**
M. W. WOOD COMPANY, 3320 Hamilton Blvd., Allentown, PA, Zip 18103; tel. 215/435-6751; Jane H. Smith, mktg. coor. **(07)**
MASTR SOFT CORPORATION, 24293 Telegraph Rd., Southfield, MI, Zip 48034; tel. 313/358-3366; Bernard R. Mannisto, pres. **(14)**
MCDONALD'S CORPORATION, One McDonalds Plaza, Re 090, Oak Brook, IL, Zip 60521; tel. 312/887-6516; Dae Abram, dir.-real estate & spec. proj. **(13)**
MEDICAL CARE INTERNATIONAL, 15110 Dallas Pkwy., Suite 600, Dallas, TX, Zip 75248; tel. 214/490-3190; William Wilcox, sr. vice-pres. **(13)**
MEDICAL LAB AUTOMATION, INC., 270 Marble Ave., Pleasantville, NY, Zip 10570; tel. 914/747-3020; Charles E. Saunders, pres. **(11)**
MEDICAL MANAGEMENT DEVELOPMENT ASSOCIATES, INC., 500 N. First Ave., Suite 7, Arcadia, CA, Zip 91006; tel. 818/446-0979; Lyman Martin, pres. **(13)**
MEDICAL PLANNING ASSOCIATES, 1601 Rambla Pacifico, Malibu, CA, Zip 90265; tel. 213/456-2084; Daniel Logan, pres. **(06)**
MEDICUS, One American Plaza, Suite 400, Evanston, IL, Zip 60201; tel. 312/570-7500; Richard C. Jelinek, chm. **(05E)**
WILLIAM M. MERCER-MEIDINGER, INC., 2600 Meidinger Tower, Louisville, KY, Zip 40202; tel. 502/561-4771; Mary H. Osborne, coor.practice dev. **(05B)**
MIRICH MEDICAL CORPORATION, 1000 W. 127th Pl., Crown Point, IN, Zip 46307; tel. 219/769-3570; Eleanor Kay-Mirich, chief exec. off. **(13)**
MISSOURI HEALTH AND EDUCATIONAL FACILITIES AUTHORITY, 515 Olive St., Suite 404, St. Louis, MO, Zip 63101; tel. 314/231-3355; Steven C. Davis, exec. dir. **(13)**
MMI COMPANIES, INC., 2275 Half Day Rd., Suite 320, Bannockburn, IL, Zip 60015; tel. 312/940-7550; Janice Marsh, educ. spec. corp. affairs **(09)**
MOTOROLA COMPUTER SYSTEMS, INC., P. O. Box A, Cupertino, CA, Zip95014; tel. 408/255-0900; Ken Sibrava **(11)**
NATIONAL ASSOCIATION OF HOSPITAL ADMITTING MANAGERS, 1101 Connecticut Ave. N.W., 700, Washington, DC, Zip 20036; tel. 202/857-1162; Carol Lively, exec. dir. **(02)**
NATIONAL HEALTHCARE LINEN SERVICE, 1180 Peachtree St. N.E., Atlanta, GA, Zip 30309; tel. 404/892-7344; Anne Dillard-McGroch, dir. mktg. sales **(12D)**
NEW YORK CITY HEALTH AND HOSPITALS CORPORATION, 125 Worth St., New York, NY, Zip 10013; tel. 212/566-7711; Jo Ivey Boufford MD, pres. **(13)**
NORTH DAKOTA STATE DEPARTMENT OF HEALTH, DIVISION OF HEALTH FACILITIES, State Capitol, Bismarck, ND, Zip 58505; tel. 701/224-2352; Joe Pratschner, dir. **(13)**
NORTHERN TELECOM, 2100 Lakeside Blvd., Richardson, TX, Zip 75081; tel. 214/437-8000; J. R. Jasenof, industry mktg. mgr. **(04)**
OLSTEN HEALTH CARE SERVICES, One Merrick Ave., Westbury, NY, Zip 11590; tel. 516/832-8200; Linda K. Duval, asst. vice-pres. **(12D)**
OMNIBUS INDUSTRIES, INC.-REVENUE SERVICE OF AMERICA, 10811 Washington Blvd., Suite 301, Culver City, CA, Zip 90232; tel. 213/204-2044; Micki Schulman, pres. **(12C)**
PAR ASSOCIATES, 27 State St., Boston, MA, Zip 02109; tel. 617/367-0320, Peter A. Rabinowitz, pres. **(12C)**
PEAT, MARWICK, MITCHELL AND COMPANY, 303 E. Wacker Dr., Chicago, IL, Zip 60601; tel. 312/938-1000; R. E. Schimmel, partner **(05A)**
PHAMIS, INC., 419 Second Ave. S., P. O. Box 3057, Seattle, WA, Zip 98104; tel. 206/622-9558; R. Lee Buechler, exec. vice-pres. **(08)**
PITTSBURGH MERCY HEALTH CORPORATION, 3333 Fifth Ave., Pittsburgh, PA, Zip 15213; tel. 412/578-6351; Sr. Joanne Marie Andiorio, pres. **(13)**
PRESBYTERIAN HEALTH RESOURCES, INC., 600 Third Ave., New York, NY, Zip 10016; tel. 212/557-7474; David L. Ginsberg, vice-pres. plng. **(05A)**
PRICE WATERHOUSE, 200 E. Randolph, Chicago, IL, Zip 60601; tel.312/565-1500; Steve Heck, partner-in-charge **(03)**
REID AND TARICS ASSOCIATES, INC., 20 Jones St., 3rd Floor, San Francisco, CA, Zip 94102; tel. 415/863-2420; Charles Schrader, pres. **(01)**
THE RENFREW CENTER, 475 Spring Lane, Philadelphia, PA, Zip 19128; tel. 215/482-5353; Samuel Menaged, pres. **(13)**
THE RITCHIE ORGANIZATION, 174 Boylston St., Chestnut Hill, MA, Zip 02167; tel. 617/969-9400; Wendell R. Morgan Jr., pres. **(01)**
RIVENDELL OF AMERICA, 5100 Poplar, Suite 2820, Memphis, TN, Zip 38137; tel. 901/685-9152; Kathleen Kennally, vice-pres. commun. **(05A)**
ROLLINS BURDICK HUNTER, 10 S. Riverside Plaza, Chicago, IL, Zip 60606; tel. 312/559-5428; J. Thomas Freidheim, vice-pres. **(09)**
ANTHONY J. J. ROURKE, INC., 550 Mamaroneck Ave., Harrison, NY, Zip 10528; tel. 914/698-9100; Anthony J. J. Rourke Jr. MD, pres. **(05C)**
SAINT JOSEPH'S CARE GROUP, INC., 707 E. Cedar St., Suite 200, South Bend, IN, Zip 46617; tel. 219/237-7990; Dennis W. Heck, pres. **(13)**
THE SALVATION ARMY NATIONAL HEADQUARTERS, 120 W. 14th St., New York, NY, Zip 10011; tel. 201/239-0606; Lt. Col. Edith A. MacLachlan, reg. dir. **(13)**
SCIENTIFIC GROWTH INC., 5030 S. Mill C-1, Tempe, AR, Zip 85282; tel. 602/897-7939; Gary M. Reed, gen. mgr. **(11)**
SECURITY PACIFIC CAPITAL MARKETS GROUP, 300 S. Grand Ave., 21st Fl, Los Angeles, CA, Zip 90071; tel. 213/229-1435; Joseph A. Boystak, vice-pres. & mgr. **(10)**
SELTZER DALEY COMPANIES, 575 Ewing St., Princeton, NJ, Zip 08540; tel. 609/924-2420; Eliot Daley, pres. **(05C)**
SERVICEMASTER INDUSTRIES, INC., 2300 Warrenville Rd., Downers Grove, IL, Zip 60515; tel. 312/964-1300; C. William Pollard, pres. **(12B)**
SHARED MEDICAL SYSTEMS, INC., 51 Valley Stream Pkwy., Malvern, PA, Zip 19355; tel. 215/296-6300; Susan B. West, mgr. pub. rel. **(13)**
SOUTH BAY HOSPITAL DISTRICT, 700 N. Pacific Coast Hwy., Suite 206A, Redondo Beach, CA, Zip 90277; tel. 213/374-3426; Kathleen Belkham, exec. dir. **(13)**
SPECTRUM COMMUNICATIONS AND ELECTRONICS CORPORATION, 62 Bethpage Rd., Hicksville, NY, Zip 11801; tel. 516/822-9810; Nancy Ledesky, adm. mktg. **(05D)**
SPECTRUM HOUSE, INC., 155 Oak St., Westboro, MA, Zip 01581; tel. 617/366-1416; Robert P. Galea Phd, pres. **(13)**
SSM REHABILITATION INSTITUTE, 6420 Clayton Rd., St. Louis, MO, Zip 63117; tel. 314/768-8850; Edward L. Rosen, exec. dir. **(13)**
STONINGTON INSTITUTE, Swantown Hill Rd., P. O. Box 216, North Stonington, CT, Zip 06359; tel. 203/535-1010; Robert Fox, adm. **(13)**
SUPERIOR CONSULTANT COMPANY, INC., 7071 Orchard Lake Rd., Suite 245, West Bloomfield, MI, Zip 48033; tel. 313/855-0960; Richard D. Helppie, pres. **(05E)**
TEXAS COMMERCE BANK NATIONAL ASSOCIATION, 712 Main, Houston, TX, Zip 77002; tel. 713/236-5016; Karen Kassouf, vice-pres. **(02)**
TEXAS DEPARTMENT OF HEALTH, 1100 W. 49th St., Austin, TX, Zip 78756; tel. 512/454-3781; Robert Bernstein MD, comr. **(13)**
TEXAS MEDICAL CENTER, 406 Jesse Jones Library Bldg., Houston, TX, Zip 77030; tel. 713/791-8805; Richard E. Wainerdi, pres. **(13)**
TEXAS STATE DEPARTMENT OF MENTAL HEALTH AND MENTAL RETARDATION, Box 12668, Capitol Sta., Austin, TX, Zip 78711; tel. 512/454-3761; Gary E. Miller MD, comr. **(13)**
3M, 3m Center, Bldg. 225-5n-03, St. Paul, MN, Zip 55144; tel. 612/733-8568; Donald V. Murray, dir. distrib. dev. **(11)**
TOUCHE ROSS AND COMPANY, 1633 Broadway, New York, NY, Zip 10019;tel. 212/489-1600 **(05H)**
TRANSAMERICA OCCIDENTAL LIFE, HEALTH CARE DELIVERY SYSTEMS, 1150 S. Olive St., T-1131, Los Angeles, CA, Zip 90015; tel. 213/742-2424; Robert L. Goldman Phd, vice-pres. **(09)**
UNITED HOSPITAL FUND OF NEW YORK, 55 Fifth Ave., 16th Floor, New York, NY, Zip 10003; tel. 212/645-2500; Bruce C. Vladeck, pres. **(13)**
U. S. AIR FORCE SCHOOL OF AEROSPACE MEDICINE, Usafsam-Ce, Brooks AFB, TX, Zip 78235; tel. 512/536-3342; Maj. Ira D. Wilson **(13)**
U. S. ARMY HEALTH SERVICES COMMAND, Fort Sam Houston, TX, Zip 78234; tel. 512/221-1211; Mgen Raymond H. Bishop Jr., cmdr. **(13)**
U. S. MEDICAL CORPORATION, 7209 E. Kemper Rd., Cincinnati, OH, Zip 45249; tel. 513/489-5595; Deborah Hermann, supv. **(11)**
U. S. WEST INFORMATION SYSTEMS, INC., 6200 S. Quebec St., Suite 3000, Englewood, CO, Zip 80111; tel. 303/889-6200; Marjorie Stoltz, mktg. mgr. **(05D)**
UNIVERSAL MEDICAL SCANNERS, INC., 349 Centerville Rd., Suite C, Warwick, RI, Zip 02886; tel. 401/732-4420; Frank M. Lubrano, pres. **(11)**
UNIVERSITY HOSPITAL CONSORTIUM, INC., One Mid America Plaza, Suite 624, Oakbrook Terrace, IL, Zip 60181; tel. 312/954-4707; Robert J. Baker, pres. **(13)**
VALLEY ACCEPTANCE CORPORATION-MIDWEST, 216 S. Jefferson, Suite 206, Chicago, IL, Zip 60606; tel. 312/583-1020; Jon H. Bradshaw, mgr. **(12D)**
VETERANS ADMINISTRATION, DEPARTMENT OF MEDICINE AND SURGERY, 810 Vermont Ave. N.W., Washington, DC, Zip 20420; tel. 202/233-2597; John A. Gronvall MD, chief med. dir. **(13)**
VETERANS ADMINISTRATION REGIONAL OFFICE, 680 Alamonna Blvd., Honolulu, HI, Zip 96801; William J. Vandervort MD, dir. **(13)**
THE VILLAGE SOUTH, INC., 3180 Biscayne Blvd., Miami, FL, Zip 33137; tel. 305/573-4357; Matthew Gissen, pres. **(13)**
VIRGINIA, COMMONWEALTH OF, DEPARTMENT OF MENTAL HEALTH AND MENTAL RETARDATION, 109 Governor St., Box 1797, Richmond, VA, Zip 23219; tel. 804/770-3915; Howard Cullum, comm. adm. **(13)**
VOLUNTARY HOSPITALS OF AMERICA, 5215 N. O'Connor Rd., P. O. Box 160909, Irving, TX, Zip 75016; tel. 214/258-1737; Don L. Arnwine, pres. **(13)**
WASTE MANAGEMENT, INC., 3003 Butterfield Rd., Oak Brook, IL, Zip 60521; tel. 312/572-8800; Robert J. Keleher, dir. oper. adm. **(12D)**
WEST TEXAS REHABILITATION CENTER, 4601 Hartford St., Abilene, TX, Zip 79605; tel. 915/692-1633; Shelley V. Smith, pres. & exec. dir. **(13)**
WESTERN NATURAL GAS AND TRANSMISSION CORPORATION, 3131 S. Vaughn Way, Suite 521, Aurora, CO, Zip 80014; Ronald D. Jones, pres. **(11)**

U.S. Associated Area

Puerto Rico

San Juan: SCHOOL OF PUBLIC HEALTH, Medical Science Campus-University of Puerto Rico, G. P. O. Box 5067, Zip 00905; tel. 809/767-9626; Carlos N. Vicens MD, dean

Canada

Alberta

Edmonton: ALBERTA DEPARTMENT OF HOSPITALS AND MEDICAL CARE, 11010 101st St., P. O. Box 2222
ALBERTA HOSPITAL ASSOCIATION, 10025 108th St., 6th Floor, Don Macgregor, pres.
CRAM HEALTH SYSTEMS, 15015 123 Ave., J. P. French, mng. prin.

British Columbia

Vancouver: COMCARE CANADA, LTD, 744 E. Broadway, Patricia Turner, adm.
Victoria: MINISTRY OF HEALTH, HOSPITAL PROGRAM, 1515 Blanshard, 6th Floor

Manitoba

Winnipeg: UNIVERSITY OF MANITOBA ELIZABETH DAFOE LIBRARY, University of Manitoba, V. M. Dechene, acq. lib.

Ontario

Kanata: MITEL CORPORATION, 350 Legget Dr., P. O. Box 13089, Lorraine Small, mgr. mktg. prog.
Mississauga: SCOTT FINANCIAL SERVICES, 6711 Mississauga Rd., Suite 702, Ken Murray, sr. mgr. mktg.
Ottawa: CANADIAN HOSPITAL ASSOCIATION, 17 York St., Suite 100, Jean-Claude Martin, exec. dir.
St. Catharines: RKT COMPUTER SERVICES LTD, 4 Queen St., 5th Floor, Arlene Hallas, off. mgr.
Toronto: COMCARE, LTD, 15 Madison Ave., Doris A. Nickerson, exec. vice-pres.
MEDIREX SYSTEMS, 499 Queen St. E., Mark D. Caskenette, consult.

Quebec

Montreal: FEDERATION DES MEDECINS OMNIPRATICIENS DU QUEBEC, 1440 W. Ste. Catherine, Suite 1100, Therese Malo, lib.
SOCIETE COMCARE DU QUEBEC, INC., 1538 Sherbrooke St. W., Suite 406, Vicki Jutras, adm.

Saskatchewan

Regina: SASKATCHEWAN HEALTH CARE ASSOCIATION, 1853 Hamilton St., Suite 307, Hewitt Helmsing, exec. dir.
SASKATCHEWAN HOSPITAL SERVICES PLAN, 3475 Albert St., E. H. Wright, exec. dir.

Foreign

Arabia

Abu Dhabi: ALLIED MEDICAL GROUP, P. O. Box 2431, M. Jones, proj. dir.
Doha Qatar: HAMAD GENERAL HOSPITAL, Box 3050, Charles I. Gustafson, adm. dir.

Australia

Deakin: AUSTRALIAN HOSPITAL ASSOCIATION, 42 Thesiger Court
Melbourne: PRINCE HENRY'S HOSPITAL, 236 St. Kilda Rd., R. G. Edwards, chief exec.
ROYAL MELBOURNE HOSPITAL, Gratton St., Parkville, G. H. Dreher MD, exec. dir.
Sydney: HEALTH COMMISSION OF NEW SOUTH WALES, McKell Bldg., Rawson Pl., Box K110, Haymarket

Brazil

Rio de Janeiro: CLINICA SAO VICENTE, Rua Joao Borges 204 -Gavea, Luiz Roberto Londres, pres.
Sao Paulo: SOCIEDADE HOSPITAL SAMARITANO, Rua Conselheiro Brotero, 1486, Edson Gomes Dos Santos, supt.

Chile

Santiago: ASOCIACION CHILENA DE SEGURIDAD, Ramon Carnicer 85, Sr. Lucy Haddad
CIDES, LTD, Luis Thayer Ojeda 393, Eugenio Balmaceda, dir.

England

Brighton: BARAKAT AND ASSOCIATES, 1 New Rd., Tayseer I. Barakat MD, chm.
London: KINGS FUND CENTRE, 126 Albert St., W. G. Cannon, dir.
PWS NORTH AMERICA LIMITED, 52, Minories, Kevin R. Sower, mng. dir.

France

Neuilly-S/Sein: AMERICAN HOSPITAL OF PARIS, 63 Blvd. Victor Hugo, M. B. Fesneau, dir. gen.

Israel

Jerusalem: HADASSAH MEDICAL ORGANIZATION, Ein Kerem, Box 12000, Samuel Penchas MD, dir. gen.

Japan

Tokyo: ST. LUKE'S INTERNATIONAL HOSPITAL, 10-1 Akashi-Cho, Chuo-Ku, Eiki Makino MD, gen. dir.

Kenya

Nairobi: AGA KHAN HOSPITAL NAIROBI, P. O. Box 30270, Azim Juam, assoc. dir.

Lebanon

Beirut: AMERICAN UNIVERSITY OF BEIRUT MEDICAL CENTER, Maamari St., 850 Third Ave., 18th Floor, Ahmad Y. Nasrallah, actg. dir.

Mexico

Guadalajara: HOSPITAL MEXICO-AMERICANO, Calle Colomos 2110, Jorge Angel Rodriquez, adm.
Mexico City: AMERICAN-BRITISH COWDRAY HOSPITAL, Sur 136 Esq Av Observatorio, Lawrence V. Meagher Jr., gen. dir.
SHRINERS HOSPITAL FOR CRIPPLED CHILDREN, Suchil 152, Col. El Rosario, Betty M. Gold, adm.

Nationalist China

Taipei: MACKAY MEMORIAL HOSPITAL, 92-sec.-2 N. Chung San Rd., Rick C. C. Huang, adm.
NATIONAL TAIWAN UNIVERSITY HOSPITAL, 1 Chang-Te St., Kuo-Sin Lin MD, dir.
VETERANS GENERAL HOSPITAL, 201 Shihpai Rd., Section II, Peitou

Pakistan

Karachi-3: MURSHID HOSPITAL AND HEALTH CENTER, 28 Abdullah Haroon Rd., Box 7484, Raja S. Chowdhry, adm.

Panama

Panama City: CLINICA SAN FERNANDO, Apartado 363, Zona 9a, Ernesto Arosemena MD, med. dir.

Philippines

Quezon City: ST. LUKE'S MEDICAL CENTER, 279 E. Rodriguez Sr. Blvd., Jose F. G. Ledesma, exec. dir.

Saudi Arabia

Al-Khobar: AL-KHALEEJ COMPUTERS AND ELECTRONICS, P. O. Box 2062, Ahmad A. Ashadawi, pres.
Bahrain: INTERNATIONAL HOSPITAL OF BAHRAIN, P. O. Box 1084, Roger McLaughlin MD, adm.
Riyadh: GREEN CRESCENT HEALTH SERVICES, P. O. Box 3096, Al-Alaya, Sarry Wael Buraik, system eng.

South Africa

Cape Town: ERNST AND WHINNEY, P. O. Box 656, Mirinda Coetsee, health care consult.

Spain

Barcelona: HOSPITAL GENERAL DE CATALUNYA, Sant Cugat, Ramon Nicolau Casellas, adm.

United Arab Republic

Cairo: NILE BADRAWI HOSPITAL, Cornishe El Nile-Maadi Rd., P. O. Box 533, Maadi, Mohamed Hamdy H. Badraoui, exec. dir.

Venezuela

Caracas: HOSPITAL PRIVADO CENTRO MEDICO DE CARACAS, Plaza Del Estanque, San Bernardino, Juan Godayol Rovira MD, pres.
Maracaibo-Zulia: FUNDACION SALUD Y. CIENCIA, HOSPITAL COROMOTO, Ave. 3c No 51, La Lago, P. O. Box 422, Ricaurte Salom-Gil MD, gen. dir.

West Germany

Wiesbaden: INTERNATIONAL ACADEMY OF HEALTH CARE MANAGEMENT, 27-29 Strasse, Anthony M. Carver, exec. dir.

West Indies

Grenada: ST. GEORGE'S UNIVERSITY SCHOOL OF MEDICINE, 1 E. Main St., Charles R. Modica, chancellor

Personal Members

This list is revised to include new members accepted prior to March 20, 1987. The number following each member's identification indicates the year membership began. Members of affiliated societies, academies, and organizations are designated as follows:

(ATTY)	*American Academy of Hospital Attorneys*
(NURS)	*American Organization of Nurse Executives*
(CS)	*American Society for Healthcare Central Service Personnel*
(EDUC)	*American Society for Healthcare Education and Training*
(PERS)	*American Society for Healthcare Human Resources Administration*
(RISK)	*American Society for Healthcare Risk Management*
(ENG)	*American Society for Hospital Engineering*
(FOOD)	*American Society for Hospital Food Service Administrators*
(PR)	*American Society for Hospital Marketing and Public Relations*
(PUR)	*American Society for Hospital Materials Management*
(VOL)	*American Society of Directors of Volunteer Services*
(ENVIRON)	*American Society of Healthcare Environmental Services*
(MGMT)	*Healthcare Information and Management Systems Society*
(PAT)	*National Society of Patient Representatives*
(AMB)	*Society for Ambulatory Care Professionals*
(PLNG)	*Society for Hospital Planning and Marketing*
(SOC)	*Society for Hospital Social Work Directors*

Special designations are:

(HON)	*Honorary member*
(LIFE)	*Life member*
(RET)	*Retired member*

A

AADALEN, SHARON PRICE, RN PhD, dir. nrsg. educ. and res., United Hospital, St. Paul, MN '86 (NURS)

AALDERKS, K. J., dir. soc. serv., St. Joseph Mercy Hospital, Mason City, IA '82 (SOC)

AALDERS, PAUL F., dir. matl. mgt., Lakewood Hospital, Lakewood, OH '86 (PUR)

AARON, FRANK J. JR., adm., Margaret R. Pardee Memorial Hospital, Hendersonville, NC '74

AARON, MARCUS II, atty., Montefiore Hospital, Pittsburgh, PA '79 (ATTY)

AARON, MARY LEE, supv. cent. sup., Dorchester General Hospital, Cambridge, MD '83 (CS)

AARON, REID, assoc. dir. prof. and mgt. serv., New York Eye and Ear Infirmary, New York, NY '85 (PUR)

AARON, ROBERT V., consult., Medical Management Associates, Arcadia, FL '61

AARONSON, DONALD W., atty., Lutheran General Hospital, Park Ridge, IL '83 (ATTY)

AARONSON, RUTH TRUNSKY, dir. soc. serv., Redford Community Hospital, Redford, MI '79 (SOC)

AASTRUP, WINONA K., RN, assoc. dir. nrsg., New England Memorial Hospital, Stoneham, MA '83 (NURS)

ABAHUSSEIN, OTHMAN A., asst. adm. med. staff affairs, King Fahad Hospital, Riyadh, Saudi Arabia '84

ABALONA, WILLIAM L., atty., Children's Hospital and Health Center, San Diego, CA '80 (ATTY)

ABARAY, D. JOAN, chief exec. off., Podiatry Hospital of Pittsburgh, Pittsburgh, PA '76

ABARBANEL, GAIL, dir. soc. serv., Santa Monica Hospital Medical Center, Santa Monica, CA '75 (SOC)

ABARNO, ELIZABETH A., instr. educ., Mary Washington Hospital, Fredericksburg, VA '86 (EDUC)

ABBATE, ANTHONY J., vice-pres. association serv., Hospital Council of Southern California, Los Angeles, CA '85

ABBETT, JUDY, asst. adm. mktg. and plng., Fairfax Hospital, Falls Church, VA '81 (PR)

ABBEY, CHARLES R., exec. dir., University Suburban Health Center, South Euclid, OH '87 (AMB)

ABBEY, LOUIS, dir. pers., Mount Sinai Hospital, Hartford, CT '70 (PERS)

ABBEY, SUZAN M., dir. soc. serv., Arkansas City Memorial Hospital, Arkansas City, KS '71 (SOC)

ABBIS, CHAIKER, Edmundston Regional Hospital, Edmundston, N.B., Canada '76 (LIFE)

ABBOTT, FRANK H., atty., Mercy Catholic Medical Center, Philadelphia, PA '68 (ATTY)

ABBOTT, GERARD R., dir. pur., Franklin Square Hospital, Baltimore, MD '71 (PUR)

ABBOTT, JEFFREY R., atty., Taylor Hospital, Ridley Park, PA '83 (ATTY)

ABBOTT, MARCIA R., RN, dir. cent. serv., Boca Raton Community Hospital, Boca Raton, FL '83 (CS)

ABBOTT, MARGARET P., (ret.), Morgantown, WV '77 (FOOD)

ABBOTT, MARIBELL, dir. matl. mgt., Clayton General Hospital, Riverdale, GA '76 (PUR)

ABBOTT, NANCY C., RN, dir. pat. care serv., Scottsdale Memorial Hospital, North Division, Scottsdale, AZ '86 (NURS)

ABBOTT, NELLIE, RN, assoc. adm. nrsg. and assoc. dean nrsg. practice, Hospital of the University of Pennsylvania, Philadelphia, PA '83 (NURS)

ABBOTT, PEGGY, dir. vol. serv., Baptist Medical Center-Montclair, Birmingham, AL '79 (VOL)

ABBOTT, RICHARD L., dir. pur., Peoples Community Hospital Authority, Wayne, MI '85 (PUR)

ABBOTT, ROBERT L., consult., Bio-Medical and Plnt Engineering, West End, NC '87 (ENG)

ABBOTT, STEPHEN L., chief exec. off., Community Hospital, Anderson, IN '72

ABBOTT, STEPHEN L., atty., John F. Kennedy Medical Center, Edison, NJ '80 (ATTY)

ABBOTT, WILLIAM J., pres., Sbw Medical Packing, Inc., Houston, TX '82 (CS)

ABBOTT, WILLIAM S., adm., Massena Memorial Hospital, Massena, NY '85

ABEL, WALTER B. JR., sr. mgt. eng., SunHealth Corporation, Charlotte, NC '83 (MGMT)

ABELS, KRISTA M., dir. corp. plng., Sutter Community Hospitals, Sacramento, CA '82 (PLNG)

ABERCROMBIE, THOMPSON T., assoc. prof., University of Alabama in Birmingham, Birmingham, AL '74 (EDUC)

ABERNETHY, KELLY D., RN, dir. nrsg.-critical care, Glendale Adventist Medical Center, Glendale, CA '82 (NURS)

ABERNETHY, PAMELA L., asst. atty. gen., Oregon Department of Justice, Salem, OR '85 (ATTY)

ABESS, JOAN E., RN, dir. nrsg., Doctors' Hospital, Coral Gables, FL '80 (NURS)

ABEYTA, CHARLES, adm. coor., St. Anthony Hospital Systems, Denver, CO '82 (PUR)

ABICH, JORGE, reg. pers. mgr., Humana, Inc.-Florida Region, Orlando, FL '72 (PERS)

ABLESON, JANICE KAY, asst. dir. qual. assur., Henry Ford Hospital, Detroit, MI '85 (RISK)

ABNER, CARL O., dir. gen. serv., Floyd Medical Center, Rome, GA '85 (PLNG)

ABOOD, FRED J., reg. vice-pres., Marriott Corporation, Marietta, GA '74 (FOOD)

ABRAHAM, JOHN E., prin., Architectural Consultants, Grandview, MO '79

ABRAHAM, MATHEW, asst. adm., Antelope Valley Hospital Medical Center, Lancaster, CA '82

ABRAHAM, ROBINSON, Silver Spring, MD '75

ABRAHAMS, DENIS M., mgr. corp. pur., United Health Services, Johnson City, NY '81 (PUR)

ABRAHAMSEN, MARIA B., atty., Hutzel Hospital, Detroit, MI '80 (ATTY)

ABRAHAMSON, JAMES W., indust. eng., Cook County Government, Chicago, IL '84 (MGMT)

ABRAHAMSON, RONALD M., supv. maint., Children's Hospital and Medical Center, Seattle, WA '86 (ENG)

ABRAHMS, LYNDA E., dir. pub. rel., Placentia-Linda Community Hospital, Placentia, CA '82 (PR)

ABRAMI, PATRICK F., vice-pres., Applied Management Systems, Inc., Burlington, MA '76 (MGMT)

ABRAMOVICH, FRIEDA, biomedical tech., Palomar Memorial Hospital, Escondido, CA '85 (ENG)

ABRAMOVITZ, ALAN L., dir. pers., Spelman Memorial Hospital, Smithville, MO '85 (PERS)

ABRAMOVITZ, EDMUND ALEXANDER, vice-pres., New Jersey Hospital Association, Princeton, NJ '76 (PERS)(ENG)

ABRAMOWITZ, SUSAN, PhD, sr. assoc. plng., Society of the New York Hospital, New York, NY '87 (AMB)

ABRAMS, ERWIN EDWARD, adm., Palms of Pasadena Hospital, St. Petersburg, FL '64

ABRAMS, LES, dir. maint. and eng., Jane Phillips Episcopal-Memorial Medical Center, Bartlesville, OK '76 (ENG)

ABRAMS, RUTH M., dir. vol. serv., New England Baptist Hospital, Boston, MA '85 (VOL)(PAT)

ABRAMS, THOMAS G., sr. installation dir., Shared Medical Systems, Inc., Schamburg, IL '79 (MGMT)

ABRAMSON, ALLEN C., vice-pres. human res., Montefiore Medical Center, Bronx, NY '70 (PERS)

ABRAMSON, HERBERT, hosp. adm. consult., New York State Health Department, New York, NY '51 (LIFE)

ABRAMSON, IRMA, dir. soc. serv., Jewish Hospital and Medical Center of Brooklyn, Brooklyn, NY '66 (SOC)

ABRAMSON, JULIE, State University of New York at Albany, Social Welfare Department, Albany, NY '85 (SOC)

ABRAMSON, MARCIA, asst. prof., Columbia University School of Social Work, New York, NY '82 (SOC)

ABREAU, CYNTHIA MARIE, adm. nuclear medicine, University of Massachusetts Medical Center, Worcester, MA '83

ABRIOLA, JOSEPH L., dir. plant oper., Episcopal Hospital, Philadelphia, PA '86 (ENG)

ABROOKIN, STEVEN ROBERT, corp. dir. mgt. support serv., Sisters of Charity Health Care System, Houston TX '80 (MGMT)

ABRUZZESE, ROBERTA STRAESSLE, RN, dir. cont. nrsg. educ., School of Nursing, Adelphi University, Garden City, NY '71 (EDUC)

ABUEG, ESPERANZA S., chief food serv., Los Angeles County-High Desert Hospital, Lancaster, CA '79 (FOOD)

ACCARDI, ANDREW E., student, Program in Hospital Administration, Texas Women's University, Denton, TX '78

ACCORDINO, ELIZABETH, dir. commun. rel. and dev., Tri-County Memorial Hospital, Gowanda, NY '85 (PR)

ACCURSO, BARBARA, RN, coor. sup., proc. and distrib., Greenwich Hospital, Greenwich, CT '82 (CS)

ACHARD, KENNETH C., mgr. maint. and security, Midland Hospital Center, Midland, MI '82 (ENG)

ACHOR, R. WINFIELD, atty., Santa Rosa Memorial Hospital, Santa Rosa, CA '77 (ATTY)

ACHORN, MARY K., med. rec. consult., Shriners Hospitals for Children, Tampa, FL '84

ACHTERMANN, REV. J. ROBERT, exec. dir., Council for Health and Human Service Ministries, Lancaster, PA '82

ACKART, JANE ANN, dir. med. rec., St. Augustine General Hospital, St. Augustine, FL '83

ACKEN, RICHARD A., sr. mgt. eng., Pacific Presbyterian Medical Center, San Francisco, CA '85 (MGMT)
ACKERMAN, BARBARA, dir. vol. serv., Riverside Hospital, Toledo, OH '86 (VOL)
ACKERMAN, CARL, dir. maint., Potomac Hospital, Woodbridge, VA '85 (ENG)
ACKERMAN, CEELY A., dir. vol. serv., Bridgeport Hospital, Bridgeport, CT '86 (VOL)
ACKERMAN, FRANKLIN KENNETH JR., sr. vice-pres. and adm. dir., Geisinger Medical Center, Danville, PA '62
ACKERMAN, LARRY, dir. safety and security, Loudoun Memorial Hospital, Leesburg, VA '80 (ENG)
ACKERMAN, ROBERT A., dir. fin. and plng., Henry County Health Center, Mount Pleasant, IA '83 (PLNG)
ACKERMAN, STANLEY, buyer, New York University Medical Center, New York, NY '86 (PUR)
ACKERMANN, ELLEN TABARY, dir. vol. serv., Memorial City Medical Center, Houston, TX '85 (VOL)
ACKLEY, ROBERT L., computer oper., Berkshire Hathaway, Omaha, NE '84
ACKOR, JEFFERSON D., corporator, Penobscot Bay Medical Center, Rockport, ME '81
ACORDAGOITIA, TINA L., RN, coor. maternal and child health nrsg. serv., Washoe Medical Center, Reno, NV '86 (NURS)
ACOSTA, MARGARITA, assoc. dir. plng. and mktg., Providence Medical Center, Portland, OR '84 (PLNG)
ACREE, CHARIS L., asst. adm., West Georgia Medical Center, La Grange, GA '77
ACTON, ALLAN, dir. mktg. and plng., Mercy Hospital, Baltimore, MD '87 (PR) (PLNG)
ACTON, CYNTHIA F., dir. staff dev., Lubbock General Hospital, Lubbock, TX '86 (EDUC)
ADAIR, JERRY D., pres. and chief exec. off., Good Shepherd Medical Center, Longview, TX '69 (PLNG)
ADAMO, M. VALETON, gyn. instr., Woman's Hospital, Baton Rouge, LA '86 (EDUC)
ADAMO, PETER J., mgt. syst. eng., Graduate Hospital, Philadelphia, PA '86 (MGMT)
ADAMS-ENDER, COL. C. L., RN MSC USA, chief nrs., Walter Reed Army Medical Center, Washington, DC '81 (NURS)
ADAMS-SHERMAN, EILEEN, student, Boston University, Boston, MA '86 (PLNG)
ADAMS, ALFRED JR., asst. dir. environ., Pennsylvania Hospital, Philadelphia, PA '87 (ENVIRON)
ADAMS, BERNICE E., dir. soc. serv., Lee Hospital, Johnstown, PA '83 (SOC)
ADAMS, BILL L., dir. commun. rel., Bromenn Healthcare, Normal, IL '81 (PR)
ADAMS, CARSBIE CLIFTON, pres. and adm., Potomac Point Health Facility, Stafford, VA '54 (LIFE)
ADAMS, CHARLES B., coor. serv., Oaks Treatment Center-Brown Schools, Austin, TX '86 (PUR)
ADAMS, CORA, vice-pres., Baptist Medical Center, Jacksonville, FL '85 (NURS)
ADAMS, DAVID W., dir. pat. rel., McMaster University Medical Centre, Hamilton, Ont., Canada '86 (PAT)
ADAMS, DENNIS D., facil. eng., Saint Alphonsus Regional Medical Center, Boise, ID '86 (ENG)
ADAMS, DOLLMESHIA H., asst. dir. soc. serv., Grady Memorial Hospital, Atlanta, GA '80 (SOC)
ADAMS, FRANK, dir. facil. and constr., Western Psychiatric Institute and Clinic, Pittsburgh, PA '87 (ENG)
ADAMS, GAIL B., plng. mgr., Sisters of Charity Health Care Systems, Cincinnati, OH '84 (PLNG)
ADAMS, GEORGE, pres. and chief exec. off., Lutheran Medical Center, Brooklyn, NY '53 (LIFE)
ADAMS, GREGORY A., RN, Beaumont, TX '83 (NURS)
ADAMS, H. E. III, vice-pres., Hospital Corporation of America, Nashville, TN '74
ADAMS, HELEN, RN, reg. adm. nrsg., Group Health Eastside Hospital, Redmond, WA '83 (NURS)
ADAMS, IRENE M., sr. consult., Grant Medical Center, Columbus, OH '87 (MGMT)
ADAMS, J. D., risk mgr. and dir. med. rec., Memorial Medical Center of Jacksonville, Jacksonville, FL '81 (RISK)
ADAMS, JANE A., dir. soc. serv., Hamilton County Public Hospital, Webster City, IA '85 (SOC)
ADAMS, JANE A., RN, asst. adm. pat. care, Hamilton Hospital, Hamilton, NJ '73 (NURS)
ADAMS, JANET T., compensation spec., Mid-Maine Medical Center, Waterville, ME '83 (PERS)
ADAMS, JAY F., dir. food serv., Presbyterian Intercommunity Hospital, Whittier, CA '80 (FOOD)
ADAMS, JENNIE HARTWICK, assoc. plng. and mktg., Methodist Health Systems Foundation, New Orleans, LA '84 (PR) (PLNG)
ADAMS, JERRY R., dir. maint., St. Francis Hospital, Columbus, GA '82 (ENG)
ADAMS, KAREN M., atty., Chesapeake General Hospital, Chesapeake, VA '86 (ATTY)
ADAMS, KATHLEEN, dir. surg. serv., Queen of the Valley Hospital, Napa, CA '87 (AMB)
ADAMS, LARRY, bd. liaison off., Lee Memorial Hospital, Fort Myers, FL '79 (MGMT)
ADAMS, LAURETTA K., RN, asst. adm. nrsg., Permian General Hospital, Andrews, TX '85 (NURS)
ADAMS, LINDA JOYCE, coor. in-service educ., St. Francis Hospital, Columbus, GA '85 (EDUC)
ADAMS, MARCIA G., adm. diet., Muhlenberg Regional Medical Center, Plainfield, NJ '81 (FOOD)
ADAMS, MARGERY F., RN, vice-pres. pat. serv., Catawba Memorial Hospital, Hickory, NC '73 (NURS)(RISK)
ADAMS, MARY F., dir. pub. rel., Humana Hospital -Westminster, Westminster, CA '85 (PR)
ADAMS, MEGAN A., dir. risk mgt., Hahnemann University Hospital, Philadelphia, PA '84 (RISK)
ADAMS, MICHAEL P., sr. vice-pres. oper., Ingalls Memorial Hospital, Harvey, IL '73
ADAMS, MICHELE S., reg. indust. eng., Kaiser Permanente Medical Center, Oakland, CA '85 (MGMT)
ADAMS, PATRICIA M., head qual. assur., Naval Hospital, Bethesda, MD '82
ADAMS, PATRICIA V., supv. sterile proc., University of California at Los Angeles Medical Center, Los Angeles, CA '86 (CS)
ADAMS, PATRICIA, supv. cent. serv., Waconia Ridgeview Hospital, Waconia, MN '83 (CS)
ADAMS, PATSY K., dir. pub. rel., Medical Center Hospital, Tyler, TX '81 (PR)
ADAMS, PAULA L., dir. soc. work serv., Conway Hospital, Conway, SC '81 (SOC)
ADAMS, PAULA, Huron Valley Hospital, Milford, MI '79 (CS)(PUR)
ADAMS, RELLA A., RN PhD, vice-pres. nrsg., Valley Baptist Medical Center, Harlingen, TX '82 (NURS)
ADAMS, RICHARD B. JR., atty., Mercy Hospital, Miami, FL '80 (ATTY)
ADAMS, RICHARD E., asst. dir. pers., Wilson N. Jones Memorial Hospital, Sherman, TX '85 (PERS)
ADAMS, RICHARD K., dir. plant oper., Riverside Community Hospital, Bossier City, LA '85 (ENG)
ADAMS, RICHARD L., asst. adm., Somerset Community Hospital, Somerset, PA '86
ADAMS, ROBERT E., exec. dir., Research Medical Center, Kansas City, MO '51 (LIFE)
ADAMS, ROBERT J., atty., Rehabilitation Institute of Chicago, Chicago, IL '87 (ATTY)
ADAMS, ROBERT T., atty., McGuire, Woods and Battle, Richmond, VA '77 (ATTY)
ADAMS, RONALD J., dir. emp. rel., Mary Greeley Medical Center, Ames, IA '73
ADAMS, SARAH B., student, University of Texas, School of Allied Health Sciences, Galveston, TX '82
ADAMS, SHEILA M., dir. pat. and family serv., Fremont Medical Center, Yuba City, CA '85 (SOC)
ADAMS, STAN R., asst. dir. matl. mgt., Cottonwood Hospital Medical Center, Murray, UT '83 (PUR)
ADAMS, SUSAN E., menu, pur. and nutr. spec., Honeywell Information Systems, Inc. -Application Systems Division, Minneapolis, MN '82 (FOOD)
ADAMS, SUSAN, dir. qual. assur., Primary Children's Medical Center, Salt Lake City, UT '84 (RISK)
ADAMS, LT. COL. THOMAS H., MSC USA, exec. off., U. S. Army Medical Research Institute, Aberdeen Proving Grounds, MD '85 (PERS)
ADAMS, WILLIAM R., pres., Management Performance International, Inc., Cincinnati, OH '84 (PERS)
ADAMSON, BEVERLY A., RN, asst. dir. nrsg., Fairview Riverside Hospital, Minneapolis, MN '86 (NURS)
ADAMSON, C. LYNN, assoc. adm. plng. and mgt. serv., St. Francis Memorial Hospital, San Francisco, CA '80 (PLNG)
ADAMSON, HAROLD W., dir. clin. eng., Wesley Medical Center, Wichita, KS '81 (ENG)
ADAMSON, M. DEBORAH, dir. commun. rel., Phoenix General Hospital, Phoenix, AZ '86 (PR)
ADAMSON, SHIRLEY, dir. pers., Midwood Community Hospital, Stanton, CA '80 (PERS)
ADAMY, DENNIS N., dir. soc. work serv., Community Memorial Hospital, Hamilton, NY '82 (SOC)
ADCOCK, GERALD C., dir. pers., Memorial Hospital, Danville, VA '72 (PERS)
ADCOCK, MARIAN S., RN, vice-pres. pat. care serv., St. Mary's Hospital and Rehabilitation Center, Minneapolis, MN '81 (PLNG)(NURS)
ADCOCK, ROBERT, dir. prof. serv., Northshore Regional Medical Center, Slidell, LA '80
ADDIS, RICK J., dir. pub. rel. and mktg., Whitley County Memorial Hospital, Columbia City, IN '85 (PR)
ADDISON, WILFRED J., adm., Saratoga Hospital, Saratoga Springs, NY '83 (PLNG)
ADE, HARRY C. JR., dir. matl. contr., Memorial Hospital, Owosso, MI '71 (PUR)
ADELL, CHERYL A., dir. vol. serv., Saint Luke's Hospital, Cleveland, OH '83 (VOL)
ADELMAN, PATRICIA D., acct. exec., Bell of Pennysylvania, Pittsburgh, PA '85 (ENG)
ADELMAN, S. ALLAN, atty., Suburban Hospital, Bethesda, MD '77 (ATTY)(RISK)
ADELSBERG, HARVEY, exec. vice-pres., Daughters of Miriam Center, Clifton, NJ '55 (LIFE)
ADELSON, JULIE GROSS, atty., Georgetown University Medical Center, Washington, DC '79 (ATTY)
ADERHOLDT, ELIZABETH L., dir. mgt. eng., Piedmont Hospital, Atlanta, GA '85 (MGMT)
ADIBI, DANA, RN, dir. educ., HCA South Arlington Medical Center, Arlington, TX '79 (EDUC)
ADIX, LANI, dir. food serv., North Detroit General Hospital, Detroit, MI '82 (FOOD)
ADKINS, BARBARA F., dir. soc. serv., West Oaks-Psychiatric Institute Houston, Houston, TX '86 (SOC)
ADKINS, F. JO, RN, vice-pres. nrsg., Memorial Medical Center, Springfield, IL '87 (NURS)
ADKINS, JANICE M., dir. commun. rel., Highland Hospital, Belvidere, IL '85 (PR)
ADKINS, LILLIAN ROSE, RN, dir. nrsg., Baptist Medical Center-DeKalb, Fort Payne, AL '85 (NURS)
ADKINS, REID, asst. dir. support serv., HCA Park View Medical Center, Nashville, TN '85 (ENG)
ADKISSON, BILLY D., pres., James Russell, Inc., Bloomington, IL '83
ADLER, ANDREA, vice-pres. adm. serv., Good Samaritan Hospital, Baltimore, MD '83
ADLER, DIANE CATHERINE, RN, clin. dir. critical care nrsg., Hospital of the University of Pennsylvania, Philadelphia, PA '86 (NURS)
ADLER, MAURITA K., mgr. info. syst., Gottlieb Memorial Hospital, Melrose Park, IL '87 (MGMT)
ADLER, ROBERT K., adm., Montefiore Medical Center, Bronx, NY '53 (LIFE)
ADOLPH, CAROL L., RN, asst. adm. nrsg., Spring Branch Memorial Hospital, Houston, TX '85 (NURS)
ADRIAN, THOMAS A., atty., Axtell Christian Hospital, Newton, KS '86 (ATTY)
ADRIAN, WILLIAM A., dir. support serv., Ebenezer Society, Minneapolis, MN '86 (ENVIRON)
ADROUNIE, DOLORES, dir. risk mgt., St. Joseph Mercy Hospital, Ann Arbor, MI '85 (RISK)
ADSIT, ROBERT F., dir. soc. work, Greater Baltimore Medical Center, Baltimore, MD '67 (SOC)
AEROLA, MARGARET A., sr. prog. dir., St. Joseph Hospital, Parry Sound, Ont., Canada '86 (EDUC)
AFFELDT, JOHN E., MD, Rancho Santa Fe, CA '84 (HON)
AFFELT, CAROL, RN, dir. nrs., Illinois Valley Community Hospital, Peru, IL '86 (NURS)
AFRICH, TONI B., dir. soc. serv., Kaiser Foundation Hospital, San Diego, CA '85 (SOC)
AFZAL, NASEERA, dir. soc. work, Coler Memorial Hospital, New York, NY '84 (SOC)
AGARD, KATHRYN A., dir. plng. and mktg., Hackley Hospital, Muskegon, MI '83 (PR)
AGARWAL, BIPIN B., dir. spec. proj., St. Francis Hospital, Milwaukee, WI '79 (MGMT)
AGEE, NANCY HOWELL, coor. health educ., Roanoke Memorial Hospitals, Roanoke, VA '87 (EDUC)
AGLE, ROY L., vice-pres., Bay Medical Center, Bay City, MI '75 (ENG)(PLNG)
AGNETTA, DANIEL E., dir. pers., Adventist Health System-Eastern and Middle America, Shawnee Mission, KS '85 (PERS)
AGNEW, NETTIE L., RN, vice-pres. nrsg., North Kansas City Hospital, North Kansas City, MO '80 (NURS)
AGOSTI, JULIE, RN, head cent. serv., Mercy Hospital, Toledo, OH '85 (CS)
AGUAS, HUGO A., dir. human res., Sharp Health System, San Diego, CA '78 (PERS)
AGUERO, ROY C. JR., asst. adm., J. C. Blair Memorial Hospital, Huntingdon, PA '73 (PUR)
AGUILERA, HECTOR, MD, assoc. med. dir., Emergency Management Systems, Evanston, IL '87 (AMB)
AGUINALDO, PAT A., dir. food serv., Central Community Hospital, Chicago, IL '82 (FOOD)
AGUIRRE, ROSARIO V., dir. food serv., Brooklyn Hospital-Caledonian Hospital, Brooklyn, NY '79 (FOOD)
AGUS, CRISTINA L., supv. sup., proc. and distrib., North Charles Hospital, Baltimore, MD '80 (CS)
AGUSTIN, MUTYA SAN, MD, dir. amb. care serv., North Central Bronx Hospital, Bronx, NY '87 (AMB)
AHAROWI, ISRAEL, dir. info. serv., Mount Sinai Hospital, Toronto, Ont., Canada '86 (MGMT)
AHEARN, AUDREY M., cent. storekeeper, Ingleside Hospital, Rosemead, CA '82 (CS)
AHERN, DANIEL W., assoc. dir. plng. and prog. dev., Mercy Catholic Medical Center, Darby, PA '86 (PLNG)
AHERN, DIANNE M., sr. consult., CHI Systems, Inc., Ann Arbor, MI '74
AHERN, SR. MARGARET A., dir. educ., Catholic Medical Center, Manchester, NH '80 (EDUC)
AHERN, PAUL L. JR., atty., Stevens Memorial Hospital, Edmonds, WA '83 (ATTY)
AHL, JOHN, mgt. syst. analyst, Samaritan Health Service, Phoenix, AZ '87 (MGMT)
AHL, RICHARD F., dir. plant serv., Phoenix Memorial Hospital, Phoenix, AZ '87 (ENG)
AHLES, CAROL A., RN, vice-pres. nrsg., Memorial Hospital of Taylor County, Medford, WI '80 (NURS)
AHLFIELD, HAROLD E., dir. plant oper., Richland Memorial Hospital, Olney, IL '83 (ENG)
AHLGREN, CYNTHIA A., atty., East Hampton, NY '84 (ATTY)
AHLGRIM, PAMELA J., asst. dir. food serv., Cedars-Sinai Medical Center, Los Angeles, CA '80 (FOOD)
AHLSCHIER, JOSEPH B., pres., Asc Health System, O'Fallon, IL '58
AHNEN, CHRISTI D. GRIFFIN, plng. analyst, New England Deaconess Hospital, Boston, MA '84
AHNERT, CHRISTA B., dir. pers., Leland Memorial Hospital, Riverdale, MD '78 (PERS)
AHO, ELIZABETH, RN, vice-pres. spec. nrsg., Lee Memorial Hospital, Fort Myers, FL '81 (NURS)
AHO, MARY JO, dir. educ. serv., Houston Medical Center, Warner Robins, GA '80 (EDUC)
AHO, NANCY A., dir. soc. serv., Freeport Memorial Hospital, Freeport, IL '78 (SOC)
AHRENS, DEBORAH, RN, head nrs. outpatient, Corpus Christi Osteopathic Hospital, Corpus Christi, TX '86 (AMB)
AHRENS, GEORGE, dir. plant, Missouri Baptist Hospital, St. Louis, MO '71 (ENG)
AHRENS, LYNN I., dir. mktg. and advertising, Adventist Health System-Eastern and Middle America, Shawnee Mission, KS '84 (PR) (PLNG)
AHTANS, JAMES M., coor. trng., Children's Hospital Medical Center, Akron, OH '84 (EDUC)
AIHARA, FLORENCE H., spec. asst. to chief exec. off., St. Francis Medical Center, Honolulu, HI '83 (RISK)
AIKEN, JOYCE W., dir. vol. serv., Lewisville Memorial Hospital, Lewisville, TX '86 (VOL)
AIKMAN, EMILYA, RN, dir. nrsg. serv., Clinton Regional Hospital, Clinton, OK '79 (NURS)
AINA, LEONA, dir. qual. assur. and risk mgt., Pacific Presbyterian Medical Center, San Francisco, CA '85 (RISK)
AINLAY, CHARLES W., atty., Goshen General Hospital, Goshen, IN '70 (ATTY)
AINORA, CATHERINE A., asst. exec. dir., Newark Beth Israel Medical Center, Newark, NJ '76 (PLNG)
AINSWORTH-PETERSON, BONNIE L., asst. adm. nrsg. serv., Children's Mercy Hospital, Kansas City, MO '85 (NURS)
AINSWORTH, THOMAS H. JR., MD, Carmel Valley, CA '73 (LIFE)
AIRD, EILEEN BERGIN, vice-pres. oper., Hackensack Medical Center, Hackensack, NJ '79
AITKEN, BONNIE J., dir. matl. mgt., Antelope Valley Hospital Medical Center, Lancaster, CA '85 (PUR)
AJAMIAN, LOIS R., student, Boston University, Boston, MA '86 (PLNG)
AKE, SUSAN M., dir. soc. serv., Community Hospital of Bedford, Bedford, OH '85 (SOC)

AKER, G. COLBURN, pres., Aker Associates, Inc., Washington, DC '85 (PR)
AKER, GLENN A., owner and consult., Health Facility Planning, Fort Worth, TX '69 (PLNG)
AKERS, ARLENE J., RN, dir. nrsg., Northwest Hospital, Seattle, WA '82 (NURS)
AKERS, MARLYN, dir. qual. assur. and risk mgt., Lewis-Gale Hospital, Salem, VA '84 (RISK)
AKIF, JOSEPH I., student, California State College, Bakersfield, CA '85
AKINS, LLOYD T., dir. biomedical serv., Athens Regional Medical Center, Athens, GA '86 (ENG)
AKLAN, JOHN C., dir. eng., Children's Specialized Hospital, Mountainside, NJ '84 (ENG)
AKRIDGE, HARVEY D., asst. dir. eng. and maint., United Hospital, Grand Forks, ND '83 (ENG)
AKRY, SHAUL, coor. mgt. eng., St. Vincent Medical Center, Los Angeles, CA '85 (MGMT)
AKSEL, EDWARD A., assoc. adm., St. Elizabeth Hospital, Utica, NY '53 (LIFE)
AKUI, JOSEPH K., supv. plant oper. and maint., Shriners Hospital for Crippled Children, Honolulu, HI '85 (ENG)
AL-AHMAD, ALI AHMAD, adm. dir., King Fahd Hospital, Al-Khobar, Saudi Arabia '83
AL-ARAYED, JAWAD SALIM, minister health, State of Bahrain, Manama Bahrain, Arabia '86
AL-FADEL, HASHEM ODEH, clin. eng., Project Hope, Cairo, United Arab Republic '86 (ENG)
AL-GASEER, MAJ. JAMILLA A., RN, prin. nrsg. off., Bahrain Defence Force Medical Service, Bahrain, Saudi Arabia '86 (NURS)
AL-JUMA'A, ADNAN SALEH, dir. med. oper., Arabian American Oil Company, Medical Department, Dhahran, Saudi Arabia '71
AL-KHALEDY, NOURY S., gen. mgr., Kama Enterprises, Inc., Portland, OR '83 (PERS)
AL-KOWSI, AHMED N., staff environ., King Faisal Specialist Hospital, Riyadh, Saudi Arabia '87 (CS)
AL-MANSOOR, ABDUL WAHAB, chief exec. off., Salmaniya Medical Center, Manama Bahrain, Arabia '86
AL-SANOUSI, MOHAMED O., vice-pres., Whittaker Saudi Arabia, Ltd., Riyadh, Saudi Arabia '82
ALA, MOHAMMAD, prof., California State University, Los Angeles, CA '87 (MGMT)
ALAM, TAREK, vice-pres. plng., Holy Cross Hospital, Silver Spring, MD '80 (PLNG)
ALANDER, ROSS P., Tampa General Hospital, Tampa, FL '80 (PERS)
ALATON, KALEV, prin. arch., Kalev Alaton Architect, Van Nuys, CA '85 (ENG)
ALBA, TIMOTHY J., mgt. eng., SunHealth Corporation, Charlotte, NC '84 (MGMT)
ALBACHTEN, DAVID R., pres., Health Line Systems, Inc., San Diego, CA '85 (PR) (PLNG)
ALBANETTI, JESSIE B., RN, dir. adm. serv., St. Mary's Hospital, Waterbury, CT '83 (NURS)
ALBANO, DAVID, dir. pers. serv., Wake Medical Center, Raleigh, NC '86 (PERS)
ALBANO, MICHAEL JAMES, asst. vice-pres. and natl. mgr., American International Companies Consultants, Inc., Boston, MA '86 (RISK)(AMB)
ALBANO, SUSAN D., assoc. plng., Hartford Hospital, Hartford, CT '86 (PLNG)
ALBER, ANN M., Casselberry, FL '75 (SOC)
ALBERGHENE, MARGUERITE F., dir., Walthamweston Hospital and Medical Center, Waltham, MA '78 (VOL)
ALBERS, RONNA HOFFMANN, dir. educ., Munson Medical Center, Traverse City, MI '86 (EDUC)
ALBERSON, CONNIE M., dir. in-service educ., Union County General Hospital, New Albany, MS '81 (EDUC)
ALBERT, BEVERLY, dir. soc. serv., St. Clare's -Riverside Medical Center, Denville, NJ '78 (SOC)
ALBERT, JOHN G., dir. clin. serv., Lynn Hospital, Lynn, MA '81
ALBERT, LAURIE A., dir. ped. lung disease, American Lung Association of Iowa, Des Moines, IA '85 (EDUC)
ALBERT, NANCY MARIE, nrs. mgr. outpat and sr. alliance, Huron Road Hospital, Cleveland, OH '87 (AMB)
ALBERT, SHARON F., dir. mktg. and dev., Doctors Hospital, New York, NY '82 (PLNG)
ALBERT, SPENCER H., dir. commun., Lenox Hill Hospital, New York, NY '64 (PR)
ALBERT, STEVEN W., atty., St. Joseph Hospital and Health Center, Lorain, OH '83 (ATTY)
ALBERT, TERRA K., dir. pers., Otsego Memorial Hospital, Gaylord, MI '86 (PERS)
ALBERT, TERRY P., consult. prod. improve prog., Health and Welfare Canada, Ottawa, Ont., Canada '87 (MGMT)
ALBERTI, ANNE M., RN, asst. vice-pres. nrsg., Newton-Wellesley Hospital, Newton, MA '84 (NURS)
ALBERTS, JERRY L., dir. dev. and commun. rel., Wheeling Hospital, Wheeling, WV '81 (PR)
ALBERTS, PATRICK J., adm. asst. and planner, Monongahela Valley Hospital, Monongahela, PA '85 (PLNG)
ALBERTSON, JOSEPH L. JR., atty., New Rochelle Hospital Medical Center, New Rochelle, NY '70 (ATTY)
ALBIN, LINDA E., PhD, vice-pres. human res., Barnert Memorial Hospital Center, Paterson, NJ '86 (PERS)
ALBORN, JOSEPH A., asst. adm., Tri-City Medical Center, Oceanside, CA '85 (MGMT)
ALBOSTA, JANE R., mgr. corp. nrs. recruitment serv., Harper Hospital, Detroit, MI '83 (PERS)
ALBRECHT, SUSAN M., mgr. oper., Brigham and Women's Hospital, Boston, MA '85 (FOOD)
ALBRECHT, WILLIAM R., atty., Dover General Hospital and Medical Center, Dover, NJ '75 (ATTY)
ALBREKTSON, ERIK, risk mgr., Jewish Hospital, Louisville, KY '86 (RISK)
ALBRIGHT, DOUGLAS E., atty., Overlake Hospital Medical Center, Bellevue, WA '83 (ATTY)
ALBRITTON, ALTHEA B., RN, dir. nrsg., Cypress Hospital, Lafayette, LA '85 (NURS)
ALCABES, JOSEPH, vice-pres. oper., Bronx-Lebanon Hospital Center, Concourse Division, Bronx, NY '73 (ENG)
ALCARAZ, FRANK T., vice-pres. mgt. serv., Germantown Hospital and Medical Center, Philadelphia, PA '78 (MGMT)
ALCAZAR, CARLA J., vice-pres. mktg. and plng., Csj Health System of Wichita, Wichita, KS '82 (PLNG)
ALCEE, DONNA L., asst. vice-pres. nrsg., Zurbrugg Memorial Hospital, Willingboro, NJ '85 (NURS)
ALCON, SONJA L., dir. soc. work, Hanover General Hospital, Hanover, PA '72 (SOC)
ALCORN, CLYDE W., mgr. matl., Valley Regional Hospital, Claremont, NH '83 (PUR)
ALDEN, BARBARA, pat. rep., Clara Maass Medical Center, Belleville, NJ '78 (PAT)
ALDEN, JANE E., coor. staff dev., Clinton Memorial Hospital, Wilmington, OH '85 (EDUC)
ALDER, JONATHAN L., atty., Manion Alder and Cohen, Pittsburgh, PA '73 (ATTY)
ALDER, MARIBETH, dir. mktg., Pocatello Regional Medical Center, Pocatello, ID '85 (PR)
ALDERMAN, SHIRLEY, dir. vol. serv., Erlanger Medical Center, Chattanooga, TN '78 (VOL)
ALDERS, KATHRYN K., diet. spec., Proficient Food Company, Arlington, TX '84
ALDRED, JIM D., dir. mktg., Shawnee Mission Medical Center, Shawnee Mission, KS '73 (PR)
ALDRICH, NANCY E., vice-pres., Telecom Management Corporation, Needham Heights, MA '81 (ENG)
ALDRICH, RONALD R., pres., Franciscan Health System, Chadds Ford, PA '64
ALDRICH, WAYNE A., dir. matl. mgt., Allen Memorial Hospital, Waterloo, IA '76 (CS)
ALDRIDGE, BRYANT T., pres., Nash General Hospital, Rocky Mount, NC '67
ALDRIDGE, GERALD W., dir. plng. and bus. dev., Michigan Health Care Corporation, Detroit, MI '81 (PLNG)
ALDRIDGE, MARCIA E., dir. mgt. eng., High Point Regional Hospital, High Point, NC '84 (MGMT)
ALDRIDGE, MARSHA W., Birmingham, AL '82 (PLNG)
ALDSTADT, DAVID E., vice-pres., Mercy Hospital, Columbus, OH '86 (PR)
ALECCI, CARMEN BRUCE, vice-pres. and sr. oper. off., New Rochelle Hospital Medical Center, New Rochelle, NY '69
ALEKSANDROWICZ, LENA IORIO, RN, vice-pres., St. Elizabeth's Hospital of Boston, Boston, MA '69 (NURS)
ALER, ZOE Z., mgr. sterile proc., Union Memorial Hospital, Baltimore, MD '78 (CS)
ALES, EDIE, adm. emer. medicine, St. Paul-Ramsey Medical Center, St. Paul, MN '87 (AMB)
ALESHIRE, BRENT C., dir. soc. serv., New Berlin Memorial Hospital, New Berlin, WI '83 (SOC)
ALESKO, MICHAEL T., mgr. media rel., Providence Medical Center, Portland, OR '84 (PR)
ALESSI, ROBERTA M., serv. dir. lab. medicine, Children's Hospital National Medical Center, Washington, DC '85
ALEWINE, CHARLES M., dir. food serv., Jo Ellen Smith Medical Center, New Orleans, LA '83 (FOOD)
ALEXANDER, A. ANN, dir. soc. serv., Blue Bird Circle Children Clinic, Houston, TX '76 (SOC)
ALEXANDER, BRUCE F., asst. dir. eng. serv., Champlain Valley Physicians Hospital Medical Center, Plattsburgh, NY '85 (ENG)
ALEXANDER, CONNI K., dir. diet. serv., Delnor Hospital, St. Charles, IL '81 (FOOD)
ALEXANDER, DEAN, mgr., Medi-Plus Laboratories, Division of Arvey Corporation, Chicago, IL '78 (CS)
ALEXANDER, G. RUMAY, dir. nrsg. prog., Tennessee Hospital Association, Nashville, TN '80 (NURS)
ALEXANDER, GEORGE A., coor. off. productivity analyst, James M. Jackson Memorial Hospital, Miami, FL '86 (MGMT)
ALEXANDER, LT. COL. GUS NICHOLAS JR., MSC USA, chief nrsg., sci. div., Academy of Health Sciences, Fort Sam Houston, TX '75
ALEXANDER, JAMES R., sr. vice-pres. fin., Tennessee Hospital Association, Nashville, TN '81 (MGMT)
ALEXANDER, JEFFERY M., atty., Strong Memorial Hospital Rochester University, Rochester, NY '83 (ATTY)
ALEXANDER, JOANN, RN, assoc. adm. nrsg., Charleston Area Medical Center, Charleston, WV '85 (NURS)
ALEXANDER, JOYCE, mgr. pat. rep., Lutheran Hospital of Fort Wayne, Fort Wayne, IN '80 (PAT)
ALEXANDER, KATHRYN L., dir. mktg., Riverview Hospital, Noblesville, IN '85 (PLNG)
ALEXANDER, KATHY M., dir. vol. serv., Craig Hospital, Englewood, CO '85 (VOL)
ALEXANDER, KEITH S., student, Boston University Health Management Programs, Boston, MA '86 (PLNG)
ALEXANDER, MARGO, dir. nutr. and food serv., Long Island College Hospital, Brooklyn, NY '79 (FOOD)
ALEXANDER, MICHAEL J., mgt. adv., Michael J. Alexander, Inc., Pittsburgh, PA '67
ALEXANDER, PETER J., exec. dir., Achievement Homes, Inc., Warren, MI '76 (PLNG)
ALEXANDER, RAYMOND B., asst. mgr. eng. serv., Lee Memorial Hospital, Fort Myers, FL '85 (ENG)
ALEXANDER, RAYMOND S., Merion, PA '54 (LIFE)
ALEXANDER, REBECCA M., mgt. eng., Acute Care Affiliates, Berkeley, CA '84 (MGMT)
ALEXANDER, SHARON L., dir. market plng., Forbes Health System, Pittsburgh, PA '85 (PLNG)
ALEXANDER, STEPHANIE C., mgt. eng. and consult., Durham County General Hospital, Durham, NC '86 (MGMT)
ALEXANDER, THOMAS L., vice-pres., Mecon Associates, Union City, CA '86 (MGMT)
ALEXANDER, W. DON, partner, Ernst and Whinney, Oklahoma City, OK '79
ALEXANDER, WENDIE, adm. asst., Aspen Valley Hospital District, Aspen, CO '85 (PERS)
ALEXANDROWICZ, THOMAS E., supv. environ., Episcopal Hospital, Philadelphia, PA '87 (ENVIRON)
ALEXSANIAN, H. R., chief soc. work serv., Audie L. Murphy Memorial Veterans Hospital, San Antonio, TX '76 (SOC)
ALF, MARILYN E., dir. soc. serv., Scripps Memorial Hospital, La Jolla, CA '82 (SOC)
ALFANO, JOHN, asst. dir. educ. serv., Florida Hospital Association, Orlando, FL '86 (ENVIRON)(EDUC)
ALFEREZ, SOCORRO B., RN, mgr. cent. serv., Walther Memorial Hospital, Chicago, IL '84 (CS)
ALFF, KATHLEEN K., dir. pat. rep., Lutheran Medical Center, Wheat Ridge, CO '86 (PAT)
ALFIREVIC, JAY, mgr., Ernst and Whinney, Chicago, IL '83 (MGMT)
ALFORD, CAROL J., dir. pub. rel., Flowers Hospital, Dothan, AL '86 (PR)
ALFORD, GEOFFREY, dir. matl. mgt., St. Francis Medical Center, La Crosse, WI '86 (PUR)
ALFORD, MARGARET M., asst. dir. nutr. serv., Monitor Systems Group, Inc., McLean, VA '83 (FOOD)
ALFORD, MARY L., RN, dir. nrsg., New Hanover Memorial Hospital, Wilmington, NC '84 (NURS)
ALFORD, PHYLLIS S., RN, student, Memphis State University, Memphis, TN '87 (AMB)
ALFREDSON, LINDA S., dir. alternative delivery syst., Kenosha Hospital and Medical Center, Kenosha, WI '86 (PERS)
ALGERI, WILLIAM F., dir. pers., Sheehan Memorial Hospital, Buffalo, NY '69 (PERS)
ALI, MOHAMED S., adm. asst., St. Mary Hospital, Quincy, IL '78 (MGMT)
ALI, SYED A., dir. plant oper., Medical Center Del Oro Hospital, Houston, TX '82 (ENG)
ALIBRANDO, ELLEN, dir. pub. rel., St. Mary's Hospital, Passaic, NJ '82 (PR) (PLNG)
ALIBRIO, EUGENE P., dir. food serv., Elliot Hospital, Manchester, NH '83 (FOOD)
ALISEDA, LUPE M., dir. soc. serv., Beeville Memorial Hospital, Beeville, TX '86 (SOC)
ALISEO, CAROLYN T., dir. cent. serv., Brookhaven Memorial Hospital Medical Center, Patchogue, NY '82 (CS)
ALKEN, KATLEEN B., sr. marketer, Jeanes Health System, Jenkintown, PA '87 (PLNG)
ALKIRE, HARRIETTE, dir. soc. serv., Camden-Clark Memorial Hospital, Parkersburg, WV '80 (SOC)
ALLABEN, ARTHUR B., adm., Scott County Memorial Hospital, Scottsburg, IN '52 (LIFE)
ALLARD, JACQUELINE, RN, coor. educ., St. Anne's Hospital, Fall River, MA '79 (EDUC)
ALLARD, SR. JOAN, adm. asst., Providence-St. Margaret Health Center, Kansas City, KS '80 (RISK)
ALLBACH, DEBORAH P., adm. dir. nrsg., Harris Methodist -HEB, Bedford, TX '84 (EDUC)(NURS)
ALLBURN, BETTY, dir. vol. serv., Saint Vincent Health Center, Erie, PA '79 (VOL)
ALLEMAN, D. SCOTT, RN, asst. adm. nrsg., Sumner Memorial Hospital, Gallatin, TN '80 (NURS)
ALLEMAN, DEBRA, mgr. matl., St. Mary's Hospital, Pierre, SD '87 (PUR)
ALLEMAN, JAMES M., dir. risk mgt., Riverside Medical Center, Kankakee, IL '80 (RISK)
ALLEMAN, MARILYN J., mgr. diet., Memorial Hospital, York, PA '86 (FOOD)
ALLEN-RYAN, ANN, sr. vice-pres., Lutheran Medical Center, Brooklyn, NY '84 (RISK)
ALLEN, BARBARA R., supv. cent. serv., Newton-Wellesley Hospital, Newton, MA '78 (CS)
ALLEN, BERNICE L., student, Program and Bureau of Hospital Administration, University of Michigan, Ann Arbor, MI '83
ALLEN, BRUCE F., atty., Sutter Community Hospitals, Sacramento, CA '68 (ATTY)
ALLEN, BRUCE H., PhD, prof., School of Business, San Francisco State University, San Francisco, CA '84 (PLNG)
ALLEN, C. TOD, vice-pres., Charlton Memorial Hospital, Fall River, MA '86 (PLNG)
ALLEN, CANDACE V., dir. plng. and mktg., Piedmont Hospital, Atlanta, GA '83 (PLNG)
ALLEN, CATHERINE B., RN, dir. nrsg. serv., E. A. Conway Memorial Hospital, Monroe, LA '86 (NURS)
ALLEN, CATHY L., RN, dir. nrsg., National Hospital for Orthopaedics, Arlington, VA '79 (NURS)
ALLEN, CORY JO, dir. educ. serv., Watsonville Community Hospital, Watsonville, CA '86 (EDUC)
ALLEN, CYNTHIA ROSS, coor. guest rel., Portsmouth General Hospital, Portsmouth, VA '87 (PAT)
ALLEN, DAVID J., mgt. eng., La Crosse Lutheran Hospital, La Crosse, WI '84 (MGMT)
ALLEN, DAVID S., atty., Methodist Hospital of Indiana, Indianapolis, IN '81 (ATTY)
ALLEN, DON B., atty., Holy Cross Hospital, Salt Lake City, UT '80 (ATTY)
ALLEN, E. MARK, dir. hskpg., St. Francis Medical Center, Cape Girardeau, MO '86 (ENVIRON)
ALLEN, ELISABETH, dir. vol., Hahnemann University Hospital, Philadelphia, PA '79 (VOL)
ALLEN, ERNEST, dist. mgr., Ohio Hospital Insurance Company, Lyndhurst, OH '87 (RISK)
ALLEN, FERN A., dir. vol. and pub. rel., Grady Memorial Hospital, Chickasha, OK '81 (VOL)
ALLEN, HENRY S. JR., atty., American College of Surgeons, Chicago, IL '75 (ATTY)
ALLEN, HERBERT J., dir. soc. work and asst. prof., University of Cincinnati Hospital, Cincinnati, OH '71 (SOC)
ALLEN, JAMES D., maint. eng., Ouachita Hospital, Camden, AR '68 (ENG)
ALLEN, JAMES S., asst. vice-pres., Erlanger Medical Center, Chattanooga, TN '85
ALLEN, JAMES W., atty., Naval Hospital, Bremerton, WA '86 (ATTY)
ALLEN, JENNIFER A., dir. commun. rel., Rutherford Hospital, Rutherfordton, NC '85 (PR) (PLNG)
ALLEN, JESSIE M., dir. pers., Southwest Detroit Hospital, Detroit, MI '87 (PERS)

ALLEN, KATHY ANN, sr. consult., Ernst and Whinney, Cleveland, OH '84
ALLEN, KAY I., dir. educ., Cottonwood Hospital Medical Center, Murray, UT '86 (EDUC)
ALLEN, KENNETH C., dir. pur., Deaconess Hospital, Cincinnati, OH '81 (PUR)
ALLEN, LORETTA J., RN, supv. cent. serv., Island Hospital, Anacortes, WA '83 (CS)
ALLEN, MARA L., supv. food serv., Baptist Memorial Hospital-Huntingdon, Huntingdon, TN '86 (FOOD)
ALLEN, MARIDEL, chief plng. off., Newport Hospital, Newport, RI '84 (PLNG)
ALLEN, MARY E., asst. dir. vol. serv., Freehold Area Hospital, Freehold, NJ '86 (VOL)
ALLEN, MERLE W., exec. dir., Memorial Medical Center Foundation, Springfield, IL '71 (PR)
ALLEN, NIKKI J., RN, dir. nrsg., Shawnee Mission Medical Center, Shawnee Mission, KS '86 (NURS)
ALLEN, NORA M., vice-pres. human res., South Bend Medical Foundation, South Bend, IN '86 (PERS)
ALLEN, NORMAN J., asst. dir. hskpg., Saint Mary Hospital, Langhorne, PA '86 (ENVIRON)
ALLEN, NORMAN L., student, University of Oklahoma, Health Sciences Center, Oklahoma City, OK '85 (PLNG)
ALLEN, PAMELA A., pres., Healthcare Education Systems, Greensboro, NC '71 (EDUC)
ALLEN, PAMELA P., RN, vice-pres. nrsg., St. Vincent Memorial Hospital, Taylorville, IL '86 (NURS)
ALLEN, PATRICIA I., dir. commun. health educ., University Medical Center Southern Nevada, Las Vegas, NV '86 (PR)
ALLEN, PATRICIA, dir., St. Joseph's Home Care, Mount Clemens, MI '86 (AMB)
ALLEN, PATRICIA, asst. mgr. ins., Avon Products, Inc., New York, NY '87 (RISK)
ALLEN, PAUL, qual. assur. and risk consult.-healthcare, Marsh and McLennan, Toronto, Ont., Canada '86 (RISK)
ALLEN, PEARL E., asst. mgr. matl., St. Luke's General Hospital, Bellingham, WA '83 (CS)
ALLEN, R. LOIS, RN, dir. surg. nrsg., Robert Packer Hospital, Sayre, PA '79 (NURS)
ALLEN, RICHARD L., Ogden, UT '76
ALLEN, RICHARD L., dir. med. logistics mgt., U. S. Air Force Hospital, APO New York, NY '76 (PUR)
ALLEN, RICHARD M., asst. dir. pers., Providence Hospital, Washington, DC '78 (PERS)
ALLEN, ROBIN B., RN, dir. surg. and amb. care nrsg., Albert Einstein Medical Center, Philadelphia, PA '85 (NURS)
ALLEN, RONALD J., pur. agt., Southeastern General Hospital, Lumberton, NC '80 (PUR)
ALLEN, ROSE M., consult. and pharm., Pharmacy Information Services, Euclid, OH '86
ALLEN, SABRINIA R., student, Roosevelt University, Chicago, IL '87 (AMB)
ALLEN, SHARON, mgr. util. review, Arkansas Blue Cross and Blue Shield, Inc., Little Rock, AR '76
ALLEN, SIMEON, dir. cent. stores and distrib., Northeast Alabama Regional Medical Center, Anniston, AL '77 (CS)
ALLEN, STEPHEN D., dir. pers., Huron Memorial Hospital, Bad Axe, MI '80 (PERS)
ALLEN, STEVEN E., adm. asst., Dover General Hospital and Medical Center, Dover, NJ '84
ALLEN, THOM, mgr. environ. serv., Long Beach Community Hospital, Long Beach, CA '86 (ENVIRON)
ALLEN, THOMAS B. JR., arch., Vanderbilt University Hospital, Nashville, TN '78
ALLEN, WALTER P., adm., Human Resource Institute, Brookline, MA '51 (LIFE)
ALLEN, WAYNE A., mgt. eng., Desert Hospital, Palm Springs, CA '86 (MGMT)
ALLEN, WILEY H., chief eng., Baldwin County Hospital, Milledgeville, GA '80 (ENG)
ALLEN, WILLIAM, asst. adm. and risk mgr., Mercy Hospital, Cedar Rapids, IA '86 (RISK)
ALLEN, ZULINE M., dir. soc. work serv., Pottstown Memorial Medical Center, Pottstown, PA '80 (SOC)
ALLENSTEIN, SALLY, dir. diet., Marquette General Hospital, Marquette, MI '78 (FOOD)
ALLEVATO, JOHN A., dir. environ. serv., United Hospital Center, Clarksburg, WV '80 (PLNG)(PUR)
ALLEY, FREDERICK DON, chief exec. off., Brooklyn Hospital-Caledonian Hospital, Brooklyn, NY '64
ALLEY, LEWIS INGRAM, adm., Community Hospital, Fairfax, MO '76
ALLEY, RICHARD G. SR., chief eng., Mount Desert Island Hospital, Bar Harbor, ME '78 (ENG)
ALLEYNE, ESMOND A., mgr., Main Hurdman, New York, NY '85 (ENG)
ALLFORD, RAY, exec. dir., Ross Associate Consultants, Fruitland Park, FL '67 (PLNG)(RISK)
ALLGEYER, ALBERT, dir. hskpg., Jewish Hospital of Cincinnati, Cincinnati, OH '86 (ENVIRON)
ALLGIER, LESLIE L., dir. spec. proj., Mercy San Juan Hospital, Carmichael, CA '86 (PLNG)
ALLHUSEN, H. JOHN, mgr. syst. eng., Rochester General Hospital, Rochester, NY '83 (MGMT)
ALLIEGRO, DEBRA C., mgr., Ernst and Whinney, Boston, MA '87 (MGMT)
ALLIEN, CHARLES, dir. bldg. serv., Dumont Masonic Home, New Rochelle, NY '86 (ENVIRON)
ALLIGOOD, JIM, mgr. hskpg. and ldry., Bay Medical Center, Bay City, MI '86 (ENVIRON)
ALLIK, DONALD, dir. eng. and maint., Sinai Hospital of Baltimore, Baltimore, MD '85 (ENG)
ALLIKER, STANFORD ARNOLD, exec. dir., Levindale Hebrew Geriatric Center, Baltimore, MD '69
ALLINSON, RUSSEL, dir. pharm. and matl., Shadyside Hospital, Pittsburgh, PA '87 (PUR)
ALLISEN, ELORA, dir. diet., Holy Cross Hospital, Calgary, Alta., Canada '79 (FOOD)
ALLISON, ALVIN W. JR., asst. adm., Brownsville General Hospital, Brownsville, PA '83 (PLNG)
ALLISON, ESTON, chief fin. off., Chippewa Valley Hospital, Durand, WI '87 (RISK)
ALLISON, FRED M., (ret.), Bells, TN '64
ALLISON, GENE N., dir. eng., Jack County Hospital, Jacksboro, TX '86 (ENG)
ALLISON, GLADYS KAY, RN, dir. nrsg., Woodland Park Hospital, Portland, OR '83 (NURS)
ALLISON, JAMES A., dir. plant serv., Clay County Hospital, Flora, IL '87 (ENG)
ALLISON, JAMES W., atty., Presbyterian Hospital, Charlotte, NC '82 (ATTY)
ALLISON, JOEL T., exec. dir., Northwest Texas Hospital, Amarillo, TX '72
ALLISON, MELODY, RN, dir. nrsg., HCA Park West Medical Centers, Knoxville, TN '79 (NURS)
ALLISON, PATRICIA A., mgr. pers., Cookeville General Hospital, Cookeville, TN '74 (PERS)
ALLISON, ROGER W., dir. outpatient serv., Tarrant County Hospital District, Fort Worth, TX '87 (AMB)
ALLISON, SARAH E., vice-pres., Methodist Rehabilitation Center, Jackson, MS '80 (NURS)
ALLISON, SHARLEEN S., dir. staff dev., Fauquier Hospital, Warrenton, VA '86 (EDUC)
ALLISON, SHERYLL, dir. risk mgt. and med. rec., St. Anthony Center, Houston, TX '86 (RISK)
ALLIVATO, JEANNE M., risk mgt. spec., Abbott-Northwestern Hospital, Minneapolis, MN '85 (RISK)
ALLMAN, JOHN J. JR., dir. psychoneurotic-soc. serv., Daniel Freeman Memorial Hospital, Inglewood, CA '72 (SOC)
ALLMAN, MARY, RN, dir. nrs., Doctors Hospital, Sarasota, FL '78 (NURS)
ALLMAN, REBECCA C., dir. plng. and mgt. eng., Frankford Hospital of the City of Philadelphia, Philadelphia, PA '80 (PLNG)
ALLMAN, ROGER J., assoc. dir., Community Hospitals of Indiana, Indianapolis, IN '80
ALLRED, DANIEL M., atty., St. Mark's Hospital, Salt Lake City, UT '81 (ATTY)
ALLRED, EDGAR D., dir. phys. plant, Lovelace Medical Center, Albuquerque, NM '80 (ENG)
ALLRED, LYNN K., dir. vol. serv., Raritan Bay Medical Center, Perth Amboy, NJ '86 (VOL)
ALLUM, EDWARD L., adm. food serv., San Joaquin General Hospital, Stockton, CA '76 (FOOD)
ALLYN, JAMES R., dir. pub. rel. serv., Samaritan Health Center, Detroit, MI '86 (PR)
ALMADA, CHARLES L., dir. environ. serv. and hskpg., Torrance Memorial Hospital, Torrance, CA '86 (ENVIRON)
ALMASY, HELEN, dir. educ., Monongalia General Hospital, Morgantown, WV '80 (EDUC)
ALMDALE, JUDITH A., student, Program in Health Administration, College of St. Francis, Joliet, IL '81
ALMEDA, ROMULO M., pres., Almeda and Associate, Seattle, WA '83 (ENG)
ALMEIDA, HUGO A., adm., East Los Angeles Children and Youth Clinic, Los Angeles, CA '74
ALMEN, MARY C., market planner, Lutheran Hospitals and Home Society, Fargo, ND '84 (PLNG)
ALMENARA, GUILLERMO, MD, Lima, Peru '55 (HON)
ALMENAS, JULIUS, dir. cent. sup., St. John's Riverside Hospital, Yonkers, NY '75 (CS)
ALMENDINGER, RUTH ANN, coor. vol. and aux., St. Ann's Hospital of Columbus, Westerville, OH '85 (VOL)
ALMGREN, GUNNAR ROBERT, dir. soc. serv., Northwest Hospital, Seattle, WA '79 (SOC)
ALMLI, CONNIE, dir. pub. rel., Cascade Valley Hospital, Arlington, WA '79 (PR)
ALMOND, LINDA K., RN, asst. adm. pat. serv., Huron Regional Medical Center, Huron, SD '81 (NURS)
ALMONEY, JOHN B., mgr. mgt. eng., York Hospital, York, PA '84 (MGMT)
ALMONRODE, SHARON, atty., William Beaumont Hospital, Royal Oak, MI '83 (ATTY)
ALMQUIST, N. JAN, atty., California Hospital Association, Sacramento, CA '82 (ATTY)
ALOISIO, MARY, dir. pur. and stores, Booth Memorial Medical Center, Flushing, NY '80 (PUR)
ALONGE, GERALD P., Horizon Health Group, Meadville, PA '76 (PLNG)
ALONSO, SHERLYL L., RN, actg. adm. nrsg. serv., Mercy Hospital, Miami, FL '85 (NURS)
ALPER, NORMAN H., dir. facil. plng., St. Francis Hospital, Wilmington, DE '79 (PLNG)
ALPERN, ANDREA G., atty., Charter Suburban Hospital, Mesquite, TX '87 (ATTY)
ALPERT, DEBI, student, Graduate School of Management, New School for Social Research, New York, NY '85
ALPERT, ELAINE L., coor. vol. serv., Sinai Hospital of Baltimore, Baltimore, MD '86 (VOL)
ALPERT, ROCHELLE D., atty., Providence Hospital, Oakland, CA '87 (ATTY)
ALPHIN, JOANNE, RN, dir. nrsg., L. W. Blake Memorial Hospital, Bradenton, FL '75 (NURS)
ALSAGER, MARY M., RN, vice-pres., Alexian Brothers Hospital San Jose, San Jose, CA '81 (NURS)
ALSCHULER, SAM, atty., Copley Memorial Hospital, Aurora, IL '71 (ATTY)
ALSEDEK, ALBERT EUGENE, asst. vice-pres., Lancaster General Hospital, Lancaster, PA '67 (RISK)
ALSENTZER, WILLIAM J. JR., atty., Phoenix Baptist Hospital and Medical Center, Phoenix, AZ '78 (ATTY)
ALSETH, KAREN, dir. educ. serv., St. Mary's Medical Center, Duluth, MN '71 (EDUC)
ALSMAN, WILLIAM H., dir. eng., St. Joseph Hospital, Lexington, KY '81 (ENG)
ALSPACH, JOANN GRIF, clin. nrs. educator-critical care nrsg., Clinical Center National Institute of Health, Bethesda, MD '83 (EDUC)
ALSTON, CLINTON A., partner and natl. dir. info. syst. consult., Ernst and Whinney, Cleveland, OH '86 (MGMT)
ALSTON, LEILA J., asst. vice-pres., Baptist Medical Center, Little Rock, AR '87 (AMB)
ALSTON, PHILLIP S. JR., mgt. eng., Jackson-Madison County General Hospital, Jackson, TN '84 (MGMT)
ALSTON, RICHARD D., dir. pers., St. Thomas Hospital, Nashville, TN '86 (PERS)
ALSUP, WILLIAM DEWITT, atty., Memorial Medical Center, Corpus Christi, TX '73 (ATTY)
ALT, HELENE A., atty., Texas Medical Association, Austin, TX '85 (ATTY)
ALT, JAMES, dir. clin. eng., Meriter Hospital, Madison, WI '81 (ENG)
ALTANO, ROSEMARY, RN, vice-pres., Community Medical Center, Scranton, PA '83 (NURS)
ALTENBURG, THOMAS, vice-pres. health care mktg., McDonald Davis and Associates, Inc., Milwaukee, WI '81 (PR)
ALTEPETER, JOANNE C., instr., St. Elizabeth's Hospital, Belleville, IL '86 (EDUC)
ALTHAUSER, DONALD K., atty., Hermann Area District Hospital, Hermann, MO '79 (ATTY)
ALTMAN, DIANE C., dir. soc. serv., Group Health Eastside Hospital, Redmond, WA '81 (SOC)
ALTMAN, JEAN, coor. pub. rel., El Camino Hospital, Mountain View, CA '80 (PR)
ALTMAN, MARIE C., mgr. matl. and supv. cent. serv. room, Community Memorial Hospital, Lisbon, ND '84 (CS)
ALTMAN, MARTHA E., dir. soc. serv., Northbay Medical Center, Fairfield, CA '82 (SOC)
ALTMAN, MURRAY L., assoc. vice-pres., Michael Reese Hospital and Medical Center, Chicago, IL '63 (PUR)
ALTMAN, RENEE, pat. rep., Peninsula Hospital Center, Far Rockaway, NY '80 (PAT)
ALTMAN, SCOTT A., dir. pub. rel., Ukiah Adventist Hospital, Ukiah, CA '85 (PR)
ALTOMARI, DEBORAH A., coor. aging serv., Jeanes Community Health Services-Vital Age, Rockledge, PA '86 (VOL)
ALTON, MARGARET ANN, RN, asst. adm. behavioral health nrsg., St. Luke's Medical Center, Phoenix, AZ '79 (NURS)
ALTOPIEDI, ALICE, dir. soc. serv., Charles Camsell Hospital, Edmonton, Alta., Canada '86 (SOC)
ALTOPIEDI, JOSEPH, mgr. soc. serv., University of Alberta Hospitals, Edmonton, Alta., Canada '82 (SOC)
ALTRINGER, MARY G., dir. vol. serv., Metropolitan Medical Center, Minneapolis, MN '76 (VOL)
ALTSCHULER, J. ANGELA, dir. vol. serv., Hackensack Medical Center, Hackensack, NJ '82 (VOL)
ALUISE, DOMINIC J., dir. data serv., Magee-Womens Hospital, Pittsburgh, PA '84 (MGMT)
ALUISE, TINA M., account mgr., Technegrowth, Inc., Milford, OH '82 (PR)
ALVAREZ, EDWARD M., atty., Alexian Brothers Hospital San Jose, San Jose, CA '73 (ATTY)
ALVAREZ, ERNESTO, dir. soc. work, Calvary Hospital, Bronx, NY '84 (SOC)
ALVAREZ, FELIX, pur. agt., Labette County Medical Center, Parsons, KS '70 (PUR)
ALVAREZ, ROBERT, dir. plant oper., Southwestern General Hospital, El Paso, TX '85 (ENG)
ALVATOR, MAJ. MARILYN HELENE, MSC USA, exec. off., U. S. Army-Fort Detrick, Frederick, MD '80 (PERS)
ALVES, SHARON M., coor. benefits, St. Joseph Hospital, Nashua, NH '86 (PERS)
ALVIN, HEATHER, supv. soc. work, Metropolitan Hospital-Springfield Division, Springfield, PA '86 (SOC)
ALVIN, WILLIAM RICHARD, adm. dir., Metropolitan Hospital and Health Centers, Detroit, MI '69
ALVORD, PATRICIA A., mgr. educ., St. Joseph's Hospital, Stockton, CA '86 (EDUC)
ALWARD, RUTH R., RN, asst. prof. nrsg. adm., Hunter-Bellevue School of Nursing, New York, NY '85 (NURS)
ALWELL, AUDREY S., coor. mktg. commun., St. Paul-Ramsey Medical Center, St. Paul, MN '86 (PR)
ALWELL, JAMES PAUL, vice-pres., Christ Hospital, Jersey City, NJ '76
ALWOOD, WILLIAM J., coor. safety and security, Carlisle Hospital, Carlisle, PA '86 (ENG)
ALY, FEKREYA, asst. dir. soc. serv., University of Kentucky Medical Center, Lexington, KY '76 (SOC)
ALZHEIMER, VERONICA C., dir. educ., Zurbrugg Memorial Hospital -Riverside, Riverside, NJ '85 (EDUC)
AMABILE, MARY, RN, coor. cent. serv., St. Francis Hospital of New Castle, New Castle, PA '84 (CS)
AMACHER, JOAN M., dir. risk mgt., Burnham Hospital, Champaign, IL '82 (RISK)
AMANI, RICK, adm. fellow, Kaiser Foundation Hospital-Sunset, Los Angeles, CA '83
AMAR, MICHEL, dir. hosp. serv., Mount Sinai Hospital Center, Ste-Agathe Des Monts, Que., Canada '85 (RISK)
AMATO, LOUIS P., vice-pres. human res., St. Mary Hospital, Hoboken, NJ '84
AMBERG, DAVID M., atty., Butterworth Hospital, Grand Rapids, MI '76 (ATTY)
AMBERGER, LARRY D., atty., Cary Medical Center, Caribou, ME '84 (ATTY)
AMBERS, FLOREID, oper. analyst, Healthlink, Portland, OR '87 (MGMT)
AMBROSE, GEORGE T. JR., RN, asst. dir. nrsg., evening shift, York Hospital, York, PA '83 (NURS)
AMBROSE, HARRY D. JR., atty., West Jersey Hospital, Northern Division, Camden, NJ '75 (ATTY)
AMBROSE, JAMES J., dir. maint., Harmarville Rehabilitation Center, Pittsburgh, PA '79 (ENG)
AMBROSE, WILLIAM T., dir. plant oper., AMI West Alabama Hospital, Northport, AL '79 (ENG)
AMBROSECCHIA, JOHN P., adm., Christian Hospital Northwest, Florissant, MO '79
AMBROSINI, V. J., vice-pres. human res., St. Joseph's Hospital and Medical Center, Paterson, NJ '85 (PERS)
AMEIGH, ANN Y., RN, adm. dir. nrsg., Geisinger Medical Center, Danville, PA '86 (NURS)
AMELOTTE, ALBERT J., mgr. matl., Graphic Controls Corporation, Buffalo, NY '85 (PUR)
AMENDOLA, WILLIAM, asst. dir. plant serv., Society of the New York Hospital, New York, NY '87 (ENG)
AMES, BEATRICE A., RN, dir. nrsg. educ. and res., Department of Health and Hospitals, Boston, MA '86 (NURS)

AMES, CHARLES F., dir. soc. serv., Augusta General Hospital, Augusta, ME '74 (SOC)
AMES, CRAIG M., vice-pres. oper., Metropolitan Medical Center, Minneapolis, MN '78
AMES, KATHERINE M., (ret.), Bath, ME '41 (LIFE)
AMES, NANCY B., dir. pub. rel., St. Joseph Hospital, Nashua, NH '77 (PR)
AMEY, ANNETTE LYNN, student, Graduate Program in Health Systems Management, Rush University, Chicago, IL '86
AMEY, VICTOR D., vice-pres. sup. serv., Peninsula General Hospital Medical Center, Salisbury, MD '78 (ENG)
AMEZAGA, CLEMENTE CARLOS, dir. plant oper., Cedars Medical Center, Miami, FL '79 (ENG)
AMICARELLA, HENRY, (ret.), Longmont, CO '50 (LIFE)
AMICO, MILDRED C., dir. pat. rel., Brooklyn Hospital-Caledonian Hospital, Brooklyn, NY '73 (PAT)
AMIDON, ROGER L., PhD, prof. and chm. pub. health adm., College of Health, University of South Carolina, Columbia, SC '65
AMMERMAN, JULIE, pat. rep., United Hospital, St. Paul, MN '79 (PAT)
AMMONS, DONNA M., pers. interviewer, East Jefferson General Hospital, Metairie, LA '85 (PERS)
AMON, JEANNINE F., RN, vice-pres. pat. serv., Riverview Hospital Association, Crookston, MN '79 (NURS)
AMORMINO, SAM, commun. eng., Vista United Telecommunications, Lake Buena Vista, FL '86 (ENG)
AMOROSI, JOSEPH A., eng., Chapel Manor Nursing and Rehabilitation Center, Philadelphia, PA '86 (ENG)
AMOROSO, LOUIS A., partner, Arthur Andersen and Company, Chicago, IL '80 (MGMT)
AMOS, JAMES L., vice-pres. and mgr., Bethesda Oak Hospital, Cincinnati, OH '71
AMOS, LINDA K., RN, assoc. dir. nrsg., University of Utah Hospital, Salt Lake City, UT '85 (NURS)
AMPARAN, OSCAR L., pres., Medplus, El Paso, TX '74
AMSDEN, JOHN R., chief eng., Campbell County Memorial Hospital, Gillette, WY '82 (ENG)
AMSLER, BARRY L., mgr. mktg., Access Battery, Butler, NJ '85 (ENG)
AMUNDSEN, JUDITH, RN, dir. acute nrsg. serv., Cleveland Metropolitan General Hospital, Cleveland, OH '86 (NURS)
AMUNDSON, PAULETTE, RN, dir. amb. care, Prairie Lakes Hosptial, Watertown, SD '80 (NURS)(AMB)
ANABLE, EDWARD W., dir. facil. dev., Flagstaff Medical Center, Flagstaff, AZ '82 (ENG)
ANCIN, LAWRENCE D., dir. eng. and maint., St. Joseph's Hospital and Medical Center, Paterson, NJ '83 (ENG)
ANDELMAN, PHYLLIS, adm. vol. serv., Rahway Hospital, Rahway, NJ '79 (VOL)
ANDER-MONAGHAN, STEPHANY J., RN, dir. med. and surg. nrsg., St. Joseph Hospital, Orange, CA '85 (NURS)
ANDERS, MAJ. MICHAEL T., MSC USA, cmdr., 2nd 421st Medical Company-Aa, APO New York, NY '83
ANDERSEN, BETTY L., supv. cent. serv., Queen of the Valley Hospital, Napa, CA '84 (CS)
ANDERSEN, CHRISTOPHER A., dir. plant oper., Meadowcrest Hospital, Gretna, LA '81 (ENG)
ANDERSEN, DAVID L., dir. plng., Amsco Group, Erie, PA '84 (PLNG)
ANDERSEN, EILEEN RUTH, RN, coor. pat. serv., St. Francis Memorial Hospital, San Francisco, CA '67 (PAT)
ANDERSEN, ELLEN, clin. soc. worker and coor. qual. assur., U. S. Public Health Service Alaska Native Medical Center, Anchorage, AK '85 (SOC)
ANDERSEN, ERLING G., mgr. syst. dev., Presbyterian Hospital in the City of New York, New York, NY '85 (MGMT)
ANDERSEN, MARK L., dir. mgt., Price Waterhouse, Detroit, MI '77 (MGMT)
ANDERSEN, MARSHA O'CHESKEY, dir. pub. rel., Presbyterian Intercommunity Hospital, Whittier, CA '84 (PR) (PLNG)
ANDERSEN, NANCY A., dir. nutr. serv., Pottstown Memorial Medical Center, Pottstown, PA '77 (FOOD)
ANDERSEN, PAUL, asst. dir. eng., Beth Israel Medical Center, New York, NY '83 (ENG)
ANDERSEN, VOGEL F., oper. room staff nrs. and charge nrs. cent. sterile sup., U. S. Air Force Medical Center Wright-Patterson, Dayton, OH '86 (CS)
ANDERSON-DELP, JULIE E., adm. coor. center for women and child, Toledo Hospital, Toledo, OH '85
ANDERSON, ALLAN R., asst. adm., Swedish Covenant Hospital, Chicago, IL '66
ANDERSON, ANITA K., coor. soc. serv., Brookside Hospital, San Pablo, CA '87 (SOC)
ANDERSON, ANN, RN, pat. rep., Cottonwood Hospital Medical Center, Murray, UT '85 (PAT)
ANDERSON, ANNA, dir. environ. serv., United Hospitals Medical Center, Newark, NJ '86 (ENVIRON)
ANDERSON, ARTHUR D., Skokie, IL '80 (ENG)
ANDERSON, ARTHUR WILLIAM, (ret.), Galesburg, IL '41 (LIFE)
ANDERSON, ARVID W., dir. plant oper. and maint., Mercy Medical Center and Hospital, Williston, ND '85 (ENG)
ANDERSON, BARBARA, pat. rep., Columbus Hospital, Chicago, IL '77 (PAT)
ANDERSON, BARRY S., dir. educ., St. Alexius Medical Center, Bismarck, ND '84 (EDUC)
ANDERSON, BETH H., instr. med. rec. adm., University of Texas, School of Allied Health Sciences, Medical Branch, Galveston, TX '80 (RISK)
ANDERSON, BETTY JANE, atty., American Medical Association, Chicago, IL '68 (ATTY)
ANDERSON, BETTY, actg. supv. cent. serv., French Hospital, San Francisco, CA '84 (CS)
ANDERSON, BOBBIE LADONNA, RN, dir. nrs., Memorial Hospital, Frederick, OK '82 (NURS)
ANDERSON, CAROL L., dir. food serv., Village Green Retirement Center, Greensboro, NC '80 (FOOD)
ANDERSON, CAROLYN ANNE, RN, dir. critical care, Providence Hospital, Mobile, AL '80 (NURS)
ANDERSON, CAROLYN C., dir. pat. rel., Park Nicollet Medical Center, St. Louis Park, MN '86 (PAT)
ANDERSON, CAROLYN MARIE, coor. pat. rel., Milwaukee County Medical Complex, Milwaukee, WI '86 (PAT)
ANDERSON, CHARLES JAY, adm. corp. and affiliate res., Tucson Medical Center, Tucson, AZ '76
ANDERSON, CHARLES R., dir. maint. and eng., St. Luke's Hospital-West, Chesterfield, MO '73 (ENG)
ANDERSON, CHRISTINE A., student, Program in Hospital Administration, Concordia College, Moorhead, MN '85
ANDERSON, CLARE, dir. urgent care serv., Phoenix General Hospital, Phoenix, AZ '87 (AMB)
ANDERSON, CLAUDIA S., dir. pub. rel., Hospital for Sick Children, Toronto, Ont., Canada '85 (PR)
ANDERSON, CORA E., dir. corp. commun., Csj Health System, Wichita, KS '82 (PR)
ANDERSON, CYNTHIA, dir. pub. rel., Missouri Hospital Association, Jefferson City, MO '86 (PR)
ANDERSON, DALE W., sect. mgr., Baxter Travenol Laboratories, Deerfield, IL '86 (MGMT)
ANDERSON, DAVID B., coor. educ. and trng., Taylor Hospital, Ridley Park, PA '79 (EDUC)
ANDERSON, DAVID C., mgr. mkt, Illinois Bell Telephone Company, Chicago, IL '86 (ENG)
ANDERSON, DAVID G., supv. bldg. craftsmen, University of Illinois at Chicago, Chicago, IL '84 (ENG)
ANDERSON, DAVID J., consult., Peat, Marwick, Mitchell and Company, Richmond, VA '80 (MGMT)
ANDERSON, DAVID S., assoc. adm., Michiana Community Hospital, South Bend, IN '70
ANDERSON, DEBORAH A. GOWER, Fort Leavenworth, KS '82
ANDERSON, DEBRA KAY, dir. plng. and mktg., Portsmouth General Hospital, Portsmouth, VA '82 (PR) (PLNG)
ANDERSON, DIANE D., RN, vice-pres. nrsg., Memorial Hospital, Burlington, WI '86 (NURS)
ANDERSON, DIANE M., assoc. adm., University Hospital, Seattle, WA '80 (NURS)
ANDERSON, DONNA J., sr. vice-pres., Veterans Administration Medical Center, Iron Mountain, MI '80 (FOOD)
ANDERSON, DOUGLAS C., vice-pres. mktg. and plng., Santa Monica Hospital Medical Center, Santa Monica, CA '77
ANDERSON, CAPT. DOUGLAS E., MSC USAF, rmo intern, U. S. Air Force Medical Service, APO New York, NY '84
ANDERSON, ELAINE F., RN, assoc. adm. and dir. nrsg., Charlton Memorial Hospital, Fall River, MA '81 (NURS)
ANDERSON, ERIC W., dir. food and nutr. serv., Reading Rehabilitation Hospital, Reading, PA '86 (FOOD)
ANDERSON, EVELYN PEARL, dir. soc. serv., Taylor County Hospital, Campbellsville, KY '85 (SOC)
ANDERSON, FRED, exec. dir., Hospital Purchasing Services, Inc., Portsmouth, VA '84 (PUR)
ANDERSON, GAIL S., RN, dir. daily oper., St. Joseph Medical Center, Burbank, CA '86 (EDUC)
ANDERSON, GERRI P., assoc. dir. human res., Good Samaritan Hospital, Cincinnati, OH '85 (PERS)
ANDERSON, GLEN E., dir. plant oper., Holmes Regional Medical Center, Melbourne, FL '84 (ENG)
ANDERSON, GLENN L., constr. eng., Health Facilities Services, Arkansas Department of Health, Little Rock, AR '83 (ENG)
ANDERSON, HAROLD L., atty., North Dakota Hospital Association, Grand Forks, ND '68 (ATTY)
ANDERSON, HARRY F., chm. and chief exec. off., Anderson, Mikos Architect, Ltd., Chicago, IL '86 (PLNG)
ANDERSON, HARRY, atty., Lake Medical Center, Leesburg, FL '81 (ATTY)
ANDERSON, HERBERT A., (ret.), Branford, CT '50 (LIFE)
ANDERSON, HERBERT H., atty., Emanuel Hospital and Health Center, Portland, OR '77 (ATTY)
ANDERSON, HOWARD F., dir. soc. serv., South Side Hospital of Pittsburgh, Pittsburgh, PA '70 (SOC)
ANDERSON, IRIS I., asst. adm., Framingham Union Hospital, Framingham, MA '46 (LIFE)
ANDERSON, IVAN D., exec. dir., Memorial Hospital of Topeka, Topeka, KS '52 (LIFE)
ANDERSON, JAMES B., dir. ins. and risk mgt., Tampa General Hospital, Tampa, FL '80 (RISK)
ANDERSON, JAMES W., dir. biomedical serv., Mary Washington Hospital, Fredericksburg, VA '84 (ENG)
ANDERSON, JANE K., dir. pub. and media rel., AMI Doctors' Hospital, Lanham, MD '86 (PR)
ANDERSON, JEROME T., consult., Biomedical Consulting Services, Corona Del Mar, CA '81 (ENG)
ANDERSON, JOAN HUMPHREY, dir. phys. rel., Baptist Hospital, Pensacola, FL '84 (PR)
ANDERSON, JOANN, RN, assoc. exec. dir. nrsg., Humana Hospital -Lexington, Lexington, KY '86 (NURS)
ANDERSON, JOE A., dir. maint., White River Medical Center, Batesville, AR '72 (ENG)
ANDERSON, JOHN G., mgr. health facil. plng., Hospital Corporation of America, Nashville, TN '85 (PLNG)
ANDERSON, JOHN H., mgr. matl., Cape Canaveral Hospital, Cocoa Beach, FL '69 (PUR)
ANDERSON, JOHN J., (ret.), Arlington, VA '46 (LIFE)
ANDERSON, JOHN K. JR., chief fin. off., Baptist Medical Center, Jacksonville, FL '84
ANDERSON, JOHN R., dir. mgt. eng., Lutheran Healthcare Network, Mesa, AZ '84 (MGMT)
ANDERSON, JOHN V., dir. plng. and mktg., Howard Community Hospital, Kokomo, IN '84 (PLNG)
ANDERSON, JULIA, dir. soc. serv., Gulf Coast Hospital, Fort Walton Beach, FL '87 (SOC)
ANDERSON, KATHLEEN F., interim dir. soc. serv., Children's Medical Center, Dayton, OH '84 (SOC)
ANDERSON, KEN E., dir. mgt. eng., Methodist Medical Center of Illinois, Peoria, IL '84 (MGMT)
ANDERSON, LARRY, dir. pub. affairs and mktg., Methodist Hospital, St. Louis Park, MN '79 (PR)
ANDERSON, LAURA, RN, dir. nrsg. serv., Scioto Memorial Hospital, Portsmouth, OH '68 (NURS)
ANDERSON, LETA N., RN, dir. nrsg., Swedish American Hospital, Rockford, IL '83 (NURS)
ANDERSON, LINDA K., dir. food serv., Bess Kaiser Medical Center, Portland, OR '79 (FOOD)
ANDERSON, LINDA P., dir. plng. and mktg., Saint Joseph's Hospital, Atlanta, GA '86 (PR) (PLNG)
ANDERSON, LOWELL C., dir. pers. serv., Community Memorial Hospital, Cheboygan, MI '74 (PERS)
ANDERSON, LUCINDA S., RN, asst. dir. nrsg. educ., West Virginia University Hospital, Morgantown, WV '85 (NURS)
ANDERSON, MARCIA RENEE, RN, dir. pat. serv., Golden Valley Health Center, Golden Valley, MN '80 (NURS)
ANDERSON, MARILYN, dir. qual. assur., Parkland Memorial Hospital, Dallas, TX '85 (RISK)
ANDERSON, MARION, dir. dev., Peekskill Hospital, Peekskill, NY '86 (PR)
ANDERSON, MARTIN E., adm., Ionia County Memorial Hospital, Ionia, MI '69
ANDERSON, MARY A., assoc. dir. nrsg., Lutheran Hospital -LaCrosse, La Crosse, WI '87 (AMB)
ANDERSON, MARY A., dir. food serv., St. Mary's Hospital, Galesburg, IL '73 (FOOD)
ANDERSON, MARYLYN P., supv. cent. serv., St. Anne's Hospital, Chicago, IL '84 (CS)
ANDERSON, MATTHEW O., pres. and chief exec. off., Marlborough Hospital, Marlborough, MA '70 (PLNG)
ANDERSON, NANCY B., vice-pres. corp. oper., General Health Services, Inc., Madison, WI '76 (PLNG)
ANDERSON, MAJ. NAOMI J., asst. chm. nrsg. educ., APO New York, NY '85 (EDUC)
ANDERSON, NORMAN P., vice-pres. commun. affairs, St. Jude Hospital, Inc., Fullerton, CA '81 (PR)
ANDERSON, ODIN W., prof. sociology, University of Wisconsin, Madison, WI '78
ANDERSON, ONITA K., assoc. dir., Bellevue Hospital Center, New York, NY '80 (CS)
ANDERSON, PAMELA REAKOFF, instr.-prof. dev. and res., Washington Hospital Center, Washington, DC '86 (EDUC)
ANDERSON, PATRICIA A., RN, dir. nrsg., LaRabida Children's Hospital, Chicago, IL '86 (NURS)
ANDERSON, PATRICIA G., pat. adv., Moss Rehabilitation Hospital, Philadelphia, PA '84 (PAT)
ANDERSON, PATRICIA J., RN, dir. nrsg., Green Hospital of Scripps Clinic, La Jolla, CA '87 (NURS)
ANDERSON, PATRICIA J., RN, dept. head med. floor and actg. dir. pat. care serv., St. Peter's Community Hospital, Helena, MT '86 (NURS)
ANDERSON, PATTI J., vice-pres. mem. and pub. rel., Minnesota Hospital Association, Minneapolis, MN '82 (PR)
ANDERSON, PEGGY S., health care consult., Laurel, MS '84 (RISK)
ANDERSON, PEHR H., adm., Rose Hospital, Rome, NY '53 (LIFE)
ANDERSON, PHILIP D., adm. dir. rad., St. Mary's Medical Center, Knoxville, TN '82 (PLNG)
ANDERSON, R. JANE, dir. corp. commun., Saint Vincent Health Center, Erie, PA '80 (PR)
ANDERSON, RHONDA, RN, adm. nrsg., Good Samaritan Medical Center, Phoenix, AZ '80 (NURS)
ANDERSON, ROGER F., asst. dir. plant oper., Deborah Heart and Lung Center, Browns Mills, NJ '84 (ENG)
ANDERSON, RUTH, dir. hskpg. and ldry. serv., Hermann Hospital, Houston, TX '86 (ENVIRON)
ANDERSON, SCOTT R., pres., North Memorial Medical Center, Robbinsdale, MN '63
ANDERSON, SHARON, adm. asst. pat. rel., Proctor Community Hospital, Peoria, IL '86 (RISK)
ANDERSON, STEPHEN P., dir. plant oper., Methodist Hospital-Central Unit, Memphis, TN '84 (ENG)
ANDERSON, SUSAN J., dir. diet. serv., Waconia Ridgeview Hospital, Waconia, MN '83 (FOOD)
ANDERSON, SUSAN L., dir. vol. serv., Fallston General Hospital, Fallston, MD '82 (VOL)
ANDERSON, THEDA K., coor. pub. rel. and mktg., De Paul Hospital, Cheyenne, WY '82 (PR)
ANDERSON, THELMA, dir. food serv., Memorial Hospital, South Bend, IN '81 (FOOD)
ANDERSON, VELMA M., dir. clin. soc. work, Los Angeles County-University of Southern California Medical Center, Los Angeles, CA '82 (SOC)
ANDERSON, VIRGINIA L., RN, dir. amb. care, Logan Regional Hospital, Logan, UT '87 (AMB)
ANDERSON, W. RICHARD, adm., Lander Valley Regional Medical Center, Lander, WY '79
ANDERSON, WAYNE, dir. syst. dev., University of Alabama Hospital, Birmingham, AL '73 (MGMT)
ANDERSON, WILLIAM A., dir. eng. serv., Providence Memorial Hospital, El Paso, TX '78 (ENG)
ANDERSON, WILLIAM C. III, atty., Rush-Presbyterian-St. Luke's Medical Center, Chicago, IL '81 (ATTY)
ANDERSON, WILLIAM D., dir. plant serv., Rahway Hospital, Rahway, NJ '78 (ENG)
ANDERSON, WILLIAM R., supv. maint., Saint Vincent Hospital, Worcester, MA '81 (ENG)
ANDERTON, LINDA, dir. amb. clin. serv., St. Thomas Hospital, Nashville, TN '87 (AMB)
ANDLER, BARBARA, dir. med. rec., Hahnemann Hospital, Boston, MA '86 (RISK)
ANDRA, RAYMOND G., dir. pers., Citizens General Hospital, New Kensington, PA '86 (PERS)
ANDRE, NICK J., dir. plant and eng., Hampton General Hospital, Hampton, VA '80 (ENG)
ANDREAE, ALAN B., supv. plant serv., Ely-Bloomenson Community Hospital, Ely, MN '81 (ENG)
ANDREAS, DAVID W., atty., William Newton Memorial Hospital, Winfield, KS '81 (ATTY)
ANDREAS, MICHAEL B., pres., Deaconess Service Corporation, Evansville, IN '80
ANDREONI, ARMAND J., asst. dir. plng., F. G. McGaw Hospital, Loyola University, Maywood, IL '85 (PLNG)
ANDREOPOULOS, SPYROS G., dir. office commun., Stanford University Medical Center, Stanford, CA '64 (PR)
ANDREW, BRIAN LEE, atty., Metlife Health Care Management Corporation, St. Louis, MO '82 (ATTY)

ANDREW, CHARLES H. JR., atty., Dr. John M. Meadows Memorial Hospital, Vidalia, GA '80 (ATTY)
ANDREW, WILLIAM F., pres., William F. Andrew and Associates, Winterhaven, FL '68 (MGMT)
ANDREWS, ALANA G., dir. pub. rel., St. Vincent Charity Hospital and Health Center, Cleveland, OH '84 (PR)
ANDREWS, ANNE K., mgr. emp., Park City Hospital, Bridgeport, CT '83 (PERS)
ANDREWS, BARBARA F., dir. soc. serv., Robert Wood Johnson University Hospital, New Brunswick, NJ '80 (SOC)
ANDREWS, C. NORMAN, (ret.), Mercer Island, WA '39 (LIFE)
ANDREWS, CAROL M., dir. vol. serv., Little Company of Mary Hospital, Evergreen Park, IL '85 (VOL)
ANDREWS, CAROLYN, instr. staff educ., Trumbull Memorial Hospital, Warren, OH '72 (EDUC)
ANDREWS, DONALD A., dir. tech. serv., American Compensation Association, Scottsdale, AZ '69 (PERS)
ANDREWS, DONALD R., mgr., Ernst and Whinney, St. Louis, MO '84 (PLNG)
ANDREWS, ERNEST C., dir. soc. serv., Baptist Hospital of Southeast Texas, Beaumont, TX '80 (SOC)
ANDREWS, FREDERIC H., adm. emer. medicine, Rhode Island Hospital, Providence, RI '87 (AMB)
ANDREWS, GWENDOLYN, RN, dir. nrsg., North Carolina Baptist Hospital, Winston-Salem, NC '75 (NURS)
ANDREWS, JAN E., dir. vol. serv., Altoona Hospital, Altoona, PA '86 (PR)(VOL)
ANDREWS, JEANNE A., dir. pur., Lancaster-Fairfield Community Hospital, Lancaster, OH '81 (PUR)
ANDREWS, JEFFREY A., atty., Alamance County Hospital, Burlington, NC '81 (ATTY)
ANDREWS, JENNIFER, supv. clin. soc. work, St. Mary Medical Center, Long Beach, CA '86 (SOC)
ANDREWS, JOAN L., pres., Visiting Nurse Service, Inc., Akron, OH '87 (AMB)
ANDREWS, JOHN H., assoc. commun. rel., Eastern Maine Medical Center, Bangor, ME '86 (PR)
ANDREWS, JOHN H., dir. health care serv., Coopers and Lybrand, Detroit, MI '71
ANDREWS, KEVIN C., supv. soc. serv., Westlake Community Hospital, Melrose Park, IL '86 (SOC)
ANDREWS, LINDA SUE, dir. guest serv. and phys. mktg., Humana Hospital -Medical City Dallas, Dallas, TX '85 (PR)(PAT)
ANDREWS, MARVIN H., sr. vice-pres., Tennessee Hospital Association, Nashville, TN '86 (PLNG)
ANDREWS, MICHAEL C., dir. pub. rel., The Shrine of North America, Tampa, FL '82 (PR)
ANDREWS, MICHAEL K., dir. pub. rel., Catawba Memorial Hospital, Hickory, NC '86 (PR)
ANDREWS, NORMAN JOSEF, adm., Clovis Community Hospital, Clovis, CA '76
ANDREWS, PAULA B., pers. adm., University of South Alabama Medical Center, Mobile, AL '85 (PERS)
ANDREWS, RAY, atty., New Britain General Hospital, New Britain, CT '84 (ATTY)
ANDREWS, RONALD T., mgr. cost center, Methodist Hospital of Indiana, Indianapolis, IN '85 (CS)
ANDREWS, WILLIAM H., (ret.), Cleveland, OH '52 (LIFE)
ANDREWS, WILLIAM H., dir. oper., Cigna Health Plan, Inc., San Diego, CA '73
ANDREWS, WILLIAM J., pres., Licking Memorial Hospital, Newark, OH '79
ANDREWS, WILLIAM RUSSELL, vice-pres., Holyoke Hospital, Holyoke, MA '72 (MGMT)(PUR)
ANDRING, GAIL E., dir. diet., Community Memorial Hospital and Convalescent and Rehabilitation Unit, Winona, MN '86 (FOOD)
ANDRIOLE, RICHARD C., sr. vice-pres., Cooley Dickinson Hospital, Northampton, MA '70
ANDRO, RONALD J., prog. dir. same day serv., Mary Hitchcock Memorial Hospital, Hanover, NH '84
ANELLO, PATRICIA J., dir. soc. serv. and cont. care, Windham Community Memorial Hospital, Willimantic, CT '85 (SOC)
ANGALICH, DANIEL T., mgt. eng., Ohio Valley Medical Center, Wheeling, WV '86 (MGMT)
ANGEL, JEAN K., dir. educ., Floyd Medical Center, Rome, GA '85 (EDUC)
ANGELL, JOSEPH P., Touche Ross and Company, Chicago, IL '81 (MGMT)
ANGELL, KATHRYN A., dir. plng., New England Medical Center, Boston, MA '84 (PLNG)
ANGELO, ANTHONY J., prod. mgr., Ppg Biomedical Systems, Pleasantville, NY '83 (ENG)
ANGELO, CHRISTOPHER E., atty., Buena Park Community Hospital, Buena Park, CA '86 (ATTY)
ANGELO, LEWIS E., dir. med. serv., Department of the Navy, Bureau of Medicine and Surgery, Washington, DC '82
ANGELO, RALPH R., assoc. dir., Veterans Administration Medical Center, Tuskegee, AL '74
ANGELONE, ELAINE M., RN, asst. vice-pres. nrsg., Newton-Wellesley Hospital, Newton, MA '86 (NURS)
ANGELOS, NICHOLAS E., dir. constr., Pacific Health Resources, Glendale, CA '86 (ENG)
ANGELOVICH, JOCELYN M., dir. vol., New Milford Hospital, New Milford, CT '86 (VOL)
ANGENY, MARK G., dir. pers., Hospital Central Service, Inc., Allentown, PA '82 (PERS)
ANGEVINE, KRYSTAL S., dir. soc. serv., Floyd Memorial Hospital, New Albany, IN '81 (SOC)(PAT)
ANGIULO, CINDY L., RN, dir. nrsg.-amb. serv., University Hospital, Seattle, WA '84 (NURS)
ANGLE, DONALD F., MD, pres., Andico, Shreveport, LA '87 (AMB)
ANGLIN, DENNIS R., chief eng., Hutchinson Community Hospital, Hutchinson, MN '83 (ENG)
ANGOOD, JOHN B., pres., Angood and Associates, San Jose, CA '83 (MGMT)
ANGOTT, GARY M., asst. contr., Rex Hospital, Raleigh, NC '84
ANGULO, ANNA, coor. qual. assur. and risk mgt., Centro Espanol Memorial Hospital, Tampa, FL '86 (RISK)
ANGULO, JESUS, dir. pub. rel. and mktg., AMI Kendall Regional Medical Center, Miami, FL '82 (PR)
ANN, SR. BARBARA, vice-pres. plng., Mary Immaculate Hospital, Newport News, VA '87 (AMB)
ANNAS, JANET E., adm. dir. food and nutr. serv., Baptist Medical Center, Columbia, SC '86 (FOOD)
ANNECCHIARICO, FRANK J., assoc. lab. adm. path. and lab. medicine, Woodhull Medical and Mental Health Center, Brooklyn, NY '79
ANNECHARICO, MARY ALICE, coor. info. syst., Jersey Shore Medical Center, Neptune, NJ '85 (MGMT)
ANNICQ, CHARLES, dir., Gasthuiszusters Van Antwerpen, Antwerpen, Belgium '80
ANNIS, CAROL M., dir. food serv., Laurelwood Hospital, The Woodlands, TX '84 (FOOD)
ANNIS, DEAN A., asst. dir., New England Deaconess Hospital, Boston, MA '73
ANNIS, HAROLD E., asst. vice-pres. matl. mgt., American Healthcare Management, Inc., Dallas, TX '86 (PUR)
ANSELL, JAMES R., atty., St. Mary's Hospital, Galveston, TX '74 (ATTY)
ANSLEY, CHARLES E., consult., Ernst and Whinney, Cleveland, OH '80
ANSLEY, D'ARCY M., RN, vice-pres. and consult., Affiliated Hosptial Systems, Houston, TX '82 (NURS)
ANSTY, ROBERT J., dir. pers., North Adams Regional Hospital, North Adams, MA '81 (PERS)
ANTAL, SUSAN D., dir. pers., York Hospital, York, ME '80 (PERS)
ANTHONY, DIANE S., dir. commun., Forbes Health System, Pittsburgh, PA '82 (PR)
ANTHONY, HARRIS C., dir. mktg., Vicksburg Medical Center, Vicksburg, MS '86 (PR) (PLNG)
ANTHONY, LEONARD S., (ret.), Naranja, FL '80
ANTHONY, MARCIE, Chicago, IL '84 (PUR)
ANTHONY, MARK R., vice-pres., Providence Hospital, Southfield, MI '78
ANTHONY, MARY K., RN, dir. critical care specialties, St. Vincent Charity Hospital and Health Center, Cleveland, OH '84 (NURS)
ANTHONY, MICHAEL F., atty., Hinsdale Hospital, Hinsdale, IL '79 (ATTY)
ANTHONY, SUSAN E., mktg. mgr., Sisters of Charity Health Care Systems, Cincinnati, OH '85 (PR)
ANTIN, JUDITH, dir. soc. serv., Tallahassee Community Hospital, Tallahassee, FL '84 (SOC)
ANTOCI, BARBARA A., mgr. matl., Shriners Hospitals for Crippled Children, Chicago, IL '81 (CS)
ANTOINE, MARY POWERS, atty., Sutter Community Hospitals, Sacramento, CA '85 (ATTY)
ANTOLICK, JOHN H., dir. food serv., Community Medical Center, Scranton, PA '83 (FOOD)
ANTOLIK, PAUL M., dir. pers., Hamot Medical Center, Erie, PA '82 (PERS)
ANTON, DAVID, consult., Pensacola, FL '47 (LIFE)
ANTON, RAY, sr. consult., Peat, Marwick, Mitchell and Company, Walnut Creek, CA '80 (MGMT)
ANTON, RICHARD E., student, Program in Health Service Administration, School of Health Professions, Governors State University, Park Forest South, IL '86
ANTONELLI, PATTIE COLLINS, dir. pub. rel., Josiah B. Thomas Hospital, Peabody, MA '82 (PR)
ANTONETTE, SR. M., RN, dir. nrsg., St. Mary's Hospital, Athens, GA '67 (NURS)
ANTONIK, JOAN M., dir. food serv., Resurrection Nursing Pavilion, Park Ridge, IL '80 (FOOD)
ANTONIO, ANTHONY A. DI, dir. environ. serv., Norwalk Community Hospital, Norwalk, CA '86 (ENVIRON)
ANTONIOU, SOPHIA, RN, asst. adm. nrsg., Concord Hospital, Concord, NH '84 (NURS)
ANTONOPOULOS, ADAM T., dir. food serv., Research Medical Center, Kansas City, MO '78 (FOOD)
ANTONSEN, JOHN R., dir. hskpg., Ravenswood Hospital Medical Center, Chicago, IL '86 (ENVIRON)
ANTRIM, RALPH C. JR., adm., Soldiers and Sailors Memorial Hospital, Wellsboro, PA '70
ANTUNA, CLAUDETTE S., dir. soc. work, Children's Hospital and Medical Center, Seattle, WA '75 (SOC)
ANTWORTH, MAUREEN R., RN, dir. surg. nrsg. serv., University Community Hospital, Tampa, FL '82 (NURS)
ANZANO, ROSEMARIE, RN, pat. adv., General Hospital Center at Passaic, Passaic, NJ '86 (PAT)
APAKA, TSUENKO, chief soc. work serv., Veterans Administration, Op Clinic, Honolulu, HI '83 (SOC)
APGOOD, CHARLOTTE, assoc. adm., Olympic Memorial Hospital, Port Angeles, WA '86 (RISK)
APILADO, PATSY D., dir. pers., Truckee Meadows Hospital, Reno, NV '85 (PERS)
APKE, DAMIAN J., mgr. oper. health, Deloitte Haskins and Sells, Chicago, IL '72 (PLNG)
APLINGTON, DAVID R., atty., St. Clement Hospital, Red Bud, IL '84 (ATTY)
APONTE, JOSEPH A., adm., Valley Park Medical Center, Canoga Park, CA '61 (PR)
APONTE, THOMAS ANTHONY, mgr. critical care, St. Luke's-Roosevelt Hospital Center, New York, NY '85
APP, JOAN, RN, exec. asst., Saint Thomas Medical Center, Akron, OH '80
APPEL, DAVID B., asst. adm., Saint Luke's Hospital, Cleveland, OH '83
APPEL, PEGGY L., student, Program in Hospital and Health Care Administration, University of Minnesota, Minneapolis, MN '86
APPELGATE, BARBARA, acct. exec., Schrews and Associate, Waterloo, IA '86 (PR)
APPENZELLER, LENORE, RN, vice-pres. nrsg., St. Luke's-Roosevelt Hospital Center, New York, NY '77 (NURS)
APPLE, IRENE B., RN, dir. nrsg. serv., Duncan Regional Hospital, Duncan, OK '79 (NURS)
APPLEBEE, BARBARA J., dir. pers., Willamette Falls Hospital, Oregon City, OR '86 (PERS)
APPLEBY, HARVEY, mgr. textiles serv., Medical Center of Delaware, Wilmington, DE '86 (ENVIRON)
APPLEBY, KENNETH, sr. risk spec., Henry Ford Hospital, Detroit, MI '86 (RISK)
APPLEBY, MARY E., adm. diet., Polyclinic Medical Center, Harrisburg, PA '83 (FOOD)
APPLEGATE, KENDALL L., asst. dir. matl. mgt., hskpg. and receiving, Mercy Hospital, Portsmouth, OH '86 (ENVIRON)
APPLEGATE, RODNEY T., pres., Walla Walla General Hospital, Walla Walla, WA '87 (AMB)
APPLEGATE, STANLEY J., dir. biomedical electronics syst. and assoc. prof., Kettering Medical Center, Kettering, OH '79 (ENG)
APPLEGEET, CAROL J., dir. outpatient surg., Jewish Hospital Ambulatory Services, Inc., Louisville, KY '85 (NURS)(AMB)
APPLEYARD, MILTON H., pres., Harrisburg Hospital, Harrisburg, PA '61
APPOLONEY, PETER EDWARD, dir. matl. mgt., Craven County Hospital, New Bern, NC '82 (PUR)
APPOLONIO, DANIEL R., dir. eng., Metropolitan Hospital-Springfield Division, Springfield, PA '85 (ENG)
APRAHAMIAN, RONALD V., Tml, Inc., Great Falls, VA '68
APRO, JAN F., dir. risk mgt., Mercy Hospital, Hamilton, OH '80 (RISK)
APTER, ROBERT L., MD, dir. emer., United General Hospital, Sedro Woolley, WA '86 (AMB)
APUZZO, JOAN J., coor. cent. sup., Shriners Hospitals for Crippled Children, Chicago, IL '83 (CS)
AQUAVIA, JOANNE M., RN, supv. cent. sup., Broward General Medical Center, Fort Lauderdale, FL '79 (CS)
AQUINO, JEANINE A., adm. res., Booth Memorial Medical Center, Flushing, NY '83
AQUINO, REYNATO S. M., mgr. broadcast syst., Morton F. Plant Hospital, Clearwater, FL '86 (EDUC)
ARAK, SYDNEY F., vice-pres. and atty., Methodist Hospital of Indiana, Indianapolis, IN '83 (ATTY)
ARAKAKI, ROY M., chief telecommun., Queen's Medical Center, Honolulu, HI '78 (ENG)
ARANGIO, EDWARD M., asst. adm. mktg. and pub. rel., Memorial Hospital, Colorado Springs, CO '80 (PR)
ARAUJO, MARIANNE, RN, vice-pres. nrsg. and gen. adm., Mercy Hospital and Medical Center, Chicago, IL '71 (NURS)
ARBEITEL, BERNICE, dir. vol. serv., St. Francis Medical Center, Lynwood, CA '75 (VOL)
ARBITMAN, DEBORAH B., pres., Peabody Consulting Group, Beachwood, OH '81 (MGMT)
ARBLASTER, MARK D., supv. maint., United Community Hospital, Grove City, PA '86 (ENG)
ARBLE, CECILIA A., RN, dir. nrsg. serv., Suburban Community Hospital, Warrensville Heights, OH '83 (NURS)
ARBOGAST, CLAIRE S., dir. pub. rel., Good Samaritan Hospital, Cincinnati, OH '83 (PR)
ARBOGAST, DONNA K., dir. human res., Thomas Memorial Hospital, South Charleston, WV '83 (PERS)
ARBONA, GUILLERMO, MD, prof., University of Puerto Rico School of Medicine, San Juan, P.R. '63 (HON)
ARBUCKLE, JANET L., dir. med. soc. serv., Community Hospitals of Indiana, Indianapolis, IN '86 (SOC)
ARCANGELI, KATHRYN K., sr. mgt. eng., Baptist Medical Centers, Birmingham, AL '85 (MGMT)
ARCENTALES, DIANA O., asst. dir. vol. serv., Mount Sinai Medical Center, Miami Beach, FL '84 (VOL)
ARCH, VINCENT JR., dir. pers., Montgomery Hospital, Norristown, PA '86 (PERS)
ARCHAMBAULT, DENNIS J., dir. pub. rel., Detroit Receiving Hospital and University Health Center, Detroit, MI '82 (PR)
ARCHAMBO, LARRY, pur. agt., Chenango Memorial Hospital, Norwich, NY '86 (PUR)
ARCHER, ANN H., dir. cont. educ., Westminster-Canterbury, Richmond, VA '84 (EDUC)
ARCHER, DEBRA A., atty., Bluefield Community Hospital, Bluefield, WV '83 (ATTY)
ARCHER, HARVEY E., consult., Department of Hospital Administration, School of Medicine, University of North Carolina, Chapel Hill, NC '56
ARCHER, HOWARD J., adm., Community Hospital Schoharie County, Cobleskill, NY '59
ARCHER, SUSAN W., asst. dir. soc. serv., Newton-Wellesley Hospital, Newton, MA '81 (SOC)
ARCHIBALD, BECKY, dir. vol., Bethesda Hospital, Zanesville, OH '79 (VOL)
ARCHIBALD, MARGARET C., dir. vol., St. Agnes Hospital, White Plains, NY '83 (VOL)
ARCHILLES, LILLIAN E., RN, Knoxville, TN '74 (NURS)
ARCHOTE, REGINA LOWERY, pat. rep., United Medical Center, New Orleans, LA '86 (PAT)
ARCHUT, JOSEPH, partner, Mirick, Pearson and Batcheler, Philadelphia, PA '78
ARCIDIACONO, KAREN, assoc. counsel and risk mgr., Greater Southeast Community Hospital, Washington, DC '86 (RISK)
ARDNER, DAVID R., contr., Madigan Army Medical Center, Tacoma, WA '84
AREHART, F. MICHARL, adm. amb. care clin., Harborview Medical Center, Seattle, WA '87 (AMB)
ARENA, PHYLLIS D., asst. dir., University of Virginia Hospitals, Charlottesville, VA '87 (AMB)
ARENDS, CHARLES W., Winter Park, FL '56 (LIFE)
ARENDSEN, DIEDERIK A., prin., Arendsen Associates, North Vancouver, B.C., Canada '86 (PLNG)
ARENDT, DIANNA, RN, dir. nrsg. serv., St. Mary's Medical Center, Duluth, MN '75 (NURS)
ARENTH, LINDA M., RN, dir. nrsg., Johns Hopkins Hospital, Baltimore, MD '81 (NURS)
ARESCO, MARK R., med. adm., Hartford Insurance Group, Hartford, CT '75
AREY, BETTE, dir. soc. serv., Bristol Hospital, Bristol, CT '86 (SOC)
ARFORD, PATRICIA H., RN, asst. prof. nrsg. serv., Medical University Hospital of the Medical University of South Carolina, Charleston, SC '85 (NURS)
ARGENTIERI, THOMAS, MD, res. assoc. cardiology, Hospital of the University of Pennsylvania, Philadelphia, PA '84

ARGES-BAKRIS, DEMETRIA M., asst. dir. food serv., St. Catherine Hospital, East Chicago, IN '87 (FOOD)
ARGOTA, OSCAR B., eng., Philips Medical Systems, Inc., Shelton, CT '74 (ENG)
ARHOS, KOSTANTINOS H., dir. bldg. serv., LaRabida Children's Hospital, Chicago, IL '80 (ENG)
ARINGTON, MARITA, dir. vol. serv., O'Connor Hospital, San Jose, CA '82 (VOL)
ARKFELD, THOMAS E., asst. adm., St. Elizabeth's Hospital, Chicago, IL '81 (RISK)
ARLISS, DAVID, chief eng., Auburn Memorial Hospital, Auburn, NY '81 (ENG)
ARMANINI, SYLVIA, dir. vol., Parma Community General Hospital, Parma, OH '77 (VOL)
ARMATO, CHARLES, Pass Christian, MS '85 (ENG)
ARMBRUST, JAMES MARTIN, off. contract med. care, Alaska Area Native Health Service, Anchorage, AK '68
ARMBRUSTER, ROBIN, dir. mktg. and commun. rel., AMI Columbia Regional Hospital, Columbia, MO '85 (PR)
ARMBRUSTER, ROMA S., dir. vol. serv., Shawnee Mission Medical Center, Shawnee Mission, KS '68 (VOL)
ARMENTI, FRANK, exec. hskpr., John T. Mather Memorial Hospital, Port Jefferson, NY '86 (ENVIRON)
ARMENTROUT, JANICE D., vice-pres., Affiliated Healthcare Systems, Bangor, ME '82 (MGMT)
ARMES, DAVID, dir. plant eng., East Texas Hospital Foundation, Tyler, TX '86 (ENG)
ARMITAGE, LOUISE HUFF, dir. soc. serv., Sibley Memorial Hospital, Washington, DC '80 (SOC)
ARMOR, LARRY M., adm. res., Winchester Medical Center, Winchester, VA '86
ARMOUR, JO ANNE, supv. pers., Palo Verde Hospital, Tucson, AZ '85 (PERS)
ARMSTRONG, AGNES H., dir. educ., Hospital Association of Pennsylvania, Camp Hill, PA '82 (EDUC)
ARMSTRONG, CAROL LEE, Elizabeth General Medical Center, Elizabeth, NJ '84
ARMSTRONG, DORIS M., RN, dir. nrsg., Hartford Hospital, Hartford, CT '71 (NURS)
ARMSTRONG, EDWARD J., pres., Jeanes Health System, Jenkintown, PA '85
ARMSTRONG, ELMER, dir. plant serv., Tillamook County General Hospital, Tillamook, OR '86 (ENG)
ARMSTRONG, FRANK W., vice-pres., Blue Cross and Blue Shield of Ohio, Cincinnati, OH '85
ARMSTRONG, H. JACK, dir. eng., St. Luke's Lutheran Hospital, San Antonio, TX '87 (ENG)
ARMSTRONG, IVA P., RN, Sacramento, CA '72 (CS)
ARMSTRONG, JOYCE L., dir. vol., Forbes Regional Health Center, Monroeville, PA '76 (VOL)
ARMSTRONG, LOIS CLAMAGE, dir. urban and reg. affairs, Sinai Health Services, Detroit, MI '77 (PR)
ARMSTRONG, MADGELEEN, RN, dir. nrsg., Bob Wilson Memorial Grant County Hospital, Ulysses, KS '80 (NURS)
ARMSTRONG, MICHAEL A., dir. plant oper., Community Hospital of Anderson and Madison County, Anderson, IN '85 (ENG)
ARMSTRONG, NEIL G., dir. fin., Divine Providence Hospital, Williamsport, PA '86
ARMSTRONG, PEGGY, dir. med. surg. nrsg., Scott and White Memorial Hospital, Temple, TX '80 (NURS)
ARMSTRONG, PHILIP R., student, Webster College, St. Louis, MO '83
ARMSTRONG, REBECCA A., dir. vol. serv., Johnson City Medical Center Hospital, Johnson City, TN '86 (VOL)
ARMSTRONG, RICHARD F., dir. plant and environ. serv., St. Cloud Hospital, St. Cloud, MN '82 (ENG)(ENVIRON)
ARMSTRONG, ROBERT RICHARD, sr. asst. adm., St. Joseph Medical Center, Burbank, CA '70 (MGMT)(PLNG)
ARMSTRONG, ROGER J., mgr. maint. and eng., Holy Family Medical Center, Manitowoc, WI '85 (ENG)
ARMSTRONG, VICTORIA M., RN, dir. nrsg., Miami County Hospital, Paola, KS '84 (NURS)
ARMSTRONG, WILLIAM BRUCE III, mgr. qual. assur. syst., Glens Falls Hospital, Glens Falls, NY '74 (RISK)
ARNBERG, WILBER H., med. rep., State of California Department of Health Care Services, South San Francisco, CA '72
ARNDT, LORI, supv. med. equip. and matl. mgt., St. Paul-Ramsey Medical Center, St. Paul, MN '84 (CS)
ARNEILL, BRUCE P., lecturer, Yale University School of Medicine, Department of Public Health and Epidemiology, New Haven, CT '75
ARNETT, DONALD D., contract adm., Falick-Klein Partnership, Houston, TX '86 (ENG)
ARNETT, EUGENE WILLIAM, pres., Memorial Hospital of Taylor County, Medford, WI '59
ARNETT, FOSTER D., atty., Fort Sanders Regional Medical Center, Knoxville, TN '68 (ATTY)
ARNETT, THOMAS M., MD, (ret.), Ormond Beach, FL '52 (LIFE)
ARNETTE, JANE L., dir. commun. rel., Terrebonne General Medical Center, Houma, LA '84 (PR)
ARNFELT, THOMAS, mgr. contract adm., Medtronics, Inc., Minneapolis, MN '79
ARNOLD, BILL, chief eng., Enid Memorial Hospital, Enid, OK '75 (ENG)
ARNOLD, BRUCE W., dir. soc. serv., Lima Memorial Hospital, Lima, OH '72 (SOC)
ARNOLD, FRANCES A., dir. cent. serv., Valley Baptist Medical Center, Harlingen, TX '80 (CS)
ARNOLD, HERKELUS L., vice-pres. plant oper. and facil., Methodist Evangelical Hospital, Louisville, KY '61 (ENG)
ARNOLD, JAY L., dir. mktg., Eppley Treatment Resources, Omaha, NE '85 (PLNG)
ARNOLD, JAY, dir. pers. and emp. rel., Selby General Hospital, Marietta, OH '80 (PERS)
ARNOLD, JOHN W., corp. mgr. educ. and mgt., Sisters of Charity Corporate Office, Houston, TX '78 (EDUC)
ARNOLD, KENT ARTHUR, exec. vice-pres., Community General Hospital of Greater Syracuse, Syracuse, NY '67
ARNOLD, LAURIE E., dir. vol. serv. and coor. commun. rel., St. Anthony's Memorial Hospital, Effingham, IL '85 (VOL)(PR)
ARNOLD, LOIS M., dir. commun. rel., Little Company of Mary Hospital, Evergreen Park, IL '81 (PR)
ARNOLD, MARGERY, dir. plng., Massachusetts Eye and Ear Infirmary, Boston, MA '79 (PLNG)
ARNOLD, MARGUERITE L., RN, asst. adm. nrsg. serv., Millard Fillmore Hospital, Buffalo, NY '81 (NURS)
ARNOLD, MARTIE, RN, asst. adm. pat. serv., Island Hospital, Anacortes, WA '76 (NURS)
ARNOLD, MARY ANNE, health care mktg. consult., Prospect, KY '85
ARNOLD, ROBERT J., dir. environ. serv., Touro Infirmary, New Orleans, LA '75 (ENG)
ARNOLD, ROBERT W., dir. eng., Cottonwood Hospital Medical Center, Murray, UT '86 (ENG)
ARNOLD, RUSSELL B., dir. facil. serv., Good Samaritan Hospital and Medical Center, Portland, OR '76 (ENG)
ARNOLD, WILBUR VOGT III, sr. consult., Deloitte Haskins and Sells, Cincinnati, OH '79
ARNOLDY, JAMES, supt. maint., St. Elizabeth Hospital, Wabasha, MN '78 (ENG)
ARNSON, FREDRICK KENNETH, mgr. plant oper., St. Charles Medical Center, Bend, OR '77 (ENG)
ARNWINE, DON L., bd. chm., Voluntary Hospitals of America, Inc., Irving, TX '73
ARONIE, SAMUEL L., asst. adm. and dir. syst. eng., St. Joseph's Hospital, Lowell, MA '70 (MGMT)
ARONSON, JANET LAMPELL, dir. amb. care center, Arkansas Children's Hospital, Little Rock, AR '80
ARONSON, LAURA R., adm. rad., Mount Sinai Medical Center, New York, NY '77
ARP, RICHARD, asst. vice-pres. pub. rel. and mktg., Hutcheson Medical Center, Fort Oglethorpe, GA '82 (PR)
ARRASMITH, LEILIA M., pat. rep., Salvation Army William Booth Memorial Hospital, Florence, KY '82 (PAT)
ARRATE, DANIEL N., dir. matl. mgt., De Paul Hospital, New Orleans, LA '86 (PUR)
ARRINGTON, BARBARA A., assoc. dir., Executive Development Laboratory, St. Louis, MO '86 (PLNG)
ARRINGTON, CAMMON I., dir. pers., University of Utah Health Sciences Center, Salt Lake City, UT '82 (PERS)
ARRINGTON, CLAUDENE TYLER, dir. pub. rel., St. Bernard Hospital, Chicago, IL '86 (PR) (PLNG)
ARRINGTON, MARTHA L., spec. asst. to pres., Lutheran Medical Center, Brooklyn, NY '85 (PR)
ARRIOLA, JOHN H., vice-pres. external oper., Nashville Memorial Hospital, Madison, TN '85 (PLNG)
ARRUDA, KATHLEEN M., dir. pers., St. Anne's Hospital, Fall River, MA '86 (PERS)
ARSHAID, SALEH A., adm. med. serv., Arabian American Oil Company, Dhahran, Saudi Arabia '80
ARTER, RONALD W., dir. security and constr. design, Fairbanks Memorial Hospital, Fairbanks, AK '81 (ENG)
ARTERBURN, J. DAVID, pres. and chief exec. off., Orthopaedic Hospital, Los Angeles, CA '86
ARTERS, LINDA B., pub. rel. consult., Arters and Associates, Tempe, AZ '80 (PR)
ARTHERHOLT, IRENE, RN, dir. nrsg., Northwest Hospital, Seattle, WA '79 (NURS)
ARTHUR, CLENNIE E. III, assoc. adm., Memorial Hospital, Charleston, WV '83
ARTHUR, DANIEL B., dir. plant oper., Greenview Hospital, Bowling Green, KY '79 (ENG)
ARTHUR, DAVID M., vice-pres., Unity Medical Center, Fridley, MN '72
ARTHUR, DIXIE, vice-pres., Health Providers Insurance Company, Chicago, IL '84 (RISK)
ARTHUR, JENNIFER, dir. mktg., Acute Care Affiliates, Berkeley, CA '84 (PLNG)
ARTHUR, JYME J., dir. nrs. educ. serv., Spohn Hospital, Corpus Christi, TX '84 (EDUC)
ARTHUR, SARAH A., asst. dir. emp. rel., Deborah Heart and Lung Center, Browns Mills, NJ '81 (PERS)
ARTHUR, TONI, liability control asst., Lutheran Hospital of Maryland, Baltimore, MD '82 (RISK)
ARTILES, NEMUEL O., adm., Bella Vista Hospital, Mayaguez, P.R. '85
ARTZ, TYLER D., Germantown, TN '79
ARVESEN, GERALDINE C., rep. pat. rel., LaPorte Hospital, LaPorte, IN '87 (PAT)
ARVIDSON, ELYCE E., dir. pat. and family serv., Naeve Hospital, Albert Lea, MN '74 (SOC)
ARVIN, VIRGINIA, dir. hskpg., Fort Hamilton-Hughes Memorial Hospital, Hamilton, OH '86 (ENVIRON)
ARWOOD, LINDA P., mgr. and dir. food serv., Area Maria Guild, Inc. of Memphis, Area Maria Home, Memphis, TN '84 (FOOD)
ARZOLA, RAUL, student, National University, San Diego, CA '83
ASADI, M. JAFAR, dir. mgt. eng., Rockford Memorial Hospital, Rockford, IL '87 (MGMT)
ASAY, NEAL D., Riverside, CA '53 (LIFE)
ASCHLIMAN, NILAH F., asst. pers., Caylor-Nickel Hospital, Bluffton, IN '86 (PERS)
ASCHLIMAN, SHARON K., dir. qual. assur. and risk mgt., Saint Anthony Medical Center, Rockford, IL '84 (RISK)
ASENDIO, SHERYLL, dir. soc. work serv., Our Lady of Mercy Medical Center, Bronx, NY '81 (SOC)
ASGHARI, FARIDEH, RN, dir. specialty nrsg., Northwestern Memorial Hospital, Chicago, IL '85 (NURS)
ASH, ANNE G., RN, dir. nrsg. serv., Lloyd Noland Hospital and Health Centers, Birmingham, AL '84 (NURS)
ASH, JAMES LYNN, pres. and chief exec. off., Santa Barbara Cottage Hospital, Santa Barbara, CA '65
ASH, JOHN P., vice-pres. corp. oper., Methodist Hospital of Chicago, Chicago, IL '85 (PR) (PLNG)
ASH, MARY LOU, dir. staff dev., Olean General Hospital, Olean, NY '86 (EDUC)
ASH, PAMELLA, assoc. dir. amb. care, Long Island College Hospital, Brooklyn, NY '87 (AMB)
ASH, SUSAN, med. soc. worker, Fort Atkinson Memorial Hospital, Fort Atkinson, WI '86 (SOC)
ASHBAUGH, ANN M., RN, chief nrs., U. S. Air Force Hospital, Las Vegas, NV '86 (NURS)
ASHBAUGH, BRUCE J., mgr. rad., St. Francis Hospital, Wilmington, DE '81
ASHBAUGH, JAMES L., assoc. exec. dir., Humana Hospital -Lexington, Lexington, KY '77
ASHBAUGH, RICHARD R., dir. med. serv., U. S. Public Health Service, Rockville, MD '82
ASHBRIDGE, DREW W., exec. dir. urgent care, St. Joseph's Hospital and Medical Center, Phoenix, AZ '84
ASHBRIDGE, JOHN R., dir. phys. plant, Pennsylvania Hospital, Philadelphia, PA '84 (ENG)
ASHBY, DILLU ANN, asst. supt., University of Wisconsin Hospital and Clinics, Madison, WI '81
ASHBY, DOUGLAS B., Academy of Health Sciences, Fort Sam Houston, TX '81
ASHBY, GLORIA COATS, dir. soc. work, Baylor Institute for Rehabilitation, Dallas, TX '84 (SOC)
ASHBY, JOHN L., District of Columbia Hospital Association, Washington, DC '79
ASHBY, JOHN ROBERT, chief eng., Veterans Administration Medical Center, Martinsburg, WV '86 (ENG)
ASHBY, MARY PAT, adm. off. emer., Greater Southeast Community Hospital, Washington, DC '86
ASHBY, ROBERT W., chief eng., Greensville Memorial Hospital, Emporia, VA '75 (ENG)
ASHE, NANCY S., asst. vice-pres., National Healthcare, Inc., Dothan, AL '85
ASHENDEN, JAMES F. JR., atty., St. Joseph Hospital, Chicago, IL '67 (ATTY)
ASHFORD, BRYTAIN L., student, West Los Angeles College, Culvert City, CA '86 (PERS)
ASHFORD, WILLIAM C., supv. maint., Eskaton Manzanita Manor, Carmichael, CA '86 (ENVIRON)
ASHJIAN, LEE THOMAS, adm., Los Banos Community Hospital, Los Banos, CA '77 (PLNG)
ASHLEY, CARROLL, pres., Riverside Hospital, Toledo, OH '77 (PERS)
ASHLEY, H. VINCENT III, adm. res., Oklahoma Osteopathic Hospital, Tulsa, OK '82
ASHLEY, PEGGY S., asst. safety off., Swain County Hospital, Bryson City, NC '86 (RISK)
ASHLEY, SHELDON, adm. med. imaging, Flushing Hospital and Medical Center, Flushing, NY '85
ASHLIN, ROBERT, supv. eng., HCA Doctors Hospital, Lake Worth, FL '86 (ENG)
ASHMAN, WILBUR M., (ret.), Naples, FL '47 (LIFE)
ASHOK-KUMAR, T. M., dir. new market dev., Hitachi-America Ltd., Norcross, GA '85 (ENG)
ASHTON, BERT, RN, assoc. adm., Saddleback Community Hospital, Laguna Hills, CA '81 (NURS)
ASHTON, JAMES W., dir. mktg., Saint Louis Memorial Hospital, St. Louis, MO '75 (PLNG)
ASHTON, RICHARD WALLACE, RN, vice-pres., Riverside Methodist Hospitals, Columbus, OH '67 (NURS)
ASHTON, STEVEN D., mgr. facil., Naval Hospital, San Diego, CA '87 (ENG)
ASHWORTH, DAVID C., vice-pres. strategic plng., Presbyterian Hospital, Dallas, TX '83 (PLNG)
ASHWORTH, JOHN W. III, exec. dir., Maryland Institute for Emergency Medical Services Systems, Baltimore, MD '80
ASHWORTH, RONALD B., partner, Peat, Marwick, Mitchell and Company, New York, NY '74
ASIMUS, ANTOINETTE, dir. vol. serv., Jewish Hospital of Cincinnati, Cincinnati, OH '82 (VOL)
ASK, PETER J., exec. dir., Farwest Council of Hospitals, Eugene, OR '82 (PLNG)
ASKEW, JOYCE MARIE, mgr. matl., River Oaks Hospital, Jackson, MS '86 (ENVIRON)
ASKIN, WARREN B., dir. eng., St. Ann's Hospital of Columbus, Westerville, OH '82 (ENG)
ASKINS, NANCY P., mgr. trng., Shore Memorial Hospital, Somers Point, NJ '84 (EDUC)
ASLAN, SY, proj. eng., Montefiore Medical Center, Bronx, NY '79 (MGMT)
ASLANIAN, MARGARET, sr. asst. dir. food serv., Cedars-Sinai Medical Center, Los Angeles, CA '80 (FOOD)
ASLINGER, JAMES S., dir. mgt. eng., Northside Hospital, Atlanta, GA '81 (MGMT)
ASMAN, TERESA COX, coor. pat. liaison, Lexington County Hospital, West Columbia, SC '80 (PAT)
ASMUSSEN, ROBERT W., sr. consult., Henry Ford Hospital, Detroit, MI '83
ASPHOLM, ELIZABETH DIANE, oncology educ., St. Joseph Health Care Corporation, Albuquerque, NM '86 (EDUC)
ASPILLAGA, MAGGIE, dir. mktg., Pan American Hospital, Miami, FL '86 (PLNG)
ASPINALL, JOYCE E., coor. trng. and dev., Memorial Hospital, Burlington, WI '86 (EDUC)
ASPIS, SAMUEL L., MD, dir., Veterans Administration Hospital, Cleveland, OH '56 (LIFE)
ASSIP, CLAIRE M., pat. rep., Methodist Hospital, Brooklyn, NY '77 (PAT)
ASTI, ROBERT J., atty., South Miami Hospital, South Miami, FL '80 (ATTY)
ASTIZ, PETER M., atty., St. Francis Memorial Hospital, San Francisco, CA '85 (ATTY)
ASTRACHAN, STEPHEN M., coor. risk mgt., Naval Hospital, San Diego, CA '82
ASTRO, BETTY A., dir. pers., Charles River Hospital, Wellesley, MA '86 (PERS)
ATCHISON, CHERYL A., dir. pers., Woodland Memorial Hospital, Woodland, CA '84 (PERS)
ATCHISON, THOMAS A., pres., Lifelong Learning Systems, Inc., Chicago, IL '77 (PERS)
ATCHLEY, JODELL C., student, Georgia State University-Institute of Health Administration, Atlanta, GA '86
ATEN, DOROTHY R., mgr. pur., Swedish American Hospital, Rockford, IL '82 (PUR)

ATER, ELIZABETH P., asst. chief diet. serv., Veterans Administration Medical Center, Minneapolis, MN '70 (FOOD)
ATHANASIUS, BROTHER, pat. rep., Alexian Brothers Hospital, St. Louis, MO '37 (LIFE)
ATHERTON, CONNIE M., dir. food and nutr. serv., AMI Barrow Medical Center, Winder, GA '84 (FOOD)
ATHERTON, MARC E., supv. maint., Metropolitan Medical Center, Minneapolis, MN '86 (ENG)
ATHWAL, SUSAN L., asst. vice-pres., Winston Personnel, New York, NY '86 (PERS)
ATKATZ, JEANNE M., assoc. dir., Bronx-Lebanon Hospital Center, Bronx, NY '86 (SOC)
ATKIN, NELSON D. II, atty., Emanuel Hospital and Health Center, Portland, OR '83 (ATTY)
ATKINS, NANCY A., student, Graduate in Epidemiology and Public Health, Yale University, New Haven, CT '87
ATKINS, THOMAS L., prin. consult., J. H. Albert International Insurance Advisors, Inc., Needham, MA '83 (RISK)
ATKINS, VICKIE S., mgr. med. staff and review, Children's Hospital of Alabama, Birmingham, AL '86 (RISK)
ATKINSON, JEAN E., RN, mgr. cent. sup., Community Hospital, Anderson, IN '80 (CS)
ATKINSON, MICHAEL WAYNE, sales eng. and energy serv., Johnson Control, Arlington Heights, IL '76 (ENG)
ATKINSON, MYRON H. JR., trustee and atty., St. Alexius Medical Center, Bismarck, ND '69 (ATTY)
ATKINSON, PAT R., RN, outpatient coor., Davie County Hospital, Mocksville, NC '86 (AMB)
ATKINSON, REGINA E., dir. soc. serv., Glades General Hospital, Belle Glade, FL '81 (SOC)
ATKINSON, SARA C., asst. dir. vol. serv., York Hospital, York, PA '86 (VOL)
ATKINSON, W. SHERWOOD, adm., St. Joseph Hospital, Augusta, GA '56 (LIFE)
ATLAS, LEWIS, assoc. adm. dir., Michigan State University Clinical Center, East Lansing, MI '87 (AMB)
ATLAS, ROBERT F., dir. mgt. serv., Jurgovan and Blair, Inc., Potomac, MD '76
ATMAR, RICHARD S., partner, Page Southerland Page, Houston, TX '85
ATOR, NANCY E., atty., Ropes and Gray, Boston, MA '78 (ATTY)
ATTAL, GENE, vice-pres. pub. affairs, Seton Medical Center, Austin, TX '81 (PR)
ATTAYA, M. LOUISE, atty., U. S. Army Health Services Command, Fort Sam Houston, TX '81 (ATTY)
ATTEBERRY, TANINA, student, University of Dallas, Irving, TX '85
ATTONITO, RALPH, dir. pur., Trinity Memorial Hospital, Cudahy, WI '67 (PUR)
ATTWOOD, DORT W., dir. human res., Mendocino Coast District Hospital, Fort Bragg, CA '86 (PERS)
ATWATER, VERN E., (ret.), Leawood, KS '66 (ENG)
ATWELL, ALECIA K. J., dir. soc. serv., Comanche County Memorial Hospital, Lawton, OK '85 (SOC)
ATWELL, BARBARA A., mgr. cent. proc. and distrib., St. Vincent Medical Center, Los Angeles, CA '82 (CS)
ATWELL, BARBARA A., dir. educ., Leland Memorial Hospital, Riverdale, MD '85 (EDUC)
ATWOOD, BETH, dir. commun., Tennessee Hospital Association, Nashville, TN '82 (PR)
ATWOOD, CAMILLE ANN, dir. allied health, Norfolk General Hospital, Norfolk, VA '84 (EDUC)
ATWOOD, D. L., vice-pres. corp. dev., Alltel Supply, Inc., Norcross, GA '85 (ENG)
ATWOOD, JANE, dir. food serv., Memorial Medical Center of Jacksonville, Jacksonville, FL '85 (FOOD)
ATWOOD, JOSEPH M., unit mgr., Fairfield Memorial Hospital, Fairfield, IL '82 (PUR)
ATWOOD, JUDITH G., RN, vice-pres. pat. care serv., Good Samaritan Hospital, Baltimore, MD '81 (NURS)
ATWOOD, SAUNDRA L., vice-pres., Communications Strategies, Inc., Coral Gables, FL '78 (PLNG)
ATZROTT, ALLAN EARL, pres., Wilkes-Barre General Hospital, Wilkes-Barre, PA '71
AUBERT, NORA E., clin. instr., Dearborn County Hospital, Lawrenceburg, IN '84 (EDUC)
AUBIN, MARY C., mktg. asst., Proffessional Counseling Association, Little Rock, AR '86 (PLNG)
AUBIN, MICHAEL D., asst. adm., H. Lee Moffit Hospital and Cancer Research Institute at the University of South Florida, Tampa, FL '80
AUBIN, NANCY L., RN, dir. nrsg., Redington-Fairview General Hospital, Skowhegan, ME '78 (NURS)
AUBIN, RAYMOND P., vice-pres., Cannon and Falkner, Washington, DC '83
AUBLE, JOHN A., atty., Cleveland Clinic Hospital, Cleveland, OH '71 (ATTY)
AUBUT, RICHARD H., RN, vice-pres. and dir. nrsg., Morton Hospital and Medical Center, Taunton, MA '82 (NURS)
AUCLAIR, PAULETTE, spec. educ. dev., Curative Rehabilitation Center, Milwaukee, WI '81 (EDUC)
AUDET, GASTON A., dir. plng. oper., St. Joseph Hospital, Orange, CA '83 (ENG)
AUDETTE, MARY M., prod. mgr., Abbott-Northwestern Hospital, Minneapolis, MN '86 (PR)
AUDITORE-GARONE, THERESA, coor. risk control, Kingsbrook Jewish Medical Center, Brooklyn, NY '86 (RISK)
AUERBACH, KIM R., student, Program in Health Care Management, Boston University, Boston, MA '86 (PLNG)
AUERBACH, SHELLEY, dir. mgt. eng., Lenox Hill Hospital, New York, NY '72 (MGMT)
AUGER, CHRISTINE, pur. agt., Kennebec Valley Medical Center, Augusta, ME '70 (PUR)
AUGER, STEPHEN R., asst. to dir. commun. rel., St. Vincent's Medical Center, Staten Island, NY '86 (PR)
AUGSBURGER, MICHEL A., vice-pres., Shady Grove Adventist Hospital, Rockville, MD '80 (PLNG)
AUGUGLIARO, RITA ENRICA, dir. vol. serv. and commun. rel., Baptist Medical Center of New York, Brooklyn, NY '84 (VOL)
AUGUST, JANE E., RN, vice-pres. nrsg., St. Peter's Medical Center, New Brunswick, NJ '82 (NURS)
AUGUSTINE, JOSEPH C., vice-pres. pers. serv., Rhode Island Hospital, Providence, RI '71 (EDUC)(PERS)
AUGUSTINE, KENT R., student, California State College, Bakersfield, CA '86 (PLNG)
AUGUSTUS, R. NEAL, dir. pers., Jackson County Schneck Memorial Hospital, Seymour, IN '84 (PERS)
AUGUSTYN, CYNTHIA L., atty., Bascom Palmer Eye Institute and Hospital, Miami, FL '85 (ATTY)
AUKER, GERALD L., RN, dir. sup., proc. and distrib., Desert Hospital, Palm Springs, CA '82 (CS)
AULD, JANELL C., dir. amb. center, Methodist Medical Center, Dallas, TX '87 (AMB)
AULT, MARK JOHNSON, MD, dir. amb. care center, Cedars-Sinai Medical Center, Los Angeles, CA '87 (AMB)
AULTMAN, TERRY V., mgr., Price Waterhouse, Atlanta, GA '85 (PLNG)
AUNGST, SHERMAN L., dir. pur., Yale-New Haven Hospital, New Haven, CT '69 (PUR)
AURAND, STEVEN A., student, Ferris State College, Big Rapids, MI '86
AURETTO, FREDERICK A., dir. pers., McKeesport Hospital, McKeesport, PA '79 (PERS)
AUSBAND, FRANK P., RN, vice-pres. and dir. nrsg., Carteret General Hospital, Morehead City, NC '83 (NURS)
AUSMAN, DORIS, RN, asst. adm. dir. nrsg., Doctors Hospital of Lakewood, Lakewood, CA '77 (NURS)
AUSMUNDSON, SANDRA, RN, head nrs. outpatient surg. unit, Cleveland Clinic Hospital, Cleveland, OH '87 (AMB)
AUSTERLITZ, DON M., dir. pers., Comanche County Memorial Hospital, Lawton, OK '77 (PERS)
AUSTIN, ANNE M., RN, asst. dir. nrsg. serv., John T. Mather Memorial Hospital, Port Jefferson, NY '81 (NURS)
AUSTIN, DALE L., RN, asst. dir. nrsg. and specialty serv., St. Marys Hospital Medical Center, Madison, WI '86 (NURS)
AUSTIN, GEORGEANN B., assoc., Anderson Debartolo Pan, Inc., Tucson, AZ '84
AUSTIN, GERALD PATRICK, dir. eng., Archbishop Bergan Mercy Hospital, Omaha, NE '75 (ENG)
AUSTIN, JAN E., mgr. human res., Suburban Hospital and Sanitarium-Cook County, Hinsdale, IL '87 (PERS)
AUSTIN, JUDY, RN, vice-pres. nrsg., Ingalls Memorial Hospital, Harvey, IL '77 (NURS)
AUSTIN, PATRICIA A., dir. commun. rel., Champlain Valley Physicians Hospital Medical Center, Plattsburgh, NY '78 (PR)
AUSTIN, ROBERT L., atty., St. John's Healthcare Corporation, Anderson, IN '82 (ATTY)
AUSTIN, ROBERT M., student, Georgia Institute of Technology, Program in Health Systems Management, Atlanta, GA '82 (MGMT)
AUSTIN, THEODORE ARNOLD, assoc. prof., Union College, Cranford, NJ '48 (LIFE)
AUSTIN, VIVIAN, RN, dir. nrsg., Parkridge Medical Center, Chattanooga, TN '76 (NURS)
AUSTIN, WILLIAM E., dir. plant oper., Muscatine General Hospital, Muscatine, IA '85 (ENG)
AUSTINSON, ARLENE, RN, dir. nrsg., Providence Medical Center, Portland, OR '72 (NURS)
AUTEN, REGINA, risk mgr., Wheelock Memorial Hospital, Goodrich, MI '85 (RISK)
AUTHEMENT, CATHERINE MONTELEPRE, guest rel. rep., Montelepre Memorial Hospital, New Orleans, LA '86 (PAT)
AUTHEMENT, NOEL P., dir. matl. mgt., Montelepre Memorial Hospital, New Orleans, LA '86 (PUR)
AUTHIER, PHILIP D., RN, dir. nrsg. serv., St. Mary's Hospital, Pierre, SD '85 (NURS)
AUTIO, DENNIS D., biomedical eng., Veterans Administration Medical Center, Minneapolis, MN '82 (ENG)
AUTREY, HAROLD L., chief exec. off., Perry Memorial Hospital, Princeton, IL '55 (PLNG)(LIFE)
AUTULLO, RALPH D., dir. plant oper. and maint., St. Anthony Hospital, Chicago, IL '86 (ENG)
AUYER, PETER V., mgr. health enhancement, Methodist Hospital-Central Unit, Memphis, TN '84
AVAKIAN, LAURA, dir. human resources, Beth Israel Hospital, Boston, MA '81 (PERS)
AVALONE, NANCY ACERBO, assoc. dir. risk mgt., Fojp Service Corporation, New York, NY '82 (RISK)
AVERBUCH, LT. COL. MICHAEL, MSC USA, dep. staff dir., Department of the Army, Office of the Surgeon General, U. S. Army Health Facilities Planning Agency, Washington, DC '85
AVERILL, RAYMOND P., supv. cent. serv., Southern Maine Medical Center, Biddeford, ME '80 (CS)
AVERITT, LINNIE B., dir. vol. serv., Portsmouth General Hospital, Portsmouth, VA '83 (VOL)
AVERY, ANTHONY G., mgt. eng. consult., The Methodist Hospital, Houston, TX '86 (MGMT)
AVERY, DAVID, consult., Providence Hospital, Washington, DC '86
AVERY, DONALD L., dir. pers., Manchester Memorial Hospital, Manchester, CT '72 (PERS)
AVERY, DONALD R., student, Program in Health and Hospital Administration, University of Florida, Gainesville, FL '84
AVERY, GWEN M., dir. qual. assur., Sheltering Arms Rehabilitation Hospital, Richmond, VA '84 (RISK)
AVERY, JOANNE S., dir. food serv., AMI Presbyterian-St. Luke's Medical Center, Denver, CO '85 (FOOD)
AVERY, LAURA BAILEY, dir. pub. rel. and dev., Raleigh Community Hospital, Raleigh, NC '80 (PR) (PLNG)
AVNER, JAY, asst. vice-pres. strategic plng., Bethesda Hospital, Inc., Cincinnati, OH '80 (PLNG)
AVVOCATO, ROY A., MD, med. dir., Caledonian Hospital, Brooklyn, NY '74
AWERKAMP, M. ANN, coor. pub. rel., Blessing Hospital, Quincy, IL '85 (PR)
AXEL, JACOB M., pres., Axel, Grube and Associates, Inc., Schaumburg, IL '76 (PLNG)
AXELROD, STEPHANIE S., dir. mktg., Children's Hospital and Medical Center, Seattle, WA '85 (PR) (PLNG)
AXELSON, NILS G., pres., Swedish Covenant Hospital, Chicago, IL '52 (LIFE)
AXLEY, ROBERT E., mgr. maint., Ontonagon Memorial Hospital, Ontonagon, MI '83 (ENG)
AXNICK, KAREN J., dir. risk mgt., Stanford University Hospital, Stanford, CA '83 (RISK)
AXT, SUZANNE E., RN, dir. critical care nrsg., Methodist Hospital of Southern California, Arcadia, CA '86 (NURS)
AYALA, JACINTO L., chief exec. off., First Hospital Cidra, San Juan, P.R. '84
AYARS, ERNEST JAMES, dir. eng., Walker Memorial Hospital, Avon Park, FL '59 (ENG)
AYCOCK, EDWARD J., asst. adm. pers. and adm. risk mgr., King's Daughters Hospital, Temple, TX '86 (RISK)
AYD, RICHARD A., asst. dir., Franklin Square Hospital, Baltimore, MD '80 (RISK)
AYERS, AMY L., RN, asst. adm. pat. care serv., Whidbey General Hospital, Coupeville, WA '78 (NURS)
AYERS, FRED A., sr. mgt. eng., Cleveland Clinic Foundation, Cleveland, OH '86 (MGMT)
AYERS, GEORGE, supv. elec. and sterilizer, Good Samaritan Medical Center, Phoenix, AZ '84 (ENG)
AYERS, LCDR JAMES L., MSC USN, contr., Naval Medical Command, Northwest Regional, Oakland, CA '76
AYERS, MARK R., student, Program in Hospital Administration, Trinity University, San Antonio, TX '84
AYERS, NANCY A., RN, assoc. dir. nrsg., South Community Hospital, Oklahoma City, OK '86 (NURS)
AYERS, NANCY R., coor. guest rel., Orangeburg-Calhoun Regional Hospital, Orangeburg, SC '87 (PAT)
AYERS, WILLIAM F., dir., Southern Illinois Consultants, Carterville, IL '77 (SOC)
AYLWARD, NANCY A., coor. qual. assur., North Colorado Medical Center, Greeley, CO '83 (RISK)
AYOTTE, BARBARA G., RN, dir. nrsg., Warren Hospital, Phillipsburg, NJ '83 (NURS)
AYRES, RICHARD A., vice-pres. human res., Mississippi Methodist Hospital and Rehabilitation Center, Jackson, MS '81 (RISK)
AYRES, RONALD M., atty., Alleghany Regional Hospital, Low Moor, VA '82 (ATTY)
AZMAT, SHAHID, dir. plant oper., Charter Hospital of Las Vegas, Las Vegas, NV '86 (ENG)

B

BAAB, KENNETH M., vice-pres., Lehigh Valley Hospital Center, Allentown, PA '73
BAAR, WILLARD J., dir. pur., Blodgett Memorial Medical Center, Grand Rapids, MI '72 (PUR)
BAASCH, LYNN A., dir. nrsg. educ., Rochester Methodist Hospital, Rochester, MN '86 (EDUC)
BABASHANIAN, MARCIA N., asst. adm., DePaul Hospital, Norfolk, VA '84 (RISK)
BABB, DONALD J., chief exec. off., Citizens Memorial Hospital, Bolivar, MO '83
BABB, RAY J., adm. dir., Good Samaritan Hospital and Medical Center, Portland, OR '72 (FOOD)
BABCOCK, BRYON D., asst. dir. eng., Edward W. Sparrow Hospital, Lansing, MI '85 (ENG)
BABCOCK, DEBORAH SUE, sr. pub. rel. off., Henry Ford Hospital, Detroit, MI '86 (PR)
BABCOCK, ERNEST J., atty., Mercy Hospital, Portland, ME '78 (ATTY)
BABCOCK, KENNETH B., MD, consult., Pompano Beach, FL '45 (LIFE)
BABCOCK, SR. MARY, RN, dir. nrsg. serv., Memorial Hospital and Health Care Center, Jasper, IN '82 (NURS)
BABCOCK, PAUL A., asst. dir., New England Deaconess Hospital, Boston, MA '79 (PLNG)
BABIARZ, JANE, vice-pres. mktg. and pub. rel., Charlton Memorial Hospital, Fall River, MA '78 (PR)
BABICH, CAROLE, RN, asst. to dir. emer. serv., St. Mary's Medical Center, Duluth, MN '87 (AMB)
BABINCHAK, PAUL, risk mgr. and dir. cent. serv., Wilson Center, Faribault, MN '86 (RISK)(CS)
BABINGTON, LYNN M., RN, assoc. dir. nrsg., Saint Cabrini Hospital of Seattle, Seattle, WA '85 (NURS)
BABUDRO, ED, Project Hope, Tegucigalpa, Honduras '85 (ENG)
BACA, EVELYN, asst. vice-pres. nrsg., St. Joseph Health Care Corporation, Albuquerque, NM '85 (NURS)
BACCI, JOYCE E., RN, dir. nrsg. serv., Auburn Faith Community Hospital, Auburn, CA '80 (NURS)
BACDAYAN, CAROLYN B., dir. plng., University Hospital, University of Kentucky, Lexington, KY '81 (PLNG)
BACH, HARRY C., Fredericksburg, VA '50 (LIFE)
BACHENHEIMER, JOAN, pres., B. B. and K. Communications, Inc., Chestnut, MA '84 (PR)
BACHLER, TRAUTE F., dir. food serv., Park Avenue Nursing, Convalescent and Retirement Home, Arlington, MA '80 (FOOD)
BACHMAN, DALE C., dir. eng. serv., Hospital Shared Services Western Pennsylvania, Warrendale, PA '73 (ENG)
BACHMAN, ROBERT J., asst. adm., Crawford Long Hospital Emory University, Atlanta, GA '79
BACHMEYER, ROBERT W., (ret.), Hot Springs Village, AR '39 (LIFE)
BACHRACH, DAVID J., dir. adm. and fin. affairs, The University of Michigan Medical School, Ann Arbor, MI '71
BACHRACH, EDGAR H., PhD, assoc. med. dir., Franklin General Hospital, Hampton, IA '87 (AMB)

BACHRODT, ANDREW K., adm. intern, Rockford Memorial Hospital, Rockford, IL '85 (PLNG)
BACIGALUPI, BARBARA A., pub. rel. and mktg. consult., Bacigalupi Associates, Emeryville, CA '78 (PR)
BACK, MARY V., RN, dir. nrsg., Baum Harmon Memorial Hospital, Primghar, IA '82 (NURS)
BACKEMEYER, GENEVA J., dir. human res. and dev., University Heights Hospital, Indianapolis, IN '83 (EDUC)
BACKMAN, COLLEEN M., dir. soc. serv., Bethesda Lutheran Medical Center, St. Paul, MN '83 (SOC)
BACKMAN, LILLIAN, dir. vol. serv., Charles A. Dana Hospital of Sidney Farber Cancer Institute, Boston, MA '78 (VOL)
BACKY, BASIL R., asst. vice-pres., Loma Linda University Medical Center, Loma Linda, CA '78 (PERS)
BACON, BRENDA J., pres., Healthteam, Inc., Clementon, NJ '82 (PLNG)
BACON, ERNEST, adm., HCA Park View Medical Center, Nashville, TN '79 (PR) (PLNG)
BACON, GLENDA L., assoc. dir. nrsg., Christ Hospital and Medical Center, Oak Lawn, IL '81 (NURS)
BACON, HAL B., coor. diet., Mercy Hospital, Davenport, IA '82 (FOOD)
BACON, JEAN G., vice-pres., Savant, Inc., Kansas City, MO '86 (AMB)
BACON, JOAN E., dir. commun. rel., Monadnock Community Hospital, Peterborough, NH '79 (PR)
BACON, SHARYN L., dept. mgr. pur., St. Francis-St. George Hospital, Cincinnati, OH '82 (PUR)
BACRARELLI, RENATO V., adm. res., Hotel Dieu Medical Center, El Paso, TX '85 (PLNG)
BACULIS, DIANA BREUER, staff asst. pub. rel., Mercy Hospital, Cedar Rapids, IA '82 (PR)
BACUS, JACQUELINE L., dir. soc. serv., Newark-Wayne Community Hospital, Newark, NY '82 (SOC)
BADACH, GINNY A., mgr. cent. serv., Leonard Hospital, Troy, NY '81 (CS)
BADALI, MELBA H., dir. pur., Doctors' Hospital, Coral Gables, FL '81 (PUR)
BADDLEY, JAMES R., sr. vice-pres., Mississippi Hospital Association, Jackson, MS '75 (EDUC)
BADE, REBECCA DUPREE, dir. soc. serv., Moberly Regional Medical Center, Moberly, MO '79 (SOC)
BADEAUX, PAMELA J., student, Program in Health Care Administration, Texas Woman's University, Houston, TX '85
BADER, BARRY S., pres., Bader and Associates, Inc., Rockville, MD '80 (RISK)
BADER, HENRY M. JR., mgr. cent. sup. serv., Holyoke Hospital, Holyoke, MA '86 (CS)
BADER, MARK P., vice-pres. oper., Jackson Park Hospital, Chicago, IL '72
BADERMAN, BETTY J., chief news bur., James M. Jackson Memorial Hospital, Miami, FL '81 (PR)
BADGETT, DENISE C., dir. prod. mgt., Tallahassee Memorial Regional Medical Center, Tallahassee, FL '85 (MGMT)
BADMAN, BEN JR., exec. vice-pres., Geisinger Wyoming Valley Medical Center, Wilkes-Barre, PA '50 (LIFE)
BADNER, BARRY, pres., Zelner and Badner, Inc., Englewood, NJ '84 (MGMT)
BADR, MUHAMMAD A., student, Union Graduate School, Cincinnati, OH '86 (PERS)(PLNG)
BAECHER, JOSEPH C., mgr. biomedical eng. and commun., Bayfront Medical Center, St. Petersburg, FL '83 (ENG)
BAEHR, CARYL S., coor. pat. care, University General Hospital, Seminole, FL '79 (SOC)
BAER, HELEN E., pres., Baer Enterprises, New York, NY '79 (PLNG)
BAER, JOHN ETHAN, PhD, pres., Center to Promote Health Care Studies, Inc., Scarsdale, NY '59
BAER, LARRY D., dir. environ. serv., Naeve Health Care Association, Albert Lea, MN '83 (ENG)
BAER, MICHELE S., dir. pub. rel., Magee-Womens Hospital, Pittsburgh, PA '81 (PR)
BAESLER, SANDRA J., dir. soc. serv., Sarasota Memorial Hospital, Sarasota, FL '85 (SOC)
BAETE, GREGORY P., dir. biomedical eng., Sioux Valley Hospital, Sioux Falls, SD '84 (ENG)
BAEZ, JAMES, adm. dir. matl. mgt., Florida Hospital Medical Center, Orlando, FL '86 (PUR)
BAGBY, CATHERINE M., health care consult., Ernst and Whinney, San Antonio, TX '81
BAGDON, BRIDGET M., mgt. eng. analyst, Detroit Osteopathic Hospital Corporation, Oak Park, MI '87 (MGMT)
BAGDONAS, MARGARET E., dir. commun. rel., Raritan Bay Medical Center, Perth Amboy, NJ '85 (PR)
BAGG, FREDERICK C., dir. pub. rel. and mktg. commun., St. Francis Hospital Center, Beech Grove, IN '79 (PR)
BAGG, HALSEY M., dir. mgt. eng., Our Lady of Lourdes Memorial Hospital, Binghamton, NY '75 (MGMT)
BAGGALEY, JOHN F., dir. pers., Delano Regional Medical Center, Delano, CA '86 (PERS)
BAGGETT, CHARLES A., pres. and dean faculty, American Institute of Medical Law, Inc., South Miami, FL '80 (RISK)
BAGGETT, MARY E., dir. pers., Phoebe Putney Memorial Hospital, Albany, GA '66 (PERS)
BAGGIO, DENISE, acct. mgr., Ncr, Chicago, IL '85
BAGINSKI, EDWARD, adm. and chief exec. off., Grace Hospital, Cleveland, OH '86
BAGINSKI, KATHI, dir., MacNeal Hospital, Berwyn, IL '87 (AMB)
BAGLEY, JAMES E., sr. exec. vice-pres., Phoenix Baptist Hospital and Medical Center, Phoenix, AZ '66 (PERS)
BAGLI, ELLEN G., coor. pub. rel., Palisades General Hospital, North Bergen, NJ '84 (PR)
BAGLIO, PETER, dir., Veterans Administration Medical Center, East Orange, NJ '47 (LIFE)
BAGNALL, JANICE ANN, RN, asst. vice-pres. nrsg., Lankenau Hospital, Philadelphia, PA '77 (NURS)
BAGNOLA, CHRISTINE, actg. dir. food serv., Westlake Community Hospital, Melrose Park, IL '80 (FOOD)
BAGSHAW, LOUISE S., RN, mgr. matl., Newark-Wayne Community Hospital, Newark, NY '80 (PUR)
BAGWELL, MARTHA ROYAL, risk mgr., Moses H. Cone Memorial Hospital, Greensboro, NC '83 (RISK)
BAGWELL, ROBERT S., mgr. ins. and investments, Eisenhower Medical Center, Rancho Mirage, CA '83 (RISK)
BAHE-HERNANDEZ, GERI, RN, dir. nrsg., U. S. Public Health Service Indian Hospital, Tuba City, AZ '87 (NURS)
BAHLKE, BARBARA, adm. dir., Leonard Morse Hospital, Natick, MA '84 (PLNG)
BAHNEMANN, STEVEN L., asst. dir. human res., St. Marys Hospital of Rochester, Rochester, MN '83 (PERS)
BAHNSON, BETH A., dir. soc. serv., Dallas County Hospital, Perry, IA '83 (SOC)
BAHR, HAZEL J., RN, chief nrsg. serv., Veterans Administration Medical Center, Asheville, NC '78 (NURS)
BAHR, M. JAMES, prin., James Bahr Associates, Ltd., Plymouth, MI '78 (MGMT)
BAHR, MELODY, head nrs. amb. serv., Richland Hospital, Richland Center, WI '87 (AMB)
BAICKER, MARTIN, asst. adm., Jersey City Medical Center, Jersey City, NJ '84 (RISK)
BAIG, MIRZA M. S., dir. food serv., Methodist Hospital of Chicago, Chicago, IL '80 (FOOD)
BAILEY-DUNBAR, KATHY L., asst. adm. nrsg., Herrick Memorial Hospital, Tecumseh, MI '86 (PR) (PLNG)
BAILEY, BARBARA, dir. soc. work, Lawrence Memorial Hospital, Lawrence, KS '78 (SOC)
BAILEY, CHANDLER, vice-pres. plng. and dev., South Florida Hospital Association, Miami, FL '85 (PLNG)
BAILEY, CHARLES WALKER, atty., Texas Hospital Association, Austin, TX '81 (ATTY)
BAILEY, CHRISTOPHER, dir. plng., Illinois Hospital Association, Naperville, IL '83
BAILEY, CLAYTON W. JR., adm. asst. eng., DeKalb General Hospital, Decatur, GA '84 (ENG)
BAILEY, DAN, dir. facil. serv., Martin Luther Hospital Medical Center, Anaheim, CA '86 (ENG)
BAILEY, DANIEL R., sr. asst. adm., bus. and fund dev., St. Mary's Hospital, Galesburg, IL '85 (PR)
BAILEY, DAVID R., exec. dir., McLean Home, Simsbury, CT '77
BAILEY, EDWARD D., supv. and exec. hskpg., Skaalen Sunset Home, Stoughton, WI '87 (ENVIRON)
BAILEY, ELISE K., buyer, Mid-Columbia Medical Center, The Dalles, OR '86 (PUR)
BAILEY, FORREST L., dir. design, Florida Hospital Medical Center, Orlando, FL '80 (ENG)
BAILEY, FRANKLIN W., dir. plant serv., Halifax Hospital Medical Center, Daytona Beach, FL '64 (ENG)
BAILEY, GEORGE C., dir. matl. mgt., Portage View Hospital, Hancock, MI '82 (PUR)
BAILEY, JACK C., pres. and chief exec. off., Southmark Retirement Corporation, Dallas, TX '81 (PLNG)
BAILEY, JAMES SCOTT, Business Risks International, Inc., Oak Brook Terrace, IL '86
BAILEY, JAMES T., dir. human res., Charter Northridge Hospital, Raleigh, NC '86 (PERS)
BAILEY, JIMMY M., Miami Beach, FL '74 (MGMT)
BAILEY, JOAN M., RN, dir. nrsg. serv., St. Mary-Rogers Memorial Hospital, Rogers, AR '83 (NURS)
BAILEY, JOHN W., adm., Divine Saviour Hospital, York, SC '54 (LIFE)
BAILEY, JOHN W., dir. pers., University Medical Center, Lebanon, TN '86 (PERS)
BAILEY, LEIGH S., asst. hosp. dir. pat. serv., Cedars Medical Center, Miami, FL '86 (NURS)
BAILEY, LINDA ELAINE, dir. soc. serv. and pat. rep., Culpeper Memorial Hospital, Culpeper, VA '78 (SOC)(PAT)
BAILEY, LYNN M., consult., Integrated Healthcare Systems, Columbia, SC '83 (PLNG)
BAILEY, MARY ALICE, RN, adm. nrsg. serv., Redding Medical Center, Redding, CA '84 (NURS)
BAILEY, MARY ANN, RN, dir. nrsg., Wooster Community Hospital, Wooster, OH '80 (NURS)
BAILEY, NORA J., vice-pres. corp. plng., Sacred Heart Health Systems, Inc., Pensacola, FL '82 (PLNG)
BAILEY, PAMELA, RN, educ. and dev. staff, University Medical Center, Lebanon, TN '86 (EDUC)
BAILEY, RALPH S., dir. pastoral and educ. serv., Candler General Hospital, Savannah, GA '85 (EDUC)
BAILEY, RICHARD R., pur. agt., Cottage Grove Hospital, Cottage Grove, OR '80 (PUR)
BAILEY, SR. ROBERT JOSEPH, coor. commun. educ., St. Rose de Lima Hospital, Henderson, NV '68 (EDUC)
BAILEY, RON C., vice-pres. clin. serv., Mobile Infirmary Medical Center, Mobile, AL '82
BAILEY, V. H., eng., St. Elizabeth Community Hospital, Baker, OR '75 (ENG)
BAILEY, VIRGINIA, dir. hostesses, Baptist Memorial Hospital, Memphis, TN '73 (PAT)
BAILEY, WILLIAM N., RN, actg. asst. adm. nrsg. and dir. nrsg., Bon Secours Hospital, Baltimore, MD '81 (NURS)
BAILEY, ZEILA W., RN, consult. nrsg. adm., Birmingham, AL '78 (NURS)
BAILIE, FRANCES R., RN, dir. nrsg. serv., Wilson Clinic and Hospital, Darlington, SC '84 (NURS)
BAILIS, SUSAN S., exec. vice-pres., Ads Management, Lawrence, MA '77 (SOC)
BAILLY, LUCI E., RN, risk mgr. and coor. nrsg. qual. assur., West Florida Hospital, Pensacola, FL '83 (RISK)
BAIN, LANDEN C., dir. mgt. plng. and analyst, Ohio State University Hospitals, Columbus, OH '83 (MGMT)
BAIN, LEWIS J., sr. assoc., Keyes Associates, Providence, RI '79 (ENG)
BAIN, NEENA L., dir. vol. serv., Methodist Hospital-Central Unit, Memphis, TN '84 (VOL)
BAINBRIDGE, MARK A., partner, Ernst and Whinney, Columbus, OH '81
BAINE, ROBERT P. JR., atty., Lindell Hospital, St. Louis, MO '84 (ATTY)
BAIR, CRAIG A., coor. commun. rel., Cape Coral Hospital, Cape Coral, FL '86 (PR)
BAIR, ED M., dir. info. syst., University of Kansas College of Health Sciences and Bell Memorial Hospital, Kansas City, KS '85 (MGMT)
BAIR, JEANETTE, dir., American Occupational Therapy Association, Rockville, MD '84
BAIR, STANLEY, dir. pub. rel., Brookdale Hospital Medical Center, Brooklyn, NY '70 (PR)
BAIRD, ANN ELIZABETH, dir. pub. info., Sampson County Memorial Hospital, Clinton, NC '85 (PR)
BAIRD, ANNA B., dir. pers. serv., Mercy Hospital, Owensboro, KY '81 (PERS)
BAIRD, BETTY, dir. vol. serv., Hadley Regional Medical Center, Hays, KS '80 (VOL)
BAIRD, BRUCE K., asst. adm. bldg. serv., Tobey Hospital, Wareham, MA '85 (ENG)
BAIRD, CHARLES F. JR., vice-pres., Main and Company, Boston, MA '86
BAIRD, JEFFREY ROSS, adm., Mercy Hospital, Toledo, OH '64
BAIRD, JOE D., dir. plant oper. and maint., Riverside Community Hospital, Riverside, CA '82 (ENG)
BAIRD, JOHN E., chm., Baird, Degroot and Associates, Inc., Gurnee, IL '84 (PERS)
BAIRD, JOSEPH A. JR., mgr. dev., American Medical International, Atlanta, GA '65
BAIRD, SHIRLEY C., spec. lecturer food serv. syst. mgt., Texas Woman's University, Houston Center, Houston, TX '68 (FOOD)
BAIRD, STEVE A., dir. facil. serv., Spelman Memorial Hospital, Smithville, MO '82 (ENG)
BAIRD, THOMAS A., dir. pers., St. Mary Hospital, Quincy, IL '70 (PERS)
BAITZEL, WILLIAM, (ret.), Broomall, PA '79 (ENG)
BAKAY, DIANE MARIE, student, Russell Sage College, Troy, NY '87
BAKER, A. J., asst. vice-pres. health educ., Baptist Medical System, Little Rock, AR '81 (EDUC)
BAKER, ANITA S., adm. assoc. clin. serv., St. Jude Children's Research Hospital, Memphis, TN '77
BAKER, BETTY M., RN, (ret.), Lansing, MI '75 (CS)
BAKER, BEVERLY, RN, adm. asst. pat. care serv., Providence Hospital, Southfield, MI '77 (NURS)
BAKER, BONNIE L., dir. pers., Pekin Memorial Hospital, Pekin, IL '84 (PERS)
BAKER, BONNIE M., dir. plng., St. Vincent Charity Hospital and Health Center, Cleveland, OH '85 (PLNG)
BAKER, BROOKS H. III, dir. maint., University of Alabama Hospital, Birmingham, AL '85 (ENG)
BAKER, BRYDIE J., RN, vice-pres. nrsg. serv., St. Luke's Hospital of New Bedford, New Bedford, MA '85 (NURS)
BAKER, C. RENE, RN, asst. vice-pres. nrsg., Bethesda Hospital, Inc., Cincinnati, OH '85 (NURS)
BAKER, CARLTON CASEY, dir. pers., Schumpert Medical Center, Shreveport, LA '80 (PERS)
BAKER, CECE, dir. nutr. serv., St. Joseph's Hospital and Health Center, Tucson, AZ '87 (FOOD)
BAKER, CHARLES R., sr. vice-pres., Baptist Memorial Hospital, Memphis, TN '65
BAKER, CHARLES RODNEY, assoc. chief staff, McClellan Memorial Veterans Hospital, Little Rock, AR '87 (AMB)
BAKER, CHARLES W., dir. food serv., Gilman Hospital, St. Marys, GA '81 (FOOD)
BAKER, CONSTANCE H., atty., Johns Hopkins Hospital, Baltimore, MD '85 (ATTY)
BAKER, DALE E., partner, Ernst and Whinney, Denver, CO '79 (PLNG)
BAKER, DALE R., asst. chief eng., St. Mary Medical Center, Hobart, IN '85 (ENG)
BAKER, DAVID M., dir. matl. mgt., St. John's Mercy Medical Center, St. Louis, MO '87 (PUR)
BAKER, DELIA WELLER, dir. soc. serv., Riverside Hospital, Jacksonville, FL '78 (SOC)
BAKER, DENISE H., dir. pers., Scott County Hospital, Oneida, TN '83 (PERS)
BAKER, DONALD A., proj. mgr. constr., Berkshire Medical Center, Pittsfield, MA '67 (ENG)
BAKER, DOROTHY, dir. vol., Marianjoy Rehabilitation Center, Wheaton, IL '73 (VOL)
BAKER, DWIGHT E., atty., Eastern Idaho Regional Medical Center, Idaho Falls, ID '86 (ATTY)
BAKER, EVELYN T., dir. vol. serv., Regional Medical Center at Memphis, Memphis, TN '85 (VOL)
BAKER, FLORENCE H., RN, (ret.), Phoenix, AZ '83 (CS)
BAKER, FLORENCE M., head mobilization and plng., Naval Hospital, Oakland, Oakland, CA '86
BAKER, FRANK E., dir. pers., Burdette Tomlin Memorial Hospital, Cape May Court House, NJ '76 (PERS)
BAKER, GEORGE F., dir. gen. serv., Amsterdam Memorial Hospital, Amsterdam, NY '73
BAKER, GORDON F., adm., Schick Shadel Hospital, Santa Barbara, CA '71
BAKER, H. BRADLEY, chief eng., Huntington Hospital, Huntington, NY '81 (ENG)
BAKER, HAROLD G. JR., atty., Anderson Hospital, Maryville, IL '79 (ATTY)
BAKER, JAMES G., atty., Missouri Hospital Association, Jefferson City, MO '79 (ATTY)
BAKER, JAMES W., dir. pur., Pacific Health Resources, Los Angeles, CA '78 (PUR)
BAKER, JANET L., dir. commun. and pub. rel., Defiance Hospital, Defiance, OH '86 (PR) (PLNG)
BAKER, JANET L., dir. food prod., Doctors Hospital, Columbus, OH '79 (FOOD)
BAKER, JANET, asst. dir. med. affairs, Valley Medical Center, Renton, WA '86 (RISK)
BAKER, JANICE R., dir. educ. serv., Peninsula Hospital and Medical Center, Burlingame, CA '84 (EDUC)
BAKER, JEAN H., RN, dir. nrsg., Dorchester General Hospital, Cambridge, MD '83 (NURS)
BAKER, JEANNE T., RN, coor. vol., St. Margaret's Hospital, Montgomery, AL '84 (VOL)
BAKER, JERRY E., assoc. exec. dir., Baptist Memorial Hospital, Gadsden, AL '76 (RISK)

BAKER, JUNE M., dir. commun., Lester E. Cox Medical Centers, Springfield, MO '79 (ENG)
BAKER, KAY R., dir. vol. serv., St. Joseph's Hospital, St. Paul, MN '84 (VOL)
BAKER, KENNETH G., vice-pres., Sullivan, Kelly and Associates, Inc., Portland, OR '86
BAKER, KENNETH R., dir. pers., Lake Charles Memorial Hospital, Lake Charles, LA '79 (PERS)
BAKER, KRISTI P., dir. mktg., St. Francis Hospital, Wilmington, DE '84 (PLNG)
BAKER, LEE L., dir. oper. and eng., Petersburg General Hospital, Petersburg, AK '85 (ENG)(ENVIRON)
BAKER, LEROY E., dir., Voluntary Hospitals of America Enterprises, Consulting Services, Tampa, FL '79 (MGMT)
BAKER, LINDA L., coor. staff dev., Shelby Memorial Hospital, Shelby, OH '86 (EDUC)
BAKER, LORI A., pub. info. off., University of California at Los Angeles Neuropsychiatric Hospital, Los Angeles, CA '86 (PR)
BAKER, MARTHA D., dir. computer serv., Baptist Memorial Hospital, Gadsden, AL '86 (MGMT)
BAKER, MARY B., mgr. pub. rel. and dev., Lincoln General Hospital, Lincoln, NE '84 (PR)
BAKER, MARY C., mgr. mktg., Marion Community Hospital, Ocala, FL '85 (PR)
BAKER, MICHAEL E., dir. plng., The Medical Center, Beaver, PA '86 (PLNG)
BAKER, MICHAEL G., mgr. food syst., Research Medical Center, Kansas City, MO '84 (FOOD)
BAKER, NANCY W., head diet., St. Anne General Hospital, Raceland, LA '86 (FOOD)
BAKER, NORMAN E., asst. dir. eng., St. Francis Hospital Center, Beech Grove, IN '84 (ENG)
BAKER, OTTO F., pur. agt., Audrain Medical Center, Mexico, MO '70 (PUR)
BAKER, PAMELA, asst. dir. nrsg. staff dev., Alexandria Hospital, Alexandria, VA '86 (EDUC)
BAKER, PHYLLIS S., RN, dir. nrsg., Page Memorial Hospital, Luray, VA '72 (NURS)
BAKER, RANDY, asst. vice-pres. human res., Valley Baptist Medical Center, Harlingen, TX '82 (PERS)
BAKER, ROBERT L., dir. pers., St. Joseph Hospital, Lexington, KY '86 (PERS)
BAKER, ROBERT S., atty., Swedish Covenant Hospital, Chicago, IL '86 (ATTY)
BAKER, RODGER H., asst. adm., Fauquier Hospital, Warrenton, VA '76
BAKER, RUTH VIRGINIA, dir. pat. serv., Shenandoah County Memorial Hospital, Woodstock, VA '80 (SOC)
BAKER, SHELLEY R., asst. dir. dining serv., Thomas Jefferson University Hospital, Philadelphia, PA '84 (FOOD)
BAKER, SHERYL L., dir. strategic plng. and commun., McG Telesis, Inc., Mount Clemens, MI '86 (PLNG)
BAKER, SUSAN E., coor. pat. rel. and vol. serv., Arlington Hospital, Arlington, VA '79 (PAT)(VOL)
BAKER, SUSAN ELIZABETH, atty., Cooper Green Hospital, Birmingham, AL '86 (ATTY)
BAKER, SUSAN KEANE, asst. adm., St. Joseph Medical Center, Stamford, CT '81 (RISK)
BAKER, SUSAN, risk mgr., Cooper Green Hospital, Birmingham, AL '86 (RISK)
BAKER, WILLIAM F., (ret.), Mesa, AZ '57 (LIFE)
BAKER, WILLIAM GARY, dir. safety and environ. serv., Clearfield Hospital, Clearfield, PA '68 (RISK)
BAKER, WILLIAM H., sr. vice-pres., Middle Atlantic Shared Services Corporation, Princeton, NJ '81 (PERS)(RISK)
BAKKEN, CRAIG, adm. and chief oper. off., Geneva General Hospital, Geneva, NY '86 (RISK)
BAKKO, ORVILLE E., Oakland, CA '48 (LIFE)
BAKOMENKO, RAYMOND M. JR., dir. matl. mgt., Alfred I. Dupont Institute, Wilmington, DE '83 (PUR)
BAKOS, JANE A., vice-pres., St. Joseph's Hospital and Health Center, Tucson, AZ '82 (RISK)
BAKSHI, SIMI, chief fin. off., Visiting Nurse Association of Trenton, West Trenton, NJ '83
BAKST, MICHAEL D., PhD, exec. dir., Community Memorial Hospital of San Buenaventura, Ventura, CA '68
BAKST, SILVIA, mktg. and pub. rel. consult., Community Health Program of Queens, Nassau, New Hyde Park, NY '65 (PR)
BAKUZONIS, CRAIG W., clin. eng., Geisinger Medical Center, Danville, PA '80 (ENG)
BALANCIA, CHARLES G., assoc. dir., Montefiore Medical Center, Bronx, NY '79 (ENG)
BALAS, JUDITH A., dir. admit., University of Michigan Hospitals, Ann Arbor, MI '82
BALASCO, ELOISE M., RN, dir. nrsg.-acute care prog., Children's Hospital, Boston, MA '84 (NURS)
BALASCO, ERNEST A., supv. clin. soc. work, St. Joseph Hospital, North Providence, RI '86 (SOC)
BALBINOT, BARBARA J., RN, dir. nrsg. serv., Fort Madison Community Hospital, Fort Madison, IA '82 (NURS)
BALDECK, GLADYS H., dir. vol. serv., Moses Taylor Hospital, Scranton, PA '81 (VOL)
BALDERSON, WILBUR JAMES, asst. chief logistics and facil., Department of the Army, Office of the Surgeon General, Washington, DC '59
BALDERSTON, MAUREEN M., dir. soc. serv., Brandywine Hospital, Caln Township, PA '86 (SOC)
BALDINI, LCDR DOMENIC A., MSC USN, Summerville, SC '74
BALDUF, MICHAEL D., dir. pub. rel., Mansfield General Hospital, Mansfield, OH '79 (PR)
BALDWIN, D. PETER, elec. tech. coor., Ellerbe Associates, Inc., Bloomington, MN '85 (ENG)
BALDWIN, DAVID LEE, dir. hskpg. and linen, Northeast Medical Center Hospital, Humble, TX '86 (ENVIRON)
BALDWIN, ELIZABETH M., soc. serv. consult., Columbia Hospital for Women, Washington, DC '70 (SOC)
BALDWIN, HERBERT J., dir. matl. mgt., Red Deer Regional Hospital Centre, Red Deer, Alta., Canada '83 (MGMT)
BALDWIN, HOWARD, chief eng., Geary Community Hospital, Junction City, KS '80 (ENG)
BALDWIN, JANE A., dir. fin. serv., Wyandotte General Hospital, Wyandotte, MI '66
BALDWIN, JO, dir. diet., Children's Hospital, Columbus, OH '72 (FOOD)
BALDWIN, JOAN, asst. dir. pub. rel., Harper Hospital, Detroit, MI '86 (PR)
BALDWIN, JOHN L., dist. mgr., ARA Services, Hospital Food Management, Environmental Service, Inc., Philadelphia, PA '75 (FOOD)
BALDWIN, JUDITH A., mgr. commun. rel., St. Joseph's Hospital, Lowell, MA '86 (PAT)
BALDWIN, KAREN L., dir. pers., Metropolitan Hospital-Springfield Division, Springfield, PA '83 (PERS)
BALDWIN, LUCILLE M., RN, asst. adm. and dir. nrsg., John C. Lincoln Hospital and Health Center, Phoenix, AZ '83 (NURS)
BALDWIN, MIRIAM T., dir. pub. rel., Florence General Hospital, Florence, SC '84 (PR)
BALDWIN, PATRICIA A., dir. vol. serv., Community Hospital, Munster, IN '83 (VOL)
BALDWIN, PAUL JR., asst. to pres., McPherson Community Health Center, Howell, MI '79 (PLNG)(RISK)
BALDWIN, RAYMOND L., mgr. matl. oper. room, Mission Community Hospital, Mission Viejo, CA '84 (PUR)
BALDWIN, ROGER A., vice-pres., St. John's Regional Medical Center, Joplin, MO '76 (ENG)
BALDWIN, STEPHEN C., sr. mgt. eng., Fairview Hospital and Healthcare Service, Minneapolis, MN '82 (MGMT)
BALE, BART D., proj. eng., Fishbeck, Thompson, Carr, Hiber and Fairbrother, Inc., Ada, MI '85 (ENG)
BALES, KATHLEEN E., dir. soc. work and qual. assur., Portland Adventist Medical Center, Portland, OR '84 (SOC)
BALES, RUTH, RN, asst. adm. nrsg., Good Samaritan Hospital, Corvallis, OR '78 (NURS)
BALES, WAYNE M., dir. bldg. and grds., St. John's Hospital, Richmond, VA '85 (ENG)
BALESKY, JEANNE RENO, dir. soc. work, Bon Secours Hospital, Grosse Pointe, MI '86 (SOC)
BALESTRIERI, ANTHONY F., partner, Goebel-Balestrieri and Associates, Architects and Engineers, Elkhorn, WI '76
BALICK, JUDITH, assoc. adm., St. Johns Episcopal Nursing Home, Far Rockaway, NY '81
BALISTRERI, JOHN, dir. gen. serv., St. Mary's Hospital, Milwaukee, WI '86 (ENVIRON)
BALISTRERI, SANDIE M., dir. vol., St. Anthony Hospital, Milwaukee, WI '79 (VOL)
BALIUS, NEAL R., mgr., Coopers and Lybrand, Minneapolis, MN '85 (ENG)
BALK, DUWAYNE, mgr. pur., Wausau Hospital Center, Wausau, WI '84 (PUR)
BALKCOM, DAVID, asst. vice-pres., Rhode Island Hospital, Providence, RI '87 (AMB)
BALKUS, GINA M., dir. pub. rel., New Hampshire Hospital Association, Concord, NH '86 (PR)
BALL, DIANE M., dir. vol. serv., Union Hospital, Union, NJ '80 (VOL)
BALL, FRANCINE JUDITH, consult. corp. human res., Faulkner Hospital, Boston, MA '86 (PERS)
BALL, FRANK E., Houston, TX '83 (ENG)
BALL, GEORGE, dir. pub. rel. and pers., Brunswick General Hospital, Amityville, NY '64 (PR)(PERS)
BALL, LARRY K., dir. med. rec., Cabell Huntington Hospital, Huntington, WV '82
BALL, LISA A., asst. dir. pub. rel., Midland Memorial Hospital, Midland, TX '86 (PR)
BALL, LOIS E., dir. vol., New England Medical Center, Boston, MA '73 (VOL)
BALL, MARY KELLER, dir. pub. rel., Children's Mercy Hospital, Kansas City, MO '83 (PR)
BALL, PAMELA A., dir. vol. serv., Memorial Northwest Hospital, Houston, TX '85 (VOL)
BALL, PATRICIA G., dir. mktg. and pub. rel., HCA Park West Medical Centers, Knoxville, TN '85 (PR)
BALL, PEGGY J., supv. commun., St. John's Regional Medical Center, Joplin, MO '83 (ENG)
BALL, ROBERT W., dir. gen. serv. and chief eng., Doctors Medical Center, Modesto, CA '83 (ENG)
BALL, TIMOTHY J., vice-pres. commun., Grandview Hospital and Medical Center, Dayton, OH '86 (PR)
BALLAM, SAMUEL H. JR., chm. trustee com., Hospital of the University of Pennsylvania, Philadelphia, PA '79
BALLANTYNE, DONNA, asst. adm. nrsg. serv., Fairview General Hospital, Cleveland, OH '80 (NURS)
BALLANTYNE, G. KENT, adm., Bay Area Hospital, Coos Bay, OR '78
BALLANTYNE, REGINALD M. III, pres., Phoenix Memorial Hospital Health Resources, Inc., Phoenix, AZ '71
BALLARD-STORCK, JAN, dir. commun. rel., Our Lady of Lourdes Health Center, Pasco, WA '83 (PR)(VOL)
BALLARD, BRYAN M., vice-pres. and adm., Fresno Community Hospital and Medical Center, Fresno, CA '73
BALLARD, DIANA, RN, vice-pres. health syst. dev., Saint Raphael Corporation, New Haven, CT '77 (NURS)
BALLARD, DIANE B., dir. vol. serv., Floyd Memorial Hospital, New Albany, IN '86 (VOL)
BALLARD, GARY D., student, Duke University, Department of Health Administration, Durham, NC '83
BALLARD, LYNETTE M., dir. vol. serv., St. Anthony's Medical Center, St. Louis, MO '84 (VOL)
BALLARD, PATRICIA W., dir. soc. work, Mary Washington Hospital, Fredericksburg, VA '86 (SOC)
BALLARD, RICHARD R., dir. amb. serv., Newington Children's Hospital, Newington, CT '87 (AMB)
BALLARD, ROBIN LYNN-THOMSON, supv. pat. rep., Saint Francis Medical Center, Peoria, IL '86 (PAT)
BALLARD, THERESE, mgr. matl., Saint John Regional Hospital, Saint John, N.B., Canada '83 (PUR)
BALLARD, VERNON L., plng. assoc. to chm., Portsmouth Regional Hospital, Portsmouth, NH '52 (PLNG)(LIFE)
BALLARD, WILLIAM C. JR., exec. vice-pres. fin. and adm., Humana Inc., Louisville, KY '70 (ATTY)
BALLENGER, MILDRED F., dir. soc. serv., John E. Fogarty Memorial Hospital, North Smithfield, RI '79 (SOC)
BALLENTINE, CRAIG MIKE, dir. mech. eng., Falick Klein Partnership, Inc., Houston, TX '86 (ENG)
BALLENTINE, JANICE M., prac. mgr., Northside Cardiology, Inc., Indianapolis, IN '81
BALLENTINE, MARY, dir. soc. serv., Huntsville Hospital, Huntsville, AL '80 (SOC)
BALLER, KENNETH NEIL SR., dir. plant oper., Mercy Hospital, Cadillac, MI '76 (ENG)
BALLI, DONALD GEORGE, mgr. benefits and compensation, Kettering Medical Center, Kettering, OH '79 (PERS)
BALLOU, DONNA R., coor. pub. rel., Prince William Hospital, Manassas, VA '85 (PLNG)
BALMAIN, THOMAS F., mgr. res., Washoe Medical Center, Reno, NV '86 (ENG)
BALMER, JANE E., RN, dir. nrsg., Hall-Brooke Hospital, Westport, CT '84 (NURS)
BALOCCA, JOSEPH J., dir. matl. mgt., Phelps Memorial Hospital Center, North Tarrytown, NY '82
BALOG, JON WALLACE, mgr. pur., St. Joseph's Medical Center, South Bend, IN '81 (CS)(PUR)
BALOH, CHRISTINE J., dir. soc. serv., Frick Community Health Center, Mount Pleasant, PA '86 (SOC)
BALSAMO, JAMES J. JR., environ. health and safety off., Tulane University Hospital and Clinics, New Orleans, LA '79 (ENG)
BALSLEY, DONNA M., RN, dir. nrsg., Waynesboro Hospital, Waynesboro, PA '86 (NURS)
BALTA, JOHN, dir. cent. serv., Anaheim Memorial Hospital, Anaheim, CA '83 (CS)
BALTAZAR, AIDA, pat. educ., Medical College of Georgia Hospital and Clinic, Augusta, GA '87 (EDUC)
BALTER, SUSAN W., atty., Travenol Laboratories, Inc., Deerfield, IL '83 (ATTY)
BALTHASER, WILLIAM F., editorial dir., Fund-Raising Institute, Ambler, PA '80 (PR)
BALTHROP, NATHANIEL R., asst. adm., Georgetown University Medical Center, Washington, DC '74
BALTUNIS, PATRICIA, dir. vol. serv., La Grange Memorial Hospital, La Grange, IL '85 (VOL)
BALTZ, FLORENCE WEAVER, (ret.), Washington, IL '44 (LIFE)
BALUSH, HELEN B., vice-pres. pub. affairs, Our Lady of Mercy Hospital, Cincinnati, OH '83 (PR)
BALZANO, DOMINIC, asst. adm., Elmer Community Hospital, Elmer, NJ '74
BALZE, MARY ANN, dir. vol., Franklin Square Hospital, Baltimore, MD '81 (VOL)
BALZER, JOHN A., dir. plant oper., Froedtert Memorial Lutheran Hospital, Milwaukee, WI '85 (ENG)
BALZER, MARY J., RN, clin. dir. nrsg., Abbott-Northwestern Hospital, Minneapolis, MN '81 (NURS)
BALZER, YVONNE C., dir. soc. serv., Bethesda Oak Hospital, Cincinnati, OH '70 (SOC)
BAMBERG, BARBARA B., RN, dir. nrsg. adm., Robinson Memorial Hospital, Ravenna, OH '85 (NURS)
BAMBRICK, MILDRED H., coor. vol., Children's Rehabilitation Hospital, Philadelphia, PA '68 (VOL)
BAMFORD, THOMAS J., dir. pub. rel., Elmhurst Memorial Hospital, Elmhurst, IL '83 (PR)
BAMPTON, DEBRA K., dir. pub. rel., Irvington General Hospital, Irvington, NJ '87 (PR)
BANACH, SR. LUCILLE M., RN, dir. nrsg. serv., Sancta Maria Hospital, Cambridge, MA '82 (NURS)
BANAHAN, PAULA J., exec. dir. administration, Arizona Heart Institute, Ltd., Phoenix, AZ '86 (PR)
BANAS, C. LESLIE, atty., Harrison Community Hospital, Mount Clemens, MI '85 (ATTY)
BANAS, GARY A., atty., Robinson Memorial Hospital, Ravenna, OH '80 (ATTY)
BANAS, RICHARD G., vice-pres. mktg., Revere Healthcare, Ltd., Palatine, IL '83 (PR)
BANASZAK, STANLEY M. JR., dir. human resources, South Suburban Hospital, Hazel Crest, IL '75 (EDUC)(PERS)
BANASZYNSKI, GREGORY A., vice-pres. adm., Louis A. Weiss Memorial Hospital, Chicago, IL '84 (PLNG)
BANCROFT, CHARLENE J., asst. dir. pub. rel., Barnes Hospital, St. Louis, MO '82 (PR)
BANCUK, JAMES B., vice-pres., Edward W. Sparrow Hospital, Lansing, MI '78 (MGMT)
BAND, IRWIN M., sr. planner, Kaiser Permanente Medical Care Program, Pasadena, CA '77
BANDA, NANCY R., dir. food serv., Hemet Valley Hospital District, Hemet, CA '83 (FOOD)
BANDER, MARTIN S., dir. news and pub. affairs, Massachusetts General Hospital, Boston, MA '70 (PR)
BANDER, RITA A., dir. vol. serv., Monmouth Medical Center, Long Branch, NJ '72 (VOL)
BANDES, JON, adm. asst. to pres. and dir. mktg. serv., Miami Children's Hospital, Miami, FL '85 (PR)
BANDMAN, ROSALYN L., dir. soc. serv., Children's Hospital, Columbus, OH '68 (SOC)
BANDYK, ANTHONY S., dir. soc. serv., Wyandotte General Hospital, Wyandotte, MI '75 (SOC)
BANE, SANDRA L., RN, dir. nrsg., Morton County Hospital, Elkhart, KS '84 (NURS)
BANGHART, STEVEN F., atty., Mercy Medical Center, Springfield, OH '86 (ATTY)
BANGS, KATHRYN A., coor. educ., Clinton Memorial Hospital, St. Johns, MI '80 (EDUC)
BANK, LESLIE G., dir. guest rel., Greenwich Hospital, Greenwich, CT '84 (PAT)
BANKA, RAYMOND L., coor. spec. proj., Port Huron Hospital, Port Huron, MI '82 (MGMT)
BANKE, LOIS E., RN EdD, dir. educ., Rogue Valley Medical Center, Medford, OR '84 (EDUC)
BANKES, RONALD C., asst. dir. eng. constr., Florida Hospital Medical Center, Orlando, FL '84 (ENG)
BANKS, ALFREDA W., RN, asst. dir. nrsg., Hampton General Hospital, Hampton, VA '86 (NURS)
BANKS, EVELYN C., asst. adm., St. Claire Medical Center, Morehead, KY '72 (PERS)

BANKS, HAROLD V. JR., chief fin. off., Falmouth Hospital, Falmouth, MA '84
BANKS, JOHN D., coor. plng. and constr., St. Francis Xavier Hospital, Charleston, SC '74 (ENG)
BANKS, JOHN E., atty., Southwest Texas Methodist Hospital, San Antonio, TX '72 (ATTY)
BANKS, MARTHANNA R., dir. pub. rel. and commun., Orangeburg-Calhoun Regional Hospital, Orangeburg, SC '73 (PR)
BANKS, REBECCA, assoc. dir. soc. work, Barnes Hospital, St. Louis, MO '84 (SOC)
BANKS, VIOLA, adm. pers., Howard University Hospital, Washington, DC '77 (PERS)
BANKSTON, DALE L., pres., Voluntary Hospitals of America Gulf States, Baton Rouge, LA '70
BANKSTON, JESSE H., pres., Bankston Associates, Baton Rouge, LA '50 (PLNG)(LIFE)
BANNERMAN, JOHN A., atty., Vista Sandia Hospital, Albuquerque, NM '83 (ATTY)
BANNICK, CAPT. RICHARD R., MSC USAF, dep. chief med. constr. prog. br., Department of Air Force Medical Service, Bolling AFB, DC '80
BANNING, FRANK, mgr. bldg. serv., The Methodist Hospital, Houston, TX '86 (ENVIRON)
BANNISTER, TIM, prin., Bannister and Company, Royal Oak, MI '76 (PR)
BANNON, GAY, dir. vol. serv., Muskogee Regional Medical Center, Muskogee, OK '82 (VOL)
BANNON, ROBERTA, RN, supv. oper. room, St. Anthony Medical Center, Columbus, OH '87 (AMB)
BANNON, THOMAS, dir. diet., Rhode Island Hospital, Providence, RI '80 (FOOD)
BANOFF, ANDREW, student, Program in Health Care Administration, Baruch College, New York, NY '86
BANSE, J. PATRICK, consult. eng., Houston, TX '83 (ENG)
BANTA, PETER G., atty., Hackensack Medical Center, Hackensack, NJ '75 (ATTY)
BANTA, WILLIAM F., atty., East Jefferson General Hospital, Metairie, LA '85 (ATTY)
BANTLE, SR. JOYCE, RN, asst. adm. pat. care, St. Francis Medical Center, La Crosse, WI '70 (NURS)
BANTUVERIS, KAREN K., student, Program in Health Administration, Tulane University, New Orleans, LA '87
BANZHAF, KATHARINE, dir. vol. serv., Children's Hospital of Wisconsin, Milwaukee, WI '77 (VOL)
BAPP, HELEN R., environ. control spec., Presbyterian Hospital in the City of New York, New York, NY '85 (ENG)
BAPTIE, LARRY N., dir. educ., Geauga Hospital, Chardon, OH '82 (EDUC)
BAPTISTA, KATHLEEN M., supv. cent. serv., John E. Fogarty Memorial Hospital, North Smithfield, RI '85 (CS)
BAPTISTE, DONALD E., dir. facil., Sturdy Memorial Hospital, Attleboro, MA '83 (ENG)
BARA, MATILDA, dir. staff dev. nrsg., Vancouver General Hospital, Vancouver, B.C., Canada '85 (EDUC)
BARAN-ETTIPIO, BARBARA J., student, Program in Hospital Administration, Trinity University, San Antonio, TX '87
BARAN, ARVELLA, RN, dir. nrsg., Garden City Osteopathic Hospital, Garden City, MI '79 (NURS)
BARAN, DEBORAH A., Franciscan Medical Center, Rock Island, IL '83 (MGMT)
BARAN, FE R., dir. food serv., Norwegian-American Hospital, Chicago, IL '72 (FOOD)
BARAN, MARY M., RN, coor. pat. serv., St. Peter's Medical Center, New Brunswick, NJ '83 (PAT)
BARAN, PAUL N., asst. dir. environ. serv., Wilkes-Barre General Hospital, Wilkes-Barre, PA '86 (ENVIRON)
BARANEK, RICHARD M., dir. pers., Midwest City Memorial Hospital, Midwest City, OK '78 (PERS)
BARANOWSKI, BONITA L., dir. soc. work, Mount Washington Pediatric Hospital, Baltimore, MD '83 (SOC)
BARANOWSKI, DANIEL F., dep. dir. prog., Project Hope, Millwood, VA '85 (EDUC)
BARANOWSKI, EDWARD J., PhD, dir. educ. and org. dev., Ingalls Memorial Hospital, Harvey, IL '84 (EDUC)
BARANSKI, HENRY, dir. plant oper., Atlantic City Medical Center, Atlantic City, NJ '73 (ENG)
BARATTA, STEVEN R., adm., St. Louis Health Center, Morgan Hill, CA '85 (PLNG)
BARB, THOMAS D., dist. vice-pres., Hospital Corporation of America, Nashville, TN '78
BARBADIAN, JOHN C., dir. pers., Hoag Memorial Hospital Presbyterian, Newport Beach, CA '81 (PERS)
BARBARO, KIMBERLY A., RN, dir. acute care nrsg. serv., Worcester Hahnemann Hospital, Worcester, MA '84 (NURS)(AMB)
BARBAROWICZ, PAT, dir. prog. plng. and mktg., Washington County Hospital, Hagerstown, MD '85 (PLNG)
BARBASSO, KATHERINE, pat. rep., Franklin General Hospital, Valley Stream, NY '86 (PAT)
BARBEE, SUE V., dir. pers., Stanly Memorial Hospital, Albemarle, NC '84 (PERS)
BARBER, ANGELA S., student, Department of Health Care Administration, George Washington University, Washington, DC '81
BARBER, CARLA, RN, supv. cent. serv., Scioto Memorial Hospital, Portsmouth, OH '84 (CS)
BARBER, DARLYNE BEVERLY, coor. pat. rep., New Rochelle Hospital Medical Center, New Rochelle, NY '85 (PAT)
BARBER, EARLE N. JR., atty., Germantown Hospital and Medical Center, Philadelphia, PA '78 (ATTY)
BARBER, ELAINE D., dir. nrsg. in-service, Kent County Memorial Hospital, Warwick, RI '79 (EDUC)
BARBER, GERARD, assoc. prof., University of Louisville, Louisville, KY '85 (SOC)
BARBER, GLENN V., dir. pat. acct., St. John's Riverside Hospital, Yonkers, NY '73 (MGMT)
BARBER, JEFFREY B., chief oper. off., Affiliated Hospital Systems, Houston, TX '86 (PLNG)
BARBER, JERRY L., dir. maint., Shelby Memorial Hospital, Shelby, OH '84 (ENG)
BARBER, COL. LEROY M. JR., MSC USA, (ret.), Chapin, SC '71
BARBER, THOMAS A., dir. plant oper. and security, Hutchinson Hospital Corporation, Hutchinson, KS '75 (ENG)
BARBERA, SHERRI L., dir. soc. serv., Lakeside Hospital, Metairie, LA '86 (SOC)
BARBERSEK, JANET R., pat. care rep., St. Luke's Hospital, Newburgh, NY '84 (PAT)
BARBETTO, DEBBIE, cent. sup. tech., Children's Seashore House, Atlantic City, NJ '86 (CS)
BARBINI, GERALD J., dir. soc. serv., Hubbard Regional Hospital, Webster, MA '85 (SOC)
BARBOUR, KIM G., dir. mktg., Doctors Regional Medical Center, Poplar Bluff, MO '86 (PR) (PLNG)
BARBOUR, PAMELA G., asst. dir. diet., Emory University Hospital, Atlanta, GA '84 (FOOD)
BARCH, CAPT. JOHN W., MSC USA, adm. medicine, Brooke Army Medical Center, San Antonio, TX '84
BARCLAY, JAMES M., atty., Baptist Hospital of Miami, Miami, FL '85 (ATTY)
BARCLAY, JEFFREY F., asst. dir., Pennsylvania Hospital, Philadelphia, PA '85 (FOOD)
BARCLAY, PETER G., pres., Pgb Associates, Phoenix, AZ '85
BARCUS, JAMES R. JR., contr., Tarrant County Hospital District, Fort Worth, TX '84
BARD, BARBARA, dir. risk mgt., Crittenton Hospital, Rochester, MI '80 (RISK)
BARDAVID, HERB, exec. dir., Alive and Well, Melville, NY '78 (SOC)
BARDEN, MARY M., RN, assoc. dir. nrsg., George Washington University Hospital, Washington, DC '82 (NURS)
BARDIN, MICHAEL D., dir. commun. and pub. affairs, Scripps Memorial Hospital, La Jolla, CA '85 (PR)
BARDO, M. RITA, dir. soc. serv., St. Luke Hospital, Fort Thomas, KY '86 (SOC)
BARDSWICH, EARL D., sr. consult., Medicus Systems of Canada, Toronto, Ont., Canada '81 (MGMT)
BARE, JAMES L., dir. prog. and serv. plng., Tampa General Hospital, Tampa, FL '76 (PLNG)
BAREN, DAVID, exec. dir. and adm., Cook-DuPage Home Health Care Service, Inc., Maywood, IL '79
BARENBERG, CHERYL A., dir. risk mgt., Community Hospital of Lubbock, Lubbock, TX '85
BARENGO, DENNIS, asst. dir. plant facil., St. Vincent's Medical Center, Jacksonville, FL '86 (ENG)
BARETICH, MATTHEW F., res. assoc., Center for Health Service Research, University of Iowa, Iowa City, IA '79 (ENG)(MGMT)
BARFIELD, LATRELL, RN, supv. cent. sup., Tift General Hospital, Tifton, GA '85 (CS)
BARG, GUY A., vice-pres., Berkshire Health Systems, Pittsfield, MA '79
BARGER, FRANCES C., dir. pers., Jane Phillips Episcopal-Memorial Medical Center, Bartlesville, OK '70 (PERS)
BARHAM, SAMUEL J., pat. rep., Stormont-Vail Regional Medical Center, Topeka, KS '41 (PAT)(LIFE)
BARIL, RONALD J., vice-pres. emp. rel., Maine Medical Center, Portland, ME '75 (PERS)
BARILLARI, RICHARD C., mgr. elec. syst., Bridgeport Hospital, Bridgeport, CT '86 (ENG)
BARISH, LAURIE ANNE, student, Program in Hospital and Service Management, Kellogg Graduate School of Management, Northwestern University, Evanston, IL '86
BARISH, STUART, asst. dir. fin., Mount Sinai Medical Center, New York, NY '79
BARKAN, ELLEN J., dir. trng. and educ., Hall-Brooke Foundation, Westport, CT '86 (EDUC)
BARKER, ALMAN JEFFERSON, dir. medicare, State Department of Health, Oklahoma City, OK '62
BARKER, BEVERLY, RN, asst. vice-pres., Good Samaritan Hospital and Health Center, Dayton, OH '77 (NURS)
BARKER, CYNTHIA, dir. mgt. syst., Clara Maass Medical Center, Belleville, NJ '86 (PLNG)
BARKER, JILL, lib., Mona Vale Hospital, Mona Vale, Australia '86 (MGMT)
BARKER, KATE J., dir. vol. serv., Whidden Memorial Hospital, Everett, MA '86 (VOL)
BARKER, LINDA M., dir. staff dev. and educ., Bethany Medical Center, Kansas City, KS '86 (EDUC)
BARKER, LOUIS, dir. nrsg., Central Louisiana Ambulatory Surgical Center, Alexandria, LA '87 (AMB)
BARKER, MARGARET A., adm. asst. pers., Angleton-Danbury General Hospital, Angleton, TX '86 (PERS)
BARKER, MARY A., RN, (ret.), Griffith, IN '82 (NURS)
BARKER, MAUREEN E., dir. pers., St. Helen's Hospital and Health Center, St. Helens, OR '84 (PERS)
BARKER, MICHELLE M., dir. pub. rel., California Medical Center-Los Angeles, Los Angeles, CA '85 (PR)
BARKER, NANCY J., chief vol. serv., Texas Department of Mental Health and Mental Retardation, Austin, TX '81 (VOL)
BARKER, PATRICIA M., qual. assur. and health educ. spec., University Hospital, London, Ont., Canada '86 (EDUC)
BARKER, ROBERT H., dir. pers., Mercy Hospital of Sacramento, Sacramento, CA '82 (PERS)
BARKER, ROSEMARY, supv. cent. sterile sup., St. Mary's Medical Center, Knoxville, TN '85 (CS)
BARKER, RUTH, dir. qual. assur. and risk mgt., St. Bernardine Medical Center, San Bernardino, CA '86 (RISK)
BARKER, SYLVIA M., nrsg. consult., Mount Sinai Medical Center, New York, NY '71 (EDUC)
BARKER, W. DANIEL, dir. hosp., Emory University Hospital, Atlanta, GA '61 (MGMT)(LIFE)
BARKLAGE, MARLIN J., dir. pers. and emp. rel., Shadyside Hospital, Pittsburgh, PA '81 (PERS)
BARKLEY, SANDRA, student, Rush University, Chicago, IL '86
BARKLEY, WILLIAM C., assoc. dir. diet., Baptist Medical Center of Oklahoma, Oklahoma City, OK '84 (FOOD)
BARKO, WILLIAM F., APO San Francisco, CA '78
BARKSDALE, A. R., atty., Rockdale Hospital, Conyers, GA '84 (ATTY)
BARKSDALE, BILL, atty., Okmulgee Memorial Hospital Authority, Okmulgee, OK '77 (ATTY)
BARKSDALE, GARY T., dir. pers., Hamilton Medical Center, Dalton, GA '85 (PERS)
BARLETTA, SR. MARIE, asst. coordinating mgr. pat. advocacy, Lincoln Medical and Mental Health Center, Bronx, NY '82 (PAT)
BARLEY, JOSEPH, dir. eng. and security, Crossroads Community Hospital, Mount Vernon, IL '85 (ENG)
BARLOW, ANDREA LYNN, student, Department of Health Services Administration, Washington, DC '86
BARLOW, CYNTHIA P., dir. soc. serv., Hinds General Hospital, Jackson, MS '83 (SOC)
BARLOW, HAROLD L., dir. hskpg., Deborah Heart and Lung Center, Browns Mills, NJ '87 (ENVIRON)
BARLOW, COL. MATTHEW J. JR., MSC USA, Alexandria, VA '76
BARLOW, PHYLLIS L., RN, dir. nrsg., Huntington Hospital, Huntington, NY '67 (NURS)
BARLOW, RULON J., asst. adm., Utah Valley Regional Medical Center, Provo, UT '72
BARLOW, TAMARA M., RN, dir. nrsg. oper. and budget, Craven County Hospital, New Bern, NC '86 (NURS)
BARNARD, DEBORAH, dir. plng. and dev., Valley Hospital and Medical Center, Spokane, WA '85 (PLNG)
BARNARD, DENNIS C., asst. to vice-pres. and reg. adm., Kaiser Foundation Hospitals, Oakland, CA '86 (MGMT)
BARNARD, FLORA B., RN, coor. staff educ., Sudbury General Hospital, Sudbury, Ont., Canada '84 (EDUC)
BARNARD, JOHN, atty., Alameda Hospital, Alameda, CA '80 (ATTY)
BARNER, JAMES W., vice-pres. fiscal and prof. serv., Altoona Hospital, Altoona, PA '79
BARNES, A. DIANE, pres., NPW Marketing, Fort Myers, FL '81 (PR)
BARNES, CRAIG A., dir. phys. ther. dept., North Mobile Community Hospital, Satsuma, AL '64
BARNES, DAVID H., atty., Mary Hitchcock Memorial Hospital, Hanover, NH '85 (ATTY)
BARNES, DEBRA A., dir. mktg., St. Mary's Hospital and Medical Center, San Francisco, CA '78 (PR)
BARNES, ELAINE T., supv. pers., Monroe County Hospital, Monroeville, AL '85 (PERS)
BARNES, ELIZABETH W., RN, dir. nrsg., Bruce Hospital, Florence, SC '76 (NURS)
BARNES, FLOYD M., dir. matl. mgt., Carlisle Hospital, Carlisle, PA '84 (PUR)
BARNES, GARY D., atty., Liberty Hospital, Liberty, MO '85 (ATTY)
BARNES, GERI H., dir. vol. serv., Rose Medical Center, Denver, CO '85 (VOL)
BARNES, GREG, owner, Health Career Resources, Houston, TX '87
BARNES, J. JOANN, dir. pers., Mercy San Juan Hospital, Carmichael, CA '83 (PERS)
BARNES, JAMES R., student, Program in Hospital and Health Administration-Business and Health Sciences, University of Florida, Gainesville, FL '85
BARNES, JIM, dir. cent. serv., HCA Doctors Hospital, Lake Worth, FL '78 (CS)
BARNES, JOHN L., vice-pres. plng. and corp. dev., Underwood-Memorial Hospital, Woodbury, NJ '71 (ENG)(PLNG)
BARNES, JOSEPH E., Raleigh, NC '50 (LIFE)
BARNES, KAREN, dir. qual. assur. and risk mgt., Mercy Hospital, Bakersfield, CA '85 (RISK)
BARNES, LEE ANNE, asst. dir. pers. and safety, United Hospital Center, Clarksburg, WV '82 (PERS)
BARNES, MARIAN M., pat. rep., Richard L. Roudebush Veterans Administration Medical Center, Indianapolis, IN '86 (PAT)
BARNES, MAUREEN P., risk mgr., Holy Redeemer Hospital and Medical Center, Meadowbrook, PA '84 (RISK)
BARNES, RICHA L., dir. vol., Norman Regional Hospital, Norman, OK '75 (VOL)
BARNES, ROBERT A., dir. mktg., Doctors Hospital, Tucker, GA '85 (PR) (PLNG)
BARNES, ROBERT L., sr. mgt. eng. syst., University of Massachusetts Medical Center, Worcester, MA '77 (MGMT)
BARNES, ROY E., atty., Kennestone Hospital, Marietta, GA '78 (ATTY)
BARNES, SHIRLEY A., dir. human res., Corona Community Hospital, Corona, CA '86 (PERS)
BARNES, TYLER L. JR., chief operating off., Oklahoma Osteopathic Hospital, Tulsa, OK '75
BARNES, WILLIAM B., sr. consult., Health Tech, Inc., Philadelphia, PA '85 (PR)
BARNETT, BETTYE J., dir. matl. mgt., HCA Parkway Medical Center, Lithia Springs, GA '83 (PUR)
BARNETT, DONNA LEE, dir. vol. serv., Holyoke Hospital, Holyoke, MA '82 (VOL)
BARNETT, EWING S., consult., Humana Hospital -Newnan, Newnan, GA '82
BARNETT, FAY S., mgr. food serv., Baton Rouge Chemical Dependency Units, Baton Rouge, LA '76 (FOOD)
BARNETT, GARY L., exec. dir., Osteopathic Hospital of Maine, Portland, ME '79
BARNETT, JAMES C., adm., HCA Greenview Hospital, Bowling Green, KY '70
BARNETT, JANE, adm. asst. risk mgt., Virginia Mason Hospital, Seattle, WA '86 (RISK)
BARNETT, LARRY H., corp. dir. human res., Normandy Osteopathic Medical Center, St. Louis, MO '85 (PERS)
BARNETT, MARK I., adm., St. Mary's Health Center, Emporia, KS '85
BARNETT, MICHAEL H., atty., Montefiore Medical Center, Bronx, NY '69 (ATTY)
BARNETT, NED B., partner, BNW Healthcare Marketing, Communications, Nashville, TN '78 (PR)
BARNETT, RICHARD J., vice-pres. mktg., Paradise Valley Hospital, National City, CA '85 (PLNG)

BARNETT, SHARON B., dir. pers., Providence Hospital, Columbia, SC '84 (PERS)

BARNETT, SUSAN T., atty., Pattie A. Clay Hospital, Richmond, KY '81 (ATTY)

BARNETT, THOMAS J., dir. plant oper., St. Mary's Medical Center, Evansville, IN '77 (ENG)

BARNETTE, CYNTHIA WEGLEY, atty., Thomas Memorial Hospital, South Charleston, WV '86 (ATTY)

BARNETTE, J. RICHARD, commun. consult., HBO and Company, Atlanta, GA '86 (ENG)

BARNETTE, PETER, dir. mktg. and pub. rel., Brunswick Hospital, Supply, NC '86 (PR)

BARNETTE, VICKIE D., assoc. dir., Duke University Hospital, Durham, NC '81 (CS)

BARNEY-VILLANO, BECKY L., dir. mktg., Charter Suburban Hospital, Paramount, CA '85 (PR)

BARNEY, CAROLYN A., dir. pub. rel., Leominster Hospital, Leominster, MA '82 (PR)

BARNHART, BRIAN N., RN, dir. nrsg. serv., Vicksburg Medical Center, Vicksburg, MS '86 (NURS)

BARNHART, ELEANOR M., dir. vol. serv., Sheppard and Enoch Pratt Hospital, Baltimore, MD '70 (VOL)

BARNHART, JEAN, RN, supv. sup., proc. and distrib., Frankford Hospital of the City of Philadelphia, Torresdale Division, Philadelphia, PA '77 (CS)

BARNHART, RALPH D., biomedical eng., Potters Medical Center, East Liverpool, OH '85 (ENG)

BARNHART, VICKI L., coor. pers., Community Hospital, Tallassee, AL '86 (PERS)

BARNHILL, JOYCE LEE, pat. rep., Baltimore County General Hospital, Randallstown, MD '76 (PAT)

BARON, ALEX M., dir. vol. and soc. serv., Metropolitan General Hospital, Pinellas Park, FL '85 (SOC)

BARON, E. JEFF, Joint Purchasing Corporation, New York, NY '84 (PUR)

BARON, LOIS E., dir. pub. affairs, Saint Luke's Hospital, Cleveland, OH '86 (PR)

BARON, MARLENE, RN, coor. qual. assur. and util. analyst, Fireman's Fund Health Care Plan, Green Bay, WI '87 (AMB)

BARON, STEVEN DAVID, exec. vice-pres., Miriam Hospital, Providence, RI '69

BAROWSKY, DIANE M., sr. assoc., Korn Ferry International, Chicago, IL '82 (PLNG)

BARR, DONALD E., dir. mgt. eng., Sisters of St. Mary, St. Louis, MO '72 (MGMT)

BARR, JACK L., dir. human res., East Alabama Medical Center, Opelika, AL '82 (PERS)

BARR, JAMES F., asst. dir., Indiana University Hospitals, Indianapolis, IN '83 (RISK)

BARR, JOHANNA T., dir. vol. serv., Providence Memorial Hospital, El Paso, TX '80 (VOL)

BARR, JUDITH A., pub. info. off., Rogue Valley Medical Center, Medford, OR '84 (PR)

BARR, KEVIN W., dir. market plng. and mktg., St. Mary's Hospital, Richmond, VA '83 (PLNG)

BARR, NORMA J., instr. educ. and trng., Barnes Hospital, St. Louis, MO '80 (EDUC)

BARR, PAMELA S., graduate asst., University of Illinois, Urbana, IL '84 (MGMT)

BARRAND, KERWOOD W., dir. maint. and eng., Providence Hospital, Washington, DC '81 (ENG)

BARRECA, MARY, atty., Querrey, Harrow, Gulanick and Kennedy, Chicago, IL '86 (RISK)

BARRER, PETER J., tech. dir., Hospital Efficiency Corporation, Boston, MA '86

BARRETT, ARLENE J., mgr. cent. sup., Memorial Hospital and Health Care Center, Jasper, IN '77 (CS)

BARRETT, CARL T., mgr. hskpg. and linen, Calvert Memorial Hospital, Prince Frederick, MD '86 (ENVIRON)

BARRETT, CHARLOTTE, asst. dir., Cedars Medical Center, Miami, FL '85 (RISK)

BARRETT, CYNTHIA R., coor. pat. educ., Jersey Community Hospital, Jerseyville, IL '86 (EDUC)

BARRETT, JOAN M., dir. consumer health educ., Community Memorial Hospital, Toms River, NJ '86 (EDUC)

BARRETT, JOHN P., pres., United Methodist Convalescent Home, Shelton, CT '58

BARRETT, JOHN P., mgr., Peat, Marwick, Mitchell and Company, Chicago, IL '83 (PERS)

BARRETT, JOY N., pat. rep. and soc. serv. asst., Beauregard Memorial Hospital, De Ridder, LA '82 (PAT)

BARRETT, MARK T., dir. pub. rel., Iowa Lutheran Hospital, Des Moines, IA '85 (PR)

BARRETT, MAUREEN E., asst. contr., Mount Sinai Hospital Medical Center, Chicago, IL '86

BARRETT, PAMELA A., mgt. eng., University Hospital and Clinic, University of Nebraska, Omaha, NE '84 (MGMT)

BARRETT, PAUL M., atty., Jordan Hospital, Plymouth, MA '84 (ATTY)

BARRETT, SR. ROSEMARIE, pat. rep., Mercy Hospital of Pittsburgh, Pittsburgh, PA '87 (PAT)

BARRETT, SUSAN R., vice-pres., Smith, Barney, Harris, Upham and Company, New York, NY '81

BARRETTE, PAUL RAYMOND, pres., Holden Hospital, Holden, MA '71

BARRETTE, SARAH C., RN, asst. adm., Spelman Memorial Hospital, Smithville, MO '77 (NURS)

BARRETTI, MICHAEL L., pres., Hospital Services of New England, Inc., Braintree, MA '80 (PUR)

BARRICK, IVAN J., dir. info. syst., Carlisle Hospital and Health Service, Inc., Carlisle, PA '81 (MGMT)

BARRIGAR, ROBERT D., dir. mktg., Resurrection Health Care Corporation, Chicago, IL '85 (PR) (PLNG)

BARRINGTON, JAMES W., sr. mgr., Ernst and Whinney, St. Louis, MO '87 (MGMT)

BARRIOS, EDGAR ANTONIO, MD, vice-pres. commun. health, New Orleans General Hospital, New Orleans, LA '80

BARRIOS, RANDY J., dir. food serv., Thibodaux General Hospital, Thibodaux, LA '84 (FOOD)

BARRIS, ROBERT W., dir. eng., Lowell General Hospital, Lowell, MA '76 (ENG)

BARRON, BARRY M., asst. vice-pres., American Home Assurance Company, New York, NY '86

BARRON, DEBORAH, dir. commun., Northwestern University Cancer Center, McGaw Pavilion, Chicago, IL '79 (PR)

BARRON, ELLEN, vice-pres. plng. and mktg., Franciscan Health System, Chadds Ford, PA '80 (PLNG)

BARRON, JOHN C., atty., St. Vincent Medical Center, Toledo, OH '85 (ATTY)

BARRON, SARA, consumer educ., St. Joseph Health Care Corporation, Albuquerque, NM '85 (EDUC)

BARROW, BARBARA, dir. pub. affairs, University Hospital, Denver, CO '86 (PR)

BARROW, WILLIAM F. II, sr. consult., Deloitte Haskins and Sells, Cincinnati, OH '86 (MGMT)

BARROWS, DONNA D., RN PhD, dir. nrsg. spec. serv., Butterworth Hospital, Grand Rapids, MI '81 (NURS)

BARROWS, JANE K., RN, coor. cont. ed., Deborah Heart and Lung Center, Browns Mills, NJ '77 (EDUC)

BARROWS, PAMELA K., RN, dir. nrsg., Weiner Memorial Medical Center, Marshall, MN '84 (NURS)

BARRY-IPEMA, CATHY, dir. pub. affairs, Lutheran General Hospital, Park Ridge, IL '78 (PR)

BARRY, BRAD, chief oper. off., Quakertown Community Hospital, Quakertown, PA '81 (MGMT)

BARRY, DAVID D., dir. human res., St. Joseph's Hospital and Health Center, Dickinson, ND '86 (PERS)

BARRY, DENNIS M., atty., Sisters of Charity Health Care Systems, Houston, TX '76 (ATTY)

BARRY, DIANA M., asst. dir. food and nutr. serv., Rush-Presbyterian-St. Luke's Medical Center, Chicago, IL '85 (FOOD)

BARRY, FRANCIS E., MD, dir. surg., Atlanticare Medical Center, Lynn, MA '87 (AMB)

BARRY, FRANK E., dir. med. soc. serv., Riverside Hospital, Wilmington, DE '77 (SOC)

BARRY, JOHN A. JR., atty., Hillcrest Hospital, Pittsfield, MA '80 (ATTY)

BARRY, JOHN P., atty., Edmundston Regional Hospital, Edmundston, N.B., Canada '83 (ATTY)

BARRY, JOHN S., dir. telecommun. group, Westec Services, Inc., San Diego, CA '85 (ENG)

BARRY, JOSEPH E., St. Barnabas Medical Center, Livingston, NJ '83 (ENG)(RISK)

BARRY, MERRILYN, dir. vol., North Country Hospital and Health Center, Newport, VT '84 (VOL)

BARRY, NELSON C. III, atty., Kaiser Foundation Hospitals, Oakland, CA '86 (ATTY)

BARRY, PAULINE M., risk mgr., Griffin Hospital, Derby, CT '84 (RISK)

BARRY, ROBERT M., vice-pres. fin., Worcester Hahnemann Hospital, Worcester, MA '82

BARRY, THOMAS F. JR., assoc. admin& chief oper. off., Jane Phillips Episcopal-Memorial Medical Center, Bartlesville, OK '79 (PLNG)

BARRY, WILLIAM D., vice-pres., Joslin Diabetes Center, Boston, MA '54 (LIFE)

BARSHINGER, BRENDA L., RN, vice-pres. pat. serv., Memorial Hospital, York, PA '81 (NURS)

BARSTAD, GLENNA L., assoc. dir. fin. serv., Hospital of the Good Samaritan, Los Angeles, CA '83

BARSZCZ, MAJ. MICHAEL E., MSC USA, adm. res., DeWitt Army Community Hospital, Fort Belvoir, VA '86 (PERS)

BART, CATHANNE, assoc. gen. dir., Albert Einstein Medical Center, Philadelphia, PA '80

BARTEE, DOUGLAS P., mgr. health care info. syst., Ernst and Whinney, Kansas City, MO '87 (MGMT)

BARTELL, NANCY KRAMER, dir. soc. work, St. James Mercy Hospital, Hornell, NY '85 (SOC)

BARTELMA, ROBERT J., mgr. mktg., Ramsey Clinic, St. Paul, MN '79 (PLNG)

BARTELME, DONNA J., pur. mgr., Hillcrest Hospital, Mayfield Heights, OH '82 (PUR)

BARTELS, BRUCE M., Essex Junction, VT '76

BARTELS, JULIE M., dir. commun., Research Health Services, Kansas City, MO '86 (PR)

BARTELS, SUZANNE M., RN, dir. nrsg., Jefferson County Memorial Hospital, Fairbury, NE '85 (NURS)

BARTELS, WALTER J., dir. maint. and hskpg., Adams County Memorial Hospital, Friendship, WI '79 (ENG)

BARTELT, VERN J., dir. commun. rel., Mercy Hospital of Janesville, Janesville, WI '81 (PR)

BARTEN, FRED J., vice-pres. plng. and mktg., Oakwood Hospital, Dearborn, MI '86 (PLNG)

BARTH, H. ALLAN, Lansing, MI '42 (LIFE)

BARTH, JEAN S., dir. commun. affairs, Cuyahoga County Hospitals, Cleveland, OH '74 (VOL)

BARTH, SANFORD M., dir. health care cost cont., Provident Life and Accident, Inc., Chattanooga, TN '75 (PLNG)

BARTH, WANDA J., RN, nrsg. adm. consult., Midlothian, VA '75

BARTHA, EILEEN M., RN, dir. nrsg., Doctors' Hospital of Staten Island, Staten Island, NY '86 (NURS)

BARTHEL, WILLIAM L., consult., Facility Planning and Management Systems, Milwaukee, WI '80 (ENG)

BARTHOLOMEW, DOROTHY, RN, dir. amb. care center activ., Forbes Regional Health Center, Monroeville, PA '87 (AMB)

BARTHOLOMEW, HELEN, dir. vol. serv., Bethesda Memorial Hospital, Boynton Beach, FL '80 (VOL)

BARTHOLOMEW, KAY, dir. mktg., Central Florida Regional Hospital, Sanford, FL '80 (PR)

BARTHOLOMEW, L. KAY, coor. health educ., Texas Children's Hospital, Houston, TX '83 (EDUC)

BARTHOLOMEW, P. RAYMOND, atty., Shenango Valley Medical Center, Farrell, PA '76 (ATTY)

BARTHULY, BETTY J., dir. cent. serv., Stormont-Vail Regional Medical Center, Topeka, KS '79 (CS)

BARTILOTTA, KATHERINE A., dir. tech. support serv., Lutheran Medical Center, Wheat Ridge, CO '83 (PLNG)

BARTLES, DONNA C., dir. pers., Humana Hospital -Sebastian, Sebastian, FL '85 (PERS)

BARTLETT, DIANA F., vice-pres. mktg. and strategic plng., Mount Sinai Medical Center, Cleveland, OH '87 (PLNG)

BARTLETT, EDWARD E., pres., Edward Bartlett Associates, Rockville, MD '84 (EDUC)

BARTLETT, EVELYN J., RN, dir. qual. assessment, Sarasota Memorial Hospital, Sarasota, FL '82 (RISK)

BARTLETT, GAIL W., coor. in-service vol., Childrens Hospital of Orange County, Orange, CA '85 (VOL)

BARTLETT, JAMES W., Strong Memorial Hospital Rochester University, Rochester, NY '83

BARTLETT, JOHN C., PhD, prin. in charge, Herman Smith Associates, Houston, TX '62

BARTLETT, JUDY A., buyer, Memorial Hospital, Colorado Springs, CO '83 (PUR)

BARTLETT, SUSANNE K., Grosse Pointe, MI '71 (SOC)

BARTLETT, WILLIAM J., dir. bldg. and grds., Kansas City College of Osteopathic Medicine, Center for the Health Sciences, Kansas City, MO '73 (ENG)

BARTLEY, SHIRLEY A., vice-pres. plng., Healtheast, Inc., Allentown, PA '77

BARTLEY, THEODORE T. JR., arch., Pennsylvania Hospital, Philadelphia, PA '71

BARTLEY, YVONNE LOUISE, tech. surg. and cent. serv., Salida Hospital, Salida, CO '83 (CS)

BARTMESS, NANCY A., RN, dir. nrsg., Boone Hospital Center, Columbia, MO '86 (NURS)

BARTNICK, DONALD C., asst. vice-pres. amb. prog., Fallston General Hospital, Fallston, MD '87 (AMB)

BARTO, ALBERT A., dir. syst. and data proc., St. Joseph's Hospital, Elmira, NY '77 (MGMT)

BARTO, MILAN A., pres., Barto Associates, Inc., Cupertino, CA '75 (PAT)

BARTOLF, BARBARA J., coor. in-service, William B. Kessler Memorial Hospital, Hammonton, NJ '85 (EDUC)

BARTOLO, DONNA M., RN, dir. oper. room and ancillary serv., Emory University Hospital, Atlanta, GA '83 (NURS)

BARTON, DONALD E., vice-pres., Consolidated Media, Jacksonville, FL '85 (PR) (PLNG)

BARTON, ESTELLE A., dir. educ., Our Lady of Lourdes Regional Medical Center, Lafayette, LA '83 (EDUC)

BARTON, JOSEPH R., RN, vice-pres., Wake Medical Center, Raleigh, NC '67 (NURS)

BARTON, KATHERINE M., asst. dir. food serv., Mease Health Care, Dunedin, FL '84 (FOOD)

BARTON, LEE, dir. biomedical eng., Citizens Medical Center, Victoria, TX '85 (ENG)

BARTON, LEON T., dir. mgt. eng., American Healthcare Management, Inc., Dallas, TX '80 (MGMT)

BARTON, RAY H. III, pres. and chief exec. off., Arrowhead Health Care System, San Bernardino, CA '84 (PLNG)

BARTON, ROBERT VINCENT JR., atty., Daughters of Charity of St. Vincent de Paul, St. Louis, MO '73 (ATTY)

BARTON, THEODORE C., chief eng., Bethany Hospital, Chicago, IL '84 (ENG)

BARTONE, VIRGINIA M., dir. matl. mgt., Metropolitan Health Center, Erie, PA '77 (PUR)

BARTS, THOMAS M., prin., Kurt Salmon Associates, Inc., Atlanta, GA '84 (MGMT)

BARTSCHT, KARL G., chief exec. off., CHI Systems, Inc., Ann Arbor, MI '67 (MGMT)(PLNG)

BARTU, PETER J., dir. maint. and eng., Elmhurst Memorial Hospital, Elmhurst, IL '81 (ENG)

BARTUSEK, WILLIAM C., vice-pres. support serv., Bromenn Healthcare, Normal, IL '75 (MGMT)

BARYLAK, JOSEPH A., asst. adm., Western Reserve Systems-Northside, Youngstown, OH '80

BASARA, LINDA K., dir. pers., St. Luke's Hospital, Duluth, MN '87 (PERS)

BASCH, JOHN W., sr. consult., Lerch Bates Hospital Group, Lutherville, MD '78 (PUR)

BASDAVANOS, REBECCA, risk mgr., Fairfax Hospital, Falls Church, VA '86 (RISK)

BASGALL, SR. AGNES CLAIRE, dir. educ. res., St. John Medical Center, Tulsa, OK '86 (PAT)(EDUC)

BASH, ROBERTA L., student, Georgia State University, Institute of Health Administration, Atlanta, GA '83

BASH, SHARON RODNING, supv. soc. serv., Metropolitan Medical Center, Minneapolis, MN '85 (SOC)

BASHAM, JAMES H., mgt. eng., Jewish Hospital, Louisville, KY '84 (MGMT)

BASHAM, VICKI GLENN, pat. liaison, Jewish Hospital, Louisville, KY '87 (PAT)

BASILE, MARY C., oper. analyst, Mount Sinai Hospital, Hartford, CT '80 (MGMT)

BASILE, SUZANNE, vice-pres., Healthmark Industries Company, St. Clair Shores, MI '80 (CS)

BASKETT, MARY L., dir. mktg. and plng., Saint Joseph Health Center Kansas, Kansas City, MO '80 (PLNG)

BASKIN, DENA S., RN, coor. pat. educ., Day Kimball Hospital, Putnam, CT '83 (EDUC)

BASKIN, MOSES, West Palm Beach, FL '68

BASKIN, SHERRY E., atty., Hospital Association of Pennsylvania, Camp Hill, PA '82 (ATTY)

BASKIN, SID, dir. soc. serv., St. Luke's Hospital, Racine, WI '84 (SOC)

BASOLIS-KOONS, CYNTHIA, asst. dir. pers. and coor. benefits, Newcomb Medical Center, Vineland, NJ '86 (PERS)

BASON, WILLIAM S., pat. rep., Memorial Sloan-Kettering Cancer Center, New York, NY '74 (PAT)

BASQUE, GUSTAVE JR., chief eng., Haverhill Municipal-Hale Hospital, Haverhill, MA '87 (ENG)

BASS, ADRIANNE BLACK, asst. adm., University of Southern California-Kenneth Norris Cancer Hospital, Los Angeles, CA '86 (RISK)

BASS, DONALD B., dir. plant oper., Doctors' Hospital, Coral Gables, FL '85 (ENG)

BASS, JIM, dir. plant oper., Christian Hospital Northwest, Florissant, MO '85 (ENG)

BASS, JOAN M., dir. soc. serv., McKenna Memorial Hospital, New Braunfels, TX '85 (SOC)

BASS, SUZANNE, dir. soc. work, Community Medical Center, Scranton, PA '77 (SOC)

BASSETT, LAWRENCE C., vice-pres., Applied Leadership Technologies, Bloomfield, NJ '65 (PERS)

BASSETT, LILLIAN PATSEL, RN, dir. nrsg. serv., Scripps Memorial Hospital-Encinitas, Encinitas, CA '81 (NURS)
BASSETT, SUZANNE S., dir. pub. rel., Georgia Baptist Medical Center, Atlanta, GA '86 (PR)
BASSI, DAVID V., dir. human res., St. Joseph Medical Center, Burbank, CA '79 (PERS)
BASSI, KATHLEEN, dir. qual. assur., St. Charles Hospital and Rehabilitation Center, Port Jefferson, NY '81 (RISK)
BASSMAN, GERSHON J., chm., Signature Corporation, Chicago, IL '81
BASSO, KATHLEEN BOOZANG, atty., St. Mary's Health Center, St. Louis, MO '84 (ATTY)
BASSO, LANE W., pres., Deaconess Medical Center, Billings, MT '83
BASSO, THOMAS J., dir. pers., Henry Heywood Memorial Hospital, Gardner, MA '83 (PERS)
BAST, DAVID, dir. soc. serv., Howard Young Medical Center, Woodruff, WI '85 (SOC)
BAST, KENNETH G., vice-pres. health serv., John Knox Village, Lee's Summit, MO '82 (PLNG)
BASTA, CALLISTA JEAN, dir. soc. serv., Nicholas H. Noyes Memorial Hospital, Dansville, NY '72 (SOC)
BASTABLE, STEPHEN JEFFREY, exec. vice-pres., Westerly Hospital, Westerly, RI '74 (PLNG)
BASTIAN, SUSAN, mgt. eng., Scott and White Memorial Hospital, Temple, TX '77 (MGMT)
BASTIEN, SHIRLEY, coor. health educ., Mid-Maine Medical Center, Waterville, ME '71 (EDUC)
BATAL, ROBERT C., adm., East Boston Neighborhood Health Center, East Boston, MA '72
BATCHELDER, SUSAN M., RN, dir. nrsg. serv., Northern Inyo Hospital, Bishop, CA '81 (NURS)
BATCHELER, GEORGE D. JR., trustee, Pennsylvania Hospital, Philadelphia, PA '83
BATCHELLER, KATHLEEN A., RN, clin. dir. rehab. serv., Abbott-Northwestern Hospital, Minneapolis, MN '83 (NURS)
BATCHELOR, DAN C., dir. eng., Beauregard Memorial Hospital, De Ridder, LA '82 (ENG)
BATCHELOR, DOROTHY G., dir. vol. serv., Washoe Medical Center, Reno, NV '81 (VOL)
BATCHELOR, DOUGLAS D. JR., atty., St. Joseph Hospital, Augusta, GA '80 (ATTY)
BATE, PAUL K., dir. soc. work, Deaconess Hospital of Cleveland, Cleveland, OH '81 (SOC)
BATEMAN, KENNETH L., dir. diet. serv., Charter Ridge Hospital, Lexington, KY '85 (FOOD)
BATEMAN, MARK T., vice-pres. and chief oper. off., Episcopal Hospital, Philadelphia, PA '86
BATEMAN, STEVEN B., vice-pres., St. Benedict's Enterprises, Ogden, UT '84 (PLNG)
BATES, ANN C., coor. pat. and family rel., Rush-Presbyterian-St. Luke's Medical Center, Chicago, IL '80 (PAT)
BATES, BARBARA J., dir. soc. serv., Victory Memorial Hospital, Waukegan, IL '86 (SOC)
BATES, DENNIS L., dir. diet., University Hospital-University of Nebraska, Omaha, NE '73 (FOOD)
BATES, DORI, pat. rep., Milford-Whitinsville Regional Hospital, Milford, MA '86 (PAT)
BATES, EVELYN L. FARRIS, Fort Leavenworth, KS '84
BATES, FRANK P., chief acct., St. Paul Medical Center, Dallas, TX '85
BATES, KAREN S., asst. mgr. food serv., Rowan Memorial Hospital, Salisbury, NC '79 (FOOD)
BATES, MALCOLM E., prin., The Freeman-White Associates, Inc., Charlotte, NC '85
BATES, PATRICIA L., RN, supv. sup., proc. and distrib., Roxborough Memorial Hospital, Philadelphia, PA '81 (CS)
BATES, RUTH A., dir. vol. serv., Arden Hill Hospital, Goshen, NY '86 (VOL)
BATES, WILLIAM F., atty., Flower Memorial Hospital, Sylvania, OH '76 (ATTY)
BATEZEL, VIRGINIA W., coor. prof. serv. and risk mgr., American Oncologic Hospital, Philadelphia, PA '76 (NURS)(RISK)
BATINA, KIT ANN, student, University of California, La Jolla, CA '86 (PERS)(MGMT)
BATISTA, DANIEL P., atty., St. Joseph Hospital and Health Center, Lorain, OH '77 (ATTY)
BATMAN, BRENT L., vice-pres., Mercy Hospital Medical Center, Des Moines, IA '75
BATORY, ROBERT J., dir. emp. rel., Gettysburg Hospital, Gettysburg, PA '82 (PERS)
BATT, ELLIE, pat. rep., Memorial Hospital for Cancer and Allied Diseases, New York, NY '85 (PAT)
BATT, RICHARD A., exec. vice-pres., Ancilla Systems, Inc., Elk Grove Village, IL '68 (MGMT)
BATTAGLIA, VICTOR F., atty., St. Francis Hospital, Wilmington, DE '81 (ATTY)
BATTAGLINI, LINDA J., corp. planner, United Health Services, Binghamton, NY '80 (PLNG)
BATTAGLIO, JAMES D., dir. pub. info., Hartford Hospital, Hartford, CT '78 (PR)
BATTEN, GWYNNELLYN R., dir. plng. and market res., Mid-Maine Medical Center, Waterville, ME '79 (PLNG)
BATTEY, MARLA S., dir. commun., SunHealth Corporation, Charlotte, NC '83 (PR)
BATTIESTE, DEMETRIC L., student, Program in Health Care Administration, Los Angeles Verne University, La Verne, CA '86
BATTISTA, S. GAIL, vice-pres. tech. serv., Alexandria Hospital, Alexandria, VA '77
BATTISTE, DANIEL P., dir. pers., Southside Hospital, Bay Shore, NY '86 (PERS)
BATTLE, MARIAN J., dir. soc. serv., Robert F. Kennedy Medical Center, Hawthorne, CA '85 (SOC)
BATTUELLO, ELAINE L., coor. nrsg. in-service, McMinnville Community Hospital, McMinnville, OR '86 (EDUC)
BATTY, JANE G., dir. environ. health and safety, Faxton Hospital, Utica, NY '73 (RISK)
BATWAY, LINDA E., dir. soc. work, Lakewood Hospital, Lakewood, OH '86 (SOC)
BATZ, DONNA LEE, dir. pers., Cape Coral Hospital, Cape Coral, FL '81 (PERS)
BAUBKUS, JEROME JOSEPH, asst. vice-pres., F. G. McGaw Hospital, Loyola University, Maywood, IL '67 (ENG)
BAUDER, DOLORES ANN, RN, asst. vice-pres. nrsg., Aultman Hospital, Canton, OH '86
BAUDERMANN, JAY, dir. cent. sterile sup., Cooley Dickinson Hospital, Northampton, MA '82 (CS)
BAUDINO, ROBERT J. JR., atty., Charter Community Hospital, Des Moines, IA '79 (ATTY)
BAUER, ANNABEL, supv. allied health, District One Technical Institute, Eau Claire, WI '85
BAUER, ANNE, claim supv., Health Providers Insurance Company, Chicago, IL '86 (RISK)
BAUER, BERT, dir. soc. serv., South Fulton Hospital, East Point, GA '87 (SOC)
BAUER, ELIZABETH R., dir. med. rec., Saint Francis Medical Center, Grand Island, NE '84
BAUER, FRANCIS X., atty., Hopkins County Memorial Hospital, Sulphur Springs, TX '86 (ATTY)
BAUER, HERMAN E., MD, dep. comr., New York City Health and Hospitals Corporation, New York, NY '42 (LIFE)
BAUER, ILONA, supv. cent. sup. and mgr. matl., Memorial Hospital of Michigan City, Michigan City, IN '81 (PUR)(CS)
BAUER, JEANNINE, mgr. staff dev., St. Elizabeth Community Health Center, Lincoln, NE '86 (EDUC)
BAUER, JOAN E., dir. vol. serv., Ingham Medical Center, Lansing, MI '82 (VOL)
BAUER, KENNETH E., dir. plant oper., West Volusia Memorial Hospital, De Land, FL '86 (ENG)
BAUER, L. DAVID, dir. eng. and security, Winter Park Memorial Hospital, Winter Park, FL '77 (ENG)
BAUER, LEE FRANKLIN, soc. worker, Cancer Treatment Center of Central Los Angeles, Alexandria, LA '86 (SOC)
BAUER, LINDA M., coor. risk mgt. and pat. rep., Anaheim Memorial Hospital, Anaheim, CA '86 (PAT)
BAUER, MARK C., asst. dir. eng., St. Luke's Hospital, Saginaw, MI '86 (ENG)
BAUER, PENNY S., dir. vol. serv., St. Joseph's Hospital, Parkersburg, WV '79 (VOL)
BAUER, RACHEL A., dir. commun., Constance Bultman Wilson Center for Adolescent Psychiatry, Faribault, MN '82 (ENG)
BAUERS, CHRISTINA M., asst. dir. soc. work, Hospital of the University of Pennsylvania, Philadelphia, PA '83 (SOC)
BAUGH, MARYMARGARET, RN, asst. dir. nrsg. and staff dev., North Dakota State Hospital, Jamestown, ND '76 (EDUC)
BAUGHMAN, MARGARET L., dir. vol. serv., Chestnut Hill Hospital, Philadelphia, PA '85 (VOL)
BAUGHMAN, RICHARD C., prin. health care recruitment, Advanced Management Systems, Inc., Brentwood, TN '79 (PERS)
BAUGHMAN, TERRY, dir. prof. dev., Hpi Health Care Services, Inc., Dallas, TX '86 (EDUC)
BAUKNIGHT, WILLIAM C., atty., Fairfax Hospital, Falls Church, VA '71 (ATTY)
BAULD, THOMAS J. III, PhD, dir. biomedical eng., Sinai Hospital of Detroit, Detroit, MI '78 (ENG)
BAULKNIGHT, DONALD, asst. dir. maint., St. Vincent Charity Hospital, Cleveland, OH '85 (ENG)
BAUM, JOHN W., dir. plant oper., Oklahoma Osteopathic Hospital, Tulsa, OK '76 (ENG)
BAUM, LARRY, vice-pres. commun. rel., Cedars-Sinai Medical Center, Los Angeles, CA '67 (PR)
BAUM, RICHARD T., partner, Jaros, Baum and Bolles, New York, NY '81 (ENG)
BAUMAN, DONALD H., vice-pres., Nashville Memorial Hospital, Madison, TN '64
BAUMAN, GARY L., dir. oper. and maint., Children's Hospital of Pittsburgh, Pittsburgh, PA '76 (ENG)
BAUMAN, RITA A., asst. adm. nrsg., Bay Area Hospital, Coos Bay, OR '80 (NURS)
BAUMAN, ROBERT D., mgr. prod. line, Kettering Medical Center, Kettering, OH '84 (PLNG)
BAUMANN, JAMES A., dir. ldry. and linen, St. Mary's Hospital, Waterbury, CT '86 (ENVIRON)
BAUMANN, MICHAEL E., sr. vice-pres., St. Joseph's Medical Center, South Bend, IN '69
BAUMANN, ROBERT EWALD, adm., Booneville City Hospital, Booneville, AR '70
BAUMANN, RON G., dir. eng., Central Montana Hospital, Lewistown, MT '85 (ENG)
BAUMANN, MAJ. RONALD C., MSC USA, chief logistics, Blanchfield Army Community Hospital, Fort Campbell, KY '85 (ENG)
BAUMGART, PAUL, mgr. natl. acct. dev., Ohmeda, Madison, WI '86 (RISK)
BAUMGARTEL, EARL A., consult., St. Francis Medical Center, Pittsburgh, PA '58 (ENG)
BAUMGARTEN, BENITA, RN, chief nrsg. serv., Veterans Administration Medical Center, Durham, NC '85 (NURS)
BAUMGARTNER, CHARLES EDWARD, atty., Elyria Memorial Hospital, Elyria, OH '76 (ATTY)
BAUMGARTNER, ROGER J., maint. control eng., Alfred I. Dupont Institute, Wilmington, DE '85 (ENG)
BAUMTROG, JOHN PATRICK, dir. cent. serv., Methodist Hospital, St. Louis Park, MN '76 (CS)
BAUN, LUANE, coor. vol., Saint Francis Hospital, Tulsa, OK '69 (VOL)
BAUSMAN, MITCHEL, asst. adm. support serv., Magic Valley Regional Medical Center, Twin Falls, ID '81 (ENG)
BAUTISTA, SOTERO, RN, head nrs. emer. room, Southwest General Hospital, San Antonio, TX '86 (NURS)
BAVASSO, RICHIE A., dir. pub. rel. and dev., Westerly Hospital, Westerly, RI '82 (PR)
BAWART, SANDRA KAY, RN, asst. adm., Marshall Hospital, Placerville, CA '80 (NURS)
BAWEL, LUCY A., RN, asst. adm. nrsg. serv., Union Medical Center, El Dorado, AR '81 (NURS)
BAXA, MICHAEL A., adm. asst., Bay Area Hospital, Coos Bay, OR '84
BAXLEY, CAROLYN M., exec. dir., Carle Medical Communications, Urbana, IL '84 (EDUC)
BAXLEY, KAREN D., RN, assoc. dir. nrsg., Baptist Medical Center, Columbia, SC '84 (NURS)
BAXT, LEONARD J., atty., Doctors Hospital of Prince George's County, Lanham, MD '75 (ATTY)
BAXTER, BETTY M., RN, dir. nrsg., Humana Hospital -Greensboro, Greensboro, NC '78 (NURS)
BAXTER, CHARLES E., atty., National Healthcare, Inc., Dothan, AL '87 (ATTY)
BAXTER, GEOFFREY A. E., dep. dir. gen., American British Cowdray Hospital, Mexico, Mexico '84 (PUR)
BAXTER, JOANNE K., dir. mktg. and pub. rel., Baptist Hospital of Miami, Miami, FL '78 (PR)
BAXTER, M. DARLENE, dir. bus. and commun. affairs, Maury County Hospital, Columbia, TN '86 (PR)
BAXTER, MARTHA P., atty., Ohio Hospital Association, Columbus, OH '86 (ATTY)
BAXTER, SANDRA, RN, asst. dir. nrsg. surg. serv., Trumbull Memorial Hospital, Warren, OH '87 (AMB)
BAXTER, THOMAS C., Good Samaritan Hospital, Lexington, KY '77 (ENG)
BAY, JOHN C., pres., Munson Medical Center, Traverse City, MI '56 (LIFE)
BAYCH, TONI I., mgr. telecommun., St. Paul Medical Center, Dallas, TX '77 (ENG)
BAYER, CHARLES M., atty., Saratoga Community Hospital, Detroit, MI '71 (ATTY)
BAYER, GERSHON, chief eng., AMI Kendall Regional Medical Center, Miami, FL '82 (ENG)
BAYES, FRANCES N., dir. pat. serv., Waianae Comprehensive Center, Waianae, HI '86 (PAT)
BAYES, VIRGINIA, supv. cent. serv., Lynchburg General Hospital, Lynchburg, VA '86 (CS)
BAYLESS, BECKY L., dir. soc. work, William F. Bowld Hospital, Memphis, TN '85 (SOC)
BAYLESS, MARION E., RN, adm. nrsg. serv., U. S. Public Health Service Alaska Native Medical Center, Anchorage, AK '83 (NURS)
BAYLEY, THOMAS W., atty., St. Joseph's Hospital, Parkersburg, WV '74 (ATTY)
BAYLIS, MARY K., adm., Baylis Home, Detroit, MI '46 (LIFE)
BAYLIS, MYRNA L., asst. vice chancellor univ rel. and dir. pub. affairs and publ, University of Massachusetts Medical Center, Worcester, MA '81 (PR)
BAYLISS, E. J., market mgr., Pac-Tel Publishing, Walnut Creek, CA '86 (PUR)
BAYLOR, REV. ROBERT L., vice-pres. health and religion, Evangelical Health Systems, Oak Brook, IL '86
BAYNE-SMITH, MARCIA, dir. soc. work serv., St. John's Episcopal Hospital, Far Rockaway, NY '85 (SOC)
BAYNE, DAVID, mgr. food and nutr. serv., Children's Hospital Medical Center, Cincinnati, OH '85 (FOOD)
BAYNES, MRS. ERIC N., chm. vol., New London Hospital, New London, NH '80 (VOL)
BAYNES, PATRICIA G., dir. med. soc. serv., Madison County Hospital, London, OH '84 (SOC)
BAYS, IRIS L., asst. dir. vol., Kaiser Foundation Hospital and Rehabilitation Center, Vallejo, CA '81 (VOL)
BAYS, KARL D., chm., Baxter Travenol Laboratories, Deerfield, IL '82 (HON)
BAYSINGER, SANDRA, risk mgt. consult., Frank B. Hall and Company of Fl, Coral Gables, FL '87 (RISK)
BAYTOS, DAVID G., pres. and chief oper. off., Holy Cross Parkview Hospital, Plymouth, IN '76
BAYZIK, BARBARA ANN, dir. food serv., Fort Sanders-Sevier Medical Center, Sevierville, TN '86
BAZZELL, CARL, asst. chief eng., Peralta Hospital, Oakland, CA '86 (ENG)
BEACH, BARBARA A., dir. soc. serv., Dartmouth Hospital, Dayton, OH '86 (SOC)
BEACH, BETTY L., dir. diet. internship, Veterans Administration Hospital, Hines, IL '75 (FOOD)
BEACH, J. MONA, vice-pres. plng. and mktg., Brattleboro Retreat, Brattleboro, VT '83 (PLNG)
BEACH, R. WALT, assoc. dir., Cape Fear Valley Medical Center, Fayetteville, NC '86
BEACH, RAYNE, RN, assoc. dir. nrsg. educ., University of Utah Health Sciences Center, Salt Lake City, UT '86 (NURS)
BEACH, RONALD A., dir., Mercy Ambulatory Care Center, Orchard Park, NY '87 (AMB)
BEACHBOARD, ROBERT L., risk mgr., The Methodist Hospital, Houston, TX '77 (RISK)
BEACHKOFSKI, JON R., gen. mgr., Madison United Hospital Laundry, Ltd., Madison, WI '83
BEACHLER, SUE J., pride coor., Methodist Medical Center of Illinois, Peoria, IL '86 (PAT)
BEAGLE, CHARLOTTE R., dir. soc. serv., St. Joseph Mercy Hospital, Ann Arbor, MI '70 (SOC)
BEAHAN, DEBBIE M., coor. emp., Mecosta County General Hospital, Big Rapids, MI '86 (PERS)
BEAL, CAROLINE M., pat. and family rep., Miami Children's Hospital, Miami, FL '79 (PAT)
BEAL, CAROLYN E., soc. worker, Saline Community Hospital, Saline, MI '82 (SOC)
BEAL, DARRELL L., dir. mktg., Cini-Grissom Associates, Schaumburg, IL '85 (FOOD)
BEAL, DONNA KAY KINNE, dir. diet., Erlanger Medical Center, Chattanooga, TN '68 (FOOD)
BEAL, JOHN W. JR., pres., J. W. B. Associates, Inc., Bristol, RI '78
BEALLOR, GERALD N., dir. soc. serv., Montefiore Medical Center, Bronx, NY '71 (SOC)
BEALS, WENDY A., asst. dir., New England Deaconess Hospital, Boston, MA '85
BEAM, INGRID, exec. dir., Provider Review Consultants, Daleville, AL '86
BEAM, J. ROBERT, atty., Good Samaritan Medical Center, Zanesville, OH '80 (ATTY)
BEAM, JOANNA MCKEE, atty., University of California San Diego Medical Center, San Diego, CA '84 (ATTY)
BEAMAN, DELORES, coor. hskpg., Moberly Regional Medical Center, Moberly, MO '87 (ENVIRON)
BEAMER, BETTE BRYANT DARDEN, pat. rep., Radford Community Hospital, Radford, VA '79 (VOL)

BEAMER, DEANE E., exec. dir., Smyth County Community Hospital, Marion, VA '61

BEAMISH, EDWARD A., dir. environ., Mercy Center for Health Care Services, Aurora, IL '86 (ENVIRON)

BEAMISH, RAHNO MARY, Kitchener, Ont., Canada '51 (LIFE)

BEAN, AMY A., dir. soc. work, Pulaski Memorial Hospital, Winamac, IN '82 (PERS)

BEAN, CLAUDETTE R., RN, dir. educ., Redington-Fairview General Hospital, Skowhegan, ME '82 (EDUC)

BEAN, DALE K., vice-pres., California College for Health Science, National City, CA '81 (EDUC)

BEAN, DAVID L., mgt. rep., Servicemaster Industries, Inc., Downers Grove, IL '86

BEAN, GORDON MICHAEL, dir. plant oper., Northshore Regional Medical Center, Slidell, LA '85 (ENG)

BEAN, KIM P., mgt. eng., Ohio State University Hospitals, Columbus, OH '83 (MGMT)

BEAN, LESLIE TERESE, dir. pat. advocacy, University of Texas System Cancer Center, Houston, TX '86 (PAT)

BEAN, NATHAN, dir. spec. serv., Merle West Medical Center, Klamath Falls, OR '86 (RISK)

BEAN, RUTH ANN, dir. matl. mgt., Hospital of the Medical College of Pennsylvania, Philadelphia, PA '80 (PUR)

BEAN, RUTH L., pat. rep., Howard University Hospital, Washington, DC '78 (PAT)

BEANE, DONNA, student, Program in Health Services Administration, George Washington University, Washington, DC '86 (RISK)

BEAR, CATHY J., dir. human res., Medical Center of Independence, Independence, MO '85 (PERS)

BEARD, BRAMLET LES, HCA West Paces Ferry Hospital, Atlanta, GA '81

BEARD, GREGORY, asst. chief biomedical, Boca Raton Community Hospital, Boca Raton, FL '84 (ENG)

BEARD, JOHN E., mgr. maint. plant, River Parishes Medical Center, Laplace, LA '83 (ENG)

BEARD, MARCIA-ANNE, student, Program in Hospital Administration, University of Michigan, Ann Arbor, MI '85

BEARDEN, ROBERT E., coor. plng., Veterans Administration Medical Center, Dallas, TX '75 (PLNG)

BEARDEN, WANDA J., asst. dir. matl. mgt., Galesburg Cottage Hospital, Galesburg, IL '86 (CS)

BEARDIN, MARY M., atty., Tomball Regional Hospital, Tomball, TX '84 (ATTY)

BEARDSLEY, CHRISTOPHER, exec. dir., Colorado Springs Osteopathic Foundation, Colorado Springs, CO '77 (PR)

BEARDSLEY, JOYCE W., dir. pers., St. Mary's Health Center, Emporia, KS '83 (PERS)

BEARDSLEY, RALPH A., mgr., Health Care Management, Inc., Oak Park, IL '82 (PLNG)

BEASLEY, EILEEN B., dir. pers., Richardson Medical Center, Richardson, TX '86 (PERS)

BEASLEY, GAIL B., RN, dir. nsrg, Lenoir Memorial Hospital, Kinston, NC '86 (NURS)

BEASLEY, MARJORIE A., dir. food and nutr., Bloomington Hospital, Bloomington, IN '71 (FOOD)

BEATON, DARROW ROSS, pres., Apex Medical Corporation, Sioux Falls, SD '86 (PR)

BEATRICE, SR. MARY, pat. rep., St. John's Queens Hospital, Flushing, NY '83 (PAT)

BEATRICE, PAUL R., risk mgr., Forty-Fifth Street Mental Health Center, West Palm Beach, FL '86 (RISK)

BEATTIE, GREGORY P., proj. off., Mercy International Health Services, Mason City, IA '84

BEATTIE, JOHN R., atty., Metropolitan Medical Center, Minneapolis, MN '84 (ATTY)

BEATTIE, NORMAN L., dir. maint., Defiance Hospital, Defiance, OH '75 (ENG)

BEATTY, BRAD A., RN, asst. dir. nrsg., Bone and Joint Hospital, Oklahoma City, OK '82 (NURS)

BEATTY, GREGG C., vice-pres. emer. plng. and trng., Sb Consultants, Inc., Olney, MD '85 (ENG)(RISK)

BEATTY, JAMES S., food serv. dir., North Carolina Baptist Hospital, Winston-Salem, NC '83 (FOOD)

BEATTY, JANE T., dir. vol. serv., Northbay Medical Center, Fairfield, CA '86 (VOL)

BEATTY, SCOTT THOMAS, consult., Ernst and Whinney, Cleveland, OH '80

BEATY, DELORIS DIAHN, pat. rep., Memorial Hospital of Laramie County, Cheyenne, WY '87 (PAT)

BEAUBIER, H. AL, mgr. health care adm., Southern California Edison Company, Rosemead, CA '87 (AMB)

BEAUCHAMP, EDITH ANN, RN, vice-pres. nrsg., St. Joseph Hospital, Bangor, ME '81 (NURS)

BEAUCHAMP, PHILLIP E., vice-pres., Alexander and Alexander of California, Inc., San Francisco, CA '82 (RISK)

BEAUCHENE, PAUL J., mgr. plant oper., Group Health Cooperative of Puget Sound, Seattle, WA '81 (ENG)

BEAUCHESNE, KAREN S., RN, vice-pres. nrsg., Hospital of Saint Raphael, New Haven, CT '84 (NURS)

BEAUCHESNE, PHILIPPE V., dir. mktg., Mount Vernon Hospital, Alexandria, VA '83 (PR) (PLNG)

BEAUDETTE, MARCELLA R., RN, dir. nrsg., Robert B. Brigham Hospital, Boston, MA '72 (NURS)

BEAUDIN, RICHARD L., vice-pres. and prin., Cini-Little International, Chagrin Falls, OH '84 (FOOD)

BEAUDOIN, GEORGIA, pat. rel. rep., Ravenswood Hospital Medical Center, Chicago, IL '77 (PAT)

BEAUDRY, STEPHEN J., field rep., Joint Commission on Accreditation of Hospitals, Chicago, IL '55 (LIFE)

BEAULIEU, ALBERT L., spec. consult. and adm. pension plan, Speare Memorial Hospital, Plymouth, NH '48 (LIFE)

BEAULIEU, AVA M., vice-pres., Maryland General Hospital, Baltimore, MD '85

BEAULIEU, PATRICIA L., RN, proj. spec., Berkshire Medical Center, Pittsfield, MA '80 (NURS)

BEAUMAN, CYNTHIA C., coor. pat. rep., St. Luke's Regional Medical Center, Sioux City, IA '83 (PAT)

BEAUMONT, CATHERINE, risk mgr., Bergen Pines County Hospital, Paramus, NJ '82 (RISK)

BEAUPRE, JOSEPH K., mgr. tele-commun., Kaiser Permanente Medical Care Program, Oakland, CA '74 (ENG)

BEAUTYMAN, MICHAEL J., atty., New England Medical Center, Boston, MA '84 (ATTY)

BEAVER, CHARLES E. JR., plant eng., North Arkansas Medical Center, Harrison, AR '74 (ENG)

BEAVERS, MARIAN G., RN, vice-pres., Mercy Health Center, Oklahoma City, OK '82 (NURS)

BEAVERSON, T. PAT, dir. human res., Ozarks Medical Center, West Plains, MO '85 (SOC)(PERS)

BEAVES, THEODORE J. SR., sr. prin. syst. analyst, Ncr Corporation, Dayton, OH '82 (MGMT)

BEAVON, JENNIE E., dir. staff dev., Grandview Hospital and Medical Center, Dayton, OH '83 (EDUC)

BEAZLEY, LAWRENCE, asst. dir. environ. serv., Oak Forest Hospital of Cook County, Oak Forest, IL '87 (ENVIRON)

BEBB, RICHARD S., atty., Alexian Brothers Hospital San Jose, San Jose, CA '80 (ATTY)

BEBEE, BETH, dir. trng. and dev., St. Mary's Hospital and Health Center, Tucson, AZ '80 (EDUC)

BEBLA, JIM, dir. pub. rel., Lewistown Hospital, Lewistown, PA '86 (PR)

BECERRIL, CARMEN TERESA, RN, assoc. exec. dir., Lincoln Medical and Mental Health Center, Bronx, NY '79 (NURS)

BECHARD, SUSAN E., dir. pub. rel., Fairview Deaconess Center, Minneapolis, MN '85 (PR)

BECHEK, JACQUELINE B., atty., Massachusetts General Hospital, Boston, MA '86 (ATTY)

BECHTEL, ALLEN D., mgr. matl., Medical Surgical Clinic, Milwaukee, WI '84 (PUR)

BECK, ANDREW A., dir. pub. rel. and dev., Manchester Memorial Hospital, Manchester, CT '77 (PR)

BECK, ARTHUR E., atty., Beck, Chaet and Loomis, Milwaukee, WI '78 (ATTY)

BECK, CAROL B., RN, vice-pres. pat. serv., Pendleton Memorial Methodist Hospital, New Orleans, LA '80 (NURS)

BECK, CHARLOTTE A., placement consult., Michigan Hospital Association Service Corporation, Lansing, MI '86 (PERS)

BECK, DOROTHY K., dir. vol. serv., North Kansas City Hospital, North Kansas City, MO '70 (VOL)

BECK, ELMER A., pur. and qual. contr. diet., Loma Linda University Medical Center, Loma Linda, CA '81 (FOOD)

BECK, JAMES M., mgr. corp. logistics, American Hospital Supply Corporation, Hayward, CA '84 (PUR)

BECK, KAREN E., Pittsburgh, PA '84 (PUR)

BECK, KENNETH ALAN, dir. pur., Good Samaritan Medical Center, Milwaukee, WI '78 (PUR)

BECK, L. HERBERT, dir. environ. serv., Bronson Methodist Hospital, Kalamazoo, MI '86 (ENVIRON)

BECK, MARY A., dir. plng. and prog. dev., North Carolina Memorial Hospital, Chapel Hill, NC '78

BECK, MARY L., risk coor., Alton Memorial Hospital, Alton, IL '83 (RISK)

BECK, RICHARD H., asst. dir. health, Nebraska State Department of Health, Lincoln, NE '70

BECK, RITA M., RN, prog. adm. ob. and gyn., Mount Sinai Medical Center, Milwaukee, WI '86 (NURS)

BECK, SANDRA J., mgr. cent. serv. and sup., York Hospital, York, PA '78 (CS)

BECK, SHARON M. H., dir. vol. serv., Medical Center at Princeton, Princeton, NJ '77 (VOL)

BECK, STEVEN E., sr. vice-pres., Fred S. James and Company of Arizona, Tucson, AZ '85 (RISK)

BECKELMAN, KENNETH, vice-pres. plng. and mktg., Sacred Heart Hospital, Allentown, PA '86 (PLNG)

BECKER-REEMS, ELIZABETH D., vice-pres. human res., Memorial Mission Hospital, Asheville, NC '83 (PERS)

BECKER, AGNES H., RN, dir. staff dev., Lebanon Community Hospital, Lebanon, OR '71 (EDUC)

BECKER, AMY G., sr. analyst, Healthcare Communications, Inc., Reston, VA '84 (ENG)

BECKER, AMY HOGUE, adm. diet. pat. serv., Mercy Hospital Medical Center, Des Moines, IA '84 (FOOD)

BECKER, BERNARD H., corp. dir. human res., Horizon Health Systems, Oak Park, MI '81 (PERS)

BECKER, BETTY, vice-pres. plng. and mktg., Parkside Home Health Services, Northbrook, IL '79 (PLNG)

BECKER, DONNA S., dir. food and nutr. serv., University of Wisconsin Hospital and Clinics, Madison, WI '78 (FOOD)

BECKER, GARY W., mgr. data proc., St. Joseph's Hospital, Parkersburg, WV '81 (MGMT)

BECKER, JEANINE ANN, RN, dir. psych. and gen. nrsg., Memorial Hospital, South Bend, IN '81 (NURS)

BECKER, JEANNE M., dir. plng., Yuma Regional Medical Center, Yuma, AZ '86 (PLNG)

BECKER, JEFFREY HOWARD, atty., Joint Diseases North General Hospital, New York, NY '81 (ATTY)

BECKER, JUDITH DEL COLLIANO, dir. pub. rel., Germantown Hospital and Medical Center, Philadelphia, PA '85 (PR)

BECKER, LENORE, RN, dir. nrsg., Community Hospital, Watervliet, MI '87 (AMB)

BECKER, MARJORIE C., adm. human res., University of Michigan Hospitals, Ann Arbor, MI '83 (PERS)

BECKER, RICHARD J., asst. adm. clin. serv., Booth Memorial Medical Center, Flushing, NY '83

BECKER, SCOTT A., pres., Butler Memorial Hospital, Butler, PA '82 (PLNG)

BECKETT, CARL C., actg. dir. bldg. serv., Memorial Hospital for Cancer and Allied Diseases, New York, NY '86

BECKETT, THOMAS ALFRED, pres., St. Elizabeth Medical Center, Dayton, OH '64

BECKHAM, DOROTHY, RN, vice-pres. nrsg. serv., Hanford Community Hospital, Hanford, CA '86 (NURS)

BECKHAM, J. DANIEL, pres., HealthMarket, Inc., Arlington Heights, IL '80 (PR) (PLNG)

BECKHAM, KAY, student, Program in Health Care Administration, University of Colorado, Boulder, CO '84

BECKHAM, SHARON L., coor. vol. resources, Stanford University Hospital, Palo Alto, CA '70 (VOL)

BECKLEY, BETTY J., student, George Washington University, Washington, DC '79

BECKMAN, CYNTHIA A., coor. risk mgt. and dir. pat. rel., Graduate Hospital, Philadelphia, PA '79 (PAT)(RISK)

BECKMAN, GREGORY L., adm. res., McLaren General Hospital, Flint, MI '81

BECKMAN, MARJORIE ANNE, dir. soc. work, Lenox Hill Hospital, New York, NY '69 (SOC)

BECKMAN, MORTON, vice-pres. oper., Flushing Hospital and Medical Center, Flushing, NY '73

BECKMAN, NANCY LEE, RN, sr. vice-pres. oper., San Pedro Peninsula Hospital, San Pedro, CA '78 (NURS)

BECKMANN, GEORGE C. JR., vice-pres., St. Joseph's Hospital, Savannah, GA '52 (PUR)(LIFE)

BECKWITH, JOHN L., adm. rehab. serv., Center General Hospital, Howard, RI '50 (LIFE)

BECO, ELOISE, supv. sterilization, Ochsner Foundation Hospital, New Orleans, LA '83 (CS)

BEDARD, BRIDGET M., mgr. pub. rel., Noble Hospital, Westfield, MA '84 (PR)

BEDARD, MARY A., RN, dir. nrsg., Tidewater Psychiatric Institute, Virginia Beach, VA '76 (NURS)

BEDDIE, DONALD J., dir. mgt. syst., Maine Medical Center, Portland, ME '79 (MGMT)

BEDDOW, JOHN H., (ret.), Melbourne, FL '49 (LIFE)

BEDDOW, SARA, mgr. cent. sup., Memorial Hospital, Colorado Springs, CO '80 (CS)

BEDELL, DIANI BICA, chief soc. worker discharge plng., New England Medical Center, Boston, MA '85 (SOC)

BEDELL, MARY B., RN, asst. adm. nrsg., Memorial Hospital of Southern Oklahoma, Ardmore, OK '86 (NURS)

BEDENKOP, BARRY T., Syrause, NY '58

BEDFORD, MARY RUTH, PhD, Boston, MA '78 (FOOD)

BEDNARCZYK, LORRAINE, RN, asst. adm. nrsg. serv., Bluefield Community Hospital, Bluefield, WV '80 (NURS)

BEDNAREK, VALERIA ANN, student, Governors State University, Program in Health Services Administration, Park Forest South, IL '81

BEDNER, CAROL A., dir. soc. serv., John C. Lincoln Hospital and Health Center, Phoenix, AZ '84 (SOC)

BEDSWORTH, GARY J., dir. food serv., Southwest Florida Regional Medical Center, Fort Myers, FL '83 (FOOD)

BEDWELL, RAYMOND T. JR., Brookfield, WI '71 (EDUC)

BEECHAMP, LYNNE E., asst. dir. prod. and food serv., Palos Community Hospital, Palos Heights, IL '87 (FOOD)

BEECHER, DONALD G., dir. cent. sup., Astoria General Hospital, Long Island City, NY '86 (CS)

BEEGLE, SANDRA C., Louisville, TN '83 (MGMT)

BEEHLER, CAROL A., RN, asst. exec. dir. pat. care serv., Saint Joseph Hospital, Mishawaka, IN '86 (NURS)

BEEHLER, CHRISTINE R., supv. cent. serv., St. Francis Hospital, Milwaukee, WI '80 (CS)

BEEKLEY, HENRY L., corp. dir. mgt. eng., Harper-Grace Hospitals, Detroit, MI '84 (MGMT)

BEEKMAN, FREDERICK, assoc. dir. vol. serv., Coney Island Hospital, Brooklyn, NY '80

BEEKMAN, MARJORY ANNE, mgr. med. and surg. nrsg., Sierra Community Hospital, Fresno, CA '86 (NURS)

BEELER, ANDREA, RN, pat. rep., Monongahela Valley Hospital, Monongahela, PA '84 (PAT)

BEELER, DON A., vice-pres., Incarnate Word Health Services, San Antonio, TX '75

BEELER, JAMES R., dir. plng. and mktg. reg. oper., Samaritan Health Service, Phoenix, AZ '83 (PLNG)

BEELER, JAY, mktg. consult., Beeler and Associates, Long Beach, CA '74 (PR)

BEELER, JOHN, dir. food serv., Bristol Hospital, Bristol, CT '85 (FOOD)

BEEM, GORDON R., adm., Hillsdale Community Health Center, Hillsdale, MI '68

BEEMAN, BARRY G., dir. human res., Rockville General Hospital, Rockville, CT '86 (PERS)

BEEMAN, CAROL, mgr. corp. wage and salary, Harper Hospital, Detroit, MI '83 (PERS)

BEEMAN, MERIAM M., coor. staff dev., Lykes Memorial Hospital, Brooksville, FL '87 (EDUC)

BEER, HELEN M., coor. pers., Magic Valley Regional Medical Center, Twin Falls, ID '83 (PERS)

BEER, MARTIN, dir. eng., High Point Hospital, Port Chester, NY '85 (ENG)

BEERS, SARAH W., RN, chief nrsg. serv., Veterans Administration Medical Center, St. Louis, MO '81 (NURS)

BEETS-GARNER, MERRY K., mgr. vol. serv., Saint Joseph Hospital, Fort Worth, TX '85 (VOL)

BEGGS, CAROL A., dir. soc. serv., Heights General Hospital, Albuquerque, NM '81 (PAT)(SOC)

BEGGS, W. LYNN, coor. vol., Heartland Hospital East, St. Joseph, MO '84 (VOL)

BEGHIN, CAROLYN V., dir. pers., Community Hospital of Sacramento, Sacramento, CA '82 (PERS)

BEGHIN, LAWRENCE PAUL, dir. plant, Sinai Hospital of Detroit, Detroit, MI '83 (ENG)

BEGHTOL, JOHN D., asst. dir. commun. affairs and cooperative serv., Western State Hospital, Staunton, VA '85 (PR)

BEGLEY, MARILU, dir. telecommun., Children's Medical Center, Dayton, OH '83 (ENG)

BEGLINGER, JOAN E., vice-pres., Good Samaritan Medical Center, Milwaukee, WI '85 (NURS)

BEHARIE-WORD, DAISY, asst. adm., Walter Reed Army Medical Center, Washington, DC '84

BEHE, ELAINE E., RN, vice-pres. nrsg., Conemaugh Valley Memorial Hospital, Johnstown, PA '77 (NURS)

BEHLING, ARLEEN V., RN, assoc. dir. nrsg., Mount Sinai Medical Center, Milwaukee, WI '83 (NURS)

BEHLING, PATRICIA L., RN, vice-pres. nrsg., Victory Memorial Hospital, Waukegan, IL '84 (NURS)

BEHLING, ROBERT J., asst. prof. health serv. adm., College of St. Francis, Joliet, IL '77

BEHM, JOHN F., asst. vice-pres., Mount Sinai Medical Center, Milwaukee, WI '80

BEHN, WALTER L., exec. vice-pres. and adm., Kapiolani Women's and Children's Medical Center, Honolulu, HI '62

BEHREND, THOMAS A., dir. pers., Mercy Medical Center, Coon Rapids, MN '74 (PERS)
BEHRENDT, ROBERT V. JR., asst. dir. plant, Good Samaritan Medical Center, Phoenix, AZ '79 (ENG)
BEHRENS, BARBARA A., RN, dir. critical care and emer. serv., Queen's Medical Center, Honolulu, HI '84 (NURS)
BEHRENS, JOHN S., dir. med. logistics mgt., U. S. Air Force Regional Hospital, Eglin AFB, FL '77
BEHRINGER, CHARLES W., exec. hskpg., Dunn Memorial Hospital, Bedford, IN '86 (ENVIRON)
BEHRMAN, CELERINA LIM, RN, asst. vice-pres. nrsg., Resurrection Hospital, Chicago, IL '77 (NURS)
BEHRMAN, EDWARD A., dir. educ., Catholic Health Association of the United States, St. Louis, MO '65 (EDUC)
BEICH, J. JEFFREY, vice-pres. prof. serv., Muhlenberg Hospital Center, Bethlehem, PA '81 (PLNG)
BEIDLER, MURRAY M., dir. matl. mgt., Mary Hitchcock Memorial Hospital, Hanover, NH '74 (PUR)(CS)
BEIER, DIANE E. AHRENS, supv. soc. serv., Lutheran Hospital of Milwaukee, Milwaukee, WI '79 (SOC)
BEIGHTOL, KEVIN E., adm., Randolph County Hospital, Roanoke, AL '76
BEIGLER, JERRY S., adm. asst., Glen Eden Hospital, Warren, MI '81 (RISK)
BEIL, CLARK R., asst. adm., King's Daughters' Hospital, Staunton, VA '86 (PERS)
BEILFUSS, LEO, dir. bldg. serv., Memorial Hospital of Taylor County, Medford, WI '78 (ENG)
BEIRNE, FRANK T., adm., Chatham Hospital, Siler City, NC '82
BEISEL, DANA L., dir. pat. commun. rel., Palmerton Hospital, Palmerton, PA '82 (SOC)
BEISHLINE, CYNTHIA E., asst. dir. pers., Mercer Medical Center, Trenton, NJ '84 (EDUC)
BEITLER, KENNETH R., sr. planner-productivity improvement, Hennepin County Medical Center, Minneapolis, MN '85 (MGMT)
BEITZ, BARBARA G., pat. advocate, Kino Community Hospital, Tucson, AZ '83 (PAT)
BEJJANI, LILI E., supv. food serv., Yale Clinic and Hospital, Houston, TX '84 (FOOD)
BEKENSTEIN, CAROL S., dir. vol., Michael Reese Hospital and Medical Center, Chicago, IL '69 (VOL)
BELAIR, HOLLY, coor. family cent. educ., Alexandria Hospital, Alexandria, VA '82 (EDUC)
BELANGER, BARRY B., asst. adm., St. Patrick Hospital, Lake Charles, LA '77 (PR)
BELANGER, BONNIE JEAN, vice-pres., Hebrew Home and Hospital, Hartford, CT '83 (PERS)(PR)
BELANICH, JOSEPH F., sr. vice-pres. oper., St. Elizabeth Medical Center, Dayton, OH '70
BELANICH, WILLIAM M., dir. pers., St. Elizabeth Medical Center, Dayton, OH '82 (PERS)
BELASIC, BONNIE, mgr. spec. proj., St. Luke's Hospital, Kansas City, MO '85 (PR)
BELBACK, CAROL ANN, RN, dir. nrsg., Cottage Hospital of Grosse Pointe, Grosse Pointe Farms, MI '77 (NURS)
BELCHER, DAVID M., Everett, WA '74 (PR)
BELCHER, GERALD W., risk mgr., McLaren General Hospital, Flint, MI '80 (RISK)
BELCHER, GOLDIE, coor. peer review and qual. assur., Fountain Valley Regional Hospital Medical Center, Fountain Valley, CA '87 (RISK)
BELCHER, KATHY E., RN, asst. vice-pres., Jewish Hospital, Louisville, KY '81 (NURS)
BELCHER, WILLIAM S., atty., All Children's Hospital, St. Petersburg, FL '71 (ATTY)
BELDEN, ALICE WILLIAMS, dir. soc. serv., Children's Hospital of Michigan, Detroit, MI '70 (SOC)
BELEMJIAN, VIRGINIA C., dir. vol. serv., Samaritan Hospital, Troy, NY '81 (VOL)
BELEN, SR. MARY JANICE, Lansing, MI '81 (PLNG)
BELEW, CHARLES D., dir. commun., Erlanger Health Services, Chattanooga, TN '85 (PR)
BELEW, GLORIA S., mgr. matl., Crawford Memorial Hospital, Robinson, IL '84 (PUR)
BELFIELD, DEEANN D., RN, adm. coor., St. Catherine Hospital on Half Moon, Moss Beach, CA '82 (NURS)
BELFLOWER, TERESA R., head nrs., HCA Coliseum Medical Centers, Macon, GA '85 (CS)
BELIN, CURTIS G., dir. eng. and maint., Sparks Regional Medical Center, Fort Smith, AR '75 (ENG)
BELING, DALE D., partner, Charles Bailly and Company, Fargo, ND '78
BELISSARY, GAIL B., RN, mgr. cent. prod., McLeod Regional Medical Center, Florence, SC '84 (CS)
BELIVEAUX, ROBERT L., dir. plant oper., Medical Center Hospital, Conroe, TX '71 (ENG)
BELK, PEGGY C., coor. educ., Schumpert Medical Center, Shreveport, LA '86 (EDUC)
BELKHAM, KATHKEEN, reg. dir., Hospital Council of Southern California, Los Angeles, CA '86 (RISK)
BELKIN, NATHAN L., dir. res. and dev., Superior Surgical Manufacturing Company, Inc., Seminole, FL '77 (CS)
BELKNAP, DEBORAH K., supv. cent. reg., Ashtabula County Medical Center, Ashtabula, OH '84 (ENG)
BELKNAP, RUTH A., RN, asst. dir. nrsg. serv., Bellevue Hospital, Bellevue, OH '83 (NURS)
BELL, ALICE T., RN, adm. dir. nrsg., St. Francis Regional Medical Center, Wichita, KS '83 (NURS)
BELL, BARBARA A., Bath Memorial Hospital, Bath, ME '85 (EDUC)
BELL, BRUCE A., dir. mktg. and dev., Hartford Memorial Hospital, Hartford, WI '84 (PR)
BELL, C. STUART, asst. adm., Marshalltown Medical and Surgical Center, Marshalltown, IA '67 (PERS)
BELL, DARRELL J., exec. vice-pres., Bryn Mawr Hospital, Bryn Mawr, PA '70
BELL, DAVID P., dir. human res., St. Joseph's Hospital, Parkersburg, WV '78 (PERS)
BELL, DAVID S., dir. biomedical serv., Children's Hospital of Philadelphia, Philadelphia, PA '86 (ENG)
BELL, DEANNE R., RN, pres., Deanne Bell and Associates, Muskogee, OK '79 (NURS)
BELL, DIANE B., pat. serv. rep., Humana Hospital -Enterprise, Enterprise, AL '82 (PAT)
BELL, DIANE D., staff asst. to chm.-surg., Washington Hospital Center, Washington, DC '83
BELL, DONALD G., mgr. facil., Hennepin County Medical Center, Minneapolis, MN '80 (ENG)
BELL, DORIS C., RN, assoc. dir. nrsg., Cape Fear Valley Medical Center, Fayetteville, NC '84 (NURS)
BELL, ELISABETH S., mktg. intern, Presbyterian Hospital, New York, NY '85 (PLNG)
BELL, ELIZABETH J., RN, vice-pres., Community Hospital of Springfield and Clark County, Springfield, OH '69 (NURS)
BELL, G. DAVID JR., student, Indiana University, Bloomington, IN '85
BELL, GLADYS H., RN, vice-pres. nrsg., Hackensack Medical Center, Hackensack, NJ '79 (NURS)
BELL, HERBERT H., Good Samaritan Hospital, Mount Vernon, IL '65
BELL, HOUSTON L. JR., exec. vice-pres., Roanoke Memorial Hospitals, Roanoke, VA '75
BELL, JACK E., asst. adm., Fairview General Hospital, Cleveland, OH '85
BELL, JAMES BRUCE, dir. maint. and eng., Northeast Medical Center Hospital, Humble, TX '86 (ENG)
BELL, JERRY A. JR., atty., Hospital Corporation of America, Nashville, TN '86 (ATTY)
BELL, JESSIE M., RN, dir. nrsg., Lost Rivers District Hospital, Arco, ID '86 (NURS)
BELL, SR. JUDITH A., RN, dir. pat. serv., St. Mary's Hospital of Blue Springs, Blue Springs, MO '81 (NURS)
BELL, KENNETH J., mgt. eng., Methodist Hospitals of Dallas, Dallas, TX '81 (MGMT)
BELL, LEONA F., dir. staff dev., Good Samaritan Hospital and Medical Center, Portland, OR '83 (EDUC)
BELL, LYNNE P., adm. sec., Cape Coral Hospital, Cape Coral, FL '82 (VOL)
BELL, MARY JANE, dir. vol. serv., Shepherd Spinal Center, Atlanta, GA '86 (VOL)
BELL, MARY, dir. vol. serv., Morristown-Hamblen Hospital, Morristown, TN '73 (VOL)
BELL, MICHAEL O., vice-pres. corp. dev., St. Vincent Hospital and Health Care Center, Indianapolis, IN '80 (PLNG)
BELL, PATRICIA R., dir. pur., Grenada Lake Medical Center, Grenada, MS '81 (PUR)
BELL, RAEFORD A., mgr. health care consult. serv., Deloitte Haskins and Sells, Atlanta, GA '79
BELL, RALPH Z., mgr. matl., DeSoto Memorial Hospital, Arcadia, FL '82 (PUR)
BELL, ROBERT G., dir. gen. serv., Houlton Regional Hospital, Houlton, ME '82 (PUR)(RISK)
BELL, SANDRA J., med. soc. worker, Baptist Hospital of Miami, Miami, FL '72 (SOC)
BELL, SUE H., pres., Bell Associates, Inc., Atlanta, GA '82 (PR)
BELL, SUSANNE S., RN, asst. adm. med. and surg. serv., Berkshire Medical Center, Pittsfield, MA '85 (NURS)
BELL, T. KNOX, atty., Sharp Cabrillo Hospital, San Diego, CA '73 (ATTY)
BELL, TERRY K., dir. matl. mgt., Lakeland Regional Medical Center, Lakeland, FL '75 (PUR)
BELL, THOMAS L., atty., Kansas Hospital Association, Topeka, KS '86 (ATTY)
BELL, WILLIAM A., atty., Florida Hospital Association, Tallahassee, FL '79 (ATTY)(RISK)
BELL, WILLIAM D., dir. plant eng., North Carolina Memorial Hospital, Chapel Hill, NC '83 (ENG)
BELL, WILLIAM H. JR., Rand Corporation, Santa Monica, CA '70
BELL, WILLIAM H., dir. environ. serv., Harper-Grace Hospitals, Detroit, MI '86 (ENVIRON)
BELLACERA, ANDY, dir. environ. serv., Lutheran Home for the Aging, Wauwatosa, WI '87 (ENVIRON)
BELLATTI, WALTER R., atty., Passavant Area Hospital, Jacksonville, IL '78 (ATTY)
BELLE, EUGENE, vice-pres., St. John's Hospital, Lowell, MA '67
BELLENDORF, PAUL C., adm., St. Elizabeth Medical Center-North, Covington, KY '51 (LIFE)
BELLENGHI, G. MICHAEL, partner, Touche Ross and Company, Philadelphia, PA '81
BELLHOUSE, DOROTHY E., staff asst. to pres., Sewickley Valley Hospital, Sewickley, PA '81
BELLICK, JACK J., dir. bur. nutr. serv., New York State Department of Health, Albany, NY '70 (FOOD)
BELLIS-SQUIRES, JAN, media rep., Kaiser Permanente, Portland, OR '85 (PR)
BELLISARIO, DOMENIC, corp. dir., Western Reserve Care System, Youngstown, OH '87 (PERS)
BELLISARIO, LT. COL. PETER C., MSC USAF, Wichita Falls, TX '75 (RISK)
BELLISTON, EDWARD GLEN, student, Brigham Young University, Provo, UT '85
BELLIVEAU, ANDREW J., dir. plant oper., York Hospital, York, ME '84 (ENG)
BELLMORE, MARY K., pat. rep., Spalding Rehabilitation Hospital, Denver, CO '83 (PAT)
BELLOR, JIM, adm., Hospital for Sick Children, Washington, DC '80
BELLOSPIRITO, FRANK, dir. hskpg., Beverly Hospital, Montebello, CA '87 (ENVIRON)
BELLOTTI, ROGUE, plant supv., Community Hospital, Anderson, IN '86 (ENG)
BELLOWS, JANET PAUL, dir. matl., Robert Wood Johnson University Hospital, New Brunswick, NJ '81 (CS)(PUR)
BELLUOMINI, FRANK S., partner, Touche, Ross and Company, San Jose, CA '72
BELMONT, ELISABETH, atty., Maine Medical Center, Portland, ME '87 (ATTY)
BELMONT, TERRY A., pres. and exec. dir., Pacific Health Resources, Los Angeles, CA '78
BELMORE, JAMES W., dir. bldg. and grds., Myrtle Werth Medical Center, Menomonie, WI '81 (ENG)
BELOFF, STEVEN H., pres., Healthcare, Inc., Bethany, CT '74 (AMB)
BELOSI, MICHAEL W., dir. matl., St. Elizabeth's Hospital, Belleville, IL '86 (PUR)
BELPERIO, DEBORAH A., RN, consult., Deloitte Haskins and Sells, Cincinnati, OH '84 (NURS)
BELSEY, GEORGE W., adm., University of Utah Health Sciences Center, Salt Lake City, UT '65
BELSEY, PAMELA D., dir. in-service educ., Stony Plain Municipal Hospital, Stony Plain, Alta., Canada '86 (EDUC)
BELSHA, ELIZABETH H., dir. plng., Mary Washington Hospital, Fredericksburg, VA '85 (PLNG)
BELSJOE, EDITH HELEN, dir. pers., St. John's Riverside Hospital, Yonkers, NY '64 (PERS)
BELSKAS, SR. M. MONICA, exec. hskpr., Good Samaritan Hospital, Mount Vernon, IL '86 (ENVIRON)
BELSKI, BARBARA, RN, supv. cent. sterilizing, St. Mary's Hospital, Rhinelander, WI '80 (CS)
BELSON, EDWARD D., mgr. food serv., Eastern Long Island Hospital, Greenport, NY '85 (FOOD)
BELT, NANCY L., dir. commun. rel., Christian Hospitals Northeast-Northwest, St. Louis, MO '86 (PR)
BELT, S. JANE, med. lib. and coor. cont. educ., Central Washington Hospital, Wenatchee, WA '77 (EDUC)
BELTZ, DOUGLAS M., dir. emp. asst. serv. and commun. rel., Psychiatric Center of Michigan, New Baltimore, MI '85 (PR)
BELTZ, NANCY M., dir. cent. sup., East Tennessee Children's Hospital, Knoxville, TN '81 (CS)
BELYUSAR, WILLIAM, asst. dir. plant oper., Youngstown Hospital Association, Youngstown, OH '86 (ENG)
BELZ, GEORGE T., dir. plant oper., Kaiser Foundation Hospital-Cleveland, Cleveland, OH '83 (ENG)
BEMIS, DONALD L., asst. dir. risk mgt., Deaconess Hospital, Evansville, IN '86 (RISK)
BEN-ZVI, SEYMOUR, ScD, dir. sci. and med. instrumentation center, State University Hospital, Downstate Medical Center, Brooklyn, NY '75 (ENG)
BENAGE, OPAL M., adm., St. Luke's Episcopal Hospital, Houston, TX '67 (NURS)
BENDA, CHARLES G., sr. assoc., Healthcare Management Counselors, New York, NY '86 (MGMT)
BENDA, GEORGE J. JR., off. mgr., Hec Energy Corporation, Palos Heights, IL '85 (ENG)
BENDA, SR. LUDMILLA, assoc. dir., Davenport Diocesan Volunteer Program, Davenport, IA '67
BENDALL, PATRICIA S., dir. vol. serv., AMI Brookwood Medical Center, Birmingham, AL '80 (VOL)
BENDER, CYNTHIA L., RN, asst. dir. nrsg., West Jersey Hospital Garden State Division, Marlton, NJ '81 (NURS)
BENDER, DONALD L., dir. maint., Loma Linda University, Loma Linda, CA '75 (ENG)
BENDER, JEAN C., dir. nrsg. educ., East Orange General Hospital, East Orange, NJ '82 (EDUC)(NURS)
BENDER, JEFFREY A., dir. pub. rel., Elmer Community Hospital, Elmer, NJ '87 (PR)
BENDER, RICHARD A., dir. facil. eng., West Valley Camelback Hospital, Glendale, AZ '85 (ENG)
BENDER, VERONICA C., RN, vice-pres. nrsg., Hyde Park Hospital, Chicago, IL '84 (NURS)(AMB)
BENDER, WILLIAM F., dept. head family and soc. serv., Saint Joseph Hospital, Reading, PA '81 (SOC)
BENDER, WILLIAM T., dir. matl. mgt., HCA Brotman Medical Center, Culver City, CA '85 (PUR)
BENDERMAN, RANDA K., dir. diet., Shelby Medical Center, Alabaster, AL '86 (FOOD)
BENDIS, RICHARD A., pres. and chief exec. off., R. A. B. Ventures, Inc., Overland Park, KS '82
BENDITT, WILMA R., dir. vol. serv., Sacred Heart Medical Center, Chester, PA '68 (VOL)
BENDLER, DEBORAH D., pub. rel. counsel, Wallis Gideon Wallis, Inc., Tulsa, OK '86 (PR)
BENDTSEN, JOAN B., coor. vol. serv., Polyclinic Medical Center, Harrisburg, PA '87 (VOL)
BENDYCKI, NADINE A., mgr. mktg., Cleveland Clinic Hospital, Cleveland, OH '86 (PLNG)
BENDZSEL, BOB M., dir. plant oper., Charter Community Hospital, Hawaiian Gardens, CA '83 (ENG)
BENEDETTO, MAJ. RAMON L., MSC USAF, adm. and chief exec. off., U. S. Air Force Clinic Spangdahlem, APO New York, NY '78
BENEDICT, JOY M., dir. pers., Pattie A. Clay Hospital, Richmond, KY '86 (PERS)
BENEDICT, LAWRENCE W., vice-pres. facil., Valley Presbyterian Hospital, Van Nuys, CA '64 (PERS)
BENEDICT, RICHARD L., student, Harvard Business School, Boston, MA '85
BENEDIKTER, HELEN, RN, vice-pres. clin. serv., Long Beach Community Hospital, Long Beach, CA '70 (NURS)
BENEFIELD, CLYDE DEWAYNE, sr. vice-pres. and chief oper. off., Good Shepherd Medical Center, Longview, TX '80
BENENSON, MICHAEL J., pres., Healthlink Systems, Inc., Calabasas, CA '86
BENESCH, KATHERINE, atty., Presbyterian-University Hospital, Pittsburgh, PA '81 (ATTY)
BENESH, STEPHEN P., proj. eng., Square D. Company, Oshkosh, WI '81 (ENG)
BENFER, BEVERLY A., RN, dir. nrsg., C. F. Menninger Memorial Hospital, Topeka, KS '73 (NURS)
BENFER, DAVID WILLIAM, chief exec. off., Henry Ford Hospital, Detroit, MI '69
BENGEL, MARGE, RN, coor. staff educ., Good Samaritan Hospital, Cincinnati, OH '77 (EDUC)
BENGTSSON, JEANNE B., student, Department of Health Service Administration, George Washington University, Washington, DC '86
BENHAM, CAROL J., dir. commun., American River Hospital, Carmichael, CA '86 (PR)
BENINTENDI, VERONICA J., dir. vol., Community Hospital of Western Suffolk, Smithtown, NY '80 (VOL)

BENITEZ, DIANE, RN, asst. exec. dir. nrsg. serv., East Jefferson General Hospital, Metairie, LA '80 (NURS)
BENJAMIN, ARNOLD, sr. maint. eng., Mount Sinai Medical Center, New York, NY '78 (ENG)
BENJAMIN, BLAIR D., atty., Samaritan Health Service, Phoenix, AZ '79 (ATTY)
BENJAMIN, HARRY W., (ret.), Philadelphia, PA '32 (LIFE)
BENJAMIN, JUSTUS JR., med. adm. off., USS Carl Vinson, San Francisco, CA '86
BENJAMIN, PHILLIS, dir. cent. proc., St. Joseph Regional Medical Center, Lewiston, ID '80 (CS)
BENNER, CAROL, chief util. review, Department of Health and Mental Hygiene, Baltimore, MD '86 (RISK)
BENNER, LARRY A., asst. dir. commercial diet. serv., Jewish Hospital, Louisville, KY '84 (FOOD)
BENNER, VIRGINIA D., atty., Sinai Hospital of Detroit, Detroit, MI '84 (ATTY)
BENNETT-SCHULTE, MARY, mgr. soc. serv., Childrens Memorial Hospital, Omaha, NE '86 (SOC)
BENNETT, ADDISON C., sr. vice-pres., Pacific Health Resources, Inc., Los Angeles, CA '65 (MGMT)(EDUC)
BENNETT, ALLEN J., exec. dir., Park West Medical Center, Inc., Baltimore, MD '83
BENNETT, ANNA L., Eldorado, IL '74 (CS)
BENNETT, ARDEN, adm., Oroville Hospital, Oroville, CA '86
BENNETT, BERNICE E., dir. pat. serv., Dallas County Hospital District-Parkland Memorial Hospital, Dallas, TX '83 (SOC)
BENNETT, BETH, risk mgr., Community General Hospital, Syracuse, NY '87 (RISK)
BENNETT, BETTY E., plng. and mktg. analyst, Desert Samaritan Hospital, Mesa, AZ '86 (PLNG)
BENNETT, CHARLES M., mgt. eng., Baptist Memorial Hospital, Memphis, TN '86 (MGMT)
BENNETT, DAVID L., atty., Holden Hospital, Holden, MA '85 (ATTY)
BENNETT, FRED N., asst. dir. plant oper., L. W. Blake Memorial Hospital, Bradenton, FL '82 (ENG)
BENNETT, GARLAND W., dir. maint., Mercy Memorial Hospital, Urbana, OH '75 (ENG)
BENNETT, H. FAYE, (ret.), Miami, FL '69 (FOOD)
BENNETT, H. MICHAEL, atty., Memorial Hospital, Clarksville, TN '86 (ATTY)
BENNETT, HELLEN E., mgt. eng., SunHealth Corporation, Charlotte, NC '83 (MGMT)
BENNETT, J. BRETT, student, Duke University, Department of Health Administration, Durham, NC '85
BENNETT, JANE F., dir. soc. serv., Memorial Hospital at Gulfport, Gulfport, MS '79 (SOC)
BENNETT, JOHN G., mgr. rad. eng., Rex Hospital, Raleigh, NC '86 (ENG)
BENNETT, JOHN R., atty., South Georgia Medical Center, Valdosta, GA '82 (ATTY)
BENNETT, KAREN A., dir. pers., Humana Hospital -St. Lukes, Richmond, VA '84 (PERS)
BENNETT, KATHLEEN, dir. hskpg., St. Luke's Hospital, Saginaw, MI '86 (ENVIRON)
BENNETT, LEON D., reg. adm., Psychiatric Institutes of America, Washington, DC '75
BENNETT, MARGARET LOUISE, dir. pat. rel., Booth Memorial Medical Center, Flushing, NY '86 (PAT)
BENNETT, MARIAN F., RN, dir. med. and surg. nrsg., Virginia Beach General Hospital, Virginia Beach, VA '86 (NURS)
BENNETT, MARK, dir. soc. work serv., St. John's Regional Health Center, Springfield, MO '87 (SOC)
BENNETT, MARY ANN D., admit. nrs. coor., St. Francis Hospital, Greenville, SC '85 (PAT)
BENNETT, MARY L., RN, dean and adm. nrsg., Eastern Maine Medical Center, Bangor, ME '85 (NURS)
BENNETT, MELVYN L., asst. adm. human resources, Primary Children's Medical Center, Salt Lake City, UT '76 (PERS)
BENNETT, NANCY H., dir. food serv., Mercy Hospital and Medical Center, San Diego, CA '84 (FOOD)
BENNETT, NEIL E., Professional Healthcare Management, Villa Park, CA '68
BENNETT, PAMELA, coor. risk mgt., Flagstaff Medical Center, Flagstaff, AZ '85 (RISK)
BENNETT, PAUL DOUGLAS, dir. matl. mgt., Crawford W. Long Memorial Hospital of Emory University, Atlanta, GA '74 (PUR)
BENNETT, PEG M., dir. consumer health educ., Bayshore Community Hospital, Holmdel, NJ '87 (EDUC)
BENNETT, RICHARD, vice-pres., R. L. B. and Associates, Novato, CA '68 (PERS)
BENNETT, SHONNA K., RN, educ., Alton Memorial Hospital, Alton, IL '84 (EDUC)
BENNETT, THOMAS F., sr. radiological eng., Danbury Hospital, Danbury, CT '83 (ENG)
BENNETT, THOMAS H., atty., Independence Regional Health Center, Independence, MO '78 (ATTY)
BENNETT, VIRGINIA A., supv. diet., Jesse Holman Jones Hospital, Springfield, TN '84 (FOOD)
BENNETT, W. C., dir. fiscal serv., Mount Sinai Medical Center, Miami Beach, FL '80
BENNETT, WILLIAM F., dist. mgr. health care serv., Blue Cross of Massachusetts, Boston, MA '79
BENNING, ANITA K., commun. rel. spec., Dearborn County Hospital, Lawrenceburg, IN '87 (PR)
BENNY, PAUL R., dir. eng. serv., St. Mary Medical Center, Gary, IN '84 (ENG)
BENOIT, JAMES G., vice-pres., Cape Cod Hospital, Hyannis, MA '71 (MGMT)
BENOIT, LESLIE C., dir. vol. serv., Yakima Valley Memorial Hospital, Yakima, WA '83 (VOL)
BENOIT, THOMAS A., assoc. dir., Staten Island Hospital, Staten Island, NY '86
BENOLKEN, CRETIA, assoc. exec. dir., Valley Community Hospital, Dallas, OR '82 (NURS)
BENONIS, JOSEPH E., asst. dir. matl. mgt., Mercy Catholic Medical Center, Darby, PA '86 (PUR)
BENSCHOP, MELVIN E., dir. plant oper., Stoughton Hospital Association, Stoughton, WI '78 (ENG)
BENSING, DONALD A., dir. soc. serv., Columbus Hospital, Chicago, IL '79 (SOC)
BENSING, GARY E., dir. pers., Our Lady of Peace Hospital, Louisville, KY '83 (PERS)
BENSON, CHARLES R., dir. maint., Sarah R. Newman Nursing Home, Mamaroneck, NY '81 (ENG)
BENSON, ELAINE K. G., dir. commun. rel., Southampton Hospital, Southampton, NY '69 (PR)
BENSON, GERARD C., sr. clin. syst. analyst, Group Health Association, Inc., Washington, DC '83 (MGMT)
BENSON, GRADIE LEE, dir. soc. serv., Huguley Memorial Hospital, Fort Worth, TX '78 (SOC)
BENSON, HARRY L. JR., dir. matl. mgt., Amarillo Hospital District, Amarillo, TX '85 (PUR)
BENSON, JAMES C., equip. planner, J. C. Benson Associates, Santa Rosa, CA '79 (PLNG)
BENSON, JAMES O., supv. oper. room, Hiawatha Community Hospital, Hiawatha, KS '86 (CS)
BENSON, JUNE, RN, coor. staff dev., Rice Memorial Hospital, Willmar, MN '79 (EDUC)
BENSON, KAREN LEE, dir. soc. serv., Stoughton Hospital Association, Stoughton, WI '83 (SOC)
BENSON, LELDON J., dir. facil., South Coast Medical Center, South Laguna, CA '85 (ENG)
BENSON, LOIS J., diet., Meeker County Memorial Hospital, Litchfield, MN '80 (FOOD)
BENSON, MARTEILE M., RN, asst. adm. nrsg., Eastern Maine Medical Center, Bangor, ME '83 (NURS)
BENSON, MICHELLE S., RN, dir., Fairview and St. Mary Emergency Center, Minneapolis, MN '86 (AMB)
BENSON, NANCY, nrs. mgr. surg., Worcester Hahnemann Hospital, Worcester, MA '87 (AMB)
BENSON, PAUL R., vice-pres. pers., Presbyterian Intercommunity Hospital, Whittier, CA '83 (PERS)
BENSON, ROSITA, adm. pers. serv., Interfaith Medical Center, Brooklyn, NY '84 (PERS)
BENSON, WARREN, sr. vice-pres., Mount Washington Pediatric Hospital, Baltimore, MD '86 (RISK)
BENTFIELD, VIOLA D., RN, coor. risk mgt., Metropolitan Medical Center, Minneapolis, MN '77 (RISK)
BENTIVEGNA, PETER I., partner, Benitivegna, Lindsay, Maron, Merlino, Architects, Bala Cynwyd, PA '83
BENTLEY, ANGELA C., asst. mgt. eng., Saint Joseph's Hospital, Atlanta, GA '83 (MGMT)
BENTLEY, CHRIS H., atty., Charter Medical Corporation, Macon, GA '85 (ATTY)
BENTLEY, LOUISE C., (ret.), Santa Ana, CA '31 (LIFE)
BENTLEY, MARSHALL G., coor. nrsg. serv. and pat. rep., Huron Valley Hospital, Milford, MI '86 (PAT)
BENTLEY, SANDRA E., atty., Bower and Gardner, New York, NY '81 (ATTY)
BENTON, BILL, supv. biomedical electronics, Holmes Regional Medical Center, Melbourne, FL '86 (ENG)
BENTON, JOAN, dir. vol., Mercy Hospital, Hamilton, OH '68 (VOL)
BENTON, KAREN R., supv. pat. educ., Wesley Long Community Hospital, Greensboro, NC '84 (EDUC)
BENZENBERG, CLAUDIA L., vice-pres. pat. serv., Cabrini Medical Center, New York, NY '75
BENZINGER, GERALD E., atty., St. Elizabeth Medical Center-North, Covington, KY '79 (ATTY)
BEQUEATH, JAN, pres., Bequeath Communications, Atlanta, GA '81 (PR)
BERAN, ANTHONY, dir. hskpg., Tawas St. Joseph Hospital, Tawas City, MI '86 (ENVIRON)
BERAN, MARY ANN, chief diet., Genesee Memorial Hospital, Flint, MI '68 (FOOD)
BERARDI, LEO E., dir. hskpg., Saint Francis Medical Center, Peoria, IL '84 (ENVIRON)
BERARDUCCI, JIM, student, Program in Health Service Administration, University of Minnesota, Minneapolis, MN '87
BERAULT, JOHN S., assoc. adm., Seventh Ward General Hospital, Hammond, LA '80
BERCH, GEORGE R., pres., South Florida Hospital Associaton, Miami, FL '71 (PLNG)
BERCK, STEVE H., dir. food serv., HCA Park View Medical Center, Nashville, TN '84 (FOOD)
BERENBERG, BARBARA, dir. soc. serv., New England Baptist Hospital, Boston, MA '86 (SOC)
BERENHOLZ, GERALDINE, med. rec. consult., Lexington, MA '76
BERENSTEIN, MARVIN S., atty., Marian Health Center, Sioux City, IA '84 (ATTY)
BERESFORD, JAN A., vice-pres. corp. dev., Meritcare, Inc., Pittsburgh, PA '80
BERESKI, EDWARD J., vice-pres., Micah Systems Inc., Reading, PA '86
BERG, BRADLEY J., atty., Stevens Memorial Hospital, Edmonds, WA '84 (ATTY)
BERG, BRUCE B., adm., Kittson Memorial Hospital, Hallock, MN '70 (MGMT)
BERG, CARLTON M., asst. dir., University of Chicago Hospitals, Chicago, IL '86 (ENG)
BERG, CHARLOTTE M., dep. chief soc. work, Clinical Center National Institutes of Health, Bethesda, MD '79 (SOC)
BERG, DAVID H., vice-pres. plng. and mktg., Mercy Health System, Burlingame, CA '77 (PLNG)
BERG, DON, mgr. biomedical eng., Cigna Health Plans, Santa Fe Springs, CA '86 (ENG)
BERG, GERALDINE B., dir. prog. dev., Alta Bates Corporation, Berkeley, CA '83 (PLNG)
BERG, GRACE D., coor. vol., Wausau Hospital Center, Wausau, WI '80 (VOL)
BERG, HELEN V., RN, vice-pres. nrsg., Catherine McAuley Health Center, Ann Arbor, MI '77 (NURS)
BERG, JUDITH G., RN, dir. nrsg., Kaweah Delta District Hospital, Visalia, CA '77 (NURS)
BERG, LOIS Y., mgr. food serv., Memorial Hospital, Burlington, WI '82 (FOOD)
BERG, MARY B., student, Concordia College, Moorhead, MN '87
BERG, MICHAEL ALLEN, pat. rep., Fairview Riverside Hospital, Minneapolis, MN '87 (PAT)
BERG, NELS H., sr. vice-pres. constr. and facil., Mount Sinai Medical Center, New York, NY '73 (PLNG)
BERG, SHARON, adm. asst. facil., Stanford University Hospital, Stanford, CA '78 (ENG)
BERG, CAPT. VALERIE J., MSC USA, Blacksburg, VA '83
BERG, SR. VERONICA, dir. human serv., Providence Hospital, Mobile, AL '84 (SOC)
BERGAILA, JOSEPH, dir. food serv., St. Luke's Episcopal Hospital, Houston, TX '72 (FOOD)
BERGDORF, MICHAEL B., mgr. matl., University of California San Francisco, South San Francisco, CA '83 (PUR)
BERGEN, STANLEY S. JR., MD, pres., University of Medicine and Dentistry of New Jersey-University Hospital, Newark, NJ '73
BERGENGREN, ERIC F., dir. phys. plant, Penobscot Bay Medical Center, Rockport, ME '81 (ENG)
BERGER, CANDYCE S., dir. soc. work, University Hospital, Seattle, WA '81 (SOC)
BERGER, DAN L., chief eng., Kaiser Foundation Hospital, Anaheim, CA '84 (ENG)
BERGER, DANIEL B., pres., D. Berger and Associates, Ltd., Chicago, IL '76 (PLNG)
BERGER, EMANUEL D., mgr. trng. and dev., Beth Israel Hospital, Boston, MA '83 (EDUC)
BERGER, FAYE E., asst. food dir. serv., West Florida Regional Medical Center, Pensacola, FL '85 (FOOD)
BERGER, GARY E., mgr. compensation and benefits, Bethesda Oak Hospital, Cincinnati, OH '79 (PERS)
BERGER, JACK, dir. plant oper., Josiah B. Thomas Hospital, Peabody, MA '86 (ENG)
BERGER, JAMES L., mgt. consult., Paoli Memorial Hospital, Paoli, PA '80 (MGMT)
BERGER, JILL T., supv. nrsg. educ., Jewish Hospital, Louisville, KY '86 (EDUC)
BERGER, KEITH L., dir. soc. work, United Hospital, Grand Forks, ND '82 (SOC)
BERGER, LEONA, adm. prof. support serv., AMI Presbyterian-St. Luke's Medical Center, Denver, CO '81 (RISK)
BERGER, MARY E., consult., Van Scoyoc Associates, Inc., Alexandria, VA '85 (PLNG)
BERGER, MELANIE L., dir. mktg., Tampa General Hospital, Tampa, FL '86 (PR) (PLNG)
BERGER, RICHARD W., pres. and bd. memb, St. Catherine's Hospital and Medical Center, Kenosha, WI '80 (PLNG)
BERGERON, CAROLYN D., RN, nrsg. educ. consult., Florida State Blood of Nursing, Jacksonville, FL '73 (PERS)
BERGERON, JAMES A., dir. matl. mgt., Lakeview Medical Center, Danville, IL '80 (PUR)
BERGERON, JANE A., dir. nutr. serv., Mount Airy Psychiatric Center, Denver, CO '84 (FOOD)
BERGERON, KAREN B., dir. pur., Jo Ellen Smith Medical Center, New Orleans, LA '79 (PUR)
BERGERON, MAURICE, dir. soc. serv., Androscoggin Valley Hospital, Berlin, NH '83 (SOC)
BERGERON, REGIS P., mechanical eng., Regis P. Bergeron, Duson, LA '86 (ENG)
BERGERON, SANDRA J., RN, dir. nrsg., Franklin Regional Hospital, Franklin, NH '81 (NURS)
BERGERSON, KAY, dir. vol., Mercy Medical Center and Hospital, Williston, ND '77 (VOL)
BERGHORN, JEANNIE M., coor. mktg. commun., Mercy Health Center, Oklahoma City, OK '86 (PR)
BERGIN, MICHAEL A., atty., Methodist Hospital of Indiana, Indianapolis, IN '81 (ATTY)
BERGIN, ROBERT C., reg. dir. mktg., plng. and pub. affairs, St. Catherine Hospital, East Chicago, IN '83 (PR)
BERGKVIST, CARL I., exec. vice-pres., Main Line Health, Inc., Radnor, PA '56 (LIFE)
BERGLUND, DONALD C., assoc. adm., Fairview Southdale Hospital, Minneapolis, MN '77
BERGLUND, RICHARD W., atty., Iowa Hospital Association, Des Moines, IA '68 (ATTY)
BERGLUND, RONALD GARY, dir., Patient Care Management System, Detroit, MI '85
BERGMAN, BRIAN C., mktg. analyst, DePaul Health Center, Bridgeton, MO '86 (PLNG)
BERGMAN, DAVID HENRY, dir. mgt. info. syst., Middlesex Memorial Hospital, Middletown, CT '74
BERGMAN, M. MARLENE, dir. food serv., Good Samaritan Hospital, Vincennes, IN '72 (FOOD)
BERGMAN, PATRICIA, coor. med. affairs, Woodhull Hospital, Brooklyn, NY '78
BERGMAN, SIGRID, dir. soc. serv., St. Elizabeth Community Health Center, Lincoln, NE '70 (SOC)
BERGMANN, CORINNE L., RN, dir. nrsg., Glendale Adventist Medical Center, Glendale, CA '81 (NURS)
BERGMANN, EDWARD W., atty., St. Marys Hospital Medical Center, Madison, WI '76 (ATTY)
BERGMANN, SUSAN S., consult., SunHealth, Inc., West Columbia, SC '86 (MGMT)
BERGOLD, IDA DULCY, soc. dir. nutr. serv., Loma Linda University Medical Center, Loma Linda, CA '73 (FOOD)
BERGOLD, WILLIAM J., partner, Ernst and Whinney, Cleveland, OH '83
BERGOUST, DONALD G., pres., Bergoust Engineers and Company, Inc., Missoula, MT '80 (ENG)
BERGS, WILLIAM F., asst. vice-pres., Underwriters Adjusting Company, Chicago, IL '83 (RISK)
BERGSEID, MARION E., coor. aux., Dakota Hospital, Fargo, ND '85 (VOL)
BERGSTEDT, SHARON S., dir. mktg. and plng., United Hospital, St. Paul, MN '87 (PLNG)
BERGSTROM, RONALD C. M., adm., Saint Cabrini Hospital of Seattle, Seattle, WA '74
BERGSVEN, DAVID A., vice-pres. human res., Deaconess Medical Center, Billings, MT '86 (PERS)
BERGVALL, MELVIN, dir. maint., Loma Linda University Medical Center, Loma Linda, CA '79 (ENG)

BERGWALL, DAVID F., prof., Department of Health Care Administration, George Washington University, Washington, DC '73
BERHANG-DOGGETT, JANET R., RN, dir. home health care and hospice, St. Joseph Hospital, Augusta, GA '85 (NURS)
BERING, EVA J., RN, vice-pres. nrsg. serv., Good Samaritan Hospital, Lebanon, PA '85 (NURS)
BERING, MARTHA J., dir. food serv., Beth Israel Hospital, Denver, CO '79 (FOOD)
BERINGER, LT. COL. GEORGE RICHARD, MSC USA, chief pat. adm., Letterman Army Medical Center, San Francisco, CA '81
BERKELEY, JANICE R., dir. vol., Hospital for Joint Diseases Orthopaedic Institute, New York, NY '70 (VOL)
BERKEYHEISER, WILLIAM L., dir. eng., Helene Fuld Medical Center, Trenton, NJ '80 (ENG)
BERKINSHAW, GEORGEANN ARADER, Annapolis, MD '75
BERKLER, MARGO S., asst. vice-pres. corp. ventures and mktg., Michael Reese Hospital and Medical Center, Chicago, IL '87 (PLNG)
BERKLEY, LEE S., dir. pub. rel., Good Shepherd Rehabilitation Hospital, Allentown, PA '85 (PR)
BERKLEY, MICHAEL T., dir. eng. serv., Cape Coral Hospital, Cape Coral, FL '86 (ENG)
BERKLEY, RALPH B., adm., Illinois Valley Community Hospital, Peru, IL '76
BERKMAN, ALLEN H., atty., Montefiore Hospital, Pittsburgh, PA '70 (ATTY)
BERKMAN, BARBARA, prof. and dir. soc. work health care prog., Massachusetts General Hospital Institute of Health Professions, Boston, MA '77 (SOC)
BERKMAN, JEROME, dir. food and nutr., Cedars-Sinai Medical Center, Los Angeles, CA '68 (FOOD)
BERKMAN, RICHARD OWEN, asst. dir. adm., Stillman Infirmary, Harvard University Health Services, Cambridge, MA '76 (MGMT)
BERKOPEC, ROBERT A., asst. mgt. eng., Fairview Hospital and Healthcare Service, Minneapolis, MN '83 (MGMT)
BERKOPEC, ROBERT N., audit partner, Peat, Marwick, Mitchell and Company, Milwaukee, WI '75
BERKOWITZ, BARRY J., pres., Hospital Communications, Inc., Westfield, NJ '86 (ENG)
BERKOWITZ, MICHAEL A., student, Program in Hospital Administration, University of Houston at Clear Lake, Clear Lake City, TX '83
BERKOWITZ, SANDRA L., atty., Johnson and Higgins, Philadelphia, PA '84 (RISK)
BERKSHIRE, STEVEN D., adm., Charter North Hospital, Anchorage, AK '73
BERKSON, PAMELA, mgr. plng. and mktg., Little Company of Mary Hospital, Torrance, CA '84 (PLNG)
BERLAGE, KEITH A., dir. pur., Lincoln General Hospital, Lincoln, NE '73 (PUR)
BERLANT, HARLEY D., asst. dir. matl. mgt., Mount Sinai Medical Center, Miami Beach, FL '81 (CS)
BERLIC, PHYLLIS J., dir. vol., St. Joseph Riverside Hospital, Warren, OH '76 (VOL)
BERLIN, LORRAINE P., RN, dir. nrsg. clin. serv., St. Joseph Mercy Hospital, Pontiac, MI '82 (NURS)
BERLINER, JOAN, asst. vice-pres., Alexander and Alexander, Los Angeles, CA '85
BERLING, BETTY, dir. vol., St. Francis-St. George Hospital, Cincinnati, OH '77 (VOL)
BERMAN, HOWARD J., pres. and chief exec. off., Blue Cross and Blue Shield of the Rochester Area, Rochester, NY '84 (LIFE)
BERMAN, JEFFREY A., atty., St. Francis Medical Center, Lynwood, CA '77 (ATTY)
BERMAN, MALCOLM F., vice-pres. plng., St. Francis Medical Center, Pittsburgh, PA '66 (PLNG)
BERMAN, PAMELA F., res. consult., Metropolitan Life, New York, NY '85 (PLNG)
BERMAN, RICHARD A., commun., New York State Housing and Community Renewal, Albany, NY '66
BERMEL, DAVID MICHAEL, dir. pur., St. Joseph Intercommunity Hospital, Cheektowaga, NY '86 (PUR)
BERMINGHAM, KENT, gen. vice-pres., Washington Adventist Hospital, Takoma Park, MD '86 (RISK)
BERMUDEZ, JOSEPH, dir. soc. work, Bayley Seton Hospital, Staten Island, NY '82 (SOC)
BERNABO, LOIS, dir. soc. work serv., Queens Hospital Center, Jamaica, NY '76 (SOC)
BERNARD, DAVID W., proj. mgr., Mercy San Juan Hospital, Carmichael, CA '63 (ENG)
BERNARD, EARL F., student, University of California at Los Angeles, School of Public Health, Program in Health Services Management, Los Angeles, CA '85
BERNARD, ELAINE, coor. qual. assur., Truman Medical Center-West, Kansas City, MO '86 (RISK)
BERNARD, JACK A., vice-pres. plng., American Health Care Systems, San Diego, CA '81 (PLNG)
BERNARD, JOSEPH L., mgr. sup., proc. and distrib., Addison Gilbert Hospital, Gloucester, MA '86 (CS)
BERNARD, LEONARD M. JR., atty., North Broward Hospital District, Fort Lauderdale, FL '84 (ATTY)
BERNARD, MOTHER LORETTO, treas., St. Vincent's Medical Center, Staten Island, NY '44 (LIFE)
BERNARD, ROBERT S., atty., Bernard, Overton and Russell, Albany, NY '69 (ATTY)
BERNARDIN, GUERIN A. JR., dir. mgt. info. syst., St. Mary's Medical Center of Evansville, Evansville, IN '85 (MGMT)
BERNARDO, ANDREANA DI, asst. chief diet., Morristown Memorial Hospital, Morristown, NJ '84 (FOOD)
BERNATZKI, ROGER A., pres. and chief exec. off., Surrey Memorial Hospital, Vancouver, B.C., Canada '81 (PLNG)
BERNDT, RICHARD O., atty., Mercy Hospital, Baltimore, MD '80 (ATTY)
BERNGARD, DEBBIE, adm. asst. to chief of staff, Veterans Administration Medical Center, Miami, FL '78
BERNHARDT, ALAN T., atty., Saint Joseph's Hospital, Atlanta, GA '84 (ATTY)
BERNHART, JANET L., Youngstown, OH '85 (PR)
BERNHOLTZ, BONNIE, dir. commun. rel., Good Samaritan Hospital, Kearney, NE '79 (PR)
BERNIER, ALBERT L., atty., Seton Hospital, Waterville, ME '70 (ATTY)
BERNIER, JANINE, asst. dir., Genesee Memorial Hospital, Flint, MI '84 (FOOD)
BERNIER, LYDIA F., safety off., Sutter Community Hospitals, Sacramento, CA '83 (RISK)
BERNIER, NANSI M., supv. sup., proc. and distrib., St. Luke's Medical Center, Phoenix, AZ '86 (CS)
BERNINGER, DOUGLAS L., mgt. eng., Rochester Methodist Hospital, Rochester, MN '85 (MGMT)
BERNREUTER, MAXINE E., RN, dir. nrsg. serv., Southwest General Hospital, San Antonio, TX '81 (NURS)
BERNS, LEWIS A., atty., Condrad Scherer and James, Fort Lauderdale, FL '83 (ATTY)(RISK)
BERNSHOCK, HAROLD ROBERT, L. B. Johnson Tropical Medical Center, Pago Pago, American Samoa '52 (LIFE)
BERNSTECKER, HARLAN A., vice-pres. fin. and adm., Marion General Hospital, Marion, OH '76 (PLNG)
BERNSTEIN, ARTHUR H., atty., Kaiser Foundation Hospitals, Oakland, CA '68 (ATTY)
BERNSTEIN, ARTHUR S., asst. adm., Sunrise Hospital, Sunrise, FL '86
BERNSTEIN, CRAIG J., vice-pres. client rel., Century Credit Service, Scarsdale, NY '84
BERNSTEIN, ERIK P., student, Program in Hospital and Health Care Administration, University of Minnesota School of Public Health, Minneapolis, MN '87
BERNSTEIN, JEFFREY I., atty., Graduate Hospital, Philadelphia, PA '86 (ATTY)
BERNSTEIN, JOYCE S., pres., Link to Life Hospital-Line, Inc., Fort Lauderdale, FL '85
BERNSTEIN, KENNETH, dir. matl. mgt., Jewish Home and Hospital for Aged, Bronx, NY '84 (PUR)
BERNSTEIN, LINDA A., asst. adm., University Hospital, Stony Brook, NY '85
BERNSTEIN, MELVIN S., student, University of Illinois Medical Center, School of Public Health, Chicago, IL '84
BERNSTEIN, NANCY P., dir. mktg. and plng., Institute of Living, Hartford, CT '81 (PLNG)
BERNSTEIN, NEIL D., Danville, CA '81 (PLNG)
BERNSTEIN, STEVEN E., atty., Hospital Association of Pennsylvania, Camp Hill, PA '80 (ATTY)
BERNSTOCK, RICHARD, dir. soc. serv., Concourse Division, Bronx, NY '81 (SOC)(PAT)
BERNZWEIG, ELI P., vice-pres. loss control, Insurance Equities Corporation, Palo Alto, CA '86 (RISK)
BERRES, BARBARA A., coor. vol., West Oaks-Psychiatric Institute Houston, Houston, TX '86 (VOL)
BERRIE, KAREN W., dir. pers., Greenville Hospital, Jersey City, NJ '86 (PERS)
BERRIER, G. ALLAN, adm., Rehabilitation Institute of San Antonio, San Antonio, TX '71
BERRIMAN, W. THOMAS, atty., Wolf, Block, Schorr and Solis-Cohen, Philadelphia, PA '70 (ATTY)(PLNG)
BERRY, BARBARA J., RN, asst. dir. nrsg., University of Kansas College of Health Sciences and Bell Memorial Hospital, Kansas City, KS '86 (NURS)
BERRY, BETTY LOUISE, RN, asst. dir. nrsg., Louisiana State University Hospital, Shreveport, LA '80 (CS)
BERRY, CATHERINE G., RN, dir. nrsg., Providence Hospital, Washington, DC '85 (NURS)
BERRY, LT. COL. CHARLES M., MSC USAF, student, University of Texas, School of Allied Health Sciences, Galveston, TX '83
BERRY, CHERYL ANNE DAVY, dir. soc. serv., Martin Luther Hospital Medical Center, Anaheim, CA '80 (SOC)
BERRY, DENISE CLARE, asst. head health benefits, Naval Medical Command, Washington, DC '78
BERRY, FRANK C., asst. dev. and pub. rel., Leland Memorial Hospital, Riverdale, MD '86 (PR)
BERRY, JAMES R., dir. pers., Meadowview Regional Hospital, Maysville, KY '86 (PERS)
BERRY, JOHN STEWART, adm., Page Memorial Hospital, Luray, VA '77
BERRY, LIONEL D., pres., The Marketing Works, Austin, TX '77 (PLNG)
BERRY, LOUISE LAVERE, mgr. pub. rel., Medivision, Inc., Boston, MA '86 (PR)
BERRY, LOUISE T., dir. vol. serv., Southwest Community Health System, Middleburg Heights, OH '78 (VOL)
BERRY, MARY ANN, supv. cent. serv., St. Mary's Hospital of Kankakee, Kankakee, IL '84 (CS)
BERRY, MARY D., RN, asst. adm., Evangelical Health Systems, Oak Brook, IL '85 (NURS)
BERRY, PETER M., dir. telecommun., Children's Hospital, Boston, MA '85 (ENG)
BERRY, RICHARD J., atty., St. Mary's Hospital, Streator, IL '83 (ATTY)
BERRY, ROBERT L., atty., Redmond Park Hospital, Rome, GA '80 (ATTY)
BERRY, SUE J., instr., Jefferson Regional Medical Center, Pine Bluff, AR '86 (EDUC)
BERRY, THOMAS P., dir. plng. and sales, Marshall Erdman and Associates, Inc., Madison, WI '84 (AMB)
BERRYMAN, JOANNE, asst. vice-pres., Jewish Hospital Ambulatory Services, Inc.-Outpatient Care Center, Louisville, KY '87 (AMB)
BERSBACH, EDWARD H., vice-pres. human res., Chilton Memorial Hospital, Pompton Plains, NJ '73 (PERS)
BERSELL, RALPH BERGH, (ret.), Chandler, AZ '48 (LIFE)
BERSHAD, HY A., Cost Control Enterprises, Inc., Staten Island, NY '67 (ENG)
BERSON, CHARLES W., vice-pres. corp. dev., Mgh Health Services, Inc., Olney, MD '85 (PLNG)
BERSON, MARK I., atty., Franklin Medical Center, Greenfield, MA '86 (ATTY)
BERT, RUSSELL R., chief biomedical and telecommun. eng., St. Peter Hospital, Olympia, WA '85 (ENG)
BERTANI, NANCY K., RN, asst. dir. nrsg. and qual. assur. prog., St. Joseph Medical Center, Joliet, IL '83 (EDUC)
BERTAUSKI, DAVID, RN, vice-pres., Robert Packer Hospital, Sayre, PA '77 (NURS)
BERTELS, EDWARD C., dir. mgt. syst., Edward W. Sparrow Hospital, Lansing, MI '86 (MGMT)
BERTERO, JAMES B., atty., California Hospital Association, Sacramento, CA '78 (ATTY)
BERTHINEE, JAN, dir. qual. assur., Doctors Hospital of Stark County, Massillon, OH '86 (RISK)
BERTILRUD, SELVIN H., dir. plant, Dakota Hospital, Fargo, ND '79 (ENG)
BERTOGLI, HEIDI SCHELLING, student, Program in Hospital and Health Administration, Washington University School of Medicine, St. Louis, MO '81
BERTOLI, SHARON, dir. soc. serv., Providence Milwaukie Hospital, Milwaukie, OR '85 (SOC)
BERTOLIN, ANNE, RN, asst. adm. nrsg., St. Peter Hospital, Olympia, WA '75 (NURS)
BERTOLINO, MARJORIE SANFORD, dir. mktg. and pub. rel., Richmond Memorial Hospital, Richmond, VA '79 (PR)
BERTRAM, DENNIS A., MD, asst. prof., State University of New York, School of Medicine, Buffalo, NY '87 (RISK)
BERTRAM, DONNA LEE, RN, vice-pres., Harris Methodist -Fort Worth, Fort Worth, TX '84 (NURS)
BERTRAM, H. HENRY, (ret.), Amagansett, NY '64 (PERS)
BERTRAND, RUSTON T., chief eng., Franklin Foundation Hospital, Franklin, LA '77 (ENG)
BERTUCCI, MADELINE, RN, dir. nrsg., Suburban General Hospital, Pittsburgh, PA '86 (NURS)
BERUBE, NORBERT E., dir. plant eng. and maint., St. Anne's Hospital, Fall River, MA '85 (ENG)
BESHEARS, JEAN, mgr. pers. serv., Nash General Hospital, Rocky Mount, NC '82 (PERS)
BESKIND, STACY S., student, Georgia State University-Institute of Health Administration, Atlanta, GA '83
BESS, LILLIAN B., dir. vol. serv., Bronx Municipal Hospital Center, Bronx, NY '83 (VOL)
BESSERER, NANCY, RN, asst. adm., Mercy-Memorial Hospital, Monroe, MI '71 (NURS)
BEST, HARRY R., contr., Franciscan Health System, Chadds Ford, PA '80
BEST, JACQUE W., atty., Community Memorial Hospital, Sidney, MT '80 (ATTY)
BEST, JAMES W. III, plant eng., Lenoir Memorial Hospital, Kinston, NC '84 (ENG)
BEST, JONATHAN, dir. emer. mgt., Park City Hospital, Bridgeport, CT '87 (AMB)
BEST, LINDA, dir. soc. work serv., Binghamton General Hospital, Binghamton, NY '83 (SOC)
BEST, PATRICIA A., dir. food serv., St. Elizabeth Hospital Medical Center, Lafayette, IN '75 (FOOD)
BEST, SUSAN J., dir. educ. and res., The Medical Center, Beaver, PA '86 (EDUC)
BESTE, JON T., vice-pres. pur. serv., Sisters of the Sorrowful Mother, Milwaukee, WI '86 (PUR)
BESTERMAN, WILLIAM L., dir. mktg., Hospital Shared Services of Western Pensylavania, Warrendale, PA '86 (PR) (PLNG)
BESTOR, WILLIAM E., vice-pres., Community Memorial Hospital, Menomonee Falls, WI '81 (MGMT)
BETANCOURT, MANUEL THOMAS JR., vice-pres. pers., Gulf Health, Inc., Mobile, AL '64 (PERS)
BETHANY, FRANK M., dir. soc. work, Halifax Hospital Medical Center, Daytona Beach, FL '73 (SOC)
BETHAY, JOHN N., exec. vice-pres., Alabama Hospital Association Trust, Montgomery, AL '84 (RISK)
BETHEA, JAMES C., mgr. providers rel., Blue Cross and Blue Shield of Mississippi, Inc., Jackson, MS '87 (AMB)
BETHEA, KARL R., asst. dir. environ. and linen serv., Hospital Center at Orange, Orange, NJ '86 (ENVIRON)
BETHEL, ANN C., adm. dir. pub. rel., Northridge Hospital Medical Center, Northridge, CA '85 (PR)
BETHEL, ANNE M., Ernst and Whinney, Chicago, IL '85 (PLNG)
BETHGE, LEO, dir. eng., Lenox Hill Hospital, New York, NY '70 (ENG)
BETHUNE, GOLDEN H., RN, vice-pres., St. Clare's Hospital, Denville, NJ '85 (NURS)
BETJEMANN, JOHN H., pres., Methodist Hospitals of Gary, Gary, IN '70
BETLER, SANDRA, acct. exec., Jansen Associates, Inc., Santa Ana, CA '86 (PR)
BETLEY, LEONARD J., atty., Community Hospitals of Indiana, Indianapolis, IN '78 (ATTY)
BETSCH, MARTY, RN, unit mgr. emer., St. Charles Medical Center, Bend, OR '87 (AMB)
BETTENCOURT, RICHARD PAUL, exec. dir., 36th Medical, Fort Devens, MA '73
BETTERS, NORMA C., RN, dir. nrsg. spec. care serv., Salem Hospital, Salem, MA '83 (NURS)
BETTERSWORTH, GRETCHEN, dir. vol. serv., Medical Center-Bowling Green, Bowling Green, KY '81 (VOL)
BETTS, JAMES A. JR., mgt. eng., SunHealth Inc., West Columbia, SC '79 (MGMT)
BETTS, JOAN, RN, sr. vice-pres., West Allis Memorial Hospital, West Allis, WI '73 (NURS)
BETTS, WILLIAM F., asst. dir. biomedical eng., University Medical Center, Tucson, AZ '84 (ENG)
BETZ, COLONEL F., atty., Skagit Valley Hospital and Health Center, Mount Vernon, WA '80 (ATTY)
BETZ, EUGENE W., assoc., Eugene W. Betz Architects, Inc., Winter Park, FL '77
BETZ, ROBERT B., pres., Robert Betz Associates, Inc., Washington, DC '82
BEUM, HELEN H., RN, coor. nrsg. staff dev., Brokaw Hospital, Normal, IL '84 (EDUC)
BEUMER, O. FRANKLIN, dir. pers., St. Mary's Medical Center, Evansville, IN '68 (PERS)
BEVERIDGE, TODD C., dir. soc. serv., Mercy Hospital Medical Center, Des Moines, IA '85 (SOC)
BEVERLY, DARREL L., dir. clin. soc. work, Southern Veterans Administration Mental Health Institute, Danville, VA '86 (SOC)
BEVERLY, JACQUELINE, asst. dir., Tricity Community Mental Health Center, East Chicago, IN '86 (AMB)

BEVERLY, MARTHA A., dir., Potomac Hospital, Woodbridge, VA '87 (CS)
BEVES, RITA, dir. vol. serv., St. Vincent's Medical Center of Richmond, Staten Island, NY '76 (VOL)
BEVIL, WILLIAM T., dir. matl. mgt., Jupiter Hospital, Jupiter, FL '81 (PUR)
BEVILACQUA, EUGENE, assoc. adm., Allegheny Valley Hospital, Natrona Heights, PA '64
BEVINGTON, E. MILTON, pres., Servidyne, Inc., Atlanta, GA '84
BEVIRT, NORMAN L., dir. diet., Heartland Hospital East, St. Joseph, MO '80 (FOOD)
BEWSMAN, MARY R., dir. pub. rel., Sister Kenny Institute, Minneapolis, MN '87 (PR)
BEY, GLORIA JONES, RN, asst. adm., Meriter Hospital, Madison, WI '80 (NURS)
BEYDLER, DWAIN E., coor. educ., Le Bonheur Children's Medical Center, Memphis, TN '86 (EDUC)
BEYER, DARLENE J., RN, dir. educ. serv., Mary Free Bed Hospital and Rehabilitation Center, Grand Rapids, MI '84 (EDUC)
BEYER, JOAN W., assoc. adm., Montefiore Hospital, Pittsburgh, PA '79 (NURS)
BEYER, ROBERT, pres., Mercy Hospital, Port Huron, MI '84
BEYER, WILLIAM H., adm. and chief exec. off., Children's Hospital National Medical Center, Washington, DC '86 (PLNG)
BEYERS, MARJORIE, RN, dir. nrsg., Sisters of Mercy Health Corporation, Farmington Hills, MI '85 (NURS)
BEYRER, NANCY E., dir. pub. rel., Central Suffolk Hospital, Riverhead, NY '86 (PR)
BEYT, THOMAS S., arch., Lafayette General Medical Center, Lafayette, LA '80
BEZELLA, DIANE M., dir. med. soc. work, St. Mary's Hospital-Ozaukee, Port Washington, WI '86 (SOC)
BHARDWAJ, NEELAM B., corp. adm., William Beaumont Hospital, Royal Oak, MI '83 (PLNG)
BHATIA, KRISHIN L., adm., Victory Memorial Hospital, Brooklyn, NY '81
BIALEK, GLORIA E., mgr. soc. serv., Westlake Community Hospital, Melrose Park, IL '80 (SOC)
BIALKIN, NEIL M., adm., Plastic Surgical Specialist, Inc., Norfolk, VA '87 (AMB)
BIANCARDI, RICK, dir. food serv., St. Anthony Hospital, Michigan City, IN '79 (FOOD)
BIANK, PATRICIA S., RN, dir. nrsg., Kaiser Permanente Medical Center, Reston, VA '84 (NURS)
BIAS, RICHARD R., dir. fin. plng., North Carolina Memorial Hospital, Chapel Hill, NC '79
BIAS, SHARON M., RN, dir. maternal-child health, Cabell Huntington Hospital, Huntington, WV '85 (NURS)
BIASKO, NANCY M., staff dev., Clinical Center National Institute of Health, Bethesda, MD '86 (EDUC)
BIASO, FRANK K. DI, student, Program in Hospital Administration, Trinity University, San Antonio, TX '86
BIBBY, JAMES J., exec. dir., Four County Counseling Center, Logansport, IN '86
BIBLE, LEROY JR., maint. eng., Holdenville General Hospital, Holdenville, OK '82 (ENG)
BIBLE, RON L., dir., Voluntary Hospital Association, Springfield, IL '83 (MGMT)
BIBO, GERALD W., pres., Northern Montana Hospital, Havre, MT '66 (PLNG)
BICK, DAVID G., exec. dir., Health Benefits Management of Ohio, Inc., Toledo, OH '86
BICKART, DAVID H., mgr. med. instrumentation, Mount Zion Hospital and Medical Center, San Francisco, CA '84 (ENG)
BICKART, RHONDA N., dir. spec. proj., Samaritan Health Service, Phoenix, AZ '85 (PLNG)
BICKEL, COLLEEN, RN, vice-pres. nrsg. serv., Memorial Hospital, Belleville, IL '73 (NURS)
BICKER, THOMAS R., dir. amb. care, Hinds General Hospital, Jackson, MS '87 (AMB)
BICKERS, CONSTANCE R., Sheffield Lake, OH '79
BICKFORD, NOEL C., consult. plng. and proj. mgt., New York City, Department of Mental Health, New York, NY '83 (PLNG)
BICKHAM, MARTI, RN, dir. emer., DePaul Health Center, Bridgeton, MO '87 (AMB)
BICKLEY, ALBERT D., dir. pers., Hartford Hospital, Hartford, CT '73 (PERS)
BICKLING, J. ALLAN, asst. adm., Memorial Hospital at Easton Maryland, Easton, MD '83 (PLNG)
BICOCCHI, BONNIE C., dir. nrsg., Children's Hospital, New Orleans, LA '81 (NURS)
BIDDLE, BEVERLY S., health syst. spec. and dist. planner, Veterans Administration Medical Center, Washington, DC '86 (PLNG)
BIDDLE, C. KEITH, dir. plng., Cabell Huntington Hospital, Huntington, WV '85 (PLNG)
BIEBEL, JOHN, adm., St. Joseph's Hospital, Tampa, FL '79 (PLNG)
BIEBER, MARGARET J., student, Alfred University, Alfred, NY '86
BIEBER, ROBERT M., pres., Ebasco Risk Management Consultants, Inc., New York, NY '86 (RISK)
BIEBERLY, ELAINE, owner, Bieberly Communications, Wichita, KS '80 (PR)
BIEBESHEIMER, JOHN G., consult., John G. Biebesheimer and Associates, Pompano Beach, FL '84 (FOOD)
BIEGLER, SHIRLEY, coor. vol., Children's Specialized Hospital, Mountainside, NJ '78 (VOL)
BIEHL, ISABEL, RN, dir. in-service educ., Cobb General Hospital, Austell, GA '73 (EDUC)
BIEHL, NOREEN A., dir. org. dev., Wentworth-Douglass Hospital, Dover, NH '85 (PR)
BIEHNER, CARL, dir. maint., grds. and security, Chesapeake General Hospital, Chesapeake, VA '78 (ENG)
BIEKER, DENNIS L., atty., St. Anthony Hospital, Hays, KS '75 (ATTY)
BIELEFELDT, EDWARD H., dir. diet., Charles S. Wilson Memorial Hospital, Johnson City, NY '69 (FOOD)
BIELENDA, WILLIAM E. JR., dir. ancillary productivity, American Medical International, Beverly Hills, CA '86 (MGMT)
BIELING, CONSTANCE V., dir. soc. serv., Gnaden Huetten Memorial Hospital, Lehighton, PA '82 (SOC)
BIEN, EILEEN ROSE, asst. corp. dir. nrsg., Grace Hospital, Detroit, MI '80
BIENEMANN, KATHERINE A., dir. pub. rel., Salem Hospital, Salem, MA '86 (PR)
BIENENFELD, JILL ANN, student, Program in Hospital and Health Care Administration, Xavier University, Cincinnati, OH '82
BIENER, PATRICIA, dir. qual. assur., St. Mary of the Plains Hospital, Lubbock, TX '86 (RISK)
BIENKOWSKI, LUCINDA L., dir. prog. plng., Robert Wood Johnson University Hospital, New Brunswick, NJ '82 (PLNG)
BIER, MICHAEL A., coor. sup. proc. and distrib., Mercy Hospital of Janesville, Janesville, WI '81 (CS)
BIER, MIKE, supv. cent. serv., Fairview General Hospital, Cleveland, OH '79 (CS)
BIERDEMAN-FIKE, JANE, dir. soc. serv., Fulton State Hospital, Fulton, MO '85 (SOC)
BIERIG, JACK R., atty., Association of Nurse Anesthetists, Park Ridge, IL '84 (ATTY)
BIERLE, DON A., atty., Sacred Heart Hospital, Yankton, SD '58 (ATTY)
BIERMAN, LAURA LADD, coor. plng. and proj., Champlain Valley Physicians Hospital Medical Center, Plattsburgh, NY '85 (PLNG)
BIERMAN, NORMAN, atty., Jewish Hospital of St. Louis, St. Louis, MO '68 (ATTY)
BIERMAN, RONALD L., adm., Mercy Hospital, Miami, FL '87 (AMB)
BIERMANN, ROBERT A., exec. dir., St. Ann Foundation, Cleveland, OH '65
BIERYLA, DOREEN M., dir. commun. and mktg., Williamson Medical Center, Franklin, TN '85 (PR)
BIESER, JAMES EDWARD, pres., Optimun Health Systems, Inc., Cincinnati, OH '80 (PR) (PLNG)
BIESTER, DORIS J., RN, sr. vice-pres. and dir. nrsg., Children's Hospital, Denver, CO '83 (NURS)
BIETER, JEROME T., sr. vice-pres.-prin., James A. Hamilton Associates, Inc., Minneapolis, MN '50 (LIFE)
BIEWEN, LOU S., dir. vol. serv., Medical Center Hospital, Conroe, TX '84 (VOL)
BIGELOW, JOHN, Seattle, WA '82 (LIFE)
BIGELOW, PETER, adm., Providence Medical Center, Seattle, WA '77
BIGGE, RUTH E., RN, adm. nrsg., Asbury Hospital, Salina, KS '86 (NURS)
BIGGERS, B. JOAN N., coor. hosp. prog., St. Paul's Cathedral, Boston, MA '77 (PAT)
BIGGERS, VIVIAN C., pat. educ. faciliator, Johnston-Willis Hospital, Richmond, VA '85 (EDUC)
BIGGERSTAFF, SHIRRELL R., dir. matl. mgt., Lake of the Ozarks General Hospital, Osage Beach, MO '82 (PUR)
BIGGS, BETH C., vice-pres., Hospital Association of Metropolitan St. Louis, St. Louis, MO '79 (PLNG)
BIGGS, BONNIE C., mgr. vol., Southeastern General Hospital, Lumberton, NC '86 (VOL)
BIGGS, JANE M., RN, dir. nrsg., Union Hospital of Cecil County, Elkton, MD '80 (NURS)
BIGGS, MAURY J., mgr. inventory stores, Memorial Hospital System, Houston, TX '85 (MGMT)
BIHARY, KRISTEN M., sr. acct. mgr., Hesselbart and Mitten-Watt Inc., Cleveland, OH '76 (PR)
BIHLDORFF, JOHN P., pres. and chief exec. off., St. Luke's Hospital of New Bedford, New Bedford, MA '78
BIKOFSKY, JAY, vice-pres. health group, Johnson and Higgins, New York, NY '86 (RISK)
BILAK, SHELIA, dir. soc. serv., HCA Grant Center Hospital North Florida, Citra, FL '86 (SOC)
BILBIE, JAMES N. II, sr. mgt. eng., St. Joseph Mercy Hospital, Ann Arbor, MI '79 (MGMT)
BILENKER, STUART A., MD, dir. emer. serv., Clara Maass Medical Center, Belleville, NJ '87 (AMB)
BILGER, LAURIE T., York Alpern-Ddb Needham, New York, NY '81 (PR) (PLNG)
BILHORN, DONALD C., exec. vice-pres., John T. Mather Memorial Hospital of Port Jefferson, Port Jefferson, NY '49 (LIFE)
BILINSKI, BLANCHE B., asst. coor. pers. recruitment, Day Kimball Hospital, Putnam, CT '81 (PERS)
BILLE, DONALD A., RN PhD, Silver Spring, MD '77 (EDUC)
BILLECI, JOAN P., RN, asst. dir. nrsg., Maimonides Medical Center, Brooklyn, NY '86 (NURS)
BILLIARD, MARY H., The Practical Approach, Kansas City, MO '81 (MGMT)
BILLIMORIA, NADIR J., mgt. eng., Sacred Heart Hospital of Pensacola, Pensacola, FL '85 (MGMT)
BILLINGSLEY, CANDACE J., dir. soc. work serv., Tampa General Hospital, Tampa, FL '86 (SOC)
BILLINGSLEY, KATHLEEN M., mgr. pat. food serv., Deaconess Hospital, St. Louis, MO '82 (FOOD)
BILLINGSLEY, WILLIAM M., assoc. exec. dir., Eastwood Hospital, Memphis, TN '83
BILLINGTON, BARBARA ANN, dir. med. serv. oper., Pennsylvania Health Corporation, Philadelphia, PA '84
BILLINGTON, GEORGE F., pres., Elizabeth General Medical Center, Elizabeth, NJ '53 (LIFE)
BILLINGTON, JOHN J., plant eng., Carteret General Hospital, Morehead City, NC '75 (ENG)
BILLINGTON, ROBERT J., prin., Billington Poon Associates Ltd., Vancouver, B.C., Canada '83 (PLNG)
BILLINGY, KELD, asst. dir. matl. mgt., Hinsdale Hospital, Hinsdale, IL '84 (PUR)
BILLIU, JO ANN, pres., Billiu Associates, Southfield, MI '86 (EDUC)
BILLMAN, RHONDA L., asst. dir. pub. rel., St. Elizabeth Hospital Medical Center, Lafayette, IN '83 (PR)
BILLS, BARBARA J., RN, assoc. dir. nrsg., Memorial Hospital, Colorado Springs, CO '83 (NURS)
BILLUPS, GAIL MILLER, dir. mktg., Charter Colonial Institute, Newport News, VA '83 (PR)
BILLUPS, JANICE F., dir. commun. rel., Community General Hospital of Thomasville, Thomasville, NC '85 (PR) (PLNG)
BIMONTE, JOHN JR., vice-pres. pers. and gen. resource group, Hospital of Saint Raphael, New Haven, CT '79 (PERS)
BINDER, LINDA S., dir. diet. serv., Sheboygan Memorial Medical Center, Sheboygan, WI '82 (FOOD)
BINFORD, DONALD D., PhD, dir. human res., Bayfront Medical Center, St. Petersburg, FL '86 (PERS)
BING, JERILYN, dir. risk mgt., Clayton General Hospital, Riverdale, GA '86 (RISK)
BINGER, JANE L., mgt. educator, Stanford University Hospital, Stanford, CA '83 (EDUC)
BINGHAM, ANTHONY J., prod. mgr., American Hospital Supply-Hospital Systems, McGaw Park, IL '86
BINGHAM, LARRY J., atty., Research Health Services, Kansas City, MO '83 (ATTY)
BINGHAM, MARCIA G., vice-pres. mktg. and plng., La Grange Memorial Hospital, La Grange, IL '77 (PR) (PLNG)
BINGNER, RICK, dir. food serv., Spartanburg Regional Medical Center, Spartanburg, SC '78 (FOOD)
BINIK, MILDRED J., dir. pub. rel., Suburban General Hospital, Norristown, PA '76 (PR)
BINION, RICHARD III, sr. mgr., Peat, Marwick, Mitchell and Company, Atlanta, GA '74 (MGMT)
BINNICKER, LARRY W., dir. soc. serv., Independence Regional Health Center, Independence, MO '83 (SOC)
BINNIG, RICHARD F., West Chester, PA '55 (LIFE)
BINNS, GREGORY S., pres., Lexecon Health Services, Chicago, IL '85
BINNS, JANE E., RN, dir. staff dev., Hilton Head Hospital, Hilton Head Island, SC '86 (EDUC)
BINNS, NANNETTE, RN, dir. emer., Botsford General Hospital, Farmington Hills, MI '87 (AMB)
BINTZ, WILLIS H., dir. pur., Waukesha Memorial Hospital, Waukesha, WI '59 (PUR)
BIRA, PATRICK G., asst. to pres. and risk mgr., St. Mary of Nazareth Hospital Center, Chicago, IL '86 (RISK)
BIRCH, SUE, student, University of Michigan School of Public Health, Ann Arbor, MI '85
BIRCH, WILLIAM H., asst. dir. nrsg., Dreyer Medical Clinic, Aurora, IL '86 (EDUC)
BIRD, MARY C., RN, dir. nrsg. serv., Cushing Regional Hospital, Cushing, OK '86 (NURS)
BIRDSELL, ROGER JR., vice-pres., Memorial Health Foundation, South Bend, IN '80 (PR)
BIRDZELL, JOHN R., exec. dir., St. Catherine Hospital, East Chicago, IN '70
BIRK, CARMEN C., Mount Sinai Medical Center, Milwaukee, WI '84
BIRKENSTOCK, MARGUERITE, RN, faculty nrsg. adm., University of Pittsburg School of Nursing, Pittsburgh, PA '80 (NURS)
BIRKS, ROBERT C., mgr. eng. and maint., Bishop Clarkson Memorial Hospital, Omaha, NE '75 (ENG)
BIRKY, MELVIN G., vice-pres. human res., Lutheran Medical Center, Wheat Ridge, CO '68 (PERS)
BIRMINGHAM, MARCIA L., dir. commun., Presbyterian Healthcare Services, Albuquerque, NM '86 (ENG)
BIRMINGHAM, WILLIAM T., atty., St. Joseph's Hospital and Medical Center, Phoenix, AZ '72 (ATTY)
BIRNBAUM, GARY, MD, dir. emer., Hillcrest Hospital, Mayfield Heights, OH '87 (AMB)
BIRNBAUM, IRWIN M., Proskauer, Rose, Goetz and Mendelsohn, New York, NY '73 (ATTY)
BIRNBAUM, PHILIP S., dean adm. affairs, George Washington University Medical Center, Washington, DC '73
BIRNBERG, JODY R., pat. rel. rep., St. Luke's Episcopal Hospital, Houston, TX '86 (PAT)
BIRNHAK, ROBIN S., vice-pres. strategic plng., Atlantic Health Systems, Chatham, NJ '79 (PLNG)
BIRO, LAWRENCE A., chief oper. off., St. Frances Xavier Cabrini Hospital, Chicago, IL '73 (EDUC)
BIRON, LAURENT J., med. logistics consult., Marlborough, NH '76
BIROS, MARILYN L., dir. mktg., Roosevelt General Hospital, Portales, NM '86 (PR) (PLNG)
BIRT, M. MAXINE, RN, dir. nrsg., Charleston General Hospital, Charleston, WV '81 (NURS)
BIRT, PAULA EAMES, mgr. pub. rel., Barnwell County Hospital and Nursing Home, Barnwell, SC '68 (PR)
BIRTY, ROBERT E., dir. eng., Citizens General Hospital, New Kensington, PA '75 (ENG)
BISAHA, JOHN P., dir. corp. plng. and mktg., St. Mary Medical Center, Gary, IN '84 (PLNG)
BISBEE, GERALD E. JR., vice-pres., Kidder, Peabody and Company, Inc., New York, NY '84
BISCHOFF, ADELE G., dir. data proc., Hospital of the Medical College of Pennsylvania, Philadelphia, PA '87
BISCHOFF, JAMES C., dir. clin. eng., Holy Name Hospital, Teaneck, NJ '86 (ENG)
BISH, BARBARA W., supv. cent. serv., Brookville Hospital, Brookville, PA '84 (CS)
BISHOP, ANNELLE C., RN, asst. adm. nrsg., Bessemer Carraway Medical Center, Bessemer, AL '68 (NURS)
BISHOP, BILL, pres., Bill Bishop and Associates, Inc., Jacksonville, FL '81
BISHOP, CINDA L., RN, dir. surg. serv., HCA Medical Center of Plano, Plano, TX '81 (AMB)
BISHOP, DIONE O., RN, dir. outpat, Shriners Hospitals for Crippled Children, Spokane, WA '87 (AMB)
BISHOP, GREGORY A., dir. amb. care serv., Vassar Brothers Hospital, Poughkeepsie, NY '87 (AMB)
BISHOP, GREGORY S., pres., Bishop and Associates, Irvine, CA '85
BISHOP, JOAN M., RN, sr. vice-pres., Children's Hospital of Pittsburgh, Pittsburgh, PA '83 (NURS)
BISHOP, JOSEPH WELLS, (ret.), Horsham, PA '48 (LIFE)
BISHOP, LINDA A., asst. diet., Meadville Medical Center, Meadville, PA '86 (FOOD)

BISHOP, MARJORIE, dir. vol. serv., Martin Memorial Hospital, Stuart, FL '78 (VOL)
BISHOP, PAUL A., asst. exec. dir., Holston Valley Hospital and Medical Center, Kingsport, TN '76
BISHOP, ROWENA, RN, chief nrsg. serv., Veterans Administration Wadsworth Medical Center, Los Angeles, CA '81 (NURS)
BISHOP, SAMUEL D., dir. security and loss prevention, Kennestone Hospital, Marietta, GA '80 (RISK)
BISHOP, SUSAN P., dir. soc. serv., Memorial Hospital at Easton Maryland, Easton, MD '86 (SOC)
BISHOP, VALERIE J., RN, dir. educ. serv., Hamilton Memorial Hospital, McLeansboro, IL '83 (EDUC)
BISHOP, WILLIAM H., dir. matl. mgt., Perry Memorial Hospital, Princeton, IL '83 (PUR)
BISHOP, WILLIAM L., asst. adm., Lake Taylor City Hospital, Norfolk, VA '71
BISI, JOSEPH A. JR., adm. asst., Interfaith Medical Center, Brooklyn, NY '73
BISKER, MARLENE A., RN, dir. clin. nrsg., Washington Hospital, Washington, PA '85 (NURS)
BISKEY, SUZETTE M., adm. mgr., Digestive Healthcare, Minneapolis, MN '87 (AMB)
BISKIN, MICHAEL A., dir. eng., St. Francis Hospital, Evanston, IL '83 (ENG)
BISSELL, JUNE L., RN, asst. adm., Allegheny Valley Hospital, Natrona Heights, PA '78 (NURS)
BISSELL, VICKI K., mgr. food serv., Methodist Hospital, Omaha, NE '84 (FOOD)
BISSEN, CASSANDRA A., mgt. eng., St. Francis Medical Center, La Crosse, WI '80 (MGMT)
BISSETT, PATRICIA D., Escondido, CA '86 (FOOD)
BISSONNET, PAT M., instructional designer, Memorial Care Systems, Houston, TX '86 (EDUC)
BITROS, BARBARA SCHAFFER, RN, dir. matl. mgt., Grand View Hospital, Sellersville, PA '83 (PUR)
BITTING, GRACE, RN, mgr. sup., proc. and distrib., Community General Osteopathic Hospital, Harrisburg, PA '87 (CS)
BITTING, NANCY J., RN, asst. adm. nrsg. serv., Queen of the Valley Hospital, West Covina, CA '83 (NURS)
BITTLE, LOIS J., pres., Bittle and Associates, Inc., Baltimore, MD '80 (RISK)
BITTLE, MARK J., mgr. amb. serv., University of Maryland Medical Systems, Baltimore, MD '86 (AMB)
BITTLE, SHELIA, RN, assoc. dir. nrsg. and psych., University of Utah Health Sciences Center, Salt Lake City, UT '86 (NURS)
BITTNER, RHONDA, supv. rad. dept., Ingalls Memorial Hospital, Harvey, IL '86
BITTNER, SUSAN J., dir. vol. serv., Overlake Hospital Medical Center, Bellevue, WA '81 (VOL)
BIVENS, P. SHARON, asst. adm., Miami General Hospital, Miami, FL '86
BIVONA, CHARLES A., biomedical eng., Greenwich Hospital, Greenwich, CT '87 (ENG)
BIXBY, NEENA B., mgr. pat. serv., Huntington Memorial Hospital, Pasadena, CA '80 (SOC)
BIXLER, MICKEY, pres., Biomedical Electronics, Inc., Amarillo, TX '86 (ENG)
BIXLER, PATRICIA A., mgr. pat. and vol. rel., Community Hospital North, Indianapolis, IN '86 (PAT)
BIZETTE, JUSTINE L., RN, dir. nrsg., Imperial Point Medical Center, Fort Lauderdale, FL '80 (NURS)
BIZZARRI, ANITA, RN, dir. nrsg. serv., Beverly Hospital, Montebello, CA '71 (NURS)
BJELICH, STEVEN C., chief oper. off., AMI Medical Center of North Hollywood, North Hollywood, CA '78
BJERKE, CRAIG M., dir. soc. serv., North Country Hospital, Bemidji, MN '76 (SOC)
BJERKE, WILLIAM D., dir. food serv., St. Joseph's Hospital, Providence, RI '77 (FOOD)
BJERKEN, ELLEN, dir. food serv., St. John's Hospital, Fargo, ND '80 (FOOD)
BJORK, JOHN W., (ret.), Oklahoma City, OK '83 (SOC)
BJORK, VIRGINIA, mgr. cent. serv., Unity Medical Center, Fridley, MN '86 (CS)
BJORK, WAYNE V., dir. matl. mgt., Providence Hospital, Washington, DC '80 (PUR)
BJORNSON, DAVID L., adm., St. Peter Hospital, Olympia, WA '65
BJORVIK, ROBERT A., exec. dir., Emergency Treatment Associates, Department Emergency Medicine, St. Francis Hospital, Pougkeepsie, NY '84
BLACK, AGNES LUCAS, RN, chief nrsg. serv., Veterans Administration Medical Center, Lexington, KY '68 (NURS)
BLACK, AILEEN, asst. dir., Medical University of South Carolina Medical Center, Charleston, SC '83 (RISK)
BLACK, ANNE S., RN, vice-pres. nrsg., Children's Hospital, Boston, MA '76 (NURS)
BLACK, BEVERLY L., student, Department of Health Services Administration, George Washington University, Washington, DC '84
BLACK, BOB L., dir. bldg. serv., Tulane University Hospital and Clinics, New Orleans, LA '85 (ENG)
BLACK, BOB, mgr. matl., Euclid Clinic Foundation, Euclid, OH '83 (PUR)
BLACK, CAROLYN S., dir. food serv., Mercy Hospital, Bakersfield, CA '85 (FOOD)
BLACK, CATHERINE T., RN, surveyor, Joint Commission on Accreditation of Hospitals, Chicago, IL '77 (NURS)
BLACK, CHRIS S., dir. soc. work, Washington-St. Tammany Charity Hospital, Bogalusa, LA '86 (SOC)
BLACK, CHRISTINA W., atty., Deaconess Hospital of Cleveland, Cleveland, OH '86 (ATTY)
BLACK, CORINNE P., RN, dir. nrsg., HCA Doctors Hospital, Conroe, TX '82 (NURS)
BLACK, DON C., chief exec. off., Children Health Corporation of America, Overland Park, KS '76 (PR) (PLNG)
BLACK, DONNA M., dir. soc. serv., Jones County Community Hospital, Laurel, MS '82 (SOC)
BLACK, DOROTHY BRIDGWATER, dir. soc. serv., Texas Children's Hospital, Houston, TX '68 (SOC)
BLACK, EMILY M., dir. food serv., Grand View Hospital, Sellersville, PA '84 (FOOD)
BLACK, HEIDI, dir. pat. care, Hamilton Medical Center, Dalton, GA '87 (AMB)
BLACK, JED M., dir. prof. dev., Rehabilitative Health Services, Inc., Indianapolis, IN '83
BLACK, JOHN L., actg. dir. food serv. and diet., University of Illinois Hospital, Chicago, IL '84 (FOOD)
BLACK, JOSEPH SANDERS JR., dir. environ. health and safety, St. Mary's Hospital, Richmond, VA '86 (ENVIRON)(ENG)
BLACK, LILY S., asst. dir. vol. serv., Mercy Catholic Medical Center, Philadelphia, PA '80 (VOL)
BLACK, MABRY LEO, dir. eng. and maint., Monroe County Hospital, Monroeville, AL '84 (ENG)
BLACK, MARCIA M., dir. soc. serv., St. Elizabeth Medical Center, Yakima, WA '87 (SOC)
BLACK, NANCY J., dir. qual. assur., Kaiser Foundation Hospital, Walnut Creek, CA '87 (RISK)
BLACK, PATRICIA F., dir. vol. serv., Brackenridge Hospital, Austin, TX '86 (VOL)
BLACK, ROBERT W., dir. plng. and bus. dev., Baxter Travenol Laboratories, McGaw Park, IL '87 (PLNG)
BLACK, SALLY A., RN, dir. nrsg., Jamestown General Hospital, Jamestown, NY '86 (NURS)
BLACK, SANDY D., dir. vol. serv. and mgr. gift shop, Baptist Medical Center Easley, Easley, SC '85 (VOL)
BLACK, THOMAS J., vice-pres. fin. affairs, St. Joseph's Hospital and Medical Center, Paterson, NJ '85
BLACK, WARREN G. JR., dir. plant oper., Medical Center Hospital, Chillicothe, OH '85 (ENG)
BLACK, WILLIAM SPENCE, arch. consult., Weston, MA '66
BLACKBURN, DAVID G., exec. vice-pres. and chief oper. off., Riverside Methodist Hospitals, Columbus, OH '75
BLACKBURN, JACKYE L., supv. oper. room serv., Valley View Regional Hospital, Ada, OK '86
BLACKBURN, KATHLEEN, dir. soc. work, Plummer Memorial Public Hospital, Sault Ste Marie, Ont., Canada '85 (SOC)
BLACKBURN, MARGUERITE T., RN, mgr. sterile proc., Franklin Square Hospital, Baltimore, MD '71 (CS)
BLACKBURN, REUBEN G., mgr. soc. serv., Nash General Hospital, Rocky Mount, NC '75 (SOC)
BLACKLEY, JOANNE G., dir. food and nutr. serv., Rochester General Hospital, Rochester, NY '86 (FOOD)
BLACKMAN, ALLAN, sr. strategic planner, Group Health Cooperative of Puget Sound, Seattle, WA '79 (PLNG)
BLACKMAN, BETTY L., dir. soc. serv., Venice Hospital, Venice, FL '79 (SOC)
BLACKMAN, JAY H., vice-pres., Methodist Hospital, Philadelphia, PA '76
BLACKMER, PATRICIA, dir. amb. and emer. serv., Faulkner Hospital, Boston, MA '87 (AMB)
BLACKMORE, TIMOTHY A., mgr. pub. rel. and dev., University of Missouri Hospital and Clinics, Columbia, MO '85 (PR)
BLACKWELL, AMY C., dir. med. rec. serv., Presbyterian Hospital, Charlotte, NC '82
BLACKWELL, BEVERLY J., mgr. product line, Hyde Park Hospital, Chicago, IL '87 (AMB)
BLACKWELL, CHARLOTTE E., clin. instr., Wake Medical Center, Raleigh, NC '85 (EDUC)
BLACKWELL, DAVID N., dir. human res., Fort Worth Children's Hospital, Fort Worth, TX '86 (PERS)
BLACKWELL, FRANK E., dir. staff dev., Hinds General Hospital, Jackson, MS '79 (EDUC)
BLACKWELL, HUGH A., atty., Valdese General Hospital, Valdese, NC '83 (ATTY)
BLACKWELL, JOHN R., dir. human res., University of California Los Angeles, Los Angeles, CA '77 (PERS)
BLACKWOOD, KATHLEEN H., RN, assoc. dir. nrsg., Mercy Hospital, Toledo, OH '83 (NURS)
BLACKWOOD, SARAH, RN, adm. nrsg., Kaiser Foundation Hospital, Fontana, CA '81 (NURS)
BLADES, BARBARA ELLEN, RN, dir. nrsg., Beebe Hospital of Sussex County, Lewes, DE '73 (NURS)
BLAES, STEPHEN M., atty., St. Joseph Medical Center, Wichita, KS '68 (ATTY)
BLAESING, SANDRA L., RN, coor. nrsg., St. Louis University School of Nursing, St. Louis, MO '84 (NURS)
BLAIES, JOAN M., RN, clin. dir. nrsg., Waukesha Memorial Hospital, Waukesha, WI '82 (NURS)
BLAINE, LEORA C., dir. commun. serv., St. Francis Memorial Hospital, San Francisco, CA '85 (ENG)
BLAINE, PHYLLIS MONICA, chief diet., Hospital for Joint Diseases and Medical Center, New York, NY '67 (FOOD)
BLAIR, BILL J., pres. and hosp. consult., McCaleb, Blair Mason, Inc., Edmond, OK '68
BLAIR, BOB, dir. mktg. and pub. rel., Horizon Health Systems, Oak Park, MI '80 (PR)
BLAIR, BONNIE L., dir. vol. serv., St. Joseph Hospital, Memphis, TN '84 (VOL)
BLAIR, CATHERINE A., asst. pub. rel. and mktg., Ohio Valley Medical Center, Wheeling, WV '87 (PR)
BLAIR, CONSTANCE S., dir. soc. serv., Jefferson Davis Hospital, Houston, TX '73 (SOC)
BLAIR, DAVID LEE, adm. res., University Hospital, Augusta, GA '84
BLAIR, DOROTHY M., RN, vice-pres. nrsg., Holyoke Hospital, Holyoke, MA '78 (NURS)
BLAIR, EUNICE M., RN EdD, prof. emeritus and div. head, School of Nursing, University of Colorado Health Sciences Center, Denver, CO '76 (NURS)
BLAIR, FREDERICK L., adm., Sloop Memorial Hospital, Crossnore, NC '76
BLAIR, JAMES D., MD, dep. exec. dir., Health and Human Services, Fin Commission, Columbia, SC '74
BLAIR, JAMES, chief soc. work serv., Veterans Administration Medical Center, Butler, PA '87 (SOC)
BLAIR, JANET M., dir. human res., Beloit Memorial Hospital, Beloit, WI '83 (PERS)
BLAIR, JANET S., dir. pub. rel. and commun., Howard Young Medical Center, Woodruff, WI '86 (PR)
BLAIR, LOUIS BLISS, Cedar Rapids, IA '40 (LIFE)
BLAIR, MARDIAN J., pres., Adventist Health System-Sunbelt, Orlando, FL '61 (PLNG)
BLAIR, MARILEE, RN, asst. dir. nrsg., Sarah Bush Lincoln Health Center, Mattoon, IL '81 (NURS)
BLAIR, MARSHA M., RN, asst. dir. nrsg., Sarah Bush Lincoln Health Center, Mattoon, IL '81 (NURS)
BLAIR, ROBERT DELMER JR., student, Program in Health Service Administration, University of California at Los Angeles School of Public Health, Los Angeles, CA '86
BLAIR, RON, dir. pur., Charles Cole Memorial Hospital, Coudersport, PA '73 (PUR)
BLAIR, SHIRLEY M., dir. pub. rel., Medina Community Hospital, Medina, OH '83 (PR)
BLAIR, SUSAN S., dir. vol. serv., Long Island Jewish-Hillside Medical Center, New York, NY '85 (VOL)
BLAIS, CYNTHIA S., plng. analyst, Anaheim Memorial Hospital, Anaheim, CA '87 (PLNG)
BLAIS, EARLE C., atty., Granada Hills Community Hospital, Granada Hills, CA '76 (ATTY)
BLAIS, JIM, asst. chief eng., Lodi Memorial Hospital, Lodi, CA '79 (ENG)
BLAISDELL, BEVERLY J., asst. adm., HCA Greenview Hospital, Bowling Green, KY '84
BLAISDELL, RICHARD W., consult., Health Care Services, Inc., Kapaa Kauai, HI '53 (LIFE)
BLAISDELL, WALLACE, Kapiolani Medical Center for Women, Honolulu, HI '86 (PERS)
BLAKE, BETTY, RN, asst. dir. and dir. nrsg., Grady Memorial Hospital, Atlanta, GA '79 (NURS)
BLAKE, BONNIE L., RN, clin. dir. med.-surg. nrsg., Fairview Riverside Hospital, Minneapolis, MN '82 (NURS)
BLAKE, CARMELITA, coor. in-service, Beekman Downtown Hospital, New York, NY '78 (EDUC)
BLAKE, CARTER F., dir. matl. mgt. and ancillary serv., Sisters of Charity of the Incarnate Word Health Care Systems, Corporate Office, Houston, TX '74 (PUR)
BLAKE, DANIEL, Tampa, FL '85
BLAKE, GEORGE H., Montgomery, AL '77 (ENG)
BLAKE, GEORGE PAUL, asst. dir. eng., Hamilton Hospital, Hamilton, NJ '86 (ENG)
BLAKE, JUDITH, coor. diet. serv., Ontario Hospital Association, Don Mills, Ont., Canada '80 (FOOD)
BLAKE, KATHERINE JANE, RN, asst. vice-pres. pat. serv., Southern Baptist Hospital, New Orleans, LA '84 (NURS)
BLAKE, LOUISE S., RN, asst. adm. nrsg., Jackson Hospital and Clinic, Montgomery, AL '80 (NURS)
BLAKE, MARIANNE C., RN, assoc. dir. nrsg., Barnes Hospital, St. Louis, MO '81 (NURS)
BLAKE, PAMELA B., asst. dir. cent. sterile sup., Mount Sinai Medical Center, New York, NY '82 (CS)
BLAKE, PAUL J., dir. mktg. and sales, Riverfront Medical Services, Tonawanda, NY '84 (RISK)
BLAKE, ROBERT L., atty., James M. Jackson Memorial Hospital, Miami, FL '87 (ATTY)
BLAKE, THOMAS C., pres., Colony Charter Life Insurance Company, Los Angeles, CA '81
BLAKELEY, BARBARA, dir. vol. serv., St. Vincent Hospital and Medical Center, Portland, OR '78 (VOL)
BLAKELY, ELTON TIMOTHY, dir. facil., Kaiser Permanente Medical Care Program, Los Angeles, CA '70 (MGMT)
BLAKELY, MICHELLE Y., student, Program and Bureau of Hospital Administration, University of Michigan, Ann Arbor, MI '86
BLAKELY, THOMAS A., dir. plant oper., Kennedy Memorial Hospitals University Medical Center, Stratford, NJ '84 (ENG)
BLAKENEY, JOE F., asst. dir., Mississippi State Hospital, Whitfield, MS '66
BLAKLEY, DIANE M., mgr. pub. rel., DuBois Regional Medical Center, Dubois, PA '84 (PR)
BLALOCK, ANDY E., asst. dir. eng. and oper., Duke University Hospital, Durham, NC '86 (ENG)
BLALOCK, JAN J., pers. off., R. T. Jones Memorial Hospital, Canton, GA '82 (PERS)
BLALOCK, ROBERT J., dir. commun., Kingsbrook Jewish Medical Center, Brooklyn, NY '85 (ENG)(PLNG)
BLANC, LAWRENCE W., dir. matl. mgt., Queen of the Valley Hospital, Napa, CA '77 (PUR)
BLANCH, KATHY A., dir. in-service educ., Clinton County Hospital, Frankfort, IN '86 (EDUC)
BLANCH, PAUL B., coor. resp. care educ., Shands Hospital, Gainesville, FL '86 (ENG)
BLANCHAR, JOAN M., student, University of Missouri-Columbia School of Industrial Engineer, Columbia, MO '86 (MGMT)
BLANCHARD, BRUCE A., dir. plant oper., St. Mary's General Hospital, Lewiston, ME '83 (ENG)
BLANCHARD, BRYAN R., dir. matl. mgt., Advanced Management Systems, Auburn, MA '78 (MGMT)(PUR)
BLANCHARD, HELEN V., mgr. matl., Frances Mahon Deaconess Hospital, Glasgow, MT '83 (PUR)
BLANCHARD, MARY S., dir. vol. serv., St. Francis Xavier Hospital, Charleston, SC '83 (VOL)
BLANCHARD, MICHAEL J., Jane Lamb Health Center, Clinton, IA '84 (PR)
BLANCHARD, STEPHEN C., asst. to chief exec. off., Philhaven Hospital, Mount Gretna, PA '71
BLANCHET, MICHAEL C., vice-pres. corp. plng., Community Hospitals of Indiana, Indianapolis, IN '82 (PLNG)
BLANCHETTE, ROBERT O., dir. pers., Crotched Mountain Rehabilitation Center, Greenfield, NH '84 (PERS)
BLANCO, JOSE A. JR., prin., Professional Group Enterprises, Bethesda, MD '68 (MGMT)
BLANCO, PATRICIA, vice-pres. and chief oper. off., Hasco, Coral Gables, FL '81 (RISK)
BLAND, ANNA L., dir. food serv., Humana Hospital -Natchez, Natchez, MS '83 (FOOD)
BLAND, LT. COL. EDWARD C., MSC USA, mission assignment off., health care plng., U. S. Army Health Services Command, Fort Sam Houston, TX '76

BLAND, JOHN W. JR., atty., Hardin Memorial Hospital, Elizabethtown, KY '78 (ATTY)
BLAND, ROENNA J., pat. rep., Greater Southeast Community Hospital, Washington, DC '78 (PAT)
BLAND, TOMMY E., adm., Bennett County Community Hospital, Martin, SD '86
BLANDFORD, DALE KIRK, sr. budget analyst, Children's Hospital National Medical Center, Washington, DC '85
BLANDING, LINDA MCCARTY, instr. staff dev., Iroquois Memorial Hospital, Watseka, IL '85 (EDUC)
BLANK, BETTY ROSE, (ret.), Cincinnati, OH '70 (EDUC)
BLANK, EDWARD C. II, atty., Baptist Hospital, Nashville, TN '87 (ATTY)
BLANK, ELLA, dir. soc. work, Long Beach Community Hospital, Long Beach, CA '70 (SOC)
BLANK, F. PHILIP, atty., United Medical Corporation, Orlando, FL '84 (ATTY)
BLANK, JUNE, dir. vol. serv., Northern Westchester Hospital Center, Mount Kisco, NY '85 (VOL)
BLANK, PEACHES G., exec. dir., Hospital Alliance of Tennessee, Inc., Nashville, TN '82
BLANKEN, HOWARD M., dir. mgt. syst., Forsyth Memorial Hospital, Winston-Salem, NC '77 (MGMT)
BLANKENSHIP, ALICIA H., dir. mktg., Greenfield Area Medical Center, Greenfield, OH '86 (PR)
BLANKENSHIP, CHARLES D. SR., maint. eng., Kosciusko Community Hospital, Warsaw, IN '85 (ENG)
BLANKENSHIP, KENNETH, Shriver and Holland Associates, Norfolk, VA '82 (ENG)
BLANKENSHIP, PEGGY S., RN, co-dir. nrsg. serv., Roanoke Memorial Hospitals, Roanoke, VA '76 (NURS)
BLANKENSHIP, ROBERT G., buyer matl. mgt., East Liverpool City Hospital, East Liverpool, OH '85 (PUR)
BLANKERTS, BETH ANN, dir. food serv., ARA Services, Hospital Food Management, Environmental Service, Inc., Westland, MI '79 (FOOD)
BLANTON, FOREST W., dir. mgt. syst., Memorial Hospital, Hollywood, FL '85 (MGMT)
BLANTON, H. M., chief adm. diet., Veterans Administration Medical Center, Omaha, NE '78 (FOOD)
BLANTON, JANSEN N., Sierra Vista, AZ '80
BLANTON, JOHN C., (ret.), Ahoskie, NC '80
BLANTON, MILLY A., dir. matl. mgt., Kissimmee Memorial Hospital, Kissimmee, FL '67 (CS)
BLASI, RITA, mgr. hskpg., Seton Medical Center, Daly City, CA '86 (ENVIRON)
BLASINGAME, BILLY, student, Program in Hospital Administration, Trinity University, San Antonio, TX '87
BLASIO, WILLIAM J. DI, chm. risk mgt. com. and atty., Deborah Heart and Lung Center, Browns Mills, NJ '85 (RISK)(ATTY)
BLATTERBAUER, SANDRA, dir. soc. work, St. Francis Hospital, Evanston, IL '79 (SOC)
BLATZ, LAWRENCE A., dir. bldg. and grds., Wayne County Memorial Hospital, Honesdale, PA '84 (ENG)
BLAU, PAUL W., asst. gen. dir., Philadelphia Psychiatric Center, Philadelphia, PA '68
BLAUER, MARK, mgr. maint., Dixie Medical Center, St. George, UT '86 (ENG)
BLAZAR, JAMES, pres., Blazar Health Care Consultants, Glenview, IL '77
BLAZEK, JUDITH J., asst. vice-pres., Hospital Corporation of America, Oklahoma City, OK '83 (PLNG)
BLAZER, BARBARA J., dir. prod. mgt., Cedars Medical Center, Miami, FL '80 (MGMT)
BLAZER, JEANNINE, RN, dir. nrsg. adm. serv., Cabell Huntington Hospital, Huntington, WV '85 (NURS)
BLAZOVIC, VINCENT P., vice-pres., St. Joseph's Hospital and Medical Center, Paterson, NJ '73
BLEAU, MARY E., dir. educ., Warren General Hospital, Warren, PA '86 (EDUC)
BLECH, JAMES A., dir. eng., L. W. Blake Memorial Hospital, Bradenton, FL '74 (ENG)
BLECHNER, RALPH E., pres., Walker Devices, Inc., Norwalk, CT '85 (PUR)
BLECKMAN, JOHN, sr. mgt. consult., New York City Health and Hospitals Corporation, New York, NY '80 (ENG)
BLEDSOE, FORREST L., pres., Healthcare Management Enterprises, Inc., Pembroke Pines, FL '78
BLEDSOE, JOHN K., asst. mgr. eng., North Colorado Medical Center, Greeley, CO '83 (ENG)
BLEDSOE, SANDRA, assoc. dir. risk mgt. and claims, Vanderbilt University Hospital, Nashville, TN '87 (RISK)
BLEEKE, MARY ANN, dir. soc. serv., St. Joseph's Medical Center, Fort Wayne, IN '85 (SOC)
BLEICH, MICHAEL R., RN, vice-pres. nrsg., St. Mary's Medical Center, Racine, WI '80 (NURS)
BLEICHER, N. LOIS, dir. pub. rel., Palms of Pasadena Hospital, St. Petersburg, FL '80 (PR)
BLEND, MARY THERESE, RN, dir. nrsg., Winthrop-University Hospital, Mineola, NY '77 (NURS)
BLENDON, ROBERT JAY, vice-pres., Robert Wood Johnson Rehabilitation Institute, Edison, NJ '65
BLESSING, CAROLYN, supv. sterile proc. tech., Good Samaritan Hospital, Kearney, NE '85 (CS)
BLESSING, WILLIAM H., exec. dir., Mary Free Bed Hospital and Rehabilitation Center, Grand Rapids, MI '71
BLETHEN, ERNEST, asst. dir. maint., Brunswick General Hospital, Amityville, NY '82 (ENG)
BLEVINS, DANIEL D., dir. human resources and commun., North Side Hospital, Johnson City, TN '82 (PR)(PERS)
BLEVINS, FRED L., mgr. matl., Servicemaster Industries, Inc., Downers Grove, IL '82 (PUR)
BLEVINS, GREGORY G., mgr., Arthur Young and Company, Los Angeles, CA '85 (PLNG)
BLEVINS, JERRY W., dir. plant oper., Parkway Medical Center Hospital, Decatur, AL '86 (ENVIRON)
BLEVINS, WILLIAM L., eng., Shriners Hospital for Crippled Children, Lexington, KY '85 (ENG)
BLEWETT, JEAN, member serv. mgr., Cigna Healthplan of Colorado, Inc., Denver, CO '86 (PAT)
BLEY, CHARLES M., partner, Ernst and Whinney, Chicago, IL '81
BLIESE, ROBERT K., adm. res., Veterans Administration West Side Medical Center, Chicago, IL '84
BLINKA, CAREN E., assoc., Wood, Lucksinger and Epstein, Houston, TX '84
BLISH, CHRISTINE S., mgr., Transition Systems, Inc., Boston, MA '85 (MGMT)
BLISS, ANTHONY H., vice-pres. and chief oper. off., Hunterdon Medical Center, Flemington, NJ '75
BLISS, DAVID, adm. asst., Rush-Presbyterian-St. Luke's Medical Center, Chicago, IL '85
BLISS, EMILY J., assoc., Cambridge Research Institute, Cambridge, MA '82 (PLNG)
BLISS, KATHLEEN ALLEN, RN, clin. dir. critical care, Beverly Hospital, Beverly, MA '86 (NURS)
BLISS, PAUL S., Seattle, WA '53 (LIFE)
BLITCH, RONALD B., pres., Blitch Architects, Inc., New Orleans, LA '85
BLITZ, ALAN, acct. exec., Abelson and Taylor, Inc., Chicago, IL '79 (PR) (PLNG)
BLITZER, GLORIA G., pat. serv. rep., New York University Medical Center, New York, NY '84 (PAT)
BLIVEN, DAVID, asst. dir. plant oper., St. Vincent Hospital, Green Bay, WI '86 (ENG)
BLIVEN, WILLIAM S., dir. plant oper., George Washington University Hospital, Washington, DC '86 (ENG)
BLIXT, JILL E., partner and creative dir., Blixt and Associates, Ann Arbor, MI '86 (PR)
BLIZZARD, RICHARD T., asst. vice-pres., United Health Services, Johnson City, NY '84 (PLNG)
BLOCH, EMILY B., vice-pres. support serv., Raritan Bay Medical Center, Perth Amboy, NJ '84
BLOCH, GREGG E., asst. dir. nrsg.-critical care and surg., Mount Sinai Medical Center, Miami Beach, FL '81 (NURS)
BLOCH, JACQUES W., dir. food serv., Montefiore Medical Center, Bronx, NY '54 (FOOD)(LIFE)
BLOCH, JOSEPH LORING, vice-pres. adm., Peninsula Hospital Center, Far Rockaway, NY '65
BLOCH, KENNETH J., vice-pres., Instant Care Centers of America, New Orleans, LA '75
BLOCH, NANCY E., RN, vice-pres. nrsg., Heights General Hospital, Albuquerque, NM '80 (NURS)
BLOCK-LOVE, LINDA A., mgr. mktg., St. Joseph Hospital and Health Center, Kokomo, IN '84 (PR) (PLNG)
BLOCK, CAROL, RN, dir. nrsg., Memorial Hospital for McHenry County, Woodstock, IL '85 (NURS)
BLOCK, CHARLES M., mgr. mkt commun., Highland Park Hospital, Highland Park, IL '86 (PR)
BLOCK, DARLENE, mgr. sup., proc. and distrib., St. Nicholas Hospital, Sheboygan, WI '86 (CS)
BLOCK, JUDITH K., dir. vol. and pat. rel., Highland Park Hospital, Highland Park, IL '86 (VOL)(PAT)
BLOCK, LEE F., pres., Lee F. Block and Partners, Inc., Chicago, IL '66 (PR)
BLOCK, LOUIS, DrPH, bd. chm., Block, McGibony and Associates, Inc., Columbia, MD '42 (LIFE)
BLOCK, MAE H., dir. commun., Cabarrus Memorial Hospital, Concord, NC '74 (ENG)
BLOCK, PAULA E., student, Department of Health Services Administration, George Washington University, Washington, DC '86
BLOCK, SUSAN KENNEDY, dir. soc. serv., Dearborn County Hospital, Lawrenceburg, IN '85 (SOC)
BLOCK, WILLIAM A., sr. sales rep., Honeywell Information Systems, Louisville, KY '86
BLOCKER, VERNITA, dir. soc. work, Episcopal Hospital, Philadelphia, PA '85 (SOC)
BLOM, DAVID PAUL, vice-pres. mgt. serv., U. S. Health Corporation, Columbus, OH '78
BLOMBERG, STEPHEN M., dir. plant serv., Grays Harbor Community Hospital, Aberdeen, WA '82 (ENG)
BLOME, MAXINE, RN, vice-pres. prof. serv., Adventist Health System-West, Roseville, CA '74 (NURS)
BLOMMER, BILL, asst. dir. plant eng., University of Wisconsin Hospital and Clinics, Madison, WI '86 (ENG)
BLOMQUIST, BOBBI, dir. hosp. rel., Medtronic, Inc., Minneapolis, MN '85
BLOMQUIST, CARL A. JR., chief oper. off., Cooperative of American Physicians, Inc., Los Angeles, CA '74
BLOMSTROM, CAROL K., vice-pres. info. syst., Palomar Pomerado Hospital District, Escondido, CA '85 (MGMT)
BLONDIN, SHAUNE M., dir. pers., Saratoga Hospital, Saratoga Springs, NY '85 (PERS)
BLOOM, GEORGE E., atty., Our Lady of Mercy Hospital, Dyer, IN '81 (ATTY)
BLOOM, LILLIAN, dir. vol. serv., Encino Hospital, Encino, CA '83 (VOL)
BLOOM, MARIA DE LOS ANGELES, dir. soc. serv., Miami General Hospital, Miami, FL '87 (SOC)
BLOOM, MARY JOEL, pat. serv. spec., Group Health, Inc., Bloomington, MN '85 (PAT)
BLOOM, MICHAEL ALAN, chief soc. work serv., Veterans Administration Medical Center, Battle Creek, MI '80 (SOC)
BLOOM, REBECCA J., student, Program in Hospital Administration, University of Minnesota, Moorhead, MN '84
BLOOM, ROBERT A., affil. adm., Montefiore Medical Center, Bronx, NY '65
BLOOM, ROBERT A., assoc. vice-pres., St. Luke's-Roosevelt Hospital Center, New York, NY '82 (ENG)
BLOOM, RUTH M., mgr. and supv. cent. proc., St. Joseph Hospitals, Mount Clemens, MI '85 (CS)
BLOOMBERG, CAROL A., dir. mktg., Georgetown University Medical Center, Washington, DC '85 (PLNG)
BLOOMBERG, DONALD STANLEY, exec. dir., Doctors' Hospital of Staten Island, Staten Island, NY '57 (LIFE)
BLOOMER, PATRICIA A., dir. vol. serv., West Hudson Hospital, Kearny, NJ '85 (VOL)
BLOOMER, RUTH A., mgr. vol. serv., Munson Medical Center, Traverse City, MI '87 (VOL)
BLOOMFIELD, EUGENE, consult., Farmers Insurance Group, Los Angeles, CA '64 (RISK)
BLOOMFIELD, ROGER E., atty., Community Hospital of Springfield, Springfield, OH '86 (ATTY)
BLOOMQUIST, MARGARET A., dir. pers., Paoli Memorial Hospital, Paoli, PA '78 (PERS)
BLOOMQUIST, MICHAEL, dir. plant oper. and maint., St. Mark's Hospital, Salt Lake City, UT '77 (ENG)
BLOOMQUIST, NEAL R., supv. biomedical electronics, Memorial Hospital, Carbondale, IL '78 (ENG)
BLOOMSTINE, WILLIAM C., pres., Insurance Management Company, Erie, PA '82 (RISK)
BLOSCHOCK, LEO A., pur. agt., Lexington County Hospital, West Columbia, SC '77 (PUR)
BLOSER, THOMAS J., mgr. biomedical commun., Memorial Hospital for Cancer, New York, NY '86 (PLNG)
BLOUIN, ANN S., RN, sr. nrsg. exec., MacNeal Hospital, Berwyn, IL '81 (NURS)
BLOUNT, BRANTON B., facil. eng., Presbyterian Hospital, Albuquerque, NM '65 (ENG)
BLOUNT, LAMAR, atty., Cobb Memorial Hospital, Royston, GA '81
BLOUNT, SYLVIA M., RN, asst. chief nrsg. serv., Veterans Administration Medical Center, Dallas, TX '86 (NURS)
BLOWER, JOHN G., vice-pres., St. Joseph's Medical Center, South Bend, IN '78 (PUR)
BLOXSOM, ALLAN P., prin., Bloxsom and Associates, Houston, TX '83 (ENG)
BLUDWORTH, BILL R., atty., Sisters of Charity of the Incarnate Word, Houston, TX '75 (ATTY)
BLUE, BEVERLY A., dir. allied health, Delta College, University Center, MI '85 (EDUC)
BLUE, CATHIE J., coor. phlebotomy trng., Riverside Methodist Hospitals, Columbus, OH '85 (EDUC)
BLUE, JAMES R., dir. safety eng. and educ., Ohio Hospital Insurance Company, Columbus, OH '81 (ENG)
BLUE, JEAN W., asst. to chm., University of Alabama Hospital, Birmingham, AL '81
BLUESTEIN, LYNDA S., dir. mktg., University of California Irvine, California College of Medicine, Irvine, CA '85 (PLNG)
BLUESTONE, BARRY, mgr. trng. and dev., Staten Island Hospital, Staten Island, NY '86 (PERS)
BLUETT, TERRENCE E., dir. pers., York Hospital, York, PA '84 (PERS)
BLUHM, JON M., asst. dir. pers., Memorial Medical Center, Springfield, IL '83 (PERS)
BLUHM, LINDA M., dir. pastoral care, soc. serv. and pat. advocate, Holy Family Hospital, Spokane, WA '86 (PAT)
BLUM, DIANE S., dir. soc. serv., Cancer Care, Inc., New York, NY '85 (SOC)
BLUM, HARRIETT, dir. pat. rel., Lenox Hill Hospital, New York, NY '77 (PAT)
BLUM, JOHN D., atty., Institute for Health Law, Loyola Law School, Chicago, IL '77 (ATTY)
BLUM, MARLENE C., coor. human res., Catherine McAuley Health Center, Ann Arbor, MI '86 (PERS)
BLUM, CAPT. ROBERT W., MSC USAF, dir. res. mgt., U. S. Air Force Clinic Bentwaters, APO New York, NY '80
BLUM, WILLIAM R., Weston, MA '82 (PAT)
BLUMBERG, MARK S., MD, dir. spec. studies, Kaiser Foundation Health Plan, Oakland, CA '67 (MGMT)
BLUMBERG, MELVIN R., int. auditor, Santa Rosa Medical Center, San Antonio, TX '70 (ATTY)
BLUME, THEODORE S., student, School of Technical Careers, Southern Illinois University, Carbondale, IL '86
BLUMENFIELD, SUSAN, dir. soc. work, Mount Sinai Medical Center, New York, NY '83 (SOC)
BLUMENSHEID, PAMELA E., pub. rel. accounts mgr., St. Elizabeth Medical Center, Dayton, OH '83 (PR)
BLUMENTHAL, DAVID, MD, assoc. medicine, Massachusetts General Hospital, Boston, MA '83 (PLNG)
BLUMETTI, JOSEPH F., asst. dir. food serv., Morristown Memorial Hospital, Morristown, NJ '75 (FOOD)
BLUNSCHI, RICKY D., adm., Riverland Medical Center, Ferriday, LA '82 (PR)
BLUSIEWICZ, GENE, fin. consult., Atlanta, GA '84
BLY, DOUGLAS A., dir. syst. eng., Medical Center of Delaware, Wilmington, DE '71 (MGMT)
BLY, JAMIE L., student, New School for Social Research Rome Division, Rome, NY '81
BLYTH, PAMELA L., dir. environ. serv., Hamilton Medical Center, Dalton, GA '86 (ENVIRON)
BLYTHE, GLEN R., dir. maint., Aultman Hospital, Canton, OH '68 (ENG)
BOAG, LYNN O., RN, asst. chief nrsg. serv., Veterans Administration Medical Center, Sheridan, WY '85 (NURS)
BOAN, ORIS, mgr. emp., Utah Valley Regional Medical Center, Provo, UT '79 (PERS)
BOARD, HELEN K., RN, dir. nrsg. serv., Southwest Mississippi Medical Center, McComb, MS '86 (NURS)
BOARDMAN, ROBERT C., exec. dir., Rockville General Hospital, Rockville, CT '59
BOASE, BEVERLY, dir. mktg., AMI Danforth Hospital, Texas City, TX '82 (PR)
BOATMAN, DANIEL W., vice-pres., Columbus Hospital, Great Falls, MT '75
BOATMAN, HELLA, dir. pub. rel. and commun. serv., Sebasticook Valley Hospital, Pittsfield, ME '83 (PR)
BOATMAN, PAMELA K., dir. commun., Mercy-Memorial Medical Center, Inc., Benton Harbor, MI '85 (PR)
BOATRIGHT, NED C., pres., Health Management Services, Inc., Columbus, OH '81
BOATTENHAMER, GREG, dir. commun., Iowa Hospital Association, Des Moines, IA '86 (PR)
BOATWRIGHT, SHARON L., RN, dir. nrsg., Wayne Memorial Hospital, Jesup, GA '81 (NURS)
BOBBE, ALAN L., dir. mktg., Nexus Healthcare Corporation, Mount Holly, NJ '87 (PLNG)
BOBBERT, PATRICIA M., RN, dir. nrs., Clarion Osteopathic Community Hospital, Clarion, PA '86 (NURS)
BOBBY, CARL M., dir. biomedical eng., Western Reserve Care Systems-Northside Medical Center, Youngstown, OH '83 (ENG)

BOBEN, JOAN H., RN, adm. supv. maternal and child health, Lancaster General Hospital, Lancaster, PA '84
BOBENG, BARBARA J., PhD, American Dietetic Association, Chicago, IL '75 (FOOD)
BOBINGER, ANN E., RN, asst. adm. and dir. nrsg., Gulf Oaks Hospital and Clinic, Biloxi, MS '86 (NURS)
BOBLITZ, CATHERINE D., dir. pers., Children's Hospital, Baltimore, MD '82 (PERS)
BOBO, CAROLYN G., dir. pub. rel., St. Joseph Hospital, Albuquerque, NM '86 (PR)
BOBROWITZ, ISIDORE D., MD, assoc. prof. med., Hospital of the Albert Einstein College of Medicine, Bronx, NY '39 (LIFE)
BOCHENEK, ROBERT C., dir. pur. and sup., St. Agnes Hospital, Baltimore, MD '86 (PUR)
BOCOOK, MICHAEL D., dir. soc. serv., King's Daughters' Medical Center, Ashland, KY '85 (SOC)
BODARY, RONALD L., adm., War Memorial Hospital, Sault Ste Marie, MI '86 (PR)
BODDY, MARGARET J., risk mgr., Port Huron Hospital, Port Huron, MI '87 (RISK)
BODE, KATHLEEN P., RN, dir. nrsg. serv., Southwest Medical Center, Liberal, KS '76 (NURS)(AMB)
BODE, SUSAN, RN, vice-pres., St. Luke's Hospital, Milwaukee, WI '76 (NURS)
BODENHAMER, BETTY NEAL, mgr. pat. serv., North Carolina Baptist Hospital, Winston-Salem, NC '76 (SOC)
BODENHORN, SUSAN M., dir. human res., St. Catherine Hospital, East Chicago, IN '83 (PERS)
BODENSTEIN, JOYCE E., RN, vice-pres. nrsg., Christ Hospital, Cincinnati, OH '84 (NURS)
BODIN, ROBERT A., dir. plant serv., Miller-Dwan Medical Center, Duluth, MN '75 (ENG)
BODINE, SANDY L., Pittsburgh, PA '81 (FOOD)
BODNAR, TIMOTHY A., dir. med. eng., Akron City Hospital, Akron, OH '86 (ENG)
BODNAR, WILLIAM L., dir. corp. plng. and dev., Mercy Hospital, Davenport, IA '75 (PR)
BODOK, STANLEY A., adm., Dr. Capriles Kliniek, Willemstad Curacao, Antilles '78
BODUCH, MARY E., dir. educ., Faxton Sunset, St. Luke's Health Related Facilities and Home, Utica, NY '71 (EDUC)
BODZEK, J. WILLIAM, dir. plng. and mktg., Hospital Corporation of America, Kingwood, TX '79 (PLNG)
BOE, GRACE, dir. pat. rep., Abbott-Northwestern Hospital, Minneapolis, MN '72 (PAT)
BOEHLER, SHARRON D., RN, chief nrsg., Oklahoma Memorial Hospital and Clinics, Oklahoma City, OK '81 (NURS)
BOEHM, BARRETT L., sr. mgr., Price Waterhouse, St. Louis, MO '85 (PLNG)
BOEHM, ELLEN F., RN, dir. med. nrsg., Illinois Masonic Medical Center, Chicago, IL '82 (NURS)
BOEHM, ERIC T., student, National University, San Diego, CA '86 (MGMT)
BOEHM, MARCIA E., dir. soc. work and cont. care, Providence Hospital, Southfield, MI '86 (SOC)
BOEHM, ROBERT J., atty., Spears, Moore, Rebman and Williams, Inc., Chattanooga, TN '80 (RISK)(ATTY)
BOEHRINGER, PAUL, asst. adm., Temple University Hospital, Philadelphia, PA '82
BOELSTLER, JUDITH L., student, Ferris State College, Big Rapids, MI '87
BOELTER, ANNMARIE B., Parkersburg, WV '86 (VOL)
BOENECKE, CLAYTON A., med. constr. liaison off., U. S. Naval Hospital, FPO New York, NY '84
BOERGADINE, PHYLLIS C., dir. vol., St. Mary's Hospital, Galesburg, IL '85 (VOL)
BOERGER, JOHN S., partner, The Design Partnership, San Francisco, CA '78 (ENG)
BOERNER, HERBERT, partner and proj. mgr., Sargent, Webster, Crenshaw and Folley, Syracuse, NY '83
BOES, CHARLES W., atty., Presbyterian Hospital, Dallas, TX '80 (ATTY)(RISK)
BOESEN, GARY J., chief eng., Douglas County Hospital, Alexandria, MN '79 (ENG)
BOETTCHER, LEAH, dir. soc. serv., Thorek Hospital and Medical Center, Chicago, IL '78 (SOC)
BOETTCHER, WILLIAM V., assoc. exec. dir., University Hospital, Seattle, WA '72 (MGMT)
BOETTE, SUSAN B., RN, asst. adm. nrsg., Moses H. Cone Memorial Hospital, Greensboro, NC '86 (NURS)
BOETTGER, DENISE M., RN, asst. dir. nrsg. and dir. educ., Saint Anthony's Hospital, Alton, IL '85 (EDUC)
BOEVERS, R. KENT, student, Oklahoma State University, Stillwater, OK '86 (MGMT)
BOGART, ELMER J., dir. maint. and plant facil., Lankenau Hospital, Philadelphia, PA '84 (ENG)
BOGDANOVE, ARTHUR J., diet., Giles Memorial Hospital, Pearisburg, VA '87 (FOOD)
BOGDEN-CIOTTI, BERNADETTE, coor. mgt. educ., Chester County Hospital, West Chester, PA '83 (EDUC)
BOGEN, ELLEN, assoc. dir. amb. serv., New York Eye and Ear Infirmary, New York, NY '87 (AMB)
BOGER, CAROLYN, RN, vice-pres. nrsg. serv., Forsyth Memorial Hospital, Winston-Salem, NC '81 (NURS)
BOGER, LINDA, dir. risk mgt. and qual. assur., St. Joseph's Medical Center, South Bend, IN '87 (RISK)
BOGGAN, BENNIE M., buyer, New York University Medical Center, New York, NY '86 (PUR)
BOGGAN, DORIS M., dir. pur., Citizens Memorial Hospital, Victoria, TX '81 (PUR)
BOGGS, ISADORA, pur. agt., Madison County Hospital, London, OH '85 (PUR)
BOGGS, JOYCE W., dir. vol. serv., Spartanburg Regional Medical Center, Spartanburg, SC '81 (VOL)
BOGGS, MICHAEL J., dir. mktg. and commun., Harris Methodist Health Services, Fort Worth, TX '80 (PR) (PLNG)
BOGLE, ELIZABETH W., RN, dir. nrsg. serv., Lewis-Gale Hospital, Salem, VA '80 (NURS)
BOGLE, MARGARET L., dir. nutr. serv., Arkansas Children's Hospital, Little Rock, AR '78 (FOOD)
BOGLE, WILLIAM J., dir. phys. facil., Arkansas Children's Hospital, Little Rock, AR '84 (ENG)
BOGLIOLI, THERESA, pres. and dir., Insurance Recovery Specialists, Inc., Fort Lauderdale, FL '84
BOGOSLAWSKI, ALICE, cent. serv. tech., St. Anthony Hospital, Michigan City, IN '86 (CS)
BOGRAD, EDWARD, atty., Union Hospital, Lynn, MA '71 (ATTY)
BOGUSLAWSKI, JOHN R., dir. soc. serv., St. Margaret Hospital, Hammond, IN '74 (SOC)
BOGUSZEWSKI, MICHAEL J., student, Program in Health Service Administration, Governors State University, Park Forest South, IL '85
BOHACH, STEPHANIE A., head nrs. outpatient, Weirton Medical Center, Weirton, WV '87 (AMB)
BOHAM, DOUGLAS J., commun. counselor, Parkview Hospital, Toledo, OH '83 (ENG)
BOHAM, PHILLIP R., dir. pers., Chelsea Community Hospital, Chelsea, MI '84 (PERS)
BOHAN, GLENDA, RN, dir. nrsg., Mercy Community Hospital, Port Jervis, NY '86 (NURS)
BOHANEK, PAUL, dir. plant eng., Marlborough Hospital, Marlborough, MA '73 (ENG)
BOHANNAN, THOMAS F., mgr. facil. design, Pacific Presbyterian Medical Center, San Francisco, CA '83 (ENG)
BOHANNON, CLAUDETTE, family advocacy off. and prog. coor., Malcolm Grow U. S. Air Force Medical Center, Camp Springs, MD '84 (SOC)
BOHART, LYNN, exec. dir. and dir. pub. rel. and dev., Central Washington Hospital Foundation, Wenatchee, WA '84 (PR)
BOHINC, THOMAS, mgr. hosp. serv., The Peabody Group, Beachwood, OH '86
BOHLIG, JOHN, mgt. eng., Hospital Association of Pennsylvania, Camp Hill, PA '79 (MGMT)
BOHMAN, MADELINE AMANDA, health consult., Apopka, FL '69 (PLNG)
BOHN, BARBARA A., plng. analyst, Louise Obici Memorial Hospital, Suffolk, VA '79 (PLNG)
BOHN, SANDRA, asst. vice-pres., Mercy Catholic Medical Center, Darby, PA '80
BOHN, WALTER G., dir. pers., Sisters of Mercy, St. Louis, MO '78 (PERS)
BOHNART, RENEE, mgr. amb. serv., Riverside Community Memorial Hospital, Waupaca, WI '87 (AMB)
BOHNER, DAVID E., adm., Shriners Hospitals for Crippled Children, Philadelphia Unit, Philadelphia, PA '65
BOHNET, NANCY L., pres. and chief exec. off., Visiting Nurses Association of Butler, Company, Butler, PA '87 (AMB)
BOHRER, JOHN L., sr. vice-pres. adm., St. Joseph Medical Center, Wichita, KS '84
BOHUSLAW, AGNES M., RN, vice-pres. nrsg., Good Samaritan Hospital, West Islip, NY '73 (NURS)(AMB)
BOHY, DAVID W., vice-pres. human res., Miriam Hospital, Providence, RI '86 (PERS)
BOINEAU, ELIZABETH, asst. to dir. pat. accounts, Georgia Baptist Medical Center, Atlanta, GA '84
BOISSONEAU, ROBERT ALLEN, prof., Wright State University, Dayton, OH '69
BOIVIN, DAVE, supv. plant oper., Westlake Community Hospital, Melrose Park, IL '85 (ENG)
BOIVIN, JOSEPH B., asst. dir., William Beaumont Hospital, Royal Oak, MI '81 (PERS)
BOIVIN, MICHAEL R., asst. adm., Washington Hospital Center, Washington, DC '78
BOJARSKI, JOHN KEVIN, mgr., Arthur Young and Company, Richmond, VA '78
BOKHARI, IJAZ M., dir. mgt. eng., Alexandria Hospital, Alexandria, VA '87 (MGMT)
BOKINSKY, GEORGE E., surveyor, Joint Commission on Accreditation of Hospitals, Chicago, IL '47 (LIFE)
BOLAN, JOHN F., dir. pers., Euclid General Hospital, Euclid, OH '81 (PERS)
BOLAND, ANNE L., asst. dir. soc. serv., St. Vincent's Hospital and Medical Center of New York, New York, NY '74 (SOC)
BOLAND, DONNA CAPOBIANCO, pat. rep., New York Hospital, New York, NY '84 (PAT)
BOLAND, GERALD L., Washington Hospital Center, Washington, DC '70
BOLAND, ISABELLE P., RN, assoc. dir. nrsg., Cleveland Clinic Hospital, Cleveland, OH '86 (NURS)
BOLAND, PAMELA K., RN, vice-pres. pat. serv., Allentown Osteopathic Medical Center, Allentown, PA '86 (NURS)
BOLANDIS, JERRY L., asst. vice-pres., St. Elizabeth Medical Center, Granite City, IL '81 (MGMT)
BOLDA, DOLORES, RN, assoc. dir. pers. and staff, St. Mary of Nazareth Hospital Center, Chicago, IL '80 (NURS)
BOLDE, TRACY ANN, student, Baruch College, New York, NY '87
BOLDER, JANE A., RN, vice-pres. nrsg. serv., Holy Cross Hospital, Silver Spring, MD '82 (NURS)
BOLDT, ALAN R., gen. mgr., Marriott Corporation, Columbia, MO '83 (FOOD)
BOLEN, DAVID A., contr., Katherine Shaw Bethea Hospital, Dixon, IL '82
BOLES, BARBARA KAYE, PhD, dir. educ., American Academy of Orthopaedic Surgeons, Park Ridge, IL '71 (EDUC)
BOLES, FAYE O., coor. in-service, Mercy Health Center, Oklahoma City, OK '80 (EDUC)
BOLEY, RUSSELL WILSON, pres., Pal-Medical Health Services, Miami Lakes, FL '71
BOLGER, T. MICHAEL, atty., Sacred Heart Hospital, Eau Claire, WI '77 (ATTY)
BOLGIANO, SUSAN H., dir. pers., Harford Memorial Hospital, Havre de Grace, MD '86 (PERS)
BOLICK, CAROLYN M., dir. vol. serv., Bethesda Lutheran Medical Center, St. Paul, MN '84 (VOL)
BOLIG, KENNETH L., dir. bldg. serv., Evangelical Community Hospital, Lewisburg, PA '82 (ENG)
BOLIN, DENNIS L., dir. mktg., Adventist Health System-North, Hinsdale, IL '81 (PR) (PLNG)
BOLIN, JANE, adm. asst. risk mgt., Mercy Hospital of Sacramento, Sacramento, CA '84 (RISK)
BOLING, MICHAEL J., partner, Arthur Young and Company, Atlanta, GA '82
BOLINGER, WARD D. III, dir. pur., Bay Harbor Hospital, Harbor City, CA '82 (PUR)
BOLL, RAYMOND JR., asst. exec. dir., Sharon Hospital, Sharon, CT '68
BOLLER, JANET E., pres., Health Education International, Inc., San Diego, CA '86 (EDUC)
BOLLIN, EDWARD H., head stationary eng., Roswell Park Memorial Institute, Buffalo, NY '86 (ENG)
BOLLING, FRANCES H., (ret.), Irving, TX '67 (FOOD)
BOLLING, GLADYS V., chief soc. work, Veterans Administration Medical Center, North Chicago, IL '66 (SOC)
BOLLINGER, MICHAEL S., fin. consult. and reimbursement spec., Wexford, PA '84
BOLMEY, ARMANDO LINO, dir. syst. support, Kaiser-Permanente Medical Care Program, Pasadena, CA '74 (MGMT)
BOLOGNA, JAMES S., sr. oper. analyst, Oakwood Hospital, Dearborn, MI '85 (MGMT)
BOLON, DOUGLAS S., Brandon, FL '83
BOLOTIN, NORMAN, dir. fin. plng., Bellevue Hospital Center, New York, NY '53 (LIFE)
BOLSER, WILLIAM A., asst. adm., Truckee Meadows Hospital, Reno, NV '85
BOLSHAZY, CDR ROBERT STEPHEN, MSC USN, asst. to med. facil., Navsaceng Committee, Alexandria, VA '68
BOLSTER, CHARLES J. JR., dir. dev., Medicus System Corporation, Evanston, IL '80 (MGMT)
BOLT, JACKIE M., dir. pers., Shriners Hospital for Crippled Children, Greenville, SC '86 (PERS)
BOLTE, COL. GORDON L., PhD MSC USA, soc. work staff off., Brooke Army Medical Center, San Antonio, TX '84 (SOC)
BOLTE, JUDGE FRANK R., atty., St. Francis Medical Center, Pittsburgh, PA '68 (ATTY)
BOLTON, JOHN S., dist. mgr. food mgt., ARA Services, Hospital Food Management, Environmental Service, Inc., Rosemont, IL '77 (FOOD)
BOLTON, LINDA BURNES, RN, dir. nrsg. res., Cedars-Sinai Medical Center, Los Angeles, CA '84 (NURS)
BOLTON, MARTHA, dir. soc. serv., Hillcrest Health Center, Oklahoma City, OK '80 (SOC)
BOLTON, MICHAEL E., dir. biomedical eng., Desert Springs Hospital, Las Vegas, NV '84 (ENG)
BOLTON, REBECCA L., dir. vol. serv., Memorial Hospital, Danville, VA '86 (VOL)
BOLTON, SHARON K., mgr. emp., Hardin Memorial Hospital, Elizabethtown, KY '82 (PERS)
BOLTON, WIMBERLY F., asst. adm. and dir. nrsg., Gulf Breeze Hospital, Gulf Breeze, FL '84 (NURS)
BOLTZ, JOHN M., dir. food serv., Church Hospital Corporation, Baltimore, MD '77 (FOOD)
BOLZ, EDWIN B., pres., Amsterdam Memorial Hospital, Amsterdam, NY '81 (PLNG)
BOLZE, RAY S., atty., Rex Hospital, Raleigh, NC '84 (ATTY)
BOMBARD, COL. CHARLES F., RN MSC USA, chief nrsg., U. S. Army Hospital Nuernberg, APO New York, NY '85 (NURS)
BOMBERGER, AUDREY S., dir. educ., St. Mary's Hospital, Reno, NV '76 (EDUC)
BOMER, BLOSSIE M., RN, student, Spertus College, Chicago, IL '86
BOMGARDNER, STEPHEN R., RN, dir. nrsg. adm., St. Catherine Hospital, Garden City, KS '80 (NURS)
BOMKAMP, JAMES E., dir. educ. serv., St. Francis Hospital Center, Beech Grove, IN '80 (EDUC)
BON, DENNIS L. DI, asst. dir. maint. and eng., North Hills Passavant Hospital, Pittsburgh, PA '85 (ENG)
BONADONNA, S. STEPHEN, vice-pres. adm., Winthrop-University Hospital, Mineola, NY '55 (LIFE)
BONANDER, EVELYN E., dir. soc. serv., Massachusetts General Hospital, Boston, MA '72 (SOC)
BONANO, GEORGE J., dir. sterile sup., State University Hospital, Downstate Medical Center, Brooklyn, NY '85 (CS)
BONAPARTE, BARBARA P., asst. dir. pat. rel., Hospital of the University of Pennsylvania, Philadelphia, PA '81 (PAT)
BONARDI, FRANCES S., RN, vice-pres. pat. serv., Martha Jefferson Hospital, Charlottesville, VA '80 (NURS)
BONAVITA, MARY A., dir. educ., St. Patrick Hospital, Lake Charles, LA '84 (EDUC)
BONAZZA, CHERYL E., asst. mgr. food serv., Marion Community Hospital, Ocala, FL '84 (FOOD)
BOND, CAROL A., diet. consult., Maury County Hospital, Columbia, TN '78 (FOOD)
BOND, DONALD J., eng., Crawford County Memorial Hospital, Denison, IA '85 (ENG)
BOND, GAY LYNN, dir. soc. serv., Charity Hospital at New Orleans, New Orleans, LA '81 (SOC)
BOND, JAMES H., dir. pers. adm., Memorial Hospital of Sweetwater County, Rock Springs, WY '82 (PERS)
BOND, JOAN, RN, asst. dir. nrsg. serv., Sewickley Valley Hospital, Sewickley, PA '77 (NURS)
BOND, SYLVIA, RN, asst. adm., Medical Center of Central Georgia, Macon, GA '79 (NURS)
BOND, WANDA W., dir. pub. affairs, St. Mary's Hospital, Richmond, VA '86 (PLNG)
BONDELLI, JACK JR., adm. asst. environ. serv., St. Mary of Nazareth Hospital Center, Chicago, IL '77 (ENG)
BONDIE, PATRICA A., RN, chief nrsg. serv., Veterans Administration Medical Center, Phoenix, AZ '83 (NURS)
BONDS, PATRICIA ANN, RN, asst. adm. nrsg., Walls Regional Hospital, Cleburne, TX '78 (NURS)
BONDURANT, FRAN W., dir. vol., Henrietta Egleston Hospital for Children, Atlanta, GA '78 (VOL)
BONDURANT, JOHN T., atty., Methodist Evangelical Hospital, Louisville, KY '80 (ATTY)
BONENFANT, ARTHUR SR., mgr. plant oper., Kennebec Valley Medical Center, Augusta, ME '71 (ENG)

BONENFANT, PETER A., dir. pers., Frederick Ferris Thompson Hospital, Canandaigua, NY '82 (PERS)
BONFANTI, RUTH L., RN, supv. cent. serv., Hunt Memorial Hospital, Danvers, MA '83 (CS)
BONGIOVANNI, ANTHONY R., assoc. vice-pres. gen. and adm. serv., St. Louis University, St. Louis, MO '77 (PERS)
BONGIOVANNI, DAVID A., mgr. compensation and benefits, Miami Children's Hospital, Miami, FL '86 (PERS)
BONGIOVANNI, ELISA A., atty., Mercy Catholic Medical Center, Darby, PA '83 (ATTY)
BONHAM, DOROTHY B., supv. cent. sup. room, Florida Keys Memorial Hospital, Key West, FL '82 (CS)
BONIFAS, JOHN H., head med. soc. serv., Alpena General Hospital, Alpena, MI '82 (SOC)
BONING, MARY R., dir. staff dev., Presbyterian Hospital, Albuquerque, NM '72 (EDUC)
BONK, SANDRA M., RN, supv. sup., proc. and distrib., Rockville General Hospital, Rockville, CT '87 (CS)
BONNEM, SHIRLEY, vice-pres. pub. rel. and dev., Children's Hospital of Philadelphia, Philadelphia, PA '68 (PR)
BONNER, MICHAEL E., adm. asst., Wesley Long Community Hospital, Greensboro, NC '83 (PERS)
BONNER, PAUL ANTHONY, vice-pres. prov. affairs, Blue Cross and Blue Shield of Maryland, Inc., Towson, MD '67
BONNER, THOMAS JR., exec. vice-pres., Hendrick Medical Center, Abilene, TX '75
BONNET, CHRISTOPHER P., Sarasota, FL '86
BONNET, EDNA, pres., Evazbo Risk Management Consulting, Old San Juan, P.R. '86 (RISK)
BONNET, JANIS I., dir. pers., Psychiatric Institute of Washington, Washington, DC '84 (PERS)
BONNET, PHILIP DIRLAM, MD, prof. emeritus, Johns Hopkins University School of Public Health and Hygiene, Baltimore, MD '42 (LIFE)
BONNEY, ROBERT S., sr. vice-pres., Research Medical Center, Kansas City, MO '83
BONNING, JANE E., RN, assoc. dir. nrsg., New England Sinai Hospital, Stoughton, MA '84 (NURS)
BONNOUGH, MICHAEL J., Independence Health Plan of Southeastern Michigan, Southfield, MI '76
BONO, JAMES D., dir. plng., St. Joseph Health Care Corporation, Albuquerque, NM '83 (PLNG)
BONSALL, ANN MARIE B., mgt. eng., Baystate Health Systems, Inc., Springfield, MA '87 (MGMT)
BONUCCELLI, JULIUS BERNARD, dir. mktg. and commun., Bethany Medical Center, Kansas City, KS '84 (PR) (PLNG)
BONUTTI, ELIZABETH M., syst. analyst, Jackson County Memorial Hospital, Altus, OK '86 (MGMT)
BONWELL, RICHARD L., exec. dir. and dir. mktg., The HMO of Oklahoma, Tulsa, OK '70 (PERS)(PLNG)
BOOHER, DIANE RUSSO, dir. soc. serv., Framingham Union Hospital, Framingham, MA '86 (SOC)
BOOHER, PAMELA SUE, site mgr., Managed Healthcare Services, Baltimore, MD '87
BOOK, LOIS J., RN, dir. pat. educ., Mercy Center for Health Care Services, Aurora, IL '79 (EDUC)
BOOKBINDER, NANCY, dir. plng. and economic analysis, Salick Health Care, Inc., Health Resources Group, Washington, DC '86 (AMB)
BOOKER, JEANIE F., sr. mgt. eng., Tampa General Hospital, Tampa, FL '86 (MGMT)
BOOKER, SAM F., pres. health care mktg. and plng., Booker and Associates, Kailua, HI '80 (PLNG)
BOOKER, SUZETTE B., dir. mktg., John D. Archbold Memorial Hospital, Thomasville, GA '85 (PR)
BOOKIN, BEVERLY R., sr. planner, Good Samaritan Hospital and Medical Center, Portland, OR '85 (PLNG)
BOON, ALICE M., actg. dir. human res., St. Louis Regional Medical Center, St. Louis, MO '86 (PERS)
BOON, CLIFFORD H. JR., (ret.), Aliquippa, PA '83
BOONE, CHARLOTTE R., dir. med. soc. serv., Akron City Hospital, Akron, OH '75 (SOC)
BOONE, DAVID JAN, vice-pres. fin., Catawba Memorial Hospital, Hickory, NC '77
BOONE, DONISE C., dir. pers., Sheltering Arms Hospital, Richmond, VA '86 (PERS)
BOONE, E. G., atty., Fawcett Memorial Hospital, Port Charlotte, FL '77 (ATTY)
BOONE, JOHN, adm., Hickman County Health Services, Centerville, TN '86
BOONE, JOHNNA MARIE, student, Program in Health Services Administration, College of Allied Health, University of Kentucky, Lexington, KY '86
BOONE, LARRY W., dir. pers., St. Joseph Regional Medical Center, Lewiston, ID '77 (PERS)
BOONE, LESTER S., pur. asst., New England Sinai Hospital, Stoughton, MA '81 (CS)
BOONE, RICHARD W., atty., Columbia Hospital for Women, Washington, DC '78 (ATTY)(RISK)
BOONE, RICHARD, corp. vice-pres. dev., St. John Medical Center, Tulsa, OK '85 (PR)
BOONE, ROBERT D., exec. asst., Hamilton Medical Center, Dalton, GA '83
BOONE, STEPHEN K., atty., Florida Hospital Medical Center, Orlando, FL '84 (ATTY)
BOORAS, PASCAL J., dir. food serv., St. Luke's Hospital, Davenport, IA '69 (FOOD)
BOOS, SR. VIRGINIA, dir. educ., St. Mary's Hospital, Saginaw, MI '74 (EDUC)
BOOSE, MARGARET S., RN, asst. adm., Charter Peachford Hospital, Atlanta, GA '83 (NURS)
BOOSE, RUTH A., RN, dir. nrsg. serv., Community Hospital of Lancaster, Lancaster, PA '86 (NURS)
BOOTE, A. JAMES, adm. and vice-pres., Berwick Hospital Center, Berwick, PA '79
BOOTH, JAMES A., dir. matl. mgt., Braddock General Hospital, Braddock, PA '74 (PUR)
BOOTH, JANE M., coor. events, Lutheran Medical Center, Omaha, NE '82 (VOL)
BOOTH, JOHN A., pres., Hospital Cost Consultants, Inc., Reewood City, CA '82 (MGMT)
BOOTH, JONATHAN, hosp. dir., Al Qassimi Hospital, Sharjah, United Arab Republic '86
BOOTH, KAY C., dir. soc. serv., AMI Brookwood Community Hospital, Orlando, FL '81 (SOC)
BOOTH, MARIAN R., dir. soc. serv., La Grange Memorial Hospital, La Grange, IL '75 (SOC)
BOOTH, MAUREEN, vice-pres. plng., Holy Family Hospital, Des Plaines, IL '81 (PLNG)
BOOTH, MILTON O., vice-pres., Gulf Health, Inc., Mobile, AL '80 (RISK)
BOOTH, PETER G., adm., Henrietta D. Goodall Hospital, Sanford, ME '68
BOOTH, RACHEL Z., RN, asst. vice-pres. health affairs and dean nrsg., Duke University Hospital, Durham, NC '84 (NURS)
BOOTS, SUSAN L., RN, asst. adm. health care serv., Black Hills Community Hospital, Olympia, WA '85 (NURS)
BOOTSRN, LINDA M., dir. nrsg., St. Anthony Hospital, Oklahoma City, OK '83 (NURS)
BOOZER, JOHN C., risk mgr., Providence Hospital, Columbia, SC '84 (RISK)
BOPP, KENNETH, lecturer health serv. mgt., University of Missouri-Columbia, Columbia, MO '79 (PLNG)
BORCHARD, RICHARD H., mgr. bio-eng. maint., University of Iowa, College of Medicine, Iowa City, IA '78 (ENG)
BORCHARDT, DIETER, dir. food serv., Kansas City College of Osteopathic Medicine, Center for Health Sciences, Kansas City, MO '80 (FOOD)
BORCHER, SHARON K., mgr. cafeteria, Cook County Hospital, Chicago, IL '83 (FOOD)
BORCHMAN, BONNIE L., RN, dir. nrsg., St. Mary of Nazareth Hospital Center, Chicago, IL '80 (NURS)
BORDEAU, ROBERT M., atty., Marquette General Hospital, Marquette, MI '77 (ATTY)
BORDEIANU, OVIDIU, biomedical eng., Newport Hospital, Newport, RI '86 (ENG)
BORDELON, SR. OLIVE, sr. vice-pres. mission serv., Sisters of Charity Health Care Systems, Houston, TX '86
BORDEN, MICHAEL D., dir. trng. and educ., Grant Medical Center, Columbus, OH '83 (EDUC)
BORDER, ROBERT L., dir. plant serv., St. Luke's Medical Center, Phoenix, AZ '67 (ENG)
BORDERS, NORMA J., dir. nutr. serv., Terre Haute Regional Hospital, Terre Haute, IN '86 (FOOD)
BORDUI, RONALD J., contr., American Osteopathic Association, Chicago, IL '78
BORDWINE, JAMES H., dir. environ. serv., Buchanan General Hospital, Grundy, VA '86 (ENVIRON)
BORELLI, MICHAEL J., vice-pres. plng., Mount Sinai Medical Center, Milwaukee, WI '80 (PLNG)
BORENSTEIN, JUDITH, atty., Swedish Covenant Hospital, Chicago, IL '85 (ATTY)
BORG, ELDEAN, dir. info. serv., University of Iowa Hospitals and Clinics, Iowa City, IA '77 (PR)
BORGESON, DOLORES, dir. matl., Citrus Memorial Hospital, Inverness, FL '74 (PUR)
BORICHEVSKY, JOAN F., dir. human res., Bellevue Maternity Hospital, Schenectady, NY '84 (PERS)
BORIN, HARLAN F., pres., Borin-Halbich, Inc., Ocean Hills, CA '83
BORING, NANCY M., coor. vol. and info., HCA Donelson Hospital, Nashville, TN '84 (VOL)
BORING, NATHAN L., dir. plng., Wilkes-Barre General Hospital, Wilkes-Barre, PA '82 (PLNG)
BORKOWSKI, ELEANOR H., RN, asst. dir. nrsg., San Bernardino County Medical Center, San Bernardino, CA '86 (NURS)
BORLAND, JAMES R., dir. food serv., Self Memorial Hospital, Greenwood, SC '72 (FOOD)
BORLAND, JUDY A., RN, asst. mgr. cent. serv., Smyrna Hospital, Smyrna, GA '79 (CS)
BORMAN, FREDERICK A., dir. eng. and maint., Suburban Hospital, Bethesda, MD '84 (ENG)
BORMAN, RHONDA S., supv. health educ., Miller Medical Group, Nashville, TN '86 (EDUC)
BORMOLINI, SUSAN J., RN, dir. educ., Porter Medical Center, Middlebury, VT '80 (NURS)(EDUC)
BORNE, SIAN R., RN, dir. nrsg. serv., Medical Plaza Hospital, Fort Worth, TX '86 (NURS)
BORNS, CLARENCE, atty., St. Mary Medical Center, Gary, IN '77 (ATTY)(RISK)
BORNSTEIN, LESTER M., exec. dir., Newark Beth Israel Medical Center, Newark, NJ '53 (LIFE)
BORNSTEIN, PHILIP R., dir. support serv., Freehold Area Hospital, Freehold, NJ '83 (FOOD)(PUR)
BORNSTEIN, ROBERT J., adm., Central General Hospital, Plainview, NY '67
BORNTRAEGER, WILHELM, arch., Bertrand Goldberg Associates, Inc., Chicago, IL '80 (PLNG)
BOROCH, MICHAEL, pres., Health Network Associates, Pearland, TX '84
BORROR, THOMAS D., chief eng., Iowa Lutheran Hospital, Des Moines, IA '82 (ENG)
BORSHUK, RICHARD D., chief fin. off., Greater Baltimore Medical Center, Baltimore, MD '86
BORSODY, ROBERT P., atty., Gracie Square Hospital, New York, NY '75 (ATTY)
BORST, DIANE G., sr. vice-pres., The Manning Organization, Inc., New York, NY '79 (PLNG)
BORST, PATRICIA FRY, RN, vice-pres. pat. care serv., Augustana Hospital and Health Care Center, Chicago, IL '84 (NURS)
BORSTAD, NANCY M., RN, dir. nrsg., Abbott-Northwestern Hospital, Minneapolis, MN '83 (NURS)
BORTHWICK, RUTH M., coor. pat. educ., Community Hospital, McCook, NE '87 (EDUC)
BORTHWICK, WILLIAM FORBES, dir. nutr. and food serv., Northwest Community Hospital, Arlington Heights, IL '83 (FOOD)
BORTNICK, JAMES F., vice-pres., Illinois Hospital Joint Ventures, Inc., Division of Illinois Hospital Association, Naperville, IL '76 (MGMT)
BORTON, KAREN A., dir. med. soc. work, Butterworth Hospital, Grand Rapids, MI '72 (SOC)
BORTVIT, DARRYL H., dir. food and nutr., Desert Hospital, Palm Springs, CA '82 (FOOD)
BOSANQUET, NOEL T., dir. human res., American Red Cross Blood Service, Northeast Regional, Dedham, MA '80 (PERS)
BOSCARINO, JOSEPH A., PhD, vice-pres., Modern Health Affiliates, Neptune, NJ '85 (PLNG)
BOSCH, MEINDERT, chief exec. off., Bethesda Hospital Association, Denver, CO '86
BOSCHERT, ELLEN M., dir. plng., Research Health Services, Kansas City, MO '84 (PLNG)
BOSCHETTO, SCOTT A., student, Emory University, Atlanta, GA '82
BOSETTI, LARRY G., dir. automation mgt., Walter Reed Army Medical Center, Washington, DC '81
BOSHARD, NICK, St. Mary's Health Center, Jefferson City, MO '79 (PLNG)
BOSHIER, MAUREEN L., RN, vice-pres. nrsg., New Mexico Hospital Association, Albuquerque, NM '85 (NURS)
BOSIC, DAVID C., dir. emp. rel., Conemaugh Valley Memorial Hospital, Johnstown, PA '71 (PERS)
BOSICA, THOMAS A. JR., dir. pers. serv., Penobscot Bay Medical Center, Rockport, ME '69 (PERS)
BOSK, NATHAN, assoc. adm., Warminster General Hospital, Warminster, PA '82 (PLNG)
BOSKIND, CONNIE M., RN, dir. med. nrsg., Loma Linda University Medical Center, Loma Linda, CA '85 (NURS)
BOSOLD, ROBERT F., dir. eng. serv., Eden Hospital Medical Center, Castro Valley, CA '80 (ENG)
BOSS, CARL, dir. eng. and maint., St. Mary's Hospital and Medical Center, Grand Junction, CO '85 (ENG)
BOSS, FREDERICK R., pres., Clinton Hospital, Clinton, MA '85 (PLNG)
BOSSAK, ERIC S., pres., Paragon Health Management, Inc., Atlanta, GA '71 (MGMT)
BOSSARD, KAREN L., RN, adm. nrsg. serv., Central Community Hospital, Elkader, IA '82 (NURS)
BOSSARD, LORI B., supv. commun., Metropolitan Medical Center, Minneapolis, MN '82 (ENG)
BOSSART, MAJ. BRUCE NORMAN, MSC USAF, adm., U. S. Air Force Clinic, APO New York, NY '80
BOSSE, PATRICIA A., coor. vol. serv. and commun. educ., Kennedy Institute for Handicapped Children, Baltimore, MD '85 (VOL)
BOSSHARDT, MARY LOUISE, dir. educ., North Valley Hospital, Whitefish, MT '85 (EDUC)
BOST, LARRY, asst. chief eng., AMI Mission Bay Hospital, San Diego, CA '86 (ENG)
BOSTER, PAUL E., dir. matl. mgt., Lawrence County General Hospital, Ironton, OH '84 (PUR)
BOSTIAN, JAMES MICHAEL, student, Program in Health Policy and Administration, University of North Carolina, Chapel Hill, NC '85
BOSTIC, FLORINE, RN, asst. dir. nrsg.-oper. room, Hutzel Hospital, Detroit, MI '82 (NURS)
BOSTIC, PAMELA A., dir. med. rec., York Hospital, York, PA '78
BOSTIN, MARVIN J., PhD, prin., M. Bostin Associates, Inc., Elmsford, NY '56 (PLNG)(LIFE)
BOSTON, CAROL A., Chicago, IL '86 (NURS)
BOSTON, ELISE K., actg. dir. advertising and commun., Cedars Medical Center, Miami, FL '86 (PLNG)
BOSTON, LINDA, RN, dir. home health serv., Fox Chase Cancer Center, Philadelphia, PA '87 (AMB)
BOSTON, RONALD FRANKLIN, dir. diet., Westminster Manor, Austin, TX '79 (FOOD)
BOSTWICK, MARY C., mgt. dev. spec., Alexandria Hospital, Alexandria, VA '85 (EDUC)
BOSWELL, AUSTIN W. II, proj. coor., Charleston Area Medical Center, Charleston, WV '84 (MGMT)
BOSWELL, DIANE, dir. soc. work, St. Catherine Hospital, East Chicago, IN '86 (SOC)
BOSWELL, J. ROBERT, pur. agt., Sewickley Valley Hospital, Sewickley, PA '82 (PUR)
BOSWELL, JOHN E., dir. eng., Chippenham Hospital, Richmond, VA '76 (ENG)
BOTON, JOSEPH L., dir. pub. rel., St. Mary of Nazareth Hospital Center, Chicago, IL '74 (PR)
BOTSFORD, ANNE, dir. soc. serv., Northern Dutchess Hospital, Rhinebeck, NY '79 (SOC)
BOTT, THOMAS H., dir. adm., Harlem Valley Psychiatric Center, Wingdale, NY '57 (LIFE)
BOTTA, WILLIAM L., dir. plant serv., Illini Hospital, Silvis, IL '79 (ENG)(ENVIRON)
BOTTGER, JOY, dir. vol. serv., Immanuel Medical Center, Omaha, NE '79 (VOL)
BOTTICELLI, JOHN, vice-pres. human res., Ellis Hospital, Schenectady, NY '86 (PERS)
BOTTINI, FRANK A., dir. mktg., Bbc Health Care Facilities, St. Louis, MO '85 (PLNG)
BOTTOMLEY, WENDY, risk mgt. consult., Quality Systems Group, Nolensville, TN '86 (RISK)
BOTTORFF, CHESTER H., dir. food serv., Pontiac General Hospital, Pontiac, MI '73 (FOOD)
BOTTORFF, JUDY A., RN, dir. nrsg., Floyd Memorial Hospital, New Albany, IN '86 (NURS)
BOTTS, DENNIS C., dir. soc. work serv., Rapides General Hospital, Alexandria, LA '82 (SOC)
BOTTS, THOMAS M., vice-pres., Community Physicians, Inc., Virginia Beach, VA '68
BOTWICK, JUDY, mgr. consult., Arthur Andersen and Company, Detroit, MI '83 (MGMT)
BOUCHARD, CRAIG T., vice-pres., First National Bank of Chicago, Chicago, IL '86
BOUCHARD, LYDIE, coor. diet. serv., Notre Dame Hospital, Montreal, Que., Canada '76 (FOOD)
BOUCHARD, RONALD A., asst. vice-pres. pers. adm., University of Virginia, Charlottesville, VA '81 (PERS)
BOUCHARD, WAYNE D., dir. control sales, Automatic Switch Company, Florham Park, NJ '86 (ENG)
BOUCHER, KEN, dir. staff dev., St. Helen Hospital, Chehalis, WA '87 (EDUC)

BOUCHER, VICTOR R., corp. dir. matl. mgt., Ancilla Systems, Inc., Elk Grove Village, IL '86 (PUR)
BOUCK, SUE A., dir. staff dev., Sarah Bush Lincoln Health Center, Mattoon, IL '87 (EDUC)
BOUDREAU, DIANE E., asst. adm. pers. and adm. serv., U. S. Air Force Medical Center Keesler, Biloxi, MS '85
BOUDREAU, EUGENE, dir. qual. assur., Manchester Memorial Hospital, Manchester, CT '86 (RISK)
BOUDREAU, NANETTE S., asst. dir. mktg. and commun. rel., Bethesda Lutheran Medical Center, St. Paul, MN '86 (PR)
BOUDREAUX, CLAUDETTE S., RN, asst. vice-pres. nrsg. serv., Phoenix General Hospital, Phoenix, AZ '84 (NURS)
BOUDREAUX, DEWEY J., risk mgr., Lakewood Hospital, Morgan City, LA '80 (PUR)(RISK)
BOUGHEY, NANCY L., dir. soc. serv., Pacific Presbyterian Hospital, San Francisco, CA '77 (SOC)
BOUGHNER, KATHLEEN A., dir. soc. serv., Franklin Regional Medical Center, Franklin, PA '75 (SOC)
BOUGHTON, ROSE M., dir. food serv., Fairview Southdale Hospital, Minneapolis, MN '70 (FOOD)
BOUGHTON, SABRA, RN, asst. adm. nrsg., Eastern Long Island Hospital, Greenport, NY '84 (NURS)
BOUILLON, MARGARET ANN, mgr. qual. assur., Extendicare Health Services, Inc., Toronto, Ont., Canada '86 (RISK)
BOUKNIGHT, ED R., dir. pers. serv., Spartanburg Regional Medical Center, Spartanburg, SC '85 (PERS)
BOULANGER, JAMES DAVID, pat. advocate, Earl K. Long Memorial Hospital, Baton Rouge, LA '85 (PAT)
BOULDEN, HERBERT B. JR., vice-pres., Pennsylvania Hospital, Philadelphia, PA '76
BOULDIN, AGNES R., asst. chief pat. affairs serv., Naval Hospital, Portsmouth, VA '82 (PERS)
BOULDIN, ERNEST F., dir. human res., Arab Hospital, Arab, AL '86 (PERS)
BOULERICE, MONIQUE, RN, dir. nrsg., Canadian Hospital Association, Ottawa, Ont., Canada '81 (NURS)
BOULEY, ALAN J., mgr. clin. eng., Norfolk General Hospital, Norfolk, VA '83 (ENG)
BOULEY, DONNA, dir. pers., Harbour Shores Hospital Lawnwood, Fort Pierce, FL '86 (PERS)
BOULT, JOHN W., atty., University Community Hospital, Tampa, FL '82 (ATTY)
BOULTER, JANE A., educator, Poudre Valley Hospital, Fort Collins, CO '79 (EDUC)
BOULTER, PAUL E., assoc. dir. eng., Helene Fuld Medical Center, Trenton, NJ '83 (ENG)
BOULTINGHOUSE, LISA ANN, asst. dir. pat. rel., Northridge Hospital Medical Center, Northridge, CA '86 (PAT)
BOULTINGHOUSE, WILLIAM G., dir. qual. assur., Deaconess Hospital, Evansville, IN '80 (RISK)
BOUMBULIAN, PAUL, vice-pres. strategic plng., Dallas County Hospital District-Parkland Memorial Hospital, Dallas, TX '79 (PLNG)
BOURDET, CATHERINE J., dir. food serv., F. Edward Hebert Hospital, New Orleans, LA '86 (FOOD)
BOURDON, JAMES A., head matl. mgt., Bay Medical Center, Bay City, MI '82 (PUR)
BOURG, LYNETTE R., pat. rep., Jo Ellen Smith Medical Center, New Orleans, LA '86 (PAT)
BOURGEAULT, JOAN C., pur. agt., Marin General Hospital, San Rafael, CA '66 (PUR)
BOURGEOIS, ALLEN, dir. food serv., Lakeside Hospital, Metairie, LA '67 (FOOD)
BOURGEOIS, ANN, mgt. serv. analyst, East Jefferson General Hospital, Metairie, LA '86 (MGMT)
BOURGEOIS, ANNE M., RN, assoc. adm. nrsg. and dir. nrsg. educ., University of Massachusetts Medical Center, Worcester, MA '85 (NURS)
BOURKE, M. CHRISTOPHER, dir. staff dev., Stella Maris Hospice, Baltimore, MD '82 (EDUC)
BOURLAND, DON, mgr. emp., St. Joseph Hospital, Bellingham, WA '80 (RISK)(PERS)
BOURLIER, ANN, coor. qual. assur., HCA Huntington Hospital, Huntington, WV '86 (RISK)
BOURNE, BRENDA K., mgr. risk, North Kansas City Hospital, North Kansas City, MO '83 (RISK)
BOUSTEAD, JOHN W., vice-pres. sales and mktg., Hamilton Industries, Manitowoc, WI '81 (PLNG)
BOUTAN, LOIS J., vol. liaison and asst. mktg., Memorial Hospital, Burlington, WI '86 (VOL)
BOUTHILLET, JULES W., chief exec. off., Lakewood Hospital, Lakewood, OH '78 (MGMT)
BOUTON, GAIL C., mgt. eng., Children's Hospital, Boston, MA '82 (MGMT)
BOUTON, JANET, ScD, vice-pres. plng., Good Samaritan Hospital, Baltimore, MD '81 (PLNG)
BOVE, CHARLES R., student, Department of Health Care Administration, George Washington University, Department of Health Services Administration, Washington, DC '86
BOVEE, PHYLLIS E., RN, vice-pres., Bryan Memorial Hospital, Lincoln, NE '83 (NURS)
BOVEN, CAROL, RN, sr. vice-pres. pat. serv., Butterworth Hospital, Grand Rapids, MI '78 (NURS)
BOW, BEVERLY A., dir. human res., Douglas Community Hospital, Roseburg, OR '83 (PERS)
BOWAR-FERRES, SUSAN L., RN, assoc. dir. nrsg., Columbia-Presbyterian Medical Center, New York, NY '84 (NURS)
BOWCUTT, MARILYN A., RN, asst. adm. nrsg. serv., University Hospital, Augusta, GA '84 (NURS)
BOWDEN, CHERYL RAE, pat. rep., Lea Regional Hospital, Hobbs, NM '86 (PAT)
BOWDOIN, DONALD E., dir. soc. serv., St. John's Hospital, Lowell, MA '78 (SOC)
BOWDOIN, MATTHEW L., adm. res., Veterans Administration Medical Center, Augusta, GA '85 (MGMT)
BOWEN, ANN L., RN, dir. nrsg., Womens Hospital, Las Vegas, NV '81 (NURS)
BOWEN, BARBARA L., dir. food serv., Bethany Methodist Terrace, Morton Grove, IL '81 (FOOD)
BOWEN, BERT L., dir. food serv., Family Hospital, Milwaukee, WI '73 (FOOD)
BOWEN, CAROLE M., dir. vol. serv., St. Agnes Hospital, Baltimore, MD '86 (VOL)
BOWEN, CLARINDA J., dir. dev., Samaritan Health Plan, Phoenix, AZ '83
BOWEN, DAVID E., dir. eng., American Sterilizer Company, Erie, PA '79 (ENG)
BOWEN, DOROTHY A., RN, asst. adm. and dir. nrsg., St. Christopher's Hospital for Children, Philadelphia, PA '84 (NURS)
BOWEN, MARNELLE S., RN, asst. adm., Kaseman Presbyterian Hospital, Albuquerque, NM '81 (NURS)
BOWEN, SR. MARY HILARY, pat. rep., Schumpert Medical Center, Shreveport, LA '84 (PAT)
BOWEN, NANCY A., dir. diet., Washington Regional Medical Center, Fayetteville, AR '84 (FOOD)
BOWEN, NANCY, risk mgr. and coor. infection control, Humana Hospital -Orange Park, Orange Park, FL '86 (RISK)
BOWEN, REBECCA D., pat. rep., Valley View Regional Hospital, Ada, OK '85 (PAT)
BOWEN, ROY, mgr. soc. serv., John Peter Smith Hospital, Fort Worth, TX '85 (SOC)
BOWEN, RUPERT W., vice-pres. adm. serv., Forsyth Memorial Hospital, Winston-Salem, NC '86 (PERS)
BOWEN, SANDRA A., RN, risk mgt. serv. rep., St. Paul Fire and Marine Insurance Company, Holyoke, MA '82 (RISK)
BOWER, BOYD O., prin., Wilmot, Bower and Associates, Inc., Rockville, MD '70
BOWER, JULIA L., student, University of Florida, Gainesville, FL '87
BOWER, KATHLEEN ANNE, RN, assoc. chm. nrsg., New England Medical Center, Boston, MA '77 (NURS)
BOWER, ROBERT B., chief eng., Lewis-Gale Hospital, Salem, VA '76 (ENG)
BOWERMAN, CATHY ROGERS, atty., Siemion, Huckabay, Et Al, Detroit, MI '78 (ATTY)
BOWERMAN, CORINNE C., pat. rep., Mount Carmel Mercy Hospital, Detroit, MI '79 (PAT)
BOWERMASTER, JON P., dir. educ. serv., Carle Foundation Hospital, Urbana, IL '81 (EDUC)
BOWERS, BARRY, (ret.), Annapolis, MD '50 (LIFE)
BOWERS, BURTON CLYDE JR., dir. eng., Wadley Regional Medical Center, Texarkana, TX '81 (ENG)
BOWERS, CAROL L., mgr. trng., Kaiser Foundation Health Plan, Dallas, TX '86 (EDUC)
BOWERS, CATHY S., dir. pub. rel., Northeast Georgia Medical Center, Gainesville, GA '81 (PR)
BOWERS, CHRISTOPHER D., dir. plng., Bronson Methodist Hospital, Kalamazoo, MI '81 (PLNG)
BOWERS, CYNTHIA, asst. contr., Stuart Circle Hospital, Richmond, VA '83
BOWERS, DIANNA, dir. diet., Mercy Hospital, Iowa City, IA '77 (FOOD)
BOWERS, DONNA, dir., Riverside Htlhcare Association, Newport News, VA '87 (AMB)
BOWERS, FLOY L., adm. asst., Memorial Hospital, Abilene, KS '86 (PERS)
BOWERS, GAYLN L., dir. pat. bus., Memorial Hospital, Manchester, KY '85
BOWERS, JAMES LEWIS, exec. vice-pres., Scripps Memorial Hospital, La Jolla, CA '75 (PR)
BOWERS, JOHN A., vice-pres., St. Ann's Hospital of Columbus, Westerville, OH '79 (PERS)
BOWERS, JOYCE M., consult., Wyncote, PA '80 (PR)
BOWERS, LYNN R., mgr. soc. serv., Southern Ocean County Hospital, Manahawkin, NJ '86 (SOC)
BOWERS, MYRTLE J., RN, vice-pres. pat. care serv., St. Luke's Methodist Hospital, Cedar Rapids, IA '86 (NURS)
BOWERS, NORENE A., RN, dir. nrsg. spec. serv., Queen of the Valley Hospital, West Covina, CA '84 (NURS)
BOWERS, T. R., IV, adm. res., Georgetown University Medical Center, Washington, DC '84
BOWERS, TIMOTHY J., vice-pres. bus. dev., St. Mary's Hill Hospital, Milwaukee, WI '86 (PLNG)
BOWERSOX, BRUCE D., adm., Pelican Valley Health Center, Pelican Rapids, MN '75
BOWERSOX, ROBERT J., pres., Sunquest Corporation, Phoenix, AZ '85 (PLNG)
BOWES, DONALD J., vice-pres. health care prog., Employers Service Corporation, Charleston, WV '76
BOWIE, THOMAS L., risk mgr., Illinois Valley Community Hospital, Peru, IL '72 (FOOD)(RISK)
BOWING, KATHIE, vice-pres., Salick Health Care, Inc., Washington, DC '84 (PLNG)(AMB)
BOWKER, CHARLES S., asst. adm. gen. serv., Lutheran General Hospital, San Antonio, TX '77
BOWKER, JOSEPH E., dir. soc. serv., Providence Hospital, Washington, DC '81 (SOC)
BOWLER, WILFRED JR., dir. food serv., Lenoir Memorial Hospital, Kinston, NC '71 (FOOD)
BOWLES, BOB J., EdD, dir. educ., St. Francis Hospital and Medical Center, Topeka, KS '83 (EDUC)
BOWLES, CHRISTINA M., dir. pat. educ., Ball Memorial Hospital, Muncie, IN '79 (EDUC)
BOWLES, GROVER C. JR., prof. pharm. adm., University of Tennessee, Memphis, TN '56 (LIFE)
BOWLES, JOHN C. JR., assoc. dir., Cabarrus Memorial Hospital, Concord, NC '73
BOWLES, MARY BRIDGEMAN, asst. dir. matl. mgt. and dir. cent. serv., Alexian Brothers Hospital, St. Louis, MO '78 (CS)
BOWLES, PAULA B., dir. pub. rel., Norman Regional Hospital, Norman, OK '82 (PR)
BOWLES, PAULA S., dir. hskpg., Muhlenberg Community Hospital, Greenville, KY '86
BOWLEY, BEVERLEY L., dir. staff dev., Queensway General Hospital, Toronto, Ont., Canada '84 (EDUC)
BOWLEY, MELANIE SIMMONS, dir. mktg. and pub. rel., Guadalupe Medical Center, Carlsbad, NM '80 (PR)
BOWLIN, TOM H., PhD, mgr., Peat, Marwick, Mitchell and Company, Kansas City, MO '79 (MGMT)
BOWLING, BERTHAL E., dir. maint. and security, Kanawha Valley Memorial Hospital, Charleston, WV '85 (ENG)
BOWLING, JOEL F., dir. matl. mgt., Middletown Regional Hospital, Middletown, OH '82 (PUR)
BOWLING, JOHN S., adm., South Georgia Medical Center, Valdosta, GA '83 (PLNG)
BOWLING, WILLIAM D., dir. pers., Princeton Community Hospital, Princeton, WV '73 (PERS)
BOWLYOW, RONALD G., Silver Spring, MD '85 (NURS)
BOWMAN, BRIAN T., vice-pres. fiscal serv., Frederick Memorial Hospital, Frederick, MD '82 (PLNG)
BOWMAN, BRUCE, supv. maint., St. Mary Medical Center, Gary, IN '86 (ENG)
BOWMAN, DAVID G., atty., Sarasota Memorial Hospital, Sarasota, FL '86 (ATTY)
BOWMAN, DENNIS L., dir. commun. affairs, Woods Memorial Hospital, Etowah, TN '86 (PR)
BOWMAN, E. JOYCE, dir. vol. serv., DeKalb General Hospital, Decatur, GA '84 (VOL)
BOWMAN, ED H. JR., vice-pres., HBO and Company, Atlanta, GA '83
BOWMAN, EUGENIA D., RN, dir. nrsg. serv., Oswego Hospital, Oswego, NY '76 (NURS)
BOWMAN, GEORGE K., dir. eng., Schwab Rehabilitation Center, Chicago, IL '84 (ENG)
BOWMAN, JACK L., dir. food serv., AMI Saint Joseph Hospital, Omaha, NE '68 (FOOD)
BOWMAN, JODY PELOZA, dir. alternative delivery syst., St. Vincent Hospital and Health Center, Indianapolis, IN '79 (PLNG)
BOWMAN, JUNE C., coor. educ., Morristown Memorial Hospital, Morristown, NJ '79 (EDUC)
BOWMAN, MARGIE H., coor. vol., Moses H. Cone Memorial Hospital, Greensboro, NC '81 (VOL)
BOWMAN, MARION THOMAS, dir. pur., Cobb General Hospital, Austell, GA '74 (PUR)
BOWMAN, MONIKA S., dir. soc. serv., Cookeville General Hospital, Cookeville, TN '85 (SOC)
BOWMAN, SALLY B., dir. commun. rel. and mktg., Alliance Community Hospital, Alliance, OH '86 (PR)
BOWMAN, SUSAN M., dir. pers. serv., HCA Oak Hill Hospital, Spring Hill, FL '83 (PERS)
BOWNE, REBECCA L., dir. oper. support, Good Samaritan Hospital and Medical Center, Portland, OR '84 (PLNG)
BOWROSEN, LOIS A., dir. commun., Winthrop-University Hospital, Mineola, NY '81 (ENG)
BOWSE, JAMES T., pres., Franklin Memorial Hospital, Farmington, ME '80 (PLNG)
BOWSER, WILLIARD M. JR., mgr. pers., St. Mary's Infant Home, Norfolk, VA '86 (PERS)
BOWYER, ELIZABETH A., RN, loss prevention and underwriting rep., Risk Management Foundation of Harvard Medical Institute, Inc., Cambridge, MA '86 (RISK)
BOWYER, MARGARET C., dir. vol. serv., Dover General Hospital and Medical Center, Dover, NJ '84 (VOL)
BOYAR, ROBERT L., vice-pres. plng. facil., St. Luke's-Roosevelt Hospital Center, New York, NY '83 (PLNG)
BOYARSKI, ROBERT P., RN, vice-pres. nrsg., Craven County Hospital, New Bern, NC '73 (NURS)
BOYARSKY, BEVERLY L., pub. rel. asst., Union Hospital, Union, NJ '86 (PR)
BOYCE-REID, KARLENE, head med. soc. work, University Hospital of the West Indies, Mona Kingston, Jamaica '86 (SOC)
BOYCE, JAMES I., facil. consult., Ohio Department of Health, Columbus, OH '53 (LIFE)
BOYCE, LORRAINE P., student, Rush University, Chicago, IL '86
BOYCE, SHARON L., reg. care coor., Personal and Professional Development, Inc., Phoenix, AZ '77 (PERS)
BOYD, ANITA SMITH, asst. vice-pres. nrsg., Methodist Hospital South-J. R. Flippin Hospital, Memphis, TN '71 (NURS)
BOYD, CAROL W., Royal Palm Beach, FL '83 (EDUC)
BOYD, DAISY J., coor. vol. serv., Lake Taylor City Hospital, Norfolk, VA '85 (VOL)
BOYD, DAVID D., adm., Lutheran Home of Southbury, Southbury, CT '54 (LIFE)
BOYD, DWIGHT A., prin., Boyd-Sobieray Associates, Inc., Indianapolis, IN '84 (ENG)(AMB)
BOYD, FLORENCE J., actg. chief diet., Norfolk Community Hospital, Norfolk, VA '70 (FOOD)
BOYD, FRED J., dir. matl. mgt., Palms West Hospital, Loxahatchee, FL '82 (PUR)
BOYD, GLORIA M., dir. vol., Bethany General Hospital, Bethany, OK '77 (VOL)
BOYD, HELEN, coor. qual. assur., Anne Arundel General Hospital, Annapolis, MD '82 (RISK)
BOYD, JOY M., supv. cent. sup., St. John's Hospital and Health Center, San Angelo, TX '82 (CS)
BOYD, JOYCE D., mgt. eng., Community Hospitals of Indiana, Indianapolis, IN '81 (MGMT)
BOYD, JUDY S., dir. commun. rel., Houston International Hospital, Houston, TX '86 (PR)
BOYD, LORETTA M., RN, dir. nrsg., Margaretville Memorial Hospital, Margaretville, NY '80 (NURS)
BOYD, MARILYN, acct. spec. risk mgt. serv., The St. Paul Companies, Fremont, CA '86 (RISK)
BOYD, MARY E., dir. nrsg., Jones Memorial Hospital, Wellsville, NY '81 (NURS)
BOYD, NORMA JEAN, RN, dir. nrsg. educ. and res., Richland Memorial Hospital, Columbia, SC '86 (NURS)
BOYD, PATTY, dir. vol. serv., Baptist Medical Center of Oklahoma, Oklahoma City, OK '79 (VOL)
BOYD, ROBERT G., (ret.), Madison, NJ '37 (LIFE)
BOYD, SUZAN D., vice-pres. amb. serv., St. Joseph Hospital, Chicago, IL '83 (AMB)
BOYD, THOMAS J., exec. vice-pres., Sisters of Charity Hospital, Buffalo, NY '57 (LIFE)
BOYDEN, JACQUELYN K., atty., Fairfax Hospital Association, Springfield, VA '84 (ATTY)
BOYER-ORQUIZA, KAAREN W., pat. rep., Reading Hospital and Medical Center, Reading, PA '86 (PAT)

BOYER, CATHERINE M., RN, vice-pres., Maine Coast Memorial Hospital, Ellsworth, ME '74 (NURS)
BOYER, CHRISTINE MESSINA, dir. pub. rel., Allentown Hospital, Allentown, PA '76 (PR)
BOYER, EDWARD R., dir. eng. and maint., Charlton Memorial Hospital, Fall River, MA '81 (ENG)
BOYER, EDWARD, sr. consult., Towers, Perrin, Forster and Crosby, Washington, DC '70 (PLNG)
BOYER, JOHN K., atty., Childrens Memorial Hospital, Omaha, NE '80 (ATTY)
BOYER, JOYCE K., RN, asst. dir. nrsg. serv., Western Pennsylvania Hospital, Pittsburgh, PA '85 (NURS)
BOYER, KATHERINE M., dir. soc. work, Rhd Memorial Medical Center, Dallas, TX '81 (SOC)
BOYER, KENNETH J., plant eng., Women and Infants Hospital of Rhode Island, Providence, RI '84 (ENG)
BOYER, LEE, dir. plant facil., Good Samaritan Hospital, Mount Vernon, IL '80 (ENG)
BOYER, LINDA E., supv. cent. serv., Muhlenberg Hospital Center, Bethlehem, PA '85 (CS)
BOYER, MIMI, dir. soc. work serv., South Highlands Hospital, Birmingham, AL '86 (SOC)
BOYER, NANCY N., RN, dir. nrsg., Park Ridge Hospital, Rochester, NY '79 (NURS)
BOYER, RUTH L., RN, asst. adm. pat. care serv., Modesto City Hospital, Modesto, CA '86 (NURS)
BOYER, WILLIAM H., reg. dir., Service Direction, Inc., Minneapolis, MN '77 (FOOD)
BOYERS, LON, dir. environ. serv., Memorial Hospital of Garland, Garland, TX '86 (ENVIRON)
BOYETT, JENNIFER L., compensation spec., Mount Airy Psychiatric Center, Denver, CO '86 (PERS)
BOYETTE, WANDA L., RN, asst. adm., Sampson County Memorial Hospital, Clinton, NC '76 (NURS)
BOYINGTON, RONALD E., vice-pres. human res., Sacred Heart Hospital, Cumberland, MD '70 (PERS)
BOYKIN, DENNIS, pur. agt., Lenoir Memorial Hospital, Kinston, NC '80 (PUR)
BOYLAN, DANIEL R., dir. eng., Illinois Masonic Medical Center, Chicago, IL '83 (ENG)
BOYLAN, GAIL B., RN, vice-pres. nrsg., Baptist Hospital, Pensacola, FL '84 (NURS)
BOYLE, ANN, RN, asst. adm. nrsg. serv., Condell Memorial Hospital, Libertyville, IL '79 (NURS)
BOYLE, ANNA M., RN, assoc. adm. and dir. nrsg. serv., University Hospital of Brooklyn-Suny Center, Brooklyn, NY '79 (NURS)
BOYLE, SR. BENJAMIN, dir. soc. serv., St. Mary's Hospital, Reno, NV '72 (SOC)
BOYLE, CAROLYN HINCKLEY, dir. commun. rel., Brackenridge Hospital, Austin, TX '86 (PR)
BOYLE, CAROLYN, RN, asst. to vice-pres. nrsg. and mgr. corp. nrsg. oper., Group Health Cooperative, Seattle, WA '85 (NURS)
BOYLE, J. BARTON, Indianapolis, IN '56 (LIFE)
BOYLE, JAMES W., pres., Tennessee Christian Medical Center, Madison, TN '81 (PLNG)
BOYLE, JEANNE M., RN, dir. nrsg. serv., Middlesex County Hospital, Waltham, MA '86 (NURS)
BOYLE, JENNINGS W. JR., supv. hskpg., Research Belton Hospital, Belton, MO '86 (ENVIRON)
BOYLE, JOHN P., coor. pat. support serv., Charity Hospital at New Orleans, New Orleans, LA '82 (PAT)
BOYLE, JOHN, dir. food serv., Holy Redeemer Hospital and Medical Center, Meadowbrook, PA '69 (FOOD)
BOYLE, JULIE P., student, Program in Industrial Engineer, Youngstown State University, Youngstown, OH '86 (MGMT)
BOYLE, MICHAEL J., atty., Divine Providence Hospital, Pittsburgh, PA '74 (ATTY)
BOYLE, TERESA E., dir. vol., Children's Hospital of Philadelphia, Philadelphia, PA '85 (VOL)
BOYLE, THOMAS E., atty., Buchanan, Ingersoll, Pittsburgh, PA '82 (ATTY)
BOYLES, JEAN WINBORNE, atty., North Carolina Memorial Hospital, Chapel Hill, NC '78 (ATTY)
BOYLES, LARRY L., dir. pers., Riverside Hospital, Newport News, VA '80 (PERS)
BOYLES, ROBERT W., Bartlett, TN '77
BOYLES, V. I. JR., asst. chief exec. off., Iredell Memorial Hospital, Statesville, NC '82 (PUR)
BOYNE, FRANCES A., RN, pur. agt., St. Anne General Hospital, Raceland, LA '70 (CS)
BOYNTON, PAUL M., exec. dir., Eastern Virginia Health Systems Agency, Norfolk, VA '86 (PLNG)
BOYNTON, RITA M., dir. adult placement and soc. serv., Westmoreland County Area Agency on Aging, Greensburg, PA '85 (SOC)
BOYTER, JERRY W., adm., Tulare District Hospital, Tulare, CA '76
BOYTER, MARY L., dir. health res., Public Health Service, Region Six, Dallas, TX '76
BOZARDT, VERNA N., dir. vol. serv., Orangeburg-Calhoun Regional Hospital, Orangeburg, SC '85 (VOL)
BOZE, SUSAN S., coor. cont. educ., Eastern Virginia Inter-Hospital, Norfolk, VA '86 (EDUC)
BOZEMAN, MARY, chief soc. serv. and med. surg. rehab., Vaco Social Work Service, Washington, DC '79 (SOC)
BOZEWICZ, THOMAS R., PhD, vice-pres. plng. and qual. assur., De Paul Rehabilitation Hospital, Milwaukee, WI '83 (PLNG)
BOZZA, RENNE R., mgr. vol. serv., AMI North Fulton Medical Center, Roswell, GA '85 (VOL)
BOZZO, AUDREY J., RN, vice-pres. nrsg., Cooley Dickinson Hospital, Northampton, MA '79 (NURS)
BRAATEN, GARLAND, maint. eng., Stanley Community Hospital, Stanley, ND '81 (ENG)
BRABSON, MAX L., chm. and chief exec. off., Columbus Regional Health Care System, Inc., Columbus, GA '70 (PLNG)
BRACEWELL, CAMILLA H., dir. vol. serv., Athens Regional Medical Center, Athens, GA '85 (VOL)
BRACEY, DAVID B., asst. dir. pub. affairs, University of Cincinnati Medical Center, Cincinnati, OH '82 (PR)
BRACEY, LUCIUS H. JR., atty., Johnston-Willis Hospital, Richmond, VA '83 (ATTY)
BRACHMAN, DANIEL F., vice-pres. mktg. and plng., Holy Family Medical Center, Manitowoc, WI '83 (PLNG)
BRACHULIS, JAMES S., mgt. eng., University of California at Los Angeles Medical Center, Los Angeles, CA '83 (MGMT)
BRACK, KELLY R., dir. pub. rel. and vol. serv., Comanche County Memorial Hospital, Lawton, OK '82 (PR)(VOL)
BRACKE, MARK RICHARD, dir. eng., Harris Methodist -HEB, Bedford, TX '75 (ENG)
BRACKEN, WILLIAM, supv. sup., proc. and distrib., St. Joseph's Hospital and Health Center, Tucson, AZ '83 (CS)
BRACKETT, MABEL B., supt. nrs., St. Andrews Hospital, Boothbay Harbor, ME '42 (LIFE)
BRACKETT, MERIANNE E., dir. diet., AMI Frye Regional Medical Center, Hickory, NC '80 (FOOD)
BRACKETT, PATRICK D., linear acceleator eng., St. Vincent's Medical Center, Jacksonville, FL '80 (ENG)
BRACKNEY, CHARLES R., adm., Valley Lutheran Hospital, Mesa, AZ '78
BRACY, DAVID N., mgr. emerging health care org., Hoechst-Roussel Pharmaceuticals, Somerville, NJ '86 (AMB)
BRADBURN, JAMES L., asst. dir. matl. mgt., Shawnee Mission Medical Center, Shawnee Mission, KS '78 (CS)
BRADBURY, CATHERINE, RN, asst. vice-pres. nrsg., Oakwood Hospital, Dearborn, MI '83 (NURS)
BRADBURY, DON C., dir. bldg. and grds., Pekin Memorial Hospital, Pekin, IL '75 (ENG)
BRADBURY, ELLEN F., dir. pub. rel., Wayne County Memorial Hospital, Honesdale, PA '86 (PR)
BRADBURY, JUDY, coor. qual. assur., Charter Hills Hospital, Greensboro, NC '86 (RISK)
BRADEE, ALICE, RN, dir. nrsg., Wausau Hospital Center, Wausau, WI '80 (NURS)
BRADEL, WILLIAM T., vice-pres. plng. and mktg., St. Joseph Medical Center, Wichita, KS '83 (PLNG)
BRADELL, SGT. ERIC A., MSC USAF, mgt. eng., U. S. Air Force Medical Management Engineering Team, Maxwell AFB, AL '84 (MGMT)
BRADFORD, DERONDA D., dir. soc. work, Roper Hospital, Charleston, SC '85 (SOC)
BRADFORD, E. EDWIN JR., pres., Bradford Communications, Inc., Hickory, NC '82 (PR)
BRADFORD, COL. JACKIE E., MSC USA, dep. cmdr. adm., Reynolds Army Community Hospital, Fort Sill, OK '72 (RISK)
BRADFORD, JAMES R., dir. nrsg., West Volusia Memorial Hospital, De Land, FL '85 (NURS)
BRADFORD, LINDA C., dir. soc. work, Thunderbird Samaritan Hospital, Glendale, AZ '86 (SOC)
BRADFORD, PATRICIA SHANNON, dir. vol. serv., Cardinal Cushing General Hospital, Brockton, MA '78 (VOL)
BRADLEY-BROWN, BARBARA A., dir. staff dev., Tyler Memorial Hospital, Tunkhannock, PA '84 (EDUC)
BRADLEY, CAROL ANN, instr. nrsg. educ., Nashville Memorial Hospital, Madison, TN '84 (EDUC)
BRADLEY, DEB R., asst. dir. pers., St. Anthony Medical Center, Columbus, OH '86 (PERS)
BRADLEY, DONALD A., pres., Morristown Memorial Hospital, Morristown, NJ '55 (LIFE)
BRADLEY, DONALD J., student, Army-Baylor University Program in Health Care Administration, Fort Sam Houston, TX '81
BRADLEY, GREGORY R., asst. dir., Mary Immaculate Hospital, Jamaica, NY '74
BRADLEY, J. FRANKLIN, pres., Stiles-Bradley, Chattanooga, TN '77 (PR)
BRADLEY, JAMES G., dir. maint., El Dorado Hospital and Medical Center, Tucson, AZ '84 (ENG)
BRADLEY, JOHN A., PhD, chm. and chief exec. off., American Healthcare Management, Inc., Dallas, TX '70
BRADLEY, JOHN A., pres. and chief exec. off., Metlife Healthcare Network of Florida, Maitland, FL '73 (MGMT)
BRADLEY, JOHNNIE S., RN, vice-pres. nrsg. serv., Hamilton Medical Center, Dalton, GA '71 (NURS)
BRADLEY, JOSEPH W., dir. pub. rel., Baystate Medical Center, Springfield, MA '86 (PR)
BRADLEY, KATHERINE J., RN, assoc. dir. nrsg., The Mason Clinic, Seattle, WA '85 (NURS)
BRADLEY, LEONARD O., MD, (ret.), Calgary, Alta., Canada '47 (LIFE)
BRADLEY, LINDA, dir. human res., John Muir Memorial Hospital, Walnut Creek, CA '78 (EDUC)(PERS)
BRADLEY, LORRAINE A., RN, asst. dir. nrsg., St. Francis Hospital, Wilmington, DE '76 (NURS)
BRADLEY, MARGARET B., RN, asst. vice-pres. nrsg., Faulkner Hospital, Boston, MA '80 (NURS)
BRADLEY, MICHAEL J., exec. dir. and vice-pres. health serv., Thomas Jefferson University Hospital, Philadelphia, PA '73 (PLNG)
BRADLEY, NELL M., dir. diet., Levi Arthritis Hospital, Hot Springs National Park, AR '74 (FOOD)
BRADLEY, PATRICK M., exec. hskpr., St. Mary's Hospital, Orange, NJ '83 (ENG)(ENVIRON)
BRADLEY, ROBERT B., atty., Mount Sinai Medical Center, Milwaukee, WI '77 (ATTY)
BRADLEY, RUTH L., mgr. prod. serv., Ingalls Memorial Hospital, Harvey, IL '80 (FOOD)
BRADLEY, SHARON E., RN, nrs. adm. surg., Pitt County Memorial Hospital, Greenville, NC '86 (NURS)
BRADLEY, TIM, dir. pub. rel., Valley Presbyterian Hospital, Van Nuys, CA '87 (PR)
BRADLEY, VIRGIL L. J., asst. dir. soc. serv., Fulton State Hospital, Fulton, MO '85 (SOC)
BRADLEY, WAYNE J., dir. bus. dev., Consolidated Media, Jacksonville, FL '81 (PR)
BRADMON, DELORES A., supv. cent. serv. sup. and distrib., Community Hospital of Bedford, Bedford, OH '85 (CS)
BRADRICK, JUDY LAKER, dir. vol. serv., Scripps Memorial Hospital-Chula Vista, Chula Vista, CA '83 (VOL)
BRADSHAW, ANDREW C., dir. eng., Humana Hospital -Desert Valley, Phoenix, AZ '85 (ENG)
BRADSHAW, CAROL E., RN, dir. nrsg., Children's Hospital at Stanford, Palo Alto, CA '82 (NURS)
BRADSHAW, D. JEFFREY, adm. ped., University of Massachusetts Medical School, Worcester, MA '78
BRADSHAW, JOHN P., atty., St. Francis Hospital of Franciscan Sisters, Cape Girardeau, MO '73 (ATTY)
BRADSHAW, MARY CLAIRE, dir. vol. serv., Tennessee Christian Medical Center, Madison, TN '82 (VOL)
BRADSHAW, OVIE, dir. hskpg., Miramar Lodge Nursing Home, Pass Christian, MS '86 (ENVIRON)
BRADY, ALICE C., RN, dir. surg. serv., Doctors Hospital of Jefferson, Metairie, LA '87 (AMB)
BRADY, BARBARA A., RN, asst. adm. nrsg. serv., Hunt Memorial Hospital, Danvers, MA '76 (NURS)
BRADY, GERALD A., mgr. maint., Piggott Community Hospital, Piggott, AR '81 (ENG)
BRADY, JAMES L., sr. vice-pres. oper., Geisinger System Services, Danville, PA '75 (ENG)
BRADY, JUDITH L., vice-pres. human res., Brookville Hospital, Brookville, PA '83 (PERS)
BRADY, MARY FRANCES, dir. food serv., St. Michael Hospital, Texarkana, AR '72 (FOOD)
BRADY, MARY, vice-pres., Bidnet, Rockville, MD '86 (PUR)
BRADY, NORMAN AIKMAN, health plng. consult., Hilton Head Island, SC '50 (PLNG)(LIFE)
BRADY, ROBERT J. JR., atty., Bowie, MD '86 (PUR)
BRADY, RONALD, dir. pur., Maryview Hospital, Portsmouth, VA '85 (PUR)
BRADY, STEVEN J., mgr. pur., Hazelden Foundation, Center City, MN '86 (PUR)
BRADY, THOMAS J., dir. plant oper., Nashoba Community Hospital, Ayer, MA '85 (ENG)
BRADY, THOMAS J., atty., Milton, Keane and Brady, Jersey City, NJ '80 (ATTY)
BRADY, VIRGINIA A., dir. soc. work, Roswell Park Memorial Institute, Buffalo, NY '71 (SOC)
BRADY, WILLIAM L., dir. pur., Greenville Regional Hospital, Greenville, PA '74 (PUR)
BRAEUTIGAM, DONALD H., chief eng., Barnes Hospital, St. Louis, MO '76 (ENG)
BRAFFORD, RONALD P., vice-pres. pub. rel. and mktg., Tallahassee Memorial Regional Medical Center, Tallahassee, FL '80 (PR) (PLNG)
BRAGAN, ELMER A., mgr. cent. serv. and linen room, Valley Presbyterian Hospital, Van Nuys, CA '77 (CS)
BRAGDON, HAROLD W., dir. clin. eng., St. Francis Hospital and Medical Center, Topeka, KS '78 (ENG)
BRAGG, JOSEPH D., dir. plant oper., St. Luke's Memorial Hospital Center, New Hartford, NY '79 (ENG)
BRAGMAN, SANFORD M., vice-pres. ins. and risk mgt., Daughters of Charity Health Systems, Baltimore, MD '80 (RISK)
BRAID, WILLIAM B., dir. bldg. oper. and serv., Mount Washington Pediatric Hospital, Baltimore, MD '85 (ENG)
BRAIDWOOD, GEORGE F., vice-pres., The Steiner Company, Ann Arbor, MI '67 (MGMT)
BRAINARD, LINDA H., legislative adm. assoc., Florida Hospital Association, Tallahassee, FL '86 (RISK)
BRAITHWAITE, BERNADINE E., exec. vice-pres., U. S. Health Corporation, Clearwater, FL '75
BRAITHWAITE, JOHN D., dir. plant serv. and chief eng., Memorial Hospital, Manchester, KY '83 (ENG)
BRAITHWAITE, LINDA J., dir. soc. serv., vol. and pat. rep., Memorial Hospital, Manchester, KY '81 (PAT)
BRAKE, SANDRA J., supv. soc. work, Veterans Administration Medical Center, Altoona, PA '82 (SOC)
BRAKE, VIVIAN S., dir. pub. rel. and educ., Ozarks Medical Center, West Plains, MO '85 (PR)
BRALEY, ELLA MARIE, dir. matl. mgt., Mercy Medical Center, Roseburg, OR '85 (PUR)
BRAMBLE, RICHARD JOSEPH, mgr. pers., Chester County Hospital, West Chester, PA '77 (PERS)
BRAMEL, JOAN M. BROWN, dir. vol. serv., Sycamore Hospital, Miamisburg, OH '79 (VOL)
BRAMER, ROBERT ANTHONY JR., student, Graduate Program in Hospital and Health Administration, Xavier University, Cincinnati, OH '85
BRAMIGK, CAPT. DAVID H., MSC USAF, dir. pat. affairs, U. S. Air Force Hospital Moody, Valdosta, GA '84
BRAMLET, MARY L., dir. pers., Marion Memorial Hospital, Marion, IL '80 (PERS)
BRAMM, LORRAINE, dir. vol. serv., Mississauga Hospital, Mississauga, Ont., Canada '81 (VOL)
BRANAGAN, CHARLES A., pharm., U. S. Public Health Service Indian Hospital, Redlake, MN '74
BRANAMAN, A. RAY, mgr. bus. off., Coral Gables Hospital, Coral Gables, FL '86
BRANCH, BARNEY M., mgr. qual. control and trng., Duke University Hospital, Durham, NC '83 (CS)
BRANCH, CHARLES R., dir. plant oper., Northbay Medical Center, Fairfield, CA '86 (ENG)
BRANCH, GENE R., dir. info. syst., Hospital Corporation of America, Houston, TX '77 (MGMT)
BRANCH, NANCY S., assoc., Health Management Systems Inc., Alpine, NJ '85 (PR)
BRANCHEAU, F. PAUL, vice-pres. human res., Mercy Hospital, Muskegon, MI '76 (PERS)
BRAND, BRYAN S., asst. adm., North Park Hospital, Chattanooga, TN '80
BRAND, CHRISTINE, pub. rel. spec., Community Health Center of Branch County, Coldwater, MI '86
BRAND, ELWIN C., dir. bldg. serv., University Hospital, St. Louis University Center, St. Louis, MO '78 (ENG)
BRAND, GEORGE F., dir. food serv., Methodist Evangelical Hospital, Louisville, KY '75 (FOOD)
BRAND, THOMAS B., atty., Salem Hospital, Memorial Unit, Salem, OR '69 (ATTY)
BRANDAU, ROSE S., RN, dir. nrsg. serv., Rutherford Hospital, Rutherfordton, NC '84 (NURS)
BRANDAU, ROSE S., RN, vice-pres. nrsg. serv., Rutherford Hospital, Rutherfordton, NC '86 (NURS)

BRANDEL, CHRISTINE C., RN, dir. pat. care, St. Mary's Health Center, Jefferson City, MO '86 (NURS)
BRANDENBURG, EDWARD MAURICE JR., dir. mgt. eng., Jewish Hospital, Louisville, KY '78 (MGMT)
BRANDENBURG, JACK L., dir., Bay Area Health Care, Annapolis, MD '81
BRANDENBURG, MAJ. JOE W., MSC USA, dir. educ. and trng. nutr. care directorate, Brooke Army Medical Center, San Antonio, TX '82 (FOOD)
BRANDENBURG, STEPHEN J., adm. dir. mgt. info. syst., Aultman Hospital, Canton, OH '85 (MGMT)
BRANDIN, PATRICIA A., atty., St. Luke's Hospital, Racine, WI '81 (ATTY)
BRANDIS, MICHAELE C., dir. vol. serv., Santa Monica Hospital Medical Center, Santa Monica, CA '85 (VOL)
BRANDON, GERALD G., dir. matl. mgt., Peninsula General Hospital Medical Center, Salisbury, MD '86 (PUR)
BRANDON, GWEN, mgr. commun., Florida Hospital Medical Center, Orlando, FL '86 (ENG)
BRANDON, JEFFREY A., dir. amb. serv., Medical College of Ohio Hospital, Toledo, OH '87 (AMB)
BRANDON, JOSEPH, dir. pur., Downtown General Hospital, Chattanooga, TN '80 (PUR)
BRANDON, LORI L., mgt. eng., Hampton General Hospital, Hampton, VA '84 (MGMT)
BRANDOW, NANCY R., dir. human res., Penobscot Valley Hospital, Lincoln, ME '86 (PERS)(PR)
BRANDSTATER, SUZANNE KAY, pat. rep., Sydney Adventist Hospital, Wahroonga, Australia '86 (PAT)
BRANDT, BEVERLY, dir. oper. room, Holy Family Medical Center, Manitowoc, WI '87 (AMB)
BRANDT, DEE, dir. pub. rel., Woman's Hospital, Baton Rouge, LA '80 (PR)
BRANDT, SR. FLORENCE, vice-pres., St. Francis Medical Center, Pittsburgh, PA '78 (MGMT)
BRANDT, JEFF D., adm., Orthopedics Physicians, Inc., Seattle, WA '87 (AMB)
BRANDT, L. SCOTT, mgr. pur., Pennsylvania State University Hospital, Hershey, PA '78 (PUR)
BRANDT, LAVERNE, mgr. plant oper., St. Mary's Regional Health Center, Roswell, NM '86 (ENG)
BRANDT, WILLIAM J., dir. med. logistics mgt., U. S. Air Force Clinic-Howard, APO Miami, FL '85
BRANDT, WILLIAM R., atty., Bromenn Healthcare, Normal, IL '87 (ATTY)
BRANHAM, JERRY, dir. environ. serv., Winter Park Memorial Hospital, Winter Park, FL '86 (ENVIRON)
BRANIGAN, JACK E., exec. dir., Centre Community Hospital, State College, PA '74
BRANING, MARGARET NORMAN, asst. dir. vol. serv., Tulane University Hospital and Clinics, New Orleans, LA '84 (VOL)
BRANN, FRANCES D., dir. soc. serv., Franklin Memorial Hospital, Farmington, ME '82 (SOC)
BRANNEN, SAM L., atty., Willingway Hospital, Statesboro, GA '83 (ATTY)
BRANNIGAN, CATHERINE A., dir. vol. serv., Cornwall Hospital, Cornwall, NY '83 (VOL)
BRANNIGAN, JOHN F., dir. food and nutr. serv., William W. Backus Hospital, Norwich, CT '81 (FOOD)
BRANNIN, RICHARD EDWARD, proj. analyst, Kaiser Foundation Health Plan, Los Angeles, CA '75 (MGMT)(PLNG)
BRANNOCK, COL. JOSEPH E. JR., MSC USA, Raleigh, NC '65
BRANNON, BRETT D., student, University of Alabama at Birmingham, School of Community and Allied Health, Birmingham, AL '86
BRANNON, CINDY, RN, clin. coor. outpatient and family practice center, Franklin Square Hospital, Baltimore, MD '87 (AMB)
BRANNON, RACHEL A., RN, dir. nrsg., Miami Valley Hospital, Dayton, OH '83 (NURS)
BRANNON, SANDRA R., RN, dir. nrsg. serv., Baylor Medical Center at Grapevine, Grapevine, TX '77 (NURS)
BRANSCOMB, LISETTE, adm. res., Piedmont Hospital, Atlanta, GA '87
BRANSCOMB, SANDRA BROOKS, pat. rel. rep., North Carolina Memorial Hospital, Chapel Hill, NC '86 (PAT)
BRANSON, RAY M., pres., Midland Memorial Hospital, Midland, TX '81
BRANSON, WILLIAM L., (ret.), Portland, OR '53 (LIFE)
BRANSTETTER, GORDON, vice-pres. eng. serv., St. Rita's Medical Center, Lima, OH '72 (ENG)
BRANSTON, MARY C., dir. food serv. and diet., McLean Hospital, Division of Massachusetts General Hospital, Belmont, MA '70 (FOOD)
BRANT, JEROME E., atty., Spelman Memorial Hospital, Smithville, MO '83 (ATTY)
BRANT, JONATHAN, atty., Beth Israel Hospital, Boston, MA '84 (ATTY)
BRANT, LAURA L., dir. soc. serv., Merle West Medical Center, Klamath Falls, OR '73 (SOC)
BRANT, PENNY L. JONES, coor. vol. serv., Berrien General Hospital, Berrien Center, MI '85 (VOL)
BRANTLEY, JAMES L., vice-pres. matl. mgt., Gulf Health, Inc., Mobile, AL '66 (PUR)
BRANTLEY, JERRY E., dir. malt mgt., Baptist Memorial Hospital, Memphis, TN '81 (PUR)
BRANTLEY, MARSHA GRACE, bus. mgr. surg. serv., Hinsdale Hospital, Hinsdale, IL '84
BRANTLEY, WAYNE, dir. bldg. serv., Pemiscot County Memorial Hospital, Hayti, MO '81 (ENG)
BRANTNER, DIANE, dir. cent. sup., Fairview Southdale Hospital, Minneapolis, MN '78 (CS)
BRANTON, CAROLINE R., dir. soc. serv., Georgia Baptist Medical Center, Atlanta, GA '86 (SOC)
BRANUM, MARJORIE, RN, dir. cent. serv., Huntsville Hospital, Huntsville, AL '80 (CS)
BRANUM, RICHARD DAVID, dir. corp. serv. educ. center, South Miami Hospital, South Miami, FL '74 (MGMT)(PLNG)
BRASIL, SANDRA, dir. soc. serv., South County Hospital, Wakefield, RI '82 (SOC)
BRASSINGTON, BARBARA, dir. util. review and risk mgt., Children's Hospital of Philadelphia, Philadelphia, PA '86 (RISK)
BRASWELL, FLOY S., assoc. dir. food serv., Medical Center Hospital, San Antonio, TX '74 (FOOD)
BRASWELL, JOHN R., dir. mgt. eng., Carondelet Health Services, Tucson, AZ '86 (MGMT)
BRASWELL, LEROY J., assoc. adm., Villa Rosa Hospital, San Antonio, TX '70
BRATBY, KATHLEEN LOVELL, RN, dir. nrsg., West Jersey Health System, Camden, NJ '76 (NURS)
BRATCHER, NELDA L., RN, assoc. dir. maternal-child health and psych. nrsg., Greater Southeast Community Hospital, Washington, DC '83 (NURS)
BRATRUD, JOY, dir. soc. work serv., Alachua General Hospital, Gainesville, FL '85 (SOC)
BRATSVEN, RANDELL R., head matl. mgt., Naval Hospital, Corpus Christi, TX '86
BRATTON, ANN, AMI Arroyo Grande Community Hospital, Arroyo Grande, CA '84 (NURS)
BRATTON, CYNTHIA S., dir. human res., Alamance County Hospital, Burlington, NC '84 (PERS)
BRAUER, ELLWOOD A., dir. maint., Lutheran Hospital of Maryland, Baltimore, MD '82 (ENG)
BRAUER, TERRY B., chief exec. and dir., George S. May International Company, Park Ridge, IL '79 (MGMT)(PLNG)
BRAULICK, GILBERT J., supv. sup., proc. and distrib., Bay Area Hospital, Coos Bay, OR '86 (CS)
BRAULT, G. LORAIN, RN, nrsg. consult., American Medical International, Western Division, Brea, CA '82 (NURS)
BRAUN, CHARLES S., sr. vice-pres., Helman Hurley Charvat Peacock-Architects, Inc., Maitland, FL '83 (PLNG)
BRAUN, HUGO E. JR., atty., Saginaw General Hospital, Saginaw, MI '68 (ATTY)
BRAUN, JANE TESSITOR, coor. pub. rel., Foothill Presbyterian Hospital, Glendora, CA '78 (PR)
BRAUN, JOHN MARTIN, vice-pres., Saginaw General Hospital, Saginaw, MI '69
BRAUN, LEWIS M., health syst. spec., U. S. Public Health Services, New York, NY '56 (LIFE)
BRAUN, PETER, atty., Beverly Hospital, Beverly, MA '84 (ATTY)
BRAUN, RONALD J., dir. plng. and mktg., St. Joseph Health Center, St. Charles, MO '82 (PLNG)
BRAUN, SYLVIA M., pur. agt. and mgr. matl., St. Anthony Hospital, Hays, KS '80 (PUR)
BRAUTH, MARVIN J., atty., South Amboy Memorial Hospital, South Amboy, NJ '83 (ATTY)
BRAVENDER, CONSTANCE, dir. vol. serv., Alamance County Hospital, Burlington, NC '86 (VOL)
BRAVER, ARNOLD R., planner, Botsford General Hospital, Farmington Hills, MI '86 (PLNG)
BRAVINDER, MONTEREY, RN, dir. soc. serv., San Antonio Community Hospital, Upland, CA '79 (SOC)
BRAWLWY, DON R., adm., Vermillion County Hospital, Clinton, IN '80 (PLNG)
BRAXTON-THOMAS, ELVERDA LAVERNE, student, Program in Hospital and Health Care Management, Strayer College, Washington, DC '85
BRAY, A. F. JR., atty., Mount Diablo Hospital Medical Center, Concord, CA '78 (ATTY)
BRAY, COLLEEN, mgr., The Nutrition Company, Colorado Springs, CO '86 (FOOD)
BRAY, DONALD C., adm., University Hospital, Augusta, GA '64
BRAY, JAMES F. JR., pres., Doctors Hospital of San Diego, Inc., San Diego, CA '64
BRAY, JAY E., mgr. soc. serv., San Jose Hospital, San Jose, CA '81 (SOC)
BRAY, KAREN A., RN, dir. critical care nrsg., Washington Hospital, Washington, PA '85 (NURS)
BRAY, LANCE WILLIAM, pur. agt., Euclid Clinic Foundation, Euclid, OH '86 (PUR)
BRAY, NANCY A., dir. pub. rel., Southeast Missouri Hospital, Cape Girardeau, MO '82 (PR)
BRAZELL, RICKY, asst. dir. eng., Methodist Hospital, Lubbock, TX '86 (ENG)
BRAZIL, ROBERT D., dir. human res., Children's Medical Center, Tulsa, OK '84 (PERS)
BRAZIS, SUSAN L., supv. vol., Fawcett Memorial Hospital, Port Charlotte, FL '84 (VOL)
BRAZITIS, MARK A., vice-pres., Grant Medical Center, Columbus, OH '87 (AMB)
BREAKER, RICHARD H., dir. eng. and tech. serv., Swedish Covenant Hospital, Chicago, IL '85 (ENG)
BREAKSTONE, JERRY, vice-pres., Stone, Marraccini and Patterson, Clayton, MO '83 (PLNG)
BREAM, TERRY L., RN, vice-pres. nrsg. serv., Daniel Freeman Memorial Hospital, Inglewood, CA '87 (NURS)
BREAZEALE, KELLY W., Voluntary Hospitals of America-Massachusetts, Waltham, MA '80
BRECHBILL, ALAN L., sr. asst. dir., Foster G. McGaw Hospital, Loyola University of Chicago, Maywood, IL '84
BRECHER, BERND, pres., Bernd Brecher and Associates, Inc., New York, NY '75 (PLNG)
BRECHT, ROBERT M., PhD, dir. biomedical commun., University of Texas Medical Branch, Galveston, TX '83
BRECK, ELAINE COLLIER, mgr. guest rel., Swedish-American Hospital, Rockford, IL '85 (PAT)
BRECKMAN, MAUREEN, chief diet. and dir. food serv., Mounds Park Hospital, St. Paul, MN '74 (FOOD)
BREDELL, FRANK F., dir. pub. rel., Harper-Grace Hospitals, Detroit, MI '78 (PR)
BREDESTAGE, DOROTHY ANNETTE, dir. trng. and educ., Mercy Hospital, Hamilton, OH '73 (EDUC)
BREDOW, RONALD, dir. matl. mgt., John T. Mather Memorial Hospital, Port Jefferson, NY '78 (PUR)
BREDTHAUER, TRUDY SAUNDERS, atty., Methodist Hospital, Omaha, NE '85 (ATTY)
BREEDEN, BETTY H., coor. risk mgt. review, University of Virginia Hospitals, Charlottesville, VA '80 (RISK)
BREEDEN, ETHEL M., dir. matl. mgt., Providence Hospital, Everett, WA '85 (CS)
BREEDEN, PATRICIA L., dir. pers. serv., Norton Sound Regional Hospital, Nome, AK '84 (PERS)
BREEDING, LARRY L., exec. dir., Iowa Health Care Association, Des Moines, IA '74
BREEDLOVE, PAUL A., mgr. matl., Swain County Hospital, Bryson City, NC '82 (PUR)
BREEDLOVE, RICHARD S. SR., maint. elec., Man Appalachian Regional Hospital, Man, WV '86 (ENG)
BREEMAN, JOHN, Deloitte Haskins and Sells, Morristown, NJ '80
BREEN, MARGARET J., educ. consult., Bishop Clarkson Memorial Hospital, Omaha, NE '87 (EDUC)
BREEN, MARIETTA, dir. soc. serv., Citrus Memorial Hospital, Inverness, FL '75 (SOC)
BREES, RAY C., adm., Newnan Hospital, Newnan, GA '81
BREHM, JAY R., contr., St. Francis Hospital Center, Beech Grove, IN '85
BREHMER, HERMAN G., vice-pres. corp. dev., Eastern Health System, Birmingham, AL '75 (PLNG)
BREIDENSTEIN, DIANE E., asst. adm., Chippenham Hospital, Richmond, VA '86
BREIEN, MICHAEL A., mgr. eng., North Colorado Medical Center, Greeley, CO '80 (ENG)
BREIGHNER, KATHRYN W., pub. affairs spec., Northern Michigan Hospitals, Petoskey, MI '85 (PR)
BREILH, CYNTHIA J., pres., Video Education Associates, Spokane, WA '86 (EDUC)
BREINDEL, CHARLES L., PhD, assoc. prof., Medical College of Virginia, Virginia Commonwealth University, Department of Health Administration, Richmond, VA '79 (PLNG)
BREINIG, K'ALICE, RN, vice-pres., Freeman Hospital, Joplin, MO '72 (NURS)(RISK)
BREISCH, ALYSON J., dir. clin. prog., Lehigh Valley Hospital Center, Allentown, PA '86 (EDUC)
BREITENBACH, JOSEPH F., asst. adm. pers. serv., Our Lady of Mercy Hospital, Cincinnati, OH '64 (PERS)
BREITMEYER, JOHN F. III, mgr. mktg., Health Alliance Plan, Detroit, MI '85 (PLNG)
BREITWEISER, SHIRLEY, dir. vol. serv., University Hospital, St. Louis University Center, St. Louis, MO '79 (VOL)
BREKKE, ARVID B., pres., Volunteer Hospital Association-Mountain States, Inc., Englewood, CO '84
BREKKE, PAULA L., prog. mgr., University Hospital, Seattle, WA '83 (EDUC)
BREMER, JOHN S., dir. biomedical eng., U. S. Air Force Medical Center, Scott AFB, IL '86 (ENG)
BREMER, LOUIS H. JR., adm., Tuomey Hospital, Sumter, SC '77
BREMER, ROBERT A., dir. emp. educ., Spartanburg Regional Medical Center, Spartanburg, SC '81 (EDUC)
BREMER, ROBERT J. JR., mgt. eng., Poudre Valley Hospital, Fort Collins, CO '78 (MGMT)
BREMNER, LESLIE, health educ., Coronado Hospital, Coronado, CA '87 (EDUC)
BRENDEL, CHERYL, RN, supv. med. amb. unit, Shadyside Hospital, Pittsburgh, PA '87 (AMB)
BRENDEL, DAVID P., coor. energy conservation, Shadyside Hospital, Pittsburgh, PA '84 (ENG)
BRENDEL, EVALYN K., coor. food serv., North Carolina Division of Mental Health and Mental Retardation Services, Raleigh, NC '78 (FOOD)
BRENDEMIHL, PATRICIA A., mgr. food serv., St. Joseph's Community Hospital, West Bend, WI '82 (FOOD)
BRENDEMUHL, KATHIE J., dir. commun. rel., Ashley Valley Medical Center, Vernal, UT '84 (PR)
BRENDSEL, MARLIN D., chief eng. serv., Veterans Administration Medical Center, Hot Springs, SD '86 (ENG)
BRENIZER, JAMES R. JR., pat. rep., St. Vincent Medical Center, Toledo, OH '78 (PAT)
BRENN, DONNA A., asst. adm., Griffin Hospital, Derby, CT '85 (PLNG)
BRENNAN, BETTY E., dir. vol. serv., Bon Secours Hospital-Villa Maria Nursing Center, North Miami, FL '85 (VOL)
BRENNAN, SR. BRIDGET MARY, pat. rep., Saint Joseph Hospital, Fort Worth, TX '85 (PAT)
BRENNAN, CHARLES F., safety eng., New York Hospital, Cornell University, New York, NY '76 (RISK)
BRENNAN, DIANE M., mgt. eng., Geisinger Systems Services, Danville, PA '86 (MGMT)
BRENNAN, DORIS J., dir. diet. serv., Otto C. Epp Memorial Hospital, Cincinnati, OH '83 (FOOD)
BRENNAN, DOROTHY M., dir. food serv., Commonwealth of Pennsylvania, Southeast Pennsylvania Institutional Area Service Unit, Cornwells Heights, PA '80 (FOOD)
BRENNAN, ELAINE M., RN, asst. dir. nrsg., Montefiore Medical Center, Bronx, NY '86 (NURS)
BRENNAN, GERALDINE L., mgr. cent. sup., University Hospital, Lexington, KY '82 (CS)
BRENNAN, JOHN T. JR., atty., Psychiatric Institute of Washington, Washington, DC '81 (ATTY)
BRENNAN, MARIE L., dir., Hospital of the University of Pennsylvania, Philadelphia, PA '68 (FOOD)
BRENNAN, MARY K. GONYA, atty., Brener Wallack and Hill, Princeton, NJ '77 (ATTY)
BRENNAN, SR. MARY, RN, dir. nrsg. serv., A. Barton Hepburn Hospital, Ogdensburg, NY '67 (NURS)
BRENNAN, MICHAEL G., atty., Our Lady of Lourdes Medical Center, Camden, NJ '80 (ATTY)
BRENNAN, MICHAEL V. B., RN, dir. nrsg., Nathan Littauer Hospital, Gloversville, NY '85 (NURS)
BRENNAN, OLIVIA G., dir. soc. serv., Doctors' Hospital of Staten Island, Staten Island, NY '78 (SOC)
BRENNAN, PAUL, Walnut Creek, CA '80
BRENNAN, RICHARD J., atty., West Suburban Hospital Medical Center, Oak Park, IL '76 (ATTY)
BRENNAN, ROBERT J., dir. food serv., Mercy Medical Center, Oshkosh, WI '74 (FOOD)
BRENNAN, THERESE M., RN, asst. exec. dir., Menorah Medical Center, Kansas City, MO '83 (NURS)

BRENNAN, THOMAS D., dir. food serv., Nathan Littauer Hospital, Gloversville, NY '68 (FOOD)
BRENNAN, WARREN T., pres., Brennan Associates, Inc., Fort Washington, PA '73 (PLNG)
BRENNEMAN, GEORGE, asst. maint. eng., Arkansas Valley Regional Medical Center, La Junta, CO '76 (ENG)
BRENNER, BARBARA L., prog. coor. mgt.-soc. work serv., Mount Sinai Medical Center, New York, NY '81 (SOC)
BRENNER, IRMA S., RN, exec. asst., Warren General Hospital, Warren, OH '83
BRENNER, JAMES W., prin., McLellan and Copenhagen, Inc., Cupertino, CA '79 (PLNG)
BRENNER, CAPT. PAUL L., MSC USAF, dir. pers. and adm. serv., U. S. Air Force Clinic, McClellan AFB, CA '82
BRENNER, SUSAN J., asst. dir. soc. work, St. Vincent's Hospital and Medical Center, New York, NY '80 (SOC)
BRENO, CHARLES J., environ. eng., Cleveland Clinic Hospital, Cleveland, OH '80 (ENG)
BRENT, A. J., atty., Richmond Eye and Ear Hospital, Richmond, VA '77 (ATTY)
BRENTNALL, ZUMA E., dir. vol. serv., St. Vincent's Hospital, Birmingham, AL '63 (VOL)
BRENTS, THOMAS E., mgr. arch. serv., Hermann Hospital, Houston, TX '84 (PLNG)
BRENTWOOD, ANN, RN, vice-pres. nrsg., Regional Medical Center, Madisonville, KY '81 (NURS)
BREON, RICHARD C., chief oper. off., Brackenridge Hospital, Austin, TX '80
BRESCIA, BONNIE A., vice-pres., Bb and K Communications, Inc., Brookline, MA '85 (PR) (PLNG)
BRESLIN, ANN E., dir. cent. serv., Flushing Hospital and Medical Center, Flushing, NY '81 (CS)
BRESLIN, JOHN B., dir. diet. serv., St. Joseph Hospitals, Mount Clemens, MI '72 (FOOD)
BRESLIN, MARY T., dir. soc. serv., St. Margaret's Hospital for Women, Boston, MA '66 (SOC)
BRESLIN, RUTH L., chief soc. worker, Yale-New Haven Hospital, New Haven, CT '75 (SOC)
BRESLIN, SUSAN W., dir. mktg., Pennsylvania State University Hospital, Hershey, PA '86 (PR)
BRESNAHAN, CATHERINE C., dir. pers., St. Mary's Hospital, Waterbury, CT '74 (PERS)
BRESSANELLI, LEO A., asst. adm., St. Luke's Hospital, Davenport, IA '68
BRESTICKER, STANLEY, MD, med. dir., Middlesex Same Day Surgical Center, East Brunswick, NJ '87 (AMB)
BRETHAUER, CRAIG V., dir. emp. rel., Mease Health Care, Dunedin, FL '74 (PERS)
BRETHERICK, JIM, dir. matl. mgt., Phoenixville Hospital, Phoenixville, PA '86 (PUR)
BRETT, ANTHONY H., atty., Forsyth Memorial Hospital, Winston-Salem, NC '81 (ATTY)
BRETT, MARY, asst. dir. soc. work, North Shore University Hospital, Manhasset, NY '81 (SOC)
BRETTMANN, BRAD, pur. agt., Bryan Memorial Hospital, Lincoln, NE '86 (PUR)
BRETZ, CORNELL, chief soc. work serv., Veterans Administration Outpatient Clinic, Boston, MA '87 (SOC)
BREUER, COLLEEN, asst. dir. diet. and food serv., St. Luke's Regional Medical Center, Sioux City, IA '83 (FOOD)
BREUNIG, KURT A., atty., Elyria Memorial Hospital, Elyria, OH '82 (ATTY)
BREUNING, JONATHAN R., atty., Methodist Hospital, Omaha, NE '82 (ATTY)
BREUNLE, COL. PHILLIP C., MSC USA, adm. and dep. cmdr. adm., Cutler Army Hospital, Fort Devens, MA '71 (PAT)
BREW, GWENDOLYN, mgr. pers., Valley Hospital Association, Palmer, AK '86 (PERS)
BREWER, ANITA, mgr. mktg. commun., Lawrence Memorial Hospital of Medford, Medford, MA '86 (PR)
BREWER, B. J., vice-pres. pub. rel. and mktg., Wadley Regional Medical Center, Texarkana, TX '86 (PR)
BREWER, DAVID L., eng. mgt., University Hospital, Augusta, GA '84 (MGMT)
BREWER, DONNA E., asst. exec. dir. pers. res., Lawrence Memorial Hospital, Lawrence, KS '82 (PERS)
BREWER, DONNA M., dir. pers., Osteopathic Hospital of Maine, Portland, ME '76 (PERS)
BREWER, ELEANOR V., vice-pres., Sisters of St. Joseph of Orange Health Systems, Orange, CA '73
BREWER, EVIA J., supv. cent. serv., W. A. Foote Memorial Hospital, Jackson, MI '84 (CS)
BREWER, GEORGE M., pres., Methodist Hospital, Lubbock, TX '56 (LIFE)
BREWER, GERALDINE H., pat. rep., Indian Path Hospital, Kingsport, TN '81 (PAT)
BREWER, JOHN J., chief eng., Bakersfield Memorial Hospital, Bakersfield, CA '87 (ENG)
BREWER, MARGARET J., dir. soc. work serv., Community Memorial Hospital, Toms River, NJ '86 (SOC)
BREWER, PAMELA K., RN, dir. nrsg. educ. and asst. dir. nrsg., Oklahoma Osteopathic Hospital, Tulsa, OK '86 (NURS)
BREWER, PATRICK A., dir. maint. and eng., Baptist Medical Center, Little Rock, AR '80 (ENG)
BREWER, REBECCA T., RN, dir. nrsg., Colleton Regional Hospital, Walterboro, SC '82 (NURS)
BREWER, ROBERT G. JR., atty., Leland Memorial Hospital, Riverdale, MD '81 (ATTY)
BREWER, VIRGINIA, dir. soc. serv., Blackwell Regional Hospital, Blackwell, OK '75 (SOC)
BREWSTER, JOHN S., atty., Franklin Hospital, Benton, IL '84 (ATTY)
BREWTON, CLARENCE MCDONAL JR., dir. oper. plng., Washington Healthcare Management Corporation, Washington, DC '75
BREYER, NORMAN, asst. adm., Hyde Park Hospital, Chicago, IL '85
BREZA, PAUL W., asst. dir. pers. serv., Walter O. Boswell Memorial Hospital, Sun City, AZ '84 (PERS)
BRICE, HAROLD, (ret.), St. Louis, MO '72 (FOOD)
BRICE, SUSAN W., dir. vol. serv., Granville C. Morton Cancer and Research Hospital, Wadley Research Institute, Dallas, TX '80 (VOL)
BRICH, SCOTT, asst. eng., Midland Memorial Hospital, Midland, TX '87 (ENG)
BRICKELL, BONNIE, prog. mgr. and health maint. org. affiliate, Memorial Medical Center, Savannah, GA '87 (AMB)
BRICKELL, MARY ANN, asst. risk mgr., Children's Hospital of Pittsburgh, Pittsburgh, PA '86 (RISK)
BRICKETT, KATHRYN M., supv. recruitment and emp., Saint Francis Hospital and Medical Center, Hartford, CT '86 (PERS)
BRICKLEY, RONALD J., vice-pres. info. serv., C. R. Bard, Inc., Murray Hill, NJ '87 (PUR)
BRICKMAN, HENRY GUSTAF, (ret.), Natick, MA '41 (LIFE)
BRICKMAN, JEFFREY L., vice-pres. med. support serv., Baystate Medical Center, Springfield, MA '80 (MGMT)
BRICKMEIER, BARBARA A., asst. dir. pers., St. Elizabeth's Hospital of Boston, Boston, MA '84 (PERS)
BRICKNER, STEPHEN M., dir. mgt. eng., Vanderbilt University Hospital, Nashville, TN '82 (MGMT)
BRIDEAU, LEO P., dir. oper., Strong Memorial Hospital of the University of Rochester, Rochester, NY '79
BRIDENSTINE, MARY LEE W., dir. food serv., Landstuhl Army Regional Medical Center, APO New York, NY '77 (FOOD)
BRIDGE, CATHY R., coor. educ., King's Daughters Hospital, Brookhaven, MS '84 (EDUC)
BRIDGE, JACK C., mgr. matl. mgt., Deaconess Medical Center, Billings, MT '82 (PUR)
BRIDGE, PAUL N., exec. vice-pres., Roanoke Memorial Hospitals, Roanoke, VA '73 (RISK)
BRIDGEFORTH-HEIDER, FERN, RN, dir. cent. serv., Barnes Hospital, St. Louis, MO '70 (CS)
BRIDGER, GENEAN C., coor. nrsg. educ. and qual. assur., Hillcrest Baptist Medical Center, Waco, TX '86 (EDUC)
BRIDGES, BARBARA J., RN, Mill Creek, WA '76 (NURS)
BRIDGES, COLLYN G., vice-pres. and dir. fin., Mary Greeley Medical Center, Ames, IA '73 (PLNG)
BRIDGES, CONNIE R., coor. pub. rel. and dev., Memorial Hospital of Dodge County, Fremont, NE '81 (PR)
BRIDGES, ROZETTA J., supv. soc. work, Botsford General Hospital, Farmington Hills, MI '86 (SOC)
BRIDGES, TERRELL, dir. phys. plant, Arkansas Mental Health Services, Benton, AR '86 (ENG)
BRIDGEWATER, C. C. JR., atty., Monticello Medical Center, Longview, WA '80 (ATTY)
BRIDGEWATER, TERRY N., Dalton, MA '81 (PUR)
BRIEN, LAURA J., dir. commun. rel., Community Hospital of Chula Vista, Chula Vista, CA '84 (PR)
BRIEN, SHIRLEY H., med. tech., Catholic Medical Center, Manchester, NH '82 (EDUC)
BRIER, DOROTHY, asst. dir. soc. work, Lenox Hill Hospital, New York, NY '73 (SOC)
BRIERE, DAVID M., mgr. prod. dev., Pacificare Health System, Cypress, CA '83
BRIERLEY, GILBERT C., dir. plant, Sacred Heart Medical Center, Spokane, WA '85 (ENG)
BRIERLEY, JANE L., dir. pub. rel., Butterworth Hospital, Grand Rapids, MI '83 (PR)
BRIETIGAM, GEORGE, dir. plant and maint., Valley Children's Hospital, Fresno, CA '81 (ENG)
BRIGANCE, LINDA C., dir. corp. commun., Regional Medical Center at Memphis, Memphis, TN '84 (PR)
BRIGGIN, THOMAS, mng. consult., The Wyatt Company, San Francisco, CA '86 (RISK)
BRIGGS, BILLIE CATHERINE, RN, dir. nrsg. serv., Maury County Hospital, Columbia, TN '80 (NURS)
BRIGGS, BRUCE T., vice-pres. plng., dev. and educ., St. Luke's Hospitals, Fargo, ND '84 (PLNG)
BRIGGS, CRAIG L., mgr. food serv., Intermountain Health Care, Inc., Salt Lake City, UT '85 (FOOD)
BRIGGS, DEBORAH S., dir. emer. and trauma serv., Borgess Medical Center, Kalamazoo, MI '87 (AMB)
BRIGGS, FRED M., dir. constr., St. John's Hospital and Health Center, Santa Monica, CA '76 (ENG)
BRIGGS, GALEN P. JR., PhD, El Camino Hospital, Mountain View, CA '76 (MGMT)
BRIGGS, JAMES A., dir. plant serv., Martin Memorial Hospital, Stuart, FL '79 (ENG)
BRIGGS, JAMES D., chief mktg. off., Lutheran Healthcare Network, Mesa, AZ '84 (PLNG)
BRIGGS, JAMES I., adm. asst. plant affairs, St. Joseph's Regional Health Center, Hot Springs National Park, AR '80 (ENG)
BRIGGS, CAPT. LEE W., MSC USA, student, Armed Force Staff College, Norfolk, VA '82
BRIGGS, M. BEVERLY, RN, assoc. vice-pres. nrsg., Baystate Medical Center, Springfield, MA '82 (NURS)
BRIGGS, SR. M. LUCY, vice-pres., Holy Redeemer Hospital and Medical Center, Meadowbrook, PA '75
BRIGGS, R. ANNETTE, dir. nutr. serv., Irving Community Hospital, Irving, TX '86 (FOOD)
BRIGGS, WAYNE, dir. adult serv., Woods Psychiatric Institute, Abilene, TX '87 (SOC)
BRIGHAM, JAMES A. JR., dir. mktg., Emergency Medical Services Associates, Plantation, FL '79
BRIGHT, LARRY E., chief elec. tech. and supv. biomedical elec. and instrumentation, Reid Memorial Hospital, Richmond, IN '85 (ENG)
BRIGHT, MAUREEN J., atty., St. Mary Desert Valley Hospital, Apple Valley, CA '80 (ATTY)
BRIGHT, SHERRY L., vice-pres. and dir. mktg., Baystate Health Systems, Inc., Springfield, MA '86 (PR)
BRIGHT, SUSAN L., pat. rep., St. Francis Regional Medical Center, Wichita, KS '83 (PAT)
BRIGHTON, BARRY LEE, student, Georgia State University, Institute of Health Administration, Atlanta, GA '85
BRIGHTWELL, LYNN W., vice-pres. plng. and mktg., Missouri Baptist Hospital, St. Louis, MO '85 (PR) (PLNG)
BRILEY, JAN L., dir. vol. serv., Brea Hospital-Neuropsychiatric Center, Brea, CA '84 (VOL)
BRILEY, JEANNINE M., dir. vol. serv., commun. rel. and pub. rel., Metropolitan Nashville General Hospital, Nashville, TN '82 (VOL)(PR)
BRILL, N. C., atty., Ozarks Medical Center, West Plains, MO '85 (ATTY)
BRILL, NEWTON C., chm. risk mgt. committee, Ozarks Medical Center, West Plains, MO '86 (RISK)
BRILLI, PATRICIA A., dir. soc. serv., St. Mary's Hospital for Children, Bayside, NY '75 (SOC)
BRILLMAN, ALLAN, dir. prop., Heritage Health Management Corporation, Rockford, IL '86 (ENG)
BRIM, ARMAND EUGENE, pres., Brim and Associates, Inc., Portland, OR '53 (LIFE)
BRIMHALL, BARBARA H., dir. pub. rel., Chico Community Hospital, Chico, CA '86 (PR)
BRINDLE, JAMES E., dir. food serv., Morristown Memorial Hospital, Morristown, NJ '67 (FOOD)
BRINES, WILLIAM STEWART, Marshfield Hills, MA '40 (LIFE)
BRINGHURST, LAREE, dir. vol., Cassia Memorial Hospital, Burley, ID '77 (VOL)
BRINK, BERNARD B., bd. chm., Tuality Community Hospital, Hillsboro, OR '80 (ATTY)
BRINK, GERALD R., exec. vice-pres., Riverside Hospital, Newport News, VA '64
BRINK, GLENDA, med. soc. worker, Berwick Hospital Center, Berwick, PA '85 (SOC)
BRINK, SUSAN, vice-pres. strategic plng., HealthOne Corporation, Minneapolis, MN '85 (PLNG)
BRINKER, BERNARD C., atty., St. John's Mercy Medical Center, St. Louis, MO '86 (ATTY)
BRINKER, DAVELLE L., dir. trng. and dev., Little Company of Mary Hospital, Evergreen Park, IL '86 (EDUC)
BRINKERT, SUSAN, RN, asst. vice-pres. nrsg., Newton-Wellesley Hospital, Newton, MA '86 (NURS)
BRINKERT, WILLIAM K., atty., St. John of God Hospital, Boston, MA '86 (ATTY)
BRINKLEY, MICHAEL C., exec. dir., Medical Center Redevelopment Corporation, Phoenix, AZ '80 (PLNG)
BRINKMAN, BRENDA C., student, Program in Hospital Administration, Trinity University, San Antonio, TX '86
BRINKMAN, JOAN C., RN, dir. vol. serv., Franklin Memorial Hospital, Farmington, ME '85 (VOL)
BRINKMAN, MICHAEL O., pres., Hospital Maintenance Consultants, Inc., Lebanon, WI '75 (ENG)
BRISBANE, MARILYN, RN, asst. dir. nrsg. serv., St. Peter Hospital, Olympia, WA '83 (NURS)
BRISBON, DELORES, adm., Hospital of the University of Pennsylvania, Philadelphia, PA '75
BRISCOE, DOUGLAS, asst. vice-pres., John D. Archbold Memorial Hospital, Thomasville, GA '87 (RISK)
BRISCOE, RICHARD J., exec. vice-pres., Bronson Methodist Hospital, Kalamazoo, MI '76
BRISELL, DAVID R., atty., Charleston Area Medical Center, Charleston, WV '82 (ATTY)
BRISLEY, DAVID T., coor. comp. ins. prog., Ontario Hospital Association, Don Mills, Ont., Canada '80 (RISK)
BRISLIN, JAMES M. JR., dir. mgt. serv., United Hospital, Grand Forks, ND '76 (MGMT)
BRISSE, THOMAS MICHAEL, student, Program in Hospital Administration, University of Michigan, Ann Arbor, MI '85
BRISSETTE-ANDERSON, SUSAN M., dir. plng. and mktg., Franklin Medical Center, Greenfield, MA '80 (PLNG)
BRISSMAN, ULRIKE, proj. mgr., American Hospital Association, Chicago, IL '83
BRISTOW, JOAN, dir. qual. assur. and risk mgt., St. Francis Medical Center, Trenton, NJ '86 (RISK)
BRITSKY, MARINA APPLEGATE, dir. mktg. pub. rel. dept., Providence Milwaukie Hospital, Milwaukie, OR '86 (PR)
BRITT, BEVERLY W., dir. diet., St. Joseph's Hospital, Savannah, GA '76 (FOOD)
BRITT, HARRY L. JR., dir. maint., Jasper County Hospital, Rensselaer, IN '82 (ENG)
BRITT, PATRICIA R., dir. pers., Sampson County Memorial Hospital, Clinton, NC '81 (PERS)
BRITT, ROSEMARY, RN, vice-pres. nrsg. serv., St. Francis Hospital Systems, Colorado Springs, CO '85 (NURS)
BRITT, STEVEN D., dir. pers., Shriners Hospitals for Crippled Children, Chicago, IL '82 (PERS)
BRITTAIN, DAVID L., mgr. eng., Busch, Inc., Virginia Beach, VA '82 (ENG)
BRITTAIN, DAVID R., dir. commun. rel., Hadley Regional Medical Center, Hays, KS '85 (PR)
BRITTEN, MARILYN J., dir. pub. rel., Emma L. Bixby Hospital, Adrian, MI '82 (PR)
BRITTENHAM, PHILLIP J., mgr. emp. rel., Washoe Medical Center, Reno, NV '83 (PERS)
BRITTIN, JOCELYN WEST, atty., Alexandria Hospital, Alexandria, VA '83 (ATTY)
BRITTON, DONALD L., asst. dir. plant and eng., Memorial Medical Center, Springfield, IL '74 (ENG)
BRITTON, ROBERT K., dir. eng. serv., St. Elizabeth Hospital, Danville, IL '82 (ENG)
BRITTS, REGINALD L., dir. pur., Giles Memorial Hospital, Pearisburg, VA '85 (PUR)
BRIWA, CHARLES III, dir. eng. serv., Winchester Hospital, Winchester, MA '81 (ENG)
BROAD, TOM L., dir. pub. rel., Trinity Lutheran Hospital, Kansas City, MO '81 (PR)
BROADSTONE, LARRY S., dir. phys. plant, St. John's Hospital, Jackson, WY '79 (ENG)
BROADWATER, JAMES B., partner, Touche Ross and Company, Louisville, KY '72
BROADWAY, CHARLES B., (ret.), Marion, IL '54 (LIFE)
BROADWAY, JAMES D., atty., Methodist Medical Center of Illinois, Peoria, IL '78 (ATTY)
BROBST, LORRAINE G., dir. educ. and trng., Kaiser Foundation Hospital, Santa Clara, CA '76 (EDUC)
BROBST, SHIRLEY M., adm. food, Western Maryland Center, Hagerstown, MD '67 (FOOD)
BROCCOLO, BERNADETTE M., atty., Rush-Presbyterian-St. Luke's Medical Center, Chicago, IL '81 (ATTY)
BROCHTRUP, CHRISTINE A., atty., Sisters of Mercy of the Union, St. Louis, MO '84 (ATTY)
BROCK, BRUCE M., PhD, pres., Information Transfer Systems, Inc., Ann Arbor, MI '86 (PLNG)

BROCK, CONNIE A., dir. commun. rel., Lebanon Community Hospital, Lebanon, OR '84 (VOL)
BROCK, DANIEL N., atty., Central Baptist Hospital, Lexington, KY '78 (ATTY)
BROCK, DONALD R., dir. eng. and maint., Bloomington Hospital, Bloomington, IN '80 (ENG)
BROCK, GARY, asst. adm., Memorial Hospital of Garland, Garland, TX '86 (RISK)
BROCK, JAMES S., atty., Central Vermont Medical Center, Berlin, VT '80 (ATTY)
BROCK, LARRY, asst. risk mgr., National Health Corporation, Marfreesboro, TN '86 (RISK)
BROCK, MARTHA L., acct. exec., Cincinnati Bell, Inc., Cincinnati, OH '79
BROCK, MARYBETH ANNE, supv. soc. serv., Christian Hospitals Northeast-Northwest, St. Louis, MO '85 (SOC)
BROCK, RICHARD B., RN, dir. nrsg.-internal medicine, Los Angeles County-University of Southern California Medical Center, Los Angeles, CA '84 (NURS)
BROCK, ROBERT W., vice-pres. fin., East Liverpool City Hospital, East Liverpool, OH '85
BROCK, SIDNEY J., chief eng., Pine Rest Christian Hospital, Grand Rapids, MI '81 (ENG)
BROCKER, SANDRA POTISH, RN, vice-pres. nrsg. serv., Ridgeview Institute, Smyrna, GA '79 (NURS)
BROCKMAN, HAROLD J., Sear Brown Associates, Albany, NY '83
BROCKMAN, JAMES H., vice-pres. corp. rel., Rushmore National Health Systems, Rapid City, SD '64 (PERS)
BROCKMAN, SUSAN B., dir. commun. rel., Methodist Hospital, Madison, WI '86
BROCKMAN, SUZANNE S., vice-pres., The Arthur Sherman Company, La Mesa, CA '85 (PR) (PLNG)
BROCKMAN, WILLIAM F. II, adm., Seven Rivers Community Hospital, Crystal River, FL '85
BROCKMEIER, FREDERICK, atty., Jewish Hospital of Cincinnati, Cincinnati, OH '77 (ATTY)
BROCKWAY, GAIL M., dir. diet., Green Hospital of Scripps Clinic, La Jolla, CA '83 (FOOD)
BROCKWAY, LAURENCE E., educ. coor., Susan B. Allen Memorial Hospital, El Dorado, KS '86 (EDUC)
BRODEEN, RAWLEY D., Ellerbe Associates, Inc., Minneapolis, MN '84 (ENG)
BRODERIC, DAVID, pres. and chief exec. off., Good Samaritan Hospital, Lebanon, PA '87 (AMB)
BRODERICK, R. J., dir. pur., St. Joseph Hospital, Orange, CA '79 (PUR)
BRODEUR, GAIL, coor. cent. sterile, Kent County Memorial Hospital, Warwick, RI '80 (CS)
BRODEUR, MARK S., asst. vice-pres., St. Anthony's Medical Center, St. Louis, MO '80
BRODIE, CAROL M., coor. staff dev., Healthcare Medical Center of Tustin, Tustin, CA '87 (EDUC)
BRODIE, STEPHEN, sr. consult., Healthcorp Affiliates, Naperville, IL '85 (EDUC)
BRODKIN, ELLEN GARTNER, dir. mktg., American Medical Buildings, Bala Cynwyd, PA '84 (PLNG)
BRODNIAK, BRIAN A., vice-pres. human res., St. Joseph Mercy Hospital, Clinton, IA '81 (PERS)
BRODOWSKI, THOMAS A., dir. eng., St. Francis Hospital, Jersey City, NJ '82 (ENG)
BRODSKY, EDWARD, consult., Flushing, NY '39 (LIFE)
BRODSKY, KAREN L., dir. mktg. res., Brookshire Group, Belair, MD '85 (PLNG)
BRODT, ANN L., RN, vice-pres. pat. care, Galesburg Cottage Hospital, Galesburg, IL '86 (NURS)
BRODY, BETH E., coor. pub. rel., Hampton Hospital, Rancocas, NJ '87 (PR) (PLNG)
BRODY, CORRINE L., consult., Arthur Andersen and Company, Miami, FL '84 (MGMT)
BRODY, E. W., pres., The Resource Group, Inc., Memphis, TN '75 (PR)
BRODZIN, CAROLYN M., chief soc. work serv., Veterans Administration Medical Center, Saginaw, MI '86 (SOC)
BROEK, DEBORAH, risk mgr., Saint Joseph's Hospital, Atlanta, GA '85 (RISK)(ENG)
BROEKEMEIER, CHLOE J., RN, Fair Oaks, CA '86 (NURS)
BROEKER, JOHN M., atty., Minnesota Association of Health Care Facilities, Minneapolis, MN '77 (ATTY)
BROELAND, GEORGE E., dir. eng., Humana Hospital -Biscayne, Miami, FL '83 (ENG)
BROGAN, BARBARA H., dir. vol. serv., Sarah Bush Lincoln Health Center, Mattoon, IL '85 (VOL)
BROGDON, GEORGIA, asst. vice-pres., Gwinnett Hospital System, Lawrenceville, GA '83 (PLNG)
BROGDON, PAUL F., coor. constr., Memorial Hospital, Hollywood, FL '76 (ENG)
BROGIOLI, MAUREEN P., dir. qual. assur., Milford-Whitinsville Regional Hospital, Milford, MA '82 (RISK)
BROHAWN, BARBARA A., pat. rep., Frederick Memorial Hospital, Frederick, MD '79 (PAT)
BROHAWN, MICHAEL T., mgt. eng., Indian River Memorial Hospital, Vero Beach, FL '84 (MGMT)
BROIHIER, JOHN C., atty., Holy Family Hospital, Des Plaines, IL '79 (ATTY)
BROKAW, DIANE J., dir. vol. serv., Trinity Regional Hospital, Fort Dodge, IA '86 (VOL)
BROKENBURR, ANNETTE, pers. off., Winter Haven Hospital, Winter Haven, FL '73 (PERS)
BROKUS, JUDITH A., mgr. food serv., Selinsgrove Center, Selinsgrove, PA '86 (FOOD)
BROLAN, DAVID J., dir. med. soc. work, Moses Taylor Hospital, Scranton, PA '85 (SOC)
BROLUND, ARNOLD J., asst. dir. plant oper., Tucson Medical Center, Tucson, AZ '86 (ENG)
BROMAN, KAY F., asst. dir. nrsg. and human res., University of Iowa Hospitals and Clinics, Iowa City, IA '86 (PERS)
BROMBERG, NELDA J., dir. mktg., Baptist Medical Center, Little Rock, AR '85 (PLNG)
BROMBERG, ROBERT S., atty., Cleveland Clinic Hospital, Cleveland, OH '72 (ATTY)
BROMLEY, GAIL E., RN, vice-pres., Lakewood Hospital, Lakewood, OH '81 (NURS)
BROMLEY, PAM L., dir. care groups, Saint Alphonsus Regional Medical Center, Boise, ID '85 (NURS)
BROMLEY, RICHARD, atty., American Hospital Association, Chicago, IL '85 (ATTY)
BRONKESH, SHERYL J., prin., Health Services Marketing, Ltd., Scottsdale, AZ '76 (PR)
BRONSON, ALFREDA T., dir. environ. serv., St. Mary's Health Center, St. Louis, MO '86 (ENVIRON)
BRONSON, JO A., dir. pat. rep., Broward General Medical Center, Fort Lauderdale, FL '82 (PAT)
BRONSTEIN, BEN, asst. adm. pub. affairs, Montefiore Hospital, Pittsburgh, PA '68 (PR)
BRONZINI, BLANCHE M., RN, State College Manor Nursing Home, State College, PA '84 (EDUC)
BROOK, EDITH, mgr. pur. and matl., Baptist Hospital, Winner, SD '87 (PUR)
BROOKE, JULIA B., atty., Baptist Medical Center, Jacksonville, FL '86 (ATTY)
BROOKE, RICHARD JR., vice-pres. and dir. group ins., Independent Life and Accident Insurance Company, Jacksonville, FL '54 (LIFE)
BROOKER, RICHARD, prin., Architects Collaborative, Cambridge, MA '72
BROOKER, THOMAS J., chief exec. off., St. Vincent's Private Hospital, Darlinghurst Sydney, Australia '86 (MGMT)
BROOKHART, JAMES L., asst. adm. pers. serv., Riverview Hospital, Noblesville, IN '81 (PERS)
BROOKINGS, MICHAEL D., dir. facil. mgt., Queen of Angels Medical Center, Los Angeles, CA '85 (ENG)(ENVIRON)
BROOKINS, CHRISTINE B., dir. qual. assur., Charter Lake Hospital, Macon, GA '86 (RISK)
BROOKLER, KATIE, mgr. qual. assur. and risk mgr., Children's Hospital, Denver, CO '82 (RISK)
BROOKS, ALMENA H., student, Boston University Health Management Programs, Boston, MA '85 (PLNG)
BROOKS, ANN MARIE T., RN, dir. nrsg., Sheppard and Enoch Pratt Hospital, Baltimore, MD '83 (NURS)
BROOKS, AUDREY, head admit. and telecommun., Bay Medical Center, Bay City, MI '82 (ENG)
BROOKS, BERNARD E., bd. mem., St. Vincent's Hospital and Medical Center of New York, New York, NY '85
BROOKS, BILL L., dir. human res., City of Hope National Medical Center, Duarte, CA '83 (PERS)
BROOKS, BRENDA HENNIG, dir. diet., Bay Area Medical Center-Menominee, Menominee, MI '80 (FOOD)
BROOKS, CAROL A., RN, vice-pres. nrsg., Long Island Jewish Medical Center, New York, NY '72 (NURS)
BROOKS, DAVID TODD, adm. fellow, Health Alliance Plan, Health Facilities Division, Detroit, MI '83 (PLNG)
BROOKS, DIANA LEE, dir. plng. and mktg., Maryvale Samaritan Hospital, Phoenix, AZ '83 (PLNG)
BROOKS, EDWARD S., asst. dir. eng. and plant oper., Mount Auburn Hospital, Cambridge, MA '85 (ENG)
BROOKS, GAIL W., dir. diet., East Tennessee Children's Hospital, Knoxville, TN '79 (FOOD)
BROOKS, GILBERT, dir. oper., Bellevue Hospital Center, New York, NY '80 (CS)
BROOKS, JAMES D., atty., Springhill Memorial Hospital, Mobile, AL '78 (ATTY)
BROOKS, JAMES F., asst. exec. dir. pat. serv., Medical Center Hospital, San Antonio, TX '85
BROOKS, CAPT. JAMES H., MSC USA, student, U. S. Army Command and General Staff College, Fort Leavenworth, KS '84
BROOKS, LOUIS, dir. eng., Georgetown Hospital, Georgetown, TX '80 (ENG)
BROOKS, LYNN R., dir. vol., Salinas Valley Memorial Hospital, Salinas, CA '84 (VOL)
BROOKS, LYNNE M., student, Widener College, Chester, PA '82
BROOKS, LYNWOOD T., dir. pers., Memorial Hospital of Southern Oklahoma, Ardmore, OK '81 (PERS)
BROOKS, MARGERY B., student, Graduate Program in Health Care Administration, Trinity University, San Antonio, TX '82
BROOKS, MARTY, risk mgr., Medical Park Hospital, Winston-Salem, NC '86 (PAT)(RISK)
BROOKS, MICHAEL G., sr. consult., Ernst and Whinney, Indianapolis, IN '86 (MGMT)
BROOKS, NANCY T., dir. soc. serv., Holy Cross Hospital, Chicago, IL '80 (SOC)
BROOKS, RICHARD J., dir. corp. dev., South Shore Hospital, South Weymouth, MA '82 (PLNG)
BROOKS, ROBERT C., dir. mktg. and video commun., University of Cincinnati Medical Center, Cincinnati, OH '86 (PR)
BROOKS, ROGER E., risk mgr., Marquette General Hospital, Marquette, MI '86 (RISK)
BROOKS, RONALD A., vice-pres. human res., Dover General Hospital and Medical Center, Dover, NJ '82 (PERS)
BROOKS, SHERI K., dir. plng. and mktg., Holden Hospital, Holden, MA '86 (PR) (PLNG)
BROOKS, SUE C., dir. vol., St. Mary's Medical Center, Knoxville, TN '81 (VOL)
BROOKS, SUSAN W., educ. adm. coor., Riverside Methodist Hospitals, Columbus, OH '82
BROOKS, TERESA A., atty., Michigan Hospital Association, Lansing, MI '79 (ATTY)
BROOKS, TERRY A., atty., Yakima Valley Memorial Hospital, Yakima, WA '77 (ATTY)
BROOKS, THORNTON H., atty., Wesley Long Community Hospital, Greensboro, NC '76 (ATTY)
BROOKS, WILLIAM J., chief eng., Greene County Memorial Hospital, Waynesburg, PA '85 (ENG)
BROOKS, WILLIAM N., chief eng., Klinker and Associates, Inc., Gambrills, MD '84
BROPHY, CHARLES J., dir. fiscal serv. and pers., Jewish Home for the Elderly, Fairfield, CT '83 (PERS)
BROPHY, CHARLOTTE D., dir. vol. serv., Westerly Hospital, Westerly, RI '74 (VOL)
BROPHY, JOHN E., exec. dir., Veterans Administration Medical Center, Erie, PA '72 (EDUC)
BROPHY, JOSEPH G., dir. support serv., Shriners Hospital for Crippled Children, Philadelphia, PA '85 (PUR)
BROPHY, KEVIN M., coor. trng., Presbyterian Hospital in the City of New York, New York, NY '83 (EDUC)
BROSCO, JAMES E., chief eng., War Memorial Hospital, Sault Ste Marie, MI '86 (ENG)
BROSNAN, SR. M. AGNESITA, adm., Schumpert Medical Center, Shreveport, LA '69
BROSNAN, MARGARET ANNE, pres., Saint Thomas Medical Center, Akron, OH '64 (ATTY)
BROSNAN, TIMOTHY J., vice-pres., Mercy Center for Health Care Services, Aurora, IL '82 (PLNG)
BROSS, GERARD ANTHONY, adm. res., Hutzel Hospital, Detroit, MI '83
BROSSEAU, TERRANCE G., pres., Medcenter One, Bismarck, ND '81 (PLNG)
BROST, PATRICIA L., coor. educ., Mount Hood Medical Center, Gresham, OR '77 (EDUC)
BROTHERS, CAROL E., chief diet. serv., Harry S. Truman Memorial Veterans Hospital, Columbia, MO '82 (FOOD)
BROTHERS, CHAUNCY P. JR., dep. cmdr. adm., Munson Army Community Hospital, Fort Leavenworth, KS '69 (PLNG)
BROTHERS, JOHN T., RN, dir. nrsg., St. Mary's Hospital, Galesburg, IL '86 (NURS)
BROTHERTON, GEORGE T., Coos Bay, OR '50 (LIFE)
BROTNOW, JAMES B., chief fin. off., AMI Medical Center of North Hollywood, North Hollywood, CA '78
BROTON, ALICE M., dir. matl. mgt., Norwegian-American Hospital, Chicago, IL '85 (CS)
BROTZ, KAREN M., supv. cent. proc., Providence Medical Center, Portland, OR '82 (CS)
BROUDE, ALAN LEE, vice-pres. fin., Jewish Hospital, Louisville, KY '78
BROUILLETTE, PEGGY W., RN, dir. nrsg., Bunkie General Hospital, Bunkie, LA '84 (NURS)
BROUSSARD, KATHRYN S., mgr. emp., Medical Center of Baton Rouge, Baton Rouge, LA '86 (PERS)
BROUSSARD, MARY E., dir. soc. serv., Abbeville General Hospital, Abbeville, LA '85 (SOC)
BROUSSARD, RIVEST JOSEPH, mgr. pur., Citizens Hospital, Talladega, AL '82 (PUR)
BROUSSARD, REV. WILLIAM L., exec. dir., Texas Conference of Catholic Health Facilities, Austin, TX '79
BROUTMAN, CHARLES A., commun. syst. consult., Rancho Palos Verdes, CA '83
BROW, MARY, dir. nrsg., Lincoln West Hospital, Chicago, IL '79 (NURS)
BROWDY, JERAD D., pres., Jerad D. Browdy, Inc., Evanston, IL '83
BROWER-BRADLEY, CAROL ANN, RN, vice-pres. clin. serv., Western Medical Center, Santa Ana, CA '86 (NURS)
BROWER, ANDREA THERESE, consult., Laventhol and Horwath, Chicago, IL '84
BROWER, FORREST A., group vice-pres., New Jersey Hospital Association, Princeton, NJ '55 (LIFE)
BROWER, KARL J., dir. pers., Glendale Adventist Medical Center, Glendale, CA '77 (PERS)
BROWER, LESTER S., sr. assoc. dir., University of Wisconsin Hospital and Clinics, Madison, WI '68 (PLNG)
BROWER, NANCY N., coor. emp., Rutland Regional Medical Center, Rutland, VT '86 (PERS)
BROWER, STANLEY G., coor. tech. support, L. W. Blake Memorial Hospital, Bradenton, FL '86 (ENG)
BROWN, ALETTA R., asst. dir. commun. serv., Brigham and Women's Hospital, Boston, MA '86 (ENG)
BROWN, ALLAN, dir. commun. serv., Methodist Hospital, Brooklyn, NY '86 (ENG)
BROWN, ALLEN, vice-pres. adm., Community Memorial Hospital, Toms River, NJ '75
BROWN, AMY S., dir. vol. serv., Sinai Hospital of Detroit, Detroit, MI '84 (VOL)
BROWN, ANDREW IRVIN, atty., Mercy Hospital of New Orleans, New Orleans, LA '83 (ATTY)
BROWN, ANN B., adm., Jefferson County Hospital, Fayette, MS '81 (PR)
BROWN, ANNA LEE, dir. soc. serv., Greenleaf Center, Inc., Shawnee, OK '86 (SOC)
BROWN, ANNE LORETTA, pat. advocate, St. Frances Cabrini Hospital, Alexandria, LA '84 (PAT)
BROWN, ANTHONY N., dir. pers., Skokie Valley Hospital, Skokie, IL '86 (PERS)
BROWN, ARTHUR E., pres., Arthur E. Brown and Associates, West Trenton, NJ '68
BROWN, AUSTIN C., sr. mgt. eng., Holy Cross Hospital, Silver Spring, MD '84 (MGMT)
BROWN, BARBARA A., dir. vol. serv., St. Cloud Hospital, St. Cloud, MN '80 (VOL)
BROWN, BARBARA J., RN, asst. adm. nrsg., Virginia Mason Hospital, Seattle, WA '74 (NURS)
BROWN, BARRY D., pres., West Jersey Hospital, Northern Division, Camden, NJ '61
BROWN, BERNARD L. JR., exec. dir., Kennestone Hospital, Marietta, GA '64
BROWN, BEVERLY J., coor. med. staff, Mercy San Juan Hospital, Carmichael, CA '81 (RISK)
BROWN, BRENDA, dir. soc. work, Holyoke Hospital, Holyoke, MA '85 (SOC)
BROWN, C. HAROLD, atty., Harris Methodist -Fort Worth, Fort Worth, TX '78 (ATTY)
BROWN, COL. CARL D., MSC USA, San Antonio, TX '81
BROWN, CARMENCITA P., dir. nutr. serv., Highlands Regional Medical Center, Sebring, FL '85 (FOOD)
BROWN, CAROL, actg. mgr. cent. serv., Harborview Medical Center, Seattle, WA '86 (CS)
BROWN, CAROLINE F., vice-pres. human res., Southern Chester County Medical Center, West Grove, PA '83 (PERS)
BROWN, CAROLYN S., Lewisville, TX '79 (FOOD)
BROWN, CATHERINE W., student, Xavier University, Program in Hospital Administration, Cincinnati, OH '82
BROWN, CHARLES R. P., atty., Lawnwood Regional Medical Center, Fort Pierce, FL '72 (ATTY)

BROWN, CHARLES R., dir. matl. mgt., Pacific Presbyterian Hospital, San Francisco, CA '67 (CS)(PUR)
BROWN, CHARLES, mgr. cent. sup., Medical Center, Columbus, GA '86 (CS)
BROWN, CHARLOTTE A., RN, supv. cent. proc., Peninsula General Hospital Medical Center, Salisbury, MD '84 (CS)
BROWN, CLIFF, dir. pub. rel., Eisenhower Medical Center, Rancho Mirage, CA '75 (PR)
BROWN, CYNTHIA L., mgr. educ., Mercy Hospital, Urbana, IL '86 (EDUC)
BROWN, D. JEANNE, dir. matl. mgt., Jane Lamb Health Center, Clinton, IA '81 (PUR)
BROWN, DALE, dir. soc. work serv., University Hospital, Augusta, GA '74 (SOC)
BROWN, DANIEL M., consult., Sun City West, AZ '64
BROWN, DAVID M., dir. maint. and risk mgr., Mercy Hospital, Columbus, OH '83 (ENG)
BROWN, DAVID W., dir. biomedical serv., Medical Plaza Hospital, Fort Worth, TX '83 (ENG)
BROWN, DAVID, vice-pres., Woods Psychiatric Institute, Abilene, TX '86 (RISK)
BROWN, DELMAR V., dir. power plant and maint., Frederick Memorial Hospital, Frederick, MD '83 (ENG)
BROWN, DENISE M., vice-pres. adm., St. Joseph Hospital, Chicago, IL '85
BROWN, DIANA G., asst. dir. soc. work, New York University Medical Center, New York, NY '79 (SOC)
BROWN, DIANE G., dir. risk mgt., Children's Hospital Medical Center of Northern California, Oakland, CA '85 (RISK)
BROWN, DONALD C., mgr. compensation, Providence Medical Center, Portland, OR '82 (PERS)
BROWN, DONALD L., exec. vice-pres., Children's Hospital National Medical Center, Washington, DC '76
BROWN, DONALD S., proj. dir., The Hysen Group, Livonia, MI '83 (FOOD)
BROWN, DONN W., dir. plant oper. and maint., Saint Joseph Health Center Kansas, Kansas City, MO '84 (ENG)
BROWN, DONNA P., RN, assoc. dir. nrsg., Methodist Hospital-Central Unit, Memphis, TN '81 (NURS)
BROWN, DOROTHY J., dir. emp. rel., Catherine McAuley Health Center, Ann Arbor, MI '84 (PERS)
BROWN, DORSYL CHAMBERS, dist. mgr., ARA Services, Hospital Food Management, Environmental Service, Inc., Omaha, NE '71 (FOOD)
BROWN, DOUGLAS R., PhD, dir., Program in Health Services Administration, Cornell University, Ithaca, NY '79 (PLNG)
BROWN, EDWARD COLEMAN, dir., University Health Service, Central Michigan University, Mount Pleasant, MI '76 (PUR)
BROWN, EDWARD, risk mgr., Newington Children's Hospital, Newington, CT '86 (RISK)
BROWN, ELIZABETH L., RN, dir. nrsg., Westview Hospital, Indianapolis, IN '82 (NURS)
BROWN, ELIZABETH VINCENT, vice-pres., Askey Associates, Keene, NH '86
BROWN, EMMA JEAN, assoc. dir. med. soc. work, University of Cincinnati Hospital, Cincinnati, OH '83 (SOC)
BROWN, ERNEST H., area supv., Florida Office of Licensure and Certification, Jacksonville, FL '57 (LIFE)
BROWN, EUGENIE V., dir. human res., Bermuda Hospitals Board, Hamilton, Bermuda '84 (PERS)
BROWN, EVELYNN G., sr. vice-pres. corp. serv., North Colorado Medical Center, Greeley, CO '80 (PR) (PLNG)
BROWN, F. FAYE, St. Helena, CA '85
BROWN, F. JUDY, dir. pur., Hospital of the Medical College of Pennsylvania, Philadelphia, PA '85 (PUR)
BROWN, FRANCES R., consult., Pannel, Kerr, Foester, Atlanta, GA '83 (MGMT)
BROWN, FRANCIS A., atty., Calais Regional Hospital, Calais, ME '77 (ATTY)
BROWN, LT. FRANCIS CHRISTOPHER, MSC USN, U. S. Naval Hospital, Subic Bay, FPO San Francisco, CA '79
BROWN, FRED T. JR., pres., Voluntary Hospitals-Carolinas, Charlotte, NC '85
BROWN, FRED W., chief eng., Carlinville Area Hospital, Carlinville, IL '81 (ENG)
BROWN, FREDERIC W. JR., adm., United Memorial Hospital, Greenville, MI '79 (PLNG)
BROWN, FREDERICK L., pres. and chief exec. off., Christian Hospitals Northeast-Northwest, St. Louis, MO '83
BROWN, GARY W., atty., Sibley Memorial Hospital, Washington, DC '83 (ATTY)
BROWN, H. DAVIDA RILEY, mgr. pers., Forbes Regional Health Center, Monroeville, PA '83 (PERS)
BROWN, HELEN INEZ, chief soc. serv., District of Columbia General Hospital, Washington, DC '77 (SOC)
BROWN, HELENE F., risk mgt. serv. rep., St. Paul Fire and Marine Insurance Company, Brookfield, WI '83 (RISK)
BROWN, HOMER L., mgr. safety and security, Daniel Drake Memorial Hospital, Cincinnati, OH '86 (RISK)
BROWN, J. MERRITT, assoc. adm., Framingham Union Hospital, Framingham, MA '74
BROWN, JACK, asst. dir. eng. and actg. dir. safety, Children's Hospital, Boston, MA '84
BROWN, JACQUELINE L., dir. commun., Children's Hospital of Philadelphia, Philadelphia, PA '77 (ENG)
BROWN, JAMES A., reg. vice-pres., Food Dimensions, Inc., Vancouver, WA '76 (FOOD)
BROWN, JAMES BROOKS, pres., Health South, Inc., Jacksonville, FL '83 (PLNG)
BROWN, JAMES W. JR., adm., Russell Hospital, Alexander City, AL '49 (LIFE)
BROWN, JAMES, dir. plant oper., Houston International Hospital, Houston, TX '85 (ENG)
BROWN, JANE E., dir. pub. rel., Mercy Medical Center, Durango, CO '86 (PR)
BROWN, JANET E., RN, dir. nrsg., Braddock General Hospital, Braddock, PA '83 (NURS)
BROWN, JANICE L., RN, dir. nrsg. serv., Cass County Memorial Hospital, Atlantic, IA '86 (NURS)
BROWN, JEAN B., dir. vol. serv., Baton Rouge General Medical Center, Baton Rouge, LA '75 (VOL)
BROWN, JERRY F., dir. strategic implementation, Healthlink, Portland, OR '83 (PLNG)
BROWN, JERRY, chief eng., Physicians Hospital, Reno, NV '86 (ENG)
BROWN, MAJ. JIMMY C., MSC USAF, adm. med. res. mgt., Wilford Hall U. S. Air Force Medical Center, Lackland AFB, TX '86 (PLNG)
BROWN, JOAN HASTINGS, dir. vol. serv., Georgetown University Medical Center, Washington, DC '83 (VOL)
BROWN, JOAN S., chief med. rec. and risk mgr., U. S. Army Community Hospital, Fort Carson, CO '81 (RISK)
BROWN, JOANNE E., bus. analyst, Humana Inc., Louisville, KY '81
BROWN, JODEE B., pub. rel. asst., Intermountain Health Care, Inc., Salt Lake City, UT '84 (PR)
BROWN, JOHN J., Jonesboro, TN '80 (ENG)
BROWN, JOHN L., pres., Community General Hospital of Greater Syracuse, Syracuse, NY '47 (LIFE)
BROWN, JOSEPH L., dir. fin. and prof. serv., Montefiore Medical Center, Bronx, NY '85
BROWN, JUDITH A., mgr. pur., Lawrence General Hospital, Lawrence, MA '86 (PUR)
BROWN, KAREN J., RN, dir. nrsg., Rockford Memorial Hospital, Rockford, IL '85 (NURS)
BROWN, KAREN M., RN, clin. mgr. maternal and child health, Bay Medical Center, Bay City, MI '84 (NURS)
BROWN, KATHERINE E., RN, dir. nrsg., Horsham Clinic, Ambler, PA '85 (NURS)
BROWN, KATHLEEN LIPIEC, dir. sales mgt., Hotel Dieu Hospital, New Orleans, LA '82 (SOC)(PR) (PLNG)
BROWN, KELLY N., atty., Pullman Memorial Hospital, Pullman, WA '85 (ATTY)
BROWN, KENNETH C., dir. plant oper., Orange Memorial Hospital, Orange, TX '85 (ENG)
BROWN, KEVIN D., vice-pres. plng. and mktg., St. Clair Memorial Hospital, Pittsburgh, PA '84 (PR) (PLNG)
BROWN, LARRY E., supv. cent. serv., Middle Tennessee Medical Center, Murfreesboro, TN '86 (CS)
BROWN, LAVERNE KINDRED, RN, vice-pres. nrsg. serv., Western Baptist Hospital, Paducah, KY '79 (NURS)
BROWN, LEAH RUBBA, dir. soc. serv., Kennedy Memorial Hospitals University Medical Center, Stratford, NJ '81 (SOC)
BROWN, LEE R., chief vol. serv., Veterans Administration Medical Center, Bay Pines, FL '86 (VOL)
BROWN, LES, vice-pres. plng., St. Joseph's Hospital, Asheville, NC '83 (PLNG)
BROWN, LIBBY, supv. pur., Monticello Medical Center, Longview, WA '85 (PUR)
BROWN, LILLIAN E., RN, dir. nrsg., University of California Irvine Medical Center, Orange, CA '68 (NURS)
BROWN, LINDA A., RN, dir. nrsg. affairs, Memorial Hospital, South Bend, IN '84 (NURS)
BROWN, LIZ, dir. pub. rel., Lloyd Noland Hospital and Health Ctrs, Birmingham, AL '86 (PR)
BROWN, LOIS W., asst. dir. nrsg., St. Mary's Hospital, Waterbury, CT '85 (EDUC)
BROWN, LORRAINE C., RN, coor. clin. and outpat serv., AMI Parkway Hospital, Houston, TX '87 (AMB)
BROWN, M. JOYCE, coor. lab. educ., St. Joseph Health Care Corporation, Albuquerque, NM '86 (EDUC)
BROWN, MADISON B., MD, (ret.), South Burlington, VT '40 (LIFE)
BROWN, MARGARET V., dir. pers., St. Joseph's Hospital, Minot, ND '85 (PERS)
BROWN, MARGE M., health care spec., Truitt Brothers Cannery, Salem, OR '84 (FOOD)
BROWN, MARIE W., dir. vol. serv., Beaufort County Hospital, Washington, NC '83 (VOL)
BROWN, MARJORIE E., RN, coor. nrsg. staff dev., Lovelace Medical Center, Albuquerque, NM '82 (EDUC)
BROWN, MARY H., RN, dir. nrsg. prac., Memorial Hospital for Cancer and Allied Diseases, New York, NY '77 (NURS)
BROWN, MARY M., mgr. vol. serv., St. Vincent Hospital and Health Center, Indianapolis, IN '75 (VOL)
BROWN, SR. MARY NOEL, RN, dir. adm. nrsg., Good Samaritan Medical Center and Rehabilitation Center, Zanesville, OH '82 (NURS)
BROWN, MARY, RN, coor. qual. assur. and risk mgt., Glynn-Brunswick Memorial Hospital, Brunswick, GA '87 (RISK)
BROWN, MICHAEL H., contr., St. Catherine Hospital on Half Moon Bay, Moss Beach, CA '83 (RISK)
BROWN, MICHAEL H., student, Program in Health Service Administration, School of Health Professions, Governors State University, Park Forest South, IL '86
BROWN, MICHAEL N., atty., Hillsborough County Hospital, Tampa, FL '77 (ATTY)
BROWN, MICHAEL S., pres., Telehealth Associates, Needham, MA '85
BROWN, MICHAEL, exec. vice-pres., Gerber Alley and Company, Norcross, GA '86
BROWN, MILLIE S., coor. pat. rep., St. Paul-Ramsey Medical Center, St. Paul, MN '87 (PAT)
BROWN, MONTAGUE, DrPH, Shawnee Mission, KS '70 (ATTY)
BROWN, MYRA R., dir. soc. work, Southern Baptist Hospital, New Orleans, LA '72 (SOC)
BROWN, NANCY A., RN, dir. nrsg., Baptist Medical Center, Columbia, SC '82 (NURS)
BROWN, NANCY G., student, Northeastern University, Boston, MA '86 (PLNG)
BROWN, NANCY R., dir. vol. serv., University of Maryland Medical Systems, Baltimore, MD '74 (VOL)
BROWN, NEAL, dir. human res., United Community Hospital, Grove City, PA '80 (PERS)
BROWN, NORMA E., RN, vice-pres. nrsg., St. Joseph's Hospital, Stockton, CA '86 (NURS)
BROWN, OLIVE JANE, (ret.), East Lansing, MI '22 (LIFE)
BROWN, PATRICIA A., dir. pub. rel., Skokie Valley Hospital, Skokie, IL '86 (PR)
BROWN, PATRICIA ALLEN, dir. soc. serv., Presbyterian Hospital, Oklahoma City, OK '79 (SOC)
BROWN, PATRICIA H., RN, asst. adm., St. Benedict's Hospital, Ogden, UT '77 (NURS)
BROWN, PATRICIA L., dir. soc. serv. and discharge plng., Valley Children's Hospital, Fresno, CA '86 (SOC)
BROWN, PATRICIA M., RN, vice-pres. pat. serv., Fallston General Hospital, Fallston, MD '81 (NURS)
BROWN, PAUL C., mech. eng., Oklahoma Health Planning Commission, Oklahoma City, OK '71 (ENG)
BROWN, PAULINE F., dir. food serv., San Clemente General Hospital, San Clemente, CA '75 (FOOD)
BROWN, PEGGY M. V., dir. pers. and educ., St. Joseph's Hospital, Minot, ND '84 (EDUC)
BROWN, PEGGY W., dir. trng., Baptist Medical Center, San Antonio, TX '86 (EDUC)
BROWN, PENNY C., med. sup. tech., Veterans Administration Medical Center, Grand Island, NE '87 (CS)
BROWN, PHILIP A. III, sr. vice-pres., Lehigh Valley Hospital Center, Allentown, PA '80
BROWN, PHILLIP B., dir. video commun., East Alabama Medical Center, Opelika, AL '85 (PR)
BROWN, RACHELLE A., RN, dir. med. and surg. nrsg., La Grange Memorial Hospital, La Grange, IL '85 (NURS)
BROWN, REBECCA C., RN, dir. nrsg. serv., Addison Gilbert Hospital, Gloucester, MA '80 (NURS)
BROWN, RENEE J., coor. mktg., Memorial Health Ventures, Houston, TX '84
BROWN, REX H., vice-pres., St. Luke's Hospital, Racine, WI '83 (PERS)
BROWN, RICHARD L., exec. vice-pres., Walthamweston Hospital and Medical Center, Waltham, MA '70
BROWN, RICHARD SCOTT, dir. legal serv., Good Samaritan Hospital and Health Center, Dayton, OH '79 (ATTY)
BROWN, RICHARD W., pres., Research Medical Center, Kansas City, MO '73
BROWN, ROBERT C., risk mgr., Flint Osteopathic Hospital, Flint, MI '83 (RISK)
BROWN, ROBERT H., mgr. pers., Lenoir Memorial Hospital, Kinston, NC '85 (PERS)
BROWN, ROBERT J., atty., York Hospital, York, PA '68 (ATTY)
BROWN, ROBERTA W., RN, asst. adm. and dir. nrsg., Grace Hospital, Detroit, MI '84 (NURS)
BROWN, RODGER, dir. pers., North Mississippi Medical Center, Tupelo, MS '81 (PERS)
BROWN, ROGER K., Clifton Park, NY '63
BROWN, LT. COL. ROGER L., MSC USA, biomedical info. syst. off., Trimis Army, Washington, DC '78
BROWN, ROSEMARY E., (ret.), Toledo, OH '69 (FOOD)
BROWN, RUSSELL W., vice-pres. matl. mgt., St. Francis Hospital, Charleston, WV '84 (PUR)
BROWN, SHEILA K., dir. vol. serv., Anderson Memorial Hospital, Anderson, SC '86 (VOL)
BROWN, SHIRLEY, supv. environ. serv., Ephraim McDowell Regional Medical Center, Danville, KY '86 (ENVIRON)
BROWN, SINOMA, RN, clin. dir. nrsg. and oper. room, Shands Hospital, Gainesville, FL '86 (NURS)
BROWN, STEVEN J., dir. bldg. serv., Presbyterian Home for Central New York, Inc., New Hartford, NY '85 (ENG)
BROWN, TED R., atty., Ball Memorial Hospital, Muncie, IN '83 (ATTY)
BROWN, THOMAS C. JR., atty., Fairfax Hospital, Falls Church, VA '74 (ATTY)
BROWN, THOMAS D., atty., Orthopaedic Hospital of Charlotte, Charlotte, NC '86 (ATTY)
BROWN, THOMAS E., Germantown, TN '86 (PLNG)
BROWN, THOMAS R., dir. pers., St. Jude Hospital, Fullerton Division, Fullerton, CA '78 (PERS)
BROWN, VENEL D., mgr. compensation and benefits, Mary Washington Hospital, Fredericksburg, VA '86 (PERS)
BROWN, VICTORIA WILLIAMS, adm. soc. serv., Rahway Hospital, Rahway, NJ '84 (SOC)
BROWN, VIRGINIA E., dir. soc. serv., Oak Hill Hospital, Joplin, MO '85 (SOC)
BROWN, WALLACE E. JR., adm. mgr. dent. and oral maxillo-facil. surg., Sinai Hospital of Detroit, Detroit, MI '81
BROWN, WALTER, atty., Jefferson Davis Memorial Hospital, Natchez, MS '84 (ATTY)
BROWN, WILLIAM A., vice-pres., Jewish Hospital, Louisville, KY '79 (PUR)
BROWN, WILLIAM C., chief exec. off., Georgia Baptist Medical Center, Atlanta, GA '69
BROWN, WILLIAM H., dir. eng., Germantown Hospital and Medical Center, Philadelphia, PA '79 (ENG)
BROWN, WILLIAM KING, Weatherford, TX '59
BROWN, WINFORD L., buyer, New York University Medical Center, New York, NY '86 (PUR)
BROWN, ZIGRIDA R., dir. staff dev., Blessing Hospital, Quincy, IL '84 (EDUC)
BROWN, ZOLTAN W., dir. pub. rel. and mktg., Carleton Memorial Hospital, Woodstock, N.B., Canada '86 (PR)
BROWNE, C. A. IRENE, vice-pres., Bond Investors Guaranty, New York, NY '78
BROWNE, JAMES P., asst. adm. facil. mgt., University of Tennessee Memorial Hospital, Knoxville, TN '81 (ENG)
BROWNE, MICHAEL, vice-pres. human res., Memorial Hospital for Cancer and Allied Diseases, New York, NY '69 (PERS)
BROWNE, PAUL E., mgr. food serv., Beth Israel Hospital, Boston, MA '84 (FOOD)
BROWNE, SHEILA T., dir. pers., Memorial Hospital, Pawtucket, RI '80 (PERS)
BROWNE, TONY, pres., Management Communications, Sacramento, CA '80 (PR)
BROWNE, YVONNE, dir. commun. rel. and vol., Mary Immaculate Hospital, Jamaica, NY '85 (VOL)
BROWNING, FRANKIE C., asst. adm., Leesburg Regional Medical Center, Leesburg, FL '80
BROWNING, GAIL C., RN, dir. nrsg., York Hospital, York, ME '71 (NURS)

BROWNING, JEWELL B. HORN, dir. soc. serv., Community Hospital of Roanoke Valley, Roanoke, VA '66 (SOC)
BROWNING, SR. M. CATHERINE, vice-pres., Saint Thomas Medical Center, Akron, OH '67
BROWNING, PATRICIA A., dir. soc. serv., Baptist Regional Medical Center, Corbin, KY '82 (SOC)
BROWNING, RAYMOND, assoc. dir. maint., St. Anthony Medical Center, Columbus, OH '79 (ENG)
BROWNING, ROBERT K., assoc. dir. plant oper., Vanderbilt University Hospital, Nashville, TN '85 (ENG)
BROWNING, SUSAN K., dir. soc. serv., Bethania Regional Health Center, Wichita Falls, TX '81 (SOC)
BROWNING, VINCENT LEE, dir. matl. mgt. and environ. serv., Providence Hospital, Anchorage, AK '67 (PUR)
BROWNLEE, WALTER W., chief exec. off., Jefferson County Hospital, Fairfield, IA '87 (AMB)
BROWNSBERGER, PATRICIA A., dir. matl. mgt., Cass County Memorial Hospital, Atlantic, IA '86 (PUR)
BROWNSTEIN, CINDY, assoc. dir. cont. educ., Hospital Association of New York State, Albany, NY '80 (EDUC)
BROWNSTEIN, MERYL, sr. consult., Network, Inc., Randolph, NJ '80
BROY, LARRY J., trng. mgr., Dow Corning Wright, Arlington, TN '85 (EDUC)
BROYLES, MAJ. THOMAS E., MSC USA, student, Command and General Staff College, Fort Leavenworth, KS '79
BROZ, WILLIAM JACK JR., dir. pub. rel., St. Joseph Hospital and Health Center, Lorain, OH '81 (PR)
BROZOWSKI, LCDR DENNIS R., MSC USN, Department of the Navy, Bureau of Medicine and Surgery, Washington, DC '83
BRUBAKER, A. FRANCES, RN, supv. nrsg., Beaches Hospital, Jacksonville Beach, FL '77 (NURS)
BRUBAKER, CRISTINA C., dir. soc. serv., St. Elizabeth Medical Center, Dayton, OH '83 (SOC)
BRUBAKER, DANIEL W., dir. pers., Robinson Memorial Hospital, Ravenna, OH '83 (PERS)
BRUBAKER, KAREN, RN, coor. outpatient surg., Tarpon Springs General Hospital, Tarpon Springs, FL '86 (AMB)
BRUBAKER, KATHY MATTHEWS, RN, dir. nrsg., Chelsea Community Hospital, Chelsea, MI '77 (NURS)
BRUCATO, ROBERT V., owner, Ceilingco, Anaheim, CA '87 (ENVIRON)
BRUCE, ALFRED D., dir. pub. affairs, Mount Ascutney Hospital and Health Center, Windsor, VT '84 (PLNG)
BRUCE, ANNE L., RN, supv., Ernst and Whinney, Chicago, IL '84 (NURS)
BRUCE, D. CHRISTINE, EdD, mgr. commun. and res. dev., Sch Health Care System, Houston, TX '83 (EDUC)(PLNG)
BRUCE, DOUGLAS A., dir. pub. affairs, University Hospital, Lexington, KY '86 (PR)
BRUCE, EDWARD C., dir. eng., proc. and distrib., Presbyterian Hospital, Oklahoma City, OK '73 (ENG)
BRUCE, KAREN, coor. pat. and commun. educ., St. Francis Hospital, Greenville, SC '84 (EDUC)
BRUCE, LEROY, dir. maint., Beaumont Neurological Hospital, Beaumont, TX '85 (ENG)
BRUCE, ROBERT O., exec. vice-pres., Sun Coast Hospital, Largo, FL '63 (PLNG)
BRUCE, SHEILA K., RN, vice-pres., Holy Cross Hospital, Mission Hills, CA '85 (NURS)
BRUCH, HARRY C., dir. ldry. and linen, Robinson Memorial Hospital, Ravenna, OH '86 (ENVIRON)
BRUCHER, WILLIAM P., dir. pers., Saint Mary Hospital, Langhorne, PA '86 (PERS)
BRUCHERT, FAY A., mgr. sup., proc. and distrib., St. Mary's Hospital and Rehabilitation Center, Minneapolis, MN '82 (CS)
BRUCKER, WILLIS H., pres., Cooley Dickinson Hospital, Northampton, MA '72
BRUCKMANN, C. ROBERT, vice-pres. fin., Baystate Medical Center, Springfield, MA '68 (MGMT)
BRUDER, PAUL T., vice-pres., Center for Applied Bioethics, McLean, VA '85
BRUDEREK, FRANK J., asst. pur., New York University Medical Center, New York, NY '86 (PUR)
BRUECKNER, GERRY, RN, adm. dir., Baylor Home Care, Dallas, TX '87 (AMB)
BRUEHL, RALPH A., asst. adm. matl. mgt., Nexus Healthcare Corporation, Mount Holly, NJ '77 (PUR)
BRUELL, ANDREA P., dir. mktg., Horsham Clinic, Ambler, PA '86 (PR)
BRUEN, SR. M. REGINA, adm. health care, Sisters of the Sorrowful Mother, Milwaukee, WI '74
BRUENGER, DONNA L., dir. pers., Memorial Hospital, Carthage, IL '83 (PERS)
BRUENING, LYNNE, dir. pers., Bon Secours Hospital, Baltimore, MD '79 (PERS)
BRUENING, PAULA L., RN, dir. nrsg., Loudoun Memorial Hospital, Leesburg, VA '86 (NURS)
BRUFF, EDWARD G., dir. matl. mgt., St. Luke's Hospital, Saginaw, MI '83 (PUR)
BRUGGMAN, RAYMOND W., RN, supv. oper., Hospital of the University of Pennsylvania, Philadelphia, PA '85 (ENG)
BRUGLER, MARY LOIS, supv. fiscal oper., Preakness Hospital, Paterson, NJ '85 (MGMT)
BRUHN, CHARLOTTE C., RN, dir. nrsg. serv., McCullough-Hyde Memorial Hospital, Oxford, OH '84 (NURS)
BRUINS, GARY F., RN, dir. nrsg., Illini Hospital, Silvis, IL '80 (NURS)
BRULET, ROBERT W., mgt. eng., Massachusetts General Hospital, Boston, MA '84 (MGMT)
BRULEY, MARILYNN, RN, dir. pat. rep., St. Joseph Hospital West, Mount Clemens, MI '78 (PAT)
BRULL-NATER, JORGE, Rio Piedras, P.R. '82 (LIFE)
BRULOTTE, ROSEMARY S., RN, dir. mental health nrsg. educ., Norwich Hospital, Norwich, CT '86 (EDUC)
BRUMBACK, BARBARA M., info. off., University of Virginia Hospitals, Charlottesville, VA '86 (PR)
BRUMBAUGH, MARK A., facil. eng., U. S. Public Health Service Alaska Native Medical Center, Anchorage, AK '86 (ENG)
BRUMBAUGH, RITA, RN, vice-pres. pat. care, Timken Mercy Medical Center, Canton, OH '79 (NURS)
BRUMFIELD, CLYDE E., asst. adm., St. Anthony Hospital, Oklahoma City, OK '74
BRUMFIELD, ROBERT W., atty., Southwest Mississippi Medical Center, McComb, MS '85 (ATTY)
BRUMLEY, DOYCE D., dir. pers., Stillwater Medical Center, Stillwater, OK '81 (PERS)
BRUMLEY, PAT M., dir. pub. rel., Marion County General Hospital, Hamilton, AL '82 (PR)
BRUMM, LIZABETH G., dir. vol. serv., Lincoln General Hospital, Lincoln, NE '75 (VOL)
BRUMMETT, PAUL O., dir. matl. support, Department of Health Administration, Duke University, Durham, NC '85 (PUR)
BRUNDAGE, VERONICA F., mgr. cent. serv., St. Mary's Hospital, Passaic, NJ '81 (CS)
BRUNE, ROGER W., dir. pers., Arkansas Children's Hospital, Little Rock, AR '84 (PERS)
BRUNELL, MICHAEL J., assoc., Dillon, Read and Company, Inc., New York, NY '85
BRUNER, DOROTHY M., RN, head nrs. sup., proc. and distrib., Penrose Hospitals, Colorado Springs, CO '85 (CS)
BRUNER, ROBERT B., pres., Mount Sinai Hospital, Hartford, CT '67
BRUNET, JUDY K., asst. dir. pers. serv., Phoenix General Hospital, Phoenix, AZ '85 (PERS)
BRUNETTE, MARIAN B., RN, asst. dir. nrsg., Fairview Riverside Hospital, Minneapolis, MN '86 (NURS)
BRUNGARD, W. ROBERT, pres., Mercy Midlands, Omaha, NE '55 (LIFE)
BRUNICK, MARK M., dir. matl. mgt., McKennan Hospital, Sioux Falls, SD '82 (CS)
BRUNING, DARLYNNE CARLTON, dir. vol. serv., Seventh Ward General Hospital, Hammond, LA '86 (VOL)
BRUNING, LORI R., coor. vol. serv., Lutheran Hospital, Moline, IL '86 (VOL)
BRUNINGS, RUTH, dir. soc. serv., Rancho Los Amigos Medical Center, Downey, CA '68 (SOC)
BRUNINI, ED JR., atty., St. Dominic-Jackson Memorial Hospital, Jackson, MS '77 (ATTY)
BRUNKOW, DEBI, serv. coor., Rehabilitation Institute of Oregon, Portland, OR '85 (PR) (PLNG)
BRUNNER, ARNOLD R., dir. matl. mgt., Hei Central Purchasing, Houston, TX '83 (PUR)
BRUNNER, NANCY A., dir. educ. serv., Mount Carmel Medical Center, Columbus, OH '86 (EDUC)
BRUNNER, SUZANNE, RN, dir. nrsg. educ., qual. assur. and res., Children's Hospital Medical Center, Cincinnati, OH '85 (NURS)
BRUNO, BARBARA K., RN, dir. nrsg. serv., Valley Regional Hospital, Claremont, NH '81 (NURS)
BRUNO, CAROL E., dir. pub. rel., Good Samaritan Hospital, West Palm Beach, FL '80 (PR)(VOL)
BRUNO, GLORIA, RN, vice-pres., Greenwich Hospital, Greenwich, CT '78 (NURS)
BRUNO, JOHN M., dir. environ. serv., Holy Redeemer Hospital and Medical Center, Meadowbrook, PA '77 (ENVIRON)
BRUNO, RICHARD J., dir. matl. mgt., Andrew Kaul Memorial Hospital, St. Marys, PA '86 (PUR)
BRUNS, ARTHUR I., dir. mktg. and long range plng., Memorial Hospital, Cambridge, MN '85 (PLNG)
BRUNS, KENNETH, MD, asst. prof., University Hospital, St. Louis University Center, St. Louis, MO '87 (AMB)
BRUNS, KRISTIN K., student, Duke University, Department of Health Administration, Durham, NC '86
BRUNS, PHYLLIS M., dir. vol., Sherman Hospital, Elgin, IL '84 (VOL)
BRUNSMANN, JULIUS B., dir. plant serv., Kaiser Foundation Mental Health Center, Los Angeles, CA '82 (ENG)
BRUNSON, PAMELA J., dir. pers., St. Clair Regional Hospital, Pell City, AL '85 (PERS)
BRUNT, BARBARA A., dir. staff dev., Aultman Hospital, Canton, OH '85 (EDUC)
BRUNTON, MARGARET J., RN, dir. prof. serv., Meadville Medical Center, Meadville, PA '78 (NURS)
BRUSCHETTE, JEROME A., Roslindale, MA '81 (ENG)
BRUSCHI, DENNIS J., asst. dir., Newark Beth Israel Medical Center, Newark, NJ '71
BRUSH, JULIA M., RN, dir. nrs., Aliquippa Hospital, Aliquippa, PA '73 (NURS)
BRUSH, THOMAS M., asst. vice-pres., Texas Hospital Association, Shared Hospital Electrical Safety Services, Waco, TX '73 (ENG)
BRUSKOF, JERROLD B., dir. matl. mgt., Frankford Hospital of the City of Philadelphia, Philadelphia, PA '72 (PUR)
BRUSS, MAJ. DONALD J., MSC USA, student, Army-Baylor University, Program in Health Care Administration, Fort Sam Houston, TX '80
BRUSS, ERNEST, mgr., Energy Productivity, Albuquerque, NM '86 (ENG)
BRUST, COLETTE KAY, RN, asst. dir. nrsg., St. Luke's Hospital, Aberdeen, SD '81 (NURS)
BRUST, CYNTHIA P., dir. pub. rel., Midland Memorial Hospital, Midland, TX '85 (PR)
BRUTLAG, JOHN A., supv. sterilization, preparation and decontamination, Veterans Administration Medical Center, Phoenix, AZ '84 (CS)
BRUTON, DONA L., dir. cont. care, Eskaton American River Healthcare Center, Carmichael, CA '67 (NURS)
BRUTON, PETER W., vice-pres., Citicorp Investment Bank, New York, NY '86
BRUZZESE, FRANK J., atty., Ohio Valley Hospital, Steubenville, OH '85 (ATTY)
BRYAN, ALFRED J. JR., exec. dir., North Arundel Hospital, Glen Burnie, MD '82 (PLNG)
BRYAN, ALICE M., RN, nrsg. adm., Madera Community Hospital, Madera, CA '87 (NURS)
BRYAN, ALICE R., risk mgr., Adventist Health Systems-West, Roseville, CA '87 (RISK)
BRYAN, HARRY, assoc. dir. soc. work serv., University Hospital, Stony Brook, NY '83 (SOC)
BRYAN, LAURA G., dir. diet., Harper Hospital, Detroit, MI '68 (FOOD)
BRYAN, LOIS G., asst. dir. food serv., Sea View Hospital and Home, Staten Island, NY '85 (FOOD)
BRYAN, MARGARET B., assoc. chief nrsg. serv. educ., Veterans Administration Medical Center, Lincoln, NE '83 (EDUC)
BRYAN, WILLIAM E., MD, asst. vice-pres. strategic plng. and mktg., Kennedy Memorial Hospitals University Medical Center, Stratford, NJ '86 (PLNG)
BRYAN, WILLIAM H., Riverside, CA '82 (ENG)
BRYAN, WILLIAM H., dir. mktg. and plng., Northeast Medical Center Hospital, Humble, TX '86 (PLNG)
BRYANT, BARBARA EVERITT, sr. vice-pres., Market Opinion Research, Detroit, MI '86 (PLNG)
BRYANT, BURT B., dir. environ. serv., Estelle Doheny Eye Hospital, Los Angeles, CA '85 (ENG)
BRYANT, CAROL A., adm., Salvation Army Booth Memorial Hospital, Cleveland, OH '86 (PLNG)
BRYANT, DIANE C., mgr. food serv., Greenville Hospital, Jersey City, NJ '80 (FOOD)
BRYANT, DIANNE F., coor. nrsg. educ., Richland Memorial Hospital, Columbia, SC '82 (EDUC)
BRYANT, DORIS M., asst. dir. educ. serv., Mississippi Baptist Medical Center, Jackson, MS '83 (EDUC)
BRYANT, GARY M., dir. support serv., Midwest City Memorial Hospital, Midwest City, OK '85 (PUR)
BRYANT, HANK, chief biomedical eng., Louis A. Weiss Memorial Hospital, Chicago, IL '82 (ENG)
BRYANT, JANE J., dir. risk mgt., Greenville Hospital System, Greenville, SC '80 (RISK)
BRYANT, L. EDWARD JR., atty., Rush-Presbyterian-St. Luke's Medical Center, Chicago, IL '73 (ATTY)
BRYANT, L. GERALD, exec. vice-pres., Baylor Health Care System, Dallas, TX '79 (PLNG)
BRYANT, LINDA Z., dir. human res., Sharp Rees-Stealy Medical Group, San Diego, CA '87 (PERS)
BRYANT, LUPE BARRERA, dir. vol. serv., Saint Joseph Health Center Kansas, Kansas City, MO '87 (VOL)
BRYANT, MARTHA S., dir. pers., Humana Hospital -Huntsville, Huntsville, AL '82 (PERS)
BRYANT, ROBERT E., (ret.), Chicago, IL '75
BRYANT, WILBUR G., eng. proj. consult., Wilson Memorial Hospital, Wilson, NC '78 (ENG)
BRYANT, WILLIAM H., dist. vice-pres., Hospital Corporation of America Management Company, Roanoke, VA '84
BRYANT, YVONNE N., atty., Mercy Hospital and Medical Center, Chicago, IL '71 (ATTY)
BRYE, PAUL E., health care consult., Hbe Corporation, St. Louis, MO '86 (PLNG)
BRYSON, JAMES M., dist. mgr., Dearborn Chemical Company, Houston, TX '84 (ENG)
BRYSON, JERRY L., pres., Medical Marketing Associates, Brentwood, TN '77 (PLNG)
BRZUZ, RICHARD W., adm., Shriners Hospitals for Crippled Children, Erie, PA '84 (PLNG)
BUBAR, MARLENE M., dir. soc. serv., Eastern Idaho Regional Medical Center, Idaho Falls, ID '87 (SOC)
BUBBA, JOSEPH A., atty., Lehigh Valley Hospital Center, Allentown, PA '87 (ATTY)
BUBLITZ, NANCY J., RN, head nrs. emer. room, outpatient and center for digestive disease, Trinity Memorial Hospital, Cudahy, WI '87 (AMB)
BUBOLTZ, CHARLES A., adm. dir. plant eng., Geisinger Medical Center, Danville, PA '82 (MGMT)
BUCALO, PATRICIA, atty., Weissburg and Aronson, Inc., San Francisco, CA '85 (ATTY)
BUCCAFURNI, ANTHONY D., adm. asst., Atlantic City Medical Center, Atlantic City, NJ '78
BUCCI-SHIFFER, CAROL, asst. exec. dir., Westmoreland Hospital, Greensburg, PA '86
BUCCI, ROBERT L., atty., Hardin Memorial Hospital, Kenton, OH '85 (ATTY)
BUCCINI, EUGENE P., PhD, mgr. labor rel., Albert Einstein College of Medicine, Bronx, NY '75 (PERS)
BUCCITELLI, FRANK, dir. pub. rel., Holy Family Hospital, Des Plaines, IL '85 (PR)
BUCH, RONALD M., dir. chaplaincy and soc. serv., Northwest Community Hospital, Arlington Heights, IL '85 (SOC)
BUCHANAN, ANCEL L., pres., Imi, Inc., Oklahoma City, OK '80
BUCHANAN, B. VIRGINIA, RN, dir. nrsg. serv., McMinnville Community Hospital, McMinnville, OR '78 (NURS)
BUCHANAN, BRUCE F., assoc. adm., Providence Medical Center, Seattle, WA '76
BUCHANAN, JERI J., mgr. emp., Regional Medical Center at Memphis, Memphis, TN '86 (PERS)
BUCHANAN, JOHN D., mgr. plant oper. and maint., Augustana Hospital and Health Care Center, Chicago, IL '84 (ENG)
BUCHANAN, JOHN D. JR., atty., Tallahassee Memorial Regional Medical Center, Tallahassee, FL '77 (ATTY)
BUCHANAN, LARRY E., atty., Martin Memorial Hospital, Stuart, FL '79 (ATTY)
BUCHANAN, LINDA, asst. adm. soc. serv., Kaiser Permenante, Downey, CA '85 (SOC)
BUCHANAN, NELLES V., bd. chm., Alberta Blue Cross Plan, Edmonton, Alta., Canada '63 (HON)
BUCHANAN, PATTY E., dir. commun. rel. and mktg., West Park Hospital, Cody, WY '86 (PR)
BUCHANAN, ROBERT P. JR., dir. eng., North Carolina Baptist Hospital, Winston-Salem, NC '77 (ENG)
BUCHANAN, ROBERT STEPHEN, supv. cent. serv., Holston Valley Hospital and Medical Center, Kingsport, TN '75 (CS)
BUCHANAN, SHIRLEY STRUTT, pat. rep., Lexington Memorial Hospital, Lexington, NC '86 (PAT)
BUCHANAN, VICTOR, atty., Memorial Mission Hospital, Asheville, NC '78 (ATTY)
BUCHANNA, RICHARD S., head matl. and sup., Methodist Hospital of Indiana, Indianapolis, IN '83 (PUR)

BUCHE, DANIEL L., dir. educ., Mercy Hospitals of Kansas, Fort Scott, KS '85 (EDUC)
BUCHER, ANN K., RN, coor. pat. health educ., McClellan Memorial Veterans Hospital, Little Rock, AR '84 (EDUC)
BUCHER, DONALD F., supv. cent. sup., Oswego Hospital, Oswego, NY '85 (CS)
BUCHER, LINDA L., dir. vol. serv., Fort Hamilton-Hughes Memorial Hospital, Hamilton, OH '79 (VOL)
BUCHER, MARILYN J., pur. asst., Hotel Dieu Hospital, New Orleans, LA '83 (PUR)
BUCHHEIM, ROGENE, pat. rep., St. Luke's Methodist Hospital, Cedar Rapids, IA '79 (PAT)
BUCHHEIT, SANDY, RN, asst. dir. nrsg., Southeast Missouri Hospital, Cape Girardeau, MO '85 (CS)
BUCHHOLZ, DIANE M., mgt. eng., St. Joseph Hospital, Flint, MI '86 (MGMT)
BUCHHOLZ, KARL E., dir. soc. work and rehab. serv., Bellevue Hospital Center, New York, NY '67 (SOC)
BUCHHOLZ, PAMELA M., RN, dir. nrsg. and pat. care serv., Waupun Memorial Hospital, Waupun, WI '85 (NURS)
BUCHMANN, ANNA MARIE, PhD, vice-pres. human res., Children's Memorial Hospital, Chicago, IL '85 (PERS)
BUCHMUELLER, DAVID P., pres. and chief exec. off., Healtheast, Inc., Allentown, PA '63 (MGMT)
BUCHNOWSKI, CAPT. RANDY P., MSC USAF, cmdr. company b., Fitzsimons Army Medical Center, Aurora, CO '82
BUCHSBAUM, KAREN FUSON, pres., Communications Strategies, Inc., Coral Gables, FL '78 (PR)
BUCK, BEVERLY, discharge planner, Richmond Heights General Hospital, Cleveland, OH '86 (SOC)
BUCK, CHARLES R. JR., ScD, staff exec. health care prog., General Electric Company, Fairfield, CT '84
BUCK, FRED P., dir. human res., Cleveland Clinic Hospital, Cleveland, OH '81 (PERS)
BUCK, JAMES G., dir. shared tech., Hospital Association of Pennsylvania, Camp Hill, PA '77 (MGMT)
BUCK, JEFFREY W., dir. pers., Incarnate Word Hospital, St. Louis, MO '82 (PERS)
BUCK, KATHRYN M., adm. coor. aux., Rochester Methodist Hospital, Rochester, MN '84 (VOL)
BUCK, MICHAEL, asst. dir. plant oper. and environ. serv., Magee Rehabilitation Hospital, Philadelphia, PA '86 (ENVIRON)
BUCK, NANCY W., supv. vol., Prince George's General Hospital and Medical Center, Cheverly, MD '85 (VOL)
BUCK, RICHARD T., atty., Silver Cross Hospital, Joliet, IL '75 (ATTY)
BUCK, ROBERT E., assoc. adm., Katherine Shaw Bethea Hospital, Dixon, IL '79
BUCK, SARAH B., dir. mktg. and info. serv., Mary Greeley Medical Center, Ames, IA '80 (PR)
BUCK, THOMAS J., Northwest Texas Hospital, Amarillo, TX '84 (ENG)
BUCK, WAYNE J., dir. support serv., HCA West Side Hospital, Nashville, TN '81 (ENG)
BUCKHOUT, CAROL H., acct. exec., Market Group One, Inc., Columbus, OH '81 (PR)
BUCKHOY, LEROY, dir. electronics, Foster G. McGaw Hospital, Loyola University of Chicago, Maywood, IL '81 (ENG)
BUCKINGHAM, PAUL STEVEN, dir. med. soc. work, Utah Valley Regional Medical Center, Provo, UT '86 (SOC)
BUCKLES, CHRISTIE ANN, risk mgr., Memorial Hospital, Colorado Springs, CO '86 (RISK)
BUCKLES, JO ANN, exec. sec., Indian Path Pavilion, Kingsport, TN '86 (PERS)
BUCKLES, LISA, RN, dir. commun. rel., Brentwood Hospital, Warrensville Heights, OH '83 (PR)(PAT)
BUCKLEY, ANN E., RN, corp. vice-pres. nrsg., Freeman Health Services, Culver City, CA '86 (NURS)
BUCKLEY, BARBARA J., unit supv. soc. serv., Massachusetts General Hospital, Boston, MA '80 (SOC)
BUCKLEY, COLLEEN F., student, Program in Health Care Administration, Temple University, Philadelphia, PA '85
BUCKLEY, DANIEL J., atty., Clinton Memorial Hospital, Wilmington, OH '83 (ATTY)
BUCKLEY, DONALD S., pres. and adm., Chesapeake General Hospital, Chesapeake, VA '60 (PLNG)
BUCKLEY, GERALDINE M., RN, vice-pres. and chm. nrsg., Abington Memorial Hospital, Abington, PA '83 (NURS)
BUCKLEY, HOWARD R., pres., Mercy Hospital, Portland, ME '64
BUCKLEY, JACK B., bd. vice chm., I. A. Naman and Associates, Consulting Engineering, Houston, TX '71
BUCKLEY, JO ANN, coor. pat. serv., Memorial Hospital, Ormond Beach, FL '86 (SOC)
BUCKLEY, JOHN J. JR., pres., St. Joseph's Hospital and Medical Center, Phoenix, AZ '68
BUCKLEY, MARY C., dir. mgt. info. serv., Brandywine Hospital, Caln Township, PA '85 (MGMT)
BUCKLEY, SR. NORA T., RN, asst. exec. dir. nrsg. serv., Cardinal Glennon Children Hospital, St. Louis, MO '73 (NURS)
BUCKLEY, PATRICK T., dir. plng., Foster G. McGaw Hospital, Loyola University of Chicago, Maywood, IL '80 (PLNG)
BUCKLEY, SHEILA A., mgr. plng. and mktg. proj., Emerson Hospital, Concord, MA '86 (PLNG)
BUCKLEY, TIMOTHY N., chief soc. work serv., Veterans Administration Medical Center, Milwaukee, WI '80 (SOC)
BUCKLEY, WILLIAM, pat. care rep., Massachusetts General Hospital, Boston, MA '80 (PAT)
BUCKLEY, YVONNE, coor. qual. assur., New York University Medical Center, New York, NY '86 (RISK)
BUCKNER, CHARLENE C., infection control practitioner, Doctors Hospital, Columbus, OH '86 (ENVIRON)
BUCKNER, JOHN, dir. eng., Woman's and Children's Hospital, Lafayette, LA '85 (ENG)
BUCKNUM, AGNES ELAINE, dir. soc. work, Foothills Provincial General Hospital, Calgary, Alta., Canada '87 (SOC)
BUCOLO, JOSEPH A., prin., Sugerman Associates, Inc., Chicago, IL '78 (PERS)
BUCUR, JOHN E., dir. pers., Php Corporation, Falls Church, VA '86 (PERS)
BUCY, SANDRA, bus. mgr., Centers for Psychotherapy, New Orleans, LA '87 (AMB)
BUCZKOWSKI, BEA, RN, dir. cent. serv., All Children's Hospital, St. Petersburg, FL '78 (CS)
BUCZKOWSKI, LEONARD E., dir. soc. serv., St. Anthony Medical Center, Crown Point, IN '74 (SOC)
BUCZYNSKI, DONNA M., student, Program in Health Care Administration, Baruch College, New York, NY '81
BUDA, EDWARD C., dir., Sioux Valley Wellness Center, Sioux Falls, SD '85 (EDUC)
BUDACKI, TIMOTHY J., mgr., M & M Protection Consultants, Pittsburgh, PA '86
BUDATZ, LOIS E., RN, dir. nrsg., Methodist Midtown, Omaha, NE '80 (NURS)
BUDAY, JON P., dir. plant eng., Traverse City Osteopathic Hospital, Traverse City, MI '85 (ENG)
BUDD, GITA B., consult., Jennings, Ryan, Federa and Company, Chicago, IL '81 (PLNG)
BUDDE, CHARLES, dir. environ. serv., Waukesha Memorial Hospital, Waukesha, WI '74 (ENG)
BUDERWITZ, JOSEPH J. JR., atty., Lawrence Hospital, Bronxville, NY '74 (ATTY)
BUDNIK, ROBERT M., exec. dir. plant serv., St. John's Hospital, Springfield, IL '83 (ENG)
BUDZA-BRODEMUS, ELAINE, mgr. soc. work serv., Our Lady of Mercy Hospital, Dyer, IN '86 (SOC)
BUE, FRANCES E., dir. guest rel., Wesley Medical Center, Wichita, KS '86 (EDUC)
BUE, JAMES A., mgr. phys. plant, St. Joseph Hospital, Augusta, GA '86 (ENG)
BUECHE, HOWARD J., atty., St. Joseph Hospital, Flint, MI '75 (ATTY)
BUECHLE, THOMAS C., vice-pres. adm., Bryn Mawr Hospital, Bryn Mawr, PA '73
BUECHNER, TERI, proj. coor., Meriter Hospital, Madison, WI '85 (ENG)
BUEGAR, DANNY O., Lower Buchanan, Liberia '84
BUEHLER, ALBERT C. III, vice-pres., Sachs Group, Ltd., Chicago, IL '81
BUEHLER, HARRY J., risk mgr., Gencon Risk Management Service, Takoma Park, MD '84 (RISK)
BUEHLER, PATRICIA, dir. soc. serv., St. Joseph's Hospital, Marshfield, WI '77 (SOC)
BUEHRLE, TONY, dir. food serv., St. Francis Medical Center, Cape Girardeau, MO '80 (FOOD)
BUELT, JOHN E., partner, Price Waterhouse, St. Louis, MO '72
BUENVIAJE, ROSALINDA T., Albuquerque, NM '80 (FOOD)
BUERGER, MARGARET A., RN, pres., Pro Tem, Inc., Michigan City, IN '74
BUERGER, RICHARD A., atty., Williamson Medical Center, Franklin, TN '80 (ATTY)
BUERKI, ROBIN C., MD, bd. mem., Henry Ford Hospital, Detroit, MI '24 (LIFE)
BUERSTATTE, GARY E., vice-pres. corp. dev., Waukesha Hospital System, Inc., Waukesha, WI '79 (PR)
BUESCHING, DON P., mkt analyst, Rockford Memorial Hospital, Rockford, IL '86 (PLNG)
BUETER, ROBERT F., dir. plant oper., Baptist Memorial Hospital, Memphis, TN '86 (ENG)
BUFALINO, NANETTE, atty., Martha Washington Hospital, Chicago, IL '87 (ATTY)
BUFF, ELIZABETH, RN, vice-pres. nrsg., Medical Center at Princeton, Princeton, NJ '79 (NURS)
BUFFINGTON, DAVID B., asst. adm. and risk mgr., Ivinson Memorial Hospital, Laramie, WY '83 (RISK)
BUFFINGTON, INEZ L., dir. sup., proc. and distrib., St. Elizabeth Hospital, Appleton, WI '82 (CS)
BUFFINGTON, JOHN, dir. pers., San Juan Regional Medical Center, Farmington, NM '78 (PERS)
BUFKIN, CARY E., atty., Mississippi Baptist Medical Center, Jackson, MS '68 (ATTY)
BUGBEE, GEORGE, (ret.), Genesee Depot, WI '36 (LIFE)
BUHITE, SUSAN E., RN, Anaheim Memorial Hospital, Anaheim, CA '77 (EDUC)
BUHR, DOROTHY C., mgr. pur., Mercy Hospital, Urbana, IL '84 (PUR)
BUHRMAN, DONALD, sr. biomedical equip. tech., Rogue Valley Medical Center, Medford, OR '87 (ENG)
BUIE, DANNY, mgr. maint., Shelby Medical Center, Alabaster, AL '86 (ENG)
BUIS, GEORGE S., consult., Wisconsin State Board of Health, Madison, WI '39 (LIFE)
BUISCH, VIVIAN M., mgr. pub. rel., Bry-Lin Hospital, Buffalo, NY '84 (PR)
BUISSON, CAROL JOY, dir. cont. educ. prog., Louisiana State University Medical Center, School of Nursing, Metairie, LA '85 (EDUC)
BUISSON, RENNEE M., pub. rel. spec., Roger Williams General Hospital, Providence, RI '86 (PR)
BUIST, JEAN MORFORD, assoc. adm., Memorial Hospital of Burlington County, Mount Holly, NJ '80
BULAND, D. BRUCE, dir. pers., Brigham City Community Hospital, Brigham City, UT '82 (PERS)
BULAVSKY, JACK D., dir. commun. affairs, Washoe Medical Center, Reno, NV '82 (PR)
BULGER, DEBORAH F., mgr. products, Adventist Health System, Arlington, TX '81 (PR)
BULGER, JANE C., RN, asst. dir. staff educ., Western Pennsylvania Hospital, Pittsburgh, PA '86 (NURS)
BULGER, MARILYN L., dir. pers., Stevens Memorial Hospital, Edmonds, WA '83 (PERS)
BULGER, WILLIAM W., dir. pub. affairs and mktg. commun., University of Chicago Hospitals, Chicago, IL '85 (PR)
BULLA, LINDA T., dir. soc. serv., Our Lady of Lake Regional Medical Center, Baton Rouge, LA '82 (SOC)
BULLARD, ANTHONY RAY, adm., Chestnut Lodge Hospital, Rockville, MD '86 (ENG)
BULLARD, BARRY W., dir. phys. plant, Penrose Hospitals, Colorado Springs, CO '81 (ENG)
BULLARD, CHERYL H., atty., Newberry County Memorial Hospital, Newberry, SC '84 (RISK)
BULLARD, NAOMI E., dir. bldg. serv., Kings County Hospital Center, Brooklyn, NY '86 (ENVIRON)
BULLARD, PATRICIA J., vice-pres. prof. affairs, Mercy Hospital of Pittsburgh, Pittsburgh, PA '85
BULLARD, WILLY, dir. vol. serv., St. Benedict's Hospital, Ogden, UT '85 (VOL)
BULLENS, DENISON K. JR., plng. consult., Monsour Medical Center, Jeannette, PA '77
BULLER, LARRY, dir. hskpg., University of Iowa Hospitals and Clinics, Iowa City, IA '86 (ENVIRON)
BULLERDICK, BEVERLY A., asst. dir. pers., Union Hospital, Terre Haute, IN '81 (PERS)
BULLITT, RUSSELL THAYER, vice-pres., Fidelity Bank, Philadelphia, PA '77
BULLOCK, BEVERLY H., dir. soc. serv., Children's Hospital, Norfolk, VA '81 (SOC)
BULLOCK, CAROL J., dir. pub. affairs, St. Anthony Medical Center, Louisville, KY '77 (PR)
BULLOCK, LEVI, evening coor. sup., proc. and distrib., St. Mary of Nazareth Hospital Center, Chicago, IL '86 (CS)
BULLOCK, LINDA METZGER, adm. asst., Beth Israel Hospital, Denver, CO '84
BULLOCK, SR. M. ADELE, dir. vol. serv., St. Elizabeth Hospital, Utica, NY '83 (VOL)
BULLOCK, REBECCA J., dir. vol. serv., Bayfront Medical Center, St. Petersburg, FL '85 (VOL)
BULLOCK, ROBERT C., asst. adm., City of Faith Hospital, Tulsa, OK '71 (MGMT)
BULLOCK, ROBERT E., dir. commun., Samaritan Hospital Foundation, Troy, NY '87 (PR)
BULYGO, JOHN C., dir. maint., University Hospital, Boston, MA '80 (ENG)
BUMBA, ROBERT R., asst. dir. plant oper., Church Hospital Corporation, Baltimore, MD '83 (ENG)
BUMGARNER, GAIL A., corp. planner, Northern Illinois Medical Center, McHenry, IL '84 (PLNG)
BUMGARNER, MARY ANN, dir. biomedical eng., Providence Hospital, Columbia, SC '86 (ENG)
BUMGARNER, RUSSELL, plant eng., Lowrance Hospital, Mooresville, NC '79 (ENG)
BUMP, WILBUR N., atty., Iowa Lutheran Hospital, Des Moines, IA '83 (ATTY)
BUMPIOUS, MARTHA M., RN, dir. pat. serv., Northeast Alabama Regional Medical Center, Anniston, AL '85 (NURS)
BUNCH, AMANDA, coor. soc. serv., Albemarle Hospital, Elizabeth City, NC '85 (SOC)
BUNDRANT, PATTI, tech. asst. risk mgt., Hendrick Medical Center, Abilene, TX '85 (RISK)
BUNDY, DOROTHY M., asst. adm., Providence Hospital, Medford, OR '85 (PR) (PLNG)
BUNDY, WILLIAM A., PhD, gen. mgr., Smith Kline Bio-Science Laboratories-Northeast Operations, King of Prussia, PA '86
BUNESS, JANET L., RN, dir. nrsg., Wrangell General Hospital, Wrangell, AK '83 (NURS)
BUNGE, ARNOLD F. JR., atty., Toledo Hospital, Toledo, OH '73 (ATTY)
BUNGER, LEN E. JR., atty., Bloomington Hospital, Bloomington, IN '69 (ATTY)
BUNKO, ELEANOR G., RN, supv. cent. serv., North Arundel Hospital, Glen Burnie, MD '84 (CS)
BUNTING, DIANE J., RN, dir. nrsg., Maryview Hospital, Portsmouth, VA '81 (NURS)
BUNTING, EDWARD D., adm., Kaiser-Permanente Medical Group, Harbor City, CA '65 (PERS)
BUNTING, MARY VIRGINIA, RN, dir. sup., proc. and distrib., St. Francis Medical Center, Trenton, NJ '83 (CS)
BUNTING, RUTH, dir. vol., Barnesville Hospital Association, Barnesville, OH '83 (VOL)
BUNTON, LAURA E., dir. pub. rel., HCA Northwest Regional Hospital, Margate, FL '86 (PR)
BUNZICK, ROBERT, dir. eng. serv., Lakeside Memorial Hospital, Brockport, NY '85 (ENG)
BUONO, JULIANNE T., dir. plng., Holy Cross Hospital, Fort Lauderdale, FL '77 (PR) (PLNG)
BUONO, RICHARD CARL, adm. res., Central Medical Center and Hospital, Pittsburgh, PA '84
BUPP, RICHARD C., safety off., Presbyterian Hospital, Albuquerque, NM '86 (ENG)
BURACK, JOSEPH, dir. soc. serv., Holden Hospital, Holden, MA '73 (SOC)
BURACK, MICHAEL E., pres., Mrm-Multi-Risk Management, Inc., Chicago, IL '76 (RISK)
BURACZYNSKI, STANLEY JR., dir. diet. serv., Staten Island Hospital, Staten Island, NY '80 (FOOD)
BURAIK, SARRY WAEL, hosp. syst. eng., Green Crescent Health Services, Riyadh, Saudi Arabia '85 (MGMT)(PUR)
BURAIK, YASMINE WAEL, soc. worker, King Abdul Aziz University Hospital, Riyadh, Saudi Arabia '86 (SOC)
BURAN, GRETCHEN, chief soc. work serv., Veterans Administration Medical Center, Minneapolis, MN '81 (SOC)
BURAU, PEGGY JO, RN, chief nrs.-critical care and heart-lung nrsg. serv., Clinical Center, National Institutes of Health, Bethesda, MD '85 (NURS)
BURCH, CHARLES C., sr. adm., Johns Hopkins Hospital, Baltimore, MD '63
BURCHARD, CHARLES W., vice-pres., University Hospitals of Cleveland, Cleveland, OH '59
BURCHARD, DONNA, mgr. hskpg. and ldry., Mercy Hospital, Bakersfield, CA '86 (ENVIRON)
BURCHARD, MARTHA, dir. emer. outpatient, Marian Health Center, Sioux City, IA '87 (AMB)
BURCHETT, LOIS H., RN, dir. surg. and amb. care, Highlands Regional Medical Center, Prestonsburg, KY '82 (NURS)
BURCHETT, MICHAEL J., chief prop. mgt., U. S. Army Hospital, APO New York, NY '83 (PUR)
BURCHILL, KEVIN R., asst. exec. dir., Parkwood Hospital, New Bedford, MA '84

BURDELL, JODY M., vice-pres. human res., Children's Hospital of Pittsburgh, Pittsburgh, PA '86 (PERS)

BURDETT, LINDA C., RN, vice-pres. nrsg., St. Joseph Hospital, Concordia, KS '86 (NURS)

BURDETT, RALPH H., dir. security and parking, The Methodist Hospital, Houston, TX '84 (RISK)

BURDETT, ROBERT JAMES JR., atty., Bethany Hospital, Chicago, IL '76 (ATTY)

BURDETT, YVELLE D., RN, dir. in-service educ., Hotel Dieu Hospital, New Orleans, LA '76 (EDUC)

BURDETTE, LINDA P., RN, vice-pres. pat. serv., Northeast Alabama Regional Medical Center, Anniston, AL '82 (NURS)

BURDICK, GINNY R., adm. human res., Sharp Cabrillo Hospital, San Diego, CA '84 (PERS)

BURDICK, TWILA, mgt. syst. analyst-res. eval., Samaritan Health Service, Phoenix, AZ '86 (MGMT)

BURDS, ANN, mgr. soc. serv., Mercy Health Center, Dubuque, IA '85 (SOC)

BURDULLIS, PATRICIA, dir. food serv., Pleasant Valley Hospital, Camarillo, CA '79 (FOOD)

BURGE, BETTY C., dir. vol., Pawating Hospital, Niles, MI '82 (VOL)

BURGE, MARGUERITE G., RN, unit dir. emer. room and med. serv., Bonner General Hospital, Sandpoint, ID '87 (AMB)

BURGE, MARJORIE I., risk mgr., St. Joseph's Hospital, Asheville, NC '68 (RISK)

BURGE, PATRICIA B., RN, dir. med.-surg. nrsg., Jewish Hospital, Louisville, KY '81 (NURS)

BURGE, ROBERT M., dir. eng., Mount Sinai Hospital, Minneapolis, MN '77 (ENG)

BURGE, WILLIAM, assoc. dir. eng., DePaul Hospital, Norfolk, VA '80 (ENG)

BURGER, BARBARA B., acct. mgr., Massachusetts Hospital Association, Burlington, MA '78 (MGMT)

BURGER, EUGENE, Bronx, NY '65 (MGMT)

BURGER, SHERRY M., RN, vice-pres., Methodist Hospitals of Gary, Gary, IN '71 (NURS)

BURGESS, ALAN J., Rockville, MD '74

BURGESS, CLIFTON C., dir. hskpg. serv., Union Memorial Hospital, Monroe, NC '86 (ENVIRON)

BURGESS, ELAINE A., dir. telecommun., St. Joseph's Hospital, Marshfield, WI '84 (ENG)

BURGESS, HARRISON W., dir. commun. rel., University of Virginia Medical Center, Charlottesville, VA '82 (PR)

BURGESS, JERRY W., asst. vice-pres. mktg. and commun., Christ Hospital, Cincinnati, OH '85 (PLNG)

BURGESS, KAREN B., pub. rel. off., St. Clare Hospital of Monroe, Monroe, WI '85 (PR)

BURGESS, PAULA, asst. risk mgr., Duke University Hospital, Durham, NC '84 (RISK)

BURGESS, PHYLLIS L., dir. soc. serv., Jones Memorial Hospital, Wellsville, NY '72 (SOC)

BURGESS, REG, vice-pres. mktg., pub. rel. and dev., Washington Adventist Hospital, Takoma Park, MD '74 (PR)

BURGESS, ROBERT J., dir. pers., Carthage Area Hospital, Carthage, NY '86 (PERS)

BURGETT, GEORGE LEONARD, atty., Chicago Osteopathic Medical Center, Chicago, IL '78 (ATTY)

BURGETT, LEONORA M., (ret.), Cincinnati, OH '74

BURGIN, CHARLES E., atty., McDowell Hospital, Marion, NC '76 (ATTY)

BURGIS, JUDITH E., sr. vice-pres., Robert Wood Johnson University Hospital, New Brunswick, NJ '84 (PLNG)

BURGMAN, TODD A., fin. analyst, Archbishop Bergan Mercy Hospital, Omaha, NE '82 (MGMT)

BURGMEIER, PAULA E., dir. med. soc. work, St. Joseph Mercy Hospital, Clinton, IA '85 (SOC)

BURGUN, J. ARMAND, pres., Rogers, Burgun, Shahine and Daschler, New York, NY '60 (ENG)

BURHANS, TIM, supv. maint., Flambeau Medical Center, Park Falls, WI '86 (ENG)

BURK, MARY LOUISE, RN, dir. nrsg. serv., New England Baptist Hospital, Boston, MA '70 (NURS)

BURK, MILDRED K., dir. diet., South Side Hospital of Pittsburgh, Pittsburgh, PA '82 (FOOD)

BURKE, ANDREW A., dir. soc. work, St. Mary-Corwin Hospital Center, Pueblo, CO '82 (SOC)

BURKE, BARBARA D., RN, asst. dir. nrsg., Charleston Memorial Hospital, Charleston, SC '83 (NURS)

BURKE, BARBARA K., mgr. wellness and health care, St. Vincent Hospital and Health Center, Indianapolis, IN '83 (EDUC)

BURKE, BEVERLY EVELYN, dir. pat., mgt. and nrsg. serv., John E. Fogarty Memorial Hospital, North Smithfield, RI '86 (PAT)

BURKE, BRENDA S., asst. dir. vol. serv., St. Luke's Medical Center, Phoenix, AZ '82 (VOL)

BURKE, BRIAN M., proj. mgr., Monmouth Ocean Regional Perinatal Center, Manasquan, NJ '85 (PLNG)

BURKE, CAREY J., asst. adm., Redmond Park Hospital, Rome, GA '84

BURKE, CARY DWIGHT, dir. risk mgt., Group Health Cooperative of Puget Sound, Seattle, WA '80 (RISK)

BURKE, DAVID J., dir. pers., Mount Vernon Hospital, Mount Vernon, NY '71 (PERS)

BURKE, DEBRA A., coor. mktg. and commun. rel., Williamsport Hospital and Medical Center, Williamsport, PA '85 (PR)

BURKE, DENNIS E., dir. dev. and plng., Portland Adventist Medical Center, Portland, OR '81 (PLNG)

BURKE, ELLEN, dir. pers., Beth Abraham Hospital, Bronx, NY '85 (PERS)

BURKE, ESTELLE L., RN, adm. dir. nrsg. serv., Northridge Hospital Medical Center, Northridge, CA '81 (NURS)

BURKE, FRAN E., dir. environ. serv., Santa Rosa Memorial Hospital, Santa Rosa, CA '86 (ENVIRON)

BURKE, FRANK W., atty., Our Lady of Peace Hospital, Louisville, KY '80 (ATTY)

BURKE, GEORGE C. III, asst. prof., Southwest Texas State University Department of Health Administration, San Marcos, TX '75

BURKE, GREG C., vice-pres. plng., Montefiore Medical Center, Bronx, NY '83 (PLNG)

BURKE, JAMES B., sr. mgt. eng., Hospital of the University of Pennsylvania, Philadelphia, PA '84 (MGMT)

BURKE, JAMES O., pres. and bd. chm., Allied Pharmacy Service, Inc., Abilene, TX '84

BURKE, JAMES, dir. biomedical eng., Lankenau Hospital, Philadelphia, PA '83 (ENG)

BURKE, JO ANN, RN, asst. dir. nrsg., Orlando Regional Medical Center, Orlando, FL '84 (NURS)

BURKE, JO-ANN T., asst. dir., Orlando Regional Medical Center, Orlando, FL '86 (MGMT)

BURKE, JOAN R., joan rathswohl burke, Grossmont District Hospital, La Mesa, CA '80 (FOOD)

BURKE, JOHN C., atty., Father Flanagan's Boys' Town, Boys Town, NE '80 (ATTY)

BURKE, JOHN G., exec. adm., Ed Fraser Memorial Hospital, MacClenny, FL '86 (RISK)

BURKE, JOHN J., vice-pres., Mercy Hospital, Scranton, PA '73 (PERS)

BURKE, JOHN J., RN, dir. med. nrsg., Morton Hospital and Medical Center, Taunton, MA '86 (NURS)

BURKE, JOSEPH K., adm. dir. emer., Barnes Hospital, St. Louis, MO '87 (AMB)

BURKE, JUDY A., dir. vol. serv., Childrens Memorial Hospital, Omaha, NE '82 (VOL)

BURKE, KATHARINE B., sr. consult., Price Waterhouse, Birmingham, AL '87 (MGMT)

BURKE, KATHLEEN M., atty., New York Hospital Office of Legal Affairs, New York, NY '85 (ATTY)

BURKE, LORETTA M., pat. rep., Christ Hospital and Medical Center, Oak Lawn, IL '86 (PAT)

BURKE, LOYAL A. JR., mgr. food serv. oper., Schneider Health Services, Bridgeville, PA '72 (FOOD)

BURKE, MARION E., RN, asst. vice-pres. nrsg., Newton-Wellesley Hospital, Newton, MA '86 (NURS)

BURKE, MARJORIE W., atty., Carney Hospital, Boston, MA '79 (ATTY)

BURKE, SR. MARY ELIZABETH, RN, asst. vice-pres. nrsg., Mercy Catholic Medical Center, Darby, PA '81 (NURS)

BURKE, MICHAEL J., dir. commun. rel., Providence Hospital, Holyoke, MA '78 (PR)

BURKE, MICHAEL P., asst. dir.-legal affairs, Providence Hospital, Southfield, MI '84 (RISK)

BURKE, MONETTE B., RN, supv. cent. sup., St. Mary's General Hospital, Lewiston, ME '80 (CS)

BURKE, NANCY E., RN, asst. dir. nsrg serv., Ohio Valley Medical Center, Wheeling, WV '81 (NURS)

BURKE, PAMELA I., mgr. food serv., Saint Therese Medical Center, Waukegan, IL '87 (FOOD)

BURKE, PETER G., atty., Phelps, Dunbar, Marks, Claverie and Sims, New Orleans, LA '70 (ATTY)

BURKE, RAYMOND J. III, manpower contr. off., Department of the Army, Office of the Surgeon General, Washington, DC '80

BURKE, REBECCA ANN, sr. consult. strategic plng. and mktg., Hospital Corporation of America Management Company, Nashville, TN '78 (PLNG)

BURKE, RICHARD E., asst. adm., Henrietta D. Goodall Hospital, Sanford, ME '76

BURKE, ROSEMARY L., exec. vice-pres., St. Michael's Hospital, Stevens Point, WI '81 (AMB)

BURKE, SR. ROSEMARY, pat. rep., Saint Joseph Hospital, Fort Worth, TX '84 (PAT)

BURKE, STEPHEN E., dir. soc. serv., Lawrence General Hospital, Lawrence, MA '79 (SOC)

BURKE, STEVEN CHARLES, vice-pres. mktg., Richland Memorial Hospital, Columbia, SC '76 (PLNG)

BURKE, THOMAS B., atty., Washington Regional Medical Center, Fayetteville, AR '75 (ATTY)

BURKE, THOMAS C., atty., Strong Memorial Hospital Rochester University, Rochester, NY '82 (ATTY)

BURKE, THOMAS R., atty., Archbishop Bergan Mercy Hospital, Omaha, NE '68 (ATTY)

BURKE, THOMAS W., mgr., Ernst and Whinney, Cincinnati, OH '85 (MGMT)

BURKENS, JAN C. J., MD, (ret.), Arnhem, Holland '67 (HON)

BURKET, ELDA KAYE, dir., Nason Hospital, Roaring Spring, PA '87 (AMB)

BURKET, WILLIAM R., chief fin. off., Hampton General Hospital, Hampton, VA '77

BURKETT, A. VAUGHN, mgt. eng., St. Vincent's Medical Center, Jacksonville, FL '80 (MGMT)

BURKETT, NORMAN D. JR., vice-pres. pat. serv., Hamilton Medical Center, Dalton, GA '86 (RISK)

BURKETT, NORMAN D. SR., pres., Hamilton Medical Center, Dalton, GA '79 (LIFE)

BURKETT, PATRICIA L., reg. environ. serv. consult., Kaiser Permanente Medical Centers, Oakland, CA '86 (PUR)

BURKHARDT, EDWARD J., asst. to exec. eng., Montefiore Medical Center, Bronx, NY '68 (ENG)

BURKHARDT, J. BLAND JR., chief exec. off., Maryview Hospital, Portsmouth, VA '67

BURKHARDT, MARY ANNE, RN, coor. in-service educ., St. Mary's Hospital, Orange, NJ '85 (EDUC)

BURKHARDT, MINNIE, atty., Texoma Medical Center, Denison, TX '84 (ATTY)

BURKHOLDER, BARBARA B., dir. health promotion, Catherine McAuley Health Center, Ann Arbor, MI '84 (EDUC)

BURKLAND, DARRELL A., dir. soc. serv., St. Luke's Hospitals, Fargo, ND '74 (SOC)

BURKLE, JULIANNA, RN, vice-pres. nrsg., Easton Hospital, Easton, PA '76 (NURS)

BURKS, HAROLD A., dir. pers., Children's Seashore House, Atlantic City, NJ '86 (PERS)

BURKS, HELEN V., mgr. emp., Tri-City Medical Center, Oceanside, CA '84 (PERS)

BURKS, PATRICIA A., dep. health comr., Philadelphia Department of Health, Philadelphia, PA '82

BURKS, R. WAYNE, partner, Coopers and Lybrand, Tampa, FL '82

BURLESON, PHILLIP R., mgr. matl., Helen Keller Memorial Hospital, Sheffield, AL '75 (PUR)

BURLESON, SCOTT D., dir. plng. serv., Memorial Hospital, Cumberland, MD '81 (PLNG)

BURLINGAME, RICHARD H., prod. analyst, Shared Medical Systems, Inc., Malvern, PA '86 (MGMT)

BURLINGAME, WILLIAM KEITH, dir. safety and risk mgt., South County Hospital, Wakefield, RI '80 (RISK)(ENG)

BURMAN, CLAIRE L., dir. strategic plng., St. Joseph Hospital, Chicago, IL '81 (PLNG)

BURMESTER, MARK A., dir. plng., Palomar Pomerado Hospital District, Escondido, CA '84 (PLNG)

BURN, ANNETTE Y., dir. soc. work, AMI Parkway Regional Medical Center, North Miami Beach, FL '86 (SOC)

BURNER, OLIVE Y., RN, asst. prof. and dir. prog. nrsg. adm., University of California at Los Angeles School of Nursing, Los Angeles, CA '86 (NURS)

BURNES, DANIEL, pres., Managed Care Corporation, Boston, MA '85

BURNET, EDWARD H., sales mgr., HBO and Company, Mount Laurel, NJ '62 (MGMT)

BURNETT, BYRON C., vice-pres. matl. mgt., The Methodist Hospital, Houston, TX '82 (PUR)

BURNETT, HENRY, atty., James M. Jackson Memorial Hospital, Miami, FL '74 (ATTY)

BURNETT, MAUREEN, dir. soc. serv., Lodi Memorial Hospital, Lodi, CA '85 (SOC)

BURNETT, TERESA L., RN, syst. consult., Herman Miller, Inc., San Francisco, CA '77 (CS)

BURNETT, WILLIAM L., mgr. food serv., Cornwall Hospital, Cornwall, NY '69 (FOOD)

BURNETTE, GEORGIA M., RN, asst. adm. nrsg., Roswell Park Memorial Institute, Buffalo, NY '87 (NURS)

BURNETTE, W. SCOTT, vice-pres., Lynchburg General Hospital, Lynchburg, VA '83

BURNEY, CHRISTOPHER M., dir. eng., Hospital of Saint Raphael, New Haven, CT '84 (ENG)

BURNHAM, SR. CORITA, dir. educ., St. John's Regional Medical Center, Oxnard, CA '83 (EDUC)

BURNHAM, JAMES T., vice-pres. adm. and plng., Riddle Memorial Hospital, Media, PA '72 (PLNG)

BURNHAM, JANET, asst. exec. dir. plng., Thomas Jefferson University Hospital, Philadelphia, PA '83 (PLNG)

BURNHAM, RICHARD B., atty., John C. Lincoln Hospital and Health Center, Phoenix, AZ '83 (ATTY)

BURNHEIMER, SHARON A., dir. pers., Somerset Community Hospital, Somerset, PA '84 (PERS)

BURNISTON, KAREN S., RN, chief oper. off., St. Catherine Hospital of East Chicago, East Chicago, IN '80 (NURS)

BURNS, BARRY, dir. soc. serv., Great Plains Regional Medical Center, North Platte, NE '86 (SOC)

BURNS, BUFF C., dir. commun., Rbd Marketing Communications, Los Angeles, CA '85 (PR)

BURNS, CHESTER S., pur. agt., Marietta Memorial Hospital, Marietta, OH '67 (PUR)

BURNS, CYNTHIA, RN, dir. nrsg., Roseland Community Hospital, Chicago, IL '79 (NURS)

BURNS, DANIEL D. JR., vice-pres., Professional Health Care Management Services, Inc., Portsmouth, VA '83 (MGMT)

BURNS, DARLENE A., RN, dir. nrsg., Rome Hospital and Murphy Memorial Hospital, Rome, NY '86 (NURS)

BURNS, DAVID C., atty., Bethel Deaconess Hospital, Newton, KS '79 (ATTY)

BURNS, DAVID H., asst. adm., York Hospital, York, PA '82

BURNS, DENNIS J., mgr. biomedical eng. serv., Queen's Medical Center, Honolulu, HI '84 (ENG)

BURNS, DENNIS R., asst. vice-pres., Hamot Medical Center, Erie, PA '80 (PUR)

BURNS, EVELYN H., asst. dir. clin. serv. and chief diet., Albert Einstein Medical Center, Philadelphia, PA '86 (FOOD)

BURNS, FREDDA P., pat. asst. rep., Kasier Permanente Medical Center, Cleveland Heights, OH '81 (PAT)

BURNS, JAMES A., pres., Tehila Associates, Ogden, UT '82 (PLNG)

BURNS, JAMES W., mgr. pur. serv., Hospital Central Service, Inc., Allentown, PA '86 (PUR)

BURNS, JODY, RN, asst. adm. nrsg., Berkshire Medical Center, Pittsfield, MA '85 (NURS)

BURNS, JOSEPH P., coor. pur., Hospital Council of the National Capital Area, Inc., Washington, DC '74 (PUR)

BURNS, KATHLEEN M., dir. risk mgt. and qual. assur., South Amboy Memorial Hospital, South Amboy, NJ '80 (RISK)

BURNS, KATHRYN T., dir. mgt. info. syst., Community Memorial Hospital, Toms River, NJ '85 (MGMT)

BURNS, LAWRENCE P., atty., St. Mary's Health Services, Grand Rapids, MI '83 (ATTY)

BURNS, LAWRENCE, dir. environ. serv., Copley Memorial Hospital, Aurora, IL '87 (ENVIRON)

BURNS, LAWTON ROBERT, Way College of Biblical Research, Rome City, IN '81

BURNS, MARY K., dir. educ., Barton Memorial Hospital, South Lake Tahoe, CA '85 (EDUC)

BURNS, MARY K., RN, dir. nrsg., St. Joseph Hospital, Port Charlotte, FL '86 (NURS)

BURNS, MARY TIERNEY, dir. soc. serv., St. Luke's Hospital of New Bedford, New Bedford, MA '66 (SOC)

BURNS, MICHAEL, mgr. pur., Providence Memorial Hospital, El Paso, TX '85 (PUR)

BURNS, MILDRED L., pat. rep., Christian Hospital Northwest, Florissant, MO '86 (PAT)

BURNS, PAMELA SMITH, dir. soc. serv., Bethel Deaconess Hospital, Newton, KS '82 (SOC)

BURNS, RITA J., dir. pub. rel. and mktg., Eisenhower Medical Center, Colorado Springs, CO '86 (PR)

BURNS, RUTH ANN, RN, dir. nrsg., Sarasota Palms Hospital, Sarasota, FL '86 (NURS)

BURNS, SHIRLEY A., dir. vol. serv., Medical Center Hospital, Chillicothe, OH '85 (VOL)

BURNS, STEPHEN P., RN, vice-pres. nrsg., Elmhurst Memorial Hospital, Elmhurst, IL '81 (NURS)

BURNSHIRE, ELSIE, dir. ldry. and linen, Grand Valley Hospital, Pryor, OK '86 (ENVIRON)

BURNSIDE, BARBARA A., dir. pub. rel., Gerbig, Snell, Weisheimer and Associates, Columbus, OH '83 (PR)
BURNSON, DIANA L., dir. pers. and pub. rel., Shriners Hospitals for Crippled Children, St. Louis, MO '86 (PERS)
BURPEE, LINDA S., mgr. nutr. serv., St. Mary's Health Services, Grand Rapids, MI '86 (FOOD)
BURR, DONALD S., syst. eng., Beth Israel Hospital, Boston, MA '78 (MGMT)
BURR, RICHARD W., pres., Burr Engineers, Inc., Houston, TX '85
BURRELLO, ANTHONY G., actg. dir. plant oper., Capitol Hill Hospital, Washington, DC '86 (ENG)
BURRIS, COL. CARSHAL A. JR., MSC USA, Springfield, VA '67
BURROUGH, CYNTHIA R., contr., Weirton Medical Center, Weirton, WV '84
BURROUGHS, BOBBY, dir. maint., Randolph County Hospital, Roanoke, AL '79 (ENG)
BURROUGHS, CHARLES E., atty., St. Joseph's Hospital, Milwaukee, WI '84 (ATTY)
BURROWS, JACK A., asst. adm., Trinity Lutheran Hospital, Kansas City, MO '74
BURROWS, LILA J., mgr. staff dev., Richland Memorial Hospital, Olney, IL '83 (EDUC)
BURROWS, PHYLLIS A., RN, dir. nrsg. serv., Alice Peck Day Memorial Hospital, Lebanon, NH '82 (NURS)
BURROWS, WILLIAM F., coor. soc. work, Marian Health Center-Division of Sisters of Mercy Health Corporation, Sioux City, IA '72 (SOC)
BURROWS, WILLIAM P., atty., Community General Hospital, Syracuse, NY '85 (ATTY)
BURSAW, ANDREA J., dir. vol. serv., Anna Jaques Hospital, Newburyport, MA '85 (VOL)
BURSON, LLOYD F. JR., mgr. cent. serv., Divine Providence Hospital, Williamsport, PA '83 (CS)
BURSTEIN, GEORGE, assoc. prof. mgt., Program in Health Care Management, California State University at Los Angeles, Los Angeles, CA '80 (EDUC)
BURSTEIN, I. GEORGE, asst. proj. dir., Finlay Medical Center HMO Corporation, Miami, FL '79 (AMB)
BURT, DENNIS L., dir. hskpg., Riddle Memorial Hospital, Media, PA '87 (ENVIRON)
BURT, H. JOSEPH, dir. pers. serv., Sisters of St. Mary Health Care Systems, St. Louis, MO '83 (PERS)
BURT, JOAN E., mgr. mktg. and pub. rel., Riverside Community Hospital, Riverside, CA '86 (PR) (PLNG)
BURT, ROBERT G., atty., Good Samaritan Hospital and Medical Center, Portland, OR '84 (ATTY)
BURT, STEPHEN A., dir. hskpg. serv., Roanoke Memorial Hospitals, Roanoke, VA '86 (ENVIRON)
BURTCH, JACK W. JR., atty., Richmond Memorial Hospital, Richmond, VA '78 (ATTY)
BURTELOW, MARY JOAN, dir. guest rel., St. Luke's Hospital West, Chesterfield, MO '80 (SOC)(PAT)
BURTNETT, FRANK, dir. pers., Parkview Memorial Hospital, Brunswick, ME '78 (PERS)
BURTON, ANNE M., pres., Anne Burton Associates, Ltd., New York, NY '86 (PR)
BURTON, CHRISTINA M., consult., Lubbock, TX '86
BURTON, GENE D., vice-pres. matl. mgt., Hospital Corporation of America, Nashville, TN '64 (PUR)
BURTON, JEAN M., dir. educ., Seventh Ward General Hospital, Hammond, LA '86 (EDUC)
BURTON, MARGIE, cent., proc. and distrib. tech., St. Elizabeth Hospital, Beaumont, TX '84 (CS)
BURTON, PAUL F., chief soc. work serv., Veterans Administration Medical Center, Sepulveda, CA '74 (SOC)
BURTON, ROBERT E., asst. adm. serv. dev., St. Mary Hospital, Port Arthur, TX '86 (PR)
BURTON, SCOTT L., dir. safety and gen. serv. asst., Children's Mercy Hospital, Kansas City, MO '84 (RISK)
BURTON, THEODORE J., adm. prop. serv., Southern Baptist Hospital, New Orleans, LA '83 (ENG)
BURWELL, JULIE A., dir. pers., Good Samaritan Hospital, Lexington, KY '86 (PERS)
BURWELL, SOPHRONIA W., adm. asst., Newport News General Hospital, Newport News, VA '78 (PR)
BURY, FRED J., adm., St. Joseph's Community Hospital, West Bend, WI '64
BURY, JAMES L., adm. consult., Colorado State Department of Health, Denver, CO '57 (LIFE)
BURZAK, ANN C., pat. rep., Northeastern Hospital of Philadelphia, Philadelphia, PA '77 (PAT)
BURZYNSKI, EUGENIA T., asst. vice-pres., Financial Guaranty Insurance Company, New York, NY '82
BURZYNSKI, REGINA, asst. vice-pres. util. mgt., Leominster Hospital, Leominster, MA '86 (RISK)
BUSAT, O. WILLIAM, exec. dir., St. Mary's Hospital, Montreal, Que., Canada '67
BUSBY, HOWARD, dir. maint., Carraway Methodist Medical Center, Birmingham, AL '86 (ENG)
BUSCH-CEJKA, DEBORAH, dir. aux. and vol. serv., DePaul Health Center, Bridgeton, MO '84 (VOL)
BUSCH, CAROL A., dir. pat. rel., Mercy Medical Center, Springfield, OH '87 (PAT)
BUSCH, CHRISTINE M., RN, dir. nrsg., Children's Hospital of King's Daughters, Norfolk, VA '81 (NURS)
BUSCH, EMERY B. JR., (ret.), University Heights, OH '64
BUSCH, HARRY J., atty., John F. Kennedy Medical Center, Chicago, IL '84 (ATTY)
BUSCH, MORGAN D., mgr. plng., Intermountain Health Care, Inc., Salt Lake City, UT '83 (PLNG)
BUSCH, NANCY E., pres., Busch and Associates, Birmingham, MI '78 (PLNG)
BUSCHLEN, SHIRLEY, mgr. pur., Hills and Dales General Hospital, Cass City, MI '84 (PUR)
BUSER, CAROLINE M., dir. pers. and educ., St. Mary's Hospital-Ozaukee, Port Washington, WI '85 (PERS)(EDUC)
BUSER, KENNETH R., exec. vice-pres., Mercy Hospital of Pittsburgh, Pittsburgh, PA '78
BUSFIELD, ROGER M. JR., pres., Arkansas Hospital Association, Little Rock, AR '64
BUSH, ANDREW J., res. scientist, Baptist Memorial Hospital, Memphis, TN '82 (MGMT)
BUSH, BETTY J., RN, dir. critical care, Mansfield General Hospital, Mansfield, OH '86 (NURS)
BUSH, CANDACE A., dir. educ., Richland Memorial Hospital, Columbia, SC '86 (EDUC)
BUSH, CARLA, mgr. soc. serv., Group Health Copp of Puget Sound, Seattle, WA '86 (SOC)
BUSH, CAROL, RN, dir. nrsg. adm., Intermountain Health Care Hospitals, Inc., Salt Lake City, UT '77 (NURS)
BUSH, F. M. III, atty., North Mississippi Medical Center, Tupelo, MS '79 (ATTY)
BUSH, GRANVILLE M., atty., Hospital District Number One of Rice County, Lyons, KS '76 (ATTY)
BUSH, RONNIE B., PhD, pres., Medical Office Services, Inc., Arlington Heights, IL '86 (PLNG)
BUSH, SANDERS, dir. human res., St. Anthony's Hospital, St. Petersburg, FL '82 (PERS)
BUSH, SHARRON N., dir. pers., Carrollwood Community Hospital, Tampa, FL '86 (PERS)
BUSH, THEON V., supv. cent. serv., Wesley Medical Center, Wichita, KS '79 (CS)
BUSH, VALERIE W., RN, dir. nrsg., Portsmouth Psychiatric Center, Portsmouth, VA '86 (NURS)
BUSHAW, CELIA J., RN, asst. adm. nrsg. serv., Centralia General Hospital, Centralia, WA '84 (NURS)
BUSHEY, JO ANNE, coor. pat. educ., Valley Regional Hospital, Claremont, NH '84 (EDUC)
BUSHMAN, JEAN H., dir. vol. serv. and pat. rel., Hutzel Hospital, Detroit, MI '74 (VOL)
BUSHNELL, CLARENCE WILLIAM, sr. consult., Health Strategy Associates, Chestnut Hill, MA '49 (PLNG)(LIFE)
BUSHONG, JEFFREY L., assoc. plng., St. Vincent Medical Center, Toledo, OH '86 (PLNG)
BUSHONG, MARY E., assoc. dir. oper. room and adm. dir. amb. surg. serv., University Hospitals of Cleveland, Cleveland, OH '87 (AMB)
BUSICH, JOHN R., mech. consult.-plant eng. serv., Southwest Community Health Services, Albuquerque, NM '85 (ENG)
BUSO, MRS. RAYMOND, dir. vol. serv., Milford Hospital, Milford, CT '71 (VOL)
BUSSARD, PAULA A., dir. health care delivery syst., Hospital Association of Pennsylvania, Camp Hill, PA '79 (PLNG)
BUSSELL, GEORGE E., dir. environ. serv., Virginia Mason Hospital, Seattle, WA '86 (ENVIRON)
BUSSENGER, JOSEPH DONALD, asst. vice-pres. matl. mgt., Germantown Hospital and Medical Center, Philadelphia, PA '61 (PUR)
BUSTAMANTE, BETSY J., RN, dir. pat. care serv., Rehoboth McKinley Christian Hospital, Gallup, NM '85 (NURS)
BUSTEED, SUSAN, asst. dir., Children's Hospital at Stanford, Palo Alto, CA '87 (AMB)
BUSTIN, JOHN C., vice-pres. plng. dev., Williamsport Hospital and Medical Center, Williamsport, PA '80 (PLNG)
BUSTOW, SHELDON, dir. gerontology programs, Ghm, Inc., East Hartford, CT '86
BUSTRAAN, JAMES A., mgt. eng., Thomas Jefferson University Hospital, Philadelphia, PA '72 (MGMT)
BUTCHER, BARBARA A., dir. mktg., St. Barnabas Hospital, Bronx, NY '86 (PR)
BUTCHER, HARRY C., dir. plant eng. and maint., Long Island Jewish Medical Center, New York, NY '76 (ENG)
BUTCHER, SANDRA, dir. soc. serv., George Washington University Hospital, Washington, DC '80 (SOC)
BUTCHER, SUSAN V., dir. food and nutr. serv., Hollywood Presbyterian Medical Center, Los Angeles, CA '85 (FOOD)
BUTCHER, THOMAS C. JR., assoc. to vice-pres. oper., Women and Infants Hospital of Rhode Island, Providence, RI '79
BUTCHERITE, CHARLES D., asst. adm., Central Washington Hospital, Wenatchee, WA '70 (MGMT)
BUTEYN-GIER, JERITH N., coor. commun. and pat. educ., Sheboygan Memorial Medical Center, Sheboygan, WI '84 (EDUC)
BUTH, MARY MCGARR, RN, dir. nrsg., Corning Hospital, Corning, NY '86 (NURS)
BUTIKOFER, LON D., RN, dir. nrsg., St. Joseph Community Hospital, New Hampton, IA '86 (NURS)
BUTKE, LT. COL. KENNETH P., MSC USA, assoc. adm., Walter Reed Army Medical Center, Washington, DC '80 (MGMT)
BUTKUS, ALEXANDER S. JR., proj. eng., Grumman-Butkus Associates, Evanston, IL '78 (ENG)
BUTLER, ANITA M., pat. advocate, Spartanburg Regional Medical Center, Spartanburg, SC '85 (PAT)
BUTLER, BEVERLEY B., dir. ped. soc. work, University of Virginia Medical Center, Charlotteville, VA '75 (SOC)
BUTLER, CAROL H., dir. cont. care, Ashtabula County Medical Center, Ashtabula, OH '84 (SOC)
BUTLER, CHARLES R., vice-pres. mktg., Tampa General Hospital, Tampa, FL '80 (PR)
BUTLER, CINDY C., asst. dir. nutr., Grossmont District Hospital, La Mesa, CA '82 (FOOD)
BUTLER, DANA L., supv. cent. sterile, Baptist Regional Health Center, Miami, OK '32 (CS)
BUTLER, DAVID L., atty., Incarnate Word Health Services, San Antonio, TX '85 (ATTY)
BUTLER, DIANE L., instr. educ., Bronson Clinic Investigation Unit, Kalamazoo, MI '86 (EDUC)
BUTLER, ELTON T. JR., dir. pers. and pub. rel., Community General Hospital, Reading, PA '74 (PERS)
BUTLER, HAROLD R., asst. dir. eng., Methodist Medical Center of Illinois, Peoria, IL '81 (ENG)
BUTLER, JILL S., dir. cent. sup., Halifax Hospital Medical Center, Daytona Beach, FL '79 (CS)
BUTLER, JOAN S., RN, vice-pres. nrsg. adm., Holy Cross Hospital, Salt Lake City, UT '83 (NURS)
BUTLER, JOE HAROLD, asst. adm., Memorial Hospital, Palestine, TX '79
BUTLER, JONATHAN P., pres., Butler Rogers Baskett Associates, Inc., New York, NY '75
BUTLER, JOSEPH M., atty., Rapid City Regional Hospital, Rapid City, SD '74 (ATTY)
BUTLER, JOSEPH P., dir. data proc., Grandview Hospital and Medical Center, Dayton, OH '85 (MGMT)
BUTLER, LEONA M., vice-pres. prov. serv., Blue Cross of California, Oakland, CA '86
BUTLER, MADLYN, dir. cont. educ., Nashville Memorial Hospital, Madison, TN '73 (EDUC)
BUTLER, MARCHITA M., RN, pres., Amicare Home Health Services, Ann Arbor, MI '78 (NURS)
BUTLER, MARCIA, RN, dir. nrsg., Central Plains Regional Hospital, Plainview, TX '80 (NURS)
BUTLER, MARILYN A., RN, dir. nrsg., Navarro Regional Hospital, Corsicana, TX '83 (NURS)
BUTLER, MARY FRANCES, infection control nrs. and risk mgr., Medical Plaza Hospital, Fort Worth, TX '86 (RISK)
BUTLER, MARY L., RN, vice-pres. pat. serv., Sacred Heart Medical Center, Spokane, WA '83 (NURS)
BUTLER, MICHAEL RYAN, atty., Musick, Peeler and Garrett, Los Angeles, CA '80 (ATTY)(PR) (PLNG)
BUTLER, NATHANIEL GLOVER, assoc. dir. soc. serv., Massachusetts General Hospital, Boston, MA '77 (SOC)
BUTLER, NORMA GENE, dir. cent. sup. room, Metropolitan Nashville General Hospital, Nashville, TN '84 (CS)
BUTLER, ROBERT A., dir. human res., Frick Community Health Center, Mount Pleasant, PA '83 (PERS)
BUTLER, ROY, dir. food serv., Methodist Hospital, Omaha, NE '82 (FOOD)
BUTLER, WILLIAM C., atty., Mount Clemens General Hospital, Mount Clemens, MI '85 (ATTY)
BUTLER, WILLIAM E., supv. maint., Presbyterian Hospital of Kaufman, Kaufman, TX '86 (ENG)
BUTLER, WILLIAM R., vice-pres. mktg. and reg. prog., Healthcare Services of New England, Braintree, MA '82 (PUR)
BUTSCHAT, DEE, dir. vol. serv., St. Alexius Medical Center, Bismarck, ND '82 (VOL)
BUTTARO, RAYMOND ANDREW, acct. mgr., Massachusetts Hospital Association, Burlington, MA '75 (MGMT)
BUTTE, KIMBERLEE E., dir. vol. serv., NKC Hospitals, Louisville, KY '86 (VOL)
BUTTERBAUGH, JEFFREY L., dir. commun., Tucson Medical Center, Tucson, AZ '79 (ENG)
BUTTERFIELD, GERALDINE M., chief cent. matl. serv., Touro Infirmary, New Orleans, LA '77 (CS)
BUTTERICK, JEFFREY S., consult., Hospital Corporation of America, Nashville, TN '86 (MGMT)
BUTTERWORTH, JOHN F., dir. food serv., Lutheran Medical Center, Wheat Ridge, CO '70 (FOOD)
BUTTERWORTH, JOHN, atty., Episcopal Hospital, Philadelphia, PA '68 (ATTY)
BUTTERY, ROBERT, supv. maint., McCullough-Hyde Memorial Hospital, Oxford, OH '79 (ENG)
BUTTNER, BRIAN R., arch., Geneva General Hospital, Geneva, NY '77
BUTTOLPH, MIRIAM R., coor. pat. serv., Deaconess Hospital of Cleveland, Cleveland, OH '86 (PAT)
BUTTS, JOE, dir. phys. plant, Lake of the Ozarks General Hospital, Osage Beach, MO '81 (ENG)
BUTTS, RHONDA M., dir. commun. rel., Glynn-Brunswick Memorial Hospital, Brunswick, GA '81 (PR)
BUTZ, RALPH O., atty., La Grange Memorial Hospital, La Grange, IL '66 (ATTY)
BUTZ, SARAH V., vice-pres. human res., St. Francis Hospital Systems, Colorado Springs, CO '78 (PERS)
BUTZLAFF-VOSS, BAMBI L., dir. pub. rel. and mktg., Lakeland Hospital, Elkhorn, WI '85 (PR)
BUVELOT, JOHN L., storekeeper, Christ Hospital, Oak Lawn, IL '80 (PUR)
BUXBAUM, RICHARD J., vice-pres., Greater Cleveland Hospital Association, Cleveland, OH '56 (PUR)(MGMT)(LIFE)
BUXTON, SHIRLEY, dir. soc. work, Providence Medical Center, Portland, OR '69 (SOC)
BUZACHERO, VICTOR V., vice-pres. human res., Baptist Medical Centers, Birmingham, AL '84 (PERS)
BUZZELL, RONALD E., mgr. plant oper., Logan County Health Center, Guthrie, OK '80 (ENG)
BYARS, ROBERT M., supv. matl. mgt., Cleveland Memorial Hospital, Shelby, NC '84 (CS)
BYASSEE, JEAN L., atty., Hospital Corporation of America, Nashville, TN '79 (ATTY)
BYCER, ROBERT ELLIOTT, dir. bus. affairs, Association of University Physicians, Seattle, WA '77
BYE, EDWARD SIDNEY, chief pat. rec., Armed Forces Institute of Pathology, Laurel, MD '85
BYERLY, BARBARA J., dir. pub. rel., St. Joseph Hospital, Kirkwood, MO '81 (PR)
BYERLY, GENE E., mgr. pur., St. John's Mercy Medical Center, St. Louis, MO '87 (PUR)
BYERS, CYNTHIA S., dir. pub. rel., Georgetown University Medical Center, Washington, DC '78 (PR)
BYERS, HELEN JEAN, RN, dir. nrsg., Swedish Hospital Medical Center, Seattle, WA '76 (NURS)
BYERS, JIMMIE CAROL, matl. mgt. serv. consult., Hospital Corporation of America, Nashville, TN '80 (PUR)
BYERS, KATHERINE CARPENTER, dir. pack room, oper. room and mktg., National Healthcare Linen Service, Atlanta, GA '85 (CS)
BYERS, LYLE W., asst. vice-pres. prov. affairs, Blue Cross of Western Pennsylvania, Pittsburgh, PA '58
BYERS, RICHARD Q., asst. adm., Southampton Hospital, Southampton, NY '73
BYERS, TALIS DALY, dir. mktg. and dev., Opelousas General Hospital, Opelousas, LA '83 (PR)
BYHAM, JAMES M., contr., Community Hospital, Kane, PA '86
BYINGTON, A. DALE, dir. plng., Roanoke Memorial Hospitals, Roanoke, VA '82 (PLNG)
BYINGTON, KATHRYN VOSS, RN, dir. nrsg. serv., Jackson Hospital, Marianna, FL '76 (NURS)
BYKER, BEN G., dir. pers., Mille Lacs Hospital, Onamia, MN '86 (PERS)
BYRD, BERNIE, supv. environ. serv., South Haven Community Hospital, South Haven, MI '79 (ENG)

BYRD, DEBORAH M., dir. educ. serv. and risk mgr., Arnot-Ogden Memorial Hospital, Elmira, NY '82 (EDUC)(RISK)
BYRD, LONNIE D. III, risk mgr., Riverside Hospital, Newport News, VA '80 (RISK)
BYRD, MABEL E., cent. serv. tech., St. Anthony Hospital, Michigan City, IN '86 (CS)
BYRD, MARIAN ARLENE, dir. soc. serv., Mercy Medical Center, Redding, CA '82 (SOC)
BYRD, RACHEL G., RN, asst. dir. nrsg., Charleston Area Medical Center, Charleston, WV '85 (NURS)
BYRD, ROBERT E., asst. adm., Alamance Memorial Hospital, Burlington, NC '77
BYRD, SAM, dir. risk mgt. and security, Portsmouth General Hospital, Portsmouth, VA '86 (RISK)
BYRD, STEPHANIE W., asst. vice-pres. fin., Christ Hospital, Cincinnati, OH '84 (RISK)
BYRD, WAVELINE SUE, dir. cent. serv., Christ Hospital, Cincinnati, OH '78 (CS)
BYRNE, DEIRDRE D., mgr., Ernst and Whinney, St. Louis, MO '85 (AMB)
BYRNE, DONNA L., asst. risk mgr. and coor. qual. assur., Morristown Memorial Hospital, Morristown, NJ '84 (RISK)
BYRNE, JO-ANN C. THOMPKINS, Charleston, SC '78 (EDUC)
BYRNE, JOHN H., dir. environ. serv., Riverside Hospital, Wilmington, DE '85 (ENG)
BYRNE, KATHERINE J., vice-pres. and chief exec. off., Southwest Catholic Health Network, Phoenix, AZ '80 (PR) (PLNG)
BYRNE, MARIAN J., adm. asst. and dir. vol. serv., James Lawrence Kernan Hospital, Baltimore, MD '86 (VOL)
BYRNE, MARY H., student, Boston University Health Management Programs, Boston, MA '86 (PLNG)
BYRNE, PAUL A., dir. neonatology, Archbishop Bergan Mercy Hospital, Omaha, NE '85 (RISK)
BYRNE, PEGGY, emp. asst. prog. mgr., Dominican Santa Cruz Hospital, Santa Cruz, CA '81 (SOC)
BYRNE, ROBERT F., MD, pres. and med. dir., Community Physicians, Inc., Virginia Beach, VA '84
BYRNE, THOMAS G., asst. adm., St. Michael Hospital, Texarkana, AR '73
BYRNES, EDWARD M., dir. soc. serv., Wyoming Medical Center, Casper, WY '86 (SOC)
BYRNES, MAUREEN, RN, Union Memorial Hospital, Baltimore, MD '77 (NURS)
BYRON, BRUCE JAMES, dir. matl. mgt., Woonsocket Hospital, Woonsocket, RI '79 (PUR)
BYRON, JOHN, dir. plant oper. and maint., St. Mary's Hospital, Orange, NJ '69 (ENG)
BYRON, WILLIAM J., dir. clin. oper., Eastern Maine Medical Center, Bangor, ME '76 (MGMT)
BYRON, WILLIAM J., adm. asst. dir., Geisinger Clinic, Danville, PA '80

C

CABALLERO, IRIS, dir. soc. serv., Kensington Hospital, Philadelphia, PA '86 (SOC)
CABBAN, PETER THOMAS, chief exec. off., CSF Australiasia, Ltd., Roseville, Australia '70 (MGMT)
CABIN, WILLIAM D., assoc., Home Health Associates, Totowa, NJ '87 (AMB)
CABLE, CLARK, partner, Coopers and Lybrand, Philadelphia, PA '80
CABLE, FRANK A., dir. plant oper., North Mississippi Medical Center, Tupelo, MS '80 (ENG)
CABOT, JEFFREY, student, Seton Hall University, Southorange, NJ '86 (PLNG)
CABRAL, JOHN, dir. hskpg., New England Baptist Hospital, Boston, MA '86 (ENVIRON)
CACCHIONE, THOMAS J., vice-pres. health care, Fitch Investors Service, Inc., Englewood, CO '80
CACCIA, ELAINE, RN, vice-pres. nrsg., Brandywine Hospital, Caln Township, PA '69 (NURS)
CACCIA, J. DONALD, Crouse-Irving Memorial Hospital, Syracuse, NY '76
CACIC, STEPHEN, coor. plng., Silver Cross Hospital, Joliet, IL '83 (PLNG)
CADA, JUDY A., RN, atty., Bailey, Polsky, Cada, Todd and Cope, Lincoln, NE '86 (RISK)
CADARET, DOUGLAS A., mgr. elec. serv., St. John Hospital, Detroit, MI '81 (ENG)
CADARIU, JOSEPH P., mgr. commun. rel., Holy Cross Hospital, Detroit, MI '86 (PR)
CADDELL, PAUL A., student, Program in Hospital Administration, University of Alabama at Birmingham, Birmingham, AL '85
CADDICK, ELIZABETH, dir. home care unit, Whidden Memorial Hospital, Everett, MA '87 (AMB)
CADDY, CAROL A., mgr. diet., Good Samaritan Hospital, Downers Grove, IL '84 (FOOD)
CADDY, E. REID, John Knox Village Medical Center, Tampa, FL '38 (LIFE)
CADEMARTORI, AUGUST D., vice-pres. pers. and labor rel., St. Luke's-Roosevelt Hospital Center, New York, NY '74 (PERS)
CADIZ, DOUGLAS R., chief soc. work serv., Veterans Administration Medical Center, Erie, PA '86 (SOC)
CADMUS, ROBERT RANDALL, MD, (ret.), Milwaukee, WI '54 (LIFE)
CADWELL, SHERWOOD S., atty., Woman's Christian Association Hospital, Jamestown, NY '68 (ATTY)
CADY, BARBARA A., assoc. pat. rep., Children's Hospital National Medical Center, Washington, DC '82 (PAT)
CADY, CHARLOTTE E., RN, vice-pres. nrsg., Children's Hospital of Philadelphia, Philadelphia, PA '83 (NURS)
CADY, HELEN M., RN, vice-pres. pat. care serv., St. Mary's Hospital, Reno, NV '87 (NURS)
CADY, JANE W., RN, asst. adm., Ontario Community Hospital, Ontario, CA '81 (NURS)
CAESAR, NEIL B., atty., Foster Medical Corporation, Home Health Care Division, Conshohocken, PA '84 (ATTY)
CAFARO, NICHOLAS J., assoc. dir., Mount Vernon Hospital, Mount Vernon, NY '49 (LIFE)
CAFER, JAYNE M., dir. vol., St. Francis Hospital and Medical Center, Topeka, KS '86 (VOL)
CAFFERKY, MICHAEL E., Upland, CA '86 (PLNG)
CAFFERTY, EARL J., asst. mgr. eng. serv., United Health Services, Johnson City, NY '56 (ENG)(LIFE)
CAFONE, ROBERT L., adm., Mount Sinai Medical Center, New York, NY '86 (MGMT)
CAFRAN, WAYNE, North Bellmore, NY '84
CAGAN, MARY ELLEN, prog. plng. spec., Baystate Medical Center, Springfield, MA '87 (AMB)
CAGE, CHARLES A., asst. adm., Kaiser Foundation Hospital, San Francisco, CA '86
CAGLE, GERALD W., dir. mgt. serv., Geisinger System Services, Danville, PA '77 (MGMT)
CAGLE, MARLIN, dir. maint., Decatur General Hospital, Decatur, AL '81 (ENG)
CAGUIAT, CARLOS J., adm. dir., Michigan State University Clinic Center, East Lansing, MI '77 (AMB)
CAHALAN, GLORIA J., RN, dir. vol. serv. and pat. advocate, Community General Hospital, Harris, NY '84 (VOL)(PAT)
CAHILL, JOHN M., dir. pub. rel. and dev., Moberly Regional Medical Center, Moberly, MO '86 (PR)
CAHILL, LTJG JOHN T., MSC USN, Naval Hospital, Groton, CT '85
CAHILL, KATHLEEN M., RN, clin. dir. maternal and child health, St. Joseph Hospital, Nashua, NH '86 (NURS)
CAHILL, MARCIA R., mgr. sup., proc. and distrib., Sherman Hospital, Elgin, IL '86 (CS)
CAHILL, PATRICIA A., atty., Department of Health and Hospital Archdiocese of New York, New York, NY '73 (ATTY)
CAHILL, TERRENCE F., dir. soc. serv., East Orange General Hospital, East Orange, NJ '81 (SOC)
CAHN, NEVA M., pat. rep. and risk mgr., Boulder Community Hospital, Boulder, CO '77 (PAT)(RISK)
CAIL, RONALD K., asst. adm., Vanderbilt University Hospital, Nashville, TN '85
CAIN, BARBARA, RN, dir. nrsg., Naples Community Hospital, Naples, FL '86 (NURS)
CAIN, C. RAY, Sherwood, OR '79 (MGMT)
CAIN, DANIEL G., mgr. matl. serv., Lankenau Hospital, Philadelphia, PA '85 (PUR)
CAIN, EVELYN A., RN, asst. adm. nrsg., St. Helen Hospital, Chehalis, WA '86 (NURS)
CAIN, JOHN L., dir. pers., University of Alabama Hospital, Birmingham, AL '83 (PERS)
CAIN, KATHI WHATLEY, dir. pur., Doctors Hospital, Tucker, GA '81 (PUR)
CAIN, MARY I., RN, dir. nrsg. serv., Mid-Valley Hospital, Omak, WA '83 (NURS)
CAIN, PEGGY C., RN, assoc. exec. dir. nrsg., Humana Hospital -Aurora, Aurora, CO '86 (NURS)
CAINE, DENNIS L., mktg. mgr. group pur., Hospital Central Service, Inc., Allentown, PA '86 (PUR)
CAINE, NORA C., dir. pub. rel. and mktg., Beaufort Memorial Hospital, Beaufort, SC '74 (PR)
CALABRESE-BOELSEN, TONI, dir. pub. rel., White Plains Hospital Medical Center, White Plains, NY '81 (PR)
CALAMAS, PAMELA K., dir. soc. serv., Tarpon Springs General Hospital, Tarpon Springs, FL '86 (SOC)
CALANDRO, ROSALIND R., dir. vol., St. John's Regional Health Center, Springfield, MO '84 (VOL)
CALBONE, ANGELO G., asst. adm., East Ohio Regional Hospital, Martins Ferry, OH '82
CALCAGNO, SHARON H., asst. adm., San Francisco General Hospital Medical Center, San Francisco, CA '86 (MGMT)
CALDERALA, FRANK E., chief bldg. mgt., Veterans Administration Medical Center, Lake City, FL '86 (ENVIRON)
CALDERIN, CAROLINA, assoc. adm., Pan American Hospital, Miami, FL '86 (RISK)
CALDERON, ELIZABETH H., vice-pres. pub. affairs, Hermann Hospital, Houston, TX '77 (PR)
CALDWELL, ADONNA, adm. dir. mktg. and health info., St. Joseph Hospital, Memphis, TN '85 (PR)
CALDWELL, DOROTHY J., cent. serv. tech., Monadnock Community Hospital, Peterborough, NH '81 (CS)
CALDWELL, GEORGE B., pres., Lutheran General Health Care Systems, Park Ridge, IL '53 (LIFE)
CALDWELL, GREGORY J., asst. dir. maint. and oper., Washington Hospital, Washington, PA '84 (ENG)
CALDWELL, HOLLY R., vice-pres., Samaritan Medical Foundation, Phoenix, AZ '83 (PLNG)
CALDWELL, MARGARET A., coor. sup., proc. and distrib., Germantown Hospital and Medical Center, Philadelphia, PA '83 (CS)
CALDWELL, MARION C., risk mgr., Bayfront Medical Center, St. Petersburg, FL '80 (RISK)
CALDWELL, MICHAEL A., atty., Kimball Medical Center, Lakewood, NJ '80 (ATTY)
CALDWELL, NAOMI RUTH, dir. matl. mgt., Community Hospital of Springfield and Clark County, Springfield, OH '75 (PUR)
CALDWELL, PATRICIA G., RN, sr. dir. nrsg., St. Francis Hospital, Greenville, SC '83 (NURS)
CALDWELL, PETER A., dir. matl. mgt. and transportation, Albert Einstein Medical Center, Philadelphia, PA '85 (PUR)
CALDWELL, PHYLLIS E., RN, dir. nrsg., St. Elizabeth's Hospital, Hannibal, MO '86 (NURS)
CALDWELL, RALPH A., asst. dir. diet., Memorial Medical Center, Springfield, IL '71 (FOOD)
CALDWELL, ROSE MARY, supv. commun., St. Mary Medical Center, Hobart, IN '86 (ENG)
CALDWELL, SANDRA, dir. mgt. eng., Fort Hamilton-Hughes Memorial Hospital, Hamilton, OH '80 (MGMT)
CALDWELL, SKIP, buyer, Memorial Hospital, Colorado Springs, CO '83 (PUR)
CALDWELL, WILLIAM, chief off. oper., John Randolph Hospital, Hopewell, VA '85 (RISK)
CALEO, LINDA S., asst. adm., Moline Public Hospital, Moline, IL '81 (PERS)
CALEY, GEORGE B., asst. adm., Winchester Medical Center, Winchester, VA '66
CALFEE, BARBARA E., atty., Saint Luke's Hospital, Cleveland, OH '85 (ATTY)
CALGI, DOMINICK R., vice-pres. oper., Nyack Hospital, Nyack, NY '77
CALGUIRE, WILLIAM J., dir. pers., Hennepin County Medical Center, Minneapolis, MN '74 (PERS)
CALHOUN, BOB, dir. matl. mgt., Riverview Hospital, Little Rock, AR '86 (PUR)
CALHOUN, CHESTER C., asst. adm., St. Elizabeth Hospital, Beaumont, TX '72
CALHOUN, D. BRAIN, dir. pub. rel., Buchanan General Hospital, Grundy, VA '86 (PR)
CALHOUN, JOSEPH E., vice-pres. fin., Sewickley Valley Hospital, Sewickley, PA '81 (PLNG)
CALHOUN, NORMA G., adm., Jesse Holman Jones Hospital, Springfield, TN '78 (PAT)
CALHOUN, ZAN F., pres., First Consulting Group, Long Beach, CA '82 (MGMT)
CALI, MARK J., asst. dir., Children's Hospital, Richmond, VA '87 (PUR)
CALI, MICHAEL D., MD, dir. emer. serv., General Hospital Center at Passaic, Passaic, NJ '86 (AMB)
CALICHMAN, MURRAY V., pres., Gbc Consulting Corporation, Huntington Station, NY '86 (MGMT)
CALIGA, LINDA B., actg. pres., St. Margaret's Hospital for Women, Boston, MA '82 (PLNG)
CALIHAN, VIRGINIA M., mgr. vol. serv., Mount Carmel Mercy Hospital, Detroit, MI '81 (VOL)
CALIP, MANOLITA S., RN, assoc. dir. maternal and child nrsg., St. Mary of Nazareth Hospital Center, Chicago, IL '83 (NURS)
CALIRI, LOUIS M., dir. matl. mgt., St. Francis Hospital, Wilmington, DE '79 (PUR)
CALKINS, JOANN R., RN, dir. nrs., Oaklawn Hospital, Marshall, MI '73 (NURS)
CALL, JIM M., dir. pat. rel., San Jose Hospital, San Jose, CA '86 (PAT)
CALLAGHAN, DONALD F., PhD, bd. mem. and health care consult., Sisters of Charity Health Care Systems, Houston, TX '68
CALLAGHAN, TRICIE, dir. med. soc. serv., Marcus Daly Memorial Hospital, Hamilton, MT '84 (SOC)
CALLAHAN, CAROL B., RN, asst. adm. nrsg., St. Anthony Hospital, Oklahoma City, OK '78 (NURS)
CALLAHAN, FRAN, dir. matl. mgt., AMI Parkway Regional Medical Center, North Miami Beach, FL '81 (PUR)
CALLAHAN, JAMES J., dir. plant oper. and maint., Jewish Hospital of St. Louis, St. Louis, MO '79 (ENG)
CALLAHAN, KEITH LAURENCE, vice-pres., Premier Hospitals Alliance, Inc., Westchester, IL '75
CALLAHAN, MARY F., RN, asst. adm., Commonwealth Hospital, Fairfax, VA '82 (NURS)
CALLAHAN, MICHAEL R., atty., Michael Reese Hospital and Medical Center, Chicago, IL '84 (ATTY)
CALLAHAN, ROD P., asst. adm. pers. serv., Washoe Medical Center, Reno, NV '82 (PERS)
CALLAHAN, SUE, Atlantic, IA '83 (PERS)
CALLAHAN, THOMAS E., asst. vice-pres. adm. serv., Lee Hospital, Johnstown, PA '86 (PLNG)
CALLAN, JAMES E. JR., dir. food serv., St. Joseph Hospital, Augusta, GA '82 (FOOD)
CALLENS, BETTYE J., supv. nrsg. and actg. asst. dir. nrsg., Cooper Green Hospital, Birmingham, AL '86 (NURS)
CALLIGARIS, CHARLES F., adm., Suny Health Science Center at Syracuse University Hospital, Syracuse, NY '54 (LIFE)
CALLISON, PRESTON H., atty., Baptist Medical Center, Columbia, SC '68 (ATTY)
CALLISON, WILLIAM LANCASTER, student, Georgia State University, Institute of Health Administration, Atlanta, GA '85
CALLOWAY, JOAN M., supv. food serv., Sloop Memorial Hospital, Crossnore, NC '77 (FOOD)
CALLOWAY, SUSAN J., coor. staff dev., Hays Memorial Hospital, San Marcos, TX '86 (EDUC)
CALLUM, JEAN R., asst. to vice-pres., Catherine McAuley Health Center, Ann Arbor, MI '84
CALMES, PAUL M., Boerne, TX '84
CALOGGERO, CONSTANCE M., asst. to prog. dev. dir., St. Elizabeth's Hospital of Boston, Boston, MA '74 (PLNG)
CALOGGERO, SUSAN, RN, student, Lesley College, Program in Health Service Management, Jamaica Plain, MA '84
CALTON, JUDGE T., pres., Methodist Hospitals of Memphis, Memphis, TN '72 (PLNG)
CALU, GAIL Z., pub. rel. asst., Rhode Island Hospital, Providence, RI '86 (PR)
CALVARUSO, JOSEPH T., corp. dev., Mount Carmel Health, Columbus, OH '86 (PLNG)
CALVERT, ANNE M., sr. consult., HealthMarket Dynamics, Louisville, KY '79 (PR)
CALVERT, JAMES W., dir. matl. mgt., Methodist Evangelical Hospital, Louisville, KY '67 (PUR)
CALVERT, LUCILLE S., coor. educ. and trng., Walker Regional Medical Center, Jasper, AL '85 (EDUC)
CALVIN, CAL, pres., Hospital Mktg Alternative, Inc., Bartlesville, OK '87 (PR)
CALVIN, RUTH W., student, London Business School-Health Economics, London, England '84
CALZONETTI, JANICE, dir. diet., Kennedy Memorial Hospitals-University Medical Center-Cherry Hill Division, Cherry Hill, NJ '84 (FOOD)
CAMACHO, MERCEDES E., assoc. adm., State University Hospital, Downstate Medical Center, Brooklyn, NY '85 (RISK)
CAMAIONI, JOHN H., vice-pres. and adm., Seton Medical Center, Daly City, CA '65

CAMBRIDGE, ELIZABETH A., asst. dir., Baptist Hospital of Miami, Miami, FL '87 (ENVIRON)
CAMCAM, GLORIA A., chief nutr. serv., St. Elizabeth's Hospital, Chicago, IL '81 (FOOD)
CAMERO, ADRIAN, dir. matl. mgt., Greater Southeast Community Hospital, Washington, DC '82 (PUR)
CAMERON, A. CRAIG, atty., Florida Hospital Medical Center, Orlando, FL '81 (ATTY)
CAMERON, DAVID BRIAN, asst. adm., Detroit Receiving Hospital, Detroit, MI '76
CAMERON, HUGH R., pres., Camtech, Inc., Indianapolis, IN '80 (ENG)
CAMERON, JEFFREY D., mgr. matl., Mercy Hospital, Port Huron, MI '84 (PUR)
CAMERON, JOHN C., vice-pres., Methodist Hospital, Philadelphia, PA '73 (ATTY)
CAMERON, KAREN LEE, adm. res., Rome Hospital and Murphy Memorial Hospital, Rome, NY '87
CAMERON, MICKEY S., diet., Atlanta Hospital, Atlanta, GA '80 (FOOD)
CAMERON, RICHARD MICHAEL, asst. adm., Henry Ford Hospital, Detroit, MI '79
CAMERON, RODERICK A., dir. eng., Lawrence and Memorial Hospital, New London, CT '84 (ENG)
CAMERON, SUSAN K., RN, dir. cent. sterilization, Grand Island Memorial Hospital, Grand Island, NE '82 (CS)
CAMERON, WILLIAM ROBERT, (ret.), Pasco, WA '66
CAMISI, DOMENICK J., group sr. vice-pres., New Jersey Hospital Association, Princeton, NJ '83
CAMMACK, THOMAS N. JR., sr. vice-pres., All Saints Episcopal Hospital, Fort Worth, TX '75
CAMMARANO, PATRICK, dir. eng., Beth Israel Hospital, Passaic, NJ '85 (ENG)
CAMOSSO, AL M., adm., Providence Hospital, Anchorage, AK '77
CAMP, BLAINE R., prod. mgr., Continental Hlthcare Systems, Overland Park, KS '86 (PUR)
CAMP, JAMES H., vice-pres. educ. serv., North Carolina Hospital Association, Raleigh, NC '73 (EDUC)
CAMP, PHYLLIS W., dir. soc. work, North Mississippi Medical Center, Tupelo, MS '86 (SOC)
CAMP, SHERIDAN, maint. mech., Memorial Hospital, Towanda, PA '85 (ENG)
CAMP, SUZANNE A., dir. vol. serv. and chaplaincy, Greater Southeast Community Hospital, Washington, DC '85 (VOL)
CAMP, SUZANNE SMALL, dir. soc. work, St. Mary's Hospital, Leonardtown, MD '78 (SOC)
CAMPANA, KAREN S., res. and dev. asst., Franciscan Sisters Health Care Corporation, Mokena, IL '83
CAMPANA, RONALD A., dir. commun. rel. and mktg., Williamsburg Community Hospital, Williamsburg, VA '84 (PR)
CAMPANE, LAWRENCE J., atty., Natchaug Hospital, Mansfield Center, CT '85 (ATTY)
CAMPANELLA, SARICE M., fin. analyst, Blue Cross and Blue Shield of Fl, Jacksonville, FL '84
CAMPANO, JOHN, asst. gen. counsel and risk mgr., Lenox Hill Hospital, New York, NY '86 (RISK)
CAMPAZZI, BETTY C., field rep., Joint Commission on Accreditation of Hospitals, Chicago, IL '83 (NURS)
CAMPBELL, ALLAN N., dir. mktg. and dev., Lee Hospital, Johnstown, PA '84 (PR) (PLNG)
CAMPBELL, BERNARD M. JR., dir. human res., Alleghany Regional Hospital, Clifton Forge, VA '86 (PERS)
CAMPBELL, BRIAN E., syst. eng., Community Hospital of Springfield and Clark County, Springfield, OH '77 (MGMT)
CAMPBELL, BRIAN W., vice-pres., Research Development Group, Kansas City, MO '82
CAMPBELL, BRUCE C., DrPH, pres., Campbell Associates, Chicago, IL '75
CAMPBELL, BRUCE E., dir. risk mgt., St. Joseph Hospital, Providence, RI '85 (RISK)
CAMPBELL, CINDY C., RN, dir. nrs., Memorial Hospital at Gulfport, Gulfport, MS '84 (NURS)
CAMPBELL, COLLEEN L., independent nrs. educ., Tacoma, WA '85 (EDUC)
CAMPBELL, CURTIS KEITH, pres. and chief exec. off., Seward General Hospital, Seward, AK '63
CAMPBELL, DANIEL J., supt. bldg. and grd., Jeanes Hospital, Philadelphia, PA '80 (ENG)
CAMPBELL, DAVID B., dir. pers., Milford-Whitinsville Regional Hospital, Milford, MA '80 (PERS)
CAMPBELL, DAVID J., pres., Allegheny General Hospital, Pittsburgh, PA '85 (PLNG)
CAMPBELL, DONALD F., pres., Howmedica Campbell Associates, Inc., York, ME '85 (PUR)
CAMPBELL, DONNA HEERN, dir. soc. serv., Missouri Delta Medical Center, Sikeston, MO '85 (SOC)
CAMPBELL, DOROTHY A., RN, nrsg. adm., Parkland Medical Center, Derry, NH '86 (NURS)
CAMPBELL, DOUGLAS W., mgr. eng. oper., John Randolph Hospital, Hopewell, VA '86 (ENG)
CAMPBELL, DUNCAN M. JR., mgr. sup., proc. and distrib., Hackley Hospital, Muskegon, MI '83 (CS)
CAMPBELL, EMILY E., asst. coor. educ., St. Luke's Hospital, San Francisco, CA '80 (EDUC)
CAMPBELL, GARETH R., assoc. dir., University of Chicago Hospitals, Chicago, IL '67 (PLNG)
CAMPBELL, GEORGE, dir. refrigeration and air conditioning, Winter Haven Hospital, Winter Haven, FL '85 (ENG)
CAMPBELL, GEORGE, dir. bldg. serv., Pottstown Memorial Medical Center, Pottstown, PA '81 (ENG)
CAMPBELL, GLENN R., vice-pres. clin. serv., Akron City Hospital, Akron, OH '80 (PLNG)
CAMPBELL, GREGORY R., student, Concordia College, Moorehead, MN '86
CAMPBELL, HENRY M. III, atty., Jennings Memorial Hospital, Detroit, MI '68 (ATTY)
CAMPBELL, IONE G., RN, assoc. dir. nrsg., Central Maine Medical Center, Lewiston, ME '86 (NURS)
CAMPBELL, JAMES G., dir. mgt. sci., UCLA Medical Center, Los Angeles, CA '78 (MGMT)
CAMPBELL, JANE A., pers. rep., Petaluma Valley Hospital, Petaluma, CA '82 (PERS)
CAMPBELL, JANIE L., RN, vice-pres. pat. serv., St. Mary of Nazareth Hospital Center, Chicago, IL '75 (NURS)
CAMPBELL, JEAN, vice-pres. and dir. corp. mktg., St. Anthony's Medical Center, St. Louis, MO '85 (PLNG)
CAMPBELL, JEANNE PHILLIPS, adm. asst., Medical Center Hospital, Odessa, TX '83
CAMPBELL, JERRY, exec. dir., Johnson County Regional Hospital, Clarksville, AR '75
CAMPBELL, JOAN T., vice-pres. human res., Borgess Medical Center, Kalamazoo, MI '84 (PERS)
CAMPBELL, JOHN A. JR., mgr. commun. rel., Rowan Memorial Hospital, Salisbury, NC '86 (PR)
CAMPBELL, JOHN BOYD JR., vice-pres. constr., American Medical International, Brea, CA '78 (ENG)
CAMPBELL, JOHN W., natl. sales mgr., Controlonics Communications, Westford, MA '87
CAMPBELL, JUDITH, dir. soc. work, Memorial Hospital, Hollywood, FL '79 (SOC)
CAMPBELL, JUNE K., asst. dir. vol. serv., Binghamton General Hospital, Binghamton, NY '85 (VOL)
CAMPBELL, KATHARINE ANN, dir. vol., Bannock Regional Medical Center, Pocatello, ID '86 (VOL)
CAMPBELL, KAY B., RN, health educ. nrs., Waterman Medical Center, Eustis, FL '85 (EDUC)
CAMPBELL, KENNETH G., vice-pres. human res., Hermann Hospital, Houston, TX '86 (PERS)
CAMPBELL, LARRY J., dir. environ. serv., Rehabilitation Institute of Pittsburgh, Pittsburgh, PA '81 (ENG)
CAMPBELL, LINDA R., RN, dir. amb. care, H. Lee Moffitt Cancer Center, Tampa, FL '87 (AMB)(NURS)
CAMPBELL, LOIS, supv. cent. serv., Craig Hospital, Englewood, CO '85 (CS)
CAMPBELL, LORIN SCOTT, asst. prof., Department of Social and Administrative Medicine, Chapel Hill, NC '66
CAMPBELL, MANIE W., sr. mgr., Ernst and Whinney, Houston, TX '83 (PLNG)
CAMPBELL, MARIANNE B., dir. commun. rel. and dev., Holzer Medical Center, Gallipolis, OH '72 (PR)
CAMPBELL, MARION W., dir. press off., Virginia Department of Mental Health and Mental Retardation, Richmond, VA '84 (PR)
CAMPBELL, MARY K., RN, vice-pres., Incarnate Word Hospital, St. Louis, MO '84 (NURS)
CAMPBELL, MAUREEN, asst. dir. matl. mgt., Bryn Mawr Hospital, Bryn Mawr, PA '85 (PUR)
CAMPBELL, MONICA T., mgr. sup., proc. and distrib., St. Joseph's Hospital and Medical Center, Phoenix, AZ '83 (CS)
CAMPBELL, NEIL D., dir. eng. serv., Emma L. Bixby Hospital, Adrian, MI '84 (ENG)
CAMPBELL, PATRICIA A., atty., Eastwood Hospital, Memphis, TN '82 (ATTY)
CAMPBELL, PATRICIA A., dir. soc. serv., Marcus J. Lawrence Memorial Hospital, Cottonwood, AZ '79 (SOC)
CAMPBELL, PEGGY, asst. prod. mgr., Commission on Professional and Hospital Activities, Ann Arbor, MI '79
CAMPBELL, R. O. SCOTT, asst. adm. pub. affairs, Grand View Hospital, Sellersville, PA '75 (PR) (PLNG)
CAMPBELL, RAY, mgr. commun., Hinsdale Hospital, Hinsdale, IL '84 (ENG)
CAMPBELL, SR. REGINA MARIE, coor. pat. rel., Holy Cross Hospital, Fort Lauderdale, FL '79 (PAT)
CAMPBELL, RICHARD O., atty., La Plata Community Hospital, Durango, CO '83 (ATTY)
CAMPBELL, ROBERT F., dir. facil. serv., Faulkner Hospital, Boston, MA '85 (ENG)
CAMPBELL, ROBERT P., MD, dir. resp. disease serv. and inhal. ther., San Antonio State Chest Hospital, San Antonio, TX '67
CAMPBELL, ROSS E., atty., Stanford University Hospital, Stanford, CA '83 (ATTY)
CAMPBELL, RUTH M., RN, dir. pat. care serv., Pekin Memorial Hospital, Pekin, IL '84 (NURS)
CAMPBELL, SAMUEL R., dir. plant serv., Metroplex Hospital, Killeen, TX '81 (ENG)
CAMPBELL, SARAH S., dir. food serv., Illinois Masonic Medical Center, Chicago, IL '79 (FOOD)
CAMPBELL, SCOTT N., plng. consult., Brim and Associates, Inc., Portland, OR '81 (PLNG)
CAMPBELL, STEPHEN J., assoc. adm., Chandler Community Hospital, Chandler, AZ '86 (RISK)
CAMPBELL, STEVE, mgr. matl., Herrick Hospital and Health Center, Berkeley, CA '83 (PUR)
CAMPBELL, TOM M., dir. pub. affairs, Oklahoma Osteopathic Hospital, Tulsa, OK '83 (PR)
CAMPBELL, WENDELL E., asst. adm., St. Francis Hospital Center, Beech Grove, IN '71 (MGMT)
CAMPBELL, WINONA H., mgr. continuity care, Saint Therese Medical Center, Waukegan, IL '86 (SOC)
CAMPEL, ROBERT J., mgr. org. analyst, Kings County Hospital Center, Brooklyn, NY '72 (MGMT)
CAMPER, ARLENE, dir. pub. rel. and mktg., St. Peter's Community Hospital, Helena, MT '79 (PR)
CAMPER, J. ROBERT, dir. facil., Stanford University Hospital, Stanford, CA '86 (ENG)
CAMPERUD, PRISCILLA A., asst. adm. human res., St. Joseph's Hospital, Stockton, CA '80 (PERS)
CAMPIGOTTO, JOHN J., dir. diet., Licking Memorial Hospital, Newark, OH '86 (FOOD)
CAMPION, BEVERLY S., dir. food and nutr. serv., Mercy Catholic Medical Center, Philadelphia, PA '86 (FOOD)
CAMPION, JANE K., Mayo Clinic, Rochester, MN '78
CAMPISANO, JOSEPH F., dir. trng. and dev., Conemaugh Valley Memorial Hospital, Johnstown, PA '78 (EDUC)
CAMPISANO, NANCY, dir. counseling serv., Cardinal Hill Hospital, Lexington, KY '86 (SOC)
CAMPMAN, KATHLEEN C., pat. rep., Penrose Hospitals, Colorado Springs, CO '82 (PAT)
CAMPOBASSO, FRED D., pres., American Medical Design Corporation, Chicago, IL '86 (PLNG)
CAMPODALL'ORTO, JANICE M., coor. pat. and prof. serv., St. Luke's Hospital, San Francisco, CA '81 (RISK)
CAMPONOVO, LT. DEBORAH L., asst. adm. and surg. dir., Naval Hospital, Bethesda, MD '83
CAMPOS, ANTHONY D., indust. eng., Data Control Corporation, Portsmouth, NH '86 (MGMT)
CAMPOS, DENNIS A., vice-pres. human res., San Pedro Peninsula Hospital, San Pedro, CA '85 (EDUC)
CAMPOS, HELGA C., asst. dir. food and nutr. care serv., R. E. Thomason General Hospital, El Paso, TX '84 (FOOD)
CAMPS, MAUREEN S., dir. commun. rel., Peoples Community Hospital Authority, Wayne, MI '81 (PR)
CAMRAS, MICHAEL J., atty., Temple Community Hospital, Los Angeles, CA '78 (ATTY)
CAMUSO, PETER C., asst. mgr. eng., Munroe Regional Medical Center, Ocala, FL '86 (ENG)
CANADY, LEROY, asst. adm., Methodist Hospital, Brooklyn, NY '73
CANALE, CATHERINE, dir. qual. assessment, Mercy Hospital of New Orleans, New Orleans, LA '87 (RISK)
CANAN, BRUCE A., atty., East Liverpool City Hospital, East Liverpool, OH '87 (ATTY)
CANBY, EUGENE, Dundas, Ont., Canada '81 (PLNG)
CANDA, KATHLEEN B., coor. pat. educ., University Hospitals of Cleveland, Cleveland, OH '87 (EDUC)
CANDAU, M. G., MD, dir. gen. emeritus, World Health Organization, Geneva, Switzerland '59 (HON)
CANDELARIA, LEANDRO JR., asst. dir. plant oper., San Juan Regional Medical Center, Farmington, NM '81 (ENG)
CANDIA, GARY R., PhD, vice-pres., Abington Memorial Hospital, Abington, PA '80 (PLNG)
CANDIDA, VINCENT L., dir. human res., Loudoun Memorial Hospital, Leesburg, VA '81 (PERS)(RISK)
CANDIOTTI, LOUIS T., mgr. review objectives, Michigan Peer Review Organization, Plymouth, MI '85 (PLNG)
CANDITO, DONALD G., mgr. plant eng., Perth Amboy Division, Perth Amboy, NJ '82 (ENG)
CANEDY, JAMES A., adm., Bishop Clarkson Memorial Hospital, Omaha, NE '52 (LIFE)
CANFIELD, AUSTIN F. JR., atty., Children's Hospital National Medical Center, Washington, DC '81 (ATTY)
CANFIELD, ERNEST E., dir. human res., St. Peter's Hospital, Albany, NY '86 (PERS)
CANIFF, CHARLES E. JR., atty., Haverford Community Hospital, Havertown, PA '75 (ATTY)
CANIGIANI, PATRICIA, RN, asst. adm. nrsg. serv., Mid-Island Hospital, Bethpage, NY '85 (NURS)
CANNA, MARILYN, coor. commun., American Medical Association, Chicago, IL '85 (PR)
CANNAMELA, ROMOLO A., exec. dir. and dir. soc. serv., Family Counseling Center, Inc., Columbus, GA '75 (SOC)
CANNIFF-GILLIAM, CATHY, RN, vice-pres. oper., Orlando Regional Medical Center, Orlando, FL '80 (NURS)
CANNIZZARO, KATHLEEN G., coor. educ. serv., Thomas Jefferson University Hospital, Philadelphia, PA '84 (EDUC)
CANNON, JANICE D., dir. food serv., Cranston General Hospital Osteopathic, Cranston, RI '83 (FOOD)
CANNON, JOHN V. III, atty., Sarasota Memorial Hospital, Sarasota, FL '79 (ATTY)
CANNON, LINDA J., mgr. pers., St. Rose de Lima Hospital, Henderson, NV '86 (PERS)
CANNON, LINDA L., risk mgr., St. Vincent's Medical Center, Bridgeport, CT '84 (RISK)
CANNON, PEGGY I., RN, vice-pres., Good Samaritan Community Healthcare, Puyallup, WA '82 (NURS)
CANNON, PEGGY, vice-pres. human res., St. Mary's Hospital and Medical Center, Grand Junction, CO '80 (PERS)(RISK)
CANNON, SUSAN A., adm., Bucktail Medical Center, Renovo, PA '86
CANNON, WILL ALBAN JR., bd. chm., Cannon Design, Inc., Grand Island, NY '63 (PLNG)
CANOVA, BERT N., vice-pres. matl. mgt., Sisters of St. Joseph Health Systems of Wichita, Wichita, KS '84 (PUR)
CANTARANO, LAWRENCE F., pur. agt., Park City Hospital, Bridgeport, CT '80 (PUR)
CANTER, HELEN J., lead cent. serv. tech., Highline Community Hospital, Seattle, WA '85 (CS)
CANTER, RICHARD J., atty., St. Michael Hospital, Milwaukee, WI '84 (ATTY)
CANTEY, EMMA O., risk mgr., Madison County Memorial Hospital, Madison, FL '86 (RISK)
CANTIN, JOHN, sr. vice-pres., Reed Stenhouse, Ltd., Montreal, Que., Canada '84 (RISK)
CANTONWINE, DIANE E., dir. vol., Middletown Regional Hospital, Middletown, OH '86 (VOL)
CANTOR, SEYMOUR M., dir. spec. proj., Botsford General Hospital, Farmington Hills, MI '83 (RISK)
CANTRELL, GREGORY Z., asst. adm., Charter Peachford Hospital, Atlanta, GA '84 (PLNG)
CANTWELL, ELIZABETH A., RN, vice-pres., Oak Ridge Hospital of the United Methodist Church, Oak Ridge, TN '71 (NURS)
CANTWELL, MARVIN L., chief eng., Baptist Regional Health Center, Miami, OK '85 (ENG)
CAPAL, DAVID F., asst. dir. plant and prop., Good Samaritan Hospital, Cincinnati, OH '86 (ENG)
CAPALDI, EVELYN A., supv. cent. serv., St. Agnes Medical Center, Philadelphia, PA '82 (CS)
CAPARCO, ANTHONY, asst. dir. plant eng., Imperial Point Medical Center, Fort Lauderdale, FL '85 (ENG)
CAPARROS, CHERYL, coor. risk mgt., Long Beach Memorial Hospital, Long Beach, NY '87 (RISK)
CAPEL, COL. WALLACE, Veterans Administration Hospital, Tuskegee, AL '71
CAPERS, MARILYN J., coor. vol. serv., Brooklyn Hospital-Caledonian Hospital, Brooklyn, NY '86 (VOL)
CAPEZIO, JOSEPH GRAHAM, dir. pers., Mountainside Hospital, Montclair, NJ '83 (PERS)
CAPIELANO, MICHAEL A., dir. maint. and environ. serv., River Oaks Hospital, New Orleans, LA '85 (ENG)
CAPILI, JOAN WOHLITKA, mgr. diet. serv., Group Health Eastside Hospital, Redmond, WA '81 (FOOD)
CAPIN, CYNTHIA J., dir. vol., Miller-Dwan Medical Center, Duluth, MN '83 (VOL)
CAPLE, PAULA G., mgt. eng., Baptist Medical System, Little Rock, AR '85 (MGMT)

CAPLES, ANNE L., RN, dir. educ., Healthcare Information Network, Princeton, NJ '77 (EDUC)
CAPOBIANCO, MICHAEL J., dir. commun. rel., Saint Joseph Hospital, Reading, PA '83 (PR)
CAPOCACCIA, MARY ANN, RN, asst. adm., St. Joseph Hospital, Memphis, TN '79 (NURS)
CAPODANNO, ANN E., asst. dir. oper. analyst, Medlantic Healthcare Group, Washington, DC '84 (MGMT)
CAPONE, AUDREY, mgr. cent. sup., Meadowlands Hospital Medical Center, Secaucus, NJ '85 (CS)
CAPONE, JOSEPH, dir. health care div., Defrank and Sons Corporation, New Haven, CT '82
CAPOZZALO, GAYLE, corp. dir. plng. and mktg., Sisters of St. Mary, St. Louis, MO '81 (PLNG)
CAPOZZI, LORRAINE S., mgr. pub. rel., St. Clair Memorial Hospital, Pittsburgh, PA '85 (PR)
CAPPEL, SAM D., dir. pers., Seventh Ward General Hospital, Hammond, LA '82 (PERS)
CAPPELLI, JAMES F., mgr. matl., Reston Hospital Center, Reston, VA '85 (PUR)
CAPPS, DICKSON M., adm., The Harbin Clinic, Rome, GA '81 (ENG)(PLNG)
CAPPS, GRADY, eng., Alamance Memorial Hospital, Burlington, NC '86 (ENG)
CAPPS, HAROLD KLINE JR., asst. chief eng., Iowa Lutheran Hospital, Des Moines, IA '85 (ENG)
CAPRETTO, ROBERT A., adm. emp. rel., Lorain Community Hospital, Lorain, OH '80 (PERS)
CAPRON, JOHN FRANCIS III, dir. safety, Cleveland Clinic Foundation, Cleveland, OH '80 (RISK)(ENG)
CAPSTICK, BRIAN, atty., Capstick, Hamer and Company, St. James's London, England '86 (ATTY)
CAPURSO, JOHN F., assoc. dir. adm.-emp. rel., Emma Pendleton Bradley Hospital, Riverside, RI '81 (PERS)
CAPUTA, MICHAEL J., dir. soc. serv., Chandler Community Hospital, Chandler, AZ '86 (SOC)
CAPUTI, MARIE A., PhD, health care consult., Midwest Center for Human Services, Madison, WI '79 (SOC)
CAPUTI, THOMAS S., dir. matl. mgt., Englewood Hospital, Englewood, FL '86 (PUR)
CAPUTO, CHARLES S. II, student, Alfred University, Alfred, NY '85
CAPUTO, FRANKLIN T., dir. sup. serv., Bristol Hospital, Bristol, CT '86 (ENVIRON)
CARABELLI, PAULA, asst. vice-pres., Santa Monica Hospital Medical Center, Santa Monica, CA '84 (RISK)
CARACCI, MARYBETH, dir. pub. rel., Zurbrugg Memorial Hospital, Riverside Division, Riverside, NJ '84 (PR)
CARACCIOLO, KEVIN J., asst. vice-pres. human res., Kennedy Memorial Hospitals University Medical Center, Stratford, NJ '86 (PERS)
CARAGHER, JAMES E., asst. adm., Saint Francis Medical Center, Peoria, IL '64 (PR)
CARALIS, GEORGE P., adm., Grace Hospital, Detroit, MI '78
CARAM, DENISE, dir. vol., Midwest City Memorial Hospital, Midwest City, OK '80 (VOL)
CARAM, LORETTA, asst. to dir. sup., proc. and distrib., Mercy Health Center, Oklahoma City, OK '86 (CS)
CARAMANICA, LAURA J., RN, asst. vice-pres. and dir. nrsg., Mount Sinai Hospital, Hartford, CT '85 (NURS)
CARAWAY, RICHARD R., chief eng., Woman's Hospital, Jackson, MS '82 (ENG)
CARB, SAUL, PhD, exec. vice-pres., Jackson Park Hospital, Chicago, IL '57 (LIFE)
CARBECK, ROBERT B., MD, exec. vice-pres., Catherine McAuley Health Center, Ann Arbor, MI '83 (PLNG)
CARBERY, STEPHEN J., asst. dir. eng., Greenwich Hospital, Greenwich, CT '86 (ENG)
CARBONE, DAVID M., assoc. exec. dir., Humana Hospital -Bennett, Plantation, FL '78
CARBONE, JOSEPH F., mgt. review off., Westmead Hospital, Westmead, Australia '85 (MGMT)
CARCHEDI, CAROLYN J., coor. vol. serv., Greater Laurel Beltsville Hospital, Laurel, MD '84 (VOL)
CARCIA, ROY, dir. mgt. eng., Manchester Memorial Hospital, Manchester, CT '84 (MGMT)
CARDEN, DONNA S., mgt. eng., Harrisburg Hospital, Harrisburg, PA '85 (MGMT)
CARDEN, JERRY A., coor. educ., Mercy Hospital, Urbana, IL '81 (EDUC)
CARDEN, TERRENCE S. JR., MD, dir. emer. serv., Highland Park Hospital, Highland Park, IL '87 (AMB)
CARDER, DENNIS L., asst. exec. dir., Pleasant Valley Hospital, Point Pleasant, WV '87 (AMB)
CARDER, ELIZABETH BYRD, atty., American Hlthcare Association, Washington, DC '80 (ATTY)
CARDER, WILLIAM W., vice-pres., Voluntary Hospitals of America-Michigan, Inc., Grand Rapids, MI '79 (PLNG)
CARDILLO, ROBERT J., asst. adm., Sacred Heart Hospital, Norristown, PA '83
CARDINALE, ANTHONY C. III, adm., Naval Medical Command Northwest, Oakland, CA '79 (PERS)
CARDINALE, KATHLEEN, RN, sr. vice-pres. nrsg., Cabrini Medical Center, New York, NY '78 (NURS)
CARDWELL, HORACE M., pres., Hospital-Medical Communications, Inc., Lufkin, TX '48 (LIFE)
CARDWELL, PAMELA, mgr. cent. sup., St. James Hospital Medical Center, Chicago Heights, IL '86 (CS)
CARDWELL, SCARLET L., dir. med. soc. work, Presbyterian Hospital, Charlotte, NC '80 (SOC)
CARELS, EDWARD J., PhD, exec. vice-pres., Comprehensive Care Corporation, Irvine, CA '86 (PLNG)
CAREY, ANNE L., dir. soc. work, William Beaumont Hospital-Troy, Troy, MI '76 (SOC)
CAREY, BLANCHE E., student, Herbert H. Lehman College, Bronx, NY '82
CAREY, GRACE R., dir. educ. serv., Wausau Hospital Center, Wausau, WI '81 (EDUC)
CAREY, MARLENE R., vice-pres. corp. commun., St. John's Healthcare Corporation, Anderson, IN '86 (PR)
CAREY, ROBERT E., consult., Medco, Inc., Langhorne, PA '83 (MGMT)
CAREY, RONALD C., atty., Clinton Memorial Hospital, Wilmington, OH '76 (ATTY)
CAREY, SALLY, dir. soc. serv., Cobb General Hospital, Austell, GA '81 (SOC)
CAREY, SHIRLEY L., dir. soc. serv., Sturgis Hospital, Sturgis, MI '79 (PAT)(SOC)
CARGILL, JAMES W. III, pur. agt., Memorial Hospital System, Houston, TX '76 (PUR)
CARGILL, VIRGINIA LEE, pat. rel. rep., Rapid City Regional Hospital, Rapid City, SD '87 (PAT)
CARGO, JACK W., dir. pers., Lee Hospital, Johnstown, PA '68 (PERS)
CARHART, HELEN D., asst. dir. environ. serv., Riverview Medical Center, Red Bank, NJ '87 (ENVIRON)
CARHART, ROBERT S., mgr. mktg., Washington Healthcare Corporation, Washington, DC '85 (PR) (PLNG)
CARISSIMI, DEREK C., asst. dir. human res., Hutzel Hospital, Detroit, MI '83 (PERS)
CARITHERS, HERBERT PAUL, dir. eng., Jellico Community Hospital, Jellico, TN '76 (ENG)
CARITHERS, ROBERT W., (ret.), Evansville, IN '51
CARL, BARTON, dir. risk mgt. and qual. assur., Oklahoma Health Network, Oklahoma City, OK '86 (RISK)
CARLBERG, DUANE A., exec. vice-pres. and dir., Inter-Community Medical Center, Covina, CA '80
CARLBERG, PAUL R., adm. asst. and dir. pers., Glover Memorial Hospital, Needham, MA '83 (PERS)
CARLE, CHRIS G., student, University of Cincinnati, Cincinnati, OH '86 (MGMT)
CARLIN, BEATRICE J., RN, dir. nrsg. serv., Lawrence Hospital, Bronxville, NY '74 (NURS)
CARLINO, ELAINE, dir. pers., Mount Zion Hospital and Medical Center, San Francisco, CA '81 (PERS)
CARLINO, ROSE T., RN, asst. vice-pres. nrsg., Lutheran Medical Center, Brooklyn, NY '67 (NURS)
CARLISLE, ACREE B., sr. partner, Page Southerland Page, Houston, TX '82
CARLISLE, HARRIETTE L., dir. med. soc. serv., Magee-Womens Hospital, Pittsburgh, PA '74 (SOC)
CARLISLE, RICHARD E., dir. eng. and maint., Sarasota Memorial Hospital, Sarasota, FL '84 (ENG)
CARLISLE, ROBERT H., group contr., Hospital Management Professionals, Inc., Naperville, IL '85
CARLISLE, VIRGINIA M., RN, dir. amb. care serv., Memorial Medical Center, Savannah, GA '87 (AMB)
CARLO, ARLENE, RN, mgr. cent. sup., Bergen Pines County Hospital, Paramus, NJ '85 (CS)
CARLQUIST, ROBERT E., dir. pur., Skokie Valley Hospital, Skokie, IL '82 (PUR)
CARLS, BETH B., dir. plng. and res., HCA Woodland Heights Medical Center, Lufkin, TX '81 (PLNG)
CARLS, LINDA A., mgt. eng., SunHealth Corporation, Charlotte, NC '86 (MGMT)
CARLSEN, MARY S., dir. soc. serv., Mount Sinai Hospital, Minneapolis, MN '86 (SOC)
CARLSON, ANDRAE E., student, Concordia College, Moorhead, MN '87
CARLSON, BARBARA J., vice-pres. pers., Dickinson County Hospitals, Iron Mountain, MI '86 (PERS)
CARLSON, BINGHAM H., dir. soc. work serv., South Highlands Hospital, Birmingham, AL '83 (SOC)
CARLSON, BOBBIE, dir. pub. rel. and mktg., Grand Island Memorial Hospital, Grand Island, NE '85 (PR)
CARLSON, BRIAN J., vice-pres. corp. dev., St. Joseph's Medical Center, Brainerd, MN '86 (PLNG)
CARLSON, CAROL A., RN, clin. dir. nrsg., Fairview-Southdale Hospital, Edina, MN '84 (NURS)
CARLSON, CRAIG E., atty., Trinity Regional Hospital, Fort Dodge, IA '81 (ATTY)
CARLSON, DIANE E., dir. pub. rel., St. Francis Hospital, Evanston, IL '85 (PR)
CARLSON, DIANE K., RN, vice-pres. and dir. nrsg., St. Joseph Hospital, Kirkwood, MO '83 (NURS)
CARLSON, DOUGLAS R., atty., Northwestern Memorial Hospital, Chicago, IL '75 (ATTY)
CARLSON, EDGAR L., dir. bldg. serv., Mercy Medical Center, Nampa, ID '83 (ENG)
CARLSON, EDWARD R. JR., dir. plant eng., St. Elizabeth Hospital Medical Center, Lafayette, IN '79 (ENG)
CARLSON, G. I., dir. pur., Northside Hospital, Atlanta, GA '78 (PUR)
CARLSON, GREG L., vice-pres. prof. serv., Ball Memorial Hospital, Muncie, IN '82 (PLNG)
CARLSON, HELEN M., asst. dir. vol. serv., Yale-New Haven Hospital, New Haven, CT '78 (VOL)
CARLSON, HERBERT L., pur. agt., Christ Hospital and Medical Center, Oak Lawn, IL '85 (PUR)
CARLSON, JEAN R., dir. nrsg., Mercy Hospital, Portsmouth, OH '87 (AMB)
CARLSON, JOCELYN E., dir. educ., Health Northeast, Manchester, NH '67 (EDUC)
CARLSON, K. CAROL, vice-pres., ARA Services, Inc.-Hospital Food Management, Philadelphia, PA '79 (FOOD)
CARLSON, KAYE K., pat. rep., Sherman Hospital, Elgin, IL '84 (PAT)
CARLSON, LEROY E., chief eng., Redwood Falls Municipal Hospital, Redwood Falls, MN '82 (ENG)
CARLSON, MAROLYN L., coor. vol., Swedish Covenant Hospital, Chicago, IL '72 (VOL)
CARLSON, PAUL W., asst. exec. dir., Trumbull Memorial Hospital, Warren, OH '78 (PERS)
CARLSON, RICHARD J., sr. vice-pres., St. Joseph's Hospital, Marshfield, WI '72
CARLSON, ROBERT G., mgt. consult., Fairview Hospital and Healthcare Service, Minneapolis, MN '81 (MGMT)
CARLSON, ROLAND R., vice-pres. adm., Western Reserve Care System, Youngstown, OH '66
CARLSON, RONALD L., supv. cent. serv., St. Joseph's Hospital, St. Paul, MN '78 (CS)
CARLSON, RUBIE M., RN, (ret.), South St. Paul, MN '40 (LIFE)
CARLSON, RUTH A., atty., Richland Hospital, Mansfield, OH '82 (ATTY)
CARLSON, STEPHEN A., dir. matl. mgt., Lankenau Hospital, Philadelphia, PA '86 (PUR)
CARLSON, STEPHEN GERARD, adm. fellow, Intermountain Health Care, Inc., Salt Lake City, UT '84
CARLSON, SUSAN, RN, assoc. dir. clin. nrsg., Hackley Hospital, Muskegon, MI '86 (NURS)
CARLSON, SUZANNE M., dir. pers., Good Samaritan Hospital, West Palm Beach, FL '84 (PERS)
CARLSON, VIRGINIA L., student, University of Alabama at Birmingham, School of Community and Allied Health, Birmingham, AL '87
CARLSON, WENDELL H., (ret.), Sheboygan, WI '39 (LIFE)
CARLSON, WILLIAM T. JR., atty., Children's Hospital, New Orleans, LA '84 (ATTY)
CARLTON, DONALD N., dir. matl. mgt., St. Joseph's Hospital, Tampa, FL '85 (PUR)
CARLTON, JOMARIE COOK, dir. soc. work, Mercy Hospital, Rockville Centre, NY '76 (SOC)
CARLTON, JOYCE P., pers. sec., Kershaw County Memorial Hospital, Camden, SC '86 (PERS)
CARLTON, THOMAS OWEN, assoc. prof. and chm. soc. work, Virginia Commonwealth University, School of Social Work, Richmond, VA '81 (SOC)
CARLUCCI, FRANCES E., RN, assoc. dir. nrsg., South Amboy Memorial Hospital, South Amboy, NJ '82 (NURS)
CARMAN, ALICE L., mgr. cent. serv., Piedmont Hospital, Atlanta, GA '85 (CS)
CARMAN, GARY M., atty., Tampa General Hospital, Tampa, FL '85 (ATTY)
CARMAN, MARY ANN T., dir. educ., Divine Savior Hospital, Portage, WI '83 (EDUC)
CARMICHAEL, BRUCE F., arch., Yale-New Haven Hospital, New Haven, CT '85 (ENG)
CARMICHAEL, BRUCE L., vice-pres. plng. and mktg., St. Francis Regional Medical Center, Wichita, KS '75 (PLNG)
CARMICHAEL, FRED M., atty., Craven County Hospital, New Bern, NC '75 (ATTY)
CARMICHAEL, THOMAS A., vice-pres., Buffalo General Hospital, Buffalo, NY '58
CARMIEN, BARBARA A., dir. pers., Huntington Memorial Hospital, Huntington, IN '86 (PERS)
CARMINE, STEPHEN R., dir. fiscal affairs, Magee Rehabilitation Hospital, Philadelphia, PA '84
CARMINES, HOPE M., RN, dir. psych. serv., Riverside Hospital, Newport News, VA '85 (NURS)
CARMODY, AMY R., dir. qual. assur., Northwestern Health Care Corporation, Valparaiso, IN '82
CARMODY, ARTHUR R. JR., atty., Schumpert Medical Center, Shreveport, LA '69 (ATTY)
CARNAHAN, PATSY J., dir. vol. serv., Bascom Palmer Eye Institute, Anne Bates Leach Eye Hospital, Miami, FL '81 (VOL)
CARNALL, NED R., atty., Wells Community Hospital, Bluffton, IN '80 (ATTY)
CARNAZZO, JOSEPH S., asst. to pres., Nebraska Methodist Health System, Inc., Omaha, NE '79 (PLNG)
CARNER, DONALD C., Tiburon, CA '47 (LIFE)
CARNES, GARY A., vice-pres. mgt. and dev., Healthcare Services of America, Inc., Birmingham, AL '83 (PLNG)
CARNES, RONALD K., dir. plant oper., South Georgia Medical Center, Valdosta, GA '86 (ENG)
CARNESECCHI, RALPH, pres., Cityside Associates, Inc., Staten Island, NY '87 (RISK)
CARNEVALE, ACHILLE A., facil. planner, Williamsport Hospital and Medical Center, Williamsport, PA '85 (ENG)
CARNEY, ANN STANDLEE, atty., Oak Park Hospital, Oak Park, IL '84 (ATTY)
CARNEY, DALE, risk mgr., St. Margaret Memorial Hospital, Pittsburgh, PA '86 (RISK)
CARNEY, DAVID J., vice-pres. emp. rel., Rochester St. Mary's Hospital, Rochester, NY '81 (PERS)
CARNEY, MICHAEL B., dir. diet., Deaconess Hospital, Evansville, IN '81 (FOOD)
CARNEY, NANCY L., dir. nutr. serv., Faxton Hospital, Utica, NY '85 (FOOD)
CARNEY, RAYMOND T., reg. vice-pres., Coastal Emergency Services, Columbus, OH '83
CARNEY, ROBERT A., spec. asst. to pres., Jewish Hospital of Cincinnati, Cincinnati, OH '49 (LIFE)
CARNEY, TERRENCE K., dir. matl. mgt., Our Lady of Lourdes Medical Center, Camden, NJ '83 (PUR)
CARNIOL, RENIE, health care consult., Murray Hill, NJ '77
CAROLAN, SHEILA M., RN, dir. nrsg. and amb. care, Lenox Hill Hospital, New York, NY '87 (NURS)
CARON, BONNIE L., coor. cent. serv., Regional Memorial Hospital, Brunswick, ME '87 (CS)
CARON, CHERYL, dir. soc. work, Charlton Memorial Hospital, Fall River, MA '86 (SOC)
CARON, JAMES F., Upper Montclair, NJ '64
CARON, JANE M., dir. soc. work serv., New Britain General Hospital, New Britain, CT '87 (SOC)
CARON, JOHN PHILIP, dir. fin., James Archer Smith Hospital, Homestead, FL '75 (MGMT)
CARON, MAUREEN A., vice-pres. adm., Chilton Memorial Hospital, Pompton Plains, NJ '85 (PLNG)
CARON, RICHARD L., dir. plant oper., St. Joseph Hospital, Bangor, ME '83 (ENG)
CARONIA, CHARLES A., pres., Caronia Corporation, Jericho, NY '81 (RISK)
CAROTENUTO, BERNARDO J., asst. adm., A. Barton Hepburn Hospital, Ogdensburg, NY '85 (PR) (PLNG)
CAROW, BERNADINE I., RN, dir. nrsg., Waukesha Memorial Hospital, Waukesha, WI '82 (NURS)
CARPENETTI, BEN W., mgt. syst. eng., North Broward and Hospital District, Fort Lauderdale, FL '84 (MGMT)
CARPENTER, CAROLYN B., dir. commun. rel., AMI Piedmont Medical Center, Rock Hill, SC '75 (PR)
CARPENTER, CHRISTOPHER S., dir. soc. work serv., Mid-Maine Medical Center, Waterville, ME '75 (SOC)
CARPENTER, CONSTANCE J., dir. pers., Hubbard Regional Hospital, Webster, MA '83 (PERS)
CARPENTER, CRAIG, risk mgt. spec., Spohn Hospital, Corpus Christi, TX '86 (RISK)

CARPENTER, DAVID R., pres. and chief exec. off., Hadley Regional Medical Center, Hays, KS '77
CARPENTER, DOYLE R., dir. vol., Parkview Memorial Hospital, Fort Wayne, IN '74 (VOL)
CARPENTER, EDWARD J., mgt. eng., North Broward Hospital District, Fort Lauderdale, FL '83 (MGMT)
CARPENTER, GAIL, mgr. pur., St. Joseph Hospital, Orange, CA '84 (PUR)
CARPENTER, HOWARD P., supt. maint., Mercy San Juan Hospital, Carmichael, CA '86 (ENG)
CARPENTER, JUDY A., off. mgr., Scioto Valley Health Foundation, Portsmouth, OH '85 (ENG)
CARPENTER, KATHLEEN E. MURPHY, supv. cent. serv., Morton Hospital and Medical Center, Taunton, MA '80 (CS)
CARPENTER, LINDA T., dir. pub. rel. and mktg., West Orange Memorial Hospital, Winter Garden, FL '85 (PR)
CARPENTER, LORENE, dir. soc. serv., Marlboro Park Hospital, Bennettsville, SC '86 (SOC)
CARPENTER, ROBERT ALLEN, dir. eng. and maint., Southern Baptist Hospital, New Orleans, LA '75 (ENG)
CARPENTER, RUSSELL BRUCE, atty., Intermedical Facilities Corporation, San Francisco, CA '75 (ATTY)
CARPENTER, SANDY, RN, dir. educ., Los Robles Regional Medical Center, Thousand Oaks, CA '84 (EDUC)
CARPENTER, STEVEN L., supv. revenue, inventory control and matl. mgt., University of New Mexico Hospital, Albuquerque, NM '86 (PUR)
CARPENTER, STEVEN LUTHER, supv. revenue contr. and matl. mgt., University of New Mexico Hospital, Albuquerque, NM '85
CARPENTER, THERESA P., syst. analyst, Fairfax Hospital Association, Springfield, VA '83 (MGMT)
CARPER, DORIS T., vice-pres. adm. affairs, Roanoke Memorial Hospitals, Roanoke, VA '64 (PR)
CARPER, ROBERT M., sr. vice-pres., Lancaster General Hospital, Lancaster, PA '83
CARPEROS, NICK W., mgr. cent. sup., Silver Cross Hospital, Joliet, IL '85 (CS)
CARR, ADELL C., dir. vol. serv., New York University Medical Center, New York, NY '75 (VOL)
CARR, ALBERT, dir. food serv., Hamilton Hospital, Hamilton, NJ '73 (FOOD)
CARR, ANDREA M., RN EdD, dir. med. surg. serv., Tri-City Medical Center, Oceanside, CA '84 (NURS)
CARR, BARBARA A., vice-pres. market res. and dev., Spectrum Health Care, Dallas, TX '82 (PLNG)
CARR, BARRY E., vice-pres., Central Medical Center and Hospital, Pittsburgh, PA '69 (PERS)
CARR, BERNARD FRANCIS, div. adm., Charter Medical Corporation, Macon, GA '50 (LIFE)
CARR, BETSY, dir. vol. serv., Mennonite Hospital, Bloomington, IL '83 (VOL)
CARR, CAROLYN WORTHINGTON, asst. dir. adm., Thomas Jefferson University Hospital, Philadelphia, PA '86 (PUR)
CARR, DARLENE A., mgr. food serv., Millcreek Community Hospital, Erie, PA '82 (FOOD)
CARR, FRANKLIN D., dir. plng. and mktg., Pacific Health Resources, Los Angeles, CA '46 (PR)(LIFE)
CARR, GERALD M., dir. amb. serv., Southview Hospital and Health Center, Dayton, OH '85
CARR, J. ANTHONY III, chief exec., The Fresno Surgery Center, Fresno, CA '82 (PLNG)
CARR, JAMES E., dir. matl. mgt., North Country Hospital and Health Center, Newport, VT '81 (PUR)
CARR, JOHN A., acct. supv., Barker Campbell and Farley, Virginia Beach, VA '87 (PR)
CARR, KATHLEEN P., budget analyst, Fox Chase Cancer Center, Philadelphia, PA '86
CARR, MARJORIE H., vice-pres., Marsh and McLennan, Inc., Kansas City, MO '80 (RISK)
CARR, MARLENE ARLENE, student, Xavier University Master of Hospital and Health Administration Program, Cincinnati, OH '86
CARR, MICHAEL R., dir. human res., St. Joseph's Medical Center, Fort Wayne, IN '86 (PERS)
CARR, R. DOUGLAS, dir. matl. mgt., Pasqua Hospital, Regina, Sask., Canada '86 (PUR)
CARR, ROBERT CALLAHAN, dir. pur., Antelope Valley Hospital Medical Center, Lancaster, CA '75 (PUR)
CARR, SUSAN L., dir. pub. affairs, Brooklyn Hospital-Caledonian Hospital, Brooklyn, NY '85 (PR)
CARRACHER, CANDACE L., RN, dir. nrsg., HCA Northwest Regional Hospital, Margate, FL '81 (NURS)
CARRAHER, DENNIS E., chief soc. work serv., Veterans Administration Outpatient Clinic, Anchorage, AK '83 (SOC)
CARRAHER, LYNDA L., dir. commun. rel., Good Shepherd Community Hospital, Hermiston, OR '86 (PR)
CARRAS, GEORGE W., exec. vice-pres., Illinois Hospital Association, Naperville, IL '68 (MGMT)
CARRASCO, MIRIAM LOUISE, dir. diet. serv., Saint Michael's Medical Center, Newark, NJ '73 (FOOD)
CARRAWAY, JUNE, adm., St. Louis Eye Clinic, Kirkwood, MO '87 (AMB)
CARREIRA, GERALD O., supv. cent. serv. and distrib., St. Francis Medical Center, Honolulu, HI '85 (CS)
CARRERA, LAVERN H., asst. dir. food serv., St. Elizabeth Hospital Medical Center, Youngstown, OH '87 (FOOD)
CARRICK, PAULA S., sr. risk mgt. consult., Virginia Hospital Association, Richmond, VA '86 (RISK)
CARRICO, FLORENCE, pur., Damon Clinical Laboratories, Tampa, FL '85 (PUR)
CARRINGER, ERNIE W., dir. oper. serv., Smyrna Hospital, Smyrna, GA '83 (ENG)
CARRINGTON, M. EDNA PARRISH, Brooklyn, NY '75 (FOOD)
CARRINGTON, SUZAN, State University Hospital, Downstate Medical Center, Brooklyn, NY '78
CARRIS, ROBERT CHARLES, mgr. oper. room, Providence Hospital, Southfield, MI '70
CARRITTE, GLORIA, asst. to pres., Laboure Junior College, Boston, MA '75 (EDUC)
CARROLL, BETSEY R., RN, dir. cent. matl. distrib., Hotel Dieu Medical Center, El Paso, TX '80 (CS)
CARROLL, BONNIE J., coor. commun. rel., River Falls Area Hospital, River Falls, WI '83 (PR)
CARROLL, CARRIE L., coor. pub. rel., Memorial Hospital, Carthage, IL '86 (PR)
CARROLL, DALE C., RN, dir. nrsg. serv., Redmond Park Hospital, Rome, GA '84 (NURS)
CARROLL, DAVID BRUCE, unit mgr., Baptist Medical Center, Columbia, SC '86 (PAT)
CARROLL, DENISE S., dir. amb. serv., Saints Mary and Elizabeth Hospital, Louisville, KY '86 (EDUC)(AMB)
CARROLL, DOROTHY C., (ret.), Riverview, FL '77 (CS)
CARROLL, FRANCIS BRIAN, MD, (ret.), Waban, MA '48 (LIFE)
CARROLL, GLADA I., dir. diet. serv., Mercy Hospital Medical Center, Des Moines, IA '70 (FOOD)
CARROLL, HAZEL J., asst. dir. food serv., Indian Path Hospital, Kingsport, TN '84 (FOOD)
CARROLL, JAMES D., mgt. eng., St. Joseph Medical Center, Wichita, KS '82 (MGMT)
CARROLL, JAMES J., asst. dir. eng., Our Lady of Mercy Medical Center, Bronx, NY '84 (ENG)
CARROLL, JOHN F., dir. environ. serv., Riverview Medical Center, Red Bank, NJ '87 (ENVIRON)
CARROLL, KEVIN J., pres. and chief exec. off., Champlain Valley Physicians Hospital Medical Center, Plattsburgh, NY '71 (ATTY)
CARROLL, MICHAEL C., vice-pres., Tribrook Group, Inc., Tampa, FL '75 (PLNG)
CARROLL, PAMELA A., RN, asst. dir. nrsg., North Broward Medical Center, Pompano Beach, FL '86 (NURS)
CARROLL, PATRICK E. JR., consult., Laventhol and Horwath, Costa Mesa, CA '79 (PUR)(MGMT)
CARROLL, PATRICK R., sr. vice-pres., Massachusetts Hospital Association, Burlington, MA '64 (ATTY)
CARROLL, R. BRUCE, dir. pers., Carle Foundation Hospital, Urbana, IL '75 (PERS)
CARROLL, RALENE G., dir. soc. serv., Central Florida Regional Hospital, Sanford, FL '81 (SOC)
CARROLL, ROBERTA, risk mgr., Premier Hospitals Alliance, Inc., Westchester, IL '75 (RISK)
CARROLL, RONALD L., PhD, dir. health educ., Lexington County Hospital, West Columbia, SC '81 (EDUC)
CARROLL, S. WILLIAM, vice-pres., Blue Cross and Blue Shield of Virginia, Richmond, VA '85 (PR)
CARROLL, SARAH BROWNE, pres., Carroll and Company, Chagrin Falls, OH '86 (PR)
CARROLL, SONJA ROSENTHAL, dir. prog. dev., Hospital Corporation of America, Clearwater, FL '80 (NURS)
CARROLL, TERRENCE P., asst. vice-pres. support serv., Magee-Womens Hospital, Pittsburgh, PA '84
CARROLL, VICKIE J., student, Program in Industrial Engineering, Youngstown State University, Youngstown, OH '86 (MGMT)
CARROTHERS, JAMES M., atty., Twin City Hospital, Dennison, OH '77 (ATTY)
CARROTHERS, MARJORIE ANN, dir. soc. serv., Harrison Community Hospital, Cadiz, OH '80 (SOC)
CARROTT, ANN L., atty., Douglas County Hospital, Alexandria, MN '84 (ATTY)
CARROZA, JOAN E., dir. pub. rel., Gaston Memorial Hospital, Gastonia, NC '86 (PR)
CARRUTH, CLAUDE Y. III, partner, Pannell Kerr Forster, Atlanta, GA '81 (PLNG)
CARSEY, MICHAEL W., mgr. spec. proc., pur. and distrib., Archbishop Bergan Mercy Hospital, Omaha, NE '85 (PUR)
CARSON, CHRISTOPHER JOHN, amb. fin. serv., Boca Raton Community Hospital, Boca Raton, FL '87 (AMB)
CARSON, GAIL, dir. discharge plng., Charlotte Memorial Hospital and Medical Center, Charlotte, NC '83 (SOC)
CARSON, HUGH M. JR., chief eng., Fish Memorial Hospital, New Smyrna Beach, FL '76 (ENG)
CARSON, JOHN T., dir., Veterans Administration Medical Center, St. Louis, MO '75
CARSON, RANDAL E., mgt. eng. health serv. res., Baptist Memorial Hospital, Memphis, TN '85 (MGMT)
CARSWELL, PEGGY A., dir. vol. serv., University of Chicago Hospitals, Chicago, IL '84 (VOL)
CARSWELL, STEVEN T., dir. med. soc. work, Grace Hospital, Morganton, NC '85 (SOC)
CARTER, AMELIA C., (ret.), Bethesda, MD '39 (LIFE)
CARTER, ANN KEELING, RN, dir. pat. serv., Doctors General Hospital, Plantation, FL '86 (NURS)
CARTER, BARBARA B. G., supv. soc. work, consult. and coor. pub. rel., Community Home Health Services, Dallas, TX '86 (SOC)
CARTER, CAROL S., dir. soc. serv., Franklin Memorial Hospital, Rocky Mount, VA '81 (SOC)
CARTER, CHRISTINE, dir. soc. serv., Berea Hospital, Berea, KY '84 (SOC)
CARTER, CLEMENT, MD, med. dir., HCA Vista Hills Medical Center, El Paso, TX '68
CARTER, DELORES, RN, dir. nrsg., Knollwood Park Hospital, Mobile, AL '82 (NURS)
CARTER, GORDON F., chief eng., Liberty Hospital, Liberty, MO '85 (ENG)
CARTER, GRANT L., vice-pres. mktg. and human res., Clinton Memorial Hospital, Wilmington, OH '79 (PLNG)
CARTER, JANE E., dir. vol. serv., Northeast Georgia Medical Center, Gainesville, GA '76 (VOL)
CARTER, JANET H., dir. educ. serv., St. John's Regional Medical Center, Joplin, MO '86 (EDUC)
CARTER, JASON M., chief fin. off., Healthcare Management Systems, Houston, TX '85 (MGMT)
CARTER, JEFFREY B., MD, Baptist Hospital, Nashville, TN '86 (PLNG)
CARTER, JERRY, dir. hskpg. serv., Memorial Medical Center of Jacksonville, Jacksonville, FL '86 (ENVIRON)
CARTER, JOAN H., RN, assoc. prof., St. Louis University, St. Louis, MO '84 (NURS)
CARTER, JOHN M., East Albany Medical Center, Albany, GA '74
CARTER, KAREN L., atty., Arizona Hospital Association, Phoenix, AZ '84 (ATTY)
CARTER, KATHLEEN B., RN, asst. dir. nrsg., Ochsner Foundation Hospital, New Orleans, LA '83 (NURS)
CARTER, LEONARD MATTHEW JR., Lancaster-Fairfield Community Hospital, Lancaster, OH '80 (PERS)
CARTER, LYNELLE D., dir. sup., proc. and distrib., Wadley Regional Medical Center, Texarkana, TX '70 (CS)
CARTER, LYNN K., dir. vol. serv., Knapp Medical Center, Weslaco, TX '85 (VOL)
CARTER, MARGARET M., supv. cent. sup., Zurbrugg Memorial Hospital -Riverside, Riverside, NJ '81 (CS)
CARTER, MARGARET O., vice-pres. commun. and pub. rel., Healthcare Services of America, Birmingham, AL '79 (PR)
CARTER, MARTHA W., sr. tech., McLeod Regional Medical Center, Florence, SC '85 (CS)
CARTER, NANCY I., dir. commun. serv., St. Francis Regional Medical Center, Wichita, KS '84 (ENG)
CARTER, NORMAN M. JR., atty., Muhlenberg Regional Medical Center, Plainfield, NJ '79 (ATTY)
CARTER, PAULA A., dir. amb. care, Moses H. Cone Memorial Hospital, Greensboro, NC '87 (AMB)
CARTER, PHILIP L., atty., Evergreen Hospital Medical Center, Kirkland, WA '76 (ATTY)
CARTER, ROBERT E., eng., Walton County Hospital, Monroe, GA '83 (ENG)
CARTER, ROBERTA F., dir. food serv., Massac Memorial Hospital, Metropolis, IL '85 (FOOD)
CARTER, THELMA S., (ret.), Randallstown, MD '67 (CS)
CARTMEL, WILLIAM E., plant eng., Indian Path Hospital, Kingsport, TN '80 (ENG)
CARTMILL, GEORGE E., Grosse Pointe Farms, MI '48 (LIFE)
CARTON, CHERIE L., supv. preparation and pack, Mercy Hospital Medical Center, Des Moines, IA '85 (CS)
CARTWRIGHT, BRENDA KAY, RN, supv. nrsg., Piqua Memorial Medical Center, Piqua, OH '85 (NURS)
CARTWRIGHT, CHARLES N., atty., Southside Community Hospital, Corpus Christi, TX '80 (ATTY)
CARTWRIGHT, DAVID H., dir. mgt. eng., Memorial Hospital, Danville, VA '82 (MGMT)
CARTWRIGHT, JOAN ALISON, pat. rep. emer. dept., York Hospital, York, PA '86 (PAT)
CARTWRIGHT, ROSEMARY, dir. soc. work and discharge plng., St. Francis Hospital, Roslyn, NY '68 (SOC)
CARTY, BARBARA A., RN, assoc. dir. nrsg., Kent County Memorial Hospital, Warwick, RI '83 (NURS)
CARTY, EDWIN E. JR., dir. matl. mgt., Republic Health Corporation, Dallas, TX '82 (PUR)
CARTY, KAREN A., asst. dir. food and nutr. serv., Catherine McAuley Health Center, Ann Arbor, MI '84 (FOOD)
CARUBIA, ROBERT J., dir. facil. plng. and constr., West Virginia University Hospital, Morgantown, WV '85 (ENG)
CARUSI, FRANK X., coor. trng., food and nutr. serv., Cedars-Sinai Medical Center, Los Angeles, CA '85 (EDUC)
CARUSO, JOANN B., dir. pat. rel. and vol., Baystate Medical Center, Springfield, MA '84 (VOL)
CARUSO, JOSEPH A., assoc. dir. plant plng. and oper., Johns Hopkins University, Baltimore, MD '82 (ENG)
CARUSO, MARY MARTHA J., pat. rep., Slidell Memorial Hospital, Slidell, LA '85 (PAT)
CARUTH, FRANCES M., coor. efficiency enhancement prog., Vancouver General Hospital, Vancouver, B.C., Canada '87 (MGMT)
CARVALHO, KEVIN, risk mgr., Roger Williams General Hospital, Providence, RI '86 (RISK)
CARVER, GERALDINE B., safety off., Seton Medical Center, Daly City, CA '84 (EDUC)(ENG)
CARVER, MAJ. MICHAEL E., MSC USAF, chief eng. and tech. serv., Air Force Medical Logistics Office, Fort Detrick, MD '83 (ENG)
CARVER, THOMAS W., dir. plant oper., Vermillion County Hospital, Clinton, IN '80 (ENG)(ENVIRON)
CARVER, WILLIAM J. JR., dir. pers., HCA Park West Medical Centers, Knoxville, TN '84 (PERS)
CARVISIGLIA, PAUL, North Kingstown, RI '56 (LIFE)
CASAD, NANCY R., pres., Nutrition Concepts, Memphis, TN '81 (FOOD)
CASADY, NORMAN L., dir. food serv., Meriden-Wallingford Hospital, Meriden, CT '78 (FOOD)
CASANO, A. ANDRES, MD, vice-pres. med. practice, Albany Medical College, Albany, NY '87 (AMB)
CASANOVA, MELVIN K., dir. eng., Hammond-Henry Hospital, Geneseo, IL '82 (ENG)
CASAS, NORMA I., RN, vice-pres. pat. serv., Our Lady of Providence Unit, St. Joseph Hospital, Providence, RI '79 (NURS)
CASCARDO, DEBRA, adm. outpatient, St. Luke's-Roosevelt Hospital Center, New York, NY '79
CASCIOLA, D. GLENN, dir. home care soc. work, Homestead Center, Homestead, PA '84 (SOC)
CASCURDO, DEBRA, Armonk, NY '86 (AMB)
CASE, ALAN R., adm. inst. serv., Henry Ford Hospital, Detroit, MI '59
CASE, DONNA L., Harrison Memorial Hospital, Bremerton, WA '81 (FOOD)
CASE, FRANCES S., RN, asst. adm. nrsg. serv., Kenmore Mercy Hospital, Kenmore, NY '85 (NURS)
CASE, COL. HARRY MICHAEL, MSC USA, dep. cmdr. adm., 5th General Hospital, APO New York, NY '67
CASE, LOTTYE L., dir. vol. serv., Kalamazoo Regional Psychiatric Hospital, Kalamazoo, MI '79 (VOL)
CASE, MARY K., mgr. matl. mgt., Orem Community Hospital, Orem, UT '86 (PUR)
CASEBOLT, DOUGLAS GERALD, chaplain and ombudsman, Takoma Adventist Hospital, Greeneville, TN '87 (PAT)
CASELEY, DONALD J., MD, Big Pine Key, FL '54 (LIFE)
CASEY, ALLAN L., atty., Polk General Hospital, Bartow, FL '80 (ATTY)
CASEY, CATHERINE A., dir. in-service educ., Desert Samaritan Hospital, Mesa, AZ '78 (EDUC)
CASEY, DENNIS A., exec. dir., Albert Lindley Lee Memorial Hospital, Fulton, NY '72 (PLNG)
CASEY, E. J. JR., dir. eng., Memorial Hospital of Martinsville, Martinsville, VA '81 (ENG)

CASEY, GLORIA, Riverside, IL '85 (PERS)
CASEY, JAMES F., adm., Shriners Hospital for Crippled Children, Philadelphia, PA '80
CASEY, JAMES R., vice-pres. human res., St. Elizabeth Medical Center-North, Covington, KY '86 (PERS)
CASEY, JOHN F., consult. eng., Maplewood, NJ '78 (ENG)
CASEY, JOHN T., pres., Methodist Health Systems, Inc., Memphis, TN '78
CASEY, JOSEPH J., corp. dir. oper. analysis, United Hospitals, Elkins Park, PA '69 (MGMT)
CASEY, LINWOOD JACKSON, chief stationary eng., Los Angeles County-University of Southern California Medical Center, Los Angeles, CA '87 (ENG)
CASEY, SR. M. JOSEPH, pat. rep., Little Company of Mary Hospital, Evergreen Park, IL '80 (PAT)
CASEY, MADELYN B., dir. pub. rel., Rapides General Hospital, Alexandria, LA '86 (PR)
CASEY, MARY JO, RN, clin. coor. surg., Humana Hospital -Abilene, Abilene, TX '87 (AMB)
CASEY, MIRIAM L., RN, asst. adm. rehab., Santa Clara Valley Medical Center, San Jose, CA '81 (NURS)
CASEY, PHYLLIS, dir. pub. rel., Floyd Medical Center, Rome, GA '75 (PR)
CASEY, WILLIAM F., pres. and chief exec. off., Mercy Hospital, Urbana, IL '84
CASH, BARBARA L., asst. dir. vol. serv., Ohio State University Hospitals, Columbus, OH '86 (VOL)
CASH, DOROTHY V., dir. soc. serv., Community Hospital of Springfield and Clark County, Springfield, OH '70 (SOC)
CASH, HENRY L., chief eng., Pacific Presbyterian Hospital, San Francisco, CA '75 (ENG)
CASH, JANET D., dir. soc. serv., Jefferson Regional Medical Center, Pine Bluff, AR '77 (SOC)
CASHDOLLAR, LARRY R., vice-pres., Fairfax Hospital Association, Springfield, VA '72 (PERS)
CASHEN, J. LARRY, atty., Hospital Corporation of America, Nashville, TN '84 (ATTY)
CASHIN, HELEN E., RN, head nrs. cent. serv., Tallahassee Memorial Regional Medical Center, Tallahassee, FL '86 (CS)
CASHION, CAROLE F., RN, vice-pres. nrsg., House of the Good Samaritan, Watertown, NY '77 (NURS)
CASHMAN, EUGENE K. JR., pres., Le Bonheur Children's Medical Center, Memphis, TN '70 (MGMT)
CASHMAN, MICHAEL J., vice-pres. corp. human res., Bethany Methodist Healthcare Corporation, Chicago, IL '84 (PERS)
CASHWELL, PAMELA K., mgr. food serv., Wake Medical Center, Raleigh, NC '78 (FOOD)
CASKEY, HERBERT T., MD, pres., Liberty Healthcare Corporation, Philadelphia, PA '78
CASLER, PAUL, dir. gen. serv., Ukiah Adventist Hospital, Ukiah, CA '87 (ENVIRON)
CASLOW, DIANE L., plng. spec., Good Samaritan Hospital, Baltimore, MD '86 (PLNG)
CASON, ARLENE K., asst. dir. pub. rel. and vol. activ., Wadley Regional Medical Center, Texarkana, TX '86 (VOL)
CASON, DEBRA J., dir. commun. rel., Olathe Medical Center, Olathe, KS '80 (PR)
CASPARIS, WILLIAM R., vice-pres., Kearney Management Consultants, San Francisco, CA '75
CASPER, LISA J., pub. rel. dir., Framingham Union Hospital, Framingham, MA '86 (PR)
CASPER, MARIE H., RN, dir. med. and surg. nrsg., Candler General Hospital, Savannah, GA '84 (NURS)
CASPER, MARTIN E., exec. dir., Greynolds Park Manor, Inc., North Miami Beach, FL '71
CASPERITE, NANCY, RN, dir. nrsg., Kennedy Memorial Hospitals-University Medical Center-Cherry Hill Division, Cherry Hill, NJ '84 (NURS)
CASS, LAVERN W., dir. risk mgt., St. Francis Medical Center, La Crosse, WI '85 (RISK)
CASS, R. MICHAEL, mgr., R. K. Carvill, Incorporated, Chicago, IL '86 (RISK)
CASSERLY, RICCI IVERS, student, Graduate Program in Health Service Administration, University of Houston at Clear Lake City, Houston, TX '80
CASSETTA, REGINA, RN, dir. nrsg., St. Mary's Hospital, Amsterdam, NY '73 (NURS)
CASSIDY, BONNIE, student, Cleveland State University, Cleveland, OH '86 (RISK)
CASSIDY, DOROTHY H., asst. dir. soc. serv., Jeanes Hospital, Philadelphia, PA '85 (SOC)
CASSIDY, REV. MSGR. JAMES P., PhD, dir., Catholic Charities, Division of Health and Hospitals, New York, NY '73
CASSIDY, JUDITH L., RN, vice-pres. nrsg. serv., Inter-Community Medical Center, Covina, CA '82 (NURS)
CASSIDY, KATHLEEN A., dir. pub. rel., Trident Regional Medical Center, Charleston, SC '86 (PR)
CASSIDY, MICHAEL A., atty., United Community Hospital, Grove City, PA '85 (ATTY)
CASSIDY, PATRICK M., RN, dir. nrsg., Annapolis Hospital, Wayne, MI '82 (NURS)
CASSIDY, PAUL W., atty., Parma Community General Hospital, Parma, OH '68 (ATTY)
CASSIDY, TERRY B., adm. asst. to pres. and pat. rep., Woonsocket Hospital, Woonsocket, RI '86 (PAT)
CASSIDY, WENDY J., dir. human res., Community Hospital of Gardena, Gardena, CA '82 (PERS)
CASSON, JOSEPH E., atty., Humana Inc., Louisville, KY '77 (ATTY)
CASSONE, KERRY S., nrsg. educ., Nashoba Community Hospital, Ayer, MA '86 (EDUC)
CASTAGNO, RONALD J., adm., Shriners Hospital for Crippled Children, San Francisco, CA '80
CASTANADA, C. ARLENE, dir. soc. serv., Heartland Hospital East, St. Joseph, MO '75 (SOC)
CASTEEL, KAREN L., dir. pers., Akron City Hospital, Akron, OH '85 (PERS)
CASTELL, JOSEFINA, dir. qual. assur., Psychiatric Hospital, Levittown, P.R. '86 (RISK)
CASTELLI, BARTOLOMEO J., adm. asst., Ssm Rehabilitation Institute, St. Louis, MO '83
CASTER, PATRICIA D., RN, vice-pres. pat. serv., Providence Milwaukie Hospital, Milwaukie, OR '80 (NURS)(RISK)
CASTERLIN, WILLIAM T., vice-pres. mgt. serv., Doylestown Hospital, Doylestown, PA '87 (AMB)
CASTERTON, SHIRLEY B., head cent. proc., Hospital of the Good Samaritan, Los Angeles, CA '82 (CS)
CASTETTER, SANDRA L., RN, vice-pres., Peninsula Hospital and Medical Center, Burlingame, CA '82 (NURS)
CASTIGLIONI, SHERRY LEE, serv. rep., Newcomb Medical Center, Vineland, NJ '85 (PAT)
CASTILLO-MENA, ERNESTO, dir. eng., Mercy Regional Medical Center, Laredo, TX '82 (ENG)
CASTILLO, MATILDE A., prof., University Catolica Devalparaiso, Valparaiso, Chile '84 (MGMT)
CASTILLO, PROBO H., MD, Prime Health Care, Inc., Richlands, VA '87 (AMB)
CASTLE-COON, CATHERINE, commun. rel. spec., American Nursing Care, Inc., Cincinnati, OH '74 (SOC)
CASTLE, CHARLES K., asst. adm., Memorial Hospital of Geneva, Geneva, OH '77 (PUR)
CASTLE, JAMES R., pres., Maine Hospital Association, Augusta, ME '70 (MGMT)
CASTLE, JOANN C., dir. pat. serv., Metropolitan Hospital and Health Centers, Detroit, MI '82 (PAT)
CASTLE, WILLIAM A. JR., dir. pers., Southwestern Vermont Medical Center, Bennington, VT '73 (PERS)
CASTLEBURY, NANCY L., dir. pat. and family counseling, Boulder Memorial Hospital, Boulder, CO '85 (SOC)
CASTLEMAN, HARRY W. JR., mgr. media rel., Brigham and Women's Hospital, Boston, MA '87 (PR)
CASTLEMAN, ROBERT D., dir. matl. mgt., Richards Medical Company, Memphis, TN '84 (PUR)
CASTLES, WILLIAM ALBERT II, dir. info. syst., College of Osteopathic Medicine-Kirksville, Kirksville, MO '80 (PR)
CASTO, BARRY L., atty., Pleasant Valley Hospital, Point Pleasant, WV '80 (ATTY)
CASTO, CARROLL W., atty., Pleasant Valley Hospital, Point Pleasant, WV '68 (ATTY)
CASTONGUAY, NORMAN F., dir. soc. serv., Farren Memorial Hospital, Montague, MA '85 (SOC)
CASTOR, BRUCE L., atty., Philadelphia, PA '78 (ATTY)
CASTOR, PAULA LAURA, dir. pharm. serv., Moss Rehabilitation Hospital, Philadelphia, PA '86
CASTRO, LUZ E., dir. pub. rel., York Plaza Hospital and Medical Center, Houston, TX '81 (PR)
CASTROP, RICHARD F., exec. dir., O'Bleness Memorial Hospital, Athens, OH '76
CATANZARO, JOSEPH J., chief biomédical eng., Methodist Hospital, Brooklyn, NY '85 (ENG)
CATE, NORMAN R., dir. pers. serv., Memorial Hospital, Chattanooga, TN '80 (PERS)
CATER, MARGARET N., adm. asst., Cannon Memorial Hospital, Pickens, SC '82 (PERS)
CATES, RICHARD S., consult., Medco, Inc., Warminster, PA '77 (MGMT)
CATES, ROY J., vice-pres. dev. and vol. rel., Texas Hospital Association, Austin, TX '85 (VOL)
CATHCART, H. ROBERT, pres., Pennsylvania Hospital, Philadelphia, PA '48 (LIFE)
CATHERINE, SR. MARY, dir. commun., St. Mary Medical Center, Gary, IN '75 (ENG)
CATHERMAN, TIM M., adm. asst., Chippenham Hospital, Richmond, VA '87
CATHEY, WILLIAM COLE, dir. safety and security, St. Thomas Hospital, Nashville, TN '86 (ENG)
CATINO, ANNETTE, asst. adm., Delaware Valley Medical Center, Langhorne, PA '79 (PLNG)
CATLETT, REBECCA FRANCES, pat. rep., St. Luke Hospital, Fort Thomas, KY '80 (PAT)
CATLIN, GAIL E., consult., Catlin Company, Carmichael, CA '84 (PR)
CATO, CHARLES W. II, atty., Tennessee Hospital Association, Nashville, TN '85 (ATTY)
CATON, ROBERT M., vice-pres. corp. plng. and dev., Franciscan Sisters Health Care, Little Falls, MN '83 (PLNG)(AMB)
CATRON, LAURIE J., atty., Hfic Management Company, Inc., Vienna, VA '84 (RISK)
CATTANACH, REXFORD K., sr. consult., Peat, Marwick, Mitchell and Company, Detroit, MI '86 (PLNG)
CAUBLE, A. ELIZABETH, coor. family serv., Shriners Hospital for Crippled Children, Minneapolis, MN '84 (SOC)
CAUBLE, J. MICHAEL, asst. adm. med. staff affairs, Melrose-Wakefield Hospital, Melrose, MA '86 (RISK)
CAUDILL, HELENE, dir. mgt. serv., Presbyterian Hospital, Dallas, TX '84 (MGMT)
CAUDILL, KELLY K., student, Temple University, Department of Health Administration, Philadelphia, PA '85
CAUDILL, MARY JO, RN, dir. nrsg., St. Mary's Health Center, Emporia, KS '86 (NURS)
CAUDLE, ALLEN S., dir. food serv., Providence Medical Center, Portland, OR '80 (FOOD)
CAULEY, JOHN H. JR., vice-pres. pub. affairs and dev., Lansing General Hospital, Lansing, MI '85 (PR) (PLNG)
CAULFIELD, GERARD J., sr. syst. analyst, Shared Medical Systems, King of Prussia, PA '81
CAUSEY, DEE A., asst. mktg., Cobb General Hospital, Austell, GA '86 (PR)
CAUSSIN, MARY J., RN, dir. nrsg., HCA Northern Virginia Hospital, Arlington, VA '79 (NURS)
CAUST-ELLENBOGEN, MELISSA R., Washington, DC '81 (PLNG)
CAVACECI, EUGENE M. JR., biomedical tech., House of the Good Samaritan, Watertown, NY '85 (ENG)
CAVAGNARO, LOUISE P., (ret.), Baltimore, MD '52 (LIFE)
CAVALIER, NIKKI, dir. soc. serv., Las Encinas Hospital, Pasadena, CA '85 (SOC)
CAVALLARO, DIANE T., coor. mktg., Albert Einstein Medical Center, Mount Sinai-Daroff Division, Philadelphia, PA '83
CAVALLARO, LIBBY, dir. matl. mgt., F. G. McGaw Hospital, Loyola University, Maywood, IL '86 (PUR)
CAVANAGH, HARRY J., atty., Good Samaritan Medical Center, Phoenix, AZ '70 (ATTY)
CAVANAGH, RICHARD R., sr. consult., Healthcare Strategies, Inc., St. Louis, MO '76 (PLNG)
CAVANAUGH, ANNE, RN, pat. rep., Bryn Mawr Hospital, Bryn Mawr, PA '81 (PAT)
CAVANAUGH, CAPT. DEBRA A., MSC USAF, adm., U. S. Air Force Clinic Zweibrucken, APO New York, NY '79
CAVANAUGH, DEE K., dir. vol., Menorah Medical Center, Kansas City, MO '68 (VOL)
CAVANAUGH, GERMAINE, coor. subscriber serv., Health Maintenance Plan, Cortland, OH '84 (PAT)
CAVANAUGH, JAMES H., PhD, Smithkline Clinical Laboratory, King of Prussia, PA '59 (HON)
CAVANAUGH, KENNETH P., vice-pres. human res., Carle Foundation Hospital, Urbana, IL '82 (PERS)
CAVANAUGH, LAURENCE D., vice-pres. pat. serv., Mount Carmel Mercy Hospital and Medical Center, Detroit, MI '68 (ATTY)(RISK)
CAVANAUGH, MARILYN B., pat. rep., HCA Medical Center of Port St. Lucie, Port St. Lucie, FL '76 (PAT)
CAVANAUGH, PAUL S., asst. adm., North Pennsylvania Hospital, Lansdale, PA '83 (PERS)
CAVANAUGH, THOMAS W., dir. phys. plant, Roper Hospital, Charleston, SC '84 (ENG)
CAVANUAGH, KATHRYN M., RN, asst. vice-pres. nrsg., Little Company of Mary Hospital, Evergreen Park, IL '86 (NURS)
CAVE, NATALIE HELENE JACOBS, chief soc. work serv., Veterans Administration Medical Center, New York, NY '84 (SOC)
CAVENDER, IRIS J., RN, dir. nrsg. serv., Jane Phillips-Memorial Medical Center, Bartlesville, OK '83 (NURS)
CAVERA, JAMES J., dir. soc. serv., St. Mary's Medical Center, Evansville, IN '76 (SOC)
CAVIN, SHIRLEY N., RN, dir. nrsg., River West Medical Center, Plaquemine, LA '86 (NURS)
CAVINESS, ARTHUR R., vice-pres. plng., Kettering Medical Center, Kettering, OH '77 (PLNG)
CAVOURAS, CAROL ANN L., RN, asst. dir. nrsg., Hermann Hospital, Houston, TX '81 (NURS)
CAWELTI, ROBERT N., chief eng., Community Hospital of Lodi, Lodi, CA '81 (ENG)
CAWLEY, MARION A., PhD, dir. environ. serv., Mercy Catholic Medical Center, Darby, PA '86 (ENVIRON)
CAWOOD, STEPHEN C., atty., Pineville Community Hospital, Pineville, KY '83 (ATTY)
CAYAN, PETER JOSEPH III, asst. dir. food serv., Glens Falls Hospital, Glens Falls, NY '80 (FOOD)
CAYER, DORIS M., assoc. dir. educ., nrsg., res., dev. and qual. assur., Malden Hospital, Malden, MA '82 (EDUC)
CAYNER, JAY JOSEPH, dir. soc. serv., University of Iowa Hospitals and Clinics, Iowa City, IA '82 (SOC)
CAYWOOD, STEVEN A., pres. and chief exec. off., Western Pennsylvania Hospital, Pittsburgh, PA '68
CEARNS, DEBRA A., mgt. eng., Magee-Womens Hospital, Pittsburgh, PA '84 (MGMT)
CEBUHAR, FRANCES O., dir. pub. info., Saint Francis Hospital, Tulsa, OK '71 (PR)
CECCHI, DIANE J., dir. soc. work, Cooper Hospital-University Medical Center, Camden, NJ '80 (SOC)
CECCHINE, MEL D., dir. risk mgt., Baylor College of Medicine, Houston, TX '84 (RISK)
CECCONI, JOHN L., assoc. vice-pres., New York Eye and Ear Infirmary, New York, NY '70 (PUR)
CECHVALA, JON F., constr. mgr., Columbia Hospital, Milwaukee, WI '87 (ENG)
CECIL, DAVID E., atty., Buchanan General Hospital, Grundy, VA '86 (ATTY)
CECILIA, JOHN L., mgr. strategic mktg. plng., McC Powers, Northbrook, IL '82 (ENG)
CEDERHOLM, BARBARA, dir. vol. serv., St. Joseph Hospital, Providence, RI '78 (VOL)
CEDRONE, SUSAN M., dir. soc. serv., All Saints' Rehabilitation Hospital, Wyndmoor, PA '86 (SOC)
CELA, MARYANN T., RN, dir. nrs., Irvington General Hospital, Irvington, NJ '83 (NURS)
CELBA, JOANNE, unit mgr. amb. care, Lake Forest Hospital, Lake Forest, IL '87 (AMB)
CELEBRE, ERNEST P., dir. dev. and mktg., St. Catherine's Hospital, Kenosha, WI '84 (PLNG)
CELEY, BARRY F., dir. plant serv., Monongalia General Hospital, Morgantown, WV '78 (ENG)
CELIBERTI, RICHARD T., partner, Ernst and Whinney, New York, NY '73
CELMER, MARK E., dir., De Graff Memorial Hospital, North Tonawanda, NY '75
CEMATE, DAVID D., assoc. vice-pres., Mercycare, Inc., Detroit, MI '78
CENDROWSKA, FRANCES S., consult., Arthur Andersen and Company, Chicago, IL '83 (PLNG)
CENTLIVRE, THOMAS P., mgr. mgt. eng., Mersco Corporation, Bloomfield Hills, MI '86 (MGMT)
CENTRELLA, SUSAN T., supv. cent. distrib. and cent. serv. room, Hospital of Philadelphia College of Osteopathic Medicine, Philadelphia, PA '83 (CS)
CERBINS, VICTOR, vice-pres. and dir. mktg. and sales, Stone Johnston Corporation, Ferrysburg, MI '86 (ENG)
CERBONE, ERMELINDA S., PhD, vice-pres., Advanced Projects, Medical Electronics, New York, NY '67
CERGIZAN, JUDITH A., RN, dir. qual. assur., Borgess Medical Center, Kalamazoo, MI '81
CERIER, HOLLIS C., coor. pat. rep. serv., Norwood Hospital, Norwood, MA '86 (PAT)
CERIER, MARTYANNE W., assoc. planner, Providence Hospital, Southfield, MI '87 (PLNG)
CERIO, JOSEPH M., dir. soc. serv., St. Joseph's Hospital Health Center, Syracuse, NY '78 (SOC)
CERNIK, JOSEPH A., pres., Wedemeyer, Cernik, Corrubia, Inc., St. Louis, MO '82
CERNY, K. C., PhD, consult., Patrick Philbin and Associates, Austin, TX '86 (PLNG)
CERONE, JAMES R., vice-pres., Duff and Phelps, Inc., Chicago, IL '78
CERRA, JOSEPH, mgr. biomedical eng., United Health Services, Johnson City, NY '86 (ENG)

CERRATO, DOMINICK A., atty., Freehold Area Hospital, Freehold, NJ '75 (ATTY)
CERRETA, DEBRA A., supv. inventory mgt., Danbury Hospital, Danbury, CT '86 (PUR)
CERRONE, SUSAN R., consult., Deloitte Haskins and Sells, Boston, MA '84 (MGMT)
CERVENAK, MICHAEL M., vice-pres. amb. serv. and prog. dev., Providence Hospital, Southfield, MI '87 (AMB)
CESA, ANGELA, asst. adm., Queens Hospital Center, Jamaica, NY '86
CETERA, MICHAEL W., risk mgt. consult., Wyatt Company, Chicago, IL '80 (RISK)
CHABALLA, PAUL V., coor. spec. serv., St. Mary's Hospital, Orange, NJ '77 (ENG)
CHABOT, KATHLEEN F., coor. guild, Mercy Hospital Medical Center, Des Moines, IA '80 (VOL)
CHABOT, LORETTA, dir. soc. serv., Jewish Hospital of Cincinnati, Cincinnati, OH '77 (SOC)
CHACHAM, YEHUDA, gen. mgr., Y. B. Electro-Mechanical Systems Maintenance, Beer-Sheva, Israel '84 (ENG)
CHACK, JOAN C., RN, dir. nrsg., Riverview Medical Center, Red Bank, NJ '85 (NURS)
CHACON, ARMANDO A., pres., Glendale Heights Community Hospital, Glendale Heights, IL '87 (RISK)
CHADBOURN, LLOYD H., (ret.), Grants Pass, OR '38 (LIFE)
CHADBOURNE, RICHARD F., dir. productivity serv., Voluntary Hospitals of America-Gulf States, Baton Rouge, LA '81 (MGMT)
CHADICK, SUSAN L., dir. soc. serv., Washington Regional Medical Center, Fayetteville, AR '82 (SOC)
CHADWICK, ALAN W., (ret.), Venice, FL '40 (LIFE)
CHADWICK, ARTHUR P. JR., dir. commun. and pub. rel., Mercy Hospital, Wilkes-Barre, PA '78 (PR)
CHADWICK, DEBRA DEE, dir. educ., Lutheran Medical Center, Richard H. Young Memorial Hospital, Omaha, NE '79 (EDUC)
CHADWICK, RAYMOND G. JR., atty., University Hospital, Augusta, GA '81 (ATTY)
CHADWICK, SHARON M., dir. human res., Lovelace Medical Center, Albuquerque, NM '86 (PERS)
CHAFETZ, LYNNE A., atty., Children's Hospital and Medical Center, Seattle, WA '85 (ATTY)
CHAIDO, MICHELLE C., dir. soc. serv., Massillon Community Hospital, Massillon, OH '77 (SOC)
CHAIKEN, ILA, supv. pat. and family counselor, Mercy Hospital and Medical Center, Chicago, IL '86 (SOC)
CHAIKIN, ERIC D., asst. adm., Parkway Hospital, Flushing, NY '83
CHAISTY, KENNETH J., dir. plant serv., Androscoggin Valley Hospital, Berlin, NH '79 (ENG)
CHAIT, LOIS H., dir. food serv., Long Beach Memorial Hospital, Long Beach, NY '86 (FOOD)
CHAIX, RONALD A., vice-pres. facil. dev., Northwestern University-Medical Hospitals, Inc., Encino, CA '79 (ENG)
CHAIX, ROSEMARY R., dir. diet., Fairview Hospital, Minneapolis, MN '72 (FOOD)
CHAKALES, JAMES M., dir. mktg., Baptist Medical Center, Columbia, SC '84 (PLNG)
CHAKVABARTY, CHINMAYEE, asst. dir., Montefiore Medical Center, Bronx, NY '77 (SOC)
CHAKWIN, JANET A., asst. dir. risk mgt., Fojp Service Corporation, New York, NY '84 (RISK)
CHALAS, BRUCE, treas., James Chalas and Sons, Inc., Ashland, MA '85 (ENG)
CHALEF, MORTON N., Boca Raton, FL '51 (LIFE)
CHALEK, HERBERT ALAN, Cornwall on Hudson, NY '78
CHALLAN, BARBARA B., asst. dir. risk mgt., Fojp Service Corporation, New York, NY '85 (RISK)
CHALMERS, STEWART, supv. order instruments, Medical Center Hospital of Vermont, Burlington, VT '86 (CS)
CHALONER, ROBERT S., bus. mgr., Lenox Hill Hospital, New York, NY '81
CHALOUPKA, ROBERT P., atty., Van Steenberg, Brower, Chaloupka, Miller and Holyoke, Scottsbluff, NE '82 (ATTY)
CHALTIEL, VICTOR, pres., Salick Health Care, Inc., Beverly Hills, CA '87 (AMB)
CHAMBERLAIN, ALVIN L., dir. matl. mgt., Methodist Hospital, Omaha, NE '85 (PUR)
CHAMBERLAIN, C. DOUGLAS, atty., Mary Rutan Hospital, Bellefontaine, OH '78 (ATTY)
CHAMBERLAIN, DIANA L., dir. compensation, Mount Carmel Mercy Hospital, Detroit, MI '86 (PERS)
CHAMBERLAIN, JACQUELYNN S., dir. soc. work, Hospital of Philadelphia College of Osteopathic Medicine, Philadelphia, PA '86 (SOC)
CHAMBERLAIN, JEANNE, adm., Northwest Medical Center, Spooner, WI '87 (AMB)
CHAMBERLAIN, JOHN C., dir. pers., J. C. Blair Memorial Hospital, Huntingdon, PA '82 (PERS)
CHAMBERLAIN, JOHN M., asst. adm., Lakeview Hospital, Bountiful, UT '84
CHAMBERLAIN, LYNE, adm. dir. outpatient clin., Erlanger Medical Center, Chattanooga, TN '85
CHAMBERLAIN, SUSAN L., RN, dir. surg. nrsg., Beth Israel Hospital, Boston, MA '87 (NURS)
CHAMBERLAIN, SUSAN M., dir. vol. serv., National Orthopedic and Rehabilitation Hospital, Arlington, VA '79 (VOL)
CHAMBERLAIN, TOMASINA ASTA, dir. hm health serv., Saint Mary Hospital, Langhorne, PA '87 (AMB)
CHAMBERLAIN, WILLIAM J., dir. pers., St. Francis Medical Center, La Crosse, WI '76 (PERS)
CHAMBERS, D. SUE, pur. agt., R. T. Jones Memorial Hospital, Canton, GA '81 (PUR)
CHAMBERS, DONNA MARIE, fellow mgt. dev., State of New York Department of Health, Albany, NY '85
CHAMBERS, J. CLARENCE JR., MD, (ret.), Santurce, P.R. '40 (LIFE)
CHAMBERS, JACQUELINE, RN, asst. adm. nrsg., St. Mary Medical Center, Long Beach, CA '78 (NURS)
CHAMBERS, JANET, dir. soc. serv., Wheeling Hospital, Wheeling, WV '86 (SOC)
CHAMBERS, JOHN W., sr. vice-pres. dev., Catholic Healthcare West, Sacramento, CA '85 (PLNG)
CHAMBERS, JUDI D., pub. rel. and alumni affairs off., Brown University, Providence, RI '85 (PR)
CHAMBERS, K. W. MICHAEL, atty., Mobile Infirmary Medical Center, Mobile, AL '86 (ATTY)
CHAMBERS, MARJORIE, dir. vol., Corning Hospital, Corning, NY '78 (VOL)
CHAMBERS, MARK W., exec. dir., Center for Mother and Children Care, Memorial Hospital, South Bend, IN '83 (PLNG)
CHAMBERS, MARTHA C., dir. vol. serv., Good Samaritan Hospital, Corvallis, OR '85 (VOL)
CHAMBERS, LT. COL. MILDRED JEAN, MSC USAF, chairperson nutr. med. serv., Malcolm Grow U. S. Air Force Medical Center, Camp Springs, MD '85 (FOOD)
CHAMBERS, PHILLIP B., dir. info. serv., Divine Providence Hospital, Williamsport, PA '86 (MGMT)
CHAMBLEE, KATRINA S., dir. human res., Children's Hospital of Alabama, Birmingham, AL '86 (PERS)
CHAMBLEE, MARIETTA E., dir. matl. mgt., West Houston Medical Center, Houston, TX '80 (PUR)
CHAMBLESS, JOHN R. JR., jr. partner, Chambless-Killingsworth and Associates, Montgomery, AL '84 (ENG)
CHAMBLESS, NANCY W., MD, dir. mktg., Phoebe Putney Memorial Hospital, Albany, GA '86 (PR)
CHAMMOUN, LILA ANN, University Hospital, Augusta, GA '79 (MGMT)
CHAMP, FRED E., dir. plant oper. and maint., Weirton Medical Center, Weirton, WV '81 (ENG)
CHAMP, RAYMOND LESTER, pres., Wake Medical Center, Raleigh, NC '64
CHAMPAGNE, A. LOUIS, dir. pers., Baton Rouge General Medical Center, Baton Rouge, LA '75 (PERS)
CHAMPAGNE, BARRY, mgr. bldg. oper., Woman's Hospital, Baton Rouge, LA '85 (ENG)
CHAMPER, JAMES, pres., Louis A. Weiss Memorial Hospital, Chicago, IL '74
CHAMPION, J. ANNE, RN, vice-pres. nrsg., Mercy Hospital, Charlotte, NC '80 (NURS)
CHAMPION, NANCY, dir. human res., St. Luke's Memorial Hospital Center, New Hartford, NY '84 (PERS)
CHAMPOUX, MICHELLE, dir. soc. serv., Gifford Memorial Hospital, Randolph, VT '85 (SOC)
CHAN, BUDDY TAK BIU, prod. dev., Buddy Electronics and Systems Ltd., Jardines Lookout, Hong Kong '86 (ENG)
CHAN, PAK MAN L., facil. eng., Community Hospital of Lancaster, Lancaster, PA '85 (ENG)
CHAN, PUI-MING SUNNY, mgt. eng., Long Island College Hospital, Brooklyn, NY '85 (MGMT)
CHAN, TERESA, dir. cost and fin. analyst, Highland Park Hospital, Highland Park, IL '85
CHANCELLOR, JOYCE M., pat. rep., Southwest Florida Regional Medical Center, Fort Myers, FL '85 (PAT)
CHANDLER, ELIZABETH BOYD, mgt. eng., Presbyterian Hospital, Charlotte, NC '81 (MGMT)
CHANDLER, GARY L., chief oper. off., Central Texas Health Plan, Austin, TX '80 (PLNG)
CHANDLER, JOAN, dir. matl. distrib., Vanderbilt University Hospital, Nashville, TN '86 (PUR)
CHANDLER, JOHN A., atty., Piedmont Hospital, Atlanta, GA '85 (ATTY)
CHANDLER, MARIE L., RN, dir. nrsg. serv., Valley Hospital Association, Palmer, AK '85 (NURS)
CHANDLER, MARY MARGARET, mgt. eng., SunHealth, Inc., Atlanta, GA '81 (MGMT)
CHANDLER, ORELLA H., coor. qual. assur., St. Joseph Hospital, Bangor, ME '83 (RISK)
CHANDLER, ROBERT L., vice-pres. and client serv. mgr., Burson-Marsteller, New York, NY '77 (PR)
CHANDLEY, DONALD J., dir. pur., Hamot Medical Center, Erie, PA '65 (PUR)
CHANEY, GERALD R., RN, dir. nrsg. serv., Ukiah Adventist Hospital, Ukiah, CA '85 (NURS)(AMB)
CHANEY, JOANN, dir. soc. serv., Bethesda Hospital, Zanesville, OH '86 (SOC)
CHANEY, WIRT M., natl. sales mgr.-process support prod., Sybron, Rochester, NY '84 (CS)
CHANG, CHIH-CHIEN JOSEPH, adm. res., French Hospital of Los Angeles, Los Angeles, CA '86
CHANG, CHIN-UN, adm., Chang Gung Memorial Hospital, Taipei, Republic of China '64
CHANG, LAURIE, student, New School for Social Research, New York, NY '84 (PERS)
CHANG, SHAO-NING, student, Graduate Program in Hospital Administration, China Medical College, Taichung City Taiwan, Republic of China '86 (PERS)
CHANG, WILLIAM B., vice-pres., Kapiolani Medical Center for Women, Honolulu, HI '87 (ENG)
CHANG, YEN-YEN, student, Graduate Program in Hospital Administration, China Medical College, Taichung, Republic of China '86 (PERS)
CHANNEL, JOANN, RN, exec. assoc., Saint Thomas Medical Center, Akron, OH '80 (NURS)
CHANNELL, KAY GLENN, dir. human resources, Baptist Medical Center-Montclair, Birmingham, AL '78 (PERS)
CHANNON, JAN LISA OWLICK, mgr. mktg., res. and plng., Highland Park Hospital, Highland Park, IL '81 (PLNG)
CHANTRY, CHRISTINE S., mgr. media rel., University of Wisconsin-Madison, Center for Health Sciences, Madison, WI '86 (PR)
CHAPA, ROBERT, dir. pers., Mercy Regional Medical Center, Laredo, TX '86 (PERS)
CHAPIN, BARBARA A., dir. soc. serv., Resurrection Hospital, Chicago, IL '78 (SOC)
CHAPIN, RONALD B., proj. dir. med. info. syst., St. Mary's Hospital and Medical Center, San Francisco, CA '73 (MGMT)
CHAPLIK, JOHN P. JR., dir. med. soc. serv., Mary Greeley Medical Center, Ames, IA '78 (SOC)
CHAPMAN, ARNOLD, dir. matl. mgt., Long Beach Memorial Hospital, Long Beach, NY '78 (PUR)
CHAPMAN, CHARLES R., exec. dir., Community Methodist Hospital, Henderson, KY '74
CHAPMAN, CHERYL A., dir. soc. serv., Pennsylvania State University Hospital, Hershey, PA '70 (SOC)
CHAPMAN, DAVID E., chief eng., Washington Adventist Hospital, Takoma Park, MD '83 (ENG)
CHAPMAN, DAVID L., syst. analyst mgt. info. serv., University Community Hospital, Tampa, FL '86 (MGMT)
CHAPMAN, DOROTHY O., dir. pers. serv., Arkansas Valley Regional Medical Center, La Junta, CO '82 (PERS)
CHAPMAN, EVELYN A., RN, dir. nrsg. educ. and paramed. trng., St. Mary's Hospital and Health Center, Tucson, AZ '83 (EDUC)
CHAPMAN, GEORGE C., atty., Methodist Hospitals of Dallas, Dallas, TX '73 (ATTY)
CHAPMAN, GLORIA S., asst. dir. matl. mgt., East Jefferson General Hospital, Metairie, LA '78 (CS)
CHAPMAN, JAMES D., asst. dir. eng., Shands Hospital, Gainesville, FL '83 (ENG)
CHAPMAN, JOANN, RN, vice-pres. pat. serv., Covenant Medical Center -St. Francis, Waterloo, IA '77 (NURS)
CHAPMAN, KATHLEEN M., RN, dir. res. and dev., La Grange Memorial Hospital, La Grange, IL '85 (NURS)(EDUC)
CHAPMAN, MARIE O., coor. qual. assur. and med. staff, Caldwell Memorial Hospital, Lenoir, NC '86 (RISK)
CHAPMAN, MAURICE, dir. maint. eng., Kennestone Hospital, Marietta, GA '80 (ENG)
CHAPMAN, MIDGE R., RN, supv. matl. mgt., Moncton Hospital, Moncton, N.B., Canada '83 (CS)
CHAPMAN, PETER A., pres., Jordan Hospital, Plymouth, MA '72
CHAPMAN, REGINA P., RN, dir. clin. serv., Fayetteville City Hospital, Fayetteville, AR '85 (NURS)
CHAPMAN, ROBERT F., mgr. maint. and biomedical, Glens Falls Hospital, Glens Falls, NY '85 (ENG)
CHAPMAN, SUSAN A., prog. mgr. amb. serv., Mount Zion Hospital and Medical Center, San Francisco, CA '87 (AMB)
CHAPMAN, SUSAN M., atty., North Carolina Hospital Association Trust Fund, Raleigh, NC '84 (ATTY)
CHAPMAN, THOMAS W., pres., Greater Southeast Community Hospital, Washington, DC '82
CHAPMAN, WILLIAM S., exec. dir., Jackson General Hospital, Ripley, WV '68
CHAPPELL, JOHN H., adm., Santa Teresa Community Hospital, San Jose, CA '55 (LIFE)
CHAPPELL, MARY L., dicharge plng., soc. serv. and pat. rep., Fayette Memorial Hospital, Connersville, IN '86 (PAT)
CHAPPELL, PATRICIA ANN, coor. qual. assur. and risk mgt., U. S. Air Force Academy Hospital, USAF Academy, CO '86 (RISK)
CHAPPELL, THOMAS T., atty., Degonge, Garrity and Fitzpatrick, Bloomfield, NJ '79 (ATTY)
CHAPPELLE, LTCOL RAYMOND J., MSC USAF, adm., U. S. Air Force Hospital, Shreveport, LA '71
CHAPPLE, LYNN E., mgr. qual. assur., Humana Inc., Louisville, KY '84
CHAPPY, EDWARD P., mgr. trng. and dev., Aga Khan Hospital and Medical College, Karachi, Pakistan '75 (EDUC)
CHARD, LORETTA, dir. staff educ., Western Memorial Regional Hospital, Corner Brook, Nfld., Canada '77 (EDUC)
CHAREST, LORRAINE PROFITA, mgr. cent. serv., Newington Children's Hospital, Newington, CT '81 (CS)
CHAREWICZ, DEBORAH J., dir. commun. rel., Whittier Rehabilitation Hospital, Haverhill, MA '86 (PR)
CHARLES, CAROL, dir. soc. serv., Ohio Valley Medical Center, Wheeling, WV '85 (SOC)
CHARLES, ETHEL M., dir. soc. serv., Brookdale Hospital Medical Center, Brooklyn, NY '86 (SOC)
CHARLES, FRANCES B., RN, vice-pres. nrsg. serv., South Shore Hospital, South Weymouth, MA '76 (NURS)
CHARLES, HELEN S., student, Mumbles Swansea, England '85 (MGMT)
CHARLES, MARK, supv. clin. eng., Highland Park Hospital, Highland Park, IL '86 (ENG)
CHARLES, MARY, dir. soc. serv., Providence Hospital, Everett, WA '86 (SOC)
CHARLES, MICHAEL CURTIS, dir. gen. serv., University of New Mexico Mental Health Center, Albuquerque, NM '86 (ENG)
CHARLES, MICHAEL F., dir. info. syst., Millard Fillmore Hospital, Buffalo, NY '85 (MGMT)
CHARLES, PAT L., dir. pub. rel., Parkridge Medical Center, Chattanooga, TN '86 (PR)
CHARLES, SUSAN M., dir. soc. serv., Humana Hospital -Davis North, Layton, UT '81 (SOC)
CHARLESTON, LETIZIA, dir. med. soc. work, North Ottawa Community Hospital, Grand Haven, MI '85 (SOC)
CHARLIP, CAPT. RALPH, MSC USAF, mgr. oper., Department of Air Force Medical Service, Bolling AFB, DC '79
CHARLSON, JEFFREY T., mgt. eng., University of Wisconsin Hospital and Clinics, Madison, WI '83 (MGMT)
CHARLTON, BARBARA A., student, Department of Health Care Administration, George Washington University, Washington, DC '86
CHARNECO, MARIA E., dir. educ., South Community Hospital, Oklahoma City, OK '86 (EDUC)
CHARNOCK, ANITA C., supv. cent. serv., Hampton General Hospital, Hampton, VA '85 (CS)
CHARPENTIER, MARCEL O., dir. soc. serv., Memorial Hospital, Pawtucket, RI '80 (SOC)
CHARTIER, RICHARD D., dir. oper. analyst, Bryan Memorial Hospital, Lincoln, NE '72 (MGMT)
CHARTIER, RICHARD N., asst. mgr. eng., AMI Memorial Hospital of Tampa, Tampa, FL '81 (ENG)
CHARYN, JEROME I., consult., Johnson and Higgins, New York, NY '67 (RISK)
CHASE, A. J., dir. eng., Edward W. Sparrow Hospital, Lansing, MI '78 (ENG)

CHASE, BEATRICE A., RN PhD, prof. nrsg. adm., Duke University Hospital, Durham, NC '66 (NURS)(EDUC)
CHASE, CYNTHIA F., coor. pub. rel. and mktg., Johnson County Regional Hospital, Clarksville, AR '86 (PR)
CHASE, DAVID D., adm., York Manor, Inc., Fredericton, Man., Canada '79 (MGMT)
CHASE, GERALDINE, dir. soc. serv., Cardinal Cushing General Hospital, Brockton, MA '85 (SOC)
CHASE, JEAN M., dir. food serv., Hunt Memorial Hospital, Danvers, MA '79 (FOOD)
CHASE, LEE J. III, atty., St. Francis Hospital, Memphis, TN '79 (ATTY)
CHASE, NEWTON K., chief facil. sect. div. plng., Department of Health and Social Services, Juneau, AK '86 (ENG)
CHASIN, SUSAN B., chief mktg. and plng. off., Camelback Hospitals, Inc., Scottsdale, AZ '78 (PLNG)
CHASSIE, MARILYN B., RN, assoc. prof. nrsg. adm. and asst. dean nrsg. practice, University of South Carolina, Columbia, SC '83 (NURS)
CHASTAIN, E. JANE, asst. dir. vol., Wesley Medical Center, Wichita, KS '83 (VOL)
CHASTAIN, JANET L., dir. soc. work serv., Arkansas Valley Regional Medical Center, La Junta, CO '80 (SOC)
CHASTANG, CHARLES J., pres., Doctors Hospital, Columbus, OH '79 (ATTY)
CHASTEEN, MAY A., dir. vol. serv., St. John's Episcopal Hospital, Smithtown, NY '83 (VOL)
CHATFIELD, DAVID E., vice-pres. plng. and mktg., Riverside Hospital, Toledo, OH '81 (PLNG)
CHATHAM, HENRY E. JR., atty., Hinds General Hospital, Jackson, MS '77 (ATTY)
CHATY, BETH, dir. plng. and spec. proj., North Adams Regional Hospital, North Adams, MA '85 (PLNG)
CHAU, HUNG, sr. mgt. eng., Straub Clinic and Hospital, Honolulu, HI '86 (MGMT)
CHAUDRY, MOE, mgr. providing affairs, Pierce County Medical Bureau, Takoma, WA '82
CHAUFOURNIER, ROGER L., asst. adm., George Washington University Hospital, Washington, DC '83 (ENG)
CHAUNCEY, PETER W., mgr. med. facil., Kaiser Foundation Health Plan North Carolina, Raleigh, NC '87 (AMB)
CHAUNCEY, SUSAN J., coor. pub. rel., Sumner Memorial Hospital, Gallatin, TN '86 (PR)
CHAUVIN, KATHY A., dir. pub. rel., Lane Memorial Hospital, Zachary, LA '86 (PR)
CHAVEZ, ALFREDO VELA, pres., Proveedora Tecnica Industrial, San Salvador, El Salvador '80 (ENG)
CHAVEZ, JUAN M., El Paso, TX '86
CHAVEZ, OLIVIA, dir. environ. care serv., Santa Teresita Hospital, Duarte, CA '86 (ENVIRON)
CHAVIS, CLAUDIA J., mgr. health serv., Atterbury Job Corps Center, Edinburgh, IN '84
CHAVIS, TIMOTHY R., sr. info. analyst, Harper-Grace Hospitals, Detroit, MI '86 (MGMT)
CHAWK, GARY W., vice-pres. and chief fin. off., St. Joseph's Hospital, Tampa, FL '82
CHAWLA, NEAL K., prog. dev. analyst, Providence Hospital, Southfield, MI '82 (MGMT)
CHEATHAM, ELIZABETH A., coor. commun., Community Memorial Hospital, Ventura, CA '87 (PR)
CHEATHAM, JAMES T., atty., Pitt County Memorial Hospital, Greenville, NC '77 (ATTY)
CHEATHAM, JUDY H., Haleiwa, HI '79 (FOOD)
CHEATWOOD, PHILIP H., atty., Highsmith-Rainey Memorial Hospital, Fayetteville, NC '86 (ATTY)
CHECK, PAMELA J., dir. pat. family serv., HCA Park View Medical Center, Nashville, TN '86 (SOC)
CHECK, ROSEMARY CAROLINA, asst. adm., Montgomery Regional Hospital, Blacksburg, VA '79
CHEEK, LOU M., dir. vol., University Hospital, Augusta, GA '84 (VOL)
CHEEK, THOMAS M., asst. supt., Fallsview Psychiatric Hospital, Cuyahoga Falls, OH '84 (MGMT)
CHEEKS, MARY JANE R., soc. work asst., Greenville Hospital, Jersey City, NJ '82 (SOC)
CHEESEMAN, GLORIA S., dir. educ. resources, St. Francis Medical Center, Trenton, NJ '86 (EDUC)
CHEESEMAN, ROBERT WILLIAM, dir. pur., St. Jerome Hospital, Batavia, NY '84 (PUR)
CHEGASH, THOMAS J., dir. diet. serv., North Carolina Memorial Hospital, Chapel Hill, NC '78 (FOOD)
CHEIFETZ, WALTER, atty., Arizona Hospital Association, Phoenix, AZ '68 (ATTY)
CHELEEN, MARY L., assoc. adm. amb. care serv., University of Minnesota Hospital and Clinic, Minneapolis, MN '87 (AMB)
CHELETTE, EVERETTE J., dir. mgt. eng., Decatur Memorial Hospital, Decatur, IL '80 (MGMT)
CHELETTE, LORENE R., mgr. food prod. and pat. serv., Hotel Dieu Hospital, New Orleans, LA '81 (FOOD)
CHELETTE, RALPH, dir. plant serv., Mary Free Bed Hospital and Rehabilitation Center, Grand Rapids, MI '75 (ENG)
CHELF, TRACY ANN, dir. mktg. and pub. rel., HCA East Pointe Hospital, Lehigh Acres, FL '87 (PR)
CHELLEW, SANDRA, student, College of William and Mary, Williamsburg, VA '86 (RISK)
CHEN, CHU JE, student, Graduate Program in Hospital Administration, China Medical College, Taichung, Republic of China '86 (PERS)
CHENEN, ARTHUR R., atty., Hirschtick, Chenen and Cavanaugh, Los Angeles, CA '80 (ATTY)
CHENEY, ALICE V., RN, vice-pres. pat. care, Parkview Memorial Hospital, Fort Wayne, IN '84 (NURS)
CHENEY, J. RICHARD, atty., The Methodist Hospital, Houston, TX '87 (ATTY)
CHENEY, LAURA A., dir. soc. work serv., Pekin Memorial Hospital, Pekin, IL '86 (SOC)
CHENG, GRACE M., vice-pres., St. Jude Hospital Yorba Linda, Yorba Linda, CA '84 (PR) (PLNG)
CHEREN, ISABEL K., spec. asst. to vice-pres. human res., Montefiore Medical Center, Bronx, NY '83 (PERS)
CHERKASKY, MARTIN, MD, consult., Montefiore Medical Center, Bronx, NY '51 (LIFE)
CHERNEFF, MARTIN H., prin., M. H. Cherneff and Associates, Inc., Deerfield, IL '84 (FOOD)
CHERNENKO, GARY C., dir. commun. affairs, Charleston Area Medical Center, Charleston, WV '84 (PR)
CHERNER, ROBERT M., vice-pres., Desert Health Resources, Inc., Sun City, AZ '70
CHERNESKY, ROSLYN H., assoc. prof., Columbia University, School of Social Work, New York, NY '78 (SOC)
CHERNOFF, SUSAN N., atty., Lutheran General Hospital, Park Ridge, IL '84 (ATTY)
CHERNOW, PATRICIA, risk mgr., Washington Adventist Hospital, Takoma Park, MD '86 (RISK)
CHERNY, CANDACE, supv. environ. serv., Memorial Hospital of Dodge County, Fremont, NE '86 (ENVIRON)
CHERRY, BRENDA SUE, risk mgr., Doctors' Hospital, Coral Gables, FL '86 (RISK)
CHERRY, LOUIS W., dir. soc. work, Pilgrim Psychiatric Center, West Brentwood, NY '85 (SOC)
CHERRY, MARILYN, dir. human res., Swedish Health Systems, Englewood, CO '86 (PERS)
CHERRY, VICTORIA A., coor. commun. rel. and mktg., Armstrong County Memorial Hospital, Kittanning, PA '86 (PR)
CHERUBINI, CELESTE, RN, assoc. dir. nrsg., St. Joseph Health Care Corporation, Albuquerque, NM '86 (NURS)
CHERVENY, JAMES A., exec. vice-pres., St. Mary's Medical Center, Duluth, MN '72
CHESKY, DEBORAH J., dir. pat., family serv. and discharge plng., Memorial Hospital, Albany, NY '85 (SOC)
CHESLOCK, RICHARD, dir. eng., Alexandria Hospital, Alexandria, VA '79 (ENG)
CHESON, CHRISTINE M., RN, dir. nrsg. mgt. syst., Providence Hospital, Washington, DC '85 (NURS)
CHESS, HOWARD C., dir. food serv., HCA North Beach Hospital, Fort Lauderdale, FL '82 (FOOD)
CHESS, NANCY, dir. soc. serv., J. D. McCarty Center for Handicapped Children, Norman, OK '85 (SOC)
CHESS, STEVEN, dir. food serv., Bascom Palmer Eye Institute-Anne Bates Leach Eye Hospital, Miami, FL '72 (FOOD)
CHESSER, RONALD, dir. equip. and syst. plng., Presbyterian Hospital in the City of New York, New York, NY '78
CHESSIN, NEIL A., dir. pers., Jameson Memorial Hospital, New Castle, PA '78 (PERS)
CHESTER, ALBERT S., pres. and dir. eng., Chester Associates, Inc., Harper Woods, MI '84 (MGMT)
CHESTER, DON W., vice-pres. dev. and commun. rel., St. Mary's Hospital, West Palm Beach, FL '78 (PR)
CHESTER, SR. MARY, dir. vol., Mercy Hospital, Altoona, PA '76 (VOL)
CHESTER, NANCY A., lead tech. cent. serv., Black Hills Community Hospital, Olympia, WA '83 (CS)
CHESTER, ROBERT D., dir. eng., South Oaks Hospital, Amityville, NY '81 (ENG)
CHESTER, SALLY D., RN, nrs. mgr. staff dev. and educ., St. Mary's Hospital, West Palm Beach, FL '85 (EDUC)
CHESTER, SANDRA M., dir. plng. and prog. dev., Hollywood Presbyterian Medical Center, Los Angeles, CA '84 (PLNG)
CHESTNUT, CHARLENE W., asst. pers., Georgia Baptist Medical Center, Atlanta, GA '74 (PERS)
CHEUNG, FRANCIS, dir. mgt. info. syst., St. Lawrence Hospital, Lansing, MI '79 (MGMT)
CHEUNG, MAN WAH, MD, supt. and med. dir., Roosevelt Hospital, Edison, NJ '67
CHEUNG, SHU-TIM, sr. mgt. eng., Ottawa Civic Hospital, Ottawa, Ont., Canada '82 (MGMT)
CHEVALIER, BERNARD R. JR., pur. agt., Biloxi Regional Medical Center, Biloxi, MS '85 (PUR)
CHEVALIER, DOROTHY, (ret.), Berkeley, CA '75 (SOC)
CHEVIGNY, JOHN E., atty., St. Margaret Hospital, Hammond, IN '73 (ATTY)
CHEW, ROY G., PhD, vice-pres. human res., Kettering Medical Center, Kettering, OH '84 (PERS)
CHEWNING, LARRY, chief oper. off., AMI Doctors Memorial Hospital, Spartanburg, SC '77
CHEZICK, LLOYD E., supv. maint., International Falls Memorial Hospital, International Falls, MN '82 (ENG)
CHIANG, PO-HUANG, student, Columbia University School of Public Health and Administrative Medicine, New York, NY '87
CHIAPPETTA, DORA, dir. food serv., Kings County Hospital Center, Brooklyn, NY '73 (FOOD)
CHIARAMONTE, JOSEPH F., chm. util. review com. and qual. assur., Ryan Medical Arts Building, Rockville Centre, NY '73
CHIARELLI, VINCENT J., dir. affil. and contract mgt., Brooklyn Hospital-Caledonian Hospital, Brooklyn, NY '76
CHIAVETTA, BARBARA, dir. vol. serv., Mercy Hospital, Buffalo, NY '86 (VOL)
CHICKERELLA, BERYL G., RN, sr. vice-pres. nrsg., Doctors Hospital, Columbus, OH '82 (NURS)
CHIDESTER, DREW A., dir. facil. mgt., Indiana Hospital, Indiana, PA '74 (ENG)
CHIEFFA, JOHN D., dir. environ. serv., Forbes Metropolitan Health Center, Pittsburgh, PA '86 (ENVIRON)
CHIEFFE, KAREN K., pat. rep., Butler Memorial Hospital, Butler, PA '85 (PAT)
CHIER, LAURENE MARIE, coor. pub. rel., Berlin Hospital Association, Berlin, WI '85 (PR)
CHIERCHIO, ELLEN S., dir. pat. rel., Montefiore Medical Center, Bronx, NY '86
CHIESA, ANN, RN, asst. adm. nrsg. and spec. serv., San Gabriel Valley Medical Center, San Gabriel, CA '77 (NURS)
CHIFFELLE, ROBERT L., dir. facil. plng., St. Joseph's Hospital and Medical Center, Phoenix, AZ '83 (PLNG)
CHILCOTE, PATTI L., student, Rush University, Chicago, IL '84
CHILD, GEORGE L., dir. pers., Shady Grove Adventist Hospital, Rockville, MD '85 (PERS)
CHILDERS, J. RICHARD, atty., Children's Memorial Hospital, Chicago, IL '80 (RISK)(ATTY)
CHILDERS, JAMES A., dir. biomedical serv., Eastwood Hospital, Memphis, TN '87 (RISK)
CHILDERS, LINDA C., dir. soc. work, Munroe Regional Medical Center, Ocala, FL '82 (SOC)
CHILDRESS, DAN S., dir. qual. assur., East Alabama Medical Center, Opelika, AL '86 (RISK)
CHILDRESS, JAMES C., dir. ldry. serv., Saint Joseph's Hospital, Atlanta, GA '86 (ENVIRON)
CHILDRESS, JIM H., dir. mktg. and commun. rel., Metropolitan Hospital, Grand Rapids, MI '86 (PR)
CHILDRESS, ROBERT L., consult., Dept. of HHS, U. S. Public Health Service, Division of Indian Health Area Office, Oklahoma City, OK '69
CHILDS, MICHAEL E., dir. eng., Lakeland Regional Medical Center, Lakeland, FL '84 (ENG)
CHILEK, MARTIN GUDEN, dir. acquisitions, Humana Inc., Louisville, KY '77
CHILES, DARBY C., Upland, CA '84 (MGMT)
CHILL, THOMAS M., dir. plant and facil., William Beaumont Hospital, Royal Oak, MI '85 (ENG)
CHIMIELINSKI, FRANK, dir. bus. analyst, Johnson and Johnson, New Brunswick, NJ '84 (PUR)
CHIMNER, NORA, RN, dir. nrsg. and rehab., Sinai Hospital of Detroit, Detroit, MI '86 (NURS)
CHIN, LT. COL. GORDON O., MSC USA, instr. pers. mgt. br., Army-Baylor University Program in Health Care Administration, Fort Sam Houston, TX '69
CHIN, MARY C., dir. soc. serv., Union Hospital, Lynn, MA '81 (SOC)
CHIN, YEN, chief soc. work, Veterans General Hospital, Taichung Taiwan, Republic of China '86 (SOC)
CHINETTI, GEORGE C., dir. food serv., Hebrew Rehabilitation Center for Aged, Boston, MA '72 (FOOD)
CHING, STANLEY K., vice-pres. fin. oper., Northwestern University-Medical Medical, Inc., Encino, CA '85
CHINN-ANDERSON, SHERRY, asst. dir. pub. rel., Newton-Wellesley Hospital, Newton, MA '86 (PR)
CHINN, CATHERINE, dir. soc. serv., Castle Medical Center, Kailua, HI '81 (SOC)
CHINNOCK, JANE, med. prod. tech., Bemis Manufacturing Company, Sheboygan, WI '85 (CS)
CHIOCCARELLI, ANTHONY, mgr., Deloitte, Haskins and Sells, New York, NY '87 (PUR)
CHIODO, ANITA LYNN, dir. soc. serv., St. Joseph's Hospital Medical Center, Bloomington, IL '79 (SOC)
CHIOU, PI-YUNG, Niles, IL '73 (FOOD)
CHIOZZA, FRANK X., coor. pharm., Methodist Hospital-Central Unit, Memphis, TN '84 (PUR)
CHIPKA, ROBERT S., dir. plant eng., Cuyahoga County Hospitals, Cleveland, OH '79 (ENG)
CHIPMAN, ANN, dir. emp. dev., Evanston Hospital, Evanston, IL '84 (EDUC)
CHIQUOINE, STEPHEN D., atty., Reedsburg Memorial Hospital, Reedsburg, WI '81 (ATTY)
CHIRCHIRILLO, ANTHONY L., partner, Peat, Marwick, Mitchell and Company, Chicago, IL '84
CHIRINOS, COLLEEN T., RN, dir. nrsg. and adm. asst. pat. serv., St. Anthony Hospital, Michigan City, IN '77 (NURS)
CHISENA, CHRIS, adm. claims and risk mgt., Hospital of the University of Pennsylvania, Philadelphia, PA '86 (RISK)
CHISHOLM, KENNETH, dir. human res., Salem Hospital, Salem, MA '83 (PERS)
CHISHOLM, MICHAEL D., dir. mktg., Trinity Lutheran Hospital, Kansas City, MO '85 (PLNG)
CHISHOLM, WILLIAM G., dir. phys. plant, Baycrest Centre-Geriatric Care, Toronto, Ont., Canada '85 (ENG)
CHITTENDEN, MICHAEL D., vice-pres., St. Vincent Hospital and Health Care Center, Indianapolis, IN '82 (ENG)
CHITWOOD, SUZANNE R., dir. pub. rel., Welborn Memorial Baptist Hospital, Evansville, IN '74 (PR)
CHLEBORAD, PATRICIA A., RN, vice-pres. in-patient serv., St. Elizabeth Community Health Center, Lincoln, NE '86 (NURS)
CHO, SUSAN A., dir. soc. work and alcohol serv., St. Francis Hospital and Medical Center, Topeka, KS '82 (SOC)
CHOATE, JAMES ROBERT, mgr. hskpg., Saint Anthony Medical Center, Rockford, IL '87 (ENG)
CHOBIN, NANCY G., RN, mgr. sup. proc. and distrib., St. Peter's Medical Center, New Brunswick, NJ '81 (CS)
CHOEFF, CAREN T., assoc. mktg., Mount Sinai Medical Center, Miami Beach, FL '86 (PLNG)
CHOI, SEYUEN, plng. analyst, Ochsner Medical Institute, New Orleans, LA '85 (PLNG)
CHOI, Y. W. BRYAN, vice-pres., Levin Porter Associates, Inc., Dayton, OH '83
CHONG, IRMA A., RN, dir. nrsg., Palmerton Hospital, Palmerton, PA '79 (NURS)
CHONKA, E. STEPHEN, dir. bldg. and facil. serv., Central Medical Center and Hospital, Pittsburgh, PA '75 (ENG)
CHOPCHITZ, ROMAN, asst. dir. food serv., Hebrew Rehabilitation Center for Aged, Boston, MA '79 (FOOD)
CHOTINER, BURTON, exec. vice-pres., Northwest Community Hospital, Arlington Heights, IL '64
CHOUDHRY, SID, asst. vice-pres. fin., Cedars-Sinai Medical Center, Los Angeles, CA '87 (MGMT)
CHOUINARD, THOMAS J., dir. matl. mgt., Multicare Medical Center, Tacoma, WA '82 (PUR)
CHOW, KAREN A., dir. pers., Chinese Hospital, San Francisco, CA '86 (PERS)
CHOW, TED G., mgr. matl., Shield Home Healthcare Center, Van Nuys, CA '85 (PUR)
CHOWDHRY, SUBODH K., dir. plant oper., Lake Charles Memorial Hospital, Lake Charles, LA '86 (ENG)
CHOWNING, JOHN S., atty., Miami Children's Hospital, Miami, FL '77 (ATTY)
CHRANIUK, SHERRY J., sr. buyer, St. John's Episcopal Hospital, Far Rockaway, NY '79 (PUR)
CHRISMAN, JUNE, vice-pres. human res., Robert F. Kennedy Medical Center, Hawthorne, CA '85 (PERS)
CHRISMAN, ROBERT C., vice-pres. human res., O'Connor Health Services, San Jose, CA '68 (PERS)(EDUC)

CHRISPELL, RICHARD J., bd. mem. qual. assur., Methodist Hospitals of Gary, Gary, IN '83 (RISK)
CHRIST, CAROLINE T., RN, sr. vice-pres. nrsg., Genesee Hospital, Rochester, NY '79 (NURS)
CHRIST, CHARLES E., proj. mgr. health facil., Bechtel International Corporation, Gaithersburg, MD '76
CHRIST, GRACE H., dir. soc. work, Memorial Hospital for Cancer and Allied Diseases, New York, NY '80 (SOC)
CHRIST, WINIFRED, chief soc. worker and lecturer, New York Hospital, Westchester Division, White Plains, NY '80 (SOC)
CHRISTAIN, EDWIN E., dir. pat. rep., Porter Memorial Hospital, Denver, CO '82 (PAT)
CHRISTEN, JEROLD W., dir. trng. and dev., St. Elizabeth's Hospital of Boston, Boston, MA '86 (EDUC)
CHRISTEN, PATSY M., RN, assoc. dir. nrsg., DePaul Health Center, Bridgeton, MO '80 (NURS)
CHRISTENSEN, CORNELIA F., RN, Methodist Hospital-Central Unit, Memphis, TN '81 (NURS)
CHRISTENSEN, M. TYCHO, dir. human res., Rocky Mountain Hospital, Denver, CO '82 (PERS)
CHRISTENSEN, MARY, risk mgr., H. Lee Moffitt Cancer Center, Tampa, FL '86 (RISK)
CHRISTENSEN, NEAL L., adm. serv., Holy Cross Hospital, Merrill, WI '75 (ENG)
CHRISTENSEN, RICHARD M., eng. consult., Doctors Hospital, Columbus, OH '75 (ENG)
CHRISTENSEN, ROBERT M., asst. vice-pres. plng. and facil., Pontiac General Hospital, Pontiac, MI '83 (PLNG)
CHRISTENSEN, ROBERT G., mgr. syst. and eng., Lutheran Medical Center, Omaha, NE '79 (ENG)
CHRISTENSEN, STEWART W., dir. food serv., University Medical Center, Tucson, AZ '69 (FOOD)
CHRISTENSEN, VAL H., adm., Mountain View Hospital, Payson, UT '74
CHRISTENSON, PEGGY D., mgt. eng., St. Marys Hospital of Rochester, Rochester, MN '86 (MGMT)
CHRISTENSON, WILLIAM C., dir. reg. 2, American Hospital Association, Princeton, NJ '66
CHRISTIAN, CAPT. E. R., MSC USN, Oviedo, FL '82
CHRISTIAN, F. ANNE, dir. pub. rel. and human res., Cassia Memorial Hospital, Burley, ID '82 (PR)(PERS)
CHRISTIAN, JOHN, dir. educ., Thorek Hospital and Medical Center, Chicago, IL '78 (RISK)(EDUC)
CHRISTIAN, MIKELL, RN, clin. dir. surg. nrsg., St. Mary-Corwin Hospital Center, Pueblo, CO '84 (NURS)
CHRISTIAN, REBECCA H., vice-pres. mktg., Wake Medical Center, Raleigh, NC '72 (PR) (PLNG)
CHRISTIAN, RODNEY V., dir. food serv., Henry Heywood Memorial Hospital, Gardner, MA '77 (FOOD)
CHRISTIANSEN, BARBARA J., RN, dir. nrsg., St. Rose de Lima Hospital, Henderson, NV '82 (NURS)
CHRISTIANSEN, EDWARD J. JR., atty., University Hospital, Boston, MA '80 (ATTY)
CHRISTIANSEN, JAY D., atty., Abbott-Northwestern Hospital, Minneapolis, MN '84 (ATTY)
CHRISTIANSEN, KEVIN, assoc. adm., Maryvale Samaritan Hospital, Phoenix, AZ '78 (PLNG)
CHRISTIANSEN, WAYNE C., MD, dir. emer., Charlton Memorial Hospital, Fall River, MA '87 (AMB)
CHRISTIANSON, DAVID E., dir. eng., Waukesha Memorial Hospital, Waukesha, WI '86 (ENG)
CHRISTIANSON, JOAN L., RN, mgr., St. Joseph's Hospital, Minot, ND '87 (AMB)
CHRISTIE, ARTHUR P., dir. matl. mgt., Houston Medical Center, Warner Robins, GA '86 (PUR)
CHRISTIE, DEBORAH L., case mgr. psych. soc. work, Christ Hospital, Cincinnati, OH '83 (SOC)
CHRISTIE, DRUE ANN, supv. memb serv., Cigna Healthplan of Texas, Inc., Dallas, TX '80 (PAT)
CHRISTIE, JANET L., dir. pers., Alachua General Hospital, Gainesville, FL '80
CHRISTIE, JOE L., vice-pres. constr. and plng., King's Daughters' Medical Center, Ashland, KY '83 (PLNG)
CHRISTIE, THOMAS C., (ret.), Petaloma, CA '80
CHRISTINA, SR. MARGARET, vice-pres., Little Company of Mary Hospital, Evergreen Park, IL '86 (ENVIRON)
CHRISTISON, EARL L., adm. dir. outpatient, LDS Hospital, Salt Lake City, UT '82
CHRISTMAN, GERALD H. SR., adm. pers., St. Joseph Hospital, Providence, RI '72 (PERS)
CHRISTMAN, LT. COL. LAURENCE M., MSC USA, adm., Andrew Rader Clinic, Fort Myer, VA '86 (PR)
CHRISTMAN, THOMAS C. JR., dir. plant oper., St. Mary's Health Center, St. Louis, MO '83 (ENG)
CHRISTNER, DON, asst. adm. prof. serv., Douglas Community Hospital, Roseburg, OR '84 (RISK)
CHRISTOFFERSEN, ELIZABETH E., Healthcare Consultants of North Texas, Irving, TX '83 (PLNG)
CHRISTOPHER, CHARISSA A., dir. pub. rel. and mktg., Beaumont Medical Surgical Hospital, Beaumont, TX '85 (PR)
CHRISTOPHER, E. WAYNE, (ret.), Port Richey, FL '67
CHRISTOPHER, ELLA J., RN, assoc. adm., Arkansas Children's Hospital, Little Rock, AR '85 (NURS)
CHRISTOPHER, MADELYN C., dir. mktg. and dev., John F. Kennedy Memorial Hospital, Atlantis, FL '81 (PR)
CHRISTOPHER, NICKOLAS, dir. eng., Maimonides Medical Center, Brooklyn, NY '84 (ENG)
CHRISTOPHER, THURMAN, dir. maint. and plant oper., Milton Community Hospital, River Rouge, MI '83 (ENG)
CHRISTY, BARBARA STEVENSON, RN, vice-pres. nrsg. serv., Butler Memorial Hospital, Butler, PA '78 (NURS)
CHRISTY, JEANNE D., coor. qual. assur. and infection control, Virginia Gay Hospital, Vinton, IA '87 (RISK)
CHROMANSKI, ANNETTE, dir. corp. plng. and mktg., St. Anne's Hospital, Fall River, MA '87 (PLNG)
CHROSTOWSKI, DOROTHY, RN, Fort Walton Beach, FL '76 (NURS)
CHRUSCIEL, MARY THERESE, asst. dir. food serv., Rutland Regional Medical Center, Rutland, VT '84 (FOOD)
CHRYMKO, GERTRUDE M., prof. and dir. diet., Erie Community College, Buffalo, NY '76 (FOOD)
CHRZANOSKI, CYNTHIA L., student, Temple University, Department of Health Administration, School of Business Administration, Philadelphia, PA '87
CHU, DAVID K. W., PhD, asst. prof., Indiana University, Indianapolis, IN '86
CHUDZYNSKI, MARY B., dir. dev. and pub. rel., LaPorte Hospital, LaPorte, IN '82 (PR)
CHULLEN, ELLA S., mgr. food serv., Franklin Hospital, Benton, IL '86 (MGMT)(FOOD)
CHUMBLEY, PENNY GORDON, dir. vol. serv., HCA Greenview Hospital, Bowling Green, KY '87 (VOL)
CHUMLEY, DAVID A., exec. vice-pres., Memorial Hospital, Belleville, IL '76
CHUMLEY, MICHAEL K., dir. pers., Union Hospital, Terre Haute, IN '86 (PERS)
CHUMSAE, PATRICIA A., dir. vol., Saint Vincent Hospital, Worcester, MA '84 (VOL)
CHURAN, JAMES F., assoc. eng., New York State Department of Health, Albany, NY '81 (ENG)
CHURCH, CHARLES F., asst. dir. eng., Holy Name Hospital, Teaneck, NJ '83 (ENG)
CHURCH, CHUCK, dir. phys. plant, Medical Center Rehabilitation Hospital, Grand Forks, ND '84 (ENG)
CHURCH, ETHEL, dir. environ. serv., Johnson City Medical Center Hospital, Johnson City, TN '86 (ENVIRON)
CHURCH, JANE E., RN, dir. nrsg., Atchison Hospital, Atchison, KS '76 (NURS)
CHURCH, JO, dir. soc. serv., Colquitt Regional Medical Center, Moultrie, GA '86 (SOC)
CHURCH, SUSAN E., asst. adm. pub. rel., St. Christopher's Hospital for Children, Philadelphia, PA '83 (PR)
CHURCH, TERRY A., dir. eng., Hermann Hospital, Houston, TX '86 (ENG)
CHURCHILL, AGGIE, dir. aux. serv., Florida Hospital Medical Center, Orlando, FL '78 (VOL)
CHURCHILL, JACK A., mgr. constr. and shared serv., Touro Infirmary, New Orleans, LA '85 (ENG)
CHURCHILL, JOAN R., dir. pub. info., Valley Regional Hospital, Claremont, NH '82 (PR)
CHURCHILL, MARY ANN, mgr. food serv., St. Elizabeth's Hospital, Belleville, IL '74 (FOOD)
CIALELLA, ROBERT F., student, Pennsylvania State University, University Park, PA '86 (PLNG)
CIAMPOLILLO, EDMUND L., coor. qual. assur., Sherrill House, Inc., Boston, MA '83 (RISK)
CIANFRANI, JAYNE, dir. vol. serv., Lower Bucks Hospital, Bristol, PA '85 (VOL)
CIARAMELLA, PAUL, exec. dir., Hospital of the Holy Family, Brooklyn, NY '85
CICATIELLO, JULIAN S. A., RN, dir. nrsg., James M. Jackson Memorial Hospital, Miami, FL '68 (NURS)
CICCHINO, VINCENT R., dir. plant oper., Ingalls Memorial Hospital, Harvey, IL '82 (ENG)
CICCOLONE, LENORA, coor. risk mgt., Roxborough Memorial Hospital, Philadelphia, PA '85 (RISK)
CICCOTOSTO, HUGO, pur. agt., North Pennsylvania Hospital, Lansdale, PA '87 (PUR)
CICERO, FRANCINE A., adm. asst., East Jefferson General Hospital, Metairie, LA '76 (RISK)
CICERO, S. SALLY, dir. vol. serv., Saint Anthony Medical Center, Rockford, IL '85 (VOL)
CICIORA, EDWIN F., supt. med. group eng., University of Chicago Hospitals, Chicago, IL '79 (ENG)
CIDRAS, JOSEPH M., dir. eng., Humana Hospital -San Antonio, San Antonio, TX '84 (ENG)
CIEPLY, JANET M., dir. commun. rel., Monongahela Valley Hospital, Monongahela, PA '86 (PR)
CIERZAN, GEORGE J., dir. pur., Kingman Regional Hospital, Kingman, AZ '82 (PUR)
CIESIELSKI, DONALD B., biomedical eng., South Suburban Hospital, Hazel Crest, IL '83 (ENG)
CIESLA, FRANK R., atty., Monmouth Medical Center, Long Branch, NJ '79 (ATTY)
CIESLAK, PAUL E., consult., Ernst and Whinney, Cleveland, OH '86 (MGMT)
CIHAK, JOAN L., dir. plng., Good Samaritan Medical Center, Phoenix, AZ '81 (PLNG)
CILIBERTO, ELLA A., RN, dir. nrsg. serv., Northern Westchester Hospital Center, Mount Kisco, NY '87 (NURS)
CILUFFO, JAMES V. JR., adm. res., Blodgett Memorial Medical Center, Grand Rapids, MI '80 (MGMT)
CIMA, LAURA E., RN, dir. nrsg.-surg. serv., Hackensack Medical Center, Hackensack, NJ '83 (NURS)
CIMINELLI, COL. LAWRENCE W., MSC USAF, adm. and chief exec. off., U. S. Air Force Hospital, Tucson, AZ '82
CIMMA, CLAUDIA A., assoc. adm. clin. serv., Memorial Hospital for Cancer, New York, NY '87 (AMB)
CINTRON, ROBERT J., El Paso, TX '82 (ENG)
CIOCCA, ALEXANDER J., atty., Mercy Hospital of Johnstown, Johnstown, PA '86 (ATTY)
CIOFFI, JOAN P., dir. educ. serv., Emory University Hospital, Atlanta, GA '86 (EDUC)
CIOLLI, DAVID E., dir. pers., Jackson Park Hospital, Chicago, IL '84 (PERS)
CIPOLLA, JOSEPH C., hosp. adm. consult., State of New York, Office of Health Systems Management, Hauppauge, NY '72
CIPOLLA, MICHAEL M., Brookfield, IL '81 (FOOD)
CIRI, ROBERT E., hosp. fin. computer application spec., Hewlett Packard, Glen Cove, NY '79
CIRILLO, ANTHONY, dir. corp. commun., Episcopal Hospital, Philadelphia, PA '85 (PR)
CIRILLO, SUSAN N., student, Program in Hospital and Health Care Administration, University of Minnesota, Minneapolis, MN '86 (PLNG)
CIRNE, M. CEU, dir. commun. rel., Saint James Hospital of Newark, Newark, NJ '85 (PR)
CIRULIS, BENITA, adm., Margaret Tietz Center for Nursing, Jamaica, NY '59
CISARIK, JAMES M., pres., James M. Cisarik and Associates, Houston, TX '77 (MGMT)
CISLER, ROBERT L., assoc. dir., Veterans Administration Medical Center, Brooklyn, NY '75
CISNEROS, RAYMOND JAMES, natl. dir. health care, Touche, Ross and Company, Boston, MA '68
CISNEY, LUCIEN, atty., Muhlenberg Community Hospital, Greenville, KY '84 (ATTY)
CITA, SARA L., coor. risk assessment, Mount Zion Hospital and Medical Center, San Francisco, CA '81 (RISK)
CITELLI, ANNE, cent. sup. tech., Burke Rehabilitation Center, White Plains, NY '83 (CS)
CITERONE, BERNARD P., mgr., Ernst and Whinney, Philadelphia, PA '78 (MGMT)
CITRINO, RICHARD A., staff eng., Cooper Hospital-University Medical Center, Camden, NJ '86 (ENG)
CITTA, ANTHONY J., dir. health and safety, Department of Sanitation Clinic, New York, NY '70
CIVALI, ANN G., RN, clin. coor. cent. serv., Memorial Hospital, Meriden, CT '81 (CS)
CIVIELLO, HAROLD J., (ret.), Bradenton, FL '61
CLADEK, LYDIA I., RN, assoc. dir. nrsg., Copley Memorial Hospital, Aurora, IL '80 (NURS)
CLADY, NELLIE, RN, dir. nrsg., Bucyrus Community Hospital, Bucyrus, OH '76 (NURS)
CLAERBAUT, RHONDA R., mgr. matl., Bethany Hospital, Chicago, IL '84 (PUR)
CLAIR, KEVIN M., corp. assoc. dir. health promotion serv., Baptist Medical Centers, Birmingham, AL '85
CLAIR, PATRICIA L., mgr. emp. rel., Charter Hospital Charlottesville, Charlottesville, VA '85 (PERS)
CLAIRE, THOMAS, sr. asst. dir., Medical College of Ohio Hospital, Toledo, OH '86 (RISK)
CLAIRMONT, THOMAS, vice-pres. oper. and fin., Lakes Region General Hospital, Laconia, NH '77
CLAMPITT, KELLI E., mgt. eng., Harper Hospital, Detroit, MI '85 (MGMT)
CLAMPITT, SHIRLEY D., dir. amb. serv., Deaconess Hospital, St. Louis, MO '87 (AMB)
CLANCY, CATHERINE ANN, dir. soc. serv., St. Luke's Episcopal Hospital, Houston, TX '85 (SOC)
CLANCY, JOSEPH DANIEL, vice-pres., Atlanticare Medical Center, Lynn, MA '62
CLANCY, LT. NANCY E., MSC USN, acct. receivable div. off., Naval Hospital, San Diego, CA '85
CLANTON, LEE M., vice-pres. pub. rel. and pers., Moore Municipal Hospital, Moore, OK '82 (PR)
CLAPP, FRANCES A., dir. vol. serv., Shady Grove Adventist Hospital, Rockville, MD '80 (VOL)
CLAPP, J. ROBERT JR., asst. adm., Mount Elizabeth Hospital Ltd., Singapore, Singapore '85 (MGMT)
CLAPP, RICHARD E., adm., Robinson Memorial Hospital, Ravenna, OH '85
CLAPPER, ROY, supv. maint. and security, Rehoboth-McKinley Christian Hospital, Gallup, NM '85 (ENG)
CLARE, SUSAN, vice-pres., Chemical Bank, New York, NY '83
CLARK, BARBARA OLIVER, supv. ped. unit and emer., Presbyterian Hospital in the City of New York, New York, NY '85 (SOC)
CLARK, BENJAMIN W., dir. clin. eng., Virginia Baptist Hospital, Lynchburg, VA '84 (ENG)
CLARK, BONNIE L., RN, adm. dir. pat. serv., Bedford Medical Center, Bedford, IN '73 (NURS)
CLARK, CAROL JEAN, pat. rep., Fairview Southdale Hospital, Minneapolis, MN '85 (PAT)
CLARK, CHARLES E. JR., CO-owner, C. E. Clark and Associates, Cottondale, AL '69 (MGMT)
CLARK, CHARLES KENNETH, vice-pres. mktg., Candler General Hospital, Savannah, GA '79 (PLNG)
CLARK, CHARLES L., dir. eng., St. Francis Medical Center, Honolulu, HI '84 (ENG)
CLARK, CHRIS, atty., Northside Hospital, Atlanta, GA '82 (ATTY)
CLARK, CLINT P., dir. eng. serv., AMI Palm Beach Gardens Medical Center, Palm Beach Gardens, FL '82 (ENG)
CLARK, DAVID M., atty., L. Richardson Memorial Hospital, Greensboro, NC '68 (ATTY)
CLARK, DAVID W., sr. vice-pres., University Hospitals of Cleveland, Cleveland, OH '87
CLARK, DENNY J., assoc. adm. commun. rel. and dev., Yuma Regional Medical Center, Yuma, AZ '84 (PR)
CLARK, DIANE A., dir. vol., New York Hospital, Westchester Division, White Plains, NY '85 (VOL)
CLARK, DICK, dir. maint., Bucyrus Community Hospital, Bucyrus, OH '85 (ENG)
CLARK, DOROTHY, RN, vice-pres., Newington Children's Hospital, Newington, CT '80 (NURS)
CLARK, EDGAR, asst. dir. bldg., St. Luke's Episcopal Hospital, Houston, TX '74 (ENG)
CLARK, ELAINE BRUSA, RN, mgr. cent. serv., Northeastern Vermont Regional Hospital, St. Johnsbury, VT '72 (CS)
CLARK, ELIZABETH HUGHES, soc. work consult., Blue Bell, PA '67 (SOC)
CLARK, GERALD W., vice-pres., Jonas and Associates, Milwaukee, WI '74 (PERS)
CLARK, GLENDA S., dir. soc. serv., St. Tammany Parish Hospital, Covington, LA '85 (SOC)
CLARK, GLENN A., atty., Valley Hospital, Ridgewood, NJ '81 (ATTY)
CLARK, HARRIETT WEDGEWORTH, atty., Kaiser Foundation Hospitals, Oakland, CA '85 (ATTY)
CLARK, HELEN, RN, vice-pres. nrsg. serv., Tempe St. Luke's Hospital, Tempe, AZ '82 (NURS)
CLARK, IDA O'GRADY, (ret.), Brooklyn, NY '66 (SOC)
CLARK, J. TOBEY, dir. clin. eng., Technical Services Program, University of Vermont, Burlington, VT '86 (ENG)
CLARK, JAMES FRANK, (ret.), Dallas, TX '52 (LIFE)
CLARK, JEFFREY A., dir. pers. and pub. rel., Gritman Memorial Hospital, Moscow, ID '86 (PERS)(PR)
CLARK, JOHN R., PhD, sr. assoc., Witt Associates, Inc., Oak Brook, IL '84
CLARK, JOSEPH D., supv. plant eng., Children's Hospital of Michigan, Detroit, MI '86 (ENG)

CLARK, JUDITH LYNN, coor. soc. serv., Clinton County Hospital, Frankfort, IN '86 (SOC)

CLARK, JUDITH W., RN, dir. nrsg., Charles Cole Memorial Hospital, Coudersport, PA '86 (NURS)

CLARK, KAREN O., diet., Johnson County Memorial Hospital, Franklin, IN '86 (FOOD)

CLARK, KATHLEEN M., dir. vol. serv., Suny Health Sciences Center at Syracuse, Syracuse, NY '84 (VOL)

CLARK, KATHY, RN, instr., Nashville Memorial Hospital, Madison, TN '85 (EDUC)

CLARK, KAY H., RN, vice-pres. nrsg. affairs, Baystate Medical Center, Springfield, MA '76 (NURS)

CLARK, KAY J., dir. vol. serv., Hilton Head Hospital, Hilton Head Island, SC '85 (VOL)

CLARK, KENNETH JOHN, dep. dir., Veterans Administration Central Office, Western Region, Washington, DC '75

CLARK, KIMBERLY, dir. soc. work, Fred Hutchinson Cancer Research Center, Seattle, WA '85 (SOC)

CLARK, LARRY, dir. plant oper., Washington County Hospital, Nashville, IL '80 (ENG)

CLARK, LAURENE L., human res. and commun. rep., Portage View Hospital, Hancock, MI '85 (PR)

CLARK, LINDA F., student, Northwestern University, Center for Nursing, Chicago, IL '86 (MGMT)

CLARK, MARILYN, adm. asst., Piedmont Hospital, Atlanta, GA '86 (RISK)

CLARK, MARTA D., reg. dir. plng., Intermountain Health Care, Inc., Salt Lake City, UT '81 (PLNG)

CLARK, MARY ANN, vice-pres. pat. serv., St. Joseph's Hospital, Minot, ND '86 (RISK)

CLARK, MARY D., PhD RN, Chicago, IL '83 (NURS)

CLARK, MARY, discharge planner, St. Peter's Community Hospital, Helena, MT '79 (SOC)

CLARK, MICHAEL A., atty., Hopkins and Sutter, Chicago, IL '86 (ATTY)

CLARK, MICHAEL J. P., vice-pres. mktg. and plng., Glendale Memorial Hospital and Health Center, Glendale, CA '83 (PLNG)

CLARK, NANCY, dir. vol. serv., Mercy Hospital, Owensboro, KY '76 (VOL)

CLARK, NORMAN F., (ret.), Columbus, OH '71 (EDUC)

CLARK, PAUL T., vice-pres. corp. dev., South Side Hospital of Pittsburgh, Pittsburgh, PA '73 (PLNG)

CLARK, PEGGY, coor. commun. educ., HCA Southern Hills Medical Center, Nashville, TN '86 (EDUC)

CLARK, PRISCILLA L., pres., P. Clark Associates, Concord, MA '84 (PLNG)

CLARK, RAIMONDA CORRADO, RN, asst. dir. nrsg., Beth Israel Medical Center, New York, NY '83 (NURS)

CLARK, REX A., asst. dir. eng., St. Joseph's Medical Center, Fort Wayne, IN '84 (ENG)

CLARK, RICHARD A., dir. res. eval., O'Connor Health Service, San Jose, CA '83 (MGMT)

CLARK, RICHARD L., prin., Arthur, Clark, Elmore Associates, Inc., Kansas City, MO '79 (PLNG)

CLARK, RONALD J., mgr. reg. mktg., Health Central Metropolitan Hospitals, Minneapolis, MN '79 (PUR)

CLARK, RONALD S., adm., Castine Community Hospital, Castine, ME '86 (PLNG)

CLARK, RONALD, design eng., Mechanical Engineers Inc., Charlotte, NC '84 (ENG)

CLARK, ROSALIE, dir. soc. serv. and util. review, Humana Hospital -Sunrise, Las Vegas, NV '84 (SOC)

CLARK, ROSEMARY GORTZ, dir. vol., Middletown Regional Hospital, Middletown, OH '77 (VOL)

CLARK, SHEILA M., RN, dir. nrsg. serv., St. Joseph's Hospital, Huntingburg, IN '80 (NURS)

CLARK, THEODORE, student, University of Michigan Program in Hospital Administration, Ann Arbor, MI '87 (PLNG)

CLARK, THOMAS C., dir. oper. and maint., Hospital of the University of Pennsylvania, Philadelphia, PA '85 (ENG)

CLARK, THOMAS W., mgr. maint., St. Joseph Health and Rehabilitation Center, Ottumwa, IA '82 (ENG)

CLARK, TRACY A., dir. soc. serv., St. Mary's Hospital, Centralia, IL '85 (SOC)

CLARK, VERNON, dir. plant eng., Memorial Hospital, Hollywood, FL '82 (ENG)

CLARK, WILLARD H. JR., dir. eng., St. Ann's Home the Heritage, Rochester, NY '79 (ENG)

CLARK, WILLIAM D., dir. facil. mgt., Mary Imogene Bassett Hospital and Clinics, Cooperstown, NY '69 (ENG)

CLARK, WILLIAM, mgt. consult., South Shore Hospital, South Weymouth, MA '68 (PLNG)

CLARKE, ALEX M., atty., Antelope Memorial Hospital, Neligh, NE '74 (ATTY)

CLARKE, BARRY L., pres., Wheelock Associates, Inc., Hanover, NH '85 (PR)

CLARKE, DAVID K., dir. food serv., Westview Hospital, Indianapolis, IN '79 (FOOD)

CLARKE, DENISE W., dir. vol. serv., Hartford Hospital, Hartford, CT '79 (VOL)

CLARKE, EDWARD O. JR., atty., Bon Secours Hospital, Baltimore, MD '68 (ATTY)

CLARKE, SR. ELAINE A., dir. vol. serv., Snoqualmie Valley Hospital, Snoqualmie, WA '85 (VOL)

CLARKE, ELIZABETH, dir. soc. serv., Seton Medical Center, Austin, TX '79 (SOC)

CLARKE, ESTON W., dir. pub. rel., McLeod Regional Medical Center, Florence, SC '73 (PR)

CLARKE, GLENN E., consult., Rodgers Construction, Nashville, TN '79 (ENG)

CLARKE, J. ROBERT, mgr. health serv. div., Furst Group, Rockford, IL '85

CLARKE, JAMES O., assoc. dir., Health Education Consortium, Inc., Manchester, NH '85 (EDUC)

CLARKE, JENNIFER ANN, mgr. pat. rel., Riverside Methodist Hospitals, Columbus, OH '84 (PAT)

CLARKE, JOSEPH P., asst. adm., DePaul Hospital, Norfolk, VA '85 (PERS)

CLARKE, KAREN B., dir. commun. rel., Winter Park Memorial Hospital, Winter Park, FL '86 (PR)

CLARKE, KATHLEEN, pat. rep., St. Mary's Hospital, Norton, VA '85 (PAT)

CLARKE, KATHRYN P., dir. diet., Calgary General Hospital, Calgary, Alta., Canada '86 (FOOD)

CLARKE, LEROY W., dir. cent. matl. serv., Winchester Hospital, Winchester, MA '79 (CS)

CLARKE, MARJIE L., coor. lifeline and vol. serv., St. Catherine Hospital, Garden City, KS '85 (VOL)

CLARKE, PATRICIA A., asst. dir. vol., Mercy Hospital of Wilkes-Barre, Wilkes-Barre, PA '85 (VOL)

CLARKE, PAULINE E., pat. rep., Cheshire Medical Center, Keene, NH '84 (PAT)

CLARKE, ROBERTA N., assoc. prof. health care mgt. prog., Boston University, Boston, MA '84 (PLNG)

CLARKE, RODNEY G., assoc. dir. eng., Baptist Medical Center-Princeton, Birmingham, AL '85 (ENG)

CLARKE, W. JOSEPH JR., dir. health support, Community Mutual Insurance Company, Cincinnati, OH '77

CLARKE, WALTER L., dir. facil., Sherman Hospital, Elgin, IL '77 (ENG)

CLARKIN, JOHN F., dir., Coopers and Lybrand, Philadelphia, PA '74 (MGMT)

CLARKSON, EDWARD H., adm. health care, Southern Baptist Hospital, New Orleans, LA '59

CLARY, GARY E., atty., Cherokee Memorial Hospital, Gaffney, SC '83 (ATTY)

CLASSEN, H. WARD, atty., University of Maryland Medical Systems, Baltimore, MD '87 (ATTY)

CLAUER, ALICE J., dir. vol., South Louisiana Medical Center, Houma, LA '80 (VOL)

CLAUS, ELEANOR G., RN, pres., Alta Bates Hospital, Berkeley, CA '73 (NURS)

CLAUSEN, CAROLYN S., RN, dir. nrsg. serv., Marian Health Center, Sioux City, IA '86 (NURS)

CLAUSEN, DARWIN G., dir. plant eng. serv., St. Francis Medical Center, La Crosse, WI '71 (ENG)

CLAUSER, MARGE, mgr. emp., Orlando Regional Medical Center, Orlando, FL '85 (PERS)

CLAUSER, NORMA JEAN, pat. rel. rep., Farmington Community Hospital, Farmington, MO '85 (PAT)

CLAUSON, ELSA J., RN, dir. nrsg., Doctors Hospital, Tucker, GA '81 (NURS)

CLAUSTRE, DWIGHT, dir. risk mgt., St. Margaret Hospital, Hammond, IN '85 (RISK)

CLAVETTE, HARVEY, supt. plant, Edmundston Regional Hospital, Edmundston, N.B., Canada '85 (ENG)

CLAVIN, DEE THERIOT, asst. dir. pers., East Jefferson General Hospital, Metairie, LA '86 (PERS)

CLAY, DANA L., consult., Ev Clay Associates, Inc., Coral Gables, FL '86

CLAY, GERALD L., reg. eng., Samaritan Health Services, Phoenix, AZ '76 (ENG)

CLAY, MARILYNN M., dir. cent. sup., Sierra Medical Center, El Paso, TX '82 (CS)

CLAY, SANDRA K., RN, asst. dir. nrsg., Charleston Area Medical Center, Charleston, WV '85 (NURS)

CLAYPOOLE, PATRICIA A., RN, asst. adm. nrsg., Redford Community Hospital, Redford, MI '83 (NURS)

CLAYTON, ANNE M., dir. vol. serv., HCA Park View Medical Center, Nashville, TN '87 (VOL)

CLAYTON, ANTHONY DONALD, dir. matl. mgt., Lions Gate Hospital, North Vancouver, B.C., Canada '86 (PUR)

CLAYTON, CURTIS A., consult., Curtis A. Clayton Consulting Company, Richmond, VA '64

CLAYTON, DOLORES M., RN, adm. mgr. nrsg., St. Luke's-Roosevelt Hospital Center, New York, NY '85 (NURS)

CLAYTON, JANICE L., dir. pers., Val Verde Memorial Hospital, Del Rio, TX '87 (PERS)

CLAYTOR, NORRIS V., assoc. exec. dir. plng., Hospital of the University of Pennsylvania, Philadelphia, PA '79 (PLNG)

CLAYWELL, JAMES C., eng., NKC Hospitals, Louisville, KY '63 (ENG)

CLEARE, HENRY O., vice-pres. eng. and facil., Good Samaritan Hospital, West Palm Beach, FL '84 (ENG)

CLEARY, CAROL J., student, University of Michigan, Ann Arbor, MI '84 (MGMT)

CLEARY, EUGENE T., dir. facil., plng. and constr., Long Island Jewish Medical Center, New York, NY '83

CLEARY, JAMES P., mgr. pers., Geisinger Medical Center, Danville, PA '81 (PERS)

CLEARY, JOAN L., exec. asst., Park Nicollet Medical Center, Minneapolis, MN '81

CLEARY, JOHN C., dir. pur., Providence Hospital, Southfield, MI '73 (PUR)

CLEARY, LT. COL. JOHN J., MSC USAF, dep. sr. med. staff off., Headquarters U. S. European Command, APO New York, NY '70

CLEARY, MARGARET S., asst. adm., Fairview Southdale Hospital, Fairview Community Hospitals, Minneapolis, MN '78

CLEARY, ROBERT J., vice-pres., Healthwest Foundation, Great Missenden, England '84

CLEARY, ROBERT J., adm. asst., St. Francis Hospital, Charleston, WV '76 (RISK)

CLEARY, THOMAS D., pres., Center for Dianostic Imaging, Minneapolis, MN '87 (AMB)

CLEARY, LT. COL. THOMAS J., MSC USAF, chief soc. work, U. S. Air Force Regional Hospital, Sheppard AFB, TX '82 (SOC)

CLEARY, WILLIAM H., dir. human res., Palos Community Hospital, Palos Heights, IL '76 (PERS)

CLEATON, GLORIA, RN, dir. nrsg. serv., Memorial Hospital of Michigan City, Michigan City, IN '77 (NURS)

CLEAVER, SANDRA M., RN, dir. nrsg., City Hospital, Martinsburg, WV '83 (NURS)

CLEAVES, DONNA L., supv. cent. serv., Nashua Memorial Hospital, Nashua, NH '86 (CS)

CLEESATTLE, DONALD A., dir. maint., Phoebe Putney Memorial Hospital, Albany, GA '85 (ENG)

CLEGHORN, PRUDENCE A., RN, coor. educ., Anderson Hospital, Maryville, IL '85 (EDUC)

CLEGHORN, RUFUS JAMES JR., dir. plant oper., Hillcrest Baptist Medical Center, Waco, TX '80 (ENG)

CLELAND, JAMES, mgr. matl., St. Mary's Hospital, Amsterdam, NY '74 (PUR)

CLELAND, MARC, dir. matl. mgt., Saratoga Community Hospital, Detroit, MI '83 (PUR)

CLELAND, VIRGINIA S., RN, prof. and coor. nrsg. adm. prog., University of California San Francisco, San Francisco, CA '86 (NURS)

CLEM, HOWARD D. JR., dir. matl. serv., George H. Lanier Memorial Hospital and Nursing Home, Valley, AL '79 (PUR)

CLEM, HUSTON, dir. environ. serv., Mesquite Community Hospital, Mesquite, TX '86 (ENVIRON)

CLEMENCE, JOYCE M., RN, dir. nrsg. qual. assur. and info. syst., St. Paul Medical Center, Dallas, TX '81 (NURS)

CLEMENS, MARTINA K., dir. mktg., Grandview Hospital and Medical Center, Dayton, OH '84 (PLNG)

CLEMENS, ROSEMARY A., PhD, asst. dir., New York Hospital, New York, NY '85 (PLNG)

CLEMENT, ALICE E., RN, supv. cent. sterile sup., Camden County Health Services Center, Blackwood, NJ '80 (CS)

CLEMENT, BARBARA J., asst. dir. food and nutr. serv., Good Samaritan Hospital and Medical Center, Portland, OR '83 (FOOD)

CLEMENT, BRYAN B., dir. mgt. eng., Air Force Management Engineer Agency, Randolph AFB, TX '82 (MGMT)

CLEMENT, DANIEL C., adm. dir. psych. and soc. work, Overlake Hospital Medical Center, Bellevue, WA '85 (SOC)

CLEMENT, JANICE F., dir. nrsg. serv., Heartland Hospital West, St. Joseph, MO '83 (NURS)

CLEMENT, JENNIFER ELAINE, mgt. consult., Arthur Andersen and Company, Dallas, TX '84

CLEMENTE, ARMANDO B., consult., Coopers and Lybrand, New York, NY '84 (MGMT)

CLEMENTE, ROBERT A., exec. dir., Hemac, Inc., Ambulatory Care Division, Marlton, NJ '79

CLEMENTS, DAVID, dir. pers., Lutheran Medical Center, Omaha, NE '80 (PERS)

CLEMENTS, FRANKLIN, chief eng., Peralta Hospital, Oakland, CA '85 (ENG)

CLEMENTS, JAMIE HAGER, atty., Scott and White Memorial Hospital, Temple, TX '64 (ATTY)

CLEMENTS, MARION D., adm. asst., Dorminy Medical Center, Fitzgerald, GA '86 (PERS)

CLEMENTS, ROBERT W., atty., Lake Charles Memorial Hospital, Lake Charles, LA '71 (ATTY)

CLEMES, JOHN J., bus. mgr. lab., University of Illinois Hospital, Chicago, IL '68 (PERS)

CLEMONS, BARBARA A., Catholic Healthcare West, Sacramento, CA '79 (PR)

CLEMONS, JOHN F., dir. safety, University Hospital, Boston, MA '66 (ENG)

CLEMONS, JOSEPH N., pres. and arch., Clemons, Rutherford and Associates, Inc., Tallahassee, FL '85 (ENG)

CLENDENEN, ANNETTE S., pat. adv., Vanderbilt University Hospital, Nashville, TN '86 (PAT)

CLENNON, MARTIN J., asst. supt. bldg., Bridgeport Hospital, Bridgeport, CT '85 (ENG)

CLERKE, NANCY C., asst. to dir. vol. serv., Manchester Memorial Hospital, Manchester, CT '86 (VOL)

CLEVELAND, HENRY C. III, atty., AMI Presbyterian-St. Luke's Medical Center, Denver, CO '72 (ATTY)

CLEVELAND, JERRY L., dir. cent. serv., St. Luke's Methodist Hospital, Cedar Rapids, IA '78 (CS)

CLEVEN, CY, dir. pat. rel., Victory Memorial Hospital, Waukegan, IL '75 (RISK)

CLEVENGER, BILL, dir. hskpg. and ldry., Deaconess Hospital, Cincinnati, OH '86 (ENVIRON)

CLEVENGER, VIRGINIA A., dir. educ., Springdale Memorial Hospital, Springdale, AR '81 (EDUC)

CLEVERLY, MAE B., adm., Harley Hospital, Boston, MA '42 (LIFE)

CLEWELL, LINDA J., RN, assoc. dir. nrsg., Rapides General Hospital, Alexandria, LA '84 (NURS)

CLEWLOW, CATHERINE M., consult., Arthur Andersen and Company, Chicago, IL '86 (MGMT)

CLIBORNE, JAMES J. JR., adm., HCA South Arlington Medical Center, Arlington, TX '78

CLICK, CATHRYN M., coor. nrsg. educ., Central Washington Hospital, Wenatchee, WA '81 (EDUC)

CLICK, LENA R., dir. environ. serv., Farmington Nursing Home, Farmington Hills, MI '86 (ENVIRON)

CLIFFORD, JOYCE C., RN, vice-pres. nrsg., Beth Israel Hospital, Boston, MA '74 (NURS)

CLIFFORD, RONALD J., chief exec. off., Henderson Memorial Hospital, Henderson, TX '85

CLIFFORD, WILLARD H., chief eng., Wadsworth-Rittman Hospital, Wadsworth, OH '68 (ENG)

CLIFT, NANCY B., pers. asst., Crawford W. Long Memorial Hospital of Emory University, Atlanta, GA '77 (EDUC)

CLIFTON, EARL B., vice-pres. oper., Elmbrook Memorial Hospital, Brookfield, WI '82 (PUR)

CLIFTON, MICHAEL F., dir. pub. rel. and mktg., Kosciusko Community Hospital, Warsaw, IN '84 (PR)

CLIFTON, VALERIE R., dir. soc. work, Methodist Hospital of Brooklyn, Brooklyn, NY '86 (SOC)

CLINE, COREEN B., asst. pers., Bay Area Hospital, Coos Bay, OR '86 (PERS)

CLINE, GERALD F., dir. sup., proc. and distrib., St. Vincent's Medical Center, Bridgeport, CT '77 (CS)

CLINE, JAMES W., dir. human res., Davis Community Hospital, Statesville, NC '75 (PERS)

CLINE, LAURA J., dir. nutr. serv., Day Kimball Hospital, Putnam, CT '72 (FOOD)

CLINE, PATRICIA J., mgr. matl., Beverly Hospital, Montebello, CA '83 (PUR)

CLINE, RONALD L., assoc. vice-pres. plng., Ingham Medical Center, Lansing, MI '85 (PLNG)(PAT)

CLINE, WALTER PATRICK, dir. plant oper., Children's Hospital of Pittsburgh, Pittsburgh, PA '68 (ENG)

CLINE, WILLIAM H., dir. pers., Washington Hospital, Washington, PA '83 (PERS)

CLINEFELTER, KATHRYN B., RN, dir. nrsg. syst., Shands Hospital, Gainesville, FL '86 (NURS)
CLINGERMAN, YVONNE, dir. outpat. St. Joseph's Hospital and Health Center, Tucson, AZ '87 (AMB)
CLINTON, HELEN G., dir. soc. serv., Children's Hospital, Boston, MA '77 (SOC)
CLINTON, JOHN B., partner, Concord Partners, New York, NY '85
CLINTON, THOMAS F. JR., vice-pres., Howard County General Hospital, Columbia, MD '82 (ATTY)
CLITES, JANET G., RN, dir. nrsg., Brookings Hospital, Brookings, SD '85 (NURS)
CLODFELTER, PHYLLIS J., clin. diet., Montgomery County Culver Union Hospital, Crawfordsville, IN '75 (FOOD)
CLONES, CHRISTOPHER, dir. cent. sup., St. Vincent's Hospital and Medical Center of New York, New York, NY '84 (CS)
CLOSE, SANDRA, coor. qual. assur., Methodist Hospital of Southern California, Arcadia, CA '86 (RISK)
CLOSS, CATHERINE A., dir. educ. serv., Children's Hospital of Eastern Ontario, Ottawa, Ont., Canada '80 (EDUC)
CLOSSIN, EARL CHARLES, dir. clin. eng., Saint Luke's Hospital, Cleveland, OH '82 (ENG)
CLOSSIN, RAYMOND JR., dir. maint., St. Luke's Hospital of the United Methodist Church, Cleveland, OH '67 (ENG)
CLOSSON, BONNIE L., asst. dir. nrsg. educ., St. Marys Hospital of Rochester, Rochester, MN '85 (EDUC)
CLOTE, SALLIE COWAN, dir. soc. serv., Moore Municipal Hospital, Moore, OK '80 (SOC)
CLOTHIER, MELVIN L., adm. med. serv., Nebraska Department of Social Services, Lincoln, NE '60
CLOUD, BENJAMIN, vice-pres., J. A. Montgomery, Inc., Wilmington, DE '85 (RISK)
CLOUGH, JUDITH ANNE, dir. risk mgt., Southwest Detroit Hospital, Detroit, MI '85 (RISK)
CLOUSER, ESTHER L., consult., Akron, OH '81 (FOOD)
CLOUTIER, THOMAS I., dir. hskpg., St. Mary's Medical Center, Duluth, MN '86 (ENVIRON)
CLOVER, CAROL S., dir. vol. serv., Oak Park Hospital, Oak Park, IL '83 (VOL)
CLOYS, JO HELEN, dir. pat. and commun. rel., Pattie A. Clay Hospital, Richmond, KY '82 (PR)
CLUBB, JOSEPH R., dir. soc. serv., Fairview Riverside Hospital, Minneapolis, MN '85 (SOC)
CLUFF, PATRICIA L., dir. commun. rel., Shands Hospital at the University of Florida, Gainesville, FL '85 (PR)
CLUMP, ADEN H., chief life safety security, Illinois Department of Public Health, Springfield, IL '79 (PLNG)
CLUMPNER, JANE L., mng. dir., Bayou Knoll Marketing Concepts, Houston, TX '86 (PLNG)
CLYATT, WILLIAM P., sr. mgt. eng., University of California at Los Angeles Management Sciences, Los Angeles, CA '79 (MGMT)
CLYMER, JOHN H., atty., Children's Hospital, Boston, MA '77 (ATTY)
CLYNE, JOYCE K., sr. mgt. syst. eng., North Broward Medical Center, Pompano Beach, FL '86 (MGMT)
CNOSSEN, ALICE, dir. commun. rel., Stormont-Vail Regional Medical Center, Topeka, KS '81 (PR)
COADY, ARTHUR F., atty., Holy Cross Hospital, Calgary, Alta., Canada '75 (ATTY)
COAKLEY, SR. COLMAN, pres., Presentation Health System, Sioux Falls, SD '76
COAKLEY, EDWARD E., RN, dir. oper. room nrsg., Massachusetts General Hospital, Boston, MA '86 (NURS)
COALSON, TOMMY C., SunHealth Corporation, Charlotte, NC '79 (MGMT)
COAR, MARLENE J., dir. commun. serv., Memorial Hospital, South Bend, IN '81 (ENG)
COATAR, JOAN M., RN, clin. dir. spec. unit, Louis A. Weiss Memorial Hospital, Chicago, IL '85 (NURS)
COATES, DAVID M., PhD, pres., Community Memorial Hospital, Monmouth, IL '82 (AMB)
COATES, JANET E., RN, adm. nrsg., Doctors Hospital, Little Rock, AR '84 (NURS)
COATES, LORI SMITH, mgr. prod. dev., San Antonio Community Hospital, Upland, CA '84 (PLNG)
COATES, STAN B., chief eng., Humana Hospital -Greensboro, Greensboro, NC '81 (ENG)
COATS, ROBERT, vice-pres. oper., Meriter Hospital, Madison, WI '70 (MGMT)
COBB, CAROLYN J., dir. emp. rel., Oconee Memorial Hospital, Seneca, SC '87 (PERS)
COBB, GREGORY G., dir. soc. serv., Stevens Memorial Hospital, Edmonds, WA '85 (SOC)
COBB, JAMES B., exec. vice-pres., Santa Barbara Medical Foundation Clinic, Santa Barbara, CA '64
COBB, KENNETH W., exec. dir. support serv., Berrien General Hospital, Berrien Center, MI '87 (ENG)(ENVIRON)
COBB, NATHALEEN, student nrs., Methodist Hospital, Lubbock, TX '85 (PAT)
COBB, WILLIAM C., eng., Lane Memorial Hospital, Zachary, LA '62 (ENG)
COBBETT, HARRY A., dir. eng. and maint., Ellwood City Hospital, Ellwood City, PA '82 (ENG)
COBBS, W. DANIEL, adm. and chief exec. off., St. Joseph's Hospital, Belvidere, IL '80 (PR)
COBEY, SR. ROSALIA, pres. health care council, Religious Hospital of St. Joseph, Kingston, Ont., Canada '85
COBLE, DAVID W., pub. rel. asst., St. Peter Hospital, Olympia, WA '82 (PR)
COBLEY, GEORGE G., assoc. dir. plant oper., Cedars-Sinai Medical Center, Los Angeles, CA '83 (MGMT)
COBOS, ANGELICA H., dir. pub. rel., Southwest General Hospital, San Antonio, TX '86 (PR)
COBURN, JOHN F., mgr., Arthur Andersen and Company, Boston, MA '85 (MGMT)
COBURN, LELAND B., dir. mgt. eng., Utah Valley Regional Medical Center, Provo, UT '82 (MGMT)
COBURN, WALTER V., sr. vice-pres. prog. dev., Bethany Medical Center, Kansas City, KS '84 (PLNG)
COCAVESSIS, PAMELA A. M., sr. mgt. eng., St. Joseph Hospital, Houston, TX '82 (MGMT)
COCAYNE, MARVIN E., mgr. environ. serv., Mercy Health Center, Dubuque, IA '86 (ENVIRON)
COCCO, JOHN G., pres., Lafayette Engineering, Inc., Lafayette Hill, PA '85 (ENG)
COCCO, WILHELMINA, mgr. eng., Lenox Hill Hospital, New York, NY '81 (ENG)
COCHARD, ROBERT E., mgt. eng., Hospital of the Medical College of Pennsylvania, Philadelphia, PA '85 (MGMT)
COCHIS, SHIRLEY J., dir. pers., Amesbury Hospital, Amesbury, MA '83 (PERS)
COCHRAN, CHARLES E., dir. mgt. eng., National Medical Enterprises, Western Region, Santa Monica, CA '80 (MGMT)
COCHRAN, GARY P., mgr. corp. plng., Nebraska Methodist Health System, Inc., Omaha, NE '79 (PLNG)
COCHRAN, MARILYN, RN, dir. educ., Baxter County Regional Hospital, Mountain Home, AR '83 (EDUC)
COCHRAN, ROGER A., mgr. plng. and operational analysis, American Medical International, Atlanta, GA '84 (PLNG)
COCHRAN, SUZANNE E., spec. telecommun., Washington Hospital, Fremont, CA '85 (ENG)
COCHRANE, DONNA M., dir. pub. rel. and fund dev., St. Joseph Mercy Hospital, Ann Arbor, MI '81 (CS)
COCHRANE, EUGENE W. JR., dir. mgt. serv., The Duke Endowment, Charlotte, NC '72
COCKBURN, PEGGY ANN, mgr. syst. ldry., Memorial Hospital System, Houston, TX '86 (ENVIRON)
COCKE, JAMES M., chief eng. plant oper., Thoms Rehabilitation Hospital, Asheville, NC '82 (ENG)
COCKE, THOMAS P., dir. bldg. maint. and grds., Johns Hopkins Hospital, Baltimore, MD '68 (ENG)
COCKERILL, HOWARD, dir., Thunderbird Samaritan Hospital, Glendale, AZ '85 (ENG)
COCKERILL, JANET L., coor. educ., Arkansas City Memorial Hospital, Arkansas City, KS '87 (EDUC)
COCKEROFT, SUE J., exec. asst., Mills Memorial Hospital, San Mateo, CA '82 (PAT)
COCKRELL, PEGGY J., risk mgt. liaison, Ashland Community Hospital, Ashland, OR '86 (RISK)
COCKRUM, CAROLYN, dir. vol., St. John Medical Center, Tulsa, OK '83 (VOL)
COCO, STANLEY A., asst. dir. eng. and plant oper., Methodist Hospital-Central Unit, Memphis, TN '85 (ENG)
COCOZZA, CAMILLE M., dir. soc. serv., Mercer Medical Center, Trenton, NJ '79 (SOC)
COCQUYT, RON, exec. vice-pres., Monarch Products, Mount Clemens, MI '85 (CS)
CODD, EDWARD B., chief info. syst. off., Catherine McAuley Health Center, Ann Arbor, MI '83 (MGMT)
CODDINGTON, BARBARA E., dir. food serv., Children's Mercy Hospital, Kansas City, MO '80 (FOOD)
CODDINGTON, MEGAN, dir. commun. resources, Lakeside Community Hospital, Lakeport, CA '82 (PERS)
CODERRE, RONALD P., dir. commun. rel. and dev., Day Kimball Hospital, Putnam, CT '85 (PR)
CODKIND, MELISSA D. MAGID, asst. vice-pres. mktg. and plng., Jeanes Health System, Jenkintown, PA '84 (PLNG)
CODY, C. WILLIAM, mgr. natl. acct., Home Nutrional Support, Inc., Pinebrook, NJ '87 (AMB)
CODY, ED, mgr., Lindsey, Crisp, Hughes and Company, Asheville, NC '84
CODY, JAMES P., prog. analyst, Veterans Administration, Department of Medicine and Surgery, Washington, DC '83
CODY, MAURICE P., dir. pub. rel., Victoria General Hospital, Halifax, N.S., Canada '83 (PR)
CODY, NANCY HILL, coor. commun. rel., Muskegon General Hospital, Muskegon, MI '85 (PR)
COE, BETTY P., RN, vice-pres., Crouse-Irving Memorial Hospital, Syracuse, NY '78 (EDUC)
COE, CLYDE E., dir. environ. serv., San Bernardino Community Hospital, San Bernardino, CA '86 (ENVIRON)
COE, FRANK M., exec. vice-pres., St. Peter's Medical Center, New Brunswick, NJ '52 (LIFE)
COE, WILLIAM G., adm., Parker Community Hospital, Parker, AZ '80 (PUR)(PLNG)
COELLO, CARLOS C., MD, chief health evaluation serv., Eastern Los Angeles Regional Center for Developmental Disabled, Alhambra, CA '65
COEN, SONDRA E., mgr. matl., Floyd County Memorial Hospital, Charles City, IA '81 (CS)
COFER, JENNIFER I., publisher, Medical Records Briefing, Marblehead, MA '86
COFF, MORRIS J., atty., American International Hospital, Zion, IL '78 (ATTY)
COFFEE, MAURICE P. JR., pres., Health Planning and Development, Inc., Princeton, NJ '60
COFFELT, KEMPER R., atty., Christian Hospitals Northeast-Northwest, St. Louis, MO '86 (ATTY)
COFFEY, ANNE M., dir. soc. serv., Valdese General Hospital, Valdese, NC '80 (SOC)
COFFEY, CHRISTOPHER H., corp. planner, Martin Memorial Hospital, Stuart, FL '83 (PLNG)
COFFEY, DANIEL B., chief fin. off., Eastern Maine Healthcare, Bangor, ME '79
COFFEY, DOROTHY C., dir. pers., Woods Psychiatric Institute, Abilene, TX '82 (PERS)
COFFEY, FRED L. JR., vice-pres., Huntsville Hospital, Huntsville, AL '87 (AMB)
COFFEY, LCDR HARRY C., MSC USN, Naval Medical Command, Washington, DC '75
COFFEY, JAMES B. JR., vice-pres., Eastern Maine Healthcare, Bangor, ME '78 (PLNG)
COFFEY, RICHARD JAMES, PhD, pres., Coffey Associates, Milan, MI '67 (MGMT)
COFFEY, VIRGINIA, supv. cent. proc., Rowan Memorial Hospital, Salisbury, NC '83 (CS)
COFFIELL, ANNE M., asst. dir. sup., proc., distrib., and matl. mgt., Our Lady of Lourdes Medical Center, Camden, NJ '83 (CS)
COFFILL, DAVID, mgr. matl. and cent. sup., Lexington Memorial Hospital, Lexington, NC '87 (CS)
COFFIN, DIANNE P., RN, asst. adm. pat. serv., South County Hospital, Wakefield, RI '85 (NURS)
COFFIN, JOHN F., dir. univ rel., University Hospital and Ambulatory Care Center, Little Rock, AR '83 (PR)
COFFIN, LARRY C., dir. plant serv., White Memorial Medical Center, Los Angeles, CA '82 (ENG)
COFFIN, RONALD F., dir. commun., Porter Memorial Hospital, Denver, CO '82 (PR)
COFFMAN, CHERYL A., vice-pres., Grant Medical Center, Columbus, OH '82
COFFMAN, LOUISE R., adm. pat. rep., Loma Linda Community Hospital, Loma Linda, CA '85 (PAT)
COFFMAN, SONJA M., coor. commun. rel., Highline Community Hospital, Seattle, WA '85 (PR)
COGAN, JOAN E., asst. supv. sup., Bergen Pines County Hospital, Paramus, NJ '85 (CS)
COGAN, STEW, atty., Providence Central Memorial Hospital, Toppenish, WA '80 (ATTY)
COGDILL, RON G., dir. environ. serv., HCA Valley Regional Medical Center, Brownsville, TX '85 (ENG)
COGGESHALL, LOWELL T., MD, Foley, AL '58 (HON)
COGSWELL, BILL, mgr. corp. logistics, American Health Facilities Inc., Subsidiary of American Hospital Supply Corporation, McGaw Park, IL '85 (PUR)
COHAGEN, CINDY, dir. commun., Sharp Healthcare, San Diego, CA '84 (PR)
COHAN, MARVIN, dir., Wagner College, Program in Health Services Administration, Staten Island, NY '51 (LIFE)
COHAN, MORT S., dir. food serv., Lawrence Memorial Hospital of Medford, Medford, MA '80 (FOOD)
COHEN-BUTLIEN, JOYCE M., Shaker Heights, OH '85 (PLNG)
COHEN, ADRENE G., RN, assoc. dir., New York City Health and Hospitals Corporation, New York, NY '78 (NURS)
COHEN, ARTHUR B., dep. exec. dir., Newark Beth Israel Medical Center, Newark, NJ '62
COHEN, BARNEY I., atty., Michael Reese Hospital and Medical Center, Chicago, IL '80 (ATTY)
COHEN, BEATRICE, dir. soc. work, Central General Hospital, Plainview, NY '86 (SOC)
COHEN, BETTY RICHARDS, assoc. dir. nrsg. educ., Swedish Covenant Hospital, Chicago, IL '85 (EDUC)
COHEN, BILL, publisher, Haworth Press, Inc., New York, NY '84 (PLNG)(AMB)
COHEN, CHRISTOPHER B., atty., Oak Park Hospital, Oak Park, IL '81 (ATTY)
COHEN, CYNTHIA E., student, Temple University, Department of Health Administration, Philadelphia, PA '86
COHEN, DAVID L., atty., Pennsylvania Hospital, Philadelphia, PA '83 (ATTY)
COHEN, DAVID S., pres., Cohen, Rutherford and Blum, Rockville, MD '77
COHEN, ELLIOT GENE, assoc. hosp. dir., Foster G. McGaw Hospital, Loyola University of Chicago, Maywood, IL '69
COHEN, HERBERT, prin., Cohen, Karydas and Associates, Inc., Washington, DC '73
COHEN, HILARY H., atty., Saint Vincent Hospital, Billings, MT '86 (ATTY)
COHEN, HIRSH J., exec. dir., University Health Plan, Inc., Cincinnati, OH '82 (PLNG)
COHEN, HUGH P., procedure analyst, State of New Jersey, Department of Human Services, Trenton, NJ '81
COHEN, IRWIN, atty., Fairfax Hospital Association, Springfield, VA '85 (ATTY)
COHEN, JANE Z., dir. commun., American Cancer Society, Culver City, CA '81 (PR)
COHEN, JEAN A., dir. soc. serv., Baptist Memorial Hospital-Union City, Union City, TN '78 (SOC)
COHEN, JEFFREY I., dir. pers., St. Agnes Hospital, Baltimore, MD '86 (PERS)
COHEN, JEROLD S., RN, dir. pat. serv., Brookhaven Memorial Hospital Medical Center, Patchogue, NY '79 (AMB)
COHEN, JUDITH L., staff acct., Ernst and Whinney, New York, NY '85
COHEN, JULIE, dir. pers., Humana Women's Hospital, Indianapolis, IN '86 (PERS)
COHEN, KATHERINE E., tech. mgt. eng., Temple University Hospital, Philadelphia, PA '80 (MGMT)
COHEN, KENNETH B., adm., Riverside General Hospital-University Medical Center, Riverside, CA '74 (PLNG)
COHEN, LARRY JAY, bus. mgr. surg. serv., Emanuel Hospital and Health Center, Portland, OR '80
COHEN, LAWRENCE A., asst. exec. dir., Friedman Hospital, Philadelphia, PA '69
COHEN, LEON N., bd. chm., LaGuardia Hospital Shared Services, New York, NY '71
COHEN, LEONARD, pres., National Medical Enterprises, Los Angeles, CA '69 (ATTY)
COHEN, LISA L., prin., Delta Health Care Consultants, Guttenberg, NJ '85 (PLNG)
COHEN, MADELINE S., dir. vol. serv., Friedman Hospital of the Home for the Jewish Aged, Philadelphia, PA '86 (VOL)
COHEN, MANUEL, consult., Manuel Cohen and Associates, Elkins Park, PA '51 (LIFE)
COHEN, MARK I., adm. analyst-risk mgt., University of California at Los Angeles Medical Center, Los Angeles, CA '86 (RISK)
COHEN, MARTIN G., coor. pub. rel. and mktg. commun., Atlanticare Medical Center, Lynn, MA '86 (PR)
COHEN, MARTIN H., arch., Armonk, NY '72 (PLNG)
COHEN, MARVIN A., vice chm. medicine, Detroit Medical Center Corporation, Detroit, MI '68 (MGMT)
COHEN, MICHAEL HENRY, dir. emp. rel. and dev., Louis A. Weiss Memorial Hospital, Chicago, IL '84 (EDUC)
COHEN, MILTON, proj. adm., Professional Staff Association, Los Angeles County Harbor, UCLA Medical Center, Torrance, CA '59
COHEN, RALPH A., atty., Community Hospitals of Indiana, Indianapolis, IN '78 (ATTY)
COHEN, REBECCA, RN, dir. nrsg. staff dev. and independent educ. consult., Sycamore Hospital, Sycamore, IL '81 (EDUC)

COHEN, ROBERT A., hlthcare benefit consult., Health Management Strategies, Washington, DC '84
COHEN, SAMUEL S., consult., Jewish General Hospital, Montreal, Que., Canada '35 (LIFE)
COHEN, SANDRA N., mgt. consult., Pacific Health Resources, Los Angeles, CA '81 (MGMT)
COHEN, SELMA S., asst. dir. soc. work and discharge plng., Bronx Municipal Hospital Center, Bronx, NY '86 (SOC)
COHEN, SHEPARD NATHAN, dir. med. educ., University of Massachusetts Medical Center, Worcester, MA '62
COHEN, SHEVA M., coor. plng., Saint Mary Hospital, Langhorne, PA '83 (PLNG)
COHEN, STEVEN M., dir. fin., Cigna Healthplan, Inc., Paramus, NY '74
COHEN, STEVEN S., dir. matl. mgt. and pharm., Good Samaritan Hospital, Baltimore, MD '84 (PUR)
COHEN, WILBUR J., prof., University of Texas, School of Public Affairs, Austin, TX '86 (HON)
COHEN, WILLIAM MICHAEL, dir. pub. affairs, St. Joseph Hospital, Bangor, ME '79 (PR)
COHEN, YOLANDA M. VALENTINO, RN, dir. med. nrsg. serv., Mercy Hospital, Charlotte, NC '83 (NURS)
COHN, GORDON, dir. pub. rel. and mktg., University of Southern California-Kenneth Norris Cancer Hospital, Los Angeles, CA '83 (PR)
COHN, IRVING A., atty., Central General Hospital, Plainview, NY '80 (ATTY)
COHN, JOANNE BRECKER, Chestnut Hill, MA '79
COHN, MARSHA R., coor. mem. serv., Community Mutual Insurance Company, Youngstown, OH '86 (PAT)
COHN, STEVEN S., pres., Medical Management Planning, Inc., Marina Del Rey, CA '73 (MGMT)
COHOLICH, ROBERT J., adm. asst., Marion General Hospital, Marion, OH '78
COHRAC, PATRICIA A., risk mgr., Anderson Memorial Hospital, Anderson, SC '86 (RISK)
COHRS, CAROLYN, dir. diet., Holy Cross Hospital, Merrill, WI '81 (FOOD)
COHRS, KENNETH D., dir. matl. mgt., St. Luke's Regional Medical Center, Sioux City, IA '79 (PUR)
COIL, VERN, mgr. loss control, Southwest Community Health Services, Albuquerque, NM '86 (RISK)
COKE, BEVERLY J., off. health analyst, Sutter Health Systems, Sacramento, CA '86 (MGMT)
COKELY, DONNA M., asst. dir. pers., Wentworth-Douglass Hospital, Dover, NH '86 (PERS)
COKER, KAREN A., RN, dir. nrsg.-psych., Baptist Medical Center, Columbia, SC '84 (NURS)
COLACHIS, SAM C. JR., dir. rehab., St. Luke's Medical Center, Phoenix, AZ '77
COLAIANNI, ALBERT J., res. fellow, Logistics Management Institute, Bethesda, MD '83 (PUR)
COLAIANNI, LOIS ANN, assoc. dir. lib. oper., National Library of Medicine, Bethesda, MD '86 (PLNG)
COLAIZZO, DOMINIC A., vice-pres. adm., Taylor Hospital, Ridley Park, PA '73
COLANGELO, PATRICK A., vice-pres. fin., Stamford Hospital, Stamford, CT '72
COLAS, AMY E., dir. diet., St. Clare Hospital of Monroe, Monroe, WI '82 (FOOD)
COLBENSON, DORA R., RN, dir. nrsg. serv., St. Anthony Hospital, Pendleton, OR '83 (NURS)
COLBERG, GARY R., vice-pres. prof. serv., Methodist Evangelical Hospital, Louisville, KY '82
COLBY, CHRISTOPHER J., programmer and analyst, Samaritan Health Service, Phoenix, AZ '86 (MGMT)
COLBY, NEAL D. JR., dir. soc. serv., St. Mary's Hospital, Kansas City, MO '72 (SOC)
COLCHER, MARIAN W., asst. adm. and dir. alcoholism prog., Valley Forge Medical Center and Hospital, Norristown, PA '79 (SOC)
COLDICUTT, BEN W., dir. pers., Hendrick Medical Center, Abilene, TX '81 (PERS)
COLE-SMITH, BARBARA, dir. info. serv. and qual. assur., General Hospital of Everett, Everett, WA '82 (RISK)
COLE, BETTIE LOUISE, soc. worker, Stringfellow Memorial Hospital, Anniston, AL '74 (SOC)
COLE, BONNIE C., dir. mgt. eng., National Medical Enterprises, Los Angeles, CA '81 (MGMT)
COLE, C. WAYNE, mktg. dir. matl. serv., SunHealth Corporation, Charlotte, NC '86 (PUR)
COLE, DAVID F., student, Program in Industrial Engineer, University of Michigan, Ann Arbor, MI '86 (MGMT)
COLE, EDWIN L., asst. adm. pers. and pub. rel., Marion General Hospital, Marion, IN '73 (PERS)
COLE, EVAN H., asst. adm., Kern Medical Center, Bakersfield, CA '72
COLE, GRETCHEN, actg. dir. corp. dev., Scripps Memorial Hospital, La Jolla, CA '86 (PR) (PLNG)
COLE, JAMES A., dir. soc. work, Rehabilitation Institute, Detroit, MI '83 (SOC)
COLE, JAMES F., mgr. environ. serv., George Washington University Hospital, Washington, DC '87 (ENVIRON)
COLE, JILL, dir. soc. work, Pacific Medical Center, Seattle, WA '85 (SOC)
COLE, JUDITH P., pat. rep., Veterans Administration Medical Center, Perry Point, MD '86 (PAT)
COLE, MARY K., RN, asst. dir. nrsg., Holladay Park Medical Center, Portland, OR '85 (NURS)
COLE, MICHAEL B., dir. plant oper., St. Joseph Hospital, Chicago, IL '80 (ENG)
COLE, MICHAEL S., adm. supv., Danbury Hospital, Danbury, CT '80 (FOOD)
COLE, MICHAEL, mgr. pers., Wythe County Community Hospital, Wytheville, VA '86 (PERS)
COLE, PATRICIA L., RN, assoc. dir. nrsg., Broadlawns Medical Center, Des Moines, IA '78 (NURS)
COLE, RICHARD L. JR., atty., United Hospitals, Inc., Cheltenham, PA '84 (ATTY)
COLE, ROBERT L., dir. plant eng., University of Wisconsin Hospital and Clinics, Madison, WI '80 (ENG)
COLE, SHIRLEY J., coor. vol., Annapolis Hospital, Wayne, MI '86 (VOL)
COLE, TEAWANA M., Chicago, IL '85
COLE, WILLIAM A., dir. commun. serv., University Hospital and Ambulatory Care Center, Little Rock, AR '85 (ENG)
COLECCHI, STEPHEN, atty., Robinson Memorial Hospital, Ravenna, OH '86 (RISK)(ATTY)
COLEGROVE, SHARYN L., dir. prof. support serv., AMI South Bay Hospital, Redondo Beach, CA '80 (RISK)
COLEMAN-MORRIS, DIANN, Naval Hospital, Philadelphia, PA '85
COLEMAN, ALANA R., pres., Arc Limited, Oakland, CA '85 (MGMT)
COLEMAN, ALLEN, asst. adm. bus. dev., Kino Community Hospital, Tucson, AZ '85 (PLNG)
COLEMAN, ANDREA Y., South Valley Inter Community Hospital, Gilroy, CA '79 (PLNG)
COLEMAN, CHERYL N., dir. pers., Swope Parkway Comprehensive Health Center, Kansas City, MO '86 (PERS)
COLEMAN, DAVID LEE, dir. eng., Orem Community Hospital, Orem, UT '86 (ENG)
COLEMAN, DELORES JUNE, asst. pur. agt., Greater Baltimore Medical Center, Baltimore, MD '74 (PUR)
COLEMAN, ELIZABETH TERRY, dir. vol., Lankenau Hospital, Philadelphia, PA '73 (VOL)
COLEMAN, FRANCIS T., atty., Holy Cross Hospital, Silver Spring, MD '74 (ATTY)
COLEMAN, GEORGIA CAROL, mgr. emp. benefits and rel., Sheppard and Enoch Pratt Hospital, Baltimore, MD '86 (PERS)
COLEMAN, SR. GERALDINE PAULA, risk mgr., Sisters of Charity Hospital, Buffalo, NY '84 (RISK)
COLEMAN, JAMES A., Slidell, LA '64
COLEMAN, JAMES O. III, dir. pers., Hebrew Home of Greater Washington, Rockville, MD '78 (PERS)
COLEMAN, JANE A., assoc. dir. food serv., Good Samaritan Medical Center, Phoenix, AZ '75 (FOOD)
COLEMAN, JELENA, assoc. dir. and risk mgr., Health and Hospitals Corporation, New York, NY '86 (RISK)
COLEMAN, JENNIFER F., coor. vol., Harold D. Chope Community Hospital, San Mateo, CA '86 (VOL)
COLEMAN, JENNIFER L., dir. pub. rel., Baylor University Medical Center, Dallas, TX '83 (PR)
COLEMAN, LEATRICE J., RN, vice-pres. pat. care serv., Our Lady of Mercy Hospital, Dyer, IN '79 (NURS)
COLEMAN, MARY R., dir. gen. serv., St. Frances Cabrini Hospital, Alexandria, LA '82 (PUR)
COLEMAN, MARYLOU K., supv. mktg., St. Joseph's Hospital and Medical Center, Phoenix, AZ '86 (PR)
COLEMAN, NANCY J., dir. soc. serv., Milton Medical Center, Milton, MA '85 (SOC)
COLEMAN, PEGGY A., dir. pub. affairs, Little Company of Mary Hospital, Torrance, CA '79 (PR)
COLEMAN, RUSSELL L., Woodbridge, VA '78
COLEMAN, LT. COL. STEVEN L., MSC USAF, APO New York, NY '71
COLEMAN, SUZY M., dir. mktg., Wadley Regional Medical Center, Texarkana, TX '86 (PR) (PLNG)
COLEMAN, VIVIAN L., dir. pur., Good Samaritan Hospital, Lexington, KY '86 (PUR)
COLEPAUGH, CEIA WEBB, vice-pres. mktg., Recourse, Inc., New Milford, CT '85 (PR)
COLES, BARBARA I., vice-pres., Oberfest Associates, Inc., Philadelphia, PA '84 (PLNG)
COLES, DON J., dir. pat. rel., Glendale Adventist Medical Center, Glendale, CA '86 (PAT)
COLES, KAREN M., dir. educ., St. Clair Regional Hospital, Pell City, AL '87 (EDUC)
COLES, RONALD THOMAS JR., pat. rep., Jewish Hospital, Louisville, KY '85 (PAT)
COLES, THOMAS BRADY JR., MD, dir. health and med. affairs, Health Alliance Plan, Detroit, MI '59
COLESON, CAREY A., student, College of William and Mary, Williamsburg, VA '84
COLEY, BYRNE L., supv. cent. serv., St. Mary's Hospital and Health Center, Tucson, AZ '85 (CS)
COLGAN, EILEEN G., dir. nrsg., Sturgis Hospital, Sturgis, MI '85 (NURS)
COLGAN, GREGORY H., dir. adm. serv., Illinois Hospital Association, Naperville, IL '86 (MGMT)
COLIN, HOLLY O'HIRE, dir. qual. assur., Children's Hospital of San Francisco, San Francisco, CA '85 (RISK)
COLIN, SHIRLEY JEAN, dir. outpatient serv., St. Mary's Medical Center, Duluth, MN '87 (AMB)
COLING, CAROLINE YOUNG, dir. soc. work, University Hospital and Clinic, Pensacola, FL '82 (SOC)
COLISON, CHARLES B., dir. food serv., Carroll County General Hospital, Westminster, MD '73 (FOOD)
COLIZZO, GERALDINE S., dir. vol., Newton Memorial Hospital, Newton, NJ '83 (VOL)
COLLAR, COLLEEN M., RN, asst. dir. nrsg., Cedars-Sinai Medical Center, Los Angeles, CA '84 (NURS)
COLLEN, LELAND H., Las Cruces, NM '78
COLLETT, LORA JEAN, dir. pers. serv., Cheshire Medical Center, Keene, NH '83 (PERS)
COLLETTE, DONALD J., RN, dir. nrsg. mgt. syst., Worcester Hahnemann Hospital, Worcester, MA '74 (NURS)
COLLEY, GWEN, dir. emp. rel., Alta Bates Hospital, Berkeley, CA '85 (PERS)
COLLEY, ROBBIE W., dir. mktg. and pub. rel., Bluefield Community Hospital, Bluefield, WV '86 (PR)
COLLICOTT, ELIZABETH C., coor. vol. serv., Fort McMurray Regional Hospital, Fort McMurray, Alta., Canada '83 (VOL)
COLLIER, ABEL CHARLES, adm., Charlotte Rehabilitation Hospital, Charlotte, NC '58
COLLIER, CHARLOTTE MEIER, dir. res., Springhouse Corporation, Springhouse, PA '84
COLLIER, CHERYL L., dir. human res., Baptist Medical Center, Kansas City, MO '85 (PERS)
COLLIER, JAMES W. JR., asst. adm., Memorial Hospital at Gulfport, Gulfport, MS '79 (PR) (PLNG)
COLLIER, SUE S., dir. pub. rel., St. Mary's Hospital, Galveston, TX '82 (PR)
COLLIER, SUE, adm. asst., Lewis County General Hospital, Lowville, NY '85 (PERS)
COLLIER, WILLIAM, asst. dir. plng. oper., St. Joseph Hospital, Baltimore, MD '80 (ENG)
COLLING, DENNIS D., dir. human resources, Catherine McAuley Health Center, Ann Arbor, MI '83 (PERS)
COLLING, DOROTHY, supv., St. Francis Hospital, Poughkeepsie, NY '77 (CS)
COLLINGWOOD, PHILLIP, cost mgr., United Healthservice, Inc., Leawood, KS '85 (ENG)
COLLINS, ALAN C., adm. dir. matl. mgt., AMI Frye Regional Medical Center, Hickory, NC '86 (PUR)
COLLINS, BENNIE MAE, asst. dir. vol., Methodist Hospitals of Gary, Gary, IN '83 (VOL)
COLLINS, BONNIE M., pat. educator, Rowan Memorial Hospital, Salisbury, NC '87 (EDUC)
COLLINS, SR. BRIGID, dir. soc. serv., St. Joseph Hospital, Bellingham, WA '76 (SOC)
COLLINS, CARSON, dir. pur., Medical Laboratory Associates, Birmingham, AL '84 (PUR)
COLLINS, COLIN C., PhD, adm., Ozarks Medical Center, West Plains, MO '84 (PLNG)
COLLINS, DENISE E., coor. spec. proj., United Hospitals, Inc., Cheltenham, PA '86 (PLNG)
COLLINS, GEORGE A., (ret.), Anchorage, AK '43 (LIFE)
COLLINS, HELEN H., dir. soc. work, AMI Central Carolina Hospital, Sanford, NC '82 (SOC)
COLLINS, J. MICHAEL, dir. educ., St. Francis Hospital, Greenville, SC '86 (EDUC)
COLLINS, JAMES W., dir. eng., St. Joseph Mercy Hospital, Ann Arbor, MI '77 (ENG)
COLLINS, JANE A., dir. clin. soc. work, Denver Department of Health and Hospitals, Denver, CO '70 (SOC)
COLLINS, JANET M., dir. soc. serv., Mary Hitchcock Memorial Hospital, Hanover, NH '76 (SOC)
COLLINS, JAY W., consult., Euclid, OH '47 (LIFE)
COLLINS, JERALD A., dir. pat. rel., University of Wisconsin Hospital and Clinics, Madison, WI '86 (PAT)
COLLINS, JERRY D., chief eng., Children's Hospital, Denver, CO '86 (ENG)
COLLINS, JO, dir. nrsg. and risk mgr., Sumter Regional Hospital, Americus, GA '86 (RISK)
COLLINS, JOHN CAMERON, Health Resources Development, Boise, ID '76 (PLNG)
COLLINS, JULIE, dir. pers., Saint Joseph's Hospital, Atlanta, GA '83 (PERS)
COLLINS, KARI, dir. soc. serv., Red Bird Mountain Medical Center, Beverly, KY '86 (SOC)
COLLINS, KAY G., educ. spec., Mercy Hospital, Port Huron, MI '83 (EDUC)
COLLINS, KEITH, asst. dir. eng., Desert Hospital, Palm Springs, CA '86 (ENG)
COLLINS, KEN, sr. dir. matl. serv., SunHealth Corporation, Charlotte, NC '77 (PUR)
COLLINS, LINDA F., dir. bldg. serv., Massachusetts Eye and Ear Infirmary, Boston, MA '86 (ENVIRON)
COLLINS, LYNDA B., dir. soc. serv., The Methodist Hospital, Houston, TX '79 (SOC)
COLLINS, MARIA, coor. vol. serv., Bronson Methodist Hospital, Kalamazoo, MI '78 (VOL)
COLLINS, MARION H., asst. chief diet. serv., Veterans Administration Medical Center, Coatesville, PA '83 (FOOD)
COLLINS, MARSHA A., dir. pers. serv., Winona Memorial Hospital, Indianapolis, IN '84 (PERS)
COLLINS, MARTIN D., mgr. environ. serv., Memorial Hospital, North Conway, NH '86 (ENG)
COLLINS, MARY ELLEN, dir. diet. and nutr., Brigham and Women's Hospital, Boston, MA '83 (FOOD)
COLLINS, MAJ. MICHAEL H., MSC USA, adm. surg., Brooke Army Medical Center, San Antonio, TX '80
COLLINS, MICHAEL K., dir. commun. serv., Evanston Hospital, Evanston, IL '74 (ENG)
COLLINS, NANCY E., media rel. coor., Children's Hospital, Boston, MA '86 (PR)
COLLINS, PHILLIP V., dir. bus. health serv., Douglas Community Hospital, Roseburg, OR '86 (PR) (PLNG)
COLLINS, LT. ROBERT V., MSC USN, chief syst., Naval Hospital, Bethesda, MD '77
COLLINS, ROBERT, dir. environ. serv., Kennedy Memorial Hospitals-University Medical Center, Cherry Hill, NJ '86 (ENVIRON)
COLLINS, ROBERTA, dir. commun. rel., University of Minnesota Hospital and Clinic, Minneapolis, MN '78 (VOL)(PR)
COLLINS, RODERICK C., dir. food serv., Community Hospital of Ottawa, Ottawa, IL '76 (FOOD)
COLLINS, STEPHEN B., vice-pres., Voluntary Hospitals of America, Irving, TX '55 (LIFE)
COLLINS, SUSAN B., RN, Petaluma Valley Hospital, Petaluma, CA '84 (EDUC)
COLLINS, SUSAN M., RN, dir. amb. and surg. care, Walthamweston Hospital and Medical Center, Waltham, MA '86 (NURS)(AMB)
COLLINS, T. GLENN, atty., Mother Frances Hospital Regional Center, Tyler, TX '68 (ATTY)
COLLINS, TERRY L., mgr. matl., Logan Memorial Hospital, Russellville, KY '83 (PUR)
COLLINS, THOMAS J., vice-pres.-corp. serv., Memorial Health Services, Long Beach, CA '84 (PLNG)
COLLINS, THOMAS M., atty., California Hospital Association, Sacramento, CA '73 (ATTY)
COLLINS, VERLA B., RN PhD, dir. nrsg. and educ., Intermountain Health Care, Inc., Salt Lake City, UT '79 (NURS)
COLLINS, VIRGIL E., dir. human res. dev., Akron City Hospital, Akron, OH '84 (EDUC)
COLLINS, WADE D., dir. cent. sup., Texas Scottish Rite Hospital for Crippled Children, Dallas, TX '76 (CS)
COLLINS, WILBUR L., atty., Bethesda Hospital, Inc., Cincinnati, OH '85 (ATTY)
COLLINS, WILLIAM H., chm., Collins, Rimer and Gordon, Architects Inc., Cleveland, OH '84

COLLINS, WILLIAM S., Stone Mountain, GA '73
COLLIS, MALISSA K., educ. coor. soc. serv., Emory University Hospital, Atlanta, GA '84 (SOC)
COLLISON, BRUCE L., dir. commun. rel., University Community Hospital, Tampa, FL '84 (PR)
COLLOTON, JOHN W., dir. and asst. vice-pres. health serv., University of Iowa Hospitals and Clinics, Iowa City, IA '56 (LIFE)
COLMAN, MARK S., dir. adm. serv., Dunlap Psychiatric Center, New York, NY '74
COLMAN, THOMAS W., exec. vice-pres., Turner Medical Building Service, Winter Park, FL '87 (AMB)
COLMANS, DAVID J., vice-pres., Cohn and Wolfe, Atlanta, GA '80 (PR)
COLOGIE, THERESA M., asst. adm., St. Elizabeth Hospital, Elizabeth, NJ '80
COLOMBO, ROSEMARY, mng. dir., St. Anthony's Hospital, St. Petersburg, FL '81 (PLNG)
COLON-CRUZ, FRANCISCO A., atty., Puerto Rico Hospital Association, Rio Piedras, P.R. '68 (ATTY)
COLON, EDGAR, assoc. dir. soc. serv. and discharge plng., Lincoln Medical and Mental Health Center, Bronx, NY '85 (SOC)
COLON, IVAN, dir. risk mgt., Hospital San Pablo, Bayamon, P.R. '86 (RISK)
COLON, KATHLEEN F., RN, asst. vice-pres. nrsg., Park Ridge Hospital, Rochester, NY '77 (NURS)
COLONE, ANN L., dir. commun., St. Joseph's Medical Center, Fort Wayne, IN '81 (PR)
COLONNA, JAMES M., dir. hskpg. and ldry., Memorial Hospital, Colorado Springs, CO '86 (ENVIRON)
COLOSI, NATALE, PhD, dir., Italian Hospital Society, New York, NY '37 (EDUC)(LIFE)
COLSON, DAVID L., atty., Farmington Community Hospital, Farmington, MO '76 (ATTY)
COLSTON, NANCY D., dir. pers., Lanier Park Hospital, Gainesville, GA '84 (PERS)
COLT, JOHN E. JR., dir. plant oper., Cedars-Sinai Medical Center, Los Angeles, CA '79 (ENG)
COLTEY, ROGER W., dir. matl. mgt., Thomas Memorial Hospital, South Charleston, WV '83 (PUR)
COLTON, DOUGLAS J., atty., Sch Health Care System, Houston, TX '82 (ATTY)
COLUCCI, LISA M., res. asst., Texas Hospital Association, Austin, TX '85 (PLNG)
COLUMBER, ROBERT E., asst. adm., Marion General Hospital, Marion, OH '74 (PUR)
COLUMBUS, CANDYCE L., pub. spec., Community Hospitals of Central California, Fresno, CA '84 (PR)
COLVERT, CHARLES C., vice-pres. bus. affairs, Baptist Medical Center-Montclair, Birmingham, AL '83 (MGMT)
COLVILLE, CAROL S., dir. soc. serv., Highland District Hospital, Hillsboro, OH '79 (SOC)
COLVILLE, SANDRA L., vice-pres. oper., Greater Baltimore Medical Center, Baltimore, MD '87 (AMB)
COLVIN, CAROLYN, RN, supv. cent. serv., St. Joseph Regional Medical Center of Northern Oklahoma, Ponca City, OK '85 (CS)
COLVIN, HAZEL, dir. support serv., St. Joseph Hospital, Del Norte, CO '87 (AMB)
COLVIN, NORTON A. JR., atty., HCA Valley Regional Medical Center, Brownsville, TX '85 (ATTY)
COLVIN, ROBERT, asst. adm., West Valley Medical Center, Caldwell, ID '86 (RISK)
COLWELL, GORDON D., mgr. matl., Redmond Park Hospital, Rome, GA '76 (PUR)
COMAN, TERRY, dir. vol. serv., St. Vincent Medical Center, Los Angeles, CA '79 (VOL)
COMAR, MARILYN R., dir. educ., Southland Medical Center, Darlington, SC '86 (EDUC)
COMBS, DON, PhD, asst. vice-pres. adm. and serv., Eastern Virginia Medical Authority, Norfolk, VA '85
COMBS, JAN L., mgr. print prod., Miami Valley Hospital, Dayton, OH '85 (PR)
COMBS, WILLIAM DENNIS, asst. adm., Onslow Memorial Hospital, Jacksonville, NC '75 (MGMT)
COMBS, WILLIAM JR., supv. eng. and maint., Daniel Drake Memorial Hospital, Cincinnati, OH '81 (ENG)
COMCOWICH, DELORES G., asst. dir. pur., Allied Services for the Handicapped, Scranton, PA '85 (PUR)
COMEAUX, PRESTON NOE III, vice-pres. spec. serv., Hamilton Medical Center, Dalton, GA '78
COMELLA, MARTIN S., adm., Scripps Memorial Hospital-Chula Vista, Chula Vista, CA '52 (LIFE)
COMER, ANN T., dir. pers., Children's Hospital of the King's Daughters, Norfolk, VA '86 (PERS)
COMER, C. CLINE, partner, Cherry, Bekaert and Holland, Charlotte, NC '79
COMER, JOHN D., atty., Medical Center of Central Georgia, Macon, GA '68 (ATTY)
COMER, KIMBERLY C., pub. rel. spec., Portsmouth General Hospital, Portsmouth, VA '85 (PR)
COMEY, SALLIE S., coor. educ., Children's Specialized Hospital, Mountainside, NJ '82 (EDUC)
COMISKEY, JOHN ANTHONY, pres., St. Michael Hospital, Milwaukee, WI '62
COMMEREE, PHYLLIS M., RN, dir. nrsg. serv., Lebanon Community Hospital, Lebanon, OR '82 (NURS)
COMO, ANTHONY V., adm. dir. food serv., Palisades General Hospital, North Bergen, NJ '82 (FOOD)
COMPAGNONE, ELENA, RN, asst. dir. nrsg. serv., Milford-Whitinsville Regional Hospital, Milford, MA '79 (NURS)
COMPAS, BRIAN J., dir. mgt. eng., Abington Memorial Hospital, Abington, PA '85 (MGMT)
COMPTON, DAVID O., dir. cont. educ., Methodist Health Systems, Inc., Memphis, TN '85 (EDUC)
CONANT, BARBARA A. SCHOOF, dir. pub. info. serv., Kansas Hospital Association, Topeka, KS '79 (PR)
CONARD, JANE REISTER, atty., Intermountain Health Care, Inc., Salt Lake City, UT '84 (ATTY)
CONATY, ROBERT B., exec. vice-pres. oper., Montefiore Medical Center, Bronx, NY '72
CONAWAY, PATTIE R., dir. diet. serv., Reynolds Memorial Hospital, Glen Dale, WV '74 (FOOD)
CONDE, MARILYN T., Chino Community Hospital, Chino, CA '83 (CS)
CONDERMAN, JOHN D., atty., St. Mary Hospital, Manhattan, KS '83 (ATTY)
CONDERY, BOBBY R., dir. maint., Baxter County Regional Hospital, Mountain Home, AR '84 (ENG)
CONDIFF, GREG, adm. aide amb. care, Riverside Hospital, Wilmington, DE '87 (AMB)
CONDIT, CHRISTINE, dir. pat. and family serv., Scripps Memorial Hospital-Chula Vista, Chula Vista, CA '85 (SOC)
CONDON, DONALD F., dir. eng., McLaren General Hospital, Flint, MI '86 (ENG)
CONDON, HUGH, vice-pres. spec. serv., Jackson Park Hospital, Chicago, IL '76 (PLNG)
CONDON, JOHN W., atty., Morris Hospital, Morris, IL '83 (ATTY)
CONDOULIS, JUDITH, dir. soc. serv., Hillsborough County Hospital, Tampa, FL '86 (SOC)
CONDRY, GARY B., vice-pres. matl. mgt., Holy Cross Health System Corporation, South Bend, IN '84 (PUR)
CONDRY, ROBERT S., assoc. dir., Foster G. McGaw Hospital, Loyola University, Maywood, IL '68
CONE, C. THOMAS, atty., Hancock Memorial Hospital, Greenfield, IN '77 (ATTY)
CONEFREY, JOHN E., asst. dir. eng., Indian River Memorial Hospital, Vero Beach, FL '83 (ENG)
CONERLY, HILDA W., dir. vol. serv., University Hospital, Jackson, MS '84 (VOL)
CONFLENTI, FRANKLYN E., atty., Mercy Hospital of Pittsburgh, Pittsburgh, PA '74 (ATTY)
CONGDON, RICHARD G., dir. clin. eng. and safety off., Massachusetts Eye and Ear Infirmary, Boston, MA '85 (ENG)
CONGER, SHIRLEY L., dir. vol. serv., West Valley Medical Center, Caldwell, ID '79 (VOL)
CONKLIN, JAMES W., dir. pur., University Hospital, Stony Brook, NY '83 (PUR)
CONKLIN, MARILYN A., RN, dir. educ. serv., Holy Family Hospital, Spokane, WA '77 (EDUC)
CONKLIN, WILLIAM E. JR., dir. pers., Deaconess Hospital, Evansville, IN '64 (PERS)
CONKLING, JACK E., vice-pres., Southwestern Memorial Hospital, Weatherford, OK '75 (PERS)
CONKLING, JOAN F., supv. cent. sterile sup., Peekskill Hospital, Peekskill, NY '82 (CS)
CONKLING, VIRGINIA KAY, Beverly Hills, CA '80 (SOC)
CONLEY, BRUCE S., dir. eng., McCuistion Regional Medical Center, Paris, TX '84 (ENG)
CONLEY, DEAN, consult., Wayne, PA '39 (HON)
CONLEY, DIANE, dir. food serv., Polk General Hospital, Bartow, FL '87 (FOOD)
CONLEY, EDWARD T., mgr. mgt. eng., Morton F. Plant Hospital, Clearwater, FL '80 (MGMT)
CONLEY, EUGENE DEAN JR., instr. sociology, Georgetown University Medical Center, Washington, DC '70
CONLEY, JAMES R., mgr. oper. and trades, University of Connecticut Health Center, Farmington, CT '86 (ENG)
CONLEY, KAREN L., coor. in-service, Saint Joseph Health Center Kansas, Kansas City, MO '80 (EDUC)
CONLEY, L. MELVIN, bd. mem., Baptist Hospital Fund, St. Paul, MN '53 (LIFE)
CONLEY, LOIS ELAINE, RN, dir. educ. and res., Musc Medical Center of Medical University of South Carolina, Charleston, SC '73 (EDUC)
CONLEY, PAT, dir. soc. serv., Iowa Methodist Medical Center, Des Moines, IA '77 (SOC)
CONLEY, RALPH L., chief soc. work serv., Veterans Administration Medical Center, Prescott, AZ '85 (SOC)
CONLEY, THOMAS C., dir. human res., Bon Secours Hospital, Grosse Pointe, MI '85 (PERS)
CONLIN, KEVIN P., sr. vice-pres. and chief oper. off., East Tennessee Baptist Hospital, Knoxville, TN '85 (AMB)
CONLIN, WILLIAM J., atty., Mercywood Neuro-Psychiatric Hospital, Ann Arbor, MI '68 (ATTY)
CONMY, TIMOTHY A., dir. mgt. and info. syst., North Shore Children's Hospital, Salem, MA '76 (MGMT)
CONN, GORDON A., asst. adm., Divine Providence Hospital, Pittsburgh, PA '82 (PLNG)
CONN, H. E., sr. vice-pres. corp. serv., Wuesthoff Memorial Hospital, Rockledge, FL '87 (AMB)
CONN, SHERRY A., dir. commun. rel., HCA Edward White Hospital, St. Petersburg, FL '84 (PR)
CONNAUGHTON, MARY J., RN, clin. dir. med. nrsg., Mount Auburn Hospital, Cambridge, MA '84 (NURS)
CONNELL, AMELIA, pat. rep., Clark County Memorial Hospital, Jeffersonville, IN '76 (PAT)
CONNELL, BERT C., dir. nutr. serv., Loma Linda University Medical Center, Loma Linda, CA '79 (FOOD)
CONNELL, CHRISTOPHER J., dir. food serv., United Helpers Management Company, Ogdensburg, NY '86 (FOOD)
CONNELL, SR. GABRIELLA, pat. rep., St. Mary's Hospital and Medical Center, Grand Junction, CO '86 (PAT)
CONNELL, H. BOYCE JR., atty., Northside Hospital, Atlanta, GA '73 (ATTY)
CONNELL, MARJORIE M., chief diet. serv., Veterans Administration Medical Center, Martinsburg, WV '73 (FOOD)
CONNELLAN, THOMAS K., PhD, exec. dir., National Center for Health Promotion, Ann Arbor, MI '81 (EDUC)(PR)
CONNELLEY, PHILLIP, dir. bldg. and grds., Seventh Ward General Hospital, Hammond, LA '85 (ENG)
CONNELLY, EDWARD J., sales rep., American Dietary Products, Shaker Heights, OH '84 (FOOD)
CONNELLY, FLOYD L., mgr. rad., Miriam Hospital, Providence, RI '80
CONNELLY, ISABEL L., dir. corp. commun., McManis Associates, Inc., Washington, DC '86
CONNELLY, JAMES P., atty., Children's Hospital of Wisconsin, Milwaukee, WI '82 (ATTY)
CONNELLY, JUDIE B., dir. vol. serv., Virginia Baptist Hospital, Lynchburg, VA '86 (VOL)
CONNELLY, MARY L., dir. pat. rep., St. Vincent's Medical Center, Bridgeport, CT '81 (PAT)
CONNELLY, MICHAEL D., pres., St. Joseph Hospital, Chicago, IL '81 (ATTY)
CONNELLY, MICHAEL J., sr. mgr. sup. serv., Mount Sinai Medical Center, New York, NY '81
CONNELLY, RITA A., chief diet., Veterans Administration Medical Center, Augusta, GA '78 (FOOD)
CONNER, DALE, mgr. ldry., St. Mary's Hospital, Streator, IL '86 (ENVIRON)
CONNER, DANIEL, risk mgr. and staff acct., Des Moines General Hospital, Des Moines, IA '86 (RISK)
CONNER, HATCIL L., dir. risk mgt., St. Vincent Hospital and Health Center, Indianapolis, IN '64 (RISK)
CONNER, WILLIAM L., dir. eng., Franciscan Medical Center, Rock Island, IL '83 (ENG)
CONNERLEY, PHYLLIS K., dir. nrsg. educ., West Florida Hospital, Pensacola, FL '72 (EDUC)
CONNERS, JOHN THOMAS JR., atty., St. Thomas Hospital, Nashville, TN '68 (ATTY)
CONNOLE, CHARLES R., chief eng., Riverside Methodist Hospitals, Columbus, OH '85 (ENG)
CONNOLEY, WILLIAM B., pres. and chief exec. off., Multicare Medical Center, Tacoma, WA '75
CONNOLLY, DAVID K., dir. plng., dev. and mktg., St. Joseph Hospital, Aberdeen, WA '85 (PLNG)
CONNOLLY, EDWARD B., atty., St. Mary Hospital, Hoboken, NJ '74 (ATTY)
CONNOLLY, GRACE G., RN, coor. health serv. mktg., Mercy Hospital, Baltimore, MD '84 (PLNG)
CONNOLLY, HUGH F., atty., Seton Medical Center, Daly City, CA '71 (ATTY)
CONNOLLY, JAMES W., asst. vice-pres., Mercy Hospital, Rockville Centre, NY '78
CONNOLLY, LEO A., pres., Leo Connolly Associates, Inc., Union, NJ '77
CONNOLLY, MARY V., RN, coor. educ., St. Mary's Medical Center, Duluth, MN '80 (EDUC)
CONNOLLY, MICHAEL P., exec. vice-pres., Health Services Association of Central New York, Inc., Baldwinsville, NY '87 (AMB)
CONNOLLY, NOREEN B., RN, vice-pres. nrsg., St. Joseph Hospital, Flint, MI '86 (NURS)
CONNOLLY, PETER C., partner, McGladrey Hendrickson and Pullen, Rochester, MN '82
CONNOLLY, RITA BUCKLEY, vice-pres. mktg. and pub. rel., Delaware County Memorial Hospital, Drexel Hill, PA '86 (PR)
CONNOLLY, ROBERT P., dir. soc. work and ger. serv., Union Memorial Hospital, Baltimore, MD '80 (SOC)
CONNOR, C. TIMOTHY, dir. med. soc. serv., Archbishop Bergan Mercy Hospital, Omaha, NE '81 (SOC)
CONNOR, CAROLYN R., mgr. vol. serv., North Carolina Baptist Hospital, Winston-Salem, NC '79 (VOL)
CONNOR, GERALD W., atty., Centinela Hospital Medical Center, Inglewood, CA '79 (ATTY)
CONNOR, J. HAL, atty., Winter Haven Hospital, Winter Haven, FL '69 (ATTY)
CONNOR, JOHN J., trng. consult., Training Resources Catalog, Boston, MA '86 (EDUC)
CONNOR, K. PATRICIA, coor. pat. serv., Fitzgerald Mercy Division, Darby, PA '79 (PAT)
CONNOR, MAUREEN, RN, asst. adm. and dir. pat. care, St. Croix Valley Memorial Hospital, St. Croix Falls, WI '76 (NURS)
CONNOR, MICHAEL S., dir. pers., Lankenau Hospital, Philadelphia, PA '84 (PERS)
CONNOR, NANCY, dir. educ. and trng., Medical Plaza Hospital, Fort Worth, TX '85 (EDUC)
CONNOR, ROBERT A., fin. analyst, Strong Memorial Hospital of the University of Rochester, Rochester, NY '78
CONNORS, DENNIS P., Williston Park, NY '82
CONNORS, EDWARD J., pres., Sisters of Mercy Health Corporation, Farmington Hills, MI '73 (LIFE)
CONNORS, JAMES P., dir. hskpg. and ldry., Newton-Wellesley Hospital, Newton, MA '86 (ENVIRON)
CONNORS, JOANNE, dir. soc. serv., Worcester Hahnemann Hospital, Worcester, MA '87 (AMB)
CONNORS, MARION Y., RN, clin. dir., Malden Hospital, Malden, MA '84 (NURS)
CONNORS, MARTIN J., dir. mktg. and plng., Mercy Hospital, Toledo, OH '86 (PLNG)
CONNORS, MARY ANN, chief diet. serv., Veterans Administration Medical Center, Togus, ME '80 (FOOD)
CONNORS, WILLIAM, assoc. adm., St. James Mercy Hospital, Hornell, NY '85 (PLNG)
CONNORTON, JOHN V. JR., atty., St. Luke's-Roosevelt Hospital Center, New York, NY '81 (ATTY)
CONOLE, CHARLES P., vice-pres., Crouse-Irving Memorial Hospital, Syracuse, NY '65
CONOVER, HELEN, RN, dir. sup., proc. and distrib., Jersey Shore Medical Center, Neptune, NJ '83 (CS)
CONOVER, JO CAROL, health care indust. mktg. mgr., Tandem Computers, Cupertino, CA '87 (MGMT)
CONRAD, ANN P., coor. mental health concentration, Catholic University of America, Washington, DC '86 (SOC)
CONRAD, ANTHONY WILLIAM, mgr. matl., Alleghany Regional Hospital, Low Moor, VA '80 (PUR)
CONRAD, BETTIE L., RN, dir. intensive care nrsg., Commonwealth Hospital, Fairfax, VA '86 (NURS)
CONRAD, CHARLES F., asst. adm. gen. serv., Skagit Valley Hospital and Health Center, Mount Vernon, WA '73 (ENG)
CONRAD, DONALD C., biomedical eng., Augustana Hospital and Health Care Center, Chicago, IL '83 (ENG)
CONRAD, GARY A., Green Springs, OH '75 (PLNG)
CONRAD, GEORGE, biomedical eng., Mercy Hospital, Scranton, PA '86 (ENG)
CONRAD, REX, atty., Memorial Hospital, Hollywood, FL '80 (ATTY)
CONRAD, SHEILA L., prin. and chief exec. off., Conrad, Spellman, Coan Associates, Inc., Granada Hills, CA '74 (PLNG)

CONRAD, STEPHEN J., dir. commun. rel. and dev., Memorial Hospital, Cumberland, MD '80 (PR)
CONRAD, YVONNE, RN, asst. adm. and dir. nrsg., St. John's Episcopal Hospital, Smithtown, NY '80 (NURS)
CONRAGAN, LANCE C., dir. plant serv., Pacific Coast Hospital, San Francisco, CA '83 (ENG)
CONRON, JANE E., dir. amb. health serv., St. Peter's Hospital, Albany, NY '87 (AMB)
CONROY, DENNIS P., commun. rel. and pres. off., Bradley Memorial Hospital, Southington, CT '81 (PR)(PERS)
CONROY, MARY A., RN, dir. nrsg., Genesee Memorial Hospital, Flint, MI '85 (NURS)
CONROY, SR. MARY PLACIDO, RN, dir. pat. rep. prog., St. Mary Hospital, Port Arthur, TX '82 (PAT)
CONROYD, S. DANIELLE, vice-pres. human res., Mount Carmel Mercy Hospital, Detroit, MI '84 (PERS)
CONSIGNY, ROBERT H., atty., Mercy Hospital of Janesville, Janesville, WI '74 (ATTY)
CONSOLINI, GILDO MICHAEL, dir. soc. work and discharge plng., Doctors Hospital, New York, NY '87 (SOC)
CONSTABLE, JOSEPH FRANCIS, San Antonio, TX '71
CONSTABLE, THOMAS W., vice-pres. human resources, Waukesha Memorial Hospital, Waukesha, WI '74 (PERS)
CONSTANTIAN, CAPT. ALAN R., MSC USAF, dir. med. logistics, U. S. Air Force Clinic San Vito Dei Normanni, APO New York, NY '85
CONSTANTINE, HERBERT P., MD, dir. amb. and commun. medicine, Rhode Island Hospital, Providence, RI '87 (AMB)
CONSTANTINE, SPENCER A., dir. culinary serv., F. Edward Hebert Hospital, New Orleans, LA '86 (FOOD)
CONSTANTINE, WILLIAM J., mgr. food and nutr., Lee Memorial Hospital, Fort Myers, FL '83 (FOOD)
CONSTON, LILLIAN, supv. cent. sup., Albert Einstein Medical Center, Philadelphia, PA '77 (CS)
CONTE, RICHARD L., gen. counsel, Community Psychiatric Centers, Santa Ana, CA '80 (ATTY)
CONTEAS, EVANTHIA L., dir. vol., St. John's Hospital and Health Center, Santa Monica, CA '83 (VOL)
CONTI, ANTHONY, mng. partner, Coopers and Lybrand, Harrisburg, PA '80
CONTI, JAMES M., pres., Ambulatory and Surgical Care Corporation, Austintown, OH '83
CONTI, MARIE, spec. asst. adm., St. Christopher's Hospital, Philadelphia, PA '84 (RISK)
CONTI, MARYBETH, actg. dir. emp. rel., Gottlieb Memorial Hospital, Melrose Park, IL '86 (PERS)
CONTI, RICHARD, adm., Norton Sound Regional Hospital, Nome, AK '87 (AMB)
CONTI, ROBERTA M., RN, asst. adm. nrsg. serv., Suburban Hospital, Bethesda, MD '82 (NURS)
CONTI, SHIRLEY E., dir. soc. serv., HCA Medical Center of Port St. Lucie, Port St. Lucie, FL '85 (SOC)
CONTRACT, NORA LISS, mgr. res. resources mgt., Memorial Hospital for Cancer, New York, NY '86
CONTRACTOR, PENELOPE A., student, Widener University, Chester, PA '86 (PLNG)
CONTRO, NANCY, dir. soc. serv., Children's Hospital at Stanford, Palo Alto, CA '86 (SOC)
CONTRUCCI, THOMAS, asst. dir., Mount Carmel Mercy Hospital, Detroit, MI '79 (PUR)
CONVERSE, REGINALD L., student, Program in Health Administration, Indiana University School of Medicine, Indianapolis, IN '81
CONWAY-CALLAHAN, MELINDA KAY, dir. vol. serv., Rehabilitation Institute, Detroit, MI '86 (VOL)
CONWAY, ALVIN J., pres., Catholic Medical Center of Brooklyn and Queens, Jamaica, NY '71
CONWAY, BARBARA, RN, asst. dir. nrsg.-clin. serv., Sibley Memorial Hospital, Washington, DC '85 (NURS)
CONWAY, DENNIS H., dir. plng. and prog. dev., St. Charles Hospital and Rehabilitation Center, Port Jefferson, NY '78 (PLNG)
CONWAY, DONNA, dir. soc. serv., Victor Valley Community Hospital, Victorville, CA '86 (SOC)
CONWAY, EDWARD M., dir. pers. and manpower, District of Columbia General Hospital, Washington, DC '85 (PERS)
CONWAY, GREGORY B., atty., Bellin Memorial Hospital, Green Bay, WI '83 (ATTY)
CONWAY, J. W., atty., Muscatine General Hospital, Muscatine, IA '76 (ATTY)
CONWAY, JAMES B., asst. to vice-pres. fin., Children's Hospital, Boston, MA '86
CONWAY, JOAN BONNER, dir. soc. serv., Hospital of the University of Pennsylvania, Philadelphia, PA '66 (SOC)
CONWAY, JOHN M., atty., Providence Hospital, Anchorage, AK '84 (ATTY)
CONWAY, KATHLEEN A., plng. assoc., Baptist Medical System, Little Rock, AR '85 (PLNG)
CONWAY, MARY JO, dir. pub. rel., Mercy Hospital, Grayling, MI '87 (PR)
CONWAY, MARY T., RN, asst. adm. and dir. nrsg., Cardinal Cushing General Hospital, Brockton, MA '81 (NURS)
CONWAY, SUSAN, mgr., Travenol Management Services, Deerfield, IL '86 (PLNG)
CONWELL, GARY K., vice-pres. pub. rel. and mktg., Providence Memorial Hospital, El Paso, TX '84 (PR)
CONWELL, RICHARD J., consult., Blue Cross of Western Pennsylvania, Pittsburgh, PA '79 (MGMT)
CONWILL, MICHAEL G., asst. dir. human res., Spohn Hospital, Corpus Christi, TX '83 (PERS)
CONYERS, JANE H., dir. vol., Cobb General Hospital, Austell, GA '84 (VOL)
COOK, AGATHA, coor. cent. serv. room, Williamson Medical Center, Franklin, TN '82 (CS)
COOK, BARBABA A., dir. vol. serv., Guernsey Memorial Hospital, Cambridge, OH '83 (VOL)
COOK, BARBARA A., RN, asst. dir. nrsg., Chilton Memorial Hospital, Pompton Plains, NJ '81 (NURS)
COOK, BEN B., asst. to dir., University of Texas Health Center, Tyler, TX '83 (PLNG)
COOK, BETTY W., dir. diet., Coral Ridge Psychiatric Hospital, Fort Lauderdale, FL '82 (FOOD)
COOK, BETTY, dir. vol. serv., Evanston Hospital, Evanston, IL '73 (VOL)
COOK, CAROL DEMOSS, pur. agt., St. Joseph Hospital, Baltimore, MD '82 (PUR)
COOK, CHARLES ROBERT, (ret.), Fripp Island, SC '46 (LIFE)
COOK, SGT. CHARLES T., State College, PA '81
COOK, CHRISTOPHER B., pres., Clearfield Hospital, Clearfield, PA '74
COOK, DONNA ANN, coor. med. soc. worker, Humana Women's Hospital-South Texas, San Antonio, TX '86 (SOC)
COOK, DORIS A., RN, assoc. dir. nrsg., Beth Israel Medical Center, New York, NY '84 (NURS)
COOK, EDWARD F., dir. strategic plng., Good Samaritan Hospital, Pottsville, PA '85 (PLNG)
COOK, ELIZABETH A., coor. vol., Metropolitan Hospital-Central Division, Philadelphia, PA '81 (VOL)
COOK, FAYE WILKERSON, dir. soc. serv., Dr. Walter Olin Moss Regional Hospital, Lake Charles, LA '86 (SOC)
COOK, GARTH D., mgt. eng., Lincoln General Hospital, Lincoln, NE '85 (MGMT)
COOK, HOWARD F., Evanston, IL '86 (LIFE)
COOK, JANE, dir. pers., H. Lee Moffitt Cancer Center, Tampa, FL '86 (PERS)
COOK, JERRY, dir. matl. mgt., Humana Hospital -St. Petersburg, St. Petersburg, FL '79 (PUR)
COOK, JOHN A., atty., Straith Memorial Hospital, Southfield, MI '85 (ATTY)
COOK, JOHN C., student, Georgia State University-Institute of Health Administration, Atlanta, GA '86
COOK, JOHN EDWIN, dir. risk mgt., Children's Medical Center of Dallas, Dallas, TX '68 (RISK)
COOK, JOHNNY R., dir. environ. serv., HCA Donelson Hospital, Nashville, TN '86 (ENVIRON)
COOK, KATHRYN L., dir. food serv., San Bernardino Community Hospital, San Bernardino, CA '82 (FOOD)
COOK, LANOVA RAE, RN, dir. nrsg. serv., Community Methodist Hospital, Henderson, KY '71 (NURS)
COOK, LAWRENCE AUSTIN, dir. sup. and distrib., St. Joseph Hospitals, Mount Clemens, MI '84 (PUR)
COOK, MARGARET COWAN, dir. pat. rep., Victoria Hospital, Miami, FL '86 (PAT)
COOK, MARIA T., pur. agt., Memorial Hospital System, Houston, TX '80 (PUR)
COOK, MARY O., RN, mgr. pat. care serv., Mercy Hospital of Pittsburgh, Pittsburgh, PA '86 (NURS)
COOK, MELINDA ANN, pat. advocate, Memorial Hospital, Fremont, OH '86 (PAT)
COOK, MICHAEL H., atty., Cooper Hospital-University Medical Center, Camden, NJ '82 (ATTY)
COOK, MONICA D., vice-pres. strategic plng., Flushing Hospital and Medical Center, Flushing, NY '87 (PLNG)
COOK, PATRICIA, RN, asst. adm., Alexian Brothers Hospital, St. Louis, MO '75 (NURS)
COOK, QUENTIN L., atty., Peninsula Hospital and Medical Center, Burlingame, CA '84 (ATTY)
COOK, CAPT. RICK C., MSC USA, clin. eng., U. S. Air Force Medical Center Wright-Patterson, Dayton, OH '76 (MGMT)
COOK, ROBERT B. JR., atty., Baylor University Medical Center, Dallas, TX '74 (ATTY)
COOK, ROBERT LYNN, asst. vice-pres. proj. serv., Hospital Corporation of America, Nashville, TN '86 (PLNG)
COOK, S. EDWARD JR., chief exec. off., St. Mary's Hospital, Saginaw, MI '85
COOK, SAM E., dir. eng., Grand Valley Hospital, Pryor, OK '78 (ENG)
COOK, STEVEN H., asst. dir. eng., McLaren General Hospital, Flint, MI '86 (ENG)
COOK, VIRGINIA D., trustee, Rogue Valley Medical Center, Medford, OR '82 (PLNG)
COOK, VIRGINIA D., dir. vol. serv., Jefferson Davis Memorial Hospital, Natchez, MS '85 (VOL)
COOK, WILLIAM JEROME, dir. eng., Pasadena Community Hospital, Pasadena, CA '87 (ENG)
COOKE, GARY M., dir. pub. info. and dev., Community Hospital Monterey Peninsula, Monterey, CA '81 (PR)
COOKE, JANETTE S., dir. plng., Staten Island Hospital, Staten Island, NY '81 (PLNG)
COOKE, JILL Y., coor. clin. educ., Visiting Nurse Services, Seattle, WA '85 (EDUC)
COOKE, SUSAN SCHWARTZ, dir. human res., Benjamin Rush Center, Syracuse, NY '85 (PERS)
COOKSEY, FRANK C., atty., Warm Springs Rehabilitation Hospital, Gonzales, TX '84 (ATTY)
COOKSEY, MARY J., res. spec. plng., St. Luke's Hospital, Kansas City, MO '83 (PLNG)
COOLER, COLIN T., sr. consult., SunHealth Services, West Columbia, SC '83 (MGMT)
COOLEY, CHARLES M. JR., vice-pres., Health Management, Memphis, TN '86 (ENG)
COOLEY, KEN, dir. plng., Wichita General Hospital, Wichita Falls, TX '80 (PLNG)
COOLEY, LUKE B., dir. soc. serv., Southeast Alabama Medical Center, Dothan, AL '82 (SOC)
COOLEY, MICHAEL T., dir. pers., Shenandoah County Memorial Hospital, Woodstock, VA '86 (PERS)
COOLEY, NORMA J., dir. commun. rel. and res. dev., Allegan General Hospital, Allegan, MI '84 (PR)
COOMBES, DAVID H., pres. and chief exec. off., University of Minnesota Clinical Associates, Minneapolis, MN '83
COOMBES, DAVID W., dir. human res., John C. Lincoln Hospital and Health Center, Phoenix, AZ '84 (PERS)
COOMLER, RITA, coor. qual. assur. and risk mgt., Our Lady of Lourdes Health Center, Pasco, WA '86 (RISK)
COON, MARY, RN, clin. dir. nrsg. serv., Fairview General Hospital, Cleveland, OH '86 (NURS)
COON, TRICIA, dir. vol. serv., Institute of Living, Hartford, CT '79 (VOL)
COONEN, ROBERT H., asst. vice-pres. bldg. and grds., St. Elizabeth Hospital, Appleton, WI '75 (ENG)
COONEY, BARBARA A., plng. and dev. asst., Lower Bucks Hospital, Bristol, PA '82 (PLNG)
COONEY, ELLEN K., sr. assoc., Booz, Allen and Hamilton, Inc., Atlanta, GA '83
COONEY, THOMAS E., atty., Oregon Medical Association, Portland, OR '83 (ATTY)
COONING, PEGGY J., dir. commun. rel., D. W. McMillan Memorial Hospital, Brewton, AL '85 (PR)
COONS, BETTY, dir. vol., Moberly Regional Medical Center, Moberly, MO '82 (VOL)
COONS, KATHRYN, dir. pat. acct., St. Francis Xavier Hospital, Charleston, SC '78
COONS, MARK, dir. mktg., Utah Valley Regional Medical Center, Provo, UT '85 (PLNG)
COOP, R. TUCKER, pres., Triad Medical, Inc., Brea, CA '85
COOPER, ALAN F., supv. soc. work, F. D. Roosevelt Veterans Administration Hospital, Montrose, NY '86 (SOC)
COOPER, ALMETA E., exec. asst. to pres. and gen. counsel, Meharry Medical College, Nashville, TN '80 (ATTY)
COOPER, ANTHONY J. JR., pres., Arnot-Ogden Memorial Hospital, Elmira, NY '74
COOPER, BONNIE, supv. cent. serv. room, Redmond Park Hospital, Rome, GA '85 (CS)
COOPER, CHARLES L., dir. hskpg. and linen serv., St. Joseph Hospital, Flint, MI '86 (ENVIRON)
COOPER, CHARLES M. JR., consult., Allen, TX '55 (LIFE)
COOPER, CHERYL J., dir. mktg., Singing River Hospital System, Pascagoula, MS '86 (PR)
COOPER, CHESTER L., dir. eng., Valley Hospital, Ridgewood, NJ '83 (ENG)
COOPER, CLINTON G., pres., Newport Hospital, Newport, NH '82 (PLNG)
COOPER, COLLEEN, mgr. matl., Community Memorial Hospital, Sidney, MT '84 (PUR)
COOPER, DARLENE, asst. dir. diet., Ball Memorial Hospital, Muncie, IN '82 (FOOD)
COOPER, DAVID J., atty., Children's Hospital of Michigan, Detroit, MI '76 (ATTY)
COOPER, DEANNA, dir. educ., Winter Haven Hospital, Winter Haven, FL '74 (EDUC)
COOPER, DELORIS, RN, dir. nrsg., Norfolk General Hospital, Norfolk, VA '86 (NURS)
COOPER, ELIZABETH B., coor. trng., Cedars-Sinai Medical Center, Los Angeles, CA '80 (EDUC)
COOPER, ELLEN, dir. environ. serv., Healthcare Rehabilitation Center, Austin, TX '86 (ENVIRON)
COOPER, ETHEL ANN, asst. dir. vol. serv., Desert Hospital, Palm Springs, CA '74 (VOL)
COOPER, FOSTER K., lead biomedical tech., Mercy Hospital, Muskegon, MI '86 (ENG)
COOPER, GLORIA, pres., Mount Carmel Hospital, Colville, WA '79 (PR)(PERS)
COOPER, HOWARD L., asst. chief food prod. and serv., Veterans Administration Medical Center Atlanta, Decatur, GA '68 (FOOD)
COOPER, JAMES C., vice-pres., Sewickley Valley Hospital, Sewickley, PA '86
COOPER, JAMES E., adm., Wayne County Hospital, Monticello, KY '83
COOPER, JAMES H., dir. nutr. serv., Woodward Hospital and Health Center, Woodward, OK '83 (FOOD)
COOPER, JANE E., RN, dir. nrsg. serv., Plateau Medical Center, Oak Hill, WV '83 (NURS)
COOPER, JEFFREY A., health care consult., Pannell, Kerr, Forster, Atlanta, GA '87 (MGMT)
COOPER, JOHN A. D., MD, pres., Association of American Medical Colleges, Washington, DC '69 (HON)
COOPER, JUDITH D., pat. rep., St. Paul-Ramsey Medical Center, St. Paul, MN '78 (PAT)
COOPER, KATHLEEN M., soc. worker, Northern Montana Hospital, Havre, MT '81 (SOC)
COOPER, KATHLEEN M., dir. educ. and staff dev., Ingham Medical Center, Lansing, MI '77 (EDUC)
COOPER, KATHY, RN, supv. cent. proc., Woodward Hospital and Health Center, Woodward, OK '85 (CS)
COOPER, LYLE F., dir. security and commun., St. Anne's Hospital, Fall River, MA '85 (ENG)
COOPER, MICHAEL E., adm., Richland Parish Hospital-Rayville, Rayville, LA '87 (AMB)
COOPER, MICHELE RONE, dir. plng. and mktg., Mercy Hospital of Pittsburgh, Pittsburgh, PA '83 (PLNG)
COOPER, PAUL S., pres., Bridgeton Hospital, Bridgeton, NJ '79
COOPER, PHYLLIS GORNEY, consult., educ. and author, Cooper Consulting, Playa Del Rey, CA '87 (EDUC)
COOPER, RUSSELL S., vice-pres., Cleveland Memorial Hospital, Shelby, NC '81 (PUR)
COOPER, SANDRA K., dir. pers. and risk mgt., Lee's Summit Community Hospital, Lees Summit, MO '85 (PERS)(RISK)
COOPER, SHARON M., pres., Sharon Cooper Associates, Ltd., Englewood, CO '81 (PR)
COOPER, STEVEN M., dir. clin. prog. mktg., University of Connecticut Health Center, John Dempsey Hospital, Farmington, CT '74 (MGMT)
COOPER, SUSAN G., supv. soc. serv., Magee Rehabilitation Hospital, Philadelphia, PA '86 (SOC)
COOPER, TERRI C., dir. soc. serv., Baptist Hospital, Pensacola, FL '82 (SOC)
COOPER, THEODORE, MD, exec. vice-pres., The Upjohn Company, Kalamazoo, MI '77 (LIFE)
COOPER, THOMAS J., MD, path., Pathology Associates, St. Louis, MO '62
COOPER, THOMAS V., mgr. matl., Long Beach Community Hospital, Long Beach, CA '79 (CS)
COOPER, W. PAUL, mgr. compensation, Lafayette Home Hospital, Lafayette, IN '84 (PERS)
COOPERIDER, LINDA L., mgr. cent. serv., Massillon Community Hospital, Massillon, OH '84 (CS)
COOPERIDER, WENDELL E., dir. plant oper., Fairbury Hospital, Fairbury, IL '82 (ENG)
COOPERSMITH, WENDY ANNE, atty., Sacred Heart Medical Center, Chester, PA '82 (ATTY)

COORPENDER, WILLIAM G., adm. asst. human res., Schumpert Medical Center, Shreveport, LA '76 (PERS)
COORS, MARY LOU, RN, asst. adm. clin. serv., St. Joseph Health Care Corporation, Albuquerque, NM '84 (NURS)
COPE, MARGARET G., dir. vol. serv., University of Massachusetts Medical Center, Worcester, MA '77 (VOL)
COPELAND, BEATRICE HOWARD, staff nrs. oper. room, Southwest Detroit Hospital, Detroit, MI '71 (CS)
COPELAND, CURTIS BRYAN, atty., Wood, Lucksinger and Epstein, Washington, DC '77
COPELAND, DOUGLAS W. JR., vice-pres. mktg., Moses H. Cone Memorial Hospital, Greensboro, NC '86 (PLNG)
COPELAND, EVERETT C., dir. cmputer info. serv., St. Elizabeth Hospital, Beaumont, TX '87 (MGMT)
COPELAND, NORVAL R., exec. dir., Riverside Hospital, Wilmington, DE '68
COPELAND, ROBERT W., atty., Incarnate Word Hospital, St. Louis, MO '85 (ATTY)
COPELAND, WANDA S., asst. dir. pers., Charleston Memorial Hospital, Charleston, SC '86 (PERS)
COPELAND, WILLIAM M., pres., St. Francis-St. George Hospital, Cincinnati, OH '78 (ATTY)
COPLAN-WEISMAN, TRUDY, dir. soc. serv., Skokie Valley Hospital, Skokie, IL '74 (SOC)
COPPENBARGER, SHERRY, supv. cent. serv., Wesley Medical Center, Wichita, KS '84 (CS)
COPPENS, ROBERT D., dir. plant mgt., St. Joseph Hospital, Kirkwood, MO '74 (ENG)
COPPOCK, BARBARA, RN, pat. rep., Wabash County Hospital, Wabash, IN '86 (SOC)
COPPOCK, MARGARET M., mgr. commun., Group Health Cooperative Hospital, Seattle, WA '82 (ENG)
COPPOCK, VIVIAN H., dir. food serv., South Community Hospital, Oklahoma City, OK '86 (FOOD)
COPPOLINO, IDA E., RN, vice-pres. nrsg., Uniontown Hospital, Uniontown, PA '87 (NURS)
CORBAN, ROBERT M., dir. soc. serv., North Mississippi Medical Center, Tupelo, MS '79 (SOC)
CORBEIL, STEPHEN E., asst. adm. clin. serv., Lutheran Medical Center, St. Louis, MO '85
CORBETT, JANET R., RN, dir. nrsg., Miles Memorial Hospital, Damariscotta, ME '80 (NURS)
CORBETT, LAURENCE PAUL, atty., Associated Hospitals of San Francisco, San Francisco, CA '68 (ATTY)
CORBETT, STANLEY M., atty., St. Luke's Regional Medical Center, Sioux City, IA '73 (ATTY)
CORBETT, STEPHEN P., vice-pres. prof. serv., Mercy Hospital, Springfield, MA '81
CORBETT, TERRY L., Phoenix, AZ '81 (PLNG)
CORBETT, W. GRAY, dir. hskpg. serv., Richmond Eye and Ear Hospital, Richmond, VA '86 (ENVIRON)
CORBEY, JOHN P., supv. biomedical serv., Horton Memorial Hospital, Middletown, NY '85 (ENG)
CORBIN, CHRISTINE M., dir. emp. and recruitment, Barnes Hospital, St. Louis, MO '85 (PERS)
CORBIN, MIKE A., plant eng., Wilson Clinic and Hospital, Darlington, SC '85 (ENG)
CORBIN, ROBERT M., atty., St. Anthony Medical Center, Crown Point, IN '86 (ATTY)
CORCORAN, BETH L., dir. soc. serv., Harris Hospital-HEB North, Bedford, TX '74 (SOC)
CORCORAN, DIANE K., RN, base mgr., U. S. Army-Academy of Health Sciences, San Antonio, TX '85 (NURS)
CORCORAN, JOHN F., dir. pers., Oneida City Hospital, Oneida, NY '86 (PERS)
CORCORAN, LARRY T., asst. vice-pres., Marsh and McLennan, Inc., St. Louis, MO '81 (RISK)
CORCORAN, SR. M. ELIZABETH ANNE, RN, vice-pres., Mercy Hospital, Baltimore, MD '76 (NURS)
CORCORAN, SR. MARIE EDANA, pat. rep., Our Lady of Lake Regional Medical Center, Baton Rouge, LA '78 (PAT)
CORCORAN, NORA MAY, RN, vice-pres. nrsg., Morristown Memorial Hospital, Morristown, NJ '72 (NURS)
CORCORAN, PAMELA L., exec. dir., Southwest Virginia Health Systems Agency, Inc., Roanoke, VA '85
CORDAN, ANNE-ELIZABETH, risk mgr., Mercy Hospital of Pittsburgh, Pittsburgh, PA '86 (RISK)
CORDEIRO, AUGUST B., dir. matl. mgt., Newport Hospital, Newport, RI '83 (PUR)
CORDELL, BARBARA J., dir. amb. care, Tampa General Hospital, Tampa, FL '83 (AMB)
CORDELL, HAROLD E., asst. dir. plant maint., Spohn Hospital, Corpus Christi, TX '83 (ENG)
CORDELL, MICHAEL J., adm. res., Virginia Ambulatory Surgery Center, Charlottesville, VA '82 (AMB)
CORDELL, NORMAN W., Goose Creek, SC '80 (FOOD)
CORDER, A. LYNN, dir. fiscal serv., United Hospital Center, Clarksburg, WV '86
CORDER, LOIS B., (ret.), Bettendorf, IA '30 (LIFE)
CORDER, THOMAS J., adm., Imperial Point Medical Center, Fort Lauderdale, FL '80 (PLNG)
CORDERMAN, DONALD P., dir. pers., Emory University, Atlanta, GA '80 (PERS)
CORDES, DAVID C., vice-pres., Strategic Resources, Inc., St. Paul, MN '87 (AMB)
CORDES, DONALD W., pres., Cordes and Associates, Inc., Des Moines, IA '44 (PLNG)(LIFE)
CORDES, WAYNE G., dir. pub. rel. and dev., Memorial Medical Center, Ashland, WI '83 (PR)
CORDOVA, DONALD E., atty., Rose Medical Center, Denver, CO '82 (ATTY)
CORDOVI, MARILYN G., promotional coor., W. A. Foote Memorial Hospital, Jackson, MI '85 (PR)
CORDRAY, DAVID E., dir. eng., St. Paul Medical Center, Dallas, TX '86 (ENG)
CORDRAY, JACQUELINE H., dir. mktg. and pub. rel., St. John Medical Center, Steubenville, OH '82 (PR) (PLNG)
CORE, THERESA E., dir. surg. serv., St. John Hospital, Detroit, MI '87 (AMB)
CORETTE, ROBERT D. JR., atty., St. James Community Hospital, Butte, MT '69 (ATTY)
COREY, JOYCE T., RN, supv. cent. serv., Aroostook Medical Center, Presque Isle, ME '83 (CS)
COREY, MARGARET A., RN, dir. nrs., McKenzie Memorial Hospital, Sandusky, MI '84 (NURS)
COREY, MARIAN L., dir. soc. serv., South Macomb Hospital, Warren, MI '79 (SOC)
CORICA, ANTHONY J., dir. pub. rel., Alameda Hospital, Alameda, CA '81 (PR)
CORIELL, HAROLD E., supv. maint. and asst. chief eng., Mercy Hospital, Portsmouth, OH '86 (ENG)
CORKIN, FRANK R. JR., vice-pres., Middlesex Memorial Hospital, Middletown, CT '65 (PERS)
CORLEY, JAMES R., atty., People's Hospital, Mansfield, OH '80 (ATTY)
CORLEY, JOAN R., Shelby Memorial Hospital, Shelbyville, IL '82 (PERS)
CORLISS, JEAN A., mgr. commun. rel., Warren General Hospital, Warren, OH '81 (PR)
CORMIER, PHILIP M., dir. matl. mgt., Atlanticare Medical Center, Lynn, MA '86 (PUR)
CORN, HEIDI J., RN, clin. dir. ped., Amarillo Hospital District, Amarillo, TX '87 (NURS)
CORN, RANDALL L., dir. sup., proc. and distrib., St. Joseph's Hospital and Health Center, Tucson, AZ '78 (CS)
CORN, REYNOLD M., vice-pres., Alliance Health Management Services, Inc., Westbury, NY '80 (RISK)
CORN, RUTH, supv. soc. serv., New York Hospital, Westchester Division, White Plains, NY '78 (SOC)
CORNACHIONE, CHERI, actg. dir. commun. rel., Providence Hospital, Anchorage, AK '84 (PR)
CORNELISON, BRIAN D., dir. plant oper. and maint., Children's Memorial Hospital, Chicago, IL '84 (ENG)
CORNELIUS, CARL RICHARD, atty., Mercy Catholic Medical Center, Darby, PA '75 (ATTY)
CORNELL, DAVID R., pres., Montana Deaconess Medical Center, Great Falls, MT '76
CORNELL, LEON M., dir. pers. serv., Elliot Hospital, Manchester, NH '79 (PERS)
CORNETT, BONNA E., dir. soc. serv., Carraway Methodist Medical Center, Birmingham, AL '87 (SOC)
CORNETT, HOMER W., atty., Homer D. Cobb Memorial Hospital, Phenix City, AL '76 (ATTY)
CORNETT, SANDRA J., coor. pat. educ., Ohio State University Hospitals, Columbus, OH '82 (EDUC)
CORNILLE, JUDITH A., dir. soc. work, Humana Hospital -Biscayne, Miami, FL '78 (SOC)
CORNING, SUSAN P., Corning and Associates, Palo Alto, CA '79 (PLNG)
CORNWELL, JEANNE MARIE, vice-pres., St. Agnes Hospital and Medical Center, Fresno, CA '77 (NURS)
CORNWELL, NANCY M., pres., Cornell and Associates, Wadesboro, NC '74 (PR)
COROMINAS, MIGUEL A., dir. matl. mgt., Cedars Medical Center, Miami, FL '80 (PUR)
CORONA, PATRICIA R., dir. pers., Middlesex Memorial Hospital, Middletown, CT '76 (PERS)
CORONADO, LINDA G., dir. vol. serv., Cook County Hospital, Chicago, IL '85 (VOL)
CORRADINO, PAMELA A., adm. surg., Lahey Clinic Hospital, Burlington, MA '85 (PLNG)
CORRADO, DIANE, supv. cent. serv., Memorial Hospital of Greene County, Catskill, NY '86 (CS)
CORRADO, KEVIN W., dir. soc. serv., Memorial Hospital, Neillsville, WI '84 (SOC)
CORREA, BARBARA FARREN, dir. nutr. serv., Laurel Grove Hospital, Castro Valley, CA '80 (FOOD)
CORREIA, KATHRYN, vice-pres. oper., Central Ohio Medical Group, Columbus, OH '87 (AMB)
CORRELL, GENE W., mgr. educ. and trng., Wyandotte General Hospital, Wyandotte, MI '72 (EDUC)
CORRELL, RICHARD, California Health Management Systems, San Francisco, CA '78 (MGMT)
CORRENTE, DONNA M., asst. dir. food serv., Winter Haven Hospital, Winter Haven, FL '84 (FOOD)
CORRENTE, JOHN D., assoc. dir., St. Vincent's Medical Center of Richmond, Staten Island, NY '70 (ENG)
CORRIE, CHRIS E., health care partner, Coopers and Lybrand, St. Louis, MO '74
CORRIEL, HILDA, dir. vol. serv., LaGuardia Hospital, Flushing, NY '71 (VOL)
CORRIERE, ANN, pur. agt., Somerville Hospital, Somerville, MA '76 (PUR)
CORRIGAN, ANNE L., dir. pub. rel., St. Mary's Hospital, Streator, IL '76 (PR) (PLNG)
CORRIGAN, DANIEL G., dir. dev. and commun. rel., Anderson Memorial Hospital, Anderson, SC '85 (PR)
CORRIGAN, JEFFREY T., vice-pres. human res., Peninsula General Hospital Medical Center, Salisbury, MD '84 (PERS)
CORRIGAN, JO ANN, dir. vol., St. Francis Hospital Systems, Colorado Springs, CO '85 (VOL)
CORRIGAN, KEVIN W., dir. environ. serv., South Miami Hospital, South Miami, FL '86 (ENVIRON)
CORRIGAN, PEGGY ANNE, dir. pers., Verdugo Hills Hospital, Glendale, CA '80 (PERS)
CORRIVEAU, CONNIE L., dir. human res., Zeeland Community Hospital, Zeeland, MI '85 (PERS)
CORRIVEAU, RICHARD A., RN, asst. adm., Jo Ellen Smith Medical Center, New Orleans, LA '80 (NURS)
CORRIVEAU, SUE T., RN, dir. surg., Brawne McHardy Clinic, Metairie, LA '84 (NURS)
CORRY, MARY E., asst. dir. vol. serv., St. Joseph's Hospital, Parkersburg, WV '87 (VOL)
CORSETTI, ROSEMARY L., atty., Mercy Hospital of Johnstown, Johnstown, PA '86 (ATTY)
CORSICK-BOYCOTT, DIANE, dir. mktg. and commun. rel., Lander Valley Regional Medical Center, Lander, WY '87 (PR)
CORSON, NORMAN P., dir. plant oper., Atlantic City Medical Center, Mainland Division, Pomona, NJ '76 (ENG)
CORTESE, BONITA B., human res. rep., Parkland Medical Center, Derry, NH '85 (PERS)
CORTEZ, DARLENE S., RN, asst. exec. dir., Weirton Medical Center, Weirton, WV '86 (NURS)
CORTHELL, MICHAEL A., trng. spec. and safety off., Goddard Memorial Hospital, Stoughton, MA '78 (EDUC)(RISK)
CORTIGLIA, ANN MARIE, coor. educ., Holy Name Hospital, Teaneck, NJ '82 (EDUC)
CORVELEYN, ELISABETH, dir. pub. rel., Arnot-Ogden Memorial Hospital, Elmira, NY '86 (PR)
CORWIN, CHARLES D. III, dir. food serv., Greenville Memorial Hospital, Greenville, SC '86 (FOOD)
CORWIN, WILLIAM L., asst. adm., Palomar Memorial Hospital, Escondido, CA '85 (RISK)
CORY, CLARENCE B., pres., Ottumwa Regional Health Center, Ottumwa, IA '84 (PLNG)
CORY, RALPH N., dir. food serv., AMI Park Plaza Hospital, Houston, TX '83 (FOOD)
CORY, RICHARD L., atty., Bucyrus Community Hospital, Bucyrus, OH '77 (ATTY)
CORYELL, BEVERLY A., mgr. matl., Columbia Memorial Hospital, Astoria, OR '82 (PUR)
CORYELL, CHARLES W., dir. telecommun., Kaiser Foundation Hospital, Bellflower, CA '87 (ENG)
CORYELL, GREGORY R., dir. pub. rel., mktg. and dev., Louis Smith Memorial Hospital, Lakeland, GA '86 (PR)
CORYELL, MARGIE E., dir. vol. serv., Mercy Hospital, Council Bluffs, IA '86 (VOL)
COSBY, ROGERS, dir. plant oper., St. Rose de Lima Hospital, Henderson, NV '85 (ENG)
COSCO, JOHN ANTHONY, asst. adm., Mercy Hospital, Tiffin, OH '73
COSENTINO, MARY JOANNE COSGROVE, gen. counsel, St. Joseph Hospital, Chicago, IL '79 (ATTY)
COSEY, ETTA L., chief adm. diet., Veterans Administration Medical Center, Seattle, WA '85 (FOOD)
COSGROVE, ELIZABETH E., Evanston, IL '80 (SOC)
COSGROVE, SYLVIA, adm. asst. oper., Community Health Plan, Inc., Latham, NY '86 (RISK)
COSHOW, ANTOINETTE L., mgt. eng., San Jose Hospital, San Jose, CA '86 (MGMT)
COSIMATI, YVONNE D., dir. vol. serv., Horton Memorial Hospital, Middletown, NY '70 (VOL)
COSMIK, BRUCE E., search consult., International Search Consultant, Inc., Cincinnati, OH '86 (MGMT)
COSSA, JOHN P., MD, vice-pres. med. affairs, St. Agnes Medical Center, Philadelphia, PA '71 (RISK)
COSTA, BRIAN J., asst. dir. pub. rel., Portland Adventist Medical Center, Portland, OR '83 (PR)
COSTA, DENISE C., RN, mgr. intensive care unit, Meridian Park Hospital, Tualatin, OR '86 (NURS)
COSTA, GAIL E., vice-pres. plng., Women and Infants Hospital of Rhode Island, Providence, RI '83 (PLNG)
COSTA, GILBERT M., mgr. new bus. dev., Medical Area Service Corporation, Boston, MA '81 (PUR)
COSTA, JANICE D., dir. trng. and dev., Cedars-Sinai Medical Center, Los Angeles, CA '71 (EDUC)
COSTA, JOHN, asst. adm. support serv., Berwick Hospital Center, Berwick, PA '77 (ENG)
COSTA, LINDA L., RN, asst. adm. med. nrsg., Washington Hospital Center, Washington, DC '86 (NURS)
COSTA, MICHAEL G., dir. human res., Daniel Drake Memorial Hospital, Cincinnati, OH '83 (PERS)
COSTA, PATRICIA A., RN, adm. nrsg., John E. Fogarty Memorial Hospital, North Smithfield, RI '76 (NURS)
COSTA, SUSAN G., dir. vol. serv., Allen Memorial Hospital, Waterloo, IA '86 (VOL)
COSTANTE, PATRICIA ANNE, dir. soc. work, St. Lawrence Rehabilitation Center, Lawrenceville, NJ '87 (SOC)
COSTANTINI, SHARON A., RN, dir. clin. nrsg., Penrose Hospitals, Colorado Springs, CO '84 (NURS)
COSTANTINO, JEANETTE, dir. soc. work, Niagara Falls Memorial Medical Center, Niagara Falls, NY '74 (SOC)
COSTANTINO, JOSEPH PETER, dir. commun. rel., Cardinal Glennon Children Hospital, St. Louis, MO '84 (PR)
COSTANZO, ROBERT A., asst. chief eng., Eden Hospital Medical Center, Castro Valley, CA '83 (ENG)
COSTELLA, ALFRED B., dir. pur., Presbyterian Hospital in the City of New York, New York, NY '73 (PUR)
COSTELLO, B. PATRICK, atty., Westmoreland Hospital, Greensburg, PA '68 (ATTY)
COSTELLO, BRIAN G., asst. vice-pres. human res., Hahnemann University Hospital, Philadelphia, PA '75 (PERS)
COSTELLO, GENE, assoc. adm., New York Hospital, Westchester Division, White Plains, NY '80 (PERS)
COSTELLO, JOHN J., dir. market res. and dev., Susquehanna American, Inc., Moosic, PA '85 (PLNG)
COSTELLO, JOHN K., pres., Costello Associates, Inc., Washington, DC '62
COSTELLO, KATHLEEN M., RN, vice-pres. nrsg., Bridgeport Hospital, Bridgeport, CT '83 (NURS)
COSTELLO, MICHAEL M., dir. commun. rel., Moses Taylor Hospital, Scranton, PA '84 (PLNG)
COSTELLO, NICHOLAS J., dir. pers. and emp. rel., Caledonian Hospital, Brooklyn, NY '86 (PERS)
COSTELLO, ROBERT E., dir. pur., St. Joseph's Hospital and Medical Center, Paterson, NJ '76 (PUR)
COSTELLO, ROBERT M., dir. commun. and health info., Mercy Hospital, Scranton, PA '83 (PR)
COSTELLO, WILLIAM A., Carbondale, IL '86 (PLNG)
COSTILL, PHYLLIS, RN, dir. nrsg., Delta Medical Center, Greenville, MS '85 (NURS)
COTE, ANNE ALEXIS, assoc. dir., Society of the New York Hospital, New York, NY '72 (PAT)
COTE, JOHN CHARLES, adm. asst., Hurley Medical Center, Flint, MI '84 (MGMT)
COTE, LOREN, dir. matl. mgt., St. Joseph Hospital, Concordia, KS '84 (PUR)
COTE, LOU, asst. dir. soc. serv., University of Texas M. D. Anderson Hospital and Tumor Institute at Houston, Houston, TX '80 (SOC)
COTE, PAULA A., dir. nrsg. educ., Nashua Memorial Hospital, Nashua, NH '81 (EDUC)
COTNER, LUCILLE E., RN, dir. nrsg. dev., Ohio Hospital Association, Columbus, OH '80 (NURS)(CS)

COTTA, CAROLYN, dir. soc. serv., Modesto City Hospital, Modesto, CA '85 (SOC)
COTTER, BONNIE A., dir. pub. rel., Kenmore Mercy Hospital, Kenmore, NY '82 (PR)
COTTER, JOHN A., atty., William W. Backus Hospital, Norwich, CT '85 (ATTY)
COTTER, KAREN T., RN, assoc., Interqual, Inc., North Hampton, NH '85 (NURS)
COTTER, NEIL HUGHES, vice-pres. plant serv., Clermont Mercy Hospital, Batavia, OH '76 (ENG)
COTTILLION, JOHN G., adm. mktg. and plng. serv., Ohio State University Hospitals, Columbus, OH '80 (PLNG)
COTTINGHAM, ALVENIA W., dir. plng. and dev., Seabrook House, Seabrook, NJ '84 (PLNG)
COTTLER, JOAN M., dir. soc. work, McLean Hospital, Belmont, MA '84 (SOC)
COTTON, GLENDA G., dir. vol. serv., Deaconess Hospital, Oklahoma City, OK '81 (VOL)
COTTON, MARCIA, clin. eng., Southwest Community Health System, Middleburg Heights, OH '86 (ENG)
COTTONE, BRIAN A., dir. environ. serv., Hospital-Philadelphia College of Osteopathic Medicine, Philadelphia, PA '86 (ENVIRON)
COTTONGIM, GARY, exec. vice-pres., Peninsula Hospital and Medical Center, Burlingame, CA '78
COTTRELL, RONALD J., dir. plng. and dev., AMI Frye Regional Medical Center, Hickory, NC '85 (PLNG)
COTTRILL, IMOGENE, head nrs. day surgery, Swedish Hospital Medical Center, Seattle, WA '87 (AMB)
COUCH, DORIS B., supv. cent. serv., Cobb General Hospital, Austell, GA '85 (CS)
COUCH, PAMELA L., pat. rep., Clermont Mercy Hospital, Batavia, OH '85 (PAT)
COUCH, ROBERT C., pres., Cumberland Medical Center, Crossville, TN '60
COUCHON, LINDA W., asst. to dir.-joint educ. and trng., Southern Tier Health Management Corporation, Elmira Heights, NY '85 (EDUC)
COUGHLIN, JANE, dir. consulting serv., American Medical Association, Chicago, IL '83 (PR)
COUGHLIN, OLIVANNE, dir. pers., Cardinal Cushing General Hospital, Brockton, MA '83 (PERS)
COUGHLIN, RPBERT, dir. soc. serv., Rehabilitation Institute of Pittsburgh, Pittsburgh, PA '85 (SOC)
COULTER, EDWARD M., adm. anes., University of Kansas Hospital, Kansas City, KS '78
COULTER, PATRICIA A., dir. vol., Holy Family Hospital, Spokane, WA '82 (VOL)
COULTER, RICHARD T., co-chief diet. serv., Pacific Medical Center, Seattle, WA '85 (FOOD)
COULTER, SHARON J., RN, vice-pres. pat. serv., Research Medical Center, Kansas City, MO '78 (NURS)
COULTON, CLAUDIA J., asst. prof., Case Western Reserve University, School of Applied Social Sciences, Cleveland, OH '78 (SOC)
COUNCIL, MARIE W., dir. trng., Lloyd Noland Hospital and Health Centers, Birmingham, AL '73 (EDUC)
COUNCIL, SUE R., dir. soc. serv., Baptist Hospital, Nashville, TN '87 (SOC)
COUNSELMAN, DALE F., supv. maint., Standish Community Hospital, Standish, MI '83 (ENG)
COUNTRYMAN, DENNIS, dir. health care serv., Sverdrup Corporation, St. Louis, MO '80 (PLNG)
COUNTS, MICHAEL M., dir. matl. mgt., Metropolitan Hospital and Health Centers, Detroit, MI '83 (PUR)
COUPAL, SALLY, dir. soc. serv., All Children's Hospital, St. Petersburg, FL '85 (SOC)
COUPE, J. LEO, atty., St. Elizabeth Hospital, Utica, NY '68 (ATTY)
COURAGE, THOMAS R., atty., Roger Williams General Hospital, Providence, RI '76 (ATTY)
COUREY, KENNETH MICHAEL, pres., St. Clare's Hospital, Denville, NJ '62
COURSON, GARDNER G., atty., Grady Memorial Hospital, Atlanta, GA '76 (ATTY)
COURTER, LEE ANN, asst. corp. dir. mktg. and pub. rel., Horizon Health Systems, Oak Park, MI '86 (PR)
COURTNEY, DENNIS K., dir. educ. and matl. mgt., Servicemaster Industries, Inc., Downers Grove, IL '80 (PUR)
COURTNEY, DON R., sr. vice-pres., Frank J. Corbett, Inc., Chicago, IL '86 (PR)
COURTNEY, MARGARET M., RN, dir. soc. serv., Hudson County Meadowview Hospital, Secaucus, NJ '77 (SOC)
COURTNEY, ROGER C., atty., Temple University Hospital, Philadelphia, PA '87 (ATTY)
COURVOISIER, JOHN JR., asst. exec. dir. fiscal serv., East Jefferson General Hospital, Metairie, LA '75
COURY, ELIZABETH A., dir. commun., Catholic Health Corporation, Omaha, NE '86 (PR)
COUSIN, GARY L., vice-pres., Mount Sinai Medical Center, Cleveland, OH '74 (ENG)
COUSINS, ANNA M., dir. food serv., Mercy Hospital, Springfield, MA '82 (FOOD)
COUSSENS, BRENT B., mgt. analyst, Saint Francis Hospital, Tulsa, OK '86
COUSTILLAC, REGIS G., assoc. adm., Kaiser Foundation Hospital, Parma, OH '87 (AMB)
COUTS, TERRY BRENT, dir. human res., Joint Township District Memorial Hospital, St. Marys, OH '78 (PERS)
COUTU, ROGER JR., dir. matl. mgt., Memorial Hospital, Pawtucket, RI '79 (MGMT)
COUTURE, EILEEN, head nrs. emer. room, Gottlieb Memorial Hospital, Melrose Park, IL '87 (AMB)
COVELL, JAMES P., dir. environ. serv., Ellis Hospital, Schenectady, NY '86
COVELL, SUSAN T., dir. vol. serv., Children's Hospital of Michigan, Detroit, MI '85 (VOL)
COVENKO, LEE M., dir. plant oper., Princeton Community Hospital, Princeton, WV '80 (ENG)
COVENTRY, JOHN A., assoc. prof., Army-Baylor University Program in Health Care Administration, Fort Sam Houston, TX '81 (MGMT)
COVERT, KATHLEEN A., dir. plng., Boulder Memorial Hospital, Boulder, CO '84 (PR) (PLNG)
COVEY, BARBARA B., dir. vol. serv., Daniel Freeman Memorial Hospital, Inglewood, CA '68 (VOL)
COVEY, LAIRD P., assoc. adm., North Country Hospital and Health Center, Newport, VT '84 (PLNG)(EDUC)
COVEY, WILLIAM E., vice-pres. fin., Huntington Memorial Hospital, Pasadena, CA '81 (PLNG)
COVILL, SHERWOOD GRANT, adm., Scripps Clinic San Diego, San Diego, CA '80
COVINGTON-SIDICANE, JANET, RN, coor. qual. assur., Fresno Community Hospital and Medical Center, Fresno, CA '86 (RISK)
COVINGTON, JIM H., dir. plant oper., Charter Southland Hospital, Mobile, AL '78 (ENG)
COVINGTON, ROBERT C., vice-pres., Alexander and Alexander, Atlanta, GA '81 (RISK)
COVONE, JOSEPH T. JR., dir. environ. and ldry. serv., St. Joseph's Hospital, Philadelphia, PA '86 (ENVIRON)
COWAN, CHERRIE L., RN, pat. advocate, Camden-Clark Memorial Hospital, Parkersburg, WV '85 (PAT)
COWAN, DALE H., atty., St. Alexis Hospital, Cleveland, OH '82 (ATTY)
COWAN, DAVID Z., mgt. syst. consult., Stone Mountain, GA '79 (MGMT)
COWAN, JAMES R., MD, pres., United Hospitals Medical Center, Newark, NJ '76
COWAN, JOHN W., coor. preventive maint., Memorial Hospital of Southern Oklahoma, Ardmore, OK '83 (ENG)
COWAN, JOSEPH L., atty., University of California San Francisco, San Francisco, CA '76 (ATTY)
COWAN, LARRY, supv. maint., Aspen Valley Hospital District, Aspen, CO '85 (ENG)
COWAN, LAURIE A., vice-pres. plng. and mktg., Lowell General Hospital, Lowell, MA '85 (PLNG)
COWAN, LILLY, student, Insurance Institute of America, Malvern, PA '86 (RISK)
COWAN, MARY ELLEN, dir. soc. work, Eye and Ear Hospital of Pittsburgh, Pittsburgh, PA '82 (SOC)
COWAN, OLIVER R., buyer, New York University Medical Center, New York, NY '86 (PUR)
COWAN, REX PHILLIP, atty., Winter Haven Hospital, Winter Haven, FL '77 (ATTY)
COWAN, RICHARD E., dir. mgt. and info. serv., St. John's Regional Medical Center, Joplin, MO '85 (MGMT)
COWAN, ROBERT S., mgr. facil. consult. serv., SunHealth Corporation, Charlotte, NC '83 (ENG)
COWARD, JANDA W., dir. diet. serv., Coryell Memorial Hospital, Gatesville, TX '78 (FOOD)
COWART, PAUL R., exec. off., Naval Aerospace Medical Institute, Pensacola, FL '84
COWART, RICHARD G., atty., Memorial Hospital at Gulfport, Gulfport, MS '85 (ATTY)
COWDREY, NANCY R., bus. mgr., Johnson and Johnson Hospital Service, Tinton Falls, NJ '85 (PUR)
COWELL, ROBERT L. G., dir. maint. and plant oper., Lincoln General Hospital, Lincoln, NE '67 (ENG)
COWELL, VICKI, dir. pub. rel., Deaconess Hospital of Cleveland, Cleveland, OH '80 (PR)
COWEN, EILEEN GROVES, plng. assoc., Episcopal Hospital, Philadelphia, PA '84 (PLNG)
COWEN, SANDRA E., atty., Evangelical Health Systems, Oak Brook, IL '85 (ATTY)
COWHIG, JOHN E., reg. vice-pres., Health East, Inc., Roanoke, VA '75
COWLES, ROBERT P., George W. Jackson Mental Health Center, Jonesboro, AR '82 (CS)
COWLESS, ELIZABETH J., RN, adm. asst. pat. care serv., Providence Hospital, Southfield, MI '81 (NURS)
COWLEY, DARON H., dir. commun. rel., Orem Community Hospital, Orem, UT '85 (PR)
COWLEY, MARGARITA M., RN, dir. nrsg., Children's Medical Center of Dallas, Dallas, TX '86 (NURS)
COWSEET, W. EUGENE, pres., Wood River Township Hospital, Wood River, IL '80 (PLNG)
COWTON, CHRISTINA A., RN, head nrs. cent. serv., Cornwall Hospital, Cornwall, NY '77 (CS)
COX, BEVERLY H., RN, asst. adm. nrsg., Jefferson Memorial Hospital, Alexandria, VA '77 (NURS)
COX, BOBBY D., adm., Eastern Oklahoma Medical Center, Poteau, OK '87 (AMB)
COX, C. ROBERT, atty., Washoe Medical Center, Reno, NV '84 (ATTY)
COX, CAROL LEE, RN, vice-pres. nrsg. serv., St. Joseph's Hospital, Stockton, CA '76 (NURS)
COX, CELESTE O., dir. commun. rel., St. Mary's Hospital, West Palm Beach, FL '85 (PR)
COX, CLYDE G., assoc. dean, University of Alabama, School of Medicine, Birmingham, AL '52 (LIFE)
COX, CONNIE J., dir. human res., LaPorte Hospital, LaPorte, IN '85 (PERS)
COX, CORA LEE, supv. cent. sterile sup., Mary Black Memorial Hospital, Spartanburg, SC '85 (CS)
COX, DIANE S., dir. dev. and commun. rel., Geneva General Hospital, Geneva, NY '78 (PR)
COX, DON H., dir. food serv., John C. Lincoln Hospital and Health Center, Phoenix, AZ '85 (FOOD)
COX, EDNA M., coor. package and sterile, St. Anthony Medical Center, Crown Point, IN '85 (CS)
COX, ELLEN, dir. nrsg. qual. assur., Scott and White Memorial Hospital, Temple, TX '85 (PAT)
COX, EUGENE M., pres., Curative Rehabilitation Center, Milwaukee, WI '72
COX, EVELYN J., coor. pub. rel., Loris Community Hospital, Loris, SC '86 (PR)
COX, FREDERIC H. JR., prin., Marcellus, Wright, Cox and Smith, Architects, Richmond, VA '77
COX, JAMES A. JR., exec. vice-pres., Carondelet Rehabilitation Center of America, Tallahassee, FL '86
COX, JAMES T., atty., Southwest Mississippi Medical Center, McComb, MS '83 (ATTY)
COX, JAN G., dir. plng. and mktg., Holy Cross Management Service, Inc., Mountain Home, ID '86 (PLNG)
COX, JOAN M., sr. mgr., Price Waterhouse, Washington, DC '77
COX, JOHN E. JR., student, Central Michigan University, Mount Pleasant, MI '86 (MGMT)
COX, JOHN W. JR., atty., Galena-Stauss Hospital, Galena, IL '79 (ATTY)
COX, JOSEF H., chief eng., St. Francis Hospital Systems, Colorado Springs, CO '76 (ENG)
COX, JULIE C., contr., HCA East Pointe Hospital, Lehigh Acres, FL '84
COX, LAVONNE A., vice-pres., Iowa Methodist Medical Center, Des Moines, IA '85 (MGMT)
COX, LESTER L., bd. chm., Lester E. Cox Medical Centers, Springfield, MO '58
COX, LINDA J., RN, coor. risk mgt., Valley Hospital and Medical Center, Spokane, WA '85 (RISK)
COX, MARGARETTE, dir. hskpg. and linen serv., HCA Coronado Hospital, Pampa, TX '86 (ENVIRON)
COX, MARK M., vice-pres., Witt Associates, Inc., Oak Brook, IL '77 (PERS)
COX, MARSHA C., RN, vice-pres. nrsg., Fort Worth Osteopathic Medical Center, Fort Worth, TX '87 (NURS)
COX, MICHAEL T., pat. serv. rep., Stormont-Vail Regional Medical Center, Topeka, KS '84 (PAT)
COX, NOVELLA ANN, RN, vice-pres. pat. serv., St. Luke Hospital, Fort Thomas, KY '81 (NURS)
COX, PAMELA H., phys. liaison, Good Samaritan Hospital and Health Center, Dayton, OH '86 (PLNG)
COX, PAUL R., dir. human res., Basic American Medical, Inc., Indianapolis, IN '86 (PERS)
COX, PAUL STAN, dir. vol., Gritman Memorial Hospital, Moscow, ID '86 (VOL)
COX, PETER T., recruiting coor., University of Texas at Arlington, Arlington, TX '73
COX, ROBERT C., adm., Mercy Hospital, Columbus, OH '53 (LIFE)
COX, ROBERT O., atty., Eliza Coffee Memorial Hospital, Florence, AL '74 (ATTY)
COX, RUTHY LOU, coor. pat. rel., Hendrick Medical Center, Abilene, TX '85 (PAT)
COX, SHARYN D., supv. cent. sterile room, North Broward Medical Center, Pompano Beach, FL '82 (CS)
COX, STEVE, coor. qual. assur. and risk mgr., Radford Community Hospital, Radford, VA '86 (RISK)
COX, THOMAS L. JR., atty., Dallas County Hospital District, Dallas, TX '81 (ATTY)
COX, TIMOTHY L., chief eng., Porter Memorial Hospital, Valparaiso, IN '86 (ENG)
COXE, PATRICIA J., RN, dir. nrsg. serv., Medina Memorial Hospital, Medina, NY '86 (NURS)
COXWELL, DIAN H., dir. pub. rel. and mktg., Gulf Coast Hospital, Baytown, TX '85 (PR)
COY, CYNTHIA TABER, dir. pub. rel., Lutheran Hospital, Moline, IL '82 (PR)
COYLE, JOHN J., mgr. matl., Saratoga Hospital, Saratoga Springs, NY '86 (PUR)
COYLE, JOHN R., chief eng., Dixon Memorial Hospital, Denham Springs, LA '81 (ENG)
COYNE, DANIEL WILLIAM, atty., St. Joseph Hospital, Chicago, IL '74 (ATTY)
COYNE, GENEVIEVE, RN, vice-pres., Hoag Memorial Hospital Presbyterian, Newport Beach, CA '73 (NURS)
COYNE, JOHN L., dir. maint., Scott County Hospital, Scott City, KS '86 (ENG)
COYNE, SHIRLEY M., dir. vol. serv., Lakeview Medical Center, Danville, IL '75 (VOL)
COYNE, THOMAS A., dir. plant eng., Sacred Heart Hospital, Norristown, PA '64 (ENG)
COZZENS, RAYMOND A., mgr. electronic dev., Florence Corporation, Chicago, IL '86 (ENG)
CRABTREE, CHARLES E., supv. cent. sup., Westerly Hospital, Westerly, RI '86 (CS)
CRABTREE, HENRY E., asst. mgr. plant and maint. serv., Walter O. Boswell Memorial Hospital, Sun City, AZ '87 (ENG)
CRABTREE, TOM R., dir. maint., ldry. and hskpg., Oak Hill Community Medical Center, Oak Hill, OH '81 (ENG)
CRACRAFT, NATHANIEL SILAS JR., supt. maint., Independence Regional Health Center, Independence, MO '74 (ENG)
CRADDICK, JOYCE W., consult. prof. liability, Marsh and McLennan, Inc., San Francisco, CA '80 (RISK)
CRAFT, WILLIAM H. III, asst. mgr. commun., Danbury Hospital, Danbury, CT '85 (ENG)
CRAGIN, CHARLES L. III, atty., Cragin for Governor Committee, Portland, ME '76 (ATTY)
CRAHAM, GEORGE W., exec. vice-pres. and adm., Torrance Memorial Hospital Medical Center, Torrance, CA '78
CRAHAN, PAULINE C., dir. pers., The Savannas Hospital, Port St. Lucie, FL '87 (PERS)
CRAIG, BARRY G., atty., Mercy Hospital, Miami, FL '82 (ATTY)
CRAIG, DONNA, assoc. adm., Oakwood Hospital, Dearborn, MI '86 (RISK)
CRAIG, E. GLEN, asst. dir. pers. serv., Richland Memorial Hospital, Columbia, SC '86 (PERS)
CRAIG, ELLA H., dir. soc. serv., Charter North Hospital, Anchorage, AK '86 (SOC)
CRAIG, EUNICE Z., coor. staff dev., Kent General Hospital, Dover, DE '86 (EDUC)
CRAIG, GAY, sr. health planner, Medical Planning Associates, Malibu, CA '79 (PLNG)
CRAIG, GLENN L., asst. vice-pres., Hendrick Medical Center, Abilene, TX '80
CRAIG, GREGORY, asst. adm., Medical Center Hospital, Odessa, TX '80
CRAIG, HOWARD R., supv. maint., White County Memorial Hospital, Monticello, IN '81 (ENG)
CRAIG, J. KATHY, dir. pers., Sonora Community Hospital, Sonora, CA '86 (PERS)
CRAIG, JANET B., RN, asst. adm., Greenville Hospital System, Greenville, SC '82 (AMB)

CRAIG, KEVIN W., asst. adm., North Shore Children's Hospital, Salem, MA '81 (MGMT)
CRAIG, MARJORIE A., med. rec. consult., Queen of Angels Medical Center, Los Angeles, CA '84
CRAIG, MARY ANN, pat. rep., Union Hospital, Terre Haute, IN '80 (PAT)
CRAIG, MAJ. MARY PAT, 128th Combat Support Hospital, APO New York, NY '86
CRAIG, MAYBLE E., RN, dir. med. nrsg., University of Michigan Hospitals, Ann Arbor, MI '83 (NURS)
CRAIG, MICHAEL, dir. ins. and risk mgt., Paracelsus Healthcare, Pasadena, CA '87 (RISK)
CRAIG, PATRICIA A., dir. soc. serv., Brownsville General Hospital, Brownsville, PA '81 (SOC)
CRAIG, PATRICIA L., RN, dir. nrsg., Hendricks County Hospital, Danville, IN '84 (NURS)
CRAIG, ROBERT J., vice-pres. mktg., Lancaster-Fairfield Community Hospital, Lancaster, OH '86 (PR) (PLNG)
CRAIG, THOMAS G., dir. plant maint., South Peninsula Hospital, Homer, AK '81 (ENG)
CRAIG, TIM, dir. bus. health center, Mercy Center for Health Care Services, Aurora, IL '80 (PLNG)
CRAIG, VIRGINIA S., dir. pub. rel. and dev., Grove General Hospital, Grove, OK '83 (PR)
CRAIG, WILLIAM H., asst. adm., Doctors' Hospital, Shreveport, LA '82
CRAIN, ALLEN, asst. dir. pers., Rapides General Hospital, Alexandria, LA '80 (PERS)
CRAIN, MARK M. II, dir. pers., Bloomington Hospital, Bloomington, IN '77 (PERS)
CRAIN, TAMARA LANE, coor. pat. rel., Firelands Community Hospital, Sandusky, OH '86 (PAT)
CRALLE, CHARLES, sr. vice-pres., Henderson and Phillips, Inc., Norfolk, VA '86 (RISK)
CRAM, ELLEN H., Ardmore, OK '83 (FOOD)
CRAMER, BRIAN J., cmdr. med. syst. sect., U. S. Air Force Clinic Randolph, San Antonio, TX '84
CRAMER, HAROLD, atty., Graduate Hospital, Philadelphia, PA '76 (ATTY)
CRAMER, JOHN S., sr. vice-pres. corp. plng., Harrisburg Hospital Health Foundation, Harrisburg, PA '68 (PLNG)
CRAMER, LINDA M., chief soc. worker, Emanuel Hospital and Health Center, Portland, OR '78 (SOC)
CRAMER, LOIS A., dir. vol. serv., Armstrong County Memorial Hospital, Kittanning, PA '72 (VOL)
CRANDALL, DEIRDRE D., mgt. eng., Thomas Jefferson University Hospital, Philadelphia, PA '85 (MGMT)
CRANDALL, F. WILLIAM, atty., Brooklyn Hospital-Caledonian Hospital, Brooklyn, NY '73 (ATTY)
CRANDALL, HARRY R., chief sup., proc. and distrib. serv., Veterans Administration Medical Center, Albany, NY '86 (CS)
CRANDALL, PATRICIA I., atty., Holy Family Hospital, Spokane, WA '80 (ATTY)
CRANDELL, KIM O., student, Brigham Young University, Provo, UT '86 (PLNG)
CRANE, DONALD H., atty., Healthwest Medical Centers, Chatsworth, CA '82 (ATTY)
CRANE, JUDY, RN, dir. nrsg., Dallas County Hospital, Perry, IA '80 (NURS)
CRANE, LANSING E., atty., Connecticut Mental Health Center, New Haven, CT '85 (ATTY)
CRANE, VICKI S., assoc. dir. pharm., Presbyterian Hospital, Dallas, TX '82
CRANEY, TOM, dir. human res., South Miami Hospital, South Miami, FL '71 (PERS)
CRANFORD, SANDRA C., dir. vol. serv., Worcester Memorial Hospital, Worcester, MA '85 (VOL)
CRANKE, GENELL H., dir. soc. work, Gaston Memorial Hospital, Gastonia, NC '81 (SOC)
CRANKSHAW, SUZANNE R., dir. diet., William Beaumont Hospital-Troy, Troy, MI '80 (FOOD)
CRANSHAW, THOMAS H., vice-pres. strategic plng., Research Health Services, Kansas City, MO '69 (PLNG)
CRAPPS, DANNY, dir. pers. serv., Hillcrest Baptist Medical Center, Waco, TX '80 (PERS)
CRAPSER, DOUGLAS M., assoc. adm., Harrington Memorial Hospital, Southbridge, MA '81 (PLNG)
CRARRY, DELWIN R., supv. matl., Anacapa Adventist Hospital, Port Hueneme, CA '83 (PUR)
CRAVEN, BEVERLY J., pur. agt., Cushing Regional Hospital, Cushing, OK '82 (PUR)
CRAVEN, JAMES A., mgr. pers. and contr., Excelsior Springs City Hospital, Excelsior Springs, MO '82 (PERS)
CRAVEN, RONALD J., reg. dir. health care, Equitable Life Insurance, Chicago, IL '75
CRAVEY, ETHELYN, head nrs. cent. sup., Jones County Community Hospital, Laurel, MS '77 (CS)
CRAVSWELL, FRED, dir. pers., Huntsville Hospital, Huntsville, AL '83 (PERS)
CRAWFIS, EWING H., adm., Mary Rutan Hospital, Bellefontaine, OH '69
CRAWFORD, A. ROBERT JR., Charlotte, NC '53 (LIFE)
CRAWFORD, BARBARA ANN, student, Program in Health Administration and Planning, Washington University School of Medicine, St. Louis, MO '83
CRAWFORD, BENJAMIN L., biomedical electronic tech., St. Vincent's Medical Center, Jacksonville, FL '79 (ENG)
CRAWFORD, BRENITA, assoc. adm., Henry Ford Hospital, Detroit, MI '80
CRAWFORD, CLAUDIA C., supv. cent. sup., HCA Sun City Hospital, Sun City Center, FL '85 (CS)
CRAWFORD, D. LEE, asst. dir. pers., Holston Valley Hospital and Medical Center, Kingsport, TN '83 (PERS)
CRAWFORD, DOUGLAS H., mgr. emp. serv., Vassar Brothers Hospital, Poughkeepsie, NY '83 (PERS)
CRAWFORD, EDWIN M., dir. pub. affairs, San Diego Hospital Association, San Diego, CA '84 (PR)
CRAWFORD, EUGENE B. JR., sr. vice-pres. adm., Medical Center of Delaware, Wilmington, DE '55 (LIFE)
CRAWFORD, GEORGE T., dir. food serv., Dominican Santa Cruz Hospital, Santa Cruz, CA '70 (FOOD)
CRAWFORD, HARRY, pres., Insurance and Risk Management, Fort Wayne, IN '86 (RISK)
CRAWFORD, JAMES S., vice-pres., Ambulatory Health Care Corporation, Austintown, OH '87 (AMB)
CRAWFORD, JEAN E., RN, adm. nrsg., Orthopaedic Hospital of Charlotte, Charlotte, NC '85 (NURS)
CRAWFORD, JILL C., RN, dir. nrsg. mgt. syst., Zurbrugg Memorial Hospital, Willingboro, NJ '86 (NURS)
CRAWFORD, COL. JOHN C., MSC USA, King Fahad Hospital, APO New York, NY '77
CRAWFORD, JOHN CLAY, sr. mgr., Peat, Marwick, Mitchell and Company, New Orleans, LA '83
CRAWFORD, JUNE, dir. mktg. and pub. rel., HCA Edgefield Hospital, Nashville, TN '85 (PR)
CRAWFORD, KENNETH E., dir. eng. and maint., Guernsey Memorial Hospital, Cambridge, OH '84 (ENG)
CRAWFORD, MARY ANN, RN, vice-pres. pat. care support, Akron General Medical Center, Akron, OH '85 (NURS)
CRAWFORD, NANCY, dir. mktg. commun., Integrated Healthcare Technicians, Travenol Laboratories, Inc., Reston, VA '86
CRAWFORD, PATRICIA R., dir. vol. serv., Welkind Rehabilitation Hospital, Chester, NJ '77 (VOL)
CRAWFORD, R. VINCENT, assoc. dir., Veterans Administration Medical Center, Ann Arbor, MI '77
CRAWFORD, SARA M., dir. commun. rel. and mktg., HCA Medical Center of Plano, Plano, TX '87 (PR) (PLNG)
CRAWFORD, SUSAN, dir. pub. info., Georgia Hospital Association, Atlanta, GA '86 (PR)
CRAWFORD, SUSAN, dir. soc. work serv., Pinal General Hospital, Florence, AZ '86 (SOC)
CRAWLEY, KEN, asst. dir. pers., Slidell Memorial Hospital, Slidell, LA '85 (PERS)
CRAY, JOHN D., atty., Burlington Medical Center, Burlington, IA '76 (ATTY)
CREAMER, DONALD R., pres. and chief exec. off., Williamsport Hospital and Medical Center, Williamsport, PA '71
CREAMER, ROBERT, vice-pres., LaGuardia Hospital Shared Service Division, New York, NY '86 (MGMT)
CREASON, KAREN, atty., McMinnville Community Hospital, McMinnville, OR '81 (ATTY)
CREASY, JOHN C., pres., Danbury Hospital, Danbury, CT '80 (PLNG)
CREBBIN, JOANN, RN, assoc. dir. nrsg. serv., Baptist Hospital of Miami, Miami, FL '79 (NURS)
CREDILLE, CECILIA, mgr., Marianjoy Rehabilitation Center, Wheaton, IL '87 (AMB)
CREECH, BERTIE, RN, vice-pres. nrsg., Community Hospital of Anderson and Madison County, Anderson, IN '76 (NURS)
CREECH, DALE E. JR., sr. vice-pres. and atty., MedAmerica Health Systems Corporation, Dayton, OH '80 (ATTY)
CREECH, DONNA L., dir. pub. rel., East Tennessee Baptist Hospital, Knoxville, TN '86 (PR)
CREECH, ROY R. JR., adm., Prepaid Health of Maryland, Baltimore, MD '58
CREED, CLARA EDMONDS, (ret.), Chelsea, MA '62
CREEDEN, MICHAEL J., asst. dir. food serv., Holy Redeemer Hospital and Medical Center, Meadowbrook, PA '86 (FOOD)
CREEKMAN, JAMES E., atty., Margaret R. Pardee Memorial Hospital, Hendersonville, NC '85 (ATTY)
CREEL, GEORGE HARRIS II, mgr. res. and dev., Health Central System, Minneapolis, MN '79 (PLNG)
CREEL, PATRICIA H., dir. soc. serv., Flowers Hospital, Dothan, AL '85 (SOC)
CREEL, WILLIAM E., dir. facil. eng., St. Joseph Hospital, Houston, TX '81 (ENG)
CREGER, BETTY J., RN, asst. adm. nrsg. and chm. risk mgt., Fresno Community Hospital and Medical Center, Fresno, CA '74 (NURS)(RISK)
CREGG, MARTIN J., dir. pers. and human res., Santa Monica Hospital Medical Center, Santa Monica, CA '71 (PERS)
CREHAN, MARGARET E., dir. vol. serv., Quincy City Hospital, Quincy, MA '86 (VOL)
CRENSHAW, MARY H., dir. matl. mgt., Lakeside Hospital, Metairie, LA '81 (PUR)
CRENWELGE, RACHEL S., RN, exec. dir., Las Encinas Hospital, Pasadena, CA '84 (RISK)
CRESCENZO, ROBERT A., dir. soc. work, Bellevue Hospital Center, New York, NY '78 (SOC)
CRESPO, IRVING, supv. cent. serv., St. Mary's Hospital and Health Center, Tucson, AZ '85 (CS)
CRESS, MARY ELIZABETH, dir. pat. and family serv., Suburban Hospital, Bethesda, MD '78 (SOC)
CRESSLER, JOHN C., MD, (ret.), Bethesda, MD '51 (LIFE)
CRESSY, CLAUDE N., sr. mgt. eng., Porter Memorial Hospital, Denver, CO '86 (MGMT)
CREUTZ, MARGARET L., dir. educ., Toledo Hospital, Toledo, OH '82 (EDUC)
CREVER, RITA M., vice-pres. pat. care serv., St. Mary's Health Services, Grand Rapids, MI '83 (NURS)
CREVIER, CAROLE A., adm. dir., Good Samaritan Medical Center, Phoenix, AZ '74
CREW, MICHAEL D., atty., Cooney, Crew and Wihtol, Portland, OR '84 (ATTY)
CREWS, CATHY S., mgt. eng., Self Memorial Hospital, Greenwood, SC '87 (MGMT)
CREWS, DEBORAH B., dir. pub. rel., DeSoto Memorial Hospital, Arcadia, FL '86 (PR)
CREWS, JOHN WILLIAM, atty., Virginia Hospital Association, Richmond, VA '76 (ATTY)
CREWS, KAY FAIR, dir. pers., Guadalupe Medical Center, Carlsbad, NM '86 (PERS)
CREWS, MERRILL W., pres., South Miami Hospital, South Miami, FL '64
CRIBBEN, LUCY F., adm. dir., New York Hospital, New York, NY '84
CRIDER, NANCY M., RN, dir. nrsg. adm. oper., Morristown Memorial Hospital, Morristown, NJ '86 (NURS)
CRIGGAR, DENNIS F., dir. facil. eng., Community Hospitals of Indiana, Indianapolis, IN '78 (ENG)
CRILL, JOHN L., atty., Durham County General Hospital, Durham, NC '76 (ATTY)
CRILLY, BETTIE A., dir. vol. serv., Burdette Tomlin Memorial Hospital, Cape May Court House, NJ '83 (VOL)
CRIMI, DENNIS F., vice-pres. mktg., St. Luke's-Roosevelt Hospital Center, New York, NY '85 (PR)
CRIMMINS, BRIAN M., asst. adm., Harper Hospital, Detroit, MI '80
CRIMMINS, SUSAN, asst. dir., Mount Sinai Medical Center, New York, NY '86 (SOC)
CRIPE, MICHAEL J., vice-pres. oper., Uci Medical Affiliates, Inc., Dallas, TX '86 (PLNG)
CRISA, NICHOLAS, pat. rep., Sea View Hospital and Home, Staten Island, NY '82 (PAT)
CRISMORE, ROSEMARY M., dir. diet., Proctor Community Hospital, Peoria, IL '81 (FOOD)
CRISP, LINDA T., dir. food and nutr. serv., Valley Presbyterian Hospital, Van Nuys, CA '81 (FOOD)
CRISPO, BRUNO, pur. agt., Sudbury Memorial Hospital, Sudbury, Ont., Canada '83 (PUR)
CRISS, JOHN P., assoc. adm., Jefferson Regional Medical Center, Pine Bluff, AR '80 (MGMT)
CRISSMAN, SUSAN, RN, vice-pres., Memorial Hospital, South Bend, IN '77 (NURS)
CRIST, JANICE D., RN, consult., Self Care Education, Olympia, WA '86 (EDUC)
CRIST, MARY JANE, dir. commun. dev., Tempe St. Luke's Hospital, Tempe, AZ '86 (VOL)
CRISWELL, LARRY W., dir. soc. serv. and discharge plng., Hollywood Presbyterian Medical Center, Los Angeles, CA '84 (SOC)
CRITTENDEN, CAROL S., supv. cent. sup., Cooper County Memorial Hospital, Boonville, MO '75 (CS)
CROCE, NICHOLAS JR., asst. vice-pres., Cooper Hospital-University Medical Center, Camden, NJ '85
CROCKER, BLAKE D., atty., Borgess Medical Center, Kalamazoo, MI '86 (ATTY)
CROCKER, DAVID G., atty., Borgess Medical Center, Kalamazoo, MI '68 (ATTY)
CROCKETT, DAVY F., RN, clin. dir. surg. nrsg., Moses H. Cone Memorial Hospital, Greensboro, NC '86 (NURS)
CROCKETT, JAMES D., CPA, partner, Laventhol and Horwath, Chicago, IL '71
CROES, LYNNE M., emp. dev. spec., Willmar Regional Treatment Center, Willmar, MN '86 (EDUC)
CROFOOT, SHIRLEY A., RN, dir. matl. mgt., Whitley County Memorial Hospital, Columbia City, IN '86 (CS)
CROFT, ALBERT C., asst. adm. gen. serv., Western Reserve Care Systems-Northside Medical Center, Youngstown, OH '84 (PUR)
CROFTON, TIMOTHY A., chief exec. off., Great Lakes Rehabilitation Hospital, Erie, PA '86
CROGHAN, M. EILEEN, dir. educ. serv., St. Patrick Hospital, Missoula, MT '81 (EDUC)
CROITORU, JUDITH M., dir. soc. work serv., Nashoba Community Hospital, Ayer, MA '86 (SOC)
CROLL, KARON J., dir. educ., New Brunswick Hospital Association, Fredericton, N.B., Canada '82 (EDUC)
CROLL, MARY, exec. dir. serv. league, Hennepin County Medical Center, Minneapolis, MN '73 (VOL)
CROMARTIE, JENNIFER S., asst. dir. pub. rel., Providence Hospital, Washington, DC '86 (PR)
CROMBIE, MARTHA HOOVER, dir. mktg., Woman's and Children's Hospital, Lafayette, LA '83 (PR)
CROMER, MARK L., dir. pur., Anderson Memorial Hospital, Anderson, SC '64 (PUR)
CROMWELL, B. JANIE, RN, vice-pres. pat. serv., De Paul Hospital, Cheyenne, WY '68 (NURS)
CROMWELL, ROBERT A., consult., St. Vincent Infirmary, Little Rock, AR '83 (ENG)
CRONEBERGER, HARRY L., plant supt., Hemet Valley Hospital District, Hemet, CA '87 (ENG)
CRONEN, RONALD L., adm., Horizon Health Corporation, Dallas, TX '81
CRONIN, CONSTANCE J., RN, asst. dir. nrsg. serv., specialty and critical care, William Beaumont Hospital, Royal Oak, MI '83 (NURS)
CRONIN, FRANCIS J., pres., Elliot Hospital, Manchester, NH '64
CRONIN, JOHN C. J., assoc. dir. clin. serv., St. Elizabeth's Hospital of Boston, Boston, MA '68 (PLNG)
CRONIN, KATHLEEN M., dir. educ., Cheshire Medical Center, Keene, NH '86 (EDUC)
CRONIN, MARILYN J., RN, assoc. dir. nrsg., Kaiser Foundation Hospital, Bellflower, CA '84 (NURS)
CRONIN, COL. MARTHA A., MSC USA, chief diet., Office of Surgeon General, Falls Church, VA '81 (FOOD)
CRONIN, MICHAEL SUE, RN, dir. nrsg., Michael Reese Hospital and Medical Center, Chicago, IL '86 (NURS)
CRONIN, SUSAN H., adm. asst., St. Paul Medical Center, Dallas, TX '78
CRONKHITE, MARLENE GLORIA, pat. rep., Eisenhower Medical Center, Rancho Mirage, CA '87 (PAT)
CROOKS, JOSEPH W., atty., Emory University Hospital, Atlanta, GA '82 (ATTY)
CROOKS, NORMA F., dir. soc. serv., Schumpert Medical Center, Shreveport, LA '85 (SOC)
CROSBY, BEN G., mgr. healthcare mktg., Oneac Corporation, Libertyville, IL '86 (ENG)
CROSBY, DOROTHY A., RN, mgr. cent. serv., Community Hospital Monterey Peninsula, Monterey, CA '84 (CS)
CROSBY, ELIZABETH G., atty., Charter Medical Corporation, Macon, GA '86 (ATTY)
CROSBY, JOHN A., dir. human res., Caldwell Memorial Hospital, Lenoir, NC '86 (PR)
CROSBY, VIRGINIA D., dir. vol., Roosevelt Hospital, New York, NY '81 (VOL)
CROSLEY, WILBUR D., adm., Williamson Appalachian Regional Hospital, South Williamson, KY '67
CROSS, HELENE M., mgr. pers., St. Vincent Stress Center, Indianapolis, IN '85 (PERS)
CROSS, JEFFERY M., atty., United Physicians Association, Arlington Heights, IL '84 (ATTY)

CROSS, JOAN E., risk mgt. consult., St. Paul Fire and Marine Insurance Company, Cincinnati, OH '84 (RISK)
CROSS, JOANNE A., RN, dir. med. and surg. nrsg., Memorial Hospital, South Bend, IN '86 (NURS)
CROSS, KAREN D., asst. to vice-pres.-advancement and commun. rel., Catherine McAuley Health Center, Ann Arbor, MI '86 (PR) (PLNG)
CROSS, RALPH E. JR., Maxicare North Texas, Dallas, TX '75
CROSS, ROBERT T., dir. commun. health, Louis A. Weiss Memorial Hospital, Chicago, IL '69 (SOC)
CROSS, RUTH R., RN, dir. nrsg., Holden Hospital, Holden, MA '75 (NURS)
CROSSIN, WILLIAM J. JR., asst. vice-pres. human res., Wilkes-Barre General Hospital, Wilkes-Barre, PA '81 (PERS)
CROSSLAND, STEPHEN MICHAEL, chief biomedical elec. tech., St. Luke's Hospital, Jacksonville, FL '79 (ENG)
CROSSMAN, PATRICIA, risk mgr., St. Luke's Episcopal Hospital, Houston, TX '86 (RISK)
CROSSON, MARGARET W., dir. vol. and pat. serv., Roanoke Memorial Hospitals, Roanoke, VA '79 (VOL)(PAT)
CROSWELL, MICHAEL T., prin., Keyplan, St. Petersburg, FL '85
CROTHALL, GRAEME A., Quornden Services, Inc., New Castle, DE '75
CROTTY, BETTY O., sr. mgr., Ernst and Whinney, Dallas, TX '86 (MGMT)
CROTTY, E. WILLIAM, atty., Halifax Hospital Medical Center, Daytona Beach, FL '81 (ATTY)
CROUCH, EDWARD C., atty., Greater Cleveland Hospital Association, Cleveland, OH '72 (ATTY)
CROUCH, JERRY D., supt. plant, Goddard Memorial Hospital, Stoughton, MA '72 (ENG)
CROUCH, LINDEN, RN, discharge planner, Ashland Community Hospital, Ashland, OR '85 (SOC)
CROUSE-WILKINSON, DIANE, risk mgt. analyst, Georgetown University Medical Center, Washington, DC '87 (RISK)
CROUSE, EDWARD F., vice-pres. human res., Jeanes Health System, Jenkintown, PA '83 (PERS)
CROUSE, JAMES G., dir. matl. mgt., Union Hospital of Cecil County, Elkton, MD '77 (PUR)
CROUSE, MARY M., dir. plng., Berrien General Hospital, Berrien Center, MI '84 (PLNG)
CROUSE, PHYLLIS E., RN, vice-pres. and dir. nrsg. serv., Mary Greeley Medical Center, Ames, IA '71 (NURS)(MGMT)
CROW, GREGORY L., asst. adm. nrsg., Peralta Hospital, Oakland, CA '85 (NURS)
CROW, SHIRLEY, supv. cent. sup., West Orange Memorial Hospital, Winter Garden, FL '78 (CS)
CROWDER, ETHEL M., (ret.), Chicago, IL '69 (FOOD)
CROWDER, KEN, dir. mktg. and pub. rel., Norton Community Hospital, Norton, VA '86 (PR) (PLNG)
CROWDER, ROBERT S., assoc. adm., King Khaled Eye Specialist Hospital, Riyadh, Saudi Arabia '67
CROWDER, ROBERT V. III, asst. exec. dir., Virginia Baptist Hospital, Lynchburg, VA '80 (PLNG)
CROWE, LESLIE, mgr. cent. sup., Southwest Community Health System, Middleburg Heights, OH '80 (CS)
CROWE, STEPHEN B., dir. soc. serv., Indian Path Hospital, Kingsport, TN '85 (SOC)
CROWE, SUZANNE, asst. adm., Suny Health Sciences Center at Syracuse, Syracuse, NY '85 (RISK)
CROWE, THOMAS, mgr. cent. sup., Community General Hospital of Sullivan County, Harris, NY '83 (CS)
CROWELL, BARBARA A., RN, actg. dir. nrsg., Missouri Delta Medical Center, Sikeston, MO '84 (NURS)
CROWELL, BARBARA A., supv. cent. serv., St. Francis Regional Medical Center, Wichita, KS '81 (CS)
CROWELL, EDWARD J., atty., Roger Williams General Hospital, Providence, RI '81 (ATTY)
CROWELL, ERIC THOMAS, vice-pres., Franciscan Medical Center, Rock Island, IL '80
CROWELL, KENNETH WAYNE, dir. matl. mgt., Nashville Memorial Hospital, Madison, TN '81 (PUR)
CROWELL, LARRY A., pres. and chief exec. off., Pottstown Memorial Medical Center, Pottstown, PA '84
CROWELL, THOMAS W., mgr., Touche Ross and Company, San Francisco, CA '81 (PUR)
CROWLEY, ARTHUR R., dir. phys. plant and grds., Foster G. McGaw Hospital, Loyola University of Chicago, Maywood, IL '82 (ENG)
CROWLEY, CHARLOTTE C., asst. dir. pub. rel., Elizabeth General Medical Center, Elizabeth, NJ '86 (PR)
CROWLEY, EDWARD, supt. plant, Carbon County Home for the Aged, Weatherly, PA '77 (ENG)
CROWLEY, JEAN, RN, vice-pres. nrsg., Highland Hospital of Rochester, Rochester, NY '79 (NURS)
CROWLEY, JOHN J., adm. eng., St. John's Hospital, Lowell, MA '75 (ENG)
CROWLEY, JOSEPH F., dir. pub. affairs, New Britain General Hospital, New Britain, CT '82 (PR)
CROWLEY, KENNETH R., exec. vice-pres., Maryland Hospital Laundry, Baltimore, MD '81
CROWLEY, LAURETTA, dir. telecommun., North Shore University Hospital, Manhasset, NY '86 (ENG)
CROWLEY, NEAL A., atty., St. Anne's Hospital, Chicago, IL '86 (ATTY)
CROWLEY, THOMAS J. JR., mgr., Ernst and Whinney, Baltimore, MD '71 (MGMT)
CROWLEY, TIMOTHY J., adm., Salida Hospital, Salida, CO '86
CROWN, NAOMI G., RN, dir. cent. serv., Palo Duro Hospital, Canyon, TX '74 (CS)
CROXTON, HARDY W., atty., St. Mary-Rogers Memorial Hospital, Rogers, AR '86 (ATTY)
CROZIER, ELMER LEWIS, (ret.), Louisa, KY '46 (LIFE)
CRUDEN, JAMES E., dir. qual. assur. and mgt. serv., CHI Systems, Inc., Ann Arbor, MI '83 (MGMT)
CRUISE, DONALD J., mgr. food prod. and qual. assur., ARA Services, Hospital Food Management, Environmental Service, Inc., Philadelphia, PA '77 (FOOD)
CRUISE, PETER L., dir., Coastal Surgical Care, Stuart, FL '84 (MGMT)
CRUIT, ROSEMARY R., dir. pub. rel., Inter-Community Medical Center, Covina, CA '83 (PR)
CRUM, CHARLES D., supv. clin. biomedical equip. tech., Durham County General Hospital, Durham, NC '85 (ENG)
CRUM, CLARK A., vice-pres. plng. and mgt. serv., North Dakota Hospital Association, Grand Forks, ND '81 (PLNG)
CRUM, FRANK O., RN, dir. nrsg., Alaska Psychiatric Institute, Anchorage, AK '83 (NURS)
CRUMLING, CHARLES ALEXANDER, dir. matl. mgt., Morton F. Plant Hospital, Clearwater, FL '68 (PUR)
CRUMP, DOROTHY J., dir. diet. serv., Friendship Village of Columbus, Columbus, OH '86 (FOOD)
CRUMP, JOHN, dir. pub. rel. and dev., Grady Memorial Hospital, Chickasha, OK '84 (PR)
CRUMP, MARGIE W., dir. vol. and commun. serv., Lincoln County Hospital, Lincolnton, NC '81 (VOL)
CRUMP, MAUREEN R., mktg. analyst, St. Mary Medical Center, Gary, IN '87 (PLNG)
CRUMP, PHILIP L., RN, dir. nrsg., King's Daughters' Hospital, Staunton, VA '74 (NURS)
CRUMP, ROBERT A., res. eng., University of Alabama in Birmingham, Birmingham, AL '81 (ENG)
CRUMP, ROBERT J., atty., Deaconess Hospital of Cleveland, Cleveland, OH '78 (ATTY)
CRUMPTON, CHARLES T., asst. vice-pres., Hospital Corporation of America, Nashville, TN '74 (MGMT)
CRUMRINE, CATHY R., soc. worker, Providence-St. Margaret Center, Kansas City, KS '87 (SOC)
CRUNKLETON, MARIE A., adm. asst., Church Hospital Corporation, Baltimore, MD '80 (RISK)
CRUSE, JANET L., dir. food serv., Wabash General Hospital District, Mount Carmel, IL '81 (FOOD)
CRUSEY, LINDA C., mgr. emp., Wilson Memorial Hospital, Sidney, OH '82 (PERS)
CRUTCHER, DAN, dir. biomedical elec., St. John's Regional Medical Center, Joplin, MO '85 (ENG)
CRUTCHER, STEPHEN L., exec. hskpg., Parkside Manor, Wenatchee, WA '87 (ENVIRON)
CRUTE, EDNA G., dir. vol. serv., DePaul Hospital, Norfolk, VA '68 (VOL)
CRUTE, RONALD E., mgr. maint., Sacred Heart-St. Mary's Hospitals, Rhinelander, WI '83 (ENG)
CRUTHIS, ROSELYN R., dir. pub. rel., Saratoga Community Hospital, Detroit, MI '81 (PR)
CRUZ-TORRES, ZORAIDA, atty., Hospital San Pablo, Bayamon, P.R. '87 (RISK)
CRUZ, JUDITH A., RN, actg. dir. emer. nrsg., Rhode Island Hospital, Providence, RI '87 (AMB)
CRUZ, PEDRO C., mgr. hosp. facil. and maint., Guam Memorial Hospital Authority, Tamuning, Guam '86 (ENG)
CRUZ, REINERIO P., head elec., Smith, Korach, Hayet and Haynie, Miami, FL '81 (ENG)
CRYSTAL, JULES I., atty., Chicago Osteopathic Medical Center, Chicago, IL '80 (ATTY)
CSATARI, THOMAS C., atty., Methodist Medical Center, Dallas, TX '85 (ATTY)
CSOTTY, STEPHEN R., dir. pers., Martin Memorial Hospital, Stuart, FL '82 (PERS)
CUBBLER, COL. CHARLES A., sr. vice-pres., Health Care Network, Inc., Falls Church, VA '49 (LIFE)
CUBER, MARILYN D., asst. mgr., MacNeal Hospital, Berwyn, IL '86 (FOOD)
CUCCI, EDWARD A., exec. vice-pres., Swedish Covenant Hospital, Chicago, IL '75
CUCURELLO, SUELLEN M., dir. food serv., Overlook Hospital, Summit, NJ '86 (FOOD)
CUDDY, RAYMOND, dir. plant eng., Armstrong County Memorial Hospital, Kittanning, PA '80 (ENG)
CUDNEY, BARBARA J., dir. med. soc. work, Arnold Gregory Memorial Hospital, Albion, NY '86 (SOC)
CUERVO, JORGE, coor. new bus. dev., Cedars Medical Center, Miami, FL '85
CUFFE, ROBIN J., RN, coor. cardiovascular health prog., Arlington Hospital, Arlington, VA '85 (EDUC)
CUFFIA, MINNIE F., soc. worker, Community Memorial Hospital, South Hill, VA '78 (SOC)
CULBERT, FREDERICK JOSEPH, mgr. pers. adm., Rochester General Hospital, Rochester, NY '81 (PERS)
CULBERTSON, LERRYN, RN, dir. clin. nrsg. days, Self Memorial Hospital, Greenwood, SC '86 (RISK)
CULBERTSON, RICHARD A., adm., Kaiser Foundation Hospital, Los Angeles, CA '73
CULBERTSON, RONALD D., dir. emp. rel., Grossmont District Hospital, La Mesa, CA '80 (PERS)
CULBRETH, WILLIAM, Bellville General Hospital, Bellville, TX '78 (ENG)
CULHANE, GERALD C., dir. pers., W. A. Foote Memorial Hospital, Jackson, MI '72 (PERS)
CULKIN, F. HOSMER, atty., Oswego Hospital, Oswego, NY '80 (ATTY)
CULLEN, BENJAMIN THOMAS JR., assoc. dean, School of Allied Health Professions, Virginia Commonwealth University, Richmond, VA '72
CULLEN, BETH SITTRE, consult., Beth Sittre Cullen and Associates, San Antonio, TX '86 (PAT)
CULLEN, ROSE MINNICK, consult., Children's Rehabilitation Hospital, Philadelphia, PA '49 (LIFE)
CULLEN, THOMAS P., coor. arch., Hospital of Saint Raphael, New Haven, CT '85 (ENG)
CULLER, GAIL S., dir. pers., Medical Park Hospital, Winston-Salem, NC '86 (PERS)
CULLIMORE, DON, asst. dir. plant oper., Resurrection Hospital, Chicago, IL '85
CULLINANE, JOHN S., atty., Chicago Osteopathic Medical Center, Chicago, IL '81 (ATTY)
CULLINS, WINIFRED A., dir. soc. serv., McLeod Regional Medical Center, Florence, SC '71 (SOC)
CULLISON, JUDITH A., vice-pres. res. and plng., South Carolina Hospital Association, West Columbia, SC '86 (PLNG)
CULLIVER, SANDRA A., dir. pers., AMI National Park Medical Center, Hot Springs, AR '75 (PERS)
CULLMAN, LENORE M., RN, assoc. adm. pat. care serv., Charter Suburban Hospital, Paramount, CA '74 (NURS)
CULLY, CHRISTOPHER P., dir. eng. serv., Williamsport Hospital and Medical Center, Williamsport, PA '80 (ENG)
CULMER, JUDITH, pat. rep., Orthopaedic Hospital, Los Angeles, CA '80 (PAT)
CULOTTA, JOHN F., dir. info., St. Marys Hospital Medical Center, Madison, WI '81 (MGMT)
CULP, JOSEPH W., dir. eng. and maint., Mercy Hospital, Charlotte, NC '85 (ENG)
CULP, KERRY E., dir. soc. work, University of Tennessee Medical Center, Memphis, TN '75 (SOC)
CULP, LARRY L., dir. matl. mgt. syst., Harris Methodist Health System, Fort Worth, TX '84 (PUR)
CULP, LINDA H., dir. med. staff serv., St. Joseph's Hospital, Parkersburg, WV '80 (RISK)
CULPEPPER, GREG, mktg. intern, White Memorial Medical Center, Los Angeles, CA '86 (PR)
CULPEPPER, REATHER D., supv. cent. sup. serv., Kennestone Hospital, Marietta, GA '72 (CS)
CULPS, DOROTHY, mgr. commun., Saint Joseph Hospital, Fort Worth, TX '84 (ENG)
CULTICE, R. DONALD, atty., Bethesda Hospital, Zanesville, OH '73 (ATTY)
CULVER, JOHN P., mgr. qual. assur. and risk mgr., St. John's Hospital, Longview, WA '81 (RISK)
CULVER, LESSIE, pur. agt., Piggott Community Hospital, Piggott, AR '86 (PUR)
CULVER, VANESSA CAROL, pat. rep., Sylacauga Hospital, Sylacauga, AL '82 (PAT)
CUMMING, AL, dir. pers., Seton Medical Center, Austin, TX '76 (MGMT)(PERS)
CUMMING, GORDON R., actg. exec. dir., California Health Facilities Commission, Sacramento, CA '73 (LIFE)
CUMMINGS, BOBBY D., assoc. dir. pur., University of Alabama Hospital, Birmingham, AL '84 (PUR)
CUMMINGS, CLAUDIA T., dir. food and diet. serv., Wilkes General Hospital, North Wilkesboro, NC '86 (FOOD)
CUMMINGS, DEBORAH A., asst. dir. soc. work, McLaren General Hospital, Flint, MI '86 (SOC)
CUMMINGS, ELLIE, dir. mktg. and dev., Delnor Hospital, St. Charles, IL '84 (PLNG)
CUMMINGS, HELEN KING, vice-pres. reimbursement, Hospital Corporation of America, Nashville, TN '84
CUMMINGS, JAMES J., dir. pers. serv., Corning Hospital, Corning, NY '80 (PERS)
CUMMINGS, JUDY S., mgt. eng., Bethesda Hospital, Inc., Cincinnati, OH '86 (MGMT)
CUMMINGS, THOMAS E., dist. vice-pres., Hospital Corporation of America Management Company, Newton, MA '63
CUMMINGS, TILDEN, Chicago, IL '59 (LIFE)
CUMMINS, ANN R., dir. diet. serv., Greenville Hospital, Jersey City, NJ '81 (FOOD)
CUMMINS, GARY J., mgr., University of Missouri Hospital and Clinics, Columbia, MO '86 (EDUC)
CUMMINS, JOAN, RN, dir. nrsg. serv., HCA West Side Hospital, Nashville, TN '81 (NURS)
CUMMINS, MARTHA CAROLYN, dir. vol. serv. and pat. rep., Doctors Hospital of Jefferson, Metairie, LA '86 (VOL)
CUMMINS, RICHARD S., dir. emp. rel., Reynolds Memorial Hospital, Glen Dale, WV '80 (PERS)
CUMMINS, ROBERT F., Vero Beach, FL '68
CUMMINS, WILLIAM H., vice-pres. human res., Western Reserve Care System, Youngstown, OH '85 (PERS)
CUNEO, ANTHONY J., mgr. soc. serv. and qual. assur., Deaconess Hospital, St. Louis, MO '73 (SOC)
CUNEO, JOHN ANDREW, exec. dir., Parkway Hospital, Forest Hills, NY '54 (LIFE)
CUNNING, JANICE E., dir. soc. work, St. Peter's Medical Center, New Brunswick, NJ '78 (SOC)
CUNNINGHAM, ALAN J., mgr. pur., Amsterdam Memorial Hospital, Amsterdam, NY '86 (PUR)
CUNNINGHAM, BRIAN A., biomedical eng., Resurrection Hospital, Chicago, IL '84 (ENG)
CUNNINGHAM, CAROL, dir. surg. nrsg. serv., Meriter Hospital, Madison, WI '87 (AMB)
CUNNINGHAM, CHERRY L., RN, dir. nrsg., Texoma Medical Center, Denison, TX '85 (NURS)
CUNNINGHAM, CYNTHIA, dir. nutr. serv., Children's Medical Center of Dallas, Dallas, TX '86 (FOOD)
CUNNINGHAM, D. RIGNEY, dir. pub. rel. and mktg., Newton-Wellesley Hospital, Newton, MA '84 (PR)
CUNNINGHAM, DANIEL PATRICK, atty., Akron General Medical Center, Akron, OH '82 (ATTY)
CUNNINGHAM, DENEICE, dir. commun. rel., Edmond Memorial Hospital, Edmond, OK '86 (PR)
CUNNINGHAM, DIANE, dir. commun. educ., St. Mark's Hospital, Salt Lake City, UT '82 (EDUC)
CUNNINGHAM, EDWARD J., atty., Memorial Medical Center, Springfield, IL '77 (ATTY)
CUNNINGHAM, HEIDI, RN, coor. qual. assur., Veterans Administration, San Francisco, CA '86 (RISK)
CUNNINGHAM, JOHN J., coor. pers., Healthcare Services Group, Inc., Huntingdon Valley, PA '86 (PERS)
CUNNINGHAM, JOHN M., dir. soc. serv., Sacred Heart Hospital, Eau Claire, WI '70 (SOC)
CUNNINGHAM, JOY V., atty., F. G. McGaw Hospital, Loyola University, Maywood, IL '86 (ATTY)
CUNNINGHAM, JOYCE V., health care and safety consult., Marsh and McLennan, Cedar Knolls, NJ '81 (RISK)
CUNNINGHAM, LYDA S., RN, vice-pres. nrsg. serv., Dover General Hospital and Medical Center, Dover, NJ '82 (NURS)
CUNNINGHAM, LYNNE, pres., Cunningham Associates, Sacramento, CA '78 (PR)
CUNNINGHAM, M. LOYD, dir. computer serv., Compucare, Tampa, FL '75
CUNNINGHAM, MARILYN, RN, vice-pres. pat. care serv., Memorial Hospital of Dodge County, Fremont, NE '80 (NURS)
CUNNINGHAM, MARSHA L., RN, assoc. exec. dir. nrsg., Humana Hospital -Tacoma, Tacoma, WA '84 (NURS)

CUNNINGHAM, MICHAEL F., acct. exec. tech. prod., Insurance Management Services, Cleveland, OH '85 (ENG)
CUNNINGHAM, MICHAEL, student, University of Pennsylvania, Philadelphia, PA '85 (RISK)
CUNNINGHAM, PATRICIA K., dir. vol. serv., Cheshire Medical Center, Keene, NH '78 (VOL)
CUNNINGHAM, PATRICIA E., RN, vice-pres. adm., Robert F. Kennedy Medical Center, Hawthorne, CA '80 (NURS)
CUNNINGHAM, PAUL, assoc. vice-pres., Arkansas Hospital Association, Little Rock, AR '80 (PLNG)
CUNNINGHAM, RIGNEY, dir. pub. rel. and mktg., Newton-Wellesley Hospital, Newton, MA '85 (PLNG)
CUNNINGHAM, ROBERT M. JR., Blue Cross and Blue Shield Association, Chicago, IL '66 (HON)
CUNNINGHAM, ROBERT WILLIAM, asst. vice-pres. plng., Memorial Medical Center, Savannah, GA '68 (PLNG)
CUNNINGHAM, SARALYN, dir. vol. serv., Bryan Memorial Hospital, Lincoln, NE '80 (VOL)
CUNNINGHAM, STEPHEN J., assoc. adm., Pocono Hospital, East Stroudsburg, PA '81 (PUR)(RISK)
CUNNINGHAM, W. B., reg. safety eng., Veterans Administration Medical Center, Waco, TX '86 (ENG)
CUNNINGHAM, WILLIAM C., MD, dir. emer., Timken Mercy Medical Center, Canton, OH '87 (AMB)
CUNNINGHAN, EILEEN, dir. spec. serv., Sunnybrook Hospital, Toronto, Ont., Canada '85 (MGMT)
CUPP, NAOMI JEAN, dir. cent. serv. proc., St. Joseph's Hospital, Parkersburg, WV '83 (CS)
CURE, KAREN G., RN, asst. adm. nrsg., Scott and White Memorial Hospital, Temple, TX '77 (NURS)
CURE, ORIN R., atty., Columbus Hospital, Great Falls, MT '74 (ATTY)
CURIEL, ANGIE B., dir. soc. serv., Spohn Kleberg Memorial Hospital, Kingsville, TX '80 (SOC)
CURL, RUBYE P., sr. buyer, Detroit Receiving Hospital, Detroit, MI '74 (PUR)
CURLEY, BETH, dir. commun., Bon Secours Hospital, Baltimore, MD '79 (ENG)
CURLEY, EDWARD F., hosp. analyst, Empire Blue Cross and Blue Shield of Greater New York, New York, NY '77
CURLEY, GERALDINE M., RN, vice-pres. nrsg. serv., La Grange Memorial Hospital, La Grange, IL '71 (NURS)
CURLEY, JAMES R., dir. maint., St. Elizabeth's Hospital of Boston, Boston, MA '83 (ENG)
CURLEY, JAMES W., vice-pres. human res., Coastal Placement, Inc., Florence, SC '70 (PERS)
CURLEY, LYSTRA A., mgr. bus. dev., Riverside Community Hospital, Riverside, CA '86 (PLNG)
CURRAN, ALAN, dir. plng. and mktg., DeKalb General Hospital, Decatur, GA '85 (PLNG)
CURRAN, CONNIE R., RN, vice-pres. nrsg., American Hospital Association, Chicago, IL '84 (NURS)
CURRAN, DENNIS C., mgr. human res., Bethesda North Hospital, Cincinnati, OH '82 (EDUC)
CURRAN, JAMES S., mgr. computer oper., University of Texas Medical Branch Hospitals, Galveston, TX '86 (MGMT)
CURRAN, LENORA J., dir. syst., Tucson Medical Center, Tucson, AZ '86 (NURS)
CURRAN, MARY LYNN, asst. vice-pres., Alexander and Alexander National Healthcare, Chicago, IL '86 (RISK)
CURRAN, VIRGINIA M., pat. adv., Oil City Area Health Center, Oil City, PA '82 (PAT)
CURRAN, WILLIAM JOHN, LLD, prof. legal medicine, Harvard School of Public Health, Boston, MA '71 (ATTY)
CURRIE, IRMA B., coor. qual. assur. and risk mgr., Bay Harbor Hospital, Harbor City, CA '83 (RISK)
CURRIE, JOHN MICHAEL, pres., Gmk-Healthcare, Columbia, SC '77
CURRIE, JOHN R., dir., Vouluntary Hospitals of America Consulting Services, Walnut Creek, CA '77 (MGMT)
CURRIE, MARGARET KIMBERLY, pat. rep., Putnam Hospital Center, Carmel, NY '86 (PAT)
CURRIE, W. A., dir. pers., Metropolitan-Calgary and Rural General Hospital, Calgary, Alta., Canada '80 (PERS)
CURRIER, DENNIS T., Ernst and Whinney, Detroit, MI '73 (PLNG)
CURRIER, DONALD L., asst. dir. human res., Toledo Hospital, Toledo, OH '80 (PERS)
CURRIER, KENNETH H., mgr. cost containment dev., Cna Insurance Companies, Chicago, IL '82
CURRIER, LLOYD R., pres., Christ Hospital, Jersey City, NJ '69
CURRIN, AMANDA J., Ambulatory Surgical Center of Danville, Danville, VA '79
CURRIN, LESLIE H., instr. educ., Merle West Medical Center, Klamath Falls, OR '86 (EDUC)
CURRY, ANDREA JEAN, coor. vol., Memorial Hospital Corporation of Topeka, Topeka, KS '84 (VOL)
CURRY, DOUGLAS L., atty., Lincoln General Hospital, Lincoln, NE '79 (ATTY)
CURRY, JAMES C., proj. arch., Lockwood Greene-Architects and Engineers, Spartanburg, SC '81
CURRY, LOU ELLA, dir. soc. serv., Hurley Medical Center, Flint, MI '79 (SOC)
CURRY, SR. MARY, guest rel. asst., St. Paul Medical Center, Dallas, TX '77 (PAT)
CURRY, PATRICIA, pat. rep., Methodist Hospital of Indiana, Indianapolis, IN '77 (PAT)
CURRY, SANDRA H., coor. staff dev., AMI Memorial Hospital of Tampa, Tampa, FL '87 (EDUC)
CURRY, WAYNE K., atty., Prince George's Hospital Center, Cheverly, MD '85 (ATTY)
CURTA, JOSEPH P., PhD, dir. pat. and family counseling, Mercy Hospital, Davenport, IA '70 (SOC)
CURTH, NICOLETTE A., mktg. spec., Good Samaritan Hospital, Downers Grove, IL '86 (PLNG)
CURTIN, DONALD E., dir. pur., Charles A. Dana Hospital of Sidney Farber Cancer Institute, Boston, MA '80 (PUR)
CURTIN, GARY M., chief eng., Resurrection Hospital, Chicago, IL '84 (ENG)
CURTIN, ZILPHA C., dir. vol. serv., Daniel Drake Memorial Hospital, Cincinnati, OH '80 (VOL)
CURTIS, ALEXANDRA, adm., Benjamin Rush Center, Syracuse, NY '86
CURTIS, ELIZABETH A., Reno, NV '83
CURTIS, HAROLD F. JR., atty., Greenville Hospital District-Citizens General Hospital, Greenville, TX '74 (ATTY)
CURTIS, HARRY C., asst. dir., Saint Vincent Hospital, Worcester, MA '57 (PUR)(LIFE)
CURTIS, JOHN, dir. staff rel., Dr. Everett Chalmers Hospital, Fredericton, N.B., Canada '75 (PERS)
CURTIS, LUCILLE H., actg. dir. vol. serv., United Hospitals Medical Center, Newark, NJ '85 (VOL)
CURTIS, MARGARET B., dir. food serv., Caldwell County Hospital, Princeton, KY '86 (FOOD)
CURTIS, MARK A., dir. pur. and stores, Henry County Memorial Hospital, New Castle, IN '84 (PUR)
CURTIS, MARY E., dir. vol. serv., San Antonio Community Hospital, Upland, CA '77 (VOL)(PR)
CURTIS, ROBERT S., exec. dir., Clara Maass Medical Center, Belleville, NJ '79
CURTIS, THOMAS B., atty., San Gabriel Valley Medical Center, San Gabriel, CA '85 (ATTY)
CURTIS, W. NORMAN, vice-pres. plng., Fort Sanders Alliance, Knoxville, TN '81 (PLNG)
CURTIS, WILLIAM G., dir. pers., Community Hospitals of Indiana, Indianapolis, IN '65 (PERS)
CURTISS, THOMAS C. JR., sr. vice-pres., F. S. James and Company, Philadelphia, PA '85 (RISK)
CUSAAC, SHIRLEY J., RN, assoc. vice-pres. nrsg., Baptist Hospital, Nashville, TN '86 (NURS)
CUSACK, JOHN, adm. pers. and labor, North Shore University Hospital, Manhasset, NY '76 (PERS)
CUSACK, WALTER, coor. telecommun. proj., Medical Area Service Corporation, Boston, MA '84 (ENG)
CUSANO, PHILIP D., pres. and chief exec. off., Stamford Hospital, Stamford, CT '71 (PLNG)
CUSCURIDA, SR. JO ANN, RN, vice-pres. nrsg. serv., St. Joseph Hospital, Chicago, IL '72 (NURS)
CUSHING, CAROLYN J., info. spec., Kennebec Valley Medical Center, Augusta, ME '86 (PR)
CUSHING, JOHN C. JR., dir. prof. serv., Aga Khan University Hospital, Karachi, Pakistan '86
CUSHMAN, CHARLES P., consult., Gonser Gerber Tinker Stuhr, Chicago, IL '84 (PR)
CUSHMAN, ORIS, RN, dir. educ., Pawating Hospital, Niles, MI '81 (EDUC)
CUSHNIE, PATRICIA B., RN, actg. dir. nrsg. serv., Medical College of Virginia Hospitals, Richmond, VA '81 (NURS)
CUSHO, WILLIAM THEODORE, dir. maint., Harrison Community Hospital, Mount Clemens, MI '86 (ENG)
CUSHSHON, LILLIE M., adm. asst. qual. assur., St. Mary's Hospital, East St. Louis, IL '81 (RISK)
CUSIMANO, MARTHA H., dir. commun. rel., St. Luke's Hospital, Bethlehem, PA '86 (PR)
CUSTER, JOHN C., Hummelstown, PA '65
CUSTIS, DONALD L., MD, Veterans Administration, Department of Medicine and Surgery, Washington, DC '82 (LIFE)
CUSTIS, REBECCA W., RN, dir. maternal, child health and emer. serv., Gwinnett Hospital System, Lawrenceville, GA '85 (NURS)
CUTCHINS, CLIFFORD A., atty., Henrico Doctor's Hospital, Richmond, VA '77 (ATTY)
CUTHBERT, GEORGIA A., pub. rel. off., St. Mark's Hospital, Salt Lake City, UT '84 (PR)
CUTHBERT, KAREN K., coor. matl. mgt., Bay Medical Center, Bay City, MI '82 (CS)
CUTHBERT, PATRICIA A., RN, asst. adm., Mercy Hospital of Johnstown, Johnstown, PA '86 (NURS)
CUTHBERTSON, JOHN, dir. eng., LDS Hospital, Salt Lake City, UT '79 (ENG)
CUTHBERTSON, ROBERT W. III, supv. cent. proc. and distrib., St. Vincent Medical Center, Los Angeles, CA '85 (CS)
CUTHRIELL, DANIEL, dir. risk mgt. and security, Louise Obici Memorial Hospital, Suffolk, VA '86 (RISK)
CUTLER, A. BUDD, atty., Mount Sinai Medical Center, Miami Beach, FL '86 (ATTY)
CUTLER, J. CHRISTOPHER, vice-pres. corp. plng., Worcester Memorial Hospital, Worcester, MA '78 (MGMT)(PLNG)
CUTLER, MARY JO, asst. dir. nutr. and food serv., Spaulding Rehabilitation Hospital, Boston, MA '86 (FOOD)
CUTLER, ROBERT M., coor. manpower control, Horizon Health Systems, Oak Park, MI '74 (MGMT)
CUTLER, STEPHEN J., dir. pers., Mount Washington Pediatric Hospital, Baltimore, MD '81 (PERS)
CUTLIP, PAUL W., corp. vice-pres. human res., Marymount Hospital, Garfield Heights, OH '70 (PERS)
CUTRONA, FRANCIS PAUL, dir. plant eng., Milford Memorial Hospital, Milford, DE '85 (ENG)
CUTSHALL, JULIA M., mgt. eng., Magee-Womens Hospital, Pittsburgh, PA '86 (MGMT)
CUTSINGER, DONALD D., dir. human res., Memorial Hospital, McPherson, KS '86 (PERS)
CUTTING, MALCOLM M., res. arch., Cleveland Clinic Hospital, Cleveland, OH '76 (PLNG)
CUZZI, LAWRENCE F., dir. soc. work, City Hospital Center at Elmhurst, Flushing, NY '81 (SOC)
CVECHKO, SUSIE, RN, supv. cent. sup. and asst. dir. nrsg., Broaddus Hospital, Philippi, WV '85 (CS)
CVETNIC, NICHOLAS I., dir. mgt. eng., Montefiore Hospital, Pittsburgh, PA '82 (MGMT)
CVIJANOVICH, ELI, vice-pres. prof. serv., Lee Hospital, Johnstown, PA '79 (PLNG)
CWIK, MARGARET E., vice-pres., Glenn, Nyhan and Associates, Rosemont, IL '84 (RISK)
CYMENT, LAWRENCE J., asst. reg. dir., Ambulatory Surgery Center, Tampa, FL '72
CYMROT, JEFFREY J., dir. plng., Carney Hospital, Boston, MA '86 (PLNG)
CYPHERT, STACEY T., Iowa City, IA '83
CYR, DOROTHY C., pat. rep., Baptist Medical Center-DeKalb, Fort Payne, AL '83 (PAT)
CYRAN, FREDRICK ANTHONY, exec. vice-pres. and chief oper. off., Memorial Hospital, Chattanooga, TN '68
CYRS, DAVID M., consult., Hansen Lind Meyer, Iowa City, IA '83
CYRUS, CHARLES H. JR., mgr. data proc. and mgt. info. syst., Nash General Hospital, Rocky Mount, NC '87 (MGMT)
CYTRON, MARVIN S., mgr. natl. acct., Du Pont Pharmaceuticals, Wilmington, DE '84
CYTRYN, DANIEL, adm. amb. care, Manhattan Eye, Ear and Throat Hospital, New York, NY '75
CZACHOWSKI, COL. ROBERT J., MSC USA, chief pers. serv. div., Department of the Army, Office of the Surgeon General, Washington, DC '83 (EDUC)
CZAJA, THERESA, supv. cent. serv., Shore Memorial Hospital, Somers Point, NJ '84 (CS)
CZAJKOWSKI, RONALD J., dir. press rel., New Jersey Hospital Association, Princeton, NJ '86 (PR)
CZAPIEWSKI, JENNIFER V., student, Program in Health Systems Management, Rush University, Chicago, IL '86
CZECH, MELANIE SUSAN, dir. nrsg., St. Francis Hospital, Blue Island, IL '86 (NURS)
CZEL, SINE W., sec. cent. sterile sup., Norwalk Hospital, Norwalk, CT '86 (PUR)(CS)
CZERWONKA, MARY ALICE, dir. pub. rel., Ramsey Clinic, St. Paul, MN '85 (PR)
CZIRAKY, MARTIN FREDERICK, asst. adm., State University Hospital, Downstate Medical Center, Brooklyn, NY '81
CZUCHRA, ELIZABETH JANE, student, College of St. Francis, Joliet, IL '84

D

D'ACIERNO, SALVATORE, asst. vice-pres., Our Lady of Lourdes Medical Center, Camden, NJ '85 (RISK)
D'ADAMO, GREGORY N., health care consult., Coopers and Lybrand, Philadelphia, PA '80
D'ADDARIO, JOSEPH P., mgr. food serv., Crouse-Irving Memorial Hospital, Syracuse, NY '85 (FOOD)
D'AGOSTINO, JAMES P., adm., Eastern New Mexico Medical Center, Roswell, NM '67
D'AGOSTINO, JANICE, dir. vol. serv. and pat. rep., Good Samaritan Hospital, Baltimore, MD '75 (VOL)(PAT)
D'AGOSTINO, RAYMOND R., atty., St. Joseph's Hospital Health Center, Syracuse, NY '83 (ATTY)
D'AGOSTINO, RUDOLPH, mgr. fin., Memorial Hospital for Cancer and Allied Diseases, New York, NY '78 (MGMT)
D'ALESSANDRO, LOUIS, dir. maint., Riddle Memorial Hospital, Media, PA '63 (ENG)
D'ALESSANDRO, MARIE, adm. asst., Clara Maass Medical Center, Belleville, NJ '68
D'ALESSANDRO, SYDNEY P., coor. pat. rep., Lee Memorial Hospital, Fort Myers, FL '85 (PAT)
D'AMARIO, MICHAEL, pat. rep., Empire Blue Cross and Blue Shield-Healthnet, Albany, NY '82 (PAT)
D'AMATO, FRANK, asst. vice-pres. info. syst., Children's Hospital of Sf, San Francisco, CA '87 (MGMT)
D'AMBROSIA, MARGARET, vice-pres. corp. dev., St. Francis Medical Center, Lynwood, CA '85 (PLNG)
D'AMBROSIO, CLARE A., dep. dir., Bayley Seton Hospital, Staten Island, NY '76 (PLNG)
D'AMBROSIO, KATHRYN M., RN, dir. nrsg., Riverside Hospital, Wilmington, DE '86 (NURS)
D'AMICO, DAVID M., audit mgr., Laventhol and Horwath, Coral Gables, FL '85
D'ANDREA, FRANK A., dir. security, safety and loss prevention, Jersey Shore Medical Center, Neptune, NJ '82 (RISK)
D'ANDREA, MICHAEL A., dir. linen serv., Greenwich Hospital, Greenwich, CT '86 (ENVIRON)
D'ANGELO-RITZ, AMELITA, dir. soc. work, Health Hill Hospital for Children, Cleveland, OH '85 (SOC)
D'AQUILA, RICHARD, vice-pres., Health Initiatives Corporation, Providence, RI '78
D'AURIA, ANTHONY J., atty., North Shore University Hospital, Manhasset, NY '79 (ATTY)
D'AURORA, G. JOHN, vice-pres. human res., Lehigh Valley Hospital Center, Allentown, PA '85 (PERS)
D'ELIA, VINCENT L., assoc. dir. corp. mktg., Riverview Medical Center, Red Bank, NJ '86 (PLNG)
D'EMILIO, LOUIS F., dir. emp. rel., Forbes Health System, Pittsburgh, PA '87 (PERS)
D'ERAMO, ANTHONY P., chm. and chief exec. off., Management Performance International, Inc., Cincinnati, OH '78 (PERS)
D'ERASMO, MARTHA J., RN, dir. clin. serv., Group Health Association, Inc., Washington, DC '85 (NURS)
D'ETTORRE, CAROL, RN, clin. dir. nrsg., Fairview General Hospital, Cleveland, OH '86 (NURS)
DA SILVA, ASSIR R., pat. rep. and dir. vol. serv., Thorek Hospital and Medical Center, Chicago, IL '86 (PAT)(VOL)
DAAKE, MARY K., dir. educ. serv., Good Samaritan Hospital, Kearney, NE '86 (EDUC)
DABBS, EUGENE W., IV, atty., AMI Griffin-Spalding Hospital, Griffin, GA '84 (ATTY)
DABIR, LIANA, student, Graduate Program in Management and Public Service, DePaul University, Chicago, IL '86 (RISK)
DABNEY, SARAH, coor. discharge plng. and soc. serv., Ivinson Memorial Hospital, Laramie, WY '86 (SOC)
DABROWSKI, PAUL C., sr. vice-pres. fin., Our Lady of Mercy Medical Center, Bronx, NY '81
DABRUSIN, SANDRA R., mgr. pers., Central General Hospital, Plainview, NY '81 (PERS)

DACEY, MICHAEL J., dir. pers. and pub. rel., Kent County Memorial Hospital, Warwick, RI '84 (PR)
DACHELET, CHRISTY Z., coor. plng., Methodist Hospital, St. Louis Park, MN '81 (PLNG)
DACHMAN, MILLICENT F., dir. pub. rel. and corp. dev., John F. Kennedy Medical Center, Chicago, IL '81 (PR)
DACK, JAMES L., adm., Boone Hospital Center, Columbia, MO '40 (LIFE)
DACSO, SHERYL T., legal counsel, Providence Hospital, Mobile, AL '84 (ATTY)
DAGENAIS, CAROLIN J., asst. mgr. matl., Royal Victoria Hospital, Montreal, Que., Canada '82 (CS)
DAGGETT, LARRY A., asst. dir. mgt. syst., Sisters of St. Joseph Health Systems of Wichita, Wichita, KS '85 (MGMT)
DAGGETT, RICHARD C., chief oper. off., Goodwin, Procter and Hoar, Boston, MA '77 (PERS)
DAHILL, KEVIN, dir. govt. and commun. rel., Presbyterian Hospital in the City of New York, New York, NY '79 (PAT)
DAHL, CAROL A., mgr. mktg., AMI Saint Joseph Hospital, Omaha, NE '83 (PR)
DAHL, CURTISS A., dir. facil., St. Alexius Medical Center, Bismarck, ND '87 (ENG)
DAHL, HANS A., adm., Rice Memorial Hospital, Willmar, MN '59
DAHL, JEFFREY S., adm., Dell Rapids Community Hospital, Dell Rapids, SD '86
DAHL, LYNNETTE M., RN, instr. pat. care educ., Baptist Medical Center, Kansas City, MO '87 (EDUC)
DAHL, OSSIE T., asst. dir. eng. and biomedical, White Plains Hospital Medical Center, White Plains, NY '85 (ENG)
DAHL, SUSAN, dir. vol. serv., Good Samaritan Community Healthcare, Puyallup, WA '80 (VOL)
DAHL, TERESA M., supv. cent. proc. and distrib., Rice Memorial Hospital, Willmar, MN '76 (CS)
DAHLEN, ALICE L., RN PhD, vice-pres. pat. serv., St. Joseph's Hospital and Health Center, Tucson, AZ '73 (NURS)
DAHLEN, GRETCHEN M., vice-pres. amb. serv., Meriter Hospital, Madison, WI '82
DAHLEN, SUSAN R., soc. worker, Lebanon Community Hospital, Lebanon, OR '86 (SOC)
DAHLKEMPER, RICHARD J., exec. vice-pres., St. Joseph's Care Group, Inc., South Bend, IN '81 (PLNG)
DAHLQUIST, CHARLES W., atty., Intermountain Health Care, Inc., Salt Lake City, UT '81 (ATTY)
DAHLSTROM, GAIL A., sr. oper. analyst, Mary Hitchcock Memorial Hospital, Hanover, NH '83 (MGMT)
DAHM, BARBARA K., dir. vol., Abraham Lincoln Memorial Hospital, Lincoln, IL '85 (VOL)
DAHMS, MARQUERITE, RN, dir. nrsg., Pico Rivera Community Hospital, Pico Rivera, CA '76 (NURS)
DAIGLE, NORMAND, dir. prof. serv., L'Industrielle-Services Techniques, Inc., Montreal, Que., Canada '79 (MGMT)
DAIGLE, OREEN, dir. maint., Northern Maine Medical Center, Fort Kent, ME '85 (ENG)
DAIGNAULT, ANDRE, dir. commun. syst., Hospital of Saint Raphael, New Haven, CT '85 (ENG)
DAIL, LINC M., dir. mktg., Lake Seminole Hospital, Seminole, FL '82 (PR)
DAILEY, BETTY L., dir. pers., Skaggs Community Hospital, Branson, MO '84 (PERS)
DAILEY, BETTY L., dir. human res. dev., Newton General Hospital, Covington, GA '64 (PERS)
DAILEY, BONNIE L., RN, dir. surg. nrsg., Hamot Medical Center, Erie, PA '85 (NURS)
DAILEY, IRENE E., asst. dir. vol. serv., Forbes Regional Health Center, Monroeville, PA '84 (VOL)
DAILEY, JANE, RN, reg. nrsg. adm., Group Health Cooperative of Puget Sound, Seattle, WA '76 (NURS)
DAILEY, JANET L., mgr. pur. and matl., Methodist Medical Center of Illinois, Peoria, IL '81 (PUR)
DAILEY, KATHRYN C., assoc. dir. pat. care, Merrithew Memorial Hospital, Martinez, CA '81 (NURS)
DAILEY, MARY S., dir. outpat serv., Providence-St. Margaret Center, Kansas City, KS '87 (AMB)
DAILEY, STEPHEN G., assoc. adm., Mercy Community Hospital, Port Jervis, NY '85
DAILY, JAMES LESTER, exec. dir., Porter Medical Center, Middlebury, VT '77 (PLNG)
DAILY, MARY ANN, asst. dir. soc. serv., Massachusetts General Hospital, Boston, MA '79 (SOC)
DAILY, NORMA, dir. cent. sup., Warner Brown Hospital, El Dorado, AR '81 (CS)
DAISEY, J. F., dir. pur., Androscoggin Valley Hospital, Berlin, NH '77 (PUR)
DAISLEY, TERENCE D., dir. staff educ., Owen Sound General and Marine Hospital, Owen Sound, Ont., Canada '83 (EDUC)
DAITCH, BOBBIE SUE, student, Fordham University, Bronx, NY '84 (MGMT)
DAJANI, AHMAD WALID K., MD, Eden Prairie Family Physicians, Eden Prairie, MN '80
DAKOPOLOS, JOHN N., chief eng., Dameron Hospital, Stockton, CA '86 (ENG)
DALANNI, DOMINICK F., dir. hskpg. serv., Alfred I. Dupont Institute, Wilmington, DE '87 (ENVIRON)
DALBA, NICHOLAS J., asst. adm. gen. serv., St. John's Regional Medical Center, Oxnard, CA '80 (ENG)
DALCERO, VERONICA, dir. soc. work, Englewood Hospital, Englewood, NJ '80 (SOC)
DALE, ERVIN B., dir. pur., Valdese General Hospital, Valdese, NC '84
DALE, LT. COL. GLYNDON A., MSC USA, exec. off., U. S. Army Dental Activity, Fort Benning, GA '78
DALE, JACQUELINE L., asst. adm., South Florida State Hospital, West Hollywood, FL '72 (PAT)
DALE, RANDY L., dir. plng., Americor Enterprises, Lansing, MI '77 (PLNG)
DALE, ROSEMARY L., RN, adm. nrsg. serv., Medical Center Hospital of Vermont, Burlington, VT '84 (NURS)
DALEY-ADAMJI, MARY, dir. oper. analysis, Rehabilitation Institute of Chicago, Chicago, IL '85
DALEY, DANIEL J., dir. matl. mgt., Meriden-Wallingford Hospital, Meriden, CT '81 (CS)
DALEY, FRANK, dir. phys. plant, Lawrence Memorial Hospital, Lawrence, KS '86 (ENG)
DALEY, FRANKLIN S. JR., mgr. plant oper., AMI Doctors' Hospital, Lanham, MD '86 (ENG)
DALEY, JOHN E., vice-pres. dev., Borgess Medical Center, Kalamazoo, MI '70 (PR)
DALINE, ANNETTE L., mgr. matl., Northern Itasca District Hospital and Convalescent and Nursing Care Unit, Bigfork, MN '79 (PUR)
DALKE, SR. PATRICIA ANN, RN, dir. staff dev., Mercy Hospital, Toledo, OH '71 (EDUC)
DALLAM, SUE, dir. vol. serv., University of Iowa Hospitals and Clinics, Iowa City, IA '81 (VOL)
DALLAVIA, LOUIS L., dir. eng., St. Mary's Medical Center, Duluth, MN '65 (ENG)
DALLERY, CARLETON, dir. soc. serv., Bryn Mawr Hospital, Bryn Mawr, PA '80 (SOC)
DALONZO, MARIANNE B., Sarasota Palms Hospital, Sarasota, FL '83 (PERS)
DALPIAZ, PATRICIA, dir. matl. control, St. Mark's Hospital, Salt Lake City, UT '77 (PUR)
DALRYMPLE, LESLIE, coor. soc. serv., Parkland Medical Center, Derry, NH '86 (SOC)
DALRYMPLE, STEPHEN T., atty., High Plains Baptist Hospital, Amarillo, TX '80 (ATTY)
DALSTON, JEPTHA WILLIAM, PhD, chief exec. off., Hermann Hospital, Houston, TX '65
DALTON, JAMES E. JR., vice-pres., Hospital Corporation of America, Arlington, TX '64
DALTON, JOHN J., pres., Health Care Business Specialist, Inc., Cranford, NJ '80
DALTON, JOHN N., atty., Henrico Doctor's Hospital, Richmond, VA '82 (ATTY)
DALTON, JOHN R., reg. dir., Charter Memorial Hospital, Santa Ana, CA '73 (ENG)
DALTON, PHILIP, vice-pres. strategic plng. and mktg., Riverside Community Hospital, Riverside, CA '83 (PLNG)
DALTON, ROBERT G., vice-pres. dev., Good Samaritan Community Healthcare, Puyallup, WA '79 (PR)
DALTON, VICTORIA L., RN, mgr. cent. sterile proc., Lawrence Hospital, Bronxville, NY '82 (CS)
DALY, CECIL F., dir. food serv., Humana Hospital -Desert Valley, Phoenix, AZ '78 (FOOD)
DALY, CHARLES ARTHUR, vice-pres., Delaware Valley Hospital Council, Philadelphia, PA '77 (PLNG)
DALY, CLARENCE W., dir. amer soc. for hosp. cent. serv. pers., American Hospital Association, Chicago, IL '81 (CS)
DALY, DENNIS S., corp. dir. mgt. serv., Fairview Community Hospitals, Minneapolis, MN '72 (MGMT)
DALY, EUGENE A., biomedical tech., Aultman Hospital, Canton, OH '83 (ENG)
DALY, HUGH F. JR., dir. soc. serv., Christ Hospital, Cincinnati, OH '71 (SOC)
DALY, JOHN M., atty., Campbell County Memorial Hospital, Gillette, WY '86 (ATTY)
DALY, KAREN, pur. agt., St. Francis Hospital, Poughkeepsie, NY '83 (PUR)
DALY, MARIANNE A., dir. soc. serv., Haverford Community Hospital, Havertown, PA '81 (SOC)
DALY, MICHAEL J., pres., Voluntary Hospitals of America, Inc., Bala Cynwyd, PA '87
DALZELL, MARGARET A., RN, dir. nrsg., Idaho Elks Rehabilitation Hospital, Boise, ID '85 (NURS)
DAMASO, CECELIA J., RN, dir. nrsg., Myers Community Hospital, Sodus, NY '85 (NURS)
DAMATO, EARL J., assoc. dir., St. Vincent's Medical Center, Staten Island, NY '73
DAMEIER, BRIAN, sr. vice-pres. mktg., Professional Research Consultants, Inc., Omaha, NE '83 (PR)
DAMEWOOD, THOMAS L., dir. environ. serv., Shawnee Mission Medical Center, Shawnee Mission, KS '86 (ENVIRON)
DAMICO, RICHARD L., mgr., Baxter Travenol Laboratories, Deerfield, IL '85 (MGMT)
DAMMERMAN, JUSTIN, coor. plant serv., Abraham Lincoln Memorial Hospital, Lincoln, IL '87 (ENG)
DAMON, JEAN, RN, asst. supt. pat. serv., Western Reserve Care System, Youngstown, OH '73 (NURS)
DAMORE, JOSEPH F., exec. vice-pres., Sisters of Mercy Health Corporation, Lansing, MI '86
DAMRON, MARY A., RN, vice-pres., St. Joseph's Hospital, Parkersburg, WV '71 (NURS)
DAMSKY, HELEN S., asst. dir., New York City Health and Hospitals Corporation, New York, NY '86 (EDUC)
DANA, BARBARA, dir. corp. dev. and commun. affairs, Hospital for Sick Children, Washington, DC '86 (PR)
DANA, KITTY HSU, dir. oper. and commun. medicine, Union Memorial Hospital, Baltimore, MD '87 (AMB)
DANA, LOOMIS G., coor. vol. serv., Southwestern Vermont Medical Center, Bennington, VT '82 (VOL)
DANA, WARREN B., dir. pub. affairs, North Hills Passavant Hospital, Pittsburgh, PA '85 (PR)
DANBURG, SANDRA, adm., Cigna Health Plans, Orange, CA '85
DANCE, GARY T., atty., Bannock Regional Medical Center, Pocatello, ID '80 (ATTY)
DANDRIDGE, THOMAS CLAY, adm., Fish Memorial Hospital at DeLand, De Land, FL '77 (RISK)(AMB)
DANE, PATRICIA J., dir. pers., Naples Community Hospital, Naples, FL '86 (PERS)
DANEHY, L. J., pres., Newark-Wayne Community Hospital, Newark, NY '71 (MGMT)
DANES, DAN C., dir. phys. plant serv., Broadlawns Medical Center, Des Moines, IA '75 (ENG)
DANFORTH, JAMES DAVIS, dir. human resources, Silver Cross Hospital, Joliet, IL '68 (PERS)
DANG, DEBORAH, RN, dir. clin. nrsg., Hospital for Women of Maryland, Baltimore, MD '86 (NURS)
DANGEL, ROBERT M., atty., Memorial Hospital of Burlington County, Mount Holly, NJ '79 (ATTY)
DANGELO, MICHAEL D., prin., Risk Strategies, Inc., Darien, CT '80 (RISK)
DANGERFIELD, DEBORAH L., student, Program in Health Service Administration, School of Health Professions, Governors State University, Park Forest South, IL '84
DANGLER, BARBARA J., RN, supv. cent. serv., Shady Grove Adventist Hospital, Rockville, MD '86 (CS)
DANHIRES, KATHLEEN ELIZABETH, lab. tech., Naval Hospital, San Diego, CA '85
DANHOF, RENEE M., dir. diet. serv., St. Joseph's Hospital, Marshfield, WI '77 (FOOD)
DANHOUSER, DAVID C., dir. matl. mgt., Freeport Memorial Hospital, Freeport, IL '83 (PUR)
DANIEL, DAVID, mgr. natl. acct., Oxford Chemicals, Inc., Atlanta, GA '87 (PUR)
DANIEL, HARVEY SYLVESTER, unit mgr., Baptist Medical Center, Columbia, SC '86 (PAT)
DANIEL, JIMMY D., chief eng., Children's Hospital of Alabama, Birmingham, AL '66 (ENG)
DANIEL, JOSEPH P. III, asst. adm., St. Anthony's Hospital, St. Petersburg, FL '81
DANIEL, JOSEPH, asst. mgr. plant oper. and maint., South Suburban Hospital, Hazel Crest, IL '84 (ENG)
DANIEL, PATRICIA BOWERS, vice-pres., Methodist Hospital, Philadelphia, PA '78 (PLNG)
DANIEL, PAUL E., comdg. off. and chief exec. off., Naval Regional Medical Clinic, Port Hueneme, CA '83
DANIEL, PRISCILLA A., RN, asst. vice-pres. clin. and ancillary serv., Western Medical Center, Santa Ana, CA '78 (NURS)
DANIEL, ROBERT O., atty., St. Luke's Methodist Hospital, Cedar Rapids, IA '68 (ATTY)
DANIEL, MAJ. RONNIE M., MSC USA, planner health facil., U. S. Army Health Facilities Planning Agency, Washington, DC '81
DANIEL, ROYAL THOMAS JR., mgr. plant oper., Wake Medical Center, Raleigh, NC '83 (ENG)
DANIEL, SUSAN M., RN, asst. adm. nrsg. syst., Kaiser Permanente, Santa Rosa, CA '83 (NURS)
DANIELD, CDR DAVID G., MSC USN, health care analyst, Naval Hospital, Okinawa, FPO Seattle, WA '85
DANIELE, THERESA, dir. soc. work, St. Vincent's Hospital, Harrison, NY '80 (SOC)
DANIELS, ANN A., assoc. dir. soc. serv., Massachusetts General Hospital, Boston, MA '84 (SOC)
DANIELS, CHANTAL PAULA, student, California State University, Long Beach, CA '83 (PLNG)
DANIELS, CHARLES, dir. pers., Sinai Hospital of Detroit, Detroit, MI '66 (PERS)
DANIELS, DUANE A., asst. exec. dir., Frick Community Health Center, Mount Pleasant, PA '85 (PR) (PLNG)
DANIELS, EDWARD B., vice-pres. mgt. serv., Gerimed of America, Inc., Denver, CO '82 (MGMT)
DANIELS, JAMES G., dir. pur., Community Medical Center, Scranton, PA '77 (PUR)
DANIELS, JOHN D., atty., St. Luke's Regional Medical Center, Sioux City, IA '85 (ATTY)
DANIELS, JOHN H., atty., St. Joseph's Hospital and Medical Center, Phoenix, AZ '82 (ATTY)
DANIELS, LAMERIAL, dir. amb. serv., Good Samaritan Hospital and Health Center, Dayton, OH '87 (AMB)
DANIELS, MARY E., mgt. consult., Methodist Hospital System, Houston, TX '86 (MGMT)
DANIELS, NANCY, dir. adm. serv., Framingham Union Hospital, Framingham, MA '86 (RISK)
DANIELS, RICHARD R., adm., Sequoia Hospital District, Redwood City, CA '69
DANIELS, RODGER LEE, vice-pres. fin., Beth Israel Hospital, Boston, MA '58
DANIELS, STEFANI, RN, asst. dir. nrsg., St. Luke's-Roosevelt Hospital Center, New York, NY '85 (NURS)
DANIELS, SYLVIA P., asst. dir. soc. serv., Magee Rehabilitation Hospital, Philadelphia, PA '82 (SOC)
DANIELS, WILLIAM J., adm., Henry County Hospital and Nursing Home, Abbeville, AL '52 (LIFE)
DANIELSON, BARBARA D., dir. matl. mgt., Indiana University Hospitals, Indianapolis, IN '85 (PUR)
DANIELSON, HARLEY J., exec. vice-pres., Walthall and Associates, Inc., Staples, MN '82 (PR)
DANIELSON, COL. JOHN JOSEPH, MSC USA, chief pat. adm., U. S. Army Health Services Command, Fort Sam Houston, TX '67
DANIELSON, NEAL E., dir. matl. mgt., Wesley Medical Center, Wichita, KS '67 (CS)
DANIELSON, WORRELL M., mgr. plant serv., St. John Hospital, Detroit, MI '81 (ENG)
DANIHEL, JANE B., risk mgr., Chestnut Hill Hospital, Philadelphia, PA '82 (RISK)
DANIHER, FRANCES ANDERSON, vice-pres., St. Francis Hospital, Evanston, IL '78
DANILO, JEFFREY, assoc. exec. dir. in-patient serv., Lincoln Medical and Mental Health Center, Bronx, NY '85
DANILOFF, MARIETTE F., plng. analyst, Intermountain Health Care, Inc., Salt Lake City, UT '86 (PLNG)
DANISH, ANN, asst. dir. soc. serv., Lankenau Hospital, Philadelphia, PA '79 (SOC)
DANKO, DOUGLAS, dir. amb. serv., Jameson Memorial Hospital, New Castle, PA '87 (AMB)
DANNEN, CAROL J., RN, dir. nrsg. serv., Alpena General Hospital, Alpena, MI '85 (NURS)
DANNER, JERI A., consult., Coopers and Lybrand, Boston, MA '86 (MGMT)
DANOFF, SANDRA N., sr. consult., John Short and Associates, Atlanta, GA '82 (MGMT)
DANSEREAU, PAUL W., student, Boston University, Boston, MA '87
DANSIE, CRAIG, chief eng., Castleview Hospital, Price, UT '85 (ENG)
DANSKER, ALAN J., atty., St. Francis Hospital Center, Beech Grove, IN '86 (ATTY)

DANSKINE, ELSA, RN, dir. staff dev., Mercy Medical Center, Roseburg, OR '82 (EDUC)
DANTZLER, LORETTA A., student, Texas University, Galveston, TX '85
DANVILLE, VIRGINIA, dir. food serv., Northern Michigan Hospitals, Petoskey, MI '75 (FOOD)
DANZIG, BERNARD, dir. soc. serv., Hospital of Einstein Medical College, Bronx, NY '80 (SOC)
DANZIGER, SHARON B., dir. soc. serv. and adolescent psych. unit, HCA Shoal Creek Hospital, Austin, TX '85 (SOC)
DAPELO, GERMAINE, mgr. pers., Schick Shadel Hospital, Santa Barbara, CA '86 (PERS)
DAPPEN, JULIE M., dir. pub. rel., West Nebraska General Hospital, Scottsbluff, NE '85 (PR)
DAPRATO, ROBERT H., vice-pres., Reid Memorial Hospital, Richmond, IN '79
DAQUIOAG, FRANCIS D., contr., Kahuku Hospital, Kahuku, HI '86 (PERS)
DARBY, CAMILIA JUNE, RN, coor. nrsg. educ. and trng., Scioto Memorial Hospital, Portsmouth, OH '84 (EDUC)
DARBY, DANIEL R., sr. vice-pres. and chief oper. off., Alexandria Health Service Corporation, Alexandria, VA '69 (MGMT)(PLNG)
DARBY, DAVID T., dir. pers., Selma Medical Center, Selma, AL '86 (PERS)
DARBY, DOUGLAS E., mgr. fin. syst. support, Burroughs Health Care Services, Charlotte, NC '84 (MGMT)
DARDEN-DEBOSE, DOROTHY, asst. adm. prog. dev. and regulatory compliance, Tarrant County Hospital District, Fort Worth, TX '86
DARDEN, DAVID B., asst. vice-pres., Health East, Inc., Roanoke, VA '83
DARDY, MARY ANN, pat. rep., Richland Memorial Hospital, Columbia, SC '86 (PAT)
DARE, CAROLINE, RN, assoc. dir. and dir. nrsg., University of California Davis Medical Center, Sacramento, CA '81 (NURS)
DARE, MILTON LEE, vice-pres. dev., Methodist Hospital, Lubbock, TX '76 (PR)
DARLING, ANTHONY H., (ret.), Bow, NH '70 (PERS)
DARLING, ELLEN J., dir. educ., Worthington Regional Hospital, Worthington, MN '82 (EDUC)
DARLING, RUSSELL CHRISTIAN, asst. adm., Edmond Memorial Hospital, Edmond, OK '84
DARLING, WILLIAM DUANE, atty., Sisters of Charity, Houston, TX '78 (ATTY)
DARR, CLAUDIA W., asst. dir. food serv. and adm. serv., Presbyterian Hospital, Dallas, TX '83 (FOOD)
DARR, KURT, ScD, prof., Department of Health Care Administration, George Washington University, Washington, DC '74
DARREY, JEFFREY A., pres., Marketing Associates, Inc., Tampa, FL '86 (PR)
DARROW, JAMES L., atty., El Centro Regional Medical Center, El Centro, CA '80 (ATTY)
DAS, EULA, RN, vice-pres., Baylor University Medical Center, Dallas, TX '81 (NURS)
DASBACH, ERIK V., mgt. eng., University of Wisconsin Hospital and Clinics, Madison, WI '85 (MGMT)
DASCHER, NORMAN EDWARD JR., asst. adm., Samaritan Hospital, Troy, NY '79
DASCOLA, JOSEPH, (ret.), Greenville, MI '48 (LIFE)
DASHEVSKY, CATHERINE, RN, dir. nrsg., Rahway Hospital, Rahway, NJ '80 (NURS)
DASHIELL, LYNDA L., dir. vol. serv., Peninsula General Hospital Medical Center, Salisbury, MD '84 (VOL)
DASKAL, MARYPAT M., Falls Church, VA '85 (PR)
DASTRUP, SHIRLEE, dir. vol. serv. and pat. rep. prog., Primary Children's Medical Center, Salt Lake City, UT '73 (VOL)(PAT)
DAUBEL, COL. KARL J., MSC USA, dir. equip., U. S. Army Environmental Hygiene Agency, Aberdeen Proving Ground, MD '75 (ENG)
DAUDLIN, PAUL T., sr. assoc., Bernie Hoffmann Associates, Inc., Southfield, MI '84 (PERS)
DAUGHENBAUGH, MARILYN, pat. rep., Unity Medical Center, Fridley, MN '78 (PAT)
DAUGHERTY, DOLORES L., dir. human res., Jefferson Memorial Hospital, Crystal City, MO '80 (PERS)
DAUGHERTY, JOE B., RN, asst. adm. nrsg., Medical Center Hospital, Odessa, TX '83 (NURS)
DAUGHERTY, JUDITH K., RN PhD, Excelcare, Ligonier, PA '76 (NURS)
DAUGHERTY, JUNE W., RN, dir. nrsg., Palms West Hospital, Loxahatchee, FL '83 (NURS)
DAUGHERTY, LEONARD W., adm., Children's Hospital of the King's Daughters, Kingwood, WV '76
DAUGHERTY, MARTIN L., Philadelphia, PA '80 (PR)
DAUGHETY, HARRY D. JR., dir. matl. mgt., Valley Hospital Medical Center, Las Vegas, NV '70 (PUR)
DAUGHTREY, MARY F., dir. pub. rel., Vicksburg Medical Center, Vicksburg, MS '86 (PR)
DAUGHTRY, CHARLOTTE J., RN, dir. nrsg. serv., Middle Georgia Hospital, Macon, GA '82 (NURS)
DAULT, DOUGLAS M., dir. soc. serv., Chelsea Community Hospital, Chelsea, MI '85 (SOC)
DAUSTER, WILLIAM C., dir. pub. rel. and mktg., Kennedy Memorial Hospitals Saddle Brook, Saddle Brook, NJ '86 (PR)
DAUT, ALAN M., atty., Altoona, IA '87
DAUTH, DONNA J., RN, asst. adm., Mother Frances Hospital Regional Center, Tyler, TX '67 (RISK)
DAVANZO, JOHN P., vice-pres. adm., Winthrop-University Hospital, Mineola, NY '84 (PLNG)
DAVE, KAILASH C., PhD, dir. educ., Labette County Medical Center, Parsons, KS '75 (EDUC)
DAVENHALL, WILLIAM F., sr. vice-pres., Methodist Evangelical Hospital, Louisville, KY '79 (PR) (PLNG)
DAVENPORT, DAVID C., atty., Vancouver General Hospital, Vancouver, B.C., Canada '84 (ATTY)
DAVENPORT, GLORIA, supv. cent. sup., St. Charles General Hospital, New Orleans, LA '78 (CS)
DAVENPORT, KEN D., head constr. adm., University of Iowa Hospitals and Clinics, Iowa City, IA '85 (ENG)
DAVENPORT, YOLANDE B., dir. soc. serv., Chestnut Lodge Hospital, Rockville, MD '86 (SOC)
DAVEY, MICHAEL D., dir. plng., Alexandria Hospital, Alexandria, VA '81 (PLNG)
DAVI, RICHARD, pres., Kapiolani Medical Center for Women, Honolulu, HI '81 (LIFE)
DAVID, BEATRICE D., (ret.), Madison, WI '73 (FOOD)
DAVID, CATHERINE H., RN, asst. adm. nrsg., Biloxi Regional Medical Center, Biloxi, MS '81 (NURS)
DAVID, IRWIN T., partner, Touche Ross and Company, Washington, DC '79
DAVID, JAMES R., asst. chief soc. work serv., Walter Reed Army Medical Center, Washington, DC '86 (SOC)
DAVID, KATHRYN, risk mgr., St. Joseph Medical Center, Burbank, CA '81 (RISK)
DAVID, LEON N. JR., dir. diet. serv., Kodiak Island Hospital, Kodiak, AK '85 (FOOD)
DAVID, LLOYD A., actg. dir. plng., Harborview Medical Center, Seattle, WA '84 (PLNG)
DAVID, MARTIN F., asst. exec. dir., Hebrew Hospital for Chronic Sick, Bronx, NY '73
DAVID, PAUL, dir. matl. mgt., Navapache Hospital, Show Low, AZ '85 (PUR)
DAVID, RECY H., dir. diet. and environ. serv., Hospital Center at Orange, Orange, NJ '86 (ENVIRON)
DAVID, RESURRECCION H., dir. diet. and environ. serv., Hospital Center at Orange, Orange, NJ '77 (FOOD)
DAVID, WILLIAM B., atty., Saint Joseph Hospital, Fort Worth, TX '76 (ATTY)
DAVIDGE, KATHERINE GENEVIEVE, dir. soc. serv., Saint Francis Hospital, Tulsa, OK '85 (SOC)
DAVIDOFF, AMY J., plng. and mktg. analyst, Children's Memorial Hospital, Chicago, IL '85 (PLNG)
DAVIDOW, BRUCE B., assoc. adm., St. John's Episcopal Hospital, Far Rockaway, NY '77
DAVIDSEN, ALBERT O., (ret.), Delray Beach, FL '43 (LIFE)
DAVIDSON, ALAN ROBERT, asst. adm., Chippenham Hospital, Richmond, VA '80
DAVIDSON, BETTY B., dir. vol. serv., James M. Jackson Memorial Hospital, Miami, FL '84 (VOL)
DAVIDSON, BRUCE N., student, University of California at Los Angeles Center for Health Policy Study, Division of Health Service Management, Los Angeles, CA '85 (PLNG)
DAVIDSON, DEREK G., asst. vice-pres., Intercare Health Systems, Edison, NJ '83 (PLNG)
DAVIDSON, DONNA A., dir. vol. serv., Valley Regional Hospital, Claremont, NH '86 (VOL)
DAVIDSON, DONNA R., RN, asst. adm., Northside Presbyterian Hospital, Albuquerque, NM '80 (NURS)
DAVIDSON, G. CLARK, vice-pres. plant oper., St. Francis Hospital, Charleston, WV '75 (ENG)
DAVIDSON, GREGG A., dir. plng. and mktg., Skagit Valley Hospital and Health Center, Mount Vernon, WA '83 (PLNG)
DAVIDSON, JOAN K., dir. human res., Metaplex, Inc., Red Bank, NJ '86 (PERS)
DAVIDSON, JOHN B., asst. dir. pub. rel., Suburban Hospital, Bethesda, MD '85 (PR)
DAVIDSON, JOHN L. JR., atty., Barnes Hospital, St. Louis, MO '68 (ATTY)
DAVIDSON, LORRAINE I., dir. vol. serv., Torrance Memorial Hospital Medical Center, Torrance, CA '68 (VOL)
DAVIDSON, LUANN, mgr. soc. serv., Lancaster-Fairfield Community Hospital, Lancaster, OH '84 (SOC)
DAVIDSON, MARGARET E., atty., St. Joseph Health Care Corporation, Albuquerque, NM '86 (ATTY)
DAVIDSON, PERRY M., sr. auditor, Hospital Corporation of America, Nashville, TN '82 (PUR)
DAVIDSON, RICHARD O., dir. eng., Guadalupe Medical Center, Carlsbad, NM '82 (ENG)
DAVIDSON, ROSLYN, pat. rep., Jewish General Hospital, Montreal, Que., Canada '85 (PAT)
DAVIDSON, SHARON S., dir. matl. mgt., Jewish Hospital, Louisville, KY '83 (PUR)
DAVIDSON, STANLEY J., atty., Ravenswood Hospital Medical Center, Chicago, IL '82 (ATTY)
DAVIDSON, STEPHANIE A., dir. util. review, St. John's Hospital, Lowell, MA '82 (RISK)
DAVIDSON, WILLIAM A., asst. adm. prof. serv., Mercy Hospital, Portsmouth, OH '82
DAVIES, ARTHUR B. III, atty., Lynchburg General-Marshall Lodge Hospitals, Lynchburg, VA '75 (ATTY)
DAVIES, DONALD A., atty., Mount Carmel Medical Center, Columbus, OH '73 (ATTY)
DAVIES, DONNA S., RN, vice-pres. pat. serv., Jameson Memorial Hospital, New Castle, PA '78 (NURS)
DAVIES, ELLEN Y., dir. mktg., pub. rel. and dev., Alice Peck Day Memorial Hospital, Lebanon, NH '86 (PR)
DAVIES, JOHN H., vice-pres. plng., mktg. and commun. rel., Our Lady of Mercy Hospital, Dyer, IN '86 (PR) (PLNG)
DAVIES, LESLIE R., dir. human res., Charter North Hospital, Anchorage, AK '86 (PERS)
DAVIES, MARIA, dir., Center Associates, Chicago, IL '82 (SOC)
DAVIES, PATRICK R., buyer, Edward Hospital, Naperville, IL '86 (PUR)
DAVIES, SUSAN DILLICK, supv. soc. work, General Hospital Center at Passaic, Passaic, NJ '84 (SOC)
DAVIGNON, ROSEMARY CONLAN, mgr. food serv., Mercy Catholic Medical Center, Fitzgerald Mercy Division, Darby, PA '68 (FOOD)
DAVILA, JOSE M., assoc. dir. med. educ., Lincoln Medical and Mental Health Center, Bronx, NY '83
DAVILA, VINCENT, dir. plant oper., Saint James Hospital, Newark, NJ '86 (ENG)
DAVIO, ELEANOR L., RN, dir. educ. and res., Providence Hospital, Holyoke, MA '86 (NURS)
DAVIS-MINTUN, MARGARET, dir. soc. serv., St. Vincent Hospital and Health Center, Indianapolis, IN '84 (SOC)
DAVIS, A. B. JR., pres., Wesley Medical Center, Wichita, KS '76
DAVIS, AARON T., risk mgr., Veterans Administration Medical Center, Chillicothe, OH '86 (RISK)
DAVIS, AL JR., dir. corp. matl., Fhp, Inc., Fountain Valley, CA '81 (PUR)
DAVIS, ALAN G., dir. mktg. and commun., HCA Gulf Coast Hospital, Panama City, FL '86 (PLNG)
DAVIS, ANDREW H. JR., atty., Emma Pendleton Bradley Hospital, Riverside, RI '78 (ATTY)
DAVIS, ANN D., dir. educ. serv. and mktg., Moore Regional Hospital, Pinehurst, NC '75 (EDUC)(PLNG)
DAVIS, ANN L., RN, dir. pat. care serv., Finley Hospital, Dubuque, IA '86 (NURS)
DAVIS, ANN L., RN, asst. adm., Trinity Lutheran Hospital, Kansas City, MO '85 (NURS)(AMB)
DAVIS, ANN M., dir. vol. serv., Bon Secours Hospital, North Miami, FL '86 (VOL)
DAVIS, BARBARA J., dir. educ., Franklin Regional Medical Center, Franklin, PA '85 (EDUC)
DAVIS, BELINDA A., asst. dir. pub. rel., DePaul Health Center, Bridgeton, MO '86 (PR)
DAVIS, BETTY H., dir. pub. rel. and vol. serv., Thunderbird Samaritan Hospital, Glendale, AZ '77 (VOL)
DAVIS, BEVERLY G., dir. mktg. and pub. rel., Warren Regional Hospital, McMinnville, TN '86 (PR)
DAVIS, BRENDA R., PhD, dir. health educ., Northwestern Memorial Hospital, Chicago, IL '86
DAVIS, BRIAN W., asst. vice-pres. health serv., Comprehensive Health Service of Detroit, Inc., Detroit, MI '66 (MGMT)
DAVIS, BRUCE R., dir. eng. serv., Alachua General Hospital, Gainesville, FL '84 (ENG)
DAVIS, C. STEVEN, coor. plng., Hinsdale Hospital, Hinsdale, IL '83 (PLNG)
DAVIS, CARL EDWARD, dir. diet., Crozer-Chester Medical Center, Chester, PA '73 (FOOD)
DAVIS, CARLA J., RN, dir. nrsg. serv., Craig General Hospital, Vinita, OK '81 (NURS)
DAVIS, CAROL COHEN, proj. mgr., Metropolitan Life Insurance Company, New York, NY '80
DAVIS, CAROLE D., pat. rep., McLeod Regional Medical Center, Florence, SC '86 (PAT)
DAVIS, CAROLE M., dir. vol. serv. and commun. serv., Logan Regional Hospital, Logan, UT '83 (VOL)
DAVIS, CATHY S., dir. outpatient serv., Presbyterian Hospital, Dallas, TX '82
DAVIS, CHARLES GRACIE JR., consult., Burlington, VT '55 (PLNG)(LIFE)
DAVIS, CHARLES S., adm., Dodge County Hospital, Eastman, GA '85
DAVIS, CHERYL S., adm. diet., Mercy Hospital, Council Bluffs, IA '85 (FOOD)
DAVIS, CHRISTOPHER T., student, Program in Hospital and Health Care Administration, University of Minnesota, Minneapolis, MN '84
DAVIS, CONRAD W., dir. hskpg. and linen serv., Charlton Memorial Hospital, Fall River, MA '86 (ENVIRON)
DAVIS, CRAIG G., vice-pres., Corporate Compensation Plans, Danbury, CT '86 (PERS)
DAVIS, DAVID W., pres., Placid Memorial Hospital, Lake Placid, NY '77 (PLNG)
DAVIS, DEBBIE A., dir. pur., Crittenden Memorial Hospital, West Memphis, AR '86 (PUR)
DAVIS, DENISE P., sr. acct. supv., Hill and Knowlton, Inc., Pittsburgh, PA '86 (PR)
DAVIS, DIANNE, RN, asst. dir. nrsg.-emer., Waterman Medical Center, Eustis, FL '87 (AMB)
DAVIS, DONALD M., dir. human res., St. Joseph Mercy Hospital, Pontiac, MI '86 (PERS)
DAVIS, DONALD W., pres. and chief exec. off., Hunterdon Medical Center, Flemington, NJ '68
DAVIS, DOUGLAS W., asst. mgr. food serv., Huggins Hospital, Wolfeboro, NH '84 (FOOD)
DAVIS, ELAINE CLAIRE, dir. med. soc. work, Self Memorial Hospital, Greenwood, SC '77 (SOC)
DAVIS, ELIZABETH J., mgr. syst. dev., Hamot Medical Center, Erie, PA '85 (MGMT)
DAVIS, ELIZABETH JOHNSON, supv. pat. rep., Roanoke Memorial Hospitals, Roanoke, VA '87 (PAT)
DAVIS, ELLEN M., atty., Methodist Health Systems, Inc., Memphis, TN '86 (ATTY)
DAVIS, ERASTINE W., dir. pat. serv., Chicago Osteopathic Medical Center, Chicago, IL '78 (PAT)
DAVIS, ESTELLE, dir. vol. serv., St. Barnabas Medical Center, Livingston, NJ '75 (VOL)
DAVIS, ETHEL DELORES, dir. med. soc. serv., Howard Community Hospital, Kokomo, IN '74 (SOC)
DAVIS, F. GORDON, pres., F. Gordon Davis and Associates, Roscommon, MI '49 (PR)(LIFE)
DAVIS, FRANK, head pur., Methodist Hospital of Indiana, Indianapolis, IN '83 (PUR)
DAVIS, FREDA E., RN, dir. nrsg., Howard County Memorial Hospital, Nashville, AR '86 (NURS)
DAVIS, GARY L., atty., St. Peter's Community Hospital, Helena, MT '86 (ATTY)
DAVIS, GARY THAYNE, adm. off., Jefferson County Health Department, Lakewood, CO '72
DAVIS, GEORGE W., dir. safety and security, St. Joseph Riverside Hospital, Warren, OH '84 (RISK)
DAVIS, GREGORY J., dir. biomedical eng., Driscoll Foundation Children's Hospital, Corpus Christi, TX '84 (ENG)
DAVIS, HARRY L., mgr. ldry., Nashoba Community Hospital, Ayer, MA '86 (ENVIRON)
DAVIS, JACK G., dir. plant oper., St. David's Community Hospital, Austin, TX '82 (ENG)
DAVIS, JAMES E. JR., atty., Humana Hospital -Huntsville, Huntsville, AL '83 (ATTY)
DAVIS, JAMES O., dir. eng., AMI Brownsville Medical Center, Brownsville, TX '86 (ENG)
DAVIS, JAMES R., vice-pres., Iowa Methodist Health System, Des Moines, IA '77 (PLNG)
DAVIS, JAMES S., dir. plant oper. and maint., St. Frances Cabrini Hospital, Alexandria, LA '81 (ENG)

DAVIS, JANE S., (ret.), Niles, MI '47 (LIFE)
DAVIS, JANICE M., mgr. pat. serv., Methodist Hospital-Central Unit, Memphis, TN '85 (FOOD)
DAVIS, JAYNE, RN, student, Memphis State University, School of Nursing, Memphis, TN '87 (AMB)
DAVIS, JEANNE M., dir. vol. and spec. serv., Methodist Medical Center of Illinois, Peoria, IL '85 (VOL)
DAVIS, JERI A., mgr. mktg., Charter Medical Corporation, Macon, GA '86 (PR)
DAVIS, JERRY N., dir. food serv., Fairview Park Hospital, Dublin, GA '80 (FOOD)
DAVIS, JERYL R., dir. pub. rel., Memorial Medical Center, Savannah, GA '86 (PR)
DAVIS, JIMMY C., dir. safety and security, South Georgia Medical Center, Valdosta, GA '86 (RISK)
DAVIS, JOALICE, adm. res., Dch Regional Medical Center, Tuscaloosa, AL '83
DAVIS, JOE S., eng., St. John's Hospital, Longview, WA '77 (ENG)
DAVIS, JOE, asst. adm., Kaiser Foundation Hospital, San Diego, CA '67 (ENG)
DAVIS, JOHN B., asst. adm., St. Francis Xavier Hospital, Charleston, SC '75 (PERS)
DAVIS, JOHN D., sr. vice-pres., Complete Health, Inc., Birmingham, AL '83 (PLNG)
DAVIS, JOHN PAUL, atty., Michigan Health Care Corporation, Detroit, MI '82 (ATTY)
DAVIS, JOHN, dir. maint., St. Joseph Regional Medical Center -Oklahoma, Ponca City, OK '80 (ENG)
DAVIS, JOSEPH W., mgr. proj. dev., Morrison-Knudsen Company, Inc., Boise, ID '84 (PLNG)
DAVIS, JOSEPHINE F., RN, asst. dir. matl. mgt. and sup., proc. and distrib., Cedars-Sinai Medical Center, Los Angeles, CA '81 (CS)
DAVIS, JUDY K., dir. vol. and spec. proj., HCA Brotman Medical Center, Culver City, CA '85 (VOL)
DAVIS, KAREN G., RN, asst. adm. nrsg., Children's Hospital, Norfolk, VA '86 (NURS)
DAVIS, KATHLEEN H., RN, vice-pres. nrsg. serv., McDonough District Hospital, Macomb, IL '86 (NURS)
DAVIS, KENNETH D., chief eng., Condell Memorial Hospital, Libertyville, IL '83 (ENG)
DAVIS, KENT K., mgr. food syst. and oper., St. Joseph Medical Center, Joliet, IL '77 (FOOD)
DAVIS, KURT H., dir. info. serv., Canadian Society of Laboratory Technologists, Hamilton, Ont., Canada '84 (PR)
DAVIS, LANT B., atty., Bradley, Arant, Rose and White, Birmingham, AL '85 (ATTY)
DAVIS, LAWRENCE C., Homosassa, FL '56 (LIFE)
DAVIS, LAWRENCE W., MD, chm. radiation ther., Montefiore Medical Center, Bronx, NY '84
DAVIS, LEONARD F., mgr. hskpg. serv., Peterson Hospitalal Center, Wheeling, WV '86 (ENVIRON)
DAVIS, LEONARD, sr. dir., Blue Cross of Greater Philadelphia, Philadelphia, PA '74
DAVIS, LOLA B., chief diet. serv., Veterans Administration Medical Center, Des Moines, IA '86 (FOOD)
DAVIS, LOUISE I., pat. rep., Joint Township District Memorial Hospital, St. Marys, OH '82 (PAT)
DAVIS, LYNN K., RN, clin. dir., Charlton Memorial Hospital, Fall River, MA '84 (NURS)
DAVIS, LYNN, dir. maint. and eng., St. John's Regional Health Center, Springfield, MO '85 (ENG)
DAVIS, M. SUSAN, RN, dir. nrsg. serv., St. Mary's Hospital, Sparta, WI '84 (NURS)
DAVIS, MAMIE B., nutr. consult., Florida Department of Health and Rehabilitation Services, Office of Licensure and Certification, Jacksonville, FL '77 (FOOD)
DAVIS, MANUEL, vice-pres. corp. plng. and dev., Sisters of the Sorrowful Mother-Ministry Corporation, Milwaukee, WI '77 (PLNG)
DAVIS, MARGE, exec. sec., Catherine McAuley Health Center, Ann Arbor, MI '84 (ENG)
DAVIS, MARIAN C., dir. nrsg. educ., The Arbour, Boston, MA '76 (EDUC)
DAVIS, MARIELLEN, dir. pat. rel., Hinsdale Hospital, Hinsdale, IL '86 (PAT)
DAVIS, MARITHA M., dir. soc. serv., Gilmore Memorial Hospital, Amory, MS '79 (SOC)
DAVIS, MARJORIE P., RN, sr. vice-pres., St. Mary's Hospital, Milwaukee, WI '72 (NURS)
DAVIS, MARY ELIZABETH, cent. sup. tech., Burke Rehabilitation Center, White Plains, NY '83 (CS)
DAVIS, MARY M., mgr. pers., University of Missouri Hospital and Clinics, Columbia, MO '86 (PERS)
DAVIS, SR. MARY STEPHEN, coor. fin., Presentation Convent, Aberdeen, SD '66
DAVIS, MICHELLE R., dir. pub. rel., Faulkner Hospital, Boston, MA '83 (PR)
DAVIS, MILBREW, dir. soc. serv., Baptist Memorial Hospital, San Antonio, TX '74 (SOC)
DAVIS, NANCY L., RN, dir. nrsg., CPC Coliseum Medical Center, New Orleans, LA '85 (NURS)
DAVIS, NOREEN I., RN, dir. pat. care serv., Olmsted Community Hospital, Rochester, MN '77 (NURS)
DAVIS, PAHL M., mgr., Ernst and Whinney, Charlotte, NC '84 (PLNG)
DAVIS, PATRICK B. JR., vice-pres., The Ritchie Organization, Sarasota, FL '83 (PLNG)
DAVIS, PAULA B., student, Johns Hopkins School of Hygiene and Health, Baltimore, MD '86 (PLNG)
DAVIS, PETER B., pres. and chief exec. off., St. Joseph Hospital, Nashua, NH '69
DAVIS, PETER W., dir. matl. syst., Geisinger Medical Center, Danville, PA '73 (PUR)
DAVIS, PHYLLIS A., dir. pub. rel., Sycamore Hospital, Sycamore, IL '82 (PR)
DAVIS, RAY H. JR., vice-pres. dev., Calais Regional Hospital, Calais, ME '73 (PERS)
DAVIS, RENDER S., asst. adm., Crawford Long Hospital Emory University, Atlanta, GA '80 (RISK)
DAVIS, ROBERT A., dir. res. and dev., Florida Hospital Association, Orlando, FL '81
DAVIS, ROBERT D., arch., Smith, Hinchman and Grylls Associates, Inc., Detroit, MI '85
DAVIS, ROBERT L., mgr. food serv., West Frankfort United Mine Workers of America Union Hospital, West Frankfort, IL '79 (FOOD)
DAVIS, ROBERT N., pres., Resource Development Associates, Hendersonville, TN '68 (MGMT)
DAVIS, ROBERT S. III, adm., Normandy Osteopathic Hospital-North, St. Louis, MO '76
DAVIS, RODNEY S., pres., Davis Partnership, Denver, CO '75 (PLNG)
DAVIS, RONALD LEWIS, asst. vice-pres., Jackson-Madison County General Hospital, Jackson, TN '77 (ENG)
DAVIS, ROSS L., chief eng., Pioneer Hospital, Artesia, CA '85 (ENG)
DAVIS, ROY E., dir. hosp. eng., Wayne Memorial Hospital, Goldsboro, NC '84 (ENG)
DAVIS, RUTH A., risk mgr., Southwest Community Health Services, Albuquerque, NM '86 (RISK)
DAVIS, SAMUEL, pres. and chief exec. off., Ecumed, New York, NY '58
DAVIS, SANDRA A., RN, dir. pat. care, Estelle Doheny Eye Hospital, Los Angeles, CA '86 (NURS)
DAVIS, SCOTT A., mgr. cent. serv., Mountain View Medical Center, Simi Valley, CA '85 (CS)
DAVIS, SCOTT P., Dallas, PA '83 (MGMT)
DAVIS, SHEILA K., mgr. outpatient surg., East Tennessee Baptist Hospital, Knoxville, TN '87 (AMB)
DAVIS, STEPHEN A., atty., Summersville Memorial Hospital, Summersville, WV '78 (ATTY)
DAVIS, STEPHEN, dir. hskpg., linen, printing, and mail, Sacred Heart General Hospital, Eugene, OR '86 (ENVIRON)
DAVIS, SUSAN M., dir. vol. serv., Fountain Valley Regional Hospital Medical Center, Fountain Valley, CA '83 (VOL)
DAVIS, SYDNOR I., atty., Bethesda Oak Hospital, Cincinnati, OH '77 (ATTY)
DAVIS, THERESA S., dir. nrsg. cent. serv., The Methodist Hospital, Houston, TX '77 (CS)
DAVIS, TROY, pur. agt., Pitt County Memorial Hospital, Greenville, NC '80 (PUR)
DAVIS, VALERIE, supv. matl. mgt., E. J. Noble Hospital of Alexandria, Alexandria Bay, NY '84 (PUR)
DAVIS, VICTORIA E., student, Georgia Institute of Technology, Program in Health Systems Engineering, Atlanta, GA '82 (MGMT)
DAVIS, VIRGINIA, Wilmington, DE '81
DAVIS, WALTER M., supv. pur., Imperial Point Medical Center, Fort Lauderdale, FL '82 (PUR)
DAVIS, WALTER WINN, atty., T. J. Samson Community Hospital, Glasgow, KY '74 (ATTY)
DAVIS, WAYNE, chief maint. and eng., Deaconess Hospital, Cincinnati, OH '71 (ENG)
DAVIS, WESLEY A., RN, vice-pres. nrsg., Elkhart General Hospital, Elkhart, IN '74 (NURS)
DAVIS, WILLIAM E., dir. environ. safety, Saline Memorial Hospital, Benton, AR '84 (ENG)
DAVIS, WILLIAM R. JR., atty., Chambersburg Hospital, Chambersburg, PA '73 (ATTY)
DAVIS, WILMONT E., dir. pers., Leominster Hospital, Leominster, MA '86 (PERS)
DAVISON-YORK, KATHERINE, asst. dir. pat. rep., Memorial Hospital for Cancer and Allied Diseases, New York, NY '86 (PAT)
DAVISON, BARBARA I., RN, dir. nrsg., Salem Hospital, Salem, MA '82 (NURS)
DAVISON, CHERYL L., dir. commun. rel. and fund dev., Marian Medical Center, Santa Maria, CA '84 (PR)
DAVISON, DONNA J., pat. rep., Glens Falls Hospital, Glens Falls, NY '82 (PAT)
DAVISON, JOHN A., sr. assoc. partner, Health Consortium, Inc., San Diego, CA '83
DAW, PAUL C., atty., Swedish Medical Center, Englewood, CO '83 (ATTY)
DAWES, KRIS M., dir. human res., Fred Hutchinson Cancer Research Center, Seattle, WA '83 (PERS)
DAWKINS, CAROLYN J., pur. agt., Gordon Memorial Hospital District, Gordon, NE '85 (PUR)
DAWSON, BARTON H., atty. and dir., University of South Dakota School of Medicine, Medical Services Plan, Sioux Falls, SD '73 (ATTY)(AMB)
DAWSON, CORNELIA MAE, dir. vol. serv., Western State Hospital, Staunton, VA '85 (VOL)
DAWSON, DAMOND, dir. matl. mgt., Riverside Community Hospital, Bossier City, LA '86 (PUR)
DAWSON, DAVID R., dir. matl. mgt., Mercy Hospital, Portsmouth, OH '86 (PUR)
DAWSON, EVELYN J., RN, dir. nrsg., HCA Palmyra Medical Centers, Albany, GA '82 (NURS)
DAWSON, MARGARET, dir. soc. serv., Sister Kenny Institute, Minneapolis, MN '74 (SOC)
DAWSON, PEGGY, RN, asst. adm. nrsg., Willamette Falls Hospital, Oregon City, OR '80 (NURS)
DAWSON, SUE, dir. market dev., Mercy Hospital, Urbana, IL '85 (PLNG)
DAWSON, TED E., dir. pur., Ashland Community Hospital, Ashland, OR '74 (PUR)
DAY, BOB R., dir. facil. mgt., St. Mary Medical Center, Long Beach, CA '83 (ENG)
DAY, CHARLOTTE M., RN, assoc. exec. dir. nrsg., Humana Hospital -Sun Bay, St. Petersburg, FL '82 (NURS)
DAY, DAN O., vice-pres. mktg., Healthmark, Cleveland, TN '87 (PR)
DAY, DENNIS M., PhD, dir. trng. and dev., University of Wisconsin Hospital and Clinics, Madison, WI '79 (EDUC)
DAY, EDWIN, dir. mgt. eng., St. Thomas Hospital, Nashville, TN '76 (MGMT)(PLNG)
DAY, FRAN, pat. asst. rep., Kaiser Foundation Hospital, Parma, OH '78 (PAT)
DAY, FRANK W., dir. pers., Wood County Hospital, Bowling Green, OH '85 (PERS)
DAY, GARY, plng. and mktg. consult., Billings, MT '80 (PLNG)
DAY, JACKSON H., student, Program in Health Policy and Administration, School of Public Health, University of North Carolina, Chapel Hill, NC '84 (MGMT)
DAY, JAMES M., dir. matl. mgt., Riverside Hospital, Toledo, OH '77 (PUR)
DAY, JANET L., dir. soc. work serv., St. Mary's Medical Center, Racine, WI '83 (SOC)
DAY, JOHN B., assoc. dir. gen. serv., St. Luke's Hospital of New Bedford, New Bedford, MA '77
DAY, JOHN R., atty., Shutts and Bowen, West Palm Beach, FL '68 (ATTY)
DAY, KAREN L., asst. dir. diet., Henry Ford Hospital, Detroit, MI '86 (FOOD)
DAY, LINWOOD L., adm. eng., Fort Hamilton Hospital, Hamilton, OH '70 (ENG)
DAY, LYMAN R., plant eng., Miles Memorial Hospital, Damariscotta, ME '83 (ENG)
DAY, MARGRETTA M., dir. vol., Somerset Community Hospital, Somerset, PA '83 (VOL)
DAY, SHARON MARIE, dir. guest rel., Good Samaritan Hospital and Medical Center, Portland, OR '86 (PAT)
DAY, STEVEN M., dir. mgt. eng., Desert Hospital, Palm Springs, CA '85 (MGMT)
DAY, VIRGINIA A., RN, vice-pres. pat. care, Rochester St. Mary's Hospital, Rochester, NY '86 (NURS)
DAY, W. LAWRENCE, asst. dir. psych. serv., Community General Hospital, Syracuse, NY '77
DAYE, REGINALD T., assoc. dir., Bellevue Hospital Center, New York, NY '86
DAYTON, DAVID S., pres., Hospital Efficiency Corporation, Boston, MA '84
DAYTON, JERRY V., mgr. biomedical, McDowell Hospital, Marion, NC '86 (ENG)
DAYTON, RICHARD S. JR., vice-pres. mktg., Healthwest Medical Centers, Chatsworth, CA '86 (PR) (PLNG)
DAYTON, WILLIAM, (ret.), Albany, GA '82 (ENG)
DE ANGELIS, BOBBI M., supv. cent. serv., Northside Hospital, Atlanta, GA '77 (CS)
DE BARD, SUSAN D., coor. nuclear medicine, New York Hospital, New York, NY '86
DE BLASI, IGNATIUS A., adm., Midtown Hospital, Atlanta, GA '86 (AMB)
DE CORREA, ANA E., chief diet., Centro Medico Paitilla, Panama 5, Panama '86 (FOOD)
DE DEBUCHY, ASTRID BOGEDAM, dir., Cires, Buenos Aires, Argentina '84 (ENG)
DE JESUS, MANUEL H., syst. analyst, Walter O. Boswell Memorial Hospital, Sun City, AZ '84 (MGMT)
DE JOHN, JAMES P., dir. capital equip. prog., Health Resources Institute, Los Angeles, CA '77 (PUR)
DE LANGE, JOYCE T., coor. vol., Coral Reef Hospital, Miami, FL '86 (VOL)
DE LEON, KAREN L., dir. environ., Doctors' Hospital of Montclair, Montclair, CA '86 (ENVIRON)
DE LOPEZ, SANDRA L. M., pres. vol. prog., Hospital Dr. Dominguez, Humacao, P.R. '85 (VOL)
DE LOUISA, NICHOLAS, assoc. dir. plant, maint. and eng., Goldwater Memorial Hospital, New York, NY '81 (ENG)
DE NIO, COLLYN L., vice-pres. human res., Rose Medical Center, Denver, CO '82 (EDUC)(PERS)
DE PAULIS, CARL E., dir. food serv., Lewistown Hospital, Lewistown, PA '81 (FOOD)
DE SANTIS, ALICE T., RN, chief nrsg. serv., William S. Middleton Memorial Veterans Hospital, Madison, WI '86 (NURS)
DE SHAYES, JOSEPH A. JR., pres., On Site Drapery Cleaning, Inc., Haddonfield, NJ '86 (ENVIRON)
DE SILVA, KATHERINE S., dir. pers., Tidewater Psychiatric Institute, Virginia Beach, VA '82 (PERS)
DE SPAIN, REV. WARREN E., chaplain, Methodist Hospital of Chicago, Chicago, IL '81 (PAT)
DE SYLVA, FRANK, dir. plant eng., Saint Joseph Hospital, Denver, CO '75 (ENG)
DE TATA, JAMES, facil. eng., St. Peter's Medical Center, New Brunswick, NJ '81 (ENG)
DE THOMAS, ART, adm. tech. serv., Fisher Scientific, Instrument Service Division, Pittsburgh, PA '86 (ENG)
DE TINE, BETH L., sr. consult., Robert Douglass Associates, Houston, TX '81 (PLNG)
DE VANEY, JEAN, risk mgr., Hemet Valley Hospital District, Hemet, CA '83 (RISK)
DE VIVO, PAUL F., assoc. adm., Providence Hospital, Oakland, CA '75
DE WEERD, ANNETTE M., dir. clin. support serv., Pine Rest Christian Hospital, Grand Rapids, MI '86 (NURS)
DE WITT, DONALD F., dir. soc. serv., McKay-Dee Hospital Center, Ogden, UT '76 (SOC)
DE YOUNG, DEBORAH A., dir. emp. rel., Nyack Hospital, Nyack, NY '83 (PERS)
DE-SOUZA, EDWARD, coor. pur., Dominion Hospital, Falls Church, VA '86 (PUR)
DEACON, CINDY S., discharge plng., counselor coor. and med. soc. work, Wilkes General Hospital, North Wilkesboro, NC '85 (SOC)
DEACON, J. C., atty., St. Bernard's Regional Medical Center, Jonesboro, AR '79 (ATTY)
DEAKINS, HOMER L. JR., atty., Grady Memorial Hospital, Atlanta, GA '68 (ATTY)
DEAL, GREGORY A., mgr. facil., U. S. Air Force Regional Hospital, Sheppard AFB, TX '86 (ENG)
DEAN, ANNA R., dir. pers., Falmouth Hospital, Falmouth, MA '83 (PERS)
DEAN, CHARLES V., vice-pres., St. Margaret's Hospital, Montgomery, AL '75
DEAN, CONSTANCE, adm. coor., Passavant Area Hospital, Jacksonville, IL '84 (RISK)
DEAN, ED, dir. maint., St. Joseph's Hospital and Health Center, Paris, TX '86 (ENG)
DEAN, ERIC WILLIAM JR., vice-pres. human res., St. Clair Memorial Hospital, Pittsburgh, PA '86 (PERS)
DEAN, HELEN, RN, mgr. cent. serv., Good Samaritan Hospital, Corvallis, OR '80 (CS)

DEAN, JAMES N., mgr. cent. serv., Palomar Memorial Hospital, Escondido, CA '83 (CS)
DEAN, JENNIFER M., mgr. food prod., University of Texas M. D. Anderson Hospital and Tumor Institute at Houston, Houston, TX '84 (FOOD)
DEAN, KATHY A., chief diet., St. Louis Regional Medical Center, St. Louis, MO '77 (FOOD)
DEAN, MARILYN M., vice-pres. plng. and mktg., Arlington Hospital, Arlington, VA '86 (PLNG)
DEAN, MARY L., vice-pres. mktg. and plng., Valley Children's Hospital, Fresno, CA '84 (PR)
DEAN, MICHAEL R., dir. matl. mgt., Castleview Hospital, Price, UT '82 (PUR)
DEAN, PATRICIA R., RN, dir. nrsg., Coronado Hospital, Coronado, CA '86 (NURS)
DEAN, PAULA P., vice-pres. and dir. human res., Green Hospital of Scripps Clinic, La Jolla, CA '84 (PERS)
DEAN, SANDI, dir. safety and chairperson, Grinnell General Hospital, Grinnell, IA '86 (RISK)
DEAN, SANDRA L., dir. pers., Grinnell General Hospital, Grinnell, IA '81 (PERS)
DEANE, PEGGY G., RN, vice-pres., Anderson Memorial Hospital, Anderson, SC '74 (NURS)
DEANER, KATE I., mktg. spec., Perry Memorial Hospital, Princeton, IL '86 (PR)
DEANGELIS, MICHAEL J., vice-pres. human res., Baystate Medical Center, Springfield, MA '74 (PERS)
DEANGELIS, SALVATORE J., dir. food serv., Worcester Hahnemann Hospital, Worcester, MA '74 (FOOD)
DEANS-HUMS, JO ANNE, RN, clin. dir. emer. serv., Moses H. Cone Memorial Hospital, Greensboro, NC '86 (NURS)
DEARBORN, MICHELE Z., coor. pat. rel., Overlook Hospital, Summit, NJ '87 (PAT)
DEAREN, DAN L., EdD, pres., Samaritan Medical Foundation, Phoenix, AZ '78
DEARING, RUTHIE H., pres., Dearing and Associates, Spokane, WA '85 (PR) (PLNG)
DEARY, LAWRENCE A., vice-pres. human res., Providence Hospital, Southfield, MI '81 (PERS)
DEASE, ONEITA, dir. environ. serv., Forsyth Memorial Hospital, Winston-Salem, NC '86 (ENVIRON)
DEATER, GARY A., asst. adm., Witham Memorial Hospital, Lebanon, IN '86 (PERS)
DEATER, RALPH E., vice-pres., Alexander and Alexander, Inc., St. Louis, MO '83 (RISK)
DEATHERAGE, JAMES W., atty., Irving Community Hospital, Irving, TX '76 (ATTY)
DEATON, KAY, dir. telecommun., Baptist Medical Center, Jacksonville, FL '86 (ENG)
DEATON, MARK D., atty., Illinois Hospital Association, Naperville, IL '85 (ATTY)
DEATON, MARSHA A., RN, dir. women's serv., Harris Methodist -Fort Worth, Fort Worth, TX '86 (NURS)
DEATS, JOHN R., dir. pub. info., New York University Medical Center, New York, NY '81 (PR)
DEBACKER, ROBERT E., assoc. adm., Schumpert Medical Center, Shreveport, LA '65
DEBAKEY, MICHAEL ELLIS, MD, pres., Baylor College of Medicine, Houston, TX '65 (HON)
DEBCZAK, LUCY, pat. advocate, Henry Ford Hospital, Detroit, MI '86 (PAT)
DEBELLE, DIANNE, dir. risk mgt., Methodist Hospital of Chicago, Chicago, IL '87 (RISK)
DEBELS, CARYOL J., dir. pers., Sacred Heart Hospital, Tomahawk, WI '74 (PERS)
DEBENHAM, BERNADETTA M., Morton County Hospital, Elkhart, KS '81 (PERS)
DEBIAISE-DIETE, RENEE G., oper. analyst, Henry Ford Hospital, Detroit, MI '86 (MGMT)
DEBIASE, CAROL A., RN, vice-pres. pat. care serv., St. Mary-Corwin Hospital Center, Pueblo, CO '82 (NURS)
DEBIASI, PATRICIA, student, Program in Hospital and Health Service Management, Kellogg Graduate School of Management, Northwestern University, Evanston, IL '84 (PLNG)
DEBOLT, ELLICE G., coor. mktg. and commun., Emanuel Medical Center, Turlock, CA '86 (PR)
DEBONNY, MARTHA A., dir. vol. serv., Providence Medical Center, Portland, OR '85 (VOL)
DEBORD, JUDITH O., asst. dir. vol. serv., Hartford Hospital, Hartford, CT '86 (VOL)
DEBORDE, FRED J., chief eng., St. Joseph's Hospital, Savannah, GA '75 (ENG)
DEBROSKY, LEO P., chief maint., Dobbs Ferry Hospital, Dobbs Ferry, NY '75 (ENG)
DEBRUEYS, JAMES W., dir. sup., proc. and distrib., Ochsner Foundation Hospital, New Orleans, LA '83 (CS)
DEBRUHL, KATHLEEN L., atty., St. Charles General Hospital, New Orleans, LA '82 (ATTY)
DEBRUN, MICHAEL D., mgt. eng., Carle Clinic, Urbana, IL '86 (MGMT)
DEBRUNNER, GERALD J., partner, Deloitte Haskins, and Sells, Cincinnati, OH '70
DEBUTTS, DAVID A., asst. dir. publications, St. Agnes Hospital and Medical Center, Fresno, CA '84 (PR)
DECAMP, J. W., dir. plant serv., Shawnee Mission Medical Center, Shawnee Mission, KS '77 (ENG)
DECAPORALE, WILLIAM P., dir. soc. serv., Westerly Hospital, Westerly, RI '84 (SOC)
DECARLO, ROBERT JOSEPH, dir. plant oper. and eng., Lassen Community Hospital, Susanville, CA '85 (ENG)
DECATOR, ERIC R., atty., Swedish Medical Center, Englewood, CO '84 (ATTY)
DECESARE, EILEEN, RN, assoc. dir. nrsg., District of Columbia General Hospital, Washington, DC '83 (NURS)
DECHANT, THOMAS A., health syst. spec., William S. Middleton Memorial Veterans Hospital, Madison, WI '86 (PLNG)
DECHENE, ARTHUR C., PhD, dir. environ. serv., Mesa Lutheran Hospital, Mesa, AZ '86 (ENVIRON)
DECHRISTOFORD, RICHARD J., assoc. vice-pres. human res., St. Luke's-Roosevelt Hospital Center, New York, NY '68 (PERS)
DECHRISTOPHER, GLORIA, dir. diet., St. Luke's Hospital, Bethlehem, PA '67 (FOOD)
DECINA, JOHN A., assoc. dir., Society of the New York Hospital, New York, NY '78 (ENG)(PLNG)
DECK, GREGORY A., atty., Riverside Medical Center, Kankakee, IL '86 (ATTY)
DECKER-BURROUS, KATHY, dir. soc. work, St. Joseph's Medical Center, South Bend, IN '85 (SOC)
DECKER, EDWARD H. III, Hall, Decker, McKibbin, Inc., Los Angeles, CA '77
DECKER, JAMES LEE, adm., Sumner Memorial Hospital, Gallatin, TN '76
DECKER, JON H., prin., Decker-Hobbs Fukui Davison, Seattle, WA '85
DECKER, MARY E., dir. diet., AMI Palm Beach Gardens Medical Center, Palm Beach Gardens, FL '78 (FOOD)
DECKER, PAMELA, dir. soc. serv., Helene Fuld Medical Center, Trenton, NJ '86 (SOC)
DECKER, PAUL J., loss control consult., Hospital Underwriters Mutual Insurance Company, Tarrytown, NY '85 (RISK)
DECKERT, NANCY L., dir. vol. serv., Bedford Medical Center, Bedford, IN '86 (VOL)
DECKERT, VERDA E., coor. educ., Bethel Deaconess Hospital, Newton, KS '86 (EDUC)
DECLUE, DONNA, dir. extended care, Kaiser Foundation Hospital, Santa Clara, CA '77 (SOC)
DECOURSEY, ROBERT A., atty., Providence-St. Margaret Center, Kansas City, KS '85 (ATTY)
DECOURSEY, STEPHEN, corp. planner, Presentation Health System, Sioux Falls, SD '85 (PLNG)
DECRAMER, DONALD L., sr. proj. eng., Mayo Clinic, Rochester, MN '82 (ENG)
DECRISTOFANO, DOMENIC A., sr. mgt. eng., Roger Williams General Hospital, Providence, RI '84 (MGMT)
DECRISTOFORO, RALPH B., assoc. dir. human res., Akron City Hospital, Akron, OH '79 (PERS)
DEDENACH, MARC T., atty., Flint Osteopathic Hospital, Flint, MI '83 (ATTY)
DEE, DENNIS C., mgr. bldg., University of California at Los Angeles Medical Center, Los Angeles, CA '85 (ENG)
DEE, PAUL T., atty., Bascom Palmer Eye Institute and Hospital, Miami, FL '85 (ATTY)
DEEHAN, OLIVER E., vice-pres. plng., Medical Center of Delaware, Wilmington, DE '73 (PLNG)
DEEKENS, BETSY T., vice-pres. corp. commun., Virginia Hospital Association, Richmond, VA '69 (PR)
DEEMER, WILLIAM T., vice-pres. and dir. natl. health care div., Alexander and Alexander, Inc., St. Louis, MO '85 (RISK)
DEEN, ROBERT B. JR., atty., Riley Memorial Hospital, Meridian, MS '71 (ATTY)
DEENY, RAYMOND M., atty., St. Mary-Corwin Hospital Center, Pueblo, CO '82 (ATTY)
DEEP, WILLIAM M., atty., Community Methodist Hospital, Henderson, KY '74 (ATTY)
DEER, WALTER G., exec. vice-pres. adm., Memorial Medical Center of East Texas, Lufkin, TX '74
DEERE, T. DIANE, coor. staff dev., Eastwood Hospital, Memphis, TN '86 (EDUC)
DEERY, JACOB R. III, dir. matl. mgt., Abington Memorial Hospital, Abington, PA '83 (PUR)
DEES, HARRY P., atty., St. Mary's Medical Center, Evansville, IN '68 (ATTY)
DEETER, E. JEAN, RN, pat. rep. and risk mgr., Harrisburg Hospital, Harrisburg, PA '68 (PAT)
DEFAIL, ANTHONY J., assoc. adm., Meadville City Hospital, Meadville, PA '73
DEFAUW, THOMAS DAVID, exec. vice-pres. oper., Rockford Memorial Hospital, Rockford, IL '75
DEFENDORF, RAY, dir. commun. rel., Corning Hospital, Corning, NY '81 (PR)
DEFEO, ANNETTE THERESA, dir. pat. rel., Cooper Hospital-University Medical Center, Camden, NJ '85 (PAT)
DEFFENDOLL, DONALD L., mgr. clin. eng., Memorial Hospital and Health Care Center, Jasper, IN '82 (ENG)
DEFILIPO, FRANK P., supt. bldg. and grds., Coney Island Hospital, Brooklyn, NY '81 (ENG)
DEFINO, PAUL J., dir. welf., Smith House Health Care Center, Stamford, CT '70
DEFLORIO, JOSEPH, asst. dir. emp. rel., Community Hospital at Glen Cove, Glen Cove, NY '83 (PERS)
DEFORD, CAMILLE A., vice-pres., Magliaro and McHaney, LaJolla, CA '86 (PR)
DEGARMO, JAMES R., contr., City Hospital, Bellaire, OH '86
DEGEN, BERNARD J. II, exec. dir., American Association of Oral and Maxillofacial Surgeons, Chicago, IL '71
DEGEN, TOBY, adm. pers. and human res., Coney Island Medical Group, Brooklyn, NY '75 (PERS)
DEGENNARO, EDNA W., dir. vol. serv., West Georgia Medical Center, La Grange, GA '79 (VOL)
DEGEORGE, ELLEN L., assoc. dir., Veterans Administration Medical Center, Marion, IL '82
DEGERSTROM, JAMES M., dir. plant oper., Copley Memorial Hospital, Aurora, IL '81 (ENG)
DEGIDIO, CHARLENE A., dir. soc. serv., St. Helen Hospital, Chehalis, WA '82 (SOC)
DEGNER, MICHAEL V., dir. med. soc. work and pastoral care, Poudre Valley Hospital, Fort Collins, CO '86 (SOC)
DEGON, SHIRLEY R., RN, dir. med. nrsg., Tucson Medical Center, Tucson, AZ '80 (NURS)
DEGRANDE, LYNNE M., dir. soc. work serv., Samaritan Health Center, Detroit, MI '75 (SOC)
DEGRANDIS, FRED M., atty., Lakewood Hospital, Lakewood, OH '80 (ATTY)
DEGRAVE, CAROL M., dir. food serv., Glenbrook Hospital, Glenview, IL '81 (FOOD)
DEGROOT, MARY A., instr. educ. trng. and dev., AMI Doctors' Hospital, Lanham, MD '86 (EDUC)
DEGROOT, MARY C., RN, asst. adm. nrsg., St. John's Hospital, Springfield, IL '85 (NURS)
DEGUZMAN, CANDELARIA, RN, asst. adm. nrsg. serv., St. Elizabeth's Hospital, Chicago, IL '79 (NURS)
DEHAAN, DOROTHY R., asst. dir. diet. and prod., United Hospital, Grand Forks, ND '86 (FOOD)
DEHART, DONNA E., vice-pres., National Center for Health Promotion, West Chester, PA '84
DEHART, RAY, vice-pres., Moore Regional Hospital, Pinehurst, NC '86 (RISK)
DEI ROSSI, JAMES A., sr. assoc., Herman Smith Associates, Redwood City, CA '80 (PLNG)
DEI-CAS, KAREN L., vice-pres. corp. commun., Monongahela Valley Hospital, Monongahela, PA '79 (PR)
DEIGNAN, PAUL B., dir. nutr. and cent. sup. serv., United Hospital, St. Paul, MN '76 (FOOD)
DEIMAN, PATRICIA A., RN, nrs. consult., Health Resources and Services Administration, Rockville, MD '84 (NURS)
DEISENROTH, KEITH, Ernst and Whinney, Los Angeles, CA '80
DEISTER, LYNNE, dir. serv. dev., Bethany Medical Center, Kansas City, KS '84 (PLNG)
DEITCH, PHILIP L., asst. vice-pres. prof. serv., Easton Hospital, Easton, PA '79
DEITENBECK, WILLIAM H., mgr. plant eng., University of Missouri-Columbia Hospital and Clinics, Columbia, MO '76 (ENG)
DEITZ, DON R., asst. dir. maint., St. Vincent Infirmary, Little Rock, AR '83 (ENG)
DEJONG, JACQUELYN D., adm. amb. care, Greenville Memorial Hospital, Greenville, SC '87 (AMB)
DEJOY, JOSEPH C., supt. bldg. and grds., New York Hospital, New York, NY '83 (ENG)
DEKKER, JEAN L., asst. dir. nutr. and diet., University of California San Diego Medical Center, San Diego, CA '84 (FOOD)
DEL BUENO, DOROTHY J., RN, asst. dean, University of Pennsylvania, School of Nursing, Philadelphia, PA '71 (NURS)
DEL CAMPO, CHARLES, exec. dir., White Memorial Medical Center, Los Angeles, CA '87 (AMB)
DEL MAURO, PEGGY, adm. asst. risk mgt., St. Barnabas Medical Center, Livingston, NJ '86 (RISK)
DEL PERCIO, ROBERT W., mgt. eng., St. Francis Hospital, Wilmington, DE '78 (MGMT)
DEL PINO, PATRICIA A., dir. soc. serv., Methodist Hospital of Southern California, Arcadia, CA '81 (SOC)
DEL POZO, JORGE, bus. mgr. cent. serv., St. Joseph Hospital, Orange, CA '78 (CS)
DEL PRINCIPE, J., mgr. facil. and eng., Good Shepherd Hospital, Barrington, IL '86 (ENG)
DEL RIO, SR. CLOTILDE, RN, dir. nrsg. serv., Auxilio Mutuo Hospital, San Juan, P.R. '78 (NURS)
DEL ROSARIO, LT. COL. LAWRENCE, hosp. spec. rep., Farmers Insurance Group, Walnut Creek, CA '51 (LIFE)
DEL SORDO, MICHAEL A., dir. soc. work, Freehold Area Hospital, Freehold, NJ '73 (SOC)
DELABY, DANIEL, mgr. plant oper., Holy Cross Hospital, Detroit, MI '85 (ENG)
DELAFOSSE, MAJ. JODIE L., MSC USA, adm. res., David Grant U. S. Air Force Medical Center, Fairfield, CA '84
DELAMAR, WILLIAM THOMAS, pres., Resource, Inc., Melrose Park, PA '67 (MGMT)
DELAMATER, GAIL H., dir. vol. serv., Weirton Medical Center, Weirton, WV '81 (VOL)
DELAND, LINDA A., RN, assoc. adm. pat. care serv., Mercy International Health Services, Majuro, Marshall Islands '87 (NURS)
DELANEY, ALICE H., consult., Ernst and Whinney, Cleveland, OH '86 (MGMT)
DELANEY, JOHN P., asst. prof., Alfred University College of Business Administration, Alfred, NY '85
DELANEY, LINDA L., RN, dir. med. and surg. nrsg., Greene Memorial Hospital, Xenia, OH '85 (NURS)
DELANEY, LLOYD, assoc. dir., Cedars-Sinai Medical Center, Los Angeles, CA '79 (FOOD)
DELANEY, MARGARET R., dir. dev., St. Helen's Hospital and Health Center, St. Helens, OR '83 (PR) (PLNG)
DELANEY, MARTIN J., atty., Winthrop-University Hospital, Mineola, NY '71 (ATTY)
DELANGE, JAMES J., dir. plng. and mktg., Community General Hospital, Sterling, IL '85 (PLNG)
DELANO, RICHARD J., pres., Albany General Hospital, Albany, OR '72
DELANOY, DRAKE, atty., Desert Springs Hospital, Las Vegas, NV '85 (ATTY)
DELANY, JACQUELINE D., consult. pub. rel., Marblehead, MA '86 (PR)
DELANY, PEGGY E., asst. adm., Cottonwood Hospital Medical Center, Murray, UT '85 (PLNG)
DELAPORTA, RICHARD I., New England Deaconess Hospital, Boston, MA '70 (MGMT)
DELARGY, PATRICIA A., asst. dir. matl. mgt., Memorial Hospital, South Bend, IN '80 (CS)
DELARM, BECKY, RN, dir. nrsg. outpatient serv., Highland Park Hospital, Highland Park, IL '84 (NURS)
DELASHAW, JERRY J., Tulsa, OK '84 (PR) (PLNG)
DELATORRE, JOE, student, Program in Health and Hospital Administration, University of Florida, Gainesville, FL '85
DELAUDER, MARLEEN M., RN, dir. med. serv., Lynchburg General Hospital, Lynchburg, VA '86 (NURS)
DELAURA, FRANK J., mgt. assoc., St. John Hospital, Detroit, MI '84 (PLNG)
DELAURA, GIL, atty., West Virginia Hospital Association, Cahrleston, WV '86 (RISK)(ATTY)
DELECKE, JANET H., dir. pers. serv., St. Joseph Mercy Hospital, Pontiac, MI '84 (PERS)
DELEO, JULIA J., adm. asst. pers., Jefferson General Hospital, Port Townsend, WA '85 (PERS)
DELEON, ARMANDO, dir. environ. serv., safety and security, Valley Presbyterian Hospital, Van Nuys, CA '86 (ENVIRON)
DELEON, BETTE S., mgr. pat. rel., White Memorial Medical Center, Los Angeles, CA '82 (PAT)
DELF, ROBERT B. JR., assoc. exec. dir., Multnomah County Medical Society, Portland, OR '82 (PLNG)
DELGADO, DAVID J., student, Columbia University School of Public Health and Administrative Medicine, New York, NY '86 (PLNG)

DELGADO, JIM W., chief vol. serv., Audie L. Murphy Memorial Veterans Hospital, San Antonio, TX '79 (VOL)
DELIJA, LOUISE CARIATI, dir. food serv., New York Infirmary, New York, NY '67 (FOOD)
DELIS, BARBARA, RN, dir. cent. and surg. serv., Euclid General Hospital, Euclid, OH '79 (CS)
DELISI, JOHN J., partner, Jls Consulting Service, Arlington Heights, IL '86 (ENG)
DELISLE, GARY R., corp. vice-pres., Daughters of Charity Health Systems-East Central, Inc., Evansville, IN '69
DELKER, JEANNE GALE, corp. diet. and dir. health care, Code, Inc., Pittsburgh, PA '73 (FOOD)
DELKS, HARRY E. III, dir. eng. serv., St. Vincent Hospital and Health Center, Indianapolis, IN '83 (ENG)
DELL, ANN MARIE, mgr. nrsg., University of California Irvine Medical Center, Orange, CA '86 (NURS)
DELL, JOHN J., dir. mgt. info. syst., Shadyside Hospital, Pittsburgh, PA '86 (MGMT)
DELL, ROBERT E., asst. vice-pres., Kettering Medical Center, Kettering, OH '77 (PERS)
DELLABADIA, MAXINE, exec. asst. and risk mgr., Astoria General Hospital, Long Island City, NY '86 (RISK)
DELLAMAR, WILLIAM, asst. dir. eng., St. Benedict's Hospital, Ogden, UT '69 (ENG)
DELLEA, EUGENE A., adm., Hillcrest Hospital, Pittsfield, MA '81
DELLIGATTI, CATHY L., RN, vice-pres. nrsg. and pat. serv., Calvert Memorial Hospital, Prince Frederick, MD '83 (NURS)
DELLINGER, ANNE M., atty., Institute of Government, University of North Carolina, Chapel Hill, NC '82 (ATTY)
DELLORUSSO, EMANUEL, syst. analyst, North Shore University Hospital, Manhasset, NY '81 (MGMT)
DELMATOFF, JOHN P., pres., Delmatoff, Gerow, Morris and Langhans, Inc., Whittier, CA '85 (PR)
DELONEY, LOY DANIEL, underwriter, Stephens, Inc., Little Rock, AR '75
DELONG, BARBARA A., corp. dir. educ., Mercy Hospital, Benton Harbor, MI '82 (EDUC)
DELONG, GEORGE E. JR., dir. support serv., HCA Park View Medical Center, Nashville, TN '81 (ENG)
DELONG, PAUL B., dir. pers., St. Luke's Regional Medical Center, Boise, ID '73 (PERS)
DELOZIER, AMY B., mgt. eng. consult., Lloyd Noland Hospital and Health Centers, Birmingham, AL '80 (MGMT)
DELSITE, DEAN E., coor. sup., proc. and distrib., Geisinger Medical Center, Danville, PA '82 (CS)
DELSORDO, JANE ANN, dir. vol. serv., St. Francis Hospital, Wilmington, DE '85 (VOL)
DELUCA, GAIL A., dir. nutr. serv., Beth Israel Hospital, Boston, MA '84 (FOOD)
DELUCA, JOSEPH M., founder and practice dir., Joseph Deluca Associates, San Francisco, CA '86 (PLNG)
DELUCA, RICHARD J., exec. vice-pres., New Mexico Hospital Association, Albuquerque, NM '79 (PLNG)
DELUCAS, ANGELINE CHRISTINE, RN, asst. adm. nrsg. serv., St. Joseph Regional Medical Center, Lewiston, ID '84 (NURS)
DELUCENAY, BETH A., Psychiatric Institutes of America, Washington, DC '84 (PLNG)
DELUCIA, DAN W., student, Alfred University, Alfred, NY '86
DELUISE, PAUL M., dir. matl. mgt., Howard Community Hospital, Kokomo, IN '82 (PUR)
DELUTIS, BARBARA A., RN, vice-pres. pat. care, Nashoba Community Hospital, Ayer, MA '85 (NURS)
DELVECCHIO, JOE, dir. eng., AMI Central Carolina Hospital, Sanford, NC '85 (ENG)
DELZER, CLARENCE, dir. matl., Medcenter One, Bismarck, ND '71 (PUR)
DEMANCHE, DENIS J., Andover, MA '53 (LIFE)
DEMAPAN, ROMAN S., plant eng., Commonwealth Health Center, Saipan, Mariana Islands '86 (ENG)
DEMARCO, FRANK JOSEPH III, adm., North Trident Regional Hospital, Charleston, SC '75
DEMARCO, MARY ROSE, Lyndhurst, OH '68 (FOOD)
DEMAREST, BARBARA L., dir. diet., McKeesport Hospital, McKeesport, PA '85 (FOOD)
DEMAREST, DONNA L. WALDRON, student, Temple University, Department of Health Administration, School of Business Administration, Philadelphia, PA '84
DEMAREST, SR. FRANCIS, supv. amb. care, St. Joseph's Hospital and Medical Center, Paterson, NJ '87 (AMB)
DEMARS, SCOTT E., dir. pur., Memorial Hospital, Fremont, OH '86 (PUR)
DEMAS, DONALD J., dir. pers., Good Samaritan Hospital, Vincennes, IN '72 (PERS)
DEMASTERS, PATTI L., adm. asst., Liberty Hospital, Liberty, MO '78 (PERS)
DEMELFY, MARY A., Newark, DE '75
DEMENGE, STANLEY D., dir. bldg. and grds., Community Memorial Hospital, Cloquet, MN '85 (ENG)
DEMEO, JOSEPH M., vice-pres. fin., Cheshire Medical Center, Keene, NH '81
DEMEREST, BARBARA A., dir. soc. work, Erie County Medical Center, Buffalo, NY '86 (SOC)
DEMERS, B. NATALIE, Waupun, WI '85 (PR)
DEMERS, DEBRA A., pur. agt., Nashua Memorial Hospital, Nashua, NH '82 (PUR)
DEMERS, PATRICIA M., RN, asst. dir. nrsg., Winthrop Hospital, Winthrop, MA '86 (NURS)
DEMES, LEANNE C., RN, dir. nrsg. serv., St. Mary's Hospital, Huntington, WV '75 (NURS)
DEMEYER, JOANNA, RN, vice-pres. pat. care, St. Luke's Regional Medical Center, Boise, ID '72 (NURS)
DEMEZA, KIMBERLY FOX, dir. mktg., St. Francis Hospital, Miami Beach, FL '83 (PR)
DEMING, ELIZABETH A., RN, dir. nrsg., Hospital of the Albert Einstein College of Medicine, Bronx, NY '75 (NURS)
DEMING, GEORGE R., dir. soc. serv., St. Joseph Medical Center, Joliet, IL '76 (SOC)
DEMING, MICHAEL S., sr. vice-pres., Silver Cross Hospital, Joliet, IL '81 (RISK)
DEMKE, JONATHAN A., student, Program in Health Services Administration, Arizona State University College of Business, Tempe, AZ '86
DEMKEE, DONALD E., MD, bd. mem., Wooster Community Hospital, Wooster, OH '80
DEMKOWICZ, JOHANNA K., RN, dir. nrsg. serv., Chilton Memorial Hospital, Pompton Plains, NJ '68 (NURS)
DEMME, LESLIE J., dir. info. serv., Peninsula Hospital and Medical Center, Burlingame, CA '85 (MGMT)
DEMONG, VANCE C., Concordia College, Morehead, MN '51 (LIFE)
DEMONT, PAMELA D., student, University of Kentucky, Lexington, KY '86
DEMOON, PATRICK S., adm., Central Community Hospital, Chicago, IL '61 (EDUC)
DEMORY, EMMA L., dir. diet., Fairmont General Hospital, Fairmont, WV '83 (FOOD)
DEMOVILLE, DIANNE B., dir. in-service, Angelo Community Hospital, San Angelo, TX '86 (EDUC)
DEMPSEY, BARRY L., dir. risk mgt., Pennsylvania Hospital, Philadelphia, PA '80 (RISK)
DEMPSEY, DESMOND J., chief exec., Federated Dublin Voluntary Hospitals, Dublin, Ireland '78
DEMPSEY, DOROTHY B., pat. ombudsperson, Amherst Medical Associates, Amherst, MA '80 (PAT)
DEMPSEY, PAUL F., atty., Massachusetts Hospital Association, Burlington, MA '75 (ATTY)
DEMPSEY, THOMAS, dir. amb. care, Riverside Hospital, Wilmington, DE '87 (AMB)
DEMPSEY, VIRGINIA B., RN, clin. dir. intensive serv., St. Joseph Hospitals, Mount Clemens, MI '86 (NURS)
DEMPSTER, MARILYN B., serv. off., University Medical Center Southern Nevada, Las Vegas, NV '87 (SOC)
DEMSTER, MICHAEL, exec. dir., Pri-Medical, Inc., Memphis, TN '80 (MGMT)
DEMURO, PAUL ROBERT, atty., Carpenter, Higgins and Simonds, Burlingame, CA '82 (ATTY)
DEMUSEY, SR. EDITH B., adm., Villa Maria Nursing Home, Villa Maria, PA '50 (LIFE)
DENARDIS, RICHARD R., prin., Kitch, Suhrheinrich, Smith, Saurbier and Drutchas, Detroit, MI '83
DENECHAUD, CHARLES I. JR., atty., Hotel Dieu Hospital, New Orleans, LA '74 (ATTY)
DENGER, E. SUE, RN, vice-pres. nrsg. serv., St. Francis Regional Medical Center, Wichita, KS '69 (NURS)
DENGLER, ELIZABETH J., RN, dir. nrsg., Union Hospital of the Bronx, Bronx, NY '68 (NURS)
DENGLER, JANE B., RN, assoc. dir. nrsg. serv., Bryn Mawr Hospital, Bryn Mawr, PA '81 (NURS)(EDUC)
DENHA, DAVID B., mgr. eng. and lab., Bascom Palmer Eye Institute and Hospital, Miami, FL '86 (ENG)
DENHOLM, WILLIAM E., asst. dir., Mount Vernon Hospital, Mount Vernon, NY '66 (RISK)
DENICOLA, PAUL JOHN, pur. mgr., St. Joseph's Hospital, Milwaukee, WI '86 (PUR)
DENIGER, DENNIS A., Servicemaster Industries, Inc., Irvine, CA '85 (PUR)
DENISE, SR. MARY, dir. soc. serv., Mercy Community Hospital, Port Jervis, NY '76 (SOC)
DENISON, JUDY E., RN, asst. adm. pat. serv., Rhd Memorial Medical Center, Dallas, TX '85 (NURS)
DENITTO, JOHN F., dir. safety, security and commun., St. Mary's Hospital, Passaic, NJ '85 (ENG)
DENMAN, PATRICIA A., assoc. dir., St. Joseph Hospital, Houston, TX '84
DENN, NANCY M., vol. serv. spec., Veterans Administration Medical Center, Albuquerque, NM '86 (VOL)
DENNEHY, DANIEL T., atty., St. Michael Hospital, Milwaukee, WI '84 (ATTY)
DENNETT, RICHARD A., atty., United Hospital, Port Chester, NY '82 (ATTY)
DENNEY, BEVERLY A., RN, asst. dir. nrs., South Community Hospital, Oklahoma City, OK '86 (NURS)
DENNIHAN, JANICE M., dir. environ. serv., Leominster Hospital, Leominster, MA '86 (ENVIRON)
DENNIK-CHAMPION, GINA M., RN, dir. nrsg., Villa Clement Nursing Home, West Allis, WI '87 (NURS)
DENNING, RICHARD A., sr. vice-pres. human res., St. Luke's Episcopal Hospital, Houston, TX '76 (PERS)
DENNIS, C. E., dir. facil., St. Luke's Hospital, Duluth, MN '79 (ENG)
DENNIS, JAMES E., D. and S. Healthcare Resources, Memphis, TN '76 (SOC)
DENNIS, LYMAN C. II, chief exec. off., Whittaker Health Services, Los Angeles, CA '69
DENNIS, NORINE M., RN, asst. dir. nrsg. serv., Addison Gilbert Hospital, Gloucester, MA '82 (NURS)
DENNIS, REBECCA D., RN, dir. cont. educ. and asst. prof. nrsg. and health sci., Western Carolina University, Cullowhee, NC '83 (EDUC)
DENNIS, TERRI L., pat. rep., Alliance Community Hospital, Alliance, OH '87 (PAT)
DENNISON, JANET E., student, Program in Hospital Administration, School of Public Health, University of Michigan, Ann Arbor, MI '84
DENNISON, VICKI P., consult., Blue Cross and Blue Shield Association, Chicago, IL '85 (PLNG)
DENNISTON, MARILYN, RN, head nrs. amb. surg., Fairmont General Hospital, Fairmont, WV '87 (AMB)
DENNY, JEANNE F., dir. soc. work, Penobscot Bay Medical Center, Rockport, ME '79 (SOC)
DENNY, MARIETTA, student, Program in Health Policy and Administration, School of Public Health, University of North Carolina, Chapel Hill, NC '86
DENOYER, JAMES R., assoc. adm. pub. affairs and mktg., Illinois Masonic Medical Center, Chicago, IL '76 (PR)
DENSER, CLARENCE H. JR., MD, path., Des Moines Medical Center, Des Moines, IA '68
DENSMORE, ROBERT C., pres., Mercy Health System, Burlingame, CA '53 (LIFE)
DENSON, ROBERT, exec. dir., Glenbeigh Hospital of Tampa, Inc., Tampa, FL '86
DENT, ALBERT W., (ret.), New Orleans, LA '64 (HON)
DENT, MARTHA J., RN, Saint Luke's Hospital, Cleveland, OH '78 (NURS)
DENT, THOMPSON S. JR., vice-pres. dev., Equicor, Nashville, TN '78 (AMB)
DENTON, CHARLES L., adm., Shelby Medical Center, Alabaster, AL '73
DENTON, RONALD I., matl. mgt. consult., Ron Denton and Associates, Inc., Knoxville, TN '78 (PUR)
DENTON, RONNIE H., mgr. surg., Wilson Memorial Hospital, Sidney, OH '87 (AMB)
DENTON, THOMAS, vice-pres. human res., Barnes Hospital, St. Louis, MO '85 (PERS)
DENUCCIO, JAMES A., vice-pres. adm., South Suburban Hospital, Hazel Crest, IL '70 (PLNG)
DEOBIL, ANTHONY, risk mgr. and dir. safety and commun., Horton Memorial Hospital, Middletown, NY '85 (RISK)
DEPA, JOHN RAYMOND, supv. sr. acct., Peat, Marwick, Mitchell and Company, Chicago, IL '74
DEPALLO, LAURA, bus. mgr., Dermatology, Ltd., Media, PA '87 (AMB)
DEPAOLO, DOMINIC J. JR., mgr. pur., Quakertown Community Hospital, Quakertown, PA '86 (PUR)
DEPASCAL, TEDDIE D., dir. pers., Sun Belt Regional Medical Center, Houston, TX '82 (PERS)
DEPASSE, CHARLES A., student, New York University, New York, NY '86 (ENG)
DEPIERRO, JOHN J., pres. and chief exec. off., Sisters of Charity Health Care Systems, Staten Island, NY '64
DEPONTE, JOE, dir. pers., St. John Hospital, Nassau Bay, TX '87 (PERS)
DEPPE, BRIAN J., atty., Johnson County Memorial Hospital, Franklin, IN '84 (ATTY)
DEPPENSMITH, DONALD L., San Antonio, TX '82
DEPUE, DARRELL, chief eng., Dallas County Hospital, Perry, IA '78 (ENG)
DEPUY, WILMA L., dir. vol. serv., Ellenville Community Hospital, Ellenville, NY '86 (VOL)
DEREMO, DOROTHY E., RN, vice-pres. pat. care serv., Hutzel Hospital, Detroit, MI '84 (NURS)
DEREZINSKI, ANTHONY A., atty., Mercy Health Services, Farmington Hills, MI '82 (ATTY)
DERINGER, JAMES, asst. vice-pres., Marsh and McLennan, Ltd., Vancouver, B.C., Canada '85 (RISK)
DERIWALLA, MASOOD, chief acct., Ministry of Health, Manama Bahrain, Arabia '86
DERKS, STEVEN M., adm. intern, Mercy Hospital, Urbana, IL '85
DEROIN, MIKE, dir. plant maint., St. Luke's Regional Medical Center, Boise, ID '80 (ENG)
DEROOS, ROGER L., PhD, dir. environ. health and safety, University of Washington, Seattle, WA '74 (ENG)
DEROSA, MARCIA S., dir. vol. serv., St. Charles Hospital, Oregon, OH '85 (VOL)
DEROSE-MEISTER, DIANE A., mgt. eng., Swedish-American Hospital, Rockford, IL '86 (MGMT)
DEROSE, ANNE K., dir. soc. serv., St. Lawrence Hospital, Lansing, MI '82 (SOC)
DEROWSKI, JEROME, syst. and dev. spec., Harper Hospital, Detroit, MI '79 (CS)(PUR)
DERR, E. ELIZABETH, RN, coor. staff dev., Frederick Memorial Hospital, Frederick, MD '71 (EDUC)
DERR, ELLY, dir. vol. serv., Medical Center Hospital, Punta Gorda, FL '85 (VOL)
DERR, RICHARD A., corp. dir., Waterbury Hospital, Waterbury, CT '52 (LIFE)
DERR, SUSAN R., dir. mktg., Charter Beacon Hospital, Fort Wayne, IN '82 (PR)
DERRICK, CORLISS GRINSTEAD, RN, assoc. exec. dir. nrsg., Humana Hospital -Augusta, Augusta, GA '86 (NURS)
DERRICK, JAMES V. JR., atty., Hermann Hospital, Houston, TX '86 (ATTY)
DERRINGE, SHARON R., dir. mktg., Welborn Memorial Baptist Hospital, Evansville, IN '85 (PR) (PLNG)
DERSTADT, RONALD T., sr. vice-pres., St. Francis-St. George Hospital, Cincinnati, OH '74
DERUOSI, DIANE, pur. off., Roger Williams General Hospital, Providence, RI '86
DERZON, GORDON M., supt., University of Wisconsin Hospital and Clinics, Madison, WI '59
DERZON, ROBERT A., vice-pres., Lewin and Associates, Inc., San Francisco, CA '54
DESALVO, THOMAS W., dir. matl. mgt., Bon Secours Health System, Inc., Columbia, MD '73 (PUR)
DESANDES, MARYJEAN, dir. vol. serv., Sacred Heart Hospital, Allentown, PA '85 (VOL)
DESANSSURE, MARYLOUISE V., mgr. telecommun., Children's Hospital of San Francisco, San Francisco, CA '86 (ENG)
DESANTA, DELNORA, RN, adm. nrsg., King's Daughters Hospital, Greenville, MS '81 (NURS)
DESAUTEL, HELEN C., RN, dir. pat. rel., Baptist Hospital of Miami, Miami, FL '74 (PAT)
DESCHAMBEAU, WAYNE G., dir. corp. affairs, St. Thomas Hospital, Nashville, TN '85 (PLNG)
DESCHENE, NORMAND E., exec. vice-pres. and chief oper. off., Lowell General Hospital, Lowell, MA '78
DESCHENE, SUSAN L., dir. soc. serv., Arthur R. Gould Memorial Hospital, Presque Isle, ME '79 (SOC)
DESCHENES, ALEXANDER M. JR., atty., Emma L. Bixby Hospital, Adrian, MI '76 (ATTY)
DESCHLER, PAULA, student, University of Cincinnati, Cincinnati, OH '87 (RISK)
DESEPTE, WILLETTA L., coor. vol., Kaiser Foundation Hospital-San Rafael, San Rafael, CA '83 (VOL)
DESHIELDS, ROSE MARIE, supv. cent. serv. proc., Abington Memorial Hospital, Abington, PA '81 (CS)
DESHONG, M. JUNE, mgr. telecommun., Mercy Hospital, Baltimore, MD '79 (ENG)
DESILVA, KATHLEEN A., atty., Institute for Rehabilitation and Research, Houston, TX '83 (ATTY)
DESIMONE, DENNIS LEWIS, pres., Reality Based Management, Inc., Derry, NH '80 (EDUC)
DESIMONE, MICHAEL A., pur. agt., Francis Scott Key Medical Center, Baltimore, MD '86 (PUR)

DESJARDINS, EDWARD R., corp. vice-pres. human res., Carondelet Health Services, Tucson, AZ '76 (PERS)
DESJARDINS, PATRICIA R., pat. rep., St. Boniface General Hospital, Winnipeg, Man., Canada '78 (PAT)
DESKIEWICZ, LAURA NEVADA, pat. rep., Roxborough Memorial Hospital, Philadelphia, PA '82 (PAT)
DESKIN, ARCHIE S., exec. dir., Jewish General Hospital, Montreal, Que., Canada '62
DESKIN, W. C. SR., mgr. plng., Medical Associates Clinic, Dubuque, IA '86
DESKOVITZ, MICHAEL H., chief fin. off., Central Michigan Community Hospital, Mount Pleasant, MI '86
DESLANDES, JOANN E., asst. dir. human res., American Red Cross, Mid-America Chapter, Chicago, IL '71 (VOL)
DESMARAIS, DENNIS R., adm. eng., Baystate Medical Center, Springfield, MA '75 (ENG)
DESMARIAS, JOHN C., chief exec. off., Medical Center-Bowling Green, Bowling Green, KY '71
DESMOND, JOANNE M., dir. vol. serv., Catherine McAuley Health Center, Ann Arbor, MI '81 (VOL)
DESMOND, STEPHEN G., dir. diet., Mount Sinai Medical Center, Cleveland, OH '86 (FOOD)
DESNOYER, JANET MEYER, asst. dir. educ. and trng., Barnes Hospital, St. Louis, MO '81 (EDUC)
DESNOYERS, DANIEL P., dir. support serv., Davie County Hospital, Mocksville, NC '79 (ENG)
DESPELDER, JAMES F., pres., Health Care Associates, Troy, MI '52 (LIFE)
DESROCHERS, I. BARGARA, mgr. matl., Lowell General Hospital, Lowell, MA '82 (PUR)
DESTAFENO, FRANCES A., mgr. matl., Kent General Hospital, Dover, DE '86 (PUR)
DESTEFANO, DONNA, dir. vol. serv., Women and Infants Hospital of Rhode Island, Providence, RI '86 (VOL)
DESTEFANO, JOSEPH A., adm., Vision Care Center, Fresno, CA '87 (AMB)
DESTEFANO, THERESA, student, Program in Health Service Administration, School of Health Professions, Governors State University, Park Forest South, IL '86
DETERING, EDMUND L., dev. consult., St. Luke's Hospital West, Chesterfield, MO '74 (PR)
DETERS, JOAN M., mgr. pub. rel., St. Mary Hospital, Quincy, IL '84 (PR)
DETESKE, MARGARET J., assoc. dir. qual. assur., Children's Hospital Medical Center, Akron, OH '72
DETHLEFS, DENNIS A., dir. educ. and staff dev., Lincoln General Hospital, Lincoln, NE '79 (EDUC)
DETHLOFF, KAREN, dir. maint., Huron Road Hospital, Cleveland, OH '81 (ENG)
DETLOR, LYNN R., vice-pres. matl. mgt., American Healthcare Systems, La Jolla, CA '75 (PUR)
DETMER, SARAH S., RN, dir. commun. health nrsg., Group Health Cooperative, Seattle, WA '82 (NURS)
DETRING, LINDA M., RN, dir. nrsg., Normandy Osteopathic Hospital, St. Louis, MO '84 (NURS)
DETTLEFF, JACK S., sr. vice-pres., Allentown Osteopathic Medical Center, Allentown, PA '82 (PLNG)
DETTLING, SHARON M., dir. diet., W. A. Foote Memorial Hospital, Jackson, MI '82 (FOOD)
DETUERK, SUZANNE C., dir. vol. serv., Centre Community Hospital, State College, PA '82 (VOL)
DETWEILER, LEON, dir. plant serv., Lebanon Community Hospital, Lebanon, OR '79 (ENG)
DETWEILER, REBECCA M., coor. emp., Grand View Hospital, Sellersville, PA '82 (PERS)
DEUCHARS, BERNARD D., head eng. serv., Sunnybrook Hospital, Toronto, Ont., Canada '86 (ENG)
DEUEL, LOLA B., supv. cent. sterilizing, University of Osteopathic, Des Moines, IA '81 (CS)
DEUSTER, MAJ. KATHRYN P., MSC USA, nrs. meth. analyst, Walter Reed Army Medical Center, Washington, DC '82
DEUTSCH, ALINE I., student, Boston University Health Management Programs, Boston, MA '86 (PLNG)
DEUTSCH, FLORENCE G., RN, vice-pres., East Liverpool City Hospital, East Liverpool, OH '75 (NURS)
DEUTSCH, GARY E., assoc. exec. dir., Staten Island Hospital, Staten Island, NY '70
DEUTSCH, GLENN, assoc. dir. pub. affairs, Mount Sinai Medical Center, New York, NY '85 (PR)
DEUTSCH, LALAN L., dir. vol. serv., Wabash County Hospital, Wabash, IN '86 (VOL)
DEUTSCH, SUZANNE Z., coor. soc. work, Massachusetts General Hospital, Boston, MA '81 (SOC)
DEVALL, BEVERLY, supv., East Jefferson General Hospital, Metairie, LA '86 (PLNG)
DEVANSKY, GARY WILLIAM, pub. rel. off., Veterans Administration Medical Center, Minneapolis, MN '77 (PR)
DEVAULT, RICHARD L., dir. pers., Providence Hospital, Washington, DC '82 (PERS)
DEVENNEY, EDMAN L., pres., Devenney Associates, Ltd., Phoenix, AZ '86
DEVENNEY, SHARON, coor. vol. serv., Carlisle Hospital, Carlisle, PA '72 (VOL)
DEVER, SR. MARY CHARLES, pres., Daughters of Charity National Purchasing Services, Inc., St. Louis, MO '84
DEVER, PHILIP R., dir. pers., Clermont Mercy Hospital, Batavia, OH '83 (PERS)
DEVEREAUX, W. C., dir. risk mgt., Blodgett Memorial Medical Center, Grand Rapids, MI '80 (RISK)
DEVET, CATHERINE M., RN, dir. educ. and staff serv., Blodgett Memorial Medical Center, Grand Rapids, MI '86 (NURS)
DEVILLIER, BECKY, RN, dir. nrsg. res. and educ., University of California San Diego Medical Center, San Diego, CA '83 (NURS)
DEVINE, DONALD E., dir. phys. plant, United Health Services, Binghamton, NY '86 (ENG)
DEVINE, EUGENE M., dir. health care info. syst., Ernst and Whinney, New York, NY '87 (MGMT)
DEVINE, GEORGE K., adm., University Hospital School, Iowa City, IA '54 (LIFE)
DEVINE, JOANNE, RN, dir. nrsg., St. Mary's Hospital, Passaic, NJ '86 (NURS)(AMB)
DEVINE, JOHN B., atty., St. Joseph Mercy Hospital, Ann Arbor, MI '68 (ATTY)
DEVINE, SANDRA, dir. soc. serv., Bay Harbor Hospital, Harbor City, CA '86 (SOC)
DEVINE, WILLIAM G., dir. plant serv., Community Medical Center, Scranton, PA '71 (ENG)
DEVINS, THOMAS B., dir. strategic plng., Addison Gilbert Hospital, Gloucester, MA '86 (PLNG)
DEVITA, GERARD, mgr. prof. liabilities, C. N. A. Insurance Company, Chicago, IL '84 (RISK)
DEVITO, PHILIP T., dir. eng., St. Luke's Hospital, Newburgh, NY '83 (ENG)
DEVITT, BENNY E., dir. eng., Hancock Memorial Hospital, Greenfield, IN '85 (ENG)
DEVITT, ROBERT L., coor. plng. and bus. dev., Saint Joseph Hospital, Mishawaka, IN '80 (PLNG)
DEVITT, VALGENE, sr. vice-pres., Portland Adventist Medical Center, Portland, OR '83 (RISK)
DEVIVO, LYNNE M., dir. vol. serv., Lakes Region General Hospital, Laconia, NH '85 (VOL)
DEVLIN, ANNE, vice-pres., Chase Manhattan Capital Markets Corporation, New York, NY '85
DEVLIN, EDWARD, exec. eng., Hunterdon Medical Center, Flemington, NJ '83 (ENG)
DEVLIN, NANCY J., commissioned off., U. S. Public Health Service, Hyattsville, MD '77
DEVOCELLE, FRANK H., adm., Olathe Medical Center, Olathe, KS '76
DEVOE, ROBERT F. SR., (ret.), Louisville, KY '59 (ENG)
DEVOLITES, PHILIP J., dir., Blue Cross and Blue Shield of Mississippi, Jackson, MS '77
DEVONO, DORIS, adm. asst. and ombudsman, United Hospital Center, Clarksburg, WV '78 (PAT)
DEVORE, JOANNE M., dir. food serv., Sturdy Memorial Hospital, Attleboro, MA '80 (FOOD)
DEVORE, KEITH A., mgr. elec. serv., Detroit Medical Center Cooperative Services, Detroit, MI '85 (ENG)
DEVORE, ROBERT W., pres., Horizon Companies, Boston, MA '84 (PLNG)
DEVORE, SARA H., coor. perinatal educ., Sutter Memorial Hospital, Sacramento, CA '80 (EDUC)
DEVOS, RONALD, risk mgr. and claims mgt., University of Medicine and Dentistry of New Jersey-University Hospital, Newark, NJ '83 (RISK)
DEVRIES, HENRY JR., chief oper. off., Bon Secours Hospital, Grosse Pointe, MI '79
DEVRIES, JOHN E., dir. mgt. eng., Carondelet Community Hospitals, Minneapolis, MN '86 (MGMT)
DEVRIES, ROBERT A., prog. dir., W. K. Kellogg Foundation, Battle Creek, MI '58 (HON)
DEW, DIANA E., dir. pat. serv., Hampton General Hospital, Hampton, VA '76 (SOC)
DEW, HERMON R., dir. eng. and maint., St. Luke's Hospital, Davenport, IA '83 (ENG)
DEWAAL, JOHN, dir. biomedical electronics, Mount Sinai Medical Center, New York, NY '86 (ENG)
DEWALSHE, DIANE, Long Beach Community Hospital, Long Beach, CA '87 (AMB)
DEWAN, ANIL, dir. elec., Bryan Memorial Hospital, Lincoln, NE '83 (ENG)
DEWAR, CATHERINE L., dir. diet., St. Boniface General Hospital, Winnipeg, Man., Canada '84 (FOOD)
DEWBERRY, MICHAEL J., atty., Riverside Hospital, Jacksonville, FL '86 (ATTY)
DEWEERD, JERALD S., dir. staff educ., Pine Rest Christian Hospital, Grand Rapids, MI '85 (EDUC)
DEWEES, DEBORAH B., dir. vol., Fort Worth Children's Hospital, Fort Worth, TX '85 (VOL)
DEWEES, EDWIN D., Main Line Health, Inc., Radnor, PA '73 (PERS)
DEWEESE, MABEL S., dir. nutr. and environ. serv., Meriter Hospital, Madison, WI '67 (FOOD)
DEWEVER, MARGARET K., RN, chief nrsg. serv., Veterans Administration Hospital, Salisbury, NC '84 (NURS)
DEWEY, MARY FRAME, dir. pub. rel. and mktg., Stuart Circle Hospital, Richmond, VA '78
DEWEY, RICHARD L., adm., A. Lindsay and Olive B. O'Connor Hospital, Delhi, NY '80
DEWEY, SUZANNE R., student, Boston University, Boston, MA '86 (PLNG)
DEWITT, JON F., atty., Kent Community Hospital, Grand Rapids, MI '80 (ATTY)
DEWITT, ROSCOE P., arch. and owner, Roscoe DeWitt, Architects and Engineers, Dallas, TX '46 (LIFE)
DEWITT, SHARON, coor. cent. serv., Wood County Hospital, Bowling Green, OH '83 (CS)
DEWOLF, LINDA, dir. pat. and commun. serv., St. Luke's Methodist Hospital, Cedar Rapids, IA '78 (PAT)
DEWOLFE, GEORGE F., atty., Suburban Hospital and Sanitarium-Cook County, Hinsdale, IL '85 (ATTY)
DEWOLFE, NORMAN S., trng. spec., Lee Memorial Hospital, Fort Myers, FL '82 (EDUC)
DEXHEIMER, WILLIAM R., chief oper. off., AMI Brookwood Primary Care Centers, Inc., Birmingham, AL '83
DEXTER, JANET, risk mgr., East Shoshone Hospital, Silverton, ID '86 (RISK)
DEXTER, SHARON ANNE, dir. environ. serv., Charter Oak Hospital, Covina, CA '86 (ENVIRON)
DEYARMIN, CARLTON W. II, mgr. pur., Lakeland Regional Medical Center, Lakeland, FL '82 (PUR)
DEYERLE, TIM, dir. soc. work serv., Elmore County Hospital, Wetumpka, AL '82 (SOC)
DEYOUNG, JOY M., adm. asst., Research Medical Center, Kansas City, MO '82
DEYOUNG, TODD M., mgt. eng., Emory University Hospital, Atlanta, GA '87 (MGMT)
DEZERN, NORMA R., supv. sterile proc., Duke University Medical Center, Durham, NC '85 (CS)
DIAMOND, DAVID H., atty., Long Island Jewish Medical Center, New York, NY '83 (ATTY)
DIAMOND, DONALD A., dir. eng., Mount Auburn Hospital, Cambridge, MA '84 (ENG)
DIAMOND, DOROTHY I., dir. vol. serv., Presbyterian Hospital in the City of New York, New York, NY '86 (VOL)
DIAMOND, EUGENE B., dir. mktg., Hospital Financial Association, New York, NY '71
DIAMOND, JAN C., asst. dir., University of California Davis Medical Center, Sacramento, CA '78
DIAMOND, LENORE J., asst. adm., HCA North Beach Hospital, Fort Lauderdale, FL '81
DIAMOND, LESTER KENT, asst. adm., Charter Plains Hospital, Lubbock, TX '84
DIAMOND, O. PATRICIA, RN, vice-pres. nrsg., Hutchinson Hospital Corporation, Hutchinson, KS '77 (NURS)
DIAMOND, P. ANN, dir. diet., Ottawa Civic Hospital, Ottawa, Ont., Canada '81 (FOOD)
DIAMOND, PAUL F., dir. compensation and benefits, Northwestern Memorial Hospital, Chicago, IL '86 (PERS)
DIAMOND, VICKIE L., adm. asst. nrsg., Penrose Hospitals, Colorado Springs, CO '85 (NURS)
DIAZ-FORNS, ISABEL L., dir. soc. serv., Victoria Hospital, Miami, FL '84 (SOC)
DIAZ, DENNIS S., atty., St. Joseph Health System, Orange, CA '85 (ATTY)
DIAZ, EDMUND M., dir. emp. and labor rel., Duke University Medical Center, Durham, NC '85 (PERS)
DIAZ, JAMES, partner, Kaplan, McLaughlin and Diaz, San Francisco, CA '79
DIAZ, JESUS RAFAEL, dir. nrsg., Coral Gables Hospital, Coral Gables, FL '85 (NURS)
DIBBLE, FREDERICK N., mgr. environ. studies and govt. health policy affairs, Smith Kline and French, Philadelphia, PA '85
DIBBLE, KERRY, dir. vol. serv., Magee Rehabilitation Hospital, Philadelphia, PA '80 (VOL)
DIBENEDETTO, MARY CATHERINE, supv. hskpg., Bridgeton Hospital, Bridgeton, NJ '86 (ENVIRON)
DIBIAS, NANCY E., dir. surg. serv., Colleton Regional Hospital, Walterboro, SC '86 (CS)
DIBIASO, CARMEN F., dir. pur., Gnaden Huetten Memorial Hospital, Lehighton, PA '83 (PUR)
DIBITETTO, GEORGE F. JR., adm. mgr. plant oper., George Washington University Hospital, Washington, DC '86 (ENG)
DICAMPLI, JOSEPH V., assoc. dir., West Park Hospital, Philadelphia, PA '72
DICARLO, SAM E., vice-pres., Hart-Freeland-Roberts, Inc., Nashville, TN '81
DICE, JEFFREY N., dir. soc. work serv., Welborn Memorial Baptist Hospital, Evansville, IN '76 (SOC)
DICHTER, ROBERT M., student, Boston University Health Management Programs, Boston, MA '84
DICICCO, ELAINE B., co-dir. educ., Griffin Hospital, Derby, CT '79 (EDUC)
DICK, CATHERINE T., student, University of Texas, School of Allied Health Sciences, Department of Health Related Studies, Galveston, TX '82
DICK, JAMES H., dir. maint. and eng., King's Daughters' Hospital, Staunton, VA '80 (ENG)
DICK, LOIS CHAPMAN, dir. soc. serv., Valley Medical Center, Renton, WA '85 (SOC)
DICK, MARTHA SUE, pat. rep., St. Mary's Hospital, Reno, NV '85 (PAT)
DICK, ROBERT E., asst. dir. eng., St. Joseph Health Center, St. Charles, MO '81 (ENG)
DICKENS, BARBARA SCHAEFER, head health and educ., Cape Coral Hospital, Cape Coral, FL '83 (EDUC)
DICKENS, KEN, chief eng., St. Rose Hospital, Hayward, CA '85 (ENG)
DICKENSON, JOAN M., dir. soc. serv., Burnaby Hospital, Burnaby, B.C., Canada '82 (SOC)
DICKENSON, NANCY A., dir. mktg. and prog. dev., Ross General Hospital, Ross, CA '86 (PR)
DICKERHOOF, PAMELA WISEMAN, dir. vol. serv., Lovelace Medical Center, Albuquerque, NM '80 (VOL)
DICKERSON, BETTY, RN, asst. dir. nrsg. serv., Radford Community Hospital, Radford, VA '80 (NURS)
DICKERSON, CLAUDIA W., atty., Hospital Corporation of America, Nashville, TN '84 (ATTY)
DICKERSON, CLINTON W., off. sup. mgt., Howard University Hospital, Washington, DC '78 (PUR)
DICKERSON, FOGER C., Carlsbad, CA '86 (MGMT)
DICKERSON, JEAN W., RN, head nrs. cent. sup., Elizabethtown Community Hospital, Elizabethtown, NY '82 (CS)
DICKERSON, JEANETTE H., rep. pat. affairs, Martin Army Hospital, Fort Benning, GA '77 (PAT)
DICKERSON, MARY E., dir. vol. serv., St. John Hospital, Cleveland, OH '84 (VOL)
DICKERSON, S. L., dir. risk mgt., safety and security, Saints Mary and Elizabeth Hospital, Louisville, KY '85 (RISK)
DICKERSON, THELMA M., EdD RN, vice-pres., Fort Sanders Regional Medical Center, Knoxville, TN '76 (NURS)
DICKES, COL. DAVID W., dir. matl. mgt., Lake Chelan Community Hospital, Chelan, WA '73 (PUR)
DICKEY, DAVID M., dir. biomedical eng., Washington Hospital Center, Washington, DC '85 (ENG)
DICKEY, DELORES, RN, dir. educ., Lodi Memorial Hospital, Lodi, CA '79 (EDUC)
DICKEY, JOHN M., asst. vice-pres. med. and dent. staff support serv., Bethesda Hospital, Inc., Cincinnati, OH '78
DICKEY, LEONARD H., dir. facil. mgt., Moses H. Cone Memorial Hospital, Greensboro, NC '82 (ENG)
DICKEY, MARY ANN, RN, assoc. dir.-med. nrsg., St. Vincent Hospital and Medical Center, Portland, OR '82 (NURS)
DICKINSON, DONALD, dir. plant oper., HCA Oak Hill Hospital, Spring Hill, FL '85 (ENG)
DICKINSON, E. FEEN, dir. amb. care, Saint Vincent Hospital, Billings, MT '87 (AMB)
DICKINSON, ELEANOR, supv. cent. serv., Andrew Kaul Memorial Hospital, St. Marys, PA '80 (CS)
DICKINSON, GEORGE A. JR., vice-pres. fin., Chenango Memorial Hospital, Norwich, NY '81 (PLNG)
DICKINSON, W. ANDREW JR., sr. vice-pres., Roanoke Memorial Hospitals, Roanoke, VA '73

DICKMAN, LINDA C., dir. vol. serv., Riverside Osteopathic Hospital, Trenton, MI '82 (VOL)
DICKMAN, VIRGINIA K., dir. soc. serv., Idaho Elks Rehabilitation Hospital, Boise, ID '86 (SOC)
DICKS, ANNE, student, Program in Health Care Administration, Baruch College Mount Sinai School of Medicine, New York, NY '86
DICKS, GARY R., dir. audit and syst., Lutheran General Hospital, San Antonio, TX '82 (MGMT)
DICKSON, ALON NANCY, pat. rep., St. Mary Medical Center, Hobart, IN '82 (PAT)
DICKSON, ELLEN, doctoral student, Program in Public Administration and Health Policy, University of Colorado, Denver, CO '86
DICKSON, HAROLD D., dir. health serv. res., Baptist Memorial Hospital, Memphis, TN '81 (MGMT)
DICKSON, JOSEPH M., adm., Scott and White Memorial Hospital, Temple, TX '61
DICKSON, LAURENCE A., corp. dir. matl. mgt., Sisters of Providence, Seattle, WA '83 (PUR)
DICKSON, MARY JANICE, RN, vice-pres. nrsg., Baptist Medical Center, Little Rock, AR '75 (NURS)
DICKSON, MELVIN, chief eng., Stevens Community Memorial Hospital, Morris, MN '80 (ENG)
DICKSON, ROBERT J., atty., Providence Hospital, Anchorage, AK '77 (ATTY)
DICOLA, JOHN F., sr. mgr., Ernst and Whinney, Milwaukee, WI '85 (PLNG)
DICUS, MICHAEL E., supv. support contr., Los Angeles County-University of Southern California Medical Center, Los Angeles, CA '81 (PUR)
DIDARIO, ALBERT R., dir. soc. work, Haverford State Hospital, Haverford, PA '77 (SOC)
DIDIER, GEORGE B., pres., Ohio Health Management Services, Inc., Worthington, OH '68 (MGMT)
DIDIER, THOMAS G., dir. plant oper., Great Plains Regional Medical Center, North Platte, NE '86 (ENG)
DIDONATO, RONALD J., AMI Town and Country Medical Center, Tampa, FL '85 (PUR)
DIEBOLD, CLAUDIA, RN, educ. consult., East Alabama Medical Center, Opelika, AL '78 (EDUC)
DIECK, ANTONIO J., PhD, asst. prof. indust. eng., St. Mary's University, San Antonio, TX '84 (MGMT)
DIECKMANN, LISA A., dir. pers., Seven Rivers Community Hospital, Crystal River, FL '84 (PERS)
DIEDRICH, STEVEN J., adm. plng., Deaconess Hospital of Cleveland, Cleveland, OH '84 (PLNG)
DIEFENDORF, JOHN J., dir. plant oper. and maint., Tallahassee Community Hospital, Tallahassee, FL '84 (ENG)
DIEFFENBACH, MARGARET HAWKINS, coor. pat. rep., Children's Hospital of King's and Daughters, Norfolk, VA '86 (PAT)
DIEHL, HAROLD JR., Mechanicsburg, PA '57 (LIFE)
DIEHL, JANE, RN, dir. nrsg., Sun Coast Hospital, Largo, FL '77 (NURS)
DIEHL, JOHN E., atty., University of Minnesota Hospital and Clinic, Minneapolis, MN '76 (ATTY)
DIEHL, JOSEPH E., dir. maint., Methodist Medical Center of Oak Ridge, Oak Ridge, TN '84 (ENG)
DIEHL, JUNE M., RN, dir. nrsg. serv., Robert Wood Johnson University Hospital, New Brunswick, NJ '68
DIEHL, KENNETH G. JR., dir. mktg., Smith Seckman Reid, Inc., Nashville, TN '85
DIEHL, PHILIP L., sr. mgt. eng., Pennsylvania Hospital, Philadelphia, PA '86 (MGMT)
DIEHL, ROBERT E., asst. dir. eng. serv., Green Hospital of Scripps Clinic, La Jolla, CA '86 (ENG)
DIEHL, ROY H., mgr. matl., Berwick Hospital Center, Berwick, PA '83 (PUR)
DIEHL, RUTH N., dir. food serv., Glendale Memorial Hospital and Health Center, Glendale, CA '80 (FOOD)
DIENEMANN, JACQUELINE A., RN, asst. prof., Graduate Program in Nursing Administration, George Mason University, Fairfax, VA '86 (NURS)
DIENER, DON D., pres., Advanced Quality Towel and Linen Company, Los Angeles, CA '87 (ENVIRON)
DIEPENBROCK, JOHN V., atty., Mercy Hospital of Sacramento, Sacramento, CA '68 (ATTY)
DIERKER, ANNE H., asst. adm., Mary Free Bed Hospital and Rehabilitation Center, Grand Rapids, MI '81 (PERS)
DIESER, JAMES G., mgt. eng., Mercy Health Care Organization, Sacramento, CA '86 (MGMT)
DIESSNER, RAND, dir. soc. serv., St. Elizabeth Medical Center, Yakima, WA '85 (SOC)
DIETERLE, DONNAH J., adm., Homecaring Service, Kettering, OH '87 (AMB)
DIETIKER, RICHARD F., dir. nutr. serv., Lutheran Hospital of Fort Wayne, Fort Wayne, IN '73 (FOOD)
DIETMANN, ELIZABETH A., coor. pub. affairs, St. Catherine Hospital, East Chicago, IN '86 (PR)
DIETRICH, DEBORAH A., dir. soc. serv., Mercer County Community Hospital, Coldwater, OH '80 (SOC)
DIETRICH, FRED J., risk mgr., Halifax Hospital Medical Center, Daytona Beach, FL '79 (RISK)
DIETRICH, RICHARD A., proj. mgr., Reynolds, Smith and Hills Architects-Engineers, Jacksonville, FL '86 (ENG)
DIETZ, FRANCIS R., pres., Memorial Hospital, Pawtucket, RI '67
DIETZ, GREGORY F., asst. dir. facil., Holy Cross Hospital, Chicago, IL '84 (ENG)
DIETZ, JOYCE A., coor. guest rel., St. Francis Hospital Center, Beech Grove, IN '85 (PAT)
DIETZEN, SHEILA A., RN, asst. adm. nrsg., Yakima Valley Memorial Hospital, Yakima, WA '77 (NURS)
DIFLUMERI, VANESSA, sr. consult., Ernst and Whinney, Miami, FL '85 (PLNG)
DIGGS, WALTER W., asst. prof., University of Tennessee, Memphis, TN '55 (LIFE)
DIGIACOMO, ENZO V., vice-pres. med. affairs, Mercy Hospital, Springfield, MA '87 (AMB)
DIGIACOMO, MARY LOU, RN, vice-pres. nrsg. affairs, Mercy Hospital, Springfield, MA '74 (NURS)
DIGIORGIO, JOHN J., proj. dir., Fallon Community Health Service, Inc., Worcester, MA '74
DIGIOVANNI, LAWRENCE, asst. dir. eng. and maint., Alexian Brothers Hospital, Elizabeth, NJ '84 (ENG)
DIIORIO, ERMENEGILDO, assoc., Skidmore, Owings and Merrill, Houston, TX '83 (ENG)
DIJULIO, FLORENCE M., coor. soc. serv., pat. and family serv., Virginia Mason Hospital, Seattle, WA '85 (SOC)
DIKEOU, GEORGE D., atty., University Hospital, Denver, CO '73 (ATTY)
DILDY, DAVID B., dir. mgt. serv., East Texas Hospital Foundation, Tyler, TX '70 (MGMT)
DILEONARDI, ROBERT J., atty., Holy Family Hospital, Des Plaines, IL '68 (ATTY)
DILG, MARILYN A., RN, dir. soc. serv., Indiana Hospital, Indiana, PA '79 (SOC)
DILL, ROBERT J., sr. mgr., Peat, Marwick, Mitchell and Company, Dallas, TX '83 (PERS)
DILL, ROSE M., dir. pub. rel., Mount Carmel Mercy Hospital, Detroit, MI '84 (PR)
DILL, SHEILA C., dir. trng. and educ., St. Joseph Hospital, Lexington, KY '82 (EDUC)
DILL, WILLIAM A., pur. agt., Sunbury Community Hospital, Sunbury, PA '82 (PUR)
DILLARD, EILEEN ELEANOR, dir. diet., C. J. Harris Community Hospital, Sylva, NC '67 (FOOD)
DILLE, BRYCE H., atty., Good Samaritan Community Healthcare, Puyallup, WA '74 (ATTY)
DILLEHAY, LAWRENCE B., Northbrook, IL '50 (LIFE)
DILLER, SAMUEL W., atty., Bluffton Community Hospital, Bluffton, OH '79 (ATTY)
DILLEY, WILLIAM S., dir. food and nutr., AMI Brookwood Community Hospital, Orlando, FL '79 (FOOD)
DILLIE, MARGARET, RN, pat. care analyst, The Methodist Hospital, Houston, TX '81 (RISK)
DILLING, JAMES A., asst. dir. info. and mgt. serv., Rochester Methodist Hospital, Rochester, MN '81 (MGMT)
DILLINGHAM, MICHAEL R., exec. vice-pres., Comsul, Ltd., Houston, TX '85 (ENG)
DILLIONE, MARILYN A., RN, vice-pres. pat. care, St. Francis Medical Center, Trenton, NJ '78 (NURS)(AMB)
DILLON, DORANCE, dir. matl. mgt., St. Luke's Medical Center, Phoenix, AZ '84 (PUR)
DILLON, EDWARD B. JR., atty., St. Vincent Infirmary, Little Rock, AR '73 (ATTY)
DILLON, EILEEN M., RN, clin. dir., Mount Auburn Hospital, Cambridge, MA '86 (NURS)
DILLON, LARRY E., asst. adm. human res., St. Elizabeth Hospital, Beaumont, TX '82 (PERS)
DILLON, MARJORIE DIANNE, dir. soc. serv., Good Samaritan Hospital, West Islip, NY '77 (SOC)
DILLON, MAURA E., asst. dir. food serv., Bayley Seton Hospital, Staten Island, NY '84 (FOOD)
DILLON, MAUREEN, med. soc. worker, Southside Hospital, Bay Shore, NY '78 (SOC)
DILLON, WALTER B., Southern Pines, NC '53 (LIFE)
DILTS, J. RUSSELL, vice-pres., St. Paul Medical Center, Dallas, TX '87 (AMB)
DILTS, WILLIAM R., vice-pres. plng. and mktg., Rockford Memorial Hospital, Rockford, IL '79 (PLNG)
DILUZIO, ALBERT J., dir. cardiopulmonary center serv., Hamot Medical Center, Erie, PA '82
DIMARCO, JOAN M., partner, Laventhol and Horwath, Burlington, NJ '75
DIMENSTEIN, MICHAEL S., supv. comp., Yale-New Haven Hospital, New Haven, CT '83 (PERS)
DIMICK, SANDRA MARRS, dir. staff dev., Fort Sanders Regional Medical Center, Knoxville, TN '76 (EDUC)
DIMINO, JAMES F., dir. eng., St. Michael Hospital, Milwaukee, WI '76 (ENG)
DIMOND, SALLY, student, Duke University, Department of Health Administration, Durham, NC '83
DIMOTT, MARYANNE, adm. dir. emer. room, rad., guest rel. and vol., Framingham Union Hospital, Framingham, MA '85 (PAT)
DIMOTTA, PATRICK J., dir. pers., Astoria General Hospital, Long Island City, NY '85 (PERS)
DIMOW, JOAN M., mgt. syst. analyst, Children's Hospital of Wisconsin, Milwaukee, WI '82 (MGMT)
DINAUER, ANNETTE HELEN, assoc. dir. nrsg. serv., Holy Cross Hospital, Salt Lake City, UT '85 (PAT)
DINEEN, MEGAN, dir. mktg., Bristol Hospital, Bristol, CT '85 (PR) (PLNG)
DINEEN, NANCY A., RN, dir. nrsg., Charlton Memorial Hospital, Fall River, MA '80 (NURS)
DINES, DAVID EUGENE, exec. dir., St. Michael's Centre, Burnaby, B.C., Canada '85 (CS)
DINGRANI, ANITA, South Laguna, CA '85 (PLNG)
DININ, BENJAMIN G., MD, (ret.), Chatham, MA '46 (LIFE)
DINIZIO, GARY, dir. plant oper., Central Suffolk Hospital, Riverhead, NY '81 (ENG)
DINNEGAN, JAMES E., asst. dir. matl. mgt., Jewish Hospital, Louisville, KY '83 (PUR)
DINOTO, GREGORY A., PhD, dir. soc. serv., Shore Memorial Hospital, Somers Point, NJ '85 (SOC)
DINSE, JOHN M., atty., Medical Center Hospital of Vermont, Burlington, VT '70 (ATTY)
DINSMORE, ROBERT W., atty., Monongalia General Hospital, Morgantown, WV '78 (ATTY)
DION, DANIEL, mktg. support rep., Burroughs Corporation, Lombard, IL '86 (MGMT)
DIONNE, CLARENCE, dir. plant oper., Bay Area Medical Center, Marinette, WI '80 (ENG)
DIONNE, MAJ. RAOUL B., MSC USN, adm., Alexandria Health Department, Alexandria, VA '78
DIOSEGY, ARLENE J., atty., Costal Group, Inc., Durham, NC '81 (ATTY)
DIPAOLA-FAZIO, ANNE, dir. pers., Southampton Hospital, Southampton, NY '74 (PERS)
DIPAOLA, LOUIS, chief eng., Jersey Shore Medical Center, Neptune, NJ '83 (ENG)
DIPASQUALE, SANDRA A., DrPH, dir. health serv. resources, Sewickley Valley Hospital, Sewickley, PA '83 (PLNG)
DIPIETRO, JOSEPH J., dir. maint. serv., Holy Cross of Silver Spring, Silver Spring, MD '85 (ENG)
DIPIETRO, MELANIE, atty., Mercy Hospital of Johnstown, Johnstown, PA '86 (ATTY)
DIPIRRO, ELAINE M., dir. diet., Surburan Hospital and Sanitarium of Cook County, Hinsdale, IL '81 (FOOD)
DIPISA, RALPH, vice-pres., St. Anne's Hospital, Fall River, MA '80
DIPPEL, DORIS A., dir. educ., Riverside Medical Center, Kankakee, IL '83 (EDUC)
DIRIENZO, DAYNAL, mgr. corp. commun., Western Reserve Systems-Northside, Youngstown, OH '87 (PR)
DIRIENZO, MARIA T., dir. commun. rel., Lower Bucks Hospital, Bristol, PA '81 (PR)
DIRKSEN, MSGR. FRANK T., dir., Diocesan Hospital Office, Springfield, IL '51 (LIFE)
DIROSARIO, INEZ E., RN, head nrs. cent. serv., Penrose Hospitals, Colorado Springs, CO '84 (CS)
DISBENNETT, DON W., assoc. adm., Dolly Vinsant Memorial Hospital, San Benito, TX '73
DISBROW, LILLIAN E., dir. vol., Northern Ocean Hospital System, Point Pleasant, NJ '79 (VOL)
DISBROW, VICTOR JOSEPH, asst. supv. cent. serv. and coor. trng., Harford Memorial Hospital, Havre de Grace, MD '86
DISCH, JOANNE M., RN, clin. dir. nrsg., emer. and dialysis serv., Hospital of the University of Pennsylvania, Philadelphia, PA '86 (NURS)
DISHAMN, PATRICIA L., dir. pub. rel., St. Joseph's Hospital and Health Center, Paris, TX '86 (PR)
DISHMAN, D. REX, dir. pers. syst., Holy Cross Health System Corporation, South Bend, IN '77 (PERS)
DISINGER, ROBERT L., dir. food serv., Lafayette Home Hospital, Lafayette, IN '82 (FOOD)
DISLEY, JOAN E., actg. mgr. food prod. and diet., St. Joseph Medical Center, Joliet, IL '84 (FOOD)
DISNEY, CATHERINE E., dir. dev. and commun. info., Copley Hospital, Morrisville, VT '86 (PR)
DISNEY, KATHRYN K., dir. counseling and referral center, Rochester St. Mary's Hospital, Rochester, NY '75 (SOC)
DISON, CHARLOTTE C., RN, asst. adm., Baptist Hospital of Miami, Miami, FL '78 (NURS)
DISPENSA, PATRICIA A., mgr. pers., Oak Forest Hospital of Cook County, Oak Forest, IL '83 (PERS)
DISSER, ANTHONY, RN, vice-pres. nrsg. serv., Brokaw Hospital, Normal, IL '80 (NURS)
DISSINGER, JOYCE A., staff writer, Good Samaritan Hospital, Lebanon, PA '81 (PR)
DISTEFANO, JANET C., dir. pub. rel., House of the Good Samaritan, Watertown, NY '84 (PR)
DISTEL, CARYL A., dir. pat. advocacy, John F. Kennedy Medical Center, Edison, NJ '83 (PAT)
DITMAR, JOHN WILLIAM, dir. matl. mgt., Butterworth Hospital, Grand Rapids, MI '77 (PUR)
DITMER, DIANNE T., asst. sr. pat. rel., Kettering Medical Center, Kettering, OH '86 (PAT)
DITOMMASO, RICHARD A., Greensburg, PA '86 (PLNG)
DITTFURTH, DENNIS ERVIN, dir. diet., Spring Branch Memorial Hospital, Houston, TX '77 (FOOD)
DITTMAN, MARK A., environ. safety off., Henry Ford Hospital, Detroit, MI '86 (ENG)
DITTMER, MICHAEL, mgr. plant eng., Providence Hospital, Cincinnati, OH '86 (ENG)
DITZHAZY, JOHN G., dir. med. soc. work, Edward W. Sparrow Hospital, Lansing, MI '84 (SOC)
DIUGLIO, LEANORA, health care serv. consult., Alg Consultants, Inc., New York, NY '85 (RISK)
DIVALERIO, DENISE A., mgr. mktg., Frank Cuneo Memorial Hospital, Chicago, IL '86 (PLNG)
DIVELLO, DOUGLAS F., adm. dir., Kennedy Memorial Hospital, Turnersville, NJ '85
DIVER, DONALD F., dir. pur., Fairview General Hospital, Cleveland, OH '76 (PUR)
DIVERS, BRENDA SHARON, dir. educ., Lewis-Gale Hospital, Salem, VA '81 (EDUC)
DIVINCENTI, MARIE P., RN, dir. nrsg. prog., Louisiana State University Medical Center, School of Nursing, New Orleans, LA '66 (NURS)
DIVINYI, JOYCE E., dir. commun. rel. and mktg., Bradley Center, Columbus, GA '86 (PR)
DIVIS, KATHY L., assoc. dir. mktg., University of Alabama Hospitals, Birmingham, AL '86 (PR)
DIX, DAVID H., dir. pers., Regional Memorial Hospital, Brunswick, ME '81 (PERS)
DIXON, BARBARA J., RN, head nrs. cent. serv., Sibley Memorial Hospital, Washington, DC '81 (CS)
DIXON, CINDY R., dir. vol. serv., Moore Regional Hospital, Pinehurst, NC '86 (VOL)
DIXON, DEBBIE, Parker, CO '78 (PERS)
DIXON, DEBORAH L., dir. pers., HCA Park View Medical Center, Nashville, TN '86 (PERS)
DIXON, GAYLE L., dir. food and nutr. serv., Presbyterian Hospital, Charlotte, NC '86 (FOOD)
DIXON, GILBERT H., dir. hosp. serv., Chicago HMO, Chicago, IL '82
DIXON, HAROLD C., chief soc. work serv., Veterans Administration Medical Center, San Diego, CA '77 (SOC)
DIXON, HELEN I., RN, assoc. dir. nrsg. adm., St. Ann's Hospital of Columbus, Westerville, OH '80 (NURS)
DIXON, INGRID L., RN, asst. adm., St. Vincent Hospital, Green Bay, WI '82 (NURS)
DIXON, IRA, supv. maint., Mercy Hospital, Merced, CA '82 (ENG)
DIXON, JAMES B., assoc. dir., St. Paul-Ramsey Medical Center, St. Paul, MN '71
DIXON, JAMES M., vice-pres. res., Louisiana Hospital Association, Baton Rouge, LA '81 (MGMT)
DIXON, JAMES PAYSON, pres., University of North Carolina, School of Public Health, Chapel Hill, NC '48 (LIFE)
DIXON, JOHN DONALD, pres., Medical Planning and Development, Inc., Portland, OR '66

DIXON, JON MICHAEL, asst. vice-pres., Bronson Methodist Hospital, Kalamazoo, MI '74 (AMB)
DIXON, MIRIAM MAGUIRE, pat. rep., Marshall Hospital, Placerville, CA '86 (PAT)
DIXON, PATRICIA J., mgr. cent. serv., Liberty Hospital, Liberty, MO '85 (CS)
DIXON, RICHARD F., dir. matl. mgt., Mississauga Hospital, Mississauga, Ont., Canada '86 (PUR)
DIXON, ROBERT H. SR., dir. environ. serv., Irving Community Hospital, Irving, TX '84 (ENVIRON)
DIXON, THERESSA, RN, dir. nrsg., Northville Regional Psychiatric Hospital, Northville, MI '74 (NURS)
DIXON, THOMAS D'WAYNE, adm., John and Mary Kirby Hospital, Monticello, IL '67
DIXON, W. MCGREGOR JR., atty., Stouder Memorial Hospital, Troy, OH '85 (ATTY)
DMYTRYCK, PAUL J., mgt. eng., Hartford Hospital, Hartford, CT '70 (MGMT)
DOAK, MARY D., dir. commun. rel., Freeport Memorial Hospital, Freeport, IL '84 (PR)
DOAK, SUZANN, clin. soc. work, Southeastern Methodist Hospital, Dallas, TX '85 (SOC)
DOAN, BARBARA J., dir. vol., Irving Community Hospital, Irving, TX '83 (VOL)
DOAN, REBECCA, dir. soc. serv. and discharge plng., Kissimmee Memorial Hospital, Kissimmee, FL '85 (SOC)
DOBAL, MAY, student, Louisiana State University Medical Center School of Nursing, New Orleans, LA '86
DOBBERSTEIN, KATHLEEN, dir. pat. educ. and media serv., Grady Memorial Hospital, Atlanta, GA '86 (EDUC)
DOBBINS, JAMES C. JR., dir. pers., Gaston Memorial Hospital, Gastonia, NC '84 (PERS)
DOBBINS, NAKETA H., dir. pub. rel., Indiana Hospital, Indiana, PA '86 (PR)
DOBBS, EDITH A., RN, (ret.), Baltimore, MD '67 (CS)
DOBBS, HUBERT L., LLD, pres. emeritus, Baptist Hospitals, Louisville, KY '36 (LIFE)
DOBBS, KATHE B., RN, exec. dir., Washington Organization of Nurse Executives, Seattle, WA '86 (NURS)
DOBIES, ANTHONY JAMES, coor. med. dist., Veterans Administration Medical Center, Gainesville, FL '75
DOBOS, GLENN THOMAS, dir. gen. serv., Orlando Regional Medical Center, Orlando, FL '86 (ENVIRON)
DOBOSENSKI, DAVID M., mgt. eng., Fairview Hospital and Healthcare Service, Minneapolis, MN '87 (MGMT)
DOBROVOLSKY, GEORGE, dir. pur., Englewood Hospital, Englewood, NJ '73 (PUR)
DOBRZYNSKI, KATHRYN R., dir. cent. proc., Saint Vincent Health Center, Erie, PA '81 (CS)
DOBSON, BETH, atty., Southern Maine Medical Center, Biddeford, ME '86 (ATTY)
DOBSON, M. GERALDINE, dir. risk mgt. and loss prevention, St. Francis Hospital Systems, Colorado Springs, CO '80 (RISK)
DOBYNS, CLIFFORD N., mgt. analyst, Medical Center East, Birmingham, AL '78 (MGMT)
DOCEKAL, KENNETH F., dir. eng. serv., Meridian Park Hospital, Tualatin, OR '81 (ENG)
DOCKEMEYER, JOSEPH R., dir. food serv., Saint Joseph Hospital and Health Center, Kokomo, IN '67 (FOOD)
DOCKERY, GLENDA, RN, dir. nrs., Levi Arthritis Hospital, Hot Springs National Park, AR '77 (NURS)
DOCKERY, ORVILLE DON, dir. environ. serv., HCA Doctors Hospital, Conroe, TX '86 (ENVIRON)
DOCKERY, VERNON J., pres., Metropolitan Medical Center Fundation, Minneapolis, MN '82
DOCKHAM, JAMES, dir. environ. serv., Harding Hospital, Worthington, OH '86 (ENVIRON)
DOCKHORN, JEAN M., (ret.), Baltimore, MD '67 (SOC)
DOCKINS, FRANCES T., pat. rep., St. Thomas Hospital, Nashville, TN '83 (PAT)
DOCKINS, PHYLLIS J., coor. pers., Ukiah Adventist Hospital, Ukiah, CA '83 (PERS)
DOCTO, AURORA TRINIDAD, dir. food serv., Broken Arrow Medical Center, Broken Arrow, OK '81 (FOOD)
DOCTOR, BERNARD H., dir. mgt. eng., Jewish Hospital of Cincinnati, Cincinnati, OH '67 (MGMT)
DOCTOR, RICHARD P., plant eng., St. Elizabeth Hospital, Elizabeth, NJ '83 (ENG)
DODD, ANN M., sr. mgr. health care fin., The Toronto-Dominion Bank, New York, NY '86
DODD, JOANNE, dir. pub. rel., Deaconess Medical Center, Billings, MT '76 (PR)
DODD, JOHNNY L., dir. pers., North Arkansas Medical Center, Harrison, AR '81 (PERS)
DODD, KATHLEEN, RN, dir., Baptist Home Care Services, Kansas City, MO '87 (AMB)
DODD, LORETTA K., RN, dir. clin. nrsg., Memorial Medical Center, Springfield, IL '82 (NURS)
DODDRIDGE, TOMMY, mgr. natl. commun. prod., Power and Telephone Supply Company, Inc., Memphis, TN '86 (ENG)
DODDS, VIRGINIA, RN, pat. serv. adv., Veterans Administration Medical Center, Durham, NC '84 (NURS)
DODERO, FRANK C., risk consult., Victor O. Schinnerer, Inc., Chicago, IL '86 (RISK)
DODGE, JILL, dir. soc. serv., Vista Hill Hospital, Chula Vista, CA '86 (SOC)
DODGE, JOHN P., mgr. Idry., Leominster Hospital, Leominster, MA '86 (ENVIRON)
DODGE, LAURA M., chief soc. worker, Champlain Valley Physicians Hospital Medical Center, Plattsburgh, NY '84 (SOC)
DODRILL, DEL H., risk mgr., Shawnee Mission Medical Center, Shawnee Mission, KS '84 (RISK)
DODRILL, MARTIN C., pres., Health Systems Association, Lima, OH '86 (PLNG)
DODSON, ARLESS JAMES, dir. soc. serv., Mercy Hospital, Altoona, PA '77 (SOC)
DODSON, DEBRA LEWIS, dir. commun. rel., Memorial Hospital, Danville, VA '82 (PR)
DODSON, DOUGLAS A., exec. dir., Lee Memorial Hospital, Fort Myers, FL '79
DODSON, LANCE S., dir. pub. rel., St. Anthony Medical Center, Crown Point, IN '81 (PR)
DODSON, LYNN M., dir. soc. serv., Mercy Hospital, Toledo, OH '85 (SOC)
DOEHLING, GLORIA J., asst. adm., Doctors Hospital of Dallas, Dallas, TX '79 (MGMT)
DOELLE, MICHAEL B., vice-pres. and assoc. gen. counsel litigation, Blue Cross and Blue Shield of Michigan, Detroit, MI '77 (ATTY)
DOERHOFF, ROGER L., dir. plant oper., St. Peters Community Hospital, St. Peters, MO '81 (ENG)
DOERING, HERMAN W., dir. mgt. eng., Porter Memorial Hospital, Denver, CO '81 (MGMT)
DOERING, WALT R., assoc. dir. human res., Saint Joseph Health Center Kansas, Kansas City, MO '86 (PERS)
DOERNER, FRED W. JR., atty., South Miami Hospital, South Miami, FL '86 (ATTY)
DOERR, DAVID R., vice-pres., Union Hospital, Terre Haute, IN '83
DOERR, TERRY, dir. matl. mgt., Providence Medical Center, Portland, OR '75 (PUR)
DOES, SR. M. STEPHEN, pat. rep., Saint Joseph Hospital, Elgin, IL '82 (PAT)
DOFFERMYRE, L. RANDOLPH III, atty., Betsy Johnson Memorial Hospital, Dunn, NC '86 (ATTY)
DOHENY, FRANK P. JR., atty., Saints Mary and Elizabeth Hospital, Louisville, KY '71 (ATTY)
DOHENY, JUSTIN E., pres., Wayne General Hospital, Wayne, NJ '74 (PLNG)
DOHERTY, HELEN T., dir. diet., Massachusetts General Hospital, Boston, MA '77 (FOOD)
DOHERTY, JAMES P. JR., atty., Opelousas General Hospital, Opelousas, LA '79 (ATTY)
DOHERTY, JANET L., dir. vol. serv., St. Joseph Hospital, Orange, CA '82 (VOL)
DOHERTY, KATHLEEN, mgr. food serv., North Kansas City Hospital, North Kansas City, MO '78 (FOOD)
DOHERTY, MARGARET A., dir. admissions, Visiting Nurse Association of Boston, Boston, MA '84 (PLNG)
DOHERTY, THOMAS B., asst. dir. pur., University of Michigan Hospitals, Ann Arbor, MI '79 (PUR)
DOHERTY, WILLIAM THOMAS, supt. plant, Saint Francis Hospital and Medical Center, Hartford, CT '62 (ENG)
DOHLEN, GILBERT E., dir. matl. mgt. serv., Swedishamerican Hospital, Rockford, IL '82 (PUR)
DOHNAL, JEANETTE T., coor. pat. educ., Piedmont Hospital, Atlanta, GA '85 (EDUC)
DOHNER, JEAN SHOTT, chm. soc. work, Philhaven Hospital, Mount Gretna, PA '86 (SOC)
DOHRMAN, MARGIE M., dep. dir. and sr. clin. soc. work, U. S. Public Health Service Alaska Native Medical Center, Anchorage, AK '80 (SOC)
DOLACK, GARY A., chief exec. off., Bertie Memorial Hospital, Windsor, NC '67
DOLAM, MARGARET B., RN, dir. nrsg., spec. care, Tulane University Hospital and Clinics, New Orleans, LA '86 (NURS)
DOLAN, ANDREW KEVIN, atty., Bogle and Gates, Seattle, WA '80 (ATTY)
DOLAN, BARBARA, dir. support serv., Glenbrook Hospital, Glenview, IL '84 (PLNG)
DOLAN, COLLEEN A., dir. trng. and dev., Providence Medical Center, Seattle, WA '86 (EDUC)
DOLAN, ELIZABETH M., RN, asst. adm. nrsg., Booth Memorial Medical Center, Flushing, NY '80 (NURS)
DOLAN, LINDA R., RN, coor. pat. care, Delaware County Memorial Hospital, Drexel Hill, PA '80 (NURS)
DOLAN, MICHAEL C., asst. vice-pres., St. Agnes Hospital and Medical Center, Fresno, CA '84 (PUR)
DOLAN, ROBERT L., assoc. adm., Jefferson Regional Medical Center, Pine Bluff, AR '83 (RISK)
DOLAN, THOMAS C., PhD, vice-pres. corp. ventures and dev., American College of Healthcare Executives, Chicago, IL '73 (PLNG)
DOLE, REBECCA A., dir. mktg. and pub. rel., Sarah Bush Lincoln Health Center, Mattoon, IL '86 (PR)
DOLE, SENATOR ROBERT J., Washington, DC '84 (LIFE)
DOLEJS, JOSEPH M., consult. eng., Dolejs and Associates, Mankato, MN '80 (ENG)
DOLES, GEORGE A., supv. preventive maint., Rochester St. Mary's Hospital, Rochester, NY '86 (ENG)
DOLFAY, THOMAS J., dir. mktg., St. Joseph Center for Mental Health, Omaha, NE '84 (PR) (PLNG)
DOLICH, CAROL L., dir. vol., Rye Psychiatric Hospital Center, Rye, NY '86 (VOL)
DOLINGER, JAMES D., dir. food serv., Spohn Hospital, Corpus Christi, TX '85 (FOOD)
DOLINICH, MARTHA E., instr. nrsg. in-service, Wheeling Hospital, Wheeling, WV '84 (EDUC)
DOLINS, DAVID, exec. vice-pres. and dir., Beth Israel Hospital, Boston, MA '66
DOLL, ANNE B., sr. vice-pres. corp. commun. and mktg., Miami Valley Hospital, Dayton, OH '83 (PR)
DOLL, GEORGE J., dir. soc. work, Levindale Geriatric Center and Hospital, Baltimore, MD '86 (SOC)
DOLL, JAMES, dir. plant oper., Holy Cross Parkview Hospital, Plymouth, IN '81 (ENG)
DOLL, JANE E., dir. mgt. eng., Grand View Hospital, Sellersville, PA '85 (MGMT)
DOLL, LES, asst. mgr. maint., N. T. Enloe Memorial Hospital, Chico, CA '86 (ENG)
DOLLARTON, MICHAEL J., mgr. pur., Chestnut Hill Hospital, Philadelphia, PA '82 (PUR)
DOLOJAN, ANA H., RN, asst. vice-pres. nrsg., Hadley Memorial Hospital, Washington, DC '85 (NURS)(RISK)
DOMAINGUE, RICHARD A., asst. vice-pres., Healthcare Service of New England, Inc., Stoughton, MA '82 (PUR)
DOMANSKI, MARGARET DIETZ, dir. soc. work, Henry Ford Hospital, Detroit, MI '84 (SOC)
DOMBKOWSKI, KEVIN J., prog. scientist, Vector Research, Inc., Arlington, VA '85 (MGMT)
DOMBRO, SANDRA B., dir. mktg. plng., Harrisburg Hospital, Harrisburg, PA '84 (PLNG)
DOMBROWSKI, DALE C., dir. pub. rel., St. Rose de Lima Hospital, Henderson, NV '85 (PR)
DOMBROWSKI, RICHARD J., dir. eng., Lower Bucks Hospital, Bristol, PA '78 (ENG)
DOMENGEAUX, BEVERLY, adm. asst. prof. affairs, Rockdale Hospital, Conyers, GA '85 (RISK)
DOMINE, ROBERT M., student, University of Pennsylvania, Philadelphia, PA '83 (MGMT)
DOMINEY, DONALD J., vice-pres. gen. serv., Children's Medical Center, Dayton, OH '73 (ENG)
DOMINGUE, DALLAS, supt. maint., Rayne-Branch Hospital, Rayne, LA '66 (ENG)
DOMINIANI, DAVID A., asst. adm. fiscal serv., Seidle Memorial Hospital, Mechanicsburg, PA '86
DOMINICK, EILEEN H., prog. supv. soc. work, Clinical Center National Institute of Health, Bethesda, MD '81 (SOC)
DOMINICK, FRANK, atty., St. Vincent's Hospital, Birmingham, AL '73 (ATTY)
DOMINIQUE, P. PIERRE, atty., Charles E. Still Osteopathic Hospital, Jefferson City, MO '74 (ATTY)
DOMINO, BOHDANNA, dir. food serv., St. Anne's Hospital, Chicago, IL '82 (FOOD)
DOMINSKY, LARRY J., mgt. syst. eng., Hahnemann University Hospital, Philadelphia, PA '85 (MGMT)
DOMKE, GENE, dir. eng. serv., Glendale Adventist Medical Center, Glendale, CA '79 (ENG)
DOMSIC, DENNIS M., adm. asst. to chief of staff, Veterans Administration Medical Center, Iowa City, IA '73
DONAHEY, RICHARD G., dir. pers., Greenville Hospital System, Greenville, SC '84 (PERS)
DONAHO, BARBARA A., RN, vice-pres. nrsg. and pat. serv., Shands Hospital at the University of Florida, Gainesville, FL '67 (NURS)
DONAHUE, ANNMARIE, RN, asst. dir. clin. nrsg., New England Sinai Hospital, Stoughton, MA '86 (NURS)
DONAHUE, JAMES A., asst. to pres., West Jersey Hospital, Northern Division, Camden, NJ '80 (RISK)
DONAHUE, JAMES F., plant eng., Abington Memorial Hospital, Abington, PA '70 (ENG)
DONAHUE, JAMES L. JR., sr. consult., Ernst and Whinney, Charlotte, NC '83 (PLNG)
DONAHUE, LINDA L., asst. vice-pres. support serv., Magee-Womens Hospital, Pittsburgh, PA '85 (AMB)
DONAHUE, MICHELLE, coor. qual. assur., Hemet Valley Hospital District, Hemet, CA '86 (RISK)
DONAHUE, PATRICA A., dir. human res., Friedman Hospital, Philadelphia, PA '84 (PERS)
DONAHUE, RUSSEL L., dir. pub. rel., Penobscot Bay Medical Center, Camden, ME '86 (PR)
DONAHUE, WILLIAM PAUL JR., dir. oper. and prov. rel., Health Preferred of Mid-America, Chicago, IL '84
DONALD, DONNA MCDONALD, adm., Surprise Valley Hospital District, Cedarville, CA '53 (LIFE)
DONALD, MICHELE R., assoc., Applied Management Systems, Inc., Burlington, MA '86 (MGMT)
DONALD, SUSAN, mgr. soc. serv., St. John's Hospital, Longview, WA '86 (SOC)
DONALDSON, BARBARA, dir. vol., Victory Memorial Hospital, Waukegan, IL '79 (VOL)
DONALDSON, CATHERINE J., dir. mktg. and pub. rel., Westview Hospital, Indianapolis, IN '83 (PR)
DONALDSON, DAVID A., vice-pres., Voluntary Hospitals of America Enterprises, Inc., Tampa, FL '74 (MGMT)
DONALDSON, E. CAROL, coor. educ., Baptist Medical Center-Princeton, Birmingham, AL '87 (EDUC)
DONALDSON, LINDA, design coor., Tanner Medical Center, Carrollton, GA '86 (PR)
DONALDSON, MARGARET L., dir. vol. serv., Bella Vista Hospital, Mayaguez, P.R. '85 (VOL)
DONALDSON, MARVIN W., mgr. matl., Holy Family Hospital, Spokane, WA '77 (PUR)
DONALDSON, ROBERTA, RN, asst. dir. pur. and matl. serv., Sinai Hospital of Detroit, Detroit, MI '81 (CS)
DONALDSON, SUSAN R., dir. matl. mgt., Children's Hospital, Baltimore, MD '78 (CS)(PUR)
DONALDSON, WILLIAM D., dir. matl. mgt., Westland Medical Center, Westland, MI '86 (PUR)
DONALDSON, WILLIAM E., atty., St. John's Hospital, Lowell, MA '80 (ATTY)
DONBAUGH, BARRY E., dir. pers., Strong Memorial Hospital of the University of Rochester, Rochester, NY '85 (PERS)
DONDONAN, CORAZON C., asst. dir. diet., William Beaumont Hospital-Troy, Troy, MI '86 (FOOD)
DONEGAN, DIANA LEE, pat. advocate, Washington County Hospital, Hagerstown, MD '87 (PAT)
DONELSON, BRUCE F., dir. eng., Methodist Hospital, Omaha, NE '76 (ENG)
DONEY, DIANE E., mgr. food serv., Scottsdale Memorial Hospital, Scottsdale, AZ '81 (FOOD)
DONEY, JOSEPH J., Bradenton, FL '51 (LIFE)
DONICA, JOHN P., consult., Donica Photography, Nashville, TN '83 (PR)
DONIEL, DEBORAH J., sr. cost containment analyst, Crownlife Insurance Company, Alexandria, VA '85
DONIN, DAVID K., exec. dir., Humana Hospital -St. Petersburg, St. Petersburg, FL '86
DONIN, ROBERT A., Fullerton, CA '80
DONLEY, JAMES E., chief eng., Ohio Valley Medical Center, Wheeling, WV '75 (ENG)
DONLIN, MICHAEL T., Naval Hospital, Great Lakes, IL '77
DONNAL, CATHERINE A., student, Medical College of Virginia, Program in Health Administration, Richmond, VA '83
DONNELLY, JAMES F. III, dir. fiscal support serv., Salem Hospital, Salem, MA '79
DONNELLY, JO ANN, coor. shared food serv., Non-Profit Hospitals Venture, Largo, FL '85 (FOOD)
DONNELLY, JOHN J., vice-pres. human res., International Medical Centers, Miami, FL '78
DONNELLY, JOSEPH MICHAEL, dir. mgt. eng., Little Company of Mary Hospital, Evergreen Park, IL '74 (MGMT)

DONNELLY, KAREN, dir. hskpg. and linen, Evergreen Hospital Medical Center, Kirkland, WA '87 (ENVIRON)
DONNELLY, KEVIN F., asst. dir., Downstate Medical Center, Brooklyn, NY '86 (CS)
DONNELLY, KEVIN J., William S. Middleton Memorial Veterans Hospital, Madison, WI '82 (SOC)
DONNELLY, MARGARET K., dir. mktg. matl. mgt. serv., Parkside Associates, Inc., Park Ridge, IL '83 (PUR)
DONNELLY, MARY E., pat. rep., Children's Hospital National Medical Center, Washington, DC '78 (PAT)
DONNELLY, MARY ELLEN, RN, dir. nrsg. serv., San Pedro Peninsula Hospital, San Pedro, CA '80 (NURS)
DONNELLY, PAUL ALOYSIUS, exec. vice-pres., Hamot Medical Center, Erie, PA '61
DONNELLY, PAUL R., PhD, pres., P. R. Donnelly and Associates, Inc., Crestwood, MO '69
DONNELLY, THOMAS B., mgr. mktg., National Association for Ambulatory Care, Dallas, TX '73
DONNELLY, THOMAS J., exec. dir., Phoenixville Hospital, Phoenixville, PA '67
DONNELLY, WILLIAM J., vice-pres., Baystate Medical Center, Springfield, MA '73
DONNENWERTH, SHARON M., dir. food serv., Oaklawn Hospital, Marshall, MI '86 (FOOD)
DONNER, AARON B., atty., South Oaks Hospital, Amityville, NY '80 (ATTY)
DONNESON, REES M., dir. med. info., University of California Davis Medical Center, Sacramento, CA '76
DONOCOFF, BRIAN C., adm. in-patient, New York Hospital, New York, NY '81
DONOFRIO, JUDITH RIEGER, RN, dir. nrsg., Aspen Valley Hospital District, Aspen, CO '86 (NURS)
DONOGHUE, SR. EILEEN M., RN, dir. nrsg., St. Agnes Hospital of the City of Baltimore, Baltimore, MD '83 (NURS)
DONOHER, NORA E., dir. human res., Irvington General Hospital, Irvington, NJ '86 (PERS)
DONOHUE, MARIA, mgr. educ. serv., Holy Family Hospital, Des Plaines, IL '79 (EDUC)
DONOVAN, BETTY, dir. vol. serv., Easton Hospital, Easton, PA '80 (VOL)
DONOVAN, DANIEL R., assoc., Ringler Associates, Inc., Detroit, MI '80 (RISK)
DONOVAN, GAIL FREDERICK, exec. asst., Methodist Hospital, Brooklyn, NY '81
DONOVAN, JAMES P., Sun Belt Regional Medical Center East, Channelview, TX '85 (PLNG)
DONOVAN, JAMES W., exec. vice-pres., Community General Osteopathic Hospital, Harrisburg, PA '86 (RISK)
DONOVAN, JOHN F., atty., Mercy Hospital, Buffalo, NY '85 (ATTY)
DONOVAN, JOHN M., dir. maint. and plant oper., St. Margaret's Hospital for Women, Boston, MA '84 (ENG)
DONOVAN, KREAG, atty., Genesee Hospital, Rochester, NY '74 (ATTY)
DONOVAN, KYM M., mgt. eng., Baptist Hospital, Pensacola, FL '86 (MGMT)
DONOVAN, LAWRENCE L., dir. risk mgt., St. Mary's Hospital, West Palm Beach, FL '84 (RISK)
DONOVAN, MARGARET, dir. soc. work serv., Children's Hospital of Wisconsin, Milwaukee, WI '79 (SOC)
DONOVAN, MARILEE I., chairperson med. nrsg., Rush-Presbyterian-St. Luke's Medical Center, Chicago, IL '84 (NURS)
DONOVAN, ROBERT A., pres., Lowell General Hospital, Lowell, MA '71
DONOVAN, WILLIAM, (ret.), Winthrop, MA '59
DOODAN, JOSEPH E., sr. mgt. eng., Bethesda Oak Hospital, Cincinnati, OH '83 (MGMT)
DOOLEN, ROBERT W., student, South West Texas State University, San Marcos, TX '78 (EDUC)
DOOLEY, JEANNINE, dir. soc. serv., St. Mary's Hospital, Streator, IL '76 (SOC)
DOOLEY, KYLE, pub. rel. rep., Good Samaritan Medical Center, Phoenix, AZ '84 (PR)
DOOLEY, MICHAEL J., dir. mktg., Rockford Memorial Hospital, Rockford, IL '85 (PLNG)
DOOLEY, RICHARD J., prin., Sippel, Glidden, Bohan and Hicks, Milwaukee, WI '81 (PUR)
DOOLEY, ROBERT L., mng. assoc., The Nbbj Group, Seattle, WA '84 (ENG)
DOOLIN, LAURA E., plng. asst., Glens Falls Hospital, Glens Falls, NY '85 (PLNG)
DOOLITTLE, ALDEN T., plan adm., Capital Area Community Health Plan, Latham, NY '86
DOOLITTLE, FRED, dir. eng., Medical Center Hospital, Punta Gorda, FL '79 (ENG)
DOONAN, JUDITH E., pres., Authors and Anthropologists Research, Kalispell, MT '82 (PR)
DOPF, GAIL M., dir. pub. and govt. rel., Good Samaritan Hospital, Suffern, NY '85 (PR) (PLNG)
DOPKO, DIANE, asst. dir. food serv., St. Elizabeth Hospital Medical Center, Lafayette, IN '82 (FOOD)
DOPLER, KATHERINE, dir. pub. rel. and mktg. commun., Anaheim Memorial Hospital, Anaheim, CA '85 (PR)
DORAME, OLIVIA ORTIZ, mgr. pat. rel., Cigna Healthplan of Arizona, Inc., Tucson, AZ '85 (PAT)
DORAN, DENNIS J., chief exec. off., St. Francis Medical Center, Breckenridge, MN '84 (PLNG)
DORAN, ELIZABETH R., dir. cent. sterile sup., Eastern Maine Medical Center, Bangor, ME '80 (CS)
DORAN, JAMES M., asst. dir. food serv., Millard Fillmore Hospital, Buffalo, NY '84 (FOOD)
DORAN, S. PETER, dir. plant eng., Horton Memorial Hospital, Middletown, NY '79 (ENG)
DORE, JOHN M., HSA Greenbrier Hospital, Covington, LA '83 (PUR)
DOREMUS, BERTHA L., Bainbridge Island, WA '68 (SOC)
DOREMUS, CELIA JANE, dir. pub. rel., Atlanticare Corporation, Lynn, MA '83 (PR)
DORF, ANITA K., mgr. manpower productivity, Wesley Medical Center, Wichita, KS '87 (EDUC)
DORFMEIER, NEIL W., mgt. eng., Fresno Community Hospital and Medical Center, Fresno, CA '86 (MGMT)
DORFNER, SR. DONNA MARIE, dir. soc. serv., Divine Providence Hospital, Pittsburgh, PA '68 (SOC)
DORINSON, RODNEY D., DrPH, adm., Ormond Beach Memorial Hospital, Ormond Beach, FL '71 (PLNG)
DORIS, ANNETTE L., adm. asst. and planner, Kessler Institute for Rehabilitation, West Orange, NJ '83
DORIS, JAMES D., dir. bldg. serv., Shallowford Community Hospital, Chamblee, GA '78 (FOOD)
DORITY, JAMES L., vice-pres., Servicemaster Industries, Inc., Santa Ana, CA '69
DORMAN, D. DOUGLAS, dir. pers., Shenango Valley Medical Center, Farrell, PA '81 (PERS)
DORMANT, DIANE, pres., Dormant and Associates, Inc., Bloomington, IN '85 (EDUC)
DORN, JANE L., dir. plng., Memorial Hospital of Laramie County, Cheyenne, WY '83 (PLNG)
DORN, TALY, dir. matl. mgt., Glendale Adventist Medical Center, Glendale, CA '81 (PUR)
DORNER, HELEN, RN, dir. sup., proc. and distrib., Northwestern Memorial Hospital, Chicago, IL '78 (CS)
DORNHEGGEN, DAVID P., asst. adm., St. Luke Hospital, Fort Thomas, KY '72
DORO, GREGORY R., consult., Kowalski Dickow and Associates, Inc., Milwaukee, WI '85 (MGMT)
DORON, TOM, dir. commun. rel., Carraway Methodist Medical Center, Birmingham, AL '76 (PR)
DORRELL, CHARLES E., assoc. dir. eng., Baylor University Medical Center, Dallas, TX '86 (ENG)
DORRIS, WAYNE L., PhD, assoc. dir. res. and educ., University of Texas M. D. Anderson Hospital and Tumor Institute at Houston, Houston, TX '82 (SOC)
DORSE, BERNICE P., chief diet. serv., Veterans Administration Medical Center, Washington, DC '86 (FOOD)
DORSET, LINDA M., mgt. eng. and planner, Bon Secours Hospital, Grosse Pointe, MI '84 (PLNG)(MGMT)
DORSEY, DOROTHY J., asst. dir. food serv., St. Mary's Hospital, Passaic, NJ '85 (FOOD)
DORSEY, JOHN J., atty., Saint Vincent Hospital, Worcester, MA '86 (ATTY)
DORSKY, DEBORAH L., sr. consult., Ernst and Whinney, Chicago, IL '80
DORSON, BILL, dir. environ. serv., Portsmouth Psychiatric Center, Portsmouth, VA '86 (ENVIRON)
DORTCH, JESSE E., adm. res., Garfield Medical Center, Monterey Park, CA '83
DORTCH, JOHN M., sr. mgt. eng., Baptist Medical Centers, Birmingham, AL '85 (MGMT)
DORTCH, VIVIAN J., dir. vol. serv., Detroit Receiving Hospital, Detroit, MI '84 (VOL)
DOSHER, JON M., asst. adm. prof. serv., Passavant Area Hospital, Jacksonville, IL '81 (MGMT)
DOSS, JACKY R., dir. trng. and educ., Lloyd Noland Hospital and Health Centers, Birmingham, AL '85 (EDUC)
DOSS, LEIGH E., dir. emp. rel., AMI Columbia Regional Hospital, Columbia, MO '86 (PERS)
DOSS, MOUNIR, dir. fin. mgt., Jamaica Hospital, Jamaica, NY '81
DOSS, RUTH A., RN, dir. educ., Pontiac Osteopathic Hospital, Pontiac, MI '86 (EDUC)
DOSSETT, PENNY, RN, head nrs. amb. care, Hermann Hospital, Houston, TX '87 (AMB)
DOSTER, CYNTHIA J., dir. pers., Doctors Hospital, Detroit, MI '83 (PERS)
DOSTER, SANFORD R. JR., assoc. reg. mgr., SunHealth Corporation, Charlotte, NC '82 (MGMT)
DOTSON, PHILIP E., chief exec. off., Athens-Limestone Hospital, Athens, AL '87
DOTTERY, GEOFFREY G., sr. mgt. eng., St. John's Hospital and Health Center, Santa Monica, CA '79 (MGMT)
DOTTI, CHRISTINA M., coor. pub., Bon Secours Hospital of Methuen, Methuen, MA '85 (PR)
DOTTS, GEORGE JR., dir. plant oper. and maint., Suburban General Hospital, Norristown, PA '79 (ENG)
DOTY, CONNIE E., RN, asst. vice-pres. ped. nrsg.-gen., Children's Medical Center, Dayton, OH '85 (NURS)
DOTY, ELIZABETH, dir. qual. assur. and risk mgt., St. John's Regional Medical Center, Oxnard, CA '86 (RISK)
DOTY, WILLIAM H., dir. mktg., Barnes Hospital, St. Louis, MO '85 (PR)
DOUBEK, ALBERT E., dir. anesthesia and surg., Sioux Valley Hospital, Sioux Falls, SD '87 (AMB)
DOUBEK, FAYOLA M., coor. educ., St. Croix Valley Memorial Hospital, St. Croix Falls, WI '83 (EDUC)
DOUCET, LAWRENCE G., prin., Doucet and Mainka, Peekskill, NY '82 (ENG)
DOUGAL, WILLIAM P., vice-pres. plng. and med. staff affairs, Rhode Island Hospital, Providence, RI '71 (PLNG)
DOUGAN, THOMAS G., mgr. matl. mgt., Servicemaster Industries, Inc., Salisbury, NC '83 (PUR)
DOUGHERTY, DARLENE A., asst. dir. diet., University of California San Francisco, San Francisco, CA '74 (FOOD)
DOUGHERTY, DAVID MICHAEL, exec. dir. hskpg., Kennestone Regional Health Care Systems, Marietta, GA '86 (ENVIRON)
DOUGHERTY, DAVID WAYNE, consult., Residential Property Management, San Antonio, TX '87 (ENG)
DOUGHERTY, ELEANOR A., RN, vice-pres. nrsg., Saints Mary and Elizabeth Hospital, Louisville, KY '83 (NURS)
DOUGHERTY, EUGENE E., sr. proj. eng., F. G. McGaw Hospital, Loyola University, Maywood, IL '83 (ENG)
DOUGHERTY, H. ROBERT, dir. environ. and ldry. serv., HCA Riveredge Hospital, Forest Park, IL '86 (ENVIRON)
DOUGHERTY, JOSEPH D., dir. plant oper., Community Hospital of Ottawa, Ottawa, IL '84 (ENG)
DOUGHERTY, MARGARET V., dir. soc. work, Southern Chester County Medical Center, West Grove, PA '86 (SOC)
DOUGHERTY, PAUL J., vice-pres. risk mgt., Mercy Hospital, Scranton, PA '83 (RISK)
DOUGHERTY, RUTH A., dir. qual. mgt., St. Vincent's Medical Center, Jacksonville, FL '86 (PAT)(RISK)
DOUGHERTY, THOMAS E., atty., Hennepin County Medical Center, Minneapolis, MN '77 (ATTY)
DOUGHTY, SUSAN D., RN, dir. critical care nrsg., Maine Medical Center, Portland, ME '86 (NURS)
DOUGLAS, CURT R., assoc. dir. bus. dev., Sharp Hospitals, San Diego, CA '82 (PLNG)
DOUGLAS, DIANE, Slidell, LA '76 (FOOD)
DOUGLAS, DONALD E., dir. human res., Wesley Homes, Inc., Atlanta, GA '86 (PERS)
DOUGLAS, ELIZABETH, educ. consult., Sharp Memorial Hospital, San Diego, CA '85 (EDUC)
DOUGLAS, ELIZABETH, coor. clin. soc. serv., Mercy Hospital of Sacramento, Sacramento, CA '85 (SOC)
DOUGLAS, JAMES, dir., Medical Faculty Group, University of California, Irvine, CA '84
DOUGLAS, STANLEY J., vice-pres. commun. rel. and fund dev., St. Joseph's Hospital, Elmira, NY '83 (PR)
DOUGLAS, VIRGINIA M., dir. pat. rep. and vol. serv., St. John Hospital, Detroit, MI '68 (VOL)(PAT)
DOUGLAS, WILHELMINA, supv. cent. sterile, Sinai Hospital of Baltimore, Baltimore, MD '83 (CS)
DOUGLASS, CLYDE M., asst. dir. facil. eng., St. Marys Hospital of Rochester, Rochester, MN '78 (ENG)
DOUGLASS, H. ROBERT, chief exec. off., Robert Douglass Associates, Inc., Houston, TX '79 (PLNG)
DOUGLASS, JOHN F., dir. educ., Valley Medical Center, Renton, WA '86 (EDUC)
DOUGLASS, MARY S., asst. adm. amb. care serv., Paulding Memorial Medical Center, Dallas, GA '81 (CS)(AMB)
DOULD, CDR PHILIP EDWARD, MSC USN, (ret.), South Weymouth, MA '70
DOURLET, JACQUELINE A., student, Michigan State University, East Lansing, MI '86 (PLNG)
DOUROUX, LEE, dir. eng., AMI Rancho Encino Hospital, Encino, CA '86 (ENG)
DOUTHITT, J. MICHAEL, exec. dir., Physicians and Surgeons Hospital, Shreveport, LA '76
DOVER, JAMES W., mgr. human res., St. Charles Medical Center, Bend, OR '85 (PERS)
DOVER, LARRY F., dir. plant serv., Humana Hospital -Gwinnett, Snellville, GA '78 (ENG)
DOVER, MARION Z., RN, dir. pat. serv., Androscoggin Valley Hospital, Berlin, NH '79 (NURS)
DOVEY, CHARLES J., chief exec. off., American Medtech, San Diego, CA '84
DOW, CANDACE F., health mgt. consult., Honeywell, Minneapolis, MN '80
DOW, DANA, mgr. pers., Boaz-Albertville Medical Center, Boaz, AL '79 (PERS)
DOW, RALPH W., mgr. food serv., Fairbanks Memorial Hospital, Fairbanks, AK '75 (FOOD)
DOW, RANDOLPH C., atty., Moore Regional Hospital, Pinehurst, NC '84 (ATTY)
DOWD, DENISE M., dir. pub. rel., Children's Hospital of the King's Daughters, Norfolk, VA '85 (PR)
DOWD, MARY ELLEN, coor. pat. rel., Framingham Union Hospital, Framingham, MA '76 (PAT)
DOWD, SHIRLEY J., clin. mgr. maternal care unit, Overlake Hospital Medical Center, Bellevue, WA '87 (MGMT)
DOWD, THOMAS J., exec. dir., Nathan Littauer Hospital, Gloversville, NY '63
DOWDELL, DIANE M., RN, head oper. and recovery room, New York Hospital, New York, NY '85 (NURS)
DOWDY, SUSAN A., dir. human res., hskpg. and ldry., Tazewell Community Hospital, Tazewell, VA '86 (ENVIRON)
DOWERY, GORDON K., proj. dir., Numed Medical, Inc., Silver Spring, MD '82 (PLNG)
DOWLING, E. J., vice-pres. human resources, Yale-New Haven Hospital, New Haven, CT '81 (PERS)
DOWLING, THOMAS C., mgr. food serv., Bethesda Oak Hospital, Cincinnati, OH '72 (FOOD)
DOWLING, WILLIAM L., PhD, vice-pres. plng. and policy dev., Sisters of Providence Health Care Corporations, Seattle, WA '59 (PLNG)
DOWNARD, SUSAN D., dir. pub. rel., Doctors Hospital of Nelsonville, Nelsonville, OH '85 (PR)
DOWNEN, MARIE H., chief diet., Franklin Square Hospital, Baltimore, MD '77 (FOOD)
DOWNER, DOROTHY, dir. soc. serv., Deaconess Hospital, Evansville, IN '86 (SOC)
DOWNER, WILLIAM J. JR., pres., Columbus Hospital, Great Falls, MT '59
DOWNES, JANICE R., RN, dir. nrsg. serv., Cottage Grove Hospital, Cottage Grove, OR '83 (NURS)
DOWNEY, LINDA J., RN, dir. nrsg., Good Samaritan Hospital and Medical Center, Portland, OR '84 (NURS)
DOWNEY, MARVIN, dir. combined serv., Methodist Hospitals of Gary, Gary, IN '78 (ENG)
DOWNEY, NANCY DENISE, asst. pat. rel., Children's Hospital, Boston, MA '85 (PAT)
DOWNEY, PATRICK J., dir. eng., International Center, New York, NY '87 (ENG)
DOWNEY, PAUL LEO, pres., Choate-Symmes Hospitals, Inc., Woburn, MA '61 (PLNG)
DOWNEY, RICHARD M., vice-pres. human res., Mountainside Hospital, Montclair, NJ '86 (PERS)
DOWNEY, WILLIAM R., mgr. mgt. eng., Cleveland Metropolitan General Hospital, Cleveland, OH '83 (MGMT)
DOWNIE, PATRICIA, risk mgr., Reynolds Memorial Hospital, Glen Dale, WV '87 (RISK)
DOWNING, ANITA R., dir. pers., Speare Memorial Hospital, Plymouth, NH '84 (PERS)
DOWNING, SR. BETTY, RN, dir. educ. serv., Good Samaritan Hospital, Cincinnati, OH '69 (EDUC)
DOWNING, BOB, dir. plant oper., HCA South Arlington Medical Center, Arlington, TX '74 (ENG)
DOWNING, SR. CECILIA, dir. vol., St. Anne's Hospital, Fall River, MA '83 (PAT)
DOWNING, DELBERT G., dir. support serv., Charter North Hospital, Anchorage, AK '86 (ENVIRON)
DOWNING, MICHAEL C., dir. plng., Greenville Regional Hospital, Greenville, PA '75 (PLNG)
DOWNING, MICHAEL J., eng., Kaiser Foundation Hospital, Martinez, CA '83 (ENG)

DOWNING, PHILIP J., partner, Laventhol and Horwath, Boston, MA '70
DOWNING, WILLIAM, risk and benefits coor., Middletown Regional Hospital, Middletown, OH '86 (RISK)(PERS)
DOWNS, ALBERTA M., RN, dir. nrsg., Grayson County Hospital, Leitchfield, KY '80 (NURS)
DOWNS, BRUCE A., sr. buyer, New York University Medical Center, New York, NY '86 (PUR)
DOWNS, CYNTHIA E., asst. dir. food serv., Kennestone Hospital, Marietta, GA '87 (FOOD)
DOWNS, FRED H., RN, sr. vice-pres., Baptist Memorial Hospital, Gadsden, AL '82 (NURS)
DOWNS, SHARON L., asst. exec. dir., John Neil Hospital, Cold Lake, Alta., Canada '86 (MGMT)
DOYLE, SR. ANNA, RN, vice-pres. nrsg., Palos Community Hospital, Palos Heights, IL '79 (NURS)
DOYLE, ARKANSAS, coor. staff dev., Provident Medical Center, Chicago, IL '71 (EDUC)
DOYLE, CATHY H., RN, dir. nrsg. serv., Orangeburg-Calhoun Regional Hospital, Orangeburg, SC '86 (NURS)
DOYLE, CATHY K., asst. to pat. care and nrsg. serv., Cincinnati General Division, Cincinnati, OH '78
DOYLE, CHARLEEN M., buyer, Providence Medical Center, Portland, OR '86 (PUR)
DOYLE, CHRISTINE B., coor. risk mgt., Daughters of Charity Health-Systems-West Central, St. Louis, MO '85 (RISK)
DOYLE, DIANA P., dir. soc. serv., James M. Jackson Memorial Hospital, Miami, FL '70 (SOC)
DOYLE, DONNA L., dir. in-service, Mount Carmel Hospital, Colville, WA '80 (EDUC)
DOYLE, JACKLYN L., RN, dir. day surg., Doctors Hospital of Tacoma, Tacoma, WA '84 (NURS)
DOYLE, JAMES J. JR., assoc. adm., Chilton Memorial Hospital, Pompton Plains, NJ '78
DOYLE, JAMES J. JR., atty., Maryland Hospital Association, Lutherville-Timonium, MD '77 (ATTY)
DOYLE, JOE, mgr. emp., Rapid City Regional Hospital, Rapid City, SD '82 (PERS)
DOYLE, JOHN D., vice-pres., MacNeal Hospital, Berwyn, IL '83 (PR) (PLNG)
DOYLE, JOHN J., asst. exec. dir. human res., Jersey City Medical Center, Jersey City, NJ '86 (PERS)
DOYLE, JOSEPH FRANCIS, pat. rep., Thomas Jefferson University Hospital, Philadelphia, PA '86 (PAT)
DOYLE, JOSEPH FRANCIS II, mgr. pat. acct., Jewish Hospital of Cincinnati, Cincinnati, OH '74
DOYLE, KENNETH K., vice-pres. human res., South Baltimore General Hospital, Baltimore, MD '86 (PERS)
DOYLE, MARY ELLEN, asst. dir., Saint Francis Hospital and Medical Center, Hartford, CT '77
DOYLE, MARY, asst. adm. mental health serv., Fairview Deaconess Center, Minneapolis, MN '86 (PLNG)
DOYLE, MICHAEL J., vice-pres., Voluntary Hospitals of America, Irving, TX '86
DOYLE, PAUL H., dir. food serv., Baker Hospital, North Charleston, SC '70 (FOOD)
DOYLE, PHILIP E., vice-pres., Johnson and Johnson Hospital Services, Piscataway, NJ '83 (PLNG)
DOYLE, SHARON, mktg. spec., Candler General Hospital, Savannah, GA '87 (PR) (PLNG)
DOYLE, THOMAS E., mgr. benefits and compensation, Memorial Hospital, South Bend, IN '83 (PERS)
DOYNE, MARK A., MD, sr. vice-pres. corp. dev., Baptist Hospital, Nashville, TN '85 (PLNG)
DOZIER, ROBERT DELANO, chief eng., Humana Hospital -Augusta, Augusta, GA '79 (ENG)
DRABIK, DENNIS M., coor. preventive maint., Hutzel Hospital, Detroit, MI '84
DRACE, CONNIE, RN, coor. amb. surg. center, St. Luke's Hospital, Kansas City, MO '87 (AMB)
DRACH, JOSEPH J., pres., Log Three, Inc., Annapolis, MD '84 (PUR)
DRAGONE, EUNICE M., RN, assoc. adm., Spaulding Rehabilitation Hospital, Boston, MA '79 (NURS)
DRAGOVITS, JOHN F., vice-pres. fin., Children's Medical Center of Dallas, Dallas, TX '86
DRAIN, DONALD L., dir. pers., St. Francis Hospital, Wilmington, DE '81 (PERS)
DRAKE, BETTY A., dir. pub. rel., Henry General Hospital, Stockbridge, GA '82 (PR)
DRAKE, DAVID F., PhD, group vice-pres. and sec.-treas., American Hospital Association, Chicago, IL '73 (LIFE)
DRAKE, DENNY, atty., Iowa Methodist Medical Center, Des Moines, IA '86 (ATTY)(RISK)
DRAKE, DIANA M., dir. vol. serv., Paoli Memorial Hospital, Paoli, PA '86 (VOL)
DRAKE, JEROME D., chief soc. serv., Veterans Administration Medical Center, Iron Mountain, MI '85 (SOC)
DRAKE, LCDR JO ANN, MSC USN, Virginia Beach, VA '80
DRAKE, JUNE L., pat. rep., Condell Memorial Hospital, Libertyville, IL '79 (PAT)
DRAKE, NORMA J., dir. diet. serv., Douglas County Hospital, Omaha, NE '86 (FOOD)
DRAKE, PAMELA, dir. mktg., The Mangelsdorf Companies, Dallas, TX '85 (RISK)
DRAKE, PHILIP Y., mgr., HBO and Company, Atlanta, GA '75 (MGMT)
DRAKE, RICHARD L., Drake Management Services, Inc., Scottsdale, AZ '70 (FOOD)
DRALLE, CLYDE D., dir. bldg. and grds., Silver Cross Hospital, Joliet, IL '68 (ENG)
DRALNICK, BARBARA A., fellow qual. assur., Department of Air Force Medical Service, Bolling AFB, DC '83 (RISK)
DRANSFIELD, N. DIANE, RN, asst. adm. nrsg., University of Alabama Hospital, Birmingham, AL '76 (NURS)
DRAPALA, MARK F., student, Program in Hospital Administration, University of Michigan School of Public Health, Ann Arbor, MI '85
DRAPALIK, JEFFREY G., consult., SunHealth Corporation, Charlotte, NC '83 (MGMT)
DRAPEAU, JACQUELINE U., dir. soc. serv., Brattleboro Retreat, Brattleboro, VT '82 (SOC)
DRAPER, BARBARA ANN, dir. telecommun., Mercy Catholic Medical Center, Darby, PA '85 (ENG)
DRAPER, BECKIE, dir. cent. serv., Presbyterian Hospital, Oklahoma City, OK '83 (CS)
DRAPER, JUDITH L., instr. in-service educ., Kennedy Memorial Hospitals-University Medical Center, Cherry Hill, NJ '85 (EDUC)
DRAPER, TAD D., atty., Intermountain Health Care, Inc., Salt Lake City, UT '86 (ATTY)
DRATLER, SANDRA J., vice-pres. corp. plng., St. Mary's Hospital and Medical Center, San Francisco, CA '76 (PLNG)
DRAUGHON, CARL A., dir. support serv., Ephraim McDowell Regional Medical Center, Danville, KY '84 (ENG)(ENVIRON)
DRAXTON, MARILYN, RN, dir. nrsg., Methodist Hospital, Brooklyn, NY '79 (NURS)
DRAY, W. PERRY, atty., Memorial Hospital of Laramie County, Cheyenne, WY '77 (ATTY)
DREACHSLIN, JANICE L., PhD, dir. consulting serv., Commission on Professional and Hospital Activities, Ann Arbor, MI '83 (PLNG)
DREBIN, MARTIN E., vice-pres. fin., Evanston Hospital, Evanston, IL '74
DRECHSLER, JANET, asst. vice-pres. human res., St. Peter's Medical Center, New Brunswick, NJ '85 (PERS)
DREES, DANIEL L., vice-pres. fin., Iowa Hospital Association, Des Moines, IA '85
DREGER, DONNA M., dir. pur., Huron Memorial Hospital, Bad Axe, MI '74 (PUR)
DREIER, DOUGLAS H., exec. vice-pres., Morse-Diesel, Inc., Chicago, IL '84
DREISER, KIRK J., mgt. eng., Kennestone Hospital, Marietta, GA '84 (MGMT)
DREISIGER, MICHAEL N., LaGuardia Hospital Shared Services, New York, NY '77
DRENNAN, ROBERT THOMAS, CO-owner, Commonwealth Vendors, Lexington, KY '85
DRENNEN, JILL A., dir. commun. serv., Community Hospital of Ottawa, Ottawa, IL '82 (PR)
DRESHER, FRANCES, dir. soc. work, Bronx-Lebanon Hospital Center, Concourse Division, Bronx, NY '74 (SOC)
DRESSEN, ROBERTA ANTOINE, adm., Shriners Hospital for Crippled Children, Minneapolis, MN '85 (PR) (PLNG)
DRESSER, EARL G., (ret.), Eden Prairie, MN '86
DRESSLER, JOANNE M., editorial asst., Riverside Medical Center, Kankakee, IL '85 (PR)
DRESSLER, JOSEPH E. SR., asst. dir. lab., Pleasant Valley Hospital, Point Pleasant, WV '84
DREW, DENISE H., mgr. matl., Chicot Memorial Hospital, Lake Village, AR '82 (PUR)
DREW, DENNIS P., dir. maint., Cary Medical Center, Caribou, ME '84 (ENG)
DREW, LESLIE A., RN, dir. nrsg., med. and surg. serv., Highland Park Hospital, Highland Park, IL '86 (NURS)
DREWA, MARCUS E., pres., Methodist Hospital, Jacksonville, FL '54 (LIFE)
DREYER, FREDERIC C. JR., chief exec. off., Charlton Memorial Hospital, Fall River, MA '64 (PLNG)
DRIGGERS, LEE I., asst. adm., Moncrief Army Community Hospital, Fort Jackson, SC '80
DRING, JOANNE SPONSLER, vice-pres., Indiana Hospital Association, Indianapolis, IN '75 (PR)
DRISCOL, BARBARA P., pres., B. P. Driscol and Associates, Inc., Shaker Heights, OH '84
DRISCOLL, FRANCES P., dir. pub. affairs, Rhode Island Group Health Association, Providence, RI '86 (PR)
DRISCOLL, J. KEVIN, dir. pers., Sutter General Hospital, Sacramento, CA '86 (PERS)
DRISCOLL, JOAN J., asst. dir. nrsg. serv. staff dev., St. Vincent's Medical Center, Staten Island, NY '69 (EDUC)
DRISCOLL, MICHAEL E., pres., Riverview Hospital Foundation, Red Bank, NJ '86 (PLNG)
DRISCOLL, PETER E., atty., Cooper Hospital-University Medical Center, Camden, NJ '72 (ATTY)
DRISCOLL, MAJ. ROBERT S., MSC USA, med. oper. and plans off., U. S. Army, Hanscom AFB, MA '85
DRISKILL, TIMOTHY WEYLAND, atty., Hillcrest Medical Center, Tulsa, OK '82 (ATTY)
DRISNER, ROBERT EUGENE, pres., Community Memorial Hospital, Menomonee Falls, WI '63
DRISS, MARILYN, dir. soc. serv., Glendale Memorial Hospital and Health Center, Glendale, CA '84 (SOC)
DRIVER, ANNA LAUMAN, RN, (ret.), Dillsboro, IN '14 (LIFE)
DRIVER, CAROL, coor. maternal, child and health, Self Memorial Hospital, Greenwood, SC '86 (RISK)
DRIVER, MARTHA, buyer, Glendale Memorial Hospital and Health Center, Glendale, CA '83 (PUR)
DROBILE, MARGARET T., student, Temple University, Department of Health Administration, School of Business Administration, Philadelphia, PA '82
DROBOT, MICHAEL D., pres., American Health Group International, Inc., Kirkland, WA '69
DROEGE, MARIE, oper. spec., Healthcor, Urbana, IL '84 (MGMT)
DROLLINGER, EARL J., chief eng., Hoopeston Regional Hospital, Hoopeston, IL '80 (ENG)
DRONE, VIRGINIA L., asst. exec. dir., St. Mary's Health Center, St. Louis, MO '86 (PLNG)
DRONSFIELD, JOHN C., vice-pres. risk mgt., Mmi Companies, Inc., Bannockburn, IL '83 (RISK)
DROSINS, C. J., dir. food serv., Lenox Hill Hospital, New York, NY '77 (FOOD)
DROSNESS, DANIEL LEED, (ret.), Lake Worth, FL '51 (LIFE)
DROW, FREDERICK L., dir. pers., Health Management Associates, Naples, FL '80 (PERS)
DROWN, B. J., chief eng., Flowers Hospital, Dothan, AL '81 (ENG)
DRUASH, MARK, vice-pres., Americare Corporation, Tallahassee, FL '86 (PLNG)
DRUE, ROGER H., exec. vice-pres., Mills Memorial Hospital, San Mateo, CA '68
DRUHAN, JULIE, dir. soc. work serv., East Alabama Medical Center, Opelika, AL '85 (SOC)
DRUMM, CAROLYN A., RN, vice-pres. pat. care serv., Highland Park Hospital, Highland Park, IL '82 (NURS)
DRUMMOND, BARBARA A., RN, dir. nrsg. serv., Flagler Hospital, St. Augustine, FL '82 (NURS)
DRUMMOND, CAROLYN L., dir. strategic plng., Providence Hospital, Southfield, MI '79 (PLNG)
DRUMMOND, CHARLES W., coor. pub. rel., Oxford-Lafayette Medical Center, Oxford, MS '85 (PR)
DRUMMOND, KAREN A., dir. food serv., Presbyterian-University of Pennsylvania Medical Center, Philadelphia, PA '84 (FOOD)
DRUMMOND, PHYLLIS A., coor. cont. educ., Santa Rosa Memorial Hospital, Santa Rosa, CA '84 (EDUC)
DRUPIESKI, NORMA J., buyer, Allegheny Valley Hospital, Natrona Heights, PA '84 (PUR)
DRURY, STEPHEN ALAN, sr. vice-pres., Thomson McKinnon Health Care Capital Markets Group, Houston, TX '61
DRUTCHAS, GREGORY, atty., Henry Ford Hospital, Detroit, MI '81 (ATTY)
DRYDEN, DAVID D., asst. adm., Onslow Memorial Hospital, Jacksonville, NC '69
DRYDEN, JAMES D., pres., Southern Medical Recruiters, Corpus Christi, TX '80
DRYE, ALVIN B. JR., dir. pat. affairs, U. S. Air Force Regional Hospital, Eglin AFB, FL '83
DRYE, RANDOLPH L., health syst. spec., Veterans Administration, Department of Medicine and Surgery, Washington, DC '80
DRYJA, KAREN A., dir. pub. rel., Children's Hospital, Buffalo, NY '84 (PR)
DUANE, CHRISTOPHER R., mgr. sup., proc. and distrib., Overlake Hospital Medical Center, Bellevue, WA '82 (CS)
DUANE, THOMAS E., dir. pers., St. Mary's Hospital, West Palm Beach, FL '73 (PERS)
DUBACH, GEORGE G., pres., Dubach and Associates, Ashtabula, OH '47 (LIFE)
DUBANEVICH, KEITH, atty., Fulbright and Jaworski, Houston, TX '86 (RISK)
DUBANSKY, CYNTHIA, dir. soc. serv., Fairview Ridges Hospital, Burnsville, MN '86 (SOC)
DUBAY, DONALD H., dir. eng., Virginia Mason Hospital, Seattle, WA '84 (ENG)
DUBAY, JACQUELINE A., coor. pat. rel., Harper Hospital, Detroit, MI '78 (PAT)
DUBBS, JOHN W. III, atty., Ravenswood Hospital Medical Center, Chicago, IL '84 (ATTY)
DUBBS, ROBERT M., atty., Universal Health Services, Inc., King of Prussia, PA '84 (ATTY)
DUBEAU, ROBERT C., atty., Rockville General Hospital, Rockville, CT '72 (ATTY)
DUBIEL, CHERYL T., West Jersey Health Systems, Eastern Division, Voorhees, NJ '79 (SOC)
DUBIS, JOHN STEVE, sr. vice-pres., Alexian Brothers Hospital, St. Louis, MO '79
DUBLIN, KARAN W., dir. cent. serv., Nan Travis Memorial Hospital, Jacksonville, TX '84 (CS)
DUBMAN, NINA J., dir. food serv., Northwest Continuing Care Center, Arlington Heights, IL '82 (FOOD)
DUBOIS, E. WAYNE, supv. sup. serv., Purdue University Student Hospital, West Lafayette, IN '86 (ENVIRON)
DUBOIS, REGINALD S., dir. food serv., Lawrence General Hospital, Lawrence, MA '76 (FOOD)
DUBOIS, RENALD A., pres., DuBois and Associates Engineering Management Resources, Inc., Biddeford, ME '74 (ENG)
DUBOSE, MARY B., dir. soc. serv., Medical Center of Central Georgia, Macon, GA '81 (SOC)
DUBZINSKI, ANNE, dir. soc. serv., Henry Heywood Memorial Hospital, Gardner, MA '87 (SOC)
DUCALO, KENNETH, dir. eng., Long Beach Memorial Hospital, Long Beach, NY '76 (ENG)
DUCEY, DONNA Y., RN, dir. nrsg., Radford Community Hospital, Radford, VA '83 (NURS)
DUCHARME, JAMES N., dir. facil., Peninsula Hospital and Medical Center, Burlingame, CA '81 (ENG)
DUCHESNEAU, SR. IRENE, asst. adm. human res., Fanny Allen Hospital, Winooski, VT '80 (PERS)
DUCHON, LISA M., mgt. analyst, Denver Health and Hospitals, Denver, CO '86 (MGMT)
DUCK, ELIZABETH B., RN, dir. nrsg., Field Memorial Community Hospital, Centreville, MS '84 (NURS)
DUCKER, FRANKLIN E., plant eng., Charter Woods Hospital, Dothan, AL '81 (ENG)
DUCKETT, DARLENE K., dir. vol. serv., St. Luke's Methodist Hospital, Cedar Rapids, IA '81 (VOL)
DUCKETT, JOHN E., mgt. eng., Pottstown Memorial Medical Center, Pottstown, PA '77 (MGMT)
DUCO, BERNARD A. JR., atty., Providence Hospital, Waco, TX '85 (ATTY)
DUCZYNSKI, JOHN M., atty., Children's Memorial Hospital, Chicago, IL '82 (ATTY)
DUDA, GEORGE G., asst. dir. pur., La Grange Memorial Hospital, La Grange, IL '82 (PUR)
DUDDING, MARY N., mgr. commun. rel., Mercy Hospital, Cadillac, MI '85 (PR)
DUDEN, IRA M., asst. adm. human res., Children's Hospital and Medical Center, Seattle, WA '85 (PERS)
DUDLEY, HARRY O., adm., West Orange Memorial Hospital, Winter Garden, FL '49 (LIFE)
DUECKER, STEVEN E., chief oper. off., Mercy Shared Services, Inc., Cincinnati, OH '85 (PLNG)
DUER, A. ADGATE, atty., Church Home and Hospital of the City of Baltimore, Baltimore, MD '73 (ATTY)
DUERR, LOUISE, RN, vice-pres. pat. serv., Baltimore County General Hospital, Randallstown, MD '75 (NURS)
DUESSEL, MARIAN, RN, instr., St. Anthony's Medical Center, St. Louis, MO '87 (EDUC)
DUET, BILLIE F., supv. cent. serv., Thibodaux General Hospital, Thibodaux, LA '80 (CS)
DUFAULT, SR. KARIN J., RN PhD, St. Elizabeth Medical Center, Yakima, WA '85 (NURS)

DUFF, CHERRY, unit coor. cent. sterile sup., United Community Hospital, Grove City, PA '84 (CS)
DUFF, LARRY R., atty., Minidoka Memorial Hospital, Rupert, ID '86 (ATTY)
DUFF, RICHARD T., asst. dir. diet. serv., Columbia Hospital for Women, Washington, DC '84 (FOOD)
DUFFE, EDWARD G., asst. adm., Iowa Lutheran Hospital, Des Moines, IA '86
DUFFETT, JOAN K., RN, pat. rep., Athens Regional Medical Center, Athens, GA '81 (PAT)
DUFFEY, SUSAN L., dir. sup., proc. and distrib., Richland Memorial Hospital, Columbia, SC '86 (PUR)
DUFFEY, TIMOTHY, adm. asst. and risk mgt. coor., Albany Medical Center Hospital, Albany, NY '86 (RISK)
DUFFNEY, VICKI M., dir. soc. serv., Mayo Clinic, Rochester, MN '85 (SOC)
DUFFUS, ALYCE JEAN, RN, asst. exec. dir. prof. nrsg., Mercy Hospital of Pittsburgh, Pittsburgh, PA '84 (NURS)
DUFFY-MEYERS, JEANNE, dir. vol. serv., Boulder Community Hospital, Boulder, CO '77 (VOL)
DUFFY, BETH, adm. coor. emer. medicine, Albert Einstein Medical Center, Philadelphia, PA '87 (AMB)
DUFFY, CHRISTINE M., dir. pub. rel., HCA Bayonet Point-Hudson Center, Hudson, FL '83 (PR)
DUFFY, DONALD A., vice-pres. pub. and commun. rel., Kaiser Foundation Health Plan, Inc., Oakland, CA '81 (PR)
DUFFY, DONNA H., RN, asst. dir. nrsg., Burbank Hospital, Fitchburg, MA '84 (NURS)
DUFFY, JAMES J., mgr. human res., South Shore Hospital, South Weymouth, MA '83 (PERS)
DUFFY, JAMES J. JR., dir. soc. serv., Easton Hospital, Easton, PA '77 (SOC)
DUFFY, JANICE I., RN, vice-pres., Mercy Hospital, Bakersfield, CA '84 (NURS)
DUFFY, LAURA C., mgr. publications, Brigham and Women's Hospital, Boston, MA '85 (PR)
DUFORT, MARY E., asst. to dir. educ., Catholic Medical Center, Manchester, NH '80 (EDUC)
DUFOUR, C. MAUREEN, dir. vol. serv., Bon Secours Hospital, Grosse Pointe, MI '77 (VOL)
DUGAL, BERT, sr. mgr. environ. serv., St. Mary's General Hospital, Lewiston, ME '86 (ENVIRON)
DUGAN, ADRON S., mgr. pur., Charter Lakeside Hospital, Memphis, TN '87 (PUR)
DUGAN, SR. LORETTA, RN, dir. pat. rel., St. Francis Hospital, Roslyn, NY '73 (PAT)
DUGAN, MARYKAY, asst. contr., Concourse Division, Philadelphia, PA '85
DUGGAN, EDITH F., dir. vol. serv., Humana Hospital -Bayside, Virginia Beach, VA '78 (VOL)
DUGGAN, SHEILA K., RN, dir. nrsg. info. syst., Brockton Hospital, Brockton, MA '86 (NURS)
DUGGAN, WILLIAM JR., atty., Henry Ford Hospital, Detroit, MI '78 (ATTY)(RISK)
DUGGER, STEPHEN E., mgr. clin. eng., Community Hospitals of Indiana, Indianapolis, IN '84 (ENG)
DUGGINS, ELIZABETH L., RN, dir. nrsg., Medical Center of Delaware, Wilmington, DE '71 (NURS)
DUGGINS, MARJORIE, dir. pharm. and mgr. matl., Marin General Hospital, San Rafael, CA '84 (PUR)
DUGGINS, MARY C., dir. diet., Heights Psychiatric Hospital, Albuquerque, NM '85 (FOOD)
DUHM, MAXINE R., RN, asst. vice-pres. nrsg., Lutheran Hospital, Moline, IL '81 (NURS)
DUIGNAN, BARRY J., dir. eng., Mount Sinai Medical Center, New York, NY '71 (ENG)
DUJARDIN, HELENE KAMEN, assoc. dir. plng., University of Medicine and Dentistry of New Jersey-University Hospital, Newark, NJ '78 (PLNG)
DUKE, ANGELEE M., coor. soc. serv. and discharge plng., Diagnostic Center Hospital, Houston, TX '86 (SOC)
DUKE, DONALD M., Riverside, CT '62
DUKE, JAMES L., Nashville, TN '75 (ENG)
DUKE, JOE B., supv. cent. sterile, Lubbock County Hospital District, Lubbock, TX '86 (CS)
DUKE, LOUISE, dir. vol. serv., Missouri Baptist Hospital, St. Louis, MO '77 (VOL)
DUKE, MICHAEL C., atty., Medscan, Inc., Philadelphia, PA '85 (ATTY)
DUKE, ROBERT E., vice-pres. tech. serv., Covenant Medical Center -St. Francis, Waterloo, IA '87 (AMB)
DUKE, VERONICA, chief soc. work, Alaska Psychiatric Institute, Anchorage, AK '86 (SOC)
DULA, M. ALYCE, vice-pres. plng. and mktg., Horizon Health System, Inc., Bethlehem, PA '86 (PLNG)
DULCIE, MICHELE M., dir. guest rel., Baylor University Medical Center, Dallas, TX '85 (PAT)
DULIK, FRANK J., mgr. cent. serv., Latrobe Area Hospital, Latrobe, PA '86 (CS)
DULIN, NANCY L., supv. oper. room and cent. serv. room, West Shore Hospital, Manistee, MI '85 (CS)
DULOHERY, SR. M. CORNILE, dir. dev., St. Joseph's Hospital, Savannah, GA '43 (PLNG)(LIFE)
DULZO, DOLORES A., mgr. cent. sup. room, Crittenton Hospital, Rochester, MI '71 (CS)
DUMACK, HELEN, (ret.), Bath, NY '38 (LIFE)
DUMAIS, GARY W., dir. food serv., Pitt County Memorial Hospital, Greenville, NC '79 (FOOD)
DUMARS, HELEN B., dir. soc. serv., Mobile Infirmary Medical Center, Mobile, AL '75 (SOC)
DUMAS, BARBARA, head nrs. and unit mgr., Winona Memorial Hospital, Indianapolis, IN '87 (AMB)
DUMAS, JANET S., coor. soc. serv., Sam Houston Memorial Hospital, Houston, TX '81 (SOC)
DUMOND, RUTH P., dir. risk mgt., Mercy Hospital and Medical Center, San Diego, CA '84 (RISK)
DUMONT, JOAN A., dir. vol. serv., Bellevue Hospital Center, New York, NY '80 (VOL)
DUNAGAN, H. LEE, vice-pres., Medical Design International, Atlanta, GA '82 (PLNG)
DUNBAR, BARBARA B., mgr. pub. affairs, Children's Hospital, New Orleans, LA '85 (PR)
DUNBAR, DERWOOD B. JR., exec. dir., Hospital Services Corporation, Camp Hill, PA '74 (PUR)
DUNBAR, PATRICIA A., dir. soc. serv., Montgomery County Memorial Hospital, Red Oak, IA '85 (SOC)
DUNBAR, THOMAS E., dir. hskpg. and ldry., Garrett County Memorial Hospital, Oakland, MD '86 (ENVIRON)
DUNBAR, WILLIAM A., dir. eng., Burbank Hospital, Fitchburg, MA '83 (ENG)
DUNCAN-ANDREWS, DEBORAH, dir. commun. rel., Peninsula Hospital, Louisville, TN '84 (PR)
DUNCAN, ALEX G. III, atty., Palo Verde Mental Health Service, Inc., Tucson, AZ '84 (ATTY)
DUNCAN, DARRYL L., student, Xavier University, Cincinnati, OH '87
DUNCAN, DAVID J., PhD, vice-pres. plng. and mktg., Central Pennsylvania Health Services Corporation, Altoona, PA '76 (PLNG)
DUNCAN, DONALD W., consult., Sun City, AZ '46 (LIFE)
DUNCAN, EDGAR N., adm. assoc., Blue Cross and Blue Shield of Greater New York, New York, NY '56 (LIFE)
DUNCAN, ELEANOR L., sr. vice-pres., St. Joseph's Hospital and Medical Center, Phoenix, AZ '70 (NURS)
DUNCAN, EVELYN M., RN, dir. med. surg., St. Margaret's Hospital, Montgomery, AL '82 (NURS)
DUNCAN, HERBERT L., dir. educ. serv., St. Joseph Hospital and Health Care Center, Tacoma, WA '71 (EDUC)
DUNCAN, JAMES E., mgr. inst. serv., University of California Davis Medical Center, Sacramento, CA '83 (ENG)
DUNCAN, KAREN A., consult., Health Informations Systems, Los Altos, CA '81
DUNCAN, LINDA L., dir. emp. rel., Wood River Township Hospital, Wood River, IL '84 (PERS)
DUNCAN, PAMELA NEFF, pat. rep. off., DeWitt Army Community Hospital, Fort Belvoir, VA '79 (PAT)
DUNCAN, RUTH B., med. soc. worker, West Georgia Medical Center, La Grange, GA '69 (SOC)
DUNCAN, SALLY A., RN, supv. cent. proc., Galesburg Cottage Hospital, Galesburg, IL '83 (CS)
DUNCAN, SUSAN K., supv. prof. nrsg. dev., St. Francis Regional Medical Center, Wichita, KS '82 (EDUC)
DUNCAN, YVONNE M., dir. educ., Polly Ryon Memorial Hospital, Richmond, TX '86 (EDUC)
DUNCHEON, MICHAEL A., atty., California Hospital Association, Sacramento, CA '77 (ATTY)
DUNEHEW, ALLEN R., mgr. matl., Cary Medical Center, Caribou, ME '85 (PUR)
DUNFORD, RUSSELL R., asst. dir. matl. mgt., sup., proc. and distrib., Doctors Hospital, Columbus, OH '86 (CS)
DUNFORD, WYNTON B., pres., Medirec, Murray, UT '82
DUNG, CAROL A., chief soc. serv., Rehabilitation Hospital of the Pacific, Honolulu, HI '80 (SOC)
DUNHAM, JANET G., pat. advocate, Massillon Community Hospital, Massillon, OH '84 (PAT)
DUNHAM, JANNE, assoc. prof., University of Akron, Akron, OH '86 (NURS)
DUNHAM, JOSEPH, corp. fire marshal, Samaritan Health Service, Phoenix, AZ '86 (ENG)
DUNHAM, NANCY L., corp. mgr. med. serv. and risk mgt., Health Corporation-Archdiocese of Newark, New Jersey, Newark, NJ '84 (RISK)
DUNIGAN, WILLIAM CLEVELAND, mgr. pat. rel., St. Bernard Hospital, Chicago, IL '85 (PAT)
DUNKEL-DAVIS, KAREN, asst. matl. mgr., Kern Medical Center, Bakersfield, CA '86 (CS)
DUNKEL, JOAN, field work consult. and lecturer, University of California, Berkeley, CA '85 (SOC)
DUNKEL, PATTY L., prog. dir., American Medical Association, Chicago, IL '85 (EDUC)
DUNKIN, STEPHEN L., dir. human res., South Community Hospital, Oklahoma City, OK '86 (PERS)
DUNKLE, LT. COL. JEFFREY H., MSC USAF, chief med. logistics and facil., Headquarters Mac-Sg, Scott AFB, IL '77
DUNKLE, MARY, dir. pub. rel., Danbury Hospital, Danbury, CT '86 (PR)
DUNKLEMAN, DENNIS C., dir. matl. mgt., Milford Memorial Hospital, Milford, DE '86 (PUR)
DUNLAP, B. WILLIAM, atty., Ohio Hospital Association, Columbus, OH '79 (ATTY)
DUNLAP, CAROLYN M., RN, adm. nrsg., Iron County General Hospital, Iron River, MI '86 (NURS)
DUNLAP, DAVID LAWRENCE, adm., Parkridge Medical Center, Chattanooga, TN '67
DUNLAP, HATTIE V., dir. pur., Hebrew Home for Aged-Riverdale, Bronx, NY '82 (PUR)
DUNLAP, JAMES A., atty., Northeast Georgia Medical Center, Gainesville, GA '69 (ATTY)
DUNLAP, RAY, adm. dir. facil. serv., AMI Saint Joseph Hospital, Omaha, NE '86 (ENVIRON)
DUNLOP, JOHN T., prof., Belmont, MA '84 (HON)
DUNMIRE, MARGARET R., asst. vice-pres. mgt. info. syst., Children's Hospital of Pittsburgh, Pittsburgh, PA '85 (MGMT)
DUNMIRE, THOMAS, dir. eng., Peninsula Hospital, Hampton, VA '85 (ENG)
DUNN, ANDREA C., dir. pers. serv., Roper Hospital, Charleston, SC '86 (PERS)
DUNN, CATHERINE, chief med. soc. worker, St. Francis Medical Center, Honolulu, HI '77 (SOC)
DUNN, CLAUDIA J., risk mgr., Northern Illinois Medical Center, McHenry, IL '86 (RISK)
DUNN, EDWARD J., vice-pres. human res., West Jersey Hospital, Northern Division, Camden, NJ '75 (PERS)
DUNN, EDWARD P., mgr. cent. sup., Northern Ocean Hospital System, Point Pleasant, NJ '85 (CS)
DUNN, ELIZABETH F., vice-pres. mktg. and plng., West Jersey Health System, Camden, NJ '85 (PLNG)
DUNN, EUGENIA M., dir. perinatology and gyn. nrsg., Sinai Hospital of Detroit, Detroit, MI '86 (NURS)
DUNN, GREGORY A., vice-pres. human res., Franklin Square Hospital, Baltimore, MD '86 (PERS)
DUNN, H. MITCHELL JR., atty., St. Joseph's Hospital, Savannah, GA '80 (ATTY)
DUNN, JEROME, dir. pers., St. Joseph Hospital, Orange, CA '77 (PERS)
DUNN, LT. COL. JOHN DAVID, MSC USA, adm., U. S. Dunham Army Hospital, Carlisle, PA '80
DUNN, JOSEPH, atty., Barnert Memorial Hospital Center, Paterson, NJ '79 (ATTY)
DUNN, KAY W., dir. pub. rel., Hoots Memorial Hospital, Yadkinville, NC '85 (PR)
DUNN, LARRY MATTHEW, mgr. cent. sup., Howard University Hospital, Washington, DC '85 (CS)
DUNN, MARIANNE G., RN, chief nrsg. serv., Veterans Administration Medical Center, Newington, CT '80 (NURS)
DUNN, MAUREEN M., dir. soc. serv., Samuel Merritt Hospital, Oakland, CA '77 (SOC)
DUNN, ROBERT E., dir. eng. facil., St. Joseph's Hospital, Parkersburg, WV '70 (ENG)
DUNN, SYLVIA G., dir. vol. serv., New Britain General Hospital, New Britain, CT '81 (VOL)
DUNN, TERI CHASE, dir. pers., Logan Regional Hospital, Logan, UT '80 (PERS)
DUNN, THOMAS A., dir. risk mgt., St. Vincent Charity Hospital and Health Center, Cleveland, OH '80 (RISK)
DUNN, TOBY, sr. consult. and mgr. cost acctg. prog., Chms, Inc., San Francisco, CA '86 (MGMT)
DUNNE, JANET K., RN, vice-pres. nrsg., St. Joseph Mercy Hospital, Clinton, IA '82 (NURS)
DUNNE, PAULETTE M., coor. pat. rel., Martin Memorial Hospital, Stuart, FL '85 (RISK)
DUNNING, FRANCES A., dir. vol. serv., Eastern Maine Medical Center, Bangor, ME '84 (VOL)
DUNNING, JANICE D., mgr. pub. rel., Hampton General Hospital, Hampton, VA '83 (PR)
DUNNING, KERRY N., dir. serv. dev., Putnam Community Hospital, Palatka, FL '86 (PR) (PLNG)
DUNPHY, DANIEL M., dir. matl. mgt., Hospital for Special Surgery, New York, NY '85 (PUR)
DUNPHY, JOANNE M., student, Department of Health Services Administration, George Washington University, Washington, DC '86
DUNPHY, MARY L., dir. soc. serv., New England Deaconess Hospital, Boston, MA '81 (SOC)
DUNPHY, PAUL T., pat. rep., Scripps Memorial Hospital, La Jolla, CA '77 (PAT)
DUNST, JOHN J., adm. gen. serv., South Hills Health System, Pittsburgh, PA '84
DUNSTON, DEBRA A., dir. pub. rel., Methodist Hospital of Dyersburg, Dyersburg, TN '85 (PAT)(PR)
DUPLINSKY, JOSEPH F., chm. and chief exec. off., Blue Cross and Blue Shield of Connecticut, North Haven, CT '84 (LIFE)
DUPONT, A. A., dir. maint. eng., Riverside Hospital, Newport News, VA '81 (ENG)
DUPONT, PAUL J., vice-pres., Peterson Associated Engineers, Portland, OR '84 (ENG)
DUPONT, ROBERT E., vice-pres. plng. and mktg., St. Joseph Hospital, Kirkwood, MO '80 (PLNG)
DUPPER, F. F., pres., Adventist Health System, West, Roseville, CA '79
DUPPER, KENNETH K., exec. vice-pres., Huguley Memorial Hospital, Fort Worth, TX '69 (PLNG)(PERS)
DUPREE, BARBARA B., dir. pub. rel. and dev., Woodland Memorial Hospital, Woodland, CA '85 (PR) (PLNG)
DUPREE, DWAYNE J., coor. mkt analyst, Baylor Health Care System, Dallas, TX '86 (PR)
DUPREE, KIRK, dir. soc. serv., East Pasco Medical Center, Zephyrhills, FL '85 (SOC)
DUPRIEST, ROBERT C., dir. commun. rel., St. Francis Hospital, Columbus, GA '85 (PR)
DUPUIS, DANIEL P., dir. environ. serv., Henry Heywood Memorial Hospital, Gardner, MA '86 (ENVIRON)
DUPUIS, DOLORES, supv. cent. serv., St. Mary's Hospital of Kankakee, Kankakee, IL '84 (CS)
DUQUE, ELIANA B., RN, coor. surg. sup. serv., University of California at Los Angeles Medical Center, Los Angeles, CA '83 (CS)
DURALL, MARTHA L., dir. pers., Westview Hospital, Indianapolis, IN '77 (PERS)
DURAN, JULIE E., dir. pub. affairs, Kaiser Foundation Hospital, Los Angeles, CA '86 (PR)
DURAN, VIRGINIA, RN, dir. qual. review, Phoenix Memorial Hospital, Phoenix, AZ '84 (RISK)
DURANCE, PAUL W., student, Program and Bureau of Hospital Administration, University of Michigan, Ann Arbor, MI '84 (MGMT)
DURAND, RAFAEL, fin. adv.-bd. of trustees, Fajardo Regional Hospital, Fajardo, P.R. '86 (PLNG)
DURANT, CAROL LYNN, dir. pub. rel., Chino Community Hospital, Chino, CA '87 (PR)
DURANTE, PETER, atty., Lutheran Medical Center, Wheat Ridge, CO '79 (ATTY)
DURBIN, DEBORAH, dir. soc. work serv., Oklahoma Children's Memorial Hospital, Oklahoma City, OK '83 (SOC)
DURBROW, TYSON V., mgr. hosp. mktg., Smithkline Bio-Science Laboratories, King of Prussia, PA '84 (PLNG)
DURBURG, SUZANNE, RN, assoc. chm. nrsg., Evanston Hospital, Evanston, IL '81 (NURS)
DURDY, BARBARA A., bus. mgr., Hartford Surgical Center, Hartford, CT '87 (AMB)
DUREJ, ALIDA L., mktg. res. spec., National Medical Enterprises, Santa Monica, CA '86 (PLNG)
DUREJ, ROBERT J., sr. mgr., Ernst and Whinney, Los Angeles, CA '73 (MGMT)
DUREL, THOMAS J., mgt. eng., Electronic Data Systems, Dallas, TX '77 (MGMT)
DURENBERGER, SENATOR DAVID F., Washington, DC '84 (LIFE)
DUREPO, KATHLEEN M., dir. soc. serv., Baystate Medical Center, Springfield, MA '85 (SOC)
DURFEE, KENT A., vice-pres. human res. syst., Sisters of St. Joseph Health Systems of Wichita, Wichita, KS '78 (MGMT)(PERS)
DURGIN, JACQUELINE S., assoc. dir. soc. work, Harborview Medical Center, Seattle, WA '82 (SOC)

DURHAM, BARBARA J., risk mgr., Hermann Hospital, Houston, TX '81 (RISK)
DURHAM, DONALD E., vice-pres. fin., Peninsula General Hospital Medical Center, Salisbury, MD '80 (PLNG)
DURHAM, JOY, dir. vol. serv., White Plains Hospital Medical Center, White Plains, NY '76 (VOL)
DURHAM, JUNE A., dir. vol., Frederick Ferris Thompson Hospital, Canandaigua, NY '85 (VOL)
DURHAM, LYNN L., coor. staff dev. and pub. rel., Baptist Medical Center Easley, Easley, SC '82 (EDUC)(PR)
DURHAM, MARY E., mgr. cent. proc. and distrib., St. Vincent Hospital and Health Center, Indianapolis, IN '83 (CS)
DURHAM, NORA L., adm. dir. human res., Bay Medical Center, Panama City, FL '76 (PERS)
DURHAM, ROBERT C., vice-pres., Fort Sanders Regional Medical Center, Knoxville, TN '84 (PLNG)
DURHAM, WILLIAM L., atty., Huntsville Memorial Hospital, Huntsville, TX '75 (ATTY)
DURIS, MILLER M., mgr. facil. plant, Tuality Community Hospital, Hillsboro, OR '87 (ENG)
DURKAN, JAMES, asst. vice-pres. mktg., West Jersey Health System, Camden, NJ '81 (PR) (PLNG)
DURKAN, MAJ. JOHN P. JR., MSC USA, dir. pat. adm., Keller Army Community Hospital, West Point, NY '75
DURKE, ROSE D., risk mgr., St. Elizabeth Hospital, Beaumont, TX '83 (RISK)
DURKEE, JAMES C., mgr. cent. sup., Memorial Hospital at Easton Maryland, Easton, MD '86 (CS)
DURKEE, TERRY L., mgr. food serv., Good Samaritan Nursing Home, Delmar, NY '82 (FOOD)
DURLING, CORA JANE, RN, dir. pat. serv., Saint Joseph Hospital, Reading, PA '76 (NURS)
DURNEY, ANN OBERDORF, dir. soc. serv., HCA New Port Richey Hospital, New Port Richey, FL '73 (SOC)
DURNIN, GEORGE W. JR., vice-pres. emp. serv., Franklin Medical Center, Greenfield, MA '78 (PERS)
DURSO, JOHN J., atty., Ravenswood Hospital Medical Center, Chicago, IL '83 (ATTY)
DURY, IRA M., pres., Executive Industries, Bala Cynwyd, PA '78
DURYEA, CLARENCE W., Bay Minette, AL '41 (LIFE)
DURYEA, NANCY W., dir. vol. serv., Coral Gables Hospital, Coral Gables, FL '85 (VOL)
DURYEE, EDWARD E. JR., dir. pat. acct., Abington Memorial Hospital, Abington, PA '80 (MGMT)
DUSEK, CATHERINE R., RN, dir. maternal and child nrsg., St. Joseph Hospital, Chicago, IL '83 (NURS)
DUSZYNSKI, MAUREEN B., RN, vice-pres. nrsg. serv., Family Hospital, Milwaukee, WI '71 (NURS)
DUTKEWYCH, JAROSLAV I., vice-pres., Fairlane Health Services, Birmingham, MI '76 (EDUC)(PERS)
DUTT, MERLE L., mgr. pur., Marion General Hospital, Marion, OH '73 (PUR)
DUTTON, JOHN T., dir. pers., Northeastern Hospital of Philadelphia, Philadelphia, PA '86 (PERS)
DUTTON, LORETTA, dir. matl. mgt., El Camino Hospital, Mountain View, CA '82 (PUR)
DUTTON, THOMAS E., atty., Riverside Methodist Hospitals, Columbus, OH '86 (ATTY)
DUTTON, TIMOTHY C., vice-pres. plng. and dev., Shelby Memorial Hospital, Shelby, OH '82 (PLNG)
DUTY, DAVID G., dir. educ., Bayfront Medical Center, St. Petersburg, FL '85 (EDUC)
DUVALL, THOMAS O. JR., atty., Georgia Baptist Medical Center, Atlanta, GA '86 (ATTY)
DUVALL, WALLACE L., PhD, health care mgt. consult., Wallace L. Duvall and Associates, Denton, TX '69
DUVALL, WILLIAM G., atty., Salisbury, MD '77 (ATTY)
DUVIVIER, ROGER, MD, dir. gyn. and amb. care, Winthrop-University Hospital, Mineola, NY '87 (AMB)
DUWEL, BERNARD F., (ret.), Charleston, SC '59
DUX, CHRISTOPHER W., vice-pres. oper., C. J. Harris Community Hospital, Sylva, NC '78 (RISK)
DVERSDAL, BETTY MINA, coor. pat. rel., Southwest Washington Hospitals, Vancouver, WA '85 (PAT)
DWAN, JOHN, dir. commun. rel., University of Utah Health Sciences Center, Salt Lake City, UT '78 (PR)
DWIGHT, MARIA B., pres., Gerontological Services, Inc., Santa Monica, CA '82
DWINELL, RICHARD L., mgr. matl., Burlington Medical Center, Burlington, IA '78 (PUR)
DWORKIN, JULIE P., student, Iona College, New Rochelle, NY '86 (PLNG)
DWORKIN, NEIL ROBERT, asst. dir., United Home for Aged Hebrews, New Rochelle, NY '71 (PLNG)
DWYER, CECILIA JULIA, dir. soc. work and asst. prof. soc. work, Cincinnati Center for Developmental Disorders, University of Cincinnati, Cincinnati, OH '66 (SOC)
DWYER, JEANNE C., coor. commun. support, Devereux Foundation-French Division, Devon, PA '85 (VOL)
DWYER, KAREN B. DAVIS, Bowie, MD '79
DWYER, LINDA H., plng. analyst, Alexandria Hospital, Alexandria, VA '83 (PLNG)
DWYER, SR. M. LYN, dir. diet. serv., Forbes Regional Health Center, Monroeville, PA '82 (FOOD)
DWYER, MARGE H., assoc. dir. info. serv., University Hospital, Boston, MA '86 (PR)
DWYER, MICHAEL J. JR., dir. campus oper., University Hospital of Arkansas, Little Rock, AR '76 (ENG)
DWYER, PATRICIA D., RN, Fremont, CA '83 (NURS)
DWYER, ROBERT G., dist. contr., Hospital Corporation of America, Albany, NY '75
DWYER, SUZANNE N., dir. vol. serv., AMI St. Joseph Center for Health, Omaha, NE '86 (VOL)
DWYER, W. G., vice-pres. mktg., St. Clare Hospital of Monroe, Monroe, WI '84 (PR) (PLNG)
DWYER, WILLIAM E., atty., Cooley Dickinson Hospital, Northampton, MA '41 (LIFE)
DWYER, WILLIAM M., student, Program in Hospital and Health Service Management, Kellogg Graduate School of Management, Northwestern University, Evanston, IL '87 (PLNG)
DYAR, NANCY A., mgr. educ. and trng., Eden Hospital Medical Center, Castro Valley, CA '83 (EDUC)
DYBDAL, GUDRUN O., mgr. educ. serv., Providence Hospital, Oakland, CA '84 (EDUC)
DYE, CARSON F., dir. pers., Ohio State University Hospitals, Columbus, OH '75 (PERS)
DYE, GUSSIE, dir. vol. serv., Riverside Methodist Hospitals, Columbus, OH '79 (VOL)
DYE, MARY JANE, pat. rep., Seaway Hospital, Trenton, MI '85 (PAT)
DYE, PATRICIA C. P., dir. commun. rel., Windham Community Memorial Hospital, Willimantic, CT '64 (PR)
DYER, BILLY D., dir. eng. serv., Emory University Hospital, Atlanta, GA '82 (ENG)
DYER, BOB G., ins. coor., Memorial Hospital System, Houston, TX '80 (RISK)
DYER, CARLA S., student, Program in Health Administration, Washington University School of Medicine, St. Louis, MO '85
DYER, JAMES A., atty., Sebaly, Shillito and Dyer, Dayton, OH '83 (ATTY)
DYER, JOAN, mgr. matl., Home for Adults and Nursing Home, Richmond, VA '79 (PUR)
DYER, PAUL F., asst. adm., Fresno Community Hospital and Medical Center, Fresno, CA '75
DYER, SHIRLEY J., coor. vol., Meridian Park Hospital, Tualatin, OR '86 (VOL)
DYER, SUSAN L., dir. pub. rel., Providence Hospital, Washington, DC '81 (PR)
DYESS, TAMMY, risk mgr., Laurelwood Hospital, The Woodlands, TX '86 (RISK)
DYKE, DOROTHY, supv. mem. serv., Lovelace Medical Center, Albuquerque, NM '85 (PAT)
DYKEMA, JOHN R., atty., Crittenton Hospital, Rochester, MI '77 (ATTY)
DYKMAN, K. RAND, exec. dir., Saratoga Community Hospital, Detroit, MI '76
DYM-SMOLER, HELEN, dir. soc. work, Lutheran General Hospital, Park Ridge, IL '86 (SOC)
DYNER, GABY A., (ret.), New York, NY '66 (SOC)
DYNES, IRENE M., adm., Broadway Medical Clinic, Portland, OR '87 (AMB)
DYSON, J. PATRICK, exec. vice-pres., Mercy Memorial Medical Center, Benton Harbor, MI '83 (PLNG)
DYSON, ROSE S., RN, adm. nrsg. adm., Pelham Bay General Hospital, Bronx, NY '81 (NURS)
DYSZLEWSKI, KIM THOMAS, dir. soc. serv., Mercy Hospital, Scranton, PA '84 (SOC)
DZIEDZIC, TERESA LOUISE, pat. serv. rep., Group Health, Inc., St. Paul, MN '85 (PAT)
DZIELAWA, MAJ. JAMES WALTER, MSC USAF, Wichita Falls, TX '74
DZIENNY, FREDERICK L., dir. shared serv., Mercy Hospital, Toledo, OH '75 (PUR)
DZIEWIONTKOSKI, RICHARD K., reg. dir. consult. serv., Illinois Hospital Association, Oak Brook, IL '80 (MGMT)
DZINGLESKI, LEE, asst. vice-pres. risk mgt., Tillinghast, Nelson and Warren, Inc., Atlanta, GA '83 (RISK)
DZWONCZYK, ROGER, head biomedical eng., Ohio State University Hospitals, Columbus, OH '86 (ENG)
DZWONKOWSKI, STANLEY J., adm. asst., Miami Heart Institute, Miami Beach, FL '80 (RISK)

E

EACKER, LISA, coor. safety and risk mgt., Mercy Medical Center, Denver, CO '85 (RISK)
EADES, JOE C., chief soc. work, Veterans Administration Medical Center, Nashville, TN '80 (SOC)
EADY, CAROLYN E., asst. adm., Providence Hospital, Anchorage, AK '77
EAGAN, ESTHER, dir. emp. health and safety, Rochester St. Mary's Hospital, Rochester, NY '82 (RISK)
EAGAN, LUCIA, coor. staff dev., Newport Hospital, Newport, RI '82 (EDUC)
EAGER, YVETTE, RN, supv. cent. sup. and oper. room, Youville Rehabilitation and Chronic Disease Hospital, Cambridge, MA '77 (CS)
EAGLES, DONALD E., pres., Blue Shield of North Dakota, Fargo, ND '43 (LIFE)
EAGLESON, WAYNE C., Pekin Memorial Hospital, Pekin, IL '82 (PLNG)
EARHART, FAY M., dir. biomedical and commun. serv., Hunterdon Medical Center, Flemington, NJ '86 (ENG)
EARL, SANDRA L., RN, vice-pres. pat. care, Franklin Medical Center, Greenfield, MA '81 (NURS)
EARLE, C. EDWARD, mgr. matl., HCA Park West Medical Centers, Knoxville, TN '83 (PUR)
EARLE, PAUL W., assoc. dir. and chief fin. off., New England Deaconess Hospital, Boston, MA '73 (LIFE)
EARLE, VIRGINIA, coor. qual. review, Martin Memorial Hospital, Stuart, FL '86 (RISK)
EARLEY, DELIA T., RN, supv. cent. serv., Mountainside Hospital, Montclair, NJ '79 (CS)
EARLEY, GENE EPHRIEM JR., dir., Naval Dental Clinic, Philadelphia, PA '79 (PERS)
EARLEY, PAUL W., dir. food serv., West Georgia Medical Center, La Grange, GA '79 (FOOD)
EARLEY, SUSAN M., dir. mktg. and pub. rel., Woodford Memorial Hospital, Versailles, KY '85 (PR)
EARLEY, THOMAS J., adm., Russell City Hospital, Russell, KS '82
EARLS, JACQUELINE C., vice-pres. logistic serv., Methodist Hospitals of Dallas, Dallas, TX '77 (FOOD)(PUR)
EARLY, ALICE M., coor. pat. educ., Botsford General Hospital, Farmington Hills, MI '87 (EDUC)
EARLY, AMES S., pres., Scripps Memorial Hospitals, La Jolla, CA '61 (PLNG)
EARLY, THAIS E., dir. soc. serv., St. Mary's Hospital, Orange, NJ '82 (SOC)
EARNEST, CHARLOTTE C., pur. agt., HSA Hill Crest Sunrise Hospital, Birmingham, AL '82 (PUR)
EARNEST, G. LANE, atty., Boulder Community Hospital, Boulder, CO '84 (ATTY)
EARNEST, SANDRA F., dir. staff dev., Memorial Hospital, South Bend, IN '81 (EDUC)
EARNHARDT, JEAN A., dir. pub. rel. and dev., Alamance Health Services, Burlington, NC '81 (PR)
EARNHARDT, TED W., mgr. plng. res., Riverside Healthcare Association, Inc., Newport News, VA '81 (MGMT)(PLNG)
EASTERDAY, SAMMY E., coor. educ., Olathe Medical Center, Olathe, KS '85 (EDUC)
EASTERLING, RAE, exec. hskpg., DeKalb General Hospital, Decatur, GA '86 (ENVIRON)
EASTHAM, JAMES E., sr. vice-pres., St. Paul Medical Center, Dallas, TX '85
EASTIN, GREGORY M., vice-pres., All Saints Episcopal Hospital, Fort Worth, TX '80 (PLNG)
EASTLICK, ALEXANDER C., sr. mgt. eng., Bethesda Hospital, Inc., Cincinnati, OH '82 (MGMT)
EASTMAN, PETER D., chief clin. eng., Children's Hospital, Norfolk, VA '86 (ENG)
EASTMOND, WILLIAM R., dir. commun. and mktg., Northern Ocean Hospital System, Point Pleasant, NJ '83 (PR)
EASTON, DENNIS T., dir. matl. mgt., New York Hospital, New York, NY '86 (PUR)
EASTON, IAN S., PhD, dir. bus. serv., Jacksonville Health Education Programs, Jacksonville, FL '75
EASTON, JAMES R., corp. dir. risk mgt., Basic American Medical, Inc., Indianapolis, IN '82 (RISK)
EASTON, MARY DON, dir. pers., Humana Hospital -Overland Park, Overland Park, KS '76 (PERS)
EASTON, RHONDA S., RN, dir. nrsg., Penrose Community Hospital, Colorado Springs, CO '86 (NURS)
EASTWOOD, LEONA C., dir. health occup. educ., Riverside Hospital, Newport News, VA '77 (EDUC)
EASTWOOD, ROSEMARY G., dir. human res., St. Elizabeth Community Health Center, Lincoln, NE '86 (PERS)
EASUM, RITA, dir. med. surg., Stormont-Vail Regional Medical Center, Topeka, KS '81 (NURS)
EATON, ANN W., atty., Mid-American Hospitals, Inc., Houston, TX '84 (ATTY)
EATON, DEBRA, mgr. health promotion programs, Hermann Hospital, Houston, TX '85
EATON, JOHN H., Unicef, New York, NY '67 (MGMT)
EATON, ROBERT C., adm., Bowdon Area Hospital, Bowdon, GA '84
EATON, STACEY, RN, student, St. Francis Hospital, Roslyn, NY '86
EAVES, DARLENE E., dir. soc. work, AMI Griffin-Spalding Hospital, Griffin, GA '86 (SOC)
EBAUGH, JAMES P., dir. fin., South Shore Hospital and Medical Center, Miami Beach, FL '85
EBB, PAUL T., vice-pres. gen. serv., United Hospital, St. Paul, MN '57 (ENG)(LIFE)
EBEL, MARION, mgr. sup., proc., distrib. and Idry., Mercy Medical Center, Durango, CO '79 (CS)
EBEL, SHARON A., dir. pub. rel., Berkshire Medical Center, Pittsfield, MA '85 (PR)
EBERHARD, JEAN, infection control and qual. assur. nrs. and asst. dir. nrsg., St. Elizabeth Hospital Medical Center, Lafayette, IN '86 (ENG)
EBERHARD, SALLY C., vice-pres. plng. and mktg., Torrance Health Association, Torrance, CA '81 (PLNG)
EBERHARDT, MARTY H., adm. asst., Sun Belt Regional Medical Center East, Channelview, TX '79 (PR)
EBERHARDT, PAUL D., dir. matl. mgt., Butler Memorial Hospital, Butler, PA '83 (PUR)
EBERHART, JAMES E., dir. clin. eng., Washington County Hospital, Hagerstown, MD '82 (ENG)
EBERLY, ROBERT, MD, med. dir. amb. care and emer., Cortland Memorial Hospital, Cortland, NY '87 (AMB)
EBERS, EARL S. JR., atty., St. Francis Hospital, Blue Island, IL '75 (ATTY)
EBERSOLE, CAROL M., asst. adm., Mary Rutan Hospital, Bellefontaine, OH '81
EBERSOLE, JO A., dir. food serv., Lincoln West Hospital, Chicago, IL '74 (FOOD)
EBERT, GEORGE W., dir. plant oper., Salida Hospital, Salida, CO '82 (ENG)
EBERT, MARIE E., coor. educ., Tampa General Hospital, Tampa, FL '82 (EDUC)
EBERTOWSKI, SUSAN K., RN, vice-pres. pat. care serv., Mercy Medical Center and Hospital, Williston, ND '85 (NURS)
EBERWINE, JAMES A., dir., Oaks Treatment Center-Brown Schools, Austin, TX '82
EBIN, SR. MARGARET, RN, dir. amb. care, St. Elizabeth Hospital Medical Center, Youngstown, OH '71 (NURS)(AMB)
EBLING, LOREEN N., mgr. cent. proc., Bartholomew County Hospital, Columbus, IN '77 (CS)
EBNER, BONNIE J., dir. cent. serv., Akron General Medical Center, Akron, OH '78 (CS)
EBNER, GEORGE H., asst. vice-pres. commun., Hospital Association of Pennsylvania, Camp Hill, PA '85 (PR)
EBORN, DYANA F., mgr. telecommun., DePaul Hospital, Norfolk, VA '86 (ENG)
EBRITE, MARGUERITE M., dir. soc. work, Lee Memorial Hospital, Dowagiac, MI '87 (SOC)
EBY, NANCY Y., pres., Nex Research, Inc., Grand Blanc, MI '85 (PLNG)
EBY, SUSAN J., dir. pers., Overlake Hospital Medical Center, Bellevue, WA '83 (PERS)
ECCARD, MARY H., RN, assoc. dir. nrsg. and asst. adm., Vanderbilt University Hospital, Nashville, TN '85 (NURS)
ECCLESTON, ARTHUR W., pres., Eccleston Associates, Inc., New York, NY '66 (PLNG)
ECHELBARGER, CHESTER M., mgr. phys. plant serv., Deaconess Medical Center-Spokane, Spokane, WA '68 (ENG)

ECHELBERRY, JOSEPH D., vice-pres. pers. serv., Marin General Hospital, San Rafael, CA '84 (PERS)
ECHEVERRIA, RAUL H., dir. maint., St. Joseph Hospital, Chicago, IL '82 (ENG)
ECHLIN, BERNARD J., atty., St. Anne's Hospital, Chicago, IL '70 (ATTY)
ECK, JOHN P., consult., Sisters of the Third Order of St. Francis, Springfield, IL '74
ECK, KATHERINE COKER, asst. dir. soc. work, University Hospital, Jackson, MS '86 (SOC)
ECKARDT, DONNA L. S., RN, dir. nrsg., Marlborough Hospital, Marlborough, MA '84 (NURS)
ECKEL, FRED M., prof., University of North Carolina, Department of Pharmacy Practice, Chapel Hill, NC '78
ECKELS, JANE S., vice-pres. pub. rel., Southeast Michigan Hospital Council, Southfield, MI '82 (PR)
ECKER, BART E., atty., Hazleton-St. Joseph Medical Center, Hazleton, PA '83 (ATTY)
ECKER, G. T. DUNLOP, exec. vice-pres., Washington Hospital Center, Washington, DC '63
ECKERLE, JAMES E., sr. planner, St. Elizabeth Medical Center, Dayton, OH '83 (PLNG)
ECKERMAN, MARCIA, coor. mktg., St. Joseph Health and Rehabilitation Center, Ottumwa, IA '86 (PR)
ECKERSALL, EDWIN R. JR., dir. mgt. eng., St. Joseph Hospital, Chicago, IL '83 (MGMT)
ECKERT, EILEEN ANN, asst. dir. educ. serv., St. Joseph Hospitals, Mount Clemens, MI '84 (EDUC)
ECKERT, H. ANN, RN, vice-pres., Huntington Memorial Hospital, Huntington, IN '79 (NURS)
ECKERT, JOHN D., asst. vice-pres. mktg. and commun., Lakeview Medical Center, Danville, IL '81 (PR)
ECKERT, NANCY K., dir. vol. serv., Freeport Memorial Hospital, Freeport, IL '82 (VOL)
ECKERY, SR. MIRIAM, dir. educ. and trng., St. Jude Hospital and Rehabilitation Center, Fullerton, CA '75 (EDUC)
ECKES, ARNOLD J., chief eng., St. Joseph's Hospital, Marshfield, WI '80 (ENG)
ECKES, DONALD P., dep. dir. dev., David Grant U. S. Air Force Medical Center, Fairfield, CA '79 (ENG)
ECKFELD, FREDERICK J., Kenton, OH '61
ECKHARDT, ALICE L., asst. adm., West Orange Memorial Hospital, Winter Garden, FL '86 (RISK)
ECKHART, JOHN E., dir. matl. mgt., St. Joseph's Hospital, Parkersburg, WV '82 (PUR)
ECKHOFF, ROSALEE, RN, dir. nrsg., Phelps Memorial Health Center, Holdrege, NE '83 (NURS)
ECKHOLM, L. KENNETH, dir. food and nutr., Mobile Infirmary Medical Center, Mobile, AL '73 (FOOD)
ECKL, W. WRAY, atty., HCA West Paces Ferry Hospital, Atlanta, GA '86 (ATTY)
ECKSTEIN, MELISSA A., dir. diet., Vanderbilt Children and Psychiatric Hospital, Nashville, TN '86 (FOOD)
ECKSTEIN, SUZAN RAY, dir. soc. serv., Martha Washington Hospital, Chicago, IL '78 (SOC)
ECKSTROM, MERCEDA J., risk mgr., Pottstown Memorial Medical Center, Pottstown, PA '84 (RISK)
ECROYD, GILDA VENTRESCA, dir. govt. affairs, New York University Medical Center, New York, NY '82 (PLNG)
ECROYD, ROBERT F., exec. vice-pres., Central Suffolk Hospital, Riverhead, NY '66 (MGMT)
ED, VICTORIA L., dir. diag. serv., Magee-Womens Hospital, Pittsburgh, PA '84
EDDER, PAUL E., dir. pers., Clarion Osteopathic Community Hospital, Clarion, PA '86 (PERS)
EDDINGTON, SR. MARY TRINITA, RN, asst. adm., St. Dominic-Jackson Memorial Hospital, Jackson, MS '68 (NURS)
EDDINS, JANICE R., dir. food serv., DeKalb General Hospital, Smithville, TN '81 (FOOD)
EDDLEMAN, GWEN S., RN, dir. nrsg., Tuomey Hospital, Sumter, SC '85 (NURS)
EDDY, CHERYL KAYE, head pat. and family rep., Lincoln General Hospital, Lincoln, NE '78 (PAT)
EDDY, J. WILLIAM, pres., Greenville Regional Hospital, Greenville, PA '57 (LIFE)
EDDY, M. LYNNE, dir. food serv., Choate-Symmes Hospitals, Woburn, MA '83 (FOOD)
EDDY, PATRICIA A., RN, adm. asst., Robinson Memorial Hospital, Ravenna, OH '84 (NURS)
EDELEN, BARBARA JOYCE, dir. vol. serv., Texoma Medical Center, Denison, TX '84 (VOL)
EDELMAN, ALVIN, atty., St. Mary's Hospital of Kankakee, Kankakee, IL '78 (ATTY)
EDELMAN, JOEL, pres., Rose Medical Center, Denver, CO '66 (ATTY)
EDELMAN, LARRY, assoc. dir. trng., Rehabilitation Institute of Pittsburgh, Pittsburgh, PA '85 (EDUC)
EDELMAN, MARC DANIEL, risk mgr., Episcopal Hospital, Philadelphia, PA '85 (RISK)
EDELMAN, ROBIN D., dir. diet., Memorial Hospital, Cumberland, MD '86 (FOOD)
EDELSON, EDWARD, pres., Kme Ltd., East Meadow, NY '83
EDELSTEIN, JOAN A., dir. soc. serv., University Community Hospital, Tamarac, FL '75 (SOC)
EDELSTEIN, LEONARD, dir. eng. serv., Dallas County Hospital District, Dallas, TX '80 (ENG)
EDELSTEIN, SAMUEL B., vice-pres. human res., Milton Medical Center, Milton, MA '81 (PERS)(RISK)
EDEN, MARITA C., dir. pers., Elliott White Springs Memorial Hospital, Lancaster, SC '70 (PERS)
EDEN, WILLIAM J., dir. eng., Saddleback Community Hospital, Laguna Hills, CA '84 (ENG)
EDENFIELD, J. FRANKLIN, atty., Emanuel County Hospital, Swainsboro, GA '81 (ATTY)
EDGAR, DANIEL M., vice-pres. oper., Cape Coral Hospital, Cape Coral, FL '81 (PLNG)
EDGAR, DONALD S., mgt. eng., University of California San Diego Medical Center, San Diego, CA '85 (MGMT)
EDGAR, ELLEN K., dir. commun. rel. and vol. serv., Westmoreland Hospital, Greensburg, PA '83 (VOL)(PR)
EDGE, DONALD R., arch., Edge Group, West Palm Beach, FL '70 (ENG)
EDGE, MURRAY C., dir. risk mgt., University of Tennessee, Knoxville, TN '81 (RISK)
EDGERTON, DOROTHY, dir. vol. serv., St. Elizabeth Medical Center, Yakima, WA '80 (VOL)
EDGERTON, JOAN P., dir. vol. serv., Medical University Hospital Medical University of South Carolina, Charleston, SC '81 (VOL)
EDGERTON, OWEN L., ARA Services, Hospital Food Management, Environmental Service, Inc., Battle Creek, MI '78 (FOOD)
EDINBURG, GOLDA, dir. soc. work, McLean Hospital, Division of Massachusetts General Hospital, Belmont, MA '68 (SOC)
EDINOFF, LYNN, dir. soc. serv., Imperial Point Medical Center, Fort Lauderdale, FL '85 (SOC)
EDISON, MARIAN S., dir. vol. serv., Gaston Memorial Hospital, Gastonia, NC '87 (VOL)
EDISON, STEVE M., pres., Edison and Associates, Santa Barbara, CA '83
EDMONDS, IRENE, supv. cent. sup., De Paul Hospital, Cheyenne, WY '83 (CS)
EDMONDS, COL. ROBERT D., MSC USAF, cmdr., U. S. Air Force McClellan-Sg, McClellan AFB, CA '79
EDMONDS, ROBERT E., atty., Memorial Hospital of Topeka, Topeka, KS '86 (ATTY)
EDMONDSON, JAMES H., dir. spec. mktg. proj., Baylor Health Affiliates Group, Dallas, TX '85
EDMONDSON, JOAN, mgr. compensation and benefits, Mercy Hospital, Scranton, PA '85 (ENG)
EDMONDSON, LINDA, dir. soc. serv., Muskogee Regional Medical Center, Muskogee, OK '85 (SOC)
EDMONSON, LEE EDWARD, dir. matl. mgt., Golden Triangle Regional Medical Center, Columbus, MS '86 (PUR)
EDMUNDS, THOMAS, mgr. soc. work serv., Community General Osteopathic Hospital, Harrisburg, PA '86 (SOC)
EDMUNDSON, R. WILLIAM, pres. healthcare nutr. serv., ARA Services, Inc., Philadelphia, PA '86 (FOOD)
EDSON, HERBERT ROBBINS, asst. adm. fin. serv., Mercy Memorial Hospital, Monroe, MI '80
EDWARDS, A. JANE, RN, mgr. nrsg., Wilson Memorial Hospital, Wilson, NC '86 (NURS)
EDWARDS, AGNES B., Madison, CT '86 (SOC)
EDWARDS, ALEXANDER L., dir. hskpg., AMI St. Joseph Center Mental Health, Omaha, NE '85 (ENVIRON)
EDWARDS, BARBA J., RN, vice-pres. nrsg., Archbishop Bergan Mercy Hospital, Omaha, NE '86 (NURS)
EDWARDS, BRADLEY K., dir. plng. and prog. dev., West Nebraska General Hospital, Scottsbluff, NE '84 (PLNG)
EDWARDS, BUDDY, dir. plng. and res., Hillcrest Baptist Medical Center, Waco, TX '79 (PLNG)
EDWARDS, BYRON M. III, arch. and health facil. planner, The Ratcliff Architects, Berkeley, CA '86 (PLNG)
EDWARDS, CAROL J., asst. adm. mktg., plng. and pub. rel., Memorial Hospital, Meriden, CT '85 (PLNG)
EDWARDS, CHARLES C., MD, pres., Scripps Clinic Research Foundation, La Jolla, CA '75 (HON)
EDWARDS, DAVID L., dir. pers., Homer D. Cobb Memorial Hospital, Phenix City, AL '83 (PERS)
EDWARDS, DAVID R., sect. head pharm., Sinai Hospital of Detroit, Detroit, MI '80
EDWARDS, DONA L., mgr. vol. serv., Appleton Medical Center, Appleton, WI '83 (VOL)
EDWARDS, FRANK E., dir. eng., Riverside Health Care Center, East Hartford, CT '85 (ENG)
EDWARDS, GRETCHEN H., dir. diet. serv., SunHealth Corporation, Charlotte, NC '86 (FOOD)
EDWARDS, JACK H., dir. plng. and mktg., South Georgia Medical Center, Valdosta, GA '86 (PLNG)
EDWARDS, JOHN W., dir. plant oper., Chilton Memorial Hospital, Pompton Plains, NJ '82 (ENG)
EDWARDS, JUANITA, chief clin. soc. work serv., Women's Hospital, Los Angeles, CA '85 (SOC)
EDWARDS, JULIE R., asst. to vice-pres. fin., Beth Israel Hospital, Boston, MA '86 (PLNG)
EDWARDS, LEWIS M., adm., Facial Surgery Institute, Phoenix, AZ '69
EDWARDS, MARGARET R., care coor., HCA Largo Medical Center Hospital, Largo, FL '85 (PAT)
EDWARDS, MARK A., dir. pers., Central Baptist Hospital, Lexington, KY '86 (PERS)
EDWARDS, MERICA J., dir. vol. serv., Antelope Valley Hospital Medical Center, Lancaster, CA '83 (VOL)
EDWARDS, MILLICENT A., pub. rel. spec., Harris Methodist -HEB, Bedford, TX '86 (PR)
EDWARDS, NANCY H., asst. dir. nrsg. educ., Central Florida Regional Hospital, Sanford, FL '81 (EDUC)
EDWARDS, NOLA K., coor. vol. serv., Pennock Hospital, Hastings, MI '83 (VOL)
EDWARDS, PATRICIA TAYLOR, dir. qual. assur., State Hospital South, Blackfoot, ID '85
EDWARDS, PATRICK A., sales mgr. health care, E. F. Bavis and Associates, Inc., Maineville, OH '84 (MGMT)
EDWARDS, ROBERT M., pres. and chief exec. off., Palomar Pomerado Hospital District, Escondido, CA '65 (PLNG)
EDWARDS, ROBERTA M., dir. vol., Pacific Hospital of Long Beach, Long Beach, CA '71 (VOL)
EDWARDS, SYLVIA W., RN, vice-pres. nrsg. serv., Marion General Hospital, Marion, OH '84 (NURS)
EDWARDS, TAMMY STOCKS, pat. rep., Lenoir Memorial Hospital, Kinston, NC '85 (PAT)
EDWARDS, WADE H., vice-pres., Florida Hospital Association, Orlando, FL '67 (PR)
EDWARDS, WANNETTA P., West Chester, PA '82 (MGMT)
EDWARDS, WARD E., vice-pres., North Memorial Medical Center, Robbinsdale, MN '51 (LIFE)
EDWARDS, WILEY, asst. dir., Providence Hospital, Southfield, MI '84
EFFINGER, LUCILLE, RN, vice-pres., Missouri Baptist Hospital, St. Louis, MO '76 (NURS)(AMB)
EFIRD, PATSY, RN, dir. nrsg., Union General Hospital, Blairsville, GA '86 (RISK)
EFTHEMIS, JOHN A., dir. matl. mgt. and food serv., Sisters of Charity Hospital, Buffalo, NY '71 (FOOD)
EFTODA, DEANNA LOVE, RN, student, Nova University, Fort Lauderdale, FL '83 (EDUC)
EFURD, JANE P., adm. pat. rep., Southeast Alabama Medical Center, Dothan, AL '83 (PAT)
EGAN-MALONE, LOUISE, risk mgr., Catholic Medical Center of Brooklyn and Queens, Jamaica, NY '80 (RISK)
EGAN, SR. DOROTHY, pat. and family advocate, Calvary Hospital, Bronx, NY '84 (PAT)
EGAN, KATHLEEN A., Criterion Health Group, Inc., Clearwater, FL '85 (EDUC)
EGAN, KEVIN J., atty., Ingalls Memorial Hospital, Harvey, IL '85 (ATTY)
EGAN, MARY ANN, dir. food serv., Allen Bennett Memorial Hospital, Greer, SC '76 (FOOD)
EGAN, MARY O'LEARY, dir. food serv. and nutr., Palos Community Hospital, Palos Heights, IL '71 (FOOD)
EGAN, PHYLLIS R., RN, dir. nrsg. serv. critical care, St. James Community Hospital, Butte, MT '86 (NURS)
EGAR, THOMAS, student, Program in Hospital and Health Administration, St. Luis University School of Law, St. Louis, MO '86 (RISK)
EGBERT, LINDA A., dir. pers. serv., Northern Westchester Hospital Center, Mount Kisco, NY '80 (EDUC)
EGEBERG, DAVID R., pres. and chief fin. off., Yuma Regional Medical Center, Yuma, AZ '84 (PLNG)
EGELSTON, FRED L., dir. eng. and facil., O'Connor Hospital, San Jose, CA '87 (ENG)
EGERTON, M. W. JR., atty., East Tennessee Baptist Hospital, Knoxville, TN '69 (ATTY)
EGGEN, ALLEN H., dir. plant oper., Children's Mercy Hospital, Kansas City, MO '83 (ENG)
EGGERS, MICHAEL ALLEN, pat. rep., Naval Hospital, Jacksonville, FL '80
EGGERS, RONALD S., adm. consult., Department of Health, Education and Welfare, Dallas, TX '59
EGGERT, GARY W., assoc. adm., Kern Medical Center, Bakersfield, CA '87 (MGMT)
EGGES, MARTHA A., dir. soc. serv., Wausau Hospital Center, Wausau, WI '85 (SOC)
EGGINS, ALBERTA ALLEN, mgr. cent. serv., Tulane University Hospital and Clinics, New Orleans, LA '78 (CS)
EGGLESTON, WILLIAM R., pres., Atlantic Health Corporation, Daytona Beach, FL '86
EGLAND, DALE H., vice-pres. fin., Alton Memorial Hospital, Alton, IL '81 (PLNG)
EHARDT, FREDERICK, health syst. consult., Alexandria, VA '52 (LIFE)
EHLERS, KENNETH L., dir. commun. syst., St. John's Hospital, Springfield, IL '79 (ENG)
EHMKA, BELLA D., dir. vol. serv., Buffalo General Hospital, Buffalo, NY '76 (VOL)
EHRAT, KAREN S., RN PhD, vice-pres. nrsg. serv., St. Joseph Hospitals, Mount Clemens, MI '79 (NURS)
EHRENFRIED, JAIMEE S., mgr., Arthur Andersen and Company, Chicago, IL '86 (MGMT)
EHRENREICH, PAUL, dir. constr., Fairfax Hospital Association, Springfield, VA '78 (PLNG)
EHRHARD, GARY E., dir. pers., Missouri Baptist Hospital, St. Louis, MO '86 (PERS)
EHRLICH, JOHN P., dir. plant serv., Mount Hood Medical Center, Gresham, OR '82 (ENG)
EICH, RITCH K., PhD, sr. vice-pres. institutional advancement and external rel., Butterworth Hospital, Grand Rapids, MI '81 (PR) (PLNG)
EICHELBERGER, PRISCILLA D., dir. vol. serv., Richmond Memorial Hospital, Richmond, VA '86 (VOL)
EICHENHOLTZ, JOHN R., dir. emp. rel., Braintree Hospital, Braintree, MA '77 (PERS)
EICHER, KIM D., adm. dir. emer. room, Altoona Hospital, Altoona, PA '78
EICHHORN, KIM M., adm. food serv., Niagara Fronteir Methodist Homes, Inc., Getzville, NY '84 (FOOD)
EICHNER, SR. VERDA CLARE, RN, vice-pres. nrsg. serv., St. Mary's Medical Center, Duluth, MN '68 (NURS)
EICHNORN, JANETTE F., RN, asst. vice-pres. med. center rel. and risk mgt., St. Francis Medical Center, Cape Girardeau, MO '81 (RISK)
EICHORN, MICHELLE D., dir. pers., Richmond Community Hospital, Richmond, VA '85 (PERS)
EIDSON, CHARLES M., dir. pers., South Georgia Medical Center, Valdosta, GA '70 (PERS)
EIFERT, DAVID C., coor. educ., St. Mary's Hospital, Centralia, IL '82 (EDUC)
EIGEN, DIANE, healthcare mktg. and pub. rel. consult., Eigen and Associates Marketing, Milwaukee, WI '83 (PR)
EIGHMEY, DOUGLAS J., vice-pres. oper., amb. serv., Children's Medical Center, Dayton, OH '80 (PLNG)
EILAND, GARY W., atty., Sisters of Charity, Houston, TX '77 (ATTY)
EILAND, GEORGIA B., RN, adm. nrsg., St. Francis Hospital, Columbus, GA '79 (NURS)
EILBACHER, DAVID J., coor. facil., Robert Wood Johnson University Hospital, New Brunswick, NJ '79 (ENG)
EILER, HARRY O., vice-pres., Precision Energy Systems, Inc., Schaumburg, IL '86 (ENG)
EILERS, ALBERT HENRY, Good Samaritan Hospital, Cincinnati, OH '79 (MGMT)
EILERS, DAVID H., dir. maint. and eng., Huron Memorial Hospital, Bad Axe, MI '84 (ENG)
EINHORN, MELVIN S., vice-pres. human res., Newton-Wellesley Hospital, Newton, MA '69 (PERS)
EINHORN, RICHARD R., dir. plng., Community Hospital of Western Suffolk, Smithtown, NY '82 (PR) (PLNG)
EINHORN, STEVEN L., pres., Einhorn, Yaffee, Prescott and Krouner, Albany, NY '83
EINHORN, THEODORE E. B., atty., St. Clare's Hospital, Denville, NJ '73 (ATTY)
EINSPANIER, JOHN K., vice-pres. mktg., Hpi Health Care Services, Inc., Los Angeles, CA '85
EISELE, C. WESLEY, MD, prog. dir., Estes Park Institute, Englewood, CO '72 (HON)

EISELE, FREDERICK R., assoc. prof., Graduate Studies in Health Planning and Administration, Pennsylvania State University, University Park, PA '86 (PLNG)
EISEMAN, ELLEN R., dir. trng. and international prog., American Medical International, Beverly Hills, CA '83 (EDUC)
EISENBAUGH, ALTA, dir. matl. mgt., St. Christopher's Hospital, Philadelphia, PA '83 (PUR)
EISENBERG, ANNE FRANCES, dir. plng. and pub. policy, Regional Medical Center at Memphis, Memphis, TN '83 (PLNG)
EISENBERG, BARRY E., PhD, mgr. trng. and dev., Memorial Sloan-Kettering Cancer Center, New York, NY '85 (PLNG)
EISENBERG, BARRY J., asst. adm. plng. and mktg., Sibley Memorial Hospital, Washington, DC '82 (PLNG)
EISENBERGER, ELIZABETH ANNE, clin. instr., South Amboy Memorial Hospital, South Amboy, NJ '77 (EDUC)
EISENBISE, MARY A., RN, asst. adm. and dir. nrsg. serv., University of Kansas Hospital, Kansas City, KS '73 (NURS)
EISENHART, ROBERT R., facil. arch. and planner, Northwestern Memorial Hospital, Chicago, IL '86 (ENG)
EISENHAUER, TERRI S., educ. instr., Kershaw County Memorial Hospital, Camden, SC '86 (EDUC)
EISENHUT, DENNIS L., dir. pulmonary serv., Bethesda Oak Hospital, Cincinnati, OH '85
EISENSTAT, DAVID H., atty., Cabrini Medical Center, New York, NY '82 (ATTY)
EISENSTAT, MARGIE A., acct., Ernst and Whinney, New York, NY '78
EISENSTEIN, ROBERT, dir. prog., Lutheran Medical Center, St. Louis, MO '86
EISFELDT, PHILIP M., supv. biomedical, Methodist Hospital, Madison, WI '79 (ENG)
EISGRUB, FRED, asst. dir. pers., Kingsbrook Jewish Medical Center, Brooklyn, NY '77 (PERS)
EISNER, J. MICHAEL, atty., Yale-New Haven Hospital, New Haven, CT '78 (ATTY)
EITAPENCE, NANCY N., dir. vol. serv., Rutland Regional Medical Center, Rutland, VT '80 (VOL)
EITEL, RICHARD K., adm. support serv., Memorial Hospital, Colorado Springs, CO '82 (PLNG)
EIZIS, JAN, student, Roosevelt University, Chicago, IL '85 (MGMT)
EIZIS, JAN, student, Roosevelt University, Chicago, IL '87 (PR)
EKDAHL, PAT E., RN, corp. dir. nrsg., Sisters of St. Mary, St. Louis, MO '82 (NURS)
EKSTRAND, MARTHA JANE, RN, dir. qual. assur. and risk mgt., Brigham and Women's Hospital, Boston, MA '78 (RISK)
EL-GAWLY, F. GEORGE, supv. pur., St. Anthony Center, Houston, TX '86 (PUR)
ELARBEE, VERNON R., dir. pers., University General Hospital, Seminole, FL '86 (PERS)
ELBAUM, ELEANOR, RN, dir. ped. nrsg., Rhode Island Hospital, Providence, RI '81 (NURS)
ELBERFELD, MARK, vice-pres., Frankford Hospital of the City of Philadelphia, Philadelphia, PA '80
ELBOW, PAUL X., adm. surveyor, Joint Commission on Accreditation of Hospitals, Chicago, IL '51 (LIFE)
ELCOCK, ESTHER K. M., (ret.), Belleville, PA '26 (LIFE)
ELDEN, DOUGLAS L., atty., Altheimer and Gray, Chicago, IL '84 (ATTY)
ELDER, DAVID E., dir. educ. and trng., Heartland Hospital West, St. Joseph, MO '82 (EDUC)
ELDER, MARY LOU, pat. rep., Mary Lanning Memorial Hospital, Hastings, NE '87 (PAT)
ELDER, MAX Q., consult., Max Q. Elder Associates, Wilmington, DE '65 (PR)
ELDER, MICHAEL R., dir. food serv., St. Bernardine Medical Center, San Bernardino, CA '83 (FOOD)
ELDER, ROSALIE T., dir. food serv., Hoag Memorial Hospital Presbyterian, Newport Beach, CA '81 (FOOD)
ELDER, SUE ANGELA, dir. risk mgt., Providence Hospital, Mobile, AL '84 (RISK)
ELDERKIN, DAVID M., atty., Mercy Hospital, Cedar Rapids, IA '68 (ATTY)
ELDERSVELD, DAVID R., planner, Borgess Medical Center, Kalamazoo, MI '79 (PLNG)
ELDREDGE, CLIFFORD MURRAY, dep. dir., University of Iowa Hospitals and Clinics, Iowa City, IA '70
ELDRIDGE, CHARLEY O., pres., Leland Memorial Hospital, Riverdale, MD '67
ELDRIDGE, RUTH A., RN, dir. corp. nrsg., Western Reserve Systems-Southside, Youngstown, OH '84 (NURS)
ELEAZAR, PAULA Y., syst. rep., Hospital Corporation of America, Nashville, TN '83
ELEFANTE, RICHARD J., dir. vol. and guest rel., Hospital for Special Surgery, New York, NY '86 (VOL)
ELGIN, DOUGLAS L., dir. soc. serv., Memorial Hospital, Danville, VA '81 (SOC)
ELGIN, JO ANN, adm. dir. mktg., HCA South Arlington Medical Center, Arlington, TX '86 (PR)
ELGIN, JOANNE C., RN, adm. pat. care, St. Joseph's Mercy Hospital, Centerville, IA '75 (NURS)
ELIAS, ANGEL L. RODRIGUEZ, dir. pers., Auxilio Mutuo Hospital, San Juan, P.R. '86 (PERS)
ELIAS, CLIFFORD E., gen. counsel, Bon Secours Hospital of Methuen, Methuen, MA '75 (ATTY)
ELIAS, HARRY, student, Program in School of Public Health, Columbia University, New York, NY '86
ELIAS, JOAN E., atty., Massachusetts General Hospital, Boston, MA '81 (ATTY)
ELIAS, KATHLEEN, student, Linfield School of Nursing, Portland, OR '87 (AMB)
ELIAS, MICHAEL D., dir. facil. plng., Mercy Hospital, Wilkes-Barre, PA '82 (PLNG)
ELIASON, CHARLES WILLIAM, pres., Consolidated Health Services, Inc., Knoxville, TN '65 (PERS)
ELICKER, JULIANNE, dir. soc. serv., Bryn Mawr Rehabilitation Hospital, Malvern, PA '86 (SOC)
ELIKAN, DINA C., soc. worker, St. Mary of Nazareth Hospital Center, Chicago, IL '87 (PAT)
ELINE, JOHN C., dir. pub. rel. and mktg., Gettysburg Hospital, Gettysburg, PA '85 (PR)
ELING, ROBERT R., asst. vice-pres. corp. facil., Grandview Hospital and Medical Center, Dayton, OH '86 (ENG)
ELION, OLA R., dir. hskpg., St. Jude Children's Research Hospital, Memphis, TN '86 (ENVIRON)
ELIOPOULOS, ANDREW J., dir. eng., Naples Community Hospital, Naples, FL '83 (ENG)
ELISEO, FRANK, exec. vice-pres., Roe-Eliseo, Oradell, NJ '81
ELKERN, KENNETH F., dir. plant oper., St. Clare Hospital, Baraboo, WI '79 (ENG)
ELKINS, BETTYE S., atty., Oakwood Hospital, Dearborn, MI '77 (ATTY)
ELKINS, NANCY W., dir. soc. work, Lee Moffitt Hospital and Cancer Research Institute at the University of South Florida, Tampa, FL '85 (SOC)
ELKINS, NANCY, supv. renal soc. work, Mount Carmel Mercy Hospital, Detroit, MI '86 (SOC)
ELKINS, REGIE G., area mgr. health care facil., Carlson Southeast Corporation, Smyrna, GA '83 (PLNG)
ELKINS, RICHARD R., dir. new constr., Pekin Memorial Hospital, Pekin, IL '69 (ENG)
ELKO, AUDREY J., coor. cent. proc., Porter Memorial Hospital, Denver, CO '76 (CS)
ELLAISSI, FATHY, unit adm., Medical College of Georgia Hospital and Clinic, Augusta, GA '87
ELLAND, M. BETH, dir. strategic plng., Mercy Medical Center, Denver, CO '85 (PLNG)
ELLEDGE, JEFFREY S., dir. inventory mgt., Tucson Medical Center, Tucson, AZ '86 (CS)
ELLENBERGER, DONNA, RN, Centre Community Hospital, State College, PA '87 (AMB)
ELLENBURG, JOHN C., constr. grds. maint., Baptist Medical Center Easley, Easley, SC '78 (ENG)
ELLENTUCK, BERTRAM, vice-pres. plng., Monmouth Medical Center, Long Branch, NJ '78 (ENG)
ELLER, ROBERT M., atty., Cedars-Sinai Medical Center, Los Angeles, CA '73 (ATTY)
ELLERBROOK, SANDRA LYNN, dir. vol. serv., Tuality Community Hospital, Hillsboro, OR '85 (VOL)
ELLETT, FRANCES KATHRYN, assoc. dir. pat. serv., University of California at Los Angeles Medical Center, Los Angeles, CA '87 (PAT)
ELLICK, ALFRED G., atty., University Hospital, University of Nebraska, Omaha, NE '68 (ATTY)
ELLINGSEN, LEIF J., supv. biomedical eng., Concord Hospital, Concord, NH '85 (ENG)
ELLINGSON, C. POLLY, atty., University of Washington Hospitals, Seattle, WA '78 (ATTY)
ELLINGTON, ELIZABETH, dir. pub. affairs, National Hospital for Orthopaedics, Arlington, VA '87 (PR)
ELLINGTON, MARVIN L. JR., coor. matl. and dir. cent. sup., St. Luke's Hospital, Kansas City, MO '77 (CS)
ELLINGWOOD, DWIGHT, partner, Phase II Consulting, Salt Lake City, UT '87
ELLIOT, GAE H., dir. pers. and payroll, Lowrance Hospital, Mooresville, NC '87 (PERS)
ELLIOT, JOAN C., RN, dir. nrsg. serv., Winsted Memorial Hospital, Winsted, CT '78 (NURS)
ELLIOTT, BARBARA B., dir. vol. serv., Memorial Hospital, York, PA '80 (VOL)
ELLIOTT, BRUCE H., dir. human res., Newington Children's Hospital, Newington, CT '83 (PERS)
ELLIOTT, CLIFTON L., atty., St. John's Regional Medical Center, Joplin, MO '78 (ATTY)
ELLIOTT, DAVID O., dir. facil. mgt., State of Connecticut, Department of Mental Retardation, East Hartford, CT '82 (ENG)
ELLIOTT, DIANE L., dir. pers., Broadlawns Medical Center, Des Moines, IA '82 (PERS)
ELLIOTT, DIANNE M., dir. soc. serv., Watsonville Community Hospital, Watsonville, CA '79 (SOC)
ELLIOTT, EUGENE LEE, bus. mgr., Gynecological and Ob Associates, College Park, MD '71
ELLIOTT, IVAN A. JR., atty., Carmi Township Hospital, Carmi, IL '75 (ATTY)
ELLIOTT, J. D., pres., Nashville Memorial Hospital, Madison, TN '58
ELLIOTT, JOHN PASCAL, student, Graduate Program in Health Systems and Hospital Administration, School of Public Health and Tropical Medicine, Tulane University, New Orleans, LA '85
ELLIOTT, JUANITA B., dir. pub. rel., Pottstown Memorial Medical Center, Pottstown, PA '72 (PR)
ELLIOTT, JUNE L., dir. qual. assur., Somerset Medical Center, Somerville, NJ '83 (RISK)
ELLIOTT, KAREN S., RN, assoc. dir. nrsg., Fairmont General Hospital, Fairmont, WV '75 (NURS)
ELLIOTT, LOUIS C. JR., atty., Newport Hospital, Newport, NH '77 (ATTY)
ELLIOTT, PATRICIA F., dir. mktg. and commun., Casa Colina, Inc., Pomona, CA '79 (PR)
ELLIOTT, PEARL K., dir. vol. serv., Hanover General Hospital, Hanover, PA '86 (VOL)
ELLIOTT, PHYLLIS J., dir. vol. and pat. rep. serv., Winona Memorial Hospital, Indianapolis, IN '70 (VOL)(PAT)
ELLIOTT, ROGER W., supv. eng., Beloit Memorial Hospital, Beloit, WI '86 (ENG)
ELLIOTT, SHELLEY, dir. commun. and comm. rel., Pendleton Memorial Methodist Hospital, New Orleans, LA '85 (PR) (PLNG)
ELLIOTT, TERRY B., coor. food serv., St. Luke's Hospital, Kansas City, MO '74 (FOOD)
ELLIOTT, TERRY L., dir. phys. plant, AMI Nacogdoches Medical Center Hospital, Nacogdoches, TX '81 (ENG)
ELLIS, ALICE M., dir. soc. serv., St. John's Hospital, Red Wing, MN '75 (SOC)
ELLIS, BETTY R., dir. food serv., Lake Shore Nursing Centre, Chicago, IL '86 (FOOD)
ELLIS, DOROTHY V., assoc. adm., Hemet Valley Hospital District, Hemet, CA '86 (NURS)
ELLIS, EDWARD DAVID, atty., St. Joseph's Hospital and Health Center, Paris, TX '76 (ATTY)
ELLIS, GEORGE R., MD, chief rehab. med. serv., Veterans Administration Medical Center, Lexington, KY '55 (LIFE)
ELLIS, JANE F., dir. plng., St. Margaret's Hospital, Montgomery, AL '74 (PLNG)
ELLIS, JANET L., dep. chief exec. off., Alabama Health Plan, Birmingham, AL '85 (PLNG)
ELLIS, JAY C., sr. mgr., Peat, Marwick, Mitchell and Company, Richmond, VA '85 (MGMT)
ELLIS, JEFFREY O., atty., Holbrook, Ellis and Heaven, Merriam, KS '82 (ATTY)
ELLIS, LEE E., coor. pat. rep., Hospital of the University of Pennsylvania, Philadelphia, PA '81 (PAT)
ELLIS, MARGARET P., dir. vol. serv., Montgomery General Hospital, Olney, MD '73 (VOL)
ELLIS, MICHAEL, MD, pres., owner, dir. and path., The Laboratory, Inc., Bossier City, LA '86
ELLIS, PATRICIA ANN, pur. agt., Ina Ross Loos Health Plans, Glendale, CA '84 (PUR)
ELLIS, RANDY L., mgr. fin. serv., Executive Consulting Group, Bellevue, WA '79 (PLNG)
ELLIS, ROGER G., atty., St. Elizabeth Hospital, Elizabeth, NJ '82 (ATTY)
ELLIS, RUTH A., adm. liaison vol. serv., Graham Hospital, Canton, IL '86 (VOL)
ELLIS, SHARON A., dir. emp. rel., Memorial Medical Center, Savannah, GA '84 (PERS)
ELLIS, SHAWN L., dir. soc. serv., Alvarado Hospital Medical Center, San Diego, CA '86 (SOC)
ELLIS, THOMAS J., dir. pers., Mount Washington Pediatric Hospital, Baltimore, MD '86 (PERS)
ELLISH, PATTI, RN, asst. dir. nrsg. and med. surg. serv., West Jefferson Medical Center, Marrero, LA '86 (NURS)
ELLISON, BARBARA C., asst. vice-pres., Kettering Medical Center, Kettering, OH '86 (PLNG)
ELLISON, CARL E., asst. vice-pres., Memorial Health Properties, Inc., South Bend, IN '82 (PLNG)
ELLISON, CAROL LOUISE, coor. pat. serv., St. Francis Memorial Hospital, San Francisco, CA '85 (PAT)
ELLISON, FRANCES D., atty., Greenville General Hospital, Greenville, SC '84 (ATTY)
ELLISON, FRED F., American Medical International, Atlanta, GA '53 (LIFE)
ELLISON, NANCY M., dir. pub. rel., Munson Medical Center, Traverse City, MI '76 (PR)
ELLISON, PAUL, exec. vice-pres. network oper., SunHealth Corporation, Charlotte, NC '78
ELLISOR, PATRICIA R., RN, Austin, TX '86 (NURS)
ELLISTON, JOELLE A. H., dir. diet., Porter Memorial Hospital, Denver, CO '83 (FOOD)
ELLMER, FRANK M., partner, Ernst and Whinney, Hartford, CT '81
ELLSON, STEVEN K., mgr. educ. serv., Memorial Hospital, South Bend, IN '85 (EDUC)
ELLSWORTH, GERALD F., RN, dir. nrsg., Brattleboro Memorial Hospital, Brattleboro, VT '78 (NURS)
ELLSWORTH, MARVIN G., dir. environ. serv., Quakertown Community Hospital, Quakertown, PA '86 (ENVIRON)
ELLSWORTH, PETER K., atty., Sharp Healthcare, San Diego, CA '78 (ATTY)
ELLWANGER, JERRY, pres. physicians res., Nebraska Methodist Health System, Inc., Omaha, NE '87 (AMB)
ELLWOOD, RICHARD L., pres., Rle Consulting, Inc., Vestavia Hills, AL '83 (PUR)
ELMAN, KATHERINE L., dir. food serv., Louis A. Weiss Memorial Hospital, Chicago, IL '67 (FOOD)
ELMENDORF, CAROL, dir. health hm care, Loudoun Services Group, Leesburg, VA '87 (AMB)
ELMENDORF, SR. MARY, dir. diet., St. Francis Hospital, Blue Island, IL '72 (FOOD)
ELMER, DAVID R., dir. soc. serv., St. Clare Hospital of Monroe, Monroe, WI '84 (SOC)
ELMER, DENISE, corp. matl. mgr., Lutheran Hospitals and Homes Society of America, Fargo, ND '79 (CS)(PUR)
ELMER, PAUL D., dir. eng., Canonsburg General Hospital, Canonsburg, PA '87 (ENG)
ELMER, RUSSELL E., MD, chm. emer. room, Swedish Covenant Hospital, Chicago, IL '84
ELMES, DIANA J., dir. qual. assur. and risk mgt., National Rehabilitation Hospital, Washington, DC '87 (RISK)
ELMHIRST, MICHAEL P., dir. human res., Leominster Hospital, Leominster, MA '85 (PERS)
ELMI, SAEID, energy coor., St. Mary's Medical Center, Evansville, IN '82 (ENG)
ELMORE, BARBARA, outreach coor., Golden Valley Memorial Hospital, Clinton, MO '85 (PR)
ELMORE, CRAIG W., prin., Arthur, Clark, Elmore and Associates, Kansas City, MO '81 (PLNG)
ELMORE, DEBORAH L., dir. pub. rel., Halstead Hospital, Halstead, KS '79 (PR)
ELMORE, ELAINE, student, Boston University Health Management Programs, Boston, MA '86 (PLNG)
ELMORE, MYRTLE, RN, supv. and dir. cent. serv. sup., Hilton Head Hospital, Hilton Head Island, SC '85 (CS)
ELMORE, PAUL, dir. pers., St. John's Regional Health Center, Springfield, MO '80 (PERS)
ELMORE, THOMAS S., dir. network serv., SunHealth Corporation, Charlotte, NC '78 (MGMT)
ELRIFAI, AMR M., MD, plng. assoc., Greater Canonsburg Health Systems, Canonsburg, PA '85
ELROD, JAMES L. JR., vice-pres., Dillon, Read and Company, Inc., New York, NY '83
ELROD, LEIGH M., coor. pers., Rockdale Hospital, Conyers, GA '83 (PERS)
ELROD, ROBERT G., atty., University Heights Hospital, Indianapolis, IN '79 (ATTY)
ELROY, WILLIAM A. JR., actg. dir. emp. and labor rel., Johns Hopkins Hospital, Baltimore, MD '86 (PERS)
ELSASS, EUGENE P., atty., Wilson Memorial Hospital, Sidney, OH '74 (ATTY)

ELSBURY, ELLEN M., RN, vice-pres. nrsg., Allen Memorial Hospital, Waterloo, IA '80 (NURS)
ELSINGER, HENRY W., Baystate Health Management Services, Inc., Springfield, MA '70 (MGMT)
ELSNER, HAROLD F., mgr. emp. and trng., Bay Medical Center, Bay City, MI '78 (EDUC)
ELSON, BARRY R., atty., Friedman Hospital, Philadelphia, PA '83 (ATTY)
ELSTER, JOHN J., dir. mktg., Children's Hospital of Pittsburgh, Pittsburgh, PA '86 (PR)
ELSTROM, THOMAS M., vice-pres. prod. dev., Coffey Communications, Inc., Walla Walla, WA '78 (PR)
ELSWICK, CALVIN W. II, chief eng., Charleston General Hospital, Charleston, WV '84 (ENG)
ELTRINGHAM, PATRICIA, dir. matl. mgt., East Liverpool City Hospital, East Liverpool, OH '83 (CS)
ELVING, JAMES L., mech. eng., Horty, Elving and Associates, Inc., Minneapolis, MN '85 (ENG)
ELY, DWIGHT COLLINS, mgr. sales plng., Philips Medical Systems, Inc., Shelton, CT '77
ELYARD, INA E., dir. vol. serv., United Hospital Center, Clarksburg, WV '86 (VOL)
EMANUEL, CATHERINE F., vice-pres. mktg., Carle Foundation Hospital, Urbana, IL '80 (PR) (PLNG)
EMANUEL, WILLIAM J., atty., Morgan, Lewis and Bockius, Los Angeles, CA '73 (ATTY)
EMANUELSON, HERBERT L. JR., atty., Masonic Hospital, Wallingford, CT '70 (ATTY)
EMANUELSON, PATRICIA G., dir. emer. care serv., Phoenix General Hospital, Phoenix, AZ '87 (AMB)
EMARD, ESTHER, RN, assoc. dir. nrsg., Morton Hospital and Medical Center, Taunton, MA '86 (NURS)
EMBRY, CHRISTINE, dir. vol. serv., University Hospital, Lexington, KY '85 (VOL)
EMBRY, REBA S., coor. qual. assur. and pat. rep., Community General Hospital, Thomasville, NC '83 (PAT)
EMCH, ELEANOR L., chief food serv., District of Columbia General Hospital, Washington, DC '81 (FOOD)
EMERMAN, ROBERT DAVID, sr. vice-pres., The Medical Center, Beaver, PA '69
EMERSON, EDWARD L., dir. human res., Group Health Cooperative of Puget Sound, Seattle, WA '82 (PERS)
EMERSON, EDWIN G., atty., St. Vincent Medical Center, Toledo, OH '77 (ATTY)
EMERSON, MARILYN P., dir. mktg., McPherson Community Health Center, Howell, MI '83 (PR) (PLNG)
EMERY, DOROTHY JANE, pat. rep., Lake Forest Hospital, Lake Forest, IL '74 (PAT)
EMERY, KENNETH R., exec. vice-pres. and chief oper. off., St. Joseph's Hospital, Elmira, NY '74 (PLNG)
EMERY, LEIGH A., actg. clin. contract mgr., University of Massachusetts Medical Center, Worcester, MA '86
EMLER, DIXIE G., RN, asst. adm. nrsg. serv., Lafayette Home Hospital, Lafayette, IN '77 (NURS)
EMMANUEL, KAREN O., atty., Sacred Heart Hospital of Pensacola, Pensacola, FL '86 (ATTY)
EMMER, ADELE R., dir. vol. serv., Botsford General Hospital, Farmington Hills, MI '82 (VOL)
EMMERICH, CHARLES E., fin. analyst, Hospital Corporation of America, Richmond, VA '83
EMMERT, KATHLEEN D., dir. food serv., Anne Arundel General Hospital, Annapolis, MD '71 (FOOD)
EMMETT, ROBERT M., chief fin. off., Wills Eye Hospital, Philadelphia, PA '78
EMMINGER, SR. MARILYNN, RN, Seton Provincialate, Los Altos Hills, CA '72 (NURS)
EMMITT, MARY, dir. soc. serv., St. Marys Hospital Medical Center, Madison, WI '68 (SOC)
EMMONS, BOBBY B., assoc. dir., Hospital of the University of Pennsylvania, Philadelphia, PA '70
EMMONS, J. ALEX, dir. matl. mgt., Hancock Memorial Hospital, Greenfield, IN '80 (PUR)
EMMONS, JANE O., coor. vol. serv., Osteopathic Hospital of Maine, Portland, ME '85 (VOL)
EMMONS, JANET S., dir. emp. rel., Swedish American Hospital, Rockford, IL '86 (PERS)
EMMOTT, LILLIAN J., dir. vol. and pat. rep. serv., Brockton Hospital, Brockton, MA '74 (VOL)(PAT)
EMORY, RICHARD J., dir. pers., John T. Mather Memorial Hospital, Port Jefferson, NY '82 (PERS)
EMRICH, HERBERT W. R., adm., Daniel Boone Clinic, Harlan, KY '51 (LIFE)
EMRIE, GLENDA M., coor. staff dev., Southwest Medical Center, Liberal, KS '86 (EDUC)
ENCHELMAYER, CARL R., asst. vice-pres. pers. adm., St. Vincent's Medical Center, Jacksonville, FL '81 (PERS)
ENDERS, STEPHEN L., dir. plng., Bexar County Hospital District, San Antonio, TX '80 (PLNG)
ENDERS, WILLIAM L., dir. matl. mgt., Natividad Medical Center, Salinas, CA '86 (PUR)
ENDRES, MARTHA WHITLOCK, coor. risk mgt., Florida Medical Center Hospital, Fort Lauderdale, FL '86 (RISK)
ENDRESEN, KAREN W., PhD, pres., Endresen Research, Seattle, WA '84 (PLNG)
ENDSLEY, DONALD L., asst. adm. plant serv., Marion General Hospital, Marion, IN '71 (ENG)
ENDSLEY, JANET L., dir. mktg. and pub. rel., Stevens Memorial Hospital, Edmonds, WA '84 (PR)
ENG, RALPH D. MCNATT DIR, dir. eng. and spec. proj., Pennsylvania State University Hospital, Hershey, PA '87 (ENG)
ENGBERG, BONNIE J., RN, dir. nrsg. serv., Woman's Christian Association Hospital, Jamestown, NY '80 (NURS)
ENGBERG, GLADYS, dir. vol., Ballard Community Hospital, Seattle, WA '86 (VOL)
ENGBRECHT, DEAN C., dir. soc. work, North Dakota State Hospital, Jamestown, ND '80 (SOC)
ENGEBRECHT, CAROLYN, dir. matl. mgt., Passavant Area Hospital, Jacksonville, IL '84 (PUR)
ENGEBRETSON, BERY, MD, dir. primary care, Broadlawns Medical Center, Des Moines, IA '87 (AMB)
ENGEBRETSON, STEVEN C., dir. environ. serv., St. Michael Hospital, Milwaukee, WI '87 (ENVIRON)
ENGEDAL, JEAN, RN, dir. nrsg. serv., National Medical Health Care Services, Santa Monica, CA '84 (NURS)
ENGEL, ARTHUR S. W., MD, past pres., Swedish Hospital Organization, Stockholm, Sweden '67 (HON)
ENGEL, CONNIE E., dir. food serv., Mary Black Memorial Hospital, Spartanburg, SC '86 (FOOD)
ENGEL, D. JOYCE, plng. and mktg. analyst, Desert Hospital, Palm Springs, CA '83 (PLNG)
ENGEL, ELMER T., dir. plant oper., St. Margaret Memorial Hospital, Pittsburgh, PA '81 (ENG)
ENGEL, INEZ B., dir. diet., Sweeny Community Hospital, Sweeny, TX '77 (FOOD)
ENGEL, MARY LU, dir. diet., North Memorial Medical Center, Robbinsdale, MN '69 (FOOD)
ENGELBY, JOHN E., dir. pers., Finley Hospital, Dubuque, IA '77 (PERS)
ENGELHARDT, IVAN, dir. inst. serv., McKee Medical Center, Loveland, CO '75 (ENG)
ENGELHART, ROBERT G., consult., Burnsville, MN '50 (LIFE)
ENGELKE, HAROLD A., MD, chm. outpatient and emer. dept., Lawrence and Memorial Hospital, New London, CT '87 (AMB)
ENGELMAN, RANKE W., chief eng., Angelo Community Hospital, San Angelo, TX '75 (ENG)
ENGELMOHR, JACK H., coor. prog. health care adm., Pace University, White Plains, NY '56 (LIFE)
ENGELS, DIANE L., coor. cent. serv., Our Lady of Fatima Hospital, North Providence, RI '81 (CS)
ENGEN, MURIEL, dir. vol. serv., Lakewood Hospital, Tacoma, WA '79 (VOL)
ENGEN, PHYLLIS J., dir. corp. human res., AMI Presbyterian-St. Luke's Medical Center, Denver, CO '83 (PERS)
ENGLAND, DORIS, RN, vice-pres. pat. care, Children's Hospital, St. Louis, MO '74 (NURS)(RISK)
ENGLAND, FRED J., dir. nrsg., Regina Continuing Care Center, Evansville, IN '81
ENGLAND, LOIS A., mgr. staff pers. serv., Washington University School of Medicine, St. Louis, MO '85 (PERS)
ENGLAND, PAUL H., supt. bldg. and grds., Jennings Community Hospital, North Vernon, IN '85 (ENG)
ENGLE, SHIRLEY H., dir. diet., Deaconess Hospital of Cleveland, Cleveland, OH '72 (FOOD)
ENGLEBARDT, SHEILA P., RN, asst. adm. nrsg., Moses H. Cone Memorial Hospital, Greensboro, NC '83 (NURS)
ENGLEMAN, HARRIET, RN, asst. adm. nrsg., Valley Medical Center of Fresno, Fresno, CA '77 (NURS)
ENGLER, GARY, asst. dir. environ. serv., Memorial Hospital, Towanda, PA '85 (ENG)
ENGLER, HIBBARD H., atty., Mercy Medical Center, Oshkosh, WI '68 (ATTY)
ENGLER, ULRICH, arch. facil. plng., Cuyahoga County Hospitals, Cleveland, OH '86 (ENG)
ENGLERT, BERNICE E., dir. in-service educ., Kennedy Memorial Hospitals-University Medical Center-Cherry Hill Division, Cherry Hill, NJ '85 (EDUC)
ENGLEY, FRANK B. JR., prof. microbiology, University of Missouri School of Medicine, Columbia, MO '84 (CS)
ENGLISH, BEVERLY J., RN, dir. nrsg., Axtell Christian Hospital, Newton, KS '85 (NURS)
ENGLISH, CHARLES E., atty., Franklin-Simpson Memorial Hospital, Franklin, KY '75 (ATTY)
ENGLISH, ESLYN D., dir. food serv., Huntington Hospital, Huntington, NY '77 (FOOD)
ENGLISH, HUGH, dir. plant oper., HCA Southern Hills Medical Center, Nashville, TN '86 (ENG)
ENGLISH, JOHN M., dir. plant oper., North Monroe Community Hospital, Monroe, LA '85 (ENG)
ENGLISH, PATRICIA A., RN, dir. adm. nrsg., St. Mary's Medical Center, Evansville, IN '80 (NURS)
ENGLISH, SAMUEL J. JR., chief eng., Chinese Hospital, San Francisco, CA '79 (ENG)
ENGSTROM, CRAIG W., dir. biomedical eng., Covenant Medical Center -St. Francis, Waterloo, IA '85 (ENG)
ENGSTROM, MARGARET, dir. commun., Oakwood Hospital, Dearborn, MI '84 (ENG)
ENGSTROM, MARK D., student, Program in Health Services Administration, University of Minnesota, Minneapolis, MN '86
ENGSTRUM-GRONEMAN, RENEE, dir. soc. serv., Dixie Medical Center, St. George, UT '86 (SOC)
ENLOE, RONALD L., dir. pers., Ashley Valley Medical Center, Vernal, UT '82 (PERS)
ENLOW, DAVID T., atty., Appalachian Regional Healthcare, Lexington, KY '76 (ATTY)
ENNIS, ALICE, asst. supv. cent. serv., Christ Hospital, Jersey City, NJ '80 (CS)
ENNIS, MARTIN, dir. hosp. serv., Mutual Assurance Society of Alabama, Birmingham, AL '84 (RISK)
ENO, EARL, eng., Scott Memorial Hospital, Lawrenceburg, TN '80 (ENG)
ENO, RONALD, dir. plant eng., Saint Joseph Hospital, Denver, CO '85 (ENG)
ENOCH, DONNA, dir. soc. serv., Glendale Memorial Hospital and Health Center, Glendale, CA '86 (SOC)
ENOCKSON, DOROTHY, dir. soc. work serv., Saline Memorial Hospital, Benton, AR '80 (SOC)
ENRIGHT, JOHN D., asst. adm., Rockingham Memorial Hospital, Bellows Falls, VT '84
ENRIGHT, TIMOTHY D., vice-pres. gen. serv. and facil. mgt., Victory Memorial Hospital, Waukegan, IL '69 (ENG)
ENSIGN, GAYLE H., pres., California Association of Catholic Hospitals, Sacramento, CA '84
ENSIGN, JAMES M., vice-pres. syst. dev., Daughters of Charity Health Systems, Los Altos Hills, CA '56
ENSINGER, G. STEVEN, RN, asst. adm. nrsg., Western Reserve Systems-Northside, Youngstown, OH '86 (NURS)
ENSOR, BARBARA A., mgr. educ. serv., Saint Joseph Hospital, Fort Worth, TX '85 (EDUC)
ENSOR, PHYLLIS P., dir. food serv., North Side Hospital, Johnson City, TN '83 (FOOD)
ENTIN, FREDRIC J., atty., Fohrman, Lurie, Sklar and Simon, Ltd., Chicago, IL '76 (ATTY)
ENZ, JOAN M., RN, assoc. exec. dir. nrsg. serv., Hahnemann University Hospital, Philadelphia, PA '86 (NURS)
EPIFANIO, PATRICIA C., coor. emer. nrs., Maryland Institute of Emergency Medical Service, Baltimore, MD '86 (EDUC)
EPKE, BARBARA J., dir. soc. work serv., Shadyside Hospital, Pittsburgh, PA '85 (SOC)
EPMEIER, BRUCE E., dir. mgt. serv., Deaconess Hospital, Evansville, IN '84 (MGMT)
EPPARD, H. KELLY JR., dir. plant oper., Martha Jefferson Hospital, Charlottesville, VA '87 (ENG)
EPPERSON, GORDON W., pres., Driscoll Foundation Children's Hospital, Corpus Christi, TX '59
EPPLER, SUE, coor. pat. serv., Springfield General Hospital, Springfield, MO '82 (PAT)
EPPLEY, DANIEL A., assoc. adm., Greenville Regional Hospital, Greenville, PA '74
EPPLEY, WANEMA A., RN, dir. nrsg. serv. critical care, Bethesda Hospital, Zanesville, OH '84 (NURS)
EPPLING, DALE W., dir. staff dev., East Jefferson General Hospital, Metairie, LA '85 (EDUC)
EPPS, C. B., dir. safety and security, Huntsville Hospital, Huntsville, AL '67 (ENG)
EPPS, JAMES A., dist. vice-pres., Hospital Corporation of America Management Company, Dallas, TX '75
EPPS, MARY E., RN, mgr. matl., HCA Aiken Regional Medical Center, Aiken, SC '79 (CS)(PUR)
EPPS, SPENCER JR., maint. and telecommun. tech., Bethany Hospital, Chicago, IL '87 (ENG)
EPSTEIN, ALAN I., atty., Fountain Valley Regional Hospital Medical Center, Fountain Valley, CA '76 (ATTY)
EPSTEIN, ANDREA BELKIN, mgr. mktg., New England Critical Care, Marlborough, MA '86 (PLNG)
EPSTEIN, FIELDING W., plng. analyst, Cleveland Clinic Foundation, Cleveland, OH '81
EPSTEIN, GAIL M., dir. telecommun., Mount Sinai Medical Center, Miami Beach, FL '84 (ENG)
EPSTEIN, J. D., atty., Sisters of Charity Health Care Systems, Houston, TX '74 (ATTY)
EPSTEIN, STEVEN B., atty., Epstein, Becker, Borsody and Green, Sacramento, CA '82 (ATTY)
EPSTEIN, WILLIAM ERIC, adm. support serv., Mount Sinai Medical Center, New York, NY '76 (MGMT)(PLNG)(PUR)
ERB, EUGENE I., vice-pres. prof. serv., Lynchburg General Hospital, Lynchburg, VA '86
ERB, PAMELA S., asst. exec. dir., Tampa General Hospital, Tampa, FL '77 (NURS)
ERBSTOESZER, MARIE J., consult., Mount Vernon, WA '75 (PLNG)
ERCEG, ANGELINA F., ombudsman, San Pedro Peninsula Hospital, San Pedro, CA '78 (PAT)
ERDMAN, BERNARD P., pres., Padgett-Thompson, Inc., Overland Park, KS '70 (MGMT)(EDUC)
ERDMAN, JUNE M., asst. dir. diet., Evergreen Hospital Medical Center, Kirkland, WA '85 (FOOD)
ERDMANN, NEAL, dir. maint. and safety, St. Clement Hospital, Red Bud, IL '86 (ENG)
ERDOS, MARGUERITE H., asst. adm. and pur. agt., Bayonne Hospital, Bayonne, NJ '47 (LIFE)
EREN, ERKAL, dir. diet. serv., Braddock General Hospital, Braddock, PA '77 (FOOD)
ERHARDT, ADELE A., dir. soc. serv., Visitors Hospital, Buchanan, MI '86 (SOC)
ERICK, JACQUELINE, RN, nrs. mgr., St. Mary Hospital, Philadelphia, PA '86 (RISK)
ERICK, REBECCA S., mgr. diet., University Heights Hospital, Indianapolis, IN '86 (FOOD)
ERICKSON, CARL E., atty., St. Joseph's Medical Center, Brainerd, MN '77 (ATTY)
ERICKSON, DARRELL R., chief eng. serv., Veterans Administration Medical Center, Salt Lake City, UT '86 (ENG)
ERICKSON, DOUGLAS S., dir. eng. and constr., American Hospital Association, Chicago, IL '80 (ENG)
ERICKSON, GARY B., mgr. mgt. eng., Intermountain Health Care, Pocatello, ID '85 (MGMT)
ERICKSON, JANE E., res. assoc., Center for Hospital Finance and Management, Baltimore, MD '86
ERICKSON, JANET C., dir. food serv., Memorial Hospital, Carbondale, IL '84 (FOOD)
ERICKSON, KATHRYN L., dir. vol. serv., The Connecticut Hospice, Inc., Branford, CT '83 (VOL)
ERICKSON, KAY D., dir. educ., North Memorial Medical Center, Robbinsdale, MN '86 (EDUC)
ERICKSON, MARLENE, dir. pers., Immanuel-St. Joseph's Hospital, Mankato, MN '78 (PERS)
ERICKSON, MARY BETH, dir. commun., North Memorial Medical Center, Robbinsdale, MN '82 (ENG)
ERICKSON, NANCY J., vice-pres., New Solutions, Inc., Hackensack, NJ '82 (PLNG)
ERICKSON, PEGGY J., RN, vice-pres. nrsg., Central Kansas Medical Center, Great Bend, KS '80 (NURS)
ERICKSON, ROBERT D., exec. vice-pres. and chief fin. off., Servicemaster Industries, Inc., Downers Grove, IL '74
ERICKSON, ROBERTA G., coor. educ., Hutchinson Community Hospital, Hutchinson, MN '85 (EDUC)
ERICKSON, ROY F., pres., Bmh Health Services, Inc., Muncie, IN '54 (LIFE)
ERICKSON, RUTH ANN, RN, dir. nrsg., St. John's Hospital, Red Wing, MN '79 (NURS)
ERICKSON, SUZANNE J., RN, dir. home health, St. Elizabeth Community Hospital, Baker, OR '87 (AMB)
ERICKSON, VERN D., dir. plng., Miami Valley Hospital, Dayton, OH '82 (PLNG)
ERICKSON, VIRGINIA, RN, dir. pat. care, Divine Savior Hospital and Nursing Home, Portage, WI '68 (NURS)
ERICSON, CHIQUITA, dir. vol. serv., AMI Palmetto General Hospital, Hialeah, FL '79 (VOL)
ERICSON, DUDLEY R., dir. pers., Woman's Christian Association Hospital, Jamestown, NY '67 (PERS)
ERICSSON, ELEANOR H., RN, adm. nrsg. serv., Bear Lake Memorial Hospital, Montpelier, ID '80 (NURS)

ERIXON, STEPHEN MICHAEL, asst. vice-pres. prof. serv., Memorial Medical Center, Springfield, IL '78
ERLENHEIM, ROSEANN K., dir. commun. rel. and mktg., Selma District Hospital, Selma, CA '84 (PR)
ERLMAN, JOHN ARTHUR, pres., Shared Health Management Experience Association, Manchester, NH '56 (LIFE)
ERMOLOWICH, WILLIAM, dir. human res., St. Mary's Hospital, Passaic, NJ '84 (PERS)
ERNE, MARY ANN, RN, dir. nrsg., Coffeyville Regional Medical Center, Coffeyville, KS '86 (NURS)
ERNST, BRENDA R., RN, vice-pres. and dir. nrsg. serv., Jewish Hospital of St. Louis, St. Louis, MO '74 (NURS)
ERNST, DEBORAH, dir. soc. serv., Northwest Medical Center, Thief River Falls, MN '79 (SOC)
ERNST, JOHN R., dir. plant oper., St. Joseph Hospital and Health Care Center, Tacoma, WA '78 (ENG)
ERNST, NORA S., planner, North Colorado Medical Center, Greeley, CO '82 (PLNG)
ERNSTROM, WAYNE P., chief soc. work serv., Veterans Administration Medical Center, Martinez, CA '75 (SOC)
ERNSTTHAL, HENRY L., exec. dir., Society of Nuclear Medicine, New York, NY '83
ERSKINE, MARGY, dir. vol., Yuma Regional Medical Center, Yuma, AZ '86 (VOL)
ERSKINE, WILLIAM R., atty., Methodist Health Systems, Inc., Memphis, TN '82 (ATTY)
ERTL, NANCY L., RN, dir. pat. care, Mercy Health Center, Dubuque, IA '82 (NURS)
ERVIN, STEVE D., EdD, dir. educ., Shawnee Mission Medical Center, Shawnee Mission, KS '84 (EDUC)
ERWIN, DUANE L., vice-pres. mktg., Good Samaritan Hospital and Health Center, Dayton, OH '85 (PR) (PLNG)
ERWIN, ELEANOR, dir. vol. serv., Mercy Hospital, Miami, FL '74 (VOL)
ERWIN, GLADYS B., pat. rep. and nrsg. off. adm. asst., Hillcrest Health Center, Oklahoma City, OK '86 (PAT)
ERWIN, JERRY W., dir. pers., Bass Memorial Baptist Hospital, Enid, OK '69 (PERS)
ERWIN, KATHRINE S., (ret.), Birmingham, MI '72 (FOOD)
ERWIN, WILLIAM R., dir. pub. rel., North Carolina Hospital Association, Raleigh, NC '81 (PR)
ERWINE, BRUCE ADRIAN, vice-pres. group health prog., Bethesda Hospital, Inc., Cincinnati, OH '73
ERYOU, DAVID, atty., Buset and Eryou, Thunder Bay, Ont., Canada '85 (RISK)
ESCH, LOUISE, (ret.), Tonkawa, OK '45 (LIFE)
ESCH, RAYMOND G. JR., atty., St. Luke's Hospital, Maumee, OH '80 (ATTY)
ESCHER, DONNA M., mgr. pers., Myrtue Memorial Hospital, Harlan, IA '82 (PERS)
ESCUETA, FRANKLIN T., adm., Brady-Green Community Health Center, San Antonio, TX '72
ESDALE, ANNE E., Lansing, MI '78 (EDUC)
ESENRICH, MARCELLA D., coor. pers. and payroll, Rice County District One Hospital, Faribault, MN '83 (PERS)
ESHAK, KENNETH, assoc. adm., St. Joseph Hospital, Houston, TX '74 (PLNG)
ESHAM, MARVIN T., dir. environ. serv., Reid Memorial Hospital, Richmond, IN '84 (ENG)
ESHELMAN, LAURIE S., dir. diet. serv., Hancock Memorial Hospital, Greenfield, IN '81 (FOOD)
ESKEDAHL, SUSAN A., asst. dir. pers., North Memorial Medical Center, Robbinsdale, MN '84 (PERS)
ESKIN, STEVEN M., chief eng. serv., Veterans Administration Medical Center, East Orange, NJ '84 (ENG)
ESKRA, FRANCES G., RN, asst. dir. med. nrsg., Western Pennsylvania Hospital, Pittsburgh, PA '86 (NURS)
ESKRIDGE, PAULA, adm. risk mgt., Eastern Virginia Medical Authority, Norfolk, VA '84 (RISK)
ESLYN, COLE C., assoc. exec. dir., Presbyterian Hospital, Dallas, TX '82 (MGMT)
ESPINOSA, ANGELICIA C., chief diet. serv., Brockton-West Roxbury Veterans Administration Center, Brockton, MA '82 (FOOD)
ESPINOZA, BARBARA A., RN, dir. nrsg., AMI Glendora Community Hospital, Glendora, CA '81 (NURS)
ESPINOZA, ERNEST J., owner, Quality Engineer Biomedical Service, Sugarland, TX '82 (ENG)
ESPOSITO, DONNA, RN, coordinating supv. nrsg., Norwalk Hospital, Norwalk, CT '87 (AMB)
ESPOSITO, TONY, asst. dir. pub. rel., Illinois Hospital Association, Naperville, IL '85 (PR)
ESQUIBEL, LORENZO A., dir. pers., Eden Hospital Medical Center, Castro Valley, CA '86 (PERS)
ESSARY, HOWARD E., dir. soc. serv., Oklahoma Osteopathic Hospital, Tulsa, OK '78 (SOC)
ESSER, DICK, supv. cent. serv., Bellin Memorial Hospital, Green Bay, WI '77 (CS)
ESSEX, ROLLIE V., student, Department of Health Care Administration, George Washington University, Washington, DC '84
ESSIG, PAUL T., atty., Saint Joseph Hospital, Reading, PA '75 (ATTY)
ESSLINGER, VIRGINIA, RN, adm. prog. and proj. dev., United Hospital, Grand Forks, ND '86 (NURS)
ESSON, WILLIAM B., (ret.), Everett, WA '48 (LIFE)
ESTA, DAN, dir. matl. mgt., Northwest Community Hospital, Arlington Heights, IL '86 (CS)
ESTABROOK, KENNETH L., atty., Kessler Institute for Rehabilitation, West Orange, NJ '69 (ATTY)
ESTABROOK, MADELEINE A., atty., Beth Israel Hospital, Boston, MA '84 (ATTY)(RISK)
ESTEP, DONALD P., dir. plant eng., Broward General Medical Center, Fort Lauderdale, FL '85 (ENG)
ESTEP, SR. EULALIA, pat. and family rep., St. Francis Hospital, Charleston, WV '83 (PAT)
ESTEP, REGINA A., dir. pub. rel., Mercy Medical Center, Springfield, OH '77 (PR)
ESTERHAI, JOHN L., trustee, Roxborough Memorial Hospital, Philadelphia, PA '79
ESTERLEIN, LOIS A., adm. asst. and dir. vol., Illini Hospital, Silvis, IL '85 (VOL)
ESTERLY, CATHY, dir. environ. serv., Haverford Community Hospital, Havertown, PA '86 (ENVIRON)
ESTES, BETH, dir. pers., Raleigh General Hospital, Beckley, WV '83 (PERS)
ESTES, DOUG, dir. eng., South Seminole Community Hospital, Longwood, FL '85 (ENG)
ESTES, LON, vice-pres. human res., Venice Hospital, Venice, FL '71 (PERS)(RISK)
ESTES, MANFORD R., adm. dir. outreach serv., Wuesthoff Memorial Hospital, Rockledge, FL '87 (AMB)
ESTES, O. C., sr. vice-pres. adm., Wesley Medical Center, Wichita, KS '52 (LIFE)
ESTEY, GRETTA P., vice-pres. mktg. and dev., Kennedy Institute for Handicapped Children, Baltimore, MD '84 (PR) (PLNG)
ESTIS, BESS R., dir. soc. work serv., Baptist Memorial Hospital, Gadsden, AL '81 (SOC)
ESTIS, JOHN ALAN, dir. human res., Baptist Medical Center-Princeton, Birmingham, AL '83 (PERS)
ESTOCK, DOUGLAS L., dir. info. mgt., St. Joseph Hospital, Lancaster, PA '87 (MGMT)
ESTOUP, W. MICHAEL, asst. dir. pur., Southern Baptist Hospital, New Orleans, LA '83 (PUR)
ESTRELLA, WILLIAM, atty., Ashford Presbyterian Community Hospital, San Juan, P.R. '79 (ATTY)
ESTRIDGE, DAVID, vice-pres. dev. and pub. affairs, Children's Hospital, Boston, MA '74 (PR)
ETCHEN, LAURA L., vice-pres. and dir. plng., Ochsner Medical Institutions, New Orleans, LA '82 (PLNG)
ETCHESON, KENNETH CARLYLE, pres., Graham Hospital, Canton, IL '53 (LIFE)
ETEN, FRANK X. JR., assoc. adm., Brookhaven Memorial Hospital Medical Center, Patchogue, NY '70
ETHELL, SHARON L., diet., Veterans Administration Medical Center, Knoxville, IA '77 (FOOD)
ETHERTON, JAMES L., asst. matl. mgt., Baptist Medical Center-Princeton, Birmingham, AL '83 (PUR)
ETHIER, CAPT. JOSEPH F. M., MSC USAF, Philadelphia, PA '82 (PUR)
ETHINGTON, LT. COL. WILLIAM, MSC USA, oper. off., 44th Medical Brigade, Fayetteville, NC '71
ETHRIDGE, MARTIN L. JR., dir. pers., North Hills Medical Center, North Richland Hills, TX '81 (PERS)
ETHRIDGE, PHYLLIS, RN, vice-pres. pat. care serv., St. Mary's Hospital and Health Center, Tucson, AZ '79 (NURS)
ETNIRE, DEANNA, clin. soc. work, Indian Health Service, Keams Canyon, AZ '84 (SOC)
ETTENHEIM, TIM M., asst. adm., New York University Medical Center, New York, NY '82
ETTER, LAVON M., coor. pat. rep., St. Margaret Hospital, Hammond, IN '81 (PAT)
ETTINGER, JOEL H., pres., Voluntary Hospitals of America of Pennsylvania, Inc., Pittsburgh, PA '80 (PLNG)
ETTMUELLER, DENNIS D., risk mgr., Miami Valley Hospital, Dayton, OH '82 (RISK)
ETUE, LAWRENCE J., dir. soc. serv., Delano Regional Medical Center, Delano, CA '85 (SOC)
ETZELMILLER, NANCY KAY, mgr. wage and salary, Good Samaritan Hospital, Kearney, NE '81 (PERS)
EUBANK, GARY J., RN, asst. adm. pat. serv., Saint Anthony Medical Center, Rockford, IL '86 (NURS)
EUBANK, PAMELA L., dir. group pur., Alabama Hospital Association, Birmingham Regional Office, Birmingham, AL '85 (PUR)
EUBANK, THOMAS F., atty., St. Mary's Hospital, Richmond, VA '83 (ATTY)
EUDES, JO ANN E., dir. educ., Baptist Medical Center-Princeton, Birmingham, AL '85 (EDUC)
EUDES, JOHN A., assoc. adm. mktg., University of Alabama Hospital, Birmingham, AL '80 (PLNG)
EUGLEY, ANNE-MARIE LOUISE, asst. dir. oper. dev. and pat. ombudsman, Salem Hospital, Salem, MA '84 (PAT)
EUSEBIO, EVELYN, RN, asst. adm., Providence Hospital, Southfield, MI '72 (NURS)
EUSTER, SONA, adm. supv., Presbyterian Hospital in the City of New York, New York, NY '84 (SOC)
EVANGELISTA, DIANE, dir. ed. serv., Samaritan Health Center, Detroit, MI '84 (EDUC)
EVANGELISTA, JAMES, mgr. emer. and amb. care, Leonard Morse Hospital, Natick, MA '87 (AMB)
EVANO, CARMELITA U., asst. mgr. food serv., Walther Memorial Hospital, Chicago, IL '86 (FOOD)
EVANS, ANN, supv. hskpg., Good Shepherd Hospital, Barrington, IL '86 (ENVIRON)
EVANS, AUSTIN J., field surveyor, Joint Commission on Accreditation of Hospitals, Chicago, IL '48 (LIFE)
EVANS, BABS C., dir. vol., Wayne Memorial Hospital, Jesup, GA '85 (VOL)
EVANS, BETHEL Q. II, asst. adm., St. Joseph Hospital, Houston, TX '75 (PUR)
EVANS, BONNIE R., coor. vol., Humana Hospital -Tacoma, Tacoma, WA '84 (VOL)
EVANS, CATHERINE, dir. pub. rel. and pat. rep., Valley View Hospital, Glenwood Springs, CO '82 (PR)
EVANS, CHARLES L., dir. environ. serv., Charter Ridge Hospital, Lexington, KY '86 (ENVIRON)
EVANS, CHARLOTTE, dir. pub. rel. and mktg., Chippenham Hospital, Richmond, VA '83 (PR)
EVANS, CHRISTINE B., RN, asst. dir. nrsg., Johns Hopkins Hospital, Baltimore, MD '85 (NURS)
EVANS, CHRISTOPHER JOHN, adm. intern, Sisters of Charity of the Incarnate Word, Inc., Houston, TX '86
EVANS, DAN, asst. dir. eng., Memorial Hospital, Carbondale, IL '82 (ENG)
EVANS, DAVID L., Danville, PA '83 (MGMT)
EVANS, DEBORAH J., vice-pres. commun. rel. and mktg., Hancock Memorial Hospital, Greenfield, IN '86 (PR)
EVANS, DOROTHEA B., dir. soc. serv., Decatur General Hospital, Decatur, AL '73 (SOC)
EVANS, E. THOMPSON JR., pres. and chief exec. off., St. Luke's Hospital, Duluth, MN '59 (PLNG)
EVANS, EDWARD J., dir. matl. mgt., Audrain Medical Center, Mexico, MO '61 (PUR)
EVANS, EDWIN E., atty., Sioux Valley Hospital, Sioux Falls, SD '81 (ATTY)
EVANS, ELIZABETH O., sr. vice-pres. corp. serv., Methodist Hospital of Southern California, Arcadia, CA '84 (PR) (PLNG)
EVANS, FRANCES N., adm. food, Buffalo Psychiatric Center, Buffalo, NY '80 (FOOD)
EVANS, SR. FRANCES, dir. soc. serv., Saint Joseph Hospital, Fort Worth, TX '72 (SOC)
EVANS, FRANK M. III, atty., St. John's Regional Health Center, Springfield, MO '81 (ATTY)
EVANS, GAIL M., assoc. adm., Rutland Regional Medical Center, Rutland, VT '82 (PLNG)
EVANS, GEORGE QUINN, atty., Hinds General Hospital, Jackson, MS '76 (ATTY)
EVANS, GRACE AILEEN, dir. qual. assur. and risk mgt., Metroplex Hospital, Killeen, TX '86 (RISK)
EVANS, HARRY H. JR., dir. telecommun., Ohio State University Hospitals, Columbus, OH '85 (ENG)
EVANS, HELEN C., Weston, MA '71 (PR)
EVANS, JAMES F. SR., dir. maint., Harding Hospital, Worthington, OH '79 (ENG)
EVANS, JAMES R., sr. mgt. eng., Humana Inc., Louisville, KY '80
EVANS, JAMES W., asst. adm., Heartland Hospital East, St. Joseph, MO '75 (ENG)
EVANS, JOAN M., dir. staff dev., Boulder Memorial Hospital, Boulder, CO '84 (EDUC)
EVANS, JOHN K., chief pat. adm., Keller Army Community Hospital, West Point, NY '82
EVANS, JOHN M. JR., RN, dir. nrsg., Metroplex Hospital, Killeen, TX '78
EVANS, LARRY D., dir. pers., Research Medical Center, Kansas City, MO '84 (PERS)
EVANS, LYNN, dir. soc. serv., Presbyterian Hospital of Kaufman, Kaufman, TX '85 (SOC)
EVANS, M. JANE, facil. adm. mktg. consult., Health and Marketing West, Billings, MT '85 (PR)
EVANS, MARIAN D., supv. cent. sterile sup., St. Joseph Hospital, Baltimore, MD '81 (CS)
EVANS, MARJORIE A., RN, dir. pat. serv., Ottumwa Regional Health Center, Ottumwa, IA '77 (SOC)
EVANS, MARJORIE B., risk mgr., HCA Santa Rosa Medical Center, Milton, FL '83 (RISK)
EVANS, MARY LOUISE, supv. cent. serv., Perry Memorial Hospital, Princeton, IL '77 (CS)
EVANS, MICHAEL B., atty., Sutter Community Hospitals, Sacramento, CA '86 (ATTY)
EVANS, MICHAEL J., exec. dir., Highlands Hospital and Health Center, Connellsville, PA '84
EVANS, MICHAEL L., RN, adm. prof. serv., Amarillo Hospital District, Amarillo, TX '85 (NURS)
EVANS, MICHELE R., PhD, occup. safety, health spec., Clinical Center National Institute of Health, Bethesda, MD '86 (ENG)
EVANS, NATALIE H., (ret.), Buffalo, NY '78 (SOC)
EVANS, ROBERT M., pres., Dietary Consultants, Inc., Hornell, NY '70 (FOOD)
EVANS, SALLY B., RN, asst. adm., Wichita General Hospital, Wichita Falls, TX '83 (NURS)
EVANS, SANDRA K., RN, vice chairperson nrsg. and pat. care mgt., North Carolina Memorial Hospital, Chapel Hill, NC '85 (NURS)
EVANS, SUSAN K., RN, dir. nrsg. serv. acute care, Bethesda Hospital, Zanesville, OH '84 (NURS)
EVANS, THOMAS D., asst. vice-pres. human res., Evanston Hospital, Evanston, IL '73 (RISK)(PERS)
EVANS, W. MICHAEL, Herman Smith Associates, Redwood City, CA '84 (PLNG)
EVANS, CAPT. WILLIAM DAVID, MSC USA, student, Army Baylor University Program in Health Care Administration, Fort Sam Houston, TX '80
EVANS, WILLIAM J. JR., mgr. natl. market, Calgon Corporation, St. Louis, MO '82 (CS)
EVANS, WILLIAM T., atty., University of Utah Health Sciences Center, Salt Lake City, UT '77 (ATTY)
EVARTS, EDWARD C., dir. matl. handling, Rochester General Hospital, Rochester, NY '84 (CS)(PUR)
EVELIUS, JOHN C., atty., Good Samaritan Hospital, Baltimore, MD '72 (ATTY)
EVERETT, EDWARD L., dir. human res., Baptist Memorial Hospital, Memphis, TN '73 (PERS)(EDUC)
EVERETT, JACQUELIN B., dir. vol., Johnston-Willis Hospital, Richmond, VA '81 (VOL)
EVERETT, JOHN CLEVELAND, head matl. mgt., Naval Hospital Okinawa, FPO Seattle, WA '85 (PUR)
EVERETT, LAWRENCE P., dir. cent. sterile proc., Overlook Hospital, Summit, NJ '80 (CS)
EVERETT, M. RONALD, vice-pres., Northside Hospital, Atlanta, GA '70 (PLNG)
EVERETT, MARLENE L., dir. pat. rep. and vol. serv., Mid-Maine Medical Center, Waterville, ME '84 (VOL)(PAT)
EVERETT, MARY LOU M., dir. med. soc. serv., Santa Rosa Medical Center, San Antonio, TX '79 (SOC)
EVERETT, MELINDA B., mgr. pub. rel., Worcester Memorial Hospital, Worcester, MA '86 (PR)
EVERHART, DAVID L., pres. and chief exec. off., Northwestern Memorial Group, Chicago, IL '51 (LIFE)
EVERHART, DIANE R., dir. human res., Charter Hills Hospital, Greensboro, NC '86 (PERS)
EVERITT, BEVERLY, mgr. soc. serv., Methodist Hospital, Omaha, NE '84 (SOC)
EVERS, THEO, spec. health and environ. protection, Royal Netherlands Embassy, Washington, DC '80
EVERSMEYER, RUTH J., dir. vol. serv., Murray-Calloway County Hospital and Convalescent Division, Murray, KY '81 (VOL)
EVERSOLE, ERMA M., mgr. inventory contr., Morton F. Plant Hospital, Clearwater, FL '84 (PUR)
EVERSON-BUTLER, MARY, plng. assoc., South Hills Health System, Pittsburgh, PA '85 (PLNG)
EVERT, DALE W., dir. food and nutr. serv., St. Michael Hospital, Milwaukee, WI '74 (FOOD)
EVERTS, RANDALL M., exec. vice-pres., Our Lady of Mercy Hospital, Cincinnati, OH '81

EVERTTS, M. ANN, mktg. info. spec., Harrisburg Hospital, Harrisburg, PA '84 (PLNG)
EVETTS, PHYLLIS A., RN, asst. adm., St. John Hospital, Nassau Bay, TX '84 (NURS)
EVJY, SHEILA A., RN, vice-pres. nrsg., Elliot Hospital, Manchester, NH '84 (NURS)
EVRARD, EUGENE E., vice-pres. plng. and oper., Dickinson County Hospitals, Iron Mountain, MI '84 (PLNG)
EWALD, GRAYDON R., dir. pers., Marcus J. Lawrence Memorial Hospital, Cottonwood, AZ '79 (PERS)
EWALT, JACK RICHARD, MD, (ret.), Tucson, AZ '61 (HON)
EWALT, MARY L., dir. nutr. serv., St. Mary's Hospital, Galesburg, IL '69 (FOOD)
EWALT, STEPHEN, mgr. soc. serv., Hemet Valley Hospital District, Hemet, CA '86 (SOC)
EWARD, ANN M., PhD, dir. kellogg cost containment proj., Butterworth Hospital, Grand Rapids, MI '87 (MGMT)
EWART, CAROLE V., EdD, mgr. emp. educ. and trng., Rhode Island Hospital, Providence, RI '78 (EDUC)
EWART, JAMES M., pres., Management Business Systems, Inc., DFW Airport, TX '84
EWELL, CHARLES M. JR., PhD, pres., The Governance Institute, La Jolla, CA '67
EWER, KENNETH L., chief eng., Bayfield County Memorial Hospital, Washburn, WI '81 (ENG)
EWIG, SUSAN M., dir. telecommun., St. Francis Hospital, Milwaukee, WI '85 (ENG)
EWING, ALTON P. JR., asst. adm., Loris Community Hospital, Loris, SC '71
EWING, ELIZABETH, dir. mktg. and pub. rel., St. John's Regional Medical Center, Oxnard, CA '83 (PR)
EWING, EVELYN JUNE, dir. soc. serv., Freeman Hospital, Joplin, MO '75 (SOC)
EWING, FRED, exec. adm., Austin Regional Clinic, Austin, TX '87 (AMB)
EWING, JOSEPH NEFF JR., atty., Bryn Mawr Hospital, Bryn Mawr, PA '75 (ATTY)
EWING, SANDRA S., dir. soc. serv., Jefferson Davis Memorial Hospital, Natchez, MS '81 (SOC)
EWOLDT, CHARLES L., dir. pub. rel., Buena Vista County Hospital, Storm Lake, IA '86 (PR)
EXENDINE, JOSEPH N., Gainesville, MO '74
EXLINE, JOAN L., vice-pres. bus. dev., Deaconess Development Corporation, Evansville, IN '81 (MGMT)(PLNG)
EXSTROM, SHEILA M., RN, asst. adm., Lincoln General Hospital, Lincoln, NE '81 (NURS)
EYLER, BONNIE, atty., HCA Northwest Regional Hospital, Margate, FL '86 (ATTY)
EYLES, MARY O., coor. educ., Kessler Institute for Rehabilitation, West Orange, NJ '86 (EDUC)
EYRE, F. JANE, RN, supv. sterile sup., Strong Memorial Hospital of the University of Rochester, Rochester, NY '78 (CS)
EYTCHESON, KELLY W., mgt. analyst, Kettering Medical Center, Kettering, OH '86 (MGMT)
EZELL, JANE, University of Texas, School of Nursing, Austin, TX '86 (NURS)
EZELL, JOCLYN, asst. chief diet., Veterans Administration Hospital, St. Louis, MO '78 (FOOD)
EZRA, LILA J., dir. soc. serv., Medical Arts Center Hospital, New York, NY '80 (SOC)
EZZI, CINDA R., dir. commun., Fawcett Memorial Hospital, Port Charlotte, FL '82 (ENG)

F

FAAS, ANITA B., dir. vol. serv., Lee Hospital, Johnstown, PA '84
FABBIANO, STEPHEN, mgr. matl., Sheehan Memorial Hospital, Buffalo, NY '86 (PUR)
FABE, BARBARA A., vice-pres. human res., Doctors Hospital, New York, NY '73 (PERS)
FABELLA, VANCE W., dir. cent. sterile sup. dept., Humana Hospital -Bennett, Plantation, FL '84 (CS)
FABER, DONALD A., international oper. exec., Hospital Corporation of America, Nashville, TN '50 (LIFE)
FABER, EMMY-LOU, mgr. educ., Northside Hospital, Atlanta, GA '75 (EDUC)
FABER, KAREN KAINE, dir. qual. assur., Sinai Hospital of Baltimore, Baltimore, MD '78
FABER, MARY HELEN, dir. pub. rel., Paulding Memorial Medical Center, Dallas, GA '86 (PR)
FABER, RICHARD A., asst. dir. plant oper., Deaconess Hospital of Cleveland, Cleveland, OH '81 (ENG)
FADELY, LYNNE, risk mgr., Carrollwood Community Hospital, Tampa, FL '86 (RISK)
FADER, HENRY C., atty., Albert Einstein Medical Center, Philadelphia, PA '86 (ATTY)
FAEHL, GEORGE W., chief eng., Frankford Hospital of the City of Philadelphia, Torresdale Division, Philadelphia, PA '76 (ENG)
FAELLA, CHARLES W., dir. plant oper., Community Memorial Hospital, Toms River, NJ '82 (ENG)
FAGAN, DEBORAH F., dir. pub. rel., Mount Sinai Medical Center, Milwaukee, WI '86 (PR)
FAGAN, JULIE A., dir. plng., Erie County Medical Center, Buffalo, NY '84 (PLNG)
FAGAN, VALERIE L., dir. soc. serv., HCA Parkway Medical Center, Lithia Springs, GA '80 (SOC)
FAGAN, WILLIAM L., dir. facil. dev. and constr., Hoag Memorial Hospital Presbyterian, Newport Beach, CA '67 (ENG)
FAGEN, JANICE, asst. adm., Spring Shadows Glen, Houston, TX '86 (RISK)
FAGERBERG, MICHAEL R., proj. eng., Memorial Hospital System, Houston, TX '77 (MGMT)
FAGG, ROBERT E., mech. eng., Anderson, Debartolo and Pan, Inc., Tucson, AZ '85 (ENG)
FAGIN, HOWARD E., PhD, pres., Fagin Advisory Services, Inc., Atlanta, GA '67 (MGMT)
FAGOT, JEFFREY D., dir. human res., St. Catherine Hospital, Garden City, KS '84 (PERS)
FAHERTY, T. J., consult., SunHealth, Inc., West Columbia, SC '84 (MGMT)
FAHEY, CATHERINE ELIZABETH, dir. soc. serv., Reynolds Memorial Hospital, Glen Dale, WV '76 (SOC)
FAHEY, KEVIN J., dir. pub. rel., St. Elizabeth's Hospital, Chicago, IL '85 (PR) (PLNG)
FAHEY, MARY C., RN, dir. nrsg. serv., Norwegian-American Hospital, Chicago, IL '76 (NURS)
FAHEY, PHILIP J., dir. pur., Indian River Memorial Hospital, Vero Beach, FL '83 (PUR)
FAHEY, THOMAS J., dir. facil. design and constr., Lutheran General and Deaconess Hospitals, Park Ridge, IL '75 (ENG)
FAHEY, THOMAS M., atty., Ravenswood Hospital Medical Center, Chicago, IL '81 (ATTY)
FAHEY, THOMAS M., adm., Castle Rest Nursing Home, Syracuse, NY '72
FAHEY, WILLIAM JOSEPH, adm. mgr. gen. serv., Paoli Memorial Hospital, Paoli, PA '76 (FOOD)(ENG)
FAHLBERG, WILLSON J. JR., sr. dir. dev., Hospital Corporation of America, Dallas, TX '72
FAHNESTOCK, MRS. HARRIS, chm. adv. bd. nrsg., Massachusetts General Hospital, Boston, MA '46 (LIFE)
FAHRENBACHER, E. F., asst. vice-pres., Borgess Medical Center, Kalamazoo, MI '84
FAHRENBRUCH, RONALD W., mgt. eng., Bronson Methodist Hospital, Kalamazoo, MI '77 (MGMT)
FAHRENHOLTZ, BETHEL ANN, King Fasial Specialist Hospital and Research Centre, Riyadh, Saudi Arabia '80 (CS)
FAIG, KENNETH W., mgr. commercial and inst. dept., International Fabricare Institute, Silver Spring, MD '75
FAILOR, KENNETH, dir. eng. and plant oper., Alta View Hospital, Sandy, UT '81 (ENG)
FAINE, STEVEN B., asst. adm., Botsford General Hospital, Farmington Hills, MI '79
FAINTER, JILL, dir. qual. assur. support, Hospital Corporation of America, Nashville, TN '84 (RISK)
FAIR, DIANNE M., RN, dir. nrsg., Atlanticare Medical Center, Lynn, MA '86 (NURS)
FAIR, WILLIAM K., vice-pres. mktg., Western Pennsylvania Hospital, Pittsburgh, PA '86 (PR) (PLNG)
FAIRBANK, LYNN, vice-pres., Faulkner Hospital, Boston, MA '73
FAIRBANKS, JANE E., RN, asst. vice-pres. and adm., Mercy Medical Center, Denver, CO '85 (NURS)
FAIRCHILD, PATRICIA, vice-pres., John Snow Public Health Group, Inc., Boston, MA '83
FAIRCHILD, ROGER C., vice-pres. syst. integration, U. S. West Information Systems, Inc., Englewood, CO '86 (PLNG)
FAIRCLOTH, DEBORAH G., dir. pub. rel., Riverside Hospital, Jacksonville, FL '84 (PR)
FAIRLEY, DANIEL J., atty., Voluntary Hospitals of America, Irving, TX '86 (ATTY)
FAJT, JOHN D., exec. dir., Putnam County Hospital, Greencastle, IN '78
FAKE, BARENT L., atty., Fairfax Hospital, Falls Church, VA '80 (ATTY)
FALAGUERRA, ROBERT J., assoc. exec. dir., Bellevue Hospital Center, New York, NY '73 (ENG)
FALAHEE, JAMES B., atty., Bronson Healthcare Group, Inc., Kalamazoo, MI '79 (ATTY)
FALARDEAU, JEANNE C., coor. nrsg. and pat. educ., Roger Williams General Hospital, Providence, RI '85 (EDUC)
FALBE, SR. MARYANN, RN, asst. adm. pat. care serv., St. Mary's Hospital Medical Center, Green Bay, WI '81 (NURS)
FALBERG, WARREN CARL, pres., Jewish Hospital of Cincinnati, Cincinnati, OH '64
FALCIONE, EDWARD J., dir. food serv., Spaulding Rehabilitation Hospital, Boston, MA '68 (FOOD)
FALCK, HANS S., head soc. work and prof., Virginia Commonwealth University School of Social Work, Richmond, VA '85 (SOC)
FALCK, R. MICHAEL, reg. adm., Intermountain Health Care, Inc., Salt Lake City, UT '69
FALCK, WILLIAM E., atty., University Hospital, Jacksonville, FL '83 (ATTY)
FALCONER, H. MICHAEL, adm. asst., Hutzel Hospital, Detroit, MI '80
FALE, ROBERT A., exec. vice-pres., Mercy Medical Center and Hospital, Williston, ND '80
FALETRA, JOSEPH L., dir. dev., St. Elizabeth Hospital, Roslindale, MA '58
FALICK, JAMES, pres., Falick and Klein Partnership, Inc., Houston, TX '76
FALISKIE, MARY KAY, dir. soc. work, St. Joseph's Hospital, Carbondale, PA '87 (SOC)
FALK, GWYNN, dir. commun. rel., Flint Osteopathic Hospital, Flint, MI '80 (PR)
FALK, JULIE D., commun. spec., Port Huron Hospital, Port Huron, MI '86 (PR)
FALK, KIMBERLEY CHARLESWORTH, pat. rep. asst., University of Iowa Hospitals and Clinics, Iowa City, IA '84 (PAT)
FALK, LAURA LEE, dir. food serv., LDS Hospital, Salt Lake City, UT '71 (FOOD)
FALK, MARY A., coor. commun., Vista Hill Foundation, San Diego, CA '86 (PR)
FALK, PATRICIA A., dir. soc. work, Marquette General Hospital, Marquette, MI '86 (SOC)
FALK, THEODORE C., atty., Healthlink, Portland, OR '86 (ATTY)
FALKE, MARGARET MARY, pat. rel. rep., Kettering Medical Center, Kettering, OH '82 (PAT)
FALKE, RICHARD A., asst. dir. eng., York Hospital, York, PA '76 (ENG)
FALKENSTEIN, NANCY D., vice-pres., Ernest Smith Insurance Agency, Sarasota, FL '86 (RISK)
FALKENSTEN, SHARON KAY, coor. info. syst., St. John's Regional Medical Center, Joplin, MO '85 (MGMT)
FALKENSTINE, ROBERT J., dir., St. Joseph Hospital and Health Center, Lorain, OH '86 (SOC)
FALKSON, JOSEPH L., PhD, pres., Continental Healthcare Corporation, Washington, DC '80
FALLEN, DENNIS K., consult., Reston, VA '84 (PLNG)
FALLERT, JENNIFER C., student, St. Louis University, St. Louis, MO '86
FALLIS, MARY K., RN, dir. nrsg., Van Wert County Hospital, Van Wert, OH '80 (NURS)
FALLON, ALICE M., student, Rush University, Chicago, IL '86
FALLON, JOHN J., atty., Shawnee Mission Medical Center, Shawnee Mission, KS '68 (ATTY)
FALOON, GERARD V., dir. plant oper., Staten Island Hospital, Staten Island, NY '83 (ENG)
FALTER, ROBERT G., assoc. vice-pres., Staten Island Hospital, Staten Island, NY '75 (MGMT)
FALVEY, ANITA L., dir. pur., Warren Hospital, Phillipsburg, NJ '80 (PUR)
FALZONE, JOSEPH, dir. safety, security and risk mgt., Indian River Memorial Hospital, Vero Beach, FL '85 (RISK)
FALZONE, MICHAEL, indust. hygienist, Veterans Administration Medical Center, Ann Arbor, MI '87 (ENG)
FAMILETTI, CAROLE A., mgr. mktg. commun., Osteopathic Medical Center of Philadelphia, Philadelphia, PA '86 (PR)
FANBURG, JANE R., sr. clin. soc. worker, Stillman Infirmary, Harvard University, Cambridge, MA '85 (SOC)
FANDL, MICHAEL R., dir. constr., St. Mary Medical Center, Gary, IN '86 (ENG)
FANELLI, JOHN C., dir. pers. serv., Pottstown Memorial Medical Center, Pottstown, PA '83 (PERS)
FANGUY, JUNIUS J., PhD, reg. dir., Cantex Medical Centers, Highlands, TX '54 (LIFE)
FANIZZI, CARYL, adm. off. amb. care, Veterans Administration Medical Center, Dallas, TX '86 (AMB)
FANNIN, JAMES C. JR., adm., Leominster Hospital, Leominster, MA '64
FANNING, JANE A., vice-pres. pat. care div., Bayfront Medical Center, St. Petersburg, FL '78 (NURS)
FANNING, ROBERT J., pres., St. John's Regional Medical Center, Joplin, MO '69 (PLNG)
FANNING, ROBERT REECE, pres., Beverly Hospital, Beverly, MA '68
FANNING, THOMAS J., dir. commun. rel., St. Francis Hospital, Wilmington, DE '79 (PR) (PLNG)
FANNING, WILLIAM J., coor. educ., St. Joseph's Hospital, Tampa, FL '85 (EDUC)
FANNING, WOODROW W., exec. vice-pres., Bristol Memorial Hospital, Bristol, TN '52 (LIFE)
FANNO, PATRICIA C., dir. mktg., Saddleback Community Hospital, Laguna Hills, CA '85 (PR)
FANOS, NICHOLAS G., assoc. exec. dir., Hospital for Joint Diseases Orthopaedic Institute, New York, NY '54 (PLNG)
FANT, JIMMIE SIMMONS, dir. soc. serv., University Hospital, Jacksonville, FL '86 (SOC)
FANTL, ROBIN, dir. human res., Wilson Clinic and Hospital, Darlington, SC '82 (SOC)
FANTUS, JAMES, chief exec. off., Sonora Laboratory Sciences, Mesa, AZ '78 (PR)
FANUIEL, CLARICE E., dir. food serv., Metropolitan Hospital Center, New York, NY '86 (FOOD)
FARAGE, ALICIA E., pat. rep., Vicksburg Medical Center, Vicksburg, MS '84 (PAT)
FARAGHER, DOUGLAS A., vice-pres. facil. and environ. serv., St. Mary's Medical Center, Duluth, MN '83 (RISK)
FARAJIANI, LETICIA A., RN, assoc. exec. dir., Sea View Hospital and Home, Staten Island, NY '75 (NURS)
FARASAT, MOHAMMAD REZA, arch., Iran Housing Company, Tehran, Iran '85 (ENG)
FARB, JOEL, dir. res. spec. and proj., Owen Healthcare, Inc., Houston, TX '87 (EDUC)
FARBER, JUDI L., mgt. info. consult., Arthur Andersen and Company, Houston, TX '83
FARBER, MARK A., planner, St. Mary's Medical Center, Knoxville, TN '82 (PLNG)
FARBER, ROSALIND, coor. risk mgt., Baltimore County General Hospital, Randallstown, MD '86 (RISK)
FARESS, MARY LYNN, RN, asst. adm. nrsg., West Georgia Medical Center, La Grange, GA '82 (NURS)
FARGIANO, CARL N., dir. data proc. and syst., Norwalk Hospital, Norwalk, CT '68 (MGMT)
FARGIE, DENNIS M., adm., Northpark Hospital, El Paso, TX '85 (MGMT)
FARGO, DAVID L., atty., Altheimer and Gray, Chicago, IL '76 (ATTY)
FARGO, JOAN M., RN, asst. dir. nrsg., Georgetown University Medical Center, Washington, DC '79 (NURS)
FARHAT, JALIL KAMAL, dir. food serv., Broadlawns Medical Center, Des Moines, IA '80 (FOOD)
FARINA, MARY ELLEN T., risk mgr., Freehold Area Hospital, Freehold, NJ '81 (RISK)
FARIS, JOYCE, RN, asst. adm., AMI Presbyterian-Denver Hospital, Denver, CO '77 (NURS)
FARKAS, LEONARD A., dir. facil. mgt., Lehigh Valley Hospital Center, Allentown, PA '75 (ENG)
FARLEY, ANTOINETTE L., assoc. consult., Kieffer, Ford and Associates, Chicago, IL '85 (PERS)(PR) (PLNG)
FARLEY, BARBARA A., RN, dir. nrsg., University of Maryland Medical Systems, Baltimore, MD '86 (NURS)
FARLEY, DONALD W., atty., St. Alexis Hospital, Cleveland, OH '77 (ATTY)
FARLEY, DONNA O., sr. vice-pres. corp. dev., Ancilla Systems, Inc., Elk Grove Village, IL '83 (PLNG)
FARLEY, FRANK A., vice-pres., Adjustco, Inc., Tarrytown, NY '86 (RISK)
FARLEY, THOMAS T., atty., Parkview Episcopal Medical Center, Pueblo, CO '76 (ATTY)
FARLEY, WILLIAM M., student, Program in Hospital and Health Administration, Temple University, Philadelphia, PA '78

FARLOW, JOHN B. JR., dir. pers., Community General Hospital, Thomasville, NC '77 (PERS)
FARMER, ADRIAN STEPHEN, asst. adm., Security Forces Hospital, Riyadh, Saudi Arabia '86
FARMER, DAWN M., supv. sup., proc. and distrib., St. Joseph's Hospital and Health Center, Tucson, AZ '82 (CS)
FARMER, EDGAR T., dir. pers. serv., Jewish Hospital, Louisville, KY '82 (PERS)
FARMER, JOHN JOSEPH, vice-pres., Blue Cross and Blue Shield of Greater New York, New York, NY '66
FARMER, LUCY A., vice-pres. plng., Mount Auburn Hospital, Cambridge, MA '84 (PLNG)
FARMER, MARGARET L., chief coor. educ. serv., Methodist Hospitals of Gary, Gary, IN '87 (EDUC)
FARMER, MICHAELENE, student, Program in Industrial and Management Systems Engineering, Arizona State University, Tempe, AZ '86 (MGMT)
FARMER, RONALD A., MD, Ronald A. Farmer and Associates, Inc., Willowdale, Ont., Canada '61
FARMER, TERRY L., supv. maint., Pennock Hospital, Hastings, MI '85 (ENG)
FARNELL, K. ELIZABETH, RN, dir. nrsg., Baptist Memorial Hospital, Memphis, TN '71 (NURS)
FARNEY, MARY RUTH, RN, head nrs. cent. serv., Hillcrest Baptist Medical Center, Waco, TX '85 (CS)
FARNHAM, CDR JOHN B., MSC USN, exec. off., Naval Medical Clinic, San Francisco, CA '68
FARNSWORTH, JAMES J., pres., Children's Health Services of Texas, Dallas, TX '52 (LIFE)
FARR, NELLIE PAUL, dir. vol. serv., Mississippi Methodist Hospital and Rehabilitation Center, Jackson, MS '79 (VOL)
FARRAR, CYDNEY E., dir. human res., Irving Community Hospital, Irving, TX '86 (PERS)
FARRAR, JUDITH A., dir. commun. rel., New England Sinai Hospital, Stoughton, MA '79 (VOL)(PR)
FARRAY, MARILYN C., atty., Howard University Hospital, Washington, DC '86 (ATTY)
FARRELL, ANNE M., sr. mgt. eng., William Beaumont Hospital, Southfiled, MI '84 (MGMT)
FARRELL, DARLA, student, Claremont Graduate School, Berkeley, CA '86 (RISK)
FARRELL, EUGENE W., Luther Manor, Wauwatosa, WI '82 (FOOD)
FARRELL, J. KIRBY JR., consult., Georgetown University Medical Center, Washington, DC '86 (ENG)
FARRELL, JAMES A., atty., Good Samaritan Hospital, West Palm Beach, FL '85 (ATTY)
FARRELL, JAMES P., vice-pres. human res., Sutter Community Hospitals, Sacramento, CA '75 (PERS)
FARRELL, JIM, dir. environ. serv., Canoga Care Center, Canoga Park, CA '87 (ENVIRON)
FARRELL, JOANNE, RN, mgr. nrsg., Frankford Hospital, Philadelphia, PA '84 (CS)
FARRELL, JOHN T., pres. and chief exec. off., St. John's Mercy Medical Center, St. Louis, MO '76
FARRELL, JOHN W., pres., Homecare Strategic Management, Inc., Ligonier, PA '84 (PLNG)
FARRELL, JOSEPH F., pres., Germantown Hospital and Medical Center, Philadelphia, PA '49 (LIFE)
FARRELL, JUDITH A., mgt. eng., Mount Sinai Hospital Medical Center, Chicago, IL '84 (MGMT)
FARRELL, KEVIN J., asst. exec. dir., Holy Redeemer Hospital and Medical Center, Meadowbrook, PA '84
FARRELL, LOUIS M., pub. rel. asst., Miriam Hospital, Providence, RI '86 (PR)
FARRELL, SR. MARY E., adm., St. Joseph's Hospital and Health Center, Paris, TX '81 (PLNG)
FARRELL, MICHAEL J., adm., Somerset Community Hospital, Somerset, PA '73
FARRELL, RAYMOND B., assoc. dir., Saint Francis Hospital and Medical Center, Hartford, CT '75 (PLNG)
FARRELL, ROBERT A., exec. vice-pres., Massachusetts Hospital Association, Burlington, MA '76
FARRELL, W. KERK, pres., National Energy Control Centers, Havertown, PA '86 (ENG)
FARRELL, WILLIAM C., vice-pres., Whi Battery, Inc., Brewster, NY '86 (ENG)
FARRIER, HAROLD V., Reynoldsburg, OH '83 (PLNG)
FARRIS, BARBARA J., diet., Pinckneyville Community Hospital, Pinckneyville, IL '81 (FOOD)
FARRIS, BRANDY D., dir. vol. serv., Woman's Hospital, Baton Rouge, LA '87 (VOL)
FARRIS, HAZEL MARIE, dir. vol. serv., Presbyterian Intercommunity Hospital, Whittier, CA '69 (VOL)
FARRIS, ROBERT C., dir. plant adm., Loudoun Memorial Hospital, Leesburg, VA '82 (ENG)
FARROW, PAUL S., asst. adm., HCA West Paces Ferry Hospital, Atlanta, GA '85 (PLNG)
FARSDAHL, DONA M., dir. commun. rel. and mktg., New Valley Osteopathic Hospital, Yakima, WA '86 (PR)
FARSTER, PAMELA R., adm. asst., St. Charles Medical Center, Bend, OR '81 (MGMT)
FARUGGIO, BARBARA, RN, vice-pres. nrsg., Community Memorial Hospital, Toms River, NJ '86 (NURS)
FARVENI, CAROLE JEAN, dir. matl. mgt., Northridge Hospital Medical Center, Northridge, CA '83 (PUR)
FARWELL, PATRICK H., asst. adm., St. Elizabeth Medical Center, Yakima, WA '79 (PLNG)
FARWIG, RICHARD, chief plant eng. and maint., Mercy Medical Center Mount Shasta, Mount Shasta, CA '86 (ENG)
FASANO, MARIE T., exec. consult., David Ross Associates, New York, NY '87
FASNACHT, LILIAN MARIA, coor. pat. serv., Ashford Presbyterian Community Hospital, San Juan, P.R. '86 (PAT)
FASNAUGH, EDELGARD, pur. agt., St. Luke's Hospital, Maumee, OH '84 (PUR)
FASS, JOEL, lab. adm., Brookhaven Memorial Hospital Medical Center, Patchogue, NY '80
FASSETT, JACQUELINE D., dir. soc. work, Sinai Hospital of Baltimore, Baltimore, MD '70 (SOC)
FASSLER, MICHAEL S., assoc. adm., Beth Abraham Hospital, Bronx, NY '77
FASSNACHT, JOHN B., dir. human res., Yavapai Regional Medical Center, Prescott, AZ '86 (PERS)
FASSO, KAY, RN, supv. cent. sup., Beth Israel Hospital, Denver, CO '83 (CS)
FASULLO, DONNA L., clin. soc. worker and interim dir. soc. serv., AMI Bellaire Hospital, Houston, TX '86 (SOC)
FASULO, ALFRED E., partner, The Douglas Group, Inc., Avon, CT '85 (PLNG)
FATKIN, LOUIS A., risk mgr., Eastern Idaho Regional Medical Center, Idaho Falls, ID '83 (RISK)
FATZINGER, ELVA G., RN, dir. nrsg., St. Margaret's Hospital, Montgomery, AL '84 (NURS)
FAUBERT, ROBERT A., adm. dir. adult serv., Mount Airy Psychiatric Center, Denver, CO '83
FAUGHT, LEE EVANS, mgr. human res. serv., Alzed Medical and Health Care, Pittsburgh, PA '86
FAUGHT, T. DON, dir. pub. rel., Sam Houston Memorial Hospital, Houston, TX '82 (PR)
FAUL, BLANCE C., RN, assoc. exec. dir. nrsg., West Jersey Hospital-Eastern Division, Voorhees, NJ '87 (NURS)
FAUL, DEBORAH G., dir. nutr. and fitness div., Dudley-Anderson-Yutzy-Public Relations, Inc., New York, NY '84 (PR)
FAULCONER, DIANE RAMY, dir. surg. serv., Boca Raton Community Hospital, Boca Raton, FL '87 (AMB)
FAULK, ALFRED DONALD JR., asst. adm., Medical Center of Central Georgia, Macon, GA '74
FAULK, LYNNE G., RN, dir. nrsg. serv.-psych., University of South Alabama Medical Center, Mobile, AL '83 (NURS)
FAULKNER, DANA M., dir. strategic plng., Yale-New Haven Hospital, New Haven, CT '86 (PLNG)
FAULKNER, DAVID W., dev. and pub. rel. consult., Tfg, Monument Beach, MA '85 (PR)
FAULKNER, JOHN F., dir. mgt. eng., Research Medical Center, Kansas City, MO '84 (MGMT)
FAULKNER, MICHAEL J., vice-pres., American Medical International, Beverly Hills, CA '83 (PLNG)
FAULKNER, R. MARK, atty., Pennsylvania State University Hospital, Hershey, PA '80 (ATTY)
FAULKNER, TOM, exec. dir., St. Joseph Ambulatory Services, Wichita, KS '87 (AMB)
FAULKNER, VIRGINIA, mgr. cent. serv., Baptist Medical Center-Montclair, Birmingham, AL '85 (CS)
FAULWELL, JAMES A., vice-pres. plng., Unity Medical Center, Fridley, MN '75 (PLNG)
FAUNCE, KAY, dir. food serv., Ingham Medical Center, Lansing, MI '80 (FOOD)
FAUNG, BETTY M., RN, adm. dir. nrsg. serv., Providence Hospital, Everett, WA '86 (NURS)
FAUSEL, DOROTHY M., dir. pub. rel. and dev., Fanny Allen Hospital, Winooski, VT '85 (PR)
FAUST, LAWRENCE L., atty., Sisters of Charity, Houston, TX '84 (ATTY)
FAUST, MARJORIE JARETTA, RN, asst. dir. nrsg. staff and supv., West Virginia University Hospital, Morgantown, WV '85 (NURS)
FAUTH-BROOKS, CAROLEE, adm. clin. affairs, Community Health Program of Queens-Nassau, New Hyde Park, NY '84 (RISK)
FAVALE, MONTSERRAT G., dir. soc. serv., Kessler Institute for Rehabilitation, West Orange, NJ '82 (SOC)
FAVILLA, STEVEN J., sr. mgt. eng., Fairview Riverside Hospital, Minneapolis, MN '87 (MGMT)
FAWBER, HEIDI L., pat. serv. rep., Magee-Womens Hospital, Pittsburgh, PA '86 (PAT)
FAWCETT, HENRY S. JR., dir. environ. serv., Tuomey Hospital, Sumter, SC '70 (ENG)
FAWCETT, JAMES, dir. matl. mgt., Lawrence General Hospital, Lawrence, MA '86 (PUR)
FAWLEY, DORMAN III, vice-pres., Sinai Hospital of Baltimore, Baltimore, MD '78
FAY, GEORGE W., mgr. mkt plng., Cleveland Clinic Hospital, Cleveland, OH '86 (PLNG)
FAY, JENNIFER, spec. health syst., Veterans Administration Medical Center, Dallas, TX '85
FAY, MARY S., RN, asst. vice-pres. nrsg., Brigham and Women's Hospital, Boston, MA '82 (NURS)
FAY, THOMAS J., rehab. and alcoholism counselor, Pilgrim Psychiatric Center, West Brentwood, NY '85
FAY, VINCENT P., dir. gen. serv., Saint Cabrini Hospital of Seattle, Seattle, WA '79 (ENG)
FAY, WILLIAM J., vice-pres. human res., Nanticoke Memorial Hospital, Seaford, DE '82 (PERS)
FAZEKAS, JOAN E., coor. pub. rel. and vol., Alton Memorial Hospital, Alton, IL '86 (PR)
FAZIO, MARILYN M., adm. dir. food serv., Autumn View Manor, Hamburg, NY '81 (FOOD)
FEAGIN, PAT, RN, dir. qual. assur., Gulf Coast Medical Center, Wharton, TX '86 (RISK)
FEARHELLER, DAVID G., mng. dir. health care fin. group, Dean Witter Reynolds, Inc., San Francisco, CA '85
FEARS, DONALD G., plng. asst., Baptist Memorial Hospital, Gadsden, AL '86 (PLNG)
FEATHERS, HOWARD J., dir. surg. serv., Monongalia General Hospital, Morgantown, WV '87 (AMB)
FEATHERSTON, DOUGLAS, asst. dir. eng. and maint., Jefferson Regional Medical Center, Pine Bluff, AR '86 (ENG)
FEATHERSTON, H. JOE, vice-pres. human res., St. Benedict's Health System, Ogden, UT '66 (PERS)
FEATHERSTONE, JAMES W. III, atty., Richmond Memorial Hospital, Richmond, VA '77 (ATTY)
FEAZEL, JAMES, asst. adm., Illinois Masonic Medical Center, Chicago, IL '86 (ENVIRON)
FEAZELL, SAMUEL G., adm., HCA West Side Hospital, Nashville, TN '64
FECHTEL, EDWARD J., adm., St. Mary's Hospital, Athens, GA '59
FECHTMEISTER, ARLENE J., dir. human res. dev., St. Mary's Medical Center, Evansville, IN '86 (EDUC)
FECK, NEVA, RN, asst. dir. nrsg., Monongalia General Hospital, Morgantown, WV '79 (NURS)
FECTEAU, GREGORY LEE, RN, dir. amb. serv., St. Luke's Hospital, Milwaukee, WI '81 (NURS)
FEDDERLY, MICHELE D., dir. mktg., Minneapolis Children's Medical Center, Minneapolis, MN '84 (PLNG)
FEDDERSEN, JEROLD VAUGHN JR., vice-pres. strategic plng. and mktg., Fairview General Hospital, Cleveland, OH '74 (PLNG)
FEDELE, JERRY J., asst. exec. dir. and atty., Western Pennsylvania Hospital, Pittsburgh, PA '86 (RISK)(ATTY)
FEDER, ERIC, assoc. gen. dir., Albert Einstein Medical Center, Philadelphia, PA '78
FEDER, JANET K., coor. pat. educ., St. Luke's Hospitals, Fargo, ND '78 (EDUC)
FEDERA, R. DANIELLE, exec. vice-pres., Jennings, Ryan, Federa and Company, Northampton, MA '83 (PLNG)
FEDERICO, MICHAEL B., mgr., Hospital Association of New York State, Albany, NY '79 (MGMT)(ENG)
FEDERMAN, LISE A., spec. asst. to pres., Winchester Hospital, Winchester, MA '85 (PR) (PLNG)
FEDEROWICZ, FELIX F., vice-pres. prof. and prov. rel., Blue Cross and Blue Shield of Northern Ohio, Cleveland, OH '85
FEDERSPILL, JEANNE, dir. vol. serv., Providence Hospital, Southfield, MI '75 (VOL)
FEDOR-BASSEMIER, JOAN E., RN, dir. surg., Deaconess Hospital, Evansville, IN '86 (NURS)
FEDOTA, STEPHEN CONRAD, dir. human res., Illinois Hospital Association, Naperville, IL '81 (PERS)
FEE, DOROTHEA L., RN, vice-pres. nrsg. serv., High Plains Baptist Hospital, Amarillo, TX '75 (NURS)
FEE, GEORGE A., chief fiscal off., Moss Rehabilitation Hospital, Philadelphia, PA '81
FEEHAN, VINCENT D., asst. vice-pres. mgt. sales support, Economics Laboratory, Inc., Van Nuys, CA '86 (FOOD)
FEELEY, JACQUELINE H., dir. human res. and vol. serv., Millville Hospital, Millville, NJ '85 (VOL)
FEELEY, PATRICIA A., chief exec. off., American Home Health Care, Inc., Newton, MA '83 (PLNG)
FEELY, WILLIAM J., PhD, St. Vincent's Medical Center, Jacksonville, FL '84
FEEMSTER, SAMUEL JR., vice-pres. human res., Spartanburg Regional Medical Center, Spartanburg, SC '77 (PERS)
FEENAN, SCOTT A., dist. mgr., Balston Filter Products, Inc., Lexington, MA '86 (CS)
FEENER, EMILY L., RN, dir. nrsg. staff dev., Salem Hospital, Salem, MA '73 (EDUC)
FEENEY, ARTHUR E., consult., Quality Systems Group, Mesa, AZ '84
FEENEY, GLENYCE, dir. food serv., Oklahoma Teaching Hospitals, Oklahoma City, OK '76 (FOOD)
FEENEY, JOAN L., RN, dir. nrsg., Miami Valley Hospital, Dayton, OH '85 (NURS)
FEENEY, PATRICK, dir. eng., St. Barnabas Hospital, Bronx, NY '84 (ENG)
FEENSTRA, TERRENCE D., vice-pres., St. Luke's Regional Medical Center, Sioux City, IA '76
FEERO, NINA, Half Moon Bay, CA '83
FEERST, DANIEL A., mgr. govt. and indust. serv., Arlington Hospital Addictions Treatment Programs, Arlington, VA '86 (PR)
FEETHAM, SUZANNE, dir. nrsg. educ. and res., Children's Hospital National Medical Center, Washington, DC '84 (EDUC)
FEGAN, KATE, supv. commun., St. Charles Hospital, Oregon, OH '81 (ENG)
FEHER, KATHLEEN H., dir. med. rec., St. Elizabeth's Hospital, Belleville, IL '87 (RISK)
FEHR, LOLA M., RN, exec. dir., Colorado Nurses Association, Denver, CO '75
FEHRING, MAJ. CHARLES F., MSC USA, chief clin. support div., General Leonard Wood Army Hospital, Fort Leonard Wood, MO '86
FEHSENFELD, E. JEAN, dir. vol. serv., Lutheran Hospital of Maryland, Baltimore, MD '86 (VOL)
FEIG, HERMAN D., dir. matl. mgt., St. John's Riverside Hospital, Yonkers, NY '86 (PUR)
FEIGE, KEN, dir. matl. mgt., St. Francis Hospital, Memphis, TN '80 (PUR)
FEIKEMA, DEBRA A., student, Program in Business Administration, Calvin College, Grand Rapids, MI '87 (MGMT)
FEIL, FREDERICK N., dir. matl. serv., McLeod Regional Medical Center, Florence, SC '85 (PUR)
FEIN, LORI A., dir. mktg. and plng., North Miami Medical Center, North Miami, FL '82 (PR)
FEIN, MITCHELL, pres., Mitchell Fein, Inc., Hillsdale, NJ '85 (MGMT)
FEIN, SANDRA M., student, Temple University, Department of Health Administration, School of Business Administration, Philadelphia, PA '85 (PLNG)
FEIN, SUSAN F., asst. dir. cent. serv., Barnes Hospital, St. Louis, MO '85 (CS)
FEINBERG, ADRIANNE, dir. soc. work serv., Piedmont Hospital, Atlanta, GA '85 (SOC)
FEINGOLD, MOIRA G., vice-pres. med. affairs, St. Vincent Medical Center, Los Angeles, CA '86 (RISK)
FEINGOLD, SUSAN, coor. mktg., Mediplex Group, Inc., New York, NY '86 (SOC)
FEINMAN, BERNICE F., dir. soc. serv., Metropolitan Hospital-Parkview Division, Philadelphia, PA '86 (SOC)
FEINMAN, MICHAEL, assoc. adm., Yonkers General Hospital, Yonkers, NY '77 (RISK)
FEINSTEIN, ALLEN L., atty., Phoenix Memorial Hospital, Phoenix, AZ '85 (ATTY)
FEINSTEIN, HOWARD E., atty., John F. Kennedy Medical Center, Chicago, IL '83 (ATTY)
FEIST, JERRY, dir. soc. serv., Medcenter One, Bismarck, ND '80 (SOC)
FEIST, TIMOTHY L., dir. soc. serv., Peninsula General Hospital Medical Center, Salisbury, MD '85 (SOC)

FEISTEL, JOHN AUGUST, adm., King James Care Center, Trenton, NJ '69
FEIT, BRIAN, commun. rel. liaison, Society of the New York Hospital, New York, NY '86 (PR)
FEITH, ANITA L., asst. dir. soc. work, Union Memorial Hospital, Baltimore, MD '86 (SOC)
FEITH, JOSEPH, exec. dir., HCA East Pointe Hospital, Lehigh Acres, FL '64 (PERS)
FELCH, JAMES F., dir. facil. eng., Arlington Hospital, Arlington, VA '85 (ENG)
FELD, JODI, mgt. consult., Health Review Systems, Chicago, IL '84
FELD, LEONARD, dir. risk mgt. serv., United Health Services, Johnson City, NY '78 (RISK)
FELD, SHERRY, dir. clin. soc. work, Cigna Hospital of Los Angeles, Los Angeles, CA '86 (SOC)
FELDER, MURIEL D., dir. soc. work, Medical College of Virginia Hospitals, Virginia Commonwealth University, Richmond, VA '70 (SOC)
FELDER, SUZANNE L., RN, dir. nrsg., critical care and surg. serv., Providence Hospital, Washington, DC '84 (NURS)
FELDMAN, ANDREW, atty., Sheehan Memorial Hospital, Buffalo, NY '84 (ATTY)
FELDMAN, EDWIN B., pres., Service Engineer Associates, Inc., Atlanta, GA '87 (ENVIRON)
FELDMAN, ELAINE, dir. diet., Heights General Hospital, Albuquerque, NM '77 (FOOD)
FELDMAN, FRANCES, dir. soc. serv., Peekskill Hospital, Peekskill, NY '85 (SOC)
FELDMAN, HARRY, atty., Parkview Hospital, Toledo, OH '76 (ATTY)
FELDMAN, IRWIN M., atty., Mount Sinai Medical Center, Cleveland, OH '73 (ATTY)
FELDMAN, JUNE, assoc. dir. soc. work, University Hospital, Stony Brook, NY '85 (SOC)
FELDMAN, KENNETH JAY, mgr., Stony Brook Orthopaedics, Stony Brook, NY '85 (AMB)
FELDMAN, MARK I., vice-pres. mktg. and plng., Dch Healthcare Authority, Tuscaloosa, AL '71 (PLNG)
FELDMAN, MICHAEL R., sr. vice-pres., Glenn, Nyhan and Associates, Inc., Columbia, MD '81 (RISK)
FELDMAN, MYRNA, coor. qual. assur., Danbury Hospital, Danbury, CT '81 (RISK)
FELDMAN, RASHEL D., student, Program in Health Administration and Planning, Washington University School of Medicine, St. Louis, MO '81
FELDMAN, RICHARD M., MD, chm. emer. medicine, Illinois Masonic Medical Center, Chicago, IL '87 (AMB)
FELDMAN, RICHARD, exec. dir., Maxicare Medical Center, Los Angeles, CA '62
FELDMAN, RON, pur. agt., Eisenhower Medical Center, Rancho Mirage, CA '84 (PUR)
FELDNER, PAUL D., dir. plant serv., St. Agnes Hospital, Fond Du Lac, WI '77 (ENG)
FELDSTEIN, CHARLES R., pres., Charles R. Feldstein and Company, Inc., Chicago, IL '81
FELDT, ROGER D., dir. eng. and maint., West Nebraska General Hospital, Scottsbluff, NE '78 (ENG)
FELER, ARMANDO, pres., The Ascot Group, Inc., Louisville, KY '83
FELGNER, LEONARD N., chief oper. off., Health Management Advisors, Inc., Ann Arbor, MI '69 (MGMT)
FELICE, GERARD F., asst. dir. food serv., St. Mary Hospital, Hoboken, NJ '80 (FOOD)
FELIS, DOROTHY C., dir. prof. serv., University of Texas Medical Branch Hospitals, Galveston, TX '79
FELIX, KURT E., dir. plant oper., Osteopathic Hospital of Maine, Portland, ME '85 (ENG)
FELIX, MICHELLE A., dir. clin. soc. work, Memorial Medical Center, Long Beach, CA '85 (SOC)
FELIX, PAUL N., dir. soc. serv., Huron Regional Medical Center, Huron, SD '80 (SOC)
FELIX, ROBERT A., adm. med. and surg., Medical and Surgical Clinic, Pennsylvania, Tyler, TX '87 (AMB)
FELKER, DEBRA B., coor. hosp. rel., Swedish Medical Center, Englewood, CO '84 (PR)
FELKNER, JOSEPH G., sr. fin. analyst, U. S. Health Corporation, Columbus, OH '80
FELL, LLOYD C., atty., Community Memorial Hospital, Cheboygan, MI '86 (ATTY)
FELL, MARIAN, dir. vol., St. Joseph Medical Center, Wichita, KS '78 (VOL)
FELLMAN, JOSEPH L., sr. vice-pres. corp. serv., Mercy Hospital of Pittsburgh, Pittsburgh, PA '79 (PLNG)
FELLNER, KENNETH M., mgt. syst. analyst, Samaritan Health Service, Phoenix, AZ '87 (MGMT)
FELLOWS, STEVEN A., adm. dir., Sutter Memorial Hospital, Sacramento, CA '81
FELSER, FRANCES Y., Miami, FL '81
FELT, CATHY A., sr. consult., Peat, Marwick and Mitchell, Kansas City, MO '83 (PLNG)
FELT, J. KAY, atty., Harper Hospital, Detroit, MI '72 (ATTY)
FELT, WESLEY D., asst. mgr. eng. and maint., Bishop Clarkson Memorial Hospital, Omaha, NE '84 (ENG)
FELTEN, JEROME, supt. plant, St. Joseph's Medical Center, Brainerd, MN '74 (ENG)
FELTES, JOSEPH J., atty., Aultman Hospital, Canton, OH '81 (ATTY)
FELTON, BERNARD L., (ret.), Mansfield Center, CT '50 (LIFE)
FELTON, JUDITH P., assoc. adm., Cambridge Research Institute, Cambridge, MA '84 (PLNG)
FELTON, LINDA B., asst. dept. head, Methodist Hospital of Indiana, Indianapolis, IN '86 (FOOD)
FELTS, ILSE, lead cent. serv. tech., Cape Coral Hospital, Cape Coral, FL '80 (CS)
FELTS, JAMES R. JR., (ret.), Pawleys Island, SC '55 (HON)
FELTS, LAURA L., dir. commun. rel., Annie Penn Memorial Hospital, Reidsville, NC '81 (PR)
FELTS, MELINDA ANNE, pat. rep., Boca Raton Community Hospital, Boca Raton, FL '85 (PAT)
FELTS, PAT S., pers. asst., York Plaza Hospital and Medical Center, Houston, TX '86 (PERS)
FELTY, LINDA L., RN, asst. dir. pat. care, Sacred Heart Hospital, Eau Claire, WI '81 (NURS)
FELZER, ANDREA C., dir. health care mktg., The Melior Group, Philadelphia, PA '84 (PLNG)
FEMRITE, MARY A., RN, clin. dir. nrsg. serv., St. Marys Hospital of Rochester, Rochester, MN '85 (NURS)
FENAROLI, PAUL J., sr. mgr., Ernst and Whinney, Cleveland, OH '86 (MGMT)
FENBERT, DOUGLAS C., asst. dir. environ. serv., Providence Hospital, Southfield, MI '84
FENDER, MICHAEL P., dir. plant oper., HCA Bayonet Point-Hudson Center, Hudson, FL '82 (ENG)
FENDER, WILLIAM I., Georgetown, IN '49 (LIFE)
FENDLEY, TERESA, pur. agt., Spartanburg Regional Medical Center, Spartanburg, SC '85 (PUR)
FENNEL, VICTORIA M., dir. educ., Parkridge Medical Center, Chattanooga, TN '82 (EDUC)
FENNELL, MARGARET E., dir. diet., Georgia Baptist Medical Center, Atlanta, GA '85 (FOOD)
FENNELL, STEVEN EUGENE, RN, asst. dir. nrsg., University of Connecticut Health Center, John Dempsey Hospital, Farmington, CT '78 (NURS)
FENNELL, WILLIAM T., dir. plant serv., Kaiser Foundation Hospital, San Diego, CA '83 (ENG)
FENNER, JOHN W., consult., Touche Ross and Company, Pittsburgh, PA '79
FENNESSY, CHARLES L., vice-pres. human res., Pitt County Memorial Hospital, Greenville, NC '71 (PERS)
FENNESSY, JOSEPH J., partner, Deloitte Haskins and Sells, New York, NY '81
FENNIGKOH, LARRY, mgr. clin. eng., St. Luke's Hospital, Milwaukee, WI '78 (ENG)
FENSTERMACHER, DAVID L., assoc. adm., University Hospital, Augusta, GA '75
FENTON, DIANNE, dir. mktg. and plng., South Coast Medical Center, South Laguna, CA '86 (PLNG)
FENTON, JOHN V., dir. rehab. serv., HCA Brotman Medical Center, Culver City, CA '75
FENTON, LEWIS L., atty., Community Hospital Monterey Peninsula, Monterey, CA '86 (ATTY)
FENTON, MICHAEL S., exec. dir. western region, McManis Associates, Inc., San Francisco, CA '86 (PR) (PLNG)
FENTON, ROBERT E., dir. matl. mgt., Altoona Hospital, Altoona, PA '80 (PUR)
FERENTINO, JOSEPH M., dir. human res., Mount Sinai Medical Center, New York, NY '79 (PERS)
FERERES, J., med. dir., Hospital Clinico, Madrid, Spain '84
FERGIONE, BOBBIE, dir. soc. work serv., Middlesex Memorial Hospital, Middletown, CT '85 (SOC)
FERGIONE, GENE, dir. soc. serv., Manchester Memorial Hospital, Manchester, CT '81 (SOC)
FERGUSON, BECKIE E., coor. health educ., Charter Suburban Hospital, Mesquite, TX '86 (EDUC)
FERGUSON, CHARLES M., pres., Medical Management Consultants, Riverside, CA '78 (PR)
FERGUSON, CHRISTOPHER, atty., Riden, Watson and Goldstein, St. Petersburg, FL '86 (ATTY)
FERGUSON, ELIZABETH, sr. mgt. eng., Vanderbilt Hospital, Nashville, TN '83 (MGMT)
FERGUSON, FRANK, dir. facil., Memorial Hospital of Dodge County, Fremont, NE '80 (ENG)
FERGUSON, G. DOUGLAS, atty., General Hospital of Everett, Everett, WA '77 (ATTY)
FERGUSON, G. THOMAS, vice-pres. human res., Bethesda Hospital, Inc., Cincinnati, OH '80 (PERS)
FERGUSON, GINGER H., RN, asst. exec. dir., Forrest County General Hospital, Hattiesburg, MS '82 (NURS)
FERGUSON, GORDON B., dir. plng., East Tennessee Baptist Hospital, Knoxville, TN '84 (PLNG)
FERGUSON, GREGORY H., sr. mech. eng., Carlson Southeast, Smyrna, GA '85 (ENG)
FERGUSON, JAMES E., Atlanta, GA '84 (LIFE)
FERGUSON, JANET L., commun. spec., King's Daughters' Medical Center, Ashland, KY '85 (PR)
FERGUSON, JOHN M., dir. plant and equip., Group Health Association, Inc., Washington, DC '80 (ENG)
FERGUSON, JOHN P., pres. and chief exec. off., Hackensack Medical Center, Hackensack, NJ '71
FERGUSON, JOSEPH WILLIAM, asst. vice-pres. oper., Good Samaritan Hospital and Health Center, Dayton, OH '77
FERGUSON, KEITH, sr. mgr. consult. serv., SunHealth, Richmond, VA '80 (MGMT)
FERGUSON, KENT, dir. hskpg. and ldry. serv., Valley Memorial Home, Grand Forks, ND '86 (ENVIRON)
FERGUSON, MARILYN, dir. telecommun., Baylor University Medical Center, Dallas, TX '84 (ENG)
FERGUSON, MARY BARSTOW, atty., Sisters of Charity Hospital, Buffalo, NY '85 (ATTY)
FERGUSON, NATHAN W., asst. adm., Chippenham Hospital, Richmond, VA '65
FERGUSON, PAUL E., exec. hskpg., St. Anne General Hospital, Raceland, LA '86 (ENVIRON)
FERGUSON, ROBERT D., dir. environ. serv., St. Mary's Hospital and Medical Center, Grand Junction, CO '86 (ENVIRON)
FERGUSON, STANLEY A., consult., University Hospitals of Cleveland, Cleveland, OH '47 (LIFE)
FERGUSON, THOMAS H., dir. matl. mgt., University of Virginia Hospitals, Charlottesville, VA '83 (PUR)
FERGUSON, VERNICE, dep. asst. chief med. dir. nrsg. prog., Veterans Administration, Department of Medicine and Surgery, Washington, DC '74 (NURS)
FERIANC, CYNTHIA M., coor. vol., Mercy Hospital and Medical Center, Chicago, IL '83 (VOL)
FERINGA, SCOTT DOUGLAS, atty., William Beaumont Hospital, Royal Oak, MI '81 (ATTY)
FERKO, JOHN M., asst. adm., Allegheny Valley Hospital, Natrona Heights, PA '81 (PLNG)
FERKOVIC, THOMAS J., dir. matl. mgt., Saint Luke's Hospital, Cleveland, OH '87 (PUR)
FERNALD, GRAHAM, atty., Valley Medical Center, Renton, WA '81 (ATTY)
FERNANDEZ, ARLEEN V., coor. educ., St. Catherine Hospital on Half Moon, Moss Beach, CA '84 (EDUC)
FERNANDEZ, BARBARA MYRES, vice-pres. plng. and mktg., St. Joseph's Hospital, Tampa, FL '79 (PR) (PLNG)
FERNANDEZ, FRANK, dir. matl. mgt., Baptist Hospital of Miami, Miami, FL '81 (PUR)
FERNANDEZ, JOSE, adm., Coral Reef Hospital, Miami, FL '85
FERNANDEZ, LOUISE, dir. soc. serv., St. Vincent Medical Center, Los Angeles, CA '82 (SOC)
FERNANDO, JOE, MD, dir. med. serv., Department of Health Services, Colombo, Laos '86
FERNIANY, WILL, vice-pres. plng., res. and dev., HSA Hill Crest Sunrise Hospital, Birmingham, AL '86
FERNS, JOYCE A., dir. vol. serv., Harrison Community Hospital, Cadiz, OH '87 (VOL)
FERO, RICHARD S., mgr. pers., Major Hospital, Shelbyville, IN '80 (PERS)
FEROW, ADELINE M., dir. pur., Herrick Memorial Hospital, Tecumseh, MI '74 (PUR)
FERRAGAMO, SALVATORE, dir. eng., Kingsbrook Jewish Medical Center, Brooklyn, NY '84 (ENG)
FERRANDIZ, GEORGE F., dir. soc. work, Coral Gables Hospital, Coral Gables, FL '86 (SOC)
FERRARA, ANGELO R., commun. spec., Lovelace Medical Center, Albuquerque, NM '84 (ENG)
FERRARA, CLAUDIA, dir. soc. work serv., Memorial Hospital, Meriden, CT '86 (SOC)
FERRARO, PETER JR., eng., Veterans Administration Medical Center, Pittsburgh, PA '78 (ENG)
FERRARO, SHERRY B., dir. commun. rel., Mercy Hospital, Springfield, MA '85 (PR)
FERREBEE, LOUISE A., dir. commun., Glendale Heights Community Hospital, Glendale Heights, IL '85 (PR)
FERRELL, KATHY S., clin. mgr. outpatient, AMI Doctors Hospital, Tulsa, OK '87 (AMB)
FERRELL, MIRIAM K., dir. pub. rel., Bristol Memorial Hospital, Bristol, TN '83 (PR)
FERRELL, ORVILLE L., Tifton, GA '53 (LIFE)
FERRER, EVA, dir. vol. serv. and pat. rep., Hospital Pavia, San Juan, P.R. '86 (VOL)(PAT)
FERRER, PATRICIA, dir. soc. work, New Rochelle Hospital Medical Center, New Rochelle, NY '86 (SOC)
FERRER, REINALDO A., MD, San Juan, P.R. '69
FERRERI, ANTHONY C., vice-pres. human res., Alexian Brothers Hospital, Elizabeth, NJ '83 (PERS)
FERRETTI, WILLIAM P., chm. and chief exec. off., Medstar Communications, Inc., Allentown, PA '72 (PR) (PLNG)
FERREY, GEORGE E. JR., dir. plng. and commun. affairs, Holy Spirit Hospital, Camp Hill, PA '67 (PLNG)
FERRI, CAROL A., atty., Jeanes Health System, Jenkintown, PA '85 (ATTY)
FERRI, EVERETT L., asst. vice-pres. phys. plant, Hahnemann University Hospital, Philadelphia, PA '82 (ENG)
FERRIEGEL, WILLIAM J., dir. pur., Lovelace Medical Center, Albuquerque, NM '84 (PUR)
FERRIN, DAVID M., sr. mgt. eng., Intermountain Health Care, Inc., Salt Lake City, UT '86 (MGMT)
FERRIS, HARRISON T., asst. adm., Trident Regional Medical Center, Charleston, SC '75
FERRIS, JEAN P., dir. vol. serv., Fairview Hospital, Great Barrington, MA '83 (VOL)
FERRIS, MICHAEL, supv. sup., proc. and distrib., Cooper Hospital-University Medical Center, Camden, NJ '84 (CS)
FERRIS, WANDA L., RN, dir. nrsg., Biloxi Regional Medical Center, Biloxi, MS '83 (NURS)
FERRO, DONNA M., adm. pers., Miles Memorial Hospital, Damariscotta, ME '84 (PERS)
FERRO, JACQUELINE ANN, coor. compensation, St. Joseph Hospital, Nashua, NH '86 (PERS)
FERRO, PAUL F., dir. food and nutr., HCA Largo Medical Center Hospital, Largo, FL '86 (FOOD)
FERRON, KENNETH R., vice-pres. and chief oper. off., St. Joseph Hospital, Nashua, NH '77 (MGMT)(PLNG)
FERRON, MARY J., mgt. syst. analyst, Samaritan Health Service, Phoenix, AZ '86 (MGMT)
FERTEL, MURRAY, exec. vice-pres., Jewish Memorial Hospital, Boston, MA '43 (LIFE)
FERTEL, STANLEY M., exec. dir., Jewish Memorial Hospital, Boston, MA '67
FERULLO, ANDRE, dir. pers., John F. Kennedy Medical Center, Edison, NJ '79 (PERS)
FESLER, WAYNE F., pres., Kishwaukee Community Hospital, De Kalb, IL '81 (PLNG)
FESTA, GUY A., dir. pur., Moss Rehabilitation Hospital, Philadelphia, PA '86 (PUR)
FETROW, PAUL B., vice-pres. res. mgt., Saint Alphonsus Regional Medical Center, Boise, ID '79 (ENG)
FETTERHOFF, ELSA M., pat. rep., University Hospital, Denver, CO '84 (PAT)
FETTERS, RONALD F., dir. pur., Walker Memorial Hospital, Avon Park, FL '82 (PUR)
FETZER, BRIAN, atty., Johnson, Cusack and Bell, Ltd., Chicago, IL '86 (RISK)
FEUER, CHERYL I., mgt. consult., The Corson Group, New York, NY '86 (PLNG)
FEUER, LOUIS CHARLES, dir. trng. and dev., Fuster Medical Corporation, Hollywood, FL '78 (SOC)
FEUER, WILLIAM W., PhD, asst. gen. council, Healthwest Medical Centers, Chatsworth, CA '68 (ATTY)
FEUGER, CAROL E., RN, dir. nrsg. specialty care, Memorial Medical Center, Savannah, GA '84 (NURS)
FEUREISEN, PERLA, dir. food serv., Rockland Community College Association, Suffern, NY '80 (FOOD)
FEURER, RUSSELL E., chief exec. vice-pres., Good Shepherd Hospital, Barrington, IL '67
FEURIG, THOMAS L., pres., St. Joseph's Hospital, Milwaukee, WI '75
FEUTZ, SHERYL A., atty., Saint Joseph Health Center Kansas, Kansas City, MO '86 (ATTY)
FEY, ROBERT A., dir. mktg., Greater Baltimore Medical Center, Baltimore, MD '85 (PLNG)

FEYEREISEN, BELVA, dir. pers., Methodist Hospital, Mitchell, SD '77 (PERS)
FFRENCH, HENRY J., dir. pur., Crozer-Chester Medical Center, Chester, PA '84 (PUR)
FIANDER, ED, vice-pres. human res., South Shore Hospital, South Weymouth, MA '82 (PERS)
FIASCHETTI, TERESA, vice-pres., St. Joseph Hospital, Chicago, IL '78
FICE, PAUL F., USN, adm., Naval Hospital, San Diego, CA '86
FICEK, RAY V., mgr. hskpg. and ldry., St. Joseph's Hospital and Health Center, Dickinson, ND '86 (ENVIRON)
FICHT, MARY A., indust. hygienist, American Hospital Association, Chicago, IL '86 (ENVIRON)
FICHTER, JACQUELINE M., coor. pat. educ., Decatur Memorial Hospital, Decatur, IL '84 (EDUC)
FICK, JOHN W., mgr. plng. and bus. dev., Holy Cross Hospital, Detroit, MI '82 (PLNG)
FICK, MARCIA A., RN, vice-pres. nrsg., Holy Family Hospital, Des Plaines, IL '78 (NURS)
FICKEN, TED, dir. educ. and qual. mgt., Golden Valley Health Center, Golden Valley, MN '86 (EDUC)
FICKENSCHER, SAUNDRA, div. sdm commun. serv. and educ., United Health Resources, Grand Forks, ND '84 (EDUC)
FICKES, ELAINE S., dir. diet. serv., Presbyterian Association on Aging, Washington, PA '84 (FOOD)
FICKLER, DORIS A., RN, dir. nrsg., Greene Memorial Hospital, Xenia, OH '85 (NURS)
FIDEN, THOMAS J., dir. eng., St. Mary's Hospital, Richmond, VA '79 (ENG)
FIDLER, JOHN E., pres. and chief exec. off., St. Mary's Hospital, West Palm Beach, FL '70 (PLNG)
FIDUCIA, KAREN A., vice-pres., Harris Methodist -HEB, Bedford, TX '83
FIEDERER, BARBARA, dir. vol. serv., Jewish General Hospital, Montreal, Que., Canada '86 (VOL)
FIEDLER, B. JOAN, RN, dir. nrsg.-maternal and child serv., St. Francis Hospital, Blue Island, IL '86 (NURS)
FIEDLER, THOMAS L., atty., Richardson Medical Center, Richardson, TX '73 (ATTY)
FIEGER, ROBERT D., dir. pers., Stormont-Vail Regional Medical Center, Topeka, KS '80 (PERS)
FIEGLE, ELIZABETH A., RN, instr. pat. educ., St. Anthony Medical Center, Crown Point, IN '86 (EDUC)
FIELD, ALLAN S., asst. adm. surg. serv., Washington Hospital Center, Washington, DC '80
FIELD, HUGH M., atty., Covenant Medical Center-Schoitz, Waterloo, IA '85 (ATTY)
FIELD, NANCY, asst. adm. mktg. and plng., Providence Medical Center, Seattle, WA '79 (PLNG)
FIELD, RICHARD J., dir. commun., Sarasota Memorial Hospital, Sarasota, FL '80 (PR)
FIELD, SELMA G., pub. rel. and mktg. consult., Field Associates, Ltd., Monticello, NY '69 (PR)
FIELD, TINA, asst. adm., Rush-Presbyterian-St. Luke's Medical Center, Chicago, IL '80
FIELD, WILLIAM CAMERON, dir. eng. and dev., American Medical International, Beverly Hills, CA '85 (ENG)
FIELDER, ANNE B., mgr. emp. rel., Lee Memorial Hospital, Fort Myers, FL '81 (PERS)
FIELDER, TIMOTHY L., atty., Hospital District Number One of Crawford County, Girard, KS '79 (ATTY)
FIELDS, ANNETTE JEAN, pat. rep., City of Hope National Medical Center, Duarte, CA '78 (PAT)
FIELDS, CLYDE D., pres., Basic American Healthcare Management, Inc., Indianapolis, IN '82
FIELDS, COREEN J., RN, assoc. dir. nrsg., Los Angeles County-University of Southern California Medical Center, Los Angeles, CA '84 (NURS)
FIELDS, FRAN, RN, dir. educ. serv., Hamilton Medical Center, Dalton, GA '78 (EDUC)
FIELDS, GLENN C., dir. human res., St. John's Medical Center, Anderson, IN '86 (PERS)
FIELDS, JUDY G., exec. sec., Providence Memorial Hospital, El Paso, TX '85 (PAT)
FIELDS, MARTHA R. A., vice-pres. human res., Massachusetts Eye and Ear Infirmary, Boston, MA '83 (PERS)
FIELDS, SR. MARY CHARLES, dir. med. soc. serv., St. Elizabeth Hospital Medical Center, Youngstown, OH '71 (SOC)
FIELDS, MAURA, RN, dir. prof. serv., North Valley Hospital, Whitefish, MT '86 (NURS)
FIELDS, PAULA M., RN, vice-pres., Baptist Hospital Highlands, Louisville, KY '78 (NURS)
FIELDS, PEGGY FAYE, serv. rep., Jess Parrish Memorial Hospital, Titusville, FL '87 (PAT)
FIELDS, RICHARD C., atty., St. Luke's Regional Medical Center, Boise, ID '78 (ATTY)
FIELDS, ROGER, student, University of Oklahoma, Oklahoma City, OK '86 (RISK)
FIELDSON, MAXINE E., RN, vice-pres. nrsg., Southwestern Vermont Medical Center, Bennington, VT '86 (NURS)
FIERRO, FRANCES M., soc. worker, Humana Hospital -St. Petersburg, St. Petersburg, FL '86 (PAT)
FIESTA, JANINE, atty., Lehigh Valley Hospital Center, Allentown, PA '80 (ATTY)
FIFE, ELVIRA S., RN, asst. adm. nrsg. serv., Ballard Community Hospital, Seattle, WA '72 (NURS)
FIFER, WILLIAM R., MD, pres., Clayton Fifer Associates, Minneapolis, MN '82
FIFIELD, BRUCE G., mgr., Baystate Health Systems, Inc., Springfield, MA '70 (MGMT)
FIFIELD, FRED F., dir. mgt. eng., Mercy Health Center, Dubuque, IA '77 (MGMT)
FIGARD, KIMBERLY J. M., RN, dir. nrsg., J. C. Blair Memorial Hospital, Huntingdon, PA '86 (NURS)
FIGEL, NANCY J., asst. vice-pres., Bronson Methodist Hospital, Kalamazoo, MI '86 (NURS)
FIGGIS, HOPE D., soc. worker and coor. soc. serv., Leelanau Memorial Hospital, Northport, MI '82 (SOC)
FIJEWSKI, MAX T., dir. human res., The Medical Center, Beaver, PA '82 (PERS)
FIKE, ROSEMARY E., coor. vol., Euclid General Hospital, Euclid, OH '86 (VOL)
FILES, BRUCE A., dir. bus. off., Mercy Hospital and Medical Center, Chicago, IL '86
FILES, LAUREL A., PhD, dir. masters prog., University of North Carolina, Department of Health Policy and Administration, Chapel Hill, NC '82
FILES, LEON O., dir. food serv., Saint Joseph Hospital, Mishawaka, IN '71 (FOOD)
FILETI, WILLIAM J., vice-pres. bus. dev., St. Joseph Mercy Hospital-Division of Sisters of Mercy Health Corporation, Ann Arbor, MI '74
FILICETTI, JANICE M., RN, asst. dir. nrsg., educ. and res., Fox Chase Cancer Center, Philadelphia, PA '86 (NURS)
FILIPIAK, NADINE M., dir. pub. rel., South Chicago Community Hospital, Chicago, IL '85 (PR)
FILIPPINI, DINA MARIE F., adm. asst., Church-Charity Foundation of Long Island, Hempstead, NY '81
FILLBACH, BETTY M., RN, coor. in-service, University General Hospital, Seminole, FL '81 (EDUC)
FILLENWORTH, THOMAS, dir. emp. rel., St. Cloud Hospital, St. Cloud, MN '69 (PERS)
FILLHABER, MITCHELL, mgr. corp. sales, Miami Valley Hospital-Medical America Health Systems, Dayton, OH '86 (PR) (PLNG)
FILLING, THOMAS FRANK, vice-pres. human res., St. Joseph Hospital, Baltimore, MD '75 (PERS)
FILLIP, DENISE A., mgr. matl. and equip., South Hills Health System, Pittsburgh, PA '82 (PUR)
FILLMORE, CATHERINE, mgr. educ. and trng., McLaren General Hospital, Flint, MI '78 (EDUC)
FILLMORE, JOSEPH H., consult., Ernst and Whinney, Chicago, IL '82 (PLNG)
FILOSA, LAWRENCE T., chief exec. off., Health Care Provider of Arizona, Phoenix, AZ '64
FILOSA, MARY E., soc. worker, St. Mary's Hospital, Galesburg, IL '85 (SOC)
FINAN, LETICIA ANN, pat. rep., Michael Reese Hospital and Medical Center, Chicago, IL '86 (PAT)
FINAZZO, PETER, dir. food serv., Anderson Memorial Hospital, Anderson, SC '70 (FOOD)
FINCANNON, KEN F., dir. plant oper., St. Eugene Community Hospital, Dillon, SC '82 (ENG)
FINCEL, B. JOYCE, RN, asst. dir. pat. sup., proc. and distrib., University of Texas Anderson Hospital, Houston, TX '83 (CS)
FINCH, BARBARA L., pub. rel. consult., Barbara L. Finch Public Relations, Kirkwood, MO '75 (PR)
FINCH, CURTIS H., asst. adm., Cornwall Hospital, Cornwall, NY '78
FINCH, MARY ELLEN, student, Program and Bureau of Hospital Administration, University of Michigan, Ann Arbor, MI '82
FINCKE, MILDRED K., RN, vice-pres., The Medical Center, Beaver, PA '84
FINE, ALLAN H., acct. exec., Rush Contract Care, Chicago, IL '81 (PLNG)
FINE, ARLENE, atty., Federation of American Hospitals, Washington, DC '79 (ATTY)
FINE, DARWIN E., chief clin. support, Cutler Army Hospital, Fort Devens, MA '86
FINE, EDGY MAY, dir. soc. work, Maricopa Medical Center, Phoenix, AZ '84 (SOC)
FINE, EVA L., RN, asst. adm., Piqua Memorial Medical Center, Piqua, OH '83 (NURS)(RISK)
FINE, PETER S., pres., Northwestern Healthcare Corporation, Chicago, IL '76
FINE, STEVEN M., vice-pres. adm., Wyman Park Medical Center, Baltimore, MD '77
FINE, STUART H., pres., Lexington Memorial Hospital, Lexington, NC '77 (PLNG)
FINEBERG, JANE, adm. med. care, New York State Department of Health, White Plains, NY '77
FINEMAN, STEPHEN J., mgt. consult., Bronxville, NY '77
FINER, NORMAN S., res. assoc., Graduate Program in Hospital Administration, Xavier University, Cincinnati, OH '52 (LIFE)
FINGERET, HAROLD, exec. dir., North Central Bronx Hospital, Bronx, NY '78
FINGERHOOD, ANN J., asst. dir. strategic plng., DePaul Health Center, Bridgeton, MO '84 (PLNG)
FINK, BARRY N., dir. plant serv., Fayetteville City Hospital, Fayetteville, AR '82 (ENG)
FINK, FREDERICK S., pres. and chief exec. off., Federation of American Clinics, Burlingame, CA '80 (PLNG)
FINK, NANCY, dir. soc. serv., Gracie Square Hospital, New York, NY '85 (SOC)
FINK, ROBERT M., atty., Smyrna Hospital, Smyrna, TN '75 (ATTY)
FINK, RONALD A., dir. matl. mgt., Good Samaritan Hospital, Kearney, NE '76 (PUR)
FINKEL, DAVID, student, Program in Health Care Administration, Bernard Baruch College, New York, NY '85
FINKELSTEIN, HOWARD H., supt. elec., Johns Hopkins Hospital, Baltimore, MD '86 (ENG)
FINKELSTEIN, JANICE, dir. strategic plng. and prog. dev., Baystate Medical Center, Springfield, MA '82 (PLNG)
FINKERNAGEL, ROBERT H. III, dir. mktg. and pub. rel., Cape Coral Hospital, Cape Coral, FL '86 (PR) (PLNG)
FINKLEIN, TERRY, sr. vice-pres. ancillary serv., Southwest Washington Hospitals, Vancouver, WA '85 (RISK)
FINLAY, JOHN A., atty., Greene Memorial Hospital, Xenia, OH '73 (ATTY)
FINLAYSON, WILLIAM C., pres. and chief exec. off., O'Connor Hospital, San Jose, CA '67
FINLEY, BILL, dir. plant oper., Lee's Summit Community Hospital, Lees Summit, MO '83 (ENG)
FINLEY, JOHN P., assoc. vice-pres. fin., F. G. McGaw Hospital, Loyola University, Maywood, IL '86
FINLEY, JOHN R., dir. pers., Mercy Hospital, Hamilton, OH '84 (PERS)
FINLEY, KATHY ANN, supv. cent. proc., Bethesda Hospital, Zanesville, OH '83 (CS)
FINLEY, MARJORIE, coor. soc. serv., St. Francis Hospital, Maryville, MO '75 (SOC)
FINN, ANDREW A., asst. dir. pers., Pendleton Memorial Methodist Hospital, New Orleans, LA '82 (PERS)
FINN, BARBARA J., dir. matl. mgt., St. Francis Hospital, Evanston, IL '86 (PUR)
FINN, BARRY, dir. fiscal serv., Northern Illinois Medical Center, McHenry, IL '86
FINN, CARL L., dir. risk mgt. and security, Methodist Evangelical Hospital, Louisville, KY '80 (RISK)
FINN, LEO J., dir. plant oper., Gettysburg Hospital, Gettysburg, PA '83 (ENG)
FINN, MARY C., coor. diagnostic related group, Mount Sinai Hospital Medical Center, Chicago, IL '84 (MGMT)
FINN, PATRICK D., dir. pur., Oswego County, Oswego, NY '71 (PUR)
FINN, THEODORA M., dir. vol. and pat. rel., Somerville Hospital, Somerville, MA '85 (VOL)
FINNE, HANS H., pres., Hans H. Finne, Inc., Wilmington, MA '75
FINNEGAN, GREGORY T., dir. mgt. syst., Robert Wood Johnson University Hospital, New Brunswick, NJ '87 (MGMT)
FINNEGAN, JEANNETTE K., dir. vol., St. Joseph Medical Center, Stamford, CT '77 (VOL)
FINNEGAN, MAURICE J. JR., Quinlivan, Pierik and Krause, Syracuse, NY '84
FINNEGAN, PATRICK L., dir. emer. serv., Metropolitan Chicago Hlthcare Council, Chicago, IL '87 (AMB)
FINNEGAN, RITA, exec. dir., American Medical Record Association, Chicago, IL '73 (EDUC)
FINNERTY, ELIZABETH E., student, Georgia State University-Institute of Health Administration, Atlanta, GA '84
FINNEY, CATHERINE K., dir. mktg., Baylor Medical Center at Grapevine, Grapevine, TX '80 (PR)
FINNEY, LYNDON, dir. pub. rel., Baptist Medical System, Little Rock, AR '86 (PR)
FINNEY, MAMIE, dir. nutr. and food serv., Bethany Brethren-Garfield Park Community Hospital, Chicago, IL '75 (FOOD)
FINNEY, MARION R., dir. pub. rel., East Ohio Regional Hospital, Martins Ferry, OH '77 (PR)
FINNIGAN, SHARON A., RN, adm. nrsg., Saint Joseph's Hospital, Atlanta, GA '81 (NURS)
FINSILVER, SHARI E., pres., Productivity Plus, Inc., West Bloomfield, MI '81 (MGMT)
FINSKI, CAROLYN F., RN, assoc. dir. nrs., Brooks Memorial Hospital, Dunkirk, NY '83 (NURS)
FINSTEIN, DONALD B., dir. cent. sup., Humana Hospital -Phoenix, Phoenix, AZ '72 (CS)(PUR)
FINUF, JUDITH L., gen. counselor, Medical University Hospital of the Medical University of South Carolina, Charleston, SC '84 (ATTY)
FINZER, LOIS C., adm. asst., Henry Ford Hospital, Detroit, MI '79
FIORE, STEVE P., mgt. eng., Memorial Hospital, Pawtucket, RI '80 (MGMT)
FIORENTINI, MONA LISA, Matrix, Philadelphia, PA '80 (PLNG)
FIORENTINO, JOSEPH A., RN, dir. nrsg. serv., Parkway Hospital, Flushing, NY '86 (NURS)
FIORI, D'ARLENE A., dir. human res., Charter Suburban Hospital, Paramount, CA '86 (PERS)
FIRIS, ROBERT M., dir. commun. rel., St. Joseph's Hospital, Parkersburg, WV '73 (PR)
FIRMAGE, JOHN H., chm., Medirec, Salt Lake City, UT '83
FIRMAN, BERNARDA, student, Graduate Program in Public Affairs and Human Services Administration, Rider College, Lawrenceville, NJ '86 (RISK)
FIRMAN, EILEEN, RN, dir. pat. care serv., Vassar Brothers Hospital, Poughkeepsie, NY '85 (PAT)
FIRSCHEIN, ISIDORE, MD, Miami Beach, FL '39 (LIFE)
FIRSCHING, RUTH A., dir. matl. mgt., Medical Center Delaware Oro Hospital, Houston, TX '82 (PUR)
FISCH, HENRY, mgr. food serv., Brookhaven Health Related Facilities, Far Rockaway, NY '76 (FOOD)
FISCHER, LT. COL. ARTHUR K., MSC USA, chief human res. mgt. br., Academy of Health Sciences, U. S. Army Medical Department, Fort Sam Houston, TX '74
FISCHER, CLIFFORD L., dir. facil. serv., St. Helena Hospital and Health Center, Deer Park, CA '84 (ENG)
FISCHER, GARY L., vice-pres., Methodist Hospital System, Houston, TX '73 (PERS)
FISCHER, JOHN W. III, atty., Deaconess Hospital, Cincinnati, OH '73 (ATTY)
FISCHER, KARLO D., asst. adm., Northfield Hospital, Northfield, MN '86 (PERS)
FISCHER, KATHLEEN M., dir. human res., St. Anthony's Medical Center, St. Louis, MO '84 (PERS)
FISCHER, KATHLEEN, coor. risk mgt., Saint Therese Medical Center, Waukegan, IL '86 (RISK)
FISCHER, MARIS S., assoc. dir., Health Education Dynamics, San Pedro, CA '83 (EDUC)
FISCHER, MARVIN J., vice-pres. facil. plng. and eng. serv., Brookdale Hospital Medical Center, Brooklyn, NY '73 (MGMT)(ENG)
FISCHER, MARYLOU MARKHAM, dir. soc. serv., Alleghany Regional Hospital, Low Moor, VA '80 (SOC)
FISCHER, ROBERT J. JR., dir. eng. and maint., St. Elizabeth Medical Center-North, Covington, KY '79 (ENG)
FISCHER, THOMAS N., vice-pres. human res., Mercy Medical Center, Oshkosh, WI '87 (PERS)
FISCHER, WILLIAM C., dir. plng., Bridgeport Hospital, Bridgeport, CT '81 (PLNG)
FISCHESSER, CHARLES M., mgr. claims, Sisters of Charity Health Care Systems, Cincinnati, OH '84 (RISK)
FISCHLER, PATRICIA B., dir. plng., Park Ridge Hospital, Rochester, NY '86 (PLNG)
FISCUS, DIANE P., RN, adm. nrsg., Community Memorial Hospital, Clarion, IA '83 (NURS)

FISCUS, SANDY L., dir. mktg., Bloomington Hospital, Bloomington, IN '82 (PR) (PLNG)
FISH, DONALD WINSTON, sr. vice-pres., Hospital Corporation of America, Nashville, TN '70 (ATTY)
FISH, FRED K., Boca Ratony, FL '44 (LIFE)
FISH, ROBERT H., plant eng., Maryland Masonic Homes, Cockeysville, MD '86 (ENG)
FISHBAUGH, CAROL, dir. human res., Alton Memorial Hospital, Alton, IL '78 (PERS)
FISHBEIN, RHONDA L., atty., American Medical International, Atlanta, GA '86 (ATTY)
FISHBEIN, VICTORIA KOLES, dir. long range plng., Carrier Foundation, Belle Mead, NJ '75 (PLNG)
FISHBONE, HERBERT, atty., Easton Hospital, Easton, PA '75 (ATTY)
FISHER, BARBARA ALLEN, RN, asst. adm. and dir. nrsg., Cottonwood Hospital Medical Center, Murray, UT '85 (NURS)
FISHER, BONNIE HELFGOTT, atty., Johns Hopkins Hospital, Baltimore, MD '86 (ATTY)
FISHER, BRADLEY W., dir. matl. mgt., LDS Hospital, Salt Lake City, UT '85 (PUR)
FISHER, BRENDA SHARON, dir. soc. serv., Grant Park Care Center, Washington, DC '86 (SOC)
FISHER, CAPT. DAVID HOWARD, MSC USN, head facil., Department of the Navy, Bureau of Medicine and Surgery, Washington, DC '68 (ENG)
FISHER, DEBBIE, coor. educ. and trng., Bryan Memorial Hospital, Lincoln, NE '80 (EDUC)
FISHER, DENA, dir. alternative health care, Presbyterian Health Resources, Inc., New York, NY '73 (SOC)
FISHER, DIANE, atty., Southwest Community Health Services, Albuquerque, NM '84 (ATTY)
FISHER, DONNA F., RN, dir. nrsg. educ. and supplementary staff, St. Elizabeth Medical Center, Granite City, IL '84 (EDUC)
FISHER, FRANCES A., RN, asst. dir., St. Elizabeth's Hospital of Boston, Boston, MA '85 (NURS)
FISHER, HARRIET R., dir. diet., Oakwood Hospital, Dearborn, MI '80 (FOOD)
FISHER, HENRY J., dir. hskpg. and ldry., Memorial Hospital of Martinsville, Martinsville, VA '86 (ENVIRON)
FISHER, JAMES BENJAMIN, mgr. health facil. standards and licensure, Utah Department of Health, Salt Lake City, UT '68
FISHER, JAMES L., mgr. corp. plng., Care One Health Systems, Zanesville, OH '75 (PLNG)
FISHER, JAMES N., sr. pub. rel. off., Henry Ford Hospital, Detroit, MI '86 (PR)
FISHER, JEANNE ELIZABETH, field rep., Maryland Hospital Association, Hospital Cost Analysis Service, Towson, MD '67
FISHER, JULIE A., adm. ped., Mount Sinai Medical Center, New York, NY '86 (PLNG)
FISHER, KAY L., RN, coor. med. unit, Castleview Hospital, Price, UT '86 (NURS)
FISHER, KENNETH L., mgt. eng., Hospital of Saint Raphael, New Haven, CT '80 (MGMT)
FISHER, MAJ. MARTIN J., MSC USA, adm. dept. of medicine, Fitzsimons Army Medical Center, Aurora, CO '82
FISHER, MARY L., RN PhD, asst. adm., University of South Alabama Medical Center, Mobile, AL '85 (NURS)
FISHER, PEARL R., trustee, St. Andrews Hospital, Boothbay Harbor, ME '37 (LIFE)
FISHER, ROBERT M., dir. pub. rel., Polyclinic Medical Center, Harrisburg, PA '84 (PR)
FISHER, ROGER K., atty., Freeman Hospital, Joplin, MO '76 (ATTY)
FISHER, SUSAN B., mktg. spec., Baylor College of Medicine, Houston, TX '86 (PLNG)
FISHER, VIRGINIA R., dist. qual. assur. spec., Veterans Administration Medical Center, Memphis, TN '82
FISHER, WILLIAM A., dir. peer review, The Taab Corporation, International Chiropractic and Consultants Division, North Myrtle Beach, SC '86
FISHER, WILLIAM HAMILTON, student, Georgia State University, Institute of Health Administration, Atlanta, GA '84
FISHMAN, LEWIS W., atty., Mercy Hospital, Miami, FL '82 (ATTY)
FISHMAN, LINDA, consult., Los Angeles, CA '66 (SOC)
FISK, DEBRA L., corp. dir. home serv., Community Hospital of Central California, Fresno, CA '87 (AMB)
FITCH, BRADFORD W., sr. mgt. eng., Hurley Medical Center, Flint, MI '83 (MGMT)
FITCH, DAVID P., dir. maint., Millinocket Regional Hospital, Millinocket, ME '85 (ENG)
FITCH, GRAHAM, atty., Swedish Hospital Medical Center, Seattle, WA '80 (ATTY)
FITCH, JONATHAN, coor. mktg. res., Bloomington Hospital, Bloomington, IN '86 (PLNG)
FITCH, JOSEPH J., pres., J. Fitch and Associates, Kansas City, MO '85
FITCH, RODERICK A., chief soc. work serv., Veterans Administration Medical Center, Ann Arbor, MI '83 (SOC)
FITCHETT, JANE, dir. food serv., Hospital of Saint Raphael, New Haven, CT '81 (FOOD)
FITCHETT, L. ERIC, staff eng., Veterans Administration Medical Center, Perry Point, MD '86 (ENG)
FITE, JONATHAN PETER, int. auditor, Athens Regional Medical Center, Athens, GA '78 (MGMT)
FITE, REBECCA F., coor. cont. care, Brown County General Hospital, Georgetown, OH '86 (SOC)
FITTIPALDI, MICHAEL F., dir. pub. rel., Our Lady of Mercy Medical Center, Bronx, NY '83 (PR)
FITTS, DAISY E., dir. pub. rel., Howard University Hospital, Washington, DC '73 (PR)
FITZ, DON L., dir. eng., Children's Medical Center of Dallas, Dallas, TX '81 (ENG)
FITZGERALD, C. B., atty., Western Missouri Medical Center, Warrensburg, MO '79 (ATTY)
FITZGERALD, CONSTANCE E., dir. vol. serv., Hunt Memorial Hospital, Danvers, MA '70 (VOL)
FITZGERALD, DENNIS L., risk mgr., St. John's Regional Medical Center, Joplin, MO '84 (RISK)
FITZGERALD, G. CARTER, mgr. pers., Watson Clinic, Lakeland, FL '84 (PERS)
FITZGERALD, GERALD DENNIS, pres., Oakwood Hospital, Dearborn, MI '64
FITZGERALD, GRETCHEN D., RN, vice-pres. nrsg., Montana Deaconess Medical Center, Great Falls, MT '84 (NURS)
FITZGERALD, JAMES P., pres., Good Samaritan Hospital and Health Center, Dayton, OH '59
FITZGERALD, JAMES P., vice-pres., Brockton Hospital, Brockton, MA '67 (PERS)
FITZGERALD, JEANNE M., vice-pres. plng. and mktg., Intermountain Health Care, Inc., Salt Lake City, UT '83 (PR) (PLNG)
FITZGERALD, JOHN E. JR., chief bldg. mgt. serv., Veterans Administration Medical Center-W. Los Angeles, Los Angeles, CA '86 (ENVIRON)
FITZGERALD, KATHLEEN, RN, chief nrsg. serv., Veterans Administration Medical Center, Tucson, AZ '85 (NURS)
FITZGERALD, MARGARET A., dir. food serv., Quakertown Community Hospital, Quakertown, PA '84 (FOOD)
FITZGERALD, MICHAEL E., exec. vice-pres., Little Company of Mary Hospital, Evergreen Park, IL '75
FITZGERALD, R. ANN, dir. pub. rel., Holy Spirit Hospital, Camp Hill, PA '86 (PR)
FITZGERALD, THERESA L., pat. rep. and risk mgr., Scripps Memorial Hospital-Chula Vista, Chula Vista, CA '82 (PAT)
FITZGERALD, WILLIAM B., atty., Detroit-Macomb Hospital Corporation, Detroit, MI '87 (ATTY)
FITZGIBBON, ROBERT E., plant serv. eng., Leominster Hospital, Leominster, MA '81 (ENG)
FITZNER, KAREN, consult., Wilmette, IL '85
FITZNER, TIM, chief eng., Southern Hills General Hospital, Hot Springs, SD '87 (ENG)
FITZPATRIC, RICHARD T., dir. emp. rel., Providence Hospital, Cincinnati, OH '78 (PERS)(ENG)
FITZPATRICK, BRUCE B., dir. pharm. and cent. serv. room, Braintree Hospital, Braintree, MA '85 (CS)
FITZPATRICK, JAMES A., atty., Champlain Valley Physicians Hospital Medical Center, Plattsburgh, NY '79 (ATTY)
FITZPATRICK, JENNIFER L., dir. vol. serv., Mercy Hospital, Portland, ME '81 (VOL)
FITZPATRICK, JUNE BOUTIN, RN, dir. nrsg. serv., Lakes Region General Hospital, Laconia, NH '69 (NURS)
FITZPATRICK, MARILYN R., dir. vol. serv., Northern Dutchess Hospital, Rhinebeck, NY '82 (VOL)
FITZPATRICK, THERESE A., RN, dir. nrsg. qual. assur., Grant Hospital of Chicago, Chicago, IL '83 (NURS)
FITZPATRICK, THOMAS B., (ret.), Pittsburgh, PA '51 (LIFE)
FITZSIMMONS, JOSEPH JAMES, dir. food serv., Pontiac Osteopathic Hospital, Pontiac, MI '81 (FOOD)
FITZSIMMONS, M. JANE, RN, vice-pres. pat. care qual. and advocacy, Massachusetts Hospital Association, Burlington, MA '78 (NURS)
FITZSIMONS, LYNDA J., dir. vol. serv., Salem Hospital, Salem, OR '72 (VOL)
FITZSIMONS, PATRICIA SUSAN, RN, vice-pres. nrsg., Miami Valley Hospital, Dayton, OH '87 (NURS)
FIVEASH, BETH, dir. mktg., Charter Woods Hospital, Dothan, AL '87 (PR)
FIXLER, JILL FRIEDMAN, dir. vol., National Jewish Center, Denver, CO '83 (VOL)
FLACH, PATTY, dir. vol., St. Luke's Medical Center, Phoenix, AZ '73 (VOL)
FLACK, HERBERT L., prof. clin. pharm. and coor. cont. educ., Philadelphia College of Pharmacy and Sciences, Philadelphia, PA '53 (LIFE)
FLACKS, ANDREW G., prog. analyst and health planner, Veterans Administration, Department of Medicine and Surgery, Washington, DC '78
FLADMO, SANDRA A., RN, mgr. surg. serv., Deaconess Medical Center, Billings, MT '86 (NURS)
FLAGG, BILL B., dir. commun. rel. and dev., Cary Medical Center, Caribou, ME '86 (PR)
FLAHERTY, JEAN M., sr. mktg. and plng. analyst, Elizabeth General Medical Center, Elizabeth, NJ '86 (PR) (PLNG)
FLAHERTY, MARJORIE ANN, RN, vice-pres. nrsg. serv., Noble Hospital, Westfield, MA '86 (NURS)
FLAHERTY, THOMAS L., vice-pres., University Health Center of Pittsburgh, Pittsburgh, PA '85 (PLNG)
FLAITZ, JACOB W. JR., mktg. analyst, Holy Cross Health System Corporation, South Bend, IN '84 (PLNG) (PR)
FLAKE, JANET D., RN, mgr. sterile sup. proc., Deaconess Hospital, Evansville, IN '86 (CS)
FLAM, MANFRED, planner, University of Miami-Jackson Memorial Hospital, Miami, FL '47 (PLNG)(LIFE)
FLAM, MARVIN A., arch., Marvin A. Flam Architect, Clearwater, FL '86 (ENG)
FLAME, PHILIP, Encino, CA '76 (ATTY)
FLANAGAN, DONALD S., asst. adm., Spohn Hospital, Corpus Christi, TX '77
FLANAGAN, JAMES B., partner, Arthur Andersen and Company, Marblehead, MA '82 (MGMT)
FLANAGAN, JANET, dir. commun. rel., St. Luke's Regional Medical Center, Sioux City, IA '81 (PR)
FLANAGAN, MAUREEN F., mgr. cent. proc. and distrib., Cape Cod Hospital, Hyannis, MA '80 (CS)(PUR)
FLANAGAN, MAUREEN J., pres., Healthcare Communications-Marketing Corporation, Colorado Springs, CO '85 (PR)
FLANAGAN, WILLIAM E. JR., dir. pur., Holy Cross Hospital of Silver Spring, Silver Spring, MD '85 (PUR)
FLANDERS, J. PAUL, dir. plant eng., Jess Parrish Memorial Hospital, Titusville, FL '84 (ENG)
FLANDERS, JOHN T., RN, dir. nrsg., St. Joseph's Community Hospital, West Bend, WI '86 (NURS)
FLANDERS, PAMELA SHELDAHL, dir. soc. serv., Allen Memorial Hospital, Waterloo, IA '75 (SOC)
FLANEGIN, JAMES, asst. adm. pers. serv., St. John Hospital, Detroit, MI '79 (PERS)
FLANIGAN, JOHN F., atty., Tallahassee Community Hospital, Tallahassee, FL '83 (ATTY)
FLANNAGAN, HANNAH ASHBY, adm. res., Roanoke Memorial Rehabilitation Center, Roanoke, VA '84
FLANNAGAN, WILLIAM H., pres., Roanoke Memorial Hospitals, Roanoke, VA '51 (LIFE)
FLANNAGAN, WILLIAM H. JR., vice-pres. oper., Potomac Hospital, Woodbridge, VA '74
FLANNERY, DONNA M., mgr. soc. work serv., East Orange General Hospital, East Orange, NJ '86 (SOC)
FLANNERY, MAJ. J. G., MSC USA, chief clin. support, Landstuhl Army Regional Medical Center, APO New York, NY '85 (PAT)
FLASCK, ESTELLE, dir. human res., Edwin Shaw Hospital, Akron, OH '86 (PERS)
FLASHER, BARBARA J., dir. diet., William Beaumont Hospital, Royal Oak, MI '73 (FOOD)
FLATH, CARL I., consult., Tampa, FL '38 (LIFE)
FLATLEY, CONN J., vice-pres., Hamot Medical Center, Erie, PA '82
FLAX, HERBERT, dir. food serv., Foothills Provincial General Hospital, Calgary, Alta., Canada '84 (FOOD)
FLECHSIG, RANDOLPH K., dir. clin. serv., Oaklawn Hospital, Marshall, MI '82
FLECK, JOHN E., dir. risk mgt., Heartland Hospital West, St. Joseph, MO '84 (RISK)
FLECKNER, JENMAN KAKO, dir. soc. work, Scottsdale Memorial Hospital, Scottsdale, AZ '85 (SOC)
FLECKNOE, MARLENE M., mgr. vol., Geisinger Wyoming Valley Medical Center, Wilkes-Barre, PA '83 (VOL)
FLEEGE, RICHARD A., supv. maint., Galena-Stauss Hospital, Galena, IL '83 (ENG)
FLEESE, EILEEN J., RN, dir. nrsg. serv., Holy Cross Hospital, Fort Lauderdale, FL '70 (NURS)
FLEHARTY, PHYLLIS J., coor. plng. and spec. serv., Boys Town National Institute for Children, Omaha, NE '82 (PERS)
FLEISCHER, ELLIOT, asst. vice-pres. matl. mgt., Palisades General Hospital, North Bergen, NJ '83 (PUR)
FLEISCHER, EVA, dir. soc. serv., Mount Vernon Hospital, Mount Vernon, NY '77 (SOC)
FLEISCHER, FRANK R., dir. eng., St. Augustine General Hospital, St. Augustine, FL '84 (ENG)
FLEISCHER, GARY R., dir. mgt. info., St. Anthony's Medical Center, St. Louis, MO '80
FLEISCHMANN, HARTLY, atty., Garden Hospital Jerd Sullivan Rehabilitation Center, San Francisco, CA '70 (ATTY)
FLEISCHMANN, MICHAEL, dir. diet., Gordon Hospital, Calhoun, GA '85 (FOOD)
FLEISHACKER, EILEEN DIXON, coor. vol., Rapid City Regional Hospital, Rapid City, SD '82 (VOL)
FLEISHER, MARY L., dir. diet. serv., Presbyterian-University of Pennsylvania Medical Center, Philadelphia, PA '81 (FOOD)
FLEIT, JOEL P., RN, asst. dir. nrsg., St. Elizabeth's Hospital of Boston, Boston, MA '86 (NURS)
FLEMING, ARLENE E., RN, dir. nrsg., Galion Community Hospital, Galion, OH '87 (NURS)
FLEMING, BENNIE M., dir. soc. serv., Fort Sanders Regional Medical Center, Knoxville, TN '73 (SOC)
FLEMING, CAROL T., dir. commun., Mercy Health Services, Farmington Hills, MI '81 (PR)
FLEMING, DAVID F., vice-pres. and exec. dir. pub. affairs, Jewish Hospital, Louisville, KY '83 (PR)
FLEMING, DAVID W., atty., Valley Presbyterian Hospital, Van Nuys, CA '84 (ATTY)
FLEMING, EDWARD H., chief eng., Arnot-Ogden Memorial Hospital, Elmira, NY '74 (ENG)
FLEMING, FREDRIC J., vice-pres. ancillary serv., Palos Community Hospital, Palos Heights, IL '75
FLEMING, JANET K., supv. cent. sterile sup., St. Elizabeth Hospital Medical Center, Lafayette, IN '83 (CS)
FLEMING, JO A., coor. pat. educ., Leonard Morse Hospital, Natick, MA '84 (EDUC)
FLEMING, JOHN J., pres., Hospital Productivity Management Service, Inc., Lake Oswego, OR '87 (MGMT)
FLEMING, JOSEPH J., adm. res., Seton Medical Center, Daly City, CA '86
FLEMING, JUDITH A., exec. vice-pres., Alternative Care Technologies, Fort Wayne, IN '84
FLEMING, LESLIE C., mgr. plng. and bus. dev., Holy Cross Hospital, Detroit, MI '86 (PLNG)
FLEMING, SR. MARY BLANDINE, adm., Saint Francis Hospital, Tulsa, OK '64 (PLNG)
FLEMING, MARY E., dir. diet., Maine Coast Memorial Hospital, Ellsworth, ME '78 (FOOD)
FLEMING, PATRICK G., dir. mktg. shared serv., Mercy Health Center, Dubuque, IA '67 (PR)
FLEMING, RICHARD F., dir. plant oper. and maint., Harrison Memorial Hospital, Bremerton, WA '85 (ENG)
FLEMING, ROBERT B. JR., atty., Children's Hospital, Buffalo, NY '82 (ATTY)
FLEMING, ROBERT B., consult., Medical Placers, Wilmington, DE '86 (MGMT)
FLEMING, ROBERT S., coor. hosp. matl. sup., Harold D. Chope Community Hospital, San Mateo, CA '86 (CS)
FLEMING, RUTH, dir. amb. nrsg. practice, Little Company of Mary Hospital, Evergreen Park, IL '87 (AMB)
FLEMING, STEVEN N., dir. pers., Scotland Memorial Hospital, Laurinburg, NC '85 (PERS)
FLEMING, T. CLIFFORD, atty., St. Anthony Medical Center, Crown Point, IN '86 (ATTY)
FLENSBORG, PATSY E., dir. qual. assur. and risk mgt., Camden-Clark Memorial Hospital, Parkersburg, WV '81 (RISK)
FLETCHER, ALFRED E., Tallahassee, FL '59
FLETCHER, BOBBY D., dir. eng., Los Robles Regional Medical Center, Thousand Oaks, CA '81 (ENG)
FLETCHER, DAVID A., chief oper. off., Elizabeth General Medical Center, Elizabeth, NJ '64
FLETCHER, ELEANOR S., dir. cent. sterile and proc., Phoebe Putney Memorial Hospital, Albany, GA '82 (CS)
FLETCHER, I. MARIE, RN, dir. nrsg., Seaway Hospital, Trenton, MI '85 (NURS)

FLETCHER, JAN, RN, dir. amb. surg. serv., Good Samaritan Hospital and Medical Center, Portland, OR '87 (AMB)
FLETCHER, RITA, asst. dir. vol. serv., Medical Center at Princeton, Princeton, NJ '84 (VOL)
FLETCHER, ROBERT L. JR., proj. mgr., Tilden, Lobnitz and Cooper, Inc., Orlando, FL '83 (ENG)
FLETCHER, SUSAN R., RN, adm. pat. care, Harms Memorial Hospital, American Falls, ID '82 (NURS)
FLETCHER, TODD N., mgt. eng., Georgetown University Medical Center, Washington, DC '85 (MGMT)
FLEURY, N. BERNADINE, Veterans Administration Medical Center, Pittsburgh, PA '71 (FOOD)
FLEXNER, WILLIAM A., pres., Flexner and Associates, Inc., Mendota Heights, MN '80 (PLNG)
FLICK, BARBARA G., coor. educ., East Alabama Medical Center, Opelika, AL '86 (EDUC)
FLICKINGER, JEAN, risk mgr., Medical Center of Delaware, Wilmington, DE '85 (RISK)
FLICKINGER, KENNETH E., vice-pres. fin., Chester County Hospital, West Chester, PA '81
FLICKINGER, THOMAS L., pres., Voluntary Hospital of America of the Midlands, Omaha, NE '86
FLIEHMAN, DEBORAH G., mgr. educ. prog. dev., Travenol Management Services, Deerfield, IL '86 (EDUC)
FLIERL, PETER J., exec. dir., Greenwich Health Association, Greenwich, CT '86 (PLNG)
FLINK, JOHN W., asst. dir. info. syst., Hermann Hospital, Houston, TX '87 (MGMT)
FLINN, JEANNE, dir. soc. work, John Randolph Hospital, Hopewell, VA '85 (SOC)
FLINT, GREGORY, dir. clin. soc. work, Childrens Hospital of Orange County, Orange, CA '81 (SOC)
FLODEN, G. SCOTT, sr. assoc. dir., University Medical Center, Tucson, AZ '86
FLOECKHER, DONALD B., dir. plant eng., Lutheran General Hospital, Park Ridge, IL '86 (ENG)
FLOHR, JUDY K., dir. food serv., Allied Services for Handicapped, Scranton, PA '86 (FOOD)
FLOMAN, JOSEPH F., asst. dir. fin., Jewish Memorial Hospital, Boston, MA '71
FLOOD, ANNETTE E., risk mgr., Lansing General Hospital, Lansing, MI '86 (RISK)
FLOOD, BRIDGET M., mkt res. mgr., St. Louis University Medical Center, St. Louis, MO '86 (PLNG)
FLOOD, JOHN A., dir. pers., St. Clare Hospital of Monroe, Monroe, WI '82 (PERS)(RISK)
FLOOD, JOSEPH, dir. soc. serv., Hartford Hospital, Hartford, CT '78 (SOC)
FLOOD, MARILYN E., RN, assoc. dean nrsg., University of California, San Francisco, CA '83 (NURS)
FLOOD, PAUL M., pres., Flr Health Resources, Atlanta, GA '85
FLOOD, PENNY E., dir. educ. and trng., Hillcrest Baptist Medical Center, Waco, TX '81 (EDUC)
FLORA, KRISTIN A., educ. consult., Kaf Enterprises, Sioux Falls, SD '87 (EDUC)
FLORENCE, AGNES F., Dixon, IL '38 (LIFE)
FLORES, HOMERO, dir. vol. serv., Santa Clara Valley Medical Center, San Jose, CA '80 (VOL)
FLORES, JEANNE R., dir. emp. rel., Cedars-Sinai Medical Center, Los Angeles, CA '86 (PERS)
FLORES, JOSEPH, vice-pres., Popov Engineers, Inc., Ontario, CA '86 (ENG)
FLORES, JUDITH Z., risk mgt. consult., Bewton Square, PA '86 (RISK)
FLORES, LESLIE A. RAINS, vice-pres., St. Luke Medical Center, Pasadena, CA '80
FLORKEY, ELLEN M., asst. dir. pers., Pontiac General Hospital, Pontiac, MI '86 (PERS)
FLORMAN, DAVID A., adm. dir. amb. serv., Mount Sinai Medical Center, New York, NY '81 (AMB)
FLORY, JOYCE, PhD, dir. commun., American College of Healthcare Executives, Chicago, IL '80 (PR)
FLORY, WILLIAM M., adm. dir. gen. serv., Long Beach Community Hospital, Long Beach, CA '84 (ENG)
FLOSS, DENNIS L. SR., maint. forman, Piqua Memorial Medical Center, Piqua, OH '87 (ENG)
FLOURNOY, CARYN, dir. risk mgt., Medical College of Ohio Hospital, Toledo, OH '87 (RISK)
FLOUTON, LUTHER H., arch., Department of Health and Human Services, Washington, DC '81
FLOWER, MARYBETH, asst. adm. educ., Pacific Presbyterian Medical Center, San Francisco, CA '77 (SOC)(EDUC)
FLOWERS, ELISE B., dir. vol. serv., Richland Memorial Hospital, Columbia, SC '86 (VOL)
FLOWERS, JAMES D., facil. eng. and safety off., U. S. Air Force Hospital Luke, Glendale, AZ '86 (ENG)
FLOWERS, LINDA P., coor. pub. rel., Durham County General Hospital, Durham, NC '86 (PR)
FLOWERS, MARY KING, dir. pers., Wayne Memorial Hospital, Jesup, GA '82 (PERS)
FLOWERS, ROBERT S., supv. biomedical eng., Nash General Hospital, Rocky Mount, NC '85 (ENG)
FLOWERS, SUSAN M., dir., National Rehabilitation Information Center, Washington, DC '85
FLOYD, CAROL Y., dir. vol. serv., Community Hospital of Springfield and Clark County, Springfield, OH '69 (VOL)
FLOYD, EDNA B., soc. worker, Mount Desert Island Hospital, Bar Harbor, ME '79 (SOC)
FLOYD, GEORGE K., mgr., Ernst and Whinney, Atlanta, GA '86 (MGMT)
FLOYD, HAROLD C., mgr. diet., Colleton Regional Hospital, Walterboro, SC '83 (FOOD)
FLOYD, NILES, exec. dir., Riverchase Hospital, Chattanooga, TN '87 (AMB)
FLOYD, RICHARD B., asst. dir., New England Deaconess Hospital, Boston, MA '85
FLOYD, ROBERT, mgr. eng., Bromenn Healthcare, Bloomington, IL '86 (ENG)
FLUKE, RICHARD M., pres., Hospital Network, Inc., Kalamazoo, MI '86
FLURY, PATRICIA A., assoc. adm., Memorial Hospital, Hollywood, FL '84 (ENG)
FLURY, RICHARD A., vice-pres. pers., Mansfield General Hospital, Mansfield, OH '83 (PERS)
FLYER, NATALIE S., dir. market res. and plng., Alexian Brothers Medical Center, Elk Grove Village, IL '82 (PLNG)
FLYER, ROBERT, dir. eng. and maint., Lake Hospital System, Painesville, OH '80 (ENG)
FLYNN-HOLLANDER, SHARON M., RN, vice-pres. nrsg. and commun. serv., Gottlieb Memorial Hospital, Melrose Park, IL '85 (NURS)
FLYNN, BARRY J., Memphis, TN '71
FLYNN, BRIAN T., student, University of Denver, Denver, CO '86 (PLNG)
FLYNN, CARROLL A., student, Program in School Business Administration, Tulane University, New Orleans, LA '86
FLYNN, DEBBIE M., adm. asst., Metropolitan Hospital-Parkview Division, Philadelphia, PA '81 (RISK)
FLYNN, EDWARD J., pres., Riddick, Flynn and Associates, Louisville, KY '86 (PLNG)
FLYNN, EDWARD JOSEPH SR., plant eng., Jackson County Schneck Memorial Hospital, Seymour, IN '75 (ENG)
FLYNN, GORDON L., dir. mgt. eng., Children's Hospital of Wisconsin, Milwaukee, WI '71 (MGMT)
FLYNN, JANE PATRICE, RN, vice-pres. nrsg. serv., Cape Cod Hospital, Hyannis, MA '81 (NURS)
FLYNN, KEVIN, dir. emp. and commun. rel., Franklin Memorial Hospital, Farmington, ME '86 (PERS)
FLYNN, LILLIAN, dir., West Jersey Home Health Care, Marlton, NJ '87 (AMB)
FLYNN, SR. M. BARBARA, chm., Gwynedd Mercy College, Gwynedd Valley, PA '79 (EDUC)
FLYNN, MARY LOUISE, dir. soc. serv., St. Francis Memorial Hospital, San Francisco, CA '85 (SOC)
FLYNN, REV. SEAN P., diocesan coor. catholic hosp., Catholic Diocese of Trenton, Manasquan, NJ '84
FLYNN, SUSAN B., dir., Carondelet Health Services, Inc., Tucson, AZ '84 (PR)
FLYNN, THOMAS J., vice-pres., gen. counsel and sec., Humana Inc., Louisville, KY '76 (ATTY)
FLYNN, THOMAS P., vice-pres. mktg., Martin Luther Hospital Medical Center, Anaheim, CA '86 (PR)
FLYNN, THOMAS W., reg. vice-pres., Adventist Health System-Eastern and Middle America, Wheaton, MD '83
FLYNN, WILLIAM J., dir. eng. and maint., Melrose-Wakefield Hospital, Melrose, MA '81 (ENG)
FLYTE, JONATHAN D., mgr. plant oper., Mercy Center for Health Care Services, Aurora, IL '85 (ENG)
FOARDE, MARY P., atty., Mount Sinai Hospital, Minneapolis, MN '86 (ATTY)
FOBAR, DOV B., owner, Health Industry Recruiters, New York, NY '84 (MGMT)
FOBES, JOHN W., student, Program in Hospital Administration, Trinity University, San Antonio, TX '80
FOCHT, M. H. SR., sr. vice-pres. eastern reg., National Medical Enterprises, Tampa, FL '83
FODEL, DOROTHY, risk mgr., Mercy Hospital, Charlotte, NC '86 (RISK)
FOGARTY, DAN, dir. hskpg. and linen serv., Wentworth-Douglass Hospital, Dover, NH '86 (ENVIRON)
FOGARTY, JOHN P., sr. vice-pres., First Interstate Mortgage Company, Pasadena, CA '78
FOGEL, LAWRENCE NEIL, pres., Capital Health Associates, Vienna, VA '62
FOGEL, LEONARD, assoc. adm., St. John's Episcopal Hospital-South Shore Division, Far Rockaway, NY '80
FOGLE, JAMES M., exec. dir., Halifax Home Health, Inc., Daytona Beach, FL '77
FOLAN, SR. M. ALFREDA, RN, rep. pat. care, Saint Joseph Hospital, Fort Worth, TX '75 (PAT)
FOLEY, SR. ANNA C., (ret.), Oakland, CA '39 (LIFE)
FOLEY, BRIAN P., inspector gen., Headquarters 18th Medical Command, APO San Francisco, CA '82
FOLEY, ELEANOR J., pat. rep., Doctors Hospital, New York, NY '84 (PAT)
FOLEY, EVERETT JR., chief eng., Helena Hospital, Helena, AR '76 (ENG)
FOLEY, GENEVIEVE V., RN, dir. surg. nrsg., Memorial Sloan-Kettering Cancer Center, New York, NY '85 (NURS)
FOLEY, JAMES T., dir. acctg. serv., Shore Memorial Hospital, Somers Point, NJ '84
FOLEY, JOSEPH J., vice-pres. mission effectiveness, Columbus-Cuneo-Cabrini Medical Center, Chicago, IL '75 (EDUC)
FOLEY, M. KAYE, RN, vice-pres. pat. care serv., North Memorial Medical Center, Robbinsdale, MN '86 (NURS)
FOLEY, MARGARET W., RN, asst. adm. nrsg. serv., Florida Keys Memorial Hospital, Key West, FL '86 (NURS)
FOLEY, LT. COL. NAOMI J., DeWitt Army Community Hospital, Fort Belvoir, VA '85
FOLEY, PENELOPE S., RN, dir. nrsg. and health care serv., Doctors Hospital, Detroit, MI '85 (NURS)
FOLEY, THOMAS G., dir. soc. serv., Brockton Hospital, Brockton, MA '68 (SOC)
FOLEY, CAPT. WILLIAM A., MSC USA, proj. consult., Headquarters 2nd U. S. Army, Fort Gillem, GA '86 (SOC)
FOLEY, WILLIAM T., vice-pres. prof. serv., Mercy Hospital, Miami, FL '86
FOLGER, JAMES C., pres., Northwest Healthcare Consulting, Eugene, OR '83 (PLNG)
FOLGER, SARA, dir. pur., DeKalb General Hospital, Decatur, GA '74 (PUR)
FOLISI, FRANK A., dir. pers., St. Vincent's Medical Center, Staten Island, NY '83 (PERS)
FOLK, JOHN A., chief eng., Kaiser Foundation Hospital, Sacramento, CA '81 (ENG)
FOLKER, DAVID ALAN, exec. vice-pres., Magee-Womens Hospital, Pittsburgh, PA '68 (MGMT)
FOLLEN, WILLIAM R., chief tech.-cent. sterile proc., Lawrence Hospital, Bronxville, NY '82 (CS)
FOLLETT, SANDRA D., asst. dir. pat. and food serv., Foothills Provincial General Hospital, Calgary, Alta., Canada '85 (FOOD)
FOLLIARD, JOHN F. JR., atty., Emanuel Hospital and Health Center, Portland, OR '80 (ATTY)
FOLLMAN, ROBERT J., National Medical Enterprises, Inc., Tampa, FL '85 (MGMT)
FOLSE, JANIE N., RN, dir. staff dev. and educ., St. Anne General Hospital, Raceland, LA '73 (EDUC)(PR)
FOLSOM, JACK E., mgr. mgt. eng., Lincoln General Hospital, Lincoln, NE '82 (MGMT)
FOLSOM, JUDITH A., RN, dir. nrsg., Hadley Regional Medical Center, Hays, KS '86 (NURS)
FOLSOM, KAREN A., RN, coor. dialysis and transplantation, St. Luke's Hospital, Kansas City, MO '80
FOLTZ, DONALD S., dir. plant serv., Taylor Hospital, Ridley Park, PA '75 (ENG)
FOLZ, GREGORY A., dir. pub. rel. and advertising, St. Mary's Medical Center, Evansville, IN '83 (PR)
FONCANNON, SUSAN E., RN, Simi Valley, CA '86 (ENVIRON)
FONGERS, CATHERINE A., RN, vice-pres., Harris Methodist Health System, Fort Worth, TX '86 (NURS)
FONT, JACQUELINE, student, Program in Hospital and Health Care Administration, St. Louis University, St. Louis, MO '85
FONTAINE, JOHN E., chief eng., Frances Mahon Deaconess Hospital, Glasgow, MT '84 (ENG)
FONTAINE, LEHARD J., adm., Houma Surgi-Center, Inc., Houma, LA '87 (AMB)
FONTAINE, MELISSA, vice-pres., Memorial Hospital, North Little Rock, AR '80
FONTANA, MICHAEL E., dir. plng., Desert Hospital, Palm Springs, CA '80 (PLNG)
FONTECCHIO, KEN A., mgr. pers., Theda Clark Regional Medical Center, Neenah, WI '85 (PERS)
FONTES, DAVID N., asst. dir. eng., St. Joseph Hospital, Providence, RI '82 (ENG)
FONVILLE, ANN M., RN, consult., Lenoir, NC '83 (NURS)
FOOTE, PATTI L., dir. vol., Holladay Park Medical Center, Portland, OR '87 (VOL)
FOOTE, WILLARD G., pres., Redwood Memorial Hospital, Fortuna, CA '84 (PLNG)
FORAN, JAMES R., student, University of New South Wales School, Carlingford, Australia '82 (MGMT)
FORBES, CHARLES F., atty., California Hospital Association, Sacramento, CA '70 (ATTY)
FORBES, D. MICHAEL, assoc. adm., St. Luke's Hospital, Chesterfield, MO '75 (PERS)
FORBES, I. HELEN, mgr. pers., Wilson Memorial Hospital, Wilson, NC '84 (PERS)
FORBES, JANE, atty., Harper Hospital, Detroit, MI '82 (ATTY)
FORBES, MAGGIE L., dir. diet., Annapolis Hospital, Wayne, MI '76 (FOOD)
FORBES, NORMA D., dir. plng., St. John's Regional Medical Center, Oxnard, CA '79 (PLNG)
FORD, ANN N., coor. qual. assur., Holy Cross Hospital of Silver Spring, Silver Spring, MD '85 (RISK)
FORD, ANTHONY, dir. food serv., DeKalb General Hospital, Decatur, GA '83 (FOOD)
FORD, CAROLYN S., asst. dir. pub. affairs, Moses H. Cone Memorial Hospital, Greensboro, NC '81 (PR)
FORD, CONNIE J., mgr. pur. serv., LaPorte Hospital, LaPorte, IN '86 (PUR)
FORD, ELIZABETH C., asst. adm., North Mississippi Medical Center, Tupelo, MS '84 (RISK)
FORD, LT. FRANK H. III, MSC USN, asst. head pat. affairs, Naval Hospital, Jacksonville, FL '83
FORD, GARY W., vice-pres. mktg., General Learning Corporation, Highland Park, IL '87 (PR)
FORD, GEORGE W., MD, med. dir., Norfolk and Western Railway Company, Roanoke, VA '70
FORD, J. DANIEL, sr. partner, Clapp, Kieffer and Associates, Chicago, IL '71 (PLNG)
FORD, JAMES H. III, mgt. eng., Baptist Memorial Hospital, Memphis, TN '82 (MGMT)
FORD, JEAN E., dir. pur., Alexander Blain Memorial Hospital, Detroit, MI '61 (PUR)
FORD, KARLA K., adm. asst., Northwest Community Hospital, Arlington Heights, IL '82 (RISK)
FORD, LEONARD T., adm., Stokes Regional Eye Center, Pee Dee Ambulatory Surgical Center, Florence, SC '87 (AMB)
FORD, LESLIE S., coor. nephrology soc. work, Greenfield Health Service Corporation, Detroit, MI '84 (SOC)
FORD, LINDA, dir. risk mgt., grants and contracts, Denver Health and Hospitals, Denver, CO '86 (RISK)
FORD, MALCOLM J., dir. matl. mgt., New Rochelle Hospital Medical Center, New Rochelle, NY '75 (PUR)
FORD, MARTHA ANN, dir. cent. serv., Children's Mercy Hospital, Kansas City, MO '82 (CS)
FORD, MARY S., dir. diet. serv., Brokaw Hospital, Normal, IL '80 (FOOD)
FORD, MERRYMAN, mgr. commun., Sheppard and Enoch Pratt Hospital, Baltimore, MD '85 (ENG)
FORD, NANCY P., dir. soc. serv., St. Luke's Hospital, Jacksonville, FL '79 (SOC)
FORD, PATRICIA C. G., mgr. health promotion, Franklin Square Hospital, Baltimore, MD '84 (EDUC)
FORD, RAYMOND L., sr. vice-pres., St. Vincent's Hospital, Birmingham, AL '77
FORD, ROBERT J. JR., div. dir. human serv., Our Lady of Lourdes Memorial Hospital, Binghamton, NY '83 (SOC)
FORD, SARA E., dir. plng. and mktg., St. Mary's Health Center, Jefferson City, MO '86 (PR) (PLNG)
FORD, W. RAYMOND C., dir. mkt strategy, Hospital Corporation of America, Nashville, TN '83 (PLNG)
FORD, WILLIAM F., dir. pers., St. Mary's Hospital, Kansas City, MO '65 (PERS)
FORD, WILLIAM HOWER, PhD, (ret.), Pittsburgh, PA '56 (LIFE)
FORDE, JANE R., RN, vice-pres. nrsg., Phoenix Baptist Hospital and Medical Center, Phoenix, AZ '84 (NURS)
FORDERHASE, SANDRA HOPE, coor. guest rel., HCA Regional Hospital of Jackson, Jackson, TN '86 (PAT)
FORDHAM, LORRAINE A., dir. info. syst., Sibley Memorial Hospital, Washington, DC '85 (MGMT)
FORDIANI, MARTHA L., atty., Danbury Hospital, Danbury, CT '83 (PLNG)(RISK)(ATTY)
FORDYCE, CONSTANCE M., supv. cent. serv., Crittenton Hospital, Rochester, MI '81 (CS)

FORE, CYNTHIA F., consult., The Wyatt Company, Washington, DC '75
FORE, DOREEN M., dir. pub. rel. and vol. serv., Ashe Memorial Hospital, Jefferson, NC '85 (PR)
FOREMAN, FRAN V., pat. rep., Akron General Medical Center, Akron, OH '87 (PAT)
FOREN, DAVID O., dir. pers., Bristol Hospital, Bristol, CT '75 (PERS)
FORER, JOHN L., pres., Forer Interests, Tenkintown, PA '79 (PR) (PLNG)
FORERO, GLADYS, dir. pur., Mercy Hospital, Miami, FL '81 (PUR)
FORESMAN, MATT P., dir. prof. serv., North Kansas City Hospital, North Kansas City, MO '81
FOREST, ANNE M., RN, dir. pat. care, Fairfield Memorial Hospital, Winnsboro, SC '85 (NURS)
FOREST, JAMES I., mgr. pur., matl. and facil., Winston-Salem Dental Care Plan, Winston-Salem, NC '86 (PUR)
FORESTALL, JACQUELINE L., dir. human res., Saint Luke's Hospital, Cleveland, OH '86 (PERS)
FORGIEL, KENNETH J., vice-pres., Boldyreff, Crosby and Forgiel, Inc., Marysville, MI '86 (ENG)
FORGUE, RUTH A., student, Rush University, Chicago, IL '86
FORGUES, ROBERT L., dir. ldry. serv., Hebrew Rehabilitation Center for Aged, Boston, MA '87 (ENVIRON)
FORINASH, LEONARD A., vice-pres. support serv., Ashtabula County Medical Center, Ashtabula, OH '80 (ENG)
FORMAN, CAROL, dir. soc. work, St. Joseph Mercy Hospital, Pontiac, MI '85 (SOC)
FORMAN, I. S., vice-pres. human res., Long Island Jewish Medical Center, New York, NY '82 (PERS)
FORMAN, JEANETTE, dir. vol., Interfaith Medical Center-Brooklyn, Brooklyn, NY '74 (VOL)
FORMAN, JEFFREY H., asst. dir. eng., Helene Fuld Medical Center, Trenton, NJ '86 (ENG)
FORMAN, JOSEPH D., dir. plant serv., Montclair Community Hospital, Montclair, NJ '79 (ENG)
FORMAN, LAWRENCE S., pres., Lawrence Forman and Associates, Miami, FL '86
FORMAN, NAOMI, head nrs. cent. serv. room, Central General Hospital, Plainview, NY '83 (CS)
FORMAN, R. C., maint. eng., Memorial Hospital, Guymon, OK '85 (ENG)
FORMAN, ROBERT A., vice-pres. human res., Emanuel Hospital and Health Center, Portland, OR '79 (PERS)
FORMICA, ANTHONY L., sr. vice-pres., Kessler Institute for Rehabilitation, West Orange, NJ '81 (PLNG)
FORNARI, RALPH J., adm. assoc., Alexian Brothers Medical Center, Elk Grove Village, IL '82
FORNEY, DEE COLLINS, dir. soc. work and pat. rep., Cass Medical Center, Harrisonville, MO '85 (SOC)(PAT)
FORR, MARY L., asst. dir. matl. mgt., University Hospitals of Cleveland, Cleveland, OH '83 (CS)
FORRAND, FLOYD C., assoc. adm., Ridgecrest Community Hospital, Ridgecrest, CA '80 (RISK)
FORREST, ARGUS D., vice-pres., Presbyterian Medical Center, Dallas, TX '71
FORREST, CHRISTOPHER R., practice plan adm., University of Wisconsin, Madison, WI '81 (AMB)
FORREST, FRANKLIN THOMAS, dir. clin. eng., Alamance Memorial Hospital, Burlington, NC '79 (ENG)
FORREST, KATHY CRUISE, dir. soc. serv., Saint Vincent Hospital, Worcester, MA '73 (SOC)
FORREST, P. RYDER, dir. plant oper., Mobile Infirmary Medical Center, Mobile, AL '79 (ENG)
FORREST, WILLIAM R., head hskpg., ldry. and linen serv., St. Peter's Community Hospital, Helena, MT '86 (ENVIRON)
FORRO, ELIZABETH G., vice-pres., Bryn Mawr Rehabilitation Hospital, Malvern, PA '87 (AMB)
FORSHEY, MAJ. DAVID L., MSC USA, exec. off., Madigan Army Medical Center, Tacoma, WA '82
FORSMAN, VERNON W., Hinsdale, IL '52 (LIFE)
FORSTENZER, STEPHEN L., Washington, DC '59
FORSTER, BONNIE A., supv. hskpg., South Peninsula Hospital, Homer, AK '86 (ENVIRON)
FORSTER, SR. FRANCIS, vice-pres. mission effectiveness, St. Benedict's Hospital, Ogden, UT '69 (PR)
FORSTER, JOHN F., RN, asst. adm. pat. care serv., AMI Griffin-Spalding Hospital, Griffin, GA '72 (NURS)
FORSTER, MIKE, dir. food serv., Boulder Community Hospital, Boulder, CO '82 (FOOD)
FORSYTH, GEORGE C., dir. fin. mgt., Vanderbilt University Hospital, Nashville, TN '78
FORSYTHE, DOROTHY M., dir. diet. serv., Frick Community Health Center, Mount Pleasant, PA '83 (FOOD)
FORSYTHE, RONALD J., assoc. adm., Western Psychiatric Institute and Clinic, Pittsburgh, PA '79 (PLNG)
FORT, JOSEPH EUGENE, sr. biomedical eng. tech., Forrest County General Hospital, Hattiesburg, MS '86 (ENG)
FORT, SUSAN R., dir. soc. work, Shands Hospital of the University of Florida, Gainesville, FL '78 (SOC)
FORTE, THEODORE, elec. eng., The Methodist Hospital, Houston, TX '84 (ENG)
FORTIN, E. JEAN, supv. cent. sup., Androscoggin Valley Hospital, Berlin, NH '83 (CS)
FORTIN, JULIE A., atty., Charter Suburban Hospital, Mesquite, TX '81 (ATTY)
FORTNER, ELLIOTT T., adm., Sycamore Hospital, Miamisburg, OH '81
FORTNER, LYNDA S., pat. rep., Indian Path Hospital, Kingsport, TN '86 (PAT)
FORTNEY, JAMES M., asst. dir. food serv. oper., York Hospital, York, PA '84 (FOOD)
FORTNEY, JERI L., dir. soc. serv., Burnham Hospital, Champaign, IL '85 (SOC)
FORTNEY, TERESA, supv. cent. sup., Dameron Hospital, Stockton, CA '80 (CS)
FORTON, GERALD T., dir. diet. serv., Durham County General Hospital, Durham, NC '67 (FOOD)
FORTSON, STACEY, vice-pres. corp. dev., Columbus-Cuneo-Cabrini Medical Center, Chicago, IL '86 (PR)
FORTUNA, GINA M., student, University of Michigan School of Public Health, Ann Arbor, MI '86 (MGMT)
FORTUNE, ANNE OSTRAND, atty., Lutheran Medical Center, Omaha, NE '78 (ATTY)
FORTUNE, KAREN L., RN, vice-pres. pat. care, Washington Adventist Hospital, Takoma Park, MD '86 (NURS)
FORTUNO, JOSE LUIS, chief eng., Hospital San Pablo, Bayamon, P.R. '77 (ENG)
FORYSTHE, JACQUELINE ANN, dir. pub. rel., Verdugo Hills Hospital, Glendale, CA '85 (PR)
FOSHER, SUSAN E., coor. human res., Bullhead Community Hospital, Bullhead City, AZ '86 (PERS)
FOSMIRE, FRANCIS GEORGE, exec. vice-pres., Brookhaven Memorial Hospital Medical Center, Patchogue, NY '67
FOSS, JEAN, pres., Jean A. Foss and Associates, Chicago, IL '86 (RISK)
FOSSE, DAVID R., vice-pres. plng., mktg. and pub. rel., South Chicago Community Hospital, Chicago, IL '86 (PLNG)
FOSSELMAN, JERRY, adm., Medical Arts Laboratory, Inc., Oklahoma City, OK '86
FOSSEN, MICHAEL D., supv. maint., Rice Memorial Hospital, Willmar, MN '84 (ENG)
FOSSIER, MICHAEL P., atty., Centinela Hospital Medical Center, Inglewood, CA '83 (ATTY)
FOSTER, ANNE, coor. qual. assur., Fountain Valley Regional Hospital Medical Center, Fountain Valley, CA '87 (RISK)
FOSTER, BETH E., RN, chm. nrsg., Howard Young Medical Center, Woodruff, WI '84 (NURS)
FOSTER, BRIAN R., acct. mgr., Illinois Hospital Association, Oak Brook, IL '77 (MGMT)
FOSTER, CAROL A., dir. telecommun., St. John and West Shore Hospital, Westlake, OH '85 (ENG)
FOSTER, LT. COL. CHARLES STEPHEN, MSC USA, Fairfax, VA '80
FOSTER, DONALD G., pres., The Planning Center, Inc., Northbrook, IL '85
FOSTER, H. E., plant eng., Hillcrest Medical Center, Tulsa, OK '71 (ENG)
FOSTER, J. DARRELL, atty., Maryview Hospital, Portsmouth, VA '83 (ATTY)
FOSTER, J. KEITH, dir. syst., United Hospital Center, Clarksburg, WV '86 (MGMT)
FOSTER, JACQUELINE G., RN, dir. nrsg. serv., Natchaug Hospital, Mansfield Center, CT '81 (NURS)
FOSTER, JAMES B., adm., Lake Shore Hospital, Irving, NY '87
FOSTER, LT. COL. JAMES M., MSC USA, pers. off., Fitzsimons Army Medical Center, Aurora, CO '76
FOSTER, JANICE M., mktg. analyst and prog. coor., Providence Medical Center, Portland, OR '86 (PLNG)
FOSTER, JEAN, dir. vol. serv., Englewood Hospital, Englewood, NJ '86 (VOL)
FOSTER, JOHN THOMAS, pres., Cheshire Medical Center, Keene, NH '57 (LIFE)
FOSTER, KENNETH L., asst. vice-pres. plng. and mktg., St. Joseph's Hospital, Marshfield, WI '82 (PLNG)
FOSTER, LAVERNE B., RN, asst. vice-pres., Methodist Manor, West Allis, WI '83 (NURS)
FOSTER, LESLIE, coor. vol. serv., Isabella Geriatric Center, New York, NY '79 (VOL)
FOSTER, LOWELL A., vice-pres., The Travelers Insurance Company, Hartford, CT '85
FOSTER, MARGARET T., dir. vol. serv., Hotel Dieu Medical Center, El Paso, TX '85 (VOL)
FOSTER, MARION J., pres., North Carolinas Hospital Association Trust Fund, Raleigh, NC '77 (ATTY)
FOSTER, NADINE ARDIS, Chicago, IL '78
FOSTER, RICHARD C., vice-pres., Fairfax Hospital Association, Springfield, VA '53 (LIFE)
FOSTER, SYLVIA K., dir. soc. serv., Morton Hospital and Medical Center, Taunton, MA '71 (SOC)
FOSTER, THOMAS J., adm. dir. path., Kettering Medical Center, Kettering, OH '84
FOSTER, WAYNE B., coor. loss prevention, Ohio Hospital Insurance Company, Columbus, OH '48 (LIFE)
FOSTER, WILLIE H., supv. cent. serv., San Pedro Peninsula Hospital, San Pedro, CA '83 (CS)
FOSTER, ZELDA P., chief soc. work serv., Veterans Administration Medical Center, Brooklyn, NY '76 (SOC)
FOTHERINGHAM, MARK R., mgr. pub. rel., Pioneer Valley Hospital, West Valley City, UT '84 (PR)
FOTIS, WILLIAM P., mgr. mktg., Belmont Community Hospital, Chicago, IL '86 (PR)
FOTOS, KATHERINE M., student, Program in Health Administration and Planning, University of New Hampshire, Durham, NH '85 (MGMT)
FOTSCHKY, ARTHUR J., dir. eng., San Antonio Community Hospital, Upland, CA '85 (ENG)
FOUGEROUSSE, FRANK G., adm., Stoughton Hospital Association, Stoughton, WI '75
FOUGEROUSSE, JACK G., health care planner, Indiana State Board of Health, Indianapolis, IN '58
FOUGEROUSSE, WILLIAM J., dir. environ. serv., Mary Sherman Hospital, Sullivan, IN '84 (ENG)
FOUGHT, RONALD J., RN, vice-pres. nrsg., St. Agnes Hospital, Fond Du Lac, WI '86 (NURS)
FOUGNIES, CHARLES R., mgr. plant oper., maint. and security, St. Vincent Hospital and Health Care Center, Indianapolis, IN '85 (ENG)
FOUKE, JUNE C., dir. commun. rel. and dev., Grinnell General Hospital, Grinnell, IA '86 (PUR)(PR)
FOULDS, WILLIAM L., dir. info. syst., St. Anthony's Hospital, St. Petersburg, FL '87 (MGMT)
FOUNTAIN, DONALD B., dir. pers., Orangeburg-Calhoun Regional Hospital, Orangeburg, SC '86 (PERS)
FOUNTAIN, JULIA M., dir. vol. serv., St. Luke's Hospital, Aberdeen, SD '84 (VOL)
FOURKAS, TED, dir. pub. info., California Hospital Association, Sacramento, CA '79 (PR)
FOURNIER, LEO R., dir. eng., Graduate Hospital, Philadelphia, PA '80 (ENG)
FOURNIER, NANCY L., coor. educ., Northern Montana Hospital, Havre, MT '86 (EDUC)
FOURNIER, ODETTE M., RN, vice-pres. nrsg., Cheshire Medical Center, Keene, NH '80 (NURS)
FOURNIER, PAULINE M., dir. vol. serv., St. Mary's General Hospital, Lewiston, ME '81 (VOL)
FOURNIER, PETER J., pres., Caesar Software Systems, Inc., Sykesville, MD '86 (MGMT)
FOUSSARD, ROGER P., chm., Foussard Econ Laboratory Management Services, Inc., St. Paul, MN '72
FOUST, KATHY, soc. worker and discharge planner, Helena Hospital, Helena, AR '85 (SOC)
FOUST, MARGARET JANE, (ret.), Kent, OH '70 (FOOD)
FOVARGUE, PETER, dir. eng., Danbury Hospital, Danbury, CT '83 (ENG)
FOWLER, MRS. EARLE B., bd. mem., Rush-Presbyterian-St. Luke's Medical Center, Chicago, IL '21 (LIFE)
FOWLER, FRANCES J., pres., Fowler Healthcare Affiliates, Atlanta, GA '82 (PLNG)
FOWLER, GLENDA DALE, Hyattsville, MD '85
FOWLER, JOANNA D., RN, dir. cent. serv., Miami Valley Hospital, Dayton, OH '79 (CS)
FOWLER, JOSEPH B., Watsonville, CA '47 (LIFE)
FOWLER, KAREN D., dir. food and nutr. serv., De Paul Rehabilitation Hospital, Milwaukee, WI '82 (FOOD)
FOWLER, LINDA M., RN, assoc. adm. and dir. nrsg., North Shore Medical Center, Miami, FL '85 (NURS)
FOWLER, MARSHALL C., dir. risk mgt., Norfolk General Hospital, Norfolk, VA '83 (RISK)
FOWLER, OMAR DEGARY, asst. adm. bldg. serv., Jefferson Regional Medical Center, Pine Bluff, AR '81 (ENG)
FOWLER, S. BENJAMIN, vice-pres., Baptist Hospital, Nashville, TN '80
FOWLER, SAM F. JR., atty., Fort Sanders Regional Medical Center, Knoxville, TN '75 (ATTY)
FOWLER, W. HOWARD, atty., Gwinnett Hospital System, Lawrenceville, GA '78 (ATTY)
FOWLER, WAYNE J., atty., Colorado Hospital Association, Denver, CO '68 (ATTY)
FOWLKES, NELSON J., dir. market res. and plng., St. Agnes Hospital and Medical Center, Fresno, CA '81 (PLNG)
FOX, ANN M., dir. vol. serv., St. Francis Regional Medical Center, Wichita, KS '83 (VOL)
FOX, LT. ARTHUR W., MSC USN, fiscal and sup. off., Naval Dental Clinic, San Francisco, CA '77 (PUR)
FOX, BENJAMIN B., health care mgt. consult., New Ventures, Boston, MA '85 (PLNG)
FOX, BETTY, dir. family serv., Kettering Medical Center, Kettering, OH '84 (SOC)
FOX, CARY ALAN, asst. adm., AMI Rancho Encino Hospital, Encino, CA '80
FOX, CHARLES F. JR., chief oper. off., Indiana University School of Medicine, Indianapolis, IN '71 (MGMT)
FOX, DAVID K., coor. pub. rel., Hackley Hospital, Muskegon, MI '86 (PR)
FOX, DELORES G., RN, dir. maternal and child nrsg., Baystate Medical Center, Springfield, MA '84 (NURS)
FOX, DIANE M., dir. pers., United General Hospital, Sedro Woolley, WA '86 (PERS)
FOX, ELEANOR H., dir. pers. dev., St. Joseph Hospital, Baltimore, MD '75 (EDUC)
FOX, ELYSE, RN, asst. adm., Grand View Hospital, Sellersville, PA '79 (NURS)
FOX, EVERETT VERNON, (ret.), New York, NY '56 (LIFE)
FOX, FRANK G. JR., dir. plng. and res., St. Joseph Hospital and Health Care Center, Tacoma, WA '86 (PLNG)
FOX, GENEVIEVE J., pat. rep., Memorial Hospital, Ormond Beach, FL '86 (PAT)
FOX, JAMES A., chief vol. serv., Veterans Administration Medical Center, Asheville, NC '80 (VOL)
FOX, SR. JANE, Detroit, MI '83
FOX, JOHN K., dir. plant oper. and eng., Kootenai Medical Center, Coeur D'Alene, ID '81 (ENG)
FOX, JOHN N. JR., partner, Touche Ross and Company, Detroit, MI '75
FOX, JULIA HAGGERTY, RN, head nrs. gen. surg., St. Joseph's Hospital and Medical Center, Phoenix, AZ '86 (CS)
FOX, LARRY K., dir. pers., Cary Medical Center, Caribou, ME '87 (PERS)
FOX, MARGARET ELIZABETH, Phoenix, AZ '76 (FOOD)
FOX, MARIAN L., (ret.), Laguna Hills, CA '67
FOX, NANCY BERNSTEIN, adm., Jeanes Hospital, Philadelphia, PA '85
FOX, PATRICIA S., dir. soc. serv., Mercy Hospital, Baltimore, MD '70 (SOC)
FOX, RANDALL H., dir. human res., Medical Center Hospital, Punta Gorda, FL '86 (PERS)
FOX, RICHARD A., dir. pub. rel., Nexus Healthcare Corporation, Mount Holly, NJ '78 (PR)
FOX, RICHARD K., (ret.), Duluth, MN '45 (LIFE)
FOX, RICHARD R., dir. facil., St. Joseph's Hospital, Alton, IL '74 (ENG)
FOX, RICHARD T., dir. plng.-serv. prog., Peoples Community Hospital Authority, Wayne, MI '85 (PLNG)
FOX, SR. RUTH ANN, dir. soc. serv., Mercy Hospital, Wilkes-Barre, PA '82 (SOC)
FOX, SHIRLEY A., RN, dir. pat. care, St. Vincent Hospital, Green Bay, WI '85 (NURS)
FOX, SUE JANE, coor. pat. health educ., Kaiser-Permanente Medical Care Program, Denver, CO '82 (EDUC)
FOX, SUE, dir. immediate care, Loudoun Memorial Hospital, Leesburg, VA '87 (AMB)
FOX, SUSAN ANN, student, Program in Health Administration, Baruch College, New York, NY '86
FOX, THOMAS C., atty., American Nursing Home Association, Washington, DC '74 (ATTY)
FOX, THOMAS G., PhD, exec. vice-pres., University Health System of New Jersey, Princeton, NJ '79 (PLNG)
FOX, THOMAS L., dir. environ. serv., Green Hospital of Scripps Clinic, La Jolla, CA '86 (ENVIRON)
FOX, WILLIAM RUSSELL, mng. dir., Sparks Family Hospital, Sparks, NV '77
FOXWELL, LEO G., dir. health care risk mgt. serv., Hartford Insurance Group, Hartford, CT '80 (RISK)

FOXWORTHY, JERRY L., dir. risk mgt., White Memorial Medical Center, Los Angeles, CA '80 (RISK)
FOY, FREDERICK C., bd. chm., Koppers Company, Inc., Pittsburgh, PA '60 (HON)
FOY, JOYCE M., RN, dir. nrsg. serv., Pomerado Hospital, Poway, CA '83 (NURS)
FOY, LINDA, risk mgr., St. John's Episcopal Hospital, Far Rockaway, NY '82 (RISK)
FRAGALA, GUY A., dir. risk mgt. and safety assur., University of Massachusetts Medical Center, Worcester, MA '80 (RISK)
FRAHER, SHIRLEY L., vice-pres. commun. rel., St. Francis Hospital and Medical Center, Topeka, KS '81 (PR)
FRAICHE, DONNA D., atty., Slidell Memorial Hospital, Slidell, LA '79 (ATTY)
FRAIN, JANE P., dir. vol. serv., Pottstown Memorial Medical Center, Pottstown, PA '84 (VOL)
FRAKER, SUZANNE, dir. practice dev. res., American Medical Association, Chicago, IL '87 (PLNG)
FRALEY, GARY F., vice-pres., Baptist Medical Center Easley, Easley, SC '80 (RISK)
FRALEY, R. REED, exec. dir., Presbyterian Hospital, Dallas, TX '85
FRALEY, WILLIAM F., ins. consult., Robert W. Lazarus and Associates, Plano, TX '81 (RISK)
FRALIC, MARYANN F., RN, sr. vice-pres. nrsg., Robert Wood Johnson University Hospital, New Brunswick, NJ '75 (NURS)
FRALICK, DENISE R., dir. vol. serv., Children's Hospital and Medical Center, Seattle, WA '86 (VOL)
FRALIX, PATTI PENNINGTON, RN, asst. dir. and nrs. exec., Rex Hospital, Raleigh, NC '81 (NURS)
FRAM, STANLEY, dir. environ. serv., Walter O. Boswell Memorial Hospital, Sun City, AZ '79 (ENG)
FRAME, JAMES M., pres., St. Joseph's Hospital, Lowell, MA '86 (PLNG)
FRANCE, ROBERT G., adm., Alleghany Center Unit, Harmarville Rehabilitation Center, Pittsburgh, PA '84
FRANCESCHI, HAROLD J., dir. pat. adm. serv., San Antonio Community Hospital, Upland, CA '73
FRANCIS, CHARLES P., dir. plng. and mktg., Evangelical Health Systems, Oak Brook, IL '80 (PLNG)
FRANCIS, DWAINE, pres., Francis and Associates, Des Moines, IA '85
FRANCIS, FREIDA A., RN, dir. nrsg. serv., St. Elizabeth Hospital Medical Center, Lafayette, IN '81 (NURS)
FRANCIS, JAMES E., dir. pharm. and matl. mgt., McKay-Dee Hospital Center, Ogden, UT '86 (PUR)
FRANCIS, JAMES R., asst. to pres., Christian Hospitals Northeast-Northwest, St. Louis, MO '85
FRANCIS, JOHN D., adm., Ashland State General Hospital, Ashland, PA '70 (PERS)
FRANCIS, JOHN J. JR., atty., Hospital Center at Orange, Orange, NJ '85 (ATTY)
FRANCIS, JOSEPHINE, coor. risk mgt., Kings Highway Hospital Center, Brooklyn, NY '87 (RISK)
FRANCIS, JUDITH A., RN, mgr. critical care, Gerald Champion Memorial Hospital, Alamogordo, NM '86 (NURS)
FRANCIS, SYLVIA, dir. hskpg. and ldry., Shriners Hospitals for Crippled Children, Spokane, WA '87 (ENVIRON)
FRANCISCO, SHIRELY R., RN, vice-pres., Leigh Memorial Hospital, Norfolk, VA '80 (NURS)
FRANCK, ROGER D., vice-pres. performance syst., Meridian Enterprises, St. Louis, MO '79 (PLNG)(PERS)
FRANCO, ISABELLE, dir. pat. rel. and soc. serv., Westchester General Hospital, Miami, FL '74 (SOC)
FRANCO, VINCENT P., dir. pers., Freeport Memorial Hospital, Freeport, IL '86 (PERS)
FRANCOIS, BRUCE E., sr. vice-pres., Wayne General Hospital, Wayne, NJ '79 (PLNG)
FRANEY, STEPHEN GREGORY, sr. assoc., Abt Associates, Inc., Cambridge, MA '78
FRANGIPANI, GERTRUDE I., RN, adm. nrsg., Kaiser Foundation Hospital, Panorama City, CA '87 (NURS)
FRANK, BRUCE R., dir. corp. strategic plng., Sisters of Mercy Health Corporation, Farmington Hills, MI '86 (PLNG)
FRANK, CLIFFORD R., Medical Center Clinic, Pensacola, FL '84
FRANK, DAVID E., pres., Frank Management, Redondo Beach, CA '70 (FOOD)
FRANK, ELLEN K., RN, assoc. dir. nrsg., Mercy San Juan Hospital, Carmichael, CA '85 (NURS)
FRANK, ERMA, Wishek Community Hospital, Wishek, ND '86 (PUR)
FRANK, FERMINA G., RN, asst. adm., St. John Hospital, Detroit, MI '83 (NURS)
FRANK, JACK C., vice-pres., Healthmark Corporation, Pittsburgh, PA '75 (PR)
FRANK, JOANNE B., internal auditor analyst, Good Samaritan Hospital, Lexington, KY '84 (MGMT)
FRANK, LINDA A., RN, asst. dir. nrsg., Luther Hospital, Eau Claire, WI '83 (NURS)
FRANK, SALLY C., student, Elmira College, Buffalo, NY '86 (PERS)
FRANKE, DONALD S., atty., Chisago Health Services, Chisago City, MN '85 (ATTY)
FRANKEBERGER, COL. ANN P., MSC USA, off., Tripler Army Medical Center, Honolulu, HI '78 (CS)
FRANKEL, BENJAMIN, student, University of Chicago, Chicago, IL '86
FRANKEL, LINDA E., dir. pub. rel., Deaconess Hospital, Cincinnati, OH '85 (PR)
FRANKEL, LOUISE R., chief diet. serv., Veterans Administration Medical Center, Waco, TX '74 (FOOD)
FRANKEL, NANCY B., dir. music ther. and vol., Children's Hospital, New Orleans, LA '79 (VOL)
FRANKEL, ROBERT R., dir. pur., American Committee for Shaare Zedek Hospital in Jerusalem, Inc., New York, NY '74 (PUR)
FRANKEL, ROGER J., asst. adm., University of Cincinnati Medical Center, Cincinnati, OH '76
FRANKEL, SOL, dir. pur., South Nassau Communities Hospital, Oceanside, NY '78 (PUR)
FRANKENFIELD, MARSHA A., RN, vice-pres., Harrisburg Hospital, Harrisburg, PA '83 (NURS)
FRANKER, PHYLLIS, dir. vol. serv., St. Luke's Regional Medical Center, Sioux City, IA '74 (VOL)
FRANKHOUSER, SUSAN E., adm. res., Jameson Memorial Hospital, New Castle, PA '86 (PLNG)
FRANKLIN, ALENE, student, University of Michigan School of Public Health, Program in Hospital Administration, Ann Arbor, MI '85
FRANKLIN, ANNIE FAYE, mgr. emer. and amb. serv., St. Vincent Hospital and Health Center, Indianapolis, IN '87 (AMB)
FRANKLIN, DAVID A., atty., Phoenixville Hospital, Phoenixville, PA '82 (ATTY)
FRANKLIN, HELEN M., dir. nutr. and diet., Henry County Memorial Hospital, New Castle, IN '81 (FOOD)
FRANKLIN, JAMES A. JR., atty., Naples Community Hospital, Naples, FL '84 (ATTY)
FRANKLIN, JAMES P. JR., vice-pres. human res., St. Francis Hospital, Greenville, SC '79 (PERS)
FRANKLIN, JEANNE W., dir. commun. affairs, Hall-Brooke Foundation, Westport, CT '75 (PR)
FRANKLIN, JOHN III, atty., DePaul Hospital, Norfolk, VA '77 (ATTY)
FRANKLIN, KATHLEEN M., nrsg. in-service educator, Appleton Medical Center, Appleton, WI '85 (EDUC)
FRANKLIN, SUSAN T., RN, vice-pres. pat. care serv., Mercy Hospital, Muskegon, MI '84 (EDUC)(NURS)
FRANKLIN, VICKI L., RN, dir. nrsg., Lake of the Ozarks General Hospital, Osage Beach, MO '80 (NURS)
FRANKOVITCH, CARL N., atty., Weirton Medical Center, Weirton, WV '85 (ATTY)
FRANKS, JULIAN GEORGE, retirement care associates, inc, Retirement Care Associates, St. Louis, MO '69
FRANKS, LAWRENCE R., dir. pers., Lutheran Hospital of Maryland, Baltimore, MD '81 (PERS)
FRANKS, LUCINDA, rehab. adm., James M. Jackson Memorial Hospital, Miami, FL '84
FRANKS, MICHAEL A., dir. pers., Proctor Community Hospital, Peoria, IL '74 (PERS)
FRANKS, STEPHEN, vice-pres. human res., St. Paul Medical Center, Dallas, TX '82 (PERS)
FRANQUEMONT, JAMES R., sr. mgr., Ernst and Whinney, Phoenix, AZ '86 (MGMT)
FRANTONIUS, MICHAEL J., dir. facil., Highland Park Hospital, Highland Park, IL '78 (ENG)
FRANTZ, DOUGLAS J., vice-pres. mktg. and support serv., Crittenton Hospital, Rochester, MI '79 (PLNG)
FRANTZ, YVETTE D., dir. vol. serv., Grossmont District Hospital, La Mesa, CA '86 (VOL)
FRANZ, KATHY, dir. pers., Yakima Valley Memorial Hospital, Yakima, WA '77 (PERS)
FRANZ, SUSAN M., student, University of Illinois School of Public Health, Chicago, IL '85
FRANZBLAU, DAVID C., mgr., Fischer Mangold, Walnut Creek, CA '86 (PLNG)
FRANZBLAU, DAVID C., consult., Walnut Creek, CA '78
FRANZE, JUDY A., RN, med. underwriter, Empire Blue Cross and Blue Shield, New York, NY '85
FRANZEN, MARGARET M., dir. vol. serv., Fairview Southdale Hospital, Minneapolis, MN '86 (VOL)
FRAPRIE, FRANK, sr. vice-pres. oper., New Britain General Hospital, New Britain, CT '55 (LIFE)
FRAPWELL, DOROTHY J., atty., Indiana University Hospitals, Indianapolis, IN '80 (ATTY)
FRARACCIO, FELIX A., adm., R. J. Reynolds-Patrick County Hospital, Stuart, VA '68
FRASCA, CATHERINE, RN, exec. dir., South Hills Health System, Pittsburgh, PA '76 (NURS)(AMB)
FRASCA, MATTHEW V., dir. environ. serv., Nashoba Community Hospital, Ayer, MA '86 (ENVIRON)
FRASER, ARLETTE, dir. vol. serv., St. Peter Hospital, Olympia, WA '80 (VOL)
FRASER, CAROLINE M., adm. dir. lab., Reading Hospital and Medical Center, Reading, PA '82
FRASER, ELAINE H., soc. worker and coor. util., University Health Services, Amherst, MA '86 (SOC)
FRASER, JAMES S., safety off., Maine Medical Center, Portland, ME '80 (ENG)
FRASER, JOHN MARTIN, sr. vice-pres. mgt. cent., St. Luke's Episcopal Hospital, Houston, TX '79 (PLNG)
FRASER, JUDITH, mgr. health care syst. and res. analyst, Blue Cross and Blue Shield of Connecticut, North Haven, CT '86
FRASER, KAYE BERYL, dir. soc. serv., St. Joseph Hospital, Mitchell, SD '78 (SOC)
FRASER, NANCY, student, University of California at Los Angeles, School of Public Health, Program in Health Service Management, Los Angeles, CA '87 (AMB)
FRASHIER, KAREN MESS, proj. coor. commun. affairs, Charleston Area Medical Center, Charleston, WV '84 (PR)
FRASURE, JOAN M., RN, Rapid City, SD '78 (NURS)
FRAUENTHAL, BETSY J., dir. plng., Matthew Thornton Health Plan, Nashua, NH '87 (PLNG)
FRAY, GEORGE S., adm., Cleburne County Hospital, Heber Springs, AR '87
FRAY, ROBERT B. JR., dir. pers., Bon Secours Hospital, North Miami, FL '85 (PERS)
FRAYNE, KEVIN F., dir. plant oper. and maint., Wills Eye Hospital, Philadelphia, PA '85 (ENG)
FRAZER, HERMLINE, asst. dir. cent. serv., Kingsbrook Jewish Medical Center, Brooklyn, NY '86 (CS)
FRAZER, JOHN P., atty., Mease Health Care, Dunedin, FL '85 (ATTY)
FRAZIER, CATHERINE H., RN, Ponca City, OK '83 (NURS)
FRAZIER, E. KENT, asst. adm. pers., Grand View Hospital, Sellersville, PA '72 (PERS)
FRAZIER, GLORIA C., RN, assoc. adm. nrsg. serv., University of Medicine and Dentistry of New Jersey-University Hospital, Newark, NJ '86 (NURS)
FRAZIER, HELEN KAY, pat. rep., Baptist Medical Center of Oklahoma, Oklahoma City, OK '84 (PAT)
FRAZIER, HOWARD T., pur. agt., Genesee Memorial Hospital, Flint, MI '71 (PUR)
FRAZIER, JOAN, mgr. clin. risk, HCA Medical Center of Port St. Lucie, Port St. Lucie, FL '86 (RISK)
FRAZIER, KENNETH S., atty., Deaconess Medical Center, Billings, MT '83 (ATTY)
FRAZIER, RENEE SHERRY, dir. mktg. and plng., Liberty Medical Center, Baltimore, MD '82 (PLNG)
FRAZIER, RICHARD H., dir. maint., HCA Edgefield Hospital, Nashville, TN '83 (ENG)
FRAZIER, SANDRA M., dir. risk mgt., Borgess Medical Center, Kalamazoo, MI '81 (RISK)
FRAZIER, WILLIAM L., dir. plng. and oper., Cleveland Clinic Foundation, Cleveland, OH '79 (PLNG)
FREAS, MICHAEL J., dir. soc. serv., Ridgecliff Hospital, Willoughby, OH '81 (SOC)
FRECK, ROY C., dir. environ. serv., Spartanburg Regional Medical Center, Spartanburg, SC '86 (ENVIRON)
FREDERIC, DONALD J., dir. matl. mgt., Hamilton Medical Center Hospital, Lafayette, LA '82 (PUR)
FREDERICK, BRUCE JAMES, RN, asst. adm. nrsg., St. Marys Hospital of Rochester, Rochester, MN '79 (NURS)
FREDERICK, CHARLES L., dir. eng., Memorial Care System, Houston, TX '86 (ENG)
FREDERICK, DARRELL R., mgr. human res., Geisinger System Services, Danville, PA '84 (PERS)
FREDERICK, DONALD B., atty., Tioga General Hospital, Waverly, NY '70 (ATTY)
FREDERICK, LYNN M., dir. soc. serv., Medical University of South Carolina Medical Center, Charleston, SC '86 (SOC)
FREDERICK, RANDY, dir. matl. mgt., Hood General Hospital, Granbury, TX '84 (PUR)
FREDERICK, REED H., vice-pres. human res., Memorial Medical Center, Long Beach, CA '80 (PERS)
FREDERICK, RONALD A., atty. and vice-pres., Management Science Associates, Inc., Kansas City, MO '78 (ATTY)
FREDERICK, SUSAN L., RN, asst. dir. nrsg. critical care, St. Elizabeth's Hospital of Boston, Boston, MA '86 (NURS)
FREDERICKS, JOHN E., dir. pers., Cortland Memorial Hospital, Cortland, NY '80 (PERS)
FREDERICKS, RAYMOND F., vice-pres. fin. plng., Intercare Health Systems, Edison, NJ '87 (PLNG)
FREDERICKSON, SUSAN C., supv. benefits and compensation, Theda Clark Regional Medical Center, Neenah, WI '86 (PERS)
FREDERIKSEN, MARY C. A., pat. educ. instr., Kaiser Foundation Hospital, Fontana, CA '86 (EDUC)
FREDETTE, SR. RITA, pat. rep., St. Joseph Hospital, Orange, CA '77 (PAT)
FREDRICKSON, GERALD K., Berkshire Physicians and Surgeons, Pittsfield, MA '64
FREDRICKSON, SHIRLEY A., RN, clin. dir., Allen Memorial Hospital, Waterloo, IA '86 (NURS)
FREDSON, SHELLEY ANN, pat. rep., University of Iowa Hospitals and Clinics, Iowa City, IA '85 (PAT)
FREE, JAN, RN, coor. cent. proc. and distrib., Memorial Hospital, Ormond Beach, FL '85 (CS)
FREE, ROSEMARY J., RN, dir. educ. and consult. serv., Los Angeles County-University of Southern California Medical Center, Los Angeles, CA '85 (NURS)
FREE, WENDY C., dir. vol. serv., California Medical Center-Los Angeles, Los Angeles, CA '82 (VOL)
FREEDMAN, ABRAHAM, (ret.), Sacramento, CA '53 (LIFE)
FREEDMAN, ANN T., mgr., Cigna Corporation, Bloomfield, CT '79
FREEDMAN, BARRY R., dir., Mount Sinai Medical Center, New York, NY '75 (MGMT)
FREEDMAN, HEIDI A., adm. res., Tobey Hospital, Wareham, MA '86 (PLNG)
FREEDMAN, LARRY, student, Georgia State University, Institute of Health Administration, Atlanta, GA '86
FREEDMAN, LARRY, adm. asst., South Georgia Medical Center, Valdosta, GA '87 (ENG)
FREEDMAN, LEONARD, dir. matl. mgt. and adm. food serv., Boca Raton Community Hospital, Boca Raton, FL '73 (FOOD)(PUR)
FREEDMAN, LUCIA D., supv. soc. work, Veterans Administration Hospital, Hines, IL '81 (SOC)
FREEDMAN, MARK ABRAHAM, MD, (ret.), Pompano Beach, FL '46 (LIFE)
FREEDMAN, S. DAVID, MD, student, Program in Health Care Administration, Rutgers-the State University of New Jersey, New Brunswick, NJ '85
FREEDOM, GERALD A., dir. prof. placement, New Medico Head Injury System, Boston, MA '87 (PLNG)
FREEHAUF, M. GRACE, assoc. dir. soc. serv., University of Chicago Hospitals, Chicago, IL '66 (SOC)
FREEHILL, MICKEY, pur. agt., Graham Hospital, Canton, IL '84 (PUR)
FREELAND, BYRON, atty., Baptist Medical Center, Little Rock, AR '85 (ATTY)
FREEMAN-BOOTS, BETTY, dir. pers., Saint Joseph Health Center Kansas, Kansas City, MO '83 (PERS)
FREEMAN, CALLIE, mgr. mem. serv., Kaiser Foundation Health Plan, Los Angeles, CA '78 (PAT)
FREEMAN, CLEO, RN, assoc. adm. nrsg., Southeast Alabama Medical Center, Dothan, AL '80 (NURS)
FREEMAN, DEWEY E., dir. mgt. syst., Baptist Medical System, Little Rock, AR '79 (MGMT)
FREEMAN, DONALD, dir. plant oper., Huron Valley Hospital, Milford, MI '86 (ENG)
FREEMAN, DORIS B., dir. mktg. and pub. rel., Jackson-Madison County General Hospital, Jackson, TN '86 (PR)
FREEMAN, ELAINE, dir. pub. affairs, Johns Hopkins Hospital, Baltimore, MD '79 (PR)
FREEMAN, HERBERT, exec. dir., Sephardic Home for the Aged, Brooklyn, NY '58
FREEMAN, JAMES M., assoc. dir. fiscal serv., Rowan Memorial Hospital, Salisbury, NC '86

FREEMAN, JAMES R., atty., National Medical Enterprises, Tampa, FL '83 (ATTY)
FREEMAN, JANE R., sr. planner pub. health, Determination of Need, Boston, MA '86 (PLNG)
FREEMAN, JEANINE, atty., Iowa Hospital Association, Des Moines, IA '84 (ATTY)
FREEMAN, KAREN K., pat. rep., North Memorial Medical Center, Robbinsdale, MN '83 (PAT)
FREEMAN, KENNETH W., dir. matl. mgt., Virginia Mason Hospital, Seattle, WA '86 (PUR)
FREEMAN, LARRY J., adm., Jacksonville Wolfson Children's Hospital, Jacksonville, FL '78
FREEMAN, LYNNE, dir. vol., Sierra Medical Center, El Paso, TX '81 (VOL)
FREEMAN, MARY ELLEN, RN, dir. nrsg. and primary care serv., St. Luke's Hospital, Milwaukee, WI '87 (NURS)
FREEMAN, MAX L., plant eng., Republic County Hospital, Belleville, KS '85 (ENG)
FREEMAN, MEIGS D., dir. human res. dev., Catholic Medical Center, Manchester, NH '81 (EDUC)
FREEMAN, PATRICIA L., dir. soc. work, Scott County Hospital, Oneida, TN '80 (SOC)
FREEMAN, S. MARVIN, pres., Syosset Community Hospital, Syosset, NY '85
FREEMAN, STUART J., vice-pres. human res., San Antonio Community Hospital, Upland, CA '86 (PERS)
FREEMAN, THOMAS M., dir. productivity mgt., St. Vincent Charity Hospital and Health Center, Cleveland, OH '84 (MGMT)
FREEMAN, VALORIE ANN, coor. soc. serv., Salem Hospital, Salem, OR '85 (SOC)
FREES, THOMAS D., dir. biomedical eng., Naples Community Hospital, Naples, FL '84 (ENG)
FREESTON, LEIGH ANNE U., sr. consult., SunHealth Corporation, Charlotte, NC '85 (MGMT)
FREGGENS, DONALD B., asst. adm., Shadyside Hospital, Pittsburgh, PA '74 (PUR)(ENG)
FREI, GENE R., adm. eng., St. Agnes Hospital, Fond Du Lac, WI '69 (ENG)(RISK)
FREIBRUN, RICHARD B., Sms Corporation, Schaumburg, IL '67 (MGMT)
FREIBURGER, OPAL A., instr. staff educ. and prof. dev., Lutheran Hospital of Fort Wayne, Fort Wayne, IN '87 (EDUC)
FREILICH, HERBERT, MD, dir. prof. serv., New York City Health and Hospitals Corporation, New York, NY '60
FREIREICH, RICHARD E., chief eng., Coronado Hospital, Coronado, CA '83 (ENG)
FREITAS, ANTHON C., pres., Criterion Systems, Inc., San Jose, CA '84
FREIWIRTH, MARTIN, dep. exec. dir., Kingsbrook Jewish Medical Center, Brooklyn, NY '56 (LIFE)
FREMBLING, CAROL, RN, dir. nrsg., Pioneer Memorial Hospital, Prineville, OR '84 (NURS)
FRENCH, C. MICHAEL, exec. vice-pres., Fairfax Hospital Association, Springfield, VA '80
FRENCH, C. TED, atty., Venice Hospital, Venice, FL '86 (ATTY)
FRENCH, DOUGLAS A., vice-pres. gen. serv., Glens Falls Hospital, Glens Falls, NY '75 (ENG)
FRENCH, EDWARD M., vice-pres., Memorial Hospital, Belleville, IL '74 (MGMT)
FRENCH, JOHN H. JR., atty., Florida League of Hospitals, Tallahassee, FL '80 (ATTY)
FRENCH, JOHN R., dir. human res., Childrens Hospital of Los Angeles, Los Angeles, CA '86 (PERS)
FRENCH, MARLENE R., dir. vol. serv., Clara Maass Medical Center, Belleville, NJ '86 (VOL)
FRENCH, MORRIS L. V., prof. path., Indiana University-Purdue University, Indianapolis, IN '84 (ENG)
FRENCH, PATRICIA B., RN, assoc. dir. and actg. dir. nrsg., Medical University of South Carolina Medical Center, Charleston, SC '86 (NURS)
FRENCH, CAPT. PATRICIA M., MSC USAF, health res. staff off., prog. analyst, Department of Air Force Medical Service, Bolling AFB, DC '80
FRENCH, ROBERT P., vice-pres., Parkside Medical Services Corporation, Park Ridge, IL '67
FRENCH, STEPHAN D., dir. eng., Saints Mary and Elizabeth Hospital, Louisville, KY '85 (ENG)
FRENCH, SUSAN C., dir. vol. serv., Hamilton Hospital, Hamilton, NJ '85 (VOL)
FRENCH, SYLVIA E., dir. soc. serv., Providence Hospital, Sandusky, OH '80 (SOC)
FRENCHIE, RICHARD J., exec. vice-pres., Geauga Hospital, Chardon, OH '81 (PLNG)
FRENN, JOHN D., Voluntary Hospitals of America, Waltham, MA '73
FRENZEL, MARK G., chief soc. work serv., Veterans Administration Medical Center, Albany, NY '82 (SOC)
FRENZEL, SARAH, dir. franchise dev., Pregnagym, Tampa, FL '87 (PLNG)
FRERICHS, KATHRYN M., RN, asst. adm., Inter-Community Memorial Hospital, Newfane, NY '80 (NURS)
FRESHER, BRIAN L., atty., Naval Hospital, Bethesda, MD '86 (ATTY)
FRESHLEY, CAROL, student, Program in Health Services Administration, University of Colorado, Boulder, CO '87
FRETZ, AMELIA, RN, dir. soc. serv., Montgomery Hospital, Norristown, PA '85 (SOC)
FREUND, CYNTHIA M., RN, prof. nrsg., University of North Carolina, Chapel Hill, NC '83 (NURS)
FREUND, EVAN, dir. amb. care serv., Michael Reese Medical Center-Mandel Clinic, Chicago, IL '67
FREUND, JANET W., counselor and consult., Highland Park Hospital, Highland Park, IL '83 (PAT)
FREUND, JERRY E., dir. educ., Tucson Medical Center, Tucson, AZ '71 (EDUC)
FREUND, NEIL F., atty., Children's Medical Center, Dayton, OH '85 (ATTY)
FREUND, R. ADELE, dir. vol. serv., Mount Sinai Medical Center, Miami Beach, FL '69 (VOL)
FREUTHAL, RENEE S., mgt. serv. tech., AMI Presbyterian-St. Luke's Medical Center, Denver, CO '85 (MGMT)
FREVERT, ELAINE I., RN, vice-pres. nrsg., Children's Hospital National Medical Center, Washington, DC '83 (NURS)
FREVERT, MYRL D., mgr. computer oper., Boone Hospital Center, Columbia, MO '84 (ENG)
FREY, JOHN ANTHONY, dir. plng. and mktg., Pascack Valley Hospital, Westwood, NJ '74 (PLNG)
FREY, LISA L., student, Tulane University, New Orleans, LA '86
FREY, MARIE E., dir. pers. serv., DeKalb Memorial Hospital, Auburn, IN '86 (PERS)
FREY, MARY ELLEN, dir. educ., Jamestown Hospital, Jamestown, ND '80 (EDUC)
FREY, MAVIS I., adm. diet., Memorial Hospital, Colorado Springs, CO '83 (FOOD)
FREY, WILLIAM R., adm. and chief exec. off., Rehabilitation Hospital for Special Services, York, PA '85
FREYER, RICHARD, MD, chief med. staff, Royal Prince Alfred Hospital, Camperdown, Australia '78 (MGMT)
FREYMANN, JOHN G., MD, pres., National Fund for Medical Education, Farmington, CT '65
FREYSINGER, EDWARD ELGIN, asst. to pres., McPherson Community Health Center, Howell, MI '84
FRIAR, ANITA L., dir. soc. work, Sunnyview Hospital and Rehabilitation Center, Schenectady, NY '85 (SOC)
FRICK, ANNE T., dir. soc. serv., Mercy Hospital of New Orleans, New Orleans, LA '84 (SOC)
FRICK, MARY C., dir. vol. serv., Charleston Area Medical Center, Charleston, WV '84 (VOL)
FRICK, RONALD, dir. environ. serv., Mercy Community Hospital, Port Jervis, NY '86 (ENG)(ENVIRON)
FRICKE, WILMA L., dir. nrsg., Memorial Medical Center, Springfield, IL '85
FRIDKIN, DAVID, assoc. adm., St. Joseph's Hospital, Flushing, NY '71
FRIDLINGTON, JAMES PATRICK, adm., Charter Grove Hospital, Corona, CA '79
FRIE, ARTHUR, adm., United Hospital, Port Chester, NY '82
FRIED, JEFFREY M., asst. vice-pres., Lancaster General Hospital, Lancaster, PA '79
FRIED, JOHN P., dir. food serv., Four Winds Hospital, Katonah, NY '73 (FOOD)
FRIED, ROBIN BETH, asst. dir. nrsg., St. Luke's-Roosevelt Hospital Center, New York, NY '86
FRIEDE, SAMUEL A., vice-pres. oper., Allegheny General Hospital, Pittsburgh, PA '73
FRIEDERICHS, MARLYS J., RN, asst. dir. nrsg. serv., Hennepin County Medical Center, Minneapolis, MN '81 (NURS)
FRIEDERS, WAYNE R., dir. staff rel., Memorial Hospital, South Bend, IN '83 (PERS)
FRIEDEWALD, DON E. SR., adm. pur. serv., James M. Jackson Memorial Hospital, Miami, FL '80 (PUR)
FRIEDLAENDER, MARTHA, asst. dir. soc. work and coor. discharge plng., Roosevelt Hospital, New York, NY '82 (SOC)
FRIEDLAND, RICHARD, dir. health care, Inteck, Inc., Denver, CO '67 (MGMT)
FRIEDLANDER, ALICE M., dir. vol., University Hospital and Clinic, University of Nebraska, Omaha, NE '74 (VOL)
FRIEDLANDER, BEVERLY, supv. soc. work serv., St. Vincent's Hospital, Birmingham, AL '82 (SOC)
FRIEDLANDER, JOHN E., exec. vice-pres. and chief oper. off., Buffalo General Hospital, Buffalo, NY '75
FRIEDLANDER, LYNNE S., commun. spec., Straub Clinic and Hospital, Honolulu, HI '86 (PR)
FRIEDMAN, BARBARA B., dir. matl. mgt., Manhattan Eye, Ear and Throat Hospital, New York, NY '83 (PUR)
FRIEDMAN, BRUCE, dir. res. and plng., Monroe County Long Term Care Program, Inc., East Rochester, NY '82 (PLNG)
FRIEDMAN, JAMES A., pres., Prime Health Services, Rolling Meadows, IL '83
FRIEDMAN, JANET S., dir. pub. rel., Coral Springs Medical Center, Coral Springs, FL '83 (PR) (PLNG)
FRIEDMAN, JEFFREY S., exec. dir., Diagnostic Imaging Services, Metairie, LA '80 (AMB)
FRIEDMAN, MARK E., dir. human res., St. Joseph's Hospital, Elmira, NY '81 (PERS)
FRIEDMAN, MARTIN A., dir. mgt. eng., Saint Luke's Hospital, Cleveland, OH '83 (MGMT)
FRIEDMAN, MARVIN B., student, Program in Hospital Administration, Baruch College Mount Sinai School of Medicine, New York, NY '86
FRIEDMAN, ROBIN C., atty., Children's Memorial Hospital, Chicago, IL '86 (ATTY)
FRIEDMAN, SHERRILL S., RN, dir. maternal and ped. nrsg., Memorial Hospital, South Bend, IN '81 (NURS)
FRIEDMAN, STEVEN H., PhD, Morton Grove, IL '69 (MGMT)
FRIEDMAN, STEVEN M., asst. adm., Montefiore Medical Center, Bronx, NY '82
FRIEDMAN, W. ROBERT JR., Montgomery Securities, San Francisco, CA '75 (PUR)
FRIEDRICH, STEPHEN J., student, Wayland Baptist University, Plainview, TX '87
FRIEL, EILEEN, supv. commun., Horton Memorial Hospital, Middletown, NY '85 (ENG)
FRIEL, JAMES W., dir. pers., Jennie Edmundson Memorial Hospital, Council Bluffs, IA '83 (PERS)
FRIEL, MATTHEW C., asst. dir. facil. and maint., State of Rhode Island, Department of Mental Health, Retardation and Hospital, Cranston, RI '79 (ENG)
FRIELING, MORRIS J., asst. dir., University of Colorado Sciences Center, Denver, CO '86 (ENG)
FRIEND, MAGGIE, coor. promotions, Southeast Missouri Hospital, Cape Girardeau, MO '86 (PR)
FRIEND, PETER M., exec. vice-pres., Highland Park Hospital, Highland Park, IL '86 (PLNG)
FRIEND, RUSSELL G., dir. plant oper., Garrett County Memorial Hospital, Oakland, MD '86 (ENG)
FRIER, ADRIENNE M., dir. human res., Richland Memorial Hospital, Columbia, SC '83 (PERS)
FRIES, JOLIE H., student, Program in Hospital Administration, Yale University, New Haven, CT '84
FRIES, TERESANN B., RN, dir. nrsg. serv. adm., Boca Raton Community Hospital, Boca Raton, FL '79 (NURS)
FRIESE, WILLIAM B., dir. matl. mgt., St. Peters Community Hospital, St. Peters, MO '83 (PUR)
FRIESEN, GORDON ARTHUR, LLD, (ret.), Arva, Ont., Canada '48 (LIFE)
FRIESEN, KAREN J., dir. educ., Henderson Community Hospital, Henderson, NE '86 (EDUC)
FRIESEN, ROBERT J., sr. consult., Peat, Marwick, Mitchell and Company, Chicago, IL '83
FRIESEN, ROGER L., asst. dir., Methodist Hospital, St. Louis Park, MN '78 (ENG)
FRIESENHAHN, MARGARET M., prog. spec. med. facil., National Easter Seal Society, Inc., Chicago, IL '84
FRIESWICK, GAIL M., RN, adm. nrsg., University of Massachusetts Medical Center, Worcester, MA '83 (NURS)
FRIETZIE, SYLVIA, RN, dir. med. and surg. serv., Mercy Hospital of Sacramento, Sacramento, CA '86 (NURS)
FRIGON, KIMBERLI K., dir. pers., Humana Hospital -Dodge City, Dodge City, KS '86 (PERS)
FRINK, ANTOINETTE P., RN, vice-pres. pat. serv., Oakland General Hospital Osteopathic, Madison Heights, MI '81 (NURS)
FRINTZILAS, LEWIS P., Pittsburgh, PA '82 (MGMT)
FRIPP, NATHANIEL E., dir. soc. serv., Herrick Hospital and Health Center, Berkeley, CA '82 (SOC)
FRIS, MARY E., dir. vol., Albany Medical Center Hospital, Albany, NY '84 (VOL)
FRISCH, JOAN E., dir. diet., Cardinal Glennon Children Hospital, St. Louis, MO '84 (FOOD)
FRISCHE, LELAND R., sr. safety off., Samaritan Health Service, Phoenix, AZ '86 (ENG)
FRISCHKORN, CARROL M., dir. pers., Indian River Memorial Hospital, Vero Beach, FL '86 (PERS)
FRISHMAN, MELANIE E., dir. network serv., Protocol, Washington, DC '82 (PLNG)
FRISLIE, BRIAN, dir. environ. serv., Alliance Community Hospital, Alliance, OH '86 (ENVIRON)
FRISONE, MARTH J., adm. asst. mktg. and plng., Johnston Memorial Hospital, Smithfield, NC '86 (PR) (PLNG)
FRITCHIE, ROGER M., atty., Our Lady of Lake Regional Medical Center, Baton Rouge, LA '81 (ATTY)
FRITH, NEVA M., dir. commun. rel. and vol. serv., Gulf Coast Community Hospital, Biloxi, MS '83 (PR)
FRITSCH, LT. COL. ROBERT G., MSC USA, Aurora, CO '71
FRITSCHLE, MILTON D. JR., sr. vice-pres. mktg. and dev., Memorial Medical Center of Jacksonville, Jacksonville, FL '86 (PR) (PLNG)
FRITTS, AUDREY SUZANNE, mgr. soc. serv., Louis A. Weiss Memorial Hospital, Chicago, IL '86 (SOC)
FRITZ, ELI, dir. reg. sales, American Hospital Publishing, Inc., New York, NY '78
FRITZ, JOHN T., dir. matl. mgt., Metropolitan Hospital-Central Division, Philadelphia, PA '76 (PUR)
FRITZ, L. RITA, pres., Corporate Systems and Images, South Bend, IN '85
FRITZ, MARTHA A., RN, vice-pres. nrsg., Methodist Medical Center of Illinois, Peoria, IL '81 (NURS)
FRITZ, MAUREEN P., student, Wayne State University, Detroit, MI '86 (EDUC)
FRITZ, MICHAEL H., adm., Harper Hospital, Detroit, MI '69
FRITZ, R. ANTHONY, dir. soc. work, Scott and White Hospital, Temple, TX '85 (SOC)
FRIZ, DELILAH A., dir. pur., Eagleville Hospital, Eagleville, PA '86 (PUR)
FROEHLKE, VICTOR P., dir. matl., St. Mary's Hospital, Athens, GA '75 (PUR)
FROELICH, GLORIA J., dir. pers., Riverside Hospital, Wilmington, DE '85 (PERS)
FROEMKE, JOHN A., student, Program in Health Service Administration, School of Health Professions, Governors State University, Park Forest South, IL '83
FROEMMING, MARY, soc. worker, Community Memorial Hospital, Menomonee Falls, WI '86 (SOC)
FROESCHLE, CHARLES F., plant eng., Bothwell Regional Health Center, Sedalia, MO '77 (ENG)
FROHARDT, ELLEN, St. Thomas More Hospital, Canon City, CO '86 (PERS)
FROHLICH, WILLIAM H., exec. dir., Beth Abraham Hospital, Bronx, NY '68
FROLLI, DOUGLAS WILLIAM, dir. eng., St. Francis Memorial Hospital, San Francisco, CA '85 (ENG)
FROMAN, HANK, supt. maint., Clinton Regional Hospital, Clinton, OK '77 (ENG)
FROME, STEVEN J., asst. adm., Jewish Institute for Geriatric Care, New Hyde Park, NY '76 (PLNG)
FROMHOLD, JOHN ANTHONY, assoc. exec. dir., Humana Hospital -Suburban, Louisville, KY '82 (PLNG)
FROMM, LINDA S., RN, asst. exec. dir. pat. care serv., Sharon Hospital, Sharon, CT '79 (NURS)
FROMMELT, JEFFREY J., prin., Herman Smith Associates, Hinsdale, IL '65
FRONCZEK, REBECCA J., risk mgr., York Hospital, York, PA '86 (RISK)
FROSH, WENDY J., dir. mktg. and plng., St. Joseph Hospital, Nashua, NH '84 (PLNG)
FROST, JACQUELINE C., RN, consult.-women and children, Butterworth Hospital, Grand Rapids, MI '83 (NURS)
FROST, JAMES H., Houston, TX '78
FROST, LEBARON, chief emp. rel., District of Columbia General Hospital, Washington, DC '84 (PERS)
FROST, VIRGINIA L., RN, asst. dir. nrsg., Northeast Medical Center Hospital, Humble, TX '86 (NURS)
FROYD, PETER W., pres., Bronson Methodist Hospital, Kalamazoo, MI '62
FRUCHTER, DANIEL S., vice-pres. and adm., Union Hospital of the Bronx, Bronx, NY '50 (LIFE)
FRUIK, LAWRENCE ARTHUR, Tinley Park, IL '58
FRUMENTI, JEANINE MARIA, adm. nrsg., New York University Medical Center, New York, NY '87

FRUSH, DIANE H., dir. diet., St. Ann's Hospital of Columbus, Westerville, OH '81 (FOOD)
FRUTH, J. RICHARD III, partner, Hayes, Large, Suckling, Fruth and Wedge, Altoona, PA '76 (ENG)
FRY, AGNES, cent. serv. tech., St. Anthony Hospital, Michigan City, IN '86 (CS)
FRY, ARTHUR J., exec. dir., Hotel Dieu Hospital, Cornwall, Ont., Canada '79
FRY, DOROTHY L., chief diet., Saint Elizabeths Hospital, Washington, DC '68 (FOOD)
FRY, L. MARCUS JR., chief exec. off., Sierra Medical Center, El Paso, TX '77
FRY, RICHARD W., chief eng., Veterans Administration Medical Center, Washington, DC '81 (ENG)
FRY, ROBERT H., mgr. telecommun., Catherine McAuley Health Center, Ann Arbor, MI '83 (ENG)
FRY, ROBERT W., mgr. soc. serv., Bellin Memorial Hospital, Green Bay, WI '75 (SOC)
FRY, SUSAN C., RN, asst. adm. nrsg., St. Francis Hospital and Medical Center, Topeka, KS '84 (NURS)
FRY, WILLIS F., pres., Covenant Medical Center -St. Francis, Waterloo, IA '69
FRYAR, PEARL S., adm., Caribou Memorial Hospital and Nursing Home, Soda Springs, ID '81 (LIFE)
FRYE, CAL, dir. matl. mgt., Asbury Hospital, Salina, KS '85 (PUR)
FRYE, JASON WILLIAM, Pierce Goodwin Alexander, Houston, TX '69
FRYE, LINDA, pat. rep., Wythe County Community Hospital, Wytheville, VA '86 (PAT)
FRYE, ROGER W., dir. soc. serv., Florida Hospital Medical Center, Orlando, FL '86 (SOC)
FRYZEL, RONALD J., adm., Jamestown General Hospital, Jamestown, NY '71
FUCHS, JONATHAN M., exec. asst. adm. serv. and dir. med. educ., San Pedro Peninsula Hospital, San Pedro, CA '73
FUCHS, PATRICIA R., dir. trng., nutr. and health care, Continental Bit of Gold Foods, Arlington Heights, IL '82 (FOOD)
FUDAILI, AHMED ABDULLAH AL, asst. dir. eng., Hamad Medical Corporation, Qatar, Saudi Arabia '86 (ENG)
FUDER, ROBERT, supv. eng., Boys Town National Institute for Children, Omaha, NE '81 (ENG)
FUELLE, MARY ANN, dir. soc. serv., Terre Haute Regional Hospital, Terre Haute, IN '73 (SOC)
FUELLER, WILLIAM H., dir. educ., Harmarville Rehabilitation Center, Pittsburgh, PA '80 (EDUC)
FUENZALIDA, MARIA, dir. med. soc. work, Natividad Medical Center, Salinas, CA '85 (SOC)
FUERCH, JOSEPH E., chief plant oper., Marian Medical Center, Santa Maria, CA '85 (ENG)
FUGATE, DARRELL W., dir. eng., Saint Alphonsus Regional Medical Center, Boise, ID '84 (ENG)
FUGAZZI, PATRICIA K., dir. food serv., Providence Hospital, Cincinnati, OH '76 (FOOD)
FUGER, VAL E., prin., Lankton, Ziegele, Terry and Associates, Inc., Austin, TX '78
FUGLIE, SUSAN J., coor. commun. rel., Dakota Hospital, Fargo, ND '82 (PR)
FUHR, LINDA BURNEY, student, Program in Hospital and Health Care Administration, Texas Woman's University, Denton, TX '78
FUHRMAN, GERALD M., dir. risk mgt., Sch Health Care System, Houston, TX '80 (RISK)
FUHRMAN, JERRIE E., pat. rep., Baptist Memorial Hospital, Gadsden, AL '82 (PAT)
FUHRMAN, KATHERINE E., coor. educ., Saint Joseph Hospital, Fort Worth, TX '86 (EDUC)
FUHRMAN, RICHARD C., dir. pur., Missouri Hospital Purchasing Council, Jefferson City, MO '81 (PUR)
FUJIMOTO, SUSUMU, MD, prof., Kitasato University, School of Hygienic Sciences, Kitasato, Japan '82 (CS)
FUJIO, IONE T., dir. membership serv., General Medical Centers Health Plan, Orange, CA '85 (PAT)
FULBRIGHT, KATHRYN J., dir. food serv., Humana Hospital -Metropolitan, San Antonio, TX '85 (FOOD)
FULBRIGHT, SUSAN L., RN, dir. nrsg., St. Francis Hospital, Marceline, MO '84 (NURS)
FULCHER, LT. LARRY M., MSC USN, head soc. work, Naval Hospital, Camp Pendleton, CA '85 (SOC)
FULFORD, RICHARD C., sr. vice-pres., Baptist Hospital, Pensacola, FL '69 (RISK)
FULGINITI, FLORENCE S., dir. vol., Pennsylvania State University Hospital, Hershey, PA '74 (VOL)
FULGINITI, JOHN V., dir. plant oper., Mercy Catholic Medical Center, Misericordia Division, Philadelphia, PA '85 (ENG)
FULKERSON, JUDY H., dir. human res., HCA Greenview Hospital, Bowling Green, KY '83 (PERS)
FULKERSON, LARRY D., dir. food serv., St. Anthony Medical Center, Louisville, KY '80 (FOOD)
FULKERT, JILL A., dir. matl. mgt., L. W. Blake Memorial Hospital, Bradenton, FL '84 (PUR)
FULKS, KATHLEEN, mgr. matl., Lapeer General Hospital, LaPeer, MI '79 (CS)
FULL, CHRISTOPHER H., consult., Health Facility Planning Services, Toronto, Ont., Canada '87
FULL, JAMES M., med. center planner, Veterans Administration West Side Medical Center, Chicago, IL '85 (PLNG)
FULLAN, RICHARD K., dir. soc. work, Abington Memorial Hospital, Abington, PA '85 (SOC)
FULLENWIDER, EILEEN, adm. dir., Memorial Medical Center of Jacksonville, Jacksonville, FL '87 (AMB)
FULLER, ANN O'GWYNN, dir. soc. serv., Selma Medical Center, Selma, AL '85 (SOC)
FULLER, BARBARA I., RN, asst. adm. nrsg. serv., Hopkins County Memorial Hospital, Sulphur Springs, TX '77 (NURS)
FULLER, BETSEY RAY, Reading, MA '65 (PERS)
FULLER, BROOKE A., dir. commun. rel., AMI Sierra Vista Regional Medical Center, San Luis Obispo, CA '82 (PR)
FULLER, CAROLYN ANN, dir. prof. serv., Hospital of the Good Samaritan, Los Angeles, CA '77
FULLER, CATHERINE MARY, asst. dir. pat. rel., Community Memorial Hospital, Toms River, NJ '85 (PAT)
FULLER, CLIFFORD C., dir. info. syst., Midland Hospital Center, Midland, MI '82 (MGMT)
FULLER, DAVID, dir. human res., Decatur General Hospital, Decatur, AL '78 (PERS)
FULLER, DEBORAH, sr. assoc. dir. and dir. human res., New York Hospital, New York, NY '67 (PERS)
FULLER, ELIZABETH, supv. cent. serv., Imperial Point Medical Center, Fort Lauderdale, FL '82 (CS)
FULLER, COL. GARY L., chief staff, Tripler Army Medical Center, Honolulu, HI '70
FULLER, HELEN R., dir. med. soc. serv., Saginaw General Hospital, Saginaw, MI '72 (SOC)
FULLER, KIM, dir. soc. serv., Saint Joseph Health Center Kansas, Kansas City, MO '86 (SOC)
FULLER, MAURICE D. L. JR., atty., St. Luke's Hospital, San Francisco, CA '77 (ATTY)
FULLER, NILA J., dir. pat. rep., Western Reserve Systems-Southside, Youngstown, OH '83 (PAT)
FULLER, RALPH N., dir. pub. rel., Lahey Clinic Medical Center, Burlington, MA '82 (PR)
FULLER, STEPHEN DALE, dir. pur., Baptist Medical Center, Montgomery, AL '84 (PUR)
FULLER, THOMAS E., asst. adm., Marion Memorial Hospital, Marion, SC '80 (RISK)
FULLMER, BARBARA H., dir. vol. serv., Community Memorial Hospital, Toms River, NJ '79 (VOL)
FULLMER, DAVID R., atty., Cleveland Clinic Hospital, Cleveland, OH '84 (ATTY)
FULLMER, SALLY, asst. mgr. cent. serv., Little Company of Mary Hospital, Torrance, CA '86 (CS)
FULTON, ARTHUR F., dir. matl. mgt., Lawrence and Memorial Hospital, New London, CT '78 (PUR)
FULTON, BRUCE M., dist. mgr., Ace Foods, Milwaukee, WI '80 (FOOD)
FULTON, DON, dir. bldg. and grds., Audrain Medical Center, Mexico, MO '85 (ENG)
FULTON, DONAL D., supv. safety eng., Veterans Administration Midwestern Region, St. Louis, MO '78 (ENG)
FULTON, JOANNE R., dir. soc. work, Boone Hospital Center, Columbia, MO '83 (SOC)
FULTON, JOHN R., dir. soc. work, Veterans Administration, Department of Medicine and Surgery, Washington, DC '84 (SOC)
FULTON, MATTHEW S., vice-pres. prof. serv., Berkshire Medical Center, Pittsfield, MA '82 (PR) (PLNG)
FULTON, SHIRLEY V., mgr. cent. serv., Ottumwa Regional Health Center, Ottumwa, IA '83 (CS)
FULTS, PHYLLIS J., RN, chief nrsg., Veterans Administration Medical Center, Birmingham, AL '79 (NURS)
FUMAI, FRANK L., adm. med. affairs, Montgomery Hospital, Norristown, PA '83 (PLNG)
FUNDERBURK, BARBARA A., dir. pers., Mercy Hospital, Charlotte, NC '84 (EDUC)(PERS)
FUNDINGSLAND, DONALD WALLACE, pres., Waukesha Memorial Hospital, Waukesha, WI '65
FUNK, ALLEN W., student, Widener University, Chester, PA '84
FUNK, MICHAEL J., reg. adm., Southwest Community Health Services, Albuquerque, NM '76
FUNK, NATALIE, vice-pres. mktg., Saint Joseph Hospital, Denver, CO '79 (PLNG)
FUNK, PATRICIA ANN, dir. educ., Pottstown Memorial Medical Center, Pottstown, PA '80 (EDUC)
FUNK, TIMOTHY J., dir. plng., Salem Hospital, Salem, OR '80 (PLNG)
FUNSTON, LINDI L., dir. pers., AMI Medical Center of North Hollywood, North Hollywood, CA '74 (PERS)
FUOCO, STEPHEN V., asst. vice-pres. facil., Methodist Hospital of Southern California, Arcadia, CA '79 (PLNG)(ENG)
FUOTI-LIVEZEY, BEVERLY A., asst. head nrs. surg. and recovery room, Saint Joseph Hospital, Reading, PA '87 (AMB)
FUREY, JAMES R., exec. dir., Finger Lake Area Hospitals Corporation, Geneva, NY '75
FUREY, NANCY J., dir. bus. dev., St. Francis Hospital, Greenville, SC '87 (PR) (PLNG)
FUREY, RAYMOND J., atty., Winthrop-University Hospital, Mineola, NY '81 (ATTY)
FURGURSON, ANNE S., coor. qual. assur., Memorial Hospital, Danville, VA '79 (PAT)(RISK)
FURHMAN, HERBERT G., vice-pres. dev. and mktg. commun., New Milford Hospital, New Milford, CT '81 (PR)
FURLER, FRANCINE M., dir. info. syst., Oregon Health Sciences University Hospital, Portland, OR '85 (MGMT)
FURMAN, BERNARD C. JR., mgr. compensation and benefits, Shands Hospital at the University of Florida, Gainesville, FL '83 (PERS)
FURMAN, EVA K., dir. pub. rel., Pomona Valley Community Hospital, Pomona, CA '83 (PR)
FURMAN, GLENN A., dir. oper., Holy Family Hospital, Spokane, WA '85 (ENG)
FURMAN, GLENN L., chief soc. work serv., Veterans Administration Medical Center, Oklahoma City, OK '79 (SOC)
FURMAN, JOAN P., dir. plng. and mktg., Union Hospital, Union, NJ '78 (PLNG)
FURMAN, JOAN, RN, dir. nrs., St. Jude Hospital-Fullerton, Fullerton, CA '76 (NURS)
FURMANCHIK, BARBARA M., RN, asst. dir. nrsg., Allegheny General Hospital, Pittsburgh, PA '84 (NURS)
FURMANSKI, ELIZABETH A., student, University of Colorado, Denver, CO '86 (MGMT)
FURR, MARY PRICE, dir. commun. rel., Kingston Hospital, Kingston, NY '85 (PR)
FURR, PATRICIA ANN, RN, head nrs. cent. serv., Roper Hospital, Charleston, SC '79 (CS)
FURROW, STEVEN J., mgr. health educ. res., Toledo Hospital, Toledo, OH '85
FURST, EMANUEL F., PhD, dir. biomedical eng., University Medical Center, Tucson, AZ '76 (ENG)(MGMT)
FURST, MARY ANN, dir. matl. mgt., Lock Haven Hospital and Extended Care Unit, Lock Haven, PA '80 (PUR)
FURTNER, WALTER J., adm. asst., Little Company of Mary Hospital, Evergreen Park, IL '62 (PUR)
FUSCHETTI, JOHN, dir. environ. serv., Eisenhower Medical Center, Rancho Mirage, CA '86 (ENVIRON)
FUSCO, RAYMOND F., vice-pres. emp. serv., Covenant Medical Center -St. Francis, Waterloo, IA '65 (PERS)
FUSEK, PAULA A., asst. dir. nurt and food serv., Long Island College Hospital, Brooklyn, NY '85 (FOOD)
FUSELIER, LOUIS A., atty., University Hospital, Jackson, MS '71 (ATTY)
FUSON, SHARON K., dir. pers., Humana Hospital -McFarland, Lebanon, TN '80 (PERS)
FUSS, BERNARD, sr. assoc. adm., Brookdale Hospital Medical Center, Brooklyn, NY '57 (LIFE)
FUSS, RICHARD U., dir. pers., Paradise Valley Hospital, National City, CA '75 (PERS)
FUSSELLE, SAMM S., dir. pub. rel., St. Joseph Hospital, Augusta, GA '84 (PR)
FUTCH, CATHERINE J., RN, asst. dir. nrsg. and dir. satellite nrsg., Emory University Hospital, Atlanta, GA '84 (NURS)
FUTCH, JOAN R., RN, sr. vice-pres. nrsg. serv., Tallahassee Memorial Regional Medical Center, Tallahassee, FL '79 (NURS)
FUTCH, JOAN WILLIAMS, RN, asst. adm. nrsg., South Georgia Medical Center, Valdosta, GA '85 (NURS)
FUTCH, TOM, sr. vice-pres., Rehabilitation Hospital Services Corporation, Coral Springs, FL '78
FUTRELL, J. WILSON JR., asst. adm., Memorial Hospital, Danville, VA '83
FUZY, EDNA M., dir. hskpg., St. Clair Memorial Hospital, Pittsburgh, PA '86 (ENVIRON)
FUZY, PAUL J., chief exec. off., Davie, FL '86 (ENG)
FYFE, ANN, vice-pres. mktg., Mills-Peninsula Corporation, San Mateo, CA '85 (PR)
FYLLING, CARELYN P., dir. clin. prog., Curatech, Inc., Minneapolis, MN '75 (EDUC)

G

GAARDSMOE, JOHN P., adm. matl., United Hospital, Grand Forks, ND '66 (PUR)
GABBERT, CHARLES CLARK, partner, Ernst and Whinney, Los Angeles, CA '72 (MGMT)
GABE, GAYE, dir. pat. rel., Santa Monica Hospital Medical Center, Santa Monica, CA '79 (PAT)
GABEL, RONALD A., MD, chm. and prof. anes., Strong Memorial Hospital of the University of Rochester, Rochester, NY '85 (MGMT)
GABER, VERONICA, dir. corp. bus. affairs, Arcventures, Inc., Chicago, IL '86 (PLNG)
GABIS, JULIA E., atty., Hahnemann University Hospital, Philadelphia, PA '83 (ATTY)
GABLE, AMY BETH, asst. adm., Magee Rehabilitation Hospital, Philadelphia, PA '80
GABLE, JAMIE SUE, dir. vol. serv., Quakertown Community Hospital, Quakertown, PA '85 (VOL)
GABOR, FRANK RICHARD, pres., Montgomery General Hospital, Olney, MD '64
GABRIEL, DONALD E., vice-pres. amb. serv., Charlotte Memorial Hospital and Medical Center, Charlotte, NC '87 (AMB)
GABRIEL, DONNA P., sr. serv. coor., St. Joseph Mercy Hospital, Clinton, IA '77 (PR)
GABRIEL, SHARON, RN, dir. nrs., Hood Memorial Hospital, Amite, LA '81 (NURS)
GABRIELSON, ANN, RN, asst. adm., Providence Hospital, Everett, WA '81 (NURS)
GABRILSKA, DEBORAH K., coor. pers., Berlin Hospital Association, Berlin, WI '86 (PERS)
GADA, DENNIS J., dir. food serv., Carney Hospital, Boston, MA '81 (FOOD)
GADDY, BEVERLY M., RN, dir. nrsg., med. and surg., Hotel Dieu Hospital, New Orleans, LA '87 (NURS)
GADDY, RICHARD C., mgt. eng., Candler General Hospital, Savannah, GA '87 (MGMT)
GAEDDERT, THEODORE JR., dir. eng. serv., University of Cincinnati Hospital, Cincinnati, OH '79 (ENG)
GAERTNER, BEVERLY K., health care mktg. spec., Grants Sysco Food Services, Inc., Saginaw, MI '81 (FOOD)
GAETANO, ROSS A., dir. facil. eng., Scottsdale Camelback Hospital, Scottsdale, AZ '85 (ENG)
GAETZ, HENRIETTA BUTTON, (ret.), Sequim, WA '39 (LIFE)
GAFFANEY, GERALD K., atty., Lake Havasu Community Hospital, Lake Havasu City, AZ '76 (ATTY)
GAFFIN, JOHN R., pres., H. R. Associates, Miami, FL '83 (PERS)
GAFFKE, JANET K., dir. diet., Veterans Administration Medical Center, Saginaw, MI '79 (FOOD)
GAFFKE, PAUL R., sr. underwriter hosp. malpractice, Shand Morahan and Company, Inc., Evanston 4360201, IL '86 (RISK)
GAFFNEY, FLORA M., dir. soc. work, Cherokee Memorial Hospital, Gaffney, SC '82 (SOC)
GAFFNEY, HALE R., gen. mgr., American Overseas Book Company, Norwood, NJ '84
GAFFNEY, JOHN C., vice-pres. and div. dir., American Medical International, Great Plains Division, Omaha, NE '81
GAFFNEY, JOHN T., dir. matl. mgt., Roosevelt Hospital, Edison, NJ '73 (PUR)
GAFFNEY, KATHLEEN K., RN, clin. dir. med. and surg. serv., Louis A. Weiss Memorial Hospital, Chicago, IL '85 (NURS)
GAFFNEY, MARY ELLEN, dir. pat. and family counseling, Hutzel Hospital, Detroit, MI '82 (SOC)

GAFFNEY, PHILIP, dir. loss prevention, St. Francis Hospital, Miami Beach, FL '80 (RISK)
GAFFNEY, SUSANNA K., dir. matl. mgt., Carthage Area Hospital, Carthage, NY '81 (PUR)
GAGE, LARRY S., atty., National Association of Public Hospitals, Washington, DC '81 (ATTY)
GAGEN, MARY A., dir. vol., Lawrence Hospital, Bronxville, NY '79 (VOL)
GAGEN, THOMAS C., adm. support serv., Deaconess Hospital of Cleveland, Cleveland, OH '83 (ENG)
GAGLIANO, ANGELO, dir. food and nutr., Society of the New York Hospital, New York, NY '67 (FOOD)
GAGLIANO, VINCENT S., dir. food serv., Pascack Valley Hospital, Westwood, NJ '82 (FOOD)
GAGLIARDI, DONNA M., dir. diet. serv., Millville Hospital, Millville, NJ '85 (FOOD)
GAGNAIRE, ALICE D., RN, assoc. adm. pat. care serv., Flagstaff Medical Center, Flagstaff, AZ '87 (NURS)
GAGNE, ANNETTE Z., asst. dir. nrsg.-qual. assur., St. Luke's Hospital of New Bedford, New Bedford, MA '84 (RISK)
GAGNE, WILFRED A., assoc. adm., University of Tennessee Medical Center, Memphis, TN '68 (PR)
GAGNON, DAVID E., exec. dir., National Perinatal Information Center, Providence, RI '81 (PLNG)
GAGNON, FRANCES, coor. qual. assur., HCA Medical Center of Port St. Lucie, Port St. Lucie, FL '86 (RISK)
GAGNON, HENRY A., dir. pur. and matl. mgt., Burbank Hospital, Fitchburg, MA '72 (PUR)
GAGNON, MARY JO, dir. hskpg. and ldry., St. Luke's Hospital, Duluth, MN '86 (ENVIRON)
GAGNON, PAULETTE L., adm. asst. and risk mgr., Catholic Medical Center, Manchester, NH '83 (RISK)
GAGO, KENDRA A., coor. educ., Magee-Womens Hospital, Pittsburgh, PA '84 (EDUC)
GAGON, LYNNE L., RN, dir. nrsg. serv., Ashley Valley Medical Center, Vernal, UT '86 (NURS)
GAHART, BETTY L., RN, coor. educ., Queen of the Valley Hospital, Napa, CA '79 (EDUC)
GAIDA, JOHN B., corp. dir. matl. mgt., Alta Bates Hospital, Berkeley, CA '80 (PUR)
GAILBREATH, JERROLD T., mgr. health center, Group Health Plan, Troy, MI '82
GAILEY, RUTH N., dir. vol., Lakeview Hospital, Bountiful, UT '70 (VOL)
GAILUNAS, CHARLES P., dir. pers., Baltimore County General Hospital, Randallstown, MD '76 (PERS)
GAINER, CHERYL, RN, dir. nrsg. and educ., Westchester County Medical Center, Valhalla, NY '86 (NURS)
GAINES, DOROTHY B., adm. coor., Fox Chase Cancer Center, Philadelphia, PA '80 (PLNG)
GAINES, HOWARD J., mgt. eng., Baystate Health Management Services, Springfield, MA '82 (MGMT)
GAINES, KENNETH W., mgr. ldry., Howard University Hospital, Washington, DC '86 (ENVIRON)
GAINES, LISA, dir. vip advantage, Amherst Associates, Inc., Los Angeles, CA '86 (PR) (PLNG)
GALA, JEFFREY A., PhD, dir. res., Jag Clinic and Research, Palm Beach, FL '85
GALACZY, ANDRE, exec. dir., Royal Edward Chest Hospital, Montreal, Que., Canada '67 (MGMT)
GALAMBOS, COLLEEN M., dir. soc. work, Stella Maris Hospice, Baltimore, MD '86 (SOC)
GALAMBOS, J. JAMES, dir. food serv., Schumpert Medical Center, Shreveport, LA '78 (FOOD)
GALANTE, ENRICO, mgr. food serv., Jewish Hospital of Cincinnati, Cincinnati, OH '83 (FOOD)
GALANTI, JEFFREY R., student, Department of Health Care Administration, George Washington University, Washington, DC '82
GALARDI, FRANCES M., dir. soc. work, Mercy Hospital of Pittsburgh, Pittsburgh, PA '74 (SOC)
GALARNEAU, MARVIN F., dir. group pur. serv., Northeast Healthshare Corporation, Augusta, ME '82 (PUR)
GALATI, MARIANNE, dir. soc. serv., St. Luke's Hospital, Newburgh, NY '86 (SOC)
GALATZER, RUTH E., vice-pres.-dir. advertising and promotion, American Medical International, Beverly Hills, CA '85 (PLNG)
GALBRAITH, ANNETTE, mgr. pur., food serv. and nutr., Northwest Community Hospital, Arlington Heights, IL '86 (FOOD)
GALBRAITH, FAITH HABER, exec. dir., Education and Auditory Research Foundation, Baptist Hospital, Nashville, TN '84 (EDUC)
GALBRAITH, JEANNE A., RN, nrs. mgr., Rapid City Regional Hospital, Rapid City, SD '85 (NURS)
GALBRAITH, LACHLAN N., PhD, vice-pres. mktg., Empire Health Services, Spokane, WA '83 (PLNG)
GALBRAITH, PAMELA, RN, dir. nrsg.-oper., University of New Mexico Hospital, Albuquerque, NM '79 (NURS)
GALEA, ROBERT P., PhD, pres., Spectrum House, Inc., Westboro, MA '85
GALEAZZI, JOSEPH A., dir. nrsg. serv., Children's Mercy Hospital, Kansas City, MO '82 (PERS)
GALELLA, ARMANDO V., vice-pres. commun. and dev., Northern Westchester Hospital Center, Mount Kisco, NY '82 (PR)
GALENES, LT. COL. ALEXANDER A., MSC USA, cmdg off., 86th Evacuation Hospital, Fort Campbell, KY '74
GALEOTA, JAMES J., dir. adm. serv., National Hospital for Orthopaedics, Arlington, VA '83 (PUR)
GALES, HARRIET, adm. educ., William Beaumont Hospital Corporation, Royal Oak, MI '84 (EDUC)
GALES, LARRY V., vice-pres. human res., St. Joseph Hospital, Concordia, KS '86 (PERS)
GALES, LYNDA S., RN, dir. nrsg., Massillon Community Hospital, Massillon, OH '87 (NURS)
GALEY, CHARLES E., atty., Lubbock County Hospital District, Lubbock, TX '79 (ATTY)
GALICA, FRANCES L., RN, mgr. pur., Middle Tennessee Medical Center, Murfreesboro, TN '84 (PUR)
GALIMORE, DON ORELL, prin., Managed Care, Inc., Fayetteville, GA '76 (MGMT)
GALIN, DANA E., adm. asst., Hospital Association of Rhode Island, Providence, RI '83 (PERS)
GALIOTTO, LINDA, survey analyst, Joint Commission on Accreditation of Hospitals, Chicago, IL '81
GALJOUR, GAIL H., dir. soc. work, Terrebonne General Medical Center, Houma, LA '84 (SOC)
GALKIN, STUART B., student, St. Joseph's University, Cherry Hill, NJ '84
GALL, LESLIE C., dir. pub. rel., Mercy Hospital, Portland, ME '85 (PR)
GALLAGHER, ALZADA H., RN, vice-pres., St. Ann's Hospital of Columbus, Westerville, OH '77 (NURS)
GALLAGHER, ANNA, RN, North Pennsylvania Hospital, Lansdale, PA '77 (CS)
GALLAGHER, CHERYL, risk mgr., St. Agnes Medical Center, Philadelphia, PA '86 (RISK)
GALLAGHER, DEBRA L., dir. soc. work, Crouse-Irving Memorial Hospital, Syracuse, NY '85 (SOC)
GALLAGHER, DIANE M., coor. vol., Memorial Hospital at Gulfport, Gulfport, MS '86 (VOL)
GALLAGHER, DIANE, dir. risk mgt., Saratoga Community Hospital, Detroit, MI '85 (RISK)
GALLAGHER, ELLEN I., student, Temple University, Philadelphia, PA '86
GALLAGHER, ELLEN M., consult., Coopers and Lybrand, San Francisco, CA '84 (PLNG)
GALLAGHER, JACK P., mgr. distrib., Saint Vincent Hospital, Billings, MT '83 (PUR)
GALLAGHER, JAMES E. JR., atty., Holy Redeemer Hospital and Medical Center, Meadowbrook, PA '74 (ATTY)
GALLAGHER, JENNIFER B., prin., Health Initiatives Corporation, Providence, RI '81 (PLNG)
GALLAGHER, JOE C., dir. plant oper., St. Anthony Hospital, Oklahoma City, OK '66 (ENG)
GALLAGHER, JOSEPH F., atty., Mercy Hospital, Wilkes-Barre, PA '77 (ATTY)
GALLAGHER, JOSEPH J., dir. educ. and trng., Community Hospital of Lancaster, Lancaster, PA '86 (EDUC)
GALLAGHER, LEO A., asst. vice-pres. emp. rel., Germantown Hospital and Medical Center, Philadelphia, PA '68 (PERS)
GALLAGHER, MARY KAY, dir. pub. rel., Humana Hospital -South Broward, Hollywood, FL '84 (PR)
GALLAGHER, MICHAEL J., vice-pres. health serv., Swedish American Corporation, Rockford, IL '83 (PLNG)
GALLAGHER, PATRICK E., pres., Service Direction, Inc., Minneapolis, MN '69 (FOOD)
GALLAGHER, PETER F., vice-pres. fin. off., Scioto Valley Health Foundation, Portsmouth, OH '85
GALLAGHER, RICHARD S., dir. food and nutr., Institute of Living, Hartford, CT '85 (FOOD)
GALLAGHER, SALLY, asst. adm., City of Hope National Medical Center, Duarte, CA '87 (AMB)
GALLAGHER, THOMAS M., pres., Central Medical Center and Hospital, Pittsburgh, PA '66 (MGMT)
GALLAGHER, WILLIAM T., vice-pres. prof. serv., Providence Hospital, Sandusky, OH '78 (PLNG)
GALLANT, BARBARA J., RN, dir. nrsg., Community Memorial Hospital, Menomonee Falls, WI '82 (NURS)
GALLANT, JOYCE A., dir. vol. serv., John Randolph Hospital, Hopewell, VA '80 (VOL)
GALLAY, LESLIE S., coor. plng. and mktg. info. serv., University of Michigan Hospitals, Ann Arbor, MI '87 (PLNG)
GALLAY, PAMELA M., dir. soc. work, Holmes Regional Medical Center, Melbourne, FL '82 (SOC)
GALLE, LILLIAN F., dir. soc. serv., Axtell Christian Hospital, Newton, KS '82 (SOC)
GALLE, LORRAINE E., psych. soc. worker and consult., Halstead Hospital, Halstead, KS '82 (SOC)
GALLEGOS, LYNN M., consult., Vadnais Heights, MN '85
GALLER, MINNIE, coor. sup., proc. and distrib., St. Joseph Hospital and Health Center, Lorain, OH '79 (CS)
GALLETLY, C. JEANNE, dir. diet., West Seattle Community Hospital, Seattle, WA '78 (FOOD)
GALLI, STEVEN R., adm. planner, Memorial Medical Center, Springfield, IL '84 (PLNG)
GALLICHOTTE, URSULA A., dir. pers., Valley Children's Hospital, Fresno, CA '85 (PERS)
GALLIGAN, THOMAS F., dir. eng. and maint., St. Luke's Hospital of New Bedford, New Bedford, MA '68 (ENG)
GALLIGHER, LARRY W., dir. dev. and mktg., Dakota Midland Hospital, Aberdeen, SD '86 (PR)
GALLIMORE, LYNNE R., mgr. benefits and compensation, Wilson Memorial Hospital, Wilson, NC '84 (PERS)
GALLIN, VIRGINIA M., adm. asst. to pres., Northern Westchester Hospital Center, Mount Kisco, NY '76 (PAT)(RISK)
GALLO, DORIS M., dir. pat. rel., Columbus Hospital, Newark, NJ '85 (PAT)
GALLO, GARY G., dir. cent. sup., Conemaugh Valley Memorial Hospital, Johnstown, PA '80 (CS)
GALLO, SIMEO J., atty., St. Clare's Hospital of Schenectady, Schenectady, NY '73 (ATTY)
GALLOGLY, LINDA C., RN, vice-pres. nrsg., Mercy Hospital, Columbus, OH '80 (NURS)
GALLOWAY, ALVIN C., dir. pers., Bruce Hospital, Florence, SC '81 (PERS)
GALLOWAY, CAROLYN L., mgr. sterilization, Winston Salem Dental Care, Winston Salem, NC '80 (CS)
GALLOWAY, JOHN M., (ret.), Columbus, GA '53 (LIFE)
GALLOWAY, MARGARET A., RN, dir. nrsg., Merle West Medical Center, Klamath Falls, OR '83 (NURS)
GALLOWAY, ROBERT C., atty., Memorial Hospital at Gulfport, Gulfport, MS '74 (ATTY)
GALLOWAY, RONALD E., dir. maint. eng., Riverside Hospital, Newport News, VA '81 (ENG)
GALTNEY, WILLIAM F. JR., Healthcare Insurance Service, Inc., Houston, TX '80 (RISK)
GALUP-TUMOLO, KAREN M., mgr. emp., Episcopal Hospital, Philadelphia, PA '86
GALVAGNI, WILLIAM, vice-pres. plng. and mktg., NKC, Inc., Louisville, KY '79 (PLNG)
GALVIN, JOSEPH MICHAEL, pres., Memorial Hospital of Salem County, Salem, NJ '70 (PLNG)
GALVIN, MARY KAY, dir. pat. rep., Mount Carmel Mercy Hospital, Detroit, MI '79 (PAT)
GALVIN, THOMAS M., dir. eng. and maint., Gottlieb Memorial Hospital, Melrose Park, IL '81 (ENG)
GALYON, BETTY PAXTON, hostess, Fort Sanders Regional Medical Center, Knoxville, TN '85 (PAT)
GAMBAL, SERGIUS B., exec. vice-pres., Deborah Heart and Lung Center, Browns Mills, NJ '65
GAMBATESE, ANTHONY J., vice-pres. info. serv., St. Vincent Charity Hospital, Cleveland, OH '86
GAMBERG, DIANE L., instr. nrsg. educ., Good Samaritan Hospital, San Jose, CA '84 (EDUC)
GAMBLE, STEPHEN W., pres., Hospital Council of Southern California, Los Angeles, CA '72
GAMBLE, WILLIAM T., atty., Holston Valley Hospital and Medical Center, Kingsport, TN '82 (ATTY)
GAMBOA, SYLVIA R., coor. risk mgt. and pat. liaison, La Grange Memorial Hospital, La Grange, IL '86 (RISK)
GAMBONE, JOSEPH L., dir. capital design, New York City Health and Hospitals Corporation, New York, NY '80 (ENG)
GAMBUCCI, PAUL, asst. adm. oper., Childrens Hospital of Los Angeles, Los Angeles, CA '68 (ENG)
GAMBUTI, GARY, pres., St. Luke's-Roosevelt Hospital Center, New York, NY '60
GAMMON, SARAH E., instr., Mount San Antonio College, Walnut, CA '87 (EDUC)
GAMMONS, BEATRICE, supv. cent. serv., Orangeburg-Calhoun Regional Hospital, Orangeburg, SC '78 (CS)
GANDEE, FAYE E., pat. rep., Charleston Area Medical Center, Charleston, WV '82 (PAT)
GANDY, DOROTHY A., asst. dir. commun. and pub. affairs, Griffin Hospital, Derby, CT '84 (PR)
GANDY, JETTA O., dir. pers., Bethany General Hospital, Bethany, OK '86 (PERS)
GANDY, M. P. JR., asst. exec. dir. external affairs, East Jefferson General Hospital, Metairie, LA '85 (PLNG)
GANELES, PAUL MORTON, bd. mem., Provider Reimbursement Review Board, Health Care Finance Administration, Dept. of HHS, Baltimore, MD '83
GANLEY, RICHARD J., dir. plant serv., San Francisco General Hospital Medical Center, San Francisco, CA '87 (ENG)
GANN, RONNY D., dir. plant oper., Children's Hospital, New Orleans, LA '82 (ENG)
GANN, ROSALIE P., dir. soc. work, Mount Sinai Hospital, Hartford, CT '82 (SOC)
GANNON, BELDON, asst. adm., Ramapo Manor Nursing Center, Suffern, NY '86 (ENVIRON)
GANNON, KATHE E., asst. dir. human res., Mercy Hospital, Iowa City, IA '86 (PERS)
GANNON, REBECCA E., dir. educ., St. Luke's Hospital, Davenport, IA '84 (EDUC)
GANNON, THOMAS J., Phoenix, AZ '80
GANNON, WILLIAM E. JR., MD, student, Department of Health Care Administration, George Washington University, Washington, DC '86 (PLNG)
GANOE, DAVID W., chief eng., Veterans Administration Medical Center, Long Beach, CA '68 (ENG)
GANOFSKY, MARY ANN, chief ped. soc. worker and unit mgr., University Hospitals of Cleveland, Cleveland, OH '85 (SOC)
GANS, MARCIA P., dir. soc. serv., Rogue Valley Medical Center, Medford, OR '81 (SOC)
GANSERT, MICHAEL R., asst. exec. dir., Fayette Memorial Hospital, Connersville, IN '83 (PERS)(PUR)
GANT, LISA J., dir. pub. rel., South Georgia Medical Center, Valdosta, GA '86 (PR)
GANTER, MARTIN J., dir. pur. matl. mgt., Yale-New Haven Hospital, New Haven, CT '86 (PUR)
GANTI, ANDREW R., vice-pres., Ohio Hospital Management Services, Worthington, OH '71 (MGMT)
GANTT, DIANE, RN, supv. matl. mgt., Grady Memorial Hospital, Chickasha, OK '80 (CS)
GANUNG, KEN W., instr. clin. educ., Good Samaritan Hospital, Downers Grove, IL '85 (EDUC)
GARABEDIAN, CAROLE F., RN, dir. nrsg., Riverside General Hospital, Secaucus, NJ '86 (NURS)
GARB, KAREN R., dir. mktg. and sales, Woodview Regional Hospital, Pineville, LA '86 (PR)
GARBELMAN, HENRY A., chief eng. serv., Veterans Administration Medical Center, Hampton, VA '72 (ENG)
GARBER, DANN D., dir. plant oper., Evergreen Hospital Medical Center, Kirkland, WA '87 (ENG)
GARBER, GREGORY J., Lutheran Hospitals and Home Society, Fargo, ND '78
GARBER, JONATHAN A., asst. adm., Charter Pacific Hospital, Torrance, CA '82
GARBER, SHELDON, vice-pres. philanthropy and commun., Rush-Presbyterian-St. Luke's Medical Center, Chicago, IL '65 (PR)
GARBOWICZ, STEVEN C., atty., Eagle River Memorial Hospital, Eagle River, WI '85 (ATTY)
GARCIA, GLORIA SARITA, dir. soc. work serv., Southwest General Hospital, San Antonio, TX '83 (SOC)
GARCIA, HILDA, dir. environ. serv., Bon Secours Hospital, North Miami, FL '86 (ENVIRON)
GARCIA, JULIA, dir. food serv., Community Hospital of Western Suffolk, Smithtown, NY '81 (FOOD)
GARCIA, JULIAN, dir. eng. and maint., Southwest Community Health Services, Albuquerque, NM '85 (ENG)
GARCIA, LAWRENCE B., atty., Catholic Healthcare West, Sacramento, CA '84 (ATTY)
GARCIA, LEYDA E., Norwalk, CT '86 (PLNG)
GARCIA, MARIA M., med. soc. worker, Pioneers Memorial Hospital, Brawley, CA '86 (SOC)
GARCIA, MITCH M., dir. soc. serv., Memorial Hospitals Association, Modesto, CA '81 (SOC)
GARCIA, RITA K., dir. diet. serv., Wheeler Hospital, Gilroy, CA '85 (FOOD)

GARCIA, ROBERT A., adm. amb. serv., Presbyterian Hlthcare Services, Albuquerque, NM '87 (AMB)
GARCIA, SANDRA V., adm. res., Bethany Hospital, Chicago, IL '84
GARCIA, VICTORIA, dir. sterile proc., Long Island College Hospital, Brooklyn, NY '86 (CS)
GARCZEWSKI, EDWARD, dir. matl. mgt., St. Vincent's Medical Center, Bridgeport, CT '79 (CS)(PUR)
GARDELLA, JOHN M., assoc. adm., Memorial Hospital, Hollywood, FL '81
GARDELLA, MARIA, dir. pat. rep., Memorial Hospital for Cancer and Allied Diseases, New York, NY '73 (PAT)
GARDENIER, MARIE, consult., Coopers and Lybrand, Philadelphia, PA '84
GARDIAN, TERESA, dir. soc. work serv., St. Luke's-Roosevelt Hospital Center, New York, NY '80 (SOC)
GARDNER, AMY J., risk mgr., Divine Providence Hospital, Williamsport, PA '85 (RISK)
GARDNER, BETTE, RN, dir. nrsg., Kings Highway Hospital Center, Brooklyn, NY '77 (NURS)
GARDNER, BILL, dir. environ. serv., Parkland Medical Center, Derry, NH '86 (ENVIRON)
GARDNER, CARL A., pres., C. A. Gardner and Company, Brentwood, TN '82
GARDNER, DAVID A., dir. prod. mgt., St. Luke's Medical Center, Phoenix, AZ '83 (MGMT)
GARDNER, DONALD J., dir. pers., St. Anthony's Memorial Hospital, Effingham, IL '82 (PERS)
GARDNER, ELIZABETH D., dir. vol. serv., Swedish Hospital Medical Center, Seattle, WA '84 (VOL)
GARDNER, GEORGIANA JANE, dir. educ., Port Huron Hospital, Port Huron, MI '82 (EDUC)
GARDNER, J. DONLEY, adm. dir., Texas Emergency Medicine Physicians, Arlington, TX '63
GARDNER, JERRY W., dir. matl. serv., St. Charles Medical Center, Bend, OR '74 (PUR)
GARDNER, JOANNE G., dir. soc. serv., Central Washington Hospital, Wenatchee, WA '82 (SOC)
GARDNER, JOHN R., dir. plng., Alliance Health System, Norfolk, VA '81 (PLNG)
GARDNER, LEVI THOMAS III, risk mgt. consult., Blue Cross and Blue Shield of Michigan, Detroit, MI '73 (RISK)
GARDNER, MARILYN, dir. vol. serv., Saint Joseph Hospital, Mishawaka, IN '78 (VOL)
GARDNER, MARY J., coor. educ., South Haven Community Hospital, South Haven, MI '86 (EDUC)
GARDNER, MICHAEL W., dir. plant oper., St. Anthony's Memorial Hospital, Effingham, IL '84 (ENG)
GARDNER, PEGGY C., PhD, dir. educ., St. Francis Regional Medical Center, Wichita, KS '81 (EDUC)
GARDNER, RAELENE M., dir. diet., Henrietta D. Goodall Hospital, Sanford, ME '85 (FOOD)
GARDNER, RICHARD L., mgr. educ. serv., Saint Alphonsus Regional Medical Center, Boise, ID '87 (EDUC)
GARDNER, ROBERT E., dir. maint., Dakota Midland Hospital, Aberdeen, SD '79 (ENG)
GARDNER, RUSSELL H., atty., Lutheran Hospital of Maryland, Baltimore, MD '77 (ATTY)
GARDNER, SARAH C., dir. soc. serv., Lewis-Gale Hospital, Salem, VA '74 (SOC)
GARDNER, STEPHEN B., dir. mktg. and pub. rel., St. Mary's Hill Hospital, Milwaukee, WI '76 (PR)
GARDNER, STEVE F., vice-pres. mktg., St. Vincent Hospital and Health Care Center, Indianapolis, IN '85 (PR) (PLNG)
GARDNER, THOMAS W., mgr. pur., Kent County Memorial Hospital, Warwick, RI '82 (PUR)
GARDNER, THOMAS, dir. environ., Brunswick Hospital, Supply, NC '86 (ENVIRON)
GARDNER, TONY, dir. environ. serv., King's Daughters Memorial Hospital, Frankfort, KY '82 (ENG)
GARDNER, VINCENT F., res. eng., Massachusetts General Hospital, Boston, MA '53 (ENG)(LIFE)
GARDNER, WANDA R., RN, dir. acute care serv., West Virginia University Hospital, Morgantown, WV '85 (NURS)
GARDNER, WILMA M., dir. pub. rel., Wilkes-Barre General Hospital, Wilkes-Barre, PA '82 (PR)
GARDON, KATHLEEN M., asst. chm. surg. nrsg., Wilford Hall U. S. Air Force Medical Center, Lackland AFB, TX '82 (NURS)
GARDSTROM, KAREN L., atty., Catherine McAuley Health Center, Ann Arbor, MI '85 (ATTY)
GARFIELD, CHRISTINE H., pub. rel. off., Nantucket Cottage Hospital, Nantucket, MA '86 (PR)
GARFINKEL, NANCY KRAMER, dir. soc. serv., Gundry Hospital, Baltimore, MD '86 (SOC)
GARFINKEL, STEPHEN M., partner, Laventhol and Horwath, Providence, RI '75
GARFUNKEL, GEORGE M., atty., Hospital for Joint Diseases and Medical Center, New York, NY '73 (ATTY)
GARGARELLA, GEORGE A., dir. mgt. info. serv., Ottawa Civic Hospital, Ottawa, Ont., Canada '84 (MGMT)
GARICH, BOB, asst. dir. maint., security and biomedical, St. Joseph Regional Medical Center -Oklahoma, Ponca City, OK '82 (ENG)
GARIKES, ARTHUR GEORGE, pres., Garikes, Wilson, Atkinson, Inc., Birmingham, AL '66 (PLNG)
GARIKES, CARLA, dir. human res., Lakeshore Hospital, Birmingham, AL '84 (PERS)
GARITY, LORRAINE GWYN, student, George State University, Institute of Health Administration, Atlanta, GA '86
GARITY, SANDRA L., RN, asst. adm. pat. care serv., Holy Cross Jordan Valley Hospital, West Jordan, UT '86 (NURS)
GARLETTS, ANTIALEE M., RN, dir. nrsg., Fairmont General Hospital, Fairmont, WV '69 (NURS)
GARLEY, SR. LOUISE, dir. pub. rel., Benedictine Hospital, Kingston, NY '86 (PR)
GARLICK, DAVID J., dir. phys. plant, Palos Community Hospital, Palos Heights, IL '80 (ENG)
GARLING, CHARLES O., dir. pur., St. Joseph Medical Center, Joliet, IL '77 (PUR)
GARLOCH, ROBERT, dir. plant oper., Arden Hill Hospital, Goshen, NY '81 (ENG)
GARLOCK, STEVEN J., vice-pres., Riverside Methodist Hospitals, Columbus, OH '82 (PLNG)
GARMAN, GILL M., atty., St. Elizabeth Hospital, Danville, IL '86 (ATTY)
GARMAN, JUDITH G., RN, vice-pres. pat. serv., Community General Hospital, Reading, PA '80 (NURS)
GARNER, BERGLIOT J., Central Point, OR '51 (LIFE)
GARNER, H. DOUGLAS, RN, asst. adm. nrsg. serv., Providence Hospital, Anchorage, AK '82 (NURS)
GARNER, JAC B., dir. pers., Methodist Hospital, Madison, WI '86 (PERS)
GARNER, JOY DIANNE, dir. med. soc. work, Cedars-Sinai Medical Center, Los Angeles, CA '73 (SOC)
GARNER, JUDY F., RN, asst. adm., Presbyterian Hospital, Albuquerque, NM '86 (NURS)
GARNER, KACKY, pat. rep., Missouri Delta Medical Center, Sikeston, MO '82 (PAT)
GARNER, LINDA, RN, asst. adm. and dir. nrsg. serv., Kennewick General Hospital, Kennewick, WA '80 (NURS)(RISK)
GARNER, MARIE, RN, asst. dir. nrsg., Ochsner Foundation Hospital, New Orleans, LA '85 (NURS)
GARNER, RICHARD C., pres., Rcg and Associates, Inc., Tucker, GA '86 (ENG)
GARNETT, JERKER L., med. claims investigator, Letterman Army Medical Center, San Francisco, CA '85 (RISK)
GAROFANO, MARY E., dir. pat. rel., Berkshire Medical Center, Pittsfield, MA '85 (PAT)
GAROFANO, SULLY, dir. soc. serv., Berkshire Medical Center, Pittsfield, MA '71 (SOC)
GARRA, DOROTHY E., asst. vol. serv., Massillon Community Hospital, Massillon, OH '86 (VOL)
GARRAS, JANE L., corp. dir. plng., Mercy Hospital Medical Center, Des Moines, IA '83 (PLNG)(AMB)
GARRELL, MARCIA E., strategic planner, Hospital of the University of Pennsylvania, Philadelphia, PA '84 (PLNG)
GARRETT, DALE M., risk mgr., Nashville Memorial Hospital, Madison, TN '80 (RISK)
GARRETT, DARLENE, RN, dir. nrsg., Caylor-Nickel Hospital, Bluffton, IN '86 (NURS)
GARRETT, DELCINA A., student, University of Il, School of Public Health, Chicago, IL '82
GARRETT, DONALD J., dir. pur., Kenmore Mercy Hospital, Kenmore, NY '69 (PUR)
GARRETT, ELEANOR H., dir. educ., Virginia Baptist Hospital, Lynchburg, VA '83 (EDUC)
GARRETT, FRANKLIN G., dir. human res., Green Hospital of Scripps Clinic, La Jolla, CA '73 (PERS)
GARRETT, JAMES H., asst. dir., All Saints Episcopal Hospital of Fort Worth, Fort Worth, TX '72 (EDUC)
GARRETT, JAMES L., Ocala, FL '82 (PR)
GARRETT, JOHN L., assoc. dir. off. of univ phys., University of Florida, Gainesville, FL '58
GARRETT, L. LOANNE, RN, dir. specialty serv., Independence Regional Health Center, Independence, MO '86 (NURS)
GARRETT, MICHAEL S., dir. mgt. eng., Washoe Medical Center, Reno, NV '78 (MGMT)
GARRETT, ROBERT, vice-pres., Meadowlands Hospital Medical Center, Secaucus, NJ '85
GARRETT, ROGER D., vice-pres. plng. and mktg., Mercy Hospital, Iowa City, IA '84 (PLNG)
GARRETT, SHARON DENISE, chief oper. off., International Medical Diagnostics Ltd., Encino, CA '75 (MGMT)
GARRETT, TERRY GLEN SR., biomedical equip. tech., Valley View Regional Hospital, Ada, OK '80 (ENG)
GARRETT, VICKIE L., RN, dir. nrsg., Riverside Community Memorial Hospital, Waupaca, WI '85 (NURS)
GARRETT, WILLIAM C. JR., adm., Franklin Memorial Hospital, Rocky Mount, VA '77
GARRETT, WILLIAM W., chief soc. work serv., Veterans Administration Medical Center, Mountain Home, TN '75 (SOC)
GARRIGAN, MICHAEL EUGENE, exec. dir., St. Eugene Community Hospital, Dillon, SC '74
GARRIGAN, SR. PATRICIA, adm., St. Francis Hospital, Columbus, GA '83 (PLNG)
GARRIOTT, MICHAEL H., asst. to chm., First Hospital Corporation, Norfolk, VA '84
GARRIS, JARVIS M., chief eng., Wayne Memorial Hospital, Goldsboro, NC '77 (ENG)
GARRIS, MAC, mgr. clin. eng., Suburban Hospital, Bethesda, MD '86 (ENG)
GARRISON, CORENNE A., dir. dev., AMI Valley Medical Center, El Cajon, CA '86 (PR)
GARRISON, JAMES E., atty., St. Joseph Medical Center, Joliet, IL '74 (ATTY)
GARRISON, JUDITH, dir. soc. serv., Flower Memorial Hospital, Sylvania, OH '85 (SOC)
GARRISON, KACEE C., dir. pers., Lincoln General Hospital, Ruston, LA '86 (PERS)
GARRISON, LOREN, chief eng., St. Ansgar Hospital, Moorhead, MN '80 (ENG)
GARRISON, MARTHA A., mgr. food serv. oper., Morton F. Plant Hospital, Clearwater, FL '85 (FOOD)
GARRISON, MYRTLE, pur. agt. and mgr. matl., Stroud Municipal Hospital, Stroud, OK '73 (PUR)
GARRISON, PAMELA J., sr. consult. and mgr., First Consulting Group, Long Beach, CA '83 (MGMT)
GARRISON, PETER, dir. automated info. syst., St. John's Hospital, Springfield, IL '78
GARRISON, RICHARD, dir., West Jersey Health System, Marlton, NJ '87 (AMB)
GARRISON, SHIRLEY COLE, dir. pat. rel., Alexian Brothers Medical Center, Elk Grove Village, IL '75 (PAT)
GARRITY, CARIE RUTH, dir. rel., pat. and family serv., University of Michigan Hospitals, Ann Arbor, MI '83 (PR) (PLNG)
GARRITY, FREDERICK J., asst. dir. soc. serv., Rhode Island Hospital, Providence, RI '80 (SOC)
GARROW, WILLIAM C., mgr., Shotz, Miller and Glusman, Philadelphia, PA '77
GARSIDE, PAMELA M., prin., The Newhealth Group, New York, NY '80 (PLNG)
GARSKE, BETTE L., dir. emp. serv., St. Ansgar Hospital, Moorhead, MN '85 (PERS)
GARSO, WILLIAM S., dir. pur., Maui Memorial Hospital, Wailuku, HI '84 (PUR)
GARSON, GERTRUDE, dir. qual. assur. and risk mgt., St. Mary's Hospital, Saginaw, MI '85 (RISK)
GARSTECKI, KATHLEEN R., student, Program in Hospital and Health Service Management, Kellogg Graduate School of Management, Northwestern University, Evanston, IL '83
GARSZCZYNSKI, SUZANNE M., PhD, dir. adm. serv., Palmerton Hospital, Palmerton, PA '86
GARTHE, ELIZABETH A., sr. consult., Arthur Andersen and Company, Baltimore, MD '84 (PLNG)
GARTLAND, MADELYN J., dir. pub. rel. and dev., Wills Eye Hospital, Philadelphia, PA '79 (PR)
GARTLAND, MICHAEL G., atty., St. Francis Hospital, Poughkeepsie, NY '81 (ATTY)
GARTON, CECILIA C., assoc. dir. soc. work, Timberlawn Psychiatric Hospital, Dallas, TX '83 (SOC)
GARVER, F. ELAINE, pat. rep., Middletown Regional Hospital, Middletown, OH '85 (PAT)
GARVER, KENNETH L. JR., dir. plng., Jameson Memorial Hospital, New Castle, PA '85 (PLNG)
GARVER, PAUL DUANE, asst. adm. nrsg. serv., St. Mary's Hospital, Decatur, IL '83 (NURS)
GARVEY, BONITA M., coor. pat. rel., Sarasota Memorial Hospital, Sarasota, FL '87 (PAT)
GARVEY, CYRIL T., atty., Sharon General Hospital, Sharon, PA '68 (ATTY)
GARVEY, SR. FRANCIS MARIE, exec. dir. and treas., Saint Francis Hospital and Medical Center, Hartford, CT '63
GARVEY, JAMES M., Hamden, CT '84 (PR)
GARVEY, JAMES M., reg. dir. strategic plng., Sisters of Mercy Health Corporation, West Des Moines, IA '86 (PLNG)
GARVEY, RUTH L., dir. soc. work, Saint Michael's Medical Center, Newark, NJ '84 (SOC)
GARVIN, F. JEANNE, RN, asst. adm. pat. serv., Muscatine General Hospital, Muscatine, IA '80 (NURS)
GARVIN, IRENE T., dir. vol. serv., Holy Redeemer Hospital and Medical Center, Meadowbrook, PA '83 (VOL)
GARVIN, KAREN M., dir. vol. serv., Covenant Medical Center-Schoitz, Waterloo, IA '82 (VOL)
GARVIN, MICHAEL, safety and hazard control adm., University of Wisconsin Hospital and Clinics, Madison, WI '86 (ENG)
GARVIN, NORMA, RN, dir. vol. serv., Nashoba Community Hospital, Ayer, MA '84 (VOL)
GARVIN, SARAH C., sr. vice-pres. corp. dev., Healthsouth Rehabilitation Corporation, Birmingham, AL '81 (PLNG)
GARVIN, VAIL P., exec. dir., Warminster General Hospital, Warminster, PA '85
GARY, BRYAN DAVID, student, Program in Health Systems and Hospital Administration, School of Public Health and Tropical Medicine, Tulane University, New Orleans, LA '84
GARY, RON, dist. mgr., Shamrock Food Service, Glendale Heights, IL '80 (FOOD)
GARZA, ROY C., partner, Phelps, Garza and Bomberger, San Antonio, TX '79
GARZARELLI, JOAN M., RN, assoc. dir. nrsg., Monsour Medical Center, Jeannette, PA '86 (NURS)
GARZINO, FRED R., consult., Health Decisions, Chicago, IL '82 (PLNG)
GARZIO, CATHERINE E., dir. plng., St. Mary's Hospital and Medical Center, San Francisco, CA '80 (PLNG)
GARZON, MARGARET J., RN, dir. nrsg., Maimonides Medical Center, Brooklyn, NY '83 (NURS)
GASCHEN, MONROE LAWRENCE JR., spec. asst. to dir., Veterans Administration Medical Center, Memphis, TN '74
GASIEWICZ, STANLEY F., asst. adm., Mercy Hospital, Buffalo, NY '84 (PLNG)
GASKEL, MICHELLE T., dir. vol. serv., St. Peter's Medical Center, New Brunswick, NJ '85 (VOL)
GASKER, MAX, dir. plant oper., Levindale Hebrew Geriatric Center, Baltimore, MD '86 (ENG)
GASKILL, IDA P., dir. nrsg. school, Jefferson Regional Medical Center, Pine Bluff, AR '84
GASPAR, KYLE M., corp. dir., Ancilla Systems, Inc., Elk Grove Village, IL '82 (MGMT)
GASPARI, RICHARD V., dir. admissions, Merle West Medical Center, Klamath Falls, OR '85 (PAT)
GASPARICH, CHRIS G., atty., Mount Zion Hospital and Medical Center, San Francisco, CA '75 (ATTY)
GASS, JOHN R. JR., pres., Englewood Community Hospital, Englewood, FL '51 (LIFE)
GASSMAN, DAVID F., Chicago, IL '86 (MGMT)
GASSMANN, RICHARD C., dir. pers., Mount Carmel Medical Center, Columbus, OH '84 (PERS)
GASTELUM, CHARLENE, pat. rep., San Ysidro Health Center, San Ysidro, CA '86 (PAT)
GASTON, CHERYL A., dir. trng. and educ., South Georgia Medical Center, Valdosta, GA '80 (EDUC)
GASTON, CLARE, coor. soc. serv., St. Clare Hospital, Baraboo, WI '80 (SOC)
GASTON, DOROTHY E., chief diet., Olean General Hospital, Olean, NY '69 (FOOD)
GATCHELL, LYDIA E., dir. diet. serv., Parkview Memorial Hospital, Fort Wayne, IN '82 (FOOD)
GATENS, MAJ. PAUL D., MSC USA, chief pat. adm., Womack Army Community Hospital, Fort Bragg, NC '72
GATES, BENTON E. JR., atty., Whitley County Memorial Hospital, Columbia City, IN '85 (ATTY)
GATES, GEORGE N., vice-pres. commun. rel. and mktg., King's Daughters' Medical Center, Ashland, KY '86 (PR)
GATES, JUDITH N., RN, vice-pres. nrsg. serv., Lynchburg General Hospital, Lynchburg, VA '80 (NURS)
GATES, JUDY A., dir. nrsg. staff dev., Loma Linda University Medical Center, Loma Linda, CA '85 (EDUC)
GATES, MARK R., dir. pers., St. Gabriel's Hospital, Little Falls, MN '76 (PERS)
GATES, MONICA P., dir. gen. serv., Slidell Memorial Hospital, Slidell, LA '85 (PUR)

GATES, N. KATHRYN, dir. mktg., Hospital Corporation of America, Kenner, LA '86 (PR)
GATHERS, BETTY J., nrsg. staff dev. instr., Stormont-Vail Regional Medical Center, Topeka, KS '87 (EDUC)
GATLIN, DELORIS, coor. pat. care, Hattiesburg Clinic, Hattiesburg, MS '86 (EDUC)
GATMAITAN, ALFONSO W., asst. adm., Memorial Hospital, Logansport, IN '86 (PR)
GATNAREK, DONNA, dir. commun., Catholic Medical Center, Manchester, NH '78 (PR)
GATOFF, HARVEY, pres., Gatoff Mechanical Group, Oceanside, NY '85 (ENG)
GATTEN, JOE, mgt. eng., Lexington County Hospital, West Columbia, SC '86 (MGMT)
GAUDET, JAMES T., pres., Terry Gaudet and Associates, Lafayette, LA '85 (ENG)
GAUDIN, ADRIANNE, guest rel., St. Joseph's Hospital, Tampa, FL '84 (PAT)
GAUDINSKI, MARION A., Philadelphia, PA '80 (RISK)
GAUDIOSI, THOMAS STEPHEN, sr. vice-pres., Milway Corporation, Radnor, PA '75 (RISK)
GAUDREAULT, J. RONALD, asst. adm., Huntington Hospital, Huntington, NY '64
GAUERKE, RONALD D., RN, asst. adm. pat. care serv., Marshalltown Medical and Surgical Center, Marshalltown, IA '76 (NURS)
GAUERKE, WILLIAM B., dir. biomedical eng., St. Elizabeth Hospital, Appleton, WI '83 (ENG)
GAUGER, DENNIS P., vice-pres. bldg. serv., St. Francis Hospital, Milwaukee, WI '79 (ENG)
GAULD-JAEGER, JEAN, dir. pat. affairs, Vanderbilt University Hospital, Nashville, TN '78 (PAT)
GAULT, DAVID L., mgr. matl., Taylor County Hospital, Campbellsville, KY '80 (PUR)
GAULT, FRED H. JR., pres., Gault and Associates, Chattanooga, TN '75 (PR)
GAUNT, CAROLYN S., dir. diet., Warner Brown Hospital, El Dorado, AR '85 (FOOD)
GAUNTT, HOLLY, dir. risk mgt., Franklin Boulevard Community Hospital, Chicago, IL '86 (RISK)
GAUSE, JACK H., dir. eng. and maint., Bruce Hospital, Florence, SC '82 (ENG)
GAUSS, BRIGITTE K., dir. food serv., Nipissing Manor Nursing Home, Corbeil, Ont., Canada '80 (FOOD)
GAUSZ-MANDELBERG, CAROL, exec. dir., Delaware Health Council, Inc., Wilmington, DE '86
GAUTHE', PEGGY E., RN, asst. adm. nrsg., Gulf Coast Community Hospital, Biloxi, MS '86 (NURS)
GAUTHIER, JEFFRY W., exec. dir., Central Oklahoma Ambulance Trust, Oklahoma City, OK '85
GAUTHIER, ROGER, plant eng., Exeter Hospital, Exeter, NH '83 (ENG)
GAUTHIER, RONALD H., dir. qual. assur. and risk mgt., Schumpert Medical Center, Shreveport, LA '81 (RISK)
GAUTHIER, YVONNE L., RN, dir. nrsg., Pipp Community Hospital, Plainwell, MI '84 (NURS)
GAUTIER, DOUGLAS A., dir. pers., St. Edward Mercy Medical Center, Fort Smith, AR '86 (PERS)
GAUTSCH, JAMES P., dir. food serv., Sacred Heart Hospital, Eau Claire, WI '74 (FOOD)
GAVAZZI, ALADINO A., (ret.), McLean, VA '53 (LIFE)
GAVIGAN, BARBARA R., dir. vol. prog., Los Angeles County-University of Southern California Medical Center, Los Angeles, CA '85 (VOL)
GAVIN, ROBERT, partner, Mason-Daugherty Agency, Wichita Falls, TX '86 (RISK)
GAVULA, ELIZABETH A., RN, asst. vice-pres. nrsg., Mercy Catholic Medical Center, Philadelphia, PA '83 (NURS)
GAWLEY, DALE, dir. contract serv., Methodist Hospital of Southern California, Arcadia, CA '85
GAWTHROP, ROBERT S. JR., atty., Chester County Hospital, West Chester, PA '69 (ATTY)
GAY, DAWN V., bd. mem., National College of Education, Lombard, IL '84
GAY, ELEANOR J., dir. pub. rel. and dev., Morton Hospital and Medical Center, Taunton, MA ' (PR)
GAY, JAMES, atty., Stevens Memorial Hospital, Edmonds, WA '68 (ATTY)
GAY, MARVA M., atty., Kentucky Hospital Association, Louisville, KY '87 (ATTY)
GAY, SALLY C., mgr. human res., Meridian Park Hospital, Tualatin, OR '86 (PERS)
GAY, TOMMY, asst. dir. plant oper., Schumpert Medical Center, Shreveport, LA '86 (ENG)
GAYA, ALEX, mgr. health care mkt, Eastman Kodak Company, Rochester, NY '87
GAYDA, FRANK G., mgr. food serv., Holy Cross Hospital, Chicago, IL '74 (FOOD)
GAYER, GORDON K., atty., Mercy Hospital, Portland, ME '87 (ATTY)
GAYNAIR, DELEON A., dir. pur., Douglas Gardens-Miami Home and Hospital for the Aged, Miami, FL '83 (PUR)
GAYNES, MARTIN J., atty., Psychiatric Institute of Washington, Washington, DC '78 (ATTY)
GAYNOR, DEBORAH, coor. lifestyle prog., Kaiser Permanente Honolulu Clinic, Honolulu, HI '86 (PR)
GAYNOR, JAMES M., atty., Rush-Presbyterian-St. Luke's Medical Center, Chicago, IL '82 (ATTY)
GAYNOR, JEANINE M., dir. qual. assur. and risk mgt., Nyack Hospital, Nyack, NY '85 (RISK)
GAYNOR, MARY E., dir. vol. serv., Wheeling Hospital, Wheeling, WV '68 (VOL)
GAYNOR, WILLIAM L., vice-pres., Good Samaritan Hospital and Medical Center, Portland, OR '87 (AMB)
GAYZIK, JOSEPH P., dir. pers., Underwood-Memorial Hospital, Woodbury, NJ '83 (PERS)
GAZALL, VICTOR JEROME, student, Program in Hospital and Health Care Administration, St. Louis University, St. Louis, MO '84
GAZZANA, THOMAS M., vice-pres. inst. and prof. rel., Blue Cross and Blue Shield United of Wisconsin, Milwaukee, WI '85
GAZZERRO, PAUL JR., vice-pres. fin. plng. and analyst, University of Pennsylvania, Philadelphia, PA '68
GAZZOLO, EUGENE F., coor. pers., El Camino Hospital, Mountain View, CA '64 (PERS)
GEACINTOV, CYRIL E., pres., Drg International, Inc., Mountainside, NJ '85 (PUR)
GEANES, RONALD EDWIN, adm., Carolina Eye Associates, Southern Pines, NC '75
GEARITY, ANNE R., sr. consult. soc. work, Minneapolis Children's Medical Center, Minneapolis, MN '86 (SOC)
GEARY, DOROTHY W., chief soc. work, Veterans Administration Medical Center, Long Beach, CA '71 (SOC)
GEARY, GERALDINE M., dir. med. rec., qual. assur. and risk mgt., Carney Hospital, Boston, MA '83 (RISK)
GEATZ, CANDACE, dir. qual. assur., risk mgt., Sacred Heart Hospital, Cumberland, MD '86 (RISK)
GEBHARDT, BARBARA LYNN, Falls Church, VA '79
GEBHART, COL. EILEEN G., RN, Beaver Creek, OH '86 (NURS)
GEBHART, KENNETH R., dir. mgt. eng., South Baltimore General Hospital, Baltimore, MD '73 (MGMT)
GEDDY, VERNON M. JR., atty., Williamsburg Community Hospital, Williamsburg, VA '78 (ATTY)
GEDNEY, CATHERINE J., RN, dir. qual. assur., Providence Hospital, Oakland, CA '86 (RISK)
GEE, BARBARA J., pat. care rep., Oak Forest Hospital of Cook County, Oak Forest, IL '73 (PAT)
GEE, DAVID ALAN, pres., Jewish Hospital of St. Louis, St. Louis, MO '50 (LIFE)
GEE, KEITH L., oper. analyst, Medical Center Hospital of Vermont, Burlington, VT '86 (MGMT)
GEE, MONIKA M., dir. telecommun., Northwest Community Hospital, Arlington Heights, IL '84 (ENG)
GEEDEY, CLOYD, dir. sup., proc. and distrib., Community Memorial Hospital, Toms River, NJ '86 (CS)(PUR)
GEER, CDR JOHN J. JR., atty., Bureau of Medicine and Surgery, Washington, DC '83 (ATTY)
GEER, RICK O., dir. benefits adm., Bronson Methodist Hospital, Kalamazoo, MI '67 (PERS)
GEER, WALTER E., mgr. sup., proc. and distrib., Roger Williams General Hospital, Providence, RI '83 (CS)
GEETTER, ISIDORE S., MD, consult., Mount Sinai Hospital, Hartford, CT '40 (LIFE)
GEHA, ALBERT J., adm. tech., Medical College of Ohio Hospital, Toledo, OH '86 (ENG)
GEHEN-BENEDICT, MELANIE, student, Department of Health Care Administration, George Washington University, Washington, DC '82
GEHLBACH, AMY L., mgr. food serv., Abraham Lincoln Memorial Hospital, Lincoln, IL '80 (FOOD)
GEHLBACH, KIRSTEN M., acct. exec., Wheelock Associates, Inc., Hanover, NH '85 (PR)
GEHLMANN, JOHN B., vice-pres. mktg. and corp. ventures, Premier Hospitals Addiance, Inc., Westchester, IL '77 (PLNG)
GEHNER, DONA, RN, dir. educ., St. John's Mercy Hospital, Washington, MO '76 (EDUC)
GEHRE, PAUL E., dir. soc. serv., Havasu Regional Hospital, Lake Havasu City, AZ '85 (SOC)
GEHRIG, LEO J., MD, Washington, DC '85 (LIFE)
GEHRING, LINDA L., student, Program in Health Care Administration, University of Wisconsin, Milwaukee, WI '87 (AMB)
GEIBEL, EDGAR L., consult., Stamford Hospital, Stamford, CT '47 (LIFE)
GEIER, AMY YEAGER, dir. vol., Brattleboro Memorial Hospital, Brattleboro, VT '86 (VOL)
GEIGER, ALLAN T., atty., Memorial Medical Center of Jacksonville, Jacksonville, FL '80 (ATTY)
GEIGER, ELAINE F., dir. pur., Jersey Shore Medical Center, Neptune, NJ '82 (PUR)
GEIL, ROBERT G., dir. maint., Goshen General Hospital, Goshen, IN '81 (ENG)
GEINZER, RAYMOND P., mgt. eng., St. Francis Medical Center, Pittsburgh, PA '82 (MGMT)
GEIS, LOUISE, RN, dir. nrsg., Good Samaritan Hospital, Vincennes, IN '75 (NURS)
GEISE, GEORGIA L., prog. regstr., Geisinger Medical Center, Danville, PA '83 (EDUC)
GEISEL, ANTHONY, dir. biomedical eng., Elmhurst Memorial Hospital, Elmhurst, IL '87 (ENG)
GEISELMAN, THOMAS D., dir., Center for Management and Organization Development, Alameda, CA '71 (EDUC)
GEISLER, RICHARD W., asst. dir. human res., City of Faith Hospital, Tulsa, OK '80 (PERS)
GEISMAN, SR. JEANNE, dir. soc. serv., Timken Mercy Medical Center, Canton, OH '80 (SOC)
GEISSLER, CURT, dir. adm. serv., Metropolitan Medical Center, Minneapolis, MN '85 (NURS)
GEIST, MARIAN, supv. cent. sup., St. Anthony Hospital, Hays, KS '77 (CS)
GEISTER, VERONICA M., RN, asst. dir. nrsg. and spec. proj., Saint Francis Hospital, Tulsa, OK '82 (NURS)
GEITHMAN, PAT, dir. mktg. and dev., St. John Hospital, Cleveland, OH '86 (PLNG)
GEKAS, ALEXANDRA, Chicago, IL '78 (PAT)
GELDER, MICHAEL A., pres., Michael A. Gelder and Associates, Evanston, IL '85
GELDER, SUSAN T., atty., Charter Medical Corporation, Macon, GA '86 (ATTY)
GELHAUS, MARK L., mktg. analyst, University of Iowa, College of Medicine Administration, Los Angeles, CA '82 (PLNG)
GELINAS, LILLEE SMITH, RN, nrsg. rep., Voluntary Hospitals of America, Irving, TX '82 (NURS)
GELINAS, MARC A., vice-pres. corp. affairs, Voluntary Hospitals of America, Irving, TX '78
GELINEAU, STEPHEN D., vice-pres., Health Northeast, Manchester, NH '74 (PLNG)
GELLATLY, DONNA L., prof., Governors State University-HSA, Park Forest South, IL '84
GELLEN, PAMELA L., atty., University of Chicago Hospitals, Chicago, IL '87 (ATTY)
GELLER, LTJG JANET S., MSC USN, head, direct care mgt. and asst. chief of staff-dent., Naval Hospital, Great Lakes, IL '86
GELLER, LAWRENCE, dir. and gen. mgr., Focus Health Care, Oak Park, MI '74 (PLNG)
GELLMAN, CHARLES, consult., Valley Stream, NY '56 (LIFE)
GELLMAN, LARRY, dir. maint., Saratoga Community Hospital, Detroit, MI '82 (ENG)
GELPI, MARY JANE G., dir. food and diet. serv., Ochsner Foundation Hospital, New Orleans, LA '80 (FOOD)
GELSER, MARY ELIZABETH, (ret.), Geneseo, NY '29 (LIFE)
GELSOMINO, VICTOR V. JR., partner, Gelsomino-Johnson, Architects, Houston, TX '75 (ENG)
GELWICKS, LOUIS E., pres., Gerontological Planning Associates, Santa Monica, CA '83
GEMBALLA, ELEANOR F., RN, dir. nrsg. serv., Citizens General Hospital, New Kensington, PA '86 (NURS)
GEMBAR, JOHN J., adm. asst. and dir. pub. rel., Robinson Memorial Hospital, Ravenna, OH '85 (PR)
GEMIGNANI, NANCY ASSUNTA, RN, vice-pres. nrsg., Kuakini Medical Center, Honolulu, HI '80 (NURS)
GEMMA, WILLIAM ROBERT, PhD, assoc. adm., Dept. of HHS, Health Services and Mental Health Administration, Rockville, MD '68
GENDRON, FRANCES G., clin. eng., Riverside Hospital, Newport News, VA '82 (ENG)
GENDRON, MARYJANE, RN, supv. cent. sup., Fuller Memorial Hospital, South Attleboro, MA '84 (CS)
GENEREUX, PATRICIA J., exec. dir. strategic plng., Fairview Hospital and Healthcare Service, Minneapolis, MN '87 (PLNG)
GENETOS, CLARA, asst. dir. soc. serv., Montefiore Medical Center, Bronx, NY '75 (SOC)
GENOVESE, CONSTANCE, dir. food serv., North Shore University Hospital, Manhasset, NY '78 (FOOD)
GENOVESE, NICHOLAS, dir. pur., New York Eye and Ear Infirmary, New York, NY '77 (PUR)
GENT, DONALD I., pres., Decatur Health System, Decatur, IL '82 (PAT)
GENTER, JOAN L., dir. pers., Las Encinas Hospital, Pasadena, CA '83 (PERS)
GENTILE, NORMA M., asst. dir. matl. mgt., sup., proc. and distrib., Allegheny General Hospital, Pittsburgh, PA '83 (PUR)
GENTILE, THOMAS S., dir. mgt. eng., Children's Hospital of Pittsburgh, Pittsburgh, PA '68 (MGMT)
GENTLEMAN, CAROLINE A., RN, vice-pres. nrsg., Mercy Hospital of Pittsburgh, Pittsburgh, PA '80 (NURS)
GENTRY, GAVIN M., atty., Methodist Hospital-Central Unit, Memphis, TN '78 (ATTY)
GENTRY, JEAN WALTON, assoc. dir. and dir. nrsg., Slidell Memorial Hospital, Slidell, LA '73 (NURS)
GENUARDI, JOSEPH G., vice-pres. group pur., Hospital Central Service, Inc., Allentown, PA '85 (PUR)
GENUNG, LEONARD L., dir. reg. oper., Hospital Corporation of America, Nashville, TN '61
GENZ, ELIZABETH C., dir. vol. serv., Doctors Hospital, Little Rock, AR '79 (VOL)
GEOGHAN, MICHAEL R., asst. dir. food and nutr. serv., Saddleback Community Hospital, Laguna Hills, CA '85 (FOOD)
GEORGE-DAVIS, GLORIA, dir. soc. work, Harlem Hospital Center, New York, NY '86 (SOC)
GEORGE, DAVID R., dir. eng., St. Clare's Hospital of Schenectady, Schenectady, NY '83 (ENG)
GEORGE, DAVID T., asst. vice-pres. matl. mgt., Bronx-Lebanon Hospital Center, Bronx, NY '81 (PUR)
GEORGE, ELAINE, dir. vol. serv., St. Francis Medical Center, La Crosse, WI '82 (VOL)
GEORGE, GERALDINE, loss control consult., Hospital Underwriters Mutual Insurance Company, Tarrytown, NY '85 (RISK)
GEORGE, GLADYS JEAN, atty., Lenox Hill Hospital, New York, NY '73 (ATTY)
GEORGE, HARRIET L., dir. food serv., Kaiser Foundation Hospital, Harbor City, CA '85 (FOOD)
GEORGE, JAMES E., MD, pres., Emergency Physician Associates, Woodbury, NJ '85
GEORGE, JAMES F., dir. tech. serv., Dickinson County Memorial Hospital, Spirit Lake, IA '77 (PR)
GEORGE, JANE L., RN, Sean Health Plan, Long Beach, CA '76 (NURS)
GEORGE, JOHN A., exec. dir., Alpha Health Network, Pittsburgh, PA '81
GEORGE, KENN S., reg. dir., American Medical International, Irving, TX '86
GEORGE, LINDA A., supv. cent. sterile serv., Bay Medical Center, Panama City, FL '87 (CS)
GEORGE, MARIE A., PhD, asst. vice-pres. human res., Mercy Hospital, Wilkes-Barre, PA '83 (EDUC)(PERS)
GEORGE, MARY LOU, dir. pers. and pub. rel., Memorial Hospital of Salem County, Salem, NJ '78 (PERS)
GEORGE, PETER R., dir. biomedical eng., Southeastern Kentucky Baptist Hospital, Corbin, KY '85 (ENG)
GEORGE, RAYMOND G., corp. dir. constr. mgt., Charleston Area Medical Center, Charleston, WV '83 (ENG)
GEORGE, SANDRA G., dir. soc. serv., Immanuel-St. Joseph's Hospital, Mankato, MN '85 (SOC)
GEORGE, SARA A., dir. spec. proj., Healtheast, Inc., Allentown, PA '86 (PR)
GEORGE, WALTER L., dir. emp. rel., AMI Presbyterian-St. Luke's Medical Center, Denver, CO '82 (PERS)
GEORGE, WILLIAM G., pres., Waynesboro Hospital, Waynesboro, PA '63 (PLNG)
GEPFORD, JON W., pres., Hyde Park Hospital, Chicago, IL '67
GEPPI, JOANNA M., mgr. vol. and commun. serv., Maryland General Hospital, Baltimore, MD '85 (VOL)
GERA, MICHAEL G., dir. info. syst., Clara Maass Medical Center, Belleville, NJ '86 (MGMT)
GERACI, AUGUST A., corp. dir. nutr. serv., Buffalo General Hospital, Buffalo, NY '78 (FOOD)
GERAGHTY, DONALD M., dir. gen. serv., Salem Hospital, Salem, MA '82 (ENG)

GERARD, JOSEPH M., dir. med. soc. work, Allied Services for Handicapped, Scranton, PA '81 (SOC)
GERARD, MARY LOUISE, vice-pres. mktg. and pub. rel., Our Lady of Lake Regional Medical Center, Baton Rouge, LA '81 (PR)
GERBER-SAIONZ, LYNNE, atty., Galfand, Berger, Senesky, Lurie and March, Philadelphia, PA '87 (ATTY)
GERBER, BARBARA S., adm. asst., Aliquippa Hospital, Aliquippa, PA '81
GERBER, DEBORAH K., RN, assoc. dir. nrsg., San Juan Regional Medical Center, Farmington, NM '85 (NURS)
GERBER, DONNA L., vice-pres., Highland Park Hospital, Highland Park, IL '84 (PLNG)
GERBER, IRWIN, PhD, adm., Mount Sinai School of Medicine, Department of Neoplastic Diseases, New York, NY '76
GERBER, KIRT, dir. sup., proc. and distrib., Northwestern Memorial Hospital, Chicago, IL '85 (PUR)
GERBER, LAWRENCE, atty., Carle Foundation Hospital, Urbana, IL '78 (ATTY)
GERBER, NED L., supv. consult., Coopers and Lybrand, Chicago, IL '80 (PUR)
GERBER, RICHARD C., proj. mgr., Eichleay Engineers Inc., Loftus Division, Pittsburgh, PA '86 (ENG)
GERBER, RON, chief eng., AMI Glendora Community Hospital, Glendora, CA '81 (ENG)
GERBERDING, STEPHEN N., sr. consult., Ernst and Whinney, Minneapolis, MN '81 (PLNG)
GERBI, RAYMOND P., dir. environ. serv., Concord Hospital, Concord, NH '84 (ENG)
GERDEMAN, JUDITH A., RN, chief nrsg. serv., Veterans Administration Medical Center, Perry Point, MD '86 (NURS)
GERDEN, HELEN V., RN, supv. cent. sterile serv., Worcester Hahnemann Hospital, Worcester, MA '80 (CS)
GERDES, JOHN W., sr. adm., Mountain States Health Corporation, Great Falls, MT '49 (LIFE)
GERFEN, MAX E., (ret.), San Carlos, CA '43 (LIFE)
GERGO, JOSEPH A. SR., dir. commun. serv., Hahnemann University Hospital, Philadelphia, PA '85 (ENG)
GERGORA, CATHERINE A., dir. pers., New England Baptist Hospital, Boston, MA '68 (PERS)
GERHARD, JOHN C., head food mgt., Naval Hospital, Bethesda, MD '83 (FOOD)
GERHARDT, ADELAIDA, mgr. commun., Children's Mercy Hospital, Kansas City, MO '83 (ENG)
GERHARDT, BARBARA JEAN, sr. mgt. eng., Alliance Health System, Norfolk, VA '78 (MGMT)
GERHARDT, JAY R., dir. data proc., St. Joseph Hospital, Lancaster, PA '86 (MGMT)
GERHOLD, JANEENE C., RN, dir. nrsg.-maternal child, Pendleton Memorial Methodist Hospital, New Orleans, LA '83 (NURS)
GERING, SUSAN, dir. vol. serv., Community Memorial Hospital, Menomonee Falls, WI '80 (VOL)
GERKE, RUSSEL, eng., St. Luke Community Hospital, Ronan, MT '86 (ENG)
GERLACH, ROBERT, eng. and proj. coor., Faith Clinic, Glennallen, AK '86 (ENG)
GERM, J. A., pres., Jns Associates, Inc., Naperville, IL '72
GERMAIN, LUCY D., (ret.), Detroit, MI '46 (LIFE)
GERMAN, DIANNE M., coor. qual. assur. and risk mgt., McKenzie-Willamette Hospital, Springfield, OR '83 (RISK)
GERMANESE, VINCENT L., partner, Ernst and Whinney, St. Louis, MO '79
GERMO, WILLIAM C., dir. eng., St. Joseph Health Center, St. Charles, MO '80 (ENG)
GERNANDER, KENT A., atty., Community Memorial Hospital and Convalescent and Rehabilitation Unit, Winona, MN '80 (ATTY)
GERNER, BETTY J., RN, dir. spec. nrsg. serv., St. Vincent's Medical Center, Bridgeport, CT '77 (NURS)
GERNER, EDWARD J. JR., vice-pres., Children's Hospital of Pittsburgh, Pittsburgh, PA '67 (MGMT)
GERNHARDT, BARBARA J., RN, dir. pat. care serv., Huggins Hospital, Wolfeboro, NH '82 (NURS)
GERNOLD, NANCY J., RN, dir. nrsg., Cypress Fairbanks Medical Center, Houston, TX '84 (NURS)
GEROL, ADOLPHE YALE, MD, Gerol Clinic for Neurological Services, Kenosha, WI '86 (RISK)
GEROLD, SR. PHYLLIS ANN, exec. dir., Mercy Hospital, Toledo, OH '67
GERON, MARILY J., RN, vice-pres. nrsg., St. Luke's Hospitals, Fargo, ND '86 (NURS)
GERONEMO, SR. LOUISE A., (ret.), Hospital of Saint Raphael, New Haven, CT '53 (LIFE)
GERRARD, DAN, adm. off., Veterans Administration Medical Center, Albuquerque, NM '84
GERRARD, PATRICK W., dir. plant oper., Roundup Memorial Hospital, Roundup, MT '85 (ENG)
GERRARD, ROBERT JOHN, dir. oper. eng. and constr., Charter Medical Corporation, Macon, GA '64 (ENG)
GERSCHEFSKE, LYNETTE, RN, dir. nrsg. serv., St. Joseph Health Center, St. Charles, MO '71 (NURS)
GERSHKOW, SHERRI L., coor. health adm., Duane, Morris and Heckscher, Philadelphia, PA '85
GERSHON, HOWARD J., exec. vice-pres., Lammers and Gershon Associates, Reston, VA '73
GERSHON, RUTH H., atty., Georgia Hospital Association, Atlanta, GA '73 (ATTY)
GERSHONE, ERNEST A., dir. qual. improvement, St. John's Eastside Hospital, St. Paul, MN '76 (MGMT)
GERST, ROBERT J., atty., Hospital Corporation of America, Nashville, TN '72 (ATTY)
GERSTEN, ELIZABETH W., pat. educ., St. Mary's Hospital and Health Center, Tucson, AZ '84 (EDUC)
GERSTENHABER, BLANCHE, coor. vol. serv., Memorial Hospital, Meriden, CT '86 (VOL)
GERSTER, JOHN W., asst. adm., St. Francis Hospital-Beacon, Beacon, NY '49 (LIFE)
GERSTNER, LORRAINE S., dir. educ., Our Lady of Mercy Medical Center, Bronx, NY '87 (EDUC)
GERTMANN, ROGER H., contract adm., Ancilla Systems, Inc., Elk Grove Village, IL '85 (PUR)
GERTZEN, HENRY B. JR., dir. pers., Atlantic City Medical Center, Atlantic City, NJ '82 (PERS)
GERVAIS, CDR DAVID R., MSC USN, asst. chief staff-logistics, Naval Medical Command, Norfolk, VA '80
GERVAIS, JERRY A., dir. tech. eng., Lutheran General Hospital, Park Ridge, IL '78 (ENG)
GERWICK, CLARA L., vice-pres., C. L. Gerwick and Associates, Inc., Overland Park, KS '75 (FOOD)
GERYK, KAREN, reg. mgr. costumer support, HBO and Company, Dallas, TX '80 (MGMT)
GESELL, CAROL W., diet., Gibson Community Hospital, Gibson City, IL '76 (FOOD)
GESHEL, PETER J., vice-pres. fin., Detroit Receiving Hospital, Detroit, MI '82 (PLNG)
GESSLER, ANNETTE, adm. dir. emer. amb. care, Greenville Regional Hospital, Greenville, PA '87 (AMB)
GESSLER, MAUREEN A., MSC USAF, U. S. Air Force Hospital, APO New York, NY '74
GESSNER, BARBARA, nrsg. spec., University Extension, University of Wisconsin Department of Nursing, Madison, WI '71 (EDUC)
GESSNER, OTTO H., vice-pres. eng., Medifac, Inc., Elkins Park, PA '77 (ENG)
GETSON, JACOB, vice-pres., Blue Cross and Blue Shield of Massachusetts, Boston, MA '79 (PLNG)
GETSON, LISA M., dir. pub. rel. and mktg., HCA Doctors Hospital, Lake Worth, FL '86 (PR)
GETTYS, RODDEY E. III, vice-pres., Baptist Medical Center Easley, Easley, SC '70 (PLNG)
GETZ, EDWIN A., atty., Northwestern Memorial Hospital, Chicago, IL '87 (ATTY)
GETZ, JAMES L., vice-pres., Ohio Hospital Management Services, Columbus, OH '81 (MGMT)
GEYER, ANNA M., asst. dir. matl. mgt., F. G. McGaw Hospital, Loyola University, Maywood, IL '80 (CS)
GEYER, ELIZABETH D., dir. commun. serv. and mktg., Coral Reef Hospital, Miami, FL '81 (PR)
GEYER, SUSAN G., mgr. cent. serv., Children's Hospital, Boston, MA '80 (CS)
GHANI, MICHAEL A., adm., Mahorner Clinic, Kenner, LA '81
GHARRITY, JAN, assoc. nrsg. resources, Indiana University Hospitals, Indianapolis, IN '86 (PERS)
GHAZI, ASIF, health care analyst, Blue Cross and Blue Shield, Cleveland, OH '79
GHEESLING, JAMES R., syst. analyst, Medical College of Georgia Hospital and Clinic, Augusta, GA '87 (ENG)
GHILARDUCCI, LAWRENCE R. JR., atty., Multicare Medical Center, Tacoma, WA '82 (ATTY)
GHILONI, NORMA F., dir. pur., Santa Teresita Hospital, Duarte, CA '83 (PUR)
GHOLSON, W. DEANE, coor. allied health cont. educ., Dodge City Community College, Dodge City, KS '86 (EDUC)
GHOLSTON, LINDA J., RN, asst. adm. nrsg. serv., North Mississippi Medical Center, Tupelo, MS '82 (NURS)
GHOSH, JATA S., dir. prod. mgt., Harrisburg Hospital, Harrisburg, PA '85 (PLNG)
GIACOBBO, JOHN N., MD, vice-pres. prof. affairs, Methodist Hospital, Philadelphia, PA '71 (EDUC)
GIACOMUZZI, BRUNO F., dir. environ. serv., Methodist Hospitals of Gary, Gary, IN '86 (ENVIRON)
GIAGNACOVO, RICHARD, dir. nutr. and food serv., All Saints Episcopal Hospital, Fort Worth, TX '82 (FOOD)
GIALANELLA, JOHN, vice-pres., University of Michigan Hospitals, Ann Arbor, MI '79 (PR) (PLNG)
GIAMBALVO, LEONARD, atty., Eastern Maine Medical Center, Bangor, ME '87 (ATTY)
GIAMBARRESI, JOHN P., dir. food serv., Carleton-Willard Village, Bedford, MA '86 (FOOD)
GIAMMALVO, PETER J., PhD, asst. adm., St. Thomas Hospital, Nashville, TN '79
GIANCOLA, DAVID M., pres., Giancola Associates, Knoxville, TN '69 (MGMT)
GIANGRANDE, LEO, dir. eng. and support serv., Greystone Park Psychiatric Hospital, Greystone Park, NJ '84 (ENG)
GIANNUNZIO, DIANE, dir. med. serv., HMO West, Inc., Battle Creek, MI '85
GIANNUZZI, DONNA, RN, dir. pat. serv., Cape Coral Hospital, Cape Coral, FL '79 (NURS)
GIARD, E. NORMAND, vice-pres., St. John Hospital, Detroit, MI '73
GIARDINA, ANTHONY J., vice-pres., Oregon Association of Hospitals, Portland, OR '70
GIARRAPUTO, DIANA, asst. matl. mgr. and dir. cent. serv., Doctors Hospital, New York, NY '84 (CS)
GIBALA, DONALD, vice-pres. plng. and mktg., Butler Memorial Hospital, Butler, PA '82 (PLNG)
GIBB, H. PHILIP, dist. vice-pres., Hospital Corporation of America Management Company, Midlothian, VA '76
GIBBENS, LORETTA O., RN, dir. cent. serv., Brothers-Menn Health Care, Bloomington, IL '82 (CS)
GIBBLE, THOMAS B., risk mgr., St. Joseph Hospital, Lancaster, PA '86 (RISK)
GIBBON, SR. M. VINCENT DE PAUL, dir. pat. rep., Mercy Hospital of Johnstown, Johnstown, PA '86 (PAT)
GIBBONS, SR. ADRIAN, pat. rep., Saint Joseph Hospital, Fort Worth, TX '75 (PAT)
GIBBONS, SR. CONSTANCE MARY, RN, dir. cent. sterile proc., St. Joseph's Hospital Health Center, Syracuse, NY '81 (CS)
GIBBONS, E. DAVID, divisional dir. mktg. and pub. rel., Providence Hospital, Columbia, SC '86 (PR)
GIBBONS, ELSA R., coor. vol., Newington Children's Hospital, Newington, CT '82 (VOL)
GIBBONS, G. HUNTER, atty., Venice Hospital, Venice, FL '73 (ATTY)
GIBBONS, JOSEPH F. JR., mgr. health care strategic plng., Blue Cross and Blue Shield, Cleveland, OH '87
GIBBONS, KAREN, RN, mgr. sterile proc., Anne Arundel General Hospital, Annapolis, MD '82 (CS)
GIBBONS, MARY PATRICIA, adm. dir., Beth Israel Hospital, Boston, MA '85 (NURS)
GIBBS, AMY LEIGH, dir. soc. serv., Guadalupe Valley Hospital, Seguin, TX '85 (SOC)
GIBBS, ELLEN MILLS, atty., Broward General Medical Center, Fort Lauderdale, FL '77 (ATTY)
GIBBS, JAMES P., dir. environ. serv., Memorial Hospital, Carbondale, IL '86 (ENVIRON)
GIBBS, KATE, RN, coor. in-service and staff dev., Shriners Hospitals for Crippled Children, St. Louis, MO '82 (EDUC)
GIBBS, MARC ALAN, adm. mgr., Bronson Methodist Hospital, Kalamazoo, MI '81
GIBBS, MARCIA PHOENIX, RN, dir. nrsg., Medical Center Del Oro Hospital, Houston, TX '78 (NURS)
GIBBS, MARK R. III, vice-pres., Crouse-Irving Memorial Hospital, Syracuse, NY '68 (RISK)
GIBBS, MELBAHU M., dir. soc. work and alcohol prog., Carney Hospital, Boston, MA '86 (SOC)
GIBBS, RICHARD F., MD, Brigham and Women's Hospital, Boston, MA '81 (RISK)
GIBBS, RICHARD S., atty., St. Mary's Hospital, Milwaukee, WI '79 (ATTY)
GIBLER, JACQUELINE A., mgt. analyst, University of Missouri Hospital and Clinics, Columbia, MO '86 (PR)
GIBOFSKY, ALLAN, MD, assoc. dir., Hospital for Special Surgery, New York, NY '83 (RISK)
GIBRALTER, BERNICE, exec. asst. to pres., Long Island College Hospital, Brooklyn, NY '73 (RISK)
GIBSON, ALLAN B., supt. powerhouse plant oper., Pontiac General Hospital, Pontiac, MI '85 (ENG)
GIBSON, DEBORAH L., dir. soc. serv., Children's Hospital Medical Center, Akron, OH '82 (SOC)
GIBSON, DON R., vice-pres. prof. rel., Baton Rouge General Medical Center, Baton Rouge, LA '80
GIBSON, FELICITTA, RN, dir. nrsg., American Legion Hospital, Crowley, LA '80 (NURS)
GIBSON, JEFFERY G., mktg. analyst, Baptist Medical Centers, Birmingham, AL '84 (PLNG)
GIBSON, JOHN H., atty., Wesley Medical Center, Wichita, KS '82 (ATTY)
GIBSON, JOYCE A., dir. mktg., General Health Enterprises, Chicago, IL '85 (PR)
GIBSON, KEN A., dir. phys. plant, Royal Alexandra Hospital, Edmonton, Alta., Canada '84 (ENG)
GIBSON, L. EDWARD, dir. plant oper., Lutheran Hospital of Fort Wayne, Fort Wayne, IN '85 (ENG)
GIBSON, MARK S., MD, dir. emer. medicine, Sherman Hospital, Elgin, IL '87 (AMB)
GIBSON, NANCY B., dir. food serv., Lonesome Pine Hospital, Big Stone Gap, VA '85 (FOOD)
GIBSON, REGINALD POWELL, assoc. adm., St. Anne's Hospital, Chicago, IL '78
GIBSON, RHONDA M., RN, assoc. dir. nrsg., Gulf Coast Community Hospital, Biloxi, MS '86 (NURS)
GIBSON, ROBERT N., pres., The Medical Center, Beaver, PA '77
GIBSON, ROBERT W. JR., vice-pres. adm. serv., Our Lady of Mercy Hospital, Dyer, IN '71
GIBSON, ROBERTA S., RN, dir. nrsg. serv., Roseau Area Hospital, Roseau, MN '83 (NURS)
GIBSON, SHARON SUE, pat. advocate, Truman Medical Center-West, Kansas City, MO '73 (PAT)
GIBSON, SUSAN, dir. educ. and trng., St. Francis Xavier Hospital, Charleston, SC '78 (EDUC)
GIBSON, THOMAS F., corp. vice-pres. human res., Columbus-Cuneo-Cabrini Medical Center, Chicago, IL '86 (PERS)
GIBSON, THOMAS W., atty., Florida Hospital Medical Center, Orlando, FL '79 (ATTY)
GIDDENS, T. K. JR., atty., Willis-Knighton Medical Center, Shreveport, LA '76 (ATTY)
GIDDINGS, LUCILLE CASSELL, RN, dir. interdepartmental serv., Our Lady of Mercy Medical Center, Bronx, NY '81
GIDEON, DAWN M., dir., Forbes Vantage Group, Pittsburgh, PA '83 (PR) (PLNG)
GIDEWALL, ELMER E., dir. hskpg., grds. and linen, St. Francis Hospital, Greenville, SC '87 (ENVIRON)
GIDLEY, THOMAS D., atty., Hospital Association of Rhode Island Comprehensive, Inc., Providence, RI '73 (ATTY)
GIDWANI, PRADEEP G., student, Webster's College, St. Louis, MO '85
GIELOW, CURTIS C., Phoenix, AZ '74
GIERHART, KATHLEEN, dir. pub. rel. and dev., O'Bleness Memorial Hospital, Athens, OH '84 (PR)
GIESE, CLINTON, corp. pub. rel. mgr., Intermountain Health Care, Inc., Salt Lake City, UT '79 (PR)
GIESEKE, SUSAN, mgr. cent. sup., Memorial Hospital Medical Center, Modesto, CA '82 (PUR)
GIESEL, RICHARD A., vice-pres. mktg., Barberton Citizens Hospital, Barberton, OH '85 (PLNG)
GIESLER, PATRICIA JANE, dir. soc. serv., St. Anthony Hospital, Michigan City, IN '80 (SOC)
GIESLER, RAYMOND H., vice-pres. plng. and mktg., Jewish Hospital of Cincinnati, Cincinnati, OH '74 (PLNG)
GIESSEL, BRUCE, adm., Refugio County Memorial Hospital, Refugio, TX '86 (PLNG)
GIESSELMAN, CHRISTINE K., Fountain Hills, AZ '74
GIEZIE, WILLIAM S., dir. emp. rel., St. Charles Hospital, Oregon, OH '82 (PERS)
GIFFIN, THOMAS W., dir. pub. rel., Sacred Heart Hospital, Cumberland, MD '86 (PR)
GIFFORD, AUDREY ANN, RN, pat. and family advocate, Morton F. Plant Hospital, Clearwater, FL '77 (PAT)
GIFFORD, HARRY C. F., lecturer, Program in Health Administration, School of Public Health, University of Massachusetts, Amherst, MA '48 (LIFE)
GIFFORD, JAY B., lead biomedical equip. tech., San Jose Hospital, San Jose, CA '84 (ENG)
GIFFORD, JOHN W., dir. mgt. eng., Tampa General Hospital, Tampa, FL '72 (MGMT)
GIFFORD, RICHARD D., exec. dir., Russell Reynolds Associates, Inc., Chicago, IL '55 (PLNG)(LIFE)
GIFFORD, SHERI C., asst. dir. soc. work serv., Graduate Hospital, Philadelphia, PA '85 (SOC)
GIFFUNE, MARY BETH, student, Northeastern University, Cambridge, MA '85 (PLNG)

GIFT, JILL M., dir. diet. serv., Mercy Hospital, Council Bluffs, IA '78 (FOOD)
GIFT, ROBERT G., vice-pres. oper. res., Catholic Health Corporation, Omaha, NE '84 (PLNG)(MGMT)
GIGANTI, EDWARD J., asst. dir. commun. rel., St. John's Hospital, Springfield, IL '86 (PR)
GIGGEY, LINDA P., supv. outpat surg., HCA Palmyra Medical Centers, Albany, GA '87 (AMB)
GIGLER, FRANK FREDRICK III, dir., Louisiana State University Hospital, Shreveport, LA '79
GIGLIA, LUCILLE, dir. vol., Rochester General Hospital, Rochester, NY '71 (VOL)
GIGLIOTTI, T. ALLEN, dir. biomedical eng., Sinai Hospital of Detroit, Detroit, MI '87 (ENG)
GIGRAY, WILLIAM F. III, atty., West Valley Medical Center, Caldwell, ID '86 (ATTY)
GILARD, LEONARD J. JR., dir. plant oper., Humana Hospital -Hoffman Estates, Hoffman Estates, IL '87 (ENG)
GILBERG, RICHARD L., pres. organizational dev. div., Personal and Professional Development, Inc., Wheeling, IL '78 (PR)(EDUC)
GILBERT, ANDREA, dir. amb. care, Hahnemann University Hospital, Philadelphia, PA '87 (AMB)
GILBERT, BARBARA F., RN, dir. qual. appraisal prog., Medical Center of Central Georgia, Macon, GA '84 (RISK)
GILBERT, BENJAMIN, atty., North Carolina Memorial Hospital, Chapel Hill, NC '83 (ATTY)
GILBERT, CAROLYN, coor. educ., University of Michigan, Ann Arbor, MI '79 (EDUC)
GILBERT, CLAUDE J., dir. plant and prop., St. Vincent Hospital, Santa Fe, NM '61 (ENG)
GILBERT, DANIEL L., dir. pers., Bradley County Memorial Hospital, Cleveland, TN '86 (PERS)
GILBERT, EDGAR W., dist. mgr. health care serv., Blue Cross of Massachusetts, Braintree, MA '72
GILBERT, GAEL, adm. asst., University Hospital, Augusta, GA '85 (NURS)
GILBERT, GAY F., RN, vice-pres. nrsg., Washington County Hospital, Hagerstown, MD '86 (NURS)
GILBERT, GAYLE, RN, asst. adm., Sacred Heart General Hospital, Eugene, OR '82 (NURS)
GILBERT, IVAN S., MD, pres., Home Health Institute, Columbus, OH '84
GILBERT, JACK A., vice-pres., Medco, Inc., Langhorne, PA '80 (MGMT)
GILBERT, JAMES F., dir. food serv., Williamsport Hospital and Medical Center, Williamsport, PA '72 (FOOD)
GILBERT, JOHN R., dir. matl. mgt., Catherine McAuley Health Center, Ann Arbor, MI '83 (PUR)
GILBERT, LEONARD H., atty., University Community Hospital, Tampa, FL '70 (ATTY)
GILBERT, MARILYN M., dir. vol., Shriners Hospital for Crippled Children, Honolulu, HI '83 (VOL)
GILBERT, MARJEAN D., RN, dir. nrsg., St. John's Hospital, Fargo, ND '86 (NURS)
GILBERT, MARY K., dir. vol. serv., Mount Auburn Hospital, Cambridge, MA '68 (VOL)
GILBERT, NEAL E., sr. mgt. eng., University of Michigan Hospitals, Ann Arbor, MI '83 (MGMT)
GILBERT, ROBERT A., dir. nutr. and diet., Harris Hospital-Hurst-Euless-Bedford North, Bedford, TX '78 (FOOD)
GILBERT, ROBERT D., pur. agt., North Broward Hospital District, Fort Lauderdale, FL '64 (PUR)
GILBERT, SHERRY, RN, risk mgr., Miami Heart Institute, Miami Beach, FL '86 (RISK)
GILBERT, WILLIAM R., mgr. const, Victory Health and Human Service, Lake Villa, IL '67 (ENG)
GILBERTSON, ELBERT EDMUND, pres., St. Luke's Regional Medical Center, Boise, ID '60 (LIFE)
GILBRIDE, DANIEL J., dir. facil., Holy Cross Hospital, Chicago, IL '79 (ENG)
GILCHRIST, RONALD G., Cypress Fairbanks Medical Center Hospital, Houston, TX '81 (ENG)
GILCHRIST, LCDR WILLIAM R., MSC USN, contr., Naval Hospital, Bethesda, MD '75 (MGMT)
GILDIN, NORMAN B., asst. dir., Jewish Home for the Elderly of Fairfield County, Fairfield, CT '75
GILDNER, JOHN L., chief exec. off., Regional Institute for Children and Adolescents-Rockville, Rockville, MD '72
GILE, TERRY JO, asst. adm. dir. lab., Barnes Hospital, St. Louis, MO '86 (ENG)
GILES, CARMA L., dir. cent. serv., Sequoia Hospital District, Redwood City, CA '82 (CS)
GILFEATHER-DYER, JANICE, RN, dir. nrsg., Hilton Head Hospital, Hilton Head Island, SC '82 (NURS)
GILFILLAN, MICHAEL S., vice-pres., Legat Architects, Schaumburg, IL '85 (ENG)
GILFOY, KATHERINE M., dir. commun. rel. and vol. serv., Glover Memorial Hospital, Needham, MA '83 (VOL)
GILGAREN, R. J., student, Program in Health Care, Southern Illinois University, Carbondale, IL '84
GILHAM, MARJORIE B., pur. agt., Willow Creek Adolescent Center, Arlington, TX '87 (PUR)
GILHAM, ROY S., sr. mgt. eng., Tri-City Medical Center, Oceanside, CA '86 (MGMT)
GILKEY, JUANITA P., RN, vice-pres. nrsg., Michiana Community Hospital, South Bend, IN '83 (NURS)
GILKEY, KATHRYN C., supv. hskpg., Armstrong County Memorial Hospital, Kittanning, PA '87 (ENVIRON)
GILKEY, PRISCILLA L., vice-pres. commun. rel., Empire Health Services, Spokane, WA '81 (PR)
GILL, ANNE G., RN, supv. cent. serv. room, Jupiter Hospital, Jupiter, FL '83 (CS)
GILL, CHARLES M., vice-pres. mktg., Zurbrugg Memorial Hospital, Willingboro, NJ '85 (PLNG)
GILL, DAVID L., dir. plant serv., Moberly Regional Medical Center, Moberly, MO '74 (ENG)
GILL, DOROTHY, dir. pers., Parkview Episcopal Medical Center, Pueblo, CO '87 (PERS)
GILL, HARRIET S., pres., H. S. Gill and Associates, Inc., Roswell, GA '87
GILL, KATHLEEN N., loss prevention consult., Health Care Insurance Exchange, Princeton, NJ '82 (RISK)
GILL, KATHRYN B., mgr. mktg., American Healthcorp, Inc., Nashville, TN '86 (PLNG)
GILL, LISA A., dir. food serv., St. Elizabeth Hospital Medical Center, Youngstown, OH '84
GILL, SHIRLEY O., asst. dir. pers., South Florida Baptist Hospital, Plant City, FL '82 (PERS)
GILLAN, PAUL J., student, Program in Health Information Sciences, University of Victoria, Victoria, B.C., Canada '85 (MGMT)
GILLEN, JANET, dir. soc. serv., Seton Medical Center, Daly City, CA '87 (SOC)
GILLENWATER, ELBA JR., risk mgr., Ohio Valley Medical Center, Wheeling, WV '83 (RISK)
GILLER, DONALD R., dir. mktg. and pub. affairs, University Hospital at Boston University Medical Center, Boston, MA '75 (PR)
GILLERMAN, GERALD, atty., Beth Israel Hospital, Boston, MA '68 (ATTY)
GILLES, KEITH E., sr. vice-pres., Tallahassee Memorial Regional Medical Center, Tallahassee, FL '78
GILLESPIE, CHRISTINE L., RN, clin. instr., Columbus Hospital, Great Falls, MT '86 (EDUC)
GILLESPIE, DONNA F., mgr. educ., American Health Consultants, Atlanta, GA '77 (EDUC)
GILLESPIE, EDWARD M., exec. dir., University Hospital, Augusta, GA '63
GILLESPIE, GERALDINE, dir. food serv., Alfred I. Dupont Institute, Wilmington, DE '77 (FOOD)
GILLESPIE, JOHNNIE L., dir. environ. serv., Lutheran Medical Center, Wheat Ridge, CO '86 (ENVIRON)
GILLETTE, BOB, dir. environ. serv. and safety off., St. Peter Hospital, Olympia, WA '86 (ENG)
GILLETTE, LEWIS R., Avalon, CA '53 (LIFE)
GILLETTE, MARILYN L., sr. mgr., Ernst and Whinney, Los Angeles, CA '87 (MGMT)
GILLETTE, PHILIP J., adm. health syst., University of Nevada, School of Medical Sciences, Reno, NV '51 (LIFE)
GILLETTE, ROBERT F., dir. environ. serv., St. Peter Hospital, Olympia, WA '86 (ENVIRON)
GILLETTE, SUSAN, atty., University of Maryland at Baltimore, Baltimore, MD '83 (ATTY)
GILLHAM, DEBBIE, student, Program in Health Systems Management, Rush University, Chicago, IL '84
GILLHAM, LANCE F., vice-pres. midwest reg., Fairview Ridges Hospital, Burnsville, MN '71 (EDUC)
GILLIAM, E. M., chief eng., Ardmore Adventist Hospital, Ardmore, OK '80 (ENG)
GILLIAM, GERALD V., coor. soc. work serv., Charity Hospital at New Orleans, New Orleans, LA '86 (SOC)
GILLIAM, JOSEPH E. JR., pur. agt., John Randolph Hospital, Hopewell, VA '70 (PUR)
GILLIAM, THOMAS H., dir. eng., Riverside Methodist Hospitals, Columbus, OH '85 (ENG)
GILLIES, MARJORIE J., dir. pub. rel., Health Sciences Centre, Winnipeg, Man., Canada '81 (PR)
GILLIG, GERALD, dir. soc. serv., Heartland Hospital West, St. Joseph, MO '84 (SOC)
GILLIGAN, RICHARD F., asst. dir. plant serv., St. Elizabeth's Hospital, Chicago, IL '82 (ENG)
GILLIGAN, RICHARD JAMES, dir. maint. and eng., Borgess Medical Center, Kalamazoo, MI '86 (ENG)
GILLILAND, EDWARD A., dir. facil., South Florida Baptist Hospital, Plant City, FL '77 (ENG)
GILLILAND, JOHN C. II, atty., Ball Memorial Hospital, Muncie, IN '74 (ATTY)
GILLILAND, MARY M., RN, asst. exec. dir., Presbyterian Hospital, Dallas, TX '86 (NURS)
GILLILAND, ROBERT, atty., Hutchinson Hospital Corporation, Hutchinson, KS '72 (ATTY)
GILLIS, GWENDOLYN LEA, dir. strategic plng., Alamance Health Services, Burlington, NC '86 (PLNG)
GILLIS, LEA, dir. strategic plng., Alamance Health Services, Burlington, NC '87 (AMB)
GILLISPIE, RICARDO, dir. psych. and soc. work serv., Meridian Regional Hospital, Meridian, MS '86 (SOC)
GILLMEISTER, DEBRA A., dir. plng. and mktg., Good Shepherd Hospital, Barrington, IL '84 (PLNG)
GILLOCK, RICHARD E., vice-pres. and adm., Lovelace Medical Center, Albuquerque, NM '83
GILLON, MARY, dir. extended care, Kaiser Foundation Hospital, Hayward, CA '85 (SOC)
GILLOOLY, FAITH F., dir. cent. sterile serv., Middlesex Memorial Hospital, Middletown, CT '77 (CS)
GILLOTTI, FREDERICK PAUL, dir. pers., St. Rita's Medical Center, Lima, OH '67 (PERS)
GILLS, KARL BENJAMIN, sr. vice-pres. oper., North Colorado Medical Center, Greeley, CO '79
GILLS, MARGARET, risk mgt. consult., Virginia Hospital Association, Richmond, VA '86 (RISK)
GILMAN, JOAN K., scrub tech. labor and delivery, Mercy Health Center, Oklahoma City, OK '85 (CS)
GILMAN, KATHLEEN M., asst. risk mgt., American Oncologic Hospital, Philadelphia, PA '86 (RISK)
GILMAN, LAWRENCE S., supv. diet., Routt Memorial Hospital, Steamboat Springs, CO '82 (FOOD)
GILMAN, LESLIE, dir., All Saints' Rehabilitation Hospital, Wyndmoor, PA '86
GILMARTIN, JAMES J., exec. vice-pres. and chief oper. off., Parkside Human Services Corporation, Park Ridge, IL '86
GILMER, ROBERT, risk mgr., Self Memorial Hospital, Greenwood, SC '86 (RISK)
GILMORE, CAROL J., asst. dir. food and nutr. serv., Cedars-Sinai Medical Center, Los Angeles, CA '82 (FOOD)
GILMORE, EARL W., dir. mgt. syst., Erlanger Medical Center, Chattanooga, TN '83 (MGMT)
GILMORE, JAMES D., dir. plant oper., Charter Pacific Hospital, Torrance, CA '86 (ENG)
GILMORE, JOHN STEVENS, atty., Mercy Hospital of Sacramento, Sacramento, CA '77 (ATTY)
GILMORE, MARY C., adm. asst., Morton County Hospital, Elkhart, KS '83 (PR)
GILMORE, PHILLIP K., vice pres., Warner Brown Hospital, El Dorado, AR '76
GILNER, MARGARET, supv. sup. and distrib., St. Francis Memorial Hospital, San Francisco, CA '83 (CS)
GILPIN, DONALD W., dir. commun. rel., Littleton Hospital, Littleton, NH '84 (PR)
GILPIN, KAREN PARK, RN, dir. nrsg., Allen County Hospital, Iola, KS '80 (NURS)
GILPIN, L. ANNETTE, dir. vol. serv., St. Vincent's Hospital and Medical Center of New York, New York, NY '73 (VOL)
GILREATH, EARL R., pres., Providence Hospital, Cincinnati, OH '64
GILROY, MARILYN P., asst. dir. food serv., Wesley Medical Center, Wichita, KS '85 (FOOD)
GILROY, PHILIP W., exec. dir., St. Elizabeth's Hospital, Chicago, IL '73
GILSON, J. MICHAEL, asst. adm., Ohio Valley Medical Center, Wheeling, WV '78 (ENG)(ENVIRON)
GILSON, JAMES W., atty., Intermountain Health Care, Inc., Salt Lake City, UT '86 (ATTY)
GILSON, JOSEPH E., supv. residential care prog., Veterans Administration Medical Center, Tacoma, WA '82 (SOC)
GILSTRAP, MICHAEL L., asst. adm., Medical Center of Central Georgia, Macon, GA '80 (RISK)
GILVARY, JAMES J., atty., Good Samaritan Hospital and Health Center, Dayton, OH '69 (ATTY)
GIMBER, JUDITH R., RN, adm. asst. nrsg. serv., Schumpert Medical Center, Shreveport, LA '86 (NURS)
GIMBERT, ALAIN R., asst. mgt. eng., Midwest Health Services, Inc., Peoria, IL '86 (MGMT)
GIMBLET, SUSAN H., dir. diet. serv., St. Anne's Hospital, Fall River, MA '84 (FOOD)
GIMLIN, N. ELAINE, dir. matl. mgt., West Florida Hospital, Pensacola, FL '80 (PUR)
GIMMILL, MAJ. ROBERT H., MSC USA, chief med. and surg. soc. work, Walter Reed Army Medical Center, Washington, DC '86 (SOC)
GINDI, HARRY E., atty., North Shore University Hospital, Manhasset, NY '86 (ATTY)
GINGRAS, GUSTAVE, MD, consult., Queen Elizabeth Hospital, Charlottetown, P.E.I. Canada '50 (LIFE)
GINGRICH, KENNETH J., dir. maint., Good Samaritan Hospital, Lebanon, PA '81 (ENG)
GINILEWICZ, STEFAN JAN, dir. oper. res., Numed, Inc., Encino, CA '78 (MGMT)
GINN, LT. COL. JAMES P., MSC USA, chief prog. and distrib. br. manpower div., Office of the Surgeon General, Washington, DC '77
GINN, TERRY, mgr. gen. sales, Leon's Bakery, Inc., Hamden, CT '86 (FOOD)
GINNARD, PATRICIA L., health promotion educ., Tulane University Hospital and Clinics, New Orleans, LA '86 (EDUC)
GINNOW, WILLIAM K., assoc. adm., St. Louis County Hospital, Clayton, MO '80
GINSBERG, ALLEN S., dir. mgt. syst. and audit, Presbyterian Hospital in the City of New York, New York, NY '87 (MGMT)
GINSBERG, ARTHUR M., adm., Belle Park Hospital, Houston, TX '79
GINSBERG, BERNARD LAWRENCE, pres., Medical Marketing and Management, West Los Angeles, CA '81
GINSBERG, DAVID L., exec. vice-pres. plng. and prog. dev., Presbyterian Hospital in the City of New York, New York, NY '77 (PLNG)
GINSBERG, DOLORES M., RN, coor. in-serv., Miller-Dwan Medical Center, Duluth, MN '84 (EDUC)
GINSBERG, ROBERT D., dir. mgt. info., Mount Sinai Medical Center, New York, NY '81
GINSBURG, BEVERLY R., assoc. exec. dir., Rolling Hill Hospital, Elkins Park, PA '85 (PR)
GINTER, GARY J. N., mgr. ancillary serv., Hospital Central Service, Inc., Allentown, PA '81 (PUR)
GINTER, ZELDA MAZEL, chief exec. off., Edgewater Hospital, Chicago, IL '84
GINTHER, MARY LOU F., dir. vol. serv., Pomona Valley Community Hospital, Pomona, CA '85 (VOL)
GINTZIG, LT. KAREN A., MSC USN, adm., Baptist Memorial Hospital-Germantown, Memphis, TN '78
GIOANNINI, KAROL D., mgt. eng., Rex Hospital, Raleigh, NC '85 (MGMT)
GIOBBE, RAPHAEL C., dir. rad., West Hudson Hospital, Kearny, NJ '85
GIORDANO, CLARE L., RN, assoc. dir. nrsg. serv., Sancta Maria Hospital, Cambridge, MA '78 (NURS)
GIORDANO, JOHN C. JR., atty., Monmouth Medical Center, Long Branch, NJ '70 (ATTY)
GIORDANO, JOHN J., vice-pres. mktg., Kimball Medical Center, Lakewood, NJ '86 (PR)
GIORDANO, LUCAS J., atty., East Jefferson General Hospital, Metairie, LA '78 (ATTY)
GIORDANO, PAUL J., dir. pers., Community Hospital at Glen Cove, Glen Cove, NY '83 (PERS)
GIORGILLI, FRANK L., mgt. eng., Thomas Jefferson University Hospital, Philadelphia, PA '82 (MGMT)
GIORGIO, CHUCK, dir. eng., Lake Seminole Hospital, Seminole, FL '83 (ENG)
GIOSA, RITAMARIE, RN, exec. dir., New Era Nursing, Inc., Cherry Hill, NJ '82 (NURS)
GIOVANNI, LOUIS DI, exec. dir. dev., Maxim Healthcare Corporation, Erdenheim, PA '77 (PLNG)
GIOVANNIELLO, MICHAEL PATRICK, asst. dir. fin., Mount Sinai Medical Center, New York, NY '78
GIPSON, FRANCES THERESE, asst. adm., William N. Wishard Memorial Hospital, Indianapolis, IN '79
GIRARD, CHERYL J., coor. mktg., Hospice of Northern Virginia, Arlington, VA '86 (PR)
GIRARD, DEAN J., asst. contr., University Community Hospital, Tamarac, FL '85
GIRARD, JOAN I., RN, coor. nrsg., Lawrence General Hospital, Lawrence, MA '82 (NURS)
GIRARD, LUCILLE M., RN, supv. and instr. nrsg., Center General Hospital, Howard, RI '82 (EDUC)
GIRARD, M. MARGARET, supv. soc. work, Veterans Administration Medical Center, Baltimore, MD '67 (SOC)

GIRARD, ROBERT D., atty., California Hospital Association, Sacramento, CA '73 (ATTY)
GIRE, MICHAEL K., atty., Riverside Methodist Hospitals, Columbus, OH '81 (ATTY)
GIRLING, JANE L., dir. matl. mgt., Good Samaritan Hospital, Suffern, NY '84 (PUR)
GIROIR, D. MICHAEL, dir. pers., Southern Baptist Hospital, New Orleans, LA '75 (PERS)
GIROMINI, CHARLENE, dir. diet. in trng., Dallas-Fort Worth Medical Center, Grand Prairie, TX '78 (FOOD)
GIRON, EDWARD D., chief oper. off., Association of Medical Group Specialists, Hawthorne, CA '85 (PLNG)
GIRONE, GERARD MICHAEL, adm., Highsmith-Rainey Memorial Hospital, Fayetteville, NC '64
GIROUARD, RONALD P., asst. vice-pres., Roger Williams General Hospital, Providence, RI '78 (MGMT)
GISCH, JAMES THOMAS, dir. plant oper., Valley View Medical Center, Plymouth, WI '86 (ENG)
GISIN, GEORGE J., doctoral student, University of Iowa, Iowa City, IA '80
GIST, HOWARD B. JR., atty., St. Frances Cabrini Hospital, Alexandria, LA '69 (ATTY)
GITCH, DAVID W., adm., Harborview Medical Center, Seattle, WA '63
GITELMAN, FRANCES M., dir. vol. serv., Jewish Home and Hospital for Aged, New York, NY '73 (VOL)
GITELSON, AILEEN, dir. soc. work, Northern Westchester Hospital Center, Mount Kisco, NY '83 (SOC)
GITTINS, DAVID A., atty., Tri-State Memorial Hospital, Clarkston, WA '83 (ATTY)
GITTLER, ROSALIE DERHAM, adm., Memorial Hospital for Cancer and Allied Diseases, New York, NY '73
GIULIANI, CHARLES J., mgt. syst. eng., St. Mary's Hospital, Milwaukee, WI '83 (MGMT)
GIUNTA, ADOLPH A., assoc. adm., Memorial Hospital, Hollywood, FL '71 (PUR)
GIURLANDO, ANGELA D., dir. pub. rel., Community Hospital of Lancaster, Lancaster, PA '85 (PR)
GIUSTI, MICHAEL G., mgr. matl., Methodist Medical Center of Illinois, Peoria, IL '81 (PUR)
GIVANS, DELORES A., supv. cent. serv. and rep., Saratoga Community Hospital, Detroit, MI '72 (CS)
GIVEN, DEBORAH, dir. pub. rel. and commun. serv., Memorial Hospital of Burlington County, Mount Holly, NJ '87 (PR)
GIVENS, JANE, dir. matl. mgt., Mary Rutan Hospital, Bellefontaine, OH '85 (CS)
GIVENS, STEPHEN K., adm., Lonesome Pine Hospital, Big Stone Gap, VA '80
GIVNER, ELEANOR S., pat. rep., Victoria General Hospital, Halifax, N.S., Canada '85 (PAT)
GIZZI, JAMES C., exec. vice-pres., St. Francis Hospital, Evanston, IL '64
GJERSETH, WAYNE H., dir. plant oper., Mount Sinai Medical Center, Milwaukee, WI '71 (ENG)
GJESDAHL, ANNETTE Z., RN, dir. med. nrsg., St. Luke's Hospitals, Fargo, ND '85 (NURS)
GJESTVANG, JON, dir. eng., Beloit Memorial Hospital, Beloit, WI '80 (ENG)
GLACE, H. DAVID, asst. exec. dir., Lewistown Hospital, Lewistown, PA '80
GLACKIN, SUSAN E., dir. food serv., St. Joseph Hospital, Lancaster, PA '80 (FOOD)
GLADDING, CAROLYN A., RN, assoc. dir. nrsg. serv., Halifax Hospital Medical Center, Daytona Beach, FL '80 (NURS)
GLADDING, MOLLY, dir. food and nutr. serv., St. Mary's Hospital, West Palm Beach, FL '82 (FOOD)
GLANSBERG-PHILLIPS, KAREN, Poway, CA '81 (SOC)
GLANZ, MARLENE R., dir. diet., Straith Memorial Hospital, Southfield, MI '82 (FOOD)
GLASER, DONALD ALAN, assoc. dir. eng., Shands Hospital, Gainesville, FL '85 (ENG)
GLASER, DONALD R., dir. plant oper., St. Mary Medical Center, Walla Walla, WA '85 (ENG)
GLASER, ROBERT E., atty., University Hospitals of Cleveland, Cleveland, OH '76 (ATTY)
GLASGOW, LOIS A., sr. mgr., Ernst and Whinney, Minneapolis, MN '80 (PLNG)
GLASMIRE, REBEKAH L., dir. diet., Texas Scottish Rite Hospital, Dallas, TX '84 (FOOD)
GLASS, ANDREW J., asst. vice-pres., Hamot Medical Center, Erie, PA '83 (ENG)
GLASS, BEVERLY A., mgr. vol. serv., Holy Cross Hospital, Detroit, MI '86 (VOL)
GLASS, CAROL P., dir. vol. serv., Saint Joseph's Hospital, Atlanta, GA '81 (VOL)
GLASS, JOEL, atty., Montefiore Medical Center, Bronx, NY '86 (RISK)(ATTY)
GLASS, NATALIE, adm. coor. soc. serv., Good Samaritan Hospital, Suffern, NY '69 (SOC)
GLASS, RICHARD W., vice-pres. mktg. and plng., Proctor Community Hospital, Peoria, IL '79 (PR) (PLNG)
GLASS, ROGER W., dir. adm. serv., Hutcheson Medical Center, Fort Oglethorpe, GA '87
GLASS, VIDULA PATEL, dir. diet. serv., Holy Cross Hospital, Silver Spring, MD '80 (FOOD)
GLASSANOS, PHILIP J., vice-pres., Amherst Associates, Inc., Lexington, MA '80 (PLNG)
GLASSCOCK, DOUGLAS J., atty., University of Texas, Office of General Counsel, Austin, TX '80 (RISK)(ATTY)
GLASSCOCK, GARY M., adm., Lloyd Noland Hospital and Health Ctrs, Birmingham, AL '73
GLASSIE, RICHARD J., chief eng., McCray Memorial Hospital, Kendallville, IN '82 (ENG)
GLASSMAN, JOHN, vice-pres., Stormont-Vail Regional Medical Center, Topeka, KS '86 (PR) (PLNG)
GLASSMIRE, JOHN W., dir. plant maint., St. Lawrence Rehabilitation Center, Lawrenceville, NJ '82 (ENG)
GLATTER, DAVID A., adm. anes., Hahnemann University Hospital, Philadelphia, PA '80 (PLNG)
GLAUBIGER, MEREL P., atty., University of California, Berkeley, CA '73 (ATTY)
GLAVIN, JAMES H. III, atty., Bellevue Maternity Hospital, Schenectady, NY '72 (ATTY)
GLAVIN, THOMAS M., dir. plng., Community Hospital Monterey Peninsula, Monterey, CA '75 (PLNG)
GLAVIN, YE-FAN WANG, PhD, dir. gerowtology center, St. Margaret Memorial Hospital, Pittsburgh, PA '87
GLAVIS, EDWARD S., asst. adm., Presbyterian Hospital, San Francisco, CA '75
GLAZA, ANTHONY M., adm. asst., William Beaumont Hospital-Troy, Troy, MI '84 (PLNG)
GLAZER, LINDA K., dir. soc. serv. and util. review, LaGuardia Hospital, Flushing, NY '86 (SOC)
GLAZER, SHARON J., atty., Hayt, Hayt and Landau, Miami, FL '82 (RISK)(ATTY)
GLEASON, DORIS E., med. rec. consult., West Allis, WI '64 (HON)
GLEASON, ERIC, mgr. qual. and risk assessment, St. Francis Hospital, Blue Island, IL '84 (RISK)
GLEASON, HILDUR M., dir. soc. work serv., Good Samaritan Community Healthcare, Puyallup, WA '77 (SOC)
GLEASON, JAMES S., atty., Our Lady of Lourdes Memorial Hospital, Binghamton, NY '79 (ATTY)
GLEASON, JOHN F., mgr., Peat, Marwick and Mitchell, New York, NY '82 (PLNG)
GLEASON, MARTIN F., partner, Ernst and Whinney, Newark, NJ '82
GLEASON, V. RANDOLPH, atty., Hermann Hospital, Houston, TX '81 (ATTY)
GLEAVE, BARBARA G., mgr. food serv., Mountain View Hospital, Payson, UT '84 (FOOD)
GLEAVES, LLOYD A., dir. nutr. and food serv., Tulare District Hospital, Tulare, CA '84 (FOOD)
GLEBA, JOANNE, rep. pub. rel., Ellis Hospital, Schenectady, NY '86 (PR)
GLEBER, CAROL A., vice-pres., Voluntary Hospitals of America Health Ventures, Irving, TX '79 (PLNG)(MGMT)
GLEICH, JAMES G., RN, dir. pur. and inventory control, Children's Hospital, St. Louis, MO '86 (PUR)
GLEISS, HENRY W., atty., Southwestern Michigan Health Association, St. Joseph, MI '84 (ATTY)
GLEITZ, HERBERT G., atty., Harris Methodist Health System, Fort Worth, TX '86 (ATTY)
GLENDINNING, ELIZABETH A., RN, asst. dir. nrsg., Norwalk Hospital, Norwalk, CT '71 (NURS)
GLENESK, ALAN E., vice-pres., John Short and Associates, Inc., Atlanta, GA '80 (PLNG)
GLENN, CHRISTOPHER A., pres., Glenn Pipeline, Inc., Kansas City, MO '84
GLENN, JAMIE C., dir. human res., St. Luke's Hospital, Maumee, OH '81 (VOL)
GLENN, JEANNETTE C., RN, dir. staff dev., McLeod Regional Medical Center, Florence, SC '86 (NURS)
GLENN, JOHN K., PhD, asst. prof., University of Missouri, School of Medicine, Columbia, MO '67 (MGMT)
GLENN, JOYCE A., dir. risk mgt., Silver Cross Hospital, Joliet, IL '82 (RISK)
GLENN, KAY, adm., Island Cardiac Corporation, Hicksville, NY '72
GLESSNER, MARY J., consult., Price Waterhouse, Chicago, IL '73 (AMB)
GLEZEN, JOSEPH W. III, dir. pers., Southeastern General Hospital, Lumberton, NC '72 (PERS)
GLICKMAN, BARBARA L., Southern Maryland Health Systems Agency, Clinton, MD '83
GLICKSMAN, EDWARD J., vice-pres., Good Samaritan Hospital, West Islip, NY '78 (MGMT)
GLIDEWELL, BARBARA L., pat. adv., University of Oregon Health Sciences Center, Portland, OR '80 (PAT)
GLIDEWELL, CALVIN E. JR., dir. mktg., Anne Arundel General Hospital, Annapolis, MD '82 (PLNG)
GLIEDT, BEVERLY, mgr. nrsg.-neonatal, Covenant Medical Center -St. Francis, Waterloo, IA '85 (RISK)
GLISSON, KATHY B., dir. hlthcare advantage, Hospital Corporation of America, Tallahassee, FL '86 (PLNG)
GLOBENSKY, NAN S., dir. pur. and pers., Albion Community Hospital, Albion, MI '58 (PUR)
GLOSSER, RITA, RN, dir. staff educ., Conemaugh Valley Memorial Hospital, Johnstown, PA '77 (EDUC)
GLOTH, FRED M. JR., atty., Blue Cross of Maryland, Inc., Baltimore, MD '78 (ATTY)
GLOVER, BEVERLY ANN, RN, pat. rep., City Hospital, Martinsburg, WV '84 (PAT)
GLOVER, CAROLYN H., RN, dir. nrsg., Lincoln County Hospital, Lincolnton, NC '87 (NURS)
GLOVER, JESSIE M., pat. rep., Hospital of the University of Pennsylvania, Philadelphia, PA '83 (PAT)
GLOVER, MARVIN H., mgr. plant oper., Schick Shadel Hospital, Santa Barbara, CA '83 (ENG)
GLOVER, NANCY L., RN, dir. cent. proc., Orangeburg-Calhoun Regional Hospital, Orangeburg, SC '81 (CS)
GLOVER, SUSAN M., coor. educ. res., Anne Arundel General Hospital, Annapolis, MD '84 (EDUC)
GLOW, ROBERT J., asst. adm., Mercy Hospital of New Orleans, New Orleans, LA '82
GLOZER, DONALD A., adm. qual. assur., Children's Hospital Medical Center of Akron, Akron, OH '85
GLUBA, ANDREW J., mgr. matl., Tuomey Hospital, Sumter, SC '82 (CS)(PUR)(ENVIRON)
GLUECKERT, BARBARA J., sr. oper. res. analyst, Michael Reese Hospital and Medical Center, Chicago, IL '85 (MGMT)
GLUECKSTEIN, SR. MARY BETH, RN, assoc. dir. qual. assur., St. Joseph's Hospital, Milwaukee, WI '73 (RISK)
GLUNZ, KARL D., consult., Children's Hospital of Wisconsin, Milwaukee, WI '58
GLUSKIN, ROBERT W., vice-pres. mktg. and bus. plng., Baxter Travenol Laboratories, Inc., Evanston, IL '83 (PLNG)
GLYMPH, JOHN DAVID, student, Duke University, Department of Health Administration, Durham, NC '86
GLYNN, ARTHUR J., dir. food serv., Iowa Lutheran Hospital, Des Moines, IA '73 (FOOD)
GLYNN, J. FREDERICK, chief soc. work serv., Veterans Administration Medical Center, Brockton, MA '73 (SOC)
GLYNN, JERRY, supt. bldg. and grds., Community Memorial Hospital and Nursing Home, Spring Valley, MN '77 (ENG)
GLYNN, MARIE, asst. dir. plng. and family counseling, Good Samaritan Hospital, Cincinnati, OH '80 (SOC)
GLYNN, MARYANNE C., RN, dir. nrsg., Bon Secours Hospital, North Miami, FL '86 (NURS)
GLYNN, RUSSELL, MD, assoc. chief, Veterans Administration Medical Center, Muskogee, OK '86 (AMB)
GNAGEY, LAUREL THOMAS, dir. pub. info., Mecosta County General Hospital, Big Rapids, MI '85 (PR)
GNASS, WILLIAM E., atty., Merced Community Medical Center, Merced, CA '83 (ATTY)
GNESDA, LINO, foreman biomedical equip. repair, Rush-Presbyterian-St. Luke's Medical Center, Chicago, IL '86 (ENG)
GOAD, BEVERLY, RN, coor. qual. care and risk mgr., Goleta Valley Community Hospital, Santa Barbara, CA '86 (RISK)
GOAD, TED O., dir. pers., Kaiser Foundation Hospital, Oakland, CA '81 (PERS)
GOANS, WILMA, mgr. cent. serv., Methodist Medical Center of Oak Ridge, Oak Ridge, TN '85 (CS)
GOBLE, BILLIE J., dir. soc. serv., Highlands Regional Medical Center, Prestonsburg, KY '81 (SOC)
GOBLE, PAUL E., vice-pres., Lee Hospital, Johnstown, PA '77
GODBER, SIR GEORGE EDWARD, MD, chm., Health Education Council, London, England '64 (HON)
GODDARD, CALVIN C., dir. pub. rel., Ingham Medical Center, Lansing, MI '86 (PR)
GODDARD, JAMES HOWARD, dir., Hall of Life, Denver, CO '80
GODDARD, NANETTE L., RN, asst. prof. nrsg. adm. prog., University of Texas Medical Branch Hospitals, Galveston, TX '80 (NURS)
GODDEN, BARBARA A., dir. vol. serv., Kaiser Foundation Hospital, Sacramento, CA '85 (VOL)
GODEK, ROBERT J., dir. pers., St. Mary Hospital, Livonia, MI '83 (PERS)
GODFREY, CYNTHIA, pat. rep., Society of the New York Hospital, New York, NY '86 (PAT)
GODFREY, DOROTHY, supv. cent. serv., St. Barnabas Hospital, Bronx, NY '86 (CS)
GODFREY, JONATHAN F., exec. dir., Houston County Hospital, Crockett, TX '75
GODFREY, JOYCE ELAINE, dir. soc. serv., Emory University Hospital, Atlanta, GA '80 (SOC)
GODFREY, MARTIN, asst. chief maint., Montefiore Hospital, Pittsburgh, PA '78 (ENG)
GODFREY, PAUL G., dir. plant oper. and maint., East Alabama Medical Center, Opelika, AL '86 (ENG)
GODFREY, COL. WILLIAM HOWARD, MSC USA, (ret.), Beaver Creek, OH '61
GODIN, ARTHUR C., adm., Sacred Heart Hospital, Norristown, PA '61
GODLESKY, VINCENT W., consult., Wellesley Hills, MA '53 (PUR)(LIFE)
GODOMSKI, PATRICIA L., Middlefield, CT '77 (MGMT)
GODSPEED, RON, dir. pub. rel., Exeter Hospital, Exeter, NH '86 (PR)
GODSTED, GLENN, dir. eng. and maint., South Chicago Community Hospital, Chicago, IL '71 (ENG)
GODWIN, JAMES C. JR., dir. pers., Richmond Memorial Hospital, Richmond, VA '83 (PERS)
GODWIN, PAUL S. II, supv. eng. and maint., Christ Hospital, Cincinnati, OH '85 (ENG)
GODWIN, ROBERT W., dir. eng., Humana Women's Hospital -Tampa, Tampa, FL '83 (ENG)
GOE, MICHAEL D., vice-pres. human res., St. Luke's Medical Center, Phoenix, AZ '82 (PERS)
GOE, STEVEN J., Scripps Memorial Hospital-Encinitas, Encinitas, CA '76 (SOC)
GOEBEL, EDWARD M., dir. plant oper., Hawthorne Hospital, Hawthorne, CA '81 (ENG)
GOEBERT, H. WILLIAM JR., atty., Queen's Medical Center, Honolulu, HI '80 (ATTY)
GOEDECK, PETER S., dir. plant serv., Goleta Valley Community Hospital, Santa Barbara, CA '81 (ENG)
GOEHLE, WILLIAM L., dir. eng., Good Samaritan Hospital, Pottsville, PA '81 (ENG)
GOEHRING, LUTHER W., vice-pres. reg. oper., Samaritan Health Service, Phoenix, AZ '80
GOEHRING, WALTER O. II, vice-pres., North Hills Passavant Hospital, Pittsburgh, PA '75 (PLNG)
GOERIGK, URSULA M., assoc. adm., Emerson Hospital, Concord, MA '74
GOERING, GRACE A., pat. rep., Bethany Medical Center, Kansas City, KS '84 (PAT)
GOERING, WALTER S., dir. hskpg. and ldry. serv., Beebe Hospital of Sussex County, Lewes, DE '86 (ENVIRON)
GOERKE, SIEGFRIED R., clin. eng., St. Joseph's Hospital, Milwaukee, WI '81 (ENG)
GOETSCH, HAROLD E., dir. hosp. affairs and coor. medicare, Blue Cross of Washington and Alaska, Inc., Seattle, WA '48 (LIFE)
GOETZE, CAROLYN MARIE, RN, vice-pres. nrsg., St. Francis Hospital, Roslyn, NY '74 (NURS)
GOFF, CARLETON N., res. arch., Massachusetts General Hospital, Boston, MA '66
GOFF, MARJORIE V., dir. nrsg. educ., Northwest Area Health Education Center, Bowman Gray School of Medicine, Winston Salem, NC '75 (EDUC)
GOFF, RODNEY C., dir. sup. serv., Memorial Hospital, York, PA '87
GOFF, RONALD, dir. matl. mgt., Takoma Adventist Hospital, Greeneville, TN '85 (PUR)
GOFF, SGM DAVID A., MSC USA, Mesquite, TX '80 (PAT)
GOGLIA, GAIL, RN, vice-pres. nrsg. serv., Blaine County Medical Center, Hailey, ID '85 (NURS)
GOGNA, OMKUMAR, chief eng., Greater Harlem Nursing Home, New York, NY '79 (ENG)
GOHDES, MARY K., RN, coor. cent. serv., Dakota Hospital, Fargo, ND '86 (CS)
GOING, JOHN E., dir. matl. mgt., Ventura County Medical Center, Ventura, CA '79 (CS)(PUR)(ENG)

GOING, ROBERT M., atty., St. Joseph Hospital, Lancaster, PA '77 (ATTY)
GOINGS, JEAN D., RN, dir. nrsg., Nicholas H. Noyes Memorial Hospital, Dansville, NY '79 (NURS)
GOINS, BILL, vice-pres., Mercy Hospital, Owensboro, KY '86 (RISK)
GOINS, LARRY L., atty., Eastern Idaho Regional Medical Center, Idaho Falls, ID '83 (ATTY)
GOLAN, BERNARD J., exec. dir., South Suburban Home Health Service, Inc., North Riverside, IL '77
GOLAN, SUE, RN, supv. cent. sterile sup., New Britain General Hospital, New Britain, CT '80 (CS)
GOLASZEWSKI, THOMAS, dir. distrib. serv., Hospital of the University of Pennsylvania, Philadelphia, PA '83 (PUR)
GOLD, BARRY A., atty., Ellis Hospital, Schenectady, NY '78 (ATTY)
GOLD, EILEEN, assoc. dir. soc. work, St. Charles Hospital and Rehabilitation Center, Port Jefferson, NY '82 (SOC)
GOLD, JULIE BETH, student, Program in Health Care, School of Business Administration, Temple University, Philadelphia, PA '85
GOLD, LAWRENCE H., vice-pres., Long Island College Hospital, Brooklyn, NY '72
GOLD, MICHAELE R., dir. pub. rel., Mallinckrodt Institute of Radiology, St. Louis, MO '86 (PR)
GOLD, MITCHELL G., mgr., Ernst and Whinney, Baltimore, MD '86 (PLNG)
GOLDA, E. ANTHONY, dir. corp. plng. and mktg. res., Brim and Associates, Inc., Portland, OR '79 (PLNG)
GOLDBAUM, CAROL S., asst. dir. soc. work, University of Illinois Medical Center, Chicago, IL '84 (SOC)
GOLDBERG-ALBERTS, AMY, student, Program in Health Care Administration, Temple University, Philadelphia, PA '85
GOLDBERG, ALAN J., pres., Applied Management Systems, Inc., Burlington, MA '73 (MGMT)
GOLDBERG, ALAN S., atty., First Healthcare Corporation, Boston, MA '79 (ATTY)
GOLDBERG, ALAN S., vice-pres. adm. serv., Gottlieb Memorial Hospital, Melrose Park, IL '78 (ENG)
GOLDBERG, BARBARA RAITT, dir. educ. and info., Center for Recovery at John F. Kennedy Hospital, Atlantis, FL '86 (PR)(AMB)
GOLDBERG, BARRY, pres. and chief exec. off., Comed HMO Headquarters, Denville, NJ '72 (MGMT)(AMB)
GOLDBERG, CATHERINE MURPHY, assoc. adm., Hospital of the University of Pennsylvania, Philadelphia, PA '79
GOLDBERG, DANA E., mgr. plng., Griffin Hospital, Derby, CT '86 (PLNG)
GOLDBERG, DANIEL, atty., Albert Einstein Medical Center, Philadelphia, PA '77 (ATTY)
GOLDBERG, ELAINE R., dir. vol. serv. and guest rel., Burbank Hospital, Fitchburg, MA '85 (VOL)
GOLDBERG, EMMET M., dir. client dev., Medicus Systems Corporation, Arlington Heights, IL '76 (MGMT)
GOLDBERG, HOWARD S., mgt. eng., Yale-New Haven Hospital, New Haven, CT '81 (MGMT)
GOLDBERG, IVAN, adm., John F. Kennedy Memorial Hospital, Atlantis, FL '87 (AMB)
GOLDBERG, JUDITH C., mgr. vol. serv., Halifax Hospital Medical Center, Daytona Beach, FL '87 (VOL)
GOLDBERG, KATHRYN E., dir. food serv., Thomas Jefferson University Hospital, Philadelphia, PA '74 (FOOD)
GOLDBERG, LAWRENCE S., dir. natl. affairs and health care, Deloitte Haskins and Sells, Washington, DC '84
GOLDBERG, MERYL A., dir. matl. mgt., Tuxedo Memorial Hospital, Tuxedo Park, NY '82 (PUR)
GOLDBERG, MICHAEL J., dir. food serv., Bon Secours Hospital, Baltimore, MD '86 (FOOD)
GOLDBERG, NEIL A., atty., Millard Fillmore Hospital, Buffalo, NY '86 (ATTY)
GOLDBERG, PEARL, dir. soc. work serv., Hospital for Joint Diseases Orthapaedic Institute, New York, NY '79 (SOC)
GOLDBERG, ROSS K., vice-pres. corp. commun., Healthwest Medical Centers, Chatsworth, CA '80 (PR)
GOLDBERG, SONIA K., dir. soc. serv., Our Lady of Mercy Hospital, Cincinnati, OH '86 (SOC)
GOLDBLATT, MAURICE, bd. chm., Goldblatt Brothers, Inc., Chicago, IL '64 (HON)
GOLDBLATT, STANFORD J., atty., University of Chicago Hospitals, Chicago, IL '78 (ATTY)
GOLDEN, BETTY M., RN, dir. nrsg., Medical College of Georgia Hospital and Clinics, Augusta, GA '71 (NURS)
GOLDEN, DIANE FAVA, coor. commun. liaison, Rhode Island Hospital, Providence, RI '85 (EDUC)
GOLDEN, DOUGLAS S., supv. biomedical, St. Mary's Medical Center, Duluth, MN '86 (ENG)
GOLDEN, JED A., in-patient adm., New York Hospital, New York, NY '78
GOLDEN, JOHN C., vice-pres. gen. serv., Chestnut Hill Hospital, Philadelphia, PA '79
GOLDEN, KIM WALTON, student, Georgia State University, Institute of Health Administration, Atlanta, GA '85
GOLDEN, NANCY S., RN, dir. nrsg., St. Louis Regional Medical Center, St. Louis, MO '82 (NURS)
GOLDEN, R. KEITH, dir. food serv., Good Shepherd Hospital, Barrington, IL '80 (FOOD)
GOLDEN, W. THOMAS, vice-pres., Northern Ocean Hospital System, Point Pleasant, NJ '77
GOLDENBERG, ROBERT B., dir. corp. ventures, Children's Hospital, Columbus, OH '85 (PR)
GOLDENBERG, SYBIL, dir. pers., Peninsula Hospital Center, Far Rockaway, NY '86 (PERS)
GOLDFARB, ROCHELLE BROOKS, dir. vol., West Park Hospital, Philadelphia, PA '72 (VOL)
GOLDFELD, ARON P., student, Baruch College, New York, NY '86
GOLDFINGER, SUSAN R., dir. soc. work, Rolling Hill Hospital, Elkins Park, PA '85 (SOC)
GOLDIE, THOMAS B., dir. plant oper., Queen of the Valley Hospital, Napa, CA '85 (ENG)
GOLDING, JOHN G., atty., Humana Specialty Hospital-Charlotte, Charlotte, NC '75 (ATTY)
GOLDMAN, C. MITCHELL, atty., Pottstown Memorial Medical Center, Pottstown, PA '86 (ATTY)
GOLDMAN, EDWARD B., atty., University Hospital, Ann Arbor, MI '80 (ATTY)
GOLDMAN, ELLEN F., prin., Lammers and Gershon Associates, Inc., Reston, VA '80 (PLNG)
GOLDMAN, JAMES O. JR., MD, dir. qual. assur., AMI Central Carolina Hospital, Sanford, NC '82
GOLDMAN, JEAN, dir. soc. serv., Bethesda Hospital, Chicago, IL '86 (SOC)
GOLDMAN, LAWRENCE, dir. pharm., Muhlenberg Regional Medical Center, Plainfield, NJ '79
GOLDMAN, MARY H., pat. rep., Kishwaukee Community Hospital, De Kalb, IL '78 (PAT)
GOLDMAN, MICHAEL ALLEN, dir. soc. serv., Cabell Huntington Hospital, Huntington, WV '79 (SOC)
GOLDMAN, MICHAEL S., sr. asst. adm., Grace Hospital, Detroit, MI '80
GOLDMAN, MYRON W., dir. soc. work, Mount Sinai Medical Center, Cleveland, OH '66 (SOC)
GOLDMAN, NAOMI L., student, Columbia University School of Public Health and Administrative Medicine, New York, NY '83
GOLDMAN, SHARON E., mgr. matl., American Oncologic Hospital, Philadelphia, PA '80 (PUR)
GOLDMAN, THOMAS, pres., Bayshore Community Hospital, Holmdel, NJ '63
GOLDMAN, TRUDY A., risk mgr., University of Illinois at the Medical Center, Chicago, IL '81 (RISK)
GOLDMAN, VIRGINIA B., RN, dir. nrsg. surg. serv., Mount Sinai Medical Center, Miami Beach, FL '82 (NURS)
GOLDSMITH, EUNICE M., dir. educ., Providence Memorial Hospital, El Paso, TX '87 (EDUC)
GOLDSMITH, JEFF C., natl. tech. adv., Ernst and Whinney, Chicago, IL '83 (PLNG)
GOLDSMITH, SHARON ANN, RN, asst. exec. dir. nrsg., Hardin Memorial Hospital, Elizabethtown, KY '79 (NURS)
GOLDSMITH, SHEILA G., RN, assoc. dir. nrs., St. Joseph Regional Medical Center, Lewiston, ID '86 (NURS)
GOLDSMITH, THOMAS, gen. foreman, Electrical Contractor, White Plains, NY '87 (ENG)
GOLDSTEIN, ALAN J., atty., Rush-Presbyterian-St. Luke Medical Center, Chicago, IL '86 (ATTY)
GOLDSTEIN, ALLAN D., atty., Central General Hospital, Plainview, NY '83 (ATTY)
GOLDSTEIN, ALVIN, mgr. biomedical eng., Long Island Jewish Medical Center, New York, NY '76 (ENG)
GOLDSTEIN, ANDREA, RN, dir., Ambulatory Surgical Center of Miami, Inc., Miami, FL '87 (AMB)
GOLDSTEIN, ARLENE J., dir. soc. work, AMI North Ridge Medical Center, Fort Lauderdale, FL '85 (SOC)
GOLDSTEIN, ARNOLD H., consult., East Norwich, NY '64
GOLDSTEIN, BARBARA A., RN, vice-pres. nrsg., Stamford Hospital, Stamford, CT '77 (NURS)
GOLDSTEIN, FREDERIC SCOTT, Farmers Branch, TX '83
GOLDSTEIN, HAROLD M., dir., Center for Medical Manpower Studies, Northeastern University, Boston, MA '77
GOLDSTEIN, JULIE A., mgr. contracts and affil., University of California Davis Medical Center, Sacramento, CA '84
GOLDSTEIN, KAREN, dir. soc. serv., Queen of the Valley Hospital, West Covina, CA '85 (SOC)
GOLDSTEIN, MARC R., bus. mgr. nrsg. serv., Hahnemann University Hospital, Philadelphia, PA '81 (MGMT)
GOLDSTEIN, MARIAN, assoc. dir. soc. work serv., Long Island Jewish Medical Center, New York, NY '85 (SOC)
GOLDSTEIN, PAUL, MD, chm., Hospital of Saint Raphael, New Haven, CT '87 (AMB)
GOLDSTEIN, ROBERT, vice-pres., Elizabeth General Medical Center, Elizabeth, NJ '81
GOLDSTEIN, STANLEY M., dir., New Medico Associates, Inc., Boston, MA '87 (PLNG)
GOLDSTEIN, TOBEY ALLERTON, dir. pers., Edgewater Hospital, Chicago, IL '68 (PERS)
GOLDSTON, MYNA, RN, dir. nrs., Community Hospital, Tallassee, AL '82 (NURS)
GOLDT, MURIEL T., liaison cardiac surveillance, Michael Reese Hospital and Medical Center, Chicago, IL '80 (PAT)
GOLEC, JOSEPHINE B., coor. staff dev., Middlesex Memorial Hospital, Middletown, CT '86 (EDUC)
GOLEMAN, W. LAYTON, sr. vice-pres., Affiliated Hospitals Systems, Houston, TX '84
GOLEMBE, ROSALIND, dir. soc. work, State University Hospital, Downstate Medical Center, Brooklyn, NY '77 (SOC)
GOLENWSKY, CAROL J., dir. commun., St. Mary's Hospital, Waterbury, CT '83 (ENG)
GOLIGOSKI, THOMAS J., dir. human res., Charter Grove Hospital, Corona, CA '86 (PERS)
GOLL, ELSIE ZARIN, consult., Beth Abraham Hospital, Bronx, NY '72 (PAT)
GOLLIHER, PAUL E., PhD, assoc. prof., Program in Hospital Administration, Trinity University, San Antonio, TX '69
GOLUBIC, HELEN D., vice-pres. commun., Conemaugh Valley Memorial Hospital, Johnstown, PA '79 (PR)
GOLUBSKI, THERESA, mgr. commun., St. Joseph's Medical Center, South Bend, IN '74 (ENG)
GOMBERG, FRANCINE G., RN, vice-pres. nrsg. serv., Southwest Florida Regional Medical Center, Fort Myers, FL '82 (NURS)
GOMBESKI, WILLIAM R. JR., dir. market res. and plng., Cleveland Clinic Hospital, Cleveland, OH '85 (PLNG)
GOMBITA, M. PATRICIA, coor. commun. educ., Somerset Community Hospital, Somerset, PA '86 (EDUC)
GOMBKOTO, JOSEPH L., adm. spec. proj., West Allis Memorial Hospital, West Allis, WI '70
GOMES, LT. FRANCINE M., MSC USN, staff civil eng., Naval Hospital, Orlando, FL '84 (ENG)
GOMES, JOSEPH M., dir. soc. serv., Mary Chiles Hospital, Mount Sterling, KY '82 (SOC)
GOMEZ, JERRY R., dir. educ., St. Tammany Parish Hospital, Covington, LA '85 (EDUC)
GOMEZ, MANUEL, dir. environ. serv., Coral Gables Hospital, Coral Gables, FL '86 (ENG)
GOMEZ, MYRTLE R., RN, dir. nrsg., District of Columbia General Hospital, Washington, DC '83 (NURS)
GOMILLER, FRANK, dir. plant serv., Shriners Burns Institute, Cincinnati, OH '86 (ENG)
GOMPERS, WILLIAM C., asst. dir., Cedars of Lebanon Health Care Center, Miami, FL '72
GONGAWARE, CAROLE ANN, dir. critical care and cardiac lab. serv., St. Mary's Hospital and Rehabilitation Center, Minneapolis, MN '80 (NURS)
GONZALES, AUGUSTINE JR., adm. asst., Yakima Valley Memorial Hospital, Yakima, WA '80 (MGMT)
GONZALES, MARY ALICE, dir. risk mgt. and dist. fin., Edna Hospital, Edna, TX '86 (RISK)
GONZALES, ROBERT, dist. mgr., St. Vincent Hospital, Santa Fe, NM '87 (ENG)
GONZALEZ, DANIEL, dir. pers., St. Joseph's Hospital, Tampa, FL '84 (PERS)
GONZALEZ, ERNESTO G., supv. cent. serv., St. Joseph's Hospital, St. Paul, MN '86 (CS)
GONZALEZ, LOUIS M., Health Strategists Ltd., Madison, CT '82 (PLNG)
GONZALEZ, SOLEDAD, dir. soc. serv., Humana Hospital -San Antonio, San Antonio, TX '85 (SOC)
GOOCH, THOMAS R., dir. plant oper., Pleasant Valley Hospital, Point Pleasant, WV '85 (ENG)
GOOD, COL. DONALD S., MSC USAF, chief med. serv. corp., Department of the Air Force, Office of the Surgeon General, Bolling AFB, DC '63
GOOD, JOHN D., asst. adm. pers. and trng., Piedmont Hospital, Atlanta, GA '78 (PERS)
GOOD, JOHN E., dir. mktg., Mercy Medical Center, Redding, CA '85 (PLNG)
GOOD, JULIAN H., atty., Touro Infirmary, New Orleans, LA '75 (ATTY)
GOOD, PATRICIA A., RN, adm. pat. care, Antelope Memorial Hospital, Neligh, NE '84 (NURS)
GOOD, ROGER S., adm., Sierra View District Hospital, Porterville, CA '80
GOODALE, JEAN R., sr. sect. mgr. oper. plng., Baxter Travenol Laboratories, Inc., Deerfield, IL '85 (PUR)
GOODALL, ROBERT, coor. educ., Shaughnessy Hospital, Vancouver, B.C., Canada '83 (EDUC)
GOODBY, MARY C., mgr. emp., Tri-City Medical Center, Oceanside, CA '83 (PERS)
GOODE, BARBARA J., dir. soc. serv., Swedish Covenant Hospital, Chicago, IL '75 (SOC)
GOODE, COLLEEN J., RN, dir. nrsg., Horn Memorial Hospital, Ida Grove, IA '80 (NURS)
GOODE, MARCIA HOLMES, asst. risk mgr., Memorial Hospital System, Houston, TX '84 (RISK)
GOODE, MARGARET C., dir. vol. serv., Faulkner Hospital, Boston, MA '82 (VOL)
GOODE, RUTH ANN, dir. soc. work, St. John Hospital, Cleveland, OH '86 (SOC)
GOODELL, ADDISON, dir. pers., Ashtabula County Medical Center, Ashtabula, OH '84 (PERS)
GOODENOUGH, MARION P., RN, asst. dir. nrsg., Somerset Medical Center, Somerville, NJ '84 (NURS)
GOODER, CHARLES E., assoc. dir., Minnesota Regional Health Associates Fund, Minneapolis, MN '86 (PLNG)
GOODFRIEND, WILLIAM, dir. eng., Memorial Medical Center, Springfield, IL '71 (ENG)
GOODHARD, NORMA J., mgr. cent. serv., Easton Hospital, Easton, PA '83 (CS)
GOODHART, LINDA J., RN, dir. nrsg., Pottsville Hospital and Warne Clinic, Pottsville, PA '83 (NURS)
GOODIRON, VANCE N., supv. cent. serv. and instrument proc., St. Mary's Hospital and Health Center, Tucson, AZ '85 (CS)
GOODMAN, ANNE S., human res. consult., Charter Medical Corporation, Richmond, VA '86 (PERS)
GOODMAN, DONNA L., mgr. pur., Wyman Park Medical Center, Baltimore, MD '84 (PUR)
GOODMAN, ELLA, dir. counseling and soc. serv., Memorial Hospital, South Bend, IN '85 (SOC)
GOODMAN, JAMES, dir. mgt. info. serv., Baptist Medical Center of Oklahoma, Oklahoma City, OK '85 (MGMT)
GOODMAN, JAY K., vice-pres. pub. rel. and mktg., Middletown Regional Hospital, Middletown, OH '84 (PR)
GOODMAN, JOSEPH C., dir. pub. affairs, Massachusetts Eye and Ear Infirmary, Boston, MA '84 (PR) (PLNG)
GOODMAN, KAREN I., atty., Sisters of Mercy Health Corporation, Farmington Hills, MI '86 (ATTY)
GOODMAN, LISA S., dir. vol. serv., Southside Regional Medical Center, Petersburg, VA '83 (VOL)
GOODMAN, LOUIS, dir. pers., Montefiore Hospital, Pittsburgh, PA '85 (PERS)
GOODMAN, MARIAN MICHL, dir. diet., LaGuardia Hospital, Flushing, NY '67 (FOOD)
GOODMAN, NANCY L., dir. cent. sup., Walter O. Boswell Memorial Hospital, Sun City, AZ '82 (CS)
GOODMAN, NANCY R., dir. vol., Children's Hospital of Pittsburgh, Pittsburgh, PA '68 (VOL)
GOODMAN, NANETTE L., dir. vol. serv., Hebrew Home and Hospital, Hartford, CT '85 (VOL)
GOODMAN, NORMAN B., pres., West Suburban Hospital Medical Center, Oak Park, IL '79
GOODMAN, PATRICIA, dir. soc. work serv., University Hospital, Stony Brook, NY '81 (SOC)
GOODMAN, PHYLLIS L., assoc. vice-pres. commun. and pub. affairs, St. Luke's-Roosevelt Hospital Center, New York, NY '86 (PR)
GOODMAN, PORTIA, coor. telecommun., Rockefeller University Hospital, New York, NY '86 (ENG)
GOODMAN, ROBERT L., MD, actg. exec. dir., Hospital of the University of Pennsylvania, Philadelphia, PA '86
GOODMAN, TERESA J., adm. res., Forrest County General Hospital, Hattiesburg, MS '84
GOODMAN, TERRI, dir. commun. liaison, Bethany Pavilion, Bethany, OK '86 (PR)
GOODMAN, VERA BOYLE, dir. vol. serv., St. Vincent's Medical Center, Jacksonville, FL '82 (VOL)
GOODRICH, PATRICIA J., mgt. eng., Pacific Presbyterian Medical Center, San Francisco, CA '84 (MGMT)

GOODRUM, NANCY M., RN, assoc. dir. nrsg., Clayton General Hospital, Riverdale, GA '85 (NURS)
GOODSON, CAROL ELIZABETH, RN, dir. surg. nrsg., Methodist Medical Center, Dallas, TX '86 (NURS)
GOODSON, JOANNE, partner, Flr Health Resources, Atlanta, GA '85
GOODSON, MARGUERITE, RN, vice-pres. nrsg., St. James Hospital Medical Center, Chicago Heights, IL '77 (NURS)
GOODSPEED, SCOTT WINANS, vice-pres., Elliot Hospital, Manchester, NH '79 (PLNG)
GOODSTEIN, JERRY, asst. dir. support serv., Bellevue Hospital Center, New York, NY '83 (PLNG)
GOODWIN, BARBARA A., coor. pers., Memorial Hospital, Owosso, MI '86 (PERS)
GOODWIN, CLAIRE K., vice-pres., Kennebec Valley Medical Center, Augusta, ME '80 (RISK)
GOODWIN, DAVID A., dir. matl. mgt., Intermountain Health Care, Inc., Salt Lake City, UT '74 (PUR)
GOODWIN, FRANK L., dir. risk mgt., John F. Kennedy Medical Center, Chicago, IL '81 (PERS)(RISK)
GOODWIN, IRA H., pres., Goodwin and Company, Inc., New York, NY '85
GOODWIN, KEITH D., dir. pat. unit mgt., Children's Hospital, Columbus, OH '84
GOODWIN, LINDA K., coor. plng., Camden-Clark Memorial Hospital, Parkersburg, WV '86 (PR) (PLNG)
GOODWIN, MEREDITH V., dir. human res., HCA Donelson Hospital, Nashville, TN '86 (PERS)
GOODWIN, MICHAEL A., maint. elec., Charter Rivers Hospital, West Columbia, SC '85 (ENG)
GOODWIN, NEVA M., Thoms Proestler, Davenport, IA '83 (FOOD)
GOODWIN, PATRICIA ANN, RN, adm. nrsg., Ferguson Hospital, Grand Rapids, MI '68 (NURS)
GOODWIN, PEGGY J., RN, vice-pres. pat. care, Central Baptist Hospital, Lexington, KY '86 (NURS)
GOODWIN, PHILLIP H., exec. vice-pres., Charleston Area Medical Center, Charleston, WV '65
GOODWIN, PHYLLIS A., dir. diet. serv., Nashville Memorial Hospital, Madison, TN '81 (FOOD)
GOODWIN, RAY A., atty., Arkansas Methodist Hospital, Paragould, AR '79 (ATTY)
GOODWIN, SR. RUTH, vice-pres. misson and ministry, Franciscan Health System, Chadds Ford, PA '86
GOODWIN, SUSAN J., RN, vice-pres. nrsg., Carroll County General Hospital, Westminster, MD '82 (NURS)
GOODWIN, WILLIAM H., dir. plant serv., Poudre Valley Hospital, Fort Collins, CO '80 (ENG)
GOODWIN, LT. COL. WILLIAM L. JR., MSC USA, chief nutr. care div., Frankfurt Army Regional Medical Center, APO New York, NY '81 (FOOD)
GOODWYNE, LUCILLE, dir., Abbott-Northwestern Home Health Care, Minneapolis, MN '87 (AMB)
GOOLSBEE, DANIEL S., dir. bldg. serv., DeKalb General Hospital, Decatur, GA '70 (ENG)
GOOSEN, SIDNEY S., (ret.), Detroit, MI '47 (LIFE)
GOOSNEY, ROSE, exec. hskpg., Syosset Community Hospital, Syosset, NY '86 (ENVIRON)
GORA, RAYMOND FRANCIS, pat. rep., Jersey City Medical Center, Jersey City, NJ '84 (PAT)
GORA, ROBERT R., vice-pres. oper., Catawba Memorial Hospital, Hickory, NC '74
GORAJ, JOSEPH RICHARD, dir. soc. serv., Sioux Valley Hospital, Sioux Falls, SD '82 (SOC)
GORAN, MARK H., atty., Barnes Hospital, St. Louis, MO '83 (ATTY)
GORCZYCA, JOANNA TERESA, dir. soc. work, Clara Maass Medical Center, Belleville, NJ '85 (SOC)
GORDETSKY, GORDON R., prin., G. R. Gordetsky Consultants, San Diego, CA '85 (ENG)
GORDON-GIRVIN, SHARON M., sr. analyst, Management of America, Tallahassee, FL '86 (PLNG)
GORDON, BARRY E., coor. resp. rehab., Catholic Medical Center, Manchester, NH '83 (EDUC)
GORDON, BAYLEE, dir. vol. serv., Montefiore Hospital, Pittsburgh, PA '84 (VOL)
GORDON, DANIEL H., dir. matl. mgt., Montgomery Regional Hospital, Blacksburg, VA '86 (PUR)
GORDON, DIANA S., asst. adm., Eastern Maine Medical Center, Bangor, ME '74 (RISK)
GORDON, DOROTHY L., RN, assoc. adm. nrsg., National Rehabilitation Hospital, Washington, DC '85 (NURS)
GORDON, EDWIN H., Convent Station, NJ '84
GORDON, ELLIOTT K., dir. pers., Wagoner Community Hospital, Wagoner, OK '84 (PERS)
GORDON, GAILORD J., mgr., Permanente Medical Group, Berkeley, CA '78 (ENG)
GORDON, JENNIFER H., dir. commun. rel., Hendrick Medical Center, Abilene, TX '79 (PR)
GORDON, JERRY, gen. mgr., Airco Medical and Special Products, Lodi, NJ '86
GORDON, JOEL E., dir. adm. syst., Hospital Corporation of America, Nashville, TN '82 (MGMT)
GORDON, JOSEPH A., Lancaster, PA '67
GORDON, L. JAMES, atty., Licking Memorial Hospital, Newark, OH '76 (ATTY)
GORDON, LOUIS E., chief exec. off., Western Missouri Medical Center, Warrensburg, MO '55 (PLNG)(LIFE)
GORDON, MARILYN, dir. vol., Palisades General Hospital, North Bergen, NJ '76 (VOL)
GORDON, MARJORIE G., dir. nutr. serv., Highlands Regional Medical Center, Sebring, FL '85 (FOOD)
GORDON, NATALIE, chief soc. serv., Jewish Home and Hospital for Aged, New York, NY '81 (SOC)
GORDON, PATRICIA H., RN, vice-pres., Baptist Medical Center of Oklahoma, Oklahoma City, OK '81 (NURS)
GORDON, PAUL A., atty., Hospital Council of Northern California, San Bruno, CA '77 (ATTY)
GORDON, R. KENNETH, atty., Houston Northwest Medical Center, Houston, TX '84 (ATTY)
GORDON, R. WARREN, dir. staff serv., Kennestone Hospital, Marietta, GA '72 (PERS)
GORDON, ROBERT S., vice-pres., Baptist Memorial Hospital, Memphis, TN '76
GORDON, SETH M., assoc. dir. prof. and regulatory serv., Hospital Association of New York State, Albany, NY '85 (PLNG)
GORDON, SHEILA RUPPRECHT, pat. advocate and coor. risk mgt., East Tennessee Baptist Hospital, Knoxville, TN '82 (PAT)(RISK)
GORDON, STEVEN ROGER, adm., Parkland Medical Center, Derry, NH '78
GORDON, COL. THOMAS J., MSC USA, sr. oper. off., 2nd Hospital Center, Hamilton AFB, CA '72
GORDON, WILLIAM H., dir. mktg. and pub. rel., Saint Mary Hospital, Langhorne, PA '84 (PR)
GORE, BARBARA A., dir. food serv., Metropolitan Hospital, Grand Rapids, MI '86 (FOOD)
GORE, BERNARD L. JR., adm., Patterson Army Community Hospital, Fort Monmouth, NJ '78
GORE, GEORGE H., atty., Holy Cross Hospital, Fort Lauderdale, FL '68 (ATTY)
GORE, JAMES E., chief eng., Memorial Hospital of Laramie County, Cheyenne, WY '76 (ENG)
GORE, JAMES G., adm., Pacific Health Associates, Seattle, WA '75
GORE, MARY C., RN, claims analyst, Encon Insurance Managers, Inc., Ottawa, Ont., Canada '85 (RISK)
GORE, SAUNDRA S., RN, dir. cardiology, San Pedro Peninsula Hospital, San Pedro, CA '82 (NURS)
GORE, THOMAS, asst. vice-pres. mktg. and pub. rel., Tulane University Hospital and Clinics, New Orleans, LA '71 (PR)
GORECKI, A. YVONNE, RN, adm. dir. pat. care serv., St. Joseph's Hospital and Health Center, Dickinson, ND '82 (NURS)
GORECKI, TRUDY, RN, assoc. adm. nrsg., Illinois Masonic Medical Center, Chicago, IL '75 (NURS)
GORELICK, SHERRI R., coor. pat. and pub. rel., University of Michigan Health Service, Ann Arbor, MI '82 (PR)
GORELIK, ELIHU A., adm., New York State Health Department, New York, NY '74
GOREN, NATHAN A., dir. commun. serv., North Broward Hospital District, Fort Lauderdale, FL '82 (PR)
GORGUZE, AMY C., student, University of Illinois School of Public Health, Chicago, IL '85
GORHAM, CONNIE, RN, dir. nrsg., Nash General Hospital, Rocky Mount, NC '77 (NURS)
GORHAM, MERRY L., RN, supv. nrsg., Bethany Hospital, Chicago, IL '86 (NURS)
GORIN, EDWARD J., vice-pres. pub. affairs, Hackensack Medical Center, Hackensack, NJ '81 (PR)
GORIN, JEANETTE, mgr. emp., St. John's Healthcare Corporation, Anderson, IN '80 (PERS)
GORIUP, LT. COL. FRANKLIN J., MSC USA, chief force dev., Walter Reed Army Medical Center, Washington, DC '77
GORMAN, EILY P., RN, asst. chief, United States Army Nurse Corps, Falls Church, VA '86 (NURS)
GORMAN, LEONARD H., risk mgr., Morton F. Plant Hospital, Clearwater, FL '80 (RISK)
GORMAN, MARY, RN, asst. adm. and dir. nrsg., Harper Hospital, Detroit, MI '85 (NURS)
GORMAN, WALLACE P., mgr. eastern zone sales, Agfa-Gevaert Rex, Inc., White Plains, NY '83
GORMAN, WILLIAM C., MD, assoc. med. dir., Southwest Community Health Services, Albuquerque, NM '81
GORMAN, ZELIA R., staff asst., New England Deaconess Hospital, Boston, MA '71 (EDUC)
GORMLEY, BARBARA C., off. mgr. amb. serv. unit, Abington Memorial Hospital, Abington, PA '84
GORMLY, WILLIAM M., pres., Consultants in Public Finance, Ltd., Scottsdale, AZ '83
GORNBERG, MYNDEE, plng. spec., Highland Park Hospital, Highland Park, IL '87 (PLNG)
GORONZY, DANIEL W., exec. vice-pres. and chief oper. off., Kettering Medical Center, Kettering, OH '74 (PLNG)
GOROPEUSCHEK, LINDA S., RN, assoc. dir. nrsg., LaGuardia Hospital, Flushing, NY '86 (NURS)
GORRELL, MARK B., adm. dir. mgt. serv., Geisinger System Services, Danville, PA '80 (MGMT)
GORSKI, DONALD L., dir. telecommun., U. S. Air Force Regional Hospital, Fort Worth, TX '84 (ENG)
GORSKI, JEANNE, dir. commun., Hospital for Special Surgery, New York, NY '85 (ENG)
GORSKI, RICHARD, risk mgr., St. Luke's Hospital, Bethlehem, PA '86 (RISK)
GORSTEIN, AVIVA, dir. vol. serv., Vanderbilt University Hospital, Nashville, TN '84 (VOL)
GORVINE, BEVERLY F., RN, vice-pres. pat. care serv., Leominster Hospital, Leominster, MA '86 (NURS)
GORYL, KATHLEEN, student, Illinois Benedictine College, Lisle, IL '86 (AMB)
GOSCH, KENNITH L., atty., Dakota Midland Hospital, Aberdeen, SD '76 (ATTY)
GOSENSKI, JOAN, vice-pres. human res., Ancilla Systems, Inc., Elk Grove Village, IL '87 (PERS)
GOSFIELD, ALICE G., atty., Rehabilitation Hospital in Mechanicsburg, Mechanicsburg, PA '80 (ATTY)
GOSHDIGIAN, VIOLET A., RN, asst. adm. nrsg., Youville Rehabilitation-Chronic Diseases Hospital, Cambridge, MA '86 (NURS)
GOSLIN, MARGARET A., dir. pers., Woodruff Hospital, Cleveland, OH '84 (PERS)
GOSNELL, SUSAN K., dir. environ. serv., Children's Hospital and Medical Center, Seattle, WA '86 (ENVIRON)
GOSPODAREK, JOHN A., dir. mktg. and plng., Two Rivers Community Hospital, Two Rivers, WI '86 (PR)
GOSS, EUGENE H., dir. phys. plant, Waterville Osteopathic Hospital, Waterville, ME '87 (ENG)
GOSS, JAMES W., dir. matl. mgt., Roper Hospital, Charleston, SC '86 (PUR)
GOSS, MONTY F., proj. coor., Mobile Infirmary Medical Center, Mobile, AL '83 (ENG)
GOSS, NANCY J., adm. nrsg. serv., St. Luke Community Hospital, Ronan, MT '86 (NURS)
GOSSELIN, CHRISTIANE, risk mgt. counsel, Quebec Hospital Association, Montreal, Que., Canada '86 (RISK)
GOSSELIN, JACK R., dir. facil., North Country Hospital and Health Center, Newport, VT '84 (ENG)
GOSSELINK, MARGARET L., atty., Seton Medical Center, Austin, TX '77 (ATTY)
GOSSETT, DANIEL E., dir. emp. and pub. commun., Haywood County Hospital, Clyde, NC '86 (PR)
GOSSMAN, RONI J., vice-pres., Anistics, Inc., Atlanta, GA '83 (RISK)
GOTT, ROBERT A., asst. dir. sup., proc. and distrib., Harper-Grace Hospitals, Detroit, MI '82 (CS)
GOTTFRIED, JERALD W., mgt. analyst, Shawnee Mission Medical Center, Shawnee Mission, KS '83 (MGMT)
GOTTFRIED, OSCAR, exec. sec., Association of Private Hospitals, Inc., New York, NY '33 (LIFE)
GOTTHART, LYNDA M., RN, dir. nrsg. oper., Lockport Memorial Hospital, Lockport, NY '84 (NURS)
GOTTLIEB, DAVID W., vice-pres. plng. and mktg., Leonard Morse Hospital, Natick, MA '86 (PLNG)
GOTTLIEB, GLORIA D., dir. vol. serv., Overlook Hospital, Summit, NJ '85 (VOL)
GOTTLIEB, HAROLD J., Papillion, NE '69
GOTTLIEB, JERRY, atty., Timken Mercy Medical Center, Canton, OH '77 (ATTY)
GOTTLIEB, LARRY, dir. soc. work, Newark Beth Israel Medical Center, Newark, NJ '86 (SOC)
GOTTLIEB, MARK A., Silver Spring, MD '81 (PLNG)
GOTTLIEB, PRISCILLA, Gadsden, AL '80 (RISK)
GOTTLIEB, RICHARD, atty., Timken Mercy Medical Center, Canton, OH '82 (ATTY)
GOTTLIEB, SYMOND R., exec. dir., Greater Detroit Area Health Council, Detroit, MI '65 (PLNG)
GOTTLIEB, TERRY WALSH, RN, asst. adm. nrsg., Yonkers General Hospital, Yonkers, NY '85 (NURS)
GOTTLIEB, WALLACE E., mgr. clin. eng., Staten Island Hospital, Staten Island, NY '84 (ENG)
GOTTSCHALK, CARL A., asst. adm. prof. serv., Hemet Valley Hospital District, Hemet, CA '83 (PLNG)
GOTTSCHALK, EVELYN M., RN, dir. nrsg., Perry Hospital, Perry, GA '82 (NURS)
GOTTSEGEN, IRVING, spec. asst. to pres., Montefiore Medical Center, Bronx, NY '46 (LIFE)
GOTTWALD, MARY HELEN, dir. soc. serv., Trinity Memorial Hospital, Cudahy, WI '79 (SOC)
GOUBLER, SHARON T., dir. vol. serv., East Jefferson General Hospital, Metairie, LA '85 (VOL)
GOUDREAU, JEANETTE BOUSQUET, dir. clin. serv., Strato Medical Corporation, Beverly, MA '85 (PUR)
GOUGH, AUDREY F., dir. vol. serv., Maine Medical Center, Portland, ME '80 (VOL)
GOUGH, JOHN F., atty., Sacred Heart Hospital, Allentown, PA '81 (ATTY)
GOUGH, JUDY, asst. vice-pres. med. staff affairs, Children's Hospital of Sf, San Francisco, CA '85 (RISK)
GOUGH, PATRICIA A., dir. educ., Humana Hospital -Audubon, Louisville, KY '86 (EDUC)
GOUGIS, THERESA A., mgr. sterile proc., Palos Community Hospital, Palos Heights, IL '82 (CS)
GOULART, THOMAS A., asst. dir. diet., food prod. and serv., Memorial Mission Hospital, Asheville, NC '85 (FOOD)
GOULD-LUCHT, PATRICIA, dir. soc. work, Grand Island Memorial Hospital, Grand Island, NE '86 (SOC)
GOULD, BRADFORD W., adm. fellow, Women and Infants Hospital of Rhode Island, Providence, RI '83
GOULD, MAUREEN BANK, RN, vice-pres. nrsg., Jordan Hospital, Plymouth, MA '82 (NURS)
GOULD, MORTON, dir. plng. and market res., Sharp Healthcare System, San Diego, CA '82 (PLNG)
GOULD, ROBERT J., dir. plng. and dev., St. Joseph's Hospital, Carbondale, PA '86 (PLNG)
GOULD, ROBERT W., asst. dir., Temple University Hospital, Philadelphia, PA '82 (SOC)
GOULD, ROBERTA L., dir. pub. rel., Deborah Heart and Lung Center, Browns Mills, NJ '82 (PR)
GOULDER, RICHARD M., dir. dev. commun., Children's Hospital Medical Center of Akron, Akron, OH '67 (PR)
GOULDING, DARLENE, mgr. commun., Edward Hospital, Naperville, IL '85 (ENG)
GOULDING, ERNA I., RN, vice-pres. pat. care, Children's Hospital of Philadelphia, Philadelphia, PA '72 (NURS)
GOULDING, THOMAS E., data syst. eng., Memorial Hospital System, Houston, TX '80 (MGMT)
GOULET, CHARLES R., exec. vice-pres., Blue Cross-Blue Shield, Chicago, IL '52 (LIFE)
GOULET, GERARD R., atty., Hospital Association of Rhode Island, Providence, RI '81 (ATTY)
GOULET, JAMES P., dir. pur., Columbus Community Hospital, Columbus, NE '86 (PUR)
GOULET, MARY C., mgt. eng., Alta Bates Corporation, Berkeley, CA '85 (MGMT)
GOUSMAN, EVELYN, RN, dir. nrsg., Union Hospital, Union, NJ '85 (NURS)
GOUTY, CAROL ANN, RN, dir. nrsg.-med. and critical care, Alexian Brothers Medical Center, Elk Grove Village, IL '84 (NURS)
GOVE, WAYNE D., dir. commun. and prof. serv., Palo Verde Hospital, Tucson, AZ '84
GOVERN, FRANK S., dir., The Harvard Joint Center, Boston, MA '87
GOWAN, CAROL M., dir. vol. serv., St. Francis Hospital, Greenville, SC '85 (VOL)
GOWEN, COLEEN, mgr. pub. rel., St. Elizabeth Community Health Center, Lincoln, NE '85 (PR)
GOWEN, RICHARD B., dir. pers. and pur., St. Joseph's Community Hospital, West Bend, WI '64 (PUR)
GOWING, ROBERT E. JR., vice-pres., Baptist Hospital, Pensacola, FL '75
GOWRIE, CHRISTOPHER M., dir. eng. and facil., St. Charles Hospital and Rehabilitation Center, Port Jefferson, NY '84 (ENG)

GOYEN, ANN E., Franklin, TN '85 (PLNG)
GOYETTE, BETSY B., dir. vol. serv., Noble Hospital, Westfield, MA '86 (VOL)
GOYMA, ELSA, RN, dir. med. surg., St. Mary of Nazareth Hospital Center, Chicago, IL '82 (NURS)
GRAB, DAVID S., med. dir., Memorial Hospital, Belleville, IL '85 (PR) (PLNG)
GRAB, EDWARD L., asst. to sr. vice-pres., Harrisburg Hospital, Harrisburg, PA '85
GRABEL, STEPHEN, adm., Long Island Jewish Medical Center, New York, NY '72
GRABER, BRAD STEVEN, dir. mktg., Providence Hospital, Southfield, MI '80 (PR) (PLNG)
GRABER, DAVID J., dir. pur., M. J. G. Nursing Home, Brooklyn, NY '86 (PUR)
GRABER, SR. KATHERINE, RN, dir. pat. care serv. and vice-pres., St. Peter's Hospital, Albany, NY '67 (NURS)
GRABOIS, MARTIN, chief phys. med., Baylor College of Medicine, Houston, TX '86
GRABOWSKI, DILPHINE, chief oper., Grace Hospital, Detroit, MI '82 (ENG)
GRACE, FRANK JR., atty., Nashville Memorial Hospital, Madison, TN '79 (ATTY)
GRACE, NANCY M., vice-pres. commun. rel., Stamford Hospital, Stamford, CT '81 (PR)
GRACI, JOSEPH J., eng., Eugenia Hospital, Lafayette Hill, PA '85 (ENG)
GRACZYK, LEONARD B., dir. admissions, Hospital of the Albert Einstein College of Medicine, Bronx, NY '74
GRACZYK, VALERIE A. THIBAUDEAU, dir. vol. serv., St. Agnes Hospital, Fond Du Lac, WI '81 (VOL)
GRADISON, REP WILLIS D. JR., Washington, DC '86 (HON)
GRADY, BETTY J., dir. vol., Oak Forest Hospital of Cook County, Oak Forest, IL '75 (VOL)
GRADY, DENNIS W., dir. matl. mgt., The Medical Center, Beaver, PA '81 (PUR)
GRADY, F. DENNIS, dir. facil., South Miami Hospital, South Miami, FL '80 (ENG)
GRADY, MARJORIE A., prog. coor. dept. educ., Catholic Medical Center, Manchester, NH '86 (EDUC)
GRADY, MICHELLE O., asst. vice-pres. pub. rel., Greenwich Hospital, Greenwich, CT '82 (PR) (PLNG)
GRADY, NANCY S., RN, dir. nrsg. serv. and asst. adm., Montclair Community Hospital, Montclair, NJ '83 (NURS)
GRADY, NIKKI, dir. matl. mgt., Henry General Hospital, Stockbridge, GA '82 (PUR)
GRADY, PATRICIA A., RN, dir. educ. and staff dev., Bon Secours Hospital, Grosse Pointe, MI '72 (EDUC)
GRADY, RAYMOND, sr. vice-pres., Evanston Hospital, Evanston, IL '80
GRADY, SUSAN M., asst. adm. human res., DuBois Regional Medical Center, Dubois, PA '84 (PERS)
GRAECA, RAYMOND A., pres., Corry Memorial Hospital, Corry, PA '72
GRAEFF, CATHERINE C., vice-pres. corp. dev., The Owen Company Hospital Pharmacies, Houston, TX '85
GRAF, BAYARD MAYHEW, atty., Friedman Hospital, Philadelphia, PA '75 (ATTY)
GRAF, CHRISTINA M., RN, dir. nrsg. mgt. syst., Massachusetts General Hospital, Boston, MA '86 (NURS)
GRAF, CURTIS G., asst. adm., Kaiser Foundation Hospitals Oregon Region, Clackamas, OR '74
GRAF, GAIL SCOTT, pat. rep., St. Vincent's Medical Center, Staten Island, NY '85 (PAT)
GRAF, RONALD B., dir. mgt. info. serv., Saint Therese Medical Center, Waukegan, IL '86
GRAFF, N. WALTER, atty., Fairview Hospital and Healthcare Service, Minneapolis, MN '75 (ATTY)
GRAFFEO, A. PAUL, dir. plant serv., Sancta Maria Hospital, Cambridge, MA '75 (ENG)(ENVIRON)
GRAFIUS, LINDA CAMPBELL, coor. guest rel., Doylestown Hospital, Doylestown, PA '86 (PAT)
GRAFTON, RUTH, RN, dir. vol., Penobscot Bay Medical Center, Rockport, ME '78 (VOL)
GRAGNOLATI, BRIAN A., coor. facil. dev. and res. plng., Medical Center Hospital of Vermont, Burlington, VT '85 (MGMT)
GRAH, JOHN A., student, Program in Hospital and Health Administration, St. Louis University, St. Louis, MO '85
GRAHAM-DAVIS, ROBBIE, dir. diet. serv., Veterans Administration Hospital, Salisbury, NC '80 (FOOD)
GRAHAM, BRENDA, supv. cent. serv., Cumberland Medical Center, Crossville, TN '85 (CS)
GRAHAM, C. MICHELLE, dir. soc. serv., Incarnate Word Hospital, St. Louis, MO '85 (SOC)
GRAHAM, CAM L. JR., consult. health care mktg., Management Science America, Inc., Atlanta, GA '78 (MGMT)
GRAHAM, CAROLE J., student, Program in Health Administration, Temple University, Philadelphia, PA '85
GRAHAM, CHRIS T., coor. compensation, Roseville Community Hospital, Roseville, CA '85 (PERS)
GRAHAM, CLARE J., dir. soc. work, Mercy Medical Center, Durango, CO '82 (SOC)
GRAHAM, DAROL L., PhD, dir.-television syst., University of Texas, Health Scince Center, Dallas, TX '83 (EDUC)
GRAHAM, DENZIL G. SR., asst. chief eng., Alhambra Community Hospital, Alhambra, CA '85 (ENG)
GRAHAM, ERIC M., dir. commun., Hinsdale Hospital, Hinsdale, IL '86 (PR)
GRAHAM, FRED EUGENE II, PhD, assoc. dir., Medical Group Management Association, Denver, CO '67
GRAHAM, FRED M. JR., dir. environ. serv., Institute of Pennsylvania Hospital, Philadelphia, PA '86 (ENVIRON)
GRAHAM, GAIL E., mgr. adm. serv., New England Deaconess Hospital, Boston, MA '78
GRAHAM, GARRETT R., pres., Greater Houston Hospital Council, Houston, TX '59
GRAHAM, GEORGE WILLIAM, MD, vice-pres., Joint Commission on Accreditation of Hospitals, Chicago, IL '54 (LIFE)
GRAHAM, GREGG D., dir., New River Mental Health Inpatient Unit, Charles A. Cannon Jr. Memorial Hospital, Banner Elk, NC '84
GRAHAM, H. JAMES, asst. adm., Chippenham Hospital, Richmond, VA '78
GRAHAM, HARROLD E., dir. pur., Trinity Lutheran Hospital, Kansas City, MO '71 (PUR)
GRAHAM, HUGH J. JR., atty., St. John's Hospital, Springfield, IL '75 (ATTY)
GRAHAM, HUGH J. III, atty., St. John's Hospital, Springfield, IL '79 (ATTY)
GRAHAM, JEFFREY J., vice-pres., Cooley Dickinson Hospital, Northampton, MA '87 (RISK)
GRAHAM, JOHN A., pres., Sherman Hospital, Elgin, IL '85
GRAHAM, JOHN K., dir. pur., Saint Joseph's Hospital, Atlanta, GA '86 (PUR)
GRAHAM, KEITH, chief biomedical and eng., Wood River Township Hospital, Wood River, IL '85 (ENG)
GRAHAM, LARRY M., assoc. adm., AMI Park Place Hospital, Port Arthur, TX '81
GRAHAM, MARY B., RN, asst. dir. nrsg., Lester E. Cox Medical Centers, Springfield, MO '85 (NURS)
GRAHAM, MAX, chief eng., Farmington Community Hospital, Farmington, MO '78 (ENG)
GRAHAM, NANCY O., RN DrPH, vice-pres. nrsg., Lenox Hill Hospital, New York, NY '81 (NURS)
GRAHAM, RALPH C. JR., biomedical eng., Our Lady of Mercy Hospital, Dyer, IN '80 (ENG)
GRAHAM, RICHARD W., assoc. adm., Fairmont General Hospital, Fairmont, WV '85
GRAHAM, ROBERT B., dir. pur., Baptist Medical Center, Jacksonville, FL '82 (PUR)
GRAHAM, ROBERTA G., RN, consult., Peat, Marwick, Mitchell and Company, Chicago, IL '82
GRAHAM, ROSEMARY, RN, mgr. pur. and cent. sup., Paris Community Hospital, Paris, IL '86 (CS)
GRAHAM, STACEY A., exec. vice-pres., Lewis Clark and Graham, Atlanta, GA '87 (PR)
GRAHAM, SUSAN, dir. soc. work, Huron Valley Hospital, Milford, MI '86 (SOC)
GRAHAM, THOMAS J., adm., Nanticoke State General Hospital, Nanticoke, PA '75
GRAINGER, SHARYN, adm. asst., Metropolitan Hospital and Health Centers, Detroit, MI '83
GRAINGER, WENDY L., mktg. analyst, Ramsey Clinic, St. Paul, MN '86 (PLNG)
GRAMBLIN, PAUL M., mgr. corp. commun., Morton F. Plant Hospital, Clearwater, FL '85 (PR)
GRAMBO, MICHAEL ALBERT, ed., St. Anthony Hospital Publications, Washington, DC '87 (PAT)
GRAMS, LYNN J., dir. nrsg. dev., Fawcett Memorial Hospital, Port Charlotte, FL '87 (EDUC)
GRAMS, ROBERT J., dir. human res., Cigna Health Plan of Arizona, Inc., Tucson, AZ '68 (PERS)
GRAMS, STANLEY, mgr. mktg. res., Technicon Data Systems Corporation, Atlanta, GA '70 (MGMT)
GRAN, LOIS, supv. oper. room and cent. serv., Gordon Memorial Hospital District, Gordon, NE '85 (CS)
GRANADO, ROBERTO, dir. hskpg. and ldry. serv., Community General Hospital, Harris, NY '86 (ENVIRON)
GRANBERG, MERLIN P., dir. food serv., Skagit Valley Hospital, Mount Vernon, WA '70 (FOOD)
GRAND, LAWRENCE N., asst. adm., Kennedy Memorial Hospitals University Medical Center, Stratford, NJ '78
GRANDA, DONNA K., RN, dir. oper. room, Barnes Hospital, St. Louis, MO '81 (NURS)
GRANDELLI, ANGELO N., Brooklyn, NY '81
GRANDIA, LARRY D., dir. mgt. syst., Intermountain Health Care, Inc., Salt Lake City, UT '72 (MGMT)
GRANGE, RONALD T., dir. nutr. serv., Tennessee Christian Medical Center, Madison, TN '81 (FOOD)
GRANGER, ELAINE, RN, supv. cent. serv., St. Luke's General Hospital, Bellingham, WA '78 (CS)
GRANGER, HARRY L., dir. food serv., Niagara Falls Memorial Medical Center, Niagara Falls, NY '76 (FOOD)
GRANGER, NANCY, dir. pers., Charles S. Wilson Memorial Hospital, Johnson City, NY '67 (PERS)
GRANGER, ROBERT CARROLL, (ret.), Palm Coast, FL '48 (LIFE)
GRANING, HARALD M., MD, (ret.), Severna Park, MD '75
GRANITZ, DONALD L., dir. educ., Elkhart General Hospital, Elkhart, IN '79 (PLNG)
GRANOFF, KAREN, sr. assoc. plng., Blue Cross of Massachusetts, Boston, MA '87 (AMB)
GRANT-THOMAS, BEVERLY PATRICIA, dir. pat. rel., Hospital of Saint Raphael, New Haven, CT '81 (PAT)(PR)
GRANT, CAROL A., dir. pers., St. Francis Medical Center, Breckenridge, MN '86 (PERS)
GRANT, DEBORAH L., dir. pub. rel. and info., Tulane Medical Center, New Orleans, LA '86 (PR)
GRANT, GENIE R., dir. plng., Sutter Health System, Sacramento, CA '80 (PLNG)
GRANT, J. R., prin., Modern Management, Inc., Lake Bluff, IL '81 (PERS)
GRANT, JAMES N., sr. dir. plant and eng., Zurbrugg Memorial Hospital, Willingboro, NJ '85 (ENG)
GRANT, JAMES T., RN, asst. adm. pat. serv., Trinity Medical Center, Carrollton, TX '86 (NURS)
GRANT, JOSEPH J., spec. emp. rel., Elmhurst Memorial Hospital, Elmhurst, IL '73 (PERS)
GRANT, JULIANA T., dir. corp. rel., Silver Cross Hospital, Joliet, IL '83 (PR)
GRANT, MARY KATHRYN, dir. sponsorship, Catholic Health Association, St. Louis, MO '83 (PLNG)
GRANT, MICHAEL D., pharm., Naval Hospital, Orlando, FL '85
GRANT, PETER N., atty., Mount Zion Hospital and Medical Center, San Francisco, CA '85 (ATTY)
GRANT, RICHARD T., dir. clin. soc. work, Cushing Hospital, Framingham, MA '85 (SOC)
GRANT, THOMAS WAYNE, (ret.), Lawrenceburg, KY '67
GRANT, WARREN C. JR., coor. loss prevention, Mutual Assurance, Birmingham, AL '87 (RISK)
GRANTHAM, JULIE R., dir. pub. rel., Rush Foundation Hospital, Meridian, MS '85 (PR)
GRAPPE, J. BERNARD, dir. pub. rel., Schumpert Medical Center, Shreveport, LA '78 (PR)
GRASKY, FRANCES, RN, dir. educ., Holy Rosary Hospital, Miles City, MT '76 (EDUC)
GRASSER, SANDRA K., vol. coor., Kenosha Hospital and Medical Center, Kenosha, WI '85 (VOL)
GRASSI, MARY E., asst. dir. soc. serv., Lehigh Valley Hospital Center, Allentown, PA '82 (SOC)
GRASSO, BRUCE, prod. syst. consult., AMI Brookwood Medical Center, Birmingham, AL '80 (MGMT)
GRASTY, FAY WALTERS, dir. vol. serv. and pat. rep., Charlotte Memorial Hospital and Medical Center, Charlotte, NC '84 (VOL)(PAT)
GRATE, MARTHA D., RN, assoc. exec. dir. nrsg., Harlem Hospital Center, New York, NY '85 (NURS)
GRATES, FREDERICK R., adm., AMI Fort Bend Community Hospital, Missouri City, TX '83
GRATTAN, GEORGE G., IV, atty., University of Virginia Hospitals, Charlottesville, VA '75 (ATTY)
GRATTAN, PATRICIA JEANNE, adm. sec., Scripps Memorial Hospital-Encinitas, Encinitas, CA '85 (PAT)
GRATTAN, SUSYN, student, Graduate Studies in Health Planning and Administration, Pennsylvania State University, University Park, PA '80
GRATTO, MARILYN, dir. soc. serv., Miller-Dwan Medical Center, Duluth, MN '77 (SOC)
GRAU, BETTY J., supv. cent. serv., Washington Medical Center, Culver City, CA '83 (CS)
GRAU, WILLIAM H., RN, adm. nrsg. critical care, Pitt County Memorial Hospital, Greenville, NC '86 (NURS)
GRAUBIT, JOAN, RN, asst. dir. nrsg., Northern Ocean Hospital System, Point Pleasant, NJ '83 (AMB)
GRAUER, KATHLEEN H., adm., Monmouth Medical Center, Long Branch, NJ '83
GRAUMANN, FRED W., sr. vice-pres. human res., Robert Wood Johnson University Hospital, New Brunswick, NJ '77 (PERS)
GRAUPENSPERGER, ROBERT, vice-pres. gen. serv., Ephrata Community Hospital, Ephrata, PA '86 (RISK)
GRAVEL, NANCY E., RN, dir. pat. care, Western Massachusetts Hospital, Westfield, MA '86 (NURS)
GRAVELLE, SUSAN E., dir. pers. and pub. rel., Cranston General Hospital Osteopathic, Cranston, RI '85 (PERS)(PR)
GRAVELY, GRETCHEN, asst. adm., Southside Regional Medical Center, Petersburg, VA '79
GRAVELY, STEVEN D., atty., Riverside Hospital, Newport News, VA '85 (ATTY)
GRAVELY, WILLIAM A. JR., pres., Culpeper Memorial Hospital, Culpeper, VA '69 (PLNG)
GRAVES, AILEEN S., dir. diet., Vanderbilt University Hospital, Nashville, TN '75 (FOOD)
GRAVES, LINDA, dir. soc. serv., St. Margaret's Hospital, Spring Valley, IL '81 (SOC)
GRAVES, MARY W., dir. diet., Ball Memorial Hospital, Muncie, IN '78 (FOOD)
GRAVES, MELVIN M. JR., asst. adm., Milwaukee County Medical Complex, Milwaukee, WI '65
GRAVES, PAMELA L., dir. soc. serv., Nashville Memorial Hospital, Madison, TN '85 (SOC)
GRAVES, ROBERT G., sr. vice-pres., St. John's Mercy Medical Center, St. Louis, MO '79
GRAVES, STEPHEN, vice-pres., Glenn, Nyhan and Asociates, Inc., Radnor, PA '86 (RISK)
GRAVESMILL, DOROTHY JANE, coor. guest rel., Holy Family Hospital, Des Plaines, IL '86 (PAT)
GRAY, ADELE, RN, vice-pres. nrsg., Northern Ocean Hospital System, Point Pleasant, NJ '79 (NURS)
GRAY, BEN L., dir. educ. serv., Hendrick Medical Center, Abilene, TX '86 (EDUC)
GRAY, BETTY S., RN, educator in-service, Oxford-Lafayette Medical Center, Oxford, MS '78 (EDUC)
GRAY, BETTY, asst. adm., Stouder Memorial Hospital, Troy, OH '86 (RISK)
GRAY, CAROLYN, asst. vice-pres. qual. assur., Good Samaritan Medical Center, Zanesville, OH '86 (RISK)
GRAY, CARROL B., dir. educ. serv., Virginia Hospital Research and Education Foundation, Richmond, VA '86 (EDUC)
GRAY, DANNY R., dir. bldg. and maint. serv., Saint Francis Medical Center, Peoria, IL '85 (ENG)
GRAY, DAVID A., mgr., B. U. P. A. Hospital, Norwich, England '83
GRAY, DAVID L., dir. pub. rel., Neponset Valley Health System, Norwood, MA '81 (PR)
GRAY, DAVID M., dir. ldry. serv., University of Iowa, Iowa City, IA '86 (ENVIRON)
GRAY, DONALD G., dir. health care, American Food Management, Inc., Marshall, MO '84
GRAY, ELAINE ROUSE, dir. soc. serv., McNairy County General Hospital, Selmer, TN '85 (SOC)
GRAY, FRED A., chief eng., Washington Hospital Center, Washington, DC '83 (ENG)
GRAY, GORDON, mem. bd. visitors, Bowman Gray School of Medicine, Washington, DC '23 (HON)
GRAY, IRWIN N., supv. support serv., Coos Bay Care Center, Coos Bay, OR '86 (ENVIRON)
GRAY, J. ROBERT, dir., Lenox Baker Children's Hospital, Durham, NC '86
GRAY, JACK H., vice-pres. and risk mgr., Lutheran Hospital of Fort Wayne, Fort Wayne, IN '73 (RISK)
GRAY, JACK S., dir. pers., Bristol Memorial Hospital, Bristol, TN '84 (PERS)
GRAY, JESSE W., dir. plant oper., Cape Canaveral Hospital, Cocoa Beach, FL '85 (ENG)
GRAY, JOHN W. JR., adm. dir. outpat serv., Latrobe Area Hospital, Latrobe, PA '87 (AMB)
GRAY, JUDITH A., adm. asst. and dir. pub. rel., Arkansas City Memorial Hospital, Arkansas City, KS '85 (PR)
GRAY, LENORA R., dir. soc. work, High Point Regional Hospital, High Point, NC '85 (SOC)

GRAY, LILLIAN W., asst. adm., Spaulding Rehabilitation Hospital, Boston, MA '86 (PLNG)
GRAY, LOIS O., risk mgr. and dir. med. and legal affairs, Jacksonville Medical Center, Jacksonville, FL '86 (RISK)
GRAY, LORRAINE, legal asst., Evangelical Health Systems, Oak Brook, IL '82 (RISK)
GRAY, M. P., dir. proj. review, Eastern Virginia Health Systems Agency, Inc., Norfolk, VA '80 (PLNG)
GRAY, MARY E., coor. human res. dev., Wabash County Hospital, Wabash, IN '84 (EDUC)
GRAY, NANCY B., dir. vol., Edgewater Hospital, Chicago, IL '71 (VOL)
GRAY, O. MICHAEL, Robinson Humphrey Company, Atlanta, GA '78 (MGMT)
GRAY, OREN L., dir. plant oper., AMI Presbyterian Aurora Hospital, Aurora, CO '76 (ENG)
GRAY, PEGGY S., dir. commun. rel., Saline Memorial Hospital, Benton, AR '85 (PR)
GRAY, RICHARD G., dir. med. staff dev., Memorial Care System, Houston, TX '85 (PR)
GRAY, ROBERT B., dir. eng. serv., Pacific Health Resources, Los Angeles, CA '75 (ENG)
GRAY, ROBERT C., reg. vice-pres., ARA Services, Hospital Food Management, Environmental Service, Inc., Irving, TX '68 (FOOD)
GRAY, ROBERT E., sr. health facil. planner, Einhorn Yaffee Prescott, Albany, NY '83
GRAY, STEVEN PAUL, pres., CHI Systems, Inc., Ann Arbor, MI '67 (PUR)
GRAY, VAL S., adm., Cornwall Hospital, Cornwall, NY '84 (ENG)
GRAY, VICKY G., vice-pres., Tidewater Health Care, Inc., Virginia Beach, VA '87 (AMB)
GRAY, WALTER J., vice-pres., St. Clair Health Corporation, Detroit, MI '77 (PUR)
GRAY, WAYNE M., consult., Ernst and Whinney, Grand Rapids, MI '80 (MGMT)
GRAY, WILLIAM J., supv. maint., Kennedy Institute for Handicapped Children, Baltimore, MD '81 (ENG)
GRAYBEAL, RICHARD R., dir. plng. and dev., Careage Investments, Inc., Bellevue, WA '82 (PLNG)
GRAYBIEL, LAURIE, dir. loss prevention, Stratton-Cheeseman Management Company, East Lansing, MI '85 (RISK)
GRAYBILL, MATTHEW P., vice-pres. human res., Children's Medical Center, Dayton, OH '79 (PERS)(MGMT)
GRAYSON, SUSAN N., dir. publications, Medical College of Virginia Hospitals, Virginia Commonwealth University, Richmond, VA '83 (PR)
GRAZE, GREGORY G., dir. commun. rel., Dallas County Hospital District-Parkland Memorial Hospital, Dallas, TX '83 (PR)
GRAZMAN, TED E., pres., Ted E. Grazman and Associates, St. Louis, MO '67 (MGMT)
GREANEY, FRANCIS JAMES, vice-pres., American General Group Insurance Company, Dallas, TX '67 (PLNG)
GREASLEY, DAVID M., dir. oper., Tie Pharmaceutical Corporation, New York, NY '84 (PUR)
GREATHOUSE, FERN L., dir. soc. work, St. Catherine Hospital, Garden City, KS '79 (SOC)
GREATHOUSE, JOAN R., coor. vol. prog., Group Health Cooperative, Seattle, WA '84 (VOL)
GREATHOUSE, JOE S., vice-pres. plng. and dev., Eastern Virginia Medical Authority, Norfolk, VA '80
GREAVES, LORRAINE F., dir. vol. serv., General Hospital Center at Passaic, Passaic, NJ '85 (VOL)
GREAVES, NICHOLAS G., vice-pres. pub. affairs, Blue Cross of Maryland, Inc., Baltimore, MD '74 (PR)
GREAVES, PATRICK D., vice-pres. human res., Detroit Receiving Hospital, Detroit, MI '86 (PERS)
GREAVES, STEWART G., dir. pur., Mercy Hospital and Medical Center, San Diego, CA '71 (PUR)
GREBB, PAUL J., dir. eng., North Pennsylvania Hospital, Lansdale, PA '82 (ENG)
GREBNER, RONI M., coor. risk mgt. and qual. assur., Mount Diablo Hospital Medical Center, Concord, CA '85 (RISK)
GRECO, JESSICA J., coor. risk mgt., DePaul Hospital, Norfolk, VA '86 (RISK)
GRECO, KATHLEEN A., RN, assoc. dir. nrsg., Allegheny Valley Hospital, Natrona Heights, PA '81 (NURS)
GRECO, MARY J., sales rep., Bergen Brunswick, Middletown, NY '79
GREDELJ, ZELJKO, sr. consult. eng., Teh Projekt-Rijeka, Rijeka, Yugoslavia '83 (ENG)
GREEBY, JOELLEN, dir. vol. serv., North Pennsylvania Hospital, Lansdale, PA '83 (VOL)
GREELY, JOSEPH W., dir. support serv., Petaluma Valley Hospital, Petaluma, CA '81 (ENG)
GREEN, ALAN R., vice-pres. oper., Polyclinic Medical Center, Harrisburg, PA '78
GREEN, ANTHONY C., dir. pers., Wyman Park Medical Center, Baltimore, MD '85 (PERS)
GREEN, BARBARA HELEN, coor. pat. rel., Emanuel Hospital and Health Center, Portland, OR '85 (PAT)
GREEN, MAJ. BARBARA M., MSC USA, Reynolds Army Community Hospital, Fort Sill, OK '82
GREEN, BARBARA, dir. cent. proc. and distrib., St. Joseph's Medical Center, Yonkers, NY '80 (CS)
GREEN, BEATRICE C., vice-pres. adm. serv., South Shore Hospital, South Weymouth, MA '86 (RISK)
GREEN, BETSY A., coor. pub. info., Asbury Hospital, Salina, KS '85 (PR)
GREEN, CARLTON SCOTT, dir. food serv., Valley Medical Center, Van Nuys, CA '84 (FOOD)
GREEN, DANIEL D., vice-pres. corp. commun., Samaritan Health Service, Phoenix, AZ '84 (PR)
GREEN, DAVID R., adm. and chief exec. off., Van Nuys Hospital, Van Nuys, CA '85 (MGMT)
GREEN, DEBBIE, dir. commun., Baptist Medical Center, Little Rock, AR '83 (ENG)
GREEN, DEBORAH KAY, asst. vice-pres. and qual. assur. mgr., American Medical International, Atlanta, GA '81 (RISK)
GREEN, DENNIS C., mgr. syst. analyst, Mount Diablo Hospital Medical Center, Concord, CA '83 (MGMT)
GREEN, DENNIS L., dir. matl. mgt., Memorial Hospital, Colorado Springs, CO '81 (PUR)
GREEN, DON E., student, Southwest Texas State University, San Marcos, TX '87 (PLNG)
GREEN, DOUGLAS M., coor. qual. assur. and risk mgt., Lapeer General Hospital, LaPeer, MI '84 (RISK)
GREEN, FRED WILLIAM, pres., Fred W. Green and Associates, Clearwater, FL '64 (MGMT)
GREEN, GAIL, supv. cent. sup., Lake Region Hospital and Nursing Home, Fergus Falls, MN '77 (CS)
GREEN, GRACE W., dir. health care plng., Chester County Hospital, West Chester, PA '82 (PLNG)
GREEN, GRANT E., dir. pers. and trng., Washington Regional Medical Center, Fayetteville, AR '79 (PERS)
GREEN, GUNNAR, strategic planner, Los Angeles County Department of Health Services, Los Angeles, CA '83 (PLNG)
GREEN, HELEN G., RN, dir. cont. educ. and trng., Timberlawn Psychiatric Hospital, Dallas, TX '77 (EDUC)
GREEN, JACOB, med. dir., Southwestern Neurodiagnostic Institute, Inc., Jacksonville, FL '85
GREEN, JAMES S., mgr. pub. rel., Psicor, Inc., Brighton, MI '85 (PR)
GREEN, JANICE R., dir. soc. serv., Edwin Shaw Hospital, Akron, OH '79 (SOC)
GREEN, JESSE, dir. res., New York University Medical Center, New York, NY '85 (PLNG)
GREEN, JOHN L., dir. legal serv. and atty., Good Samaritan Hospital and Health Center, Dayton, OH '83 (ATTY)
GREEN, JOHN L., exec. vice-pres. corp. serv., Medlantic Healthcare Group, Washington, DC '83 (PLNG)
GREEN, JOHN R., atty., Duncan Regional Hospital, Duncan, OK '77 (ATTY)
GREEN, LARRY G., dir. environ. serv., Humana Hospital -St. Petersburg, St. Petersburg, FL '86 (ENVIRON)
GREEN, LOIS, asst. vice-pres. corp. dev., Lutheran Hospital Society, Los Angeles, CA '79 (PLNG)
GREEN, MARTHA, consult., Coopers and Lybrand, Washington, DC '86
GREEN, MARY P., assoc. dir. pub. rel., Shands Hospital, Gainesville, FL '84 (PR)
GREEN, MICHAEL R., atty., Virginia Mason Hospital, Seattle, WA '70 (ATTY)
GREEN, MYRA J., atty., Brigham and Women's Hospital, Boston, MA '82 (ATTY)
GREEN, NANCY M., dir. vol. serv., William W. Backus Hospital, Norwich, CT '86 (VOL)
GREEN, NANCY, asst. coor. pat. rel., University of Minnesota Hospital and Clinic, Minneapolis, MN '76 (PAT)
GREEN, NAOMI F., RN, supv. cent. sterilization, Veterinary Clinic, Michigan State University, East Lansing, MI '77 (CS)
GREEN, PATRICIA A., RN, dir. nrsg., Bry-Lin Hospital, Buffalo, NY '81 (NURS)
GREEN, PATRICIA T., dir. soc. serv., Community Hospital of Chula Vista, Chula Vista, CA '83 (SOC)
GREEN, PHILIP D., atty., Mount Sinai Medical Center, Miami Beach, FL '85 (ATTY)
GREEN, RAYMOND R., asst. adm., Meadowlands Hospital Medical Center, Secaucus, NJ '85
GREEN, ROBERT F., pres. health facil. design, Hospital Bureau, Inc., Pleasantville, NY '72
GREEN, ROGER E., vice-pres. mktg. and plng., Healtheast, St. Paul, MN '81 (PLNG)
GREEN, RONALD A., assoc. dir. mktg., The Ratcliff Architects, Berkeley, CA '85 (PLNG)
GREEN, RONALD, supv. clin. eng. and biomedical equip. tech., Deaconess Hospital, Cincinnati, OH '85 (ENG)
GREEN, S. JANE, coor. vol. serv., Unity Medical Center, Fridley, MN '80 (VOL)
GREEN, SHIRLEY L., RN, asst. adm. nrsg., Washoe Medical Center, Reno, NV '75 (NURS)
GREEN, TARRAZONIA, dir. vol. serv., Milwaukee County Medical Complex, Milwaukee, WI '83 (VOL)
GREEN, THOMAS E., asst. adm. and dir. pub. rel., Dobbs Ferry Hospital, Dobbs Ferry, NY '81 (PR)
GREEN, THOMAS, dir. biomedical eng., Stormont-Vail Regional Medical Center, Topeka, KS '86 (ENG)
GREEN, W. T., atty., Citrus Memorial Hospital, Inverness, FL '77 (ATTY)
GREEN, WARREN A., pres., Mount Sinai Hospital, Minneapolis, MN '71
GREEN, WILLIAM H. JR., adm., Fauquier Hospital, Warrenton, VA '58
GREEN, YVONNE V., dir. diet., Stanton Yellowknife Hospital, Yellowknife, N.W.T., Canada '83 (FOOD)
GREENAGE, KAREN, mgr. matl., Northwest Institute of Psychiatry, Fort Washington, PA '84 (PUR)
GREENAN, EUGENE H., asst. adm., Bayonne Hospital, Bayonne, NJ '85
GREENAWALT, IVY B., market info. analyst, Harrisburg Hospital, Harrisburg, PA '86 (PLNG)
GREENBERG, CAROL C., dir. soc. work, Stamford Hospital, Stamford, CT '81 (SOC)
GREENBERG, DAVID, dir. food serv., St. Elizabeth's Hospital, Chicago, IL '70 (FOOD)
GREENBERG, DIANE C., banking off., First American National Bank Nashville, Nashville, TN '87
GREENBERG, JANETT C., vice-pres., Massachusetts Mutual Life Insurance Company, Springfield, MA '81
GREENBERG, PENELOPE C., atty., Peninsula Hospital and Medical Center, Burlingame, CA '84 (ATTY)
GREENBERG, SANDY, dir. environ. serv., Los Robles Regional Medical Center, Thousand Oaks, CA '86 (ENVIRON)
GREENBLATT, FRANCES, dir. staff dev., Jewish Hospital and Rehabilitation Center, Jersey City, NJ '85 (EDUC)
GREENBLATT, LAURENCE V., Los Angeles, CA '76
GREENBURG, DAVID, exec. dir., National Health Lawyers Association, Washington, DC '71 (ATTY)
GREENBUSH, ANGELA R., dir. food serv., Eger Nursing Home, Staten Island, NY '83 (FOOD)
GREENE, ALBERT LAWRENCE, sr. vice-pres. adm., Harper Hospital, Detroit, MI '72
GREENE, ANDREW, asst. treas., Robert Wood Johnson Foundation, Princeton, NJ '76
GREENE, BARBARA F., student, Roosevelt University, Chicago, IL '86
GREENE, CHRISTOPHER T., atty., Sheehan Memorial Hospital, Buffalo, NY '82 (ATTY)
GREENE, GAIL A., adm. coor. rehab. medicine, North Central Bronx Hospital, Bronx, NY '83
GREENE, GEORGANNE, RN, dir. pat. care serv., Plumas District Hospital, Quincy, CA '86 (NURS)
GREENE, HARRIET, mgr. cent. serv., Waukesha Memorial Hospital, Waukesha, WI '83 (CS)
GREENE, ILENA, student, Program in Health Care Administration, Bernard M. Baruch College Mount Sinai School of Medicine, New York, NY '86
GREENE, JAMES E., dir. educ., Baptist Medical Center, Montgomery, AL '77 (EDUC)
GREENE, JEROME G. JR., Dayton, OH '73
GREENE, MARY L., coor. soc. serv., Jefferson Memorial Hospital, Alexandria, VA '81 (SOC)
GREENE, MICHAEL E., vice-pres., Bethesda Hospital, Zanesville, OH '75 (MGMT)
GREENE, PAUL F., atty., Rhode Island Hospital, Providence, RI '76 (ATTY)
GREENE, RALEIGH W. III, atty., Allegany Health System, St. Petersburg, FL '87 (ATTY)
GREENE, RICHARD D., pres., Rochester Health Network, Rochester, NY '64
GREENE, RICHARD HARVEY, exec. vice-pres., Cheshire Medical Center, Keene, NH '71 (PLNG)
GREENE, ROBERT E., dir. soc. serv., St. Anthony's Hospital, St. Petersburg, FL '82 (SOC)
GREENE, ROBERT J., dir. plng. and dev., National Medical Enterprises, Tampa, FL '82 (PLNG)
GREENE, ROBERT MICHAEL, atty., Sisters of Charity Hospital, Buffalo, NY '86 (ATTY)
GREENE, SANDRA L., RN, coor. pat. educ., St. Patrick Hospital, Missoula, MT '81 (EDUC)
GREENE, STEVEN J., chief oper. off., AMI Palmetto General Hospital, Hialeah, FL '84
GREENE, TY B., med. soc. worker, Finley Hospital, Dubuque, IA '77 (SOC)
GREENE, WILLIAM MAYNARD, Traverse City, MI '67
GREENE, WILLIAM TEIDI, asst. dir., Society of the New York Hospital, New York, NY '78
GREENEBAUM, WILLIAM M., asst. dir.-dev. plans, Oregon Health Sciences University Hospital, Portland, OR '85 (PLNG)
GREENFIELD, CARY, area off. health care fin., The Toronto-Dominion Bank, New York, NY '86
GREENFIELD, RICHARD S., pres., Syosset Community Hospital, Syosset, NY '62
GREENFIELD, TIMOTHY, vice-pres. fin., Albany General Hospital, Albany, OR '80
GREENFIELD, ZELA S., supv. casework, Booth Memorial Medical Center, Flushing, NY '71 (SOC)
GREENFOGEL, VIVIAN T., dir. pat. rel., Hospital of Saint Raphael, New Haven, CT '83 (PAT)
GREENHILL, JAMES T., dir. nutr., Crawford Long Hospital Emory University, Atlanta, GA '74 (FOOD)
GREENHOUSE, WILLIAM J., reg. dir., Hospital Council of Southern California, Los Angeles, CA '84 (SOC)
GREENING, ANDREW B., dir. soc. serv., St. Elizabeth's Hospital, Hannibal, MO '73 (SOC)
GREENLEE, ARTHUR I., plng. assoc., Detroit Medical Center, Detroit, MI '80 (PLNG)
GREENLEE, NANCY C., (ret.), Marion, NC '69 (FOOD)
GREENLEY, DON, mgr. food serv., Eisenhower Medical Center, Rancho Mirage, CA '77 (FOOD)
GREENLY, LAURA L., RN, dir. nrsg., Chalmette General Hospital, Chalmette, LA '84 (NURS)
GREENMAN, ROGER E. W., mgr., Cabrini Hospital, Malvern, Australia '80 (MGMT)
GREENQUIST, GARY, dir. plng. and mktg., St. Joseph's Hospital and Health Center, Dickinson, ND '75 (PLNG)
GREENSLADE, DON, reg. commercial mgr., Wessex Regional Health Authority, Winchester, England '85 (PUR)
GREENSPAN, MYRON J., vice-pres., Baptist Medical Center, Jacksonville, FL '73 (FOOD)
GREENSTEIN, DEBRA, sr. pat. rel. rep., Muhlenberg Regional Medical Center, Plainfield, NJ '86 (PAT)
GREENSTEIN, L. M., coor. commun. rel., Bon Secours Hospital of Methuen, Methuen, MA '86 (PR)
GREENWELL, RICHARD D., vice-pres. plng., Sparrow, Inc., Lansing, MI '81 (PLNG)
GREENWOOD, BARBARA S., team leader amb. surg., Penobscot Bay Medical Center, Rockport, ME '87 (AMB)
GREENWOOD, JACK R., dir. emp. rel., Robert Packer Hospital, Sayre, PA '77 (PERS)
GREENWOOD, SHERRY E., diet., Nutricare, London, Ont., Canada '86 (FOOD)
GREER, BONNIE H., RN, dir. nrsg. serv., Mount Graham Community Hospital, Safford, AZ '85 (NURS)
GREER, DAVID C., atty., Miami Valley Hospital, Dayton, OH '76 (ATTY)
GREER, JAMES W., RN, Holy Family Medical Center, Manitowoc, WI '78 (NURS)
GREER, JOHN H., dir. health facil., Charter Medical Corporation, Macon, GA '86 (PR) (PLNG)
GREER, JUDITH, dir. info. syst., Maryvale Samaritan Hospital, Phoenix, AZ '86 (MGMT)
GREER, ROLLI PAUL, adm. asst. and mgr. risk control, St. Francis Medical Center, Honolulu, HI '84 (RISK)
GREGER, RICHARD GEORGE, mgr. pur., Edward Hospital, Naperville, IL '84 (PUR)
GREGERSEN, TERI L., RN, coor. nrsg. educ., Mary Greeley Medical Center, Ames, IA '85 (EDUC)
GREGG, JACK E., dir. maint., St. Vincent Infirmary, Little Rock, AR '75 (ENG)

GREGG, JOHN W., supt. bldg. and grds., River District Hospital, St. Clair, MI '81 (ENG)
GREGG, PAULA V., dir. vol. serv. and pub. rel., St. Luke's Hospital, Columbus, NC '68 (VOL)
GREGG, RICHARD H., mng. dir., Seltzer Daley Companies, Princeton, NJ '85 (PLNG)
GREGG, STEPHEN A., pres., Metrocare, Inc., Portland, OR '85
GREGO, CHARLES, dir. plant serv., Mercy Memorial Hospital, Monroe, MI '85 (ENG)
GREGO, JULIE ANN, adm. asst., Rush-Presbyterian-St. Luke's Medical Center, Chicago, IL '82
GREGORIC, FLORENCE I., ed., National Cancer Institute, Bethesda, MD '55 (LIFE)
GREGORICH, PAULINE M., dir. pers., Louis A. Weiss Memorial Hospital, Chicago, IL '64 (PERS)
GREGORICH, THOMAS H., dir. mgt., St. John Hospital, Detroit, MI '86 (MGMT)
GREGORIO, LOUIS J., dir. pers., Valley Presbyterian Hospital, Van Nuys, CA '83 (RISK)
GREGORY, BARBARA A., RN, adm. asst. cent. serv., Monmouth Medical Center, Long Branch, NJ '83 (CS)
GREGORY, BERNARD C., dir. pers., Passavant Area Hospital, Jacksonville, IL '83 (PERS)
GREGORY, CAROL A., asst. adm., Memorial Hospital at Easton Maryland, Easton, MD '66
GREGORY, CHERRY L., RN, mgr. educ., Providence Hospital, Medford, OR '79 (EDUC)
GREGORY, CONNIE, coor. vol., Pembina County Memorial Hospital, Cavalier, ND '82 (VOL)
GREGORY, DAVID W., supv. cent. sup., St. Peters Community Hospital, St. Peters, MO '85 (CS)
GREGORY, DORIE ANN D., tech. serv. chemist, Calgon Corporation Subsidary of Merck and Company, St. Louis, MO '86 (CS)
GREGORY, DOUGLAS D., PhD, prin., Booz, Allen and Hamilton, Inc., Chicago, IL '81 (PLNG)
GREGORY, JAMES A., dir. pur., Mercy Hospital, Wilkes-Barre, PA '77 (PUR)
GREGORY, JAMES P., atty., Danbury Hospital, Danbury, CT '85 (ATTY)
GREGORY, JANE W., pub. rel. coor., New Jersey Hospital Association, Princeton, NJ '84 (PR)
GREGORY, JON C., buyer, Scripps Memorial Hospital, La Jolla, CA '82 (PUR)
GREGORY, LYNNE W., dir., St. Joseph Hospital, Augusta, GA '87 (AMB)
GREGORY, ROBERT E., dir. food serv., Howard University Hospital, Washington, DC '77 (FOOD)
GREGORY, TERRI A., RN, dir. educ., Broken Arrow Medical Center, Broken Arrow, OK '84 (EDUC)
GREGORY, WILLIS III, asst. dir. pers., McLeod Regional Medical Center, Florence, SC '77 (PERS)
GREGSON, C. MARK, vice-pres. oper., Phoenix Baptist Hospital and Medical Center, Phoenix, AZ '81
GREIDER, GEORGE M., vice-pres. and dir. mktg., Hospital Efficiency Corporation, Boston, MA '85 (ENG)
GREIG, LESLIE M., dir. phys. plant, Cape Cod Hospital, Hyannis, MA '79 (ENG)(RISK)
GREINER, FRANK L. III, Erie, PA '85 (PLNG)
GREIS, R. TED JR., asst. vice-pres. outpatient serv., St. John's Regional Medical Center, Joplin, MO '87 (AMB)
GREISBERGER, JOHN L., atty., Rochester St. Mary's Hospital, Rochester, NY '71 (ATTY)
GREISCH, JAMES R., sr. mgr., Peat, Marwick, Mitchell and Company, Omaha, NE '86
GREKO, CHARLOTTE, RN, dir. matl. mgt., Scottsdale Camelback Hospital, Scottsdale, AZ '76 (PUR)
GRELYAK, ANN, risk mgr. and dir. qual. assur., Norwegian-American Hospital, Chicago, IL '86 (RISK)
GREMILLION, BRUCE, dir. soc. serv., Baton Rouge General Medical Center, Baton Rouge, LA '82 (SOC)
GREMILLION, GINNY, dir. pat. rel., Hermann Hospital, Houston, TX '81 (PAT)
GRENELL, BARBARA H., PhD, dir. health serv. dev., Blue Cross Blue Shield, New York, NY '83
GRENELL, RUTH E., RN, dir. nrsg. oper., Hackley Hospital, Muskegon, MI '83 (NURS)
GRENVILLE, WILLIAM, tech. dir., Sita Corporation, Philadelphia, PA '86 (PUR)
GRESHAM, JAMES E., atty., North Arkansas Medical Center, Harrison, AR '83 (ATTY)
GRESHAM, PAULETTA A., dir. pur., Boone Hospital Center, Columbia, MO '80 (PUR)
GRESKO, MATTHEW C., chief exec. off., Suburban Community Hospital, Warrensville Heights, OH '70 (PLNG)
GRESSER, EVE W., dir. vol. serv., Columbia Hospital for Women, Washington, DC '84 (VOL)
GRESSER, OTTO, (ret.), Paris, France '54 (LIFE)
GRETHEL, SUE, dir. vol. serv., Clermont Mercy Hospital, Batavia, OH '85 (VOL)
GRETZINGER, JOHN R., bd. mem., McLaren General Hospital, Flint, MI '84 (PLNG)
GREULE, JANE E., dir. info. serv., Newark-Wayne Community Hospital, Newark, NY '86 (MGMT)
GREVE, CHARLES F., dir. matl. mgt., St. Francis Hospital Center, Beech Grove, IN '82 (PUR)
GREVE, RENSKE, educ. dev. eng., Servicemaster Management Services Corporation, Downers Grove, IL '86 (CS)
GREW, ROBERT R., atty., Hospital for Special Surgery, New York, NY '84 (ATTY)
GREY, BILL F., asst. fin. oper., American Medical International, Dallas, TX '84
GRICIUS, EILEEN T., dir. vol. serv., Saint Mary Hospital, Langhorne, PA '78 (VOL)
GRIEM, J. MICHAEL, vice-pres., A. T. Kearney, Chicago, IL '86 (PLNG)
GRIENER, MARGARET M., RN, dir. nrsg., Children's Hospital, New Orleans, LA '84 (NURS)
GRIER, ROBERT C., dir. pub. affairs, Sydenham Neighborhood Family Care Center, New York, NY '85 (PAT)
GRIERSON, CHARLES W., exec. dir., Western Rehabilitation Society, Vancouver, B.C., Canada '60
GRIESEMER, VICKY S., sr. vice-pres. corp. dev., Virginia Beach General Hospital, Virginia Beach, VA '83 (PLNG)
GRIESHABER, DAWN M., RN, dir. school nrsg., Mercy Hospital, Miami, FL '84 (EDUC)
GRIEST, NANCY LEE, mgr. plng., Saint Joseph Hospital, Fort Worth, TX '81 (PLNG)
GRIFF, STEVEN L., pres., Home Health Associates, Totowa, NJ '68
GRIFFEL, RICHARD B., hlthcare prog. planner and analyst, New York City Health and Hospital Corporation, New York, NY '87 (PLNG)
GRIFFEN, JAMES V., eng., General Arabian Medical and Allied Services, Ltd., Riyadh, Saudi Arabia '87 (ENG)
GRIFFETH, TERESA BLOUNT, sr. consult., Ernst and Whinney, St. Louis, MO '85
GRIFFIN, BOBBY H., atty., Union Memorial Hospital, Monroe, NC '71 (ATTY)
GRIFFIN, DAN G., atty., St. Mary's Hospital and Medical Center, Grand Junction, CO '73 (ATTY)
GRIFFIN, JANE MARIE, RN, assoc. adm. nrsg., Harborview Medical Center, Seattle, WA '68 (NURS)
GRIFFIN, JEANNE, supv. vol. serv., Griffin Hospital, Derby, CT '86 (VOL)
GRIFFIN, JEANNETTE P., dir. soc. serv., Montgomery General Hospital, Montgomery, WV '75 (SOC)
GRIFFIN, JOHN T., pres., Thermocycle International, Inc., New York, NY '82 (ENG)
GRIFFIN, JUANITA W., dir. diet. serv., Albert Einstein Medical Center, Philadelphia, PA '77 (FOOD)
GRIFFIN, KELLY L., dir. pub. rel., Carrier Foundation, Belle Mead, NJ '85 (PR)
GRIFFIN, LELAND J., pur. agt., Schick Shadel Hospital, Santa Barbara, CA '82 (PUR)
GRIFFIN, LEO P., asst. vice-pres. pub. rel., Montana Deaconess Medical Center, Great Falls, MT '81 (PR)
GRIFFIN, MARY ANN, dir. soc. work serv., Good Samaritan Medical Center, Phoenix, AZ '87 (SOC)
GRIFFIN, MARYA D., dir. vol. serv., St. Joseph Hospital, Bellingham, WA '79 (VOL)
GRIFFIN, OTTO, mgr. matl., Southwestern Medical Center, Lawton, OK '83 (PUR)
GRIFFIN, PATRICK T., dir. plant oper., Elkhart General Hospital, Elkhart, IN '75 (ENG)
GRIFFIN, ROBERT G., arch. and health planner, Odell Associates, Inc., Richmond, VA '82
GRIFFIN, ROSE E., RN, charge nrs. sup., proc. and distrib., Northern Michigan Hospitals, Petoskey, MI '83 (CS)
GRIFFIN, SANDRA K., dir. mktg., Georgia Baptist Medical Center, Atlanta, GA '86 (PLNG)
GRIFFIN, TERESA H., dir. plng. and res., Central Texas Health Plan, Austin, TX '86 (PLNG)
GRIFFIN, WILLIAM H., acquisitions lib., Southwest Texas State University, San Marcos, TX '86 (PLNG)
GRIFFITH, A. ANNE, med. soc. worker, Good Samaritan Hospital, Corvallis, OR '84 (SOC)
GRIFFITH, C. ANDERSON, atty., Emanuel Hospital and Health Center, Portland, OR '80 (ATTY)(RISK)
GRIFFITH, CYNTHIA A., dir. food serv., York Plaza Hospital and Medical Center, Houston, TX '84 (FOOD)
GRIFFITH, FAYNE J., mgr. plant, Broadlawns Medical Center, Des Moines, IA '85 (ENG)
GRIFFITH, GRETA, mgr. cent. sup., Lutheran Medical Center, Brooklyn, NY '80 (CS)
GRIFFITH, JACK H., dir. eng., Washington Regional Medical Center, Fayetteville, AR '74 (ENG)
GRIFFITH, JOHN C., student, Southern Illinois University, School of Technical Careers, Carbondale, IL '86
GRIFFITH, JOHN R., prof. and dir., School of Public Health, University of Michigan, Ann Arbor, MI '55 (MGMT)(LIFE)
GRIFFITH, JOYCE L., dir. mktg., Kennewick General Hospital, Kennewick, WA '86 (PR) (PLNG)
GRIFFITH, LINDA MAE, dir. soc. serv., Lawrence County General Hospital, Ironton, OH '85 (SOC)
GRIFFITH, LOREN H., dir. soc. serv., St. Luke's Hospital, Kansas City, MO '73 (SOC)
GRIFFITH, MARY ELLEN, RN, adm. nrsg., Deaconess Hospital, Oklahoma City, OK '73 (NURS)
GRIFFITH, RICHARD L., atty., Saint Joseph Hospital, Fort Worth, TX '85 (ATTY)
GRIFFITH, ROBERT W., syst. analyst mgt. eng., St. Francis-St. George Hospital, Cincinnati, OH '83 (MGMT)
GRIFFITH, SALLY ANNE, dir. vol., Kennedy Memorial Hospitals-University Medical Center, Cherry Hill, NJ '83 (VOL)
GRIFFITH, THERESA ANN, dir. rad., Charleston Area Medical Center, Charleston, WV '86
GRIFFITH, WILBUR, pur. agt., Marion General Hospital, Marion, IN '68 (PUR)
GRIFFITH, WILLIAM W., proj. analyst, St. Francis-St. George Hospital, Cincinnati, OH '82 (PLNG)
GRIFFITHS, DORIS, dir. vol. serv., Germantown Hospital and Medical Center, Philadelphia, PA '79 (VOL)
GRIFT, STEVEN L., pres., Home Care Information Systems, Inc., Totowa, NJ '87 (AMB)
GRIGA, LAURA M., mgt. eng., Good Samaritan Hospital, Cincinnati, OH '86 (MGMT)
GRIGGERS, PAT R., coor. vol. serv., University of New Mexico Mental Health, Albuquerque, NM '84 (VOL)
GRIGGS, DOROTHELLE M., dir. vol. serv., John F. Kennedy Medical Center, Edison, NJ '70 (VOL)
GRIGGS, GENNEY A., dir. human res., Des Moines General Hospital, Des Moines, IA '86 (PERS)
GRIGGS, JAMES A., dir. clin. eng. serv., Shore Memorial Hospital, Somers Point, NJ '84 (ENG)
GRIGGS, KATHERINE E., dir. staff dev. and educ., Sutter General Hospital, Sacramento, CA '68 (EDUC)
GRIGGS, PHYLLIS, coor. in-service, Stewart Memorial Community Hospital, Lake City, IA '72 (EDUC)
GRIGGS, THOMAS E., dir. plant oper., Salem Community Hospital, Salem, OH '85 (ENG)
GRILLO, BARBARA ANN, exec. dir., Exeter Hospital, Exeter, NH '80
GRILLO, JOHN J., dir. matl. mgt. and pur., Kingsbrook Jewish Medical Center, Brooklyn, NY '83 (PUR)
GRIM, WILLIAM W., chm., Devon Manor, Devon, PA '84
GRIMA, JOHN A., dir. plng., McKay-Dee Hospital Center, Ogden, UT '86 (PLNG)
GRIMA, JOHN J., chief med. info., Veterans Administration Medical Center, Palo Alto, CA '83
GRIMALDI, LOUIS, mgr. facil., Johnson Memorial Hospital, Stafford Springs, CT '85 (ENG)
GRIMES, CATHERINE M., dir. diet., Saint Francis Hospital and Medical Center, Hartford, CT '77 (FOOD)
GRIMES, EDWARD E., dir. phys. plant, Uniontown Hospital, Uniontown, PA '76 (ENG)
GRIMES, JOAN D., corp. vice-pres. plng., Carondelet Health Services, Inc., Tucson, AZ '85 (PR) (PLNG)
GRIMES, JOHN H., dir. phys. facil., Florida Keys Memorial Hospital, Key West, FL '83 (ENG)
GRIMES, SAMUEL H., dir. food serv., St. Mary's Hospital, Passaic, NJ '81 (FOOD)
GRIMES, TERESA, dir. mktg. and commun. rel., Medical Center-Bowling Green, Bowling Green, KY '86 (PR)
GRIMM, ANDREW E., atty., Bishop Clarkson Memorial Hospital, Omaha, NE '73 (ATTY)
GRIMM, DALE L., risk mgt. consult., Illinois Hospital Association, Naperville, IL '82 (RISK)
GRIMMELMANN, FRANK J., pres., F. J. Grimmelmann and Associates, Inc., San Francisco, CA '78
GRIMSHAW, KENNETH A., dir. environ. serv., Putnam Community Hospital, Palatka, FL '77 (ENG)
GRIMSLEY, EDWARD J., dir. commun. rel. and dev., Clifton Springs Hospital and Clinic, Clifton Springs, NY '81 (PR)
GRIMSLEY, HATTIE, Oak Park, IL '84 (RISK)
GRIMSLEY, JAN BATCHELOR, Decature, GA '81 (MGMT)
GRIMSLEY, LINDA P., RN, dir. nrsg., Worth Community Hospital, Sylvester, GA '82 (NURS)
GRIMSTAD, DUANE E., dir. pat. rel. and chaplaincy, St. Helena Hospital and Health Center, Deer Park, CA '87 (PAT)
GRIMWOOD, CHARLES G., dir. educ., Asbury Hospital, Salina, KS '84 (EDUC)(PLNG)
GRINAGER, CLAIRE L., RN, clin. dir., Fairview Southdale Hospital, Minneapolis, MN '83 (NURS)
GRINDE, STANLEY E., dir. eng., Swedish Medical Center, Englewood, CO '83 (ENG)
GRINDSTAFF, EVELYN S., dir. corp. mktg., CHI Systems, Inc., Ann Arbor, MI '84 (PR) (PLNG)
GRING, LAURA JEAN, dir. soc. work serv., White County Memorial Hospital, Monticello, IN '85 (SOC)
GRINNELL, STEVEN S., vice-pres. prof. serv., St. Agnes Hospital, Fond Du Lac, WI '80
GRINNELL, SUE, exec. dir., Friends of Strong Memorial Hospital, Rochester, NY '81 (VOL)
GRINNEY, JAY, sr. vice-pres., Methodist Hospital System, Houston, TX '84 (PLNG)
GRIPNE, JANET B., adm. diet., Idaho State School and Hospital, Nampa, ID '86 (FOOD)
GRISCAVAGE, MARYANNE, dir. vol. serv., Soldiers and Sailors Memorial Hospital, Wellsboro, PA '80 (VOL)
GRISCHY, ROBERT J., adm. emp. policy and benefits, Sears, Roebuck and Company, Dallas, TX '53 (LIFE)
GRISCOM, DOROTHY L., RN, dir. nrsg., Regional Medical Center at Memphis, Memphis, TN '80 (NURS)
GRISCOM, W. DAVID, dir. pers., Doctors General Hospital, Plantation, FL '85 (PERS)
GRISHAM, TRUDY M., dir. dev. and pub. rel., Decatur General Hospital, Decatur, AL '83 (PR)
GRISHMAN, MELANIE H., chief soc. work, Veterans Administration Medical Center, San Juan, P.R. '79 (SOC)
GRISOLA, JOSEPH E., dir. vol. serv., The Medical Center, Beaver, PA '80 (VOL)
GRISOLANO, JAMES E., facil. planner, Burlington Medical Center, Burlington, IA '76
GRISSINGER, STANLEY E., vice-pres., Suburban General Hospital, Norristown, PA '85 (RISK)
GRISSLER, BRIAN G., sr. vice-pres., Morristown Memorial Hospital, Morristown, NJ '86
GRISSOM, GARTH C., atty., Swedish Medical Center, Englewood, CO '79 (ATTY)
GRIST, ALICE C., diet., Richard L. Roudebush Veterans Administration Medical Center, Indianapolis, IN '76 (FOOD)
GRIST, W. SAMUEL, vice-pres., Louis A. Weiss Memorial Hospital, Chicago, IL '67 (ENG)
GRISWOLD, PAUL L., dir. pur., Copley Hospital, Morrisville, VT '81 (PUR)
GRISWOLD, ROBERT P., dir. pers. serv., Wyandotte General Hospital, Wyandotte, MI '76 (PERS)
GRITTON, EVELYN B., RN, vice-pres. nrsg., Methodist Evangelical Hospital, Louisville, KY '79 (NURS)
GRITTON, KAY N., dir. vol., Fairview Riverside Hospital, Minneapolis, MN '83 (VOL)
GROAH, LINDA K., RN, dir. nrsg. oper. and recovery room, University of California San Francisco, San Francisco, CA '81 (NURS)
GROARKE, HELEN J., RN, Wolfboro, NH '82 (NURS)
GROB, CHARLES E., chief exec. off., Medco Media, Inc., Point Pleasant, NJ '84 (EDUC)
GROB, GAIL GREEN, assoc. dir. soc. work serv., City Hospital Center at Elmhurst, Flushing, NY '83 (SOC)
GROBSMITH, MICHAEL S., Lincoln, NE '46 (LIFE)
GROCE, ROBERT B., asst. dir. eng., Hermann Hospital, Houston, TX '64 (ENG)
GROCH, JEROME, adm. dir. food serv. and catering, Carondelet Health Care, Tucson, AZ '75 (FOOD)
GROCHOLSKI, JAMES F., mgr. matl., Muskogee Regional Medical Center, Muskogee, OK '86 (PUR)
GROCHOWSKI, JEAN R., coor. in-service vol., Presbyterian Intercommunity Hospital, Whittier, CA '86 (VOL)
GRODE, STEPHEN J., vice-pres. support serv., Theda Clark Regional Medical Center, Neenah, WI '80 (ENG)

GROE, JOAN F., dir. diet., St. Joseph's Hospital, Chippewa Falls, WI '77 (FOOD)
GROEBER, SR. HELEN, dir. vol., Good Samaritan Hospital and Health Center, Dayton, OH '76 (VOL)
GROESCHEL, AUGUST H., MD, Sea Girt, NJ '49 (LIFE)
GROGAN, BRUCE E., dir. plng. and mktg., St. Mary's Medical Center, Knoxville, TN '86 (PLNG)
GROGAN, EDWARD J., actg. dir. biomedical eng., Alexandria Hospital, Alexandria, VA '82 (ENG)
GROGAN, HAROLD N., dir. pers., Hospital for Special Surgery, New York, NY '86 (PERS)
GROGAN, MARY B., dir. vol. serv., Le Bonheur Children's Medical Center, Memphis, TN '78 (VOL)
GROGAN, PAUL M., dir., Medical Center of Central Georgia, Macon, GA '84 (AMB)
GROGAN, SYLVIA S., dir. mktg., Morehead Memorial Hospital, Eden, NC '82 (PR)
GROH, DONNA H., RN, asst. dir. nrsg., Childrens Hospital of Los Angeles, Los Angeles, CA '83 (NURS)
GROHN, CHERYL L., RN, dir. maternal-child health, Poudre Valley Hospital, Fort Collins, CO '82 (NURS)
GROMALA, GUY R., dir. plant oper., Sacred Heart Rehabilitation Hospital, Milwaukee, WI '79 (ENG)
GROMKO, ALLEN R., dir. food serv., Salem Hospital, Salem, MA '79 (FOOD)
GROMOSKY, LAURA E., asst. dir. food and nutr. serv., Hamilton General Hospital, Hamilton, Ont., Canada '84 (FOOD)
GRONBACH, ROBERT C., asst. dir. and dir. emp. rel., Hartford Hospital, Hartford, CT '64 (PERS)
GRONDIN, GARY D., vice-pres., Fairlane Health Services Corporation, Birmingham, MI '85 (PLNG)
GRONE, JOSEPH L., dir. matl. mgt., Children's Hospital and Health Center, San Diego, CA '82 (PUR)
GRONER, FRANK SHELBY, pres. emeritus, Baptist Memorial Hospital, Memphis, TN '45 (LIFE)
GRONER, PAT NEFF, pres. emeritus, Baptist Care, Inc., Pensacola, FL '48 (LIFE)
GRONKIEWICZ, EDMUND, atty., Saint Mary of Nazareth Hospital Center, Chicago, IL '70 (ATTY)
GROOM, ROBERT W., dir. external affairs, Milford Memorial Hospital, Milford, DE '85 (PR)
GROOMS, SHARON, RN, vice-pres. nrsg., Licking Memorial Hospital, Newark, OH '79 (NURS)
GROOVER, B. VIRGINIA, RN, charge nrs. sterile proc., Firelands Community Hospital, Sandusky, OH '86 (CS)
GROOVER, CAROLYN J., coor. staff dev., Winter Haven Hospital, Winter Haven, FL '85 (EDUC)
GROOVER, DAN C. JR., dir. mgt. serv., Northeast Georgia Medical Center, Gainesville, GA '84 (MGMT)
GROOVER, ROBERT J., coor. commun. health educ., Baptist Hospital of Miami, Miami, FL '64 (PR)
GROSE, FRED M., pres., Impac, Inc., Braintree, MA '82
GROSE, KAREN S., RN, dir. nrsg., Beaver County Memorial Hospital, Beaver, OK '85 (SOC)
GROSKOPF, JOHN E., atty., Mmi Companies, Inc., Bannockburn, IL '85 (ATTY)
GROSS, ARTHUR E., dir. mktg., Johnson County Memorial Hospital, Franklin, IN '86 (PR)
GROSS, BENJAMIN GARY, reg. dir., ARA Health Care Nutrition Services, Philadelphia, PA '73
GROSS, CHARLIE, dir. eng., Lake Wales Hospital, Lake Wales, FL '84 (ENG)
GROSS, DOLORES M., RN, dir. nrsg. adm., Trumbull Memorial Hospital, Warren, OH '77 (NURS)
GROSS, DORIS E., dir. soc. work, River Garden Home for the Aged, Jacksonville, FL '80 (SOC)
GROSS, IRIS MACHLAN, coor. staff dev., educ. and trng., Hospital of the University of Pennsylvania, Philadelphia, PA '79 (EDUC)
GROSS, JANE A., risk mgr., Doctors General Hospital, Plantation, FL '85 (RISK)
GROSS, SR. M. LEONTINE, RN, dir. nrsg. serv., St. Joseph Intercommunity Hospital, Cheektowaga, NY '76 (NURS)
GROSS, M. MADELINE, dir. vol. serv., Milford-Whitinsville Regional Hospital, Milford, MA '86 (VOL)
GROSS, MARIE F., dir. regulatory serv., Massachusetts Hospital Association, Burlington, MA '85 (PLNG)
GROSS, MARK H., dir. loss prevention, Affiliated Risk Control Administration, New York, NY '79 (ENG)
GROSS, MARK S., natl. dir. health care info. syst. consult., Ernst and Whinney, Cleveland, OH '84 (MGMT)
GROSS, MICHAEL G., dir. support serv., Allegheny Valley Hospital, Natrona Heights, PA '75 (ENG)
GROSS, MICHEAL D., mgt. eng., Baptist Medical System, Little Rock, AR '86 (MGMT)
GROSS, MORRIS, asst. vice-pres., Danbury Health Systems, Danbury, CT '77
GROSS, PAUL A., exec. vice-pres., Humana Inc., Louisville, KY '63
GROSS, PHILIP H., tech. dir. facts dept., Laventhol and Horwath, Los Angeles, CA '83 (MGMT)
GROSS, RICHARD E., student, Boston University Health Management Programs, Boston, MA '86 (PLNG)
GROSSFELD, BEA, dir. soc. serv., Franklin Square Hospital, Baltimore, MD '85 (SOC)
GROSSI, RICHARD A., asst. dean to adm., Johns Hopkins Hospital, Baltimore, MD '87 (AMB)
GROSSMAN, BARBARA C., dir. vol. serv., St. Joseph Hospital, Lexington, KY '84 (VOL)
GROSSMAN, HARVEY L., dir. mktg., East Liverpool City Hospital, East Liverpool, OH '82 (PLNG)
GROSSMAN, MARTIN, chief facil. mgt., Department of Health and Human Services, New York, NY '85 (ENG)
GROSSMAN, PAUL J., consult., Ernst and Whinney, Tampa, FL '86 (MGMT)
GROSSMAN, RANDOLPH M., PhD, pres., Health-Care Market Metrics, Foster, CA '79 (PLNG)
GROSSMAN, RISA S., asst. dir. diet., St. Charles Hospital and Rehabilitation Center, Port Jefferson, NY '76 (FOOD)
GROSSMAN, TERRI ANN, mgr. sup., proc. and distrib., Spelman Memorial Hospital, Smithville, MO '85 (CS)
GROST, THOMAS M., dir. plant oper., St. Lawrence Hospital, Lansing, MI '81 (ENG)
GROSZ, ARLYSS LOKEN, mgr. educ., Boulder Community Hospital, Boulder, CO '86 (EDUC)
GROSZ, SUSAN, coor. nrsg. staff educ., St. Alexius Medical Center, Bismarck, ND '83 (EDUC)
GROTH, DONALD P., asst. dir. corp. procurement, Harper-Grace Hospitals, Detroit, MI '82 (PUR)
GROTH, HOWARD S., adm., Shriners Hospital for Crippled Children, Portland, OR '64
GROTH, THOMAS J., adm. dir. oper., Henry Ford Hospital-Maple Grove, West Bloomfield, MI '84
GROTHAUS, CRAIG L., dir. risk mgt. and safety, Elmhurst Memorial Hospital, Elmhurst, IL '81 (RISK)
GROTHEER, EUGENE, vice-pres. adm., Mount Carmel Medical Center, Pittsburg, KS '86 (RISK)
GROTKE, FREDERICK J., asst. dir. plant eng., John F. Kennedy Memorial Hospital, Atlantis, FL '84 (ENG)
GROTKE, LINDA B., dir. pub. rel., Medical Center Hospital, Punta Gorda, FL '82 (PR)
GROTNES, MILFORD S., exec. vice-pres., Sisters of Mercy Health Corporation, Iowa and Indiana Regional Office, West Des Moines, IA '69
GROTTING, JOHN B., sr. vice-pres. oper., Healthlink, Portland, OR '73
GROTTON, LINDA L., mgr. mktg., Concord Hospital, Concord, NH '86 (PLNG)
GROUDLE, SANDRA J., RN, vice-pres. pat. care serv., St. John and West Shore Hospital, Westlake, OH '84 (NURS)
GROUNDS, GENEVA M., adm. food serv., Morgan County Memorial Hospital, Martinsville, IN '68 (FOOD)
GROUNDWATER, ROBERT B., vice-pres. human res., Winchester Medical Center, Winchester, VA '83 (PERS)
GROVE, GARTH W., dir. educ., Sacred Heart Hospital of Pensacola, Pensacola, FL '82 (EDUC)
GROVE, HOMER N., asst. to pres., Adventist Health System-Sunbelt, Orlando, FL '86
GROVEMAN, HELEN L., vice-pres., Healthcare Management Counselors, New York, NY '80 (MGMT)
GROVES, ANNE, asst. dir. soc. work, Brigham and Women's Hospital, Boston, MA '76 (SOC)
GROVES, CAROL M., RN, coor. qual. assur., Northeastern Regional Hospital, Las Vegas, NM '80 (RISK)
GROVES, DENNIS M., vice-pres. human res., St. Francis Hospital and Medical Center, Topeka, KS '80 (PERS)
GROVES, JOANNE K., coor. in-service, Huron Regional Medical Center, Huron, SD '83 (EDUC)
GROVES, JOHN, PhD, Alma, MI '84
GROVES, ROBERT J., exec. dir., Southeastern Pennsylvania High Blood Pressure Control Program, Inc., Philadelphia, PA '82
GRUBB, ALLEN W., EdD, dir. human res. dev., Community Hospitals of Indiana, Indianapolis, IN '71 (EDUC)
GRUBB, JESSE I., dir. eng., West Park Hospital, Philadelphia, PA '82 (ENG)
GRUBB, TERRY J., dir. pat. acctg., Parkview Memorial Hospital, Fort Wayne, IN '84
GRUBBER, KATHERINE J., pur. agt., Swedish Covenant Hospital, Chicago, IL '77 (PUR)
GRUBBS, DEE E., RN, assoc. adm. pat. serv., University Medical Center Southern Nevada, Las Vegas, NV '86 (NURS)
GRUBBS, ELAINE, dir. vol., Huntsville Hospital, Huntsville, AL '77 (VOL)
GRUBBS, JAMES M., chief eng., Logan County Hospital, Sterling, CO '85 (ENG)
GRUBBS, ZELDA A., (ret.), Los Angeles, CA '79 (SOC)
GRUBE, MARK E., sr. consult., Ernst and Whinney, Chicago, IL '84 (PLNG)
GRUBER, NANCY L., dir. pur., Good Samaritan Hospital, Baltimore, MD '83 (PUR)
GRUBER, STEPHEN J., dir. support serv., Valley Hospital Association, Palmer, AK '86 (ENG)
GRUBER, SUZIE, dir. mktg. and commun., St. Joseph's Hospital, Tampa, FL '86 (PR)
GRUBER, THOMAS H. JR., dir. matl. and support serv., Mercy Hospital, Portland, ME '86 (ENG)
GRUDZIEN, MICHAEL A., supv. biomedical eng., Tucson General Hospital, Tucson, AZ '86 (ENG)
GRUENEWALD, MARY M., mgt. dev. spec., Group Health Cooperative of Puget Sound, Seattle, WA '83 (EDUC)
GRUHLKE, JERRY S., mgr. matl., Alton Memorial Hospital, Alton, IL '82 (PUR)
GRUJIC, OLGA, coor. qual. assur. and risk mgt., Augustana Hospital and Health Care Center, Chicago, IL '86 (RISK)
GRUMBINE, ROBERT, pat. rep., Franklin Square Hospital of the City of Baltimore, Baltimore, MD '74 (PAT)
GRUMET, JULES, dir. matl. mgt., Children's Hospital of Pittsburgh, Pittsburgh, PA '73 (PUR)
GRUMMER, LINDA L., dir. nrsg. res., St. Mary's Hospital and Rehabilitation Center, Minneapolis, MN '84 (EDUC)
GRUNDIN, ROBERT E., atty., Methodist Hospital of Chicago, Chicago, IL '76 (ATTY)
GRUNDSTROM, DAVID A., vice-pres. adm. serv., St. Joseph's Hospital, Marshfield, WI '83
GRUNKE, ARTHUR G., atty., Bogle and Gates, Seattle, WA '69 (ATTY)
GRUSSING, CHERYL R., dir. hskpg., Mount Sinai Hospital, Minneapolis, MN '86 (ENVIRON)
GRUTTEMEYER, PATRICIA H., mgr. commun. rel., Concord Hospital, Concord, NH '86 (PR)
GRYCKIEWICZ, FREDERIC C., dir. eng., DePaul Hospital, Norfolk, VA '86 (ENG)
GRYZBEK, THOMAS JOSEPH, atty., St. Margaret Hospital, Hammond, IN '80 (RISK)(ATTY)
GRZEGORCZYK, PHYLLIS, dean health and pub. serv., Washtenaw Community College, Ann Arbor, MI '79 (EDUC)
GRZYWA, JUDITH A., asst. vice-pres., St. Charles Hospital, Oregon, OH '83 (PLNG)
GSTUNDTNER, KAREN MCCARTHY, dir. food serv., Cleveland Memorial Hospital, Shelby, NC '79 (FOOD)
GUALCO, FRANK, Alcohol and Drug Treatment Center, Pomona, CA '86 (PR)
GUALTIERI, CARMEN V., dir. soc. work, Methodist Hospital of Chicago, Chicago, IL '85 (SOC)
GUANCI, MARIE T., pat. rep., Bascom Palmer Eye Institute, Anne Bates Leach Eye Hospital, Miami, FL '77 (PAT)
GUARDIANI, LOUIS J., assoc. dir. bldg. serv., Pottstown Memorial Medical Center, Pottstown, PA '83 (ENG)
GUARE, THOMAS R., dir. matl. mgt., Maine Medical Center, Portland, ME '84 (PUR)
GUARINO, JOHN P., dir. corp. serv., Framingham Union Hospital, Framingham, MA '85 (PR) (PLNG)
GUARINO, KATHY, dir. soc. serv., Lower Bucks Hospital, Bristol, PA '82 (SOC)
GUARISCO, TOM, mgr. human resource, AMI Westpark Community Hospital, Hammond, LA '85 (PERS)
GUARRERA, VINCENT J., dir. soc. work, North Shore University Hospital, Manhasset, NY '78 (SOC)
GUASCONI, J., dir., St. Peter's Hospital, Albany, NY '87 (AMB)
GUASTELLA, JENNIE M., dir. pat. serv., Boca Raton Community Hospital, Boca Raton, FL '77 (PAT)
GUBBELS, JOSEPH GERARD, adm. fellow, Mercy Health Center, Oklahoma City, OK '84
GUBBELS, LARRY D., vice-pres. human resources, St. Francis Medical Center, Cape Girardeau, MO '79 (PERS)
GUBBINS, JUDITH A., asst. supv. cent. sup., Midway Hospital, St. Paul, MN '86 (CS)
GUBIN, LLOYD BARRY, atty., Deaconess Hospital, St. Louis, MO '82 (ATTY)
GUBRUD, JERRY, dir. plant oper. and maint., Mercy Hospital of Sacramento, Sacramento, CA '82
GUDEMAN, JOYCE, asst. dir. mktg. and plng., Choate-Symmes Health Services, Arlington, MA '85 (PLNG)
GUDEX, BEVERLEY, dir. soc. serv., Waupun Memorial Hospital, Waupun, WI '81 (SOC)
GUDMUNDSON, LENORE C., RN, asst. dir. nrsg., Day Kimball Hospital, Putnam, CT '80 (NURS)
GUDZ, ORYST EUGENE, dir. aux. serv., Reddy Memorial Hospital, Montreal, Que., Canada '83 (ENG)
GUELLICH, FRANK G., MD, hand surg., Beverly Hospital, Montebello, CA '83 (RISK)
GUEN, AMY C., dir. soc. serv., Youville Rehabilitation and Chronic Diseases Hospital, Cambridge, MA '72 (SOC)
GUERIN, JEREMIAH J., vice-pres. human res., Marshal Hale Memorial Hospital, San Francisco, CA '84 (PERS)
GUERIN, MICHAEL D. JR., med. insp., Health Service Administration, Norton AFB, CA '58
GUERRA, ARNOLD, supv. eng. and bldg. maint. III, Arizona State Hospital, Phoenix, AZ '86 (ENG)
GUERRA, BETTY L., RN, asst. dir. nrsg., Children's Mercy Hospital, Kansas City, MO '86 (NURS)
GUERRA, MARYANN, RN, dir. nrsg., Lawndale Community Hospital, Philadelphia, PA '82 (NURS)
GUERRANT, STEVE, dir. biomedical elec. serv., Hinds General Hospital, Jackson, MS '85 (ENG)
GUERRETTE, SHARA A., dir. mktg., Community Hospital and Rehabilitation Center, Los Gatos, CA '85 (PR) (PLNG)
GUEST, JOHN A., exec. dir., Bexar County Hospital District, San Antonio, TX '75
GUETHLEIN, WILLIAM O., atty., Hardin Memorial Hospital, Elizabethtown, KY '73 (ATTY)
GUEVREMONT, FRANCES A., dir. commun. rel., Woonsocket Hospital, Woonsocket, RI '78 (PR)
GUFFY, THELMA R., dir. vol., San Jose Hospital, San Jose, CA '82 (VOL)
GUGIN, ALAN H., dir. pers., Mercy Medical Center, Redding, CA '76 (PERS)
GUGIN, CARMEN, vice-pres. plng. and mktg., St. Francis Regional Medical Center, Shakopee, MN '84 (PR) (PLNG)
GUGLIELMO, LEONARD R., asst. adm., Putnam Hospital Center, Carmel, NY '84 (ENG)
GUIBORD, DEBORAH L., student, Masters Program of Health Services Administration, University of Michigan, Ann Arbor, MI '85 (PLNG)
GUIDA, MARY L., dir. human res., St. Joseph Memorial Hospital, Murphysboro, IL '86 (PERS)
GUIDO, ALBERT J., dir. pers., St. Joseph Medical Center, Stamford, CT '67 (PERS)
GUIDROZ, M. ELAINE, trng. off., University Medical Center, Lafayette, LA '78 (EDUC)
GUIDRY, GREG, atty., Franklin Foundation Hospital, Franklin, LA '83 (ATTY)
GUIDRY, RONALD C., mgt. eng., Lake Charles Memorial Hospital, Lake Charles, LA '82 (MGMT)
GUIDRY, WILLIAM D., atty., Memorial Hospital, Nacogdoches, TX '85 (ATTY)
GUIGNET, PAUL D., dir. plant oper., Muhlenberg Hospital Center, Bethlehem, PA '85 (ENG)
GUILBAULT, CLAUDE R., dir. soc. work, Ottawa General Hospital, Ottawa, Ont., Canada '81 (SOC)
GUILETTE, GAYLORD G., eng., Bellin Memorial Hospital, Green Bay, WI '78 (ENG)
GUILFORD, JOAN, sr. mgr. mktg., Acute Care Affiliates, Berkeley, CA '86 (PLNG)
GUILFOYLE, FRANCIS, chief soc. work serv., Veterans Administration Medical Center, Tomah, WI '85 (SOC)
GUILFOYLE, WILLIAM A., atty., Memorial Hospital, Abilene, KS '76 (ATTY)
GUILIANO, CARMINE, dir. eng. and maint., North Shore University Hospital, Manhasset, NY '81 (ENG)
GUILLE, CLARE H., dir. vol., Winthrop-University Hospital, Mineola, NY '80 (VOL)
GUILLEMETTE, HELEN H., coor. nrs., Catholic Medical Center, Manchester, NH '86 (EDUC)
GUILLEN, EDGARDO, plant eng., Mennonite General Hospital, Aibonito, P.R. '84 (ENG)
GUILLETT, WARREN V. JR., mgr. health syst. consult., Coopers and Lybrand, Detroit, MI '77 (MGMT)
GUILLORY, MARY, actg. exec. dir. plng., University of Texas Health Sciences Center, Houston, TX '85 (PLNG)
GUIN, MICHAEL W., dir. clin. eng., telecommun. and safety, Jefferson Regional Medical Center, Pine Bluff, AR '86 (ENG)

GUINN, DANIEL B., mgr. oper. and productivity dev., Pacific Health Resources, Los Angeles, CA '84 (MGMT)
GUINN, ROBERT MONROE, vice-pres., prin., Heery Architects and Engineers, Inc., Atlanta, GA '83 (PLNG)
GULEY, MICHAEL G., pres. and chief exec. off., Bradford Hospital, Bradford, PA '74 (RISK)
GULINSON, SHELDON KEITH, pres., Hospital Council of Northern California, San Mateo, CA '68
GULKO, EDWARD, adm., Montclair Medical Group, Montclair, NJ '73
GULLA, MARY ANN, dir. vol., Calvary Hospital, Bronx, NY '85 (VOL)
GULLEDGE, CATHERINE M., dir. pur., Western Medical Center, Santa Ana, CA '66 (PUR)
GULLETT, BETTE M., asst. mgr. matl., Ottumwa Regional Health Center, Ottumwa, IA '84 (PUR)
GULLEY, EILEEN S., coor. vol. serv., Regional Institute for Children and Adolescents, Baltimore, MD '74 (VOL)
GULLEY, OLIVIA J., dir. vol. serv., Salvation Army William Booth Memorial Hospital, Florence, KY '84 (VOL)
GULLIKSEN, EVELYN M., RN, assoc. dir. nrsg., Bayley Seton Hospital, Staten Island, NY '82 (NURS)
GUMAER, MYRTLE L., RN, asst. dir. sup., proc., distrib. and matl. mgt., United Health Services, Johnson City, NY '83 (CS)
GUMBERICH, LOTHAR D., vice-pres. mktg. and sales, Inter Metropolitan Industry, Wilkes-Barre, PA '82 (FOOD)
GUMPERT, NORMAN F., pres. and owner, Educational Affiliates, Torrance, CA '80 (EDUC)
GUMPERTZ, BETTY, dir. soc. serv., Beth Israel Hospital, Boston, MA '77 (SOC)
GUNDEN, ELIZABETH A., RN, div. dir. surg. nrsg., Memorial Hospital, South Bend, IN '81 (NURS)
GUNDERSON, DENISE, mgr. soc. work serv., Holy Cross Hospital, Detroit, MI '86 (SOC)
GUNDERSON, SHIRLEY A., coor. pat. rep., Sacred Heart Hospital, Yankton, SD '85 (PAT)
GUNDLACH, ANN-MICHELE, dir. org. dev., Johns Hopkins Hospital, Baltimore, MD '85 (EDUC)
GUNN, CHRISTINA B., adm., University of New Mexico Children Psychiatric Hospital, Albuquerque, NM '84 (PLNG)
GUNN, JAMES F., atty., St. Joseph Hospital, Kirkwood, MO '68 (ATTY)
GUNN, JOHN R., sr. vice-pres., Memorial Hospital for Cancer and Allied Diseases, New York, NY '81 (PLNG)
GUNN, ROBERT D., oper. improvement, Daughters of Charity Data Center, Grand Prairie, TX '76 (MGMT)
GUNN, THOMAS WILLIAM, pres. and arch., Gunn LeVine Associates, Inc., Detroit, MI '75 (MGMT)
GUNN, WILLIAM J., atty., Jeff Anderson Regional Medical Center, Meridian, MS '68 (ATTY)
GUNTER, CHARLES P., dir. plant oper. and maint., Blount Memorial Hospital, Maryville, TN '80 (ENG)
GUNTER, H. CLAIR, RN, dir. nrsg. serv., South Highlands Hospital, Birmingham, AL '74 (NURS)
GUNTER, KAREN, asst. vice-pres., Memorial Health Systems, Inc., South Bend, IN '87 (AMB)
GUNTER, ROBERT L., dir. eng., Memorial Medical Center of East Texas, Lufkin, TX '81 (ENG)
GUNTZ, ALLEN H., asst. dir. matl. serv., Mary Hitchcock Memorial Hospital, Hanover, NH '81 (PUR)
GUPTA, AVINASH, partner, Smith, Korach, Hayet and Haynie, Miami, FL '82
GUPTA, HARISH C., proj. eng., University of Chicago, Chicago, IL '78 (ENG)
GUPTA, VINOD C., sr. mgt. syst. eng., Memorial Hospital, Hollywood, FL '85 (MGMT)
GUPTIL, WALTER S., dir. safety, Medical Center Hospital of Vermont, Burlington, VT '66 (RISK)
GUPTILL, JANET I., vice-pres. mktg. and sales, The Sachs Group, Ltd., Chicago, IL '77 (PLNG)
GUPTILL, PAUL B., dir. plng., Missouri Hospital Association, Jefferson City, MO '70 (PLNG)(ENG)
GURAL, KIMBERLY A., coor. educ. serv., Prince William Hospital, Manassas, VA '86 (EDUC)
GURCHIK, ROBERT J., dir. bldgs. and grds., Fairview General Hospital, Cleveland, OH '86 (ENG)
GURDAK, BARBARA ANN, RN, chief amb. nrsg., Arabian American Oil Company, Dhahran, Saudi Arabia '86 (NURS)
GURIAN, CHARLES, mgr. mgt. serv., Blackman, Kallick and Company, Ltd., Chicago, IL '86 (PLNG)
GURKA, RICHARD, supv. maint., Marymount Hospital, Garfield Heights, OH '71 (ENG)
GURKIN, BEVERLY A., dir. soc. work and human serv., Good Hope Hospital, Erwin, NC '82 (SOC)
GURNEY, ELLEN K., dir. vol. serv., Kennebec Valley Medical Center, Augusta, ME '86 (VOL)
GURNICK, DOLORES A., student, University of California, Berkeley, CA '80
GURSKI, HENRY S., dir. plant oper., St. Joseph Hospital, Baltimore, MD '75 (ENG)
GUSACK, DIANE M., dir. soc. serv., Overlook Hospital, Summit, NJ '78 (SOC)
GUSFA, ANNE M., RN, dir. nrsg. serv., St. Mary Hospital, Livonia, MI '76 (NURS)
GUSIC, JOAN C., RN, vice-pres., Mount Auburn Hospital, Cambridge, MA '80 (NURS)
GUSSERT, JEFFREY R., mgr. emer. and trauma serv., Borgess Medical Center, Kalamazoo, MI '87 (AMB)
GUSTAFSON, ALBERT H., supt. plant, Roswell Park Memorial Institute, Buffalo, NY '84 (ENG)
GUSTAFSON, BONNIE L., asst. pers., Sarasota Palms Hospital, Sarasota, FL '86 (PERS)
GUSTAFSON, EDWARD C., dir. hskpg., Spring Shadows Glen, Houston, TX '86 (ENVIRON)
GUSTAFSON, EUGENE L., supv. maint., Abbott-Northwestern Hospital, Minneapolis, MN '82 (ENG)
GUSTAFSON, FRANCES, dir. vol., Baptist Medical Center, San Antonio, TX '74 (VOL)
GUSTAFSON, GERRIE, dir. comm. rel. and commun., Saint Anthony Medical Center, Rockford, IL '79 (PR)
GUSTAFSON, LEE A., mgr. pers. and payroll, Sanford Memorial Hospital and Nursing Home, Farmington, MN '86 (PERS)
GUSTAFSON, NANCY FELLGER, dir. pub. rel., Fairview Southdale Hospital, Minneapolis, MN '80 (PR)
GUSTAFSON, RICHARD P., pres., Lutheran General Health Care Systems, Park Ridge, IL '70 (AMB)
GUSTAFSON, VERN, dir. eng., Washington Hospital, Fremont, CA '86 (ENG)
GUSTAVSON, TEXAS A., RN, dir. nrsg. serv., Desert Springs Hospital, Las Vegas, NV '82 (NURS)
GUSTER, RICHARD, atty., Saint Thomas Medical Center, Akron, OH '74 (ATTY)
GUTEKUNST, WILLIAM J., dir. fin., Lake Wales Hospital, Lake Wales, FL '85 (RISK)
GUTHERY, PETER C., atty., AMI Presbyterian-St. Luke's Medical Center, Denver, CO '78 (ATTY)
GUTHRIE, GEORGE G. II, atty., Charleston Area Medical Center, Charleston, WV '75 (ATTY)
GUTHRIE, J. KENNETH, dir. eng., Davis Community Hospital, Statesville, NC '82 (ENG)
GUTHRIE, JUDI H., adm., Plaquemines Parish General Hospital, Port Sulphur, LA '79
GUTHRIE, KATHLEEN A., asst. coor. educ. and staff dev., Good Samaritan Hospital, Corvallis, OR '87 (EDUC)
GUTHRIE, LOUIS T., atty., Hanover General Hospital, Hanover, PA '86 (ATTY)
GUTHRIE, RICHARD, dir. support serv., Illini Community Hospital, Pittsfield, IL '83 (ENG)
GUTHRIE, ROBERT L., vice-pres., Frankford Hospital, Philadelphia, PA '77
GUTHRIE, S. W., dir. matl. handling, Health Sciences Centre, Winnipeg, Man., Canada '83 (PUR)
GUTIERREZ, DORIS M., dir. pers., Belmont Community Hospital, Chicago, IL '86 (PERS)
GUTIERREZ, FREDERIC S., mng. dir. eng., Sharp Cabrillo Hospital, San Diego, CA '83 (ENG)
GUTIERREZ, NESTOR, biomedical elec. tech., Lovelace Medical Center, Albuquerque, NM '86 (ENG)
GUTOS, STEVAN N., vice-pres. mktg., General Health, Inc., Baton Rouge, LA '81 (PR)
GUTSTADT, BARBARA J., exec. dir., Professional Strategies, Marlton, NJ '87 (EDUC)
GUTTCHEN, EMILY S., dir. vol., New Rochelle Hospital Medical Center, New Rochelle, NY '80 (VOL)
GUTTENPLAN, PATSY A., dir. clin. data, Raritan Bay Medical Center, Perth Amboy, NJ '82 (MGMT)
GUTTING, PAUL, dir. risk mgt., St. Paul Medical Center, Dallas, TX '85 (RISK)
GUTTMAN, ELLIOTT S., vice-pres. facil., eng. and constr., Catherine McAuley Health Center, Ann Arbor, MI '72 (ENG)
GUTTORMSEN, NEIL F., atty., Kenosha Hospital and Medical Center, Kenosha, WI '82 (ATTY)
GUY, DOUGLAS I., vice-pres., Mercy Catholic Medical Center, Fitzgerald Mercy Division, Darby, PA '76
GUY, EDWARD T., coor. safety, Childrens Hospital of Los Angeles, Los Angeles, CA '79 (ENG)
GUY, JOHN E., atty., Evanston Hospital, Evanston, IL '68 (ATTY)
GUY, MARY ELLEN, head nrs. surg. reproc, F. G. McGaw Hospital, Loyola University, Maywood, IL '86 (CS)
GUY, PAUL W., dir. human resources, Parkview Memorial Hospital, Fort Wayne, IN '68 (PERS)
GUY, ROBERT A., proj. mgr., Daverman Associates, Inc., Austin, TX '84
GUY, WILLIAM T. JR., dir. bldg. serv., Elizabeth General Medical Center, Elizabeth, NJ '68 (ENG)
GUYER, LIBBY, dir. pat. and guest rel., Tampa General Hospital, Tampa, FL '77 (PAT)
GUYOL, DAVID M., sr. assoc., Herman Smith Associates, Hinsdale, IL '83 (PUR)
GUYRE, MARK J., vice-pres., Roc Scientific Supply Inc., Marlboro, NJ '86 (PUR)
GUYTON, BETTY, asst. mgr. sup., University of Missouri Hospital and Clinics, Columbia, MO '86 (CS)
GUYTON, LORETTA, supv. distrib., Ochsner Foundation Hospital, New Orleans, LA '83 (CS)
GUZEWSKI, RITA L., mgr. emp., Chestnut Hill Hospital, Philadelphia, PA '83 (PERS)
GUZMAN, RICHARD M., Naval Hospital, Oak Harbor, WA '81
GUZZARDI, MARY ANN, dir. educ., Children's Hospital of Pittsburgh, Pittsburgh, PA '83 (EDUC)
GUZZI, RICHARD S., mgr. proc. and distrib., Pomona Valley Community Hospital, Pomona, CA '86 (CS)
GUZZO, ELIZABETH A., dir. pers., Mary Black Memorial Hospital, Spartanburg, SC '86 (PERS)
GWALTNEY, BEVERLY, RN, assoc. adm. nrsg. serv., Ventura County Medical Center, Ventura, CA '86 (NURS)
GWARTNEY, BILL D., pres., Vha Oklahoma, Oklahoma City, OK '86 (PLNG)
GWIAZDOWSKI, DEBRA REGAN, supv. bus. off., Women and Infants Hospital of Rhode Island, Providence, RI '84
GWIN, LOIS F., RN, dir. nrsg. serv., Mercy Hospital of New Orleans, New Orleans, LA '84 (NURS)
GWIN, WILMA C., dir. vol., Community Hospital of Roanoke Valley, Roanoke, VA '73 (VOL)
GYGI, JUDY C., dir. soc. work, West Florida Hospital, Pensacola, FL '78 (SOC)

H

HAAG, HERSCHEL L. III, atty., Southern Baptist Hospital, New Orleans, LA '77 (ATTY)
HAAG, KEITH, coor. eng. and maint., Bay Medical Center, Bay City, MI '85 (ENG)
HAAG, PETER B., dir. codes and standards consult. serv., Michigan Hospital Association, Lansing, MI '78 (ENG)
HAAG, SHAWN J., vice-pres., Mount Sinai Hospital of Cleveland, Cleveland, OH '79
HAAG, WANDA L., RN, vice-pres. pat. serv., Midwest City Memorial Hospital, Midwest City, OK '86 (NURS)
HAAN, RICHARD V., dir. plant oper., St. Mary's Hospital of Kankakee, Kankakee, IL '83 (ENG)
HAAR, CLARE A., vice-pres., Buffalo General Hospital, Buffalo, NY '75
HAAS, CHRISTINA LEONE, RN, div. mgr., Home Care America, Cosmopolitan Care Corporation, New York, NY '80 (NURS)(AMB)
HAAS, DENNIS A., atty., Charter Medical Corporation, Macon, GA '84 (ATTY)
HAAS, DONI, RN, dir. risk mgt. and qual. review, Martin Memorial Hospital, Stuart, FL '86 (RISK)
HAAS, JAN M., dir. strategic plng., St. Francis Hospital, Wilmington, DE '83
HAAS, JO LYNN, RN, dir. clin. info. syst., St. Joseph Hospital East, Mount Clemens, MI '83
HAAS, MARK I., dir. soc. work, Saint Luke's Hospital, Cleveland, OH '84 (SOC)
HAAS, PHILLIP J., pres., First Choice Health Plan, Bellevue, WA '72
HAAS, RAYMOND R., dir. human res., Sarah Bush Lincoln Health Center, Mattoon, IL '87 (PERS)
HAAS, RICHARD A., dir. pers., Shawnee Mission Medical Center, Shawnee Mission, KS '83 (PERS)
HAAS, ROBERT L., MD, consult., Florida Regional Medical Program, Tampa, FL '72
HAAS, SHEILA A., RN, asst. prof. med. and surg. nrsg., Niehoff School of Nursing, Loyola University, Chicago, IL '86 (NURS)
HAAS, STEVEN C., atty., House of the Good Samaritan, Watertown, NY '81 (ATTY)
HAAS, WOLFGANG, chief health syst. initiatives, Silas B. Hays Army Community Hospital, Fort Ord, CA '83
HAASE, DIANE A., adm. dir. mktg., Spring Branch Memorial Hospital, Houston, TX '85 (PLNG)
HAASE, FRANCES, dir. pers., St. Mary's Hospital of Kankakee, Kankakee, IL '84 (PERS)
HAASE, JUDY A., coor. comm. rel., St. Luke's Hospital, Kansas City, MO '83 (PR)
HABEGGER, DYANNE H., dir. aux. rel., National Medical Enterprises, Los Angeles, CA '85 (VOL)
HABER, A. J., plant eng., Mercy Medical Center, Roseburg, OR '78 (ENG)
HABER, MARTHA E., RN, vice-pres. nrsg., Presbyterian Hospital in the City of New York, New York, NY '74 (NURS)
HABER, PERRY Z., spec. asst. to pres. off., Beth Israel Medical Center, New York, NY '73 (PLNG)
HABGOOD, STEPHEN P., asst. dir. pub. rel., Baylor University Medical Center, Dallas, TX '84 (PR)
HABICH, LOUIS C., dir. plng. and mktg. serv., Dover General Hospital and Medical Center, Dover, NJ '85 (PLNG)
HACHEY, JOSEPH E., dir. pur. and matl. mgt., Northside Hospital, Atlanta, GA '83 (PUR)
HACK, JUDITH L., asst. prof., Purdue University, Hammond, IN '73 (FOOD)
HACKENBURG, DOROTHY R., dir. soc. serv., Evangelical Community Hospital, Lewisburg, PA '82 (SOC)
HACKER, JAMES O., dir. mktg., Mercy Hospital, Charlotte, NC '84 (PLNG)
HACKER, JOHN R., dir. eng. and planner oper., Good Samaritan Medical Center, Milwaukee, WI '82 (ENG)
HACKER, WILLIAM A., (ret.), McKeesport, PA '41 (LIFE)
HACKETT, CHARLES J., exec. dir., Garden City Imaging Center, Garden City, NY '64
HACKETT, DAVID RODNEY, atty., Nanticoke Memorial Hospital, Seaford, DE '76 (ATTY)
HACKETT, KAREN L., dir. tech. serv., Healthcare Financial Management Association, Oak Brook, IL '85
HACKETT, THOMAS E., atty., Mercy Medical Center, Springfield, OH '73 (ATTY)
HACKLER, EUGENE T., pres., American Association of Homes for the Aging, Olathe, KS '68 (ATTY)
HACKLER, PATRICIA H., RN, risk mgr., Smyrna Hospital, Smyrna, GA '82 (RISK)
HACKMAN, MICHAEL, atty., Hyatt Medical Enterprises, Encino, CA '79 (ATTY)
HACKNEY, HAZEL LOUISE, pat. rep., HCA Park West Medical Centers, Knoxville, TN '86 (PAT)
HACKNEY, VIRGINIA H., atty., Chippenham Hospital, Richmond, VA '80 (ATTY)
HADDAD, ERNEST M., atty., Massachusetts General Hospital, Boston, MA '77 (ATTY)
HADDAD, LARRY J., dir. environ. serv., Moses H. Cone Memorial Hospital, Greensboro, NC '86 (ENVIRON)
HADDAD, LOUIS JR., asst. adm., Natchaug Hospital, Mansfield Center, CT '86 (PERS)
HADDICK, MARGARET K., dir. soc. work, Beyer Memorial Hospital, Ypsilanti, MI '74 (SOC)
HADDIX, ROBERT G., dir. diet., Kennedy Memorial Hospitals-University Medical Center, Cherry Hill, NJ '80 (FOOD)
HADDON, ROSALINDA M., RN, asst. adm. and dir. nrsg., Newark Beth Israel Medical Center, Newark, NJ '80 (NURS)
HADFORD, CAROL ANDERSON, dir. vol. serv., Childrens Hospital of Los Angeles, Los Angeles, CA '84 (VOL)
HADLEY, MAJ. RALPH R., MSC USA, adm. res., General Leonard Wood Army Hospital, Fort Leonard Wood, MO '84
HADY, JAMES A. JR., mgr. matl., Scripps Memorial Hospital-Encinitas, Encinitas, CA '81 (PUR)
HAEDO, JORGE A., pres., Shifa Services, Inc., Hackensack, NJ '87
HAEFFNER, SARAH I., dir. vol., Ballard Community Hospital, Seattle, WA '75 (VOL)
HAELEN, DOROTHY B., pat. rep., Highland Hospital of Rochester, Rochester, NY '87 (PAT)
HAEMER, DOROTHY L., RN, asst. adm. nrsg. serv., Our Lady of Compassion Center, Anchorage, AK '85 (NURS)

HAEUSER, JAMIE L., dir. mktg. commun., East Jefferson General Hospital, Metairie, LA '84 (PR)
HAFER, TAMAREE, RN, adm. dir. emer. serv., Kettering Medical Center, Kettering, OH '87 (AMB)
HAFEY, JOSEPH M., exec. dir., Western Consortium for Health Professions, Inc., San Francisco, CA '82 (PLNG)
HAFF, EDWIN W., dir. plant oper., Kaiser Foundation Hospital, Los Angeles, CA '83 (ENG)
HAFFA, DEAN A., dir. environ. serv., Russell City Hospital, Russell, KS '81 (ENG)
HAFFENREFFER, CAROL P., asst. dir. mktg., Newton-Wellesley Hospital, Newton, MA '85 (PLNG)
HAFFERTY, VERONICA N., RN, dir. nrsg. and spec. serv., Memorial Hospital at Gulfport, Gulfport, MS '83 (NURS)
HAFFNER, WILLIAM J., mgr. cent. proc. and distrib., Westlake Community Hospital, Melrose Park, IL '81 (CS)
HAFFY, THOMAS III, dir. biomedical eng., Hackensack Medical Center, Hackensack, NJ '77 (ENG)
HAFNER, FRED W., dir. soc. serv., St. Mary Desert Valley Hospital, Apple Valley, CA '86 (SOC)
HAFNER, ROBERT R. III, atty., Birmingham Regional Hospital Council, Birmingham, AL '76 (ATTY)
HAGAN, DOROTHY W., dir. diet. internship, Veterans Administration Medical Center, Portland, OR '80 (FOOD)
HAGAN, COL. FAYE T., MSC USAF, chm. nrsg., U. S. Air Force Medical Center Keesler, Biloxi, MS '78 (NURS)
HAGAN, PATRICIA K., vice-pres. adm., Doctors Hospital of San Diego, San Diego, CA '70
HAGAN, PATRICK J., vice-pres. med. serv., Children's Hospital Medical Center of Akron, Akron, OH '81
HAGAN, ROBERT J., dir. mgt. syst., Hamad General Hospital, Doha Qatar, Arabia '83 (MGMT)
HAGBERG, ANNA G., dir. matl. mgt., Thorek Hospital and Medical Center, Chicago, IL '70 (PUR)
HAGELE, GLENN F. JR., dir., Creative Marketing Design, Sacramento, CA '86 (PR) (PLNG)
HAGELIOS, ANNA MARIA, mgt. eng., SunHealth Corporation, Charlotte, NC '86 (MGMT)
HAGEN, ANGELA, dir. soc. serv., Gwinnett Medical Center, Lawrenceville, GA '85 (SOC)
HAGEN, DONALD L., dir. matl. mgt., Sisters of St. Mary-Third Order of St. Francis, St. Louis, MO '75 (PUR)
HAGEN, JOYCE A., mgr. food serv., Midland Hospital Center, Midland, MI '79 (FOOD)
HAGEN, LINDA LORRAINE, dir. plng. syst., Groote Schuur Hospital, Cape, South Africa '85
HAGEN, SUE M., dir. pat. rel., Richland Memorial Hospital, Columbia, SC '82 (PAT)
HAGENLOCHER, JANICE A., coor. comm. rel., Swedish-American Hospital, Rockford, IL '84 (PR)
HAGENSTAD, ROBERTA R., coor. educ., Santa Rosa Memorial Hospital, Santa Rosa, CA '87 (EDUC)
HAGER, ALLEN, dir. mktg., United Hospital Center, Clarksburg, WV '86 (PR)
HAGER, KENNETH C., asst. adm., Saint Francis Hospital, Tulsa, OK '85 (PLNG)
HAGER, RITA R., dir. cent. serv., Presbyterian Hospital, Dallas, TX '85 (CS)
HAGER, ROBERT E., dir. mgt. syst., Fairfax Hospital Association, Springfield, VA '78 (MGMT)
HAGERSTROM, THOMAS A., supv. cent. serv., Franklin Memorial Hospital, Farmington, ME '80 (CS)
HAGERTY, AGNES D., atty., Mercy Health Services, Farmington Hills, MI '86 (ATTY)
HAGERTY, BONNIE M. K., student, University of Michigan, Ann Arbor, MI '84 (EDUC)
HAGERTY, DOREEN COOK, dir. mgt. eng., University of Chicago Hospitals, Chicago, IL '79 (MGMT)
HAGERTY, GERALD F., dir. pub. affairs, Hamot Medical Center, Erie, PA '79 (PR)
HAGERTY, GRETCHEN VEDDER, dir. food serv., Valley Baptist Medical Center, Harlingen, TX '77 (FOOD)
HAGERTY, ROBERT G., vice-pres. constr. and gen. serv., Valley Baptist Medical Center, Harlingen, TX '86 (ENG)
HAGES, ROBERTA M., dir. soc. serv., Aliquippa Hospital, Aliquippa, PA '79 (SOC)
HAGG, SHEILA, asst. vice-pres., Memorial Hospital, Belleville, IL '83 (RISK)
HAGGAR, SUSAN E., nrsg. coor. human res., North Memorial Medical Center, Robbinsdale, MN '84 (PERS)
HAGGARD, ALBERT L., dir. risk mgt., Scott and White Clinic, Temple, TX '86 (RISK)
HAGGARD, LYLA L., vice-pres. corp. commun., Bethesda Hospitals, Cincinnati, OH '82 (PR)
HAGGARTY, J. AUDREY, coor. qual. assur., Good Shepherd Hospital, Barrington, IL '81 (RISK)
HAGGERTY, LOIS J., dir. plng. and market res., St. Francis Memorial Hospital, San Francisco, CA '85 (PLNG)
HAGGERTY, PATRICK E., pres., Allied Medical Services, Inc., Metairie, LA '82
HAGGLUND, ROBERT A., pres., Military Imaging, Northbrook, IL '86
HAGIE, NANCY D., RN, asst. adm. nrsg. serv., Johnson City Medical Center Hospital, Johnson City, TN '76 (NURS)
HAGIST, DARCY L., student, University of Oklahoma, Norman, OK '85 (MGMT)
HAGLE, MARY E., doctoral student, University of Illinois-Chicago, Chicago, IL '84
HAGLUND, CLAUDIA L., health policy analyst, Sisters of Providence, Seattle, WA '84 (PLNG)
HAGMAN, LYNDA W., supv. educ. serv., Richmond Memorial Hospital, Richmond, VA '85 (EDUC)
HAGSTRAND, CHARLES P., dir. info. serv., St. Peter's Hospital, Albany, NY '81 (MGMT)
HAGUE, JAMES E., San Diego, CA '75 (LIFE)
HAGUE, JEAN G., head pat. rep., Allegheny General Hospital, Pittsburgh, PA '79 (PAT)
HAGWOOD, L. CARL, atty., Delta Medical Center, Greenville, MS '76 (ATTY)
HAHN, ALICE, dir. hskpg., Mary McClellan Hospital, Cambridge, NY '86 (ENVIRON)
HAHN, BETTY L., dir. vol., Mesa Lutheran Hospital, Mesa, AZ '73 (VOL)
HAHN, DELLA L., dir. aux. vol., Defiance Hospital, Defiance, OH '86 (VOL)
HAHN, FRED J., supv. mech. eng., Yandell and Hiller, Inc., Fort Worth, TX '85 (ENG)
HAHN, HOWARD FREDRICK, atty., Omaha, NE '80 (ATTY)
HAHN, JACK A. L., (ret.), Indianapolis, IN '48 (LIFE)
HAHN, JAMES H., mgt. eng., Harrisburg Hospital, Harrisburg, PA '85 (MGMT)
HAHN, KENNETH K., consult., Torrance, CA '66 (MGMT)
HAHN, LIDA, exec. adm., Everett A. Gladman Memorial Hospital, Oakland, CA '67
HAHN, SR. NORA, vice-pres. prof. affairs, Ancilla Systems, Inc., Elk Grove Village, IL '83
HAHN, PHIL H., dir. pur., Mercy Hospital Medical Center, Des Moines, IA '86 (PUR)
HAHN, WILLIAM E., atty., St. Joseph's Hospital, Tampa, FL '78 (ATTY)
HAI, DR. SAMANDAR M., assoc. prof. fin., University of Wisconsin, La Crosse, WI '76
HAIBACH, MARTIN J., dir., University of Chicago, Chicago, IL '87 (AMB)
HAIDUK, STANLEY, Dover, DE '84 (FOOD)
HAIGLER, STEVEN V. III, dir. emp. rel., Baptist Medical Center, Jacksonville, FL '75 (PERS)
HAIKALIS, SUSAN W., asst. dir. soc. work, Mount Zion Hospital and Medical Center, San Francisco, CA '71 (SOC)
HAILE, GAIL A., mgr., Archbishop Bergan Mercy Hospital, Omaha, NE '84 (EDUC)
HAIMANN, CAROLYN A., atty., Jewish Hospital of St. Louis, St. Louis, MO '78 (ATTY)
HAINES, ARTHUR C., sr. assoc., Executive Consulting Group, Bellevue, WA '81 (PLNG)
HAINES, BEVERLY J., RN, dir. nrsg., Western Pennsylvania Hospital, Pittsburgh, PA '87 (NURS)
HAINES, BONNIE K., vice-pres. governmental and pub. rel., Idaho Hospital Association, Boise, ID '76 (PR)
HAINES, JOHN F., exec. vice-pres., Unity Medical Center, Fridley, MN '57 (LIFE)
HAINES, NANCY F., dir. vol. serv., Memorial Hospital, Manhattan, KS '60 (VOL)
HAINES, PATRICK H., sr. vice-pres., Florida Hospital Association, Orlando, FL '73 (PLNG)
HAINES, RAYMOND E., vice-pres. safety serv., Crump Special Services, Inc., Altamonte Springs, FL '80 (RISK)
HAINES, RICHARD C. JR., pres., Medical Design International, Atlanta, GA '82
HAINES, ROGER A., dir. bldg. and grds., Community Memorial Hospital and Convalescent and Rehabilitation Unit, Winona, MN '83 (ENG)
HAINES, RONALD L., dir. mktg., Grand Valley Health Plan, Grand Rapids, MI '85 (PLNG)
HAINES, WILLIAM G., dir. pers., Diagnostic Center Hospital, Houston, TX '83 (PERS)
HAINO, A. ADELE, ins. mgr., Santa Rosa Medical Center, San Antonio, TX '80 (RISK)
HAIR, REBECCA E., dir. soc. serv., Northeast Georgia Medical Center, Gainesville, GA '73 (SOC)
HAIR, ROBERT L., pres., Hospital Homecare, Santa Ana, CA '83
HAIRE, ELMER, dir. facil. and eng., New Center Hospital, Detroit, MI '86 (ENG)
HAIRE, WILLIAM J., Capitol Hill Hospital, Washington, DC '68
HAIRR, SUE, supv. cent. serv., Sampson County Memorial Hospital, Clinton, NC '83 (CS)
HAIRSTON, MARTHA C., dir. vol., Spring Shadows Glen, Houston, TX '83 (VOL)
HAISLER, DORIS H., dir. vol. serv., Centinela Hospital Medical Center, Inglewood, CA '86 (VOL)
HAITHCOCK, KIM T., dir. educ., Palisades General Hospital, North Bergen, NJ '85 (EDUC)
HAJEK, HOLLY L., serv. mgr., University Hospitals of Cleveland, Cleveland, OH '86 (MGMT)
HAJER, ROB, dir. soc. serv., Charles River Hospital, Wellesley, MA '82 (SOC)
HAJNOSZ, PATRICIA, dir. risk mgt., Our Lady of Mercy Medical Center, Bronx, NY '86 (RISK)
HAJNY, JOAN MARIE, RN, assoc. dir. risk mgt., Cedars-Sinai Medical Center, Los Angeles, CA '82 (RISK)
HAKES, PATRICIA P., consult., Yoakum Catholic Hospital, Yoakum, TX '72 (SOC)
HAKIM, PATRICIA P., coor. commun. health educ., Southern Baptist Hospital, New Orleans, LA '86 (EDUC)
HAKUSA, NORMA S., dir. soc. serv., New York Hospital, Westchester Division, White Plains, NY '79 (SOC)
HALBARDIER, RENE E., equip. spec., Falick-Klein Partnership, Inc., Houston, TX '83 (ENG)
HALBERSTADT, DONALD E., consult., Touche Ross and Company, Philadelphia, PA '85 (PLNG)
HALBERSTADT, SR. RUTH, adm. asst., Daughters of Charity, Eastern Cooperative Services, Washington, DC '47 (LIFE)
HALBERT, BETTYE L., RN, dir. nrsg. serv., Oktibbeha County Hospital, Starkville, MS '86 (NURS)
HALBERT, JAMES W., dir. gen. serv., Keswick-Home for Incurables, Baltimore, MD '84
HALBERT, NANCY E., RN, dir. nrsg., Shriners Hospital for Crippled Children, Honolulu, HI '83 (NURS)
HALBERT, VIRGIL ALLEN, Baltimore, MD '51 (LIFE)
HALD, DAVID L., mgt. eng., University Hospital-University of Nebraska, Omaha, NE '87 (MGMT)
HALE, BARBARA A., RN, asst. adm. nrsg. serv., Riverview Hospital, Noblesville, IN '86 (NURS)
HALE, DONNA DITTMAN, student, Medical College of Virginia, Virginia Commonwealth University, Department of Health Administration, Richmond, VA '82
HALE, EARL F. JR., atty., St. Paul Medical Center, Dallas, TX '77 (ATTY)
HALE, FREDERICK A., vice-pres. fin., Medical Center Hospital of Vermont, Burlington, VT '61
HALE, HARRY H., asst. dir. eng., Memorial Hospital of Dodge County, Fremont, NE '81 (ENG)
HALE, JEFFREY J., mgr., Ernst and Whinney, Baltimore, MD '86 (MGMT)
HALE, KAY R., RN, dir. educ. serv., Kansas Hospital Association, Topeka, KS '81 (EDUC)(NURS)
HALE, NOREEN, academic coor., National College of Education, McLean, VA '81 (PR)
HALE, PATRICIA E., dir. mktg., Lykes Memorial Hospital, Brooksville, FL '86 (PLNG)
HALE, POLLY, dir. pers., Samaritan Hospital, Moses Lake, WA '86 (PERS)
HALE, VICKI J., RN, asst. adm., Grady Memorial Hospital, Delaware, OH '83 (NURS)
HALECHKO, ANNA D., MD, dir. emer. serv., South Hills Health System, Pittsburgh, PA '86 (AMB)
HALES, DOROTHY L., coor. educ., Royal Inland Hospital, Kamloops, B.C., Canada '80
HALES, THOMAS M., assoc. exec. dir. fin., Children's Hospital of Alabama, Birmingham, AL '84
HALEY-SMITH, CHERYL A., dir. vol. serv., Fresno Community Hospital and Medical Center, Fresno, CA '86 (VOL)
HALEY, BARBARA L., acct. exec., Miami Valley Hospital, Dayton, OH '86 (PR)
HALEY, DOROTHY M., dir. human res., St. Marys Hospital of Rochester, Rochester, MN '83 (PERS)
HALEY, DOROTHY, asst. dir. pers., Parkridge Medical Center, Chattanooga, TN '79 (PERS)
HALEY, GLADYS ANNE, RN, asst. adm. nrsg., AMI Presbyterian-St. Luke's Medical Center, Denver, CO '71 (NURS)
HALEY, PAULETTE JO, RN, nrsg. consult., Our Lady of Lourdes Hospital, Norfolk, NE '78 (EDUC)
HALEY, ROBERT W., MD, University of Texas Health Scienc Center, Department of Internal Medicine, Dallas, TX '85
HALEY, SHERRY, RN, actg. dir. nrsg., Lake Charles Memorial Hospital, Lake Charles, LA '86 (NURS)
HALEY, VINCENT P., atty., Mercy Catholic Medical Center, Darby, PA '74 (ATTY)
HALFAR, ALLAN C., asst. dir. corp. plng., Sisters of St. Mary, St. Louis, MO '85 (PLNG)
HALFERTY, ELAINE M., head soc. serv., Our Lady of Lourdes Hospital, Norfolk, NE '82 (SOC)
HALFON, PETER B., mng. dir., The Eggers Group, New York, NY '84 (PLNG)
HALFORD, CATHY A., RN, dir. nrsg., Medical Personnel Pool, Tulsa, OK '86 (PAT)
HALFORD, NANCY K., RN, dir. nrs. and coor. nrsg., North Iowa Medical Center, Mason City, IA '85 (NURS)
HALFORD, ROBERT LEE, dir. pers., St. Francis Hospital, Memphis, TN '77 (PERS)
HALKO, MAVIS B., RN, asst. adm. nrsg., East Alabama Medical Center, Opelika, AL '81 (NURS)
HALL, ANNA G., mgr. pub. rel., Massillon Community Hospital, Massillon, OH '86 (PR)
HALL, ARLIE, supv. maint., Scott County Memorial Hospital, Scottsburg, IN '81 (ENG)
HALL, AUGUST W., mgr. pers., Salem Hospital, Salem, OR '75 (PERS)
HALL, AUSTIN S., vice-pres. and gen. mgr., Mrt Systems Corporation, Inc., Los Angeles, CA '63
HALL, BARBARA A., dir. vol., St. Clare Hospital of Monroe, Monroe, WI '80 (VOL)
HALL, BERTHA M., dir. amb. care and gen. support serv., Harold D. Chope Community Hospital, San Mateo, CA '87 (AMB)
HALL, BETTY J., dir. pat. rel., Sid Peterson Memorial Hospital, Kerrville, TX '80 (PR)
HALL, CAROL J., chief diet. serv., Veterans Administration Hospital, Hines, IL '68 (FOOD)
HALL, CHARLES P. JR., PhD, prof., Temple University School of Business Administration, Philadelphia, PA '70
HALL, CLAI MOREHEAD, dir. vol. serv., Arkansas Children's Hospital, Little Rock, AR '83 (VOL)
HALL, DAVID CHARLES, dir. guest rel., Memorial Hospital of Laramie County, Cheyenne, WY '84 (PR)
HALL, DAVID M., dir. hskpg. and food serv., Hahnemann Hospital, Boston, MA '86 (ENVIRON)
HALL, DAVID, dir., Care Programs, Baltimore, MD '84
HALL, DONNA JEAN, dir. soc. serv., Desert Springs Hospital, Las Vegas, NV '74 (SOC)
HALL, DOUGLAS, dir. med. soc. work, Borgess Medical Center, Kalamazoo, MI '86 (SOC)
HALL, ELIZABETH, RN, med. surg. educ., Jefferson Davis Memorial Hospital, Natchez, MS '82 (EDUC)
HALL, COL. ELLIS F. JR., (ret.), Greenville, NC '71
HALL, ERMAN JR., dir. bldg. and grds., Winona Memorial Hospital, Indianapolis, IN '77 (ENG)
HALL, EUGENE C., atty., St. Mary's Hospital, Kansas City, MO '80 (ATTY)
HALL, F. RILEY, atty., Marion General Hospital, Marion, OH '75 (ATTY)
HALL, F. ROGER, adm. outpatient res., Tucson Medical Center, Tucson, AZ '86 (AMB)
HALL, FRANK S., sr. plng. consult., Hbe Corporation, St. Louis, MO '74
HALL, FRED C., consult. risk mgt., Lockton Insurance Agency, Prairie Village, KS '85 (RISK)
HALL, FRED C., dir. pers. serv., Resurrection Hospital, Chicago, IL '71 (PERS)
HALL, GARY E., dir. emp. serv., Peninsula Hospital and Medical Center, Burlingame, CA '71 (EDUC)(PERS)
HALL, GARY M., vice-pres., Wyoming Medical Center, Casper, WY '76
HALL, HILDRED A., pur. agt., Cheshire Medical Center, Keene, NH '78 (PUR)
HALL, JAMES D., adm. consult., University Hospital, Lexington, KY '85 (MGMT)
HALL, JAMES I., dir. food serv., Medical Center Hospital, Odessa, TX '81 (FOOD)
HALL, JAMES L. JR., atty., Baptist Medical Center of Oklahoma, Oklahoma City, OK '81 (ATTY)
HALL, JAMES L., dir. human res., Mid-Columbia Medical Center, The Dalles, OR '80 (PERS)
HALL, JESSE B. JR., dir. eng., Mount Vernon Hospital, Alexandria, VA '80 (ENG)

HALL, JOEL THOMAS, dir. cent. serv., Baldwin County Hospital, Milledgeville, GA '87 (CS)
HALL, JOHN THOMAS JR., RN, asst. adm. nrsg., St. Paul Medical Center, Dallas, TX '80 (NURS)
HALL, JOHN W. JR., dir. pat. sup., proc. and distrib., University of Texas M. D. Anderson Hospital and Tumor Institute at Houston, Houston, TX '82 (CS)
HALL, JOYCE G., mgr. matl., Share Development Corporation, Bloomington, MN '82 (PUR)
HALL, JUDITH ANN, dir. pat. rel., Community Memorial Hospital, Toms River, NJ '85 (PAT)
HALL, KAREN O., dir. food serv., Charter Canyon Hospital, Orem, UT '86 (FOOD)
HALL, KATHY M., Samuel Merritt Hospital, Oakland, CA '83 (PR)
HALL, LARRY J., dir. pub. rel., Bethesda Hospital, Zanesville, OH '81 (PR)
HALL, LOIS M., RN, dir. nrsg., Burbank Hospital, Fitchburg, MA '71 (NURS)
HALL, LUCY N., chief diet. serv., Veterans Administration Medical Center, Minneapolis, MN '78 (FOOD)
HALL, MARK A., atty., College of Law, Arizona State University, Tempe, AZ '83 (ATTY)
HALL, MARSHA A., dir. pub. rel., Delta County Memorial Hospital, Delta, CO '84 (PLNG)
HALL, SR. MARY ST. JOHN, chief exec. off., Mercy San Juan Hospital, Carmichael, CA '68
HALL, MICHAEL A., clin. cost analyst, South Shore Hospital, South Weymouth, MA '86 (MGMT)
HALL, NANCY A., loss control consult., Hospital Underwriters Mutual Insurance Company, Albany, NY '85 (RISK)
HALL, NANCY, asst. adm. amb. care, Illinois Masonic Medical Center, Chicago, IL '87 (AMB)
HALL, PATRICK R., dir. support serv., Servicemaster Industries, Inc., Chesterfielde, MO '86 (ENG)
HALL, PAULA J., adm. diet. and actg. mgr., South Suburban Hospital, Hazel Crest, IL '83 (FOOD)
HALL, PEGGY J., pat. rep. and coor., New Hanover Memorial Hospital, Wilmington, NC '82 (PAT)
HALL, RALPH E., exec. vice-pres., Morningside House Nursing Home Company, Inc., Bronx, NY '83
HALL, RALPH R. JR., vice-pres., Pitt County Memorial Hospital, Greenville, NC '78 (ENG)
HALL, RANDY, spec. proc. stores, Holy Cross Hospital, Salt Lake City, UT '80 (CS)
HALL, REED E., atty., Marshfield Clinic, Marshfield, WI '76 (ATTY)
HALL, RICHARD W., chief eng., Melrose-Wakefield Hospital, Melrose, MA '81 (ENG)
HALL, ROBERT M., MD, Raleigh, NC '73
HALL, RUTH A., RN, asst. vice-pres., Mercy Memorial Medical Center, St. Joseph, MI '87 (AMB)
HALL, SHARON A., dir. cont. educ., Charleston Area Medical Center, Charleston, WV '86 (EDUC)
HALL, STARLING E., dir. procurement serv., Richland Memorial Hospital, Columbia, SC '77 (PUR)
HALL, STEPHEN R., vice-pres. info. syst., MedAmerica Health Systems, Dayton, OH '85
HALL, TERRI G., dir. vol. serv., St. Joseph Regional Medical Center -Oklahoma, Ponca City, OK '86 (VOL)
HALL, UDELLA EDNA, student, University of Nevada, Las Vegas, NV '86 (MGMT)
HALL, WALTER A. III, dir. environ. serv., Phoebe Putney Memorial Hospital, Albany, GA '86 (ENVIRON)
HALL, WALTER L., supv. chemistry sect., U. S. Public Health Service Indian Hospital, Fort Defiance, AZ '84
HALL, WALTER R. JR., adm., Mount Sinai Medical Center, New York, NY '79 (CS)
HALL, WENDY A., dir. vol. serv., Grady Memorial Hospital, Delaware, OH '85 (VOL)
HALL, WILLIAM S., atty., Indiana Hospital Association, Indianapolis, IN '68 (ATTY)
HALL, COL. WILLIAM, bd. mem., Harborview Medical Center, Seattle, WA '71
HALL, WILMA RUSH, chief diet. serv., Veterans Administration Medical Center, Saginaw, MI '72 (FOOD)
HALLAN, T. JAMES JR., dir. pub. rel., Butler Hospital, Providence, RI '83 (PR)
HALLAS, JUDY, Delmore Systems, Rochester, MI '82 (EDUC)
HALLEEN, NATALIE, dir. risk mgt., Multi-Risk Management, Chicago, IL '87 (RISK)
HALLEN, CAROL J., dir. comm. rel., Highline Community Hospital, Seattle, WA '86 (PR)
HALLENBECK, MICHAEL E., dir. soc. work, AMI Anclote Manor Psychiatric Hospital, Tarpon Springs, FL '84 (SOC)
HALLENBECK, ROBERT M., atty., Nixon, Hargrave, Devens and Doyle, Rochester, NY '87 (ENG)
HALLER, LINDA S., student, University of Minnesota, Duluth, MN '87 (PLNG)
HALLERON, JOHN J. III, atty., Good Samaritan Hospital, West Islip, NY '77 (ATTY)
HALLEY, ANN, vice-pres. risk mgt., Methodist Hospital, Jacksonville, FL '86 (RISK)
HALLEY, ELEANOR, mgr. emp., Mount Sinai Medical Center, New York, NY '83 (PERS)
HALLEY, FRANKLIN D., dir. cont. educ., Providence Hospital, Sandusky, OH '84 (EDUC)
HALLEY, JAMESETTA A., RN, chief nrs., Veterans Administration Medical Center, East Orange, NJ '85 (NURS)
HALLGREN, HUGH R., pres., St. Vincent Hospital, Santa Fe, NM '77
HALLIGAN, MARY T., RN, dir. clin. nrsg., St. Joseph Hospital, Flint, MI '85 (NURS)
HALLINAN, EDWARD J., intern, Presbyterian-University Hospital, Pittsburgh, PA '86 (PERS)
HALLINAN, RICHARD J., dir. trng. and dev., St. Barnabas Medical Center, Livingston, NJ '85 (EDUC)
HALLMAN, NANCY, pat. rep., Crozer-Chester Medical Center, Chester, PA '75 (PAT)
HALLOCK, DAVID R., dir. pers., Nashville Metropolitan Bordeaux Hospital, Nashville, TN '85 (PERS)
HALLOCK, MICHAEL D., dir. matl. mgt., Kewanee Public Hospital, Kewanee, IL '86 (PUR)
HALLORAN, EDWARD J., RN PhD, sr. vice-pres. and dir. nrsg., University Hospitals of Cleveland, Cleveland, OH '77 (NURS)
HALLORAN, GLORIA J., adm. mgr., Hospital of the Albert Einstein College of Medicine, Bronx, NY '81
HALLSTROM, JANET L., asst. adm., Abbott-Northwestern Hospital, Minneapolis, MN '82
HALPER, H. ROBERT, atty., Crozer-Chester Medical Center, Chester, PA '82 (ATTY)
HALPERN, MINDY, dir. soc. work serv., Humana Hospital -Westminster, Westminster, CA '86 (SOC)
HALPRYN, LOUIS J., assoc. dir. hosp. and med. care, Connecticut State Department of Health, Hartford, CT '64
HALSE, DAVID L., vice-pres. matl. mgt., Albany Medical Center Hospital, Albany, NY '80 (PUR)
HALSEY, NANCY A., dir. comm. rel., Reid Memorial Hospital, Richmond, IN '81 (PR)
HALSTEAD, EDWARD GREY, sr. partner, Halstead Consulting Group, San Antonio, TX '48 (LIFE)
HALSTEAD, MICHAEL J., chief fin. off., Ellis Hospital, Schenectady, NY '85
HALSTED, ARLENE CHECH, RN, asst. adm. nrsg., HCA Northwest Regional Hospital, Margate, FL '83 (NURS)
HALSTED, JOHN S., atty., Brandywine Hospital, Caln Township, PA '79 (ATTY)
HALSTROM-CREST, SALLY A., mgr. cent. serv., Holy Family Medical Center, Manitowoc, WI '81 (CS)
HALTER, DAVID W., dir. pers., Saint Alphonsus Regional Medical Center, Boise, ID '85 (PERS)
HALTERMAN, MICHAEL W., exec. dir. home health care serv., Christian Hospitals Northeast-Northwest, St. Louis, MO '87 (AMB)
HALTOM, JEAN V., RN, assoc. dir. nrsg., Memorial Hospital, Belleville, IL '85 (NURS)
HALVERSON, JAN DONALD, atty., University of Minnesota Hospital and Clinic, Minneapolis, MN '83 (ATTY)
HALVERSON, KARL E., supv. cent. plant, Washoe Medical Center, Reno, NV '86 (ENG)
HALVERSON, PAUL K., chief exec. off., Central Michigan Community Hospital, Mount Pleasant, MI '82
HALVORSON, BETTY C., RN, adm. reg. nrsg., Group Health Cooperative of Puget Sound, Tacoma, WA '85 (NURS)
HALVORSON, TOM R., sr. mgr., Ernst and Whinney, Kansas City, MO '87 (MGMT)
HALWIG, JEAN L., dir. vol. serv. and actg. pat. rep., Newport Hospital, Newport, RI '76 (VOL)(PAT)
HAM, ANN LILLEY, dir. comm. rel., St. Mary's Regional Health Center, Roswell, NM '83 (PR)
HAM, JANE E., dir. vol. serv., Central Maine Medical Center, Lewiston, ME '83 (VOL)(PAT)
HAMADA, ANNA C., asst. vice-pres., American Medical International, Beverly Hills, CA '78 (FOOD)
HAMAMOTO, DENNIS K., mgr. elec. syst., San Antonio Community Hospital, Upland, CA '86 (ENG)
HAMANN, JANEAN K., dir. diet., Poudre Valley Hospital, Fort Collins, CO '81 (FOOD)
HAMANN, KURT P., dir. bldg. and grds., Fairview Southdale Hospital, Minneapolis, MN '79 (ENG)
HAMANN, LAWRENCE R. JR., chief eng., H. B. Magruder Memorial Hospital, Port Clinton, OH '81 (ENG)
HAMANN, MARILYN KAY, supv. cent. proc., Lutheran Hospital, Moline, IL '78 (CS)
HAMANN, RAENETTE L., mgr. trayline, Saint Joseph Hospital, Denver, CO '81 (FOOD)
HAMBLIN, LEONARD W., (ret.), Princeton, IL '43 (LIFE)
HAMBLING, WILLIAM T., mgr. maint., St. Joseph's Medical Center, South Bend, IN '79 (ENG)
HAMBRICK, JACK, dir. pub. rel., Baptist Medical Center, Columbia, SC '80 (PR)
HAMBURG, ALVIN Z., adm., Princeton University McCosh Health Center, Princeton, NJ '53 (LIFE)
HAMBURG, DAVID A., MD, dir., Division of Health Policy Research and Education, Harvard University, Cambridge, MA '77 (HON)
HAMED, ISSAM A., adm. and consult., Issam Hamed Musa Health Consultation and Management, Inc., Amman, Jordan '84 (MGMT)
HAMEL, HELENE, pat. rep., Hotel-Dieu D'Arthabaska, Arthabaska, Que., Canada '78 (PAT)
HAMEL, PAT, dir. vol. serv., Wyandotte General Hospital, Wyandotte, MI '78 (VOL)
HAMEL, PIERRETTE, dir. diet., Jewish General Hospital, Montreal, Que., Canada '70 (FOOD)
HAMEL, SHEILA E., RN, dir. nrsg., Georgetown University Medical Center, Washington, DC '84 (NURS)
HAMER, FAISAL YACOUB AL, dean, College of Health Sciences, Manama, Saudi Arabia '86 (EDUC)
HAMER, THOMAS P., dir. pub. rel. and mktg., Apple River Hospital, Amery, WI '86 (PR)
HAMES, WINTERS B. JR., pres., University of Southern California Associates, Inc., Center Harbor, NH '79 (PLNG)
HAMILL, DAVE H., chief exec. off., Memorial Hospital of Southern Oklahoma, Ardmore, OK '85
HAMILL, PATRICIA, dir. educ., Saint Mary Hospital, Langhorne, PA '79 (EDUC)
HAMILT, MILTON W., prof. health adm., Temple University, School of Business Administration, Philadelphia, PA '52 (LIFE)
HAMILTON, ANNE C., dir. soc. serv., West Orange Memorial Hospital, Winter Garden, FL '85 (SOC)
HAMILTON, BILL L., constr. exec., Hackensack Medical Center, Hackensack, NJ '56 (LIFE)
HAMILTON, D. KIRK, partner, Watkins, Carter and Hamilton, Bellaire, TX '80
HAMILTON, DEBORAH A., dir. pers., Devereux Foundation-California, Santa Barbara, CA '86 (PERS)
HAMILTON, ELIZABETH A., RN, asst. adm. pat. serv., Kennestone Hospital, Marietta, GA '82 (NURS)
HAMILTON, ESTHER M., RN, vice-pres. pat. serv., Medical Center Hospital, Punta Gorda, FL '68 (NURS)
HAMILTON, GABRILLE M., RN, dir. nrsg., Lonesome Pine Hospital, Big Stone Gap, VA '80 (NURS)
HAMILTON, JAMES C., dir. plant oper., Overlake Hospital Medical Center, Bellevue, WA '82 (ENG)
HAMILTON, JAMES C., PhD, adm. medicine prog., St. Luke's Regional Medical Center, Sioux City, IA '77
HAMILTON, JOHN B., asst. adm., Antelope Valley Hospital Medical Center, Lancaster, CA '81 (PLNG)
HAMILTON, JOHN C., dir. matl. mgt., Hampton General Hospital, Hampton, VA '83 (PUR)
HAMILTON, JOSEPH E., atty., Minnesota Hospital Association, Minneapolis, MN '69 (ATTY)
HAMILTON, KATHRYN, dir. plng. and dev., Providence Hospital, Everett, WA '81 (PLNG)
HAMILTON, LOIS J., RN, asst. exec. dir. nrsg. serv., Fayette Memorial Hospital, Connersville, IN '82 (NURS)
HAMILTON, MARK ALLEN, asst. dir., Indiana University Hospitals, Indianapolis, IN '79 (RISK)
HAMILTON, MARY LINN, RN, exec. dir., Thomas Memorial Hospital, South Charleston, WV '87 (AMB)
HAMILTON, MARY, asst. dir. sup., proc. and distrib., Desert Hospital, Palm Springs, CA '86 (CS)
HAMILTON, MELINDA S., dir. comm. rel., Arab Hospital, Arab, AL '83 (PR)
HAMILTON, MELVINA P., asst. adm., Blue Ridge Hospital, Charlottesville, VA '83 (RISK)
HAMILTON, NANCY E., dir. diet., High Plains Baptist Hospital, Amarillo, TX '83 (FOOD)
HAMILTON, PAT R., atty., Plateau Medical Center, Oak Hill, WV '81 (ATTY)
HAMILTON, RAE E., mgr. risk, HCA Sun Towers Hospital, El Paso, TX '82 (RISK)
HAMILTON, REED CHARLES, atty., Blank, Rome, Comisky and McCauley, Philadelphia, PA '82 (ATTY)
HAMILTON, RICHARD A., dir., Michigan Hospital Association, Lansing, MI '78 (MGMT)
HAMILTON, ROBERT M., chief eng., HCA Midway Park Medical Center, Lancaster, TX '79 (ENG)
HAMILTON, ROGER N., coor. plng., Deaconess Hospital, Milwaukee, WI '63
HAMILTON, RUTH A., dir. vol. serv., Memorial Medical Center of West Michigan, Ludington, MI '84 (VOL)
HAMILTON, SAMUEL S., pres. oper., New Medi Company Associates, Middlebury, CT '75
HAMILTON, T. STEWARD, MD, pres. emeritus, Hartford Hospital, Hartford, CT '42 (LIFE)
HAMILTON, TODD C. JR., dir. plng. and mktg., Medical Center of Baton Rouge, Baton Rouge, LA '84 (PLNG)
HAMKE, KURT A., student, University of Massachusetts, Amherst, MA '86 (MGMT)
HAMLEN, DIANE, dir. pat. rel., Atlanticare Medical Center, Lynn, MA '85 (PAT)
HAMLIN, ANGELA L., coor. comm. rel., Houston Healthcare Complex, Warner Robins, GA '83 (PR)
HAMLIN, HELEN R., consult., New York, NY '81 (SOC)
HAMLIN, JEFFREY W., corp. mgr. emp. benefits, Sisters of Charity of the Incarnate Word, Houston, TX '77 (PERS)
HAMLIN, LINDA, dir. pub. rel., Memorial Hospital, Hollywood, FL '81 (PR)
HAMLIN, MARY DAVIS, pat. rep., University of Virginia Hospitals, Charlottesville, VA '87 (PAT)
HAMM, GREGORY L., economic analyst, Applied Decision Analysis, Menlo Park, CA '86 (PLNG)
HAMM, MICHAEL A., buyer, Riverside Hospital, Toledo, OH '86 (PUR)
HAMM, THELMA, adm. dir. pat. care, Mount Airy Psychiatric Center, Denver, CO '85 (PAT)
HAMMACK, ANN L., dir. pub. rel., St. Francis Hospital, Charleston, WV '76 (EDUC)(PR)
HAMMAN, DAWN R., pub. affairs and dev. off., University of Illinois College of Medical, Peoria, IL '85 (PR)
HAMME, JOEL M., atty., Holy Cross Hospital, Silver Spring, MD '80 (ATTY)
HAMMEL, ALLEN L., dir. food serv., Alexian Brothers Medical Center, Elk Grove Village, IL '77 (FOOD)
HAMMEL, ERNEST M., PhD, exec. dir., Oakland Health Education Program, Rochester, MI '80 (EDUC)
HAMMER, DOUGLAS J., atty., Intermountain Health Care, Inc., Salt Lake City, UT '79 (ATTY)
HAMMER, JOHN H. II, vice-pres. support serv., Lakeview Medical Center, Danville, IL '78 (PERS)
HAMMER, LYDIA, dir. plng. and mktg., Hahnemann University, Philadelphia, PA '84 (PLNG)
HAMMER, PATTY A., dir. educ. and trng., St. Elizabeth Medical Center, Dayton, OH '83 (EDUC)
HAMMER, STEPHEN J., vice-pres., Meta Software, New York, NY '75
HAMMERAN, KEVIN RICHARD, adm. dir. oper., Geisinger Medical Center, Danville, PA '80
HAMMERGREN, CARL K., dir. plng., University of Colorado Health Sciences Center, Denver, CO '81 (PLNG)
HAMMERS, BILLY EUGENE, dir. plant serv., F. Edward Hebert Hospital, New Orleans, LA '86 (ENG)
HAMMERS, MARYANN, dir. pub. rel., San Gabriel Valley Medical Center, San Gabriel, CA '83 (PR)
HAMMERSBERG, SUZANNE S., dean pub. serv., allied health and nrsg., Moraine Valley Community College, Palos Hills, IL '86 (EDUC)
HAMMERSCHMIDT, BRUCE C., counsel and bd. of dir., Memorial Hospital, South Bend, IN '74 (ATTY)
HAMMES, BETTY, RN, mgr. cent. serv., Mercy Hospital Medical Center, Des Moines, IA '83 (CS)
HAMMETT, CYNDEE L., dir. soc. work, Baptist Medical Center Easley, Easley, SC '78 (SOC)
HAMMETT, WARREN E., student, University of Alabama at Birmingham, School of Community and Allied Health, Birmingham, AL '81
HAMMON, GARY L., San Antonio, TX '64
HAMMOND, ALICE R., dir. comm. rel., Randolph Hospital, Asheboro, NC '82 (PR)
HAMMOND, BRUCE JR., dir. human res., Holy Cross Hospital, Salt Lake City, UT '84 (PERS)

HAMMOND, C. RANDY, exec. dir., Medical Laboratory Associates, Birmingham, AL '76
HAMMOND, CAROL L., supv. oper. room, Madison County Hospital, London, OH '85 (CS)
HAMMOND, JARIS, dir. soc. serv., Hancock Memorial Hospital, Greenfield, IN '84 (SOC)
HAMMOND, RICHARD W., atty., Euclid Clinic Foundation, Euclid, OH '85 (ATTY)
HAMMOND, VIVI, dir. vol. serv., Riverton Hospital, Seattle, WA '78 (VOL)
HAMMONDS, JEROME, serv. mgr., American Medical International, Carrollton, TX '86 (ENG)
HAMNER, CANDACE, dir. qual. assur., Lutheran Hospital of Maryland, Baltimore, MD '82 (RISK)
HAMON, B. IMOGENE, asst. dir. soc. work and rehab., Ohio State University Hospitals, Dodd Hall, Columbus, OH '84 (SOC)
HAMPER, SANDRA LEE, mgr. mktg., Dornier Medical Systems, Inc., Marietta, GA '79
HAMPTON, ANDRE, atty., Eastwood Hospital, Memphis, TN '87 (ATTY)
HAMPTON, DANIEL W., adm. asst., Jane Phillips-Memorial Medical Center, Bartlesville, OK '85 (PLNG)
HAMPTON, DEBRA C., RN, dir. nrsg. critical care, St. Joseph Hospital, Lexington, KY '85 (NURS)
HAMPTON, JACQUELINE R., sr. consult., Ernest and Whinney, Los Angeles, CA '86 (MGMT)
HAMPTON, KAY S., RN, asst. dir. nrsg., Redmond Park Hospital, Rome, GA '83 (NURS)
HAMPTON, LARRY H., pres., Help International, Plano, TX '83
HAMPTON, RITA C., mgr. telecommun., Valley Presbyterian Hospital, Van Nuys, CA '81 (ENG)
HAMRICK, WILLIAM D., consult., San Antonio, TX '53 (LIFE)
HAMRY, DAVID K., exec. dir., Good Samaritan Community Healthcare, Puyallup, WA '66
HANACEK, BETTY, dir. soc. serv., South Seminole Community Hospital, Longwood, FL '85 (SOC)
HANAK, JOAN P., dir. diet. serv., Oak Cliff Medical and Surgical Hospital, Dallas, TX '86 (FOOD)
HANAN, JEFFERY D., dir. pers. serv., Meriter Hospital, Madison, WI '83 (PERS)
HANAWALT, ANN K., RN, Jacksonville, FL '80 (EDUC)
HANCKEL, FRANCES S., dir. plng. and spec. proj., Temple University Hospital, Philadelphia, PA '86 (PLNG)
HANCOCK, CLAIRE C., dir. soc. serv., Copley Hospital, Morrisville, VT '86 (SOC)
HANCOCK, EDWARD HUGH, adm., University of Maryland Medical Systems, Baltimore, MD '74
HANCOCK, J. WAYNE, coor. educ. and trng., Hinsdale Hospital, Hinsdale, IL '85 (EDUC)
HANCOCK, K. N., dir. human res., Fairmount Institute, Philadelphia, PA '86 (PERS)
HANCOCK, LARRY, contr., Jellico Community Hospital, Jellico, TN '86
HANCOCK, ROBERT LYNDON, adm., Chippenham Hospital, Richmond, VA '66
HANCOCK, ROSE MARY, RN, dir. nrsg., Lake Forest Hospital, Lake Forest, IL '79 (NURS)
HANCOCK, CDR SUSAN H., MSC USN, head dev. and educ., Naval Hospital, Bethesda, MD '86 (EDUC)
HANCOCK, WALTON M., prof., University of Michigan, Ann Arbor, MI '78 (MGMT)
HANCOX, SUSAN C., dir. pers., Beverly Hospital, Beverly, MA '78 (PERS)
HANDA, BINA R., adm. res., Staten Island Hospital, Staten Island, NY '86
HANDEL, MAURICE P., dir. corp. plng., Newton-Wellesley Hospital, Newton, MA '82 (PLNG)
HANDERHAN, DONALD A. SR., dir. food serv., Cohoes Memorial Hospital, Cohoes, NY '79 (FOOD)
HANDLER, CAROLYN M., student, Rush University, Chicago, IL '84
HANDY, STEVEN P., asst. contr., Conemaugh Valley Memorial Hospital, Johnstown, PA '86
HANE, SUE S., mktg. analyst, Wake Medical Center, Raleigh, NC '86 (PLNG)
HANEBERG, ALFRED CRAIG, adm. clin. serv., Deaconess Hospital of Cleveland, Cleveland, OH '81
HANEKE, WILLIAM G., exec. dir., Aetna Choice Healthcare Plan, Richmond, VA '74
HANEMANN, CARL C., atty., Pendleton Memorial Methodist Hospital, New Orleans, LA '86 (ATTY)
HANEN, BARBARA L., coor. plng. and mktg., Memorial Hospital of Dodge County, Fremont, NE '83 (PR) (PLNG)
HANES, JUDITH D., coor. staff dev., Meridian Park Hospital, Tualatin, OR '86 (EDUC)
HANEY, CHARLES A. III, Natick, MA '53 (LIFE)
HANEY, MICHAEL L., vice-pres., Cps Business Systems, Inc., Wichita Falls, TX '85 (MGMT)
HANEY, ROBERT W., dir. soc. work serv., Baptist Medical Center, Columbia, SC '83 (SOC)
HANEY, RODNEY, asst. dir. pur., Charleston Area Medical Center, Charleston, WV '86 (PUR)
HANEY, WILLIAM S., dir. matl. mgt., Saint Anthony Medical Center, Rockford, IL '86 (PUR)
HANGES, SUSAN J., mgt. eng. intern, Thomas Jefferson University Hospital, Philadelphia, PA '85 (MGMT)
HANGGI, MICHAEL J., proj. dir. and adm., Finlay Medical Center HMO Corporation, Miami, FL '87 (AMB)
HANIGAN, MARY L., med. spec., Pioneer Hi-Bred International, Inc., Johnston, IA '87 (AMB)
HANIGHEN, CECELIA N., mgt. eng., Good Samaritan Hospital, Cincinnati, OH '85 (MGMT)
HANKAMMER, HMC CURTIS G., MSC USN, Naval Hospital, Millington, TN '79
HANKAMP, STEPHEN G., asst. to vice-pres. mental health, Catherine McAuley Health Center, Ann Arbor, MI '81
HANKE, LOREN D., asst. mgr. plant serv., Fresno Community Hospital and Medical Center, Fresno, CA '85 (ENG)
HANKEY, JANICE A., dir. food serv., Good Samaritan Hospital, Kearney, NE '81 (FOOD)
HANKIN, ERROL P., vice-pres. adm., Winthrop-University Hospital, Mineola, NY '87 (AMB)
HANKIN, LOUISE C., dir. soc. serv., Norwood Hospital, Norwood, MA '74 (SOC)
HANKINS, ROBERT W., asst. prof. health syst. mgt., Tulane University Hospital and Clinics, New Orleans, LA '86 (MGMT)
HANKINS, WARREN, dir. educ., Welborn Memorial Baptist Hospital, Evansville, IN '79 (EDUC)
HANKINS, WILLIAM L., asst. dir., Bon Secours Hospital, Baltimore, MD '67
HANKINSON, KATHRYN, dir. counseling and discharge plng., Presbyterian Hospital, Albuquerque, NM '84 (SOC)
HANKLEY, SANDRA N., dir. mktg. and commun. rel., Twin County Community Hospital, Galax, VA '86 (PR)
HANKO, LT. COL. JAMES F., MSC USAF, chief staffing, manpower educ. and biometrics, Headquarters Military Airlift Command, Scott AFB, IL '74
HANKS, BARBARA J., RN, sr. dir. clin. serv., Lehigh Valley Hospital Center, Allentown, PA '78 (NURS)(AMB)
HANKTON, WILLIE L., dir. environ. serv., University of California San Francisco, San Francisco, CA '86 (ENVIRON)
HANKWITZ, A. WALTER, vice-pres. strategic bus. dev., Centinela Hospital Medical Center, Inglewood, CA '69
HANLEY, MARGIE, RN, vice-pres. nrsg., Good Samaritan Hospital and Medical Center, Portland, OR '76 (NURS)
HANLEY, SHEILA, dir. plng., Mercy Hospital, Portland, ME '85 (PLNG)
HANLEY, THOMAS J., dir. pub. rel., Mount Sinai Hospital, Hartford, CT '87 (PR)
HANLIN, DAVID C., dir. plng. and mktg., Arnot-Ogden Memorial Hospital, Elmira, NY '79 (PLNG)
HANLON, C. ROLLINS, MD, dir., American College of Surgeons, Chicago, IL '76 (HON)
HANLON, CARL E., asst. dir. facil. serv., Medical Park Hospital, Winston-Salem, NC '77 (PUR)
HANLON, JAMES F., vice-pres. plng. and dev., Timken Mercy Medical Center, Canton, OH '80 (PLNG)
HANLON, MARY ANN, dir. soc. work serv., Bay Area Hospital, Coos Bay, OR '86 (SOC)
HANN, BARBARA A., mgr. pers., Pocono Hospital, East Stroudsburg, PA '85 (PERS)
HANN, MARTIN JAY III, pres., Hanna Engineering Corporation, Baltimore, MD '79 (ENG)
HANNA, ALBERT R., adm., Dettmer Hospital, Troy, OH '47 (LIFE)
HANNA, DIANNE, dir. vol. serv., Mercy Medical Center, Denver, CO '86 (VOL)
HANNA, DOROTHY, RN, asst. dir., William Beaumont Hospital, Royal Oak, MI '82 (NURS)
HANNA, IVAN E., dir. plant serv., St. Joseph's Hospital and Health Center, Tucson, AZ '75 (ENG)
HANNA, S. SUE, RN, consult., Pittsburgh, PA '76
HANNA, TERRY R., atty., Baptist Medical Center of Oklahoma, Oklahoma City, OK '87 (ATTY)
HANNAH, ARNOLD V. JR., dir. eng., Saint Joseph's Hospital, Atlanta, GA '87 (ENG)
HANNAH, GENE A., vice-pres. med. staff dev., Baptist Medical Center, Montgomery, AL '72 (PR)
HANNAH, JOE E., dir. pers., Muskogee Regional Medical Center, Muskogee, OK '63 (PERS)
HANNAN, C. PHILLIP, RN, vice-pres. nrsg., Ravenswood Hospital Medical Center, Chicago, IL '69 (NURS)
HANNAN, DAVID T., pres., South Shore Hospital, South Weymouth, MA '69
HANNAN, JUDITH E., dir. pur., Titus County Memorial Hospital, Mount Pleasant, TX '84 (PUR)
HANNAS, RALSTON R. JR., MD, dir. emer. serv., Saint Joseph Health Center Kansas, Kansas City, MO '73 (LIFE)
HANNASCH, JO ANNE, RN, dir. nrsg., Iowa Hospital Association, Des Moines, IA '76 (NURS)
HANNAWAY, JANET A., prin., Hannaway and Associates, Lemont, IL '86
HANNEMANN, WILLIAM C. JR., asst. dir. matl. mgt., Peninsula General Hospital Medical Center, Salisbury, MD '74 (PUR)
HANNIGAN, HARRIET R., RN, dir. nrsg. serv., Josiah B. Thomas Hospital, Peabody, MA '72 (NURS)
HANNON, PATRICIA A., sr. unit serv. mgr. oper. room and matl. mgt., Yale-New Haven Hospital, New Haven, CT '86 (PUR)
HANNON, RICHARD M., atty., Phoenix Children's Hospital, Phoenix, AZ '85 (ATTY)
HANNON, TRISH L., health care mktg. consult., San Diego, CA '85 (PLNG)
HANOLD, WAYNE L., atty., Methodist Medical Center of Illinois, Peoria, IL '74 (ATTY)
HANOVER, KEN, sr. vice-pres. plng. and mktg., Healthlink, Portland, OR '84 (PLNG)
HANPETER, JOHN A., dir. biomedical eng., Barnes Hospital, St. Louis, MO '84 (ENG)
HANRAHAN, ELENA M., dir. vol., New York Eye and Ear Infirmary, New York, NY '78 (VOL)
HANRAHAN, MARY ELLEN, dir. counseling serv., Albany Medical Center Hospital, Albany, NY '78 (SOC)
HANSBURG, TINA B., dir. vol. serv., Maryvale Samaritan Hospital, Phoenix, AZ '85 (VOL)
HANSCHMIDT, JOSEPH J., dir. eng., Lindell Hospital, St. Louis, MO '80 (ENG)
HANSCOM, PERCY R., dir. phys. plant, Regional Memorial Hospital, Brunswick, ME '76 (ENG)
HANSEN, ANNE SPENCER, mgr. mktg., Sutter General Hospital, Sacramento, CA '83 (PR)
HANSEN, ANNETTE M., RN, assoc. dir. nrsg., Northeastern Hospital of Philadelphia, Philadelphia, PA '86 (NURS)
HANSEN, BARBARA, asst. dir. vol. serv., Presbyterian Hlthcare Services, Albuquerque, NM '86 (VOL)
HANSEN, CAROL, dir. soc. serv., St. John's Hospital and Health Center, Santa Monica, CA '79 (SOC)
HANSEN, CHARLOTTE MORAN, supv. soc. work, Winona Memorial Hospital, Indianapolis, IN '85 (SOC)
HANSEN, DANA LYNN, student, Georgia State University-Institute of Health Administration, Atlanta, GA '85
HANSEN, DOLORES, educator in-service, Magic Valley Regional Medical Center, Twin Falls, ID '71 (EDUC)
HANSEN, DONALD K., vice-pres., Dynamic Isolation Systems, Inc., Berkeley, CA '86 (ENG)
HANSEN, EMIL C., (ret.), St. Paul, MN '42 (LIFE)
HANSEN, FLORA, dir. vol. serv., Mercy Community Hospital, Port Jervis, NY '74 (VOL)
HANSEN, FLORENCE M., (ret.), Omaha, NE '68 (SOC)
HANSEN, GENE E., RN, dir. nrsg. serv., West Valley Medical Center, Caldwell, ID '85 (NURS)
HANSEN, GENE, mgr. biomedical syst., Appleton Medical Center, Appleton, WI '85 (ENG)
HANSEN, HELEN, RN, assoc. adm. and dir. nrsg. serv., Saint Joseph Health Center Kansas, Kansas City, MO '77 (NURS)
HANSEN, JANE, dir. vol. serv., South Macomb Hospital, Warren, MI '79 (VOL)
HANSEN, KRIS, dir. mktg. and pub. rel., South Fulton Hospital, East Point, GA '86 (PR)
HANSEN, KRISTEN E., staff spec. pub. rel., American Hospital Association, Chicago, IL '82 (PR)
HANSEN, LORETTA B., RN, asst. adm., Antelope Valley Hospital Medical Center, Lancaster, CA '68
HANSEN, MARIA C., dir. comm. rel., AMI Fort Bend Community Hospital, Missouri City, TX '84 (PR)
HANSEN, MARION J., dir. educ., Tri-County Hospital, Wadena, MN '86 (EDUC)
HANSEN, MARJORIE J., RN, asst. exec. dir., Shawnee Mission Medical Center, Shawnee Mission, KS '68 (NURS)
HANSEN, MITCHELL J., mgr. info. serv., Goddard Memorial Hospital, Stoughton, MA '86 (MGMT)
HANSEN, REBECCA L., dir. soc. serv., Phoenix Memorial Hospital, Phoenix, AZ '83 (SOC)
HANSEN, RICHARD D., vice-pres. mktg. dev., Mercy Hospital and Medical Center, San Diego, CA '85 (PLNG)
HANSEN, LT. COL. RICHARD N., MSC USA, assoc. adm., LaRabida Children's Hospital, Chicago, IL '72
HANSEN, ROBERT E., dir. eng., Children's Hospital and Health Center, San Diego, CA '84 (ENG)
HANSEN, RUSSEL M., asst. dir. cent. serv., St. Francis Regional Medical Center, Wichita, KS '84 (CS)
HANSEN, RUSSELL J., dir. pers., Riverview Medical Center, Red Bank, NJ '85 (PERS)
HANSEN, SUSAN M., exec. vice-pres., Jeanes Health System, Jenkintown, PA '82 (PLNG)
HANSEN, THOMAS H., sr. vice-pres. corp. plng. and mktg., Burbank Hospital and Centmass Systems Corporation, Fitchburg, MA '80 (PLNG)
HANSFORD, C. L., asst. dir. plant oper., Bethania Regional Health Care Center, Wichita Falls, TX '85 (ENG)
HANSON, ANDREA R., dir. pers., Malden Hospital, Malden, MA '71 (PERS)
HANSON, BRUCE E., atty., United Hospital, St. Paul, MN '76 (ATTY)
HANSON, BRYANT R., exec. dir., St. Francis Hospital, Blue Island, IL '73
HANSON, CLAUDINE J., syst. analyst, Servantcor, Urbana, IL '84 (MGMT)
HANSON, DAVID L., assoc. adm. fiscal affairs, Goddard Memorial Hospital, Stoughton, MA '77
HANSON, DENNIS M., sr. consult., Honeywell, St. Louis Park, MN '74
HANSON, DENNIS R., dir. pers. serv., Rochester Methodist Hospital, Rochester, MN '78 (PERS)
HANSON, ERICK E., gen. mgr., Key Care Health Resources, Zionville, IN '87 (AMB)
HANSON, HENRY G. JR., sr. vice-pres. prop. serv., Tallahassee Memorial Regional Medical Center, Tallahassee, FL '84 (ENG)
HANSON, LARRY J., mgt. eng., Community Hospitals of Indiana, Indianapolis, IN '84 (ENG)
HANSON, LINDA J., dir. emp. rel., Braddock General Hospital, Braddock, PA '86 (PERS)
HANSON, MARGARET R., Farmington Hills, MI '85 (EDUC)
HANSON, MARY B., RN, vice-pres. nrsg., St. Luke's Hospital, Duluth, MN '86 (NURS)
HANSON, MICHAEL P., asst. adm. oper., Berlin Hospital Association, Berlin, WI '82
HANSON, PAUL W., dir., Genesee Hospital, Rochester, NY '62
HANSON, PHILIP J., dir. pers. serv., Walter O. Boswell Memorial Hospital, Sun City, AZ '64 (PERS)
HANSON, RAYMOND J. JR., vice-pres., Medicus Systems Corporation, Johnston, RI '74 (MGMT)
HANSON, RICHARD, adm., Leigh Memorial Hospital, Norfolk, VA '79
HANSON, ROBERT L., owner and consult., Health Systems Management Service, Seattle, WA '79 (MGMT)
HANSON, RUTH A., dir. in-service educ., St. Luke's Hospitals, Fargo, ND '86 (EDUC)
HANSON, SUSAN RUTH, risk mgr. and qual. assur., Kino Community Hospital, Tucson, AZ '84 (RISK)
HANSON, SYLVIA B., dir. vol., St. Luke's Hospital, Racine, WI '82 (VOL)
HANSON, TERRY C., dir. plng., Pomona Valley Community Hospital, Pomona, CA '78 (PLNG)
HANSSON, AGNES G., dir. vol. serv., Mount Vernon Hospital, Mount Vernon, NY '84 (VOL)
HANSZ, R. LARRY, dir. matl. mgt., Munson Medical Center, Traverse City, MI '80 (PUR)
HANYAK, DIANA C., dir. mktg. and pub. rel., Charter Community Hospital, Hawaiian Gardens, CA '84 (PR)
HAPP, DOUGLAS W., consult., Happ and Happ, New Rochelle, NY '80 (MGMT)
HAPSHIE, EDWARD L., dir. matl. mgt. and environ. serv., Plantation General Hospital, Plantation, FL '83 (PUR)
HARAF, SHERRI L., RN, dir. nrsg., Elmhurst Extended Care Center, Elmhurst, IL '86 (NURS)

HARALSON, BOBBY J., asst. dir. phys. plant, University Hospital of Arkansas, Little Rock, AR '81 (ENG)
HARAN, MARIE LOIS, RN, dir. nrsg., Brookdale Hospital Medical Center, Brooklyn, NY '76 (NURS)
HARB, OMAR FUAD, asst. to adm., American University of Beirut Medical Center, Beirut, Lebanon '79 (CS)(PUR)
HARBARGER, CLAUDE W., adm., University Medical Center, Lebanon, TN '83
HARBART, R. DONALD, staff planner, Tucson Medical Center, Tucson, AZ '81 (PLNG)
HARBER, NANCY J., RN, assoc. adm., Sharp Memorial Hospital, San Diego, CA '80 (NURS)
HARBERT, GENEVA F., dir. food serv., Marshall I. Pickens Hospital, Greenville, SC '84 (FOOD)
HARBERT, KENNETH R., mgr. phys. extenders, Geisinger Medical Center, Danville, PA '83 (EDUC)
HARBERT, PEGGEEN O., dir. dev., Evangelical Community Hospital, Lewisburg, PA '83 (PLNG)
HARBERT, TERRY LEE, Topeka, KS '77 (SOC)
HARBIN, NANCY J., qual. assur. nrs. and pat. rep., Baptist Medical Center, Jacksonville, FL '86 (PAT)
HARBISON, CHERYL M., RN, asst. dir. cent. serv., Allegheny Valley Hospital, Natrona Heights, PA '86 (CS)
HARBISON, EDWARD A., dir. spec. serv., Suny Health Sciences Center at Syracuse, Syracuse, NY '82 (CS)
HARBOLD, CYNTHIA S., asst. exec. dir. staff serv., St. Joseph's Medical Center, Fort Wayne, IN '83 (PERS)
HARBOLD, JUDITH C., risk mgr., Visiting Nurse Association of Central Massachusetts, Inc., Worcester, MA '86 (RISK)
HARBOUR, KARLENE S., dir. pat. and family counseling, St. Joseph Hospital East, Mount Clemens, MI '85 (SOC)
HARCEK, MICHAEL S., dir. bldg. and grd., Estes Park Medical Center, Estes Park, CO '87 (ENG)
HARCROW, E. EARL, atty., Shannon, Gracey, Ratliff and Miller, Fort Worth, TX '82 (ATTY)
HARDAWAY, JAMES RICHARD, dir. comm. rel., Hackettstown Community Hospital, Hackettstown, NJ '86 (PR)
HARDEN, DONNA H., risk mgr., Penrose Hospitals, Colorado Springs, CO '80 (RISK)
HARDEN, JIMMIE W., adm., Cobb Memorial Hospital, Royston, GA '79
HARDEN, RICHARD R., dir. prog. dev., Rehabilitation Institute of Pittsburgh, Pittsburgh, PA '83
HARDER, FRED M., pres. and chief exec. off., Paradise Valley Hospital, National City, CA '84 (PLNG)
HARDER, KATHLEEN K., asst. mgr. pur. and stores, Appleton Medical Center, Appleton, WI '84
HARDER, COL. RICHARD C., adm., Alamo Heights University, Methodist Church, San Antonio, TX '82 (PERS)
HARDER, RICHARD, dir. pers., Inter-Community Medical Center, Covina, CA '67 (PERS)
HARDESTY, PATSY W., dir. diet., Hays Memorial Hospital, San Marcos, TX '85 (FOOD)
HARDESTY, STELLA M., supv. cent. serv., N. T. Enloe Memorial Hospital, Chico, CA '79 (CS)
HARDIE, MILES C., dir. gen., International Hospital Federation, London, England '82 (HON)
HARDIN, HARRY S. III, atty., Tulane University Hospital and Clinics, New Orleans, LA '83 (ATTY)
HARDIN, MARVIN C., vice-pres., Methodist Hospital, Lubbock, TX '72
HARDIN, STEPHEN H., mgr. and owner, Western Medical Technical Service, Inc., Modesto, CA '84 (ENG)
HARDIN, SUSAN H., asst. adm., McKenna Memorial Hospital, New Braunfels, TX '86 (PLNG)
HARDINE, RICHARD GRANT, dir. matl. mgt., Marianjoy Rehabilitation Center, Wheaton, IL '78 (PUR)
HARDING, HARRY F., dir. vol. serv., Braintree Hospital, Braintree, MA '86 (VOL)
HARDING, JAMES G., pres. emeritus, Medical Center of Delaware, Wilmington, DE '53 (LIFE)
HARDING, JANE E., RN, dir. critical care nrsg., Carney Hospital, Boston, MA '86 (NURS)
HARDING, LU HILL, asst. adm., Mississippi Baptist Medical Center, Jackson, MS '68 (PERS)
HARDING, RICHARD A., coor. pur., St. Jude Hospital-Fullerton, Fullerton, CA '80 (PUR)
HARDING, SCOTT R., dir. plant oper., Oaklawn Hospital, Marshall, MI '82 (ENVIRON)(ENG)
HARDING, WILLIAM W., pres., Union Hospital, Dover, OH '77 (PLNG)
HARDISSON, JOSEPH L., adm. food serv., Lutheran Medical Center, Brooklyn, NY '69 (FOOD)
HARDMAN, R. KIM, dir. mktg. and pub. rel., American Fork Hospital, American Fork, UT '85 (PR) (PLNG)
HARDT, KEITH E., dir. eng., Fairfax Hospital, Falls Church, VA '74 (ENG)
HARDT, LUKE W., supv. maint., Holy Family Hospital, Des Plaines, IL '86 (ENG)
HARDTMAN, SCOTT, asst. adm., St. Catherine Hospital of East Chicago, East Chicago, IN '80
HARDWICK, DARLENE, RN, supv. sup., proc. and distrib., Shriners Hospital for Crippled Children, Shriners Burns Institute, Cincinnati Unit, Cincinnati, OH '85 (CS)
HARDWICK, MARCIA G., dir. vol. serv. and pat. rep., Valley Medical Center, Renton, WA '84 (PAT)
HARDWICK, WILLARD ELI, health planner, State of Indiana, Indianapolis, IN '66
HARDY, C. THOMPSON, adm. dir., Akron Clinic, Akron, OH '87 (AMB)
HARDY, DENNIS M., sales rep., Concept, Inc., Clearwater, FL '86 (PUR)
HARDY, FREDERICK C., account mgr., Flower Memorial Hospital, Sylvania, OH '86 (ENVIRON)
HARDY, FREDERICK CHARLES, student, School of Technical Careers, Southern Illinois University, Carbondale, IL '81
HARDY, JACK S., dir. mktg. and commun. unit, Hill and Knowlton, Inc., Atlanta, GA '76 (PR)
HARDY, LINDA LEE, dir. mktg., Pineridge Hospital, Lander, WY '86 (PR) (PLNG)
HARDY, MARILYN E., asst. dir. cent. sup., Westchester County Medical Center, Valhalla, NY '79 (CS)
HARDY, MAUREEN L., RN, dir. nrs., Athol Memorial Hospital, Athol, MA '80 (NURS)
HARDY, MICHAEL J., mgr. risk mgt. serv., Michigan Hospital Association Mutual Insurance Company, Lansing, MI '84 (RISK)
HARDY, MURIEL, dir. pub. rel., Southwest Community Health System, Middleburg Heights, OH '80 (PR)
HARDY, RONALD M., dir. pur., Bethesda Hospital, Zanesville, OH '83 (PUR)
HARDY, RUTH E., dir. pub. rel., St. Mary's Hospital, West Palm Beach, FL '72 (PR)
HARDY, THOMAS J. JR., St. Paul Medical Center, Dallas, TX '78
HARDY, VALERIE S., RN, dir. nrsg., Franklin Square Hospital, Baltimore, MD '86 (NURS)
HARDY, WILLIAM E., dir. soc. serv., Lander Valley Regional Medical Center, Lander, WY '84 (SOC)
HARDYCK, NANCY A., nrsg. coor., El Camino Hospital, Mountain View, CA '83 (VOL)
HARDYMON, SANDRA M., pres. and creative dir., Hardymon and Associates, Columbus, OH '86 (PR) (PLNG)
HARE, SALLY A., actg. dir. staff dev. and commun. educ., Galesburg Cottage Hospital, Galesburg, IL '86 (EDUC)
HARE, SYLVIA, mktg. assoc., Mercy Hospital, Toledo, OH '85 (PLNG)
HARE, WILLIAM A., dir. eng. and maint., Indiana Hospital, Indiana, PA '85 (ENG)
HARGADON, TERRY, dir. plng., University of Texas Health Center, Tyler, TX '83 (PLNG)
HARGER, PATRICIA S., vice-pres. consumer health oper., Inter Health, St. Paul, MN '76 (PLNG)
HARGER, WILLIAM G., adm., Surgical Center Associates, Winter Park, FL '86 (AMB)
HARGIS, CAROL, RN, nrs. adm., Camelback Hospitals, Inc., Scottsdale, AZ '83 (NURS)
HARGIS, PAMELA SUE, dir. commun., St. Agnes Hospital and Medical Center, Fresno, CA '75 (PR)
HARGRAVE, ALFRED E. JR., asst. adm., HCA Doctors Hospital, Lake Worth, FL '83
HARGRAVE, MARYLLYN, dir. vol. serv., St. Paul Medical Center, Dallas, TX '77 (VOL)
HARGREAVES, BETTY J., supv. cent. store room, Martin Memorial Hospital, Stuart, FL '83 (CS)
HARGROVE, BEN T., dir. pers., Leesburg Regional Medical Center, Leesburg, FL '86 (PERS)
HARGROVE, PAUL A., dir. cent. serv., Bossier Medical Center, Bossier City, LA '83 (CS)
HARKER, ARICHA T., dir. food serv., Mercy Hospital, Rockville Centre, NY '85 (FOOD)
HARKER, BETTY, coor. vol., Mercy Medical Center, Nampa, ID '71 (VOL)
HARKER, JAY E., dir. pat. and family counseling, Holy Cross Hospital, Salt Lake City, UT '82 (SOC)
HARKER, KENNETH W., dir. energy mgt. and syst. design, American Medical International, Beverly Hills, CA '84 (ENG)
HARKER, LINDA Z., dir. vol., Island Hospital, Anacortes, WA '82 (VOL)
HARKER, RENEE S., dir. food serv., Bellevue Hospital Center, New York, NY '81 (FOOD)
HARKIN, WALTER J., dir. human res., Calvary Hospital, Bronx, NY '86 (PERS)
HARKINS, PAMELA E., dir. commun. rel., Our Lady of Bellefonte Hospital, Ashland, KY '86 (VOL)
HARKINS, THOMAS A., mgt. analyst, Mount Sinai Medical Center, New York, NY '87 (PLNG)
HARKNESS, RUTH, dir. pur., White County Memorial Hospital, Monticello, IN '83 (PUR)
HARLAN, JOHN F. JR., asst. vice-pres., University of Virginia Medical Centers, Charlottesville, VA '53 (PLNG)(LIFE)
HARLAN, KATHY, risk mgr., California Emergency Physicians, Oakland, CA '84 (RISK)
HARLOW, GEORGE D., adm. eng., New England Medical Center, Boston, MA '67 (ENG)
HARLOW, NAVAH, dir. pat. rep. prog., Beth Israel Medical Center, New York, NY '79 (PAT)
HARLOWE, JOHN T., exec. dir., Ruskin Health Center, Ruskin, FL '84
HARM, RONALD C., dir. accred and regulation, Kaiser Foundation Hospitals, Oakland, CA '87 (RISK)
HARMALA, ETHEL, dir. med. rec., Cottage Hospital of Grosse Pointe, Grosse Pointe Farms, MI '79
HARMAN, DONALD L., dir. nrsg. staff educ., Meriter Hospital, Madison, WI '81 (EDUC)
HARMAN, JOHN R., atty., Elkhart General Hospital, Elkhart, IN '77 (ATTY)
HARMAN, KAREN M., vice-pres. pub. rel., Hospital of Saint Raphael, New Haven, CT '87 (PR)
HARMAN, LAWRENCE J., dir. soc. serv., Alexian Brothers Medical Center, Elk Grove Village, IL '86 (SOC)
HARMAN, COL. LOUIS E. JR., MSC USA, chief qual. assur.-clin. serv., U. S. Army Health Services Command, Fort Sam Houston, TX '84
HARMAN, PATRICK R., dir. sup., proc. and distrib., Carroll County General Hospital, Westminster, MD '81 (CS)
HARMAN, R. M., assoc. adm., Martin Memorial Hospital, Stuart, FL '80
HARMENING, JANET B., RN, asst. adm. pat. care, Union Hospital, Terre Haute, IN '86 (NURS)
HARMER, CAROL D., mgr. mktg. and pub. rel., Phoenix Baptist Hospital and Medical Center, Phoenix, AZ '83 (PR)
HARMEYER, GARY R., student, Naval Postgraduate School, Monterey, CA '85 (MGMT)
HARMON, ALEXANDER, exec. dir., Christ Hospital, Cincinnati, OH '53 (LIFE)
HARMON, CHERYL JEAN, spec. pers., Kaiser Foundation Hospitals Oregon Region, Portland, OR '72 (PERS)
HARMON, EDWIN L., MD, (ret.), Grosse Pointe Park, MI '31 (LIFE)
HARMON, GARY F., fin. planner, Mayo Foundation, Rochester, MN '86
HARMON, GREGORY JOHN, dir. plng. and mktg., St. Anthony Hospital, Oklahoma City, OK '64 (PLNG)
HARMON, JOEL A., Naval Hospital, Camp Pendleton, CA '83
HARMON, MARVELLA J., dir. vol., Walker Memorial Hospital, Avon Park, FL '83 (VOL)
HARMON, MONA GAY, mgr. pers., National Health Laboratories, Inc., Dallas, TX '74 (PERS)
HARMON, PATRICIA, RN, sr. asst. dir., Medical College of Ohio Hospital, Toledo, OH '80 (NURS)
HARMON, SCOTT M., health care planner, Veterans Administration Wadsworth Medical Center, Los Angeles, CA '78
HARMOUNT, SCOTT T., asst. dir. bldg. and grds., Fairview General Hospital, Cleveland, OH '86 (ENG)
HARMS, HELEN E., RN, dir. nrsg., United Memorial Hospital, Greenville, MI '76 (NURS)
HARMS, JOHN W., dir. plant oper., Community Hospital, Geneva, IL '79 (ENG)
HARMS, RONALD H., pres., Lake Shore HMO, Holland, MI '80 (PLNG)
HARNDEN, PHILIP H. JR., dir. plant oper., Mercy Hospital, Council Bluffs, IA '80 (ENG)
HARNED, MARY ANN, RN, dir. cont. educ., Jesse Holman Jones Hospital, Springfield, TN '75 (EDUC)
HARNESS, BARBARA ZEL, mgr., Prentice Women's Hospital and Maternity Center of Northwestern Memorial Hospital, Chicago, IL '85
HARNESS, CAROL, dir. vol., Stormont-Vail Regional Medical Center, Topeka, KS '81 (VOL)
HARNESS, CONSTANCE T., dir. pers., Wabash General Hospital District, Mount Carmel, IL '85 (PERS)
HARNESS, WILLIAM M., RN, chief nrsg. serv., Veterans Administration Medical Center, Togus, ME '85 (NURS)
HARNETIAUX, DARLENE, RN, coor. in-service educ., Edward A. Utlaut Memorial Hospital, Greenville, IL '80 (EDUC)
HARNETT, SR. MICHAEL FRANCES, pat. rep., St. Patrick Hospital, Lake Charles, LA '78 (PAT)
HARNEY, CARMEN E., dir. human res., Tri-City Medical Center, Oceanside, CA '84 (PERS)
HARNEY, JOHN P., assoc. exec. dir. amb. care, Lincoln Medical and Mental Health Center, Bronx, NY '77
HARNEY, MARILYN, RN, assoc. dir. pat. care, Union Hospital, Terre Haute, IN '77 (NURS)
HARNISH, THOMAS I., vice-pres., Health Options, Inc., Chillicothe, OH '83
HARNS, JAMES F., dir. pers., Saline Community Hospital, Saline, MI '86 (PERS)
HAROLD, JANE W., coor. vol. serv., Bon Secours Hospital of Methuen, Methuen, MA '86 (VOL)
HARPER, ALAN G., asst. dir., Veterans Administration Medical Center, Dayton, OH '74
HARPER, BARBARA O., RN, chief nrsg., Dhahran Health Center, Dhahran, Saudi Arabia '86 (NURS)
HARPER, GERARD, risk mgr., South Shore Hospital, Chicago, IL '86 (RISK)
HARPER, GWENDOLYN, dir. nrsg., Harris Hospital, Newport, AR '86 (NURS)
HARPER, HELEN E., RN, asst. prof., Jacksonville Health Education Program, University of Florida College of Nursing, Jacksonville, FL '68 (NURS)
HARPER, HENRY O. JR., MD, pres., Medical Networks, Inc., Houston, TX '80 (AMB)
HARPER, JEAN G., coor. nrsg., McLeod Regional Medical Center, Florence, SC '85 (EDUC)
HARPER, JERRY L., exec. vice-pres. and chief oper. off., Medical Networks, Inc., Houston, TX '83 (AMB)
HARPER, LILAH M., RN, asst. adm. serv., Palomar Memorial Hospital, Escondido, CA '77 (NURS)
HARPER, SR. M. EMMANUEL, dir. educ., Mercy Regional Medical Center, Vicksburg, MS '78 (EDUC)
HARPER, M. SUZANNE, coor. pub. rel., Moses Taylor Hospital, Scranton, PA '84 (PR)
HARPER, MARY PATRICIA, asst. dir. nrsg. rehab. and recruitment, Jewish Hospital of St. Louis, St. Louis, MO '86 (NURS)
HARPER, NORMAN E., pres., Church Homes, Inc., Hartford, CT '64
HARPER, PATRICIA C., supv. soc. serv., Ralph K. Davies Medical Center-Franklin Hospital, San Francisco, CA '83 (SOC)
HARPER, PEGGY K., dir. soc. work, Rochester General Hospital, Rochester, NY '85 (SOC)
HARPER, ROBERT L., dir. mktg., Medical Center East, Birmingham, AL '80 (PR)
HARPER, STUART, dir. pur., Charter Hospital Charlottesville, Charlottesville, VA '84 (PUR)
HARPER, THOMAS B. III, atty., Holy Redeemer Hospital and Medical Center, Meadowbrook, PA '80 (ATTY)
HARPER, WALTER G., atty., Hillcrest Hospital, Mayfield Heights, OH '85 (ATTY)
HARPER, WILLIAM H., chief soc. work, Veterans Administration Medical Center, Omaha, NE '85 (SOC)
HARPSTER, ALEXANDRA, dir. vol. serv., Timken Mercy Medical Center, Canton, OH '80 (VOL)
HARPSTER, LINDA M., dir. legal, Sisters of Charity Health Care Systems, Cincinnati, OH '80 (RISK)
HARR, MAURICE A., chief hosp. police, University of Texas Medical Branch, Galveston, TX '83 (RISK)
HARRAL, PAUL K., vice-pres. mktg., Baptist Medical Center, Jacksonville, FL '85 (PLNG)
HARRELL, GARY P., RN, dir. nrsg. serv., Grande Ronde Hospital, La Grande, OR '83 (NURS)
HARRELL, HELEN VIRGINIA, student, Georgia State University, Institute of Health Administration, Atlanta, GA '85
HARRELL, R. KEN SR., dir. matl. mgt., Lutheran Medical Center, Wheat Ridge, CO '75 (PUR)
HARRELL, WALLACE E., atty., Glynn-Brunswick Memorial Hospital, Brunswick, GA '74 (ATTY)
HARREN, MARILYN GRONES, plng. analyst, Hillcrest Baptist Medical Center, Waco, TX '85 (PLNG)
HARRIFF, JOHN R., dir. human res., Pine Rest Christian Hospital, Grand Rapids, MI '82 (PERS)

HARRIGAN, ROBERT D., chief human res. off., North Broward Hospital District, Fort Lauderdale, FL '86
HARRIGAN, STEPHEN WILCOX, student, Program in Health Policy and Management, New York Medical College, Valhalla, NY '84
HARRINGTON, B. NOEL, dir. food serv., Waterbury Hospital, Waterbury, CT '71 (FOOD)
HARRINGTON, BARBARA V., dir. food serv., J. C. Blair Memorial Hospital, Huntingdon, PA '78 (FOOD)
HARRINGTON, BETTY J., dir. educ. serv., Sacred Heart Medical Center, Spokane, WA '72 (EDUC)
HARRINGTON, DAVID V., dir. soc. serv., Cape Cod Hospital, Hyannis, MA '82 (SOC)
HARRINGTON, DAVID, dir. med. eng., New England Medical Center, Boston, MA '76 (ENG)
HARRINGTON, DENNIS R., mgr. cent. serv., Cedars Medical Center, Miami, FL '82 (CS)
HARRINGTON, GEOFFREY, asst. adm. plng., Mercy Community Hospital, Port Jervis, NY '83 (PLNG)
HARRINGTON, GEORGIANNA V., RN, asst. dir. matl. mgt., Hamot Medical Center, Erie, PA '80 (CS)
HARRINGTON, JUDITH M., supv. med. soc. serv., Southern Maine Medical Center, Biddeford, ME '82 (SOC)
HARRINGTON, MARGARET R., RN, assoc. dir. and dir. nrsg., Brooklyn Hospital-Caledonian Hospital, Brooklyn, NY '85 (NURS)
HARRINGTON, MARY ELLEN, dir. vol. serv., Northwest Community Hospital, Arlington Heights, IL '86 (VOL)
HARRINGTON, ROBERT L., dir. environ. serv., St. John's Regional Medical Center, Joplin, MO '85 (ENVIRON)
HARRINGTON, SARA J., vice-pres. plng., Worcester Memorial Hospital, Worcester, MA '83 (PLNG)
HARRINGTON, SHARON G., student, Program in Health Administration, University of Miami, Miami, FL '86 (PLNG)
HARRINGTON, TONI, RN, vice-pres. nrsg., Culpeper Memorial Hospital, Culpeper, VA '85 (NURS)
HARRIOTT, BERYL E., dir. diet. serv., Metropolitan Hospital and Health Centers, Detroit, MI '72 (FOOD)
HARRIS, ANDREW M., sr. consult., Price Waterhouse, Tampa, FL '86 (PLNG)
HARRIS, ANN H., dir. soc. serv., St. Joseph Hospital, Flint, MI '81 (SOC)
HARRIS, BARBARA H., dir. vol. serv., Cottonwood Hospital Medical Center, Murray, UT '82 (VOL)
HARRIS, BECKY, RN, coor. pat. educ., Covenant Medical Center -St. Francis, Waterloo, IA '78 (EDUC)
HARRIS, BETTY TREHERNE, dir. vol. serv., Hubbard Hospital Meharry Medical College, Nashville, TN '86 (VOL)
HARRIS, BEVERLY A., atty., Kaiser Foundation Hospital-Cleveland, Cleveland, OH '81 (ATTY)
HARRIS, BEVERLY J., coor. vol. serv., Alexandria Hospital, Alexandria, VA '86 (VOL)
HARRIS, BRIAN M., dir. bldg. serv., Baystate Medical Center, Springfield, MA '86 (ENVIRON)
HARRIS, BRUCE C., mgr., Ernst and Whinney, Detroit, MI '86 (MGMT)
HARRIS, BRUCE E., dir. eng. and maint., Doctors Hospital, Columbus, OH '79 (ENG)
HARRIS, CAROLINE C., pat. rep., St. Mary's Medical Center, Knoxville, TN '80 (PAT)
HARRIS, CHARLOTTE M., mgr. pers., Shelby Medical Center, Alabaster, AL '86 (PERS)
HARRIS, CLARENCE E., vice-pres. human res., Lifespan, Inc., Minneapolis, MN '85 (PERS)
HARRIS, CLAUDE, dir. maint., Wells Community Hospital, Bluffton, IN '81 (ENG)
HARRIS, DANIEL M., dir. mktg. res. and prog. dev., Healthlink, Portland, OR '84 (PLNG)
HARRIS, DARRELL L., asst. mgr. food serv., Saint Alphonsus Regional Medical Center, Boise, ID '82 (FOOD)
HARRIS, DAVID MICHAEL, atty., Sisters of St. Mary, St. Louis, MO '83 (ATTY)
HARRIS, DEAN M., atty., Rex Hospital, Raleigh, NC '83 (ATTY)
HARRIS, DENNIS W., Muskegon, MI '84 (RISK)
HARRIS, DONALD L., sr. vice-pres., Fairfax Hospital Association, Springfield, VA '77 (PLNG)
HARRIS, DORIS E., RN, dir. nrsg. serv., St. Luke's Hospital, Kansas City, MO '78 (NURS)
HARRIS, DOROTHY J., supv. cent. serv., Trinity Regional Hospital, Fort Dodge, IA '80 (CS)
HARRIS, EDWARD E., dir. human res., Baptist Medical Center, Columbia, SC '84 (PERS)
HARRIS, FONDA B., dir. educ. and pub. rel., Blue Ridge Hospital System, Spruce Pine, NC '85 (PR)
HARRIS, GARY R., dir. risk mgt. and ins., University of Cincinnati Hospital-University Hospital, Cincinnati, OH '85 (RISK)
HARRIS, H. PATTERSON, MD, dir., Fairfield Health Department, Fairfield, CT '41 (LIFE)
HARRIS, HARRY J., dir. ldry. and linen serv., University of Kansas Hospital, Kansas City, KS '86 (ENVIRON)
HARRIS, JAMES R., dir. clin. serv., Candler General Hospital, Savannah, GA '80 (ENG)
HARRIS, JAMES ROBERT SR., dir. amb. serv., Medical Center of Central Georgia, Macon, GA '84
HARRIS, JEAN N., asst. vice-pres. nrsg., Aurelia Osborn Fox Memorial Hospital, Oneonta, NY '85 (NURS)
HARRIS, JEANNE A., vice-pres. pub. rel., Numed Hospitals, Inc., Encino, CA '83 (PR)
HARRIS, JEFFREY P., vice-pres. pub. affairs, The Medical Center, Beaver, PA '85 (PR)
HARRIS, JERRY L., pres., Community General Hospital of Greater Syracuse, Syracuse, NY '69
HARRIS, JOAN, dir. commun., Providence Central Memorial Hospital, Toppenish, WA '86 (PR)
HARRIS, JOHN D., supv. biomedical and plant maint., Mercy Center for Health Care Services, Aurora, IL '80 (ENG)
HARRIS, JOYCE B., supv. cent. serv., Onslow Memorial Hospital, Jacksonville, NC '82 (CS)
HARRIS, JUANITA M., RN, dir. plng. and dev., Richland Memorial Hospital, Olney, IL '79 (EDUC)(PLNG)
HARRIS, KATHLEEN A., sr. consult., Ernst and Whinney, Washington, DC '86 (PLNG)
HARRIS, KATHY, dir. pers., Marian Health Center, Sioux City, IA '81 (PERS)
HARRIS, LINDA A., RN, dir. nrsg., Bone and Joint Hospital, Oklahoma City, OK '83 (NURS)
HARRIS, LINDA M., dir. pub. rel., Children's Medical Center of Dallas, Dallas, TX '82 (PR)
HARRIS, LOUISE T., asst. vice-pres. emp. rel., Roanoke Memorial Hospitals, Roanoke, VA '73 (PR)
HARRIS, LYMAN H., atty., Medical Center East, Birmingham, AL '75 (ATTY)
HARRIS, MALCOLM, atty., Providence Memorial Hospital, El Paso, TX '84 (ATTY)
HARRIS, MARGARET J., mgr. contr., University Medical Center, Tucson, AZ '82
HARRIS, MARJORIE, dir. vol. serv., Mease Health Care, Dunedin, FL '80 (VOL)
HARRIS, MARY F., dir. soc. serv., HCA Vista Hills Medical Center, El Paso, TX '84 (SOC)
HARRIS, MARY KATHERINE, dir. matl. mgt., Lawnwood Regional Medical Center, Fort Pierce, FL '74 (PUR)(CS)
HARRIS, MITCH, dir. commun., Mercy Hospital Medical Center, Des Moines, IA '78 (ENG)
HARRIS, MORRIS RAY JR., adm., Northeast Baptist Hospital, San Antonio, TX '69
HARRIS, NORMA A., prog. analyst-mgt. eng. staff, Veterans Administration Medical Center, Houston, TX '82 (MGMT)
HARRIS, PAMELA L., coor. educ., University Hospital and Clinic, Pensacola, FL '86 (EDUC)
HARRIS, PAT, dir. vol., Presbyterian Hospital, Dallas, TX '68 (VOL)
HARRIS, PATRICIA M., RN, adm. nrsg. serv., Wyckoff Heights Hospital, Brooklyn, NY '86 (NURS)
HARRIS, PATTIE C., dir. med. soc. serv., University of Texas Health Center at Tyler, Tyler, TX '85 (SOC)
HARRIS, PAUL S., dir. mktg. and pub. rel., Magee Rehabilitation Hospital, Philadelphia, PA '74 (PR) (PLNG)
HARRIS, RICHARD J., asst. vice-pres. risk mgt., Alabama Hospital Associate Trust Fund, Montgomery, AL '83 (RISK)
HARRIS, RICHARD L., sales consult., Industrial Disposal Supply Company, Plano, TX '85 (ENG)
HARRIS, RICHARD V., exec. vice-pres., Western Kentucky Hospital Services, Madisonville, KY '83 (PUR)
HARRIS, ROBERT L., pres., Ingalls Memorial Hospital, Harvey, IL '84
HARRIS, ROBERT L., asst. adm., Outer Drive Hospital, Lincoln Park, MI '81
HARRIS, ROBERT P., dir. matl. mgt., St. Mary's Hospital, Galesburg, IL '82 (PUR)
HARRIS, ROBERT, dir. emer. and amb. care center, Medical Center of Central Georgia, Macon, GA '87 (AMB)
HARRIS, RONALD B., dir. eng., Memorial Hospital at Gulfport, Gulfport, MS '86 (ENG)
HARRIS, RONALD E., vice-pres., Phillips Swager Associates, Inc., Peoria, IL '85 (ENG)
HARRIS, RUFUS F., consult., Tribrook Group, Inc., Oak Brook, IL '73
HARRIS, RUTH N., soc. worker, Mountain States Tumor Institute, Boise, ID '77 (SOC)
HARRIS, SANDY D., dir. commun. rel., Beaufort County Hospital, Washington, NC '86 (PR)
HARRIS, SELMA JEAN, RN, vice-pres. nrsg., C. J. Harris Community Hospital, Sylva, NC '77 (NURS)
HARRIS, STEVEN D., adm. dir. diagnostic serv. and commun., Hillcrest Medical Center, Tulsa, OK '83 (ENG)
HARRIS, STEVEN WILLIAM, foreman eng. and maint., Mercy Hospital, Davenport, IA '87 (ENG)
HARRIS, SUSAN, dir. legal affairs, American Health Care Association, Washington, DC '85 (RISK)
HARRIS, TED M., dir. pur., St. Margaret's Hospital, Montgomery, AL '81 (PUR)
HARRIS, W. C. JR., atty., North Carolina Hospital Association, Raleigh, NC '79 (ATTY)
HARRIS, W. DANIEL, asst. pat. rel., Kettering Medical Center, Kettering, OH '86 (PAT)
HARRIS, WEN, dir. mktg., River Wood Hospital, Provo, UT '83 (PR)
HARRIS, WILLIAM M., exec. asst. amb. serv., St. Rose Hospital, Hayward, CA '85
HARRIS, WILLIAM T., adm., Oakwood Springwells Health Center, Dearborn, MI '68
HARRISON, BERNICE L., ombudsman, St. Joseph's Medical Center, Fort Wayne, IN '73 (PAT)
HARRISON, BETTIE M., dir. pers., Mercy Hospital, Bakersfield, CA '86 (PERS)
HARRISON, CINDY H., asst. dir. pers., Chelsea Community Hospital, Chelsea, MI '81 (PERS)
HARRISON, CONSTANCE T., RN, assoc. dir. nrsg. mgt. sup. syst., St. Vincent Hospital and Medical Center, Portland, OR '86 (NURS)
HARRISON, DAVID D., asst. dir., Ingham Medical Center, Lansing, MI '84 (FOOD)
HARRISON, DEAN M., vice-pres., Medical Networks, Inc., Houston, TX '79
HARRISON, DOROTHY M., dir. pat. and family counseling, St. Francis Hospital, Greenville, SC '73 (SOC)
HARRISON, DOROTHY, dir. pur., Granville C. Morton Hospital, Dallas, TX '79 (PUR)
HARRISON, ERNEST JR., assoc. vice-pres. clin. serv., Methodist Rehabilitation Center, Jackson, MS '84 (ENG)
HARRISON, EVELYN H., dir. matl. mgt., AMI Griffin-Spalding Hospital, Griffin, GA '69 (PUR)
HARRISON, GAY L. R., mgr. plant oper., Rehabilitation Institute of West Florida, Pensacola, FL '83 (ENG)
HARRISON, GEORGE B., vice-pres. plng. and dev., St. Joseph's Hospital, Parkersburg, WV '85 (PLNG)
HARRISON, GLADYS M., dir. vol., Highline Community Hospital, Seattle, WA '80 (VOL)
HARRISON, HOWARD DOUGLAS, dir. pers., Leigh Memorial Hospital, Norfolk, VA '78 (PERS)
HARRISON, HOWARD W., dir. eng. and proj. coor., Muhlenberg Community Hospital, Greenville, KY '83 (ENG)
HARRISON, JAMES F., dir. plng., Sutter Health System, Sacramento, CA '84 (PLNG)
HARRISON, JEANNE, dir. res. and syst. dev., The Hysen Group, Livonia, MI '79 (FOOD)
HARRISON, JOHN A., Marblehead, MA '54 (LIFE)
HARRISON, JOHN D., coor. pur., Memorial Hospital, Ormond Beach, FL '81 (PUR)
HARRISON, JUDITH R., RN, asst. vice-pres. nrsg. serv., Midwest City Memorial Hospital, Midwest City, OK '86 (NURS)
HARRISON, JUDY A., coor. soc. serv., Bethesda North Hospital, Cincinnati, OH '86 (SOC)
HARRISON, KATHRYN D., dir. telecommun., Alachua General Hospital, Gainesville, FL '84 (ENG)
HARRISON, KIMBERLEY A., customer cost analyst, Blue Cross and Blue Shield of Michigan, Detroit, MI '86
HARRISON, LAWRENCE J., dir. facil., Chicago College of Osteopathic Medicine, Chicago, IL '76
HARRISON, LISA S., dir. pub. rel., South Highlands Hospital, Birmingham, AL '85 (PLNG)
HARRISON, MARCY, mgt. eng., Georgetown University Medical Center, Washington, DC '81 (MGMT)
HARRISON, MARY LU, dir. soc. serv., Ohio State University Hospitals, Columbus, OH '78 (SOC)
HARRISON, MARY STARMANN, vice-pres. med. serv., St. Luke's Medical Center, Phoenix, AZ '78
HARRISON, MATTHEW W. III, mgr., Ernst and Whinney, Dallas, TX '78 (MGMT)
HARRISON, MICHELLE L. DILLEN, student, Program in Hospital and Health Administration, University of Florida, Gainesville, FL '84
HARRISON, ROBERT C., pres. and chief exec. off., St. Luke's Hospital, Jacksonville, FL '78 (PLNG)
HARRISON, ROGER D., dir. safety and security, Mississippi Baptist Medical Center, Jackson, MS '84 (RISK)
HARRISON, SUSAN C., dir. human res., Jess Parrish Memorial Hospital, Titusville, FL '86 (PERS)
HARRISON, SUZANNE D., asst. to dir. human resource, Institute of Living, Hartford, CT '85 (MGMT)
HARRISON, TOM, asst. dir. maint. and grds., Saint Michael's Medical Center, Newark, NJ '86 (ENG)
HARRISON, W. T. JR., atty., Doctors Hospital, Sarasota, FL '68 (ATTY)
HARRITY, ANDREW D., hskpg. off., Naval Hospital, Beaufort, SC '87 (ENVIRON)
HARRON, TERESA M., dir. pur., Cape Cod Hospital, Hyannis, MA '82 (PUR)
HARROUN, JAMES JOSEPH, dir. spec. diagnostics, safety and risk mgt., Wausau Hospital Center, Wausau, WI '80 (RISK)
HARROW, THOM W., prin., Morgan Stanley and Company Inc., New York, NY '84
HARRY, ANN, RN, dir. educ. serv., West Georgia Medical Center, La Grange, GA '76 (EDUC)
HARRY, KAYE S., dir. soc. work, Giles Memorial Hospital, Pearisburg, VA '86 (SOC)
HARSH, LOREE LYNN, pat. rep., Platte County Memorial Hospital, Wheatland, WY '86 (PAT)
HARSHMAN, AMY, dir. mktg., Vanderbilt University-School of Nursing, Nashville, TN '85 (PR)
HARSTAD, CAROL Y., mgr., Hennepin Faculty Associates, Minneapolis, MN '87 (AMB)
HART, ARLENE, asst. dir. cent. serv., Hinsdale Hospital, Hinsdale, IL '85 (CS)
HART, BONITA ELLEN, Kent, WA '67 (FOOD)
HART, CAROL H., dir. nutr. serv., Monongalia General Hospital, Morgantown, WV '77 (FOOD)
HART, D. SCOTT, partner, Peat, Marwick, Mitchell and Company, Peoria, IL '76
HART, DIANE M., dir. pers., Moses Ludington Hospital, Ticonderoga, NY '86 (PERS)
HART, DIANE MARIE, pat. rep., Mercy Hospital, Miami, FL '85 (PAT)
HART, GARY L., vice-pres. manpower plng. and dev., Intermountain Health Care, Inc., Salt Lake City, UT '86 (PERS)
HART, GEORGE E., atty., Washington Hospital Center, Washington, DC '71 (ATTY)
HART, GINA S., coor. soc. serv., H. B. Magruder Memorial Hospital, Port Clinton, OH '80 (SOC)
HART, GREGORY P., chief med. recruiting div., U. S. Air Force Recruiting Service, Randolph AFB, TX '77
HART, JOEL A., adm., Edmond Memorial Hospital, Edmond, OK '75
HART, JOHN W., coor. med. staff, Lehigh Valley Hospital Center, Allentown, PA '85
HART, JUDY, vice-pres. and dir. natl. health care sales and serv., Alexander and Alexander, Clayton, MO '86 (RISK)
HART, K. MICHAEL, corp. account mgt., Virtual Imaging Company, Indianapolis, IN '86
HART, KATHARINE P., coor. risk mgt. proj., Morton F. Plant Hospital, Clearwater, FL '84 (RISK)
HART, KATHLEEN H., dir. food and nutr., Caylor-Nickel Hospital, Bluffton, IN '80 (FOOD)
HART, M. CATHERINE, RN, adm. nrsg. affairs, York Hospital, York, PA '74 (NURS)
HART, MARGARET ELOISE, dir. vol., Clinton Memorial Hospital, Wilmington, OH '82 (VOL)
HART, MARY M., RN, dir. nrsg., Bayshore Community Hospital, Holmdel, NJ '84 (NURS)
HART, NANCY CONLEE, exec. vice-pres., Interhealth, St. Paul, MN '79 (PLNG)
HART, PAT, RN, mgr. cent. serv., Hinds General Hospital, Jackson, MS '86 (CS)
HARTER, RONALD E., dir. eng., Lester E. Cox Medical Center, Springfield, MO '85 (ENG)
HARTER, SUSAN BROOKS, RN, vice-pres. nrsg. serv., Rehabilitation Institute of Santa Barbara, Santa Barbara, CA '86 (NURS)

HARTER, SUSAN C., dir. pat. care fin., budget and staffing, Tucson Medical Center, Tucson, AZ '85 (NURS)

HARTFORD, LYLE STEPHEN, (ret.), Setagayaku, Tokyo, Japan '52 (LIFE)

HARTIG, KATHLEEN M., dir. vol. serv., Norwood Hospital, Norwood, MA '80 (VOL)

HARTIGAN, DONNA M., dir. corp. rel., Healthcare Financial Management Association, Oak Brook, IL '84 (PR)

HARTIGAN, EVELYN G., RN EdD, vice-pres. nrsg. serv., Little Company of Mary Hospital, Evergreen Park, IL '71 (NURS)

HARTIGAN, MICHAEL J., dir. food serv., Naples Community Hospital, Naples, FL '84 (FOOD)

HARTIN, DANA S., dir. diet., HSA Hill Crest Sunrise Hospital, Birmingham, AL '83 (FOOD)

HARTIN, THOMAS J., dir. soc. work serv., Community Memorial Hospital, Oconto Falls, WI '85 (SOC)

HARTING, JAMES J., pres., Health Resources, Fairview Heights, IL '85

HARTKE, KENNETH N., dir. matl. mgt., Saint Francis Medical Center, Peoria, IL '83 (CS)(PUR)

HARTL, CRAIG, dir. plant oper. and maint., Rogue Valley Medical Center, Medford, OR '80 (ENG)

HARTLEY, BRODES H. JR., exec. dir., Community Health of South Dade, Miami, FL '67

HARTLEY, DORA J., dir. pub. rel., Bulloch Memorial Hospital, Statesboro, GA '84 (PR)

HARTLEY, JACK L., pres., Midwest Management Service, Inc., Shawnee Mission, KS '86 (PLNG)

HARTLEY, JAMES A., atty., Giles Memorial Hospital, Pearisburg, VA '81 (ATTY)

HARTLEY, JOHN, dir. qual. assur., util. review and risk mgt., Atlanticare Medical Center, Lynn, MA '85 (RISK)

HARTLEY, MARJORIE E., coor. commun. dev., Giles Memorial Hospital, Pearisburg, VA '86 (PR) (PLNG)

HARTLEY, PATTY M., mgr. corp. mktg., Care One Health Systems, Zanesville, OH '80 (EDUC)(PR) (PLNG)

HARTLEY, PEGGY A., RN, dir. nrsg. serv., HCA Santa Rosa Medical Center, Milton, FL '86 (NURS)

HARTLEY, RICHARD, eng. consult., Robert J. Sigel, Inc., Narberth, PA '81 (ENG)

HARTLEY, ROBERT C., vice-pres. plng., mktg. and pub. rel., Mercy Health Systems of the Gulf South, New Orleans, LA '85 (PLNG)

HARTLEY, SELWYN, MD, chm. emer., Clayton General Hospital, Riverdale, GA '87 (AMB)

HARTLEY, WILLIAM L., dir. food serv., HCA Gulf Coast Hospital, Panama City, FL '80 (FOOD)

HARTLIEB, CATHERINE T., vice-pres., Alexander and Alexander, Inc., Chicago, IL '80 (RISK)

HARTLINE, DAVID S., dir. plant oper. mgt., Heights General Hospital, Albuquerque, NM '79 (ENG)

HARTLINE, JAMES R., atty., Montefiore Hospital, Pittsburgh, PA '87 (ATTY)

HARTMAN, A. EDWIN, vice-pres., Health Services Corporation of America, Springfield, IL '83 (PUR)

HARTMAN, BONNIE J., RN, dir. nrsg. serv., Abraham Lincoln Memorial Hospital, Lincoln, IL '84 (NURS)

HARTMAN, CLYDE M., dir. maint. and eng., Sycamore Hospital, Sycamore, IL '85 (ENG)

HARTMAN, CYNTHIA J., RN, dir. nrsg. serv., Grenada Lake Medical Center, Grenada, MS '85 (NURS)

HARTMAN, G. JANE, food serv. consult., Dietary Management Advisory, Rosemont, PA '47 (FOOD)(LIFE)

HARTMAN, GERHARD, PhD, Billings, MT '36 (LIFE)

HARTMAN, GWYN L., mgr., Deloitte Haskins and Sells, Costa Mesa, CA '86 (MGMT)

HARTMAN, HAROLD W., adm. and chief oper. off., Sharp Cabrillo Hospital, San Diego, CA '63 (PLNG)

HARTMAN, JANET, exec. dir., Miller-Dwan Medical Center, Duluth, MN '78 (EDUC)

HARTMAN, KENATH, Wilmette, IL '47 (LIFE)

HARTMAN, MARK A., atty., Cabrini Medical Center, New York, NY '82 (ATTY)

HARTMAN, SARA E., vice-pres. plng., Rochester Area Hospitals Corporation, Rochester, NY '80 (PLNG)

HARTMANN, BETH F., dir. soc. serv., La Crosse Lutheran Hospital, La Crosse, WI '81 (SOC)

HARTMANN, DIAN N., coor. vol., Sutter Memorial Hospital, Sacramento, CA '81 (VOL)

HARTMANN, ELENA F., med. lib., Forbes Regional Health Center, Monroeville, PA '86

HARTMANN, JAMES C., vice-pres. human res., Toledo Hospital, Toledo, OH '76 (PERS)

HARTMANN, SR. MARIE, reg. counselor, Sisters of Mercy Provincialate, Cincinnati, OH '80

HARTMANN, MARLENE A., RN, dir. nrsg., Barnes Hospital, St. Louis, MO '80 (NURS)

HARTNESS, JANE B., coor. vol. serv., Rowan Memorial Hospital, Salisbury, NC '84 (VOL)

HARTNETT, GEORGE D., pres., Zurbrugg Memorial Hospital, Willingboro, NJ '69

HARTSFIELD, DOROTHY B., dir. vol. serv., Mercer Medical Center, Trenton, NJ '86 (VOL)

HARTSFIELD, GAIL J., vice-pres. strategic plng. and mktg., Baylor Health Care System, Dallas, TX '79 (PLNG)

HARTTER, CHARLOTTE M., RN, asst. vice-pres. nrsg., Northern Michigan Hospitals, Petoskey, MI '84 (NURS)

HARTUNG, DENNIS A., dir. stores, proc. and distrib., Western Pennsylvania Hospital, Pittsburgh, PA '74 (PUR)(CS)

HARTUNG, ERIC D., pres., Edh and Associates, Redondo Beach, CA '86 (MGMT)

HARTUNG, JAMES S., sr. buyer, Carondelet Community Hospitals, Minneapolis, MN '82 (PUR)

HARTWELL, DAVID, atty., Maine Medical Center, Portland, ME '86 (ATTY)

HARTWELL, JOHN S., atty., Valley Memorial Hospital, Livermore, CA '77 (ATTY)

HARTY, PAULA E., dir. soc. work serv., Guadalupe Medical Center, Carlsbad, NM '87 (SOC)

HARTZELL, FRANKLIN M., atty., Memorial Hospital, Carthage, IL '68 (ATTY)

HARVEGO, KELLY L., student, Program in Hospital Administration, Concordia College, Moorhead, MN '87

HARVEL, GEORGE W., dir. maint., Marion Memorial Hospital, Marion, IL '74 (ENG)

HARVEY, ANN GRAY, plng. analyst, Greenville Hospital System, Greenville, SC '84 (PLNG)

HARVEY, COLLEEN K., RN, nrs. analyst info. syst., Hospital Corporation of America, Nashville, TN '86 (NURS)

HARVEY, DIANE M., dir. pat. educ., Scott and White Memorial Hospital, Temple, TX '85 (EDUC)

HARVEY, ESTELE, dir. pur., St. Albans Psychiatric Hospital, Radford, VA '87 (PUR)

HARVEY, ETHEL, supv. cent. serv., Louis A. Weiss Memorial Hospital, Chicago, IL '86 (CS)

HARVEY, JACK, mgt. consult., Methodist Hospital System, Houston, TX '82 (MGMT)

HARVEY, JAMES D., pres., Hillcrest Medical Center Foundation, Tulsa, OK '51 (LIFE)

HARVEY, JAMES R., mgr. elec. eng. design, University of Michigan Hospitals, Ann Arbor, MI '86 (ENG)

HARVEY, JANNA L., dir. pers., Gulf Coast Medical Center, Wharton, TX '85 (PERS)

HARVEY, JUDITH, RN, dir. nrsg., Massachusetts Eye and Ear Infirmary, Boston, MA '80 (NURS)

HARVEY, LUTHER B., adm. food serv., Labette County Medical Center, Parsons, KS '70 (FOOD)

HARVEY, MADELINE J., dir. pub. rel. and dev. asst. to adm., Children's Seashore House, Atlantic City, NJ '81 (PR)

HARVEY, MARY A., dir. vol. serv., St. Mary's Hospital and Health Center, Tucson, AZ '72 (VOL)

HARVEY, MARY BENNETT, acct. exec., William Cook Advertising, Inc., Jacksonville, FL '86

HARVEY, REED A., dir. pers. serv., Baylor University Medical Center, Dallas, TX '82 (PERS)

HARVEY, STEPHANIE L., mgr. emp. dev., Greater Southeast Community Hospital, Washington, DC '81 (EDUC)

HARVEY, THOMAS E. JR., proj. dir., Harwood K. Smith and Partners, Los Angeles, CA '76

HARVEY, WILLIAM C., consult., Webster, MA '67

HARVEY, WILLIAM LEE, asst. adm., Mount Vernon Hospital, Alexandria, VA '78 (PLNG)

HARVIEUX, ANNE M., dir. med. soc. serv., Beloit Memorial Hospital, Beloit, WI '82 (SOC)

HARWELL, AMY, pres., Amy Harwell, Ltd., Chicago, IL '85

HARWELL, CHARLIE, atty., Springdale Memorial Hospital, Springdale, AR '85 (ATTY)

HARWELL, HENRY R., asst. to pres. and dir. mktg., St. Mark's Hospital, Salt Lake City, UT '86 (PLNG)

HARWELL, JOHN D., atty., Centinela Hospital Medical Center, Inglewood, CA '84 (ATTY)

HARWELL, W. KATHLEEN, RN, vice-pres. nrsg., Gaston Memorial Hospital, Gastonia, NC '80 (NURS)

HARWIG, LEAH T., dir. vol. serv., AMI Town and Country Medical Center, Tampa, FL '84 (VOL)

HARWOOD, CANDY M. GRAVES, assoc. dir. soc. work, Portland Adventist Medical Center, Portland, OR '83 (SOC)

HARWOOD, VERN, student, New School for Social Research, New York, NY '74 (PERS)

HASBROUCK, GAIL DURHAM, atty., Evangelical Health Systems, Oak Brook, IL '79 (ATTY)

HASCALL, NEVA Z., asst. pub. rel., Cass County Memorial Hospital, Atlantic, IA '83 (PR)

HASEK, JANE E., vice-pres. educ., Allen Memorial Hospital, Waterloo, IA '83 (EDUC)

HASELHORST, JUDY A., dir. mktg., Palos Community Hospital, Palos Heights, IL '85 (PLNG)

HASELHUHN, GERALD R., sr. vice-pres., Schmidt, Garden and Erikson, Inc., Chicago, IL '79

HASELROTH, STEPHEN M., student, Oklahoma City College, McAlester, OK '85 (PLNG)

HASENPUSCH, PETER H., sr. eng., Roswell Park Memorial Institute, Buffalo, NY '82 (ENG)

HASERICK, HARVEY F., dir. environ. serv., Masonic Home and Charity Fund, Burlington, NJ '86 (ENVIRON)

HASKELL, CAROL R., RN, mgr. cent. serv., Franklin Medical Center, Greenfield, MA '80 (CS)

HASKELL, JEAN E., mgr. pers., Mercy Hospital, Merced, CA '86 (PERS)

HASKELL, ROBERT E., Shared Medical Systems, Inc., Malvern, PA '83 (PLNG)

HASKELL, TRUEMAN L. JR., dir., Medlantic Healthcare Group, Washington, DC '82 (RISK)

HASKIN, G. MARK, risk mgr., St. Luke's Hospital, Kansas City, MO '81 (RISK)

HASKINS, ANN M., dir. plng., Rockford Memorial Hospital, Rockford, IL '81 (PLNG)

HASKINS, CRAIG S., dir. food serv., Central Washington Hospital, Wenatchee, WA '77 (FOOD)

HASLAG, DANIEL, supv. hskpg., St. Mary's Health Center, Jefferson City, MO '86 (ENVIRON)

HASLER, LINDA SUE, pat. rep., Lawrence Memorial Hospital, Lawrence, KS '84 (PAT)

HASLER, V. DIANE, vice-pres., Memorial Hospitals Association, Modesto, CA '81

HASLINGER, TERRY, coor. in-service, Munson Medical Center, Traverse City, MI '80 (EDUC)

HASPEDIS, BETTY L., RN, dir. risk mgt., Sacred Heart Medical Center, Spokane, WA '76 (RISK)

HASS, JOEL W., vice-pres. mktg. and commun., Adventist Health System, Arlington, TX '76 (PR) (PLNG)

HASSAN, JO ANN, student, Program in Health Service Administration, School of Health Professions, Governors State University, Park Forest South, IL '84

HASSAN, REFAT O., dir. food serv., Havenwyck Hospital, Auburn Hills, MI '83 (FOOD)

HASSAN, RICHARD C., dir. pur., Bronson Methodist Hospital, Kalamazoo, MI '68 (PUR)

HASSAN, WILLIAM E. JR., atty., Brigham and Women's Hospital, Boston, MA '85 (ATTY)

HASSARD, PATRICIA C., commun. consult., Resources, Inc., Richmond, VA '83 (PR)

HASSEL, MARIA L., dir. diet., Cook County Hospital, Chicago, IL '82 (FOOD)

HASSEL, MARILYN J., RN, vice-pres. nrsg., Malden Hospital, Malden, MA '83 (NURS)

HASSEL, PATRICIA A., RN, vice-pres. and dir. nrsg., Benedictine Hospital, Kingston, NY '85 (NURS)

HASSELBRACK, CAROL, RN, vice-pres. nrsg., St. Helena Hospital and Health Center, Deer Park, CA '82 (NURS)

HASSELL, LEROY R., atty., Richmond Community Hospital, Richmond, VA '81 (ATTY)

HASSEMER, ROBERT J., dir. pers., Sacred Heart Hospital, Eau Claire, WI '80 (PERS)

HASSEN, ETHEL D., pat. rep., Rogue Valley Medical Center, Medford, OR '82 (PAT)

HASSON, JAMES K. JR., atty., Piedmont Hospital, Atlanta, GA '78 (ATTY)

HASTING, JOHN L., plant eng., Madison County Hospital, London, OH '86 (ENG)

HASTINGS, DOUGLAS A., atty., SunHealth Corporation, Charlotte, NC '86 (ATTY)

HASTINGS, FLORIS, RN, coor. educ., Gulf Coast Medical Center, Wharton, TX '84 (EDUC)

HASTINGS, G. RICHARD II, exec. dir. oper., St. Luke's Hospital, Kansas City, MO '76

HASTINGS, JAMES T., dir. matl. mgt., St. Mary's Hospital and Medical Center, San Francisco, CA '85 (PUR)

HASTINGS, JOHN H., asst. dir. distributed computing dev., University of Washington Hospitals, Seattle, WA '85 (MGMT)

HASTINGS, LAVONE, RN, coor. pat. and family educ., St. Alexius Medical Center, Bismarck, ND '79 (EDUC)

HASTINGS, MARGARET M., PhD, exec. dir., Illinois Commission on Mental Health and Developmental Disabilities, Chicago, IL '84

HASTON, LENORA R., RN, asst. exec. dir. nrsg. serv., Rolling Hill Hospital, Elkins Park, PA '86 (NURS)

HATCH, EDWARD W., vice-pres. plng., Holy Family Hospital, Des Plaines, IL '82 (PR) (PLNG)

HATCH, NANCY D., dir. vol. serv., Copley Hospital, Morrisville, VT '85 (VOL)

HATCH, STEPHEN W., exec. vice-pres., CHI Systems, Inc., Chicago, IL '74 (PLNG)

HATCH, VINCENT J., atty., St. Elizabeth's Hospital, Belleville, IL '74 (ATTY)

HATCHER, CALVIN P., dir. ancillary serv., Presbyterian Hospital in the City of New York, New York, NY '52 (LIFE)

HATCHER, JAMES F., dir. mktg. and dev., Craven County Hospital, New Bern, NC '86 (PLNG)

HATCHER, JAN M., actg. dir. mktg., Morton F. Plant Hospital, Clearwater, FL '86 (PLNG)

HATCHER, JERROLD W., mgr. equip. acquisition and redistribution, Medical Resources International, Phoenix, AZ '77 (ENG)

HATCHER, JOHN M., adm., Whitley County Memorial Hospital, Columbia City, IN '85

HATCHER, MARY LOUISE, RN, coor. commun. health educ., Morristown Memorial Hospital, Morristown, NJ '84 (EDUC)

HATCHER, ROBERT W., Fayetteville, NC '83 (SOC)

HATCHETT, BLAIR M., dir. educ., Helen Keller Memorial Hospital, Sheffield, AL '85 (EDUC)

HATFIELD, DAVID M., dir., Mary Breckinridge Hospital-Frontier Nursing Service, Wendover, KY '58

HATFIELD, DONALD L., dir. cent. proc., Hospital of the University of Pennsylvania, Philadelphia, PA '86 (CS)

HATFIELD, JOHN N. II, Walters Health Clinic, Independence, MO '83

HATFIELD, MARY FRANCES, loss control consult., Hospital Underwriters Mutual Insurance Company, Albany, NY '85 (RISK)

HATFIELD, RICHARD, vice-pres. commun. rel. and mktg., Burlington Medical Center, Burlington, IA '84 (PR)

HATHAWAY, DAVID B., plant eng., Lawrence Memorial Hospital of Medford, Medford, MA '76 (ENG)

HATHAWAY, ROSEMARY J., RN, assoc. dir. nrsg., Windham Community Memorial Hospital, Willimantic, CT '83 (NURS)

HATHCOCK, PATRICIA H., dir. mktg., Mississippi Methodist Hospital and Rehabilitation Center, Jackson, MS '85 (PR)

HATHCOCK, TEDDIE S., dir. pat. and family serv., Caldwell Memorial Hospital, Lenoir, NC '86 (SOC)

HATKOFF, MAJ. PAUL, MSC USA, chief pat. adm., U. S. Army Hospital Heidelberg, APO New York, NY '84

HATON, STEVEN L., asst. vice-pres., Professional Risk Management of California, Los Angeles, CA '81 (RISK)

HATT, MARTHA A., pub. info. off., Bass Memorial Baptist Hospital, Enid, OK '81 (PR)

HATTABAUGH, FRANCIE M., dir. vol., Pratt Regional Medical Center, Pratt, KS '86 (VOL)

HATTEN, CARL D., dir. soc. serv., Trinity Lutheran Hospital, Kansas City, MO '71 (SOC)

HATTLEY, EVELYN H., asst. mgr. cent. serv., Craven County Hospital, New Bern, NC '83 (CS)

HATTMAN, TIM, dir. plant oper., Ohio Valley General Hospital, McKees Rocks, PA '86 (ENG)

HATTON, DANIEL, PhD, dir. ambulance serv., Bay Medical Center, Bay City, MI '73

HATTON, JEAN, RN, dir. nrsg., St. Mary's Hospital, Streator, IL '80 (NURS)

HATTON, JESSE R., eng., Memorial Hospital, Bainbridge, GA '83 (ENG)

HATTON, TERRY ANNE, RN, dir. med.-surg. nrsg., Cabell Huntington Hospital, Huntington, WV '85 (NURS)

HATZ, DANIEL F., pur. agt., Child's Hospital, Albany, NY '83 (PUR)

HATZIS, CAROLYN, Evanston, IL '82 (SOC)

HAUBENSTOCK, LORI ANN, dir. govt. rel., Tampa General Hospital, Tampa, FL '86

HAUBER, KARL W., student, Cleveland State University, Cleveland, OH '86 (MGMT)

HAUBNER, RUTH L., RN, dir. critical care, St. Mary's Medical Center, Knoxville, TN '87 (NURS)

HAUBOLD, CAROL, mgr. membership serv., Kaiser Health Plan of Colorado, Denver, CO '86 (PAT)

HAUCH, MARY L., dir. mktg., Lutheran General Hospital, Park Ridge, IL '84 (PR) (PLNG)
HAUCK, FRED E., vice-pres. human res. dev., New England Memorial Hospital, Stoneham, MA '86 (PERS)
HAUCK, KAYRL S., dir. human res., Waterman Medical Center, Eustis, FL '80 (PERS)
HAUCK, MELANIE, dir. corp. commun., Pacific Presbyterian Medical Center, San Francisco, CA '86 (PR)
HAUCK, REGINA, coor. cent. sup., Reading Rehabilitation Hospital, Reading, PA '79 (CS)
HAUER, ROSE M., RN, vice-pres. nrsg. serv., Beth Israel Hospital, New York, NY '68 (NURS)
HAUG, SR. JEAN FRANCES, health care consult., St. Joseph Hospital, Kirkwood, MO '77
HAUG, WILLIAM F., pres., California Medical Center-Los Angeles, Los Angeles, CA '75
HAUGABROOK, EDDIE, vice-pres. gen. serv., Tallahassee Memorial Regional Medical Center, Tallahassee, FL '77 (PUR)
HAUGE, JAMES E., vice-pres., North Carolina Hospital Association, Raleigh, NC '83
HAUGE, JUNE, dir. soc. serv., Moline Public Hospital, Moline, IL '72 (SOC)
HAUGEN, JANICE R., dir. pers., Good Samaritan Hospital, Corvallis, OR '81 (PERS)
HAUGEN, KAREN A., dir. diet., Luther Hospital, Eau Claire, WI '78 (FOOD)
HAUGEN, MAJ. LAWRENCE A., MSC USA, Bayne-Jones Army Community Hospital, Fort Polk, LA '72
HAUGEN, T. MARIE, dir. environ. and hskpg. serv., Valley View Hospital, Glenwood Springs, CO '86 (ENVIRON)
HAUGEN, WILLIS G., atty., Newnan Hospital, Newnan, GA '74 (ATTY)
HAUGER, LINDA KAY, mgr. data proc., Frick Community Health Center, Mount Pleasant, PA '85 (MGMT)
HAUGHNEY, BRENDA R., dir. pers., Memorial Medical Center, Savannah, GA '86 (PERS)
HAUGHT, JANET K., RN, asst. dir. nrsg., Charleston Area Medical Center, Charleston, WV '83 (NURS)
HAUKAP, GERALDINE D., dir. soc. serv., St. Joseph's Hospital, Breese, IL '81 (SOC)
HAUKE, ROBERT, adm. dir. amb. serv., Sacred Heart General Hospital, Eugene, OR '87 (AMB)
HAUPT, ROBERT K., exec. vice-pres. and treas., Cahmplin-Haupt, Inc., Cincinnati, OH '84
HAURELECHKO, NELL, coor. educ. and staff dev., Good Samaritan Hospital, Corvallis, OR '81 (EDUC)
HAUSER, HARRY E., dir. eng., Forsyth Memorial Hospital, Winston-Salem, NC '79 (ENG)
HAUSER, JACK, Larkspur, CA '56 (LIFE)
HAUSER, JOHN M., dir. safety, University Hospital-University of Nebraska, Omaha, NE '85 (ENG)
HAUSER, LES J., vice-pres. corp. plng. and mktg., DePaul Health Center, Bridgeton, MO '86 (PLNG)
HAUSER, MARTHA BREWER, RN, asst. adm. nrsg., Davis Community Hospital, Statesville, NC '79 (NURS)
HAUSMAN, ALICE, dir. vol. serv., United Hospital, St. Paul, MN '80 (VOL)
HAUSMAN, LYDIA B., asst. vice-pres. commun., Children's Medical Center, Dayton, OH '84 (PR)
HAUSMANN, RALPHA J., soc. worker, St. Elizabeth Medical Center, Granite City, IL '72 (SOC)
HAUSS, DEVORAH J., cardiac rehab. clin. spec., Mount Auburn Hospital, Cambridge, MA '84 (EDUC)
HAUSSLER, GERTRUDE, RN, vice-pres., Loma Linda University Medical Center, Loma Linda, CA '77 (NURS)
HAUSSMANN, R. K. DIETER, vice-pres., Booz, Allen and Hamilton, Inc., Chicago, IL '77 (MGMT)(PLNG)
HAUSSMANN, ROBERT S., vice-pres. mktg., Maryland General Hospital, Baltimore, MD '81 (PR)
HAUTZINGER, JAMES E., atty., Mercy Medical Center, Denver, CO '82 (ATTY)
HAUTZINGER, REBECCA ANN, coor. qual. assur. and util., Rockyview General Hospital, Calgary, Alta., Canada '86 (PAT)
HAVEL, MARK T., dist. dir. commun. rel., Tri-City Medical Center, Oceanside, CA '84 (PR) (PLNG)
HAVEMAN, BARBARA, dir. soc. serv., St. Bernardine Medical Center, San Bernardino, CA '82 (SOC)
HAVEN, CARL O., dir. mktg. and oper., A. Kuhlman and Company, Saline, MI '70
HAVEN, CHARLES E., dir. matl. mgt., Doctors Medical Center, Modesto, CA '86 (PUR)
HAVENER, DARRELL L., atty., Golden Valley Memorial Hospital, Clinton, MO '77 (ATTY)
HAVENS, FRANCES LAMOYNE, RN, dir. nrsg. serv., Brownwood Regional Hospital, Brownwood, TX '86 (NURS)
HAVERLY, BEVERLY, dir. soc. serv., Lakeview Medical Center, Rice Lake, WI '80 (SOC)
HAVERS, ELLEN M., asst. dir. food serv., Scripps Memorial Hospital, La Jolla, CA '76 (FOOD)
HAVILAND, JUDITH ANN, RN, vice-pres. pat. care serv., Mercy Medical Center, Coon Rapids, MN '79 (NURS)
HAVILAND, WILLIAM R., asst. dir. diet. serv., Antelope Valley Hospital Medical Center, Lancaster, CA '82 (FOOD)
HAVRILLA, MARY H., RN, chief nrsg. serv., Veterans Administration Medical Center, Butler, PA '79 (NURS)
HAVRYLUK, BETTY, vice-pres. pub. affairs, Hospital Council of Western Pennsylvania, Warrendale, PA '70 (PR)
HAW, MARY A., RN PhD, assoc. prof., San Francisco State University, San Francisco, CA '84 (EDUC)
HAWES, SR. MARYANN V., dir. vol. serv., Saint Cabrini Hospital of Seattle, Seattle, WA '86 (VOL)
HAWES, NANCY J., ger. clin. spec., St. Luke's Regional Medical Center, Boise, ID '87 (EDUC)
HAWK, ESTHER M., RN, vice-pres. pat. serv., Scripps Memorial Hospital, La Jolla, CA '80 (NURS)
HAWK, JEAN A., RN, coor. pat. care, Northside Presbyterian Hospital, Albuquerque, NM '86 (NURS)
HAWK, RANDY S., oper. dir., Whittaker Health Services, Fresno, CA '79
HAWK, WILLIAM C., pres., Teamcare, Inc., Laurel, MD '86 (PR) (PLNG)
HAWKINS, CYNTHIA, mgr. pub. rel., Mercy Hospital, Owensboro, KY '85 (PR)
HAWKINS, HOWARD K., mgr. loss prevention, Michigan Hospital Association, Lansing, MI '82 (ENG)(RISK)
HAWKINS, JOHN O. III, exec. vice-pres., Sarasota Memorial Hospital, Sarasota, FL '80
HAWKINS, LT. COL. LOWELL F., MSC USAF, cost analyst, Ehrling Bergquist U. S. Air Force Regional Hospital, Omaha, NE '86 (MGMT)
HAWKINS, MARILYN A., RN, dir. nrsg., Sierra Community Hospital, Fresno, CA '86 (NURS)
HAWKINS, MARK S., exec. dir., First Source Corporation, Albuquerque, NM '85
HAWKINS, LT. COL. ROBERT T., MSC USA, dep. cmdr. adm., Hawley U. S. Army Community Hospital, Indianapolis, IN '77
HAWKINS, SANDRA A., asst. dir. soc. work, Presbyterian-University Hospital, Pittsburgh, PA '83 (SOC)
HAWKINS, SHARON, dir. hskpg., Maryvale Samaritan Hospital, Phoenix, AZ '87 (ENVIRON)
HAWKINS, TIMOTHY F., dir. matl. mgt., Mercy Hospital, Miami, FL '83
HAWKS, R. E., adm. dir. support serv., Sheehan Memorial Hospital, Buffalo, NY '78 (ENG)
HAWKSLEY, VIRGINIA, RN, dir. nrsg. serv., Memorial Hospital, Pawtucket, RI '79 (NURS)
HAWLEY, BARBARA L., atty., Lake Hospital System, Painesville, OH '85 (ATTY)
HAWLEY, DENNIS B., dir. pers., Patrick Henry Hlthcare Center, Newport News, VA '86 (PERS)
HAWLEY, DONNA L., dir. vol. serv., Memorial Medical Center, Long Beach, CA '84 (VOL)
HAWLEY, GEORGE H., dir. eng., Hebrew Rehabilitation Center for Aged, Boston, MA '76 (ENG)
HAWLEY, HELEN M., Decatur, IL '74 (PAT)
HAWLEY, JANET J., RN, chief nrs., Veterans Administration Medical Center, Lake City, FL '80 (NURS)
HAWN, NEAL, dir. matl. mgt., Henrietta Egleston Hospital for Children, Atlanta, GA '83 (PUR)
HAWORTH, WILLIAM BURTON, Lake Elsinore, CA '80
HAWRYLAK, CHRISTINE, asst. dir. pub. rel., Park Ridge Hospital, Rochester, NY '86 (PR)
HAWTHORNE, GORDON W., sr. vice-pres., Baptist Medical System, Little Rock, AR '80 (ATTY)
HAWTHORNE, WILLIAM B., pres., Hawthorne Associates, Inc., Arlington, MA '82
HAXHE, JEAN-JACQUES, MD, med. dir., Cliniques Universitaires St. Luc, Bruxelles, Belgium '67
HAY, AUDREY M., RN, asst. exec. dir., Western Pennsylvania Hospital, Pittsburgh, PA '83 (NURS)
HAY, BILL H., vice-pres. mktg. and commun. rel., Lovelace Medical Center, Albuquerque, NM '85 (PR)
HAY, DAVID G., asst. vice-pres. matl. mgt., Winthrop-University Hospital, Mineola, NY '83 (PUR)
HAY, LELSIE ANNE, sr. underwriter, American Home Assurance Company, New York, NY '87
HAY, MARGARET, RN, mgr. pat. care, Ortonville Area Health Services, Ortonville, MN '79 (NURS)
HAY, MARJORIE A., RN, dir. nrsg., Harding Hospital, Worthington, OH '86 (NURS)
HAYAS, S. RANDOLPH, vice-pres., Center for Health Affairs, Cleveland, OH '75 (PUR)
HAYASHI, CHARLES Y., dir. educ. and trng., Ballard Community Hospital, Seattle, WA '80 (EDUC)
HAYAUX, PAUL L., asst. vice-pres. facil. and eng., Cooper Hospital-University Medical Center, Camden, NJ '76 (ENG)
HAYCOCK, SCOTT M., dir. plant serv., Valley View Medical Center, Cedar City, UT '80 (ENG)
HAYDEN, ADALINE C., (ret.), Indianapolis, IN '47 (LIFE)
HAYDEN, FISK, adm. dir. food serv., Orlando Regional Medical Center, Orlando, FL '81 (FOOD)
HAYDEN, JOHN T., dir. pers. and benefits, Henry Ford Hospital, Detroit, MI '79 (PERS)
HAYDEN, KENNETH T., dir. eng., Baylor University Medical Center, Dallas, TX '81 (ENG)
HAYDEN, MARCELLA M., dir. pub. rel., Bergen Pines County Hospital, Paramus, NJ '79 (PR)
HAYDEN, MARTIN J., dir. eng., Hospital for Special Surgery, New York, NY '79 (ENG)
HAYDEN, RICHARD ALLAN, group pres., Holy Cross Health System, Vienna, VA '70
HAYDEN, SHARON L., dir. soc. work serv., Westchester County Medical Center, Valhalla, NY '79 (SOC)
HAYDON, GLEN E., pres., Mercy International Health Service, Mason City, IA '86
HAYEK, THOMAS J., clin. eng., Christian Health Services Development Corporation, St. Louis, MO '85 (ENG)
HAYES, ALAN L., vice-pres. human res., Holy Family Hospital, Des Plaines, IL '82 (PERS)
HAYES, ALICE MARIE, dir. guest rel., Metropolitan Hospital-Central Division, Philadelphia, PA '81 (PAT)
HAYES, BARBARA D., RN, Lexington, SC '85 (NURS)
HAYES, BOBBIE H., dir. pub. rel., Clayton General Hospital, Riverdale, GA '81 (PR)(VOL)
HAYES, GARY N., dir. human res. dev., Church Charity Foundation of Long Island, Hempstead, NY '83 (EDUC)
HAYES, GEORGE E., sr. assoc. dir., St. Luke's Hospital, Kansas City, MO '80
HAYES, J. MICHAEL, dir. info. syst., Memorial Medical Center, Springfield, IL '85 (MGMT)
HAYES, JAMA J., RN, asst. to pres., Clinton Memorial Hospital, Wilmington, OH '80 (NURS)(PAT)
HAYES, JAMES E., atty., Memorial Hospital for Cancer and Allied Diseases, New York, NY '77 (ATTY)
HAYES, COL. JAMES H., MSC USA, chief insp. gen. evaluation, U. S. Army Health Services Command, Fort Sam Houston, TX '67
HAYES, JOHN S., atty., New Jersey Society of Hospital Attorneys, Princeton, NJ '79 (ATTY)
HAYES, LARRY R., dir. plant serv. and mgr. safety, Shorewood Osteopathic Hospital, Seattle, WA '85 (ENG)
HAYES, LYNDA, asst. dir. pub. rel., St. Mary's Hospital, Passaic, NJ '86 (PR)
HAYES, MARJORIE, dir. qual. assur., Our Lady of Mercy Medical Center, Bronx, NY '86 (RISK)
HAYES, MARY JANE, RN, dir. cent. serv., St. Joseph's Hospital Medical Center, Bloomington, IL '84 (CS)
HAYES, NONA M., dir. food serv., St. Lawrence Hospital, Lansing, MI '82 (FOOD)
HAYES, PAMELA W., adm. res., Program and Bureau of Hospital Administration, University of Michigan, Ann Arbor, MI '84
HAYES, RHONDA RADER, dir. matl. mgt., Framingham Union Hospital, Framingham, MA '78 (PUR)
HAYES, ROBBIE, dir. environ. serv., Lakeland Regional Medical Center, Lakeland, FL '86 (ENVIRON)
HAYES, ROBERT W., dep. dir. and adm., Wilton Developmental Center, Wilton, NY '51 (LIFE)
HAYES, STEVE A., dir. matl. mgt., Illinois Valley Community Hospital, Peru, IL '81 (PUR)
HAYES, THOMAS E., dir. matl., Sumter Regional Hospital, Americus, GA '81 (PUR)
HAYES, THOMAS M. JR., atty., St. Francis Medical Center, Monroe, LA '81 (ATTY)
HAYES, WILLIAM J., dir. pers., Delaware Valley Medical Center, Langhorne, PA '86 (PERS)
HAYES, MRS. WILLIE, mgr. food serv., Wilson Memorial Hospital, Wilson, NC '77 (FOOD)
HAYHURST, ROBERT E., asst. dir. pat. sup., proc. and distrib., University of Texas Anderson Hospital, Houston, TX '86 (CS)
HAYMAN, BARBARA A., RN, dir. educ. serv., Methodist Hospital, Hattiesburg, MS '82 (EDUC)
HAYMAN, JOYCE L., RN PhD, coor. health promotion, Providence Hospital, Washington, DC '80 (EDUC)
HAYMOND, JAMES T., student, Cleveland State University, Cleveland, OH '86 (MGMT)
HAYMONS, DAN LESTER JR., pres., North Kansas City Hospital, North Kansas City, MO '62
HAYNER, AGGIE, dir. commun. rel., St. John's Hospital, Springfield, IL '82 (PR)
HAYNES, BERNARD, dir. fiscal affairs, Victoria Hospital, Miami, FL '76
HAYNES, JEANNE P., dir. vol. serv., Alleghany Regional Hospital, Low Moor, VA '80 (VOL)
HAYNES, JEPTHA T., dir. mgt. info. syst., St. Francis Hospital and Medical Center, Topeka, KS '86 (MGMT)
HAYNES, JOYCE C., dir. vol. serv., Paradise Valley Hospital, National City, CA '75 (VOL)
HAYNES, LINDA A., dir. pub. rel., HCA Coronado Hospital, Pampa, TX '85 (PR)
HAYNES, PATRICIA K., dir. pur., Providence Hospital, Sandusky, OH '85 (PUR)
HAYNES, PATRICIA, mgt. educ. consult., Lewis-Gale Hospital, Salem, VA '74 (EDUC)
HAYNIE, CELINA M., dir. hskpg. and linen, Lafayette General Medical Center, Lafayette, LA '86 (ENVIRON)
HAYNIE, MARY E., dir. vol. serv., Children's Seashore House, Atlantic City, NJ '69 (VOL)
HAYNIE, MARY J., RN, chief nrsg. serv., Veterans Administration Medical Center, Waco, TX '79 (NURS)
HAYNOR, PATRICIA M., vice-pres. nrsg., Crozer-Chester Medical Center, Chester, PA '77 (NURS)
HAYS, ALMA R., coor. pat. educ., Johns Hopkins Hospital, Baltimore, MD '85 (EDUC)
HAYS, HOWARD C., dir. food serv., Marriott-the Tamalpais, Greenbrae, CA '81 (FOOD)
HAYS, JAMES F., health syst. spec., Veterans Administration Medical Center, Brooklyn, NY '82 (PLNG)(MGMT)
HAYS, JANET A., RN, assoc. dir. in-patient serv., Pacific Medical Center, Seattle, WA '86 (NURS)
HAYS, MARY A., RN, dir. nrsg., Scottsdale Memorial Hospital, Scottsdale, AZ '82 (NURS)
HAYS, NANCY M., RN, clin. dir. amb. care, Mount Auburn Hospital, Cambridge, MA '86 (NURS)
HAYTER, MARGARET E., mktg. spec., Health Corporation-Archdiocese of Newark, Newark, NJ '86 (PLNG)
HAYWARD, CYNTHIA, vice-pres., CHI Systems, Inc., Ann Arbor, MI '78 (MGMT)
HAYWARD, JOHN F., atty., Medical College of Ohio Hospital, Toledo, OH '74 (ATTY)
HAYWARD, LEONARD W. JR., vice-pres. plant serv. and security, Newport Hospital, Newport, RI '72 (ENG)
HAYWARD, NANCY C., mktg. res. and plng. asst., Munson Medical Center, Traverse City, MI '83 (PLNG)
HAYWOOD, BARRY PAUL, dir. soc. serv., Forrest County General Hospital, Hattiesburg, MS '73 (SOC)
HAYWOOD, JEAN L., chief sup., proc. and distrib., Veterans Administration Medical Center, Tucson, AZ '85 (CS)
HAYWORTH, DAVID MICHAEL, chief diet. serv., Veterans Administration Medical Center, Dallas, TX '81 (FOOD)
HAZARD, BRUCE D., assoc. dir. matl. mgt., Rose Medical Center, Denver, CO '82 (PUR)
HAZARD, FRANKLIN C., exec. dir., Kenny Michigan Rehabilitation Foundation, Southfield, MI '85
HAZARD, JAMES M., risk mgr., Resurrection Health Care Corporation, Chicago, IL '82 (RISK)
HAZEL, JAMES, supv. maint., Munising Memorial Hospital, Munising, MI '70 (ENG)
HAZEL, JOHN M., asst. dir. human resources, Holy Cross Hospital, Fort Lauderdale, FL '81 (PERS)
HAZEL, JOHN M., dir. pers., Burbank Hospital, Fitchburg, MA '70 (PERS)
HAZELL, NORMA BARBER, dir. mktg. and enrollment, Newark Comprehensive Health Services Plan, Newark, NJ '74
HAZELRIGG, HAROLD T., dir. commun. rel., North Lincoln Hospital, Lincoln City, OR '86 (PR)
HAZELTON, ELEANOR V., pat. rep., Union Hospital, Union, NJ '81 (PAT)
HAZEN, KAY A., dir. mktg., Galesburg Cottage Hospital, Galesburg, IL '81 (PR) (PLNG)

HAZI, DAVID, dir. maint. and eng., Greenville Regional Hospital, Greenville, PA '80 (ENG)
HAZLE, DONNA BAKER, dir. pub. rel., Humana Hospital -Audubon, Louisville, KY '86 (PR)
HAZLETT, ALLEN KIRK, mgr. pub. rel., Medical Area Service Corporation, Boston, MA '87 (PR)
HAZLETT, ALVIN GUY II, adm., Lockney General Hospital, Lockney, TX '78
HAZLETT, DONALD P., dir. food serv., Mercy Memorial Hospital, Monroe, MI '68 (FOOD)
HEAD, DONNA W., RN, vice-pres. pat. serv., St. Mary's Hospital and Medical Center, Grand Junction, CO '77 (NURS)
HEAD, JOSEPH H. JR., atty., Christ Hospital, Cincinnati, OH '80 (ATTY)
HEAD, SALLIE K., dir. pers., Community Hospital, Geneva, IL '86 (PERS)
HEAD, LT. COL. WILLIAM C., MSC USAF, pres., U. S. Air Force Hospital, Panama City, FL '68
HEADINGTON, JOAN I., RN, clin. dir., Allen Memorial Hospital, Waterloo, IA '80 (NURS)
HEADLEY, LORRAINE F., RN, asst. dir., William Beaumont Hospital-Troy, Troy, MI '83 (NURS)
HEAGEN, GAIL P., atty., Hampton General Hospital, Hampton, VA '85 (ATTY)
HEAGLE, GLEN L., pres. and chief exec. off., Burlington Medical Center, Burlington, IA '76
HEALEY, FRANK T., atty., St. Mary's Hospital, Waterbury, CT '68 (ATTY)
HEALEY, HENRY M., consult. eng., Florida Alternative Energy Corporation, Merritt Island, FL '87 (ENG)
HEALEY, LAWRENCE A., asst. mgr. environ. serv., Salem Hospital, Salem, MA '86 (ENVIRON)
HEALION, SR. MARY VERONICA, pat. rep., Saint Joseph Hospital, Fort Worth, TX '75 (PAT)
HEALY, CANDACE M., dir. soc. work, Kaiser Foundation Hospital, San Francisco, CA '77 (SOC)
HEALY, ELIZABETH, asst. dir. soc. serv., St. Vincent's Hospital and Medical Center, New York, NY '77 (SOC)
HEALY, KEITH E., asst. adm., St. Mary Hospital, Port Arthur, TX '85 (RISK)
HEALY, MARIE, dir. soc. serv., Park City Hospital, Bridgeport, CT '74 (SOC)
HEALY, MARY F., lab. mgr., Phelps Memorial Hospital Center, North Tarrytown, NY '85
HEALY, MARY M., coor. vol. serv., Valley Hospital, Ridgewood, NJ '85 (VOL)
HEALY, SONYA A., RN, assoc. dir. and dir. pat. care serv., University of California San Diego Medical Center, San Diego, CA '76 (NURS)
HEANEY, C. E. JR., atty., AMI Saint Joseph Hospital, Omaha, NE '68 (ATTY)
HEANEY, THOMAS A. JR., dir. eng., Long Beach Memorial Hospital, Long Beach, NY '72 (ENG)
HEANEY, VIRGINIA G., RN, dep. dir. nrsg., Westchester County Medical Center, Valhalla, NY '87 (NURS)
HEARING, PHILIP, vice-pres. adm., Guernsey Memorial Hospital, Cambridge, OH '85 (PERS)
HEARN, CURTIS R., atty., American Medical International, Beverly Hills, CA '82 (ATTY)
HEARN, DIANE, dir. vol. serv., Silver Hill Foundation Hospital, New Canaan, CT '86 (VOL)
HEARN, SHIRLEY W., (ret.), Dallas, TX '70 (FOOD)
HEATER, FLOYD R., assoc. adm., Franklin Regional Medical Center, Franklin, PA '82
HEATH, ALISON M., sr. assoc., Amherst Associates, Inc., Tampa, FL '86 (PLNG)
HEATH, ELLEN, mgr. pub. affairs, Methodist Hospital System, Houston, TX '85 (PR)
HEATH, JAMES R., Crabtree, PA '84
HEATH, SR. KAREN SUE, MD, med.-family phys., Sisters of St. Mary, St. Louis, MO '81
HEATH, MARGERY S., asst. vice-pres., Mother Frances Hospital Regional Center, Tyler, TX '87 (AMB)
HEATH, R. TERRY, atty., St. Vincent Hospital and Health Center, Indianapolis, IN '86 (ATTY)
HEATH, ROBERT L., atty., St. Joseph Medical Center, Wichita, KS '80 (ATTY)
HEATH, WALDO D., dir. bldg. serv., Winsted Memorial Hospital, Winsted, CT '80 (ENG)
HEATH, WILLIAM C., asst. supt. eng., Rush-Presbyterian-St. Luke's Medical Center, Chicago, IL '85 (ENG)
HEATHERLY, JOHN D., dir. pers., Texoma Medical Center, Denison, TX '82 (PERS)
HEATON, CAROL S., dir. mktg. and pub. rel., Davenport Medical Center, Davenport, IA '86 (PR)
HEATON, MONICA BAYER, dir. pub. rel. and audiovisuals, Catholic Health Association of the United States, St. Louis, MO '85 (PR)
HEATON, RUTH C., RN, asst. dir. nrsg., University of Kansas College of Health Sciences and Bell Memorial Hospital, Kansas City, KS '85 (NURS)
HEAVENER, DEAN W., dir. matl. mgt., Johnson City Medical Center Hospital, Johnson City, TN '83 (PUR)
HEAVEY, MARTHA M., Medway, MA '86 (CS)
HEAVRIN, TERRY L., dir. matl. mgt., Memorial Hospital, Carbondale, IL '84 (PUR)
HEAYN, JOSEPH A., student, Program in Health Care Administration, Los Angeles Salle University, Philadelphia, PA '86
HEBDA, CYNTHIA R., dir. human resources, Lutheran Hospital, Moline, IL '80 (PERS)
HEBERT, ALBERT G., dir. maint. and eng., St. Joseph's Hospital, Lowell, MA '82 (ENG)
HEBERT, KATHRYN B., supv. pur., East Jefferson General Hospital, Metairie, LA '83 (PUR)
HEBERT, PIERRE, dir. soc. work, Chester County Hospital, West Chester, PA '85 (SOC)
HEBERT, SCOTT JAMES, student, Dalhousie University, Halifax, N.S., Canada '85
HECHENBERGER, A. J. JR., adm. coor. pat. and staff affairs, St. Joseph Hospital, Baltimore, MD '80 (RISK)
HECHT, ANDREA P., pres., Hecht Communications, Sepulveda, CA '86 (PR)
HECHT, DOLORES E., mgr. cent. sup., St. Mary's Regional Health Center, Roswell, NM '79 (CS)
HECHT, GEORGE J., dir. pur., Long Island College Hospital, Brooklyn, NY '59 (PUR)
HECK, WILLIAM H., dir. pers., National Jewish Center, Denver, CO '86 (PERS)
HECKATHORN, THEODORE P., dir. matl., Lewistown Hospital, Lewistown, PA '66 (PUR)
HECKEMEYER, SR. M. RALPH, dir. soc. serv., St. John's Mercy Medical Center, St. Louis, MO '71 (SOC)
HECKERT, DONALD E., asst. vice-pres. plant oper., St. Luke's Hospital, Bethlehem, PA '56 (ENG)(LIFE)
HECKERT, MAJ. ROBERT JAMES JR., MSC USA, chief clin. support directorate, William Beaumont Army Medical Center, El Paso, TX '80
HECKLER, MARTIN G., atty., Albert Einstein Foundation, Philadelphia, PA '86 (ATTY)
HECKLER, THOMAS M., vice-pres., Hamilton Associates, Inc., San Mateo, CA '84
HECKMAN, FRANK D., vice-pres., Professional Risk Management, Inc., Long Beach, CA '80 (RISK)
HEDBLOM, JANICE E., asst. dir. soc. work, Johns Hopkins Hospital, Baltimore, MD '80 (SOC)
HEDDING, BEA, dir. pers., Mercy Hospital of Janesville, Janesville, WI '80 (PERS)
HEDEMAN, MARY C., dir. vol. serv., Keswick-Home for Incurables, Baltimore, MD '85 (VOL)
HEDERMAN, CECILIA C., (ret.), St. Louis, MO '73 (FOOD)
HEDGE, THOMAS L., dir. facil. and bldg. serv., Queen's Medical Center, Honolulu, HI '84 (ENG)
HEDGEPETH, JAY H., atty., Baptist Medical Center, Jacksonville, FL '82 (ATTY)
HEDGES, CALVIN L., RN, dir. nrsg., Perry County Memorial Hospital, Tell City, IN '84 (NURS)
HEDGES, CAROLYN A., dir. human res., Charter Westbrook Hospital, Richmond, VA '85 (PERS)
HEDGES, CLARICE, RN, asst. dir. matl. mgt., San Antonio Community Hospital, Upland, CA '83 (CS)
HEDGES, DIANA L., dir. legal off.-risk mgt., Mills Memorial Hospital, San Mateo, CA '84 (RISK)
HEDGES, RICHARD H., PhD, asst. prof., University of Kentucky, Lexington, KY '85
HEDLUND, CAREL THEILGARD, atty., Spartanburg Regional Medical Center, Spartanburg, SC '85 (ATTY)
HEDMAN, LYLE D., dir. mgt. sci., St. Margaret Hospital, Hammond, IN '85 (MGMT)
HEDRICK, MARGARET, RN, dir. nrsg. educ., Washington County Hospital, Nashville, IL '81 (EDUC)
HEDRICK, NANCY, dir. pers. and vol., Prairie View Mental Health Center, Newton, KS '73 (PERS)
HEDSTROM, LUD J., dir. plant oper., St. John Hospital, Leavenworth, KS '74 (ENG)
HEEGER, ELEANOR GOODLEY, assoc. dir. vol. serv., Century City Hospital, Los Angeles, CA '83 (VOL)
HEEKE, JOHN W., student, Villanova University, Villanova, PA '86
HEETER, JAMES A., atty., Trinity Lutheran Hospital, Kansas City, MO '81 (ATTY)
HEFFELFINGER, PEGGY R., dir. vol. serv., Alpena General Hospital, Alpena, MI '86 (VOL)
HEFFERAN, HARRY H. JR., atty., Norwalk Hospital, Norwalk, CT '74 (ATTY)
HEFFERNAN, ELINOR D., dir. support serv., Rahway Hospital, Rahway, NJ '74 (PLNG)
HEFFERNAN, JAMES L., vice-pres. fin., St. John and West Shore Hospital, Westlake, OH '80
HEFFERNAN, PAUL F., dir. human res., Waterbury Hospital, Waterbury, CT '86 (PERS)
HEFFERNAN, PHYLIS, dir. vol. serv., Robert Wood Johnson University Hospital, New Brunswick, NJ '79 (VOL)
HEFFERNAN, RAYMOND E., dir. eng., St. Anthony's Medical Center, St. Louis, MO '79 (ENG)
HEFFERNAN, THOMAS E., asst. to pres., Holy Cross Health System Corporation, South Bend, IN '80 (PLNG)
HEFFERS, MARGARET A., coor. human res., Geisinger Wyoming Valley Medical Center, Wilkes-Barre, PA '83 (PERS)
HEFFNER, CAROL J., asst. dir., Baystate Medical Education and Research Foundation, Inc., Springfield, MA '87 (AMB)
HEFFNER, JOHN C., proj. dir., Psychiatric Institute of America, Washington, DC '85 (PLNG)
HEFKE, SUZANNE, dir. vol. serv., Marquette General Hospital, Marquette, MI '83 (VOL)
HEFLEY, JUDITH TAYLOR, dir. commun. rel., Lawrence Memorial Hospital, Lawrence, KS '83 (PR)
HEFLIN, BARBARA, soc. worker, Memorial Hospital, Clarksville, TN '77 (SOC)
HEFNER, RONALD L., asst. vice-pres., United Health Services, Johnson City, NY '78 (PUR)
HEGARTY, STEPHEN J., pres., Massachusetts Hospital Association, Burlington, MA '78
HEGARTY, W. KEVIN, vice chm.-bd. of dir., Huntington Memorial Hospital, Pasadena, CA '86
HEGARTY, WILLIAM J., atty., Melrose-Wakefield Hospital, Melrose, MA '69 (ATTY)
HEGEDUS, JOSEPH R., dir. pers., St. Margaret Memorial Hospital, Pittsburgh, PA '84 (PERS)
HEGEMAN, EARL W., adm., Havenwyck Hospital, Auburn Hills, MI '83
HEGEMAN, KAREN M., coor. staff dev., Dover General Hospital and Medical Center, Dover, NJ '86 (EDUC)
HEGGESTAD, CONNIE R., RN, adm. nrsg. serv., Baptist Hospital, Winner, SD '83 (NURS)
HEGGIE, WILLIAM GRANT JR., pres., Voluntary Hospitals of America Mid-Atlantic States, Inc., Alexandria, VA '65 (PLNG)
HEGSTAD, RICHARD S., dir. pers., Porter Memorial Hospital, Denver, CO '81 (PERS)
HEGYI-GIOIA, DONNA MAE, dir. med. rec., Helene Fuld Medical Center, Trenton, NJ '84
HEHER, JOHN ROBERT, atty., New Jersey Hospital Association, Princeton, NJ '68 (ATTY)
HEIBERGER, CARMELLA, RN, instr., University of California at Los Angeles, School of Nursing, Los Angeles, CA '77 (NURS)
HEID, KARL JACK, dir. pur., American Healthcare Systems, La Jolla, CA '82 (PUR)
HEID, RALPH F., dir. food serv., Warren General Hospital, Warren, PA '82 (FOOD)
HEIDEL, THOMAS D., mgt. eng. analyst, Kaiser Permanente-Southern California Regional, Pasadena, CA '85 (MGMT)
HEIDELBAUGH, HELEN F., staff spec. prof. serv., The Hospital Association of Pennsylvania, Camp Hill, PA '85 (NURS)
HEIDELBERG, ROWLAND W., atty., Forrest County General Hospital, Hattiesburg, MS '71 (ATTY)
HEIDEMAN, CAROL A., RN, dir. nrsg. and cardiovascular, Abbott-Northwestern Hospital, Minneapolis, MN '84 (NURS)
HEIDEMAN, EDITH M., RN, pres., Nursing Management Analysts, Inc., Medford, MA '78 (NURS)
HEIDENHEIM, CAPT. RENE A., MSC USA, chief prop. mgt., Tripler Army Medical Center, Honolulu, HI '84
HEIDENREICH, JAMES C., adm., Kaiser Foundation Hospital, Harbor City, CA '50 (LIFE)
HEIDKAMP, DONALD E., vice-pres. mktg. and dev. serv., Westlake Community Hospital, Melrose Park, IL '73 (PR) (PLNG)
HEIDLEBAUGH, TIM C., mgr. bldg. and grds., Northern Montana Hospital, Havre, MT '84 (ENG)
HEIDTMAN, TERRY L., dir. diet., Saginaw General Hospital, Saginaw, MI '81 (FOOD)
HEIDTMANN, SUSAN A., RN, vice-pres. nrsg. serv., Flushing Hospital and Medical Center, Flushing, NY '86 (NURS)
HEIL, JACK, mgr. mgt. consult., Touche Ross and Company, St. Louis, MO '80 (PLNG)
HEILIG, ALAN B., chm. and chief exec. off., Ambassador Healthcare, Inc., Baltimore, MD '64 (PLNG)
HEILMAN, DIANE C., mgr. diet., Susan B. Allen Memorial Hospital, El Dorado, KS '86 (FOOD)
HEILMAN, ROBERT O., exec. vice-pres., Gmk Associates, Columbia, SC '76 (ENG)
HEIMANN, KATHLEEN J., dir. in-service, St. Joseph's Hospital, Breese, IL '85 (EDUC)
HEIMARCK, JAMES, exec. dir., Regent Health Group, Edison, NJ '76
HEIMARCK, THEODORE, dir. hosp. adm. prog., Concordia College, Moorhead, MN '71
HEIMKE, HOWARD H., dir. pers., Alpena General Hospital, Alpena, MI '76 (PERS)
HEIN, JOYCE GROVER, mgr. human res., Virginia Regional Medical Center, Virginia, MN '82 (PERS)
HEIN, MARK H., corp. dir. mktg., Western Reserve Care System, Youngstown, OH '79 (PLNG)
HEIN, SALLY L., PhD, dir. educ. serv., Dallas County Hospital District-Parkland Memorial Hospital, Dallas, TX '84 (EDUC)
HEINE, ALICE E., pat. rep., J. C. Blair Memorial Hospital, Huntingdon, PA '77 (PAT)
HEINEMAN, THOMAS C., vice-pres. adm., Ingalls Memorial Hospital, Harvey, IL '81
HEINEMANN, CHARLES ALAN, consult., James A. Hamilton Associates, Inc., Minneapolis, MN '65
HEINEMANN, CINDY F., student, Business School and School of Public Health, University of Michigan, Ann Arbor, MI '85
HEINEMANN, I. B., exec. vice-pres., Roanoke Memorial Hospitals, Roanoke, VA '71 (PR)
HEINEN, RAYMOND W., health care consult., Johnson and Higgins, St. Louis, MO '80 (RISK)
HEINEY, DAVID M., EdD, dir. emp. rel. and educ., Williamsport Hospital and Medical Center, Williamsport, PA '83 (PERS)
HEINICKE, SR. MARCELLA, Covenant Medical Center -St. Francis, Waterloo, IA '70 (CS)
HEINLEN, RONALD E., atty., Our Lady of Mercy Hospital, Cincinnati, OH '74 (ATTY)
HEINRICH, BRYAN P., vice-pres. prog. dev., Overlake Hospital Medical Center, Bellevue, WA '85 (PR) (PLNG)
HEINRICH, EDWARD, dir. eng., Engineering Managements Service, Olney, MD '81 (ENG)
HEINRICH, GARY W., dir. emp. rel., National Medical Enterprises, Santa Monica, CA '78 (PERS)
HEINRICH, PAUL E., dir. soc. work, Texas Tech University Health Sciences Center, Ambulatory Clinic, Lubbock, TX '72 (SOC)
HEINRICH, REJEANA R., dir. commun. rel., St. Mary's Hospital, Saginaw, MI '82 (PR)
HEINRICH, TINA, head nrs. emer. room, Gordon Hospital, Calhoun, GA '87 (AMB)
HEINRICHS, LEE, dir. maint. and grds., Kings View Hospital, Reedley, CA '79 (ENG)
HEINS, BARBARA, dir. qual. assur., University Hospital, Seattle, WA '87 (RISK)
HEINS, ROBERT W., dir. med. serv. plan, University of Texas Health Sciences Center, Dallas, TX '83 (RISK)
HEINSOHN, JOHN G., chief exec. off., Visalia Medical Clinic, Inc., Visalia, CA '87 (AMB)
HEINTZ, DUANE H., pres., McNerney, Heintz and Associates, Barrington, IL '74
HEINZ, BONNIE J., sr. mgt. eng., Mersco, Bloomfield Hills, MI '78 (MGMT)
HEINZ, KAY H. SOHN, dir. diet., HCA New Port Richey Hospital, New Port Richey, FL '81 (FOOD)
HEINZELLER, MANFRED, partner, Deloitte Haskins and Sells, Minneapolis, MN '78
HEINZELMAN, LYNN A., dir. commun. rel. and advertising, Bethesda Hospital, Inc., Cincinnati, OH '85 (PR)
HEINZLER, JEROLD J., partner, Denman and Company, West Des Moines, IA '83
HEISE, M. DOUG, dir. bldg. serv., Providence Hospital, Columbia, SC '85 (ENG)

HEISEN, CATHY M., RN, Portland, OR '84 (NURS)
HEISEY, MARY E., RN, mgr. nrs., Rapid City Regional Hospital, Rapid City, SD '84 (NURS)
HEISEY, VIRGINIA E., (ret.), Topeka, KS '70 (SOC)
HEISKELL, ALICE J., asst. vice-pres., Saint Mary Hospital, Langhorne, PA '83
HEISLER, NANCY A., asst. vice-pres., Froedtert Memorial Lutheran Hospital, Milwaukee, WI '84 (PERS)
HEISLER, ROBERT P., Orange Park, FL '73 (FOOD)
HEITHOFF, JAN, asst. pur. agt., Antelope Memorial Hospital, Neligh, NE '84 (PUR)
HEITLER, GEORGE, atty., Kaye, Scholer, Fierman, Et Al, New York, NY '65 (ATTY)
HEITSCH, ROBERT H., sr. pub. rel. spec., University of Chicago Hospitals, Chicago, IL '85 (PR)
HEIWIG, NAOMI NAU, dir. vol. serv., Jackson County Schneck Memorial Hospital, Seymour, IN '83 (VOL)
HEJNA, WILLIAM J., mgt. syst. eng., Foster G. McGaw Hospital, Loyola University, Maywood, IL '80 (MGMT)
HEKHUIS, FRANCES M., asst. adm. psych. and ob. clin. nrsg., Washington Hospital Center, Washington, DC '86 (NURS)
HEKMAN, CALVIN, dir. pat. and family serv., Mercy Hospital, Muskegon, MI '83 (SOC)
HELD, FRED W., dir. plant eng., Good Samaritan Medical Center, Phoenix, AZ '77 (ENG)
HELD, PAUL F., dir. pers., United Hospital, Port Chester, NY '79 (PERS)
HELD, SAMUEL E., chief eng., College Hospital, Cerritos, CA '84 (ENG)
HELFAND, ARTHUR E., co-chief podiatry and dir. podiatry educ., St. Lukes and Children's Medical Center, Philadelphia, PA '66
HELFENSTEIN, CAROLYN J. B., dir. pat. and commun. rel., Rushmore National Health System, Rapid City, SD '81 (PR)
HELFER-AMIRA, SHELLEY, consult., Blue Cross and Blue Shield of Massachusetts, Boston, MA '77
HELFRICH, RICHARD A., reg. contr., Healthamerica of Georgia, Atlanta, GA '79
HELFRICK, GARY M., dir. sup., proc., distrib. and matl. mgt., Harper Hospital, Detroit, MI '81 (CS)
HELIN, ERNEST B., dir. pers., Good Shepherd Medical Center, Longview, TX '67 (PERS)
HELINSKI, DONALD MICHAEL, dir. soc. work serv., Memorial Medical Center of West Michigan, Ludington, MI '85 (SOC)
HELLARD, DANIEL, dir. hskpg., Hardin Memorial Hospital, Elizabethtown, KY '86 (ENVIRON)
HELLE, JUDITH W., RN, dir. nrsg., Graham Hospital, Canton, IL '84 (NURS)
HELLEBRAND, BARBARA A., pat. rep., Good Samaritan Hospital and Health Center, Dayton, OH '85 (PAT)
HELLENBRAND, MICHAL S., RN, dir. nrsg., Fair Oaks Hospital, Summit, NJ '81 (NURS)
HELLER, ALBERTO, sr. vice-pres. fin., Holy Family Hospital, Des Plaines, IL '81 (PLNG)
HELLER, CAREN A., MD, mktg. rel. spec., University of Chicago Hospitals, Chicago, IL '86 (PLNG)
HELLER, ILEEN, dir. vol., Newton-Wellesley Hospital, Newton, MA '77 (VOL)(PAT)
HELLER, J. JEAN, dir. food and nutr. serv., Harrisburg Hospital, Harrisburg, PA '83 (FOOD)
HELLER, MARIANNE J., dir. pat. care coor., Dover General Hospital and Medical Center, Dover, NJ '77 (SOC)
HELLER, RICHARD H., dir. mktg. serv., West Suburban Hospital Medical Center, Oak Park, IL '86 (PR) (PLNG)
HELLINGER, MARTIN B., dir. budget and plng.-nrsg., Newark Beth Israel Medical Center, Newark, NJ '70 (MGMT)
HELLINGMAN, TRICIA A., pub. rel. off., Chedoke-McMaster Hospitals, Hamilton, Ont., Canada '85 (PR)
HELLMAN, RICHARD, dir. pat. and family serv., Green Hospital of Scripps Clinic, La Jolla, CA '86 (SOC)
HELLMER, FRED W., Pacific Palisades, CA '65
HELLSTROM, JANE D., dir. mktg. and pub. rel., Lawnwood Regional Medical Center, Fort Pierce, FL '83 (PR)
HELLZEN, GUSTAF, eng., Kanabec Hospital, Mora, MN '79 (ENG)
HELM, ANN, mgr. qual. assur., Veterans Administration Medical Center, Portland, OR '84 (RISK)
HELM, JEFFREY M., mgr., Ernst and Whinney, Washington, DC '81 (PLNG)
HELM, MICHAEL D., exec. vice-pres., Sparks Regional Medical Center, Fort Smith, AR '72
HELMAN, NATHAN W., (ret.), Chicago, IL '42 (LIFE)
HELMBOLD, RICHARD, chief clin. support, Martin Army Community Hospital, Fort Benning, GA '78
HELMER, ROSEMARIE, RN, dir. nrsg., Northwest Mississippi Regional Medical Center, Clarksdale, MS '79 (NURS)
HELMINSKI, FRANCIS, atty., Harper-Grace Hospitals, Detroit, MI '83 (ATTY)
HELMS, CAROLYN K., dir. soc. serv., Kennestone Hospital, Marietta, GA '74 (SOC)
HELMS, JUDITH G., RN, asst. adm. nrsg. serv., Burbank Community Hospital, Burbank, CA '85 (NURS)
HELMS, NANCY B., dir. pers., R. J. Reynolds-Patrick County Memorial Hospital, Stuart, VA '77 (PERS)
HELMSTETTER, EUGENE C., pur. agt., Hotel Dieu Hospital, New Orleans, LA '83 (PUR)
HELMUTH, KATHRYN M., dir. commun. rel., University General Hospital, Seminole, FL '82 (PR)
HELRIEGEL, BRUCE J., pres., Helriegel-Keenan Advertising, Allentown, PA '86 (PR)
HELSER, COL. CARL W., MSC USA, Fort Sheridan, IL '68
HELSETH, CANDICE A., pub. rel. spec., St. Joseph's Hospital, Minot, ND '84 (PR)
HELSINGER, IRENE S., dir. pers., Spring Branch Memorial Hospital, Houston, TX '77 (PERS)
HELSLEY, SHARON M., RN, nrsg. educ., Midland Memorial Hospital, Midland, TX '86 (EDUC)
HELT, ERIC H., MD, pres., Eric Helt and Associates, Michigan City, IN '86
HELTMAN, MARGARET E., dir. soc. serv., St. Mark's Hospital, Salt Lake City, UT '77 (SOC)
HELVESTINE, WILLIAM A., atty., American Hospital Association, Sacramento, CA '84 (ATTY)
HELVEY, RICHARD, dir. hskpg., St. Charles Hospital, Oregon, OH '86 (ENVIRON)
HELWEG, JAKOB H., dir. arch. serv., Daniel Freeman Memorial Hospital, Inglewood, CA '83
HELZER, JAMES DENNIS, pres., Fresno Community Hospital and Medical Center, Fresno, CA '64
HEMBREE, WILLIAM E., dir., Health Research Institute, Concord, CA '87
HEMELT, LEO, atty., Northshore Regional Medical Center, Slidell, LA '85 (RISK)
HEMLER, FRANK T., pres., Seaboard Energy Systems, Virginia Beach, VA '77 (ENG)
HEMMER, LEWIS E., dir. soc. serv., Pocono Hospital, East Stroudsburg, PA '82 (SOC)
HEMMERLING, BARBARA J., adm. dir., Midwest Center for Day Surgery, Downers Grove, IL '86 (AMB)
HEMNESS, RAY L., adm., HCA Northern Virginia Hospital, Arlington, VA '67
HEMP, SUZANNE M., dir. soc. work serv., Atlantic City Medical Center, Atlantic City, NJ '85 (SOC)
HEMPHILL, DELORES J., dir. vol. serv., AMI Columbia Regional Hospital, Columbia, MO '85 (VOL)
HEMPHILL, JAMES W., vice-pres., Servicemaster Industries, Inc., Downers Grove, IL '74 (FOOD)
HEMPHILL, MICHAEL ROSS, asst. dir. matl. mgt., Charlotte Memorial Hospital and Medical Center, Charlotte, NC '80 (PUR)
HEMRICK, FRANK J., vice-pres. mktg., St. Francis Hospital, Poughkeepsie, NY '86 (PLNG)
HENAULT, RICHARD A., exec. vice-pres., Methodist Health Systems Foundation, Inc., New Orleans, LA '73
HENCH, DOUGLAS G., dir. biomedical eng., Baptist Hospital of Miami, Miami, FL '83 (ENG)
HENCKE, W. RICHARD, MD, dir. emer. medicine, San Jose Hospital, San Jose, CA '87 (AMB)
HENDEE, MICHAEL N., student, Alfred University, Alfred, NY '85
HENDEL, BETTY G., coor. educ., Lutheran Medical Center, St. Louis, MO '85 (EDUC)
HENDELA, MARY, dir. staff dev., Elisabeth Bruyere Health Centre, Ottawa, Ont., Canada '85 (EDUC)
HENDERSON-DAMON, CONNIE S., pres., Henderson-Damon and Associates, Chicago, IL '86 (PLNG)
HENDERSON, ALMARIE, dir. soc. work, Memorial Hospital, Nacogdoches, TX '85 (SOC)
HENDERSON, BRENDA T., dir. vol. serv., Saints Mary and Elizabeth Hospital, Louisville, KY '84 (VOL)
HENDERSON, BROOKS E., dir. biomedical eng., Lutheran General Hospital, Park Ridge, IL '80 (ENG)
HENDERSON, BUNNY SMITH, dir. soc. work, St. Frances Cabrini Hospital, Alexandria, LA '82 (SOC)
HENDERSON, CAROLYN E., RN, mgr. staff educ. and dev., Durham County General Hospital, Durham, NC '82 (EDUC)
HENDERSON, CHRISTINE, dist. dir. educ., Tri-City Medical Center, Oceanside, CA '86 (EDUC)
HENDERSON, CLYDE, dir. pers., Group Health Plan of Southeast Michigan, Troy, MI '80 (PERS)
HENDERSON, CONNIE J., dir. pub. rel. and mktg., Citizens Medical Center, Colby, KS '86 (PLNG)
HENDERSON, DEWEY L., chief eng., Rogue Valley Medical Center, Medford, OR '86 (ENG)
HENDERSON, DONALD G., dir. pers., Beltway Community Hospital, Pasadena, TX '8 (PERS)
HENDERSON, F. JEAN, dir. pub. rel., Washington State Hospital Association, Seattle, WA '79 (PR)
HENDERSON, GEORGE H., atty., Providence Memorial Hospital, El Paso, TX '81 (ATTY)
HENDERSON, GITTENS, assoc. dir. food serv., Brooklyn Hospital-Caledonian Hospital, Brooklyn, NY '79 (FOOD)
HENDERSON, GLENDA SUE, RN, mgr. cent. serv., Wesley Medical Center, Wichita, KS '76 (CS)
HENDERSON, JAMES A., atty., American Hospital Association, Chicago, IL '85 (ATTY)
HENDERSON, JAMES D., adm. asst. to chief of staff, Veterans Administration Medical Center, Iowa City, IA '82
HENDERSON, JOAN KITCHEN, pat. serv. rep., Oak Creek Medical Center-Health Alliance Plan, Livonia, MI '85 (PAT)
HENDERSON, JOSIE L., mgr. matl. mgt., Georgetown University Medical Center, Washington, DC '85 (CS)
HENDERSON, KALEN D., dir. pub. info., Henry County Health Center, Mount Pleasant, IA '82 (PR)
HENDERSON, LINDA CAROL, pat. rep., Terrebonne General Medical Center, Houma, LA '85 (PAT)
HENDERSON, LINDSEY, dir. commun., Detroit Medical Center Corporation, Detroit, MI '79 (ENG)
HENDERSON, LISA C., dir. pub. rel., Sun Coast Hospital, Largo, FL '86 (PR)
HENDERSON, LISA K., staff dev. instr., Golden Triangle Regional Medical Center, Columbus, MS '85 (EDUC)
HENDERSON, M. JAMES, exec. vice-pres., The Methodist Hospital, Houston, TX '73
HENDERSON, MARION, RN, dir. educ., Saint Therese Medical Center, Waukegan, IL '76 (EDUC)
HENDERSON, PRESTON D., dir. maint., Sam Houston Memorial Hospital, Houston, TX '81 (ENG)
HENDERSON, RICHARD F., vice-pres. and gen. mgr., Cigna Hlthplan of Kansas City, Overland Park, KS '86
HENDERSON, ROBERT F. JR., dir. pers., Jackson-Madison County General Hospital, Jackson, TN '82 (PERS)
HENDERSON, ROBERT STEPHAN, util. contracting off., Veterans Administration, Washington, DC '86 (ENG)
HENDERSON, SAMUEL R., atty., Memorial Hospital, St. Joseph, MI '74 (ATTY)(RISK)
HENDERSON, SHELLY, coor. soc. serv., St. Rose de Lima Hospital, Henderson, NV '86 (SOC)
HENDERSON, TEENIA H., dir. pers., Kings Mountain Hospital, Kings Mountain, NC '81 (PERS)
HENDERSON, TERRIE L., dir. pers., Hood General Hospital, Granbury, TX '83 (PERS)
HENDERSON, WILLIAM F. III, dir. pub. rel., Quincy City Hospital, Quincy, MA '82 (PR)
HENDLISZ, JACQUES, dir. gen., Jewish Rehabilitation Hospital, Laval, Que., Canada '83 (PLNG)
HENDRICK, FRANCIS X., asst. vice-pres., Mercy Catholic Medical Center, Darby, PA '84
HENDRICK, LARRY F., mgr. plant, eng. and maint., St. Mary's Health Services, Grand Rapids, MI '80 (ENG)
HENDRICKS, DAVID, assoc. chief amb. care, Veterans Administration Medical Center, Cincinnati, OH '86 (AMB)
HENDRICKS, JANE E., atty., St. Francis Hospital, Miami Beach, FL '82 (ATTY)
HENDRICKS, MARK, asst. vice-pres. and risk mgr., East Tennessee Baptist Hospital, Knoxville, TN '86 (RISK)
HENDRICKS, SHERMAN, exec. vice-pres., Baptist Medical Center Easley, Easley, SC '65
HENDRICKS, SUSAN O., org. dev. spec., University Hospital-University of Nebraska, Omaha, NE '87 (EDUC)
HENDRICKSON, KAREN S., RN, asst. adm. pat. care, Southeast Missouri Hospital, Cape Girardeau, MO '82 (NURS)
HENDRICKSON, MARK L., mktg. commun. spec., Center for Health Sciences, Madison, WI '86 (PLNG)
HENDRICKSON, ROBERT M., PhD, dir. clin. soc. work, St. Albans Psychiatric Hospital, Radford, VA '85 (SOC)
HENDRICKSON, WILLIAM WILSON, pres., Grant Medical Center, Columbus, OH '69
HENDRIX, BARBARA M., risk mgr., Duke University Hospital, Durham, NC '80 (RISK)
HENDRIX, GLORIA JEAN, pat. rep. emer., York Hospital, York, PA '86 (PAT)
HENDRIX, JANET M., consult. food and nutr., Decatur Community Hospital, Decatur, TX '82 (FOOD)
HENDRIX, KAREN A., dir. vol. serv., Cedars Medical Center, Miami, FL '87 (VOL)
HENDRIXSON, TERRI JO, student, Department of Health Services Administration, George Washington University, Washington, DC '85
HENDRY, ROGER S., dir. mgt. eng., Vanderbilt University Hospital, Nashville, TN '80 (MGMT)
HENDRY, VAN C., adm. fellow, Forbes Health System, Pittsburgh, PA '83
HENDY, CAROLYN C., dir. matl. mgt., Charter Northside Community Hospital, Macon, GA '84 (PUR)
HENERY, JOSEPH J., adm., Mount Hood Medical Center, Gresham, OR '77 (PLNG)
HENGEHOLD, PAUL D., dir. pers., Little Traverse Hospital, Petoskey, MI '75 (PERS)
HENGEL, GERALD E., mgr. matl., St. Joseph's Hospital, Stockton, CA '85 (PUR)
HENICAN, CASWELL ELLIS, atty., Mercy Hospital of New Orleans, New Orleans, LA '68 (ATTY)
HENINGER, RALPH H., atty., Mercy Hospital, Davenport, IA '73 (ATTY)
HENISA, HAROLD, dir. maint., Memorial Hospital, Logansport, IN '76 (ENG)
HENK, NANCY E., asst. dir. trng. and educ., John F. Kennedy Medical Center, Chicago, IL '86 (EDUC)
HENKE-DERSHAM, LISA, mgr. bus. unit, Bird Products Corporation, Palm Springs, CA '87
HENKE, CHARLES A., mgr. pur., Huron Valley Hospital, Milford, MI '78 (PUR)
HENKE, MARCELLA V., adm., Memorial Southwest Hospital-Day Surgery Center, Houston, TX '80
HENKE, MARILEE, supv. pat. rel., Deaconess Hospital, Evansville, IN '73 (PAT)
HENKE, SUSAN M., dir. vol. serv., St. Mary's Medical Center, Duluth, MN '87 (VOL)
HENKEL, ARTHUR J. JR., vice-pres., Kidder, Peabody and Company, Inc., New York, NY '73
HENLEY, AMY S., RN, mgr. cent. sup., Regional Medical Center at Memphis, Memphis, TN '85 (CS)
HENLEY, BARBARA M., dir. soc. serv., Ben Taub General Hospital, Houston, TX '68 (SOC)
HENLEY, DONALD EMERSON, family counselor and soc. worker, United Community Hospital, Grove City, PA '85 (SOC)
HENLEY, JOHN T. JR., MD, dir., Fayetteville Ambulatory Services, Inc., Fayetteville, NC '86 (AMB)
HENLEY, CAPT. STEPHEN R., MSC USA, Washington, DC '81
HENLEY, T. L., PhD, dir., Gem City Emergency Association, Beavercreek, OH '87 (AMB)
HENNE, JUDY C., dir. diet., Glenwood State Hospital School, Glenwood, IA '81 (FOOD)
HENNEBERRY, BARBARA OWEN, dir. soc. work, Holy Family Hospital, Spokane, WA '75 (SOC)
HENNEMAN, JOHN T., chief vol. serv., Richard L. Roudebush Veterans Administration Medical Center, Indianapolis, IN '83 (VOL)
HENNEN, RUTH E., dir. vol. serv., Burke Rehabilitation Center, White Plains, NY '83 (VOL)
HENNENFENT, VICTORIA K., dir. pub. rel., Community Memorial Hospital, Monmouth, IL '82 (PR)
HENNES, SR. KARA, RN, vice-pres. nrsg., St. Cloud Hospital, St. Cloud, MN '80 (NURS)
HENNES, RONALD K., RN, vice-pres. nrsg., Mercy Hospital, Merced, CA '85 (NURS)
HENNESSEY, ELIZABETH A., nrs. coor. surg., Kaiser Permanente, East Hartford, CT '87 (EDUC)
HENNESSEY, THOMAS FORD, pres., Lawrence General Hospital, Lawrence, MA '54 (LIFE)
HENNESSY, A. GORDON, assoc. adm., University of New Mexico Hospital-Bernalillo County Medical Center, Albuquerque, NM '71
HENNESSY, JAMES M., dir. mktg., Mesquite Physicians Hospital, Mesquite, TX '86 (PR)
HENNESSY, KIM HASCHER, dir. human res. oper., Catherine McAuley Health Center, Ann Arbor, MI '84 (PERS)
HENNESSY, MARGARET B., student, Rush Presbyterian University, Chicago, IL '85 (PLNG)

HENNESSY, PAT E., vice-pres. plng. and mktg., Lakeland Regional Medical Center, Lakeland, FL '84 (PLNG)
HENNESSY, SUZANNE E., atty., Norton Sound Regional Hospital, Nome, AK '85 (ATTY)
HENNING, EMILY S., dir. mktg., Alliance Health System, Norfolk, VA '87 (PR)
HENNING, GREGORY T., asst. dir. food serv., Albert Einstein Medical Center, Philadelphia, PA '83 (FOOD)
HENNING, SUSAN E., atty., Southern Baptist Hospital, New Orleans, LA '85 (ATTY)
HENNING, WILLIAM K., proj. dir., American Hospital Supply, Equipping and Consulting, Northbrook, IL '73
HENNING, WILLIAM P., vice-pres. human res., St. James Hospital Medical Center, Chicago Heights, IL '86 (PERS)
HENNINGSEN, ANNA M., RN, nrsg. adm. consult. and mem. proj. faculty, St. Xavier College School of Nursing, Chicago, IL '76 (NURS)
HENNINGSEN, LINDA J., coor. pat. educ., Hiawatha Community Hospital, Hiawatha, KS '83 (EDUC)
HENNKE, ROBERT J., dir. plant eng., Kirksville Osteopathic Hospital, Kirksville, MO '85 (ENG)
HENNON, RALPH E. JR., dir. plant oper., Western Reserve Systems-Southside, Youngstown, OH '80 (ENG)
HENRICKS, DEWITT J., mgr. corp. commun., United Health Services, Binghamton, NY '85 (PR)
HENRIETTA, REV. MOTHER, Baton Rouge, LA '36 (LIFE) (RET)
HENRIETTA, SR. MARY, RN, dir. nrsg. serv., Good Samaritan Hospital, Mount Vernon, IL '68 (NURS)
HENRIQUEZ, ANN C., pat. rep., Pendleton Memorial Methodist Hospital, New Orleans, LA '85 (PAT)
HENRY, BEVERLY M., RN, assoc. prof. nrsg. adm., University of Florida, College of Nursing, Gainesville, FL '85 (NURS)
HENRY, CAROLE L., dir. soc. serv., Evergreen Hospital Medical Center, Kirkland, WA '82 (SOC)
HENRY, CATHERINE T., dir. pers., AMI Park Plaza Hospital, Houston, TX '81 (PERS)
HENRY, CHARLES A., dir. pur., Crouse-Irving Memorial Hospital, Syracuse, NY '81 (PUR)
HENRY, CHARLES, dir. hskpg. and ldry. serv., Santa Clara Valley Medical Center, San Jose, CA '86 (ENVIRON)
HENRY, CRAIG CHARLES, student, Graduate Program in Health and Hospital Administration, Tulane University School of Public Health and Tropical Medicine, New Orleans, LA '87
HENRY, DAVID R., dir. eng., Mercy Community Hospital, Port Jervis, NY '86 (ENG)
HENRY, DEBORAH B., dir. vol. serv., Beth Israel Hospital, Boston, MA '81 (VOL)
HENRY, ELIZABETH B., RN, vice-pres. nrsg. serv., Our Lady of Lake Regional Medical Center, Baton Rouge, LA '86 (NURS)
HENRY, JAMES B., dir. pers., Harrisburg Hospital, Harrisburg, PA '74 (PERS)
HENRY, JOANNA A., (ret.), Milton, MA '51 (LIFE)
HENRY, JOHN DUNKLIN, adm. and chief exec. off., Crawford W. Long Memorial Hospital of Emory University, Atlanta, GA '64 (MGMT) (PUR) (ENG) (PLNG)
HENRY, JOSEPH M., Hospital Research and Educational Trust of New Jersey, Princeton, NJ '51 (LIFE)
HENRY, KAREN HAWLEY, atty., Mount Zion Hospital and Medical Center, San Francisco, CA '80 (ATTY)
HENRY, KAROLYN G., dir. pub. rel., HCA Regional Hospital of Jackson, Jackson, TN '84 (PR)
HENRY, MERRELL L., vice-pres. matl. mgt., Healthcor Corporation, Kankakee, IL '80 (PUR)
HENRY, NADINE B., consult., Public Relations and Marketing Communications, Newport Beach, CA '83 (PR)
HENRY, OLGA, supv. telecommun., Columbia Hospital, Milwaukee, WI '80 (ENG)
HENRY, PAUL H., dir. pers., Saddleback Community Hospital, Laguna Hills, CA '82 (PERS)
HENRY, RIC, asst. dir. soc. serv., Loma Linda University Medical Center, Loma Linda, CA '80 (SOC)
HENRY, ROBERTA R., dir. nutr. and food serv., Children's Hospital, Boston, MA '84 (FOOD)
HENRY, RUBY I., coor. staff dev., Salem Hospital, Salem, OR '84 (EDUC)
HENRY, SALLY, RN, dir. educ., Bridgeton Hospital, Bridgeton, NJ '81 (EDUC)
HENRY, VALERIE NICOLE, Memorial Medical Center, Savannah, GA '86
HENRY, WAYNE MARTIN, pres., Brockton Hospital, Brockton, MA '54 (LIFE)
HENRY, WILLIAM F., adm., International Diabetes Center-Park Nicollet Medical Foundation, Minneapolis, MN '86
HENRY, WILLIAM J., dir. pur., Chestnut Lodge Hospital, Rockville, MD '81 (PUR)
HENSE, GERMAINE A., mgr. cent. serv., Finley Hospital, Dubuque, IA '79 (CS)
HENSEL, RONALD R., biomedical eng., Memorial Hospital, Cumberland, MD '83 (ENG)
HENSEY, JOHN J., sr. mgt. eng., University of Wisconsin Hospital and Clinics, Madison, WI '81 (MGMT)
HENSKE, TERRY E., corp. mgr. human res., Sch Health Care System, Houston, TX '86 (PERS)
HENSLEE, JO ANN BUSBEE, coor. pat. rel., Bristol Memorial Hospital, Bristol, TN '86 (PAT)
HENSLEE, R. KENT, atty., Baptist Memorial Hospital, Gadsden, AL '83 (ATTY)
HENSLER, WILLIAM, mgr. plant, Sun Coast Hospital, Largo, FL '81 (ENG)
HENSLEY, ALICE L., pat. rep., Veterans Administration Hospital, Salisbury, NC '86 (PAT)
HENSLEY, CHARLES WARNER, sr. mgt. eng., Fresno Community Hospital and Medical Center, Fresno, CA '80 (MGMT)
HENSLEY, DIANNE, RN, dir. nrsg., Deaconess Hospital, Evansville, IN '85 (NURS)
HENSLEY, DOLA JEAN, asst. dir. pur., Presbyterian Hospital, Oklahoma City, OK '86 (PUR)
HENSLEY, DORIS N., RN, dir. pat. rel., Methodist Evangelical Hospital, Louisville, KY '86 (PAT)
HENSLEY, JACK F., Wayne County Memorial Hospital, Honesdale, PA '49 (PR)(LIFE)
HENSLEY, SR. MARY PAUL, guest rel. rep., St. Elizabeth Medical Center, Granite City, IL '81 (PAT)
HENSLEY, MIKAL P., dir. pur., Chisago Health Services, Chisago City, MN '86 (PUR)
HENSLIN, ARLENE FRANCES, dir. diet., Bethesda Hospital, Chicago, IL '80 (FOOD)
HENSON, E. BRYAN JR., atty., Century Healthcare Corporation, Tulsa, OK '86 (ATTY)
HENSON, FRED T., dir. food serv., Hartselle Medical Center, Hartselle, AL '82 (FOOD)
HENSON, GLORIA A., dir. human res., Spohn Hospital, Corpus Christi, TX '83 (PERS)
HENSON, PATRICIA A., RN, dir. pat. care, Keokuk Area Hospital, Keokuk, IA '85 (NURS)
HENSON, ROBERT, dir. facil., Northridge Hospital Medical Center, Northridge, CA '87 (ENG)
HENTHORN, MARK A., mgt. eng., Colonel Florence A. Blanchfield Army Community Hospital, Fort Campbell, KY '86 (ENG)
HENTSCHEL, LINDA CHRISTINE CLOYD, dir. food serv., ARA Services, Health Care Nutrition Services, Chicago, IL '78 (FOOD)
HENWOOD, ROBERT E., Los Angeles, CA '49 (LIFE)
HENZ, KAREN R., dir. food serv., AMI Presbyterian-St. Luke's Medical Center, Denver, CO '76 (FOOD)
HENZE, CAROLYN W., dir. mgt. serv., Emergency Physician Associates, Woodbury, NJ '87 (AMB)
HENZE, HOWARD M., asst. dir. emer. medicine, Hospital of the University of Pennsylvania, Philadelphia, PA '84 (PLNG)(AMB)
HEPKIN, NORMA, dir. soc. serv., Franklin Boulevard Community Hospital, Chicago, IL '77 (PAT)(SOC)
HEPLER, CHARLES E., dir. hskpg. and ldry., Ashtabula County Medical Center, Ashtabula, OH '86 (ENVIRON)
HEPLER, MERRILEE, dir. human res., Hyde Park Hospital, Chicago, IL '86 (PERS)
HEPNER, BARBARA L., dir. pub. rel., Lodi Memorial Hospital, Lodi, CA '84 (PR)
HEPNER, JAMES O., PhD, dir. health care adm., Washington University School of Medicine, Graduate Program in Hospital Administration, St. Louis, MO '57 (LIFE)
HEPNER, LARRY F., RN, asst. dir. nrsg., National Hospital for Orthopaedics and Rehabilitation, Arlington, VA '85 (NURS)
HEPP, DENNIS C., mgr. transcare venture, Medtronic, Inc., Minneapolis, MN '86 (ENG)
HERALD, BEVERLY T., dir. pers. and commun. rel., Muhlenberg Community Hospital, Greenville, KY '86 (PR)
HERB, WANDA C., RN, dir. vol. serv., Holy Cross Hospital, Silver Spring, MD '79 (VOL)
HERBA, CHERYL, RN, asst. adm., Bon Secours Hospital, Grosse Pointe, MI '80 (NURS)
HERBECK, DANIEL, supv. maint., Straith Memorial Hospital, Southfield, MI '81 (ENG)
HERBER, WILLIAM E. JR., adm., Muncie Eye Surgi-Center, Muncie, IN '73 (PUR)
HERBERMANN, CHARLES G. JR., atty., Bronxville, NY '73 (ATTY)
HERBERT, ELEANOR, RN, dir. nrsg., Manhattan Eye, Ear and Throat Hospital, New York, NY '86 (NURS)
HERBERT, JAMES ADAM, RN, dir. nrsg., Opelousas General Hospital, Opelousas, LA '69 (NURS)
HERBERT, JOHN W., pres., Blue Cross and Blue Shield of Florida, Inc., Jacksonville, FL '49 (LIFE)
HERBERT, KATHY D., pat. rep., Methodist Hospital of Middle Mississippi, Lexington, MS '86 (PAT)
HERBERT, SR. PAULINE, RN, vice-pres. nrsg., Providence Hospital, Sandusky, OH '82 (NURS)
HERBERT, STEPHEN W., pres., Royal Victoria Hospital, Montreal, Que., Canada '67
HERBOLD, CARL F. JR., atty., California Hospital Association, Sacramento, CA '81 (ATTY)
HERBRECHTMEIER, HELMUT, chief eng., St. Mary's Hospital, Reno, NV '83 (ENG)
HERBRUCK, GRETCHEN S., assoc., Heidrick and Struggles, Inc., Cleveland, OH '86 (MGMT)
HERBST, ALAN LEWIS, pur. agt., Sibley Memorial Hospital, Washington, DC '76 (PUR)
HERBST, DOROTHY B., RN, coor. pat. educ., Newark-Wayne Community Hospital, Newark, NY '83 (EDUC)
HERBST, RICHARD E., dir. plant eng., Menorah Medical Center, Kansas City, MO '85 (ENG)
HERBST, ROBERT HOWARD, chief eng., Fisher-Titus Medical Center, Norwalk, OH '72 (ENG)
HERBY, DIANE J., dir. vol. serv., California Hospital Association, Sacramento, CA '81 (VOL)
HERCHER, MONA R., student, Program in Health Care Administration, University of Houston at Clear Lake City, Houston, TX '83
HERDA, INGRID VIVIANNE, asst. dir. pat. rel., Northridge Hospital Medical Center, Northridge, CA '86 (PAT)
HERDELIN, SANDRA J., dir. matl. mgt., Spartanburg Regional Medical Center, Spartanburg, SC '85 (PUR)
HERDINA, ANNE E., asst. dir. mktg., West Oaks Hospital-Fort Bend, Sugar Land, TX '86 (PR)
HERDT, BARBRA A., RN, asst. dir. nrsg., Penrose Community Hospital, Colorado Springs, CO '86 (NURS)
HERFINDAHL, LOWELL D., adm., Tioga Community Hospital, Tioga, ND '73
HERGENREDER, DONALD W., proj. mgr., Healthmark Corporation, Pittsburgh, PA '78 (ENG)
HERIOT, RICHARD M., vice-pres. pat. care serv., North Carolina Baptist Hospital, Winston-Salem, NC '68
HERKALA, WILLIAM J., dir. human res., Loretto Geriatric Center, Syracuse, NY '82 (PERS)
HERLIHY, BRENDAN P., mgr. cent. serv., Lowell General Hospital, Lowell, MA '75 (CS)
HERLIHY, JEROME O., atty., Riverside Hospital, Wilmington, DE '85 (ATTY)
HERLIHY, PATRICIA A., RN, assoc. dir. surg., Presbyterian Hospital in the City of New York, New York, NY '85 (NURS)
HERMALIK, GEORGE E., proj. mgr., Hayes, Large, Suckling and Fruth, Altoona, PA '76
HERMALYN, DEBORAH PIZER, dir. soc. serv., Edgewater Hospital, Chicago, IL '77 (SOC)
HERMAN, ALLEN I., chief exec. off., Nephrology Fund of Brooklyn, Brooklyn, NY '76
HERMAN, ANITA A., dir. food serv., ARA Hlthcare Nutrition Service, Stockton, CA '86 (FOOD)
HERMAN, B. MICHAEL, atty., Blue Cross and Blue Shield of Southwestern Virginia, Roanoke, VA '82 (ATTY)
HERMAN, BERNARD J., exec. vice-pres., Mercy Hospital, Bakersfield, CA '75
HERMAN, CARLA E., sr. consult. health care practice, Peat, Marwick, Mitchell and Company, New York, NY '84 (PLNG)
HERMAN, DANIEL S., Medicus, Evanston, IL '84 (MGMT)
HERMAN, ELMER W., dir. matl. mgt., Harmarville Rehabilitation Center, Pittsburgh, PA '81 (PUR)
HERMAN, FRAN, mgr. cent. serv., Hendricks County Hospital, Danville, IN '83 (CS)
HERMAN, GORDON R., mgr. constr., Mercy Center for Health Care Services, Aurora, IL '86 (ENG)
HERMAN, JAMES JOSEPH, pres., Daughters of Charity Health Systems-West, Los Altos Hills, CA '55 (LIFE)
HERMAN, JAY R., atty., Jersey Shore Medical Center, Neptune, NJ '79 (ATTY)
HERMAN, JOHN WILLIAM, vice-pres., Methodist Hospital, St. Louis Park, MN '79
HERMAN, KENNETH H., supv. maint., Smith County Memorial Hospital, Smith Center, KS '82 (ENG)
HERMAN, LAUREL A., owner, Laurel Design-Direction, Pittsburgh, PA '86 (PR) (PLNG)
HERMAN, OLIVIA S., dir. vol., Allentown Osteopathic Medical Center, Allentown, PA '80 (VOL)
HERMAN, PATRICIA K., RN, dir. nrsg., St. Luke's Memorial Hospital Center, New Hartford, NY '84 (NURS)
HERMAN, RICHARD G., dir. soc. serv., St. Joseph's Hospital and Medical Center, Phoenix, AZ '73 (SOC)
HERMAN, WAYNE JAMES, clin. eng., Southwest Community Health Services, Albuquerque, NM '81 (ENG)
HERMANN, DONALD H. J., atty., DePaul University College of Law, Evanston, IL '85 (ATTY)
HERMANN, HELEN M., dir. pers., St. Lukes Hospital of Middleborough, Middleboro, MA '83 (PERS)
HERMANN, JOAN F., dir. soc. work, American Oncologic Hospital, Philadelphia, PA '77 (SOC)
HERMANN, KENNETH G., exec. dir., Omaha Council Bluffs Hospital Association, Omaha, NE '69
HERMANSON, JERRY, mgt. consult., North Federal Management Group, Inc., Deerfield Beach, FL '72
HERMIDA, ROBERT J., dir. diet. serv., AMI Twelve Oaks Hospital, Houston, TX '82 (FOOD)
HERN, KARIN J., atty., Alta Bates Hospital, Berkeley, CA '82 (ATTY)
HERN, TIMOTHY M., dir. plant serv., Tucson Medical Center, Tucson, AZ '84 (ENG)
HERNANDEZ, ANTONIO J., elec. eng., Pan American Health Organization, San Jose, Costa Rica '84 (ENG)
HERNANDEZ, GILBERT, mgr. matl., Huguley Memorial Hospital, Fort Worth, TX '78 (PUR)
HERNANDEZ, HANK, affil. adm., Beth Israel Medical Center, New York, NY '74
HERNANDEZ, JOHN ANTHONY, assoc. exec. dir., Woodhull Medical and Mental Health Center, Brooklyn, NY '76 (PERS)
HERNANDEZ, JOSIE M., dir. environ. serv., Monterey Park Hospital, Monterey Park, CA '86 (ENVIRON)
HERNANDEZ, JOYCE, cent. serv. tech., St. Anthony Hospital, Michigan City, IN '86 (CS)
HERNANDEZ, RALPH C., dir. soc. serv. and home health care, San Bernardino County Medical Center, San Bernardino, CA '85 (SOC)
HERNANDEZ, ROBERTO, Hospital San Pablo, Bayamon, P.R. '79
HERNANDEZ, RUDY A., dir. eng., King William Health Care Center, San Antonio, TX '85 (ENG)
HERNDON-CROSS, LYNDA L., dir., Cape Surgery Center, Sarasota, FL '87 (AMB)
HERNDON, GAY B., pat. rep., Shawnee Mission Medical Center, Shawnee Mission, KS '85 (PAT)
HERNDON, JACK D., dir. matl. mgt., Medical Center of Central Georgia, Macon, GA '86 (PUR)
HERNDON, THERESA A., coor. prod. dev., Mercy Hospital Medical Center, Des Moines, IA '86 (PLNG)
HEROD, WALTER R., dir. matl. mgt., West Nebraska General Hospital, Scottsbluff, NE '82 (PUR)
HERONIME, MYRTLE D., RN, dir. nrsg.-staff and support serv., Stormont-Vail Regional Medical Center, Topeka, KS '85 (NURS)
HERPICH, BRUCE J., sr. mgt. eng., Temple University Hospital, Philadelphia, PA '76 (MGMT)
HERPICH, MARY E., corp. risk mgr., Universal Health Services, Inc., King of Prussia, PA '85 (RISK)
HERPOLSHEIMER, KAREN S., RN, asst. chief nrsg. serv., Veterans Administration Medical Center, Manchester, NH '83 (NURS)
HERR, GREGORY L., dir. clin. eng., Christ Hospital, Cincinnati, OH '84 (ENG)
HERR, GUY C., assoc., Michaud, Cooley, Erickson and Associates, Inc., Minneapolis, MN '83 (ENG)
HERREN, PHILLIP W., dir. mgt. serv., Michigan Hospital Association, Lansing, MI '80 (MGMT)
HERRERA, BENNETT, dir. soc. work, Coney Island Hospital, Brooklyn, NY '82 (SOC)
HERRERA, CHARLES R., dir. eng. serv., Antelope Valley Hospital Medical Center, Lancaster, CA '80 (ENG)
HERRERA, JEAN E., supv. soc. worker, Veterans Administration Medical Center, Portland, OR '81 (SOC)

HERRERA, PRISCILLA, dir. vol. serv., Los Lunas Hospital and Training School, Los Lunas, NM '81 (VOL)
HERRICK, DENNIS ROBERT, corp. contr., William Beaumont Hospital, Royal Oak, MI '86
HERRICK, MARGE J., dir. matl. mgt., Wyoming Medical Center, Casper, WY '82 (PUR)
HERRICK, MICHAEL W., mgr., Ernst and Whinney, St. Louis, MO '78
HERRIG, GREG, dir. biomedical serv., Mother Frances Hospital Regional Center, Tyler, TX '85 (ENG)
HERRIN, COL. DANIEL M. JR., MSC USAF, consult. health care mgt., Gambier, OH '48 (PLNG)(LIFE)
HERRIN, SAMMY H., dir. eng., Forrest County General Hospital, Hattiesburg, MS '79 (ENG)
HERRIN, SIMMIE P., dir. pur., Gulf Coast Community Hospital, Biloxi, MS '82 (PUR)
HERRING, ANN SMITH, dir. soc. work, Burke Rehabilitation Center, White Plains, NY '77 (SOC)
HERRING, DEBRA, clin. investigator, Northwestern Memorial Hospital, Chicago, IL '85 (RISK)
HERRING, DONALD CLAY, mgr. comp., St. Luke's-Roosevelt Hospital Center, New York, NY '68 (PERS)
HERRING, EMLA, RN, dir. sup., proc. and distrib., Desert Samaritan Hospital, Mesa, AZ '87 (PUR)
HERRING, GAIL MARIE, Goldwater Memorial Hospital, New York, NY '79 (SOC)
HERRING, MICHAEL S., adm., South Peninsula Hospital, Homer, AK '78
HERRING, NEIL C., dir. bus. dev., Damon Clinical Laboratory, Needham Heights, MA '85 (PLNG)
HERRING, R. MARK, pres., Mha Marketing Services, Inc., Overland Park, KS '84 (EDUC)(PR)
HERRING, ROSELMA, dir. food serv., Culpeper Memorial Hospital, Culpeper, VA '78 (FOOD)
HERRING, WAYNE, asst. dir. environ. serv., Abington Memorial Hospital, Abington, PA '86 (ENVIRON)
HERRINGER, SR. ANNE, pat. rep., Dominican Santa Cruz Hospital, Santa Cruz, CA '78 (PAT)
HERRINGTON, BETTY, dir. vol. serv., Lake West Hospital, Willoughby, OH '78 (VOL)
HERRINGTON, RICHARD, dir. pub. rel., St. Anthony Hospital, Oklahoma City, OK '85 (PR)
HERRMAN, CASSANDRA C., coor. vol. serv., Phelps County Regional Medical Center, Rolla, MO '85 (VOL)
HERRMAN, JAMES M., sr. vice-pres., Fred S. James and Company of Illinois, Chicago, IL '86 (RISK)
HERRMANN, HARRY, dir. maint. eng., Basic American Medical, Inc., Fort Myers, FL '84 (ENG)
HERRMANN, KARYN A., mgt. eng., William Beaumont Hospital, Southfield, MI '84 (MGMT)
HERRMANN, RICHARD C., exec. vice-pres., Mercy Hospital, Rockville Centre, NY '59
HERRMANN, WILLIAM RONALD, mgr. pat. and family serv., St. Anthony Hospital Systems, Denver, CO '87 (PAT)
HERROLD, STUART R., exec. vice-pres., Frederick Memorial Hospital, Frederick, MD '69
HERRON, JAY S., audit mgr., Arthur Andersen and Company, Albuquerque, NM '85
HERRON, JOHN C., vice-pres., ARA Services, Inc.-Hospital Food Management, Philadelphia, PA '70 (FOOD)
HERRON, KATHRYN, student, Program in Hospital Administration, University of Michigan, School of Public Health, Ann Arbor, MI '85
HERRON, LAWRENCE D., dir. risk mgt., Sisters of Mercy Health Corporation, Southfield, MI '80 (RISK)
HERRON, ROBIN T., asst. dir. pub. rel., Alexandria Hospital, Alexandria, VA '86 (PR)
HERRUP, CAROLE, dir. corp. commun., Atlantic City Medical Center, Atlantic City, NJ '86 (PR)
HERSBERGER, ROBERT W., RN, vice-pres. clin. serv., Bethesda Hospital, Zanesville, OH '76 (NURS)
HERSCH, GEORGE Y., dir. matl. mgt., Fairfax Hospital Association, Springfield, VA '78 (PUR)
HERSCHER, MARY, dir. soc. serv., Riverside Hospital, Toledo, OH '85 (SOC)
HERSCOVICI, LEONARD, exec. dir., United Surgi-Center, Warminster, PA '84 (AMB)
HERSHBERG, MARSHALL A., dir. bus. res., South Hills Health System, Pittsburgh, PA '86 (PLNG)
HERSHBERGER, HERB L., dir. matl. mgt., Children's Hospital Medical Center, Akron, OH '86 (PUR)
HERSHBERGER, KENNETH E., dir. commun. rel. and mktg., St. Luke's Hospital, Newburgh, NY '86 (PR)
HERSHER, BETSY S., pres., Hersher Associates, Ltd., Northbrook, IL '81 (MGMT)
HERSHEY, NATHAN, res. prof. law, Graduate School of Public Health, University of Pittsburgh, Pittsburgh, PA '68 (ATTY)
HERSKOVITZ, DELMA, dir. vol., Bon Secours Hospital, Baltimore, MD '77 (VOL)
HERTEL, JANICE, dir. vol. serv., Saratoga Community Hospital, Detroit, MI '83 (VOL)
HERTER, BARBARA J., supv. cent. serv., St. Joseph Medical Center, Wichita, KS '87 (CS)
HERTKO, VICTORIA A., RN, dir. emer. and critical care, Iowa Methodist Medical Center, Des Moines, IA '83 (NURS)
HERTZ, DENNIS J., adm. asst. and of mgr. medicine, Buffalo General Hospital, Buffalo, NY '85
HERTZ, PAUL, dir. food serv., HCA Riveredge Hospital, Forest Park, IL '77 (FOOD)
HERTZBERG, DEBRA, adm., Kenosha Visiting Nurse Association, Inc., Kenosha, WI '86 (AMB)
HERTZING, VONNIE, dir. human res., Charter Springs Hospital, Ocala, FL '86 (PERS)
HERTZLER, CLAIRE, asst. dir. vol. serv., Grady Memorial Hospital, Atlanta, GA '84 (VOL)
HERTZLER, DONALD E., dir. pers., Mercy Memorial Hospital, Urbana, OH '87 (PERS)
HERTZOG, JEAN M., dir. vol. serv., Community General Hospital, Reading, PA '86 (VOL)
HERWATT, ROSALIE, RN, exec. assoc., Saint Thomas Medical Center, Akron, OH '80
HERZ, RALPH JR., MD, med. dir., Corson Group, New York, NY '79
HERZBERG, VIRGINIA NORMA, dir. soc. serv., Community General Hospital, Harris, NY '78 (SOC)
HERZEL, MAX, adm. asst. to chief of staff, Veterans Administration Medical Center, Birmingham, AL '78
HERZER, DAVID L., atty., Lorain Community Hospital, Lorain, OH '72 (ATTY)
HERZFELD, JOAN, asst. vice-pres., Baptist Medical Center, Jacksonville, FL '86
HERZIG, ROBERT W., vice-pres. corp. dev., Summit Health, Ltd., Los Angeles, CA '85
HERZOG, BARRY, adm., Fayetteville Diagnostic Clinic, Ltd., Fayetteville, AR '87 (AMB)
HERZOG, MARK P., adm. res., Healthmark Corporation, Pittsburgh, PA '81
HERZOG, PAUL F., dir. support serv., Yavapai Regional Medical Center, Prescott, AZ '80 (PUR)
HERZOG, THOMAS, RN, vice-pres. pat. care serv., Ingalls Memorial Hospital, Harvey, IL '74 (NURS)
HESALTINE, ROBERT G., dir. facil. and plng., National Hospital for Orthopaedic and Rehabilitation, Arlington, VA '63 (ENG)
HESCH, FREDERICK P., dir. facil. dev., St. Joseph Hospital, Eureka, CA '79 (ENG)
HESEN, BENEDICT E., exec. dir., Livingston County Hospital, Salem, KY '64
HESKETT, MARVIN D., RN, dir. nrsg. serv., North Lincoln Hospital, Lincoln City, OR '80 (NURS)
HESS, ANN M., asst. exec. dir. pat. serv., St. John Hospital, Leavenworth, KS '83 (NURS)
HESS, CAROLYN K., RN, dir. nrsg., Pocahontas Community Hospital, Pocahontas, IA '83 (NURS)
HESS, CHERYL ANN, dir. soc. serv., Saint Thomas Medical Center, Akron, OH '84 (SOC)
HESS, DEAN K., dir. food serv., Humana Hospital -Cypress, Pompano Beach, FL '81 (FOOD)
HESS, E. GLENN, dir. facil. eng., Cleveland Clinic Hospital, Cleveland, OH '80 (ENG)
HESS, ESMERALDA S., student, Texas Woman's University, Dallas, TX '85
HESS, FURF, dir. pub. rel. and mktg. commun., Timken Mercy Medical Center, Canton, OH '82 (PR)
HESS, GEORGIA L., dir. vol. serv., St. Mary's Hospital of Kankakee, Kankakee, IL '84 (VOL)
HESS, JOHN J., owner, Biomedical Services of Santa Barbara, Santa Barbara, CA '73 (ENG)
HESS, LOIS K., atty. and dir. pat. serv., University Hospital, St. Louis University Center, St. Louis, MO '86 (ATTY)(RISK)
HESS, MARY H., supv. sterile proc., Vaughan Regional Medical Center, Selma, AL '75 (CS)
HESS, MARY LOU, RN, dir. nrsg. adm., St. Benedict's Hospital, Ogden, UT '82 (NURS)
HESS, OLIVIA V., mgr. pers., John Randolph Hospital, Hopewell, VA '81 (PERS)
HESS, PAUL E., pres., St. Elizabeth Hospital Medical Center, Lafayette, IN '84 (PR) (PLNG)
HESS, SANDY, dir. vol., Bryn Mawr Hospital, Bryn Mawr, PA '86 (VOL)
HESSBERG, ALBERT II, atty., Albany Medical Center Hospital, Albany, NY '73 (ATTY)
HESSE, GORDON L., dir. pub. rel., Kimball Medical Center, Lakewood, NJ '86 (PR)
HESSE, J. FRANCIS, exec. vice-pres. and atty., St. Francis Regional Medical Center, Wichita, KS '68 (ATTY)
HESSE, JAMES P., student, Program in Hospital Administration, University of Houston at Clearlake City, Houston, TX '83
HESSE, JERALEA F., dir. soc. serv., Silver Hill Foundation Hospital, New Canaan, CT '86 (SOC)
HESSE, NORLA, dir. educ., Immanuel-St. Joseph's Hospital, Mankato, MN '76 (EDUC)
HESSERT, PETER L., atty., Wausau Hospital Center, Wausau, WI '82 (ATTY)
HESSING, DAVID F., atty., Henry County Medical Center, Paris, TN '80 (ATTY)
HESSION, EILEEN M., RN, student, Boston University Health Management Programs, Boston, MA '86 (PLNG)
HESSION, SR. MAGDALEN, pat. rep., Saint Joseph Hospital, Fort Worth, TX '79 (PAT)
HESSLER, DONA M., assoc. adm. nrsg., Oak Forest Hospital of Cook County, Oak Forest, IL '69 (NURS)
HESSON, JOHN D. JR., matl. mgt. consult., Hospital Corporation of America, Nashville, TN '82 (PUR)
HESSON, WILLIAM W., atty., University of Iowa Hospitals and Clinics, Iowa City, IA '80 (ATTY)
HESTER, CHARLES R., asst. dir., Clarendon Memorial Hospital, Manning, SC '80 (RISK)
HESTER, CURTIS L., dir. soc. serv., St. Elizabeths Hospital, Washington, DC '83 (SOC)
HESTER, DOLORES, coor. educ. and trng., St. Joseph's Hospital, Highland, IL '79 (EDUC)
HESTER, JAMES A. JR., asst. prof., University of Lowell, Department of Health, Lowell, MA '75 (MGMT)
HESTER, JOEY A., dir. matl. mgt., Flowers Hospital, Dothan, AL '86 (PUR)
HESTER, SUSAN M., dir. vol. serv., Wake Medical Center, Raleigh, NC '78 (VOL)
HESTNESS, GARY E., mgr. outreach serv., Hazelden Foundation, Center City, MN '85 (PR)
HESTON, HARRY E., vice-pres., Pennsylvania Hospital, Philadelphia, PA '76
HETHCOCK, ALVA D., exec. consult., Warm Springs Services Corporation, Victoria, TX '65
HETHERINGTON, BETTY J., dir. pers., AMI Nacogdoches Medical Center Hospital, Nacogdoches, TX '84 (PERS)
HETHERINGTON, J. GEORGE, atty., Kuakini Medical Center, Honolulu, HI '84 (ATTY)
HETHERITON, AL, dir. plant oper. and maint., Central Kansas Medical Center, Great Bend, KS '86 (ENG)
HETLAGE, C. KENNON, assoc. vice-pres., Barnes Hospital, St. Louis, MO '87 (AMB)
HETNER, JAMES F., dir. soc. work serv., Outer Drive Hospital, Lincoln Park, MI '81 (SOC)
HETRICK, DONNA P., dir. pub. rel. and mktg., Mary Washington Hospital, Fredericksburg, VA '85 (PR)
HETSON, LINDA L., mktg. and plng. assoc., Children's Hospital Medical Center, Akron, OH '83 (PLNG)
HETT, PAMELA A., mktg. analyst, MacNeal Hospital, Berwyn, IL '85 (PLNG)
HETZEL, ROBERT WILLIAM, dir. pers., St. Luke Hospital, Fort Thomas, KY '76 (PERS)
HETZEL, STEPHEN WALTER, dir. human res., Iowa Lutheran Hospital, Des Moines, IA '79 (PERS)
HETZLER, W. P., mgr. eng. and maint., Medical Center Hospital, Odessa, TX '85 (ENG)
HEUBEL, MADELINE L., prog. coor., U. S. Army Hospital, APO New York, NY '82
HEUCK, JAMES M., dir. pers. and pub. rel., West Volusia Memorial Hospital, De Land, FL '73 (PERS)
HEUEL, NORBERT W., dir. pers., Foster G. McGaw Hospital, Loyola University of Chicago, Maywood, IL '78 (PERS)
HEUER, PAT, RN, mgr. qual. assur. and util. review, Lutheran General Health Plan, Park Ridge, IL '87 (AMB)
HEUERMAN, JAMES N., mng. vice-pres., Korn-Ferry International, San Francisco, CA '79 (PLNG)
HEUMANN, JANET, RN, asst. vice-pres. human res., American Medical International, Los Angeles, CA '83 (NURS)
HEUSEY, GARY L., mgt. eng., Western Pennsylvania Hospital, Pittsburgh, PA '83 (MGMT)
HEWITT, ARLENE MAY, dir. soc. work, Alexandria Hospital, Alexandria, VA '68 (SOC)
HEWITT, BENJAMIN N., atty., Niagara Falls Memorial Medical Center, Niagara Falls, NY '79 (ATTY)
HEWITT, DAVID R., dir. mktg. and pub. rel., Gerber Memorial Hospital, Fremont, MI '85 (PR)
HEWITT, TIMOTHY NEAL, student, Tulane University, School of Public Health and Tropical Medicine, New Orleans, LA '85
HEWLETT, ELIZABETH M., atty., Prince George's Hospital Center, Cheverly, MD '86 (ATTY)
HEWLETT, PAUL, dir. plant serv., Boulder Memorial Hospital, Boulder, CO '86 (ENG)
HEWSON, THEODORE S., asst. vice-pres. info. serv., Our Lady of Lourdes Medical Center, Camden, NJ '86 (MGMT)
HEYD, DONNA A., RN, dir. nrsg., F. Edward Hebert Hospital, New Orleans, LA '82 (NURS)
HEYD, EDWARD H., (ret.), Hampton Bays, NY '50 (LIFE)
HEYD, GWEN, dir. vol. serv., Dakota Midland Hospital, Aberdeen, SD '78 (VOL)
HEYDE, JORGE A., student, University of Tennessee, Nashville, TN '86
HEYDEMANN, HELAINE, atty., Northwestern Memorial Hospital, Chicago, IL '75 (ATTY)
HEYDINGER, THOMAS A., atty., Mary Rutan Hospital, Bellefontaine, OH '78 (ATTY)
HEYER, CAROLYN A., sr. tech., New Milford Hospital, New Milford, CT '81 (CS)
HEYMAN, LYNN, dir. vol. serv., AMI Kendall Regional Medical Center, Miami, FL '84 (VOL)
HEYMAN, NEIL F., adm. asst., St. Joseph Hospital and Health Care Center, Tacoma, WA '81
HEYWOOD, GRACE C., coor. vol. serv., Roxborough Memorial Hospital, Philadelphia, PA '86 (VOL)
HIATT, LEIGH ANNE H., dir. mktg. and pub. rel., Marymount Hospital, London, KY '82 (PR)
HIBBARD, CURT E., St. Joseph Regional Medical Center, Lewiston, ID '81 (ENG)
HIBBARD, GEORGE L., legal counsel, Willamette Falls Hospital, Oregon City, OR '76 (ATTY)
HIBBARD, JAN C., dir. pur., Underwood-Memorial Hospital, Woodbury, NJ '84
HIBBITT, JANE H., dir. vol. serv., Walter O. Boswell Memorial Hospital, Sun City, AZ '78 (VOL)
HIBBS, C. WAYNE, vice-pres., Performance Network, Dallas, TX '86 (ENG)
HIBBS, JOHN E., pur. agt., Fairmont General Hospital, Fairmont, WV '72 (PUR)
HIBBS, JOHN S., atty., Fairview Hospital and Healthcare Service, Minneapolis, MN '82 (ATTY)
HIBBS, PATRICIA S., instr. staff dev., Tidewater Psychiatric Institute, Virginia Beach, VA '86 (EDUC)
HIBIT, DENISE L., dir. food serv., Odd Fellow and Rebekah Nursing Home, Lockport, NY '84 (FOOD)
HICE, DANA C., student, Program in Health Service Administration, School of Health Professions, Governors State University, Park Forest South, IL '84
HICKEY, CINDY L., coor. mktg. commun., Timken Mercy Medical Center, Canton, OH '86 (PR)
HICKEY, DONALD F., asst. dir. nutr., Bronx-Lebanon Hospital Center, Bronx, NY '68 (FOOD)
HICKEY, GEORGE JOSEPH JR., asst. vice-pres., Rhode Island Hospital, Providence, RI '62 (EDUC)
HICKEY, JUDITH E., dir. mktg., St. Elizabeth's Hospital of Boston, Boston, MA '86 (PLNG)
HICKEY, KAREN J., dir. human resources, Valley Medical Center, Renton, WA '85 (PERS)
HICKEY, KEVIN F., exec. vice-pres., First Health Associates, Inc., Chicago, IL '82 (ATTY)
HICKEY, LAURA MARIE, supv. soc. serv., St. Vincent's Medical Center, Jacksonville, FL '79 (SOC)
HICKEY, LOUISE A., RN, asst. adm. pat. serv., Melrose-Wakefield Hospital, Melrose, MA '71 (NURS)
HICKEY, MARY W., RN, dir. nrsg., Gaylord Hospital, Wallingford, CT '84 (NURS)
HICKEY, MIV, dir. vol. serv., Baptist Hospital, Nashville, TN '76 (VOL)
HICKEY, ROBERT C., vice-pres. emp. rel., Baptist Medical Center of Oklahoma, Oklahoma City, OK '85 (PERS)
HICKEY, ROBERT J., atty., Providence Hospital, Washington, DC '71 (ATTY)
HICKEY, ROSE M., dir. mktg. and pub. rel., Sloop Memorial Hospital, Crossnore, NC '85 (PR)
HICKEY, SHARON L., staff dev. nrs., St. Peters Community Hospital, St. Peters, MO '85 (EDUC)

HICKLE, ELIZABETH J., corp. mgr., University Dermatologist, Inc., Cleveland, OH '87 (AMB)
HICKMAN, DEWEY C., dir. plng., Medical College of Virginia Hospitals, Richmond, VA '81 (PLNG)
HICKMAN, GEORGE THOMAS JR., mgr., Price Waterhouse, Pittsburgh, PA '82 (MGMT)
HICKMAN, WILL A., atty., Oxford-Lafayette Medical Center, Oxford, MS '73 (ATTY)
HICKMAN, WILLIAM J. JR., dir. pers., Temple University Hospital, Philadelphia, PA '83
HICKS, CAMILLA K., RN, asst. dir. nrsg., Illini Hospital, Silvis, IL '81 (NURS)
HICKS, GERALD S., PhD, dir. pers., Kissimmee Memorial Hospital, Kissimmee, FL '84 (PERS)
HICKS, H. JAMES JR., sr. vice-pres., East Tennessee Baptist Hospital, Knoxville, TN '68 (MGMT)
HICKS, JAMES THOMAS, atty., Oak Park Hospital, Oak Park, IL '77 (ATTY)
HICKS, JOANNA PARKER, dir. educ., St. Joseph Hospital, Augusta, GA '85 (EDUC)
HICKS, JUDITH, RN, vice-pres. nrsg., Children's Memorial Hospital, Chicago, IL '78 (NURS)
HICKS, SR. MARY VINCENT, Hot Springs, AR '67 (PERS)
HICKS, MICHAEL E., mgr. matl., Alamance Health Services, Burlington, NC '84 (PUR)(PERS)
HICKS, STEVE E., atty., Louisiana Public Facilities Authority, Baton Rouge, LA '79 (ATTY)
HICKS, SUSAN LYNN BOWMAN, dir. soc. work and pat. rel., Crittenton Hospital, Rochester, MI '79 (SOC)(PAT)
HIEBEL, LINDA L., mgt. eng., Akron General Medical Center, Akron, OH '82 (MGMT)
HIEBERT, CHERYLE J., RN, dir. nrsg., Blackwell Regional Hospital, Blackwell, OK '86 (NURS)
HIERS, JANE L., RN, dir. nrsg. serv. and asst. adm., Putnam Community Hospital, Palatka, FL '81 (NURS)
HIERS, RETA H., dir. educ., East Tennessee Children's Hospital, Knoxville, TN '85 (EDUC)
HIETT, ROBERT L., pres., KCA Research, Inc., Alexandria, VA '81 (PR)
HIETT, TEE H., PhD, prof., School of Community and Allied Health Resources, University of Alabama in Birmingham, Birmingham, AL '67 (MGMT)
HIGBIE, J. RICHARD, exec. vice-pres., Children's Hospital Medical Center, Akron, OH '65
HIGBIE, JEFFREY J., dir. pub. rel., St. Francis Hospital, Escanaba, MI '85 (PR)
HIGDON, CAMILLE S., assoc. dir. diet., Albert Einstein Medical Center, Philadelphia, PA '81 (FOOD)
HIGDON, DONALD LYNN, dir. human res., Stringfellow Memorial Hospital, Anniston, AL '86 (PERS)
HIGDON, PATRICIA R., dir. spec. proj., Hartselle Medical Center, Hartselle, AL '84 (VOL)
HIGDON, SAMUEL THOMAS II, assoc. adm. oper., Lafayette Home Hospital, Lafayette, IN '69
HIGGERSON, NANCY J., RN, assoc. adm. nrsg., Children's Hospital of Michigan, Detroit, MI '73 (NURS)
HIGGES, KAREN S., dir., Norfolk General Hospital, Norfolk, VA '87 (AMB)
HIGGINBOTHAM, DIANNE I., prod. coor., Duke University Hospital, Durham, NC '86 (PUR)
HIGGINBOTHAM, FREDERICK RHODES, chief exec. off., Blue Cross and Blue Shield of Georgia, Atlanta, GA '70
HIGGINBOTHAM, SARA, dir. educ., Baptist Memorial Hospital, Gadsden, AL '71 (EDUC)
HIGGINS, CLAYTON A., dir. safety and security, Concord Hospital, Concord, NH '82 (RISK)
HIGGINS, DUANE ADELNO, vice-pres. pur. and matl. mgt., Adventist Health System-Sunbelt, Orlando, FL '65 (PUR)
HIGGINS, GEORGE L. III, MD, chief emer. medicine, Maine Medical Center, Portland, ME '87 (AMB)
HIGGINS, GLENDA M., coor. educ., Methodist Medical Center, Dallas, TX '86 (EDUC)
HIGGINS, JAMES E., dir. diet., Eastern Idaho Regional Medical Center, Idaho Falls, ID '84 (FOOD)
HIGGINS, JAMES J., student, University of Houston-Clear Lake City, Houston, TX '83
HIGGINS, MARY K., pat. rep., St. Margaret Hospital, Hammond, IN '86 (PAT)
HIGGINS, MARYANN, dir. soc. serv., Venice Hospital, Venice, FL '82 (SOC)
HIGGINS, NANCY M., dir. vol. serv., Desert Samaritan Hospital, Mesa, AZ '86 (VOL)
HIGGINS, WALTER E., vice-pres. human res., Walker Regional Medical Center, Jasper, AL '71 (PERS)
HIGH, MAJ. BLANCO T., MSC USA, chief health clin. support br., 97th General Hospital, APO New York, NY '71
HIGH, LORETTE, dir. vol. serv., Vancouver Memorial Hospital, Vancouver, WA '78 (VOL)
HIGHLAND, JAMES P., consult., Arthur Andersen and Company, San Francisco, CA '83
HIGHLEN, MARY E., dir. vol. serv., Caylor-Nickel Hospital, Bluffton, IN '85 (VOL)
HIGHTOWER, THOMAS R., adm., Woman's Hospital, Baton Rouge, LA '82 (PLNG)
HIGIE, WILLIAM F., atty., Bradford Hospital, Bradford, PA '78 (ATTY)
HILBERT, WILLIAM A., dir., Hermann Hospital, Houston, TX '83 (PUR)
HILDEBRAND, JAMES L., mgr. eng. serv., Columbia Hospital, Milwaukee, WI '83 (ENG)
HILDEBRAND, VIRGINIA M., dir. pers., Washington County Hospital, Nashville, IL '82 (PERS)
HILDEBRANDT, KAREN L., RN, asst. adm. and dir. nrsg., Pocatello Regional Medical Center, Pocatello, ID '83 (NURS)
HILDMAN, GENE P., chief eng., Scott and White Memorial Hospital, Temple, TX '76 (ENG)
HILDRETH, MARY ANN, chief adm. food serv. and diet., Shriners Burns Institute, Galveston, TX '79 (FOOD)
HILDRETH, RHONDA, dir. soc. serv., Our Lady of Lake Regional Medical Center, Baton Rouge, LA '87 (SOC)
HILEMAN, BYRON P., atty., Summerlin and Connor Law Offices, Winter Haven, FL '86
HILEMAN, DAVID M., asst. to pres., Mercy Hospital of Pittsburgh, Pittsburgh, PA '78
HILES, GLORIA F., dir. pers., Kennedy Institute for Handicapped, Baltimore, MD '81 (PERS)
HILF, LAURA A., RN, consult., Cortland, NY '82 (NURS)
HILFERTY, JAMES P., adm. dir., Sequoia Hospital District, Redwood City, CA '86 (PLNG)
HILFIKER, JAMES F., dir. health center eng., Howard University Hospital, Washington, DC '73 (ENG)
HILGEFORD, WILLIAM, dir. mgt. eng., Jefferson Regional Medical Center, Pine Bluff, AR '86 (MGMT)
HILGERS, THOMAS J., dir. pur., Froedtert Memorial Lutheran Hospital, Milwaukee, WI '80 (PUR)
HILKER, TERRY, adm. and chief exec. off., Peninsula Medical Center, Ormond Beach, FL '85
HILL, ALDEN V., atty., Poudre Valley Hospital, Fort Collins, CO '74 (ATTY)
HILL, ANTHONY W., matl. mgt. consult., Daughters of Charity National Purchasing, Inc., Daughters of Charity Health Systems-West Central, St. Louis, MO '83 (PUR)
HILL, BARBARA M., RN, adm. nrsg.-clin. serv., Catherine McAuley Health Center, Ann Arbor, MI '84 (NURS)
HILL, BARBARA, dir. vol. serv., Olathe Medical Center, Olathe, KS '86 (VOL)
HILL, BEATRICE M., dir. pers., Our Lady of Mercy Hospital, Cincinnati, OH '82 (PERS)
HILL, BEVERLY B., RN, coor. spec. serv., Holy Name of Jesus Medical Center, Gadsden, AL '87 (AMB)
HILL, CAROL A., dir. vol. serv. and pub. rel., Community Memorial Hospital and Convalescent and Rehabilitation Unit, Winona, MN '78 (VOL)(PR)
HILL, CHRISTA FALINE, mgt. eng., Jewish Hospital, Louisville, KY '83 (MGMT)
HILL, DAVID A., chief eng. serv., Canandaigua Veterans Administration Medical Center, Canandaigua, NY '85 (ENG)
HILL, DAVID C., pat. rep., St. James Hospital Medical Center, Chicago Heights, IL '86 (PAT)
HILL, DAVID N., dir. plant serv., St. Elizabeth Community Health Center, Lincoln, NE '80 (ENG)
HILL, DONALD, dir. med. elec., Divine Providence Hospital, Williamsport, PA '85 (ENG)
HILL, DOUGLAS J., mgr. bus. dev., Daverman Associates, Inc., Grand Rapids, MI '81 (PLNG)
HILL, DOUGLAS J., atty., Methodist Hospital of Indiana, Indianapolis, IN '68 (ATTY)
HILL, EARL W., atty., Hancock County Memorial Hospital, Britt, IA '83 (ATTY)
HILL, EDWARD W., dir. info. syst., Winchester Hospital, Winchester, MA '87 (MGMT)
HILL, ELAINE M., dir. vol., North Carolina Memorial Hospital, Chapel Hill, NC '68 (VOL)
HILL, ELLIOTT E., mgr. plant oper., South Suburban Hospital, Hazel Crest, IL '83 (ENG)
HILL, GARY, dir. plant serv. and maint., Bethany Medical Center, Kansas City, KS '82 (ENG)
HILL, GERALD G., chief pat. adm. div., Reynolds Army Community Hospital, Fort Sill, OK '86
HILL, H. H., pres., Pacific Living Centers, Roseville, CA '68
HILL, J. DWIGHT, dir. human res., Northside Hospital, Atlanta, GA '82 (PERS)
HILL, JAMES FOXX, vice-pres. syst., Saskatoon City Hospital, Saskatoon, Sask., Canada '68 (MGMT)
HILL, JANE HARCUS, sr. consult., Ernst and Whinney, Charlotte, NC '85 (PLNG)
HILL, JEFFREY A., RN, dir. nrsg., Charter Lake Hospital, Macon, GA '82 (NURS)
HILL, JOHN J., pers. off., Veterans Administration Medical Center, East Orange, NJ '82 (PERS)
HILL, JUDY L., dir. soc. serv., Community General Hospital, Sterling, IL '82 (SOC)
HILL, KATHLEEN S., dir. soc. serv., St. Joseph Hospital, Orange, CA '86 (SOC)
HILL, LAWRENCE A., exec. vice-pres., Care America Health Plans, Inc., Chatsworth, CA '61
HILL, M. EARLE, vice-pres., Parkview Community Hospital, Riverside, CA '72
HILL, M. KING JR., atty., Union Memorial Hospital, Baltimore, MD '75 (ATTY)
HILL, MARIAN SHIRLEY, dir. vol. serv., Spelman Memorial Hospital, Smithville, MO '85 (VOL)
HILL, MICHAEL J., vice-pres., New Hampshire Hospital Association, Concord, NH '82 (PLNG)
HILL, NANCY H., RN, dir. nrsg., Margaret R. Pardee Memorial Hospital, Hendersonville, NC '86 (NURS)
HILL, PAMELA J., mgr. mgt. dev., Health Central Human Resources, Minneapolis, MN '81 (EDUC)
HILL, PEGGY A., dir. vol. serv., Kaiser Medical Center, Richmond, CA '85 (VOL)
HILL, RONALD W., dir. mktg. and prog. dev., Stanford University Hospital, Stanford, CA '81 (PLNG)
HILL, SANDY, dir. pub. rel., Kingman Regional Hospital, Kingman, AZ '86 (PR)
HILL, TERRI L., dir. educ. serv., Union Hospital, Terre Haute, IN '86 (EDUC)
HILL, W. WALLACE, dir. soc. work, North Carolina Memorial Hospital, Chapel Hill, NC '66 (SOC)
HILL, WALTER A., dir. plng., Children's Hospital National Medical Center, Washington, DC '84 (PLNG)
HILL, WAYNE, mgr. ldry., Hillcrest Baptist Medical Center, Waco, TX '86 (ENVIRON)
HILL, WENDY PAULEN, asst. adm., Guadalupe Valley Hospital, Seguin, TX '85
HILL, WILLIAM H., dir. soc. serv. psych. mgt. center, University Hospitals of Cleveland, Cleveland, OH '85 (SOC)
HILLARD, GEORGIA F., coor. staff serv., Ephraim McDowell Regional Medical Center, Danville, KY '85 (VOL)
HILLARY, CLAUDIA B., dir. pur., St. Francis Memorial Hospital, San Francisco, CA '87 (PUR)
HILLE, ROBERT A., sr. vice-pres., Baylor University Medical Center, Dallas, TX '67
HILLEBRAND, JEFFREY H., vice-pres., Evanston Hospital, Evanston, IL '78 (PLNG)
HILLENBRAND, HAROLD, DDS, exec. dir., American Dental Association, Chicago, IL '62 (HON)
HILLERMAN, MARCY A., dir. soc. serv., Harrison Memorial Hospital, Bremerton, WA '84 (SOC)
HILLES, WILLIAM C., adm., Georgetown University Medical Center, Washington, DC '84
HILLESTAD, STEVEN G., vice-pres. mktg., Life Span, Minneapolis, MN '77
HILLI, MARY E., RN, vice-pres. nrsg. serv., Joseph P. Kennedy Jr. Memorial Hospital, Boston, MA '85 (NURS)
HILLIARD, JUDI L., dir. pers., University Hospital, Boston, MA '86 (PERS)
HILLIARD, PETER L., dir. soc. serv., Kaiser Permanente Medical Center, Sacramento, CA '86 (SOC)
HILLIARD, LT. COL. ROBERT W., MSC USA, br. chief, Department of Defense, Health Affairs, Arlington, VA '67
HILLIER, ROBERT K., dir. cost and budget, Harris County Hospital District, Houston, TX '83 (MGMT)
HILLIER, STEVEN D., arch., Sinai Hospital of Detroit, Detroit, MI '82 (PLNG)
HILLING, LEVI N., exec. vice-pres., Baystate Medical Center, Springfield, MA '73
HILLIS, DAVID W., pres. and chief exec. off., Doctors Hospital of Worcester, Worcester, MA '86
HILLMAN, DEBRA S., coor. hosp. serv., Clarke Hospital, Jackson, AL '86 (PR)
HILLMAN, JO L., RN, vice-pres. nrsg., Pekin Memorial Hospital, Pekin, IL '84 (NURS)
HILLMAN, LISA, dir. pub. rel. and dev., Anne Arundel General Hospital, Annapolis, MD '83 (PR)
HILLMAN, WILMA C., spec. proj. nrs., University of Cincinnati Hospital, Cincinnati, OH '84 (MGMT)
HILLMER, HARLAN A., adm., Family Practice and Surgical Clinic, Huntsville, TX '87 (AMB)
HILLSINGER, GEORGE R., atty., Downey Community Hospital, Downey, CA '83 (ATTY)
HILLYER, SARAH A., health adm., Prucare-Northcare Medical Group, Chicago, IL '86
HILMER, JAY R., adm. dir. rehab. serv., La Palma Intercommunity Hospital, La Palma, CA '84
HILPIPRE, STEVEN L., adm., Swift County-Benson Hospital, Benson, MN '86
HILS, NELMA L., dir. food serv., Bethesda Scarlet Oaks, Dayton, KY '75 (FOOD)
HILTERBRAND, CYNTHIA K., sr. mgt. analyst, Oklahoma Teaching Hospitals, Oklahoma City, OK '86 (MGMT)
HILTNER, BEVERLY D., dir. soc. serv., Deaton Hospital and Medical Center, Baltimore, MD '82 (SOC)
HILTON, DONNA J., Barberton Citizens Hospital, Barberton, OH '72 (VOL)
HILTON, J. PAUL, vice-pres. human res., Middle Tennessee Medical Center, Murfreesboro, TN '82 (PERS)
HILTON, NANCY H., dir. educ., Trident Regional Medical Center, Charleston, SC '84 (EDUC)
HILTON, RICHARD, asst. dir., Oktibbeha County Hospital, Starkville, MS '71
HILTZ, SR. GRACE MARIE, pres., Sisters of Charity Health Care Systems, Inc., Cincinnati, OH '79 (LIFE)
HILTZ, JUDITH L., RN, dir. nrsg., Stephens Memorial Hospital, Norway, ME '83 (NURS)
HILVERS, ELEANOR J., coor. prog., St. Luke's Regional Medical Center, Boise, ID '85 (EDUC)
HILYARD, TERESA D., RN, dir. nrsg., Elkhart General Hospital, Elkhart, IN '83 (NURS)
HILYER, ALAN C., health care mgt. consult., Ernst and Whinney, Atlanta, GA '84 (MGMT)
HIMEDA, KATHLEEN R., pat. rel. rep., Kuakini Medical Center, Honolulu, HI '84 (PAT)
HIMEGARNER, A. H., dir. human res., St. Luke's Hospital, Kansas City, MO '72 (PERS)
HIMMELSBACH, WILLIAM A. JR., pres., Holy Cross Health System Corporation, South Bend, IN '69
HINCHEY, JAMES J. JR., atty., St. Vincent Hospital, Green Bay, WI '82 (ATTY)
HINCHEY, MARY ANNE, RN, vice-pres. nrsg. serv., Saint Francis Medical Center, Grand Island, NE '84 (NURS)
HINCKLEY, BRIAN J., dir. pur., Bradford Hospital, Bradford, PA '80 (PUR)
HINCKLEY, DEBORAH L., asst. mgr. food serv., Saint Vincent Hospital, Billings, MT '81 (FOOD)
HINCKLEY, FRANK O., sr. consult. mktg. and plng., Baptist Medical Centers, Birmingham, AL '78 (PLNG)
HIND, CAROL A., RN, dir. nrsg. serv., Newman Memorial County Hospital, Emporia, KS '82 (NURS)
HINDBAUGH, FLOYD C., dir. pers., Lee Memorial Hospital, Dowagiac, MI '85 (PERS)
HINDE, LORRIE R., dir. soc. serv., Sherman Hospital, Elgin, IL '77 (SOC)
HINDELANG, MARY L., dir. educ., Traverse City Osteopathic Hospital, Traverse City, MI '82 (EDUC)
HINDEN, RICHARD A., atty., Altheimer and Gray, Chicago, IL '82 (ATTY)
HINDERLITER, MARGARET T., dir. soc. serv., Crozer-Chester Medical Center, Chester, PA '78 (SOC)
HINDIN, EDWARD M., exec. vice-pres., Healtheast, Inc., Allentown, PA '79 (PR) (PLNG)
HINDMAN, GARY, supv. maint., Sparta Community Hospital, Sparta, IL '85 (ENG)
HINDSMAN, PEGGY L., RN, dir. pat. care, HCA West Paces Ferry Hospital, Atlanta, GA '86 (NURS)
HINE, CYNTHIA B., atty., Daughters of Charity Health Systems, St. Ann, MO '86 (ATTY)
HINENBURG, MORRIS, MD, (ret.), North Miami Beach, FL '30 (LIFE)
HINER, BILL, dir. human res., Imperial Point Medical Center, Fort Lauderdale, FL '84 (PERS)
HINER, JOHN W., dir. mktg. and dev., Stonewall Jackson Hospital, Lexington, VA '86 (PR)
HINES, GRACE R., adm. dir. rad. commun. and neurologist, Hampton General Hospital, Hampton, VA '85
HINES, H. FRANCIS, dir. commun. rel., Frankford Hospital, Philadelphia, PA '80 (PR)
HINES, JOHN C., dir. bldg. and grds., St. John's Home, Rochester, NY '80 (ENG)

HINES, LISA R., asst. dir. food serv., Norfolk Community Hospital, Norfolk, VA '86 (FOOD)
HINES, MARSHA MORGAN, coor. info. serv., University of Arkansas, Medical Sciences Campus, Little Rock, AR '80 (PR)
HINES, RICHARD H., dir. eng., Pasadena Bayshore Medical Center, Pasadena, TX '79 (ENG)
HINES, TRISA C., coor. educ., Cleveland Memorial Hospital, Shelby, NC '86 (EDUC)
HINKE, JAMES F., mgr. cent. sup., Good Shepherd Medical Center, Longview, TX '85 (CS)
HINKEL, BARBARA K., risk mgr., Richland Memorial Hospital, Olney, IL '82 (RISK)
HINKEL, SUE A., RN, dir. adult nrsg., Baptist Medical Center, Jacksonville, FL '84 (NURS)
HINKES, JULES M., pres. and chief exec. off., Miami Children's Hospital, Miami, FL '56 (PLNG)(LIFE)
HINKLE, CARL D., dir. pers., Onslow Memorial Hospital, Jacksonville, NC '80 (PERS)
HINKLE, PATRICIA, dir. diet., Mercer Medical Center, Trenton, NJ '81 (FOOD)
HINKLEY, GERALD M., atty., Pacific Presbyterian Medical Center, San Francisco, CA '84 (ATTY)
HINKSON, PAMELA A., student, Program in Health Care Management, Boston University, Boston, MA '85 (PLNG)
HINMAN, EDWARD J., MD, St. Leonard, MD '84
HINMAN, INGE, pat. rep., Alice Hyde Hospital Association, Malone, NY '80 (PAT)
HINNEN, DONALD J., vice-pres. corp. adm., Voluntary Hospitals of America, Irving, TX '82
HINNENKAMP, JOHN B. III, dir. maint., St. John's Hospital, Salina, KS '83 (ENG)
HINSDALE, LAURENCE C., asst. adm., HCA Park View Medical Center, Nashville, TN '86
HINSDALE, S. BROOKE, asst. dir. mktg., Medical Park Hospital, Winston-Salem, NC '85 (PR)
HINSHAW, EDWARD A., atty., Santa Clara County Medical Society, San Jose, CA '84 (ATTY)
HINSON, DAVID E., dir. food serv., Lake Taylor City Hospital, Norfolk, VA '84 (FOOD)
HINSON, JEAN MARIE, head nrs. cent. sterile sup., Midwest City Memorial Hospital, Midwest City, OK '77 (CS)
HINSON, KATHY, dir. health educ., Florida Hospital Medical Center, Orlando, FL '79 (EDUC)
HINSON, ROBIN L., atty., Charlotte Memorial Hospital and Medical Center, Charlotte, NC '83 (ATTY)
HINTERMISTER, JOHN H., dir. food serv., HCA North Florida Regional Medical Center, Gainesville, FL '76 (FOOD)
HINTHORN, BELVA JEAN, dir. pat. rep., Menorah Medical Center, Kansas City, MO '85 (PAT)
HINTON, COLLIE, dir. vol. serv., University of New Mexico Hospital, Albuquerque, NM '72 (VOL)
HINTON, JACK RAYMOND, assoc. adm., Chippenham Hospital, Richmond, VA '74
HINTON, MARGARET A., dir. soc. serv., Hi-Desert Medical Center, Joshua Tree, CA '85 (SOC)
HINTON, PATRICIA A., RN, assoc. dean and adm. assoc., School of Nursing-Emory University Hospital, Atlanta, GA '80 (EDUC)(NURS)
HINTON, WARREN S., pres., Heartland Hospital West, St. Joseph, MO '51 (LIFE)
HINYTZKE, JAN, instr. educ., La Crosse Lutheran Hospital, La Crosse, WI '81 (EDUC)
HINZ, MARY ROSELLEN, coor. cent. sterile sup., Regional Memorial Hospital, Brunswick, ME '82 (CS)
HINZMAN, TERRI L., mgr. sterile preparation, Indian River Memorial Hospital, Vero Beach, FL '85 (CS)
HIPKENS, T. P., sr. consult., Home for Crippled Children-the Regional Comprehensive Rehabilitation Center for Children and Youth, Pittsburgh, PA '75
HIPP, FRED L. JR., dir. commun. rel., Muhlenberg Regional Medical Center, Plainfield, NJ '80 (PR)
HIRAMOTO, ELIZABETH H., mgr. ped. pers., Department of Pediatrics, University of California at Los Angeles, Los Angeles, CA '86 (PERS)
HIRAMOTO, YURIKO, asst. chief soc. serv., Tripler Army Medical Center, Honolulu, HI '70 (SOC)
HIRANO, BENJAMIN N., assoc. adm., Good Samaritan Hospital of Santa Clara Valley, San Jose, CA '54 (LIFE)
HIRCH, JANE E., RN, assoc. dir. nrsg., University of California San Francisco, San Francisco, CA '81 (NURS)
HIRD, ELLEN M., dir. food serv., National Jewish Center, Denver, CO '82 (FOOD)
HIRE, RICHARD L., mgr. environ. and linen serv., Children's Hospital, Denver, CO '86 (ENVIRON)
HIRLEMAN, JEAN, dir. food serv., Chandler Hall Nursing Home, Newton, PA '81 (FOOD)
HIRN, MARVIN J., atty., Humana, Inc., Louisville, KY '74 (ATTY)
HIRSCH, GLENN J., chief oper. off., Community Hospital of Western Suffolk, Smithtown, NY '81
HIRSCH, LT. COL. KATHLEEN M., MSC USA, chief nutr. care div., Darnall Army Community Hospital, Fort Hood, TX '80 (FOOD)
HIRSCH, MARY E., student, Graduate Program in Management Public Services, DePaul University, Chicago, IL '84
HIRSCH, SIDNEY, (ret.), Kew Garden Hills, NY '72 (SOC)
HIRSCH, VIRGINIA L., dir. qual. assur., Ottumwa Regional Health Center, Ottumwa, IA '83 (RISK)
HIRSCHWALD, JUDITH FRANK, dir. soc. serv., Magee Rehabilitation Hospital, Philadelphia, PA '70 (SOC)
HIRSCHY, JULIET A., RN, adm. nrsg. serv., Ridgecrest Community Hospital, Ridgecrest, CA '78 (NURS)
HIRSEKORN, ROBERT DEAN, vice-pres. fin., Healthwatch Medical Centers, Boulder, CO '78
HIRSH, KAY S., asst. adm.-oper., University Hospital and Clinic, Pensacola, FL '85
HIRSHBERG, MARK IRWIN, vice-pres. prof. serv., Galesburg Cottage Hospital, Galesburg, IL '80 (RISK)
HIRT, ANNIE M., adm. health serv., Clinica San Agustin, Manati, P.R. '85
HIRT, DONALD, dir. market res., Henry Ford Hospital, Detroit, MI '82 (PLNG)
HIRT, JACQUELYN K., dir. pub. rel., St. Francis-St. George Hospital, Cincinnati, OH '82 (PR)
HISCOE, NANCY H., vice-pres. corp. and commun. dev., Cabell Huntington Hospital, Huntington, WV '84 (PR)
HISE, MARIE ANNETTE, dir. diet., Gaylord Hospital, Wallingford, CT '81 (FOOD)
HISER, ROGER BRUCE, adm. and chief exec. off., Quakertown Community Hospital, Quakertown, PA '82 (PLNG)
HISEY, MARK A., sr. mgt. eng., St. Joseph's Medical Center, Fort Wayne, IN '86 (MGMT)
HISSOM, CAROL ANN, dir. diet., Presbyterian Association on Aging, Oakmont, PA '84 (FOOD)
HITCH, HORACE ERVIN, atty., St. Barnabas Hospital, Minneapolis, MN '68 (ATTY)
HITCHCOCK, ADRIENNE C., RN, asst. dir. nrsg. and dir. educ., Memorial Hospital, Cambridge, MN '83 (NURS)
HITCHCOCK, BRIAN K., dir. matl. mgt., Desert Springs Hospital, Las Vegas, NV '86 (PUR)
HITCHCOCK, DOUGLAS J., atty., California Hospital Association, Sacramento, CA '84 (ATTY)
HITCHCOCK, EARL S. JR., dir. diet. serv., Adirondack Regional Hospital, Corinth, NY '86 (FOOD)
HITCHCOCK, JACK E., dir. environ. serv., St. Marys Hospital Medical Center, Madison, WI '86 (ENVIRON)
HITCHCOCK, KARLA A., dir. plng., Greater Baltimore Medical Center, Baltimore, MD '86 (PLNG)
HITCHCOCK, WILLIAM FRED, actg. chief vol. serv., Department of Health and Mental Hygiene-Division of Volunteer Service, Baltimore, MD '86 (VOL)
HITCHENS, DAVID W., dir. matl. mgt., Children's Hospital, Denver, CO '86 (PUR)
HITCHINGS, ROY A. JR., pres. and chief exec. off., Falmouth Hospital, Falmouth, MA '79 (PLNG)
HITCHNER, CARL H., atty., Mount Zion Hospital and Medical Center, San Francisco, CA '76 (ATTY)
HITE, CHARLES L., dir. plng. and design serv., Duke Endowment, Hospital and Child Care Sections, Charlotte, NC '54 (PLNG)(LIFE)
HITT, ALAN S., assoc. dir., Veterans Administration Medical Center, Lyons, NJ '73
HITT, IOLA, dir. diet. serv., Chilton Memorial Hospital, Pompton Plains, NJ '74 (FOOD)
HITT, PETER, vice-pres., Marshall Erdman and Associates, Inc., Richardson, TX '86
HITTLE, DEBORAH K., pat. rel. rep., White Memorial Medical Center, Los Angeles, CA '85 (PAT)
HITTNER, JAMES, pur. syst. spec., Providence Medical Center, Portland, OR '86 (PUR)
HITZEMANN, MARY F., vice-pres. human res., Golden Valley Health Center, Golden Valley, MN '80 (PERS)
HITZHUSEN, WILLIAM JON, asst. to exec. dir., Hermann Hospital, Houston, TX '75
HIXENHEISER, DAWN M., dir. diet., Evangelical Congregational Church Retirment Village, Myerstown, PA '87 (FOOD)
HIXON, JANET K., dir. educ., Association of Operating Room Nurses, Denver, CO '83 (EDUC)
HIXSON, DOROTHY H., RN, mgr. cent. proc. and sterilization, Grande Ronde Hospital, La Grande, OR '85 (CS)
HIXSON, RICK, dir. matl. mgt., St. John's Regional Medical Center, Oxnard, CA '71 (PUR)
HIXSON, WILLIAM L., dir. oper. support serv., Western Pennsylvania Hospital, Pittsburgh, PA '85 (PUR)
HIZER, RONALD V., dir. environ. serv., Indian River Memorial Hospital, Vero Beach, FL '86 (ENVIRON)
HLAVATY, RENEE, RN, dir. critical care, St. Margaret Hospital, Hammond, IN '80 (NURS)
HLUCHAN, DEBORAH M., atty., Mercy Catholic Medical Center, Philadelphia, PA '85 (ATTY)
HOADLEY, PAMLA K., dept. head diet. serv., Saint Joseph Hospital, Reading, PA '82 (FOOD)
HOAG, CHARLES A., plant eng. and dir. security, Albion Community Hospital, Albion, MI '87 (ENG)
HOAG, MARIANNE UNDERWOOD, RN, vice-pres. nrsg., Hinsdale Hospital, Hinsdale, IL '78 (NURS)
HOAK, BARBARA J., RN, dir. nrsg., Rockville General Hospital, Rockville, CT '87 (NURS)
HOARD, JACK D., exec. adm., Shriners Hospital for Crippled Children, Tampa, FL '86
HOBAN, BARBARA LOUISE, pat. advocate, Veterans Administration Treatment Center for Children, Richmond, VA '86 (PAT)
HOBAN, DEBORAH, dir. risk mgt., Yakima Valley Memorial Hospital, Yakima, WA '86 (RISK)
HOBAN, ROBERT, mgr. audit div., Arthur Andersen and Company, Grand Rapids, MI '77 (ATTY)(PLNG)
HOBART, CHRISTENE ELIZABETH, dir. mktg. and new bus. dev., Hospital Corporation of America Network, Chattanooga, TN '83 (PR) (PLNG)
HOBART, DEAN, interior arch., Design Consultant-Aia, Atlanta, GA '86
HOBART, WILLIAM M., mgr. maint. and eng., Saint Vincent Hospital, Worcester, MA '86 (ENVIRON)
HOBBS, ALYCE J., dir. human res., University Hospital, Stony Brook, NY '86 (PERS)
HOBBS, GAIL K. NOAH, coor. vol., Marin General Hospital, San Rafael, CA '86 (VOL)
HOBBS, ROY E., dir. eng., Mercy Hospital and Medical Center, San Diego, CA '83 (ENG)
HOBERECHT, KAREN L., supv. facil. analysis and plng., Humana Inc., Louisville, KY '87 (PLNG)
HOCH, FRANCIS L., Camden, DE '86 (ENG)
HOCH, LEWIS JARVIS, atty., Decatur Memorial Hospital, Decatur, IL '81 (ATTY)
HOCHBAUM, SOLOMON R., MD, chm., Sinai Hospital of Detroit, Detroit, MI '87 (AMB)
HOCHENBERG, PAUL S., adm., Craig House Hospital, Beacon, NY '78
HOCHHEISER, MARVIN, asst. exec. dir., Metropolitan Jewish Geriatric Center, Brooklyn, NY '67
HOCHKAMMER, WILLIAM O., atty., Sinai Hospital of Detroit, Detroit, MI '75 (ATTY)
HOCHMAN, RUTH A., dir. health educ., Memorial Medical Center of Jacksonville, Jacksonville, FL '83 (EDUC)
HOCKEMA, MARIANNE L., dir. pub. affairs, St. Marys Hospital of Rochester, Rochester, MN '79 (PR)
HOCKENSMITH, JANICE M., dir. soc. serv., St. Mary's Hospital of Kankakee, Kankakee, IL '77 (SOC)
HOCKETT, PAUL B. JR., dir. mktg. and commun., Highland Hospital, Shreveport, LA '73 (PR)
HOCKING, JEANIE L., adm., North Big Horn Hospital, Lovell, WY '82
HODAVANCE, GALE SCHMIDT, hosp. and health care commun. consult., Emmaus, PA '76 (PR)
HODAVANCE, ROBERT S., atty., Delaware Valley Hospital Council, Philadelphia, PA '71 (ATTY)
HODDER, GAIL B., coor. vol. serv., Northwest Hospital, Tucson, AZ '85 (VOL)
HODESH, RICA S., pres., Kinder Cash, Cincinnati, OH '86
HODGDON, DOLORES M., Hialeah, FL '82 (FOOD)
HODGE-JONES, JUEL L., asst. to comr. legislative affairs, Westchester County Medical Center, Valhalla, NY '83 (PLNG)
HODGE, BRIAN, corp. commun., Physicians Insurance Company of Michigan, Okemos, MI '81 (PR)
HODGE, CHARLES C., PhD, coor. prog. plng. and evaluation, Gowanda Psychiatric Center, Helmuth, NY '83 (PLNG)
HODGE, JEAN A., supv. cent. sup., Methodist Hospital, Madison, WI '76 (CS)
HODGE, JEANNETTE W., dir. vol. serv., Middlesex Memorial Hospital, Middletown, CT '81 (VOL)
HODGE, KATHY M., dir. pub. rel., Murray-Calloway County Hospital, Murray, KY '77 (PR)
HODGE, KATHY, asst. pub. rel., Crossroads Community Hospital, Mount Vernon, IL '86 (PR)
HODGE, LILLIAN C., dir. pers., Loudon County Memorial Hospital, Loudon, TN '86 (PERS)
HODGE, LINDA F., RN, dir. surg. and cent. serv., Wallace Thomson Hospital, Union, SC '86 (CS)
HODGE, MAX, asst. dir. eng., Methodist Hospital, Lubbock, TX '84 (ENG)
HODGE, ROBERT H. JR., MD, dir., University of Virginia Hospitals, Charlottesville, VA '87 (AMB)
HODGE, WANDA B., RN, dir. nrsg. serv., Diagnostic Center Hospital, Chattanooga, TN '82 (NURS)
HODGE, YVONNE M., RN, dir. nrsg., Riverton Memorial Hospital, Riverton, WY '82 (NURS)
HODGES, BETTY M., dir. vol. serv., Baptist Medical Center, Kansas City, MO '70 (VOL)(PAT)
HODGES, CHARLES E., dir. maint. and eng., Westerly Hospital, Westerly, RI '84 (ENG)
HODGES, JUDITH L., RN, vice-pres. pat. serv., Riverside Community Hospital, Riverside, CA '87 (NURS)
HODGES, LARRY F., dir. pers., Clayton General Hospital, Riverdale, GA '80 (PERS)
HODGKINS, MARY E., mgr. human res., Health Central System, Minneapolis, MN '86 (PERS)
HODGMAN, BETTY LOU, dir. vol. serv., Lankenau Hospital, Philadelphia, PA '86 (VOL)
HODGSON, HUGH C., vice-pres., Baptist Memorial Hospital East, Memphis, TN '73
HODGSON, JUDY, vice-pres. human res., Mercy Medical Center, Roseburg, OR '78 (PERS)
HODGSON, LOUIS A., mgr. maint. and eng., Chenango Memorial Hospital, Norwich, NY '74 (ENG)
HODLER, DONALD L., dir. plng. and facil., Winter Haven Hospital, Winter Haven, FL '82 (ENG)
HODLIN, ADELE S., mgr. qual. assur., Nathan Littauer Hospital, Gloversville, NY '83 (RISK)
HODNIK, ROBERT M., dir. hskpg., Presbyterian-University Hospital, Pittsburgh, PA '87 (ENVIRON)
HODOROWICZ, MARY ANN, asst. mgr. food serv., Little Company of Mary Hospital, Evergreen Park, IL '79 (FOOD)
HODSDON, JAMES R. III, dir. pub. rel., Lonesome Pine Hospital, Big Stone Gap, VA '85 (PR)
HODUR, GREGORY, legislative asst., United States Congress, Washington, DC '82
HOEFLE, EMELIA, mgr. matl., Fort Worth Osteopathic Medical Center, Fort Worth, TX '86 (PUR)
HOEFT, THOMAS M., asst. adm., Huntington Hospital, Huntington, NY '73
HOEGE, BEVERLY L., RN, asst. adm. pat. care serv., Reedsburg Memorial Hospital, Reedsburg, WI '83 (NURS)
HOEGL, JANE A., dir. lab. school, St. John's Hospital, Springfield, IL '82 (EDUC)
HOEKENDORF, KURT M., dir. plng., mktg. and pub. rel., Mountain View Medical Center, Simi Valley, CA '85 (PR)
HOEKSEMA, JANICE, dir., Surgical Center, Grand Rapids, MI '87 (AMB)
HOEKSTRA, KATHERINE, dir. qual. assur. and risk mgt., Southeastern General Hospital, Lumberton, NC '86 (RISK)
HOEKWATER, SUE, mgr. med. soc. work, Gratiot Community Hospital, Alma, MI '85 (SOC)
HOELL, LOIS E., dir. cont. educ., Deaconess Medical Center-Spokane, Spokane, WA '85 (EDUC)
HOELLER, SR. MARY LOUISE S., coor. nrsg. educ. res., Seton Medical Center, Austin, TX '86 (EDUC)
HOELMAN, BRENDA, exec. dir., Medical Resource Group, Blue Bell, PA '84 (RISK)
HOELTKE, EDWIN H., asst. vice-pres., Christ Hospital, Cincinnati, OH '70 (ENG)
HOELZEL, CHARLOTTE B., RN, dir. nrsg. serv., Cape Fear Memorial Hospital, Wilmington, NC '80 (NURS)
HOEMANN, NANCY J., med. soc. worker, Abraham Lincoln Memorial Hospital, Lincoln, IL '80 (SOC)
HOENACK, AUGUST F., hosp. arch., Dalton, Dalton, Little and Newport, Bethesda, MD '53 (LIFE)
HOEPPNER, BRIAN S., dir. hskpg. and linen serv., Waukesha Memorial Hospital, Waukesha, WI '86 (ENVIRON)
HOERLING, AVANEL, dir. food serv., Tacoma General Hospital, Tacoma, WA '74 (FOOD)

HOESING, HELEN, RN, vice-pres. nrsg., Methodist Hospital, Omaha, NE '73 (NURS)
HOESMAN, TED L., dir. soc. serv., Mercy Hospital, Bakersfield, CA '84 (SOC)
HOEY, ARTHUR, planner and arch., George Washington University Hospital, Washington, DC '83
HOEY, IRENE, RN, dir. nrsg., Community Hospital of Chula Vista, Chula Vista, CA '82 (NURS)
HOEY, MARY JANE, coor. educ., Christian Hospitals Northeast-Northwest, St. Louis, MO '85 (EDUC)
HOEY, PATRICK JR., asst. adm., St. John's Hospital, Springfield, IL '79
HOEY, THOMAS F., chief eng., Cornwall Hospital, Cornwall, NY '68 (ENG)
HOFER, LEONARD P., adm. asst., Mercy Hospital, Toledo, OH '61
HOFF, CHARLES, dir. pers., Forty-Fifth Street Mental Health Center, West Palm Beach, FL '84 (PERS)
HOFF, DAVID, asst. adm. prof. serv., Heritage Hospital, Taylor, MI '80
HOFF, JOHN S., atty., Swidler, Berlin and Strelow, Washington, DC '75 (ATTY)
HOFF, JUDY, RN, trng. spec., Red Line Supply, Minneapolis, MN '77 (EDUC)
HOFFERBER, BEVERLY E., asst. adm., Evergreen Hospital Medical Center, Kirkland, WA '83 (NURS)
HOFFERBERT, DONALD Y., dir. plant oper., Community Hospital and Health Care Center, St. Peter, MN '83 (ENG)
HOFFMAN, CHARLENE R., RN, dir. nrsg., St. Elizabeth Hospital, Beaumont, TX '84 (NURS)
HOFFMAN, CHARLES C. III, dir. protective serv., Bexar County Hospital District, San Antonio, TX '86 (RISK)
HOFFMAN, CHARLES F., vice-pres., Multicare Medical Center, Tacoma, WA '82
HOFFMAN, CHARLES S., asst. vice-pres. adm., St. Charles Hospital and Rehabilitation Center, Port Jefferson, NY '65 (PUR)
HOFFMAN, DENNIS K., dir. vol. human res., Marymount Hospital, Garfield Heights, OH '83 (VOL)
HOFFMAN, FAE E., mgr. human res., Kaiser Permanente, Pasadena, CA '78 (PERS)
HOFFMAN, FERNE S., dir. vol. serv., Sacred Heart General Hospital, Eugene, OR '79 (VOL)
HOFFMAN, FRANK J., dir. safety and security, Union Hospital, Terre Haute, IN '84 (RISK)
HOFFMAN, FRANK J., pres., Hall Decker McKibbin, Inc., Englewood Cliffs, NJ '85 (AMB)
HOFFMAN, GARY D., dir. trng. and dev., Hartgrove Hospital, Chicago, IL '85 (EDUC)
HOFFMAN, HARVEY E., vice-pres., Diversified Health Services-Mental Healthcare, Plymouth Meeting, PA '86
HOFFMAN, HENRY STEVEN, adm., Long Island Jewish-Hillside Medical Center, Glen Oaks, NY '69
HOFFMAN, IRVING, atty., Gottlieb Memorial Hospital, Melrose Park, IL '69 (ATTY)
HOFFMAN, JACK S., dist. mgr., ARA Services, Hospital Food Management, Environmental Service, Inc., Hunt Valley, MD '81 (FOOD)
HOFFMAN, JACKIE L., RN, dir. nrsg. serv., Walton County Hospital, Monroe, GA '82 (NURS)
HOFFMAN, JAMES R., dir. eng., Children's Hospital National Medical Center, Washington, DC '84 (ENG)
HOFFMAN, JOHN L., dir. environ. serv., Mercy Hospital, Urbana, IL '77 (ENG)
HOFFMAN, KAY D., RN, dir. nrsg., Mercy Hospital, Altoona, PA '84 (NURS)
HOFFMAN, KENNETH F., atty., Memorial Medical Center of Jacksonville, Jacksonville, FL '79 (ATTY)
HOFFMAN, KENNETH, dir. prof. rel., Blue Cross and Blue Shield of Greater New York, New York, NY '85
HOFFMAN, LADONNA L., coor. media, University Hospital-University of Nebraska, Omaha, NE '86 (PR)
HOFFMAN, LUCY, supv. cent. proc. and distrib., Holland Community Hospital, Holland, MI '84 (CS)
HOFFMAN, LYNNE, coor. vol. and pat. rep. serv., Westview Hospital, Indianapolis, IN '85 (VOL)(PAT)
HOFFMAN, MARGARET S., RN, vice-pres. nrsg., Jess Parrish Memorial Hospital, Titusville, FL '85 (NURS)
HOFFMAN, MERLE, pres., Choices Women's Medical Center, Inc., Forest Hills, NY '87 (AMB)
HOFFMAN, NATALIE, dir. soc. work serv., Kaiser Foundation Hospital-San Rafael, San Rafael, CA '85 (SOC)
HOFFMAN, PAUL, dir. supportive health, Eskaton Health Corporation, Sacramento, CA '79
HOFFMAN, ROBERT JR., dir. food and nutr. serv., Leesburg Regional Medical Center, Leesburg, FL '85 (FOOD)
HOFFMAN, RONALD S., dir. plant oper., Pembroke Pines General Hospital, Pembroke Pines, FL '82 (ENG)
HOFFMAN, WILLIAM C. JR., assoc. dir. human res., Children's Hospital, Boston, MA '71 (PERS)
HOFFMAN, WILLIAM F., dir. clin. eng., Providence Hospital, Sandusky, OH '80 (ENG)
HOFFMAN, WILLIAM L., supv. biomedical tech., Aultman Hospital, Canton, OH '83 (ENG)
HOFFMAN, WILLIAM R., coor. biomedical, Bethany Brethren Hospital, Chicago, IL '84 (ENG)
HOFFMANN, DANIEL F., chief exec. off., Northeast Rehabilitation Hospital, Salem, NH '78
HOFFMANN, JOHN P., dir. maint., Mercy Medical Center, Oshkosh, WI '79 (ENG)
HOFFMANN, KAY F., mgr. nutr., Mercy Health Center, Dubuque, IA '79 (FOOD)
HOFFMANN, TIM, RN, Penobscot Bay Medical Center, Rockport, ME '79 (NURS)
HOFFMANN, WILLIAM E. JR., atty., Charter Medical Corporation, Macon, GA '85 (ATTY)
HOFFMANN, WILLIAM E., dir. emp. rel., Lenox Hill Hospital, New York, NY '80 (EDUC)
HOFFMASTER, JEAN M., dir. vol. serv., Rehabilitation Institute of Chicago, Chicago, IL '79 (VOL)
HOFFMEISTER, DOLORES J., dir. pers., Fort Madison Community Hospital, Fort Madison, IA '78 (PERS)
HOFFNER, CLAUDIA W., dir. educ., HCA Park West Medical Centers, Knoxville, TN '77 (EDUC)
HOFMANN, GRETCHEN A., dir. pers. serv., West Virginia University Hospital, Morgantown, WV '86 (PERS)
HOFMANN, MAJ. JACK J., MSC USAF, atty., Wilford Hall U. S. Air Force Medical Center, Lackland AFB, TX '87 (ATTY)
HOFMANN, LINDA K., dir. vol. serv., Good Samaritan Hospital, Kearney, NE '86 (VOL)
HOFMANN, PAUL B., exec. dir., Emory University Hospital, Atlanta, GA '64
HOFMEISTER, LINDA R., coor. food serv. oper., Lutheran General Hospital, Park Ridge, IL '79 (FOOD)
HOFSTAD, PAUL A., exec. dir. commun. rel., Fairview Deaconess Center, Minneapolis, MN '50 (LIFE)
HOFSTRA, PATRICIA S., atty., St. James Hospital Medical Center, Chicago Heights, IL '83 (ATTY)
HOFTIEZER, HELEN L., RN, dir. acute care, Prairie Lakes Hospital West, Watertown, SD '83 (NURS)
HOGAN, ERIC W., dir. mktg. and dev., National Medical Enterprises, San Monica, CA '85 (PLNG)
HOGAN, JAMES M., dir. admissions and rec., Clatsop Community College, Astoria, OR '72
HOGAN, JEANNE M., partner, Coopers and Lybrand, Los Angeles, CA '79 (PLNG)
HOGAN, JOANNE, RN, nrs. mgr. amb. care, Brockton Hospital, Brockton, MA '87 (AMB)
HOGAN, KEN, pur. agt., Salvation Army William Booth Memorial Hospital, Florence, KY '84 (PUR)
HOGAN, MARTHA I., RN, asst. vice-pres., St. Elizabeth Medical Center, Granite City, IL '84 (NURS)
HOGAN, NORMA SHAW, dir. pat. rel. serv., Presbyterian Hospital in the City of New York, New York, NY '72 (PAT)(RISK)
HOGAN, PATRICIA L., RN, dir. nrsg., Jefferson General Hospital, Port Townsend, WA '86 (NURS)
HOGAN, SUZY, mgr. cent. serv., St. John's Regional Medical Center, Joplin, MO '77 (CS)
HOGAN, TIMOTHY J., asst. vice-pres. clin. serv., Presbyterian-University Hospital, Pittsburgh, PA '86
HOGANCAMP, MARLENE M., dir. pers., Dominion Hospital, Falls Church, VA '85 (PERS)
HOGE, LAWRENCE B., dir. educ., St. Joseph's Hospital, Tampa, FL '77 (EDUC)
HOGG, JAMES R., vice-pres., Citicorp Industrial Credit, Inc., Atlanta, GA '81
HOGGLE, ROBIN L., dir. soc. work serv., AMI West Alabama Hospital, Northport, AL '81 (SOC)
HOGIN, NANCY JO, dir. soc. serv., Flagstaff Medical Center, Flagstaff, AZ '77 (SOC)
HOGUE, LARRY L., eng., Myrtue Memorial Hospital, Harlan, IA '81 (ENG)
HOGUE, LAURIE A., dir. plng. and mktg., Samaritan Health Service, Phoenix, AZ '85 (PLNG)
HOHEISEL, RUDOLF B., chief eng., HCA Gulf Coast Hospital, Panama City, FL '84 (ENG)
HOHL, SUSAN Y., syst. analyst, Children's Hospital Medical Center of California, Oakland, CA '86 (MGMT)
HOHLE, SHIRLEY, mgr. sup., proc. and distrib., Memorial General Hospital, Las Cruces, NM '85 (CS)
HOHMAN, JOHN D., vice-pres., Saint Joseph Hospital, Reading, PA '66
HOIDAL, L. PAT, RN, dir. nrsg., Methodist Hospital, Omaha, NE '85 (NURS)
HOIL, JOAN, mgr. qual. assur. and risk mgt., St. John's Episcopal Hospital, Smithtown, NY '83 (RISK)
HOKE, K. C., dir. eng., Harford Memorial Hospital, Havre de Grace, MD '82 (ENG)
HOKE, LOIS JEAN, dir. oper. rooms, Northwestern Memorial Hospital, Chicago, IL '86 (NURS)
HOKE, SALLY R., dir. food serv., Crawford Memorial Hospital, Robinson, IL '84 (FOOD)
HOLB, JAMES A., prin. diet., Holb, Gunckel and Associates, Fort Wayne, IN '80 (FOOD)
HOLBERT, CHARLEEN, dir. pers., Grand Valley Hospital, Pryor, OK '79 (PERS)
HOLBERT, CHARLES R., dir. plng., Braddock General Hospital, Braddock, PA '74 (PLNG)
HOLBROOK, ALFRED S. III, sr. consult., Pannell, Kerr and Forster, Atlanta, GA '81
HOLBROOK, FRED K., Midvale, UT '54 (LIFE)
HOLBROOK, JOHN A., asst. dir., Greenwich Hospital, Greenwich, CT '55 (ENG)(LIFE)
HOLBROOK, REID F., atty., University of Kansas Hospital, Kansas City, KS '76 (ATTY)
HOLCOMB, DAVID, sr. assoc. adm., Jennie Edmundson Memorial Hospital, Council Bluffs, IA '86 (RISK)
HOLCOMB, DELORES M., dir. matl. mgt., Platte County Memorial Hospital, Wheatland, WY '80 (PUR)
HOLCOMB, JAMES A., atty., Community Hospital, Munster, IN '85 (ATTY)
HOLCOMB, LESTER W., vice-pres. prof. serv., Tampa General Hospital, Tampa, FL '83 (MGMT)
HOLCOMB, PAUL, asst. dir. biomedical eng., Baptist Medical Center, Little Rock, AR '86 (ENG)
HOLDEN, ARTHUR L., sr. mktg. mgr. home ther. group, Baxter Travenol Laboratories, Winnetka, IL '83
HOLDEN, JOSEPH M., atty., Children's Hospital Medical Center, Akron, OH '68 (ATTY)
HOLDEN, MARGUERITE L., dir. vol., House of the Good Samaritan, Watertown, NY '84 (VOL)
HOLDEN, MARY O., asst. dir. soc. work, Georgetown University Medical Center, Washington, DC '80 (SOC)
HOLDEN, STEPHEN J., dir. diet., Springhill Memorial Hospital, Mobile, AL '85 (FOOD)
HOLDENRIED, JOHN R., atty., Methodist Hospital, Omaha, NE '78 (ATTY)
HOLDER, ANGELA R., atty., Yale-New Haven Hospital, New Haven, CT '77 (ATTY)
HOLDER, JAMES O., mgr. matl., Warrick Hospital, Boonville, IN '83 (CS)
HOLDER, JENNIE LYNN, proj. coor., The Methodist Hospital, Houston, TX '80 (PUR)
HOLDER, LYNNETTE MARIE, RN, dir. critical care nrsg., Albert Einstein Medical Center, Philadelphia, PA '83 (NURS)
HOLDER, MARGARET E., RN, vice-pres., St. John Medical Center, Tulsa, OK '86 (NURS)
HOLDER, ROBERT L., atty., Ohio State University Hospitals, Columbus, OH '86 (ATTY)
HOLDER, WILLIAM L., consult., Fort Smith, AR '68
HOLDERFIELD, DANNY W., chief eng., Baptist Memorial Hospital, Gadsden, AL '84 (ENG)
HOLDERLE, KARL E. JR., atty., Lutheran Medical Center, St. Louis, MO '62 (ATTY)
HOLDERLE, KARL EDWARD III, atty., Lutheran Medical Center, St. Louis, MO '79 (ATTY)
HOLDFORD, ARTHUR A., dir. matl. mgt., East Jefferson General Hospital, Metairie, LA '82 (PUR)
HOLDSWORTH, MICHAEL P., sr. vice-pres. and treas., Grant Medical Center, Columbus, OH '86
HOLE, F. MARVIN, EdD, prof., Alaska Pacific University, Anchorage, AK '71 (EDUC)
HOLES, JOHN E., dir. dev. and constr., David Grant U. S. Air Force Medical Center, Fairfield, CA '87 (ENG)
HOLFELNER, BARBARA A., RN, vice-pres. pat. serv., Our Lady of Lourdes Medical Center, Camden, NJ '82 (NURS)
HOLIDAY, PHYLLIS E., RN, dir. clin. nrsg., Providence Hospital, Anchorage, AK '85 (NURS)
HOLLADAY, ELLEN H., mgr. mgt. consult. serv., Ernst and Whinney, Birmingham, AL '87 (MGMT)
HOLLADAY, GEORGE A. JR., asst. chief bldg. mgt. serv., Dorn Veterans Hospital, Columbia, SC '84 (ENVIRON)
HOLLADAY, MARY ANN, dir. human res., Cottonwood Hospital Medical Center, Murray, UT '82 (PERS)
HOLLAND, CHRISTIANA DAVIDSON, spec. proj. consult., Memorial Hospital, Charleston, WV '82 (PLNG)
HOLLAND, DEAN ANTHONY, assoc. adm., Memorial Hospital-San Leandro, San Leandro, CA '85
HOLLAND, DONNA J., dir. pub. rel., Genesee Memorial Hospital, Flint, MI '85 (PR)
HOLLAND, DOROTHY M., dir. soc. serv., Henrietta Egleston Hospital, Atlanta, GA '83 (SOC)
HOLLAND, DOUGLAS M., asst. dir. plant serv., St. Thomas Hospital, Nashville, TN '86 (ENG)
HOLLAND, E. J. JR., atty., Kansas City Area Hospital Association, Kansas City, MO '80 (ATTY)
HOLLAND, EARL P., sr. vice-pres., Hospital Management Associates, Naples, FL '85
HOLLAND, IOLENE C., RN, dir. nrsg. serv., South Chicago Community Hospital, Chicago, IL '69 (NURS)
HOLLAND, J. C., corp. risk mgr., William Beaumont Hospital, Royal Oak, MI '80 (RISK)
HOLLAND, KATE, dir. pub. rel., Overlake Hospital Medical Center, Bellevue, WA '82 (PR)
HOLLAND, COL. LEON L., MSC USA, dep. cmdr., U. S. Army Medical Materiel Agency, Frederick, MD '77 (PUR)
HOLLAND, MARC, vice-pres. syst. res. serv., Information Planning Associates, Inc., Spring Valley, NY '80 (MGMT)
HOLLAND, NANCY E., atty., Whittaker Corporation, Los Angeles, CA '80 (ATTY)
HOLLAND, NANCY S., dir. pers., Edmond Memorial Hospital, Edmond, OK '81 (PERS)
HOLLAND, RANDY J., atty., Milford Memorial Hospital, Milford, DE '78 (ATTY)
HOLLAND, SALLY A., dir. vol. serv., Waveny Care Center, New Canaan, CT '86 (VOL)
HOLLAND, THOMAS W., atty., Wood River Township Hospital, Wood River, IL '77 (ATTY)
HOLLAND, VINCENT, dir. eng., Jordan Hospital, Plymouth, MA '80 (ENG)
HOLLAND, WALTER G., adm. plant mgt., Los Angeles County-University of Southern California Medical Center, Los Angeles, CA '78 (ENG)
HOLLANDER, DEBRA, corp. exec. diet., Dietary Management Advisory, Inc., Rosemont, PA '78 (FOOD)
HOLLANDER, ELLEN C., asst. dir. human resources, Southwest Texas Methodist Hospital, San Antonio, TX '72 (EDUC)
HOLLANDER, FRED, vice-pres., United Hospitals, Inc., Elkins Park, PA '72
HOLLANDER, ROLAND M., sr. vice-pres. policy and plng., Massachusetts Hospital Association, Burlington, MA '83 (PLNG)
HOLLANDS, JOHN C., chief eng., Good Samaritan Hospital, Corvallis, OR '85 (ENG)
HOLLE, JUDITH R., diet. consult. and coor., Southwest Community Health Services, Albuquerque, NM '80 (FOOD)
HOLLEFREUND, BARBARA H., vice-pres. nrsg., Mount Sinai Medical Center, Cleveland, OH '81 (NURS)
HOLLEN, ELOISE W., dir. food serv., Davis Memorial Hospital, Elkins, WV '79 (FOOD)
HOLLENBACH, DALE T., dir. food serv., Pennsylvania State University Hospital, Hershey, PA '82 (FOOD)
HOLLENBAUGH, FLORENCE A., epidemiologist, Southwest Community Health System, Middleburg Heights, OH '82 (ENG)
HOLLEY, ALAN C., mgt. eng., Baton Rouge General Medical Center, Baton Rouge, LA '86 (MGMT)
HOLLEY, ALAN F., Wake Medical Center, Raleigh, NC '81 (ENG)
HOLLIDAY-ABBOTT, ANNE, dir. pub. rel. and mktg., Casa Grande Regional Medical Center, Casa Grande, AZ '84 (PR)
HOLLIDAY, DAVID P., supt. facil., Fenwick Hall Hospital, Johns Island, SC '83 (ENG)
HOLLIDAY, MARY, dir. matl. mgt., Edmond Memorial Hospital, Edmond, OK '83 (PUR)
HOLLIDAY, ROBERT J., asst. dir. plant oper., Ball Memorial Hospital, Muncie, IN '85 (ENG)
HOLLIDAY, VIRGINIA, RN, dir. nrsg. serv., Memorial Hospital, Danville, VA '79 (NURS)
HOLLIDGE, EDWARD W., dir. eng., Maine Medical Center, Portland, ME '77 (ENG)
HOLLIDGE, JAMES B., dir. matl. mgt., George Washington University Hospital, Washington, DC '81 (PUR)

HOLLIE, VIVIAN M., supv. cent. room, Metropolitan Hospital and Health Centers, Detroit, MI '85 (CS)
HOLLIFIED, KENNETH R., mgr. sterile proc., Spartanburg Regional Medical Center, Spartanburg, SC '83 (CS)
HOLLIMAN, KATIE O., dir. pers., Erlanger Medical Center, Chattanooga, TN '84 (PERS)
HOLLINGER, JANET L., acct. exec., Diversified Food Sales System, Newbury Park, CA '82 (FOOD)
HOLLINGSWORTH, JERRY W., mgr. matl., Pattie A. Clay Hospital, Richmond, KY '82 (PUR)
HOLLINGSWORTH, JERRY L., mgr. emp. and emp. rel., North Carolina Baptist Hospital, Winston-Salem, NC '87 (PERS)
HOLLINGWORTH, DIANNA R., vice-pres. human res., Holy Family Hospital, Spokane, WA '81 (PERS)
HOLLINSWORTH, GARY R., adm. med. staff serv., Rhode Island Hospital, Providence, RI '71 (MGMT)
HOLLIS, AMY V., mgr. mktg. commun., Holy Cross Health System Corporation, South Bend, IN '85 (PR)
HOLLIS, JOHN W., dir. eng., Fairfield Memorial Hospital, Winnsboro, SC '86 (ENG)
HOLLIS, JOYCE C., RN, vice-pres. nrsg., Hadley Memorial Hospital, Washington, DC '85 (NURS)
HOLLIS, P. DANIEL III, atty., Northern Westchester Hospital Center, Mount Kisco, NY '84 (ATTY)
HOLLIS, RONALD F., dir. matl. mgt., Westmoreland Hospital, Greensburg, PA '66 (PUR)
HOLLIS, WILLIAM C. III, asst. adm., Long Beach Memorial Hospital, Long Beach, NY '82 (MGMT)(AMB)
HOLLIS, WILLIAM G., asst. dir. pers., Baptist Memorial Hospital, Memphis, TN '85 (PERS)
HOLLON, KIM NORTON, vice-pres., Baylor University Medical Center, Dallas, TX '77
HOLLOWAY, BETTY W., RN, dir. in-service educ., Woman's Hospital, Baton Rouge, LA '71 (EDUC)
HOLLOWAY, CHRISTINA G., mgr. pub. rel., Munroe Regional Medical Center, Ocala, FL '86 (PR)
HOLLOWAY, DAN, dir. maint., Chelsea Community Hospital, Chelsea, MI '87 (ENG)
HOLLOWAY, MAGGIE H., mgr. food serv., West Georgia Medical Center, La Grange, GA '81 (FOOD)
HOLLOWAY, MARGARET A., dir. mktg. and pub. rel., Moore Municipal Hospital, Moore, OK '86 (PR)
HOLLOWAY, PATRICIA, dir. risk mgt., Mercy Health System, Burlingame, CA '85 (RISK)
HOLLOWAY, ROBERT G., pres., Holloway Health Management Group, Ltd., Chicago, IL '71 (EDUC)(PERS)
HOLLOWAY, SALLY T., prin., Healthcare Consultancy, Santa Rosa, CA '71 (PLNG)
HOLLOWELL, EDWARD E., atty., North Carolina Hospital Association, Raleigh, NC '68 (ATTY)
HOLLOWELL, ROBERT P., dir. plant serv., Childrens Hospital of Los Angeles, Los Angeles, CA '84 (ENG)
HOLLY, BARBARA A., staff nrs. oper. room, U. S. Air Force Medical Center Wright-Patterson, Dayton, OH '82 (EDUC)
HOLLY, CLAUDETTE, dir. surg. serv., North Country Hospital, Bemidji, MN '87 (AMB)
HOLLY, SCOTT R., chief clin. eng., St. Mary Medical Center, Gary, IN '85 (ENG)
HOLM, AUDREY C., assoc. exec. dir., Booth Memorial Medical Center, Flushing, NY '84 (PLNG)
HOLM, DENNIS D., dir. environ. serv., Ohio State University Hospitals, Columbus, OH '86 (ENVIRON)
HOLM, ELLEN, asst. dir. risk mgt., Group Health Cooperative of Puget Sound, Seattle, WA '85 (RISK)
HOLM, JEFFREY N., dir. mgt. eng., Saint Vincent Hospital, Worcester, MA '85 (MGMT)
HOLM, RICHARD N. D., dir. pers., North Memorial Medical Center, Robbinsdale, MN '70 (PERS)
HOLMAN, BELVIN T., supv. cent. sup. and infection control nrs., Allen Bennett Memorial Hospital, Greer, SC '78 (CS)
HOLMAN, BETTY L., dir. vol., St. Joseph Regional Medical Center, Lewiston, ID '86 (VOL)
HOLMAN, ELAINE, RN, coor. staff dev., North Arundel Hospital, Glen Burnie, MD '79 (EDUC)
HOLMAN, GERALD HALL, MD, dir., St. Anthony's Hospital, Amarillo, TX '87 (AMB)
HOLMAN, LANSING L., dir. plng., Interfaith Medical Center, Brooklyn, NY '85 (PR) (PLNG)
HOLMAN, PENNEY C., RN, dir. nrsg. serv., United General Hospital, Sedro Woolley, WA '82 (NURS)
HOLMAN, SANDRA H., RN, coor. nrsg. educ., Riley Memorial Hospital, Meridian, MS '82 (EDUC)
HOLMAN, WILLIAM R., vice-pres., University Hospitals of Cleveland, Cleveland, OH '77
HOLMBERG, LAURIE JEAN, pat. serv. spec., Group Health, Inc., Brooklyn Center, MN '85 (PAT)
HOLMES, ALINE M., RN, vice-pres. nrsg., Jersey Shore Medical Center, Neptune, NJ '83 (NURS)
HOLMES, CHARLOTTE B., dir. pub. rel., Johnston Memorial Hospital, Smithfield, NC '86 (PR)
HOLMES, DAVID A., field mgr., Kettering Affiliated Health Service, Dayton, OH '82 (PERS)
HOLMES, DAVID E., dir. pers., Hancock Memorial Hospital, Greenfield, IN '80 (PERS)
HOLMES, DIANE, mgr. pur., Henrietta Egleston Hospital, Atlanta, GA '83 (PUR)
HOLMES, ELMORE III, atty., Le Bonheur Children's Medical Center, Memphis, TN '79 (ATTY)
HOLMES, GLENN EDWARD, dir. pat. and commun. rel., Lexington Memorial Hospital, Lexington, NC '86 (PAT)
HOLMES, HANSEL F., Largo, FL '67
HOLMES, HOWARD F., asst. adm., Genesee Memorial Hospital, Flint, MI '77 (PERS)
HOLMES, JAMES T., atty., Pepper, Hamilton and Scheetz, Philadelphia, PA '80 (ATTY)
HOLMES, LAURENCE B., dir. pers., Mary Hitchcock Memorial Hospital, Hanover, NH '72 (PERS)
HOLMES, MARY J., RN, dir. cent. serv., Golden Triangle Regional Medical Center, Columbus, MS '82 (CS)
HOLMES, RICHARD, dir. environ. serv., AMI Westbury Hospital, Houston, TX '86 (ENVIRON)
HOLMES, ROSALIE, supv. cent. matl. serv., Hotel Dieu Hospital, New Orleans, LA '81 (CS)
HOLMES, THELMA F., pat. and family rep., Grant Medical Center, Columbus, OH '80 (PAT)
HOLMES, VIRGINIA JEAN, RN, dir. nrsg., Covenant Medical Center-Schoitz, Waterloo, IA '74 (NURS)
HOLMES, WILLIAM M., atty., St. Charles Medical Center, Bend, OR '74 (ATTY)
HOLMGRAIN, FLOYD H. JR., EdD, exec. dir., National Academy of Opticianry, Bowie, MD '78
HOLMGREN, JOHN H., exec. dir., Catholic Health Association of Kansas, Topeka, KS '67
HOLMSTEAD, RANDY, pur. agt., LDS Hospital, Salt Lake City, UT '84 (PUR)
HOLOD, JOHN M., dir. food and environ. serv., Arlington Hospital, Arlington, VA '80 (FOOD)
HOLSCLAW, PHYLLIS M., dir. diet., Woodland Memorial Hospital, Woodland, CA '86 (FOOD)
HOLSTEIN, BETTE LOU, RN, clin. dir. spec. care, Easton Hospital, Easton, PA '86 (NURS)
HOLSTON, JEANETTE L., dir. telecommun., Cedars-Sinai Medical Center, Los Angeles, CA '83 (ENG)
HOLSTON, MARY PATRICIA, duty adm., Regional Medical Center at Memphis, Memphis, TN '85
HOLT, BEATRICE, risk mgr., Connecticut Medical Insurance Company, Wallingford, CT '86 (RISK)
HOLT, CALVIN A., dir. bldg. and grds., Greater Baltimore Medical Center, Baltimore, MD '81 (ENG)
HOLT, CAROL P., coor. pers. serv., St. Claire Medical Center, Morehead, KY '83 (PERS)
HOLT, E. BERRY III, atty., St. Thomas Hospital, Nashville, TN '84 (ATTY)
HOLT, GEORGE H., dir. bldg. and grds., University of South Alabama Medical Center, Mobile, AL '67 (ENG)
HOLT, HYATT H., vice-pres. human res., Queen of the Valley Hospital, Napa, CA '86 (PERS)
HOLT, IRA R., mgr. fin. analyst, Michigan Hospital Association Service Corporation, Lansing, MI '86 (MGMT)
HOLT, J. ROBERT, pres., American Health Development, Pasadena, CA '82
HOLT, JACQUELINE D., adm. asst. risk mgt. and staff educ., St. David's Community Hospital, Austin, TX '84 (RISK)
HOLT, JERRY LEE, dir. commun., Kettering Medical Center, Kettering, OH '83 (PR)
HOLT, JOANN L., RN, vice-pres., Akron General Medical Center, Akron, OH '84 (NURS)
HOLT, JOHN DOUGLAS, exec. dir., Premier Health Plan, Midland, TX '73
HOLT, JOSEPHINE ARENA, dir. pat. rel., Hospital of the University of Pennsylvania, Philadelphia, PA '76 (PAT)
HOLT, LARRY K., dir. matl. mgt., Riverside Community Hospital, Riverside, CA '77 (PUR)
HOLT, NANCYE B., RN, vice-pres. nrsg., Rehabilitation Institute of Chicago, Chicago, IL '83 (NURS)
HOLT, PHILIP B., dir. ins. and pers., Lutheran Hospitals and Homes Society of America, Fargo, ND '74 (RISK)
HOLT, SHIRLEY, RN, nrsg. consult., Hospital Corporation of America, Dallas, TX '78 (NURS)
HOLTEN, JERRY, dir. gen. serv., Minnewaska District Hospital, Starbuck, MN '79 (ENG)
HOLTERS, ROBERT W., asst. vice-pres., Georgetown University Medical Center, Washington, DC '50 (LIFE)
HOLTHAUS, KATHY D., mkt analyst, Porter Memorial Hospital, Denver, CO '86 (PLNG)
HOLTROP, JAN, dir. amb. care, Blodgett Memorial Medical Center, Grand Rapids, MI '87 (AMB)
HOLTSHOPPLE, ROBERT G., dir. eng., Meriter Hospital, Madison, WI '81 (ENG)
HOLTZ, JEANNA M., sr. consult., Ernst and Whinney, Chicago, IL '83
HOLTZ, PAMELA, student, Hofstra University, Hempstead, NY '86
HOLTZBERG, SYLVIA N., vice-pres. plng., Nyack Hospital, Nyack, NY '82 (PLNG)
HOLUB, GREGORY S., exec. vice-pres., Mercy Medical Center, Oshkosh, WI '84
HOLVECK, DOROTHY ANN, RN, asst. dir. nrsg., Muhlenberg Hospital Center, Bethlehem, PA '86 (NURS)
HOLWAY, WILLIAM K., chief logistics div., U. S. Army Medical Department Activity, Fort Wainwright, AK '86 (ENG)
HOLYFIELD, MARY, dir. educ. serv., Mississippi Baptist Medical Center, Jackson, MS '73 (EDUC)
HOLZ, ROBERT F., atty., Iowa Health Systems Agency, Inc., Des Moines, IA '79 (ATTY)
HOLZER, AL J., dir. matl. res., St. Alexius Medical Center, Bismarck, ND '86 (PUR)
HOLZER, JAMES F., vice-pres. loss prevention and underwriting, Risk Management Foundation of Harvard Medical Institute, Cambridge, MA '71 (RISK)
HOLZMAN, MICHELE J., corp. planner, Sacred Heart Rehabilitation Hospital, Milwaukee, WI '85 (PLNG)
HOLZMAN, ROBIN B., asst. to adm., Medical Center Del Oro Hospital, Houston, TX '76 (PAT)
HOMAN, RICK, student, Rush University, Chicago, IL '86
HOMANS, MARTHA K., dir. diet. serv., City of Hope National Medical Center, Duarte, CA '80 (FOOD)
HOMBERG, JOANN M., RN, mgr. educ. res., Munson Medical Center, Traverse City, MI '86 (EDUC)
HOMER, GERALD M., assoc. adm., Nashua Hospital Association-Memorial Hospital, Nashua, NH '72
HOMER, JUDITH D., RN, dir. nrsg., Stokes-Reynolds Memorial Hospital, Danbury, NC '85 (NURS)
HOMER, KENNETH J., dir. risk mgt., Sarasota Memorial Hospital, Sarasota, FL '81 (RISK)
HOMER, LEONARD C., atty., Ober, Grimes and Shriver, Baltimore, MD '75 (ATTY)
HOMEYER, EVE, dir. pub. rel. and mktg., Aspen Valley Hospital District, Aspen, CO '81 (PR)
HON, RONALD R., mgr. soc. serv., Swedish-American Hospital, Rockford, IL '85 (SOC)
HONAKER, JAN, dir. plng., Saint Francis Medical Center, Peoria, IL '85 (PLNG)
HONAKER, SHARON K., RN, dir. nrsg., LaGrange Hospital, LaGrange, IN '76 (NURS)
HONE, JIM, eng., Mountain View Hospital, Payson, UT '79 (ENG)
HONEY, LLOYD N., mgr. matl., General Hospital, Sault Ste Marie, Ont., Canada '85 (CS)
HONEYCUTT, DOROTHY B., coor. staff dev., Holly Hill Hospital, Raleigh, NC '84 (EDUC)
HONEYCUTT, LYNN D., hosp. revenue spec., Mid South Business Forms, Memphis, TN '82 (CS)
HONEYFIELD, ROBERT M., chief soc. work, Veterans Administration Medical Center, Leavenworth, KS '72 (SOC)
HONEYMAN, JUANITA, RN, asst. dir. nrsg. serv., Saint Francis Hospital, Tulsa, OK '80 (NURS)
HONG, JOHN S., MD, chm. family practice and commun. medicine, Catholic Medical Center, Jamaica, NY '87 (AMB)
HONIBERG, BARBARA LYNN, planner, Arizona Health Care Cost Containment Systems, Phoenix, AZ '83 (PLNG)
HONKANEN, CLARENCE D., St. Clair Shores, MI '56 (LIFE)
HONKOMP, MARIA, dir. market res., Millard Fillmore Hospital, Buffalo, NY '86 (PLNG)
HONN-PURCELLA, KAREN L., ultrasound supv., Multicare Medical Center, Tacoma, WA '86 (PLNG)
HONSAKER, JOHN J., clin. eng., Mercy Hospital, Hamilton, OH '83 (ENG)
HONTS, GARY L., dir. matl. serv., AMI Saint Joseph Hospital, Omaha, NE '85 (CS)
HOOD, BARBARA A., asst. adm. plng. and mktg., Providence Medical Center, Portland, OR '79 (PLNG)
HOOD, CHARLES S., dir. soc. work, University Hospital of Arkansas, Little Rock, AR '77 (SOC)
HOOD, CHARLES STEWART, dir. food serv., River Oaks Hospital, New Orleans, LA '86 (FOOD)
HOOD, CHRISTOPHER, MD, Presbyterian Hospital, Charlotte, NC '85 (RISK)
HOOD, HELEN I., mgr. nutr. serv., Toronto General Hospital, Toronto, Ont., Canada '84 (FOOD)
HOOD, J. WILSON, dir. diet., Wadley Regional Medical Center, Texarkana, TX '74 (FOOD)
HOOD, JAMES L., Hampton, NH '56 (LIFE)
HOOD, M. MICHELLE, asst. dir., Emory University Hospital, Atlanta, GA '81
HOOK, ROSEMARY LOUISE, RN, asst. adm. nrsg., St. Elizabeth Medical Center-North, Covington, KY '79 (NURS)
HOOKER, ANITA S., pub. rel. asst., Sisters of St. Mary, St. Louis, MO '86 (PR)
HOOKER, CLAUDE L., dir. matl. serv., Baylor University Medical Center, Dallas, TX '73 (PUR)
HOOKER, JOHN DWIGHT, dir. adm. serv., Windham Community Memorial Hospital, Willimantic, CT '76 (MGMT)
HOOKER, PAUL, mgr. matl., Golden Triangle Regional Medical Center, Columbus, MS '76 (PUR)
HOOKER, SANDRA L., RN, dir. nrsg., Roger Williams General Hospital, Providence, RI '87 (NURS)
HOOKER, SUE H., dir. educ., Golden Valley Memorial Hospital, Clinton, MO '86 (EDUC)
HOOKS, FAITHE, dir. food serv., Mercy Hospital, Columbus, OH '76 (FOOD)
HOOKS, GLADYS MAE, dir. pers. serv., Tucson Medical Center, Tucson, AZ '65 (PERS)
HOOLEY, PATRICIA A., dir. nrsg. educ. and res., Tulane University Hospital and Clinics, New Orleans, LA '81 (EDUC)
HOOLEY, SUSAN, dir. vol. serv., Swedish-American Hospital, Rockford, IL '80 (VOL)
HOOPER, LEON W., vice-pres., Hospital Corporation of America, Westlake Village, CA '66
HOOPER, MICHELE J., vice-pres. strategy dev., Travenol Laboratories Inc., Deerfield, IL '84 (PLNG)
HOOPER, THOMAS M., dir. eng., Mercy Hospital and Medical Center, Chicago, IL '79 (ENG)
HOOPES, JOHN J., adm., The Thoracic Clinic, Portland, OR '66
HOOPES, MARGARET, mgr. matl., Metropolitan Hospital-Springfield Division, Springfield, PA '85 (PUR)
HOOSE, JEFFORY, dir. maint., Memorial Hospital, Owosso, MI '78 (ENG)
HOOT, FLORENCE M., RN, dir. educ., HCA Medical Center of Port St. Lucie, Port St. Lucie, FL '84 (EDUC)
HOOTEN, EXA FAY, U. S. Air Force Hospital, Abilene, TX '67 (FOOD)(LIFE)
HOOVER, CRAIG A., student, School of Health Care Sciences, Sheppard AFB, TX '86
HOOVER, JAMES A. III, mgr., Ernst and Whinney, Baltimore, MD '80 (MGMT)
HOOVER, JAMES C., atty., Miami Children's Hospital, Miami, FL '80 (ATTY)
HOOVER, JAMES WILLIAM, student, Graduate Program in Health Care Administration, Golden Gate University, San Francisco, CA '80
HOOVER, KAREN F., RN, asst. dir. educ., Hinsdale Hospital, Hinsdale, IL '85 (NURS)
HOOVER, LINDA K., RN, dir. pat. care serv., Carson Tahoe Hospital, Carson City, NV '83 (NURS)
HOOVER, M. JOSIAH III, atty., New Kent, VA '83 (ATTY)
HOOVER, MARGARET L., dir. pers., Our Lady of the Way Hospital, Martin, KY '81 (PERS)
HOOVER, MARSHA J., dir. mktg. support serv., Saints Mary and Elizabeth Hospital, Louisville, KY '86 (PR)
HOOVER, MICHAEL J., dir. soc. serv., Washoe Medical Center, Reno, NV '77 (SOC)
HOOVER, STEPHEN E., med. facil. consult., Ohio Department of Health, Columbus, OH '83
HOOVER, STEPHEN M., supv., Ernst and Whinney, Worthington, OH '80
HOOVER, VICKI LYNN, dir. pers., Williamson Medical Center, Franklin, TN '80 (PERS)
HOOVER, W. JEFFREY, mgr. audit, Coopers and Lybrand, Pittsburgh, PA '86

HOPE, AVIS O., coor. pers. serv., Woman's Hospital, Baton Rouge, LA '77 (PERS)
HOPE, HENRY W., atty., Hermann Hospital, Houston, TX '80 (ATTY)
HOPE, JEAN T., dir. soc. work, Memorial Hospital, Towanda, PA '86 (SOC)
HOPE, MICHAEL L., dir. matl. mgt., Chesterfield General Hospital, Cheraw, SC '82 (PUR)
HOPEN, STUART NEIL, atty., Memorial Hospital, Hollywood, FL '81 (ATTY)
HOPKINS, BETTY, dir. emp. rel., Stella Maris Hospice, Baltimore, MD '86 (PERS)
HOPKINS, C. TIMOTHY, atty., Eastern Idaho Regional Medical Center, Idaho Falls, ID '78 (ATTY)
HOPKINS, CHARLEY, dir. environ. serv., HCA Edward White Hospital, St. Petersburg, FL '81 (ENG)
HOPKINS, COLLEEN, dir. vol. serv., Tucson Medical Center, Tucson, AZ '76 (VOL)(PAT)
HOPKINS, DOLORES, dir. diet., HCA Raulerson Hospital, Okeechobee, FL '76 (FOOD)
HOPKINS, EDWARD J., atty., Dallas-Fort Worth Hospital Council, Dallas, TX '86 (ATTY)
HOPKINS, GWENDOLYN D., asst. dir. diet., Riverside Medical Center, Kankakee, IL '82 (FOOD)
HOPKINS, JOANNE P., atty., Hermann Hospital, Houston, TX '84 (ATTY)
HOPKINS, JULIAN H., atty., Lincoln General Hospital, Lincoln, NE '68 (ATTY)
HOPKINS, JULIE L., dir. qual. assur. serv., White Memorial Medical Center, Los Angeles, CA '85 (RISK)
HOPKINS, MARGARET, asst. exec. dir., Millinocket Regional Hospital, Millinocket, ME '86 (RISK)
HOPKINS, MARGARET, sr. vice-pres. and legal serv., All Saints Health Care, Inc., Fort Worth, TX '86 (RISK)
HOPKINS, MARY ANN, dir. vol. serv., HCA Palmyra Medical Centers, Albany, GA '76 (VOL)
HOPKINS, NELSON E., dir. food serv., Waterville Osteopathic Hospital, Waterville, ME '84 (FOOD)
HOPKINS, WILLARD G., exec. dir., Euclid Clinic Foundation, Euclid, OH '76
HOPP, BARBARA A., dir. mktg. and pub. rel., St. Joseph's Hospital and Medical Center, Paterson, NJ '82 (PR)
HOPPE, KATHLEEN J., soc. worker, Hartford Memorial Hospital, Hartford, WI '85 (SOC)
HOPPE, WILLIAM C., pres., Long Beach Hospital, Long Beach, CA '51 (LIFE)
HOPPEL, LIN, coor. commun. rel., Saint Joseph Hospital, Mishawaka, IN '86 (PR)
HOPPENWORTH, GARY L., plant consult., Mercy Coordinating Center, Oakbrook Terrace, IL '70 (ENG)
HOPPER, FAYE D., dir. vol. serv., Maury County Hospital, Columbia, TN '87 (VOL)
HOPPER, PAUL C., dir. pur., Bethesda Memorial Hospital, Boynton Beach, FL '81 (PUR)
HOPPER, PAUL L., dir. plant oper., St. Elizabeth Medical Center, Granite City, IL '73 (ENG)
HOPPER, THERESA L., mgt. eng., Parkview Memorial Hospital, Fort Wayne, IN '85 (MGMT)
HOPPS, JAMES K., atty., Adventist Health System-Sunbelt, Orlando, FL '85 (ATTY)
HORAN, BEV, RN, dir. nrsg., HCA Bayonet Point-Hudson Center, Hudson, FL '86 (NURS)
HORAN, EUGENE F., vice-pres. commun. rel., Robert Wood Johnson University Hospital, New Brunswick, NJ '81 (PR)
HORAN, GARY STEPHEN, dir., St. Vincent's Medical Center of Richmond, Staten Island, NY '71
HORAN, KATHRYN V., supv. cent. serv., Mercy Hospital, Rockville Centre, NY '67 (CS)
HORAN, THOMAS J., atty., Southwest Community Health Services, Albuquerque, NM '81 (ATTY)
HORAN, TIMOTHY J., dir. diet., Hartford Hospital, Hartford, CT '76 (FOOD)
HORBIAK, PATRICIA LYNN, student, School of Hygiene and Public Health, Johns Hopkins University, Baltimore, MD '84
HOREJSI, GLORIA A., dir. soc. serv., Missoula Community Hospital, Missoula, MT '79 (SOC)
HORGAN, JUDITH T., dir. vol. serv., Magee-Womens Hospital, Pittsburgh, PA '84 (VOL)
HORGER, ROBERT R., atty., Orangeburg-Calhoun Regional Hospital, Orangeburg, SC '83 (ATTY)
HORLANDER, FRED J., dir. pers., Clark County Memorial Hospital, Jeffersonville, IN '84 (PERS)
HORLANDER, MARGARET A., acct. mgr., K. Shaver Advertising and Public Relations, Louisville, KY '86 (PR)
HORLICK, KAREN A., dir. soc. serv., California Medical Center-Los Angeles, Los Angeles, CA '86 (SOC)
HORN, ALBERTA LUECKE, owner and mgr., Dunhill of Everett, Everett, WA '85
HORN, ALTON L., dir. plant oper., Morton Hospital and Medical Center, Taunton, MA '82 (ENG)
HORN, LEAGENE G., dir. soc. serv., Sacred Heart Medical Center, Spokane, WA '85 (SOC)
HORN, LYNN M., assoc., Herman Smith Associates, Hinsdale, IL '86
HORN, MICHAEL P., mgr. inplementation, HBO and Company, Evanston, IL '85 (MGMT)
HORN, PAUL, dir. eng., Northern Michigan Hospitals, Petoskey, MI '77 (ENG)
HORN, RAYMOND, sr. vice-pres. and treas., Norwalk Hospital, Norwalk, CT '68
HORN, SHIRLEY, dir. matl. mgt., Calgary General Hospital, Calgary, Alta., Canada '86 (PUR)
HORNBACH, TERRI S., coor. pub. rel. acct., Christ Hospital, Cincinnati, OH '86 (PR)
HORNBRUCH, RAYMOND E., dir. plant eng., Imperial Point Medical Center, Fort Lauderdale, FL '83 (ENG)
HORNE, ELIZABETH B., asst. dir. plng., Shands Hospital, Gainesville, FL '85 (PLNG)
HORNELL, JAMES T., dir. oper., Northwest Hospital, Seattle, WA '83 (RISK)
HORNFECK, SHIRLEY J., RN, asst. dir. nrsg., Western Pennsylvania Hospital, Pittsburgh, PA '86 (NURS)
HORNICKLE, RICHARD J., dir. info. serv., Pennsylvania Hospital, Philadelphia, PA '85 (MGMT)
HORNING, DUANE E., exec. dir., Allen Memorial Hospital, Oberlin, OH '80
HORNSBY, RUDY L., dir. plant oper., Huntsville Hospital, Huntsville, AL '81 (ENG)
HORNSTROM, ROGER L., asst. dir. diet. serv., Southwest Community Health System, Middleburg Heights, OH '80 (FOOD)
HORNUNG, KATHLEEN, sr. vice-pres., Libra Health Technology, Rockville, MD '84
HORNUNG, MARTIN O., dir. matl., Mercy Health Systems of the Gulf South, New Orleans, LA '86 (PUR)
HORNYAK, BARBARA A., dir. diet. serv., St. Alexis Hospital, Cleveland, OH '70 (FOOD)
HORNYAK, BRENDA, supv. amb. care, Kosciusko Community Hospital, Warsaw, IN '87 (AMB)
HORRALL, THOMAS V., dir. mgt. eng., Mercy Hospital, Toledo, OH '85 (MGMT)
HORRELL, WAYNE A., vice-pres. mktg. and plng., Baltimore County General Hospital, Randallstown, MD '84 (PLNG)
HORRISBERGER, KAREN E., RN, dir. critical care and spec. units, Mansfield General Hospital, Mansfield, OH '83 (NURS)
HORSH, DONALD J., (ret.), Glendale, MO '53 (ATTY)(LIFE)
HORSHAM-BRATHWAITE, STEVE, dir. hskpg., Daughters of Jacob Geriatric, Bronx, NY '86 (ENVIRON)
HORST, CECIL, dir. plng., St. Joseph Hospital, Flint, MI '82 (PLNG)
HORST, TOM E., student, Central Michigan University, Mount Pleasant, MI '84
HORSTKOTTE, DON A., assoc. vice-pres., Sisters of Mercy Health Corporation, Southfield, MI '82
HORSTMANN, DEBORAH S., adm. asst., Mercy Regional Medical Center, Vicksburg, MS '86 (PERS)
HORTENSTINE, PAMELA A., RN, asst. dir. nrsg., Sarah Bush Lincoln Health Center, Mattoon, IL '85 (NURS)
HORTON, CAROL E., RN, dir. psych. nrsg. serv., Framingham Union Hospital, Framingham, MA '84 (NURS)
HORTON, CATHERINE, dir. qual. assur. and risk mgt., St. Mary Hospital, Philadelphia, PA '86 (RISK)
HORTON, CHARLIE MILTON, vice-pres. sup. serv., Rutherford Hospital, Rutherfordton, NC '78
HORTON, CONSTANTINA L., mgr. pub. rel., Children's Hospital of Alabama, Birmingham, AL '85 (PR)
HORTON, DAVID A., dir. mktg. and bus. mgr., Helen Keller Memorial Hospital, Sheffield, AL '85 (PR)
HORTON, ELAINE E., student, Alfred University, Alfred, NY '85
HORTON, HOMER JR., adm., Hunt Memorial Hospital District, Greenville, TX '83 (RISK)
HORTON, JAMES ALAN, asst. adm., Clayton General Hospital, Riverdale, GA '78 (MGMT)
HORTON, JODI, vice-pres. pub. rel. and dev., St. Joseph's Medical Center, Yonkers, NY '81 (PR)
HORTON, LOTTIE F., dir. plng., Santa Barbara Cottage Hospital, Santa Barbara, CA '82 (PLNG)
HORTON, PATRICIA, RN, assoc. dir. nrsg., North Carolina Baptist Hospital, Winston-Salem, NC '79 (NURS)
HORTON, SUSAN R., dir. cardiac rehab., Catholic Medical Center, Manchester, NH '81 (EDUC)
HORTON, THOMAS A., dir. human res., Mercy Health Care System, Cincinnati, OH '76 (PERS)
HORTY, JOHN F., partner, Horty, Springer and Mattern, Pittsburgh, PA '68 (ATTY)(LIFE)
HORTY, THOMAS, pres., Horty, Elving and Associates, Minneapolis, MN '67
HORVAT, FRANK P., dir. tech. support serv. and regional mgr., Medical Instrumentation Systems, Mount Clemens, MI '86 (ENG)
HORVATH, BONNIE JOYCE, student, Department of Health Services Administration, George Washington University, Washington, DC '83 (PLNG)
HORVATH, JERRI L., dir. diet., Silvercreek Manor, San Antonio, TX '84 (FOOD)
HORVATH, JOSEPH A., adm. asst. and dir. matl. mgt., Somerset Medical Center, Somerville, NJ '84 (PUR)
HORVITZ, DEBORAH J., dir. pub. rel., Hebrew Rehabilitation Center for Aged, Boston, MA '86 (PR)
HORWATH, LAWRENCE J. JR., dir. eng. and maint., Warren Hospital, Phillipsburg, NJ '70 (ENG)
HORWITZ, DEANNA M., mgr. med. info. syst., Henry Ford Hospital, Detroit, MI '85 (MGMT)
HORWITZ, JAMES D., atty., Glens Falls Hospital, Glens Falls, NY '86 (ATTY)
HORWITZ, THEODORE H., pres., Meriden-Wallingford Hospital, Meriden, CT '66
HOSFELD, ANNE L., RN, asst. adm. pat. care, Novato Community Hospital, Novato, CA '86 (NURS)
HOSICK, ARLENE D., RN, dir. nrsg., Clay County Hospital, Flora, IL '74 (NURS)
HOSICK, JUNE E., dir. trng., Christ Hospital, Cincinnati, OH '71 (EDUC)
HOSIE, ISABELLA C., dir. vol. serv., St. Joseph Hospital, Baltimore, MD '72 (VOL)
HOSKING, JAMES E., prin., Herman Smith Associates, Hinsdale, IL '72 (MGMT)
HOSKING, PHYLLIS M., aux. coor., St. Marys Hospital of Rochester, Rochester, MN '86 (VOL)
HOSKINS, ELIZABETH A., coor. pat. rep., St. Luke's Methodist Hospital, Cedar Rapids, IA '87 (PAT)
HOSKINS, GERALDINE, RN, vice-pres., Jewish Hospital of Cincinnati, Cincinnati, OH '74 (NURS)
HOSKINS, JAMES E., dir. risk mgt., Iowa Methodist Medical Center, Des Moines, IA '80 (RISK)
HOSLER, STEVE G., dir. pers., G. N. Wilcox Memorial Hospital, Lihue, HI '82 (RISK)(PERS)
HOSLTEIN, ELLEN A., asst. dir. vol. serv., Bryan Memorial Hospital, Lincoln, NE '82 (VOL)
HOSPERS, COLEE J., RN, dir. surg. nrsg. serv., Ottumwa Regional Health Center, Ottumwa, IA '82 (NURS)
HOSPODAR, JOYCE A., dir. plng., St. Mark's Hospital, Salt Lake City, UT '82 (PLNG)
HOSS, SCHUYLER F., vice-pres. commun. dev., Visiting Nurse Association, Portland, OR '86 (PLNG)
HOST, NANCY H., dir. mktg. and plng., Memorial Hospital, Fremont, OH '83 (PLNG)
HOSTAGE, SUSAN DUNCAN, vice-pres. prof. serv., New Milford Hospital, New Milford, CT '81 (PLNG)
HOSTERT, ARTHUR H., prog. mgt., Hahnemann University Hospital, Philadelphia, PA '85 (MGMT)
HOSTETLER, PHILIP M., RN, asst. dir. nrsg., Providence Medical Center, Portland, OR '83 (NURS)
HOSTETLER, ROSEMARY, dir. vol. and commun. rel., LaPorte Hospital, LaPorte, IN '80 (VOL)(PR)
HOSTINSKY, LT. CATHY, MSC USN, U. S. Naval Hospital, Norfolk, VA '86 (EDUC)
HOSTLER, PAT, coor. telecommun., St. Luke's Hospital, Chesterfield, MO '86 (ENG)
HOTCHKISS, DIANA K., dir. matl. mgt., Alamosa Community Hospital, Alamosa, CO '81 (PUR)
HOTCHKISS, JAY, dir. human res., Osteopathic Hospital of Maine, Portland, ME '86 (PERS)
HOTT, DAVE, dir. gen. serv., Holy Family Hospital, Spokane, WA '83 (ENG)
HOTTENDORF, CATHERINE, RN, asst. hosp. dir. nrsg. serv., Nassau County Medical Center, East Meadow, NY '84 (NURS)
HOTTENSTEIN, PAUL A., dir. mech. eng., Medlantic Healthcare Group, Washington, DC '85 (ENG)
HOTZ, ROBERT W., dir. maint. and eng., Gordon Memorial Hospital District, Gordon, NE '85 (ENG)
HOUCHIN, LEO, dir. maint., Osceola Memorial Hospital, Osceola, AR '71 (ENG)
HOUCK, EDWARD W., vice-pres., Sarasota Memorial Hospital, Sarasota, FL '83 (PLNG)
HOUCK, EDWIN J., mgr. plant oper., West Nebraska General Hospital, Scottsbluff, NE '78 (ENG)
HOUCK, GLORIA J., RN, dir. clin., Abington Memorial Hospital, Abington, PA '86 (NURS)
HOUDEK, FRED J., Prospect Heights, IL '74
HOUDEK, JAMES JR., assoc. dir., American Hospital Association, Washington, DC '80
HOUDYSHELL, BERTA M., RN, dir. nrsg., Methodist Hospital, Jacksonville, FL '81 (NURS)
HOUGAARD, JUDY, RN, asst. adm. and dir. nrsg. serv., St. Mark's Hospital, Salt Lake City, UT '80 (NURS)
HOUGEN, INGRID FRANK, dir. pers., Virginia Mason Hospital, Seattle, WA '68 (PERS)
HOUGH, ADELE, RN, asst. adm. nrsg., Moses H. Cone Memorial Hospital, Greensboro, NC '80 (NURS)
HOUGH, CHARLES S. JR., vice-pres. & adm., Bryn Mawr Hospital, Bryn Mawr, PA '84 (PLNG)
HOUGH, DOROTHY A., chief vol. serv., Veterans Administration Medical Center, Baltimore, MD '85 (VOL)
HOUGH, FREDERICK A., exec. dir., Braddock General Hospital, Braddock, PA '66
HOUGH, MARGARET B., student, Program and Bureau of Hospital Administration, University of Michigan, Ann Arbor, MI '84
HOUGH, MARTHA, dir. qual. and util. mgt., Maryland Hospital Education Institute, Lutherville, MD '85 (RISK)
HOUGH, STEPHEN R., mgr. market analysis, Scott and White, Temple, TX '82 (PLNG)
HOUGHKIRK, ELLEN, chief soc. work serv., Veterans Administration Medical Center, Grand Island, NE '80 (SOC)
HOUGHTON, DONNA A., consulting mgr., Denver Tech Group, Denver, CO '81
HOUGHTON, JACK F., adm., HCA Vista Hills Medical Center, El Paso, TX '69
HOUGHTON, LISBETH, (ret.), Elmhurst, IL '66 (SOC)
HOUGHTON, MARY ALICE, dir. vol. serv. and pat. rep., Princeton Community Hospital, Princeton, WV '77 (PAT)(VOL)
HOUK, MARVIN R., Healthcare Equipment and Services, Plano, TX '78
HOULE, SHEILA A., dir. mktg., St. Ann's Hospital, Watertown, SD '84 (PR) (PLNG)
HOULIHAN, KATHY, adm., American Red Cross Blood Service, Portland, OR '85
HOULIHAN, SIMON J., pers. and labor rel. consult., Colorado Hospital Association, Denver, CO '84 (PERS)
HOUSE, EVA J., dir. outpatient serv., Bronson Methodist Hospital, Kalamazoo, MI '87 (AMB)
HOUSE, IRMA P., dir. educ. serv., Bon Secours Hospital, Baltimore, MD '86 (EDUC)
HOUSE, MILTON V., coor. constr., Providence Memorial Hospital, El Paso, TX '84 (ENG)
HOUSE, ROY C., (ret.), Mesa, AZ '48 (LIFE)
HOUSER, CHARLOTTE R., dir. food serv., Texoma Medical Center, Denison, TX '77 (FOOD)
HOUSER, DOUGLAS R., adm. children and youth proj., Children's Hospital, Columbus, OH '80
HOUSER, KATHLEEN W., dir. commun. rel., St. Margaret Memorial Hospital, Pittsburgh, PA '83 (PR)
HOUSER, WILLIAM R., mech. eng., U. S. Army Environmental Hygiene Agency, Aberdeen Proving Grd, MD '86 (ENG)
HOUSTON, JOAN, vice-pres. nrsg. serv., Texas Hospital Association, Austin, TX '80 (NURS)
HOUSTON, LINDSAY, dir. commun., Swedish Medical Center, Englewood, CO '85 (ENG)
HOUSTON, RICHARD, student, University of Dallas, Irving, TX '85
HOUSTON, ROBIN R., dir. pers., Valley General Hospital, Monroe, WA '86 (PERS)
HOUSTON, W. SCOTT, dir. pers. serv., Health and Hospital Services, Bellevue, WA '80 (PERS)(RISK)
HOUSTON, WILLIAM A., co-dir. emer. serv., Osteopathic Hospital of Maine, Portland, ME '87 (AMB)
HOUTLER, WAYNE T., dir. plant oper., Saint Anthony Medical Center, Rockford, IL '85 (ENG)(ENVIRON)
HOUTS, CLARENCE JR., chief eng., Silverton Hospital, Silverton, OR '81 (ENG)

HOUY, MARGARET L., asst. prof., New England School of Law, Boston, MA '80 (ATTY)
HOUYOUX, NANCY LEACH, exec. dir., Northwestern Institute of Psychiatry, Fort Washington, PA '83
HOVANCE, ANDREA J., instr. trng. and educ., St. Joseph Riverside Hospital, Warren, OH '86 (EDUC)
HOVANEC, GEORGE P., corp. proj. spec., Blue Cross and Blue Shield of Northern Ohio, Cleveland, OH '85 (MGMT)
HOVE, BARTON A., adm., Beaches Hospital, Jacksonville Beach, FL '77
HOVERKAMP, JOHN DUANE, mgr. mgt. eng., Medical College of Georgia, Division of Systems and Computer Services, Augusta, GA '77 (MGMT)
HOVEY, MONROE A., dir. pers., Lawrence Hospital, Bronxville, NY '69 (PERS)
HOWARD-ZYVOLOSKI, BARBARA E., commun. consult., Port Washington, WI '84 (PR)
HOWARD, BEVERLY K., dir. educ., Holston Valley Hospital and Medical Center, Kingsport, TN '76 (EDUC)
HOWARD, BRENDA C., dir. soc. work, North Arundel Hospital, Glen Burnie, MD '82 (SOC)
HOWARD, CAROLE, dir. soc. serv., Beverly Hospital, Beverly, MA '81 (SOC)
HOWARD, CHRISTOPHER, dir. food serv., Cardinal Hill Hospital, Lexington, KY '76 (FOOD)
HOWARD, CLARENCE A., asst. exec. dir., Mary Immaculate Hospital, Jamaica, NY '87 (AMB)
HOWARD, CLARISSA ANN, vice-pres. qual. assur. and risk mgt., Licking Memorial Hospital, Newark, OH '76 (RISK)
HOWARD, DAVID, chief eng., High Plains Baptist Hospital, Amarillo, TX '78 (ENG)
HOWARD, DEIRDRE, student, New School of Social Research, New York, NY '86
HOWARD, DENNIS D., student, Program in Hospital Administration, University of Michigan, Ann Arbor, MI '85
HOWARD, ELAYNE B., mgr. mktg. prog., Shared Medical Systems, King of Prussia, PA '76
HOWARD, ELLY, assoc. dir. human res., Cedars Medical Center, Miami, FL '82 (PERS)
HOWARD, ERNEST B., MD, Palatine, IL '70 (HON)
HOWARD, GERALD L., student, University of Kansas, Wichita, KS '84
HOWARD, H. LAMAR, adm., Gamble Brothers and Archer Clinic, Greenville, MS '87 (AMB)
HOWARD, IVAN D., adm. support div., Sutter Community Hospitals, Sacramento, CA '86
HOWARD, J. KENT, sr. vice-pres., Research Medical Center, Kansas City, MO '85
HOWARD, JANELLE R., mktg. commun. spec., Hillcrest Medical Center, Tulsa, OK '86 (PR)
HOWARD, JOHN R., consult., Newton Associates, Walnut Creek, CA '86
HOWARD, KATHY, dir. soc. serv., Leonard Morse Hospital, Natick, MA '81 (SOC)
HOWARD, MIKE D., supv. maint., Archer County Hospital, Archer City, TX '85 (ENG)
HOWARD, MILDRED D., Blue Bell, PA '75
HOWARD, PATRICK C., asst. dir. food serv., Flower Memorial Hospital, Sylvania, OH '85 (FOOD)
HOWARD, RAYMOND A., dir. plng., Memorial Health System, Inc., South Bend, IN '83 (PLNG)
HOWARD, REX H., dir. educ., St. Anthony's Hospital, Amarillo, TX '80 (EDUC)
HOWARD, RICHARD S., Kansas City, MO '73
HOWARD, ROBERT L. JR., dir. support serv., Merle West Medical Center, Klamath Falls, OR '69 (ENG)
HOWARD, ROBERT M., dir. plng., Children's Hospital Medical Center, Akron, OH '84 (PLNG)
HOWARD, SHERRY L., RN, exec. dir. in-patient nrsg., Holy Family Hospital, Spokane, WA '84 (NURS)
HOWARD, STEPHEN C., dir. human res., Good Samaritan Hospital, Lexington, KY '85 (PERS)
HOWARD, STEVEN M., dir. matl. mgt., Sacred Heart General Hospital, Eugene, OR '82 (PUR)
HOWARD, THOMAS J., dir. plant oper., Eastwood Hospital, Memphis, TN '83 (ENG)
HOWARD, WESLEY W., asst. adm. eng., St. Joseph's Hospital, Stockton, CA '72 (ENG)
HOWARD, WILLIAM E., dir. eng., Boone Hospital Center, Columbia, MO '74 (ENG)
HOWARTH, MARGARET JOYCE, dir. vol. serv., Cross Cancer Institute, Edmonton, Alta., Canada '82 (VOL)
HOWE, COLLEEN M., mgt. eng., William Beaumont Hospital, Southfield, MI '84 (MGMT)
HOWE, DAVID D., dir. plant oper., Memorial Hospital, Cumberland, MD '80 (ENG)
HOWE, FREDRICK GORDON JR., dir. mktg., Lewistown Hospital, Lewistown, PA '83 (PR)
HOWE, LINDA A., coor. educ., Montgomery General Hospital, Montgomery, WV '86 (EDUC)
HOWE, VICTOR, dir. matl. mgt., Memorial Hospital of Burlington County, Mount Holly, NJ '86 (PUR)
HOWEL, CLAUDETTE H., dir. vol. serv. and mktg., Doctors Hospital, Tucker, GA '86 (VOL)(PR)
HOWELL, BETTY J., RN, asst. dir. spec. proj., Salvation Army William Booth Memorial Hospital, Florence, KY '86 (NURS)
HOWELL, CAROL A., sr. vice-pres., Custom Management Corporation, Kingston, PA '82 (FOOD)
HOWELL, DENNIS R., mgr. matl., Longmont United Hospital, Longmont, CO '82 (CS)(PUR)
HOWELL, ED, dir. mgt. eng., Bloomington Hospital, Bloomington, IN '80 (MGMT)
HOWELL, JAMES F., atty., Midwest City Memorial Hospital, Midwest City, OK '84 (ATTY)
HOWELL, JOHN J., dir. pur., St. Francis Xavier Hospital, Charleston, SC '75 (PUR)
HOWELL, JULIANNE R., PhD, assoc. dir., University of California San Diego Medical Center, San Diego, CA '81 (PLNG)
HOWELL, KYLE E., asst. adm., University Hospital, Augusta, GA '76
HOWELL, LADSON FISHBURNE, atty., Beaufort Memorial Hospital, Beaufort, SC '81 (ATTY)
HOWELL, RONALD JAY, student, Program in Health Services Administration, Indiana University, Indianapolis, IN '86
HOWELL, SALLY B., dir. diet., Kootenai Medical Center, Coeur D'Alene, ID '79 (FOOD)
HOWELL, SALLY S., dir. vol. serv., Christian Hospital Northeast-Northwest, St. Louis, St. Louis, MO '81 (VOL)
HOWELL, SUSAN HALLIDAY, dir. pur., Irving Community Hospital, Irving, TX '85 (PUR)
HOWELL, VIRGINIA T., dir. matl. mgt., Elizabeth General Medical Center, Elizabeth, NJ '85 (PUR)
HOWELLS, JOHN E. III, San Diego, CA '83
HOWERTON, PEGGY, asst. dir. cent. serv., St. John's Regional Medical Center, Joplin, MO '83 (CS)
HOWERTON, RICHARD T., sr. vice-pres., Presbyterian Hospital, Charlotte, NC '85 (PLNG)
HOWERTON, ROBERT B. III, dir. dev. oper., Methodist Health Systems, Inc., Memphis, TN '85
HOWERTON, ROBERT F., corp. dir. pub. rel., Baptist Medical Centers, Birmingham, AL '79 (PR)
HOWES, INEZ, RN, dir. nrsg. serv., Pleasant Valley Hospital, Point Pleasant, WV '76 (NURS)
HOWES, WILLIAM R., (ret.), Harwich, MA '49 (LIFE)
HOWICK, ANDREW R., sr. mgt. eng., University of Wisconsin Hospital and Clinics, Madison, WI '87 (MGMT)
HOWIE, ELIZABETH WEINSCHENK, RN, San Jose, CA '51 (LIFE)
HOWILER, ANN M., RN, mgr. amb. nrsg. serv., Meridian Park Hospital, Tualatin, OR '86 (NURS)
HOWITT, KATHLEEN M., dir. diet., Piqua Memorial Medical Center, Piqua, OH '82 (FOOD)
HOWLAND, ELVIN B., exec. vice-pres., Community Medical Center, Scranton, PA '71
HOWLETT, MARLENE S., RN, dir. nrsg., Brunswick Hospital, Supply, NC '81 (NURS)
HOWLIN, JOYCE, RN, vice-pres. nrsg., Valley Hospital, Ridgewood, NJ '70 (NURS)
HOWSER, DAVID M., eng., Memorial Hospital, McPherson, KS '84 (ENG)
HOXIE, DAVID EVANS, sr. vice-pres., Methodist Health Care Network, Houston, TX '61
HOY, MICHAEL J., atty., Evangelical Health Systems, Oak Brook, IL '84 (ATTY)
HOYE, ELLEN F., student, Rush University, Chicago, IL '84
HOYT, JEANNE K., instr., Baptist Medical Center, Kansas City, MO '87 (EDUC)
HOYT, JOHN B., mgt. eng., St. Joseph's Hospital and Medical Center, Phoenix, AZ '86 (MGMT)
HOYT, JOHN T., vice-pres., Englewood Community Hospital, Englewood, FL '62
HOYT, PAUL A., exec. vice-pres., Somerset Medical Center, Somerville, NJ '76
HOYT, PAULA J., asst. pub. info., Sturdy Memorial Hospital, Attleboro, MA '86 (PR)
HOYT, ROBERT A., dir. soc. serv., Saint Francis Medical Center, Peoria, IL '80 (SOC)
HOYT, V. A. W., RN, adm. nrsg., Rockdale Hospital, Conyers, GA '83 (NURS)
HRANAC, LOUISE A., student, Idaho State University, Pocatello, ID '85
HREACHMACK, C. PATRICK, St. John's Healthcare Corporation, Anderson, IN '81
HRIC, AILENE M., pat. rep., Sinai Hospital of Detroit, Detroit, MI '78 (PAT)
HRISOMALOS, BECKY, dir. med. soc. serv., Bloomington Hospital, Bloomington, IN '85 (SOC)
HRITZ, WILLIAM ROBERT, mgr. adm. serv., Mercy Hospital, Miami, FL '77 (MGMT)
HRONCHEK, KATHLEEN M., pat. serv. rep. and discharge planner, HCA Palmyra Medical Centers, Albany, GA '85 (PAT)
HRUSOVSKY, JEROME, dir. new bus., Abbott Laboratories, North Chicago, IL '84
HSU, JUI-SHAN S., student, Program in Health Systems, Shcl of Industrial and Systems Engineer, Georgia Institute of Technology, Atlanta, GA '87 (MGMT)
HUANG, CHING CHAW, RN, assoc. dir. nrsg., Howard University Hospital, Washington, DC '83 (NURS)
HUANG, JAUE-HWA J., dir. diet., Seaway Hospital, Trenton, MI '83 (FOOD)
HUANG, SHEILA H., asst. mgr. educ. and trng., Northwest Hospital, Seattle, WA '80 (EDUC)
HUARD, GARRY B., dir. pers., Leila Hospital and Health Center, Battle Creek, MI '71 (PERS)
HUBBARD, BERNARD RAWLINGS, RN, dir. risk mgt. and safety, Middle Tennessee Medical Center, Murfreesboro, TN '85 (RISK)
HUBBARD, CHARLES A., pres., Allied Adjustment Service, Needham, MA '85 (RISK)
HUBBARD, DOROTHY MARY, Shreveport, LA '78
HUBBARD, HELEN F., dir. soc. serv., Stephens Memorial Hospital, Norway, ME '81 (SOC)
HUBBARD, KATHERINE, head nrs. outpatient, University Medical Center of Southern Nevada, Las Vegas, NV '86 (AMB)
HUBBARD, KAY B., RN, dir. pat. serv., Northeast Alabama Regional Medical Center, Anniston, AL '85 (NURS)
HUBBARD, KAY, instr. educ. serv., University Hospital, London, Ont., Canada '79 (EDUC)
HUBBARD, KIM S., dir. mktg. and commun. rel., Rockdale Hospital, Conyers, GA '83 (PR)
HUBBARD, LYNN, RN, dir. nrs., Stonewall Jackson Memorial Hospital, Weston, WV '86 (NURS)
HUBBARD, MARK, dir. risk mgt., Loma Linda University Medical Center, Loma Linda, CA '85 (RISK)
HUBBARD, MICHAL A., dir. bus. dev., HCA Medical Center of Plano, Plano, TX '84 (PLNG)
HUBBARD, ROBERT E., dir. mktg., American Medical International, Washington, DC '85 (PR)
HUBBARD, RODNEY C., energy conservation consult., Engineering Sciences, Inc., Memphis, TN '86 (ENG)
HUBBART, CAROLYN GAY, pat. rep. and proj. mgr., Kaseman Presbyterian Hospital, Albuquerque, NM '85 (PAT)
HUBBART, JAMES A., asst. adm., Lutheran General Hospital, San Antonio, TX '69
HUBBELL, ANNMARIE B., supv. sterile cent. serv., Doctors Hospital of Jefferson, Metairie, LA '85 (CS)
HUBBELL, MARK B., mgt. analyst, Red Deer Regional Hospital Centre, Red Deer, Alta., Canada '83 (MGMT)
HUBBLE, JON C., dir. mgt. eng., Scott and White Memorial Hospital, Temple, TX '75 (MGMT)
HUBER, CAROL A., dir. pub. rel., St. Francis Hospital, Poughkeepsie, NY '85 (PR)
HUBER, CONNIE S., RN, asst. adm. pat. serv., Meridian Park Hospital, Tualatin, OR '81 (NURS)
HUBER, GEORGE A., atty., Western Psychiatric Institute and Clinic, Pittsburgh, PA '72 (MGMT)(ATTY)
HUBER, KAREN M., coor. staff dev., Community General Hospital, Sterling, IL '86 (EDUC)
HUBER, KATHRYN, coor. risk mgt., Dallas County Hospital District, Dallas, TX '85 (RISK)
HUBER, MARILYN J., mktg. coor., Christian Hospitals Northeast-Northwest, St. Louis, MO '85 (PR)
HUBER, MARY LOUISE, asst. adm., St. John Hospital, Detroit, MI '82 (EDUC)(NURS)
HUBER, MICHAEL R., asst. dir. plng., Lifespan, Inc., Minneapolis, MN '79 (PLNG)(AMB)
HUBER, ROBERT F., dir. pur., Newington Children's Hospital, Newington, CT '83 (PUR)
HUBER, STAN A., pres., Stan A. Huber Consultants, Inc., New Lenox, IL '74
HUBER, SUSAN M., sr. consult., Peat, Marwick, Mitchell and Company, Kansas, MO '86 (PLNG)
HUBERT, DAVID C., mgr. mktg. and commun. rel., Black Hills Community Hospital, Olympia, WA '84 (PR)
HUBERTY, DANIEL J., partner, Zimmer, Gunsul and Frasca Partnership, Portland, OR '83
HUBLER, JOYCE, dir. vol. serv., St. Joseph Hospital, Eureka, CA '83 (VOL)
HUBNER, MARY G., dir. pub. rel., Nashville Memorial Hospital, Madison, TN '85 (PR)
HUCH, ROBERT E., adm., Tazewell Community Hospital, Tazewell, VA '83
HUCHKO, JOSEPH E., Southwest, PA '75
HUCK, JAMES M. JR., atty., Central DuPage Hospital, Winfield, IL '74 (ATTY)
HUCK, RICHARD J., assoc. adm. human resources, Mercy Hospital, Baltimore, MD '81 (PERS)
HUCKLEBERRY, CHARLES R., dir. eng., Floyd Memorial Hospital, New Albany, IN '85 (ENG)
HUCKLEBRIDGE, MARK H., dir. commun. rel., Watsonville Community Hospital, Watsonville, CA '81 (PR)
HUCKSTEP, STEPHEN CHARLES, RN, student, Webster College, St. Louis, MO '84
HUDAK, RONALD P., mgr. pers. policy, Department of the Army, Office of the Surgeon General, Washington, DC '79
HUDDERS, JOHN R., atty., Allentown Hospital, Allentown, PA '74 (ATTY)
HUDDLESTON, KIMBERLY, coor. risk mgt., St. Mary's Medical Center, Knoxville, TN '84 (RISK)
HUDDLESTON, THOMAS L., mgr. pur., Christian Hospitals Northeast-Northwest, St. Louis, MO '84 (PUR)
HUDEC, MARY SUZANNE, RN, chief nrsg. serv., Veterans Administration Medical Center, Washington, DC '80 (NURS)
HUDES, JACK H., PhD, Kaiser Permanente, Los Angeles, CA '82 (MGMT)
HUDES, NEIL, dir. educ. serv., Memorial General Hospital, Union, NJ '86 (EDUC)
HUDGENS, A. NEIL, atty., Providence Hospital, Mobile, AL '81 (ATTY)
HUDGINS, ROBERT W., dir. pers., Southside Mental Health and Mental Retardation, Petersburg, VA '76 (PERS)
HUDGINS, THOMAS J., vice-pres. oper., Galion Community Hospital, Galion, OH '74
HUDIK, BERNARD JAMES, dir. food serv., Saint Mary of Nazareth Hospital Center, Chicago, IL '72 (FOOD)
HUDIK, MARTIN FRANCIS, asst. adm., Illinois Masonic Medical Center, Chicago, IL '77 (ENG)(RISK)
HUDOCK, COL. JOHN M., MSC USA, mgr. pers., U. S. Army Office of Surgeon General, Falls Church, VA '77
HUDSON, BETTY G., sr. consult. adv., Ernst and Whinney, Chicago, IL '85 (MGMT)
HUDSON, DONALD, asst. adm. support serv., American River Hospital, Carmichael, CA '86 (RISK)
HUDSON, E. W., chief eng., Kaiser Foundation Hospital, San Francisco, CA '86 (ENG)
HUDSON, FAYE K., dir. soc. work serv., Roseland Community Hospital, Chicago, IL '75 (SOC)
HUDSON, FRANCES H., RN, dir. nrsg. serv., North Side Hospital, Johnson City, TN '80 (NURS)
HUDSON, FRANK C., pres. and chief exec. off., Seton Medical Center, Daly City, CA '86
HUDSON, GARY MIKEAL, assoc. adm., Timberlawn Psychiatric Hospital, Dallas, TX '75
HUDSON, JAMES H., adm., Vernon Memorial Hospital, Viroqua, WI '85
HUDSON, JANE A., RN, assoc. dir., University of Tennessee Memorial Hospital, Knoxville, TN '83 (NURS)
HUDSON, KENNETH L., asst. exec. dir., Children's Hospital Guidance Center, Columbus, OH '82
HUDSON, LINDA K., RN, dir. nrsg. serv., Methodist Hospital, Hattiesburg, MS '86 (NURS)
HUDSON, LOWELL G., dir. plant oper., Hamilton Medical Center Hospital, Lafayette, LA '82 (ENG)
HUDSON, NANCY G., dir. pers., Riverside Hospital, Jacksonville, FL '82 (PERS)
HUDSON, NANCY RICE, atty., Memorial Hospital System, Houston, TX '84 (ATTY)
HUDSON, PAUL L. JR., atty., Cobb Memorial Hospital, Royston, GA '82 (ATTY)
HUDSON, RANNIE S., dir. plant oper., Beebe Hospital of Sussex County, Lewes, DE '85 (ENG)

HUDSON, RAY, MD, bd. mem., Walker Regional Medical Center, Jasper, AL '81
HUDSON, RICHARD E., adm. and chief exec. off., Baker Hospital, North Charleston, SC '80
HUDSON, WILLIAM F., dir. diet., Medical Center of Delaware, Wilmington, DE '80 (FOOD)
HUDSPETH, BARRY E., dir. pur. mgt., Baptist Hospital, Pensacola, FL '87 (PUR)
HUDSPETH, INGRID FOX, RN, dir. nrsg. serv., St. Benedict's Family Medical Center, Jerome, ID '84 (NURS)
HUDSPETH, TODD R., student, Iowa State University, Ames, IA '87 (MGMT)
HUEBERT, JAMES H., dir. soc. serv., Williamsport Hospital and Medical Center, Williamsport, PA '86 (SOC)
HUEBNER, DONALD P., Rochester Hills, MI '81 (MGMT)
HUEBNER, JACK L., exec. dir., Teco, Houston, TX '77 (ENG)
HUEBNER, STEPHEN, dir. matl. mgt., Waterbury Hospital, Waterbury, CT '77 (PUR)
HUEBNER, THOMAS W., vice-pres. mktg. and strategic plng., Choate-Symmes Health System, Arlington, MA '84 (PLNG)
HUESTON, RALPH MARSHALL, (ret.), Cedar Rapids, IA '26 (LIFE)
HUETTIG, JANET E., adm. supv. soc. serv., Massachusetts Eye and Ear Infirmary, Boston, MA '83 (SOC)
HUEY, ELIZABETH A., vice-pres., Piper, Jaffray and Tower, Minneapolis, MN '82
HUEY, J. P., McKinney, TX '53 (LIFE)
HUEY, LLOYD RAY, chief eng., Lourdes Hospital, Paducah, KY '75 (ENG)
HUEY, WILLIAM R., dir. mktg., Brazosport Memorial Hospital, Lake Jackson, TX '86 (PR)
HUFF, CONNIE C., RN, asst. adm. nrsg. serv., Mercy San Juan Hospital, Carmichael, CA '82 (NURS)
HUFF, DIANA L. NOLTE, commun. health nrs., Health Care at Home, Hinsdale, IL '86 (RISK)
HUFF, DIANA S., dir. commun. rel., United Community Hospital, Grove City, PA '86 (PR)
HUFF, GLEN D., atty., Norman Regional Hospital, Norman, OK '80 (ATTY)
HUFF, JOYCE E., dir. commun. rel., Northwestern Medical Center, St. Albans, VT '86 (PR)
HUFF, MICHAEL H., adm. asst., Shannon Healthcare Services, San Angelo, TX '86
HUFF, SARA DAVIS, nrs. consult., Atlanta, GA '86
HUFF, SHARON A., RN, asst. adm. nrsg., Utah Valley Regional Medical Center, Provo, UT '84 (NURS)
HUFF, WILLIAM J., adm. shared serv., Christian Hospitals Northeast-Northwest, St. Louis, MO '75
HUFFMAN, CATHERINE L., dir. pur., Pleasant Valley Hospital, Point Pleasant, WV '85 (PUR)
HUFFMAN, HENRY S. JR., mgr. bldg. serv., Fruco Engineers, Inc., Ballwin, MO '85 (ENG)
HUFFMAN, MYRON, dir. pur., Adventist Health Systems, U. S., Arlington, TX '86 (PUR)
HUFFMAN, PAUL E., chief eng., Saint James Hospital, Pontiac, IL '75 (ENG)
HUFFMAN, ROBIN B., dir. mktg., Middle Georgia Hospital, Macon, GA '86 (PR)
HUFFSTETLER, J. FRANK, dir. plant oper., La Hacienda Treatment Center, Hunt, TX '71 (ENG)
HUFFSTETLER, NOAH H., atty., Rex Hospital, Raleigh, NC '82 (ATTY)
HUFFSTUTLER, C. DAVID, dir. and chief exec. off. staff serv., The Methodist Hospital, Houston, TX '79
HUFSCHMID, NANCY K., RN, dir. nrsg., South Community Hospital, Oklahoma City, OK '82 (NURS)
HUFSTEDLER, RICHARD, dir. mgt. syst., Augustana Hospital and Health Care Center, Chicago, IL '82 (ENG)
HUFTON, WILFRID L., Saginaw Osteopathic Hospital, Saginaw, MI '56 (LIFE)
HUG, LINDA S., mgt. eng., Northside Hospital, Atlanta, GA '83 (MGMT)
HUGER, BERNARD C., atty., St. Mary's Health Center, St. Louis, MO '72 (ATTY)
HUGGETT, BARBARA, dir. pub. rel. and vol. serv., Lawndale Community Hospital, Philadelphia, PA '83 (VOL)
HUGGINS, HARRY L., mgr. phys. facil., Healthcare International Inc., Austin, TX '86 (ENG)
HUGGINS, MICHAEL L., coor. human res., Our Lady of Lourdes Medical Center, Lafayette, LA '80 (RISK)
HUGGINS, PAMELA J., dir. soc. serv., Ssm Rehabilitation Institute, St. Louis, MO '87 (SOC)
HUGGINS, SUSAN J., Birmingham, AL '80 (FOOD)
HUGHES, ALFRED E., atty., St. Joseph Sanitarium, Dubuque, IA '79 (ATTY)
HUGHES, ANNETTE H., supv. cent. proc., St. Mary's Hospital, Athens, GA '83 (CS)
HUGHES, ARTHUR F. JR., sr. consult., Hospital Association of New York State, Albany, NY '83 (MGMT)
HUGHES, BARBARA D., RN, dir. critical care nrsg., Candler General Hospital, Savannah, GA '84 (NURS)
HUGHES, CHARLES M., dir. food serv., Mercy Medical Center, Roseburg, OR '83 (FOOD)
HUGHES, CHARLES S., dir. soc. serv., Liberty Hospital, Liberty, MO '82 (SOC)
HUGHES, CHRISTINE M., consult., International Imaging, Inc., Bannockburn, IL '86 (PLNG)
HUGHES, CLAUDIA J., dir. vol. serv., Crozer-Chester Medical Center, Chester, PA '85 (VOL)
HUGHES, DAVID J., matl. mgr., Valley Community Hospital, Dallas, OR '87 (PUR)
HUGHES, DORA F., dir. pat. serv., Memorial City Medical Center, Houston, TX '84 (PAT)
HUGHES, DOROTHEA A., RN, vice-pres. nrsg. serv., Bon Secours Hospital of Methuen, Methuen, MA '76 (NURS)
HUGHES, DOROTHY M., div. dir. nrsg. serv., Community General Hospital, Sterling, IL '81 (NURS)
HUGHES, EILEEN D., RN, dir. surg. and intravenous ther. nrsg., Fairfax Hospital, Falls Church, VA '79
HUGHES, ELLEN, RN, mgr. qual. assur., Memorial General Hospital, Las Cruces, NM '86 (RISK)
HUGHES, ERNEST L., dir. food serv., Saint Alphonsus Regional Medical Center, Boise, ID '77 (FOOD)
HUGHES, GEORGE M., atty., New England Deaconess Hospital, Boston, MA '76 (ATTY)
HUGHES, J. DEBORAH, RN, clin. asst. to med. dir., Forbes Regional Health Center, Monroeville, PA '86
HUGHES, JAMES E., (ret.), Lancaster, CA '68
HUGHES, JAMES J., atty., Ohio Hospital Association, Columbus, OH '68 (ATTY)
HUGHES, JAMIE R., RN, dir. nrsg., Charter Hospital of Jackson, Jackson, MS '72 (NURS)
HUGHES, JANE F., dir. educ., Shady Grove Adventist Hospital, Rockville, MD '83 (EDUC)
HUGHES, JEAN, pat. rep., Charleston Area Medical Center, Charleston, WV '86 (PAT)
HUGHES, JEFFREY B., dir. plng., Danbury Hospital, Danbury, CT '84 (PLNG)
HUGHES, JOHN WILLIAM, dir. diet. serv., Beth Sholom Home of Virginia, Richmond, VA '86 (FOOD)
HUGHES, JONAH, exec. vice-pres., Daughters of Charity National Purchasing Services, St. Louis, MO '86
HUGHES, JUDY, cent. serv. tech., St. Joseph's Hospital, Asheville, NC '86 (CS)
HUGHES, KATHLEEN E., consult., Jennings, Ryan, Federa and Company, Northampton, MA '81 (AMB)
HUGHES, KEVIN J., atty., St. Cloud Hospital, St. Cloud, MN '68 (ATTY)
HUGHES, LEWIS A., RN, asst. dir. med. and surg. nrsg., University of Cincinnati Hospital, Cincinnati, OH '84 (NURS)
HUGHES, LLOYD L., pres., Rhode Island Hospital, Providence, RI '51 (LIFE)
HUGHES, LU ANN, pat. serv. rep., Fisher-Titus Medical Center, Norwalk, OH '85 (PAT)
HUGHES, MARILYN A., consult., Kaiser Permanente Medical Care Program, Oakland, CA '86 (MGMT)
HUGHES, MARILYN J., dir. food mgt. and nutr. serv., Valley Medical Center, Renton, WA '77 (FOOD)
HUGHES, MARY E., RN, Long Island Jewish Medical Center, New York, NY '86 (PR) (PLNG)
HUGHES, MARYANN, vice-pres. human res., Berkshire Medical Center, Pittsfield, MA '83 (PERS)
HUGHES, MAUREEN J., dir. commun. rel., Childrens Hospital of Orange County, Orange, CA '83 (PR)
HUGHES, MELBA BOYETT, dir. clin. matl. mgt., Rapides General Hospital, Alexandria, LA '80 (CS)
HUGHES, MICHAEL D., atty., Mercy Hospital of Pittsburgh, Pittsburgh, PA '86 (ATTY)
HUGHES, MICHAEL H., asst. adm. fin., Norton Community Hospital, Norton, VA '86
HUGHES, NED B. JR., adm., Gerber Memorial Hospital, Fremont, MI '72
HUGHES, PETER R., asst. adm. mktg. and plng., Franklin Regional Medical Center, Franklin, PA '86 (PLNG)
HUGHES, RANDY R., dir. mktg. serv., Metropolitan Health Center, Erie, PA '86 (PLNG)
HUGHES, RUTH K., dir. vol. serv., Jeannette District Memorial Hospital, Jeannette, PA '74 (VOL)
HUGHES, STEVEN L., adm., Kansas City Women's Clinic, Overland Park, KS '86 (PLNG)
HUGHES, SUE E., dir. clin. soc. work, Children's Hospital of Pittsburgh, Pittsburgh, PA '82 (SOC)
HUGHES, SUSAN L., mktg. commun., Emergency Physician Associates, Woodbury, NJ '83 (PR)
HUGHES, THOMAS, mgr. matl., New England Medical Center, Boston, MA '79 (PUR)
HUGHES, WILLIAM L., asst. to pres., Hospital of the Good Samaritan, Los Angeles, CA '82
HUGHEY, P. JAN, sr. vice-pres., Santa Fe Healthcare System, Gainesville, FL '86 (PR)
HUGLY, MARGARET, dir. soc. serv., Lincoln Regional Center, Lincoln, NE '81 (SOC)
HUGUENIN, ROLAND L., chief eng., Kent County Memorial Hospital, Warwick, RI '76 (ENG)
HUIE, ROBERT D., vice-pres. fin., Willis-Knighton Medical Center, Shreveport, LA '78
HUL, MARINUS VANDEN, pres., Health Care Management Consultants, Inc., Colorado Springs, CO '86 (MGMT)
HULA, CARL J., University Hospital, Jacksonville, FL '75
HULGAN, ROGER M., mgr. bldg. serv., Milwaukee Medical Center, Milwaukee, WI '86 (ENVIRON)
HULL, EUGENE F., fin. analyst, Washington Adventist Hospital, Takoma Park, MD '86 (MGMT)
HULL, LANCE E., analyst and planner strategic mgt., Washington Hospital, Fremont, CA '86 (PLNG)
HULL, PEGGY K., RN, asst. dir. staff dev., Ohio State University Hospitals, Columbus, OH '71 (EDUC)
HULL, WILLIAM R., Boca Raton, FL '80 (FOOD)
HULLIHAN, DORIS A., dir. food serv., Foster G. McGaw Hospital, Loyola University of Chicago, Maywood, IL '71 (FOOD)
HULLIHEN, LYNN, mgr. vol. serv., Geisinger Medical Center, Danville, PA '79 (VOL)
HULS, LYNN FLERMOEN, student, Program in Health Planning and Hospital Administration, University of Michigan, Ann Arbor, MI '85 (PLNG)
HULSE, EDGAR, dir. food serv., East Ohio Regional Hospital, Martins Ferry, OH '78 (FOOD)
HULSE, RONALD E., dir. eng., Southwest Washington Hospitals, Vancouver, WA '81 (ENG)
HULSEBUS, JOHN B., sr. vice-pres. human res., Catholic Healthcare West, Sacramento, CA '72 (PERS)
HULSEY, DONNA M., asst. to pres., Children's Hospital, Norfolk, VA '87 (PR) (PLNG)
HULSEY, MARK, atty., Baptist Medical Center, Jacksonville, FL '68 (ATTY)
HULSEY, REBECCA S., dir. pur., Hardee Memorial Hospital, Wauchula, FL '86 (PUR)
HULSEY, RENEE L., mgr. food serv., Bishop Clarkson Memorial Hospital, Omaha, NE '85 (FOOD)
HULSHOF, PATRICIA K., dir. soc. serv., West Side Hospital, Nashville, TN '84 (SOC)
HULSTON, JOHN K., atty., Lester E. Cox Medical Center, Springfield, MO '69 (ATTY)
HULTIN, JANE D., unit coor., Holston Valley Hospital and Medical Center, Kingsport, TN '87 (AMB)
HULTMAN, KRISTINE L., dir. food serv., St. Joseph Mercy Hospital, Clinton, IA '85 (FOOD)
HUM, BETTY J., dir. soc. serv., Cleveland Metropolitan General Hospital, Cleveland, OH '71 (SOC)
HUMAN, F. WILLIAM JR., atty., St. John's Mercy Medical Center, St. Louis, MO '72 (ATTY)
HUMBLE, JERRY W., dir. soc. work serv., St. David's Community Hospital, Austin, TX '74 (SOC)
HUME, CAROLE, dir. aux., Mercy Health Center, Oklahoma City, OK '80 (VOL)
HUME, ROSEMARY K., mgr. educ. serv., St. Vincent Hospital and Health Center, Indianapolis, IN '87 (EDUC)
HUMENUK, WILLIAM A., atty., Children's Hospital of Philadelphia, Philadelphia, PA '77 (ATTY)
HUMINIAK, LOIS M., RN, assoc. dir. adm. serv. and nrsg., Swedish Covenant Hospital, Chicago, IL '84 (NURS)
HUMMEL, ALBERT L., dir. food serv., Lancaster General Hospital, Lancaster, PA '67 (FOOD)
HUMMEL, DIANE A., dir. vol. serv., Good Samaritan Hospital, Lebanon, PA '78 (VOL)
HUMMEL, ELWOOD JOSEPH JR., vice-pres. oper., Kennedy Memorial Hospitals University Medical Center, Stratford, NJ '81
HUMMEL, PATRICIA A., dir. mktg. commun., Central DuPage Hospital, Winfield, IL '84 (PR)
HUMMEL, STUART K., (ret.), Lake Geneva, WI '32 (LIFE)
HUMMER, MARY ANN, distrib. facil. spec., Veterans Administration Medical Center, Washington, DC '84 (CS)
HUMPHREY, BRUCE W., dir. soc. serv. and admissions, Kansas Masonic Home, Wichita, KS '74 (SOC)
HUMPHREY, CLARK M., dir. plant oper., Baton Rouge General Medical Center, Baton Rouge, LA '83 (ENG)
HUMPHREY, JAMES ALLEN, adm. mgr. nrsg. serv., Ellis Hospital, Schenectady, NY '85
HUMPHREY, JEREL THOMAS, asst. vice-pres. adm., Carle Foundation Hospital, Urbana, IL '78
HUMPHREY, P. TOBEY, chief eng., Valley Crest, Wilkes-Barre, PA '79 (ENG)
HUMPHREYS, DONALD C., dir. plant serv., Portland Adventist Medical Center, Portland, OR '86 (ENG)
HUMPHREYS, JAMES B., vice-pres., St. Luke's Hospital West, Chesterfield, MO '68
HUMPHRIES, JIM E., dir. bus. serv., Baylor University Medical Center, Dallas, TX '80 (RISK)
HUMPHRIES, MARTHA A., mgr. cent. proc., Memorial Medical Center, Savannah, GA '84 (CS)
HUMPHRIES, SUSAN E., dir. vol., Arnot-Ogden Memorial Hospital, Elmira, NY '85 (VOL)
HUNCE, MARIE D., adm. food serv., Mount Vernon Hospital, Mount Vernon, NY '75 (FOOD)
HUNDELT, CRAIG T., mgr. plant oper., Normandy Osteopathic Hospital-South, St. Louis, MO '85 (ENG)
HUNDLEY, ELEANOR, dir. soc. serv., North Broward Medical Center, Pompano Beach, FL '70 (SOC)
HUNGERFORD, MELISSA LEVY, vice-pres., Kansas Hospital Association, Topeka, KS '83 (PLNG)
HUNSAKER, RICHARD WILSON, Dayton, OH '57 (LIFE)
HUNSAKER, SUSAN L., student, Graduate School of Management, Boston University, Brookline, MA '85 (PLNG)
HUNSBERGER, ARTHUR G., sr. dir. plng. serv., Hospital Council of Western Pennsylvania, Meadville, PA '82 (PLNG)
HUNSBERGER, RANDALL S., sr. facil. eng., Emergency Care Research Institute, Plymouth Meeting, PA '79 (ENG)
HUNSE, PATRICIA, RN, clin. mgr., cent. sup., Los Angeles Grange Memorial Hospital, La Grange, IL '83 (CS)
HUNSTIGER, CYNTHIA A., RN, dir. cent. serv., St. Marys Hospital of Rochester, Rochester, MN '78 (CS)
HUNSTON, THOMAS J., (ret.), Gaithersburg, MD '37 (LIFE)
HUNT, BETTY J., supv. food serv., Wayne Hospital, Greenville, OH '76 (FOOD)
HUNT, CAROL A., adm. orthopedic surg., Methodist Hospital, Houston, TX '76 (PERS)
HUNT, DOROTHY R., pers. assoc., Coney Island Hospital, Brooklyn, NY '85 (PERS)
HUNT, EDWARD D., dir. diet. and nutr., Burbank Hospital, Fitchburg, MA '84 (FOOD)
HUNT, ELIZABETH S., dir. pers., North Shore Children's Hospital, Salem, MA '81 (PERS)
HUNT, HELEN D., San Diego, CA '76 (LIFE)
HUNT, JACK R., dir. hskpg., St. Francis Hospital Systems, Colorado Springs, CO '80 (FOOD)(ENVIRON)
HUNT, JEAN L., consult., Sanders, Hunt and Associates, Edison, NJ '68
HUNT, JOHANNA C., dir. plng., Eastern Maine Healthcare, Bangor, ME '83 (PLNG)
HUNT, JOHN W., risk mgr., University Hospital, Lexington, KY '86 (RISK)
HUNT, KATHY E., dir. phys. serv., East Jefferson General Hospital, Metairie, LA '85 (PR) (PLNG)
HUNT, LINDA A. S., RN, asst. dir. nrsg. serv., University Hospital, Denver, CO '85 (NURS)
HUNT, MARGARET A., dir. food serv., Frederick Ferris Thompson Hospital, Canandaigua, NY '78 (FOOD)
HUNT, MARY THERESE, dir. qual. assur., St. Joseph's Medical Center, South Bend, IN '83 (RISK)
HUNT, MOLLY A., pub. rel. asst., Samaritan Health Center, Detroit, MI '85 (PR)
HUNT, MRS. PAULAJO, pat. rep., Niagara Falls Memorial Medical Center, Niagara Falls, NY '75 (PAT)
HUNT, VIRGINIA A., vice-pres. commun. and pub. affairs, Shands Hospital at the University of Florida, Gainesville, FL '81 (PR)
HUNTER, BETTY HOLWERDA, dir. soc. serv. and discharge plng., Lindsborg Community Hospital, Lindsborg, KS '86 (PAT)
HUNTER, BRUCE M., dir. spec. proj., Montefiore Medical Center, Bronx, NY '82 (MGMT)

HUNTER, CLAUDETTE ARLENE, RN, pat. rep., Kaiser Foundation Hospital-Sunset, Los Angeles, CA '84 (PAT)
HUNTER, DAVID M., exec. vice-pres., M. Bostin Associates, Inc., Elmsford, NY '59 (PLNG)
HUNTER, DAVID PAUL, pres., Voluntary Hospitals of America, Irving, TX '69
HUNTER, DEBORAH A., adm. res., Sancta Maria Hospital, Cambridge, MA '85
HUNTER, FORREST W., atty., Grady Memorial Hospital, Atlanta, GA '86 (ATTY)
HUNTER, JERRY, dir. nutr. serv., St. Vincent Hospital and Medical Center, Portland, OR '81 (FOOD)
HUNTER, JOHNIE, dir. plant and grds., Lexington Clinic, Lexington, KY '81 (ENG)
HUNTER, JUDITH PITT, chief soc. work serv., Veterans Administration Medical Center, Fort Howard, MD '85 (SOC)
HUNTER, JULIA, RN, mgr. cent. serv., Milford Hospital, Milford, CT '70 (CS)
HUNTER, JUNE B., dir. pers., Dr. John M. Meadows Memorial Hospital, Vidalia, GA '84 (PERS)
HUNTER, M. MICHELE, dir. sup. proc. distrib., Taylor Hospital, Ridley Park, PA '78 (CS)
HUNTER, MARGARET, dir. soc. work, Thomas Jefferson University Hospital, Philadelphia, PA '78 (SOC)
HUNTER, MARVIN R., dir. eng. and facil. dev., Providence Hospital, Cincinnati, OH '80 (ENG)
HUNTER, NANCY B., dir. mktg. and pub. rel., St. Thomas More Hospital, Canon City, CO '86 (PR)
HUNTER, NANCY H., dir. pers., Grace Hospital, Morganton, NC '85 (PERS)
HUNTER, OSCAR BENWOOD JR., MD, consult., Sibley Memorial Hospital, Washington, DC '46 (LIFE)
HUNTER, PAMELA K., ed., Medical Center of Central Georgia, Macon, GA '85 (PR)
HUNTER, ROBERT B., MD, Sedro Woolley, WA '80 (LIFE)
HUNTER, STEPHEN G., dir. plant oper., Wood County Hospital, Bowling Green, OH '84 (ENG)
HUNTER, STEVEN L., vice-pres., St. Elizabeth Medical Center, Granite City, IL '82 (PLNG)
HUNTER, SUE, dir. soc. serv., Cumberland County Hospital System, Fayetteville, NC '78 (SOC)
HUNTER, SUSAN, consult., Lake Luzerne, NY '79 (PLNG)
HUNTER, VIRGINIA M., dir. food serv., University of New Mexico Mental Health, Albuquerque, NM '86 (FOOD)
HUNTER, WILLIAM JEFFREY, vice-pres. mktg., McKenzie-Willamette Hospital, Springfield, OR '79 (PLNG)
HUNTINGTON, JEAN R., dir. plng., Glens Falls Hospital, Glens Falls, NY '83 (PLNG)
HUNTINGTON, LINDA K., RN, asst. dir. nrsg., St. John's Regional Medical Center, Oxnard, CA '85 (NURS)
HUNTINGTON, RICHARD R., partner, Advanced Risk Management Techniques, Laguna Hills, CA '82 (RISK)
HUNTLEY, LEE S., assoc. adm., Baptist Hospital of Miami, Miami, FL '77 (PLNG)
HUNTOON, DANIEL T. V., sr. staff assoc., Massachusetts Hospital Association, Burlington, MA '80 (MGMT)
HUNTOWSKI, AURELIA, RN, asst. vice-pres. nrsg., Ravenswood Hospital Medical Center, Chicago, IL '78 (NURS)
HUNTRESS-RATHER, BARBARA, dir. qual. assur. and risk mgt., Melrose-Wakefield Hospital, Melrose, MA '86 (RISK)
HUNTSMAN, ANN J., dir. human res., El Camino Hospital, Mountain View, CA '75 (EDUC)(PERS)
HUNTZICKER, MARGARET S., dir. vol. serv., St. Francis Hospital, Memphis, TN '86 (VOL)
HUNYADY, JOAN, RN, vice-pres. nrsg., Altoona Hospital, Altoona, PA '73 (NURS)
HUOTARI, MICHAEL E., atty., Humana Hospital -Aurora, Aurora, CO '83 (ATTY)
HUPART, LYNN, dir. vol. serv., Norwalk Hospital, Norwalk, CT '74 (VOL)
HUPCEJ, DORA, asst. dir. nrs., Parma Community General Hospital, Parma, OH '80 (NURS)
HUPP, LOIS ANN, dir. vol., Medical College of Ohio Hospital, Toledo, OH '70 (VOL)
HURD, EDWARD D., proj. eng., Longmont United Hospital, Longmont, CO '77 (ENG)
HURD, MICHAEL J., adm., Monsour Medical Center, Jeannette, PA '68 (MGMT)
HURD, PHILLIPS C., health care planner, Washington Healthcare Management Corporation, Washington, DC '85 (PLNG)
HURD, THOMAS C., sales mgr. med., Waterloo Industries, Inc., Waterloo, IA '83
HURDER, RICHARD J., assoc. dir., Rowan Memorial Hospital, Salisbury, NC '71
HURLEY, MARY ANNE, RN, dir. nrsg., New York Hospital, Westchester Division, White Plains, NY '73 (NURS)
HURLEY, NAVARRO, chief cent. serv. tech., Stamford Hospital, Stamford, CT '80 (CS)
HURLEY, PATRICK D., dir. plng., St. Mary's Hospital, Milwaukee, WI '82 (PLNG)
HURLEY, PATRICK E., atty., Tallahassee Memorial Regional Medical Center, Tallahassee, FL '83 (ATTY)
HURLEY, WILLIAM P., atty., Catholic Charities of the Archdiocese, New York, NY '83 (ATTY)
HURLEY, ZENOBIA, dir. vol. serv., St. Joseph Health Care Corporation, Albuquerque, NM '76 (VOL)
HURN, ELLEN S., dir. educ., Covenant Medical Center-Schoitz, Waterloo, IA '84 (EDUC)
HURR, WANDA L., adjunct prof., Sacred Heart University, Bridgeport, CT '87 (RISK)
HURSEY, STEVEN C., eng. serv., Veterans Administration Medical Center, Washington, DC '85 (ENG)
HURST, CAROL W., vice-pres. human res., Good Samaritan Medical Center, Zanesville, OH '82 (PERS)
HURST, HAZEL A., RN, asst. adm. nrsg. serv., St. Joseph Hospital and Health Care Center, Tacoma, WA '76 (NURS)
HURST, JOHN J., dir. food serv., Martin Memorial Hospital, Stuart, FL '78 (FOOD)
HURST, MARY ELLEN, dir. soc. serv., Dunlap Memorial Hospital, Orrville, OH '85 (SOC)
HURST, O. RAY, pres., Texas Hospital Association, Austin, TX '56 (LIFE)
HURST, TERRANCE G., dir. risk mgt. and ins., Western Pennsylvania Hospital, Pittsburgh, PA '80 (RISK)
HURST, TIM T., consult. to exec. dir., University of Michigan Hospitals, Ann Arbor, MI '77 (ENG)
HURT, DORALYN B., RN, asst. chief nrsg. serv., Canandaigua Veterans Administration Medical Center, Canandaigua, NY '84 (NURS)
HURT, MARY J., exec. hskpg., Ohio Valley Medical Center, Wheeling, WV '86 (ENVIRON)
HURT, SARA C., vice-pres. tech. serv., United Service Equipment Company, Murfreesboro, TN '72 (FOOD)
HURTADO, HENRY, mgr. cent. serv., Los Robles Regional Medical Center, Thousand Oaks, CA '82 (CS)
HURTEAU, PHYLLIS, assoc. dir., Veterans Administration Medical Center, Syracuse, NY '79
HURTT, CLAUDE D., asst. vice-pres. fin., Baptist Medical Centers, Birmingham, AL '84 (RISK)
HURWITZ, DEBRA, mgt. syst. eng.-nrsg., Haricomp, Inc., Providence, RI '85 (MGMT)
HUSBANDS, RANDALL T., asst. to adm. fin. serv., Presbyterian Home, Philadephia, PA '82
HUSEINI, TEDDI, dir. pub. rel., O'Connor Hospital, San Jose, CA '77 (PR)
HUSKA, EMIL A., dir. diet. serv., Memorial Mission Hospital, Asheville, NC '71 (FOOD)
HUSKEY, RAYMOND, dir. clin. equip., Servicemaster Industries, Inc., Downers Grove, IL '83 (ENG)
HUSNEY, SAMUEL, dir. pers., Brookdale Hospital Medical Center, Brooklyn, NY '77 (PERS)
HUSON, ED, dir., Canteen Health Care Service, Inc., Portland, OR '76 (FOOD)
HUSS, JUNE K., adm. coor. vol. serv., St. Anthony Hospital Systems, Denver, CO '77 (VOL)
HUSSAIN, ARSHAD, contr., Saudi Medical Services Ltd., Riyadh, Saudi Arabia '86
HUSSEINI, SAMY, dir. proj. and renovations, Children's Hospital of Michigan, Detroit, MI '87 (ENG)
HUSSERL, BRETT B., vice-pres., South Community Hospital, Oklahoma City, OK '86
HUSSEY, JAN, soc. worker and discharge planner, HCA Grand Strand General Hospital, Myrtle Beach, SC '85 (SOC)
HUSSEY, JOE W. JR., dir. biomedical eng., St. John Medical Center, Tulsa, OK '85 (ENG)
HUSSEY, THEODORE A., sr. vice-pres., Maine Hospital Association, Augusta, ME '64 (PLNG)
HUSSION, GEORGE J., dir. mgt. eng., St. John's Regional Medical Center, Joplin, MO '77 (MGMT)
HUSSON, JOHN J., pres., Meralex Corporation, Marietta, GA '77 (RISK)
HUSTED, ELAINE, RN, dir. nrsg., Phoenixville Hospital, Phoenixville, PA '74 (NURS)
HUSTON, THERESA, RN, asst. adm. pat. care, Ivinson Memorial Hospital, Laramie, WY '84 (NURS)
HUSTWICK, JOHN, sr. vice-pres., Riverside Health Group, Toledo, OH '79 (PLNG)
HUTCHENS, STEVE R., coor. info. syst., Memorial Hospital, Danville, VA '82 (MGMT)
HUTCHERSON, RENE R., dir. med. soc. work, University Hospital, Denver, CO '83 (SOC)
HUTCHESON, MARK A., atty., Virginia Mason Hospital, Seattle, WA '76 (ATTY)
HUTCHINGS, BARRY BRENT, Dallas, TX '69 (FOOD)
HUTCHINGS, LARRY N., asst. dir. human res., Children's Hospital of Alabama, Birmingham, AL '77 (PERS)
HUTCHINGS, MARGARET, dir. vol. serv., Cottage Hospital of Grosse Pointe, Grosse Pointe Farms, MI '71 (VOL)
HUTCHINGS, THOMAS W., asst. exec. dir., Children's Hospital, Columbus, OH '75 (ENG)
HUTCHINS, JANET N., risk consult., North Carolina Hospital Association Trust Fund, Raleigh, NC '86 (RISK)
HUTCHINS, MARGARET R., dir. soc. serv., HCA Huntington Hospital, Huntington, WV '82 (SOC)
HUTCHINS, RALPH G., adm., Skokie Valley Hospital, Skokie, IL '47 (LIFE)
HUTCHINSON, ALAN E., adm., Al-Mutabagani Health Service, Ltd., Taif, Saudi Arabia '81 (PLNG)
HUTCHINSON, BARBARA J., dir. info. syst., Taylor Hospital, Ridley Park, PA '85 (MGMT)
HUTCHINSON, DONALD C., partner, Main Hurdman, Pittsburgh, PA '83
HUTCHINSON, GERRI, asst. dir. vol., Illini Hospital, Silvis, IL '86 (VOL)
HUTCHINSON, JAMES A., dir. plant oper., Twin Cities Hospital, Niceville, FL '83 (ENG)
HUTCHINSON, JOHN D., atty., Community Health Center of Branch County, Coldwater, MI '84 (ATTY)
HUTCHINSON, LOUISE, dir. pub. info., National Association of Children's Hospitals and Related Institutions, Inc., Alexandria, VA '85 (PR)
HUTCHINSON, PATRICIA ANNE, coor. nrsg. educ., Augusta General Hospital, Augusta, ME '79 (EDUC)
HUTCHINSON, ROBIN D., dir. commun. rel., Bruce Hospital, Florence, SC '84 (PLNG)
HUTCHINSON, THOMAS E. JR., asst. adm. and chief oper. off., St. Mary's Hospital Medical Center, Green Bay, WI '79 (RISK)
HUTCHISON, DOUGLAS P., atty., Silver Cross Hospital, Joliet, IL '85 (ATTY)
HUTCHISON, PATRICIA ARLEEN, dir. pat. rel., Washington Adventist Hospital, Takoma Park, MD '85 (PAT)
HUTCHISON, R. BRUCE, dir. commun. rel., Norwalk Hospital, Norwalk, CT '80 (PR)
HUTCHISON, RANDALL L., mgt. eng., Geisinger System Services, Danville, PA '84 (MGMT)
HUTCHISON, ROBIN D., dir. pub. rel. and coor. vol. serv., Bruce Hospital, Florence, SC '87 (PR)
HUTELMYER, CAROL M., RN, vice-pres. pat. care, Graduate Hospital, Philadelphia, PA '85 (NURS)
HUTSELL, JOHN G., dir. food and nutr. serv., Leigh Memorial Hospital, Norfolk, VA '86 (FOOD)
HUTSELL, MICHAEL W., dir. eng. serv., Regional Medical Center at Memphis, Memphis, TN '85 (ENG)
HUTSON, GAYNELL J., mgr. food serv., Logan Regional Hospital, Logan, UT '86 (FOOD)
HUTSON, JUDY, RN, same day serv. supv., Vermillion County Hospital, Clinton, IN '87 (AMB)
HUTTON-SEREDA, SHERYL L., dir. commun., Greater Cleveland Hospital Association, Cleveland, OH '84 (PR) (PLNG)
HUTTON-VEENSTRA, KRISTIE, student, Program in Health Service Management, Ferris State College, Big Rapids, MI '82
HUTTON, DAVID D., vice-pres. adm. oper., Carlisle Hospital, Carlisle, PA '83
HUTTON, DEBORAH, dir. risk mgt., St. Anthony's Medical Center, St. Louis, MO '85 (RISK)
HUX, VICKIE, dev. assoc., Mental Health Management, McLean, VA '85 (PLNG)
HUYCK, TERESA A., asst. vice-pres., Good Samaritan Hospital, Cincinnati, OH '87 (AMB)
HUZINEC, GEORGE D., sr. syst. consult., George Washington University Hospital, Washington, DC '83 (MGMT)
HYATT, CDR C. SUSAN, MSC USN, coor. nrsg. educ., Naval Hospital, Camp Pendleton, CA '81 (EDUC)
HYATT, JAMES B., dir. eng. serv., Stuart Circle Hospital, Richmond, VA '77 (ENG)
HYATT, THOMAS K., atty., Mercy Hospital, Wilkes-Barre, PA '83 (ATTY)
HYBBEN, LOIS B., RN, vice-pres., St. Vincent Hospital, Santa Fe, NM '78 (NURS)
HYDE, CRAIG S., dir. food serv., Bon Secours Extended Care Facility, Ellicott City, MD '84 (FOOD)
HYDE, FRANCES G., dir. in-service, Webster General Hospital, Eupora, MS '84 (EDUC)
HYDE, FRED, MD, atty., Stephens and Hyde, Inc., Beverly Hills, CA '74 (PLNG)(ATTY)
HYDE, G. COLLIN, dir. plng., NKC Hospitals, Louisville, KY '70 (PLNG)
HYDE, JAMES A., atty., Bone and Joint Hospital, Oklahoma City, OK '75 (ATTY)
HYDE, JOHN L., dir. mgt. eng., The Medical Center, Beaver, PA '79 (MGMT)
HYDE, RICHARD DEAN, RN, dir. nrsg., Tuomey Hospital, Sumter, SC '80 (NURS)
HYDE, ROBERT J., partner, Touche, Ross and Company, Minneapolis, MN '78
HYER, GRANT K., dir. soc. work serv., LDS Hospital, Salt Lake City, UT '74 (SOC)
HYLAND, DENNIS G., staff arch. and proj. eng., Baptist Medical Center, Little Rock, AR '83 (ENG)
HYLTON, SUE, dir. qual. assur., Baptist Medical Center, Little Rock, AR '86 (RISK)
HYMAN, YVETTE, dir. qual. assur., Catholic Medical Center, Jamaica, NY '86 (RISK)
HYMANS, DANIEL J., adm., Riverview Hospital, Wisconsin Rapids, WI '76
HYMANSON, PATRICIA B., dir. pers., Sparks Family Hospital, Sparks, NV '85 (VOL)(PERS)
HYMSON, DAVID, asst. branch mgr., Norwich Eaton Pharmaceuticals, Norwich, NY '86 (RISK)
HYNSON, NANCY B., RN, assoc. chief nrsg. serv. for amb. care, Veterans Administration Medical Center, Lexington, KY '86 (NURS)
HYSEN, PAUL, pres., The Hysen Group, Livonia, MI '75 (FOOD)
HYSLIP, JOHN E., asst. adm., Kalispell Regional Hospital, Kalispell, MT '85 (ENG)(RISK)(ENVIRON)
HYTOFF, RONALD A., exec. dir., Humana Hospital Wellington, London, England '73

I

IACCINO, JAMES A., dir. environ. serv., Pleasant Valley Hospital, Camarillo, CA '86 (ENVIRON)
IACOI, VINCENT J., dir. food serv., Norwich Hospital, Norwich, CT '84 (FOOD)
IACONO, ROSE LOUISE, dir. food serv., San Pedro Peninsula Hospital, San Pedro, CA '68 (FOOD)
IADANZA, GENEVIEVE D., dir. pur., Southampton Hospital, Southampton, NY '79 (PUR)
IAMS, FRANKLIN P., (ret.), Sarasota, FL '49 (LIFE)
IANDOLO, SHARON, dir. soc. serv., St. Mary Hospital, Manhattan, KS '75 (SOC)
IANNETTI, PATRICIA L., mgr. cent. sterile serv., Presbyterian-University Hospital, Pittsburgh, PA '82 (CS)
IANUZI, BEVERLY R., RN, dir. nrsg. serv., Oneida City Hospital, Oneida, NY '85 (NURS)
IAPICHINO, RALPH W., dir. diet. serv., Holy Cross Hospital, Fort Lauderdale, FL '82 (FOOD)
IAQUINTA, LAWRENCE J., mgt. eng., Central Baptist Hospital, Lexington, KY '83 (MGMT)
IBACH, PAUL E., atty., Tampa, FL '68 (ATTY)
ICENHOWER, DAVID J., dir. matl. mgt., Michiana Community Hospital, South Bend, IN '83 (PUR)
IDLEMAN, ROSEMARY J., dir. vol., Decatur Memorial Hospital, Decatur, IL '82 (VOL)
IERARDI, JOSEPH A., pres. and chief exec. off., Methodist Hospital, Philadelphia, PA '73 (MGMT)
IGLESIAS, AGUSTIN L., supv. inventory control, Mercy Hospital, Miami, FL '83 (PUR)
IGNACIO, FRANCES L., dir. cent. sup. and linen serv., Boone Hospital Center, Columbia, MO '83 (CS)
IGNACIO, FRANK W., dir. plant oper., Redbud Community Hospital, Clearlake, CA '87 (ENG)

IGNASH, TIMOTHY J., sr. assoc., Bernie Hoffman Associates, Inc., Southfield, MI '86 (PERS)
IGNASIAK, CONNIE M., supv. food serv., Psychiatric Center of Michigan, New Baltimore, MI '81 (FOOD)
IGO, PATRICIA A., asst. dir., Naval Hospital, Portsmouth, VA '84 (FOOD)
IHDE, GARY L., sr. vice-pres. external affairs, Blue Cross and Blue Shield, Kansas City, MO '78
IHENACHO, MERCY M. I., University of Nigeria, Enugu, Nigeria '81 (NURS)
IHLE, LUTHER, exec. dir., Ohio Heart Institute, Youngstown, OH '58
IHLE, ROGER L., dir. eng. and maint., Good Samaritan Hospital, Kearney, NE '75 (ENG)
IHNOT, SR. ANDRIENE, RN, assoc. dir. nrsg., St. Elizabeth Hospital Medical Center, Youngstown, OH '84 (NURS)
IKEDA, CLAUDETTE, RN, chief in-service educ., Norwalk Hospital, Norwalk, CT '78 (NURS)
IKELER, R. STEPHEN, asst. adm., Riddle Memorial Hospital, Media, PA '84
IKER, MIKE, contract mgr., Turner Construction Company, San Francisco, CA '84
ILCYN, JOHN, sr. dir. fin., Visiting Nurses Association of Butler Company, Butler, PA '87 (AMB)
ILGES, HERMAN J., dir. eng. and maint., Incarnate Word Hospital, St. Louis, MO '81 (ENG)
IMBESE, HELEN K., dir. vol., San Bernardino County Medical Center, San Bernardino, CA '85 (VOL)
IMES, HAROLD K., adm. food serv., Central Peace General Hospital, Spirit River, Alta., Canada '82 (FOOD)
IMHOF, JULIE L., RN, mgr. cent. serv., St. John's Hospital and Health Center, Santa Monica, CA '85 (CS)
IMHOFF, JOHN C., pres., Galion Community Hospital, Galion, OH '51 (LIFE)
IMIRIE, JOHN F. JR., exec. vice-pres. adm., Medical College of Ohio Hospital, Toledo, OH '74 (MGMT)
IMLAY, SHERYL, dir., Carle Home Care, Urbana, IL '87 (AMB)
IMMERMAN, BRUCE, Potomac, MD '70
IMMING, GERALD L., dir. facil. plng., University of Kansas Hospital, Kansas City, KS '79 (ENG)
IMMORDINO, KATHLEEN D., RN, dir. nrsg., Northeastern Hospital of Philadelphia, Philadelphia, PA '86 (NURS)
IMPELLIZERI, GAIL L., mgr. pur., Somerset Medical Center, Somerville, NJ '83 (PUR)
INCE, GEORGE A., chief eng., Aitkin Community Hospital, Aitkin, MN '82 (ENG)
INCORVATI, ROBERT A., dir. serv., Deloitte, Haskins and Sells, Pittsburgh, PA '78
INDELICATO, CHARLES A., adm., Methodist Hospital, Brooklyn, NY '73
INDICTOR, RHODA B., dir. pub. rel., Southern Chester County Medical Center, West Grove, PA '84 (PR)
INFANTE, JOSEPHINE, mktg. spec., Health Care Plus, Brooklyn, NY '86 (PR)
INFERRERA, JO-ANNA, dir. soc. serv., William B. Kessler Memorial Hospital, Hammonton, NJ '77 (SOC)
INGALZ, JAMES A., dir. food serv., Inter-Community Medical Center, Covina, CA '71 (FOOD)
INGBAR, MARY LEE, PhD, prin. res. assoc. preventive and soc. medicine, Harvard Medical School, Boston, MA '61
INGERMAN, MICHAEL L., pres., Discern, Inc., Nicasio, CA '75 (PLNG)
INGISON, CHRISTA J., dir. pub. rel., Children's Hospital, St. Paul, MN '85 (PR)
INGLETT, VAN W., RN, assoc. adm. nrsg. serv., University Hospital, Augusta, GA '83 (NURS)(AMB)
INGOGLIA, RICHARD P., exec. dir., American Hospital Equipment Company, Inc., Ferndale, MI '83 (SOC)
INGOLD, SUSAN PLAYFAIR, Bettendorf, IA '82 (MGMT)
INGRAM, BETTY E., dir. mktg. and pub. rel., Baptist Medical Center-Princeton, Birmingham, AL '84 (PR)
INGRAM, BOBBIE J., dir. qual. assur., Intermountain Health Care, Inc., Salt Lake City, UT '83 (RISK)
INGRAM, CHARLES M., atty., Duplin General Hospital, Kenansville, NC '84 (ATTY)
INGRAM, G. SCOTT, dir. plng., St. Boniface General Hospital, Winnipeg, Man., Canada '83 (PLNG)
INGRAM, JEAN, asst. dir. diet., St. Thomas Hospital, Nashville, TN '78 (FOOD)
INGRAM, MARJORIE J., dir. mktg., Memorial Health Services, Huntington Beach, CA '86 (PR) (PLNG)
INGRAM, REGINA I., dir. soc. serv., Lakewood Hospital, Tacoma, WA '79 (SOC)
INGRAM, VIRGINIA M., dir. vol. serv., Walker Regional Medical Center, Jasper, AL '83 (VOL)
INGRASSIA, LAURA J., student, University of Michigan Program in Hospital Administration, Ann Arbor, MI '84
INNISS, WILBUR H., dir. risk mgt. and environ. health, Bayley Seton Hospital, Staten Island, NY '82 (RISK)
INNOCENZO, LYNN S., pat. rep., West Jersey Health System, Camden, NJ '83 (PAT)
INNS, JAMES E., dir. health care consult., Arthur Young and Associates, Chicago, IL '85 (MGMT)
INSEL, ELYSE MINDY, adm. anes., Mount Sinai Medical Center, New York, NY '78
INSINGER, ANNE, dir. univ rel., Thomas Jefferson University, Philadelphia, PA '81 (PR)
INSKEEP, HERVEY H., soc. serv. consult., Chino Community Hospital, Chino, CA '79 (SOC)
INWALD, JOSEPH M., atty., Seidman and Seidman, Troy, MI '85 (ATTY)
INZER, ANN, risk mgr., Baptist Hospital of Southeast Texas, Beaumont, TX '86 (RISK)
IOBBI, LOUIS A., corp. dir. matl. mgt., United Hospitals, Inc., Cheltenham, PA '86 (PUR)
IOBST, STACY A., mktg. rep., Hospital Central Service, Inc., Allentown, PA '86 (PUR)
IORFIDA, DIANE M., asst. vice-pres., Ravenswood Health Care Corporation, Chicago, IL '79 (PERS)
IPPEL, DAVID A., asst. vice-pres. amb. serv., Oakwood Hospital, Dearborn, MI '87 (AMB)
IRBY, PATRICIA W., RN, chief nrsg. serv., Veterans Administration Medical Center, Muskogee, OK '73 (NURS)
IREDALE, SR. MARCELLA, vice-pres. plng. and dev., St. Joseph's Health Centre, Toronto, Ont., Canada '80 (PLNG)
IRELAND, ELIZABETH R., mgr. med. soc. serv., Good Samaritan Hospital, San Jose, CA '84 (SOC)
IRELAND, JIM, supv. hskpg., Ellsworth Municipal Hospital, Iowa Falls, IA '86 (ENVIRON)
IRELAND, ORIN L., vice-pres. fin., Carle Foundation Hospital, Urbana, IL '84
IRELAND, RICHARD C., pres., The Ireland Corporation, Englewood, CO '82 (PLNG)
IRENIA, SR. MARY, RN, mgr. sterile proc., Marymount Hospital, Garfield Heights, OH '69 (CS)
IRICK, JEROME H., dir. eng. and bldg. serv., Millville Hospital, Millville, NJ '81 (ENG)
IRIGOYEN, DAVID E., adm. asst., Baptist Hospital Highlands, Louisville, KY '85
IRISH, GARY G., vice pres., Adventist Health System-North, Hinsdale, IL '83 (PLNG)
IRISH, KAREN L., dir. med. staff mktg., Hinsdale Hospital, Hinsdale, IL '83
IRIZARRY, FERNANDO, arch., Dr. Pila's Hospital, Ponce, P.R. '78
IRLAND, DOLORES M., asst. dir. diet., Germantown Hospital and Medical Center, Philadelphia, PA '79 (FOOD)
IRONSIDE, ALANA, coor. group pur., Health and Hospital Services, Bellevue, WA '86 (PUR)
IRR, WILLIAM G., vice-pres. plant serv., Niagara Falls Memorial Medical Center, Niagara Falls, NY '74 (ENG)
IRSIK, LEANNE M., assoc. dir. nrsg., St. Catherine Hospital, Garden City, KS '85 (NURS)
IRVEN, ROBERT, mgt. eng., Sharp Health System, San Diego, CA '83 (MGMT)
IRVIN, E. JEAN, dir. pat. and family serv., Moore Regional Hospital, Pinehurst, NC '85 (SOC)
IRVIN, JAMES K., atty., Southern Baptist Hospital, New Orleans, LA '84 (ATTY)
IRVIN, THOMAS M., asst. adm. pers., Medcenter Hospital, Marion, OH '80 (PERS)
IRVIN, WAYNE J., dir. eng. and maint., Metropolitan Hospital-Central Division, Philadelphia, PA '86 (ENG)
IRVINE, EDWARD B., dir. facil. serv., Kaiser Permanente Medical Care Program, Honolulu, HI '85 (ENG)
IRVINE, JAMES P. JR., dir. maint., Central Georgia Eye Center, Macon, GA '86 (ENG)
IRVINE, JERELYN F., proj. asst., University of Iowa Hospitals and Clinics, Iowa City, IA '85 (PR)
IRWIN, BYRON, dir., Apm, Inc., South San Francisco, CA '67
IRWIN, DENNIS E., chief exec. off., Broad Top Area Medical Center, Broad Top, PA '86
IRWIN, GREGORY D., dir. food serv., Medcenter Hospital, Marion, OH '83 (FOOD)
IRWIN, JAMES S., atty., Mercy Hospital, Hamilton, OH '75 (ATTY)
IRWIN, JOHN R., MD, atty., Cleveland Clinic Hospital, Cleveland, OH '86 (ATTY)
IRWIN, JUDITH A., mgr. pub. rel., Northern Illinois Medical Center, McHenry, IL '85 (PR)
IRWIN, PAMELA H., coor. prod., Emory University Hospital, Atlanta, GA '75 (CS)
IRWIN, RENA E., dir. pers., Ballard Community Hospital, Seattle, WA '80 (PERS)
IRWIN, THOMAS A., dir. soc. serv., Bates County Memorial Hospital, Butler, MO '74 (SOC)
ISAAC, E. JOANNA, dir. commun. rel., Thomas Memorial Hospital, South Charleston, WV '77 (PR)
ISAAC, LINDA MARY, dir. soc. work, Community General Hospital, Syracuse, NY '84 (SOC)
ISAACS, LINDA A., dir. pers., Booth Memorial Medical Center, Flushing, NY '86 (PERS)
ISAACSON, JEAN K., dir. mktg. and pub. rel., Gulf Coast Hospital, Baytown, TX '86 (PR)
ISAACSON, SANDRA K., RN, prin., nrs. consult., Isaacson and Associates, Washington, DC '83 (NURS)
ISAACSON, WILLIAM M., dir. human res., St. Vincent Hospital and Medical Center, Portland, OR '79 (PERS)
ISACK, ARTHUR G., exec. dir., Faculty Practice Plan, Yale University School of Medicine, New Haven, CT '74
ISACKSON, CAROL, atty., Grossmont District Hospital, La Mesa, CA '84 (ATTY)
ISAIA, JOHN P., asst. vice-pres., Borgess Medical Center, Kalamazoo, MI '74 (PERS)
ISCH, CAROLYN A., asst. exec. dir., Dietary Managers Association, Hillside, IL '67 (FOOD)
ISCHAR, ROSEMARY, RN, asst. dir. nrsg., Cedars-Sinai Medical Center, Los Angeles, CA '83 (NURS)
ISELE, WILLIAM P., atty., Robert Wood Johnson University Hospital, New Brunswick, NJ '86 (ATTY)
ISEMAN, J. M., exec. dir., Richmond Memorial Hospital, Rockingham, NC '78
ISENBERG, NANCY ANN, dir. vol. serv. and pat. rel., Memorial Medical Center of Jacksonville, Jacksonville, FL '86 (VOL)
ISENSTEIN, WILLIAM D., dir. alternative delivery syst., Providence Hospital, Southfield, MI '79 (MGMT)
ISGAN, CHARLES R., asst. chief maint., Lee Hospital, Johnstown, PA '84 (ENG)
ISHAM, OPAL LYNANN, RN, dir. med. and surg. nrsg., Hackley Hospital, Muskegon, MI '83 (NURS)
ISKEN, MARK W., student, Program in Industrial and Operation Engineering, University of Michigan, Ann Arbor, MI '86 (MGMT)
ISLEY, DERIA D., dir. pers., Alamance Memorial Hospital, Burlington, NC '82 (PERS)
ISOM, HEIDI M., dir. pub. rel., Kennestone Regional Health Care Systems, Marietta, GA '86 (PR)
ISOM, JAMES S., adm., Orthopaedic Surgeons East, Birmingham, AL '87 (AMB)
ISOM, LEROY, dir. maint., Warner Brown Hospital, El Dorado, AR '85 (ENG)
ISRAEL, AMI, dir. vol. serv., University Hospital, Boston, MA '83 (VOL)
ISRAEL, KAREN L., RN, asst. chief nrsg. serv., Veterans Administration Medical Center, Buffalo, NY '86 (NURS)
ISSACS, JAMES W., exec. vice-pres., St. Elizabeth Medical Center, Dayton, OH '84
ISSENDORF-BROWN, CLEO, RN, dir. commun. serv., University of Minnesota Hospitals and Clinics, Minneapolis, MN '77 (EDUC)
ISSERMAN, JOAN L., risk mgr., Lutheran Medical Center, Wheat Ridge, CO '81 (RISK)(ATTY)
ISTORICO, ALBERT J., mgr., Ernst and Whinney, New York, NY '87 (MGMT)
IULIANO, ANNE B., RN, asst. dir. nrsg., Brockton Hospital, Brockton, MA '82 (NURS)
IULLO, NINO DI, MD, dir. emer., St. Anthony Medical Center, Columbus, OH '86 (AMB)
IULO, LINDA, RN, supv. cent. serv., St. Francis Hospital-Beacon, Beacon, NY '86 (CS)
IVAN, JOYCE M., RN, asst. adm. nrsg. serv., Saline Community Hospital, Saline, MI '86 (NURS)
IVER, MARTHA N., Bradford, PA '49 (LIFE)
IVERSEN, GORDON W., dir. hskpg. and ldry., Sequoia Hospital District, Redwood City, CA '86 (ENVIRON)
IVERSEN, JULIA N., Ithaca, NY '86 (PR)
IVERSON, CAROLYN A., dir. dev. and pub. rel., Eastern New Mexico Medical Center, Roswell, NM '85 (PR)
IVERSON, DONNA, RN, dir. nrsg., Burke Rehabilitation Center, White Plains, NY '83 (NURS)
IVES, BARBARA C., dir. soc. serv., Pender Memorial Hospital, Burgaw, NC '80 (SOC)
IVES, JOHN E., exec. vice-pres., Shands Hospital, Gainesville, FL '54 (LIFE)
IVES, SHARON H., dir. soc. serv., George H. Lanier Memorial Hospital, Valley, AL '81 (SOC)
IVEY, HORACE S., dir. soc. serv. and assoc. prof., Suny Health Sciences Center at Syracuse, Syracuse, NY '68 (SOC)
IVEY, KAY W., adm. rep., Southeast Alabama Medical Center, Dothan, AL '83 (PAT)
IVIE, DIANNE, RN, dir. qual. assur. and risk mgt., Central Michigan Community Hospital, Mount Pleasant, MI '78 (EDUC)
IVIE, JACK, asst. exec. dir., Glendale Memorial Hospital and Health Center, Glendale, CA '80 (RISK)
IVY, ROBERT A., Columbus, MS '47 (LIFE)
IVY, WANDA, dir. med. info. syst., Queen of Angels Medical Center, Los Angeles, CA '86 (RISK)
IWAMOTO, RAYMOND S., atty., Straub Clinic and Hospital, Honolulu, HI '84 (ATTY)
IWANE, CHRISTINE K., RN, asst. adm. and dir. nrsg. serv., Whittier Hospital Medical Center, Whittier, CA '80 (NURS)
IWANSKI, JOHN P., fin. off., Arthur Andersen and Company, San Francisco, CA '79
IYENGAR, SHIKHA, mgt. syst. eng., Presbyterian-University Hospital, Pittsburgh, PA '84 (MGMT)
IZEMAN, PAULA, assoc. adm. plng. and mktg., Emma Pendleton Bradley Hospital, Riverside, RI '85 (PLNG)
IZMIRLIAN, ANN, supv. soc. work, Florida Hospital Medical Center, Orlando, FL '87 (SOC)
IZYK, KENNETH A., dir. pur., Milton Medical Center, Milton, MA '81 (PUR)
IZZO, KATHLEEN H., dir. commun. affairs, Saratoga Hospital, Saratoga Springs, NY '85 (PR)

J

JAASSEN, LORI BATES, mgr. matl., Eastern New Mexico Medical Center, Roswell, NM '84 (PUR)
JABLONSKI, MARK A., mgt. dev. consult., San Diego, CA '83 (EDUC)
JABLONSKI, ROBERT J., sr. consult., Ernst and Whinney, Los Angeles, CA '86 (MGMT)
JACK, BILLY C., atty., Maury County Hospital, Columbia, TN '69 (ATTY)
JACK, CAROLINE J., dir. pur., Children's Hospital, Columbus, OH '85 (PUR)
JACK, HOWARD J., dir. pers., St. John's Hospital, Springfield, IL '64 (PERS)
JACK, MAX, asst. adm., Mercy Hospital of Sacramento, Sacramento, CA '84 (RISK)
JACK, RICHARD L., sr. consult., ARA-Hospital Nutrition Services, Rosemont, IL '70 (FOOD)
JACK, WILLIAM W. JR., atty., Ingham Medical Center, Lansing, MI '86 (ATTY)
JACKE, JOSEPH A., dir. eng. and constr., Saint Francis Medical Center, Peoria, IL '84 (ENG)
JACKIER, LAWRENCE S., atty., Huron Valley Hospital, Inc., Milford, MI '85 (ATTY)
JACKMAN, BARBARA ANNE, asst. adm., Johnston-Willis Hospital, Richmond, VA '80
JACKMUFF, STEVEN W., sr. vice-pres., Underwood-Memorial Hospital, Woodbury, NJ '78
JACKNOW, AMY S., sr. consult., Plante and Moran, Southfield, MI '86 (PLNG)
JACKOVITZ, DONALD S., sr. mgt. eng., Cleveland Clinic Hospital, Cleveland, OH '81 (MGMT)
JACKS, MASTON T., atty., Veterans Administration Department of Health, Commonwealth of Veterans Administration, Richmond, VA '86 (ATTY)
JACKSON, ANTHONY K., pres., A. K. Jackson and Associates, Inc., Hickory, NC '80 (PERS)
JACKSON, BARBARA ROBERTSON, RN, infection control surveillance nrs. and emp. health nrs., Delta Medical Center, Greenville, MS '86 (ENG)
JACKSON, BARBARA W., spec. plng., Flint Osteopathic Hospital, Flint, MI '86 (PLNG)
JACKSON, BARBARA, evening supv. sterile proc., St. Francis Memorial Hospital, San Francisco, CA '83 (CS)

JACKSON, C. LINDLEY, (ret.), Las Vegas, NV '52 (LIFE)
JACKSON, CHARLES L., DrPH, dir. bus. dev.-cent. div., American Medical International, Houston, TX '83 (PLNG)
JACKSON, CHERYL WINDERS, prod. dev. analyst, Blue Cross and Blue Shield of North Carolina, Durham, NC '80
JACKSON, CONSTANCE, dir. pat. and family counseling, Saint Joseph Hospital, Denver, CO '74 (SOC)
JACKSON, CORKY, mgr. food, Atchison Hospital, Atchison, KS '73 (FOOD)
JACKSON, CRAIG R., asst. dir. soc. work, Loma Linda University Medical Center, Loma Linda, CA '85 (SOC)
JACKSON, DAVID P., dir. health care plng., Health Care Innovations, Salt Lake City, UT '81 (PLNG)
JACKSON, DIANA C., RN, asst. dir. nrsg., Brooklyn Hospital-Caledonian Hospital, Brooklyn, NY '84 (NURS)
JACKSON, DOLORES E., RN, dir. nrsg. serv., Woodhull Medical and Mental Health Center, Brooklyn, NY '84 (NURS)
JACKSON, DOUGLAS E., dir. plant eng., Winter Haven Hospital, Winter Haven, FL '85 (ENG)
JACKSON, LT. COL. DUANE L., MSC USA, Opm-Sang, APO New York, NY '84 (PLNG)
JACKSON, DURIA JEAN, supv. cent. sterile proc., Gulf Coast Medical Center, Wharton, TX '83 (CS)
JACKSON, ERVIN, dir. food serv., Lea Regional Hospital, Hobbs, NM '81 (FOOD)
JACKSON, FREDERICK LOUIS, asst. dir., Indiana University Hospitals, Indianapolis, IN '79 (PUR)
JACKSON, GARY S., dir. support serv., Humana Hospital-Mountain View, Thornton, CO '85 (ENG)
JACKSON, GORDON E., atty., Community Hospital, Anderson, IN '77 (ATTY)
JACKSON, HARPER S., sr. vice-pres., The Methodist Hospital, Houston, TX '78
JACKSON, IRETHA, unit coor. cent. serv., AMI Brookwood Community Hospital, Orlando, FL '85 (CS)
JACKSON, JAMES H., dir. pers., Kansas Institute, Olathe, KS '86 (PERS)
JACKSON, JAMES K., assoc. exec. dir., Children's Hospital, Columbus, OH '70 (MGMT)
JACKSON, JANET Y., RN, vice-pres. nrsg., Munson Medical Center, Traverse City, MI '79 (NURS)
JACKSON, JERALDINE, dir. educ., William Beaumont Hospital-Troy, Troy, MI '85 (EDUC)
JACKSON, JERRY R., adm. dir. bldg. mgt., Blessing Hospital, Quincy, IL '86 (ENG)
JACKSON, JOHN C., coor. med. educ., Baptist Medical Center, Jacksonville, FL '84 (EDUC)
JACKSON, JULIE S., assoc. dir. food serv., Greenville Memorial Hospital, Greenville, SC '86 (FOOD)
JACKSON, KAREN A., dir. food serv., Saratoga Community Hospital, Detroit, MI '80 (FOOD)
JACKSON, KATHRYN M., dir. commun. rel., Riverside Medical Center, Kankakee, IL '81 (PR)
JACKSON, KATHY GAMM, dir. diet. serv., Careunit Hospital of Cincinnati, Cincinnati, OH '86 (FOOD)
JACKSON, LAMAR F. JR., vice-pres. pub. rel. and consumer affairs, Tennessee Hospital Association, Nashville, TN '72 (PR)
JACKSON, LEE S., student, Graduate Studies in Health Planning and Administration, Pennsylvania State University, University Park, PA '83
JACKSON, LLOYD L., adm., Mount Graham Community Hospital, Safford, AZ '86 (RISK)
JACKSON, MARIE B., dir. food serv., Radford Community Hospital, Radford, VA '84 (FOOD)
JACKSON, PATRICIA A., dir. human res. dev., Mercy Catholic Medical Center, Darby, PA '82 (EDUC)
JACKSON, PAUL A., dir. plant oper., Saint Cabrini Hospital of Seattle, Seattle, WA '81 (ENG)
JACKSON, RANDOLPH M., MD, med. dir., Surgi-Center of Winchester, Inc., Winchester, VA '87 (AMB)
JACKSON, RICHARD M., pres., Health Services Consultants, Inc., Evergreen, CO '68 (MGMT)
JACKSON, ROBERT G., dir. soc. serv., Jordan Hospital, Plymouth, MA '71 (SOC)
JACKSON, ROBERT W., gen. mgr., The Imaging Center of Elkins Park, Inc., Elkins Park, PA '85
JACKSON, RUSSELL, sr. ed., American Health Consultants, Atlanta, GA '87 (RISK)
JACKSON, SARA L., student, Phoenix Camelback Hospital, Phoenix, AZ '83 (RISK)
JACKSON, SARAH, asst. dir. pers., Goddard Memorial Hospital, Stoughton, MA '85 (PERS)
JACKSON, SHARON S., dir. emp. rel., Children's Hospital of Wisconsin, Milwaukee, WI '86 (PERS)
JACKSON, SHERYL S., dir. pub. info., Gwinnett Hospital System, Lawrenceville, GA '84 (PR)
JACKSON, TIMOTHY J., dir. food serv., Morris View Nursing Home, Morris Plains, NJ '78 (FOOD)
JACKSON, TOBY LYNN, dir. pur., Delta County Memorial Hospital, Delta, CO '85 (PUR)
JACKSON, VALERIE A., supv. soc. work, Plantation General Hospital, Plantation, FL '81 (SOC)
JACKSON, WENDY C., dir. mktg., Antelope Valley Hospital Medical Center, Lancaster, CA '86 (PR)
JACKSON, WILLIAM C., dir. mktg., Southwest Community Health Services, Albuquerque, NM '80 (PLNG)
JACKSON, WILMA G., dir. adm. serv., Tomball Regional Hospital, Tomball, TX '80 (PAT)(VOL)
JACOB, CENON G., student, Southern Illinois University, School of Technical Careers, Carbondale, IL '86
JACOB, SALLY T., dir. diet., Dover General Hospital and Medical Center, Dover, NJ '78 (FOOD)
JACOB, SALLY W., dir. vol. serv., Danbury Hospital, Danbury, CT '81 (VOL)
JACOB, THOMAS M., consult., Ernst and Whinney, Boston, MA '82
JACOB, WALTER M., vice-pres. human res., Memorial Medical Center, Savannah, GA '72 (PERS)
JACOBES, JOSEPH J., chief eng., Quakertown Community Hospital, Quakertown, PA '81 (ENG)
JACOBOWITZ, DONALD M., asst. adm., State University Hospital, Downstate Medical Center, Brooklyn, NY '81
JACOBS, ALFRED S., dir. food serv., West Oaks-Psychiatric Institute Houston, Houston, TX '86 (FOOD)
JACOBS, BEN, mgt. eng., St. Michael Hospital, Milwaukee, WI '77 (MGMT)
JACOBS, CAROL C., dir. vol. serv., John F. Kennedy Memorial Hospital, Atlantis, FL '83 (VOL)
JACOBS, DIANE E., dir. compensation and mgt. eng., Charleston Area Medical Center, Charleston, WV '80 (MGMT)
JACOBS, EDWARD L., dir. maint., Elmcrest Psychiatric Institute, Portland, CT '83 (ENG)
JACOBS, ESTA B., dir. educ., Braintree Hospital, Braintree, MA '84 (EDUC)
JACOBS, HOLLY S., dir. commun. rel., St. Eugene Community Hospital, Dillon, SC '81 (PLNG)
JACOBS, JO A., dir. vol., Kettering Medical Center, Kettering, OH '78 (VOL)
JACOBS, JOHN E., vice-pres. human res., Winsted Memorial Hospital, Winsted, CT '85 (PERS)
JACOBS, M. ORRY, dir. strategic plng., Strong Memorial Hospital Rochester University, Rochester, NY '69 (PLNG)
JACOBS, MARIAN, pub. rel. counselor, Dameron Hospital, Stockton, CA '79 (PR)
JACOBS, NANCY, dir. commun. serv., Bloomington Hospital, Bloomington, IN '85 (ENG)
JACOBS, NORENE D., atty., Iowa Hospital Association, Des Moines, IA '78 (ATTY)
JACOBS, NORMA B., coor. vol., Los Angeles County-Olive View Medical Center, Sylmar, CA '83 (VOL)
JACOBS, PATRICK S., dir. eng., Mercy Hospital, Bakersfield, CA '84 (ENG)
JACOBS, PATSY R., adm. asst. and pat. rep., Medical Center Hospital, Conroe, TX '84 (RISK)
JACOBS, PAUL C., pres., Geauga Hospital, Chardon, OH '60
JACOBS, PHILIP B., asst. dir. cent. serv., Horton Memorial Hospital, Middletown, NY '80 (CS)
JACOBS, PHYLLIS CAROLYN, RN, assoc. exec. dir. and pat. care, Highlands Regional Medical Center, Sebring, FL '86 (NURS)
JACOBS, RICHARD B., Voluntary Hospitals of America West, Inc., Los Angeles, CA '79 (PLNG)
JACOBS, ROBERT HYDE JR., plng. consult., Craig, Zeidler and Strong, Toronto, Ont., Canada '67 (MGMT)
JACOBS, ROBERT M., atty., Hackensack Medical Center, Hackensack, NJ '82 (ATTY)
JACOBS, ROBERT S., atty., Mary Thompson Hospital, Chicago, IL '75 (ATTY)
JACOBS, ROBERT V., corp. vice-pres., Manatee Memorial Hospital and Health Systems, Bradenton, FL '75 (PLNG)
JACOBS, SETH A., atty., Akron City Hospital, Akron, OH '84 (ATTY)
JACOBS, SHEILA J., consult., Healthcare Images, Baton Rouge, LA '78 (PR)
JACOBS, SHERYL J., asst. dir. soc. work serv., Hospital for Joint Diseases Orthopaedic Institute, New York, NY '85 (SOC)
JACOBS, STANLEY E., (ret.), Highwood, IL '71 (MGMT)
JACOBS, THOMAS H., atty., Southwestern Vermont Medical Center, Bennington, VT '79 (ATTY)
JACOBSEN, LARS A., mgr. constr., Lovelace Medical Center, Albuquerque, NM '81 (ENG)
JACOBSEN, ROBERT C., dir. pat. counseling, Jennie Edmundson Memorial Hospital, Council Bluffs, IA '82 (SOC)
JACOBSEN, WILLIAM D., dir. mgt. eng., Riverside Hospital, Newport News, VA '82 (MGMT)
JACOBSON, EDWARD A., assoc., Amherst Associates, Chicago, IL '86 (PERS)
JACOBSON, ERIC PAUL, adm. health facil., State Prison of Southern Michigan, Jackson, MI '70
JACOBSON, GERALD, vice-pres. plng. and prog. dev., Moss Rehabilitation Hospital, Philadelphia, PA '85 (PLNG)
JACOBSON, HERB, owner, Advance Communication Service, Denver, CO '86 (ENG)
JACOBSON, JEROLD D., atty., Hebrew Home for Aged-Riverdale, Bronx, NY '83 (ATTY)
JACOBSON, JOHN L., asst. dir. prof. serv., Waconia Ridgeview Hospital, Waconia, MN '78 (PLNG)
JACOBSON, JOHN M., student, Program in Health Administration, Portland State University, Portland, OR '86
JACOBSON, JOHN S., dir. commun. rel., Mercy Medical Center, Redding, CA '77 (PR)
JACOBSON, KAREN J., tech. writer, Alexandria, VA '84 (MGMT)
JACOBSON, MARJORIE R., student, Xavier University, Graduate Program in Hospital and Health Administration, Cincinnati, OH '84
JACOBSON, NEWTON J., Chicago, IL '82 (LIFE)
JACOBSON, PAULINE H., Mashpee, MA '75 (VOL)
JACOBSON, ROBERT M., pres., United Hospital, Grand Forks, ND '57 (LIFE)
JACOBSON, ROSEMARY B., RN, vice-pres. pat. care, United Hospital, Grand Forks, ND '66 (NURS)
JACOBSON, SARA LEE, rep. pat. serv., Sinai Hospital of Baltimore, Baltimore, MD '77 (PAT)
JACOBSON, SYLVIA J., dir. pers., Oak Hill Hospital, Joplin, MO '86 (PERS)
JACOBUS, JAMES W., asst. dir. food serv., University of Wisconsin Hospital and Clinics, Madison, WI '81 (FOOD)
JACOBY, CAROLYN P., atty., Beth Israel Hospital, Boston, MA '86 (ATTY)
JACOBY, JENNIFER, RN, asst. adm. nrsg. serv., Roseville Community Hospital, Roseville, CA '85 (NURS)
JACOBY, JILL, dir., Wyman Park Medical Center, Baltimore, MD '87 (AMB)
JACOBY, LORRAINE, mgr. food serv., St. Vincent Medical Center, Los Angeles, CA '68 (FOOD)
JACOBY, MICHAEL, student, Program in Health Care Administration, St. Francis College, Brooklyn, NY '85
JACOCKS, J. DAVID, sr. mgr., Price Waterhouse, Dallas, TX '83 (MGMT)
JACOVELLI, PATRICIA A., dir. vol. serv., Wayne General Hospital, Wayne, NJ '84 (VOL)
JACQUES, ERNEST B., chief eng., HCA Doctors Hospital, Lake Worth, FL '83 (ENG)
JACQUES, H. BENJAMIN, asst. adm. pub. affairs, St. Joseph's Hospital, Lowell, MA '81 (PR)
JACQUES, SUSAN L., dir. pers., Springfield Hospital, Springfield, VT '83 (PERS)
JAEGER, BOI JON, exec. dir., Cooperative Health Plan, Inc., Oak Brook, IL '61
JAEGER, JUDITH M., RN, dir. dev., City of Faith Hospital, Tulsa, OK '82 (NURS)
JAEGER, L. PAUL, dir. pub. rel. and dev., Wausau Hospital Center, Wausau, WI '85 (PR)
JAFFE, JACK E., clin. supv. psych. soc. serv., Coral Reef Hospital, Miami, FL '85 (SOC)
JAFFE, JOEL, sr. vice-pres., Rochlin and Baran Associates, Inc., Los Angeles, CA '85
JAGELS, MICHAEL W., asst. dir. pers., Crittenton Hospital, Rochester, MI '74 (PERS)
JAGER, MARK D., mgr. educ., Pennock Hospital, Hastings, MI '86 (EDUC)
JAGGER, THOMAS E., atty., St. Mary-Corwin Hospital Center, Pueblo, CO '76 (ATTY)
JAGIELA, STEVEN W., mgt. syst. eng., Graduate Hospital, Philadelphia, PA '85 (MGMT)
JAGNOW, LAWRENCE V., dir. pub. rel. and mktg. commun., Evangelical Health Systems, Oak Brook, IL '86 (PR)
JAHI, JABARI, dir. pers., California Hospital Association, Sacramento, CA '86 (PERS)
JAHRAUS, SHIRLEY, dir. pers., St. Luke's Hospital, Aberdeen, SD '75 (PERS)
JAIXEN, DONNA J., dir. mktg. and pub. rel., Saint Francis Medical Center, Grand Island, NE '86 (PR)
JAKACKI, MARGARET, counsel risk mgt., Medical Liability Mutual Insurance Company, New York, NY '85 (RISK)
JAKIELKO, PATRICIA M., dir. plng. and regulatory affairs, Central DuPage Hospital, Winfield, IL '87 (PLNG)
JAKUB, GREGORY T., dir. mktg. and pub. rel., Bon Secours Hospital, Grosse Pointe, MI '84 (PR)
JAKUBOWSKI, HENRY T., dir. eng. and maint., Genesee Memorial Hospital, Batavia, NY '78 (ENG)
JALOWIEC, STEVEN, asst. dir. plant oper., St. Vincent's Medical Center, Bridgeport, CT '86 (ENG)
JAMBA, NANCY N., dir. vol. serv., Catholic Medical Center, Manchester, NH '83 (VOL)
JAMERSON, BETSY, RN, adm. nrsg., Virginia Baptist Hospital, Lynchburg, VA '71 (NURS)
JAMERSON, CARLENE, RN, dir. nrsg., Takoma Adventist Hospital, Greeneville, TN '77 (NURS)
JAMES, ANN N., atty., The Methodist Hospital, Houston, TX '81 (ATTY)
JAMES, BARBARA, dir. pers., Swedish Hospital Medical Center, Seattle, WA '70 (PERS)
JAMES, CAROLYN C., mgr. automated off. syst., Abington Memorial Hospital, Abington, PA '86 (MGMT)
JAMES, CLEVELAND A. JR., (ret.), West Chester, PA '52 (LIFE)
JAMES, CRAIG B., dir. matl. mgt., Caldwell Memorial Hospital, Lenoir, NC '86 (PUR)
JAMES, DAVE E., dir. food serv., West Virginia University Hospital, Morgantown, WV '81 (FOOD)
JAMES, DONATH, prin., Donath James Associates, Radnor, PA '83
JAMES, EDWARD EVANS, pres., James Associates, Inc., Port St. Lucie, FL '47 (LIFE)
JAMES, EVAN R., vice-pres. mktg., Hamot Health Systems, Inc., Erie, PA '85 (PR) (PLNG)
JAMES, FAYE F., coor. vol. serv., Oklahoma Memorial Hospital and Clinics, Oklahoma City, OK '81 (VOL)
JAMES, GARTH F., vice-pres. mktg., Baylor Health Care System, Dallas, TX '86 (PLNG)
JAMES, GERALDINE Y., coor. blood bank, King Fadah Hospital, Riyadh, Saudi Arabia '80 (EDUC)
JAMES, GORDON III, atty., HCA Northwest Regional Hospital, Margate, FL '82 (ATTY)
JAMES, HENRY JR., assoc. dir., Risk Mangement Services, Tacoma Park, MD '86 (RISK)
JAMES, JOHN Y., pres., Hospital Planning Associates, San Francisco, CA '52 (LIFE)
JAMES, LINDA B., assoc. dir. spec. proj.-off. of pres., Memorial Sloan Kettering Cancer Center, New York, NY '82 (PLNG)
JAMES, LINDA L., asst. dir. food serv., Baton Rouge General Medical Center, Baton Rouge, LA '79 (FOOD)
JAMES, MAE BELLE, RN, dir. nrsg. serv., Timberlawn Psychiatric Hospital, Dallas, TX '80 (NURS)
JAMES, MARY J., dir. vol. serv., John C. Lincoln Hospital and Health Center, Phoenix, AZ '84 (VOL)
JAMES, SR. MARY, dir. food serv., Santa Teresita Hospital, Duarte, CA '81 (FOOD)
JAMES, PHYLLIS C., dir. cent., proc. and distrib., John F. Kennedy Memorial Hospital, Atlantis, FL '79 (CS)
JAMES, REESE E., Highland Beach, FL '48 (LIFE)
JAMES, ROBERT L., asst. adm., St. Francis Memorial Hospital, San Francisco, CA '53 (LIFE)
JAMES, SCOTT A., bus. mgr. nrsg., AMI Saint Joseph Hospital, Omaha, NE '85 (MGMT)
JAMESON, HELEN, RN, assoc. adm., Rochester Methodist Hospital, Rochester, MN '76 (NURS)
JAMESON, MARIAN C., RN, vice-pres. nrsg. serv., Rockingham Memorial Hospital, Harrisonburg, VA '76 (NURS)
JAMISON, CINDY A., dir. pub. rel., Angelo Community Hospital, San Angelo, TX '86 (PLNG)
JAMISON, FRED C., asst. adm. fin., Kadlec Medical Center, Richland, WA '86 (EDUC)
JAMISON, JANE, supv. cent. serv., University of Iowa Hospitals and Clinics, Iowa City, IA '82 (CS)
JAMISONRN, ELEANOR A., dir. cent. serv., St. Vincent Medical Center, Toledo, OH '77 (CS)

JAMPOLE, DANIEL, dir. environ. serv., Baton Rouge General Medical Center, Baton Rouge, LA '86 (ENVIRON)
JAMRO, SR. MARY EDMUND, dir. vol. serv., Holy Family Health Center, Des Plaines, IL '83 (VOL)
JAMRON, KENNETH S., pres. and chief exec. off., Good Samaritan Medical Center, Milwaukee, WI '57 (PLNG)(PR)(LIFE)
JAMSA, KENNETH, dir. soc. serv., Saint Joseph Hospital, Elgin, IL '79 (SOC)
JANAS, JUDITH B., mgr. vol. serv., Memorial Hospital of Burlington County, Mount Holly, NJ '83 (VOL)
JANATKA, LUCILLE, RN, asst. dir. nrsg. serv., St. Mary's Hospital, Waterbury, CT '82 (NURS)
JANCO, SCOTT, dir. mktg., South Chicago Community Hospital, Chicago, IL '85 (PR)
JANDASEK, EUNICE E., dir. mktg. serv., William Beaumont Hospital, Troy, MI '81 (PR)
JANECK, MARJORIE M., RN, asst. adm. pat. serv., Northridge Hospital Medical Center, Northridge, CA '72 (NURS)
JANEK, JAMES D., asst. dir. eng., Valley Baptist Medical Center, Harlingen, TX '83 (ENG)
JANELL, JOSEPH E., vice-pres. human res., Bridgeport Hospital, Bridgeport, CT '72 (PERS)
JANETAKOS, JAMES D., dir. soc. work, Roger Williams General Hospital, Providence, RI '80 (SOC)
JANICK, BERYL JEAN, vice-pres. and chief exec. off., Phoenix Camelback Hospital, Phoenix, AZ '80 (RISK)
JANICK, JOE, eng. facil., Phoenix Area Indian Health Service, Phoenix, AZ '81 (ENG)
JANKO, GARY M., pres., Bay State Health Care, Inc., Cambridge, MA '73 (PLNG)
JANKOWSKI, THERESA E., partner, Pannell Kerr Forster, New York, NY '82 (PLNG)(AMB)
JANNEY, ROBERT S., atty., Page Memorial Hospital, Luray, VA '80 (ATTY)
JANOFF, ROCHELLE L., vice-pres. plng., Albert Einstein Health Care Foundation, Philadelphia, PA '78 (PLNG)
JANOWICZ, CAROL JOYCE, coor. mem. rel., Health Circle, Kalamazoo, MI '85 (PAT)
JANOWSKI, RAYMOND J., dir. pers., St. Francis Medical Center, Trenton, NJ '86 (PERS)
JANSA, LOUIS J., spec. hosp. and clin., University of California, Berkeley, CA '70
JANSON, JOYCE, pat. rep., Chestnut Hill Hospital, Philadelphia, PA '80 (PAT)
JANSON, ROBERT L., mgr., Ernst and Whinney, Cleveland, OH '83 (PUR)
JANSSEN, ALAN P., coor. educ., St. Francis Regional Medical Center, Wichita, KS '83 (EDUC)
JANSSEN, SR. DISMAS, asst. adm., St. Joseph Medical Center, Joliet, IL '78
JANSSEN, GARY M., dir. matl. mgt., Iowa Methodist Medical Center, Des Moines, IA '80 (PUR)
JANSZEN, HARRIET, asst. to pres., Good Samaritan Hospital, Cincinnati, OH '65 (PR)
JANTY, ANNE M., sr. consult., Ernst and Whinney, Milwaukee, WI '85 (PLNG)
JANUSKIEWICZ, THELMA T., dir. environ. serv., Wilkes-Barre General Hospital, Wilkes-Barre, PA '86 (ENVIRON)
JANZ, KATHRYN C., dir. clin. soc. work and discharge plng., Stanford University Hospital, Stanford, CA '87 (SOC)
JANZIK, LINDA CANESTRARO, asst. to pres. commun., Montgomery General Hospital, Olney, MD '85 (PR)
JAPHA, AMY COHEN, student, University of Alabama at Birmingham, School of Community and Allied Health, Birmingham, AL '85
JAPP, NYLA F., RN, mgr. cent. proc., St. Catherine Hospital, Garden City, KS '83 (CS)
JAQUEZ-BELL, COL. VIRGINIA, RN MSC USA, dir. nrsg., Bassett Army Community Hospital, Fairbanks, AK '86 (NURS)
JAQUEZ, JUDI W., dir. nutr. serv., HCA Sun Towers Hospital, El Paso, TX '81 (FOOD)
JARAMILLO, IDA, mgr. cent. serv., Christ Hospital, Jersey City, NJ '80 (CS)
JARASEK, NANCY, loss control acct. exec., Cna Insurance Companies, Chicago, IL '86 (RISK)
JARDINA, J. M., dir. matl. mgt., McKeesport Hospital, McKeesport, PA '72 (PUR)
JAREK, ALOYSIUS, dir. soc. serv., Washington Hospital, Washington, PA '78 (SOC)
JAREM, CORINNE, pat. advocate, El Dorado Hospital and Medical Center, Tucson, AZ '79 (PAT)
JARETT, PAUL S., pres., Jarett Associates, Inc., Van Nuys, CA '51 (LIFE)
JARL, RAYMOND N., exec. dir., Texas Department of Corrections, University of Texas Medical Branch, Galveston, TX '76 (PUR)
JARLENSKI, MORRIS J., chief bldg. mgt. serv., Veterans Administration Medical Center, Albany, NY '86 (ENVIRON)
JARMUZ, PAUL L., asst. dir. environ. serv., St. Joseph Intercommunity Hospital, Cheektowaga, NY '86 (ENVIRON)
JARNAGIN, JOHN S., head facil. mgt., Naval Hospital, San Diego, CA '87 (ENG)
JAROSZEWICZ, ALFRED R., dir. maint., Bellevue Hospital Center, New York, NY '86 (ENG)
JAROWEY, CONSTANCE M., staff assoc., Applied Management Systems, Inc., Burlington, MA '86 (MGMT)
JARRELL, CARTER F. C., RN, vice-pres. pat. serv., Mercy Hospital, Miami, FL '81 (NURS)
JARRELL, SCOTT MCCANTS, adm. res., Floyd Medical Center, Rome, GA '83
JARRETT, MARY S., asst. dir. matl. handling, Riverside Methodist Hospitals, Columbus, OH '81 (CS)
JARVI, ELIZABETH H., dir. soc. work, Mount Ascutney Hospital and Health Center, Windsor, VT '74 (SOC)
JARVIS, CAROL J., RN, dir. nrsg. serv., Goshen General Hospital, Goshen, IN '81 (NURS)
JARVIS, SR. MARGARET MARY, treas., St. Mary's Group of Hospitals, St. Louis, MO '63
JARVIS, NANCY J., dir. vol., William Newton Memorial Hospital, Winfield, KS '84 (VOL)
JARY, LUANN LEE, dir. soc. work, Grape Community Hospital-Southwest Medical Center, Hamburg, IA '86 (SOC)
JASKULA, STANLEY W., asst. dir. plant oper. and maint., Louis A. Weiss Memorial Hospital, Chicago, IL '73 (ENG)
JASKULSKI, CHEERYL, buyer, Pottstown Memorial Medical Center, Pottstown, PA '86 (PUR)
JASPAL, S. SINGH, pres., Jaspal Engineering Service, Inc., Madison, WI '87 (ENG)
JASPER, LAURA GINTZ, dir. commun. rel., Luther Hospital, Eau Claire, WI '86 (PR)
JASPER, PAULA M., student, University of Houston, Clear Lake City, TX '83
JASPER, ROBERT, vice-pres., Marketeam Associates, St. Louis, MO '86 (PLNG)
JASTER, ELIZABETH A., RN, dir. nrs., Meeker County Memorial Hospital, Litchfield, MN '82 (NURS)
JASTRZEBSKI, JOZEF S., mgr. biomedical, Cape Cod Hospital, Hyannis, MA '83 (ENG)
JAUDON, JOSEPH C., atty., Saint Joseph Hospital, Denver, CO '80 (ATTY)
JAVIE, KAREN E., RN, asst. dir. nrsg., Presbyterian-University of Pennsylvania Medical Center, Philadelphia, PA '86 (NURS)
JAY, STEPHEN J., MD, vice-pres. academic affairs, Methodist Hospital of Indiana, Indianapolis, IN '82
JAYE, DAVID R., pres., St. Joseph's Hospital, Marshfield, WI '53 (LIFE)
JAYNES, KATHY, dir. pers., Elko General Hospital, Elko, NV '83 (PERS)
JEAN, JUNE F., dir. nutr. serv., Anna Jaques Hospital, Newburyport, MA '85 (FOOD)
JEANNETTE, MARK T., asst. dir. matl. mgt. sup., proc. and distrib., Polyclinic Medical Center, Harrisburg, PA '82 (CS)
JEANSONNE, PHILIP J., dir. hskpg., Southern Baptist Hospital, New Orleans, LA '86 (ENVIRON)
JEDDELOH, STEVEN C., staff trng. and dev. spec., Hazelden Foundation, Center City, MN '85 (EDUC)
JEDNORSKI, CHARLES A., atty., Baltimore County General Hospital, Randallstown, MD '87 (ATTY)
JEFFCOAT, DERRIS P., supv. fire and safety protection, Allegheny General Hospital, Pittsburgh, PA '84 (ENG)
JEFFERS, SR. JANET, sector supr., Generalate of Ihm, Scranton, PA '80
JEFFERSON, TERRELL S., dir. matl. mgt., Presbyterian-University Hospital, Pittsburgh, PA '86 (PUR)
JEFFERSON, THOMAS C., student, Program in Health Care Administration, Trinity University, San Antonio, TX '86
JEFFERY, LINDA, dir. pub. rel., Doctors Hospital of Pinole, Pinole, CA '85 (PR)
JEFFES, CAROL, coor. qual. assur., Genesee Memorial Hospital, Flint, MI '86 (RISK)
JEFFRES, TED, dir. matl. mgt., Great Plains Regional Medical Center, North Platte, NE '83 (PUR)
JEFFREY, ROBERT, dir. outpatient, Holdenville General Hospital, Holdenville, OK '87 (AMB)
JEFFRIES, ROBERT GEORGE, adm., Albemarle Hospital, Elizabeth City, NC '64
JEFFRIES, ROSALIND, sr. trainer, Washington Hospital Center, Washington, DC '86 (EDUC)
JEFFRIES, RUTH M., dir. vol., Toledo Hospital, Toledo, OH '85 (VOL)
JEGIERSKI, SYLVIA J., dir. hskpg. serv., Roswell Park Memorial Institute, Buffalo, NY '86 (ENVIRON)
JEGLUM, EDWARD L., dir. mktg., Seapharm, Inc., Princeton, NJ '86
JELINEK, RICHARD CARL, PhD, chm., Medicus, Evanston, IL '67 (MGMT)
JELLEN, BETTE, pat. rep., North Pennsylvania Hospital, Lansdale, PA '78 (PAT)
JELLISON, M. DEAN, atty., Kalispell Regional Hospital, Kalispell, MT '73 (ATTY)
JELONEK, BETTY WADE, dir. emp. rel., The Methodist Hospital, Houston, TX '75 (PERS)
JEMTRUD, LINDA LOE, dir. mktg. commun., St. John's Hospital, Fargo, ND '83 (PR)
JENDRASIAK, T. JOHN, dir. pers., Millard Fillmore Hospital, Buffalo, NY '73 (PERS)
JENEVEIN, STELLA THERESA, pat. rep., Chalmette General Hospital, Chalmette, LA '85 (PAT)
JENEY, JEFFREY S., mgr. distrib., Saint Luke's Hospital, Cleveland, OH '82 (PUR)
JENIKE, GEORGE M., Long Beach, CA '76
JENKIN, LESLIE S., dir. food and nutr. serv., Saddleback Community Hospital, Laguna Hills, CA '86 (FOOD)
JENKINS, BONNIE, RN, asst. dir. nrsg., Community Hospital of Ottawa, Ottawa, IL '75 (NURS)
JENKINS, CHARLES D., pres., Union Memorial Hospital, Baltimore, MD '52 (LIFE)
JENKINS, CHERYLE A., dir. pat. rel., Rehabilitation Institute, Detroit, MI '81 (PAT)
JENKINS, DEANNA DUNCAN, dir. educ., Huntsville Hospital, Huntsville, AL '86 (EDUC)
JENKINS, DON ROGER, partner, Pannell Kerr Forster, Los Angeles, CA '84 (PLNG)
JENKINS, DOROTHY P., RN, chief nrsg. serv., Veterans Administration Medical Center, Ann Arbor, MI '83 (NURS)
JENKINS, ELEANOR J., supv. cent. serv., Ellis Hospital, Schenectady, NY '82 (CS)
JENKINS, GLEN, asst. vice-pres., East Tennessee Baptist Hospital, Knoxville, TN '72 (ENG)
JENKINS, HARRY P., dir. properties and facil., John C. Lincoln Hospital and Health Center, Phoenix, AZ '87 (ENG)
JENKINS, JENNIFER ELAINE, RN, vice-pres. nrsg., Le Bonheur Children's Medical Center, Memphis, TN '78 (NURS)
JENKINS, KENNETH C., dir. food serv., Jewish Home for the Aged, New Haven, CT '85 (FOOD)
JENKINS, MARK R., dir. pers., Oakwood Hospital, Dearborn, MI '82 (PERS)
JENKINS, PAMELA A., asst. dir. commun. rel., Hamilton Medical Center, Dalton, GA '86 (PR)
JENKINS, ROBERT L. III, vice-pres. adm., St. Joseph Hospital East, Mount Clemens, MI '77
JENKINS, SUSAN S., (ret.), Kansas City, MO '66 (PR)(LIFE)
JENKINS, THOMAS L. JR., dir. educ. serv., Bronson Methodist Hospital, Kalamazoo, MI '76 (EDUC)
JENKINS, VIRGINIA W., RN, asst. adm. nrsg. serv., Pattie A. Clay Hospital, Richmond, KY '85 (NURS)
JENKINS, WILLIAM N., dir. pers., University Hospital, Augusta, GA '72 (PERS)
JENKS, G. LYN, vice-pres., Northern Michigan Hospitals, Petoskey, MI '82 (PR)
JENKS, MICHAEL T., exec. dir., Medina County Mental Health Board, Medina, OH '86
JENKS, RUSSELL C., dir. pers., Lowell General Hospital, Lowell, MA '86 (PERS)
JENKS, WILLIAM J., atty., St. Charles Hospital, Oregon, OH '86 (ATTY)
JENNE, RONALD A., dir. plant oper., Cleveland Memorial Hospital, Shelby, NC '87 (ENG)
JENNER, JULIE, dir. commun. rel., Saint Anthony's Hospital, Alton, IL '85 (PR)
JENNETTE, JOHN F., supv. bldg. serv., New England Medical Center, Boston, MA '81 (ENG)
JENNINGS, ANNETTE L., dir. soc. serv., Raleigh General Hospital, Beckley, WV '82 (SOC)
JENNINGS, FITZROY H., mgr. cent. sterile sup., Lincoln Medical and Mental Health Center, Bronx, NY '86 (CS)
JENNINGS, GARY L., chief exec. off., Meridian Research, Inc., Panama City, FL '86
JENNINGS, HAROLD R., dir. commun., Baptist Memorial Hospital, Memphis, TN '81 (PR)
JENNINGS, JAN R., pres., Millard Fillmore Hospital, Buffalo, NY '78
JENNINGS, JAROLD J., dir. environ. serv., McMinnville Community Hospital, McMinnville, OR '85 (ENG)
JENNINGS, JENNILYN, RN, student, Memphis State University, Memphis, TN '87 (AMB)
JENNINGS, KATHRYN S., dir. matl. mgt., Highland Hospital, Shreveport, LA '80 (CS)(PUR)
JENNINGS, L. THOMAS, chief soc. work serv., Veterans Administration Medical Center, Durham, NC '82 (SOC)
JENNINGS, LARRY W., assoc. adm., Russell Hospital, Alexander City, AL '80
JENNINGS, MARIAN C., pres., Jennings, Ryan, Federa and Company, Chicago, IL '82 (PLNG)
JENNINGS, MARIE E., dir. soc. serv., Catholic Medical Center, Manchester, NH '80 (SOC)
JENNINGS, MERRY E., RN, dir. nrsg. serv., Simi Valley Adventist Hospital, Simi Valley, CA '87 (NURS)
JENNINGS, PETER G., dir. plng., Good Samaritan Hospital and Health Center, Dayton, OH '78 (PLNG)
JENNINGS, R. LARRY, mgr. pur., Methodist Hospital, Philadelphia, PA '82 (PUR)
JENNINGS, RALPH E., pres., Durham County General Hospital, Durham, NC '57 (LIFE)
JENNINGS, ROBERT PAUL, vice-pres., Baptist Medical Center, Jacksonville, FL '84 (RISK)(AMB)
JENNISON, HAROLD, dir. plng., Framingham Union Hospital, Framingham, MA '79 (PLNG)
JENSEN-O'NEIL, BOBBIE, pat. rep., Sharp Memorial Hospital, San Diego, CA '77 (PAT)
JENSEN, AASE S., RN, head nrs. cent. serv., Community Hospital, Santa Rosa, CA '85 (CS)
JENSEN, ALLEN C., stationary eng., Holy Family Hospital, Des Plaines, IL '87 (ENG)
JENSEN, BRUCE C., pres., Grinnell General Hospital, Grinnell, IA '81
JENSEN, CHRISTINE C., dir. pub. rel. and publications, Rochester Methodist Hospital, Rochester, MN '86 (PR)
JENSEN, DEBORAH A., RN, dir. phys. health, Southeastern District Health Department, Pocatello, ID '85 (NURS)
JENSEN, DENNIS L., mgr. constr. and maint., Jennie Edmundson Memorial Hospital, Council Bluffs, IA '82 (ENG)
JENSEN, ELAINE, coor. cent. serv., Jane Lamb Health Center, Clinton, IA '83 (CS)
JENSEN, EVARTS P., dir. plant oper., Deaconess Hospital, Evansville, IN '75 (ENG)
JENSEN, GARY C., dir. biomedical eng., Victory Memorial Hospital, Waukegan, IL '85 (ENG)
JENSEN, GREG, asst. dir. soc. serv., University of Iowa Hospitals and Clinics, Iowa City, IA '86 (SOC)
JENSEN, JAMES AL, chief human res., Washington Hospital, Fremont, CA '73 (PERS)
JENSEN, JAMES MARTIN, adm., Omega Medical Clinic, Inc., Walnut Creek, CA '87 (AMB)
JENSEN, JAMES R., dir. qual. assur., Saint Alphonsus Regional Medical Center, Boise, ID '85 (RISK)
JENSEN, JOHN E., mgr. receiving stores, University Medical Center, Tucson, AZ '81 (CS)
JENSEN, JOYCE C., vice-pres., National Research Corporation, Lincoln, NE '84 (PR) (PLNG)
JENSEN, JULIE, RN, claims and risk mgt. consult., Hssi Agency, Inc., San Rafael, CA '86 (RISK)
JENSEN, KATHY, RN, asst. adm. pat. care serv., Douglas Community Hospital, Roseburg, OR '83 (NURS)
JENSEN, KEN E., adm., Hills and Dales General Hospital, Cass City, MI '64
JENSEN, LYNDON S., dir. mgt. syst., St. Joseph Mercy Hospital, Mason City, IA '85 (MGMT)
JENSEN, MARILYN F., dir. food serv., Cass County Memorial Hospital, Atlantic, IA '74 (FOOD)
JENSEN, NANCY W., dir. pub. rel., Mount Sinai Hospital, Minneapolis, MN '84 (PR)
JENSEN, PAUL M., dir. soc. serv., Bryan Memorial Hospital, Lincoln, NE '86 (SOC)
JENSEN, PHYLLIS A., dir. mgt. eng., Immanuel-St. Joseph's Hospital, Mankato, MN '83 (MGMT)

JENSEN, ROSE M., human res. spec. and coor. vol., Bellin Memorial Hospital, Green Bay, WI '86 (VOL)
JENSEN, SUSAN SCHLANSKY, dir. pat. rel. and soc. serv., Humana Hospital -Metropolitan, San Antonio, TX '75 (PAT)
JENSEN, SUZANN, risk mgt. consult., Virginia Insurance Reciprocal, Richmond, VA '86 (RISK)
JENSON, ANDREA A., dir. sales, Hollister, Inc., Libertyville, IL '85 (PUR)
JEPPSON, DAVID H., exec. vice-pres., Intermountain Health Care, Inc., Salt Lake City, UT '64
JEPSON, AMY A., coor. educ., Borgess Medical Center, Kalamazoo, MI '86 (EDUC)
JEPSON, JEANNE A., dir. pers., Fuller Memorial Hospital, South Attleboro, MA '85 (PERS)
JERARDI, JOSEPH V., dir. soc. serv., York Hospital, York, PA '79 (SOC)
JERGE, DONALD W., dir. pers., Eastern New Mexico Medical Center, Roswell, NM '81 (PERS)
JERGER, EMILY REMINGTON, pat. rep., John D. Archbold Memorial Hospital, Thomasville, GA '65 (PAT)
JERGESEN, ALLAN D., atty., Hospital Council of Northern California, San Bruno, CA '79 (ATTY)
JERIE, ROBERT V., dir. pur., St. Mary of Nazareth Hospital Center, Chicago, IL '78 (PUR)
JERINE, ALLEN, vice-pres. staff and clin. serv., Bronx-Lebanon Hospital Center, Bronx, NY '80
JERMANO, MARTHA G., RN, adm. nrsg., Amsterdam Memorial Hospital, Amsterdam, NY '85 (NURS)
JERNER, MARY F., mgr. pur., Emanuel Medical Center, Turlock, CA '81 (PUR)
JERNIGAN, MICHEAL D., dir. plng., Naples Community Hospital, Naples, FL '82 (PLNG)
JERNIGAN, SUSAN C., mgr. compensation and benefits, Durham County General Hospital, Durham, NC '85 (PERS)
JEROME, FRANK A. JR., dir., Jerome Consulting, Ruston, LA '58
JEROUSEK, FLORENCE A., mgr., Valley View Community Hospital, Youngtown, AZ '81 (SOC)
JERZYK, RONALD J., dir. emp. rel., St. Margaret Hospital, Hammond, IN '80 (PERS)
JESCHKE, SANDRA L., dir. risk mgt., Aps Facilities Management, Inc., Austin, TX '84 (RISK)
JESSE, JOHN J. JR., mech. eng., Henningson Durham and Richardson, Omaha, NE '83 (ENG)
JESSE, JOHN W., dir. res. and plng., St. Joseph Regional Medical Center, Lewiston, ID '86 (PLNG)
JESSE, WILLIAM, dir. environ. serv., Shriners Hospital for Crippled Children, Philadelphia, PA '86 (ENVIRON)
JESSEE, KENNETH H., mgr. data proc., Woodland Memorial Hospital, Woodland, CA '87 (MGMT)
JESSEN, JANICE M., dir. pers., Guadalupe Valley Hospital, Seguin, TX '86 (PERS)
JESSER, SANDRA L., RN, asst. vice-pres. qual. assur. and risk mgt., Western Medical Center, Santa Ana, CA '85 (NURS)(RISK)
JESSUP, STEPHEN M., atty., Howard Community Hospital, Kokomo, IN '83 (ATTY)
JESTER, WILLIAM E., mgt. sup. consult., Sch Health Care System, Houston, TX '86 (MGMT)
JESTER, WINNIE, dir. vol., Portland Adventist Medical Center, Portland, OR '78 (VOL)
JETER, NORMAN W., atty., Hadley Regional Medical Center, Hays, KS '69 (ATTY)
JETT, ALMA M., (ret.), Fredericksburg, VA '67 (CS)
JETT, BARRY L., dir. risk mgt., Christ Hospital, Cincinnati, OH '85 (RISK)
JETT, SARAH H., dir. vol. serv., Medical Center Hospitals, Leigh Memorial Hospital Division, Norfolk, VA '78 (VOL)
JEWELL, ARLICE R., dir. vol. serv., Mercy Hospital, Benton Harbor, MI '85 (VOL)
JEWELL, ROBERT E., asst. vice-pres., Jewish Hospital of St. Louis, St. Louis, MO '86 (PERS)
JEWETT, DAVID M., sr. mgt. eng., Presbyterian Hospital in the City of New York, New York, NY '73 (MGMT)
JEWETT, JOAN M., RN, dir. nrsg., Newport Hospital, Newport, NH '83 (NURS)
JEWS, WILLIAM L., pres., Liberty Medical Center, Baltimore, MD '79
JEZEK, JUDITH, RN PhD, dir. undergraduate nrsg. prog. and asst. prof., Rush University College of Nursing, Chicago, IL '82 (NURS)
JEZEWSKI, JIM, supv. hskpg., Hills and Dales General Hospital, Cass City, MI '86 (ENVIRON)
JEZYCKI, CHARLES W. S., asst. adm., Queen of the Valley Hospital, Napa, CA '66 (RISK)
JHALA, JOE H., consult., Health Care Systems Management Service, Vancouver, B.C., Canada '87 (MGMT)
JILLIONS, JOHN E., dir. mktg., Methodist Hospital, Philadelphia, PA '86 (PR) (PLNG)
JIMENEZ, SUSANA C., coor. commun. rel., Crawford Long Hospital Emory University, Atlanta, GA '86 (PR)
JIMESON, MERRIE SUE, dir. mktg., Memorial Hospital System, Houston, TX '84 (PLNG)
JIMPSON, GLORIA E., RN, dir. nrsg., Leonard Hospital, Troy, NY '83 (NURS)
JINKERSON, GREGORY L., dir. commun. rel. and mktg., Alexian Brothers Hospital, St. Louis, MO '80 (PR)
JINKS, WILLIAM PAUL, vice-pres. human resources, Memorial Medical Center, Springfield, IL '78
JINNEMAN, ROBERT C., dir. food serv., St. James Community Hospital, Butte, MT '74 (FOOD)
JIRASAKHIRAN, EVELYN Q., RN, dir. nrsg., Smyrna Hospital, Smyrna, GA '86 (NURS)
JIRU, LT. COL. MICHAEL W., MSC USAF, Headquarters Air Force Medical Service, Brooks AFB, TX '80 (PUR)
JO, SUNG KEE, dir., Department of Hospital Engineering and Research of Seoul Adventist Hospital, Seoul, South Korea '84 (ENG)
JOACHIM, RALPH B., dir. food serv., Wyandotte General Hospital, Wyandotte, MI '74 (FOOD)
JOACHIM, ROBERT, dir. dev. and pub. affairs, Staten Island Hospital, Staten Island, NY '83 (PR)
JOBE, ALICE WIEDLE, asst. dir., St. Luke's Hospital, Chesterfield, MO '77 (CS)
JOBES, MARGARET O., RN, assoc. adm. nrsg. serv., Maryvale Samaritan Hospital, Phoenix, AZ '75 (NURS)
JODOIN, PAMELA, dir. cent. sup., Downey Community Hospital, Downey, CA '83 (CS)
JOENS, CAPT. KEITH L., MSC USAF, U. S. Air Force Hospital, APO New York, NY '81
JOERS, LAWRENCE E. C. II, asst. pub. rel. and mktg., Huguley Memorial Hospital, Fort Worth, TX '85 (PR)
JOHANNIDES, DAVID F., pres., Tri-County Community Hospital, LaGrange, KY '64 (MGMT)
JOHANSON, CAROL R., dir. diet. serv., West Allis Memorial Hospital, West Allis, WI '74 (FOOD)
JOHN, BARBARA G., RN, dir. nrsg., River Park Hospital, McMinnville, TN '82 (NURS)
JOHN, EMILIO A., student, Program in Health Services Administration, University of Kansas, Lawrence, KS '84
JOHN, JOSEPH ROBERT III, adm. res., Veterans Administration Medical Center, Birmingham, AL '84
JOHN, MERVYN, dir. support serv., Washington Adventist Hospital, Takoma Park, MD '86 (FOOD)
JOHN, PERI A., coor. risk mgt., Bethany Medical Center, Kansas City, KS '86 (RISK)
JOHN, ROGER S., dir. educ., Great Plains Health Alliance, Phillipsburg, KS '85 (EDUC)
JOHN, SHERWINE PATRICIA, RN, asst. dir. cent. proc. and distrib., Washington Adventist Hospital, Takoma Park, MD '85 (CS)
JOHNCOUR, BARBARA G., dir. vol. serv., Charles Cole Memorial Hospital, Coudersport, PA '81 (VOL)
JOHNDROW, KATHRYNE M., dir. vol. and aux., Holy Cross Hospital and Health Center, Nogales, AZ '86 (VOL)
JOHNEN, LOUIS K., mgr. plant oper. and maint., St. Elizabeth Medical Center, Yakima, WA '78 (ENG)
JOHNS, DANNY E., coor. safety, Jewish Hospital of St. Louis, St. Louis, MO '86 (ENG)
JOHNS, EDWIN R., health care consult., New Milford Hospital, New Milford, CT '48 (LIFE)
JOHNS, EILEEN, med. rec. consult., Shelter Island, NY '62
JOHNS, JUDITH S., dir. amb. serv., West Suburban Hospital Medical Center, Oak Park, IL '87 (AMB)
JOHNS, MICHAEL E., MD, assoc. dean to clin. practice, Johns Hopkins Hospital, Baltimore, MD '87 (AMB)
JOHNS, RICHARD WARRENS, atty., Loma Linda University Medical Center, Loma Linda, CA '83 (ATTY)
JOHNS, ROY L., dir. maint., White County Memorial Hospital, Monticello, IN '86 (ENG)
JOHNS, TERESA S., dir. soc. serv., Florida Hospital-Altamonte, Altamonte Springs, FL '85 (SOC)
JOHNS, WARREN L., atty., Adventist Health System, Shawnee Mission, KS '78 (ATTY)
JOHNSEN, CAROL, supv. ob., Anderson Hospital, Maryville, IL '86 (RISK)
JOHNSEN, GORDON N., pres., General Health Services, Inc., Madison, WI '58
JOHNSEN, VICKIE, adm. dir. amb. serv., American Fork Hospital, American Fork, UT '87 (AMB)
JOHNSON-ARNEY, INDIA, dir. qual. assr, Smyrna Hospital, Smyrna, GA '86 (RISK)
JOHNSON, AL, dir. pers., Abbott-Northwestern Hospital, Minneapolis, MN '84 (PERS)
JOHNSON, ALICE S., RN, dir. in-service educ., Jefferson Memorial Hospital, Crystal City, MO '76 (EDUC)
JOHNSON, ALLEN S., dir. mgt. eng., Iowa Methodist Medical Center, Des Moines, IA '86 (MGMT)
JOHNSON, ALTON C., assoc. dir., Center for Advanced Study in Health Care Fiscal Management, Organization and Control, Graduate School of Business, University of Wisconsin-Madison, Madison, WI '78
JOHNSON, ANITA T., vice-pres. commun. serv., St. Michael Hospital, Milwaukee, WI '81 (PR)
JOHNSON, ANN MOND, mgr. prod. plng. and dev., Health Central Enterprises, Minneapolis, MN '81 (PLNG)
JOHNSON, ANNE BURNS, dir. plng., Eden Hospital Medical Center, Castro Valley, CA '82 (PLNG)
JOHNSON, ANNETTE B., atty., New York University Medical Center, New York, NY '83 (ATTY)
JOHNSON, ANNETTE, student, Southern Illinois University, School of Technical Careers, Carbondale, IL '86
JOHNSON, ARLO L., vice-pres., Servicemaster Industries, Inc., Downers Grove, IL '75
JOHNSON, ARTHUR M., mgt. eng., St. Luke's-Roosevelt Hospital Center, New York, NY '83 (MGMT)
JOHNSON, B. GERALD, atty., Pacific Medical Center, Seattle, WA '86 (ATTY)
JOHNSON, BARBARA A., sr. mgr. human res. serv., Michigan Hospital Association Service Corporation, Lansing, MI '85 (PERS)(PAT)
JOHNSON, BARBARA JO, RN, clin. dir., Grant Hospital of Chicago, Chicago, IL '79 (NURS)
JOHNSON, BERTIL, dir. maint., Corry Memorial Hospital, Corry, PA '81 (ENG)
JOHNSON, BETTY M., RN, pat. and family educator and discharge planner, Madison Memorial Hospital, Rexburg, ID '83 (EDUC)
JOHNSON, BILL, telecommun. consult., Coopers and Lybrand, St. Louis, MO '86 (ENG)
JOHNSON, BOBBY D., dir. plant oper., Burlington Medical Center, Burlington, IA '77 (ENG)
JOHNSON, BONNIE J., mgr., University of Kentucky, Communications Opererations-Voice, Lexington, KY '86 (ENG)
JOHNSON, BRENDA, dir. soc. serv., Cumberland Memorial Hospital, Cumberland, WI '81 (SOC)
JOHNSON, BRUCE, atty., St. Joseph Hospital, Florence, CO '77 (ATTY)
JOHNSON, CAROL ANN, dir. pat. rel., Children's Hospital of Wisconsin, Milwaukee, WI '84 (PAT)
JOHNSON, CAROL JEAN, dir. vol. serv., West Allis Memorial Hospital, West Allis, WI '82 (VOL)
JOHNSON, CATHERINE R., RN, coor. nrsg. educ., Immanuel Medical Center, Omaha, NE '86 (EDUC)
JOHNSON, CECELIA, dir. soc. work, St. Joseph Hospital, Augusta, GA '86 (SOC)
JOHNSON, CECILIA T., dir. soc. serv., Harmarville Rehabilitation Center, Pittsburgh, PA '83 (SOC)
JOHNSON, CECYL, mgr. pers., Sierra Nevada Job Corps, Reno, NV '85 (PERS)
JOHNSON, CHARLES D., student, Texas A. and M. University, College Station, TX '65 (EDUC)
JOHNSON, CHARLES F., pres., Lawrence Memorial Hospital of Medford, Medford, MA '58
JOHNSON, CHARLES P., mgr. area oper., Servicemaster Industries, Inc., Plymouth, MN '79
JOHNSON, CLARE JOAN MILNER, dir. soc. work, East Tennessee Baptist Hospital, Knoxville, TN '83 (SOC)
JOHNSON, CLIFFORD W., chief plant oper., Missoula Community Hospital, Missoula, MT '85 (ENG)
JOHNSON, CRAIG L., dir. soc. serv., Charter Pacific Hospital, Torrance, CA '87 (SOC)
JOHNSON, CYNDE L., student, Ohio State University, Columbus, OH '83
JOHNSON, CYNTHIA H., dir. vol. serv., St. Joseph Hospital, Memphis, TN '80 (VOL)
JOHNSON, DALE B., dir. soc. serv., El Dorado Hospital and Medical Center, Tucson, AZ '85 (SOC)
JOHNSON, DAVID A., pres., Deaconess Development Corporation, Evansville, IN '54 (LIFE)
JOHNSON, DAVID L., adm. dir. matl. mgt., Presbyterian Hospital, Charlotte, NC '84 (PUR)
JOHNSON, DAVID R., dir. mktg. and plng., Queen of the Valley Hospital, Napa, CA '79 (PLNG)
JOHNSON, DAVID, coor. risk mgt., Naval Hospital, Charleston, SC '86 (RISK)
JOHNSON, DEAN L., atty., Selma District Hospital, Selma, CA '84 (ATTY)
JOHNSON, DEBORAH C., RN, asst. adm. nrsg., Eastern Maine Medical Center, Bangor, ME '83 (NURS)
JOHNSON, DEEANN, dir. pers., Woodland Community Hospital, Cullman, AL '84 (PERS)
JOHNSON, DENISE A., RN, asst. dir. nrsg. serv., Alexian Brothers Hospital San Jose, San Jose, CA '85 (NURS)
JOHNSON, DOLLY M., dir. vol. serv., Northwestern Memorial Hospital, Chicago, IL '70 (VOL)
JOHNSON, DONALD E. L., pres., Donald E. L. Johnson and Associates, Chicago, IL '86
JOHNSON, DONALD P., consult., Johnti, Inc.-Consultants, Philadelphia, PA '73
JOHNSON, DONNA K., dir. soc. serv., Northwest General Hospital, Milwaukee, WI '85 (SOC)
JOHNSON, DONNA M., dir. educ., Sacred Heart Hospital, Eau Claire, WI '85 (EDUC)
JOHNSON, DOREEN HILLARY, hostess, Tri-City Medical Center, Oceanside, CA '85 (PAT)
JOHNSON, DOROTHY C., RN, dir. pat. rep., McLeod Regional Medical Center, Florence, SC '86 (PAT)
JOHNSON, DOROTHY M., dir. pers., Morrison Community Hospital, Morrison, IL '81 (PERS)
JOHNSON, REV. DOUGLAS P., Lexington, MO '86
JOHNSON, DUFFY JR., assoc. dir. matl. mgt., William N. Wishard Memorial Hospital, Indianapolis, IN '80 (PUR)
JOHNSON, DWIGHT, St. Francis Hospital and Medical Center, Topeka, KS '85 (ENG)
JOHNSON, E. OTIS JR., atty., Mississippi Methodist Hospital and Rehabilitation Center, Jackson, MS '72 (ATTY)
JOHNSON, EDITH P., RN, dir. nrsg., Peninsula General Hospital Medical Center, Salisbury, MD '71 (NURS)
JOHNSON, EDWARD L., adm., Midwest Medical Management, Inc., Indianapolis, IN '87 (AMB)
JOHNSON, ELLEN C., mktg. assoc., Health Central System, Minneapolis, MN '79 (PR)
JOHNSON, ERIC H., RN, asst. dir. matl. mgt. syst., General Hospital of Everett, Everett, WA '84 (CS)
JOHNSON, EVERETT A., dir., The E. J. Group, Inc., Marietta, GA '50 (LIFE)
JOHNSON, FARRELL E., mgr. plant oper., Community Hospital of Gardena, Gardena, CA '83 (ENG)
JOHNSON, FRAN, dir. soc. serv., Henry County Memorial Hospital, New Castle, IN '86 (SOC)
JOHNSON, FRANCES A., dir. diet. and hskpg., Charter Hospital of Kingwood, Kingwood, TX '85 (FOOD)
JOHNSON, FRANK HAYES, atty., Sacred Heart Medical Center, Spokane, WA '72 (ATTY)
JOHNSON, GARY A., dir. matl. mgt., Poudre Valley Hospital, Fort Collins, CO '86 (PUR)
JOHNSON, GARY L., spec. qual. assur., environ. serv., Manor Healthcare Corporation, Arlington, TX '86 (ENVIRON)
JOHNSON, GEORGE ODIN, PhD, dir., Program in Hospital and Health Care Administration, University of Minnesota, Minneapolis, MN '62
JOHNSON, GEORGE W., student, Medical College of Virginia, Virginia Commonwealth University, Richmond, VA '86
JOHNSON, GEORGIANNE, vice-pres. prof. serv., Hillcrest Medical Center, Tulsa, OK '78 (NURS)
JOHNSON, GRACE ELLEN, dir. soc. work, St. David's Community Hospital, Austin, TX '85 (SOC)
JOHNSON, HAROLD A., dir. matl. mgt., Woman's Christian Association Hospital, Jamestown, NY '57 (PUR)(LIFE)
JOHNSON, HEIDI E., atty., Kennebec Valley Medical Center, Augusta, ME '85 (ATTY)
JOHNSON, HELEN D., pat. advocate, Saint Vincent Hospital, Worcester, MA '78 (PAT)
JOHNSON, HELEN, mgr. health care prog., Smith Kline and French Laboratory, Philadelphia, PA '86 (AMB)
JOHNSON, HERBERT B., dir. pers., Saint Francis Medical Center, Peoria, IL '69 (PERS)
JOHNSON, HERBERT H., dir. maint., Franklin Memorial Hospital, Rocky Mount, VA '82 (ENG)
JOHNSON, HOWARD L., vice-pres. pers. serv., St. Michael's Hospital, Stevens Point, WI '87 (PERS)
JOHNSON, HOWARD P., asst. adm., Lakeview Medical Center, Rice Lake, WI '86 (PERS)

JOHNSON, J. RICHARDSON, atty., Borgess Medical Center, Kalamazoo, MI '82 (ATTY)
JOHNSON, JAMES A., dir. house serv., Beaver Dam Community Hospitals, Beaver Dam, WI '80 (ENG)
JOHNSON, JAMES D., dir. pur., Farmington Community Hospital, Farmington, MO '86 (PUR)
JOHNSON, JAMES K., adm., John F. Kennedy Memorial Hospital, Atlantis, FL '81 (PLNG)
JOHNSON, JAMES M., MD, pres., Emergency Consultants, Inc., Traverse City, MI '80 (AMB)
JOHNSON, JAN R., coor. vol. serv., Washoe Medical Center, Reno, NV '86 (VOL)
JOHNSON, JAN, dir. commun., Providence Medical Center, Seattle, WA '86 (PR) (PLNG)
JOHNSON, JANE, supv., Sherman Hospital, Elgin, IL '85
JOHNSON, JANET M., pat. rep., Wausau Hospital Center, Wausau, WI '86 (PAT)
JOHNSON, JANICE G., RN, dir. nrsg. serv., St. Charles Hospital, Luling, LA '86 (NURS)
JOHNSON, JEAN H., asst. vice-pres., Professional Risk Management, Santa Ana, CA '82 (RISK)
JOHNSON, JEAN T., asst. dir., St. Thomas Hospital, Nashville, TN '85 (EDUC)
JOHNSON, JERRY D., atty., Doctors Hospital of Dallas, Dallas, TX '84 (ATTY)
JOHNSON, JIM H., vice-pres. corp. plng., St. Vincent de Paul Community Stewardship Services, Inc., Jacksonville, FL '83 (PLNG)
JOHNSON, JO ANNE M., RN, instr. med. and surg., Forrest County General Hospital, Hattiesburg, MS '85 (EDUC)
JOHNSON, JO, corp. contr., Samaritan Health Service, Phoenix, AZ '78
JOHNSON, JOANN, vice-pres., Bellin Memorial Hospital, Green Bay, WI '86 (AMB)
JOHNSON, JOE, dir. plant oper., HCA Santa Rosa Medical Center, Milton, FL '85 (ENG)
JOHNSON, JOHN C., MD, dir. emer. med. serv., Porter Memorial Hospital, Valparaiso, IN '87 (AMB)
JOHNSON, JOHN CHARLES, pres., Berkshire Medical Center, Pittsfield, MA '70
JOHNSON, JOHN E., asst. dir. eng., University Community Hospital, Tamarac, FL '84 (ENG)
JOHNSON, JOHN F., dir. matl. mgt., St. Francis Hospital Systems, Colorado Springs, CO '80 (PUR)
JOHNSON, JOHN J., clin. soc. worker, U. S. Public Health Service Indian Hospital, Wagner, SD '72 (SOC)
JOHNSON, JOHN M., dir. cent. serv., Mainland Center Hospital, Texas City, TX '78 (CS)
JOHNSON, JOHN R., chief soc. serv., West Texas Rehabilitation Center, Abilene, TX '82 (SOC)
JOHNSON, JOHN RICHARD, (ret.), Sycamore, IL '46 (LIFE)
JOHNSON, JOSEPH H. JR., atty., Walker Regional Medical Center, Jasper, AL '78 (ATTY)
JOHNSON, JOSEPHINE GOODE, RN, dir. risk mgt., University of Maryland Hospital, Baltimore, MD '81 (RISK)
JOHNSON, JOY E., dir. mktg. and commun., Lutheran Hospitals and Home Society, Fargo, ND '84 (PLNG)
JOHNSON, JOYCE ALINE, mgr., Huntington Memorial Hospital, Pasadena, CA '77 (EDUC)
JOHNSON, JOYCE E., RN, assoc. adm., Washington Hospital Center, Washington, DC '81 (NURS)
JOHNSON, JOYCE L., RN, vice-pres. pat. care serv., Spohn Hospital, Corpus Christi, TX '77 (NURS)
JOHNSON, JUDITH A., atty., New England Medical Center, Boston, MA '84 (ATTY)
JOHNSON, JUDITH C., O'Fallon, IL '78 (FOOD)
JOHNSON, JUDITH I., RN, Turlock, CA '84 (NURS)
JOHNSON, JUDY J., dir. educ., HCA Parkway Medical Center, Lithia Springs, GA '85 (EDUC)
JOHNSON, JULIANNE, dir. diet., Mercy Hospital, Baltimore, MD '83 (FOOD)
JOHNSON, KAREN E., dir. commun. rel. and mktg., Sun Valley Regional Hospital, El Paso, TX '82 (PR)
JOHNSON, KAREN S., supv. oper. room and cent. serv., Richmond Memorial Hospital and Health Center, Staten Island, NY '79 (CS)
JOHNSON, KARLA J., mgt. eng., Jewish Hospital, Louisville, KY '85 (MGMT)
JOHNSON, KATHERINE A., RN, adm. nrsg., Pitt County Memorial Hospital, Greenville, NC '86 (NURS)
JOHNSON, KATHLEEN A., mgr., Price Waterhouse, Chicago, IL '83 (PLNG)
JOHNSON, KENNETH F., consult., Winthrop, ME '78
JOHNSON, KENNETH H., mgr. plant oper., Holyoke Hospital, Holyoke, MA '76 (ENG)
JOHNSON, KRISTEN M., adm. otolaryngology, Manhattan Eye, Ear and Throat Hospital, New York, NY '85
JOHNSON, L., coor. pat. rel., Memorial Hospital, Hollywood, FL '78 (PAT)
JOHNSON, LAWRENCE A., dir. food serv., North Gables Hospital, Coral Gables, FL '81 (FOOD)
JOHNSON, CAPT. LAWRENCE M., MSC USA, student, U. S. Army Command and General Staff College, Fort Leavenworth, KS '83
JOHNSON, LEE J., atty., St. Vincent's Hospital and Medical Center, New York, NY '84 (RISK)(ATTY)
JOHNSON, LEE R., dir. pub. affairs, Sioux Valley Hospital, Sioux Falls, SD '83 (PR) (PLNG)
JOHNSON, LEE S., chief soc. work serv., Veterans Administration Medical Center, Gainesville, FL '73 (SOC)
JOHNSON, LESLIE R., supv. maint., Mason General Hospital, Shelton, WA '79 (ENG)
JOHNSON, LESTER ELWIN, (ret.), Willmar, MN '52 (LIFE)
JOHNSON, LISA H., mgr. mktg. and primary care serv., MacNeal Hospital, Berwyn, IL '86 (PR)(AMB)
JOHNSON, LOIS Y., RN, vice-pres. pat. care serv., Rose Medical Center, Denver, CO '83 (NURS)
JOHNSON, LORIE M., RN, asst. dir. nrsg., Francis Scott Key Medical Center, Baltimore, MD '82 (NURS)
JOHNSON, LORNA J., dir. diet., United Hospital, Grand Forks, ND '77 (FOOD)
JOHNSON, LYNDEN H., dir., St. Francis Campus Services, Little Falls, MN '69 (ENG)
JOHNSON, M. R. JR., atty., Greenville Hospital System, Greenville, SC '75 (ATTY)
JOHNSON, MARCIA A., supv. cent. serv., St. Joseph Hospital, Concordia, KS '74 (CS)
JOHNSON, MARGARET E., RN, assoc. vice-pres. nrsg. serv., Metropolitan Medical Center, Minneapolis, MN '85 (NURS)
JOHNSON, MARGARET K., dir. vol., Exeter Hospital, Exeter, NH '81 (VOL)
JOHNSON, MARGARET L., corp. planner, Christian Health Services Development Corporation, St. Louis, MO '83 (PLNG)
JOHNSON, MARIA E., dir. soc. serv., Huntsville Memorial Hospital, Huntsville, TX '85 (SOC)
JOHNSON, MARIAN R. LEE, dir. pub. rel., Hanover General Hospital, Hanover, PA '85 (PR)
JOHNSON, MARIANN L., pres., Hospital Consultant International, Ltd., Barrington, IL '81 (PLNG)
JOHNSON, MARIE T., dir. pub. rel., Falmouth Hospital, Falmouth, MA '86 (PR)
JOHNSON, MARJORIE J., RN, dir. nrsg., St. Mary Hospital, Port Arthur, TX '87 (NURS)
JOHNSON, MARJORIE, dir. risk mgt. and qual. assur., National Emergency Service, Inc., Toledo, OH '87 (RISK)
JOHNSON, MARK D., dir. matl. mgt., St. Mary's Hospital Medical Center, Green Bay, WI '82 (PUR)
JOHNSON, MARK F., dir. matl. mgt., Miami Valley Hospital, Dayton, OH '87 (PUR)
JOHNSON, MARTHA M., dir. food serv., Medical College of Ohio Hospital, Toledo, OH '81 (FOOD)
JOHNSON, MARVIN A., chm. soc. work, Lutheran General Hospital, Park Ridge, IL '77 (SOC)
JOHNSON, MARY F., supv. cent. serv., Waupun Memorial Hospital, Waupun, WI '86 (CS)
JOHNSON, MARY H., dir. vol., Barnes Hospital, St. Louis, MO '85 (VOL)
JOHNSON, MARY L., emp. commun. spec., St. John and West Shore Hospital, Westlake, OH '85 (PR)
JOHNSON, MARY L., dir. diet., St. Joseph Health Center, St. Charles, MO '74 (FOOD)
JOHNSON, MICHAEL L., dir. pers., Norman Regional Hospital, Norman, OK '80 (PERS)
JOHNSON, MIKE A., biomedical eng., Menorah Medical Center, Kansas City, MO '85 (ENG)
JOHNSON, MITCHELL L., asst. vice-pres. mktg., Memorial Medical Center, Springfield, IL '80 (PLNG)
JOHNSON, MOLLIE S., plng. spec., Bronson Healthcare Group, Inc., Kalamazoo, MI '85 (PLNG)
JOHNSON, NETTE JANE, asst. dir. pat. affairs, Chippenham Hospital, Richmond, VA '85 (PAT)
JOHNSON, NORMAN S., dir. phys. plant, University South Florida Psychiatric Center, Tampa, FL '80 (ENG)
JOHNSON, PAMELA, RN, asst. adm. pat. care and dir. nrs., Mesquite Community Hospital, Mesquite, TX '86 (NURS)
JOHNSON, PATRICIA ANN, dir. matl. mgt., St. John Medical Center, Tulsa, OK '81 (PUR)
JOHNSON, PATRICIA L., sr. dir. prov. serv., Blue Cross of California, Van Nuys, CA '78
JOHNSON, PAULETTE DEJOIE, dir. pat. rel., Hospital of the Medical College of Pennsylvania, Philadelphia, PA '83 (PAT)
JOHNSON, PETER K., vice-pres. mktg., Kendrick Johnson and Associates, Inc., Minneapolis, MN '86 (FOOD)
JOHNSON, PHILIP D., corp. vice-pres. facil. plng., Mount Carmel Health, Columbus, OH '87 (ENG)
JOHNSON, PHILIP JOHN, exec. vice-pres., Malden Hospital, Malden, MA '69
JOHNSON, PIERRENE K., assoc. dir. nrsg., Baptist Medical Center, Columbia, SC '82 (NURS)
JOHNSON, RAND D., atty., Church Charity Foundation of Long Island, Hempstead, NY '83 (ATTY)
JOHNSON, RAY, adm. dir. plant oper., Lakeshore Hospital, Birmingham, AL '86 (RISK)
JOHNSON, RAYLENE J., clin. diet., Memorial Hospital of San Gorgonio Pass, Banning, CA '84 (FOOD)
JOHNSON, REBECCA D., dir. nrsg. pat. care serv., Iredell Memorial Hospital, Statesville, NC '85 (NURS)
JOHNSON, REGINALD D. A., Columbia, MD '71
JOHNSON, RICHARD D., vice-pres., Mercy Hospital Association, Columbus, OH '86 (PERS)
JOHNSON, RICHARD E., dir. matl. mgt., Frick Community Health Center, Mount Pleasant, PA '70 (PUR)
JOHNSON, RICHARD F., dir. plant oper., Immanuel Medical Center, Omaha, NE '85 (ENG)
JOHNSON, RICHARD L., risk mgr., University of California, San Francisco, CA '83 (RISK)
JOHNSON, RICHARD L., pres., Tribrook Group, Inc., Oak Brook, IL '49 (LIFE)
JOHNSON, RICHARD P., consult., Deloitte Haskins and Sells, Minneapolis, MN '85 (NURS)
JOHNSON, RICHARD R., dir. pers., Institute of Living, Hartford, CT '64 (PERS)
JOHNSON, RITA B., atty. and sr. assoc., Management Sciences Associates, Inc., Kansas City, MO '83 (ATTY)(NURS)
JOHNSON, ROBERT A., adm., Worcester City Hospital, Worcester, MA '64
JOHNSON, ROBERT E., dir. eng., Leonard Morse Hospital, Natick, MA '82 (ENG)
JOHNSON, ROBERT E., adm. consult., Geneva General Hospital, Geneva, NY '48 (LIFE)
JOHNSON, ROBERT H., RN, charge nrs. emer., Du Bois Hospital, Du Bois, PA '85
JOHNSON, ROBERT J., atty., Lehigh Valley Hospital Center, Allentown, PA '77 (ATTY)
JOHNSON, ROBERT L., dir. matl. mgt., Galesburg Cottage Hospital, Galesburg, IL '84 (PUR)
JOHNSON, ROBERT L., vice-pres., Mercy Health System, Burlingame, CA '73 (ATTY)
JOHNSON, ROBERT R., dir. matl. mgt., Dakota Hospital, Fargo, ND '80 (PUR)
JOHNSON, ROBERT W., dir. commun. rel. and mktg., Bethesda Lutheran Medical Center, St. Paul, MN '85 (PR)
JOHNSON, ROBERT, asst. vice-pres. commun., Neponset Valley Health Systems, Norwood, MA '84 (PR)
JOHNSON, ROBERT, asst. dir., Good Samaritan Hospital, West Islip, NY '84 (ENG)
JOHNSON, ROGER P., chief eng., St. Gabriel's Hospital, Little Falls, MN '81 (ENG)
JOHNSON, RONALD J., dir. food serv., St. Joseph Hospital, Concordia, KS '73 (FOOD)
JOHNSON, ROWENA F., dir. cent. sup., Boulder Memorial Hospital, Boulder, CO '86 (CS)
JOHNSON, RUTH A., dir. in-service, Magnolia Hospital, Corinth, MS '81 (EDUC)
JOHNSON, SAM K., vice-pres., Oklahoma Hospital Association, Tulsa, OK '65
JOHNSON, SANDRA K. C., RN, dir. risk mgt., Delaware County Memorial Hospital, Drexel Hill, PA '84 (RISK)
JOHNSON, SARAH ANN, pers. mgt. spec., Miners' Colfax Medical Center, Raton, NM '82 (PERS)
JOHNSON, SHEILA A., RN, dir. cent. serv., Our Lady of Lake Regional Medical Center, Baton Rouge, LA '85 (CS)
JOHNSON, SHIRLEY LEE, RN, dir. staff dev., Albany General Hospital, Albany, OR '80 (EDUC)
JOHNSON, SIDNEY S., dir. pers., Radford Community Hospital, Radford, VA '84 (PERS)
JOHNSON, STAN Q., staff asst. to dir., Veterans Administration Medical Center, Iowa City, IA '82
JOHNSON, STEVE, mgr. security and risk mgt., Kennestone Hospital at Windy Hill, Marietta, GA '85 (RISK)
JOHNSON, STEVEN D., student, University of Minnesota, Program in Health Care Administration, Minneapolis, MN '82
JOHNSON, STEVEN P., dir. pur. and matl. mgt., Williamsport Hospital and Medical Center, Williamsport, PA '85 (PUR)
JOHNSON, SUE LANE, RN, mgr. cent. serv., Ohio Valley Medical Center, Wheeling, WV '80 (CS)
JOHNSON, SUE, dir. soc. serv., Clermont Mercy Hospital, Batavia, OH '80 (SOC)
JOHNSON, SUSAN L., asst. pub. rel., Mercer Medical Center, Trenton, NJ '86 (PR)
JOHNSON, THEODORE H., adm. asst., Illinois Masonic Medical Center, Chicago, IL '56 (LIFE)
JOHNSON, THOMAS B., partner, Touche Ross and Company, Chicago, IL '69 (PLNG)
JOHNSON, THOMAS M., vice-pres., Harrisburg Hospital, Harrisburg, PA '85
JOHNSON, TRACY K., consult., Oberfast Associates, Inc., Philadelphia, PA '87 (AMB)
JOHNSON, VIRGINIA K., dir. vol. serv., St. John's Riverside Hospital, Yonkers, NY '83 (VOL)
JOHNSON, VIRGINIA M., dir. soc. serv., St. Joseph's Medical Center, Brainerd, MN '77 (SOC)
JOHNSON, WADE C., (ret.), Providence, RI '47 (LIFE)
JOHNSON, WALTER H., dir. plng. and constr., Goddard Memorial Hospital, Stoughton, MA '68 (ENG)
JOHNSON, WILLARD H. JR., pres., Chelsea Community Hospital, Chelsea, MI '71
JOHNSON, LT. COL. WILLIAM CLARENCE, MSC USN, head mgt. info., Naval Medical Command Northwest Region, Oakland, CA '75
JOHNSON, WILLIAM E. JR., pres., Methodist Hospital, Madison, WI '59
JOHNSON, WILLIAM HUGH JR., chief exec. off., University of New Mexico Hospital, Albuquerque, NM '65
JOHNSON, WILMA H., RN, vice-pres. nrsg., St. Francis Hospital, Greenville, SC '82 (NURS)
JOHNSTAL, LAWRENCE M., mgt. trainee, Bethesda Hospital, Inc., Cincinnati, OH '84
JOHNSTON, A. JOYCE, RN, vice-pres. nrsg., Sewickley Valley Hospital, Sewickley, PA '70 (NURS)
JOHNSTON, BEVERLY B., dir. soc. serv., Hillcrest Baptist Medical Center, Waco, TX '74 (SOC)
JOHNSTON, BILL, chief eng., William W. Backus Hospital, Norwich, CT '86 (ENG)
JOHNSTON, BRIAN M., risk mgr., Sacred Heart Rehabilitation Hospital, Milwaukee, WI '84 (RISK)
JOHNSTON, CHARLES E., asst. adm., Kaiser Foundation Hospital, Los Angeles, CA '71 (MGMT)
JOHNSTON, DAVID M., dir. pers., St. Joseph Intercommunity Hospital, Cheektowaga, NY '76 (PERS)
JOHNSTON, DEBRA KENNINGTON, RN, vice-pres. nrsg., South Miami Hospital, South Miami, FL '81 (NURS)
JOHNSTON, DONALD R., vice-pres. human res., Hospital Sisters Health System, Springfield, IL '73 (PERS)
JOHNSTON, ELIZABETH B., prog. adm., Mary Hitchcock Memorial Hospital, Hanover, NH '86 (PLNG)
JOHNSTON, ELLEN B., coor. vol. serv., Providence Hospital, Mobile, AL '86 (VOL)
JOHNSTON, G. DAVID, atty., Flowers Hospital, Dothan, AL '86 (ATTY)
JOHNSTON, GARY, prof. eng., Nicholas and Johnston Associates, State College, PA '86 (ENG)
JOHNSTON, HAROLD R., dir. maint., Meadville City Hospital, Meadville, PA '83 (ENG)
JOHNSTON, LENA IVERS, (ret.), Keene, NH '28 (LIFE)
JOHNSTON, LINDA S., dir. vol. serv., Nanticoke Memorial Hospital, Seaford, DE '86 (VOL)
JOHNSTON, MALCOLM W., chief eng., Marion Community Hospital, Ocala, FL '82 (ENG)
JOHNSTON, NORMA, RN, vice-pres. pat. care serv., New England Memorial Hospital, Stoneham, MA '80 (NURS)
JOHNSTON, PHILLIPPA L., RN, asst. adm., Capitol Hill Hospital, Washington, DC '79 (NURS)
JOHNSTON, R. JOE, vice-pres. oper., Community Hospital of Anderson and Madison County, Anderson, IN '81
JOHNSTON, SCOTT H., contr., Marion Memorial Hospital, Marion, IL '87 (MGMT)
JOHNSTON, SHYRL D., dir. oper., Presbyterian Hospital, Dallas, TX '87
JOHNSTON, SYLVIA S., dir. productivity mgt., St. Vincent Charity Hospital, Cleveland, OH '81 (MGMT)
JOHNSTON, THOMAS C., atty., Eastern Maine Medical Center, Bangor, ME '85 (ATTY)

JOHNSTON, WAYNE W., vice-pres. oper., Sharon General Hospital, Sharon, PA '86
JOHNSTON, WILLIAM E., dir. environ. serv., Tyler Memorial Hospital, Tunkhannock, PA '82 (ENG)
JOHNSTONE, DONALD M., contr., Prosser Memorial Hospital, Prosser, WA '72
JOHNSTONE, JAMES R., dir. eng., Daughters of Miriam Center, Clifton, NJ '79 (ENG)
JOHNSTONE, MILDRED, RN, dir. nrsg. serv., St. Elizabeth Community Hospital, Red Bluff, CA '82 (NURS)
JOHNSTONE, PETER HAMPTON, atty., St. Joseph Health Care Corporation, Albuquerque, NM '86 (ATTY)
JOHNSTONE, ROBBI, dir. psychoneurotic-soc. serv., Daniel Freeman Memorial Hospital, Inglewood, CA '86 (SOC)
JOHSON, CHRISTINE M., RN, vice-pres. nrsg., New England Baptist Hospital, Boston, MA '85 (NURS)
JOINER, MARILYN S., dir. health care mktg., Dolph Miller and Associates, Shreveport, LA '83 (PR)
JOINER, RON, mgr. bldg. and grd., Comanche County Memorial Hospital, Lawton, OK '81 (ENG)
JOINES, JACK L., mgr. maint. eng., Houston Medical Center, Warner Robins, GA '86 (ENG)
JOKERST, LAWRENCE J., exec. vice-pres., St. Mary's Hospital and Medical Center, Grand Junction, CO '74
JOLIN, TERI L., exec. vice-pres., Horizon Hospital, Clearwater, FL '86 (PR) (PLNG)
JOLLEY, DAVID A., vice-pres. pub. affairs, Geisinger Wyoming Valley Medical Center, Wilkes-Barre, PA '81 (PR)
JOLLEY, SUE U., RN, dir. nrsg. serv., Arab Hospital, Arab, AL '86 (NURS)
JOLLY, BETTY H., pres., Marketing Services, Harrisonburg, VA '86 (PR)
JOLLY, BLANCHARD E., pres. and treas., Harvard, Jolly and Associates, St. Petersburg, FL '75
JOLLY, JULIE, dir., Shenandoah Shared Hospital Services, Inc., Harrisonburg, VA '79
JOMAOAS, DAVID B., mgr. environ. serv., St. Joseph's Hospital, Stockton, CA '86 (ENVIRON)
JONAITIS, DAVID, dir. matl. mgt., Saint Therese Medical Center, Waukegan, IL '86 (PUR)
JONAS, JOHN W., dir. contr. and maint., Mercy Hospital, Hamilton, OH '81 (ENG)
JONAS, STANLEY WARREN, dir. mgt. eng., Memorial Medical Center, Springfield, IL '77 (MGMT)
JONAS, STEVEN, MD, assoc. prof. commun. medicine, State University of New York, Health Sciences Center, Stony Brook, NY '68
JONASSEN, JAMES O., partner, Naramore, Bain, Brady and Johanson, Seattle, WA '82
JONCAS, DEBORAH R., dir. commun., Hackensack Medical Center, Hackensack, NJ '81 (ENG)
JONES-SCHENK, JANEA S., RN, asst. dir. nrsg. gen. care, St. Mark's Hospital, Salt Lake City, UT '85 (NURS)
JONES, ALBERT W., Denver, CO '77
JONES, ALICE W., dir. plng. and dev., Lakeshore Hospital, Birmingham, AL '86 (PR) (PLNG)
JONES, ALLEN L., mgr. ldry., Sibley Memorial Hospital, Washington, DC '86 (ENVIRON)
JONES, ALLEN, mgr. claims, Totura and Company, Tampa, FL '87 (RISK)
JONES, ANN A., PhD, sr. mgr., Ernst and Whinney, Baltimore, MD '86
JONES, B. GAYLE, dir. matl. mgt., St. David's Community Hospital, Austin, TX '82 (PUR)
JONES, BARBARA M., RN, vice-pres. nrsg., Swedish Covenant Hospital, Chicago, IL '81 (NURS)
JONES, BETTY J., RN, dir. nrsg. serv., Henry General Hospital, Stockbridge, GA '82 (NURS)
JONES, BETTY JO, supv. cent. serv. room, HCA Park West Medical Centers, Knoxville, TN '85 (CS)
JONES, BEVERLY A., RN, vice-pres. nrsg. serv., Samaritan Health Center, Detroit, MI '83 (NURS)
JONES, BEVERLY A., RN, dir. nrsg., Bayshore Community Hospital, Holmdel, NJ '75 (NURS)
JONES, BEVERLY M., RN, dir. nrsg., Longmont United Hospital, Longmont, CO '73 (NURS)
JONES, BILLIE MARIE, cent. serv. tech., St. Elizabeth Hospital, Beaumont, TX '82 (CS)
JONES, BILLY R., chief eng., Good Shepherd Hospital, Barrington, IL '86 (ENG)
JONES, BONNYE K., dir. soc. serv., Hotel Dieu Hospital, New Orleans, LA '85 (SOC)
JONES, BRENDA B., supv. sterile proc., National Rehabilitation Hospital, Washington, DC '86 (CS)
JONES, BRENDA, adm. dir. emer. serv., Poudre Valley Hospital, Fort Collins, CO '87 (AMB)
JONES, BRYANT P., dir. commun. rel. and dev., Kennebec Valley Medical Center, Augusta, ME '81 (PR)
JONES, BUD E., dir. educ. and pub. info., South Dakota Hospital Association, Sioux Falls, SD '85 (PR)
JONES, CECILY A., Rolla, MO '77 (PR)
JONES, CHARLES S., dir. clin. eng., Oakwood Hospital, Dearborn, MI '86 (ENG)
JONES, CHARLES W., asst. adm., Jackson Park Hospital, Chicago, IL '54 (LIFE)
JONES, CHARLES WILTON JR., chief eng., Willingway Hospital, Statesboro, GA '75 (ENG)
JONES, CHARLES JR., atty., Rolling Plains Memorial Hospital, Sweetwater, TX '86 (ATTY)
JONES, CLAIRE, dir. vol. serv., Northern Ocean Hospital System, Point Pleasant, NJ '87 (VOL)
JONES, CLAUDIA A., RN, sr. assoc., Amherst Associates, Atlanta, GA '85 (NURS)
JONES, CLAUDIA, dir. soc. serv., Community Hospital of Springfield, Springfield, OH '86 (SOC)
JONES, CYNTHIA, mgr. pub. rel., St. Anne's Hospital, Chicago, IL '86 (PR)
JONES, DANNETTE, coor. qual. assur., St. Eugene Community Hospital, Dillon, SC '86 (RISK)
JONES, DAVID E., pres., David E. Jones and Associates, Hopkinsville, KY '78
JONES, DAVID O. JR., mgr. mktg. support, HBO and Company, Atlanta, GA '73 (MGMT)
JONES, DAVID R., dir. eng., Pacific Medical Center, Seattle, WA '84 (ENG)
JONES, DEE W., dir. pub. rel., Swedish Hospital Medical Center, Seattle, WA '81 (PR)
JONES, DENNIS R., mgr. health care, Burroughs Corporation, Bloomfield, NJ '86 (MGMT)
JONES, DERYL L., pres., Tillamook County General Hospital, Tillamook, OR '84 (PLNG)
JONES, DON M., mgr. matl., Sharp Cabrillo Hospital, San Diego, CA '81 (PUR)
JONES, DONA S., dir. diet. serv., Humana Hospital -Westminster, Westminster, CA '83 (FOOD)
JONES, DONALD D., dir. mktg. and sales, Normandy Osteopathic Hospital-North and South, St. Louis, MO '84 (PR) (PLNG)
JONES, DONNA L., dir. food and nutr. serv., Colonel Belcher Hospital, Calgary, Alta., Canada '85 (FOOD)
JONES, DORIS E., asst. adm., Winthrop-University Hospital, Mineola, NY '76 (PAT)
JONES, DOROTHY M., dir. vol. serv., Parkview Community Hospital, Riverside, CA '83 (VOL)
JONES, DOROTHY M., mktg. spec., Curative Rehabilitation Center, Milwaukee, WI '85 (PR) (PLNG)
JONES, EARLE C., pres., Consultaserve, Inc., St. Joseph, MO '66 (ENG)
JONES, EDGAR W., atty., Aultman Hospital, Canton, OH '68 (ATTY)
JONES, EDITH S., dir. diet., East Tennessee Baptist Hospital, Knoxville, TN '78 (FOOD)
JONES, EILEEN M., RN, asst. adm. nrsg., Geneva General Hospital, Geneva, NY '86 (NURS)
JONES, ELAINE M., mgr. phys. ther., West Georgia Medical Center, La Grange, GA '86 (EDUC)
JONES, ERNESTINE GRIFFIN, supv. cent. sup., St. Mary Hospital, Port Arthur, TX '82 (CS)
JONES, EUGENE D. III, mgr. human res., Bethesda Oak Hospital, Cincinnati, OH '81 (PERS)
JONES, EVERETT W., consult., Corvallis, OR '39 (MGMT)(LIFE)
JONES, GEORGE H., Brim and Associates, Inc., Minnetonka, MN '84
JONES, GEORGE H., dir. plant oper., Research Medical Center, Kansas City, MO '72 (ENG)
JONES, GEORGE W. JR., adm. asst., St. John's Healthcare Corporation, Anderson, IN '78 (ENG)
JONES, GERALD MARSHALL, atty., Tucson Medical Center, Tucson, AZ '68 (ATTY)
JONES, GERALDINE E., supv. sterile proc., Union Memorial Hospital, Baltimore, MD '83 (CS)
JONES, GERRY C., risk mgr. and supv. util. review, St. Mary's Hospital, Passaic, NJ '84 (RISK)
JONES, GLENDA D., asst. human res., Baptist Medical Center-DeKalb, Fort Payne, AL '84 (PERS)
JONES, GLENN D., exec. dir., Arizona Hospital Association-Cooperative Purchasing, Phoenix, AZ '67 (PUR)
JONES, GLORIA J., dir. pur., Weirton Medical Center, Weirton, WV '86 (PUR)
JONES, GROVER N. JR., pres., Quoin, Inc., San Anselmo, CA '83 (MGMT)
JONES, GUYNELLE B., coor. pat. rel., Memorial Medical Center, Savannah, GA '86 (PAT)
JONES, H. DIANA, coor. plng. and market res., St. Luke's Hospital, Kansas City, MO '84 (PR) (PLNG)(AMB)
JONES, HAL O., mgr. emp., Northeast Georgia Medical Center, Gainesville, GA '84 (PERS)
JONES, HOWARD B., dir. maint., Retreat Hospital, Richmond, VA '83 (ENG)
JONES, HOWARD P., dir. pers., Valdese General Hospital, Valdese, NC '82 (PERS)
JONES, JAMES C., dir. hskpg., Santa Rosa Medical Center, San Antonio, TX '86 (ENVIRON)
JONES, JAMES E., dir. mktg. commun., HCA Aiken Regional Medical Center, Aiken, SC '87 (PR)
JONES, JAMES H., pur. agt., South Baldwin Hospital, Foley, AL '74 (PUR)
JONES, JAMES H. III, adm. asst., Baptist Memorial Hospital, Memphis, TN '87 (AMB)
JONES, JAN T., asst. dir. matl. mgt., Loudoun Memorial Hospital, Leesburg, VA '84 (PUR)
JONES, JANA L., student, Program in Health Systems Management, Rush University, Chicago, IL '86
JONES, JANE P., dir. food and nutr. serv., Hendrick Medical Center, Abilene, TX '82 (FOOD)
JONES, JANICE S., RN, mgr. pat. care serv., Mercy Hospital of Pittsburgh, Pittsburgh, PA '85 (NURS)
JONES, JANIS M., RN, dir. nrsg., Hancock Medical Center, Bay St. Louis, MS '86 (NURS)
JONES, JEAN W., vice-pres. pat. serv., Taylor Hospital, Ridley Park, PA '86 (NURS)
JONES, JENNIFER M., Columbia, MO '84 (PLNG)
JONES, JILL A., student, Xavier University, Graduate Program in Hospital and Health Administration, Cincinnati, OH '85
JONES, JIM, assoc. dir. soc. work, Timberlawn Psychiatric Hospital, Dallas, TX '86 (SOC)
JONES, JO ANNE, natl. dir. mission effectiveness, Catholic Health Association, St. Louis, MO '85 (PR) (PLNG)
JONES, JO CAROL, dir. commun. rel. and pub. educ., Wayne Memorial Hospital, Goldsboro, NC '85 (PR)
JONES, JUDITH A., RN, sr. vice-pres., All Saints Episcopal Hospital of Fort Worth, Fort Worth, TX '81 (NURS)
JONES, JUDY B., dir. pers., Bolivar County Hospital, Cleveland, MS '86 (PERS)
JONES, JUDY C., dir. educ. and trng., HCA Medical Center of Plano, Plano, TX '82 (EDUC)
JONES, JUDY C., assoc. dir. matl. serv., Greenville Hospital System, Greenville, SC '86 (CS)
JONES, JUDY, RN, dir. surg. nrsg., Temple University Hospital, Philadelphia, PA '86 (NURS)
JONES, JULIA V., atty., Rex Hospital, Raleigh, NC '85 (ATTY)
JONES, JULIE A., coor. commun. rel. and foundation, Good Samaritan Hospital, Corvallis, OR '85 (PR)
JONES, KATHLEEN A., RN, clin. dir. emer. room, amb. care and intravenous team, Cedars-Sinai Medical Center, Los Angeles, CA '85 (NURS)
JONES, KENNETH C. III, dir. mgt. serv., Healthlink, Portland, OR '85 (MGMT)
JONES, KENNETH E., dir. eng., Allentown Hospital, Allentown, PA '84 (ENG)
JONES, KERMA, vice-pres. human res., Ihc Hospitals, Salt Lake City, UT '79 (PERS)
JONES, KIMBERLY, dir. telecomm, Fairfax Hospital, Falls Church, VA '86 (ENG)
JONES, LANE S., dir. plant oper., Arlington Memorial Hospital, Arlington, TX '86 (ENG)
JONES, LEM T. JR., atty., Research Medical Center, Kansas City, MO '72 (ATTY)
JONES, LEONARD JR., dir. bldg. serv., Manhattan Eye, Ear and Throat Hospital, New York, NY '86 (ENVIRON)
JONES, LINDA M., dir. soc. work, Golden Valley Memorial Hospital, Clinton, MO '84 (SOC)
JONES, LOIS C., RN, supv. cent. distrib., Mercy Hospital, Hamilton, OH '85 (CS)
JONES, LU ANN, supv. cent. serv., St. Jude Hospital-Fullerton, Fullerton, CA '85 (CS)
JONES, M. R. JR., claims adm., Broward General Medical Center, Fort Lauderdale, FL '80 (RISK)
JONES, MARC, adm. dir., Sutter Surgery Center, Sacramento, CA '87 (AMB)
JONES, MARCY, asst. vice-pres., Tennessee Christian Medical Center, Madison, TN '87 (RISK)
JONES, MARIE TRUITT, dir. staff dev., Jackson-Madison County General Hospital, Jackson, TN '82 (EDUC)
JONES, MARK A., student, Georgia State University-Institute of Health Administration, Atlanta, GA '84
JONES, MARK T., vice-pres., Presbyterian-University Hospital, Pittsburgh, PA '82
JONES, MARSHALL F., dir. human res., Mercy Health Center, Oklahoma City, OK '81 (PERS)
JONES, MARY ELIZABETH K., dir. vol. serv., Alvarado Hospital Medical Center, San Diego, CA '85 (VOL)
JONES, MARY S., dir. vol. serv., Mercy Hospital, Charlotte, NC '86 (VOL)
JONES, MICHAEL C., atty., Chandler Community Hospital, Chandler, AZ '81 (ATTY)
JONES, MICHAEL G., dir. plant oper., Redmond Park Hospital, Rome, GA '80 (ENG)
JONES, MILDRED P., dir. nrsg. educ., Commonwealth Hospital, Fairfax, VA '84 (EDUC)
JONES, MINNIE H., dir. soc. serv., Thomas Memorial Hospital, South Charleston, WV '77 (SOC)
JONES, MOLLY MITCHELL, asst. adm., Bradley Center, Columbus, GA '82
JONES, MYRTISS C., RN, assoc. dir. nrsg. serv., Grace Hospital, Detroit, MI '84 (NURS)
JONES, NORMA P., dir. soc. serv., Mount Carmel Mercy Hospital and Medical Center, Detroit, MI '66 (SOC)
JONES, NORMA, coor. staff dev., Tillsonburg District Memorial Hospital, Tillsonburg, Ont., Canada '77 (EDUC)
JONES, NORMAN L., dir. info. serv., Morton F. Plant Hospital, Clearwater, FL '81 (MGMT)
JONES, ORLANDO G., assoc. dir. clin. serv., Cook County Hospital, Chicago, IL '83 (MGMT)
JONES, PATTI M., dir. pub. rel., Marshall County Hospital, Benton, KY '84 (PR)
JONES, PEGGY K., RN, assoc. exec. dir. nrsg., West Jersey Hospital Garden State, Marlton, NJ '84 (NURS)
JONES, PHYLLIS A., RN, nrs. surveyer, Joint Commission on Accreditation of Hospitals, Chicago, IL '74 (NURS)
JONES, POLLY A., dir. outreach serv., Saint Joseph Hospital and Health Center, Kokomo, IN '79 (SOC)
JONES, RACHEL JEANETTE, coor. pat. rep. emer. area, University Hospital, Augusta, GA '82 (PAT)
JONES, RAY, atty., Community Hospital, Elk City, OK '86 (ATTY)
JONES, MAJ. RICHARD I., MSC USA, chief pers., Darnall Army Community Hospital, Fort Hood, TX '83 (PERS)
JONES, RICHARD L., vice-pres. adm., Abington Memorial Hospital, Abington, PA '63
JONES, RICHARD L., dir. prog. dev. and plng., Wuesthoff Memorial Hospital, Rockledge, FL '86 (PLNG)
JONES, RICHARD M., vice-pres. gen. serv. and risk mgr., Ball Memorial Hospital, Muncie, IN '77 (PUR)(CS)(RISK)
JONES, RICHARD P., dir. soc. serv., Underwood-Memorial Hospital, Woodbury, NJ '71 (SOC)
JONES, RICHARD S., mgt. eng. and consult., Terrebonne General Medical Center, Houma, LA '86 (MGMT)
JONES, RICHARD T., atty., Alachua General Hospital, Gainesville, FL '77 (ATTY)
JONES, RICHARD W., dir. commun. rel., Wayne General Hospital, Wayne, NJ '77 (PR)
JONES, ROBERT M., vice-pres. oper., Horton Memorial Hospital, Middletown, NY '73 (MGMT)(PLNG)
JONES, ROBERT TERRY, pres., Arnot-Ogden Memorial Hospital, Elmira, NY '52 (LIFE)
JONES, ROBERT, dir. maint., Capistrano By the Sea Hospital, Dana Point, CA '85 (ENG)
JONES, ROBERT, soc. work consult., Broaddus Hospital, Philippi, WV '86 (SOC)
JONES, ROBERTA E., dir. vol., St. John and West Shore Hospital, Westlake, OH '82 (VOL)
JONES, RONALD D., RN, asst. adm. and dir. nrsg., Elmbrook Memorial Hospital, Brookfield, WI '82 (NURS)
JONES, RONALD W., asst. adm., Montefiore Hospital, Pittsburgh, PA '79 (MGMT)
JONES, ROSE M., asst. dir. diet., Mississippi Baptist Medical Center, Jackson, MS '86 (FOOD)
JONES, RUDOLPH A., dir. linen serv., South Fulton Hospital, East Point, GA '86 (ENVIRON)
JONES, RUSSELL G. JR., assoc. exec. dir. plng. and dev., Truman Medical Center-West, Kansas City, MO '84 (PLNG)

JONES, RUSSELL, sr. vice-pres. health care, Sugerman Associates, Inc., Chicago, IL '86 (PERS)
JONES, SALLY B., asst. dir., Rowan Memorial Hospital, Salisbury, NC '70 (PERS)
JONES, SALLY HORTON, RN, sr. vice-pres. pat. care, Cleveland Memorial Hospital, Shelby, NC '75 (NURS)
JONES, SANDRA A., asst. adm., Burnham Hospital, Champaign, IL '78 (PLNG)(ENG)
JONES, SHARON, mgr. perinatal nrsg., St. Vincent's Hospital, Birmingham, AL '86 (RISK)
JONES, STANLEY S. JR., atty., Hospital Corporation of America, Nashville, TN '82 (ATTY)
JONES, SUSAN K., coor. commun. rel., Jamestown General Hospital, Jamestown, NY '83 (PR)
JONES, SUSAN N., asst. mktg. and plng., Johnston Memorial Hospital, Smithfield, NC '84 (PR)
JONES, TERRI M., coor. guest rel., St. Vincent Charity Hospital, Cleveland, OH '87 (PAT)
JONES, THERESA M., RN, supv. cent. sup., Hospital of Philadelphia College of Osteopathic Medicine, Philadelphia, PA '85 (CS)
JONES, THOMAS R., atty., Meridian Regional Hospital, Meridian, MS '84 (ATTY)
JONES, TOM, asst. dir. commun. rel., South Miami Hospital, South Miami, FL '86 (PR)
JONES, VICTORIA L., mgr. prod. line, Swedish Medical Center, Englewood, CO '86 (PR)
JONES, VICTORIA W., dir. pub. rel. and dev., Jackson Hospital and Clinic, Montgomery, AL '83 (PR)
JONES, VIRGINIA N., dir. vol. serv., Wichita General Hospital, Wichita Falls, TX '86 (VOL)
JONES, WILLIAM D., dir. facil., Hunterdon Medical Center, Flemington, NJ '71 (ENG)
JONES, WILLIAM L., assoc. chief fiscal off., Falmouth Hospital, Falmouth, MA '84
JONSSON, KJARTAN A., pres., Energy and Value Consultant, Inc., Scotia, NY '86
JONTZ, DOUGLAS C., vice-pres. emp. rel., St. Agnes Hospital, Fond Du Lac, WI '81 (PERS)
JOOSTEN, ELIZABETH D. BURN, consult., Baxter Travenol Laboratories, Deerfield, IL '85 (NURS)
JORDAL, JACK N., dir. plant oper., Rehabilitation Institute of Chicago, Chicago, IL '77 (ENG)
JORDAN, BERNADETTE M., PhD, vice-pres., The Medical Center, Beaver, PA '80 (EDUC)
JORDAN, BETTY LOU, assoc. dir. nutr., Arizona Health Sciences Center, Tucson, AZ '72 (FOOD)
JORDAN, CARL R., MD, dir. surg., Jordan Clinic, Savannah, GA '87 (AMB)
JORDAN, CHARLOTTE L., supv. cent. sterile, HCA West Paces Ferry Hospital, Atlanta, GA '85 (CS)
JORDAN, DENNIS, dir. matl. serv., Imperial Point Medical Center, Fort Lauderdale, FL '86 (PUR)
JORDAN, DOROTHY L., RN, dir. oper. room nrsg., Commonwealth Hospital, Fairfax, VA '86 (NURS)
JORDAN, ELIZABETH J., RN, vice-pres. pat. serv., Ellis Hospital, Schenectady, NY '86 (NURS)
JORDAN, FRANCE F., Arlington, VA '80
JORDAN, HARMON PAUL BUFFUM JR., consult., Lincoln, RI '48 (LIFE)
JORDAN, HARRY, dir. eng., Humana Hospital -Cypress, Pompano Beach, FL '85 (ENG)
JORDAN, IMEL JEAN, dir. vol., St. Joseph Medical Center, Burbank, CA '74 (VOL)
JORDAN, JACQUELINE L., coor. reg. trauma, Bronson Methodist Hospital, Kalamazoo, MI '86 (EDUC)
JORDAN, JANICE A., dir. pers., Cape Canaveral Hospital, Cocoa Beach, FL '85 (PERS)
JORDAN, JOHN R. JR., atty., AMI Brookwood Medical Center, Birmingham, AL '78 (ATTY)
JORDAN, JOHN S., sr. mgt. analyst and mgt. eng., Norfolk General Hospital, Norfolk, VA '83 (MGMT)
JORDAN, JUDITH, dir. soc. serv., Newington Children's Hospital, Newington, CT '86 (SOC)
JORDAN, JULIA, mgr. cent. serv., South Side Hospital of Pittsburgh, Pittsburgh, PA '85 (CS)
JORDAN, KATHLEEN M., student, Program in Health Service Administration, School of Health Professions, Governors State University, Park Forest South, IL '86
JORDAN, KENNETH R., dir. pers., Forrest County General Hospital, Hattiesburg, MS '72 (PERS)
JORDAN, LAVERNE C., asst. dir. cent. sterile, Sinai Hospital of Baltimore, Baltimore, MD '82 (CS)
JORDAN, LINDA C., mgr. healthplus, Presbyterian Hospital, Charlotte, NC '85 (PR) (PLNG)
JORDAN, MARILYN A., RN, dir. nrsg. serv., Christ Hospital, Jersey City, NJ '75 (NURS)
JORDAN, MARION DOROTHY, supv. pat. serv., Oak Creek Medical Center-Health Alliance Plan, Livonia, MI '85 (PAT)
JORDAN, ROBERT F., mng. dir., Marketing Corporation of America, Westport, CT '86
JORDAN, STEPHEN, sr. mgt. eng., Yale-New Haven Hospital, New Haven, CT '85 (MGMT)
JORDAN, THOMAS E., pres., Thomas E. Jordan and Associates, Newton Highlands, MA '85
JORDAN, WILLIAM A., corp. dir. matl. mgt., Scripps Memorial Hospital, La Jolla, CA '75 (PUR)
JORDAN, WINIFRED E., supv. cent. serv., Mary Hitchcock Memorial Hospital, Hanover, NH '67 (CS)
JORDE, ARLENE, RN, dir. clin. serv., St. Joseph Mercy Hospital, Mason City, IA '80 (NURS)
JORGENSEN, DENNIS, dir. plant oper., Rapid City Regional Hospital, Rapid City, SD '75 (ENG)
JORGENSEN, FARRELL J., dir. educ., Hollywood Presbyterian Medical Center, Los Angeles, CA '81 (EDUC)
JORGENSEN, JORGEN L., consult. construction and eng., Greater Cincinnati Hospital Council, Cincinnati, OH '86 (ENG)
JORGENSEN, LAWRENCE R., asst. dir., Nassau County Medical Center, East Meadow, NY '64
JORGENSEN, SCOTT M., dir. pub. rel., Harding Hospital, Worthington, OH '84 (PR)
JORGENSON, BRUCE K., student, Program in Health Care Administration, Texas Women's University, Denton, TX '85
JORGENSON, ROGER D., vice-pres. and contr., Metropolitan Medical Center, Minneapolis, MN '85
JORIA, JOANNE H., dir. pers., Tuomey Hospital, Sumter, SC '86 (PERS)
JORLETT, JEAN E., dir. educ. and pat. care serv., Providence Hospital, Southfield, MI '79 (EDUC)
JORNS, MARY LOU, nrs. consult. mgt. syst., Southwest Community Health Services, Albuquerque, NM '85 (MGMT)
JORSTAD, VIRGINIA A., student, University of Iowa, Iowa City, IA '86 (EDUC)
JOSEPH, LT. ALAN W., MSC USN, Naval Hospital, Long Beach, CA '83 (PLNG)
JOSEPH, BERNICE B., asst. adm. amb. care, St. Joseph Hospital, Houston, TX '87 (AMB)
JOSEPH, ELEANOR A., atty., Venice Hospital, Venice, FL '86 (ATTY)
JOSEPH, ELLIOT, vice-pres. plng. and mktg., Mercy Hospital and Medical Center, Chicago, IL '79 (PLNG)
JOSEPH, FRANKLIN G., mgr. pers., Beyer Memorial Hospital, Ypsilanti, MI '82 (PERS)
JOSEPH, KAROL, dir. clin. mgt., Massachusetts Hospital Association, Burlington, MA '86 (RISK)
JOSEPH, LINDA B., pur. agt., Portsmouth Psychiatric Center, Portsmouth, VA '85 (PUR)
JOSEPH, LOUIS R. III, adm. res., Greenville Hospital System, Greenville, SC '83
JOSEPH, MARY, asst. dir. vol. serv., St. Lawrence Dimondale Stress Reduction Center, Dimondale, MI '86 (VOL)
JOSEPH, MICHAEL E., atty., Presbyterian Hospital, Oklahoma City, OK '80 (ATTY)
JOSEPH, MUPPATHIL K., contr., Shriners Burns Institute, Galveston, TX '86
JOSEPHS, SHELDON B., adm. asst., Mount Sinai Medical Center, Cleveland, OH '79
JOSTWORTH, BARBARA L., Acme Restaurant Supply, Charleston, SC '85 (FOOD)
JOUINI, MARILYN B., dir. nutr. and diet., Sutter Community Hospitals, Sacramento, CA '81 (FOOD)
JOURDONAIS, LEONARD F., MD, Sun City, AZ '73 (LIFE)
JOURNEY, WILLIAM R., chief eng., Mercy Hospital, Portsmouth, OH '82 (ENG)
JOVICK, ROBERT L., atty., Livingston Memorial Hospital, Livingston, MT '82 (ATTY)
JOWERS, BRIAN JOSEPH, assoc. adm. outpatient clin., Richland Memorial Hospital, Columbia, SC '87 (AMB)
JOY, BARBARA A., dir. soc. serv., St. Luke's Hospital, Milwaukee, WI '79 (SOC)
JOY, LOUISE M., asst. adm., Southwest General Hospital, San Antonio, TX '84 (RISK)
JOY, PAUL W., vice-pres. pat. care adm., University of Texas Health Science Center, Dallas, TX '71
JOYCE, AMY L., dir. pub. rel., Jameson Memorial Hospital, New Castle, PA '85 (PR)
JOYCE, DAVID L., prin., Health Care Specialists, Inc., Chesterfield, MO '85 (PLNG)
JOYCE, JAMES R., safety off., Oregon Health Sciences University, Portland, OR '86 (ENG)
JOYCE, ROBERT H., atty., Northwestern Memorial Hospital-Wesley Pavilion, Chicago, IL '69 (ATTY)
JOYCE, THEODOSIA, dir. matl. mgt., Marcus J. Lawrence Memorial Hospital, Cottonwood, AZ '80 (PUR)
JOYNER, ROBERT C., atty., National Medical Enterprises, Los Angeles, CA '79 (ATTY)
JOYNSON-SAMMONS, ROSALYN, asst. vice-pres. prof. serv., St. Bernard Hospital, Chicago, IL '86 (RISK)
JOZKOWSKI, STANLEY, chief eng., Booth Memorial Medical Center, Flushing, NY '81 (ENG)
JOZWIK, MARY T., asst. vice-pres., Providence Hospital, Washington, DC '81 (RISK)
JUBAN, AZUCENA C., dir. food serv., Alexian Brothers Hospital, Elizabeth, NJ '77 (FOOD)
JUBINVILLE, ANN, mgr. qual. assur., util. review and risk mgt., Holyoke Hospital, Holyoke, MA '86 (RISK)
JUCAS-FELSCH, VIDA, dir. diet. serv., Milwaukee Psychiatric Hospital, Milwaukee, WI '78 (FOOD)
JUDD, DIANE C., dir. soc. serv., Providence Hospital, Holyoke, MA '78 (SOC)
JUDD, ELEANOR S., RN, coor. qual. assur., House of the Good Samaritan, Watertown, NY '81 (RISK)
JUDD, JEFFREY M., adm., Milford Memorial Hospital, Milford, DE '75
JUDD, MARTIN H., dir. mktg., Health Ventures, Inc., Hinsdale, IL '85 (PLNG)
JUDD, PAUL D., dir. pers., Rutland Regional Medical Center, Rutland, VT '84 (PERS)
JUDD, SANDRA, dir. pub. affairs, Children's Hospital, Boston, MA '85 (PR)
JUDD, THOMAS M., clin. eng., Baptist Medical Center, Jacksonville, FL '79 (ENG)
JUDGE, DOUGLAS E., dir. hskpg., Community Medical Center, Scranton, PA '86 (ENVIRON)
JUDGE, KATHLEEN M., vice-pres. mktg., Sutter Health System, Sacramento, CA '69 (PLNG)
JUDGE, MARGARET A., RN, vice-pres. nrsg., Lancaster General Hospital, Lancaster, PA '84 (NURS)
JUDGE, MARY E., RN, chief cent. serv., District of Columbia General Hospital, Washington, DC '85 (CS)
JUDGE, MICHAEL J., dir. plant oper., Mount Elizabeth Hospital, Singapore, Singapore '75 (ENG)
JUDKINS, DEAN R., mgr. med. staff support serv., Bethesda Hospital and Deaconess Association, Cincinnati, OH '79
JUDY, MARY MARGARET, student, Millsaps College, Jackson, MS '87 (PLNG)
JUDY, WILLIAM K., dir. phys. rel., Doctors Hospital, Columbus, OH '84 (PLNG)
JUEDES, GREGORY S., sr. syst. rep., Burroughs Corporation, Woburn, MA '80 (MGMT)
JUENEMANN, SR. JEAN, RN, chief exec. off., Queen of Peace Hospital, New Prague, MN '68
JUHREN, JOHN H., dir. food serv., St. Clare's Hospital of Schenectady, Schenectady, NY '78 (FOOD)
JUILLET, EDWINA L., dir. risk mgt. and safety, Waynesboro Community Hospital, Waynesboro, VA '83 (RISK)
JULIAN, ARAXI PAUL, pat. rep., Alexandria Hospital, Alexandria, VA '85 (PAT)
JULIAN, CHARLES M., dir. pastoral and vol. serv., Good Samaritan Hospital, Vincennes, IN '86 (VOL)
JULIAN, JANET, dir. soc. serv., Dettmer Hospital, Troy, OH '86 (SOC)
JULIAN, ROBERT L., assoc. exec. dir., Humana Hospital -Clear Lake, Webster, TX '80 (RISK)
JULIEN, SALLY A., prov. plng. coor., Unity Health Plan, Park Ridge, IL '86 (PR)
JUMONVILLE, GEORGE R., mng. prin., Lockwood-Andrews and Newnam, Inc., Houston, TX '83
JUNG, ANN BARRETT, dir. hosp. rel., Lakeside Hospital, Kansas City, MO '85 (PERS)
JUNG, GENE, supt. maint., St. Elizabeth's Hospital, Belleville, IL '79 (ENG)
JUNKINS, FRANCI, dir. diet. serv., Charter Grove Hospital, Corona, CA '86 (FOOD)
JURA, WALTER J., asst. adm., Chilton Memorial Hospital, Pompton Plains, NJ '78
JURACEK, EDWARD J., pres., Precision Energy Systems, Inc., Schaumburg, IL '86 (ENG)(ENVIRON)
JURLINA, PAMELA ELAINE HESS, student, Program in Health Care Administration, Texas Woman's University, Denton, TX '84
JURON, DEBRA, coor. risk mgt., Kaiser Sunnyside Medical Center, Clackamas, OR '86 (RISK)
JURSA, M. RUTH, RN, assoc. dir. nrsg. serv., Lawrence and Memorial Hospital, New London, CT '78 (NURS)
JUSSILA, STEPHANIE L., dir. mktg., Central Minnesota Group Health Plan, St. Cloud, MN '85 (PAT)
JUST, BARBARA M., RN, dir. util. mgt., Brooklyn Hospital-Caledonian Hospital, Brooklyn, NY '84 (NURS)
JUST, CARL R., dir. mktg., Wyandotte General Hospital, Wyandotte, MI '76 (PR) (PLNG)
JUSTEN, NANCY SCHERWITZ, vice-pres. mktg. and plng., Northern Illinois Medical Center, McHenry, IL '83 (PR) (PLNG)
JUSTER, HOWARD H., pres., Larsen-Juster, Architects and Planners, New York, NY '76 (PLNG)
JUSTESEN, JOAN A., loss control and qual. assur. consult., Hospital Underwriters Mutual Insurance Company, Tarrytown, NY '85 (RISK)
JUSTICE, GLORIA JANE S., dir. commun., National Renal Administration Association, Port Huron, MI '79 (PR)
JUSTICE, JESSE W., adm. dir., Medical Center Hospital, Punta Gorda, FL '81 (SOC)
JUSTICE, LORRAINE, dir. human res., Humana Hospital -Abilene, Abilene, TX '86 (PERS)
JUSTICE, PATRICIA T., dir. pers., Houston Northwest Medical Center, Houston, TX '83 (PERS)
JUSTINIANA, SR. MARY, RN, supv. cent. serv., St. Joseph Intercommunity Hospital, Cheektowaga, NY '63 (CS)
JUSTIS, BOB, dir. corp. rel., Allen Memorial Hospital, Waterloo, IA '81 (PR)
JUSTISON, PAUL R., sr. health care consult., Stone, Marraccini and Patterson, San Francisco, CA '83 (PLNG)
JUTT, EDWARD J., acct. exec., Shared Medical Systems, Indianapolis, IN '86
JUVENAL, MICHAEL, chief soc. work serv., Veterans Administration Medical Center, Iowa City, IA '80 (SOC)
JYDSTRUP, RONALD A., plng. off., Group Health Association, Inc., Washington, DC '50 (LIFE)

K

KABALA, EDWARD J., atty., United Community Hospital, Grove City, PA '80 (ATTY)
KABAN, STEVEN, dep. exec. dir., Neponsit Health Care Center, Rockaway Park, NY '86
KABIALIS, RICHARD D., recruiter, Cook Associates, Inc., Chicago, IL '87 (PERS)
KABOT, LORRAINE B., pres., Aurelia Osborn Fox Memorial Hospital, Oneonta, NY '73 (RISK)(PR) (PLNG)
KACHEL, NANCY L., coor. pat. rep., Mount Sinai Hospital, Minneapolis, MN '81 (PAT)
KACHMARIK, CHARLES H. JR., partner, Coopers and Lybrand, Syracuse, NY '85
KACZINSKI, DOROTHY T., mgr. food serv., Walther Memorial Hospital, Chicago, IL '73 (FOOD)
KADAS, RICHARD M., dir. strategic plng., Christian Health Service Development Corporation, St. Louis, MO '83 (PLNG)
KADIM, MAJID HASAN, dir. fin. pers., Ministry of Health, Manama Bahrain, Arabia '86
KADING, DAVID R., mgt. eng., Iowa Methodist Medical Center, Des Moines, IA '84 (MGMT)
KADLEC, BEVERLY A., mgr. telemarketing health pub., Stamats Communications, Inc., Cedars Rapids, IA '86 (PR)
KADOGUCHI, GEORGE A., asst. adm., Kaiser Foundation Hospital, Honolulu, HI '80 (RISK)
KADOW, MICHAEL K., arch., Somerville Associates, Green Bay, WI '87 (PLNG)
KADROVACH, DAN GEORGE, dir., Veterans Administration Medical Center, Fayetteville, AR '53 (LIFE)
KAEMMERLING, JEAN, dir. matl., Harris Hospital-HEB North, Bedford, TX '70 (PUR)
KAERCHER, ROBERT D., assoc. dir. food serv., Children's Hospital Medical Center, Cincinnati, OH '85 (FOOD)
KAESER, ELIZABETH P., RN, mgr. trng. and dev., Arlington Hospital, Arlington, VA '86 (EDUC)
KAFASIS, NICHOLAS P., vice-pres. oper., Rochester St. Mary's Hospital, Rochester, NY '77 (ENG)

KAFER, TIMOTHY C., student, Program in Health Systems Management, Tulane University, New Orleans, LA '84
KAGAN, GARY A., pres., Horizon Health Management Company, Oak Brook, IL '76 (PR) (PLNG)
KAHAN, LLOYD, student, Program in Health Care Administration, C. W. Post College, Greenvale, NY '77
KAHANE, MILDRED, coor. accreditation and regulations, Kaiser-Permanente Medical Centers, Oakland, CA '86 (RISK)
KAHARL, PETER D., supt. med. facil. maint., Aramco Medical Unit, Houston, TX '82 (ENG)
KAHL, KENNETH L., mgr. mgt. eng., St. Joseph's Hospital, Milwaukee, WI '77 (MGMT)
KAHLE, DEBORAH D., dir. diet., University Hospital, Seattle, WA '84 (FOOD)
KAHLER, KAREN E., asst. dir. vol. serv., Tulane University Hospital and Clinics, New Orleans, LA '86 (VOL)
KAHLINE, R. JOAN, dir. vol. serv., Baltimore County General Hospital, Randallstown, MD '80 (VOL)
KAHN, BENJAMIN R., asst. vice-pres., Baptist Medical Center-Montclair, Birmingham, AL '82 (PLNG)
KAHN, BERNARD A., adm. mgr. bldg., safety and constr., Warminster General Hospital, Warminster, PA '83 (ENG)
KAHN, MYRNA, asst. dir. soc. serv., Fox Chase Cancer Center, Philadelphia, PA '83 (SOC)
KAHRE, DEAN A., mgr. mgt. eng., St. Mary's Medical Center, Evansville, IN '86 (MGMT)
KAHWAJY-ANDERSON, JOAN, dir. educ., Halifax-South Boston Community Hospital, South Boston, VA '82 (EDUC)
KAI, EDWARD W., dir. pers., Kingswood Hospital, Ferndale, MI '86 (PERS)
KAIDER, TIM R., dir. pers., Spencer Hospital, Meadville, PA '83 (PERS)
KAIN, ROBERT L., dir. food serv., Brookside Hospital, San Pablo, CA '82 (FOOD)
KAINER, MARY NELLE, pres., M. Kainer Associates, Cedar Falls, IA '80 (PR)
KAIRIS, MICHAEL E., dir. pub. rel., St. John Hospital, Detroit, MI '82 (PR)
KAISER, ANN, RN, dir. nrsg., Huntington Memorial Hospital, Pasadena, CA '76 (NURS)
KAISER, ELAINE, student, Governs State University, Health Service Administration, Park Forest South, IL '81
KAISER, GARY J., dir. food and nutr. serv., Catherine McAuley Health Center, Ann Arbor, MI '86 (FOOD)
KAISER, GINA, atty., Hillcrest Medical Center, Tulsa, OK '80 (ATTY)
KAISER, JEANNE M., dir. pers., River Falls Area Hospital, River Falls, WI '80 (PERS)
KAISER, JOHN D., vice-pres. plng., mktg. and facil. dev., Nexus Healthcare Corporation, Mount Holly, NJ '79 (PLNG)
KAISER, LUCIA C., dir. nutr. serv., Union Hospital, Terre Haute, IN '81 (FOOD)
KAISER, WILLIAM M., dir. maint. and plant eng., Bryn Mawr Hospital, Bryn Mawr, PA '69 (ENG)
KAISER, WILLIAM S., vice-pres. human res., Roxborough Memorial Hospital, Philadelphia, PA '78
KAITELL, DONELLA R., dir. commun. rel., Children's Hospital E. Ontario, Ottawa, Ont., Canada '79 (PR)
KAITZ, EDWARD J., mgr. proj., Shooshanian Engineering Associates, Inc., Holliston, MA '84 (ENG)
KAKTIS, JEAN V., RN, vice-pres. nrsg., St. John's Mercy Medical Center, St. Louis, MO '84 (NURS)
KALAFAT, JOHN, PhD, dir. consult. and educ., St. Clare's -Riverside Medical Center, Denville, NJ '86 (EDUC)
KALAJIAN, GARY G., dir. human res., McLean Hospital, Belmont, MA '86 (PERS)
KALASHIAN, ELIZABETH M., dir. commun. rel., Usf Psychiatry Center, Tampa, FL '83 (PR)
KALB, ESTHER L., RN, asst. adm. pat. serv., Ottumwa Regional Health Center, Ottumwa, IA '80 (NURS)
KALB, ROLAND J., pres., Roland J. Kalb Associates, Inc., Scarsdale, NY '79
KALDOR, DENNIS C., dir. matl. serv., Mount Sinai Medical Center, Milwaukee, WI '80 (PUR)
KALDOR, PATRICIA KALLWEIT, RN, asst. dir. nrsg. serv.-critical care, St. Joseph's Hospital, Milwaukee, WI '85 (NURS)
KALDOR, RONALD E., atty., Children's Hospital and Health Center, San Diego, CA '81 (ATTY)
KALEDA, GEORGE, supv. plant oper., Holy Name Hospital, Teaneck, NJ '84 (ENG)
KALER, MARLENE, RN, dir. data base mgt., Mercy Hospital, Urbana, IL '86 (MGMT)
KALI, CHRISTINA K., asst. to exec. hskpr., Shriners Hospital for Crippled Children, Honolulu, HI '86 (ENVIRON)
KALICAK, DONALD E., vice-pres., St. Anthony's Medical Center, St. Louis, MO '82 (PR) (PLNG)
KALIES, ANNE, risk mgr., De Poo Memorial Doctors Hospital, Key West, FL '86 (RISK)
KALIN, PHILIP B., exec. vice-pres. and chief oper. off., Mount Sinai Medical Center, Cleveland, OH '81
KALINOCK, STEPHEN, dir. plant oper., Montgomery General Hospital, Olney, MD '74 (ENG)
KALKHOF, CHRISTOPHER J., health care consult., Emst and Whinney, Buffalo, NY '82
KALKINES, GEORGE, atty., Bronx-Lebanon Hospital Center, Bronx, NY '69 (ATTY)
KALLA, SYRIETTA JUNE, dir. vol. serv., Polly Ryon Memorial Hospital, Richmond, TX '73 (PAT)(VOL)
KALLAL, SYLVIA ANN, dir. nrsg., Jersey Community Hospital, Jerseyville, IL '80 (NURS)
KALLSTROM, ROBERT E., arch., Daverman Associates, Inc., Austin, TX '85 (ENG)
KALMAN, EDWARD D., atty., Massachusetts General Hospital, Boston, MA '80 (ATTY)
KALMANSON, ALVIN, atty., Desert Hospital, Palm Springs, CA '84 (ATTY)
KALMBACH, MIRIAM K., RN, dir. cent. serv., Scott and White Memorial Hospital, Temple, TX '68 (CS)
KALOUSTIAN, ROBERT O., supt. eng. and maint., Providence Medical Center, Seattle, WA '81 (ENG)
KALTENBACH, KATHERINE M., corp. mktg. spec., Hospital Sisters Health System, Springfield, IL '86 (PLNG)
KALTSCHMIDT, ALICE, dir. cent. serv., Crouse-Irving Memorial Hospital, Syracuse, NY '77 (CS)
KALVZNY, WALTER L., dir. plant oper., Hamilton Hospital, Hamilton, NJ '85 (ENG)
KAM, RALPH T., vice-pres. mktg., Wahiawa General Hospital, Wahiawa, HI '85 (PR)
KAMAN, MARK J., vice-pres. fin., Regional Medical Center at Memphis, Memphis, TN '84
KAMANTAS, VYTAUTAS, dir. plant oper., Butterworth Hospital, Grand Rapids, MI '82 (ENG)
KAMENCIK, JO-ANN, RN, dir. nrsg. serv., Carthage Area Hospital, Carthage, NY '86 (NURS)
KAMENICKY, ROSALYNE A., dir. mktg. commun., Maryview Hospital, Portsmouth, VA '82 (PR)
KAMHI, VICTORIA D., planner, Memorial Medical Center, Springfield, IL '82 (PLNG)
KAMINS, JOHN M., atty., Sinai Hospital of Detroit, Detroit, MI '79 (ATTY)
KAMINSKAS, CINDY, dir. pers., Hampton Hospital, Rancocas, NJ '86 (PERS)
KAMINSKI, KAREN A., risk mgr., Franklin Square Hospital, Baltimore, MD '85 (RISK)
KAMINSKI, LEON R., atty., LaPorte Hospital, LaPorte, IN '74 (ATTY)
KAMINSKI, MICHAEL STEPHEN JR., pres. and chief exec. off., Flushing Hospital and Medical Center, Flushing, NY '71
KAMINSKY, BARBARA, mgr. mgt. serv., B. C. Hospitals Shared Systems Society, Vancouver, B.C., Canada '86 (MGMT)
KAMM, STANLEY BRANDON, vice-pres., Roanoke Memorial Hospitals, Roanoke, VA '61 (PLNG)
KAMMER, EARL H., (ret.), Boynton Beach, FL '48 (LIFE)
KAMMERER, MARILYN, dir. vol. serv., Little Company of Mary Hospital, Torrance, CA '80 (VOL)
KAMOWSKI, DAVID B., mgr., Ernst and Whinney, Chicago, IL '87 (MGMT)
KAMP, PHIL H., mgt. eng., Peat, Marwick, Mitchell and Company, Detroit, MI '84 (MGMT)
KAMPMANN, CHARLES L., partner, Arthur Young and Company, Portland, OR '82
KAMPS, EVERETT C., vice-pres. and chief fin. off., Newport Hospital, Newport, RI '72
KAMPWERTH, SR. GEORGIA, RN, asst. vice-pres. nrsg., St. Clement Hospital, Red Bud, IL '79 (NURS)
KAMPWIRTH, RONALD A., vice-pres. human res. serv., St. Joseph's Hospital, Milwaukee, WI '83 (PERS)
KAMSON, ROSA, asst. adm., Harrison Community Hospital, Mount Clemens, MI '85
KANA, CATHERINE G., vice-pres. and account supv., Aloysius, Butler and Clark, Wilmington, DE '86 (PR)
KANDARIAN, MICHAEL A., supt. bldg. and grds., Kaiser Foundation Hospital, Santa Clara, CA '81 (ENG)
KANDEFER, THOMAS R., mgr. eng., Charlotte Hungerford Hospital, Torrington, CT '84 (ENG)
KANDEL, LYNN E., pres., Lynn Kandel and Associates, Inc., Indianapolis, IN '64 (PR)
KANDLE, ELEANOR M., RN, dir. staff, Hospital of the Medical College of Pennsylvania, Philadelphia, PA '85 (NURS)
KANE, DANIEL A., pres. and chief exec. off., Miriam Hospital, Providence, RI '64
KANE, EDWARD T. JR., dir. pers., Holy Redeemer Hospital and Medical Center, Meadowbrook, PA '83 (PERS)
KANE, HELEN S., RN, asst. dir. nrsg. and critical care, Brandywine Hospital, Caln Township, PA '83 (NURS)
KANE, JACQUELINE F., exec. dir., St. Luke's Heart Plan, Milwaukee, WI '83
KANE, JAMES F., vice-pres. emp. rel., Glens Falls Hospital, Glens Falls, NY '78 (PERS)
KANE, KELLY A., vice-pres., Kane and Kane, Inc., Birmingham, MI '86 (PR)
KANE, MARTIN W., mgr. equip. group, Gaston Memorial Hospital, Gastonia, NC '85 (ENG)
KANE, MARY M., dir. admit., Bethesda Memorial Hospital, Boynton Beach, FL '80 (PAT)
KANE, MIRIAM, dir. soc. serv., Durham County General Hospital, Durham, NC '73 (SOC)
KANE, PATRICIA K., RN, dir. nrsg., Riverview Medical Center, Red Bank, NJ '82 (NURS)
KANE, ROBERT E. JR., dir. sup., proc. and distrib., Williamsport Hospital and Medical Center, Williamsport, PA '85 (CS)
KANE, ROBERT M., atty., Jane Phillips Episcopal-Memorial Medical Center, Bartlesville, OK '77 (ATTY)
KANE, VALERIA E., dir. soc. serv., Flushing Hospital and Medical Center, Flushing, NY '68 (SOC)
KANELOS, JIM, RN, dir. cent. proc., Children's Hospital of Sf, San Francisco, CA '82 (CS)
KANER, CRAIG, adm., Southeast Medical Center, Huntington Park, CA '80
KANET, JOAN A., dir. qual. assur. and risk mgt., Mercy Hospital, Urbana, IL '83 (RISK)
KANFER, MICHAEL J., dir. nutr. serv., Medical Center Hospital of Vermont, Burlington, VT '85 (FOOD)
KANGERY, ROSEMARIE, RN, vice-pres. nrsg., St. Francis Hospital, Milwaukee, WI '74 (NURS)
KANICH, DONNA G., student, Duke University, Department of Health Administration, Durham, NC '82
KANMIK, HARRY, dir. eng. and maint., St. Christopher's Hospital, Philadelphia, PA '86 (ENG)
KANNITZER, JAMES D., dir. bldg. and grds., St. Peter Hospital, Olympia, WA '73 (ENG)
KANOSKI, JOHN A., dir. phys. plant, University Hospital and Ambulatory Care Center, Little Rock, AR '74 (ENG)
KANT, DEAN A., atty., Carle Foundation Hospital, Urbana, IL '85 (ATTY)
KANTERMAN, LAWRENCE R., atty., Presbyterian Hospital in the City of New York, New York, NY '81 (ATTY)
KANTOR, DAVID A., vice-pres. mktg. and sales, Bethesda Hospital, Inc., Cincinnati, OH '86 (PR) (PLNG)
KANTOR, STANLEY, partner, London, Kantor, Umland and Associates, Elmwood Park, NJ '85 (ENG)
KANTOR, WILLIAM E., chief soc. work serv., Veterans Administration Medical Center, Lebanon, PA '78 (SOC)
KANTUTIS, CONNIE A., sr. mgt. analyst, Rush-Presbyterian-St. Luke's Medical Center, Chicago, IL '87 (MGMT)
KANYA, MARY JEAN, mgr. food serv., Bi-County Community Hospital, Warren, MI '80 (FOOD)
KAPEGHIAN, NELL B., RN, coor. pat. educ., Deborah Heart and Lung Center, Browns Mills, NJ '83 (EDUC)
KAPILOFF, HELEN B., chief soc. serv., Veterans Administration Medical Center, Houston, TX '70 (SOC)
KAPLAN, BARBARA B., RN, asst. dir. nrsg., University Hospital-University of Nebraska, Omaha, NE '86 (NURS)
KAPLAN, BURTON, Cotuit, MA '60
KAPLAN, CARYN K., dir. plng., Mountainside Hospital, Montclair, NJ '82 (PLNG)
KAPLAN, EDWARD M., dir. corp. mgt. contracts, Massachusetts General Hospital, Boston, MA '77
KAPLAN, HAROLD E., adm., Sunrise Hospital, Sunrise, FL '73
KAPLAN, HOWARD GORDON, atty., Lincoln West Hospital, Chicago, IL '69 (ATTY)
KAPLAN, JONATHAN H., sr. mgr., Ernst and Whinney, New York, NY '86 (MGMT)
KAPLAN, JUDITH A., RN, clin. coor., St. John's Health and Hospital Center, Pittsburgh, PA '83 (NURS)
KAPLAN, KIPTON, exec. dir., Southeastern Wisconsin Health Systems Agency, Inc., Milwaukee, WI '80 (PLNG)
KAPLAN, LAURENCE, dir. food serv., St. Peter's Medical Center, New Brunswick, NJ '80 (FOOD)
KAPLAN, MARY, dir. soc. serv., Indian River Memorial Hospital, Vero Beach, FL '82 (SOC)
KAPLAN, MORTON M., mgt. eng., Milford Memorial Hospital, Milford, DE '76 (MGMT)
KAPLAN, RICHARD A., assoc. adm., Coney Island Medical Group Professional Corporation, Coney Island Hospital, Brooklyn, NY '71 (MGMT)
KAPLAN, WALTER, prin., Walter Kaplan Architects, Rome, Italy '73
KAPOLKA, GUS F., dir. eng. and maint., North Detroit General Hospital, Detroit, MI '84 (ENG)
KAPOOR, MARIE, asst. treas., Mount Sinai Hospital, Hartford, CT '81 (RISK)
KAPP, MARSHALL BARRY, atty., Wright State University, Dayton, OH '81 (ATTY)
KAPPER, TRUDY D., dir. dev. and commun. rel., Akron City Hospital, Akron, OH '86 (PR)
KAPUSTA, KATHLEEN M., dir. soc. serv., Parma Community General Hospital, Parma, OH '82 (SOC)
KAPUSTIAK, MARGARET M., chief diet. serv., Veterans Administration Lakeside Medical Center, Chicago, IL '81 (FOOD)
KARABAICH, NICK J., adm. oper., New York City Department of Sanitation Medical Clinic, New York, NY '52 (LIFE)
KARAKO, JEFFREY J., dir. plng., Virginia Beach General Hospital, Virginia Beach, VA '84 (PLNG)
KARAM, JOHN, adm. asst. matl. mgt., Henry Ford Hospital, Detroit, MI '86 (PUR)
KARAM, MARTHA L., asst. dir. diet., Good Samaritan Hospital and Health Center, Dayton, OH '81 (FOOD)
KARAM, ROBERT C., dir. surg. serv., Northern Michigan Hospitals, Petoskey, MI '87 (AMB)
KARASAWA, STEPHEN K., mgr. cent. serv., Cigna Hospital of Los Angeles, Los Angeles, CA '85 (CS)
KARASIK, STUART G., PhD, healthcare educ. consult., San Diego, CA '80 (EDUC)(PERS)
KARBS, DONNA G., vice-pres. mktg. serv., Saint Joseph Hospital, Fort Worth, TX '83 (PLNG)
KARBUSICKY, JENNIFER, RN, dir. nrsg. serv., Lincoln West Hospital, Chicago, IL '84 (NURS)
KARCH, SUSAN A., dir. mgt. dev., American Medical International, Brea, CA '82 (MGMT)
KARCSH, FRANCIS J., exec. dir., Camden County Health Services Center, Blackwood, NJ '86
KARDASEN, IRENE M., coor. vol., Michiana Community Hospital, South Bend, IN '86 (VOL)
KARDES, FERIDUN, Munster, IN '80 (ENG)
KAREL, THOMAS L., mgr. human res., Butterworth Hospital, Grand Rapids, MI '79 (PERS)
KARHOFF, CARMELITA, dir. qual. assur., Paoli Memorial Hospital, Paoli, PA '82 (RISK)
KARIHER, PETER W., dir. corp. strategic plng., Moses H. Cone Memorial Hospital, Greensboro, NC '85 (PLNG)
KARIS, JOANN, coor. nrsg. unit and amb. surg., Amsterdam Memorial Hospital, Amsterdam, NY '87 (AMB)
KARKER-JENNINGS, KATHERINE, atty., Frank, Bernstein, Conaway and Goldman, Baltimore, MD '87
KARKI, MYRON, mgr. matl. mgt., Group Health Plan, Inc., Eden Prairie, MN '74 (CS)
KARKOS, JACQUELINE H., vice-pres., National Law Publishing Corporation, Owings Mills, MD '85
KARL, ANNE S., chm. intensive care nrsg., Massachusetts General Hospital, Boston, MA '86 (NURS)
KARL, TOBYE, dir. vol. serv., Mount Sinai Hospital, Hartford, CT '82 (VOL)
KARLING, JAMES W., Arthur Young and Company, Walnut Creek, CA '82
KARLSBERGER, ROBERT L., pres., Karlsberger Companies, Columbus, OH '76
KARLSEN, CHRISTINE A., dir. commun. rel., Holy Cross Hospital, Mission Hills, CA '85 (PLNG)
KARMIRE, KENNETH R., dir. matl. mgt., Welborn Memorial Baptist Hospital, Evansville, IN '86 (PUR)
KARN, CHERYL S., dir. pub. rel., DePaul Health Center, Bridgeton, MO '82 (PR)
KARNIEWICZ, ALFRED J. JR., exec. dir., Strategic Health Development Corporation, Miami Shores, FL '66
KARNITZ, SUZANNE L., dir. diet. and hskpg., Sioux Valley Hospital, New Ulm, MN '80 (ENVIRON)
KAROL, ROBERT V., sr. indust. eng., Montefiore Medical Center, Bronx, NY '84 (MGMT)

KAROLCZAK, MIKE, dir. plant oper., Kent General Hospital, Dover, DE '83 (ENG)
KARP, DAVID, pres., David Karp Associates, San Rafael, CA '80 (RISK)
KARPAN, BOB, mgr. cost acct., Mercy Hospital Medical Center, Des Moines, IA '86 (PLNG)
KARPE, CHARLOTTE KALMUS, sr. adm. consult., Administrators on Call, Baldwin, NY '82
KARPE, HENRY R., prin. consult., Administrators on Call, Baldwin, NY '51 (LIFE)
KARR, ADRIENNE J., dir. diet. serv., Philadelphia Psychiatric Center, Philadelphia, PA '85 (FOOD)
KARR, J. THOMAS, vice-pres., Gwinnett Hospital System, Lawrenceville, GA '83
KARRAS, ROBERT SR., eng., River Falls Area Hospital, River Falls, WI '72 (ENG)
KARRER, E. KATHERINE, mental health educator, University Psychiatric Serivces, Omaha, NE '86 (EDUC)
KARRIS, MARTIN, assoc. adm., Long Island Jewish Medical Center, New Hyde Park, NY '85
KARSE, MYRA ROCHELLE, pat. rep., Bay Medical Center, Bay City, MI '85 (PAT)
KARSON, LILLIAN PLAYER, mgr. underwriting and risk mgt., Hospital Insurance Services, Inc., Los Angeles, CA '85 (RISK)
KARTHEISER, JANE L., plng. and mktg. res. analyst, St. Mary's Hospital, Kansas City, MO '84 (PLNG)
KARTONIS, MARYELLEN D., sr. consult., Deloitte Haskins and Sells, Miami, FL '86 (PLNG)
KARUSCHAK, MICHAEL JR., asst. adm. emp. rel., Northwest General Hospital, Milwaukee, WI '76 (PERS)
KARWOSKI, TIM, asst. dir. eng. serv., Antelope Valley Hospital Medical Center, Lancaster, CA '83 (ENG)
KASANG, GEORGE J., asst. dir. maint. and eng., South Chicago Community Hospital, Chicago, IL '78 (ENG)
KASBEER, STEPHEN FREDERICK, atty., Loyola University, Chicago, IL '74 (ATTY)
KASBOHM, ROBERT K., vice-pres. strategies and syst. dev., Carondelet Community Hospitals, Minneapolis, MN '61
KASCSAK, MARGARET, RN, supv. cent. serv., Winthrop-University Hospital, Mineola, NY '78 (CS)
KASER, PAMELA RUTH, RN, assoc. dir. nrsg. and surg. serv., Pacific Medical Center, Seattle, WA '86 (NURS)
KASHNIG, RANDI, mgr. reg. mktg., New Medico Combined Rehabilitation Services of Chicago, Downers Grove, IL '85 (PLNG)
KASHUBA, KATHRYN M., RN, vice-pres. nrsg., Glendale Memorial Hospital and Health Center, Glendale, CA '82 (NURS)
KASHUBA, MARY M., dir. food and nutr. serv., Pomona Valley Community Hospital, Pomona, CA '82 (FOOD)
KASKEL, PHYLLIS J., asst. dir. food serv., New York University Medical Center, New York, NY '85 (FOOD)
KASMANN, CORA ZOAN, coor. qual. assur., Maxicare Illinois, Chicago, IL '86
KASNER, EDMUND S., dir. soc. work serv., Bess Kaiser Medical Center, Portland, OR '73 (SOC)
KASONIC, JOHN F., pres., Executive Consulting Group, Bellevue, WA '78
KASPARIE, BETTY J., adm. coor. plng., Blessing Hospital, Quincy, IL '81 (PLNG)
KASPER, ANDREA, mgr. mktg., Gc Services Corporation, New York, NY '86
KASPER, DOROTHY, dir. vol. serv., St. Joseph's Medical Center, Yonkers, NY '85 (VOL)
KASPER, JOSEPH THOMAS JR., dir. food serv., HCA Brotman Medical Center, Culver City, CA '74 (FOOD)
KASPER, SANDRA G., dir. mktg., Weston Ganoff Marini, Inc., Fort Lauderdale, FL '85 (PR)
KASPERBAUER, DWIGHT, vice-pres., Allegheny General Hospital, Pittsburgh, PA '87 (PERS)
KASPOR, ANNELLE M., coor. pat. educ., Munson Medical Center, Traverse City, MI '85 (EDUC)
KASS, GAIL, asst. dir. prof. serv., Presbyterian-University of Pennsylvania Medical Center, Philadelphia, PA '84
KASS, JOEL T., consult., Los Gatos, CA '61
KASS, WARNER N., exec. dir., AMI National Park Medical Center, Hot Springs, AR '64
KASSELMANN, ROBERT L., exec. vice-pres., Comprehensive Care Corporation, Irvine, CA '74 (MGMT)
KAST, KEVIN F., vice-pres., Baptist Medical Center, Kansas City, MO '76 (PLNG)
KAST, LARRY E., dir. commun. rel. and mktg., Tulare District Hospital, Tulare, CA '84 (PR)
KASTELIC, FRANK A., dir. soc. work, University of California San Diego Medical Center, San Diego, CA '78 (SOC)
KASTEN, JACK, Arthur D. Little, Inc., Cambridge, MA '54 (LIFE)
KASTER, DEAN C., assoc. dir. corp. affairs, Touro Infirmary, New Orleans, LA '77 (PLNG)
KASTER, DONALD B., supv. hskpg. and ldry., St. Joseph's Mercy Hospital, Centerville, IA '72 (ENG)(ENVIRON)
KASTER, JULIA KENNEDY, supv. mgt. consult., Ernst and Whinney, New Orleans, LA '80 (MGMT)
KASTING, BELLE, RN, adm. dir. nrsg. serv., Dunn Memorial Hospital, Bedford, IN '86 (NURS)
KASTNER, MICHAEL JOHN, asst. vice-pres., Mercy Memorial Medical Center, St. Joseph, MI '67
KASTNER, ROSEMARY, plng. analyst, Torrance Health Association, Torrance, CA '84 (PLNG)
KASTRUP, GARY L., arch., Henningson, Durham and Richardson, Omaha, NE '71
KASZAS, JOSEPH K., mgr. proj., Northwestern Memorial Hospital, Chicago, IL '81
KATARSKI, LOIS, RN, dir. staff educ., Walther Memorial Hospital, Chicago, IL '77 (EDUC)
KATCH, SARA, lib., Aorn Library, Denver, CO '86 (EDUC)
KATEN, DONNA M., assoc. dir., University Hospital and Clinic, University of Nebraska, Omaha, NE '81 (PLNG)
KATES, GEORGE W., atty., Tehachapi Hospital, Tehachapi, CA '80 (ATTY)
KATES, JOHN C., RN, asst. dir. nrsg., Detroit Psychiatric Institute, Detroit, MI '87 (NURS)
KATES, JUDITH A., PhD, sr. consult., Health Business Strategic, Shickshinny, PA '82 (PLNG)
KATH, STEVEN R., exec. vice-pres., Wisconsin Hospital Purshasing, Inc., Milwaukee, WI '79 (PUR)
KATHAN, GILBERT GORDON, chief eng., Walter O. Boswell Memorial Hospital, Sun City, AZ '77 (ENG)
KATHRINS, RICHARD J., dir. phys. ther. and coor. rehab., Betty Bacharach Rehabilitation Hospital, Pomona, NJ '86
KATHURIA, MALTI, coor. vol., Matheny School, Peapack, NJ '86 (VOL)
KATO, KATHY M., dir. soc. serv., Riverside Psychiatric Hospital, Portland, OR '82 (SOC)
KATONA, CHARLOTTE M., RN, asst. adm., St. Luke's Medical Center, Phoenix, AZ '70 (NURS)
KATTAK, GEORGE, dir. matl. mgt., St. Barnabas Medical Center, Livingston, NJ '72 (PUR)
KATZ, ALAN S., dir. human res., SunHealth Corporation, Charlotte, NC '82 (PERS)
KATZ, BARBARA F., atty., Massachusetts Eye and Ear Infirmary, Boston, MA '81 (ATTY)
KATZ, ELI G., eng. consult., North Miami, FL '66 (ENG)
KATZ, GERALD, partner, Peat, Marwick, Mitchell and Company, Philadelphia, PA '79 (AMB)
KATZ, HAROLD M., Bayville, NY '78
KATZ, IRWIN B., dir. corp. bus. dev., Catholic Medical Center of Brooklyn and Queens, Jamaica, NY '76 (AMB)
KATZ, JEANNE L., supv. pat. and family serv., Penrose Community Hospital, Colorado Springs, CO '86 (SOC)
KATZ, JEFFREY R., dir., Diversified Health Service, Inc., Baltimore, MD '87 (AMB)
KATZ, L. WILLIAM, Arthur D. Little, Inc., Cambridge, MA '66
KATZ, MARILYN B., dir. soc. serv., AMI Tarzana Regional Medical Center, Tarzana, CA '87 (SOC)
KATZ, MARJORIE, RN, assoc. dir. nrsg., Shands Hospital, Gainesville, FL '80 (NURS)
KATZ, MARK J., sr. mgt. eng., Johns Hopkins Hospital, Baltimore, MD '84 (MGMT)
KATZ, MIRIAM, (ret.), Cincinnati, OH '86 (PAT)
KATZ, MOSHE, vice-pres. plng., Montefiore Medical Center, Bronx, NY '85 (PLNG)
KATZ, SHELDON SIDNEY, dir. food serv., Mid-Island Hospital, Bethpage, NY '58 (FOOD)
KATZENSTEIN, DOROTHEA E., mgr. commun., Children's Hospital, Vancouver, B.C., Canada '86 (PR)
KATZENSTEIN, MICHAEL, asst. vice-pres. facil. serv., Children's Memorial Hospital, Chicago, IL '77
KAUCZKA, JOSEPH F., mgr. food serv., Allied Services-John Heinz Institute of Rehabilitation Medicine, Wilkes-Barre, PA '86 (FOOD)
KAUD, FAISAL A., assoc. supt., University of Wisconsin Hospital and Clinics, Madison, WI '72 (FOOD)
KAUFFMAN, BETTY C., (ret.), Apopka, FL '69
KAUFFMAN, JOHN W., (ret.), Key Largo, FL '44 (LIFE)
KAUFFMAN, ROBERT G., dir. eng., Massillon Community Hospital, Massillon, OH '76 (ENG)
KAUFFMAN, THOMAS L., pat. rep., Miami Valley Hospital, Dayton, OH '83 (PAT)
KAUFHOLD, GLENN H., mgr. pub. rel., Chilton Memorial Hospital, Pompton Plains, NJ '86 (PR)
KAUFHOLZ, MARY R., mgr. sup., proc. and distrib., Charlotte Hungerford Hospital, Torrington, CT '70 (CS)
KAUFMAN, DAVID P., exec. vice-pres., Deliverex Service Centers, San Jose, CA '86 (MGMT)
KAUFMAN, FAY GLORIA, Brighton, MA '64 (PERS)
KAUFMAN, HELEN, dir. pat. and family serv., Verdugo Hills Hospital, Glendale, CA '85 (SOC)
KAUFMAN, JERILYN A., coor. pub. rel., New Berlin Memorial Hospital, New Berlin, WI '85 (PR)
KAUFMAN, KENNETH, mng. dir., Kaufman, Hall and Associates, Northfield, IL '87 (AMB)
KAUFMAN, LAURA B., dir. soc. serv., Moses H. Cone Memorial Hospital, Greensboro, NC '82 (SOC)
KAUFMAN, LLOYD, dir. soc. serv., Broadlawns Medical Center, Des Moines, IA '77 (SOC)
KAUFMAN, LOUIS J., dir. bldg. and grds., Southeastern Virginia Training Center, Chesapeake, VA '85 (ENG)
KAUFMAN, MARY J., dir. soc. serv., Boca Raton Community Hospital, Boca Raton, FL '85 (SOC)
KAUFMAN, MELISSA W., asst. dir. medicine, Cooper Hospital-University Medical Center, Camden, NJ '85
KAUFMAN, MICHELLE S., atty., Trinity Lutheran Hospital, Kansas City, MO '86 (ATTY)
KAUFMAN, ROBERT B., adm. fellow, Fairview Riverside Hospital, Minneapolis, MN '83
KAUFMAN, ROBERT L., dir. pharm. serv., Miriam Hospital, Providence, RI '67
KAUFMAN, ROBERT M., atty., Greater New York Hospital Association, New York, NY '73 (ATTY)
KAUFMAN, SAMUEL, clin. eng., Beth Israel Medical Center, New York, NY '75 (ENG)
KAUFMAN, SHARON A., asst. adm. plng. and mktg., National Hospital Health Systems, Arlington, VA '81 (PLNG)
KAUFMAN, SHIRLEY A., dir. pat. rel. and vol. serv., Johns Hopkins Hospital, Baltimore, MD '83 (VOL)
KAUFMAN, THOMAS D., dir. mktg. and pub. rel., Hendricks County Hospital, Danville, IN '85 (PR)
KAUHN, JOHN, dir. plant oper., Crittenton Hospital, Rochester, MI '81 (ENG)
KAULFERS, ALFRED, prog. mgr., University of Virginia Hospitals, Charlottesville, VA '87 (RISK)
KAUNITZ, KAREN KOPPEL, atty., Methodist Hospital, Inc., Jacksonville, FL '84 (ATTY)
KAUPA, MICHAEL, risk mgr., Methodist Hospital, St. Louis Park, MN '86 (RISK)
KAUTTO, MARY E., coor. vol., Shriners Hospital for Crippled Children, Minneapolis, MN '83 (EDUC)(VOL)
KAUTZER, KENNETH A., assoc. adm., Mother Frances Hospital Regional Center, Tyler, TX '83
KAUTZMANN, EUNICE, RN, asst. adm. nrsg., Georgetown University Medical Center, Washington, DC '79 (NURS)
KAVA, JOANNE, asst. dir. pers., St. Mary's Hospital and Medical Center, San Francisco, CA '80 (PERS)
KAVAL, VINCENT R., vice-pres. alternative delivery syst., Blue Cross and Blue Shield of Northeast Ohio, Cleveland, OH '68 (PLNG)
KAVANAGH, WILLIAM J., assoc. dir., New England Medical Center, Boston, MA '72
KAVANAUGH, MARY E., pat. rep., Christian Hospitals Northeast-Northwest, St. Louis, MO '85 (PAT)
KAVCAK, ELIZABETH A., RN, dir. soc. serv., Guernsey Memorial Hospital, Cambridge, OH '85 (SOC)
KAVET, JOEL, ScD, assoc., National Center for Health Service Research, Rockland, MD '66
KAVINSKI, JODI, student, University of Wisconsin, Masters of Health Systems Engineer, Madison, WI '86 (MGMT)
KAVINSKY, ANN M., dir. mktg., Milwaukee Psychiatric Hospital, Milwaukee, WI '83 (PR)
KAVOIS, JUDITH A., mgr., Medicus, Evanston, IL '83 (MGMT)
KAWAHARADA, MATSUKO, dir. diet. serv., Kapiolani Medical Center for Women, Honolulu, HI '74 (FOOD)
KAWAKITA, HIROBUMI, MD, chief exec. off., Kawakita General Hospital, Tokyo, Japan '86
KAWASE, ANN M., dir. food serv., Hospital of the Good Samaritan, Los Angeles, CA '85 (FOOD)
KAWATERS, ALAN J., mgr. sales and mktg., R. S. Landauer, Jr. and Company, Glenwood, IL '83 (RISK)
KAWULA, GARY, dir. food and environ. serv., Children's Hospital, Denver, CO '73 (FOOD)
KAWWASS, BASSAM A., assoc. plng. and dev., First Hospital Corporation, Norfolk, VA '79
KAY, DIANE, dir. commun. and commun. rel., Marian Health Center, Sioux City, IA '86 (PR)
KAY, JEFFREY A., Pittsburgh, PA '73 (ATTY)
KAY, LAUREL D., RN, adm., Orem Community Hospital, Orem, UT '83 (NURS)
KAY, LINDA L., prin., Corning and Associates, Palo Alto, CA '79 (PLNG)
KAY, ROBERT L., adm., Johnston Memorial Hospital, Abingdon, VA '67
KAYE, COL. GEORGE A., asst. dir. plng., Ohio State University, Office of Health Sciences, Columbus, OH '57 (LIFE)
KAYE, GEORGE H., vice-pres. human res., Brigham and Women's Hospital, Boston, MA '80 (PERS)
KAYE, NORMAN L., field rep., Joint Commission on Accreditation of Hospitals, Chicago, IL '51 (LIFE)
KAYE, PHYLLIS E., student, Boston University Health Management Programs, Boston, MA '86 (PLNG)
KAYE, SUSAN, dir. soc. serv., Kaiser Foundation Hospital, Redwood City, CA '82 (SOC)
KAYLOR, RICK, dir. pers. serv., Anderson Memorial Hospital, Anderson, SC '85 (PERS)
KAYS, KENNETH D., supv. maint., Craig General Hospital, Vinita, OK '84 (ENG)
KAYSER, DORIS L., mgr. soc. serv., Fresno Community Hospital and Medical Center, Fresno, CA '82 (SOC)
KAZEE, DORIS L., RN, assoc. dir. nrsg., St. Anthony Medical Center, Columbus, OH '86 (NURS)
KAZEE, HASKEL R., mgr. clin. eng. and telecommun., Massillon Community Hospital, Massillon, OH '85 (ENG)
KAZEL, KAREN A., RN, vice-pres. nrsg., Saint Luke's Hospital, Cleveland, OH '85 (NURS)
KAZMIERSKI, JACK E., dir. mgt. eng., St. John Medical Center, Tulsa, OK '74 (MGMT)
KAZWELL, ANTHONY J., contr., Good Shepherd Hospital, Barrington, IL '84
KEADLE, REGINA L., dir. hskpg., Raleigh General Hospital, Beckley, WV '86 (ENVIRON)
KEAHEY, KENT A., adm., St. Paul Medical Center, Dallas, TX '79
KEAL, IRENE A., PhD, exec. dir., Ridgecliff Hospital, Willoughby, OH '73
KEANE, BARBARA, RN, vice-pres. pat. care serv., Walter O. Boswell Memorial Hospital, Sun City, AZ '80 (NURS)
KEANE, KERRY J., dir. commun. rel. and dev., Mercy Hospital, Rockville Centre, NY '79 (PR)
KEANE, MARY, (ret.), White Plains, NY '74 (SOC)
KEANE, SANDRA L., asst. dir. vol. serv., West Jersey Hospital Southern Division, Berlin, NJ '86 (VOL)
KEANE, VIRGINIA H., (ret.), Washington, DC '76 (SOC)
KEARN, DONNA J., RN, charge nrs. outpatient surg., Josephine Memorial Hospital, Grants Pass, OR '87 (AMB)
KEARNEY, LOIS, adm. coor., Newark Beth Israel Medical Center, Newark, NJ '83 (ENG)
KEARNEY, LORETTA M., student, New School for Social Research, New York, NY '86
KEARNEY, LYNN, mgr. matl., Shelby Memorial Hospital, Shelbyville, IL '83 (PR)
KEARNEY, PEGGY R., staff asst. health care fin., Blue Cross and Blue Shield of the National Capital Area, Washington, DC '86 (MGMT)
KEARNEY, W. MICHAEL, vice-pres. prof. serv., Mary Washington Hospital, Fredericksburg, VA '75
KEARNS, CAROL D., RN, dir. nrsg. serv., Community Memorial Hospital, Deer River, MN '87 (NURS)
KEARNS, LT. COL. JAMES R., MSC USA, chief commun. serv., Headquarters, Tradoc, Fort Monroe, VA '75 (SOC)
KEARNS, LYN J., dir. vol., John F. Kennedy Medical Center, Chicago, IL '78 (VOL)
KEARNS, PAUL M., exec. hskpg., Preston Memorial Hospital, Kingwood, WV '86 (ENVIRON)
KEARNS, RICHARD R., dir. pub. rel., Hospital for Special Surgery, New York, NY '85 (PR)
KEAST, CLAUDIA, mgr. matl. and dir. cent. sup., Kentfield Medical Hospital, Kentfield, CA '86 (CS)
KEATES, GLENN T., facil. eng., Catherine McAuley Health Center, Ann Arbor, MI '82 (ENG)
KEATING, DEIRDRE, student, University of Michigan School of Public Health, Ann Arbor, MI '86
KEATING, J. MICHAEL, vice-pres. syst. dev., Alliance Health System, Norfolk, VA '86 (PLNG)
KEATING, MARGARET A., pat. rep., Long Island College Hospital, Brooklyn, NY '67 (PAT)
KEATING, MICHAEL, dir. risk mgt., St. Elizabeth Hospital Medical Center, Youngstown, OH '86 (RISK)

KEATING, ROBERT M., atty., Woodland Park Hospital, Portland, OR '80 (ATTY)
KEATING, SHARON S., coor. in-service, Community General Hospital, Reading, PA '80 (EDUC)
KEATING, W. LEO, atty., Warren General Hospital, Warren, OH '76 (ATTY)
KEATON, FRAN, RN, asst. adm. and dir. nrsg., Stevens Memorial Hospital, Edmonds, WA '86 (NURS)
KEATON, JOE, supv. maint., Stuttgart Memorial Hospital, Stuttgart, AR '83 (ENG)
KEATON, WILLIAM C., chief eng., Grossmont District Hospital, La Mesa, CA '83 (ENG)
KEAVENEY, SR. ELIZABETH JOSEPH, pres. and chief exec. off., St. Francis Medical Center, Lynwood, CA '85 (MGMT)
KEBLUSEK, JOSEPHINE, dir., Little Company of Mary Hospital, Evergreen Park, IL '78 (SOC)
KECK, LEE K., asst. vice-pres., Community Medical Center, Scranton, PA '82
KECK, RICHARD K. JR., reg. dir. plng. and mktg., Cooper and Lybrand, Detroit, MI '75 (PLNG)
KECKLEY, PAUL H., PhD, pres., The Keckley Group, Nashville, TN '85 (PR) (PLNG)
KEE, DAVID E., dir. sup. and equip. mgt., Bexar County Hospital District, San Antonio, TX '85 (PUR)
KEE, HELEN K., RN, asst. adm., University of Utah Health Sciences Center, Salt Lake City, UT '73 (NURS)
KEEDY, JOHN A., design eng., University of Michigan Hospitals, Ann Arbor, MI '86 (ENG)
KEEFE, DONALD E., mgr. phys. plant oper., AMC Cancer Research Center, Lakewood, CO '78 (ENG)
KEEFE, DONNA J., coor. pat. educ., Imperial Point Medical Center, Fort Lauderdale, FL '82 (EDUC)
KEEFE, MARSHA S., sr. consult., Ernst and Whinney, Hartford, CT '85 (PLNG)
KEEFE, THOMAS M., assoc. exec. dir., Humana Hospital -Medical City Dallas, Dallas, TX '71
KEEFER, MARY ANN, RN, dir. commun. serv., Grady Memorial Hospital, Delaware, OH '75 (PR)
KEEFER, MICHAEL R., adm. and proj. dir., First Hospital-Clarion, Clarion, PA '85
KEEFER, ROGER L., dir. eng., Cass Medical Center, Harrisonville, MO '84 (ENG)
KEEFER, RUSSEL L., dir. compensation and benefits, Multicare Medical Center, Tacoma, WA '85 (PERS)
KEEGAN, BERNARD T., vice-pres., St. Joseph Medical Center, Wichita, KS '66 (ENG)
KEEGAN, NANCY, asst. dir. prov. contract, Blue Cross of Western Pennsylvania, Pittsburgh, PA '87 (AMB)
KEEHAN, SR. CAROL, RN, vice-pres. nrsg., Sacred Heart Hospital, Cumberland, MD '79 (NURS)
KEEL, RONALD D., vice-pres., Baptist Health Systems, Kansas City, MO '87 (AMB)
KEELE, SARA J., RN, dir. nrsg. adm., Jefferson Davis Hospital, Houston, TX '83 (NURS)
KEELER, JOY G., mgr. prod., Annson Systems, Northbrook, IL '87 (MGMT)
KEELER, ROGER K., mgr. contr., Bronx Municipal Hospital Center, Bronx, NY '82 (ENG)
KEELEY, BRIAN E., pres. and chief exec. off., Baptist Hospital of Miami, Miami, FL '68
KEELEY, DONALD F., dir. pers., St. Mary's Hospital, Streator, IL '78 (PERS)
KEELEY, G. CHRIS, dir. pers., Indiana University-Purdue University at Indianapolis, Indianapolis, IN '84 (PERS)
KEELING, MAUD W., dir. soc. work, Driscoll Foundation Children's Hospital, Corpus Christi, TX '73 (SOC)
KEELY, BETH R., dir. clin. and mgt. educ., St. Joseph Hospital, Orange, CA '86 (EDUC)
KEEN, BARBARA A., pat. serv. rep., Healthcare Medical Center of Tustin, Tustin, CA '82 (PAT)
KEEN, KATHLEEN A., student, Program and Bureau of Hospital Administration, University of Michigan, Ann Arbor, MI '81
KEEN, KATHY, prod. mgr., Positive Promotions, Brooklyn, NY '85 (PR)
KEENA, JAMES E., dir. pers., Faxton Hospital, Utica, NY '84 (PERS)
KEENAN, BRIDGET T., RN, asst. exec. dir. nrsg., Caledonian Hospital, Brooklyn, NY '82 (NURS)
KEENAN, LARRY E., atty., Central Kansas Medical Center, Great Bend, KS '68 (ATTY)
KEENAN, PATRICIA A., RN, supv. cent. serv., Lakeland Hospital, Elkhorn, WI '83 (CS)
KEENAN, PATRICIA GAYLE, actg. dir. commun. rel., Sutter Solano Medical Center, Vallejo, CA '69 (PR)
KEENAN, SANDRA H., RN, dir. surg. nrsg., Grady Memorial Hospital, Atlanta, GA '85 (NURS)
KEENE, BEVERLY A., RN, asst. adm. nrsg., University Community Hospital, Tampa, FL '76 (NURS)
KEENE, JACK R., asst. dir. eng., Fairfax Hospital, Falls Church, VA '81 (ENG)
KEENE, LEE DOUGLAS, adm., Methodist Hospital of Kentucky, Pikeville, KY '63
KEENE, ROSE C., dir. vol. serv., Fairfax Hospital, Falls Church, VA '76 (VOL)
KEENE, WILLIAM F., chief vol. serv., Veterans Administration Medical Center, Cleveland, OH '83 (VOL)
KEENER, CARLA P., proj. mgr. plng. and mktg., Peninsula Hospital and Medical Center, Burlingame, CA '86 (PLNG)
KEENER, TIMOTHY J., dir. bus. affairs, Ochsner Foundation, New Orleans, LA '81
KEENEY, JOSEPH D., pres., Sea View Hospital and Home Auxiliary, Staten Island, NY '44 (LIFE)
KEERAN, R. JOHN, dir. food serv., Carle Foundation Hospital, Urbana, IL '76 (FOOD)
KEESEE, RANDY A., dir. food serv., Brunswick Hospital, Supply, NC '86 (FOOD)
KEETLE, ROGER S., atty., Nebraska Hospital Association, Lincoln, NE '79 (ATTY)
KEETON, ROSETTA, pat. rep. and pat. rel., St. Louis Regional Medical Center, St. Louis, MO '86 (PAT)
KEEZER, M. P., dir. ldry. serv., Montefiore Medical Center, Bronx, NY '86 (ENVIRON)
KEGLER, ARTHUR L., dir. bldg. and grds., Jeannette District Memorial Hospital, Jeannette, PA '79 (ENG)
KEHOE, DANIEL, vice-pres. auto and natl. mktg., Blue Cross and Blue Shield of Michigan, Detroit, MI '54 (LIFE)
KEHOE, KAREN K., coor. vol., Iowa Methodist Medical Center, Des Moines, IA '85 (VOL)
KEHOE, WILLIAM D. JR., dir. pub. info. and govt. rel., Mississippi Hospital Association, Jackson, MS '82 (PR)
KEHR, WILLIAM P., dir. soc. serv., Charles Cole Memorial Hospital, Coudersport, PA '84 (SOC)
KEHRER, GEORGE F., dir. pub. rel. and dev., Ohio Valley Hospital, Steubenville, OH '73 (PR)
KEHUS, FRANK W., staff asst. to assoc. dir., William Jennings Bryan Dorn Veterans Hospital, Columbia, SC '82 (MGMT)
KEID, PEARL Y., RN, dir. educ., Mansfield General Hospital, Mansfield, OH '84 (NURS)
KEIL, JOAN DEE, dir. vol. serv., Thomas Memorial Hospital, South Charleston, WV '68 (VOL)
KEILSON, LEONARD, MD, dir. amb. medicine, Maine Medical Center, Portland, ME '87 (AMB)
KEIM, CHARLES L., pres., Easton Hospital, Easton, PA '61
KEIM, CINDY K., dir. pat. advocate, Research Psychiatric Center, Kansas City, MO '87 (PAT)
KEIR, DOUGLAS CHARLES, adm., Southeastern Eye Center, Greensboro, NC '74 (RISK)
KEIRN, WILLIAM C., dir. soc. serv., College Hospital, Cerritos, CA '78 (SOC)
KEISER, PAUL H., pres., York Hospital, York, PA '52 (LIFE)
KEITH-SWENSON, ANNA H., RN, dir. nrsg., Jamaica Hospital, Jamaica, NY '73 (NURS)
KEITH, ANDREW P., mktg. dir., Community Hospital of Bedford, Bedford, OH '86 (PR) (PLNG)
KEITH, DWIGHT N., partner, Peat, Marwick, Mitchell, Company, Lincoln, NE '87
KEITH, ELIZABETH L., RN, dir. nrsg., All Children's Hospital, St. Petersburg, FL '76 (NURS)
KEITH, F. EUGENE JR., atty., Mountainside Hospital, Montclair, NJ '71 (ATTY)
KEITH, JANET CAROL, dir. gen. serv., Sierra Community Hospital, Fresno, CA '78 (FOOD)
KEITH, KARLA J., sr. planner, Mount Sinai Medical Center, Miami Beach, FL '85 (PLNG)
KEITH, NORMA J., dir. pers., Helena Hospital, Helena, AR '70 (PERS)
KEITH, PERRY R., dir. pub. rel., Physicians and Surgeons Hospital, Shreveport, LA '82 (PR)
KEIZER, LUCIENNE D., cent. serv. educ. consult., Hanover Park, IL '79 (CS)
KELAHER, THOMAS F., atty., Community Memorial Hospital, Toms River, NJ '77 (ATTY)
KELDER, CHERYL ANN, dir. vol. serv., Tucson General Hospital, Tucson, AZ '86 (VOL)
KELEMAN, FRANK, dir. plant oper., Brentwood Hospital, Warrensville Heights, OH '86 (ENG)
KELEMEN, GEORGE STEPHEN JR., atty., Rose Medical Center, Denver, CO '83 (ATTY)
KELIUS, JUDITH S., coor. commun. rel., Friends Hospital, Philadelphia, PA '79 (PR)
KELL, PHILIP H., pres., Gratiot Community Hospital, Alma, MI '71
KELL, VETTE E., atty., Memorial Hospital for McHenry County, Woodstock, IL '80 (ATTY)
KELLAM, JOHN M. JR., sr. vice-pres., Texas Hospital Insurance Exchange, Austin, TX '83 (RISK)
KELLEGREW, RACHEL JUNE, pat. rep., Spaulding Rehabilitation Hospital, Boston, MA '75 (PAT)
KELLEHER, CAPT. CHRISTOPHER M., MSC USAF, med. prog. analyst, Headquarters Afmpc-Sgy, Randolph AFB, TX '83
KELLEHER, KATHLEEN P., health care loss control consult., Cigna Loss Control Services, Philadelphia, PA '79 (RISK)
KELLEHER, STEPHEN J. JR., vice-pres., Frankford Hospital, Philadelphia, PA '72 (RISK)
KELLEHER, VERONICA, vice-pres. pers., Cabrini Health Care Center-Columbus Hospital Division, New York, NY '74 (PERS)(EDUC)
KELLER, BARBARA A., dir. commun. rel., Joseph P. Kennedy Jr. Memorial Hospital, Boston, MA '86 (PR)
KELLER, BARBARA F., RN, dir. in-service educ., Phelps County Regional Medical Center, Rolla, MO '78 (EDUC)
KELLER, BARBARA J., RN, vice-pres. and assoc. dir. nrsg., Children's Hospital, Denver, CO '83 (NURS)
KELLER, CHARLES C., atty., Monongahela Valley Hospital-Charleroi Division, Monongahela, PA '68 (ATTY)
KELLER, CHERYL B., dir. mktg., North Monroe Community Hospital, Monroe, LA '86 (PR)
KELLER, DIANE R., dir. in-service educ., Memorial Hospital, Aurora, NE '75 (EDUC)
KELLER, DONALD A., dir. pers., Winthrop Hospital, Winthrop, MA '83 (PERS)
KELLER, JACK, student, Program in Hospital Administration, Trinity University, San Antonio, TX '87
KELLER, JACQUELINE A., dir. vol., Oneida City Hospital, Oneida, NY '83 (VOL)
KELLER, JANET R., dir. soc. serv., Mease Health Care, Dunedin, FL '85 (PAT)
KELLER, JOHN J., exec. hskpg., St. Elizabeth's Hospital, Belleville, IL '86 (ENVIRON)
KELLER, KAREN J., RN, University of Washington, Seattle, WA '83 (NURS)
KELLER, KENNETH K., dir. pers., St. Francis Rehabilitation Hospital and Nursing Home, Green Springs, OH '82 (PERS)
KELLER, LARUE S., dir. staff dev., HCA Gulf Coast Hospital, Panama City, FL '76 (EDUC)
KELLER, SR. M. ANNUNCIATE, dir. soc. serv., Saint Anthony's Hospital, Alton, IL '73 (SOC)
KELLER, MARK L., dir. ldry. serv., Metropolitan Medical Center, Minneapolis, MN '86 (ENVIRON)
KELLER, MARLO, dir. educ. serv., Memorial Hospital, Fremont, OH '72 (EDUC)
KELLER, NELLIE, risk mgr., dir. in-service educ. and asst. dir. nrsg., Jackson County Hospital, Scottsboro, AL '85 (RISK)
KELLER, SHIRLEY M., asst. dir. med. soc. serv., Akron City Hospital, Akron, OH '80 (SOC)
KELLER, WARD E., pres., Support Management Systems, Inc., Scottsdale, AZ '83 (MGMT)
KELLER, WAYNE P., dist. contr., Hospital of Corporation of America, Dallas, TX '87
KELLETT, NANCY R., RN, dir. nrsg., William W. Backus Hospital, Norwich, CT '84 (NURS)
KELLETT, SABINE A., student, Central Michigan University, Mount Pleasant, MI '83 (PERS)
KELLEY, CATHERINE B., dir. mktg., Willowbrook Hospital, Waxahachie, TX '86 (PR)
KELLEY, CHARLES, dir. plant and safety, Southeast Alabama Medical Center, Dothan, AL '86 (RISK)
KELLEY, DANIEL J., pres., ARA, Environmental Services, Inc., Philadelphia, PA '81
KELLEY, DEBRA S., prin., Hall Kelley, Inc., Minneapolis, MN '81 (PR)
KELLEY, ERNIE, biomedical eng., Flagler Hospital, St. Augustine, FL '87 (ENG)
KELLEY, EUGENIA L., dir. vol. serv., St. Joseph's Hospital, Tampa, FL '78 (VOL)
KELLEY, JOHN R., exec. dir., St. Mary's Hospital, Amsterdam, NY '75
KELLEY, KENNETH M., pres., Roseville Community Hospital, Roseville, CA '63 (MGMT)
KELLEY, KEVIN FRANCIS, Tracy, CA '84
KELLEY, LAURIE ANN, dir. health promotion center, St. Thomas Hospital, Nashville, TN '85 (EDUC)
KELLEY, MARIANNE E., atty., Hemet Valley Hospital District, Hemet, CA '87 (ATTY)
KELLEY, MARY E., dir. vol. serv., Oklahoma Memorial Hospital and Clinics, Oklahoma City, OK '86 (VOL)
KELLEY, MARY ELLEN, dir. soc. serv., Lahey Clinic Hospital, Burlington, MA '82 (SOC)
KELLEY, MAURA J., student, Georgia State University-Institute of Health Administration, Atlanta, GA '83
KELLEY, PATRICK S., dir. matl. mgt., Medical Center of Independence, Independence, MO '84 (PUR)
KELLEY, RANDALL, vice-pres., Emma L. Bixby Hospital, Adrian, MI '85 (PERS)
KELLEY, SARAH POWELL, dir. food serv., Southwest Washington Hospitals, Vancouver, WA '76 (FOOD)
KELLEY, STEVEN M., supv. biomedical eng., Knollwood Park Hospital, Mobile, AL '86 (ENG)
KELLMAN, ELLIOTT A., dir. human res., Yale-New Haven Hospital, New Haven, CT '80 (PERS)
KELLNER, EILEEN W., adm. mgr., Presbyterian Hospital in the City of New York, New York, NY '83
KELLOGG, FRANK B., dir. hskpg. serv., Los Alamitos Medical Center, Los Alamitos, CA '86 (ENVIRON)
KELLOGG, KATHARINE, dir. vol., Sharon Hospital, Sharon, CT '80 (VOL)
KELLOGG, MEG A., dir. policy and strategic plng., Kaiser Foundation Hospitals, Oakland, CA '80 (PLNG)
KELLY, ALAN B., atty., West Jersey Health System, Camden, NJ '84 (ATTY)
KELLY, BARBARA, RN, dir. nrsg. serv., Hospital for Special Surgery, New York, NY '76 (NURS)
KELLY, BETTY Y., dir. vol. serv., Eastmoreland Hospital, Portland, OR '79 (VOL)
KELLY, BONNIE DAVIS, dir. soc. serv., Dorminy Medical Center, Fitzgerald, GA '85 (SOC)
KELLY, BRIAN J., Pointe Claire, Que., Canada '84 (ENG)
KELLY, BRUCE JAMES, pres., Bruce J. Kelly and Associates, Inc., Prairie Village, KS '68 (MGMT)
KELLY, CAROL A., coor. ins. prog., Quebec Hospital Association, Montreal, Que., Canada '86 (RISK)
KELLY, CONNIE, dir. commun. rel., Bayshore Community Hospital, Holmdel, NJ '82 (PR)
KELLY, DANA JAMES, arch., Winsor-Faricy Architects, Inc., St. Paul, MN '86 (ENG)
KELLY, DYAN DOUGHTY, dir. human res., Presbyterian-University of Pennsylvania Medical Center, Philadelphia, PA '87 (PERS)
KELLY, E. MICHAEL, atty., St. Bernard Hospital, Chicago, IL '80 (ATTY)
KELLY, EDWARD P., asst. dir. human res., American Red Cross Blood Services-Northeast Region, Dedham, MA '86 (PERS)
KELLY, ELINORE, RN, dir. qual. assur., Albert Einstein Hospital, Bronx, NY '75
KELLY, FRANK J., vice-pres. plng., Danbury Hospital, Danbury, CT '80 (PLNG)
KELLY, JACQUELINE R., dir. dev., Jerrimed Business Center, Philadelphia, PA '84 (PLNG)
KELLY, JAMES E., dir. plant eng., Self Memorial Hospital, Greenwood, SC '84 (ENG)
KELLY, JAMES M., dir. pers., Mobile Infirmary Medical Center, Mobile, AL '83 (PERS)
KELLY, JAMES P., atty., Blount Memorial Hospital, Maryville, TN '79 (ATTY)
KELLY, JAMES S., dir. clin. eng., Basic American Medical, Inc., Fort Myers, FL '86 (ENG)
KELLY, KAREN A., assoc. dir. emp. rel., Jameson Memorial Hospital, New Castle, PA '81 (PERS)
KELLY, KAREN M., dir. commun., Witt Associates, Inc., Oak Brook, IL '86 (PR)
KELLY, KATHLEEN M., food and nutr. consult., MacNeal Hospital, Berwyn, IL '83 (FOOD)
KELLY, LAWRENCE, assoc. dir., Queens Hospital Center, Jamaica, NY '87 (CS)
KELLY, LESLIE C., mgr. vol. and receptionist, Winchester Medical Center, Winchester, VA '85 (VOL)
KELLY, LESLIE M., commun. spec., Kennestone Regional Health Care Systems, Marietta, GA '77 (PR)
KELLY, MARY ANN, dir. vol., Holy Spirit Hospital, Camp Hill, PA '81 (VOL)

KELLY, MARY C., RN, dir. nrsg., Mercy Hospital, Rockville Centre, NY '77 (NURS)
KELLY, MARY E., coor. educ. and dir. spec. serv., Pocatello Regional Medical Center, Pocatello, ID '85 (EDUC)
KELLY, SR. MARY, RN, vice-pres. bd. trustee, Hospital Sisters Health System, Springfield, IL '74 (NURS)
KELLY, MICHAEL P., dir. commun. rel. and mktg., St. Anthony Hospital, Michigan City, IN '84 (PR)
KELLY, NAOMI GAIL, dir. educ., McDonough District Hospital, Macomb, IL '84 (EDUC)
KELLY, PAMELA S., mgr. soc. serv., Memorial Northwest Hospital, Houston, TX '87 (SOC)
KELLY, PATRICIA C., dir. commun. rel., East Tennessee Children's Hospital, Knoxville, TN '85 (PR)
KELLY, PATRICIA M., asst. dir. soc. work, Lenox Hill Hospital, New York, NY '79 (SOC)
KELLY, PATRICIA, vice-pres. plng., mktg. and commun. rel., North Country Hospital, Bemidji, MN '80 (PR) (PLNG)
KELLY, PAUL M., dir. pers. serv., Eastern Maine Medical Center, Bangor, ME '83 (PERS)
KELLY, PETER A., adm. medicine, Beth Israel Medical Center, New York, NY '83
KELLY, RICHARD J., supv. gen. eng., Veterans Administration, Region Seven, Grand Prairie, TX '85 (ENG)
KELLY, RITA M., RN, assoc. dir. nrsg., Mason Clinic, Seattle, WA '84 (NURS)
KELLY, ROBERT, dir. diet. serv., St. Mary Hospital, Hoboken, NJ '79 (FOOD)
KELLY, RONALD F., dir. plant maint., Preston Memorial Hospital, Kingwood, WV '87 (ENG)
KELLY, STEVEN R., dir. plng., South Side Hospital of Pittsburgh, Pittsburgh, PA '82 (PLNG)
KELLY, SYLVIA K., vice-pres. mktg. and dev., National Medical Enterprises, Santa Monica, CA '83 (PLNG)
KELLY, THEODORE E. JR., asst. adm., St. Thomas Hospital, Nashville, TN '69 (MGMT)
KELLY, THOMAS J., dir. food serv., Lemuel Shattuck Hospital, Boston, MA '82 (FOOD)
KELLY, THOMAS W., exec. vice-pres., Hospitals Laundry Association, Inc., Boston, MA '86
KELLY, TIMOTHY P., dir. risk mgt., Howard County General Hospital, Columbia, MD '84 (RISK)
KELLY, WILLIAM A. JR., asst. dir. mgt. eng., Lutheran Healthcare Network, Mesa, AZ '87 (MGMT)
KELM, EUNICE E., RN, dir. nrsg., Rosewood Medical Center, Houston, TX '86 (NURS)
KELMAN, ERVIN H., mgr. clin. and commun. equip., Wesley Long Community Hospital, Greensboro, NC '79 (ENG)
KELMAN, SUE C., dir. pub. rel., Somerville Hospital, Somerville, MA '77 (PR)
KELMENSON, CAROLYN, asst. dir. mktg. and plng., Northside Hospital, Atlanta, GA '82 (PLNG)
KELSAY, EDWARD, legal counsel, Oklahoma State Medical Association, Oklahoma City, OK '80 (RISK)
KELSEY, CAROL, dir. pat. care and clin. syst., HealthOne Corporation, Minneapolis, MN '78 (EDUC)
KELSEY, DAVID W., dir. emp. rel., University Community Hospital, Tampa, FL '64 (PERS)
KELSEY, GRETCHEN, publisher, Optimal Health Magazine, Madison, WI '84
KELSEY, MAUREEN, RN, asst. adm. nrsg. serv., Saratoga Hospital, Saratoga Springs, NY '81 (NURS)
KELSKY, ALAN E., chief exec. off., Massapequa General Hospital, Seaford, NY '70
KELTZ, FRANCES R., asst. dir. food serv., Shadyside Hospital, Pittsburgh, PA '84 (FOOD)
KEMBALL-COOK, RICHARD M., student, University of Houston, Houston, TX '87
KEMER, JAMES M., asst. exec. dir., Androscoggin Valley Hospital, Berlin, NH '86
KEMERY, JACK, mgr., Peat, Marwick, Mitchell and Company, West Chester, PA '83 (MGMT)
KEMMERES, CHARLES E., sr. clin. eng., Shands Hospital, Gainesville, FL '84 (ENG)
KEMMERLING, PHYLLIS M., dir. pers., All Saints' Rehabilitation Hospital, Wyndmoor, PA '86 (PERS)
KEMP, ROY P., dir. plant oper. and support serv., North Valley Hospital, Whitefish, MT '83 (ENG)(PUR)
KEMP, THOMAS A., dir. info. syst., Mary Imogene Bassett Hospital and Clinics, Cooperstown, NY '78
KEMP, THOMAS R., dir. matl. mgt., Richardson Medical Center, Richardson, TX '85 (PUR)
KEMPE, PAUL W., (ret.), Midlothian, VA '48 (LIFE)
KEMPER, JAMES D., atty., Community Hospitals of Indiana, Indianapolis, IN '82 (ATTY)
KEMPER, LISA M., dir. soc. serv., Mercy Hospital, Owensboro, KY '82 (SOC)
KEMPF, GERALD T., Colorado Springs, CO '84 (EDUC)
KEMPF, JAMES E., dir. biomedical eng., William N. Wishard Memorial Hospital, Indianapolis, IN '86 (ENG)
KEMPF, LEO MICHAEL, dir. plant oper., Tri-County Hospital, Wadena, MN '78 (ENG)
KEMPINSKI, PAUL D., student, Rush University, Chicago, IL '83
KEMPPAINEN, A. W., dir. plant oper., St. Francis Medical Center, Trenton, NJ '68 (ENG)
KENDAL, LAYNE LUCAS, risk mgr. and safety dir., South Miami Hospital, South Miami, FL '75 (RISK)
KENDALL, CHARLES E., vice-pres., Geupel Demars, Inc., Indianapolis, IN '86
KENDALL, EDWARD THOMAS, vice-pres., Engineering Design and Management, Inc., St. Louis, MO '86 (ENG)
KENDALL, JAMES W., dir. pur. serv., Jameson Memorial Hospital, New Castle, PA '81 (PUR)
KENDALL, KAROLYN K., RN, dir. nrs., Meadowcrest Hospital, Gretna, LA '83 (NURS)
KENDALL, PATRICIA S., asst. dir. diet., Palms of Pasadena Hospital, St. Petersburg, FL '84 (FOOD)
KENDALL, RAYMOND E. JR., dir. facil. mgt., University of Texas Health Center, Tyler, TX '82 (ENG)
KENDALL, ROBERT L., constr. mgr., Chelsea Community Hospital, Chelsea, MI '79 (ENG)
KENDALL, WAYNE, dir. pur., Bridgeport Hospital, Bridgeport, CT '74 (PUR)
KENDRA, DOROTHY A., RN, assoc. dir., St. Mary of Nazareth Hospital Center, Chicago, IL '82 (NURS)
KENDRICK, CHERI A., dir. soc. serv., Rehabilitation Institute, Kansas City, MO '81 (SOC)
KENDRICK, HARRY, mgr. pur. and syst., Newton-Wellesley Hospital, Newton, MA '83
KENDRICK, LINDA L., dir. diet., St. Mary's Health Center, St. Louis, MO '84 (FOOD)
KENDRICK, MARTHA M., atty., Fairfax Hospital Association, Springfield, VA '86 (ATTY)
KENDRICK, RAY, dir. pers. serv., Cardinal Glennon Children's Hospital, St. Louis, MO '85 (PERS)
KENEFICK, JOHN R., atty., St. Mary's Hospital and Rehabilitation Center, Minneapolis, MN '79 (ATTY)
KENIRY, SR. M. JEAN, RN, vice-pres. nrsg., Lourdes Hospital, Paducah, KY '77 (NURS)
KENISTON, KAREN, dir. med. rec., Magee-Womens Hospital, Pittsburgh, PA '84
KENNAN, ALEX, dir. environ. serv., Windber Hospital and Wheeling Clinic, Windber, PA '86 (ENVIRON)
KENNAN, SEAN A., asst. dir. pub. rel. and commun., Rehabilitation Institute of Chicago, Chicago, IL '86 (PR)
KENNARD, MARY LEE, qual. assur. staff sec. and pat. rep., Dixon Memorial Hospital, Denham Springs, LA '86 (PAT)
KENNEDY, ALTHEA, RN, vice-pres. pat. care serv., Glendale Adventist Medical Center, Glendale, CA '78 (NURS)
KENNEDY, BARBARA B., RN, asst. dir. nrsg., Moore Regional Hospital, Pinehurst, NC '83 (NURS)
KENNEDY, BILL, assoc. exec. dir., R. E. Thomason General Hospital, El Paso, TX '80
KENNEDY, CHARLES E., vice-pres., St. Luke's Regional Medical Center, Boise, ID '79 (PLNG)
KENNEDY, CLARINE E., pat. rep., New England Memorial Hospital, Stoneham, MA '83 (PAT)
KENNEDY, DANIEL EDWARD, vice-pres., Riddle Memorial Hospital, Media, PA '71
KENNEDY, DENNIS L., atty., Humana Hospital -Sunrise, Las Vegas, NV '80 (ATTY)
KENNEDY, DONALD A., PhD, vice-pres. res., Xicom, Inc., Tuxedo, NY '86
KENNEDY, DONNA L., RN, dir. critical care, med. and ped. nrsg., Baystate Medical Center, Springfield, MA '83 (NURS)
KENNEDY, EVELYN B., RN, supv. cent. serv. room and oper. room, Dorminy Medical Center, Fitzgerald, GA '83 (CS)
KENNEDY, FRANK C., dir. sup. and pad., Kenmore Mercy Hospital, Kenmore, NY '60 (PUR)
KENNEDY, HAROLD EDWARD, maint. eng., Frederick Ferris Thompson Hospital, Canandaigua, NY '58 (ENG)
KENNEDY, HELEN M., adm., Meadowlands Hospital Medical Center, Secaucus, NJ '85
KENNEDY, JACK D., dir. mktg., Baptist Hospital, Nashville, TN '83 (PR)
KENNEDY, JAMES F., (ret.), Belvidere, IL '62 (LIFE)
KENNEDY, SR. JANE FRANCES, pres., Sisters of Charity of Nazareth Health Corporation, Louisville, KY '70 (PLNG)
KENNEDY, JEANNE, dir. commun. and pat. rel., Stanford University Hospital, Stanford, CA '80 (PAT)(PR)
KENNEDY, JOANNA B., adm., Hahnemann Hospital, Boston, MA '86 (PLNG)
KENNEDY, JUDY A., vice-pres. pat. serv., St. Mary's General Hospital, Lewiston, ME '85 (NURS)
KENNEDY, KATHLEEN A., RN, vice-pres. nrsg., Glens Falls Hospital, Glens Falls, NY '84 (NURS)
KENNEDY, LAUREL A., pres., The Kennedy Organization, Inc., Chicago, IL '86 (PR)
KENNEDY, LAWRENCE E., vice-pres. commun. affairs, Winthrop-University Hospital, Mineola, NY '77 (PR)
KENNEDY, LAWRENCE P., dir. pur., Middlesex Memorial Hospital, Middletown, CT '84 (PUR)
KENNEDY, LINDA A., dir. soc. serv., Community General Hospital, Reading, PA '82 (SOC)
KENNEDY, LYNNE L., vice-pres. prof. serv., Bayfront Medical Center, St. Petersburg, FL '79 (PLNG)
KENNEDY, MARY U., dir. nutr. and food serv., Newton-Wellesley Hospital, Newton, MA '69 (FOOD)
KENNEDY, MARY, asst. to exec. vice-pres., Massachusetts Eye and Ear Infirmary, Boston, MA '85 (RISK)
KENNEDY, CAPT. MICHAEL H., MSC USA, 2nd General Hospital, APO New York, NY '84
KENNEDY, N. DAVID, risk mgr., Memorial Hospital at Easton Maryland, Easton, MD '86 (RISK)
KENNEDY, O. GEORGE, PhD, pres., The Kennedy Group, Menlo Park, CA '72 (MGMT)
KENNEDY, PAMELA C., vice-pres. pub. affairs, Sun Health Corporation, Sun City, AZ '83 (PR)
KENNEDY, PATRICIA B., coor. soc. serv., Chippenham Hospital, Richmond, VA '74 (SOC)
KENNEDY, PATRICIA D., atty., Harper-Grace Hospitals, Detroit, MI '80 (ATTY)
KENNEDY, RAYMOND W., supv., HBO and Company, Southfield, MI '83 (MGMT)
KENNEDY, RENNA A., RN, asst. adm., Cottage Hospital of Grosse Pointe, Grosse Pointe Farms, MI '74 (NURS)
KENNEDY, RUSSELL E., dir. market commun., St. Joseph's Care Group, South Bend, IN '80 (PR)
KENNEDY, SARAH JANE, dir. human res., Easton Hospital, Easton, PA '86 (PERS)
KENNEDY, SHEILA, supv. soc. serv., Sequoia Hospital District, Redwood City, CA '79 (SOC)
KENNEDY, LT. COL. TERRIS ELLEN, RN MSC USA, nrs. staff off., U. S. Army Health Services Command, Fort Sam Houston, TX '85 (NURS)
KENNEDY, THOMAS F., asst. to governing bd., Saint Mary on the Mount Hospital Rehabilitation Center, St. Louis, MO '77 (PLNG)
KENNEDY, THOMAS F., adm., Baptist Memorial Hospital-Forrest City, Forrest City, AR '71
KENNEDY, WANDA, mgr. pers. serv. off., University of California Davis Medical Center, Sacramento, CA '83 (PERS)
KENNEDY, WILLIAM CRAIG, atty., Phoenixville Hospital, Phoenixville, PA '80 (ATTY)
KENNEDY, WILLIAM F. JR., dir. staff dev. and health res., Monmouth Medical Center, Long Branch, NJ '84 (EDUC)
KENNEDY, WILLIAM J., dist. mgr., ARA Hospital Food Management, Cohoes, NY '80 (FOOD)
KENNELLY, JOHN R., atty., Lutheran Hospitals and Home Society, Fargo, ND '85 (ATTY)
KENNELLY, JOHN, dir. plant oper., Roosevelt Hospital, Edison, NJ '81 (ENG)
KENNELLY, SR. MARGARET, dir. pat. rep., St. Vincent's Hospital and Medical Center, New York, NY '80 (PAT)
KENNEMORE, INEZ A., RN, vice-pres. nrsg., Self Memorial Hospital, Greenwood, SC '86 (NURS)
KENNERDELL, EDWARD H. JR., asst. vice-pres. risk mgt., safety and qual. assur., Suburban General Hospital, Pittsburgh, PA '86 (RISK)
KENNERLY, PEGGY A., dir. vol. serv., University Hospitals of Cleveland, Cleveland, OH '78 (VOL)
KENNEY, ELIZABETH F., dir. soc. serv., Winchester Hospital, Winchester, MA '70 (SOC)
KENNEY, HAROLD T., eng., Doctors Hospital, Corpus Christi, TX '77 (ENG)
KENNEY, JEREMIAH J., partner, Kitch, Saurbier, Drutchas, Wagner and Kenney, Detroit, MI '83
KENNEY, JOHN J., asst. dir. soc. work, Washington Hospital Center, Washington, DC '86 (SOC)
KENNEY, JOSEPH W., pres., Mednet Management, Inc., Minneapolis, MN '83
KENNEY, NANCY M., pres., Kenney Associates Insurance Advisers, Inc., Boston, MA '86 (RISK)
KENNEY, STEPHANIE K., dir. plng., Valley Presbyterian Hospital, Van Nuys, CA '77 (PLNG)
KENNEY, THOMAS W., student, University of Wisconsin, Whitewater, WI '86 (RISK)
KENNEY, WILLIAM O., student, University of Minnesota Program in Hospital and Health Care Administration, Minneapolis, MN '85
KENNIKER, JUDY A., clin. res. nrs., Finley Hospital, Dubuque, IA '86 (EDUC)
KENNISON, REBA LOIS, pat. rep., Sam Rayburn Memorial Veterans Center, Bonham, TX '85 (PAT)
KENNY, CAROLYN, mgr. area plng., Kaiser Permanente Medical Care Organization, Pasadena, CA '87 (AMB)
KENNY, DENNIS E., atty., Virginia Mason Hospital, Seattle, WA '81 (ATTY)
KENNY, SR. EILEEN M., chm. bd. dir., O'Connor Hospital, San Jose, CA '81
KENNY, LEE, dir. pur., Mid-Valley Hospital, Peckville, PA '79 (CS)
KENNY, MARY ELLEN, coor. vol., HCA Riveredge Hospital, Forest Park, IL '86 (VOL)
KENNY, PAUL L., atty., Hunt Memorial Hospital, Danvers, MA '78 (ATTY)
KENNY, SUSAN, asst. dir. outpatient nrsg., Jewish Hospital of St. Louis, St. Louis, MO '87 (AMB)
KENT, ANNABELLE H., (ret.), Skokie, IL '56 (SOC)(LIFE)
KENT, CAROL J., asst. vice-pres., St. Mary's Medical Center, Evansville, IN '74 (NURS)
KENT, DONALD L., dir. matl. mgt. and adm. asst., Bethany Medical Center, Kansas City, KS '70 (PUR)
KENT, SUSAN G., dir. human res., Black Hills Community Hospital, Olympia, WA '86 (VOL)
KENT, WAYNE L., dir. pers., St. Mary's Hospital, Athens, GA '82 (PERS)
KENTERA, AMY, vice-pres., Griffin Hospital, Derby, CT '78
KENYON, EDWARD T., atty., Overlook Hospital, Summit, NJ '79 (ATTY)
KENYON, ELIZABETH S., asst. dir. educ. and res., West Jersey Health System, Camden, NJ '85 (EDUC)
KENYON, SUSAN G., dir. food serv., Ballard Community Hospital, Seattle, WA '85 (FOOD)
KEOCHEKIAN, CAROL, mgr. commun. serv. and dir. mktg. commun., Golden Health System, Camarillo, CA '86 (PR)
KEOMALU, MARILYN K., mgr. pers., Wahiawa General Hospital, Wahiawa, HI '86 (PERS)
KEON, ARTHUR P., dir. eng., Maimonides Medical Center, Brooklyn, NY '71 (ENG)
KEOUGH, ELIZABETH, dir. vol. serv., Medical Center Hospital of Vermont, Burlington, VT '77 (VOL)
KEOUGH, FRANCIS, mgt. syst. analyst, Samaritan Health Service, Phoenix, AZ '75 (MGMT)
KEOUGH, MICHAEL P., coor. contract commun. nrsg. home care prog., Veterans Administration Medical Center, Albuquerque, NM '85 (SOC)
KEOUGHAN, MARY E., RN, asst. chief nrsg. serv., Veterans Administration Outpatient Clinic, Brooklyn, NY '80 (NURS)
KEPCHAR, DENNIS M., vice-pres. plng. and mktg., Children's Memorial Hospital, Chicago, IL '78 (PLNG)
KEPHART, DENNIS W., dir. bldg. serv., Carroll County General Hospital, Westminster, MD '72 (ENG)
KEPLER, JOHN R., dir. pers., Mercy Hospital, Altoona, PA '86 (PERS)
KEPLER, RICHARD R., dir. bldg. and grds., Southwest Texas Methodist Hospital, San Antonio, TX '83 (ENG)
KEPLEY, DAVID H., asst. adm., Henry Ford Hospital, Detroit, MI '79 (MGMT)
KEPLEY, T. ALVIN, dir. bldg. mgt. serv., Veterans Administration, Central Office, Washington, DC '87 (ENVIRON)
KEPLINGER, SUSAN M., RN, vice-pres. pat. care serv., Marin General Hospital, San Rafael, CA '81 (NURS)
KERBER, LOUIS J. JR., dir. bus. and fin., Sisters of St. Mary, St. Louis, MO '73
KERBIS, LYNNE M., asst. adm., Yakima Valley Memorial Hospital, Yakima, WA '82 (PLNG)
KERCH, JANIS B., dir. food and nutr. serv., Fairview General Hospital, Cleveland, OH '78 (FOOD)
KERCHER, LOIS L., RN, assoc. dir. nrsg., George Washington University Hospital, Washington, DC '80 (NURS)
KERCHER, PHILIP J., chief eng., Mount Carmel Hospital, Colville, WA '82 (ENG)

KERELUK, DELORIS B., coor. vol. serv., Hunterdon Medical Center, Flemington, NJ '84 (VOL)
KERFOOT, KARLENE M., RN, sr. vice-pres. nrsg., St. Luke's Episcopal Hospital, Houston, TX '82 (NURS)
KERKERING, KAREN M., planner and analyst, Seton Medical Center, Austin, TX '79 (PLNG)
KERKHOFF, LARRY P., dir. matl. mgt., Theda Clark Regional Medical Center, Neenah, WI '80 (PUR)
KERLIKOWSKE, ALBERT C., MD, (ret.), Ann Arbor, MI '40 (LIFE)
KERN, DELORES A., mgr. pers., Cascade Community Hospital, Central Point, OR '85 (PERS)
KERN, HARVEY D., asst. dir. qual. assur., Los Angeles County Department of Health Services, Los Angeles, CA '77
KERN, JON S., mgr. sup., proc. and distrib., Phoenix General Hospital, Phoenix, AZ '82 (CS)
KERN, KENNETH W. II, reg. mgr., Diversicare Corporation, Clearwater, FL '74
KERN, LEE, coor. educ., Good Samaritan Hospital, Mount Vernon, IL '78 (EDUC)
KERN, RICHARD A., vice-pres. environ. serv., Memorial Hospital, Belleville, IL '78 (ENG)
KERN, STEPHEN V., dir. emp. rel., Welborn Memorial Baptist Hospital, Evansville, IN '76 (PERS)
KERNAN, MAY, dir. pub. rel. and mktg., Women and Infants Hospital of Rhode Island, Providence, RI '83 (PR)
KERNAN, THOMAS J. JR., proj. mgr., Memorial Hospital of Burlington County, Mount Holly, NJ '78 (ENG)
KERNAN, WILLIAM, dir. eng., St. Elizabeth Hospital, Utica, NY '72 (ENG)
KERNEY, JANE D., dir. commun. rel., Medical Center at Princeton, Princeton, NJ '81 (PR)
KERPCHAR, CAROLYN J., RN, asst. adm., St. Mary's Hospital, Galveston, TX '78 (NURS)
KERR, ANN S., RN, asst. adm. pat. care serv., St. John's Hospital, Longview, WA '82 (NURS)
KERR, GLEN G., clin. eng., Sheboygan Memorial Medical Center, Sheboygan, WI '77 (ENG)
KERR, JOHN THOMAS, exec. vice-pres., Mount Carmel Mercy Hospital, Detroit, MI '67
KERR, KERRY W., mgr. maint., Anne Arundel General Hospital, Annapolis, MD '81 (ENG)
KERR, LOIS, mgr. mktg., University Hospital-Health Central, Augusta, GA '86 (PR)
KERR, MARIAN L., RN, dir. nrsg. serv., Mary Lanning Memorial Hospital, Hastings, NE '83 (NURS)
KERR, MICHAEL, asst. adm., Doctors Hospital of Lakewood, Lakewood, CA '85
KERR, MINA HOOVER, instr. health adm. and plng., University of New Hampshire, Durham, NH '84
KERR, PATRICIA KOKORA, cafeteria mgr., University of Texas M. D. Anderson Hospital and Tumor Institute at Houston, Houston, TX '84 (FOOD)
KERR, PHILLIPS H., dir. human res., Medical Center Hospital of Vermont, Burlington, VT '83 (PERS)
KERR, SALLIE TARRY, dir. mktg. and pub. rel., SunHealth Corporation, Charlotte, NC '83 (PR) (PLNG)
KERR, TED M., atty., Midland Memorial Hospital, Midland, TX '80 (ATTY)
KERRIDGE, GRAEME R., student, Deakin University, Wollongong Nsw, Australia '86 (MGMT)
KERRIGAN, JAMES V., assoc. dir., St. Elizabeth's Hospital of Boston, Boston, MA '63
KERRIGAN, MAGARET A., RN, dir. nrsg., HCA Riveredge Hospital, Forest Park, IL '84 (NURS)
KERSAVAGE, ROSEANNA M., psych. nrs. instr., Selinsgrove Center, Selinsgrove, PA '87 (EDUC)
KERSCHNER, MORLEY I., vice-pres., Amherst Associates, Chicago, IL '83 (PLNG)
KERSEY, DONNA M., head nrs. cent. serv., Bethesda Memorial Hospital, Boynton Beach, FL '77 (CS)
KERSEY, DOYLE, maint. eng., Emanuel County Hospital, Swainsboro, GA '80 (ENG)
KERSEY, THOMAS E., dir. matl. mgt., Sarah Bush Lincoln Health Center, Mattoon, IL '82 (PUR)
KERSHAW, REBECCA, dir. soc. serv., Golden Triangle Regional Medical Center, Columbus, MS '83 (SOC)
KERSHEN, FAYE ANN, Health and Hospital Planning Council of Southern New York, New York, NY '69
KERSHNER-SLACK, KAREN, pres., Communication Plus, Houston, TX '86 (PR)
KERSTETTER, ANN L., vice-pres. and adm., Rehabilitation Institute of Chicago, Chicago, IL '80 (PLNG)(MGMT)
KERSTETTER, BARRY A., dir. rehab. and cardiac serv., Maryview Hospital, Portsmouth, VA '86
KERTZMAN, KATHERINE SUE, dir. mktg. and pub. rel., Angleton-Danbury General Hospital, Angleton, TX '86 (PR)
KERTZMAN, PHYLLIS R., RN, nrs. mgr., Rapid City Regional Hospital, Rapid City, SD '85 (NURS)
KERWOOD, GAIL F., RN, vice-pres. nrsg., Berkshire Medical Center, Pittsfield, MA '80 (NURS)
KESNER, BERNARD J., Voorheesville, NY '75
KESNER, DOROTHY, RN, supv., Presbyterian Hospital, Dallas, TX '79
KESS, THOMAS W., vice-pres. human res., Methodist Hospital, Omaha, NE '86 (PERS)
KESSEL, TEDD H., dir. educ., Stevens Memorial Hospital, Edmonds, WA '82 (EDUC)
KESSELMAN, CAROL L., asst. dir., Kaiser Foundation Health Plan of Colorado, Denver, CO '83
KESSENICK, LAURENCE W., atty., Hospital Council of Northern California, San Francisco, CA '74 (ATTY)
KESSLER, E. MICHAEL, dir. soc. serv., Mercy Medical Center, Springfield, OH '84 (SOC)
KESSLER, HERMAN A., dir. plant oper., Good Samaritan Hospital, Suffern, NY '79 (ENG)
KESSLER, IRA, dir. health care facil., Dalton-Dalton-Newport, Cleveland, OH '80
KESSLER, JOHN B., asst. adm., St. Margaret Hospital, Hammond, IN '84 (PR)
KESSLER, JOHN R. JR., vice-pres. plng. and mktg., Lutheran General Hospital, Park Ridge, IL '82 (PLNG)
KESSLER, PAUL R., adm., Long Island Jewish-Hillside Medical Center, Schneider Children's Hospital, New York, NY '70
KESSLER, RENEE A., adm. asst., Grace Hospital, Detroit, MI '82
KESSLER, ROBERT M., dir. food serv., Boca Raton Community Hospital, Boca Raton, FL '84 (FOOD)
KESSLER, THOMAS J., asst. dir. med. soc. work, Ingham Medical Center, Lansing, MI '85 (SOC)
KESSLER, WARREN C., pres., Kennebec Valley Medical Center, Augusta, ME '65
KESSLER, WILLIAM E., exec. dir., Saint Anthony's Hospital, Alton, IL '74 (PLNG)
KEST, SHIRLEY A., instr., Ncr Corporation, Dayton, OH '86 (EDUC)
KESTENBAUM, MARIANNE Z., mgr. mktg. serv., Sinai Health Services, Detroit, MI '85 (PR)
KESTER, RICHARD G., dir. soc. serv., St. Agnes Hospital, Fond Du Lac, WI '67 (SOC)
KESTING, MICHAEL DAVID, dir. gen. council, St. Mary's Hospital, Leonardtown, MD '75 (ENG)
KESTLY, JOHN J., vice-pres. prof. serv., St. Elizabeth Hospital, Appleton, WI '72 (MGMT)
KESTNER, SUSAN G., counselor, Ohio State University, Columbus, OH '86 (EDUC)
KETCHAM, JULIA L., dir. commun. rel., Medical Center of Independence, Independence, MO '83 (PR)
KETCHENS, DAVID R., dir. bldg. oper., East Pasco Medical Center, Zephyrhills, FL '85 (ENG)
KETCHERSID, WAYNE L., student, Central Michigan University, Mount Pleasant, MI '85
KETROW, L. E., dir. plant serv., St. Elizabeth's Hospital, Belleville, IL '77 (ENG)
KETSCHEK, CATHERINE WHITAKER, RN, asst. gen. dir., Albert Einstein Medical Center, Philadelphia, PA '86 (NURS)
KETTEN, JOYCE KAY, dir. pur., Edward A. Utlaut Memorial Hospital, Greenville, IL '83 (PERS)(PUR)
KETTERING, KATE, med. surg. educ., Southwest Community Health Services, Albuquerque, NM '87 (EDUC)
KETTLER, DONALD, chief eng., Sheboygan Memorial Medical Center, Sheboygan, WI '78 (ENG)
KETTLESON, ARTHUR D., supv. maint. and eng., Rochelle Community Hospital, Rochelle, IL '86 (ENG)
KETTLING, VIRGINIA, RN, sr. asst. vice-pres., Mount Sinai Medical Center, Milwaukee, WI '76 (NURS)
KETTNER, CAROL E., RN, instr. educ., St. Joseph Health Center, St. Charles, MO '82 (EDUC)
KEUNING, KATHY S., dir. plng. and mktg., Good Samaritan Hospital, Downers Grove, IL '83 (PLNG)
KEVAK, THERESA M., mgr. diet., Geisinger Wyoming Valley Medical Center, Wilkes-Barre, PA '81 (FOOD)
KEVER, DORIS A., dir. matl. mgt., Memorial Community Hospital, Jefferson City, MO '86 (PUR)
KEY, BONNIE J., coor. vol. serv., Clark County Memorial Hospital, Jeffersonville, IN '85 (VOL)
KEY, DENNIS M., dir. pers., Central Washington Hospital, Wenatchee, WA '84 (PERS)
KEY, EDNA SUE, RN, supv., Beaches Hospital, Jacksonville Beach, FL '78 (NURS)
KEY, GLENN SHELTON, dir. soc. work, Children's Memorial Hospital, Chicago, IL '66 (SOC)
KEY, JAMES R., dir. eng., St. Francis Hospital, Memphis, TN '79 (ENG)
KEY, MARION T., atty., Methodist Hospital, Lubbock, TX '76 (ATTY)
KEYES, MARY ANNE K., assoc. dir., William Beaumont Hospital, Royal Oak, MI '86 (NURS)
KEYES, MAURA ANN, pat. rep., Nashua Memorial Hospital, Nashua, NH '86 (PAT)
KEYES, CAPT. TOM N., MSC USA, chief cent. matl., U. S. Army MEDDAC, Fort Hood, TX '86 (CS)
KEYMES, DUANE, supv. bio-elec., Fairview Southdale Hospital, Minneapolis, MN '78 (ENG)
KEYS, JONATHAN G., mgr. plant oper., Salem Hospital, Salem, MA '84 (ENG)
KEYS, PATRICIA L., RN, dir. specialty nrsg., Barnes Hospital, St. Louis, MO '81 (NURS)
KEYS, VICKY C., coor. staff dev., Eliza Coffee Memorial Hospital, Florence, AL '84 (EDUC)
KEYS, WILLIAM H., atty., Driscoll Foundation Children's Hospital, Corpus Christi, TX '78 (ATTY)
KEYSER, BONNIE L., dir. amb. care, St. Francis Hospital, Wilmington, DE '86
KEYSER, COL. COLLETTE P., MSC USA, consult. and asst. oper. room sup., Walter Reed Army Medical Center, Washington, DC '84 (CS)
KHAN, MICHAEL H., mng. dir. med. matl., Washington Hospital Center, Washington, DC '85 (PUR)
KHEDER, SUSAN, assoc. dir. soc. work, St. Joseph Mercy Hospital, Ann Arbor, MI '87 (SOC)
KHLYAVICH, MIKHAIL, dir. facil. plng. and constr., Mount Sinai Medical Center, New York, NY '86 (ENG)
KHOURI, GEORGE S., mgr. sales and dev., St. Joseph Health System, Laguna Hills, CA '85 (PLNG)
KHOURI, RATEB I., MD, student, Program in Health Service Administration, School of Health Professions, Governors State University, Park Forest South, IL '85
KHOURY, RAYMOND J., adm., St. John Hospital, Nassau Bay, TX '75
KHOURY, SUSAN, student, Northern Michigan University, Ann Arbor, MI '87 (AMB)
KHOUZAM, NERMINE N., student, Program in Hospital Administration, University of Florida, Gainesville, FL '85
KIBBEE, PRISCILLA, coor. qual. assur., Brattleboro Retreat, Brattleboro, VT '84 (RISK)
KICHEFSKI, CAROL M., dir. nutr. serv., Silver Cross Hospital, Joliet, IL '80 (FOOD)
KICK, JEANNE G., dir. soc. serv., Manhattan Eye, Ear and Throat Hospital, New York, NY '79 (SOC)
KICKER, JO D., RN, assoc. exec. dir., AMI Brookwood Medical Center, Birmingham, AL '76 (NURS)
KICKLIGHTER, LEILANI, RN, dir. corp. risk mgt., Sisters of Charity of the Incarnate Word, Houston, TX '80 (RISK)
KIDD, ANNETTE L., dir. vol. serv., Deaconess Hospital, Cincinnati, OH '86 (VOL)
KIDD, KATHRYN S., RN, co-dir. nrsg. serv., Roanoke Memorial Hospitals, Roanoke, VA '73 (NURS)
KIDD, ROBERT C. II, pres., Wyoming Hospital Association, Cheyenne, WY '69
KIDD, TOMMY, RN, supv. amb. surg. and services, Memorial Hospital, North Little Rock, AR '87 (AMB)
KIEFFER, ANN W., dir. matl. mgt., East Orange General Hospital, East Orange, NJ '75 (PUR)
KIEFFER, EILEEN T., RN, asst. exec. dir., St. Mary's Hospital, Waterbury, CT '77 (NURS)
KIEFFER, JOHN J., dir. pers., St. Mary's Regional Health Center, Roswell, NM '83 (PERS)
KIEHNE, LYNN S., dir. amb. care, Strong Memorial Hospital of the University of Rochester, Rochester, NY '77
KIELAS, LINDA M., RN, Schaumburg, IL '79 (NURS)
KIELMAN, RICHARD C., vice-pres., Memorial Hospital of Dodge County, Fremont, NE '78 (PLNG)
KIELY, ROBERT GERARD, sr. vice-pres., Stamford Health Management, Stamford, CT '76 (PLNG)
KIENE, PAUL C., healthcare consult., Douglass Kiene Associates, Port Allen, LA '63
KIER, CHERYL JOHNSON, RN, discharge coor., Ukiah General Hospital, Ukiah, CA '79 (EDUC)(SOC)
KIERNAN, THOMAS B. JR., dir. clin. eng., Holy Redeemer Hospital and Medical Center, Meadowbrook, PA '85 (ENG)
KIESEL, NEIL A., dir. pub. rel., St. Mary's Health Center, St. Louis, MO '83 (PR)
KIESELBACH, BENEDICT J., dir. environ. serv., St. John's Hospital, Fargo, ND '87 (ENVIRON)
KIETUR, LOIS M., Bethesda, MD '80
KIFFMEYER, WILLIAM J., dir. mgt. eng., Mercy Hospital of Hamilton, Hamilton, OH '75 (MGMT)
KIGER, ARLENE A., RN, asst. dir. nrsg., Western Pennsylvania Hospital, Pittsburgh, PA '86 (NURS)
KIGER, CHARYL ANN, asst. adm. plng. and mktg., Georgetown University Medical Center, Washington, DC '80 (PLNG)
KIGER, N. JOAN, dir. pur., St. Elizabeth Hospital Medical Center, Lafayette, IN '81 (PUR)
KIGER, RANDALL E., student, Wayland Baptist University, Kaneohe, HI '86
KILBANE, BERNADETTE E., coor. outpatient surg. unit, Los Robles Regional Medical Center, Thousand Oaks, CA '87 (AMB)
KILBANE, NANCY C., RN, vice-pres. pat. care serv., Doctors Hospital of Stark County, Massillon, OH '86 (NURS)
KILBORN, VINCENT F. III, atty., Providence Hospital, Mobile, AL '76 (ATTY)
KILBRIDE, DENISE A., dir. educ., Gwinnett Hospital System, Lawrenceville, GA '78 (EDUC)
KILBY, EDGAR G., exec. dir., Masonic Hospital, Wallingford, CT '57 (LIFE)
KILDUFF, RONALD, supv. cent. serv., Mount Auburn Hospital, Cambridge, MA '80 (CS)
KILDUFF, RUTH L., risk mgr., New England Medical Center, Boston, MA '85 (RISK)
KILESKY, FLORENCE A., RN, vice-pres. nrsg., Moses Taylor Hospital, Scranton, PA '73 (NURS)
KILEY, BEVERLY, mgr. cent. serv., Leonard Morse Hospital, Natick, MA '85 (CS)
KILEY, DENNIS J., sr. vice-pres., Tennessee Christian Medical Center, Madison, TN '78 (MGMT)
KILFOYLE, REGINA S., asst. dir. pub. affairs, Massachusetts Eye and Ear Infirmary, Boston, MA '84 (PR)
KILGALLON, TIMOTHY K., atty., Charter Suburban Hospital, Mesquite, TX '87 (ATTY)
KILGO, JOYCE E., dir. vol., Barberton Citizens Hospital, Barberton, OH '77 (VOL)
KILGORE, CYNTHIA ANN, dir. matl. mgt., Tanner Medical Center, Carrollton, GA '84 (PUR)
KILGORE, KARL M., Anderson Debartolo Pan, Inc., Tucson, AZ '84
KILIAN, THOMAS A., vice-pres. human res., Wausau Hospital Center, Wausau, WI '74 (PERS)
KILIANEK, LT. COL. ROBERT M., MSC USAF, chief med. oper., plans and prog., Office of Command Surgeon, Honolulu, HI '70 (ENG)
KILKER, ELIZABETH, RN, instr. in-service, Mercy Hospital, Scranton, PA '71 (EDUC)
KILLAM, ROBERT C., dir. plant oper., Dallas Family Hospital, Dallas, TX '83 (ENG)
KILLEBREW, E. ANN, dir. vol. serv., Memorial Hospital, Chattanooga, TN '84 (VOL)
KILLEBREW, KATHRYN D., mgr. food prod., HCA West Side Hospital, Nashville, TN '85 (FOOD)
KILLEN, HARRY LEE, biomedical tech. and eng., Good Samaritan Medical Center, Zanesville, OH '86 (ENG)
KILLEN, JOHN J. JR., atty., St. Mary's Medical Center, Duluth, MN '73 (ATTY)
KILLEN, LYNETTE M., asst. dir. soc. work, Methodist Hospital, Philadelphia, PA '81 (SOC)
KILLIAN, MICHAEL C., dir. mktg. and pub. affairs, William Beaumont Hospital Corporation, Royal Oak, MI '78 (PR)
KILLIAN, REX P., atty., St. Vincent Hospital and Health Center, Indianapolis, IN '73 (ATTY)
KILLIAN, WALTER H., atty., Johns Hopkins Hospital, Baltimore, MD '86 (ATTY)
KILLILA, BARBARA A., mgr. qual. assur. and risk mgt., William N. Wishard Memorial Hospital, Indianapolis, IN '87 (RISK)
KILLINGSWORTH, BOBBIE, dep. dir. amb. serv., University of California at Los Angeles Medical Center, Los Angeles, CA '87 (AMB)
KILLIP, THOMAS, MD, exec. vice-pres., Beth Israel Medical Center, New York, NY '86
KILLOUGH, ROZ, RN, supv. cent. serv., Lincoln General Hospital, Ruston, LA '86 (CS)
KILMARTIN, JAMES T., dir. pur., Winthrop-University Hospital, Mineola, NY '72 (PUR)

KILMARTIN, MICHAEL, assoc. vice-pres. fin., Maine Medical Center, Portland, ME '71

KILMARTIN, RITA, RN, dir. matl. serv., St. John Medical Center, Steubenville, OH '83 (PUR)

KILMON, DORRIS T., dir. pur., Northampton-Accomack Memorial Hospital, Nassawadox, VA '61 (PUR)

KILPATRICK, JOE D., Anaheim, CA '86 (ENG)

KILPATRICK, MARIE, dir. soc. serv., St. Mary's Hospital, West Palm Beach, FL '74 (SOC)

KILPATRICK, R. J., atty., St. Mary Medical Center, Long Beach, CA '70 (ATTY)

KILPATRICK, STEPHANIE, RN, dir. nrsg. serv., King's Daughters Hospital, Brookhaven, MS '76 (NURS)

KILPATRICK, WILLIAM A., exec. dir., Moncton Hospital, Moncton, N.B., Canada '82

KILROY, JOHN M., atty., Research Medical Center, Kansas City, MO '77 (ATTY)

KILROY, PAT A., mgr. educ., Visiting Nurse Service Home Care, Flushing, NY '85 (EDUC)

KIM, ALICE Y., dir. vol. serv., St. Francis Medical Center, Honolulu, HI '85 (VOL)

KIM, HENDRICA, dir. psych. soc. serv., Carrier Foundation, Belle Mead, NJ '72 (SOC)

KIM, KENAM, pres., Wahiawa General Hospital, Wahiawa, HI '86 (RISK)

KIM, WINIFRED S. O., mgr. cent. sup. and distrib., St. Francis Medical Center, Honolulu, HI '80 (CS)

KIMBALL, BARBARA J., RN, assoc. dir. nrsg., Choate-Symmes Hospitals, Woburn, MA '82 (NURS)

KIMBALL, EDITH LEAH, asst. dir. educ., Mercy Hospitals of Kansas, Fort Scott, KS '87 (EDUC)

KIMBALL, MANSON JR., dir. risk mgt., Good Samaritan Hospital, Cincinnati, OH '82 (RISK)

KIMBALL, MARY ELLEN, dir. pub. rel., Charter Community Hospital, Des Moines, IA '82 (PR)

KIMBALL, SHEILA ELIZABETH, coor. guest rel., Smyrna Hospital, Smyrna, GA '85 (PAT)

KIMBELL, CHARLES W. III, dir. res. dev. and pub. rel., St. John's Episcopal Hospital-South Shore, Far Rockaway, NY '86 (PR) (PLNG)

KIMBLE, ROBERT M., dir. pers., Crawford W. Long Memorial Hospital of Emory University, Atlanta, GA '74 (PERS)

KIMBLER, CHRISTINE M., RN, dir. pat. care serv., United District Hospital and Home, Staples, MN '86 (NURS)

KIMBROUGH, BILLY J., asst. dir. pers. trng., University of Texas Medical Branch Hospitals, Galveston, TX '71 (EDUC)

KIMBROUGH, JAMES, dir. matl. mgt., Baptist Regional Health Center, Miami, OK '82 (PUR)

KIMES, WILLIAM J., sr. vice-pres., South Side Hospital of Pittsburgh, Pittsburgh, PA '51 (LIFE)

KIMMEL, C. DAVID, dir. hosp. and commun. rel., Mercy Hospital, Altoona, PA '83 (PR)

KIMMEL, ROBERT B., vice-pres. corp. mktg. and commun., Albert Einstein Medical Center, Philadelphia, PA '86 (PLNG)

KIMMERLY, DEAN L., vice-pres. human resources, Michael Reese Hospital and Medical Center, Chicago, IL '79 (PERS)

KIMMINAU, ERNA M., dir. educ. res., Sisters of St. Mary Health Care Systems, St. Louis, MO '80 (EDUC)

KIMMONS, ROBERT W., dir. plng. and mktg., St. Mary's Hospital, Decatur, IL '83 (PLNG)

KIMOTO, CHIE, dir. nrs. educ., Los Angeles County King-Drew Medical Center, Los Angeles, CA '75 (EDUC)

KIMOTO, RAYMOND S., biomedical equip. tech., Louis A. Weiss Memorial Hospital, Chicago, IL '76 (ENG)

KIMPSON, HAZEL B., coor. med. policy, Blue Cross and Blue Shield of Michigan, Detroit, MI '82

KIMSEY, BOB, asst. adm., Medical Center of Central Georgia, Macon, GA '87 (AMB)

KIMSEY, MARCUS LAFAYETTE III, asst. adm., Medical Center of Central Georgia, Macon, GA '78

KINCAID, A. DOUGLAS JR., consult., James A. Hamilton Associates, Inc., Charlotte, NC '50 (LIFE)

KINCAID, LAURILYN, student, Rosary College, River Forest, IL '86

KINCAID, LYNDA R., asst. dir. pat. rep., Mount Sinai Medical Center, Cleveland, OH '83 (PAT)

KINCAID, MARLENE L., dir. matl. mgt., St. Francis Hospital, Olean, NY '71 (PUR)

KINCAID, PATRICIA F., dir. vol. serv., Alexian Brothers Medical Center, Elk Grove Village, IL '85 (VOL)

KINCAID, WILLIAM H., Association for Healthcare Quality, Ann Arbor, MI '63

KINCEY, KENT, reg. mgr. sales, General Telephone of California, Norwalk, CA '86

KIND, BARBARA, plng. assoc., Health Central Systems, Minneapolis, MN '79 (MGMT)

KIND, THOMAS L., dir. food serv., St. Nicholas Hospital, Sheboygan, WI '85 (FOOD)

KINDER, BETTY R., assoc. vice-pres. pat. care serv., Women and Infants Hospital of Rhode Island, Providence, RI '86 (NURS)

KINDER, W. PERRY, adm., Doctors Hospital, Little Rock, AR '74

KINDERVATER, NANCY A., RN, dir. in-service educ., Retreat Hospital, Richmond, VA '83 (EDUC)

KINER, DRINDA J., dir. soc. serv., St. Vincent Charity Hospital and Health Center, Cleveland, OH '78 (SOC)

KING, A. DONNA, dir. soc. work, Medical Care Group of St. Louis, St. Louis, MO '77 (SOC)

KING, AL B., vice-pres., Baptist Memorial Hospital, Memphis, TN '76

KING, ALICE B., mktg. rep., Crothall American, Inc., Norwell, MA '81 (PLNG)(ENG)

KING, ANDREW THOMAS, reg. dir., Medical Care International, Marietta, GA '85

KING, ANNE C., head vol. serv., St. John Regional Hospital, Saint John, N.B., Canada '82 (VOL)

KING, ANNE E., dir. pub. rel., Dorchester General Hospital, Cambridge, MD '86 (PR)

KING, BASIL L., (ret.), Fort Pierce, FL '53 (LIFE)

KING, BETTY N., dir. food serv., Lawnwood Regional Medical Center, Fort Pierce, FL '77 (FOOD)

KING, BOBBY JEAN, RN, asst. vice-pres., The Methodist Hospital, Houston, TX '83 (NURS)

KING, CAROL A., dir. commun. rel., Mount Diablo Hospital Medical Center, Concord, CA '84 (PR)

KING, CHARLES M. JR., asst. vice-pres., Hospital Corporation of America, Nashville, TN '83

KING, CLARENCE CARLETON JR., adm., Crawford Memorial Hospital, Robinson, IL '78

KING, CYNTHIA DAY, atty., Southwest Texas Methodist Hospital, San Antonio, TX '85 (ATTY)

KING, DAMON D., adm., Medical Center of Central Georgia, Macon, GA '65

KING, DANIEL D., atty., St. Luke's Episcopal Hospital, Houston, TX '86 (ATTY)

KING, DIANA, dir. pub. rel., Tabitha, Inc., Lincoln, NE '86 (PR)

KING, DON D., dir. plant support serv., University of Michigan Hospitals, Ann Arbor, MI '86 (ENG)

KING, DONALD B., dir. pur., AMI Anclote Manor Psychiatric Hospital, Tarpon Springs, FL '81 (PUR)

KING, DONNA, dir. soc. work, Medical Care Associates, Inc., St. Louis, MO '87 (AMB)

KING, EDGAR L., chief fin. off., Hospital of Englewood, Chicago, IL '85

KING, EDWARD A., dir. soc. work, Saginaw Community Hospital, Saginaw, MI '78 (SOC)

KING, ELEANOR RAE, dir. vol. serv., St. Anthony's Hospital, St. Petersburg, FL '86 (VOL)

KING, ELIZABETH A., mgt. eng., South Chicago Community Hospital, Chicago, IL '86 (MGMT)

KING, ESTHER, RN, asst. exec. dir. pat. care serv., Allen Memorial Hospital, Oberlin, OH '76 (NURS)

KING, EVA M., RN, mgr. matl. distrb, Nash General Hospital, Rocky Mount, NC '81 (CS)

KING, FLORENCE, pur. mgr., Orlando Regional Medical Center-St. Cloud, St. Cloud, FL '85 (CS)

KING, G. ROGER, atty., Riverside Methodist Hospitals, Columbus, OH '79 (ATTY)(PERS)

KING, GERALD E., student, Program in Health Service Administration, School of Health Professions, Governors State University, Park Forest South, IL '86

KING, HOLLIS F., Olean, NY '79

KING, JACQUELYN S., student, Trinity University, San Antonio, TX '86

KING, JAMES J. JR., sr. res. analyst, Merrill Lynch Pierce Fenner and Smith, Inc., New York, NY '85

KING, JANET L., atty., St. Anthony's Hospital, Amarillo, TX '86 (ATTY)

KING, JAY F., dir. pers., Fresno Community Hospital and Medical Center, Fresno, CA '79 (PERS)

KING, JEFFREY W., mgt. eng. consult., SunHealth Corporation, Charlotte, NC '85 (MGMT)

KING, JERRY W., dir. plant oper. and maint., Horizon Hospital, Clearwater, FL '87 (ENG)

KING, JOHN E. JR., acct. mgr., Applied Management Systems, Burlington, MA '79 (MGMT)

KING, JOHN L., dir. pers., Rehabilitation Institute, Detroit, MI '86 (PERS)

KING, JOHN M., dir. plng., Motion Picture and Television Hospital, Woodland Hills, CA '83 (ENG)

KING, JOHN R., asst. adm. and dir. pers., Jellico Community Hospital, Jellico, TN '85 (PERS)

KING, JUDITH A., coor. staff dev., Memorial Southwest Hospital, Houston, TX '86 (EDUC)

KING, KAREN M., RN, dir. nrsg. serv., Olean General Hospital, Olean, NY '86 (NURS)

KING, KARIN J., dir. mktg. and traumatic head injury prog., Braintree Hospital, Braintree, MA '86 (PR) (PLNG)

KING, KATHY, mgr. pur., Careunit Hospital of Cincinnati, Cincinnati, OH '85 (CS)

KING, LOREN O., RN, vice-pres. nrsg. serv., Louise Obici Memorial Hospital, Suffolk, VA '74 (NURS)

KING, LOUISA C. M., dir. soc. serv. and discharge plng., Sonora Community Hospital, Sonora, CA '86 (SOC)

KING, LUCY H., pat. registration, St. Mark's Hospital, Salt Lake City, UT '87 (VOL)

KING, MARIE T., RN, liaison nrs., Oak Ridge Hospital of the United Methodist Church, Oak Ridge, TN '77 (SOC)

KING, MARILOU MEEHAN, atty., Mercy Hospital, Wilkes-Barre, PA '83 (ATTY)

KING, MARION D., dir. pers., Brookline Hospital, Brookline, MA '78 (PERS)

KING, MARJORIE, RN, Veterans Administration Medical Center, Northport, NY '77 (NURS)

KING, MARTIN F., dir. pub. rel. and mktg., Community Hospital, Anderson, IN '77 (PR)

KING, MARY D., RN, coor. educ., Gulf Coast Community Hospital, Biloxi, MS '86 (EDUC)

KING, SR. MARY GRACE, RN, (ret.), Cresson, PA '45 (LIFE)

KING, MARYANNE C., proj. asst., Lee Memorial Hospital, Fort Myers, FL '84

KING, MAUREEN L., dir. vol., Monticello Medical Center, Longview, WA '84 (VOL)

KING, MICHAEL A., dir. soc. work, St. Francis Hospital, Roslyn, NY '73 (SOC)

KING, MICHELE, dir. soc. serv., Brownwood Regional Hospital, Brownwood, TX '84 (SOC)

KING, MILES B., PhD, partner and western reg. mgr., Hay Associates, Walnut Creek, CA '81

KING, NANCY J., cent. serv. supv., North Adams Regional Hospital, North Adams, MA '84 (CS)

KING, NORMAN C., supv. cent. serv., Marion Memorial Hospital, Marion, IL '81 (CS)

KING, PATRICIA M., pat. educ. coor., Clinton Memorial Hospital, Wilmington, OH '84 (EDUC)

KING, PAUL C. JR., pres., St. Francis Hospital, Wilmington, DE '86

KING, RAJ AHUJA, vice-pres., Universal Home Health Service of Chicago, Inc., Des Plaines, IL '85

KING, RALPH E. SR., dir. environ. serv., Frick Community Health Center, Mount Pleasant, PA '70 (ENVIRON)

KING, RITA M., coor. nutr. and food serv., Palos Community Hospital, Palos Heights, IL '82 (FOOD)

KING, ROBERTA L., mgr. soc. work serv., Our Lady of Mercy Hospital, Dyer, IN '81 (SOC)

KING, RONALD E., vice-pres., Brookville Hospital, Brookville, PA '85 (PLNG)

KING, ROSS L., asst. mgr. soc. work, Queen's Medical Center, Honolulu, HI '85 (SOC)

KING, ROSS R., dir. hskpg., Newman Memorial Hospital, Shattuck, OK '86 (ENVIRON)

KING, ROYSTON A., dir. mktg. commun., Mission Community Hospital, Mission Viejo, CA '84 (PR)

KING, RUSSELL A., partner, King and King, Architects, Manlius, NY '75

KING, SANDRA FITZGERALD, dir. info. serv., Newport Hospital, Newport, RI '70 (PR)

KING, SANDRA YOUNG, dir. educ. serv., West Valley Medical Center, Caldwell, ID '79 (EDUC)

KING, SHELDON S., pres., Stanford University Hospital, Stanford, CA '55 (LIFE)

KING, STEVE, atty., Harris Methodist -Fort Worth, Fort Worth, TX '86 (ATTY)

KING, SUSAN, risk mgr., Southern Maryland Hospital, Clinton, MD '86 (RISK)

KING, THOMAS C., pur. supv., Martin Memorial Hospital, Stuart, FL '79 (PUR)

KING, WILLIAM D., atty., St. Luke's Hospital, Jacksonville, FL '83 (ATTY)

KING, WILLIAM E., dir. risk mgt., Aultman Hospital, Canton, OH '80 (RISK)

KINGAN, BESSIE R., RN, dir. nrsg., Orange Memorial Hospital, Orange, TX '70 (NURS)

KINGFIELD, KEVIN C., dir. proj., Jsa, Columbia, MD '76

KINGHORN, STEVE A., dir. pub. rel. and market commun., Medical Center of Baton Rouge, Baton Rouge, LA '82 (PR)

KINGSBURY, JAMES A., pres., Visiting Nurse Association of Greater St. Louis, St. Louis, MO '84

KINGSLEY, BONNIE J., RN, vice-pres. nrsg., St. John Medical Center, Steubenville, OH '86 (NURS)

KINGSLEY, DANIEL B., mgr., Medco, Inc., Warminster, PA '77 (MGMT)

KINGSOLVER, JACQUELINE C., atty., Research Medical Center, Kansas City, MO '84 (ATTY)

KINGSTON, BARBARA H., asst. to dir., vol. and commun. serv., Sheppard and Enoch Pratt Hospital, Baltimore, MD '83 (VOL)

KINGSTON, SUSAN H., RN, adm. dir. nrsg., St. Joseph Hospital, Memphis, TN '86 (NURS)

KINKADE, MICHAEL H., pres. and chief exec. off., Iowa Methodist Bio-Technical Engineering Services, Inc., Des Moines, IA '86 (ENG)

KINLOCK, PATRICIA B., pat. rep., Hoag Memorial Hospital Presbyterian, Newport Beach, CA '84 (PAT)

KINMAN, THOMAS EARL, dir. eng., Children's Hospital Medical Center, Cincinnati, OH '83 (ENG)

KINNAIRD, CHARLES R., atty., St. John Hospital, Detroit, MI '76 (ATTY)

KINNAIRD, LEAH S., coor. pat. educ., Baptist Hospital of Miami, Miami, FL '79 (EDUC)

KINNE, KATHLEEN L., adm. amb. care serv., Memorial Hospital for Cancer, New York, NY '87 (AMB)

KINNEAR, PATRICIA C., RN, assoc. dir. nrsg. serv., Ohio Valley Medical Center, Wheeling, WV '81 (NURS)

KINNEBERG, ROBERT L., Kenner, LA '78

KINNEEN, KATHLEEN, asst. dir. soc. serv., Lawrence General Hospital, Lawrence, MA '80 (SOC)

KINNEY, ARDIS A., RN, dir. med.-surg. nrsg., Washoe Medical Center, Reno, NV '83 (NURS)

KINNEY, BRENDA CARLSON, atty., Lankenau Hospital, Philadelphia, PA '79 (ATTY)

KINNEY, CATHERINE F., adm. commun. health serv., Catherine McAuley Health Center, Ann Arbor, MI '86 (PLNG)

KINNEY, CHARLES S., pres., Tobey Hospital, Wareham, MA '79

KINNEY, DONALD L., dir. human res., West Orange Memorial Hospital, Winter Garden, FL '73 (PERS)

KINNEY, ELEANOR D., atty., Indianapolis, IN '83 (ATTY)

KINNEY, JOYCE ELIZABETH, pat. rep., St. Luke's Hospital, Kansas City, MO '86 (PAT)

KINNEY, STERLING E., atty., Amarillo Hospital District, Amarillo, TX '85 (ATTY)

KINNEY, TERRI B., coor. pub. rel., Mercy Center for Health Care Services, Aurora, IL '86 (PR)

KINNIBURGH, PATRICIA A., asst. vice-pres. human res., Phoenix Baptist Hospital and Medical Center, Phoenix, AZ '86 (PERS)

KINNUCAN, JACK, mgr. commun. syst., Munson Medical Center, Traverse City, MI '85 (ENG)

KINSELLA, DANIEL F., mgr. mgt. info. and consult. div., Arthur Andersen and Company, Chicago, IL '82 (MGMT)

KINSEY, DAVID J., vice-pres., Kettering Medical Center, Kettering, OH '84 (PR)

KINSEY, JANICE, coor. qual. assur., Edward W. Sparrow Hospital, Lansing, MI '86 (EDUC)

KINSLEY, MARTIN DONALD, supv. biomedical eng., Yuma Regional Medical Center, Yuma, AZ '83 (ENG)

KINSMAN, SUSAN H., RN, dir. educ., St. Catherine Hospital on Half Moon Bay, Moss Beach, CA '84 (NURS)

KINTOPF, NANCY JO, coor. pat. rep., Mercy Medical Center, Oshkosh, WI '83 (PAT)

KINZEL, C. DENNIS, consult., The McCormick Group, Washington, DC '86 (PLNG)

KINZER, DAVID M., lecturer, Harvard School of Public Health, Boston, MA '83 (LIFE)

KINZER, DUANN F., dir. vol. serv., Loma Linda University Medical Center, Loma Linda, CA '84 (VOL)

KINZER, EDWARD M., dir. plant oper., Ridgecliff Hospital, Willoughby, OH '86 (ENG)

KINZER, ELIZABETH L., dir. soc. serv., Maryvale Samaritan Hospital, Phoenix, AZ '82 (SOC)

KINZER, RONALD J., dir. eng. serv., Lorain Community Hospital, Lorain, OH '76 (ENG)
KIPE, AUDREY C., dir. soc. serv., Lake Wales Hospital, Lake Wales, FL '77 (SOC)
KIPP, C. WILLIAM, supv. clin. soc. work, Mount Sinai Medical Center, Miami Beach, FL '85 (SOC)
KIRBY, BARBARA A., dir. amb. care serv., Deborah Heart and Lung Center, Browns Mills, NJ '87 (AMB)
KIRBY, CHARLES M., mgr. loss contr., Daughters of Charity Health Systems, St. Louis, MO '80 (RISK)
KIRBY, INGE T., student, Amber University, Garland, TX '86 (PERS)
KIRBY, JUDITH A., RN, risk mgt., St. Luke's Hospital, Davenport, IA '85 (RISK)
KIRBY, KAREN K., RN, adm. nrsg., University Hospital, Boston, MA '82 (NURS)
KIRBY, RICHARD, RN, dir. surg. serv., Presbyterian Hospital, Oklahoma City, OK '86 (NURS)
KIRBY, ROBERT W., asst. adm., Madison County Hospital, London, OH '73 (ENG)
KIRBY, ROY, atty., Coffeyville Regional Medical Center, Coffeyville, KS '74 (ATTY)
KIRCH, MARY, asst. mgr. pur. serv., Meriter Hospital, Madison, WI '86 (PUR)
KIRCHER, LINDA D., RN, clin. dir. and shift supv., Saint Joseph Health Center Kansas, Kansas City, MO '76 (NURS)
KIRCHHOFER, JAMIE A., dir. nutr. and food serv., Palos Community Hospital, Palos Heights, IL '85 (FOOD)
KIRCHHOFF, GLENDA L., dir. mktg. and pat. serv., Diagnostic Clinic, Largo, FL '86 (PR)
KIRCHHOFFER, ELAINE BIAGINI, exec. dir., Association of California Hospital Districts, Inc., San Rafael, CA '83
KIRCHMEIER, THOMAS E., Physicians Insurance, Seattle, WA '82 (RISK)
KIRCHNER, LINDA D., mgr. commun., Princeton Insurance Company, Princeton, NJ '82 (PR)
KIRIAKOS, ROBERT S., mgr. pub. rel., Memorial Medical Center, Springfield, IL '86 (PR)
KIRK, ALFRED S., dir. phys. plant, Sacred Heart Hospital of Pensacola, Pensacola, FL '73 (ENG)
KIRK, DELIGHT K., RN, vice-pres. pat. care serv., Castle Medical Center, Kailua, HI '86 (NURS)
KIRK, DIANE, RN, dir. qual. assur. and util. review, San Antonio Community Hospital, Upland, CA '86 (RISK)
KIRK, JAMES C., bd. chm., Pottsville Hospital and Warne Clinic, Pottsville, PA '47 (LIFE)
KIRK, JEAN, RN, pat. rep., Metropolitan General Hospital, Pinellas Park, FL '77 (PAT)
KIRK, JOHN B., dir. labor rel., Northwestern Memorial Hospital, Chicago, IL '81 (PERS)
KIRK, KATY H., dir. pers., Pulaski Community Hospital, Pulaski, VA '85 (PERS)
KIRK, MAUREEN A., RN, assoc. dir., Montefiore Medical Center, Bronx, NY '85 (NURS)
KIRK, MAUREEN, coor. soc. serv., Sauk Prairie Memorial Hospital, Prairie Du Sac, WI '86 (SOC)
KIRK, NANCY H., dir. mktg., Methodist Medical Center of Oak Ridge, Oak Ridge, TN '84 (PR) (PLNG)
KIRK, ROGER L., vice-pres. oper., Voluntary Hospitals of America, Tampa, FL '80
KIRK, W. RICHARD, dir. membership, American College of Hospital Administrators, Chicago, IL '54 (LIFE)
KIRKEL, HUGH P., Westerville, OH '58
KIRKEY, DAVID L. J., supv. biomedical eng., Condell Memorial Hospital, Libertyville, IL '82 (ENG)
KIRKHAM, G. DUANE, dir. pers., El Camino Hospital, Mountain View, CA '84 (PERS)
KIRKLAND, BARBARA BURKHARDT, dir. soc. serv., McPherson Community Health Center, Howell, MI '76 (SOC)
KIRKLAND, DON, dir. commun. serv., Samaritan Health Service, Phoenix, AZ '80 (PR)
KIRKLAND, JAMES REED, chm. health educ., Staley Junior High, Rome, NY '75
KIRKLAND, MARLIENE B., Waterman Medical Center, Eustis, FL '85 (CS)
KIRKLAND, REBECCA T., MD, head amb. serv., Texas Children's Hospital, Houston, TX '87 (AMB)
KIRKLEY, J. LYNDELL, atty., All Saints Episcopal Hospital, Fort Worth, TX '84 (ATTY)
KIRKMAN, JOYCE C., mgr. educ. serv., Rowan Memorial Hospital, Salisbury, NC '87 (EDUC)
KIRKPATRICK, ANN L., atty., Flagstaff Medical Center, Flagstaff, AZ '85 (ATTY)
KIRKPATRICK, DONNA T., dir. pub. rel., Indian Path Hospital, Kingsport, TN '83 (PR)
KIRKPATRICK, PATTY L., dir. pub. rel., St. Luke's Hospital, Aberdeen, SD '84 (PR)
KIRKPATRICK, PHILIP S., vice-pres. mktg., St. John's Hospital and Health Center, San Angelo, TX '87 (PR) (PLNG)
KIRKPATRICK, STEWART R., vice-pres. pub. rel. and adv., Intermountain Health Care, Inc., Salt Lake City, UT '77 (PR)
KIRKS, PAMELA, risk mgt. consult., North Carolina Hospital Association Trust Fund, Raleigh, NC '86 (RISK)
KIRKSEY, BELL, buyer, Hospital of Englewood, Chicago, IL '83 (PUR)
KIRKWOOD, LOUISE J., assoc. dir. soc. serv., Nassau County Medical Center, East Meadow, NY '74 (SOC)
KIRKWOOD, WILLIAM E., adm. asst., Good Samaritan Hospital, Cincinnati, OH '80
KIRLE, LESLIE, dir. qual. assur. and risk mgt., Beth Israel Hospital, Boston, MA '86 (RISK)
KIRLIN, MICHAEL H., exec. mgr., Groover, Christie and Merritt, Bethesda, MD '80
KIRN, JANET J., RN, clin. dir., St. Marys Hospital of Rochester, Rochester, MN '81 (NURS)(AMB)
KIRSCH, BERNARD W., mgr. soc. serv., Good Samaritan Hospital, Vincennes, IN '77 (SOC)
KIRSCH, EDWARD, MD, Long Boat Key, FL '43 (LIFE)
KIRSCH, JO, EdD, assoc. prof. and prog. dir. nrsg. adm., Hunter College School of Nursing, New York, NY '85 (NURS)
KIRSCH, MARY, Middletown Regional Hospital, Middletown, OH '84 (EDUC)
KIRSCH, SUE, supv., St. Mary's Health Services, Grand Rapids, MI '85 (SOC)
KIRSCHENBAUM, DAVID A., sr. vice-pres., L. F. Rothschild, Unterberg, Towbin, New York, NY '80
KIRSCHENMANN, DONNA F., RN, clin. dir., Allen Memorial Hospital, Waterloo, IA '86 (NURS)
KIRSCHMAN, MARY KAY, RN, asst. adm. nrsg., Roosevelt Hospital, Edison, NJ '81 (NURS)
KIRSHNER, ARTHUR N., adm. res., Roanoke Memorial Hospitals, Roanoke, VA '82
KIRSHNIT, HERBERT IRA, dir. diet., Massachusetts Eye and Ear Infirmary, Boston, MA '77 (FOOD)
KIRSNER, MELISSA B., dir. mktg. and adm. chemical dependency, Coral Reef Hospital, Miami, FL '83 (PLNG)
KIRSNER, WAYNE F., energy consult. and proj. mgr., Jones, Nall and Davis, Atlanta, GA '84 (ENG)
KIRSTEIN, JERROLD I., dir. soc. work, Beth Israel Medical Center, New York, NY '75 (SOC)
KIRTANE, MOHAN V., vice-pres. ancil and bus. serv., St. Thomas Hospital, Nashville, TN '73 (MGMT)
KIRTLAND, ANTHONY B., Birghamton, NY '80 (MGMT)
KIRTLEY, SUSAN, dir. soc. serv., Carle Foundation Hospital, Urbana, IL '73 (SOC)
KIRVEN, WILLIAM J. III, atty., AMI Presbyterian-Denver Hospital, Denver, CO '78 (ATTY)
KIRVIN, MADELIN M., dir. vol. and pat. rel. consult., Hillcrest Hospital, Pittsfield, MA '84 (VOL)
KISER, KAREN J., dir. food serv., St. Agnes Hospital, Fond Du Lac, WI '79 (FOOD)
KISER, SHARON A., dir. vol. serv., Grandview Hospital and Medical Center, Dayton, OH '79 (VOL)
KISH, ERICA H., educ. instr., Lancaster-Fairfield Community Hospital, Lancaster, OH '87 (EDUC)
KISH, GEORGE W., asst. adm., West Georgia Medical Center, La Grange, GA '76 (PERS)
KISHORE, PUNYAMURTULA S., student, Lesley College, Cambridge, MA '86
KISNER, RICHARD J., asst. vice-pres., Allentown Hospital, Allentown, PA '81
KISRO, FRED N., mgr. cent. proc., Tucson Medical Center, Tucson, AZ '74 (CS)
KISS, LOIS E., assoc. dean external affairs, Ohio University College Osteopathic Medicine, Athens, OH '87
KISSAM, RAYMOND F., dir. soc. serv., Lutheran Medical Center, Brooklyn, NY '71 (SOC)
KISSEL, NEAL, supv. plant oper., Beverly Hospital, Montebello, CA '86 (ENG)
KISSEL, STANLEY J. JR., dir. soc. work, Clinical Center, National Institutes of Health, Bethesda, MD '71 (SOC)
KISSIN, BARBARA, dir. soc. work, Winthrop-University Hospital, Mineola, NY '77 (SOC)
KISSINGER, KERRY W., info. syst. consult., Ernst and Whinney, Cleveland, OH '86 (MGMT)
KISSINGER, LEE, dir. maint. and plant eng., Woonsocket Hospital, Woonsocket, RI '87 (ENG)
KISTNER, ROBERT F., sr. consult., Bate Associates, South Bend, IN '72 (PR)
KITCH, RICHARD A., atty., University of Michigan Hospitals, Ann Arbor, MI '74 (ATTY)
KITCHEN, CHARLES W., atty., St. Joseph Hospital and Health Center, Lorain, OH '83 (ATTY)
KITCHEN, LIANNE M., RN, dir. med. surg. nrsg., Lourdes Hospital, Paducah, KY '86 (NURS)
KITCHEN, MARVA, dir. vol. serv., Berwick Hospital Center, Berwick, PA '77 (VOL)
KITCHEN, RUTH, dir. pub. rel. and dev., New Rochelle Hospital Medical Center, New Rochelle, NY '80 (PR)
KITCHENS, PHILIP R., med. adm. off., USS Dwight D. Eisenhower, FPO New York, NY '81
KITE, BRUCE R., atty., Columbue-Cuneo-Cabrini Health Group, Chicago, IL '80 (ATTY)
KITE, LANDON, pres., Reading Rehabilitation Hospital, Reading, PA '81 (PLNG)
KITSON, JAY C., actg. asst. dir. human res., Hurley Medical Center, Flint, MI '86 (PERS)
KITTELL, PATRICK M., mgt. info. syst. proj. adm., University of California at Los Angeles Medical Center, Los Angeles, CA '80
KITTLE, CLIFTON R., dir. matl. mgt., St. Joseph Hospital, Flint, MI '83 (PUR)
KITTREDGE, EDWARD F., adm., Hunt Memorial Hospital, Danvers, MA '71 (MGMT)
KITTRIDGE, DONNA A., asst. dir. diet., Presbyterian-University Hospital, Pittsburgh, PA '85 (FOOD)
KITWANO, RUKIYA, student, Program in Hospital Administration, Mercy College of Detroit, Detroit, MI '84
KIVELA, JANIS K., pub. rel. assoc., Unity Medical Center, Fridley, MN '84 (PR)
KJAR, WANDA L., RN, dir. nrs., Tri-County Area Hospital, Lexington, NE '83 (NURS)
KJELLBERG, BETTY J., adm. med. staff serv., Good Samaritan Medical Center, Phoenix, AZ '84 (PLNG)
KJELLBERG, CLIFFORD, eng., Ness County Hospital District Two, Ness City, KS '82 (ENG)
KLABUNDE, CARRIE N., mgt. eng., Tampa General Hospital, Tampa, FL '84 (PLNG)(MGMT)
KLAGES, DENNIS F., mgr. amb. care, Staten Island Hospital, Staten Island, NY '80 (AMB)
KLAHN, ROLLAND J., vice-pres. constr., Bellin Memorial Hospital, Green Bay, WI '76 (ENG)
KLAHN, WALTER G., mgr. compensation and benefits, Welborn Memorial Baptist Hospital, Evansville, IN '67 (PERS)
KLAMAN, EDWARD M., adm., Doctors Hospital of Lakewood, Lakewood, CA '71
KLANCER, PATRICIA J., dir. matl. mgt., Silver Cross Hospital, Joliet, IL '86 (PUR)
KLANFER, GERI, dir. vol. serv., AMI Tarzana Regional Medical Center, Tarzana, CA '82 (VOL)(PAT)
KLAPPER, ROGER, supv. pur., St. Vincent Hospital, Green Bay, WI '85 (PUR)
KLARER, KARIN J., mgt. eng., Harper-Grace Hospitals, Detroit, MI '86 (MGMT)
KLARICH, GERALDINE, dir. vol. serv., Washington Hospital, Fremont, CA '80 (VOL)
KLASCIUS, AL S., coor. pat. health educ., Veterans Administration Medical Center, Portland, OR '86 (EDUC)
KLASEK, ROBERT J., dir. hkpg. Northwest Community Hospital, Arlington Heights, IL '86
KLASS, JOAN, RN, vice-pres. nrsg., Monmouth Medical Center, Long Branch, NJ '83 (NURS)
KLASSEN, LORETTA V., RN, dir. pat. care serv., Hartford Memorial Hospital, Hartford, WI '85 (NURS)
KLATT, LAURA WALLACE, med. soc. worker, Sartori Memorial Hospital, Cedar Falls, IA '86 (SOC)
KLATT, PATRICIA MARY, pat. rep., Christ Hospital and Medical Center, Oak Lawn, IL '85 (PAT)
KLAUBERT, CHARLOTTE A., dir. vol. serv., Malden Hospital, Malden, MA '81 (VOL)
KLAUS, DAVID W., pres., McMullen, Klaus and Associates, Ltd., Lakewood, CO '83
KLAUS, FRANK M., asst. adm., Euclid Clinic Foundation, Euclid, OH '79
KLAUS, GLENN E., dir. bldg. serv., Lutheran General Hospital, San Antonio, TX '86 (ENVIRON)
KLAUS, HUBERT, dir. bldg. and grds., Loretto Hospital, Chicago, IL '59 (ENG)
KLAUS, JOHN R., atty., Mary Greeley Medical Center, Ames, IA '75 (ATTY)
KLAUSMEYER, THOMAS H., (ret.), Berkley, MI '67
KLAUZEK, RAYMOND E., dir. risk mgt. and loss control, Columbus-Cuneo-Cabrini Medical Center, Chicago, IL '80 (RISK)
KLECHA, DENISE T., dir. pers., St. Lawrence Hospital, Lansing, MI '82 (PERS)
KLECHA, MARGARET M., risk mgr., Wilkes-Barre General Hospital, Wilkes-Barre, PA '83 (RISK)
KLECKNER, JAMES R., pres., Universal Communications, Los Angeles, CA '83 (PR)
KLEEB, TERESA E., RN, dir. nrsg. serv., Bryan Memorial Hospital, Lincoln, NE '86 (AMB)
KLEEBERG, KLAUS G., dir. food serv., St. Francis Memorial Hospital, San Francisco, CA '80 (FOOD)
KLEGERMAN, DOROTHY, dir. pers., St. Francis Hospital, Evanston, IL '85 (PERS)
KLEGON, DOUGLAS A., assoc. adm. plng. and mktg., Henry Ford Hospital, Detroit, MI '82 (PLNG)
KLEIN, ALICIA D., mgt. eng., Harris Methodist -Fort Worth, Fort Worth, TX '83 (MGMT)
KLEIN, AUDREY R., Duarte, CA '76 (FOOD)
KLEIN, SR. BLANCHE, pat. rep., St. Francis Medical Center, La Crosse, WI '87 (PAT)
KLEIN, BURTON R., health care and fire protection eng., National Fire Protection Association, Quincy, MA '76 (ENG)
KLEIN, DANIEL L., atty., All Saints Episcopal Hospital, Fort Worth, TX '86 (ATTY)
KLEIN, DAVID H., sr. vice-pres., Blue Cross and Blue Shield of the Rochester Area, Rochester, NY '72 (PLNG)
KLEIN, DONNA G., atty., Tulane University Hospital and Clinics, New Orleans, LA '84 (ATTY)
KLEIN, ELEANOR, (ret.), Costa Mesa, CA '74 (SOC)
KLEIN, GENE, mgr. pur., Providence Medical Center, Portland, OR '86 (PUR)
KLEIN, GEOFFREY L., adm. res., North Shore Children's Hospital, Salem, MA '77
KLEIN, GERALD H., asst. adm. and dir. fiscal serv., St. Joseph Riverside Hospital, Warren, OH '82 (PLNG)
KLEIN, HANNE K., assoc. dir. pub. affairs, Granville C. Morton Hospital, Wadley Research Institute, Dallas, TX '85 (PR)
KLEIN, JOEL I., atty., Psychiatric Institute of Washington, Washington, DC '83 (ATTY)
KLEIN, JOHN NICHOLAS III, atty., Northampton-Accomack Memorial Hospital, Nassawadox, VA '86 (ATTY)
KLEIN, KAREN, asst. coor. cent. serv., St. Luke's Hospital, Kansas City, MO '86 (CS)
KLEIN, MARIAN B., RN, dir. nrsg., Providence Hospital, Washington, DC '86 (NURS)
KLEIN, MARILYN, dir. vol. serv., Flushing Hospital and Medical Center, Flushing, NY '82 (VOL)
KLEIN, MARTIN S., dir., Harvard Community Health Plan, Cambridge, MA '80 (PLNG)
KLEIN, MARVIN B., pres., Michael Reese Hospital and Medical Center, Chicago, IL '58
KLEIN, MARY, dir. family serv., Shriners Hospital for Crippled Children, Tampa, FL '84 (SOC)
KLEIN, MARY, RN, coor. staff dev., Lower Bucks Hospital, Bristol, PA '84 (EDUC)
KLEIN, MURRAY J., atty., Holy Name Hospital, Teaneck, NJ '81 (ATTY)
KLEIN, NANCY R., mgr. mktg., Good Samaritan Hospital, Cincinnati, OH '86 (PR)
KLEIN, RICHARD D., dir. div. membership, American College of Hospital Administrators, Chicago, IL '75
KLEIN, ROBERT A., atty., United Hospital Association, Los Angeles, CA '77 (ATTY)
KLEIN, ROBERT N., adm. res., Baptist Medical Center-Montclair, Birmingham, AL '86
KLEIN, ROLAND C., exec. dir. plant oper. and maint., Fairview Community Hospitals, Minneapolis, MN '75 (ENG)
KLEIN, SANDRA J., dir. soc. work, Presbyterian Intercommunity Hospital, Whittier, CA '85 (SOC)
KLEIN, SELMA S., dir. soc. serv., Memorial Hospital of Laramie County, Cheyenne, WY '73 (SOC)
KLEIN, STEVE A., asst. adm. med. logistics, U. S. Air Force Hospital, Wichita, KS '81
KLEIN, STEVEN M., vice-pres. prof. and med. affairs, Riverview Medical Center, Red Bank, NJ '74 (PLNG)

KLEIN, STUART L., dir. spec. proj., Graduate Hospital, Philadelphia, PA '83
KLEIN, SUSAN, dir. qual. and risk mgt., Mercy Medical Center, Coon Rapids, MN '85 (RISK)
KLEIN, TIM, chief eng., Tri-State Memorial Hospital, Clarkston, WA '85 (ENG)
KLEIN, WALTER F., dir. educ. and trng., Barnes Hospital, St. Louis, MO '74 (EDUC)
KLEIN, WILLIAM K., MD, consult., Punta Gorda, FL '42 (RISK)(LIFE)
KLEINBAUER, ROBERT C., adm. rad., St. Joseph's Medical Center, Yonkers, NY '79 (MGMT)
KLEINBERG, SUSAN B., PhD, dir. plng. and prog. dev., Mount Washington Pediatric Hospital, Baltimore, MD '86 (PLNG)
KLEINBERG, WARREN M., MD, dir. ped. amb. serv., Family Health Plan, Toledo, OH '87 (AMB)
KLEINER, GIL, dir. commun. rel., Union Memorial Hospital, Baltimore, MD '83 (PR)
KLEINERT, EDWARD L., tech. recruiter, Memorial Hospital for Cancer and Allied Dieseases, New York, NY '83 (PERS)
KLEINHOFFER, D. J., chief eng., St. Joseph Medical Center, Joliet, IL '79 (ENG)
KLEINMANN, AARON JOSEPH, pres., Atede, Inc., Peekskill, NY '85
KLEINPETER, THERESA, RN, dir. nrsg., San Diego Physicians and Surgical Hospital, San Diego, CA '85 (NURS)
KLEINSCHMIDT, JERRI, dir. soc. serv., Potomac Hospital, Woodbridge, VA '85 (SOC)
KLEINSORGE, KRISTINE E., soc. worker, West Shore Hospital, Manistee, MI '82 (SOC)
KLEINSORGE, SUSAN J., asst. commun. rel., Audrain Medical Center, Mexico, MO '82 (PR)
KLEITER, THEODORE E., exec. vice-pres. and adm. outreach serv., Palomar Pomerado Hospital District, Escondido, CA '87 (AMB)
KLEMAN, VIRGINIA A., dir. commun., Frick Community Health Center, Mount Pleasant, PA '81 (PR)
KLEMES, SUSAN J., dir. pub. rel., Maryvale Samaritan Hospital, Phoenix, AZ '86 (PR)
KLEMESRUD, NORMAND, atty., Floyd County Memorial Hospital, Charles City, IA '78 (ATTY)
KLEMZ, RONALD A., mgr. acquisition and dev., Health Central System, Minneapolis, MN '80 (PLNG)
KLENE, DONALD A., atty., St. Anthony Hospital Systems, Denver, CO '73 (ATTY)
KLENWOSKI, JOHN R., assoc. exec. dir., Community Mental Health Services, St. Clairsville, OH '85 (SOC)
KLEREKOPER, WILLIAM P., adm., Saginaw Medical Center, Saginaw, MI '80
KLERX, ROBERT P., dir. oper. and soc. work serv., Hahnemann University Hospital, Philadelphia, PA '85 (SOC)
KLETZIEN, RALPH WILLIAM, exec. vice-pres. and chief exec. off., Memorial Hospital, South Bend, IN '67
KLEVGARD, CHARLES N., dir. med. soc. work, Annapolis Hospital, Wayne, MI '85 (SOC)
KLEVIT, SARAH, atty., Group Health Cooperative of Puget Sound, Seattle, WA '86 (ATTY)
KLIAGUINE, ALLA NICHOLAS, Kaiser Permanente Medical Care Program, Honolulu, HI '71 (PR)
KLICK, PEARL A., RN, (ret.), Center for Living, Fort Lauderdale, FL '30 (LIFE)
KLICK, STEPHEN R., pres., Dairyland Computer and Consulting Company, Sauk Centre, MN '85
KLIMA, DENNIS E., pres., Kent General Hospital, Dover, DE '67
KLIMA, SANDRA M., RN, coor. pat. educ., Kent General Hospital, Dover, DE '85 (EDUC)
KLIMAN, CATHERINE, dir. soc. serv., Columbia Hospital, Milwaukee, WI '73 (SOC)
KLIMKOWSKY, RITA, RN, dir. nrsg. and pat. care, Morristown Memorial Hospital, Morristown, NJ '83 (NURS)(AMB)
KLIMON, ELLEN L., dir. risk mgt., University of Pennsylvania, Philadelphia, PA '83 (RISK)
KLINC, MARY ELLEN, dir. nutr. serv., East Liverpool City Hospital, East Liverpool, OH '86 (FOOD)
KLINE, DANIEL B., coor. plng. and mktg., University Hospital-University of Nebraska, Omaha, NE '86 (PLNG)
KLINE, KAREN, coor. staff dev.-nrsg., Kaweah Delta District Hospital, Visalia, CA '82 (EDUC)
KLINE, MICHAEL J., atty., Deborah Heart and Lung Center, Browns Mills, NJ '84 (ATTY)
KLINE, RICHARD M., asst. dir. eng., Sparks Regional Medical Center, Fort Smith, AR '82 (ENG)
KLINE, SABRA L., dir. educ., Visiting Nurses Association of Greater Kansas City, Kansas City, MO '84 (EDUC)
KLING, DAVID M., Sea Service Company, Brooklyn, NY '79 (PUR)
KLING, FREDERICK A., asst. vice-pres., Hackensack Medical Center, Hackensack, NJ '73 (ENG)
KLING, JAMES D., vice-pres., Deeter, Ritchey and Sippel Associates, Pittsburgh, PA '82
KLINGBEIL, KARIL S., asst. adm. and dir. soc. work, Harborview Medical Center, Seattle, WA '75 (SOC)
KLINGELSMITH, WAYNE D., dir. plant oper., Lee Memorial Hospital, Fort Myers, FL '78 (ENG)
KLINGENSMITH, JUDITH D., RN, asst. adm., Shadyside Hospital, Pittsburgh, PA '82 (NURS)
KLINGMAN, ROBERT, clin. adm., Pasadena Dispensary, Pasadena, CA '87 (AMB)
KLINGMANN, ESTHER C., RN, (ret.), Watertown, WI '32 (LIFE)
KLINK, MARGARET A., dir. food and nutr. serv., Good Samaritan Medical Center, Milwaukee, WI '74 (FOOD)
KLINKENBERG, JULIA, diet., Central Michigan Community Hospital, Mount Pleasant, MI '78 (FOOD)
KLINKHAMMER, N. M., dir. facil. serv., Providence Medical Center, Portland, OR '72 (ENG)
KLISE, R. JACK, dir. mgt. consult. serv., Chicago Hospital Council, Chicago, IL '71 (MGMT)
KLISIEWICZ, VIRGINIA A., dir. health educ., Youville Rehabilitation-Chronic Diseases Hospital, Cambridge, MA '80 (EDUC)
KLOBASSA, DONALD J., dir. human res., Franciscan Sisters Health Care, Little Falls, MN '86 (PERS)
KLOEPFEL, ELAINE A., RN, vice-pres. nrsg., Waukesha Memorial Hospital, Waukesha, WI '79 (NURS)
KLOEPPING, JANET A., supv. cent. serv., Freeport Memorial Hospital, Freeport, IL '82 (CS)
KLOOSTERHUIS, DAVID J., asst. mgr., Kettering Medical Center, Kettering, OH '84
KLOPPENBURG, KAREN, mgr. oper. and emer. room, Northern Montana Hospital, Havre, MT '87 (AMB)
KLOTHEN, KENNETH L., atty., Mercy Catholic Medical Center, Philadelphia, PA '84 (ATTY)
KLOTZ, CHRISTINE R., dir. mktg., National Jewish Center, Denver, CO '84 (PLNG)
KLOVER, JON A., asst. prof., St. Louis University, St. Louis, MO '61
KLUCKMAN, STACY J., dir. pub. rel., Scripps Memorial Hospital-Chula Vista, Chula Vista, CA '85 (PR)
KLUG, MARTHA L., RN, dir. nrsg., Memorial Hospital at Oconomowoc, Oconomowoc, WI '86 (NURS)
KLUG, MARTI, RN, dir. nrsg., Memorial Hospital at Oconomowoc, Oconomowoc, WI '87 (AMB)
KLUG, MARY C., dir. food serv., Wheeling Hospital, Wheeling, WV '83 (FOOD)
KLUG, YVONNE, dir. diet., Washington Hospital, Washington, PA '83 (FOOD)
KLUGE, THOMAS SCOTT, student, Medical College of Virginia, Virginia Commonwealth University, Department of Health Administration, Richmond, VA '84
KLUGE, YVONNE, dir. res. serv., Royal Oaks Lifecare Center, Sun City, AZ '85 (VOL)
KLUMPP, THEODORE G., MD, (ret.), Charlottesville, VA '56 (HON)
KLUSMANN, RICHARD W., adm., HCA East Pointe Hospital, Lehigh Acres, FL '84 (PLNG)
KMAK, LEONARD P., dir. soc. serv., St. James Hospital Medical Center, Chicago Heights, IL '72 (SOC)
KMETZ, FRANK D., mgr. matl., East Cooper Community Hospital, Mount Pleasant, SC '82 (PUR)
KMETZ, THOMAS D., student, University of Kentucky, Lexington, KY '84
KMETZO, KAREN A., mgr. med. serv., Blue Cross and Blue Shield of Ct, North Haven, CT '86
KNAB, DAVID K., dir. matl. mgt., Portsmouth Psychiatric Center, Portsmouth, VA '86 (PUR)
KNAB, LINDA A., dir. pub. rel. and pers., Lakeside Memorial Hospital, Brockport, NY '82 (PR)(PERS)
KNAPP, BRIAN ALLEN, asst. adm., Fairview Riverside Hospital, Minneapolis, MN '78
KNAPP, DENNIS C., mgr. matl., AMI Memorial Hospital of Tampa, Tampa, FL '74 (PUR)
KNAPP, ELLEN G., dir. soc. serv., North Adams Regional Hospital, North Adams, MA '76 (SOC)
KNAPP, JOHN A., atty., Bryn Mawr Hospital, Bryn Mawr, PA '85 (ATTY)
KNAPP, LAURA S., dir. food serv., New Hanover Memorial Hospital, Wilmington, NC '81 (FOOD)
KNAPP, MARY M., med. buyer, Universiyt of Rochester Purchasing Service, Rochester, NY '82 (PUR)
KNAPP, NANCY J., RN, asst. dir. nrsg., St. Nicholas Hospital, Sheboygan, WI '85 (NURS)
KNAPP, RICHARD M., dir. teaching, Association of American Medical Colleges, Washington, DC '64
KNAPP, SPENCER R., atty., Medical Center Hospital of Vermont, Burlington, VT '84 (ATTY)
KNAPP, SUSAN GINGRICH, coor. educ., Lehigh Valley Hospital Center, Allentown, PA '78 (EDUC)
KNAPTON, JOAN K., dir. commun. rel. and vol. serv., Beloit Memorial Hospital, Beloit, WI '87 (VOL)
KNARR, MARY L., RN, instr. staff educ., Good Samaritan Hospital, Cincinnati, OH '81 (EDUC)
KNATZ, JAMES C., dir. matl. mgt., St. Clare Hospital of Monroe, Monroe, WI '76 (PUR)
KNAUSS, ALBERT C., pres. and chief exec. off., Altoona Hospital, Altoona, PA '75 (PLNG)
KNAUTH, DAVID, chm. risk mgt. and vice-pres. human res., St. James Community Hospital, Butte, MT '86 (RISK)
KNECHT, BRIAN J., mgr. mgt. eng., San Jose Hospital, San Jose, CA '81 (MGMT)
KNECHT, COLETTA A., dir. diet., St. John Hospital, Cleveland, OH '79 (FOOD)
KNECHT, FRANK A. JR., dir. bldg. and grds. serv., Good Samaritan Hospital, Baltimore, MD '71 (ENG)
KNECHT, MICHAEL E., student, Temple University, Department of Health Administration, Philadelphia, PA '86
KNECHT, WAYNE, dir. fin., Ingleside Hospital, Rosemead, CA '86 (RISK)
KNECHTGES, PAUL T., dir. maint., Protestant Episcopal Church Home, Rochester, NY '83 (ENG)
KNEELAND, MARY B., RN, dir. nrsg. and family health care, Waltham Weston Hospital and Medical Center, Waltham, MA '86 (NURS)
KNEEN, JAMES R., dir. mental health serv., Parkview Memorial Hospital, Fort Wayne, IN '80
KNEEN, RUSSELL P., chief exec. off. and chm., Bronson Healthcare Group, Inc., Kalamazoo, MI '84
KNEPLEY, GREGG G., sr. vice-pres. mktg., dev. and plng., Saint Luke's Hospital, Cleveland, OH '85 (PLNG)
KNEPP, GERALD E., adm., Redding Medical Center, Redding, CA '80
KNERR, DOROTHY R., (ret.), Hot Springs, AR '64
KNEWITZ, ANN L., dir. matl. mgt., Marion Memorial Hospital, Marion, IL '82 (PUR)
KNEZOVICH, JOHN, asst. contr., McKeesport Hospital, McKeesport, PA '82 (MGMT)
KNICK, SHARON E., coor. membership serv., Blue Cross and Blue Shield Health Maintenance Plan, Dayton, OH '84 (PAT)
KNICKERBOCKER, G. GUY, chief scientist, Emergency Care Research Institute, Plymouth Meeting, PA '73 (ENG)
KNICKERBOCKER, MAX EUGENE, adm., Rouse-Warren County Home, Youngsville, PA '55 (LIFE)
KNICKERBOCKER, WILLIAM W., dir. soc. serv., St. Francis Regional Medical Center, Wichita, KS '72 (SOC)
KNIGHT, ALAN D., pres., St. Anne's Hospital, Fall River, MA '72 (MGMT)
KNIGHT, BARBARA J., adm. asst. and coor. vol. serv., St. John's Hospital, Salina, KS '83 (VOL)
KNIGHT, BERNARD J. JR., atty., Alexian Brothers Medical Center, Elk Grove Village, IL '85 (ATTY)
KNIGHT, CATHERINE A., cardio-pulmonary resuscitation prog. coor., Geisinger Medical Center, Danville, PA '86 (EDUC)
KNIGHT, DAN, proj. mgr., Hord, Coplan, Macht Architects, Baltimore, MD '86 (ENG)
KNIGHT, ED, dir. soc. work serv., Hendrick Medical Center, Abilene, TX '83 (SOC)
KNIGHT, ELSIE M., asst. supv. food serv., Massac Memorial Hospital, Metropolis, IL '85 (FOOD)
KNIGHT, JACK L., pres., Roundtable Associates, Tucson, AZ '70
KNIGHT, JAMES C., dir. oper. analyst, Washington Health Care Corporation, Washington, DC '82 (MGMT)
KNIGHT, JOAN T., adm. dir. soc. work, Orlando Regional Medical Center, Orlando, FL '79 (SOC)
KNIGHT, JOHN E., dir., Lake Shore Hospital, Lake City, FL '64 (PERS)
KNIGHT, KENNETH E., mgr. plant and facil., Bethesda Oak Hospital, Cincinnati, OH '78 (ENG)
KNIGHT, MARIAN, vice-pres. pub. rel., Children's Hospital Medical Center, Cincinnati, OH '84 (PR)
KNIGHT, MARIE RAY, RN, asst. adm., Oakwood Hospital, Dearborn, MI '82 (NURS)
KNIGHT, NELLIE, mgr. sup., proc. and distrib., University Hospital, Boston, MA '86 (CS)
KNIGHT, CDR PAUL L., MSC USN, cmdr. med. serv. corps., Bureau of Medicine and Surgery, Washington, DC '79
KNIGHT, RICHARD H. JR., atty., Hospital Corporation of America, Nashville, TN '83 (ATTY)
KNIGHT, RUSSELL M., asst. dir., Latrobe Area Hospital, Latrobe, PA '76
KNIGHT, SIDNEY S., risk mgr., City of Faith Hospital, Tulsa, OK '81 (RISK)
KNIGHT, SUSANNE SMITH, dir. soc. serv., Doctors Hospital of Jefferson, Metairie, LA '81 (SOC)
KNIGHTON, JOAN M., RN, assoc. dir. nrsg., Staten Island Hospital, Staten Island, NY '85 (NURS)
KNIPE, WILMA B., supv. commun., Blessing Hospital, Quincy, IL '76 (ENG)
KNIPP, BERNADINA, asst. exec. dir.-plng., Visting Nurse Association of Greater Kansas City, Kansas City, MO '81 (PLNG)
KNISELY, LINNAEA K. S., asst. to vice-pres., St. Joseph Hospital, Baltimore, MD '83 (PLNG)
KNISELY, MERTON E., (ret.), Milwaukee, WI '43 (LIFE)
KNOBLE, JAMES K., pres., Methodist Medical Center of Illinois, Peoria, IL '64
KNOBLE, SANDRA M., dir. plng., Lewistown Hospital, Lewistown, PA '80 (PLNG)
KNOBLOCH, JEAN R., RN, staff instr., St. Clement Hospital, Red Bud, IL '86 (EDUC)
KNOCHEL, THERESA M., dir. soc. serv., Palomar Pomerado Hospital District, Poway, CA '86 (SOC)
KNOEBER, VINCENT J., dir. risk mgt. and security, Saint Joseph Hospital, Denver, CO '76 (RISK)
KNOEPP, MEL P., sr. vice-pres. mktg., Palomar Pomerado Hospital District, Escondido, CA '85 (PR)
KNOESEL, SANDRA L., dir. plng., mktg. and dev., Licking Memorial Hospital, Newark, OH '82 (PR)
KNOL, LOIS E., coor. in-service, St. Luke's Methodist Hospital, Cedar Rapids, IA '79 (EDUC)
KNOLL, F. HOWARD JR., asst. vice-pres. eng., Rose Medical Center, Denver, CO '82 (ENG)
KNOPE, LOIS A., vice-pres. nrsg. serv., St. Michael's Hospital, Stevens Point, WI '85 (NURS)
KNOPP, JAMES F., pres., Westview Hospital, Indianapolis, IN '67 (MGMT)
KNORR, RONALD J., asst. dir. maint., Wilkes-Barre General Hospital, Wilkes-Barre, PA '85 (ENG)
KNOTT, FRED, dir. cent. serv., Butterworth Hospital, Grand Rapids, MI '85 (CS)
KNOTT, FREELOVE SHERRILL, dir. cent. serv., Maryland General Hospital, Baltimore, MD '73 (CS)
KNOUSE, SANDRA J., dir. educ., Wilkes-Barre General Hospital, Wilkes-Barre, PA '77 (EDUC)
KNOWLAND, SHIRLEY C., RN, vice-pres. nrsg., Newton-Wellesley Hospital, Newton, MA '84 (NURS)
KNOWLES, DELLA, coor. vol., University of California Davis Medical Center, Sacramento, CA '80 (VOL)
KNOWLES, EDWIN WILKS JR., exec. vice-pres., Hamilton-Ksa, Fairfax, VA '76 (PLNG)
KNOWLES, STEPHEN L., atty., St. Mary's Hospital, Milwaukee, WI '82 (ATTY)
KNOWLTON, GRANT W., dir. mktg., Charter Springs Hospital, Ocala, FL '79 (PR)
KNOWLTON, JOHN C. JR., asst. adm. human res., Athens Regional Medical Center, Athens, GA '84 (PERS)
KNOWLTON, WILLIAM A., atty., New England Medical Center, Boston, MA '84 (ATTY)
KNOX, AARON R., pur. mgr., Winter Park Memorial Hospital, Winter Park, FL '84 (PUR)
KNOX, JOHN M., dir. pub. rel., St. Mary's Hospital and Medical Center, San Francisco, CA '83 (PR)
KNOX, MARY LOU, mgr. pers., Union Hospital of Cecil County, Elkton, MD '81 (PERS)
KNOX, PHILLIP MCLAUGHLIN, dir. matl. mgt., St. Elizabeth Hospital, Beaumont, TX '74 (PUR)
KNOX, PHYLLIS A., dir. in-service, Muscatine General Hospital, Muscatine, IA '78 (EDUC)
KNOX, STUART W., (ret.), West Dennis, MA '48 (LIFE)

KNOX, THOMAS A., vice-pres. plng. and mktg., Health Central System, Minneapolis, MN '75 (PLNG)
KNOX, WYCK A. JR., atty., University Hospital, Augusta, GA '77 (ATTY)
KNUDSEN, HELEN L., MD, (ret.), Minneapolis, MN '63 (HON)
KNUDSEN, LES, vice-pres. human res., Methodist Hospital of Southern California, Arcadia, CA '86 (PERS)
KNUDSEN, ROBERT N., mgr. emp. rel., Voluntary Hospitals of America, Irving, TX '87 (PERS)
KNUDSON, ALVIN B. C., MD, asst. dir. health, Fairfax County Department of Health, Falls Church, VA '48 (LIFE)
KNUERR, JOHN, asst. dir. org. dev., Sisters of Mercy Health Corporation, Farmington Hills, MI '80 (EDUC)
KNUPP, HAROLD E., dir. plant oper., St. Rita's Medical Center, Lima, OH '79 (ENG)
KNUTH, KERRY L., mgr. oper., Defiance Clinic, Defiance, OH '87 (AMB)
KNUTSON, LEROY, dir. matl. mgt., United Hospital, Grand Forks, ND '72 (PUR)
KNUTSON, STEVEN J., adm. intern, Bethesda Lutheran Medical Center, St. Paul, MN '83
KNUTSON, VERNON A., dir. facil. and plng., Fairview Hospital and Healthcare Service, Minneapolis, MN '56 (ENG)(LIFE)
KNUTZEN, BARBARA, dir. surg., St. Agnes Hospital, Fond Du Lac, WI '87 (AMB)
KO, VINCENT, MD, vice-pres., Methodist Hospitals of Gary, Gary, IN '87
KOBAYASHI, GENICHI, MD, Elgin, IL '53 (LIFE)
KOBER, THOMAS E., asst. dean, Cincinnati Technical College, Cincinnati, OH '86 (EDUC)
KOBES, DAVID, chief fin. off., Health Plus, Bethesda, MD '80
KOBLENZ, STUART, MD, assoc. exec. dir., City Hospital Center at Elmhurst, Flushing, NY '66
KOBRITZ, BRUCE, pres., Strategic Healthcare Planning Associates, Santa Monica, CA '80 (PLNG)
KOBS, ANN E. J., RN, dir. nrsg., surg. and maternal child, Alexian Brothers Medical Center, Elk Grove Village, IL '81 (NURS)
KOCH, ANN F., RN, dir. nrsg. syst., St. Joseph Hospitals, Mount Clemens, MI '86 (NURS)
KOCH, BARBARA, dir. mktg. and plng., Humana Hospital -Suburban, Louisville, KY '85 (PLNG)
KOCH, CAROLYN, dir., Maplewood Surgery Center, Maplewood, MN '87 (AMB)
KOCH, EDWARD L., dir. pub. rel., St. Mary's Medical Center, Duluth, MN '87 (PR)
KOCH, FRANKLIN J., dir. commun. rel., Taylor Hospital, Ridley Park, PA '83 (PR)
KOCH, KAREN M., dir. pub. rel., HCA West Paces Ferry Hospital, Atlanta, GA '84 (PR)
KOCH, KAREN, dir. pub. rel., Barberton Citizens Hospital, Barberton, OH '86 (PR)
KOCH, MARJORIE M., supv. cent. serv., Moline Public Hospital, Moline, IL '81 (CS)
KOCH, MARY ELLEN, adm. asst., Mother Frances Hospital Regional Center, Tyler, TX '79 (PLNG)
KOCH, ROBERT J., asst. dir. phys. plant and facil., Parma Community General Hospital, Parma, OH '81 (ENG)
KOCH, W. JOHN, dir. soc. serv., Royal Alexandra Hospital, Edmonton, Alta., Canada '77 (SOC)
KOCHANOWSKI, MARK M., asst. dir. human res., McLean Hospital, Belmont, MA '75 (PERS)
KOCHAVI, PHYLLIS, dir. vol. serv., Northridge Hospital Medical Center, Northridge, CA '80 (VOL)
KOCHLIN, MARK W., chief eng., Queen of Peace Hospital, New Prague, MN '68 (ENG)
KOCI, HELEN, dir. soc. serv., Everett A. Gladman Memorial Hospital, Oakland, CA '77 (SOC)
KODA, CHET, mgr. info. syst., Providence Hospital, Anchorage, AK '81 (MGMT)
KODES, FRED V., dir. food serv., Mercy Hospital, Urbana, IL '69 (FOOD)
KODMAN, FRANK, assoc. exec. dir. fin. and facil. dev., Lorain Community Hospital, Lorain, OH '81 (PLNG)
KODWEIS, WILLIAM F., chief eng., Kentfield Medical Hospital, Kentfield, CA '87 (ENG)
KOEBENSKY, JOSEPH S., dir. gen. serv., Virginia Regional Medical Center, Virginia, MN '82 (PUR)
KOECH, GARY S., supv. eng., Victoria Hospital, Miami, FL '86 (ENG)
KOECHEL, PAUL C., dir. commun. and pub. affairs, South Hills Health System, Pittsburgh, PA '85 (PR)
KOEFFLER, DEBORAH P., atty., Cedars-Sinai Medical Center, Los Angeles, CA '83 (ATTY)
KOEHLER, CHRISTINE, gen. counsel, Johns Hopkins Hospital, Baltimore, MD '86 (RISK)
KOEHLER, GERALD D., mgr. phys. plant, Fort Logan Mental Health Center, Denver, CO '83 (ENG)
KOEHLER, HAROLD A., actg. dir. plant oper. and maint., Shadyside Hospital, Pittsburgh, PA '81 (ENG)
KOEHLER, ROBERT, dir. hskpg., St. Joseph's Hospital, Chippewa Falls, WI '86 (ENVIRON)
KOEHN, SANDRA M., dir. human res., Timken Mercy Medical Center, Canton, OH '82 (PERS)
KOEHN, SUSAN B., atty., Montefiore Medical Center, Bronx, NY '81 (ATTY)
KOELBL, THOMAS R., dir. emp. rel., Riverside Medical Center, Kankakee, IL '83 (PERS)
KOENIG, ANNA, RN, dir., St. Vincent's Medical Center, Jacksonville, FL '87 (AMB)
KOENIG, DAVID SCOTT, adm. fellow, Memorial Hospital System, Houston, TX '86
KOENIG, EUGENE A., asst. to dir. constr. and phys. facil., Sisters of St. Mary, St. Louis, MO '75 (ENG)
KOENIG, EVELYN J., dir. soc. serv., Ingham Medical Center, Lansing, MI '73 (SOC)
KOENIG, KRISTINE A., dir. pers. serv., Kaiser Foundation Hospital, Redwood City, CA '84 (PERS)
KOENIG, LYNN R., RN, asst. adm. pat. care serv., General Hospital of Everett, Everett, WA '80 (NURS)
KOENIG, MARK W., dir. plng., Iowa Lutheran Hospital, Des Moines, IA '75 (PLNG)
KOENIG, MARVELLA G., soc. worker, Wesley Long Community Hospital, Greensboro, NC '76 (SOC)
KOENIG, STEVEN B., gen. mgr., DeLand Medical Foundation, De Land, FL '86
KOENIGSHOFER, DAN, pres., Integrated Energy Systems, Inc., Chapel Hill, NC '85 (ENG)
KOEPKE, GERALD D., dir. pur., Incarnate Word Hospital, St. Louis, MO '74 (PUR)
KOERNER, JOELLEN, RN, vice-pres. pat. serv., Sioux Valley Hospital, Sioux Falls, SD '84 (NURS)
KOERNER, JOSEPH A., pres., Koerner Associates Market Research and Planning, St. Louis, MO '85 (PLNG)
KOESER, LELAND WILLIAM, dir. fiscal facil., Bronson Methodist Hospital, Kalamazoo, MI '64 (ENG)
KOFF, THEODORE H., EdD, dir., Long Term Care Gerontology Center, University of Arizona, Tucson, AZ '74
KOFFSKY, ROBERT M., sr. bio-eng., Mount Sinai Medical Center, New York, NY '84 (MGMT)
KOFL, ANDREA S., RN, dir. surg. nrsg., Riverside Community Hospital, Riverside, CA '85 (NURS)
KOFORD, JONE LAW, pres., St. Benedict's Enterprises Corporation, Ogden, UT '80 (PLNG)
KOGEL, MARCUS D., MD, dean emeritus, Hospital of the Albert Einstein College of Medicine, Bronx, NY '34 (LIFE)
KOGER, PENNY L., RN, vice-pres. nrsg. serv., Henry County Memorial Hospital, New Castle, IN '85 (NURS)
KOHAN, SONIA M., adm. res., Association of American Medical Colleges, Washington, DC '85
KOHL, MICHELE L., RN, chief nrsg., U. S. Ireland Army Community Hospital, Fort Knox, KY '85 (NURS)
KOHLBRENNER, JANIS C., RN, asst. dir. nrsg., St. Joseph's Hospital Health Center, Syracuse, NY '86 (NURS)
KOHLENBERG, SHARON H., adm. res., Medical College of Virginia Hospitals, Richmond, VA '85
KOHLER, ANTONE, consult., Corte Madera, CA '71
KOHLER, DONALD J., dir. oper. and maint., Hospital of the University of Pennsylvania, Philadelphia, PA '64 (ENG)
KOHLER, SWANN, dir. commun. and pub. info., St. Vincent Infirmary, Little Rock, AR '73 (PR)
KOHLERT, STEVEN D., sr. vice-pres., Intermountain Health Care, Inc., Salt Lake City, UT '76 (PLNG)
KOHLMAN, HERMAN A., pres., Memorial Hospital and Health Care Center, Jasper, IN '64
KOHLMEIR, MARGARET T., dir. nrsg., Hospital of the Medical College of Pennsylvania, Philadelphia, PA '87 (AMB)
KOHLRUSS, CHARLES D., dir. pers., Bon Secours Hospital, Grosse Pointe, MI '76 (PERS)
KOHN, GREGORY F., mgr. elec. eng., Falick-Klein Partnership, Inc., Houston, TX '83 (ENG)
KOHN, LINDA T., vice-pres. plng. and dev. serv., Samaritan Health Center, Detroit, MI '80 (PLNG)
KOHN, RON, dir. plant mgt., Straub Clinic and Hospital, Honolulu, HI '85 (ENG)
KOHNEN, DAVID A., atty., Christ Hospital, Cincinnati, OH '80 (ATTY)
KOHNKE, MARY ANN, RN, dir. risk mgt. and qual. assur., St. Patrick Hospital, Lake Charles, LA '81 (RISK)
KOHORST, JANICE R., mgt. eng., Good Samaritan Hospital, Cincinnati, OH '85 (MGMT)
KOHOUT, RANDOLPH J., supv. biomedical, Good Shepherd Hospital, Barrington, IL '86 (ENG)
KOKJOHN, FRANK T., plant eng., Fort Madison Community Hospital, Fort Madison, IA '77 (ENG)
KOKKO, WESLEY E., adm. human res., Henry Ford Hospital, Detroit, MI '76 (PERS)
KOLANDA, SYLVIA K., RN, matl. mgt. liaison and expeditor, Naples Community Hospital, Naples, FL '80 (CS)
KOLAR, PATRICIA S., dir. soc. serv., Braddock General Hospital, Braddock, PA '82 (SOC)
KOLASKY, DAVID JOEL, exec. dir., Medical College of Ohio Hospital, Toledo, OH '68
KOLB, DAVID E., pres. and chief exec. off., Healthfirst Network, Inc., Oak Brook, IL '79 (PLNG)
KOLB, DEBORAH S., vice-pres., Jennings, Ryan, Federa and Company, Atlanta, GA '85 (PLNG)
KOLB, DIANE H., pres., Kolb and Associates, Inc., Louisville, KY '85 (PLNG)
KOLB, JACOB S., atty., Muhlenberg Hospital Center, Bethlehem, PA '68 (ATTY)
KOLB, MARGUERITE D., dir. cent. serv., Burnham Hospital, Champaign, IL '83 (CS)
KOLB, NANCY A., RN, vice-pres. pat. care serv., Shelby Memorial Hospital, Shelby, OH '81 (NURS)
KOLBE, HENRY W., MD, supt., Southwood Community Hospital, Norfolk, MA '39 (LIFE)
KOLBE, MAYOLA C., dir. mktg., Morris Hospital, Morris, IL '83 (PERS)
KOLBERG, GARY, exec. hskpr., Kaiser Foundation Hospital, Richmond, CA '86 (ENVIRON)
KOLDAN, GREGORY M., dir. pers., St. John's Home, Rochester, NY '71 (PERS)
KOLDE, SANDRA L., vice-pres. shared serv., Hospital Association Shared Services, Inc., St. Louis, MO '86 (PUR)
KOLEDO, NICOLA S., mgt. eng. consult., AMI Presbyterian-St. Luke's Medical Center, Denver, CO '84 (MGMT)
KOLESAR, ANNE E., risk mgr., Long Island Jewish Medical Center, New York, NY '82 (RISK)
KOLESAR, DAVID M., pres., Kolesar and Hartwell, Minneapolis, MN '87 (PLNG)
KOLK, SUSAN D., dir. qual. assur., Highland Park Hospital, Highland Park, IL '81 (RISK)
KOLLAR, JEANNETTE T., dir. pers., Franklin Regional Hospital, Franklin, NH '80 (PERS)
KOLLATH, JOHN R., mgr. matl., Union Hospital, Dover, OH '85 (PUR)
KOLLEDA, RICHARD E., Jacksonville, FL '82
KOLLER, GEORGE, exec. vice-pres., St. John's Hospital, Lowell, MA '87
KOLLER, JANET N., dir. food serv., Meadville City Hospital, Meadville, PA '77 (FOOD)
KOLLER, KATHLEEN J., Glendale, CA '86 (MGMT)
KOLLER, MARY C., dir. vol. serv., St. Mary's Hospital, Amsterdam, NY '80 (VOL)
KOLLER, NORMAN C., proj. mech. eng., Kling Lindquist Partnership, Inc., Philadelphia, PA '86 (ENG)
KOLLER, ROBERT M. SR., vice-pres. support serv., Robert Wood Johnson University Hospital, New Brunswick, NJ '78 (ENG)
KOLLMAN, SCOTT D., dir. info. syst. serv., Travenol Laboratories, Inc., Deerfield, IL '86 (MGMT)
KOLMAN, BRADLEY K., atty., Delta County Memorial Hospital, Delta, CO '78 (ATTY)
KOLMODIN, LINDA K., dir. commun. rel., Albion Community Hospital, Albion, MI '85 (PR)
KOLODKIN, CHARLES, dir. risk mgt., Harris Methodist Health System, Fort Worth, TX '86 (RISK)
KOLODNER, SUSAN M., dir. vol. serv., Mount Washington Pediatric Hospital, Baltimore, MD '86 (VOL)
KOLODY, JOHN T., Whitestone, NY '47 (LIFE)
KOLSETH, CAMALA S., student, St. Marys Hospital Medical Center, Madison, WI '85 (MGMT)
KOLSTAD, MARLENE M., dir. diet., Winchester Medical Center, Winchester, VA '86 (FOOD)
KOLT, GAYLE, dir. qual. assur. and risk mgt., Nyack Hospital, Nyack, NY '87 (RISK)
KOLWITZ, SUSAN E., chief med. mgt. analyst br., U. S. Air Force, Hq Sac-Sgam, Offutt AFB, NE '79
KOMAREK, ALLAN G., RN, dir. nrsg. serv., Lindsay Hospital Medical Center, Lindsay, CA '85 (NURS)
KOMINE, RAYMOND, dir. food serv., St. Mary Medical Center, Long Beach, CA '82 (FOOD)
KOMJATHY-SALYER, NANCY C., vice-pres., Memorial Hospitals Association, Modesto, CA '78 (NURS)
KOMLINE, CHERYL CHANDO, chief clin. diet., Saratoga Hospital, Saratoga Springs, NY '83 (FOOD)
KOMUREK, CHARLES, sr. vice-pres. fin., Presbyterian Homes of New York, Williamsville, NY '86 (RISK)
KONATSOTIS, NICHOLAS W., mgr. food serv., Merrill Lynch and Company, Inc., New York, NY '74 (FOOD)
KONCHAN, EDWARD J., dir. environ., Dba Medi-Care Nursing Home, Cleveland, OH '87 (ENVIRON)
KONCUR, PATTI G., supv. cent. serv., Orthopaedic Hospital, Los Angeles, CA '82 (CS)
KONDE, MARY S., dir. vol. serv., St. Francis Memorial Hospital, San Francisco, CA '85 (VOL)
KONECKO, EILEEN M., RN, supv. risk mgt., University Hospital, Newark, NJ '83 (RISK)
KONIAR, JAMES, sr. assoc., Diversified Health Resources, Chicago, IL '79 (PLNG)
KONICK, JOYCE A., dir. vol. serv., Virginia Mason Hospital, Seattle, WA '85 (VOL)
KONKEL, DAVID P., mgr. data proc., West Allis Memorial Hospital, West Allis, WI '83 (MGMT)
KONNAGAN, ROBERT D., USA, adm., U. S. Army Tropic Test Center, APO Miami, FL '64
KONOPASEK, FRED J., dir. pers., Grant Hospital of Chicago, Chicago, IL '83 (PERS)
KONOPKA, MARIANNE E., RN, adm., Western Reserve Care System, Youngstown, OH '81
KONRADE, JANICE L., dir. soc. serv., Memorial Hospital, Abilene, KS '86 (SOC)
KONSOER, TOM, mgr. matl. serv., Glenbrook Hospital, Glenview, IL '85 (PUR)
KONZAK-JONES, KIM, RN, vice-pres. pat. care, Mercy Hospital, Devils Lake, ND '85 (NURS)
KOOB, SHARON, risk mgt. spec., Chicago Hospital Risk Pooling Program, Chicago, IL '86 (RISK)
KOONTER, PAUL A., asst. dir. soc. work, Detroit Receiving Hospital and University Health Center, Detroit, MI '85 (SOC)
KOONTZ, IDALENE, dir. soc. serv. and pat. rel., Pana Community Hospital, Pana, IL '81 (SOC)
KOONTZ, JAMES L., dir. human res., Lewistown Hospital, Lewistown, PA '85 (PERS)
KOOSER, RONALD P., vice-pres., Cini and Little International, Inc., Chagrin Falls, OH '81 (FOOD)
KOOY, DONALD, dir. mgt. syst., Providence Hospital, Southfield, MI '84 (MGMT)
KOPACZEWSKI, TED J., asst. dir. eng. and maint., Holy Redeemer Hospital and Medical Center, Meadowbrook, PA '86 (ENG)
KOPCHO, MICHAEL J., serv. unit dir., Verne E. Gibbs Health Center, Poplar, MT '69
KOPEC, ANNA P., RN, supv. cent. serv. room and infection control, Nashoba Community Hospital, Ayer, MA '84 (CS)
KOPELMAN, JANICE P., dir. soc. work serv., Carlisle Hospital, Carlisle, PA '85 (SOC)
KOPER, VICKI, dir. soc. serv., Daniel Drake Memorial Hospital, Cincinnati, OH '76 (SOC)
KOPETCHNY, MATTHEW D., adm. asst. to med. dir., Polyclinic Medical Center of Harrisburg, Harrisburg, PA '73 (MGMT)
KOPETSKY, EDWARD, dir. info. syst., Sharp Healthcare, San Diego, CA '80 (MGMT)
KOPF, CHRISTINE LYNN KADLEC, oper. auditor, Alexian Brothers Health Systems Inc., Elk Grove Village, IL '83
KOPF, ROSEMARY L., sr. proj. assur. analyst, Rush-Presbyterian-St. Luke's Medical Center, Chicago, IL '83 (MGMT)
KOPICKI, JOHN R., sr. vice-pres. and chief oper. off., Muhlenberg Regional Medical Center, Plainfield, NJ '73
KOPIT, WILLIAM G., atty., Epstein, Becker, Borsody and Green, Washington, DC '80 (ATTY)
KOPMAN, ALAN, pres. and chief exec. off., Westchester Square Medical Center, Bronx, NY '71
KOPP, CHARLENE D., dir. mktg., John F. Kennedy Medical Center, Chicago, IL '86 (PR)
KOPPA, MARIE, dir. pub. rel., Jersey Shore Medical Center, Neptune, NJ '77 (PR)
KOPPEL, DARLENE M., asst. mgr. mkt, A. T. and T. Communications, Basking Ridge, NJ '86

KOPPEL, ROBERT F., adm., East Tennessee Children's Hospital, Knoxville, TN '72
KOPPELMAN, LESLI K., dir. commun. rel., Jewish Hospital of St. Louis, St. Louis, MO '85 (PR)
KOPPEN, MARK A., adm. res., Hutzel Hospital, Detroit, MI '86 (PLNG)
KOPPING, VIVIAN C., RN, supv. cent. sup. room, Sacred Heart Hospital, Yankton, SD '80 (CS)
KOPROWSKI, MICHAEL J., adm. dir. cardiology, Community Hospital, Munster, IN '87
KORAL, JACQUELINE, vice-pres. mktg., pub. affairs and dev., Park City Hospital, Bridgeport, CT '83 (PR)
KORAN, VANEESA J., asst. head food mgt., Naval Hospital, Great Lakes, IL '85 (FOOD)
KORANDA, CAROL, coor. pat. rel., Good Samaritan Hospital and Medical Center, Portland, OR '72 (PAT)
KORB, RUTH H., asst. adm., Burnham Hospital, Champaign, IL '78 (PERS)
KORBELAK, KATHLEEN, RN, vice-pres. nrsg. serv., St. John Hospital, Detroit, MI '83 (NURS)
KORDECKI, CHRISTINE S., student, Program in Health Systems, Georgia Institute of Technology School of Industrial Engineering, Atlanta, GA '86 (MGMT)
KORDUCKI, STANLEY R., asst. dir. mktg., Children's Health System, Milwaukee, WI '84 (PLNG)
KORENEK, GERE H., RN, asst. adm. nrsg. serv., Pasadena Bayshore Medical Center, Pasadena, TX '83 (NURS)
KORETSKY, JACK, consult., Brooklyn, NY '62
KORETZ, DIANE S., dir. matl. mgt., Rochester St. Mary's Hospital, Rochester, NY '84 (PUR)
KORFF, DONALD H., vice-pres., Henningson, Durham and Richardson, Omaha, NE '68
KORFF, KEN, asst. adm. serv., West Florida Regional Medical Center, Pensacola, FL '82 (PERS)
KORLESKI, DEBORAH, risk mgr., Thomas Jefferson University Hospital, Philadelphia, PA '86 (RISK)
KORN, JEFFREY W., bus. mgr., Ochsner Foundation Hospital, New Orleans, LA '86
KORN, MARY JO, asst. adm. amb. care, Illinois Masonic Medical Center, Chicago, IL '87 (AMB)
KORN, RISA, RN, coor. qual. assur., St. Joseph's Hospital and Medical Center, Phoenix, AZ '82 (RISK)
KORNAFEL, JUDITH LYNN, RN, head nrs. cent. sterilizing, Community Hospital, Munster, IN '85 (CS)
KORNASIEWICZ, JOAN H., mgr. matl., Parkview Hospital, Toledo, OH '82 (PUR)
KORNBLUM, DAVID, Laventhol and Horwath, San Francisco, CA '80
KORNEMAN, JUDITH L., RN, dir. nrs., Cass Medical Center, Harrisonville, MO '86 (NURS)
KORNREICH, EDWARD S., atty., St. Luke's-Roosevelt Hospital Center, New York, NY '85 (ATTY)
KORORUDA, THOMAS G., atty., Research Medical Center, Kansas City, MO '82 (ATTY)
KOROTKIN, BRUCE M., commun. bus. off., West Seneca Developmental Center, West Seneca, NY '73
KORSAK, ANDREW J., risk mgt. serv. consult., The Wyatt Company, Chicago, IL '85 (RISK)
KORTE, JOHN J., dir. corp. plng., St. Francis-St. George Hospital, Cincinnati, OH '84 (PLNG)
KORTE, COL. THOMAS H., MSC USA, adm., DeWitt Army Community Hospital, Fort Belvoir, VA '83
KORTEMEYER, LEE A., facil. planner, St. Luke's Hospital, Kansas City, MO '85 (ENG)
KORTEN, ROBERT S., Saginaw Community Hospital, Saginaw, MI '78 (FOOD)
KORTH, WILLIAM M., dir. food serv., Bay Area Hospital, Coos Bay, OR '85 (FOOD)
KORTZ, HERB J., corp. plant eng., Detroit-Macomb Hospital Corporation, Detroit, MI '77 (ENG)
KOSANOVICH, JOHN P., Madison, WI '74 (MGMT)
KOSAR, DENNIS M., supv. cent. proc., Wills Eye Hospital, Philadelphia, PA '82 (CS)
KOSCHO, EILEEN G., plng. and mktg. consult., Houston, TX '78
KOSHAR, THEDA, coor. infection control and supv. cent. proc., Community Hospital, Watervliet, MI '79 (CS)
KOSHINSKI, SR. BARBARA ANN, vice-pres. plng., Mary Immaculate Hospital, Newport News, VA '86 (PR) (PLNG)
KOSIBA, WALTER, chief plant oper., Du Bois Hospital, Du Bois, PA '83 (ENG)
KOSICH, DEANNA T., phys. rep., Swedish Medical Center, Englewood, CO '86 (PR)
KOSINSKI, KAY, adm. plng., John Peter Smith Hospital, Fort Worth, TX '85
KOSKEY, LOREEN Z., coor. commun. rel., Marquette General Hospital, Marquette, MI '86 (PLNG)
KOSKIE, JOSEPH F., dir. diet., Ashtabula County Medical Center, Ashtabula, OH '85 (FOOD)
KOSS, DAWN COUCH, vice-pres. nrsg., Sarasota Memorial Hospital, Sarasota, FL '84 (NURS)
KOSS, MARY KAY, coor. pat. educ., Medical Center of Beaver County, Beaver Falls, PA '86 (EDUC)
KOSTENKO, MICHAEL L., dir. pur., Kettering Medical Center, Kettering, OH '67 (PUR)
KOSTEVA, DAVID B., vice-pres., CHI Systems, Inc., Ann Arbor, MI '86 (PERS)
KOSTOPOULOS, MARGARET R., RN, asst. dir. nrsg. serv., AMI Doctors' Hospital, Lanham, MD '81 (NURS)
KOSZALKA, MARIA VICTORIA, RN, dir. nrsg. serv., Brunswick General Hospital, Amityville, NY '85 (NURS)
KOTCHER, SHIRLEY J., legal counselor risk mgt., Booth Memorial Medical Center, Flushing, NY '77 (ATTY)(RISK)
KOTEK, DONALD H., dir. linen serv., St. Francis Medical Center, La Crosse, WI '86 (ENVIRON)
KOTERBSKI, EUGENE, asst. dir. food serv., Alexian Brothers Medical Center, Elk Grove Village, IL '82 (FOOD)
KOTESKI, DOROTHY R., coor. diet. prog., Community College of Philadelphia, Philadelphia, PA '78 (FOOD)
KOTHE, PATRICIA, dir. mktg., MacNeal Hospital, Berwyn, IL '85 (PLNG)
KOTHEIMER, SR. MARY CARL, RN, dir. nrsg. serv., St. Elizabeth Hospital Medical Center, Youngstown, OH '71 (NURS)
KOTNOUR, LEE MARIE, RN, vice-pres. pat. care, Westlake Community Hospital, Melrose Park, IL '71 (NURS)
KOTSCH, CHARLES S., supv. maint., Marlette Community Hospital, Marlette, MI '86 (ENG)
KOTZEN, JOYCE K., corp. dir. pub. rel. and mktg., Kennedy Memorial Hospitals-University Medical Center, Cherry Hill, NJ '78 (PR)
KOTZEN, SANFORD, Baltimore, MD '49 (LIFE)
KOUGHAN, WILLIAM P., pres., Horizon Health System, Inc., Bethlehem, PA '70
KOUKOL, SUSAN M., mgr. mktg., Ecko Products, Wheeling, IL '85 (FOOD)
KOUKOLA, PETER W., Columbia, MO '75 (MGMT)
KOURY, SUZANNE D., clin. instr., University of Iowa Hospitals and Clinics, Iowa City, IA '84 (FOOD)
KOURY, VICTOR, supv. cent. sup., St. Mary Hospital, Quincy, IL '80 (CS)
KOUTRAKIS, PETER G., assoc. vice-pres., B. R. and A. Consulting Engineers, Inc., Brighton, MA '80 (ENG)
KOVACEK, PETER R., Samaritan Health Center, Detroit, MI '81 (EDUC)
KOVACH, ELEANOR R., dist. mgr., ARA Services, Hospital Food Management, Environmental Service, Inc., Coventry, RI '70 (FOOD)
KOVACH, SANDRA F., dir. hskpg. serv., Pottstown Memorial Medical Center, Pottstown, PA '86 (ENVIRON)
KOVACS, OLIVER R., atty., Raritan Bay Medical Center, Perth Amboy, NJ '73 (ATTY)
KOVAL, BERNARD G., pres. and chief exec. off., Mountainside Hospital, Montclair, NJ '73
KOVANIC, MARILYN, RN, vice-pres. nrsg. serv., Lakeview Medical Center, Danville, IL '77 (NURS)
KOVAR, MARY L., cent. serv. tech., St. Elizabeth Hospital, Beaumont, TX '83 (CS)
KOVATS, ERNEST, sr. vice-pres., Freehold Area Hospital, Freehold, NJ '83 (PLNG)
KOVENER, RONALD R., vice-pres., Healthcare Financial Management Association, Washington, DC '76
KOWAL, STEPHEN A., assoc. dir., Queens Hospital Center, Jamaica, NY '84
KOWALCZYK, JAMES J., dir. hosp. info. syst., Illinois Hospital Association, Oak Brook, IL '81
KOWALCZYK, THOMAS J., mgr. plant oper. and new proj. dev., Loretto Hospital, Chicago, IL '80 (ENG)
KOWALESKI, MARY R., asst. dir. cent. sterile serv., Middlesex Memorial Hospital, Middletown, CT '81 (CS)
KOWALSKI, BARBARA, dir. soc. serv., Leila Hospital and Health Center, Battle Creek, MI '85 (SOC)
KOWALSKI, CHERYL CORINNE, dir. pur., Saint Joseph Hospital, Elgin, IL '74 (PUR)
KOWALSKI, JAMIE C., pres., Kowalski Dickow Associates, Inc., Milwaukee, WI '79 (PUR)
KOWALSKI, LANA C., supv. cent. serv., Nathan Littauer Hospital, Gloversville, NY '82 (CS)
KOWALSKI, PAUL D., dir. pers., Methodist Hospital of Kentucky, Pikeville, KY '78 (PERS)
KOWALSKI, PEGGY B., dir. vol., Ravenswood Hospital Medical Center, Chicago, IL '68 (VOL)
KOWALSKI, RICHARD SHELDON, adm. and exec. dir., St. Mary's Hospital, Galesburg, IL '69
KOWALSKI, ROBERT B., sr. consult., Ernst and Whinney, Houston, TX '78 (MGMT)
KOWALSKI, TERRY, asst. vice-pres. plng. and prog. dev., Roxborough Memorial Hospital, Philadelphia, PA '84 (PLNG)
KOWALYSKO, DESIA ALLY, mgt. consult. and eng., Akron City Hospital, Akron, OH '87 (PLNG)
KOWIESKI, JOHN, mgr. mktg., Professional Tape Company, Burr Ridge, IL '86 (PUR)
KOWN, CHARLES L., atty., Hospital Corporation of America, Nashville, TN '75 (ATTY)
KOWOLS, JOE, asst. dir. eng., Evanston Hospital, Evanston, IL '85 (ENG)
KOYADA, SACHIO, dir. hskpg., Kuakini Medical Center, Honolulu, HI '86 (ENVIRON)
KOZAK, JOHN H., atty., West Virginia Health Care Cost Review Authority, Charleston, WV '84 (ATTY)
KOZIEL, GERARD J., assoc. exec. dir., Forbes Regional Health Center, Monroeville, PA '79 (PLNG)
KOZIOL, SUSAN, dir. hm care, St. Margaret Hospital, Hammond, IN '87 (AMB)
KOZLOWSKI, JEAN, RN, asst. adm., St. Joseph Medical Center, Joliet, IL '80 (NURS)
KOZO, SUSAN B., assoc. dir. vol. serv., John F. Kennedy Medical Center, Edison, NJ '78 (VOL)
KOZUB, GEORGE M., dir. eng. and maint., Holy Redeemer Hospital and Medical Center, Meadowbrook, PA '81 (ENG)
KRAATZ, JOHN F., sr. mgr., Ernst and Whinney, Dallas, TX '86 (MGMT)
KRABACH, MONA LEE, dir. vol. serv., Mercy Medical Center, Springfield, OH '77 (VOL)
KRACH, DEBORAH A., RN, nrs. coor., Good Samaritan Hospital of Maryland, Baltimore, MD '85 (CS)
KRACHINSKE, KATHLEEN, adm. home health care, St. Anthony Hospital, Michigan City, IN '87 (AMB)
KRACKALL, GENEVIEVE L., pat. rep., Brooke Army Medical Center, San Antonio, TX '86 (PAT)
KRAEGEL, JANET M., RN, spec., University of Wisconsin, School of Nursing, Milwaukee, WI '69
KRAFF, M. MICHAEL, PhD, dir. risk mgt., Missouri Professional Liability Insurance Association, Jefferson City, MO '80 (RISK)
KRAFFT, JOAN, risk mgr., Lea Regional Hospital, Hobbs, NM '84 (RISK)
KRAFT, ARLENE G., dir. vol. serv., Dammasch State Hospital, Wilsonville, OR '83 (VOL)
KRAFT, CHARLES S., dir. eng., Valley Hospital Medical Center, Las Vegas, NV '83 (ENG)
KRAFT, DAN R., vice-pres. dev. and commun. rel., Horizon Health System, Inc., Bethlehem, PA '83 (PR)
KRAFT, GEORGE J., diet. consult., Greenwich Hospital, Greenwich, CT '79
KRAFT, SHERRY, dir. med. soc. serv., Evanston Hospital, Evanston, IL '85 (SOC)
KRAFT, WILLIAM, exec. vice-pres. fin., Baptist Medical Centers, Birmingham, AL '81 (RISK)
KRAGE, OLIVER D., asst. exec. dir., St. Anne's Hospital, Chicago, IL '82
KRAH, LEE H., asst. dir. plant serv., Taylor Hospital, Ridley Park, PA '86 (ENG)
KRAIL, KRISTINA A., RN, assoc. dir. nrsg., Hospital of Saint Raphael, New Haven, CT '84 (NURS)
KRAKOFF, ROBERTA Y., asst. dir. soc. work serv., Presbyterian Hospital in the City of New York, New York, NY '85 (SOC)
KRAKOWSKI, JOHN A., dir. food and nutr. serv., Neponsit Healthcare Center, Neponsit, NY '82 (FOOD)
KRALL, CHARLOTTE M., mgr. commun., HMO of Western Pennsylvania, Cheswick, PA '86 (PR)
KRAMAR, JOHN, adm., Woodruff Community Hospital, Long Beach, CA '85
KRAMAROW, FREDERICK, coor. tv, Englewood Hospital, Englewood, NJ '72 (PERS)
KRAMER, BARRY A., dir. plng., Shawnee Mission Medical Center, Shawnee Mission, KS '81 (PLNG)
KRAMER, C. RICHARD, dir. oper., Geisinger Medical Management Corporation, Danville, PA '84
KRAMER, CAROL A., adm. dir. pub. rel., Healthwest Medical Centers, Chatsworth, CA '84 (PR)
KRAMER, ELLEN W., dir. dev., United Cerebral Palsy of North Jersey, East Orange, NJ '84 (PR)
KRAMER, HELENE, RN, dir. qual. assur., St. Lawrence Rehabilitation Center, Lawrenceville, NJ '83 (RISK)
KRAMER, HENRY E., atty., Sarah Bush Lincoln Health Center, Mattoon, IL '81 (ATTY)
KRAMER, LANCE D., South Windsor, CT '85 (PLNG)
KRAMER, LAWRENCE J., partner, Deloitte Haskins and Sells, New York, NY '80
KRAMER, SR. LORETTA, dir. soc. serv. and pastoral care, Choctaw Memorial Hospital, Hugo, OK '82 (SOC)
KRAMER, MARIAN D., dir. pub. info., Burlington Medical Center, Burlington, IA '78 (PR)
KRAMER, PAUL, Carrolton, TX '81 (ENG)
KRAMER, RICHARD J., exec. vice-pres., Lifespan, Inc., Minneapolis, MN '79 (PLNG)
KRAMER, SANDRA L., atty., Richmond Memorial Hospital, Richmond, VA '83 (ATTY)
KRAMER, SUZANNE CARTER, asst. to the dir., Mount Sinai Medical Center, New York, NY '86
KRANE, CYNTHIA R., RN, dir. ob.-gyn. nrsg., Beth Israel Hospital, Boston, MA '81 (NURS)
KRANTZ, COLLETTE A., RN, coor. pat. care, Lodi Community Hospital, Lodi, OH '83 (SOC)
KRANTZ, DIANA, dir. plng., Children's Seashore House, Philadelphia, PA '86 (PLNG)
KRANTZ, GERALD M., adm., Chilton Memorial Hospital, Pompton Plains, NJ '58
KRANTZ, JEFFREY A., dir. plng., Southeast Missouri Hospital, Cape Girardeau, MO '86 (PR) (PLNG)(AMB)
KRANTZ, LINDA M., dir. pat. and qual. assur. serv., Henry Mayo Newhall Memorial Hospital, Valencia, CA '87 (PAT)
KRANTZ, MILTON L., med. tech. sup., proc. and distrib., Veterans Administration Medical Center, Walla Walla, WA '86 (CS)
KRANZ, HAROLD JR., dir. corp. commun., Children's Hospital National Medical Center, Washington, DC '72 (PR)
KRANZUSCH, ANNA, St. Mary's Hospital Medical Center, Green Bay, WI '79 (CS)
KRASIK, ELLEN R., asst. vice-pres. plng., University of Florida, J. Hillis Miller Health Center, Gainesville, FL '84 (PLNG)
KRASNAUSKAS, RICHARD J., sr. vice-pres. fin., Miriam Hospital, Providence, RI '82 (PLNG)
KRASNER, MICHAEL B., ins. agt. risk mgt., Louis D. Krasner, Inc., Rockville Centre, NY '83 (RISK)
KRASOVEC, EMRO F., vice-pres. human res., United Hospitals Medical Center, Newark, NJ '70 (PERS)
KRATUNIS, GEORGE, dir. food serv., Long Beach Memorial Nursing Home, Long Beach, NY '72 (FOOD)
KRATZKE, SUSAN R., dir. soc. serv., Pelican Valley Health Center, Pelican Rapids, MN '85 (SOC)
KRATZNER, JUDITH E., dir. human resources dev., St. John's Healthcare Corporation, Anderson, IN '79 (EDUC)
KRAU, DEBORAH L., dir. mgt. info. serv., Lahey Clinic Hospital, Burlington, MA '81 (MGMT)
KRAUKLIS, GENE J., asst. adm., Lakeland Hospital, Elkhorn, WI '76 (PERS)
KRAUS, ANNA J., dir. med. rec., Clarion Osteopathic Community Hospital, Clarion, PA '77
KRAUS, BARBARA J., RN, vice-pres. nrsg. serv., New Rochelle Hospital Medical Center, New Rochelle, NY '86 (NURS)
KRAUS, CATHERINE T., dir. clin. educ., Home Nutritional Support, Inc., Pine Brook, NJ '87 (EDUC)
KRAUS, GARY P., atty. and risk mgr., University of Missouri Graduate Studies in Health Services Management, Columbia, MO '67 (ATTY)(RISK)
KRAUS, IMOGENE K., supv. cent. sup., Western Psychiatric Institute and Clinic, Pittsburgh, PA '86 (CS)
KRAUS, SR. IRENE, pres., Daughters of Charity National Health Systems, Normandy, MO '82 (LIFE)
KRAUS, JOSEPH S. JR., student, Idaho State University, College of Allied Health Professions, Potacatello, ID '84
KRAUS, LEROY D., asst. adm. commun. rel., Cedars-Sinai Medical Center, Los Angeles, CA '72 (PAT)
KRAUS, LOIS B., dir. vol. serv., American Oncologic Hospital, Philadelphia, PA '77 (VOL)
KRAUS, MARIA L., laser coor., Pennsylvania Hospital, Philadelphia, PA '86 (PR)
KRAUS, PEGGY D., mgr. commun. rel., St. Mary's Medical Center, Racine, WI '84 (PR)
KRAUS, RICHARD A., dir. environ. serv., Community Memorial Hospital, Menomonee Falls, WI '79 (ENG)
KRAUSE, BRYAN D., dir. bus. dev., Hospital Corporation of America, Richmond, VA '86 (PR) (PLNG)

KRAUSE, CAROL, mgr. pat. and phys. serv., University of Missouri Hospital and Clinics, Columbia, MO '87 (PAT)
KRAUSE, KATHERINE, RN, asst. vice-pres. nrsg., Froedtert Memorial Lutheran Hospital, Milwaukee, WI '82 (NURS)
KRAUSE, LINDA A., mktg. assoc., St. Francis Hospital, Milwaukee, WI '85 (PR)
KRAUSE, MYRON, dir. cent. proc. and distrib., Portland Adventist Medical Center, Portland, OR '86 (CS)
KRAUSE, ROBERT L., chief soc. work serv., Veterans Administration Medical Center, Lexington, KY '83 (SOC)
KRAUSE, RONALD D., pres. and chief exec. off., Voluntary Hospitals of America-Illinois, Springfield, IL '86
KRAUSE, THOMAS J., adm. dir. prof. serv., Berkshire Medical Center, Pittsfield, MA '84 (PR) (PLNG)
KRAUSE, THOMAS WILLIAM, asst. vice-pres., Methodist Hospitals of Dallas, Dallas, TX '74 (MGMT)
KRAUSE, TRUDY MILLARD, dir. mktg. and commun. rel., Parkland Hospital, Baton Rouge, LA '84 (PR) (PLNG)
KRAUSE, WALTER E., pres., Interface Medicus Incorporated, Farmington, CT '75
KRAUSHAAR, JEAN, mgr. cent. serv., Washington Regional Medical Center, Fayetteville, AR '86 (CS)
KRAUSS, HERBERT M., Northbrook, IL '48 (LIFE)
KRAUSS, JAMES D., asst. dir. plng., Baptist Hospital of Miami, Miami, FL '85 (PLNG)
KRAUT, JEFFREY A., sr. consult., Peat, Marwick, Mitchell and Company, New York, NY '80
KRAVITZ, MELVA D., RN, assoc. dir. nrsg. practice, critical care area, University of Utah Health Sciences Center, Salt Lake City, UT '86 (NURS)
KRAWCZYNSKI, MARGARET E., head cent. serv., New Britain Memorial Hospital, New Britain, CT '87 (CS)
KRAYBILL, WALTER T., mgt. eng., Abington Memorial Hospital, Abington, PA '86 (MGMT)
KRAYER, KATHLEEN M., dir. vol. serv., Mercy Hospital and Medical Center, San Diego, CA '86 (VOL)
KREBS, ALICE M., dir. vol., Froedtert Memorial Lutheran Hospital, Milwaukee, WI '81 (VOL)
KREBS, PRISCILLA J., dir. pers., Sutter Memorial Hospital, Sacramento, CA '78 (PERS)
KRECH, PETER P., dir. pers., Crozer-Chester Medical Center, Chester, PA '83 (PERS)
KREER, CAROL L., RN, asst. dir. nrsg., University of California San Francisco, San Francisco, CA '85 (NURS)
KREGER, DAVID CHARLES, exec. vice-pres. and chief oper. off., Westland Medical Center, Westland, MI '53 (LIFE)
KREGER, JUDITH A., RN, instr. trng. and staff dev., Little Company of Mary Hospital, Torrance, CA '77 (EDUC)
KREHER, ERICH, dir. legal-risk mgt., Raritan Bay Medical Center, Perth Amboy, NJ '84 (ATTY)(RISK)
KREIDER, EVERETTE FRANCIS III, adm. asst., Audie L. Murphy Memorial Veterans Hospital, San Antonio, TX '85
KREIENKAMP, DALE E., mgr. pers., St. Anthony's Medical Center, St. Louis, MO '86 (PERS)
KREIGER, DAVID A., assoc. vice-pres. oper., Ingham Medical Center, Lansing, MI '79 (PLNG)
KREIKEMEIER, SAMUEL J., dir. food serv., Brother James' Court, Springfield, IL '76 (FOOD)
KREISLER, AARON L., MD, student, University of Dallas, Irving, TX '86
KREISS, SUSAN B., dir. pur., Bronx-Lebanon Hospital Center, Bronx, NY '78 (PUR)
KREITZ, COREY JOHN, assoc. dir. mktg., Hospital Central Service, Inc., Allentown, PA '83 (PUR)
KREJCI, RONALD J., vice-pres. pers. serv., St. Michael Hospital, Milwaukee, WI '82 (PERS)
KREKLING, VIRGINIA M., RN, dir. educ., Douglas General Hospital, Douglasville, GA '84 (EDUC)
KRELL, GEORGE I., dir. soc. work, Mount Sinai Medical Center, Miami Beach, FL '70 (SOC)
KREN, FRANK G., dir. textile serv., St. Alexis Hospital, Cleveland, OH '86 (ENVIRON)
KRESS, ROBERT E., mgr., Arthur Andersen and Company, Chicago, IL '84
KREUSCHER, ELAINE, supv. cent. sup., Franklin General Hospital, Valley Stream, NY '83 (CS)
KREUSCHER, IRENE KATZ, assoc. adm. clin. info. serv., Memorial Hospital for Cancer and Allied Diseases, New York, NY '76 (PLNG)
KREUTZ, GAIL L., dir. vol., Mercy Hospital, Columbus, OH '83 (VOL)
KREUTZER, CY A., dir. plant oper., Platte Valley Medical Center, Brighton, CO '83 (ENG)
KREUTZINGER, HENRY J., vice-pres., Health First Network, Oak Brook, IL '79 (PLNG)
KREUZER, JAY, asst. exec. dir., St. Francis Hospital, Blue Island, IL '85
KREVITZ, LEAH R., RN, dir. med. delivery, Share Health Plan of Illinois, Inc., Itasca, IL '77
KREWSON, CHARLES FLEMING III, spec. health syst., Veterans Administration Medical Center, Albany, NY '71
KREY, NATHALIE A., consult., Greater New York Hospital Food Administration Association, New York, NY '67 (FOOD)
KRICKBAUM, KEN, dist. mgr., ARA Services, Hospital Food Management, Environmental Service, Inc., Norman, OK '80 (FOOD)
KRIEBEL, CHRISTINE, dir. discharge plng. and soc. serv., Germantown Hospital and Medical Center, Philadelphia, PA '86 (SOC)
KRIEDMAN, WILLIAM R., exec. eng., Cabrini Medical Center, New York, NY '76 (ENG)
KRIEG, GARELD F., atty., Saint Vincent Hospital, Billings, MT '74 (ATTY)
KRIEG, KENNETH ALAN, adm., Hospital of University of Pennsylvania Medical Group, Philadelphia, PA '74
KRIEGEL, ELIZABETH, dir. diet., Michigan Osteopathic Medical Center, Detroit, MI '86 (FOOD)
KRIEGER, MARY L., dir. soc. work, South Hills Health System, Pittsburgh, PA '82 (SOC)
KRIEGER, ROBERT M., exec. dir., Humana Hospital -Biscayne, Miami, FL '86
KRIER, NANCY C., RN, dir. nrsg., Illinois Hospital Association, Naperville, IL '85 (NURS)
KRIER, PATRICIA A., student, H. Division USS Lexington Avt 16, FPO Miami, FL '86
KRIESEL, ROSEMARIE, dir. soc. serv., Centinela Hospital Medical Center, Inglewood, CA '82 (SOC)
KRIFF, GERTRUDE, dir. vol., Alice Hyde Hospital Association, Malone, NY '78 (VOL)
KRILL, BRENDA J., asst. dir. info. syst., Franciscan Health System, Chadds Ford, PA '85 (RISK)
KRISS, PATRICIA A., dir. pub. rel., mktg. and dev., Lawrence Hospital, Bronxville, NY '86 (PR) (PLNG)
KRISTEN, SR. M., vice-pres., St. Joseph's Hospital, Savannah, GA '85
KRISTENSEN, OLE B., dir. human res., Battle Creek Adventist Hospital, Battle Creek, MI '80 (EDUC)(PERS)
KRISTOFEK, DAISY R., dir. diet. serv., Johnson City Medical Center Hospital, Johnson City, TN '83 (FOOD)
KRISTOFFERSEN, ELSIE, dir. sup., Centinela Hospital Medical Center, Inglewood, CA '75 (CS)
KRIZ-MORTON, NANCY L., asst. dir. commun. rel., Nyack Hospital, Nyack, NY '83 (PR)
KRIZAN, LEONARD I., dir. pers., Stamford Hospital, Stamford, CT '72 (PERS)
KRIZANC, RENE A., adm., Cottage Hospital, Uxbridge, Ont., Canada '81 (PLNG)
KRIZELMAN, SHELDON L., prin., Hospital Management Professionals, Brentwood, TN '79
KRIZMAN, FREDERICK EDWARD, atty., Euclid, OH '50 (LIFE)
KROCHMAL, CHARLES F., mgt. analyst, Veterans Administration, Department of Medicine and Surgery, Washington, DC '77 (MGMT)
KROEGER, HILDA HERTHA, MD, Pittsburgh, PA '47 (LIFE)
KROEGER, LINDA A., coor. nrsg. educ., Sacred Heart General Hospital, Eugene, OR '83 (EDUC)
KROENING, GARY L., dir. food and nutr. serv., Columbia Hospital, Milwaukee, WI '83 (FOOD)
KROESCH, RANDI HERR, dir. emer. serv., Grossmont District Hospital, La Mesa, CA '87 (AMB)
KROLICKI, RICHARD W., adm. phys. facil., Henry Ford Hospital, Detroit, MI '82 (ENG)
KROLL, DANIELLE M., dir. risk mgt., Kapiolani Women's and Children's Medical Center, Honolulu, HI '78 (RISK)
KRONK, CAROLYN A., RN, dir. educ. and staff dev., St. Mary's Hospital, Richmond, VA '77 (EDUC)
KRONMAN, BRUCE, mgr. mgt. syst., Ernst and Whinney, Chicago, IL '78 (MGMT)
KROO, DONNA G., dir. commun. rel. and dev., Meridian Park Hospital, Tualatin, OR '77 (VOL)(PR)
KROOK, JOYCE D., mgr. commun., pat., emp. rel. and spec. events, Abbott-Northwestern Hospital, Minneapolis, MN '82 (PR)
KROP, MARIANNE E., RN, dir. nrsg., Norfolk General Hospital, Norfolk, VA '85 (NURS)
KROPF, ROGER, PhD, assoc. prof., New York University Graduate School of Public Administration, New York, NY '85 (PLNG)
KROPP, DAVID, mgr. tech. serv., Aseptic-Thermo Indicator, North Hollywood, CA '83 (CS)
KROPP, WILLIAM J., dir. admissions and dev., Graydon Manor, Leesburg, VA '86 (PLNG)
KROUPA, RAYMOND C., dir. environ. serv., St. Luke's Hospital, Milwaukee, WI '85 (ENVIRON)
KRUCKENBERG, KARNA K., RN PhD, coor. pat. educ. and clin. nrs., University of Missouri Hospital and Clinics, Columbia, MO '84 (EDUC)
KRUCZLNICKI, DAVID G., exec. vice-pres., Glens Falls Hospital, Glens Falls, NY '86 (MGMT)
KRUEGER, BETTY JANE, mgr. food serv., St. Mary's Hospital-Ozaukee, Port Washington, WI '81 (FOOD)
KRUEGER, CHARLOTTE I., asst. dir. pers. and budget, Rush-Presbyterian-St. Luke Medical Center, Chicago, IL '86 (FOOD)
KRUEGER, CHRISTINE A., coor. pub. rel., Washington Regional Medical Center, Fayetteville, AR '81 (PR)
KRUEGER, DEBORAH J., consulting serv. mgr., Amherst Associates, Inc., Tampa, FL '85 (PR) (PLNG)
KRUEGER, GEORGE J. III, student, Governors State University-HSA, Park Forest South, IL '84
KRUEGER, JAMES, atty., Maui Memorial Hospital, Wailuku, HI '78 (ATTY)
KRUEGER, JANELLE C., RN, prof., Arizona State University College of Nursing, Tempe, AZ '82 (NURS)
KRUEGER, JOHN W., dir. commun. rel., Mease Health Care, Dunedin, FL '82 (PR)
KRUEGER, KAREN E., clin. nrs. spec., St. Elizabeth Medical Center, Yakima, WA '83 (EDUC)
KRUEGER, KENNETH G., partner, Deloitte Haskins and Sells, Minneapolis, MN '74
KRUEGER, LORI D., asst. dir. pub. rel., DePaul Health Center, Bridgeton, MO '85 (PR)
KRUEGER, MARY MCCORMICK, atty., St. Vincent Medical Center, Toledo, OH '81 (ATTY)
KRUEGER, NANETTE M., RN, mgr. cent. serv. and sterile proc., St. Luke's Hospital, Milwaukee, WI '85 (CS)
KRUEGER, ROGER R., supv. biomedical equip. tech., Martin Memorial Hospital, Stuart, FL '85 (ENG)
KRUEGER, WILLIAM E., risk mgr., Ravenswood Hospital Medical Center, Chicago, IL '80 (RISK)
KRUG, MARJORIE B., coor. pat. rel., St. Luke's-Roosevelt Hospital Center, New York, NY '83 (PAT)
KRUG, MICHAEL J., St. Francis Hospital and Medical Center, Topeka, KS '84 (MGMT)
KRUGER, GLEN W., dir. maint., Jones Memorial Hospital, Wellsville, NY '84 (ENG)
KRUGER, KENNETH, dir. labor rel., Mount Sinai Medical Center, New York, NY '78 (PERS)
KRUGER, MARGARET D., pres., Maggie Springer and Assocs, Inc., Appleton, WI '86 (PR)
KRULL, PATRICIA, RN, assoc. chief nrsg. serv. for educ., Veterans Administration Medical Center Atlanta, Decatur, GA '71 (EDUC)
KRULL, ROBERT D., adm. coor., Memorial Hospitals Association, Modesto, CA '75 (ENG)
KRUMAN, BETTY J., asst. adm., Rehabilitation Institute of Pittsburgh, Pittsburgh, PA '81 (PLNG)
KRUMEL, FRED E., dir. pat. affairs, Riverside Methodist Hospitals, Columbus, OH '84 (RISK)
KRUMREY, NORMAN A., corp. dir. matl., Normandy Osteopathic Hospital-North and South, St. Louis, MO '72 (PUR)
KRUMWIEDE, AUDREY, asst. mgr. diet., Governor Samuel H. Shapiro Developmental Center, Kankakee, IL '82 (FOOD)
KRUPANSKY, FRANK J., dir. matl. mgt., Pontiac General Hospital, Pontiac, MI '81 (PUR)
KRUPCZAK, PETER, dir. human res., California Medical Center-Los Angeles, Los Angeles, CA '83 (PERS)
KRUPILSKI, JEROME J., dir. corp. mktg., NKC Hospitals, Louisville, KY '84 (PLNG)
KRUPPENBACHER, GERALDINE C., emp. rel. spec., Greenwich Hospital, Greenwich, CT '85 (PERS)
KRUSE, GRACE I., asst. dir., University of Chicago Medical Center, Chicago, IL '83 (FOOD)
KRUSE, LOWELL C., chief exec. off., Heartland Health System, Inc., St. Joseph, MO '84
KRUSE, STEPHANIE S., dir. commun. rel., St. Mary's Health Care Corporation, Reno, NV '80 (PR)
KRUSE, THEODORE F. JR., adm., Northwoods Hospital, Phelps, WI '67
KRUSEE, JOSEPH, dir. pers., Woodview-Calabasas Hospital, Calabasas, CA '84 (RISK)
KRUTSINGER, RUTH M., mgr. matl., Lucas County Health Center, Chariton, IA '80 (PUR)
KRUTZ, ROBERT C., pres. and chief exec. off., Correlated Health Services, Ravenna, OH '55 (LIFE)
KRUZE, THOMAS, adm., Bay Vista Convalescent Hospital, Santa Monica, CA '86
KRYGOWSKI, STANLEY W., pres., Malden Hospital, Malden, MA '67 (MGMT)(PLNG)
KRZACZEK, PATSY L., RN, dir. nrsg., Underwood-Memorial Hospital, Woodbury, NJ '74 (EDUC)(NURS)
KRZASTEK, SUSAN L. T., dir. pers., Waynesboro Community Hospital, Waynesboro, VA '86 (PERS)
KRZMARZICK, DONNA, RN, dir. mental health nrsg., Metropolitan Medical Center, Minneapolis, MN '78 (NURS)
KRZYS, BARBARA, supv. cent. serv., St. Mary's Hospital, Amsterdam, NY '79 (CS)
KRZYSTON, DIANE M., head nrs. emer. serv., Sinai Hospital of Detroit, Detroit, MI '86 (RISK)
KUBALA, CYNTHIA L., dir. pub. rel., Haverford Community Hospital, Havertown, PA '85 (PR)
KUBANY, PATRICIA S., dir. pub. rel., Chelsea Community Hospital, Chelsea, MI '86 (PR)
KUBASEK, KIM MARIE, student, Program in Health Care Administration, Baruch College-Mount Sinai School of Medicine, New York, NY '86
KUBE, FRANKLIN T., asst. adm. constr. and maint., St. Francis Medical Center, La Crosse, WI '68 (ENG)
KUBERRY, BARBARA E., loss analyst, Doctor's Management Company, Santa Monica, CA '87 (RISK)
KUBIAK, KATHLEEN M., dir. food serv., Buffalo Columbus Hospital, Buffalo, NY '83 (FOOD)
KUBICA, ANTHONY J., vice-pres., Rhode Island Hospital, Providence, RI '83
KUBIT, DONALD E., atty., Miami Heart Institute, Miami Beach, FL '80 (ATTY)
KUBIT, LUCILLE A., dir. vol. serv., St. Francis Medical Center, Pittsburgh, PA '84 (VOL)
KUBY, ALMA M., dir. mktg., American Society of Clinical Pathologists, Chicago, IL '77
KUBZANSKY, JUDITH S., assoc. adm. amb. care, Cambridge Hospital, Cambridge, MA '85 (PLNG)(AMB)
KUCERA, WILLIAM R., atty., Ravenswood Hospital Medical Center, Chicago, IL '71 (ATTY)
KUCHARZ, JOSEPH G., asst. adm., Good Samaritan Hospital, Downers Grove, IL '83
KUCHINSKY, LAURA JANE, dir. soc. work, Southside Regional Medical Center, Petersburg, VA '84 (SOC)
KUCKER, MILES, dir. pers., Lutheran Medical Center, Brooklyn, NY '80 (PERS)
KUCZKOWSKI, J. C., coor. health educ., Akron General Medical Center, Akron, OH '83 (EDUC)
KUEBLER, CHARLES E., adm., Plateau Medical Center, Oak Hill, WV '70
KUEBLER, MARCIE M., asst. dir. cent. sterile sup., Boca Raton Community Hospital, Boca Raton, FL '84 (CS)
KUEFLER, NANCY J., pat. advocate, Mount Clemens General Hospital, Mount Clemens, MI '87 (PAT)
KUEMPEL, ANNE M., RN, vice-pres., St. David's Community Hospital, Austin, TX '83 (NURS)
KUESTER, JOY B., dir. vol. serv., Kaiser Foundation Hospital, Fontana, CA '87 (VOL)
KUGEL, H. LYNDA, Philadelphia, PA '81
KUGLER, GEORGE F. JR., atty., West Jersey Hospital, Northern Division, Camden, NJ '75 (ATTY)
KUHAR, RONALD R., adm. dev. serv., Euclid General Hospital, Euclid, OH '81 (PLNG)
KUHARICH, PATRICIA ANNE, RN, vice-pres. nrsg., Graham Hospital, Canton, IL '84 (NURS)
KUHL, MOIRA H., dir. educ., Hyde Park Hospital, Chicago, IL '73 (EDUC)
KUHLMAN, MARY E., dir. soc. serv., St. Mary's Hospital and Medical Center, Grand Junction, CO '76 (SOC)
KUHLMANN, JOHN E., coor. vol. serv., Milford Memorial Hospital, Milford, DE '80 (VOL)
KUHN, LELAND V., dir. matl. mgt., Lakeview Medical Center, Danville, IL '85 (PUR)
KUHN, MICHAEL J., mgr., Methodist Hospital System, Houston, TX '84 (MGMT)
KUHN, VERNON F., dir. plant oper., Columbus Community Hospital, Columbus, WI '84 (ENG)
KUHNS, LYNNE L., dir. commun. rel., Brookville Hospital, Brookville, PA '83 (PR)
KUHNS, VERLIN V., dir. pur., Arkansas Valley Regional Medical Center, La Junta, CO '81 (PUR)
KUJAWA, GREGORY, actg. dir. facil., University of Minnesota Hospital and Clinic, Minneapolis, MN '87 (ENG)

KUKUK, TERRY L., atty., Health and Hospital Services, Bellevue, WA '81 (RISK)(ATTY)
KULA, DAVID H., sr. mgt. eng., Queen's Medical Center, Honolulu, HI '84 (MGMT)
KULAJA, JERRY, hosp. consult., San Clemente, CA '67
KULASA, DOROTHEA, dir. commun. rel., McKeesport Hospital, McKeesport, PA '81 (PR)
KULCZYCKI, MICHAEL T., dir. mktg., Healthcare Financial Management Association, Oak Brook, IL '77 (PR) (PLNG)
KULESA, CATHY A., regulatory analyst, Massachusetts Hospital Association, Burlington, MA '83 (PLNG)
KULESA, LEONARD L., asst. dir. hskpg., Community Medical Center, Scranton, PA '86 (ENVIRON)
KULESHER, ROBERT R., vice-pres., Germantown Hospital and Medical Center, Philadelphia, PA '75 (RISK)
KULIK, DEBRA R., adm. res., St. John's Mercy Medical Center, St. Louis, MO '83
KULIK, JEFF A., mgt. eng., Good Samaritan Hospital and Health Center, Dayton, OH '84 (MGMT)
KULIK, RICHARD S., biomedical eng., St. Elizabeth Medical Center, Dayton, OH '75 (ENG)
KULIKOWSKI, NADINE A., RN, assoc. adm. nrsg., L. W. Blake Memorial Hospital, Bradenton, FL '87 (NURS)
KULIKOWSKI, SANDRA L., RN, assoc. exec. dir. nrsg., Humana Hospital -Enterprise, Enterprise, AL '81 (NURS)
KULKARNI, PRAFUL M., Urs Corporation, Long Beach, CA '83
KULLBOM, JUDITH A., RN, dir. nrsg., Lapeer General Hospital, LaPeer, MI '81 (NURS)
KULLMAN, ROCHELLE, vice-pres. corp. dev., Queen of the Valley Hospital, West Covina, CA '79 (PLNG)
KULPINSKI, MARY L., asst. dir. food serv., Wausau Hospital Center, Wausau, WI '86 (FOOD)
KULWIN, MAURY H., dir. market res. and plng., MacNeal Hospital, Berwyn, IL '85 (PR) (PLNG)
KULYS, REGINA, assoc. prof., Jane Addams College of Social Wk, University of Illinois, Chicago, IL '86 (SOC)
KUMAR, NAGALAKSHMI B., dir. diet. serv. and ther. diet., Centro Asturiano Hospital, Tampa, FL '84 (FOOD)
KUMMER, FRED S., pres., Hbe Corporation, St. Louis, MO '74
KUMMICK, PATTY, dir. commun. rel. and fund dev., East Liverpool City Hospital, East Liverpool, OH '85 (PR) (PLNG)
KUMPH, DANA M., dir. matl. mgt., Athol Memorial Hospital, Athol, MA '85 (PUR)
KUMURA, THOMAS S., mgr. market res. and census dev., National Medical Enterprises, Inc., Santa Monica, CA '81 (PR) (PLNG)
KUNDEL, C. DOUGLAS, dir. mgt. serv., Hospital Association of New York State, Albany, NY '85 (MGMT)
KUNDRAVI, RICHARD M., qual. assur. asst. and risk mgr., Braddock General Hospital, Braddock, PA '86 (RISK)
KUNIEWICZ, JANE, dir. amb. serv., Children's Hospital of Philadelphia, Philadelphia, PA '87 (AMB)
KUNKLE, VI M., RN, asst. adm. pat. serv., Saint Francis Medical Center, Peoria, IL '82 (NURS)
KUNSELMAN, ROBERT B., mgr. pur., Southwest Washington Hospitals, Vancouver, WA '80 (PUR)
KUNTZ, EDWARD C., supv. maint., Monsour Medical Center, Jeannette, PA '86 (ENG)
KUNTZ, FRANK R., chief eng., Trinity Lutheran Hospital, Kansas City, MO '70 (ENG)
KUNTZ, LOUIS E., student, Trinity University, Atlanta, GA '84
KUNZ, MARY ELLEN, RN, assoc. clin. chief surg. nrsg., Strong Memorial Hospital Rochester University, Rochester, NY '84 (NURS)
KUNZ, REGINA M., student, Program in Hospital and Health Service Management, Kellogg Graduate School of Management, Northwestern University, Evanston, IL '87
KUNZ, REX G., dir. matl. serv., Memorial Medical Center of Jacksonville, Jacksonville, FL '81 (PUR)
KUNZ, WILLIAM L., chief maint. eng., Fairview Southdale Hospital, Minneapolis, MN '71 (ENG)
KUNZE, GLORIA ANN, RN, vice-pres. nrsg. serv., LaPorte Hospital, LaPorte, IN '87 (NURS)
KUO, GEORGE F., dir. soc. serv., Barberton Citizens Hospital, Barberton, OH '87 (SOC)
KUPCHAK, WALTER J., partner, Touche Ross and Company, New York, NY '71
KUPERBER, JAMES, PhD, comr., Wisconsin Hospital Rate Stetting Commission, Madison, WI '67
KUPETZKY, BARBARA, adm. rheumatic diseases, Hospital for Joint Diseases Orthopaedic Institute, New York, NY '80
KUPFERLE, NICK H. III, adm., Walls Regional Hospital, Cleburne, TX '74
KUPPER, BRUCE P. D., asst. adm., Chesapeake General Hospital, Chesapeake, VA '79 (PR) (PLNG)
KUPPLER, KARL J., asst. exec. dir., Trumbull Memorial Hospital, Warren, OH '78
KURAITIS, VINCENT T., dir. reg. mktg., National Medical Enterprises, Santa Monica, CA '85 (PLNG)
KURAMITSU, YAYOE G., dir. soc. serv., Sacred Heart General Hospital, Eugene, OR '82 (SOC)
KURDWANOWSKI, FRANCES C., RN, risk mgr., St. Joseph's Hospital and Medical Center, Paterson, NJ '84 (RISK)
KURIMCAK, MARY LOU, risk mgr., Frick Community Health Center, Mount Pleasant, PA '86 (RISK)
KUROWSKI, BETTINA D., assoc. dir., University Hospital, Denver, CO '84 (PLNG)
KUROWSKI, EUGENE L., pres., Cba, Inc., Chicago, IL '66
KURRASCH, TERRIE L., dir. plng., Providence Hospital, Oakland, CA '79 (PLNG)
KURREN, GAILE M., chief soc. worker, Queen's Medical Center, Honolulu, HI '76 (SOC)
KURS, MATTHEW A., reg. dir. adm., American Medical International, Denver, CO '76
KURSBAN, PATRICIA, RN, asst. dir. nrs., Sibley Memorial Hospital, Washington, DC '85 (NURS)
KURTH, JANICE M., dir. environ. serv., Hospital of the University of Pennsylvania, Philadelphia, PA '83 (ENG)(ENVIRON)
KURTIN, EVE M., chief fin. off. and vice-pres., Admit Services, Inc., Los Angeles, CA '83
KURTZ, EILEEN T., RN, dir. spec. serv., Bass Memorial Baptist Hospital, Enid, OK '76 (NURS)(PAT)
KURTZ, JO ANN, vice-pres. human res., Greater Southeast Community Hospital, Washington, DC '87 (PERS)
KURTZ, LEWIS A. JR., dir. plant oper., Dunn Memorial Hospital, Bedford, IN '83 (ENG)
KURTZ, MARJORIE, RN, dir. pat. care, St. Charles Medical Center, Bend, OR '77 (NURS)
KURTZ, MYERS RICHARD, supt., Central State Hospital, Milledgeville, GA '68
KURTZ, NANCY C., atty., Salem Hospital, Salem, MA '85 (ATTY)
KURTZ, THOMAS FRANCIS JR., pres., Clinton Memorial Hospital, Wilmington, OH '75
KURYSH, SUSAN, pat. serv. rep., Group Health, Inc., Maplewood, MN '86 (PAT)
KURZ, LINDA K., assoc. dep. dir. med. and surg., Veterans Administration Medical Center, Albany, NY '82 (MGMT)
KURZ, PATRICIA A., RN, student, Program in Health Care Administration, New School for Society Research, New York, NY '86
KURZAWA, EDMUND J., health care compensation consult., Union Lake, MI '85 (PERS)
KURZEKNABE, LOUIS F., dir. mgt. eng., Pennsylvania Hospital, Philadelphia, PA '71 (MGMT)
KURZER, MARTIN J., atty., AMI Palmetto General Hospital, Hialeah, FL '73 (ATTY)
KURZMAN, STEPHEN, atty., Strong Memorial Hospital Rochester University, Rochester, NY '76 (ATTY)
KUSCH, FRED C., dir. educ., Lutheran Hospital -LaCrosse, La Crosse, WI '86 (EDUC)
KUSHIDA, ROBERT, dir. nutr. serv., Loretto Hospital, Chicago, IL '80 (FOOD)
KUSHINKA, GEORGE, atty., Houston Medical Center, Warner Robins, GA '77 (ATTY)
KUSHINS, LEONARD, dir. data serv., Massachusetts Hospital Association, Burlington, MA '84 (PLNG)
KUSHMEREK, GRAYCE, dir. pub. rel., Beverly Hospital, Beverly, MA '76 (PR)
KUSHUBAR, MARIAN E., RN, vice-pres. nrsg., Franklin Square Hospital, Baltimore, MD '79 (NURS)
KUSS, B. ANN, RN, asst. dir. nrsg. and med. surg., Ochsner Foundation Hospital, New Orleans, LA '83 (NURS)
KUTCH, JOHN M., MD, dir. serv. unit, Red Lake Hospital, Redlake, MN '86 (AMB)
KUTHER, JANET M., dir. soc. serv., Central Maine Medical Center, Lewiston, ME '82 (SOC)
KUTLER, GORDON E., pres., I. P. O. Associates, Ltd., Flourtown, PA '77 (EDUC)
KUTNER, NATALIE, dir. soc. serv., Inter-Community Medical Center, Covina, CA '85 (SOC)
KUTSUFLAKIS, GUST, dir. matl. mgt., Monongalia General Hospital, Morgantown, WV '82 (PUR)
KUTTERER, DALE C., dir. pers., Montana Deaconess Medical Center, Great Falls, MT '73 (PERS)
KUTZ, LINDA MAXWELL, coor. soc. serv., Brookville Hospital, Brookville, PA '86 (SOC)
KUTZ, WAYNE J., sr. vice-pres. and chief oper. off., Bethany Medical Center, Kansas City, KS '82 (PLNG)
KUTZMAN, GERALD, PhD, sr. psychologist, Searcy Hospital, Mount Vernon, AL '86
KUTZSCHER, SHIRLEY, supv. cent. serv. and outpatient, Community Hospital Schoharie County, Cobleskill, NY '81 (CS)
KUVLESKY, MICHAEL C., student, Program in Industrial Engineer, Texas A. and M. University, College Station, TX '86 (MGMT)
KUYKENDALL, GEORGE ALBERT, sr. vice-pres., San Antonio Community Hospital, Upland, CA '76 (PLNG)
KUYKENDALL, PATRICIA A., exec. dir. surg. oper., acute care support serv. and dir. nrsg., University of Texas Medical Branch Hospitals, Galveston, TX '81 (NURS)
KUYKENDALL, RONALD D., pres., Servicemaster Industries, Inc., Wayne, PA '78
KUYPER, THEODORE R., dist. mgr., Edward Department of the Navy, Bureau of Medicine and Surgery and Company, North Riverside, IL '86 (ENVIRON)
KUYPERS, ARNIE, vice-pres., Witt Associates Library, Oakbrook, IL '82 (PLNG)
KUZIEL, MARVIN L., mgr. hskpg. and ldry., Huron Memorial Hospital, Bad Axe, MI '86 (ENVIRON)
KUZNIAR, RICHARD, student, University of Illinois at Chicago, Chicago, IL '86
KUZNICKI, JAMES JOSEPH, dir. environ. serv., Kootenai Medical Center, Coeur D'Alene, ID '86 (ENVIRON)(ENG)
KVAPIL, DAVID, coor. risk mgt., Bryan Memorial Hospital, Lincoln, NE '80 (RISK)
KVIDERA, VINCENT J., eng., Ortonville Area Health Services, Ortonville, MN '85 (ENG)
KVITTEM-BARR, DALE A., student, Arizona State University, Tempe, AZ '85 (PERS)
KWENTUS, K. SUE, RN, dir. nrsg., Northampton-Accomack Memorial Hospital, Nassawadox, VA '81 (NURS)
KWESKIN, MARGARET, dir. vol. serv., Stamford Hospital, Stamford, CT '78 (VOL)
KWIATEK, MARY, RN, dir. nrsg. serv., Bertrand Chaffee Hospital, Springville, NY '82 (NURS)
KWONG-WIRTH, STELLA, pat. advocate, New York Inf-Beekman Downtown Hospital, New York, NY '86 (PAT)
KYBARTAS, JOE, chief oper. eng., Good Samaritan Hospital, Downers Grove, IL '86 (ENG)
KYLE, CAROL M., RN, dir. nrsg. serv., Spohn Kleberg Memorial Hospital, Kingsville, TX '80 (NURS)
KYLE, ELLEN T., RN, dir. nrsg. serv., Bossier Medical Center, Bossier City, LA '74 (NURS)
KYLE, JOSEPH W., head lab., Wheelock Memorial Hospital, Goodrich, MI '85 (PR) (PLNG)
KYLE, JUDY A., RN, dir. educ. and trng., Providence Hospital, Anchorage, AK '79 (EDUC)
KYLE, MONTE R., asst. vice-pres. matl. mgt., St. Francis Medical Center, Cape Girardeau, MO '86 (PUR)
KYRIACOU, GEORGE M., adm. dir. med. serv., Baystate Medical Center, Springfield, MA '84 (PLNG)
KYROUAC, JEANNE, dir. mktg. and pub. rel., Iroquois Memorial Hospital, Watseka, IL '85 (PR)
KYSAR, GARY L., mgr. supportive serv., Broadwater Community Hospital, Townsend, MT '84 (ENG)
KYTE, BARBARA A., dir. outpatient and clin. serv., Casa Colina Hospital for Rehabilitation Medical, Pomona, CA '87 (AMB)
KYWI, ALBERTO, asst. dir. mgt. and info. syst., Little Company of Mary Hospital, Torrance, CA '81 (MGMT)

L

L'HEUREUX, DENNIS P., vice-pres. clin. support serv., Leonard Morse Hospital, Natick, MA '75 (MGMT)
L'HEUREUX, SUSAN, asst. mgr. matl., York Hospital, York, ME '80 (CS)
LA CLAIR, JOHN F., dir. pers., Community Hospital of Lancaster, Lancaster, PA '82 (PERS)
LA CRUZ, INDEPENDENCIA DE, RN, asst. dir. cent. serv., The Methodist Hospital, Houston, TX '86 (CS)
LA FORTUNE, MARIE A., RN, dir. pat. care serv., Memorial Medical Center, Long Beach, CA '77 (NURS)
LA MANTIA, SUSAN, health care consult., Johnson and Higgins, New York, NY '87 (RISK)
LA MONICA, AL, dir. commun. rel. and dev., Queen of the Valley Hospital, Napa, CA '81 (PR)
LA MORA, DONALD E., atty., Penrose Hospitals, Colorado Springs, CO '86 (ATTY)
LA PARO, HENRY C., dir. trng. and staff dev., Presbyterian Hospital in the City of New York, New York, NY '84 (EDUC)
LAAVEG, JOEL, dir. matl. mgt., St. Joseph Mercy Hospital, Mason City, IA '85 (PUR)
LABADIE, ALICE J., RN, dir. prof. nrsg., Hillcrest Medical Center, Tulsa, OK '86 (NURS)
LABARBA, FRANK J., br. mgr. bus. dev. and med. equip. fin., McDonnell Douglas Finance Corporation, Long Beach, CA '85
LABAT, CONSTANCE R., adm. clin. path., Beth Israel Medical Center, New York, NY '85
LABAUGH, THOMAS DONALD, dir. mktg., St. Mary's Hospital, Grand Rapids, MI '85 (PR) (PLNG)
LABBE, MAURICE L., pres., Russell Park Manor, Lewiston, ME '76
LABBE, PAUL W., adm. dir. human res., Slidell Memorial Hospital, Slidell, LA '85 (RISK)
LABELLE, LESLIE J., dir. educ., evaluation and res., Little Company of Mary Hospital, Evergreen Park, IL '86 (NURS)
LABENZ, SR. M. CONCETTA, RN, vice-pres. nrsg., Sacred Heart Medical Center, Chester, PA '74 (NURS)
LABERTEW, LAWRENCE R., dir. human res., Good Samaritan Hospital, Mount Vernon, IL '73 (PERS)
LABONTE, DOROTHY H., RN, dir. pat. care, Leonard Morse Hospital, Natick, MA '76 (NURS)
LABOON, SR. JOAN, coor. vol. serv., Mercy Hospital of Pittsburgh, Pittsburgh, PA '86 (VOL)
LABORANTI, JAMES, eng. consult., Sisters of Charity-St. Vincent DePaul, Bridgeport, CT '71
LABOUTELEY, ROGER B., Woodstock, VT '53 (LIFE)
LABOYTEAUX, JANICE M., sales mgr., Ball Memorial Hospital, Muncie, IN '86 (PR)
LABRECQUE, MARK A., adm. dir. amb. serv., Mercy Hospital, Urbana, IL '87 (AMB)
LACALAMITA, MICHAEL, asst. vice-pres., White Plains Hospital Medical Center, White Plains, NY '79 (PUR)
LACASSE, RUTH, RN, vice-pres. nrsg., St. John's Regional Medical Center, Oxnard, CA '81 (NURS)
LACAVA, FREDERICK W., atty., Lutheran Hospital of Fort Wayne, Fort Wayne, IN '80 (ATTY)
LACEY, LEROY M., atty., Howard Community Hospital, Kokomo, IN '73 (ATTY)
LACEY, PATRICIA, RN, mgr. emer. and outpat, Saint Cabrini Hospital of Seattle, Seattle, WA '87 (AMB)
LACEY, STEPHEN E., asst. adm. human res., St. Mary Medical Center, Gary, IN '85 (PERS)
LACHER, PAMELA K., dir. soc. serv., Mercy Hospital, Valley City, ND '82 (SOC)
LACHMAN, LOIS, asst. dir. pers., Saint Joseph Hospital, Denver, CO '82 (PERS)
LACHMAN, VICKI D., RN PhD, dir. nrsg. mgt., Center for Health Care Management, Camden, NJ '81 (EDUC)(NURS)
LACHNER, BERNARD JOSEPH, pres. and chief exec. off., Evanston Hospital, Evanston, IL '52 (LIFE)
LACHTRUP, BONNIE HILLSBERG, dir. hosp. mgt. org. oper., Cigna Health Plan, St. Louis, MO '84
LACINA, BRIGETTA C., coor. risk mgt., St. Joseph Mercy Hospital, Ann Arbor, MI '84 (RISK)
LACKETT, JEANNETTE C., RN, asst. adm., St. Joseph Hospital, Eureka, CA '82 (NURS)
LACKEY, GLORIA W., dir. pub. rel., Wabash Valley Hospital, West Lafayette, IN '84 (PR)
LACKEY, MICHAEL J., vice-pres., Towers, Perrin, Forsb and Crosby, St. Louis, MO '85 (PERS)
LACKEY, NOLAN R., pres., Hospital Services, Inc., Lafayette, IN '75 (PLNG)
LACKEY, ROBERT A., dir. pers., Visiting Nurse Association of Brooklyn, Inc., Brooklyn, NY '66 (PERS)
LACKEY, ROBERT L., dir. pers., Haywood County Hospital, Clyde, NC '81 (PERS)
LACKEY, TERRY, safety off., Eisenhower Medical Center, Rancho Mirage, CA '86 (ENG)
LACKORE, LINDA, dir. educ., Clermont Mercy Hospital, Batavia, OH '86 (EDUC)
LACLAIR, BERNARD W., adm., Albany Orthopedic Clinic, Albany, GA '78
LACOME, ELAINE C., dir. vol., Sioux Valley Hospital, Sioux Falls, SD '81 (VOL)

LACOSTE, SR. ANDREA, mgt. analyst, St. Paul Medical Center, Dallas, TX '71 (MGMT)
LACROIX, ARLENE RITA, admit. nrs. and pat. rep., Santa Ana Hospital Medical Center, Santa Ana, CA '86 (PAT)
LACUSTA, MICHAEL P., consult., Touche Ross and Company, Detroit, MI '84 (MGMT)
LACY, DONALD B., dir. environ. serv., Metropolitan Hospital, Richmond, VA '86 (ENVIRON)
LACY, KIM G., dir. pub. rel., St. Joseph Hospital, Lexington, KY '81 (PR)
LADD, DAVID G., dir. plng., William Beaumont Hospital, Royal Oak, MI '79 (PLNG)
LADD, HELEN E., dir. vol., Wood County Hospital, Bowling Green, OH '74 (VOL)
LADD, JANET W., RN, dir. nrsg. med., surg. and psych., St. Joseph's Hospital, Asheville, NC '86 (NURS)
LADD, JEFFREY R., atty., Northern Illinois Medical Center, McHenry, IL '83 (ATTY)
LADD, KENT D., dir. pers., Genesee Memorial Hospital, Batavia, NY '78 (PERS)
LADD, RONALD D., corp. dir. mgt. eng., Western Reserve Care Systems-Southside Medical Center, Youngstown, OH '80 (MGMT)
LADENBURGER, JEFFREY PAUL, fin. analyst, Sisters of Charity Health Care Systems, Cincinnati, OH '80
LADEVICH, MICHAEL R., dir. rehab. and affiliated satellite oper., The Watson Clinic, Lakeland, FL '83
LADOUCEUR, LEE JR., asst. adm. human res., Memorial Hospital, Albany, NY '80 (PERS)
LAEDTKE, RALPH H., visiting asst. prof. and prog. coor., Southern Illinois University, School of Technical Careers, Carbondale, IL '74 (EDUC)
LAETZ, ERNEST C., (ret.), Ann Arbor, MI '44 (LIFE)
LAFALCE, JOYCE B., dir. vol. serv., Hurley Medical Center, Flint, MI '81 (VOL)
LAFAVE, BETTY, mgr. pur., Kenosha Hospital and Medical Center, Kenosha, WI '84 (PUR)
LAFFERTY, DOUGLAS L., vice-pres., Hinsdale Hospital, Hinsdale, IL '80
LAFFERTY, PATRICIA, RN, pat. rep., White Plains Hospital Medical Center, White Plains, NY '77 (PAT)
LAFFERTY, WILLIAM A., dir. bldgs. and grds., St. Joseph's Hospital, Elmira, NY '77 (ENG)
LAFFEY, WILLIAM J., pres., Providence Hospital, Holyoke, MA '77 (PLNG)
LAFOND, JEAN B., reg. mgr., The Packer Group, Los Angeles, CA '70
LAFOND, RUTH E., dir. data proc., Northeast Rehabilitation Hospital, Salem, NH '84 (MGMT)
LAFONTAINE, DAVID P., matl. mgt., Sherrill House, Inc., Boston, MA '84 (PUR)
LAFRAZIA, FLORENCE T., student, Northeast University, Boston, MA '86 (PLNG)
LAGALSKI, NANCY, RN, asst. dir. nrsg., Lapeer General Hospital, LaPeer, MI '84 (NURS)
LAGASSE, ROBERT F., vice-pres. human resources, Walthamweston Hospital and Medical Center, Waltham, MA '85 (PERS)
LAGATTA, DENNIS C., sr. assoc., Heery and Heery Architects and Engineer, Atlanta, GA '78
LAGE, DEAN, dir. food serv., St. Joseph's Hospital and Medical Center, Paterson, NJ '67 (FOOD)
LAGE, JANE, RN, dir. nrsg., McPherson Community Health Center, Howell, MI '83 (NURS)
LAGERBERG, ALAN K., adm. asst., Bronson Healthcare Group, Inc., Kalamazoo, MI '79 (PLNG)
LAGERGREN, BRENT A., dir. plng. and mktg., Loudoun Memorial Hospital, Leesburg, VA '85 (PR) (PLNG)
LAGERMAN, DANIEL, dir. matl. mgt., California Medical Center-Los Angeles, Los Angeles, CA '82 (PUR)
LAGING, JON, dir. pers., St. John's Hospital, Salina, KS '86 (PERS)
LAGOMARSINO, W. LUIS, indust. eng., Hvac-Electrical and Mechanical, Montevideo, Uruguay '86 (ENG)
LAGONI, BETTY J., dir. vol., Kaiser Foundation Hospital and Rehabilitation Center, Vallejo, CA '81 (VOL)
LAGRONE, STEPHEN L., dir. plng. and mktg., Munroe Regional Medical Center, Ocala, FL '85 (PLNG)
LAGROTTERIA, VINCENT L., dir. food serv., Fallston General Hospital, Fallston, MD '80 (FOOD)
LAGUE, RICHARD C., atty., Hackley Hospital, Muskegon, MI '76 (ATTY)
LAHAYNE, ROGER W., proj. mgr., St. Mary of Nazareth Hospital Center, Chicago, IL '81 (MGMT)
LAHAZA, YOLANDA MARIA, asst. dir. pers., Medical Center at Princeton, Princeton, NJ '83 (PERS)
LAHEY, GARY, dir. prog. and plng., Payette Associates, Inc., Boston, MA '82 (PLNG)
LAHEY, MICHAEL SCOTT, student, Program in Hospital and Personnel Management, Madonna College, Livonia, MI '85
LAHEY, ROBERT W., dir. eng., Concourse Division, Bronx, NY '85 (ENG)
LAHMEYER, CONNIE B., mgr., mgt. consulting, Ernst and Whinney, Chicago, IL '79
LAIBACH, ROBERT W., dir. info. syst. dev., Brookdale Hospital Medical Center, Brooklyn, NY '84 (MGMT)
LAIBLE, ROBERT J., pres. and chief exec. off., Redford Community Hospital, Redford, MI '74 (PUR)
LAIGN, MICHAEL B., exec. vice-pres., Frankford Hospital, Philadelphia, PA '77
LAIL, SAM D., asst. dir. eng. serv., Providence Memorial Hospital, El Paso, TX '86 (ENG)
LAINE, ROSS W., dir. eng. serv., Providence Medical Center, Portland, OR '85 (ENG)
LAINE, THOMAS R., consult., Cincinnati, OH '79 (PLNG)
LAING-CURTIS, CYNTHIA, dir. mktg. and pub. rel., HCA Grand Strand General Hospital, Myrtle Beach, SC '86 (PR)
LAING, DENNIS O., atty., Richmond Eye and Ear Hospital, Richmond, VA '80 (ATTY)
LAING, SR. EDITH, dir. vol. serv., St. Francis Hospital, Charleston, WV '80 (VOL)
LAING, HARRY L., phys. asst. and mgr., Canton-Potsdam Hospital, Potsdam, NY '87 (AMB)
LAING, JACQUELINE A., dir. human serv., St. Vincent Hospital, Santa Fe, NM '83 (SOC)
LAIRD, BIRGIT S., pat. rep., Montgomery General Hospital, Montgomery, WV '82 (PAT)
LAIRD, RICHARD A., vice-pres. and dir. amb. serv., University Hospitals of Cleveland, Cleveland, OH '87 (AMB)
LAIRD, WILLIAM G., chief fin. off., Western Psychiatric Institute and Clinic, Pittsburgh, PA '86
LAITY, ANNE R., dir. vol. serv., Orthopaedic Hospital, Los Angeles, CA '85 (VOL)
LAJCZAK, CHRISTINE A., dir., Samaritan Health Service, Phoenix, AZ '81
LAJONE, LYNNE M., atty., Rush-Presbyterian-St. Luke's Medical Center, Chicago, IL '82 (ATTY)
LAKATTA, PATRICIA L., dir. pub. affairs, North Charles Hospital, Baltimore, MD '84 (PR)
LAKE, H. M., dir. matl. mgt., St. Marys Hospital of Rochester, Rochester, MN '70 (PUR)
LAKE, KAY A., RN, dir. educ. serv., Marion General Hospital, Marion, IN '72 (EDUC)
LAKE, REBECCA S., RN, student, Loyola University, Chicago, IL '82
LAKERNICK, PHILIP STEPHEN, adm., Good Hope Hospital, Erwin, NC '67 (PLNG)
LAKES, STEVEN L., dir. risk mgt., Parkview Memorial Hospital, Fort Wayne, IN '83 (RISK)
LAKEY, LT. COL. GENE A., Bakersfield, CA '67
LAKIER, NANCE S., RN, vice-pres. pat. care, Childrens Memorial Hospital, Omaha, NE '83 (NURS)
LAKIN, MELANIE, dir. pat. rel., Central DuPage Hospital, Winfield, IL '84 (RISK)
LAKRITZ, ADAM, La Jolla, CA '85 (FOOD)
LALIBERTE, BRUCE, supv. med. elec., Dickinson County Hospitals, Iron Mountain, MI '79 (ENG)
LALIBERTE, MARILYN G., soc. worker, Mesabi Regional Medical Center, Hibbing, MN '83 (SOC)
LALIBERTY, RENE, vice-pres. pers. and emp. rel., Mid-Maine Medical Center, Waterville, ME '67 (PERS)
LALLY, PAUL P., vice-pres. adm. med. serv., Wuesthoff Memorial Hospital, Rockledge, FL '80 (RISK)
LALLY, RICHARD, dir. hskpg. and ldry., Trinity Regional Hospital, Fort Dodge, IA '86 (ENVIRON)
LALONDE, ROGER J., vice-pres. commun. rel. and dev., Silver Cross Hospital, Joliet, IL '80 (PR)
LAM, BLAINE P., dir. pub. rel., Borgess Medical Center, Kalamazoo, MI '85 (PR)
LAM, CECILIA K., asst. dir. med. soc. serv., Cedars-Sinai Medical Center, Los Angeles, CA '85 (SOC)
LAMAR, STEVEN R., spec. asst. adm., Naval Hospital, Bethesda, MD '84 (FOOD)
LAMARRE, FERNAND, asst. dir. aux. serv., Montreal General Hospital, Montreal, Que., Canada '85 (ENG)
LAMB, CATHY, dir. pat. scheduling and registration, University of Iowa Hospitals and Clinics, Iowa City, IA '79
LAMB, DARRELL J., dir. eng., Mercy Hospital, Iowa City, IA '79 (ENG)
LAMB, DIANA K., mgr. info. proc., Queen of the Valley Hospital, West Covina, CA '85 (MGMT)
LAMB, DOYLE L., adm., Malone and Hogan Clinic, Big Spring, TX '87 (AMB)
LAMB, JAMES A., pres. and chief exec. off., Washoe Medical Center, Reno, NV '67
LAMB, LUAN FOREMAN, dir. pub. rel., Mary Rutan Hospital, Bellefontaine, OH '80 (PR) (PLNG)
LAMB, LCDR MARTHA JANE DICKERSON, MSC USN, head food mgt., Naval Hospital, Great Lakes, IL '84 (FOOD)
LAMB, MICHAEL J., dir. pat. and family serv., St. Mary's Hospital and Health Center, Tucson, AZ '86 (SOC)
LAMB, RODNEY J., adm., Santa Barbara Cottage Hospital, Santa Barbara, CA '54 (LIFE)
LAMB, RONALD L., assoc. vice-pres. human res., Aultman Hospital, Canton, OH '80 (PERS)
LAMB, SUSAN K., asst. vice-pres., Doctor's Management Company, Santa Monica, CA '86 (RISK)
LAMB, VIRGINIA A., atty., St. Francis Hospital, Memphis, TN '79 (ATTY)
LAMBERT, ARTHUR ALFRED, asst. vice-pres., Applied Management Systems, Inc., Burlington, MA '75 (MGMT)
LAMBERT, BARBARA LYNN, mgr. vol. serv., Our Lady of Mercy Hospital, Dyer, IN '86 (VOL)
LAMBERT, BOBBIE, RN, asst. adm. nrsg., Samaritan Hospital, Moses Lake, WA '81 (NURS)
LAMBERT, CARL, adm., Health Scan, Ltd., Philadelphia, PA '86
LAMBERT, DOROTHY A., (ret.), Augusta, GA '80 (SOC)
LAMBERT, MRS. GERARD B., chm., Board of Gerard B. Lambert Awards, Princeton, NJ '74 (HON)
LAMBERT, JAMES M., dir. matl. mgt., Rogue Valley Medical Center, Medford, OR '82 (PUR)
LAMBERT, JANIS, RN, asst. dir. nrsg., White Memorial Medical Center, Los Angeles, CA '78 (NURS)
LAMBERT, JOHN W. JR., pres., John Lambert Associates, Roanoke, VA '81 (PR)
LAMBERT, JONATHAN E., dir. eng. serv., St. Catharines General Hospital, St. Catharines, Ont., Canada '83 (ENG)
LAMBERT, MARY H., Falls Church, VA '80
LAMBERT, NORMA, dir. environ. serv., Crawford County Memorial Hospital, Van Buren, AR '86 (ENVIRON)
LAMBERT, ROBERT J., atty., Worcester Memorial Hospital, Worcester, MA '81 (ATTY)
LAMBERT, ROBERT, asst. adm. phys. plant, University of California at Los Angeles Medical Center, Los Angeles, CA '85 (ENG)
LAMBERT, RUTH C., RN, dir. nrsg., Children's Hospital, Boston, MA '82 (NURS)
LAMBERT, SHIRLEY I., dir. commun., DePaul Health Center, Bridgeton, MO '84 (ENG)
LAMBERT, VON, supr. biomed. eng., Carle Foundation Hospital, Urbana, IL '85 (ENG)
LAMBERTI, CLAIRE G., dir. dev. and commun. affairs, Yonkers General Hospital, Yonkers, NY '83 (PR)
LAMBERTSEN, ELEANOR C., RN, consult., New York, NY '61 (NURS)(LIFE)
LAMBRIGHT, WARREN D., MD, chm. amb. care, Abington Memorial Hospital, Abington, PA '87 (AMB)
LAMDIN, MARJORIE S., adm., Presidential Woods-Healthcare Retirement Corporation, Baltimore, MD '82
LAMERE, BAMBI E., mgr. pers., Copley Hospital, Morrisville, VT '83 (PERS)
LAMET, JEROME S., atty., Columbus Hospital, Chicago, IL '85 (ATTY)
LAMME, MARY L., coor. soc. serv., John Muir Memorial Hospital, Walnut Creek, CA '77 (SOC)
LAMONT, CHARLES ALASTAIR, exec. dir., Applied Management Consultants, Fredericton, N.B., Canada '80 (MGMT)
LAMONTAGNE, JOAN, dir. vol., Montreal General Hospital, Montreal, Que., Canada '80 (VOL)
LAMONTAGNE, MARGARET E., RN, dir. ob., gyn. and neonatal nrsg., Brigham and Women's Hospital, Boston, MA '86 (NURS)
LAMONTAGNE, ROGER R., dir. soc. serv., Harrington Memorial Hospital, Southbridge, MA '83 (SOC)
LAMOTHE, OMER G., dir. maint. and renovation, Humana, Inc., Louisville, KY '67 (ENG)
LAMOTTE, THOMAS M., pres. and chief exec. off., Fairview General Hospital, Cleveland, OH '66 (PLNG)
LAMOUREAUX, MICHAEL R., dir. maint., Edinburg General Hospital, Edinburg, TX '86 (ENG)
LAMPE, MARGERY J., dir. diet. serv., South Haven Community Hospital, South Haven, MI '86 (FOOD)
LAMPE, NORENE D., dir. info. syst., Sherman Hospital, Elgin, IL '85 (MGMT)
LAMPETER, RICHARD P., elec. proj. eng., Meyer, Strong and Jones, New York, NY '86 (ENG)
LAMPKIN, STEVEN B., adm., White River Medical Center, Batesville, AR '84
LAMPLEY, MARGIE W., RN, dir. nrs., Stanly Memorial Hospital, Albemarle, NC '72 (NURS)
LAMPMAN, CYNTHIA C., dir. soc. serv., Good Samaritan Hospital, West Palm Beach, FL '85 (SOC)
LAMPORT, LT. COL. JAMES E., MSC USA, dep. cmdr. and adv., 338 Medical Group, Folsom, PA '70
LAMPOS, MICHAEL W., dir. food serv., Bronson Methodist Hospital, Kalamazoo, MI '72 (FOOD)
LAMPREY, J., sr. vice-pres., Interqual, Inc., North Hampton, NH '87 (AMB)
LAMPSON, MARGELENE, supv. sterile proc., St. Vincent Charity Hospital, Cleveland, OH '83 (CS)
LAMSON, KATHERINE GRAHAM, dir. qual. assur. and risk mgt., Veterans Administration Medical Center, Miami, FL '79
LANATA, JOSEPH L., dir. cent. serv., George Washington University Hospital, Washington, DC '76 (CS)
LANAVA, FRANK C. JR., asst. dir., St. Luke's Hospital, Newburgh, NY '85 (PERS)
LANCASTER-RUSH, BOBBIE K., dir. diet., Selma Medical Center, Selma, AL '81 (FOOD)
LANCASTER, NANCY R., RN, dir. nrsg., Notre Dame Hospital, Central Falls, RI '86 (NURS)
LANCASTER, RALPH I., atty., Mercy Hospital, Portland, ME '68 (ATTY)
LANCE, DAVID S., vice-pres. human res., Faulkner Hospital, Boston, MA '74 (PERS)
LANCIANO, ANNE M., dir. med. rec., North Pennsylvania Hospital, Lansdale, PA '84
LAND, PAUL I., dir. plant oper., Bartholomew County Hospital, Columbus, IN '83 (ENG)
LAND, TRUDY, coor. soc. serv., Proctor Community Hospital, Peoria, IL '79 (SOC)
LANDA, DAVID A., mgr., Hospital Association of New York State, Albany, NY '83 (MGMT)
LANDAU, JOANNA, dir. staff dev., Four Winds Hospital, Katonah, NY '85 (EDUC)
LANDAUER, GEORGE H., pres., Generator Development Corporation Medical Electronics, Garden City, NY '79 (ENG)
LANDEFELD, CHARLES W., atty., St. Luke's Hospital of the United Methodist Church, Cleveland, OH '75 (ATTY)
LANDEN, F. GIFFORD, atty., Huron Road Hospital, Cleveland, OH '82 (ATTY)
LANDEN, MARY JANE, dir. pers., Jo Ellen Smith Medical Center, New Orleans, LA '79 (PERS)
LANDEN, RICHARD W., asst. adm., New York Infirmary-Beekman Downtown Hospital, New York, NY '79
LANDER, WALTER E. JR., RN, dir. nrsg., Fuller Mental Health Center, Boston, MA '79 (NURS)
LANDERS, GREGORY J., dir. matl. mgt., Hoag Memorial Hospital Presbyterian, Newport Beach, CA '79 (PUR)
LANDIN, DAVID CRAIG, atty., University of Virginia Hospitals, Charlottesville, VA '83 (ATTY)
LANDINI, SR. MARY TERRENCE, pat. rep., Little Company of Mary Hospital, Torrance, CA '82 (PAT)
LANDIS, DAVID W., mgr. cent. serv. room, Beyer Memorial Hospital, Ypsilanti, MI '85 (CS)
LANDIS, GEORGE F., dir. food serv., Good Samaritan Hospital, Lebanon, PA '84 (FOOD)
LANDIS, JOHN B., dir. mgt. serv., Medical University of South Carolina Medical Center, Charleston, SC '86 (MGMT)
LANDIS, MARY F., pur. agt., H. Lee Moffitt Hospital and Cancer Research Institute at the University of South Florida, Tampa, FL '82 (PUR)
LANDON, FRED B., risk mgr., Good Samaritan Hospital, West Islip, NY '84 (RISK)
LANDON, MORGAN M., proj. mech. eng., Daverman Associates, Grand Rapids, MI '85 (ENG)
LANDON, PERRY L., dir. soc. serv., Divine Providence Hospital, Williamsport, PA '86 (SOC)
LANDRAU, YOLANDA C., vice-pres. nrsg., Bridgeport Hospital, Bridgeport, CT '85 (NURS)

LANDRUM, H. BRITT JR., owner and mgr., Landrum Personnel Resources, Pensacola, FL '82
LANDRUM, JOY M., dir. educ., Columbus Hospital, Columbus, MS '86 (EDUC)
LANDRUM, SCOTT M., adm., Allen County War Memorial Hospital, Scottsville, KY '79
LANDRY, B. J., consult., B. J. Landry and Associates, Lafayette, LA '65
LANDRY, BRIAN T., dir. mktg., Children's Hospital, New Orleans, LA '85 (PR)
LANDRY, JAMES A., PhD, consult. and reg. health care practice leader, Towers, Perrin, Forster and Crosby, Houston, TX '85 (PERS)
LANDRY, ROGER A., asst. exec. dir., St. Mary's Hospital, Waterbury, CT '80 (MGMT)
LANDRY, ROSEMARY, dir. environ. serv., St. Vincent's Medical Center, Jacksonville, FL '87 (ENVIRON)
LANDRY, WILFRED A., pur. agt., Lawrence Memorial Hospital of Medford, Medford, MA '72 (PUR)
LANDSKROENER, MARIA A., dir. pers., Kent and Queen Anne's Hospital, Chestertown, MD '86 (PERS)
LANDSTROM, JOHN F., dir. corp. human res., Franciscan Sisters Health Care Corporation, Mokena, IL '81 (EDUC)
LANDVOY, ALAN B., dir. pub. rel. and dev., Hubbard Regional Hospital, Webster, MA '84 (PR)
LANDY, BARBARA, student, Program in Health and Hospital Administration, University of Florida, Gainesville, FL '85
LANE-DETMAN, DARLENE, dir. mktg., Erlanger Medical Center, Chattanooga, TN '86 (PR)
LANE-MCGRAW, CHARLOTTE W., RN, dir. nrsg. serv., Petaluma Valley Hospital, Petaluma, CA '86 (NURS)
LANE, BRUCE M., atty., Evangelical Health Systems, Oak Brook, IL '86 (ATTY)
LANE, CAROLE, mgr. linen control, Swedish American Hospital, Rockford, IL '86 (ENVIRON)
LANE, DANIEL W., mgr. hskpg., Trinity Medical Center, Minot, ND '86 (ENVIRON)
LANE, DOROTHY S., MD, chm. commun. medicine, Brookhaven Memorial Hospital Medical Center, Patchogue, NY '74
LANE, GREGORY R., atty., McLaren General Hospital, Flint, MI '86 (ATTY)
LANE, J. DAVID, gen. mgr., M. D. Industries, Inc.-Division of Chris-Craft Industrial Products, Northbrook, IL '86 (ENVIRON)
LANE, M. LUANNE, pat. advocate and dir. vol. serv., HCA Sun City Hospital, Sun City Center, FL '86 (VOL)(PAT)
LANE, MOLLY MESSNER, mgr. pub. rel., St. Francis-St. George Hospital, Cincinnati, OH '86 (PR)
LANE, NANCY M., vice-pres., Planning and Design Associates, Raleigh, NC '85
LANE, RICHARD, vice-pres., Hinsdale Hospital, Hinsdale, IL '64 (PLNG)
LANE, RUTH H., exec. dir. natl. pers. and labor rel., National Board, YWCA of United States, New York, NY '52 (LIFE)
LANE, SALLEY C., RN, dir. nsrg, Marion Memorial Hospital, Marion, SC '86 (NURS)
LANE, SAM D., MD, dir., Reno Diagnostic Center, Reno, NV '87 (AMB)
LANE, SHERRI L., sr. mgt. eng., Presbyterian Medical Center, Dallas, TX '82 (MGMT)
LANE, WILLIAM LIONETTE, pres., Bon Secours Hospital of Methuen, Methuen, MA '64
LANE, WILLIAM, dir. hskpg. and ldry., Jewish Home and Hospital for Aged, Bronx, NY '86 (ENVIRON)
LANESSKOG, TURID, dir. vol., Delnor Hospital, St. Charles, IL '85 (VOL)
LANG, BARBARA ALEXANDER, dir. soc. work, Pontiac General Hospital, Pontiac, MI '79 (SOC)
LANG, CARMENCITA B., dir. diet., Woodruff Hospital, Cleveland, OH '74 (FOOD)
LANG, CHARLES J., exec. adm., Michael Reese Hospital and Medical Center, Chicago, IL '82
LANG, DAN BENNETT, asst. adm., Halifax Hospital Medical Center, Daytona Beach, FL '79
LANG, ELAINE M., asst. dir. nrsg., Parma Community General Hospital, Parma, OH '80 (NURS)
LANG, FRED L., sr. vice-pres., Barnert Memorial Hospital Center, Paterson, NJ '72
LANG, GARY A., vice-pres. fin. and chief fin. off., St. Peter's Hospital, Albany, NY '82
LANG, HARRY H. JR., dir. eng. and maint., Mount St. Mary's Hospital, Lewiston, NY '78 (ENG)
LANG, JAMES R., dir. diet. serv., Grace Hospital, Detroit, MI '78 (FOOD)
LANG, JANICE K., RN, asst. dir. nrsg. serv., St. Francis Hospital, Blue Island, IL '82 (NURS)
LANG, JUDITH B., dir. pers., Memorial City Medical Center, Houston, TX '80 (PERS)
LANG, JUDY, mgr. external rel., St. Vincent Medical Center, Toledo, OH '86 (PR)
LANG, K. JOAN, asst. to exec. dir., Fallston General Hospital, Fallston, MD '79 (PAT)(RISK)
LANG, MARLENE, vice-pres. human res., Research Medical Center, Kansas City, MO '79 (PERS)
LANGAN, PATRICK J., risk mgr., Unity Medical Center, Fridley, MN '85 (RISK)
LANGBERG, SIMON M., partner, Vitetta Group, Architects and Engineers, Philadelphia, PA '82 (PLNG)
LANGDON, RICK, dir. matl. mgt., Wright Memorial Hospital, Trenton, MO '85 (PUR)
LANGE, GERALD A., clin. eng. serv., Mercy Health Center, Dubuque, IA '81 (ENG)
LANGE, JOHN E., dir. hskpg. serv., Louis A. Weiss Memorial Hospital, Chicago, IL '84 (ENG)(ENVIRON)
LANGE, JOHN E. III, atty., St. Luke Hospital, Fort Thomas, KY '80 (ATTY)
LANGE, PATRICE, student, Program in Hospital Administration, Bluefield State College, Bluefield, WV '85
LANGE, ROGER A., dir. pur., Health Hill Hospital for Children, Cleveland, OH '81 (PUR)
LANGELIERS, TIMOTHY R., adm. plng. and mktg., United Hospital, Grand Forks, ND '84 (PLNG)
LANGENFELD, MARY L., RN, vice-pres. nrsg., Mercy Medical Center, Nampa, ID '74 (NURS)
LANGER, CLIFFORD L., adm. cardiology, Montefiore Medical Center, Bronx, NY '75
LANGER, HENRY J., mktg. spec., Deaconess Hospital, St. Louis, MO '86 (PR)
LANGER, IRWIN, adm., Peninsula Hospital Center, Far Rockaway, NY '86 (RISK)
LANGER, MARIA P., dir. pub. rel., Northeastern Hospital of Philadelphia, Philadelphia, PA '86 (PR) (PLNG)
LANGER, THOMAS M., corp. vice-pres. mktg., Bronson Healthcare Group, Inc., Kalamazoo, MI '86 (PLNG)
LANGERMAN, VERNA M., supv. cent. serv., Eastern Idaho Regional Medical Center, Idaho Falls, ID '82 (CS)
LANGEVIN, DALLAS J., dir. psych. hosp. info. syst., New Hampshire Hospital, Concord, NH '87 (MGMT)
LANGFORD, BILL, exec. dir., Conway Regional Hospital, Conway, AR '80 (PLNG)
LANGFORD, MARGARET ANN, pat. rep., Baton Rouge General Medical Center, Baton Rouge, LA '84 (PAT)
LANGHAM, WES, PhD, vice-pres. prof. serv., High Plains Baptist Hospital, Amarillo, TX '86 (RISK)
LANGLAND, PHILIP, dir. clin. eng., University of New Mexico Hospital, Albuquerque, NM '80 (ENG)
LANGLEY, DOROTHY D., assoc. dir., Catholic Conference of Ohio, Department of Health Affairs, Columbus, OH '75
LANGLEY, ELIZABETH L., RN, dir. nrsg., Mission Oaks Hospital, Los Gatos, CA '77 (NURS)
LANGLEY, JAMES CRAWFORD JR., dir. med. serv., Southwest Florida Regional Medical Center, Fort Myers, FL '85
LANGLEY, WILLIAM O. JR., dir. plng., Morton F. Plant Hospital, Clearwater, FL '86 (PLNG)
LANGLIE, JOANN K., dir. soc. work amb. care, University of Michigan Hospitals, Ann Arbor, MI '79 (SOC)
LANGLOIS, ROBERT LEONARD, pres., Langlois and Associates Consultant Group, Quincy, MA '65
LANGPAAP, ELEANOR M., exec. vice-pres., St. John's Hospital and Health Center, Santa Monica, CA '62
LANGSAM, DAVID E., vice-pres., Chase Manhattan Capital Markets Corporation, New York, NY '85
LANGWORTHY, DORCAS E., asst. sec., Lakewood Hospital Foundation, Inc., Lakewood, OH '56 (VOL)(LIFE)
LANIER-AUSTIN, JOAN, dir. pub. rel., Highland Hospital of Rochester, Rochester, NY '85 (PR)
LANIER, DANA L., RN, dir. nrsg. serv., De Paul Hospital, Cheyenne, WY '86 (NURS)
LANIER, JACK O., vice-pres. corp. and commun. dev., Greater Southeast Corporate Office, Washington, DC '68
LANIGAN-CARTER, FRANKE, dir. commun. and pat. rel., HCA Riverton Hospital, Riverton, WY '84 (PR) (PLNG)
LANIGAN, EDMOND J., Elmhurst, IL '73 (LIFE)
LANIGAN, JUDY M., RN, actg. assoc. dir. nrsg., Stanford University Hospital, Stanford, CA '86 (NURS)
LANKFORD, JOEL J., vice-pres. mgt. serv., Columbus Hospital, Great Falls, MT '86 (PR)
LANKFORD, WILL E., assoc. dep. dir., Emory University Hospital, Atlanta, GA '59
LANNEN, RICHARD M., atty., Shiloh Park Hospital, Garland, TX '81 (ATTY)
LANNING, JOYCE A., student, University of Alabama in Birmingham, School of Community and Allied Health, Birmingham, AL '83
LANNING, LARRY, dir. bldg. and grds., Lima Memorial Hospital, Lima, OH '76 (ENG)
LANNON, MADELINE, dir. vol. serv., Our Lady of Mercy Medical Center, Bronx, NY '86 (VOL)
LANNOYE, CRAIG, dir. eng., Saginaw General Hospital, Saginaw, MI '78 (ENG)
LANSER, JOAN A., RN, dir. nrsg., St. Joseph's Hospital, Milwaukee, WI '78 (NURS)
LANSFORD, JIMMIE D., asst. adm., St. Mary's Hospital, Streator, IL '81 (PLNG)
LANSKY, GOLDIE Y., dir. bus. dev., Evangelical Health Systems, Oak Brook, IL '81 (PLNG)
LANT, THOMAS W., RN, vice-pres. pat. care serv., Saint Vincent Hospital, Worcester, MA '77 (NURS)
LANTRY, JOHN H., dir. commun., Torrance Memorial Hospital Medical Center, Torrance, CA '84 (ENG)
LANTTO, DAVID A., vice-pres. fin., Sinai Hospital of Detroit, Detroit, MI '79
LANTZ, BONNIE C., dir. dev. and pub. rel., Waterville Osteopathic Hospital, Waterville, ME '86 (PR)
LANTZ, NANCY C., dir. food serv., Charter Beacon Hospital, Fort Wayne, IN '86 (FOOD)
LANUM, THEODORE H. JR., sr. buyer, California Medical Center-Los Angeles, Los Angeles, CA '85 (PUR)
LANYON, GLORIA JEAN, dir. soc. serv., St. Luke's Hospital West, Chesterfield, MO '77 (SOC)
LANZA, ALICE, coor. qual. assur., St. Joseph of the Pines Hospital, Southern Pines, NC '86 (RISK)
LAPIDES, ALBERT M., pres., Replacement Parts Industries, Inc., Chatsworth, CA '85 (ENG)
LAPIN, JODI L., mgt. eng., University Hospitals of Cleveland, Cleveland, OH '87 (MGMT)
LAPIN, LEO, dir. phys. facil. and mgr. constr., Chestnut Lodge Hospital, Rockville, MD '86 (ENG)
LAPINE, JAY M., chief oper. off., AMI Bellaire Hospital, Houston, TX '83 (PLNG)(ATTY)
LAPINSKI, JOHN J., dir. plant oper., Walther Memorial Hospital, Chicago, IL '77 (ENG)
LAPLANTE, JOHN GUY, dir. pub. rel. and mktg., Worcester City Hospital, Worcester, MA '86 (PR)
LAPLANTE, JOSEPH PAUL, MD, (ret.), Montreal, Que., Canada '49 (LIFE)
LAPOINT, ARTHUR R., vice-pres., Methodist Hospital, St. Louis Park, MN '86 (PERS)
LAPOINT, DAVID L., adm. dir. environ. control, Joint Township District Memorial Hospital, St. Marys, OH '85 (ENG)
LAPP, ROBERT E., pres., Robert E. Lapp and Associates, Winnetka, IL '74 (MGMT)
LAPPINO, BENJAMIN A., vice-pres. corp. facil., Intercare Health Systems, Edison, NJ '83 (ENG)
LAPREZIOSA, DAVID, coor. pur., Pottstown Memorial Medical Center, Pottstown, PA '86 (PUR)
LARAMY, KIMBERLYNN, dir. mktg. and pub. rel., Bath Memorial Hospital, Bath, ME '86 (PR) (PLNG)
LARDINO, MIKE, mgr. facil., Bethany Hospital, Chicago, IL '81 (ENG)
LARDO, PASQUALE, asst. dir. eng., Jamaica Hospital, Jamaica, NY '86 (ENG)
LARE, JOHN C., dir. pub. rel., River Oaks Hospital, New Orleans, LA '80 (PR)
LARET, MARK R., assoc. dir. and dir. mktg. and plng., UCLA Medical Center, Los Angeles, CA '86 (PR)
LARGENT, KAY P., dir. in-service educ., Warren Memorial Hospital, Front Royal, VA '85 (EDUC)
LARGENT, SHARON, dir. pers., Lourdes Hospital, Paducah, KY '80 (PERS)
LARICCIA, MARIA E., assoc. vice-pres. amb. care, Staten Island Hospital, Staten Island, NY '87 (AMB)
LARIMER, KRISTI D., dir. soc. serv., Hocking Valley Community Hospital, Logan, OH '86 (SOC)
LARKIN-LEIGHTON, ELAINE M., prog. dir., Arthritis Foundation, Chicago, IL '87 (EDUC)
LARKIN, CHARLES J., atty., Office of County Counsel, San Bernardino, CA '84 (ATTY)
LARKIN, FRANK J., pres., Metropolitan Medical Center, Minneapolis, MN '67 (PLNG)
LARKIN, MARY L., RN, dir. nrsg. serv., Black River Memorial Hospital, Black River Falls, WI '77 (NURS)
LARKIN, MARYANN, dir. vol. serv., Community Hospital Schoharie County, Cobleskill, NY '87 (VOL)
LARKIN, PEG, dir. commun., Port Huron Hospital, Port Huron, MI '86 (PR)
LARKIN, TERRY, vice-pres., Johnson and Higgins, Minneapolis, MN '87 (RISK)
LARKWORTHY, WILLIAM E., dir. commun. rel., South Nassau Communities Hospital, Oceanside, NY '69 (PR)
LAROCCA, RONALD M., atty., Victory Memorial Hospital, Brooklyn, NY '82 (ATTY)
LAROCK, CAROL, dir. commun., United Hospital, St. Paul, MN '85 (ENG)
LARONDELLE, DAVID, dir. soc. serv., Walla Walla General Hospital, Walla Walla, WA '85 (SOC)
LAROVERE, JOSEPH C., Alachua General Hospital, Gainesville, FL '81 (FOOD)
LARRABEE, M. GLADYS, (ret.), Orchard Lake, MI '24 (LIFE)
LARRIMORE, PATSY GADD, RN, dir. nrsg., Bon Secours Hospital, Baltimore, MD '78 (NURS)
LARSEN, DOROTHY, dir. qual. assessment and risk mgt., Baptist Medical Center, Kansas City, MO '85 (RISK)
LARSEN, EDWARD R., pres., A. Squibb Company, Princeton, NJ '86
LARSEN, FRANK L., Southern Pines, NC '51 (LIFE)
LARSEN, JANET A., dir. food serv., Memorial Hospital of Dodge County, Fremont, NE '82 (FOOD)
LARSEN, JANICE M., coor. pers., Northbay Medical Center, Fairfield, CA '83 (PERS)
LARSEN, JOHN C., atty., Sartori Memorial Hospital, Cedar Falls, IA '86 (ATTY)
LARSEN, MABEL E., dir. pers., Redington-Fairview General Hospital, Skowhegan, ME '78 (PERS)
LARSEN, PAUL W., biomedical eng., Universal Hospital Service, Inc., Minneapolis, MN '76 (ENG)
LARSEN, PEG, dir. amb. care, Silver Cross Hospital, Joliet, IL '87 (AMB)
LARSEN, TIMOTHY G., PhD, dir., College of Osteopathic Medicine of the Pacific, Pomona, CA '87 (AMB)
LARSON-WHITE, KAREN, dir. pub. rel., St. Paul-Ramsey Medical Center, St. Paul, MN '86 (PR)
LARSON, BARBARA A., RN, asst. adm. nrsg. serv., Providence Medical Center, Seattle, WA '82 (NURS)
LARSON, BRENT L., coor. corp. pub. rel., Bronson Healthcare Group, Inc., Kalamazoo, MI '85 (PR)
LARSON, CAROL N., asst. dir. nrsg. serv., University of Kansas Hospital, Kansas City, KS '69 (CS)
LARSON, CAROLYN, mgr. mgt. serv., St. Joseph's Hospital and Medical Center, Phoenix, AZ '78 (MGMT)
LARSON, CHRISTINE A., RN, dir. clin. med. and surg. nrsg., Lahey Clinic Hospital, Burlington, MA '86 (NURS)
LARSON, DALLAS KEITH, Portsmith, OH '68
LARSON, DONALD K., Elk Grove Village, IL '61
LARSON, GAIL C., assoc. adm., Huntington Memorial Hospital, Pasadena, CA '85 (PLNG)
LARSON, GERALDINE K., RN, dir. nrsg. serv., Clark Fork Valley Hospital, Plains, MT '80 (NURS)
LARSON, GLENN A., dir. food serv., Northwestern Memorial Hospital, Chicago, IL '73 (FOOD)
LARSON, HERBERT O. JR., dir. pers., Delaware County Memorial Hospital, Drexel Hill, PA '71 (PERS)
LARSON, JEAN ANN, value improvement analyst and mgt. eng., William Beaumont Hospital, Royal Oak, MI '86 (MGMT)
LARSON, JOAN S., dir. soc. serv., Salem Community Hospital, Salem, OH '81 (SOC)
LARSON, JON F., dir. diet., Boone Hospital Center, Columbia, MO '74 (FOOD)
LARSON, KAREN LILLER, asst. vice-pres., Roanoke Memorial Hospitals, Roanoke, VA '86 (PLNG)
LARSON, LAVERNE A., pers. off., Baystate Medical Center, Springfield, MA '82 (PERS)
LARSON, MAE, dir. soc. serv., St. Ansgar Hospital, Moorhead, MN '71 (SOC)
LARSON, MARION L., coor. health educ., St. Catherine Hospital of East Chicago, East Chicago, IN '85 (EDUC)
LARSON, MARY A., adm. asst., Sandwich Community Hospital, Sandwich, IL '81 (PR)(PERS)
LARSON, MARY ANN, RN, dir. nrsg., Columbia Memorial Hospital, Astoria, OR '78 (NURS)
LARSON, MICHAEL DUANE, tech. cent. serv., St. Mary Hospital, Port Arthur, TX '84 (CS)

LARSON, NANCY K., RN, mgr. cent. proc., Munson Medical Center, Traverse City, MI '86 (CS)
LARSON, NANCY V., exec. asst. commun. rel. and dev., Kishwaukee Community Hospital, De Kalb, IL '85 (PR)
LARSON, O. C., dir. proj. contr., AMI Presbyterian-St. Luke's Medical Center, Denver, CO '78 (ENG)
LARSON, PATRICIA K., RN, dir. nrsg., Denali Center, Fairbanks, AK '86 (NURS)
LARSON, PHILIP P., dir. ldry., University of Minnesota, Minneapolis, MN '69
LARSON, ROBERT H., vice-pres. adm., Morristown Memorial Hospital, Morristown, NJ '56 (LIFE)
LARSON, SHIRLEY A., vice-pres. pat. care, St. Catherine's Hospital, Kenosha, WI '85 (NURS)
LARSON, STEPHANIE S., dir. pub. rel. and dev., St. Nicholas Hospital, Sheboygan, WI '84 (PR) (PLNG)
LARSON, SUSAN R., asst. dir. vol. serv., La Crosse Lutheran Hospital, La Crosse, WI '83 (VOL)
LARSON, THOMAS, dir. eng., Citrus Memorial Hospital, Inverness, FL '75 (ENG)
LARUE, GAYNETTE, asst. adm., Children's Hospital, Norfolk, VA '82 (RISK)
LARUE, LARRY, dir. eng., DePaul Health Center, Bridgeton, MO '81 (ENG)
LARY, CAPT. GEORGE F. III, MSC USAF, trng. eval. off., U. S. Air Force School of Health Care Sciences, Sheppard AFB, TX '79
LASAGNA, M. ANGELA, atty., Research Medical Center, Kansas City, MO '86 (ATTY)
LASATER, JOE B., dir. trng. and safety, Baroness Erlanger Hospital, Chattanooga, TN '72 (EDUC)
LASATER, W. ROBERT JR., atty., Southwest Community Health Services, Albuquerque, NM '84 (ATTY)
LASCARI, CHARLES A., dir. plng., Muhlenberg Regional Medical Center, Plainfield, NJ '83 (PLNG)
LASCARI, CHARLES E., RN, dir. nrsg., Hackensack Medical Center, Hackensack, NJ '83 (NURS)
LASCH, FRANK J., dir. constr. mgt., St. Joseph Hospital, Chicago, IL '78 (ENG)
LASCO, JOHN JR., Quincy, IL '84 (MGMT)
LASCU, EUGEN B., exec. vice-pres., Associated Retinal Consultants, Livonia, MI '81
LASH, C. PATRICK, dir. fin., Western Medical Center, Santa Ana, CA '77
LASH, CIA COLABELLA, coor. pub. affairs, Sharp Cabrillo Hospital, San Diego, CA '82 (PR)(AMB)
LASH, JAMES O., asst. adm., Howard County General Hospital, Columbia, MD '72 (ENG)
LASH, MYLES P., exec. consult., The Lash Group, Washington, DC '76
LASHIER, BETTY S., dir. food and nutr., Emanuel Hospital and Health Center, Portland, OR '72 (FOOD)
LASHLEE, LT. COL. LYNNE V., MSC USA, insp. gen. team, U. S. Army Health Services Command, Fort Sam Houston, TX '80
LASKA, LEWIS L., atty., Tennessee Association of International Physicians, Nashville, TN '83 (ATTY)(RISK)
LASKER, MARTIN B., exec. vice-pres., Hospital Learning Centers, Inc., Van Nuys, CA '71 (EDUC)
LASKOW, LYNDA T., RN, dir. acute care nrsg., Metropolitan Medical Center, Minneapolis, MN '85 (NURS)
LASKY, PAUL C., atty., Aspen Publishers, Inc., Rockville, MD '77 (ATTY)
LASLAVIC, JOHN D., dir. res. and dev., Hospital Shared Services Western Pennsylvania, Warrendale, PA '84 (PUR)
LASORSA, FRANK J., dir. pub. rel. and commun. affairs, Mount Vernon Hospital, Mount Vernon, NY '72 (PR)
LASSER, ANDREW A., assoc. adm., West Virginia University Hospital, Morgantown, WV '73
LASSIG, DONNIS E., RN, clin. dir. nrsg., St. Marys Hospital of Rochester, Rochester, MN '86 (NURS)
LASSITER, JAMES THOMAS, adm., Community Hospital of Lodi, Lodi, CA '64
LASSITER, LYNN, dir. outpat serv., Jackson-Madison County General Hospital, Jackson, TN '87 (AMB)
LASSITER, PHIL, dir. maint., Magnolia Hospital, Corinth, MS '87 (ENG)
LASSLEBEN, WILLIAM M. JR., atty., Presbyterian Intercommunity Hospital, Whittier, CA '70 (ATTY)
LAST, AMY E., student, Program in Health Care Administration, Baruch College, New York City, NY '86
LASTOWKA, TERRY M., coor. vol. and dir. pat. spec. serv., Alfred I. Dupont Institute, Wilmington, DE '86 (VOL)
LASTRAPES, GERALDINE B., RN, dir. nrsg. serv., St. Luke General Hospital, Arnaudville, LA '77 (NURS)
LATACZ, SUZANNE, RN, vice-pres. nrsg., Barnert Memorial Hospital Center, Paterson, NJ '86 (NURS)
LATAS, LAWRENCE E., coor. eng. and maint., John F. Kennedy Medical Center, Chicago, IL '86 (ENG)
LATCHAM, JOHN F., Trumbull Memorial Hospital, Warren, OH '39 (LIFE)
LATESSA, PHILIP, vice-pres., Iowa Hospital Association, Des Moines, IA '80 (RISK)
LATHAM, EMELDA M., dir. educ., Dominguez Medical Center, Long Beach, CA '85 (EDUC)
LATHAM, JAMES R., dir. plant oper. and safety, Pickens County Medical Center, Carrollton, AL '84 (ENG)
LATHAM, LEE, dir. cent. sup., Hillcrest Health Center, Oklahoma City, OK '85 (CS)
LATHAM, COL. ROBERT M., MSC USA, (ret.), North Port, FL '64
LATHROP, DONNA T., RN, dir. nrsg. serv., St. Luke's Hospital, Racine, WI '77 (NURS)
LATHROP, J. PHILIP, vice-pres., Booz, Allen and Hamilton, Inc., Atlanta, GA '74
LATIMER, EDWIN P., atty., Prince William Hospital, Manassas, VA '70 (ATTY)
LATIMER, ROBERT SCOTT, mgr. mgt. consulting serv., Coopers and Lybrand, Philadelphia, PA '80
LATIMER, SUZANNE, dir. pat. sup. serv. and risk mgt., Bellevue Maternity Hospital, Schenectady, NY '85 (RISK)
LATO, JANICE M., consult., St. Joseph's Hospital, Milwaukee, WI '82
LATSCHA, WALTER V., mgr. acctg. and budget, St. Francis-St. George Hospital, Cincinnati, OH '86 (MGMT)
LATSKO, JOHN M., atty., Miami Valley Hospital, Dayton, OH '79 (ATTY)
LATTAL, LISA, mgr. amb. serv., Johns Hopkins Oncology Center, Baltimore, MD '79
LATTIMORE, WILSON, dir. soc. work serv., St. Mary's Hospital, Athens, GA '85 (SOC)
LATTNER, FREDRIC P. G., (ret.), Des Moines, IA '31 (LIFE)
LAU, LOT T., asst. vice-pres., Kuakini Medical Center, Honolulu, HI '79 (PLNG)
LAUBACH, THOMAS, vice-pres. commun. and indust. serv., Holy Family Hospital, Des Plaines, IL '87 (AMB)
LAUBE, LARAINE B., dir. soc. serv., Memorial Hospital and Health Care Center, Jasper, IN '70 (SOC)
LAUBENTHAL, ROSE MARY, RN, assoc. dir. hosp. accreditation prog., Joint Commission on Accreditation of Hospitals, Chicago, IL '76 (NURS)
LAUDAN, BONNIE S., dir. pers., Memorial Hospital, Chester, IL '81 (PERS)
LAUDENBACH, DOUGLAS J., mgr. environ. serv., St. Joseph's Home for Children, Minneapolis, MN '86 (ENVIRON)
LAUDER, GREGG R., dir. matl. mgt., Bryn Mawr Hospital, Bryn Mawr, PA '85 (PUR)
LAUDO, FRANK M., dir. food serv., Shenango Valley Medical Center, Farrell, PA '82 (FOOD)
LAUER, BRUCE W., vice-pres. plng. and mktg., Good Samaritan Medical Center, Zanesville, OH '82 (PLNG)
LAUER, JUDIE, risk mgr., Emanuel Hospital and Health Center, Portland, OR '86 (RISK)
LAUESEN, WILLIAM D., consult., San Jose, CA '86 (MGMT)
LAUFER, MARIAN P., RN, dir. nrsg. serv., Riddle Memorial Hospital, Media, PA '81 (NURS)
LAUFER, TOM, dir. syst. and computer serv., Baycrest Centre-Geriatric Care, Toronto, Ont., Canada '83 (MGMT)
LAUGHEAD, ELIZABETH D., RN, asst. supv. sup., proc. and distrib., Bryn Mawr Hospital, Bryn Mawr, PA '79 (CS)
LAUGHLIN, DONALD E., chief fin. off. and asst. adm. fin., Sierra Medical Center, El Paso, TX '86
LAUGHLIN, DONALD L., pres., Riddle Memorial Hospital, Media, PA '62
LAUGHLIN, JERRY, vice-pres. plng. and mktg., St. John's Regional Medical Center, Joplin, MO '79 (PR)
LAUGHLIN, RAYMOND E. JR., adm., Wayne Hospital, Greenville, OH '61
LAUGHTON, BARBARA L., dir. pub. affairs, Strong Memorial Hospital of the University of Rochester, Rochester, NY '85 (PR)
LAUGHTON, COLLEEN, student, Program in Business Administration, Lakehead University, Toronto, Ont., Canada '86 (RISK)
LAUHOFF, KAREN JANIS, student, Program and Bureau of Hospital Administration, University of Michigan, Ann Arbor, MI '84
LAUNER, DEBORAH, mgr. mgt. syst. group, North Broward Hospital District, Fort Lauderdale, FL '86 (MGMT)
LAURENCE, KENNETH, atty., Peter Bent Brigham Hospital, Boston, MA '75 (ATTY)
LAURENDI, VIENNA E., dir. mktg. and strategic plng., Brandywine Health Services, Caln Township, PA '86 (PLNG)
LAURENT, FREDA B., RN, dir. nrsg. serv., Taunton State Hospital, Taunton, MA '86 (NURS)
LAURENT, LOU G., asst. coor. food serv., St. Luke's Hospital, Kansas City, MO '85 (FOOD)
LAURENTZ, NANCY B., RN, vice-pres. nrsg., Frisbie Memorial Hospital, Rochester, NH '76 (NURS)
LAURES, E. JOANN, dir. soc. serv., Franciscan Medical Center, Rock Island, IL '79 (SOC)
LAURETANO, LUKE V., dir. soc. serv., Gaylord Hospital, Wallingford, CT '77 (SOC)
LAURI, JOHN P., adm., Miami Heart Institute, Miami Beach, FL '72
LAURICELLA, CHARLES, chief soc. work serv., Veterans Administration Medical Center, Dayton, OH '81 (SOC)
LAURRO, LINDA, asst. dir. matl. mgt., AMI Palm Beach Gardens Medical Center, Palm Beach Gardens, FL '84 (PUR)
LAUTER, WALTER O., asst. vice-pres. bus. dev., HCA Eastern Operations, Clearwater, FL '85 (PR)
LAUTERBACH, JOHN W. JR., pres., Pyramid Environ Services, Inc., Baltimore, MD '87 (ENVIRON)
LAUTON, SUZANNE C., supv. pers., Larkin General Hospital, South Miami, FL '86 (PERS)
LAUVER, KAREN M., RN, dir. in-service, Soldiers and Sailors Memorial Hospital, Wellsboro, PA '75 (EDUC)
LAUZON, DYANN E., RN, dir. nrsg., Columbus Community Hospital, Columbus, TX '85 (NURS)
LAVACCHI, RICHARD J., mgr. maint. and eng., Westlake Community Hospital, Melrose Park, IL '84 (ENG)
LAVALLEE, DEBORAH A., supv. commun., Michiana Community Hospital, South Bend, IN '86 (ENG)
LAVALLEE, LEO G., loss control consult., Scott Wetzel Services, Inc., Seattle, WA '81 (ENG)
LAVALLEY, BRIAN R., dir. mktg. and plng., Bradford Hospital, Bradford, PA '85 (PLNG)
LAVANHAR, PATRICIA S., coor. health educ., Lutheran General Hospital, Park Ridge, IL '81 (EDUC)
LAVANTURE, RICHARD E., adm. asst., Holy Spirit Hospital, Camp Hill, PA '87 (AMB)
LAVELLE, JOSEPH D., asst. dir. support serv., Muhlenberg Regional Medical Center, Plainfield, NJ '85
LAVENDER, SYDNEY L., atty., Baptist Medical Center-Princeton, Birmingham, AL '68 (ATTY)
LAVENE, SHARON E., dir. mktg. and pub. rel., AMI Tarzana Regional Medical Center, Tarzana, CA '81 (PR)
LAVENGOOD, SANDRA J., dir. plng., District of Columbia Hospital Association, Washington, DC '83 (PLNG)
LAVENTHOL, JOSEPHINE, dir. pat. educ., Montefiore Medical Center, Bronx, NY '77 (EDUC)
LAVERTY, EILEEN, dir. commun. serv., Easton Hospital, Easton, PA '86 (PR)
LAVERY, THOMAS V., dir. matl. mgt., Chester County Hospital, West Chester, PA '82 (PUR)
LAVERY, WILLIAM, adm., Saline Community Hospital, Saline, MI '75
LAVIGNE, AMBROSE LOUIS, Inverness, FL '66
LAVIGNE, DONALD W., dir. ldry. and linen serv., Mississippi Baptist Medical Center, Jackson, MS '86 (ENVIRON)
LAVIN, ELIZABETH B., RN, vice-pres. nrsg., Nyack Hospital, Nyack, NY '82 (NURS)
LAVIN, HOWARD Z., adm., Victorian Manor, Scappoose, OR '84
LAVIN, JEANNE M., dir. pat. educ., Holy Family Hospital, Spokane, WA '85 (EDUC)
LAVIN, JOSEPH F., dir. pur., St. Agnes Medical Center, Philadelphia, PA '85 (PUR)
LAVIN, PATRICIA K., dir. outpatient serv., Memorial City Medical Center, Houston, TX '87 (AMB)
LAVIN, PATRICIA, dir. soc. serv., Seton Medical Center, Daly City, CA '78 (SOC)
LAVINE, DIANE C., dir. pers., Lutheran General Hospital, Park Ridge, IL '81 (PERS)
LAVINE, JUDITH A., dir. soc. serv., Beaumont Medical Surgical Hospital, Beaumont, TX '82 (SOC)
LAVOIE, ELLEN J., dir. pub. rel., Holy Cross Hospital, Fort Lauderdale, FL '85 (PR)
LAVOIE, REGINALD J., vice-pres. clin. serv., Copley Hospital, Morrisville, VT '86
LAVOY, KRISTINE, pat. rep., dir. qual. assur. and risk mgt., Washington Hospital, Fremont, CA '85 (PAT)
LAW, DALE A., dir. matl. mgt., St. Joseph's Medical Center, Fort Wayne, IN '74 (PUR)
LAW, JOHN D., dir. pub. rel., Raleigh General Hospital, Beckley, WV '86 (PR)
LAW, RICHARD A., biomedical eng., Ravenswood Hospital Medical Center, Chicago, IL '85 (ENG)
LAWHEAD, WILLIAM G., asst. exec. dir., Holston Valley Hospital and Medical Center, Kingsport, TN '75 (ENG)
LAWHON, DONNA S., RN, coor. staff serv.-div. nrsg., Methodist Hospital-Central Unit, Memphis, TN '85 (NURS)
LAWLER, KATHRYN M., RN, dir. nrsg. serv., John T. Mather Memorial Hospital, Port Jefferson, NY '81 (NURS)
LAWLER, SHIRLEY M., RN, asst. dir. nrsg., St. Mary's Hospital, Passaic, NJ '82 (NURS)
LAWLER, TIMOTHY G., atty., Northwest Community Hospital, Arlington Heights, IL '82 (ATTY)
LAWLEY, ALBERT E., dir. plant oper., Betty Bacharach Rehabilitation Hospital, Pomona, NJ '79 (ENG)
LAWLOR, SR. MARY EVANGELISTA, pat. rep., St. Patrick Hospital, Lake Charles, LA '83 (PAT)
LAWLOR, PEGGY, assoc. dir. pub. affairs, St. Mary's Hospital, Waterbury, CT '78 (PR)
LAWRANCE, FRANCES P., dir. soc. work, Johns Hopkins Hospital, Baltimore, MD '80 (SOC)
LAWRENCE, ARTHUR M., (ret.), Pittsburgh, PA '69 (PR)
LAWRENCE, BARBARA M., dir. pers., St. Paul-Ramsey Medical Center, St. Paul, MN '83 (PERS)
LAWRENCE, BRUCE A., mgr. sup., proc. and distrib., Grace Hospital, Detroit, MI '86 (CS)
LAWRENCE, CHARLES L., dir. environ. serv., Alaska Psychiatric Institute, Anchorage, AK '86 (ENVIRON)
LAWRENCE, DANIEL G., prin. health care prac., The Wyatt Company, Dallas, TX '84 (PERS)
LAWRENCE, DAVID L., dir. plng., Saint Thomas Medical Center, Akron, OH '86 (PLNG)
LAWRENCE, DENNY G., dir. food serv., Holladay Park Medical Center, Portland, OR '80 (FOOD)
LAWRENCE, ISABELLE M., asst. adm., Meadowlands Hospital Medical Center, Secaucus, NJ '78
LAWRENCE, JAMES DAVID JR., asst. adm., Doctors Hospital, Tucker, GA '80
LAWRENCE, JANE A., dir. educ., HCA Woodland Heights Medical Center, Lufkin, TX '85 (EDUC)
LAWRENCE, JOHN T. SR., reg. dir. matl. mgt., National Medical Enterprises, Inc., Santa Monica, CA '80 (PUR)
LAWRENCE, MARK W., pres., Information Partners, Inc., Nashville, TN '84
LAWRENCE, PAT M., dir. educ., Southwest Texas Methodist Hospital, San Antonio, TX '80 (EDUC)
LAWRENCE, RENATE H., dir. human res., Puget Sound Hospital, Tacoma, WA '83 (PERS)
LAWRENCE, CAPT. SCOTT E., MSC USAF, chief corp. plans and prog., School of Health Care Sciences, Sheppard AFB, TX '86 (PUR)
LAWRENCE, SHERI JOHNSON, vice-pres., Infopartners, Inc., Nashville, TN '82 (MGMT)
LAWRENCE, WM D. JR., atty., Medical Center Hospital, Tyler, TX '80 (ATTY)
LAWRENZ, EUNICE I., RN, consult., Nursing Management Services, Montclair, NJ '83 (NURS)
LAWRIE, HENRY JR., atty., Alexian Brothers Medical Center, Elk Grove Village, IL '85 (ATTY)
LAWRIMORE, JIM, vice-pres., Drexel Toland and Associates, Inc., Memphis, TN '79 (PLNG)
LAWRY, THOMAS C., vice-pres., Scottsdale Memorial Health Systems, Scottsdale, AZ '79 (PR)
LAWS, JAY C., dir. pers., Kaiser Foundation Hospital, Hayward, CA '78 (PERS)
LAWSON, ALICE, dir. pur., Hawkins County Memorial Hospital, Rogersville, TN '81 (PUR)
LAWSON, BETTY N., RN, dir. nrsg., Lockport Memorial Hospital, Lockport, NY '83 (NURS)
LAWSON, CHARLES W., APO New York, NY '78
LAWSON, ELEANOR M., dir. educ. serv., Lions Gate Hospital, North Vancouver, B.C., Canada '86 (EDUC)
LAWSON, EVERETT L., eng., St. Joseph's Medical Center, Fort Wayne, IN '62 (ENG)
LAWSON, JAMES M., adm. eng., Medical Center Hospital of Vermont, Burlington, VT '63 (ENG)
LAWSON, JEANANNE LOUISE, pat. rep., Ottumwa Regional Health Center, Ottumwa, IA '85 (PAT)
LAWSON, JEFFORY, mgr. commun. rel., Geneva General Hospital, Geneva, NY '83 (PR)
LAWSON, LOUISE T., mgr., Amherst Associates, Chicago, IL '82 (PLNG)

LAWSON, MADGE BARON, dir. pub. rel., St. Joseph Mercy Hospital, Pontiac, MI '79 (PR)
LAWSON, MARY A., dir. pub. rel. and dev., Virginia Baptist Hospital, Lynchburg, VA '84 (PR)
LAWSON, MICHAEL J., student, Bowling Green State University, Bowling Green, OH '86 (PERS)
LAWSON, MICHAEL P., vice-pres. prof. serv., Herrick Hospital and Health Center, Berkeley, CA '78
LAWSON, PAGE, dir. vol. serv., University of Texas M. D. Anderson Hospital and Tumor Institute at Houston, Houston, TX '76 (VOL)
LAWSON, PATRICIA J., RN, dir. nrsg., Stillwater Medical Center, Stillwater, OK '85 (NURS)
LAWSON, RALPH E., partner, Deloitte, Haskins and Sells, Denver, CO '81
LAWSON, THOMAS C., Touche Ross and Company, Cleveland, OH '81 (PLNG)
LAWTON, EILEEN, vice-pres. commun. rel., St. Peter's Medical Center, New Brunswick, NJ '85 (PR)
LAWTON, ROBERT P., consult., Sarasota, FL '49 (LIFE)
LAWTON, THOMAS S. JR., exec. dir., Jersey Shore Hospital, Jersey Shore, PA '82 (PLNG)
LAY, ARLINE, dir. soc. work, Nyack Hospital, Nyack, NY '86 (SOC)
LAY, FRED JR., adm. asst., Abington Memorial Hospital, Abington, PA '86 (PLNG)
LAYCOCK, RITA J., RN, supv. cent. sup., Tucson General Hospital, Tucson, AZ '78 (CS)
LAYDEN, CHARLES MAX, atty., St. Elizabeth Hospital Medical Center, Lafayette, IN '78 (ATTY)
LAYDEN, DENNIS, dir. phys. facil., St. Francis Memorial Hospital, San Francisco, CA '80 (ENG)
LAYER, JAY E., facil. risk mgr., Blue Ridge Hospital Systems, Spruce Pine Community Hospital Division, Spruce Pine, NC '85 (RISK)
LAYFIELD, L. MARTELLE JR., atty., Medical Center, Columbus, GA '76 (ATTY)
LAYFIELD, VIRGINIA B., adm. risk mgr., Peninsula General Hospital Medical Center, Salisbury, MD '86 (RISK)
LAYLON, BETSY REYNOLDS, dir. vol. serv., St. Luke's Hospital, Bethlehem, PA '78 (VOL)
LAYMAN, EDNA, asst. educ. res., Clinton Memorial Hospital, Wilmington, OH '82 (EDUC)
LAYMAN, GERALD L., dir. pers. and emp. rel., Wesley Medical Center, Wichita, KS '83 (PERS)
LAYMON, PHILIP K., dir. pur., G. N. Wilcox Memorial Hospital, Lihue, HI '81 (PUR)
LAYNE, DALENE A., dir. surg. and amb., Huron Road Hospital, Cleveland, OH '87 (AMB)
LAYTON, DIANE G., mgr. mgt. eng., British Columbia Shared Systems Society, Victoria, B.C., Canada '82 (MGMT)
LAYTON, LINDA ANN, student, Program in Health Policy and Administration, University of North Carolina at Chapel Hill, Chapel Hill, NC '84
LAYTON, M. JEAN, RN, risk mgr., St. John's Mercy Medical Center, St. Louis, MO '85 (RISK)
LAYTON, SUE, dir. mktg. and commun. rel., Southwest Florida Regional Medical Center, Fort Myers, FL '81 (PR)
LAZA, DOMINICA C., mgr. matl. mgt., Detar Hospital, Victoria, TX '81 (PUR)
LAZAR, MARCIA L., dir. med. rec., Methodist Hospital, Sacramento, CA '82 (RISK)
LAZAR, PAUL S., student, Boston University Health Management Programs, Boston, MA '86 (PLNG)
LAZARNICK, RICHARD F., vice-pres. mktg., Care Enterprises, Orange, CA '86 (PR)
LAZARUS, IAN RODNEY, dir. mktg. and bus. dev., Voluntary Hospitals of America-Mountain States, Inc., Englewood, CO '83
LAZARUS, MARC, assoc. adm., Fairmount Institute, Philadelphia, PA '74
LAZARUS, CAPT. MARK A., MSC USAF, APO San Francisco, CA '80
LAZARUS, SHIRLEY, dir. commun. and media rel., Dover General Hospital and Medical Center, Dover, NJ '84 (PR)
LAZZARO, FRANK A. III, dir. pers. serv., Johns Hopkins Hospital, Baltimore, MD '86 (PERS)
LE PERE, HAROLD L., pres., Harold L. Le Pere and Associates, Inc., St. Louis, MO '84
LE VINE, BRAD K., supv. pur., Community Memorial Hospital, Menomonee Falls, WI '82 (PUR)
LEA, DEAN E., dir. qual. assur., Medical Center Hospital of Vermont, Burlington, VT '86 (RISK)
LEA, WILLIAM, sales rep., Alberto Culver Company-Milani Foods Institute, Melrose Park, IL '82 (FOOD)
LEACH, JAMES A., dir. commun. rel. and resources, Burbank Hospital, Fitchburg, MA '76 (PR)
LEACH, KENNETH M., applications consult., HBO and Company, Atlanta, GA '83 (MGMT)
LEACH, MARY ANNE, mgr. health care info. syst., Ernst and Whinney, Kansas City, MO '87 (MGMT)
LEACH, NEIL KELLY, supv. soc. work serv., Veterans Administration Medical Center, Marion, IL '80 (SOC)
LEACH, PATRICIA A., dist. mgr., ARA Services, Hospital Food Management, Evironmental Service, Inc., Omaha, NE '72 (FOOD)
LEACH, ROBERT F., mgr. field serv., Mueller Associates, Inc., Baltimore, MD '71 (ENG)
LEACH, RON, chief eng., Fresno Community Hospital and Medical Center, Fresno, CA '85 (ENG)
LEACH, TERRY W., supv. gen. maint., University of Minnesota, Minneapolis, MN '86 (ENG)
LEACH, LT. COL. WILLIAM O., MSC USA, Harrodsburg, KY '68
LEADBETTER, RONALD C., atty., University of Tennessee, Knoxville, TN '76 (ATTY)
LEADHOLM, BARBARA A., Boston, MA '86
LEAHIGH, ALAN K., sr. vice-pres., Public Communications, Inc., Wheaton, IL '83 (PR)
LEAHY, ADRIENNE L., dir. food serv., Frankford Hospital, Philadelphia, PA '87 (FOOD)
LEAHY, IRENE M., coor. pat. rel., Mercy Hospital, Rockville Centre, NY '80 (RISK)
LEAHY, JOHN C., commun. coor., St. John's Mercy Medical Center, St. Louis, MO '86 (ENG)
LEAHY, JOHN M., atty., St. Rita's Medical Center, Lima, OH '74 (ATTY)
LEAK, ALLISON G., asst. exec. dir., Western Pennsylvania Hospital, Pittsburgh, PA '84 (NURS)
LEAKE, KAREN V., mgr. vol. and coor. commun., pat. rel. and gift shop, Northshore Regional Medical Center, Slidell, LA '85 (VOL)
LEAMING, LARRY E., vice-pres. plng. and mktg., St. Mary's Hospital and Medical Center, Grand Junction, CO '86 (PLNG)
LEANDER, MARY E., RN, asst. dir. pat. care serv., Waconia Ridgeview Hospital, Waconia, MN '82 (NURS)
LEAP, SYLVIA M., dir. diet. serv., New London Hospital, New London, NH '86 (FOOD)
LEARNED, HAROLD, supv. maint., Franklin Hospital, Benton, IL '79 (ENG)
LEARY, DANIEL L., asst. dir. hskpg. serv., St. Marys Hospital Medical Center, Madison, WI '86 (ENVIRON)
LEARY, GARY L., atty., Valley Presbyterian Hospital, Van Nuys, CA '78 (ATTY)
LEARY, SHAWN P., mgr. reg. oper., Food Dimensions, Inc., Whittier, CA '87 (FOOD)
LEATHERMAN, SUSAN K., RN, dir. nrsg., Nemaha County Hospital, Auburn, NE '85 (NURS)
LEATHERS, NANCY A., student, Department of Health Services Administration, George Washington University, Washington, DC '84
LEATHERWOOD, DOROTHY L., dir. human res., Cleveland Memorial Hospital, Shelby, NC '84 (PERS)
LEATHERWOOD, JOE LYNN, dir. biomedical eng., Methodist Hospital-Central Unit, Memphis, TN '83 (ENG)
LEAVELL, PIERRE MAURICE, student, Xavier University, Graduate Program in Hospital and Health Administration, Cincinnati, OH '86
LEAVENS, AMY C., prog. mgr., Mediq Mobile Services, Inc., Pennsauken, NJ '85 (PLNG)
LEAVENWORTH, ROGER S., mgr. corp. advertising and satellite promotion, Henry Ford Hospital, Detroit, MI '81 (PR)
LEAVER, DONALD E., vice-pres. human res., Central Maine Medical Center, Lewiston, ME '75 (PERS)
LEAVITT, GERALD F., exec. dir., Montana Hospital Rate Review Systems, Helena, MT '63
LEBBIN, MARTIN A., mgt. eng., Borgess Medical Center, Kalamazoo, MI '86 (MGMT)
LEBDA, FRANK SR., dir. plant serv., Tucson General Hospital, Tucson, AZ '80 (ENG)
LEBEAU, GEORGIA E., RN, dir. nrsg. serv., HCA Doctors Hospital, Lake Worth, FL '80 (NURS)
LEBEAUX, ARLIE E. JR., B. Company, 2nd Medical Branch, APO San Francisco, CA '86 (PUR)
LEBEIKO, RONALD L., consult., Worthington, OH '79 (PLNG)
LEBERGEN, SUSAN J., commun. rel. coor., Appleton Medical Center, Appleton, WI '83 (PR)
LEBERT-SUESS, DENISE M., dir. plng., Carondelet Community Hospitals, Minneapolis, MN '86 (PLNG)
LEBISH, DANIEL JAY, asst. vice-pres. fin., Magee-Womens Hospital, Pittsburgh, PA '77
LEBLANC, DONALD J., mgr. eng. and maint., Union Memorial Hospital, Baltimore, MD '72 (ENG)
LEBLANC, LILLIAN J., dir. pers. serv., Carney Hospital, Boston, MA '82 (PERS)
LEBLANC, MARY L., vice-pres., Alexander and Alexander of Connecticut, Inc., Hartford, CT '84 (RISK)
LEBLANC, ROBERT E., dir. eng., Rutland Regional Medical Center, Rutland, VT '85 (ENG)
LEBLANC, RONALD, mgr. environ. serv., Jacksonville Medical Center, Jacksonville, FL '86 (ENG)
LEBLANG, THEODORE RAYMOND, atty., Southern Illinois University School of Medicine, Springfield, IL '81 (ATTY)
LEBO, OPAL I., RN, vice-pres. pat. serv., Reading Rehabilitation Hospital, Reading, PA '76 (NURS)
LEBOVITZ, MIRIAM M., dir. pers., St. Joseph Hospital, Houston, TX '87 (PERS)
LEBOW, BARBARA H., atty., Office of District Counsel, Veterans Administration, Phoenix, AZ '84 (ATTY)
LEBRUN, HENRY R., mgr. matl., Heritage Hospital, Taylor, MI '71 (PUR)
LEBRUN, ROBERT, syst. mgr., Walthamweston Hospital and Medical Center, Waltham, MA '71 (ENG)
LEBSON, DONNA B., RN, dir. perinatal and ped. nrsg. serv., Framingham Union Hospital, Framingham, MA '83 (NURS)
LECH-KAMIN, CARYN T., RN, student, Program in Hospital Administration, Sangamon State University, Springfield, IL '82
LECIEJEWSKI, ROSEMARY, dir. home health serv., Deaconess Hospital, Evansville, IN '87 (AMB)
LECLAIR, HELEN T., RN, dir. nrsg. serv., Munroe Regional Medical Center, Ocala, FL '82 (NURS)
LECLERC, KATHRYN, (ret.), Fargo, ND '70 (SOC)
LECLERE, JON D., dir. mgt. eng., St. Mary's Medical Center, Evansville, IN '80 (MGMT)(PLNG)
LECO, ARMAND P., sr. vice-pres., Rhode Island Blue Cross and Blue Shield, Providence, RI '64
LECOMPTE, ROGER B., vice-pres. plng., Middlesex Memorial Hospital, Middletown, CT '81 (PLNG)
LEDBETTER, JOHN W., coor. cent. serv. and oper. room, St. Vincent Infirmary, Little Rock, AR '82 (CS)
LEDBETTER, LEE R., exec. dir., Humana Hospital -Orange Park, Orange Park, FL '70
LEDBETTER, VIVIAN EARLINE, dir. vol., North Shore Medical Center, Miami, FL '71 (VOL)
LEDDEN, EDWIN L., adm. asst. pers., Baptist Memorial Hospital-Union City, Union City, TN '83 (PERS)
LEDDY, LINDA JOYCE, dir. vol. serv., Lehigh Valley Hospital Center, Allentown, PA '80 (VOL)
LEDENE, AIDA A., asst. dir. staff dev., Ravenswood Hospital Medical Center, Chicago, IL '77 (EDUC)
LEDERER, ANDREW R., dir. plng., El Camino Hospital, Mountain View, CA '83 (PLNG)
LEDERER, JANET R., instr. staff dev., El Camino Hospital, Mountain View, CA '83 (EDUC)
LEDERMAN, BONNIE G., atty., Mercy Hospital and Medical Center, Chicago, IL '82 (ATTY)
LEDESMA, JOSE FORTUNATO G., exec. dir., St. Luke's Hospital, Quezon City, Philippines '82 (PERS)(PLNG)
LEDFORD, CAROL A., adm. asst., Community Hospital, Anderson, IN '85 (ENG)
LEDFORD, ROY C., staff eng., Memorial Hospital, Hollywood, FL '86 (ENG)
LEDOUX, MARIE M., RN, assoc. dir. nrsg., Marlborough Hospital, Marlborough, MA '83 (NURS)
LEDOUX, ROBERT A., atty., North Shore Children's Hospital, Salem, MA '78 (ATTY)
LEDWIN, NORMAN A., pres., Brandywine Hospital, Caln Township, PA '80
LEDWIN, THOMAS, dir. eng., Humana Hospital-Northside, St. Petersburg, FL '87 (ENG)
LEDWITCH, VIRGINIA LYNN, mgt. eng., Parkview Memorial Hospital, Fort Wayne, IN '84 (MGMT)
LEE, BARBARA B., asst. dir. cont. educ., Good Samaritan Hospital and Health Center, Dayton, OH '83 (EDUC)
LEE, BARBARA JEFFREY, Branford, CT '51 (LIFE)
LEE, BONNIE J., RN, dir. nrsg., HCA East Pointe Hospital, Lehigh Acres, FL '78 (NURS)
LEE, CARMEL D., dir. plant eng., Cookeville General Hospital, Cookeville, TN '81 (ENG)
LEE, CAROLE A., RN, dir. nrsg., Hillside Hospital, San Diego, CA '86 (NURS)
LEE, CAROLYN A., vice-pres., Baptist Hospital and Health Systems, Phoenix, AZ '75
LEE, CHIYON, vice-pres. environ. serv., St. Mary's Hospital of Kankakee, Kankakee, IL '76 (ENG)(MGMT)
LEE, CLAIRE, RN, dir. nrsg. serv., Mercy Hospital, Elwood, IN '76 (NURS)
LEE, DALTON N., student, National University of San Diego, San Diego, CA '83 (PLNG)
LEE, MAJ. DANIEL G., MSC USAF, dir. med. plans and readiness, Malcolm Grow U. S. Air Force Medical Center, Camp Springs, MD '74
LEE, DAVID O., mgt. eng., SunHealth Corporation, Charlotte, NC '85 (MGMT)
LEE, DIANE B., coor. in-service, Jackson Park Hospital, Chicago, IL '86 (EDUC)
LEE, DOROTHY C., dir. diet., St. Luke's Hospital West, Chesterfield, MO '74 (FOOD)
LEE, DOROTHY, dir. pub. rel. and mktg., Jane Phillips Episcopal-Memorial Medical Center, Bartlesville, OK '70 (PR) (PLNG)
LEE, E. WAYNE, vice-pres. fin. serv., Valley Baptist Medical Center, Harlingen, TX '86
LEE, EFFIE J., supv. res. application center, Lincoln Manufacturing Company, Fort Wayne, IN '86 (FOOD)
LEE, ELAINE E., coor. risk mgt., Naval Hospital, Portsmouth, VA '86 (RISK)
LEE, ERNEST M., dir. maint., Ellis Hospital, Schenectady, NY '71 (ENG)
LEE, FAY C., RN, dir. nrsg., Doctors Hospital, Columbus, GA '81 (NURS)
LEE, G. AUBREY, dir. pers. and commun. rel., Johnson City Medical Center Hospital, Johnson City, TN '83 (PERS)(PR)
LEE, GERALD R., dir. ombudsman, Harper-Grace Hospitals, Detroit, MI '82 (PAT)
LEE, IRA F., vice-pres. emp. rel., Shannon West Texas Memorial Hospital, San Angelo, TX '82 (PERS)
LEE, J. MICHAEL, Wilhelmina Medical Center, Mena, AR '84 (PLNG)
LEE, JAMES A., sr. assoc. adm. fin., University of Alabama Hospital, Birmingham, AL '84
LEE, JAMES TERRY, dir. pub. rel., Methodist Health Systems, Inc., Memphis, TN '86 (PR)
LEE, JARENE FRANCES, dir. vol. serv., Memorial Hospital for Cancer and Allied Diseases, New York, NY '74 (VOL)
LEE, JEAN A., RN, asst. dir. cent. serv., St. Marys Hospital of Rochester, Rochester, MN '86 (CS)
LEE, JENNIE R., asst. dir. pat. care serv. and staff dev., Shriners Hospital for Crippled Children, Portland, OR '82 (EDUC)
LEE, JOEL M., assoc. prof., Univeristy of Kentucky, Lexington, KY '87 (AMB)
LEE, JOHN M., pres., Health Care Mktg Innovations, Inc., Omaha, NE '84 (PLNG)
LEE, JOHN MICHAEL, coor. qual. assur., Veterans Administration Medical Center, Tuscaloosa, AL '83
LEE, KAI-MING, chief soc. work, Veterans General Hospital, Taipei, Republic of China '85 (SOC)
LEE, KAREN G., RN, mgt. consult., Penn Valley, CA '81 (NURS)
LEE, KAREN L., coor. vol., Bishop Clarkson Memorial Hospital, Omaha, NE '74 (VOL)
LEE, KENNETH E., prin., Lee, Burhart and Liu, Inc., Santa Monica, CA '79 (PLNG)
LEE, KENNETH S., gen. mgr. and consult., Pittsx Management Associates, Indianapolis, IN '82 (PLNG)
LEE, KEVIN, dir. hskpg., Bon Secours Hospital of Methuen, Methuen, MA '87 (ENVIRON)
LEE, LACY P., dir. vol. serv., Phoebe Putney Memorial Hospital, Albany, GA '83 (VOL)
LEE, LORETTA LILLIAN, vice-pres. nrsg., Little Company of Mary Hospital, Evergreen Park, IL '78 (NURS)
LEE, LYNNE M., student, Graduate Program in Health Systems and Hospital Administration, School of Public Health and Tropical Medicine, Tulane University, New Orleans, LA '85
LEE, MARIE D., RN, dir. support serv., Irving Community Hospital, Irving, TX '84 (NURS)
LEE, MARILYN L., asst. pub. rel., Riverview Hospital, Wisconsin Rapids, WI '86 (PR)
LEE, MARVIN N. T., eng., Minnesota Department of Health, Minneapolis, MN '80 (ENG)
LEE, MARY A., RN, dir. nrsg. serv., Alamosa Community Hospital, Alamosa, CO '81 (NURS)
LEE, PAMELA J., dir. adm. serv., Hospital of the Good Samaritan, Los Angeles, CA '79

LEE, PHYLLIS, (ret.), South Burlington, VT '64 (PR)
LEE, RICHARD W., dir. sup., proc. and distrib., University of Utah Health Sciences Center, Salt Lake City, UT '81 (CS)
LEE, ROBERT C. SR., dir. plant serv., Holly Hill Hospital, Raleigh, NC '82 (ENG)
LEE, ROBERT E., dir. mktg., Community Hospital of Lancaster, Lancaster, PA '85 (PR)
LEE, ROBERT E. JR., asst. vice-pres., Health East, Inc., Roanoke, VA '86
LEE, ROBERT J., risk mgr., St. John's Hospital, Springfield, IL '81 (RISK)
LEE, ROBIN JAN, dir. soc. serv., Medical Center Delaware Oro Hospital, Houston, TX '86 (SOC)
LEE, ROGER A., atty., Wichita General Hospital, Wichita Falls, TX '73 (ATTY)
LEE, SANDRA A., RN, mgr. prof. serv., Castle-Divison of Sybron Corporation, Rochester, NY '80 (CS)
LEE, SHARON A., adm. partner, Alaska Neonatal Perinatal Associates, Anchorage, AK '87 (AMB)
LEE, SHARON A., RN, vice-pres. nrsg., Penrose Hospitals, Colorado Springs, CO '76 (NURS)
LEE, THOMAS D., dir. educ., St. Rose Hospital, Hayward, CA '79 (EDUC)
LEE, THOMAS E., sr. consult., John Short and Associates, Atlanta, GA '86 (PLNG)
LEE, WALTER J. JR., asst. vice-pres. eng. serv., United Hospitals Medical Center, Newark, NJ '74 (ENG)
LEE, WOODROW, adm., Levering Hospital, Hannibal, MO '65
LEEBOV, WENDY, vice-pres. and gen. mgr., Eintein Consulting Group, Inc., Philadelphia, PA '80 (EDUC)(PAT)
LEECH, JOHN D., atty., Hillcrest Hospital, Mayfield Heights, OH '80 (ATTY)
LEEDY, VALERIE M., adm. coor. rehab. unit, Mercy Catholic Medical Center, Darby, PA '84
LEEMIS, RICHARD A., Hospital Corporation of America, Nashville, TN '82 (MGMT)
LEENHOUTS, SHARON L., adm. res., St. Mary's Hospital, Saginaw, MI '82
LEER, PETER KIRK, dir. mgt. serv. and plng., Sparks Regional Medical Center, Fort Smith, AR '78 (MGMT)
LEES, JAMES E., dir. oper., Cleveland Clinic Foundation, Cleveland, OH '72
LEES, KEITH M., risk mgr., Peoples Community Hospital Authority, Wayne, MI '80 (RISK)
LEES, WILLIAM T. JR., Sanibel, FL '46 (LIFE)
LEET, CAROLINE B., coor. pat. rel., Prince William Hospital, Manassas, VA '85 (PAT)
LEEVER, LINDA MARIE, pat. rep., Thomas Jefferson University Hospital, Philadelphia, PA '86 (PAT)
LEEWE, THOMAS W., dir. pers., Montgomery General Hospital, Olney, MD '82 (PERS)
LEFEBRE, LARRY A., mgr. matl., Pine Rest Christian Hospital, Grand Rapids, MI '83 (PUR)
LEFEBVRE, A., adm. fin. serv., Metropolitan Hospital and Health Centers, Detroit, MI '86 (MGMT)
LEFEVER, E. GAILE, mgr. cent. serv., Community Hospital of Lancaster, Lancaster, PA '83 (CS)
LEFEVER, PARKE M., dir. plant oper., Philhaven Hospital, Mount Gretna, PA '80 (ENG)
LEFEVRE, EUGENE, mgr. plant oper., Marin General Hospital, San Rafael, CA '79 (ENG)
LEFEVRE, GENE, dir. plant oper., Marin General Hospital, San Rafael, CA '87 (ENVIRON)
LEFEVRE, HELEN R., staff pat. rep., Albany Medical Center Hospital, Albany, NY '79 (PAT)
LEFEVRE, THOMAS D., asst. to vice-pres. plng., Hospital of Saint Raphael, New Haven, CT '83 (PLNG)
LEFFARD, JANET S., coor. commun., Gulf Health, Inc., Mobile, AL '85 (PR)
LEFFEL, RONNY, chief eng., Memorial Northwest Hospital, Houston, TX '84 (ENG)
LEFKO, JEFFREY J., vice-pres. plng., Greenville Hospital System, Greenville, SC '80 (PLNG)
LEFKO, LEWIS A., atty., Affiliated Hospital Systems, Houston, TX '81 (ATTY)
LEFKOWITZ, STUART, dir. soc. work, Cedars Medical Center, Miami, FL '85 (SOC)
LEFORGE, LARRY P., mgr. maint., Gratiot Community Hospital, Alma, MI '81 (ENG)
LEFROY, SHARON, risk mgr., Royal Victoria Hospital, Montreal, Que., Canada '86 (RISK)
LEFTWICH, HAL WEST, Titusville, FL '78
LEGENDZIEWICZ, HENRY, dir. fin., Nathan Littauer Hospital, Gloversville, NY '81
LEGER, RENEE, dir. food serv., Parkwood Hospital, New Bedford, MA '80 (FOOD)
LEGG, MYRON, asst. chief eng., Henrotin Hospital Corporation, Chicago, IL '84 (ENG)
LEGG, ROY G., dir. pers., Wilson Memorial Hospital, Wilson, NC '83 (PERS)
LEGGETT, JAMES H., head nrs., Lakeland Regional Medical Center, Lakeland, FL '87 (AMB)
LEGGETT, RUTH, dir. vol. serv., Elmhurst Memorial Hospital, Elmhurst, IL '80 (VOL)
LEGIER, WILLIAM B., adm. dir. amb. care serv., Regional Medical Center at Memphis, Memphis, TN '87 (AMB)
LEGREID, DONALD W., atty., Lutheran Hospitals and Homes Society of America, Fargo, ND '80 (ATTY)
LEGUM, DIANE, Fairfax Hospital Association, Springfield, VA '82
LEHLBACH, FREDERICK B., atty., Overlook Hospital, Summit, NJ '78 (ATTY)
LEHMAN, DONALD W., proj. dir. arch. div., Sverdrup Corporation, St. Louis, MO '81
LEHMAN, GARY J., adm., Madison County Hospital, London, OH '82 (PERS)
LEHMAN, MERRILL W., consult., M. W. Lehman Associates, St. Louis Park, MN '72 (MGMT)
LEHMAN, ROSS M., dir. pers., Deaconess Medical Center-Spokane, Spokane, WA '73 (PERS)
LEHMAN, THOMAS W., dir. eng., Mercy Center for Health Care Services, Aurora, IL '76 (ENG)
LEHMANN, CHARLOTTE, vice-pres., Deaconess Hospital, St. Louis, MO '80
LEHMANN, HILDE MARGARET, mgr. pat. and family serv., Sharp Memorial Hospital, San Diego, CA '77 (SOC)
LEHNERT, KAREN K., mgt. eng., Mediflex System Corporation, Cleveland, OH '84 (MGMT)
LEHNING, DAVID L., actg. dir. soc. work, Rochester General Hospital, Rochester, NY '86 (SOC)
LEHR, CAROL W., dir. mktg. and pub. rel., St. Joseph Hospital and Health Care Center, Lancaster, PA '84 (PR) (PLNG)
LEHR, LEWIS W., St. Paul, MN '82 (HON)
LEHR, S. RUTH, atty., Baptist Medical Center, Kansas City, MO '84 (ATTY)
LEHRMAN, ADDIE ALAMIA, dir. soc. serv., Spohn Hospital, Corpus Christi, TX '76 (SOC)
LEHTO, CAROL A., dir. diet., Dickinson County Hospitals, Iron Mountain, MI '87 (FOOD)
LEHTOLA, JEROME J., supv. maint., Ellsworth Municipal Hospital, Iowa Falls, IA '81 (ENG)
LEIBERT, MICHAEL, dir. pers., Memorial Hospital of Dodge County, Fremont, NE '79 (PERS)
LEIBOFF, MICHAEL D., prof. commun. and pub. rel., Mansfield University, Mansfield, PA '85 (PR)
LEIBOLD, KENNETH J., dir. pers., Allen Memorial Hospital, Waterloo, IA '86 (PERS)
LEIBOVITZ, NORMAN, atty., Albert Einstein Medical Center, Philadelphia, PA '84 (ATTY)
LEICHT, JOAN D., pat. rep., Bellin Memorial Hospital, Green Bay, WI '80 (PAT)
LEICK, SR. MARYBELLE, reg. dir., American Hospital Association, Region Seven, Irving, TX '74 (LIFE)
LEIFER, JOHN, pres., John Leifer, Ltd., Shawnee Mission, KS '85 (PR) (PLNG)
LEIGH, CYNTHIA M., RN, dir. nrsg. and pat. serv., St. Vincent Carmel Hospital, Carmel, IN '84 (NURS)
LEIGH, JUNE, acct. exec.-prof. liability loss control, Cna Insurance Companies, Chicago, IL '86 (RISK)
LEIKVOLD, JOAN, head nrs., Thunderbird Samaritan Hospital, Glendale, AZ '87 (AMB)
LEIMBACH, BARBARA JEAN, RN, asst. vice-pres. nrsg. serv., Herrick Hospital and Health Center, Berkeley, CA '81 (NURS)
LEIMBACH, ELIZABETH F., dir. med. soc. serv., Covenant Medical Center -St. Francis, Waterloo, IA '81 (SOC)
LEINENWEVER, MARK, sr. designer, Lowry, Sorensen, Willcoxon Engineers, Inc., Phoenix, AZ '85 (ENG)
LEINES, BRIAN O., student, Concordia College, Moorhead, MN '86
LEINGANG, MARY E., coor. commun. rel., St. Joseph's Hospital, Minot, ND '87 (PR)
LEINHART, AUGUST J., MD, dir. emer. and outpat, Arnot-Ogden Memorial Hospital, Elmira, NY '87 (AMB)
LEININGER, KENNETH S., plant eng., Sunbury Community Hospital, Sunbury, PA '79 (ENG)
LEIS, JAMES L. JR., Greenleaf Center, Valdosta, GA '83 (PERS)
LEISHMAN, MARGUERITE H., Association of the Advancement of Medical Instrumentation, Arlington, VA '86 (ENG)
LEISING, CINDY S., coor. pub. rel., Washoe Medical Center, Reno, NV '84 (PR)
LEISRING, JOSEPH P., dir. maint. and constr., Good Samaritan Hospital and Health Center, Dayton, OH '77 (ENG)
LEISS, ANN, coor. pat. rep., Danbury Hospital, Danbury, CT '87 (PAT)
LEISSA, CATHERINE, assoc. chief nrsg. serv. educ., Veterans Administration Medical Center, Cleveland, OH '86 (EDUC)
LEISTEN, WILLIAM H. JR., partner, Pannell Kerr Forster, Chicago, IL '85
LEITCH, JAMES W., (ret.), Melbourne, FL '69 (ENG)
LEITERMAN, THEODORE J., exec. vice-pres., Children's Memorial Hospital, Chicago, IL '86
LEITING, MARILYN A., RN, asst. vice-pres. nrsg. serv. and qual. assur., Marian Health Center, Sioux City, IA '83 (NURS)
LEITNER, PAUL R., atty., Memorial Hospital, Chattanooga, TN '78 (ATTY)
LEITNER, RAYMOND W., pres., John C. Lincoln Hospital and Health Center, Phoenix, AZ '66
LEJA, ANNE H., dir. vol., North Adams Regional Hospital, North Adams, MA '82 (VOL)
LEKANIDES, JOHN J., adm. food serv., Providence Hospital, Columbia, SC '79 (FOOD)
LEKORENOS, CHRIS, RN, vice-pres. pat. care, Guernsey Memorial Hospital, Cambridge, OH '68 (NURS)
LEMAIRE, SHARON J., RN, dir. nrsg. serv., Allegan General Hospital, Allegan, MI '82 (NURS)
LEMAN, NADA, dir. educ., Carle Clinic Association, Urbana, IL '79 (EDUC)
LEMAR, LAURENCE J., mgr. sup., proc. and distrib., San Jose Hospital, San Jose, CA '83 (CS)
LEMARR, LYNN, dir. linen serv., Good Samaritan Hospital, Lexington, KY '86 (PUR)
LEMAY, RICHARD G., dir. pers., John E. Fogarty Memorial Hospital, North Smithfield, RI '80 (PERS)(EDUC)
LEMIEUX, JOAN, dir. commun. rel., St. John's Hospital, Longview, WA '86 (PR)
LEMIEUX, KAREN G., RN, assoc. dir. nrsg. and surg. div., George Washington University Hospital, Washington, DC '84 (NURS)
LEMIRE, JUDITH A., RN, dir. nrsg., Oklahoma Children's Memorial Hospital, Oklahoma City, OK '85 (NURS)
LEMIRE, NORMA J., dir. vol. serv., Elliot Hospital, Manchester, NH '86 (VOL)
LEMISCH, ANTHONY, dir. plant oper. and maint., Brookhaven Memorial Hospital Medical Center, Patchogue, NY '85 (ENG)
LEMKAU, MARLYNN E., RN, vice-pres. pat. care serv., Memorial Medical Center, Savannah, GA '79 (NURS)
LEMKE, GLENNA, RN, vice-pres., St. Ansgar Hospital, Moorhead, MN '74 (NURS)
LEMKE, HENRY R., phys. asst. and risk mgr., U. S. Air Force Medical Center Wright-Patterson, Dayton, OH '87 (RISK)
LEMKIN, JEFFREY W., atty., Centinela Hospital Medical Center, Inglewood, CA '79 (ATTY)
LEMLEY, CRAIG L., catering mgr. food serv., State University Hospital, Downstate Medical Center, Brooklyn, NY '85 (FOOD)
LEMMERS, BARBARA J., mgr. pers., San Antonio Children's Center, San Antonio, TX '85 (PERS)
LEMMERS, DEAN P., asst. adm., Southwest General Hospital, San Antonio, TX '72
LEMOINE, DAVE H., partner, Peat, Marwick, Mitchell and Company, Phoenix, AZ '80
LEMON, FAYE T., RN, dir. nrsg. serv., Hampton General Hospital, Hampton, VA '84 (NURS)
LEMON, LEE, dir. matl. mgt., Alamance County Hospital, Burlington, NC '86 (PUR)
LEMON, MARY LINN, dir. food serv., West Valley Medical Center, Caldwell, ID '83 (FOOD)
LEMON, ROBERT B., mgt. consult., Arthur Andersen and Company, Seattle, WA '81 (MGMT)
LEMON, ROBERT K., dir. bldg. serv., Hamot Medical Center, Erie, PA '81 (ENG)
LEMON, SUSAN CHANDLER, dir. soc. serv., Hendricks County Hospital, Danville, IN '86 (SOC)
LEMON, VIRGINIA E., RN, dir. nrsg., Anne Arundel General Hospital, Annapolis, MD '85 (NURS)
LEMONS, SANDRA J., dir. soc. work, Lincoln County Hospital, Lincolnton, NC '86 (SOC)
LEMOYNE, JACKIE, pur. agt., Tuomey Hospital, Sumter, SC '84 (PUR)
LEMP, PAMELA A., dir. vol. serv., St. Luke's Episcopal Hospital, Houston, TX '82 (VOL)
LENAHAN, JANE T., dir. soc. work, Cuyahoga County Hospital-Chronic Illness Center, Cleveland, OH '72 (SOC)
LENAHAN, SR. MARIE, corp. consult., Mercy Catholic Medical Center, Darby, PA '81
LENAHAN, SARAH E., vice-pres. human res., Devereux Foundation, Devon, PA '86 (PERS)
LENARD, GARY, dir. pers., Hendricks County Hospital, Danville, IN '85 (PERS)
LENCE, ROBERT L., student, Program in Health Care Administration, University of Mississippi, Oxford, MS '84
LENDERMAN, HARRY, vice-pres. human res., United Health Service, Newark, DE '81 (EDUC)
LENDVAY, JOSEPH A., exec. off. corp. facil. plng., Metropolitan Hospital, Philadelphia, PA '82 (PLNG)
LENERTZ, BRADLEY THOMAS, student, Moorhead State University, Moorhead, MN '86
LENGYEL, NICK T., mgr. eng., Charlton Methodist Hospital, Dallas, TX '84 (ENG)
LENHARD, CHARLES G., pres., Galen Systems Corporation, Plano, TX '80 (RISK)
LENHARDT, LAURA J., sr. mgt. eng., SunHealth Corporation, Charlotte, NC '80 (MGMT)
LENHART, DONALD W., MD, med. dir. and adm., Sandusky Surgeons Amb Surgery Facilities, Sandusky, OH '86 (AMB)
LENHART, LOWELL C., adm., Oklahoma Teaching Hospitals, Oklahoma City, OK '82
LENIHAN, ISABEL A., vice-pres. pers., Neponset Valley Health System, Norwood, MA '86 (PERS)
LENIO, DONALD P., dir. facil., Moses Taylor Hospital, Scranton, PA '77 (ENG)
LENKMAN, SHEILA, RN, dir. nrsg. serv., Normandy Osteopathic Medical Center, St. Louis, MO '77 (NURS)
LENN, EDWARD J., dir. plant, St. Nicholas Hospital, Sheboygan, WI '81 (ENG)
LENNERT, DONALD F., mgr. data proc., Yuma Regional Medical Center, Yuma, AZ '85 (MGMT)
LENNEY, JILL R., chief clin. soc. work, James M. Jackson Memorial Hospital, Miami, FL '77 (SOC)
LENNON, JOYCE M., coor. pub. rel., Riverside Hospital, Wilmington, DE '85 (PR)
LENNON, LISA ANN, adm. res., Catherine McAuley Health Center, Ann Arbor, MI '85
LENNON, ROBERT R., atty., Pipp Community Hospital, Plainwell, MI '81 (ATTY)
LENNON, ROSLYN J., RN, clin. chm. nrsg., Lutheran General Hospital, Park Ridge, IL '82 (NURS)
LENNOX, ANDREW T., dir. pers., Craig House Hospital, Beacon, NY '86 (PERS)
LENNOX, FREDERICK E., asst. dir. gen. serv., McLean Hospital, Division of Massachusetts General Hospital, Belmont, MA '78 (ENG)
LENNOX, LINDA A., RN, asst. adm., Washington Hospital Center, Washington, DC '84 (NURS)
LENOX, PATRICIA, dir. soc. work, Hunterdon Medical Center, Flemington, NJ '86 (SOC)
LENSIE, WILLIAM B., dir. maint., Conemaugh Valley Memorial Hospital, Johnstown, PA '83 (ENG)
LENSKI, BRUCE M., pharm., St. Joseph Hospital, Houston, TX '85
LENTINE, SALVATORE T., dir. pers., Southwest Detroit Hospital, Detroit, MI '70 (PERS)
LENTZ, EDWARD A., vice-pres. plng. and corp. dev., Mount Carmel Health, Columbus, OH '80 (PLNG)
LENTZ, LANA, dir. risk mgt., University Medical Center, Tucson, AZ '84 (RISK)
LENTZ, MARCIA, RN, asst. dir. nrsg., San Bernardino County Medical Center, San Bernardino, CA '86 (NURS)
LENTZ, PHILIP C., facil. planner, St. Luke's Hospital, Kansas City, MO '85 (ENG)
LENTZ, ROBERT M., dir. inst. rel., Blue Cross of Maryland, Inc., Baltimore, MD '68
LENZ, MARY S., RN, dir. nrsg., Salem Hospital, Salem, OR '81 (NURS)
LEO, JAMES W., asst. mgr. cent. sup., Methodist Hospital of Indiana, Indianapolis, IN '81 (CS)
LEON, GAYLE, RN, dir. nrsg., Parkway Medical Center Hospital, Decatur, AL '83 (NURS)

LEONARD, EDWARD J., vice-pres. gen. adm., Covenant Medical Center -St. Francis, Waterloo, IA '75 (ENG)
LEONARD, EDWARD M. JR., atty., Lakewood Hospital, Morgan City, LA '75 (ATTY)
LEONARD, GARY P., dir. procurement and matl. handling, North Shore University Hospital, Manhasset, NY '82 (PUR)
LEONARD, HELEN E., head diet., Fayette Memorial Hospital, Connersville, IN '77 (FOOD)
LEONARD, INA B., atty., University of Alabama in Birmingham, School of Community and Allied Health, Birmingham, AL '75 (ATTY)
LEONARD, JEAN R., sr. staff instr., Greenwich Hospital, Greenwich, CT '85 (EDUC)
LEONARD, JUDITH E., atty., University of North Carolina Medical Center-School of Medicine, Chapel Hill, NC '84 (ATTY)
LEONARD, LARRY L., syst. analyst, Burroughs Health Care Services, Charlotte, NC '86 (PUR)
LEONARD, SR. MARY ASCENSION, St. Michael Hospital, Texarkana, AR '84 (PAT)
LEONARD, MARY KATHRYN, RN, asst. adm., Fish Memorial Hospital, New Smyrna Beach, FL '81 (NURS)
LEONARD, MICHAEL STEVEN, PhD, chm., University of Missouri, Department of Industrial Engineering, Columbia, MO '74 (MGMT)
LEONARD, PAMELA K., RN, mgr. cent. sup., Denver Health and Hospitals, Denver, CO '85 (CS)
LEONARD, PAT, dir. hskpg. serv., Doctors Nursing Foundation, Inc., Dallas, TX '86 (ENVIRON)
LEONARD, SARAH, dir. prof. support serv., Gottlieb Memorial Hospital, Melrose Park, IL '86 (RISK)
LEONARD, STEVEN C., dir. pers., Abbeville General Hospital, Abbeville, LA '82 (PERS)
LEONARD, TERESA D., dir. soc. serv., Stonewall Jackson Hospital, Lexington, VA '86 (SOC)
LEONARD, MAJ. THOMAS E., chief clin. support, MEDDAC Nuernberg, APO New York, NY '81
LEONARDO, MARION H., RN, asst. dir. nrsg., Richmond Memorial Hospital and Health Center, Staten Island, NY '86 (NURS)
LEONE, ANTHONY J., vice-pres. client support serv., Mersco Corporation, Bloomfield Hills, MI '86 (MGMT)
LEONE, DOLORES M., dir. educ., Bethesda Psychealth System, Denver, CO '85 (EDUC)
LEONE, J. N., asst. dir., Medical College of Georgia, Augusta, GA '84 (PUR)
LEONE, MARY B., instr. educ., Deaconess Medical Center, Billings, MT '86 (EDUC)
LEONES, VICTOR S., dir. eng., Waterman Medical Center, Eustis, FL '84 (ENG)
LEONIS, RICHARD R., buyer, New York University Medical Center, New York, NY '86 (PUR)
LEONOVICZ, MARY A., mgr. spec. serv., Douglas County Hospital, Omaha, NE '86 (CS)
LEPAGE, ANN MARIE, RN, dir. nrsg., Brookhaven Memorial Hospital Medical Center, Patchogue, NY '73 (NURS)
LEPINOT, ARTHUR A., pres., Lepinot Associates, Inc., East Lansing, MI '49 (ENG)(LIFE)(PR) (PLNG)
LEPLER, MALVENA M., clin. mgr., Princeton Medical Clinic, Ltd., Princeton, MN '86 (AMB)
LEPLEY, CYNTHIA J., RN, dir. maternal and child care, St. Francis Regional Medical Center, Wichita, KS '85 (NURS)
LEPLEY, LAWRENCE W. JR., atty., Tennessee Hospital Association, Nashville, TN '84 (ATTY)
LEPORE, MARTHA S., coor. pub. rel., Malden Hospital, Malden, MA '86 (PR)
LEPP, ROBERT, supv. psychosocial serv., Courage Center, Golden Valley, MN '80 (SOC)
LEPPERT, BEVERLY, supv. cent. serv., Nason Hospital, Roaring Spring, PA '82 (CS)
LEPSKY, HENRIETTA, RN, vice-pres. and dir. nrsg., White Plains Hospital Medical Center, White Plains, NY '76 (NURS)
LEPTUCK, CARY F., pres. and chief exec. off., Chestnut Hill Hospital, Philadelphia, PA '69
LEQUE, JOHN A., asst. atty., Bartlett Memorial Hospital, Juneau, AK '86 (ATTY)
LERMAN, STUART J., dir. emer. outpatient satellites, St. Joseph Hospital, Nashua, NH '79
LERNER-ADAMS, ALICIA, mgr. ins. prog., Ancilla Systems, Inc., Elk Grove Village, IL '85 (RISK)
LERNER, EDWARD, asst. adm., Florida Medical Center Hospital, Fort Lauderdale, FL '86 (RISK)
LERNER, IRA S., dir. pur., Mount Sinai Medical Center, New York, NY '83 (PUR)
LERNER, JOHN D., biomedical eng., Porter Memorial Hospital, Valparaiso, IN '82 (ENG)
LERNER, ROSE, pres., Health Record Resources, Inc., Burlington, MA '87
LERNER, WAYNE M., vice-pres. adm. affairs, Rush-Presbyterian-St. Luke's Medical Center, Chicago, IL '72
LEROY, LISA, Brigham and Women's Hospital, Boston, MA '85 (PLNG)
LEROY, MARTHA A., dir. soc. work, Anderson Memorial Hospital, Anderson, SC '82 (SOC)
LESAR, KATHY W., adm., Armenian Nursing Home, Jamaica Plain, MA '86
LESCHBER, PATRICK A., dir. eng., Good Samaritan Hospital Association, Rugby, ND '84 (ENG)
LESHER, RICHARD, PhD, pres., Chamber of Commerce of U. S., Washington, DC '80 (LIFE)
LESICA, MARTIN, dir. soc. serv., Sacred Heart Rehabilitation Hospital, Milwaukee, WI '85 (SOC)
LESKA, MARLENE F., risk mgr., Akron City Hospital, Akron, OH '83 (RISK)
LESNESKI, GARY J., atty., Elmer Community Hospital, Elmer, NJ '85 (ATTY)
LESNEVICH, KATHY, asst. adm., Extended Care Facility, Augusta, GA '87 (AMB)
LESNICK, JOAN F., coor. vol. activ., St. Catherine Hospital, East Chicago, IN '80 (VOL)
LESOING, TOM MICHAEL, dir. mgt. and plng. serv., Lincoln General Hospital, Lincoln, NE '78 (MGMT)
LESON, SUZANNE M., dir. food and nutr. serv., Saint Joseph Hospital, Elgin, IL '83 (FOOD)
LESPARRE, MICHAEL, Washington, DC '73 (LIFE)
LESS, DALE A., dir. mgt. eng., Brackenridge Hospital, Austin, TX '82 (MGMT)
LESSER, DORIS, assoc. adm., Long Island Jewish Medical Center, New York, NY '74
LESSER, EDWARD R., supv. consult., Coopers and Lybrand, Boston, MA '82
LESSIG, LESLIE L., dir. pers., AMI West Alabama Hospital, Northport, AL '86 (PERS)
LESSMAN, SYLVIA, dir. soc. medicine, Kaiser Foundation Hospital, Anaheim, CA '84 (SOC)
LESSNER, JANET E., PhD, asst. dean, University of Illinois College of Nursing and University Hospital Department of Nursing, Chicago, IL '84 (EDUC)
LESTER, ELOUISE, buyer, New York University Medical Center, New York, NY '86 (PUR)
LESTER, GREGG H., exec. hskpg., West Allis Memorial Hospital, West Allis, WI '86 (ENVIRON)
LESTER, JOAN, Schiller Park, IL '82 (SOC)
LESTER, SYLVIA M., chm. pat. rel., North Shore University Hospital, Manhasset, NY '77 (PAT)
LESURE, GEORGE G., Charlton Memorial Hospital, Fall River, MA '73 (PERS)
LETAVISHI, MARK F., interim dir. pers., Kent General Hospital, Dover, DE '86 (PERS)
LETELLIER, LEONARD D., Zumbrota, MN '83 (ENG)
LETIZIA, PAT P., dir. eng., St. Luke's Hospital, Racine, WI '82 (ENG)
LETIZIO, ANTHONY V., mgr. facil. and serv., Michigan Osteopathic Medical Center, Detroit, MI '82 (ENG)
LETT, SHERRI J., coor. qual. assur., Pulaski Memorial Hospital, Winamac, IN '83 (RISK)
LETT, WILLIAM S., atty., St. Joseph's Hospital, Huntingburg, IN '77 (ATTY)
LETTOFSKY, LT. COL. HARVEY R., MSC USAF, mgr. med. readiness, Air Force Medical Material Field Office, Frederick, MD '84
LETTS, PATRICIA, pat. rep., Central Community Hospital, Chicago, IL '81 (PAT)
LEUKEFELD, CARL G., chief off. htlh serv., U. S. Public Health Service, Rockville, MD '86 (SOC)
LEUPP, FRED E., pres., Fred E. Leupp and Associates, Pickerington, OH '75 (MGMT)
LEURCK, STEPHEN OTT, pres., St. Anthony Medical Center, Crown Point, IN '69
LEVADAS, PAULE G., spec. asst. to exec. dir.-legal affairs and risk mgr., District of Columbia General Hospital, Washington, DC '86 (RISK)
LEVALLEY, JOSEPH D., dir. commun. rel. and dev., St. Joseph Mercy Hospital, Mason City, IA '84 (PR)
LEVANDER, BERNHARD W., atty., Bethesda Lutheran Medical Center, St. Paul, MN '70 (ATTY)
LEVENS, PHYLLIS, (ret.), Chicago, IL '44 (PLNG)(LIFE)
LEVEQUE, SHARON H., dir. vol. serv., Kelowna General Hospital, Kelowna, B.C., Canada '75 (VOL)
LEVER, ROBERT A., dir. plant oper. and plant eng., Immaculate Mary Home, Philadelphia, PA '85 (ENG)
LEVERENZ, JOAN M., mgt. eng., University of Wisconsin Hospital and Clinics, Madison, WI '83 (MGMT)
LEVERETT, CONNIE H., mgr. food serv., Memorial Hospital of Washington County, Sandersville, GA '77 (FOOD)
LEVERTY, MARY M., asst. dir. nutr. serv., Bethesda Lutheran Medical Center, St. Paul, MN '86 (FOOD)
LEVESQUE, DARRELL, mgt. eng., American River Hospital, Carmichael, CA '85 (MGMT)
LEVESQUE, GEORGE E., dir. mgt. eng., Massachusetts General Hospital, Boston, MA '79 (MGMT)
LEVESQUE, JEFFRY D., dir. soc. work, Montebello Rehabilitation Hospital, Baltimore, MD '85 (SOC)
LEVETT, DAVID R., atty., St. Vincent's Medical Center, Bridgeport, CT '72 (ATTY)
LEVEY, ANNETTE, pres., Annette Levey and Associates, Marina Del Rey, CA '86
LEVEY, RENEE ROCHELLE, exec. diet., Barnert Memorial Hospital Center, Paterson, NJ '67 (FOOD)
LEVEY, SAMUEL, PhD, prof. and head, Graduate Program in Hospital and Health Administration, University of Iowa, Iowa City, IA '57 (PLNG)(LIFE)
LEVI, ALLAN H., assoc. dir. matl. mgt., Michael Reese Hospital and Medical Center, Chicago, IL '74 (PUR)
LEVI, ELIZABETH D., dir. vol. serv., Baptist Hospital of Miami, Miami, FL '79 (VOL)
LEVI, W. CHRISTOPHER, dir. pub. rel. and mktg., Winchester Medical Center, Winchester, VA '81 (PR)
LEVIJOKI, M. STEPHANIE, chief and dir. vol. serv., University of Michigan Hospitals, Ann Arbor, MI '86 (VOL)
LEVIN, BRUCE B., reimbursement analyst, New Rochelle Hospital Medical Center, New Rochelle, NY '84
LEVIN, DAVID A., atty., Holy Cross Hospital, Silver Spring, MD '79 (ATTY)
LEVIN, FRANCIS L., dir. emer. serv., Kennedy Memorial Hospitals University Medical Center, Stratford, NJ '87 (AMB)
LEVIN, LAURIE J., atty., Children's Hospital National Medical Center, Washington, DC '81 (ATTY)
LEVIN, MARLYS E., dir. commun., Oregon Health Sciences University, Portland, OR '86 (PR)
LEVIN, PATRICIA, adm. med. affairs, Francis Scott Key Medical Center, Baltimore, MD '86 (RISK)
LEVIN, PETER J., ScD, dean, College of Public Health, University of South Florida, Tampa, FL '67
LEVIN, RONALD, dir. soc. work, Glenrose Rehabilitation Hospital, Edmonton, Alta., Canada '82 (SOC)
LEVINE-JORDANO, NANCY, dir. clin. soc. work, Children's Hospital Medical Center of California, Oakland, CA '86 (SOC)
LEVINE, ANNE L., mgr. govt. rel., New England Medical Center, Boston, MA '84 (PLNG)
LEVINE, DAVID, dir. gen., Centre Hospitalier de Verdun, Verdun, Que., Canada '82
LEVINE, DONNA E., dir. pat. serv., Ochsner Foundation Hospital, New Orleans, LA '79 (SOC)
LEVINE, GLENN B., adm. dir. lab., St. Francis Hospital, Poughkeepsie, NY '80 (MGMT)
LEVINE, GWENN KAREL, dir. prog. plng., St. Joseph's Hospital and Medical Center, Paterson, NJ '82 (PLNG)
LEVINE, HAROLD A., dep. exec. dir., Bronx Municipal Hospital Center, Bronx, NY '73
LEVINE, HARVEY, vice-pres., Gunn LeVine Associates, Inc., Detroit, MI '85 (ENG)
LEVINE, HELEN L., dir. matl. mgt., Symmes Hospital, Arlington, MA '77 (PUR)
LEVINE, HOWARD H., sr. assoc. dir. oper., Beth Israel Medical Center, New York, NY '75
LEVINE, HOWARD I., atty., Memorial Hospital, Chattanooga, TN '82 (ATTY)
LEVINE, JAY K., prin., Executive Consulting Grp. Inc., Bellevue, WA '87 (AMB)
LEVINE, JERRY, dir. matl. mgt., Arden Hill Hospital, Goshen, NY '86 (PUR)
LEVINE, JULES I., PhD, asst. vice-pres. health affairs, University of Virginia Hospitals, Charlottesville, VA '74 (MGMT)
LEVINE, LAWRENCE L., vice-pres. strategic plng. and mktg., Emerson Hospital, Concord, MA '79 (PLNG)
LEVINE, LEONARD A., sr. mgt. eng., Medicus, Evanston, IL '84
LEVINE, NAT L., asst. dir. eng., Kingsbrook Jewish Medical Center, Brooklyn, NY '60 (ENG)
LEVINE, REBECCA P., dir. vol. serv., St. Mary's Hospital for Children, Bayside, NY '86 (VOL)
LEVINE, ROBERT V., vice-pres., Flushing Hospital and Medical Center, Flushing, NY '79
LEVINE, RUTH, dir. soc. serv., Angeles Home Health Care Agency, Los Angeles, CA '85 (SOC)
LEVINE, S. LEE, supv. psych. soc. serv., Allentown Hospital, Allentown, PA '86 (SOC)
LEVINE, SANDRA YOUNG, student, Program in Health Services Administration, New School for Social Research, New York, NY '86
LEVINE, SANFORD H., atty., University Hospital of Brooklyn-Suny Center, Brooklyn, NY '80 (ATTY)
LEVINGSTON, ALFRED A., atty., Bolivar County Hospital, Cleveland, MS '75 (ATTY)
LEVINS, JEAN M., asst. dir. food serv., Mount Auburn Hospital, Cambridge, MA '79 (FOOD)
LEVINS, LESTER R., asst. dir. plant maint., Providence Hospital, Mobile, AL '84 (ENG)
LEVINSOHN, DAVID, publisher, Health Education Publications, Inc., Chicago, IL '82 (PR) (PLNG)
LEVINSON, DALE, dir. pers., Hebrew Home for Aged-Riverdale, Bronx, NY '76 (PERS)
LEVINSON, EDWARD E., atty., South Shore Hospital and Medical Center, Miami Beach, FL '73 (ATTY)
LEVINSON, IRVING WALTER, mgr. human res., Saint Therese Medical Center, Waukegan, IL '75 (PERS)
LEVINSON, SARAH ANN, atty., United States Government-Federal Magistrates Office, Columbus, OH '86 (ATTY)
LEVISON, BRUCE E., dir. commun. health, Griffin Hospital, Derby, CT '76 (SOC)
LEVISON, LOUISE, bus. plng. consult., Corporation Planning and Small Business Management, Sherman Oaks, CA '82 (PLNG)
LEVIT-SILVER, JAN, dir. soc. serv., Children's Hospital, New Orleans, LA '85 (SOC)
LEVITAN, MARK S., pres., Albert Einstein Health Care Foundation, Philadelphia, PA '78
LEVITSKY, STEVEN, chief oper. off., Emerson Hospital, Concord, MA '71
LEVITT, FLORENCE M., vice-pres., Magnet Communication, New York, NY '85 (PR) (PLNG)
LEVITT, MORTON H., MD, vice-pres. med. affairs, Jewish Hospital, Louisville, KY '82
LEVITT, NANCY G., vice-pres. mktg., Iowa Methodist Health Systems, Des Moines, IA '80 (PLNG)
LEVITUS, SHERYL, West Salem, WI '83 (SOC)
LEVOY, BETTY WINTER, dir. soc. serv., St. Anthony Hospital, Oklahoma City, OK '72 (SOC)
LEVRINI, GERALDINE C., RN, Reston, VA '85 (NURS)
LEVULIS, A. EUGENE, dir. facil. mgt. and eng., Providence Hospital, Anchorage, AK '80 (ENG)
LEVY, ALAN M., vice-pres., Crss Constructors, Inc., Washington, DC '86 (ENG)
LEVY, CYNTHIA, dir. vol. serv., Mount Sinai Medical Center, New York, NY '80 (VOL)
LEVY, DAVID L., vice-pres., Booz, Allen and Hamilton, Inc., San Francisco, CA '82
LEVY, ELAINE A., coor. pat. asst., Kaiser-Permanente Medical Group, Fremont, CA '85 (PAT)
LEVY, ELIZABETH, student, Program in Health Care Administration, University of Minnesota, Minneapolis, MN '86
LEVY, GLENN D., vice-pres., MT. Sinai Hospital of Cleveland, Cleveland, OH '80
LEVY, JACK, dir. biomedical prog., Texas Hospital Association, Waco, TX '74 (ENG)
LEVY, JANINA, mktg. consult., Rynne Marketing Group, Chicago, IL '84 (PLNG)
LEVY, KEITH J., mgr. mgt. consult. group, San Pedro Peninsula Hospital, San Pedro, CA '80 (MGMT)
LEVY, LESLIE, MD, pres., Aetna Healthcare Systems, Hartford, CT '79
LEVY, LOIS S., dir. pub. rel., Moss Rehabilitation Hospital, Philadelphia, PA '85 (PR)
LEVY, MARTHA, dir. res. and prog. dev., University of California-Irvine, California College of Medicine, Irvine, CA '84 (PLNG)
LEVY, RALPH DAVID, dir., Alta California Regional Center, Sacramento, CA '68
LEVY, SHARI E., assoc. vice-pres., United Hospital, St. Paul, MN '81 (RISK)
LEWANDOSKI, ROBERT, dir. diet. serv., Winthrop-University Hospital, Mineola, NY '81 (FOOD)
LEWANDOWSKI, J. A., exec. dir., Amherst Hospital, Amherst, OH '76

LEWANDOWSKI, JAMES G., dir., Metropolitan Chicago Hlthcare Council, Chicago, IL '86 (PERS)

LEWANDOWSKI, JAN CHARLES, dir. matl. mgt., AMI Brookwood Community Hospital, Orlando, FL '79 (PUR)

LEWANDOWSKI, RICHARD J., atty., Wisconsin Hospital Association, Madison, WI '81 (ATTY)

LEWELLEN, BRENDA G., pres., Lewellen and Associates, Dallas, TX '86 (PR)

LEWELLEN, GARY L., dir. mgt. eng., Community Hospitals of Indiana, Indianapolis, IN '87 (MGMT)

LEWELLEN, WANDA P., dir. pers., Hillcrest Health Center, Oklahoma City, OK '77 (PERS)

LEWIN, BARBARA ANN, RN, Cedars-Sinai Medical Center, Los Angeles, CA '82 (NURS)

LEWIN, DAVIDA K., RN, mgr. nrsg. serv., Hospital Corporation of America, Nashville, TN '84 (NURS)

LEWIN, MARGARET A., RN, dir. nrsg., Hunt Memorial Hospital, Danvers, MA '87 (NURS)

LEWINE, SIDNEY, consult., Mount Sinai Medical Center, Cleveland, OH '50 (LIFE)

LEWIS, ALICE S., dir. vol. serv., Blount Memorial Hospital, Maryville, TN '81 (VOL)

LEWIS, ANN P., RN, dir. maternal child nrsg. and soc. serv., St. Vincent Hospital, Santa Fe, NM '84 (NURS)

LEWIS, ANNIE HOLT, RN, dir. nrsg., Pioneer Valley Hospital, West Valley City, UT '85 (NURS)

LEWIS, AVROM D., head standards and criteria, Department of Naval Facilities Engineering Command, Alexandria, VA '74

LEWIS, BARBARA, dir. hosp. and commun. rel., Sinai Hospital of Detroit, Detroit, MI '82 (PR)

LEWIS, BARBARA, dir. educ., DeKalb General Hospital, Decatur, GA '76 (EDUC)

LEWIS, BECKY SENSEMAN, atty., Sisters of St. Mary, St. Louis, MO '86 (ATTY)

LEWIS, C. ANGIE, RN, asst. dir. nrsg. serv., Langley Porter Psychiatric Institute, San Francisco, CA '86 (NURS)

LEWIS, CAROL A., health rec. consult., Bethesda, MD '84

LEWIS, CAROL J., asst. vice-pres. qual. and compliance, St. Joseph Health Care Corporation, Albuquerque, NM '86 (ENG)

LEWIS, CHARLES E., asst. dir. pur., Baptist Memorial Hospital, Memphis, TN '82 (PUR)

LEWIS, LT. COL. CHARLES H., MSC USA, inspector gen., U. S. Army Health Services Command, Fort Sam Houston, TX '81

LEWIS, CLYDE E., atty., Grady Memorial Hospital, Delaware, OH '82 (ATTY)

LEWIS, CYNTHIA S., pat. rep., F. Edward Hebert Hospital, New Orleans, LA '85 (PAT)

LEWIS, DAVE, dir. eng., Anderson Hospital, Maryville, IL '81 (ENG)

LEWIS, DAVID M., Sheldon Dorenfest and Associates, Northbrook, IL '83 (MGMT)

LEWIS, DAVID T., atty., University of Tennessee Memorial Hospital, Knoxville, TN '86 (ATTY)

LEWIS, DEBRA MARY, coor. pat. rel., AMI Parkway Regional Medical Center, North Miami Beach, FL '86 (PAT)

LEWIS, DONALD C., chief exec. off., Northeastern Vermont Regional Hospital, St. Johnsbury, VT '77 (PR) (PLNG)

LEWIS, DOUGLAS B., vice-pres. domestic dev., Hospital Corporation of America, Nashville, TN '70 (ATTY)

LEWIS, ELIZABETH N., RN PhD, chief consult., Elizabeth N. Lewis Associates, San Rafael, CA '83 (NURS)

LEWIS, ELLEN M., RN, assoc. dir., University of California Irvine Medical Center, Orange, CA '76 (NURS)

LEWIS, FRANCES H., dir. soc. serv., West Volusia Memorial Hospital, De Land, FL '79 (SOC)

LEWIS, G. MICHAEL, atty., St. John Medical Center, Tulsa, OK '78 (ATTY)

LEWIS, GEORGE T., dir. biomedical eng. syst. team, Mercy Hospital, Urbana, IL '75 (ENG)

LEWIS, GEORGE W., mktg. rep., Bay Medical Center, Bay City, MI '87 (PR) (PLNG)

LEWIS, GEORGIA K., RN, sr. vice-pres., Nash General Hospital, Rocky Mount, NC '71 (NURS)

LEWIS, HAZEL A., dir., Medicus Systems Corporation, Houston, TX '78

LEWIS, HELEN H., dir. vol., St. Joseph Hospitals, Mount Clemens, MI '68 (VOL)

LEWIS, JAMES R., atty., West Georgia Medical Center, La Grange, GA '77 (ATTY)

LEWIS, JANET F., RN, assoc. chief nrsg. serv., Veterans Administration Medical Center, Minneapolis, MN '79 (NURS)

LEWIS, JEANE T., coor. pub. rel., Riverside Methodist Hospitals, Columbus, OH '87 (PR)

LEWIS, JEANNE, RN, dir. nrsg. serv., Harlan Appalachian Regional Hospital, Harlan, KY '78 (NURS)

LEWIS, JILL P., coor. vol. serv., Medical Center of Baton Rouge, Baton Rouge, LA '85 (VOL)

LEWIS, JO F., RN, adm. dir. pat. serv., Community Hospital of Rocky Mount, Rocky Mount, NC '86 (NURS)

LEWIS, JOAN H., vice-pres. commun., District of Columbia Hospital Association, Washington, DC '85 (PR)

LEWIS, JOHN, vice-pres. oper., Butler Memorial Hospital, Butler, PA '86 (RISK)

LEWIS, JONATHAN C., atty., Grady Memorial Hospital, Delaware, OH '82 (ATTY)

LEWIS, JOSEPH OLIN II, asst. adm., West Houston Medical Center, Houston, TX '73

LEWIS, JOSEPHINE, dir. pur., South Shore Hospital, Chicago, IL '81 (PUR)

LEWIS, JUDITH M., student, Program in Health Administration, Baruch College, New York, NY '86

LEWIS, JULIA C., RN, chief exec. off., Florida Eye Clinic Ambulatory Surgical Center, Altamonte Springs, FL '83 (NURS)

LEWIS, KATHY, dir. mktg., Kessler Institute for Rehabilitation, West Orange, NJ '85 (PR) (PLNG)

LEWIS, LINDA F., assoc. dir. food serv., Naval Hospital, Portsmouth, VA '76 (FOOD)

LEWIS, M. RICHARD JR., atty., Baptist Medical Center, Jacksonville, FL '82 (ATTY)

LEWIS, MARTHA A., RN, dir. nrsg. serv., Riley Memorial Hospital, Meridian, MS '82 (NURS)

LEWIS, MILDRED, mgr. vol. serv., Alexian Brothers Hospital, Elizabeth, NJ '81 (VOL)

LEWIS, MORLAN B., chief exec. off. and mng. dir., Voluntary Hospitals of America, Irving, TX '80 (PLNG)

LEWIS, PEGGY, RN, dir. nrsg., Saint Anthony Medical Center, Rockford, IL '86 (NURS)

LEWIS, ROBERT B., dir. info. syst., Health East, Inc., Roanoke, VA '85 (MGMT)

LEWIS, ROBERT CHARLES, mgr. commun., Beth Israel Hospital, Boston, MA '86 (ENG)

LEWIS, ROBERT E., actg. dir. plant eng., North Broward Medical Center, Pompano Beach, FL '85 (ENG)

LEWIS, ROBERT E., exec. dir. prof. serv., University of Texas Medical Branch Hospitals, Galveston, TX '70

LEWIS, RONALD L., vice-pres. corp. serv., Evangelical Health Systems, Oak Brook, IL '77 (PUR)

LEWIS, RONALD R., dir. maint. and constr., Horton Memorial Hospital, Middletown, NY '84 (ENG)

LEWIS, SCOTT HOWARD, mgr. matl., Good Samaritan Hospital, Downers Grove, IL '86 (PUR)

LEWIS, SHARON K., RN, adm. asst. prof. serv., Kingswood Hospital, Ferndale, MI '80 (RISK)

LEWIS, SHARON, atty., Baptist Hospital and Health Systems, Phoenix, AZ '82 (ATTY)

LEWIS, SHERYL L., dir. outpatient serv., Holy Cross Hospital, Mission Hills, CA '87 (AMB)

LEWIS, SUE, dir. vol. serv., Methodist Hospital, Lubbock, TX '86 (VOL)

LEWIS, SUSAN L., dir. soc. serv., Mercy San Juan Hospital, Carmichael, CA '81 (SOC)

LEWIS, TED I., Brazos Psychiatric Hospital, Waco, TX '86 (ENG)

LEWIS, TED M., dir. pers. and plng., Hadley Memorial Hospital, Washington, DC '83 (PLNG)(PERS)

LEWIS, THOMAS FRANKLIN JR., atty., St. Joseph's Medical Center, South Bend, IN '73 (ATTY)

LEWIS, THOMAS R., atty., Rogers City Hospital, Rogers City, MI '81 (ATTY)

LEWIS, TOM, dir. facil., New England Baptist Hospital, Boston, MA '85 (ENG)

LEWIS, WILLIAM F., dir. human res., Clinton County Hospital, Frankfort, IN '86 (PERS)

LEWIS, WILLIAM H., atty., Bryan Memorial Hospital, Lincoln, NE '78 (ATTY)

LEWIS, WILLIAM R., Chicago Hospital Risk Planning, Chicago, IL '86 (PLNG)

LEWISSON, L. KIM, dir. environ. serv., Northeast Georgia Medical Center, Gainesville, GA '86 (ENVIRON)

LEWISTON, ALLAN, dir. facil. plng. and dev., Robert F. Kennedy Medical Center, Hawthorne, CA '83 (ENG)

LEWITT, MAURICE, atty., Numed, Inc., Encino, CA '77 (ATTY)

LEWKOWITZ, JACK I., mgr. underwriting, American Home Assurance Company, New York, NY '86

LEWTON, KATHLEEN L., vice-pres. pub. rel., St. Vincent Medical Center, Toledo, OH '83 (PR) (PLNG)

LEWYCKYJ, GLORIA, mgr. matl., Cohoes Memorial Hospital, Cohoes, NY '85 (MGMT)

LEY, AUDREY, dir. vol. serv., Braddock General Hospital, Braddock, PA '69 (VOL)

LEYLAND, DIANE, dir. home care, University of New Mexico Hospital, Albuquerque, NM '87 (AMB)

LEYVA, GERMAN, dir. food serv., Sequoia Hospital District, Redwood City, CA '86 (FOOD)

LEYVA, SUSAN J., dir. cent. distrib., Tucson Medical Center, Tucson, AZ '79 (CS)(MGMT)

LHYLE-MCDONALD, KATE, PhD, Scottsdale, AZ '83 (EDUC)

LIAKAKOS, CHRIS E., proj. dir., Hansen Lind Meyer, Chicago, IL '85

LIBBIN, MICHAEL D., dir. human res., Calumet Memorial Hospital, Chilton, WI '86 (PERS)

LIBERATOR, JACK B., asst. vice-pres., Aultman Hospital, Canton, OH '87 (AMB)

LIBERATORE, ROSEMARIE E., RN, vice-pres. nrsg. affairs, St. Joseph Hospital, Baltimore, MD '77 (NURS)

LIBERATORE, TERESA A., dir. plng., McKeesport Hospital, McKeesport, PA '83 (PLNG)

LIBERMAN, SUSAN S., dir. mktg. and pub. rel., LaGuardia Hospital-Shared Services, New York, NY '83 (PR)

LICATA, ANTHONY F., proj. mgr. info. mgt., St. Mary of Nazareth Hospital Center, Chicago, IL '82 (MGMT)

LICCIARDELLO, MICHELLE A., student, St. John's University, Jamaica, NY '85

LICCIO, BARBARA ANN, dir. vol. serv., St. Christopher's Hospital, Philadelphia, PA '87 (VOL)

LICCIONE, LOUIE A., dir. food serv., Brownwood Regional Hospital, Brownwood, TX '78 (FOOD)

LICHLITER, ROBERT L., chief biomedical eng., Harrisburg Hospital, Harrisburg, PA '84 (ENG)

LICHLYTER, VIRGINIA E., adm. coor. mgt. eng., Massachusetts General Hospital, Boston, MA '87 (MGMT)

LICHTENBERG, KATHRYN J., atty., De Paul Hospital, New Orleans, LA '86 (ATTY)

LICHTENBERG, MARY ANN, mgr. sup., proc. and distrib., Proctor Community Hospital, Peoria, IL '83 (CS)

LICHTENSTEIN, DORIS HARRIS, asst. vice-pres. emp. rel., Missouri Baptist Hospital, St. Louis, MO '75 (PERS)

LICHTER, KAREN G., Ann Arbor, MI '79 (PLNG)

LICHTERMAN, MICHAEL S., vice-pres. plng., Little Company of Mary Hospital, Evergreen Park, IL '81 (PLNG)

LICHTMAN, RANDY BRAIN, adm. res., University of Miami Hospital and Clinics, Miami, FL '86

LICHTY, CARL, chief eng., North Gables Hospital, Coral Gables, FL '81 (ENG)

LICHTY, JOSEPH S., MD, (ret.), Akron, OH '47 (LIFE)

LICKHALTER, MERLIN E., sr. vice-pres., Stone, Marraccini and Patterson, St. Louis, MO '73

LICORISH, JEANETTE F., RN, dir. risk mgt., Kennedy Memorial Hospital, Stratford, NJ '72 (NURS)(RISK)

LIDDELL, ANN T., dir. vice-pres., Santa Fe Healthcare System, Inc., Gainesville, FL '85 (PLNG)

LIDDELL, FELIX H., dir. mktg., Joint Commission on Accreditation of Hospitals, Chicago, IL '78

LIDDELL, J. LARRY, dir. pub. rel., AMI-St. Jude Medical Center, Kenner, LA '81 (PR)

LIDDELL, MARIANNE A., dir. pub. rel., dev. and mktg., Alpena General Hospital, Alpena, MI '83 (PR)

LIDEN, ROBERT C., sr. vice-pres., Ziegler Securities, Altamonte Springs, FL '87 (AMB)

LIEB, EVELYN, bus. mgr., Presbyterian Hospital in the City of New York, New York, NY '76

LIEB, MICHAEL T., asst. adm. pers., Cobb General Hospital, Austell, GA '82 (PERS)

LIEBENTRITT, FRANCES, RN, dir. nrsg. acute care and maternal child, Lake Forest Hospital, Lake Forest, IL '82 (NURS)

LIEBENTRITT, MARTIN, mgr. matl. mgt., Bishop Clarkson Memorial Hospital, Omaha, NE '86 (PUR)

LIEBER, ALAN R., assoc. dir. prof. serv., Medical College of Virginia Hospitals, Virginia Commonwealth University, Richmond, VA '84 (MGMT)

LIEBER, MICHAEL B., mgr. commun. rel., Wilson Memorial Hospital, Sidney, OH '83 (PR)

LIEBERMAN, CINDY S., Skokie, IL '85 (PR)

LIEBHABER, LOUIS, asst. adm., Beth Israel Medical Center, New York, NY '80

LIEBICH, LILLIAN A., dir. med. rec., North Adams Regional Hospital, North Adams, MA '64

LIEBOWITZ, BERNARD, exec. vice-pres., Geriatric Center-Friedman Hospital of Home for Jewish Aged, Philadelphia, PA '81 (PLNG)

LIEBSCH, CATHY J., asst. adm., Grand View Hospital, Sellersville, PA '83 (MGMT)

LIEDTKE, WILLIAM E., plant facil. eng., Connecticut Mental Health Center, New Haven, CT '86 (ENG)

LIEDY, WILLIAM J., dir. eng., Mercy Hospital, Rockville Centre, NY '79 (ENG)

LIEFFERS, BETTY, asst. dir. matl. mgt., Blodgett Memorial Medical Center, Grand Rapids, MI '80 (CS)

LIEKWEG, RICHARD JOSEPH, student, Program and Bureau of Hospital Administration, University of Michigan, Ann Arbor, MI '84

LIEM, TRACY K., dir. pub. rel., Phoenix Children's Hospital, Phoenix, AZ '84 (PR)

LIEN, JANE A., RN, dir. nrsg. serv., Hutchinson Community Hospital, Hutchinson, MN '83 (NURS)

LIENTZ, JOHN G., atty., Candler General Hospital, Savannah, GA '80 (ATTY)

LIESE, SHARON N., mktg. analyst, Olathe Medical Center, Olathe, KS '86 (PLNG)

LIESINGER, KARL ROBERT, dir. matl. mgt., Grant Medical Center, Columbus, OH '80 (PUR)

LIETZKE, E. THOMAS, adm., Paul Larson Obstetric and Gynecology Clinic, Minneapolis, MN '87 (AMB)

LIFSHUTZ, EMANUEL, MD, Los Angeles, CA '37 (LIFE)

LIFSHUTZ, MELANIE J., coor. pat. educ., Parker County Surgical Clinic, Weatherford, TX '85 (EDUC)

LIFTO, BARBARA A., dir. educ., Emma L. Bixby Hospital, Adrian, MI '71 (EDUC)

LIFTON, JAMES, sr. mgr., Ernst and Whinney, Chicago, IL '74 (PLNG)

LIFVERGREN, ALLEN E., asst. dir., Hebrew Rehabilitation Center for Aged, Boston, MA '83 (PLNG)

LIGGETT, CHARLOTTE R., dir. food serv., Evangelical Community Hospital, Lewisburg, PA '86 (FOOD)

LIGGINS, JUNE, RN, Redington Shores, FL '73 (NURS)

LIGHT, DENNIS SIMON, consult., Dennis S. Light and Associates, Inc., Reston, VA '66

LIGHT, GILES A. JR., dir. pers., Manatee Memorial Hospital, Bradenton, FL '73 (PERS)

LIGHT, LUCINDA, adm. res., Chestnut Hill Hospital, Philadelphia, PA '83

LIGHT, PATRICIA M., assoc. dir. mktg., Hospital for Joint Diseases Orthopaedic Institute, New York, NY '85 (PR) (PLNG)

LIGHTIZER, BARBARA F., pat. rep., Marlborough Hospital, Marlborough, MA '86 (PAT)

LIGHTSTONE, JACK, atty., Jewish General Hospital, Montreal, Que., Canada '86 (ATTY)

LIGO, LINDA M., dir. nutr. serv., Franklin Regional Medical Center, Franklin, PA '87 (FOOD)

LIGON, RODDEY M. JR., atty., Medical Park Hospital, Winston-Salem, NC '73 (ATTY)

LIGUORI, SALVATORE, PhD, vice-pres. mktg. and corp. serv., Robert Wood Johnson University Hospital, New Brunswick, NJ '84 (PLNG)

LIKENS, KIM J., coor. pat. serv. sup., Sun Coast Hospital, Largo, FL '86 (PAT)

LIKES, CREIGHTON E. JR., adm., Hilton Head Hospital, Hilton Head Island, SC '71 (EDUC)(AMB)

LILAVOIS, JUDITH M., student, St. John's University, Jamaica, NY '86

LILEK, RONALD P., asst. dir. pers. serv., Elmhurst Memorial Hospital, Elmhurst, IL '81 (PERS)

LILENFIELD, IRWIN, dir. amb. care center, Doctors Hospital of Stark County, Massillon, OH '86

LILES, BRENDA L., dir. soc. serv., Walker Memorial Hospital, Avon Park, FL '79 (SOC)

LILGA, DIANE, asst. cent. serv. room supv., Bertrand Chaffee Hospital, Springville, NY '79 (CS)

LILLE, MARY R., dir. vol., Children's Hospital, Norfolk, VA '80 (VOL)

LILLEP, KOIT, (ret.), West Nyack, NY '76

LILLEY, DAVID F., assoc. dir., New England Deaconess Hospital, Boston, MA '73

LILLEY, JERRY D., adm., Labette County Medical Center, Parsons, KS '86 (PR) (PLNG)

LILLEY, PATRICK J., RN, dir. nrsg. serv., HCA Midway Park Medical Center, Lancaster, TX '86 (RISK)(NURS)

LILLIBRIDGE, WILLIAM, asst. dean, University of Iowa College of Medicine, Iowa City, IA '59

LILLO, RICHARD J., mgr. hskpg., Brandywine Hospital, Caln Township, PA '86 (ENVIRON)

LILLY, DONALD J., sr. mgt. analyst, Deaconess Hospital, Evansville, IN '87 (MGMT)

LILLY, KAREN L., dir. diet. and food serv., Eye Foundation Hospital, Birmingham, AL '84 (FOOD)
LILYQUIST, GEORGE R., supv. cent. serv., St. Michael's Hospital, Stevens Point, WI '81 (CS)
LIMING, DONALD W., dir. matl. mgt., Harrison Community Hospital, Cadiz, OH '83 (PUR)
LIMMER, JAMES M., dir. plant oper., St. Francis Medical Center, Breckenridge, MN '84 (ENG)
LIMPUS, FRANK M., mgr. hosp. rel., Hospital Corporation of America, Nashville, TN '83 (PR)
LINBERG, MARY A., mgr. soc. serv., Walter O. Boswell Memorial Hospital, Sun City, AZ '84 (SOC)
LINCOLN, BEVERLY C., dir. pers., St. John's Hospital, Longview, WA '86 (PERS)
LINCOLN, DAVID R., exec. vice-pres. and chief oper. off., Covenant Health Systems, Inc., Lexington, MA '79 (PLNG)
LINCOLN, FAYE, RN, assoc. dir. nrsg. home care, University of Utah Health Sciences Center, Salt Lake City, UT '86 (NURS)
LIND, CARL JOHN JR., MD, reitired, Houston, TX '61
LIND, JOHN H., chm., Hansen, Lind and Meyer, Iowa City, IA '63
LIND, JOHN H., vice-pres., Mediplex Medical Building Corporation, Wellesley, MA '79 (PLNG)
LINDAHL, ALICE M., dir. commun., Bethesda Lutheran Medical Center, St. Paul, MN '82 (ENG)
LINDAHL, WARREN, dir. pers., Emanuel Medical Center, Turlock, CA '75 (PERS)
LINDAUER, RANDY L., dir. eng., Perry County Memorial Hospital, Tell City, IN '86 (ENVIRON)
LINDBERG, BERNARD L., dir. eng., St. Luke's Regional Medical Center, Sioux City, IA '71 (ENG)
LINDBERG, CHARLES D., atty., Good Samaritan Hospital, Cincinnati, OH '76 (ATTY)
LINDBERG, CURT, pres., Voluntary Hospitals of America New Jersey, Cranbury, NJ '76 (PLNG)
LINDBERG, ROBERT E., supv. cent. proc., St. Mary's Hospital and Medical Center, Grand Junction, CO '80 (CS)
LINDBLOM, TODD L., Edina, MN '82
LINDE, ROBERT E., staff mgr., Chicago Hospital Council, Chicago, IL '55 (LIFE)
LINDELL, LORETTA J., coor. vol., St. Peter's Community Hospital, Helena, MT '84 (VOL)
LINDELL, RICHARD G., adm. asst., Gillette Children's Hospital, St. Paul, MN '85 (ENG)
LINDEMAN, BARRY K., student, Program in Health Administration, University of Kentucky, Lexington, KY '86
LINDEMAN, STEVEN, dir. plant oper., St. Joseph's Hospital, Park Rapids, MN '87 (ENG)
LINDEMANN, ALOYSIUS J., chief oper. off., AMI Community Hospital of Santa Cruz, Santa Cruz, CA '82 (PERS)
LINDEN, JEAN O., asst. dir., Veterans Administration Medical Center, Miami, FL '71
LINDEN, ROBERT F., dir. food serv., Northeastern Hospital of Philadelphia, Philadelphia, PA '72 (FOOD)
LINDENBAUM, HERMAN, dir. plant oper., Jersey City Medical Center, Jersey City, NJ '85 (ENG)
LINDENMUTH, MARY E., coor. spec. serv. and educ., Levindale Hebrew Geriatric Center, Baltimore, MD '83 (CS)
LINDER, JEFFREY M., mgr. stores, proc. and distrib., Sacred Heart Hospital, Cumberland, MD '82 (CS)
LINDER, MARIE E., (ret.), South Haven, MI '36 (LIFE)
LINDER, MICHAEL C., dir. soc. serv., St. Croix Valley Memorial Hospital, St. Croix Falls, WI '76 (SOC)
LINDER, ROSEANN, coor. educ., Major Hospital, Shelbyville, IN '84 (EDUC)
LINDERMAN, RICHARD D., atty., Pottstown Memorial Medical Center, Pottstown, PA '83 (ATTY)
LINDERNBORN, ROBERT N., dir. ins. and loss prevention, Baptist Regional Health Services, Inc., Pensacola, FL '86 (RISK)
LINDGREN, MARY, dir. mktg. and commun. rel., Saint Joseph Hospital and Health Center, Kokomo, IN '79 (PR) (PLNG)
LINDGREN, WILBUR J., vice-pres. emp. rel., Kaiser Foundation Health Plan, Oakland, CA '76 (PERS)
LINDIE, MAUREEN JORDAN, dir. nrsg. and asst. adm., Rusk Institute, New York, NY '83 (NURS)
LINDL, WILLIAM, dir. plant oper., Kenosha Hospital and Medical Center, Kenosha, WI '80 (ENG)
LINDLEY, NELSON O., (ret.), Falmouth, MA '48 (LIFE)
LINDLOFF, P. KEITH, dir. extramural affairs, University of Texas Health Science Center at Houston, Houston, TX '84 (RISK)
LINDNER, APRIL, ed. clin. affairs, University Hospital, Boston, MA '86 (PR)
LINDNER, CARL A., dir. oper. improvement, University Community Hospital, Tampa, FL '84 (MGMT)
LINDNER, SR. CLARE, asst. adm., St. Agnes Hospital of the City of Baltimore, Baltimore, MD '85 (VOL)
LINDNER, DANIEL R., dir. matl. mgt., Northwest General Hospital, Milwaukee, WI '78 (PUR)
LINDNER, MARY K., RN, vice-pres. nrsg., Overlook Hospital, Summit, NJ '80 (NURS)
LINDNER, MARY V., dir. vol., Sacred Heart Hospital, Cumberland, MD '85 (VOL)
LINDOW, KAY D., supv. maint., Utah Valley Regional Medical Center, Provo, UT '86 (ENG)
LINDQUIST-KLEISSLER, KATHY, dir. plng., Lutheran Medical Center, Wheat Ridge, CO '84 (PLNG)
LINDQUIST, MARY A., RN, dir. nrsg., Grinnell General Hospital, Grinnell, IA '80 (NURS)
LINDSAY, MARLA C., cardiovascular pat. educ., Cedars Medical Center, Miami, FL '84 (EDUC)
LINDSAY, RICHARD J., exec. off., Naval Medical Clinic, Pearl Harbor, HI '87
LINDSAY, ROGER EUGENE, tech. biomedical equip., Onslow Memorial Hospital, Jacksonville, NC '76 (ENG)
LINDSEY, BEVERLY S., RN, assoc. chairperson, Avila College, Kansas City, MO '86 (NURS)
LINDSEY, DONNA J., dir. soc. serv., Redmond Park Hospital, Rome, GA '79 (SOC)
LINDSEY, GLORIA, supv. cent. serv., Glens Falls Hospital, Glens Falls, NY '86 (CS)
LINDSEY, REV. HENRY A., dir. environ. serv., Radford Community Hospital, Radford, VA '86 (ENVIRON)
LINDSEY, LARRY N., corp. dir. mgt. eng., Baptist Medical Centers, Birmingham, AL '77 (MGMT)
LINDSEY, MARY S., Family Medical Center, Little Rock, AR '82 (SOC)
LINDSEY, ROBERT S., atty., Doctors Hospital, Little Rock, AR '79 (ATTY)
LINDSKOG, NORBERT F., assoc. prof. mgt. and chm. bus. dept., City College of Chicago, Loop College, Chicago, IL '58 (EDUC)
LINDSTRAND, KEITH D., loss control consult., Sentry Insurance Company, Stevens Point, WI '86 (RISK)
LINE, S. DIANNE, RN, vice-pres. pat. serv., Mary Rutan Hospital, Bellefontaine, OH '86 (NURS)
LINEBARGER, MARGARET A., dir. vol., St. Vincent Infirmary, Little Rock, AR '83 (VOL)
LINENDOLL, MARTIN, risk mgt. ins. off., Hamot Medical Center, Erie, PA '86 (RISK)
LINES, JANETTE, supv. cent. serv., Archbishop Bergan Mercy Hospital, Omaha, NE '85 (CS)
LINEY, MURIEL E., dir. commun. rel., Holy Redeemer Hospital and Medical Center, Meadowbrook, PA '80 (PR)
LINGLE, ALFRED, chief eng., Union County Hospital, Anna, IL '81 (ENG)
LINHART, BARBARA A., RN, asst. vice-pres. nrsg., Highland Hospital of Rochester, Rochester, NY '86 (NURS)
LINHART, DEBORAH WILLIAMS, pres. partnership div., Healthmark Corporation, Pittsburgh, PA '77 (PLNG)
LINK, HANS M., Immanuel Medical Center, Omaha, NE '64 (PLNG)
LINK, JOHN M., adm. res., Milwaukee County Medical Complex, Milwaukee, WI '83 (PLNG)
LINK, KENNETH G., mgr. maint., Doctors Hospital, Detroit, MI '85 (ENG)
LINKOGLE, JOHN E., dir. pur., Clark County Memorial Hospital, Jeffersonville, IN '74 (PUR)
LINKOUS, JOSEPHINE A., RN, vice-pres. nrsg. adm., Our Lady of Bellefonte Hospital, Ashland, KY '82 (NURS)
LINLEY, YVONNE D., assoc. dir. food and nutr. serv., Tri-City Medical Center, Oceanside, CA '81 (FOOD)
LINN, JEAN T., mgt. eng., Ohio State University Hospitals, Columbus, OH '87 (MGMT)
LINN, LT. LARRY D., MSC USN, head fiscal dept., Naval Dental Clinic, Pearl Harbor, HI '84
LINN, MARTHA W., RN, dir. nrsg. and maternal child serv., Baptist Medical Center, Columbia, SC '86 (NURS)
LINN, TERRY H., partner, Ernst and Whinney, Charlotte, NC '78
LINNELL, KATHLEEN E., coor. pat. health educ., Virginia Mason Clinic, Seattle, WA '75 (EDUC)
LINNEMANN, SR. MARY ALBERT, exec. dir., Mercy Medical Center, Springfield, OH '52 (LIFE)
LINNET, MARY W., dir. soc. serv., Ashland State General Hospital, Ashland, PA '77 (SOC)
LINSDAY, SARA C., mgr. food serv., Brookville Hospital, Brookville, PA '86 (FOOD)
LINSE, RICHARD C., dir. pers., Saint Vincent Health Center, Erie, PA '78 (PERS)
LINSENMEYER, BETTY, pat. rep., Humana Hospital-Mountain View, Thornton, CO '80 (PAT)
LINSON, DENNIS R., vice-pres., Methodist Hospital of Southern California, Arcadia, CA '84 (MGMT)
LINSON, WILLIAM E. JR., dir. pub. info., Lester E. Cox Medical Centers, Springfield, MO '80 (PR)
LINSTER, RUTH A., dir. corp. commun., Memorial Hospital, South Bend, IN '82 (PR)
LINT, J. GARY, mgr. commun., St. Luke's Hospital, Kansas City, MO '84 (ENG)
LINTJER, GREGORY W., pres., Copley Memorial Hospital, Aurora, IL '79
LINTON, BARBARA A., dir. matl. mgt., Eastern Idaho Regional Medical Center, Idaho Falls, ID '86 (PUR)
LINTON, MORRIS D., atty., Intermountain Health Care, Inc., Salt Lake City, UT '84 (ATTY)
LINVILLE, BEA, dir. vol. serv., Glendale Memorial Hospital and Health Center, Glendale, CA '83 (VOL)
LINYEAR, MINNIE, dir. human res., St. Mary's Hill Hospital, Milwaukee, WI '86 (PERS)
LION, RUTH DEBORAH, consult., Vincertury Group, Los Angeles, CA '85 (PR) (PLNG)
LIOTARD, PAUL A., dir. eng., St. Mary's Hospital, Passaic, NJ '82 (ENG)
LIPELES, EDWARD, vice-pres. fin., Albert Einstein Medical Center, Philadelphia, PA '77
LIPINSKI, NANCY C., vice-pres. econ. and plng., Kentucky Hospital Association, Louisville, KY '84 (PLNG)
LIPKA, LOUISE, dir. vol. serv., Atlantic City Medical Center, Atlantic City, NJ '76 (VOL)
LIPKA, MARILYN, dir. fin. serv., Saint Thomas Medical Center, Akron, OH '86
LIPKIN, MARK A., mgt. eng., El Camino Hospital, Mountain View, CA '84 (MGMT)
LIPMAN, CAROL S., dir. plng., LaGuardia Hospital, New York, NY '85 (PLNG)
LIPMAN, HENRY D., vice-pres. prof. serv., Lakes Region General Hospital, Laconia, NH '81 (MGMT)
LIPOWSKI, DEBRA A., sr. mgr., Ernst and Whinney, Detroit, MI '87 (MGMT)
LIPPARELLI, DON W., mgr. plant serv., Josephine Memorial Hospital, Grants Pass, OR '84 (ENG)
LIPPER, MARGARET S., vice-pres. plng., Alta Bates Corporation, Berkeley, CA '85 (PLNG)
LIPPERT, L. BRANDT, dir. pers., St. Joseph Mercy Hospital, Mason City, IA '81 (PERS)
LIPPNER, LEWIS, adm., Sheridan Road Hospital, Chicago, IL '70
LIPSCHELTZ, ALAN, clin. eng., Waterbury Hospital, Waterbury, CT '79 (ENG)
LIPSCHULTZ, FAY, health care consult., Johnson and Higgins, Philadelphia, PA '86 (RISK)
LIPSCOMB, CARMELITA K., dir. food serv., Mercy Hospital, Portsmouth, OH '84 (FOOD)
LIPSCOMB, CAROL R., RN, asst. adm. pat. care, Metropolitan Hospital, Richmond, VA '80 (NURS)
LIPSCOMB, GWEN, RN, dir. qual. assur., Harris Methodist -Fort Worth, Fort Worth, TX '86 (RISK)
LIPSCOMB, JAMES S., student, University of Michigan Program in Hospital Administration, Ann Arbor, MI '85
LIPSCOMB, KATHLEEN, bus. mgr., Inhome Health Care Chicago North, Chicago, IL '87 (AMB)
LIPSCOMB, ROBERT E., dir. bldg. serv., Virginia Baptist Hospital, Lynchburg, VA '84 (ENG)
LIPSITZ, ALAN J., Wood, Lucksinger and Epstein, Washington, DC '81 (RISK)
LIPSITZ, HELYN K., dir. vol. serv., Henrico Doctor's Hospital, Richmond, VA '81 (VOL)
LIPSKY, HANNAH K., asst. dir. soc. serv., Mount Sinai Medical Center, New York, NY '73 (SOC)
LIPSKY, KATHERINE, dir. clin. soc. work, Children's Medical Center of Dallas, Dallas, TX '84 (SOC)
LIPSON, FRAN, vice-pres. human res., Choate-Symmes Hospitals, Woburn, MA '76 (PERS)
LIPSON, STEPHEN H., exec. vice-pres., Ohio Hospital Association, Columbus, OH '67
LIPSTEIN, STEVEN H., dir. prog. dev. and mktg., Johns Hopkins Hospital, Baltimore, MD '85 (PLNG)(AMB)
LIPTAK, WILLIAM J., dir. pers. and human res. dev., Brentwood Hospital, Warrensville Heights, OH '86 (PERS)
LIPTON, HAROLD, dir. dept. soc. work, Children's Hospital National Medical Center, Washington, DC '74 (SOC)
LIPTON, M. STEVEN, atty., California Hospital Association, Sacramento, CA '78 (ATTY)(PLNG)
LIPTON, SUSAN B., dir. soc. serv., Frankford Hospital of the City of Philadelphia, Philadelphia, PA '85 (SOC)
LIRA, LINDA KEY, dir. pers., Albemarle Hospital, Elizabeth City, NC '86 (PERS)
LIROT, CAROL J., dir. vol. serv., Masonic Home and Hospital, Wallingford, CT '74 (VOL)
LIROT, CHARLES E., dir. hosp. serv., Gaylord Hospital, Wallingford, CT '65
LISA, JUDITH A., RN, dir. nrsg., Humana Hospital -East Montgomery, Montgomery, AL '81 (NURS)
LISCHAK, JOHN M., mgt. eng., Bethesda Hospital, Inc., Cincinnati, OH '83 (MGMT)
LISCHUE, DEBORAH GWENTHER, dir. plng. and mktg., Winneshiek County Memorial Hospital, Decorah, IA '86 (PLNG)
LISCIANDRO, DIANE S., coor. mktg., Santa Rosa Memorial Hospital, Santa Rosa, CA '86 (PR)
LISENRING, HELEN, asst. dir. soc. work, Hospital for Special Surgery, New York, NY '82 (SOC)
LISET, J. ROBERT, atty., California Hospital Association, Sacramento, CA '77 (ATTY)
LISI, FRANK JAMES, dir. mgt. syst., Haricomp, Inc., Providence, RI '78 (MGMT)
LISNIK, JOHN, dir., Northern Maine Raise, Presque Isle, ME '85 (EDUC)
LISNITZER, IVAN M., asst. vice-pres. facil. mgt. and dev., University Hospital of Brooklyn-Suny Center, Brooklyn, NY '86 (ENG)
LISS, ROBERT, mgr. oper. plant, St. Francis Hospital, Escanaba, MI '85 (ENG)
LIST, WILLIAM A., dir. eng., Sharon General Hospital, Sharon, PA '75 (ENG)
LISTER, FANITA, dir. soc. serv., Humana Hospital -West Hills, Canoga Park, CA '85 (SOC)
LISTON, EDWARD T., proj. mgr., New England Medical Center, Boston, MA '77 (ENG)
LISTON, ELLEN M., RN, dir. med. nrsg. serv., Beth Israel Hospital, Boston, MA '83 (NURS)
LISWOOD, SIDNEY, pres., Mount Sinai Institute, Toronto, Ont., Canada '43 (LIFE)
LISY, DELORES P., RN, dir. med. nrsg., St. Joseph Hospital, Chicago, IL '82 (NURS)
LISZEWSKI, MAJ. RICHARD S., MSC USAF, assoc. adm., U. S. Air Force Regional Hospital, Hampton, VA '84 (PLNG)
LITHERLAND, JERRY L., dir. human res., John D. Archbold Memorial Hospital, Thomasville, GA '85 (PERS)
LITHERLAND, KAY, RN, vice-pres. nrsg., Lutheran General Hospital, Park Ridge, IL '72 (NURS)
LITLE, KAREN L., student, Georgia State University-Institute of Health Administration, Atlanta, GA '83
LITSKY, BERTHA YANIS, PhD, res. assoc. and consult. microbiologist, University of Massachusetts, Amherst, MA '62 (CS)
LITTAUER, DAVID, MD, (ret.), San Diego, CA '46 (LIFE)
LITTKE, JOHN, dir. plant serv., Richmond Community Hospital, Richmond, VA '81 (ENG)
LITTLE, EDWIN G., unit mgr., Baptist Medical Center, Columbia, SC '80 (PAT)
LITTLE, GAYLE A., RN, mgr. sterile proc., Manchester Memorial Hospital, Manchester, CT '82 (CS)
LITTLE, JUDITH M., compensation spec., Greater Southeast Community Hospital, Washington, DC '86 (PERS)
LITTLE, KAREN G., dir. food and nutr. serv., St. John's Hospital, Springfield, IL '86 (FOOD)
LITTLE, KENNETH J. JR., dir. matl. mgt., Orthopaedic Hospital, Los Angeles, CA '82 (PUR)
LITTLE, LOU ANN, asst. soc. serv.-pat. rep., Veterans Administration Medical Center, Dallas, TX '84 (PAT)
LITTLE, M. CARMEL, mgr. educ. prog., St. John's Hospital, Longview, WA '86 (EDUC)
LITTLE, MARGRETTE M., dir. pur., Baptist Memorial Hospital, Gadsden, AL '77 (PUR)
LITTLE, NANCY, RN, dir. nrsg., Hartgrove Hospital, Chicago, IL '79 (NURS)
LITTLEFIELD, ARTHUR E., RN, vice-pres. nrsg. serv., Bronson Methodist Hospital, Kalamazoo, MI '83 (NURS)
LITTLEFIELD, DEXTER D., dir. plant oper., maint. and hskpg., Live Oak Treatment Center, Victoria, TX '86 (ENG)
LITTLEFIELD, DWIGHT R., dir. sup., proc. and distrib., Kennebec Valley Medical Center, Augusta, ME '85 (CS)
LITTLESON, STEVEN G., asst. adm., Hampton General Hospital, Hampton, VA '84

LITTLETON, EDDIE JAMES, dir. plant oper., Coastal Communities Hospital, Bunnell, FL '80 (ENG)
LITTMAN, FRANCES SODINI, dir. soc. serv., St. Mary's Hospital, Richmond, VA '78 (SOC)
LITTRELL, HELEN C., dir. pub. rel., St. Luke Hospital, Fort Thomas, KY '85 (PR)
LITVACK, JACK T., vice-pres. plng. and prof. serv., St. Boniface General Hospital, Winnipeg, Man., Canada '80 (PLNG)
LITVIN, JUDITH E., dir. vol. serv., Sancta Maria Hospital, Cambridge, MA '85 (VOL)
LITVIN, MARY T., RN, vice-pres. pat. serv., Quakertown Community Hospital, Quakertown, PA '83 (NURS)
LITWACK, HERMAN L., dir. soc. work, Jewish Hospital of St. Louis, St. Louis, MO '77 (SOC)
LITZ, THOMAS H., exec. dir., West Jersey Hospital-Eastern Division, Voorhees, NJ '75
LITZINGER, JULIE, risk mgr., University of South Alabama, Mobile, AL '86 (RISK)
LIU, CHOU-SHU, MD, phys., Shaung Yuan Clinic, Taipei, Republic of China '74
LIU, GRACE L., mgr. acctg., MacKay Memorial Hospital, Taipei Taiwan, Republic of China '86 (PLNG)
LIU, MING HWANG, student, China Medical College, Taichung, Republic of China '86 (PERS)
LIU, MING-HAW, adm. dir. clin. and matl. serv., Bayshore Community Hospital, Holmdel, NJ '85 (PUR)
LIU, YEA YING, student, Graduate Program in Hospital Administration, China Medical College, Taichung City Taiwan, Republic of China '86 (PERS)
LIVELY, AMY E., dir. pub. rel., Northwest Community Hospital, Arlington Heights, IL '81 (PR)
LIVELY, CAROL A., exec. dir., Forum for Healthcare Planning, Washington, DC '81 (PLNG)
LIVELY, ELIZABETH A., dir. commun., Thorek Hospital and Medical Center, Chicago, IL '82 (PR)
LIVELY, JEAN, RN, vice-pres. and dir. nrsg., Rapides General Hospital, Alexandria, LA '76 (NURS)
LIVENGOOD, MARK D., dir. soc. work and commun. serv., Tacoma General Hospital, Tacoma, WA '74 (SOC)
LIVENGOOD, RICHARD V., pres., Lakeview Medical Center, Danville, IL '69
LIVERS, ELLEN M., supv. educ. serv., St. Peter's Community Hospital, Helena, MT '83 (EDUC)
LIVESAY, STEPHEN N., dir. pub. rel. and mktg., Shenandoah County Memorial Hospital, Woodstock, VA '85 (PR)
LIVINGSTON, A. BROADDUS, atty., University Community Hospital, Tampa, FL '82 (ATTY)
LIVINGSTON, ANN M., pur. agt., Coshocton County Memorial Hospital, Coshocton, OH '82 (PUR)
LIVINGSTON, BOYNTON P., consult., Mason, Fenwick, and Lawrence, Washington, DC '75 (LIFE)
LIVINGSTON, HELEN L., supv. sup., proc. and distrib., Tempe St. Luke's Hospital, Tempe, AZ '82 (CS)
LIVINGSTON, JEAN, RN, dir. clin. nrsg. serv., Fairview General Hospital, Cleveland, OH '86 (NURS)
LIVINGSTON, ROSALEE, dir. util. review and control, Blue Cross and Blue Shield of Michigan, Detroit, MI '85
LIVINGSTON, WILLIAM A., chief eng., Mendocino Coast District Hospital, Fort Bragg, CA '82 (ENG)
LIVINGSTONE, KERRY, RN, asst. dir. nrsg. adm., Cedars-Sinai Medical Center, Los Angeles, CA '85 (NURS)
LIVINGSTONE, ROBERT A., asst. dir. eng., Mercy Hospital, Rockville Centre, NY '81 (ENG)
LIWAG, LIWANAG R., asst. dir. food serv., Florida Hospital Medical Center, Orlando, FL '86 (FOOD)
LIZER, KENNETH C. JR., exec. dir., Lutheran Hospital Foundation, Fort Wayne, IN '80 (PR) (PLNG)
LLACER, VINCE, regional indust. hygienist, Veterans Administration Medical Center, St. Louis, MO '86 (ENVIRON)
LLEWELLYN, ELIZABETH A., asst. exec. dir. mktg. and plng., St. Mary's Hospital, Kansas City, MO '81 (PLNG)
LLEWELLYN, LOLA H., RN, vice-pres. nrsg., Methodist Hospital-Central Unit, Memphis, TN '82 (NURS)
LLEWELLYN, SARAH B., dir. soc. serv., Charleston Area Medical Center, Charleston, WV '80 (SOC)
LLOYD, ALEX, atty., Hartford Hospital, Hartford, CT '77 (ATTY)
LLOYD, CAROLYN SUE, mgr. hosp. serv. prog., University Medical Center Southern Nevada, Las Vegas, NV '81 (SOC)
LLOYD, DONALD H. II, dir. human res., Laurens District Hospital, Laurens, SC '86 (PERS)
LLOYD, GLENN C., chief eng., St. Joseph Health Care Corporation, Albuquerque, NM '87 (ENG)
LLOYD, J. ANTONY, vice-pres. pub. affairs, Beth Israel Hospital, Boston, MA '81 (PR)
LLOYD, KAREN D., PhD, dir. psych. and soc. serv., Mercy Center for Health Care Services, Aurora, IL '86 (SOC)
LLOYD, MARKLAND G., vice-pres. corp. pub. affairs, Geisinger System Services, Danville, PA '83 (PR)
LLOYD, RONALD S., dir. ldry. serv., Ohio Valley Hospital, Steubenville, OH '86 (ENVIRON)
LLOYD, SAMUEL J., MD, (ret.), Trenton, NJ '71
LLOYD, SCOTT F., sr. market analyst, Intermountain Health Care, Inc., Salt Lake City, UT '84 (PLNG)
LO, ELAINE, dir. med. soc. serv., Kaiser Foundation Hospital, Honolulu, HI '84 (SOC)
LOADER, WILLIAM F., dir. pub. rel., NKC Hospitals, Louisville, KY '83 (PR)
LOBAUGH, LCDR LARRY G., MSC USN, San Diego, CA '76 (FOOD)(PUR)
LOBDELL, M. ELAINE, dir. nrsg. staff dev. and educ., Portland Adventist Medical Center, Portland, OR '84 (EDUC)
LOBERG, RHONDA, corp. market planner, Lutheran Hospitals and Home Society, Fargo, ND '86 (PLNG)
LOBIANCO, JOAN S., health care consult., Quality Systems Group, Chandler, AZ '82 (RISK)
LOBNITZ, EDWARD A., chief exec. off., Tilden, Lobnitz and Cooper, Inc., Orlando, FL '82
LOBO, PAUL G., mgr. matl., Coral Gables Hospital, Coral Gables, FL '81 (PUR)
LOCHBAUM, LINDA R., coor. staff dev. and pat. educ., Centre Community Hospital, State College, PA '86 (EDUC)
LOCHTE, ELIZABETH, dir. soc. work, University Hospital, Boston, MA '74 (SOC)
LOCK, ANNE E., adm. asst., Memorial Community Hospital, Jefferson City, MO '86 (PR)
LOCKAMY, DEXTER, consult., Apm, Inc., New York, NY '82
LOCKARD, THOMAS L., adm., Lodi Community Hospital, Lodi, OH '73 (PAT)
LOCKE, BARRY K., dir. diet., Saint Vincent Health Center, Erie, PA '77 (FOOD)
LOCKE, LINDA D., student, Program in Hospital Care Administration, Trinity University, San Antonio, TX '86
LOCKEMEYER, DAVID S., asst. dir. vol. serv., Miami Valley Hospital, Dayton, OH '86 (VOL)
LOCKER, LETITIA A., corp. adm. asst., Methodist Health Systems, Inc., Memphis, TN '86 (PLNG)
LOCKETT, GRIFFIN DAVID, asst. chief soc. work serv., Tripler Army Medical Center, Honolulu, HI '85 (SOC)
LOCKETTE, IRENE, dir. telecommun., Metropolitan Hospital, Detroit, MI '76 (ENG)
LOCKHART, ANTOINETTE, dir. risk mgt., St. Michael Hospital, Texarkana, AR '86 (RISK)
LOCKHART, CAROL O., dir. vol. serv., Lee Memorial Hospital, Fort Myers, FL '85 (VOL)
LOCKHART, GREER E., atty., Abbott-Northwestern Hospital, Minneapolis, MN '77 (ATTY)
LOCKINGTON, JEAN, RN, head nrs. emer. room, Hamilton Hospital, Hamilton, NJ '87 (AMB)
LOCKMAN, STUART M., atty., Sinai Hospital of Detroit, Detroit, MI '80 (ATTY)
LOCKOM, WILLIAM A., exec. vice-pres., Phelps Memorial Hospital Center, North Tarrytown, NY '73
LOCKRIDGE, DIXIE, dir. soc. serv., Starke Memorial Hospital, Knox, IN '80 (SOC)
LOCKRIDGE, ROSE, cent. serv. tech., St. Anthony Hospital, Michigan City, IN '86 (CS)
LOCKWOOD, BRIAN C., pres., St. Luke's Health System, Phoenix, AZ '69
LOCKWOOD, CECIL JR., risk mgr., Caylor-Nickel Hospital, Bluffton, IN '81 (RISK)
LOCKWOOD, MARY ANN A., dir. univ rel. and exec. asst. to pres., Oregon Health Sciences University, Portland, OR '75 (PR)
LOCKWOOD, RHODES G., atty., Peter Bent Brigham Hospital, Boston, MA '74 (ATTY)
LOCKWOOD, ROSAMOND D., dir. educ., Newton Memorial Hospital, Newton, NJ '84 (EDUC)
LOCKWOOD, VALERIE J., dir. mktg. and pub. rel., Pembroke Pines General Hospital, Pembroke Pines, FL '85 (PR)
LOCKWOOD, WILLIAM M., bd. chm., Howard Bank, Burlington, VT '47 (LIFE)
LODER, ROBERT A. JR., vice-pres. pub. rel. and mktg., Intercare Health Systems, Edison, NJ '79 (PR)
LODGE, DENVER A., dir. clin. eng., Holy Rosary Hospital, Miles City, MT '86 (ENG)
LODGE, HELEN, dir. diet., Charleston General Hospital, Charleston, WV '72 (FOOD)
LODGE, ROSELEAH H., dir. pers., Schuyler Hospital, Montour Falls, NY '82 (PERS)
LODGE, TERESA ANN, supv., St. Joseph Hospital West, Mount Clemens, MI '85 (CS)
LODICO, SALVATORE D., vice-pres. pers. serv., Charleston General Hospital, Charleston, WV '82 (PERS)
LODOWSKY, JOSEPH P. JR., dir. pers., Roger Williams General Hospital, Providence, RI '80 (PERS)
LOEB, CHARLES W., atty., Montgomery General Hospital, Montgomery, WV '82 (ATTY)
LOEBEL, RON, mgr. plant oper., Memorial Hospital at Oconomowoc, Oconomowoc, WI '82 (ENG)
LOEBENBERG, WALTER P., pres., U. S. Enterprises, Inc., Clearwater, FL '77
LOEBS, STEPHEN F., chm. and assoc. prof., Hospital and Health, Columbus, OH '87 (PLNG)
LOEFFLER, KAREN M., dir. pat. serv., Conemaugh Valley Memorial Hospital, Johnstown, PA '79
LOEFFLER, KERRY K., mgr. human res., Greater Cincinnati Hospital Council, Cincinnati, OH '86 (EDUC)
LOEFFLER, WILLIAM E., dir. rad., Shands Hospital at the University of Florida, Gainesville, FL '74
LOEHR, A. WILLIAM JR., asst. adm., Catawba Memorial Hospital, Hickory, NC '73 (PLNG)
LOEHR, KATHLEEN R., plng. and fin. analyst, Northern Illinois Medical Center, McHenry, IL '85 (PLNG)
LOEHR, THERESA, dir. food serv., Children's Hospital, Richmond, VA '80 (FOOD)
LOEMKER, JEAN L., dir. soc. serv., Memorial Hospital, Carbondale, IL '85 (SOC)
LOEPP, ROBERT A. JR., asst. vice-pres., Southern Baptist Hospital, New Orleans, LA '77 (PUR)
LOESCH-FRIES, ROBERT, facil. planner, Flad and Associates, Madison, WI '83
LOESCH, CAROLE C., RN, asst. vice-pres. nrsg., Toledo Hospital, Toledo, OH '85 (NURS)
LOESCH, MARION W., RN, dir. nrsg., Lakeview Hospital, Bountiful, UT '81 (NURS)
LOESCHER, KRISTIE J., plng. and mktg. analyst, Providence Hospital, Mobile, AL '84 (PLNG)
LOEWE, NANCY A., Cambridge, MA '86 (PLNG)
LOFARO, JACQUELINE A., dir. commun. rel., New York Hospital, New York, NY '85 (PR)
LOFFER, LENA D., dir. vol. serv., Ohio Hospital Association, Columbus, OH '78 (VOL)(PAT)
LOFLIN, C. T., sr. vice-pres., Tennessee Hospital Association, Nashville, TN '79 (PLNG)
LOFQUIST, MYRON J., chief eng. serv., Veterans Administration Medical Center, St. Cloud, MN '77 (ENG)
LOFTIN, AUDREY FAYE, dir. pur., St. David's Community Hospital, Austin, TX '82 (PUR)
LOFTUS, DANIEL, analyst and planner health care market, A. T. and T. Communications, Basking Ridge, NJ '86 (PR) (PLNG)
LOFTUS, JUDITH H., coor. soc. serv., Alice Peck Day Memorial Hospital, Lebanon, NH '82 (SOC)
LOFTUS, LORETTA C., mgr. vol. serv., Northern Montana Hospital, Havre, MT '80 (VOL)
LOFTUS, ROGER, dir. adm. serv., St. Francis Regional Medical Center, Shakopee, MN '86 (RISK)
LOGAN, BRENDA C., RN, dir. nrsg., HCA Sun City Hospital, Sun City Center, FL '84 (NURS)
LOGAN, SR. MARY, exec. dir. health, Office of Health Ministry, Roman Catholic Diocese of Rockville Centre, Rockville Centre, NY '86
LOGAN, SARA J., head diet., St. Peter's Community Hospital, Helena, MT '82 (FOOD)
LOGANBILL, ESTHER L., dir. educ., St. Helena Hospital and Health Center, Deer Park, CA '85 (EDUC)
LOGE, DAVID D., contr., Los Angeles Hotel-Restaurant Health and Welfare Fund, Los Angeles, CA '66 (MGMT)(PLNG)
LOGGANS, LATEENA G., RN, mgr. nrsg. serv., Rowan Memorial Hospital, Salisbury, NC '81 (NURS)
LOGIE, JOHN H., atty., Blodgett Memorial Medical Center, Grand Rapids, MI '74 (ATTY)
LOGSDON, ANN W., dir. soc. work, Franklin General Hospital, Valley Stream, NY '74 (SOC)
LOGSDON, CLIFTON O., mgr. pers., Halifax Memorial Hospital, Roanoke Rapids, NC '85 (PERS)
LOGSDON, KAREN, RN, asst. adm., Valley Memorial Hospital, Livermore, CA '80 (NURS)
LOGUE, KAREN R., vice-pres., Johnson and Higgins, Pittsburgh, PA '84 (RISK)
LOHMAN, JULIETTE S., dir. pat. care serv., Hudson Medical Center, Hudson, WI '73 (NURS)
LOHMANN, CHESTER R., warehouse mgr., North Broward Medical Center, Pompano Beach, FL '80 (CS)
LOHMANN, ROSE, mgr. cent. sterile proc., University of Minnesota Hospital and Clinic, Minneapolis, MN '85 (CS)
LOHR, JANE B., coor. pat. rep. prog., St. Luke's-Roosevelt Hospital Center, New York, NY '80 (PAT)
LOIACONO, LCDR FRANK EDWARD, MSC USN, health facil. planner, Naval Medical Command, Washington, DC '76
LOK, JAN MICHAEL, pres., Marketing Resources, Atlanta, GA '83 (PR)
LOKKE, SHARON A., pers. asst., Sioux Valley Hospital, Sioux Falls, SD '83 (PERS)
LOMAN, LARRY ALLEN, corp. dir. diet. serv., National Medical Enterprises, Orange, CA '82 (FOOD)
LOMAS, SUZANNE M., dir. soc. serv., Crawford Long Hospital Emory University, Atlanta, GA '79 (SOC)
LOMBARD, JOHN C., atty., Planned Parenthood Association of Miami Valley, Dayton, OH '73 (ATTY)
LOMBARDI, ANTHONY M. JR., pres. and chief exec. off., Monongahela Valley Hospital, Monongahela, PA '61
LOMBARDI, DONALD L., vice-pres. mktg. and bus. dev., University Community Hospital, Tampa, FL '86 (PLNG)
LOMBARDINI, MARC A., student, Hospital of the University of Pennsylvania, Philadelphia, PA '84 (PLNG)
LOMBARDO, ANTHONY, dir. matl. mgt., St. Joseph Hospital, Lancaster, PA '80 (PUR)
LOMBARDO, DANIELLE M., atty., Children's Hospital, New Orleans, LA '84 (ATTY)
LOMBARDO, NANCY W., dir. diet., Naples Research and Counseling Center, Naples, FL '86 (FOOD)
LOMNITZER, ALLAN, dir. eng., Long Island Jewish-Hillside Medical Center-Manhasset Division, Manhasset, NY '82 (ENG)
LONDIS, DOLORES KENNEDY, dir. vol. serv., Washington Adventist Hospital, Takoma Park, MD '85 (VOL)
LONDON, HENRY A. II, spec. educ. support, Burroughs Health Care Services, Charlotte, NC '74
LONDON, JOAN R., mgr. news and info., Texas Children's Hospital, Houston, TX '86 (PR)
LONDON, JORDAN, Brooklyn, NY '64
LONDON, JUDITH B., RN, dir. nrsg., Mercy Health Center, Oklahoma City, OK '86 (NURS)
LONDON, MORRIS L., actg. dir. prog. review, Dept. of HHS, U. S. Public Health Service, Health Facilities Planning and Construction Service, Region Two, New York, NY '53 (LIFE)
LONERGAN, THOMAS C., atty., Mendocino Coast District Hospital, Fort Bragg, CA '77 (ATTY)
LONG, BARBARA L., RN, dir. nrs., Amador Hospital, Jackson, CA '84 (NURS)
LONG, BETTY G., dir. commun. rel., Shadyside Hospital, Pittsburgh, PA '83 (PR)
LONG, CAMERON E., Warner Robbins, GA '74 (ENG)
LONG, CLAIRE J., pat. rep., Somerset Medical Center, Somerville, NJ '86 (PAT)
LONG, DAN, dir. plant oper., Charter Westbrook Hospital, Richmond, VA '87 (ENG)
LONG, DAVID H., dir. food serv., Orthopaedic Hospital of Charlotte, Charlotte, NC '86 (FOOD)
LONG, DEBRA J., mgr. matl. mgt., Portsmouth Psychiatric Center, Portsmouth, VA '86 (PUR)
LONG, DELBERT E., vice-pres. pers., Edward Hospital, Naperville, IL '82 (PERS)
LONG, EDWARD GENE, dir. plant oper., Sun Belt Regional Medical Center, Houston, TX '83 (ENG)
LONG, F. MICHAEL, coor. plant maint., University Hospital of Arkansas, Little Rock, AR '85 (ENG)
LONG, FRANCIS J., dir. pers., Milford Memorial Hospital, Milford, DE '72 (PERS)
LONG, HERALDINE M., RN, pat. educ., Akron General Medical Center, Akron, OH '85 (EDUC)
LONG, JEFFREY J., dir. environ. serv., Hunterdon Medical Center, Flemington, NJ '86 (ENVIRON)
LONG, JIM ROBERT, mgr. mgt. serv., Hospital Corporation of America, Nashville, TN '75 (MGMT)
LONG, JOAN E., coor. vol., St. Mary's Medical Center, Knoxville, TN '83 (VOL)
LONG, KAREN S., dir. vol. serv., Memorial Hospital, Marysville, OH '81 (VOL)
LONG, SR. KATHLEEN MARY, pat. rep., St. Agnes Hospital, White Plains, NY '86 (PAT)

LONG, LAWRENCE C., adm., Tuolumne General Hospital, Sonora, CA '79
LONG, MARGIE A., mgr. pers., Bartholomew County Hospital, Columbus, IN '82 (PERS)
LONG, MARJORIE A., RN, assoc. dir. nrsg., Lenox Hill Hospital, New York, NY '82 (NURS)
LONG, MICHAEL L., sr. fin. analyst, Lutheran Hospitals and Home Society, Fargo, ND '81
LONG, PATRICIA A., dir. vol. and pat. rep., Stouder Memorial Hospital, Troy, OH '73 (VOL)(PAT)
LONG, PEARLENE B., supv. telecommun. center, St. Marys Hospital of Rochester, Rochester, MN '84 (ENG)
LONG, RUSSELL D., asst. exec. dir. bus. dev., St. Joseph's Medical Center, Fort Wayne, IN '75 (PLNG)
LONG, SANDRA L., exec. dir., St. Luke's Hospital, Racine, WI '85 (MGMT)
LONG, SCHELIA W., RN, dir. nrsg., North Hills Medical Center, North Richland Hills, TX '81 (NURS)
LONG, THURSTON H., (ret.), Salem, MA '51 (LIFE)
LONG, VIRGINIA A., RN, asst. dir. psych., Mount Sinai Medical Center, New York, NY '86 (NURS)
LONG, WALLACE G., atty., Detroit-Macomb Hospital Corporation, Detroit, MI '87 (ATTY)
LONG, WILL, dir. plant eng., Columbus Hospital, Great Falls, MT '79 (ENG)
LONG, WILLIAM H., pur. agt. and pharm., Conway Hospital, Conway, SC '69 (PUR)
LONGACRE, PAUL, mgt. eng., St. Agnes Hospital and Medical Center, Fresno, CA '81 (MGMT)
LONGDEN, JOEL, coor. educ., Good Samaritan Hospital and Medical Center, Portland, OR '86 (CS)
LONGEST, BEAUFORT BROWN JR., PhD, dir., Health Policy Institute, School of Public Health, University of Pittsburgh, Pittsburgh, PA '70
LONGLEY, DORAL E., pat. rep., Franciscan Medical Center, Rock Island, IL '85 (PAT)
LONGLEY, ELLA K., RN, consult., Memorial Medical Center of West Michigan, Ludington, MI '41 (LIFE)
LONGMIRE, ERNESTINE P., mgr. cent. sup., Mary Thompson Hospital, Chicago, IL '81 (CS)
LONGMIRE, GORDON DAVID, dir. pub. rel., Mercy Regional Medical Center, Vicksburg, MS '86 (PR)
LONGO, SALVADOR E., PhD, pres., Dr. Salvador E. Longo and Associates, Metairie, LA '79 (ENG)
LONGORIA, SYLVIA G., adm. asst., McAllen Medical Center, McAllen, TX '82 (PAT)(PR)
LONGRIGG, JOSEPH, dir. food serv., Pasadena Bayshore Medical Center, Pasadena, TX '76 (FOOD)
LONGSHORE, GEORGE F., partner, Fulton, Longshore and Assocs, Inc., Haverford, PA '84
LONGSINE, MARQUERITE, dir. in-service and pat. educ. coor., Phelps Memorial Health Center, Holdrege, NE '86 (EDUC)
LONGSTRETH, CAROL S., dir. pers., Weirton Medical Center, Weirton, WV '82 (PERS)
LONGTINE, LARAYNE J., student, University of Minnesota, Minneapolis, MN '87
LONQUIST, BERT A., vice-pres., Environmental Systems Design, Inc., Chicago, IL '85 (ENG)
LOOKE, WOLFGANG H., asst. dir. food serv., Norwegian-American Hospital, Chicago, IL '76 (FOOD)
LOOMIS, JAMES F., dir. med. soc. work, Bronson Methodist Hospital, Kalamazoo, MI '79 (SOC)
LOOMIS, ROGER L., asst. adm. eng., Johnson City Medical Center Hospital, Johnson City, TN '81 (ENG)
LOOMIS, TERRY, dir. hskpg. and ldry. serv., Friendship Manor, Roanoke, VA '86 (ENVIRON)
LOONEY, SR. ELIZABETH D., dir. nutr. serv., Calvary Hospital, Bronx, NY '81 (FOOD)
LOONEY, GERALD L., MD, dir. emer., Orthopaedic Hospital, Los Angeles, CA '86 (AMB)
LOOP, BONNIE L., dir. vol. serv. and commun. rel., Harrison Memorial Hospital, Bremerton, WA '80 (VOL)(PR)
LOOP, CAROLYN J., academic coor. radiol prog., St. Francis Regional Medical Center, Wichita, KS '84 (EDUC)
LOPATIN, MICHAEL A., syst. mgr., U. S. Public Health Service, Chicago, IL '74 (MGMT)
LOPER, CHARLOTTE M., pat. rel. rep., Shannon West Texas Memorial Hospital, San Angelo, TX '86 (PAT)
LOPER, EDITH L., student, School of Business, University of Chicago, Chicago, IL '85
LOPEZ-BLAZQUEZ, ANA A., student, Program in Hospital Administration, University of Florida, Gainesville, FL '85
LOPEZ, ANNEMARIE B., RN, asst. dir. nrsg. serv., William Beaumont Hospital, Royal Oak, MI '83 (NURS)
LOPEZ, AURELIO, dir. telecommun., Rose Medical Center, Denver, CO '81 (ENG)
LOPEZ, CHESTER H. JR., atty., Nashua Memorial Hospital, Nashua, NH '80 (ATTY)
LOPEZ, DAVID S., asst. adm., Bexar County Hospital District, San Antonio, TX '81
LOPEZ, EDUARDO, asst. dir. bldg. serv., Morristown Memorial Hospital, Morristown, NJ '86 (ENVIRON)
LOPEZ, FRANK W., dir. mktg. and pub. affairs, Beth Israel Medical Center, New York, NY '86 (PR)
LOPEZ, IVETTE MARIA, student, Georgia Institute of Technology, Atlanta, GA '85 (MGMT)
LOPEZ, SR. MADELEINE, dir. vol. serv., St. Mary's Hospital, Huntington, WV '85 (VOL)
LOPEZ, CAPT. MARY SULLIVAN, MSC USA, chief occup. ther., Irwin Army Community Hospital, Fort Riley, KS '85
LOPEZ, MILI A., dir. vol. serv., Reynolds Memorial Hospital, Glen Dale, WV '85 (VOL)
LOPEZ, SHIRLEY, dir. pers., Children's Medical Center of Dallas, Dallas, TX '74 (PERS)
LOPEZ, TOMMY F., dir. vol. serv., Bronx Children's Psychiatric Center, Bronx, NY '85 (VOL)
LOPEZ, VIVIAN J., dir. human res., Fair Havens Lutheran Retirement and Nursing Center, Miami Springs, FL '83 (PERS)
LOPMAN, ABE, asst. dir., Hermann Hospital, Houston, TX '86 (ENG)
LOPPNOW, BRUCE G., assoc. vice-pres. plng. and mktg., Theda Clark Regional Medical Center, Neenah, WI '84 (PLNG)(AMB)
LORANGER, ROBERT A., phys. plant mgr., New England Medical Center, Boston, MA '86
LORANGER, ROLAND C., dir. risk mgt., Rhode Island Hospital, Providence, RI '80 (RISK)
LORCH, LYNN B., sr. vice-pres. oper., Beth Israel Medical Center, New York, NY '69
LORD, ROBERT H., dir. plant oper., Parkview Memorial Hospital, Brunswick, ME '83 (ENG)
LORD, ROBERT S., dir. res. dev. and pub. rel., Nassau Suffolk Hospital Council, Hauppauge, NY '86 (PLNG)
LORD, TODD M., exec. dir., York Health Services, York, PA '82
LORE, MARY A., Fairmount Institute, Philadelphia, PA '76 (PERS)
LOREI, LISA A., student, Program in Industrial Engineer, Iowa State University, Ames, IA '86 (MGMT)
LOREN, ROSLYN M., dir. vol. and aux. serv., Syosset Community Hospital, Syosset, NY '85 (VOL)
LORENC, JULIE, dir. vol., St. Joseph Medical Center, Joliet, IL '81 (VOL)
LORENCE, GERALD C., adm., Grace Hospital, Cleveland, OH '55 (LIFE)
LORENZ, FRED J., pres., Fred J. Lorenz and Associates, Seattle, WA '73 (PERS)
LORENZ, KENNETH W., dir. equip., Voluntary Hospitals of America Supply Company, Irving, TX '82 (PUR)
LORENZ, MARK J., National Medical Enterprises, Los Angeles, CA '85
LORENZEN, TIMOTHY L., inventory mgr., Tucson Medical Center, Tucson, AZ '85 (CS)
LORENZO, NICHOLAS F. JR., atty., Punxsutawney Area Hospital, Punxsutawney, PA '79 (ATTY)
LORGEREE, EDWARD, chief oper. off., Walther Memorial Hospital, Chicago, IL '82 (PLNG)
LORIA, LANCE S., vice-pres., Amherst Associates, Houston, TX '80
LORITZ, ROBERT W., RN, dir. pat. serv., St. Rose de Lima Hospital, Henderson, NV '81 (NURS)
LORTIE, MICHAEL, dir. pur., Washington Hospital Center, Washington, DC '83 (PUR)
LORUSSO, SR. ANN M., RN, assoc. dir. nrsg., Hospital of Saint Raphael, New Haven, CT '80 (NURS)
LORY, MARC H., chief exec. off. and vice-pres., University of Medicine and Dentistry of New Jersey, Newark, NJ '87
LOSBY, HEIDI R., coor. pub. rel., United Hospital, Grand Forks, ND '85 (PR)
LOSE, LINNEA E., dir. pub. rel., Bethesda Hospital, Inc., Cincinnati, OH '84 (PR) (PLNG)
LOSEE, ROBERT J., dir. sup., proc., distrib., ldry. and store room, Mercy Hospital, Cedar Rapids, IA '86 (CS)
LOSITO, FRANK P., dir. food serv., Valley View Community Hospital, Youngtown, AZ '82 (FOOD)
LOSKA, ELNA L., RN, dir. nrsg., Methodist Hospital of Chicago, Chicago, IL '78 (NURS)
LOSOFF, MARTIN, adm., Sycamore Hospital, Sycamore, IL '71 (PERS)
LOSSEN, REBECCA L., RN, dir. nrsg., Community Memorial Hospital and Convalescent and Rehabilitation Unit, Winona, MN '83 (NURS)
LOTRECK, CHARLES T., Norwich, CT '51 (LIFE)
LOTT, KEN, dir. human res., East Alabama Medical Center, Opelika, AL '86 (PERS)
LOTTERHOS, ROBERT, dir. soc. work serv., St. Francis Medical Center, Trenton, NJ '85 (SOC)
LOUBIER, EUGENE E., pres., Winchester Hospital, Winchester, MA '72
LOUCHIOS, ANDREAS, dir. food serv., Condell Memorial Hospital, Libertyville, IL '75 (FOOD)
LOUCKS, J. RICHARD, Durango, CO '82
LOUCKS, JAMES H., MD, pres., Crozer-Chester Health Systems, Chester, PA '68
LOUCKS, KARL F., assoc., Ringler Associates, Inc., Radnor, PA '86 (RISK)
LOUDEN, DAVID F., dir. amb. and admit. serv., St. Vincent Hospital and Health Center, Indianapolis, IN '87 (AMB)
LOUDEN, PHYLLIS C., dir. vol., Camden-Clark Memorial Hospital, Parkersburg, WV '81 (VOL)
LOUDEN, TERI L., pres., Louden and Company, Chicago, IL '80 (PLNG)
LOUDON, JOHN, partner, Dulaney, Johnston and Priest Insurance, Wichita, KS '84 (RISK)
LOUGHERY, RICHARD M., exec. consult., Washington Hospital Center, Washington, DC '54 (LIFE)
LOUGHNANE, DAVID, atty., Gottlieb Memorial Hospital, Melrose Park, IL '82 (ATTY)
LOUGHNEY, KEVIN, asst. chief eng., Boca Raton Community Hospital, Boca Raton, FL '86 (ENG)
LOUGHRAN, GEORGE W., dir. food serv., HCA Doctors Hospital, Lake Worth, FL '79 (FOOD)
LOUIE, DENISE, mgr. health care bus. plng. practice, Ernst and Whinney, Los Angeles, CA '82 (PLNG)
LOUIE, KATHY, mgt. eng., Pacific Presbyterian Medical Center, San Francisco, CA '85 (MGMT)
LOUK, RODNEY D., dir. info. syst., Washington Hospital, Washington, PA '85 (MGMT)
LOUTFI, THORA J., adm. coor. vol., Alta Bates Hospital, Berkeley, CA '81 (VOL)
LOUVIERE, MICHAEL L., dir. matl. mgt., Good Shepherd Medical Center, Longview, TX '79 (PUR)
LOVALLO, NANCY, dir. trng., Booth Memorial Medical Center, Flushing, NY '82 (EDUC)
LOVASY, EUGENE E., dir. info. serv., Parma Community General Hospital, Parma, OH '81 (ENG)
LOVASZ, DON J., dir. plng., Carle Foundation, Urbana, IL '84 (PLNG)
LOVE, ANN BURNSIDE, owner, Ann Burnside Love and Associates, Frederick, MD '87 (PR)
LOVE, ANNA J., dir. mgt. eng., Iowa Methodist Medical Center, Des Moines, IA '86 (MGMT)
LOVE, BENJAMIN F., asst. dir. plant serv., Tucson Medical Center, Tucson, AZ '78 (ENG)
LOVE, DEBORAH F., RN, asst. dir. nrsg. oper. room and amb. care, Crozer-Chester Medical Center, Chester, PA '86 (NURS)
LOVE, DEBORAH, RN, asst. dir. nrsg. critical care serv., Sibley Memorial Hospital, Washington, DC '85 (NURS)
LOVE, DONALD JAMES, adm., Gill Memorial Eye, Ear, Nose and Throat Hospital, Roanoke, VA '78 (MGMT)(PERS)
LOVE, LCDR DOUGLAS, MSC USN, head food mgt., Naval Hospital, Oakland, CA '84 (FOOD)
LOVE, ESTHER, asst. dir. nrsg., Albert Einstein Medical Center-Northern Division, Philadelphia, PA '77 (EDUC)
LOVE, GAIL D., dir. emp. rel., Geneva General Hospital, Geneva, NY '81 (PERS)
LOVE, GLENN I., asst. dir. eng. serv., Iowa Methodist Medical Center, Des Moines, IA '82 (ENG)
LOVE, VANNA H., adm. rep., Southeast Alabama Medical Center, Dothan, AL '82 (PAT)
LOVE, WENDY S., exec. dir., Southern Tier Health Management Corporation, Elmira Heights, NY '86 (PLNG)
LOVECCHIO, DIANA L., dir. pers., Hampton General Hospital, Hampton, VA '81 (FOOD)(PERS)
LOVEDAY, MARTYN, dir. eng., King Fahad Hospital, Al Baha Kingdom, Saudi Arabia '86 (ENG)
LOVEDAY, WILLIAM J., exec. vice-pres., Memorial Hospital Medical Center of Long Beach, Long Beach, CA '69
LOVEJOY, LYNN S., PhD, risk mgr., University Hospitals of Cleveland, Cleveland, OH '86 (RISK)
LOVEJOY, NANCY LEE, dir. soc. serv., Beth Israel Hospital, Passaic, NJ '67 (SOC)
LOVEJOY, ROBERT RAYMOND, chm., Hospital President's Association, Concord, MA '57 (PLNG)(LIFE)
LOVEJOY, SANDRA G., clin. spec. diabetes and pat. teaching, Christ Hospital, Cincinnati, OH '86 (EDUC)
LOVELACE, TINA V., field rep., Joint Commission on Accreditation of Hospitals, Chicago, IL '58
LOVELAND, DAVID C., vice-pres., The Sturm Communications Group, Chicago, IL '85 (PLNG)
LOVELAND, SALLY A., phys. liaison, Phoenix Memorial Hospital, Phoenix, AZ '86 (PR)
LOVELAND, SUSAN H., dir. commun. rel., City Hospital, Martinsburg, WV '84 (PR) (PLNG)
LOVELL, JOAN A., atty., Irvington General Hospital, Irvington, NJ '80 (ATTY)
LOVELL, PAULA, vice-pres., Madden and Goodrum and Associates, Nashville, TN '86 (PR)
LOVERIDGE, GARY F., atty., McDonough, Holland, Schwartz and Allen, Sacramento, CA '77 (ATTY)
LOVERING, LEALAND LLOYD, atty., Wuesthoff Memorial Hospital, Rockledge, FL '68 (ATTY)
LOVETT, JOHN F. X., div. vice-pres. health affairs, Blue Cross and Blue Shield of Greater New York, New York, NY '77 (ATTY)
LOVETT, MARTHA A., consult., Virchow, Krause and Company, Madison, WI '84 (MGMT)
LOVIN, CAROL A., student, University of Michigan Program in Hospital Administration, Ann Arbor, MI '85
LOVING, CHARLOTTE M., asst. exec. dir. aux., St. Mary's Hospital, Richmond, VA '84 (VOL)
LOVING, W. M. JR., div. vice-pres., Hospital Corporation of America, Austin, TX '83
LOVING, WILLIAM L., consult., WII Associates, Lake Forest, IL '54 (PLNG)(LIFE)
LOVULLO, MARTIN S., student, Department of Health Care Administration, George Washington University, Washington, DC '82 (MGMT)
LOW, DEBRA K., prin., Debra Low and Associates, Mesa, AZ '77 (PLNG)
LOW, MARIAN E., asst. dir. nrsg. and pat. educ., Timken Mercy Medical Center, Canton, OH '86 (EDUC)
LOWD, HARRY M. III, dir., New London Hospital, New London, NH '72 (PLNG)
LOWE, ADONNA F., RN, asst. vice-pres. nrsg., Baylor Health Care System, Dallas, TX '82 (NURS)
LOWE, DAVID A., vice-pres. health care, Society National Bank, Cleveland, OH '84
LOWE, GARY B., asst. dir. eng., Fairfax Hospital, Falls Church, VA '80 (ENG)
LOWE, JANE ISAACS, prog. coor. discharge plng., Mount Sinai Medical Center, New York, NY '81 (SOC)
LOWE, LAWRENCE P., chief exec. off., Lawrence Lowe Companies, Louisville, KY '85 (PR) (PLNG)
LOWE, PHILLIP W., asst. adm. plng. and support serv., Dixie Medical Center, St. George, UT '85 (PLNG)
LOWE, STEPHEN M., asst. dir. phys. plant, University of Texas Health Center, Tyler, TX '83 (ENG)
LOWE, TERRANCE A., dir. food serv., Victory Memorial Hospital, Waukegan, IL '79 (FOOD)
LOWE, WILLIAM R., auditor fin. mgt., Charles A. Dana Hospital of Sidney Farber Cancer Institute, Boston, MA '81
LOWELL, LISA, coor. qual. assur., Children's Hospital, Boston, MA '84 (RISK)
LOWELL, MARY KATHERINE, dir. nutr. serv., St. Elizabeth Medical Center-South, Edgewood, KY '86 (FOOD)
LOWENSTEIN, ARLENE J., RN, Augusta, GA '82 (NURS)
LOWER, JOHN E., dir. matl. mgt., St. Lawrence Hospital, Lansing, MI '80 (PUR)
LOWERY, ANNETTE TAYLOR, mktg. and commun. spec., Columbia Hospital for Women Medical Center, Washington, DC '85 (PR)
LOWERY, COL. ANTOINETTE T., RN, chief nrs., David Grant U. S. Air Force Medical Center, Fairfield, CA '83 (NURS)
LOWERY, GLENN E., pres. and chief exec. off., Huron Valley Hospital, Milford, MI '62
LOWERY, MILLIE, pat. rep., Rapides General Hospital, Alexandria, LA '78 (PAT)
LOWERY, WILLIAM H., bd. mem., Paoli Memorial Hospital, Paoli, PA '72 (ATTY)
LOWMAN, REBECCA C., dir. vol. serv., St. David's Community Hospital, Austin, TX '86 (VOL)
LOWMASTER, BETTY J., mgr. matl., Palmerton Hospital, Palmerton, PA '78 (PUR)

LOWRANCE, WILLIAM W., (ret.), Morganton, NC '46 (LIFE)
LOWRIE, JAMES S., atty., Hospital Corporation of America, Nashville, TN '81 (ATTY)
LOWRY, BETTY E., exec. dir., Management Information Systems Project, Ottawa, Ont., Canada '85 (MGMT)
LOWRY, ELLIS R., partner, Baskervill and Son-Architects and Engineers, Richmond, VA '83
LOWRY, M. ELEANOR C., coor. pat. rel., New England Deaconess Hospital, Boston, MA '80 (PAT)
LOWRY, SR. MAUREEN, pres., Mercy Catholic Medical Center, Darby, PA '87
LOWRY, MELISSA ANN, student, Harvard University School of Public Health, Cambridge, MA '84
LOWS, MARY, RN, dir. pat. serv., Dearborn County Hospital, Lawrenceburg, IN '80 (RISK)
LOWY, MARTIN, affil. adm. and assoc. dir., Beth Israel Medical Center, New York, NY '71
LOY, ROBERT LEO, consult., Mercy Health Center, Oklahoma City, OK '29 (LIFE)
LOYD, RANDY L., dir. sup. serv., Denver Health and Hospitals, Denver, CO '83 (PUR)
LOYNES, PATRICIA L., mgr. sup., proc. and distrib., St. Lawrence Hospital, Lansing, MI '81 (CS)
LUALLEN, E. GENEVIEVE, asst. dir. educ., Poudre Valley Hospital, Fort Collins, CO '79 (EDUC)
LUBAWAY, WILLIAM J., vice-pres. fin., Botsford General Hospital-Osteopathic, Farmington Hills, MI '73
LUBAWSKI, JAMES L., vice-pres. bus. dev., Evangelical Health Systems, Oak Brook, IL '87 (PLNG)
LUBAWY, HARRY J., dir. hskpg., ldry. and commun., Shadyside Hospital, Pittsburgh, PA '84 (ENG)
LUBER, LARRY B., atty., Barnes Hospital, St. Louis, MO '83 (ATTY)
LUBER, PHYLLIS R., dir. commun. rel. and vol. serv., Garden State Rehabilitation Hospital, Toms River, NJ '82 (PR)(VOL)
LUBERDA, ANNE MARIE, asst. adm., Michigan Osteopathic Medical Center, Detroit, MI '79 (PLNG)
LUBIC, WILLIAM JAMES, atty., New York Infirmary, New York, NY '73 (ATTY)
LUBIN, IRVIN C., dir. bldg. serv., Greater Southeast Community Hospital, Washington, DC '72 (ENG)
LUBOTSKY, THOMAS M., assoc. vice-pres., Metropolitan Medical Center, Minneapolis, MN '80
LUCAS, CARLENE, dir. soc. work, North Detroit General Hospital, Detroit, MI '86 (SOC)
LUCAS, ERNEST A., dir. soc. serv. and util. review, Medical Center Hospital, Chillicothe, OH '86 (SOC)
LUCAS, GAYLE K., asst. vice-pres., Frankford Hospital, Philadelphia, PA '86
LUCAS, J. CURTIS, student, Program in Health Service Administration, School of Health Professions, Governors State University, Park Forest South, IL '83
LUCAS, LISA M., coor. mktg., Portland Adventist Medical Center, Portland, OR '86 (PLNG)
LUCAS, RAYMOND A. JR., vice-pres., St. Luke's Hospital of New Bedford, New Bedford, MA '83 (PERS)
LUCAS, RICHARD B., dir. pub. rel., Singing River Hospital System, Pascagoula, MS '81 (PR)
LUCAS, ROBERT T., asst. adm., Wythe County Community Hospital, Wytheville, VA '85
LUCAS, SANDRA E., dir. food and nutr., Goodman Hill Hospital, Paducah, KY '86 (FOOD)
LUCAS, STEPHEN D., asst. dir. plant oper., Deaconess Hospital, Evansville, IN '80 (ENG)
LUCAS, W. R., adm., Fort Sheridan Area Army Health Clinics, Fort Sheridan, IL '83
LUCAS, WILLIAM M. JR., atty., Lakeside Hospital, Metairie, LA '84 (ATTY)
LUCASH, PETER D., asst. adm., Montefiore Hospital, Pittsburgh, PA '79
LUCCHESI, JANE, dir. soc. work, Le Bonheur Children's Medical Center, Memphis, TN '77 (SOC)
LUCCI, LT. COL. FRANK J., (ret.), APO New York, NY '64
LUCE, GREGORY M., atty., Norfolk General Hospital, Norfolk, VA '82 (ATTY)
LUCENTE, FRANK S., pres., Meyersdale Community Hospital, Meyersdale, PA '68 (ATTY)
LUCERO, MAJ. JOHN, MSC USA, chief soc. work serv., Bayne-Jones Army Community Hospital, Fort Polk, LA '86 (SOC)
LUCHI, THOMAS A., mgr. health care mgt. adv. serv., Laventhol and Horwath, Minneapolis, MN '79 (PLNG)
LUCHSINGER, ROBERT D., adm. asst., Parkview Hospital, Toledo, OH '83 (PERS)
LUCHT, GRETCHEN G., coor. vol. serv., Mercy Hospital, Iowa City, IA '85 (VOL)
LUCIA, PEGGY A., dir. mktg., Mary Thompson Hospital, Chicago, IL '85 (PLNG)
LUCIANI, F. D., mgr. reg. indust. eng., Kaiser Permanente Medical Care Program, Oakland, CA '86 (PUR)
LUCIANI, FRANK D., mgr. reg. indust. eng., Kaiser Permanente Medical Care Program, Oakland, CA '80 (MGMT)
LUCIANI, KERRY F., oper. res. analyst and mgt. eng., Community Hospital Monterey Peninsula, Monterey, CA '87 (MGMT)
LUCIANO, KATHY, RN, vice-pres. nrsg. serv., Presbyterian Intercommunity Hospital, Whittier, CA '76 (NURS)
LUCIANO, NORMA L., RN, dir. nrsg., Princeton Community Hospital, Princeton, WV '76 (NURS)
LUCICH, NICHOLAS L. JR., atty., Fresno Community Hospital and Medical Center, Fresno, CA '83 (ATTY)
LUCK, MICHAEL F., PhD, pres. trust fund, Healtheast, Inc., Allentown, PA '85 (PR)
LUCKEY, THOMAS A., mgr. commun., Providence Memorial Hospital, El Paso, TX '85 (ENG)
LUCKMAN, PAUL T., asst. counsel and risk mgr., United Hospitals, Inc., Cheltenham, PA '85 (RISK)
LUCKSINGER, THOMAS S., atty., Sisters of Charity Health Care Systems, Houston, TX '74 (ATTY)
LUCZKA, GERALD D., adm. asst. human res., Prince William Hospital, Manassas, VA '86 (PERS)
LUDDY, PATRICK M., adm. dir. emer. serv., Yale-New Haven Hospital, New Haven, CT '80 (MGMT)
LUDKE, ROBERT L., PhD, asst. prof., Graduate Program in Hospital and Health Administration, University of Iowa, Iowa City, IA '74 (MGMT)
LUDLAM, JAMES E., atty., California Hospital Association, Sacramento, CA '68 (ATTY)(LIFE)
LUDLAM, STEVEN H., asst. dir. mktg., University Hospital, Jackson, MS '79 (PLNG)
LUDOWITZ, DANIEL L., pat. rep., Mercy Health Center, Dubuque, IA '79 (PAT)
LUDWICK, JAMES F., student, Program in Hospital and Health Care Administration, University of Minnesota, Minneapolis, MN '81
LUDWICK, JOHN H., atty., Swedish Hospital Medical Center, Seattle, WA '80 (ATTY)
LUDWIG, BARBARA A., coor. pat. educ., St. Luke's Regional Medical Center, Sioux City, IA '84 (EDUC)
LUDWIG, EDWARD, reg. eng., Crothall American, Inc., Des Plaines, IL '85 (ENG)
LUDWIG, KAREN K., dir. pers., Holy Rosary Hospital, Ontario, OR '84 (PERS)
LUDWIG, LEE, vice-pres. plng., Norwalk Hospital, Norwalk, CT '83 (PLNG)
LUDWIG, MICHAEL J., dir. phys. plant, University of Southern California-Kenneth Norris Cancer Hospital, Los Angeles, CA '84 (ENG)
LUDWIG, PATRIC E., Bronson Healthcare Group, Inc., Kalamazoo, MI '64 (MGMT)
LUEBKER, JUERGEN, dir. facil. and contstr mgt., Brooklyn Hospital-Caledonian Hospital, Brooklyn, NY '79 (ENG)
LUEDECKE, KAREN, RN, clin. supv. nrs., Harborview Medical Center, Seattle, WA '79 (NURS)
LUEDTKE, PAUL F., dir. hotel and environ. serv., Mercy Hospital, Urbana, IL '86 (ENVIRON)
LUEHRS, PAUL R., asst. vice-pres., Methodist Hospitals of Dallas, Dallas, TX '75
LUEKEN, PATTY W., dir. diet., Arkansas Rehabilitation Institute, Little Rock, AR '79 (FOOD)
LUETHY, ELLIE P., mgt. eng. ancillary serv., St. Francis Hospital, Greenville, SC '86 (MGMT)
LUEVANO, THOMAS R., vice-pres. human res., Eskaton Health Corporation, Carmichael, CA '80 (PERS)
LUFKIN, SYLVIA R., RN EdD, asst. adm., Rochester Methodist Hospital, Rochester, MN '79 (NURS)
LUFT, JOHN, dir. hskpg. and ldry. serv., Montana Deaconess Medical Center, Great Falls, MT '86 (ENVIRON)
LUFTMAN, JACOB, University of Medicine and Dentistry of New Jersey-University Hospital, Newark, NJ '80 (MGMT)
LUGENBEEL, ARCH, dean, Trident Technical College, Health Sciences Technology, Charleston, SC '71 (EDUC)
LUGINBUHL, DAVID CARL, exec. dir., Grace Hospital, Women's Health Centre, Calgary, Alta., Canada '81 (PR)
LUGO, LYNNE C., dir. pers., Doctors Hospital of Lakewood, Lakewood, CA '86 (PERS)
LUHANEY, RUDY, dir. maint. and plant oper., St. Joseph Riverside Hospital, Warren, OH '69 (ENG)
LUHRING, PAUL C., dir. eng., Scripps Memorial Hospital-Encinitas, Encinitas, CA '87 (ENG)
LUIS, CHERYL S., nrs. mgr. clin., St. Luke's Hospital, Bethlehem, PA '87 (AMB)
LUIS, HELEN J., dir. pat. rel., Straub Clinic and Hospital, Honolulu, HI '83 (PAT)
LUKACH, JOSEPH A., dir. soc. serv., Holy Redeemer Hospital and Medical Center, Meadowbrook, PA '83 (SOC)
LUKAS, CAROLYN, RN, assoc. exec. dir., John F. Kennedy Community Hospital, Edison, NJ '76 (NURS)
LUKASIEWICZ, LORI J. MELLON, asst. adm., Lormar, New City, NY '83
LUKE, JANET C., student, Georgia State University-Institute of Health Administration, Atlanta, GA '85
LUKE, KENNETH J., pres., Milford-Whitinsville Regional Hospital, Milford, MA '73
LUKENBILL, ROSANNA E., dir. vol. serv., St. Elizabeth Hospital Medical Center, Lafayette, IN '70 (VOL)
LUKENS, PAUL J., dir. food serv., Bethel Methodist Home, Ossining, NY '85 (FOOD)
LUKOFF, ROGER, assoc. plng., Albert Einstein Hlthcare Foundation, Philadelphia, PA '86 (PLNG)
LULACS, JANET L., mgr. outpat center, Phoenix Children's Hospital, Phoenix, AZ '87 (AMB)
LULEY, JAMES F., exec. dir., Slocum Dickson Medical Group, Utica, NY '87 (AMB)
LULL, ROBERT W., chief prop. mgt. br., U. S. Army Health Services Command, Fort Sam Houston, TX '84 (PUR)
LUMB, KAREN J., RN, vice-pres. pat. care, Leland Memorial Hospital, Riverdale, MD '83 (NURS)
LUMMUS, ROBERT A. III, mgt. eng., Medical Center of Central Georgia, Macon, GA '79 (MGMT)
LUMP, IRENE M., mgr. natl. health affairs, Smith Kline and French Laboratory, Philadelphia, PA '86
LUMPKIN, ILENE G., adm. dir. commun. rel. and mktg., Palisades General Hospital, North Bergen, NJ '82 (PR)
LUMPKIN, KATHLEEN, mgr. cent. sup., Floyd Medical Center, Rome, GA '79 (CS)
LUMPKIN, RITA F., mgr. cent. serv., Smyrna Hospital, Smyrna, GA '82 (CS)
LUMPP, KAREN E., partner, Touche Ross and Company, Newark, NJ '82
LUMSDEN, CHRIS A., asst. adm., Halifax-South Boston Community Hospital, South Boston, VA '83
LUNA, CAROLYN F., RN, clin. dir. critical care and psych. nrsg., St. Vincent Hospital, Santa Fe, NM '76 (NURS)
LUNA, ELAINE V., dir. discharge plng. and soc. serv., Northeastern Regional Hospital, Las Vegas, NM '85 (SOC)
LUND, ARTHUR K., atty., O'Connor Hospital, San Jose, CA '70 (ATTY)
LUND, DIANE S., dir. food serv., Doctors Hospital of Pinole, Pinole, CA '77 (FOOD)
LUND, ELDONNA M., RN, in-service dir., Community Memorial Hospital, Lisbon, ND '83 (EDUC)
LUND, GRAHAM C., vice-pres., Saint Vincent Health Center, Erie, PA '73
LUND, LOREN D., dir. bldg. and grds., Golden Valley Health Center, Golden Valley, MN '78 (ENG)
LUND, PATRICIA E., RN, vice-pres. nrsg. affairs, Wyman Park Medical Center, Baltimore, MD '85 (NURS)
LUND, SUSAN M. L., vice-pres. nrsg., Westland Medical Center, Westland, MI '84 (NURS)
LUNDBERG, DONALD J., mgt. eng., Sinai Hospital of Detroit, Detroit, MI '87 (MGMT)
LUNDBERG, LOWELL W., atty., St. Luke's Hospitals, Fargo, ND '77 (ATTY)
LUNDBERG, ROBERT H., atty., Medcenter One, Bismarck, ND '69 (ATTY)
LUNDBERG, THOMAS CHARLES, pres., Lundberg and Associates, Inc., Portland, OR '74
LUNDBLAD, CARL R. JR., dir. res. analyst, Samcor-Samaritan Research Institute, Phoenix, AZ '83
LUNDBLAD, MILO W., atty., Swedish Covenant Hospital, Chicago, IL '86 (ATTY)
LUNDBLAD, MILO, partner, Pellett, Lundblad and Baker, Chicago, IL '86 (RISK)
LUNDCHILD, NANCY A., dir. diet., Alberta Children's Hospital, Calgary, Alta., Canada '85 (FOOD)
LUNDE, ROBERT D., chief eng., New Rochelle Hospital Medical Center, New Rochelle, NY '65 (ENG)
LUNDEEN, DAVID E., plant eng., Trinity Regional Hospital, Fort Dodge, IA '78 (ENG)
LUNDEEN, JOHN V., pres., American Medical Bldgs, Inc., Milwaukee, WI '87 (AMB)
LUNDEEN, MERLE, dir. commun. serv., Bexar County Hospital District, San Antonio, TX '85 (ENG)
LUNDGREN, JOHN R., dir. risk mgt., Worcester Memorial Hospital, Worcester, MA '80 (RISK)
LUNDGREN, ROBERT F., dir. eng., Texas Scottish Rite Hospital for Crippled Children, Dallas, TX '79 (ENG)
LUNDIN, DIANA E., dir. commun. rel., Hemet Valley Hospital District, Hemet, CA '86 (PR)
LUNDIN, DONALD, student, Department of Health Services, George Washington University, Washington, DC '86
LUNDIN, ROBERT J. II, vice-pres. mktg., Health Systems Group, Vancouver, WA '77 (PR)
LUNDON, MICHELLE M., diet. spec., The Burrows Company, Brunswick, OH '85 (FOOD)
LUNDQUIST, DANA RICHARD, pres., Hamot Medical Center, Erie, PA '65
LUNDQUIST, MARJORIE A., asst. vice-pres. mktg., St. Michael's Hospital, Stevens Point, WI '86 (PR) (PLNG)
LUNDQUIST, CAPT. NANCY L., Alexandria, VA '83 (NURS)
LUNDSKOW, J. GORDON, eng., Rochester Methodist Hospital, Rochester, MN '66 (ENG)
LUNDWALL, TANYA LUEEN, pat. rep., University of Cincinnati Hospital-Christian R. Holmes Division, Cincinnati, OH '85 (PAT)
LUNDY, E. JANE, coor. vol., Mount Sinai Medical Center, Milwaukee, WI '83 (VOL)
LUNN, LINDA A., dir. cent. sup., Memorial Hospital, Hollywood, FL '82 (CS)
LUNN, ROBERT O. JR., PhD, dir., University of Florida Clinics, University of Florida, Gainesville, FL '77 (AMB)
LUNSFORD, LESLIE M., sr. consult., SunHealth Corporation, Charlotte, NC '86 (ENG)
LUONGO, STEPHEN E., atty., Philadelphia College of Osteopathic Medical, Philadelphia, PA '78 (ATTY)
LUPASCU, DOROTHY M., EdD, dir. staff educ. and prof. dev., Lutheran Hospital of Fort Wayne, Fort Wayne, IN '84 (EDUC)
LUPICA, CHARLES T., dir. pur., St. Joseph's Hospital, Savannah, GA '82 (PUR)
LUPO, THERESE C., RN, dir. clin. nrsg., Middletown Regional Hospital, Middletown, OH '86 (NURS)
LUPPOLD, LESLIE M., RN, vice-pres. nrsg., Emerson Hospital, Concord, MA '86 (NURS)
LUPTON, CHARLES H. III, Washington, DC '83 (PLNG)
LURIE, ABRAHAM, PhD, (ret.), Jericho, NY '70 (SOC)
LURIE, MICHAEL R., dir. plng., Community Memorial Hospital, Ventura, CA '81 (PLNG)
LUROS, ELLYN C., pres., Fsc Management Company, Chatsworth, CA '86 (FOOD)
LURTZ, JANE L., dir. pub. rel. and commun., St. Joseph Hospital, Port Charlotte, FL '82 (PR)
LUSBY, LINDA L., dir. food serv., Park Lane Medical Center, Kansas City, MO '84 (FOOD)
LUSE, ROBERT H., pres., Valdese General Hospital, Valdese, NC '72 (MGMT)
LUSIGNAN, LAURIE J., mgr. soc. serv., Emerson Hospital, Concord, MA '86 (SOC)
LUSK, CHARLES B., dir. mktg., Lee's Summit Community Hospital, Lees Summit, MO '86 (PLNG)
LUSK, DENISE P., asst. dir. commun. and prof. rel., Oconee Memorial Hospital, Seneca, SC '86 (PR)
LUSSIER, DONNA B., RN, dir. pat. care serv., Sch Health Care System, Houston, TX '86 (NURS)
LUSSIER, MARJORIE J., mgr. commun. rel., St. Charles Medical Center, Bend, OR '81 (PR)(EDUC)
LUSTIG, LILLIAN M., supv. nrsg., Central Florida Home Health Service, Inc., Daytona Beach, FL '75
LUSTIG, MERLE A., dir. plng., Children's Hospital Medical Center of California, Oakland, CA '84 (PLNG)
LUTHER, BARBARA ANN, dir. soc. serv., Humana Hospital -Enterprise, Enterprise, AL '83 (SOC)
LUTHER, CYNTHIA H., asst. dir. nrsg. serv. and coor. staff dev., Rush Foundation Hospital, Meridian, MS '85 (EDUC)
LUTHER, OSCAR D., (ret.), Newburgh, IN '51 (LIFE)
LUTHER, PATRICIA, assoc. planner, Southwest Community Health Services, Albuquerque, NM '84 (PLNG)
LUTHRINGER, THOMAS F., asst. adm., Charter Hospital of Lafayette, Lafayette, IN '86
LUTKE, MARLENE J., RN, dir. perioperative nrsg., Blodgett Memorial Medical Center, Grand Rapids, MI '85 (NURS)
LUTKEVICH, ROBERT, dir. matl. mgt., Winchester Hospital, Winchester, MA '86 (PUR)
LUTON, DORIS D., pat. rep., Tuomey Hospital, Sumter, SC '83 (PAT)
LUTON, MARY KATHRYN, dir. pat. rel. serv., Presbyterian Hospital, Oklahoma City, OK '77 (PAT)

LUTTBEG, ALICE T., RN, asst. adm. nrsg. serv., St. Joseph Hospital and Health Center, Bryan, TX '82 (NURS)
LUTTER, MARILYN W., dir. soc. serv., Hospital for Sick Children, Washington, DC '80 (SOC)
LUTTERMAN, WILMA JEAN, pur. agt., T. J. Samson Community Hospital, Glasgow, KY '68 (PUR)
LUTTICKEN, CAROLYN A., mgr. gen. educ. and audio visual serv., El Camino Hospital, Mountain View, CA '79 (EDUC)
LUTTRELL, RICHARD C., exec. vice-pres., Hospital Casualty Company, Oklahoma City, OK '86
LUTZ, JAY K., vice-pres. human res. serv., Samaritan Health Center, Detroit, MI '86 (PERS)
LUTZ, JOAN T., dir. vol. serv., South Nassau Communities Hospital, Oceanside, NY '81 (VOL)
LUTZ, LOUISE A., consult., Mediq Healthcare Resources, Pennsauken, NJ '80 (PLNG)
LUTZ, MADELINE A., PhD, dir. educ., Walter O. Boswell Memorial Hospital, Sun City, AZ '83 (EDUC)
LUZER, MARTHA R., RN, assoc. vice-pres., Presbyterian-University Hospital, Pittsburgh, PA '86 (NURS)
LYALL, MARIANNE J., dir. diet., Hinds General Hospital, Jackson, MS '77 (FOOD)
LYBERG, JOHN E., mgr. matl., Rogers City Hospital, Rogers City, MI '79 (PUR)
LYDA, JACK, dir. resp. ther., Rochester General Hospital, Rochester, NY '80
LYDEN, KATHLEEN, dir. commun., University of California at Los Angeles Medical Center, Los Angeles, CA '86 (ENG)
LYDEN, SHAWN M., atty., Rush-Presbyterian-St. Luke's Medical Center, Chicago, IL '86 (ATTY)
LYDIC, JACQUELYN SUE, dir. pub. rel., Springdale Memorial Hospital, Springdale, AR '83 (PR)
LYDIC, JEFF, sr. mech. eng., Cleveland Clinic Foundation, Cleveland, OH '82 (ENG)
LYERLA, MEL E. JR., dir. eng., Wesley Medical Center, Wichita, KS '82 (ENG)
LYLE, JEFFREY E., asst. adm., Harborview Medical Center, Seattle, WA '83
LYLES, VIRGINIA H., dir. pat. and commun. affairs, Newnan Hospital, Newnan, GA '81 (PR)(PERS)
LYMAN, BONNIE K., mgr. matl., Portsmouth General Hospital, Portsmouth, VA '83 (PUR)
LYMAN, LAURA BARRETT, pat. rep., Francis Scott Key Medical Center, Baltimore, MD '86 (PAT)
LYMAN, TERRY T., RN, asst. adm. nrsg. serv., Hospital of the Medical College of Pennsylvania, Philadelphia, PA '86 (NURS)
LYMBURNER, ANITA G., RN, vice-pres. nrsg. serv., Walthamweston Hospital and Medical Center, Waltham, MA '81 (NURS)
LYNCH, ANN M., RN, assoc. dir. nrsg., Meriden-Wallingford Hospital, Meriden, CT '86 (NURS)
LYNCH, CHARLOTTE A., sr. consult., SunHealth, Inc., Louisville, KY '79 (PLNG)
LYNCH, EDNA ELLEN, mgt. lecturer, Indiana University, School of Nursing, Indianapolis, IN '75 (NURS)
LYNCH, ELIZABETH A., diet., Community Hospital of Gardena, Gardena, CA '83 (FOOD)
LYNCH, ELIZABETH A., vice-pres. human res., Bristol Hospital, Bristol, CT '85 (PERS)
LYNCH, FRANCIS PATRICK, pres., Mount Auburn Hospital, Cambridge, MA '70
LYNCH, HARRELL, mgr. matl., Park Ridge Hospital, Fletcher, NC '83 (PUR)
LYNCH, JAMES FREDERICK, asst. adm., Norris Cotton Cancer Center, Mary Hitchcock Memorial Hospital, Hanover, NH '77
LYNCH, JAMES M., sr. vice-pres. corp. dev., Holy Cross Hospital, Silver Spring, MD '81 (PLNG)
LYNCH, JOHN A., pres., Medical Diagnostics, Inc., Burlington, MA '82 (PLNG)
LYNCH, JOHN F., dir. maint., Malden Hospital, Malden, MA '81 (ENG)
LYNCH, JOHN J., MD, chm. qual. assur., Washington Hospital Center, Washington, DC '84 (RISK)
LYNCH, JOHN K., pat. rep., Bayley Seton Hospital, Staten Island, NY '82 (PAT)
LYNCH, JOHN, mech. supv., Ashtabula County Medical Center, Ashtabula, OH '85 (ENG)
LYNCH, JUDITH K., mgr. commun. serv., University of Virginia Hospitals, Charlottesville, VA '81 (ENG)
LYNCH, KAREN J., RN, assoc. adm. pat. serv., Mary Bridge Children's Health Center, Tacoma, WA '79 (NURS)
LYNCH, KAREN L., dir. vol. serv., East Pasco Medical Center, Zephyrhills, FL '86 (VOL)
LYNCH, LAURA J., coor. pat. serv., Health Services Association, Baldwinsville, NY '86 (PAT)
LYNCH, LINDA J., dir. pub. rel., Owensboro-Daviess County Hospital, Owensboro, KY '77 (PR)
LYNCH, LORI A., dir. educ., St. Catherine Hospital, Garden City, KS '85 (EDUC)
LYNCH, MARILYN ANNE, RN, vice-pres. nrsg., Wayne General Hospital, Wayne, NJ '67 (NURS)
LYNCH, MARK J., dir. commun. rel. and dev., Sewickley Valley Hospital, Sewickley, PA '86 (PR)
LYNCH, MARTHA E., dir. med. lib., Methodist Hospital, Brooklyn, NY '83 (EDUC)
LYNCH, MEREDITH A., dir. pers., Monadnock Community Hospital, Peterborough, NH '84 (PERS)
LYNCH, PATRICIA A., RN, exec. vice-pres., Union Hospital, Union, NJ '80 (NURS)
LYNCH, PATRICK KELLY, clin. eng. and coor. clin. eng. serv., SunHealth Corporation, Charlotte, NC '84 (ENG)
LYNCH, PAULETTE NOSAL, assoc. dir. soc. serv., Mercy Catholic Medical Center, Philadelphia, PA '81 (SOC)
LYNCH, ROBIN A., nrsg. educ., St. Joseph Hospital, Providence, RI '86 (EDUC)
LYNCH, SHEILA A., adm., Community Health Care Plan, Bridgeport, CT '87 (AMB)
LYNCH, THOMAS J. JR., exec. vice-pres., St. Anne's Hospital, Fall River, MA '75
LYNE, WICKLIFFE S., adm., Johnston-Willis Hospital, Richmond, VA '70
LYNN, GEORGE F., pres., Atlantic City Medical Center, Atlantic City, NJ '79 (PLNG)
LYNN, KATHLEEN, mgr. soc. work, Mary Free Bed Hospital and Rehabilitation Center, Grand Rapids, MI '79 (SOC)
LYNN, RICHARD G., vice-pres. eng., Corporate Energy Consultants, Overland Park, KS '86 (ENG)
LYNN, WILLIAM R., dir. mgt. serv., Mercy Hospital, Scranton, PA '86 (MGMT)
LYNOTT, MAUREEN P., vice-pres. plng., Northern Westchester Hospital Center, Mount Kisco, NY '86 (PLNG)
LYON, BARBARA J., dir. vol. serv., Jane Phillips Episcopal Hospital and Ltc Division, Bartlesville, OK '81 (VOL)
LYON, JANETTE C., dir. soc. serv., Ephrata Community Hospital, Ephrata, PA '86 (SOC)
LYON, JEFFERY T., atty., Community Memorial Hospital, Cheboygan, MI '85 (ATTY)
LYON, MARION A., dir. vol. serv., Santa Teresa Community Hospital, San Jose, CA '82 (VOL)
LYON, NORMA A., dir. vol., LDS Hospital, Salt Lake City, UT '86 (VOL)
LYONNAIS, CAROL E., dir. pur., Falmouth Hospital, Falmouth, MA '83 (PUR)
LYONS, BETTE, dir. commun. rel., Long Beach Memorial Hospital, Long Beach, NY '83 (PR)
LYONS, DUDLEY E., mng. dir., Marketing Corporation of America, Westport, CT '86
LYONS, EDWIN F., dir. matl. mgt., Marlborough Hospital, Marlborough, MA '86 (PUR)
LYONS, JAMES E., pres. and chief exec. off., New Berlin Memorial Hospital, New Berlin, WI '82
LYONS, JOHN J. JR., vice-pres. mgt. serv., New Britain General Hospital, New Britain, CT '77 (PLNG)
LYONS, JOSEPH P., exec. dir., Lake Medical Center, Leesburg, FL '85
LYONS, KENNETH W., mgr. plng., Providence Hospital, Washington, DC '85 (PUR)
LYONS, MARLENE, dir. mktg., St. Anthony Hospital, Chicago, IL '85 (PLNG)
LYONS, MARY C., dir. vol., Citizens Medical Center, Victoria, TX '83 (VOL)
LYONS, ROBERT EDWARD, RN, assoc. adm., Dch Regional Medical Center, Tuscaloosa, AL '77 (NURS)
LYONS, ROBERT T., vice-pres., Department of the Navy, Bureau of Medicine and Surgery Rowe Associates, Inc., Mineola, NY '86 (PERS)
LYONS, RODGER V., pres., Lyons Associates, Inc., Aspen, CO '76
LYONS, WARREN L., vice-pres. corp. plng., Victory Memorial Hospital, Waukegan, IL '77 (PLNG)
LYSOWSKI, NANCY J., dir. plng. and mktg., Warren General Hospital, Warren, OH '81 (PLNG)
LYTLE, SHIRLIANNE, dir. pur., Mount Sinai Hospital, Toronto, Ont., Canada '78 (PUR)
LYTZ, HUBERT B. JR., sr. mgt. eng., Cleveland Clinic Hospital, Cleveland, OH '69 (MGMT)

M

M, JOSEPH, facil. adm., Northern Virginia Mental Health Institute, Falls Church, VA '86 (RISK)
MAAG, MICHAEL, dir. safety, Western State Hospital, Staunton, VA '86 (RISK)
MAAKESTAD, MARTHA A., RN, vice-pres. nrsg., Lutheran Medical Center, Brooklyn, NY '82 (NURS)
MAAS, LAWRENCE A., adm., Tri-City Medical Center, Oceanside, CA '84
MAAS, SR. ROSANNE, coor. educ., St. James Community Hospital, Butte, MT '81 (EDUC)
MAASSEN, STEPHEN E., vice-pres. plng. and mktg., St. Francis Hospital and Medical Center, Topeka, KS '79 (PLNG)
MABARY, WANDA F., Texoma Medical Center, Denison, TX '85 (CS)
MABBOTT, RICHARD N., dir. phys. plant, Deaconess Medical Center-Spokane, Spokane, WA '75 (ENG)
MABES, MARYJEAN S., coor. educ. resources, St. Francis Medical Center, Trenton, NJ '86 (EDUC)
MABLE, RICHARD, dir. corp. plng., Medical Center Hospital of Vermont, Burlington, VT '83 (PLNG)
MABLEY, ALAN W., dir. adm. serv., Motion Picture and Television Fund, Woodland Hills, CA '81
MABREY, EDDYE D., coor. soc. serv., St. Luke's Hospital, Maumee, OH '79 (SOC)
MABRY, NANCY C., asst. dir. vol. serv., Alexandria Hospital, Alexandria, VA '81 (VOL)
MAC ARTHUR, ANN, mgr. clin., Brockton Hospital, Brockton, MA '87 (AMB)
MACALUSO, C. P., vice-pres. environ. serv., John F. Kennedy Medical Center, Chicago, IL '87 (ENVIRON)
MACALUSO, JOSEPH, dir. soc. serv., Kaiser Foundation Hospital and Rehabilitation Center, Vallejo, CA '79 (SOC)
MACBAIN, NANCIE, dir. vol. serv., Abington Memorial Hospital, Abington, PA '68 (VOL)
MACCA, JOHN T., chief exec. off., Dobbs Ferry Hospital, Dobbs Ferry, NY '87 (AMB)
MACCALLUM, ANNE W., RN, dir. educ. and prof. dev., Children's Hospital, Norfolk, VA '84 (EDUC)
MACCALLUM, JAMES M., exec. vice-pres., Hillcrest Health Center, Oklahoma City, OK '83
MACCANNON, DORIS K., dir. vol., St. Mary-Corwin Hospital Center, Pueblo, CO '82 (VOL)
MACCOUN, MALCOLM D., pres., Northwest Community Hospital, Arlington Heights, IL '52 (LIFE)
MACCRACKEN, LINDA H., asst. to pres. plng. and mktg., Beth Israel Hospital, Boston, MA '84 (PLNG)
MACDIARMID, PAMELA A., dir. emp. rel., Eye, Ear, Nose and Throat Hospital, New Orleans, LA '81 (PERS)
MACDONALD, DOROTHY, dir. pers., Houlton Regional Hospital, Houlton, ME '75 (PERS)
MACDONALD, GENE L., dir. plng., Bethesda Hospital, Zanesville, OH '82 (PLNG)
MACDONALD, JOHN S., dir. pub. affairs, Lawrence F. Quigley Memorial Hospital, Chelsea, MA '84 (PR)
MACDONALD, JULIE A., RN, asst. adm. nrsg. serv., La Crosse Lutheran Hospital, La Crosse, WI '84 (NURS)
MACDONALD, LINDA L., assoc. dir. pub. affairs, University of Texas Medical Branch Hospitals, Galveston, TX '82 (PR)
MACDONALD, MICHAEL G., vice-pres. and atty., Mount Sinai Medical Center, New York, NY '73 (ATTY)
MACDOUGALL, BRENDA E., RN, coor. res. proj., Methodist Hospital, St. Louis Park, MN '79 (NURS)
MACDOUGALL, ELIZABETH, Denver, CO '80 (SOC)
MACDOUGALL, JOHN, mgr. reprocessing and sterilization, Bronson Methodist Hospital, Kalamazoo, MI '85 (CS)
MACDOUGALL, RONALD F., asst. adm., Anaheim Memorial Hospital, Anaheim, CA '70 (PUR)
MACDOWELL, BARRY S., exec. vice-pres., Reid Memorial Hospital, Richmond, IN '70
MACE, RICK D., exec. dir., Florida Heart Institute, Orlando, FL '84 (PR) (PLNG)
MACEACHERN, ROBERT, supv. environ. serv., New England Sinai Hospital, Stoughton, MA '87 (ENVIRON)
MACEK, SUSAN B., dir. commun., Children's Hospital and Medical Center, Seattle, WA '80 (PR)
MACER, DAN J., prof., University of Oklahoma, Oklahoma City, OK '46 (RISK)(LIFE)
MACFARLANE, DEBORAH M., asst. vice-pres. mktg. commun., National Medical Enterprises, Santa Monica, CA '85 (PR)
MACFARLANE, GLORIA M., chief diet., Monongahela Valley Hospital, Monongahela, PA '70 (FOOD)
MACFARLANE, MICHAEL C., dir. pub. rel., McKay-Dee Hospital Center, Ogden, UT '83 (PR)
MACFEIGGAN, ROSE M., dir. vol., St. Joseph's Hospital, Elmira, NY '68 (VOL)
MACGRATH, EDWARD W., vice-pres. eng., Quornden Services, Inc., Wilmington, DE '86 (ENG)
MACGREGOR, DENISE M., dir. commun., Hospital Sisters Health System, Springfield, IL '86 (PR)
MACGREGOR, ROBERT C., vice-pres. plng. and mktg. dev., Mercy Hospital, Scranton, PA '79 (PLNG)
MACGUIRE, ROSLYN R., soc. work consult., Caldwell Memorial Hospital, Lenoir, NC '81 (SOC)
MACHA, JUDITH A., adm. asst. and staff coor., Oak Forest Hospital of Cook County, Oak Forest, IL '85 (NURS)
MACHADO, LT. COL. JOSEPH ANTHONY III, MSC USAF, dep. chief health affairs and plans, Headquarters U. S. Air Force, Bolling AFB, DC '68
MACHAN, JAMES, sr. buyer, Suburban Hospital and Sanitarium-Cook County, Hinsdale, IL '85 (PUR)
MACHAVER, HARVEY, exec. dir., Hospital for Joint Diseases and Medical Center, New York, NY '54 (LIFE)
MACHOL, LT. KATHERINE HOWELL, MSC USN, head soc. work, Naval Hospital, Portsmouth, VA '85 (SOC)
MACHUL, AUDREY, dir. soc. serv., St. Mary's Hospital, Saginaw, MI '80 (SOC)
MACIAS-YBARRA, SOCORRO, mgr. educ. and dev., Santa Marta Hospital, Los Angeles, CA '86 (EDUC)
MACIAS, CONNIE, supv. cent. serv. sup., Bethany Medical Center, Kansas City, KS '83 (CS)
MACIAS, SANDRA L., supv. cent. serv., Kaiser Foundation Hospital, South San Francisco, CA '81 (CS)
MACIEKOWICH, MICHAEL F., mgr. compensation serv., Omni Group, Lynnfield, MA '84 (PERS)
MACINNIS, FREDERICK J., chief eng., Cooley Dickinson Hospital, Northampton, MA '67 (ENG)
MACINO, CARL V., dir. pat. rel. rep., Forbes Regional Health Center, Monroeville, PA '80 (PAT)
MACINTOSH, ANU M., dir. qual. assur. and risk mgt. prog., Victoria General Hospital, Halifax, N.S., Canada '84 (RISK)
MACINTOSH, CHARLES ARCHIBALD, consult., John F. Rich Company, Philadelphia, PA '59
MACK, ANNE BRODY, asst. adm. prof. and support serv., Huron Valley Hospital, Milford, MI '82
MACK, ARLENE, RN, exec. vice-pres., Medcenter One, Bismarck, ND '68 (NURS)(RISK)(AMB)
MACK, CEIL S., dir. pub. rel., St. Clare's Hospital of Schenectady, Schenectady, NY '81 (PR)
MACK, CHARLES T., mgr. plant oper., Highland Park Hospital, Highland Park, IL '77 (ENG)
MACK, FRANK A., Walpole, NH '54 (PR)(LIFE)
MACK, JOSEPH M., assoc. res. and dev., St. Vincent Medical Center, Los Angeles, CA '86 (PLNG)
MACK, KEN E., pres., Discover Marketing Innovations, Macedonia, OH '84 (PR) (PLNG)
MACK, LORRAINE, supv. med. surg. proc., Mount Sinai Hospital, Hartford, CT '79 (CS)
MACK, RENEE B., mgr. org. dev., Forbes Health System, Pittsburgh, PA '86 (EDUC)
MACK, ROBERT L., adm. eng., San Jose Hospital, San Jose, CA '67 (ENG)
MACK, ROBERT, exec. dir., Inland Health Plan, Loma Linda, CA '85 (PLNG)
MACK, STEPHEN S., dir. tech. serv., Johns Hopkins Hospital, Baltimore, MD '84 (ENG)
MACK, WILLIAM, chief psych. soc. work, Fairfield Hills Hospital, Newtown, CT '78 (SOC)
MACKAY, PETER J., dir. soc. serv., Nantucket Cottage Hospital, Nantucket, MA '85 (SOC)
MACKELVIE, CHARLES F., atty., Palos Community Hospital, Palos Heights, IL '79 (ATTY)
MACKENZIE, CHRISTIAN, dir. pur., Walther Memorial Hospital, Chicago, IL '82 (PUR)
MACKENZIE, GALE A., RN, vice-pres. nrsg. affairs, Chester County Hospital, West Chester, PA '82 (NURS)
MACKENZIE, KIP F., dir. food serv., Walter O. Boswell Memorial Hospital, Sun City, AZ '85 (FOOD)
MACKENZIE, ROBERT W., mgr. hlthcare oper., Ernst and Whinney, Minneapolis, MN '87 (MGMT)
MACKENZIE, T. WILLIAM, dir. med. soc. serv., Calgary General Hospital, Calgary, Alta., Canada '81 (SOC)

MACKESKI, DEBORAH, asst. dir. soc. serv., Charter Hospital of Long Beach, Long Beach, CA '80 (SOC)
MACKESSY, JUDITH C., clin. mgr., Good Samaritan Medical Center, Milwaukee, WI '78 (FOOD)
MACKESY, RICHARD, dir. mktg. and bus. plng., Watson Clinic, Lakeland, FL '85 (PLNG)
MACKEWICE, RICHARD, vice-pres. human res. and rel., Albany Medical Center Hospital, Albany, NY '73 (PERS)
MACKEY, DEBRA B., RN, vice-pres. nrsg., Community Memorial Hospital, Monmouth, IL '81 (NURS)
MACKEY, JOAN, health care rep. and risk mgt. serv., St. Paul Companies, Bloomington, IL '85 (RISK)
MACKEY, ROSEMARY W., dir. strategic plng., University of Texas Systems Cancer Center, M. D. Anderson Hospital and Tumor Institute, Houston, TX '84 (PLNG)
MACKEY, WILLIA MAE, coor. pat. rep., Alexandria Hospital, Alexandria, VA '78 (PAT)
MACKEY, WILLIAM R., dir. food serv., Christ Hospital, Jersey City, NJ '84 (FOOD)
MACKIE, DAVID SANFORD, RN, vice-pres. nrsg. serv., Desert Hospital, Palm Springs, CA '75 (NURS)
MACKIE, LT. COL. KENNETH J. JR., MSC USAF, exec. off., dir. prof. affairs and qual. assur., Department of Air Force Medical Service, Bolling AFB, DC '68
MACKIE, ROBERT JOSEPH, facil. dir., Elgin Mental Health Center, Elgin, IL '50 (LIFE)
MACKINNON, BARRY N., mgt. eng., Elliot Hospital, Manchester, NH '74 (MGMT)
MACKLER, ROBERT O., dir. hosp. conference, Hospital Council of Northern California, San Mateo, CA '83 (PLNG)
MACKLIN, LOIS, mgr. cent. sup., proc. and distrib., Providence Hospital, Southfield, MI '82 (CS)
MACKS, GERALD CHARLES, mgt. analyst, Clinical Center, National Institutes of Health, Bethesda, MD '69 (MGMT)
MACKUNIS, ANNA MAE M., coor. commun., Shore Memorial Hospital, Somers Point, NJ '84 (ENG)
MACLAUCHLAN, STEVEN V., dir. risk mgt., North Shore Medical Center, Miami, FL '80 (RISK)
MACLAUCHLIN, ANNA MARGARET, dir. soc. serv., Faulkner Hospital, Boston, MA '79 (SOC)
MACLEAN, ANN E., dir. food serv., Garden City Osteopathic Hospital, Garden City, MI '86 (FOOD)
MACLEAN, ELIZABETH, asst. emp. and commun. rel., Franklin Memorial Hospital, Farmington, ME '86 (PERS)
MACLEAN, MALCOLM R., atty., Memorial Medical Center, Savannah, GA '69 (ATTY)
MACLEAN, VINCENT M., chief eng., Wayne General Hospital, Wayne, NJ '72 (ENG)
MACLEOD, FLORENCE E., vice-pres. nrsg. serv., Carney Hospital, Boston, MA '71 (NURS)
MACLEOD, KRISTI L., dir. soc. serv., Providence Hospital, Oakland, CA '80 (SOC)
MACLEOD, ROBERT J., dir. support serv., Speare Memorial Hospital, Plymouth, NH '83 (PUR)
MACLIN, J. MARK, atty., Marshall Browning Hospital, Du Quoin, IL '82 (ATTY)
MACMILLAN, DONNA H., coor. lab. serv., McLean Hospital, Belmont, MA '82
MACMILLAN, DOUGLAS F., vice-pres., Charlotte Memorial Hospital and Medical Center, Charlotte, NC '85
MACMITCHELL, MELANIE, assoc. dir., Children's Hospital at Stanford, Palo Alto, CA '81 (PLNG)
MACMONAGLE, CAROLYN, vice-pres. human res., Children's Hospital and Health Center, San Diego, CA '84 (PERS)
MACNAMARA, LISA A., mktg. and plng. analyst, Mercer Medical Center, Trenton, NJ '85 (PLNG)
MACNEIL, DOUGLAS J., advanced staff consult., Ernst and Whinney, Grand Rapids, MI '84 (MGMT)
MACNINCH, LINDA L., dir. matl. mgt., Northside Presbyterian Hospital, Albuquerque, NM '86 (ENG)
MACNISH, PATRICIA A., dir. commun. rel., Freehold Area Hospital, Freehold, NJ '85 (PR)
MACNIVEN-YOUNG, M., atty., Comprehensive Care Corporation, Irvine, CA '86 (ATTY)
MACOMBER, WILLIAM C., mgr. plant, Francis Scott Key Medical Center, Baltimore, MD '83 (ENG)
MACON, REID P., dir. matl. mgt., Robert F. Kennedy Medical Center, Hawthorne, CA '82 (PUR)
MACPHEE, PAULA S., RN, assoc. dir. clin. nrsg., Hackley Hospital, Muskegon, MI '83 (NURS)
MACPHERSON, SCOT, maint. eng., Harbor Beach Community Hospital, Harbor Beach, MI '86 (ENG)
MACRAE, GAIL L., RN, assoc. dir. med. nrsg., Clara Maass Medical Center, Belleville, NJ '86 (NURS)
MACRAE, JOHN D., dir. food serv., Sisters of St. Joseph, Brentwood, NY '68 (FOOD)
MACSTRAVIC, ROBIN SCOTT, PhD, vice-pres. plng. and mktg., Sisters of St. Joseph of Peace Health and Hospital Services, Bellevue, WA '79 (PR) (PLNG)
MACVEAN, KENNETH A., atty., Horton Memorial Hospital, Middletown, NY '74 (ATTY)
MACVICAR, KAY L., nrs. educ., Rahway Hospital, Rahway, NJ '87 (EDUC)
MACY, HILDRETH A., assoc. dir. diet., Henry Ford Hospital, Detroit, MI '83 (FOOD)
MADANI, MAHMOOD-ADEL, sr. biomedical eng., King Faisal Specialist Hospital and Research Center, Riyadh, Saudi Arabia '86 (ENG)
MADANICK, CHARLES E., vice-pres. and dir. mktg. and pub. affairs, Ochsner Foundation Hospital, New Orleans, LA '86 (PR)
MADDEN, BETTYE H., dir. diet. serv., AMI Katy Community Hospital, Katy, TX '82 (FOOD)
MADDEN, CAROLYN WATTS, assoc. prof., Graduate Program in Health Services Administration and Planning, University of Washington, Seattle, WA '86 (PLNG)
MADDEN, DONNA M., vice-pres. commun., Wheaton Franciscan Services, Inc., Wheaton, IL '81 (PR)
MADDEN, EDWARD E. JR., pres., Edward Madden and Associates, Metairie, LA '79
MADDEN, EDWARD, risk mgr., Southwest Community Health Services, Albuquerque, NM '84 (RISK)
MADDEN, JEAN H., RN, clin. dir. ob., gyn. and ped. nrsg., Yale-New Haven Hospital, New Haven, CT '82 (NURS)
MADDEN, JOHN D., dir. matl. mgt., Detroit Receiving Hospital and University Health Center, Detroit, MI '82 (PUR)
MADDEN, MARY JANE, asst. prof., University of Minnesota, St. Paul, MN '83 (NURS)
MADDEN, MICHAEL J., dir. matl. mgt., Southwest Washington Hospitals, Vancouver, WA '82 (PUR)
MADDEN, PATRICK, atty., Capistrano By the Sea Hospital, Dana Point, CA '77 (ATTY)
MADDEN, PAUL R., atty., Phoenix Baptist Hospital and Medical Center, Phoenix, AZ '79 (ATTY)
MADDEN, THOMAS R., adm., Carney Hospital, Boston, MA '78
MADDIGAN, ROGER F., chief soc. work serv., Veterans Administration Medical Center, Buffalo, NY '71 (SOC)
MADDOCK, CHARLES W., dir. gen. serv., Clinton County Hospital, Frankfort, IN '81 (RISK)
MADDOCK, JAMES D. JR., dir. pur., Sinai Hospital of Baltimore, Baltimore, MD '84 (PUR)
MADDOX, A. CHERYL, dir. vol. serv., Woman's Hospital of Texas, Houston, TX '86 (VOL)
MADDOX, LARRY H., dir. pers., NKC Hospitals, Louisville, KY '64 (PERS)
MADDRELL, PAUL D., asst. vice-pres. amb. care dev., Northwestern Memorial Hospital, Chicago, IL '78 (PLNG)(AMB)
MADDREN, DOROTHY M., dir. nrsg. educ. and res. div., Rhode Island Hospital, Providence, RI '77 (EDUC)
MADDUX, MARILYN E., assoc. prof., University of Missouri School of Social Work, Columbia, MO '80 (SOC)
MADDY, CHARLES W., asst. dir. matl. mgt., Hampton General Hospital, Hampton, VA '84 (ENG)
MADELEINE, SR. MARIE, bookkeeper, St. Francis Home, Worcester, MA '36 (LIFE)
MADEO, MAJ. PETER D., MSC USA, chief pers., 5th General Hospital, APO New York, NY '86 (PERS)
MADER, CHARLES, vice-pres. outreach serv., Independence Regional Health Center, Independence, MO '87 (AMB)
MADER, MARK E., atty., Internist, Inc., Richmond, IN '84 (ATTY)
MADIGAN, BRIAN RICHARD, atty., St. Michael's Hospital, Toronto, Ont., Canada '81 (ATTY)
MADISON, JEANNE RUTH, RN, dir. nrsg., St. Mary Desert Valley Hospital, Apple Valley, CA '82 (NURS)
MADISON, MARY KAY, adm. fellow, St. Agnes Hospital and Medical Center, Fresno, CA '84
MADL, FRANK M., vice-pres. oper., St. Joseph Hospital, Chicago, IL '82 (MGMT)
MADONNA, HARRY D., atty., Blank, Rome, Comisky and McCauley, Philadelphia, PA '76 (ATTY)
MADORE, MARY E., assoc. dir. admit., Salem Hospital, Salem, MA '85
MADORE, RONALD A., dir. matl. mgt., Aroostook Medical Center, Presque Isle, ME '85 (PUR)
MADRICK, CAROL NOEL, dir. mktg., Northern Michigan Hospitals, Petoskey, MI '86 (PR)
MADRONERO, ENRIQUE, underwriter mgr., American Home Assurance Company, New York, NY '87
MADSEN, HELEN H., atty., University of Wisconsin, Madison, WI '78 (ATTY)
MADSEN, PAT, dir. fund dev. and vol. serv., Carle Foundation Hospital, Urbana, IL '84 (VOL)
MADTES, MELINDA, RN, coor. surg., Moses H. Cone Memorial Hospital, Greensboro, NC '87 (AMB)
MAEDA, RIEKO, dir. matl. mgt., Queen's Medical Center, Honolulu, HI '83 (PUR)
MAEHL, BARBARA A., RN, nrs. educ., Children's Specialized Hospital, Mountainside, NJ '86 (EDUC)
MAEHLER, KATHLEEN, dir. food serv., Jewish Hospital of Cincinnati, Cincinnati, OH '87 (FOOD)
MAES, WILLIAM E., chief eng., St. Joseph Memorial Hospital, Murphysboro, IL '82 (ENG)
MAFFEI, JOHN J., atty., Riddle Memorial Hospital, Media, PA '77 (ATTY)
MAFFIA, ANTHONY J., dir. soc. work, Jamaica Hospital, Jamaica, NY '85 (SOC)
MAFFLY, ALFRED E., (ret.), Berkeley, CA '35 (LIFE)
MAG, LILLIAN, pat. advocate, Mount Sinai Hospital, Hartford, CT '77 (PAT)
MAGANA, SHIRLEY P., RN, vice-pres. pat. serv., Bryn Mawr Hospital, Bryn Mawr, PA '81 (NURS)
MAGANTE, BEVERLY VILLASENOR, supv. hskpg., Marshal Hale Memorial Hospital, San Francisco, CA '86 (ENVIRON)
MAGAOAY, MICHAEL, mgr. eng., facil. and bldg. serv., Queen's Medical Center, Honolulu, HI '87 (ENG)
MAGARIAN, MYDA, RN, asst. adm. pat. serv., St. Vincent Medical Center, Los Angeles, CA '75 (NURS)
MAGAVERN, SAMUEL D., atty., Buffalo General Hospital, Buffalo, NY '77 (ATTY)
MAGAZINE, CHARLES, dir. qual. assur., Eastern State Hospital, Williamsburg, VA '86 (RISK)
MAGDALENO, JULIAN M., mgr., Sheldon I. Dorenfest and Associates, Northbrook, IL '86 (MGMT)
MAGDZIARZ, FRANK, supv. maint., Catholic Medical Center, Manchester, NH '81 (ENG)
MAGEE, G. GWINN, asst. adm., Mississippi Baptist Medical Center, Jackson, MS '84 (RISK)
MAGEE, WILLIAM T., dir. pers., Silver Hill Foundation Hospital, New Canaan, CT '86 (PERS)
MAGER, RICHARD DONALD, Clifton Park, NY '74 (MGMT)
MAGER, SANDRA E., adm., Consumer Health Advocacy Information Network, Oyster Bay, NY '84 (PAT)
MAGES, LOREN J., pres., Forces, Inc., Naperville, IL '85 (ENG)
MAGGAY, LISA R., student, Program in Business Administration and Health Service Management, National University, Chula Vista, CA '85
MAGGIORE, JEANNE, biomedical eng., Antelope Valley Hospital Medical Center, Lancaster, CA '86 (ENG)
MAGIE, MARLENE R., chief adm., Hollywood, FL '83
MAGILL, JUDITH RILEY, sr. assoc., Herman Smith Associates, Hinsdale, IL '79 (PLNG)
MAGIN, BERNICE A., vice-pres. human res., McDonough District Hospital, Macomb, IL '72 (PERS)
MAGINOT, JAMES F. JR., asst. dir. nutr. medicine and chief food procurement-production serv., Wilford Hall U. S. Air Force Medical Center, Lackland AFB, TX '86 (FOOD)
MAGLIANO, JOHN V., vice-pres. and chief elec. eng., Syska and Hennessy, Inc., New York, NY '83 (ENG)
MAGNANT, MARGARET R., dir. telecommun., Kent County Memorial Hospital, Warwick, RI '75 (ENG)
MAGNER, MONICA M., RN, mgr. cont. educ., Visiting Nurse Service, New York, NY '71 (EDUC)
MAGNUSON, RUTH F., dir. qual. assur. and risk mgt., Mercy Center for Health Care Services, Aurora, IL '86 (RISK)
MAGOWAN, MARILYN, assoc. dir. qual. assur., Sherman Hospital, Elgin, IL '85 (RISK)
MAGPAYO, ROSE J., RN, asst. adm. amb. care, Illinois Masonic Medical Center, Chicago, IL '87 (AMB)
MAGRAW, THOMAS W., consult., Arthur Young and Company, Atlanta, GA '82
MAGSAMEN, GARNET E., mgr. equal emp. opportunity, Johns Hopkins Hospital, Baltimore, MD '86 (PERS)
MAGUIRE, ANNE S., actg. dir. pers., Phoenixville Hospital, Phoenixville, PA '84 (PERS)
MAGUIRE, JAMES A., asst. adm. plant, St. Christophers Hospital for Children, Philadelphia, PA '81 (ENG)
MAGUIRE, MAUREEN K., RN, asst. adm., Tulane University Hospital and Clinics, New Orleans, LA '77 (NURS)
MAGUIRE, PATRICIA, RN, asst. dir. nrsg. serv., Virginia Mason Hospital, Seattle, WA '84 (NURS)
MAGUIRE, WILLIAM J. JR., pers. off., Colorado State Hospital, Pueblo, CO '64 (PERS)
MAHACZEK, VALERIA B., dir. commun. rel., William Beaumont Hospital, Royal Oak, MI '86 (PR)
MAHADEVA, MANORANJAN, chief fin. off., Dallas Memorial Hospital, Dallas, TX '86
MAHAN, CAROL K., dir. ped. soc. work, Rainbow Babies and Children's Hospital, Cleveland, OH '86 (SOC)
MAHAN, DIANNE D., dir. soc. serv., St. Mary's Hospital and Medical Center, San Francisco, CA '86 (SOC)
MAHAN, MICHELLE K., mgr., Arthur Young and Company, Washington, DC '86 (MGMT)
MAHAN, PAUL B., asst. to pres.-pers., California Hospital Association, Sacramento, CA '79 (PERS)
MAHAN, RAYMOND M., dir. eng., Lester E. Cox Medical Centers, Springfield, MO '59 (ENG)
MAHAN, STEPHEN W., asst. adm., West Florida Regional Medical Center, Pensacola, FL '77 (MGMT)
MAHAR, CLAUDETTE L., RN, asst. exec. dir. nrsg., St. Joseph Hospital, Nashua, NH '77 (NURS)
MAHER, BARBARA A., dir. qual. assur., Yavapai Regional Medical Center, Prescott, AZ '85 (RISK)
MAHER, CHARLES E. JR., dir. phys. plant, Hotel Dieu Hospital, New Orleans, LA '78 (ENG)
MAHER, GLEN L., La Crosse, WI '41 (LIFE)
MAHER, HUGH J., exec. vice-pres., Germantown Hospital and Medical Center, Philadelphia, PA '58
MAHER, ILLA R. E., pat. educ. instr., Foothills Hospital, Calgary, Alta., Canada '85 (EDUC)
MAHER, PATRICIA M., RN, asst. dir. matl. mgt. and sup., proc. and distrib., St. Vincent's Medical Center, Jacksonville, FL '85 (CS)
MAHER, SYLVIA A., RN, vice-pres. nrsg., Bethany Medical Center, Kansas City, KS '80 (NURS)
MAHIN, LCDR PATRICK L., MSC USN, health care planner, Naval Medical Command, Nas Barbers Point, HI '73
MAHLER, BECKY, dir. soc. serv., Sheltering Arms Hospital, Richmond, VA '80 (SOC)
MAHLER, JOAN E., plng. spec., St. Vincent Hospital and Medical Center, Portland, OR '84 (PLNG)
MAHLER, SR. THERESA M., RN, dir. nrsg., Mercy Hospital of Janesville, Janesville, WI '67 (NURS)
MAHMOODI, AFSHAN, student, Corcordia College, Moorhead, MN '86
MAHN, EDWARD F., asst. adm. mktg. and plng., St. John's Hospital, Longview, WA '80 (PLNG)
MAHON, PAMELA YOUNG, RN, asst. chief nrsg. serv. and commun. health, Veterans Administration Medical Center, Brooklyn, NY '86 (NURS)
MAHON, RITA A., RN, dir. nrsg., Pontiac Osteopathic Hospital, Pontiac, MI '84 (NURS)
MAHON, SANDY, mgr. emp., Washoe Medical Center, Reno, NV '85 (RISK)
MAHONE, DAVID, adm. fellow, Oklahoma Osteopathic Hospital, Tulsa, OK '84
MAHONEY, CARYL B., vice-pres. human res., Mary Hitchcock Memorial Hospital, Hanover, NH '84
MAHONEY, CECILIA M., pat. rep. and dir. vol. serv., Charlton Memorial Hospital, Fall River, MA '77 (VOL)(PAT)
MAHONEY, ELIZABETH S., buyer, Chestnut Hill Hospital, Philadelphia, PA '84 (PUR)
MAHONEY, GEORGE F. III, atty., Silver Cross Hospital, Joliet, IL '86 (ATTY)
MAHONEY, KEVIN B., dir. qual. assur. and risk mgt., Episcopal Hospital, Philadelphia, PA '84 (RISK)
MAHONEY, LINDA E., chief med. soc. serv., Fairmont Hospital, San Leandro, CA '83 (SOC)
MAHONEY, M. DIANE, dir. group health prog., Bethesda Hospital, Inc., Cincinnati, OH '85 (PLNG)
MAHONEY, MARY D., dir. pub. rel., H. Lee Moffitt Cancer Center and Research Institute at the University of South Florida, Tampa, FL '85 (PR)
MAHONEY, MAUREEN C., RN, dir. nrsg., Miller-Dwan Medical Center, Duluth, MN '84 (NURS)
MAHONEY, NORMA J., adm. coor., Spaulding Rehabilitation Hospital, Boston, MA '87 (AMB)
MAHONEY, WILLIAM J., dir. plant eng. and maint., Long Island Jewish Medical Center, New York, NY '81 (ENG)
MAHONY, JEREMIAH F., Fanwood, NJ '75
MAHONY, MICHAEL F., atty., Union Medical Center, El Dorado, AR '73 (ATTY)
MAHR, TAMARA F., chief diet., Person County Memorial Hospital, Roxboro, NC '82 (FOOD)
MAHR, TERRENCE D., atty., Newberg Community Hospital, Newberg, OR '86 (ATTY)

MAI, LINDA K., coor. vol., West Nebraska General Hospital, Scottsbluff, NE '82 (VOL)
MAICHLE, JANINE, RN, risk mgr., St. Francis Hospital, Wilmington, DE '86 (RISK)
MAIDEN, ROBERT V., dir. path., Alachua General Hospital, Gainesville, FL '81
MAIER, GAIL, dir. commun., Rochester St. Mary's Hospital, Rochester, NY '80 (ENG)
MAIER, GERALD W., dir. pers., Eye and Ear Hospital of Pittsburgh, Pittsburgh, PA '77 (PERS)
MAIL, PATRICIA D., dep. chief field oper., Bhcda-National Health Service Corps, Rockville, MD '83 (EDUC)
MAILLOUX, JOSEPH R., adm. sup. serv., Medical Center Hospital of Vermont, Burlington, VT '61
MAILLOUX, JULIE M., cent. sup. tech., Carson Tahoe Hospital, Carson City, NV '86 (CS)
MAILLOUX, MARK, dir. plng. and dev., Southwest Detroit Hospital Corporation, Detroit, MI '78 (PLNG)
MAIN, DAVID C., atty., American Hospital Association, Washington, DC '84 (ATTY)
MAIN, GERALD A., dir. mktg., Gaylord Hospital, Wallingford, CT '86 (PR) (PLNG)
MAIN, SR. MARIE A., RN, asst. adm. and dir. nrsg., Mercy Hospital, Buffalo, NY '85 (NURS)
MAIN, ROBERT P., exec. vice-pres., Marianjoy Rehabilitation Center, Wheaton, IL '71
MAIN, SANDRA, dir. vol. serv., Lutheran General Hospital, Park Ridge, IL '78 (VOL)
MAINEZ, LARRY M., supt. bldg., San Bernardino County Medical Center, San Bernardino, CA '83 (ENG)
MAINWARING, ROSSER L., MD, dir. path. and lab., Oakwood Hospital, Dearborn, MI '67
MAIOLATESI, PAMELA ANN, pat. rep., Moses Taylor Hospital, Scranton, PA '85 (PAT)
MAIR, BETTY G., RN, dir. nrsg.-maternal and child health, University of South Alabama Medical Center, Mobile, AL '81 (NURS)
MAIS, PHYLLIS, mgr. cent. sup., St. Joseph Medical Center, Stamford, CT '81 (CS)
MAISAK, MARJORIE B., curriculum coor., St. Joseph Hospital, Baltimore, MD '86 (EDUC)
MAISLIN, ISIDORE, consult., Scranton, PA '52 (LIFE)
MAITLAND, JOHN BRUCE, asst. exec. dir., Humber Memorial Hospital, Toronto, Ont., Canada '78
MAITLAND, LEAH, MD, dir., Gettysburg Hospital, Gettysburg, PA '86 (AMB)
MAJEED, KADER, dir. eng. and facil., Grant Hospital of Chicago, Chicago, IL '67 (ENG)
MAJESKE, HOPE L., RN, asst. exec. dir. pat. care, San Juan Regional Medical Center, Farmington, NM '81 (NURS)
MAJEWSKI, EUGENE J., dir. eng., Sun Valley Regional Hospital, El Paso, TX '82 (ENG)
MAJEWSKI, LILLIAN, supv. cent. proc., Samaritan Health Center, Detroit, MI '79 (CS)
MAJKA, LAWRENCE J., assoc. adm. fin., St. Mary's Hospital and Medical Center, San Francisco, CA '80
MAJOR, DEBORAH R., dir. food serv., Clark County Memorial Hospital, Jeffersonville, IN '85 (FOOD)
MAJOR, DONALD H., mgr. environ. serv., LaPorte Hospital, LaPorte, IN '86 (ENVIRON)
MAJOR, TRACEY, risk mgr., Inter-Community Memorial Hospital, Newfane, NY '86 (RISK)
MAJORS, CHARLES H., atty., Memorial Hospital, Danville, VA '80 (ATTY)
MAJORS, JAMES MICHAEL, dir. food and nutr., Barnes Hospital, St. Louis, MO '86 (FOOD)
MAJORS, MARY JO, RN, asst. adm., Martin Memorial Hospital, Stuart, FL '78 (NURS)
MAJORS, ROBERT B., dir. matl. mgt., William N. Wishard Memorial Hospital, Indianapolis, IN '77 (PUR)
MAJZOUB, MONA K., atty., Kitch, Suhrheinrich, Et Al, Detroit, MI '82
MAKI, JERROLD A., assoc. adm., Mercy Medical Center, Springfield, OH '85
MAKIN, JOCELYN C., dir. food serv., Polyclinic Medical Center, Harrisburg, PA '82 (FOOD)
MAKLEFF, RACHEL H., planner, HMO, Family Health Plan, Elm Grove, WI '85 (PLNG)
MAKOFSKY, CATHERINE V., adm. asst. out-pat. serv., East Jefferson General Hospital, Metairie, LA '75 (MGMT)
MAKOVEC, STEVE W., supv. maint., Mercy Health Center, Dubuque, IA '85 (ENG)
MAKOVITZKY, MIMI L., dir. vol. serv., Methodist Hospital, Brooklyn, NY '82 (VOL)
MAKOWICZ, DORIS, vice-pres. human res., Hackensack Medical Center, Hackensack, NJ '76 (PERS)
MAKOWSKY, BERNARD, dir. commun. rel., Scottsdale Camelback Hospital, Scottsdale, AZ '85 (PR)
MAKSIM, JOSEPH S. SR., supv. maint., Doctors Hospital of Dallas, Dallas, TX '86 (ENG)
MAKSYMOWICZ, ZYGMUNT A., assoc. adm., Kent County Memorial Hospital, Warwick, RI '72 (PLNG)
MALACINA, JOSEPH S., dir. eng., Alexian Brothers Medical Center, Elk Grove Village, IL '79 (ENG)
MALAKOUTI-DANA, MOHAMMAD Z., RN, coor. staff nrs., Children's Hospital, Denver, CO '84
MALANEY, SCOTT C., vice pres. human resoues, St. Lawrence Hospital, Lansing, MI '82 (PERS)
MALANUK, ROBERT, MD, dir. emer. serv., Emergency Physicians Group Northwest, Columbia, SC '86 (AMB)
MALARD, MAYSIL M., instr. and coor. diabetes educ., Medcenter One, Bismarck, ND '86 (EDUC)
MALASKY, JUDY, dir. ins. and risk mgt., Strategic Health Systems, Mayfield Village, OH '86 (RISK)
MALAVASE, ROBERT H., dir. food and environ. serv., Nantucket Cottage Hospital, Nantucket, MA '86 (ENVIRON)
MALAVASE, ROBERT, dir. food serv., Nantucket Cottage Hospital, Nantucket, MA '76 (FOOD)
MALBAN, JOHN R., asst. prof. and coor. mental health, Mental Health Administration Training, Program in Hospital and Health Care Administration, St. Paul, MN '55 (LIFE)
MALBON, SCOTT H., assoc. plng., Healtheast, Inc., Roanoke, VA '86 (PLNG)
MALCOLM, FAY E., RN, dir. nrsg., North Central Bronx Hospital, Bronx, NY '86 (NURS)
MALCOLM, GAIL BAUMGAERTEL, adm. data base, Hospital of the University of Pennsylvania, Philadelphia, PA '77 (MGMT)
MALDONADO, RUTH N., coor. mktg. and vol. serv., Hospital San Pablo, Bayamon, P.R. '84 (VOL)
MALE, BRUCE M., exec. dir., Traveling Nurse Corps, Inc., Malden, MA '80
MALE, ROY, chm. natl. council, National Association of Health Service Pers Office, National Health Authority, Norwich, England '86 (PERS)
MALEIKE, HERTA, RN, instr. staff dev., Valley Medical Center, Renton, WA '82 (EDUC)
MALEK, RUTHANNE, coor. pub. rel., Sartori Memorial Hospital, Cedar Falls, IA '86 (PR)
MALENSEK, WILLIAM R., dir. matl. mgt., Cleveland Clinic Hospital, Cleveland, OH '72 (PUR)
MALESKI, CYNTHIA M., atty., Mercy Hospital of Pittsburgh, Pittsburgh, PA '77 (ATTY)
MALEWSKI, EDWARD, adm., Sitka Community Hospital, Sitka, AK '78
MALEY, MELODY J., dir. soc. serv., St. Elizabeth Hospital, Danville, IL '83 (SOC)
MALEY, ROBIN A., healthcare consult., Johnson and Higgins, Inc., New York, NY '82 (RISK)
MALIEKEL, V. GEORGE, sr. mktg. mgr., Baxter Travenol Laboratories, Deerfield, IL '87 (PUR)
MALIK, UMER R., mgr. matl., Abduallah Fouad Hospital, Dammam, Saudi Arabia '86 (PUR)
MALINEE, JAMES E., dir. mgt. eng., St. Joseph Health Center, St. Charles, MO '82 (MGMT)
MALINKY, ROBERT, mgr. qual. assur. and risk mgt., Health Options, Inc., Jacksonville, FL '86 (RISK)
MALISON, MARY, exec. dir., Home Health Services, Inc., Milwaukee, WI '86
MALKEMES, LOIS C., RN, tech. adv., Ernst and Whinney, Dallas, TX '85 (NURS)
MALKIN, BONNIE H., dir. prof. practices, Food and Drug Administration, Rockville, MD '86 (EDUC)
MALKIN, SUE A., clin. instr., Downey Community Hospital, Downey, CA '83 (EDUC)
MALLEGOL, JOHN P., dir. matl. mgt., Lawrence Hospital, Bronxville, NY '81 (PUR)
MALLEK, JOSEPH, dir. plant oper., Riverview Hospital, Wisconsin Rapids, WI '75 (ENG)
MALLIN, ELLEN D., dir. pers., Northwest Institute of Psychiatry, Fort Washington, PA '86 (PERS)
MALLIN, SANDRA, coor. pat. rel., St. Mary's Hospital and Medical Center, San Francisco, CA '78 (PAT)
MALLIS, NICHOLAS JR., asst. adm., Bayonne Hospital, Bayonne, NJ '78
MALLIS, SOPHIA G., RN, dir. nrsg., Good Samaritan Hospital, Downers Grove, IL '81 (NURS)
MALLISON, GEORGE F., environ. and infection contr. consult., Glen Rock, NJ '63 (ENG)
MALLON, FRANCIS J., atty., American Physical Therapy Association, Alexandria, VA '83 (ATTY)
MALLON, LIZ, coor. consumer rel., Group Health Eastside Hospital, Redmond, WA '83 (PAT)
MALLONE, SUSAN, RN, dir. nrsg., Northeastern Ohio General Hospital, Madison, OH '81 (NURS)
MALLORY, JAMES R., asst. dir. facil., Providence Hospital, Southfield, MI '83 (ENG)
MALLORY, LT. COL. LLOYD M., MSC USA, insp. gen., Walter Reed Army Medical Center, Washington, DC '71
MALLORY, MARCELLA, aide cent. sup., Lakeshore Hospital, Detroit, MI '77 (CS)
MALLOY, LEATRICE O., pat. rep., Yale-New Haven Hospital, New Haven, CT '74 (PAT)
MALLOY, MICHAEL E., atty., Washoe Medical Center, Reno, NV '84 (ATTY)
MALLOY, R. EARL, dir. eng., Southwest Community Health System, Middleburg Heights, OH '85 (ENG)
MALLOY, R. LOUIS, Albany, NY '34 (LIFE)
MALLOY, THEODORE D., mgr. facil. eng., Stanford University Hospital, Stanford, CA '84 (ENG)
MALLUK, SUSAN, dir. soc. serv., French Polyclinic Health Center, New York, NY '73 (SOC)
MALLY, EDWARD J., Catholic Health Association, St. Louis, MO '76 (PLNG)
MALM, CRAIG B., dir. soc. serv., Unity Medical Center, Fridley, MN '85 (SOC)
MALM, HARRY M., Omaha, NE '61 (LIFE)
MALM, ROGER C., atty., Brink, Sobolik, Severson and Vroom, Hallock, MN '78 (ATTY)
MALON, GEORGE E., dir. mgt. eng., Victory Memorial Hospital, Waukegan, IL '82 (MGMT)
MALONE, JOE D., dir. matl. mgt., University of Alabama, College of Community Health Sciences, Tuscaloosa, AL '85 (PUR)
MALONE, PATRICK S., staff consult., Arthur Andersen and Company, Dallas, TX '86
MALONEY, ARTHUR J., atty., Millard Fillmore Hospital, Buffalo, NY '70 (ATTY)
MALONEY, JUDITH ANN, dir. soc. serv., Fairview Southdale Hospital, Minneapolis, MN '78 (SOC)
MALONEY, MARY B., dir. diet., Community Hospital of Bedford, Bedford, OH '84 (FOOD)
MALONEY, MARY K., dir. vol. serv., Holy Cross Hospital, Fort Lauderdale, FL '78 (VOL)
MALONEY, RICHARD J., dir. nutr. serv., Trumbull Memorial Hospital, Warren, OH '70 (FOOD)
MALONEY, SEAN ELIZABETH, dir. plng. and tech. assessment, University Hospital, St. Louis University Center, St. Louis, MO '82 (PLNG)
MALONOSKI, JOSEPH F., vice-pres. human res., Mercy Catholic Medical Center, Darby, PA '87 (PERS)
MALOTTE, REBECCA, RN, dir. nrsg., Deaconess Hospital, Evansville, IN '85 (NURS)
MALOUFF, FRANK J., exec. dir., Ohio Podiatry Association, Columbus, OH '75 (EDUC)
MALOY, MARY J., mgr. food serv., Pike Community Hospital, Waverly, OH '84 (FOOD)
MALY, JOSEPH R., vice-pres. distrib. oper., Johnson and Johnson, New Brunswick, NJ '84 (PUR)
MAMER, STUART M., atty., Carle Foundation Hospital, Urbana, IL '74 (ATTY)
MAMER, WILLIAM L., asst. to pres., St. Joseph's Hospital, Savannah, GA '87
MAMI, ARTHUR A., vice-pres. support serv., Sacred Heart Hospital, Norristown, PA '64 (PUR)(RISK)
MAMICH, JANICE, RN, coor. staff dev., Parma Community General Hospital, Parma, OH '81 (EDUC)
MAMIYA, MAY L., dir. soc. serv., Vassar Brothers Hospital, Poughkeepsie, NY '79 (SOC)
MANADE, CHARLES, dir. eng. and maint., Sid Peterson Memorial Hospital, Kerrville, TX '87 (ENG)
MANAHAN, DAVID BRIAN, adm., Charles A. Dean Memorial Hospital, Greenville, ME '74
MANAK, ROBERT, dir. plant oper., Elmbrook Memorial Hospital, Brookfield, WI '81 (ENG)
MANANSALA, MICHAEL R., dir. strategic plng. and dev., St. Jude Hospital, Fullerton, CA '85 (PLNG)
MANARD, YVETTE M., dir. plng., Austin Company, Irvine, CA '83 (PLNG)
MANARDO, ROBERT, dir. corp. serv., Doctors Hospital, Detroit, MI '81 (PR)
MANAWAR, SYED A., asst. dir. mgt. serv., Hurley Medical Center, Flint, MI '79 (MGMT)
MANCARI, JOSEPH, vice-pres., Altoona Hospital, Altoona, PA '83
MANCHESTER, DAVID, vice-pres. plng. and commun. rel., Palos Community Hospital, Palos Heights, IL '79 (PLNG)
MANCHESTER, 1ST LT. KATHRYN SUE, MSC USAF, resource mgt. off., U. S. Air Force Clinic Florennes-Sgm, APO New York, NY '83
MANCINI, LYNN J., coor. health educ., Greater Cleveland Hospital Association, Cleveland, OH '78 (EDUC)
MANCINI, MARY E., RN, vice-pres. nrsg. adm., Dallas County Hospital District-Parkland Memorial Hospital, Dallas, TX '86 (NURS)
MANCINO, DOUGLAS M., atty., California Hospital Association, Sacramento, CA '79 (ATTY)
MANCIONE, COLUMBIA, dir. diet., St. Charles Hospital and Rehabilitation Center, Port Jefferson, NY '76 (FOOD)
MANCO, CAROL A., mgr. matl., Millcreek Community Hospital, Erie, PA '85 (PUR)
MANCUSO, ALBERT J., vice-pres. prof. affairs, Crozer-Chester Medical Center, Chester, PA '69 (PUR)
MANCUSO, FRANCIS X. JR., Greenwich Hospital, Greenwich, CT '76 (MGMT)
MANCUSO, MICHAEL ANTHONY, coor. lab. computer, White Plains Hospital Medical Center, White Plains, NY '83
MAND, MARY JEAN, coor. nrsg. in-service educ., St. Marys Hospital Medical Center, Madison, WI '77 (EDUC)
MANDEL, BARRY, dir. soc. work serv., St. John's Queens Hospital, Flushing, NY '82 (SOC)
MANDEL, KEITH EVAN, student, University of Pittsburgh, Pittsburgh, PA '86
MANDEL, MARTHA PINK, atty., Northwestern University Medical Associates, Chicago, IL '75 (ATTY)
MANDELBAUM, RUTH J., dir. vol. serv., South Miami Hospital, South Miami, FL '82 (VOL)
MANDELL, DENNIS G., atty., Montefiore Medical Center, Bronx, NY '80 (ATTY)
MANDELLA, PHYLLIS ANN, dir. nutr. serv., Rehabilitation Institute of Pittsburgh, Pittsburgh, PA '82 (FOOD)
MANDERSON, SHEILA, RN, Kaiser Foundation Hospital, Richmond, CA '78 (EDUC)
MANDEVILLE, HANK, supv. electronics, Desert Hospital, Palm Springs, CA '83
MANDICH, TERESA C., RN, vice-pres. nrsg., Children's Hospital of Wisconsin, Milwaukee, WI '81 (NURS)
MANDIGO, PHYLLIS, RN, coor. in-service educ., Sturgis Hospital, Sturgis, MI '76 (EDUC)
MANDRAVELIS, PATRICIA J., RN, dir. nrsg., Nashua Memorial Hospital, Nashua, NH '81 (NURS)
MANDULA, SANDOR A., asst. to dir. constr. and phys. facil., St. Mary's Health Center, St. Louis, MO '83 (ENG)
MANESS, GARRY A., adm. pers., Le Bonheur Children's Medical Center, Memphis, TN '77 (PERS)
MANESS, JUDITH A., vice-pres. adm. serv., Riverside Hospital, Jacksonville, FL '82 (RISK)
MANESS, SYLVIA, RN, dir. pat. care, Independence Regional Health Center, Independence, MO '79 (NURS)
MANEVICH, MARTHA BIL, student, Boston University Health Management Programs, Boston, MA '79 (PLNG)
MANEY, MARILYN M., evening coor. matl. serv., St. Elizabeth Community Health Center, Lincoln, NE '86 (CS)
MANEZ, JULIE L., RN, adm. dir. nrsg., Mercy Center for Health Care Services, Aurora, IL '83 (NURS)
MANFREDI, GERALD J., dir. plant oper., St. John's Episcopal Hospital, Smithtown, NY '82 (ENG)
MANFREDI, MICHAEL JOHN, atty., Divine Providence Hospital, Williamsport, PA '86 (ATTY)
MANGEOT, KAROLYN K., coor. mktg. and pub. rel., Phoenixville Hospital, Phoenixville, PA '86 (PR)
MANGIANTE, FRANK A., adm. asst., Jewish Memorial Hospital, Boston, MA '74 (PUR)
MANGIARACINA, KATHLEEN B., RN, coor. pat. care sup., Saint Anthony Medical Center, Rockford, IL '76 (CS)
MANGINI, MICHAEL A., adm. and chief exec. off., Bellevue Maternity Hospital, Schenectady, NY '85
MANGINI, NANCY, RN, dir. nrsg. serv., St. Joseph Regional Medical Center -Oklahoma, Ponca City, OK '79 (NURS)
MANGINO, JOSEPH, dir. matl. mgt., Lourdes Hospital, Paducah, KY '86 (PUR)
MANGION, RICHARD M., exec. vice-pres. and adm., Harrington Memorial Hospital, Southbridge, MA '71
MANGONI, AUGUST M., atty., Chicago, IL '84 (ATTY)
MANGUM, RONALD SCOTT, atty., Penrose Hospitals, Colorado Springs, CO '74 (ATTY)
MANGUS, MIRIAM L., coor. educ., Tawas St. Joseph Hospital, Tawas City, MI '86

MANIATIS, SUZANNE IRENE, asst. dir. diet., Tacoma General Hospital, Tacoma, WA '75 (FOOD)
MANIS, KAREN S., chief diet., Reid Memorial Hospital, Richmond, IN '75 (FOOD)
MANISCALCO, LAWRENCE J., dir. pub. info. and mktg., Santa Rosa Memorial Hospital, Santa Rosa, CA '79 (PLNG)
MANKE, TERRENCE N., prin., Medicon, Inc., Pittsburgh, PA '82 (PLNG)
MANKIEWICH, PEGGY M., RN, dir. nrsg., Wellington Regional Medical Center, West Palm Beach, FL '87 (NURS)
MANKIN, DOUGLAS C., exec. vice-pres., Western Hospital Corporation, Alameda, CA '74
MANKIN, WENDY L., mgt. eng., Baystate Health Management Services, Inc., Springfield, MA '84 (MGMT)
MANLEY, CARL L., dir. matl. mgt., Muhlenberg Hospital Center, Bethlehem, PA '83 (PUR)
MANLEY, EDWARD H. JR., dir. food serv., North Broward Medical Center, Pompano Beach, FL '82 (FOOD)
MANLEY, JOHN J., mgr. soc. serv., St. Francis-St. George Hospital, Cincinnati, OH '78 (SOC)
MANLEY, KEVIN M., exec. dir., West Jersey Hospital Garden State, Marlton, NJ '82 (PLNG)
MANLEY, MARY JO, dir. nrsg. educ., dev. and res., St. Luke's-Roosevelt Hospital Center, New York, NY '77 (EDUC)
MANN, ALLAN, dir. pub. affairs, Kaiser Permanente Southern California, Pasadena, CA '86 (PR)
MANN, CRAYTON E., assoc. adm., St. Margaret Hospital, Hammond, IN '47 (LIFE)
MANN, DAVID D., sr. consult., Telecommunications Management, Inc., Houston, TX '83 (ENG)
MANN, ETHEL, asst. adm., Southwest Hospital and Medical Center, Atlanta, GA '86 (RISK)
MANN, GEORGE E., vice-pres. plng., Mercy Catholic Medical Center, Darby, PA '81 (PLNG)
MANN, J. GAYLE, RN, enterostomal ther., Southeast Alabama Medical Center, Dothan, AL '86 (RISK)
MANN, JAMES K., RN, dir. nrsg., Beth Israel Hospital, Boston, MA '77 (NURS)
MANN, LINDA M., RN, dir. nrsg., University of California, San Francisco Medical Center, San Francisco, CA '86 (NURS)
MANN, MARY C., head commun. rel. and vol. serv., Lafayette Home Hospital, Lafayette, IN '85 (VOL)
MANN, PEGGY A., RN, asst. adm. nrsg. serv., Halifax Memorial Hospital, Roanoke Rapids, NC '86 (NURS)
MANN, THOMAS W., dir. human res., Hospital Corporation of America, Nashville, TN '83 (PERS)
MANNEL, JOHN A., dir. human res., Sarah Bush Lincoln Health Center, Mattoon, IL '86 (PERS)
MANNI, JOSEPH R., dir. matl. mgt., Deborah Heart and Lung Center, Browns Mills, NJ '84
MANNING, ALAN M., dir. matl. mgt., Brooklyn Hospital-Caledonian Hospital, Brooklyn, NY '83 (PUR)(CS)
MANNING, ARLENE C., asst. dir. soc. serv., District of Columbia General Hospital, Washington, DC '85 (SOC)
MANNING, BETH HOTARD, dir. soc. serv., Woman's Hospital, Baton Rouge, LA '84 (SOC)
MANNING, BONNIE L., RN, coor. staff dev., Ukiah Adventist Hospital, Ukiah, CA '85 (EDUC)
MANNING, DAVID B., student, Concordia College, Moorhead, MN '87
MANNING, DOLORES HAROLD, mgr. environ. serv., Swedish Covenant Hospital, Chicago, IL '86 (ENVIRON)
MANNING, E. T. JR., atty., St. Anthony's Hospital, Amarillo, TX '86 (ATTY)
MANNING, FLORENCE, dir. pers., Ridgeview Institute, Smyrna, GA '86 (PERS)
MANNING, FRED M., coor. biomedical serv., St. Luke's Hospital, Kansas City, MO '81 (ENG)
MANNING, JAMES ALLEN, mgr. eng. and plant oper., Our Lady of Mercy Hospital-Division of Sisters of Mercy Health Corporation, Dyer, IN '73 (ENG)
MANNING, JANE E., RN, mgr. clin. instr. unit, Methodist Hospital of Indiana, Indianapolis, IN '81 (EDUC)
MANNING, MARTIN, mgr., Ernst and Whinney, Chicago, IL '86
MANNING, MICHAEL, atty., Coshocton County Memorial Hospital, Coshocton, OH '84 (ATTY)
MANNING, RAY, sanitarian, Charity Hospital at New Orleans, New Orleans, LA '79 (ENG)
MANNING, THOMAS M., dir. soc. work, Sharon General Hospital, Sharon, PA '76 (SOC)
MANNISTO, BERNARD R., pres., Micro Business Applications, Inc., Southfield, MI '86 (ENG)
MANNIX, JOHN R., health serv. consult., Cleveland, OH '24 (LIFE)
MANNIX, MARY T., asst. adm., St. Mary's Hospital, Athens, GA '85 (PLNG)
MANNIX, PATRICIA H., chief soc. worker, Grady Memorial Hospital, Atlanta, GA '86 (SOC)
MANNIX, ROBERT THOMAS JR., dir. fiscal serv., Havasu Regional Hospital, Lake Havasu City, AZ '78
MANNON, PERRY H., supv. hskpg., Sierra Vista Hospital, Truth Or Consequences, NM '86 (ENVIRON)
MANNS, CHARLES F., vice-pres., Loudoun Services Group, Leesburg, VA '83 (PUR)
MANNS, CHARLES F., vice-pres., Loudoun Services Group, Leesburg, VA '87 (AMB)
MANNS, SHARON JEAN, mgr. educ. and trng., St. Luke's Hospital, Duluth, MN '80 (EDUC)
MANO, ROBIN F., coor. pat. rel., Presbyterian-University of Pennsylvania Medical Center, Philadelphia, PA '86 (PAT)
MANOLAKIS, R. MICHAEL, dir. pur., Porter Memorial Hospital, Valparaiso, IN '86 (PUR)
MANOLES, MICHAEL L., safety coor., Presbyterian Hospital, Oklahoma City, OK '80 (RISK)
MANROW, WILLIAM E., exec. dir., Western Mutual Investment Company, Sunnymead, CA '52 (LIFE)
MANS, LARRY H., dir. pers., St. Luke's General Hospital, Bellingham, WA '82 (PERS)
MANSFIELD, CHRISTOPHER J., student, Florida State University, Tallahassee, FL '86 (PERS)
MANSFIELD, CHRISTOPHER J., coor. vol., Harris County Psychiatric Center, Houston, TX '86 (VOL)
MANSFIELD, EDGAR O., DrPH, (ret.), Naples, FL '54 (LIFE)
MANSFIELD, H. D., corp. dir. mktg., Research Health Services, Kansas City, MO '75 (PLNG)
MANSFIELD, PETER T., dir. info. serv., St. Luke's Hospital, Bethlehem, PA '85 (MGMT)
MANSFIELD, RICHARD E., vice-pres. pers. serv., DePaul Health Center, Bridgeton, MO '79 (PERS)
MANSFIELD, STEPHEN J., vice-pres. plng., mktg. and serv. dev., Northeast Health, Camden, ME '87 (PLNG)
MANSMANN, J. JEROME, atty., Mercy Hospital of Johnstown, Johnstown, PA '86 (ATTY)
MANSON, FREDERICK G., dir. human res. dev., Miami Valley Hospital, Dayton, OH '75 (EDUC)
MANSON, JULIE N., atty., Ravenswood Hospital Medical Center, Chicago, IL '79 (ATTY)
MANSON, LAWRENCE A., atty., Sisters of Charity Health Care Systems, Houston, TX '77 (ATTY)
MANSOUR, VIRGINIA, RN, sr. vice-pres. nrsg., Providence Memorial Hospital, El Paso, TX '79 (NURS)
MANSUKHANI, MOHAN, staff eng. consult., Condell Memorial Hospital, Libertyville, IL '80 (ENG)
MANSUR, RON, pres., American Clinic Laboratory, Inc., Flint, MI '86
MANSURE, JOHN FAULKNER, asst. adm., Greenville Hospital System, Greenville, SC '78
MANTAY, DONALD W., mgr. safety, U. S. Public Health Services, Food and Drug Administration, Rockville, MD '85 (ENG)
MANTER, JOAN M., sr. mgr. mktg., Riverside Methodist Hospitals, Columbus, OH '86 (PR)
MANTER, MARCIA A., vice-pres. and dir. trng. and dev., Lawrence-Letter and Company, Kansas City, MO '84 (EDUC)
MANTEY, CARL W., adm., Cibola General Hospital, Grants, NM '77
MANTHEY, MARIE E., dir. pat. care, Creative Nursing Management, Inc., Minneapolis, MN '82 (NURS)
MANTON, GEORGE W., vice-pres. prov. affairs, Blue Cross and Blue Shield of Central New York, Syracuse, NY '79 (PLNG)
MANTONI, BERTHA MARIE, asst. adm. ob. and gyn., Georgetown University Medical Center, Washington, DC '84
MANTTA, JAMES E., dir. food serv., St. Vincent Hospital, Green Bay, WI '80 (FOOD)
MANTZ, PAT, RN, nrs. mgr. amb. surg. center, St. Luke's Hospital, Bethlehem, PA '87 (AMB)
MANUEL, JOE E., atty., Leitner, Warner, Moffitt, Williams, Dooley, Carpenter and Napolitan, Chattanooga, TN '86 (ATTY)
MANUEL, PAULA M., coor. group pur., Southeast Louisiana Hospital Service Corporation, Metairie, LA '86 (PUR)
MANUELE, GAETANA M., supv. soc. work, St. Vincent's Hospital and Medical Center, New York, NY '81 (SOC)
MANUS, BARRY R., dir. human res. dev., St. John's Episcopal Hospital, Far Rockaway, NY '77 (PERS)
MANYPENNY, JOSEPH PERRY, dir. cent. proc., Weirton Medical Center, Weirton, WV '84 (CS)
MANZELLA, V. JAMES, MD, Cocoa Beach, FL '69
MANZI, GABRIELLA M., RN, dir. pat. care, Morristown Memorial Hospital, Morristown, NJ '83 (NURS)
MANZI, PINO, mgr. cent. sup., Methodist Hospital, Philadelphia, PA '80 (CS)
MANZO, ARNOLD D., dir. pers., St. Barnabas Medical Center, Livingston, NJ '86 (PERS)
MANZO, JOHN A. JR., chief indust. eng., New England Medical Center, Boston, MA '70 (MGMT)
MAPLE, K. LOUISE, dir. pub. rel., Broward General Medical Center, Fort Lauderdale, FL '82 (PR)
MAPLES, ARTHUR FRANKLIN, mgt. eng., Baptist Memorial Hospital, Memphis, TN '77 (MGMT)
MAPSTONE, SARA JEAN, RN, asst. dean, University of Virginia Hospitals, Charlottesville, VA '78 (NURS)
MARA, ELEANOR A., RN, dir. maternal, child and adolescent nrsg., Worcester Hahnemann Hospital, Worcester, MA '84 (NURS)
MARA, TOM, pres., Victor Kramer Company, Inc., New York, NY '86
MARABLE, KATHY, head nrs. cardiac care, Deaconess Hospital, Evansville, IN '86 (NURS)
MARAM, BARRY S., exec. dir., Illinois Health Facilities Authority, Chicago, IL '83
MARANZANO, ANGELINA, head diet.-in-service trng., Queens Hospital Center, Jamaica, NY '83 (EDUC)
MARAS, MARILYN K., dir. vol. serv., Warren General Hospital, Warren, OH '83 (VOL)
MARASHI, OMAR F., pres., Westmark, Inc., Grand Rapids, MI '85 (CS)
MARBLE, WARREN E., vice-pres. eng., Danbury Hospital, Danbury, CT '60 (ENG)
MARCANO, ENRIQUE, pat. advocate, St. Joseph Hospital, Chicago, IL '84 (PAT)
MARCANTUONO, DANIEL L., pres. and chief exec. off., General Hospital Center at Passaic, Passaic, NJ '66
MARCET, ENRIQUE M., vice-pres., Harvard, Jolly, Marcet and Associates, St. Petersburg, FL '75
MARCH, ELIZABETH A., dir. soc. work, Mount Vernon Hospital, Alexandria, VA '86 (SOC)
MARCH, ELIZABETH BURTON, RN, dir. nrsg. syst. resources, Northwestern Memorial Hospital, Chicago, IL '84 (NURS)
MARCH, GEORGIANNA B., asst. dir. soc. serv., Western Medical Center, Santa Ana, CA '78 (SOC)
MARCHANTE, LAZARA, dir. pers., AMI Kendall Regional Medical Center, Miami, FL '84 (PERS)
MARCHETTI, ANNEMARIE OLECKO, dir. soc. serv., Southside Hospital, Bay Shore, NY '73 (SOC)
MARCHEWKA, ANN E., RN, vice-pres. nrsg., Copley Hospital, Morrisville, VT '86 (NURS)
MARCHIONNO, PAULA M., RN, asst. adm., Shadyside Hospital, Pittsburgh, PA '86 (NURS)
MARCIL-SKIER, BARBARA J., pat. rep., Kaiser Foundation Hospital, Panorama City, CA '86 (RISK)
MARCINIAK, MARY ANN, dir. educ. serv., Houlton Regional Hospital, Houlton, ME '86 (EDUC)
MARCKX, ELAINE W., RN, dir. nrsg., Salem Hospital, Salem, OR '80 (NURS)
MARCON, MICHAEL E., vice-pres. gen. serv., Rahway Hospital, Rahway, NJ '77 (PUR)
MARCOT, CAROLE E., student, Western State College of Law, Fullerton, CA '86 (RISK)
MARCOTTE, REO J., (ret.), Belmont, MA '39 (LIFE)
MARCUM, MARVIN, dir. pers. and emp. rel., Glynn-Brunswick Memorial Hospital, Brunswick, GA '86 (PERS)
MARCUM, MONICA E., dir. vol. serv., Children's Hospital, Baltimore, MD '86 (VOL)
MARCUS-WEISS, ANNE, soc. worker, Children's Hospital, Baltimore, MD '86 (SOC)
MARCUS, LEONARD, vice-pres. human resources, Sinai Hospital of Baltimore, Baltimore, MD '80 (PERS)
MARCUS, RHODA S., dir. vol. serv., University of Connecticut Health Center, Farmington, CT '81 (VOL)
MARCUS, RICHARD C., atty., Millard Fillmore Hospital, Buffalo, NY '68 (ATTY)
MARCUS, ROBERT M., dir. soc. work, Western Reserve Systems-Southside, Youngstown, OH '80 (SOC)
MARCUS, STEPHEN G., dir. oper., Rehabilitation Hospital Services Corporation, Fort Lauderdale, FL '76
MARCUS, TOBY, dir. soc. serv., Long Beach Memorial Hospital, Long Beach, NY '79 (SOC)
MARCUS, WARREN S., exec. dir., Clinical Medical Network, Utica, NY '71 (PLNG)
MARCY, GLORIA H., dir. pers., Mercy Medical Center and Hospital, Williston, ND '80 (PERS)
MARE, GREGORY, dir. med. serv., Butler Rogers Baskett, New York, NY '86
MAREK, JOHN, vice-pres., Thomas A. Greene and Company, Inc., New York, NY '80 (RISK)
MAREK, NEIL, asst. dir. group pur., New Jersey Hospital Association, Princeton, NJ '78 (PUR)
MARELLA, MEDEA M., RN, vice-pres. nrsg. serv., Sinai Hospital of Baltimore, Baltimore, MD '77 (NURS)
MARES, EDWARD F. JR., vice-pres. human res., Good Samaritan Community Healthcare, Puyallup, WA '82 (PERS)
MARESCA, TECKLA ANN, supv. cent. serv., Dover General Hospital and Medical Center, Dover, NJ '78 (CS)
MARGALIS, ROBERT J., Spring Hill, FL '84 (PUR)
MARGARIT, SUSAN L., oper. analyst, Oakwood Hospital, Dearborn, MI '83 (MGMT)
MARGASON, LYNN C., vice-pres. health care mktg., McDonald Davis and Associates, Milwaukee, WI '84 (PLNG)
MARGELLO, MARGARET A., asst. exec. dir., Children's Hospital, Columbus, OH '79 (PUR)
MARGENTHALER, DONALD R., mgr. health care serv., Deere and Company, Moline, IL '83
MARGOLIS, ALICE, adm. diet., Saint Francis Hospital and Medical Center, Hartford, CT '80 (FOOD)
MARGOLIS, GAIL LOREN, atty., Daniel Freeman Memorial Hospital, Inglewood, CA '78 (ATTY)
MARGOLIS, LAWRENCE W., sr. vice-pres., Storandt, Kay and Pann, Inc., Chicago, IL '78 (PLNG)
MARHALIK, MAURITA K., instr. educ., West Park Hospital, Philadelphia, PA '86 (EDUC)
MARIAK, KATHLEEN A., RN, assoc. adm. nrsg., Medical Center Hospital of Vermont, Burlington, VT '85 (NURS)
MARIANI, JEANNE L., RN, vice-pres. nrsg., Mercy Hospital, Scranton, PA '82 (NURS)
MARIE, SR. FRANCES, exec. vice-pres., Sisters of the Third Order of St. Francis, Peoria, IL '79
MARIE, JULIE A. PROCHNIAK, dir. diet. serv., Riverview Hospital, Wisconsin Rapids, WI '82 (FOOD)
MARIE, SR. THERESA, dir. matl. mgt., Hazleton-St. Joseph Medical Center, Hazleton, PA '79 (PUR)
MARIENCHECK, SARAH, coor. qual. assur., St. Joseph Hospital, Memphis, TN '86 (RISK)
MARIETTA, DONNA, dir. mktg. and pub. rel., Humana Hospital -Newnan, Newnan, GA '82 (PR)
MARIK, JAROMIR, pres. and chief exec. off., Doylestown Hospital, Doylestown, PA '55 (LIFE)
MARIMOW, KENNETH, dir. gen. serv., Hospital for Sick Children, Washington, DC '77 (PUR)
MARINACCIO, RAYMOND J., vice-pres., Lenox Hill Hospital, New York, NY '74
MARINAKOS, PLATO A., exec. vice-pres., Mercy Catholic Medical Center, Darby, PA '60
MARINE, ROSS P., Leavenworth, KS '72 (PLNG)
MARINELLI, MICHAEL A., chief maint., Louis A. Weiss Memorial Hospital, Chicago, IL '80 (ENG)
MARINER, JOHN M., vice-pres., Southside Hospital, Bay Shore, NY '86 (PR)
MARINER, STEVEN A., assoc. adm., Greene County Memorial Hospital, Waynesburg, PA '72 (PERS)
MARING, JAMES, dir. facil. mgt., United Hospital, St. Paul, MN '83 (ENG)
MARINGER, MICHALENE D., RN, asst. dir. critical care, Christ Hospital and Medical Center, Oak Lawn, IL '86 (NURS)
MARINI, ANNE K., asst. dir. food and nutr. serv., HCA Largo Medical Center Hospital, Largo, FL '85 (FOOD)
MARINI, HERMAN R., supv. pharm., Citizens General Hospital, Oakmont, PA '85
MARINIELLO, JOSEPH R., atty., Bergen Pines County Hospital, Paramus, NJ '86 (ATTY)
MARINO, EMILY H., dir. pers., Ridgecliff Hospital, Willoughby, OH '82 (PERS)
MARINO, JOSEPH R., dir. food serv., Memorial Hospital, Hollywood, FL '76 (FOOD)
MARINO, PATRICIA GAIL, RN, vice-pres. nrsg., Franklin Memorial Hospital, Farmington, ME '82 (NURS)
MARINO, PHYLLIS B., dir. mktg., St. Vincent Charity Hospital, Cleveland, OH '85 (PLNG)

MARION, CHARLES G., adm., Yonkers Professional Hospital, Yonkers, NY '47 (LIFE)
MARION, DANIEL J., vice-pres., Cottage Hospital of Grosse Pointe, Grosse Pointe Farms, MI '73
MARION, ED, dir. plant oper., St. Michael Hospital, Texarkana, AR '80 (ENG)
MARION, STEPHEN R., vice-pres. plng., Mary Hitchcock Memorial Hospital, Hanover, NH '82 (PLNG)
MARIOTTI, JOEL F., consult., Ohio Department of Health, Division of Medical Facilities, Columbus, OH '78
MARK, AVRA K., dir. soc. serv., Lawrence Hospital, Bronxville, NY '75 (SOC)
MARK, JESS L. III, dir. biomedical eng., North Mississippi Medical Center, Tupelo, MS '83 (ENG)
MARKARIAN, ARMEN, dir. advertising and commun., Saint John's Hospital and Health Center, Santa Monica, CA '86 (PR)
MARKEGARD, ROD, mgr. bldg. serv., Deaconess Medical Center, Billings, MT '77 (ENG)
MARKER, JULEE, RN, dir. qual. assessment, St. Elizabeth Community Health Center, Lincoln, NE '86 (RISK)
MARKERT, RITA L., dir. soc. serv., Akron General Medical Center, Akron, OH '81 (SOC)
MARKEY, WILLIAM ALAN, health serv. consult., Sonoma, CA '52 (LIFE)
MARKEZIN, ELAINE T., dir. corp. plng. and mktg., John Hancock Health Plans, Wayne, PA '83 (PLNG)
MARKI, PAUL P. JR., dir. food serv., St. Joseph's Medical Center, Fort Wayne, IN '75 (FOOD)
MARKIEWICZ, DENNIS P., vice-pres., St. John Hospital, Detroit, MI '72
MARKIEWICZ, JOHN J., assoc. dir., Westchester County Medical Center, Valhalla, NY '83 (PUR)
MARKLE, JOHN E., dir. pers., Community Memorial Hospital, Toms River, NJ '73 (PERS)
MARKLE, RICHARD, dir. hskpg., Warren Hospital, Phillipsburg, NJ '86 (ENVIRON)
MARKLEY, WILLIAM E., partner and proj. mgr., Sargent, Webster, Crenshaw and Folley, Syracuse, NY '83
MARKMAN, DUANNE P., RN, dir. nrsg., maternal and infant care, University Hospital of Arkansas, Little Rock, AR '86 (NURS)
MARKO, DAVID E., dir. matl. mgt., Hackley Hospital, Muskegon, MI '81 (PUR)
MARKO, PATRICIA ANNE, mgr. sup., San Antonio Community Hospital, Upland, CA '86 (CS)
MARKOWICH, M. MICHAEL, dir. pers., United Hospitals, Inc., Cheltenham, PA '72 (PERS)
MARKOWITZ, BRUCE J., pres. and chief exec. off., Park City Hospital, Bridgeport, CT '86 (PLNG)
MARKOWITZ, ROBERT, pres., Fojp Service Corporation, New York, NY '56 (LIFE)
MARKOWITZ, STUART, adm. computer programmer phys. plant, pur. and procurement, George Washington University Hospital, Washington, DC '86 (ENG)
MARKS, CHARLES H., proj. mgr., Camp Dresser and McKee, Inc., Boston, MA '85 (ENG)
MARKS, CRAIG, student, Program in Health Administration, University of Minnesota, Minneapolis, MN '84
MARKS, J. BARRETT, atty., Providence Hospital, Medford, OR '78 (ATTY)
MARKS, JACK F., dir. pers., Pontiac Osteopathic Hospital, Pontiac, MI '87 (PERS)
MARKS, JOHN COURTNEY, Bowling Green, KY '71 (MGMT)
MARKS, JOHN F. JR., student, University of Pittsburgh, Pittsburgh, PA '87 (PERS)
MARKS, MARY J., dir. nutr. and food serv., Milwaukee County Medical Complex, Milwaukee, WI '87 (FOOD)
MARKS, ROGER N., atty., Church-Charity Foundation of Long Island, Hempstead, NY '85 (RISK)(ATTY)
MARKS, RONNIE E., dir. plng., Healthwest Medical Centers, Chatsworth, CA '85 (PLNG)
MARKS, STEVEN M., pub. rel. asst., Ingalls Memorial Hospital, Harvey, IL '83 (PR)
MARKS, WILLIAM P., atty., Sturgis Hospital, Sturgis, MI '75 (ATTY)
MARKUN, FRANK O., dir. food serv., Cabell Huntington Hospital, Huntington, WV '81 (FOOD)
MARKUS, BARBARA M., risk mgr., Washington University School of Medicine, St. Louis, MO '80 (RISK)
MARKUSZKA, THOMAS J., dir. matl. mgt., Waterman Medical Center, Eustis, FL '86 (PUR)
MARKWARD, JOHN A., dir. eng., St. Bernard Hospital, Chicago, IL '85 (ENG)
MARLAND, KENDALL L., dir. pers., Lawrence and Memorial Hospital, New London, CT '77 (PERS)
MARLAR, GARY G., dir. pub. rel., Holston Valley Hospital and Medical Center, Kingsport, TN '85 (PR)
MARLBOROUGH, CYNTHIA HOGAN, dir. pub. rel., Braintree Hospital, Braintree, MA '82 (PR)
MARLER, MARY M., Kaiser Permanente, Oakland, CA '84 (MGMT)
MARLER, PHILLIP L., dep. dir. med. and strategy mgt., Asst Secretary of Defense and Health Aff, Pentagon, Washington, DC '76
MARLETT, LIZABETH WARING, dir. soc. serv., Presbyterian Hospital, Oklahoma City, OK '87 (SOC)
MARLEY, AMELIA LEE, sr. consult., Ernst and Whinney, Washington, DC '87 (MGMT)
MARLEY, SARA P., dir. vol., Moncrief Army Community Hospital, Fort Jackson, SC '87 (VOL)
MARLIN, CAROLYN, mgr. hskpg., Putnam Community Hospital, Palatka, FL '86 (ENVIRON)
MARLIN, JOSEPH R., dir. soc. serv., Mount Sinai Hospital Medical Center, Chicago, IL '72 (SOC)
MARLOW, CAROL A., dir. educ., Memorial Hospital, Manchester, KY '87 (EDUC)
MARLOWE, BARBARA, mgr. soc. serv. and cont. care, Burbank Hospital, Fitchburg, MA '84 (SOC)
MARLOWE, DAVID L., dir. mktg., South Baltimore General Hospital, Baltimore, MD '80 (PLNG)
MARLOWE, HAROLD E., risk mgr., Memorial Hospital, Chattanooga, TN '80 (RISK)
MARMEN, ANDRE P., vice-pres., Miriam Hospital, Providence, RI '73 (PR)
MARMER, ELLEN B., mgr. mktg., Optimum Services, Cincinnati, OH '81 (PLNG)
MARMISH, MAJ. JOHN E., MSC USAF, adm., U. S. Air Force Clinic Brooks, Sga, Brooks AFB, TX '81 (PLNG)
MARMUREK, STEVEN R., dir., Voluntary Hospitals of America, Tampa, FL '79
MARNELL, MARJORIE A., dir. matl. mgt. and pharm. serv., Ohio Valley Health Services and Education Corporation, Wheeling, WV '84 (PUR)
MARNER, AGNES, RN, dir. nrsg. serv., St. Francis Medical Center, Pittsburgh, PA '76 (NURS)
MARNIE, MAUREEN, mng. dir. qual. assur., Washington Hospital Center, Washington, DC '86 (RISK)
MAROHN, ANN E., asst. prof. med. rec. adm., Medical University of South Carolina, Charleston, SC '85
MAROIS, DANIEL R., dir. commun. rel. and dev., Stephens Memorial Hospital, Norway, ME '85 (PR)
MAROLD, JEFF D., student, University of La Verne, West Covina, CA '85 (PLNG)
MAROULIS, FLORENA, tech. cent. serv., Ionia County Memorial Hospital, Ionia, MI '78 (CS)
MAROVICH, J. MICHAEL, mgr. matl., Preston Memorial Hospital, Kingwood, WV '86 (PUR)
MARQUAND, ROGER W., (ret.), Chagrin, OH '44 (LIFE)
MARQUARDT, EMIL C. JR., atty., Morton F. Plant Hospital, Clearwater, FL '81 (ATTY)
MARQUART, DENNIS G., maint. eng., Bluffton Community Hospital, Bluffton, OH '75 (ENG)
MARQUART, JOSEPH P. JR., dir. educ. serv., Iowa Methodist Medical Center, Des Moines, IA '81 (EDUC)
MARQUES, KAREN M., vice-pres. pub. rel., Edward Leroux Group, Woburn, MA '81 (PR)
MARQUEZ, MICHAEL, asst. adm. mktg. and bus. dev., AMI Parkway Regional Medical Center, North Miami Beach, FL '84 (PLNG)
MARQUEZ, RAMIRO, dir. pat. rep., South Chicago Community Hospital, Chicago, IL '85 (PAT)
MARQUIS, JOHN R., atty., Holland Community Hospital, Holland, MI '85 (ATTY)
MARQUIS, ROGER A., clin. eng., Catholic Medical Center, Manchester, NH '81 (ENG)
MARR, MARILYN R., asst. vice-pres. corp. commun., Riverside Methodist Hospitals, Columbus, OH '79 (PR)
MARRA, MARY ELLEN, acct. exec., A. T. and T. Communications, Oak Brook, IL '84
MARRACINO, WILLIAM G., clin. eng., St. John Medical Center, Steubenville, OH '77 (ENG)
MARRAPESE, RICHARD L., partner and dir. health care consult., Ernst and Whinney, Cleveland, OH '83
MARREN, DAN, vice-pres. adm. and support serv., St. Luke's Hospitals, Fargo, ND '77 (MGMT)
MARREN, JOHN P., atty., St. Frances Xavier Cabrini Hospital, Chicago, IL '84 (ATTY)
MARRERO, JEANNETTE, RN, assoc. dir. nrsg. serv., Hospital for Joint Diseases Orthopaedic Institute, New York, NY '84 (NURS)(AMB)
MARRINER-TOMEY, ANN L., RN, prof., Indiana University, School of Nursing, Indianapolis, IN '87 (NURS)
MARRONE, EUGENE A., Smyrna, GA '82 (FOOD)
MARRS, FRANK O., partner, Peat, Marwick, Mitchell and Company, Amarillo, TX '85
MARRS, JUDY H., dir. environ. serv., Blue Ridge Hospital, Charlottesville, VA '86 (ENVIRON)
MARSALLO, JANE O., partner, Healthmark, Syracuse, NY '85 (PR)
MARSAN, ELAYNE R., vice-pres. ancilliary serv., Howard Young Medical Center, Woodruff, WI '86 (PERS)
MARSCHALL, MARLENE E., exec. dir., St. Paul-Ramsey Medical Center, St. Paul, MN '77
MARSCHNER, JOSEPH A., dir. educ., Washington County Hospital, Hagerstown, MD '71 (EDUC)
MARSDEN, JEAN M., pat. rep., Little Company of Mary Hospital, Evergreen Park, IL '81 (PAT)
MARSELLA, SAMUEL A., atty., Springfield Hospital, Springfield, MA '70 (ATTY)
MARSH, ANNE R., student, University of Arkansas, Little Rock, AR '82 (PR)
MARSH, DONALD E., dir. food and nutr. serv., Pennsylvania Hospital, Philadelphia, PA '70 (FOOD)
MARSH, DONALD G., dir. pers., Metropolitan Hospital, Grand Rapids, MI '84 (PERS)
MARSH, DOUGLAS R., dir. res. and dev., St. Vincent Medical Center, Los Angeles, CA '82 (PLNG)
MARSH, JUDITH A., RN, vice-pres. nrsg., Hays Memorial Hospital, San Marcos, TX '86 (NURS)
MARSH, KAREN L., asst. adm., Walter Reed Army Medical Center, Washington, DC '80
MARSH, KAY, dir. commun. rel. and dev., Kishwaukee Community Hospital, De Kalb, IL '76 (PR) (PLNG)
MARSH, LOIS J., coor. pat. educ., Rockford Memorial Hospital, Rockford, IL '83 (EDUC)
MARSH, MARTHA H., pres., Matthew Thornton Health Plan, Inc., Nashua, NH '80 (PLNG)
MARSH, ROBERT J., consult., Candler General Hospital, Savannah, GA '59
MARSH, VIRGIL W., dir. alternate delivery syst., Blue Shield Association, Chicago, IL '56 (LIFE)
MARSH, WILLIAM A., product res. and dev. spec., Lutheran Healthcare Network, Mesa, AZ '83 (PR)
MARSHALL, CAROLYN A., dir. educ., Halstead Hospital, Halstead, KS '86 (EDUC)
MARSHALL, CHRISTOPHER, counsel, Mullikin Medical Center, Cerritos, CA '86 (RISK)
MARSHALL, CLARKE L., med. eng. spec., Ohmeda Company, Littleton, CO '80 (ENG)
MARSHALL, DIANNE, dir. vol. serv., Methodist Hospital of Indiana, Indianapolis, IN '85 (VOL)
MARSHALL, DONALD R., dir. food serv., Huntsville Hospital, Huntsville, AL '68 (FOOD)
MARSHALL, DOUGLASS A., atty., Saint Francis Medical Center, Peoria, IL '80 (ATTY)
MARSHALL, MRS. E. C., Atlanta, GA '48 (HON)
MARSHALL, COL. EDGARD A., MSC USA, dir. facil. eng., Walter Reed Army Medical Center, Washington, DC '86 (ENG)
MARSHALL, GARY A., mgt. eng., East Jefferson General Hospital, Metairie, LA '83 (MGMT)
MARSHALL, GEORGE L. III, asst. adm., Sumter Regional Hospital, Americus, GA '82
MARSHALL, HEMAN A. III, atty., Community Hospital of Roanoke Valley, Roanoke, VA '84 (ATTY)
MARSHALL, IRENE A., RN, asst. adm. and dir. nrsg., Waldo County General Hospital, Belfast, ME '83 (NURS)
MARSHALL, JEFFREY A., atty., Jersey Shore Hospital, Jersey Shore, PA '84 (ATTY)
MARSHALL, JO TAYLOR, dir. soc. serv., Morristown Memorial Hospital, Morristown, NJ '79 (SOC)
MARSHALL, JOHN A., asst. adm., St. Augustine General Hospital, St. Augustine, FL '84
MARSHALL, JON B., dir. matl. mgt., St. Joseph Medical Center, Joliet, IL '86 (PUR)
MARSHALL, JOSEPH S., assoc. adm. amb. serv., Lower Bucks Hospital, Bristol, PA '86 (AMB)
MARSHALL, JOYCE, supv. cent. serv., Northwest General Hospital, Detroit, MI '80 (CS)
MARSHALL, JULIE R., practitioner and teacher, Rush-Presbyterian-St. Luke's Medical Center, Chicago, IL '86
MARSHALL, MARILYN J., dir. soc. serv., Good Samaritan Hospital, Lebanon, PA '79 (SOC)
MARSHALL, PAMELA ANN, dir. pat. rel., The Fronk Clinic, Honolulu, HI '86 (PAT)
MARSHALL, RICHARD KENNERLY JR., contractor experimentation staff, Social Security Administration, Bureau of Health Insurance, Baltimore, MD '74
MARSHALL, SANDRA B., dir. gen. surg., Washington Hospital Center, Washington, DC '85 (NURS)
MARSHALL, SHARON D., dir. educ., Kaiser Foundation Hospital, Sacramento, CA '76 (EDUC)
MARSHALL, SUSAN K., coor. health educ., Memorial Hospital System, Houston, TX '86 (EDUC)
MARSHALL, TERRY M., coor. commun. health educ., Surrey Health Education Center, Division of Washington County Hospital, Hagerstown, MD '85 (EDUC)
MARSHALL, WILLIAM P., dir. maint., St. Francis-St. George Hospital, Cincinnati, OH '79 (ENG)
MARSINKO, STEVEN A., mgr. human res. and pub. affairs, Highlands Hospital and Health Center, Connellsville, PA '86 (PERS)
MARSOLAIS, RITA, RN, vice-pres. nrsg., Hebrew Rehabilitation Center for Aged, Boston, MA '80 (NURS)
MARSTELLER, BRENT A., adm., East Ohio Regional Hospital, Martins Ferry, OH '79 (PLNG)(MGMT)
MARSTERS, IRENE, dir. vol. serv., St. Vincent's Medical Center, Bridgeport, CT '73 (VOL)
MARSTERS, JUDSON F., assoc. adm., Spohn Hospital, Corpus Christi, TX '53 (LIFE)
MARSTERS, TED, vice-pres. plng., Healthnet, Inc., Salem, MA '85 (PLNG)
MARSTON, J. KENNETH, assoc. mktg., Jackson-Madison County General Hospital, Jackson, TN '86 (PR)
MARSTON, JOHN P., vice-pres. and partner, Executive Health Search Consultants, Inc., Atlanta, GA '87
MARSTON, PENNY W., coor. pat. assistance, University of California Davis Medical Center, Sacramento, CA '86 (PAT)
MARSTON, ROBERT Q., MD, pres., University of Florida, Gainesville, FL '69 (HON)
MARSZALEK-GAUCHER, ELLEN, assoc. dir. amb. care, University of Michigan Hospitals, Ann Arbor, MI '87 (AMB)
MARTEL, GABRIELLE DENISE, RN, (ret.), Chicago, IL '67 (NURS)
MARTEL, J. RICHARD, chief soc. work serv., Veterans Administration Medical Center, Des Moines, IA '84 (SOC)
MARTEL, JEANNETTE M., RN, dir. nrsg., Riverside Osteopathic Hospital, Trenton, MI '77 (NURS)
MARTEL, LT. COL. PAUL T. JR., MSC USA, chief efficiency review and manpower standards off., U. S. Army Health Services Command, Fort Sam Houston, TX '75
MARTELL, SR. BETTY, dir. soc. serv., St. Francis Medical Center, Breckenridge, MN '80 (SOC)
MARTELLO, MARSHA, med. soc. work, Deborah Heart and Lung Center, Browns Mills, NJ '86 (SOC)
MARTENS, GENE W., dir. matl. mgt., Immanuel-St. Joseph's Hospital, Mankato, MN '82 (PUR)
MARTENS, MARCIA A., dir. pur., St. Anthony's Medical Center, St. Louis, MO '85 (PUR)
MARTENS, SHARLA R., dir. commun. rel. and mktg., Southwestern Memorial Hospital, Weatherford, OK '86 (PR)
MARTICHUSKI, RITA A., dir. soc. serv., Superior Memorial Hospital, Superior, WI '86 (SOC)
MARTIN, ALVAH T., atty., Illinois Masonic Medical Center, Chicago, IL '69 (ATTY)
MARTIN, ANN L., RN, dir. nrsg., Windham Community Memorial Hospital, Willimantic, CT '82 (NURS)
MARTIN, ANNA O., dir. vol. serv., St. Anthony Medical Center, Crown Point, IN '80 (VOL)
MARTIN, BEVERLY A., dir. vol. serv., Pottsville Hospital and Warne Clinic, Pottsville, PA '83 (VOL)
MARTIN, BILL B., exec. dir., Franklin County Memorial Hospital, Meadville, MS '87
MARTIN, BONNIE, dir. soc. serv., Edward Hospital, Naperville, IL '83 (SOC)
MARTIN, BRENDA, asst. dir. of qual. risk mgt., Bay Medical Center, Panama City, FL '86 (RISK)
MARTIN, BRUCE A., dir. human res., Baptist Regional Health Services, Inc., Pensacola, FL '83 (PERS)
MARTIN, BRUCE G., atty., Great Northwest Federal Savings and Loan Association, Bremerton, WA '82 (ATTY)
MARTIN, CARL R. SR., dir. ldry. and linen serv., Clark County Memorial Hospital, Jeffersonville, IN '86 (ENVIRON)

MARTIN, CARLA H., asst. dir. matl. mgt., Blodgett Memorial Medical Center, Grand Rapids, MI '83 (PUR)
MARTIN, CATHERINE S., dir. emp. dev. and pub. rel., Graduate Hospital, Philadelphia, PA '77 (PAT)
MARTIN, CHERI G., pat. serv. rep., Group Health, Inc., Brooklyn Center, MN '85 (PAT)
MARTIN, CONNIE L., asst. mgr. pers., Scottish Rite Children's Hospital, Atlanta, GA '86 (PERS)
MARTIN, CONSTANCE L., RN, coor. home health serv., Williamsport Hospital and Medical Center, Williamsport, PA '87 (AMB)
MARTIN, CONSTANCE, risk mgr., Long Island College Hospital, Brooklyn, NY '87 (RISK)
MARTIN, DARLENE M., dir. pers., Carlisle Hospital, Carlisle, PA '86 (PERS)
MARTIN, DARRELL W., mgr. plant oper., Beaufort County Hospital, Washington, NC '85 (ENG)
MARTIN, DAVID M., mgr. pers., Rhode Island Hospital, Providence, RI '85 (PERS)
MARTIN, DAVID T., assoc. adm., Doctors Hospital of Lakewood, Lakewood, CA '85
MARTIN, DAVID, dir. risk mgt., Empire Health Services, Spokane, WA '87 (RISK)
MARTIN, DOLORIS VON DOELTZ, dir. soc. work serv., St. Joseph Hospital and Health Care Center, Tacoma, WA '75 (SOC)
MARTIN, DONALD W., dir. eng., Sewickley Valley Hospital, Sewickley, PA '79 (ENG)
MARTIN, EDWARD G., exec. hskpg., Wausau Hospital Center, Wausau, WI '86 (ENVIRON)
MARTIN, EDWARD M., mgr. matl., Granville C. Morton Cancer and Research Hospital, Wadley Research Institute, Dallas, TX '84 (PUR)
MARTIN, ELIZABETH A., supv. pat. and family serv., Ellis Hospital, Schenectady, NY '82 (SOC)
MARTIN, ELLEN, dir. pat. rel., St. Luke's-Roosevelt Hospital Center, New York, NY '80 (PAT)
MARTIN, EVELYN, dir. pers., Medical Center Hospital, Conroe, TX '77 (PERS)
MARTIN, FRANCES S., RN, asst. adm. nrsg. serv., Twin Cities Community Hospital, Templeton, CA '83 (NURS)
MARTIN, G. ROGER, exec. dir., Jeanes Hospital, Philadelphia, PA '63
MARTIN, GAIL, coor. nrsg. educ., Anna Jaques Hospital, Newburyport, MA '85 (EDUC)
MARTIN, GREG L., dir. pers. and safety, Shawnee Medical Center Hospital, Shawnee, OK '80 (PERS)
MARTIN, HAZEL M., coor. qual. assur., Scottish Rite Children's Hospital, Atlanta, GA '83 (RISK)
MARTIN, J. D., vice-pres. mktg. health care, Vollrath Company, Memphis, TN '84
MARTIN, JAMES A. JR., atty., Morton F. Plant Hospital, Clearwater, FL '79 (ATTY)
MARTIN, JAMES B., assoc. prof., University of Michigan, Department of Hospital Administration, Ann Arbor, MI '80 (MGMT)
MARTIN, JAMES M., dir. environ. serv., University of Alabama Hospital, Birmingham, AL '86 (ENVIRON)
MARTIN, JAMES, dir. maint., Memorial Hospital, Siloam Springs, AR '75 (ENG)
MARTIN, JARED H., dir. gen. serv., Huntsville Memorial Hospital, Huntsville, TX '80 (ENG)
MARTIN, JEFFREY M., assoc. adm., Long Island Jewish-Hillside Medical Center, Glen Oaks, NY '78
MARTIN, JOAN M., chm.-steering committee, National Association of Hospital Hospitality Houses, Saginaw, MI '85
MARTIN, JOAN R., budget analyst, Memorial Hospital, Colorado Springs, CO '84 (RISK)
MARTIN, JOEL M., risk mgr., Suburban Community Hospital, Warrensville Heights, OH '76 (PUR)(RISK)
MARTIN, KAREN R., mgt. eng., Orangeburg-Calhoun Regional Hospital, Orangeburg, SC '86 (MGMT)
MARTIN, KATHLEEN J., nrsg. instr., Kaiser Permanente Medical Care Program, Oakland, CA '85 (EDUC)
MARTIN, LINDA C., atty., St. John Medical Center, Tulsa, OK '84 (ATTY)
MARTIN, LOIS ANN, RN, sr. vice-pres., Burlington Medical Center, Burlington, IA '70 (NURS)
MARTIN, LUCY Z., pres., Lucy Z. Martin and Associates, Portland, OR '81 (PR)
MARTIN, M. CAROLINE, sr. vice-pres., Riverside Hospital, Newport News, VA '80
MARTIN, MAC J., dir. mgt. serv., St. Francis Hospital Center, Beech Grove, IN '85 (MGMT)
MARTIN, MARGARET L., dir. educ., Harris Methodist -Fort Worth, Fort Worth, TX '81 (EDUC)
MARTIN, MARILYN S., dir. pers., Children's Specialized Hospital, Mountainside, NJ '81 (PERS)
MARTIN, MARTHA M., dir. soc. work, Grace Hospital, Detroit, MI '85 (SOC)
MARTIN, NANCY K., RN, adm. nrsg. serv. and nrsg. educ., Ohio Valley Medical Center, Wheeling, WV '75 (NURS)
MARTIN, NAOMI M., mgr. pharm., Rush-Presbyterian-St. Luke's Medical Center, Chicago, IL '82
MARTIN, NORMAN H., proj. dir., Graduate Hospital, Philadelphia, PA '69 (ENG)
MARTIN, PAMELA A., dir. mktg. and pub. rel., Community Hospital of Lodi, Lodi, CA '85 (PR)
MARTIN, PATRICIA D., RN, asst. vice-pres. nrsg., St. Vincent's Medical Center, Jacksonville, FL '84 (NURS)
MARTIN, PATRICIA M., dir. pers., West Allis Memorial Hospital, West Allis, WI '86 (PERS)
MARTIN, PAUL, dir. eng., Columbia Hospital, Milwaukee, WI '79 (ENG)
MARTIN, PEGGY B., dir. qual. assur. and risk mgt., Children's Hospital, Boston, MA '82 (RISK)
MARTIN, PETER J., chief exec. off., Phoenix Memorial Hospital, Phoenix, AZ '73
MARTIN, PHILIP E., asst. adm. human res., Sch Entercorp, Houston, TX '72 (PERS)
MARTIN, RACHEL L., student, Georgia Institute of Technology, Atlanta, GA '86 (MGMT)
MARTIN, RICHARD E., sr. mgr., Peat, Marwick, Mitchell and Company, Raleigh, NC '84
MARTIN, RICHARD J., adm., St. Mary's Hospital, Leonardtown, MD '72
MARTIN, ROBERT D., mgr. sup., proc. and distrib., St. Francis Hospital, Wilmington, DE '83 (CS)
MARTIN, ROBERT L., atty., Centre Community Hospital, State College, PA '78 (ATTY)
MARTIN, ROGER S., atty., University of Virginia Hospitals, Charlottesville, VA '82 (ATTY)
MARTIN, ROXANNE N., dir. commun. rel., Englewood Community Hospital, Englewood, FL '85 (PR) (PLNG)
MARTIN, RUBY MAE, RN, dir. nrsg. serv., Ohio State University Hospitals, Columbus, OH '59 (NURS)
MARTIN, RUTH E., RN, dir. nrsg., Centre Community Hospital, State College, PA '71 (NURS)
MARTIN, SANDRA H., mgr., Coopers and Lybrand, Syracuse, NY '87 (AMB)
MARTIN, SHARON A., adm., Mercy Hospital, Baltimore, MD '82 (RISK)
MARTIN, STANLEY W., (ret.), Orilla, Ont., Canada '49 (LIFE)
MARTIN, STEVE, vice-pres. mktg., St. Luke's Health System, Phoenix, AZ '86 (PR)
MARTIN, SUSAN A., liason vol., Decatur County Memorial Hospital, Greensburg, IN '85 (VOL)
MARTIN, SUSAN ANNE, coor. pat. rel., Sutter Memorial Hospital, Sacramento, CA '83 (PAT)
MARTIN, TERRENCE F., (ret.), Caldwell, NJ '56 (ENG)(LIFE)
MARTIN, W. CARL, asst. exec. dir., East Jefferson General Hospital, Metairie, LA '79 (MGMT)
MARTIN, WILLA D., mgr. pur., Piggott Community Hospital, Piggott, AR '80 (PUR)
MARTIN, WILLARD G. JR., atty., Lakes Region General Hospital, Laconia, NH '74 (ATTY)
MARTIN, WILLIAM COLLIER SR., Pensacola, FL '55 (LIFE)
MARTIN, WILLIAM J., dir. commun., University Hospital, Augusta, GA '82 (ENG)
MARTINDELL, DONALD, plant eng., Chilton Memorial Hospital, Pompton Plains, NJ '86 (ENG)
MARTINE, JOHN, dir. food serv., Moses H. Cone Memorial Hospital, Greensboro, NC '79 (FOOD)
MARTINEAU, FAYE L., RN, dir. nrsg. serv., Placid Memorial Hospital, Lake Placid, NY '87 (NURS)
MARTINET, STEPHANIE A., dir. nutr. and food serv., Delaware County Memorial Hospital, Drexel Hill, PA '81 (FOOD)
MARTINEZ, EDWARD, student, Program in Health Care Administration, Baruch College, New York, NY '86
MARTINEZ, FERNANDO, mgr. pers. serv., Community Hospital, Munster, IN '86 (PERS)
MARTINEZ, FRAN, dir. risk mgt., Lutheran General Hospital, Park Ridge, IL '84 (RISK)
MARTINEZ, HENRY J., supv. soc. work, Audie L. Murphy Memorial Veterans Hospital, San Antonio, TX '85 (SOC)
MARTINEZ, JEANNE L., pat. rep., Medical College of Virginia Hospitals, Richmond, VA '82 (PAT)
MARTINEZ, JOSEPH, mgr. mktg. health maint., Blue Cross and Blue Shield, Cleveland, OH '80
MARTINEZ, LINDA M., atty., Washington University Medical School, St. Louis, MO '83 (ATTY)
MARTINEZ, MARY, dir. diet., Illini Hospital, Silvis, IL '80 (FOOD)
MARTINEZ, MAUREEN F., RN, dir. nrsg., Memorial Hospital, North Conway, NH '86 (NURS)
MARTINEZ, RENE C., dir. food and nutr. serv., AMI Riverside Hospital, Corpus Christi, TX '84 (FOOD)
MARTINEZ, ROBERTA E., mgr. commun., San Jose Hospital, San Jose, CA '81 (ENG)
MARTINEZ, ROLANDO T., asst. dir., Hartford Hospital, Hartford, CT '86 (SOC)
MARTINEZ, STEVE L., dir. pat. rel. and risk mgr., St. Mary-Corwin Hospital Center, Pueblo, CO '81 (RISK)
MARTINEZ, SUZANNE E., RN, mgr. nrsg., University of California Irvine Medical Center, Orange, CA '86 (NURS)
MARTINI, CHARLES C., pres., Martini Associates, Secane, PA '85 (PR)
MARTINI, DAVID M., atty., Albert Einstein Medical Center, Philadelphia, PA '86 (ATTY)
MARTINI, MICHAEL E., mgr. bldg. serv., Coney Island Hospital, Brooklyn, NY '86 (ENVIRON)
MARTINI, PAUL, dir. phys. plant oper., St. Joseph's Hospital Health Center, Syracuse, NY '81 (ENG)
MARTINICH, JANET, risk mgr., Louis A. Weiss Memorial Hospital, Chicago, IL '83 (RISK)
MARTINO, GRACE MARIE, dir. human res., Mercy Hospital, Rockville Centre, NY '77 (PERS)
MARTINO, MARGARET MCSHERRY, RN, asst. dir. nrsg., Beth Israel Medical Center, New York, NY '83 (NURS)
MARTINSON, CARL T., dir. mktg., Christian Health Services Development Corporation, St. Louis, MO '86 (PR) (PLNG)
MARTINSON, NORMAN L., (ret.), San Diego, CA '73 (ENG)
MARTINSON, REBECCA A., head diet., Mary Bridge Children Health Center, Tacoma, WA '74 (FOOD)
MARTINSON, STEVE, pur. agt., Quincy City Hospital, Quincy, MA '82 (PUR)
MARTISH, KENNETH R., mgr. environ. serv., Methodist Hospital, Mitchell, SD '80 (ENG)
MARTLING, ELLE L., asst. adm., Mount Airy Psychiatric Center, Denver, CO '85 (PERS)
MARTONCIK, THOMAS E., coor. soc. serv., Uniontown Hospital, Uniontown, PA '86 (SOC)
MARTSON, WILLIAM F., atty., Carlisle Hospital, Carlisle, PA '79 (ATTY)
MARTTALA, IRENE, RN, dir. qual. assur., Jameson Memorial Hospital, New Castle, PA '86 (RISK)
MARTUCCI, ERNEST A., Jeffersonville, PA '82 (ENG)
MARTUCCI, JOANNE BELL, prog. mgr. care unit, Hendrick Medical Center, Abilene, TX '86
MARTURANO, GERALDINE, dir. med. soc. serv., Mount Clemens General Hospital, Mount Clemens, MI '85 (SOC)
MARTURANO, MICHAEL C., sr. biomedical spec., St. Luke's Hospital, Duluth, MN '81 (ENG)
MARTYN, DOROTHY, RN, dir. nrsg., Somerville Hospital, Somerville, MA '71 (NURS)
MARTYNA, JOSEPH C., vice-pres., Falmouth Hospital, Falmouth, MA '81 (ENG)
MARUCA, WILLIAM H., atty., Mercy Hospital of Pittsburgh, Pittsburgh, PA '87 (ATTY)
MARVEL, RAY, dir. eng. and maint., Delta County Memorial Hospital, Delta, CO '84 (ENG)
MARVIN, BERNARD A. JR., dir. pub. rel., Cottage Hospital, Woodsville, NH '84 (PR) (PLNG)
MARVIN, ROBERT B., MD, adm. and chief exec. off., Hamilton County Memorial Hospital, Jasper, FL '87 (AMB)
MARX, KEVIN T., vice-pres. mktg. and plng., Katherine Shaw Bethea Hospital, Dixon, IL '78 (PR) (PLNG)
MARX, RICHARD C., dir. fin. and long range plng., Baptist Hospital of Miami, Miami, FL '81 (PLNG)
MARY, SR. TERESA, pres., Holy Cross Hospital, Chicago, IL '85
MARYLANDER, STUART J., pres., Cedars-Sinai Medical Center, Los Angeles, CA '64
MARYOL, GLADYS, RN, asst. adm., HCA Medical Center of Plano, Plano, TX '77 (RISK)
MARZOCCO, NICHOLAS J., adm., Lutheran Medical Center, St. Louis, MO '77
MASAR, DONALD WILLIAM, (ret.), Tucson, AZ '57 (LIFE)
MASCALI, DAVID, dir. food serv., Nesbitt Memorial Hospital, Kingston, PA '73 (FOOD)
MASCHEK, JOSEPH J., vice-pres. amb. care, Ingalls Family Care Center, Tinley Park, IL '87 (AMB)
MASCHGER, DAVID J., chief exec. off., Lee's Summit Community Hospital, Lees Summit, MO '83 (PLNG)
MASCHING, JO ANN M., dir. matl. mgt., Saint James Hospital, Pontiac, IL '83 (PUR)
MASCIA, FRANK C., dir. pers., Hospital of Saint Raphael, New Haven, CT '85
MASCITELLI, SUSAN, coor. pat. serv., Society of the New York Hospital, New York, NY '79 (PAT)
MASEK, TERRY, dir. pers., Illini Hospital, Silvis, IL '79 (PERS)(PR)
MASER, MAE JANE, dir. soc. serv., Delray Community Hospital, Delray Beach, FL '84 (SOC)
MASHBURN, LEWIS M., adm., Coffee Medical Center, Manchester, TN '85 (MGMT)
MASHBURN, PEGGY, mgt. eng., Hermann Hospital, Houston, TX '82 (MGMT)
MASHINSKI, JOHN J., dir. human resources, Geisinger Wyoming Valley Medical Center, Wilkes-Barre, PA '83 (PERS)
MASHNER, MARVIN, pres., Roxborough Memorial Hospital, Philadelphia, PA '81
MASIMILLA, JOHN P., asst. gen. dir., Albert Einstein Medical Center, Philadelphia, PA '86 (PLNG)(AMB)
MASINO, PATRICK J., dir. food serv., St. James Hospital Medical Center, Chicago Heights, IL '80 (FOOD)
MASKE, JOY Y., RN, dir. nrsg., Mercy Hospital, Iowa City, IA '81 (NURS)
MASLANKA, KATHLEEN M., dir. pub. rel., Cottage Hospital of Grosse Pointe, Grosse Pointe Farms, MI '85 (PR)
MASLOWSKI, WILLIAM M., pres., Project Development Construction, Inc., Milwaukee, WI '85 (PLNG)(ENG)
MASNICK, JEFFREY L., adm. fin., University of Pittsburgh Western Psychiatric Institute and Clinic, Pittsburgh, PA '75
MASON, ANN, adm. dir., Medical Center, Beaver Falls, PA '87 (AMB)
MASON, BEVERLY J., dir. commun. affairs, Mother Frances Hospital Regional Center, Tyler, TX '85 (PLNG)
MASON, CAROL C., dir. soc. serv., St. Mary's Hospital, Norton, VA '86 (SOC)
MASON, CHARLES H. JR., adm. and chief exec. off., Peninsula Hospital and Medical Center, Burlingame, CA '64
MASON, DARIA V., vice-pres. prof. serv., Central Vermont Hospital, Berlin, VT '81 (PLNG)
MASON, DEBBIE, dir. mktg., Martin Memorial Hospital, Stuart, FL '83 (PR)
MASON, ED, dir. environ. serv., Baptist Medical Center-Montclair, Birmingham, AL '86 (ENVIRON)
MASON, ETSIL S., dir. vol. serv., Pitt County Memorial Hospital, Greenville, NC '82 (VOL)
MASON, FLORENCE W., dir. food serv., Nanticoke Memorial Hospital, Seaford, DE '82 (FOOD)
MASON, FLOYD JR., sr. mgt. syst. eng., Humana Inc., Louisville, KY '80 (MGMT)
MASON, JAMES J., atty., Rehoboth McKinley Hospital, Gallup, NM '84 (ATTY)
MASON, JAMES K., adm., Jackson County Hospital, Scottsboro, AL '72
MASON, JOE M., arch. consult., Oklahoma State Department of Health, Oklahoma City, OK '83 (ENG)
MASON, KEVIN L., asst. dir. maint., Harding Hospital, Worthington, OH '86 (ENG)
MASON, LUCILLE P., dir. pers., Moss Rehabilitation Hospital, Philadelphia, PA '86 (PERS)
MASON, MARGARET D., RN, dir. nrsg., Kosciusko Community Hospital, Warsaw, IN '84 (NURS)
MASON, MARGARET E., asst. vice-pres. corp. educ., Bethesda Hospital, Inc., Cincinnati, OH '86 (EDUC)
MASON, MATTHEW C., dir. eng. mgt., Holmes Regional Medical Center, Melbourne, FL '85 (ENG)
MASON, PATRICIA T., dir. plng., mktg. and dev., Good Samaritan Hospital, Lexington, KY '82 (PLNG)
MASON, PATRICIA, dir. vol. serv., Abbott-Northwestern Hospital, Minneapolis, MN '73 (VOL)
MASON, REA RAE, coor. pat. rel., Midland Hospital Center, Midland, MI '78 (PAT)
MASON, RICHARD S., asst. adm. support serv., Western Reserve Systems-Northside, Youngstown, OH '79 (ENG)
MASON, CAPT. ROBERT J., MSC USA, chief health prof. recruiter, 3512th Recruiting Squadron, Westover AFB, MA '74
MASON, ROBERT STANLEY, exec. vice-pres., Scott and White Memorial Hospital, Temple, TX '52 (LIFE)

MASON, RUTH E., (ret.), Cleveland, OH '68 (SOC)
MASON, SCOTT A., pres., National Health Advisors, Ltd., McLean, VA '75 (PLNG)
MASON, SUSAN INGRID, student, Program in Hospital Administration, University of Minnesota School of Public Health, Minneapolis, MN '86
MASON, SUSAN L., RN, unit mgr. med. and surg., Ukiah Adventist Hospital, Ukiah, CA '87 (NURS)
MASON, THOMAS B. JR., dir. eng., Mercy Health Center, Oklahoma City, OK '80 (ENG)
MASON, WALTER E., asst. chief eng. and plant eng., Broward General Medical Center, Fort Lauderdale, FL '79 (ENG)
MASON, WILLIAM C., pres. and chief exec. off., Baptist Medical Center, Jacksonville, FL '86 (PLNG)
MASON, WILLIAM M., vice-pres. prog. dev., Sutter Community Hospitals, Sacramento, CA '86 (RISK)
MASONE, JOHN, dir. matl. mgt., Memorial Hospital at Easton Maryland, Easton, MD '83
MASS, DOROTHY JANE, RN, exec. dir. nrsg., James M. Jackson Memorial Hospital, Miami, FL '85 (NURS)
MASS, SHARON, dir. soc. serv., Western Medical Center, Santa Ana, CA '80 (SOC)
MASSA, ALBERT A., chief eng., AMI North Ridge Medical Center, Fort Lauderdale, FL '67 (ENG)
MASSA, ANNA MAE, RN, dir. cent. serv., Sacred Heart Hospital, Allentown, PA '82 (CS)
MASSA, ELIZABETH P. WOLFF, audio-visual coor., Bridgeport Hospital, Bridgeport, CT '73 (EDUC)
MASSA, GLADYS, RN, dir. nrsg., Community Memorial Hospital, Sturgis, SD '80 (NURS)
MASSAD, PETER, dir. pharm. serv. and risk mgt., Hahnemann Hospital, Boston, MA '87 (RISK)
MASSENGILL, ROBERT L., adm. res., Rex Hospital, Raleigh, NC '83
MASSER, PAUL G., asst. dir. risk mgt. and legal affairs, Greater Baltimore Medical Center, Baltimore, MD '85 (RISK)
MASSEY, ANNABELLE, dir. pub. rel. and advertising, All Saints Health Care, Inc., Fort Worth, TX '77 (PR)
MASSEY, BOBBY D., dir. bldg. and grds., Martha Washington Hospital, Chicago, IL '82 (ENG)
MASSEY, LCDR GEORGE CORT, MSC USA, med. adm. off., USS Carl Vinson Cvn-70, FPO San Francisco, CA '79
MASSEY, JOSEPH T. JR., coor. commun., Crawford Long Hospital Emory University, Atlanta, GA '78 (ENG)
MASSEY, ROBERT A., vice-pres., Providence Hospital, Washington, DC '77
MASSEY, TOM, dir. food serv., St. Mary's Hospital, Reno, NV '80 (FOOD)
MASSIE, LUCILLE, mgr. vol. serv., Nash General Hospital, Rocky Mount, NC '74 (VOL)
MASSMANN, ELMER O., Hayward, CA '40 (LIFE)
MASSOF, DEBORAH M., Bethel, CT '86 (ENG)
MASSON, STANLEY F., sr. mgt. consult., Orlando Regional Medical Center, Orlando, FL '49 (LIFE)
MASTA-GORNIC, VICKEY, dir. ins. and risk mgt., Albany Medical Center Hospital, Albany, NY '86 (RISK)
MASTANTUONO, ANTHONY C., dir. med. eng. lab., Strong Memorial Hospital Rochester University, Rochester, NY '84 (ENG)
MASTEJ, J. MICHAEL, exec. dir., Humana Hospital-Fort Walton Beach, Fort Walton Beach, FL '86
MASTEN, MARY, vice-pres. legal serv., Rushmore National Health Systems, Inc., Rapid City, SD '81 (ATTY)(RISK)
MASTERS, DONNA L., educ. spec., Maryland General Hospital, Baltimore, MD '85 (EDUC)
MASTERS, JOANN G., head nrs. day care, Stoughton Hospital Association, Stoughton, WI '87 (AMB)
MASTERS, PATRICIA A., dir. educ., North Broward Medical Center, Pompano Beach, FL '84 (EDUC)
MASTERSON, JAMES, dir. pub. rel., Union Hospital, Union, NJ '81 (PR)
MASTRANGELO, ANTHONY GEORGE, exec. dir., St. Anne's Hospital, Chicago, IL '64
MASTROIANNI, FRANK M., dir. safety, Memorial Hospital for Cancer, New York, NY '86 (ENG)
MASTROIANNI, MICHAEL D., dir. emp. rel., Saint Anthony Medical Center, Rockford, IL '86 (PERS)
MASTRORIO, PETER, pres., Communicare, Inc., North Miami Beach, FL '86 (ENG)
MATA, HOPE, supv. cent. serv., Woodland Memorial Hospital, Woodland, CA '77 (CS)
MATCHETTE, RICHARD A., mgr. sup., proc. and distrib., St. Joseph's Medical Center, South Bend, IN '83 (CS)
MATEER, WILLIAM G., atty., Holiday Hospital, Orlando, FL '75 (ATTY)
MATEICKA, BERNICE A., asst. dir. diet., Meriter Hospital, Madison, WI '68 (FOOD)
MATELIC, FREDERICK R., dir. hskpg., Outer Drive Hospital, Lincoln Park, MI '86 (ENVIRON)
MATESSINO, JOHN A., vice-pres. educ., Louisiana Hospital Association, Baton Rouge, LA '80 (EDUC)
MATEVISH, ROBERT A., dir. matl. mgt., Medical Center Hospital of Vermont, Burlington, VT '80 (PUR)
MATHEIN, J. DANIEL, exec. dir. pers. mgt. syst., Forest Hospital, Des Plaines, IL '80 (EDUC)
MATHEIS-KRAFT, CAROL E., RN, dir. nrsg., McKee Medical Center, Loveland, CO '84 (NURS)
MATHENA, BOB G., dir. plant eng., Lynchburg General Hospital, Lynchburg, VA '84 (ENG)
MATHENY, EDWARD T., atty., St. Luke's Hospital, Kansas City, MO '75 (ATTY)
MATHENY, LARRY DALE, vice-pres., St. Luke's Hospital West, Chesterfield, MO '76 (PLNG)
MATHERLEE, MICHAEL D., asst. adm., Southside Regional Medical Center, Petersburg, VA '86
MATHERLEE, THOMAS R., sr. vice-pres., Voluntary Hospitals of America, Wasington, DC '58 (LIFE)
MATHERLY, MARY, mgr. environ. serv., Ephraim McDowell Regional Medical Center, Danville, KY '86 (ENVIRON)
MATHERS, BRADLEY R., coor. claims, Sisters of Mercy Health Corporation, Southfield, MI '86 (RISK)
MATHES, ED, dir. plant oper., St. Anthony's Hospital, Amarillo, TX '87 (ENG)
MATHESIUS, JEANNE M., dir. pat. rep., St. Barnabas Medical Center, Livingston, NJ '75 (PAT)
MATHESON, CY R., dir. pers. and affirmative action off., North Carolina Memorial Hospital, Chapel Hill, NC '84 (PERS)
MATHESON, KAREN S., coor. vol. serv., Caulfield Hospital, Caulfield, Australia '86 (VOL)
MATHEWS, BYRON B. JR., atty., Cedars Medical Center, Miami, FL '78 (ATTY)
MATHEWS, DIANA S., RN, dir. nrsg., Rutland Regional Medical Center, Rutland, VT '80 (NURS)(AMB)
MATHEWS, GEORGE A., adm., Methodist Medical Center of Oak Ridge, Oak Ridge, TN '58
MATHEWS, JEANNE A., dir. vol. serv., HCA Doctors Hospital, Conroe, TX '82 (VOL)
MATHEWS, JOHN TED, American Hospital Association, Chicago, IL '79 (MGMT)
MATHEWS, PATRICIA A., coor. pat. and commun. health educ., Warren Hospital, Phillipsburg, NJ '78 (EDUC)
MATHEWS, THOMAS A., dir. pub. rel., Bessemer Carraway Medical Center, Bessemer, AL '81 (PR)
MATHEY, GAIL O., dir. diet., Dallas Rehabilitation Institute, Dallas, TX '81 (FOOD)
MATHIAS, ANN G., mgr. alterative syst., South Hills Health System, Pittsburgh, PA '82
MATHIAS, DAVID E., atty., Shands Teaching Hospital and Clinics, Gainesville, FL '81 (ATTY)
MATHIAS, ROSEMARY GERTY, Phoenix, AZ '84 (PLNG)
MATHIEN, ROBERT JOHN, vice-pres. sup. serv., Kennebec Valley Medical Center, Augusta, ME '77
MATHIES, SHIRLEY J., dir. pur., Cigna Health Plans of California, Los Angeles, CA '84 (PUR)
MATHIEU, MICHAEL, computer syst. dev. off., Armed Forces Institute of Pathology, Washington, DC '86
MATHIS, BETTY, mktg. and pub. rel. consult., Mathis and Bondurant, Fort Lauderdale, FL '65 (PR)
MATHIS, GALE, acct. exec., Myron F. Steves and Company, Houston, TX '82 (RISK)
MATHIS, L. J., maint. eng., Logan General Hospital, Logan, WV '78 (ENG)
MATHIS, LARRY L., pres. and chief exec. off., The Methodist Hospital, Houston, TX '84
MATHIS, MARK C. JR., dir. environ. and eng. serv., University of Iowa Hospitals and Clinics, Iowa City, IA '75 (ENG)
MATHIS, SALLY A., RN, dir. nrsg., University of Iowa Hospitals and Clinics, Iowa City, IA '80 (NURS)
MATILSKY, MARY LYNN, mgr. pat. rel., Cigna Healthplan of Arizona, Phoenix, AZ '86 (PAT)
MATISKA, LILLIAN R., dir. matl. mgt., Jeannette District Memorial Hospital, Jeannette, PA '62 (PUR)
MATNEY, DOUGLAS A., spec. proj., Manatee Memorial Hospital, Bradenton, FL '80 (MGMT)
MATOCHA, GEORGE R. JR., pres., Matocha Associates, Clarendon Hills, IL '83 (ENG)
MATONAK, NANCY L., coor. mktg., Hermann Hospital, Houston, TX '85 (PR) (PLNG)
MATORIN, SUSAN, dir. soc. work, Society of the New York Hospital, New York, NY '82 (SOC)
MATRICCIANI, ALBERT J. JR., atty., Johns Hopkins Hospital, Baltimore, MD '86 (ATTY)
MATRONE, JEANETTE SUSAN, RN, nrs. in chief, Miriam Hospital, Providence, RI '78 (NURS)
MATSIK, ALLISON, pat. rep., Saratoga Hospital, Saratoga Springs, NY '86 (PAT)
MATSON, KIMBERLY G., dir. mktg. and corp. plng., Northwest Community Hospital, Arlington Heights, IL '79 (PLNG)
MATSON, PATRICIA MICHELLE, coor. pat. asst. prog., Wellesley Hospital, Toronto, Ont., Canada '86 (PAT)
MATSUNAGA, GRACE, RN, dir. nrsg., New York City Health and Hospitals Corporation, New York, NY '77 (NURS)
MATSUNOBU, IRIS S. N., soc. worker, Maluhia Hospital, Honolulu, HI '86 (SOC)
MATTE, CORINNE C., coor. staff educ., Sudbury Memorial Hospital, Sudbury, Ont., Canada '84 (EDUC)
MATTE, MARILYN W., RN, dir. nrsg., Massachusetts Mental Health Center, Boston, MA '68 (NURS)
MATTE, MARY J., dir. nrsg., Muhlenberg Hospital Center, Bethlehem, PA '81 (NURS)
MATTEA, CHARLES L., asst. vice-pres., National Medical Enterprises, Santa Monica, CA '76 (MGMT)
MATTEI, DAVID S., exec. vice-pres., Mercy Hospital, Scranton, PA '73 (MGMT)
MATTEIS, ANDREW, coor. revenue bond prog., New York State Medical Care Facilities, New York, NY '85
MATTEN, MARLENE R., dir. educ., Memorial Hospital, Carbondale, IL '82 (EDUC)
MATTERN, DEAN, dir. pers., St. Joseph's Hospital, Minot, ND '71 (PERS)
MATTERN, THOMAS D., mgr. facil. and supt. phys. plant, UCLA Center for the Health Sciences, Los Angeles, CA '80 (ENG)
MATTESON, BARBARA, assoc. dir. human res., Long Island Jewish Medical Center, New York, NY '86 (PERS)
MATTESON, BARBARA, coor. pub. rel., Crawford Memorial Hospital, Robinson, IL '86 (PR)
MATTHEI, EDWARD H., partner, Matthei and Colin Architect-Engineers, Chicago, IL '76
MATTHESON, JANICE KINDER, dir. mktg. and pub. affairs, Bon Secours Hospital of Methuen, Methuen, MA '86 (PR)
MATTHEWS, COL. CHARLES D., MSC USA, chief nrs., U. S. Army Hospital, Atlanta, GA '73
MATTHEWS, CHRISTOPHER J., coor. med. soc. work, AMI Frye Regional Medical Center, Hickory, NC '86 (SOC)
MATTHEWS, CINDY B., dir. mktg., Baylor Institute for Rehabilitation, Dallas, TX '85 (PR)
MATTHEWS, DAVID B., asst. dir. pur., Kennestone Regional Health Care Systems, Marietta, GA '85 (PUR)
MATTHEWS, DONALD M., food serv. dir., Good Shepherd Medical Center, Longview, TX '83 (FOOD)
MATTHEWS, ELEANOR G., dir. vol. serv., Symmes Hospital, Arlington, MA '85 (VOL)
MATTHEWS, FRANCES M., supv. diet., Wagner General Hospital, Palacios, TX '79 (FOOD)
MATTHEWS, HELEN R., dir. pub. rel., Lutheran Medical Center, Wheat Ridge, CO '80 (PR)
MATTHEWS, JAKE, dir. vol., Moore Municipal Hospital, Moore, OK '80 (VOL)
MATTHEWS, JEAN A., educ. consult., Archbishop Bergan Mercy Hospital, Omaha, NE '86 (EDUC)
MATTHEWS, LORRAINE E., dir. food serv., Philadelphia Nursing Home, Philadelphia, PA '84 (FOOD)
MATTHEWS, LYNNE H., dir. pub. rel., Doctors Hospital, Little Rock, AR '81 (PR)
MATTHEWS, M. EILEEN, PhD, prof. food serv. adm., University of Wisconsin-Madison, Department of Fd Sciences, Madison, WI '71 (FOOD)
MATTHEWS, MARNEL, dir. guest rel., Community Memorial Hospital, Toms River, NJ '85 (EDUC)
MATTHEWS, MICHAEL B., vice-pres. corp. plng., Akron City Hospital, Akron, OH '82 (PLNG)
MATTHEWS, PAMELA V., mgt. eng., DeKalb General Hospital, Decatur, GA '83 (MGMT)
MATTHEWS, PATRICIA A., mgr. prod. mktg., Nellcor, Inc., Hayward, CA '85 (RISK)
MATTHEWS, PHIL E., vice-pres., Arkansas Hospital Association, Little Rock, AR '84
MATTHEWS, ROBERT C., supv. cent. sup., Albany Medical Center Hospital, Albany, NY '83 (CS)
MATTHEWS, ROBERT J., exec. vice-pres., Northern Ocean Hospital System, Point Pleasant, NJ '73
MATTHEWS, SCOTT D., health planner, Swedish Health Systems, Englewood, CO '85 (PLNG)
MATTHEWS, WILLIAM E., dir. gen. serv., Tampa General Hospital, Tampa, FL '73
MATTHEWS, WILLIAM G., dir. facil., Pittsburgh Board of Education, Pittsburgh, PA '74 (ENG)
MATTHEWS, WILLIAM T., dir. facil., Bethany Hospital, Chicago, IL '82 (ENG)
MATTHIAS, HAROLD, dir. eng., Commonwealth Hospital, Fairfax, VA '85 (ENG)
MATTHYS, ALVIN A., dir. plant oper., Gulf Coast Medical Center, Wharton, TX '68 (ENG)
MATTINGLY, FRANK H., asst. adm., Arlington Hospital, Arlington, VA '75
MATTLEMAN, BARBRA, adm. coor., Albert Einstein Medical Center, Philadelphia, PA '84
MATTOCKS, RON, dir. res. prod. dept., Center for Health Affairs, Princeton, NJ '84 (PR)
MATTOON, COLLEEN Y., mgr. food serv., Queen of Angels Medical Center, Los Angeles, CA '86 (FOOD)
MATTOON, ELLEN K., mgr. matl., McMinnville Community Hospital, McMinnville, OR '82 (PUR)
MATTOON, PETER M., atty., Temple University Hospital, Philadelphia, PA '77 (ATTY)
MATTOS, CHARLENE A., coor. vol., Children's Hospital at Stanford, Palo Alto, CA '84 (VOL)
MATTSON, CHRISTOPHER W., atty., Barley, Synder, Cooper and Barber, Lancaster, PA '82 (ATTY)
MATTSON, GLENN A., dir. plant oper., St. John's Hospital, Red Wing, MN '81 (ENG)
MATTSON, JUDITH W., pres., Judith Mattson Incorporated, Bethesda, MD '85
MATTSON, LUCILLE B., dir. matl. and food serv., Mount Sinai Medical Center, Milwaukee, WI '79 (FOOD)(PUR)
MATTSON, PATRICIA SHAFFER, dir. vol., Mesabi Regional Medical Center, Hibbing, MN '85 (VOL)
MATTSON, PHYLLIS, RN, dir. cent. sup., Sacred Heart Hospital, Eau Claire, WI '74 (CS)
MATTSON, WAYNE, mgr. matl., Hartford Memorial Hospital, Hartford, WI '81 (PUR)
MATUSH, JOANNE E., Mayfield Heights, OH '72 (FOOD)
MATUSHAK, NICKI A., student, University of North Carolina, Chapel Hill, NC '86
MATUSZAK, BARBARA K., dir. cent. serv., Massapequa General Hospital, Seaford, NY '84 (CS)
MATUSZEWSKI, KARL, adm. asst., Sheridan Road Hospital, Chicago, IL '86
MATZ, KAREN KISIOLEK, student, Program in Hospital and Health Care Administration, University of Minnesota, Minneapolis, MN '83
MATZ, THOMAS C., dir. pers., Muskegon General Hospital, Muskegon, MI '86 (PERS)
MATZA, JACK, dir. food serv., New Rochelle Hospital Medical Center, New Rochelle, NY '81 (FOOD)
MATZNER, GARY C., atty., Cedars Medical Center, Miami, FL '75 (ATTY)
MAUDIN, BEVERLY A., educ. instr., St. Anthony Medical Center, Crown Point, IN '83 (EDUC)
MAUER, GEORGE W., assoc. adm. and dir. human res., Cedars-Sinai Medical Center, Los Angeles, CA '71 (PERS)
MAUFORT, PATRICIA, dir. vol., St. Vincent Hospital, Green Bay, WI '80 (VOL)
MAUGHAN, KERRY, dir. biomedical, St. Joseph Regional Medical Center, Lewiston, ID '86 (ENG)
MAUL, GEORGE, dir. eng., Community Hospital of Western Suffolk, Smithtown, NY '86 (ENG)
MAULDIN, DAVID J., dir. pur., Kennestone Hospital, Marietta, GA '80 (PUR)
MAULDIN, DIANE, dir. soc. work serv., Shands Hospital, Gainesville, FL '86 (SOC)
MAULE, JANET G., mgr. customer serv., mktg. and pub. rel., Multicare Medical Center, Tacoma, WA '85 (PR)
MAULE, JOHN R., dir. plant oper., Burgess Memorial Hospital, Onawa, IA '84 (ENG)
MAULL, JILL E., RN, asst. dir. pat., Northside Hospital, Atlanta, GA '81 (NURS)
MAUPIN, ALYCE M., risk mgr., West Nebraska General Hospital, Scottsbluff, NE '82 (RISK)
MAUPIN, HOLLI, coor. pers., Russell City Hospital, Russell, KS '85 (PERS)
MAURAIS, EDWARD A., mgr. food serv., Henrietta D. Goodall Hospital, Sanford, ME '84 (FOOD)

MAUREL, KATHLEEN C., dir. human res., Northwest Hospital, Seattle, WA '86 (PERS)
MAURER, EDITH S., RN, asst. adm., Joint Township District Memorial Hospital, St. Marys, OH '73 (NURS)
MAURER, SR. ELERNORA MARIE, dir. vol., St. Mary's Hospital, Streator, IL '86 (VOL)
MAURER, LYNN H., dir. pers. and safety, Fairmont General Hospital, Fairmont, WV '75 (ENG)
MAURER, MICHAEL P., prin., Maurer and Associates, Dublin, CA '73 (PLNG)
MAURER, NANCY S., dir. vol. serv., St. Joseph's Medical Center, South Bend, IN '82 (VOL)
MAURER, ROBERT J., adm., Hospital of Philadelphia College of Osteopathic Medicine, Philadelphia, PA '84
MAURER, ROBERT PAUL JR., sr. assoc., Herman Smith Associates, Hinsdale, IL '74 (PLNG)
MAURER, ROBERT T., sr. consult., Flr Health Resources, Irving, TX '86 (PLNG)
MAURER, WILLIAM P., dir. pub. rel., Mercy Hospital Medical Center, Des Moines, IA '86 (PR)
MAURICE, LESLIE E., RN, consult., SunHealth, Marietta, GA '86 (MGMT)
MAURO, ANTHONY E., dir. soc. work, Children's Hospital of Philadelphia, Philadelphia, PA '77 (SOC)
MAURO, BEATRICE, asst. dir. nrsg., Bronx-Lebanon Hospital Center, Fulton Division, Bronx, NY '68
MAURO, LAURA K., dir. pur., Community Hospital of Bedford, Bedford, OH '85 (PUR)
MAURO, MICHAEL A., dir. plant serv., AMI Anclote Manor Psychiatric Hospital, Tarpon Springs, FL '80 (ENG)
MAUSZYCKI, JAMES E., dir. food serv., Lester E. Cox Medical Centers, Springfield, MO '74 (FOOD)
MAUTZ, ROBERT K., sr. mgr., Deloitte Haskins and Sells, Chicago, IL '77 (PLNG)
MAVROVIC, LESLEE NYMAN, dir. soc. work, Jewish Institute for Geriatric Care, New Hyde Park, NY '86 (SOC)
MAWDSLEY, JAMES J., chief elec. eng., New York Hospital, New York, NY '83 (ENG)
MAWHORTER, TERRY E., dir. pers., Bethesda Hospital, Zanesville, OH '83 (PERS)
MAXAM, JOYCE, health serv. consult., American Medical International, Houston, TX '85 (PLNG)
MAXCY, MARY ALICE, supv. pat. rep., Cigna Healthplan of Arizona, Phoenix, AZ '84 (PAT)
MAXFIELD, M. MAUREEN, dir. educ., Sisters of Charity Health Care Systems, Cincinnati, OH '86 (EDUC)
MAXWELL, CAROL FRAZIER, mgr. soc. work, Methodist Medical Center, Dallas, TX '85 (SOC)
MAXWELL, CAROL HALL, dir. soc. serv., Glens Falls Hospital, Glens Falls, NY '82 (SOC)
MAXWELL, CLYDE E. JR., adm., South Fulton Hospital, East Point, GA '70
MAXWELL, DONALD G., mgr. biomedical serv., Heritage Health Management Corporation, Rockford, IL '85 (ENG)
MAXWELL, DONNA M., dir. vol. serv., Good Samaritan Hospital, Cincinnati, OH '80 (VOL)
MAXWELL, KAREN F., compensation analyst, St. Francis-St. George Hospital, Cincinnati, OH '84 (PERS)
MAXWELL, KATHRYN A., dir. pers., All Saints Episcopal Hospital, Fort Worth, TX '86 (PERS)
MAXWELL, MARY C., adm. diet. and asst. dir., Deaconess Hospital, St. Louis, MO '81 (FOOD)
MAXWELL, RICHARD B. III, vice-pres. oper., Alamance County Hospital, Burlington, NC '76
MAXWELL, ROBERT A., atty., St. Joseph Mercy Hospital, Pontiac, MI '74 (ATTY)
MAY, BOB G., dir. maint. and eng., Williamson Appalachian Regional Hospital, South Williamson, KY '66 (ENG)
MAY, CAROL A. HENDERSON-LE, dir. human res., Family Health Program Hospital, Fountain Valley, CA '79 (PERS)
MAY, CURTIS H., mgr. pur., Holy Cross Hospital, Chicago, IL '82 (PUR)
MAY, DOROTHY M., dir. matl. mgt., Centre Community Hospital, State College, PA '72 (PUR)
MAY, EDDIE, dir. plant eng., Fort Sanders Regional Medical Center, Knoxville, TN '80 (ENG)
MAY, GREG, dir. environ. serv., Pomerado Hospital, Poway, CA '86 (ENVIRON)
MAY, J. JOEL, PhD, Titusville, NJ '62 (MGMT)
MAY, JEAN B., dir. pub. rel., Mississippi Baptist Medical Center, Jackson, MS '78 (PR)
MAY, KATHRYN ANN, pat. rep., Arkansas Children's Hospital, Little Rock, AR '85 (PAT)
MAY, LINNEA S., student, University of Illinois School of Public Health, Chicago, IL '83
MAY, MAURICE I., chief exec. off., Hebrew Rehabilitation Center for Aged, Boston, MA '58
MAY, MERIL A. JR., consult., Christian and Timbers, Inc., Cleveland, OH '83
MAY, TIMOTHY, health syst. spec., Veterans Administration, Department of Medicine and Surgery Western Regional, San Francisco, CA '84
MAY, WANDA KEYSER, mgt. eng., Spartanburg Regional Medical Center, Spartanburg, SC '79 (MGMT)
MAYBAUM, ELIZABETH A., dir. diet., McKee Medical Center, Loveland, CO '86 (FOOD)
MAYBERRY, C. KEITH, risk mgr. spec. proj., Bay Medical Center, Bay City, MI '83 (RISK)
MAYER, CHRISTINE R., Wellesley, MA '80 (ATTY)
MAYER, DONALD A., dir. pers., Portsmouth Regional Hospital, Portsmouth, NH '77 (PERS)
MAYER, F. ROBERT, dir. publicity, Morristown Memorial Hospital, Morristown, NJ '80 (PR)
MAYER, GLORIA G., RN, faculty, University of Phoenix, Costa Mesa, CA '86 (NURS)
MAYER, JAMES A. II, Chicago, IL '83 (FOOD)
MAYER, JAMES J., Ligonier, PA '51 (LIFE)
MAYER, JEAN M., sr. consult., Brighton Consulting Group, Salt Lake City, UT '81 (PLNG)
MAYER, JOYCE S., dir. mktg. and dev., Metroplex Hospital, Killeen, TX '86 (PR)
MAYER, LEONARD, exec. dir., Medifac Architects, Inc., Alexandria, VA '76 (PLNG)
MAYER, LINDA J., dir. programming and hosp. rel., Princeton American Communications Corporation, Princeton, NJ '85 (EDUC)
MAYER, SUSAN MADERIOUS, mgr. mktg., Cleveland Clinic Foundation, Cleveland, OH '86 (PLNG)
MAYERCIK, STEPHANIE, RN, asst. adm. pat. serv., St. Margaret Hospital, Hammond, IN '80 (NURS)
MAYERS, HAROLD J., Washington, DC '46 (LIFE)
MAYERS, M. VIRGINIA, dir. vol. serv., Swedish Medical Center, Englewood, CO '79 (VOL)
MAYERS, MARY LOU, atty., Greater Southeast Community Hospital, Washington, DC '83 (ATTY)
MAYERSOHN, ALISON RUDOLPH, Seal Beach, CA '80 (PR)
MAYES, ELMER S., chief bldg. mgt. serv., Veterans Administration Medical Center, Bath, NY '86 (ENVIRON)
MAYEWSKI, JOAN, RN, vice-pres. nrsg., Woonsocket Hospital, Woonsocket, RI '86 (NURS)
MAYEWSKI, RAYMOND, MD, dir. emer. serv., Strong Memorial Hospital Rochester University, Rochester, NY '87 (AMB)
MAYFIELD, BARBARA K., dir. diet., Henry General Hospital, Stockbridge, GA '82 (FOOD)
MAYFIELD, JANA F., dir. pers. serv., Mother Frances Hospital Regional Center, Tyler, TX '81 (PERS)
MAYFIELD, MARTHA N., RN, nrsg. consult., NKC Management, Louisville, KY '86 (NURS)
MAYFIELD, MARTINE J., asst. dir. food and nutr. serv., Hampton General Hospital, Hampton, VA '85 (FOOD)
MAYHEW, MELINDA L., Washington, DC '86 (MGMT)
MAYHILL, JOE, chief eng., Everett A. Gladman Memorial Hospital, Oakland, CA '86 (ENVIRON)
MAYNARD, BENITA D., asst. dir. vol., Baptist Hospital of Miami, Miami, FL '87 (ATTY)
MAYNARD, DERRILL B., dir. matl. mgt., South County Hospital, Wakefield, RI '82 (CS)(PUR)
MAYNARD, GARY D., MD, vice-pres. med. affairs, Bronson Healthcare Group, Inc., Kalamazoo, MI '84
MAYNE, WILLIAM R., assoc. adm., Rutland Regional Medical Center, Rutland, VT '69
MAYO, ALEX T. JR., atty., Alliance Health System, Norfolk, VA '75 (ATTY)
MAYO, CHARLES M., dir. commun., Forrest County General Hospital, Hattiesburg, MS '84 (PR)
MAYO, JIM L., vice-pres., Baptist Memorial Hospital, Gadsden, AL '81 (PLNG)
MAYO, ROBERT W., dir. pers., American International Hospital, Zion, IL '81 (PERS)
MAYO, STEPHEN, adm. mgr. telecommun., University of Michigan, Ann Arbor, MI '86 (ENG)
MAYOR, SHERMAN B., atty., Desert Springs Hospital, Las Vegas, NV '85 (ATTY)
MAYS, BARBARA F., asst. dir. adm. diet., Christ Hospital, Cincinnati, OH '84 (FOOD)
MAYS, BILL, asst. exec. dir., Presbyterian Hospital of Dallas Extended Care Facility, Dallas, TX '81
MAYS, DELORSE, dir. risk mgt., Regional Medical Center at Memphis, Memphis, TN '85 (RISK)
MAYS, TINA, nrs. anes. instr., Charity Hospital at New Orleans, New Orleans, LA '83
MAYSENT, H. W., pres., Rockford Memorial Hospital, Rockford, IL '52 (LIFE)
MAYWORM, DANIEL E., pres., Mayworm Associates, Inc., Libertyville, IL '78 (CS)
MAZAK, MARK E., vice-pres. plng., Melrose-Wakefield Hospital, Melrose, MA '83 (PLNG)
MAZAR-ROBERTS, DIANE MARY, dir. educ. and trng., Hospital of Saint Raphael, New Haven, CT '85 (EDUC)
MAZER, ROBERT E., atty., St. Vincent's Medical Center, Jacksonville, FL '82 (ATTY)
MAZIE, LISA BETH, student, University of Colorado, Denver, CO '86
MAZUR, JOHN R., atty., St. Mary's Hospital, Saginaw, MI '77 (ATTY)
MAZUR, JOSEPH L. R., mgr. mgt. info. syst. and plng., Ohio Department of Mental Health and Mental Retardation, Columbus, OH '55 (LIFE)
MAZUR, ROBERT A., dir. pers. adm., Elizabeth General Medical Center, Elizabeth, NJ '86 (PERS)
MAZUREK, PRISCILLA M., RN, asst. dir. nrsg., Metropolitan Hospital and Health Centers, Detroit, MI '84 (NURS)
MAZZA, LEON S., adm. off., U. S. Air Force Hospital, Tucson, AZ '76
MAZZIE, SANDRA A., RN, dir. pat. care serv., St. Francis Hospital, Poughkeepsie, NY '85 (NURS)
MAZZOLA, PATRICIA A., RN, actg. chm. nrsg., Memorial Hospital for Cancer, New York, NY '82 (NURS)
MAZZOLLA, D. PATRICK, sr. vice-pres. corp. and shared serv., Hospital Association of Pennsylvania, Camp Hill, PA '71 (MGMT)
MAZZONE, MARGARET C., atty., Hospital Corporation of America, Nashville, TN '83 (ATTY)
MAZZONE, MARY ANN, asst. dir. support serv. and risk mgt., Manhattan Eye, Ear and Throat Hospital, New York, NY '86 (RISK)
MAZZOTTA, BRUNO R., dir. risk mgt., St. Louis University, St. Louis, MO '81 (RISK)
MAZZULLA, WILLIAM, dir. safety, Brooklyn Hospital-Caledonian Hospital, Brooklyn, NY '86 (ENVIRON)
MCADAMS, ALAN, consult., Lerch Bates Hospital Group, Inc., Fairfax, VA '76 (PUR)
MCADAMS, JEAN M., RN, dir. med. and surg. nrsg., Providence Hospital, Mobile, AL '80 (NURS)
MCADOO, CAROL A., dir. pat. rel., University of Kansas Hospital, Kansas City, KS '84 (PAT)
MCAFEE, JAMES T. JR., exec. vice-pres., Charter Medical Corporation, Macon, GA '69
MCAFEE, THOMAS J., student, Xavier University, Graduate Program in Hospital and Health Administration, Cincinnati, OH '87
MCAFOOSE, RAYMOND CHARLES, adm., New England Baptist Hospital, Boston, MA '68
MCALEE, RICHARD G., atty., University of Maryland Medical Systems, Baltimore, MD '87 (ATTY)
MCALILEY, ALEXANDER, pres., North Hills Passavant Hospital, Pittsburgh, PA '50 (LIFE)
MCALISTER, ELIZABETH Z., dir. plng. and mktg., Columbia Hospital for Women Medical Center, Washington, DC '84 (PLNG)
MCALISTER, JAMES G., vice-pres. mktg. and dev., Treatment Centers of America, Arcadia, CA '84 (PR)
MCALISTER, RODGER REID, dir. const, St. Thomas Hospital, Nashville, TN '68 (ENG)
MCALLESTER, SPEARS L., clin. eng., Erlanger Medical Center, Chattanooga, TN '86 (ENG)
MCALLISTER, DANITA C., adm., U. S. Air Force Regional Hospital, Eglin AFB, FL '83
MCALLISTER, DENNIS M., RN, assoc. dir. nrsg., Memorial Hospital, Hollywood, FL '84 (NURS)
MCALLISTER, J. ROBERT III, atty., Arlington Hospital, Arlington, VA '84 (ATTY)
MCALLISTER, NANCY, RN, dir. cent. decontamination proc. and distrib., Lenox Hill Hospital, New York, NY '78 (CS)
MCALONEY, CAROLE LYNN, RN, dir. environ. serv., St. Charles Hospital and Rehabilitation Center, Port Jefferson, NY '80 (CS)(ENVIRON)
MCALPINE, CHRISTOPHER A., dir. risk mgt., Health Northeast, Manchester, NH '84 (RISK)
MCALPINE, LINDA L., coor. vol., St. Nicholas Hospital, Sheboygan, WI '84 (VOL)
MCANDREW, MICHAEL K., pres., Flaget Memorial Hospital, Bardstown, KY '80
MCANELLY, MARVIN L., mgr. matl., Baptist Memorial Hospital-Union City, Union City, TN '81 (PUR)
MCANINCH, MARLENE C., coor. educ., Willamette Falls Hospital, Oregon City, OR '86 (EDUC)
MCARDLE, MICHAEL J., chief fin. off., Luther Hospital, Eau Claire, WI '72 (MGMT)
MCARDLE, MICHAEL K., RN, dir. nrsg., Julia L. Butterfield Memorial Hospital, Cold Spring, NY '85 (NURS)
MCARTHUR, JOHN R., atty., Health Care and Retirement Corporation, Lima, OH '85 (ATTY)
MCATEE, JANE A., atty., University of Chicago Hospitals, Chicago, IL '85 (ATTY)
MCAULIFFE, BEVERLY, mgr. environ. serv., New England Sinai Hospital, Stoughton, MA '87 (ENVIRON)
MCAULIFFE, ROBERT E., vice-pres., Barnes Hospital, St. Louis, MO '72 (RISK)
MCAULIFFE, WILLIAM FRANCIS, dir. pat. spec. serv., Harbor View Medical Center, San Diego, CA '82 (SOC)
MCAVOY, ELSA C., dir. pat. rep., Burke Rehabilitation Center, White Plains, NY '84 (PAT)
MCAVOY, WILLIAM H., dir. health care mgt. consult. serv., Coopers and Lybrand, Syracuse, NY '85 (PLNG)
MCBARNETTE, LORNA H., dep. comr. oper., New York State Department of Health, Albany, NY '80
MCBEATH, GRETCHEN, atty., Riverside Methodist Hospitals, Columbus, OH '83 (ATTY)
MCBEE, LUCY B., dir. vol. serv., Church Hospital Corporation, Baltimore, MD '76 (VOL)
MCBETH, ANNETTE J., RN, dir. nrsg., Lake Region Hospital and Nursing Home, Fergus Falls, MN '85 (NURS)
MCBETH, SYLVIA M., dir. mktg. and commun. rel., Cheshire Medical Center, Keene, NH '85 (PR) (PLNG)
MCBRIDE, ANDREW F. III, atty., St. Mary's Hospital, Passaic, NJ '80 (ATTY)
MCBRIDE, AUDREY P., RN, dir. nrsg., Day Kimball Hospital, Putnam, CT '73 (NURS)
MCBRIDE, BARRY SR., mgr. matl., Wadsworth-Rittman Hospital, Wadsworth, OH '85 (PUR)
MCBRIDE, BETTY, dir. med. info. syst., Muskogee Regional Medical Center, Muskogee, OK '86 (RISK)
MCBRIDE, BRENDA B., RN, clin. dir. women and children's serv., Moses H. Cone Memorial Hospital, Greensboro, NC '86 (NURS)
MCBRIDE, JAMES W. JR., pres., The Meade Company, Inc., Topeka, KS '86 (RISK)
MCBRIDE, JAN, vice-pres. oper., Toledo Hospital, Toledo, OH '79 (NURS)
MCBROOM, RON D., asst. adm., Takoma Adventist Hospital, Greeneville, TN '84 (PERS)
MCBRYDE, KELLY E., adm., Transmed, Nashville, TN '82
MCCABE, SR. DANIEL MARIE, adm., St. Joseph Medical Center, Stamford, CT '62
MCCABE, GRACE, adm. govt. rel., Blue Cross Blue Shield of Greater New York, New York, NY '86
MCCABE, JACK H., adm. res., Harris Methodist -Fort Worth, Fort Worth, TX '83
MCCABE, JAMES L., facil. eng., Gallup Indian Medical Center, Gallup, NM '86 (ENG)
MCCABE, JEFFREY C., Reston Hospital Center, Reston, VA '84 (ENG)
MCCABE, JIM, mgr. telecommun., Edward W. Sparrow Hospital, Lansing, MI '85 (ENG)
MCCABE, KATHERINE A., loss prevention consult., Michigan Hospital Association Service Corporation, Lansing, MI '86 (ENVIRON)
MCCABE, KATHERINE KUNDRAT, network mgr., Children's Hospital and Medical Center, Seattle, WA '84 (PLNG)
MCCABE, SUSAN A., mgr. amb. serv., Notre Dame Hospital, Central Falls, RI '87 (AMB)
MCCAFFERTY, DONALD N., energy mgt. eng., Methodist Hospital-Central Unit, Memphis, TN '85 (ENG)
MCCAGH, BRIAN E., dir. mktg., Health Management Strategies, Inc., Washington, DC '86
MCCAIN, LEONARD, asst. dir., University of Connecticut Health Center, Farmington, CT '87 (RISK)
MCCAIN, LINN H., atty., Hospital Corporation of America, Nashville, TN '85 (ATTY)
MCCAIN, MAVIS B., dir. food serv., Southeast Alabama Medical Center, Dothan, AL '80 (FOOD)
MCCAIN, SANDRA E., RN, pat. educ. coor., Morristown Memorial Hospital, Morristown, NJ '84 (EDUC)
MCCALEB, W. BRENT, adm. fellow, Memorial Care System, Houston, TX '87
MCCALL, ANN K., RN, dir. nrsg., Eastwood Hospital, Memphis, TN '81 (NURS)

MCCALL, BILLY G., dep. exec. dir. and sec., Duke Endowment, Charlotte, NC '55 (LIFE)
MCCALL, CAROLYN, mgr. proc., Henrietta Egleston Hospital, Atlanta, GA '83 (CS)
MCCALL, FRED A., dir. med. rec., Bloomsburg Hospital, Bloomsburg, PA '84
MCCALL, KAREN A., mgt. analyst, Carraway Methodist Medical Center, Birmingham, AL '84 (MGMT)
MCCALL, LEWIS GROVER, dir. plant oper., Santa Barbara Cottage Hospital, Santa Barbara, CA '78 (ENG)(ENVIRON)
MCCALL, RAYMOND, coor. constr., Southwest Community Health Services, Albuquerque, NM '87 (ENG)
MCCALL, WALTER J., vice-pres. mktg. and sales, Ppo Alliance, Cypress, CA '84 (PLNG)
MCCALLAN, KATHLEEN F., dir. soc. serv., Suburban General Hospital, Pittsburgh, PA '85 (SOC)
MCCALLIE, THOMAS SPENCER, exec. vice-pres., Community Hospital of Roanoke Valley, Roanoke, VA '62
MCCALLIG, PATRICK E., dir. pub. rel., St. Margaret Hospital, Hammond, IN '86 (PR) (PLNG)
MCCALLISTER, PAUL E., dir. soc. serv., Putnam General Hospital, Hurricane, WV '85 (SOC)
MCCALLUM, CHARLES E., atty., Blodgett Memorial Medical Center, Grand Rapids, MI '83 (ATTY)
MCCALLUM, HERBERT M., sr. health planner, North Carolina Health Planning and Development Agency, Raleigh, NC '59
MCCALLUM, NEIL D., arch., Henningson, Durham and Richardson, Alexandria, VA '78
MCCALLUM, PATRICIA J., proj. mgr., HCA North Okaloosa Medical Center, Crestview, FL '82 (PR)
MCCALLUM, W. EDWARD JR., dir. adm. serv., Wake County Alcoholism Treatment Center, Raleigh, NC '85
MCCALPIM, BILL, dir. plant oper. and maint., Henderson Memorial Hospital, Henderson, TX '86 (ENG)
MCCALPIN, JAMES F., dir. pur., Faith Hospital Association, St. Louis, MO '86 (PUR)
MCCAMEY, TOM, vice-pres. pers., Baptist Medical Center, Little Rock, AR '81 (PERS)
MCCAMMITT, J. RUSSELL, vice-pres. sales, Contract Cleaners Supply, Inc., West Conshohocken, PA '86 (ENVIRON)
MCCAMPBELL, SUZANNE B., dir. commun. serv., Loudon County Memorial Hospital, Loudon, TN '80 (SOC)(PR)
MCCAMPBELL, WILLIAM B., dir. plant, St. Patrick Hospital, Missoula, MT '75 (ENG)
MCCAN, CHARLES D., asst. vice-pres. bldg. serv., Freehold Area Hospital, Freehold, NJ '81 (ENG)
MCCAN, GLADYS L., RN, dir. oper. and recovery room serv., Lovelace Medical Center, Albuquerque, NM '84 (NURS)
MCCANDLESS, FLORENCE R., RN, mgr. clin. care nrsg., Wyandotte General Hospital, Wyandotte, MI '82 (NURS)
MCCANDLISH, THOMAS W., atty., Johnston-Willis Hospital, Richmond, VA '81 (ATTY)
MCCANN, CAPT. CARL JOHN, MSC USAF, San Antonio, TX '79
MCCANN, GARY THOMAS, adm., Kenny Michigan Rehabilitation Foundation, Southfield, MI '86
MCCANN, JACK C., mgr. maint. and eng., Frank Cuneo Memorial Hospital, Chicago, IL '81 (ENG)
MCCANN, MARILYN G., mgt. eng., St. Luke's-Roosevelt Hospital Center, New York, NY '87 (MGMT)
MCCANN, THOMAS J., dir. food and nutr., Bronx Municipal Hospital Center, Bronx, NY '80 (FOOD)
MCCANNA, DAVID E., clin. eng., Trumbull Memorial Hospital, Warren, OH '80 (ENG)
MCCANNA, HENRY A. III, dir. soc. serv., North Kansas City Hospital, North Kansas City, MO '70 (SOC)
MCCANNON, LTJG CHARLES E., MSC USN, adm. off. and dir. ancillary serv., Naval Hospital, Bethesda, MD '86
MCCANSE, THAD C., atty., St. John's Regional Medical Center, Joplin, MO '78 (ATTY)
MCCANTS, LEONARD L., atty., District of Columbia General Hospital, Washington, DC '81 (ATTY)
MCCARNEY, JUNE, pat. rep., University of Iowa College of Dentistry, Iowa City, IA '80 (PAT)
MCCARROLL, EDWIN P., oper. analyst, Medical College of Ohio Hospital, Toledo, OH '84 (MGMT)
MCCART, JOYCE S., RN, chief cent. sterile, Rockdale Hospital, Conyers, GA '83 (CS)
MCCARTER, MARILYN F., dir. surg. nrsg., William Beaumont Hospital, Royal Oak, MI '84 (PLNG)
MCCARTHY, AGNES D., RN, coor. educ., St. Mary's Hospital, Waterbury, CT '77 (EDUC)
MCCARTHY, BENNETT J., chm. and chief exec. off., Blue Cross and Blue Shield of Michigan, Detroit, MI '40 (LIFE)
MCCARTHY, SR. CELESTINE, atty., Sisters of Charity of St. Joseph's, Emmitsburg, MD '68 (ATTY)
MCCARTHY, CHRISTOPHER J., mgr. trng. and dev., Hahnemann University Hospital, Philadelphia, PA '71 (EDUC)
MCCARTHY, DENNIS J., dir. pub. rel., Sisters of Charity Hospital, Buffalo, NY '85 (PR) (PLNG)
MCCARTHY, EDWARD D., atty., Cambridge Hospital, Cambridge, MA '75 (ATTY)
MCCARTHY, ELIZABETH A., RN, vice-pres. pat. care serv., Saint Vincent Hospital, Worcester, MA '86 (NURS)
MCCARTHY, EUGENE L., staff assoc., Applied Management Systems, Inc., Burlington, MA '84 (MGMT)
MCCARTHY, JAMES E., dir. pers., Saint Vincent Hospital, Billings, MT '83 (PERS)
MCCARTHY, JEANNE M., dir. educ. serv., Kennestone Regional Health Care Systems, Marietta, GA '82 (EDUC)
MCCARTHY, JOSEPH B., dir. alternative delivery syst., Daughters of Charity Health Systems, St. Louis, MO '79 (PLNG)
MCCARTHY, KATHLEEN A., Ochsner Foundation Hospital, New Orleans, LA '83 (PERS)
MCCARTHY, KATHLEEN H., adm. res., Strong Memorial Hospital of the University of Rochester, Rochester, NY '86 (PLNG)
MCCARTHY, KEVIN JOHN, atty., Suburban Hospital, Bethesda, MD '79 (ATTY)
MCCARTHY, LAURENCE R., PhD, Baltimore, MD '84
MCCARTHY, LINDA A., dir. telecommun., Park Ridge Hospital, Rochester, NY '81 (ENG)
MCCARTHY, MANDY L., dir. mktg., Sacred Heart Service Network, Milwaukee, WI '86 (PR)
MCCARTHY, MARLENE F., coor. commun. outreach, Columbia Hospital, Milwaukee, WI '86 (PR)
MCCARTHY, MARY A., vice-pres. and dir. health serv. group, Hamilton, Carver and Lee, Chicago, IL '86 (PR)
MCCARTHY, MARY KATHERINE, RN, dir. nrsg. prac., Skokie Valley Hospital, Skokie, IL '78 (NURS)
MCCARTHY, MARY P., dir. spec. proj., Marian Health Center, Sioux City, IA '85 (VOL)
MCCARTHY, MICHAEL J., atty., Great Plains Regional Medical Center, North Platte, NE '83 (ATTY)
MCCARTHY, MICHAEL S., atty., Lutheran General Health Care Systems, Park Ridge, IL '81 (ATTY)
MCCARTHY, MILLIE M., dir. soc. serv., Braintree Hospital, Braintree, MA '82 (SOC)
MCCARTHY, NANCY, dir. telecommun., Multicare Medical Center, Tacoma, WA '84 (ENG)
MCCARTHY, NANCY, student, St. John's University, Jamaica, NY '85
MCCARTHY, PATRICIA J., asst. dir. proc., University of Wisconsin Hospital and Clinics, Madison, WI '83 (CS)
MCCARTHY, PATRICIA R., dir. corp. pub. rel. and commun. affairs, Henry Ford Hospital, Detroit, MI '75 (PR) (PLNG)
MCCARTHY, SHEILA M., RN, dir. nrsg., George Washington University Hospital, Washington, DC '76 (NURS)
MCCARTHY, TERRANCE O., dir. matl. mgt., McLaren General Hospital, Flint, MI '70 (PUR)
MCCARTNEY, FRANK H., atty., Fleming County Hospital, Flemingsburg, KY '80 (ATTY)
MCCARTNEY, LOIS F., dir. soc. serv., Butler Hospital, Providence, RI '82 (SOC)
MCCARTNEY, MARILYN L., pres., Marvik Educational Services, Inc., San Diego, CA '85 (EDUC)
MCCARTNEY, MICHAEL J., atty., St. Francis Medical Center, Breckenridge, MN '80 (ATTY)
MCCARTY, LUCILLE C., RN, vice-pres. nrsg., Saint Vincent Health Center, Erie, PA '82 (NURS)
MCCARTY, WILLIAM L., atty., Piedmont Hospital, Atlanta, GA '86 (ATTY)
MCCASKEY, AARON, RN, Enid, OK '68 (NURS)
MCCASKILL, LINDA ANN WELLINGTON, First Hospital-Milwaukee, Milwaukee, WI '82
MCCASKILL, RICHARD H. JR., vice-pres. mktg., Hospital Corporation of America, Nashville, TN '79 (PLNG)
MCCASLAND, COL. NICKEY, MSC USA, Hqda, Dasg-Psq, Falls Church, VA '70 (RISK)
MCCASLINE, GLADYS T., dir. food serv., St. Mary's Hospital, Brooklyn, NY '80 (FOOD)
MCCAUGHEY, MARCIA E., RN, asst. adm. nrsg., Skokie Valley Hospital, Skokie, IL '74 (NURS)
MCCAUGHEY, PATRICIA E., dir. food serv., Calvin Manor, Des Moines, IA '83 (FOOD)
MCCAUGHEY, TERENCE R., dir. matl., St. Mary Hospital, Quincy, IL '82 (PUR)
MCCAUL, MARGARET T., qual. assur. consult., Marsh and McLennan, Inc., San Francisco, CA '82 (RISK)
MCCAULEY, JEANETTE M., RN, org. dev. consult., Milwaukee County Mental Health, Milwaukee, WI '86 (NURS)
MCCAULEY, NELLE R., dir. vol. serv., Greenville Memorial Hospital, Greenville, SC '77 (VOL)
MCCAULEY, PATRICIA E., dir. food serv., Roosevelt Hospital, New York, NY '70 (FOOD)
MCCAULEY, PATRICIA, asst. dir. nrsg. serv. and clin. dir. psych. nrsg., Cedars-Sinai Medical Center, Los Angeles, CA '84 (NURS)
MCCAULEY, ROBERT F., dir. supv. cent. serv., King Fahad Hospital, Riyadh, Saudi Arabia '85 (CS)
MCCAULEY, WILLIAM, vice-pres. staff serv., Church Charity Foundation of Long Island, Hempstead, NY '64 (PERS)
MCCAUSLAND, MAUREEN P., RN, vice-pres. psych.-mental health nrsg., University Hospitals of Cleveland, Cleveland, OH '83 (NURS)
MCCAUSLIN, JOHN RAY, MSC USAF, APO New York, NY '79
MCCHESNEY, EVELYN C., atty., Department of Health and Human Services, Seattle, WA '84 (ATTY)
MCCLAIN, BETTIE SUITT, dir. food serv., John D. Archbold Memorial Hospital, Thomasville, GA '80 (FOOD)
MCCLAIN, MARY, coor. staff dev., Akron General Medical Center, Akron, OH '76 (EDUC)
MCCLAIN, MILDRED ARDELLA, Tucson, AZ '79 (SOC)
MCCLAIN, PAT, coor. pat. rel., Methodist Hospital-Central Unit, Memphis, TN '84 (PAT)
MCCLANAHAN, S. A., sr. vice-pres. nrsg., Grant Medical Center, Columbus, OH '86 (NURS)
MCCLARY, ANN E. RYAN, mgr. pub. rel., Bloomington Hospital, Bloomington, IN '85 (PR)
MCCLATCHEY, DENNIS L., sr. vice-pres., Baptist Medical Center, Kansas City, MO '81 (PLNG)
MCCLAVE, CAPT. CHRISTOPHER C., MSC USAF, Department of Air Force Medical Service, Bolling AFB, DC '84 (PLNG)
MCCLEARY, BOYD T., asst. dir. matl. mgt., University of Michigan Hospitals, Ann Arbor, MI '83 (PUR)
MCCLEARY, RICHARD C., pres., Mulhauser, McCleary Associates, Inc., Houston, TX '76 (FOOD)
MCCLELLAN, NORMAN, vice-pres., Marsh and McLennan, Waterford, MI '85 (RISK)
MCCLELLAN, REGAN A., RN, mgr. nrsg. serv. and qual. assur., Hospital Corporation of America, Nashville, TN '85 (NURS)
MCCLELLAND, KELLY L., atty., Baptist Medical Center, Kansas City, MO '85 (ATTY)
MCCLELLAND, KERMIT J., proj. dir., New England Baptist Hospital, Boston, MA '71 (ENG)
MCCLELLAND, MRS. L. D., dir. vol. serv., Texas Children's Hospital, Houston, TX '76 (VOL)
MCCLELLAND, MARY R., RN, dir. nrsg., Parma Community General Hospital, Parma, OH '77 (NURS)
MCCLENAHAN, EDWARD W., dir. eng. serv., Mercy Hospital, Muskegon, MI '86 (ENG)
MCCLENAHAN, JANE NOBBE, administrative asst. medicine, Grant Hospital of Chicago, Chicago, IL '85 (PLNG)
MCCLENDON, ROBERTA, RN, supv. cent. serv., Wichita General Hospital, Wichita Falls, TX '85 (CS)
MCCLERNON, SUSAN E., student, Graduate in Hlthcare Administration, University of Minnesota, Duluth, MN '86
MCCLINTOCK, LINDA J., student, University of Wisconsin, Milwaukee, WI '86 (PR)
MCCLINTOCK, STEPHEN, dir., National Institute Cardiovascular Technology, Newport Beach, CA '85
MCCLINTOCK, WILLIAM T., adm., Schick Shadel Hospital, Fort Worth, TX '61
MCCLOSKEY, LYNNE C., mgr. cardiology and neuro-pulmonary serv., St. Mary's Health Services, Grand Rapids, MI '86
MCCLOSKEY, NANCY N., publications coor., City of Hope National Medical Center, Duarte, CA '85 (PR)
MCCLOUD, RON, mgr. risk mgt., Norwegian-American Hospital, Chicago, IL '81 (RISK)
MCCLURE, CLAIRE W., RN, asst. dir. nrsg., Magic Valley Regional Medical Center, Twin Falls, ID '86 (NURS)
MCCLURE, ELAINE M., RN, asst. dir. nrsg. adm., Jewish Hospital of St. Louis, St. Louis, MO '84 (NURS)
MCCLURE, GAIL BENTLEY, coor. pat. rel., W. A. Foote Memorial Hospital, Jackson, MI '85 (PAT)
MCCLURE, GEORGANN, dir. vol. serv., Children's Hospital, St. Paul, MN '81 (VOL)
MCCLURE, HUGH A., atty., Washington Hospital, Washington, PA '82 (ATTY)
MCCLURE, KENNETH E., dir. environ. serv., Novato Community Hospital, Novato, CA '78 (ENVIRON)
MCCLURE, LAURIE G., pur. agt., Parry Sound General Hospital, Parry Sound, Ont., Canada '67 (PUR)
MCCLURE, MARGARET L., RN EdD, exec. dir. nrsg., New York University Medical Center, New York, NY '75 (NURS)
MCCLURE, WILLIAM G. III, atty., Retreat Hospital, Richmond, VA '82 (ATTY)
MCCLURG, CATHY A., dir. pers., Golden Plains Community Hospital, Borger, TX '86 (PERS)
MCCLUSKEY, GERTRUDE K., dir. commun., vol. and admit., Nashville Memorial Hospital, Madison, TN '70 (VOL)
MCCLUSKEY, MARGARET, dir. diet., St. Mary's Hospital, Saginaw, MI '70 (FOOD)
MCCLUSKY, D. O. JR., Gulf Shores, AL '76 (LIFE)
MCCLUTCHY, JUDITH A., RN, Wauwatosa, WI '85 (NURS)
MCCOLLUM, JOSEPH D. JR., atty., Idaho Hospital Association, Boise, ID '78 (ATTY)
MCCOLLUM, W. ERNIE, pres., Emcol, Atlanta, GA '80 (RISK)
MCCOMB, JOHNELLE FOLEY, exec. dir., Minnesota Associates of Public Teaching Hospitals, St. Paul, MN '73
MCCOMB, JOYCE, risk mgr., Northwest Community Hospital, Arlington Heights, IL '85 (RISK)
MCCOMB, TRUDI G., dir. food and nutr. serv., Beverly Glen Hospital, Los Angeles, CA '84 (FOOD)
MCCOMBER, MICHAEL, syst. analyst, Notre Dame Hospital, Montreal, Que., Canada '71 (MGMT)
MCCOMBS, MIKE W., supv. eng. and security, Clearview Hospital, Midland, TX '86 (ENG)
MCCONACHIE, AUDREY N., dir. pub. rel., St. Mary Hospital, Livonia, MI '85 (PR)
MCCONAHEY, THOMAS M., coor. dev. and trng., Alton Mental Health Center, Alton, IL '79 (EDUC)
MCCONDRA, JEANNE, RN, asst. dir. home health serv., John C. Lincoln Hospital and Health Center, Phoenix, AZ '87 (AMB)
MCCONE, ERNIE, dir. matl. mgt., Humber Memorial Hospital, Toronto, Ont., Canada '86 (PUR)
MCCONNEL, CAROL S., RN, dir. surg. serv., East Tennessee Baptist Hospital, Knoxville, TN '84 (AMB)
MCCONNELL, CAROL P., dir. soc. work, St. Mary of Nazareth Hospital Center, Chicago, IL '85 (SOC)
MCCONNELL, CHARLES R., vice-pres. emp. affairs, Genesee Hospital, Rochester, NY '81 (PERS)
MCCONNELL, JANE CARROLL, vice-pres. risk mgt., Fojp Service Corporation, New York, NY '83 (RISK)
MCCONNELL, JERRY R., dir. qual. assur. and risk mgt., Northeast Georgia Medical Center, Gainesville, GA '82 (RISK)
MCCONNELL, MARY C., dir. res. and dev., Bronson Methodist Hospital, Kalamazoo, MI '85 (PLNG)
MCCONNELL, NICHOLAS S., atty., Greater Southeast Community Hospital, Washington, DC '84 (ATTY)
MCCONNELL, RICHARD O., mgr. matl., East Alabama Medical Center, Opelika, AL '85 (PUR)
MCCONNELL, SUE A., RN, asst. adm. and dir. nrsg., Chicago Osteopathic Medical Center, Chicago, IL '86 (NURS)
MCCONNELL, THOMAS D., vice-pres., Suburban General Hospital, Pittsburgh, PA '74
MCCONVILLE, JAMES J., dir. food serv., John T. Mather Memorial Hospital, Port Jefferson, NY '81 (FOOD)
MCCONVILLE, LT. KELLY J., MSC USN, head mgt. info., Naval Hospital, Long Beach, CA '86 (MGMT)
MCCOOEY, TIMOTHY ALEXANDER, dir. risk mgt., Millard Fillmore Hospital, Buffalo, NY '83 (RISK)
MCCORD, JESTENE, RN, corp. dir. nrsg., St. Luke's Samaritan Health Care, Inc., Milwaukee, WI '85 (NURS)
MCCORD, JOHN P., atty., Good Samaritan Hospital of Pottsville, Pennsylvania, Pottsville, PA '68 (ATTY)
MCCORD, NORMA J., dir. human res., Southwest Medical Center, Liberal, KS '83 (PR)
MCCORKLE, ROBERT, dir. eng., Rebsamen Regional Medical Center, Jacksonville, AR '85 (ENG)
MCCORKLE, SALLY J., dir. vol. serv., Stevens Memorial Hospital, Edmonds, WA '85 (VOL)
MCCORMACK, DANIEL J., adm. asst. and chief exec. off. staff serv., The Methodist Hospital, Houston, TX '85
MCCORMACK, JOHN JOSEPH, exec. dir., Cary Medical Center, Caribou, ME '65
MCCORMACK, KATHLEEN, pres., Health Services Development, Marietta, GA '84 (PR)
MCCORMACK, MARK A., dir. support serv., Vanderbilt Children and Adolescent Psychiatric Hospital, Nashville, TN '86 (ENG)

MCCORMICK, ALVIN R., dir. plant oper., McLeod Regional Medical Center, Florence, SC '85 (ENG)
MCCORMICK, CAROL A., asst. dir. clin. data and pat. serv., Good Samaritan Hospital and Health Center, Dayton, OH '86 (SOC)
MCCORMICK, DANIEL ERNEST, dir. plng. and spec. proj., St. Anthony Medical Center, Columbus, OH '83 (PR) (PLNG)
MCCORMICK, EDWARD G., atty., Fairview Hospital, Great Barrington, MA '80 (ATTY)
MCCORMICK, JERRY L., vice-pres. pers. serv., St. Francis Hospital, Milwaukee, WI '76 (PERS)
MCCORMICK, LELIA M., dir. pub. rel., Montgomery Regional Hospital, Blacksburg, VA '78 (PR)
MCCORMICK, RICHARD C., dir. phys. plant, Hurley Medical Center, Flint, MI '78 (ENG)
MCCORMICK, RICHARD M., RN, asst. adm., Hinds General Hospital, Jackson, MS '80 (NURS)
MCCORMICK, RUTH S., mgr. wage and salary, St. Luke's-Roosevelt Hospital Center, New York, NY '86 (PERS)
MCCORMICK, SANDRA J., asst. adm. commun. serv., La Crosse Lutheran Hospital, La Crosse, WI '76 (SOC)
MCCORMICK, VICTORIA S., RN, vice-pres. nrsg., Trinity Memorial Hospital, Cudahy, WI '83 (NURS)
MCCORMICK, WETZEL, adm., Illinois Masonic Medical Center, Warren Barr Pavilion, Chicago, IL '67 (PERS)
MCCORMICK, WILLIAM F. JR., Geisinger Wyoming Valley Medical Center, Wilkes-Barre, PA '81 (ENG)
MCCORMICK, WILLIAM J., atty., Healthmark Corporation, Pittsburgh, PA '79 (ATTY)
MCCORRISTIN, BARBARA, assoc. dir. pub. rel., Zurbrugg Memorial Hospital, Riverside, NJ '86 (PR)
MCCOURT, JOHN, dir. plant oper. and maint., St. Mary's Hospital, Streator, IL '85 (ENG)
MCCOY, BRUCE A., asst. plant eng., Cambridge Hospital, Cambridge, MA '83 (ENG)
MCCOY, CAROLYN J., mgr. pers. serv., Burnham Hospital, Champaign, IL '85 (PERS)
MCCOY, GEORGE H., chief exec. off., Erie County Medical Center, Buffalo, NY '73
MCCOY, GERALDINE A., dir. educ. and trng., Kaiser Foundation Hospital, Martinez, CA '85 (EDUC)
MCCOY, JANICE M., RN, vice-pres. nrsg. serv., Proctor Community Hospital, Peoria, IL '81 (NURS)
MCCOY, L. KENT, pres., Huntington Memorial Hospital, Huntington, IN '84
MCCOY, LAURA E., plng. and mktg. spec., Halifax Hospital Medical Center, Daytona Beach, FL '86 (PLNG)
MCCOY, MARY, dir. vol., Seton Medical Center, Daly City, CA '71 (VOL)
MCCOY, PAUL, chief eng., Reading Hospital and Medical Center, Reading, PA '81 (ENG)
MCCOY, REBECCA K., dir. vol. serv., Delray Community Hospital, Delray Beach, FL '86 (VOL)
MCCOY, SHARON, dir. amb. care, Medical Plaza Hospital, Fort Worth, TX '87 (AMB)
MCCOY, VIRGINIA H., mgr. cent. serv., Lexington County Hospital, West Columbia, SC '85 (CS)
MCCRACKEN, JOHN B., atty., St. Mary's Hospital, West Palm Beach, FL '86 (ATTY)
MCCRACKEN, W. M., RN, adm. nrsg. serv., Williamsburg Community Hospital, Williamsburg, VA '79 (NURS)
MCCRACKEN, WILLIAM EDWARD II, RN, vice-pres. pat. care serv., Medical Center East, Birmingham, AL '77 (NURS)
MCCRACKIN, WILLIAM H., consult., Houston, TX '78 (ENG)
MCCRADY, CATHLEEN E., mktg. rep., Normandy Osteopathic Medical Center, St. Louis, MO '85 (PLNG)
MCCRARY, ELIZABETH H., dir. vol. serv., Rex Hospital, Raleigh, NC '72 (VOL)
MCCRARY, THERESA, dir. cent. serv., Alachua General Hospital, Gainesville, FL '86 (PUR)
MCCRAW, MARGARET ANN, dir. soc. work and discharge plng., St. Agnes Hospital, Baltimore, MD '86 (SOC)
MCCRAY, STEPHEN S., atty., Good Samaritan Hospital, San Jose, CA '83 (ATTY)
MCCREADY, CATHRYN S., asst. adm., University of Michigan Hospitals, Ann Arbor, MI '82 (MGMT)
MCCREARY, SALLY M., RN, chief nrsg. serv., Veterans Administration Medical Center, St. Cloud, MN '83 (NURS)
MCCRICKARD, RUBY A., RN, sr. vice-pres., Lynchburg General-Marshall Lodge Hospitals, Lynchburg, VA '73 (NURS)
MCCRIMMON, JANICE A., coor. staff dev., Charter North Hospital, Anchorage, AK '86 (EDUC)
MCCRONE, RICHARD A., chief eng. serv., Louis A. Johnson Veterans Administration Medical Center, Clarksburg, WV '84 (ENG)
MCCRORY, NORA M., coor. pub. rel., Magee Rehabilitation Hospital, Philadelphia, PA '83 (PR)
MCCRORY, ROB, dir. telecommun., Samaritan Health Service, Phoenix, AZ '86 (ENG)
MCCUE, JEAN, dir. dev. and mktg., Abraham Lincoln Memorial Hospital, Lincoln, IL '72 (PR)
MCCUE, THOMAS, head hskpg., Rutland Heights Hospital, Rutland, MA '86 (ENVIRON)
MCCUISTION, PEG O., exec., Hospice of Southeastern Michigan, Southfield, MI '69
MCCULLAR, CHARLOTTE C., student, Texas Woman's University, Denton, TX '86 (FOOD)
MCCULLAR, FRANCES MAXINE, dir. soc. work serv., Hamilton Medical Center, Dalton, GA '84 (SOC)
MCCULLOCH, JAYANNA, dir. educ., St. Vincent Infirmary, Little Rock, AR '75 (EDUC)
MCCULLOCH, PATRICIA M., risk mgr., Geisinger Wyoming Valley Medical Center, Wilkes-Barre, PA '84 (RISK)
MCCULLOCH, WAYNE B., dir. environ. serv., Chester County Hospital, West Chester, PA '86 (ENVIRON)
MCCULLOUGH, CHRISTINE, nrs. mgr., St. Luke's Hospital, Chesterfield, MO '86 (AMB)
MCCULLOUGH, JACQUELINE, supv. cent. sup., Freehold Area Hospital, Freehold, NJ '85 (CS)
MCCULLOUGH, JOHNNY L., dir. plant eng., John L. Hutcheson Memorial Tri-City Hospital, Fort Oglethorpe, GA '85 (ENG)
MCCULLOUGH, MARGARET M., dir. plng., St. Agnes Hospital, Fond Du Lac, WI '86 (PLNG)
MCCULLOUGH, MARK A., bio-environ. eng., U. S. Air Force Hospital, Plattsburgh, NY '86 (ENG)
MCCULLOUGH, MARY L., dir. vol. serv., University of Tennessee Memorial Hospital, Knoxville, TN '80 (VOL)
MCCULLOUGH, TERRY M., chief manpower staff and trng. br., Headquarters Military Airlift, Scott AFB, IL '79
MCCULLY, BILL H., dir. plant eng., Springdale Memorial Hospital, Springdale, AR '77 (ENG)
MCCULLY, JANET B., dir. vol. serv., Harborview Medical Center, Seattle, WA '84 (VOL)
MCCULLY, MARY E., dir. pers., Springdale Memorial Hospital, Springdale, AR '81 (PERS)
MCCULLY, THOMAS R., atty., Lafayette Home Hospital, Lafayette, IN '83 (ATTY)
MCCUNE, FRANK B., MD, chief exec. off., Serve-U-Home Health Agency, Jackson, MS '86 (AMB)
MCCUNE, JAMES A., dir. plng., University Medical Center, Tucson, AZ '81 (PLNG)
MCCUNE, RUSSELL, head pur., St. Mary's Hospital, Galesburg, IL '86 (PUR)
MCCUNE, SUSAN E., asst. dir. plng. and mktg., Hahnemann University Hospital, Philadelphia, PA '85 (PLNG)
MCCUNE, WILLIAM, asst. vice-pres., Lankenau Hospital, Philadelphia, PA '81 (PLNG)
MCCURDY, ROBERT A., dir. eng. and maint., Hutzel Hospital, Detroit, MI '86 (ENG)
MCCURDY, ROBERT CLARK, atty., Lee Memorial Hospital, Fort Myers, FL '76 (ATTY)
MCCURDY, ROBERT K., atty., Mercy Hospital, Portsmouth, OH '74 (ATTY)
MCCURRY, SPENCER L., mgr. adm. serv., Kaiser Permanente, Pasadena, CA '82 (MGMT)
MCCUTCHEON, HUGH, atty., Trinity Medical Center, Minot, ND '80 (ATTY)
MCCUTCHEON, STEPHANIE S., assoc. vice-pres. corp. strategic plng. and prog. dev., Sisters of Mercy Health Corporation, Farmington Hills, MI '84 (PLNG)
MCCUTCHON, FRANCES, mgr., Systemetric, Inc., Santa Barbara, CA '83 (PLNG)
MCDADE, RITA, coor. pat. care, Grossmont District Hospital, La Mesa, CA '86 (RISK)
MCDANIEL, ANN B., dir. diet., Seventh Ward General Hospital, Hammond, LA '85 (FOOD)
MCDANIEL, BARBARA L., RN, dir. nrsg., Story City Memorial Hospital, Story City, IA '82 (NURS)
MCDANIEL, BRANDY, dir. ped. soc. work, Duke University Hospital, Durham, NC '86 (SOC)
MCDANIEL, CAMILLUS DUANE, RN, dir. in-service educ., Val Verde Memorial Hospital, Del Rio, TX '84 (EDUC)
MCDANIEL, DIANE, RN, dir. soc. serv., Valley Hospital and Medical Center, Spokane, WA '83 (SOC)
MCDANIEL, G. MICHAEL, partner, Coopers and Lybrand, Des Moines, IA '80
MCDANIEL, JANE B., dir. staff dev., St. Bernard's Regional Medical Center, Jonesboro, AR '76 (EDUC)
MCDANIEL, JIM, dir. spec. serv., Cape Coral Hospital, Cape Coral, FL '87 (AMB)
MCDANIEL, JOANNE W., dir. mktg. and commun., Hughston Sports Medicine Hospital, Columbus, GA '81 (PR)
MCDANIEL, LEE G., vice-pres. and chief fin. off., King's Daughters' Medical Center, Ashland, KY '85
MCDANIEL, NANCY L., adm., U. S. Air Force Hospital, Holloman AFB, NM '78
MCDANIEL, RUSSELL L., adm., Memorial Hospital, Craig, CO '86 (PERS)
MCDANIEL, SHEILA D., dir. mktg. serv., Memorial Medical Center of Jacksonville, Jacksonville, FL '86 (PR)
MCDANIEL, STEPHEN W., atty., Good Shepherd Medical Center, Longview, TX '81 (ATTY)
MCDANIELS, DIANE B., dir. soc. serv., Newcomb Medical Center, Vineland, NJ '79 (SOC)
MCDAVID, SALLY, atty., Blue Cross and Blue Shield of Mississippi, Jackson, MS '71 (ATTY)
MCDERMID, WILLIAM B., dir. matl. mgt., Bon Secours Hospital, Baltimore, MD '83 (PUR)
MCDERMOTT, BRIAN J., chief oper. off., Abraham Lincoln Memorial Hospital, Lincoln, IL '84 (RISK)
MCDERMOTT, CAROLE, RN, vice-pres. nrsg. serv., LaGuardia Hospital, Flushing, NY '75 (NURS)
MCDERMOTT, JOSEPH, dir. bldg. and grd., Human Resource Institute, Brookline, MA '86 (ENVIRON)
MCDERMOTT, THOMAS E., atty., Cottage Grove Hospital, Cottage Grove, OR '82 (ATTY)
MCDEVITT, EDWARD J., vice-pres. mgt. info. syst., Easton Hospital, Easton, PA '77 (MGMT)
MCDIARMID, ROY W., bd. pres., Beverly Hospital, Montebello, CA '70
MCDILL, LOREE VERMILLE, sr. instr. educ., Southern Baptist Hospital, New Orleans, LA '83 (EDUC)
MCDONAGH, KATHRYN J., RN, asst. adm., Saint Joseph's Hospital, Atlanta, GA '84 (NURS)
MCDONALD-SMITH, MARILYN, mgr. corp. commun., Good Samaritan Hospital and Medical Center, Portland, OR '84 (PR)
MCDONALD, BRIAN K., proj. coor. strategic plng., Hospital Corporation of America, Nashville, TN '84 (PLNG)
MCDONALD, BRIAN, dir. soc. work, Children's Seashore House, Atlantic City, NJ '80 (SOC)
MCDONALD, SR. CATHLEEN M., dir. soc. serv., Mercy Hospital, Portland, ME '85 (SOC)
MCDONALD, CHARLES E., mgr. internal audit, The Methodist Hospital, Houston, TX '86 (MGMT)
MCDONALD, DENISE YERDON, dir. med. soc. work, Sinai Hospital of Detroit, Detroit, MI '80 (SOC)
MCDONALD, DIANE M., RN, vice-pres. pat. care serv., Lowell General Hospital, Lowell, MA '84 (NURS)
MCDONALD, DONNA J., vice-pres., Manatee Memorial Hospital, Bradenton, FL '83
MCDONALD, FRANCIS L., asst. dir. plant oper., Mobile Infirmary Medical Center, Mobile, AL '83 (ENG)
MCDONALD, IONA B., dir. vol. serv., Phoenix Children's Hospital, Phoenix, AZ '85 (VOL)
MCDONALD, ISOBEL A., RN, vice-pres. nrsg., Sisters of Charity Hospital, Buffalo, NY '86 (NURS)
MCDONALD, JOHN J., adm., Schuyler Hospital, Montour Falls, NY '80 (PLNG)
MCDONALD, JOSEPH D., sr. vice-pres., St. Mary's Medical Center, Knoxville, TN '86
MCDONALD, JOSEPH D., dir. food serv., Sancta Maria Hospital, Cambridge, MA '74 (FOOD)
MCDONALD, JOSEPH, vice-pres., Wilkes-Barre General Hospital, Wilkes-Barre, PA '80 (ENG)
MCDONALD, KAREN R., sr. mgt. syst. eng., University of Massachusetts Medical Center, Worcester, MA '86 (MGMT)
MCDONALD, KENNETH J., atty., Management Science Association, Kansas City, MO '74 (ATTY)
MCDONALD, KENNETH W., plant eng., Terrell State Hospital, Terrell, TX '81 (ENG)
MCDONALD, KEVIN R., dir. plng., Akron City Hospital, Akron, OH '85 (PLNG)
MCDONALD, LOIS M., soc. serv. worker, Kennewick General Hospital, Kennewick, WA '80 (SOC)
MCDONALD, MAUREEN, assoc. vice-pres. pub. affairs, Roger Williams General Hospital, Providence, RI '81 (PR)
MCDONALD, MICHAEL L., chief outpatient adm. serv., U. S. Naval Hospital, FPO New York, NY '75
MCDONALD, NEIL J., PhD, exec. dir., Area Health Education Center, Wilmington, NC '64
MCDONALD, PAULA A., dir. mktg. and sales support serv., Cycare Practice Management, East Meadow, NY '86 (PLNG)
MCDONALD, ROBERT J., dir. emp. rel., Frankford Hospital, Torresdale Division, Philadelphia, PA '73 (PERS)
MCDONALD, ROY, bd. chm., Blue Cross-Blue Shield of Tennessee, Chattanooga, TN '65 (HON)
MCDONALD, SUE, RN, dir. cont. educ., Good Samaritan Hospital and Health Center, Dayton, OH '80 (EDUC)
MCDONALD, THOMAS R., sr. mgt. eng., Fairfax Hospital Association, Springfield, VA '82 (MGMT)
MCDONALD, WILLIAM F., chief eng., Tri-City Medical Center, Oceanside, CA '80 (ENG)
MCDONNELL, SR. GERALDINE, RN EdD, coor. pat. rel., Mercy Hospital and Medical Center, San Diego, CA '85 (PAT)
MCDONNELL, KENNETH L., mgr. prod., Nellcor, Hayward, CA '84 (RISK)
MCDONNELL, KEVIN T., mgr., Ernst and Whinney, Charlotte, NC '84 (PLNG)
MCDONNELL, MARGARET, RN, coor. outreach, Lehigh Valley Hospital Center, Allentown, PA '77 (NURS)
MCDONNELL, NEAL JR., dir. pers., Bryn Mawr Hospital, Bryn Mawr, PA '81 (PERS)
MCDONNELL, WILLIAM V., MD, vice-pres. med. affairs, West Jersey Hospital, Northern Division, Camden, NJ '61
MCDONOUGH, JAMES D., atty., Martha Washington Hospital, Chicago, IL '86 (ATTY)
MCDONOUGH, REV. JAMES T., dir., Catholic Social Services, Philadelphia, PA '67
MCDONOUGH, MARY T., supv. med. and surg. soc. work, Saint Vincent Hospital, Worcester, MA '85 (SOC)
MCDONOUGH, MICHAEL J., spec. asst. to pres., Hospital Center at Orange, Orange, NJ '78 (PLNG)
MCDONOUGH, MICHAEL W., dir. hskpg. serv., Greenwich Hospital, Greenwich, CT '86 (ENVIRON)
MCDONOUGH, THOMAS MONROE, dir. food serv., St. Luke Hospital, Fort Thomas, KY '67 (FOOD)
MCDOUGAL, TOMMY R., pres. and chief exec. off., Alabama Hospital Association, Montgomery, AL '69
MCDOUGALL, CHARLES W., sr. vice-pres., Royal Victoria Hospital, Montreal, Que., Canada '83 (PLNG)
MCDOUGALL, MARK D., mgt. eng., Evangelical Health Systems, Oak Brook, IL '83 (MGMT)
MCDOUGALL, NANCY L., dir. pers., William B. Kessler Memorial Hospital, Hammonton, NJ '78 (PERS)
MCDOUGLE, DAVID E., dir. human res., HCA Deer Park Hospital, Deer Park, TX '86 (PERS)
MCDOW, DANIEL R., sr. support analyst, Continental Healthcare Systems, Overland Park, KS '85 (PUR)
MCDOWELL, CAROL B., outpatient rep., DePaul Hospital, Norfolk, VA '85 (PAT)
MCDOWELL, DAVID R., sr. vice-pres. and chief fin. off., St. Luke's Hospital of the United Methodist Church, Cleveland, OH '74
MCDOWELL, DENNIS L., asst. to exec. dir.-plng. and dev., Prince George's Hospital Center, Cheverly, MD '77
MCDOWELL, DONALD L., exec. vice-pres. and treas., Maine Medical Center, Portland, ME '81
MCDOWELL, ELLEN, RN, dir. educ., St. Francis Medical Center, Cape Girardeau, MO '80 (EDUC)
MCDOWELL, ERNEST R., sr. vice-pres. corp. rel., Harrisburg Hospital Health Foundation, Harrisburg, PA '72 (PR)
MCDOWELL, JAMES E., asst. adm., Corvallis Clinic, Corvallis, OR '83
MCDOWELL, JAMES W., dir. eng., Arkansas Mental Health Services, Little Rock, AR '76 (ENG)
MCDOWELL, JERRY A., atty., Knollwood Park Hospital, Mobile, AL '84 (ATTY)
MCDOWELL, NANCY R., mgr. cent. sup., Richland Memorial Hospital, Olney, IL '82 (CS)
MCDOWELL, TWYLA RAE, pat. rep., Rose Medical Center, Denver, CO '80 (PAT)
MCDUFF, DOUGLAS A., atty., South Miami Hospital, South Miami, FL '82 (ATTY)
MCDUFFY, ALLISON H., dir. commun. rel., Lenoir Memorial Hospital, Kinston, NC '85 (PR)
MCDURMON, ROY, dir. support serv., Floyd Medical Center, Rome, GA '75 (PUR)
MCEACHEN, EDMUND D., atty., Methodist Hospital, Omaha, NE '68 (ATTY)

MCEACHEN, IRENE C., RN, vice-pres. nrsg., St. Barnabas Medical Center, Livingston, NJ '83 (NURS)
MCELHINNEY, NEIL C., asst. adm., Swedish Medical Center, Englewood, CO '82 (RISK)
MCELLIGOTT, MARILYN A., dir. vol. serv., La Crosse Lutheran Hospital, La Crosse, WI '77 (VOL)
MCELMURRY, PHYLLIS L., RN, asst. vice-pres., Loma Linda University Medical Center, Loma Linda, CA '82 (NURS)
MCELRONE, CHARLES, pub. rel. assoc., Graduate Hospital, Philadelphia, PA '86 (PR)
MCELROY, CRISTY J., dir. soc. serv., Saint Francis Medical Center, Grand Island, NE '83 (SOC)
MCELROY, MARIA ELENA, dir. pers., El Dorado Hospital and Medical Center, Tucson, AZ '79 (PERS)
MCELROY, THOMAS P., atty., United Hospital, Grand Forks, ND '73 (ATTY)
MCELVEEN, CHARLES W., area supv. nutr. and food, MacNeal Hospital, Berwyn, IL '83 (FOOD)
MCELYEA, DOROTHY C., dir. human res., University of Tennessee Memorial Hospital, Knoxville, TN '82 (EDUC)
MCENANEY, JOHN B., dir. cent. serv., Grant Hospital of Chicago, Chicago, IL '83 (CS)
MCENROE, JOHN E. JR., vice-pres. fin., Northeast Alabama Regional Medical Center, Anniston, AL '83
MCERLEAN, GEORGE JOSEPH, proj. dir., University Hospital, Stony Brook, NY '79 (ENG)
MCEWAM, GEORGE E., dir. med. soc. work, Arnot-Ogden Memorial Hospital, Elmira, NY '82 (SOC)
MCEWAN, ETTA S., dir. soc. work, Baycrest Centre-Geriatric Care, Toronto, Ont., Canada '77 (SOC)
MCEWEN, DAVID S., adm. res., William Beaumont Hospital, Royal Oak, MI '86 (PLNG)
MCEWEN, MARCIA J., dir. pub. rel., Washington Hospital, Washington, PA '81 (PR)
MCFADDEN, DAVID L., dir. corp. rel., Hospital Corporation of America, Nashville, TN '81 (PR)
MCFADDEN, FRANCES O., RN, supv. nrsg. home care, Veterans Administration Medical Center, Coatesville, PA '81 (NURS)
MCFADDEN, GARY P., assoc. dir. matl. mgt., Florida Hospital Medical Center, Orlando, FL '83 (PUR)
MCFADDEN, IRENE F., vice-pres. amb. serv., Mercy Hospital of Pittsburgh, Pittsburgh, PA '82 (PLNG)(AMB)
MCFADDEN, JOHN W., mgt. analyst, Veterans Administration Medical Center, Dallas, TX '81 (MGMT)
MCFADDEN, MARTIN J. JR., mng. dir., Marsh and McLennan, Inc., Chicago, IL '87 (RISK)
MCFADDEN, MARVIN, dir. cent. sterile proc., North Mississippi Medical Center, Tupelo, MS '77 (CS)
MCFADDEN, MARY F., USAF, K I Sawyer AFB, MI '85 (CS)
MCFADDEN, ROSE C., mgr. matl., Wallkill Valley General Hospital, Sussex, NJ '80 (PUR)
MCFALL, DONALD B., atty., Humana Inc., Louisville, KY '86 (ATTY)
MCFALL, EDITH M., dir. cent. serv., Wyoming Medical Center, Casper, WY '83 (CS)
MCFARLAN, TIMOTHY K., gen. mgr., Entech, Phoenix, AZ '80 (ENG)
MCFARLAND, BRADFORD, mng. dir. int. syst., Washington Hospital Center, Washington, DC '81 (MGMT)
MCFARLAND, MARGARET K., supv. cent. serv., Franklin Regional Medical Center, Franklin, PA '79 (CS)
MCFARLAND, MARJORIE K., RN, dir. educ., St. Dominic-Jackson Memorial Hospital, Jackson, MS '79 (EDUC)
MCFARLANE, DAVID E., atty., Methodist Hospital, Madison, WI '83 (ATTY)
MCFAUL, WILLIAM, pres., McFaul and Lyons, Inc., Trenton, NJ '86 (PUR)
MCFEE, RICHARD S., dir. matl. mgt., Georgetown University Medical Center, Washington, DC '82 (PUR)
MCFERRON, JOSEPH R., New Stanton, PA '57 (PLNG)(LIFE)
MCFETRIDGE, JOHN C., exec. dir., Boulder Community Hospital, Boulder, CO '61
MCGAFFEY, DAN A., proprietor, McGaffey Management Associates, Marion, MA '85 (MGMT)
MCGAFFEY, PEGGY A., pres., McGaffey Associates, Appleton, WI '72 (PLNG)
MCGALL, EDWARD C., dir. soc. serv., St. Francis Medical Center, Pittsburgh, PA '73 (SOC)
MCGARITY, J. MICHAEL, atty., Gwinnett Hospital System, Lawrenceville, GA '86 (ATTY)
MCGARRAGAN, MICHAEL, asst. adm. risk mgt., St. John Hospital, Detroit, MI '86 (RISK)
MCGARRAH, KAREN, mgr. matl., Baptist Medical Center-Montclair, Birmingham, AL '80 (PUR)
MCGARRY, DONNA J., dir. soc. serv., Mercy Memorial Hospital, Monroe, MI '74 (SOC)
MCGARRY, PAULA E., sr. consult., Ernst and Whinney, Dallas, TX '87 (MGMT)
MCGARRY, THOMAS WILLIAM, dir. pub. rel., Eden Hospital Medical Center, Castro Valley, CA '80 (PR)
MCGAUGH, STEPHAN L., dir. healthcare serv., Parson Bishop Company, Cincinnati, OH '85
MCGAUVRAN-HRUBY, STACY L., sr. coor. pub., University Hospital-University of Nebraska, Omaha, NE '86 (PR)
MCGEE, DIANNE J., student, Program in Health Care Management, Southern Illinois University, Carbondale, IL '85
MCGEE, JOSEPH D., adm., Midwest Medical Center, Palos Heights, IL '87
MCGEE, LARRY T., RN, vice-pres. nrsg. serv., St. James Community Hospital, Butte, MT '86 (NURS)
MCGEE, MARGUERITE G., dir. vol. serv., Frankford Hospital, Torresdale Division, Philadelphia, PA '82 (VOL)
MCGEE, TERENCE T., dir. diet., St. Joseph's Hospital, Philadelphia, PA '74 (FOOD)
MCGEE, THOMAS H., dir. pers., Lower Bucks Hospital, Bristol, PA '84 (PERS)
MCGETTIGAN, BARBARA, asst. dir. educ. serv., Children's Hospital of Sf, San Francisco, CA '85 (EDUC)
MCGHEE, JOHN ROBERT, Homosassa, FL '59
MCGIBANY, SUSIE, vice-pres. fin. and treas., Boca Raton Community Hospital, Boca Raton, FL '80
MCGIBONY, CAPT. CHARLES M., MSC USA, adm. res., U. S. Ireland Army Community Hospital, Fort Knox, KY '83 (PERS)(PR)
MCGIBONY, LT. COL. JAMES THOMAS JR., MSC USA, asst. chief off. procurement div., Army Medical Department Personnel Support Agency, Washington, DC '66
MCGILL, PATRICIA M., RN, asst. dir. nrsg. and clin. nrs. spec., Charleston Area Medical Center, Charleston, WV '85 (NURS)
MCGILL, WENDY G., coor. pat. rep. serv., Long Island Jewish Medical Center, New York, NY '85 (PAT)
MCGILLIVRAY, MARGARET, RN, dir. nrsg. proj. mgt. and oper., Rhode Island Hospital, Providence, RI '80 (NURS)
MCGINLEY, MARY ANN C., RN, actg. dir. nrsg., Thomas Jefferson University Hospital, Philadelphia, PA '84 (NURS)
MCGINLEY, MICHAEL A., dir. plng., Finger Lakes Area Hospital Corporation, Geneva, NY '82 (PLNG)
MCGINN, PETER V., PhD, vice-pres. human res., United Health Services, Johnson City, NY '85 (PERS)
MCGINNIS, LORRAINE I., RN, vice-pres. pat. care serv., St. Francis Hospital, Jersey City, NJ '82 (NURS)
MCGINNIS, RICHARD, RN, dir. nrsg., Littleton Hospital, Littleton, NH '80 (NURS)
MCGINNIS, SUSAN M., RN, dir. nrsg., Milford Hospital, Milford, CT '71 (NURS)
MCGINNIS, THOMAS E., vice-pres. fin., Mansfield General Hospital, Mansfield, OH '87 (MGMT)
MCGINNISS, NEIL, Cincinnati, OH '54 (LIFE)
MCGINTY, SR. JEAN MARIE, RN, asst. vice-pres. nrsg., St. Peter's Hospital, Albany, NY '84 (NURS)
MCGIRT, MARY ANN, dir. trng. and dev., HSA Cumberland Hospital, Fayetteville, NC '82 (EDUC)
MCGIVERON, DONNA M., RN, nrsg. instr., Ingham Medical Center, Lansing, MI '86 (EDUC)
MCGLADE, JANE, pres., Jane McGlade and Associates, Sneads Ferry, NC '84
MCGLASSON, MARY M., dir. matl. mgt., Mount Washington Pediatric Hospital, Baltimore, MD '83 (PUR)
MCGLAUGHLIN, ANN, RN, assoc. dir. nrsg., St. Luke's Hospital, Kansas City, MO '77 (NURS)
MCGLONE, MARITA, dir. environ. serv., Abington Memorial Hospital, Abington, PA '86 (ENVIRON)
MCGLONE, ROBERT O. JR., dir. pers., St. Mary's Hospital and Health Center, Tucson, AZ '82 (PERS)
MCGLOTHIN, DENNIS, dir. maint., Woodlawn Hospital, Rochester, IN '80 (ENG)
MCGLOTHLIN, LESLIE BEERS, student, University of Tampa, Tampa, FL '79 (PLNG)
MCGOUN, JOHN H., asst. dir. food serv., Waukesha Memorial Hospital, Waukesha, WI '80 (FOOD)
MCGOVERN, FRANK W., dir. commun. rel., Eastern Idaho Regional Medical Center, Idaho Falls, ID '81 (PR)
MCGOVERN, JOAN E., RN, dir. nrsg., Hollywood Community Hospital, Hollywood, CA '85 (NURS)
MCGOVERN, JOHN J., mgr. matl., Downey Community Hospital, Downey, CA '70 (PUR)
MCGOVERN, MARY, consult., Health Care Management, Inc., Oak Park, IL '83
MCGOVERN, MICHAEL T., dir. corp. dev., Children's Hospital, Columbus, OH '82 (PR) (PLNG)
MCGOWAN, CRISTI A., mgt. eng., St. Joseph's Hospital, Stockton, CA '78 (MGMT)
MCGOWAN, DANIEL T., exec. dir., Nassau-Suffolk Health Systems Agency, Inc., Plainville, NY '80 (PLNG)
MCGOWAN, EDGAR T., dir. soc. serv., Booth Memorial Medical Center, Flushing, NY '77 (SOC)
MCGOWAN, HARRY T., dir. sterilization sup. and mgr. matl., King Khaled Eye Spec Hospital, Riyadh, Saudi Arabia '86 (CS)(PUR)
MCGOWAN, JERRY M., vice-pres., Dallas County Hospital District, Dallas, TX '80 (PERS)
MCGOWAN, PATRICIA E., dir. pub. rel. and dev., Brockton Hospital, Brockton, MA '85 (PR) (PLNG)
MCGOWAN, R. GARRETT, sr. vice-pres. prof. serv., Proctor Community Hospital, Peoria, IL '77
MCGOWAN, TERENCE F., student, Program in Health Administration, University of Massachusetts, Amherst, MA '86
MCGOWEN, PATRICIA A., RN, nrs. educ., Presbyterian Hospital, Dallas, TX '86 (EDUC)
MCGRADY, ELIZABETH S., dir. mktg., Methodist Health Systems Foundation, New Orleans, LA '85 (PR) (PLNG)
MCGRADY, JOHN E. JR., sr. vice-pres., Blue Cross of Western Pennsylvania, Pittsburgh, PA '68
MCGRAIL, WILLIAM T., atty., Massachusetts Hospital Association, Burlington, MA '77 (ATTY)(RISK)
MCGRAN, TRIXIE HARVEY, dir. pers., Ivinson Memorial Hospital, Laramie, WY '83 (PERS)
MCGRANE, HELEN F., RN PhD, dir. pat. and commun. health educ., St. Joseph Medical Center, Burbank, CA '82 (EDUC)
MCGRANE, MILES A. III, atty., North Miami Medical Center, North Miami, FL '81 (ATTY)
MCGRANN, KATHLEEN, dir. soc. work serv., Pennsylvania Hospital, Philadelphia, PA '86 (SOC)
MCGRATH, ANN MARIE, RN, Tampa, FL '75
MCGRATH, BARBARA K., RN, asst. adm. nrsg., West Shore Hospital, Manistee, MI '77 (NURS)
MCGRATH, BRENDAN P., asst. adm., Bridgeport Hospital, Bridgeport, CT '80 (RISK)
MCGRATH, DONALD F., dir. food, St. Francis Health Resort, Denville, NJ '81 (FOOD)
MCGRATH, EDWARD J., student, Program in Hospital and Health Care Administration, St. Louis University, St. Louis, MO '84
MCGRATH, EDWARD J., supv. cent. serv., Medical Center Hospital of Vermont, Burlington, VT '86 (CS)
MCGRATH, EDWARD T., asst. to pres., Pekin Memorial Hospital, Pekin, IL '55 (LIFE)
MCGRATH, GARRETT O., adm. dir., Conifer Park, Scotia, NY '77
MCGRATH, GLENN E., vice-pres. pers. adm., Lynchburg General-Marshall Lodge Hospitals, Lynchburg, VA '79 (PERS)
MCGRATH, HAROLD E., supv. elec. and electronic maint., Pomona Valley Community Hospital, Pomona, CA '83 (ENG)
MCGRATH, JOHN HILL, dir. human res., Hewitt Management Corporation, Shelton, CT '68 (PERS)
MCGRATH, LINDA K., dir. soc. serv., Manatee Memorial Hospital, Bradenton, FL '81 (SOC)
MCGRATH, THOMAS, dir. plant oper., District Memorial Hospital, Forest Lake, MN '82 (ENG)
MCGRAW, CATHERINE, dir. soc. serv., Humana Hospital -Aurora, Aurora, CO '86 (SOC)
MCGRAW, KENNETH W., assoc. dir. maint. and eng., Lake County Memorial Hospital, Willoughby, OH '82 (ENG)
MCGRAW, MARTIN T., mgr., Palos Community Hospital Primary Care Center, Orland Park, IL '87 (AMB)
MCGREEVEY, MARYELLEN, dir. soc. serv., Lincoln West Hospital, Chicago, IL '73 (SOC)
MCGREGOR, MARTHA, RN, dir. staff dev., Bayshore Community Hospital, Holmdel, NJ '83 (EDUC)
MCGREGOR, WILLIAM F., asst. adm., Reading Rehabilitation Hospital, Reading, PA '75 (PERS)
MCGROARTY, SR. CATHERINE, RN, chief exec. off., Mercy Hospital, Port Huron, MI '77
MCGROARTY, SR. MAUREEN, ombudsman, Mercy Hospital, Wilkes-Barre, PA '78 (PAT)
MCGUANE, SR. CORNELIA ANN, RN, dir. nrsg. serv., St. Joseph's Hospital Health Center, Syracuse, NY '86 (NURS)
MCGUCKIN, MARILYN, dir. vol. serv., Children's Hospital Medical Center, Akron, OH '78 (VOL)
MCGUINNESS, DEIRDRE C., dir. mgt. eng., SunHealth, Columbia, SC '85 (MGMT)
MCGUIRE, DIANE M., actg. dir. subscriber serv., Health Insurance Plan of Greater New York, New York, NY '86 (PAT)
MCGUIRE, DOROTHY H., supv. sup., proc. and distrib., Geary Community Hospital, Junction City, KS '77 (CS)
MCGUIRE, HILDA J., vice-pres. commun. and res. dev., Women's College Hospital, Toronto, Ont., Canada '81 (PR)
MCGUIRE, JAMES C., atty., Lawrence and Memorial Hospital, New London, CT '81 (ATTY)
MCGUIRE, JAMES I., Pittsburgh, PA '49 (MGMT)(LIFE)
MCGUIRE, JOAN, RN, dir. nrsg., Northwest Hospital, Seattle, WA '79 (NURS)
MCGUIRE, JOHN M., MD, dir. rad., Gerald Champion Memorial Hospital, Alamogordo, NM '82
MCGUIRE, JOHN P., vice-pres., Jewish Hospital of St. Louis, St. Louis, MO '81
MCGUIRE, LEWIS R., mktg. spec., Cumberland A. Hospital for Children, New Kent, VA '86 (PR)
MCGUIRE, MARK R., mgt. eng., Hendrick Medical Center, Abilene, TX '85 (MGMT)
MCGUIRE, MARY HELEN, (ret.), Beattyville, KY '67 (FOOD)
MCGUIRE, MICHAEL R., dir. food serv., HCA Hendersonville Hospital, Hendersonville, TN '86 (FOOD)
MCGUIRE, T. RICHARD, indust. eng., LDS Hospital, Salt Lake City, UT '75 (MGMT)
MCGUIRE, TERENCE J. III, oper. analyst, Mount Sinai Hospital, Hartford, CT '83 (MGMT)
MCGUIRE, WILLIAM D., pres. and chief exec. off., Mercy Health Care System, Dallas, PA '74
MCGUIRE, WILLIAM H., dir. eng., AMI Tarzana Regional Medical Center, Tarzana, CA '77 (ENG)
MCGURK, LINDA, mgr. cent. serv., St. Mary's Hospital, Streator, IL '85 (CS)
MCGURL, PAUL, mgr. eng. and bldg. serv., Fox Chase Cancer Center, Philadelphia, PA '87 (ENG)
MCHALE, CHARLES E. JR., atty., Pendleton Memorial Methodist Hospital, New Orleans, LA '73 (ATTY)
MCHALE, JACQUELINE H., vice-pres. pat. serv., Mercy Hospital, Wilkes-Barre, PA '83 (NURS)
MCHALE, SANDRA J., dir. commun., Iredell Memorial Hospital, Statesville, NC '86 (PR)
MCHANEY, JAMES E. JR., chm., Magliaro and McHaney, La Jolla, CA '81 (PR)
MCHENRY, BETTY J., dir. telecommun., Memorial Medical Center, Springfield, IL '76 (ENG)
MCHENRY, JESS P. III, sr. mgt. eng., St. Margaret Hospital, Hammond, IN '87 (MGMT)
MCHENRY, LAURA ANGELA, pat. rel. rep., Potomac Hospital, Woodbridge, VA '87 (PAT)
MCHENRY, WILLIAM P., mgr. govt. rel., Coopers and Lybrand, Washington, DC '80
MCHOUL, ROSALIE, RN, head nrs. cent. sup., Chester County Hospital, West Chester, PA '85 (CS)
MCHUGH, GERALD J., assoc. prof., Indiana University School of Medicine, Department of Health Administration, Indianapolis, IN '68
MCILHANY, CORDELIA RANE, (ret.), Santa Fe, MO '23 (LIFE)
MCILMAIL, DEBORAH, dir. soc. serv., Northeastern Hospital of Philadelphia, Philadelphia, PA '85 (SOC)
MCILWAIN, G. MICHAEL, dir. plant maint., Crestwood Hospital, Huntsville, AL '85 (ENG)
MCINALLY, KATHLEEN F., supv. commun., Pontiac General Hospital, Pontiac, MI '83 (ENG)
MCINERNEY, BRIAN F., vice-pres. plng. and corp. dev., Bethesda Lutheran Medical Center, St. Paul, MN '80 (PLNG)
MCINERNEY, KATHLEEN, exec. dir., Memorial Health System, Inc., South Bend, IN '85 (PAT)
MCINERNEY, SHERYL LOCKE, sr. analyst strategic plng., Medtronic, Inc., Minneapolis, MN '78 (PLNG)
MCINNES, J. DOUGLAS, dir. emp. rel., McLaren General Hospital, Flint, MI '75 (PERS)
MCINNIS, MARILYN L., dir. pat. rel., Eastern Maine Medical Center, Bangor, ME '85 (PAT)
MCINNIS, MARTHA, head nrs. cent. serv., Tallahassee Memorial Regional Medical Center, Tallahassee, FL '79 (CS)
MCINTEE, MICHAEL R., atty., Mercy Medical Center and Hospital, Williston, ND '73 (ATTY)

MCINTIER, MICHAEL T., asst. vice-pres. oper., Phoenix General Hospital, Phoenix, AZ '83 (PUR)
MCINTOSH, C. VERN, mgr. environ. serv., St. Charles Medical Center, Bend, OR '86 (ENVIRON)
MCINTOSH, D. LAURENCE, atty., McLeod Regional Medical Center, Florence, SC '77 (ATTY)
MCINTURF, LANELL J., mgr. vol. serv., St. Elizabeth Community Health Center, Lincoln, NE '85 (VOL)
MCINTYRE, ANNE S., RN, asst. adm., Northwest Hospital, Tucson, AZ '86 (NURS)
MCINTYRE, NANCY A., dir. commun. rel. and vol. serv., Memorial Hospital, Owosso, MI '81 (PR)(VOL)
MCINTYRE, ROBERT L., arch., Turner Construction Company, New York, NY '75
MCKAY, DEL, dir. comm. rel., Douglas Community Hospital, Roseburg, OR '86 (PR)
MCKAY, E. SUSAN, dir. pub. rel., St. Anthony's Hospital, Amarillo, TX '86 (PR)
MCKAY, GARY H., Veterans Administration Hospital, Wichita, KS '85 (SOC)
MCKAY, KATHLEEN A., dir. pers., Santa Barbara Cottage Hospital, Santa Barbara, CA '82 (PERS)
MCKAY, MICHAEL B., dir. mgt. eng., Santa Fe Healthcare Systems, Inc., Gainesville, FL '84 (MGMT)
MCKAY, SHARON D., dir. pers., Anaheim Memorial Hospital, Anaheim, CA '85 (PERS)
MCKAY, SHARON L., dir. food serv., Cypress Gardens Baptist Hospital, Riverside, CA '86 (FOOD)
MCKAY, WILLIAM J., dir. matl. mgt., Flower Memorial Hospital, Sylvania, OH '81 (PUR)
MCKAY, WILLIAM S., dir. environ. serv., Exeter Hospital, Exeter, NH '86 (ENG)
MCKEAN, SR. MARY FAITH, pres., St. Joseph's Hospital, Savannah, GA '85
MCKEE, ARTHUR J., dir. plant oper. and maint., St. Paul-Ramsey Medical Center, St. Paul, MN '81 (ENG)
MCKEE, DORIS B., dir. plng. and mktg., Beverly Hospital, Montebello, CA '85 (PLNG)
MCKEE, JUDITH M., dir. commun. rel., Wilson N. Jones Memorial Hospital, Sherman, TX '82 (PR)
MCKEE, ROBERT D., coor. mktg., Kewanee Public Hospital, Kewanee, IL '86 (PR)
MCKEE, SHARON J., mgr. mktg. healthcare, Organizational Dynamics, Inc., Burlington, MA '86 (PERS)
MCKEEHAN, LUCINDA, dir. pub. rel., Memorial Mission Hospital, Asheville, NC '85 (PR)
MCKEEVER, RONALD G., dir. pers., St. Patrick Hospital, Lake Charles, LA '82 (PERS)
MCKEIGHAN, SHERI M., dir. guilds and vol. serv., Valley Children's Hospital, Fresno, CA '86 (VOL)
MCKELL, DOUGLAS C., Physicians Development Resources, Dayton, OH '82 (PR) (PLNG)
MCKELVEY, ANNE B., RN, assoc. dir. nrsg., Presbyterian Hospital, Charlotte, NC '84 (NURS)
MCKELVEY, JANICE O., asst. vice-pres. human res., St. Luke's-Roosevelt Hospital Center, New York, NY '85 (PERS)
MCKELVEY, JO K., educ. consult., McH Associates, Garland, TX '86 (EDUC)
MCKELVEY, LARRY D., food serv. dir., Presbyterian Hospital, Albuquerque, NM '84 (FOOD)
MCKELVIE, CHRISTINE, dir. pub. rel., Routt Memorial Hospital, Steamboat Springs, CO '85 (PR)
MCKELVIE, DON, mgr. ldry., HCA Group Properties, Inc., Bountiful, UT '86 (ENVIRON)
MCKEMY-MITCHELL, SUE, mgr. emp., Asbury Hospital, Salina, KS '86 (PERS)
MCKENNA, BRIAN J., student, Lisley College, Graduate School, Cambridge, MA '84
MCKENNA, JOHN J., dir. maint., Zurbrugg Memorial Hospital -Riverside, Riverside, NJ '87 (ENG)
MCKENNA, JUDITH M., asst. adm., Flowers Hospital, Dothan, AL '82 (NURS)
MCKENNA, LT. MICHAEL ROBERT, MSC USN, med. adm. off., Naval School of Health Sciences, Bethesda, MD '78
MCKENNA, OWEN, vice-pres., Travenol Management Services, Deerfield, IL '85 (PLNG)
MCKENNA, WES, mgr. distrib., St. Francis Xavier Hospital, Charleston, SC '87 (CS)
MCKENNEY, JERRY W., mgr. eng., Major Hospital, Shelbyville, IN '84 (ENG)
MCKENNEY, LINDA B., RN, dir. educ., Floyd Memorial Hospital, New Albany, IN '77 (EDUC)
MCKENNEY, VIRGINIA L., supv. cent. serv., Harrison Memorial Hospital, Cynthiana, KY '68 (CS)
MCKENZIE, SR. ANNA MARIE, chm. soc. work, Mercy Catholic Medical Center, Fitzgerald Mercy Division, Darby, PA '68 (SOC)
MCKENZIE, FRANCES E., RN, dir. clin. nrsg., Penrose Hospitals, Colorado Springs, CO '84 (NURS)
MCKENZIE, FRANKLIN C. JR., atty., Jones County Community Hospital, Laurel, MS '86 (ATTY)
MCKENZIE, JOE C., asst. adm. and dir. human res., St. Mary's Hospital and Medical Center, San Francisco, CA '83 (PERS)
MCKENZIE, MARY L., dir. med. rec.-adm. prog., Indiana University Medical Center, Indianapolis, IN '84
MCKENZIE, SYDNEY H. II, atty., Venice Hospital, Venice, FL '86 (ATTY)
MCKENZIE, V. C., supv. eng., University Hospital, Seattle, WA '81 (ENG)
MCKEON, JOHN, contr., Our Lady of Mercy Medical Center, Bronx, NY '86
MCKEON, KATHRYN L., RN, chief mental health and alcohol nrsg. serv., Clinical Center National Institute of Health, Bethesda, MD '85 (NURS)
MCKEON, PATRICIA A., dir. qual. assur. and risk mgt., Hospital for Joint Diseases Orthopaedic Institute, New York, NY '83 (RISK)
MCKEON, WARREN J., Virginia Hospital Rate Review Program, Richmond, VA '80
MCKEOWN-MOYNIHAH, CARMEL, RN, asst. dir. pat. serv., St. John of God Hospital, Boston, MA '82 (NURS)
MCKEOWN, FRANK J. JR., atty., HCA Doctors Hospital, Lake Worth, FL '72 (ATTY)
MCKEOWN, HELEN B., nrs. educator, St. Joseph Hospital, Providence, RI '84 (EDUC)
MCKEOWN, MARIE G., supv. cent. sup., Dr. John Warner Hospital, Clinton, IL '82 (CS)
MCKEOWN, ROBERT, mgr. matl., Penobscot Bay Medical Center, Rockport, ME '79 (PUR)
MCKEOWN, THOMAS E., vice-pres. fiscal serv., Holy Cross Hospital, Fort Lauderdale, FL '78
MCKERNAN, FRANK G., dir. matl. mgt., St. Joseph Medical Center, Stamford, CT '82 (PUR)
MCKEVITT, PATRICIA M., dir. soc. work, Wohl-Washington University Clinics, St. Louis, MO '81 (SOC)
MCKIBBEN, ROBERT A., pur. agt., Emanuel Hospital and Health Center, Portland, OR '77 (PUR)
MCKIERNAN, PATRICIA A., vice-pres. pub. affairs, Hunterdon Medical Center, Flemington, NJ '81 (PR)
MCKIMMY, DOYLE L., asst. dir. pers., St. Joseph Medical Center, Wichita, KS '76 (PERS)
MCKINDLES, TIMOTHY J., mgt. trng., Columbus Hospital, Chicago, IL '86 (EDUC)
MCKINLEY, CATHIE M., RN, asst. dir. nrsg., Westview Hospital, Indianapolis, IN '81 (NURS)
MCKINLEY, COLLEEN, atty., Hospital Corporation of America, Nashville, TN '84 (ATTY)
MCKINLEY, ESTHER C., mgr. info. syst. and supv. lab., Santa Barbara Cottage Hospital, Santa Barbara, CA '83
MCKINLEY, JOSEPH W., exec. vice-pres. and chief exec. off., Phoenix Memorial Hospital, Phoenix, AZ '73
MCKINLEY, MIKE, dir. security and unit mgt., Mary Greeley Medical Center, Ames, IA '83
MCKINLEY, RUDOLPH JR., adm., Morristown-Hamblen Hospital, Morristown, TN '77
MCKINNEY, JANE S., diet. consult., L. J. Minor Corporation, Indianapolis, IN '83 (FOOD)
MCKINNEY, JERRY A., dir. matl. mgt., Doctors Hospital, Little Rock, AR '81 (PUR)
MCKINNEY, JOHN DAVID, dir. eng., Beverly Hospital, Beverly, MA '74 (ENG)
MCKINNEY, KATHLEEN, dir. commun., Verdugo Hills Hospital, Glendale, CA '84 (ENG)
MCKINNEY, LUCY, supv. ldry., South Peninsula Hospital, Homer, AK '86 (ENVIRON)
MCKINNEY, MARGARET P., coor. vol. serv., University of Missouri Hospital and Clinics, Columbia, MO '84
MCKINNEY, MARY ANNE, dir. commun., Atlantic City Medical Center, Pomona, NJ '79 (ENG)
MCKINNEY, PAMELA, atty., Hinsdale Hospital, Hinsdale, IL '86 (ATTY)
MCKINNEY, SALLY P., dir. pers., HCA Woodland Heights Medical Center, Lufkin, TX '82 (PERS)
MCKINNEY, SHEILA A., vice-pres. clin. serv., Radford Community Hospital, Radford, VA '84 (PLNG)
MCKINNEY, THOMAS D., dir. med. educ., U. S. Air Force Medical Center Keesler, Biloxi, MS '81
MCKINNIE, JEANNE, RN, supv. oper., emer. room and outpatient clin., Madison County Memorial Hospital, Winterset, IA '87 (AMB)
MCKINNON, JAMES J. JR., dir. food serv., Veterans Home and Hospital, Rocky Hill, CT '80 (FOOD)
MCKINNON, LINDA M., coor. vol., Wentworth-Douglass Hospital, Dover, NH '87 (VOL)
MCKINNON, WILLIAM D., vice-pres., Baylor University Medical Center, Dallas, TX '78
MCKITTRICK, RICHARD A., atty., Penobscot Bay Medical Center, Rockport, ME '80 (ATTY)
MCKITTRICK, THOMAS J. JR., vice-pres. support serv., Sacred Heart Medical Center, Chester, PA '80
MCKIVERGAN, TIM, dir. risk mgt., St. Francis Medical Center, Lynwood, CA '84 (RISK)
MCKNEW, LINDA A., RN, dir. nrsg., Alachua General Hospital, Gainesville, FL '85 (NURS)
MCKNEW, THOMAS G., market analyst mgt. serv., Geisinger System Services, Danville, PA '82 (MGMT)
MCKNIGHT, BETH W., dir. pub. rel. and pers., King's Daughters Hospital, Greenville, MS '86 (PR)
MCKNIGHT, KATHLEEN, atty. and off., Naval Hospital, Camp Pendleton, CA '87
MCKNIGHT, NEAL L., mgt. eng., Riverside Hospital, Newport News, VA '86 (MGMT)
MCKNIGHT, RICHARD S., RN, dir. nrsg.-proj. dev., Rockford Memorial Hospital, Rockford, IL '84 (NURS)
MCKNIGHT, SHIRLEY A., dir. pur., Montefiore Medical Center, Bronx, NY '75 (PUR)
MCKOWN, DEBORAH, asst. vice-pres., Clinton Memorial Hospital, Wilmington, OH '87 (AMB)
MCKOWN, JAMES A., atty., Marion General Hospital, Marion, IN '74 (ATTY)
MCKOY, MALCOLM G., reg. eng. consult., National Medical Enterprises, Dallas, TX '85 (ENG)
MCKRELL, JOHN H., dir. pers., Magee-Womens Hospital, Pittsburgh, PA '69 (PERS)
MCLACHLAN, GORDON, sec., Nuffield Provincial Hospital Trust, London, England '76 (LIFE)
MCLAIN, ANNE H., mgr. emp., Community Memorial Hospital, Toms River, NJ '83 (PERS)
MCLAIN, I. JANEIL, dir. pub. rel., Duncan Regional Hospital, Duncan, OK '83 (PR)
MCLAIN, JERRI, vice-pres. mktg. and corp. dev., Huntsville Hospital, Huntsville, AL '76 (PR) (PLNG)
MCLAIN, MARY ANN, dir. matl. mgt., San Antonio Community Hospital, Upland, CA '80 (PUR)(CS)
MCLAMB, PEYTON F., dir. market res., Baxter Travenol Laboratories, Inc., Deerfield, IL '84
MCLAMB, WINONA, instr. in-service, HCA Grand Strand General Hospital, Myrtle Beach, SC '85 (EDUC)
MCLANAHAN, MARK A., RN, dir. nrsg., St. John's Regional Health Center, Springfield, MO '83 (NURS)
MCLANE, JAMES ARTHUR JR., adm. dir. facil., Methodist Hospital-Central Unit, Memphis, TN '78 (ENG)
MCLANE, SHARON M., RN, dir. nrsg., Doctors Hospital of Stark County, Massillon, OH '82 (NURS)
MCLAREN, MELESA H., RN, vice-pres. nrsg., De Soto General Hospital, Mansfield, LA '85 (NURS)
MCLAREN, PATRICK J., dir. sup., proc. and distrib., Mercy Hospital, Buffalo, NY '81 (CS)
MCLAREN, TERESA, dir. soc. serv., Park Lane Medical Center, Kansas City, MO '80 (SOC)
MCLARNEY, KAY, RN, dir. cent. serv., Children's Hospital and Medical Center, Seattle, WA '86 (CS)
MCLARNEY, SR. ROSE, vice-pres. plng. and mktg., St. Joseph Center for Life, Inc., Augusta, GA '71 (PLNG)
MCLARNEY, V. JAMES, Bourbonnais, IL '81 (ENG)
MCLARTY, JIMMY D., RN, asst. vice-pres. nrsg., St. Anthony's Hospital, Amarillo, TX '84 (NURS)
MCLAUGHLIN, COLLEEN, RN, vice-pres. pat. care serv., Valley Presbyterian Hospital, Van Nuys, CA '79 (NURS)
MCLAUGHLIN, EDWARD F., atty., Cape Cod Hospital, Hyannis, MA '79 (ATTY)
MCLAUGHLIN, GEORGE H., vice-pres. shared serv. and mktg., Dickinson County Hospitals, Iron Mountain, MI '86 (PR)
MCLAUGHLIN, JOANNE JARDING, instr. staff educ., St. Mary's Hospital and Rehabilitation Center, Minneapolis, MN '80 (EDUC)
MCLAUGHLIN, JOHN J., atty., Youville Rehabilitation and Chronic Diseases Hospital, Cambridge, MA '69 (ATTY)
MCLAUGHLIN, JOSEPH R., dir. bldg. and grds., Youville Rehabilitation and Chronic Diseases Hospital, Cambridge, MA '81 (ENG)
MCLAUGHLIN, KATHRYN A., vice-pres. adm. serv., St. Luke Hospital, Fort Thomas, KY '82 (PLNG)
MCLAUGHLIN, M. ELIZABETH, supv. admit., The Methodist Hospital, Houston, TX '85
MCLAUGHLIN, MARK F., vice-pres. dev. and commun. rel., Holy Family Medical Center, Manitowoc, WI '83 (PR)
MCLAUGHLIN, NELLIE J., RN, dir. nrsg. serv., Burnham Hospital, Champaign, IL '84 (NURS)
MCLAUGHLIN, SUZANNE G., RN, vice-pres. nrsg., Goddard Memorial Hospital, Stoughton, MA '80 (NURS)
MCLAUGHLIN, WELDON EUGENE JR., asst. adm. gen. serv., Wilson N. Jones Memorial Hospital, Sherman, TX '80
MCLAURIN, JUANITA, mgr. cent. serv., Cleveland Psychiatric Institute, Cleveland, OH '87
MCLAURIN, MONTY E., adm., Northeast Medical Center Hospital, Humble, TX '79
MCLEAN, ALICE, RN, dir. nrsg., Trident Regional Medical Center, Charleston, SC '84 (NURS)
MCLEAN, ANN H., dir. vol. serv., Putnam Community Hospital, Palatka, FL '86 (VOL)
MCLEAN, ANN W., dir. mktg., Southeastern General Hospital, Lumberton, NC '85 (PR)
MCLEAN, CHARLES M., (ret.), Douglas, AK '47 (LIFE)
MCLEAN, DICKSON JR., atty., Southeastern General Hospital, Lumberton, NC '70 (ATTY)
MCLEAN, CAPT. GEORGE II, MSC USN, San Antonio, TX '76
MCLEAN, JANET G., RN, asst. dir. nrsg. serv., Medical Plaza Hospital, Fort Worth, TX '82 (NURS)
MCLEAN, KENNETH R., San Francisco, CA '80
MCLEAN, LOIS D., RN, dir. nrsg. serv.-med., Trumbull Memorial Hospital, Warren, OH '82 (NURS)
MCLEAN, MARGARET J., dir. dev. and commun. rel., Mountainside Hospital, Montclair, NJ '85 (PR) (PLNG)
MCLEAN, MARILYN R., atty., Hospital Corporation of America, Nashville, TN '85 (ATTY)
MCLEAN, NANCY L., asst. dir. pat. care serv., Providence Hospital, Southfield, MI '83
MCLEAN, NEDA F., RN, dir. med., surg. and chemical dependency serv., Irving Community Hospital, Irving, TX '84 (NURS)
MCLEAVE, DONNA F., dir. human res., Charter Hospital of Jackson, Jackson, MS '85 (PERS)
MCLEES, PETER C., mgr. phys. rel., Charter Medical Corporation, El Monte, CA '86 (PR)
MCLEES, WILLIAM A., PhD, exec. dir., Medical University Hospital of the Medical University of South Carolina, Charleston, SC '53 (RISK)(LIFE)
MCLELLAN, JACK E., asst. adm. human rel., McKay-Dee Hospital Center, Ogden, UT '79 (PERS)
MCLELLAN, TERRY L., dir. matl. mgt., Sparks Regional Medical Center, Fort Smith, AR '86 (PUR)
MCLENDON, MARY L., asst. dir. pat. rep., Immanuel Medical Center, Omaha, NE '78 (PAT)
MCLEOD, KATHRYN JACKSON, dir. soc. work, Sacred Heart Hospital of Pensacola, Pensacola, FL '80 (SOC)
MCLEOD, LARRY V., atty., St. Mary's Hospital, Athens, GA '70 (ATTY)
MCLEOD, ROBERT M., atty., San Diego Hospital Association, San Diego, CA '86 (ATTY)
MCLEOD, WILLIAM R., exec. vice-pres., South Chicago Community Hospital, Chicago, IL '69
MCLEROY, ELOISE H., dir. matl. mgt., Medical Center Hospital, Tyler, TX '66 (PUR)
MCLORAINE, JACKIE N., RN, supv. cent. proc., distrib. and linen, Gottlieb Memorial Hospital, Melrose Park, IL '83 (CS)
MCLOUGHLIN, JAMES P., sr. mgt. consult., Pacific Health Resources, Los Angeles, CA '80 (MGMT)
MCLOUGHLIN, VIRGINIA A., dir. human res. serv., Porter Medical Center, Middlebury, VT '84 (PERS)
MCMAHAN, HOWARD D., sr. vice-pres., Harris Methodist Health System, Fort Worth, TX '84 (PLNG)
MCMAHILL, R. ANNETTE, assoc. plng., Research Health Services, Kansas City, MO '87 (PLNG)
MCMAHON, DAVID J., supt. int. info., U. S. Air Force Regional Hospital, Hampton, VA '87 (PR)
MCMAHON, SR. HELEN, Seton Medical Center, Daly City, CA '38 (PR)(LIFE)
MCMAHON, J. ALEXANDER, chm., Duke University, Department of Health Administration, Durham, NC '85 (LIFE)
MCMAHON, JEAN M., RN, Children's Medical Center of Dallas, Dallas, TX '84 (NURS)
MCMAHON, JOHN F., Blytheville, AR '82
MCMAHON, LYNN M., asst. dir. pub. rel., Children's Hospital of Pittsburgh, Pittsburgh, PA '87 (PR) (PLNG)

MCMAHON, PAUL F., vice chm. mgt. consult. serv., Ernst and Whinney, Cleveland, OH '86 (MGMT)
MCMAHON, STEVE, vice-pres., The Zivic Group, San Francisco, CA '85 (PERS)
MCMANIC, JAMES, mgr. mktg., Ohmeda Medical Engineering, Norcross, GA '86 (ENG)
MCMANN, DEBORAH H., asst. dir. pat. rel., University Hospital of Jacksonville, Jacksonville, FL '85 (PAT)
MCMANUS, JOSEPH S., exec. vice-pres., Lawrence General Hospital, Lawrence, MA '78
MCMANUS, KATHLEEN M., atty., Eau Claire, WI '82 (ATTY)
MCMANUS, KATHRYN ELIZABETH, dir. cont. care, St. Elizabeth's Hospital of Boston, Boston, MA '86 (SOC)
MCMANUS, MARCIA R., mgr. pat. rel. and vol. serv., United Health Services, Binghamton, NY '83 (PAT)
MCMANUS, PATRICK F., Memorial Medical Center, Savannah, GA '80 (MGMT)
MCMANUS, SHIRLEY, RN, mgr. cent. serv., Oak Park Hospital, Oak Park, IL '68 (CS)
MCMANUS, SUE S., RN, dir. environ. serv., St. Joseph's Hospital, Asheville, NC '80 (CS)(ENVIRON)
MCMARTIN, BARBARA J., dir. vol. serv., Champlain Valley Physicians Hospital Medical Center, Plattsburgh, NY '81 (VOL)
MCMARTIN, COL. GEORGE M., MSC USA, chief pat. adm., U. S. Army Health Service Command, Fort Sam Houston, TX '62
MCMASTER, WILLIAM, mgr. plant, St. Joseph Hospital, Bellingham, WA '60 (ENG)
MCMASTERS, SUZANNE C., asst. dir. pub. rel., Bryan Memorial Hospital, Lincoln, NE '82 (PR)
MCMEECHAN-LODGE, KAREN, RN, clin. coor.-ob., Bay Harbor Hospital, Harbor City, CA '85 (RISK)
MCMEEKIN, JOHN C., pers. and chief exec. off., Crozer-Chester Medical Center, Chester, PA '77
MCMENAMY, SR. JANE, adm. dir., Potter's Clay Ministries, Blacksburg, VA '83
MCMILLAN, DAVID W., vice-pres. plng., Forsyth Memorial Hospital, Winston-Salem, NC '73 (PLNG)
MCMILLAN, JAMES, asst. dir. plant eng., Tallahassee Memorial Regional Medical Center, Tallahassee, FL '84 (ENG)
MCMILLAN, MARK A., dir. bldg. serv., Episcopal Church Home, St. Paul, MN '84 (ENG)
MCMILLAN, MICHAEL C., dir. corp. plng., Lutheran Medical Center, Omaha, NE '84 (PLNG)
MCMILLAN, PATRICIA, asst. adm., Portsmouth Psychiatric Center, Portsmouth, VA '86 (RISK)
MCMILLEN, CAROL E., dir. vol. serv., Chandler Community Hospital, Chandler, AZ '85 (VOL)
MCMILLEN, LYNN, Shrewsbury, MA '75 (SOC)
MCMILLEN, ROBERT S., atty., Elizabethtown Community Hospital, Elizabethtown, NY '77 (ATTY)
MCMONIGAL, W. M., atty., Berlin Hospital Association, Berlin, WI '73 (ATTY)
MCMORROW, DIANTHA R., RN, asst. exec. dir., Lawrence and Memorial Hospital, New London, CT '75 (NURS)
MCMULLAN, LINDA B., adm. res., Good Samaritan Hospital, Suffern, NY '82
MCMULLEN, BETTE JO, dir. matl. mgt., AMI Brookwood Community Hospital, Orlando, FL '84 (PUR)
MCMULLEN, HUGH A., atty., Sacred Heart Hospital, Cumberland, MD '74 (ATTY)
MCMULLEN, MARSHALL A. JR., atty., Charleston Area Medical Center, Charleston, WV '86 (ATTY)
MCMULLEN, WILLIAM R., prov. contr., Mercy Coordinating Center, Oak Brook Terrace, IL '71
MCMUNN, C. DAVID, atty., United Hospital Center, Clarksburg, WV '84 (ATTY)
MCMURRAY, ALAN R., asst. dir. pub. rel., Holston Valley Hospital and Medical Center, Kingsport, TN '86 (PR)
MCMURRAY, MICHAEL, consult., Milliman and Robertson, Inc., Pasadena, CA '86 (RISK)
MCMURRY, PRESTON V. JR., exec. vice-pres., Baptist Hospital and Health Systems, Phoenix, AZ '85 (PR) (PLNG)
MCNAB, MELVIN E., (ret.), North Tonawanda, NY '47 (LIFE)
MCNABB, DEBORAH L., dir. pub. rel. and mktg., L. W. Blake Memorial Hospital, Bradenton, FL '85 (PR) (PLNG)
MCNAIR, GRAYDON A., dir. pers., Hospital for Sick Children, Toronto, Ont., Canada '83 (PERS)
MCNAIR, JERRY L., dir. eng., East Orange General Hospital, East Orange, NJ '79 (ENG)
MCNAIR, JOHN W., vice-pres., Lowell General Hospital, Lowell, MA '54 (PERS)(LIFE)
MCNAIR, LOREEN, dir. soc. serv., Psychiatric Institute of Washington, Washington, DC '86 (SOC)
MCNAIR, ROBERT MALCOLM JR., atty., Allegheny General Hospital, Pittsburgh, PA '80 (ATTY)
MCNAIR, SUSANAH M., dir. diet., Emory University Hospital, Atlanta, GA '81 (FOOD)
MCNALLY, DANIEL P., adm., Brookline Visiting Nurse Service, Brookline, MA '70
MCNALLY, GEORGE J., mgr. maint., Lankenau Hospital, Philadelphia, PA '84 (ENG)
MCNALLY, JOHN H., mgr. maint., Riverside Hospital, Jacksonville, FL '86 (ENG)
MCNALLY, PATRICIA C., dir. pers., De Paul Hospital, New Orleans, LA '86 (PERS)
MCNALLY, SARAH E., student, Boston University Health Management Programs, Boston, MA '86 (PLNG)
MCNAMARA, BONNIE, dir. food, nutr. serv. and cent. sup., St. Lawrence Dimondale Center, Dimondale, MI '86 (FOOD)
MCNAMARA, EVELYN M., Glen Cove, NY '85 (SOC)
MCNAMARA, FRED A., consult., Washington, DC '46 (LIFE)
MCNAMARA, IRENE, dir. vol. serv., Pontiac General Hospital, Pontiac, MI '73 (VOL)
MCNAMARA, JAMES J., PhD, dir. soc. work, University of Utah Health Sciences Center, Salt Lake City, UT '77 (SOC)
MCNAMARA, JOSEPH JAMES, supv. biomedical eng., Memorial Hospital at Gulfport, Gulfport, MS '86 (ENG)
MCNAMARA, JUDITH S., dir. pat. and vol. serv., Thomas Jefferson University Hospital, Philadelphia, PA '77 (PAT)(VOL)
MCNAMARA, JUNE E., coor. qual. assur. and risk mgr., Kingman Regional Hospital, Kingman, AZ '83 (RISK)
MCNAMARA, KATHLEEN A., asst. mgr. pers. serv., Holy Cross Hospital, Detroit, MI '86 (PERS)
MCNAMARA, SR. MARGARET MARYJOAN, dir. pat. affairs, St. Michael's Hospital, Toronto, Ont., Canada '86 (PAT)
MCNAMARA, MOTHER MARY ANNE, exec. dir., St. Joseph Medical Center, Wichita, KS '46 (LIFE)
MCNAMARA, OWEN, dir. info. serv., University Hospital, Boston, MA '86 (PR)
MCNAMARA, REGINA F., RN, asst. vice-pres. nrsg., Bristol Hospital, Bristol, CT '84 (NURS)
MCNAMARA, SUE, dir. soc. serv., Saint Cabrini Hospital of Seattle, Seattle, WA '86 (SOC)
MCNAMES, KENNETH M., vice-pres. and acct. exec., Alexander and Alexander of Texas, Inc., Houston, TX '84 (RISK)
MCNAMIRE, CONNIE S., RN, dir. nrsg. serv., Dallas Medical and Surgical Clinic-Hospital, Dallas, TX '83 (NURS)(PERS)
MCNARY, DAVID D., vice-pres., Ancilla Development Group, Elk Grove Village, IL '78
MCNARY, WILLIAM S., (ret.), Sun City, AZ '29 (LIFE)
MCNASH, MARK L., mgr., Ernst and Whinney, Detroit, MI '83 (MGMT)
MCNAUGHTON, JOHN C., dir. plant oper. and security, St. Anthony's Hospital, St. Petersburg, FL '73 (ENG)
MCNEAL, BENNETT M., assoc. dir.-dept. standards, Joint Commission on Accreditation of Hospitals, Chicago, IL '81
MCNEAL, BILL, dir. mktg., Allied Pharmacy Service, Inc., Abilene, TX '84
MCNEAL, KATHLEEN D., vice-pres. plng., Ridgeview Institute, Smyrna, GA '83 (PLNG)
MCNEAL, LISA L., dir. media rel., University of Tennessee Memorial Research Center and Hospital, Knoxville, TN '86 (PR)
MCNEAL, MARY JANE, dir. diet., St. Luke's Hospitals, Fargo, ND '78 (FOOD)
MCNEAL, R. RICHARD, pres., R. Richard McNeal Associates Company, Columbus, OH '86 (RISK)
MCNEAL, TOM R., adm., McKenna Memorial Hospital, New Braunfels, TX '72
MCNEAR, ANN, mgr. telecommun., Baptist Memorial Hospital, Memphis, TN '86 (ENG)
MCNEELY, DENNIS C., planner, Whidbey General Hospital, Coupeville, WA '85 (PLNG)
MCNEELY, FRANCES, asst. mgr. food serv., Rowan Memorial Hospital, Salisbury, NC '71 (FOOD)
MCNEELY, JANICE D., supv. med. soc. work, Charlotte Rehabilitation Hospital, Charlotte, NC '85 (SOC)
MCNEELY, WILLIAM JR., bio-med. eng., Cabell Huntington Hospital, Huntington, WV '78 (ENG)
MCNEIL, LINDA J., RN, dir. nrsg., Washington County Hospital, Washington, IA '83 (NURS)
MCNEIL, MARGARET W., coor. vol. serv., St. John's Nursing and Convalescing Home, Springfield, OH '81 (VOL)
MCNEIL, RICHARD J., mgr. acctg., Applied Management Systems, Inc., Burlington, MA '75 (MGMT)
MCNEIL, VIRGINIA, coor. cent. sup. and pat. care, Medical Plaza Hospital, Fort Worth, TX '84 (CS)
MCNEILL, DOUGLAS WILLIAM, pres. and chief exec. off., Emma L. Bixby Hospital, Adrian, MI '76
MCNEILL, MALCOLM JR., pres., McNeill Group, Inc., St. Louis, MO '86
MCNEILL, SAMUEL P., MD, dir. emer. serv., Pleasant Valley Hospital, Point Pleasant, WV '86 (AMB)
MCNEILL, STEPHANIE D., dir. pub. affairs, Washington Hospital Center, Washington, DC '75 (PR)
MCNEILLY, LARRY D., vice-pres. pers. serv., East Tennessee Baptist Hospital, Knoxville, TN '76 (PERS)
MCNEILY, KAREN MARIE, dir. vol. serv. and pat. rel., West Suburban Hospital Medical Center, Oak Park, IL '74 (VOL)(PAT)
MCNELIS, NANCY R., pat. rep., Ingalls Memorial Hospital, Harvey, IL '77 (PAT)
MCNELLEY, JAMES E., consult., Overload Service Health Care Management, San Juan, CA '49 (LIFE)
MCNERNEY, WALTER J., Winnetka, IL '50 (LIFE)
MCNICHOL, BETH, vice-pres., Bryn Mawr Rehabilitation Hospital, Malvern, PA '87 (AMB)
MCNICHOL, PATRICIA, dir. pub. rel., Alfred I. Dupont Institute, Wilmington, DE '81 (PR)
MCNICHOLAS, JAMES D., atty., Baptist Hospital of Southeast Texas, Beaumont, TX '75 (ATTY)
MCNICHOLS, EDNA T., RN, vice-pres. pat. serv., St. Charles Hospital, Oregon, OH '83 (NURS)
MCNICHOLS, EDWIN J., atty., St. Vincent Medical Center, Toledo, OH '85 (ATTY)
MCNICHOLS, WILLIAM R., corp. dir. info. syst., Columbus Hospital, Chicago, IL '86 (ENG)
MCNIERNEY, M. JANE, dir. commun. rel., Titusville Hospital, Titusville, PA '84 (PR)
MCNINCH, JOSEPH H., MD, (ret.), St. Peterburg, FL '62 (LIFE)
MCNITT, ROLAND A., (ret.), Dover, NH '51 (LIFE)
MCNULTY, JOHN L., mgr. mgt. info., Arthur Andersen and Company, Tulsa, OK '86
MCNULTY, JOHN T., vice-pres. fin., Ravenswood Hospital Medical Center, Chicago, IL '76
MCNULTY, JOSEPH D., assoc. dir. plant and gen. serv., Maricopa Medical Center, Phoenix, AZ '81 (ENG)
MCNULTY, MATTHEW FRANCIS JR., ScD, Teoc Pentref, Ocean Springs, MS '45 (LIFE)
MCNULTY, PATRICIA L., acct. mgr. pub. rel., University Hospitals of Cleveland, Cleveland, OH '83 (PR)
MCNULTY, THOMAS F., chief fin. off., Henry Ford Hospital, Detroit, MI '83
MCNUTT, MICHAEL, mgr. storeroom, Louis A. Weiss Memorial Hospital, Chicago, IL '77 (PUR)
MCPARLAND, JAMES E., atty., St. Mary of Nazareth Hospital Center, Chicago, IL '78 (ATTY)
MCPARLAND, MARY, dir. educ., qual. assur. and risk mgt., San Jacinto Methodist Hospital, Baytown, TX '86 (RISK)
MCPEAK, ELLEN A., adm., Hospital-Philadelphia College of Osteopathic Medical, Philadelphia, PA '82 (RISK)
MCPHEE, BERNICE, dir. educ. and trng., Emerson Hospital, Concord, MA '79 (EDUC)
MCPHEE, SR. JOHN GABRIEL, pres., Daughters of Charity Health Systems-W. Central, St. Ann, MO '69
MCPHEE, SR. MARY ROSE, pres., Daughters of Charity Health Systems-West Central, St. Ann, MO '83 (PLNG)
MCPHEETERS, JAMES W. III, adm., McCune-Brooks Hospital, Carthage, MO '66
MCPHERON, GENEVIEVE, vice-pres. amb. care, Mary Rutan Hospital, Bellefontaine, OH '87 (AMB)
MCPHERSON, BARBARA J., exec. dir., Central Kansas Medical Center, Great Bend, KS '87 (EDUC)
MCPHERSON, ELIZABETH E., RN, dir. nrsg. div., Georgetown University Medical Center, Washington, DC '83 (NURS)
MCPHERSON, JOHN, dir. soc. serv., Humana Hospital -St. Petersburg, St. Petersburg, FL '75 (SOC)
MCPHERSON, MICHAEL L., atty., Montana Deaconess Medical Center, Great Falls, MT '85 (ATTY)
MCPIKE, JULIE M., mgr., Ernst and Whinney, St. Louis, MO '86 (MGMT)
MCPROUD, LUCY M., assoc. prof., Department of Nutrition Foods and Dietetics, San Jose State University, San Jose, CA '77 (FOOD)
MCQUADE, PAUL J., adm., South Coast Medical Center, South Laguna, CA '69
MCQUAID, JAMES E., dir. commun. rel. and dev., St. Francis Hospital, Blue Island, IL '82 (PR)
MCQUEARY, CHERYL L., mem. membership corp., Morristown Memorial Hospital, Morristown, NJ '83
MCQUEARY, JOHN D., pres. and chief exec. off., Shared Services for Southern Hospitals, Inc., Marietta, GA '76 (PUR)
MCQUEEN, KERRY EDWARD, atty., Southwest Medical Center, Liberal, KS '84 (ATTY)
MCQUEEN, RONALD J. C., consult., Agnew, Peckham and Associates, Toronto, Ont., Canada '53 (LIFE)
MCQUEENEY, HENRY L., sr. assoc. adm., Georgetown University Medical Center, Washington, DC '86 (PERS)
MCQUILLAN, DAVID B., adm., Veterans Home and Hospital, Rocky Hill, CT '70
MCQUILLAN, JOHN F. JR., coor. energy and safety eng., Montgomery Hospital, Norristown, PA '70 (ENG)
MCQUILLEN, MARIANNE K., dir. commun. rel., Community General Hospital, Reading, PA '85 (PR)
MCQUISTON, RICHARD C., dir. eng. and maint., Bethania Regional Health Center, Wichita Falls, TX '78 (ENG)
MCRAE, PATRICIA W., RN, nrsg. adm. med. div., Pitt County Memorial Hospital, Greenville, NC '86 (NURS)
MCRAE, RUTH A., dir. environ. serv., Morton Hospital and Medical Center, Taunton, MA '86 (ENVIRON)
MCRAE, SANDY M., coor. staff dev., Shriners Hospital for Crippled Children, Tampa, FL '85 (EDUC)
MCRAY, GARY J., atty., Edward W. Sparrow Hospital, Lansing, MI '82 (ATTY)
MCREE, EDWARD B., pres., Ingham Medical Center, Lansing, MI '58
MCSHANE, FRANKLIN JOHN JR., vice-pres., Our Lady of Lourdes Memorial Hospital, Binghamton, NY '71
MCSHERRY, CYNTHIA ANN, dir. vol. serv., Methodist Hospital of Chicago, Chicago, IL '86 (VOL)
MCSHERRY, MARY E., RN, dir. nrsg. serv., Kent County Memorial Hospital, Warwick, RI '75 (NURS)
MCSORLEY, BARBARA, RN, assoc. dir. nrsg., Cape Cod Hospital, Hyannis, MA '82 (NURS)
MCSORLEY, JIM, dir. food serv., St. Vincent Hospital, Santa Fe, NM '78 (FOOD)
MCSPADDEN, GERI, dir. staff dev., St. Mary's Hospital and Medical Center, Grand Junction, CO '80 (EDUC)
MCSPEDDEN, JUANITA M., dir. mktg., HCA Parthenon Pavilion, Nashville, TN '83 (PR)
MCSTAY, ROSS W. JR., dir. pers. serv., East Jefferson General Hospital, Metairie, LA '77 (PERS)
MCSURDY, JOYCE Y., RN, dir. nrsg.-critical care, Geisinger Medical Center, Danville, PA '86 (NURS)(AMB)
MCSWAIN, JOSEPH, dir. matl. mgt., St. Vincent's Medical Center, Jacksonville, FL '84 (PUR)
MCSWEENEY, ALLEN W., dir. med. soc. work, Munson Medical Center, Traverse City, MI '86 (SOC)
MCSWEENEY, JOAN, RN, asst. clin. nrs. mgr., Northwestern Memorial Hospital, Chicago, IL '87 (AMB)
MCTAGGART, TENA, asst. dir. pers., Shawnee Mission Medical Center, Shawnee Mission, KS '86 (PERS)
MCTERNAN, KEVIN J., asst. vice-pres. support serv., Robert Wood Johnson University Hospital, New Brunswick, NJ '83 (ENG)
MCVEIGH, CHARLES B., dir., Western Reserve Care System, Boardman, OH '87 (AMB)
MCVEIGH, JAMES T., publications ed., Good Samaritan Medical Center, Phoenix, AZ '85 (PR)
MCVISK, WILLIAM K., atty., Children's Memorial Hospital, Chicago, IL '85 (ATTY)
MCWATERS, CAROL L., dir. vol. serv., St. Luke's Hospital, Jacksonville, FL '85 (VOL)
MCWHIRTER, LARRY M., dir. area oper., Ch Health Technologies, Inc., Pine Bluff, AR '84 (ENG)
MCWHORTER, ANN, dir. soc. serv., Porter Memorial Hospital, Valparaiso, IN '77 (SOC)
MCWILLIAMS, CATHERINE A., reg. adm., New Medi Company Associate, Inc., Middlebury, CT '81 (MGMT)
MCWILLIAMS, EUGENIA A., health care consult., Ernst and Whinney, Birmingham, AL '82 (PLNG)
MCWILLIAMS, FRANK G., RN, dir. nrsg. serv., Mease Hospital Countryside, Safety Harbor, FL '82 (NURS)
MCWILLIAMS, GORDON B., pres., Middlesex Memorial Hospital, Middletown, CT '57 (LIFE)
MCWILLIAMS, PAUL A., PhD, asst. provost and exec. dir., University of Pittsburgh, Pittsburgh, PA '77

MCWILLIAMS, ROSE MARIE, RN, dir. oper. room and critical care and asst. dir. pat. care serv., University of California San Diego Medical Center, San Diego, CA '86 (NURS)
MEACHAM, VERNA S., vice-pres., Methodist Hospitals of Gary, Gary, IN '83 (PR) (PLNG)
MEAD, ALICE P., atty., Providence Hospital, Oakland, CA '87 (ATTY)
MEAD, CATHIE, dir. pat. rep. and vol. serv., LaGrange Hospital, LaGrange, IN '87 (PAT)
MEAD, EDWARD C., dir. pur., Jackson County Schneck Memorial Hospital, Seymour, IN '74 (PUR)
MEAD, ROBERT M., Ernst and Whinney, Atlanta, GA '84 (MGMT)
MEAD, RONALD L., mgr., Peat, Marwick, Mitchell and Company, Kansas City, MO '84 (PLNG)
MEADE, CHRISTINE, dir. commun. rel. and mktg., Pulaski Community Hospital, Pulaski, VA '83 (PR)(VOL)
MEADE, THOMAS P., dir. plant oper. and maint., Rochester St. Mary's Hospital of the Sisters of Charity, Rochester, NY '76 (ENG)
MEADERS, JOHN DENNIS, Forum Health Investors, Inc., Atlanta, GA '74
MEADOR, PATRICIA T., atty., Duke University Hospital, Durham, NC '86 (ATTY)
MEADOR, SANDY, dir. risk mgt., Hendrick Medical Center, Abilene, TX '82 (RISK)
MEADORS, ALLEN C., PhD, exec. dir., Northwest Arkansas Radiation Therapy Institute, Springdale, AR '73
MEADOW, BETSY, coor. benefits, HCA Palmyra Medical Centers, Albany, GA '85 (PERS)
MEADOWS, BOBBY R., pres., Genesis Medical Corporation, Denver, CO '62
MEADOWS, C. ALLEN, dir. mktg. and pub. rel., Princeton Community Hospital, Princeton, WV '85 (PR)
MEADOWS, DAVID L., assoc. adm., Norwood Hospital, Norwood, MA '65
MEADOWS, JOAN M., RN, asst. dir. nrsg., Children's Hospital, New Orleans, LA '86 (NURS)
MEADOWS, PAMELA ANN, adm. off. and chief medicine, Veterans Administration Medical Center, Birmingham, AL '84
MEADOWS, PATRICIA S., dir. soc. serv., Miami Valley Hospital, Dayton, OH '75 (SOC)
MEADOWS, ROD G., atty., Henry General Hospital, Stockbridge, GA '85 (ATTY)
MEADOWS, SARAH WALKER, dir. soc. serv., William N. Wishard Memorial Hospital, Indianapolis, IN '80 (SOC)
MEADOWS, STEVE, mgr. matl. mgt., Lexington Clinic, Lexington, KY '85 (PUR)
MEALER, VICKIE, head nrs. maternity care, Hamilton Medical Center, Dalton, GA '86 (RISK)
MEANEY, KATHLEEN H., dir. diet., Fair Oaks Hospital, Summit, NJ '83 (FOOD)
MEANEY, LAUREL M., pat. rep., Walter Reed Army Medical Center, Washington, DC '84 (PAT)
MEANEY, MARY H., dir. pers., New Britain General Hospital, New Britain, CT '64 (PERS)
MEANS, ELIZABETH, RN, vice-pres. spec. serv., University Hospital of Jacksonville, Jacksonville, FL '83 (NURS)
MEANS, JOE, dir. matl. mgt., Memorial Hospital of Dodge County, Fremont, NE '86 (PUR)
MEANS, MARGIE MOORE, RN, supv. cent. proc. and distrib., Cabarrus Memorial Hospital, Concord, NC '76 (CS)
MEANS, OTTILIE C., (ret.), Florissant, MO '67 (SOC)
MEARNS, SHERRI M., dir. commun. rel., Chesapeake General Hospital, Chesapeake, VA '85 (PR) (PLNG)
MEARS, BERTHA W., (ret.), Lutherville, MD '29 (LIFE)
MEARS, PAMELA ANN, dir. plng., Durham County General Hospital, Durham, NC '77 (PLNG)
MEATS, MARVA D., supv. cent. sterile sup., St. Francis Regional Medical Center, Wichita, KS '87 (CS)
MEBANE, PATRICIA ORR, dir. commun. rel. and dev., St. Joseph's Hospital, Asheville, NC '73 (PR)
MECCIA, NEIL R., student, University of Southern California, Los Angeles, CA '81
MECHALEY, SONDRA H., asst. vice-pres., St. David's Community Hospital, Austin, TX '81 (FOOD)
MECHAM, GLENN J., atty., St. Benedict's Hospital, Ogden, UT '79 (ATTY)
MECHLER, KATHLEEN K., coor. educ., San Antonio State Chest Hospital, San Antonio, TX '86 (EDUC)
MECHLING, GLENN C., vice-pres. pers. serv., St. Francis Hospital, Charleston, WV '76 (PERS)
MECHTENBERG, BARBARA K., dir. soc. serv. and emp. assistance prog., Sacred Heart Hospital, Yankton, SD '85 (SOC)
MECKLEY, KATHY, prof. liability risk mgt. rep., Phico Insurance Company, Mechanisburg, PA '86 (RISK)
MECKLIN, JEANNE, dir. pub. rel. and mktg., Tanner Medical Center, Carrollton, GA '84 (PR)
MECKSTROTH, GEORGE R., PhD, dir. prof. support serv., Charity Hospital at New Orleans, New Orleans, LA '79 (PLNG)
MECUM, JUDY C., dir. commun. rel., Providence Hospital, Southfield, MI '81 (PR)
MEDBOURN, CAPT. JAMES W., MSC USAF, chief support div., directorate eng. and housing, U. S. Air Force Regional Medical Center, APO New York, NY '82 (ENG)
MEDDERS, B. SUZANNE, commun. rel. spec., HCA Parkway Medical Center, Lithia Springs, GA '86 (PAT)
MEDEIROS, CLAYTON, vice-pres. plng. and mktg., St. Joseph Health Care Corporation, Albuquerque, NM '84 (AMB)
MEDEIROS, GAIL H., mgt. eng., Elliot Hospital, Manchester, NH '80 (MGMT)
MEDFORD, DARLENE R., pers. rep., Memorial Hospital, Colorado Springs, CO '86 (PERS)
MEDFORD, WILLIAM D. JR., adm., Texas Department of Human Resources, Austin, TX '64
MEDINA, RAYMOND P., asst. adm., Milwaukee County Medical Complex, Milwaukee, WI '86 (PUR)
MEDINA, STEVEN ROBERT, Naval Regional Medical Center, FPO Seattle, WA '84
MEDKEFF, JACK A., dir. matl. mgt., Athens Regional Medical Center, Athens, GA '81 (PUR)
MEDLEN, EDWARD L., dir. plant oper., Monte Vista Community Hospital, Monte Vista, CO '84 (ENG)
MEDLOCK, THOMAS P., dir. matl. mgt., University Hospital, Jacksonville, FL '84 (PUR)
MEDVEC, BARBARA, nrs. mgr., University of Michigan Hospitals, Ann Arbor, MI '87 (AMB)
MEDVED, CHRISTOPHER K., coor. mgt. syst. eng., Shands Hospital, Gainesville, FL '86 (MGMT)
MEDVIGY, VIRGINIA, dir. pur., Alliance Distrib Center, Inc., Edison, NJ '86 (PUR)
MEEHAN, CHARLES H., dir. health plng., Providence Hospital, Columbia, SC '82 (PLNG)
MEEHAN, EDWARD F., exec. dir., Dorothy Rider Pool Health Care Trust, Allentown, PA '84
MEEHAN, JEAN R., RN, dir. nrsg., Baldwin County Hospital, Milledgeville, GA '68 (NURS)
MEEHAN, MAHALA, coor. risk mgt. and qual. assur., St. Mary's Hospital, Athens, GA '87 (RISK)
MEEHAN, MICHAEL J., atty., Cleveland Clinic Hospital, Cleveland, OH '82 (ATTY)
MEEHAN, THELMA A., mgr. diet., Presbyterian-University Hospital, Pittsburgh, PA '83 (FOOD)
MEEKER, GARY, dir. eng., Humana Hospital -Sun Bay, St. Petersburg, FL '86 (ENG)
MEEKER, ROBERT A., health plng. consult., Michigan Hospital Association Service Corporation, Lansing, MI '82 (PLNG)
MEEKER, VERA J., (ret.), Wichita, KS '40 (LIFE)
MEEKS, J. BYRON, atty., Lutheran Hospital Association, Kinsley, KS '76 (ATTY)
MEEKS, JANET S., dir. mktg. and dev., North Mississippi Medical Center, Tupelo, MS '84 (PR)
MEEKS, MICHAEL W., dir. human res., Bossier Medical Center, Bossier City, LA '79 (PERS)(RISK)
MEGEHEE, H. MARK, sr. mgt. eng., Baylor University Medical Center, Dallas, TX '86 (MGMT)
MEGGERS, RICHARD, mgr. cent. serv., Swedish-American Hospital, Rockford, IL '80 (CS)
MEGINNES, BRIAN J., atty., Methodist Health Services Corporation, Peoria, IL '84 (ATTY)
MEGLIOLA, DONALD E., dir. plant serv., McLean Hospital, Belmont, MA '78 (ENG)
MEGUR, MARTIN, asst. dir. med. affairs, Catholic Medical Center of Brooklyn and Queens, Jamaica, NY '70
MEHAFFEY, ELIZABETH JANE, pat. rep., Capitol Hill Hospital, Washington, DC '86 (PAT)
MEHAFFY, NANCY L., RN, dir. surg. serv., Martin Luther Hospital Medical Center, Anaheim, CA '86 (NURS)
MEHALL, CAROL A., dir. pur., Lee Hospital, Johnstown, PA '80 (PUR)
MEHEARG, MARGARET S., dir. pub. rel., St. Margaret's Hospital, Montgomery, AL '85 (PR)
MEHL, BERNARD, dir., Mount Sinai Medical Center, New York, NY '67
MEHL, BRUCE, dir. emp. rel., Saint James Hospital, Pontiac, IL '85 (PERS)
MEHL, PAUL E., dir. federal grants proj., American Hospital Association, Chicago, IL '81
MEHLBERG, JOANNE C., dir. vol., St. Marys Hospital Medical Center, Madison, WI '81 (VOL)
MEHLE, MARION L., supv. cent. sup., Mary Greeley Medical Center, Ames, IA '82 (CS)
MEHLING, DOUG R., pres., Norrell Health Care, Tyler, TX '78
MEHLING, IRENE A., RN, vice-pres. nrsg., Phelps Memorial Hospital Center, North Tarrytown, NY '82 (NURS)
MEHLMAN, GERSON B., atty., Harford Memorial Hospital, Havre de Grace, MD '85 (ATTY)
MEHLMAN, MAXWELL J., atty., Case Western Reserve University School of Law, Cleveland, OH '86 (ATTY)
MEHROTRA, ASHOK K., prin. syst. analyst, University of Minnesota Hospital and Clinic, Minneapolis, MN '81 (MGMT)
MEIDINGER, MARY ANN, vice-pres., Medcenter One, Bismarck, ND '80 (PR)
MEIER, CRAIG A., dir. soc. serv., Rockford Memorial Hospital, Rockford, IL '82 (SOC)
MEIER, HERMAN, dir. environ. serv., Holy Family Hospital, Spokane, WA '87 (ENVIRON)
MEIER, RICHARD E., dir. matl. mgt., St. Catherine Hospital, Garden City, KS '82 (PUR)
MEIERS, COL. RICHARD EDWARD, MSC USA, chief of staff, Fitzsimons Army Medical Center, Aurora, CO '71
MEIJER, THEO A., dir. plant eng., Morristown Memorial Hospital, Morristown, NJ '86 (ENG)
MEINDERS, TERESA ANN, atty., Hillcrest Medical Center, Tulsa, OK '85 (ATTY)
MEINDL, J. NICHOLSON, atty., Sisters of Charity Health Care Systems, Houston, TX '86 (ATTY)
MEINERS, SHIRLEY E., RN, vice-pres. nrsg., Mansfield General Hospital, Mansfield, OH '80 (NURS)
MEINS, WILLIAM, dir. eng., Lawrence General Hospital, Lawrence, MA '82 (ENG)
MEINTZ, SHARON L., RN, dir. reproductive and ped. nrsg. and asst. dir. pat. care serv., University of California San Diego Medical Center, San Diego, CA '86 (NURS)
MEIRING, ANNE, coor. soc. serv., Waterman Medical Center, Eustis, FL '86 (SOC)
MEIRINK, THOMAS O., adm. amb. care, St. Mary of Nazareth Hospital Center, Chicago, IL '81
MEIS, FRED J., vice-pres. pers., St. Anthony Hospital, Hays, KS '86 (PERS)
MEIS, SUSAN A., analyst fin. cost, St. Luke's Regional Medical Center, Sioux City, IA '85 (MGMT)
MEISEL, ALAN, atty., Montefiore Hospital, Pittsburgh, PA '84 (ATTY)
MEISELS, JAN ANDREA, consult., Agoura, CA '72
MEISER, SR. M. ADELE, consult., St. Francis Medical Center, Pittsburgh, PA '38 (LIFE)
MEISER, RITA A., atty., St. Joseph's Hospital and Medical Center, Phoenix, AZ '83 (ATTY)
MEISLER, ISADORE, chief pharm., Newark Beth Israel Medical Center, Newark, NJ '41 (LIFE)
MEISNER, CHARLES T., sr. assoc. dir., All Saints Episcopal Hospital, Fort Worth, TX '83 (RISK)
MEISS, MICHAEL S., coor. matl. mgt., Touro Infirmary, New Orleans, LA '80
MEISSNER, VICTORIA L. C., RN, asst. dir. nrsg., Childrens Hospital of Los Angeles, Los Angeles, CA '83 (NURS)
MEISTER, JOHN K., vice-pres. amb. serv., Sherman Hospital, Elgin, IL '75 (AMB)
MELANCON, RONALD A., dir. soc. serv., Slidell Memorial Hospital, Slidell, LA '83 (SOC)
MELARAGNO, JOSEPH V., sr. mgt. eng., Oakland Associates, Inc., Pittsburgh, PA '82 (MGMT)
MELASHENKO-JOHNS, GAYLENE, Silver Spring, MD '79 (PAT)
MELBERG, LEROY C., dir. plant oper., Saint Cabrini Hospital of Seattle, Seattle, WA '87 (ENG)
MELBERG, MARC J., dir. pers., Medical Center Rehabilitation Hospital, Grand Forks, ND '83 (PERS)
MELBY, PATRICK E., atty., St. Peter's Community Hospital, Helena, MT '86 (ATTY)
MELCHIORRE, LT. COL. JOSEPH E. JR., MSC USAF, student, Armed Forces Staff College, Norfolk, VA '81
MELENDY, KATHRYN, RN, vice-pres. pat. serv., Choate-Symmes Hospitals, Woburn, MA '80 (NURS)
MELENDY, L. ROBERT, dir. pers., St. Luke's Hospital, Davenport, IA '86 (PERS)
MELFI, MITCH H., atty., Children's Hospital, Columbus, OH '86 (ATTY)(RISK)
MELIKANT, JOSEPH P., dir. cardiology serv., Western Reserve Care Systems-Northside Medical Center, Youngstown, OH '85 (PLNG)
MELING, ROBERT T., vice-pres. mgt. serv., Riverside Medical Center, Kankakee, IL '79 (MGMT)
MELINO, JUDITH A., chief soc. work serv., Johnson Veterans Memorial Hospital, Sioux Falls, SD '86 (SOC)
MELKUS, DIXIE LEE, mgr. vol. serv., Scottsdale Memorial Hospital, Scottsdale, AZ '85 (VOL)
MELL, EDWARD L., mgt. consult., Ernst and Whinney, Memphis, TN '81
MELLEIN, MARY, dir. safety, University Hospital, St. Louis University Center, St. Louis, MO '79 (ENG)
MELLEM, ROGER C., partner, Metcalf and Associates, Washington, DC '68
MELLER, MARWIN, PhD, Brooklyn, NY '70
MELLETT, RITA M., med. soc. worker, St. Francis Memorial Hospital, San Francisco, CA '86 (SOC)
MELLING, JAMES V., dir. redevelopment, Hospital for Sick Children, Toronto, Ont., Canada '67
MELLO, JOSEPH C., sr. mgr., Peat, Marwick, Mitchell and Company, Walnut Creek, CA '85 (MGMT)
MELLO, MICHAEL, dir. environ. serv., Childrens Hospital of Orange County, Orange, CA '86 (ENVIRON)
MELLO, WILLIAM J. JR., arch., Daniel F. Tully Assocites, Inc., Melrose, MA '86
MELLOH, MARY ANN, coor. staff educ., Luther Manor, Wauwatosa, WI '85 (EDUC)
MELLON, JAMES T., atty., Bon Secours Hospital, Grosse Pointe, MI '85 (ATTY)
MELLOR, ELEANOR M., RN, instr., Graduate Program in Nursing Administration, School of Nursing, Boston University, Boston, MA '79 (NURS)
MELLOR, JOEL C., coor. video productions, St. Clare Hospital of Monroe, Monroe, WI '86 (EDUC)
MELLOTT, PAMELA J. HARKRIDER, dir., Public Relations Support Services, West Covina, CA '85 (PR)
MELOCHE, DANIEL J., proj. elec. eng., Harley, Ellington, Pierce and Yee Associates, Inc., Southfield, MI '86 (ENG)
MELONIO, DONALD E., exec. vice-pres., Jameson Memorial Hospital, New Castle, PA '75 (PLNG)
MELQUIST, NANCEE R., staff asst. risk mgt., Swedishamerican Hospital, Rockford, IL '84 (RISK)
MELROSE, J. PETER, assoc. dir. info. serv., Institute of Living, Hartford, CT '87 (MGMT)
MELROY, CHERYL SENSKE, dir. food and nutr. serv., Mercy Hospital, Grayling, MI '85 (FOOD)
MELSHEIMER, PAMELA G., coor. commun. rel., St. Dominic-Jackson Memorial Hospital, Jackson, MS '74 (PR)
MELTON, DAN L., chief eng., Cooper Green Hospital, Birmingham, AL '79 (ENG)
MELTON, JACKSON D., U. S. Army Health Services Command, Fort Sam Houston, TX '76
MELTON, PEGGY, dir. nrsg., Reston Hospital Center, Reston, VA '86 (NURS)
MELTON, RONALD P., Biosafety Systems, Inc., San Diego, CA '87
MELTZER, NEIL MARK, vice-pres., Emerson Hospital, Concord, MA '80
MELUM, MARA, pres., Mara Melum and Associates, Inc., St. Paul, MN '76 (PLNG)
MELUSO, JOSEPH LOUIS, dir. food serv., Methodist Hospital, Philadelphia, PA '86 (FOOD)
MELVILLE, CAROL, dir. pers., Houston International Hospital, Houston, TX '80 (PERS)
MELVIN, ANDREW SHAW JR., coor. commun., North Carolina Memorial Hospital, Chapel Hill, NC '78 (ENG)
MELVIN, DUANE T., supt. plant, Olmsted Community Hospital, Rochester, MN '79 (ENG)
MELVIN, PATRICIA A., dir. plng. and mktg., South Hills Health System, Pittsburgh, PA '85 (PLNG)
MELVIN, PETER H., prin. adm. analyst and inst. plng., University of California Davis Medical Center, Sacramento, CA '82 (PLNG)
MELVIN, R. MARTIN, atty., Morehead Memorial Hospital, Eden, NC '77 (ATTY)
MELZER, DOUGLAS L., assoc. adm., Long Beach Memorial Hospital, Long Beach, NY '77 (PLNG)
MELZER, JOHN A., dir. phys. plant, Methodist Medical Center, Dallas, TX '86 (ENG)

MEMEL, SHERWIN L., atty., Memel, Jacobs and Ellsworth, Los Angeles, CA '67 (ATTY)(LIFE)
MEMZOFF, JOSHUA A., sr. mgr., Peat, Marwick, Mitchell and Company, Miami, FL '87 (PR)
MENA, HELEN, RN, dir. nrsg. serv., HCA South Arlington Medical Center, Arlington, TX '81 (NURS)
MENA, JUDY L., RN, vice-pres., Stormont-Vail Regional Medical Center, Topeka, KS '80 (NURS)
MENADUE, JAMES, dir. eng., Children's Hospital, Boston, MA '75 (ENG)
MENAPACE, HERMAN N., adm., Greene Memorial Hospital, Xenia, OH '72
MENARD, KATHY, asst. dir. pat. and qual. assur. serv., Henry Mayo Newhall Memorial Hospital, Valencia, CA '86 (RISK)
MENCARINI, ROBERT JOHN, dir. facil. plng. and syst. dev., Northern Westchester Hospital Center, Mount Kisco, NY '72 (ENG)
MENCER, ANDREW E., dir. eng., Westfield Memorial Hospital, Westfield, NY '82 (ENG)
MENCK, PATRICIA C., RN, dir. nrsg., Charter Mandala Center Hospital, Winston-Salem, NC '86 (NURS)
MENDEL, EMILY S., atty., Hospital Council of Northern California, San Bruno, CA '79 (ATTY)
MENDELL, MELANIE M., mktg. assoc., New Medico, Clawson, MI '86 (PLNG)
MENDELOFF, ALAN M., adm. medicine, Ramsey Clinic, St. Paul, MN '82
MENDELSOHN, MARC R., planner, Community General Hospital, Harris, NY '82 (PLNG)
MENDENHALL, MARLENE J., coor. cont. educ., Hadley Memorial Hospital, Washington, DC '86 (EDUC)
MENDES, J. PATRICK, PhD, dir. cont. educ., Northwest Community Hospital, Arlington Heights, IL '80 (EDUC)
MENEILLY, J. KEVIN, atty., Massapequa General Hospital, Seaford, NY '80 (ATTY)
MENENDEZ, MARGARITA L., dir. vol., Meadowcrest Hospital, Gretna, LA '85 (VOL)
MENGELT, KRISTI E., dir. pers. and commun. rel., Mercy Hospital, Elwood, IN '86 (PERS)
MENGELT, LINDA, mgr. mktg. prog., Baxter Travenol Laboratories, Deerfield, IL '86 (PLNG)
MENGERING, MARK E., dir. soc. serv. and rehab. counselor, Johnson County Memorial Hospital, Buffalo, WY '86 (SOC)
MENGWASSER, MARTHA J., RN, dir. nrsg. syst. and res., Jewish Hospital of St. Louis, St. Louis, MO '86 (NURS)
MENICHETTI, ADRIAN JOHN, pres., Newington Children's Hospital, Newington, CT '68
MENIFEE, ROBERT J., atty., Santa Clara Valley Medical Center, San Jose, CA '84 (ATTY)
MENKE, JANE K., staff mgt. eng., University of California at Los Angeles Medical Center, Los Angeles, CA '85 (MGMT)
MENKE, KATHY L., coor. pat. educ., University Hospital-University of Nebraska, Omaha, NE '85 (EDUC)
MENKE, WILLIAM J., adm., Private Care Associates, Lithia Springs, GA '83 (PLNG)
MENKEN, JOHN W., mgr. plng. syst., Morton F. Plant Hospital, Clearwater, FL '86 (PLNG)
MENN, JOHN B., atty., Appleton Medical Center, Appleton, WI '68 (ATTY)
MENNE, JAMES A., dir. human res., Graham Hospital, Canton, IL '86 (PERS)
MENNING, WALTER R., asst. vice-pres., Rush-Presbyterian-St. Luke's Medical Center, Chicago, IL '81 (MGMT)
MENNITI, MARY LOUISE A., pat. rep., Allentown Osteopathic Medical Center, Allentown, PA '83 (PAT)
MENON, VANITA K., consult., Ernst and Whinney, Cincinnati, OH '87
MENSING, RAYMOND F. JR., atty. and dir. fin. affairs, Oregon Association of Hospitals, Lake Oswego, OR '76 (ATTY)
MENTON, JOHN C., risk mgr., Broward General Medical Center, Fort Lauderdale, FL '80 (RISK)
MENZEL, TONI W., dir. vol. serv., Magnolia Hospital, Magnolia, AR '86 (VOL)
MERCADANTE, LUCILLE, RN, Miami, FL '73 (NURS)
MERCEDE, JOSEPH N., asst. dir. eng., Friedman Hospital, Philadelphia, PA '82 (ENG)
MERCER-SELLS, SARA J., RN, asst. dir. nrsg., Grady Memorial Hospital, Delaware, OH '86 (NURS)(EDUC)
MERCER, JUDITH W., dir. mktg. serv., AMI Medical Center of Garden Grove, Garden Grove, CA '82 (PLNG)
MERCER, LCDR LARRY TILMON, MSC USN, adm. asst., Naval Hospital, Portsmouth, VA '78
MERCER, LOIS ANN, RN, asst. dir. nrsg. serv., Union Hospital of Cecil County, Elkton, MD '80 (NURS)
MERCER, MARTYN C. III, dir., Voluntary Hospitals of America Management Services, Tampa, FL '81 (MGMT)
MERCER, TIMOTHY D., dir. commun. rel. and mktg., San Juan Regional Medical Center, Farmington, NM '84 (PR)
MERCHANT, JOHN, mgr. plant oper., Valley Regional Hospital, Claremont, NH '82 (ENG)(ENVIRON)
MERCHANT, ROLAND S. SR., dir. off. mgt. plng., Stanford University Hospital, Stanford, CA '76 (PLNG)
MERCIER, CHERYL GRADY, off. pub. rel. and mktg., Memorial Hospital of Burlington County, Mount Holly, NJ '85 (PR)
MERCIER, MURRY I., consult., Ernst and Whinney, Columbus, OH '86 (MGMT)
MERCIER, NANCY LEE, mgr. nrsg. and pat. educ., Little Company of Mary Hospital, Torrance, CA '84 (EDUC)
MERCIER, PIERRE P., dir. fin., Montreal General Hospital, Montreal, Que., Canada '81 (MGMT)
MERCIER, ROGER R., sr. vice-pres., Catholic Medical Center, Manchester, NH '80 (MGMT)
MERCIER, SR. ROSELDA, pat. rep., St. Joseph's Hospital, Chippewa Falls, WI '80 (PAT)
MERCKE, CAROL, dir. vol. serv., St. Anthony Medical Center, Louisville, KY '79 (VOL)
MERCURY, RALPH J., (ret.), West Haverstraw, NY '84 (ENG)
MEREDITH, ELEANOR B., partner, Monroe Partners Incorporated, New York, NY '86
MEREDITH, GREGORY, RN, dir. pat. care serv., Muncy Valley Hospital, Muncy, PA '86 (NURS)
MEREDITH, KATRINA ELIZABETH, dir. mem. serv., Healthplans Management Corporation of Texas, San Antonio, TX '85 (PAT)
MEREDITH, SANDY RAY, dir. acute care serv., University of Texas Medical Branch Hospitals, Galveston, TX '80
MEREL, JUDITH A., analyst plng. and mktg., Lowell General Hospital, Lowell, MA '84 (PLNG)
MERENBLOOM, ROBERT, adm. dept. of medicine, Johns Hopkins Hospital, Baltimore, MD '84
MERHAR, RICHARD L., dir. info. syst., Hospital-Philadelphia College of Osteopathic Medical, Philadelphia, PA '87 (MGMT)
MERIT, LESLIE R., pur. agt., Jennie Edmundson Memorial Hospital, Council Bluffs, IA '81 (PUR)
MERITHEW, RENA LORRAINE BOTT, dir. soc. serv., St. Peter Hospital, Olympia, WA '76 (SOC)
MERK, JOSEPH A., dir. human res., Carrier Foundation, Belle Mead, NJ '86 (PERS)
MERKELBACH, DONALD W., atty., Montclair Community Hospital, Montclair, NJ '83 (ATTY)
MERKER, LAURA R., RN, vice-pres., Ogden Allied Service Corporation, New York, NY '80
MERKOW, JEFFREY H., vice-pres. mktg. and pub. rel., Daniel Freeman Memorial Hospital, Inglewood, CA '85 (PR)
MERLIS, LAURENCE M., pres., East Orange General Hospital, East Orange, NJ '86
MERLO, JUDY A., dir. soc. serv., Midwest City Memorial Hospital, Midwest City, OK '82 (SOC)
MERMELSTEIN, PAUL D., mgr. acctg., Medicus, Evanston, IL '76 (MGMT)
MERMIS, NORMAN A., mgr. ldry., Hadley Regional Medical Center, Hays, KS '86 (ENVIRON)
MERNYK, KRYSTYNA, RN, coor. cent. serv., Hospital for Special Surgery, New York, NY '80 (CS)
MEROS, GEORGE N. JR., atty., University Community Hospital, Tampa, FL '85 (ATTY)
MERRICK, FRANK S., vice-pres., MacNeal Hospital, Berwyn, IL '86 (PERS)
MERRIFIELD, JAMES L., adm., Wedgewood Medical Center, Lincoln, NE '87 (AMB)
MERRILL, AMBROSE P. JR., MD, consult., A. P. Merrill and Associates, Delmar, NY '38 (LIFE)
MERRILL, BAERBEL T., coor. educ., Campbell County Memorial Hospital, Gillette, WY '86 (EDUC)
MERRILL, CHARLES R., atty., Overlook Hospital, Summit, NJ '79 (ATTY)
MERRILL, LORIE, mgr. vol. and aux. serv., Long Beach Community Hospital, Long Beach, CA '82 (VOL)
MERRILL, MARK H., asst. to pres., Medlantic Healthcare Group, Washington, DC '86
MERRILL, MARY ALICE, adm. dir. soc. serv., Orlando Regional Medical Center, Orlando, FL '71 (SOC)
MERRIMAN, STAN, vice-pres., McDonald Davis and Associates, Houston, TX '86 (PLNG)
MERRITT, EDITH A., RN, asst. adm. oper. room, Oakwood Hospital, Dearborn, MI '85 (NURS)
MERRITT, ELMER J., dir. pat. rel., AMI Palmetto General Hospital, Hialeah, FL '84 (PAT)
MERRITT, MARCIA D., asst. adm., Atlantis, FL '83 (AMB)
MERRITT, MARK W., atty., Charlotte Memorial Hospital and Medical Center, Charlotte, NC '85 (ATTY)
MERRITT, RICHARD E., dir. pers. and mgt. serv., St. Elizabeth Hospital Medical Center, Lafayette, IN '81 (PERS)
MERRY, PATRICIA M., dir. diet. serv., Sarah Bush Lincoln Health Center, Mattoon, IL '84 (FOOD)
MERRYMAN, LENTON R., pres., Rogue Valley Health Services, Medford, OR '81 (PLNG)
MERRYMAN, PRISCILLA J., RN, vice-pres. pat. care serv., Mercy Hospital, Urbana, IL '83 (NURS)
MERSCHAT, MARY B., mgr. cent. sup., Kaiser Foundation Hospital, Walnut Creek, CA '85 (CS)
MERSHON, KATHRYN, RN, vice-pres. nrsg., Humana Inc., Louisville, KY '73 (NURS)
MERSON, MICHAEL R., pres. and chief exec. off., Franklin Square Hospital, Baltimore, MD '70 (PLNG)
MERTEN, CHARLES DAN, supv. plant, Riverview Hospital Association, Crookston, MN '77 (ENG)
MERTZ-HART, DIANE, dir. pers., Central Suffolk Hospital, Riverhead, NY '80 (PERS)
MERTZ, GREGORY J., dir. dev., First Hospital Corporation, Norfolk, VA '86 (PR) (PLNG)
MERTZ, MAURY, dir. eng. and constr., Research Medical Center, Kansas City, MO '81 (ENG)
MERTZ, PAUL A., adm. asst., Hospital Center at Orange, Orange, NJ '83 (PLNG)
MERVAU, RICHARD C., dir. eng., Woodview-Calabasas Hospital, Calabasas, CA '84 (ENG)
MERVIN, DONNA L., coor. cent. serv. staff dev., Lutheran Medical Center, Wheat Ridge, CO '83 (CS)
MERVINE, JEFFREY D., dir. emp. rel., Greenwich Hospital, Greenwich, CT '82 (PERS)
MERVINE, JOAN F., cardio-pulmonary resuscitation prog. instr., Geisinger Medical Center, Danville, PA '86 (EDUC)
MERWITZ, ROSEMARIE, dir. educ. and trng., Delaware Valley Medical Center, Langhorne, PA '85 (EDUC)
MERZ, ROBERT, vice-pres., Alexander and Alexander, Inc., Chicago, IL '86 (RISK)
MESA, ANTONIO A., mgr. mktg., Nash Engineering Company, Norwalk, CT '85 (ENG)
MESA, JULIO R., adm. transplant div., University of Miami School of Medicine, Miami, FL '85
MESARICH, TRICIA, dir. human res., Columbia Hospital, Milwaukee, WI '86 (PERS)
MESARVEY, JOSEPH E., asst. dir. pur., Mercer County Joint Township Community Hospital, Coldwater, OH '85 (PUR)
MESERVE, RICHARD M., asst. adm., Down East Community Hospital, Machias, ME '81 (PUR)
MESKIMEN, CARL J., vice-pres. oper., Miami Valley Hospital, Dayton, OH '74 (PUR)
MESKIMEN, JACQUELYN E., dir. pur., Lake Shore Hospital, Irving, NY '81 (PUR)
MESNER, DELBERT, Mountain View, AR '79
MESS, MICHAEL A., atty., Riverside Methodist Hospitals, Columbus, OH '86 (ATTY)
MESSER, ADDISON LEE III, Circle Soft, Charlotte, NC '70 (MGMT)
MESSER, EVA J., dir. matl. mgt., St. Joseph Hospital and Health Center, Lorain, OH '78 (PUR)
MESSER, GUY ANTHONY, student, Southern Illinois University, School of Technical Careers, Carbondale, IL '87
MESSER, HENRY R., dir. pur., Southern Baptist Hospital, New Orleans, LA '63 (PUR)
MESSER, J. N., plant eng., Rockford Memorial Hospital, Rockford, IL '85 (ENG)
MESSER, T. J., dir. cent. serv., South Community Hospital, Oklahoma City, OK '79 (CS)
MESSERSCHMIDT, COL. MARY LOUISE, RN MSC USA, Hq. Seventh Medical Command, APO New York, NY '67 (NURS)
MESSERSCHMIDT, MILLIE M., dir. vol. serv., Memorial Hospital, Carbondale, IL '86 (VOL)
MESSERSMITH, MICHAEL F., clin. adm., Concord Clinic-Hitchcock Clinic, Concord, NH '77
MESSICK, LINDA C., sr. sec., North Carolina Baptist Hospital, Winston-Salem, NC '86 (CS)
MESSICK, PAUL J., dir. pers., Maury County Hospital, Columbia, TN '77 (PERS)
MESSIER, EDWARD A., sr. assoc. dir., Staten Island Hospital, Staten Island, NY '66 (PLNG)
MESSIER, KIRK E., mgr. matl., Mercy Hospital, Iowa City, IA '77 (PUR)
MESSINEO, GUS, dir. facil. serv., Anna Jaques Hospital, Newburyport, MA '86
MESSING, FRED M., exec. vice-pres. and chief oper. off., Baptist Hospital of Miami, Miami, FL '73
MESSNER, SCOTT B., consult., Shared Materiel Management Services, San Francisco, CA '80 (CS)
MESSNER, ZELLA C., asst. dir. licensure and certification, South Dakota State Health Department, Pierre, SD '51 (LIFE)
MESTERHARM, FELIX J., RN, dir. nrsg. and support serv., Michael Reese Hospital and Medical Center, Chicago, IL '83 (NURS)
MESZAROS, ETHEL ANN, mgr. food serv., South Lake Memorial Hospital, Clermont, FL '68 (FOOD)
METCALF, DONNA LEE, mgr. vol., Carson Tahoe Hospital, Carson City, NV '86 (PR) (PLNG)
METCALF, JAMES E., vice-pres. info. syst., Worcester Memorial Hospital, Worcester, MA '71 (EDUC)
METCALF, MARION L., RN, vice-pres. nrsg., Brigham and Women's Hospital, Boston, MA '67 (NURS)
METCALF, WILLIAM H. JR., partner, Metcalf and Associates, Washington, DC '63
METCALFE, GERALD B., Emanuel Medical Center, Turlock, CA '76 (ENG)
METCALFE, JOHN C., dir. pat. affairs and serv., Memorial Medical Center, Long Beach, CA '80 (RISK)
METHENY, CARRIE L., oper. analyst, Henry Ford Hospital, Detroit, MI '81 (MGMT)
METHENY, KIMBERLY, dir. soc. serv., Preston Memorial Hospital, Kingwood, WV '85 (SOC)
METRIK, PETER F. JR., dir. risk mgt., Edgewater Hospital, Chicago, IL '81 (RISK)
METZ, DOUGLAS E., atty., St. Vincent Medical Center, Toledo, OH '85 (ATTY)
METZ, G. ALLEN, dir. plng., Children's Hospital of Michigan, Detroit, MI '79 (PLNG)
METZ, HERB H., dir. eng. and maint., Manatee Memorial Hospital, Bradenton, FL '84 (ENG)
METZ, JERRY L., asst. dir. maint., St. Anthony Medical Center, Columbus, OH '76 (ENG)
METZ, RICHARD, adm. dir., Phoenix Transplant Center, Phoenix, AZ '72
METZ, RICHARD, dir. plant oper., Christian Hospital Northwest, Florissant, MO '79 (ENG)
METZDORF, BRUCE R., contract adm., Holy Cross Health System Corporation, South Bend, IN '82 (PUR)
METZGER, ANN M., dir. pub. rel., Presbyterian-University Health System, Inc., Pittsburgh, PA '84 (PR)
METZGER, DONALD E., mgr. maint., Kino Community Hospital, Tucson, AZ '86
METZGER, ELAINE, Alta Bates Corporation, Berkley, CA '80 (RISK)
METZGER, FLOYD E. JR., asst. vice-pres., Guthrie Clinic, Ltd., Sayre, PA '81
METZGER, GLORIA P., dir. prof. serv., Missouri Hospital Association, Jefferson City, MO '80 (NURS)
METZGER, JOSEPH P., atty., Good Samaritan Hospital, West Palm Beach, FL '77 (ATTY)
METZGER, NORMAN, vice-pres. labor rel., Mount Sinai Medical Center, New York, NY '65 (PERS)
METZGER, SALLY STEELE, dir. pub. rel., Rose Medical Center, Denver, CO '84 (PR)
METZGER, THOMAS O., exec. vice-pres., Northwest Healthcare Corporation, Kalispell, MT '80 (PLNG)
METZINGER, HARRY J., CPA, pres., Metzinger Associates, Inc., Erial, NJ '77
METZLER, MICHAEL W., asst. dir. and dir. pers., St. Elizabeth's Hospital of Boston, Boston, MA '85 (PERS)
METZNER, KURT W., sr. vice-pres. oper., Fairview Hospital and Healthcare Service, Minneapolis, MN '66
MEUDELL, M. BONNER, mgr. budgeting and reporting syst., Kaiser Permanente Health Foundation, Pasadena, CA '85 (MGMT)
MEUNIER, MARCEL H., risk mgr., Baystate Medical Center, Springfield, MA '74 (RISK)
MEUSBORN, LISA A., mgr. food prod., St. Elizabeth Medical Center, Yakima, WA '86 (FOOD)
MEWBOURNE, MARTHA N., dir. mktg., Philadelphia Psychiatric Center, Philadelphia, PA '85 (PR)

MEXIA, DOREE L., dir. human res., Little Company of Mary Hospital, Torrance, CA '86 (PERS)
MEYER, COL. A. FELIX, MSC USAF, U. S. Air Force Office of the Surgeon General, Fort Detrick, MD '73
MEYER, ALAN D., dir. plant serv., Methodist Hospital, Madison, WI '84 (ENG)
MEYER, CATHERINE M., dir. plng., St. John's Hospital, Springfield, IL '84 (PLNG)
MEYER, CATHERINE M., atty., Rose Medical Center, Denver, CO '83 (ATTY)
MEYER, CHARLES H., pres. and chief exec. off., Brookdale Hospital Medical Center, Brooklyn, NY '56 (MGMT)(LIFE)
MEYER, CHARLOTTE LOIS, dir. soc. serv., Jewish Home for the Aged, Longmeadow, MA '75 (SOC)
MEYER, CYNTIA ANN, Northern Illinois Medical Center, McHenry, IL '85 (SOC)
MEYER, DAVID P., atty., Elmhurst Memorial Hospital, Elmhurst, IL '81 (ATTY)
MEYER, DAWN, risk mgr., Jewish Hospital of St. Louis, St. Louis, MO '86 (RISK)
MEYER, DONNA H., dir. pers., Antelope Valley Hospital Medical Center, Lancaster, CA '83 (PERS)
MEYER, EARL L., asst. vice-pres. facil. and tech. dev., Overlook Hospital, Summit, NJ '84
MEYER, ELAINE FALLS, RN, New Smyrna Beach, FL '77 (NURS)
MEYER, EMIL A., asst. dir. maint., Deaconess Hospital, Cincinnati, OH '85 (ENG)
MEYER, FRANCES, RN, coor. educ. and trng., Good Samaritan Community Healthcare, Puyallup, WA '77 (EDUC)
MEYER, GAIL J., dir. nrsg. and pat. serv., Iowa Hospital Association, Des Moines, IA '85 (NURS)
MEYER, HELEN, adm. diet., Little Company of Mary Hospital, Evergreen Park, IL '84 (FOOD)
MEYER, JAMES EUGENE, pres., Mansfield General Hospital, Mansfield, OH '70 (RISK)
MEYER, JEANETTE J., coor. publ, St. Mary-Corwin Hospital Center, Pueblo, CO '84 (PR)
MEYER, JOHN C., dir. safety and security, Good Samaritan Hospital and Medical Center, Portland, OR '86 (ENG)
MEYER, JOHN W., dir. mktg., Fountain Valley Regional Hospital Medical Center, Fountain Valley, CA '79 (PLNG)
MEYER, JUDITH A., RN, dir. med. nrsg., Theda Clark Regional Medical Center, Neenah, WI '86 (NURS)
MEYER, JUDITH P., dir. vol. serv., Jersey Shore Medical Center, Neptune, NJ '84 (VOL)
MEYER, JUDY C., asst. dir., American Journal of Nursing Company, New York, NY '85 (EDUC)
MEYER, JUDY, RN, head nrs. outpatient, Northfield Hospital, Northfield, MN '87 (AMB)
MEYER, KATHRYN C., gen. counsel, Beth Israel Medical Center, New York, NY '82 (ATTY)
MEYER, KAY F., dir. vol. serv., Virginia Beach General Hospital, Virginia Beach, VA '85 (VOL)
MEYER, KURT A., asst. adm., Franklin Regional Medical Center, Franklin, PA '80 (PLNG)
MEYER, MARY SUZANNE, dir. soc. work serv., Truman Medical Center-West, Kansas City, MO '82 (SOC)
MEYER, MICHAEL F., pres., Medsell, Inc., New York, NY '75 (PR)
MEYER, NANCY I., student, Program in Health Administration, St. Joseph's University, Philadelphia, PA '83
MEYER, NANCY L., mgt. trainer, El Camino Hospital, Mountain View, CA '81 (EDUC)
MEYER, NANCY R., asst. unit leader, Rush-Presbyterian-St. Luke Medical Center, Chicago, IL '79 (EDUC)
MEYER, NANCY, exec. dir., Mid Florida Home Health Service, Inc., Winter Haven, FL '87 (AMB)
MEYER, NORMAN H., asst. to pres., Lovelace Medical Center, Albuquerque, NM '65 (RISK)
MEYER, PAMELA K., assoc. adm., Christ Hospital, Oak Lawn, IL '73
MEYER, PATRICIA A., RN, asst. adm., Dettmer Hospital, Troy, OH '73 (RISK)
MEYER, PAUL G., MD, student, Trinity University, Program in Hospital Administration, San Antonio, TX '87
MEYER, PAUL J., staff consult., Deloitte Haskins and Sells, Denver, CO '86 (MGMT)
MEYER, PERRY J., data analyst, Iowa Hospital Association, Des Moines, IA '85 (PLNG)
MEYER, RAE, asst. adm., St. Joseph's Hospital, Philadelphia, PA '76
MEYER, RAYMOND C., atty., Chisago Health Services, Chisago City, MN '86 (ATTY)
MEYER, RICHARD, facil. planner, Alaska Department Health and Social Services, Anchorage, AK '86 (ENG)
MEYER, ROBERT G., Staten Island, NY '83 (ENG)
MEYER, ROBERT H. JR., student, Program in Hospital and Health Care Administration, University of Minnesota, Moorehead, MN '85
MEYER, RON H., vice-pres. sup. serv., St. Catherine's Hospital, Kenosha, WI '80 (ENG)
MEYER, SCOTT D., biomedical equip. tech., Louis A. Weiss Memorial Hospital, Chicago, IL '86 (ENG)
MEYER, SHELDON L., asst. adm. human resources, Bay Area Hospital, Coos Bay, OR '84 (EDUC)(PERS)
MEYER, STEVEN M., mgt. consult., Comprehensive Medical Services, Ann Arbor, MI '84
MEYER, SUE E., exec. dir., Oakland County Medical Society, Birmingham, MI '83 (PLNG)
MEYER, SUZAN H., RN, dir. nrsg., Brigham City Community Hospital, Brigham City, UT '87 (NURS)
MEYER, THOMAS W., supv. cent. serv., Kaiser Foundation Hospital, Panorama City, CA '79 (CS)
MEYER, VALERIE W., dir. pub. rel., Community Hospital of Springfield, Springfield, OH '84 (PR)
MEYER, WILBERT E., dir. pers. and asst. adm., Cooper County Memorial Hospital, Boonville, MO '82 (PERS)
MEYER, WILLIAM DALE, corp. dir. matl. mgt., Harper-Grace Hospitals, Detroit, MI '70 (CS)(PUR)
MEYERHOLZ, SONJA, RN, chm. nrsg., Norwalk Hospital, Norwalk, CT '77 (NURS)
MEYERS, ANNIKA C., coor. guest rel., MedAmerica Health Systems, Dayton, OH '85 (PAT)
MEYERS, DARYL L., dir. commun. rel., Platte Valley Medical Center, Brighton, CO '85 (PR)
MEYERS, DOUG, mgr. ldry., Deaconess Medical Center-Spokane, Spokane, WA '86 (ENVIRON)
MEYERS, EUGENE D., coor. health care adm. prog., Western Kentucky University, Program in Health Care Administration, Department of Health and Safety, Bowling Green, KY '79
MEYERS, GILBERT, owner, Gilbert Meyers P. E., New York, NY '84 (ENG)
MEYERS, GREGORY ALAN, dir. cont. med. educ., Saint Francis Hospital, Tulsa, OK '79 (EDUC)
MEYERS, LARRY L., adm. consult., Office of Health Systems Management, New York, NY '68
MEYERS, LAWRENCE P., assoc. dir., University of Kansas Hospital, Kansas City, KS '86 (ENG)
MEYERS, MARY L., dir. environ. serv., Mary Rutan Hospital, Bellefontaine, OH '86 (ENVIRON)
MEYERS, RUTH, mgr. environ. serv., Primary Children's Medical Center, Salt Lake City, UT '86 (ENVIRON)
MEYERS, STEVEN J., student, University of Dallas, Dallas, TX '86
MEYERSON, STEVEN, vice-pres. mktg. and bus. dev., Alexandria Hospital, Alexandria, VA '77 (PLNG)
MEYTROTT, WILLIAM B., (ret.), Pennington, NJ '40 (LIFE)
MIAO, JUDY C., vice-pres. mktg., Meadox Surgimed, Inc., Oakland, NJ '85 (PR) (PLNG)
MICALE, SALVATORE L., asst. vice-pres. gen. serv., Barnert Memorial Hospital Center, Paterson, NJ '78 (ENG)(MGMT)
MICCICHE, FRANK V., dir. matl. mgt., Mount Vernon Hospital, Mount Vernon, NY '83 (PUR)
MICCO, DONALD L., dir. maint., Jameson Memorial Hospital, New Castle, PA '80 (ENG)
MICHAEL, BRYAN J., mgr. matl., Shriners Hospital for Crippled Children, Minneapolis, MN '87 (PUR)
MICHAEL, CATHERINE WHITTEN, RN, vice-pres. nrsg. serv. and educ., Bronx-Lebanon Hospital Center, Bronx, NY '77 (NURS)
MICHAEL, J. COLLEEN, RN, coor. nrsg. prog. and qual. review, Central Washington Hospital, Wenatchee, WA '84 (NURS)
MICHAEL, JOHN H., supt. bldg. and grds., Tarpon Springs General Hospital, Tarpon Springs, FL '80 (ENG)
MICHAEL, MARTIN F., sr. assoc., Booz, Allen and Hamilton, Atlanta, GA '85 (PLNG)
MICHAEL, MIKI A., adm. asst., Fairmont General Hospital, Fairmont, WV '84 (PR)
MICHAEL, RICHARD J., atty., St. Mary Hospital, Livonia, MI '77 (ATTY)
MICHAEL, TIMOTHY, supv. bldg. maint., Providence Hospital, Anchorage, AK '85 (ENG)
MICHAELIS, STEVEN R., pres., Sme Consulting Engineers, Inc., Rockville, MD '85 (ENG)
MICHAELS, CATHLEEN L., RN PhD, staff spec., National Commission on Nursing Implementation Project, Milwaukee, WI '83 (NURS)
MICHAELS, CHRYSTAL A., mgr. vol. serv. and commun. rel. asst., Memorial Hospital, Cumberland, MD '85 (VOL)
MICHAELS, DORRIS JEANNE, dir. food serv., St. Joseph Hospital, Orange, CA '82 (FOOD)
MICHAELS, EILEEN M., prog. planner, Presbyterian Hospital in the City of New York, New York, NY '87 (PLNG)
MICHAELS, RUTH A., dir. risk mgt. and qual. assur., Phelps Memorial Hospital Center, North Tarrytown, NY '82 (RISK)
MICHAELSON, DENA, dir. pub. rel., St. Elizabeth Medical Center, Dayton, OH '84 (PR)
MICHAELSON, PATRICIA L., RN, clin. dir. med. and surg., Waconia Ridgeview Hospital, Waconia, MN '84 (NURS)
MICHALAK, MARY ANN, coor. food serv., Saratoga Community Hospital, Detroit, MI '81 (FOOD)
MICHALEK, MAUREEN T., RN, assoc. dir. nrsg., MacNeal Hospital, Berwyn, IL '85 (NURS)
MICHALSKI, MARY ANN, buyer, Metropolitan Hospital and Health Centers, Detroit, MI '83 (PUR)
MICHAUD, REGINALD J., dir. matl. mgt., Waterville Osteopathic Hospital, Waterville, ME '76 (PUR)(CS)
MICHEL, MELINDA, coor. surg., Lakewood Hospital, Morgan City, LA '87 (AMB)
MICHELEN, NASRY, MD, dir. hosp. prog., State Department of Health New York City, New York, NY '63
MICHELI, MICHAEL, pres. and atty., Riskcon, Inc., Zanesville, OH '86 (RISK)
MICHELIZZI, FRANK G., atty., Antelope Valley Hospital Medical Center, Lancaster, CA '79 (ATTY)
MICHELS, DENNIS C., risk mgr., Richland Memorial Hospital, Columbia, SC '78 (ENG)
MICHELSON, SHELLEY A., vice-pres., Ambac Indemnity Corporation, New York, NY '85
MICHELSON, SHERYL A., coor. nrsg. educ., Stanford University Hospital, Stanford, CA '87 (EDUC)
MICK, CYNTHIA, RN, University Medical Center, Tucson, AZ '83
MICKELSON, JANELLE M., dir. health and treatment, St. Joseph Hospitals, Mount Clemens, MI '87 (AMB)
MICKLE, ANNETTE P., dir. oper., Reichert Health Building, Ann Arbor, MI '85
MICUCCI, JOSEPH N., dir. human res., Haverford Community Hospital, Havertown, PA '79 (PERS)
MIDDLEBROOK, GRACE, RN, corp. dir. ed., Samaritan Health Service, Phoenix, AZ '71 (EDUC)
MIDDLEBROOKS, MUSETTE, (ret.), Columbus, OH '79 (SOC)
MIDDLEDITCH, LEIGH B., atty., Johnston-Willis Hospital, Richmond, VA '83 (ATTY)
MIDDLESWORTH, LONNIE R., dir. matl. serv., Reid Memorial Hospital, Richmond, IN '81 (PUR)
MIDDLETON, ARTHUR W., dir. pers., Baptist Memorial Hospital, Gadsden, AL '83 (PERS)
MIDDLETON, DALE P., vice-pres. pers. serv., Carroll County General Hospital, Westminster, MD '82 (PERS)
MIDDLETON, H. WOODWARD, pres., Middleton, McMillen, Architects, Inc., Charlotte, NC '77
MIDDLETON, JOE R., dir. eng., Carle Foundation Hospital, Urbana, IL '82 (ENG)
MIDDLETON, MARY B., RN, asst. adm. nrsg. serv., Tri-City Medical Center, Oceanside, CA '82 (NURS)(AMB)
MIDKIFF, JOAN M., pur. agt., Shriners Burns Institute, Galveston, TX '82 (PUR)
MIDKIFF, COL. JOHN L., MSC USA, sr. med. adv., Kimbrough Army Community Hospital, Fort George G. Meade, MD '64
MIDURA, MARY ANNE B., dir. pub. rel., St. Francis Medical Center, Trenton, NJ '82 (PR)
MIELAK, GARY, asst. adm., Christ Hospital and Medical Center, Oak Lawn, IL '81 (PLNG)
MIELING, TERENCE M., vice-pres., John Nuveen and Company, Los Angeles, CA '84 (PLNG)
MIESLE, DANIEL J., asst. dir. plng. and mktg., Indiana University Hospitals, Indianapolis, IN '84 (PLNG)
MIGLIORE, ROBERT, student, Polytechnic Institute of New York, Brooklyn, NY '86 (ENG)
MIGLIORE, SHERRY L., sr. assoc. corp. plng., Harrisburg Hospital Health Foundation, Harrisburg, PA '85 (PLNG)
MIGLIORINI, ERNEST B., vice-pres. plant oper. and maint., Servicemaster Industries, Inc., Downers Grove, IL '80 (ENG)
MIGLIOZZI, PHYLLIS A., RN, asst. adm. nrsg., Worcester City Hospital, Worcester, MA '86 (NURS)
MIGNANO, MARIAN, RN, dir. nrsg., New York University Medical Center, New York, NY '86 (NURS)
MIGNELLA, JEANNE, mgr. pub. rel. and mktg., Kennedy Memorial Hospitals-University Medical Center, Cherry Hill Division, Cherry Hill, NJ '83 (PR)
MIGNOGNA, CLARA DURANT, dir. diet. serv., Lee Hospital, Johnstown, PA '69 (FOOD)
MIGNOTT, IRWIN A., assoc. dir., Coney Island Hospital, Brooklyn, NY '84 (PAT)
MIHAILOFF, NANCY J., RN, dir. nrsg. oper., Susan B. Allen Memorial Hospital, El Dorado, KS '83 (NURS)
MIHALICK, STEVE A., mgr. food serv. and asst. dir., The Medical Center, Beaver, PA '82 (FOOD)
MIHALOPULOS, GUS, partner, Laventhol and Horwarth, Carbondale, IL '85
MIHARA, AMY, mgr. cent. sup. and distrib., Queen's Medical Center, Honolulu, HI '77 (CS)
MIHAS, JOYCE, asst. dir. vol. serv., University of Utah Health Sciences Center, Salt Lake City, UT '85 (PAT)
MIHATOV, BARBARA A., mgr. recruitment, Hospital of the University of Pennsylvania, Philadelphia, PA '86 (PERS)
MIHELICH, DONALD L., pres., Urban Oregon, Inc., Tulsa, OK '83 (ENG)
MIHEVC, JEAN, dir. pers., Little Falls Hospital, Little Falls, NY '82 (PERS)
MIK, JUDITH A., dir. vol. serv., Meriden-Wallingford Hospital, Meriden, CT '81 (VOL)
MIKA, MELANIE R., prog. adm., Mary Hitchcock Memorial Hospital, Hanover, NH '83 (PLNG)
MIKE, PETER C., asst. adm., Tucson Medical Center, Tucson, AZ '76 (PUR)
MIKELL, DIANE L., RN, dir. qual. assur. and risk mgt., Muhlenberg Regional Medical Center, Plainfield, NJ '82 (RISK)
MIKITARIAN, GEORGE JR., asst. adm., West Virginia University Hospital, Morgantown, WV '81 (PLNG)(ENG)
MIKKELSEN, MARK E., asst. contr., Medical Center of Independence, Independence, MO '82 (PUR)
MIKKELSON, HAZEL ELLEN, supv. sup., proc. and distrib., Mount Sinai Hospital, Minneapolis, MN '74 (CS)
MIKOLOWSKI, LINDA M., dir. diet., St. Joseph Hospital, Flint, MI '84 (FOOD)
MIKULA, EDWARD I., vice-pres. human res., Western Reserve Care System, Youngstown, OH '87 (PERS)
MIKULKA, THOMAS JOHN, dir. food serv., C. F. Menninger Memorial Hospital, Topeka, KS '67 (FOOD)
MILAM, CATHEY D., atty., Samcor, Inc., Phoenix, AZ '86 (ATTY)(RISK)
MILAM, J. RUSH III, atty., Edinburg General Hospital, Edinburg, TX '85 (ATTY)
MILAM, STEVE, atty., University Hospital, Seattle, WA '77 (ATTY)
MILANESI, ALFRED A., dir. pur., Mercy Hospital, Altoona, PA '81 (PUR)
MILANESI, FRANK, risk mgr., Holy Cross Hospital, Fort Lauderdale, FL '80 (RISK)
MILANOVICH, PENNY, vice-pres. hm health serv., Visiting Nurses Association of Butler Company, Butler, PA '87 (AMB)
MILBERG, SUSAN B., dir. vol. serv., Jewish Home, Atlanta, GA '85 (VOL)
MILBRANDT, DOROTHEA, RN, vice-pres. nrsg. serv., Ingham Medical Center, Lansing, MI '76 (NURS)
MILBURN, NEAL T., adm., Careunit Hospital of Portland, Portland, OR '69
MILBURN, SUE, dir. qual. assur. and educ. serv., Ephraim McDowell Regional Medical Center, Danville, KY '86 (RISK)
MILBY, KATHLEEN, RN, asst. dir. nrsg. serv., Norman Regional Hospital, Norman, OK '81 (NURS)
MILCH, ERIC M., dir. trng., Alachua General Hospital, Gainesville, FL '85 (EDUC)
MILD, LINDA J., RN, vice-pres. nrsg., Wesley Medical Center, Wichita, KS '78 (NURS)
MILD, RICHARD E., student, Wichita State University, Wichita, KS '81
MILDENBERGER, JAY, vice-pres. mktg., Silver Cross Hospital, Joliet, IL '85
MILDER, ADRIENNE, mgr. telemktg, Aims Media, Van Nuys, CA '86 (EDUC)
MILDNER, WILLIAM F., adm. asst., Zurbrugg Memorial Hospital-Riverside Division, Riverside, NJ '84
MILER, RONALD O., RN, vice-pres. pat. care, Good Samaritan Medical Center, Zanesville, OH '81 (NURS)

MILES, ANNIE, dir. soc. serv., Methodist Hospitals of Gary, Gary, IN '82 (SOC)
MILES, JOHN J., atty., Alexandria Hospital, Alexandria, VA '83 (ATTY)
MILES, MARVIN C., pres. and chief exec. off., Allentown Osteopathic Medical Center, Allentown, PA '82
MILES, SYLVIA M., dir. trng. and dev., West Virginia University Hospital, Morgantown, WV '83 (EDUC)
MILEWSKI, FRANK J. JR., asst. exec. dir., Thomas Jefferson University Hospital, Philadelphia, PA '76 (MGMT)
MILHOAN, PHILIP L., vice-pres. mktg., Rivergroup, Inc., Jacksonville, FL '75 (PR) (PLNG)
MILHON, MARILYN S., dir. vol. serv. and pub. info., Susan B. Allen Memorial Hospital, El Dorado, KS '80 (VOL)(PR)
MILICEVIC, JAMES V., dir. plant oper., Humana Hospital -Sunrise, Las Vegas, NV '86 (ENG)
MILINAZZO, MOIRA M., mgt. analyst, St. John's Hospital, Lowell, MA '84 (MGMT)
MILITZER, LAURA, dir. emp. rel., Union Hospital, Lynn, MA '78 (PERS)
MILITZER, MARGARET A., student, Graduate Studies in Health Services Management, University of Missouri, Columbia, MO '83
MILLAR, JAMES M., dir. diet. and food serv., Middletown Regional Hospital, Middletown, OH '81 (FOOD)
MILLAR, RHONA, dir. prof. affairs, Greater Cleveland Hospital Association, Cleveland, OH '86 (PLNG)
MILLAR, WILLIAM I., atty., Haywood County Hospital, Clyde, NC '83 (ATTY)
MILLARD, ELLEN M., coor. commun. health educ., Abington Memorial Hospital, Abington, PA '86 (EDUC)
MILLARD, JOHN C., dir. phys. plant, West Shore Hospital, Manistee, MI '82 (ENG)
MILLARD, LINDA J., coor. pat. educ., St. Joseph's Hospital, Chatham, Ont., Canada '84 (EDUC)
MILLBERN, MARY LOU, asst. dir. nutr. serv., Colorado State Hospital, Pueblo, CO '86 (FOOD)
MILLEN, ROBERT P., vice-pres. mktg., St. Charles Hospital, Oregon, OH '85 (PR)
MILLER, ALICE J., dir. vol. serv., St. Luke's Hospital, Saginaw, MI '83 (VOL)
MILLER, ALLAN J., trng. off., 452nd General Hospital-U. S. Army Reserve, Milwaukee, WI '83
MILLER, ALLEN L., asst. vice-pres. corp. serv., Christ Hospital, Cincinnati, OH '79 (PLNG)(MGMT)
MILLER, AMY R., dir. pub. rel., Porter Memorial Hospital, Valparaiso, IN '84 (PR)
MILLER, ANDREA W., dir. plng. and mktg., Mercer Medical Center, Trenton, NJ '83 (PLNG)
MILLER, ANNE B., mgr. pub. rel., Greater Cincinnati Hospital Council, Cincinnati, OH '85 (PR)
MILLER, LT. ARTHUR R., MSC USN, Naval Medical Command, Washington, DC '87
MILLER, B. YVONNE, RN, asst. dir. nrsg., Washington County Hospital, Hagerstown, MD '77 (NURS)
MILLER, BARBARA G., asst. dir. pers., Orthopaedic Hospital of Charlotte, Charlotte, NC '82 (PERS)
MILLER, BARBARA L., RN, actg. vice-pres. nrsg., Louis A. Weiss Memorial Hospital, Chicago, IL '84 (EDUC)
MILLER, BARBARA S., RN, rep. pat. care, Polyclinic Medical Center, Harrisburg, PA '78 (PAT)
MILLER, LT. BERNARD T., MSC USN, student, Department of Health Care Administration,, George Washington University, Washington, DC '84
MILLER, BETSY, dir. vol. serv., St. Mary's Hospital and Medical Center, San Francisco, CA '73 (VOL)
MILLER, BETTY CORSETTE, dir. educ., Wadley Regional Medical Center, Texarkana, TX '71 (EDUC)
MILLER, BRIGITTE W., dir. pers., Fisher-Titus Medical Center, Norwalk, OH '72 (PERS)
MILLER, C. A. SEARCY, atty., Presbyterian Hospital, Dallas, TX '71 (ATTY)
MILLER, MAJ. CAROL MOURTISEN, MSC USA, Bellvue, CO '81 (FOOD)
MILLER, CAROL TITTA, dir. cent. serv., Mercy Hospital of Sacramento, Sacramento, CA '82 (CS)
MILLER, CAROL, lib., Hewlett Packard, Andover, MA '84
MILLER, CATHERINE O., RN, vice-pres. nrsg., Mary Black Memorial Hospital, Spartanburg, SC '85 (NURS)
MILLER, LT. CHARLES E., MSC USN, asst. head pat. adm., Naval Hospital, Great Lakes, IL '84
MILLER, CHARLES L., pres., C. L. Miller and Associates, Beaverton, OR '67
MILLER, CHLOE A., dir. commun. serv., Parkview Memorial Hospital, Fort Wayne, IN '81 (ENG)
MILLER, CHRISTINE, dir. pers., Hahnemann Hospital, Boston, MA '86 (PERS)
MILLER, CLAIR L., (ret.), Dunedin, FL '73 (SOC)
MILLER, CLAIRE, mgr. compensation, Orlando Regional Medical Center, Orlando, FL '84 (PERS)
MILLER, CRAIG, vice-pres., St. Joseph Hospital, Flint, MI '83
MILLER, CUSHMAN N., dir. mgt. eng., St. Francis Regional Medical Center, Wichita, KS '80 (MGMT)
MILLER, DANIEL A., mgr., Arthur Andersen and Company, Chicago, IL '87 (MGMT)
MILLER, DAVID A., adm. promis lab., Medical Center Hospital of Vermont, Burlington, VT '55 (LIFE)
MILLER, DAVID B., head matl. mgt., Naval Hospital, Agana, Guam '83
MILLER, DAVID W., mgr. matl., Munroe Regional Medical Center, Ocala, FL '80 (PUR)
MILLER, DAVID, dir. hskpg. and linen serv., Southwest Texas Methodist Hospital, San Antonio, TX '86 (ENVIRON)
MILLER, DEBORAH, dir. pur., Franklin General Hospital, Valley Stream, NY '80 (PUR)
MILLER, DEE V., dir. sup., proc. and distrib., Union Hospital, Terre Haute, IN '81 (CS)
MILLER, DENNIS R., sr. mgt. eng., Mercy Hospital of Pittsburgh, Pittsburgh, PA '83 (MGMT)
MILLER, DENNIS R., dir. vol. serv., Dettmer Hospital, Troy, OH '83 (VOL)
MILLER, DIANE D., RN, assoc. exec. dir., Harrison County Hospital, Corydon, IN '69 (PERS)
MILLER, DIANE, RN, assoc. dir. nrsg. serv., St. James Hospital Medical Center, Chicago Heights, IL '70 (NURS)
MILLER, DONNA, supv. hskpg., Community Hospital and Health Care Center, St. Peter, MN '86 (ENVIRON)
MILLER, DONNA, RN, dir. nrsg. serv., River Falls Area Hospital, River Falls, WI '78 (NURS)
MILLER, DOROTHY M., dir. environ. serv., Magic Valley Regional Medical Center, Twin Falls, ID '86 (ENVIRON)
MILLER, DOUGLAS E., dir. pharm. and drug info. serv., Hospital of the University of Pennsylvania, Philadelphia, PA '84
MILLER, E. JUDD, dir. sup. proc. and distrib., Baltimore County General Hospital, Randallstown, MD '83 (PUR)
MILLER, E. L., atty., Kootenai Medical Center, Coeur D'Alene, ID '80 (ATTY)
MILLER, ELIZABETH S., coor. risk control, Bower and Gardner, New York, NY '82 (RISK)
MILLER, FRANCES C., asst. dir. soc. work, Hospital of the University of Pennsylvania, Philadelphia, PA '85 (SOC)
MILLER, FREDERICK R., proj. mgr., American Medical International, Beverly Hills, CA '83 (PLNG)
MILLER, G. JAMES, dir. pers., Memorial Hospital at Easton Maryland, Easton, MD '80 (PERS)
MILLER, GEOFFREY S., proj. eng., Mses Consultants, Inc., Clarksburg, WV '87 (ENG)
MILLER, GEORGE E., chief oper. off., Diagnostic Center Hospital, Chattanooga, TN '85 (MGMT)
MILLER, GERALD, sr. vice-pres. oper., Crozer-Chester Medical Center, Chester, PA '81
MILLER, GLENN WILLIAMS, assoc. exec. dir., Presbyterian Hospital, Dallas, TX '80
MILLER, GLORIA J., RN, dir. nrsg. and medicine, Sinai Hospital of Detroit, Detroit, MI '83 (NURS)
MILLER, GLORIA M., dir. pers., Mennonite General Hospital, Aibonito, P.R. '85 (PERS)
MILLER, GRACE L., mgr. staff educ. and dev., University of California San Diego Medical Center, San Diego, CA '76 (EDUC)
MILLER, GRANT J., southwestern reg. mgr., Coffey Communications, Inc., Ontario, CA '77 (PR)
MILLER, GREGORY R., chief exec. off., Keokuk Area Hospital, Keokuk, IA '84
MILLER, GUY JOSEPH, vice-pres., Northside Hospital, Atlanta, GA '80
MILLER, HANNAH E., (ret.), Taylor Ridge, IL '81 (CS)
MILLER, HARLEY S., mgr. cent. sterile sup., Ingham Medical Center, Lansing, MI '81 (CS)
MILLER, HELEN M., dir. pers., Morgan County War Memorial Hospital, Berkeley Springs, WV '85 (PERS)
MILLER, HENRY B. JR., dir. matl. mgt., Verdugo Hills Hospital, Glendale, CA '81 (PUR)
MILLER, IRWIN, prof., Governors State University-HSA, Park Forest South, IL '86 (AMB)
MILLER, J. SAM, dir. biomedical eng., Millard Fillmore Hospital, Buffalo, NY '81 (ENG)
MILLER, JACK R., supv. tech. serv., Follett Corporation, Easton, PA '87 (ENG)
MILLER, JACKIE, RN, staff spec., Hospital Association of Pennsylvania, Camp Hill, PA '82 (NURS)
MILLER, JACQUELINE J., RN, assoc. dir. nrsg., University of Illinois Hospital, Chicago, IL '78 (NURS)
MILLER, JACQUELINE R., asst. mgr. nutr. and diet., West Virginia University Hospital, Morgantown, WV '84 (FOOD)
MILLER, JAMES N., pres., Eaton Rapids Community Hospital, Eaton Rapids, MI '86 (PR)
MILLER, JAMES W., supv. maint., Central Blood Bank, Pittsburgh, PA '84 (ENG)
MILLER, JANE A., RN, asst. adm. nrsg., Christ Hospital, Oak Lawn, IL '80 (NURS)
MILLER, JANET D., dir. soc. serv., Memorial Medical Center of East Texas, Lufkin, TX '82 (SOC)
MILLER, JANET L., dir. nutr., Good Samaritan Hospital, Cincinnati, OH '76 (FOOD)
MILLER, JANET M., RN, dir. nrsg., Lawrence General Hospital, Lawrence, MA '82 (NURS)
MILLER, JAROLD C., asst. dir., University of Iowa, Iowa City, IA '86 (ENVIRON)
MILLER, JEAN A., dir. commun. and mktg., Alexian Brothers Hospital, Elizabeth, NJ '86 (PR)
MILLER, JEAN R., info. spec., Beckman Instruments, Inc., Fullerton, CA '79
MILLER, JEANNE E., student, James Madison University, Harrisonburg, VA '86 (PLNG)
MILLER, JENROSE M., dir. mktg. serv., Lawrence Lowe Companies, Louisville, KY '86 (PAT)
MILLER, JERRY L., dir. pers., St. Luke's Regional Medical Center, Sioux City, IA '76 (PERS)
MILLER, JOAN M., RN, dir. nrsg., St. Mary's Hospital, Leonardtown, MD '83 (NURS)
MILLER, JOAN M., mgr. commun., Kaweah Delta District Hospital, Visalia, CA '86 (PR)
MILLER, JOE D., consult., J. and M. Associates, Frankfort, KY '52 (LIFE)
MILLER, JOE, vice-pres. pub. affairs, Robert F. Kennedy Medical Center, Hawthorne, CA '82 (PR)
MILLER, JOHN F., supv. maint., Shore Memorial Hospital, Somers Point, NJ '86 (ENG)
MILLER, JOHN G., vice-pres. amb. care and surg. serv., Good Samaritan Hospital, Portland, OR '66
MILLER, JOHN M., asst. dir., University of Chicago Hospitals and Clinics, Chicago, IL '78
MILLER, JOHN T., atty., St. Anthony Medical Center, Louisville, KY '68 (ATTY)
MILLER, JOHN W., dir. maint., Windber Hospital and Wheeling Clinic, Windber, PA '83 (ENG)
MILLER, JOSEPH J., atty., Charleston Area Medical Center, Charleston, WV '83 (ATTY)
MILLER, JUDITH R., assoc. dir. and chief nrsg. off., New England Deaconess Hospital, Boston, MA '79 (NURS)
MILLER, JULI, dir. pub. rel. and mktg., Marshall Hospital, Placerville, CA '85 (PR)
MILLER, JULIE J., Rex Hospital, Raleigh, NC '86 (MGMT)
MILLER, KAREN A., RN, dir. nrsg., Chandler Community Hospital, Chandler, AZ '86 (NURS)
MILLER, KAREN L., RN, asst. dir. nrsg., Lutheran Medical Center, Wheat Ridge, CO '85 (NURS)
MILLER, KAREN L., dir. soc. serv., Ball Memorial Hospital, Muncie, IN '86 (SOC)
MILLER, KAREN M., RN, assoc. adm. nrsg. serv., St. Catherine Hospital, East Chicago, IN '83 (NURS)
MILLER, CAPT. KATHARINE D., MSC USA, adm., Brooke Army Medical Center, San Antonio, TX '84
MILLER, KATHY D., pur. agt., Bath County Community Hospital, Hot Springs, VA '84 (PUR)
MILLER, KAY, asst. vice-pres. univ rel. and dir. pub. rel., Duke University Medical Center, Durham, NC '83 (PR)
MILLER, KEVIN J., dir. mktg., Bromenn Healthcare, Bloomington, IL '82 (PLNG)
MILLER, KEVIN K., dir. mgt. eng., St. Francis Hospital, Blue Island, IL '81 (MGMT)
MILLER, KURT B., coor. mktg. commun., Bay Medical Center, Bay City, MI '85 (PR) (PLNG)
MILLER, L. ELAINE, mgr. mktg., McKay-Dee Hospital Center, Ogden, UT '85 (PLNG)
MILLER, LAVON E., vice-pres., Parkview Memorial Hospital, Fort Wayne, IN '80 (PLNG)
MILLER, LAWRENCE A., atty., Greater Southeast Community Hospital, Washington, DC '73 (ATTY)
MILLER, LEE, asst. dir. bldgs. and grds., St. John's Eastside Hospital, St. Paul, MN '84 (ENG)
MILLER, LENZO, proj. eng., Tucson Medical Center, Tucson, AZ '85 (ENG)
MILLER, LEO EDWARD, atty., Saint Alphonsus Regional Medical Center, Boise, ID '85 (ATTY)
MILLER, LILLIAN R., sr. oper. analyst, William Beaumont Hospital, Royal Oak, MI '86 (MGMT)
MILLER, LOWELL K., mgr. plant oper., Sarah Bush Lincoln Health Center, Mattoon, IL '81 (ENG)
MILLER, LYNN L., asst. vice-pres. mktg. and dev., Geauga Hospital, Chardon, OH '85 (PR)
MILLER, SR. M. GERALDINE, dir. bur. of aging, Diocese of Pittsburgh, Pittsburgh, PA '76
MILLER, M. LUKE, group pres., Holy Cross Health System, Englewood, CO '85
MILLER, MARCIA M., dir. ancillary serv., Fort Stanton Hospital, Fort Stanton, NM '83 (SOC)
MILLER, MARGARET L., RN, dir. nrsg., Lucas County Health Center, Chariton, IA '82 (NURS)
MILLER, MARGARET W., student, Duke University, Department of Health Administration, Durham, NC '84
MILLER, MARGARET, pat. rep., St. Luke's Methodist Hospital, Cedar Rapids, IA '79 (PAT)
MILLER, MARIBESS L., partner, Coopers and Lybrand, Fort Worth, TX '84
MILLER, MARK R., dir. environ. serv., Midwood Community Hospital, Stanton, CA '86 (ENG)
MILLER, MARK W., dir. adm. serv., Community General Hospital, Syracuse, NY '71
MILLER, MARTIN K., atty., Medical Center Hospital of Vermont, Burlington, VT '79 (ATTY)
MILLER, MARY ANN, dir. staff dev., South Hills Home Health Agency, Homestead, PA '85 (EDUC)
MILLER, MARY KATHERINE, dir. soc. serv., Sun Coast Hospital, Largo, FL '83 (SOC)(PAT)
MILLER, MARY, coor. qual. assur., HCA Doctors Hospital, Lake Worth, FL '86 (RISK)
MILLER, MAUREEN A., asst. vice-pres. affairs, West Jersey Health System, Camden, NJ '86 (PLNG)
MILLER, MAUREEN, RN, vice-pres., Summit Surgical Center at Voorhees, Voorhees, NJ '87 (AMB)
MILLER, MELCENA F., pat. rep., South Baltimore General Hospital, Baltimore, MD '83 (PAT)
MILLER, MELINDA J., adm., Wilson Rehabilitation Center, Fishersville, VA '85
MILLER, SR. MIRIAM CLARE, RN, dir. nrsg. serv., St. Joseph Health and Rehabilitation Center, Ottumwa, IA '76 (NURS)
MILLER, MORRIS S., RN, adm. pat. care, Queen of Peace Hospital, New Prague, MN '78 (NURS)
MILLER, NANCY B., dir. corp. commun., North Memorial Medical Center, Robbinsdale, MN '83 (PR)
MILLER, NANCY C., RN, asst. vice-pres. nrsg. serv., Grandview Hospital and Medical Center, Dayton, OH '79 (NURS)
MILLER, NANCY G., dir. vol. serv., Community General Hospital, Syracuse, NY '78 (VOL)
MILLER, NANCY L., dir. plng., University Hospital, Jacksonville, FL '86 (PLNG)
MILLER, NANCY, mgr. food serv., North Colorado Medical Center, Greeley, CO '79 (FOOD)
MILLER, NEAL F., dir. eng. and maint., St. John and West Shore Hospital, Westlake, OH '81 (ENG)
MILLER, NOELLE, asst. dir. vol. serv., Daniel Freeman Memorial Hospital, Inglewood, CA '86 (VOL)
MILLER, PAULETTE J., mgr. educ., Mercy Hospital, Urbana, IL '82 (EDUC)
MILLER, PHILIP E., dir. plant oper., St. Clair Memorial Hospital, Pittsburgh, PA '78 (ENG)
MILLER, PHILIP L., asst. dir. plant serv., Shawnee Mission Medical Center, Shawnee Mission, KS '84 (ENG)
MILLER, PHYLLIS J., coor. educ., Greater Southeast Community Hospital, Washington, DC '81 (EDUC)
MILLER, PHYLLIS R., dir. vol. serv., North Charles Hospital, Baltimore, MD '81 (VOL)
MILLER, R. COLEMAN, atty., Hospital Corporation of America, Nashville, TN '86 (ATTY)
MILLER, R. PAUL, dir. food serv., Greenwich Hospital, Greenwich, CT '75 (FOOD)
MILLER, RALPH, asst. adm. human res., Torrance Memorial Hospital Medical Center, Torrance, CA '86 (PERS)
MILLER, RHONA, dir. prof. affairs, Greater Cleveland Hospital Association, Cleveland, OH '86 (PLNG)
MILLER, RICHARD A., Oaklawn, IL '86 (PERS)

MILLER, RICHARD E., chief eng., Two Rivers Community Hospital and Hamilton Memorial Home, Two Rivers, WI '85 (ENG)
MILLER, RICHARD E., adm. and chief exec. off., Bannister Nursing Care Center, Providence, RI '69
MILLER, ROBERT A., dir. soc. serv., Froedtert Memorial Lutheran Hospital, Milwaukee, WI '83 (SOC)
MILLER, ROBERT ALLEN, soc. work consult., Huerfano Memorial Hospital, Walsenburg, CO '86 (SOC)
MILLER, ROBERT D., atty., John F. Kennedy Memorial Hospital, Atlantis, FL '76 (ATTY)
MILLER, ROBERT E., pres., Lansing General Hospital Corporation Office, Lansing, MI '68 (PLNG)
MILLER, ROBERT G., pres. and chief exec. off., Riverside Medical Center, Kankakee, IL '53 (PLNG)(LIFE)(AMB)(LIFE)
MILLER, ROBERT J., dir. eng. and maint., Holy Cross Hospital, Fort Lauderdale, FL '69 (ENG)
MILLER, ROBERT T., atty., Community General Hospital, Reading, PA '73 (ATTY)
MILLER, ROBERT W., atty., King and Spalding, Atlanta, GA '76 (ATTY)
MILLER, ROBERTA L., mgr. cent. proc., Albany General Hospital, Albany, OR '81 (CS)
MILLER, ROBERTA R., dir., Visiting Nurses Association, Greenwood, SC '87 (AMB)
MILLER, ROGER E., sr. vice-pres., York Hospital, York, PA '71 (PLNG)
MILLER, ROGER G., dir. plant oper., Resurrection Hospital, Chicago, IL '84 (ENG)
MILLER, RONALD M., dir. rad. and support serv., Hamot Medical Center, Erie, PA '72
MILLER, ROSA L., RN, assoc. adm., Truman Medical Center-West, Kansas City, MO '86 (NURS)
MILLER, RUTH EILEEN, adm. nutr., Bronx-Lebanon Hospital Center, Bronx, NY '75 (FOOD)
MILLER, RUTH S., RN, vice-pres. prof. standards, Healthstar Corporation, Houston, TX '84 (RISK)
MILLER, SADIE L., Memorial Hospital, McPherson, KS '82 (PR)
MILLER, SALLY WILLIAMS, soc. worker, Beaufort County Hospital, Washington, NC '79 (SOC)
MILLER, SCOTT R., dir. matl. mgt., Coral Reef Hospital, Miami, FL '85 (PUR)
MILLER, SHARON K., adm. asst., Corning Community Hospital, Corning, AR '86 (PR)
MILLER, SHARON, dir. unit sup., Methodist Hospitals of Dallas, Dallas, TX '86 (CS)
MILLER, SHELDON A., consult., Silver Spring, MD '46 (LIFE)
MILLER, SHIRLEY M., dir. educ. serv., Overlake Hospital Medical Center, Bellevue, WA '81 (EDUC)
MILLER, SIGMUND L., atty., Park City Hospital, Bridgeport, CT '69 (ATTY)
MILLER, STAN, dir. pers., Wilson N. Jones Memorial Hospital, Sherman, TX '80 (PERS)
MILLER, STEPHEN WILLIAM, proj. mgr., Acml Operations, Don Hills, Ont., Canada '85 (ENG)
MILLER, STEWART F., MD, dir. lab., St. Francis Hospital, Poughkeepsie, NY '86
MILLER, SUE E., asst. adm., Mercy Hospital of Folsom, Folsom, CA '80 (PLNG)
MILLER, SUZANNE G., dir. vol. serv., Jordan Hospital, Plymouth, MA '78 (VOL)
MILLER, TED M., asst. dir. phys. plant, Hotel Dieu Hospital, New Orleans, LA '85 (ENG)
MILLER, THERESA A., dir. educ., Gulf Coast Hospital, Baytown, TX '86 (EDUC)
MILLER, THOMAS D., mgr. gen. support syst., Hospital Corporation of America, Dallas, TX '79 (MGMT)
MILLER, THOMAS J., plant eng., Saint Vincent Health Center, Erie, PA '78 (ENG)
MILLER, TIMOTHY, dir. mgt. dev., Humana Inc., Louisville, KY '86 (EDUC)
MILLER, TOBIE G., dir., Mountain Medical Affiliates, Denver, CO '80
MILLER, ULRICK R. III, student, Graduate Program in Health Systems and Hospital Administration, School of Public Health and Tropical Medicine, Tulane University, New Orleans, LA '85
MILLER, WILLIAM R., mgr. facil., House of the Good Samaritan, Watertown, NY '81 (ENG)
MILLER, WILLIAM, pres., Bill Miller and Associates, Inc., San Diego, CA '84 (PLNG)
MILLER, WILLIAM III, dir. human res., Terrebonne General Medical Center, Houma, LA '86 (PERS)
MILLGARD, JACK, adm. rehab. med., Emory University Center for Rehabilitation Medicine, Atlanta, GA '85
MILLHAM, MRS. NEWTON, Glen Cove, NY '70 (HON)
MILLICH, SOPHIA, dir. vol. serv., Trumbull Memorial Hospital, Warren, OH '72 (VOL)
MILLIGAN, ANGELA T., RN, adm. dir. nrsg., White Mountain Community Hospital, Springerville, AZ '86 (NURS)
MILLIGAN, BENNIE, head hskpg., Bay Medical Center, Bay City, MI '81 (ENG)
MILLIGAN, DAVID C., asst. dir. eng. and maint., Pomona Valley Community Hospital, Pomona, CA '81 (ENG)
MILLIGAN, JOHN T., atty., Trumbull Memorial Hospital, Warren, OH '70 (ATTY)
MILLIGAN, MARILYN J., dir. soc. serv., Personal Care Health Services, Westminster, CA '72 (SOC)
MILLIKAN, DIANE E., dir. corp. commun., New England Medical Center, Boston, MA '87 (PR)
MILLIKEN, JUDY LAW, dir. vol. serv., HCA Greenview Hospital, Bowling Green, KY '83 (VOL)
MILLIMAN, MARY BETH, sr. mgt. eng., Munson Medical Center, Traverse City, MI '83 (MGMT)
MILLINGTON, SHEILA DONALD, mgt. eng., Kaiser Georgetown Community Health Plan, Washington, DC '84 (MGMT)
MILLIRONS, DENNIS CARL, vice-pres., Presbyterian Hospital, Oklahoma City, OK '74
MILLIRONS, ROGER, dir. environ. serv., Saint Luke's Hospital, Cleveland, OH '86 (ENVIRON)
MILLIS, JOHN S., PhD, chancellor, Case Western Reserve University, Cleveland, OH '65 (HON)
MILLISON, BEVERLY E., dir. soc. work, St. Joseph Hospital, Chicago, IL '85 (SOC)
MILLMAN, CAROL M., vice-pres., Harold Green and Associates, Rockville, MD '77
MILLNER, LAWRENCE M., PhD, dir. plng., Deaconess Hospital, St. Louis, MO '80 (PLNG)
MILLS, BRIAN P., mgr. sup., Sir Charles Gairdner Hospital, Nedlands, Australia '80 (PUR)
MILLS, CRAIG J., dir. pers., Providence Hospital, Anchorage, AK '84 (PERS)
MILLS, DALLAS JR., (ret.), Albany, GA '71
MILLS, DEBORAH B., coor. pat. and commun. educ., HCA Regional Hospital of Jackson, Jackson, TN '85 (EDUC)
MILLS, DENNIS J., dir. pers., Washington Hospital, Fremont, CA '86 (PERS)
MILLS, DON H., supt. bldg. and grds., Kaiser Foundation Hospital, Sacramento, CA '74 (ENG)
MILLS, DON HARPER, atty., Los Angeles County-University of Southern California Medical Center, Los Angeles, CA '70 (ATTY)
MILLS, G. FRANK, vice-pres., Mills and Mills, Inc., Architects, Dallas, TX '81
MILLS, GEORGE, dir. environ. serv., Rice Memorial Hospital, Willmar, MN '86 (ENVIRON)
MILLS, GORDON E., vice-pres., The Durrant Group, Inc., Dubuque, IA '76 (PLNG)
MILLS, GREGORY D., chief eng., Watsonville Community Hospital, Watsonville, CA '86 (ENG)
MILLS, H. EUGENE, adm. asst., Robinson Memorial Hospital, Ravenna, OH '85 (MGMT)
MILLS, JANET I., dir. diet., St. Luke's Hospital, Saginaw, MI '79 (FOOD)
MILLS, JOSEPH C., coor. equip. mgt., Providence Medical Center, Portland, OR '86 (PUR)
MILLS, MARYETTA C., RN, assoc. dir. nrsg. serv., University of Maryland Medical Systems, Baltimore, MD '83 (NURS)
MILLS, RANDY, dir. amb. adm. serv., Metropolitan Nashville General Hospital, Nashville, TN '87 (AMB)
MILLS, RICHARD H., adm., Memorial Hospital of Carbon County, Rawlins, WY '66
MILLS, SID L., mgr. pur. and stores, Mercy Hospital, Iowa City, IA '85 (PUR)
MILLS, STEPHEN S., exec. asst., Society of the New York Hospital, New York, NY '73
MILLS, STEPHEN W., mgr. loss prevention, Butterworth Hospital, Grand Rapids, MI '86 (ENG)
MILLS, WILLIAM D., dir. plng., Our Lady of Lourdes Medical Center, Camden, NJ '83
MILLS, WILLIAM H., pers. off., Veterans Administration Medical Center, Beckley, WV '85 (PERS)
MILLS, WILLIAM L., mgr. cent. sterile, Sinai Hospital of Baltimore, Baltimore, MD '78 (CS)
MILLSTEAD, IVAN E., dir. pers., Lester E. Cox Medical Centers, Springfield, MO '67 (PERS)
MILLSTEIN, ELEANORE L., dir. pur., Jewish Institute for Geriatric Care, New Hyde Park, NY '74 (PUR)
MILLSTINE, JAMES R., staff consult., CHI Systems, Inc., Ann Arbor, MI '84 (MGMT)
MILMAN, ROBERTA J., vice-pres. plng., Wyman Park Medical Center, Baltimore, MD '82 (PLNG)
MILNE, JUDY M., RN, head nrs., AMI Brookwood Community Hospital, Orlando, FL '86 (NURS)
MILNE, LOIS A., dir. vol. serv., Alberta Children's Hospital, Calgary, Alta., Canada '84 (VOL)
MILNER, CONNIE FAYE, mgr. matl., Starke Memorial Hospital, Knox, IN '85 (CS)
MILNER, LT. ELIZABETH, MSC USA, coor. nutr. care div., Noble Army Community Hospital, Fort McClellan, AL '86 (FOOD)
MILNES, M. L., dir. clin. serv., Good Samaritan Hospital, Mount Vernon, IL '86 (RISK)
MILNOR, ANN C., dir. soc. serv., Baylor University Medical Center, Dallas, TX '72 (SOC)
MILOVICH, DAVID N., vice-pres. human res., American Medical International, Long Beach, CA '82 (PERS)
MILTON, ALYCE E., dir. vol., Windham Community Memorial Hospital, Willimantic, CT '85 (VOL)
MILTON, JOHN ELLSWORTH, dir., Joint Commission on Accreditation of Hospitals, Chicago, IL '54 (LIFE)
MILTON, PAUL ARTHUR, asst. vice-pres. oper., Stamford Hospital, Stamford, CT '85
MILTON, RENEE, consult. i., SunHealth, Inc., Burlington, NC '87 (ENG)
MILUM, JOAN L., RN, vice-pres. nrsg. serv., Gwinnett Hospital System, Lawrenceville, GA '82 (NURS)
MIMBS, SHARON ELIZABETH, student, Georgia State University-Institute of Health Administration, Atlanta, GA '86
MIMI, FOSTER D., dir. vol. serv., Straub Clinic and Hospital, Honolulu, HI '86 (VOL)
MIMS, EDWIN T., dir. maint., Hinds General Hospital, Jackson, MS '84 (ENG)
MINARD, BERNIE F., sr. vice-pres., The Methodist Hospital, Houston, TX '84 (MGMT)
MINARD, THOMAS ROBERT, dir. environ. serv., Santa Rosa Memorial Hospital, Santa Rosa, CA '86 (ENVIRON)
MINCEMOYER, ROBERT R. JR., dir. pat. care serv., Clifton Springs Hospital and Clinic, Clifton Springs, NY '74
MINCH, DAVID A., pres., Health Technology Strategic Systems, Concord, CA '80 (MGMT)
MINCKLER, CHERYL D., dir. pub. rel. and mktg., Valley Medical Center, Renton, WA '85 (PR) (PLNG)
MINDELL, HAROLD L., assoc. adm. eng., Yale-New Haven Hospital, New Haven, CT '79 (ENG)
MINEHART, BILLY J., asst. mgr. cent. serv., Mercy Hospital of Sacramento, Sacramento, CA '86 (CS)
MINER, ALLISON A., dir. food serv., Hospital for Sick Children, Toronto, Ont., Canada '85 (FOOD)
MINER, STEPHEN M., dir. strategic plng., Methodist Hospital, Philadelphia, PA '83
MINETTE, HENRI G., vice-pres., Iowa Methodist Health System, Des Moines, IA '83 (PLNG)
MINGEE, ESTHER, RN, head nrs. outpatient serv., Jefferson Davis Memorial Hospital, Natchez, MS '87 (AMB)
MINI, REBECCA BRAY, dir. commun., Proctor Community Hospital, Peoria, IL '87 (PR)
MINICUCCI, RICHARD F., atty., Hospital for Joint Diseases and Medical Center, New York, NY '78 (ATTY)
MINICUCCI, THOMAS D., adm., Horsham Clinic, Ambler, PA '76
MININNI, SUSAN A., equip. maint. tech., University Hospital-University of Nebraska, Omaha, NE '86 (CS)
MINISTER, MICHAEL E., atty., Grant Medical Center, Columbus, OH '75 (ATTY)
MINISTRELLI, JEAN R., risk mgt. spec., Mount Carmel Mercy Hospital, Detroit, MI '85 (RISK)
MINK, RICHARD C., dir. pers., Columbus Hospital, Great Falls, MT '75 (PERS)
MINKALIS, CHESTER A., vice-pres., Tribrook Group, Inc., Oak Brook, IL '73
MINKIN, ROBERT A., vice-pres., Memorial Hospitals Association, Modesto, CA '83 (ENG)
MINKLER, PATRICIA P., atty., Aultman Hospital, Canton, OH '82 (ATTY)
MINKOFF, HARVEY, dir. human res., University Hospitals of Cleveland, Cleveland, OH '86 (PERS)
MINNICK, CHARLENE M. D., dir. risk mgt., St. Luke's Hospital, San Francisco, CA '86 (RISK)
MINNICK, KRISTINE E., Olney, MD '83 (EDUC)
MINOGUE, SHARON A., vice-pres. clin. serv., Robert Wood Johnson University Hospital, New Brunswick, NJ '87 (AMB)
MINOGUE, WILLIAM F., MD, med. dir., George Washington University Hospital, Washington, DC '84
MINOR, J. CHRISTOPHER, atty., Pacific Communities Hospital, Newport, OR '71 (ATTY)
MINOR, JOHN T. III, atty., Hamilton Medical Center, Dalton, GA '81 (ATTY)
MINOR, SR. MARY ANN, vice-pres., Hospital Sisters Health System, Springfield, IL '84
MINOR, RICHARD J., pres. and chief exec. off., Grandview Hospital and Medical Center, Dayton, OH '64 (PLNG)
MINORS, PATRICIA M., dir. mgt. eng., Saint Joseph's Hospital, Atlanta, GA '77 (MGMT)
MINSENT, CAPT. DENNIS, MSC USAF, APO San Francisco, CA '83 (ENG)
MINSKY, BART R., dir. emp. rel., Leonard Hospital, Troy, NY '83 (PERS)
MINSLOFF, MARK R., pres. health care assoc., Meriter Hospital, Madison, WI '87 (AMB)
MINTEL, MAURA B., RN, vice-pres. nrsg., New Britain General Hospital, New Britain, CT '85 (NURS)
MINTON, FRANCES B., dir. in-service, Buchanan General Hospital, Grundy, VA '86 (EDUC)
MINTON, RICK N., adm. dir. support serv., AMI Frye Regional Medical Center, Hickory, NC '82 (ENG)
MINTON, ROBERT H., assoc. adm., Lahey Clinic Hospital, Burlington, MA '70 (ENG)
MINTZ, ALBERT, atty., Touro Infirmary, New Orleans, LA '71 (ATTY)
MINTZ, HOWARD, adm., Miami Medical Personnel Pool, Miami, FL '74 (MGMT)
MINTZ, MICHAEL D., pres., International Technidyne Corporation, Edison, NJ '82
MINTZ, STEVEN W., consult., Swm Management Consultant, New City, NY '69
MINYARD, KAREN J., RN, dir. maternal-child nrsg., Medical Center of Central Georgia, Macon, GA '83 (NURS)
MIODOVSKI, ROBERT, asst. vice-pres. educ. and trng., South Coast Medical Center, South Laguna, CA '83 (EDUC)
MIPOS, DEBRA, coor. trng., Kaiser Foundation Hospital, Hayward, CA '77 (EDUC)
MIRABILE, MARY PAT, coor. claims, J. Hillis Miller Health Center Insurance Trust Fund, Gainesville, FL '87 (RISK)
MIRACLE, LARRY L., dir. human res., Marion General Hospital, Marion, OH '86 (PERS)
MIRACLE, SARAH J., adm. diet., Valley View Regional Hospital, Ada, OK '85 (FOOD)
MIRAFLOR, CLARITA, RN, dir. nrsg. serv., Covina Valley Community Hospital, West Covina, CA '80 (NURS)
MIRAGLIA, SALVATORE J., mgr. educ., Anon-Anew, Inc., Boca Raton, FL '86 (EDUC)
MIRANDA, HECTOR NOEL, dir. pers., Boston City Hospital, Boston, MA '83 (PERS)
MIRASOLA, SHERRY E., prog. mgr. pub. affairs, Michigan Hospital Association, Lansing, MI '85 (PR)
MIRAVITE, ALEXANDER A., mech. eng., U. S. Army Health Facilities Planning Agency, Washington, DC '83 (ENG)
MIRCHANDANI, DEEPAK B., dir. info. serv., Lexington County Hospital, West Columbia, SC '87 (MGMT)
MIRICH, ELEANOR KAY, chief exec. off., Mirich Medical Corporation, Merrillville, IN '83 (PLNG)
MIRICK, RICHARD W., atty., Worcester Memorial Hospital, Worcester, MA '68 (ATTY)
MIRICK, LT. COL. STEVEN C., MSC USAF, mgr. health policies prog., Department of Air Force Medical Service, Bolling AFB, DC '71
MIRMOBINI, MARYAM, mgt. eng., Methodist Hospital of Southern California, Arcadia, CA '86 (MGMT)
MIRON, NANCY B., dir. mktg. commun., Vincentian Health Services, Los Angeles, CA '82 (PR)
MIRRIELEES, ARCH F., pres., F. Mirrielees Company, Clearwater, FL '84 (MGMT)
MIRSKY, MICHAEL B., dir. biomedical eng., St. Luke's-Roosevelt Hospital Center, New York, NY '81 (ENG)
MIRTO, NANCY, dir. plng. and util. serv., Hospital Association of Rhode Island, Providence, RI '85 (PLNG)
MISCHLEY, JOANNE, dir. staff dev., Chelsea Community Hospital, Chelsea, MI '86 (EDUC)
MISENER, GERALDINE A., asst. supv. cent. serv., Fairview General Hospital, Cleveland, OH '79 (CS)

MISENER, JOHN H., asst. vice-pres. partnership, dev. and plng., Voluntary Hospitals of America Management Services, Tampa, FL '84 (PLNG)

MISENKO, JOSEPH F. JR., dir. in-service educ., Mercy Center for Health Care Services, Aurora, IL '76 (EDUC)

MISEVETH, PAUL A., adm. off., Department of Family Medicine, Wayne State University, Detroit, MI '76

MISHEK, MARK G., atty., Metropolitan Medical Center, Minneapolis, MN '81 (ATTY)

MISHRA, HARRY H., mng. dir., Houston, TX '83

MISHREKI, ELIZABETH A., dir. mktg., pub. rel. and vol. serv., Doctors Hospital of Santa Ana, Santa Ana, CA '86 (VOL)

MISKE, JAMES L., supv. clin. eng. and biomedical, Lutheran General Hospital, Park Ridge, IL '87 (ENG)

MISKELL, GAYLA P., mgr. pers., Flowers Hospital, Dothan, AL '80 (PERS)

MISNER, JAMES D., adm. asst., HCA West Paces Ferry Hospital, Atlanta, GA '86 (PLNG)

MISRA, VINOD K., pres., The Burlington Group, Burlington, MA '82 (PLNG)

MISSILDINE, SYBLE F., RN, dir. nrsg. and asst. adm., Northeast Medical Center Hospital, Humble, TX '86 (NURS)(AMB)

MISTOVICH, DESPINA, dir. pat. rel. and vol. serv., Osteopathic Medical Center, Philadelphia, PA '86 (PAT)

MISTRANGELO, JOHN, dir. soc. work, Fallston General Hospital, Fallston, MD '85 (SOC)

MITBY, JOHN C., atty., Columbus Community Hospital, Columbus, WI '80 (ATTY)

MITCHAM, DEBORAH S., mgt. eng., Northeast Georgia Medical Center, Gainesville, GA '87 (MGMT)

MITCHEL, MONROE, pres., Centers for Living, Inc., North Miami Beach, FL '61

MITCHELL, ABBY, exec. assoc. to dean, University of Texas Medical School, Houston, TX '79 (PLNG)

MITCHELL, ADA I., (ret.), Montpelier, OH '48 (LIFE)

MITCHELL, BARBARA R., dir. food serv., University of New Mexico Hospital-Bernalillo County Medical Center, Albuquerque, NM '81 (FOOD)

MITCHELL, BEVERLY J., mgr. vol. serv., Scottsdale Memorial Hospital, Scottsdale, AZ '84 (VOL)

MITCHELL, DAVID A., RN, asst. adm. nrsg., Doctors Hospital, Little Rock, AR '87 (NURS)

MITCHELL, DEE ANNA, mgr. pur., Berlin Memorial Hospital, Berlin, WI '82 (PUR)

MITCHELL, DELMER, atty., Blessing Hospital, Quincy, IL '85 (ATTY)

MITCHELL, EDNA S., asst. dir. nrsg., Mount Sinai Medical Center, Milwaukee, WI '82 (EDUC)

MITCHELL, EDWIN L., atty., Medcenter Hospital, Marion, OH '75 (ATTY)

MITCHELL, ELIZABETH, health serv. rep., St. Paul Fire and Marine Insurance, Portland, OR '85 (RISK)

MITCHELL, EUGENE P., atty., Saint Joseph Health Center Kansas, Kansas City, MO '77 (ATTY)

MITCHELL, GAIL, adm. dir., St. Paul Health Care Center, The Colony, TX '87 (AMB)

MITCHELL, GARETH HEEFNER, adm., Detroit Memorial Hospital, Detroit, MI '58

MITCHELL, GARY W., dir. pharm. and matl., Newman Memorial Hospital, Shattuck, OK '85 (PUR)

MITCHELL, GLENN R., exec. dir., Alliance Health System, Norfolk, VA '67

MITCHELL, H. S., dir. plant oper., Cook-Fort Worth Children Medical Center, Fort Worth, TX '86 (ENG)

MITCHELL, HELEN, dir. mktg. and pub. rel., Los Robles Regional Medical Center, Thousand Oaks, CA '80 (PR)

MITCHELL, JACK G., student, New School for Social Research, New York, NY '87

MITCHELL, JOANNE, dir. soc. serv., St. Margaret Memorial Hospital, Pittsburgh, PA '71 (SOC)

MITCHELL, JOHN A., St. Francis Hospital, Santa Barbara, CA '85 (ENG)

MITCHELL, JOHN ALBERT, atty., Maine Medical Center, Portland, ME '68 (ATTY)

MITCHELL, JOHN F., atty., Harrison Memorial Hospital, Bremerton, WA '87 (ATTY)

MITCHELL, JON KEITH, pres. and chief exec. off., Empire Health Services, Spokane, WA '73

MITCHELL, JUDITH C., asst. vice-pres. pub. rel., Phelps Memorial Hospital Center, North Tarrytown, NY '79 (PR)

MITCHELL, JUDY L., pat. rep., Parkview Episcopal Medical Center, Pueblo, CO '86 (PAT)

MITCHELL, KAREN, RN, assoc. dir. nrsg., Mercy Hospital and Medical Center, San Diego, CA '86 (NURS)

MITCHELL, KENNETH M., arch., Detroit, MI '78

MITCHELL, LEANN, supv. matl. mgt., Healthamerica, Indianapolis, IN '84 (PUR)

MITCHELL, LIZ, RN, asst. vice-pres., St. Joseph's Hospital, Stockton, CA '79 (NURS)(AMB)

MITCHELL, MALINDA S., RN, assoc. dir. nrsg., Stanford University Hospital, Stanford, CA '85 (NURS)

MITCHELL, MARK, adm. asst., Crozer-Chester Medical Center, Chester, PA '71

MITCHELL, MARY KAY, dir. pub. rel., Mercer Medical Center, Trenton, NJ '86 (PR)

MITCHELL, MARYANN W., dir., Owensboro-Daviess County Hospital, Owensboro, KY '83 (VOL)

MITCHELL, MAURA A., RN, assoc. dir. and asst. dir. pat. care serv., Brookline Hospital, Brookline, MA '82 (NURS)(PLNG)

MITCHELL, MERVIN, dir. plant eng., Rappahannock General Hospital, Kilmarnock, VA '80 (ENG)

MITCHELL, MICHAEL D., dir. plng. and dev., Oak Hill Hospital, Joplin, MO '82 (PLNG)

MITCHELL, MICHAEL WESLEY, Toledo, OH '79 (CS)

MITCHELL, NANCY B., coor. commun. rel., St. Eugene Community Hospital, Dillon, SC '86 (PLNG)

MITCHELL, O. RUTH, coor. human res. and exec. sec. adm., North Hills Medical Center, North Richland Hills, TX '85 (PAT)

MITCHELL, PATRICIA C., supv. emp., Tucson General Hospital, Tucson, AZ '82 (PERS)

MITCHELL, PHILIP H., atty., Cook County Hospital, Chicago, IL '85 (ATTY)

MITCHELL, R. JAMES, sr. vice-pres. human res., Wesley Medical Center, Wichita, KS '71 (PERS)

MITCHELL, REBECCA S., risk mgt. consult., North Carolina Hospital Association Trust Fund, Raleigh, NC '82 (RISK)

MITCHELL, ROBERT A., adm. legal affairs and staff serv., Henry Ford Hospital, Detroit, MI '77 (ATTY)(RISK)

MITCHELL, ROBERT E. SR., dir. protective serv., Holmes Regional Medical Center, Melbourne, FL '81 (RISK)

MITCHELL, SIDNEY E., dep. dir. clin. serv., University Hospital, Stony Brook, NY '85

MITCHELL, STELLA J., pur. agt., Beebe Hospital of Sussex County, Lewes, DE '79 (PUR)

MITCHELL, SYLVIA B., dir. diet., St. Francis Xavier Hospital, Charleston, SC '80 (FOOD)

MITCHELL, TOM, chief fin. off., Joan Glancy Memorial Hospital, Duluth, GA '83

MITCHELL, WILLIAM C., dir. environ. serv., Mount Sinai Medical Center, Miami Beach, FL '86 (ENVIRON)

MITCHELL, WILLIAM G., exec. dir., Jefferson Davis Memorial Hospital, Natchez, MS '73

MITCHELL, LT. WILLIAM L., MSC USN, student, Department of Health Care Administration, George Washington University, Washington, DC '85

MITCHEM, W. SPENCER, atty., Baptist Hospital, Pensacola, FL '71 (ATTY)

MITCHESON, JACK L. SR., chief maint. eng., East Liverpool City Hospital, East Liverpool, OH '75 (ENG)

MITRI, JAN A., head soc. serv., Whidbey General Hospital, Coupeville, WA '84 (SOC)

MITRISIN, GARY, dir. discharge plng., Marymount Hospital, Garfield Heights, OH '85 (SOC)

MITSUHATA, KENNETH T., asst. dir. pat. and family serv., Childrens Hospital of Los Angeles, Los Angeles, CA '86 (SOC)

MITTEER, BRIAN R., pres., Delaware Valley Hospital, Walton, NY '87 (AMB)

MITTEER, WAYNE C., mgr. amb. serv., Our Lady of Lourdes Memorial Hospital, Binghamton, NY '87 (AMB)

MITTEN, R. C., atty., Fennemore, Craig, Von Ammon, Udall and Powers, Cottonwood, AZ '75 (ATTY)

MITTICA, ROCCO C., exec. vice-pres., Whidden Memorial Hospital, Everett, MA '53 (LIFE)

MITTON, LISA A., dir. soc. serv., Providence Hospital, Medford, OR '85 (SOC)

MITTS, WILLA M., RN, coor. soc. serv., Barton Memorial Hospital, South Lake Tahoe, CA '81 (SOC)

MIX, DONALD, supv. bldg. and grds., Youville Rehabilitation and Chronic Disease Hospital, Cambridge, MA '77 (ENG)

MIXON, ELIZABETH R., RN, sr. vice-pres., Research Medical Center, Kansas City, MO '80 (NURS)

MIYAGISHIMA, DUANE H., asst. vice-pres. municipal res., Morgan Guaranty Trust Company of New York, New York, NY '82 (PLNG)

MIYAJI, ROGER W., atty., Bess Kaiser Medical Center, Portland, OR '75 (ATTY)

MIYAKE, RAYMOND I., dir. soc. serv., Bay Medical Center, Bay City, MI '71 (SOC)

MIYAMOTO, JAN M., coor. emp. and benefits, G. N. Wilcox Memorial Hospital, Lihue, HI '82 (PERS)

MIZE, JOHN W., atty., Asbury Hospital, Salina, KS '80 (ATTY)

MIZELL, DENNIS G., mgr. ldry., McLaren General Hospital, Flint, MI '86 (ENVIRON)

MIZELL, RODERICK D., asst. adm., Hunt Memorial Hospital District-Citizens General Hospital, Greenville, TX '77

MIZRAHI, REUBEN N., dir. pers., Laurel Oaks Hospital, Orlando, FL '83 (PERS)

MKITARIAN, RITA E., coor. vol., Northeastern Hospital of Philadelphia, Philadelphia, PA '83 (VOL)

MLAWSKY, JENNY R., adm. urology, Mount Sinai Medical Center, New York, NY '86

MOAKLER, THOMAS JOSEPH, vice-pres. prof. serv., Dover General Hospital and Medical Center, Dover, NJ '76

MOAT, MARY E., RN, asst. dir. nrsg., St. Joseph's Hospital, Milwaukee, WI '84 (NURS)

MOATS, JEAN, vice-pres. qual. assur. and med. staff serv., St. Agnes Hospital and Medical Center, Fresno, CA '86 (RISK)

MOAZZAMI, SETAREH, consult. mgt. eng., Health Systems Technology, Alexandria, VA '83 (MGMT)

MOBBERLEY, BRUCE D., chief soc. work serv., Veterans Administration Medical Center, Albuquerque, NM '75 (SOC)

MOBLEY, DON, mgr. commun., Arlington Hospital, Arlington, VA '86 (ENG)

MOBLEY, JOHN R., dir. pers., Missouri Delta Medical Center, Sikeston, MO '86 (PERS)

MOBLEY, MARY L., dir. vol., St. Joseph Hospital, Houston, TX '82 (VOL)

MOBLEY, SARA I., vice-pres. matl. serv., Winter Park Memorial Hospital, Winter Park, FL '57 (PUR)(LIFE)

MOBURG, KENNETH DEAN, pres., Lutheran Hospital, Moline, IL '52 (LIFE)

MOCARSKI, CDR FRANCES J., coor. inpat. educ., Naval Hospital, Bethesda, MD '86 (EDUC)

MOCHEL, MARTY, assoc. adm. prof. serv., Oak Forest Hospital of Cook County, Oak Forest, IL '80 (PLNG)

MOCKO, EDWARD P., sr. proj. leader-syst. dev., St. Vincent's Hospital and Medical Center, New York, NY '86 (MGMT)

MOCKUS, CHARLENE A., coor. health educ., Michael Reese Health Plan, Chicago, IL '84 (EDUC)

MOCZYDLOWSKY, MARY, dir. pat. and family counselor, Mercy Medical Center, Denver, CO '86 (SOC)

MODANY, DIANE LYNN, dir. commun. rel. and dev., Aliquippa Hospital, Aliquippa, PA '82 (PR)

MODER, DENNIS H., dir. food serv., Gulf Coast Community Hospital, Biloxi, MS '85 (FOOD)

MODERY, ELIZABETH C., dir. vol. serv., Mercy Hospital, Scranton, PA '68 (VOL)

MODICA, ROSE S., spec. asst. pat. serv., St. Mary's Hospital, Brooklyn, NY '78 (PAT)

MODLIN, ELIHU H., atty., Franklin General Hospital, Valley Stream, NY '77 (ATTY)

MOE, CHARLES ALLAN, vice-pres., Dakota Hospital, Fargo, ND '72 (PERS)

MOEBUS, RALPH, Spring Lake, MI '83 (MGMT)

MOED, LEON, partner, Skidmore, Owing and Merrill, New York, NY '76

MOEDING, JAMES, exec. hskpr., St. Luke's Hospital, Aberdeen, SD '86 (ENVIRON)

MOELLENBECK, CHARLOTTE A., dir. vol. serv., Morristown Memorial Hospital, Morristown, NJ '85 (VOL)

MOELLER, A. DIANE, pres., Catholic Health Corporation, Omaha, NE '71

MOEN, JULIANNE R., pub. rel. consult., Duluth, MN '81 (PR)

MOEN, LILA, nrs. mgr. emer., St. Joseph's Medical Center, Brainerd, MN '87 (AMB)

MOEN, VICTORIA J., RN, coor. commun. outreach, Memorial Hospital of Lafayette County, Darlington, WI '86 (VOL)

MOENICH, RAYMOND A., asst. vice-pres., Carle Foundation Hospital, Urbana, IL '71 (ENG)

MOESCHING, CAROL M., mgr. sup., proc. and distrib., California Medical Center-Los Angeles, Los Angeles, CA '83 (CS)

MOESER, JOEY, dir. vol., Sacred Heart Medical Center, Spokane, WA '82 (VOL)

MOFFA, DOMINIC S., dir. plng., Atlantic City Medical Center, Atlantic City, NJ '83 (PLNG)

MOFFATT, DOROTHY J., dir. pers., Millinocket Regional Hospital, Millinocket, ME '83 (PERS)

MOFFET, GARY T., exec. assoc. plng., dev. and outreach, Saint Thomas Medical Center, Akron, OH '86 (PLNG)

MOFFET, JAMES F., vice-pres. corp. pub. rel., Health Central System, Minneapolis, MN '81 (PR)

MOFFETT, GLEN DAVID, atty., West Virginia University Hospital, Morgantown, WV '83 (ATTY)

MOFFITT, TERESA A., sec. risk mgt., Phico Insurance Company, Mechanicsburg, PA '82 (RISK)

MOG, GLORIA J., dir. clin. soc. work, Dominion Hospital, Falls Church, VA '85 (SOC)

MOGGACH, G. PAUL, supv. risk mgt., University of Michigan Hospitals, Ann Arbor, MI '84 (RISK)

MOHLER, AL, dir. phys. plant, University of Alberta Hospital, Edmonton, Alta., Canada '86 (ENG)

MOHLER, DANIEL RONALD, asst. adm., Northern Itasca District Hospital, Bigfork, MN '86 (PERS)

MOHN, CHRISTINE V., dir. human res., Hilton Head Hospital, Hilton Head Island, SC '86 (PERS)

MOHN, FRANK STEPHEN, atty., Healthmark Corporation, Pittsburgh, PA '76 (ATTY)(PLNG)

MOHR, JOSEPH N., asst. adm. prof. and anciliary serv., St. Joseph Hospital, Chicago, IL '79

MOHR, VICKI H., RN, dir. nrsg., Southwest Community Health System, Middleburg Heights, OH '84 (NURS)(RISK)

MOHRMANN, JOANNE, dir. food serv., Silver Hill Foundation Hospital, New Canaan, CT '86 (FOOD)

MOHS, WALLACE, chief eng., Lake Region Hospital and Nursing Home, Fergus Falls, MN '84 (ENG)

MOILAN, BRUCE A., Presbyterian-University Hospital, Pittsburgh, PA '79 (FOOD)

MOLANO, ANITA T., atty., Keck, Mahin and Cate, Chicago, IL '78 (ATTY)

MOLARIS, BASIL, adm., Beth Israel Hospital, Passaic, NJ '55 (LIFE)

MOLEN, TIMOTHY LEE VANDER, dir. phys. facil., Evanston Hospital, Evanston, IL '80 (ENG)

MOLENAAR, ANN, adm. critical care serv., United Hospital, Grand Forks, ND '87 (AMB)

MOLER, CHARLES L., prin. dev. eng., UCLA Hospital, Los Angeles, CA '79 (ENG)

MOLES, BENJAMIN, dir. environ. serv., Rehabilitation Hospital for Special Services, Bellefonte, PA '80 (ENG)

MOLINARO, JANET L., assoc. dir. mktg., Leigh Memorial Hospital, Norfolk, VA '84 (PR)

MOLINE, CONSTANCE, RN, (ret.), St. Cloud, MN '69 (NURS)

MOLINE, ROGER A., dir. pers., La Crosse Lutheran Hospital, La Crosse, WI '71 (PERS)

MOLINELLI, DONALD J., dir. pub. affairs, Catholic Medical Center, Jamaica, NY '83 (PR)

MOLITOR, EUGENE E., dir. corp. plng. and mktg., Franciscan Health System, Inc., La Crosse, WI '84 (PLNG)

MOLITORIS, LILLIAN S., dir. vol. serv., Greystone Park Psychiatric Hospital, Greystone Park, NJ '85 (VOL)

MOLK, ROBERT ALAN, dir. soc. work serv., Baptist Medical Center of New York, Brooklyn, NY '85 (SOC)

MOLLENKOPF, ROBERT L., plant eng., Western Reserve Systems-Northside, Youngstown, OH '83 (ENG)

MOLLER, BARBARA L., supv. cent. sup., Northern Ocean Hospital System, Brick Division, Bricktown, NJ '85 (CS)

MOLLER, GERALD R., assoc. dir., Stanford University Hospital, Stanford, CA '63 (ENG)

MOLLER, WILLI, dir. eng. and maint., Capitol Hill Hospital, Washington, DC '81 (ENG)

MOLLET, CHRIS J., atty., Lutheran General Health Care Systems, Park Ridge, IL '82 (ATTY)

MOLLINS, AMY TARA, adm. res., Long Island Jewish Medical Center, New York, NY '84

MOLNAR, DEBORAH K., RN, dir. hosp. educ., Jewish Hospital, Louisville, KY '83 (NURS)(EDUC)

MOLNAR, LISA J., consult., CHI Systems, Inc., Ann Arbor, MI '85 (PLNG)

MOLNAR, TERRY S., mgr. med. equip., Naval Hospital, Bremerton, WA '82

MOLODOVSKY, ELIZABETH, atty., Brigham and Women's Hospital, Boston, MA '87 (ATTY)

MOLONEY, ELINORE G., asst. adm. plng. and mktg., Northbay Medical Center, Fairfield, CA '82 (PLNG)

MOLONEY, SR. ELLEN MARIE, pat. rep., St. Joseph's Hospital and Health Center, Paris, TX '83 (PAT)

MOLONEY, PHILIP J., dir. mktg., Beverly Hospital, Beverly, MA '87 (PLNG)
MOLTER, PETER J., clin. eng., Kenosha Hospital and Medical Center, Kenosha, WI '85 (ENG)
MOLTHEN, BARBARA A., dir. pers., New Berlin Memorial Hospital, New Berlin, WI '86 (PERS)
MOLZAHN, GWYNN M., chief diet. serv., Veterans Administration Medical Center, Houston, TX '81 (FOOD)
MOLZOW, TRICIA M., dir. vol. serv., Southwest Florida Regional Medical Center, Fort Myers, FL '86 (VOL)
MOMBERG, JOEL, dir. pub. rel., All Children's Hospital, St. Petersburg, FL '81 (PR)
MOMICH, CHRISTINE E., dir. mktg., Renshaw-Heilman and Assocs, Inc., Columbia, SC '86 (PLNG)
MOMIYAMA, AUGUSTINE T., dir. med. soc. serv., St. Francis Medical Center, Honolulu, HI '86 (SOC)
MONACO, ANTHONY J., Springfield, VA '57 (LIFE)
MONACO, ROSE ANN M., RN, adm. nrsg. serv., Harrington Memorial Hospital, Southbridge, MA '82 (NURS)
MONAGAN, DEBRA JOAN, mgr. guest rel., Riverside Hospital, Toledo, OH '86 (PAT)
MONAGAN, MARGUERITE K., dir. vol. and commun., St. Mary's Hospital, Waterbury, CT '78 (VOL)
MONAGHAN, MELINDA J., adm. food serv., Mohawk Valley Psychiatric Center, Utica, NY '85 (FOOD)
MONAGHAN, PETER A., dir. pers., St. Mary's Hospital of Troy, Troy, NY '78 (PERS)
MONAGLE, WILLIAM JOHN, pres., Somerset Medical Center, Somerville, NJ '61
MONAHAN, JACK F. JR., exec. dir., Florida Hospital Association, Orlando, FL '48 (LIFE)
MONAHAN, SR. MARGARET D., dir. vol. serv., St. Francis Hospital, Miami Beach, FL '85 (VOL)
MONAHAN, NANCY L., dir. vol., St. Paul-Ramsey Medical Center, St. Paul, MN '78 (VOL)
MONAHAN, PETER J., asst. dir. pers., Our Lady of Mercy Medical Center, Bronx, NY '86 (PERS)
MONARDO, GEORGE D., pres., Ralph K. Davies Medical Center-Franklin Hospital, San Francisco, CA '50 (LIFE)
MONBOUQUETTE, KATHLEEN, dir. commun. serv., Brigham and Women's Hospital, Boston, MA '86 (ENG)
MONCK, CHRISTOPHER, dir. mktg., University Hospital, St. Louis University Center, St. Louis, MO '84 (PLNG)
MONCRIEF, JESSE D., dir. oper. analyst, St. Joseph's Hospital, Tampa, FL '80 (MGMT)
MONDADORI, EDNA D., dir. commun. rel., Meadowlands Hospital Medical Center, Secaucus, NJ '80 (VOL)
MONDER, GRACE, RN, dir. nrsg., Kimball Medical Center, Lakewood, NJ '79 (NURS)
MONDRY, GALE, atty., Pacific Presbyterian Medical Center, San Francisco, CA '84 (ATTY)
MONE, THOMAS D., asst. adm. mgt. syst., San Gabriel Valley Medical Center, San Gabriel, CA '85 (MGMT)
MONEDERO, C. CHARLES, pres. and adm., Jones Convalescent Hospital, San Leandro, CA '58
MONES, GEORGE M., adm. asst., St. Dominic-Jackson Memorial Hospital, Jackson, MS '75 (PERS)
MONGILLO, JOAN, RN, adm. asst. nrsg., Bradford Hospital, Bradford, PA '76 (NURS)
MONICA, DANNY J., dir. pur., Winter Haven Hospital, Winter Haven, FL '80 (PUR)
MONIODIS, GEORGE JOHN, dir. pub. rel., St. Agnes Hospital of the City of Baltimore, Baltimore, MD '69 (PR)
MONIUS, FRANK, dir. plng., Maryland Hospital Association, Lutherville-Timonium, MD '79 (PLNG)
MONIZ, ALICE S., mgr. pur., Miami Children's Hospital, Miami, FL '77 (PUR)
MONKUSKY, MELANIE S., consult., SunHealth Corporation, Charlotte, NC '86 (MGMT)
MONROE, LORINDA G., supv. cent. serv., Wesley Medical Center, Wichita, KS '80 (CS)
MONROE, MICHAEL J., atty., Tucson General Hospital, Tucson, AZ '83 (ATTY)
MONROE, ROGER G., vice-pres. commun. rel., Methodist Medical Center of Illinois, Peoria, IL '80 (PR)
MONROE, RUTH M., RN, dir. med. and surg., Mercy Medical Center and Hospital, Williston, ND '86 (NURS)
MONROSE, BECKY H., pub. rel. rep., Lafayette General Medical Center, Lafayette, LA '84 (PR)
MONSELL, SUE ELLEN, dir. food and diet. serv., Children's Hospital Medical Center, Akron, OH '72 (FOOD)
MONSKY, CYNTHIA L., pub. rel. asst., Union Hospital, Union, NJ '86 (PR)
MONSON, ERIC M., sr. vice-pres. corp. strategy, Lutheran Hospitals and Home Society, Fargo, ND '81 (PLNG)
MONSON, KAREN E., sr. syst. analyst, Children's Hospital Medical Center of California, Oakland, CA '86 (MGMT)
MONSON, KERRY W., asst. vice-pres., Sherman Hospital, Elgin, IL '78
MONSON, PATRICIA A., adm. orthopedic associates, Rush-Presbyterian-St. Luke's Medical Center, Chicago, IL '83 (PLNG)
MONTAGUE, DOROTHY P., dir. soc. serv., Brooklyn Hospital-Caledonian Hospital, Brooklyn, NY '79 (SOC)
MONTAGUE, FRANK D. JR., atty., Methodist Hospital, Hattiesburg, MS '79 (ATTY)
MONTALBANO, RICHARD, vice-pres. corp. serv., Newton-Wellesley Hospital, Newton, MA '81 (PLNG)
MONTALVO, MARIAM, dir. vol. serv., Temple University Hospital, Philadelphia, PA '84 (VOL)
MONTANO, EILEEN, RN, asst. adm. and dir. nrsg., Fairbanks Memorial Hospital, Fairbanks, AK '86 (NURS)
MONTAVON, ROSE ANN, pat. rep., Miami Valley Hospital, Dayton, OH '85 (PAT)
MONTEIRO, AMY M., dir. soc. work, Prince George's Hospital Center, Cheverly, MD '75 (SOC)
MONTEITH, MARILYN, dir. pur., Baptist Hospital, Pensacola, FL '72 (PUR)
MONTELEONE, JOSEPH A., dir. human res., St. Jerome Hospital, Batavia, NY '85 (PERS)
MONTEMOINO, CLARA LUZ, pat. rep., Montefiore Medical Center, Bronx, NY '85 (PAT)
MONTES, GEORGE SR., dir. eng., Lea Regional Hospital, Hobbs, NM '87 (ENG)
MONTEUFEL, GLORIA M., asst. dir. food mgt. and nutr. serv., Valley Medical Center, Renton, WA '71 (FOOD)
MONTGOMERY, ALLEN K. JR., atty., Baptist Healthcare, Inc., Louisville, KY '87 (ATTY)
MONTGOMERY, ARLENE J., risk mgr., Hampton General Hospital, Hampton, VA '82 (RISK)
MONTGOMERY, BARRY D., risk mgr., Republic Health Corporation, Dallas, TX '84 (RISK)
MONTGOMERY, BRADLEY C., adm. res., Anderson Memorial Hospital, Anderson, SC '85
MONTGOMERY, CHERYL L., dir. pers., Baptist Specialty Hospital, Memphis, TN '86 (PERS)
MONTGOMERY, DALE A., dir. pur., Hadley Regional Medical Center, Hays, KS '74 (PUR)
MONTGOMERY, DONNA C., dir. soc. serv., Regional Medical Center, Madisonville, KY '85 (SOC)
MONTGOMERY, ESTELLE M., dir. human res., St. Joseph's Medical Center, South Bend, IN '78 (PERS)
MONTGOMERY, ESTELLE, dir. transport and commun., St. Joseph's Hospital and Medical Center, Paterson, NJ '85 (ENG)
MONTGOMERY, EVERETT DEXTER, assoc. dir., Baptist Medical Center, Jacksonville, FL '68
MONTGOMERY, LT. COL. GORDON, (ret.), Edmond, OK '72
MONTGOMERY, IRENE, budget dir., Cook County Hospital, Chicago, IL '84
MONTGOMERY, JOYCE, adm. dir. amb. serv., California Medical Center-Los Angeles, Los Angeles, CA '87 (AMB)
MONTGOMERY, KATHLEEN B., dir. vol. serv., Meriter Hospital, Madison, WI '77 (VOL)
MONTGOMERY, LESLIE D., Roswell, NM '75
MONTGOMERY, LOE RESSIE, coor. pat. care, Seton Medical Center, Daly City, CA '86 (AMB)
MONTGOMERY, RAYMOND W. II, dir. mktg., St. Elizabeth Hospital, Beaumont, TX '84 (PLNG)
MONTGOMERY, RENEE J., atty., Humana Inc., Louisville, KY '84 (ATTY)
MONTGOMERY, RICHARD A., exec. vice-pres., Memorial Health Technology, Huntington Beach, CA '81
MONTGOMERY, RICHARD D., adm., North Adams Regional Hospital, North Adams, MA '70
MONTGOMERY, ROBERT W., RN, dir. environ. serv., Concord Hospital, Concord, NH '80 (ENG)
MONTGOMERY, S. KAY, RN, vice-pres., Iowa Methodist Medical Center, Des Moines, IA '75 (NURS)
MONTGOMERY, SALLY H., dir. vol. serv., Frederick Memorial Hospital, Frederick, MD '82 (VOL)
MONTGOMERY, STEPHEN H., asst. adm., Williamsburg Community Hospital, Williamsburg, VA '74
MONTGOMERY, W. KENT, dir. emp. rel., Worcester Memorial Hospital, Worcester, MA '69 (PERS)
MONTGOMERY, WILLIAM E., dir. pers. and risk mgr., Marietta Memorial Hospital, Marietta, OH '65 (PERS)
MONTGOMERY, WILLIAM G., prod. mgr., Stanley-Vidmar, Inc., Allentown, PA '86 (CS)
MONTGOMERY, WILLIAM L., vice-pres. info. mgt., Albany Medical Center Hospital, Albany, NY '87 (MGMT)
MONTGOMERY, WILLIAM B., vice-pres. pers., Bethesda Hospital, Zanesville, OH '69 (PERS)(RISK)
MONTI, JOY E., RN, asst. dir. and dir. nrsg., West Jefferson Medical Center, Marrero, LA '77 (NURS)
MONTILIO, WILLIAM G., pub. rel. spec., Franklin Medical Center, Greenfield, MA '84 (PR)
MONTOYA, JERRY, chief eng., Seton Medical Center, Daly City, CA '85 (ENG)
MONTOYA, VICTOR, dir. soc. serv., Platte Valley Medical Center, Brighton, CO '86 (SOC)
MONTY, DENNIS G., supv. eng. and maint., New England Deaconess Hospital, Boston, MA '86 (ENG)
MOOD, ROBERT, assoc. dir. matl. serv., Baylor University Medical Center, Dallas, TX '79 (CS)
MOODY, ALICE C., RN, asst. dir. nrsg., Regional Medical Center, Madisonville, KY '85 (NURS)
MOODY, CAROLYN M., dir. vol. serv., St. Luke's General Hospital, Bellingham, WA '81 (VOL)
MOODY, DANA L., dir. cent. serv., Stamford Hospital, Stamford, CT '84 (CS)
MOODY, EDWARD A., dir. maint., Doctors Hospital, Little Rock, AR '81 (ENG)
MOODY, GARRY A., buyer, Sch Health Care System, Houston, TX '86 (PUR)
MOODY, JOE, dir. plant oper., Doctors Hospital of Mobile, Mobile, AL '81 (ENG)
MOODY, JUDY G., critical care educ., Jefferson Davis Memorial Hospital, Natchez, MS '85 (EDUC)
MOODY, LOUISE M., RN, pub. health analyst, Dept. of HHS, U. S. Public Health Service, Division of Indian Health, Health Care Administration Branch, Rockville, MD '68
MOODY, M. LEE, supv. cent. sup., Cape Canaveral Hospital, Cocoa Beach, FL '82 (CS)
MOODY, MARK S., dir. biomedical eng., Johnson City Medical Center Hospital, Johnson City, TN '85 (ENG)
MOODY, MARY L., dir. vol. serv., St. Francis Hospital, Poughkeepsie, NY '80 (VOL)
MOODY, TOM, vice-pres. and chief oper. off., Lovelace Medical Center, Albuquerque, NM '86 (PR)
MOODY, YVONNE K., RN, chief nrsg. prog., Veterans Administration Medical Center, Washington, DC '74 (NURS)
MOOERS, MARY ANN, dir. mktg. and pub. rel., Margaret R. Pardee Memorial Hospital, Hendersonville, NC '86 (PLNG)
MOOMAW, MARGOT S., vice-pres. plng., Berkshire Medical Center, Pittsfield, MA '84 (PLNG)
MOON, ALLEN W., adm., Charter Woods Hospital, Dothan, AL '81
MOON, DAVID L., dir. trng. and dev., Robinson Memorial Hospital, Ravenna, OH '80 (EDUC)
MOON, DEWEY H., chief eng., Piedmont Hospital, Atlanta, GA '75 (ENG)
MOON, FRANK R., supv. cent. serv., St. Alexis Hospital, Cleveland, OH '86 (CS)
MOON, GENE, dir. eng., Northeast Georgia Medical Center, Gainesville, GA '82 (ENG)
MOON, GERALDINE P., RN, dir. nrsg., St. Francis Medical Center, Trenton, NJ '86 (NURS)
MOON, KATHY, mgr. matl., Chamberlain Memorial Hospital, Rockwood, TN '86 (PUR)
MOON, MAXINE, dir. matl. mgt., Leesburg Regional Medical Center, Leesburg, FL '84 (PUR)
MOON, RICHARD A., arch., Richard A. Moon and Associates, Wellesley, MA '66
MOON, RODNEY D., dir., Hospital Shared Services, Columbus, OH '82 (CS)
MOON, WAYNE R., sr. vice-pres. and reg. mgr., Kaiser Foundation Health Plan, Inc., Oakland, CA '63
MOONEY, FRASER D., MD, (ret.), Pompano Beach, FL '27 (LIFE)
MOONEY, SR. JOAN FRANCIS, RN, vice-pres. nrsg., St. Joseph Medical Center, Stamford, CT '83 (NURS)
MOONEY, MORRIS A., mgr. matl., Humana Hospital -Davis North, Layton, UT '82 (PUR)
MOONEY, PAUL J., pur. agt., Monadnock Community Hospital, Peterborough, NH '83 (PUR)
MOONEY, ROBERT R. JR., student, Baruch College, New York, NY '87
MOONEY, ROBERT T., assoc. prof., Southwest Texas State University, San Marcos, TX '86 (EDUC)
MOONEY, SONDRA J., RN, sr. vice-pres. nrsg., Sacred Heart Hospital of Pensacola, Pensacola, FL '85 (NURS)
MOONEY, YVETTE, RN, dir. nrsg., South Nassau Communities Hospital, Oceanside, NY '84 (NURS)
MOORE-GREENE, GRACIE, dir. soc. work and home care, North Charles Hospital, Baltimore, MD '86 (SOC)
MOORE, ALICE J., dir. food serv., Humana Hospital -Lake Cumberland, Somerset, KY '84 (FOOD)
MOORE, ALVIN O., atty., Baroness Erlanger Hospital, Chattanooga, TN '68 (ATTY)
MOORE, ANNE A., (ret.), Brooklyn, NY '76 (SOC)
MOORE, BARRY G., Seattle, WA '76 (MGMT)
MOORE, BEVERLY J., RN, assoc. adm. and dir. nrsg., Whidden Memorial Hospital, Everett, MA '86 (NURS)
MOORE, BONNIE L., supv. cent. serv., Columbia Memorial Hospital, Hudson, NY '84 (CS)
MOORE, BURT H., sr. vice-pres. oper., Greenville Hospital System, Greenville, SC '65
MOORE, CAROL BRYDEN, pres., Moore-Johnson, Inc., Washington, DC '84 (PLNG)
MOORE, CARRIE M., dir. vol. serv., St. Lawrence Rehabilitation Center, Lawrenceville, NJ '77 (VOL)
MOORE, CHARLOTTE, risk mgr., Coronado Hospital, Coronado, CA '86 (RISK)
MOORE, CHERYL L., med. soc. worker, HCA Doctors Hospital, Lake Worth, FL '81 (SOC)
MOORE, CRAIGE L., dir. pers., South Haven Community Hospital, South Haven, MI '80 (PERS)
MOORE, DAVID L., dir. plant oper., De Graff Memorial Hospital, North Tonawanda, NY '82 (ENG)
MOORE, DAWN C., dir. pers., Littleton Hospital, Littleton, NH '81 (PERS)
MOORE, DELLOYD W., dir. maint., Memorial Community Hospital, Blair, NE '83 (ENG)
MOORE, DELORES Z., RN, dir. nrsg., Detroit Osteopathic Hospital, Highland Park, MI '82 (NURS)
MOORE, DENNIS P., dir. sup., proc. and distrib., Medical Center Hospital of Vermont, Burlington, VT '78 (CS)
MOORE, DOLORES J., RN, asst. adm. and dir. nrsg., Jackson-Madison County General Hospital, Jackson, TN '81 (NURS)
MOORE, DONALD E. JR., PhD, exec. dir., Eastern Virginia Inter-Hospital Medical Education, Norfolk, VA '81 (EDUC)
MOORE, EDWARD H., vice-pres. prof. serv., Newton-Wellesley Hospital, Newton, MA '75
MOORE, ERNEST C. III, atty., Queen's Medical Center, Honolulu, HI '84 (ATTY)
MOORE, FLORRIE G., dir. soc. serv., Candler General Hospital, Savannah, GA '85 (SOC)
MOORE, FRANCES A., RN, assoc. exec. dir. nrsg., Humana Hospital -Huntsville, Huntsville, AL '82 (NURS)
MOORE, FRANCIS J., hosp. adv., St. Louis Labor Health Institute, St. Louis, MO '47 (LIFE)
MOORE, FRED A., southeastern reg. mgr., Coffey Communications, Inc., Altamonte Springs, FL '80 (PR)
MOORE, FRED HENRY, atty., Baroness Erlanger Hospital, Chattanooga, TN '76 (ATTY)
MOORE, GARY D., dir. human res., St. Anthony's Hospital, Amarillo, TX '78 (PERS)
MOORE, GEORGIA M., head educ., Baptist Hospital of Southeast Texas, Beaumont, TX '86 (EDUC)
MOORE, GERALD E., pres., Holy Cross Hospital, Detroit, MI '75 (MGMT)(PLNG)
MOORE, GWYNNE E., dir. commun. rel., Trumbull Memorial Hospital, Warren, OH '87 (PR)
MOORE, HAROLD G., assoc. adm. surg., Johns Hopkins Hospital, Baltimore, MD '86
MOORE, JAMES MONROE, asst. chief eng., Baptist Medical Center-Montclair, Birmingham, AL '85 (ENG)
MOORE, JAMES S., chief eng., Upson County Hospital, Thomaston, GA '85 (ENG)
MOORE, JAMES T., dir. nutr. and food serv., Texas Department of Mental Health and Mental Retardation, Austin, TX '79 (FOOD)
MOORE, JAN L., Athens, AL '78 (VOL)
MOORE, JANET SILLIMAN, RN, assoc. vice-pres. and assoc. dean, Rush-Presbyterian-St. Luke's Medical Center, Chicago, IL '84 (NURS)
MOORE, JANICE W., RN, asst. dir. nrsg. and interim dir. nrsg., Northeastern Vermont Regional Hospital, St. Johnsbury, VT '87 (NURS)
MOORE, JASON H., adm., Coral Springs Medical Center, Coral Springs, FL '76
MOORE, JOAN B., RN, dir. nrsg., Our Lady of Lourdes Health Center, Pasco, WA '75 (NURS)

MOORE, JOAN P., adm. asst., Community Memorial Hospital, Toms River, NJ '84 (RISK)
MOORE, JOHN R., adm., Ottawa County Riverview Nursing Home, Oak Harbor, OH '68
MOORE, JOHN T., vice-pres., Hospital Services of Newengland, Braintree, MA '83 (PUR)
MOORE, JOYCE A., dir. vol. serv., Hillcrest Baptist Medical Center, Waco, TX '80 (VOL)
MOORE, JUDI S., dir. vol. serv., Phoenix Memorial Hospital, Phoenix, AZ '84 (VOL)
MOORE, JUDY L., RN, dir. clin. nrsg., HCA Grant Center Hospital North Florida, Citra, FL '81 (NURS)
MOORE, KAREN A., supv. cent. serv., Parkview Hospital, Toledo, OH '83 (CS)
MOORE, KATHERINE D., dir. soc. serv., Beverly Hospital, Montebello, CA '74 (SOC)
MOORE, KATHLEEN E., RN, actg. dir. educ. serv., Riverside Hospital, Toledo, OH '80 (EDUC)
MOORE, KEVIN G., chief pat. adm., Noble Army Community Hospital, Fort McClellan, AL '86
MOORE, LOIS M., dir. telecommun., Bronx-Lebanon Hospital Center, Bronx, NY '85 (ENG)
MOORE, MAE JEAN, dir. matl. mgt., Central Community Hospital, Chicago, IL '77 (CS)(PUR)
MOORE, MARCIA G., dir. pers., Tomball Regional Hospital, Tomball, TX '82 (PERS)
MOORE, MARGARET C., dir. vol. serv. and dev., Bethesda Oak Hospital, Cincinnati, OH '68 (VOL)
MOORE, SR. MARGUERITE, dir. vol. serv., Mercy Hospital of Pittsburgh, Pittsburgh, PA '78 (VOL)
MOORE, MARIE C., RN, dir. nrsg., Daniel Drake Memorial Hospital, Cincinnati, OH '86 (NURS)
MOORE, MARILYN, dir. vol., Trinity Medical Center, Minot, ND '80 (VOL)
MOORE, MARY ANN, RN, asst. adm. pat. care, Mason Clinic, Seattle, WA '82 (NURS)
MOORE, MARYANNE S., vice-pres. plng., St. Joseph Hospital West, Mount Clemens, MI '80 (PLNG)
MOORE, MCKINLEY D., asst. vice-pres. bus. dev., Hospital Corporation of America, Arlington, TX '81 (PLNG)
MOORE, MICHAEL T., exec. dir., William W. Backus Hospital, Norwich, CT '73
MOORE, MIRIAM R., dir. vol., New England Memorial Hospital, Stoneham, MA '71 (VOL)
MOORE, NANCY C., dir. vol. serv., Humana Hospital -Augusta, Augusta, GA '79 (VOL)
MOORE, NORMA NADINE, dir. vol. serv., Community Methodist Hospital, Henderson, KY '78 (VOL)
MOORE, P. SUSAN, consult., Peat, Marwick, Mitchell, Medford, MA '79 (MGMT)
MOORE, PATRICIA A., dir. strategic plng., DePaul Health Center, Bridgeton, MO '82 (PLNG)
MOORE, PATRICIA ANN, instr. and health prof. prog. consult., Northeastern University, Boston, MA '80 (EDUC)
MOORE, PATRICIA M., dir. ins., Church-Charity Foundation of Long Island, Hempstead, NY '80 (RISK)
MOORE, ROBERT J., vice-pres. mktg., Pekin Memorial Hospital, Pekin, IL '80 (PR)
MOORE, ROCHELLE EDEN, asst. vice-pres. fin.-pat. acct. serv., Tampa General Hospital, Tampa, FL '86
MOORE, RUBY, risk mgr., Mary Breckinridge Hospital, Hyden, KY '86 (RISK)
MOORE, RUSSELL A., dir. food serv., Rockford Memorial Hospital, Rockford, IL '75 (FOOD)
MOORE, RUSSELL G., lab. adm., Woonsocket Hospital, Woonsocket, RI '80 (RISK)
MOORE, RUSSELLINE C., RN, asst. dir. nrsg. and trng., Arabian American Oil Company, Dhahran, Saudi Arabia '71 (EDUC)(NURS)
MOORE, RUTH J., chm. cont. educ. for health prof., Broward Community College, Fort Lauderdale, FL '85 (EDUC)
MOORE, RUTH L., mgr. cafeteria, catering and nutr. serv., Swedish Hospital Medical Center, Seattle, WA '87 (FOOD)
MOORE, SALLY A., asst. dir. matl. mgt., Iowa Methodist Medical Center, Des Moines, IA '87 (CS)
MOORE, SHARON J., Lighthouse Point, FL '72 (FOOD)
MOORE, SHIRLEY A., dir. soc. serv., Platte County Memorial Hospital, Wheatland, WY '85 (SOC)
MOORE, STERLING, vice-pres. corp. serv. and dev., Scioto Valley Health Foundation, Portsmouth, OH '86 (PLNG)
MOORE, SUSAN C., RN, asst. adm. nrsg. serv., DuBois Regional Medical Center, Dubois, PA '87 (NURS)
MOORE, SUSAN L., dir. mktg., St. Joseph Hospital, Baltimore, MD '84 (PR) (PLNG)
MOORE, SUSAN W., risk mgr., SunHealth Corporation, Sun City, AZ '86 (RISK)
MOORE, TERESA M., sr. mgt. eng. analyst, Kaiser Permanente, Pasadena, CA '80 (MGMT)
MOORE, TERRY, pres. and owner, Moore and Associates, Brandon, MS '86 (ENG)
MOORE, THOMAS J., dir. human res., Medical University Hospital of the Medical University of South Carolina, Charleston, SC '84 (PERS)
MOORE, THOMAS K., mgr. proc. syst., Sybron Corporation Medical Products Division, Rochester, NY '80 (CS)
MOORE, VICKIE MULLINS, adm. nrsg., Saint Joseph's Hospital, Atlanta, GA '86 (NURS)
MOORE, WESLEY J., vice-pres., Underwood, Neuhaus and Company, Inc., Houston, TX '67
MOORE, WILLIAM B., chief eng. and dir. eng. serv., Crawford Long Hospital Emory University, Atlanta, GA '78 (ENG)
MOORE, LT. COL. WILLIAM ELLIS, MSC USA, U. S. Army Health Services Command, Fort Sam Houston, TX '71
MOORE, WILLIE E., dir. plant oper., Cottage Hospital of Grosse Pointe, Grosse Pointe Farms, MI '77 (ENG)
MOOREHEAD, JAMES E., asst. adm. risk mgt. and constr., St. Joseph Hospital, Augusta, GA '82 (ENG)(RISK)
MOORES, JOHN A., dir. human res. and trng., Washington Regional Medical Center, Fayetteville, AR '86 (PERS)
MOOREY, LINDA D., dir. pub. rel., Lee Memorial Hospital, Fort Myers, FL '83 (PR)
MOORHEAD, JULIANA R., Purcellville, VA '82 (PR)
MOORMAN, LUCIA DIANE, adm. mgr., Conner Medical Center, Detroit, MI '85
MOORMAN, MARY MARGARET, vice-pres., Good Samaritan Hospital, Cincinnati, OH '79 (PLNG)
MOORMAN, PAUL U., dir. pers., Joint Township District Memorial Hospital, St. Marys, OH '83 (PERS)
MOORMAN, THEODORE J., mgr. emp. serv., St. Francis-St. George Hospital, Cincinnati, OH '85 (PERS)
MOOTZ, B. LEE, adm., Medical Plaza Hospital, Fort Worth, TX '59
MOPPERT, DARLENE K., dir. diet. serv., Plantation General Hospital, Plantation, FL '82 (FOOD)
MOQUIN, DAVID A., mgr. hskpg. serv., Barstow Community Hospital, Barstow, CA '86 (ENVIRON)
MORABITO, JANE, dir. nrsg. serv., Peekskill Hospital, Peekskill, NY '87 (AMB)
MORAHAN, JOHN R., dir. plng. and mktg., Mercy Hospital, Buffalo, NY '86 (PLNG)
MORALES, ARMANDO, PhD, prof. and chief clin. soc. work, University of California at Los Angeles Neuropsychiatric Hospital, Los Angeles, CA '85 (SOC)
MORALES, HILBERT, dir. plng. and maint., Santa Clara Valley Medical Center, San Jose, CA '85 (ENG)
MORALES, MARK A., mgr. pers. serv., Tri-City Medical Center, Oceanside, CA '86 (PERS)
MORALES, VIRGINIA V., dir. environ. serv., Anaheim General Hospital, Anaheim, CA '87 (ENVIRON)
MORAN, DENNIS J., asst. dir. hosp. and clin., University of California San Diego Medical Center, San Diego, CA '83 (PLNG)
MORAN, JAMES KEITH, int. auditor, Providence Hospital, Mobile, AL '84
MORAN, JOHN WILLIAM, dir. soc. work serv., St. Joseph Hospital, Nashua, NH '79 (SOC)
MORAN, MARY JO, RN, asst. dir. adm. nrsg. syst., Washington Hospital Center, Washington, DC '86 (NURS)
MORAN, MAXINE LOUIS, asst. dir. nrsg. and pat. serv., Alpena General Hospital, Alpena, MI '87 (PAT)
MORAN, PAMELA A., dir. plng., Community Methodist Hospital, Henderson, KY '82 (PLNG)
MORAN, VICKI MCINTOSH, student, Duke University, Department of Health Administration, Durham, NC '86
MORAN, WILLIAM M., exec. dir., St. Vincent's Foundation, Birmingham, AL '79
MORANO, 1ST LT. FRANK A., MSC USAF, dir. med. facil. mgt., U. S. Air Force Hospital, Homestead, FL '80
MORATH, JULIANNE M., RN, consult., University of Cincinnati Hospital, Cincinnati, OH '83 (NURS)
MORATTI, GERALDINE ADELAIDE, pat. rep., St. Joseph's Hospital, Flushing, NY '84 (PAT)
MORCK, KATHLEEN M., dir. pers., General Hospital of Everett, Everett, WA '78 (PERS)
MOREAU, DIANE J., coor. pat. rel. and vol. serv., Copley Memorial Hospital, Aurora, IL '78 (PAT)(VOL)
MOREAU, RAY G., partner, Ernst and Whinney, Dallas, TX '86 (MGMT)
MOREHEAD, CAROL L., RN, dir. educ., Huntington Memorial Hospital, Huntington, IN '77 (EDUC)
MOREHOUSE, MILLICENT IRENE, adm. asst., Tri-County Memorial Hospital, Gowanda, NY '68 (PERS)
MORELAND, PATRICIA L., dir. food serv., Boulder Good Samaritan, Boulder, CO '71 (FOOD)
MORELAND, RUTH ANN, dir. soc. serv., Willard Area Hospital, Willard, OH '86 (SOC)
MORELAND, WILLIAM F., pres. and chief oper. off., Health Resources Corporation of America, Gatesville, TX '65
MORELL, JAMES CLIFFORD, mgr. mgt. consult. serv., Ernst and Whinney, Chicago, IL '77 (PLNG)
MORELLI, CHERYL A., asst. pers., East Ohio Regional Hospital, Martins Ferry, OH '84 (PERS)
MORELLO, JEANNE M., vice-pres. syst. plng. and dir. risk mgt., Neponset Valley Health Systems, Norwood, MA '86 (RISK)(PLNG)
MORENO, RODRIGO ALBERTO T., adm., Centro Medico Paitilla, Panama, Panama '56 (MGMT)
MORETTINI, JUNE, dir. soc. serv., St. John's Hospital, Springfield, IL '71 (SOC)
MORETTO, JANE A., RN, dir. nrsg., G. W. Long Hansen's Disease Center, Carville, LA '82 (NURS)
MOREY, CHRIS, mgr. pur., Marshfield Clinic, Marshfield, WI '87 (PUR)
MOREY, JAMES HAROLD, vice-pres. oper., Geri-Trenos Corporation, Breesport, NY '69
MOREY, LORI, clin. dir., Kennewick General Hospital, Kennewick, WA '87 (AMB)
MORFORD, SANDY D., dir. plant, tech. and safety mgt., Council Shared Services, Van Nuys, CA '85 (ENG)
MORGAN, A. DALE, adm., St. John's Hospital, Jackson, WY '65
MORGAN, BARBARA E., RN, dir. cent. serv., Community Medical Center, Scranton, PA '82 (CS)
MORGAN, BOBBY R., adm., Electra Memorial Hospital, Electra, TX '86
MORGAN, BRYAN L., dir. maint., Lakeshore Lutheran Home, Duluth, MN '85 (ENG)
MORGAN, CHARLES A., dir. bus. serv., AMI Lake City Medical Center, Lake City, FL '74 (PUR)
MORGAN, DAVID EDWARD, Summit Health, Ltd., Los Angeles, CA '74
MORGAN, DAVID R., assoc. adm., Tobey Hospital, Wareham, MA '81 (MGMT)
MORGAN, DICK, chief buyer, Texoma Medical Center, Denison, TX '86 (PUR)
MORGAN, DOROTHY M., nrsg. journalist, Canadian Hospital Association, Ottawa, Ont., Canada '49 (LIFE)
MORGAN, EDWARD F. JR., sr. vice-pres. health care serv., Servicemaster Industries, Inc., Downers Grove, IL '78
MORGAN, ELIZABETH I., asst. dir. food serv., Bloomington Hospital, Bloomington, IN '83 (FOOD)
MORGAN, FRANCES N., dir. soc. serv., Magnolia Hospital, Corinth, MS '77 (SOC)
MORGAN, HARRIET M., dir. pers., Jefferson Memorial Hospital, Alexandria, VA '83 (PERS)
MORGAN, HARRY B., dir. plant oper., L. B. Johnson Tropical Medical Center, Pago Pago, American Samoa '83 (ENG)
MORGAN, HARRY S., arch., Harry S. Morgan Associates, Glenview, IL '57 (LIFE)
MORGAN, JAMES A., adm. dir. risk mgt., Little Company of Mary Hospital, Evergreen Park, IL '74 (RISK)
MORGAN, JEANNETTE M., student, Program in Industrial Engineer, University of Tennessee, Knoxville, TN '87 (MGMT)
MORGAN, JERRY, asst. adm. emp. serv., St. Anthony Medical Center, Louisville, KY '72 (PERS)
MORGAN, JOHN, adm. dir., Gottlieb Memorial Hospital, Melrose Park, IL '73 (RISK)
MORGAN, KATHLEEN L., RN, dir. educ., Goleta Valley Community Hospital, Santa Barbara, CA '71 (EDUC)
MORGAN, LOUIS NELSON, adm. dir. nuclear medicine, Prince George's Hospital Center, Cheverly, MD '79
MORGAN, LYNNESSA G., mgr. educ. and trng., St. Joseph Hospital, Albuquerque, NM '85 (EDUC)
MORGAN, MARCIA J., buyer, Riverside Hospital, Toledo, OH '86 (PUR)
MORGAN, MARGIE, mgr. sup., proc. and distrib., Moore Regional Hospital, Pinehurst, NC '83 (CS)
MORGAN, MICHAEL L., adm. asst., Murray-Calloway County Hospital, Murray, KY '86 (PLNG)
MORGAN, MICHAEL S., asst. mgr. plant serv., Halifax Hospital Medical Center, Daytona Beach, FL '86 (ENG)
MORGAN, NANCY F., dir. pub. rel., St. Elizabeth Hospital, Beaumont, TX '86 (PR) (PLNG)
MORGAN, NANCY MALEK, adm. asst., Morgan County Appalachian Hospital, West Liberty, KY '84
MORGAN, PETER L., consult., Arthur Young and Company, Seattle, WA '84 (MGMT)
MORGAN, PHILIP W., dir. mgt. dev., Geisinger Medical Center, Danville, PA '71 (EDUC)
MORGAN, ROBERT B., student, Program in Health Service Administration, George Washington University, Washington, DC '86
MORGAN, ROBERT J., Lawrence and Memorial Hospital, New London, CT '68 (FOOD)
MORGAN, SCOTT J., dir. pub. rel., Ohio Valley General Hospital, McKees Rocks, PA '86 (PR)
MORGAN, SHARON M., dir. educ., High River General Hospital, High River, Alta., Canada '83 (EDUC)
MORGAN, VICKIE A., asst. dir. vol. serv., Williamsport Hospital and Medical Center, Williamsport, PA '87 (VOL)
MORGAN, VICTORIA M., revenue syst. analyst and consult., Healthwest Medical Centers, Chatsworth, CA '83 (MGMT)
MORGANSON, LINDA S., educator, St. Mary's Hospital, Reno, NV '84 (EDUC)
MORGENSTERN, LYNN E., atty., Jewish Hospital of St. Louis, St. Louis, MO '86 (ATTY)
MORGRET, ROY B., asst. supt. plant, Lock Haven Hospital and Extended Care Unit, Lock Haven, PA '79 (ENG)
MORIARTY, JEANNE MARIE, RN, vice-pres. pat. serv., West Nebraska General Hospital, Scottsbluff, NE '78 (NURS)
MORIARTY, KEVIN P., dir. commun. rel., St. Mary's Hospital, Orange, NJ '82 (PR)
MORIARTY, PATRICIA A., pers. asst., Haverhill Municipal-Hale Hospital, Haverhill, MA '83 (PERS)
MORIARTY, SR. RITA, RN, dir. nrsg. serv., Holy Spirit Hospital, Camp Hill, PA '78 (NURS)
MORICONI, JOANNE A., RN, vice-pres., Pennsylvania Hospital, Philadelphia, PA '73 (NURS)
MORIN, BRUCE LEONARD, vice-pres., Amherst Associates, Atlanta, GA '78 (MGMT)
MORIN, EMILY C., dir. vol. serv., Marion General Hospital, Marion, IN '83 (VOL)
MORIN, FRANK F., consult., Palm Desert, CA '73
MORIN, GERARD T., dir. pers., Marcotte Nursing Home, Lewiston, ME '79 (PERS)
MORIN, JACK E., student, Department of Health Care Administration, George Washington University, Washington, DC '82
MORIN, JULIE, asst. vice-pres. paramed., Bethesda North Hospital, Cincinnati, OH '84
MORIN, LINDA ANN, head soc. serv., Maine Coast Memorial Hospital, Ellsworth, ME '75 (SOC)
MORIN, SCOTT E., adm., Sleepy Eye Municipal Hospital, Sleepy Eye, MN '77 (MGMT)
MORIN, THOM H., dir. matl. mgt., Oak Forest Hospital of Cook County, Oak Forest, IL '82 (PUR)
MORING, ANNE, RN, charge nrs. cent. sterile, Baxter County Regional Hospital, Mountain Home, AR '83 (CS)
MORISSETTE, MARTIN J., asst. mgr. cent. sterile sup., William W. Backus Hospital, Norwich, CT '86 (CS)
MORISSETTE, SYLVIA J., supv. cent. sterile sup., Mid-Maine Medical Center, Waterville, ME '80 (CS)
MORITZ, CLAIRE L., atty., Wake Medical Center, Raleigh, NC '86 (ATTY)
MORIUCHI, MORRIS HATSUO, reg. mgr., Medicus Systems Corporation, San Francisco, CA '76 (MGMT)
MORK, DAVID L., asst. vice-pres., Alexandria Hospital, Alexandria, VA '83
MORLAN, ALFRED K., atty., Saint Francis Hospital, Tulsa, OK '80 (ATTY)
MORLEY, CLYDE E., dir. plant oper., HCA Doctors Hospital, Conroe, TX '82 (ENG)
MORLEY, GEORGE E., dir. biomedical eng., Polyclinic Medical Center, Harrisburg, PA '86 (ENG)
MORLEY, MICHAEL I., asst. dir. pat. serv., Brandywine Hospital, Caln Township, PA '70 (FOOD)
MORLEY, TAD A., dir. human res., Castleview Hospital, Price, UT '85 (PERS)
MORLEY, THERESE, RN, asst. adm. pat. serv., Granada Hills Community Hospital, Granada Hills, CA '86 (NURS)
MORLINO, STEVEN M., dir. environ. serv., Richmond Memorial Hospital and Health Center, Staten Island, NY '83 (ENG)

MORLOCK, CATHIE KOHL, mgr. healthcare prog., Moore Business Forms and Systems Division, Glenview, IL '86
MORLOK, WILLIAM C., dir. health care arch., Ewing Cole Cherry Parsky, Philadelphia, PA '79 (PLNG)
MORMAN, GLADY, dir. pers., HCA Parkway Medical Center, Lithia Springs, GA '81 (PERS)
MORNIN, CAROLE J., RN, dir. nrsg., University Hospital, St. Louis University Center, St. Louis, MO '86 (NURS)
MORO, JOHN, mgr. plant, Sheppard and Enoch Pratt Hospital, Baltimore, MD '80 (ENG)
MORO, KARL G., safety off., University of Illinois Hospital, Chicago, IL '87 (ENVIRON)
MOROOKA, KOZI, prof. mgt. eng., Tokai University, Management Engineering Department, Hiratsuka, Japan '78 (MGMT)
MOROSS, SR. KATHLEEN MARY, RN, dir. nrsg. serv., Mercy Hospital, Toledo, OH '85 (NURS)
MORPHEW, JOHNNY E., dir. phys. plant, State Training School, Plankinton, SD '83 (ENG)
MORR, ROBERT E. JR., commun. rel. mgr., Howard Community Hospital, Kokomo, IN '80 (PR)
MORRELL, BURTON H., Great Barrington, MA '46 (LIFE)
MORRELL, DOUGLAS K., mgt. eng., Sch Health Care System, Houston, TX '85 (MGMT)
MORRELL, RICHARD A., dir. environ. serv., Norfolk General Hospital, Norfolk, VA '86 (ENVIRON)
MORRICAL, WILMA L., coor. staff dev., McPherson Community Health Center, Howell, MI '84 (EDUC)
MORRIER, EDWARD J., Veterans Administration Medical Center, Manchester, NH '84 (SOC)
MORRILL, CHARLES R., dir. pers., St. Anne's Hospital, Fall River, MA '81 (PERS)
MORRILL, MICHAEL, chief eng., Memorial Hospitals Association, Modesto, CA '86 (ENG)
MORRILL, MICHELE D., coor. staff educ. and dev., Brandywine Hospital, Caln Township, PA '84 (EDUC)
MORRIS-COFFEY, GRETCHEN, dir. food serv., Watsonville Community Hospital, Watsonville, CA '86 (FOOD)
MORRIS, ANNE, dir. pub. rel. and mktg., West Georgia Medical Center, La Grange, GA '85 (PR)
MORRIS, BARBARA H., dir. pub. rel., Methodist Evangelical Hospital, Louisville, KY '74 (PR)
MORRIS, BARBARA W., dir. vol., Methodist Hospital, St. Louis Park, MN '73 (VOL)
MORRIS, BEN F., dir. eng., Green Hospital of Scripps Clinic, La Jolla, CA '80 (ENG)
MORRIS, C. FRANK, assoc. matl. mgt. consult., Daughters of Charity National Pur Service, St. Louis, MO '82 (PUR)
MORRIS, CAROLINE M., registered rec. adm., Glendale Adventist Medical Center, Glendale, CA '78
MORRIS, CHARLES C., dir. plant serv., University Hospital of Jacksonville, Jacksonville, FL '85 (ENG)
MORRIS, DANA M., dir. soc. work, Gulf Coast Community Hospital, Biloxi, MS '86 (SOC)
MORRIS, DAVID H., mgr. matl., Stanly Memorial Hospital, Albemarle, NC '82 (PUR)
MORRIS, DAVID M., dir. matl. mgt., Mount Sinai Medical Center, Miami Beach, FL '81 (PUR)
MORRIS, DORIS E., RN, dir. nrsg., Tipton County Memorial Hospital, Tipton, IN '79 (NURS)
MORRIS, DUDLEY E., dir., American Practice Management, New York, NY '81 (PLNG)
MORRIS, GERALD M., atty., Holy Cross Hospital, Fort Lauderdale, FL '83 (ATTY)
MORRIS, GERRY, risk mgt. rep., McKee Medical Center, Loveland, CO '83 (RISK)
MORRIS, HAROLD R., Concord Plaza, Northlake, IL '83
MORRIS, HELEN O'NEILL, dir. soc. serv., Holy Spirit Hospital, Camp Hill, PA '79 (SOC)
MORRIS, HENRY J., interim pres. and chief exec. off., Mercy Hospital of Wilkes-Barre, Wilkes-Barre, PA '57 (LIFE)
MORRIS, HENRY J. III, Laplace, LA '85 (PUR)
MORRIS, IRA J., dir. matl. mgt., Shepherd Spinal Center, Atlanta, GA '83 (PUR)
MORRIS, JEANETTE L., clin. diet., HCA Gulf Coast Hospital, Panama City, FL '84 (FOOD)
MORRIS, JENNY W., RN, assoc. dir. nrsg., North Carolina Baptist Hospital, Winston-Salem, NC '86 (NURS)
MORRIS, JOANN J., RN, chief nrsg. serv., Veterans Administration Medical Center, Iron Mountain, MI '85 (NURS)
MORRIS, JOHN E. III, atty., Nesbitt Memorial Hospital, Kingston, PA '81 (ATTY)
MORRIS, JOHN W., dir. maint., St. Albans Psychiatric Hospital, Radford, VA '85 (ENG)
MORRIS, JULIA CALDWELL, atty., Vanderbilt University Hospital, Nashville, TN '83 (RISK)(ATTY)
MORRIS, JULIE, dir. soc. work serv., Phelps Memorial Hospital Center, North Tarrytown, NY '84 (SOC)
MORRIS, KEN, dir. plant oper., Memorial Hospital at Easton Maryland, Easton, MD '87 (ENG)
MORRIS, LEIGH E., dir. pub. rel., Children's Hospital of Wisconsin, Milwaukee, WI '85 (PR)
MORRIS, MARK D., atty., Hospital Association of New York State, Albany, NY '74 (ATTY)
MORRIS, MARY H., RN, adm. nrsg. serv., Henry Ford Hospital, Detroit, MI '71 (NURS)
MORRIS, MARY J., dir. pub. rel., Redding Medical Center, Redding, CA '84 (PR)
MORRIS, MICHAEL E., dir. fiscal serv., Hunt Memorial Hospital, Danvers, MA '86
MORRIS, MICHAEL W., atty., St. John's Hospital, Lowell, MA '84 (ATTY)
MORRIS, MONICA, coor. pat. rel., Lankenau Hospital, Philadelphia, PA '80 (PAT)
MORRIS, NANCY A., dir. vol. serv., South Hills Health System, Pittsburgh, PA '76 (VOL)
MORRIS, NANCY R., RN, dir. nrsg. serv., Kent and Queen Anne's Hospital, Chestertown, MD '84 (NURS)
MORRIS, NANCY, supv. soc. serv., Portsmouth Regional Hospital, Portsmouth, NH '86 (SOC)
MORRIS, PATRICIA A., educ. nrsg. staff dev., Loma Linda University Medical Center, Loma Linda, CA '87 (EDUC)
MORRIS, R. CRAWFORD, atty., Fairview General Hospital, Cleveland, OH '69 (ATTY)
MORRIS, ROBERT F., coor. risk mgt. and qual. assur., The Arbour, Boston, MA '84 (RISK)
MORRIS, ROBERT K., assoc. adm. human res., West Virginia University Hospital, Morgantown, WV '71 (PERS)
MORRIS, ROLAND, atty., Hospital Association of Pennsylvania, Camp Hill, PA '80 (ATTY)
MORRIS, RONALD J., dir. risk serv., St. Mary Medical Center, Gary, IN '86
MORRIS, RONDAH M., dir. pub. rel., River Oaks Hospital, Jackson, MS '86 (PR)
MORRIS, RUTH ANN, RN, dir. nrsg., Community Hospitals of Indiana, Indianapolis, IN '80 (NURS)
MORRIS, RUTH JELLINE, sr. acct. exec., Hutchins, Young and Rubicam, Rochester, NY '78 (PR)
MORRIS, SIDNEY L., dir. phys. plant, National Hospital for Orthopaedics, Arlington, VA '79 (ENG)
MORRIS, STEPHEN M., pres., Inco Incorporated, Phoenix, AZ '52 (LIFE)
MORRIS, SUSAN P., dir. bus. dev., Village Oaks Regional Hospital, San Antonio, TX '85 (PR) (PLNG)
MORRIS, TAMI C., vice-pres. pub. rel., Northbay Medical Center, Fairfield, CA '84 (PR)
MORRIS, VICTOR, vice-pres., Corroon and Black of Illinois, Inc., Chicago, IL '80 (RISK)
MORRIS, WAYNE A., asst. dir. maint., Trumbull Memorial Hospital, Warren, OH '79 (ENG)
MORRIS, WAYNE W., mgr. matl., St. Joseph Hospital and Health Care Center, Tacoma, WA '85 (PUR)
MORRISEY, PHYLLIS, dir. amb. care unit, Memorial Hospital, Fremont, OH '87 (AMB)
MORRISON-FALLON, BARBARA R., dir. pub. rel., Ingalls Memorial Hospital, Harvey, IL '74 (PR)
MORRISON, CHARLES F., (ret.), Baltimore, MD '64 (ENG)
MORRISON, CLAIRE R., atty. and risk mgr., Veterans Administration Lakeside Medical Center, Chicago, IL '84 (ATTY)(RISK)
MORRISON, CYNTHIA J., dir. family serv., Shriners Hospitals for Crippled Children, Erie, PA '83 (PLNG)
MORRISON, DAVID G., div. dir., Villaview Community Hospital, San Diego, CA '84 (ENG)(ENVIRON)
MORRISON, DEBORAH K., vice-pres. pat. care serv., Holland Community Hospital, Holland, MI '77 (NURS)
MORRISON, DIANE R., dir. soc. serv., University of Southern California-Kenneth Norris Jr. Cancer Hospital, Los Angeles, CA '84 (SOC)
MORRISON, DONALD K., territory mgr., Therma System Corporation, South Plainfield, NJ '72 (FOOD)
MORRISON, DONNA J., mgr. diet. and food serv., Memorial Hospital at Oconomowoc, Oconomowoc, WI '86 (FOOD)
MORRISON, ELIZABETH F., RN, supv. cent. serv., Pitt County Memorial Hospital, Greenville, NC '81 (CS)
MORRISON, ELIZABETH A., health educ., Bryn Mawr Hospital, Bryn Mawr, PA '86 (EDUC)
MORRISON, FRANCINE U., dir. vol. and commun. serv., Eye and Ear Hospital of Pittsburgh, Pittsburgh, PA '83 (VOL)
MORRISON, GABRIELLE J., asst. exec. dir., Grace Maternity Hospital, Halifax, N.S., Canada '84 (MGMT)
MORRISON, JOHN C., asst. adm., St. Luke's Hospital West, Chesterfield, MO '85 (PLNG)
MORRISON, KATHLEEN D., asst. head food mgt., Naval Hospital, Bethesda, MD '85 (FOOD)
MORRISON, MARGUERITE, RN, asst. adm. nrsg. serv., Sutter Memorial Hospital, Sacramento, CA '81 (NURS)
MORRISON, MARILYN J., dir. commun. rel., Methodist Hospital of Southern California, Arcadia, CA '83 (PR)
MORRISON, MARTHA J., student, Program in Hospital Administration, University of Houston at Clear Lake City, Houston, TX '82
MORRISON, MARTHA L., RN, dir. ped. nrsg. serv., Massachusetts General Hospital, Boston, MA '79 (NURS)
MORRISON, MARVEL L., adm. diet., Maricopa Medical Center, Phoenix, AZ '79 (FOOD)
MORRISON, PATTY M., dir. human res., Lloyd Noland Hospital and Health Ctrs, Birmingham, AL '86 (PERS)
MORRISON, RICHARD E., asst. vice-pres., Florida Hospital Medical Center, Orlando, FL '82 (PLNG)
MORRISS, CURTIS W., student, Georgia State University, Institute of Health Administration, Atlanta, GA '86
MORRISS, CYNTHIA H., atty., Gardner, Carton and Douglas, Dallas, TX '85 (ATTY)
MORRISSEY, CHARLENE D., dir. vol. serv., Leonard Morse Hospital, Natick, MA '82 (VOL)
MORRISSEY, MICHAEL J., atty., Evangelical Health Systems, Oak Brook, IL '82 (ATTY)
MORRO, BEVERLY CUSHEN, coor. soc. work, Hospital of Saint Raphael, New Haven, CT '86 (SOC)
MORROW, DONALD L., dir. matl. mgt., Saint Joseph Hospital and Health Center, Kokomo, IN '85 (PUR)
MORROW, KATHLEEN R., dir. soc. serv., Research Medical Center, Kansas City, MO '67 (SOC)
MORROW, LOUISE M., dir. pat. and family serv., Grandview Hospital and Medical Center, Dayton, OH '85 (SOC)
MORROW, MARGARET A., RN, asst. adm. pat. serv., Lee Memorial Hospital, Dowagiac, MI '67 (NURS)
MORROW, MICHAEL R., dir. hskpg., Mercy Memorial Medical Center, St. Joseph, MI '86 (ENVIRON)
MORROW, ORA M., dir. vol. serv., Roper Hospital, Charleston, SC '70 (VOL)
MORROW, OTIS WARREN, atty., Arkansas City Memorial Hospital, Arkansas City, KS '76 (ATTY)
MORROW, RICHARD V., adm., Richmond Orthopaedic Clinic, Inc., Richmond, VA '87 (AMB)
MORROW, WILLIAM T., dir. plant oper. and maint., Holy Name of Jesus Medical Center, Gadsden, AL '81 (ENG)
MORROW, WINONA R., adm. asst., Baylor Medical Center at Waxahachie, Waxahachie, TX '86 (PAT)
MORSE-CLOUGH, JOANN, dir. soc. work, Corning Hospital, Corning, NY '85 (SOC)
MORSE, CYNTHIA H., coor. mental health, Prime Health, Kansas City, MO '84 (SOC)
MORSE, DONNA K., dir. food serv., Hinsdale Hospital, Hinsdale, IL '84 (FOOD)
MORSE, MAXINE K., dir. commun. rel., Lake Shore Hospital, Manchester, NH '86 (PR)
MORSE, NANCY M., corp. coor. pub. rel. and mktg., Kennedy Memorial Hospitals-University Medical Center, Cherry Hill, NJ '81 (PR)
MORSE, NORMAN A., RN, chief nrsg. serv., Veterans Administration Medical Center, Baltimore, MD '85 (NURS)
MORSE, SUSAN, mgr., Normedco Home Care, Greeley, CO '87 (AMB)
MORSE, TIMOTHY R., sr. mktg. off., St. Paul Fire and Marine Insurance Company, St. Paul, MN '82 (RISK)
MORSELANDER, SHARON, adm. nrsg. surg. serv., Saint Joseph's Hospital, Atlanta, GA '87 (AMB)
MORSHARE, LINDA J., RN, dir. med. nrsg., Methodist Hospital, St. Louis Park, MN '83 (NURS)
MORTELL, EDWIN E., atty., Lutheran General Hospital, Park Ridge, IL '72 (ATTY)
MORTENSEN, EUGENE P., vice-pres., St. Joseph's Hospital and Medical Center, Paterson, NJ '80
MORTENSEN, IRVAL LAFAUN, atty., Mount Graham Community Hospital, Safford, AZ '84 (ATTY)
MORTENSEN, LARRY W., dir. matl. mgt., Rochester Methodist Hospital, Rochester, MN '84 (PUR)
MORTENSON, SYLVIA A., dir. nutr. and food serv., South Shore Hospital, South Weymouth, MA '84 (FOOD)
MORTENSSON, MARCIA, dir. human res., Kaweah Delta District Hospital, Visalia, CA '86 (PERS)
MORTON, LT. COL. EDWARD C., MSC USA, chief exec. off., U. S. Air Force Hospital, Tucson, AZ '72
MORTON, JUDITH I., coor. vol., Medical Plaza Hospital, Fort Worth, TX '85 (VOL)
MORTON, KELLY J., Columbus, OH '84 (PR)
MORTON, KEVIN D., student, Southern Illinois University, Carbondale, IL '85
MORTON, REED LAIRD, PhD, assoc. dir., University of Chicago, Program in Health Administration, Graduate School of Business, Chicago, IL '71 (PLNG)
MORTON, WILLOW SEKIYA, dir. soc. serv., Kapiolani Medical Center for Women, Honolulu, HI '80 (SOC)
MORVAY, TZIPORA, student, University of Southern California, Los Angeles, CA '86 (SOC)
MORYKEN, JOHN M., adm. lab. serv., St. Margaret Memorial Hospital, Pittsburgh, PA '86 (PLNG)
MOSBACHER, KARL J., dir. cent. serv., University of Cincinnati Hospital, Cincinnati, OH '82 (CS)
MOSCHINI, JAMES G., pres., Todd Associates, Farmington Hills, MI '85
MOSCOU, JACK, coor. educ. serv., Hackensack Medical Center, Hackensack, NJ '80 (EDUC)
MOSEBACH, JEAN M., dir. med. rec., Westlake Community Hospital, Melrose Park, IL '86
MOSELE, ELIZABETH STARNES, dir. soc. serv., Memorial Hospital System, Southeast Unit, Houston, TX '82 (SOC)
MOSELEY, JERRILYN, dir. matl. mgt., Coastal Communities Hospital, Santa Ana, CA '86 (PUR)
MOSELEY, S. KELLEY, DrPH, dir. prog., Program in Health Services Administration, University of Houston, Clear Lake, Houston, TX '76
MOSENA, ROBERT G., dir. human resources, Burlington Medical Center, Burlington, IA '72 (PERS)
MOSENKIS, ROBERT, vice-pres. pub., Emergency Care Research Institute, Plymouth Meeting, PA '74 (ENG)
MOSER, CYNTHIA C., atty., Marian Health Center, Sioux City, IA '84 (ATTY)
MOSER, DENNIS R., pres., Dennis R. Moser and Associates, Inc., Kingwood, TX '69 (PLNG)
MOSER, JOAN P., RN, dir. med. nrsg., Riverside Methodist Hospitals, Columbus, OH '86 (NURS)
MOSER, KATHERINE R., mgr. mktg., Stanford University Hospital, Stanford, CA '86 (PLNG)
MOSER, LARRY, dir. maint., Hahnemann University Hospital, Philadelphia, PA '83 (ENG)
MOSER, M. PETER, atty., Sinai Hospital of Baltimore, Baltimore, MD '86 (ATTY)
MOSER, THOMAS ALAN, asst. adm., Providence Hospital, Anchorage, AK '80 (ENG)
MOSES, JAMES J., asst. adm. matl. and support serv., St. John's Hospital, Springfield, IL '86 (PUR)
MOSES, RENY F., mgr. cent. serv., Mid-Maine Medical Center, Waterville, ME '80 (CS)
MOSES, ROBERT J., atty., Pacific Presbyterian Medical Center, San Francisco, CA '86 (ATTY)
MOSES, WILLIAM S., dir. arch. serv., St. Luke's Episcopal Hospital, Houston, TX '86 (ENG)
MOSESMAN, BARRY, pres., Health Facilities Planning, Inc., Montecito, CA '73
MOSESMAN, LEONARD, San Antonio, TX '84
MOSHER, CARL LEE, pres., Presbyterian-University of Pennsylvania Medical Center, Philadelphia, PA '52 (LIFE)
MOSHER, LT. COL. JOHN E., MSC USA, adv. med. forces, Department of Air Force Medical Service, Bolling AFB, DC '60
MOSHER, JUDITH W., risk mgr., St. Mary's Hospital, Reno, NV '83 (RISK)
MOSHER, ROBERT G., dir. food serv., Mount St. Joseph Nursing Home, Waterville, ME '76 (FOOD)
MOSHER, SHERRA A., RN, asst. adm. nrsg., Muskegon General Hospital, Muskegon, MI '86 (NURS)
MOSIER, LUCY M., mgr. nutr. serv., Hazelden Foundation, Center City, MN '77 (FOOD)
MOSIER, SYLVAJEAN, dir. vol. serv., Kent Community Hospital, Grand Rapids, MI '84 (VOL)
MOSIER, WILLARD WARREN, MD, med. dir., Cardiopulmonary Ancillary Service, Titusville, FL '86 (ENG)
MOSKAL, WILLIAM F., EdD, William F. Moskal Associates, Inc., Sterling Heights, MI '80 (EDUC)(PERS)
MOSLENER, MARY LOU, nrs. educ., Presbyterian Hospital, Dallas, TX '82 (EDUC)

MOSLEY, FREIDA, supv. vol., Oklahoma Children's Memorial Hospital, Oklahoma City, OK '74 (VOL)
MOSLEY, JOSEPH WILLIAM, adm., Baptist Memorial Health Care Group, Memphis, TN '85
MOSLEY, PAULINE, exec. hskpg., Shelby Memorial Hospital, Shelby, OH '87 (ENVIRON)
MOSLEY, SCOTT D., dir. mktg., Baptist Medical System, Little Rock, AR '86 (PR) (PLNG)
MOSQUEIRA, CHARLOTTE, dir. diet., Fresno Community Hospital and Medical Center, Fresno, CA '76 (FOOD)
MOSQUERA, JIM J., student, University of Missouri, Columbia, MO '86 (MGMT)
MOSS, BETTY C., sr. mgt. eng., Queen's Medical Center, Honolulu, HI '83 (MGMT)
MOSS, HARVEY A., dir. mktg., Mercy Medical Center, Oshkosh, WI '83 (PR)
MOSS, J. C., dir. food serv., Huguley Memorial Hospital, Fort Worth, TX '78 (FOOD)
MOSS, JAMES L., dir. eng., Glendive Community Hospital, Glendive, MT '86 (ENG)
MOSS, JAMES T., pres., Jackson-Madison County General Hospital, Jackson, TN '74
MOSS, JANET C., dir. mktg., Catawba Memorial Hospital, Hickory, NC '85 (PLNG)
MOSS, JILL L., Cigna Health Plan of Illinois, Des Plaines, IL '85 (PLNG)
MOSS, JOHN H., dir. pers., Illinois Valley Community Hospital, Peru, IL '73 (PERS)
MOSS, MARGARET M., dir. commun. rel., Burke Rehabilitation Center, White Plains, NY '85 (PR)
MOSS, PEGGY J., RN, coor. pat. rep., St. Mary's Hospital, Athens, GA '81 (PAT)
MOSS, ROBERT W., partner-in-charge, Pannell Kerr Forster, Denver, CO '86
MOSS, SUSAN L., RN, asst. dir. nrsg., Veterans Administration Medical Center, Durham, NC '84 (NURS)
MOSS, WILLIAM H., dir. matl. syst., Tri-City Medical Center, Oceanside, CA '86 (PUR)
MOSS, WILLIAM MASON, pres., Potomac Hospital, Woodbridge, VA '65
MOSS, WILLIAM R., atty., Highland Hospital, Lubbock, TX '76 (ATTY)
MOSSER, JOANN DENISE, dir. reg. dev., Optima Health Plan, Norfolk, VA '79 (PLNG)
MOSSING, KATHLEEN A., RN, dir. nrsg., Saint Cabrini Hospital of Seattle, Seattle, WA '85 (NURS)
MOSSOP, ROBERT A., dir. food serv., Samaritan Hospital, Troy, NY '79 (FOOD)
MOTA, JORGE DANIEL, dir., R. E. Thomason General Hospital, El Paso, TX '86
MOTA, MERCEDES B., dir. food serv., Bayley Seton Hospital, Staten Island, NY '84 (FOOD)
MOTE, JOHN R., dir. human resources, Childrens Hospital of Los Angeles, Los Angeles, CA '64 (PERS)
MOTEN, PENELLA, dir. plng., Health Alliance Plan, Health Facilities Division, Detroit, MI '81 (PLNG)
MOTES, MAC, dir. bldg. and grds., Baptist Medical Center-Montclair, Birmingham, AL '85 (ENG)
MOTLEY, ELAINE E., supv. food, St. Mary's Hospital, Orange, NJ '67 (FOOD)
MOTT, ANTHONY T., vice-pres. corp. staff, Baystate Medical Center, Springfield, MA '65 (PLNG)
MOTT, CAROLYN N., student, Indiana University, Graduate School of Hospital Administration, Indianapolis, IN '80
MOTT, GREGORY P., mgr. matl., W. A. Foote Memorial Hospital, Jackson, MI '80 (PUR)
MOTT, JAN, RN, supv. cent. serv., St. John's Hospital, Longview, WA '86 (CS)
MOTT, KENNETH K., chief eng., Bradford Hospital, Starke, FL '82 (ENG)
MOTT, LOUISE K., supv. sup. and distrib., El Dorado Hospital and Medical Center, Tucson, AZ '81 (CS)
MOTT, PHYLLIS L., RN, asst. exec. dir. and dir. nrsg. serv., Wayne County Memorial Hospital, Honesdale, PA '81 (NURS)
MOTT, RITA, dir. soc. work, Heather Hill, Chardon, OH '80 (SOC)
MOTT, ROBERT E., student, Department of Health Service Administration, George Washington University, Washington, DC '86
MOTTET, ROBERT J., dir. human res., Jackson County Public Hospital, Maquoketa, IA '83 (PERS)
MOTZEL, KATHERINE R., pat. rel. rep., Washington Adventist Hospital, Takoma Park, MD '85 (PAT)
MOTZER, EARL JAMES, pres., Tempe St. Luke's Hospital, Tempe, AZ '67 (PERS)
MOU, THOMAS W., MD, pres., Educational Commission for Foreign Medical Graduates, Philadelphia, PA '86
MOULDEN, AARON R. JR., Kaiser Foundation Hospital, Los Angeles, CA '84
MOULDER, DAVID W., dir. soc. serv. and discharge plng., Jesse Holman Jones Hospital, Springfield, TN '85 (SOC)
MOULDING, STEPHEN L. B., dir. electronics, University of Utah Health Sciences Center, Salt Lake City, UT '86
MOULTHROP, M. LYNN, RN, dir. parent-child nrsg., Maine Medical Center, Portland, ME '85 (NURS)
MOULTON, SANDY, dir. policy analyst and plng., Metropolitan Chicago Hlthcare Council, Chicago, IL '86 (PLNG)
MOULTON, SHARON G., consult. health care, Ernst and Whinney, Cincinnati, OH '84 (MGMT)
MOUNSEY, JILLANNE C., mgr. commun. rel., St. Francis Hospital Center, Beech Grove, IN '85 (PR)
MOUNT, ADELE, dir. vol., Saginaw Community Hospital, Saginaw, MI '72 (VOL)
MOUNT, BARBARA A., RN, assoc. adm., Griffin Hospital, Derby, CT '82 (NURS)
MOUNTZ, WADE, pres., NKC Hospitals, Louisville, KY '75 (LIFE)
MOUR, ALBERT C., atty., United Hospital Association, Los Angeles, CA '78 (ATTY)
MOUSA, BARRY L., fin. consult., Health East, Inc., Roanoke, VA '78
MOUSE, DONNA G., dir. loss contr., Research Health Services, Kansas City, MO '81 (RISK)
MOUSSEAU, JAMES J., mgr. food serv., Horizon Hospital, Clearwater, FL '86 (FOOD)
MOUSTAKAKIS, JOHN, syst. analyst, Northern Westchester Hospital Center, Mount Kisco, NY '85 (MGMT)
MOUTON, ARTHUR D., atty., Lafayette General Medical Center, Lafayette, LA '86 (ATTY)
MOUTON, GLORIA J., dir. staff dev. and trng., Lee Memorial Hospital, Fort Myers, FL '80 (EDUC)
MOUTON, TOM S., dir. mgt. eng., Baylor University Medical Center, Dallas, TX '70 (MGMT)
MOUTON, WELTON P. JR., atty., Our Lady of Lourdes Medical Center, Lafayette, LA '76 (ATTY)
MOUTRAY, PHYLLIS J., dir. soc. serv., Good Samaritan Hospital, Mount Vernon, IL '77 (SOC)
MOUTRIE, ROBERT R., asst. vice-pres., University of Medicine and Dentistry of New Jersey-University Hospital, Newark, NJ '85 (PLNG)
MOWER, JO ANN, adm., Hospital of the Medical College of Pennsylvania, Philadelphia, PA '79
MOWKA, PATRICIA M., supv. cent. serv., St. Luke's Hospital, Maumee, OH '82 (CS)
MOXLEY, SHARON M., coor. vol., Alta View Hospital, Sandy, UT '84 (VOL)
MOYER, ALFRED D., Beaver Falls, PA '51 (LIFE)
MOYER, CHARLES L., asst. vice-pres. matl. mgt., Palos Community Hospital, Palos Heights, IL '80 (PUR)
MOYER, DELORES C., asst. vice-pres., Regional Rehabilitation Center, Memphis, TN '77
MOYER, FLORENCE E., student, Graduate Program in Health and Medical Service Administration, Widener University, Chester, PA '84
MOYER, HARRY E., dir. emer. serv., Smyrna Hospital, Smyrna, GA '87 (AMB)
MOYER, JOHN H., vice-pres. mktg. and plng., Harrisburg Hospital, Harrisburg, PA '84 (PLNG)
MOYER, K. E., adm. and chief exec. off., Grape Community Hospital-Southwest Medical Center, Hamburg, IA '86 (AMB)
MOYER, SHIRLEY, RN, dir. util. mgt. and qual. assur., St. Jude Hospital-Fullerton, Fullerton, CA '85 (RISK)
MOYER, SONJA R., dir. pur., Grand View Hospital, Sellersville, PA '64 (PUR)
MOYER, WARREN J., mgt. analyst, National Institutes of Health, Office of Clinical and Management Systems, Clinical Center, Bethesda, MD '80 (MGMT)
MOYES, PETER M. A., arch., Salt Lake City, UT '66
MOYLAN, CATHERINE M. FISHER, dir. vol. serv., Kaiser Foundation Hospital, Redwood City, CA '86 (VOL)
MOYNIHAN, MICHAEL J., mgt. eng., Massachusetts General Hospital, Boston, MA '86 (MGMT)
MOZDY, FRANK D., dir. matl. mgt. and pharm. serv., Spencer Hospital, Meadville, PA '79 (PUR)
MOZENA, SUSAN D'OLIVE, asst. adm., Detroit Receiving Hospital and University Health Center, Detroit, MI '79
MOZOLAK, STEVEN J., D. T. Watson Home for Crippled Children, Sewickley, PA '65
MOZUR, DAVID, partner, Cosentini Associates, New York, NY '81 (ENG)
MRAZ, PATRICIA, dir. home health, Daniel Freeman Memorial Hospital, Inglewood, CA '87 (AMB)
MROCZKOWSKI, THOMAS C., dir. support serv., Hackley Hospital, Muskegon, MI '79 (MGMT)
MROSS, CHARLES D., exec. vice-pres. and chief oper. off., Greater Baltimore Medical Center, Baltimore, MD '73 (MGMT)
MRUK, ELIZABETH, dir. pers., Wing Memorial Hospital and Medical Centers, Palmer, MA '80 (PERS)
MUCCIFORI, THOMAS J., atty., Community Memorial Hospital, Toms River, NJ '78 (ATTY)
MUCEK, DOLORES, RN, pat. rep., Oak Forest Hospital of Cook County, Oak Forest, IL '76 (PAT)
MUCHA, CHRISTINE R., mgr. commun. rel., Our Lady of Mercy Hospital, Dyer, IN '86 (PR)
MUCHA, JOHN R., staff atty. legal affairs, Henry Ford Hospital, Detroit, MI '80 (RISK)
MUCHERINO, KENNETH, dir. eng., New Milford Hospital, New Milford, CT '86 (ENG)
MUCHISKY, LINDA, mgr. oper. and amb. serv., Program in Health Administration and Planning, Washington University School of Medicine, St. Louis, MO '87 (AMB)
MUCHMORE, JEAN MARIE, ombudsman, Blue Cross of Northeastern New York, Inc., Albany, NY '74 (PAT)
MUCHOW, DAVID A., vice-pres. eng., Phillips Swager Associates, Inc., Peoria, IL '85 (ENG)
MUCK, TIM B., chief eng., plant oper. and maint., Centinela Hospital Medical Center, Inglewood, CA '83 (ENG)
MUCKALA, TERESA L., coor. mktg., St. Joseph's Hospital and Health Center, Dickinson, ND '85 (PR)
MUCKIN, LORA A., asst. dir. commun. rel., St. Peter's Medical Center, New Brunswick, NJ '82 (PR)
MUDANO, MARIO A., vice-pres. prof. serv., St. Mary's Hospital, West Palm Beach, FL '80
MUDD, SUSAN, supv. outpatient, Flaget Memorial Hospital, Bardstown, KY '87 (AMB)
MUDER, BETTY L., dir. vol. serv., Providence-St. Margaret Health Center, Kansas City, KS '80 (VOL)
MUDGE, PAUL T., consult. dir.-adv. bd., Fairchild Aircraft Corporation, San Antonio, TX '87
MUDGETT, CAROL ANN, PhD, dir. plng., Central Arizona Health Systems Agency, Phoenix, AZ '84 (PLNG)
MUDLER, GORDON A., pres. and chief exec. off., Hackley Hospital, Muskegon, MI '77
MUDRY, DARIA M., dir. soc. work, St. Vincent's Medical Center, Staten Island, NY '78 (SOC)
MUEHL, MARY P., vice-pres. amb. and diagnostic serv., West Suburban Hospital Medical Center, Oak Park, IL '87 (AMB)
MUEHLENBEIN, JUNE, dir. matl. mgt., Richland Memorial Hospital, Olney, IL '77 (PUR)
MUEHLFELD, KARL, supt. maint., Saginaw Community Hospital, Saginaw, MI '80 (ENG)
MUELLER, BEVERLY M., RN, dir. nrsg., Paynesville Community Hospital, Paynesville, MN '86 (NURS)
MUELLER, CHARLES R., dir. safety and protection, Elmhurst Memorial Hospital, Elmhurst, IL '84 (ENG)
MUELLER, ELAINE M., dir. vol., St. Ansgar Hospital, Moorhead, MN '83 (VOL)
MUELLER, ERVIN R., sr. vice-pres., Our Lady of Mercy Hospital, Cincinnati, OH '72
MUELLER, GERALD A. SR., dir. bldg. and grd., Fayette Memorial Hospital, Connersville, IN '75 (ENG)(ENVIRON)
MUELLER, JENNIFER F., RN, adm. nrsg., Temple University Hospital, Philadelphia, PA '85 (NURS)
MUELLER, JO-ANN, coor. vol., Des Moines General Hospital, Des Moines, IA '84 (VOL)
MUELLER, JOAN A., dir. pub. affairs, Franciscan Health System, Inc., La Crosse, WI '86 (PR) (PLNG)
MUELLER, KRIS, dir. commun., Heartland Health System, St. Joseph, MO '85 (PR)
MUELLER, L. ERIC, dir. eng., Munson Medical Center, Traverse City, MI '79 (ENG)
MUELLER, LANCE L., mgr. eng., Group Health Eastside Hospital, Redmond, WA '84 (ENG)
MUELLER, LINDA A., RN, asst. dir. nrsg., St. Ann's Hospital, Watertown, SD '86 (EDUC)
MUELLER, LINDA J., adm. res., Mercy Hospital and Medical Center, Chicago, IL '86 (PLNG)
MUELLER, MAUDIE J., dir. pat. rel., Northeast Medical Center Hospital, Humble, TX '83 (PAT)
MUELLER, PAMELA J., pers. spec., Oaklawn Hospital, Marshall, MI '86 (PERS)
MUELLER, SUSAN A., coor. amb., South Miami Hospital, South Miami, FL '87 (AMB)
MUELLER, VIRGINIA C., adm. asst.-rad., Washington University Medical Center, St. Louis, MO '79 (PUR)
MUENCH, MARK R., mgr., Arthur Andersen and Company, Chicago, IL '84 (MGMT)
MUETH, BARBARA J., dir. pub. rel., Arkansas Children's Hospital, Little Rock, AR '81 (PR)
MUETH, JOHN A., dir. hosp. and commun. rel., Memorial Hospital, Belleville, IL '78 (PR)
MUGFORD, COL. FRANK M., MSC USAF, dir. health serv. mgt., U. S. Air Force Hospital Robins, Robins AFB, GA '74
MUHICH, MARTHA BULLEN, mgt. eng., Jewish Hospital, Louisville, KY '86 (MGMT)
MUHLBAUER, LARRY P., dir. eng. and maint., West Florida Hospital, Pensacola, FL '82 (ENG)
MUHLENTHALER, P. DONALD, pres., Marion General Hospital, Marion, OH '71
MUHLETHALER, SHARON C., dir. mktg. commun., Mercy Center for Health Care Services, Aurora, IL '86 (PR) (PLNG)
MUI, W. ASHLEY, plng. analyst, Beth Israel Medical Center, New York, NY '86 (PLNG)
MUIR-HUTCHINSON, LOUANN, dir. data proc., Bon Secours Hospital of Methuen, Methuen, MA '84 (MGMT)
MUIR, JACQUELINE L., RN, dir. nrsg. in-patient serv., Children's Hospital National Medical Center, Washington, DC '85 (NURS)
MUIR, JOANNE P., proj. mgr. performance improvememt, Cedars-Sinai Medical Center, Los Angeles, CA '84 (EDUC)
MUIR, RICHARD G., sr. vice-pres., Southwestern Michigan Health Care Association, St. Joseph, MI '85
MUIR, RICHARD J., dir. maint., Bartow Memorial Hospital, Bartow, FL '84 (ENG)
MUIRHEAD, SARA, student, Program in Health Care Administration, Texas Woman's University, Denton, TX '86
MULCAHY, MICHAEL J., atty., St. Joseph's Community Hospital, West Bend, WI '75 (ATTY)
MULCAHY, NICHOLAS, press off., Hospital of the University of Pennsylvania, Philadelphia, PA '87 (PR)
MULCAHY, ROBERT J., dir. eng. and maint., Christ Hospital, Jersey City, NJ '76 (ENG)
MULCAHY, SANDRA C., pat. rep., Martin Memorial Hospital, Stuart, FL '85 (PAT)(RISK)
MULDER, CALVIN D., sr. vice-pres., Butterworth Hospital, Grand Rapids, MI '70
MULDER, PAUL T., vice-pres. mktg., Memorial Hospital, Owosso, MI '80 (PR) (PLNG)
MULDOON, GARY E., mgr. pers. human res., Beverly Hospital, Beverly, MA '85 (PERS)
MULDOWNEY, HELEN M., health educ., Lankenau Hospital, Philadelphia, PA '86 (EDUC)
MULDROW, EDWARD J., asst. vice-pres., Jersey Shore Medical Center, Neptune, NJ '86 (PLNG)
MULFORD, CATHERINE J., dir. commun. rel., St. John's Regional Health Center, Springfield, MO '85 (PR)
MULFORD, JENENE A., RN, dir. nrsg., Mangum City Hospital, Mangum, OK '83 (NURS)
MULFORD, PETER L., assoc. adm., City Hospital, Martinsburg, WV '73
MULHOLLAND, DOROTHY A., asst. dir. soc. work, Flushing Hospital and Medical Center, Flushing, NY '86 (SOC)
MULHOLLAND, GARY A., acct. mgr., Genix Corporation, Pittsburgh, PA '84 (MGMT)
MULHOLLEM, ROBERT E. JR., plant eng., Clearfield Hospital, Clearfield, PA '85 (ENG)
MULKERN, NORBERT, dir. maint. and oper., Washington Hospital, Washington, PA '84 (ENG)
MULKEY, OREN A. JR., asst. prof. and dir. health adm., Houston-Galveston Area Council, Health Systems Agency, Houston, TX '75
MULL, CONNIE H., RN, dir. nrsg., Meadows Psychiatric Center, Centre Hall, PA '86 (NURS)
MULL, DEANNA B., dir. pers., HCA Largo Medical Center Hospital, Largo, FL '86 (PERS)
MULLANE, MICHAEL C., asst. vice-pres. exec. affairs, University of Maryland Medical Systems, Baltimore, MD '87
MULLEN, GRAHAM C., atty., Gaston Memorial Hospital, Gastonia, NC '79 (ATTY)
MULLEN, J. MICHAEL, mgr. cent. sup., Malden Hospital, Malden, MA '82 (CS)

MULLEN, JAMES A., RN, dir. nrsg. serv., Wentworth-Douglass Hospital, Dover, NH '81 (NURS)
MULLEN, JEANNE, supv. pat. and family serv., Covenant Medical Center-Schoitz, Waterloo, IA '78 (SOC)
MULLEN, LAWRENCE R., atty., Hermann Hospital, Houston, TX '83 (ATTY)
MULLEN, MARILYN S., dir. soc. serv., Valley Regional Hospital, Claremont, NH '76 (SOC)
MULLEN, PAUL E., actg. dir. hosp. accreditation prog., Joint Commission on Accreditation of Hospitals, Chicago, IL '75
MULLENBACH, KEREEN, RN, assoc. dir. and dir. nrsg., Cedars Medical Center, Miami, FL '78 (NURS)
MULLER, BARBARA W., supv. vol. serv., Holland Community Hospital, Holland, MI '86 (VOL)
MULLER, ELIZABETH A., dir. pat. serv., Northern Ocean Hospital System, Point Pleasant, NJ '72 (PAT)
MULLER, KRISTIE A., mgr. matl., HCA Edward White Hospital, St. Petersburg, FL '84 (PUR)
MULLER, PATRICIA ANN, RN, asst. dir. nrsg., Saint Francis Hospital, Tulsa, OK '79 (EDUC)(NURS)
MULLER, PAUL J., dir. human res. consulting, Ernst and Whinney, Chicago, IL '80 (PERS)
MULLER, RALPH W., vice-pres., University of Chicago Hospitals, Chicago, IL '86
MULLER, RICK, dir. mktg., Community Hospital, Grand Junction, CO '81 (PR)
MULLER, SANDRA K., RN, dir. nrsg. and asst. adm., Manchester Memorial Hospital, Manchester, CT '82 (NURS)
MULLETT, ANN, RN, coor. in-service, Community Memorial Hospital, Cheboygan, MI '74 (EDUC)
MULLIGAN, ANN T., dir. commun. rel., Watson Clinic, Lakeland, FL '80 (PR)
MULLIGAN, ANNE MARIE, RN, vice-pres. pat. care serv., Mercy Hospital and Medical Center, San Diego, CA '80 (NURS)
MULLIGAN, ELIZABETH H., mgr. eng., Scientific Insturment Division, University of Washington, Seattle, WA '83 (ENG)
MULLIGAN, GRACE I., dir. pers., Centre Community Hospital, State College, PA '85 (PERS)
MULLIGAN, MARION J., dir. prov. contr., Blue Cross of Western Pennsylvania, Pittsburgh, PA '75
MULLIGAN, SUSAN O., dir. food serv., Methodist Medical Center, Dallas, TX '84 (FOOD)
MULLIKIN, R. ANTHONY, asst. dir., Floyd Memorial Hospital, New Albany, IN '70 (PERS)
MULLINGS, MARY D., dir. nrsg., William Beaumont Hospital, Royal Oak, MI '84 (MGMT)(AMB)
MULLINS, ANNA C., RN, asst. vice-pres. pat. care serv., Children's Hospital of Sf, San Francisco, CA '82 (NURS)
MULLINS, DIANA STEVENS, RN, dir. nrsg., Clayton General Hospital, Riverdale, GA '85 (NURS)
MULLINS, DONALD J., dir. pur., St. Luke Hospital, Fort Thomas, KY '75 (PUR)
MULLINS, DONNA M., dir. pers., HCA North Clark Community Hospital, Charlestown, IN '83 (PERS)
MULLINS, NANCY, natl. sales asst. and consult., Anistics, Inc., New York, NY '84 (RISK)
MULLINS, TOMMY H., adm., Boone Memorial Hospital, Madison, WV '72
MULLIS, SYLVIA B., RN, dir. nrsg., Flowers Hospital, Dothan, AL '86 (NURS)
MULRAIN, JOANELLE WOOD, vice-pres. pub. rel. and advertising, Baptist Medical Center, Jacksonville, FL '81 (PR)
MULREANEY, BERNARD J., dir. soc. work, St. Luke's Hospital, Bethlehem, PA '77 (SOC)
MULREANY, ROBERT H., atty., Presbyterian Hospital in the City of New York, New York, NY '68 (ATTY)
MULRONEY-LEITCH, RITA A., dir. diet., Victoria General Hospital, Halifax, N.S., Canada '83 (FOOD)
MULVEHILL, SR. M. CRESCENTIA, exec. vice-pres., South Hills Health System, Pittsburgh, PA '65
MULVIHILL, SR. LENORE, adm. dir., Mercy Hospital and Medical Center, Chicago, IL '87 (AMB)
MULVIHILL, VINCENT, assoc. dir. surg., Kings County Hospital Center, Brooklyn, NY '84
MULYK, MICHAEL ANDREW, student, Program in Business Administration Health Care, Baruch College, New York, NY '87
MUMAW, GRACE N., RN, night supv., George Washington University Hospital, Washington, DC '74 (NURS)
MUMFORD, JACK M., atty., Hospital Association of Pennsylvania, Camp Hill, PA '81 (ATTY)
MUMFORD, MARY B., coor. vol. serv., Montclair Community Hospital, Montclair, NJ '85 (VOL)
MUMPER, MARY S., consult., Community Health Management Corporation, Skokie, IL '83
MUNAFO, DOLORES J., RN, asst. dir. nrsg., Mercy Hospital, Baltimore, MD '81 (NURS)
MUNDAHL, HELEN T., mgt. eng., Rochester Methodist Hospital, Rochester, MN '85 (MGMT)
MUNDIE, GENE E., RN, assoc. dir. nrsg. and staff dev., University Hospital, Stony Brook, NY '82 (NURS)
MUNDT, DAVID F., supv. matl., Christ Hospital and Medical Center, Oak Lawn, IL '86 (PUR)
MUNDY, KATHLEEN, dir. health care commun., Arthur Young and Company, Wahington, DC '82
MUNDY, LOIS J., dir. vol. serv., St. Helena Hospital and Health Center, Deer Park, CA '83 (VOL)
MUNGER, JOANNE S., chief med. equip. repair, U. S. Air Force Medical Center Wright-Patterson, Dayton, OH '85 (ENG)
MUNHOFEN, NICHOLAS B. II, adm., Mohawk Valley General Hospital, Ilion, NY '74
MUNKVOLD, STEVEN R., student, Program in Health Services Management, Ferris State College, Big Rapids, MI '83
MUNN, GEORGE L. JR., vice-pres., Baton Rouge General Medical Center, Baton Rouge, LA '79
MUNN, YVONNE L., RN, assoc. gen. dir. and dir. nrsg., Massachusetts General Hospital, Boston, MA '76 (NURS)
MUNOZ, BERTHA, adm. sec. and risk mgr., Sierra Medical Center, El Paso, TX '86 (RISK)
MUNRO, ANN P., mgr. pat.-staff rel., University of Michigan Hospitals, Ann Arbor, MI '81 (RISK)
MUNRO, STEPHANIE K., RN, vice-pres. pat. serv., St. Francis Regional Medical Center, Shakopee, MN '86 (NURS)
MUNSHOWER, DOROTHEA L., RN, dir. nrsg., Long Beach Memorial Hospital, Long Beach, NY '82 (NURS)
MUNSON, CECIL E., chief soc. work serv., Veterans Administration Medical Center, Togus, ME '75 (SOC)
MUNSON, CHARLES H., dir. emp. and pub. rel. and mktg., Baxter County Regional Hospital, Mountain Home, AR '81 (PR)
MUNSON, DOROTHY M., dir. vol. serv., Butterworth Hospital, Grand Rapids, MI '80 (VOL)
MUNSON, KRISTAN F., dir. pers., The Arbour, Boston, MA '81 (PERS)
MUNSON, LESTER E., atty., Swedish Covenant Hospital, Chicago, IL '68 (ATTY)
MUNZINGER, RICHARD G., atty., Sierra Medical Center, El Paso, TX '76 (ATTY)
MUOIO, PETER A., dir. food and nutr. serv., Harper Hospital, Detroit, MI '69 (FOOD)
MURAMOTO, PAUL T., dir. pur., Kuakini Medical Center, Honolulu, HI '69 (PUR)
MURASKI, MICHAEL A., vice-pres. matl. mgt., Holy Family Hospital, Des Plaines, IL '74 (CS)(PUR)
MURAVEZ, NANCY E., dir. nrsg. serv., N. T. Enloe Memorial Hospital, Chico, CA '85 (NURS)
MURDAKES, PETER, asst. vice-pres. matl. mgt., Ravenswood Hospital Medical Center, Chicago, IL '82 (PUR)
MURDEN, WILLIAM A. JR., dir. pers., Portsmouth General Hospital, Portsmouth, VA '75 (PERS)
MURDOCH, DUNCAN B., dir. matl. mgt., New Britain General Hospital, New Britain, CT '81 (PUR)
MURDOCK, JOAN, vice-pres. amb. care, Deaconess Hospital, Cincinnati, OH '80 (AMB)
MURDOCK, KENNETH R., chief eng., Medical Center of Independence, Independence, MO '78 (ENG)
MURDOCK, LOUINE M., dir. vol. serv., Baylor University Medical Center, Dallas, TX '71 (VOL)
MURER, CHERYL G., pres., Murer Consultants, Joliet, IL '87
MURK, ROBERTA C., coor. vol., McDonough District Hospital, Macomb, IL '86 (VOL)
MURMAN, TRENT B., tech., St. Anthony Hospital, Michigan City, IN '86 (CS)
MURNANE, SR. MARIE JOSEPH, pat. rep., St. Patrick Hospital, Lake Charles, LA '83 (PAT)
MURNANE, ROBERT J., dir. soc. work, Santa Rosa Memorial Hospital, Santa Rosa, CA '74 (SOC)
MURPHY-NELSON, ROSEMARY BJORLIN, health educ. coor., Health Edu Tech, Minneapolis, MN '80 (EDUC)
MURPHY, CAROLE A., dir. soc. serv., Laguna Honda Hospital and Rehabilitation Center, San Francisco, CA '85 (SOC)
MURPHY, DANIEL C. JR., assoc. dir. facil. plng., Beth Israel Hospital, Boston, MA '79 (ENG)
MURPHY, DANIEL P., atty., Pulaski Memorial Hospital, Winamac, IN '85 (ATTY)
MURPHY, DEBORA P., dir. food serv., Szabo Food Service, Radnor, PA '85 (FOOD)
MURPHY, DEBORAH L., assoc. dir. pub. affairs, University Hospital-University of Nebraska Medical Center, Omaha, NE '84 (PR)
MURPHY, DONALD FRANCIS, exec. vice-pres., St. Francis Hospital, Poughkeepsie, NY '68
MURPHY, ELIZABETH M., RN, dir. nrsg. amb. care, Mount Sinai Medical Center, New York, NY '87 (NURS)
MURPHY, ELLEN M., dir. vol. serv., Beth Abraham Hospital, Bronx, NY '85 (VOL)
MURPHY, FRANK V. III, sr. vice-pres., NKC Hospitals, Louisville, KY '76
MURPHY, GLYNN N., dir. facil. plng., Santa Rosa Medical Center, San Antonio, TX '71 (ENG)
MURPHY, GREGORY J., dir. pers., Anne Arundel General Hospital, Annapolis, MD '81 (PERS)
MURPHY, JAMES L., RN, Methodist Medical Center, Dallas, TX '79 (NURS)
MURPHY, JEFFREY J., vice-pres. bus. dev., Evangelical Health Systems, Oak Brook, IL '81 (PLNG)
MURPHY, JOHN A., arch., The Aldrich Company, Cochituate, MA '85 (ENG)
MURPHY, JOHN E., asst. chief eng., Community Hospital at Glen Cove, Glen Cove, NY '85 (ENG)
MURPHY, JOHN F., acct. mgr., Massachusetts Hospital Association, Burlington, MA '81 (MGMT)(PUR)
MURPHY, JOHN F., dir. oper. plng. and budgets, Johns Hopkins Hospital, Baltimore, MD '79 (MGMT)
MURPHY, JOHN RICHARD, vice-pres., Unity Medical Center, Fridley, MN '77
MURPHY, JOSEPH J., coor. pur. and matl. mgr., Louise Obici Memorial Hospital, Suffolk, VA '87 (PUR)
MURPHY, JOSEPH P., exec. vice-pres., Morton F. Plant Hospital, Clearwater, FL '84 (PR)
MURPHY, JUDITH A., pat. care syst. analyst, St. Luke's Hospital, Milwaukee, WI '87 (MGMT)
MURPHY, KAY L., dir. pub. affairs, Huntington Memorial Hospital, Pasadena, CA '81 (PR)
MURPHY, LARRY M., chief eng., Colquitt Regional Medical Center, Moultrie, GA '81 (ENG)
MURPHY, LEON G., dir. environ. serv., St. John's Hospital and Health Center, San Angelo, TX '86 (ENVIRON)
MURPHY, LINDA F., dir. diet. serv., University Community Hospital, Tamarac, FL '86 (FOOD)
MURPHY, M. VIRGINIA, dir. soc. serv., Hackensack Medical Center, Hackensack, NJ '80 (SOC)
MURPHY, SR. MARY CORNELIUS, Gonzaga University, Spokane, WA '77
MURPHY, MARY LOU, RN, asst. dir. nrsg., Stanford University Hospital, Stanford, CA '86 (NURS)
MURPHY, MAUREEN A., mgr., Price Waterhouse, Chicago, IL '81 (PLNG)
MURPHY, MICHAEL C., cent. sup. serv. serv., University of Iowa Hospitals and Clinics, Iowa City, IA '84 (CS)
MURPHY, MICHAEL D., dir. pers., HCA Doctors Hospital, Conroe, TX '84 (PERS)
MURPHY, MICHAEL J., dist. gen. mgr., Interstate United-Canteen, Tonawanda, NY '86 (FOOD)
MURPHY, MICHAEL J., atty., Highland Park Hospital, Miami, FL '86 (ATTY)
MURPHY, MICHELE A., Centerville, OH '85 (MGMT)
MURPHY, MICHELLE MARY, pat. serv. spec., Group Health, Inc., Plymouth, MN '85 (PAT)
MURPHY, MIKE, dir. hskpg., HCA Southern Hills Medical Center, Nashville, TN '86 (ENVIRON)
MURPHY, MIRIAM J., RN, adm. dir. hm health network, St. Joseph Hospital, Orange, CA '82 (AMB)
MURPHY, NELLIE J., dir. pur., Park Lane Medical Center, Kansas City, MO '84 (PUR)
MURPHY, PATRICIA S., Oregon, OH '85
MURPHY, PAUL L., dir. hskpg. serv., Memorial Hospital, Hollywood, FL '86 (ENVIRON)
MURPHY, PAUL S., atty., Herrin Hospital, Herrin, IL '86 (ATTY)
MURPHY, REBECCA R., asst. dir. soc. serv., Presbyterian Hospital in the City of New York, New York, NY '81 (SOC)
MURPHY, RICHARD E., mgr. bldg. serv., Southern Ocean County Hospital, Manahawkin, NJ '70 (ENG)
MURPHY, RICHARD K., dir. plant and maint., Timken Mercy Medical Center, Canton, OH '79 (ENG)
MURPHY, RITA, RN, asst. dir. nrsg., Montefiore Medical Center, Bronx, NY '79 (NURS)
MURPHY, LT. COL. ROBERT F., MSC USA, adm. coor., Madigan Army Medical Center, Tacoma, WA '80
MURPHY, ROBERT N., vice-pres., Visitors Hospital, Buchanan, MI '86
MURPHY, RONNIE D., dir. eng., Flagler Hospital, St. Augustine, FL '81 (ENG)
MURPHY, SHIRLEY A., RN, assoc. adm. nrsg., Multicare Medical Center, Tacoma, WA '86 (NURS)
MURPHY, SUZANNE S., sr. mgr. health care, Deloitte Haskins and Sells, Baltimore, MD '81
MURPHY, T. ANNE, RN, actg. vice-pres. nrsg., Kennebec Valley Medical Center, Augusta, ME '78 (NURS)
MURPHY, THOMAS M., atty., St. Mary's Hospital and Health Center, Tucson, AZ '76 (ATTY)
MURPHY, THOMAS W., partner, Ernst and Whinney, Chicago, IL '86 (MGMT)
MURPHY, WILLIAM J., vice-pres. pers., Galesburg Cottage Hospital, Galesburg, IL '81 (PERS)
MURRAY, ARTHUR P., asst. dir. plant oper., Copley Memorial Hospital, Aurora, IL '82 (ENG)
MURRAY, BETTE M., dir. pers., Providence Central Memorial Hospital, Toppenish, WA '83 (PERS)
MURRAY, BEVERLY SCHNEIDER, dir. soc. serv., East Tennessee Children's Hospital, Knoxville, TN '82 (SOC)
MURRAY, CATHLEEN M., dir. vol. serv., Bayshore Community Hospital, Holmdel, NJ '84 (VOL)
MURRAY, CHARLES W., sr. vice-pres. mktg. and plng., Children's Health Services of Texas, Dallas, TX '77 (PLNG)(AMB)
MURRAY, CLAIRE, RN, vice-pres. nrsg. serv., St. Mary's Hospital of Troy, Troy, NY '79 (NURS)
MURRAY, EDMOND, chief eng., French Hospital, San Francisco, CA '85 (ENG)
MURRAY, ELVIRA, RN, supv. cent. sup., St. Clare's Hospital of Schenectady, Schenectady, NY '80 (CS)
MURRAY, GAY G., dir. vol. serv., Humana Hospital -Desert Valley, Phoenix, AZ '86 (VOL)
MURRAY, JAMES PATRICK, dir. prof. serv., Lake Charles Memorial Hospital, Lake Charles, LA '76
MURRAY, SR. JANET, exec. coor. health care, Sisters of St. Joseph, Willowdale M2m 3s4, Ont., Canada '82 (PLNG)
MURRAY, JUDITH T., RN, asst. vice-pres. nrsg. serv., Wilkes-Barre General Hospital, Wilkes-Barre, PA '86 (NURS)
MURRAY, KATHLEEN MARIE, dir. med. rec., Frederick Ferris Thompson Hospital, Canandaigua, NY '80
MURRAY, KATHLEEN, RN, vice-pres. pat. serv., Northwestern Memorial Hospital, Chicago, IL '79 (NURS)
MURRAY, KEVIN CHARLES, atty., Methodist Hospital of Indiana, Indianapolis, IN '84 (ATTY)
MURRAY, LINDA LOUISE, adm. res., St. Anthony Medical Center, Columbus, OH '84
MURRAY, LOIS K., coor. staff educ., St. Mary Medical Center, Gary, IN '82 (EDUC)
MURRAY, M. JOSEPH, chief eng. serv., Veterans Administration Medical Center, Boston, MA '81 (ENG)
MURRAY, MALCOLM, dir. info. syst., Children's Hospital, Columbus, OH '83 (MGMT)
MURRAY, MARGARET M., gen. mgr., Ontario Hospital Association, Don Mills, Ont., Canada '71 (EDUC)
MURRAY, MARY MCHUGH, asst. vice-pres., Washington Hospital, Washington, PA '81
MURRAY, MAUREEN D., atty., Moses H. Cone Memorial Hospital, Greensboro, NC '84 (ATTY)
MURRAY, MAUREEN E., student, Georgia State University-Institute of Health Administration, Atlanta, GA '86
MURRAY, NATHANIEL B., asst. dir. plant oper., Southwest Florida Regional Medical Center, Fort Myers, FL '86 (ENG)
MURRAY, NORMAN A., mgr. liability control, Winthrop-University Hospital, Mineola, NY '80 (RISK)
MURRAY, PAULA S., mgr. mktg. and pub. rel., Saint Joseph Health Center Kansas, Kansas City, MO '84 (PR)
MURRAY, RICHARD C., div. mgr., health care svcs, A. T. and T. Communications, Basking Ridge, NJ '86
MURRAY, ROBERT S., exec. vice-pres., Cape Cod Hospital, Hyannis, MA '83 (PLNG)
MURRAY, SEAN M., mgt. eng., Deaconess Medical Center, Billings, MT '84 (MGMT)
MURRAY, SHIRLEY J., RN, vice-pres. pat. serv. and educ., St. Agnes Medical Center, Philadelphia, PA '75 (NURS)

MURRAY, THOMAS E., EdD, pres., Seversten Murray, Inc., Chicago, IL '79 (PLNG)
MURRAY, TOM, dir. matl. mgt., HCA Sun City Hospital, Sun City Center, FL '86 (PUR)
MURRAY, W. JANE, RN, adm. nrsg., Mercy Hospital, Bakersfield, CA '67 (NURS)
MURRAY, W. SCOTT, pres., Taylor Hospital, Ridley Park, PA '66
MURRAY, WANDA B., mgt. eng., Christian Hospitals Northeast-Northwest, St. Louis, MO '83 (MGMT)
MURRELL, HARRIET HALL, dir. vol., Ochsner Foundation Hospital, New Orleans, LA '81 (VOL)
MURRELL, JOHN JOSEPH, asst. adm., Baptist Regional Medical Center, Corbin, KY '84
MURRELL, LUCILLE M., mgr. oper. and data proc., Lawrence General Hospital, Lawrence, MA '85 (MGMT)
MURREY, GREGORY J., pers. off., Naval Hospital, Bremerton, WA '87 (PERS)
MURRO, LINDA G., dir. mktg. commun., Lutheran Healthcare Network, Mesa, AZ '83 (PR)
MURTHA, LINDA L., atty., Cape Cod Hospital, Hyannis, MA '82 (ATTY)
MURTIASHAW, SHERER M., asst. adm. oper., Desert Vista Hospital, Mesa, AZ '84 (PERS)(MGMT)
MURTISHAW, KEN W., assoc. nrsg. adm., Antelope Valley Hospital Medical Center, Lancaster, CA '83 (ENG)
MURTO, MARILYN, asst. vice-pres. pat. serv., Mercer Medical Center, Trenton, NJ '86 (RISK)
MURZYN, JANICE C., adm. dir. nuclear medicine, Methodist Medical Center of Illinois, Peoria, IL '84
MUSCHAL, JUDITH A., pur. agt., Freehold Area Hospital, Freehold, NJ '77 (PUR)
MUSCHAMP, WILLIAM G., dir. food serv., Regional Memorial Hospital, Brunswick, ME '77 (FOOD)
MUSELER, MARIA C., assoc. prof. and dir. diet. tech. prog., Suffolk County Community College, Riverhead, NY '72 (FOOD)
MUSELIN, BRENDA KEITH, asst. adm. res. care serv., Quaker Heights Freedom Home, Waynesville, OH '83
MUSGRAVE, DONNA M., RN, dir. vol. serv., Tahlequah City Hospital, Tahlequah, OK '75 (VOL)
MUSGROVE, T. JANET, dir. pers., Trinity Medical Center, Carrollton, TX '85 (PERS)
MUSHOLT, KATHRYN S., RN, dir. nrsg., Shenango Valley Medical Center, Farrell, PA '82 (NURS)
MUSIAL, STEPHEN B., student, Webster University, St. Louis, MO '86 (PLNG)
MUSIC, MARVIN, dir. facil. serv., Ivinson Memorial Hospital, Laramie, WY '86 (ENG)
MUSICH, MARELYN R., RN, asst. adm. nrsg. serv., Warrick Hospital, Boonville, IN '75 (NURS)
MUSICH, PHYLLIS, RN, asst. head nrs. oper. room and reprocessing, F. G. McGaw Hospital, Loyola University, Maywood, IL '86 (CS)
MUSIKANTOW, CINDY L., dir. plng. and dev., Forest Hospital, Des Plaines, IL '85 (PR)
MUSOLINO, JOSEPH P., asst. chief eng., Manhattan Eye, Ear and Throat Hospital, New York, NY '82 (ENG)
MUSSARD, SUZY, dir. vol. serv., Helen Keller Memorial Hospital, Sheffield, AL '81 (VOL)
MUSSELLS, F. LLOYD, MD, exec. dir., Kingston Health Sciences Complex, Kingston, Ont., Canada '51 (LIFE)
MUSSER, A. WENDELL, MD, chief staff, Veterans Administration Medical Center Atlanta, Decatur, GA '74
MUSSER, M. VIRGINIA, dir. soc. serv., Grand View Hospital, Sellersville, PA '76 (SOC)
MUSSER, SYLVIA M., staff planner, Swedish American Hospital, Rockford, IL '84 (PLNG)
MUSSLEWHITE, BONNIE, dir. environ. serv., Slidell Memorial Hospital, Slidell, LA '86 (ENVIRON)
MUSSO, LEWIS C., dir. pers., Ohio Valley Hospital, Steubenville, OH '76 (EDUC)
MUSTALISH, ANTHONY C., MD, chief emer. serv., Lenox Hill Hospital, New York, NY '87 (AMB)
MUSTIAN, PERRY, dir. commun. and emp. rel., Cape Canaveral Hospital, Cocoa Beach, FL '86 (PR)
MUSTON, LINDA K., dir. commun. rel., Mercy Hospital, Iowa City, IA '81 (PR)
MUTCH, CINDY, mgr. home health prog., North Memorial Medical Center, Robbinsdale, MN '86 (AMB)
MUTH, SUSAN M. MURPHY, sr. healthcare consult., Deloitte Haskins and Sells, Cincinnati, OH '80
MUTSCHELKNAUS, REBECCA L., dir. soc. serv., Joel Pomerene Memorial Hospital, Millersburg, OH '80 (SOC)
MUZYCHENKO, MARILYN C., RN, asst. adm. nrsg., St. Mary's Hospital, Reno, NV '80 (NURS)
MUZZIO, ROBERT J., consult., Maximus, Inc., McLean, VA '66
MYATT, BEVERLY, dir. soc. serv., Brownfield Regional Medical Center, Brownfield, TX '86 (SOC)
MYER, RITA M., RN, dir. commun. health educ., Good Samaritan Hospital, Lebanon, PA '78 (EDUC)
MYERS-HUMPHREY, JEANNE, dir. educ., Centralia General Hospital, Centralia, WA '86 (EDUC)
MYERS, ALDUS C. III, consult., Peat, Marwick, Mitchell and Company, Atlanta, GA '86 (MGMT)
MYERS, ARNOLD B., atty., Salinas Valley Memorial Hospital, Salinas, CA '74 (ATTY)
MYERS, CHARLES F., atty., University of Kansas College of Health Sciences and Bell Memorial Hospital, Kansas City, KS '80 (ATTY)
MYERS, DAVID A., dir. maint., Fostoria City Hospital, Fostoria, OH '87 (ENG)
MYERS, DAVID L., dir. eng., Vassar Brothers Hospital, Poughkeepsie, NY '81 (ENG)
MYERS, DOUGLASS NELSON, pres., Irvine Medical Center, Irvine, CA '75 (PLNG)
MYERS, EDWARD W., vice-pres., Memorial Northwest Hospital, Northwest Unit, Houston, TX '84
MYERS, GENE PAUL, dir. plant oper., St. Catherine Hospital, Garden City, KS '86 (ENVIRON)
MYERS, GERALD C., dir. food serv., Good Samaritan Community Healthcare, Puyallup, WA '79 (FOOD)
MYERS, GERALDINE, asst. dir. food serv., Cedars-Sinai Medical Center, Los Angeles, CA '80 (FOOD)
MYERS, H. JAMES, adm., Cypress Hospital, Lafayette, LA '81
MYERS, HELEN A., RN, dir. nrsg. serv., James Lawrence Kernan Hospital, Baltimore, MD '76 (NURS)
MYERS, JOEL J., pres., Joel Myers and Associates, Memphis, TN '87 (PERS)
MYERS, JON, clin. coor. risk mgt., Cary Medical Center, Caribou, ME '86 (RISK)
MYERS, JOSEPH M., vice-pres. adm., Morristown Memorial Hospital, Morristown, NJ '64
MYERS, JUDY LYNN, staff asst. consumer affairs, Veterans Administration Medical Center, Ann Arbor, MI '85 (PAT)
MYERS, KENNETH A., reg. med. facil. adm., Kaiser Foundation Hospitals Oregon Region, Portland, OR '62
MYERS, KENNETH G., prin., Peat, Marwick, Mitchell and Company, Detroit, MI '69
MYERS, LANE A., dir. soc. serv., Southwest Washington Hospitals, Vancouver, WA '84 (SOC)
MYERS, LEE M., adm., Moshannon Valley Medical Group, Philipsburg, PA '80
MYERS, LOUISE C., asst. adm., George Washington University Hospital, Washington, DC '78
MYERS, M. GAIL, dir. pub. rel., Christ Hospital, Cincinnati, OH '83 (PR)
MYERS, MARILYN R., RN, asst. adm. nrsg., Tompkins Community Hospital, Ithaca, NY '86 (NURS)
MYERS, MARY H., RN, vice-pres. nrsg., Central Maine Medical Center, Lewiston, ME '83 (NURS)
MYERS, MARY J., RN, dir. nrsg. serv., Chesapeake General Hospital, Chesapeake, VA '78 (NURS)
MYERS, MICHAEL J., exec. dir., St. Marys Hospital of Rochester, Rochester, MN '70 (ATTY)
MYERS, P. EUGENE, dir. soc. serv., Conemaugh Valley Memorial Hospital, Johnstown, PA '79 (SOC)
MYERS, PAUL H., (ret.), Oklahoma City, OK '58
MYERS, RANDY C., dir. pers., St. Mary's Hospital of Blue Springs, Blue Springs, MO '84 (PERS)
MYERS, RICHARD D., dir. plant rel. and environ. serv., Bessemer Carraway Medical Center, Bessemer, AL '72 (ENG)
MYERS, RICHARD, eng., Genesee Memorial Hospital, Flint, MI '75 (ENG)
MYERS, ROBERT D., dir. eng., St. Elizabeth Medical Center, Dayton, OH '69 (ENG)
MYERS, RUTH FEY, dir. soc. work, St. Charles Hospital and Rehabilitation Center, Port Jefferson, NY '70 (SOC)
MYERS, SHARON S., dir. soc. serv., HCA Greenview Hospital, Bowling Green, KY '82 (SOC)
MYERS, STUART SHAW, dir. soc. work, University of Texas M. D. Anderson Hospital and Tumor Institute at Houston, Houston, TX '83 (SOC)
MYERS, SUSAN A., mgr. soc. work and discharge plng., Franklin Medical Center, Greenfield, MA '80 (SOC)
MYERS, SUSAN M., dir. mktg., Pennsylvania Hospital, Philadelphia, PA '86 (PR)
MYERS, THOMAS M., dir. pub. rel. and commun., Swedishamerican Hospital, Rockford, IL '87 (PR)
MYERS, WARREN G., dir. eng. and maint., Riverside Hospital, Toledo, OH '76 (ENG)
MYERS, WILLIAM P., dir. plant oper., AMI Presbyterian-Denver Hospital, Denver, CO '84 (ENG)
MYERSON, JUDD A., vice-pres. fin., Easton Hospital, Easton, PA '86
MYETTE, VICTOR J., consult., West Palm Beach, FL '85 (MGMT)
MYLCHREEST, WILLIAM F., consult., Miami, FL '52 (LIFE)
MYLENBUSCH, THEODORE VINCENT, asst. adm., Southwest General Hospital, San Antonio, TX '82 (PR) (PLNG)
MYLES, KENNETH J., atty., Tawas St. Joseph Hospital, Tawas City, MI '80 (ATTY)
MYLES, LEO THOMAS II, asst. exec. dir., Cary Medical Center, Caribou, ME '76
MYLNICZENKO, ANDREW, dir. maint. serv., St. Mary of Nazareth Hospital Center, Chicago, IL '78 (ENG)
MYNES, MARTHA H., supv. diet., Charleston Area Medical Center, Charleston, WV '86 (FOOD)
MYNSTER, FREDERICK E., dir. maint. and grds., St. John Medical Center, Steubenville, OH '82 (ENG)
MYRBERG, E. VEE, dir. pub. info., Shenandoah Memorial Hospital, Shenandoah, IA '85 (PR)
MYRIANTHOPOULOS, MARIA L., mgr. adm. syst., University of Chicago Hospitals, Chicago, IL '82 (MGMT)
MYRICK, JUSTIN A., PhD, assoc. prof., Georgia Institute of Technology, Health Systems Research Center, Atlanta, GA '75 (MGMT)
MYRICK, REBECCA, instr. educ. serv., Moore Regional Hospital, Pinehurst, NC '86 (EDUC)
MYSTROM, BARBARA C., dir., Daniel Drake Memorial Hospital, Cincinnati, OH '86 (PR)

N

NAAMAN, MARIANNE L., assoc. dir., Houston Children Guidance Center, Houston, TX '73 (PAT)
NAAS, PAULA, coor. qual. assur., Harrisburg Medical Center, Harrisburg, IL '86 (RISK)
NABORS, CHARLES E., adm., Bryan W. Whitfield Memorial Hospital, Demopolis, AL '86 (RISK)
NABORS, EDITH, dir. soc. serv.-discharge plng., Coast Plaza Medical Center, Norwalk, CA '85 (SOC)
NABORS, JOHN B., dir. emp. rel., Mid-South Hospital, Memphis, TN '81 (PERS)
NACE, KAREN E., pat. rep., York Hospital, York, PA '86 (PAT)
NACEY, GENE, exec. dir., Environmental Service Specialist, Latrobe, PA '86 (MGMT)(ENVIRON)
NACHMAN, M. ROLAND JR., atty., Baptist Medical Center, Montgomery, AL '68 (ATTY)
NACKEL, JOHN G., PhD, prin., Ernst and Whinney, Cleveland, OH '77 (MGMT)
NACMAN, MARTIN, dir. soc. serv., Strong Memorial Hospital of the University of Rochester, Rochester, NY '67 (SOC)
NADEAU, JOSEPH E., pres., Computerx Consulting, Miami, FL '75 (MGMT)
NADEL, MARK A., pres., Timken Mercy Medical Center, Canton, OH '74
NADELL, BERNARD B., MD, med. adm., Coler Memorial Hospital, New York, NY '39 (LIFE)
NADENICHEK, JAMES JOSEPH, dir. plng. and mgt. eng., South Chicago Community Hospital, Chicago, IL '75 (MGMT)(PLNG)
NADER, JOANN, media spec. pub. affairs, St. Francis Health System, Pittsburgh, PA '86 (PR)
NADONLEY, STANLEY J., atty., Holy Cross Hospital of Silver Spring, Silver Spring, MD '73 (ATTY)
NADZAM, JOHN T., dir. mgt. syst., Butler Memorial Hospital, Butler, PA '82 (MGMT)
NAEF, MARIE ELIZABETH, (ret.), Mendham, NJ '61
NAFTANAIL, GEORGE, mgr. emp. rel., Kaiser Foundation Health Plan, Cleveland, OH '86 (PERS)
NAFZIGER, JOE, supv. cent. serv., Children's Hospital at Stanford, Palo Alto, CA '82 (CS)
NAGAPRASANNA, BANGALORE R., dir. mgt. eng., Mount Sinai Medical Center, Miami Beach, FL '83 (MGMT)
NAGEL, JUDITH F., asst. mgr. food and nutr. serv., MacNeal Hospital, Berwyn, IL '83 (FOOD)
NAGEL, LEONARD E., assoc. dir. food serv., Cedars-Sinai Medical Center, Los Angeles, CA '68 (FOOD)
NAGEL, PATRICIA M., partner, Moye, Giles, O'Keefe, Vermiere and Gorrell, Denver, CO '75 (ATTY)
NAGEL, PETER B., atty., Rose Medical Center, Denver, CO '82 (ATTY)
NAGEL, THERESA M., RN, dir. nrsg., Presbyterian Hospital, Oklahoma City, OK '82 (NURS)
NAGELVOORT, LISA, coor. pub. rel., Christian Health Care Center, Wyckoff, NJ '86 (PR)
NAGLE, CONSTANCE B., consult., Peat, Marwick, Mitchell and Company, Atlanta, GA '87 (MGMT)
NAGLE, MARY M., dir. soc. serv., St. Luke's Hospital, Davenport, IA '72 (SOC)
NAGLER, MILDRED J., RN, fielp rep., Joint Commission on Accreditation of Hospitals, Chicago, IL '81 (NURS)
NAGLIC, CVETKO, dir. eng., St. Vincent's Hospital, Harrison, NY '84 (ENG)
NAGLIERI, JOHN E., dir. food serv., Northern Westchester Hospital Center, Mount Kisco, NY '71
NAGY, ALPINE LEWIS, dir. human res., Riverside Osteopathic Hospital, Trenton, MI '81 (PERS)
NAGY, ANGELINE B., dir. vol. and pat. rep., St. Margaret Hospital, Hammond, IN '74 (PAT)(VOL)
NAGY, ANN, dir. soc. work, Mount Sinai Medical Center, Milwaukee, WI '87 (SOC)
NAGY, EMIL J., pres., Arkos Associates, Idaho Springs, CO '67 (MGMT)
NAGY, JUDITH D., dir. outpatient serv., Rehabilitation Institute of Pittsburgh, Pittsburgh, PA '82
NAGY, JUNE E., dir. commun. rel., Allegheny Valley Hospital, Natrona Heights, PA '85 (VOL)
NAGY, ROSE MARIE, supv. cent. sup., Sacred Heart Rehabilitation Hospital, Milwaukee, WI '70 (CS)
NAHN, MARI E., atty., Wisconsin Hospital Association, Madison, WI '85 (ATTY)
NAIDOFF, STEPHANIE W., atty., Thomas Jefferson University Hospital, Philadelphia, PA '81 (ATTY)
NAIL, FRANKIE C., nrsg. consult., National Medical Enterprises, New Orleans, LA '77 (NURS)
NAIMAN, MICHAEL L., student, Program in Health Service Administration, School of Health Professions, Governors State University, Park Forest South, IL '85
NAKAMOTO, ANN, risk mgr., Children's Hospital and Medical Center, Seattle, WA '85 (ATTY)
NAKAMOTO, HARRIS, mgr. hskpg. and ldry. serv., Queen's Medical Center, Honolulu, HI '87 (ENVIRON)
NAKAMURA, CLIFFORD A., dir. ldry. and linen serv., Kuakini Medical Center, Honolulu, HI '86 (ENVIRON)
NAKANO, NAOMI, RN, dir. emer. medicine, San Jose Hospital, San Jose, CA '87 (AMB)
NAKATSUKASA, WENDY C., student, Program in Health Administration, University of Minnesota, Minneapolis, MN '86
NALEPA, SUSAN G., dir. pub. rel., Premier Hospitals Alliance, Westchester, IL '87 (PR)
NALLY, JAMES, dir. plant oper., Mercy Hospital of Janesville, Janesville, WI '79 (ENG)
NALON, PAUL F., Augusta, GA '46 (LIFE)
NALTY, PAUL A., atty., Eye, Ear, Nose and Throat Hospital, New Orleans, LA '82 (ATTY)
NANCE, BETTY J., dir. pers., Memorial Hospital, Siloam Springs, AR '86 (PERS)
NANCE, DEBBIE, dir. risk control, Methodist Health System, Memphis, TN '86 (RISK)
NANCE, ELIZABETH K., dir. pub. rel., Mount Vernon Hospital, Alexandria, VA '85 (PR)
NANCE, JOHN C., dir. emer. serv., Mercy Center for Health Care Services, Aurora, IL '87 (AMB)
NANCE, JUDITH, tech. cent. serv., Metropolitan Ambulatory Surgery, Inc., Phoenix, AZ '86 (CS)
NANCE, THOMAS A., adm., Atlanta Memorial Hospital, Atlanta, TX '80 (PR)
NANK, SHARON L., dir. food serv., Princeton Community Hospital, Princeton, WV '81 (FOOD)
NANNEY, EDWARD W., assoc. dir. eng., Baptist Memorial Hospital, Memphis, TN '86 (ENG)
NANNEY, JOHN H., dir. eng., Jackson-Madison County General Hospital, Jackson, TN '83 (ENG)
NANNINI, KATHLEEN L., dir. diet. serv., Dr. John Warner Hospital, Clinton, IL '84 (FOOD)

NANOPOULOS, PETER, asst. dir., Sequoia Hospital District, Redwood City, CA '81 (ENVIRON)
NANSTIEL, BARBARA L., dir. educ. and lib. serv., Mercy Hospital, Wilkes-Barre, PA '86 (EDUC)
NANTS-SHARP, KATHERINE B., Milford, CT '84
NAPIERALA, EDWARD A., vice-pres., St. Mary's Hospital, Saginaw, MI '72 (MGMT)(PLNG)(ENG)
NAPIERALA, RICHARD A., dir. eng. and maint., Mercy Hospital, Toledo, OH '87 (ENG)
NAPIEWOCKI, JOANNE, RN, atty., Providence Hospital, Southfield, MI '80 (RISK)(ATTY)
NAPOLILLI, JOAN M., RN, asst. dir. critical care and nrsg. fiscal affairs, Longmont United Hospital, Longmont, CO '84 (NURS)
NAPOLITANI, MARIE A., commun. mgr., Phelps Memorial Hospital Center, North Tarrytown, NY '83 (ENG)
NAPOLITANO, ANDREW P., atty., Hackensack Medical Center, Hackensack, NJ '86 (ATTY)
NARAYANAN, MANICKAM, course dir. mgt., Scs Kothari Academy for Women, Madras, India '86
NARAYANSWAMI, A. N., vice-pres. manufacturing, Hancock Laboratories, Inc., Huntington Beach, CA '75 (MGMT)
NARBUTIS, EGLE M., staff dev. educator, Los Angeles Grange Memorial Hospital, La Grange, IL '86 (EDUC)
NARGANG, WAYNE R., vice-pres., Blodgett Memorial Medical Center, Grand Rapids, MI '79 (PLNG)
NARIMATSU, SUSAN M., RN, clin. nrs. mgr., Northwestern Memorial Hospital, Chicago, IL '87 (AMB)
NARRELL, WILLIAM DAVID, plant eng., Oak Hill Hospital, Joplin, MO '85 (ENG)
NARWOLD-LEVINE, SALLY, mem. advocate and head mem. serv., The HMO of Delaware, Inc., Newark, DE '85 (PAT)
NASCA, EDWARD N., adm., Greenleaf Center, Shawnee, OK '83
NASETH, DIANE M., mgr. commun., Merle West Medical Center, Klamath Falls, OR '86 (PR)
NASH, BECKY A., dir. vol., Jennie Edmundson Memorial Hospital, Council Bluffs, IA '85 (VOL)
NASH, CAROLYN EASTMOND, supv. soc. work serv., Long Island College Hospital, Brooklyn, NY '84 (SOC)
NASH, DAVID ALLEN JR., assoc. exec. dir. oper., Highlands Regional Medical Center, Sebring, FL '71
NASH, FLORA JEAN, dir. soc. serv., Northern Inyo Hospital, Bishop, CA '86 (SOC)
NASH, KERMIT B., dir. soc. serv., University of North Carolina School of Social Work, Chapel Hill, NC '77 (SOC)
NASH, LARRY J., proj. mgr., Riverside Methodist Hospital, Columbus, OH '86 (MGMT)
NASH, MARY G., RN, asst. adm. nrsg., Sinai Hospital of Detroit, Detroit, MI '84 (NURS)
NASH, SHARON K., dir. educ. serv., Boca Raton Community Hospital, Boca Raton, FL '73 (EDUC)
NASH, STEPHEN P., atty., Eye and Ear Hospital of Pittsburgh, Pittsburgh, PA '81 (ATTY)
NASON, FRANCES, dir. soc. serv., Massachusetts Eye and Ear Infirmary, Boston, MA '83 (SOC)
NASRALLA, ANTHONY J., adm. and chief exec. off., Perry County Memorial Hospital, Tell City, IN '80
NASSAR-RIZEK, ENRIQUE, atty., Hospital Dr. Dominguez, Humacao, P.R. '85 (ATTY)
NASSIEF, RAY, asst. to dir. oper., Childrens Hospital of Los Angeles, Los Angeles, CA '82
NAST, ROBERT J., vice-pres., Voluntary Hospitals of America, Tampa, FL '74
NATAL, BARBARA A., mgr., Ernst and Whinney, Chicago, IL '77 (PLNG)
NATALE, DAVID A., clin. eng., Air Force Medical Logistics Office, Frederick, MD '84 (ENG)
NATARAJAN, ENGAN V., corp. budget dir., Eisenhower Medical Center, Rancho Mirage, CA '74 (MGMT)
NATARO, JOSEPH F., MD, vice-pres. med. affairs, St. Francis Hospital, Poughkeepsie, NY '85
NATEMAN, BARRY A., coor. hosp. wide activ., Mercy Hospital, Columbus, OH '85 (EDUC)
NATHANSON, STEVEN D., assoc. dir. plng., Riverside Hospital, Toledo, OH '84 (PLNG)
NATIELLO, MARY STEWART, asst. adm. and dir. mktg. and pub. rel., South Shore Hospital and Medical Center, Miami Beach, FL '86 (PR) (PLNG)
NATIELLO, THOMAS A., PhD, prof. and dir. health adm., University of Miami, Coral Gables, FL '84
NATIONS, DAVID W., vice-pres., Jewish Hospital of St. Louis, St. Louis, MO '80 (PERS)
NATIONS, KATHERINE H., dir. food serv., Mississippi County Hospitals, Blytheville, AR '67 (FOOD)
NATIVO, GLORIA, dir. environ. and ldry. serv., Suburban Hospital and Sanitarium-Cook County, Hinsdale, IL '86 (ENVIRON)
NAUFUL, ERNEST J. JR., atty., Lexington County Hospital, West Columbia, SC '75 (ATTY)
NAUGLE, GARY R., dir. human res., Altoona Hospital, Altoona, PA '84 (PERS)
NAUJOKAS, VICTOR J. JR., dir. eng., Central General Hospital, Plainview, NY '81 (ENG)
NAUMANN, RONALD J., dir. matl. mgt., King's Daughters' Medical Center, Ashland, KY '85 (PUR)
NAURATIL, KATHLEEN L., dir. pers., Spalding Rehabilitation Hospital, Denver, CO '83 (PERS)
NAVERA, ANN R., RN, Chicago, IL '85 (NURS)
NAVETTA, VIOLA M., supv. commun., Bon Secours Hospital, Grosse Pointe, MI '83 (ENG)
NAVIN, BETTY JANE, dir. diet., Bon Secours Hospital, Grosse Pointe, MI '71 (FOOD)
NAVIN, E. PATRICIA, (ret.), Grosse Pointe Park, MI '70 (FOOD)
NAVIN, TERRANCE P., dir. maint., Wilkes-Barre General Hospital, Wilkes-Barre, PA '82 (ENG)
NAWOJCZYK, GABRIEL J., dir. eng., Clara Maass Medical Center, Belleville, NJ '79 (ENG)
NAYDOCK, HARRY T., asst. vice-pres. gen. serv., Good Samaritan Hospital of Pottsville, Pennsylvania, Pottsville, PA '67 (RISK)
NAYEBAZIZ, HAMID, doctoral student, University of Minnesota, Doctoral Studies in Hospital and Health Administration, Minneapolis, MN '79
NAYLOR, CHARLES A., mgr. trng., St. Francis Hospital, Wilmington, DE '76 (EDUC)
NAYLOR, RICHARD A., environ. serv. coor., Hospital Corporation of America, Nashville, TN '83 (ENG)
NAYLOR, VI B., RN, dir. prof. serv., Georgia Hospital Association, Atlanta, GA '86 (NURS)
NAZARETH, EDWARD R. L., gen. mgr., Hospital Linen Service Facility, Pittsburgh, PA '83
NAZAREY, PEGGY, RN, dir. nrsg., Los Angeles County Harbor-University of California at Los Angeles Medical Center, Torrance, CA '81 (NURS)
NAZZARO, SAMUEL G., adm., Wheeling Hospital, Wheeling, WV '52 (LIFE)
NEAFUS, RICHARD P., dir. matl. mgt., United Hospital, St. Paul, MN '77 (PUR)
NEAL, CHARLES T. III, adm., HCA Coliseum Medical Centers, Macon, GA '86
NEAL, F. BRENT, atty., Richmond Memorial Hospital, Rockingham, NC '80 (ATTY)
NEAL, HELEN C., spec. pat. rel., Halifax Hospital Medical Center, Daytona Beach, FL '80 (PAT)
NEAL, JAMES H., adm. facil. mgt., Memorial Hospital, Colorado Springs, CO '75 (ENG)
NEAL, KENNETH, La Habra, CA '78 (ENG)
NEAL, LAVONE, mgt. eng., Baylor University Medical Center, Dallas, TX '83 (MGMT)
NEAL, NANCY B., dir. pat. and family serv., Central DuPage Hospital, Winfield, IL '80 (SOC)
NEAL, ORVILLE C., asst. chief eng., Prince William Hospital, Manassas, VA '82 (ENG)
NEAL, PAT, dir. television, American Medical International, Beverly Hills, CA '83 (PR)
NEAL, ROGER, dir. eng. and bio-med. serv., Tidewater Memorial Hospital, Tappahannock, VA '85 (ENG)
NEAL, THOMAS R., atty., William N. Wishard Memorial Hospital, Indianapolis, IN '79 (ATTY)
NEALE, ROBERT J., mgr. pers., Polk General Hospital, Bartow, FL '86 (PERS)
NEALE, THOMAS E., dir. mktg. and commun. rel., Camden-Clark Memorial Hospital, Parkersburg, WV '81 (PR) (PLNG)
NEALE, TIMOTHY A., adm. prof. serv., Medical Center Hospital of Vermont, Burlington, VT '79
NEALE, WILLIAM R., atty., Fairbanks Hospital, Indianapolis, IN '79 (ATTY)
NEALEY, LEONA HANSEN, dir. vol. serv., University of California San Francisco, San Francisco, CA '69 (VOL)
NEAMAN, MARK R., asst. vice-pres., Evanston Hospital, Evanston, IL '74
NEASE, REGINALD, pres., Medical Gas Services, Inc., Lenexa, KS '79 (ENG)
NEATHAWK, ROGER D., pres., Market Strategies, Inc., Richmond, VA '68 (PR)
NEAULT, NORMAN G., dir. food serv., Goddard Memorial Hospital, Stoughton, MA '83 (FOOD)
NEAVEILL, ROD S., dir. commun. rel. and mktg., Ravenswood Hospital Medical Center, Chicago, IL '83 (PR)
NEBBITT, MRS. GEORGE E., dir. vol. serv., Covenant Medical Center -St. Francis, Waterloo, IA '77 (VOL)
NEBLETT, RUTH D., vice-pres. pur., Walter O. Boswell Memorial Hospital, Sun City, AZ '77 (PUR)
NECK, MARY C., adm. asst., St. Frances Cabrini Hospital, Alexandria, LA '80 (RISK)
NEDELMAN, HELEN L., dir. soc. serv., St. Joseph Medical Center, Burbank, CA '84 (SOC)
NEDER, NORMAN T., adm., Baldwin County Hospital, Milledgeville, GA '79 (PLNG)
NEEDHAM, JAMES P., mgr., Arthur Young and Company, Seattle, WA '86 (MGMT)
NEEDHAM, MARK L., sr. consult., SunHealth Corporation, Charlotte, NC '81 (MGMT)
NEEDLE, ANNETTE, dir. soc. serv., Cambridge Hospital, Cambridge, MA '83 (SOC)
NEEL, LEONARD G., mgr. plant facil., Morton F. Plant Hospital, Clearwater, FL '73 (ENG)
NEEL, SHIRLEY, supv. hskpg., Bellville General Hospital, Bellville, TX '86 (ENVIRON)
NEELY, JAMES E., mgr. facil. eng., Humana Inc., Louisville, KY '68 (ENG)
NEELY, JAMES R., dir., The Equitable, Coraopolis, PA '50 (LIFE)
NEELY, JOSEPH H., exec. vice-pres., South Community Hospital, Oklahoma City, OK '76
NEELY, MICHAEL B., dir. pur., Mobile Infirmary Medical Center, Mobile, AL '84 (PUR)
NEELY, WALTER E., atty., Humana Inc., Louisville, KY '80 (ATTY)
NEENAN, MARY M., RN, adm. nrsg. serv., University General Hospital, Seminole, FL '79 (NURS)(RISK)
NEER, GENE, rep. emp. rel., Queen of the Valley Hospital, West Covina, CA '73 (PERS)
NEERING, PATRICK D., atty., Bay Medical Center, Bay City, MI '74 (ATTY)
NEES, CANDACE L., RN, dir. nrsg., Buena Vista County Hospital, Storm Lake, IA '85 (NURS)
NEFF, DAVID C., assoc. exec. dir., Children's Hospital, Columbus, OH '80 (AMB)
NEFF, JOHN B., pres., Frankford Hospital of the County of Philadelphia, Philadelphia, PA '58
NEFF, JUDITH A., dir. mktg. serv., Pro-Wellness, Inc., Dayton, OH '77 (PAT)
NEFF, PAULA E., atty., St. Catherine Hospital, East Chicago, IN '86 (ATTY)
NEFF, RALPH K., adm., Rolling Plains Memorial Hospital, Sweetwater, TX '71
NEGLES, BARBARA A., RN, assoc. chief nrsg. serv., Veterans Administration Hospital, Hines, IL '84 (NURS)
NEGRON, HECTOR R., chief soc. work serv., Veterans Administration Medical Center, San Juan, P.R. '67 (SOC)
NEHRING, NORA A., co-dir. vol. serv., Southlake Campus, Merrillville, IN '76 (VOL)
NEHRT, LUCY, RN, supv. cent. sup., St. Anthony's Memorial Hospital, Effingham, IL '85 (CS)
NEIDENBERG, CAROL A., dir. mktg., Magliaro and McHaney, La Jolla, CA '86 (PR)
NEIDLINGER, SUSAN H., RN, asst. prof. commun. and adm. nrsg., University of California San Francisco, San Francisco, CA '85 (NURS)
NEILAN, WILLIAM A., treas., Charlton Memorial Hospital, Fall River, MA '72
NEILL, MARGARET M., RN, dir. nrsg., University of California at Los Angeles Medical Center, Los Angeles, CA '74 (NURS)
NEILSON, JAMES G., asst. adm., Sparta Community Hospital, Sparta, IL '69 (ENG)
NEILSON, M. MARJORIE, dir. vol. serv., Harrisburg Hospital, Harrisburg, PA '86 (VOL)
NEIMAN, BENNETT A., partner, Neiman, Maring and Kanfield, Inc., St. Louis, MO '86 (PLNG)
NEIMAN, HELEN T., adm., Concourse Nursing Home, Bronx, NY '76 (PUR)
NEIMAN, JUDITH S., Glencoe, IL '79 (PLNG)
NEIMAN, STANLEY L., MD, dir. amb. care, Methodist Hospital, Brooklyn, NY '87 (AMB)
NEIPRIS, JONATHAN P., atty., Pennsylvania Department of Health, Harrisburg, PA '86 (ATTY)
NEITZ, M. EDWINA, coor. staff dev., Aultman Hospital, Canton, OH '78 (EDUC)
NEITZKE, BARBARA KAREN, RN, dir. nrsg., Loring Hospital, Sac City, IA '82 (NURS)
NELDNER, FREDERICK E., mgt. eng., Society of the New York Hospital, New York, NY '80 (MGMT)
NELKIN, CAROL E., dir. soc. serv., Menorah Medical Center, Kansas City, MO '80 (SOC)
NELL, JOHN D., atty., Terre Haute Regional Hospital, Terre Haute, IN '83 (ATTY)
NELLIS, JEFF, asst. mgr. pur., Northern Illinois Medical Center, McHenry, IL '86 (PUR)
NELSEN, ROBERT D., corp. dir. pers., American Health Group International, Kirkland, WA '83 (PERS)
NELSON, ALVERTA M., dir. vol., Riverside Hospital, Newport News, VA '73 (VOL)
NELSON, ARTHUR D., MD, chm. exec. committee, Scottsdale Memorial Health Systems, Scottsdale, AZ '66
NELSON, BARBARA J., assoc. dir. nrsg., St. Luke's Regional Medical Center, Boise, ID '85 (NURS)
NELSON, BARBARA, RN, dir. nrsg., South Suburban Hospital, Hazel Crest, IL '77 (NURS)
NELSON, BETH N., dir. mktg., Pitt County Memorial Hospital, Greenville, NC '85 (PR)
NELSON, BEVERLY A., dir. vol. serv., Mercy Medical Center, Coon Rapids, MN '85 (VOL)
NELSON, BRUCE L., vice-pres. med. serv., Wyandotte General Hospital, Wyandotte, MI '64
NELSON, BRYAN T., student, Program in Health Care Administration, University of Minnesota, Minneapolis, MN '86
NELSON, DAVID A., Pekin, IL '72 (PERS)
NELSON, DEAN W., sr. vice-pres., Methodist Hospital, Madison, WI '66
NELSON, DIANE, mgr. health care syst., Gte, General Telephone Company of Indiana, Inc., Carmel, IN '86
NELSON, DIRK H., student, Program in Hospital and Health Care Administration, University of Minnesota, St. Paul, MN '85
NELSON, DONALD A., dir. constr., Providence Hospital, Mobile, AL '82 (ENG)
NELSON, DONALD O., assoc. exec. dir., Providence-St. Margaret Health Center, Kansas City, KS '66 (PLNG)
NELSON, DONALD W., dir. pub. affairs, Scott and White Memorial Hospital, Temple, TX '82 (PR)
NELSON, EDMUND K., chm., Nelson International Medical Services Corporation, White Bear Lake, MN '56 (LIFE)
NELSON, ELIZABETH, dir. matl. mgt., St. Mary's Regional Health Center, Roswell, NM '83 (PUR)
NELSON, ETHEL MARIE, RN, dir. nrsg., St. Luke Hospital, Fort Thomas, KY '81 (NURS)
NELSON, GEORGE, dir. hskpg. and linen serv., St. Mary Hospital, Philadelphia, PA '86 (ENVIRON)
NELSON, GERALDINE, mgr. proc. and distrib., Huron Road Hospital, Cleveland, OH '86 (CS)
NELSON, GREGORY C., student, Program in Hospital and Health Administration, University of Iowa, Iowa City, IA '85
NELSON, HARRIET S., dir. vol., St. John's Episcopal Hospital-South Shore Division, Far Rockaway, NY '76 (VOL)
NELSON, HELEN R., RN, dir. educ., Canoga Park Hospital, Canoga Park, CA '80 (EDUC)
NELSON, IRIS FAYE, RN, chief exec. nrs., St. Mary Medical Center, Hobart, IN '80 (NURS)
NELSON, IVY M., dir. vol. serv., Sharp Memorial Hospital, San Diego, CA '76 (VOL)
NELSON, JACKLYN A., dir. matl. mgt., Lee's Summit Community Hospital, Lees Summit, MO '86 (PUR)
NELSON, JAMES E., atty., Vassar Brothers Hospital, Poughkeepsie, NY '85 (ATTY)
NELSON, JEFFREY PETER, dir. pat. and family serv., St. Francis Medical Center, La Crosse, WI '79 (SOC)
NELSON, JOAN M., asst. dir. diet. serv., University Community Hospital, Tampa, FL '86 (FOOD)
NELSON, JOHN A., exec. dir., Community Health Care Center Plan, Inc., New Haven, CT '55 (LIFE)
NELSON, JOHN A., atty., St. Joseph's Hospital, Milwaukee, WI '86 (ATTY)
NELSON, JONATHAN D. F., atty., HCA South Arlington Medical Center, Arlington, TX '83 (ATTY)
NELSON, JOSEPH A. III, PhD, dir. clin. syst. eng., Charity Hospital at New Orleans, New Orleans, LA '85 (ENG)
NELSON, JOSEPH C., vice-pres., Midland Hospital Center, Midland, MI '80 (RISK)
NELSON, K. DWIGHT, dir. fin., Stony Plain Municipal Hospital, Stony Plain, Alta., Canada '86 (PERS)(MGMT)

NELSON, KATHY J., dir. in-service, Madison Memorial Hospital, Rexburg, ID '83 (EDUC)
NELSON, KAYE LYNN, mgr. risk and qual. assur., Deaconess Medical Center, Billings, MT '84 (RISK)(PAT)
NELSON, LANI CORRINE, RN, dir. nrsg. serv., Bozeman Deaconess Hospital, Bozeman, MT '84 (NURS)
NELSON, LARRY A., vice-pres. human res., St. Joseph's Medical Center, Brainerd, MN '80 (PERS)
NELSON, LAWRENCE J., PhD, atty., Bioethics Consultation Group, Berkeley, CA '84 (ATTY)
NELSON, LINDA MAE, RN, pres., Administrative Strategies, Inc., Woodland Hills, CA '75 (MGMT)
NELSON, LINDA MCNEW, RN, dir. oper. room, Mansfield General Hospital, Mansfield, OH '83 (NURS)
NELSON, LISA, student, Program in Hospital Administration, University of Minnesota, Minneapolis, MN '87
NELSON, MARY A., RN, vice-pres. pat. serv., Queen of the Valley Hospital, Napa, CA '77 (NURS)
NELSON, MARY B., dir. vol. serv., Saint Vincent Hospital, Billings, MT '75 (VOL)
NELSON, MARY J. E., dir. diet., Naeve Hospital, Albert Lea, MN '85 (FOOD)
NELSON, PHILIP L., atty., Josephine Memorial Hospital, Grants Pass, OR '86 (ATTY)
NELSON, ROBERT C., mgr. pers., Bishop Clarkson Memorial Hospital, Omaha, NE '83 (PERS)
NELSON, ROBERT JAMES, health analyst, Dept. of HHS, Bureau of Health Planning and Resource Development, Rockville, MD '68
NELSON, ROBERT W., chm. mgt. eng., Lutheran General Hospital, Park Ridge, IL '68 (MGMT)
NELSON, RUSSELL A., MD, pres. emeritus, Johns Hopkins Hospital, Baltimore, MD '52 (LIFE)
NELSON, SHARON M., RN, dir. risk mgt. and qual. assur., Capitol Hill Hospital, Washington, DC '82 (RISK)
NELSON, STANLEY R., pres., Henry Ford Health Care Corporation, Detroit, MI '82 (LIFE)
NELSON, STEPHEN A., mgt. eng. consult., SunHealth, Richmond, VA '85 (MGMT)
NELSON, SUZANNE, dir. vol. serv., University of Utah Health Sciences Center, Salt Lake City, UT '84 (VOL)
NELSON, TIMOTHY P., cost analyst, Hamot Medical Center, Erie, PA '86 (MGMT)
NELSON, VIRGIL W., (ret.), Palm Harbor, FL '42 (LIFE)
NELSON, VIRGINIA A., coor. cont. educ., Park Lane Medical Center, Kansas City, MO '86 (EDUC)
NELSON, W. EUGENE, vice-pres., Health Strategies, Tallahassee, FL '85 (PLNG)
NELSON, WILLARD C., arch., Utah Valley Regional Medical Center, Provo, UT '80
NELSON, WILLIAM H., vice-pres. fin., Intermountain Health Care, Inc., Salt Lake City, UT '76
NELSON, WILLIAM R., student, Program in Health Administration, University of Minnesota, Minneapolis, MN '86
NEMACHECK, WILLIAM R., asst. adm., Marquette General Hospital, Marquette, MI '85 (MGMT)
NEMANN, LUELLEN J., RN, dir. nrsg., Lansing General Hospital, Lansing, MI '83 (NURS)
NEMECEK, ROY G., chief eng., Edward Hospital, Naperville, IL '70 (ENG)
NEMETH, LYNDA L., RN, risk mgr., Norwalk Hospital, Norwalk, CT '83 (NURS)(RISK)
NEMETH, MATTIE J., dir. commun., Broward General Medical Center, Fort Lauderdale, FL '84 (ENG)
NEMETH, RICHARD R., dir. eng., Greenwich Hospital, Greenwich, CT '67 (ENG)
NENE, LOUISE M., coor. educ., North Hills Passavant Hospital, Pittsburgh, PA '80 (EDUC)
NENNER, VICTORIA ANNA, vice-pres., Marvik Educational Services, San Diego, CA '80 (EDUC)
NENNI, LINDA J., atty., Millard Fillmore Hospital, Buffalo, NY '86 (ATTY)
NESBIT, JANA P., coor. pat. rel., South Miami Hospital, South Miami, FL '81 (PAT)
NESBITT, CHARLES, plant eng., Community Hospital, Mayfield, KY '87 (ENG)
NESHEM, GORDON L., sup. cent. sup. room, Permanente Medical Center, San Francisco, CA '81 (CS)
NESPER, SARA BREWSTER, dir. corp. commun., Methodist Hospital of Chicago, Chicago, IL '85 (PR)
NESPOLI, JOHN L., vice-pres. mktg. and plng., Saint Vincent Hospital, Worcester, MA '79
NESS, CARLENE K., dir. pub. rel., Arlington Memorial Hospital, Arlington, TX '82 (PR)
NESSEL, MARK P., planner, Frankford Hospital, Philadelphia, PA '86 (PLNG)
NESSELROAD, JUDY A., RN, dir. nrsg. serv., Mercy Hospital, Hamilton, OH '83 (NURS)
NESTEL, WILLIAM B., dir. nutr., Bryn Mawr Hospital, Bryn Mawr, PA '86 (FOOD)
NESTINGEN, JAN I., dir. commun. rel., Rogers Memorial Hospital, Oconomowoc, WI '86 (PR)
NESTLERODE, STEPHANIE L., dir. plng. and mktg. res., Lexington County Hospital, West Columbia, SC '81 (PLNG)
NESTOR, KATHRYN, RN, dir. nrsg. serv., Ohio Valley Hospital, Steubenville, OH '84 (NURS)
NESTOR, NINA, dir. soc. serv., Saddleback Community Hospital, Laguna Hills, CA '86 (SOC)
NETHERLAND, SUSAN B., dir. nrsg., R. J. Reynolds-Patrick County Hospital, Stuart, VA '82 (NURS)
NETTI, DOMNICK M., dir. pers., Moses Taylor Hospital, Scranton, PA '80 (PERS)
NETZEL, SR. JOAN, supv. matl. mgt., Foster G. McGaw Hospital, Loyola University of Chicago, Maywood, IL '78 (CS)
NEU, JACK L. JR., mgr. mktg. res., Sisters of Charity Health Care Systems, Cincinnati, OH '86 (PR) (PLNG)
NEU, MARLENE T., coor. commun. rel., Shreveport Eye Research Foundation, Shreveport, LA '86 (PR)
NEUBAUER, MARY, risk mgr. and coor. qual. assur., Morristown Memorial Hospital, Morristown, NJ '80 (RISK)
NEUBER, PAULETTE R., dir. hskpg., Merle West Medical Center, Klamath Falls, OR '86 (ENVIRON)
NEUENS, COLETTA M., RN, assoc. adm., Christ Hospital, Oak Lawn, IL '79 (NURS)
NEUHARD, CONNIE D., dir. commun. rel., Bloomsburg Hospital, Bloomsburg, PA '84 (PR)
NEUHART, SUE ANN, dir. educ. serv., Fairview Southdale Hospital, Minneapolis, MN '80 (EDUC)
NEUHAUS, EVELYN R., sr. planner, University of Michigan Hospitals, Ann Arbor, MI '85 (PLNG)
NEUHAUS, JOAN E., dir. plng., Archbishop Bergan Mercy Hospital, Omaha, NE '86 (PLNG)
NEUHAUSEL, DARRELL J., clin. eng., Bethesda Oak Hospital, Cincinnati, OH '80 (ENG)
NEUHAUSER, DUNCAN V. B., PhD, prof. commun. health, Case Western Reserve University, School of Medicine, Cleveland, OH '62
NEUHAUSER, PEG C., pres., Pcn Associates, Nashville, TN '86 (EDUC)
NEUJAHR, LEETTA M., sales rep., Roy Asmussen and Associates, Inc., Des Plaines, IL '86 (FOOD)
NEUMAN, CATHERINE E., RN, dir. nrsg., Memorial Hospital, Carbondale, IL '74 (NURS)
NEUMAN, KERMIT, atty., Mercer County Community Hospital, Coldwater, OH '76 (ATTY)
NEUMANN, CYNTHIA J., coor. pat. and commun. health educ., Salem Hospital, Salem, MA '85 (EDUC)
NEUMANN, ERNEST F., asst. dir., Gaston Memorial Hospital, Gastonia, NC '66
NEUMANN, ROBERTA, coor. pers., Butler Hospital, Providence, RI '79 (PERS)
NEUMANN, SHERYL J., dir. nrsg., Franciscan Medical Center, Rock Island, IL '77 (NURS)
NEUMANN, WILLIAM D., dir. diet. serv., San Antonio Community Hospital, Upland, CA '85 (FOOD)
NEUREITHER, GEORGE R., asst. pers. off., Hunter Holmes McGuire Veterans Administration Medical Center, Richmond, VA '83 (PERS)
NEUSCH, MICHAEL W., adm. asst.-dir., Veterans Administration Medical Center, Pittsburgh, PA '80
NEUSCH, RICHARD D., supv. cent. serv., Suburban General Hospital, Pittsburgh, PA '83 (CS)
NEVELOFF, BERNARD, actg. dir. pur., Montefiore Medical Center, Bronx, NY '81 (PUR)
NEVENS, ROBERT J., vice-pres. claims, Parthenon Insurance Company, Hospital Corporation of America, Nashville, TN '82 (RISK)
NEVERS, MARTIN F., dir. matl. mgt., St. Francis Hospital, Milwaukee, WI '64 (PUR)
NEVERS, RICK L., sr. consult., Ernst and Whinney, Milwaukee, WI '81 (MGMT)(PUR)
NEVILLE, ANDREZ H., RN, chief nrsg. serv., Veterans Administration Medical Center, Kerrville, TX '81 (NURS)
NEVILLE, FRED J. JR., dir. pers., Lawrence County General Hospital, Ironton, OH '83 (PERS)
NEVILLE, THOMAS J., Avon, CT '84
NEVIN, JOSEPH B., dir. soc. serv., Hebrew Hospital for Chronic Sick, Bronx, NY '73 (SOC)
NEVLING, HARRY R., dir. pers., Longmont United Hospital, Longmont, CO '79 (PERS)
NEW, NANCY A., RN, coor. qual. assur., Pacific Presbyterian Medical Center, San Francisco, CA '85 (NURS)
NEW, WAYNE C., asst. adm., Grady Memorial Hospital, Atlanta, GA '73
NEWBERRY, JUDITH M., asst. dir. fin., University of Missouri Hospital and Clinics, Columbia, MO '87 (PUR)
NEWBILL, MATTHEW C., vice-pres. mktg., Nashville Memorial Hospital, Madison, TN '85 (PLNG)
NEWBOLD, PHILIP A., pres., Baptist Medical Center of Oklahoma, Oklahoma City, OK '85 (PLNG)
NEWBOULD, RICHARD A., vice-pres. adm. serv., Lakeview Medical Center, Danville, IL '80 (RISK)
NEWBRANDER, WILLIAM C., prog. mgt. off., World Health Organization, Pt Moresby, Papua, New Guinea '76
NEWBURY, GEORGE A., (ret.), Flagler Beach, FL '73 (LIFE)
NEWBURY, JEANNE B., RN, dir. clin. support serv., Westerly Hospital, Westerly, RI '77 (EDUC)(RISK)
NEWCOMB, CAROL S., oper. analyst, Henry Ford Hospital, Detroit, MI '86 (PLNG)(MGMT)
NEWCOMB, DONALD L., vice-pres. human res., St. Mary's Hospital, Richmond, VA '84 (PERS)
NEWCOMER, BERNARD W., dir. food serv., Central General Hospital, Plainview, NY '81 (FOOD)
NEWELL, DANIEL A., dir. eng. serv., Hospital Corporation of America, Nashville, TN '82 (ENG)
NEWELL, EDWARD T. JR., MD, chief of staff, Downtown General Hospital, Chattanooga, TN '39 (LIFE)
NEWELL, MARSHA K., dir. pers., Hadley Regional Medical Center, Hays, KS '74 (PERS)
NEWELL, MICHELLE J., coor. pers., Shriners Hospital for Crippled Children, Tampa Unit, Tampa, FL '85 (PERS)
NEWELL, ROLAND A., dir. mktg., Mercy Hospital of New Orleans, New Orleans, LA '86 (PR)
NEWHALL, BLANCHE B., chief clin. soc. work, Lac-King-Drew Medical Center, Los Angeles, CA '77 (SOC)
NEWHOUSE, JOHN J., PhD, dir. mktg., Bryn Mawr Rehabilitation Hospital, Malvern, PA '82 (EDUC)
NEWINGHAM, KEVIN W., student, Sangamon State University, Springfield, IL '86 (PLNG)
NEWKIRK, HARLAN H., pres., South Chicago Community Hospital, Chicago, IL '54 (LIFE)
NEWKIRK, THOMAS, asst. vice-pres. ancillary serv., Froedtert Memorial Lutheran Hospital, Milwaukee, WI '86
NEWLAND, DONNA L., RN, asst. adm. pat. care serv., Hawaii-Desert Medical Center, Joshua Tree, CA '85 (NURS)
NEWLANDS, BARBARA, RN, coor. cent. serv., St. Elizabeth Hospital, Utica, NY '78 (CS)
NEWLIN, EDWARD S., atty., Tyrone Hospital, Tyrone, PA '79 (ATTY)
NEWMAN, ANTOINETTE BARKER, London, England '77 (PLNG)
NEWMAN, BARBARA J., nrs. educ., Presbyterian Hospital, Dallas, TX '86 (EDUC)
NEWMAN, DIANA L., pat. advocate, Community Hospital Association, Battle Creek, MI '84 (PAT)
NEWMAN, GAIL A., pat. rep., Syosset Community Hospital, Syosset, NY '86 (PAT)
NEWMAN, HOWARD N., atty., Alexandria Hospital, Alexandria, VA '82 (ATTY)
NEWMAN, JACK A. JR., partner, Peat, Marwick, Mitchell and Company, Kansas City, MO '80 (PLNG)
NEWMAN, JEAN M., dir. diet. serv., Brea Hospital-Neuropsychiatric Center, Brea, CA '86 (FOOD)
NEWMAN, JOHN MARSHALL, atty., St. Elizabeth Hospital Medical Center, Youngstown, OH '68 (ATTY)
NEWMAN, LARRY K., adm. reg. serv., St. Luke's Regional Medical Center, Sioux City, IA '74 (FOOD)
NEWMAN, M. ANN, dir. soc. work, St. Paul-Ramsey Medical Center, St. Paul, MN '72 (SOC)
NEWMAN, MARC S., proj. mgr. and dir. design and constr., Presbyterian Hospital in the City of New York, New York, NY '81 (MGMT)(ENG)
NEWMAN, MARIE T., student, Department of Health Care Administration, George Washington University, Washington, DC '82
NEWMAN, MARSHA D., dir. diet., Riverside Medical Center, Franklinton, LA '78 (FOOD)
NEWMAN, MARY ANN, adm. analyst, University of Texas Medical School at Houston, Houston, TX '78 (PLNG)
NEWMAN, MARY ANN, dir. pat. serv., Golden Valley Health Center, Golden Valley, MN '78 (NURS)
NEWMAN, MICHAEL A., dir. bldg. prog., Albert Einstein Medical Center, Philadelphia, PA '83 (PLNG)
NEWMAN, RAISA, dir. soc. serv., Human Resource Institute, Brookline, MA '82 (SOC)
NEWMAN, RAY G., partner, Ernst and Whinney, Dallas, TX '78 (PLNG)
NEWMAN, RICHARD E., dir. educ., Washoe Medical Center, Reno, NV '75 (EDUC)
NEWMAN, RICHARD G., supv. eng., William B. Kessler Memorial Hospital, Hammonton, NJ '85 (ENG)
NEWMAN, SUSAN E., dir. soc. serv., University Medical Center, Tucson, AZ '79 (SOC)
NEWMAN, SUZANNE F., dir. pub. rel. and mktg., Medical Center of Central Georgia, Macon, GA '85 (PR)
NEWMAN, THOMAS J., dir. diet. serv., Baltimore County General Hospital, Randallstown, MD '80 (FOOD)
NEWMEYER, C. EDWARD JR., dir. commun. rel., Sharon General Hospital, Sharon, PA '81 (PR)
NEWREN, MERRILL C., fin. analyst, University of Utah Health Sciences Center, Salt Lake City, UT '75 (MGMT)
NEWROTH, BENNIE, dir. med. soc. work, Medical Center, Columbus, GA '81 (SOC)
NEWSOM, JOHN E., dir. nutr. serv., Shawnee Mission Medical Center, Shawnee Mission, KS '86 (FOOD)
NEWSOME, ROBERT G., pres., Rehabilitation Service of Mid-America, Inc., Joliet, IL '83
NEWSWANGER, ANN E., RN, vice-pres. nrsg., St. Francis Hospital, Wilmington, DE '78 (NURS)
NEWTON-DARDEN, OSSIE, RN, dir. nrsg. clin. practice, East Orange General Hospital, East Orange, NJ '83 (NURS)
NEWTON, BETTY L., instr. staff educ., Lutheran Hospital of Fort Wayne, Fort Wayne, IN '87 (EDUC)
NEWTON, CAROLYN A., syst. analyst, St. Mary's Hospital, Waterbury, CT '82 (MGMT)
NEWTON, DAVID J., vice-pres. plng., Butterworth Hospital, Grand Rapids, MI '79 (PLNG)
NEWTON, DAVID R., vice-pres. adm., Charlotte Hungerford Hospital, Torrington, CT '85 (PLNG)
NEWTON, JOHN C., exec. dir., Graduate Medical Education, Inc., Lansing, MI '59
NEWTON, MARK, adm. asst. prop. serv., Southern Baptist Hospital, New Orleans, LA '86 (ENG)
NEWTON, MARK, vice-pres. plng. and mktg., Highland Park Hospital, Highland Park, IL '87 (PLNG)
NEWTON, MEG, dir. soc. serv., Union Memorial Hospital, Monroe, NC '86 (SOC)
NEWTON, PATRICIA D., mgr. cent. sup., LaGuardia Hospital, Flushing, NY '76 (CS)
NEWTON, ROBERT L., dir. fin. serv., Moses H. Cone Memorial Hospital, Greensboro, NC '81 (MGMT)
NEWTON, VIKKI, pub. rel. spec., Montefiore Hospital, Pittsburgh, PA '86 (PR)
NEWTON, WILLIAM HOWELL, vice-pres., Memorial Medical Center, Corpus Christi, TX '62
NEY, BAINE M., RN, chief nrsg. serv., Veterans Administration Medical Center, Altoona, PA '86 (NURS)
NG, JONATHAN TIAT-KHUAN, dir. pub. rel., Youngberg Memorial Adventist Hospital, Singapore 1334, Singapore '83 (PR)
NGOI, SUSAN POTTER, asst. vice-pres., Kettering Medical Center, Kettering, OH '79 (PLNG)
NICE, NANCY, dir. environ. serv., Wetzel County Hospital, New Martinsville, WV '86 (ENVIRON)
NICELY, BARBARA L., coor. pers., Memorial Hospital, Belleville, IL '85 (PERS)
NICELY, PATRICIA A., dir. vol. serv., AMI North Ridge Medical Center, Fort Lauderdale, FL '82 (VOL)
NICEWARNER, VIDA TONERI, dir. food serv., Moritz Community Hospital, Sun Valley, ID '79 (FOOD)
NICHOLAS, DONALD L., atty., Crouse-Irving Memorial Hospital, Syracuse, NY '84 (ATTY)
NICHOLAS, DORIS, mgr. soc. serv., West Virginia University Hospital, Morgantown, WV '85 (SOC)
NICHOLAS, DOUGLAS J., prod. mgr. and maint., Dfm Software Systems, Inc., West Des Moines, IA '87 (ENG)
NICHOLAS, IRVIN D., pres., Applied Risk Management, Inc., Berkeley, CA '82 (RISK)
NICHOLAS, JAY A., dir. food serv., Michiana Community Hospital, South Bend, IN '77 (FOOD)
NICHOLAS, MILDRED ANN, supv. cent. sup., Seventh Ward General Hospital, Hammond, LA '82 (CS)
NICHOLLS, CHARLES, dir. pers., Monongahela Valley Hospital, Monongahela, PA '80 (PERS)

NICHOLS, ALAN HAMMOND, atty., California College of Podiatric Medicine, San Francisco, CA '80 (ATTY)
NICHOLS, BARBARA LAURAINE, dir. in-service educ., St. Marys Hospital Medical Center, Madison, WI '71 (EDUC)
NICHOLS, BUDDY, sr. vice-pres. risk mgt. and qual. assur., Methodist Health Systems, Inc., Memphis, TN '85 (RISK)
NICHOLS, CAROLYN, sr. vice-pres., Utah Hospital Association, Salt Lake City, UT '81 (ATTY)
NICHOLS, EARL E., chief eng. and maint., Noble Hospital, Westfield, MA '79 (ENG)
NICHOLS, EVELYN F., RN, vice-pres., Swedish American Hospital, Rockford, IL '82 (NURS)
NICHOLS, GEORGE N., atty., Hall-Brooke Hospital, Westport, CT '86 (ATTY)
NICHOLS, GEORGE W., actg. dir. matl. mgt., Fawcett Memorial Hospital, Port Charlotte, FL '82 (PUR)
NICHOLS, JACK L., dir. matl. mgt., Truman Medical Center-West, Kansas City, MO '86 (PUR)
NICHOLS, JAKE, dir. plant oper., West Texas Hospital, Lubbock, TX '85 (ENG)
NICHOLS, LEONARD C., supv. cent. serv. sup., Concord Hospital, Concord, NH '83 (CS)
NICHOLS, LOIS J., dir. vol., William Beaumont Hospital, Royal Oak, MI '68 (VOL)
NICHOLS, MARY JUDITH, dir. med. soc. work, Bi-County Community Hospital, Warren, MI '75 (SOC)
NICHOLS, MINNIE RUTH, dir. vol. serv., Providence Hospital, Columbia, SC '85 (VOL)
NICHOLS, NANCY GROVE, student, Program in Hospital and Health Administration, Ohio State University, Columbus, OH '82
NICHOLS, PAMELA J., dir. mktg., Lloyd Noland Hospital and Health Ctrs, Birmingham, AL '85 (PLNG)
NICHOLS, RONALD D., adm. pers., Le Bonheur Children's Medical Center, Memphis, TN '81 (PERS)
NICHOLS, SANDRA L., dir. pur., Beaumont Shared Services, Inc., Southfield, MI '85 (PUR)
NICHOLS, SUSAN, dir. commun. rel., Blount Memorial Hospital, Maryville, TN '77 (PR)
NICHOLSEN, GENE R., mgr. mgt. eng., Bishop Clarkson Memorial Hospital, Omaha, NE '72 (MGMT)
NICHOLSON, DAN R., med. and surg. mgr., Health Central Metropolitan Hospitals, Minneapolis, MN '81 (PUR)
NICHOLSON, DOROTHEA E., dir. diet. serv., St. Elizabeth Medical Center, Yakima, WA '76 (FOOD)
NICHOLSON, FAYE A., coor. commun. dev., Giles Memorial Hospital, Pearisburg, VA '86 (PR) (PLNG)
NICHOLSON, JOAN E., dir. vol., Motion Picture and Tel Hospital, Woodland Hills, CA '86 (VOL)
NICHOLSON, JUNE, asst. dir. human res. mgt., University of Chicago Hospitals, Chicago, IL '77 (EDUC)(PERS)
NICHOLSON, LINDA G., RN, actg. vice-pres. adm. and dir. nrsg., Rochester General Hospital, Rochester, NY '86 (NURS)
NICHOLSON, LOUIS F. JR., pres., Telecommunications Management, Inc., Houston, TX '82 (ENG)
NICHOLSON, MEL, asst. exec. dir., Cardinal Glennon Memorial Hospital for Children, St. Louis, MO '79 (PLNG)
NICHOLSON, OLGA J., dir. trng. and dev., HSA Cumberland Hospital, Fayetteville, NC '86 (EDUC)
NICHOLSON, PAUL S., student, Program in Hospital Administration, Concordia College, Moorhead, MN '86
NICHOLSON, WILLIAM F., dir. plant serv., Presbyterian Hospital, Albuquerque, NM '77 (ENG)
NICK, ELISE D., dir. educ. and trng., Saint Vincent Health Center, Erie, PA '78 (EDUC)
NICKEL, LOIS L., RN, asst. to assoc. dir. nrsg., University of Maryland Medical Systems, Baltimore, MD '80 (NURS)
NICKEL, PAMELA J., mgr. vol., St. Luke's Hospitals, Fargo, ND '86 (VOL)
NICKEL, VERNA M., RN, asst. chief nrsg. serv., Veterans Administration Medical Center, San Diego, CA '85 (NURS)
NICKELL, GREGORY R., asst. vice-pres. oper., Hospital Association of Central Ohio, Dublin, OH '87 (MGMT)
NICKELLS, FRANK, mgr. oper., Sisters of Charity Health Care Systems Corporation, Monroe, OH '85 (ENG)
NICKENS, ANNA, dir. soc. work, Methodist Rehabilitation Center, Jackson, MS '86 (SOC)
NICKENS, DOLORES POWELL, dir. soc. work, St. Benedict's Hospital, Ogden, UT '87 (SOC)
NICKERSON, DOROTHY E., dir. vol. serv., Morton Hospital and Medical Center, Taunton, MA '77 (VOL)
NICKERSON, KENNETH H., mgr. pers., North Colorado Medical Center, Greeley, CO '77 (PERS)
NICKERSON, ROBERT A., div. dir. facil., Parkview Memorial Hospital, Fort Wayne, IN '80 (ENG)
NICKLAS, CHARLES E., vice-pres. tech. serv., Aladdin Synergetics, Inc., Nashville, TN '72 (FOOD)
NICKLAS, DEBORAH SIMON, vice-pres. plng. and mktg., Inter-Community Medical Center, Covina, CA '80 (PLNG)
NICKLES, MARY J., supv. cent. serv., Alvarado Hospital Medical Center, San Diego, CA '85 (CS)
NICKLESS, STERLING M., dir. environ. serv., Littleton Hospital, Littleton, NH '80 (ENG)
NICKOLAY, LILLIAN A., supv. cent. serv., Mille Lacs Hospital, Onamia, MN '78 (CS)
NICODEMUS, ROBERT A., dir. pers., Sparks Regional Medical Center, Fort Smith, AR '82 (PERS)
NICOL, CAROL A., RN, assoc. dir., Mount Sinai Medical Center, New York, NY '84 (NURS)
NICOL, CYNTHIA J., dir. commun. rel., Flagstaff Medical Center, Flagstaff, AZ '86 (PR)
NICOL, ROBBIE, dir. plng. and mktg., Yavapai Regional Medical Center, Prescott, AZ '86 (PLNG)
NICOLAOU, PHYLLIS C., RN EdD, vice-pres. pat. serv., Borgess Medical Center, Kalamazoo, MI '80 (NURS)
NICOLAY, JOHN R., sr. vice-pres., McDevitt and Street Company, Charlotte, NC '83
NICOLET, PAULA A., dir. soc. serv., St. Joseph's Hospital, Highland, IL '72 (SOC)
NICOLL, PETER, MD, dep. med. supt., Princess Alexandra Hospital, Brisbane, Australia '76
NICOLO, DANA J., pat. rep. and coor. vol., Pulaski Community Hospital, Pulaski, VA '83 (PAT)(VOL)
NICOLO, TONY J., dir. eng., Pulaski Community Hospital, Pulaski, VA '81 (ENG)
NICOLOFF, R. JASON, territory mgr., Milcare, Inc., Chicago, IL '86 (PUR)
NIDEY, REBECCA L., supv. food serv., Crawford Memorial Hospital, Robinson, IL '84 (FOOD)
NIEBERGALL, ROBERT H., mgr. info. syst., Park Ridge Hospital, Rochester, NY '81 (MGMT)
NIEDERMAN, GERALD A., atty., Rose Medical Center, Denver, CO '83 (ATTY)
NIEDERMYER, DENNIS JOHN, dir. facil., St. Alexis Hospital, Cleveland, OH '69 (ENG)
NIEDERT, KATHLEEN C., dir. outreach and shared serv., Covenant Medical Center-Schoitz, Waterloo, IA '79 (FOOD)
NIEDERT, WILLIAM, dir. resp. home care, Covenant Medical Center -St. Francis, Waterloo, IA '87 (AMB)
NIEDT, CAROL Y., RN, loss prevention consult., Health Care Insurance Exchange, Princeton, NJ '80 (RISK)
NIEDT, EILEEN A., chief diet. serv., Veterans Administration Medical Center, Charleston, SC '84 (FOOD)
NIEHAUS, ERIC B., sr. consult., Hospital Association of New York State-Maps, Albany, NY '84 (MGMT)
NIELANDER, GRETCHEN M., dir. diet. serv., B. A. Railton and Sysco, Northlake, IL '84 (FOOD)
NIELD, MARAGRET, RN, dir. nrsg., South Shore Hospital, Chicago, IL '85 (NURS)
NIELSEN-SWANSON, VERBELEE, phys. liaison, Florida Hospital-Altamonte, Altamonte Springs, FL '86
NIELSEN, CAROL, dir. pers., Mountain View Hospital, Payson, UT '73 (PERS)
NIELSEN, DAVID I., atty., Carson Tahoe Hospital, Carson City, NV '81 (ATTY)
NIELSEN, DEANN, telecommun. spec., Ihc Hospitals, Inc., Salt Lake City, UT '85 (ENG)
NIELSEN, JAMES N., pres., Nielsen P. M. Associates, Inc., Leroy, NY '86 (ENG)
NIELSEN, LAWRENCE E., exec. dir., North San Joaquin Valley Health Systems Agency, Modesto, CA '82 (PLNG)
NIELSEN, MARGARET, adm. diet., Robert Wood Johnson University Hospital, New Brunswick, NJ '82 (FOOD)
NIELSEN, NIELS F., vice-pres. med. support serv., St. Cloud Hospital, St. Cloud, MN '83 (RISK)
NIELSEN, PAUL E., adm. gen. surg., Cleveland Clinic Hospital, Cleveland, OH '82
NIELSEN, RONALD J., dir. pers., Rice Memorial Hospital, Willmar, MN '84 (PERS)
NIELSEN, SHERRY, mgr. mktg., Pioneer Park Hospital, Irving, TX '85 (PLNG)
NIELSEN, STANLEY KENNETH, dir. pat. serv., Meriter Hospital, Madison, WI '69 (SOC)
NIELSON, BRADLEY D., asst. adm., Health Maintenance Plan, Dayton, OH '85
NIELSON, DIANE, dir. pers., Pioneer Valley Hospital, West Valley City, UT '82 (PERS)
NIELSON, JACK C., adm., Montana Health Facility Authority, Helena, MT '85
NIELUBOWICZ, COMO MARY J., RN MSC USN, dir. nrsg. serv., Naval Hospital, Portsmouth, VA '73 (NURS)
NIEMAN, CHRISTINE, risk mgr., Veterans Administration Medical Center, Allen Park, MI '86 (RISK)
NIEMI, ANN M., dir. soc. serv., Allegan General Hospital, Allegan, MI '78 (SOC)
NIEMI, ROBERT J., reg. prog. adv., U. S. Public Health Service, Health Research Development, Chicago, IL '77
NIEMIEC, DAVID A., consult., Ernst and Whinney, Cleveland, OH '85 (MGMT)
NIEMIEC, LEON J., PhD, adm. health sci., National Institute of Child Health and Human Development, Baltimore, MD '52 (LIFE)
NIEMIERA, JOANNE M., RN, asst. dir. res. and dev., Wills Eye Hospital, Philadelphia, PA '86 (NURS)
NIENABER, DONNA S., atty., Bethesda Hospital, Inc., Cincinnati, OH '85 (ATTY)
NIENBERG, MARCIA LOUISE, mgr. pat. rel., Phoenix Children's Hospital, Phoenix, AZ '86 (PAT)
NIES, SUE ANN, pat. rep., Frostburg Community Hospital, Frostburg, MD '86 (PAT)
NIEVES, WILFREDO, RN, asst. chief nrsg., Cutler Army Hospital, Fort Devens, MA '86 (NURS)
NIEZER, BERNARD A., vice-pres. bus. dev., LaPorte Hospital, LaPorte, IN '85 (PLNG)
NIGAGLIONI, ADAN LOYOLA, MD, chancellor, University of Puerto Rico, Medical Sciences Campus, San Juan, P.R. '68 (HON)
NIGHTMAN, DIANA L., coor. pub. rel., Uniontown Hospital, Uniontown, PA '82 (PR)
NIGRELLO, FRANCINE R., dir. risk mgt., Westchester County Medical Center, Valhalla, NY '83 (RISK)
NIGRO, ALBERTA M., RN, asst. vice-pres. nrsg., Winchester Hospital, Winchester, MA '82 (NURS)
NIKETH, RONALD KURT, coor. biomedical elec., St. Anthony Medical Center, Crown Point, IN '85 (ENG)
NIKIRK, JOSEPH D., RN, vice-pres., Methodist Hospital, Philadelphia, PA '74 (PERS)
NIKOLSY, STEVEN T., asst. dir. hskpg., Norfolk County Hospital, Braintree, MA '86 (ENVIRON)
NILES, ELIZABETH A., dir. pur. and cent. sup., Sutter Davis Hospital, Davis, CA '86 (CS)
NILSEN, LINNEA M., student, Program in Health Care Administration, Concordia College, Moorhead, MN '85
NILSEN, LISA A., student, Carson City, NV '82 (PERS)
NIMMO, STEPHEN H., atty., Shadyside Hospital, Pittsburgh, PA '86 (ATTY)
NIMOCKS, A. BYRON, asst. vice-pres., E. F. Hutton and Company, Inc., New York, NY '86
NIMSKY, JOHN D., dir. plng., Scottsdale Memorial Health Systems, Inc., Scottsdale, AZ '81 (PLNG)
NINNEMANN, JUNE H., dir. soc. work, St. Joseph Hospital, Chicago, IL '73 (SOC)
NIPP, CINDY H., RN, dir. nrsg.-critical care, Erlanger Medical Center, Chattanooga, TN '85 (NURS)
NIPPER, WILLIAM D., mgt. eng., Vanderbilt University Hospital, Nashville, TN '84 (MGMT)
NIRO, FRANK A., exec. vice-pres., Choate-Symmes Hospitals, Woburn, MA '83 (PLNG)
NISHINAKA, LINDA, dir. soc. work, Orthopaedic Hospital, Los Angeles, CA '84 (SOC)
NISONGER, LOIS MAE, dir. vol., Children's Medical Center, Dayton, OH '68 (VOL)
NITSCHKE, DAVID MARTIN, Winchester, TN '69
NITTA, DIANE E., RN, assoc. dir. nrsg., University of California Irvine Medical Center, Orange, CA '85 (NURS)
NITTINGER, MARGENE, RN, spec. dir., Robert Packer Hospital, Sayre, PA '79 (NURS)
NITTLE, TERRY L., dir. plng. and dev., Cigna Health Plan of Arizona, Inc., Phoenix, AZ '82 (PLNG)
NITZ, RODNEY G., atty., St. John's Hospital, Salina, KS '76 (ATTY)
NIX, JEAN, dir. nrsg., mental health and rehab., Glendale Adventist Medical Center, Glendale, CA '71 (NURS)
NIX, MICHAEL EUGENE, sr. staff assoc., Massachusetts Hospital Association, Burlington, MA '80 (MGMT)
NIX, MILTON E., dir. biomedical eng., Memorial Medical Center, Long Beach, CA '84 (ENG)
NIX, THOMAS W., vice-pres. mktg., Baptist Medical Centers, Birmingham, AL '81 (PLNG)
NIXON, DIANE L., adm. mgr. phys. medicine and rehab., University of Michigan Hospitals, Ann Arbor, MI '82
NIXON, GEORGE A., asst. dir. matl. serv., McLeod Regional Medical Center, Florence, SC '84 (PUR)
NIXON, KEYTON H., pres., Silver Cross Hospital, Joliet, IL '53 (PLNG)(LIFE)
NIXON, MARY B., dir. vol. serv., Verdugo Hills Hospital, Glendale, CA '74 (VOL)
NIZER, KATHRYN A., dir. soc. serv., F. Edward Hebert Hospital, New Orleans, LA '85 (SOC)
NIZZARDINI, CAROL, RN, dir. critical care nrsg., North Charles Hospital, Baltimore, MD '87 (NURS)
NOACK, GENE L., dir. plant oper., Community General Hospital, Sterling, IL '81 (ENG)
NOAH, GARY G., dir. bldg. serv., West Allis Memorial Hospital, West Allis, WI '78 (ENG)
NOAKES, WALTER, vice-pres. prof. serv., De Paul Hospital, Cheyenne, WY '86 (RISK)
NOBLE, CLAIRE J., risk mgr., Mary Hitchcock Memorial Hospital, Hanover, NH '80 (RISK)
NOBLE, DARRYLL L., dir. maint., Allen Memorial Hospital, Waterloo, IA '81 (ENG)
NOBLE, KATHRYN M., dir. soc. serv., St. Mary's Medical Center, Duluth, MN '75 (SOC)
NOBLE, LINDA J., coor. educ. serv., St. Mary Medical Center, Walla Walla, WA '85 (EDUC)
NOBLE, MILNER E., actg. dir., Mary Hitchcock Memorial Hospital, Hanover, NH '86 (PR)
NOBLE, PATRICIA A., RN, dir. nrsg. serv., Memorial Hospital at Easton Maryland, Easton, MD '85 (NURS)
NOBLE, RAYMOND, dir. food serv., Robert Wood Johnson University Hospital, New Brunswick, NJ '80 (FOOD)
NOBLES, MOLLY S., dir. plng., Baptist Regional Health Services, Inc., Pensacola, FL '81 (PLNG)
NOCELLA, ALBERT J. JR., asst. adm., Dominican Santa Cruz Hospital, Santa Cruz, CA '82 (PERS)
NOCILLA, JOSEPH J. JR., student, Program in Health Service Administration, New School for Social Research, New York, NY '85
NOCTON, GERARD H., exec. dir., Winthrop Hospital, Winthrop, MA '76
NODAL, MARTHA, risk mgr., DeKalb General Hospital, Decatur, GA '84 (RISK)(ENG)
NODELL, JOAN, dir., Wing Memorial Hospital and Medical Centers, Palmer, MA '87 (AMB)
NODZENSKI, THADDEUS J., atty., Rush-Presbyterian-St. Luke Medical Center, Chicago, IL '85 (ATTY)
NOE, CARL W., dir. food serv., Harding Hospital, Worthington, OH '80 (FOOD)
NOEDING, NICHOLAS J., atty., Presbyterian Hospital, Albuquerque, NM '79 (ATTY)
NOEL, LINDA, asst. adm. plant serv., Fayetteville City Hospital, Fayetteville, AR '86 (ENVIRON)
NOEL, PHILIP J. III, asst. adm., Imperial Point Medical Center, Fort Lauderdale, FL '75
NOELLER, DONALD L., dir. matl. mgt., Midlands Community Hospital, Papillion, NE '81 (PUR)
NOESEN, GEORGE WILLIAM, dir. pur. and maint., Sisters of St. Benedict, Crookston, MN '65 (PUR)
NOETZEL, TERRENCE J., sr. consult., Touche Ross and Company, Detroit, MI '81 (MGMT)(PLNG)
NOGA, J. JOAN, RN, vice-pres. nrsg., Mount Carmel Mercy Hospital, Division of Sisters of Mercy Health Corporation, Detroit, MI '76 (NURS)
NOGOSKY, DAVID, asst. dir. plant oper., Ravenswood Hospital Medical Center, Chicago, IL '87 (ENG)
NOH, ALEXANDER, exec. hskpr., Shriners Hospital for Crippled Children, Honolulu, HI '86 (ENVIRON)
NOHA, ROBERT M., dir. plant oper. and maint., Little Company of Mary Hospital, Evergreen Park, IL '82 (ENG)
NOHAVA, JANE C., dir. clin. soc. work, Leigh Memorial Hospital, Norfolk, VA '82 (SOC)
NOHLGREN, SUSAN P., coor. vol., LaRabida Children's Hospital, Chicago, IL '85 (VOL)
NOIE, NANCIE E., search consult., Kieffer, Ford and Associates, Chicago, IL '85
NOIROT, BARBARA A., RN, dir. nrsg., Otsego Memorial Hospital, Gaylord, MI '84 (NURS)
NOLAN, JANIECE S., vice-pres., John Muir Memorial Hospital, Walnut Creek, CA '78
NOLAN, KEVIN CHRISTOPHER, dir. health care plng., mid-atlantic reg., Ernst and Whinney, Washington, DC '79 (PLNG)
NOLAN, KEVIN E., exec. vice-pres., United Health Services, Johnson City, NY '73

NOLAN, LUCILLE I., dir. vol. serv., Huron Road Hospital, Cleveland, OH '85 (VOL)
NOLAN, SR. M. MAGDALEN, dir. vol. serv., Memorial Hospital and Health Care Center, Jasper, IN '86 (VOL)
NOLAN, MARGARET M., dir. pers., Physicians Memorial Hospital, La Plata, MD '75 (PERS)
NOLAN, MARY GILL, RN, vice-pres., Memorial Medical Center, Long Beach, CA '79 (NURS)
NOLAN, MICHAEL L., sr. vice-pres., Southside Hospital, Bay Shore, NY '74
NOLAN, TIMOTHY J., dir. eng. and plant serv., Winchester Medical Center, Winchester, VA '81 (ENG)
NOLAN, WILLIAM C. JR., atty., Warner Brown Hospital, El Dorado, AR '74 (ATTY)
NOLD, DIANE S., asst. vice-pres., Midland Hospital Center, Midland, MI '86 (ENVIRON)
NOLDE, MARY LOUISE, dir. diet. serv., Deaconess Hospital, St. Louis, MO '75 (FOOD)
NOLEN, ROSEMARY S., dir. diet., Baptist Memorial Hospital-Tipton, Covington, TN '80 (FOOD)
NOLIN, JAMES L., bus. mgr. and dir. dev., Alameda Hospital, Alameda, CA '85 (PR)
NOLL, ANN BARKER, dir. cont. educ., Community Hospital of Springfield, Springfield, OH '81 (EDUC)
NOLON, ANN KAUFFMAN, exec. dir., Peekskill Area Health Center, Inc., Peekskill, NY '87 (AMB)
NOON, CHARLES A. III, dir. mktg., Portsmouth Regional Hospital, Portsmouth, NH '83 (PR)
NOONAN, MARGARET E., dir. guest rel., Burbank Hospital, Fitchburg, MA '85 (PAT)
NOONE, MARTIN J., dir. environ. serv., Faxton Hospital, Utica, NY '84 (ENG)
NOONE, MARY ELEANOR, vice-pres. nrsg., Providence Hospital, Washington, DC '84 (NURS)
NOONE, MICHAEL P., dir. mktg. and pub. rel., Memorial Hospital, Towanda, PA '86 (PR)
NOORDHOEK, WILLEM H., dir. eng., St. Francis Medical Center, Lynwood, CA '76 (ENG)
NOORIAN, SHERI, mgt. eng., John Muir Memorial Hospital, Walnut Creek, CA '86 (MGMT)
NORBOM, LEIF ERIK, vice-pres., Medtrac Court International, St. Paul, MN '75
NORBOM, MARILYN, sr. assoc. mktg. and plng., Mercy Medical Center, Coon Rapids, MN '86 (PLNG)
NORBY, RONALD B., RN, chief nrsg. serv., Veterans Administration Medical Center, San Diego, CA '83 (NURS)
NORBY, TIMOTHY R., student, Program in Health Systems Management, School of Public Health, Tulane University, New Orleans, LA '84
NORCROSS, DAVID R., vice-pres. mktg. and serv. dev., North Central Health Services, Lafayette, IN '73 (PR)
NORCROSS, JOE C., prin., Blass, Chilcote, Carter, Lanford and Wilcox, Architects and Engineers, Little Rock, AR '78
NORDAHL, SUSAN L., coor. educ., Black River Memorial Hospital, Black River Falls, WI '87 (EDUC)
NORDELL, NANCY R., dir. nutr. serv., HCA Vista Hills Medical Center, El Paso, TX '86 (FOOD)
NORDEN, DENNIS A., atty., St. Mary's Hospital of Kankakee, Kankakee, IL '83 (ATTY)
NORDFORS, VINCENT B., vice-pres., Mahlum and Nordfors Architects, Seattle, WA '84
NORDGAARD, WILLIAM D., mgr. sup., proc. and distrib., Southwest Washington Hospitals, Vancouver, WA '83 (CS)
NORDMARK, ANNETTE LEAH, RN, vice-pres. nrsg., Lake Forest Hospital, Lake Forest, IL '77 (NURS)
NORDQUIST, REBECCA A., dir. food serv., Valley Lutheran Hospital, Mesa, AZ '84 (FOOD)
NORDQUIST, SARAH, assoc. dir., University of California at Los Angeles Medical Center, Los Angeles, CA '87 (AMB)
NORDSTROM, SUSAN M., asst. adm., Illinois Masonic Medical Center, Chicago, IL '81
NORDYKE, BILL, supv. maint. and constr., Maryvale Samaritan Hospital, Phoenix, AZ '87 (ENG)
NOREM, PATRICIA L., coor. commun. rel., Fort Madison Community Hospital, Fort Madison, IA '85 (PR)
NOREN, LILLIAN, dir. vol. serv., Graduate Hospital, Philadelphia, PA '76 (VOL)
NORIEGA, RUDY J., exec. vice-pres., American Hospital Management Corporation, Miami, FL '72
NORLING, RICHARD A., exec. vice-pres. and chief oper. off., Lutheran Hospital Society of Southern California, Los Angeles, CA '70
NORMAN, D. KENT, adm., University of Texas Mental Sciences Institute, Houston, TX '85
NORMAN, DONALD A., dir. matl. mgt., De Paul Hospital, Cheyenne, WY '82 (PUR)
NORMAN, JUDITH M., atty., Strong Memorial Hospital Rochester University, Rochester, NY '77 (ATTY)
NORMAN, PAUL MICHAEL, adm. dir. amb. care, Hinsdale Hospital, Hinsdale, IL '80
NORMAN, RONALD E., exec. vice-pres., Kansas City Area Hospital Association, Kansas City, MO '84 (PERS)
NORMANDT, JEANETTE, consult., Blue Cross-Blue Shield, Chicago, IL '82
NORMILE, MARY T., RN, pat. rep., Our Lady of Lourdes Memorial Hospital, Binghamton, NY '72 (PAT)
NOROIAN, EDWARD H., pres., Presbyterian Health Resources, New York, NY '86 (MGMT)(AMB)
NORRED-KIDD, PAMELA, dir. soc. serv., West Georgia Medical Center, La Grange, GA '87 (SOC)
NORRICK, BRAD, vice-pres., Johnson and Higgins of Washington, Inc., Seattle, WA '86 (RISK)
NORRIS-BROADY, PATRICIA, dir. soc. work serv., Kadlec Medical Center, Richland, WA '86 (SOC)
NORRIS, ANNE M., Houston Northwest Medical Center, Houston, TX '81
NORRIS, CARRIE F., RN, dir. nrsg., Glynn-Brunswick Memorial Hospital, Brunswick, GA '81 (NURS)
NORRIS, ELIZABETH, dir. hskpg., Little Company of Mary Hospital, Evergreen Park, IL '86 (ENVIRON)
NORRIS, HENRY H., dir. for adm., Naval Hospital, Beaufort, SC '85
NORRIS, JOYCE A., RN, chief nrsg. serv., Veterans Administration Medical Center, Nashville, TN '80 (NURS)
NORRIS, LILLIAN D., dir. educ. and trng. center, Charleston Area Medical Center, Charleston, WV '85 (EDUC)
NORRIS, MARGERY T., adm. soc. serv., alcohol and drug recovery, Kaiser Foundation Hospital, Harbor City, CA '85 (SOC)
NORRIS, REBECCA M., dir. mgt. eng., Kennestone Regional Health Care Systems, Marietta, GA '83 (MGMT)
NORRIS, SANDRA L., PhD, Highlands Ranch, CO '79 (EDUC)
NORRIS, SERENA A., mgr. emp., Massillon Community Hospital, Massillon, OH '84 (PERS)
NORRISH, JOYCE A., Pittsburgh, PA '86 (PR) (PLNG)
NORTH, FOSTER D., pres., Home Health Plus, Minneapolis, MN '87 (AMB)
NORTH, JANICE A., RN, dir. nrsg.-medicine, psych. and transport, Hackensack Medical Center, Hackensack, NJ '86 (NURS)
NORTHARD, ERIC D., asst. dir. vol. serv., Johnston R. Bowman Health Center for the Elderly, Chicago, IL '86 (VOL)
NORTHCUTT, CHERYL, med. off. adm., Kaiser Permanente, Dallas, TX '87 (AMB)
NORTHERN, DAVID H., adm. res., Humana Hospital-East Montgomery, Montgomery, AL '85
NORTHINGTON, KATHERINE B., dir. soc. serv., Sid Peterson Memorial Hospital, Kerrville, TX '81 (SOC)
NORTHRUP, JEAN W., student, Program in Health Sciences Information Administration, Western Washington University, Bellingham, WA '85 (RISK)
NORTHRUP, JOSEPH E., dir. eng. and maint., Gaylord Hospital, Wallingford, CT '82 (ENG)
NORTHWOOD, KAREN J., RN, assoc. chief nrsg. and intermediate care, Veterans Administration Medical Center, Dayton, OH '86 (NURS)
NORTON-LOZIER, ELIZABETH, dir. hskpg., St. Mary's Hospital, Waterbury, CT '86 (ENVIRON)
NORTON, ANNE T., coor. educ., Good Samaritan Hospital, San Jose, CA '86 (EDUC)
NORTON, BARBARA M., assoc. dir. educ., John Muir Memorial Hospital, Walnut Creek, CA '86 (EDUC)
NORTON, DAVID C., sr. mech. eng., University of Michigan Hospitals, Ann Arbor, MI '87 (ENG)
NORTON, EDWARD V., atty., University of Michigan Hospitals, Ann Arbor, MI '86 (ATTY)
NORTON, ELIZABETH F., consult., Arthur Young and Company, Washington, DC '83 (PLNG)(MGMT)
NORTON, ERIC D., asst. dir. food serv., Children's Hospital of Wisconsin, Milwaukee, WI '81 (FOOD)
NORTON, ETHEL T., coor. guest rel. and vol., Tidewater Memorial Hospital, Tappahannock, VA '85 (PAT)
NORTON, JANET E., dir. institutional rel., University of California San Francisco, San Francisco, CA '80 (PR) (PLNG)
NORTON, JOHN W., pres. and chief exec. off., Horton Memorial Hospital, Middletown, NY '52 (LIFE)
NORTON, L. CHARNETTE, dir. nutr. and food serv., University of Texas M. D. Anderson Hospital and Tumor Institute at Houston, Houston, TX '78 (FOOD)
NORTON, LARRY E., dir. pur., Driscoll Foundation Children's Hospital, Corpus Christi, TX '82 (PUR)
NORTON, MALCOLM E., asst. adm., Southwest Texas Methodist Hospital, San Antonio, TX '70
NORTON, MARJORIE S., dir. spec. serv., Lexington County Hospital, West Columbia, SC '72 (VOL)
NORTON, MARLEEN, dir. vol. serv., Providence Hospital, Anchorage, AK '85 (VOL)
NORTON, MARTIN L., MD, anes., University of Michigan Hospitals, Ann Arbor, MI '80 (ATTY)
NORTON, PAMALA, student, University of Pittsburgh, Pittsburgh, PA '86
NORTON, RALPH E., dir. pub. rel., Lee Hospital, Johnstown, PA '86 (PR)
NORULAK, FRANK J., mgt. eng., St. John's Hospital and Health Center, Santa Monica, CA '82 (MGMT)
NOSEWORTHY, G. EDWARD C., asst. dir. diet., Florida Hospital Medical Center, Orlando, FL '81 (FOOD)
NOSKIN, DIANA E., student, Rush University, Chicago, IL '83
NOSKY, CINDY, human res. consult., Hospital Corporation of America, Nashville, TN '77 (PERS)
NOTARIANNI, ROBERT G., adm., Richmond Eye and Ear Hospital, Richmond, VA '68
NOTCH, DIANE K., chief clin. soc. work serv., Broadlawns Medical Center, Des Moines, IA '85 (SOC)
NOTDURFT, LT. COL. NORMAN E., MSC USAF, chief, Air Force Health Facilities Office Western Regional, San Francisco, CA '74
NOTEBOOM, KEN JR., exec. dir., AMI Coastal Bend Hospital, Aransas Pass, TX '79
NOTHERN, AUSTIN, atty., St. Francis Hospital and Medical Center, Topeka, KS '78 (ATTY)
NOTKIN, LEONARD, prin. and vice-pres., Architects Collaborative, Inc., Cambridge, MA '81
NOTO, GLORIA, dir. vol. serv., Newcomb Medical Center, Vineland, NJ '84 (VOL)
NOTO, REGINA F., RN, asst. adm. pat. care, Larkin General Hospital, South Miami, FL '81 (NURS)
NOTT, SYLVIA G., RN, dir. nsrg amb. serv., New England Deaconess Hospital, Boston, MA '87 (AMB)
NOTTE, WILLIAM G., mgr. food serv., Saint Vincent Hospital, Worcester, MA '81 (FOOD)
NOTTESTAD, KENNETH, dir. plant and prop., Deaconess Hospital, St. Louis, MO '73 (ENG)
NOURY, PAUL H., plant eng., St. Mary's Hospital, Waterbury, CT '77 (ENG)
NOVACEK, VERA, dir. family serv., Spalding Rehabilitation Hospital, Denver, CO '87 (SOC)
NOVAK, CONSTANCE W., dir. speech and hearing, McLaren General Hospital, Flint, MI '84
NOVAK, SR. DOLORES ANNE, RN, dir. nrsg. adm., St. Anthony Hospital, Michigan City, IN '83 (NURS)
NOVAK, IRA S., atty., Robert Wood Johnson University Hospital, New Brunswick, NJ '77 (ATTY)
NOVAK, JAMES G., dir. human res., Sherman Hospital, Elgin, IL '86 (PERS)
NOVAK, JAMES J., adm. bus. serv. and telecommun., United Hospital, Grand Forks, ND '86 (ENG)
NOVAK, JAMES R., dept. mgr., St. Joseph's Hospital and Medical Center, Phoenix, AZ '79 (ENG)
NOVAK, JAMES T., asst. vice-pres. and dir. nrsg. productivity, American Medical International, Beverly Hills, CA '87 (MGMT)
NOVAK, JILL SWYER, asst. dir. nrsg. adm. serv., M. J. G. Nursing Home, Brooklyn, NY '81
NOVAK, NINA, atty., Virginia Hospital Association, Richmond, VA '81 (ATTY)
NOVAK, RONALD A., dir. pers., Iroquois Memorial Hospital and Resident Home, Watseka, IL '78 (PERS)
NOVAK, SUSAN S., RN, dir. nrsg., Memorial Regional Rehabilitation Center, Jacksonville, FL '83 (NURS)
NOVAKOFF, SHARON, adm. dir. mktg. and plng., Presbyterian Intercommunity Hospital, Whittier, CA '84
NOVELLO-JOHNSON, THERESA, supv. sup., proc. and distrib., St. Clare Hospital of Monroe, Monroe, WI '85 (CS)
NOVEY, JUDYTHE, asst. coor., Veterans Administration Medical Center, Philadelphia, PA '81 (PLNG)
NOVICK, BARRY WELS, vice-pres., Joint Purchasing Corporation, New York, NY '75 (PUR)
NOVIELLO, JOSEPH S., pres., St. Francis Hospital of New Castle, New Castle, PA '65
NOVINSKI, EDWARD J., spec. contract, Physicians of Minnesota, Minneapolis, MN '82
NOVOTNY, BERNADETTE L., RN, assoc. dir. nrsg., Memorial Hospital, Colorado Springs, CO '83 (NURS)
NOWAK, ALFREDA L., dir. vol. serv., Mercy Hospital, Springfield, MA '75 (VOL)
NOWAK, DAVID M., dir. commun. rel., St. Joseph's Hospital, Alton, IL '85 (PR)
NOWAK, HENRY J., MD, (ret.), Danville, IL '57 (LIFE)
NOWAKOWSKI, DIANNE, RN, mgr. cent. sup., Roseland Community Hospital, Chicago, IL '80 (CS)
NOWERS, BURTON A., dir. pers., Nashville Memorial Hospital, Madison, TN '80 (PERS)
NOWICKI, KATHLEEN A., vice-pres. commun. serv., St. Joseph Mercy Hospital, Pontiac, MI '85 (PR)
NOWLIN, CATHY, RN, actg. dir. nrsg. serv., Jones County Community Hospital, Laurel, MS '80 (NURS)
NOWLING, ANTARA S., dir. pub. rel., Monroe County Hospital, Monroeville, AL '86 (PR)
NOWOHOLNIK, MARTIN H., mgr., First Consulting Group, Hudson, OH '76 (MGMT)
NOWOSAD, RONALD PETER, dir. plng. and mktg., St. Luke's Hospital, Racine, WI '79 (PLNG)
NOWOSLAWSKI, JOSEPH A., MD, pres., Trauma Service Group, Philadelphia, PA '78 (PR)(AMB)
NOYES, ALTON W., pres., Phelps Memorial Hospital Center, North Tarrytown, NY '60
NOYES, CHERYL L., dir. pers., Mercy Hospital Medical Center, Des Moines, IA '85 (PERS)
NOYES, DORIS E., RN, asst. dir. nrsg., Wentworth-Douglass Hospital, Dover, NH '86 (NURS)
NOYES, SUE ANN, prog. dir., San Francisco Heart Institute, Daly City, CA '85 (PLNG)
NUCKOLLS, TRACY P., atty., Tucson Medical Center, Tucson, AZ '83 (ATTY)
NUDELL, BARBARA L., student, Program in Hlthcare Management, Concordia College, Moorhead, MN '85
NUDO, RUDOLPH, dir. eng., Memorial Medical Center of Jacksonville, Jacksonville, FL '67 (ENG)
NUELLE, THOMAS D., atty., Memorial Hospital for McHenry County, Woodstock, IL '82 (ATTY)
NUETZEL, CAREN R., risk mgr., Sacred Heart Hospital of Pensacola, Pensacola, FL '82 (RISK)
NUGENT, EDWARD S., EdD, Bergen Pines County Hospital, Paramus, NJ '74
NUGENT, JAMES H., dir. plant oper., Community General Hospital, Syracuse, NY '79 (ENG)
NUGENT, JANE E., dir. bus. dev., Allegany Pharmaceutical, Irvine, CA '84 (PLNG)
NUGENT, LT. COL. JERRY J., MSC USAF, adm., Department of the Air Force, Office of the Surgeon General, Mather AFB, CA '75
NUGENT, LOLA C., RN, asst. adm. nrsg. serv., Lakewood Hospital, Tacoma, WA '85 (NURS)
NUHRING, PAULINE B., coor. educ., Miller Dwan Foundation, Duluth, MN '86 (EDUC)
NULL, JAMES A., dir. educ., AMI Park Plaza Hospital, Houston, TX '81 (EDUC)
NULL, MATTHEW, vice-pres. plng., Greater Baltimore Medical Center, Baltimore, MD '80 (PLNG)
NULTON, WILLIAM C., atty., Research Medical Center, Kansas City, MO '82 (ATTY)
NUMANN, SANDRA J., dir. amb. care, Harris Methodist -HEB, Bedford, TX '87 (AMB)
NUMEROF, RITA E., PhD, asst. prof., Washington University, St. Louis, MO '79 (EDUC)
NUNERY, MARY, mgr. cent. sup., Los Altos Hospital and Health Center, Long Beach, CA '82 (CS)
NUNN, PETER M., partner, Coopers and Lybrand, Washington, DC '80
NUNN, RUTH B., RN, dir. nrsg. serv., AMI Anclote Manor Psychiatric Hospital, Tarpon Springs, FL '84 (NURS)
NUNNELEE, SHARON R., dir. soc. serv., Spelman Memorial Hospital, Smithville, MO '75 (SOC)
NURICK, PAUL E., sr. vice-pres., Allentown Hospital, Allentown, PA '80 (MGMT)
NURRE, PAUL R., vice-pres. prof. and ancillary serv., Lock Haven Hospital and Extended Care Unit, Lock Haven, PA '84 (PLNG)
NURSE, CROSBY, RN, supv. nrsg., St. Rita Hospital, Sydney, N.S., Canada '74 (NURS)
NUSBAUM, CARL, consult., Carefree, AZ '49 (LIFE)

NUSBAUM, GAIL, dir. emer. serv. and flight medicine, Florida Hospital Medical Center, Orlando, FL '87 (AMB)
NUSBAUM, PAUL L., consult., Charleston, WV '74
NUSBAUM, S. RICHARD, pres., Pennsylvania Engineering Company, Philadelphia, PA '78 (CS)
NUSS, EILEEN F., mgr. sup., proc. and distrib., Providence Hospital, Anchorage, AK '83 (CS)
NUSS, LARRY D., atty., Mercy Hospitals of Kansas, Fort Scott, KS '71 (ATTY)
NUSSER, MARGARET, pat. rep., University of Iowa Hospitals and Clinics, Iowa City, IA '76 (PAT)
NUSSMAN, HOWARD B., sr. mgt. eng., Carolinas Hospital and Health Services, Inc., West Columbia, SC '79 (MGMT)
NUTE, ROBERT J., mgr. serv., Rehabilitation Hospital of the Pacific, Honolulu, HI '85 (ENG)
NUTE, ROBERT, mgr. plant oper., Rehabilitation Hospital of the Pacific, Honolulu, HI '86 (ENVIRON)
NUTTER, CLIFFORD A., dir. eng., United Hospital Center, Clarksburg, WV '79 (ENG)
NUTTER, DENNIS W., sr. vice-pres., SRI Gallup Hospital Market Research, Lincoln, NE '80 (PR) (PLNG)
NUTTER, WILLIAM T., dir. eng. serv., Children's Hospital, Columbus, OH '82 (ENG)
NYBERG, JANET J., RN, asst. vice-pres. and dir. nrsg., Lutheran Medical Center, Wheat Ridge, CO '83 (NURS)
NYBERG, KATHLEEN A., Fresno, CA '81 (EDUC)
NYBERG, SUSAN C., dir. vol. serv., Minneapolis Children's Medical Center, Minneapolis, MN '85 (VOL)
NYCUM, WILLIAM M., pres., William Nycum and Associates Ltd., Halifax, N.S., Canada '85 (PUR)
NYDAM, WILLIAM J., vice-pres. fin., American Healthcare Systems, La Jolla, CA '86
NYE, BARBARA G., sr. vice-pres. mktg., plng. and dev., University Hospitals of Cleveland, Cleveland, OH '86 (PR)
NYE, JERRY, pres., North Central Development Company, Fridley, MN '76 (PLNG)
NYE, SHARON KAY, dir. matl. mgt., Riverview Hospital, Wisconsin Rapids, WI '78 (PUR)(CS)
NYGAARD, GARY D., mgr. sup., proc. and distrib., Meriter Hospital, Madison, WI '81 (CS)
NYHAN, BARTHOLOMEW G., pres., Glenn, Nyhan and Associates, Inc., San Francisco, CA '80 (RISK)
NYIRI, JACK P., adm., HCA Edgefield Hospital, Nashville, TN '75
NYMAN, ADRIENNE Y., sr. consult. strategic plng. and mktg., Hospital Corporation of America, Dallas, TX '84 (PLNG)
NYSTROM, APRIL COYLE, dir. vol. serv., Emma L. Bixby Hospital, Adrian, MI '85 (VOL)
NYSTROM, CAROL A., RN, dir. nrsg. serv., Two Rivers Community Hospital, Two Rivers, WI '80 (NURS)

O

O'BRIEN, A. J., dir. phys. plant, St. Michael's Hospital, Toronto, Ont., Canada '80 (ENG)
O'BRIEN, ANNE F., asst. adm., West Orange Memorial Hospital, Winter Garden, FL '78 (NURS)
O'BRIEN, SR. BERNADETTE, ombudsman, O'Connor Hospital, San Jose, CA '78 (PAT)
O'BRIEN, CAROLYN, assoc. dir. food serv., Mills Memorial Hospital, San Mateo, CA '86 (FOOD)
O'BRIEN, DONALD E., Fort Gordon, GA '85 (SOC)
O'BRIEN, DONALD J., dir., Doctors Personnel of Los Angeles, Inc., Los Angeles, CA '67
O'BRIEN, ELEANORE R., corp. dir. vol. serv., West Jersey Health System, Camden, NJ '82 (VOL)
O'BRIEN, ELIZABETH B., dir. plng., C. V. Mosby Company, St. Louis, MO '82
O'BRIEN, FRED, soc. worker III and prog. mgr., Harborview Medical Center, Seattle, WA '86 (SOC)
O'BRIEN, J. PHILLIP, atty., American Hospital Association, Chicago, IL '83 (ATTY)
O'BRIEN, JEREMIAH F., dir. bldg. and grds., Jupiter Hospital, Jupiter, FL '87 (ENG)
O'BRIEN, JEROME J., dir. matl. mgt., Moses Taylor Hospital, Scranton, PA '77 (PUR)
O'BRIEN, JOHN E., dir. pers. serv., Massachusetts Hospital Association, Burlington, MA '76 (PERS)
O'BRIEN, JOSEPH DANIEL, exec. assoc. adm., Saint Thomas Medical Center, Akron, OH '82
O'BRIEN, KATHERINE, RN, dir. staff dev., Samaritan Keep Home, Watertown, NY '80 (EDUC)
O'BRIEN, KATHLEEN, RN, dir. nrsg. serv., Heritage Hospital, Taylor, MI '74 (NURS)
O'BRIEN, LINDA Z., asst. exec. dir. plng., Tampa Hospital Authority of Hillsborough County, General Hospital, Tampa, FL '80 (PLNG)
O'BRIEN, MARILYN A., RN, dir. nrsg. and asst. adm., Shriners Hospitals for Crippled Children, Los Angeles, CA '83 (NURS)
O'BRIEN, MARY B., dir. vol. serv. and pat. rep., Lawrence General Hospital, Lawrence, MA '81 (VOL)(PAT)
O'BRIEN, MARY T., dir. soc. serv., Good Samaritan Hospital of Pottsville Pennsylvania, Pottsville, PA '80 (SOC)
O'BRIEN, MICHAEL J., vice-pres., Johnson and Higgins, San Francisco, CA '82 (RISK)
O'BRIEN, MICHAEL P., exec. dir., Patient Assistant Foundation, San Francisco, CA '79 (SOC)
O'BRIEN, ORLIN P., dir., Bio-Sentry Engineering, Inc., Whitmore Lake, MI '82 (ENG)
O'BRIEN, PAULA A., coor. educ., Health Central of Owatonna, Owatonna, MN '85 (EDUC)
O'BRIEN, R. WILLIAM, adm. dir. mktg. and commun. rel., Louise Obici Memorial Hospital, Suffolk, VA '86 (PR) (PLNG)
O'BRIEN, REBECCA B., dir. amb. care serv., Saint Francis Medical Center, Peoria, IL '87 (AMB)
O'BRIEN, ROBERT J., vice-pres. prov. rel., Equicor, Wichita, KS '64 (AMB)
O'BRIEN, SHARON A., vice-pres. mktg. and dev., Eye, Ear, Nose and Throat Hospital, New Orleans, LA '81 (PR)
O'BRIEN, THOMAS W., atty., Columbia Hospital, Milwaukee, WI '84 (ATTY)
O'BRIEN, TIMOTHY S., dir. food serv., Southwest Memorial Hospital, Cortez, CO '85 (FOOD)
O'BRIEN, VERY REV MSGR TIMOTHY E., St. Martins, San Jose, CA '60 (LIFE)
O'BURKE, JOHN E., med. risk mgr., Sch Health Care System, Houston, TX '83 (RISK)
O'BYRNE, STEPHEN M., atty., Burnham Hospital, Champaign, IL '79 (ATTY)
O'CALLAGHAN, ELIZABETH ANNE, mgr. soc. serv., Scottish Rite Children's Hospital, Atlanta, GA '86 (SOC)
O'CONNELL, ANN H., atty., Sutter Community Hospitals, Sacramento, CA '78 (ATTY)
O'CONNELL, ANN MARIE, dir. plng. and mktg., Providence Hospital, Holyoke, MA '85 (PLNG)
O'CONNELL, CONLETH S., risk mgr., Victoria Hospital, Miami, FL '65 (PAT)(RISK)
O'CONNELL, DANIEL F., atty., Somerset Medical Center, Somerville, NJ '75 (ATTY)
O'CONNELL, DANIEL R., dir. pers., Holy Name Hospital, Teaneck, NJ '73 (PERS)
O'CONNELL, DANIEL T., dir. food serv., Baptist Medical Center of Oklahoma, Oklahoma City, OK '74 (FOOD)
O'CONNELL, DANIEL W., atty., St. Joseph Regional Medical Center, Lewiston, ID '74 (ATTY)
O'CONNELL, EILEEN M., asst. mgr. cent. serv. sup., Lahey Clinic Hospital, Burlington, MA '83 (CS)
O'CONNELL, ELIZABETH G., RN, corp. dir. qual. assur., Overlook Center, Columbia, MD '76 (NURS)(RISK)
O'CONNELL, GEORGE H., vice-pres. matl. mgt., St. Clare's Hospital of Schenectady, Schenectady, NY '78 (PUR)
O'CONNELL, GLORIA I., dir. commun. rel., St. John Medical Center, Tulsa, OK '86 (PR)
O'CONNELL, JOHN A., exec. dir., Holy Cross Shared Services, Inc., Notre Dame, IN '65 (RISK)
O'CONNELL, JOHN WILLIAM, exec. vice-pres., St. Joseph Hospitals, Mount Clemens, MI '70
O'CONNELL, MARTIN J., dir. mktg. and plng., Palms West Hospital, Loxahatchee, FL '86 (PR) (PLNG)
O'CONNELL, MICHAEL, student, St. Louis University Medical Center, Center for Health Services Education and Research, St. Louis, MO '85 (PLNG)
O'CONNELL, PAT, asst. vice-pres., Rehabilitation Institute of Chicago, Chicago, IL '83
O'CONNELL, WILLIAM R., pres., O'Connell Robertson Grobe, Austin, TX '48 (LIFE)
O'CONNOR, ANDREA, pub. rel. spec., Medical Center Hospital of Vermont, Burlington, VT '86 (PR)
O'CONNOR, ANN D., RN, clin. dir., Malden Hospital, Malden, MA '85 (NURS)
O'CONNOR, ANNE-ELISE, assoc. prod. and mktg. spec., Beth Israel Hospital, Boston, MA '86 (EDUC)
O'CONNOR, BEVERLY G., chief amb. care nrsg., Norwalk Hospital, Norwalk, CT '87 (AMB)
O'CONNOR, CAROL A., dir. mgt. dev., William Beaumont Hospital, Royal Oak, MI '82 (EDUC)
O'CONNOR, CATHLEEN, RN, coor. util. review and risk mgt., Children's Hospital, New Orleans, LA '84 (RISK)
O'CONNOR, DAVID J., RN, vice-pres. nrsg., Memorial Hospital, St. Joseph, MI '80 (NURS)
O'CONNOR, F. JAMES, Lynn Haven, FL '84 (FOOD)
O'CONNOR, FOTINE D., RN, dir. nrsg. serv. and educ., Los Angeles County-University of Southern California Medical Center, Los Angeles, CA '83 (NURS)
O'CONNOR, GARY M., assoc. dir. human res., Good Samaritan Hospital, West Islip, NY '86 (PERS)
O'CONNOR, JAMES P., dir. corp. procurement, Harper Hospital, Detroit, MI '82 (PUR)
O'CONNOR, JOHN P., mgt. eng., Thomas Jefferson University Hospital, Philadelphia, PA '87 (MGMT)
O'CONNOR, JOHN, pur. agt., Venice Hospital, Venice, FL '74 (PUR)
O'CONNOR, KATHI L., dir. nutr. serv., Health Hill Hospital for Children, Cleveland, OH '82 (FOOD)
O'CONNOR, SR. M. DAMIEN, pat. rep., Holy Name Hospital, Teaneck, NJ '79 (PAT)
O'CONNOR, MARILYN R., RN, dir. educ., Champlain Valley Physicians Hospital Medical Center, Plattsburgh, NY '71 (EDUC)
O'CONNOR, MARK S., atty., Mary Rutan Hospital, Bellefontaine, OH '78 (ATTY)
O'CONNOR, MARLENE, RN, dir. nrsg., Olympia Fields Osteopathic Medical Center, Olympia Fields, IL '80 (NURS)
O'CONNOR, MAUREEN L., sr. vice-pres., Martin Luther Hospital Medical Center, Anaheim, CA '80
O'CONNOR, NEIL J., dir. soc. serv., St. Nicholas Hospital, Sheboygan, WI '84 (SOC)
O'CONNOR, PATRICIA A., RN, vice-pres. nrsg., Danbury Hospital, Danbury, CT '79 (NURS)
O'CONNOR, PATRICIA, RN, assoc. adm. nrsg., University of Cincinnati Hospital, Cincinnati, OH '80 (NURS)
O'CONNOR, PATRICK J., PhD, asst. prof., Indiana University of Pennsylvania, Indiana, PA '85 (PLNG)
O'CONNOR, RALPH, dir. plant serv., St. Joseph Health Care Corporation, Albuquerque, NM '84 (ENG)
O'CONNOR, REBECCA C., atty., Mercy Hospital of Pittsburgh, Pittsburgh, PA '87 (ATTY)
O'CONNOR, RODERICK B., mgr. pat. and family serv., Wake Medical Center, Raleigh, NC '82 (SOC)
O'CONNOR, ROGER, dir. mktg. and pub. rel., American International Hospital, Zion, IL '86 (PR)
O'CONNOR, STEPHEN J., consult., Spring Valley, MN '81
O'CONNOR, STEPHEN, student, University of Dallas, Dallas, TX '84
O'CONNOR, VERONICA E., dir. human res., St. Mary's Hospital and Rehabilitation Center, Minneapolis, MN '85 (EDUC)
O'CONNOR, VINCENT J. JR., pres. and chief exec. off., Memorial Hospital of Dodge County, Fremont, NE '77
O'CONOR, HERBERT R. JR., atty., South Baltimore General Hospital, Baltimore, MD '75 (ATTY)
O'DAY, ALMA Y. C., dir. food serv., Straub Clinic and Hospital, Honolulu, HI '81 (FOOD)
O'DAY, CHARLES W., dir. eng., Beverly Enterprises, Virginia Beach, VA '80 (ENG)
O'DAY, M. LYNNE, RN, vice-pres., St. Vincent Hospital and Health Care Center, Indianapolis, IN '83 (NURS)
O'DEA, PATRICIA M., dir. vol. serv., Warren General Hospital, Warren, PA '77 (VOL)
O'DEA, THOMAS J., dir. eng., University of Minnesota Hospital and Clinic, Minneapolis, MN '84 (ENG)
O'DELL, CONSTANCE J., dir. soc. serv., Clifton Springs Hospital and Clinic, Clifton Springs, NY '81 (SOC)
O'DELL, JESSE R., coor. maint., Bay Medical Center, Bay City, MI '81 (ENG)
O'DELL, LUANNE, mgr. advertising and promotion, Research Health Services, Kansas City, MO '86 (PR)
O'DELL, MARGARET LOUISE, asst. chief nrs. trng. prog., Veterans Administration Medical Center, New York, NY '82
O'DONNELL, JAMES, pres., Associated Pharmacist Consultant, Inverness, IL '86 (RISK)
O'DONNELL, JERI A., dir. soc. serv., Grant Medical Center, Columbus, OH '80 (SOC)
O'DONNELL, JOHN H., Silver Spring, China '80 (ENG)
O'DONNELL, JOHN W., atty., Medical Center Hospital of Vermont, Burlington, VT '85 (ATTY)
O'DONNELL, KAREN S., RN, asst. dir. nrsg., West Virginia University Hospital, Morgantown, WV '85 (NURS)
O'DONNELL, MARGARET, risk mgr., St. Joseph Hospital, Houston, TX '86 (RISK)
O'DONNELL, MARK J., vice-pres. corp. plng., Ingalls Health System, Harvey, IL '85 (PLNG)
O'DONNELL, PATRICIA A., RN, dir. nrsg. serv., Monongahela Valley Hospital, Monongahela, PA '77 (NURS)
O'DONNELL, ROBERT RICHARD, dir. pers., Central Vermont Medical Center, Berlin, VT '69 (PERS)
O'DONNELL, SANDRA, adm. asst.-surg. and psychiatry, Alvin C. York Veterans Administration Medical Center, Murfreesboro, TN '86
O'DONNELL, SUELLYN, RN, dir. nrsg. critical care div., University of California San Francisco, San Francisco, CA '83 (NURS)
O'DONNELL, THOMAS V., vice-pres., Mount Auburn Hospital, Cambridge, MA '71 (MGMT)
O'DONNELL, THOMAS SR., dir. maint. and eng., St. Mary Hospital, Philadelphia, PA '79 (ENG)
O'DONNELL, TIMOTHY R., atty., Waterville Osteopathic Hospital, Waterville, ME '79 (ATTY)
O'DONNELL, TOM, atty., Mitchell, Kristl and Lieber, Kansas City, MO '84 (PLNG)
O'DONNELL, VALERIE M., RN, asst. dir. sup., proc. and distrib., Thomas Jefferson University Hospital, Philadelphia, PA '80 (PUR)
O'DONNELL, VIVIAN N., RN, chm. nrsg., Lutheran General Hospital, Park Ridge, IL '77 (NURS)
O'DONNELL, WILLIAM J., chief eng., St. Mary Hospital, Hoboken, NJ '69 (ENG)
O'DONOGHUE, SR. CARMELLA, RN, pres., Sch Health Care System, Houston, TX '80 (NURS)
O'DONOGHUE, PAUL J., sr. mgr. natl. health care info. syst., Ernst and Whinney, Cleveland, OH '86 (MGMT)
O'DONOHUE, NANCY F., RN, assoc. dir. nrsg., Kings County Hospital Center, Brooklyn, NY '84 (NURS)
O'DONOVAN, PATRICK G., plng. spec., William Beaumont Hospital, Royal Oak, MI '85 (PLNG)
O'DONOVAN, THOMAS R., pres., American Academy of Medical Administrators, Southfield, MI '64
O'FALLON, BARBARA, mgr. amb. info. syst., Jewish Hospital of St. Louis, St. Louis, MO '87 (AMB)
O'FARRELL, THOMAS M., sr. staff spec., American Hospital Association, Chicago, IL '71
O'GARA, BRIDGET M., ed., coor. media and med. rel., St. Joseph's Hospital and Medical Center, Phoenix, AZ '84 (PR)
O'GARA, EILEEN M., pres., First Health Associates, Inc., Chicago, IL '82 (PLNG)
O'GARRA, BEVERLY J., dir. pur., Virginia Beach General Hospital, Virginia Beach, VA '77 (PUR)
O'GRADY, ANN G., coor. vol., Addison Gilbert Hospital, Gloucester, MA '84 (VOL)
O'GRADY, TIMOTHY PORTER, RN, pres., Dynamic Healthcare, Norcross, GA '78 (NURS)
O'GUIN, KATHLEEN A., dir. pub. rel., Ingleside Hospital, Rosemead, CA '85 (PR)
O'HALLORAN, SEAMUS T., Jefferson Memorial Hospital, Alexandria, VA '83 (PLNG)
O'HANLEY, RONALD P., dir. pur., St. Mary's Hospital, Waterbury, CT '81 (PUR)
O'HARA, CONSTANCE J., mgr. vol. serv., University of Minnesota Hospital and Clinic, Minneapolis, MN '85 (VOL)
O'HARA, DAVID M., dir. soc. work, The Kennedy Institute for Handicapped, Baltimore, MD '85 (SOC)
O'HARA, EDWARD F., dir. matl. mgt., Sarasota Memorial Hospital, Sarasota, FL '75 (PUR)
O'HARA, FRANCIS P., atty., Sacred Heart Hospital, Norristown, PA '75 (ATTY)
O'HARA, GERALDINE, dir. vol. serv., Camelback Hospitals, Inc., Scottsdale, AZ '77 (VOL)
O'HARA, MICHAEL R., dir. new bus., Mayo Clinic, Rochester, MN '85 (PR)
O'HARA, NORMA K., dir. vol. serv., Mercy Hospital of New Orleans, New Orleans, LA '82 (VOL)
O'HARE, KATHARINE J., RN, pat. adv., Flushing Hospital and Medical Center, Flushing, NY '83 (PAT)
O'HARE, KEVIN B., dir. pub. rel., Holyoke Hospital, Holyoke, MA '86 (PR)

O'HARE, LINDA P., pres., The Bridge Organization, Inc., Chicago, IL '86
O'HARE, THOMAS P., dir. health care mgt. prog., Health Insurance Association of America, Washington, DC '75
O'HARO, JAMES P., student, University of Missouri, Graduate Studies in Health Services Management, Columbia, MO '86
O'HAVER, DONALD M., pur. agt., Lawrence County Memorial Hospital, Lawrenceville, IL '77 (PUR)
O'HEA, MICHAEL J., dir. pers., St. Elizabeth Hospital, Elizabeth, NJ '86 (PERS)
O'HEARN, JAMES C., asst. supt. maint., University of Minnesota Hospital and Clinic, Minneapolis, MN '83 (ENG)
O'KANE, KATHIE A., dir. vol. serv., Children's Hospital, Boston, MA '82 (VOL)
O'KANE, STEPHEN R., asst. vice-pres. prof. and outpatient serv., Valley Children's Hospital, Fresno, CA '87 (AMB)
O'KEEFE, DENNIS, dir. mental health and soc. serv., U. S. Public Health Service Indian Hospital, Rosebud, SD '86 (SOC)
O'KEEFE, MICHAEL F., chief oper. off., Irving Community Hospital, Irving, TX '73
O'KEEFE, PEG, dir. pub. affairs and trustee rel., Colorado Hospital Association, Denver, CO '84 (PR)
O'KEEFE, SHARON L., RN, assoc. adm. and dir. nrsg., Montefiore Medical Center, Bronx, NY '80 (NURS)
O'KEEFE, TWYLA KAY, dir. educ., Mercy Health Center, Oklahoma City, OK '78 (EDUC)
O'KEIFF, HELAYNE FISHER, RN, pres., Mason-Raskel, Inc., St. Louis, MO '85 (NURS)
O'KEIFF, MAJ. JAMES R. JR., MSC USA, exec. off., U. S. Army Health Clinic, Schofield Barracks, HI '80
O'KELLEY, SUSAN, dir. mktg., Allied Pharmacy Service, Inc., Abilene, TX '84
O'KELLY, ELIZABETH S., atty., Alexian Brothers Medical Center, Elk Grove Village, IL '86 (ATTY)
O'LEARY, ANN DREW, RN, asst. exec. dir., Memorial Hospital of Sweetwater County, Rock Springs, WY '86 (NURS)
O'LEARY, JAMES A., dir. ob., University Hospital of Jacksonville, Jacksonville, FL '85
O'LEARY, JAMES M., atty., Medical Center Hospital, Odessa, TX '81 (ATTY)
O'LEARY, JOAN G., RN, assoc. prof., Villanova University, Villanova, PA '75 (NURS)
O'LEARY, JOSEPH A., exec. dir., Frick Community Health Center, Mount Pleasant, PA '75
O'LEARY, MARY M., RN, dir. nrsg. educ., evaluation and res., Michael Reese Hospital and Medical Center, Chicago, IL '84 (NURS)
O'LEARY, THOMAS M., atty., Port Huron Hospital, Port Huron, MI '85 (ATTY)
O'LEARY, THOMAS M., vice-pres. fin., Boca Raton Community Hospital, Boca Raton, FL '78
O'LEARY, WILLIAM T., util. eng., Hunterdon Medical Center, Flemington, NJ '83 (ENG)
O'LOUGHLIN, ELAYNE, assoc. dir. nrsg., District of Columbia General Hospital, Washington, DC '86 (RISK)
O'MAHONEY, WILLIAM P., atty., Saint Joseph Hospital and Health Center, Kokomo, IN '69 (ATTY)
O'MAHONY, MARY, adm. amb. care, Manhattan Eye, Ear and Throat Hospital, New York, NY '86
O'MALEY, KEVIN J., dir. plant oper. and maint., Catholic Medical Center, Manchester, NH '84 (ENG)
O'MALLEY, JAMES P., dir. sup., proc. and distrib., Cooper Hospital-University Medical Center, Camden, NJ '78 (CS)
O'MALLEY, JAMIE, RN, dir. in-patient nrsg., Children's Memorial Hospital, Chicago, IL '84 (NURS)
O'MALLEY, PENNY, Beverly Hills, CA '85 (PLNG)
O'MARRAH, PHILLIP, Greater Baltimore Medical Center, Baltimore, MD '80 (ENG)
O'MEARA-WYMAN, KATHLEEN, dir. commun. rel., St. Elizabeth Medical Center, Yakima, WA '78 (PR)
O'MEARA, ANN R., dir. soc. serv., Goddard Memorial Hospital, Stoughton, MA '72 (SOC)
O'MEARA, EUGENE J., pres., Sharon General Hospital, Sharon, PA '53 (LIFE)
O'MEARA, SHARON A., RN, dir. surg. serv., Mount Auburn Hospital, Cambridge, MA '86 (NURS)
O'NEAL, CAPT. EDWARD A. JR., MSC USA, areomedical evacuation off., U. S. Lyster Army Hospital, Fort Rucker, AL '84
O'NEAL, HELEN H., pat. rep., St. Joseph Hospital, Lexington, KY '83 (PAT)
O'NEAL, L. BURKE, asst. scientist, University of Wisconsin, Madison, WI '77 (ENG)
O'NEAL, MARCIA S., dir. pub. rel., McDonough District Hospital, Macomb, IL '84 (PR)
O'NEAL, NANCYE H., dir. plng. and mktg., Baptist Regional Medical Center, Corbin, KY '84 (PLNG)
O'NEAL, SANDI, RN, dir. in-service and pat. educ., Halifax Hospital Medical Center, Daytona Beach, FL '79 (EDUC)
O'NEAL, TEREEN E., pat. rep., Tri-City Medical Center, Oceanside, CA '86 (PAT)
O'NEAL, WILLIAM LARRY, RN, Kansas City, MO '79 (NURS)
O'NEIL, DENNIS D., atty., Hoag Memorial Hospital Presbyterian, Newport Beach, CA '84 (ATTY)
O'NEIL, EILEEN KINSELLA, RN, assoc. dir. nrsg., Beth Israel Medical Center, New York, NY '83 (NURS)
O'NEIL, GERALD T., vice-pres. and exec. dir., Avmed Health Plan, Miami, FL '74
O'NEIL, JACK, vice-pres., Fru-Con Construction Corporation, Ballwin, MO '86
O'NEIL, NANCY I., dir. soc. serv. and cont. care, Sturdy Memorial Hospital, Attleboro, MA '82 (SOC)
O'NEIL, ROBERT J., atty., Charleston Area Medical Center, Charleston, WV '84 (ATTY)
O'NEILL-RATICA, MARY, coor. discharge plng. and dir. soc. serv., Hillcrest Hospital, Mayfield Heights, OH '85 (SOC)
O'NEILL, DAVID D., reg. vice-pres., Voluntary Hospital of America, Inc., Walnut Creek, CA '82
O'NEILL, DENNIS M., dir. soc. serv., University Hospital-University of Nebraska, Omaha, NE '83 (SOC)
O'NEILL, EDWARD S., corp. vice-pres. reg. affairs, Saint Raphael Corporation, New Haven, CT '87 (AMB)
O'NEILL, ELFRIEDE M., dir. pub. rel., Quakertown Community Hospital, Quakertown, PA '82 (PR)
O'NEILL, JANET, coor. pub. affairs, Santa Barbara Cottage Hospital, Santa Barbara, CA '85 (PR)
O'NEILL, JOHN P., adm. res., Thomas Jefferson University Hospital, Philadelphia, PA '84 (MGMT)
O'NEILL, LAVERNE T., dir. nutr. and food serv., AMI Parkway Regional Medical Center, North Miami Beach, FL '86 (FOOD)
O'NEILL, MARK A., pres., Hospital Utilization Project, Monroeville, PA '86
O'NEILL, PATRICIA T., RN, dir., Mercy Home Health Care, Chicago, IL '80 (NURS)(AMB)
O'NEILL, PATRICK J., dir. mktg., St. Mary's Medical Center, Evansville, IN '84 (PLNG)
O'NEILL, ROBERT W., dir. commun. rel., St. Mary's Hospital of Troy, Troy, NY '82 (PR)
O'NEILL, THOMAS MICHAEL, dir. human resources, Mercy Hospital and Medical Center, Chicago, IL '76 (PERS)
O'NEILL, WILLIAM P., atty., West Park Hospital, Philadelphia, PA '68 (ATTY)
O'OLEARY, ALICE M., (ret.), Peabody, MA '50 (LIFE)
O'QUINN, MARVIN ROCHELLE, asst. adm. mktg. and plng., Willamette Falls Hospital, Oregon City, OR '80 (PR) (PLNG)
O'REILLY, CLARE FRANCIS, diet. tech., Frankford Hospital, Philadelphia, PA '86 (PAT)
O'REILLY, COLLEEN, dir. risk mgt., Michigan Health Care Corporation, Detroit, MI '86 (RISK)
O'REILLY, HUGH F., dir. diet. serv., Roger Williams General Hospital, Providence, RI '79 (FOOD)
O'REILLY, JOHN, chm. qual. assur., Natchaug Hospital, Mansfield Center, CT '86 (RISK)
O'REILLY, MADELINE E., RN, asst. dir. nrsg., Brockton Hospital, Brockton, MA '86 (NURS)
O'ROURKE, BARBARA S., dir. soc. serv. and post-hosp. plng., Hospital Center at Orange, Orange, NJ '82 (SOC)
O'ROURKE, MARIA W., RN, asst. dean clin. affairs and dir. staff dev. and res. nrsg., San Francisco General Hospital Medical Center, San Francisco, CA '86 (NURS)
O'ROURKE, MARY K., dir. vol. serv., Our Lady of Lourdes Memorial Hospital, Binghamton, NY '76 (VOL)
O'ROURKE, NANCY, sr. compensation consult., A. S. Hansen, Inc., Dallas, TX '86 (PERS)
O'ROURKE, MAJ. PATRICK J., MSC USAF, adm., U. S. Air Force Clinic McChord, Sga, McChord AFB, WA '80
O'ROURKE, TERRENCE MICHAEL, pres., Blodgett Memorial Medical Center, Grand Rapids, MI '67
O'ROURKE, THOMAS E., (ret.), Hyannis Port, MA '47 (LIFE)
O'SHAUGHESSEY, TIMOTHY J., atty., Campbell Memorial Hospital, Weatherford, TX '85 (ATTY)
O'SHAUGHNESSY, JOHN J., supv. skilled trades, Oak Forest Hospital of Cook County, Oak Forest, IL '80 (ENG)
O'SHAUGHNESSY, KATHRYN L., mgr. matl., Missapequa General Hospital, Seaford, NY '84 (CS)
O'SHEA, ELIZABETH, dir. mktg., Memorial Hospital at Gulfport, Gulfport, MS '85 (PLNG)
O'SHEA, JOYCE, RN, vice-pres., Church Home and Hospital of the City of Baltimore, Baltimore, MD '75 (NURS)
O'SULLIVAN, ELAINE, dir. matl. mgt., Roger Williams General Hospital, Providence, RI '79 (PUR)
O'SULLIVAN, SR. KATHLEEN, pat. advocate, Seton Medical Center, Daly City, CA '81 (PAT)
O'SULLIVAN, THOMAS C., mgr. plng., eng. and telecommun., Kaiser Permanente Health Plan, Pasadena, CA '86 (ENG)
OAKES, JAMES L. JR., vice-pres., HBO and Company, San Mateo, CA '72 (MGMT)
OAKES, WILLIAM C., dir. pub. rel., West Suburban Hospital Medical Center, Oak Park, IL '81 (PR)
OAKLAND, GERALD D., dir. phys. ther., Methodist Hospital, Philadelphia, PA '84
OAKLEY, DAVID S., pres., Haynes and Oakley, Architects, Inc., South Pasadena, CA '77
OAKLEY, DOYLE W., dir. pur. and mgr. oper., Western Kentucky Hospital Services, Madisonville, KY '81 (PUR)
OAKLEY, VERNON BRADSHER JR., atty., Community Memorial Hospital, South Hill, VA '82 (ATTY)
OAKS, GINGER, dir. soc. work, Johnson City Medical Center Hospital, Johnson City, TN '84 (SOC)
OAST, EDWARD L. JR., atty., DePaul Hospital, Norfolk, VA '73 (ATTY)
OATES, ROBERT J., dir. pers., Blanchard Valley Hospital, Findlay, OH '76 (PERS)
OBADE, CLAIRE CONNOR, atty., Bryn Mawr Hospital, Bryn Mawr, PA '85 (ATTY)
OBAYASHI, SUE S., dir. commun. rel. and mktg., Community Hospital of Gardena, Gardena, CA '84 (PR)
OBENAUF, MARLENE, dir. qual. assur. and risk mgt., Condell Memorial Hospital, Libertyville, IL '84 (RISK)
OBER, JUDITH A., RN, dir. critical care, Jewish Hospital, Louisville, KY '81 (NURS)
OBERBECK, RICHARD E., adm. plant oper., Middlesex Memorial Hospital, Middletown, CT '63 (ENG)
OBERDECK, EILEEN R., RN, asst. supv., DeKalb General Hospital, Decatur, GA '84 (CS)
OBERFEST, PETER J., pres., Oberfest Associates, Inc., Philadelphia, PA '79 (PLNG)
OBERG, ALBIN H., (ret.), Lebanon, NJ '59
OBERG, ROGER B., dir. plng., Hamot Medical Center, Erie, PA '81 (PLNG)
OBERLANDER, CARL, dir. plant oper., Eagle River Memorial Hospital, Eagle River, WI '70 (ENG)
OBERLIESEN, THOMAS J., vice-pres. plng., Ohio Hospital Association, Columbus, OH '79 (PLNG)
OBERMAN, KIM R. MCFARLANE, asst. dir. diet., Texas Scottish Rite Hospital, Dallas, TX '86 (FOOD)
OBERMAN, SANDRA C., coor. friends of the child, Musc Medical Center of Medical University of South Carolina, Charleston, SC '84 (VOL)
OBERMARK, WILLIAM J., dir. soc. serv., Cardinal Glennon Children Hospital, St. Louis, MO '80 (SOC)
OBERMIRE, LOIS F., dir. pur., Nanticoke Memorial Hospital, Seaford, DE '85 (PUR)
OBERRECHT, PHILLIP S., atty., St. Luke's Regional Medical Center, Boise, ID '82 (ATTY)
OBERWEIS, JOSEPH, dir. matl. mgt., St. Joseph's Hospital, Chippewa Falls, WI '78 (PUR)
OBERWEIS, RITA, soc. worker, St. Joseph's Hospital, Chippewa Falls, WI '86 (SOC)
OBIE, MARCIE, dir. risk mgt., Mount Clemens General Hospital, Mount Clemens, MI '84 (RISK)
OBOHOSKI, LEONARD A., sr. mgt. eng., Thomas Jefferson University Hospital, Philadelphia, PA '81 (MGMT)
OBRIECHT, JAMES H., assoc. adm. fin., Illinois Masonic Medical Center, Chicago, IL '85
OCHSNER, ALBERT JOHN III, adm. clin. affairs, University of Wisconsin Medical School, Madison, WI '78
OCKERT, COL. CARROLL A., MSC USA, I. G., APO New York, NY '74
ODANIELL, JEANNE, dir. soc. work, Bridgeport Hospital, Bridgeport, CT '79 (SOC)
ODDIS, JOSEPH MICHAEL, vice-pres. prof. serv., Peninsula General Hospital Medical Center, Salisbury, MD '79
ODDY, EDITH M., (ret.), Milford, CT '37 (LIFE)
ODELL, MYRON G., dir. mgt. syst., Forbes Health System, Pittsburgh, PA '83 (MGMT)
ODEN, L. PATRICK, mng. dir., First Boston Corporation, New York, NY '79
ODENWELLER, GERARD F., Troy, MI '59
ODER, DONALD R., sr. vice-pres., Rush-Presbyterian-St. Luke's Medical Center, Chicago, IL '73
ODIER, THAYNE M., RN, dir. nrsg., educ. and qual. assur., Waukesha Memorial Hospital, Waukesha, WI '82 (RISK)
ODIORNE, JUDITH, RN, dir. nrsg., Mount Carmel Mercy Hospital, Detroit, MI '77 (NURS)
ODLE, SAMUEL L., vice-pres. prof. serv., Methodist Hospital of Indiana, Indianapolis, IN '82
ODOM, CRYSTINE MCLEOD, adm. asst., St. Mary's Hospital, Athens, GA '81 (RISK)
ODOM, ROBERT W., atty., Stanly Memorial Hospital, Albemarle, NC '82 (ATTY)
ODOM, VIRGINIA L., bus. mgr., Western Lane Hospital, Florence, OR '84
ODUARDO, JOHN, dir. mktg. and pub. rel., Elmcrest Psychiatric Institute, Portland, CT '77 (PR)
OECHSLE, PEGGY R., pat. liaison, University of California San Diego Medical Center, San Diego, CA '79 (PAT)
OEHLMAN, ROBERT A., prin., Main Hurdman, Los Angeles, CA '85 (MGMT)
OELSCHLAGER, TED H., mgr. hskpg. serv., St. Vincent's Hospital, Birmingham, AL '86 (ENVIRON)
OERLY, DENNIS F., sr. vice-pres. corp. dev., High Point Regional Hospital, High Point, NC '79 (PR) (PLNG)
OERTER, VESTA M., coor. vol., Great Plains Regional Medical Center, North Platte, NE '81 (VOL)
OETJEN, CHRISTINE A., dir. soc. serv., Charleston Area Medical Center, Charleston, WV '84 (SOC)
OFFUTT, DANE W., Panhandle Diagnostic Center, Amarillo, TX '76 (AMB)
OFFUTT, GEORGE W., chief eng., Jefferson Memorial Hospital, Ranson, WV '81 (ENG)
OFFUTT, JULIE ANN, coor. nrsg. oper. and mgr. staff, St. Vincent Hospital and Health Center, Indianapolis, IN '84
OFODILE, JANET B., dir. new bus. dev., Comprehensive Health Service of Detroit, Inc., Detroit, MI '85
OGAWA, YURI J. A., RN, pat. rel. rep., Cedars-Sinai Medical Center, Los Angeles, CA '86 (PAT)
OGBURN, SUSAN L., risk mgt. consult., Barrington, RI '80 (RISK)
OGBURN, WAYNE LEE, vice-pres., Hendrick Medical Center, Abilene, TX '72
OGDEN, ANNE P., dir. plng. and evaluation, Mount Sinai Hospital, Minneapolis, MN '84 (PLNG)
OGDEN, DAVID E., dir. environ. serv., North Mississippi Medical Center, Tupelo, MS '86 (ENVIRON)
OGDEN, JEAN R., asst. dir. bldg. and grds., Providence Hospital, Southfield, MI '78 (ENG)
OGDEN, LOUANN M., asst. dir. food serv., Timberlawn Psychiatric Hospital, Dallas, TX '86 (FOOD)
OGDEN, ROBERT C., dir. med. soc. work, Cleveland Memorial Hospital, Shelby, NC '84 (SOC)
OGGERO, WILLIAM, adm., Link Clinic, Mattoon, IL '87 (AMB)
OGLE, DAVID A., dir. cent. serv., Memorial City Medical Center, Houston, TX '87 (CS)
OGLE, MARK W., dir. commun., plng. and dev., Neosho Memorial Hospital, Chanute, KS '85 (PR) (PLNG)
OGLE, MARY ELLEN, RN, vice-pres. nrsg., St. Agnes Hospital and Medical Center, Fresno, CA '83 (NURS)
OGLESBEE, M. ROSS, dir. claims and risk mgt., North Carolina Memorial Hospital, Chapel Hill, NC '82 (RISK)
OGLESBY, BURT, mgr. matl., Charter Community Hospital of Cleveland, Cleveland, TX '86 (PUR)
OGNALL, MICHAEL J., MD, consult., Physician House Call Services, Portland, OR '81
OGREN, KENNETH M., adm., Patrick Henry Hospital for the Chronically Ill, Newport News, VA '77
OGREN, STUART DONALD, exec. vice-pres., Virginia Hospital Association, Glen Allen, VA '56 (LIFE)
OH, RONALD, dir. pers., Loma Linda University Medical Center, Loma Linda, CA '78 (PERS)
OHANESIAN, JOHN R., vice-pres. plng., St. John's Hospital and Health Center, Santa Monica, CA '85 (PLNG)
OHE, GREGORY P., asst. adm., Bradford Hospital, Bradford, PA '84 (PLNG)
OHKI, ANNE, RN, risk mgr., Santa Rosa Memorial Hospital, Santa Rosa, CA '86 (RISK)
OHLEN, ROBERT BRUCE, exec. dir., Lawrence Memorial Hospital, Lawrence, KS '67
OHLENKAMP, EDWARD, dir. educ., Lakeview Medical Center, Danville, IL '85 (EDUC)

OHLER, JOHANNE L., dir. mktg. and commun. rel., Knox Community Hospital, Mount Vernon, OH '86 (PR)
OHM, BRENDA E., pres., Network Health Communications, Inc., Philadelphia, PA '86 (EDUC)
OILER, SALLY A., dir. soc. serv., Doctors Hospital, Columbus, OH '84 (SOC)
OJALA, JOYCE ANN, dir. vol. serv., Grady Memorial Hospital, Atlanta, GA '73 (VOL)
OJAR, AVIS S., dir. food and nutr. serv., Physicians Hospital, New York, NY '86 (FOOD)
OJEDA, ANTONIO M., dir. sales and mktg., AMI Town and Country Medical Center, Tampa, FL '85 (PR) (PLNG)
OKA, SEISHI W., PhD, exec. dir., Lancaster Cleft Palate Clinic, Lancaster, PA '83
OKAMURA, GAIL C., dir. educ., St. Francis Medical Center, Honolulu, HI '86 (EDUC)
OKASHIMA, MARK A., mgr. market res., St. Mary's Health Care Corporation, Reno, NV '82 (PLNG)
OKINAKA, STANLEY K., mgr. ins. mgt. and loss contr., Queen's Medical Center, Honolulu, HI '78 (RISK)
OKORAFOR, HELEN IJEOMA, RN, Olympia Fields, IL '77
OKUDA, SUSAN M., chief med. soc. worker, Royal Columbian Hospital, New Westminster, B.C., Canada '78 (SOC)
OKUN, JUDITH, dir. commun. rel., Bayley Seton Hospital, Staten Island, NY '83 (PR)
OLBERDING, ROBERT J., dir. plant oper., Mercy Hospital, Cedar Rapids, IA '85 (ENG)
OLDANI, DAN J., exec. dir. oper., University of Texas M. D. Anderson Hospital and Tumor Institute at Houston, Houston, TX '83 (RISK)
OLDBERG, CARL M., exec. vice-pres., Ruder, Finn and Rotman, Inc., Chicago, IL '83 (PR)
OLDEN, JOHN A., asst. dir. food serv., Presbyterian Hospital in the City of New York, New York, NY '79 (FOOD)
OLDEN, PETER C., assoc. dir., Southside Regional Medical Center, Petersburg, VA '86
OLDENBURG, EILEEN, consult. med. facil., State Department of Health and Social Service, Division of Health and Medical Services, Cheyenne, WY '85 (MGMT)
OLDENHOEFT, MARGIE C., dir. vol. serv., Mary Greeley Medical Center, Ames, IA '83 (VOL)
OLDENIKAMP, GARY A., dir. plant oper., St. Joseph Medical Center, Burbank, CA '86 (ENG)
OLDER, HARVEY, asst. exec. dir., Arizona Hospital Association, Phoenix, AZ '71
OLDER, MOLLY, dir. soc. serv., South Shore Hospital, Chicago, IL '86 (SOC)
OLDFIELD, DAVID A., atty., LeFevre, Zeman and Oldfield Law Group, Ltd., Vandalia, IL '83
OLDFORD, CATHERINE L., dir. diet. serv., St. Mary's Hospital, Waterbury, CT '83 (FOOD)
OLDHAM, STEVE, vice-pres. pers., Elmbrook Memorial Hospital, Brookfield, WI '86 (PERS)
OLDHAM, WILLIAM M., atty., Akron General Medical Center, Akron, OH '84 (ATTY)
OLDMAN, NELSON W., dir. educ. and trng., University Medical Center Southern Nevada, Las Vegas, NV '72 (EDUC)
OLEJKO, MITCHELL J., atty., Virginia Mason Hospital, Seattle, WA '81 (ATTY)
OLEN, ROLAND D., pres., St. Mary Hospital, Quincy, IL '63
OLENDER, LOTTIE, coor. educ. res., Saint James Hospital, Newark, NJ '74 (EDUC)
OLENICK, EVELYN M., RN, dir. med. and adult psych. nrsg., Western Reserve Systems-Northside, Youngstown, OH '86 (NURS)
OLENIK, MICHAEL J., dir. plant oper., St. Vincent Charity Hospital, Cleveland, OH '68 (ENG)
OLESEN, DORIS K., coor. commun. and syst., Swedish Covenant Hospital, Chicago, IL '79 (ENG)
OLEX, STEPHEN A., dir. eng. and maint., Mercy Hospital, Wilkes-Barre, PA '76 (ENG)
OLGUIN, CORINA, dir. vol. serv., White Memorial Medical Center, Los Angeles, CA '85 (VOL)
OLINDER, JOAN CLAIRE, coor. pat. serv., Worcester City Hospital, Worcester, MA '86 (PAT)
OLINGER, RONALD D., atty., St. Mary's Hospital, Pierre, SD '79 (ATTY)
OLIO, KATHLEEN M., RN, asst. dir. nrsg.-med. and psych. div., St. Elizabeth's Hospital of Boston, Boston, MA '86 (NURS)
OLIVA, ANN MACHIN, dir. pat. educ., Overlook Hospital, Summit, NJ '81 (EDUC)
OLIVE, JAMES T., mgr., Blue Cross and Blue Shield of Fl, Jacksonville, FL '80 (MGMT)
OLIVE, MARGARET M., asst. dir. diet. serv., Plantation General Hospital, Plantation, FL '81 (FOOD)
OLIVEIRA, MYRA, dir. pers., Kapiolani Medical Center for Women, Honolulu, HI '69 (PERS)
OLIVER, CHARLES R., asst. vice-pres. commun. rel., Riverview Medical Center, Red Bank, NJ '79 (PR)
OLIVER, G. ROBERT, atty., Clayton General Hospital, Riverdale, GA '74 (ATTY)
OLIVER, HARRIET, dir. vol., Flagler Hospital, St. Augustine, FL '78 (VOL)
OLIVER, HERBERT B., dir. matl. mgt., Richmond Community Hospital, Richmond, VA '82 (PUR)
OLIVER, IRENE E., (ret.), Twin Falls, ID '34 (LIFE)
OLIVER, JAMES, dir. matl. mgt., University Hospital, Boston, MA '86 (PUR)
OLIVER, JOHN D. JR., asst. adm., Martin Memorial Hospital, Stuart, FL '82
OLIVER, KAY F. STEVENS, dir. nrsg., Willapa Harbor Hospital, South Bend, WA '84 (NURS)
OLIVER, REA A., adm., West Sands Hospital, Miami, FL '81
OLIVER, SANDRA L., assoc. dir. plng. and mgt. coordination, Metropolitan Hospital Center, New York, NY '85 (PLNG)
OLIVER, SUSAN W., dir. soc. serv., U. S. Public Health Service Indian Hospital, Whiteriver, AZ '77 (SOC)
OLIVER, TIMOTHY J., prog. dir. and soc. worker, U. S. Public Health Service Indian Hospital, Belcourt, ND '86 (SOC)
OLIVER, VINCENT C., dir. eng., Servicemaster Industries, Santa Clara, CA '82 (ENG)
OLIVERIO, EVELYN M., dir. diet., Conemaugh Valley Memorial Hospital, Johnstown, PA '69 (FOOD)
OLIVERIO, NORMA L., asst. dir. diet., Conemaugh Valley Memorial Hospital, Johnstown, PA '69 (FOOD)
OLIVERIUS, SARAH, dir. food serv., Stormont-Vail Regional Medical Center, Topeka, KS '72 (FOOD)
OLIVIER, CONNIE L., pat. rep., South Louisiana Medical Center, Houma, LA '86 (PAT)
OLLAR, CECIL D., dir. plant eng., All Saints Episcopal Hospital, Fort Worth, TX '84 (ENG)
OLLIVIERRE, CYRIL C., partner, Ernst and Whinney, New York, NY '85 (MGMT)
OLMSCHENK, DANIEL J., RN, dir. nrsg. serv., St. Michael's Hospital, Sauk Centre, MN '81 (NURS)
OLMSTED, MALCOLM, vice-pres., Nutri-Group, Inc., Roseville, CA '80 (FOOD)
OLPIN, JACK GORDON, exec. dir., Germantown Community Hospital-Methodist East, Germantown, TN '61
OLSEN, BONNIE KLIMA, dir. vol., Lutheran Medical Center, Brooklyn, NY '68 (VOL)
OLSEN, DIANE M., mgr. food prod., AMI St. Joseph Center for Health, Omaha, NE '87 (FOOD)
OLSEN, EDWARD VINCENT JR., mgr. environ. serv., St. Vincent Hospital and Health Center, Indianapolis, IN '86 (ENG)
OLSEN, GEORGE G., atty., University of Michigan Hospitals, Ann Arbor, MI '83 (ATTY)
OLSEN, HERLUF V. JR., vice-pres., American Hospital Association, Chicago, IL '52 (LIFE)
OLSEN, JOANNE, RN, vice-pres. nrsg. serv., St. Luke's Hospital, San Francisco, CA '86 (NURS)(AMB)
OLSEN, KENNETH JAMES, asst. dir. oper., Metropolitan Hospital Mental Health, New York, NY '70
OLSEN, REX N., Chicago, IL '85 (LIFE)
OLSEN, RONALD M., dir. phys. plant, St. Joseph's Hospital and Health Center, Dickinson, ND '81 (ENG)
OLSON, AUDREY G., dir. vol. serv., Children's Mercy Hospital, Kansas City, MO '77 (VOL)
OLSON, BETTY J., coor. vol. serv., Memorial Hospital at Oconomowoc, Oconomowoc, WI '80 (VOL)
OLSON, BONNIE L., dir. food serv., Holmstad, Inc., Batavia, IL '78 (FOOD)
OLSON, CHARLES H., consult. indust. eng., Scotts Valley, CA '72 (MGMT)
OLSON, CHARLOTTE G., chief med. info. and adm. med. rec., Veterans Administration Medical Center, Mountain Home, TN '85
OLSON, CONRAD WILLIAM, student, Webster University, Northfield, IL '86
OLSON, DAVID A., partner, Arthur Andersen and Company, Minneapolis, MN '84
OLSON, DENNIS G., chief eng., AMI Southeastern Medical Center, North Miami Beach, FL '82 (ENG)
OLSON, DON, mgr. purchased serv., Stanford University Hospital, Stanford, CA '86 (PUR)
OLSON, DONALD P., mgr. health benefit analysis, Blue Cross and Blue Shield of Connecticut, North Haven, CT '83 (PLNG)
OLSON, DONALD R., adm., Virginia Mason Hospital, Seattle, WA '77
OLSON, DONNA, pres. aux., St. John's Lutheran Hospital, Libby, MT '86 (VOL)
OLSON, EDWARD A., vice-pres. adm., Waukesha Memorial Hospital, Waukesha, WI '82 (PLNG)
OLSON, EUGENE E., atty., Des Moines General Hospital, Des Moines, IA '85 (ATTY)
OLSON, GARY ROGER, exec. vice-pres., St. Luke's Hospital West, Chesterfield, MO '76
OLSON, GERALD W., atty., Pocatello Regional Medical Center, Pocatello, ID '76 (ATTY)
OLSON, GLADYS, pur. agt., Two Rivers Municipal Hospital and Hamilton Memorial Home, Two Rivers, WI '67 (PUR)
OLSON, GLORIA JEAN, dir. outpatient clin., Ingham Medical Center, Lansing, MI '86 (NURS)
OLSON, JANE M., RN, vice-pres. nrsg., St. Joseph's Medical Center, Brainerd, MN '83 (NURS)
OLSON, JILLIANN, student, Southern Illinois University, Carbondale, IL '85
OLSON, JUDITH FREIMAN, dir. soc. work, Mount Auburn Hospital, Cambridge, MA '74 (SOC)
OLSON, KIM A., adm. clin. prog. mgt., Leonard Morse Hospital, Natick, MA '85 (MGMT)
OLSON, LAUREL L., plng. analyst, Northwestern Memorial Hospital, Chicago, IL '83 (PLNG)
OLSON, LEE J., eng., St. Mary's Hospital, Decatur, IL '76 (ENG)
OLSON, MARK D., atty., Siegan, Barbakoff, Gomberg and Gordon, Ltd., Chicago, IL '74 (ATTY)
OLSON, MELANIE J., student, Southern Illinois University, School of Technical Career, Carbondale, IL '86
OLSON, NEVA M., asst. adm. plng. and mktg., Hemet Valley Hospital District, Hemet, CA '82 (PLNG)
OLSON, PAUL A., chief eng., Burnett General Hospital, Grantsburg, WI '81 (ENG)
OLSON, ROBERT D., dir. pub. affairs and dev., Jennie Edmundson Memorial Hospital, Council Bluffs, IA '79 (PR)
OLSON, ROBERT H. JR., atty., Lake Hospital System, Painesville, OH '77 (ATTY)
OLSON, ROGER WILBERT, assoc. vice-pres., Metropolitan Medical Center, Minneapolis, MN '76 (ENG)
OLSON, RON L., dir. plng. and constr., Metropolitan-Calgary and Rural General Hospital District Northern 93, Calgary, Alta., Canada '79 (PLNG)
OLSON, SANDRA K., RN, vice-pres. nrsg., Williamsport Hospital and Medical Center, Williamsport, PA '83 (NURS)
OLSON, SCOTT D., assoc. pub. rel. and publications, Rochester Methodist Hospital, Rochester, MN '86 (PR)
OLSON, SHERRY B., mgr. food serv., St. Jude Children's Research Hospital, Memphis, TN '83 (FOOD)
OLSON, LT. COL. STEVEN J., MSC USAF, dir. prof. standards, School of Health Care Sciences, Wichita Falls, TX '81
OLSON, STEVEN R., atty., Hinsdale Hospital, Hinsdale, IL '82 (ATTY)
OLSON, SUSAN COCHRAN, mktg. spec., Georgetown University Hospital, Washington, DC '86 (PR)
OLSON, SUSAN L., mgr. consumer mktg., Georgetown University Medical Center, Washington, DC '87 (PLNG)
OLSON, TED, dir. matl. mgt., Bossier Medical Center, Bossier City, LA '77 (PUR)
OLSON, THOMAS H., dir. mgt. dev. and pschologist, San Pedro Peninsula Hospital, San Pedro, CA '86 (EDUC)
OLSON, THOMAS W., atty., St. Vincent Hospital, Santa Fe, NM '86 (ATTY)
OLSSON, CLIFFORD L., dir. bus. and mktg.-surg. serv., AMI Saint Joseph Hospital, Omaha, NE '85
OLSTEN, MARION K., dir. cent. sup. and distrib., Grace Hospital, Vancouver, B.C., Canada '79 (CS)
OLSZEWSKI, ANNA C., mgr. vol. serv., Shadyside Hospital, Pittsburgh, PA '86 (VOL)
OLSZEWSKI, JERRY, dir. matl. mgt., St. Paul Medical Center, Dallas, TX '83 (PUR)
OLSZEWSKI, JON J., dir. bldg. serv., Kingswood Hospital, Ferndale, MI '85 (ENG)
OLTMAN, SYLVIA, RN, nrs. epidemiologist and supv. cent. sup., Pekin Memorial Hospital, Pekin, IL '83 (CS)
OLYARNIK, ROBIN D., mgt. eng., South Hills Health System, Pittsburgh, PA '84 (MGMT)
OLYNICK, MARY V., dir. vol. serv., Raleigh Community Hospital, Raleigh, NC '83 (VOL)
OMAR, EMRAN HASAN, MD, gen. mgr., Shama Health Developing Company, Ltd., Riyadh, Saudi Arabia '82
OMEL, JOHN C., vice-pres. human res., Good Samaritan Hospital and Health Center, Dayton, OH '82 (PERS)
OMER, LEASEL M., RN, vice-pres., Weigh to Go, Inc., Torrence, CA '76 (NURS)
OMERNIK, TODD A., dir. mktg., Hood General Hospital, Granbury, TX '86 (PLNG)
OMETER, JANE L., dir. diet. serv., Geisinger Medical Center, Danville, PA '84 (FOOD)
OMIECINSKI, CHESTER J., adm., South Oaks Hospital, Amityville, NY '64
OMLOR, NANCY J., RN, dir. nrsg. serv., Grandview Hospital and Medical Center, Dayton, OH '79 (EDUC)(NURS)
OMORI, M. SUZANNE, acct. exec., Miami Valley Hospital, Dayton, OH '86 (PR)
ONDOV, RAYMOND B., atty., St. Olaf Hospital, Austin, MN '78 (ATTY)
ONDRIZEK, SANDRA S., dir. food serv., Reading Rehabilitation Hospital, Reading, PA '80 (FOOD)
ONG, REBECCA L., mgr. vol. serv., Good Shepherd Hospital, Barrington, IL '86 (VOL)
ONIEAL, ROBERT M., vice-pres. support serv., St. Joseph's Hospital, Asheville, NC '86 (ENVIRON)
ONKS, JULIA T., pat. rep. and qual. assur. tech., Veterans Administration Medical Center, Mountain Home, TN '87 (PAT)
ONTOG, JANE PADULA, dir. human res., St. Joseph Hospital, Port Charlotte, FL '82 (PERS)
OOLEY, RONALD L., dir. human res., Charter Medical Corporation, Macon, GA '83 (PERS)
OOSTENBRUG, PAUL G., student, Boston University, School of Management, Boston, MA '85 (PLNG)
OOSTING, TIMOTHY M., staff arch., Lee Memorial Hospital, Fort Myers, FL '84 (PLNG)
OPALECKY, MARYGALE, RN, dir. nrsg., Loretto Hospital, Chicago, IL '77 (NURS)
OPATRNY, BETH A., coor. nrsg. educ., Wooster Community Hospital, Wooster, OH '84 (EDUC)
OPFAR, SUZANNE P., pat. rep., Somerset Community Hospital, Somerset, PA '83 (PAT)
OPFER, WILLIAM L. JR., pres., Medical Center of Dundalk, Baltimore, MD '80 (PLNG)
OPP, PAUL FRANKLIN JR., vice-pres. oper., Community Hospital of Ottawa, Ottawa, IL '62
OPPEL, JERALD J., atty., Sacred Heart Hospital, Cumberland, MD '82 (ATTY)
OPPENHEIMER, LARRY M., dir. proj. mgt., Hansen Lind Meyer, Chicago, IL '85
OPPER, ROBERTA, dir. soc. work, Henrico Doctor's Hospital, Richmond, VA '86 (SOC)
OPPERMAN, BERTA, dir. vol. and student serv., Medical Center of Delaware, Wilmington, DE '70 (VOL)
OPPERMANN, GUS J., IV, exec. dir. bus. affairs, University of Texas Medical Branch Hospitals, Galveston, TX '82
OPSTAD, ELWOOD A., exec. dir., Huntington Hospital, Huntington, NY '48 (LIFE)
ORBAN, BARBARA LANGLAND, asst. to dir., Shands Hospital, Gainesville, FL '83 (PLNG)
ORBAN, LOUIS J., dir. plng. and mktg., Halifax Hospital Medical Center, Daytona Beach, FL '79 (PLNG)
ORCUTT, GARY, dir. matl. mgt., Faulkner Hospital, Boston, MA '86 (PUR)
ORCUTT, STEVE G., asst. adm. oper., Mary Thompson Hospital, Chicago, IL '83 (PLNG)
ORDON, CHRISTINE M., dir. food serv., Moore Regional Hospital, Pinehurst, NC '69 (FOOD)
OREBAUGH, C., mgr. bldg. serv., St. Francis Regional Medical Center, Wichita, KS '81 (ENG)
OREFICE, JOHN, pres., J. J. O. Enterprises, Chicago, IL '77 (MGMT)
ORELLA, FRANCIS G., vice-pres. bldg. serv., St. Michael's Hospital, Stevens Point, WI '74 (PUR)
OREY, LON A., mgr. pers. serv., University of California San Diego Medical Center, San Diego, CA '83 (PERS)
ORFANON, EMANUEL V., natl. dir.-health care consult., Arthur Young and Company, Washington, DC '86
ORIDE, EDITH Y., supv. cent. sup. and oper. room, Kauai Veterans Memorial Hospital, Waimea, HI '82 (CS)
ORKIN, FREDERICK K., assoc. prof. anes., University of California San Francisco, San Francisco, CA '86
ORKINS, LAWRENCE G., dir. eng., Norwalk Hospital, Norwalk, CT '62 (ENG)
ORLANDO, ANTHONY P., dir. eng. and tech. serv., Desert Samaritan Hospital and Health Center, Mesa, AZ '85 (ENG)

ORLECK, JAN C., soc. work consult., Tennessee Hospital Association, Nashville, TN '86 (SOC)
ORLEY, EDWARD I., pres. and chief exec. off., Michigan Health Care Corporation, Detroit, MI '84
ORLOFF, DEBORAH M., corp. dir. commun. health prog., Harper Hospital, Detroit, MI '84 (EDUC)
ORLOWSKI, CAROLYN M., dir. nrsg. educ., Valley Children's Hospital, Fresno, CA '87 (EDUC)
ORME, CAROLYN B., dir. aux. serv., Leesburg Regional Medical Center, Leesburg, FL '86 (VOL)
ORME, THOBURN L., dir. eng., St. Francis Hospital Center, Beech Grove, IN '73 (ENG)
ORNDOFF, CHRISTIAN, dir. hskpg. and ldry., Memorial Hospital, Cumberland, MD '86 (ENVIRON)
ORNSTEEN, JEROME E., atty., Albert Einstein Medical Center, Philadelphia, PA '75 (ATTY)
ORNSTEIN, SHELDON, RN, dir. nrsg., Jewish Home and Hospital for Aged, New York, NY '80 (NURS)
ORODENKER, NORMAN G., atty., Miriam Hospital, Providence, RI '73 (ATTY)
OROPOLLO, MICHAEL B., atty., St. Peter's Medical Center, New Brunswick, NJ '80 (ATTY)
OROZCO, ANTONIO V., eng., Winslow Memorial Hospital, Winslow, AZ '82 (ENG)
OROZCO, DEBRA ROSAS, coor. soc. serv., Memorial General Hospital, Las Cruces, NM '85 (SOC)
ORR, AGNES B., student, New School of Social Research, Program in Health Care Administration, New York, NY '84
ORR, CORLETT, mgr. facil. programming, Stone, Merraccini and Patterson, St. Louis, MO '79 (PLNG)
ORR, DEBRA Y., dir. diet., Medical Center of Central Georgia, Macon, GA '86 (FOOD)
ORR, DIANE, supv. hskpg., HSA Heartland Hospital, Nevada, MO '86 (ENVIRON)
ORR, JEANNE W., RN, dir. risk mgt., St. Mary's Hospital, Richmond, VA '73 (RISK)
ORR, KAY N., RN, dir. nrsg.-reg. prog., Alexian Brothers Medical Center, Elk Grove Village, IL '84 (NURS)
ORR, PAM J., dir. pub. rel., Butler Memorial Hospital, Butler, PA '82 (PR)
ORREN, GUILDA, soc. worker, North Side Hospital, Johnson City, TN '84 (SOC)
ORSAK, PETER M., APO New York, NY '73
ORSATTI, LOUIS R., mgr. pur., St. Francis Hospital, Wilmington, DE '86 (PUR)
ORSBAN, ANN S., RN, vice-pres. pat. care serv., Spartanburg Regional Medical Center, Spartanburg, SC '82 (NURS)
ORSENA, JOANNE M., student, Department of Health Services Administration, George Washington University, Washington, DC '80
ORSETTI, GARY C., asst. dir., Hospital of the Holy Family, Brooklyn, NY '73
ORSHER, STUART, MD, atty., Gracie Square Hospital, New York, NY '84 (ATTY)
ORSO, CAMILLE L., dir. prog. analysis, Catherine McAuley Health Center, Ann Arbor, MI '84
ORTBALS, GERALD R., atty., Barnes Hospital, St. Louis, MO '83 (ATTY)
ORTEGA, J. ROBERT, prin., J. R. Ortega-Architect, Montgomery, AL '86 (ENG)
ORTENBERG, KAREN, student, Program in Health Systems Management, Tulane University, New Orleans, LA '84
ORTENZIO, ROBERT A., pres., Rehabilitation Hospital for Special Services, Camp Hill, PA '83 (ATTY)
ORTH, ALBERT M., dir. pers., St. Francis Hospital, Charleston, WV '84 (PERS)
ORTH, NORMAN P., dist. dir. environ. serv., Tri-City Medical Center, Oceanside, CA '86 (ENVIRON)
ORTHAUS, DENIS E., dir. pers., Sinai Hospital of Baltimore, Baltimore, MD '80 (PERS)
ORTIZ, ARTHUR P. JR., constr. mgr., Lovelace Medical Center, Albuquerque, NM '86 (ENG)
ORTIZ, HERNAN, supv. eng., Rio Grande Regional Hospital, McAllen, TX '87 (ENG)
ORTIZ, JAMES, reg. indust. hygienist, Hunter Holmes McGuire Veterans Administration Center, Richmond, VA '85 (ENG)
ORTIZ, JOHN P., dir. mgt. serv., St. Joseph Hospital, Houston, TX '81 (MGMT)
ORTIZ, MANUEL J., atty., Community Hospital, Anaconda, MT '82 (ATTY)
ORTMAN, CHARLES F., sr. mgt. eng., Heartland Health Systems, Inc., St. Joseph, MO '85 (MGMT)
ORTOLANI, PHILIP A., mgr. acct., Massachusetts Hospital Association, Burlington, MA '79 (MGMT)
ORTON, JANE O., dir. pat. rel., Medical Center at Bowling-Green, Bowling Green, KY '85 (SOC)
ORVEDAHL, DAVID H., chief soc. worker, Veterans Home of California, Yountville, CA '85 (SOC)
ORWIG, CHERIE, vice-pres. commun., Miami Valley Hospital, Dayton, OH '79 (PR)
ORWOLL, GREGG S. K., atty., Mayo Clinic, Rochester, MN '68 (ATTY)
OSBORN, ALMA P., dir. vol., Pike Community Hospital, Waverly, OH '69 (VOL)
OSBORN, BARBARA L., dir. vol. serv., Okmulgee Memorial Hospital Authority, Okmulgee, OK '86 (VOL)
OSBORN, BONNIE J., RN, dir. nrsg. serv., University of Texas Health Center at Tyler, Tyler, TX '81 (NURS)
OSBORN, CYNTHIA D., mgr., Ernst and Whinney, Detroit, MI '84 (MGMT)
OSBORN, LINDSAY T., student, Program and Bureau of Hospital Administration, University of Michigan, Ann Arbor, MI '83
OSBORN, LOUISE B., RN, vice-pres. pat. care serv., Tidewater Memorial Hospital, Tappahannock, VA '86 (NURS)
OSBORN, RICHARD, dir. risk mgt., East Pasco Medical Center, Zephyrhills, FL '85 (PERS)(RISK)
OSBORN, ROBERT F., supt. bldg. and grds., Schuyler Hospital, Montour Falls, NY '79 (ENG)
OSBORN, ROBYN A., dir. diet. serv., Decatur County Memorial Hospital, Greensburg, IN '86 (FOOD)
OSBORN, THOMAS M., pres., T. M. Osborn Associates, Inc., Gaithersburg, MD '75 (PLNG)
OSBORNE, ALBERT B. JR., Quakertown, PA '53 (LIFE)
OSBORNE, ART R., supv. pat. info.-enrollment, The Group Health Centre, Sault Ste Marie, Ont., Canada '81 (PR)
OSBORNE, BRUCE W., med. air and vacuum spec., Ittx Pneumotive, Monroe, LA '84 (ENG)
OSBORNE, DORIS I., mgr. commun. serv., Johns Hopkins Hospital, Baltimore, MD '84 (ENG)
OSBORNE, DREMA M., RN, dir. nrsg. serv., Highlands Regional Medical Center, Prestonsburg, KY '80 (NURS)
OSBORNE, ELAINE M., RN, assoc. nrs. in chief, Miriam Hospital, Providence, RI '83 (NURS)
OSBORNE, JAMES C., plant eng., Our Lady of the Way Hospital, Martin, KY '81 (ENG)
OSBORNE, RALPH W., constr. and proj. rep., Sutter Community Hospitals, Sacramento, CA '75 (ENG)
OSBORNE, TERRY W., dir. pers., American Legion Hospital, Crowley, LA '83 (PERS)
OSBORNE, ZEBULON L., atty., Waterman Medical Center, Eustis, FL '76 (ATTY)
OSBUN, RAYMOND JUSTUS, adm., F. Edward Hebert Hospital, New Orleans, LA '77
OSBURN, ED, dir. facil. and eng., Good Shepherd Hospital, Barrington, IL '87 (ENG)
OSGOOD, AL, plant eng., Winthrop Hospital, Winthrop, MA '85 (ENG)
OSGOOD, JOHN F., asst. dir. emp. rel., Frankford Hospital, Philadelphia, PA '76 (PERS)
OSGOOD, WINTHROP BANCROFT, MD, (ret.), Hollis, NH '38 (LIFE)
OSHEROW, PHYLIS ROSALIE, mgr. guest rel., St. Louis University Hospitals, St. Louis, MO '85 (PAT)
OSHIRO, ROBERT C., atty., Wahiawa General Hospital, Wahiawa, HI '71 (ATTY)
OSMAN, ADIL, dir. environ. serv., Henrico Doctor's Hospital, Richmond, VA '79 (ENVIRON)
OSMUS, RICHARD D., sr. vice-pres., Erlanger Medical Center, Chattanooga, TN '85
OSSMAN, ELLEN E., RN, dir. nrsg., Franklin Square Hospital, Baltimore, MD '86 (NURS)
OST, SANDRA K., dir. soc. serv., Herrick Memorial Hospital, Tecumseh, MI '82 (SOC)
OSTASIEWSKI, DONALD A., adj. asst. prof. and staff mem., Program in Community Health Plan Administration, University of Cincinnati, Cincinnati, OH '77
OSTASIEWSKI, PAUL P., Delta Group, Bellaire, OH '82 (PLNG)
OSTBY, SANDY J., adm. diet., Baptist Memorial Hospital, Memphis, TN '86 (FOOD)
OSTEEN, DEBBIE K., dir. mktg., The Bridgeway, North Little Rock, AR '85 (PR) (PLNG)
OSTER, JAMES C., atty., Childrens Hospital and Rehabilitation Center, Utica, NY '77 (ATTY)
OSTERMAN, LEANA, asst. adm., University Hospital, Seattle, WA '76 (RISK)
OSTERMAN, LISA E., coor. benefits, Washington Hospital, Fremont, CA '86 (PERS)
OSTMAN, PHYLLIS B., RN, assoc. dir. nrsg., Haverford Community Hospital, Havertown, PA '80 (NURS)
OSTNER, RUTH ELLEN, PhD, (ret.), Albany, NY '75 (EDUC)
OSTREICH, STEVEN B., consult. health care serv., Deloitte Haskins and Sells, Miami, FL '85 (PLNG)
OSTRO, HANS, asst. chief soc. work serv., Veterans Administration Medical Center, Martinez, CA '86 (SOC)
OSTROFF, MERYLE STEPHANIE, vice-pres., Episcopal Hospital, Philadelphia, PA '79 (PR) (PLNG)
OSTROW, LYNN C., RN, dir. nrsg., Silver Hill Foundation Hospital, New Canaan, CT '82 (NURS)
OSTROWSKY, BARBARA E., plng. asst., Newark Beth Israel Medical Center, Newark, NJ '84 (PLNG)
OSTWALD, RICHARD B., RN, vice-pres. nrsg., Wausau Hospital Center, Wausau, WI '86 (NURS)
OSTWALD, SUSAN L., dir. vol. serv., Faxton Hospital, Utica, NY '86 (VOL)
OSWALD, D. DUANE, chief exec. off., Kings View Hospital, Fresno, CA '87
OSWALD, EILEEN M., dir. risk mgt. and qual. assur., University of Chicago Hospitals, Chicago, IL '85 (RISK)
OSWALD, LYNN M., student, Xavier University, Graduate Program in Hospital and Health Administration, Cincinnati, OH '84
OSWALD, WILLIAM H., gen. counselor, Foster G. McGaw Hospital, Loyola University, Maywood, IL '73 (ATTY)
OSWALT, LARRY, dir. environ. serv., Baptist Medical Center, Little Rock, AR '86 (ENVIRON)
OSZUSTOWICZ, RICHARD, vice-pres. fin., Abbott-Northwestern Hospital, Minneapolis, MN '66
OTANEZ, HEATHER, RN, asst. dir. nrsg., Pacific Presbyterian Hospital, San Francisco, CA '82 (NURS)
OTEY, ELMER MILTON, dir. soc. serv., St. Mary's Hospital, East St. Louis, IL '86 (SOC)
OTHS, RICHARD PHILIP, vice-pres., American Health Capital, Inc., New York, NY '71
OTIS, DEBRA K., clin. instr. and pat. educ., Lykes Memorial Hospital, Brooksville, FL '87 (EDUC)
OTSTOT, ERIC F., dir. soc. serv., St. Joseph's Hospital, Parkersburg, WV '86 (SOC)
OTT, DAVID R., vice-pres., United Hospital Fund of New York, New York, NY '81
OTT, EUGENE J., vice-pres. prov. serv., Blue Cross of Greater Philadelphia, Philadelphia, PA '84
OTTAWAY, LARRY D., atty., Presbyterian Hospital, Oklahoma City, OK '82 (ATTY)
OTTERSTEDT, COL. CHARLES C. JR., MSC USA, dep. dir. health care oper., Office of the Surgeon General, Washington, DC '84
OTTO, CAROL E., RN, dir. pat. serv., New London Family Medical Center, New London, WI '74 (NURS)
OTTO, FRANK B., chief eng., Lykes Memorial Hospital, Brooksville, FL '82 (ENG)
OTTO, JERRY W., mgr. continuity care, Leila Hospital and Health Center, Battle Creek, MI '82 (SOC)
OTTO, MARGARET ANNE, dir. soc. serv., Clinicare Family Health Services, Kansas City, KS '84 (SOC)
OTTO, MARY K., dir. amb. serv., Bryn Mawr Rehabilitation Hospital, Malvern, PA '83
OTTO, OLNEY F., partner, Deloitte, Haskins and Sells, St. Louis, MO '84
OTTO, PATRICIA A., risk mgr., Allegheny General Hospital, Pittsburgh, PA '86 (RISK)
OTTO, PATRICIA E., dir. matl. mgt., Memorial Medical Center of West Michigan, Ludington, MI '86 (PUR)
OTTO, RUTH M., RN, coor. cent. serv., Larkin General Hospital, South Miami, FL '82 (CS)
OTTO, WILBUR M., atty., Presbyterian-University Hospital, Pittsburgh, PA '86 (ATTY)
OTTOBONI, JOHN M., atty., Alexian Brothers Hospital San Jose, San Jose, CA '80 (ATTY)
OUBRE', JAMES P., med. facil. planner, Oubre' Associates, Architects, New Orleans, LA '79 (PLNG)
OUDENS, GERALD F., prin., Oudens and Knoop, Architects and Planners, Washington, DC '76
OUELLET, L. JAMES, dir. per, University Community Hospital, Tamarac, FL '73 (PERS)
OUELLETT, JEANINE G., RN, dir. qual. assur. and risk mgt., Brockton Hospital, Brockton, MA '86 (NURS)
OUELLETTE, GERMAINE, pur. agt., Edmundston Regional Hospital, Edmundston, N.B., Canada '77 (PUR)
OUELLETTE, JANE N., RN, asst. dir. nrsg., University of Virginia Hospitals, Charlottesville, VA '86 (EDUC)(NURS)
OUELLETTE, PHILIPPE W. JR., vice-pres. adm., Brandywine Hospital, Caln Township, PA '76
OUELLETTE, RICHARD ALAN, adm. dir. lab., Burbank Hospital, Fitchburg, MA '81
OUIMETTE, ANNE MARIE, mgt. eng., Baystate Health Management Services, Inc., Springfield, MA '85 (MGMT)
OULTON, RICHARD J., vice-pres., Virginia Hospital Insurance Reciprocal, Glen Allen, VA '74 (ATTY)(RISK)
OUNSWORTH, JAMES A., atty., Hahnemann University Hospital, Philadelphia, PA '83 (ATTY)
OURACH, LINDA M., Wayne, PA '84 (EDUC)
OUTHOUSE, CYNTHIA L., pub. rel. asst., Tobey Hospital, Wareham, MA '86 (PR)
OUTLAW, SHEILA I., dir. pers., Rappahannock General Hospital, Kilmarnock, VA '81 (PERS)
OUTTEN, MARY CORNELIA, student, Tulane University, School of Public Health and Tropical Medicine, New Orleans, LA '83
OUTTEN, RALPH L., exec. adv., South Side Hospital of Pittsburgh, Pittsburgh, PA '49 (LIFE)
OVER, DAIN, mgr. pur., Easton Hospital, Easton, PA '84 (PUR)
OVERBY, JANICE, dir. food serv., Rapid City Regional Hospital, Rapid City, SD '74 (FOOD)
OVERBY, LISA, dir. soc. work, St. Paul Medical Center, Dallas, TX '85 (SOC)
OVERBY, ROBERT, dir. risk mgt., safety and security, Welborn Memorial Baptist Hospital, Evansville, IN '85 (RISK)
OVERFELT, FRANK C., mng. partner, International Health Care Consultant Group, Salt Lake City, UT '80 (MGMT)
OVERLA, CAPT. MARILOU DORIS, MSC USA, chief serv., Letterman Army Medical Center, San Francisco, CA '86 (PUR)
OVERMAN, LINDA, supv. pur., Wyoming Medical Center, Casper, WY '86 (PUR)
OVERSTREET, CHARLES WALKER, sr. vice-pres., SunHealth Corporation, Charlotte, NC '71 (MGMT)
OVERSTREET, GARY F., atty., California Association of Hospitals & Health Systems, Sacramento, CA '80 (ATTY)
OVERVAAG, DONNA, RN, asst. adm., Dell Rapids Community Hospital, Dell Rapids, SD '81 (NURS)
OVIATT, VINSON R., coor. prog., Special Program on Safety Measures in Microbiology, World Health Organization, Division of Communicable Diseases, Geneve, Switzerland '66 (ENG)
OWEN, CATHERINE E., mgr., Ernst and Whinney, Baltimore, MD '80 (MGMT)
OWEN, DAVID A., rad. eng., University of Iowa Hospitals and Clinics, Iowa City, IA '78 (ENG)
OWEN, JACK W., American Hospital Association, Washington, DC '82 (LIFE)
OWEN, MARY H., mgr. commun. rel. and vol., St. Vincent Stress Center, Inc., Indianapolis, IN '83 (PR)(VOL)
OWEN, MARY WELSH, mgr. diet. serv., Hospital Corporation of America, Nashville, TN '86 (FOOD)
OWEN, RIPLEY P., adm., Bath County Community Hospital, Hot Springs, VA '83 (PLNG)(RISK)
OWEN, ROBERT P., asst. vice-pres. pers., Mercy Hospitals of Kansas, Independence, KS '85 (PERS)
OWEN, RONALD L., dir. plant serv., Olathe Medical Center, Olathe, KS '80 (ENG)
OWEN, RONALD S., assoc. adm., Huntsville Hospital, Huntsville, AL '73
OWEN, SR. RUTH, pat. rep., United Hospital Center, Clarksburg, WV '81 (PAT)
OWEN, VALERIE A., mgt. eng., SunHealth Corporation, Charlotte, NC '86 (MGMT)
OWENS, ARLENE A., dir. mgt. trng., King's Daughters Hospital, Temple, TX '86 (EDUC)
OWENS, DAVID LEE, asst. dir. environ. serv., Saint Luke's Hospital, Cleveland, OH '86 (ENVIRON)
OWENS, HARRY S., assoc. exec. dir. fin. affairs, Thomas Jefferson University Hospital, Philadelphia, PA '76
OWENS, HELENA, mgr. discharge plan, St. John's Healthcare Corporation, Anderson, IN '86 (SOC)
OWENS, JAMES FRANKLIN, atty., Grady Memorial Hospital, Atlanta, GA '87 (ATTY)
OWENS, MARGARET L., adm. pat. serv., Scripps Clinic, La Jolla, CA '79 (RISK)
OWENS, MARILYN, risk mgr., Washington Hospital Center, Washington, DC '80 (RISK)

OWENS, PATRICIA S., RN, nrs. adm., Mesa Lutheran Hospital, Mesa, AZ '84 (NURS)
OWENS, PHYLLIS J., vice-pres. nrsg., Bethesda Hospital, Zanesville, OH '83
OWENS, RICHARD R., dir. mgt. eng., Tri-City Medical Center, Oceanside, CA '85 (MGMT)
OWENS, STEVEN O., atty., Loudoun Memorial Hospital, Leesburg, VA '86 (ATTY)
OWENS, SUSAN S., dir. soc. serv. and pat. care, Doctors Hospital, Tucker, GA '80 (SOC)(PAT)
OWENS, WILLIAM DAVID JR., Port Arthur, TX '47 (LIFE)
OWREY, ROSALIE, dir. soc. serv., Princeton Community Hospital, Princeton, WV '79 (SOC)
OXENDALE, SHARON J., asst. dir. plng., Lancaster General Hospital, Lancaster, PA '82 (PLNG)
OXLEY, JOANN V., dir. commun. rel., Burdette Tomlin Memorial Hospital, Cape May Court House, NJ '80 (PR)
OZA, RAJESH C., prog. analyst, Worth, Auger and Associates, Oakland, CA '87 (MGMT)
OZINGA, SUZANNE, RN, vice-pres. prof. serv., Crittenton Hospital, Rochester, MI '73 (NURS)
OZOG, JUDITH G., RN, dir. nrsg. serv., Bath Memorial Hospital, Bath, ME '87 (NURS)

P

PAAP, ANTONIE HERBERT, pres. and chief exec. off., Children's Hospital Medical Center of Northern California, Oakland, CA '68 (ATTY)
PACCAPANICCIA, DOMINIC, mgr. emp. rel., Our Lady of Lourdes Medical Center, Camden, NJ '85 (PERS)
PACE, DONALD W., dir. food serv., Motion Picture and Television Hospital, Woodland Hills, CA '81 (FOOD)
PACE, HARLAN E., asst. dir. diet., Edgewater Hospital, Chicago, IL '81 (FOOD)
PACE, LINDA, RN, asst. dir. nrsg.-critical care, Muscatine General Hospital, Muscatine, IA '86 (NURS)
PACE, MARY A., pat. advocate, University Hospital, Jackson, MS '85 (PAT)
PACERA, JOSEPH A., vice-pres. prog. dev. and mktg., Osteopathic Medical Center of Philadelphia, Philadelphia, PA '79 (PLNG)
PACETTI, MADISON F., atty., Good Samaritan Hospital, West Palm Beach, FL '68 (ATTY)
PACIOUS, MARY ANNE, student, Duke University, Department of Health Administration, Durham, NC '82
PACK, CAROL J., dir. soc. serv., St. Vincent Medical Center, Toledo, OH '81 (SOC)
PACK, MARIANNE, dir. food serv., Houston Northwest Medical Center, Houston, TX '79 (FOOD)
PACKARD, DAVID W., atty., Mercy Medical Center, Redding, CA '71 (ATTY)
PACKARD, JAMES L., vice-pres. plng. and mktg., Mercy Hospital, Grayling, MI '84 (PLNG)
PACKARD, KAREN L., dir. mktg., University Hospital Consortium, Inc., Oakbrook Terrace, IL '85 (PLNG)
PACKARD, ROBERTA S., RN, dir. nrsg., Gulf Coast Medical Center, Wharton, TX '86 (NURS)
PACKARD, SUE A., dir. soc. serv., Grady Memorial Hospital, Delaware, OH '77 (SOC)
PACKER-FREEBORG, ALICE S., RN, vice-pres. nrsg., St. Joseph's Hospital, Marshfield, WI '82 (NURS)
PACKER, KATHLEEN P., RN, dir. qual. assur., Munson Medical Center, Traverse City, MI '78 (RISK)
PACKNETT, THUSTON L., dir. food serv., Saint Joseph Health Center Kansas, Kansas City, MO '81 (FOOD)
PADDEN, TERRANCE J., dir. nrsg. serv., Okmulgee Memorial Hospital Authority, Okmulgee, OK '76
PADEK, CHARLOTTE, trustee, Mount Sinai Medical Center, Miami Beach, FL '85
PADGETT, CHARLES E., vice-pres. plng. and dev., Lexington County Hospital, West Columbia, SC '79 (PLNG)
PADGETT, DEBRA L., dir. pers., HCA Andalusia Hospital, Andalusia, AL '86 (PERS)
PADGETT, MARY, dir. diet., Rehabilitation Institute, Detroit, MI '80 (FOOD)
PADGHAM, DANIEL R., adm. res., U. S. Naval Hospital, FPO Seattle, WA '85
PADILLA, ANTONIO A., chief exec. off., Oklahoma Teaching Hospitals, Oklahoma City, OK '72
PADILLA, GILBERT R., mgr. biomedical eng., Southwest Community Health Services, Albuquerque, NM '86 (ENG)
PADILLA, JOE, mgr. hskpg., Fresno Community Hospital and Medical Center, Fresno, CA '86 (ENVIRON)
PADNOS, DONNA M., adm. asst., Glen Ellyn Clinic, Glen Ellyn, IL '82 (PLNG)
PADOVANI, GREGORY A., dir. mktg., Northwestern Medical Faculty Foundation, Chicago, IL '78 (PR)
PAE, JANICE B., adm. asst., Emerald Health Network, Inc., Cleveland, OH '86
PAEN, BETTY HAZEN, dir. vol., United Hospital, Port Chester, NY '79 (VOL)
PAER, ANDREW B., student, Baruch College, New York, NY '85
PAESE, THOMAS G., corp. counsel, Rehabilitation Hospital Services Corporation, Camp Hill, PA '86
PAETH-HAAS, BARBARA, coor. vol. serv., Douglas Community Hospital, Roseburg, OR '86 (VOL)
PAFUNDI, TED J., dir. pers., Tarpon Springs General Hospital, Tarpon Springs, FL '85 (PERS)
PAGANO, ANN MARIE, dir. med. and surg. nrsg., Bon Secours Hospital, Grosse Pointe, MI '87 (AMB)
PAGANO, JOHN E., asst. dir. food serv., Waterbury Hospital, Waterbury, CT '82 (FOOD)
PAGANO, MARIA, vice-pres. pat. serv., Freehold Area Hospital, Freehold, NJ '87 (AMB)
PAGANO, RAYMOND M., asst. vice-pres. pers., Overlook Hospital, Summit, NJ '86 (PERS)
PAGE, B. BERNICE, dir. vol., Riddle Memorial Hospital, Media, PA '79 (VOL)
PAGE, DEAN R., adm. asst., C. F. Menninger Memorial Hospital, Topeka, KS '84 (RISK)
PAGE, FLORENE, RN, chief nrsg. serv., Veterans Administration Medical Center, Alexandria, LA '83 (NURS)
PAGE, GEORGE P., dir. diet., Kenmore Mercy Hospital, Kenmore, NY '74 (FOOD)
PAGE, JACQUELYN L., RN, student, Program in Health Care Administration, National University, San Diego, CA '86
PAGE, JEANETTE S., dir. vol. serv., Baptist Medical Center, Columbia, SC '78 (VOL)
PAGE, JERRY A., dir. meth., Community Health Systems, Jasper, AL '73 (MGMT)
PAGE, JOHN A., dir. mgt. eng., University Hospital-University of Nebraska, Omaha, NE '82 (MGMT)
PAGE, KATHRYN, dir. cent. serv., St. Francis Hospital, Charleston, WV '83 (CS)
PAGE, KEITH ALLEN, vice-pres., Alexian Brothers Medical Center, Elk Grove Village, IL '81
PAGE, LYLE M., atty., Biloxi Regional Medical Center, Biloxi, MS '75 (ATTY)
PAGE, PATTI J., coor. pub. rel., Hinds General Hospital, Jackson, MS '83 (PR)
PAGE, ROBERT G., chief maint., Barnes-Kasson County Hospital, Susquehanna, PA '81 (ENG)
PAGE, ROSEWELL III, atty., Johnston-Willis Hospital, Richmond, VA '77 (ATTY)
PAGEL, PAUL R., dir. soc. and commun. serv., Maimonides Medical Center, Brooklyn, NY '71 (SOC)
PAGEL, ROSEMARIE B., res. eval. analyst, Samaritan Health Service, Phoenix, AZ '83 (MGMT)
PAGLIA, CELESTE, plng. and mktg. spec., Emerson Hospital, Concord, MA '86 (PLNG)
PAGLIARINI, ANN M., RN, adm. surg. nrsg., John E. Fogarty Memorial Hospital, North Smithfield, RI '77 (NURS)(EDUC)(AMB)
PAGLIARO, ANTHONY PETER, adm., Summit Convalescent and Nursing Home, Lakewood, NJ '63
PAGLIARO, BELINDA, asst. dir. food, Valley Hospital Medical Center, Van Nuys, CA '86 (FOOD)
PAGLIARO, MICHAEL, vice-pres. and dir. pers., White Plains Hospital Medical Center, White Plains, NY '86 (PERS)
PAGOTELIS, JESSE JEAN, mgr. soc. work, Good Samaritan Hospital, Downers Grove, IL '77 (SOC)
PAIGE, ALFRED G. JR., dir. cent. sup. serv., Lawrence Memorial Hospital of Medford, Medford, MA '81 (CS)
PAINE, BARBARA A. BERTZOLD, adm. diet., St. Mary's Hospital, Centralia, IL '79 (FOOD)
PAINE, RALPH A., Birmingham, AL '83 (PERS)
PAINE, ROBERT A., dir. plng., Memorial Hospital, Ormond Beach, FL '83 (PLNG)
PAINTER, ARIS A., RN, asst. adm., Mount Hood Medical Center, Gresham, OR '77 (NURS)
PAINTER, DONALD A., vice-pres. facil. oper., Henry County Memorial Hospital, New Castle, IN '79 (ENG)
PAINTER, FRANK R., dir. biomedical eng., Bridgeport Hospital, Bridgeport, CT '83 (ENG)
PAINTER, JOHN VALDO, exec. vice-pres., DePaul Corporation, Washington, DC '65 (PLNG)(RISK)
PAINTER, SARA A., RN, vice-pres. pat. care serv., Good Samaritan Hospital, Pottsville, PA '82 (NURS)
PAIVANAS, THOMAS, planner, Alexandria Hospital, Alexandria, VA '82 (PLNG)
PAJU, JOHN A., pres., Worldwide Anesthesia Associates, Inc., Ukiah, CA '82
PAKAN, RICHARD A., pres., North Shore Medical Center, Miami, FL '86
PAKE, PHYLLIS J., dir. vol., Medcenter One, Bismarck, ND '86 (VOL)
PAKSTIS, LEE, head soc. serv., Melrose-Wakefield Hospital, Melrose, MA '84 (SOC)
PALAGI, RICHARD L., pres., Prism Consulting, Nampa, ID '78 (PR)
PALANDRANI, POLLY J., coor. customer pat. rel., Twin City Hospital, Dennison, OH '86 (PAT)
PALANZO, RICHARD M., mgr. eng. adm., Danbury Hospital, Danbury, CT '86 (ENVIRON)
PALASZESKI, LYNN, St. Joseph Hospital, Flint, MI '84
PALENCAR, WILLIAM, dir. eng., Our Lady of Lourdes Memorial Hospital, Binghamton, NY '81 (ENG)
PALENGAT, KAREN, dir. risk mgt. serv. and corp. rel., St. Mary's Hospital and Medical Center, San Francisco, CA '85 (RISK)
PALEOLOGOS, JAMES P., mgr., Gerald J. Sullivan and Associates of Arizona, Inc., Phoenix, AZ '81 (RISK)(AMB)
PALERMINO, BEVERLY ANN, pat. rep., St. Joseph Hospital West, Mount Clemens, MI '80 (PAT)
PALESTRO, RICHARD, dir. plant serv., National Jewish Center, Denver, CO '82 (ENG)
PALEY, RENEE E., coor. commun. rel., Community Hospital at Glen Cove, Glen Cove, NY '85 (PR)
PALLEN, MICHAEL S., dir. matl. mgt., St. Michael Hospital, Milwaukee, WI '69 (PUR)
PALLERA, NENE A., RN, assoc. dir. nrsg., Brookline Hospital, Brookline, MA '86 (NURS)
PALLESEN, CHARLES M. JR., atty., St. Elizabeth Community Health Center, Lincoln, NE '72 (ATTY)
PALLESEN, JEAN A., dir. vol. serv., St. Joseph Center for Mental Health, Omaha, NE '82 (VOL)
PALLEY, JONATHAN, coor. soc. serv., Washington Hospital, Fremont, CA '86 (SOC)
PALLIN, ARISTIDES, mgt. eng., Mercy Hospital, Miami, FL '86 (MGMT)
PALMA, LAVAUGHN M., dir. mktg., Blodgett Memorial Medical Center, Grand Rapids, MI '86 (PLNG)
PALMA, SUSAN G., dir. vol. serv., Mountainside Hospital, Montclair, NJ '86 (VOL)
PALMA, THOMAS V., dir. commun., United Way of Wyandotte County, Kansas City, KS '86 (PR)
PALMARO, JACK C., mgr. rehab. serv., Overlook Hospital, Summit, NJ '83
PALMATIER, CHARLENE S., RN, dir. nrs., A. Lindsey and O. B. O'Connor Hospital, Delhi, NY '86 (NURS)
PALMER, ALAN W., dir. mktg. and commun. rel., HCA Greenview Hospital, Bowling Green, KY '81 (PR)
PALMER, ARTHUR G., dir. mgt. serv., Tucson Medical Center, Tucson, AZ '84 (MGMT)
PALMER, AUGUSTUS, asst. to vice-pres.-health affairs, Howard University Hospital, Washington, DC '86 (RISK)
PALMER, BARBARA ANN, dir. staff serv., Henry Ford Hospital, Detroit, MI '83 (PERS)
PALMER, BARBARA J., dir. soc. serv., United Hospital Center, Clarksburg, WV '79 (SOC)
PALMER, BETSEY F., asst. dir. vol. serv., Waterbury Hospital, Waterbury, CT '85 (VOL)
PALMER, CAROL A., supv. soc. work, Barnes Hospital, St. Louis, MO '84 (SOC)
PALMER, CRAIG J., chief exec. off., Reproductive Medicine Consultant, Minneapolis, MN '85 (RISK)
PALMER, DAUNE M., dir. commun. rel., Brooks Memorial Hospital, Dunkirk, NY '81 (PR)
PALMER, DEBRA L., coor. staff dev., Medical Center Hospital, Chillicothe, OH '82 (EDUC)
PALMER, EVELYN B., Troy, NY '73 (SOC)
PALMER, G. BRADFORD JR., atty., Waterbury Hospital, Waterbury, CT '68 (ATTY)
PALMER, GARRY D., eng., Mount Druitt Hospital, Sydney, Australia '85 (ENG)
PALMER, GREG, adm., Medical Center South, Broadview Heights, OH '87
PALMER, JANA SEALE, pat. rep., Rankin General Hospital, Brandon, MS '85 (PAT)
PALMER, JASON R., coor. media and advertising, Mercy Center for Health Care Services, Aurora, IL '86 (PR)
PALMER, JUDIE, asst. dir. cent. sterile sup., University Hospital of Arkansas, Little Rock, AR '83 (CS)
PALMER, KATHLEEN W., mgr. pur., Ohio Valley Medical Center, Wheeling, WV '85 (PUR)
PALMER, KATHRYN, assoc. adm. risk mgt., Provident Medical Center, Chicago, IL '86 (RISK)
PALMER, KENNETH MARTIN, asst. adm., Memorial Hospital, Clarksville, TN '68
PALMER, KRISTIN E., RN, dir., Mercy Health Center, Oklahoma City, OK '87 (AMB)
PALMER, LINDA T., RN, dir. nrsg., Daniel Freeman Marina Hospital, Marina Del Rey, CA '86 (NURS)
PALMER, MARY E., RN, dir. nrsg. serv., Beverly Hospital, Beverly, MA '72 (NURS)
PALMER, PETER H., mgr. matl., Morristown Memorial Hospital, Morristown, NJ '81 (PUR)
PALMER, PHIL, chief exec. off., G. N. Wilcox Memorial Hospital, Lihue, HI '76 (PLNG)
PALMER, 2ND LT. RONALD E., MSC USAF, Biloxi, MS '82
PALMER, SARAH E., prog. analyst, Determination of Need Program, Boston, MA '86 (PLNG)
PALMER, SCOTT C., dir. mktg., plng. and dev., Mount Hood Medical Center, Gresham, OR '85 (PLNG)
PALMER, THOMAS T., atty., Roanoke Memorial Hospitals, Roanoke, VA '85 (ATTY)
PALMER, WARD B., asst. mgr. matl. distrib., Danbury Hospital, Danbury, CT '86 (PUR)
PALMER, WILLIAM E. SR., atty., Arnot-Ogden Memorial Hospital, Elmira, NY '74 (ATTY)
PALMERO, FRANCISCO J., assoc., Herman Smith Associates, Redwood City, CA '83 (ENG)
PALMISANO, PAUL V., dir. pers., Saint Joseph Hospital, Denver, CO '71 (PERS)
PALMOUR, FRANK M., atty., South Seminole Community Hospital, Longwood, FL '84 (ATTY)
PALMQUIST, JEANNE M., student, Program in Hospital and Hlthcare Administration, University of Minnesota, Minneapolis, MN '87
PALSMEIER, SR. TERESA, dir. vol. serv., St. Mary's Hospital, Enid, OK '73 (VOL)
PAMBIANCHI, WAYNE, vice-pres., Fritzche Pambianchi and Assocs, Inc., Somerville, NJ '84
PAMPERIN, JOHN CHARLES, dir. environ. serv., St. Francis Hospital Systems, Colorado Springs, CO '85 (ENG)
PAMPHILIS, THEODORA M., coor. health educ. and off. educ. res., St. Luke's Episcopal Hospital, Houston, TX '86 (EDUC)
PANAS, CDR BRUCE RICHARD, MSC USN, exec. off., Naval Hospital, Lemoore, CA '70 (FOOD)(RISK)
PANCZYKOWSKI, CARLA, RN, clin. dir. nrsg., Frank Cuneo Memorial Hospital, Chicago, IL '86 (NURS)
PANDELARAS, CONSTANTINE, dir. info. serv., Suburban Hospital, Bethesda, MD '86 (MGMT)
PANDL, THERESE B., RN, vice-pres. in-patient serv., St. Mary's Hospital, Milwaukee, WI '86 (NURS)
PANDOLFO, ANTHONY, adm. dir. emer. serv., Montefiore Medical Center, Bronx, NY '81
PANDOLFO, JEANETTE B., dir. vol., Westchester County Medical Center, Valhalla, NY '83 (VOL)
PANDORA, FRANK T. II, atty., Riverside Methodist Hospitals, Columbus, OH '79 (ATTY)
PANDORF, WALTER, dir. plant oper., New York Hospital, Westchester Division, White Plains, NY '83 (ENG)
PANE, THERESA E., dir. ob. and gyn., St. Joseph Hospital, Orange, CA '85 (NURS)
PANEBAKER, SUSAN P., supv. clin. soc. work, Geisinger Medical Center, Danville, PA '72 (SOC)
PANEK, RICHARD K., asst. vice-pres., Johnston Memorial Hospital, Smithfield, NC '84 (RISK)
PANG, CATHERINE Y. H., San Antonio, TX '83
PANG, SLEW M., student, Nepean College of Advance Education, Sydney Nsw, Australia '86 (MGMT)
PANGBORN, KAREN M., RN, dir. maternal and child nrsg., St. Margaret Hospital, Hammond, IN '82 (NURS)
PANGBORN, VERNE A., dir. hosp. and med. facil., Nebraska State Department of Health, Lincoln, NE '33 (LIFE)
PANICO, JOANN, student, University of Connecticut, Program in Health Systems Management, Storrs, CT '82 (MGMT)

PANKAN, BETTY A., adm. dir. emp. rel. and educ., Mercy Hospital, Urbana, IL '86 (EDUC)
PANKAU, BARBARA, atty., University Community Hospital, Tampa, FL '82 (ATTY)
PANKAU, ELIZABETH, dir. emp. rel., Mercy Hospital, Urbana, IL '79 (PERS)
PANKAU, JOSEPH W., PhD, White Heath, IL '77 (EDUC)
PANKRATZ, DENNIS L., dir. health serv., Swedishamerican Hospital, Rockford, IL '73
PANKRATZ, JOSIE A., coor. educ., St. Luke Hospital, Marion, KS '87 (EDUC)
PANLILIO, SALUD GUIA P., student, Case Western Reserve University, Cleveland, OH '86 (MGMT)
PANSA, LEONARD F., dir. pers., Nashua Memorial Hospital, Nashua, NH '77 (PERS)
PANTOJAS, PURA, RN, dep. dir. nrsg., University Hospital, Stony Brook, NY '86 (NURS)
PANZARELLA, CAROLINE L., student, Program in Health Administration, Columbia University School of Public Health, New York, NY '84
PANZER, HERBERT, vice-pres. and chief sanitary eng., Syska and Hennessy, New York, NY '81 (ENG)
PANZIRONI, RICHARD J., adm. assoc., Ohio State University Hospitals, Columbus, OH '86 (PLNG)
PAOLINI, N. VINCENT, dir. pers., Human Resource Institute, Brookline, MA '67 (PERS)
PAPALE, GEORGE M., atty., West Jefferson Medical Center, Marrero, LA '79 (ATTY)
PAPARELLA, CATHERINE A., RN, assoc. dir. nrsg. serv., Worcester Memorial Hospital, Worcester, MA '80 (NURS)
PAPE, PAUL A., mgr. food serv., Norman Regional Hospital, Norman, OK '75 (FOOD)
PAPELEUX, PATTI, risk mgr., University of California Davis Medical Center, Sacramento, CA '85 (RISK)
PAPENHAUSEN, ELVIN H., dir. plant oper., Fairview Princeton Hospital, Princeton, MN '81 (ENG)
PAPENHAUSEN, FREDERICK P., mgr. plant serv., Wayne Hospital, Greenville, OH '83 (ENG)
PAPER, RAYMOND, dir. diet., Doctors General Hospital, Plantation, FL '85 (FOOD)
PAPES, LUCILLE M., dir. soc. serv., Community Memorial Hospital, Marysville, KS '75 (SOC)
PAPESH, JERRY, dir. environ. serv., Health Hill Hospital for Children, Cleveland, OH '87 (ENG)
PAPILION, JULIANA, exec. hskpr., Temple Community Hospital, Los Angeles, CA '87 (ENVIRON)
PAPIT, HENRY U., dir. emp. rel., Pennsylvania Hospital, Philadelphia, PA '64 (PERS)
PAPLACZYK, DOUGLAS S., mgr. acct. and media rel., Miami Valley Hospital, Dayton, OH '81 (PR)
PAPLOW, JOHN E., (ret.), Ojai, CA '49 (LIFE)
PAPOLA, JOSEPH, vice-pres. human res., Valley Hospital, Ridgewood, NJ '72 (PERS)
PAPP, JAMES M., dir. pers., Clearfield Hospital, Clearfield, PA '83 (PERS)
PAPPAS, CHRISTINE A., RN, vice-pres. nrsg., Memorial Medical Center, Long Beach, CA '77 (NURS)
PAPPAS, JAMES J., dir. food serv., Nash General Hospital, Rocky Mount, NC '68 (FOOD)
PAPPAS, PETER C., Cleveland Heights, OH '82
PAPPELIS, RUTH W., dir. vol. serv., Lenox Hill Hospital, New York, NY '71 (VOL)
PAQUETTE, WALTER, dir. commun. rel., Sacred Heart Hospital, Norristown, PA '80 (PR)
PARADIS, PHILIP, dir. plant serv., Newton-Wellesley Hospital, Newton, MA '85 (ENG)
PARCELLS, C. WILLIAM, asst. dir., William Beaumont Hospital, Royal Oak, MI '74 (ENG)
PARCHMAN, YVONNE MORR, dir. vol. serv., St. Elizabeth Medical Center-North, Covington, KY '74 (VOL)(PAT)
PARCO, BOB, asst. dir. plant oper., Charter Community Hospital, Hawaiian Gardens, CA '85 (ENG)
PARDEE, GEORGANN HAYES, dir. food serv., Elmhurst Memorial Hospital, Elmhurst, IL '70 (FOOD)
PARDEN, ALFRED A. JR., vice-pres. fin., Southern Baptist Hospital, New Orleans, LA '85
PARDINI, ULISSE C., vice-pres. plng. and dev., Health Systems Group, Vancouver, WA '82 (PLNG)
PARDO, BRUCE, dir. emp. rel., New York University Medical Center, New York, NY '81 (PERS)
PARDO, JOHN, dir. eng., Stamford Hospital, Stamford, CT '76 (ENG)
PARDO, RALPH, dir. pur., Pontiac General Hospital, Pontiac, MI '79 (PUR)
PARDON, CHARLES D., dir. manpower and educ., Missouri Hospital Association, Jefferson City, MO '78 (EDUC)
PARDUE, WILLIAM M., dir. matl. mgt., Florida Keys Memorial Hospital, Key West, FL '86 (PUR)
PARE, ANN K., dir. food serv., Melrose-Wakefield Hospital, Melrose, MA '86 (FOOD)
PAREDES, JOSEPH R., sr. vice-pres. health plan network syst., International Medical Centers, Miami, FL '83 (PLNG)
PAREIGIS, JOYCE ANN, RN, vice-pres., St. Thomas Hospital, Nashville, TN '75 (NURS)
PARENT, PAULA, supv. cent. sup., St. Mary's Hospital, Waterbury, CT '77 (CS)
PARENT, SANDRA LEE, dir. soc. serv., Hunt Memorial Hospital, Danvers, MA '68 (SOC)
PARENTE, WILLIAM D., pres., Glendale Memorial Hospital and Health Center, Glendale, CA '84
PARET, CAROL JO, mgr. facil. and commun. health plng., Memorial Care Systems, Houston, TX '83 (PLNG)
PARGULSKI, JOSEPH A., asst. dir. data proc., Ancilla Systems, Inc., Elk Grove Village, IL '71 (MGMT)
PARILLO, BARBARA V., dir. vol. serv., Rhode Island Hospital, Providence, RI '77 (VOL)(PAT)
PARIMUCHA, JOSEPH P., vice-pres., Menningson, Durham and Richardson, Omaha, NE '87
PARIS, EARL, chief eng., Cole Hospital, Champaign, IL '82 (ENG)
PARIS, HERBERT, adm., Regional Memorial Hospital, Brunswick, ME '79
PARIS, KATHERINE F., dir. vol. serv., Healthsouth, Humble, TX '86 (VOL)
PARIS, LOUIS T., dir. emp. rel., Park Ridge Hospital, Rochester, NY '81 (PERS)
PARISO, PHILIP P., owner, Pariso Consulting Services, Buffalo, NY '82 (ENG)
PARK, BEVERLY G., dir. office of pub. info., University of Connecticut Health Center, John Dempsey Hospital, Farmington, CT '85 (PR)
PARK, DOROTHY ANN, RN, assoc. adm. hosp. serv., Straub Clinic and Hospital, Honolulu, HI '80 (NURS)
PARKAR, KHALIL DAWOOD, MD, med. adv., Rk Nursing Home and Iccu, Bombay-55, India '86 (PLNG)
PARKE, VERDIA, RN, dir. nrsg. serv., Morgan County Memorial Hospital, Martinsville, IN '86 (NURS)
PARKER-COOK, NANCY E., student, University of Connecticut, Hartford, CT '87 (AMB)
PARKER, ANNE B., exec. dir., Charter Hospital of Tucson, Tucson, AZ '84
PARKER, ANNE E., RN, dir. amb., surg. and psych. nrsg., Choate-Symmes Hospitals, Woburn, MA '80 (NURS)(AMB)
PARKER, BARBARA KEEVIL, PhD, Lilburn, GA '79 (EDUC)
PARKER, BARRY WAYNE, vice-pres. commun. rel., Hamilton Medical Center, Dalton, GA '81 (PR)
PARKER, BERNARD R., dir. plant and grds., Homer D. Cobb Memorial Hospital, Phenix City, AL '76 (ENG)
PARKER, CAROL T., dir. pub. rel. and mktg., Habersham County Medical Center, Demorest, GA '86 (PR)
PARKER, CAROLINE E. JONES, RN, assoc. adm. nrsg., Children's Hospital of Michigan, Detroit, MI '78 (NURS)
PARKER, CHARLES R., atty., Lifemark Corporation, Houston, TX '82 (ATTY)
PARKER, CHARLES, dir. bldg. serv., Richland Parish Hospital-Rayville, Rayville, LA '85 (ENG)
PARKER, DAVID W., PhD, pres., Parker Productions, Inc., Los Altos Hills, CA '86 (PAT)
PARKER, DAVID W., adm., American Red Cross Blood Services, Central California Region, San Jose, CA '79
PARKER, DIANA D., Encino, CA '76
PARKER, ELIZABETH A., pat. rep., Licking Memorial Hospital, Newark, OH '85 (PAT)
PARKER, ELLEN, asst. dir. soc. serv., New England Medical Center, Boston, MA '82 (SOC)
PARKER, FRED, adm. eng., Good Samaritan Hospital, San Jose, CA '78 (ENG)
PARKER, GENE H., pur. agt., St. Ann's Hospital of Columbus, Westerville, OH '70 (PUR)
PARKER, HANNA B., dir. med. soc. work, Tuomey Hospital, Sumter, SC '82 (SOC)
PARKER, HARVEY L., dir. pers., Heartland Hospital East, St. Joseph, MO '82 (PERS)
PARKER, JANE M., pat. rep., Goddard Memorial Hospital, Stoughton, MA '86 (PAT)
PARKER, JANE, asst. prof. and coor. internship and recruitment, Tulane University, New Orleans, LA '84 (SOC)
PARKER, JANICE E., adm. diet., Arlington Memorial Hospital, Arlington, TX '86 (FOOD)
PARKER, JEFFREY J., dir. matl. and mgt. eng., Stormont-Vail Regional Medical Center, Topeka, KS '85 (MGMT)
PARKER, JEFFREY S., dir. soc. work, Holy Family Hospital, Des Plaines, IL '83 (SOC)
PARKER, JERRY S., dir. sup., proc. and distrib., Washoe Medical Center, Reno, NV '87 (CS)
PARKER, JOHN H. JR., atty., Duke University Hospital, Durham, NC '79 (ATTY)
PARKER, JOSIE A., dir. educ., Exeter Hospital, Exeter, NH '86 (EDUC)
PARKER, JUDITH ELAINE, RN, assoc. adm. nrsg., Kern Medical Center, Bakersfield, CA '81 (NURS)
PARKER, KATHRYN, adm. asst. prof. serv., Arlington Hospital, Arlington, VA '85 (RISK)
PARKER, KENNETH A., vice-pres., Seaboard Adjustment Bureau, Inc., Melville, NY '83 (RISK)
PARKER, LESTER B., Anchorage, AK '63
PARKER, LINDA C., dir. pers., Wallace Thomson Hospital, Union, SC '78 (PERS)
PARKER, LOUIS FRANCIS, exec. dir., St. John's Riverside Hospital, Yonkers, NY '69
PARKER, LUCILLE, RN, dir. nrsg., King Edward VII Memorial Hospital, Hamilton, Bermuda '82 (NURS)
PARKER, LYNNE C., RN, assoc. dir. nrsg. serv., Baptist Medical Center, Montgomery, AL '83 (NURS)
PARKER, MADELYN K., asst. dir. vol., Jennie Edmundson Memorial Hospital, Council Bluffs, IA '79 (VOL)
PARKER, MARCIA E., RN, instr., University of Virginia, School of Nursing, Charlottesville, VA '76 (EDUC)
PARKER, MARGARET COOK, vice-pres. nrsg., St. Joseph's Hospital, Asheville, NC '84 (NURS)
PARKER, MICHAEL J., vice-pres. environ. serv., Licking Memorial Hospital, Newark, OH '82 (ENG)
PARKER, MILDRED, dir. diet. and hskpg., Lake Livingston Medical Center, Livingston, TX '86 (ENVIRON)
PARKER, NORA, pres., Wuesthoff Memorial Hospital, Rockledge, FL '86 (VOL)
PARKER, PAMELA A., RN, vice-pres., Community Memorial Hospital, Menomonee Falls, WI '70 (NURS)
PARKER, PAMELA J., coor. pub. rel., Milwaukee Psychiatric Hospital, Milwaukee, WI '85 (PR)
PARKER, PATSY ANNE, RN, dir. nrsg., Sierra Medical Center, El Paso, TX '80 (NURS)
PARKER, RALPH E., adm. food serv., Flint Osteopathic Hospital, Flint, MI '84 (FOOD)
PARKER, RICKY D., pat. rep. amb. serv., Rowan Memorial Hospital, Salisbury, NC '82 (PAT)
PARKER, ROBERT C., MD, vice-pres. plng. and clin. serv., Copley Hospital, Morrisville, VT '83 (PLNG)
PARKER, ROGER A., asst. dir. eng., Hospital of Saint Raphael, New Haven, CT '85 (ENG)
PARKER, ROGER N., RN, vice-pres., Memorial Hospital for Cancer and Allied Diseases, New York, NY '79
PARKER, SAM, eng. mgt., Baystate Health Management Service, Inc., Springfield, MA '85 (MGMT)
PARKER, SANDRA, dir. matl. mgt., Larkin General Hospital, South Miami, FL '81 (PUR)
PARKER, SHERRY S., dir. soc. work, Portsmouth General Hospital, Portsmouth, VA '80 (SOC)
PARKER, SUSANNAH M., student, Program and Bureau of Hospital Administration, University of Michigan, Ann Arbor, MI '84
PARKER, T. GRAY JR., adm. res., AMI Brookwood Medical Center, Birmingham, AL '83
PARKER, TERRY L., buyer, Children's Hospital, Richmond, VA '87 (PUR)
PARKER, TERRY P., coor. pat. educ., Freehold Area Hospital, Freehold, NJ '84 (EDUC)
PARKER, THOMAS J., mgr. syst. plng., Antelope Valley Hospital Medical Center, Lancaster, CA '85 (MGMT)
PARKER, THOMAS W., asst. dir. pers., Foster G. McGaw Hospital, Loyola University of Chicago, Maywood, IL '84 (PERS)
PARKER, WILL, dir. pat. soc. serv., Lovelace Medical Center, Albuquerque, NM '83 (SOC)
PARKER, WILLIAM J., dir. ldry. and linen, Borgess Medical Center, Kalamazoo, MI '86 (ENVIRON)
PARKER, WILLIAM J., atty., HCA Greenview Hospital, Bowling Green, KY '75 (ATTY)
PARKER, WILLIE B., adm. pat. rep., Southeast Alabama Medical Center, Dothan, AL '84 (PAT)
PARKEVICH, TAMAR J., RN, dir. nrsg., Children's Hospital, Columbus, OH '73 (NURS)
PARKHURST, EDWIN WALLACE JR., prin., Herman Smith Associates, Hinsdale, IL '68
PARKINSON, JAN, dir. plng., St. Joseph's Hospital, Tampa, FL '86 (PLNG)
PARKINSON, JEFFREY, vice-pres., Voluntary Hospitals of America Management Services, Tampa, FL '73 (MGMT)
PARKINSON, KAREN L., dir. soc. serv., Lawrence and Memorial Hospital, New London, CT '82 (SOC)
PARKISON, GLENDA MARIE, asst. adm., Medical Center of Southeastern Oklahoma, Durant, OK '84
PARKS, BARBARA A., charge nrs., Methodist Hospital, Madison, WI '87 (AMB)
PARKS, BURTON O. III, adm., West Shore Hospital, Manistee, MI '83 (PLNG)
PARKS, CHRISTINE, coor. educ. serv., Borgess Medical Center, Kalamazoo, MI '82 (EDUC)
PARKS, DORIS S., supv. cent. sterile, Wayne Memorial Hospital, Jesup, GA '82 (CS)
PARKS, ELMER L., pat. rep., North Hills Passavant Hospital, Pittsburgh, PA '83 (PAT)
PARKS, HARVEY R., dir. master plng., Charter Medical Corporation, Macon, GA '85 (PLNG)
PARKS, JAMES ROBERT II, vice-pres. support serv., Gaston Memorial Hospital, Gastonia, NC '71
PARKS, JO H., dir. amb. surg., Higgins General Hospital, Bremen, GA '86 (AMB)
PARKS, KENNETH KNOX JR., med. serv. corp. off., Naval Hospital, Oak Harbor, WA '75
PARKS, MARITA L., dir. cent. serv., Our Lady of Lourdes Memorial Hospital, Binghamton, NY '82 (CS)
PARKS, MARY P., Oceanside, CA '78 (PR)
PARKS, NORMAN D., dir. environ. eng., St. Francis Medical Center, Cape Girardeau, MO '83 (ENG)
PARKS, POLLY KATHLEEN, student, Georgia State University, Atlanta, GA '87
PARLETT, 2ND LT. LAWRENCE R., MSC USAF, dir. med. res. mgt., U. S. Air Force Hospital Whiteman, Whiteman AFB, MO '86
PARLIER, CHARLES, asst. adm., Caldwell Memorial Hospital, Lenoir, NC '85 (RISK)
PARM, GENEVIEVE, RN, prov. rel. rep., American Medical International Health Services, Orlando, FL '80
PARMELEE, PAMELA D., RN, dir. nrsg., Pacific Presbyterian Hospital, San Francisco, CA '77 (NURS)
PARMENTER, EDWARD C., asst. chief sup. serv., Veterans Administration Medical Center, Syracuse, NY '86 (PUR)
PARMENTER, JAMES W., dir. eng., St. Lukes Hospital of Middleborough, Middleboro, MA '80 (ENG)
PARMER, CAROLYN, dir. fin., District of Columbia Hospital Association, Washington, DC '85
PARNABY, HELEN, dir. soc. serv., Memorial Hospital for McHenry County, Woodstock, IL '85 (SOC)
PARNELL, JOANNE C., consult., Carthage Area Hospital, Carthage, NY '70 (SOC)
PARNELL, TIMOTHY M., dir. matl. mgt., Our Lady of Bellefonte Hospital, Ashland, KY '83 (PUR)
PARNES, H. ELLIOT, atty., Horizon Health Systems, Oak Park, MI '79 (ATTY)
PAROO, IQBAL F., vice-pres. health affairs, Hahnemann University Hospital, Philadelphia, PA '74
PARRELLA, PAUL D., vice-pres. human res., Lawrence and Memorial Hospital, New London, CT '73 (PERS)
PARRINGTON, MARK, vice-pres. corp. plng., Sutter Health System, Sacramento, CA '75 (PLNG)
PARRINO, ROSE, dir. vol. serv., Hillcrest Hospital, Mayfield Heights, OH '86 (VOL)
PARRIS, JILL, dir. pers., University of Cincinnati Medical Center, Cincinnati, OH '85 (PERS)
PARRIS, JOSEPH GEORGE, Slidell, LA '78
PARRIS, SUSAN M., dir. soc. serv., Citizens General Hospital, New Kensington, PA '86 (SOC)
PARRISH, ALICE C., RN, field rep., Joint Commission on Accreditation of Hospitals, Chicago, IL '68 (NURS)
PARRISH, GAIL H., vice-pres. mktg. and plng., St. Clair Health Corporation, Detroit, MI '85 (PR) (PLNG)
PARRISH, HEATHER A., mgr. pers., Palmdale Hospital Medical Center, Palmdale, CA '87 (PERS)
PARRISH, HUDSON E., mgr. matl., Cape Fear Memorial Hospital, Wilmington, NC '83 (CS)
PARRISH, JAMES G., mgr. matl., Mid-Columbia Medical Center, The Dalles, OR '86 (PUR)
PARRISH, SHERYL M., assoc. adm., Wyman Park Medical Center, Baltimore, MD '83 (SOC)
PARRISH, VESTAL JR., ScD, asst. dean health serv. adm. and prof. behavorial med., Mercer University School of Medicine, Macon, GA '82

PARRISH, WILLIAM C., dist. vice-pres., Hospital Corporation of America, Cincinnati, OH '68
PARROT, DONALD L., dir. mktg. res., Orlando Regional Medical Center, Orlando, FL '79 (PLNG)
PARROTT, BONNIE, mgr. treatment center, Bellin Memorial Hospital, Green Bay, WI '86 (AMB)
PARROTT, C. WARREN, dir. matl. mgt., Porter Memorial Hospital, Denver, CO '79 (PUR)
PARROTT, MARGARET M., exec. hskpr., Dameron Hospital, Stockton, CA '86 (ENVIRON)
PARROTT, TAMI B., vice-pres., Hoag Memorial Hospital Presbyterian, Newport Beach, CA '83 (PLNG)
PARRY, EDWIN J., dir. eng., Hanover General Hospital, Hanover, PA '85 (ENG)
PARRY, WAYNE C., plant eng., Mount Ascutney Hospital and Health Center, Windsor, VT '85 (ENG)
PARSEK, JAMES D., RN, Alexian Brothers Medical Center, Elk Grove Village, IL '79 (NURS)
PARSELS, DAVID L., supv. plant oper., Methodist Hospital-Central Unit, Memphis, TN '85 (ENG)
PARSEY, JOSEPH WILLIAM, student, St. Louis University, St. Louis, MO '86
PARSINEN, PAT, coor. soc. serv., Waconia Ridgeview Hospital, Waconia, MN '86 (SOC)
PARSKY, ROBERT M., pres., Ewing Cole Cherry Parsky, Philadelphia, PA '77
PARSLEY, ROBERT H., atty., St. Joseph Hospital, Houston, TX '71 (ATTY)
PARSON, DON, asst. dir. plant facil., Baptist Medical Center, Jacksonville, FL '85 (ENG)
PARSONS, CHARLES A., coor. eng. and maint., Bay Medical Center, Bay City, MI '85 (ENG)
PARSONS, DENIS W., vice-pres. support serv., Waterman Medical Center, Eustis, FL '76 (ENG)(PLNG)
PARSONS, FRANK R. JR., adm., Charleston Area Medical Center, Charleston, WV '57 (LIFE)
PARSONS, JOHN E., dir. matl. mgt., St. Vincent Hospital, Green Bay, WI '80 (PUR)
PARSONS, KATHLEEN M., student, School of Public Health, University of Michigan, Ann Arbor, MI '85
PARSONS, LEONA M., RN, asst. vice-pres., Florida Hospital-Altamonte, Altamonte Springs, FL '86 (NURS)
PARSONS, LYDIA L. M., dir. pat. and family serv., Redington-Fairview General Hospital, Skowhegan, ME '85 (SOC)
PARSONS, MALCOLM S., risk mgr., Doctors Hospital, Columbus, OH '86 (RISK)
PARSONS, MARTIN D., dir. pers., Navapache Hospital, Show Low, AZ '85 (PERS)
PARSONS, MICKEY L., RN, asst. adm., University of New Mexico Hospital, Albuquerque, NM '81 (NURS)
PARSONS, PATRICIA A., asst. dir. commun. rel., Deaconess Hospital, Evansville, IN '86 (VOL)
PARSONS, RAY L., dir. plant, Laurelwood Hospital, The Woodlands, TX '83 (ENG)
PARSONS, RAY W., supv. bldg. and grds., Bayview Manor, Seattle, WA '84 (ENG)
PARSONS, RICHARD J., pres., Performance Health, Inc., Danville, CA '84 (MGMT)
PARSONS, ROBERT J., prof. health adm., Brigham Young University, Provo, UT '83 (PLNG)
PARTEKA, LOUISE RITA, RN, dir. cardiac nrsg., St. Luke's Hospital, Milwaukee, WI '80 (NURS)
PARTHEMORE, WARRENETTE, dir. mktg. and pub. rel., St. Francis Rehabilitation Hospital and Nursing Home, Green Springs, OH '86 (PR)
PARTLOW, PATRICIA A., coor. educ., Meridian Park Hospital, Tualatin, OR '86 (EDUC)
PARTRIDGE, DAVE, dir. pub. rel., Greenville Hospital System, Greenville, SC '81 (PR)
PARTRIDGE, DOLLY C., dir. educ., Baptist Hospital, Pensacola, FL '71 (EDUC)
PARTRIDGE, TIM R., Schaumburg, IL '81 (PUR)
PARVEN, ALVIN S., asst. vice-pres., medicare adm., Aetna Life and Casualty, Hartford, CT '81
PARVIS, PETER P., atty., Howard County General Hospital, Columbia, MD '83 (ATTY)
PASCARELLA, HARRIETT, dir. soc. serv., Warren General Hospital, Warren, OH '80 (SOC)
PASCH, DEBORAH, head nrs. outpatient clin., Jewish Hospital of St. Louis, St. Louis, MO '87 (AMB)
PASCH, JOHN E., (ret.), New York Mills, MN '52 (PR)(LIFE)
PASCHALI, ROBERT L., mgr. plant serv., Fresno Community Hospital and Medical Center, Fresno, CA '85 (ENG)
PASCO, NANCY B., asst. dir. soc. serv., St. John's Mercy Medical Center, St. Louis, MO '86 (SOC)
PASCOE, MARY A., mgr. cent. proc. and distrib., Western Medical Center Anaheim, Anaheim, CA '80 (CS)
PASCUALY, RODRIGO A., vice-pres. support serv., Northwest Community Hospital, Arlington Heights, IL '83
PASETTI, ALAN C., Miami, FL '86 (PUR)
PASH, BETTY J., RN, dir. nrsg., St. Agnes Hospital and Medical Center, Fresno, CA '86 (NURS)
PASKEWICH, BONNIE T., loss control consult., Hospital Underwriters Mutual Insurance Company, Albany, NY '85 (RISK)
PASKIE, CAROLE A., sec. and pat. rep., Hospital of the University of Pennsylvania, Philadelphia, PA '84 (PAT)
PASSARELLI, RAFFAELE M., dir. sup., proc. and distrib., Mercy Center for Health Care Services, Aurora, IL '81 (CS)
PASSEN-BURNS, LT. ELIZABETH A., MSC USN, Cape Canaveral, FL '84 (SOC)
PASSERI, ANDREW J., dir., Bayley Seton Hospital, Staten Island, NY '73
PASSERI, ROSANNE M., RN, dir. nrsg., James C. Giuffre Medical Center, Philadelphia, PA '81 (NURS)
PASSETT, BARRY A., pres., Greater Southeast Community Hospital Foundation, Washington, DC '73
PASSMORE, RUTH V., RN, dir. educ., St. Joseph Regional Medical Center, Lewiston, ID '72 (EDUC)
PASTEL, ANTHONY L., dir. procurement, Cuyahoga County Hospitals, Cleveland, OH '61 (PUR)
PASTER, PHYLLIS ANN, adm. amb. serv., Children's Hospital, Boston, MA '83
PASTORS, CALVIN R., atty., Hospital Corporation of America, Nashville, TN '85 (ATTY)
PASWINSKI, RONALD, dir. phys. plant serv., St. Catherine Hospital, East Chicago, IN '87 (ENG)
PATA, JOANN, consult., Medical Record Review Services, Philadelphia, PA '79
PATAIL, BRYANNE M., dir. clin. eng., Horizon Health Systems, Oak Park, MI '81 (ENG)
PATCH, LINDA L., adm. asst., University Community Hospital, Tamarac, FL '84
PATCHKE, ERIC R., dir. phys. plant, Geneva General Hospital, Geneva, NY '83 (ENG)
PATE, ALFRED S., asst. dir. trainee, Veterans Administration West Side Medical Center, Chicago, IL '77
PATE, EARL C., vice-pres. plng., Porter Memorial Hospital, Denver, CO '81 (PLNG)
PATE, MARGARITA M., dir. mktg., St. Joseph Hospital, Baltimore, MD '86 (PR) (PLNG)
PATEL, COWAS G., dir. eng. serv., Henry Mayo Newhall Memorial Hospital, Valencia, CA '85 (ENG)
PATEL, DEVIPRASAD I., sr. proj. mgr., Queens Hospital Center, Jamaica, NY '85 (ENG)
PATEL, KIRTI, MD, med. dir., Wockhardt Medical Centre, Bombay, India '85
PATELLA, HELEN K., dir. vol. serv., John Heinz Institute-Rehabilitation Medicine, Wilkes-Barre, PA '86 (VOL)
PATERNOSTER, MICHAEL D., mgr. environ. serv., Middletown Regional Hospital, Middletown, OH '86 (ENVIRON)
PATERSON, VERNICE B., RN, vice-pres. pat. care serv., Mercy Medical Center, Roseburg, OR '72 (NURS)
PATERSON, W. MURRAY, asst. dir. soc. serv., Royal Alexandra Hospital, Edmonton, Alta., Canada '87 (SOC)
PATINO, MARGARET M., student, Georgia Institute of Technology, Atlanta, GA '84 (MGMT)
PATISAUL, WILTON, dir. cent. sup., Baldwin County Hospital, Milledgeville, GA '82 (CS)
PATRIARCA, MINA RAE, dir. qualiy assur. and risk mgt., St. Vincent Medical Center, Toledo, OH '80 (RISK)
PATRICK, CINDY C., assoc. dir. plng., res. and dev., Methodist Health Systems, Inc., Memphis, TN '86 (PR) (PLNG)
PATRICK, DEBORAH A., dir. pers., Gnaden Huetten Memorial Hospital, Lehighton, PA '86 (PERS)
PATRICK, DON C., dir. educ., St. Anthony Medical Center, Columbus, OH '76 (EDUC)
PATRICK, DWYNE RHODES, sr. mgt. eng. and mgr. mgt. eng., Forbes Health System, Pittsburgh, PA '85 (MGMT)
PATRICK, ELEANOR L., supv. sterile proc., Francis Scott Key Medical Center, Baltimore, MD '78 (CS)
PATRICK, PATRICIA F., supv. nrsg., Good Samaritan Hospital, Downers Grove, IL '86 (NURS)
PATRICK, PEGGY, coor. vol., Bethesda Psychealth System, Denver, CO '77 (VOL)
PATRICK, PHYLLIS A., dir. plng. and mktg., Mercy Hospital, Bakersfield, CA '81 (PLNG)
PATRICK, WILLIAM B. JR., atty., Self Memorial Hospital, Greenwood, SC '85 (ATTY)
PATRIZI, BRUNO J., mgr. matl., Mercy Hospital, Scranton, PA '63 (PUR)
PATRONE, CAROLE M., dir. commun. rel. and dev. assoc., St. John's Episcopal Hospital, Smithtown, NY '86 (PLNG)
PATRY, PATRICIA L., dir. educ. and trng., Eastern Maine Medical Center, Bangor, ME '85 (EDUC)
PATTEN, CONSTANCE S., RN, vice-pres. nrsg., Raritan Bay Medical Center, Perth Amboy, NJ '86 (NURS)
PATTEN, EILEEN D., dir. pub. affairs, Hospital Center at Orange, Orange, NJ '85 (PR)
PATTEN, NEAL J., atty., Mary Immaculate Hospital, Newport News, VA '81 (ATTY)
PATTEN, TIMOTHY R., asst. to pres., Glendale Heights Community Hospital, Glendale Heights, IL '84 (PR) (PLNG)
PATTERSON, ANNE M., adm. res., New Hanover Memorial Hospital, Wilmington, NC '84
PATTERSON, BRUCE W., dir. plant oper., Peninsula General Hospital Medical Center, Salisbury, MD '85 (ENG)
PATTERSON, CAROLE H., RN, nrsg. standards spec., Joint Commission on Accreditation of Hospitals, Chicago, IL '78 (NURS)
PATTERSON, CHARLES, chief matl. mgt., National Institutes of Health, Bethesda, MD '78 (PUR)
PATTERSON, CLAUDIA B., RN, asst. vice-pres. prof. serv., Memorial Medical Center of Jacksonville, Jacksonville, FL '84 (NURS)
PATTERSON, DEBORAH A., RN, dir. nrsg.-critical care serv., St. Francis Hospital, Blue Island, IL '86 (NURS)
PATTERSON, DEBORAH L., exec. hskpg., Cleveland Memorial Hospital, Shelby, NC '86 (ENVIRON)
PATTERSON, ELIZABETH, dir. commun. rel., Catherine McAuley Health Center, Ann Arbor, MI '85 (PR)
PATTERSON, J. ANTHONY JR., atty., Harris Methodist -Fort Worth, Fort Worth, TX '81 (ATTY)
PATTERSON, JAMES WILLIAM, dir. pers., Driscoll Foundation Children's Hospital, Corpus Christi, TX '77 (PERS)
PATTERSON, JANET L., dir. vol., Sharon General Hospital, Sharon, PA '81 (VOL)
PATTERSON, JEAN M., dir. commun. affairs, Ballard Community Hospital, Seattle, WA '85 (PR)
PATTERSON, JEAN, asst. dir. pub. rel., Southern Baptist Hospital, New Orleans, LA '85 (PR)
PATTERSON, KAREN A., RN, coor. educ., East Alabama Medical Center, Opelika, AL '85 (EDUC)
PATTERSON, M. CLARE JR., dir. matl. mgt., Newton Memorial Hospital, Newton, NJ '66 (PUR)
PATTERSON, PAUL W. JR., dir. educ. and trng., Cook County Hospital, Chicago, IL '85 (EDUC)
PATTERSON, RONALD E., dir. eng., Biloxi Regional Medical Center, Biloxi, MS '81 (ENG)(ENVIRON)
PATTERSON, RUTH ANN, dir. educ., Milford-Whitinsville Regional Hospital, Milford, MA '78 (EDUC)
PATTERSON, STAN F., vice-pres. corp. dev., Mercy Hospital, Charlotte, NC '82 (PLNG)
PATTERSON, SUE MCCAULEY, dir. pub. rel. and mktg., Suburban Hospital, Bethesda, MD '85 (PR) (PLNG)
PATTERSON, SUE, dir. food serv., York Hospital, York, ME '82 (FOOD)
PATTERSON, W. E., asst. dir. eng. serv., St. Elizabeth Hospital, Danville, IL '86 (ENG)
PATTERSON, WILLIAM M., vice-pres., Lourdes Hospital, Paducah, KY '79
PATTERSON, WILLIAM, atty., Lapeer General Hospital, LaPeer, MI '74 (ATTY)
PATTISON, DOUGLAS B., mgt. analyst, British Columbia Ministry of Health, Victoria, B.C., Canada '80 (MGMT)
PATTIZ, JILL FREEBAIRN, assoc. consult., Pittsburgh Management Associates, Atlanta, GA '84
PATTON, CHARLES M., maint. eng., Lawrence County Memorial Hospital, Lawrenceville, IL '87 (ENG)
PATTON, KATHLEEN, head maternal and child health, Saint Joseph Hospital, Reading, PA '85 (RISK)
PATTON, KEVIN C., vice-pres. educ. serv., Greater Cleveland Hospital Association, Cleveland, OH '77 (EDUC)
PATTON, LEDEL J., mgr. hskpg., Logan County Health Center, Guthrie, OK '86 (ENVIRON)
PATTON, MARIANNE, mgr. pub. rel., Mercy Medical Center, Nampa, ID '85 (PR)
PATTON, PHILIP R., dir. compensation, Hospital Corporation of America, Nashville, TN '81 (PERS)
PATTON, RANDALL L., dir. med. rec., Holy Spirit Hospital, Camp Hill, PA '84 (RISK)
PATTON, ROBERT F., student, University of Colorado, Denver, CO '86 (MGMT)
PATTON, SUSAN H., atty., Catherine McAuley Health Center, Ann Arbor, MI '87 (ATTY)
PATTON, SUZANNE F., dir. commun. rel., St. Michael Hospital, Texarkana, AR '82 (PR)
PATTULLO, ANDREW, (ret.), Battle Creek, MI '44 (LIFE)
PATWELL, ROBERT, dir. plant serv., Salinas Valley Memorial Hospital, Salinas, CA '85 (ENG)
PAUL, ALISON E., adm. asst. and dir. bus. dev., Dauterive Hospital, New Iberia, LA '86 (PR) (PLNG)
PAUL, LT. COL. C. PETER, MSC USA, asst. adm., Milwaukee County Medical Complex, Milwaukee, WI '69
PAUL, CAROL, vice-pres. legal and external affairs, Morristown Memorial Hospital, Morristown, NJ '79 (PLNG)
PAUL, JACK, vice-pres. and dir. pers., Bethany Medical Center, Kansas City, KS '80 (PERS)
PAUL, JANN E., dir. plng., Suburban Hospital, Bethesda, MD '81 (PR) (PLNG)
PAUL, JERRY W., exec. vice-pres. and chief oper. off., Deaconess Hospital, St. Louis, MO '85
PAUL, JOHN W., assoc. adm., Western Psychiatric Institute and Clinic, Pittsburgh, PA '83
PAUL, JUDY, dir. commun. rel., Waterman Medical Center, Eustis, FL '80 (PR)
PAUL, KITTY B., pres. and prin., Kitty Brooks-Paul Associates, Ltd., Wayne, NJ '86
PAUL, MARY ELIZABETH, RN, dir. nrsg. serv., Hospital for Joint Diseases Orthopaedic Institute, New York, NY '84 (NURS)
PAUL, ROBERT C., dir. eng. and maint., Baylor University Medical Center, Dallas, TX '56 (ENG)(LIFE)
PAULAUSKIS, MARY LOUISE, dir. diet. serv., Blessing Hospital, Quincy, IL '79 (FOOD)
PAULETTE, SR. MARY, dir. cent. serv., Providence Hospital, Sandusky, OH '67 (CS)
PAULEY, ALTA L., coor. vol., Flowers Hospital, Dothan, AL '86 (VOL)
PAULEY, DONNA L., dir. soc. serv. and coor. pain mgt., Elmbrook Memorial Hospital, Brookfield, WI '84 (SOC)
PAULEY, VERNA, RN, dir. nrsg., Douglas County Hospital, Alexandria, MN '73 (NURS)
PAULEY, WILLIAM E., reg. dir. matl. mgt., Kaiser Sunnyside Medical Center, Clackamas, OR '65 (PUR)
PAULSEN, MAJ. NORMAN W., MSC USAF, chief allied health educ. br., U. S. Air Force Clinic Randolph, Randolph AFB, TX '75
PAULSEN, SUSAN C., mgr. pers., Northridge Hospital Medical Center, Northridge, CA '87 (PERS)
PAULSON, AUDENE L., coor. educ., Bryn Mawr Rehabilitation Hospital, Malvern, PA '86 (EDUC)
PAULSON, BETTY, coor. vol. serv., Candler General Hospital, Savannah, GA '75 (VOL)
PAULSON, JOHN E., asst. vice-pres., Sioux Valley Hospital, Sioux Falls, SD '74 (PLNG)
PAULSON, MICHAEL J., RN, dir. qual. assur. and risk mgt., Park Lane Medical Center, Kansas City, MO '80 (RISK)
PAULSON, NANCY E., supv. proc., Lutheran Medical Center, Wheat Ridge, CO '86 (CS)
PAULSON, PATRICK T., vice-pres., Affiliated Hospitals Systems, Houston, TX '76
PAULSON, WALTER A., atty., Arkansas Children's Hospital, Little Rock, AR '86 (ATTY)
PAULUCCI, PHILIP MARK, asst. dir. soc. work and psych., Ohio State University Hospitals, Columbus, OH '86 (SOC)
PAUPARD, RICHARD D., dir. matl. mgt., Utah Valley Regional Medical Center, Provo, UT '84 (PUR)
PAVARINI, PETER A., atty., St. Ann's Hospital of Columbus, Westerville, OH '82 (ATTY)
PAVEK, JOYCE, RN, dir. clin. serv., St. Joseph Mercy Hospital, Mason City, IA '80 (NURS)
PAVEY, ANNETTE, dir. soc. serv., Dukes Memorial Hospital, Peru, IN '73 (SOC)
PAVEY, MARIE CECILE, coor. pat. rep., Bannock Regional Medical Center, Pocatello, ID '80 (PAT)
PAVIA, LOTTIE, dir. admissions and discharges, Terence Cardinal Cook Health Care Center, New York, NY '85 (SOC)
PAVLAKIS, GEORGE A., chief eng., St. Charles General Hospital, New Orleans, LA '85 (ENG)
PAVLO, PETER W., dir. mgt. info. syst., Children's Hospital of Philadelphia, Philadelphia, PA '85 (MGMT)

PAVLOU, SUSAN B., dir. pers., Sisters of Providence, Seattle, WA '87 (PERS)
PAVLOW, SHARA T., dir. clin. affairs, University of Miami School of Medicine, Miami, FL '79 (PLNG)
PAWLEWSKI, DAVID, coor. safety, Mercy Hospital Medical Center, Des Moines, IA '86 (RISK)
PAWLOWSKI, EUGENE P., adm., Bluefield Community Hospital, Bluefield, WV '85
PAXSON, CHARLES S. JR., consult., State College, PA '42 (LIFE)
PAXTON, FRAN, RN, dir. nrsg., St. John's Hospital, Salina, KS '77 (NURS)
PAYNE, BROOKS E., vice-pres. emp. rel., Leonard Morse Hospital, Natick, MA '84 (PERS)
PAYNE, CAMILLE L., dir. vol. serv., John D. Archbold Memorial Hospital, Thomasville, GA '86 (VOL)
PAYNE, CAPT. CARY J., chief clin. support, Fox Army Community Hospital, Huntsville, AL '81
PAYNE, DALE F., asst. adm., Mid-Valley Hospital, Omak, WA '83 (PERS)
PAYNE, DENISE A., adm. renal serv., Newark Beth Israel Medical Center, Newark, NJ '81
PAYNE, DONALD L., vice-pres., Drexel Burnham Lambert, Inc., Atlanta, GA '85
PAYNE, DONNA C., chief soc. worker, Fuller Memorial Hospital, South Attleboro, MA '84 (SOC)
PAYNE, DORIS S., dir. educ., Cleveland Memorial Hospital, Shelby, NC '81 (EDUC)
PAYNE, GENE-PAUL, RN, dir. nrsg. serv., Centro Asturiano Hospital, Tampa, FL '84 (NURS)
PAYNE, JOSEPH M., dir. soc. serv., Rush-Presbyterian-St. Luke's Medical Center, Chicago, IL '82 (SOC)
PAYNE, JUDY, RN, dir. cent. sup., Newnan Hospital, Newnan, GA '79 (CS)
PAYNE, LAWRENCE R., (ret.), Green Valley, AZ '46 (LIFE)
PAYNE, MARY ANN, dir. commun., Union Hospital of Cecil County, Elkton, MD '79 (PR)
PAYNE, MICHAEL E., dir. pers., North Kansas City Hospital, North Kansas City, MO '83 (PERS)
PAYNE, MICHAEL G., supv. maint., St. Jude Hospital-Fullerton, Fullerton, CA '78 (ENG)
PAYNE, ROSEMARIE, atty., Evangelical Health Systems, Oak Brook, IL '86 (ATTY)
PAYNE, TRACY T., exec. vice-pres., University Community Hospital, Tampa, FL '75
PAYNE, WILLIAM T. JR., exec. vice-pres., Presbyterian-University of Pennsylvania Medical Center, Philadelphia, PA '66
PAYNTER, JOHN W., White Cottage, OH '73 (LIFE)
PAYSON, MRS. CHARLES S., (ret.), Manhasset, NY '48 (HON)
PAYTON, JAMES R., dir. pers., St. Elizabeth Medical Center, Granite City, IL '73 (PERS)
PAYTON, KEVIN J., supv. biomedical eng., St. Elizabeth Medical Center, Granite City, IL '82 (ENG)
PAZAK, LUCILLE M., RN, dir. trng. and dev., Jameson Memorial Hospital, New Castle, PA '78 (EDUC)(PLNG)
PAZAK, SUSANNE T., asst. dir. diet., St. Francis Hospital, Blue Island, IL '86 (FOOD)
PAZDRY, PATRICIA, dir. diet., University Hospital, Saskatoon, Sask., Canada '67 (FOOD)
PCSOLYAR, NANCY KRILL, dir. food serv., Magee Rehabilitation Hospital, Philadelphia, PA '81 (FOOD)
PEABODY, BRADLEY, pres., National Garages, Inc., Detroit, MI '80
PEABODY, MICHAEL N., asst. vice-pres. matl. serv., Children's Medical Center, Dayton, OH '81 (PUR)
PEACE, JEANNE F., clin. dir., Moses H. Cone Memorial Hospital, Greensboro, NC '86 (NURS)
PEACH, ANNE G., mgr. educ., Orlando Regional Medical Center, Orlando, FL '85 (EDUC)
PEACH, KENNETH R., dir. pub. rel. and mktg., South Lake Memorial Hospital, Clermont, FL '86 (PR)
PEACOCK, JANE M., dir. vol. serv., Columbia Hospital, Milwaukee, WI '80 (VOL)
PEACOCK, NANCY K., vice-pres., St. Luke's Episcopal Hosp., Texas Heart Institute, Houston, TX '73 (PR)
PEACOR, GAYLE S., hostess, Tri-City Medical Center, Oceanside, CA '85 (PAT)
PEAK, GEORGE H., mgt. eng., East Texas Hospital Foundation, Tyler, TX '86 (MGMT)
PEAKE-REHM, JEAN, dir. pur., Wilson Memorial Hospital, Wilson, NC '65 (PUR)
PEARCE, BENJAMIN M., arch., Snoddy and McCulloch Associates, Charlotte, NC '76
PEARCE, DONNA B., dir. soc. serv., St. Joseph Riverside Hospital, Warren, OH '86 (SOC)
PEARCE, ERNEST R., reg. dir., Datis Corporation, Laguna Hills, CA '87 (PLNG)
PEARCE, HAROLD G., pres., Blue Cross of Utah, Salt Lake City, UT '48 (LIFE)
PEARCE, JOHN G., chief exec. off., Health America of Kentucky, Louisville, KY '82
PEARCE, JONATHAN W., Laventhol and Horwath, Philadelphia, PA '72 (MGMT)
PEARCE, MARILYN J., risk mgr., Childrens Hospital of Los Angeles, Los Angeles, CA '86 (RISK)
PEARCE, ROSEMARY H., RN, dir. nrsg. serv., Grandview Hospital and Medical Center, Dayton, OH '77 (NURS)
PEARL, ARLENE, dir. soc. serv., St. Rose Hospital, Hayward, CA '78 (SOC)
PEARLMUTTER, DEANNA R., RN, chm. psych., genitourinary and gyn. nrsg. serv., Massachusetts General Hospital, Boston, MA '85 (NURS)
PEARS, JAMES E., adm., Memorial Hospital, Marshall, TX '57 (LIFE)
PEARSALL, ROBERT S. JR., dir. pur. and matl. mgt., Kaiser Foundation Health Plan of Mid Atlantic States, Inc., Washington, DC '86 (PUR)
PEARSON, BRUCE E., asst. adm., Good Samaritan Medical Center, Phoenix, AZ '83 (AMB)
PEARSON, DONALD C. JR., dir. emp. educ. and trng., Ochsner Foundation Hospital, New Orleans, LA '75 (EDUC)(PERS)
PEARSON, EDITH F., chief soc. work, Veterans Administration Medical Center, Los Angeles, CA '74 (SOC)
PEARSON, ELLEN M., assoc., HBO-Amherst Associates, Chicago, IL '85 (PLNG)
PEARSON, GEORGE B., (ret.), Tyler, TX '48 (PLNG)(LIFE)
PEARSON, GEORGE R. JR., dir. mgt. eng., Durham County General Hospital, Durham, NC '78 (MGMT)
PEARSON, GERALD P., vice-pres., Franciscan Sisters Health Care Corporation, Mokena, IL '68 (PLNG)
PEARSON, J. VAUGHN, dir. mgt. serv., East Jefferson General Hospital, Metairie, LA '81 (MGMT)
PEARSON, JOHN A., dir. soc. serv., General Hospital of Everett, Everett, WA '80 (SOC)
PEARSON, KENNETH L., assoc. dir., Montefiore Medical Center, Bronx, NY '78
PEARSON, LINDA A., pat. care rep., AMI Circle City Hospital, Corona, CA '82 (PAT)
PEARSON, LINDA M., RN, dir. nrsg. educ., Maine Medical Center, Portland, ME '81 (NURS)(EDUC)
PEARSON, RALPH S., corp. mgr., Beverly Surgical Associates, Inc., Beverly, MA '87 (AMB)
PEARSON, ROGER W., dir. matl. mgt., St. Elizabeth Hospital Medical Center, Lafayette, IN '80 (PUR)
PEARSON, SUSAN L., RN, dir. nrsg., Mercer County Hospital, Aledo, IL '82 (NURS)
PEARSON, VIRGINIA M., dir. pub. rel. and commun., Sisters of the Sorrowful Mother-Ministry Corporation, Milwaukee, WI '86 (PR)
PECCHIO, PIERRE G., indust. eng.-oper. plng., Memorial Hospital for Cancer, New York, NY '85 (MGMT)
PECK, ALLIE, food serv. mgr., Little Company of Mary Hospital, Evergreen Park, IL '78 (FOOD)
PECK, CHERYL J., sr. med. syst. spec., Commission on Professional and Hospital Activities, Ann Arbor, MI '85 (PLNG)
PECK, CHUCK, vice-pres. mktg. and plng., Adventist Living Centers, Hinsdale, IL '87 (PR) (PLNG)
PECK, DEBORAH L., info. spec., Mary Greeley Medical Center, Ames, IA '85 (PR)
PECK, GARY V., dir. gen. serv., Deaconess Medical Center-Spokane, Spokane, WA '86 (ENVIRON)
PECK, GLENNA L., dir. mktg. and pub. rel., Freeman Hospital, Joplin, MO '80 (PR)
PECK, JOHN E., adm., Windham Community Memorial Hospital, Willimantic, CT '74 (PERS)
PECK, KAY, exec. dir., West Oaks-Psychiatric Institute Houston, Houston, TX '86
PECK, ROBERT F., pres., St. Luke's Regional Medical Center, Sioux City, IA '58 (PLNG)
PECK, STANLEY B., vice-pres. consumer and prof. rel., Health Insurance Association of America, Washington, DC '79 (PLNG)
PECK, STEVEN C., dir. mktg. and commun., East Tennessee Baptist Hospital, Knoxville, TN '86 (PR) (PLNG)
PECK, THOMAS R., dir. mktg. and pat. commun., Harris Methodist -Fort Worth, Fort Worth, TX '81 (PR)
PECKAT, C. A., cent. serv. tech., St. Anthony Hospital, Michigan City, IN '86 (CS)
PECKHAM, ARTHUR H. JR., pres., Agnew, Peckham and Associates Ltd., Marblehead, MA '71
PECKHAM, ROLAND L., mgr. matl., Giles Memorial Hospital, Pearisburg, VA '84 (PUR)
PECONIO, ORONZO, dir. matl. mgt., Mary Thompson Hospital, Chicago, IL '80 (PUR)
PECORELLI, RALPH, dir. maint. and plant oper., Brattleboro Retreat, Brattleboro, VT '84 (ENG)
PECORINO, D. JOHN, consult., Tolland, CT '82 (RISK)
PECOT, JEAN P., RN, assoc. exec. dir. nrsg., Iberia General Hospital and Medical Center, New Iberia, LA '85 (NURS)
PEDDECORD, MICHAEL, asst. prof., San Diego State University, Graduate School of Public Health, San Diego, CA '82
PEDERSEN, CDR ARTHUR STANLEY, (ret.), Bremerton, WA '69
PEDERSEN, CHERYL A., RN, nrsg. mgt. consult., University of Wisconsin Hospital and Clinics Regional Services, Madison, WI '83 (NURS)
PEDERSEN, CHERYL A., dir. commun. rel., Rahway Hospital, Rahway, NJ '85 (PR)
PEDERSEN, DAN, dir. plant serv., Community Hospital, Wickenburg, AZ '87 (ENG)
PEDERSEN, MERRILL, dir. eng., Stormont-Vail Regional Medical Center, Topeka, KS '80 (ENG)
PEDERSEN, PAUL G., sr. vice-pres., Falick-Klein Partnership, Inc., Houston, TX '83 (ENG)
PEDERSEN, T. J., vice-pres. oper. and mktg., Nmr Centers, Inc., Newport Beach, CA '85
PEDERSON, BRUCE E., dir. chaplaincy and soc. serv., Mercy Medical Center, Coon Rapids, MN '84 (SOC)
PEDERSON, MARK ALLEN, student, Concordia College, Moorhead, MN '86
PEDIGREE, RICHARD B. JR., vice-pres. clin. serv. and risk mgt., St. John's Hospital, Lowell, MA '82 (RISK)
PEDRICK, RICHARD L. JR., dir. matl. mgt., Portsmouth Regional Hospital, Portsmouth, NH '82 (PUR)
PEDROSO, ODAIR P., MD, dir., School of Public Health, Sao Paulo, Brazil '43 (HON)
PEDROTTY, JUDY HODGEN, dir. vol. serv., Massillon Community Hospital, Massillon, OH '85 (VOL)
PEEBLES, PATRICE C., RN, assoc. adm., Eye and Ear Hospital of Pittsburgh, Pittsburgh, PA '81 (NURS)(AMB)
PEEL, BARBARA K., head hskpg., Long Island Developmental Center, Melville, NY '86 (ENVIRON)
PEEL, EDWIN B., Atlanta, GA '47 (LIFE)
PEEL, KATHRYN COMER, asst. adm. human res., Henrietta Egleston Hospital, Atlanta, GA '86 (PERS)
PEEL, ROBERT STEPHEN, mgr. pers. serv., Emory Clinic, Atlanta, GA '79 (PERS)
PEFFERS, G. WILLIAM, dir. diet. serv., Ingalls Memorial Hospital, Harvey, IL '67 (FOOD)
PEFFLEY, BRAD, vice-pres. oper., Mansfield General Hospital, Mansfield, OH '79 (PLNG)
PEGLOW, TIMOTHY M., vice-pres. eng., LaPorte Hospital, LaPorte, IN '80 (ENG)
PEGUES, LOUIS E., buyer, New York University Medical Center, New York, NY '86 (PUR)
PEHANICK, KENNETH, dir. matl. mgt., Allied Services for Handicapped, Scranton, PA '86 (PUR)
PEHL, RICHARD E., dir. human res. dev., Midland Memorial Hospital, Midland, TX '84 (PERS)
PEHLE, JAMES L., dir. pub. rel., St. Joseph's Hospital, Breese, IL '84 (PR)
PEHRINGER, JOSEPH F. III, mgt. eng., Milwaukee County Medical Complex, Milwaukee, WI '86 (MGMT)
PEIFER, NATASHA D., plng. and mktg. analyst, Memorial Hospital, South Bend, IN '83 (PLNG)
PEIFFER, CARROLL E. JR., contr., Pottstown Memorial Medical Center, Pottstown, PA '69
PEIFFER, PHYLLIS F., asst. dir. nutr. serv., York Hospital, York, PA '83 (FOOD)
PEIMER, SYDNEY CARL, (ret.), Southfield, MI '52 (LIFE)
PEISER, PATRICIA L., dir. soc. serv., Texas Scottish Rite Hospital for Crippled Children, Dallas, TX '72 (SOC)
PEKAR, NANCY A., dir. soc. serv., Robinson Memorial Hospital, Ravenna, OH '85 (SOC)
PEKLEWSKY, COLLYN S., dir. pers. and pub. rel., Northern Montana Hospital, Havre, MT '79 (PERS)
PEKO, MATYAS JR., assoc. dir. plant oper., St. Vincent Charity Hospital, Cleveland, OH '82 (ENG)
PELC, ANNE, dir. soc. serv., Mercy Hospital of Franciscan Sisters, Oelwein, IA '86 (SOC)
PELESCHKA, WOLFGANG F., dir. matl. mgt., Ihc Hospitals, Inc., Salt Lake City, UT '80 (PUR)
PELIGIAN, ALEXANDER, dir. plant eng. serv., Rhode Island Hospital, Providence, RI '81 (ENG)
PELILLO, MICHAEL A., dir. food serv., Eagle Hill Alcoholic Rehabilitation Facility, Sandy Hook, CT '84 (FOOD)
PELIZZONI, VIRGINIA M., dir. pub. rel., Welkind Rehabilitation Hospital, Chester, NJ '85 (PR)
PELKEY, DONNA, mgr. mgt. trng. and dev., St. Joseph Hospital West, Mount Clemens, MI '81 (PERS)
PELKOWSKI, JOHN J., dir. matl. mgt., Bethesda Hospital, Zanesville, OH '82 (PUR)
PELLE, DENISE, RN, dir. nrsg., qual. assur. and nrsg. syst., Beth Israel Hospital, Boston, MA '84 (NURS)
PELLEGRINI, WILLIAM, actg. dir. oper., Montefiore Medical Group, Bronx, NY '76
PELLEGRINO, LOIS, dir. ther. activ. and vocational rehab. serv., St. Vincent's Hospital and Medical Center of New York, Westchester Branch, Harrison, NY '85
PELLEGRINO, THOMAS W., dir. food and beverage serv., Flagship Athletic Club, Eden Prairie, MN '83 (FOOD)
PELLENZ, KAREL JUHL, mgr. mktg. communications, Lansing General Hospital, Lansing, MI '83 (PR)
PELLETIER, CHARLOTTE M., asst. adm., Swedish Medical Center, Englewood, CO '80 (NURS)
PELLETIER, EILEEN, infection control practitioner, St. Anne's Hospital, Fall River, MA '84 (ENG)
PELLETIER, JEANNETTE, RN, asst. dir. nrsg., St. Mary's General Hospital, Lewiston, ME '84 (EDUC)
PELLETT, CLARK D., atty., Swedish Covenant Hospital, Chicago, IL '86 (ATTY)
PELOQUIN, ROGER, chief fin. off., Saint Francis Hospital and Medical Center, Hartford, CT '84
PELOSI, PATTI K., dir. educ., Mount Diablo Hospital Medical Center, Concord, CA '85 (EDUC)
PELOSI, RALPH T. JR., dir. eng. and maint., Whidden Memorial Hospital, Everett, MA '81 (ENG)
PELTON, RICHARD P., exec. vice-pres., Rehabilitative Care Systems of America, Stafford, TX '84
PELTON, RONALD W., dir. commun. rel., Parkview Memorial Hospital, Brunswick, ME '86 (PR)
PELTON, SUSAN W., dir. commun. serv., Concord Hospital, Concord, NH '81 (PR)
PELTZER, VERNON A., atty., Fallbrook Hospital District, Fallbrook, CA '78 (ATTY)
PELTZIE, KENNETH G., pres., Affiliated Hospitals of Indianapolis, Indianapolis, IN '56 (PLNG)(LIFE)
PELUSO, JOSEPH J., pres. and chief exec. off., Southwest Health System, Greensburg, PA '79 (PLNG)
PEMBERTON, RICHARD L., atty., Lake Region Hospital and Nursing Home, Fergus Falls, MN '80 (ATTY)
PEMBERTON, ROGER B., vice-pres., Santa Rosa Medical Center, San Antonio, TX '80 (RISK)
PENA, JESUS J., sr. vice-pres., Saint Michael's Medical Center, Newark, NJ '70
PENALIGON, JOHN J., pres. and chief exec. off., Queensway General Hospital, Toronto, Ont., Canada '86
PENCE, ROBERT D., asst. dir., New England Deaconess Hospital, Boston, MA '73
PENDERGAST, JOHN J. III, atty., Westerly Hospital, Westerly, RI '77 (ATTY)
PENDERGRAFT, FRANCES, actg. dir. soc. work, Institute for Rehabilitation and Research, Houston, TX '84 (SOC)
PENDERGRAFT, HARRY H., asst. vice-pres., Boone Hospital Center, Columbia, MO '84 (PERS)
PENDERGRASS, ALLEN, dir. pur., Spartanburg Regional Medical Center, Spartanburg, SC '85 (PUR)
PENDERGRASS, HAYWOOD M., clin. eng., North Carolina Memorial Hospital, Chapel Hill, NC '86 (ENG)
PENDLETON, JUDITH A., mgr. pers., Blue Hill Memorial Hospital, Blue Hill, ME '86 (PERS)
PENDOLA, CHARLES J., partner, Saverin, Pendola and Sandler, New York, NY '73
PENDON, LUCY N., RN, dir. staff dev., Brazosport Memorial Hospital, Lake Jackson, TX '77 (EDUC)
PENFIELD, ABBIE G., University Health Center, Burlington, VT '86 (PR)
PENFIELD, JANE A., coor. vol. serv., St. Agnes Hospital and Medical Center, Fresno, CA '83 (VOL)
PENG-CHEONG, LEE, adm., Hospital Pakar Johore, Johore, Malaysia '86
PENIX, DAVID, dir. hskpg. and ldry., Glacier Hills Nursing Center, Ann Arbor, MI '86 (ENVIRON)

PENKA, STEVEN, coor. alternative delivery syst., Antelope Valley Hospital Medical Center, Lancaster, CA '87
PENKHUS, MARK L., pres. and chief exec. off., St. Joseph Hospitals, Mount Clemens, MI '73
PENLAND, RUSSELL A., dir. gen. serv., Las Encinas Hospital, Pasadena, CA '81 (ENG)
PENMAN, LARRY D., dir. pers. and pub. rel., Richland Memorial Hospital, Olney, IL '80 (PERS)
PENN, ALAN TERRENCE, adm., HSA Desert Vista Hospital, Mesa, AZ '68
PENN, MARY E., mgr. pur., Robert F. Kennedy Medical Center, Hawthorne, CA '85 (PUR)
PENNER, BRENDA S., RN, dir. nrsg., Columbia Hospital for Women, Washington, DC '82 (NURS)
PENNER, NORMAN R., dir. champus psych. peer review proj., American Psychiatric Association, Washington, DC '62
PENNER, SAUL M., MD, (ret.), New York, NY '31 (LIFE)
PENNEY, MABEL R., educ. nrsg. and assoc. adm. nrsg. educ., United Hospital, St. Paul, MN '86 (EDUC)
PENNINGTON, DOLORES, RN, dir. in-service educ., Indiana Hospital, Indiana, PA '71 (EDUC)
PENNINGTON, DONNA M., coor. pub. rel., Chester County Hospital, West Chester, PA '85 (PR)
PENNINGTON, F. DANIEL, dir. info. syst., Medical Center East, Birmingham, AL '86 (MGMT)
PENNINGTON, LUCILE M., dir. commun. rel., East Alabama Medical Center, Opelika, AL '85 (PR)
PENROD, PHILLIP E., vice-pres., Ohio Hospital Management Services, Worthington, OH '80 (MGMT)(PLNG)
PENTAL, ELAINE, RN, asst. adm., Helene Fuld Medical Center, Trenton, NJ '80 (NURS)
PENTON, RICHARD, dir. human res., Golden Triangle Regional Medical Center, Columbus, MS '83 (PERS)
PENUEL, LEE S., dir. pub. affairs, St. Thomas Hospital, Nashville, TN '85 (PR)
PENZA, LAZARUS P., dir. eng., St. John's Queens Hospital, Elmhurst, NY '67 (ENG)
PEPE, ANTHONY L., sr. vice-pres. fiscal affairs, Frankford Hospital of the County of Philadelphia, Torresdale Division, Philadelphia, PA '68 (MGMT)
PEPE, JO ANN, dir. vol. serv., St. Joseph Mercy Hospital, Pontiac, MI '84 (VOL)
PEPE, STEPHEN P., atty., Mercy Hospital of Sacramento, Sacramento, CA '78 (ATTY)
PEPPARD, DAVID G., dir. mgt. serv., Abbott-Northwestern Hospital, Minneapolis, MN '85 (MGMT)
PEPPIN, PAUL T., vice-pres. plng. and mktg., Mercy Hospital, Muskegon, MI '82 (PLNG)
PEPPING, ALLEN J., reg. sales mgr., Burroughs Corporation, Lombard, IL '84
PERCIAK, TONI K., dir. vol. serv., St. Joseph Hospital and Health Center, Lorain, OH '84 (VOL)
PERDONCIN, PETER A., asst. dir., Montefiore Medical Center, Bronx, NY '70 (ENG)
PERDUE, BONNIE J., dir. vol. serv., St. Francis Medical Center, Cape Girardeau, MO '78 (VOL)
PERDUE, DENNIS, mgr. matl. serv., Morris Hospital, Morris, IL '86 (PUR)
PERDUE, JEANETTE D., dir. soc. work, Arkansas Children's Hospital, Little Rock, AR '81 (SOC)
PERERA, FELIX, dir. environ. serv., Presbyterian Hospital, Dallas, TX '86 (ENVIRON)
PEREZ, ANNE MARIE, mgr. food serv., Far Rockaway Nursing Home, Far Rockaway, NY '67 (FOOD)
PEREZ, CAROL ZELIS, U. S. Embassy, APO New York, NY '80
PEREZ, ENRIQUE C., cent. proc. tech., Samuel Merritt Hospital, Oakland, CA '83 (CS)
PEREZ, ERNEST H. JR., inventory contr., Denver Health and Hospitals, Denver, CO '83 (PUR)
PEREZ, FRANCISCO J., assoc. adm., Hospital San Pablo, Bayamon, P.R. '73
PEREZ, HIRAM, biomedical eng., Ryder Memorial Hospital, Humacao, P.R. '84 (ENG)
PEREZ, RICHARD, dir. sterile proc., Humana Hospital -Metropolitan, San Antonio, TX '86 (CS)
PERHAM, DEBORAH J., Perham Associates, Honolulu, HI '83 (PLNG)
PERIASWAMY, BENEDICT A., dir. educ., St. James Hospital Medical Center, Chicago Heights, IL '77 (EDUC)
PERICH, GEORGE H., dir. pers. serv., Presbyterian-University Hospital, Pittsburgh, PA '86 (PERS)
PERIN, MARDEEN L., dir. sup., proc. and distrib., Iowa Lutheran Hospital, Des Moines, IA '86 (CS)
PERIN, ROBIN LEE, atty., University Physicians, Inc., Tucson, AZ '82 (RISK)(ATTY)
PERINO, ANTHONY, dir. plant oper., Jewish Institute for Geriatric Care, New Hyde Park, NY '81 (ENG)
PERINO, ARLENE, coor. pat. educ., Morristown Memorial Hospital, Morristown, NJ '81 (EDUC)
PERIS, BARBARA A., exec. dir., The Surgery Center, Cleveland, OH '86 (AMB)
PERKEL, LINDA K., RN, dir. nrsg.-adm. serv., Mount Sinai Medical Center, Miami Beach, FL '86 (NURS)
PERKINS, ARTHUR H., MD, (ret.), South Weymouth, MA '28 (LIFE)
PERKINS, GEORGE W., atty., Redington-Fairview General Hospital, Skowhegan, ME '80 (ATTY)
PERKINS, GUY W., atty., Bluefield Community Hospital, Bluefield, WV '77 (ATTY)
PERKINS, KATHLEEN CARY, supv. customer rel., Pomona Valley Community Hospital, Pomona, CA '86 (PAT)
PERKINS, MARY J., dir. cent. sterile serv., North Carolina Baptist Hospital, Winston-Salem, NC '81 (CS)
PERKINS, MARY M., dir. commun. rel., Hancock Medical Center, Bay St. Louis, MS '82 (PR)
PERKINS, MAUREEN A., supv. vol. serv., Soldiers' Home in Holyoke, Holyoke, MA '85 (VOL)
PERKINS, MAURICE D., dir. eng., Tazewell Community Hospital, Tazewell, VA '84 (ENG)
PERKINS, NANCY S., chief food mgt. and diet., U. S. Naval Hospital, FPO New York, NY '81 (FOOD)
PERKINS, PARKER, dir. bldg. serv., Longmont United Hospital, Longmont, CO '86 (ENG)
PERKINS, PATRICIA A., supv. sup., proc. and distrib., Marlborough Hospital, Marlborough, MA '82 (CS)
PERKINS, PATRICK W., mgt. analyst, St. Francis Regional Medical Center, Wichita, KS '87 (MGMT)
PERKINS, PEGGY B., RN, asst. adm. pat. care serv., Golden Triangle Regional Medical Center, Columbus, MS '80 (NURS)
PERKINS, RALPH L., (ret.), Drexel Hill, PA '51 (LIFE)
PERKINS, RICHARD H., adm., St. Francis Hospital-Beacon, Beacon, NY '75 (PERS)
PERKINS, WANDA SUE, RN, Wyoming Medical Center, Casper, WY '87 (AMB)
PERKO, CARL V., dir., Grace Hospital, Detroit, MI '86 (PERS)
PERKO, DANA J., dir. matl. mgt., Miami Heart Institute, Miami Beach, FL '80 (PUR)
PERKOSKY, JOANNE E., coor. info. syst., Methodist Hospital, Philadelphia, PA '81 (MGMT)
PERKS, HEATHER J., dir. surg., Good Samaritan Hospital, Corvallis, OR '82 (NURS)
PERLBERG, ANNA, dir. soc. rehab., Johnston R. Bowman Health Center, Chicago, IL '82 (SOC)
PERLEY, BARBARA L., RN, adm. dir. nrsg., Valley Hospital Medical Center, Van Nuys, CA '86 (NURS)
PERLIA, MILDRED M., RN, dir. nrsg., Sheridan Road Hospital, Chicago, IL '85 (NURS)
PERLIN, MITCHELL PHILLIP, dir. mgt. eng., Good Samaritan Hospital of Maryland, Baltimore, MD '78 (MGMT)
PERLMAN, ELLEN, dir. risk mgt. and coor. qual. assur., White Plains Hospital Medical Center, White Plains, NY '86 (RISK)
PERLMAN, JOANNE, dir. pers., Victoria Hospital, Miami, FL '86 (PERS)
PERLMAN, MARK J., asst. contr., New York University Medical Center, New York, NY '78 (MGMT)
PERLMUTTER, IRVING, exec. dir., Health Employers, Inc., Minneapolis, MN '75 (PERS)
PERMANN, NADINE J., dir. pers., St. Mary Desert Valley Hospital, Apple Valley, CA '82 (PERS)
PERNA, LEIGH M., dir. vol. serv., Hospital Center at Orange, Orange, NJ '80 (VOL)
PERNO, LOUIS D., asst. dir., Norwalk Hospital, Norwalk, CT '85 (VOL)
PEROLDO, MARIA M., Health South Rehabilitation, Miami, FL '86 (SOC)
PEROUTKA, PEGGY ANN, asst. adm., Duke University Hospital, Durham, NC '83
PERRECO, BARBARA J., dir. hskpg., Suffolk Infirmary, Yaphank, NY '86 (ENVIRON)
PERREIRA, CELIA N., dir. cent. commun., Kapiolani Medical Center for Women, Honolulu, HI '84 (ENG)
PERRELLI, NANCY A., dir. legal affairs, Fairfax Hospital Association, Springfield, VA '83 (RISK)
PERRETTA, DEBRA M., RN, dir. util. and soc. serv., Jameson Memorial Hospital, New Castle, PA '86 (SOC)
PERRI, CARL M., dir. matl. mgt., Calvary Hospital, Bronx, NY '80 (PUR)
PERRIER, ANITA J., supv. pat. and family serv., St. Mary's General Hospital, Lewiston, ME '86 (SOC)
PERRIN, CHRISTINE H., coor. commun. and pub. affairs, Children's Hospital, New Orleans, LA '86 (PR)
PERRIN, FRANCES, RN, Kansas City, MO '87
PERRIN, MARTHA C., atty., DeKalb General Hospital, Smithville, TN '82 (ATTY)
PERRIN, MARY R., dir. human res., Children's Hospital, New Orleans, LA '84 (PERS)
PERRIN, RICHARD A., exec. vice-pres., Healthcare Concepts, Inc., Riverdale, MD '75 (PUR)
PERRIS, JANE C., dir. vol. serv., Barnert Memorial Hospital Center, Paterson, NJ '84 (VOL)
PERRITTE, JANIS, RN, dir. home health serv., Memorial Hospital, Nacogdoches, TX '87 (AMB)
PERRON, EILEEN M., RN, mgr. cent. sup., St. Francis Hospital, Escanaba, MI '77 (CS)
PERRY-GARGIULO, BARBARA, dir. pub. rel. and mktg., Kings Mountain Hospital, Kings Mountain, NC '86 (PR)
PERRY-SHERIDAN, NANCY, clin. coor., Health America, Inc., San Francisco, CA '85 (PAT)
PERRY, ANTHONY J., Perry Associates, Decatur, IL '51 (LIFE)
PERRY, BARRY L., vice-pres. human res., All Saints Episcopal Hospital, Fort Worth, TX '74 (PERS)
PERRY, BRUCE M., pres., Risk, Inc., Potomac, MD '67
PERRY, BUDDY W., dir. eng., AMI North Texas Medical Center, McKinney, TX '86 (ENG)
PERRY, CHRISTINE P., mgt. and plng. serv. consult., Hospital Association of New York State, Albany, NY '81 (MGMT)
PERRY, DAVID R., mgr. ldry. serv., Indiana Hospital, Indiana, PA '87 (ENVIRON)
PERRY, DIANNE L., RN, risk mgr., Jefferson Memorial Hospital, Crystal City, MO '86 (RISK)
PERRY, JANET K., mgr. mktg. and commun., Christ Hospital and Medical Center, Oak Lawn, IL '81 (PR)
PERRY, JEANNE L., dir. vol. serv., Lima Memorial Hospital, Lima, OH '75 (VOL)
PERRY, JOHN R., dir. eng., Moore Municipal Hospital, Moore, OK '85 (ENG)
PERRY, JUDITH A., RN, asst. vice-pres. nrsg., Holy Family Hospital, Des Plaines, IL '80 (NURS)
PERRY, KATE C., Excelsior, MN '85 (SOC)
PERRY, LINDA B., mgr. human res., HSA Greenbrier Hospital, Covington, LA '85 (PERS)
PERRY, LOU, dir. eng., Good Samaritan Hospital, Downers Grove, IL '78 (ENG)
PERRY, LYNNE G., mgr. vol. serv., St. Peter's Hospital, Albany, NY '84 (PAT)(VOL)
PERRY, MARGARET R., dir. human res., Warren General Hospital, Warren, OH '86 (PERS)
PERRY, MICHAEL, risk mgr., Elmcrest Psychiatric Institute, Portland, CT '87 (RISK)
PERRY, MILLA R., assoc. dir. nutr. serv., Baylor University Medical Center, Dallas, TX '85 (FOOD)
PERRY, PATRICIA C., RN, dir. nrsg. serv., Chenango Memorial Hospital, Norwich, NY '86 (NURS)
PERRY, PEGGY H., supv. oper. room, Granville Medical Center, Oxford, NC '86 (CS)
PERRY, ROBERT H., dir. matl. mgt., Winchester Medical Center, Winchester, VA '82 (PUR)
PERRY, ROBERT P., vice-pres., Faulkner Hospital, Boston, MA '79
PERRY, SUSAN M., RN, assoc. asst. adm. nrsg., University of South Alabama Medical Center, Mobile, AL '81 (NURS)
PERRY, WADE B. JR., atty., Mobile Infirmary Medical Center, Mobile, AL '83 (ATTY)
PERRY, WESLEY, pur. agt., Wayne County Memorial Hospital, Honesdale, PA '75 (PUR)
PERRYMAN, MARGARET, vice-pres. adm., Minneapolis Children's Medical Center, Minneapolis, MN '87 (AMB)
PERSAUD, JOHN, dir. pers., labor rel. and trng., Coney Island Hospital, Brooklyn, NY '73 (PERS)
PERSILY, NANCY ALFRED, pres., Nancy Alfred Persily Associates, Inc., Coral Gables, FL '80 (PLNG)
PERSIN, MARCIA N., assoc. adm., Sinai Hospital of Detroit, Detroit, MI '82
PERSIO, DINO S., atty., Miners Hospital Northern Cambria, Spangler, PA '86 (ATTY)
PERSIO, GASPER A., dir. hskpg., Miners Hospital Northern Cambria, Spangler, PA '86 (ENVIRON)
PERSKY, MARLA S., atty., Northwestern Memorial Hospital, Chicago, IL '83 (ATTY)
PERSON, EVERETT I., dir. adm. serv., Manhattan Psyc Center-Ward's Island, New York, NY '86
PERSSON, JOHN A. H., dir. maint. and eng., Pendleton Memorial Methodist Hospital, New Orleans, LA '84 (ENG)
PERTUZ, ALVARO E., vice-pres. support serv. and syst., Group Health Plan, Inc., Minneapolis, MN '70 (MGMT)(AMB)
PERTZBORN, ROBERT J., dir. pur., Meriter Hospital, Madison, WI '72 (PUR)
PERUN, EDMUND LAWRENCE, Charlotte, NC '63
PERVEZ, NAJMUDDIN, sr. vice-pres. prof. and fin. serv., Beth Israel Medical Center, New York, NY '82 (PLNG)
PERVEZ, SAOOD A., dir. lab., Firelands Community Hospital, Sandusky, OH '80 (EDUC)
PERVIN, BRADFORD F., dir. matl. mgt., Saint Joseph Hospital, Denver, CO '81 (PUR)
PESAVENTO, DAVID R., biomedical elec. spec., Scottsdale Memorial Hospital, Scottsdale, AZ '82 (ENG)
PESEK, ZORY, dir. environ. serv., St. Frances Xavier Cabrini Hospital, Chicago, IL '86 (ENVIRON)(ENG)
PESETSKI, LT. COL. JUDITH R., RN, Letterman Army Medical Center, San Francisco, CA '85
PESEZ, PHILIP G., mgr. pers., Sunnyview Hospital and Rehabilitation Center, Schenectady, NY '83 (PERS)
PESSIN, NACHUM, dep. dir. gen. and adm., Shaare Zedek Medical Center, Jerusalem, Israel '78
PESUT, DANIEL J., RN, assoc. dir. nrsg. serv., W. S. Hall Psychiatric Institute, Columbia, SC '86 (NURS)
PETER, MARY ANN, RN, dir. nrsg. serv., Duke Hospital North, Durham, NC '79 (NURS)
PETERMAN, AUDREY K., dir. vol. serv., Hackley Hospital, Muskegon, MI '83 (VOL)
PETERMAN, CATHERINE A., nrs. mgr. surg. center, Monongalia General Hospital, Morgantown, WV '87 (AMB)
PETERMAN, JANICE, mgr. cent. serv., Asbury Hospital, Salina, KS '79 (CS)
PETERS-STOKES, BERTHA L., vice-pres. ancillary serv., St. Mary's Hospital, Orange, NJ '86
PETERS, ADOLPHE J., mgt. syst. eng., Rhode Island Hospital, Providence, RI '71 (MGMT)
PETERS, DAVID A., MD, asst. adm. prof. serv., Alexandria Hospital, Alexandria, VA '56 (LIFE)
PETERS, DIANE M., RN, asst. adm. nrsg. serv., Door County Memorial Hospital, Sturgeon Bay, WI '85 (NURS)
PETERS, DON, chief eng., Coastal Communities Hospital, Bunnell, FL '86 (ENG)
PETERS, J. DOUGLAS, atty., American Lung Association, Detroit, MI '77 (ATTY)
PETERS, JAMES W., dir. corp. commun. and dev., Mid-Maine Medical Center, Waterville, ME '81 (PR)
PETERS, JEFFRY A., pres., Ingalls Health Ventures, Harvey, IL '83 (PLNG)(AMB)
PETERS, JERRY J., dir. eng. and maint., Magee-Womens Hospital, Pittsburgh, PA '85 (ENG)
PETERS, JOHN D., asst. adm. support serv., Bexar County Hospital District, San Antonio, TX '71 (MGMT)
PETERS, JOSEPH P., Philadelphia, PA '48 (PLNG)(LIFE)
PETERS, KAREN S., RN, dir. nrsg., Alpha Home Health Agency, Green Bay, WI '81 (NURS)
PETERS, KENNETH W., sr. vice-pres. plng. and oper., Texas Hospital Association, Austin, TX '57 (PLNG)(LIFE)
PETERS, LARRY R., coor. educ., St. Joseph Hospital, Chicago, IL '74 (EDUC)
PETERS, LORETTA A., dir. qual. assur., St. Joseph Hospital, Kirkwood, MO '83 (RISK)
PETERS, MARY ANN, RN, asst. adm. nrsg., St. Anthony Hospital, Oklahoma City, OK '79 (NURS)
PETERS, N. KIM, Bloomfield Hills, MI '76
PETERS, PATRICIA A., student, Program in Health Care Administration, University of Minnesota, Minneapolis, MN '86 (AMB)
PETERS, SR. PHYLIS L., RN, vice-pres., Seton Medical Center, Austin, TX '78 (NURS)
PETERS, ROBERT J., supv. gen. maint., Holmes Regional Medical Center, Melbourne, FL '86 (ENG)
PETERS, ROBERT J., pres., Teknow International, Inc., Miami, FL '87 (ENG)
PETERS, ROBERT M., coor. telecommun., Verdugo Hills Hospital, Glendale, CA '84 (ENG)
PETERS, ROBERT W., dir. plng., Bryan Memorial Hospital, Lincoln, NE '71 (PLNG)
PETERS, SHARON R., dir. mktg., Irving Community Hospital, Irving, TX '84 (PLNG)
PETERS, SUZANNE K., dir. human res., Munson Medical Center, Traverse City, MI '85 (PERS)

PETERS, SYLVIA H., asst. vice-pres. mktg., Victory Memorial Hospital, Waukegan, IL '81 (PR) (PLNG)
PETERS, LCDR VERNON M., MSC USN, chm. risk mgt., Naval Hospital, Bremerton, WA '83 (RISK)
PETERS, WILLIAM D., dir. pur., Leominster Hospital, Leominster, MA '83 (PUR)
PETERS, WILLIAM W., (ret.), Millwood, VA '51 (LIFE)
PETERSEN, EMILY M., dir. plng., Lester E. Cox Medical Centers, Springfield, MO '82 (PLNG)
PETERSEN, GARY L., coor. elec., Butterworth Hospital, Grand Rapids, MI '84 (ENG)
PETERSEN, INGO, vice-pres. emp. rel., Perth Amboy Division, Perth Amboy, NJ '73 (PERS)
PETERSEN, KAAREN L., adm., Children Development Center, Chicago, IL '80
PETERSEN, KARL J., dir. pers., Beebe Hospital of Sussex County, Lewes, DE '86 (PERS)
PETERSEN, LINDA L., dir. info. serv., Woodlawn Hospital, Rochester, IN '86 (PR)
PETERSEN, LINDA M., RN, dir. nrsg., Dickinson County Memorial Hospital, Spirit Lake, IA '82 (NURS)
PETERSEN, MADELINE, asst. adm., San Francisco General Hospital Medical Center, San Francisco, CA '86 (RISK)
PETERSEN, MARILYN J., RN, dir. nrsg., Medical Center Hospital, Punta Gorda, FL '84 (NURS)
PETERSEN, MARSHA C., mgr. pub. rel., Queen's Medical Center, Honolulu, HI '86 (PR)
PETERSEN, NEIL R., assoc. adm., Fairmont Hospital, San Leandro, CA '71 (FOOD)
PETERSEN, NORMA K., RN, dir. nrsg. serv., Dameron Hospital, Stockton, CA '80 (NURS)
PETERSEN, SCOTT R., asst. dir. pur., Evanston Hospital, Evanston, IL '84
PETERSEN, TERRY A., dir. mktg. and commun. rel., Northern Montana Hospital, Havre, MT '86 (PR) (PLNG)
PETERSEN, VIRGINIA L., RN, asst. adm. nrsg. serv., Kaiser Foundation Hospital, Vallejo, CA '81 (NURS)
PETERSON, AMY J. MINICK, mgr. mktg. commun., Community Hospitals of Indiana, Indianapolis, IN '85 (PR)
PETERSON, ANTHONY A., acct. exec., Marsh and McLenan, Milwaukee, WI '84 (RISK)
PETERSON, BRIAN A., contr., Swedish Medical Center, Englewood, CO '86
PETERSON, CAROLYN LOUISE, pat. rel. rep., Kettering Medical Center, Kettering, OH '81 (PAT)
PETERSON, DEBORAH KIFFIN, dir. soc. serv., Memorial Hospital of Dodge County, Fremont, NE '76 (SOC)
PETERSON, ELAINE L., mkgt serv. spec., St. Luke's Hospital of New Bedford, New Bedford, MA '87 (PR)
PETERSON, ELIZABETH A., atty., Memorial Medical Center, Long Beach, CA '84 (ATTY)
PETERSON, FRED L., mgr. pub. rel. and mktg. commun., Bethany Hospital, Chicago, IL '86 (PR) (PLNG)
PETERSON, GEORGE E., dir. plant oper., Newcomb Medical Center, Vineland, NJ '81 (ENG)
PETERSON, GERALDINE, RN, assoc. dir. nrsg., Methodist Hospital, St. Louis Park, MN '80 (NURS)
PETERSON, GLENN F., vice-pres. adm., James M. Jackson Memorial Hospital, Miami, FL '69
PETERSON, GRACE G., RN, (ret.), Sun City, AZ '74 (NURS)
PETERSON, GREGORY P., exec. dir., E. G. Todd Associates, Inc., Overland Park, KS '81 (PLNG)
PETERSON, GRETCHEN M., dir. pub. rel., commun. rel. and guest rel., Charter Grove Hospital, Corona, CA '82 (PR)(VOL)
PETERSON, H. DENNIS, asst. vice-pres., Bethany Enterprises, Inc., Phoenix, AZ '85 (PUR)
PETERSON, HAROLD L., (ret.), Lookout Mountain, TN '52 (LIFE)
PETERSON, HOWARD JOHN, dir., Pennsylvania State University Hospital, Hershey, PA '80
PETERSON, HUBERT O., dir. soc. serv., Harrisburg Hospital, Harrisburg, PA '72 (SOC)
PETERSON, HUGH JR., atty., Charter Medical Corporation, Macon, GA '86 (ATTY)
PETERSON, J. J. JR., pres., Peterson Associates, Charlotte, NC '75
PETERSON, JACK K., dir. pers. and labor rel., Community Hospital Association, Battle Creek, MI '73 (PERS)
PETERSON, JANET M., asst. dir. vol. serv., United Hospital, St. Paul, MN '84 (VOL)
PETERSON, JOAN L., dir. vol. serv., Rice Memorial Hospital, Willmar, MN '82 (VOL)
PETERSON, KRISTINE E., pres., K. E. Peterson and Associates, Chicago, IL '79 (PR)
PETERSON, LAURENCE J., adm. path. lab., El Paso Medical Center, El Paso, TX '70
PETERSON, LAWRENCE R., dir. mktg. and commun., Oil City Area Health Center, Oil City, PA '84 (PR) (PLNG)
PETERSON, LINDA N., dir. med. soc. serv., Mercy Hospital, Charlotte, NC '86 (SOC)
PETERSON, LOIS, dir. soc. serv., Bethesda Memorial Hospital, Boynton Beach, FL '77 (SOC)
PETERSON, MARGARET M., dir. soc. serv., Hospital of Saint Raphael, New Haven, CT '82 (SOC)
PETERSON, MARGARET S., dir. pub. affairs, St. Joseph's Hospital, Marshfield, WI '82 (PR)
PETERSON, MARILEE A., dir. human res., St. John's Hospital, Jackson, WY '83 (PERS)
PETERSON, MARLENE, dir. vol. serv., United Hospital, Grand Forks, ND '70 (VOL)
PETERSON, MARY CHARLES H., RN, asst. dir. nrsg. serv., Southwest Mississippi Medical Center, McComb, MS '86 (NURS)
PETERSON, MARY E., dir. mgt. syst., Mother Frances Hospital Regional Center, Tyler, TX '83 (MGMT)
PETERSON, MARY, RN, dir. nrsg. serv., St. Joseph Medical Center, Wichita, KS '73 (NURS)
PETERSON, PHILIP N., pres., Professional Resources Management, Inc., New Berlin, WI '82 (EDUC)
PETERSON, R. SCOTT, spec. asst. to pres., Orlando Regional Medical Center, Orlando, FL '83
PETERSON, RICHARD C., mgr., Arthur Andersen and Company, Chicago, IL '77 (MGMT)
PETERSON, RICHARD NORMAN, atty., American Hospital Association, Chicago, IL '82 (ATTY)
PETERSON, ROBERT E., atty., Woodlawn Hospital, Rochester, IN '76 (ATTY)
PETERSON, ROBERT L., dir. eng. and maint., Pomona Valley Community Hospital, Pomona, CA '80 (ENG)
PETERSON, SANDRA B., RN, dir. med. and surg. nrsg., Michael Reese Hospital and Medical Center, Chicago, IL '87 (NURS)
PETERSON, SHERRY, dir. risk mgt. and qual. assur., Pasadena Bayshore Medical Center, Pasadena, TX '83 (RISK)
PETERSON, SHIRLEY A., dir. cent. proc. and distrib., Illini Hospital, Silvis, IL '80 (CS)
PETERSON, SHIRLEY LOUISE, Altamonte Springs, FL '82 (SOC)
PETERSON, SHIRLEY S., coor. educ., St. Joseph Mercy Hospital, Pontiac, MI '83 (EDUC)
PETERSON, SUSAN G., dir. plng. and commun. rel., Beebe Hospital of Sussex County, Lewes, DE '86 (PR)
PETERSON, THOMAS L., RN, dir. nrsg. serv., Lakeview Medical Center, Rice Lake, WI '80 (NURS)(AMB)
PETERSON, THOMAS R., dir. pers., Independence Regional Health Center, Independence, MO '76 (PERS)
PETERSON, TODD L., assoc. dir., University of California Davis Medical Center, Sacramento, CA '73
PETHICK, LIBBY, mgr. emer., Thomas Jefferson University Hospital, Philadelphia, PA '87 (AMB)
PETIT, CONNIE C., RN, dir. nrsg.-amb. serv., Children's Hospital National Medical Center, Washington, DC '85 (NURS)
PETIT, CONSTANCE C., dir. nrsg. amb. serv., Children's Hospital National Medical Center, Washington, DC '87 (AMB)
PETIT, ROBERT R., med. adm., Student Health Center, Eugene, OR '65
PETRAGLIA, F. J., mgr. loss control, Industrial Indemnity, San Francisco, CA '87
PETRE, COURTNEY GRAHAM, atty., Valley View Hospital, Glenwood Springs, CO '81 (ATTY)
PETRELLA, PAUL P., asst. dir. plant oper., Atlantic City Medical Center, Atlantic City, NJ '79 (ENG)
PETRETTA, HOWARD M., dir. biomedical commun., Cooper Hospital-University Medical Center, Camden, NJ '84 (ENG)
PETRICH, FRANK A., pres., DePaul Health Center, Bridgeton, MO '70 (ATTY)
PETRICH, KENNETH L., vice-pres. dev. and pub. rel., Bensenville Home Society, Bensenville, IL '83 (PR)
PETRICH, LISE, assoc. vice-pres., United Hospital, St. Paul, MN '83 (PLNG)
PETRIE, FRANCIS M., (ret.), Westerly, RI '48 (LIFE)
PETRIE, JOHN A., assoc. adm., Booth Memorial Medical Center, Flushing, NY '83
PETRIE, LYNN, coor. soc. work psych., St. Boniface General Hospital, Winnipeg, Man., Canada '83 (SOC)
PETRIK, JOANNE J., RN, dir. clin., Penrose Hospitals, Colorado Springs, CO '84 (NURS)
PETRING, MARSHALL C., chief logistics serv. div., Fitzsimons Army Medical Center, Aurora, CO '56 (LIFE)
PETRO, PENNY L., dir. vol. serv., Grand View Hospital, Sellersville, PA '82 (VOL)
PETROCELLY, KENNETH L., dir. plant oper., United Community Hospital, Grove City, PA '86 (ENG)
PETROCHUK, MICHAEL AARON, adm. res., Community Medical Center, Scranton, PA '83 (PLNG)
PETRONIS, KENNETH, consult., Ernst and Whinney, Chicago, IL '85
PETROSKI, WALTER J., sr. dir. contract mgt., Blue Cross and Blue Shield Association, Chicago, IL '52 (LIFE)
PETROSS, BUCILLA A., RN, adm. nrsg., Kaiser Permanente, Pasadena, CA '76 (NURS)
PETROW, JOAN ELEANOR, pat. rel. rep., Presbyterian Hospital in the City of New York, New York, NY '87 (PAT)
PETRUCELLI, CAROL A., adm. oper., Kaiser Permanente, Akron, OH '87 (AMB)
PETRUCELLI, JOSEPH A., dir. plant eng., Genesee Hospital, Rochester, NY '86 (ENG)
PETRUNAK, JOHN E., dir. trng. and educ., St. Joseph Riverside Hospital, Warren, OH '86 (EDUC)
PETRUNIS, MARY, dir. vol. serv., Shore Memorial Hospital, Somers Point, NJ '72 (VOL)
PETRUZZI, ANTHONY, assoc. dir. eng., Mercy Hospital, Rockville Centre, NY '87 (ENG)
PETTERS, OLGA E., dir. med. plng., Neptune and Associates, San Diego, CA '77
PETTI, MARY M., RN, asst. adm. nrsg. serv., Hospital Center at Orange, Orange, NJ '85 (NURS)
PETTICK, BARBARA G., sr. plng. assoc., Beth Israel Medical Center, New York, NY '86 (PLNG)
PETTIGREW, PHILIP ALLEN, corp. dir. matl. mgt. and mgt. serv., AMI Presbyterian-St. Luke's Medical Center, Denver, CO '77 (MGMT)
PETTIGREW, STEVEN L., corp. dir. res. eval., Samaritan Health Service, Phoenix, AZ '73 (MGMT)
PETTINGER, CANDI, dir. vol. serv., Humana Hospital -Biscayne, Miami, FL '82 (VOL)
PETTIS, RICHARD C., coor. constr., Genesee Hospital, Rochester, NY '79 (ENG)
PETTIT, SARA L., assoc. dir. educ. serv., Parkview Memorial Hospital, Fort Wayne, IN '85 (EDUC)
PETTUS, WILLIAM H., dir. plant serv., University of California San Diego Medical Center, San Diego, CA '85 (ENG)
PETTY, DALE H., mgr. med. eng. sect., William Beaumont Hospital, Royal Oak, MI '80 (ENG)
PETTY, JACK E., vice-pres. adm., Wesley Medical Center, Wichita, KS '85
PETTY, JACK S., mgr. pers. and payroll, Knoxville Area Community Hospital, Knoxville, IA '86 (PERS)
PETTY, KEITH A., dir. matl. mgt., Chestnut Hill Hospital, Philadelphia, PA '85 (PUR)
PETTY, PEGGY J., RN, dir. nrsg., AMI Fort Bend Community Hospital, Missouri City, TX '85 (NURS)
PETTY, STEPHEN L., chief soc. work serv., Jerry L. Pettis Memorial Veterans Hospital, Loma Linda, CA '75 (SOC)
PETUCK, CLAIRE A., RN, mgr. cent. serv. and sup., Valley Regional Hospital, Claremont, NH '82 (CS)
PETWAY, JOSEPH K. JR., head ped. dept., Naval Hospital, Long Beach, CA '86 (RISK)
PETZELT, BETH, exec. dir., Atlanta Surgi-Center, Inc., Atlanta, GA '87 (AMB)
PEUGH, DELBERT D., asst. adm. support serv., Lutheran Medical Center, St. Louis, MO '80 (ENG)
PEVERLY, PATRICIA A., RN, dir. nrsg. serv., Anderson Hospital, Maryville, IL '85 (NURS)
PEW, R. ANDERSON, pres., Helios Capitol Corporation, Radnor, PA '76 (HON)
PEYTON, FAY B., RN, adm. nrs., Memorial Hospital System, Houston, TX '74 (NURS)
PEYTON, THOMAS G., adm., McPherson Hospital, Durham, NC '57 (MGMT)(LIFE)
PFAEHLER, KARL H., RN, chief nrsg., Moncrief Army Community Hospital, Fort Jackson, SC '85 (NURS)
PFAELZER, ANN G., bd. vice-pres., Boston Hospital for Women, Lying-in Division, Boston, MA '45 (LIFE)
PFAFFENBERGER, STEVE, supv. eng., Henry Ford Hospital, Detroit, MI '85 (ENG)
PFAFFENROTH, LINDA C., dir. plng., Mercy Medical Center, Oshkosh, WI '79 (PLNG)
PFALZER, JAMES Z., dir. diet. serv., Germantown Hospital and Medical Center, Philadelphia, PA '75 (FOOD)
PFANNENSCHMIDT, MARY ANN, dir. diet., St. Clair Memorial Hospital, Pittsburgh, PA '82 (FOOD)
PFARRER, STEPHEN M., atty., Grandview Hospital and Medical Center, Dayton, OH '74 (ATTY)
PFAU, WILLIAM E. JR., atty., Pfau, Comstock and Springer, Youngstown, OH '80 (ATTY)
PFEFERMAN, MARION C., mgr., Cohen, Rutherford and Blum, Rockville, MD '83 (PLNG)
PFEFFER, IRIS A., dir. soc. serv., Villaview Community Hospital, San Diego, CA '85 (SOC)
PFEFFER, MARGARET J., coor. nrsg. for res. and eval., Atlanticare Medical Center, Lynn, MA '86 (MGMT)
PFEIFFENBERGER, ROBERT G., vice-pres., Good Samaritan Hospital, Cincinnati, OH '86 (MGMT)
PFEIFFER, CAROL QUINN, student, Department of Health Services Administration, George Washington University, Washington, DC '86
PFEIFFER, ELAINE V., RN, clin. dir. maternal-child health, Waukesha Memorial Hospital, Waukesha, WI '82 (NURS)
PFEIFFER, PHYLLIS LEE, adm. food, Gowanda Psychiatric Center, Helmuth, NY '82 (FOOD)
PFEIFFER, RICHARD G., sr. underwriting off. med. serv., St. Paul Fire and Marine Insurance Company, St. Paul, MN '83 (RISK)
PFEIFFER, RICHARD R., dir. eng., Cobb General Hospital, Austell, GA '81 (ENG)
PFEIL, LEANN, asst. dir. pers., Roseville Community Hospital, Roseville, CA '85 (PERS)
PFIFFNER, PAMELA J., mgr. vol. serv., Mercy Health Center, Dubuque, IA '82 (VOL)
PFIRMAN, HOWARD S., (ret.), Avon, CT '38 (LIFE)
PFLUGER, JAMES D., arch., Pfluger Associates, Austin, TX '83 (ENG)
PFLUM, DONNA J., coor. vol. serv., Mercy Hospital, Grayling, MI '86 (VOL)
PFOHL, JAMES C. JR., dir. human res., Moses H. Cone Memorial Hospital, Greensboro, NC '85 (PERS)
PFRANK, KYM A., dir. info. serv., Union Hospital, Terre Haute, IN '85 (MGMT)
PFURR, DAVID J., dir. food serv., HCA Valley Regional Medical Center, Brownsville, TX '85 (FOOD)
PHAFF, JUDITH, dir. risk mgt., St. Peter's Hospital, Albany, NY '86 (RISK)
PHARES, LEATRICE TURLIS, RN, coor. in-service, Imperial Point Medical Center, Fort Lauderdale, FL '80 (EDUC)
PHARISS, STANLEY K., dir. pers., Lakeview Medical Center, Danville, IL '85 (PERS)
PHARR, JOHN K. JR., assoc. dir. prof. serv., Northeast Georgia Medical Center, Gainesville, GA '72
PHELAN, CAROL J., RN, prog. dir. cont. educ. and commun. serv., Lansing Community College, Department of Health Careers, Lansing, MI '71 (EDUC)
PHELAN, CISSY, atty., Methodist Hospital-Central Unit, Memphis, TN '84 (ATTY)
PHELAN, JOHN L., consult., Chicago, IL '85 (PLNG)
PHELAN, RITA M., spec. asst. to vice-pres., Brookdale Hospital Medical Center, Brooklyn, NY '85 (RISK)
PHELAN, WILLIAM V., atty., Mercy Hospital, Iowa City, IA '68 (ATTY)
PHELPS, BARRY JUDSON, dir. matl. mgt., Northeastern Vermont Regional Hospital, St. Johnsbury, VT '86 (PUR)
PHELPS, DAVID M., dir. ldry. serv., Tucson Medical Center, Tucson, AZ '86 (ENVIRON)
PHELPS, DENNIS O., dir. pers., Pomona Valley Community Hospital, Pomona, CA '73 (PERS)
PHELPS, DOLORES, risk mgr. and adm. assoc., Anderson Hospital, Maryville, IL '86 (RISK)
PHELPS, GARY L., chief oper. off., Doctors Memorial Hospital, Atlanta, GA '85
PHELPS, MARY JANE, RN, staff nrs., West Houston Medical Center, Houston, TX '82 (EDUC)
PHELPS, MICHAEL K., dir. risk mgt., St. Vincent Infirmary, Little Rock, AR '83 (RISK)
PHELPS, REGINA L., Ochsner Foundation Hospital, New Orleans, LA '83 (EDUC)
PHELPS, ROGER W., med. soc. worker, Community Hospital, Santa Rosa, CA '86 (SOC)
PHEMISTER, R. GLADYS, dir. educ., Goshen General Hospital, Goshen, IN '82 (EDUC)
PHEND, MARIELLEN W., dir. vol. serv., Goshen General Hospital, Goshen, IN '81 (VOL)

PHERSON, SUSAN J., assoc. dir. pat. care serv., Strong Memorial Hospital Rochester University, Rochester, NY '78
PHILBEE, MICHAEL, dir. plant oper., Whitley County Memorial Hospital, Columbia City, IN '87 (ENG)
PHILBIN, PATRICK W., pres., Patrick Philbin and Associates, Inc., Austin, TX '79 (PLNG)
PHILBIN, RICHARD J., asst. adm., Suny Health Sciences Center at Syracuse, Syracuse, NY '79 (PUR)
PHILEN, JILL G., dir. plng. and mktg., Spohn Hospital, Corpus Christi, TX '84 (PLNG)
PHILIBEN, LT. COL. ANNE N., MSC USA, 97th General Hospital, APO New York, NY '85 (NURS)
PHILIBERT, M. BARBARA, RN, assoc. adm., Mercy Hospital, Cedar Rapids, IA '84 (NURS)
PHILIPPS, KURT A., atty., St. Francis-St. George Hospital, Cincinnati, OH '87 (ATTY)
PHILIPS, ROSE MARIE, asst. to vice-pres., University of Texas Medical Branch Hospitals, Galveston, TX '83
PHILL, MAJ. CHARLES M., MSC USAF, dir. pers. and adm. serv., U. S. Air Force Hospital, Lompoc, CA '74
PHILLIPI, DAVID, adm., Aurora Community Hospital, Aurora, MO '87 (AMB)
PHILLIPPE, JAMES R. II, adm., Lake View Community Hospital, Paw Paw, MI '78
PHILLIPPI, GENE P., RN, asst. adm. pat. serv., Memorial Medical Center of West Michigan, Ludington, MI '75 (NURS)
PHILLIPS, ANNA W., vice-pres., Garofolo Curtiss and Company, Washington, DC '86 (PLNG)
PHILLIPS, BARBARA A., supv., Memorial Hospital of Dodge County, Fremont, NE '86 (ENVIRON)
PHILLIPS, BETTY J., (ret.), Newark, NJ '57 (LIFE)
PHILLIPS, BETTY JANE, mgr. cent. serv., Huntington Hospital, Huntington, NY '78 (CS)
PHILLIPS, BONNIE, dir. pers., Saratoga Community Hospital, Detroit, MI '86 (PERS)
PHILLIPS, BRONWEN M., dir. med. soc. serv., Lafayette Home Hospital, Lafayette, IN '86 (SOC)
PHILLIPS, CELESTE P., coor. pat. educ., McLeod Regional Medical Center, Florence, SC '86 (EDUC)
PHILLIPS, CHARLES D., EdD, pres., American Protestant Health Association, Schaumburg, IL '74
PHILLIPS, DAN, dir. pers., Community Methodist Hospital, Henderson, KY '74 (PERS)
PHILLIPS, EDITH J., RN, vice-pres. nrsg., Baptist Medical Center Easley, Easley, SC '80 (NURS)
PHILLIPS, GEORGE C. JR., pres., Healthnetwork, Inc., Oak Brook, IL '79
PHILLIPS, IZELL, supv. cent. serv., St. Frances Xavier Cabrini Hospital, Chicago, IL '81 (CS)
PHILLIPS, JAMES A., dir. benefits and compensation, East Jefferson General Hospital, Metairie, LA '83 (PERS)
PHILLIPS, JANE, RN, assoc. adm., Hennepin County Medical Center, Minneapolis, MN '79 (NURS)
PHILLIPS, JAQUITA D., mktg. and commun. assoc., St. Vincent Infirmary, Little Rock, AR '86 (PLNG)
PHILLIPS, JOHN F., contr., Gravette Medical Center Hospital, Gravette, AR '85
PHILLIPS, JOHN J., staff asst., Veterans Administration Medical Center, Washington, DC '79
PHILLIPS, KAY R., vice-pres. plng. and mktg., Boulder Community Hospital, Boulder, CO '77 (PR) (PLNG)
PHILLIPS, LANA C., mgr. cost center, Methodist Hospital of Indiana, Indianapolis, IN '84 (CS)
PHILLIPS, LILA H., dir. pub. rel., Warner Brown Hospital, El Dorado, AR '85 (PR)
PHILLIPS, LOUIS A., dir. eng., Phoenix General Hospital, Phoenix, AZ '84 (ENG)
PHILLIPS, MARILYN, adm. asst. pat. rel. and coor. vol., Royal Columbian Hospital, New Westminster, B.C., Canada '82 (PAT)
PHILLIPS, MARK STEVEN, adm. outpatient res., Tucson Medical Center, Tucson, AZ '78 (RISK)
PHILLIPS, MAXINE, dir. pers., Mercy Hospitals of Kansas, Fort Scott, KS '69 (PERS)
PHILLIPS, MONICA M., RN, dir. nrsg. serv., Pottstown Memorial Medical Center, Pottstown, PA '71 (NURS)
PHILLIPS, PAUL W., asst. adm., Eye and Ear Clinic, Wenatchee, WA '81 (ENG)
PHILLIPS, PHYLLIS A., dir. soc. serv., Wayne County Memorial Hospital, Honesdale, PA '86 (SOC)
PHILLIPS, RAY ELLEN, RN, vice-pres., Harris Methodist -HEB, Bedford, TX '82 (NURS)
PHILLIPS, RICHARD E., dir. food serv., Peninsula General Hospital Medical Center, Salisbury, MD '76 (FOOD)
PHILLIPS, ROSALIE R., vice-pres. plng., Harvard Community Health Plan, Brookline Village, MA '86 (MGMT)
PHILLIPS, SAMUEL F., dir. plant oper. and maint., Washington County Hospital, Hagerstown, MD '83 (ENG)
PHILLIPS, SHARON, mgr. maternity serv., St. Joseph's Hospital, Stockton, CA '86 (RISK)
PHILLIPS, SHERRY A., dir. mgt. serv., Capitol Hill Hospital, Washington, DC '85 (MGMT)
PHILLIPS, SHIRLEY B., RN, supv. oper. room, HCA Greenview Hospital, Bowling Green, KY '87 (AMB)
PHILLIPS, STEVEN J., pres., Steven Phillips International, Ltd., Buffalo Grove, IL '81 (PUR)
PHILLIPS, THOMAS, dir. pers., Benedictine Hospital, Kingston, NY '83 (PERS)
PHILLIPS, VALERIE J., dir. diet., St. Mary's Hill Hospital, Milwaukee, WI '85 (FOOD)
PHILLIPS, WHIT, arch., Page, Southerland and Page, Austin, TX '76
PHILLIPSON, CHRISTINE A., dir. diet. serv., Memorial Hospital of Iowa County, Dodgeville, WI '82 (FOOD)
PHILO, BEVERLY B., dir. pat. rel., Memorial Hospital System, Houston, TX '81 (PAT)
PHILO, ROGER F., prin., Philo Architects, Houston, TX '78
PHILPOTT, BLYE W., supv. vol., Memorial Southwest Hospital, Houston, TX '86 (VOL)
PHINNEY, THERESE, RN, dir. nrsg. support serv. and pat. adv., Addison Gilbert Hospital, Gloucester, MA '86 (PAT)
PHIPPS, ANITA L., asst. dir. matl. mgt., Chesapeake General Hospital, Chesapeake, VA '85 (PUR)
PHIPPS, DARRELL E. SR., supv. power plant, Martin Memorial Hospital, Stuart, FL '85 (ENG)
PHIPPS, JACKIE G., mgr. emp., Bristol Memorial Hospital, Bristol, TN '83 (PERS)
PHIPPS, WILLIAM, asst. adm. external affairs, Takoma Adventist Hospital, Greeneville, TN '86 (PR)
PI, CLARA M. L., asst. dir. food serv., Burnaby Hospital, Burnaby, B.C., Canada '86 (FOOD)
PIACENTINI, EUGENE, vice-pres. and treas., Creative Gourmets, Ltd., Boston, MA '82 (FOOD)
PIANO, NOEL C., RN, asst. to adm. affairs, Children's Hospital National Medical Center, Washington, DC '86 (NURS)
PIANTANIDA, MARIA, dir. educ. dev., Allegheny General Hospital, Pittsburgh, PA '78 (EDUC)
PIASECKI, LINDA, dir. food serv., Southside Hospital, Bay Shore, NY '76 (FOOD)
PIATKOWSKI, STANLEY J., dir. eng. and maint., Hutzel Hospital, Detroit, MI '80 (ENG)
PIAZZA, C. RICHARD, dir. med. prod. and serv., Radius Health Care System, Inc., Madison Heights, MI '85 (PLNG)
PIAZZA, DEBRA A., consult., Laventhol and Horwath, Philadelphia, PA '84 (PLNG)
PIAZZA, KENNETH P., adm. asst., chief of staff and pub. rel. off., Veterans Administration Medical Center, Bath, NY '86 (PR)
PIAZZA, PRESTON D., dir. human res., River Oaks Hospital, Jackson, MS '87 (PERS)
PICADASH, GARRY J., dir. biomedical electronics, Southern Baptist Hospital, New Orleans, LA '86 (ENG)
PICCOLI, LEONARD RALPH, spec. consult. to pres., St. Barnabas Hospital, Bronx, NY '59
PICCONE, JOSEPH A., mgr. design dev., Baptist Hospital and Health Systems, Phoenix, AZ '80 (MGMT)
PICHA, NORBERT O., Colorado Springs, CO '71
PICHA, PATRICIA KAYE, sr. consult., Ernst and Whinney, Miami, FL '84
PICHE, GREGORY R., atty., Cedar Springs Psychiatric Hospital, Colorado Springs, CO '77 (ATTY)
PICHE, SR. MARY A., pat. rep., Carney Hospital, Boston, MA '85 (PAT)
PICHEO, LOUIS JAMES, dir. food serv., Baptist Hospital East, Louisville, KY '72 (FOOD)
PICHEY, BRENDA A., cent. serv. tech., Lockport Memorial Hospital, Lockport, NY '84 (CS)
PICHLER, JOHN A., dir. lab. syst. and serv., Michael Reese Hospital and Medical Center, Chicago, IL '81
PICK, LENARD I., atty., St. John's Hospital and Health Center, Santa Monica, CA '82 (ATTY)
PICKARD, MYRNA R., dean, University of Texas at Arlington, School of Nursing, Arlington, TX '83 (NURS)
PICKARD, NANCY ALTEMUS, asst. vice-pres. external affairs, Chestnut Hill Hospital, Philadelphia, PA '81 (PLNG)
PICKEL, KATHY M., coor. commun., plng. and mktg., Indian River Memorial Hospital, Vero Beach, FL '86 (PR)
PICKENHEIM, JANICE S., asst. dir. food serv. mgt., Geisinger Medical Center, Danville, PA '81 (FOOD)
PICKENS, CANDICE W., dir. food and nutr. serv., AMI Terrell Community Hospital, Terrell, TX '85 (FOOD)
PICKENS, JAMES F. II, dir. pers., Saint Francis Hospital, Tulsa, OK '69 (PERS)
PICKENS, MARSHALL I., chm., Duke Endowment, Charlotte, NC '54 (HON)
PICKEREL, JO ANN, RN, dir. nrsg. serv., Heartland Hospital East, St. Joseph, MO '82 (NURS)
PICKERING, ARTHUR D. JR., MSC USA, amedd procurement counselor, Office of Surgeon General, Fort Sheridan, IL '84 (PERS)
PICKERSGIL, JACK W., dir. matl. mgt., Millard Fillmore Hospital, Buffalo, NY '84 (PUR)
PICKERT, ALTON E., exec. vice-pres., Baltimore County General Hospital, Randallstown, MD '52 (MGMT)(LIFE)(PLNG)(LIFE)
PICKETT, WILLIAM E., dir. environ. hazards off., University of Connecticut Health Center, John Dempsey Hospital, Farmington, CT '84 (ENG)
PICKING, HOWARD M. III, pres. and chief exec. off., Miller-Picking Corporation, Johnstown, PA '86 (ENG)
PICKLE, JERRY R., atty., Scott and White Memorial Hospital, Temple, TX '78 (ATTY)
PICO-SILVA, TERESITA, atty., Teresita Pico-Silva Law Office, San Juan, P.R. '86 (RISK)
PICO, JAMES F., atty., St. Rose de Lima Hospital, Henderson, NV '69 (ATTY)
PICO, STEVEN A., dir. safety, University of Chicago Hospitals, Chicago, IL '82 (ENG)
PICONE, GERALDINE F., dir. soc. serv., Samaritan Hospital, Ashland, OH '86 (SOC)
PICTOR, JOSEPH, dir. educ. and trng., Methodist Hospital of Indiana, Indianapolis, IN '71 (EDUC)
PIDHIRNY, PAMELA, vice-pres., Crouse-Irving Memorial Hospital, Syracuse, NY '76 (PR)
PIEART, MARC A., dir. human res., Delnor Hospital, St. Charles, IL '85 (PERS)
PIECH, CATHERINE TAK, mktg. planner, Sandoz Pharmaceuticals Corporation, East Hanover, NJ '86
PIEGARI, ROBERT M., asst. adm., Staten Island Center for Developmental Disabilities, Staten Island, NY '72
PIEKARSKI, JAMES LEE, staff asst., Westchester County Medical Center, Valhalla, NY '87 (CS)
PIEL, CHERYL ANN, dir. soc. serv., Wayne Hospital, Greenville, OH '86 (SOC)
PIEL, WALTER A., dir. gen. serv., Finley Hospital, Dubuque, IA '86 (ENG)
PIENKIEWICZ, ANTHONY, dir. eng., Holy Name Hospital, Teaneck, NJ '84 (ENG)
PIENOVI, SILVIO L., pres., Health Enterprise Associates, Portland, OR '79 (PLNG)
PIEPENBRING, MARY L., dir. soc. work and discharge plng., Richland Memorial Hospital, Columbia, SC '85 (SOC)
PIEPENBRINK, POLLY, vice-pres. mktg. and plng., St. Joseph Hospital, Flint, MI '81 (PLNG)
PIEPER, KATHIE GARRETT, dir. pat. rel., C. J. Harris Community Hospital, Sylva, NC '83 (PAT)
PIERCE, CAROL, exec. dir. amb. serv., Presbyterian Hlthcare Services, Albuquerque, NM '87 (AMB)
PIERCE, CHARLES F., pres., Delaware Valley Hospital Council, Inc., Philadelphia, PA '79 (PLNG)
PIERCE, CYNTHIA, dir. risk mgt., St. Mary Hospital, Port Arthur, TX '86 (RISK)
PIERCE, DONALD F., atty., Doctors Hospital of Mobile, Mobile, AL '76 (ATTY)
PIERCE, DOVE A., prin., Health Planning Consultants, Oakland, CA '79 (PLNG)
PIERCE, EILEEN C., RN, assoc. chief nrsg. serv., Veterans Administration Hospital, Hines, IL '84 (NURS)
PIERCE, JAMES M., vice-pres. prof. serv., Horton Memorial Hospital, Middletown, NY '76
PIERCE, JANIS L., RN, asst. adm. nrsg., St. Luke's General Hospital, Bellingham, WA '81 (NURS)
PIERCE, JEANNIE M., supv. sup., proc. and distrib., Good Samaritan Medical Center, Phoenix, AZ '86 (CS)
PIERCE, JOHN F., mgt. eng., Lankenau Hospital, Philadelphia, PA '74 (MGMT)
PIERCE, JOHN, consult., Park Ridge, IL '85 (RISK)
PIERCE, KAREN ELLEN, dir. mktg., Portsmouth Pavilion, Portsmouth, NH '85 (PR)
PIERCE, LANE T., dir. dev. plant oper. and maint., Servicemaster Industries, Inc., Downers Grove, IL '85 (ENG)
PIERCE, MARIE A., dir. vol. serv., St. Mary's Hospital, Orange, NJ '85 (VOL)
PIERCE, MELLANIE, risk mgt. consult., Rahn and Company, Inc., Seattle, WA '86 (RISK)
PIERCE, SAMUEL P. JR., atty., HCA Parkway Medical Center, Lithia Springs, GA '86 (ATTY)
PIERCE, SHARON I., dir. guest and phys. rel., Rockford Memorial Hospital, Rockford, IL '87 (PAT)
PIERCE, SUSAN QUINN, coor. soc. work, Duke University Hospital, Durham, NC '86 (SOC)
PIERCE, SYLVIA, dir. soc. work, Community Hospital at Glen Cove, Glen Cove, NY '78 (SOC)
PIERCE, WADE, dir. soc. work, Logan Regional Hospital, Logan, UT '86 (SOC)
PIERCE, WALTER R., dir. plant oper., Health Care Agency, Ventura, CA '86 (ENG)
PIERCE, WILLARD R. JR., dir., Piedmont Geriatric Hospital, Burkeville, VA '73
PIERCE, WILLIAM A. JR., asst. dir. facil. plng. and dev., Thomas Jefferson University Hospital, Philadelphia, PA '87 (ENG)
PIERRE, SANDRA T., asst. analyst, Mercy Hospital, Scranton, PA '83 (MGMT)
PIERROZ, BERT B., dir. educ. and org. dev., Sutter Community Hospitals, Sacramento, CA '85 (EDUC)
PIERSON, EUGENE E., dir. plant serv., Huguley Memorial Hospital, Fort Worth, TX '81 (ENG)
PIERSON, GERALD A., exec. dir., Metropolitan Hospital-Springfield Division, Springfield, PA '86
PIERSON, JOHN L., adm. dir. path., Abington Memorial Hospital, Abington, PA '67 (MGMT)
PIERSON, JULIE E., vice-pres., Franklin Square Hospital, Baltimore, MD '81
PIERSON, LOUISE M., RN, dir. nrsg., Brockton Hospital, Brockton, MA '79 (NURS)
PIERSON, ONETIA T., dir. vol. serv., Crouse-Irving Memorial Hospital, Syracuse, NY '78 (VOL)
PIERSON, TIMOTHY J., dir. eng. and maint., Hospital Of Philadelphia College of Osteopathic Medicine, Philadelphia, PA '83 (ENG)
PIES, GAY S., mgr. sup., proc. and distrib., Mesa Lutheran Hospital, Mesa, AZ '81 (CS)
PIES, HARVEY E., atty. and spec. counselor health indust. serv., Blue Cross and Blue Shield of Fl, Jacksonville, FL '75 (ATTY)
PIESCHEL, JUNE P., dir. human res., Hinds General Hospital, Jackson, MS '86 (PERS)
PIEST, PAULA J., supv. telecommun., Anaheim Memorial Hospital, Anaheim, CA '86 (ENG)
PIESTER, RICHARD B., dir. pub. rel., Hampton General Hospital, Hampton, VA '81 (PR)
PIETRAS, MICHAEL S., sr. mgt. eng., Catherine McAuley Health Center, Ann Arbor, MI '84 (MGMT)
PIETRO, JOSEPH ANTHONY DI, asst. adm., Kent County Memorial Hospital, Warwick, RI '77 (RISK)
PIETRODANGELO, DONATO A., producer and pres., D. and L. Communications, Tallahassee, FL '86 (PR)
PIETRUSIAK, JEROME, mgr. soc. serv., Frank Cuneo Memorial Hospital, Chicago, IL '80 (SOC)
PIETRZAK, DEBORAH L., dir. pers. and pub. rel., Salem Community Hospital, Salem, OH '87 (PR)
PIETRZYK, BARBARA J., mgr. diet., Aurora Presbyterian Hospital, Aurora, CO '79 (FOOD)
PIETTE, CAROL A., RN, dir. nrsg., Appleton Medical Center, Appleton, WI '85 (NURS)
PIETZ, JACQUELYN H., pat. rep., Caylor-Nickel Hospital, Bluffton, IN '81 (PAT)
PIETZSCH, PAUL M., pres., Health Policy Corporation of Iowa, Des Moines, IA '80
PIHA, RUBIN M., Atlanta, GA '69
PIKE, FRED D., atty., Caldwell Memorial Hospital, Lenoir, NC '85 (ATTY)
PIKE, FRED M., dir. pub. rel., Mercy Hospital, Miami, FL '81 (PR)
PIKE, KAREN A., dir. cont. educ., Lakewood Community College, White Bear Lake, MN '76 (EDUC)
PIKE, RON S., dir. educ. and trng., St. Mary-Corwin Hospital Regional Medical and Health Center, Pueblo, CO '85 (EDUC)
PIKL, BARBARA HILL, vice-pres. nrsg., Winchester Hospital, Winchester, MA '86 (NURS)

PIKSER, SUSAN P., New Hyde Park, NY '80 (EDUC)
PILARCZYK, PENNY, mgr. vol. serv., Good Samaritan Hospital, Downers Grove, IL '86 (VOL)
PILAT, GREGORY L., dir. diagnostic imaging center, Good Samaritan Hospital, Downers Grove, IL '87 (AMB)
PILE, MARK T., dir. soc. serv., Somerset Community Hospital, Somerset, PA '79 (SOC)
PILEGRENE, DIANA L., mgr. risk, Lovelace Medical Center, Albuquerque, NM '83 (RISK)
PILETTE, PATRICIA CHEHY, EdD RN, org. dev. spec., St. Elizabeth's Hospital of Boston, Boston, MA '85 (NURS)
PILEWSKI, VICTOR J., dir. food serv., Oil City Area Health Center, Oil City, PA '81 (FOOD)
PILGERMAYER, THOMAS J., vice-pres. human res., Saints Mary and Elizabeth Hospital, Louisville, KY '74 (PERS)
PILGRIM, GRETCHEN, dir. pers., Memorial Hospital at Gulfport, Gulfport, MS '73 (PERS)
PILGRIM, MINNIET M., RN, asst. adm. nrsg. serv., Tobey Hospital, Wareham, MA '86 (NURS)
PILKINGTON, WILMA, supv. asst. escorts, Johnson City Medical Center Hospital, Johnson City, TN '78 (CS)
PILLA, DAN, coor. cent. proc., Children's Hospital, St. Louis, MO '85 (CS)
PILLA, FELIX M., pres. and chief exec. off., Abington Memorial Hospital, Abington, PA '60 (PLNG)
PILLA, MARK D., sr. vice-pres., Community Memorial Hospital, Toms River, NJ '77
PILLE, BARBARA L., syst. mgt. analyst, University Hospital-University of Nebraska, Omaha, NE '82 (MGMT)
PILLE, RICHARD H., atty., United Health Services, Johnson City, NY '84 (ATTY)
PILLIOD, CHARLES J. JR., bd. chm., Goodyear Tire and Rubber Company, Akron, OH '77 (LIFE)
PILOTTE, GREGORY A., sales rep., HBO and Company, Louisville, KY '81 (MGMT)(PLNG)
PINA, EVA E., instr. nrsg. staff dev., Driscoll Foundation Children's Hospital, Corpus Christi, TX '86 (EDUC)
PINANSKI, VIOLA R., trustee, Beth Israel Hospital, Boston, MA '51 (HON)
PINCHBECK, BRUCE P., dir. soc. serv., The Medical Center, Beaver, PA '76 (SOC)
PINCKNEY, FRANK D., adm., Greenville Memorial Hospital, Greenville, SC '67
PINDER, MARK STEPHEN, dir. matl. mgt., St. Mary's Hospital of Blue Springs, Blue Springs, MO '85 (PUR)
PINE, JULIAN, dir. soc. serv., Medical Center of Independence, Independence, MO '86 (SOC)
PINE, RICHARD M., dir. mktg. and dev., R. J. Caron Foundation, Wernersville, PA '80 (PR) (PLNG)
PINELLI, RICHARD A., consult., Blue Cross and Blue Shield Association, Chicago, IL '84 (RISK)
PINER, NORMAN R., eng., Memorial Hospital of Sweetwater County, Rock Springs, WY '77 (ENG)
PINGLE, RAYMOND, vice-pres. med. and prov. serv., Family Health Program, Fountain Valley, CA '80
PINK, ROBERT A., mgr. constr., University Hospital-University of Nebraska, Omaha, NE '82 (ENG)
PINKARD, DONNIE, asst. dir. plant oper., Bessemer Carraway Medical Center, Bessemer, AL '75 (ENG)
PINKELMAN, JANET M., dir. pers., Lutheran Community Hospital, Norfolk, NE '86 (PERS)
PINKERMAN, CHARLES FREDERICK, dir., Madison Community Hospital, Madison Heights, MI '64
PINKERT, MICHAEL S., pres., Mental Health Management, Inc., McLean, VA '67 (MGMT)
PINKERTON, SUEELLEN, RN, vice-pres. pat. serv., St. Michael Hospital, Milwaukee, WI '82 (NURS)
PINKHAM, MICHAEL STEPHEN, plant eng., Bath Memorial Hospital, Bath, ME '85 (ENG)
PINKHAM, SARAH L., Long Beach, CA '74
PINKSTER, JERRY A., vice-pres., Tower, Pinkster and Titus Associates, Kalamazoo, MI '83 (ENG)
PINKSTON, KENNETH, sr. vice-pres., Corroon and Black, Nashville, TN '86 (RISK)
PINNELLI, MARY R., dir. vol. serv., St. Agnes Medical Center, Philadelphia, PA '86 (VOL)
PINNER, BLANCA E., RN, assoc. dir. nrs., McAllen Medical Center, McAllen, TX '86 (NURS)
PINNER, DONALD R., vice-pres. mktg. and dev., Nanticoke Memorial Hospital, Seaford, DE '86 (PR)
PINNEY, A. SEARLE, atty., Danbury Hospital, Danbury, CT '80 (ATTY)
PINNEY, DOUGLAS, asst. dir. risk mgt., California Association of Hospitals and Health Systems, Sacramento, CA '78 (RISK)
PINNEY, SIDNEY G., mgt. eng., Mercy Hospital Medical Center, Des Moines, IA '86 (MGMT)
PINO, P. STEPHEN, assoc. adm., Good Samaritan Hospital, Corvallis, OR '85 (PR) (PLNG)
PINSEN, JACK, Englewood, NJ '72 (SOC)
PINSINCE, DONNA W., dir. soc. serv. and discharge plng., Milford Hospital, Milford, CT '82 (SOC)
PINSKER, LINDA S., mgr. new prod., Krames Communications, Daly City, CA '84 (EDUC)
PINSON, ELIZABETH S., dir. vol., Eugene Talmadge Memorial Hospital and Clinics-Medical College of Georgia, Augusta, GA '73 (VOL)
PINTER, JEAN, RN, dir. nrsg. serv., Hot Springs County Memorial Hospital, Thermopolis, WY '85 (NURS)
PINTERICH, SHIRLEY J., RN, vice-pres. nrsg., Huguley Memorial Hospital, Fort Worth, TX '81 (NURS)
PINZONE, SARAH R., Forest Hills, NY '82
PIONTEK, ANNEMARIE B., dir. commun. serv., South Coast Medical Center, South Laguna, CA '86 (PR)
PIOTROWSKI, MAJ. STANLEY L., MSC USA, manpower mgt. off., Office of the Surgeon General, Washington, DC '71
PIPE, NANCY L., coor. family aid prog., Montreal Children's Hospital, Montreal, Que., Canada '76 (PAT)
PIPER, ARTHUR H. JR., assoc. exec. dir. fin., Hospital of the University of Pennsylvania, Philadelphia, PA '76
PIPER, DAVID R., atty., East Tennessee Children's Hospital, Knoxville, TN '77 (ATTY)
PIPER, GEORGE C., atty., Good Samaritan Hospital, Lexington, KY '84 (ATTY)
PIPER, JAMES H. JR., asst. vice-pres. private reimbursement, Blue Cross and Blue Shield of Georgia, Inc., Atlanta, GA '79 (MGMT)
PIPER, JANE S., dir. risk mgt. and qual. assur., John F. Kennedy Medical Center, Edison, NJ '83 (RISK)
PIPER, JEAN ANN, RN, dir. nrsg.-primary care, Brandywine Hospital, Caln Township, PA '83 (NURS)
PIPER, SALLY A., RN, dir. nrsg. serv., Dukes Memorial Hospital, Peru, IN '85 (NURS)
PIPES, JOHN W., dir. nutr. serv., Marcus J. Lawrence Memorial Hospital, Cottonwood, AZ '77 (FOOD)
PIPKIN, HARRY W., mktg. staff asst., Vanderbilt University Medical Center, Nashville, TN '83 (PR)
PIPPIN, EULA MAE, dir. vol., Pasadena Bayshore Medical Center, Pasadena, TX '70 (VOL)
PIRAINO, ANN MARIE, asst. dir. food and nutr. serv., Memorial Hospital, Hollywood, FL '86 (FOOD)
PIRAINO, CARLO A., dir. facil. plng., St. John's Episcopal Hospital, Smithtown, NY '79 (ENG)
PIRELLI, THOMAS, pres., Enterprise Systems, Inc., Bannockburn, IL '85 (PUR)
PIRIZ, J. E., adm. asst., Memorial Hospital, Hollywood, FL '86
PIROLLO, DIANE M., dir. matl. mgt., Methodist Hospital, Philadelphia, PA '84 (PUR)
PIROZEK, MICHAEL A., mgr. educ., Bard-Parker, Division of Becton Dickinson and CO, Lincoln Park, NJ '86 (EDUC)
PISACANO, THERESA M., asst. dir. pur., Church-Charity Foundation of Long Island, Hempstead, NY '73 (PUR)
PISANO, ROBERT M., pur. agt., Jamestown General Hospital, Jamestown, NY '84 (PUR)
PISARRA, VIRGINIA M., asst. vice-pres., Washington Adventist Hospital, Takoma Park, MD '84 (PLNG)
PISCHNER, TERESA W., RN, asst. dir. nrsg., medicine and oncology, Medical College of Virginia Hospitals, Richmond, VA '83 (NURS)
PISCIOTTO, NILA F., dir. pub. rel. and vol. serv., Shriners Hospital for Crippled Children, Tampa, FL '86 (VOL)
PISCITELLI, EARLINE K., corp. planner, Bayfront Medical Center, St. Petersburg, FL '85 (PLNG)
PISHKO, GALE A., dir. matl. mgt., Crittenton Hospital, Rochester, MI '84 (PUR)
PISHKO, LEONARD A., sr. mgr., Ernst and Whinney, Chicago, IL '86 (MGMT)
PITCHER, PATRICIA, pat. rep., Good Samaritan Hospital and Health Center, Dayton, OH '81 (PAT)
PITCHER, ROBERT, plant oper. planner, Tampa General Hospital, Tampa, FL '86 (ENG)
PITCHLYNN, GARY S., atty., Norman Regional Hospital, Norman, OK '84 (ATTY)
PITCHON, REGINA D., asst. to exec. vice-pres., Memorial Hospital for Cancer and Allied Diseases, New York, NY '81 (PLNG)
PITHAN, LARRY, dir. soc. serv., St. Luke's Regional Medical Center, Sioux City, IA '79 (SOC)
PITNEY, ANN M., coor. staff dev., Milford Hospital, Milford, CT '86 (EDUC)
PITT, HELEN K., assoc. dir. nrsg., University of Minnesota Hospitals and Clinics, Minneapolis, MN '86 (NURS)
PITT, ROBERT W., dir. pers., Hotel Dieu Medical Center, El Paso, TX '86 (PERS)
PITTMAN-LINDEMAN, MARY, student, University of California, Berkeley, CA '84 (PLNG)
PITTMAN, CHARLES A. JR., dir. plant oper., Thomas Memorial Hospital, South Charleston, WV '79 (ENG)
PITTMAN, CHARLES E. JR., dir. environ. serv., Nemours Children's Hospital, Jacksonville, FL '81 (ENG)
PITTMAN, GALEN W., atty., St. Francis Medical Center, La Crosse, WI '86 (ATTY)
PITTMAN, J. W., br. mgr. data proc., Central State Griffin Memorial Hospital, Norman, OK '86
PITTMAN, JAMES E., adm. dir. prof. serv., Bedford Medical Center, Bedford, IN '84 (PERS)
PITTMAN, JEFFERY P., plant eng., Kennewick General Hospital, Kennewick, WA '86 (ENG)
PITTMAN, KATHRYN L., dir. soc. serv., Highsmith-Rainey Memorial Hospital, Fayetteville, NC '86 (SOC)
PITTMAN, MICHAEL T., reg. rep. sup., Voluntary Hospital of America, Atlanta, GA '84 (PUR)
PITTMAN, SIDNEY E., dir. environ. serv., West Volusia Memorial Hospital, De Land, FL '86 (ENVIRON)
PITTMAN, THOMAS D., adm., Harding Hospital, Worthington, OH '67
PITTONI, LUKE M., atty., Society of the New York Hospital, New York, NY '83 (ATTY)
PITTS, DAVID R., pres., Pitts Management Associates, Inc., Baton Rouge, LA '70
PITTS, WAYNE H., dir. plant oper., Milton Medical Center, Milton, MA '85 (ENG)
PITTS, WILLIAM, dir. matl. mgt., St. Anthony Medical Center, Columbus, OH '77 (PUR)
PITZER, THELMA I., dir. vol. serv., Saint Francis Medical Center, Peoria, IL '85 (VOL)
PITZER, VANNESSA L., dir. pers., AMI Odessa Women's-Children Hospital, Odessa, TX '86 (PERS)
PIVER-SAVIGNANO, ANNE T., RN, dir. nrsg., Department of Health and Hospitals, Boston, MA '86 (NURS)
PIVER, SUSAN M., dir. risk mgt., Children's Hospital, Buffalo, NY '85 (RISK)(ATTY)
PIXLER, LYNNE C., dir. risk mgt., Hinsdale Hospital, Hinsdale, IL '86 (RISK)
PIXLEY, DONALD K., dir. safety and security, Our Lady of Lourdes Memorial Hospital, Binghamton, NY '81 (ENG)
PIZZA, NORMAND F., atty., Slidell Memorial Hospital, Slidell, LA '83 (ATTY)
PIZZINO, DAN J., dir. pub. rel. and mktg., Valley View Regional Hospital, Ada, OK '83 (PR)
PIZZORERRATO, MARDELL, mgr. soc. serv., Desert Hospital, Palm Springs, CA '86 (SOC)
PIZZUTI, LINDA J., plng. assoc., Methodist Medical Center of Illinois, Peoria, IL '85 (PLNG)
PLAATSMAN, JAMES P., dir. human res., Maryview Hospital, Portsmouth, VA '86 (PERS)
PLACE, RICHARD J., consult. loss control, Hartford Insurance Group, Indianapolis, IN '80 (RISK)
PLACEK, MARJORIE Y., coor. qual. assur., Western Pennsylvania Hospital, Pittsburgh, PA '85
PLACEK, ROSE S., dir. pers., Parkside Human Service Corporation, Park Ridge, IL '86 (PERS)
PLACELLA, LOUIS E., vice-pres. shared serv., Medlantic Healthcare Group, Washington, DC '69 (MGMT)
PLACHY, ROBERT, mgr. facil., Alexian Brothers Medical Center, Elk Grove Village, IL '86 (ENG)
PLACIDES, DELFADO SEBASTIAN, dir. food serv., Baptist Hospital of Miami, Miami, FL '68 (FOOD)
PLACIDO, GERARD M., dir. gen. serv., Glover Memorial Hospital, Needham, MA '77 (PUR)
PLAGATA, MILAGROS G., dir. diet. serv., Geauga Hospital, Chardon, OH '83 (FOOD)
PLAKOS, WILLIAM CHARLES, vice-pres. human res., Butterworth Hospital, Grand Rapids, MI '69 (PERS)
PLANK, ROBERT K., dir. maint., Maryview Hospital, Portsmouth, VA '77 (ENG)
PLANT, CUPIDEAN O., dir. pers., Sumter Regional Hospital, Americus, GA '68 (PERS)
PLANT, MARETTA M., dir. mktg. commun., Somerset Medical Center, Somerville, NJ '80 (PR)
PLANTE, BARBARA D., dir. pers., Framingham Union Hospital, Framingham, MA '82 (PERS)
PLANTE, EVERETT G., dir. health care serv., Szabo Food Service, Oakbrook, IL '77 (FOOD)
PLANTE, MICHELE M., hazardous waste off., New England Medical Center, Boston, MA '84 (ENG)
PLANTE, PAUL R., mgr. plant oper., Matheny School, Peapack, NJ '87 (ENG)
PLANTE, ROBERT A., asst. dir. human res. mgt., Rhode Island Medical Center, Howard, RI '80 (PERS)
PLANTENBERG, THOMAS M., adm. dir. mktg. and pub. rel., St. Mary's Hospital Medical Center, Green Bay, WI '84 (PR)
PLANTIER, ANTHONY J., Colton, CA '85
PLANTIER, CAROL, RN, coor. staff dev., Waterbury Hospital, Waterbury, CT '78 (EDUC)
PLATE, DAVID H., pres., Hillcrest Hospital, Mayfield Heights, OH '72
PLATE, EARL L., asst. to vice-pres., Arnot-Ogden Memorial Hospital, Elmira, NY '75 (ENG)
PLATMAN, STANLEY R., MD, clin. prof. psych., University of Maryland Medical Systems, Baltimore, MD '84
PLATNER, FERN, asst. adm., Riverside General Hospital-University Medical Center, Riverside, CA '78
PLATOCK, SANDI F., dir. vol. serv., Wellington Regional Medical Center, West Palm Beach, FL '86 (VOL)
PLATOU, CARL N., pres., Fairview Hospital and Healthcare Service, Minneapolis, MN '51 (LIFE)
PLATT, LT. A. CHARLES, MSC USAF, med. mgt. eng. off., Air Force Medical Management Engineering Team, Maxwell AFB, AL '81 (MGMT)
PLATT, M. ANNE, dir. diet., Lima Memorial Hospital, Lima, OH '83 (FOOD)
PLATT, ROBERT, vice-pres., Elizabeth General Medical Center, Elizabeth, NJ '70
PLATT, WILLIAM, dir. strategic plng., Anaheim Memorial Hospital, Anaheim, CA '79 (PLNG)
PLAUMANN, MARK L., sr. vice-pres. and chief exec. off., American Healthcare Management, Inc., Dallas, TX '80
PLAUT, JUDITH M., dir. soc. work, Baltimore Medical Systems, Inc., Baltimore, MD '79 (SOC)
PLAVICH, LILLIE E., mgr. matl., Doctors Memorial Hospital, Atlanta, GA '86 (PUR)
PLAVNER, BETH W., assoc. adm., Howard County General Hospital, Columbia, MD '83 (PLNG)
PLAVNICK, CHERYL J., dir. soc. work, Harper Hospital, Detroit, MI '86 (SOC)
PLEASANT, JOSEPH MARION JR., vice-pres. corp. serv., SunHealth Corporation, Charlotte, NC '76 (MGMT)
PLEASANTS, CAPT. RICHARD D., MSC USAF, chief facil. and contracting, U. S. Air Force Regional Hospital, Hampton, VA '84
PLEINES, KAREN M., adj. instr. and assoc. exec. dir., Ohio State University, Columbus, OH '73 (PLNG)
PLESHA, JEANNE, risk mgr., South Chicago Community Hospital, Chicago, IL '87 (RISK)
PLESKOW, LEONARD, pres., Bry-Lin Hospital, Buffalo, NY '61
PLEVAK, SR. SUSAN, coor. and instr. med. rec. tech., College of Lake County, Grayslake, IL '80
PLEWIK, DEANNA MARIE, dir. educ. serv., Mercy San Juan Hospital, Carmichael, CA '86 (EDUC)
PLILER, BARBARA, supv. cent. proc., Los Medanos Community Hospital, Pittsburg, CA '82 (CS)
PLODZIK, STANLEY J. JR., RN, asst. adm. pat. serv., Portsmouth Regional Hospital, Portsmouth, NH '82 (NURS)
PLOEN, ERIC L., pres., Affiliated Risk Control Administrators, Inc., New York, NY '80 (RISK)
PLONKA, JOSEPH T., chief eng., Reedsburg Memorial Hospital, Reedsburg, WI '77 (ENG)
PLOURD, JIM, mgr. soc. serv., Dominican Santa Cruz Hospital, Santa Cruz, CA '83 (SOC)
PLOURDE, ALFRED E. JR., chief clin. eng., U. S. Air Force Medical Center Keesler, Biloxi, MS '85 (ENG)
PLOURDE, KATHERINE M., dir. vol. serv., Bristol Hospital, Bristol, CT '85 (VOL)
PLOWMAN, JACQUELINE L., coor. ed., Washoe Medical Center, Reno, NV '85 (EDUC)
PLOWMAN, SHIRLEY J., dir. matl. mgt., Gettysburg Hospital, Gettysburg, PA '84 (PUR)
PLUM, JEAN H., Winter Park, FL '73 (PAT)
PLUMER, SANDRA S., dir. soc. work, Oakwood Downriver Medical Center, Lincoln Park, MI '76 (SOC)
PLUMLEE, W. TRAVIS, dir. soc. serv., All Saints Episcopal Hospital, Fort Worth, TX '80 (SOC)
PLUMMER, BRUCE H., dir. matl. mgt., Franklin Memorial Hospital, Farmington, ME '81 (PUR)
PLUMMER, JAMES B., dir. eng., St. Francis Hospital, Greenville, SC '85 (ENG)

PLUMMER, JEAN A., RN, dir. nrsg., James M. Jackson Memorial Hospital, Miami, FL '82 (NURS)
PLUMMER, PHILIP J., asst. dir. soc. serv., James M. Jackson Memorial Hospital, Miami, FL '78 (SOC)
PLUMMER, TERRY K., dir. pers., St. Francis Hospital, Escanaba, MI '85 (PERS)
PLUNKETT, DONALD F., dir. bus. affairs, Sisters of St. Joseph of Concordia Nazareth Convent and Academy, Concordia, KS '51 (LIFE)
PLUNKETT, JAMES G., arch., Plunkett, Keymar and Reginato, Architects, Milwaukee, WI '76
PLYMALE, BARBARA R., dir. human res., St. Luke's Regional Medical Center, Sioux City, IA '87 (PERS)
POACH, SHAUNA L., RN, student, Widener University, Chester, PA '83
POCHAL, AUDREY, dir. mktg., Jewish Hospital of St. Louis, St. Louis, MO '84 (PLNG)
POCHEKAILO, M. ELLEN, dir. mktg., Potomac Hospital, Woodbridge, VA '85 (PR)
POCHEREVA, MELE W., pub. rel. consult., Stryker Weiner Assocs, Inc., Honolulu, HI '83 (PR)
POCKRUS, ELIZABETH, mgr. cent. sup., Norman Regional Hospital, Norman, OK '84 (CS)
PODELL, ALLEN, PhD, consult., Edison, NJ '56 (LIFE)
PODESCHI, DONNA J., in-service dir., St. Vincent Memorial Hospital, Taylorville, IL '83 (EDUC)
PODEST, MARK, dir. human res., Clinton Regional Hospital, Clinton, OK '83 (PERS)
PODESZWIK, RANDY M., mgr. environ., California Medical Center-Los Angeles, Los Angeles, CA '87 (ENVIRON)
PODIETZ, FRANK, adm., Philadelphia Geriatric Center, Philadelphia, PA '75
PODKIN, ALBERT, vice-pres. human res., Northbay Medical Center, Fairfield, CA '65 (PERS)
PODKUL, THEODORE B. JR., mgt. analyst, Veterans Administration Medical Center, Buffalo, NY '73
PODOLIN, LEE J., exec. dir., University Physicians Milwaukee Clinical Campus Practice Plan, Inc., Milwaukee, WI '69
POE, FRANCES T., dir. soc. serv., Hospital for Joint Diseases and Medical Center, New York, NY '72 (SOC)
POELS, VICKI L., mgr. mgt. dev. and trng., Swedishamerican Hospital, Rockford, IL '84 (EDUC)
POETAIN, THOMAS C., chief soc. work, Veterans Administration Medical Center, Pittsburgh, PA '85 (SOC)
POETZSCHER, CHERYL E., mgr. food serv., Christian Hospital Northeast, St. Louis, MO '81 (FOOD)
POGANY, ANCA, RN, dir. ob. and gyn. nrsg., Michael Reese Hospital and Medical Center, Chicago, IL '84 (NURS)
POGOLOFF, DONALD DAVID, atty., Kings View Hospital, Reedley, CA '74 (ATTY)
POHL, DOROTHY G., dir. vol. serv., Conemaugh Valley Memorial Hospital, Johnstown, PA '76 (VOL)
POHLOD, RAYMOND A., dir. commun. rel., Bayley Seton Hospital, Staten Island, NY '74 (PR)
POHREN, ALLEN E., chief exec. off., Montgomery County Memorial Hospital, Red Oak, IA '81 (PLNG)
POINDEXTER, JAMES A., supv. maint., Marcus J. Lawrence Memorial Hospital, Cottonwood, AZ '82 (ENG)
POINDEXTER, RITA M., RN, asst. adm. and dir. nrsg., Marcus J. Lawrence Memorial Hospital, Cottonwood, AZ '75 (NURS)
POIRIER, JOSEPH W., dir. soc. serv., Woonsocket Hospital, Woonsocket, RI '82 (SOC)
POIRIER, LOUISE A., student, Program in Business Administration, University of Rhode Island, Kingston, RI '85
POIRIER, THOMAS A., staff asst., Veterans Administration Medical Center, Louisville, KY '75
POKER, PAMELA A., student, University of Wisconsin-Madison, Program in Health Service Administration, Madison, WI '84
POKORNY, JOHN A., mgr. eng. and maint. oper. and exec. assoc. ancillary, Saint Thomas Medical Center, Akron, OH '86 (ENG)
POKORSKI, A. J., contr., Holy Cross Hospital, Detroit, MI '73 (RISK)
POKOYSKI, MARCIA A., chief diet. serv., Veterans Administration Medical Center, Philadelphia, PA '80 (FOOD)
POLACEK, JAMES M., student, Governors State University, Program in Health Services Administration, School of Health Professions, Park Forest South, IL '82
POLACHECK, JOAN F., atty., Rush-Presbyterian-St. Luke's Medical Center, Chicago, IL '84 (ATTY)
POLANSKY, EVAN W., vice-pres. plng. and mktg., Alexian Brothers Medical Center, Elk Grove Village, IL '82 (MGMT)(PLNG)
POLCYN, ROGER F., PhD, dir. corp. plng., Erlanger Medical Center, Chattanooga, TN '79 (PLNG)(MGMT)
POLEN, GEOFFREY M., dir. pers. and pub. rel., Pleasant Valley Hospital, Point Pleasant, WV '85 (PR)(PERS)
POLETO, MARIA C., healthcare consult., Coopers and Lybrand, Syracuse, NY '83 (MGMT)
POLEZOES, NANCY, asst. adm. clin. serv., South Haven Community Hospital, South Haven, MI '85 (RISK)
POLFUS, ELLEN, dir. nrsg. serv., Woodland Memorial Hospital, Woodland, CA '80 (NURS)
POLGAR, ROBERT S., supv. oper., New England Medical Center, Boston, MA '79 (ENG)
POLHEMUS, BARBARA J., dir. plng. and mktg., Reston Hospital Center, Reston, VA '86 (PLNG)
POLICASTRO, ANTHONY M., Shaw AFB, SC '83 (EDUC)
POLICH, VICTOR JOHN JR., RN, dir. eng. and maint., Methodist Hospital, St. Louis Park, MN '81 (ENG)
POLICICCHIO, BENJAMIN J., staff arch., Conemaugh Valley Memorial Hospital, Johnstown, PA '83 (ENG)
POLIMER, BETTE, pat. rep., Jewish Memorial Hospital, Boston, MA '70 (VOL)
POLING, MARY M., RN, asst. adm. pat. serv., Mercy Hospital of Franciscan Sisters, Oelwein, IA '86 (NURS)
POLITO, ALBERT P., student, School of Social Research, Loch Sheldrake, NY '84
POLK, JEAN ELLEN, adm. res., Southwest Community Health System and Hospital, Middleburg Heights, OH '85
POLKINGHORN, JAMES B., partner, Polkinghorn, Chapman, Cline and Guy Architect, Austin, TX '76
POLKINGHORN, JAMES W., proj. dir., Maternal and Infant Health Planning Project, Atlanta, GA '50 (LIFE)
POLKOW, WILMA, dir. diet. serv., Memorial Hospital, South Bend, IN '80 (FOOD)
POLLACK, ELLIOTT B., atty., Mount Sinai Hospital, Hartford, CT '76 (ATTY)
POLLACK, RICHARD, assoc. dir., American Hospital Association, Washington, DC '85 (SOC)
POLLAK, JOANNE E., atty., Bon Secours Hospital, Baltimore, MD '77 (ATTY)
POLLAK, SARAH STRAAS, exec. dir., Broward Preferred Providers, Inc., Pompano Beach, FL '83 (PLNG)
POLLARD, ALICE M., asst. dir. food serv. syst., Mount Carmel East Hospital, Columbus, OH '78 (FOOD)
POLLARD, JEANNE A., dir. pur., Cameron Community Hospital, Cameron, MO '82 (PUR)
POLLARD, LINDA K., dir. matl. mgt., New Milford Hospital, New Milford, CT '80 (PUR)
POLLARD, PATRICK J., pres., P. J. Pollard Associates, Inc., Warren, MI '84 (MGMT)
POLLARD, SHARI E., dir. pers., Columbia Hospital for Women, Washington, DC '81 (PERS)
POLLARD, TERRI, dir. group pur., Health and Hospital Services, Bellevue, WA '86 (PUR)
POLLARD, VERY REV MSGR RAYMOND J., dir., Archdiocese of Newark, East Orange, NJ '64
POLLARD, WILLIAM A., atty., Providence Hospital, Columbia, SC '78 (ATTY)
POLLEY, ALICE L., mgt. analyst for off. of med. dir., Sturdy Memorial Hospital, Attleboro, MA '86 (PLNG)
POLLICK, ALBERT P., pres., Pottstown Memorial Medical Center, Pottstown, PA '66 (PLNG)
POLLICK, DEBRA S., consult., Health Industry Consultants, Inc., Englewood, CO '86
POLLMANN, JUDITH W., dir. nrsg. educ., St. Joseph Hospital, Lexington, KY '86 (EDUC)
POLLOCK, COL. ARCHIE D. JR., MSC USA, student, Texas A. and M. University, College Station, TX '69
POLLOCK, JOHN G., pres., Servicemaster West Central Management Services, Inc., Chesterfield, MO '77
POLLOCK, LINDA S., risk mgr., Naval Hospital, Bethesda, MD '79 (EDUC)(RISK)
POLLOCK, MARK P., dir. pur., Good Samaritan Community Healthcare, Puyallup, WA '77 (PUR)
POLLOCK, RALPH S., exec. dir., Health Systems Agency of North Central Connecticut, Hartford, CT '74
POLLOK, CLEMENTINE S., dir. school nrsg., Southside Regional Medical Center, Petersburg, VA '85
POLLY, DIANNE K., dir. food and nutr. serv., R. E. Thomason General Hospital, El Paso, TX '83 (FOOD)
POLO, SERGIO, dir. phys. assets, Augustana Hospital and Health Care Center, Chicago, IL '80 (ENG)
POLONSKY-LEVENTHAL, BINNIE C., consult., Jenkintown, PA '86 (EDUC)
POLOWCHENA, DONNA L., dir. vol. serv., Canton-Potsdam Hospital, Potsdam, NY '83 (VOL)
POLSENBERG, DANIEL F., atty., Boulder City Hospital, Boulder City, NV '84 (ATTY)
POLSKI, SHERYL L., mgr. mktg., Group Health, Inc., Minneapolis, MN '81 (PLNG)
POLSTER, ROLAND, dir. bldg. maint., Winter Haven Hospital, Winter Haven, FL '85 (ENG)
POLSTON, CATHERINE, RN, asst. dir. nrsg., Resurrection Hospital, Chicago, IL '83 (NURS)
POLTAWSKY, JEFFREY S., asst. adm. dir. oper., Geisinger Medical Center, Danville, PA '82 (PLNG)
POLUNSKY, BLANCHE, (ret.), Houston, TX '70 (FOOD)
POMA, FRANK W., dir. med. soc. serv., St. John Hospital, Detroit, MI '84 (SOC)
POMERANCE, DAVID M., pres., Dynamic Control, Longwood, FL '73 (MGMT)
POMERANCE, WILLIAM, pres., Advanced Hospital Systems Corporation, Bethesda, MD '85 (PUR)
POMERANTZ, JACK, dir. pur., Jewish Hospital and Rehabilitation Center, Jersey City, NJ '86 (PUR)
POMERANTZ, PAUL, assoc. adm., Hospital of the Medical College of Pennsylvania, Philadelphia, PA '86 (AMB)
POMERANZ, NANCY POND, dir. soc. work, Val Verde Memorial Hospital, Del Rio, TX '85 (SOC)
POMERLEAU, PATRICIA M., RN, vice-pres. nrsg. serv., Champlain Valley Physicians Hospital Medical Center, Plattsburgh, NY '79 (NURS)
POMERVILLE, RAYMOND, vice-pres. strategic plng. and prog. dev., St. Joseph Mercy Hospital, Pontiac, MI '84 (PLNG)
POMPHREY, MINA E., dir. sup., proc. and distrib., Riverview Medical Center, Red Bank, NJ '86 (CS)
POMPOCO, JOHN L., dir. eng. and maint., St. Elizabeth Hospital Medical Center, Youngstown, OH '83 (ENG)
PONCE, LARRY J., dir. soc. serv., St. Mary's Hospital, Decatur, IL '80 (SOC)
PONCE, LUIS R., dir. mktg., Southeast Alabama Medical Center, Dothan, AL '85 (PR)
POND, BRUCE WALTER, eng., Upper Connecticut Valley Hospital, Colebrook, NH '87 (ENG)
POND, PEGGY P., vice-pres., Market Strategies, Inc., Washington, NC '68 (PR)
POND, RONALD W., adm., Blue Hill Memorial Hospital, Blue Hill, ME '83 (PLNG)
PONDER-DALTON, PATSY A. MOORE, dir. mktg., Boone Hospital Center, Columbia, MO '81 (PR)
PONETA, JAN E., dir. data proc., Ingham Medical Center, Lansing, MI '85 (MGMT)
PONTARELLI, JOHN, dir. health sciences commun., University of California at Los Angeles Medical Center, Los Angeles, CA '75 (PR)
PONTBRIAND, CHARLENE F., dir. commun. rel., Rutland Regional Medical Center, Rutland, VT '86 (PR)
PONTBRIAND, JOYCE G., RN, assoc. dir. nrsg., United Hospital, Port Chester, NY '77 (NURS)
PONTE, RONALD, dir. soc. work, St. Anne's Hospital, Fall River, MA '80 (SOC)
PONTELLO, FRANK A., exec. dir., Portage Path Community Mental Health Center, Akron, OH '68
PONTICELL, RUTH K., RN, asst. adm. and dir. nrsg., Good Shepherd Hospital, Barrington, IL '72 (NURS)
PONTICELLO, SHARON L., dir. vol., St. Elizabeth Hospital, Elizabeth, NJ '81 (VOL)
PONTILILO, BRIAN, dir. mktg., Rehabilitation Hospital Service Corporation, Camp Hill, PA '86 (PR)
PONTON, KEVIN T., asst. vice-pres., Financial Guaranty Insurance Company, New York, NY '86
PONTYNEN, JANICE M., dir. med. staff dev., Adventist Health System-North, Hinsdale, IL '86
POOL, PATRICIA W., mgr. telecommun., Texoma Medical Center, Denison, TX '85 (ENG)
POOLE, CURTIS W. JR., atty., Oakwood Hospital, Dearborn, MI '81 (ATTY)
POOLE, DENNIS L., PhD, assoc. prof., Virginia Commonwealth University School of Social Wk, Richmond, VA '86 (SOC)
POOLE, DIANE A., RN, asst. vice-pres. nrsg. serv., Pitt County Memorial Hospital, Greenville, NC '85 (NURS)
POOLE, JENNIFER L., mgr. vol. serv., Munroe Regional Medical Center, Ocala, FL '84 (VOL)
POOLE, L. ERIC, adm. dir. emp. rel., Sequoia Hospital District, Redwood City, CA '81 (PERS)
POOLE, SAMUEL L., dir. plant oper., Joseph P. Kennedy Jr. Memorial Hospital, Boston, MA '84 (ENG)
POORE, CHRISTINA P., mgr. pers., Humana Hospital -Davis North, Layton, UT '82 (PERS)
POORE, MICHAEL L., Interact Performance Systems, Inc., Midvale, UT '82 (EDUC)
POORE, ROBERT G., pur. agt., Southside Regional Medical Center, Petersburg, VA '84 (PUR)
POORMAN, MARGARET J., coor. staff dev., Mary Greeley Medical Center, Ames, IA '82 (EDUC)
POORTEN, KEVIN P., adm., Page Hospital, Page, AZ '86
POORVIN, GLORIA C., RN, dir. nrsg. critical care and spec. serv., St. Mary's Hospital, West Palm Beach, FL '86 (NURS)
POPA, VIRGILIU, MD, Altamonte Springs, FL '87 (AMB)
POPARAD, PAUL C., RN, vice-pres. pat. care serv., Midland Memorial Hospital, Midland, TX '77 (NURS)
POPAY, BENJAMIN S., dir. plant facil., Floyd Medical Center, Rome, GA '75 (ENG)
POPE, ANNIE R., Veterans Administration Hospital, Hines, IL '81 (SOC)
POPE, B. F., asst. chief eng. and interim dir. eng., Mary Black Memorial Hospital, Spartanburg, SC '85 (ENG)
POPE, DAN W., dir. human resources, C. F. Menninger Memorial Hospital, Topeka, KS '76 (PERS)
POPE, JAMES W., vice-pres. support serv., Saints Mary and Elizabeth Hospital, Louisville, KY '83
POPE, JANA L., prog. mgr. mktg. and strategic mgt., Baylor Health Care System, Dallas, TX '80 (PR)
POPE, JOAN, dir. med. soc. work, Port Huron Hospital, Port Huron, MI '84 (SOC)
POPE, KATHERINE, RN, dir. nrsg. serv., Crawford Long Hospital Emory University, Atlanta, GA '77 (NURS)
POPE, PATRICIA F., tech. spec., First Consulting Group, Indianapolis, IN '80 (FOOD)
POPE, ROBERT DEAN, atty., Richmond Memorial Hospital, Richmond, VA '80 (ATTY)
POPE, RONALD C., assoc. dir. sup., proc. and distrib., St. Peter's Hospital, Albany, NY '78 (CS)
POPE, RONALD L., dir. biomedical elec., Valley Children's Hospital, Fresno, CA '84 (ENG)
POPE, SHARON A., adm. asst., Suburban Community Hospital, Warrensville Heights, OH '85 (SOC)
POPE, WILLIAM L., vice-pres. prop. serv., Tallahassee Memorial Regional Medical Center, Tallahassee, FL '70 (ENG)
POPIEK, HARRIMAN, reg. food serv. consult., Coast Plaza Medical Center, Norwalk, CA '84 (FOOD)
POPKIN, SAMUEL D., vice-pres., Albert Kahn Associates, Detroit, MI '80
POPLIN, SHERRY S., soc. worker, Stanly Memorial Hospital, Albemarle, NC '86 (SOC)
POPOVICH, PETER MARTIN, dir. pat. acct., St. John Hospital, Cleveland, OH '76
POPP, DORIS J., dir. vol. serv., Grant Medical Center, Columbus, OH '80 (VOL)
POPP, KENNETH J., asst. dir. prof. serv., University of Connecticut Health Center, John Dempsey Hospital, Farmington, CT '70 (MGMT)
POPPE, CAROL L., dir. in-service, Brodstone Memorial Nuckolls County Hospital, Superior, NE '85 (EDUC)
POPPE, CECIL L., dir. plant serv., Southwest Community Health Services, Albuquerque, NM '66 (ENG)
POPPER, JOSEPH A., asst. mktg. mgr., Popper and Sons, Inc., New Hyde Park, NY '85 (CS)
POPPITZ, CHRISTINE M., dir. pers. and payroll, Waconia Ridgeview Hospital, Waconia, MN '82 (PERS)
POPPL, DIANNE T., RN, vice-pres. nrsg., Saint Joseph Hospital, Elgin, IL '78 (NURS)
POPPLEWELL, VYN G., proj. coor. and facil. planner, Methodist Hospital of Indiana, Indianapolis, IN '79 (ENG)
POPS, BARBARA A., dir. vol. serv., University of California at Los Angeles Medical Center, Los Angeles, CA '86 (VOL)
POPSON, MICHAEL J., dir. eng. and facil. maint., Westmoreland Hospital, Greensburg, PA '68 (ENG)
POQUETTE, GARY R., exec. dir., Memorial Hospital, North Conway, NH '74 (PLNG)
PORCARO, JOAN M., asst. vice-pres. satellite serv., Phoenix General Hospital, Phoenix, AZ '87 (AMB)
PORCINO, ANN T., Mosman, Australia '80
PORELLE, M. JUDITH, RN, assoc. dir. nrsg. serv., Catholic Medical Center, Manchester, NH '83 (NURS)
POREMBA, MICHAEL P., dir. risk mgt., Forbes Health Systems-Forbes Healthmark, Pittsburgh, PA '80 (RISK)
POREMSKI, JANE M., RN, vice-pres. nrsg. serv., Frank Cuneo Memorial Hospital, Chicago, IL '86 (NURS)

PORES, JEANNE H., asst. vice-pres. risk mgt., Flushing Hospital and Medical Center, Flushing, NY '83 (PAT)(RISK)
PORRETTO, JOHN P., vice-pres. adm. and fin., University of Texas Health Sciences Center at Houston, Houston, TX '71
PORRETTO, NICHOLAS A., dir. food serv., Northern Westchester Hospital Center, Mount Kisco, NY '81 (FOOD)
PORTELL, GARY, dir. hskpg. and linen, Cardinal Glennon Children Hospital, St. Louis, MO '86 (ENVIRON)
PORTELLI, ANDREW R., vice-pres. pers. and labor rel., St. Vincent's Hospital and Medical Center of New York, New York, NY '64 (PERS)
PORTER, CARROLL JOELYN, RN, chief nrsg. serv., Veterans Administration Medical Center, Walla Walla, WA '82 (NURS)
PORTER, CARSON P., atty., NKC Hospitals, Louisville, KY '81 (ATTY)
PORTER, DONNA A., RN, dir. nrsg., Everett A. Gladman Memorial Hospital, Oakland, CA '83 (NURS)
PORTER, EUGENE R., dir. plant serv., Woodward Hospital and Health Center, Woodward, OK '85 (ENG)
PORTER, G. NIKKI, coor. staff educ. and wellness, Methodist Hospital, Mitchell, SD '86 (EDUC)
PORTER, INEZ, Vero Beach, FL '80 (FOOD)
PORTER, JACQUE, Dallas, TX '84 (RISK)
PORTER, JANET ELAINE, instr., Program in Hospital Administration, University of Minnesota, Minneapolis, MN '76
PORTER, JOAN E., dir. west bay home care and hospice serv., Seton Medical Center, Daly City, CA '86 (AMB)
PORTER, JOHN M. JR., pres., Ephrata Community Hospital, Ephrata, PA '81 (PR) (PLNG)
PORTER, JOHN T., atty., Sacred Heart Hospital, Yankton, SD '75 (ATTY)
PORTER, JOYCE L., student, Southern Illinois University, School of Technical Careers Program, Health Care Management, Carbondale, IL '86
PORTER, LISANNE, adm. fellow, Guthrie Medical Center, Sayre, PA '84
PORTER, NANCY HARRIS, instr. staff dev., Divine Providence Hospital, Williamsport, PA '87 (EDUC)
PORTER, PAMELA J., RN, vice-pres., Riverside Medical Center, Kankakee, IL '84 (NURS)
PORTER, PHILIP J., sr. consult., Peat, Marwick, Mitchell and Company, Atlanta, GA '81 (MGMT)(PR) (PLNG)
PORTER, RICHARD A., pres., Metropolitan Home Health Care Services, Inc., Dearborn, MI '84
PORTER, ROBERT E., PhD, phys. mgt. educ., Geisinger Medical Center, Danville, PA '81 (EDUC)
PORTER, ROBERT SHIG, vice-pres. commun. and pub. affairs, Memorial Medical Center, Savannah, GA '83 (PR)
PORTER, SARAH MONTGOMERY, dir. pub. rel., Bossier Medical Center, Bossier City, LA '86 (PR)
PORTER, THOMAS C., assoc. adm., Morton Hospital and Medical Center, Taunton, MA '69
PORTERFIELD, JIM WELDON, assoc. prod. and serv. res., Baylor University Medical Center, Dallas, TX '84
PORTERFIELD, JOHN D. III, MD, vice-pres., Hyatt Medical Management Services, Inc., Encino, CA '70 (HON)
PORTERFIELD, MARY JILL, asst. dir. vol. serv., Wheeling Hospital, Wheeling, WV '86 (VOL)
PORTH, CHARLES H., mgt. facil. plng., Scott and White Memorial Hospital, Temple, TX '78 (MGMT)
PORTILLO, DIANA L., RN, asst. dir. nrsg., Braddock General Hospital, Braddock, PA '73 (NURS)
PORTMAN, DAVID, exec. vice-pres., Medical Communications, Woodbridge, NJ '76
PORTMAN, ELAINE, rep. pat. asst., Kaiser Foundation Hospital-Cleveland, Cleveland, OH '77 (PAT)
PORTMANN, REVEREND FATHER FREDERICK III, (ret.), St. Joseph Catholic Church, Williams, AZ '63 (PERS)
PORTNOFF, LOIS R., dir. soc. serv., Albert Einstein Medical Center, Philadelphia, PA '75 (SOC)
PORTNOY, STEVEN, pres., Amicus, Inc., Radnor, PA '79 (PLNG)
PORTO, GRENA, risk mgr., University Hospital, Stony Brook, NY '86 (RISK)
PORTUGAL, BARRY, pres., Health Care Development Services, Northbrook, IL '81 (PLNG)
PORTWOOD, CHERYL B., RN, dir. nrsg., Germantown Hospital and Medical Center, Philadelphia, PA '85 (NURS)
PORTWOOD, DAVID A., adm. asst., Middle Georgia Hospital, Macon, GA '82
PORWAL, MANILAL S., assoc. exec. dir., Group Health Plan of Southeast Michigan, Troy, MI '83 (MGMT)
POSA, PAUL P., atty., Washington Hospital, Washington, PA '73 (ATTY)
POSHUNS, ELAINE, EdD, mgr. emp. educ., Toronto General Hospital, Toronto, Ont., Canada '83 (EDUC)
POSNER, DAVID H., atty., Clara Maass Medical Center, Belleville, NJ '74 (ATTY)
POSNER, JAMES R., PhD, Irving, TX '79 (RISK)
POSSIN, CHARLES E., dir. matl. serv. and pharm. serv., Meriter Hospital, Madison, WI '85 (PUR)
POST, ANNMARIE, coor. vol. serv., St. Mary's Health Services, Grand Rapids, MI '84 (VOL)
POSTAI, KRISTA K., vice-pres. commun. rel. and mktg., Mount Carmel Medical Center, Pittsburg, KS '82 (PR)
POSTER, ANNE T., RN, coor. nrsg. amb. care, Veterans Administration Medical Center, Boston, MA '86 (AMB)
POSTERICK, RAY, dir. bldg. serv., Shriners Hospital for Crippled Children, Minneapolis, MN '85 (ENG)
POSTMA, RICHARD, atty., Pine Rest Christian Hospital, Grand Rapids, MI '86 (ATTY)
POSTMA, SID JR., dir. eng., Toledo Hospital, Toledo, OH '76 (ENG)
POSTON, ANITA O., atty., Children's Hospital, Norfolk, VA '83 (ATTY)
POSTON, PAT, sr. vice-pres. plng. and commun., SunHealth Corporation, Charlotte, NC '79 (PR) (PLNG)
POTASH, MARY-ELLEN, vice-pres. corp. plng., Walter O. Boswell Memorial Hospital, Sun City, AZ '82 (PLNG)
POTEET, ANNA J., dir. pub. rel., Baton Rouge General Medical Center, Baton Rouge, LA '85 (PR)
POTENZO, RONALD, dir. plant oper., West Suburban Hospital Medical Center, Oak Park, IL '87 (ENG)
POTETZ, KARLA K., PhD, asst. to vice-pres. nrsg., Deaconess Hospital of Cleveland, Cleveland, OH '86 (PLNG)
POTLER, DEBORAH J., supv. telecommun., Peninsula General Hospital Medical Center, Salisbury, MD '86 (ENG)
POTOCNY, A. ROBERT, dir. pers., Robert Wood Johnson University Hospital, New Brunswick, NJ '76 (PERS)
POTTENGER, CONSTANCE R., dir., Indiana University Hospitals, Indianapolis, IN '87 (ENG)
POTTER, DONALD P., pres., Southeast Michigan Hospital Council, Southfield, MI '79 (PLNG)
POTTER, DONNA SCHONFELD, dir. pub. rel., St. Frances Cabrini Hospital, Alexandria, LA '84 (PR)
POTTER, E. J., dir. phys. plant, Trumbull Memorial Hospital, Warren, OH '83 (ENG)
POTTER, ERNESTINE A., dir. commun. affairs and vol. serv., District of Columbia General Hospital, Washington, DC '86 (VOL)
POTTER, GLORIA, dir. cent. serv., Divine Providence Hospital, Pittsburgh, PA '74 (CS)
POTTER, HARRY C., dir., Veterans Administration Medical Center, Reno, NV '49 (LIFE)
POTTER, LAURENCE A. III, Richardson, TX '73
POTTER, RENEE, dir. qual. review, St. Anne's Hospital, Chicago, IL '86 (RISK)
POTTER, SARA, risk mgr., Albert Einstein Hlthcare Foundation, Philadelphia, PA '86 (RISK)
POTTHAST, ANITA J., Chicago, IL '70 (FOOD)
POTTS, EDWARD J., mgr. human resource dev., Methodist Hospital, Philadelphia, PA '82 (EDUC)
POTTS, L. DELDEE, pres., Medical and Management Services Company, Newbury Park, CA '85 (MGMT)
POTTS, SUSAN, assoc. dir. pers., Peninsula General Hospital Medical Center, Salisbury, MD '75 (PERS)
POTVIN, DIANE GUZINSKI, sr. mgr. prof. ancillary serv., St. Mary's General Hospital, Lewiston, ME '83 (PLNG)
POTYRAJ, JAMES J., asst. adm., HCA Medical Center of Port St. Lucie, Port St. Lucie, FL '83
POTZMANN, MARY ANN, dir. plng. and mktg., Aspen Medical Group, St. Paul, MN '82 (PLNG)
POUCHER, JAMES W., adm., South Seminole Community Hospital, Longwood, FL '76
POULIDES, PAUL C., dir. matl. mgt. serv., University of Texas M. D. Anderson Hospital and Tumor Institute at Houston, Houston, TX '86 (PUR)
POULSEN, MARSHALL M., vice-pres. mktg., South Community Hospital, Oklahoma City, OK '84 (PR) (PLNG)
POUNCY, CURTIS, supv. cent. proc. and distrib., Westlake Community Hospital, Melrose Park, IL '83 (CS)
POUND, THEODORE E. G., atty., HCA West Paces Ferry Hospital, Atlanta, GA '86 (ATTY)
POUNDERS, GAIL, dir. soc. serv., Southwest Texas Methodist Hospital, San Antonio, TX '75 (SOC)
POUNDERS, JOHN H., dir. pub. affairs, Baptist Medical System, Little Rock, AR '81 (PR)
POUNDERS, JOHN N., sr. mgt. eng., Baptist Medical Centers, Birmingham, AL '85 (MGMT)
POUTOUS, WILLIAM, dir. group pur., Hospital Shared Services Western Pennsylvania, Warrendale, PA '85 (PUR)
POVLITZ, RALPH F. II, mgr. cent. serv., Rehabilitation Institute of Chicago, Chicago, IL '81 (CS)
POWANDA, WILLIAM C., asst. adm., Griffin Hospital, Derby, CT '76 (PR)
POWELL, BOONE JR., pres., Baylor University Medical Center, Dallas, TX '59
POWELL, BOONE SR., sr. consult., Baylor University Medical Center Foundation, Dallas, TX '76 (LIFE)
POWELL, CHARLENE MARIE, dir. soc. serv., McMinnville Community Hospital, McMinnville, OR '77 (SOC)
POWELL, DENNY W., exec. dir., Kissimmee Memorial Hospital, Kissimmee, FL '75
POWELL, DIANA DENISE, coor. pat. rep., Central Baptist Hospital, Lexington, KY '86 (PAT)
POWELL, DON R., PhD, exec. dir., American Institute for Preventive Medicine, Southfield, MI '82 (EDUC)(PR)
POWELL, EDWARD K., spec. environ. care, Veterans Administration, Department of Medicine and Surgery, Washington, DC '86 (ENVIRON)
POWELL, EDWARD T., vice-pres. pers. and labor rel., Children's Hospital of Philadelphia, Philadelphia, PA '80 (PERS)
POWELL, JOE, maint. spec., Harris Methodist -HEB, Bedford, TX '86 (ENG)
POWELL, JOSEPH HERBERT, pres., Baptist Memorial Hospital, Memphis, TN '54 (LIFE)
POWELL, JOY D., asst. dir. diet. and food adm., East Tennessee Baptist Hospital, Knoxville, TN '85 (FOOD)
POWELL, KENNETH W., asst. mgr. mech. maint., Bronson Methodist Hospital, Kalamazoo, MI '84 (ENG)
POWELL, KERSTIN B., dir. human res., Anne Arundel General Hospital, Annapolis, MD '86 (PERS)
POWELL, MARY L., RN, prod. analyst nrsg. adm., Hospital Corporation of America, Nashville, TN '86 (NURS)
POWELL, NANCY L., coor. vol., South Baltimore General Hospital, Baltimore, MD '86 (VOL)
POWELL, NANCY MACKENZIE, RN, vice-pres., Good Samaritan Hospital, Cincinnati, OH '77 (NURS)
POWELL, PRESTON L., (ret.), Oakland, CA '50 (LIFE)
POWELL, RONALD E., assoc. adm., Huntington Memorial Hospital, Pasadena, CA '64 (PERS)
POWELL, STEPHEN D., dir. pers. serv., Presbyterian Hospital, Oklahoma City, OK '83 (PERS)
POWELL, THOMAS S., (ret.), Pittsburgh, PA '77
POWELL, VIVIAN E., dir. diet. serv., Mercy Hospital, Toledo, OH '79 (FOOD)
POWELL, WILLIAM D., atty., Deaconess Hospital, Evansville, IN '68 (ATTY)
POWELL, YVONNE, dir. matl. mgt., Healthwest Medical Centers, Chatsworth, CA '83 (PUR)
POWER-BARNES, MARIE R., dir. pub. rel. and mktg., Hamilton Hospital, Hamilton, NJ '83 (PR)
POWER, LYNDA S., dir. diet. serv., Public Hospital of the Town of Salem, Salem, IL '81 (FOOD)
POWERS, BRUCE L., dir. pers., Harding Hospital, Worthington, OH '85 (PERS)
POWERS, DANIEL, Tamarac, FL '51 (LIFE)
POWERS, DARRELL, sr. vice-pres., Lynchburg General-Marshall Lodge Hospital, Lynchburg, VA '82
POWERS, GALEN D., atty., Walter O. Boswell Memorial Hospital, Sun City, AZ '79 (ATTY)
POWERS, JAMES M., dir. mktg., Holy Redeemer Health System, Meadowbrook, PA '85 (PR) (PLNG)
POWERS, JANE A., dir., Self Memorial Hospital, Greenwood, SC '78 (EDUC)
POWERS, JEANNE, dir. vol. serv., Mercer Medical Center, Trenton, NJ '87 (VOL)
POWERS, LINDA BAYS, dir. pub. rel., Freedman Advertising, Inc., Cincinnati, OH '85 (PR)
POWERS, M. CLAIRE, dir. pub. rel., Harrisburg Hospital, Harrisburg, PA '86 (PR)
POWERS, MARGARET A., RN, dir. nrsg.-med. and surg., Anne Arundel General Hospital, Annapolis, MD '86 (NURS)
POWERS, RICHARD S., atty., North Shore Medical Center, Miami, FL '84 (ATTY)
POWERS, SHIRLEY B., RN, vice-pres., NKC Hospitals, Louisville, KY '76 (NURS)
POWERS, THOMAS D. JR., mgr. cent. sup. and linen, Doylestown Hospital, Doylestown, PA '84 (CS)
POWERS, TRUDE C., dir. soc. serv., Delta Medical Center, Greenville, MS '81 (SOC)
POWERS, WILLIAM H., dir. matl. mgt., Deaconess Hospital, Evansville, IN '76 (PUR)
POWLESS, KENNETH, bd. pres., Marion Memorial Hospital, Marion, IL '70 (ATTY)
POYLIO, TRISH J., RN, dir. nrsg., Mercy Hospital, Moose Lake, MN '86 (NURS)
POYNER, DIANE M., diet. consult., Hospital Corporation of America, Nashville, TN '86 (FOOD)
POYSS, LEO F., dir. plng., Mercy Hospital, Scranton, PA '82 (PLNG)
POZEN, JANET T., PhD, sr. res. mgr., Decision Research, Lexington, MA '86 (PLNG)
POZGAR, GEORGE DANIEL, adm., St. John's Episcopal Hospital, Smithtown, NY '66
POZO, JAIME A., dir. eng. serv., Bascom Palmer Eye Institute, Anne Bates Leach Eye Hospital Hospital, Miami, FL '81 (ENG)
POZY, ROSEMARY J., RN, asst. dir. nrsg., St. Nicholas Hospital, Sheboygan, WI '82 (NURS)
PRAEGER, ANDREA M., atty., Montefiore Medical Center, Bronx, NY '86 (ATTY)
PRAGER, B. GAYLE, Houston, TX '85 (PAT)
PRAGER, FRANCINE, RN, vice-pres. pat. care serv., Long Island College Hospital, Brooklyn, NY '82 (NURS)
PRAINITO, BERNARDO, sr. vice-pres., Urban Association, Inc., New York, NY '86
PRAINO, INGRID S., coor. risk control, Bower and Gardner, New York, NY '84 (RISK)
PRAKKEN, SYBIL M., chief diet. serv., Veterans Administration Medical Center, Allen Park, MI '83 (FOOD)
PRANSKI, JOYCE G., mgr. syst. plng. and dev., Huntington Memorial Hospital, Pasadena, CA '82 (MGMT)
PRASERTSOM, MAJ. GEN. SA-ARD, MD, dep. surg. gen., Royal Thai Army Medical Department, Bangkok, Thailand '78
PRATER, CHARLES WAYNE, bldg. eng., Stillwater Medical Center, Stillwater, OK '77 (ENG)
PRATER, TED, mgr. pur., St. John's Regional Medical Center, Joplin, MO '86 (PUR)
PRATER, VALERIE S., dir. mktg., Lewis-Gale Hospital, Salem, VA '84 (PR)
PRATHER, GRANT W., vice-pres., Baptist Medical Center, Columbia, SC '80 (PAT)
PRATHER, ROBERT J., Phoenix, AZ '71
PRATHER, THEODORE W., assoc. dir. food serv., New York University Medical Center, New York, NY '85 (FOOD)
PRATO, ANTHONY C., dir. human res., Mesa Lutheran Hospital, Mesa, AZ '84 (PERS)
PRATO, SUE ANN, RN, clin. dir., med. nrsg. and emer. serv., Shands Hospital, Gainesville, FL '86 (NURS)
PRATT-THOMAS, E. DOUGLAS, atty., Trident Regional Medical Center, Charleston, SC '82 (ATTY)
PRATT, BONNIE F., RN, dir. nrs., Memorial General Hospital, Las Cruces, NM '83 (NURS)
PRATT, CHARLES A., dir. pharm. and matl. mgt., Millinocket Regional Hospital, Millinocket, ME '86 (PUR)
PRATT, EARL H., dir. plant oper., Eaton Rapids Community Hospital, Eaton Rapids, MI '81 (ENG)
PRATT, HENRY CHARLES, dir. matl. mgt., St. Helen Hospital, Chehalis, WA '86 (PUR)
PRATT, JEAN DIANE, mgr., New York City Department of Mental Health, New York, NY '75
PRATT, JOHN R., exec. dir., Lakeville Hospital, Lakeville, MA '64
PRATT, JOY, bus. mgr., Radiology Associates of Santa Rosa Medical Grp, Santa Rosa, CA '87 (AMB)
PRATT, MARY BETH, discharge planner and soc. serv., Margaret Mary Community Hospital, Batesville, IN '87 (SOC)
PRATT, WILLIAM A., chief eng., St. John's Hospital, Longview, WA '71 (ENG)
PREBIL, RICHARD L., atty., Alexian Brothers Health Systems Inc., Elk Grove Village, IL '82 (ATTY)
PREGIBON, COLIN P., student, Program in Industrial Engineering, Youngstown State University, Youngstown, OH '86 (MGMT)
PREGMON, MICHAEL, dir. pers., Saint Joseph Hospital, Reading, PA '67 (PERS)

PREIB, BARBARA A., RN, vice-pres. nrsg., Columbus Hospital, Chicago, IL '81 (NURS)
PREIKSAT, JON, vice-pres. and atty., Shercorp, Pittsburgh, PA '85 (ATTY)
PREISINGER, JOANNE M., dir. soc. serv., St. John Hospital, Leavenworth, KS '82 (SOC)
PREISLER, ROBIN D., assoc. dir. mktg., University Hospital, Newark, NJ '82 (PLNG)
PREJUSA, MAURO C. JR., dir. food serv., Morrison Management Services, Dallas, TX '86 (FOOD)
PREKUP, JOSEPH T., reg. vice-pres., Affiliated Hospital Consultants, Phoenix, AZ '61
PRELESNIK, WARREN L., pres., Manchester Memorial Hospital, Manchester, CT '65
PRENATT, ANN B., assoc. dir. pers., Greenville Hospital System, Greenville, SC '87 (PERS)
PRENDERGAST, JOHN G., atty., Sinai Hospital of Baltimore, Baltimore, MD '87 (ATTY)
PRENDERGAST, MARY ELIZABETH, RN, vice-pres. nrsg., Mary Hitchcock Memorial Hospital, Hanover, NH '82 (NURS)
PRENDERGAST, RICHARD W. JR., vice-pres., St. James Hospital Medical Center, Chicago Heights, IL '72 (ENG)(PLNG)
PRENZEL, DOLLY J., dir. matl. mgt., University of Virginia, Charlottesville, VA '82 (PUR)
PRESBURY-SMITH, JO, dir. soc. serv., Tri-City Medical Center, Oceanside, CA '84 (SOC)
PRESCOTT, JAMES R., plng. analyst, McKay-Dee Hospital Center, Ogden, UT '76 (PLNG)
PRESCOTT, JAYNE M., RN, dir. nrsg., Central General Hospital, Plainview, NY '68 (NURS)
PRESLEY, R. CARLTON, atty., St. Joseph Hospital, Houston, TX '86 (ATTY)
PRESOL, MARY C., RN, dir. nrsg., Gritman Memorial Hospital, Moscow, ID '82 (NURS)
PRESS, IRWIN, pres., Press, Ganey Associates, Inc., Notre Dame, IN '85 (PAT)
PRESSER, JOY A., dir. risk mgt. and spec. serv., Cape Canaveral Hospital, Cocoa Beach, FL '82 (RISK)
PRESSER, KENNETH F., adm. asst., University Medical Center Southern Nevada, Las Vegas, NV '81 (RISK)
PRESSER, STEWART M., dir. pat. acct., Presbyterian Hospital in the City of New York, New York, NY '78
PRESSLEY, DAVID L., dir. food serv., St. John Hospital, Leavenworth, KS '84 (FOOD)
PRESSMAN, ERNEST, adm. dir. human res., Providence Hospital, Everett, WA '82 (PERS)
PRESSMAN, NEIL MARC, mgt. consult., Travelers Insurance Company, Hartford, CT '78
PREST, ALAN P., asst. vice-pres., Health East, Roanoke, VA '84
PRESTON, DOREEN A., RN, asst. dir. pat. educ., Grace Hospital, Detroit, MI '84 (EDUC)
PRESTON, GINA G., asst. dir. food serv., Oklahoma Memorial Hospital, Oklahoma City, OK '81 (FOOD)
PRESTON, JOAN L., dir. vol., Lawrence and Memorial Hospital, New London, CT '72 (VOL)
PRESTON, R. CRAIG, asst. adm. plng., Utah Valley Regional Medical Center, Provo, UT '80 (PLNG)
PRESTON, WINTON R., pres., Healthmark, Cleveland, TN '72 (PR)
PRESUTTO, LORETTA, dir. cent. sterile proc., Robert Wood Johnson University Hospital, New Brunswick, NJ '87 (CS)
PRETE, F. EDWARD, Kaiser Foundation Hospital, Oakland, CA '76 (ENG)
PRETSCH, PAUL G., dir. mktg. and bus. dev., Presbyterian-St. Luke's Medical Center, Denver, CO '70 (PR) (PLNG)
PRETTYMAN, WILLIAM O. JR., exec. dir., Eastern Pennsylvania Health Care Foundation, Bethlehem, PA '61
PREWITT, THOMAS R. JR., atty., Methodist Hospital-Central Unit, Memphis, TN '79 (ATTY)
PRIBICH, MARY E., dir. diet., Doctors Hospital of Stark County, Massillon, OH '83 (FOOD)
PRICE, ANDREA R., asst. vice-pres. adm. affairs, Children's Hospital National Medical Center, Washington, DC '82 (AMB)
PRICE, CAROLE RUNYAN, assoc. dir., Stanford University Hospital, Stanford, CA '82 (RISK)
PRICE, CHARLES W., eng., Memorial Hospital of Washington County, Sandersville, GA '79 (ENG)
PRICE, DELBERT L., pres., Delaware Price Associates, Oakton, VA '48 (LIFE)
PRICE, E. RAY, dir. eng., Auburn General Hospital, Auburn, WA '80 (ENG)
PRICE, EDNA D., (ret.), Bridgetown, N.S., Canada '31 (LIFE)
PRICE, JACK E., dir. soc. serv., Flint Osteopathic Hospital, Flint, MI '78 (SOC)
PRICE, JACK E. SR., dir. food serv., Immanuel Medical Center, Omaha, NE '80 (FOOD)
PRICE, JAMES L., atty., Frankford Hospital of the County of Philadelphia, Philadelphia, PA '69 (ATTY)
PRICE, JAMES O., dir. facil. mgt., Fort Worth Osteopathic Medical Center, Fort Worth, TX '84 (ENG)
PRICE, JAMES, dir. plant oper., St. Mary of the Plains Hospital and Rehabilitation Center, Lubbock, TX '81 (ENG)
PRICE, JANE F., RN, asst. adm. nrsg., Mercy Hospital, Portsmouth, OH '86 (NURS)
PRICE, JIM F., dir. plant oper. and maint., Victoria Regional Medical Center, Victoria, TX '84 (ENG)
PRICE, LARUE M., gen. mgr., Healthserv, Scottsdale, AZ '83 (MGMT)
PRICE, LAURA, sr. consult., Ernst and Whinney, Chicago, IL '84
PRICE, SR. MARY LOUIS, dir. soc. serv., Hotel Dieu Medical Center, El Paso, TX '84 (SOC)
PRICE, OSCAR G. JR., dir. human res., Gwinnett Hospital System, Lawrenceville, GA '82 (PERS)
PRICE, PAUL E., risk mgr., Fairview Hospital and Healthcare Service, Minneapolis, MN '82 (RISK)
PRICE, PEGGY, dir. info. syst., Mount Sinai Medical Center, Miami Beach, FL '85 (MGMT)
PRICE, PHILIP B., adm., Kirkhaven, Rochester, NY '63
PRICE, ROGER S., syst. consult., Shared Medical Systems, Burlington, MA '76 (MGMT)
PRICE, SHARON, soc. worker, Mercy Hospital, Council Bluffs, IA '86 (SOC)
PRICE, STANLEY, dir. security, New York University Medical Center, New York, NY '78
PRICE, THOMAS D. JR., atty., Group Health Cooperative, Seattle, WA '83 (ATTY)
PRICE, THOMAS H. JR., arch., John R. McGovern and Associates, New York, NY '75 (PLNG)
PRICE, THOMAS ROWE III, dir. pub. and commun. rel., Maryland General Hospital, Baltimore, MD '74 (PR)
PRICE, W. F. NICK, student, Program Master of Science in Health Services Administration, College of St. Francis, Joliet, IL '86
PRICE, WALTER L., atty., Johnson City Medical Center Hospital, Johnson City, TN '75 (ATTY)
PRICHARD, RALPH H. III, food serv. mgr., Franklin Square Hospital, Baltimore, MD '83 (FOOD)
PRICHARD, YVETTE M., coor. qual. assur. and mgr. risk, Pinecrest Hospital, Santa Barbara, CA '83 (RISK)
PRICHETT, WILSON, dir. mgt. serv., Albert Einstein Medical Center, Philadelphia, PA '78 (PUR)
PRICKETT, MICHAEL J., dir. maint., Ashtabula County Medical Center, Ashtabula, OH '85 (ENG)
PRICKETT, THOMAS H., exec. dir., McKeesport Hospital, McKeesport, PA '77
PRIDDY, LINDA I., RN, dir. nrsg. serv., William Bee Ririe Hospital, Ely, NV '83 (NURS)
PRIDDY, LINDA R., dir. pat. and family serv., HCA Donelson Hospital, Nashville, TN '86 (SOC)
PRIDDY, MARY K., RN, adm. pat. care, University Hospital of Arkansas, Little Rock, AR '86 (NURS)
PRIDDY, MARY M. H., atty., Chippenham Hospital, Richmond, VA '86 (ATTY)
PRIDDY, ROBERT F., dir. mktg., Decatur Memorial Hospital, Decatur, IL '83 (PR) (PLNG)
PRIDDY, SANDRA D., adm., Stokes-Reynolds Memorial Hospital, Danbury, NC '87 (AMB)
PRIDGEN, LEE JR., adm., Sampson County Memorial Hospital, Clinton, NC '57 (LIFE)
PRIDGON, WILLIAM L., supv. cent. serv., Colquitt Regional Medical Center, Moultrie, GA '81 (CS)
PRIEST, MARTHA G., coor. educ., Spartanburg Regional Medical Center, Spartanburg, SC '86 (EDUC)
PRIETO, PEDRO A. SOLIS, gen. mgr., Seguros Unidos de Salud S. A., San Isidro, Peru '86
PRIGIONI, RITA E., pub. health educator, Division of Health, Center for Health Statistics, Madison, WI '83 (MGMT)
PRIGOFF, MILTON, atty., Englewood Hospital, Englewood, NJ '83 (ATTY)
PRIMEAU, PAUL F., assoc. adm. satellite and prepayment programs, Henry Ford Hospital, Detroit, MI '82 (MGMT)
PRIMROSE, CLAIRE H., contr., Sea Level Hospital, Sea Level, NC '86
PRIMROSE, DENNIS E., dir. plant eng., University Hospital, Augusta, GA '85 (ENG)
PRIMROSE, VICKI, risk mgr., Wyoming Medical Center, Casper, WY '86 (RISK)
PRINCE, BARBARA, coor. staff dev., St. Peter Hospital, Olympia, WA '76 (EDUC)
PRINCE, JOHN W., adm. asst. plng., Sacred Heart Hospital, Eau Claire, WI '70 (PLNG)
PRINCE, KAY, dir. soc. serv., St. Ann's Hospital of Columbus, Westerville, OH '86 (SOC)
PRINCE, THOMAS R., prof. acctg., Kellogg Graduate School of Management, Northwestern University, Evanston, IL '80
PRINCING, MARY W., pres., Princing and Ewend Associates, Saginaw, MI '84 (PR)
PRINCIPATO, VINCENT R., dir. matl. mgt., Rolling Hill Hospital, Elkins Park, PA '86 (PUR)
PRINCIPE-CROCKETT, NAN, coor. staff dev., Charter Rivers Hospital, West Columbia, SC '85 (EDUC)
PRINCIPE, MAJ. RICHARD, student, Army-Baylor University Program in Health Care Administration, Fort Sam Houston, TX '86
PRINDLE, JOAN H., dir. vol. serv., Germantown Community Hospital, Germantown, TN '86 (VOL)
PRINTUP, ROBERT H., dir. environ. serv., St. John's Hospital and Health Center, Santa Monica, CA '86 (ENVIRON)
PRINZING, SR. PATRICIA, coor. pub. rel., St. James Mercy Hospital, Hornell, NY '85 (PR)
PRIOR, HELEN, dir. sup. and equip., Virginia Mason Hospital, Seattle, WA '67 (CS)
PRISELAC, ROBERT J., vice-pres. adm. and fiscal serv., Englewood Community Hospital, Englewood, FL '85
PRISELAC, THOMAS M., sr. vice-pres. oper., Cedars-Sinai Medical Center, Los Angeles, CA '79 (PLNG)
PRISTAVE, ROBERT J., atty., Rush-Presbyterian-St. Luke's Medical Center, Chicago, IL '84 (ATTY)
PRISTER, JAMES RICHARD, student, Program and Bureau of Hospital Administration, University of Michigan, Ann Arbor, MI '83
PRISTER, RICHARD ANTHONY, exec. eng., Hutzel Hospital, Detroit, MI '67 (ENG)
PRITCHARD, GAIL J., RN, dir. nrsg., Moberly Regional Medical Center, Moberly, MO '86 (NURS)
PRITCHARD, JANIS L., dir. vol. serv., Stuart Circle Hospital, Richmond, VA '84 (VOL)
PRITCHARD, TERI B., dir. pub. rel., St. Charles Hospital, Oregon, OH '83 (PR)
PRITCHETT, ALLEN M., dir. pers., Memorial Hospital, Carbondale, IL '84 (PERS)
PRITCHETT, DEBORAH SUE, dir. food serv., Lewisville Memorial Hospital, Lewisville, TX '81 (FOOD)
PRITCHETT, GERALD L., dir. pur., Alpena General Hospital, Alpena, MI '74 (PUR)
PRITTS, ROBERT W., adm., Jewish Hospital of St. Louis, St. Louis, MO '86
PRIVER, JULIEN, MD, San Diego, CA '47 (LIFE)
PRIVETT, ALICE J., adm. res., Shands Hospital at the University of Florida, Gainesville, FL '84
PRIZIO, JOSEPH J., mgr. biomedical eng., New Milford Hospital, New Milford, CT '84 (ENG)
PROCHNOW, ARTHUR G., dir. pur., Garden City Osteopathic Hospital, Garden City, MI '78 (PUR)
PROCKNOW, MARY E., corp. dir. plng., Horizon Health Systems, Oak Park, MI '81 (PLNG)
PROCTOR, JAMES, vice-pres. plant oper., Middle Tennessee Medical Center, Murfreesboro, TN '78 (ENG)
PROCTOR, RICHARD W., dir. prof. serv., Overlook Hospital, Summit, NJ '74
PROFITA, CDR SALVATORE J., MSC USN, Woodbridge, VA '74
PROGER, PHILLIP A., atty., Baker and Hostetler, Washington, DC '78 (ATTY)
PROHOV, LAURA W., assoc. plng., Diversified Health Resources, Chicago, IL '86 (PLNG)
PROKO, THOMAS J., health care fin. syst. consult., Rush-Presbyterian-St. Luke's Medical Center, Chicago, IL '85
PROM, STEPHEN G., atty., St. Luke's Hospital, Jacksonville, FL '83 (ATTY)
PROMER, KAREN B., Empire Blue Cross and Blue Shield, New York, NY '83
PROMINSKI, JOHN E., atty., Columbia Hospital for Women, Washington, DC '82 (ATTY)
PRONKO, DONNA LOUISE BUXTON, coor. pat. rel., Stanford University Hospital, Stanford, CA '84 (PAT)
PROOST, ROBERT L., dir. constr. and phys. facil., Sisters of St. Mary, St. Louis, MO '82 (ENG)
PROPOTNIK, TONI, RN, asst. adm. nrsg. serv., LDS Hospital, Salt Lake City, UT '82 (NURS)
PROSAK, LINDA J. N., coor. info., Lorain Community Hospital, Lorain, OH '83 (PR)
PROSPERI, PATRICK H., sr. oper. analyst, United Hospitals, Inc., Cheltenham, PA '86 (MGMT)
PROSSER, JILL A., dir. soc. serv., Mason District Hospital, Havana, IL '85 (SOC)
PROSSER, JOHN, asst. dir. plant oper., St. Margaret's Hospital, Montgomery, AL '87 (ENG)
PROSSER, RAYMOND J., atty., Cook County Hospital, Chicago, IL '82 (ATTY)
PROTZ, WILLIAM D., vice-pres., Akron General Medical Center, Akron, OH '82 (PERS)
PROTZIK, STEPHEN W., assoc. dir. eng. and maint., St. Francis Medical Center, Pittsburgh, PA '83 (ENG)
PROTZMAN, PAULINE A., RN, vice-pres. nrsg. serv., Gettysburg Hospital, Gettysburg, PA '86 (NURS)
PROUD, DEBRA I., dir. pub. rel., Arlington Hospital, Arlington, VA '85 (PR)
PROUD, GEOFFREY F., pres., Marketing Communications, Inc., Southold, NY '85 (PR)
PROUD, HELEN G., asst. dir. and dir. pat. care serv., Suffolk County Department of Health Services, Hauppauge, NY '65
PROUD, JAMES D., dir. pers., Uniontown Hospital, Uniontown, PA '86 (PERS)
PROULX, JOSEPH R., RN, prof., University of Maryland, School of Nursing, Baltimore, MD '85 (NURS)
PROUT, JOHN S., exec. vice-pres., Washoe Medical Center, Reno, NV '73
PROUTY, GENE E., dir. phys. plant, Thomas Jefferson University Hospital, Philadelphia, PA '79 (ENG)
PROUTY, MARILYN P., RN, adm. nrsg., Mary Hitchcock Memorial Hospital, Hanover, NH '68 (NURS)
PROVANZANO, JOSEPH STEPHEN, atty., Beekman Downtown Hospital, New York, NY '82 (ATTY)
PROVENZANO, PAUL A., asst. matl. control mgr., Geisinger Wyoming Valley Medical Center, Wilkes-Barre, PA '84 (PUR)
PROVO, JUDITH E., dir. vol. serv., Akron City Hospital, Akron, OH '85 (VOL)
PROVOST, HARRY D. JR., adm., Medical Center of Southeastern Oklahoma, Durant, OK '74 (PERS)
PRUDDEN, DAVID N., dir. sup., proc. and distrib., Bronson Methodist Hospital, Kalamazoo, MI '83 (PUR)
PRUDENTE, STEPHEN C., partner, Maynard, O'Connor and Smith, Albany, NY '81 (ATTY)
PRUE, DEMARIS K., mgr., Providence Milwaukie Hospital, Milwaukie, OR '85 (CS)
PRUENTE, THOMAS F., dir. maint., St. Joseph Mercy Hospital, Pontiac, MI '75 (ENG)
PRUETT, WESLEY L., Fairmont Community Hospital, Fairmont, MN '83 (PERS)
PRUITT, IRA D. JR., atty., Rush Foundation Hospital, Meridian, MS '84 (ATTY)
PRUITT, JOHN D., asst. adm. facil., Truman Medical Center-East, Kansas City, MO '78 (ENG)
PRUNIER, KENNETH R., Good Samaritan Hospital and Health Center, Dayton, OH '83 (MGMT)
PRUSINSKI, SR. DIANE D., dir., Our Lady of Mercy Medical Center, Bronx, NY '68
PRUTTING, WILLIAM J., eng., Philips Medical Systems, Inc., Larchmont, NY '81 (ENG)
PRYBIL, LAWRENCE D., PhD, exec. vice-pres., Daughters of Charity, Evansville, IN '64
PRYBYL, LORI, mktg. and health care spec., Sysco Food Services, Houston, TX '70 (FOOD)
PRYCE, RICHARD J., pres., Aultman Hospital, Canton, OH '72
PRYDE, JAMES P., atty., Trinity Lutheran Hospital, Kansas City, MO '86 (ATTY)
PRYLINSKI, ROBERT E., dir. eng. serv., Brandywine Hospital, Caln Township, PA '84 (ENG)
PRYOR, MARY C., RN, dir. nrsg., St. John's Riverside Hospital, Yonkers, NY '81 (NURS)
PRYOR, R. L., dir. pers., St. Joseph Hospital and Health Care Center, Tacoma, WA '80 (PERS)
PRYOR, STANLEY G., dir. risk mgt. and ins., Miami Children's Hospital, Miami, FL '80 (RISK)

PRYZBYLKOWSKI, SHIRLEY, RN, adm. asst. vol. and commun. educ., Kennedy Memorial Hospitals University Medical Center, Stratford, NJ '84 (VOL)
PRZELOMIEC, MICHAEL JOHN, RN, supv. cent. serv., Windham Community Memorial Hospital, Willimantic, CT '86 (CS)
PRZESTRZELSKI, DAVID R., RN, assoc. chief nrsg. serv., Veterans Administration Hospital, Hines, IL '86 (NURS)
PRZYBYLA, JOHN E., supv. biomedical, St. Joseph's Hospital and Health Center, Tucson, AZ '82 (ENG)
PTAK, MARY ANN, corp. dir. mgt. eng., Evangelical Health Systems, Oak Brook, IL '84 (MGMT)
PUBLOW, PETER E., vice-pres. plng. and mktg., Saint Joseph Hospital and Health Center, Kokomo, IN '82 (PLNG)
PUCHER, TAMAS F., dir. health plng., Williams, Tazewell, Cooke and Associates, Inc., Norfolk, VA '78 (PLNG)
PUCKETT, CLEVE, dir. maint. and eng., Our Lady of Mercy Hospital, Cincinnati, OH '85 (ENG)
PUCKETT, GEORGE L., dir. matl. mgt., Bristol Memorial Hospital, Bristol, TN '82 (PUR)
PUCKETT, RUBY P., dir. food and nutr. serv., Shands Hospital, Gainesville, FL '68 (FOOD)
PUCKETT, THOMAS C., dir. shared serv., Evangelical Health Systems, Oak Brook, IL '84 (MGMT)
PUCKORIS, STEPHEN, chief eng., Community Hospital of North Las Vegas, North Las Vegas, NV '86 (ENG)
PUCOSSI, MARILYN J., RN, vice-pres. nrsg., Unity Medical Center, Fridley, MN '80 (NURS)
PUDLIN, HELEN P., atty., Pennsylvania Hospital, Philadelphia, PA '83 (ATTY)
PUENT, DAVID L., dir. eng., St. James Hospital Medical Center, Chicago Heights, IL '75 (ENG)
PUETZ, BELINDA E., ed.-in-chief, Journal of Nursing Staff Development, Indianapolis, IN '85 (EDUC)
PUFAHL, MOLLY, RN, dir. nrsg., Wesley Medical Center, Wichita, KS '83 (NURS)
PUFAL, SANDRA, student, Southern Illinois University, Carbondale, IL '85
PUFF, LINDA A., student, Graduate in School of Architecture and Planning, Columbia University School of Public Health, New York, NY '86 (PR)
PUGH, DALE III, dir. pub. rel., University Medical Center Southern Nevada, Las Vegas, NV '86 (PR)
PUGH, DAVID E., assoc. dir. eng. serv., Emory University Hospital, Atlanta, GA '83 (ENG)
PUGH, DELBERT L., (ret.), Columbus, OH '45 (LIFE)
PUGH, DENISE MCLAURINE, dir. med. soc. work, Kaiser Foundation Hospital, Oakland, CA '82 (SOC)
PUGH, DONNA NOBLIN, coor. pat. rel. and soc. serv., Baptist Memorial Hospital-Lauderdale, Ripley, TN '87 (PAT)
PUGH, ESTHER M., dir. diet., Medical Center of Independence, Independence, MO '78 (FOOD)
PUGH, LARRY W., pres., Allen Memorial Hospital, Waterloo, IA '58 (PLNG)
PUGH, PAUL M., chief exec. off., Fox Army Community Hospital, Huntsville, AL '71
PUGH, RICHARD A., dir. eng. and maint., Salem Hospital, Salem, OR '85 (ENG)
PUGH, RICHARD E., exec. dir., New Milford Hospital, New Milford, CT '81
PUGMIRE, DON G., vice-pres., Holy Cross Hospital, Salt Lake City, UT '74 (PERS)
PUHALLA, JOYCE, RN, dir. educ., Berkshire Medical Center, Pittsfield, MA '75 (EDUC)
PUISIS, SR. M. PAULISSA, pat. rep., Loretto Hospital, Chicago, IL '79 (PAT)
PULASKI, BARBARA, mgr. cent. serv., Yavapai Regional Medical Center, Prescott, AZ '85 (CS)
PULASKI, C. ROBERT, student, Program in Health Administration, Governors State University, Park Forest South, IL '85
PULCINI, DINO J., dir. sup., proc. and distrib., Pennsylvania Hospital, Philadelphia, PA '85 (CS)(PUR)
PULEO, PATRICIA M., dir. vol., Doctors Hospital, New York, NY '83 (VOL)
PULIA, DOROTHY, asst. dir. nrsg., Loretto Hospital, Chicago, IL '80 (NURS)
PULLEN, FRANK EDWARD, dir. hskpg., Greenville Memorial Hospital, Greenville, SC '86 (ENVIRON)
PULLEN, KATHLEEN S., vice-pres. pat. care serv., Feather River Hospital, Paradise, CA '84 (NURS)
PULLEN, LEON C., consult., Herman Smith Associates, Hinsdale, IL '41 (PLNG)(LIFE)
PULLI, JOHN J., adm. asst. to chief staff, Veterans Administration Medical Center, Buffalo, NY '78
PULLIAM, CLAIRE R., RN, dir. nrsg., Oxford-Lafayette Medical Center, Oxford, MS '81 (NURS)
PULLIAM, SALLY A., exec. off., Headquarters Tactical Air Command, Hampton, VA '86
PULLICINO, KATHERINE A., RN, dir. nrsg., Onslow Memorial Hospital, Jacksonville, NC '80 (NURS)
PULLING, MICHAEL O., pres., Health Care Management Associates, Lynnfield, MA '74
PULLUM, BILLY J., dir. maint., McAlester Regional Hospital, McAlester, OK '81 (ENG)
PULS, DENNIS M., mgt. eng., Community Hospital of Central California, Fresno, CA '86 (MGMT)
PULSE, JOAN T., dir. vol. serv., Charles S. Wilson Memorial Hospital, Johnson City, NY '79 (VOL)
PULVERMACHER, CDR HAROLD, (ret.), Gurnee, IL '79
PURCELL, DAVID V., atty., St. Agnes Hospital, Fond Du Lac, WI '69 (ATTY)
PURCELL, DOROTHY I., risk mgr., DePaul Health Center, Bridgeton, MO '82 (RISK)
PURCELL, EDITH G., RN, coor. in-service, Milford Memorial Hospital, Milford, DE '75 (EDUC)
PURCELL, JEANNE M., adm. diet., Saints Mary and Elizabeth Hospital, Louisville, KY '81 (FOOD)
PURCELL, MARTIN C., sr. mgt. eng., Baystate Medical Center, Springfield, MA '83 (MGMT)
PURCELL, MIKEL LEMUAL, atty., Georgia Baptist Medical Center, Atlanta, GA '85 (ATTY)
PURDOM, WAYNE C., dir. plng. oper., Nashville Memorial Hospital, Madison, TN '57 (ENG)(LIFE)
PURDUE, MARIAN R., RN, vice-pres. nrsg., St. Luke's Hospital, Saginaw, MI '84 (NURS)
PURDY, PATRICIA A., RN, chief nrs., U. S. Air Force Hospital, Homestead, FL '86 (NURS)
PURDY, WILLIAM G., atty., Rogue Valley Medical Center, Medford, OR '74 (ATTY)
PURKINS, JENNIE, RN, supv., Winthrop-University Hospital, Mineola, NY '78 (CS)
PURSELL, ROBERT H., PhD, pres., Hospital Consulting Organization, Pasadena, TX '83 (ENG)
PURSER, NOELINE I., dir. vol. serv., Spaulding Rehabilitation Hospital, Boston, MA '85 (VOL)
PURTELL, DENNIS J., atty., Trinity Memorial Hospital, Cudahy, WI '68 (ATTY)
PURVIS, J. J., pres. and chief exec. off., Good Samaritan Hospital, Lexington, KY '82
PURVIS, MICHAEL, asst. adm., Tri-City Medical Center, Oceanside, CA '86 (RISK)
PURVIS, MILDRED ANN, dir. environ. control, Saints Mary and Elizabeth Hospital, Louisville, KY '86 (ENVIRON)
PUST, GEORGE I., reg. vice-pres., Hospital Corporation of America Management Company, Nashville, TN '83
PUTERBAUGH, ROBERT E., atty., Lakeland Regional Medical Center, Lakeland, FL '86 (ATTY)
PUTNAM, BEVERLY J., dir. soc. serv., West Valley Medical Center, Caldwell, ID '82 (SOC)
PUTZIER, FREDERICK J., atty., St. John's Eastside Hospital, St. Paul, MN '76 (ATTY)
PUTZLER, RANDY J., dir. human res., Ephraim McDowell Regional Medical Center, Danville, KY '78 (PERS)
PYATT, WILLIAM S., inspector, planner and estimator, University of California San Diego Medical Center, San Diego, CA '86 (ENG)
PYBURN, RICK J., vice-pres., St. Luke's Regional Medical Center, Sioux City, IA '83 (PLNG)
PYE, MARY FULP, dir. soc. work, Baptist Medical Center, Montgomery, AL '86 (SOC)
PYKE, MARCELLA MISSAR, adm., Temple University Hospital, Philadelphia, PA '81
PYLAND, DAVID J., sr. mgr., Peat, Marwick, Mitchell and Company, Austin, TX '86
PYLE, DONALD, dir. mgt. eng., Middlesex Memorial Hospital, Middletown, CT '69 (MGMT)
PYLE, GERALDINE E., RN, asst. adm. nrsg., St. Francis Hospital of Santa Barbara, Santa Barbara, CA '85 (NURS)
PYLE, RICHARD G., dir. plng., Bon Secours Hospital, Baltimore, MD '82 (PLNG)
PYLES, JAMES C., atty., Powers, Pyles, Sutter and O'Hare, Washington, DC '81 (ATTY)
PYNE, THOMAS P., student, Program in Health Service Administration, University of Houston at Clear Lake City, Houston, TX '82
PYNN, MARY FEMRITE, asst. adm. nrsg., Bethesda Lutheran Medical Center, St. Paul, MN '81 (NURS)
PYPER, BARBARA J., dir. diet. serv., Swedish Hospital Medical Center, Seattle, WA '80 (FOOD)
PYRCE, JANICE MARGARET, dir. mktg. serv., HCA Psychiatric Company, Forest Park, IL '82 (PLNG)
PYWELL, RICHARD A., dir. bldg. and grds., Hadley Regional Medical Center, Hays, KS '76 (ENG)
PYZYK, SHARON R., RN, vice-pres. nrsg., Froedtert Memorial Lutheran Hospital, Milwaukee, WI '82 (NURS)

Q

QUADE, STEVEN R., dir. plng., Swedish American Hospital, Rockford, IL '82 (PLNG)
QUAIFE, KATHLEEN, dir. soc. serv., St. John's Hospital, Fargo, ND '74 (SOC)
QUALEY, THOMAS L., (ret.), Slidell, LA '51 (LIFE)
QUALEY, THOMAS L. JR., adm., Jefferson Davis Nursing Home, Jennings, LA '75
QUALLS, SARA, mgr. telecommun., Methodist Hospital-Central Unit, Memphis, TN '86 (ENG)
QUAMME, SHERRY, RN, dir. nrs., Columbus Community Hospital, Columbus, WI '77 (NURS)
QUAN, EDWARD C., dir. mgt. info. syst., Children's Hospital Medical Center of California, Oakland, CA '77 (MGMT)
QUAN, JOANNE M. J., vice-pres. fin., New York University Medical Center, New York, NY '83 (PLNG)
QUAN, KELVIN, assoc. adm. fin., Chinese Hospital, San Francisco, CA '81
QUARTIER, MICHAEL J., asst. adm., Huntington Hospital, Huntington, NY '76
QUATTLEBAUM, DANA P., student, Southern Illinois University, Bethesda, MD '86 (PERS)
QUATTLEBAUM, SANDRA E., diet., Gladewater Municipal Hospital, Gladewater, TX '84 (FOOD)
QUATTRUCCI, TERESA C., asst. vol. and pat. rel. serv., Rhode Island Hospital, Providence, RI '82 (VOL)
QUAY, CHARLES, dir. diet., Metropolitan Hospital-Parkview Division, Philadelphia, PA '69 (FOOD)
QUAY, E. WANDA, dir. nrsg. school, Lankenau Hospital, Philadelphia, PA '74 (EDUC)
QUEBE, JERRY L., Vvrr, Inc., Alexandria, VA '85
QUEEN, CELESTE E., nrsg. practice spec., Parma Community General Hospital, Parma, OH '86 (EDUC)
QUEEN, PAUL, dir. plant oper., Huntington Memorial Hospital, Huntington, IN '81 (ENG)
QUERAM, CHRISTOPHER J., vice-pres., Methodist Hospital, Madison, WI '81 (PLNG)
QUERRIAGROSSA, JANICE M., RN, mgr. sterile proc., Saint Francis Medical Center, Peoria, IL '86 (CS)
QUIAT, ANDREW L., atty., Beth Israel Hospital, Denver, CO '76 (ATTY)
QUICK, BRUCE W., dir. pers., Lodi Memorial Hospital, Lodi, CA '86 (PERS)
QUICK, DEWEY, dir. plant oper., Bluefield Community Hospital, Bluefield, WV '83 (ENG)
QUICK, JANICE E., dir. nrsg. serv., Baptist Medical Center-Princeton, Birmingham, AL '83 (AMB)
QUICK, JOHN CRAIG, commun. rel. and dev. off., Pitt County Memorial Hospital, Greenville, NC '80 (PR)
QUICK, PAUL M., dir. maint. and eng., Prince George's Hospital Center, Cheverly, MD '86 (ENG)
QUICKEL, CHARLES C., dir. eng., York Hospital, York, PA '75 (ENG)
QUICKLE, HAROLD V., dir. matl. mgt., HCA North Okaloosa Medical Center, Crestview, FL '81 (PUR)
QUIDONE, THOMAS J., dir. matl. mgt., Mercy Hospital, Rockville Centre, NY '70 (PUR)
QUIGLEY, BARBARA WETZLER, dir. health educ., Lankenau Hospital, Philadelphia, PA '78 (EDUC)
QUIGLEY, CORRINE M., diet., St. Croix Valley Memorial Hospital, St. Croix Falls, WI '81 (FOOD)
QUIGLEY, DONALD E., atty., Maine Medical Center, Portland, ME '86 (ATTY)
QUIGLEY, EVELYN D., RN, dir. neuropsych. nrsg., St. Luke's Hospitals, Fargo, ND '85 (NURS)
QUIGLEY, JOAN M., vice-pres. corp. affairs, Franciscan Health Systems of New Jersey, Jersey City, NJ '81 (PR)
QUIGLEY, JOHN E., pres., Quigley Associates, Burr Ridge, IL '85
QUIGLEY, JOHN L., reg. dir., American Hospital Association, Burlington, MA '63 (MGMT)(LIFE)
QUIGLEY, NELDA M., dir. vol. serv., Beverly Hospital, Beverly, MA '84 (VOL)
QUIJANO, KATHLEEN M., dir. safety assur., St. Luke's Regional Medical Center, Boise, ID '84 (RISK)
QUILICI, SUSANNE S., dir. soc. serv., Catawba Memorial Hospital, Hickory, NC '81 (SOC)
QUILL, THOMAS H. JR., vice-pres., Johnson and Higgins, Minneapolis, MN '87 (RISK)
QUILLEN, JACK L., plant eng., Outer Drive Hospital, Lincoln Park, MI '71 (ENG)
QUILLEN, LT. WILLIAM S., MSC USN, student, Central Michigan University, Mount Pleasant, MI '84
QUILLIAM, WILLIAM C., student, University of Central Florida, Orlando, FL '85 (PLNG)
QUILLIN, MARY L., asst. adm. staff serv. and legal affairs, Torrance Memorial Hospital Medical Center, Torrance, CA '83 (ATTY)
QUILLMAN, JEROLYN S., RN, dir. nrsg., Floyd Memorial Hospital, New Albany, IN '84 (NURS)
QUINBY, ROBIN W., RN, nrsg. serv. adm., Lakeside Hospital, Metairie, LA '85 (NURS)
QUINEALTY, ROBERT G., mgr. eng. and biomedical serv., Terrebonne General Medical Center, Houma, LA '79 (ENG)
QUINLAN, ARDATH D., actg. dir. qual. assur. and risk mgt., University of Massachusetts Medical School and Teaching Hospital, Worcester, MA '82 (RISK)
QUINLAN, DENIS E., vice-pres. human res., Mercy Hospital, Miami, FL '76 (PERS)
QUINLAN, JAMES L., atty., Childrens Memorial Hospital, Omaha, NE '82 (ATTY)
QUINLAN, JOSEPH W. JR., mktg. consult., Mid-America Health Network, Kansas City, MO '85 (PLNG)
QUINLAN, KATHLEEN M., student, Program in Health Care Administration, Texas Women's University, Houston, TX '83
QUINLAN, LAWRENCE J., dir. matl. mgt., Providence Hospital, Southfield, MI '81 (CS)
QUINLAN, RICHARD S., pres., Melrose-Wakefield Hospital, Melrose, MA '64
QUINLIVAN, KATHLEEN K., instr. educ., Reid Memorial Hospital, Richmond, IN '78 (EDUC)
QUINN, ANNE BOWES, RN, mgr. med. malpractice, Beltran Alexander and Alexander, Miami, FL '80 (RISK)
QUINN, BRENT L., dir. plant oper. and maint., Mount Graham Community Hospital, Safford, AZ '85 (ENG)
QUINN, DAVID V., pur. agt., Crozer-Chester Medical Center, Chester, PA '86 (PUR)
QUINN, EDWARD J., atty., St. Joseph's Hospital, Philadelphia, PA '85 (ATTY)
QUINN, FRANK, asst. vice-pres. matl. mgt., Good Samaritan Hospital, West Islip, NY '64 (ENG)
QUINN, JAMES P., mgr. maint., Lutheran General Hospital, Park Ridge, IL '82 (ENG)
QUINN, JOHN B., atty., American Medical International, Beverly Hills, CA '82 (ATTY)
QUINN, JOHN F., dir. eng., Hospital for Sick Children, Washington, DC '82 (ENG)
QUINN, JOHN J., adm., Santa Barbara General Hospital, Santa Barbara, CA '56 (LIFE)
QUINN, JOHN J., adm. off., Charity Hospital at New Orleans, New Orleans, LA '87 (ENVIRON)
QUINN, JOHN M. SR., atty., Saint Vincent Health Center, Erie, PA '83 (ATTY)
QUINN, JOHN, night adm., Hermann Hospital, Houston, TX '81
QUINN, KEVIN W., dir. fiscal serv., Retreat Hospital, Richmond, VA '84
QUINN, MAUREEN, chief off. human res., Visiting Nurse Service of New York, New York, NY '85 (PERS)
QUINN, LCDR PAUL VINCENT, MSC USN, dir. adm. serv., Naval Hospital, Newport, RI '76
QUINN, RICHARD K., atty., Kapiolani Medical Center for Women, Honolulu, HI '80 (ATTY)
QUINN, ROBERT G., dir. pat. affairs, Ehrling Bergquist U. S. Air Force Regional Hospital, Omaha, NE '81 (PUR)
QUINN, SUSAN, dir. nrsg. and amb. care, Fox Chase Cancer Center, Philadelphia, PA '87 (AMB)(NURS)
QUINN, THOMAS D. JR., atty., Georgetown University Medical Center, Washington, DC '68 (ATTY)
QUINN, VITA, pat. advocate, St. Catherine Hospital, East Chicago, IN '82 (PAT)
QUINSEY, BRIGITTE O., vice-pres. corp. rel., Northeast Health, Camden, ME '78 (PR)

QUINT, LINDA M., asst. dir. pub. affairs and mktg., Hermann Hospital, Houston, TX '85 (PR) (PLNG)
QUINTANA, LT. COL. JOSE BOOTH, MSC USAF, dir. health affairs and plans, Department of Air Force Medical Service, Office of the Surgeon General, U. S. Air Force, Bolling AFB, DC '73
QUINTIN, THERESA L., asst. dir. nrsg. educ., House of the Good Samaritan, Watertown, NY '81 (EDUC)
QUINTON, GRACE H., RN, clin. dir. med. and surg., Hotel Dieu Hospital, New Orleans, LA '81 (NURS)
QUINTON, PETER D., dir. eng., Anne Arundel General Hospital, Annapolis, MD '84 (ENG)
QUIRARTE, JOSEPH D., dir. pur., St. Vincent Charity Hospital, Cleveland, OH '74 (PUR)
QUIRK, BARBARA, RN PhD, dir. pat. care, Truman Medical Center-East, Kansas City, MO '79 (NURS)
QUISENBERRY, MARY F., dir. soc. serv., Baptist Medical Center of Oklahoma, Oklahoma City, OK '82 (SOC)
QUITKIN, ELIZABETH B., mgr. soc. work, Long Island Jewish Medical Center, New York, NY '87 (SOC)
QUYLE, JOY, adm., Community Ltd. Care Dialysis Center, Cincinnati, OH '86

R

RAAK, KENNETH W., dir. matl. mgt., Worthington Regional Hospital, Worthington, MN '80 (PUR)
RABADI, SHAW H., mgr., Ernst and Whinney, Albany, NY '80 (MGMT)
RABALAIS, CAROL L., PhD RN, vice-pres. nrsg. serv., St. Luke's Hospital, Maumee, OH '76 (NURS)
RABAS, GERARD J., asst. dir. plant serv., Methodist Hospital, Madison, WI '79 (ENG)
RABB, LINDA DIANNE, adm. asst., Huntsville Hospital, Huntsville, AL '80
RABBOTT, LISA, adm. asst., St. Mary's Hospital, Waterbury, CT '86 (RISK)
RABIDOUX, ROBERT A., chief fin. off. and treas., Texas Children's Hospital, Houston, TX '84 (PLNG)
RABIN, MICHAEL, dir. plng., Presbyterian Hospital in the City of New York, New York, NY '86 (PR) (PLNG)
RABINER, DONNA J., student, Duke University, Department of Health Administration, Durham, NC '83
RABINOVITCH, NITA, coor. soc. work serv., Norman Regional Hospital, Norman, OK '80 (SOC)
RABINOWE, MAXINE K., dir. soc. work serv., Shaughnessy Chronic Disease Hospital, Salem, MA '85 (SOC)
RABINOWITZ, MICHAEL J., Willow Creek Adolescent Center, Arlington, TX '83
RABKIN, MITCHELL T., MD, pres., Beth Israel Hospital, Boston, MA '84 (PLNG)
RABLEY, LOIS L., dir. vol. serv., St. Rita's Medical Center, Lima, OH '83 (VOL)
RABOIN, WILLIAM L., dir. hskpg., St. Agnes Hospital, Fond Du Lac, WI '86 (ENVIRON)(CS)
RABORN, MONA, RN, dir. nrsg., Jefferson Davis Memorial Hospital, Natchez, MS '79 (NURS)
RABUKA, MICKEY M., vice-pres. pur. serv., Adventist Health System, Arlington, TX '87
RABY, TONDA C., RN, dir. nrsg., Baylor University Medical Center, Dallas, TX '84 (NURS)
RACHMAN, ANITA, dir. vol., M. J. G. Nursing Home, Brooklyn, NY '83 (VOL)
RACINE, ANN M., dir. vol. serv., Leominster Hospital, Leominster, MA '84 (VOL)
RACIOPPE, LOUIS A., sr. vice-pres., Mountainside Hospital, Montclair, NJ '74
RACKLEY, SHELLEY B., dir. pers., Franklin Foundation Hospital, Franklin, LA '86 (PERS)
RACLEY, MICHAEL, assoc. adm., Arkansas Children's Hospital, Little Rock, AR '83 (RISK)
RACZ, DONNA M., dir. vol. serv., Kessler Institute for Rehabilitation, West Orange, NJ '83 (VOL)
RACZKA, MICHAELINE, asst. dir. food serv., Huron Valley Hospital, Milford, MI '85 (FOOD)
RACZKIEWICZ, FRANK, dir. pub. rel., Eye and Ear Hospital of Pittsburgh, Pittsburgh, PA '85 (PR)
RACZKIEWICZ, PAUL E., exec. vice-pres., St. Elizabeth Medical Center, Granite City, IL '80 (RISK)
RADABAUGH, STEVE L., dir. eng., Camden-Clark Memorial Hospital, Parkersburg, WV '81 (ENG)
RADAKOVICH, MARCEE, liaison, Falk Clinic, Pittsburgh, PA '87 (AMB)
RADCLIFFE, JAMES F., dir. environ. serv., South Miami Hospital, South Miami, FL '86 (ENVIRON)
RADCLIFFE, TERRY, dir. educ., Saint Vincent Hospital, Billings, MT '81 (EDUC)
RADEMACHER, T. C., dir. maint., Bon Secours Hospital of Methuen, Methuen, MA '80 (ENG)
RADER, MAJ. HERBERT C., MD MSC USA, dir. amb. care, Booth Memorial Medical Center, Flushing, NY '87 (AMB)
RADER, JANICE L., dir. risk mgt. and qual. assur., Abington Memorial Hospital, Abington, PA '80 (RISK)
RADER, JOHN A., atty., Community Hospital, Williamsport, IN '82 (ATTY)
RADER, JOSEPH A., dir. pers. serv., Scottsdale Camelback Hospital, Scottsdale, AZ '83 (PERS)
RADER, PAUL E., mgr. biomedical, Technical Services Division, Ogden, UT '84 (ENG)
RADER, PAUL M., chief exec. off., Chinese Hospital, San Francisco, CA '86 (PLNG)
RADEY, HARVEY M. JR., adm., Clifton-Fine Hospital, Star Lake, NY '52 (LIFE)
RADFORD, JUDITH T., pat. advocate and adm. asst., Rutherford Hospital, Rutherfordton, NC '85 (PAT)
RADKE, MICHAEL W., PhD, assoc. dir. med. educ., Edward W. Sparrow Hospital, Lansing, MI '81 (EDUC)
RADOIU, DENYSE M., dir. soc. work, Cottage Hospital of Grosse Pointe, Grosse Pointe Farms, MI '87 (SOC)
RADONICH, JOHN N., atty., Community Hospital of Anaconda, Anaconda, MT '74 (ATTY)
RADOSZEWSKI, ANDREW, adm., Valley Community Hospital, Willows, CA '80
RADOV, LYNN P., student, Case Western Reserve University, Cleveland, OH '83 (MGMT)
RADOWILL, MARTIN, adm., West Park Hospital, Philadelphia, PA '58
RADOYEVICH, MYRA, sr. mgt. eng., Catherine McAuley Health Center, Ann Arbor, MI '85 (MGMT)
RADTKE, GARY K., facil. mgt. eng., Indian Health Service, Bemidji, MN '84 (ENG)
RADTKE, NANCE, adm. dir., W. A. Foote Memorial Hospital, Jackson, MI '87 (AMB)
RADTKE, RALPH H., sr. vice-pres., Prime Capital Corporation, Rolling Meadows, IL '86
RADZEVICH, GAIL N., dir. pub. affairs, Acute Care Affiliates, Berkeley, CA '82 (PR)
RADZIK, JANETTE, pat. rep., Lake Forest Hospital, Lake Forest, IL '80 (PAT)
RADZVICKAS, PETER G., corp. dir. pers., Southwestern Michigan Health Care Association, St. Joseph, MI '82 (PERS)
RADZVILOWICZ, EDWARD J., dir. facil. mgt., Choate-Symmes Hospitals, Woburn, MA '86 (ENG)
RADZYNER, MARK H., atty., Memorial Hospital for Cancer and Allied Diseases, New York, NY '86 (ATTY)
RAE, ALICE S., dir. plng. and mktg., Baptist Medical Center, Kansas City, MO '84 (PLNG)
RAEL, CRISTOBAL, chief biomedical tech., St. Vincent Hospital, Santa Fe, NM '85 (ENG)
RAETTIG, VILMA M., RN, clin. dir., Porter Memorial Hospital, Denver, CO '85 (NURS)
RAFFAELE, VIRGINIA, asst. dir. pers., Winthrop-University Hospital, Mineola, NY '81 (PERS)
RAFFERTY, DENISE C., RN, assoc. vice-pres. nrsg. in-service educ., Presbyterian-University Hospital, Pittsburgh, PA '86 (NURS)
RAFFERTY, JANE P., dir. soc. serv., Luther Hospital, Eau Claire, WI '86 (SOC)
RAFFERTY, JOHN P., supv. sup., proc. and distrib., Nesbitt Memorial Hospital, Kingston, PA '83 (CS)
RAFFERTY, JULIE, dir. commun. rel., Joslin Diabetes Center, Boston, MA '87 (PR)
RAFFERTY, MARY L., dir. vol., St. Luke Hospital, Fort Thomas, KY '84 (VOL)
RAFFERTY, RICHARD R., dir. informational serv., Portsmouth General Hospital, Portsmouth, VA '83 (RISK)
RAFFETY, CLYDE R., dir. eng., Takoma Adventist Hospital, Greeneville, TN '85 (ENG)
RAFFETY, JOHN E., orth surg., Kaiser Foundation Hospital, Sacramento, CA '75
RAFFURTY, GERRY E., dir. cent. serv., Saint Joseph Health Center Kansas, Kansas City, MO '83 (CS)
RAFIQ, KHALID, student, Program in Health Care Administration, University of Minnesota, Minneapolis, MN '85
RAFKIN, LAURIE, asst. dep. dir. amb. care, University Hospital, Stony Brook, NY '87 (AMB)
RAFKY, JANET, dir. soc. serv., Franklin Square Hospital, Baltimore, MD '80 (SOC)
RAFULS, SILVIA C., asst. dir. soc. work serv., Miami Children's Hospital, Miami, FL '84 (SOC)
RAGALIE, PEARL E., sec. pub. rel., Rehabilitation Institute of Chicago, Chicago, IL '87 (PR)
RAGAN, DAVID TIMOTHY, treas., Crestview Center, Sylvania, OH '85
RAGGIO, WILLIAM J., atty., Mount Grant General Hospital, Hawthorne, NV '74 (ATTY)
RAGLAND, KENNETH E., adm., Beaufort County Hospital, Washington, NC '86
RAHAMAN, SUSAN M. J., asst. dir. diet.-pat. serv., Memorial Care System, Houston, TX '84 (FOOD)
RAHILLY, LOUISE, supv. cent. sup., Cape Fear Valley Medical Center, Fayetteville, NC '78 (CS)
RAHLFS, JOHN W. JR., dir. pers. and staff dev., Mental Health and Mental Retardation Authority, Houston, TX '81 (PERS)
RAHM, CARL W., asst. dir. plant and prop., Good Samaritan Hospital, Cincinnati, OH '86 (ENG)
RAHM, NANCY S., nrs. consult. corp. serv., Deaconess Medical Center, Billings, MT '83 (EDUC)
RAHN, EMMA LOUISE, RN, vice-pres. nrsg., Reading Hospital and Medical Center, Reading, PA '70 (NURS)
RAHN, J. GAIL, atty., Trident Regional Medical Center, Charleston, SC '82 (ATTY)
RAIBLE, PATRICIA A., coor. vol., Sacred Heart Hospital, Cumberland, MD '86 (VOL)
RAICA, ROBERT J., asst. adm. pat. and commun. rel., Marquette General Hospital, Marquette, MI '80 (PAT)(PR)
RAIGER, JOHN R., Electronic Systems, Orland Park, IL '78 (ENG)
RAIHA, CAPT. GLENN N., MSC USA, adm. res., Madigan Army Medical Center, Tacoma, WA '84
RAIL, SHIRLEY A., RN, (ret.), Albuquerque, NM '77 (NURS)
RAILEY, JANET M., vice-pres. human res., LaGuardia Hospital, Flushing, NY '65 (PERS)
RAINEAULT, DOUGLAS P., asst. dir. eng., Middlesex Memorial Hospital, Middletown, CT '85 (ENG)
RAINES, KATHRYN M., asst. exec. dir., Clark County Memorial Hospital, Jeffersonville, IN '77
RAINES, LOU, RN, asst. adm., Phoebe Putney Memorial Hospital, Albany, GA '79 (NURS)
RAINES, MURRAY A., atty., Medical Center-Bowling Green, Bowling Green, KY '86 (ATTY)
RAINES, NORMA W., dir. staff dev., Riverside Hospital, Newport News, VA '77 (EDUC)
RAINEY, BAZELLA GIOTTO III, dir. commun., University of Michigan Hospitals, Ann Arbor, MI '77 (ENG)
RAINEY, CLAUDE G., pres., Health Care of Texas, Inc., Fort Worth, TX '60
RAINEY, MARY ORTOLANO, dir. food serv., St. Joseph's Hospital and Medical Center, Phoenix, AZ '70 (FOOD)
RAINEY, SHARON ANN, coor. pat. rel., Catherine McAuley Health Center, Ann Arbor, MI '86 (PAT)
RAINIER, WARREN G., consult., Robert Wood Johnson University Hospital, New Brunswick, NJ '48 (LIFE)
RAINS, ANNA PEARL, RN, exec. dir. in-patient nrsg. serv., University of Texas Medical Branch Hospitals, Galveston, TX '80 (NURS)
RAINTREE, SHAWN, vice-pres., American Healthcare Plans, La Lolla, CA '79 (PR) (PLNG)
RAJ, DEEPAK D., vice-pres., Merrill Lynch, New York, NY '85
RAJOKOVICH, MARILYN J., RN, asst. dir. adm. and dir. nrsg. serv., Langley Porter Psychiatric Institute, San Francisco, CA '83 (NURS)
RAK, ARLENE A., RN, Tampa, FL '81 (NURS)
RAKES, GERALD M., dir. loss control, Hospital Corporation of America, Nashville, TN '83 (RISK)
RAKES, SHERRY L., RN, adm. nrsg., Olathe Medical Center, Olathe, KS '79 (NURS)
RAKOFSKY, STEPHANIE L., dir. soc. serv., South Miami Hospital, South Miami, FL '77 (SOC)
RAKSHYS, JAMES E., vice-pres. fin., Wilkes-Barre General Hospital, Wilkes-Barre, PA '85 (MGMT)
RALEY, A. HARRIET H., dir. diet., Frederick Memorial Hospital, Frederick, MD '77 (FOOD)
RALLISON, STEPHEN J., vice-pres. adm., Carle Foundation Hospital, Urbana, IL '78
RALOFF, THERESA A., coor. family health educ., Presbyterian Hospital, Albuquerque, NM '85 (EDUC)
RALPH, CHANDLER M., mgr., Ernst and Whinney, Albany, NY '80 (ENG)
RALSTON, SPENCER D., spec. asst. to the dir., Veterans Administration Medical Center, Kansas City, MO '85 (PAT)
RAMAGE, RICHARD B., dir. pub. affairs, Hospital Association of Metropolitan St. Louis, St. Louis, MO '85 (PR)
RAMBACHER, PENNY, dir. food serv., Hollywood Medical Center, Hollywood, FL '85 (FOOD)
RAMBUSCH, ANN W., RN, dir. nrsg. and critical care, Phoebe Putney Memorial Hospital, Albany, GA '86 (NURS)
RAMEY, DARLENE M., dir. educ., Benedictine Health Center, Duluth, MN '86 (EDUC)
RAMEY, EVELYN J., dir. pur., Logan General Hospital, Logan, WV '82 (PUR)
RAMEY, MARSHA BROUSSARD, dir. plng., Mount Carmel Mercy Hospital, Detroit, MI '85 (PLNG)
RAMEY, MEDFORD G. JR., dir. pub. rel. and mktg., Riverside Hospital, Newport News, VA '83 (PR)
RAMEY, PAUL B., dir., Hospital Shared Services Association, Seattle, WA '69 (PUR)
RAMIREZ, BERNARDO DE J., eng., Hospital de La Concepcion, San German, P.R. '85 (ENG)
RAMIREZ, JERRY JR., dir. matl. mgt., Southwest General Hospital, San Antonio, TX '80 (PUR)
RAMIREZ, JOHN S., dir. qual. assur. and lost control, Holy Cross Shared Services, Inc., Notre Dame, IN '82 (RISK)
RAMIREZ, OTTO J., vice-pres. hosp. serv., Mercy Hospital, Miami, FL '69
RAMIREZ, PITA, mgr. ldry., Valley Medical Center of Fresno, Fresno, CA '86 (ENVIRON)
RAMLOW, MARGARET JOSEPHINE, dir. educ., Baptist Hospital Fund, St. Paul, MN '86 (EDUC)
RAMON, ADOLPH I., asst. prof. and dir. med. rec., Program in Health Administration, Southwest Texas State University, San Marcos, TX '66 (EDUC)
RAMONES, ALVARO P. JR., mgr. matl., West Hudson Hospital, Kearny, NJ '86 (PUR)
RAMOS, ARNETTA B., mgr. food prod., Piedmont Geriatric Hospital, Burkeville, VA '80 (FOOD)
RAMOS, MONICA, dir. pub. rel., Tracy Community Memorial Hospital, Tracy, CA '86 (PR)
RAMP, NINA, dir. vol. serv., Medical Center East, Birmingham, AL '75 (VOL)
RAMPINO, FRANK A., asst. adm., St. John's Queens Hospital, Flushing, NY '82
RAMPONE, SHARI K., dir. pat. rel., Northridge Hospital Medical Center, Northridge, CA '81 (PAT)
RAMSAY, JOHN R., eng., Cortland Memorial Hospital, Cortland, NY '75 (ENG)
RAMSDEN, RANDY, dir. food serv., Pitt County Memorial Hospital, Greenville, NC '84 (FOOD)
RAMSER-YOUNG, KARLA, dir. human res., Charter North Hospital, Anchorage, AK '86 (PERS)
RAMSEUR, J. DAVID, prin., Odell Associates, Inc., Charlotte, NC '73
RAMSEY, BARBARA, RN, coor. pat. rep., McKeesport Hospital, McKeesport, PA '86 (PAT)
RAMSEY, BETTY N., dir. vol. serv., Hinds General Hospital, Jackson, MS '86 (VOL)
RAMSEY, DAVID L., sr. vice-pres., Baton Rouge General Medical Center, Baton Rouge, LA '81
RAMSEY, DAVID S., vice-pres. and adm., Iowa Methodist Medical Center, Des Moines, IA '61
RAMSEY, KEVIN D., EdD, dir. educ. serv., Copley Memorial Hospital, Aurora, IL '85 (EDUC)
RAMSEY, LINDA J., student, Dickinson School of Law, Carlisle, PA '86 (RISK)
RAMSEY, M. ELIZABETH, RN, dir. nrsg., Springdale Memorial Hospital, Springdale, AR '84 (NURS)
RAMSEY, MARIBEN, atty., St. David's Community Hospital, Austin, TX '85 (ATTY)
RAMSEY, MARION H., vice-pres. pat. care serv., New Milford Hospital, New Milford, CT '76 (NURS)
RAMSEY, MARY G., dir. food serv., coor. qual. assur. and diet. serv., North Carolina Memorial Hospital, Chapel Hill, NC '85 (FOOD)
RAMSEY, REBECCA L., dir. outpatient serv., East Tennessee Baptist Hospital, Knoxville, TN '87 (AMB)
RAMSEY, ROBERT B. III, atty., Mercy Hospital of Johnstown, Johnstown, PA '86 (ATTY)
RAMSEY, SAMUEL L., sr. mgr., Ernst and Whinney, Nashville, TN '84

RAMSEYER, JANE E., RN, asst. dir. nrsg. serv., Cedars-Sinai Medical Center, Los Angeles, CA '84 (NURS)
RAMSEYER, ROBERT R., dir. med. soc. work, Detroit Memorial Hospital, Detroit, MI '75 (SOC)
RANCURET, RAY E., risk mgr., St. Francis Regional Medical Center, Wichita, KS '83 (RISK)
RAND, BRUCE S., mgt. eng., Saint Joseph's Hospital, Atlanta, GA '87 (MGMT)
RAND, MARGARET, dir. risk mgt., Sinai Hospital of Detroit, Detroit, MI '86 (RISK)
RANDALL, CHARLOTTE, adm., Orthopedic Cente, Lake Worth, FL '87 (AMB)
RANDALL, DALE D., dir. pur., Northbay Medical Center, Fairfield, CA '78 (PUR)
RANDALL, DEBORAH A., atty., Washington, DC '82 (ATTY)
RANDALL, GWENDOLYN E., coor. pat. educ., St. Luke's Methodist Hospital, Cedar Rapids, IA '86 (EDUC)
RANDALL, JOAN POLLOCK, RN, risk mgt. consult., Los Alamitos Medical Center, Los Alamitos, CA '82 (RISK)
RANDALL, JOSEPH, dir. pat. acctg., Memorial Hospital, Ormond Beach, FL '86
RANDALL, LYNNE D., mgr. telecommun., Medical Center Hospital, Odessa, TX '85 (ENG)
RANDALL, MALCOM, dir., Veterans Administration Medical Center, Gainesville, FL '65
RANDALL, RALPH X., asst. adm., Medical College of Georgia Hospital and Clinic, Augusta, GA '87 (AMB)
RANDALL, RITA M., St. Luke's Hospitals, Fargo, ND '83 (PUR)
RANDALL, ROGER K., dir. risk mgt., Loma Linda University Medical Center, Loma Linda, CA '80 (RISK)
RANDALL, SANDRA K., RN, adm. nrsg. serv., Waupun Memorial Hospital, Waupun, WI '81 (NURS)
RANDEL, SUE, dir. phys. serv., Community Hospital -Onaga, Onaga, KS '86 (ENG)
RANDLE, JENNIFER B., dir. pers. serv., St. Mary's Hospital, Kansas City, MO '86 (PERS)
RANDOL, SHERYL E., mgr. pub. rel., Memorial Hospital, York, PA '84 (PR)
RANDOLPH, JANICE, soc. worker, Lenox Hill Hospital, New York, NY '74 (SOC)
RANDOLPH, JOAN S., RN, asst. vice-pres. and dir. nrsg., Jeanes Hospital, Philadelphia, PA '83 (NURS)
RANDOLPH, LARRY A., asst. dir., William Beaumont Hospital, Royal Oak, MI '70 (MGMT)
RANDOLPH, MARIE JANETTE, RN, mgr., St. Vincent Medical Center, Los Angeles, CA '74 (EDUC)
RANDOLPH, PATRICIA S., dir. educ. prog., Medical Care Development, Inc., Augusta, ME '83 (EDUC)
RANDOLPH, ROSA, asst. dir. oper., Grace Hospital, Detroit, MI '83 (FOOD)
RANELLI, F. EDWARD, vice-pres., Baptist Regional Health Services, Pensacola, FL '84 (PLNG)
RANERE, KATHRINE C., RN, dir. mktg. and pub. rel., Sancta Maria Hospital, Cambridge, MA '85 (PR)
RANEY, J. DAVID, asst. to exec. adm., Straub Clinic and Hospital, Honolulu, HI '78 (MGMT)
RANEY, JAMES EDWARD, pres., Northern Michigan Hospitals, Petoskey, MI '69
RANGE, ROBERT P., sr. vice-pres. dev., St. Vincent Charity Hospital, Cleveland, OH '84 (PLNG)
RANGEL, MAJ. HELEN L., RN, chief nrsg., U. S. Air Force Clinic Spangdahlem, APO , NY '86 (NURS)
RANIERI, ALFONSE F., dir. matl. mgt., Phoenixville Hospital, Phoenixville, PA '75 (PUR)
RANIERI, ELIZABETH, head nrs. cent. serv., Parma Community General Hospital, Parma, OH '79 (CS)
RANIERI, MARTHA J., dir. staff educ., Sewickley Valley Hospital, Sewickley, PA '79 (EDUC)
RANKIN, ELIZABETH ANN, dir. vol. serv., Hendrick Medical Center, Abilene, TX '80 (VOL)
RANKIN, LINDA, Morgan Hill, CA '80 (EDUC)
RANKIN, MARGERY E., dir. diet., St. Elizabeth Hospital, Appleton, WI '85 (FOOD)
RANKIN, PHYLLIS D., RN, dir. nrsg. serv., Haverford Community Hospital, Havertown, PA '76 (NURS)
RANKIN, RONALD LEE, dir. environ. serv., Shelby Memorial Hospital, Shelbyville, IL '79 (ENG)(ENVIRON)
RANKIN, SHIRLEY, mgr. vol. serv., Phoenix Baptist Hospital and Medical Center, Phoenix, AZ '81 (VOL)
RANNELLS, JEAN C., dir. soc. serv., Coronado Hospital, Coronado, CA '70 (SOC)
RANNEY, BETH A., dir. commun. rel., Medina Memorial Hospital, Medina, NY '86 (PR)
RANNEY, KAREN M., coor. commun. rel., Park Ridge Hospital, Rochester, NY '86 (PR)
RANSOHOFF, JERRY N., consult., Greater Cincinnati Hospital Council, Cincinnati, OH '83
RANSOM, MARGERY K., dir. human res. adm., Faulkner Hospital, Boston, MA '84 (PERS)
RANSOM, SALLY JANE, dir. educ., Good Samaritan Hospital of Maryland, Baltimore, MD '85 (EDUC)
RANTZ, HAZEL PATRICIA, dir. vol., Jo Ellen Smith Medical Center, New Orleans, LA '83 (VOL)
RAPHAEL, GLORIA B., dir. soc. work serv., Hebrew Home and Hospital, Hartford, CT '82 (SOC)
RAPHAELI, MARIAN, dir. vol. serv., Humana Hospital -Cypress, Pompano Beach, FL '82 (VOL)
RAPISARDA, PATRICIA, RN, dir. nrsg., Mount Holly Center, Mount Holly, NJ '86 (NURS)
RAPOPORT, KATHY, vice-pres. plng., Medical Center of Beaver County, Consolidated Healthcare Service, Inc., Beaver, PA '81 (PLNG)
RAPP, DONNA J., vice-pres., Mid-Michigan Health Care Systems, Inc., Midland, MI '80 (PR)
RAPP, KATHY R., dir. diet. serv., Jewish Hospital, Louisville, KY '80 (FOOD)
RAPP, PAMELA, RN, vice-pres., St. Joseph Hospital, Lexington, KY '80 (NURS)
RAPPAPORT, BERNARD, San Antonio, TX '55 (LIFE)
RAPPAPORT, CYRIL M., dir. mgt. and pers. serv., Jewish Vocational Service, Chicago, IL '64 (PERS)
RAPPAPORT, MARK J., asst. vice-pres., Jersey Shore Medical Center, Neptune, NJ '81
RAPPEPORT, IRA J., atty., Centinela Hospital Medical Center, Inglewood, CA '83 (ATTY)
RAPPOPORT, BRUCE A., asst. dir., Our Lady of Lourdes Medical Center, Camden, NJ '75
RAPS, MITCHELL R., staff consult., Arthur Andersen and Company, Dallas, TX '82
RASCHE, DAN S., dir. bldg. and grd., Grant Medical Center, Columbus, OH '69 (ENG)
RASCO, BERTIS C., prin., Stone, Marraccihi and Patterson, San Francisco, CA '68
RASCO, JEFFREY K., West Virginia University Hospital, Morgantown, WV '84 (RISK)
RASEKH, BEHZAD I., mgt. eng., St. Vincent's Hospital and Medical Center, New York, NY '84 (MGMT)
RASELY, LOLA F., RN, supv. cent. serv., Modesto City Hospital, Modesto, CA '82 (CS)
RASK, SHARON J., dir. educ. and prof. standards, Medical Center Rehabilitation Hospital, Grand Forks, ND '84 (PR)
RASKIN, FLORENCE B., adm. asst. to phys.-in-chief, Kaiser Foundation Hospital, Hayward, CA '83 (PLNG)
RASKIN, MARYL, atty., St. Mary Medical Center, Long Beach, CA '81 (ATTY)
RASKIN, MICHAEL M., atty., St. Francis Hospital, Miami Beach, FL '86 (ATTY)
RASLEY, ROBERT A., dir. staff rel., University of Iowa Hospitals and Clinics, Iowa City, IA '73 (PERS)
RASMUSSEM, ROD, mgr. steam plant, F. G. McGaw Hospital, Loyola University, Maywood, IL '87 (ENG)
RASMUSSEN, BRIAN R., acct. exec., Barenz Associates, Salt Lake City, UT '86 (PR)
RASMUSSEN, CHRISTINE B., dir. vol. serv., Portsmouth Regional Hospital, Portsmouth, NH '83 (VOL)
RASMUSSEN, DENNIS L., vice-pres. mktg., Holy Cross Health System Corporation, South Bend, IN '85 (PLNG)
RASMUSSEN, DIANE G., dir. human res., Sioux Valley Hospital, New Ulm, MN '80 (PERS)(PR)
RASMUSSEN, ERIK H., dir. risk mgt. and safety, Multicare Medical Center, Tacoma, WA '86 (RISK)
RASMUSSEN, ERVIN M., mgr. mgt. eng. serv., Ancilla Development Group, Ltd., Elk Grove Village, IL '86 (MGMT)
RASMUSSEN, HOMER, mgr. maint., Miami Children's Hospital, Miami, FL '79 (ENG)
RASMUSSEN, MARLENE, RN, asst. adm. nrsg., Marianjoy Rehabilitation Center, Wheaton, IL '74 (NURS)
RASMUSSEN, MILTON DALE, Minnetonka, MN '72
RASMUSSEN, OWEN L., dir. eng., Samaritan Hospital, St. Paul, MN '84 (ENG)
RASMUSSEN, PAMELA A., mgr. corp. commun., Lake Forest Hospital, Lake Forest, IL '82 (PR)
RASMUSSEN, RICHARD W., dir. mktg., Phoenix Memorial Hospital, Phoenix, AZ '86 (PR)
RASPER, ALAN F., asst. vice-pres. gen. serv., St. Francis-St. George Hospital, Cincinnati, OH '81 (MGMT)
RASPER, DEBORAH Y., asst. adm. pat. and staff serv., University of Cincinnati Hospital, Cincinnati, OH '78 (FOOD)
RASSIN, BARRY JONATHAN, adm., Rassin Hospital, Nassau, Bahamas '72
RATCLIFF, RANCE SCOTT JR., dir. soc. serv., Mississippi Baptist Medical Center, Jackson, MS '80 (SOC)
RATELIFF, KATHY G., dir. commun. affairs, Central Arkansas Radiation Therapy Institute, Little Rock, AR '83 (PR)
RATHBONE, THOMAS A., exec. dir., Health Hill Hospital for Children, Cleveland, OH '78
RATHBUN, TURID A., dir. vol. serv., McKee Medical Center, Loveland, CO '86 (VOL)
RATHER, DORIS D., vice-pres. human res., Greene County Medical Center, Jefferson, IA '84 (PERS)
RATHERT, JOHN W., atty., Allen Memorial Hospital, Waterloo, IA '68 (ATTY)
RATHFON, JAY E., vice-pres. support oper., Community General Osteopathic Hospital, Harrisburg, PA '78 (ENG)
RATHGEB, JEAN M., coor. vol. serv., Boone Hospital Center, Columbia, MO '83 (VOL)
RATHIE, JUDY C., RN, dir. nrsg. serv., Samaritan Hospital, Troy, NY '87 (NURS)
RATHKE, DEBRA A., dir. plng., Flower Memorial Hospital, Sylvania, OH '82 (PLNG)
RATHSACK, CLARENCE W., dir. diet. serv., Centreville Township Hospital, Centreville, IL '81 (FOOD)
RATLIFF, CHARLES L., dir. maint., Highland Hospital, Lubbock, TX '83 (ENG)
RATLIFF, JUDITH H., dir. pat. asst., Fair Oaks Hospital, Fairfax, VA '80 (SOC)
RATLIFF, MARIA E., dir. pur., Pan American Hospital, Miami, FL '81 (PUR)
RATLIFF, MARY L., RN, dir. critical care nrsg., Blodgett Memorial Medical Center, Grand Rapids, MI '83 (NURS)
RATLIFF, PAULA M., dir. staff educ., Golden Triangle Regional Medical Center, Columbus, MS '85 (EDUC)
RATLIFF, ROBIN, asst. vice-pres. plng., Hackensack Medical Center, Hackensack, NJ '86 (PLNG)
RATLIFF, RONALD, prog. supv., James A. Haley Veterans Hospital, Tampa, FL '86 (SOC)
RATTENBURY, BRUCE, assoc. vice-pres. philanthropy and commun., Rush-Presbyterian-St. Luke's Medical Center, Chicago, IL '83 (PR)
RATTNER, DIANE C., dir. med. soc. serv., St. Luke's Methodist Hospital, Cedar Rapids, IA '78 (SOC)
RATTO, JERILYN A., RN, div. mgr. nrsg. serv., St. Joseph's Hospital, Stockton, CA '82 (NURS)
RATTRAY, DANIEL N., dir. environ., Jewish Hospital, Louisville, KY '87 (ENVIRON)
RAU, CAROLE E., dir. soc. work, Howard County General Hospital, Columbia, MD '77 (SOC)
RAU, SR. CHRISTINA F., asst. to exec. vice-pres., Mercy Hospital, Rockville Centre, NY '67
RAU, WILLIAM A., vice-pres. fin., treas. and chief fin. off., Mercy Hospital, Portsmouth, OH '81 (MGMT)(RISK)(PLNG)(PUR)
RAUCH, CARL M., dir. med. info. syst., Borgess Medical Center, Kalamazoo, MI '85 (MGMT)
RAUCH, JOAN E., RN, dir. nrsg., Leominster Hospital, Leominster, MA '74 (NURS)
RAUCH, ROBERT J., supv. maint. and constr., Southern Baptist Hospital, New Orleans, LA '81 (ENG)
RAUDEBAUGH, HELEN, RN, head nrs. amb. care, Wooster Community Hospital, Wooster, OH '87 (AMB)
RAUDENBUSH, SAMUEL G., dir. matl. mgt., Pottstown Memorial Medical Center, Pottstown, PA '70 (PUR)
RAUFFENBART, MARY, RN, (ret.), Moorestown, NJ '54 (NURS)(LIFE)
RAUSCH, CDR JACK LEE, MSC USN, asst. chief staff res. mgt., Navmedcom, Nereg, Great Lakes, IL '77
RAVERTY, PATRICK J., dir. human res., Salvation Army William Booth Memorial Hospital, Florence, KY '82 (PERS)
RAVICH, RUTH, dir. pat. rep., Mount Sinai Medical Center, New York, NY '72 (PAT)
RAVIN, ROBERT L., assoc. adm., St. Joseph Mercy Hospital, Ann Arbor, MI '80
RAWLINGS, ALAN D., dir. plant oper., St. Mary's Hospital and Rehabilitation Center, Minneapolis, MN '85 (ENG)
RAWLINGS, C. A., Electrical Science and Systems Engineering, Carbondale, IL '75 (ENG)
RAWLINGS, JAMES E., adm. dir. amb. serv., Yale-New Haven Hospital, New Haven, CT '87 (AMB)
RAWLINSON, BETTY E., dir. vol. serv., Misericordia Hospital, Edmonton, Alta., Canada '73 (VOL)
RAWLS, ROBIN D., dir. pub. rel., Alabama Hospital Association, Montgomery, AL '83 (PR)
RAWSON, JOSEPH J., asst. dir. maint., Albert Einstein Medical Center, Philadelphia, PA '83 (ENG)
RAY, BARBARA F., adm. pat. rep., Samuel Merritt Hospital, Oakland, CA '81 (PAT)
RAY, BARBARA, dir. vol. serv., Group Health Cooperative Hospital, Seattle, WA '84 (VOL)
RAY, ELIZABETH S., student, Department of Health Care Administration, George Washington University, Washington, DC '82
RAY, HARVEY E., chief eng., Bob Wilson Memorial Grant County Hospital, Ulysses, KS '80 (ENG)
RAY, JAMES D., dir. emp. rel., St. Luke's Medical Center, Phoenix, AZ '82 (PERS)
RAY, LINDA SCHLICHTING, chief soc. work serv., Veterans Administration Medical Center, Phoenix, AZ '77 (SOC)
RAY, MARKHAM LESLIE, Atlanta, GA '84
RAY, NORRETA, dir. soc. work, Kingsboro Psychiatric Center, Brooklyn, NY '82 (SOC)
RAY, ROBERT F., dir. adm. serv., University of Illinois, Chicago, IL '80 (ENG)
RAY, SHERYL HAMM, vice-pres. commun. and educ., Oklahoma Hospital Association, Oklahoma City, OK '82 (PR)
RAYALA, JEROME R., adm. mgr., St. Michael's Hospital, Stevens Point, WI '81 (MGMT)
RAYBURN, ROSEMARY R., RN, dir. nrsg. serv. and asst. adm., Doctors Hospital of Dallas, Dallas, TX '81 (NURS)
RAYFIELD, JACK, asst. dir. eng., Holy Cross Hospital, Fort Lauderdale, FL '84 (ENG)
RAYFORD, OPHELIA S., dir. sup., proc. and distrib., Huguley Memorial Hospital, Fort Worth, TX '82 (CS)
RAYLE, MAX E., atty., Wood County Hospital, Bowling Green, OH '85 (ATTY)
RAYMAKER, GAIL, pres., Time Resource, Inc., Oak Park, IL '84
RAYMAN, JUDITH, exec. dir., Southwest Michigan Health Systems Agency, Inc., Kalamazoo, MI '85
RAYMAN, NANCY ANN, asst. adm., Somerset Community Hospital, Somerset, PA '71 (PLNG)
RAYMOND, DAVID V., coor. facil., Catherine McAuley Health Center, Ann Arbor, MI '83 (ENG)
RAYMOND, LAURIER T. JR., atty., St. Mary's General Hospital, Lewiston, ME '82 (ATTY)
RAYMOND, SPENCER H., atty., Skokie Valley Hospital, Skokie, IL '69 (ATTY)
RAYNAUD, CAPT. EUGENE H., MSC USAF, chief, Headquarters Tactical Air Command, Europe and Pacific Plans Division, Langley AFB, VA '86
RAYNE, EMMY S., vice-pres. mktg., Doctors' Hospital, Coral Gables, FL '86 (PR)
RAYNER, THOMAS J., sr. vice-pres. oper., Newcomb Medical Center, Vineland, NJ '79
RAYNOR, MARGARET D., head vol. serv., St. Mary's Hospital, Reno, NV '85 (VOL)
RAYNOR, STUART E., San Antonio, TX '79
RAYON, DAVID JR., dir. pers., Monmouth Medical Center, Long Branch, NJ '83 (PERS)
RAYSOR, THOMAS M., atty., Sibley Memorial Hospital, Washington, DC '68 (ATTY)
REA, VIRGINIA, RN, dir. cent. serv., Valley Children's Hospital, Fresno, CA '86 (CS)
READ, CHERI D., dir. vol., St. Joseph's Hospital, Milwaukee, WI '85 (VOL)
READ, CHERYL L., dir. mktg. and pub. rel., HCA West Side Hospital, Nashville, TN '84 (PR)
READ, ELLEN, RN, div. dir. nrsg., St. Joseph's Hospital, Stockton, CA '79 (NURS)
READ, HOWARD KENNETH, prin., Hkr Associates, Orange, NH '53 (LIFE)
READ, PETER K., exec. vice-pres. and chief oper. off., Bayfront Medical Center, St. Petersburg, FL '72
READ, SANDRA L., vice-pres. prog. dev. and trng., Affiliated Risk Control Administrators of Pennsylvania, Pittsburgh, PA '82 (RISK)
READ, TERRI, dir. pub. rel., Memorial General Hospital, Las Cruces, NM '82 (PR)
READING, DAWN, dir. vol. serv., Presbyterian-University Hospital, Pittsburgh, PA '75 (VOL)
READING, ROBERT P., dir. eng., McKay-Dee Hospital Center, Ogden, UT '83 (ENG)
READY, JEAN L., RN, dir. educ., Holy Cross Hospital, Fort Lauderdale, FL '77 (EDUC)

REAGAN, BENNY M., risk mgr., Vanderbilt University Hospital, Nashville, TN '80 (RISK)
REAGAN, JOHN E., dir. soc. serv., Cooley Dickinson Hospital, Northampton, MA '74 (SOC)
REAMY, OLLIE C. III, asst. dir. bldg. serv., Mainland Center Hospital, Texas City, TX '85 (ENG)
REARDON, CAROL L., dir. vol., Harrington Memorial Hospital, Southbridge, MA '72 (VOL)
REARDON, EDWARD J., vice-pres. human res., St. Joseph Hospital, Kirkwood, MO '64 (PERS)
REARDON, TIMOTHY F., adm., Morgan County War Memorial Hospital, Berkeley Springs, WV '75
REARICK, JEANNE C., dir. in-service educ., Citizens General Hospital, New Kensington, PA '71 (EDUC)
REASE, MARY E., chief nrsg. off., Hamad General Hospital Corporation, Doha Qatar, Arabia '86 (NURS)
REASONER, HELEN, RN, dir. pat. care, AMI Presbyterian-St. Luke's Medical Center, Denver, CO '76 (NURS)
REASOR, CLARENCE L., dir. maint. and eng., University of Tennessee Memorial Research Center and Hospital, Knoxville, TN '75 (ENG)
REAVES, GEORGE D., dir. food serv., South Oaks Hospital, Amityville, NY '83 (FOOD)
REAVES, PAMELA J., ed.-healthwaves magazine, St. Paul Medical Center, Dallas, TX '86 (PR)
REAVIS, RODNEY C., dir. eng., Edward A. Utlaut Memorial Hospital, Greenville, IL '81 (ENG)
REAVIS, THOMAS M., dir. commun. rel., Tucson Medical Center, Tucson, AZ '83 (PR)
REBERG, ALAN J., pres. and chief exec. off., Mercy Hospital, Muskegon, MI '81 (PLNG)
REBIC, JUDITH, dir. vol. serv., Good Samaritan Medical Center, Zanesville, OH '82 (VOL)
REBIDUE, JAMES S., mgr. pur., Saint Vincent Hospital, Worcester, MA '75 (PUR)
REBMAN, ALAN J., vice-pres. facil., Sisters of Charity Hospital, Buffalo, NY '74 (ENG)
REBUCK, ANNE M., dir. vol. serv., Sunbury Community Hospital, Sunbury, PA '82 (VOL)
RECH, RONALD E., dir. food serv., St. Joseph Hospital, Chicago, IL '77 (FOOD)
RECHIS, GEORGE, asst. vice-pres., LaGuardia Hospital, Flushing, NY '82 (PUR)
RECHNER, JOHN A., asst. dir., Burke Ambulatory Care Center, Loyola University of Chicago, Foster G. McGaw Hospital, Maywood, IL '78 (PLNG)
RECHSTEINER, BRUCE C., dir. logistics mgt., St. Francis Memorial Hospital, San Francisco, CA '82 (PUR)
RECK, HERBERT W., dir. pers., St. Joseph Medical Center, Wichita, KS '81 (PERS)
RECKARD, TERENCE H., pharm., Lenox Hill Hospital, New York, NY '79
RECKER, DONNA G., supv. cent., proc. and distrib., Appleton Medical Center, Appleton, WI '85 (CS)
RECKMEYER, CATHERINE N., dir. vol. serv., Saint Alphonsus Regional Medical Center, Boise, ID '87 (VOL)
RECORD, MARJORIE E., dir. matl. mgt., Los Alamitos Medical Center, Los Alamitos, CA '79 (PUR)
RECTOR, PATSY P., RN, clin. dir. amb. care, Lloyd Noland Hospital and Health Centers, Birmingham, AL '87 (AMB)
RECTOR, PHILIP G., dir. phys. res., University of Arizona, Tucson, AZ '80 (ENG)
RECZEK, STANLEY L., dir. corp. plng., Salem Hospital, Salem, MA '83 (PLNG)
REDD, JUDITH GRIMES, dir. pers., Timberlawn Psychiatric Hospital, Dallas, TX '79 (PERS)
REDDICK, BETSY, dir. mktg., Charter Hospital of Overland Park, Overland Park, KS '85 (PR) (PLNG)
REDDICK, WARREN W., dir. plant serv., Cottage Grove Hospital, Cottage Grove, OR '84 (ENG)
REDDINGTON, MICHAEL J. JR., proj. eng., Fosdick and Hilmer, Inc., Cincinnati, OH '85 (ENG)
REDDY, ANSA B., chief diet., Al-Adan Hospital, Rikkah, Kuwait '86
REDDY, COL. CHARLES J., RN MSC USA, chief nrsg., Headquarters U. S. Army Health Services Command, Fort Sam Houston, TX '71 (NURS)
REDEMPTA, SR. MARY, dir. educ. and trng., Mercy Hospitals of Sacramento, Carmichael, CA '80 (EDUC)
REDFERN, ROBERT J., dir. food and nutr. serv., St. Francis Regional Medical Center, Wichita, KS '86 (FOOD)
REDGATE, STEPHEN V., dir. matl. mgt., Memorial Hospital of Laramie County, Cheyenne, WY '84 (PUR)
REDING, MARY GAIL, dir. soc. serv., Medical Personnel Pool, Oak Park, IL '85 (SOC)
REDMAN, ANDREA J., RN, mgr. aux. serv., Saint Joseph Hospital, Mishawaka, IN '82 (NURS)
REDMAN, DONALD G., supv. hskpg. and ldry., Marlette Community Hospital, Marlette, MI '86 (ENVIRON)
REDMAN, RICHARD W., RN, assoc. prof. and area dir. nrsg. adm., State University of New York at Buffalo, Buffalo, NY '86 (NURS)
REDMOND, DEBORAH KELLY, dir. case mix analysis and syst., Brigham and Women's Hospital, Boston, MA '82
REDMOND, MAUREEN ELLEN, student, Program in Health Services Administration, Indiana University, Bloomington, IN '86
REDPATH, RANDOLPH A., atty., Caldwell Memorial Hospital, Lenoir, NC '84 (ATTY)
REDUS, BURLEIGH L., dir. environ. serv., HCA Shoal Creek Hospital, Austin, TX '81 (ENG)
REEBER, BRENDA J., coor. pat. educ., Sinai Hospital of Detroit, Detroit, MI '85 (EDUC)
REECE, ROBERT V., dir., Cambridge Research Institute, Cambridge, MA '83 (PLNG)
REECE, SHELBY P., RN, dir. nrsg. critical care serv., Baptist Medical Center, Columbia, SC '84 (NURS)(AMB)
REED, ANGELA Y., asst. adm. prof. serv., Metropolitan Hospital and Health Centers, Detroit, MI '79
REED, ANN D., RN, dir. nrsg., Calais Regional Hospital, Calais, ME '86 (NURS)
REED, BARBARA J., RN, dir. nrsg. and asst. adm. pat. care serv., Baxter County Regional Hospital, Mountain Home, AR '83 (NURS)
REED, CHARLES HARMON JR., dir. oper., Odell Associates, Inc., Tampa, FL '84
REED, DAVID A., pres., Samaritan Health Service, Phoenix, AZ '59
REED, DENISE E., vice-pres., First Health Associates, Inc., New York, NY '82
REED, DON, dir. bldg. serv., Community Hospital, Santa Rosa, CA '84 (ENG)
REED, DONNA V., dir. vol. serv., Miami Children's Hospital, Miami, FL '81 (VOL)
REED, ELIZABETH K., RN, chief nrsg. serv., Veterans Administration Medical Center, Marion, IN '85 (NURS)
REED, ELSIE J., dir. vol. serv., Presbyterian-University of Pennsylvania Medical Center, Philadelphia, PA '73 (VOL)
REED, FRED A., dir. matl. mgt., Servicemaster Industries, Inc., Downers Grove, IL '83 (PUR)
REED, GARY E., vice-pres. support serv., New England Baptist Hospital, Boston, MA '86
REED, GLEN A., atty., Charter Suburban Hospital, Mesquite, TX '78 (ATTY)
REED, JANET, cent. proc. tech., Clinton Memorial Hospital, Wilmington, OH '82 (CS)
REED, JOAN ALEXIS, dir. nrsg. serv., Hospital for Sick Children, Washington, DC '80 (NURS)
REED, JOEL E., chief soc. work serv., Veterans Administration Medical Center, Bedford, MA '83 (SOC)
REED, JOHN L., dir. soc. work, Betty Bacharach Rehabilitation Hospital, Pomona, NJ '84 (SOC)
REED, KATHLEEN M., dir. vol. serv., Frankford Hospital of the City of Philadelphia, Philadelphia, PA '85 (VOL)
REED, LANDER G., mgr. environ. serv., Highlands Hospital and Health Center, Connellsville, PA '86 (ENVIRON)
REED, LORI E., atty., Tampa General Hospital, Tampa, FL '85 (ATTY)
REED, MARIE A., RN, asst. adm. and dir. nrsg., Mount Vernon Hospital, Alexandria, VA '77 (NURS)
REED, MARY C., trainer info. syst., Abbott-Northwestern Hospital, Minneapolis, MN '85 (EDUC)
REED, MARY LOU, dir. sterile proc., Fairfax Hospital, Falls Church, VA '85 (CS)
REED, MICHAEL E., atty., American College of Surgeons, Chicago, IL '77 (ATTY)
REED, NOREEN, dir. risk mgt. and qual. assur., Monmouth Medical Center, Long Branch, NJ '86 (RISK)
REED, PATRICIA K., RN, vice-pres. and exec. dir. nrsg., Albany Medical Center Hospital, Albany, NY '79 (NURS)
REED, PAUL D., dir. phys. plant, Sacred Heart General Hospital, Eugene, OR '81 (ENG)
REED, PAULINE S., RN, supv. cent. serv., Twin County Community Hospital, Galax, VA '85 (CS)
REED, RICHARD O., student, Southern Illinois University, School of Technical Careers, Carbondale, IL '85
REED, ROBERT L., mgr. matl., Doctors Hospital of Stark County, Massillon, OH '82 (PUR)
REED, ROBERT R. JR., matl. proj. dir., College Hospital of the College of Medicine and Dentistry of New Jersey, Newark, NJ '77 (PUR)
REED, RONALD L., dir. pers., Lexington County Hospital, West Columbia, SC '79 (PERS)
REED, SALLIE F., dir. pat. serv., Hospital of the Medical College of Pennsylvania, Philadelphia, PA '73 (FOOD)
REED, STEVEN, dir. safety and security, Florida Hospital-Altamonte, Altamonte Springs, FL '86
REED, SYDNEY, RN, assoc. adm., Seton Medical Center, Daly City, CA '77 (NURS)
REED, V. JEAN, dir. vol., Geauga Hospital, Chardon, OH '81 (VOL)
REED, WILLIAM C., vice-pres. mgt. info. syst., Geisinger System Services, Danville, PA '85 (MGMT)
REEDER, GRETCHEN A., dir. vol. serv., Methodist Hospital, Omaha, NE '86 (VOL)
REEDER, SUSAN C., actg. dir. pub. rel., Childrens Hospital of Los Angeles, Los Angeles, CA '82 (PR)
REEDY, ISABELLE M., dir. environ. serv., Riverside Medical Center, Kankakee, IL '86 (ENVIRON)
REEDY, THOMAS A., dir. human serv., Muhlenberg Regional Medical Center, Plainfield, NJ '84 (SOC)
REEL, TODD E., mgt. eng., Parkview Memorial Hospital, Fort Wayne, IN '85 (MGMT)
REELEY, GEORGE STANLEY, unit mgt. and pat. rep., Baptist Medical Center, Columbia, SC '86 (PAT)
REEMELIN, ANGELA N., dir. food serv., ARA Services, Hospital Food Management, Environmental Service, Inc., Orange Park, FL '74 (FOOD)
REEN, PEGGY M., RN, coor. qual. assur., St. Elizabeth Hospital Medical Center, Lafayette, IN '80 (RISK)(ENG)
REEP, JAMES A., vice-pres., First Consulting Group, Long Beach, CA '82 (MGMT)
REES, GARY C., vice-pres. human res., Lourdes Hospital, Paducah, KY '81 (PERS)
REES, LUCY M., (ret.), Columbus, OH '70 (FOOD)
REES, MARRIAM L., coor. vol., Community Hospital Medical Center, Phoenix, AZ '86 (VOL)
REES, RICHARD T., EdD, dir. educ., Lakeland Regional Medical Center, Lakeland, FL '80 (EDUC)
REES, ROBERT B., assoc. adm., Baptist Hospital of Miami, Miami, FL '75 (MGMT)
REESE, CYNTHIA L., sr. consult., Price Waterhouse, Chicago, IL '86 (MGMT)
REESE, D. SUE, RN, dir. nrsg., Wilson Memorial Hospital, Sidney, OH '86 (NURS)
REESE, DAVID E., dir. productivity eng., Kuakini Medical Center, Honolulu, HI '84 (MGMT)
REESE, DIANE D., dir. pers. and commun. rel., Community Hospital, Mayfield, KY '82 (PR)
REESE, DOROTHY, dir. soc. serv., Pendleton Memorial Methodist Hospital, New Orleans, LA '86 (SOC)
REESE, ELEANOR A., dir. vol., Arthur R. Gould Memorial Hospital, Presque Isle, ME '78 (VOL)
REESE, ELTON A., (ret.), Alamosa, CO '50 (LIFE)
REESE, KAREN L., RN, dir. nrsg., Grand Island Memorial Hospital, Grand Island, NE '82 (NURS)
REESE, LYNDA T., dir. cent. serv., St. Francis Hospital, Blue Island, IL '81 (CS)
REESE, MYRNA B., RN, asst. exec. dir. nrsg., St. Eugene Community Hospital, Dillon, SC '86 (NURS)
REESE, PATTI W., RN, adm. dir. med. and surg. nrsg., AMI Brookwood Medical Center, Birmingham, AL '86 (NURS)
REESE, RALPH J. JR., exec. vice-pres. and chief oper. off., Mercy Hospital of Watertown, Watertown, NY '81
REESE, RUTH, RN, dir. nrsg., Community Medical Center, Scranton, PA '68 (NURS)
REESE, STEPHEN J., asst. dir. adm., Bayley Seton Hospital, Staten Island, NY '74
REEVE, JOHN J. JR., exec. eng., Menorah Medical Center, Kansas City, MO '68 (ENG)
REEVES, BARNEY JAMES, atty., Memorial General Hospital, Las Cruces, NM '79 (ATTY)
REEVES, CARROL A., dir. pers., Kennewick General Hospital, Kennewick, WA '86 (PERS)
REEVES, CHARLES B. JR., atty., James Lawrence Kernan Hospital, Baltimore, MD '76 (ATTY)
REEVES, DENNIS J., dir. mktg., John F. Kennedy Memorial Hospital, Indio, CA '85 (PLNG)
REEVES, DONALD K., Katy, TX '74
REEVES, GLENN ROBIN, sr. consult., SunHealth Corporation, Charlotte, NC '77 (MGMT)
REEVES, HELEN H., dir. vol. serv., Kaiser Foundation Hospital, Los Angeles, CA '85 (VOL)
REEVES, JIM, asst. adm. amb. care, University Hospital, Augusta, GA '76
REEVES, NANCY ROBINSON, dir. soc. serv., Montfort Jones Memorial Hospital, Kosciusko, MS '85 (SOC)
REEVES, PHILIP N., prof., Department of Health Services Administration, George Washington University, Washington, DC '67 (PLNG)
REEVES, REBECCA R., dir. commun. and pub. rel., Good Samaritan Medical Center, Zanesville, OH '75 (PR)
REFIEUNA, JOHN T., dir. plant oper. and maint., Central DuPage Hospital, Winfield, IL '79 (ENG)
REGAL, WILLIAM A., dir. pers., Chesapeake General Hospital, Chesapeake, VA '68 (PERS)
REGAN, A. P., reg. med. care adm., New York State Department of Health, New York, NY '83
REGAN, BRIAN K., risk mgr., Montefiore Medical Center, Bronx, NY '84 (RISK)
REGAN, HOPE M. JUCKEL, RN, assoc. dir. nrsg., Doctors Hospital, New York, NY '83 (NURS)
REGAN, JERRILYNN, Naperville, IL '79 (MGMT)
REGEDANZ, RICHARD, dir. soc. serv., Parkview Memorial Hospital, Fort Wayne, IN '85 (SOC)
REGEL, ROBERT A., adm. mgr., St. Mary's Medical Center, Evansville, IN '84 (ENG)
REGER, MICHAEL F., asst. vice-pres. pub. rel. and pro-graphics, Baptist Medical Center of Oklahoma, Oklahoma City, OK '81 (PR)
REGIS, ANNETTE E., RN, coor. clin. review, Chesapeake Physicians, Baltimore, MD '82 (RISK)
REGISTER, GLENDA C., dir. pers., Bon Secours Hospital, North Miami, FL '86 (PERS)
REGLI, LINDA K., dir. food serv., Carlinville Area Hospital, Carlinville, IL '81 (FOOD)
REGOTTI, JOANNE M., dir. diet., Westmoreland Manor, Greensburg, PA '84 (FOOD)
REHAK, THOMAS J., vice-pres., American Portfolio Advisory Service, Inc., Lisle, IL '72
REHDER, HENRY PHILIP, RN, vice-pres. risk mgt., Deaconess Medical Center-Spokane, Spokane, WA '68 (RISK)
REHILL, MARIE, dir. matl. mgt., Roxborough Memorial Hospital, Philadelphia, PA '86 (PUR)
REHM, ALICE, RN, dir. educ. and pub. affairs, American Association of Critical-Care Nursing, Newport Beach, CA '81 (NURS)
REHM, DOROTHY A., assoc. exec. dir., Bronx Municipal Hospital Center, Bronx, NY '68
REHM, SUSAN J., dir. clin. soc. work, UCLA Hospitals and Clinics, Los Angeles, CA '80 (SOC)
REHN, RAE R., dir. educ., Santa Rosa Memorial Hospital, Santa Rosa, CA '78 (EDUC)
REHR, HELEN, (ret.), New York, NY '72 (SOC)
REIBER, JAMES W., exec. vice-pres., St. John Medical Center, Tulsa, OK '67
REICH, DAVID G., dir. pers., Kalispell Regional Hospital, Kalispell, MT '86 (PERS)
REICH, JANET L., pat. educ., St. Luke's Hospital, Aberdeen, SD '84 (EDUC)
REICH, JANET, emer. consult., Rose Medical Center, Denver, CO '87 (AMB)
REICH, JOEL J., MD, chm. emer. and amb. care serv., Manchester Memorial Hospital, Manchester, CT '86 (AMB)
REICHARD, THOMAS H., dir. pers., Somerville Hospital, Somerville, MA '84 (PERS)
REICHBAUM, CAROL L., dir. plng., North Broward Hospital District, Fort Lauderdale, FL '81 (PLNG)
REICHEL, RICHARD G., atty., Massillon Community Hospital, Massillon, OH '76 (ATTY)
REICHENTHAL, JAY J., assoc. dir. environ. serv., Cedars-Sinai Medical Center, Los Angeles, CA '85 (ENVIRON)
REICHERT, FRANK J., assoc. adm., Edgewater Hospital, Chicago, IL '68
REICHERT, MARIMARGARET, RN, dir. cent. sterile reprocessing, Robinson Memorial Hospital, Ravenna, OH '79 (CS)
REICHMAN, JOE V., risk mgr., St. Anthony Medical Center, Columbus, OH '80 (RISK)
REICHMAN, MICHELA ROBBINS, asst. chancellor commun., University of California, San Francisco, CA '64 (PR)
REICHMAN, SUSAN, pat. rep., Fairfax Hospital, Falls Church, VA '85 (PAT)
REID, ADA I., dir. pub. rel. and vol. serv., Memorial Hospital at Gulfport, Gulfport, MS '72 (PR)
REID, ALFRED D. JR., chm., Reid and Stuhldreher, Pittsburgh, PA '85 (ENG)
REID, BRENDA S., atty., California Association of Hospitals and Health Systems, Sacramento, CA '86 (ATTY)

REID, DOROTHY JEAN, RN, vice-pres. nrsg. serv., Northern Michigan Hospitals, Petoskey, MI '83 (NURS)
REID, ELIZABETH A., RN, asst. adm. nrsg., National Hospital for Orthopaedics, Arlington, VA '85 (NURS)
REID, JOANNE M., dir. diet. serv., Hutzel Hospital, Detroit, MI '86 (FOOD)
REID, JOHN, eng., Charley and Bisset, Ltd., London, Ont., Canada '86 (ENG)
REID, JON S., atty., Archbishop Bergan Mercy Hospital, Omaha, NE '85 (ATTY)
REID, PEGGY, dir. pat. rep., Medical Center East, Birmingham, AL '79 (PAT)
REID, SHERIDAN A., dir. mktg., Affiliated Healthcare System, Bangor, ME '85 (PLNG)
REID, THOMAS J., supv. sterile proc., Merle West Medical Center, Klamath Falls, OR '86 (CS)
REIDER, ALAN EVAN, atty., St. John's Healthcare Corporation, Anderson, IN '82 (ATTY)
REIDY, DAVID B., asst. adm., St. Joseph's Hospital, Lowell, MA '77
REIDY, DIANE P., RN, dir. nrsg., Medical Center of Baton Rouge, Baton Rouge, LA '86 (NURS)
REIDY, JEAN M., RN, sr. asst. dir. adm. and dir. nrsg., Saint Vincent Hospital, Worcester, MA '80 (NURS)(PAT)
REIF, BEVERLY B., vice-pres., Bay Medical Center, Bay City, MI '67 (RISK)
REIF, ROBERT D., atty., American Hospital Association, Chicago, IL '82 (ATTY)
REIFERT, ROBERT G., pur. agt., Mercy Hospital, Toledo, OH '86 (PUR)
REIGART, MARY C., dir. vol. serv., York Hospital, York, PA '86 (VOL)
REIGEL, PATRICIA, RN, asst. adm. nrsg. and risk mgr., Seidle Memorial Hospital, Mechanicsburg, PA '86 (RISK)
REILAND, KATHERINE W., dir. vol., Cape Cod Hospital, Hyannis, MA '78 (PAT)(VOL)
REILING, EDMUND C., exec. dir., National Board for Cardiovascular and Pulmonary Credentialing, Inc., Dayton, OH '84 (PERS)
REILLY, CHARLES H., sr. exec. vice-pres. and chief dev. off., American Medical International, Beverly Hills, CA '85 (MGMT)
REILLY, CHARLES JOHN, RN, asst. dir. nrsg. serv., Crozer-Chester Medical Center, Chester, PA '86 (NURS)
REILLY, DONNA JEANNETTE, RN, dir. perinatal, St. Margaret's Hospital, Montgomery, AL '85 (NURS)
REILLY, GARY W., asst. adm., Millard Fillmore Hospital, Buffalo, NY '78
REILLY, HELEN D., dir. matl. mgt., Windber Hospital and Wheeling Clinic, Windber, PA '82 (CS)(PUR)
REILLY, JOSEPH J., asst. dir. res., Greater Detroit Area Health Council, Detroit, MI '84 (PLNG)
REILLY, MARIAN A., asst. contr. syst., St. James Hospital Medical Center, Chicago Heights, IL '80 (ENG)
REILLY, MARY ELEANOR, dir. cent. serv., Cleveland Clinic Hospital, Cleveland, OH '64 (CS)
REILLY, SUSAN, RN, dir. nrsg., Xavier Hospital, Dubuque, IA '77 (NURS)
REILLY, WILLIAM, dir. plant oper., Medina Community Hospital, Medina, OH '87 (ENG)
REIMEL, MIRIAM, atty., Lower Bucks Hospital, Bristol, PA '82 (ATTY)
REIMER, DAVID B., dir. safety and security, Southwest Medical Center, Liberal, KS '84 (ENG)
REIMER, ELIZABETH D., RN, dir. maternal and child serv., Tucson Medical Center, Tucson, AZ '83 (NURS)
REIMER, GEORGIA, dir. vol., St. Joseph's Hospital and Health Center, Tucson, AZ '77 (VOL)
REIMER, SR. GLENDA R., RN, dir. nrsg., Good Samaritan Hospital, Cincinnati, OH '81 (NURS)
REIMER, JUDY E., coor. staff dev., Mary Lanning Memorial Hospital, Hastings, NE '85 (EDUC)
REIMERS, TONI, student, Program in Health Administration, University of Colorado, Denver, CO '86 (MGMT)
REIMLINGER, GEORGE, oper. mgr. amb. care serv., Methodist Hospital of Indiana, Indianapolis, IN '87 (AMB)
REIN, SUZANNE P., RN, supv. nrsg. serv., Ohio Valley Medical Center, Wheeling, WV '80 (NURS)
REINACH, CAROLYN S., atty., Hayt, Hayt and Landau, Great Neck, NY '81 (RISK)
REINACHER, MARK H., dir. cent. pur., St. Joseph Hospitals, Mount Clemens, MI '84
REINBOLT, OREN L., dir. facil., Pacific Presbyterian Medical Center, San Francisco, CA '77 (ENG)
REINBRECHT, JEANETTE, mgr. food serv., Warrick Hospital, Boonville, IN '80 (FOOD)
REINDERS, JOANNE, RN, dir. sterile proc., Washington Hospital Center, Washington, DC '83 (CS)
REINECK, LT. COL. THEODORE C. JR., MSC USA, University of the Health Sciences, Uniformed Service, Washington, DC '71
REINECKE, DOROTHY, dir. pur., Glendale Heights Community Hospital, Glendale Heights, IL '84 (PUR)
REINECKE, NADEEN, dir. vol. serv., AMI Presbyterian-Denver Hospital, Denver, CO '86 (VOL)
REINEKE, DORI A., supv. health serv. advice, Community Health Center Plan, Inc., New Haven, CT '83 (PAT)
REINEKE, LINDA M., dir. diet., St. Joseph Health Care Corporation, Albuquerque, NM '83 (FOOD)
REINEMANN, ROBERT, dir. fin. mgt. and nrsg., Overlook Hospital, Summit, NJ '84
REINER, FRANK, assoc. exec. dir., St. Elizabeth's Hospital, Chicago, IL '64
REINER, RICHARD, vice-pres., Florida Hospital Medical Center, Orlando, FL '85 (RISK)
REINER, YVETTE, dir. amb. and therapeutic serv., Good Samaritan Hospital, Downers Grove, IL '87 (AMB)
REINERT, PAMELA S., RN, dir. pat. care, AMI Presbyterian-St. Luke's Medical Center, Denver, CO '84 (NURS)
REINERTS, SKAIDRITE, dir. food serv., Wayne General Hospital, Wayne, NJ '76 (FOOD)
REINERTSEN, JOHN A., exec. dir., University of Utah Health Sciences Center, Salt Lake City, UT '54 (LIFE)
REINGOLD, DANIEL, atty., Long Island Jewish Medical Center, New York, NY '82 (ATTY)
REINHARD, JANE F., coor. vol., Bryn Mawr Rehabilitation Hospital, Malvern, PA '85 (VOL)
REINHARDT, BARBARA L., RN, dir. nrsg., Illini Community Hospital, Pittsfield, IL '83 (NURS)
REINHARDT, JOHN B. JR., pres., Blue Cross of Central Ohio, Columbus, OH '83
REINHARDT, MARTHA, EdD, asst. to pres. pub. affairs, West Virginia University Hospital, Morgantown, WV '85 (PR)
REINHART, ROBERT S., consult., Catherine McAuley Health Center, Ann Arbor, MI '76 (ENG)
REINHART, STEPHEN P., student, Program in Industrial and Operations Engineering, University of Michigan, Ann Arbor, MI '86 (MGMT)
REINOLD, KEITH C., mgt. eng., Choate-Symmes Hospitals, Woburn, MA '84 (MGMT)
REINOSO, M. DIANNE, risk mgr., Mercy Hospital, Charlotte, NC '84 (RISK)
REINOSO, R. CRANSTON, Asheville, NC '80
REINSCHMIDT, RICHARD J., student, University of Illinois-Chicago Circle, Chicago, IL '82 (PLNG)
REINSMA, THOMAS R., atty., North Ottawa Community Hospital, Grand Haven, MI '68 (ATTY)
REINSTATLE, JACK A., dir. emp. rel., Providence Hospital, Cincinnati, OH '71 (EDUC)
REIS, MARY L., dir. soc. serv., Parkland Medical Center, Derry, NH '79 (SOC)
REISDORFER, GLORIA A., dir. vol. serv., St. Francis Medical Center, Breckenridge, MN '85 (VOL)
REISERT, MARY CATHERINE, student, Hofstra University, Hempstead, NY '86
REISIG, BETH L., student, Department of Health Care Administration, George Washington University, Washington, DC '82
REISINGER, HARRY S., sr. eng., SunHealth Corporation, Charlotte, NC '86 (ENG)
REISINGER, MARIE-LOUISE T., supv. fin. counselor, Providence Hospital, Anchorage, AK '85 (PAT)
REISLER, MARY G., mktg. spec., Rehabilitation Institute of Pittsburgh, Pittsburgh, PA '84 (PLNG)
REISNER, PAULINE, dir. cent. prog., Commission on Professional and Hospital Activities, Ann Arbor, MI '87 (AMB)
REISNOUR, DENNIS A., dir. plng. and mktg., Methodist Hospitals of Dallas, Dallas, TX '85 (PLNG)
REISS, BARBARA A., pres. and mgt. consult., Reiss and Associates, Inc., San Francisco, CA '81 (PLNG)
REISS, JOHN B., atty., Jeanes Hospital, Philadelphia, PA '83 (ATTY)
REISS, PATRICIA P., dir. vol. serv., Sheboygan Memorial Medical Center, Sheboygan, WI '78 (VOL)
REISS, TERRENCE W., dir. pers., Family Hospital, Milwaukee, WI '68 (PERS)
REIST, KAREN L., asst. commun., Holy Cross Health System Corporation, South Bend, IN '86 (PR)
REITAN, MARK, student, University of California Los Angeles, Los Angeles, CA '80
REITZ, DENNIS WILLIAM, dir. plant oper., Baltimore County General Hospital, Randallstown, MD '77 (ENG)
REITZ, ELLA G., vice-pres. human res., Children's Hospital Medical Center, Akron, OH '67 (PERS)
REKATE, MARY WARREN, atty., Scottsdale Memorial Hospital, Scottsdale, AZ '83 (ATTY)
RELIC, JOHN, vice-pres., Presbyterian Intercommunity Hospital, Whittier, CA '86
RELKIN, CARYN, dir. human res., St. Joseph Health Care Corporation, Albuquerque, NM '85 (PERS)
REMBIS, MICHAEL A., adm., Eisenhower Medical Center, Rancho Mirage, CA '84
REMBOLD, MICHAEL J., asst. adm. human res., Mercy Hospital, Portsmouth, OH '79 (PERS)
REMBOLDT, DARWIN R., pres., Simi Valley Adventist Hospital, Simi Valley, CA '76 (ATTY)
REMBRANDT, STEPHEN, exec. dir., Associate Physicians of Medical College, Toledo, OH '63
REMEIKA, JOSEPH G., dir. plng. serv., Audrain Medical Center, Mexico, MO '79 (PLNG)
REMER, SIOUX E., dir. plng., Santa Fe Healthcare Systems, Inc., Gainesville, FL '86 (PLNG)
REMER, STANLEY G., chief soc. work, Veterans Administration Medical Center, Kansas City, MO '81 (SOC)
REMIG, WAYNE D., RN PhD, vice-pres. nrsg., St. Luke's Hospital, Bethlehem, PA '80 (NURS)
REMINGER, RICHARD T., atty., Cleveland Clinic Hospital, Cleveland, OH '77 (ATTY)
REMINGTON, CHARLES B., prin., Ernst and Whinney, Cleveland, OH '75
REMKUS, THOMAS A., dir. matl. mgt., Mesquite Community Hospital, Mesquite, TX '86 (PUR)
REMMEL, DIANE M., dir. diet. serv., Delray Community Hospital, Delray Beach, FL '74 (FOOD)
REMMLINGER, ELAINE S., proj. mgr., Mount Sinai Medical Center, New York, NY '83
REMSBERG, JILL S., asst. adm., St. Luke's Hospital, Kansas City, MO '82
REMSCHEL, HENRY H. JR., dir. clin. eng., St. Joseph Hospital, Houston, TX '85 (ENG)
REMUND, RENE J., atty., St. Helen Hospital, Chehalis, WA '80 (ATTY)
REN, SIMON J., design eng., University of Michigan Hospitals, Ann Arbor, MI '84 (ENG)
RENAGHAN, EILEEN A., assoc. dir., Compucare, Tampa, FL '85 (MGMT)
RENAUD, KERRY A., student, Boston University Health Management Programs, Boston, MA '85
RENAUD, RENEE, student, Program in Health Services Administration, College of Allied Health , University of Kentucky, Lexington, KY '85
RENCH, JAMES L., atty., Stark and Knoll, Akron, OH '84 (ATTY)
RENDA, PHILIP M., dir. mgt. eng., Waterbury Hospital, Waterbury, CT '85 (MGMT)
RENDACK, JAMES M., sr. mgt. eng., Fairview Community Hospital, Minneapolis, MN '78 (MGMT)
RENDE, DAVID G., mgr. clin. eng., St. Joseph Mercy Hospital, Ann Arbor, MI '79 (ENG)
RENDER, JOHN C., atty., Indiana Hospital Association, Indianapolis, IN '72 (ATTY)
RENDLE, JAMES B., dir. pub. rel., Malden Hospital, Malden, MA '69 (PR)
RENDLEMAN, RHONDA M., coor. environ. serv., Union County Hospital, Anna, IL '86 (ENVIRON)
RENEAU, DALE, atty., Midwest City Memorial Hospital, Midwest City, OK '79 (ATTY)
RENEGAR, BRENDA S., coor. matl., McAlester Regional Hospital, McAlester, OK '86 (PUR)
RENEGAR, LAUREL P., mgt. eng., Orlando Regional Medical Center, Orlando, FL '84 (MGMT)
RENFRO, ROBERT M., chief eng., Union Hospital, Terre Haute, IN '76 (ENG)
RENFRO, TOM B., atty., Harris Methodist -Fort Worth, Fort Worth, TX '75 (ATTY)
RENFROE, WANDA, RN, dir. med. surg. nrsg. serv., Westlake Community Hospital, Melrose Park, IL '80 (NURS)(AMB)
RENFROW, CHRIS R., mgt. analyst, Shriners Hospital for Crippled Children, Tampa, FL '87
RENN, JOSEPH B. JR., dir. plant serv., Central Washington Hospital, Wenatchee, WA '78 (ENG)
RENN, PATRICIA K., asst. vice-pres. commun. rel., Valley Memorial Hospital, Livermore, CA '86 (PR)
RENN, STEVEN C., atty., Johns Hopkins University Center for Fin, Baltimore, MD '86 (ATTY)
RENNEKAMP, JOAN, dir. human res. dev., Penrose Hospitals, Colorado Springs, CO '86 (PERS)
RENNER, JEAN C., dir. pub. rel., Delnor Community Health Systems, Geneva, IL '86 (PR)
RENNIE, GEORGE A., dir. matl. mgt., Concord Hospital, Concord, NH '85 (PUR)
RENNINGER, ELEANOR K., RN, asst. vice-pres. and dir. nrsg. serv., Roxborough Memorial Hospital, Philadelphia, PA '86 (NURS)
RENO, DONNA J., dir. pers. and pur. agt., Bartow Memorial Hospital, Bartow, FL '67 (PERS)
RENO, DONNA JOYCE, dir. risk mgt., Mount Sinai Medical Center, Miami Beach, FL '86 (RISK)
RENO, GLENN M., consult., University of Massachusetts Medical School, Worcester, MA '47 (LIFE)
RENSBERGER, TERRY L., dir. matl. mgt., Goshen General Hospital, Goshen, IN '83 (PUR)
RENSCH, EDWARD JR., exec. dir., Central Arkansas Radiation Therapy Institute, Little Rock, AR '57 (LIFE)
RENSING, SUE GILLETTE, RN, adm. asst., Edward W. Sparrow Hospital, Lansing, MI '79 (NURS)
RENSTROM, PAUL A. JR., vice-pres. mktg. and pub. affairs, HealthOne Corporation, Minneapolis, MN '85 (PR)
RENTON, DAVID C., asst. adm., Mercy Hospital, Toledo, OH '71
RENTSCHLER, ALVIN E., oper. and maint. eng., Rochester Methodist Hospital, Rochester, MN '78 (ENG)
RENTSCHLER, CORRINE A., supv. cent. sup. serv., Aramco-Dhahran Health Center, Dhahran, Saudi Arabia '82 (CS)
RENTSCHLER, GRETCHEN, mgr. cent. proc., Robert Packer Hospital, Sayre, PA '85 (CS)
RENTSCHLER, WALTER R., pres. and chief exec. off., Community Hospital at Glen Cove, Glen Cove, NY '63
RENTZ, CAROLYN B., RN, dir. educ. and trng., South Fulton Hospital, East Point, GA '87 (EDUC)
RENTZ, CHARLOTTE C., mgr. human res. dev., Orlandc Regional Medical Center, Orlando, FL '85 (PERS)(EDUC)
RENY, MARC J., dir. plant eng., Mercy Hospital, Portland, ME '86 (ENG)
RENZ, JOHN J., dir. plng., St. Joseph's Hospital, Elmira, NY '81 (PLNG)
RENZI, ANTHONY M., buyer, Methodist Hospital, Philadelphia, PA '84 (PUR)
REPA, GEORGE, adm., Hoots Memorial Hospital, Yadkinville, NC '77
REPASS, JUDITH H., RN, dir. nrsg., Chippenham Hospital, Richmond, VA '74 (NURS)
REPETTI, BARBARA D., assoc. plng. and mktg., Hahnemann University Hospital, Philadelphia, PA '82 (PLNG)
REPETTI, GREGORY G., asst. to adm., Hospital of the Medical College of Pennsylvania, Philadelphia, PA '82
REPKA, EDITH, pat. rep., Saint Joseph Hospital, Denver, CO '79 (PAT)
REPLOGLE, KEVIN, dir. hskpg., Vanderbilt Children Psychiatric Hospital, Nasville, TN '86 (ENVIRON)
RESCH, MARY LYNN, dir. prof. serv., Elk County General Hospital, Ridgway, PA '86 (PERS)
RESCH, PAULETTE, coor. adm. proj., Medical Center of Independence, Independence, MO '86 (PLNG)
RESNICK, BARBARA G., dir. food serv., Kaiser Foundation Hospital, San Diego, CA '84 (FOOD)
RESNICK, PETER V., vice-pres. oper., Good Samaritan Hospital of Maryland, Baltimore, MD '70
RESNIK, DIANA, dir. commun. rel., Seton Medical Center, Austin, TX '82 (PR)
RESNIKOFF, JOEL, coor. pat. and family serv., Mount Diablo Hospital Medical Center, Concord, CA '82 (SOC)
RESS, GEORGE C., dir. pur., Barron Memorial Medical Center, Barron, WI '82 (PUR)
RESSLER, RICKIE L., RN, dir. proj. and syst., Abbott-Northwestern Hospital Corporation, Minneapolis, MN '86 (NURS)
RESTAD, SUZIE H., partner, Headlines, Phoenix, AZ '83 (PR)
RESTIFO, VALERIE, RN, instr., AMI Doctors' Hospital, Lanham, MD '83 (EDUC)
RESTREPO, JAIRO, eng., Hospiser-Shaio, Bogota, Colombia '85 (ENG)

RETFORD, EARLENE J., actg. dir. staff dev. and cont. educ., Christ Hospital, Cincinnati, OH '85 (EDUC)
RETORT, RITA A., RN, vice-pres. pat. care serv., Little Company of Mary Hospital, Torrance, CA '81 (NURS)
RETOSKE, ROBERT P., dir. matl. mgt., Community Hospital at Glen Cove, Glen Cove, NY '65 (PUR)
RETTER, SUE ANN, RN, sr. asst. adm., St. Joseph Medical Center, Burbank, CA '76 (NURS)
RETTEW, KATHRYN A., dir. commun. rel., High Point Regional Hospital, High Point, NC '85 (PR)
RETTINGER, BONITA O., RN, asst. dir. nrsg., Regional Medical Center, Madisonville, KY '85 (NURS)
RETTINGER, SR. STEPHANIE, RN, asst. exec. dir. pat. serv., St. Joseph's Hospital, Sarnia, Ont., Canada '79 (NURS)
RETZLOFF, JAMES, dir. matl. mgt., Mercy Medical Center, Oshkosh, WI '85 (PUR)
REUBEN, ELLEN B., asst. adm., Magee Rehabilitation Hospital, Philadelphia, PA '82 (PLNG)
REUBEN, SOPHIE, supv. soc. work and dir. comp. seizure, St. Paul-Ramsey Medical Center, St. Paul, MN '79 (SOC)
REUSCHEL, JAMES P., adm. dir., De Goesbriand Memorial Hospital, Burlington, VT '76
REUSCHER, FREDERICKA CARLENE, RN, vice-pres. nrsg., Torrance Memorial Hospital Medical Center, Torrance, CA '77 (NURS)
REUTER, MARY ANN, dir. nutr. serv., Chandler Community Hospital, Chandler, AZ '84 (FOOD)
REUTLINGER, CRAIG A., dir. legal affairs, Charlotte Memorial Hospital and Medical Center, Charlotte, NC '79 (ATTY)
REVAK, ALEIGRA J., RN, mgr. pur., Northern Illinois Medical Center, McHenry, IL '71 (PUR)
REVELS, MARK A., dir. eng., Hardin Memorial Hospital, Elizabethtown, KY '82 (ENG)
REVELS, THOMAS WILLIAM, dir. eng., Humana Hospital -Orange Park, Orange Park, FL '71 (ENG)
REVERE, GLEN PAUL, mgr. diet., Fort Worth Osteopathic Medical Center, Fort Worth, TX '85 (FOOD)
REVERS, JAN E., adm. res., Pacifica Health Systems, Cypress, CA '86
REVIS, HAZEL V., supv. cent. sterile tech., AMI Garden Park Community Hospital, Gulfport, MS '83 (CS)
REVOIR, ERNEST C., vice-pres. plng., Kimball Medical Center, Lakewood, NJ '76 (PLNG)
REVOLDT, ELAINE B., dir. soc. serv., Aultman Hospital, Canton, OH '66 (SOC)
REW, ROBERT W., dir. bldg. and grds. and chief eng., AMI Parkway Regional Medical Center, North Miami Beach, FL '85 (ENG)
REX, DAN L., pres. and chief exec. off., Newcomb Medical Center, Vineland, NJ '64
REXFORD, LINDA, dir. educ. serv., Hamilton Medical Center, Dalton, GA '86 (EDUC)
REXILIUS, EUGENE HERMAN, Lake Placid, NY '70
REXROAD, JEFFREY D., atty., Trumbull Memorial Hospital, Warren, OH '74 (ATTY)
REXROAT, FRANCES ROSE, RN, dir. nrsg. orth and neurosurgical serv., St. Joseph Hospital, Lexington, KY '84 (NURS)
REXRODE, ROBERT W., dir., Walter Reed Army Medical Center, Washington, DC '87
REY, DON, coor. pat. rel., Christ Hospital and Medical Center, Oak Lawn, IL '77 (PAT)
REYES, MADELEINE, dir. food and nutr. serv., Childrens Hospital of Los Angeles, Los Angeles, CA '83 (FOOD)
REYES, ROGELIO DIAZ, adm., Font Martelo Hospital, Humacao, P.R. '70
REYMANN, ISABELLE, RN, vice-pres. pat. care serv., Akron City Hospital, Akron, OH '78 (NURS)
REYNOLDS-DIOT, DEBBIE, dir. health care serv., National Planning Data Corporation, Dallas, TX '85 (PLNG)
REYNOLDS, AMOS B., dir. environ. serv. and supv. plant eng., Sutter Davis Hospital, Davis, CA '85 (ENG)
REYNOLDS, ANN B., dir. soc. serv., Owensboro-Daviess County Hospital, Owensboro, KY '84 (SOC)
REYNOLDS, ANN R., RN, asst. vice-pres. nrsg., Carle Foundation Hospital, Urbana, IL '80 (NURS)
REYNOLDS, DAVID C., spec. asst. to sec., State Medical Society of Wisconsin, Madison, WI '47 (LIFE)
REYNOLDS, DEAN, dir. risk mgt., St. Joseph Health System, Orange, CA '86 (RISK)
REYNOLDS, DONALD J., asst. adm. fin., Alpena General Hospital, Alpena, MI '86
REYNOLDS, DONNA S., RN, dir. plng. and mktg., Morton F. Plant Hospital, Clearwater, FL '85 (NURS)(PLNG)
REYNOLDS, DOROTHY B., mng. dir. qual. assur. and risk mgt., Sharp Memorial Hospital, San Diego, CA '81 (RISK)
REYNOLDS, EUGENE A., chief soc. serv., U. S. Public Health Service Alaska Native Medical Center, Anchorage, AK '74 (SOC)
REYNOLDS, EUGENE S., sr. mgt. eng., Baptist Medical Centers, Birmingham, AL '86 (MGMT)
REYNOLDS, GARY, consult., Nicholas H. Noyes Memorial Hospital, Dansville, NY '75 (FOOD)
REYNOLDS, H. TIM, mgr. cent. serv., Good Samaritan Hospital, Lexington, KY '86 (CS)
REYNOLDS, HARRIET M., dir. diet., Ohio Valley Medical Center, Wheeling, WV '84 (FOOD)
REYNOLDS, IRWIN, dir. soc. serv., Hinsdale Hospital, Hinsdale, IL '76 (SOC)
REYNOLDS, JAMES E., atty., Jewish Hospital of St. Louis, St. Louis, MO '83 (ATTY)
REYNOLDS, JAMES, pres., J. X. Reynolds and Company, Inc., New York, NY '71 (MGMT)(PLNG)
REYNOLDS, JANE, sr. designer, Medifac, Pennsauken, NJ '86 (ENG)
REYNOLDS, KERRY F., dir. commun. rel., St. Luke's Hospital, San Francisco, CA '86 (PR)
REYNOLDS, LARRY D., consult., J. L. Schanilec and Associates, Houston, TX '80
REYNOLDS, CAPT. MARGARET B., MSC USAF, dir. pat. affairs, U. S. Air Force Clinic Ramstein, APO Ramstein, Germany '85
REYNOLDS, MARILYN K., asst. dir. adm. serv. and mktg., University of Missouri Hospital and Clinics, Columbia, MO '83 (PR) (PLNG)
REYNOLDS, MARY L., mgr. educ., Midland Hospital Center, Midland, MI '82 (EDUC)
REYNOLDS, MARY LOU, RN, vice-pres. pat. care, Albany General Hospital, Albany, OR '77 (NURS)
REYNOLDS, NORMAN K., adm., San Augustine Memorial Hospital, San Augustine, TX '64
REYNOLDS, PHILIP L., RN, asst. adm. nrsg. serv., Holy Rosary Hospital, Ontario, OR '85 (NURS)
REYNOLDS, PHYLLIS J., RN, asst. vice-pres. nrsg. serv., Hutzel Hospital, Detroit, MI '86 (NURS)
REYNOLDS, RICHARD COE, dir. mgt. serv., University of Wisconsin Hospital and Clinics, Madison, WI '74 (MGMT)
REYNOLDS, ROGER T., mgr. plant maint., Swedish American Hospital, Rockford, IL '79 (ENG)
REYNOLDS, SHIRLEY C., coor. pat. rel., Womack Army Community Hospital, Fort Bragg, NC '76 (PAT)
REYNOLDS, STEPHEN CURTIS, vice-pres., Baptist Memorial Hospital, Memphis, TN '72
REYNOLDS, THOMAS S., adm., Ingham Medical Center, Lansing, MI '86 (PR)
REYNOLDS, TRAVIS C., dir. maint., Appalachian Hall, Asheville, NC '83 (ENG)
REZENDES, ERNEST F., consult., Florida Department of Health and Rehabilitation Services, Tallahassee, FL '67 (MGMT)
REZNIK, MAJ. RICHARD THOMAS, MSC USA, chief soc. work serv., exceptional family mem. dept., Landstuhl Army Regional Medical Center, APO New York, NY '85 (SOC)
RHEA, FLO, vice-pres., Tuality Management Systems, Hillsboro, OR '82 (PLNG)
RHEE, JURRAL C. P., adm., Lake View Medical Center, Lake View Terrace, CA '51 (LIFE)
RHEIN, LOUISE G., dir. vol. serv., Olympia Fields Osteopathic Medical Center, Olympia Fields, IL '76 (VOL)
RHEMAN, MARJORIE J., dir. vol. serv., Diagnostic Center Hospital, Houston, TX '85 (VOL)
RHOAD, DONALD B., dir. pur., Bethesda Hospital, Inc., Cincinnati, OH '80 (PUR)
RHOADES, JOYCE ANN, RN, vice-pres. nrsg., Welborn Memorial Baptist Hospital, Evansville, IN '76 (NURS)
RHOADES, MICHAEL J., dir. human resources, Sisters of Charity of Houston, Houston, TX '72 (PERS)
RHOADES, STEPHANIE, pur. agt., Brookville Hospital, Brookville, PA '87 (PUR)
RHOADS, GARY R., vice-pres. oper., Stamford Hospital, Stamford, CT '80 (PLNG)
RHOADS, VICTOR W., exec. vice-pres., Baptist Memorials Geriatric Center, San Angelo, TX '82 (PLNG)
RHODES, ANN MARIE, atty., University of Iowa Hospitals and Clinics, Iowa City, IA '84 (ATTY)
RHODES, BETTY LOU, RN, head cent. sup., Owensboro-Daviess County Hospital, Owensboro, KY '78 (CS)
RHODES, DAVID H., dir. human res., Baptist Hospital Highlands, Louisville, KY '79 (PERS)
RHODES, GENE A., dir. pers., Riverside Methodist Hospitals, Columbus, OH '87 (PERS)
RHODES, HERBERT G., dir. eng., University of Utah Health Sciences Center, Salt Lake City, UT '75 (ENG)
RHODES, JOHN DAVID, atty., Montefiore Hospital, Pittsburgh, PA '78 (ATTY)
RHODES, LANE, mktg. plans spec., East Jefferson General Hospital, Metairie, LA '86 (PR) (PLNG)
RHODES, LINDA L., asst. vice-pres. nrsg., Henry County Memorial Hospital, New Castle, IN '85 (NURS)
RHODES, MARDIE E., dir. pub. rel., Virginia Mason Hospital, Seattle, WA '86 (PR)
RHODES, MARILYN K., RN, vice-pres. nrsg. serv., Pitt County Memorial Hospital, Greenville, NC '73 (NURS)
RHODES, MARILYN, supv. cent. sup., St. Francis Regional Medical Center, Wichita, KS '87 (CS)
RHODES, MARVIN L., dir. food serv., Alexian Brothers Hospital San Jose, San Jose, CA '80 (FOOD)
RHODES, RALPH B., atty., Franklin Memorial Hospital, Rocky Mount, VA '76 (ATTY)
RHODES, THEODORE J., dir. data proc., Associated Catholic Hospitals, Inc., Brighton, MA '78
RHODES, THOMAS E., vice-pres., Skyland Hospital Supply, Bluefield, WV '85 (PUR)
RHODES, WARREN D., exec. dir., Mercy Coordinating Center, Oak Brook Terrace, IL '64 (PUR)
RHODUS, DEBRA D., dir. soc. work, Beaufort Memorial Hospital, Beaufort, SC '85 (SOC)
RHOE-JONES, JANE, actg. dir. plng., North Carolina Memorial Hospital, Chapel Hill, NC '85 (PLNG)
RHUDE, JOHN H., vice-pres. pub. issues and mktg., St. John's Mercy Medical Center, St. Louis, MO '63 (PR)
RHYNE, CAROLYN, RN, adm. dir. critical care, Utah Valley Regional Medical Center, Provo, UT '87 (NURS)
RIALL, CHARLES T., dir., Operating Room Research Institute, Allendale, NJ '58
RIAN, FRANCIS J., mgr. matl., St. Joseph's Medical Center, Brainerd, MN '68 (PUR)
RIBAUDO, VICTOR, dir. plng. and mktg., Kent General Hospital, Dover, DE '83 (PLNG)
RICCI, DAVID ANTHONY, vice-pres. oper., Abington Memorial Hospital, Abington, PA '79 (PLNG)
RICCI, ROCCO J., Health Education Consortium, Manchester, NH '80 (EDUC)
RICCIARDI, ANN MARIE, coor. nrsg. educ., St. Mary's Hospital, Passaic, NJ '86 (EDUC)
RICCIO, THOMAS R., dir. eng. and maint., Newington Children's Hospital, Newington, CT '86 (ENG)
RICCO, EDWARD, atty., Southwest Community Health Services, Albuquerque, NM '82 (ATTY)
RICE-COPLIN, KAREN J., RN, dir. nrsg., Haemo-Stat, Inc., North Hollywood, CA '85 (NURS)
RICE, ALAN J., vice-pres., Adventist Health System/west, Roseville, CA '82 (PLNG)
RICE, ALFRED L., dir. plant oper., Woodland Memorial Hospital, Woodland, CA '81 (ENG)
RICE, ALMA P., dir. nutr. serv., University Hospital of Arkansas, Little Rock, AR '87 (FOOD)
RICE, BARBARA B., supv. cent. serv., Sewickley Valley Hospital, Sewickley, PA '85 (CS)
RICE, BETTY JEAN, coor. pat. and guest rel., Akron General Medical Center, Akron, OH '84 (PAT)
RICE, C. WAYNE, pres., Greater Cleveland Hospital Association, Cleveland, OH '65
RICE, DAVID J., atty., Rush-Presbyterian-St. Luke's Medical Center, Chicago, IL '85 (ATTY)
RICE, DON A., adm. new bus. dev., Comprehensive Health Service of Detroit, Inc., Detroit, MI '86 (PLNG)
RICE, EDWARD P., dir. commun. rel. and mktg., Millinocket Regional Hospital, Millinocket, ME '86 (PR)
RICE, EVERETT E., syst. analyst, Mayo Clinic, Rochester, MN '83 (MGMT)
RICE, HARRY G., dir. biomedical eng., Church Charity Foundation of Long Island, Hempstead, NY '77 (ENG)
RICE, HELEN R., dir. nrsg. educ., Labette County Medical Center, Parsons, KS '86 (EDUC)
RICE, JAMES A., pres., Health Central International, Minneapolis, MN '79 (PLNG)
RICE, JAMES D., vice-pres. pub. affairs and commun., Research Health Services, Kansas City, MO '79 (PR)
RICE, JAMES LELAND JR., assoc. dir., Indiana University Hospitals, Indianapolis, IN '57 (LIFE)
RICE, JAMES WEBSTER, atty., ARA Services, Inc., Houston, TX '79 (ATTY)
RICE, JOHN C., vice-pres. pers., Milwaukee Psychiatric Hospital, Milwaukee, WI '86 (PERS)
RICE, JOHN M., dir. emp. rel., Mount Carmel Mercy Hospital, Detroit, MI '84 (PERS)
RICE, JOHN T., asst. dir. plant oper. and maint., St. Mary's Medical Center, Duluth, MN '84 (ENG)
RICE, JOHN T., asst. coor. and mgr. nrsg., Goldwater Memorial Hospital, New York, NY '85
RICE, JUDITH M., vice-pres., William Collins Associates Public Relations, Buffalo, NY '77 (PR)
RICE, KATHY A., dir. pers., Spaulding Rehabilitation Hospital, Boston, MA '84 (PERS)
RICE, KATIE SEAY, dir. pub. rel., Mary Black Memorial Hospital, Spartanburg, SC '80 (PR)(VOL)
RICE, LINDA DARBY, dir. emp. and labor rel., Evergreen Hospital Medical Center, Kirkland, WA '80 (PERS)
RICE, LYDIA ANN, Long Beach, MS '81
RICE, MARGARET A., coor. staff dev., Elliot Hospital, Manchester, NH '81 (EDUC)
RICE, NANCY K., chief ped. soc. worker, Strong Memorial Hospital of the University of Rochester, Rochester, NY '71 (SOC)
RICE, PATRICIA, dir. vol. serv., Palos Community Hospital, Palos Heights, IL '79 (VOL)
RICE, S. ILENE, RN, vice-pres. pat. serv., Good Shepherd Medical Center, Longview, TX '82 (NURS)
RICE, WILLIAM RUSSELL, atty., Jackson-Madison County General Hospital, Jackson, TN '73 (ATTY)
RICE, WILLIAM W., pres., W. W. Rice and Associates, Inc., Alexandria, VA '85 (PUR)
RICH, ANN SCHROERING, mgt. consult., Tribrook Group, Inc., Oak Brook, IL '76
RICH, BEN ARTHUR, atty., University of Colorado Health Sciences Center, Denver, CO '84 (ATTY)
RICH, CHARLES E., dir. risk mgt., Hospital for Sick Children, Washington, DC '78 (RISK)
RICH, DARLENE S., dir. pers., United Memorial Hospital, Greenville, MI '84 (PERS)
RICH, EDWARD M., dir., Jannx Medical Systems, Inc., St. Louis, MO '81 (ENG)
RICH, ELLEN C., vice-pres. mktg. and plng., Saint Vincent Hospital and Health Center, Billings, MT '85 (PLNG)
RICH, GARVIS GENE, staff planner, University of Alabama Hospital, Birmingham, AL '80 (PLNG)
RICH, JERRY, dir. matl. mgt., Deaconess Hospital, Oklahoma City, OK '84 (PUR)
RICH, SHARI, dir. soc. serv., Bethany Medical Center, Kansas City, KS '75 (SOC)
RICH, SHARON L., dir., St. John's Healthcare Corporation, Anderson, IN '86 (AMB)
RICH, TIMOTHY J., mgr. oper., Good Samaritan Medical Center, Phoenix, AZ '86 (CS)
RICHARD, CHARLENE J., dir. pers., Harrington Memorial Hospital, Southbridge, MA '74 (PERS)
RICHARD, DONALD C., dir. food serv., Glens Falls Hospital, Glens Falls, NY '85 (FOOD)
RICHARD, J. EDWARD JR., dir. eng., Baystate Medical Center, Springfield, MA '79 (ENG)
RICHARD, MARY ANN HOLLOWAY, atty., Presbyterian Hospital, Oklahoma City, OK '74 (ATTY)
RICHARD, STEVEN ROGER, dir. matl. mgt., Jamestown Hospital, Jamestown, ND '86 (PUR)
RICHARDI, DANIEL G., adm. health serv., County of Marin, San Rafael, CA '61
RICHARDS, ANNETTA K., dir. diet. dept., Fillmore County Hospital, Geneva, NE '84 (FOOD)
RICHARDS, BARBARA E., dir. soc. serv., San Joaquin General Hospital, Stockton, CA '77 (SOC)
RICHARDS, CHARLES H., dir. pub. rel., Venice Hospital, Venice, FL '73 (PR)
RICHARDS, CLARA D., RN, instr. in-service, St. Joseph Riverside Hospital, Warren, OH '74 (EDUC)
RICHARDS, DOUGLAS, atty., Springfield Hospital, Springfield, VT '81 (ATTY)
RICHARDS, EARL G., arch. facil. plng., Kaiser Foundation Hospitals, Los Angeles, CA '71
RICHARDS, EDWARD A., dir., St. Vincent Hospital, Green Bay, WI '79 (ENG)
RICHARDS, JAN D., RN, dir. pat. care serv., Baptist Medical Center of Oklahoma, Oklahoma City, OK '85 (NURS)
RICHARDS, JIM, risk mgr., King's Daughters' Hospital, Staunton, VA '86 (RISK)

RICHARDS, JOAN K., RN, vice-pres. nrsg. serv., Crozer-Chester Medical Center, Chester, PA '86 (NURS)
RICHARDS, JOANN, RN, dir. nrsg., Harrison Community Hospital, Mount Clemens, MI '86 (NURS)
RICHARDS, LYNN E., atty., Brown Memorial Hospital, Conneaut, OH '69 (ATTY)
RICHARDS, MARGARET M., dir. pers. and pub. rel., Holden Hospital, Holden, MA '86 (PERS)(PR)
RICHARDS, MINDY L., asst. adm., Oakwood Hospital, Dearborn, MI '82
RICHARDS, PAMELA C., asst. vice-pres., Hutcheson Medical Center, Fort Oglethorpe, GA '78
RICHARDS, RONALD L., asst. dir. matl. mgt., Grossmont District Hospital, La Mesa, CA '83 (PUR)
RICHARDS, WANDA, dir. environ. serv., Riverside Community Hospital, Riverside, CA '86 (ENVIRON)
RICHARDS, WILLIAM R., mng. dir., Harris Methodist Health System, Fort Worth, TX '80
RICHARDSON, BEN J., consult., Risk Management Services, Decatur, GA '86 (RISK)
RICHARDSON, BESSIE G., RN, dir. nrsg. serv., Grace Cottage Hospital, Townshend, VT '84 (NURS)
RICHARDSON, C. H. JR., trustee and atty., Baptist Hospital Highlands, Louisville, KY '74 (ATTY)
RICHARDSON, CHARLES A., Boca Raton, FL '45 (LIFE)
RICHARDSON, CONNIE L., dir. staff dev. and pat. educ., Greenville Regional Hospital, Greenville, PA '82 (EDUC)
RICHARDSON, D. NIKKI, vice-pres. commun. rel., Milton Medical Center, Milton, MA '85 (PR)
RICHARDSON, DANIEL G., dir. food serv., Lester E. Cox Medical Centers, Springfield, MO '86 (FOOD)
RICHARDSON, DONALD V., atty., Richland Memorial Hospital, Columbia, SC '74 (ATTY)
RICHARDSON, DOROTHY, dir. hskpg., St. John's Mercy Hospital, Washington, MO '86 (ENVIRON)
RICHARDSON, HON. ELLIOT L., Washington, DC '70 (HON)
RICHARDSON, GERALD M., atty., Barnes Hospital, St. Louis, MO '83 (ATTY)
RICHARDSON, GLADYS, (ret.), Akron, OH '69 (VOL)
RICHARDSON, GREGG S., dir. gen. serv., Hurley Medical Center, Flint, MI '83 (PUR)
RICHARDSON, IRENE, dir. educ. and trng., St. Clare's Hospital, Denville, NJ '83 (EDUC)
RICHARDSON, JACQUE W., dir. soc. work, Mullins Hospital, Mullins, SC '82 (SOC)
RICHARDSON, JAMES W., adm. risk mgt., Samaritan Health Service, Phoenix, AZ '84 (RISK)
RICHARDSON, JON S., atty., Elliot Hospital, Manchester, NH '81 (ATTY)
RICHARDSON, JOY F., exec. dir., Eastern Veterans Administration Medical Authority, Norfolk, VA '86 (EDUC)
RICHARDSON, KITTY J., asst. dir. pub. rel., Texoma Medical Center, Denison, TX '86 (PR)
RICHARDSON, LAWRENCE R., vice-pres. prof. serv., Columbia Hospital, Milwaukee, WI '82 (PLNG)
RICHARDSON, MARK MUNRO, partner, Flr Health Resources, Atlanta, GA '79 (PLNG)
RICHARDSON, MARVIN E., chief eng., Roseville Community Hospital, Roseville, CA '70 (ENG)
RICHARDSON, MELISSA B., dir. mktg. and pub. rel., Wyman Park Medical Center, Baltimore, MD '84 (PR)
RICHARDSON, PATRICIA ELLEN, RN, dir. nrsg. serv., Warren Memorial Hospital, Front Royal, VA '76 (NURS)
RICHARDSON, ROBERT C., dir. hosp. activ., Medical Sterilization, Inc., Syosset, NY '78 (CS)
RICHARDSON, ROSS, Doctor's Management Company, Santa Monica, CA '84 (RISK)
RICHARDSON, STEPHEN L., supv. maint., Riverside Medical Center, Franklinton, LA '81 (ENG)
RICHARDSON, VIRGINIA G., med. pub. affairs consult., Guilford, CT '72 (PR)
RICHARDSON, WILLIAM TRAVIS, adm., Bulloch Memorial Hospital, Statesboro, GA '76
RICHARDT, ERIC, proj. coor., The Weisenbach Architects, Seattle, WA '85 (ENG)
RICHEL, WILLIAM, vice-pres. mgt. info., St. Luke's-Roosevelt Hospital Center, New York, NY '71 (MGMT)
RICHER, EUGENE D., supv. maint., Conejos County Hospital, La Jara, CO '83 (ENG)
RICHER, GARY, dir. biomedical and clin. eng., Arnot-Ogden Memorial Hospital, Elmira, NY '86 (ENG)
RICHEY, BARBARA A., asst. dir. soc. work, Temple University Hospital, Philadelphia, PA '82 (SOC)
RICHEY, DON L., adm., Guadalupe Valley Hospital, Seguin, TX '75
RICHEY, LINDA, dir. risk mgt. and qual. assur., Saint Mary Hospital, Langhorne, PA '86 (RISK)
RICHEY, WIN R., atty., Alta Bates Hospital, Berkeley, CA '83 (ATTY)
RICHINS, SUZANNE, RN, dir. surg. center, Intermountain Health Care, Inc., Salt Lake City, UT '87 (AMB)
RICHMAN, DONNALINE, counselor risk mgt., Donald J. Fager Associates, Inc., Syracuse, NY '85 (RISK)
RICHMAN, HENRY, exec. dir., Interfaith Medical Center-Brooklyn, Brooklyn, NY '68
RICHMAN, MITCHELL L., adm., Stenton Hall Nursing-Convalescent Home, Philadelphia, PA '84
RICHMOND, CHARLES A., asst. dir., Indiana University Hospitals, Indianapolis, IN '71
RICHMOND, CORA A., mgr. pur., Emerson Hospital, Concord, MA '85 (PUR)
RICHMOND, EVELYN M., RN, dir. nrsg. serv., Bannock County Nursing Home, Pocatello, ID '79 (NURS)
RICHMOND, JACK A., vice-pres. human res., St. Mary-Corwin Hospital Center, Pueblo, CO '81 (PERS)
RICHMOND, JOSEPH W. JR., atty., Martha Jefferson Hospital, Charlottesville, VA '77 (ATTY)
RICHMOND, KENNETH ARNOLD, sr. assoc., Keiffer, Ford, Chicago, IL '69
RICHMOND, LOIS, RN, asst. vice-pres., Bronson Methodist Hospital, Kalamazoo, MI '86 (NURS)
RICHMOND, ROBERT L., mgr. cent. serv., Central Florida Regional Hospital, Sanford, FL '85 (CS)
RICHTARSIC, CAROL S., dir. med. soc. serv., Cuyahoga County Hospitals-Sunny Acres Skilled Nursing Facilities, Warrensville, OH '82 (SOC)
RICHTER-ZEUNIK, MARY M., RN, adm. asst. to vice-pres. nrsg., Grant Hospital of Chicago, Chicago, IL '83
RICHTER, BONNIE, RN, nrs. supv., University of Minnesota Hospital and Clinic, Minneapolis, MN '87 (AMB)
RICHTER, DEBORAH A., dir. soc. serv., Kewanee Public Hospital, Kewanee, IL '86 (SOC)
RICHTER, TODD B., securities analyst, Morgan Stanley and Company, Inc., New York, NY '82
RICHWAGEN, JOHN P., Steamboat Springs, CO '58 (MGMT)
RICHWALSKY, MARIBETH C., sr. mgt. analyst, Miami Valley Hospital, Dayton, OH '85 (MGMT)
RICHWINE, ANITA, dir. pub. rel., Kettering Medical Center, Kettering, OH '77 (PR)
RICKARD, CHARLES M., asst. to vice-pres. facil. dev., Kaiser Foundation Health Plan, Inc., Oakland, CA '80 (ENG)
RICKARD, DIANE L., coor. staff dev., Western Reserve Systems-Northside, Youngstown, OH '82 (EDUC)
RICKEL, GREGORY H., student, University of Arkansas at Little Rock, Little Rock, AR '83 (PERS)
RICKER, JEAN H., asst. dir. food serv., Bon Secours Hospital, Grosse Pointe, MI '80 (FOOD)
RICKETT, SHIRLEY A., RN, coor. sterile proc., Northeast Medical Center Hospital, Humble, TX '85 (CS)
RICKEY, MARJORIE P., coor. food prod., Hamilton Hospital, Hamilton, NJ '86 (FOOD)
RICKLE, SR. ANNE WILLIAM, adm. asst. qual. assur. and risk mgt., St. Agnes Hospital, Baltimore, MD '83 (RISK)
RICKMAN, BOB N., mgr. matl., Newnan Hospital, Newnan, GA '74 (PUR)
RICKS, CHARLES S., vice-pres., Adventist Health System, Arlington, TX '82
RICKS, SIDNEY F. JR., supv. matl. distrib. serv., Fairfax Hospital, Falls Church, VA '87 (PUR)
RICKSECKER, ROBERT S., atty., Galion Community Hospital, Galion, OH '68 (ATTY)
RICKSON, LOIS G., dir. pers., Westerly Hospital, Westerly, RI '77 (PERS)
RICKWOOD, PATRICIA KIM, dir. pub. rel., Mercy Health Services, Charlotte, NC '87 (PR)
RICZKO, JOHN A., exec. dir., Passaic Valley Professional Standards Review Organization, Wayne, NJ '85
RICZO, STEVE, vice-pres. mgt., Lutheran Medical Center, Cleveland, OH '80
RIDDELL, DAVID C., dir. pur., Charleston Area Medical Center, Charleston, WV '86 (PUR)
RIDDELL, ROBERT C., atty., Methodist Hospital of Indiana, Indianapolis, IN '81 (ATTY)
RIDDELL, TALLY D. SR., atty., H. C. Watkins Memorial Hospital, Quitman, MS '77 (ATTY)
RIDDER, EDNA LAVONNE, dir. educ., Liberty Hospital, Liberty, MO '86 (EDUC)
RIDDLE, CHARLOTTE J., assoc. dir. diet. serv., Meriter Hospital, Madison, WI '81 (FOOD)
RIDDLE, JOHN L., dir. soc. work serv., Hillcrest Medical Center, Tulsa, OK '84 (SOC)
RIDEN, THOMAS K., atty., Humana Hospital-Northside, St. Petersburg, FL '81 (ATTY)
RIDEOUT, JOHN B., RN, dir. nrs., Danvers State Hospital, Hathorne, MA '68 (NURS)
RIDER, GEORGE, exec. vice-pres. and chief oper. off., St. Joseph's Hospital, Parkersburg, WV '78
RIDER, MARY ELLEN, RN, vice-pres. nrsg., Bristol Memorial Hospital, Bristol, TN '83 (NURS)
RIDGE, RICHARD A., dir. pers., Mary Washington Hospital, Fredericksburg, VA '79 (PERS)
RIDGEWAY, DEBBIE, pur. agt., St. Francis Hospital, Greenville, SC '84 (PUR)
RIDGEWAY, LOIS, mgr. pur., St. Mary's Hospital, Athens, GA '83 (PUR)
RIDGWAY, MALCOLM G., PhD, vice-pres., Health Resources Institute Engineering Service, Van Nuys, CA '74 (ENG)
RIDINGER, KATHERINE M., dir. soc. work serv., Columbia Hospital for Women, Washington, DC '83 (SOC)
RIDLEY-JOHNSON, SYLVIA A., dir. amb. care, Orlando Regional Medical Center, Orlando, FL '87 (AMB)
RIDLEY, ELTON T., assoc. prof., Indiana University School of Medicine, Indianapolis, IN '51 (LIFE)
RIDLEY, GORDON T., assoc. supt., University of Wisconsin Hospital and Clinics, Madison, WI '77
RIDLEY, LARRY, mgr. facil., St. Vincent Medical Center, Los Angeles, CA '81 (ENG)
RIDLEY, MARY ANN, dir. soc. serv., Oak Forest Hospital of Cook County, Oak Forest, IL '72 (SOC)
RIDLEY, RAYMOND C., dir. eng., Spohn Kleberg Memorial Hospital, Kingsville, TX '80 (ENG)
RIDLEY, SUSAN J., asst. dir. diet., St. Marys Hospital Medical Center, Madison, WI '84 (FOOD)
RIDOUT, DAVID A., dir. pharm. and pur., Ferguson Hospital, Grand Rapids, MI '81 (PUR)
RIEB, BORIVOJ JAN EMIL, consult., Hospitalia International, Frankfurt, Germany '70
RIECKMAN, LOIS E., adm. medicine, Memorial Hospital for Cancer and Allied Diseases, New York, NY '67
RIEDEL, DANA D., dir. pers., McKenna Memorial Hospital, New Braunfels, TX '86 (PERS)
RIEDER, JAMES L., pres. and chief exec. off., Horizon Health Systems, Oak Park, MI '64
RIEDINGER, MARK, dir. diversified serv., Christ Hospital, Cincinnati, OH '80
RIEFKOHL, SSGT VICTOR M., MSC USAF, mgr. facil., U. S. Air Force Hospital, Yokota, Japan '86 (ENG)
RIEG, LINDA S., RN, dir. pat. serv., Shriners Burns Institute, Cincinnati, OH '79 (NURS)
RIEGER, ELAINE J., RN, dir. nrs., St. John's Regional Medical Center, Oxnard, CA '85 (NURS)
RIEGER, JOSEPH, dir. eng. serv., Alta Bates Hospital, Berkeley, CA '67 (ENG)
RIEGER, KAREN S., atty., Baptist Medical Center of Oklahoma, Oklahoma City, OK '85 (ATTY)
RIEHLE, KAAREN J., dir. prof. rel., Providence Hospital, Anchorage, AK '80 (PLNG)
RIEHS, STEVEN P., sr. mgt. analyst, Rush-Presbyterian-St. Luke's Medical Center, Chicago, IL '85 (MGMT)
RIEKE, SUSAN E., dir. educ. serv., Burnham Hospital, Champaign, IL '84 (EDUC)
RIEL, EVELYN J., asst. dir. matl. mgt., San Antonio Community Hospital, Upland, CA '80 (PUR)
RIEMANN, VERA D., adm. food serv., Southwest Health Center, Platteville, WI '77 (FOOD)
RIEMER, JOYCE, staff assoc., Blue Cross and Blue Shield of Greater New York, New York, NY '84
RIEMER, WILLIAM EDWARD, MD, path., Baptist Hospital of Miami, Miami, FL '63
RIENIETS, GARY, dir. qual. work life, Mercy Health Center, Dubuque, IA '71 (PERS)
RIENZO, PATRICIA G., RN, dir. nrsg. serv., New London Hospital, New London, NH '86 (NURS)
RIES, MARY ELLEN D., mgr. food prod., Pennsylvania Hospital, Philadelphia, PA '80 (FOOD)
RIES, WILLIAM A., pres., William A. Ries and Associates, Kitty Hawk, NC '83 (PR)
RIESS, HOWARD, mgr. oper., Rochester Methodist Hospital, Rochester, MN '86 (ENG)
RIESZ, GEORGE J., exec. dir., AMI Rancho Encino Hospital, Encino, CA '54 (LIFE)
RIFAS, ELLENE M., RN, dir. educ., American River Hospital, Carmichael, CA '86 (EDUC)
RIFE, JEANNE B., dir. mktg. commun., Mercy Hospital, Toledo, OH '86 (PR)
RIFFEL, EDITH A., pat. rep., Pleasant Valley Hospital, Camarillo, CA '85 (PAT)
RIFKIN, GENE C., Palm City, FL '72 (SOC)
RIGATTI, JAMES R., dir. pur., Community Hospital of Roanoke Valley, Roanoke, VA '84 (PUR)
RIGBY, JAMES B., vice-pres., Memorial Medical Center, Springfield, IL '69
RIGGALL, RODNEY, (ret.), Prairie Grove, AR '65 (LIFE)
RIGGS, LAWRENCE, dir. diet., Brunswick General Hospital, Amityville, NY '71 (FOOD)
RIGGS, LEW, EdD, prin., The Lew Riggs Company, Phoenix, AZ '74 (PR)
RIGNEY, CORAL L., med. dist. coor., Veterans Administration Medical Center, Castle Point, NY '75
RIGNEY, JUDY, supv. cent. serv., Welborn Memorial Baptist Hospital, Evansville, IN '84 (CS)
RIGNEY, JULIE MICHELLE, asst. dir. mktg., Charter Brook Hospital, Atlanta, GA '86 (PR) (PLNG)
RIGNEY, NANCY, dir. vol. serv., Mercy Catholic Medical Center, Darby, PA '76 (VOL)
RIGOT, LEAH J., dir. pers. serv., Highland Park Hospital, Miami, FL '86 (PERS)
RIGSBY, DEBORAH G., pat. rep., Veterans Administration Medical Center, Lexington, KY '87 (PAT)
RIGSBY, JAMES E., pres., Jerico Telecommunications Consulting, Inc., Columbus, OH '79 (ENG)
RIGSBY, RAYMOND E., supt. bldg., Southern Hills Hospital, Portsmouth, OH '84 (ENG)
RIHN, JOSEPH A. JR., dir. eng., Polyclinic Medical Center, Harrisburg, PA '84 (ENG)
RIINA, DANIEL CHARLES, asst. adm., Norfolk General Hospital, Norfolk, VA '79
RIISAGER, CHRIS K., plant eng., Tuomey Hospital, Sumter, SC '83 (ENG)
RIKER, DENNIS E., dir. plng., St. Mary's Hospital Medical Center, Green Bay, WI '82 (PLNG)
RIKER, JOAN L., dir. nrsg. serv., Newton Memorial Hospital, Newton, NJ '73 (NURS)
RIKER, MARY LOU, RN, asst. dir. nrsg. serv., Malden Hospital, Malden, MA '79 (NURS)
RILEE, DIANE R., dir. vol. and adm. coor., Walter Reed Memorial Hospital, Gloucester, VA '83 (VOL)
RILEY, BELLE, coor. vol. serv., Walter O. Boswell Memorial Hospital, Sun City, AZ '86 (VOL)
RILEY, CATHERINE A., generic screening analyst, North Memorial Medical Center, Robbinsdale, MN '84 (RISK)
RILEY, CHRISTOPHER, asst. dir. bldg. serv., McLean Hospital, Belmont, MA '86 (ENVIRON)
RILEY, DONALD R., dir. constr. and maint., Children's Mercy Hospital, Kansas City, MO '85 (ENG)
RILEY, GLORIA D., dir. biomedical eng., Boston City Hospital, Boston, MA '86 (ENG)
RILEY, HERMAN, dir. hskpg. and ldry., Terre Haute Regional Hospital, Terre Haute, IN '86 (ENVIRON)
RILEY, JAMES B. JR., atty., Rush-Presbyterian-St. Luke's Medical Center, Chicago, IL '85 (ATTY)
RILEY, JEAN A., RN, dir. extended care and commun., Scott and White Memorial Hospital, Temple, TX '86 (NURS)
RILEY, KAREN E., dir. environ. serv., St. John's Lutheran Hospital, Libby, MT '86 (ENVIRON)
RILEY, MAMIE L., dir. hskpg., Bascom Palmer Eye Institute and Hospital, Miami, FL '86 (ENVIRON)
RILEY, MAVIS P., dir. soc. serv., Newberry County Memorial Hospital, Newberry, SC '86 (SOC)
RILEY, PAMELA JEANNE, adm. diet., Riverside Methodist Hospitals, Columbus, OH '77 (FOOD)
RILEY, PATRICIA A., Blue Cross of Massachusetts, Boston, MA '75
RILEY, PATTY A., coor. pub. rel., Fairmont General Hospital, Fairmont, WV '86 (PR) (PLNG)
RILEY, PAUL B., dir. pers., Mountain View Medical Center, Simi Valley, CA '86 (PERS)
RILEY, PAUL, dir. environ. serv., New England Sinai Hospital, Stoughton, MA '87 (ENVIRON)
RILEY, RICHARD E., chief exec. off., Chenango Memorial Hospital, Norwich, NY '72
RILEY, SHIRLEY K., dir. diet., Palomar Memorial Hospital, Escondido, CA '82 (FOOD)
RILEY, STEVENS L., atty., Luther Hospital, Eau Claire, WI '78 (ATTY)

RILEY, THOMAS K., dir. maint., Pontiac General Hospital, Pontiac, MI '86 (ENG)
RILEY, TIMOTHY J., mgr. matl., Appleton Medical Center, Appleton, WI '80 (PUR)
RILEY, TIMOTHY P., dir. pub. rel., Flower Memorial Hospital, Sylvania, OH '86 (PR)
RILEY, VERNETTE, RN, vice-pres., Mercy Hospital Medical Center, Des Moines, IA '79 (NURS)
RILEY, WILLIAM J., sr. assoc. dir., St. Paul-Ramsey Medical Center, St. Paul, MN '81 (PLNG)
RILEY, WILLIAM T., dir. eng. and maint., St. Peter's Hospital, Albany, NY '75 (ENG)
RILL, ROGER A., vice-pres., Hospital Association of Central Ohio, Dublin, OH '78
RIMAKIS, VALENTINA, asst. dir. pers., Community Memorial Hospital, Toms River, NJ '83 (PERS)
RIMLER, MARSHA S., assoc. dir. soc. serv., Metropolitan Hospital Center, New York, NY '87 (SOC)
RIMMER, MURRAY, adm., Gracie Square Hospital, New York, NY '72
RINALDI, ANTHONY J. JR., contr., Hillcrest Hospital, Pittsfield, MA '85 (PLNG)
RINALDI, NICHOLAS, dir. eng., Booth Memorial Medical Center, Flushing, NY '86 (ENG)
RINALDO, JOSEPH A. JR., MD, dir., Providence Hospital, Southfield, MI '66
RINAS, DEBBIE L., RN, dir. med. and surg. serv., Independence Regional Health Center, Independence, MO '86 (NURS)
RINDE, ANDREW S., pres., Rinde Enterprises, Phoenix, AZ '69 (MGMT)
RINDE, MARY JAYNE, dir. vol., St. Joseph Hospital, Kirkwood, MO '83 (VOL)
RINDER, CARL T., coor. plng., Children's Memorial Hospital, Chicago, IL '82 (PLNG)
RINDNER, EDNA, vice-pres. mktg., North Kansas City Hospital, North Kansas City, MO '84 (PLNG)
RINE, CHRISTINE, coor. soc. serv., East Ohio Regional Hospital, Martins Ferry, OH '80 (SOC)
RINE, WILLIAM E., mgr. sup., University Hospital, Augusta, GA '86 (CS)
RINEHART, JO ANN, pur. agt., St. Luke's Hospital, Bethlehem, PA '83 (PUR)
RINEHIMER, ROBERT E., consult., Health Insurance Administration, Camp Hill, PA '82 (LIFE)
RINELL, MARIE J., dir. food serv., Lutheran Social Services, Jamestown, NY '75 (FOOD)
RINES, JUDITH A., mgr. matl., Exeter Hospital, Exeter, NH '82 (CS)
RING, G. STARR W., dir. soc. serv., Lexington County Hospital, West Columbia, SC '73 (SOC)
RING, RITA M., dir. vol. serv., North Memorial Medical Center, Robbinsdale, MN '84 (VOL)
RINGER, JOHN WILLIAM, atty., Dexter Memorial Hospital, Dexter, MO '84 (ATTY)
RINGER, MARLENE V., RN, corp. nrs., Adventist Health System, Hayesville, NC '86 (NURS)
RINGER, TERENCE T., dir. eng. and maint., Lahey Clinic Hospital, Burlington, MA '82 (ENG)
RINGERMAN, EILEEN S., RN, asst. dir., Providence Hospital, Oakland, CA '81 (NURS)
RINGL, KAREN K., RN, assoc. chairperson, Glenbrook Hospital, Glenview, IL '81 (NURS)
RINGLER, JULIE A., dir. pers., Samaritan Hospital, Ashland, OH '86 (PERS)
RINGO, WILLIAM P., PhD, vice-pres., Jewish Hospital, Louisville, KY '80 (PLNG)
RINGWALD, JOHN F., supv. eng., South Miami Hospital, South Miami, FL '84 (ENG)
RINI, JOSEPH C., dir. matl. mgt., Hillcrest Hospital, Mayfield Heights, OH '73 (PUR)
RINIKER, BARBARA A., dir. nutr. serv., Shriners Hospital for Crippled Children, Minneapolis, MN '86 (FOOD)
RINIKER, JOSEPH WILLIAM, dir. safety and plant serv., Memorial Hospital, Manhattan, KS '76 (ENG)
RINKE, LYNN T., dir. home care accreditation, National League for Nursing, New York, NY '87 (AMB)
RINKER, FRANKLIN M., adm., Gwinnett Hospital System, Lawrenceville, GA '70
RINKER, GEORGE A., atty., Lafayette Home Hospital, Lafayette, IN '68 (ATTY)
RIOFSKI, GERTRUDE M., dir. vol. serv., Riverside Hospital, Jacksonville, FL '83 (VOL)
RIOJAS, MARGARITO I., chief eng., Southeast Baptist Hospital, San Antonio, TX '83 (ENG)
RIOLO, MARY MICHOS, dir. soc. work, Jamestown General Hospital, Jamestown, NY '84 (SOC)
RIORDAN, CAROL JAY, PhD, proj. dir., Stanford Medical School, M. 121, Stanford, CA '85
RIORDAN, M. LUCILLE, RN, vice-pres. nrsg., Mercy Center for Health Care Services, Aurora, IL '71 (NURS)
RIOS, JOSEPH ANTHONY, supt. bldg. and grds., Kaiser Foundation Hospital, Vallejo, CA '85 (ENG)
RIOUX, PATRICK F., coor. commun., St. Francis Health Services, Little Falls, MN '86 (PR)
RIPLEY, FRANCES L., dir. vol. serv., Cuyahoga Falls General Hospital, Cuyahoga Falls, OH '83 (VOL)
RIPP, VIRGINIA L., RN, dir. nrsg. serv., Santiam Memorial Hospital, Stayton, OR '81 (NURS)
RIPPE, ROBERT D., pres., Robert Rippe and Associates, Inc., Minnetonka, MN '82 (FOOD)
RIPPEL, JULIUS A., pres. and dir., Fannie E. Rippel Foundation, Madison, NJ '72 (HON)
RIPPINGER, MARY J., health educ., Saint Joseph Hospital, Elgin, IL '87 (EDUC)
RIPPKE, SUSAN L., med. soc. worker, Good Samaritan Hospital, Kearney, NE '82 (SOC)
RIPPLE, HELEN B., RN, assoc. dir. hosp. and clin., University of California San Francisco, San Francisco, CA '76 (NURS)
RIPSCH, SUE A., RN, dir. maternal-child health, Brokaw Hospital, Normal, IL '86 (NURS)
RISER, JIMMY R., mgt. syst. eng., Humana, Inc., Louisville, KY '74 (MGMT)
RISK, RICHARD R., vice-pres. plng., Evangelical Health Systems, Oak Brook, IL '73 (PLNG)
RISKE, PHIL R., corp. dir. advertising and pub. rel., St. Luke's Health System, Phoenix, AZ '83 (PR)
RISLEY, FERN S., dir. pub. rel., Sherman Hospital, Elgin, IL '65 (PR)
RISLEY, JOHN F., dir. pers., L. W. Blake Memorial Hospital, Bradenton, FL '75 (PERS)
RISLEY, KATHERINE A., RN, dir. nrsg. res., maternal, child and mental health, Morton F. Plant Hospital, Clearwater, FL '84 (NURS)
RISLEY, SUEMMA, RN, Springfield, IL '80 (NURS)
RISLEY, WAINE L., coor. facil. eng., Kaiser Foundation Health Plan of Colorado, Denver, CO '81 (ENG)
RISOR, ROBERT L., adm. asst., Warner Brown Hospital, El Dorado, AR '81 (PR)
RISTAU, DANIEL D., consult., Mercy Midlands, Omaha, NE '77
RISTIG, LYNN E., atty., Valley Medical Center, Renton, WA '86 (ATTY)
RISTINO, ROBERT J., vice-pres. corp. pub. rel., Worcester Memorial Hospital, Worcester, MA '78 (PR)
RISVOLD, ROBERT A., asst. dir. plant serv. and eng., Riverside Medical Center, Kankakee, IL '86 (ENG)
RITCHIE, ALICE A., supv. cent. serv., Dominican Santa Cruz Hospital, Santa Cruz, CA '82 (CS)
RITCHIE, ANN C., dir. pers., St. Anne General Hospital, Raceland, LA '83 (PERS)
RITCHIE, CRAIG H., mgr. pur., St. Mary's Medical Center, Evansville, IN '77 (PUR)
RITCHIE, DONALD, bd. chm., The Ritchie Organization, Chestnut Hill, MA '48 (LIFE)
RITCHIE, J. WAYNE, chief eng., University Hospital, Lexington, KY '83 (ENG)
RITCHIE, JUDITH A., dir. plng., Salem Hospital, Salem, MA '85 (PLNG)
RITT, DAVID C., pat. rep., Jersey Shore Medical Center, Neptune, NJ '87 (PAT)
RITTENHOUSE, BELINDA, actg. dir. pers., Dr. John Warner Hospital, Clinton, IL '82 (PERS)
RITTENHOUSE, JUDITH A., ed., Fdr Publications, Allentown, PA '86 (PR)
RITTENMEYER, PATRICIA ANN MCDANIEL, RN, dir. nrsg. serv., Kaiser-Permanente, Reston, VA '83 (NURS)
RITTER, EUGENE R., dir. plant oper., St. Charles Hospital, Oregon, OH '81 (ENG)
RITTER, MICHAEL W., dir. safety and risk mgr., Lafayette General Medical Center, Lafayette, LA '85 (RISK)
RITTER, RALPH G., dir. plant oper., Union Hospital of Cecil County, Elkton, MD '83 (ENG)
RITTER, RANDALL E., chief eng., Veterans Administration Medical Center, Ann Arbor, MI '81 (ENG)
RITTER, SWANSON A., chief eng., Tri-City Hospital, Oceanside, CA '71 (ENG)
RITTER, WILLIAM G., pres., Permian Medical, Odessa, TX '85 (PUR)
RITTMAN, CHERYL, dir. educ., Spelman Memorial Hospital, Smithville, MO '76 (EDUC)
RITTNER, IRENE C., RN, chief cent. sterile sup., Norwalk Hospital, Norwalk, CT '85 (CS)(PUR)
RITZ, BARBARA, asst. adm., Washington Hospital Center, Washington, DC '87 (AMB)
RITZ, GEORGE J., South Euclid, OH '76 (ENG)
RITZI, CHERYL, Chicago, IL '86 (PUR)
RIVALL, JACK W., Minneapolis, MN '52 (LIFE)
RIVARA, J'MAY B., assoc. dir. soc. work, University Hospital, Seattle, WA '85 (SOC)
RIVARD, JUDITH A., RN, dir. med., surg. and maternal childcare, St. Joseph Hospitals, Mount Clemens, MI '86 (NURS)
RIVENBARK, LOLA S., dir. vol., New Hanover Memorial Hospital, Wilmington, NC '73 (VOL)
RIVENBURG, DENNIS L., dir. pur., Quakertown Community Hospital, Quakertown, PA '82 (PUR)
RIVERA, DAVID A., MD, chief ob. serv., Mercy Hospital, Grayling, MI '85 (RISK)
RIVERA, LUIS A., supv. cent. serv., Thorek Hospital and Medical Center, Chicago, IL '80 (CS)
RIVERA, NORMA I., mgr. human res., Cedar Springs Psychiatric Hospital, Colorado Springs, CO '86 (PERS)
RIVERA, PETE, dir. hskpg. serv., Straub Clinic and Hospital, Honolulu, HI '86 (ENVIRON)
RIVERS, CYNTHIA D., dir. soc. serv., Lakeland Regional Medical Center, Lakeland, FL '86 (SOC)
RIVERS, G. L. B. JR., atty., Roper Hospital, Charleston, SC '75 (ATTY)
RIVERS, JOHN R., prin., Ziegler Cooper, Inc., Houston, TX '86 (ENG)
RIVERS, MARILYN L., dir. pub. rel. and mktg., Wing Memorial Hospital and Medical Centers, Palmer, MA '86 (PR)
RIVERS, WILLIAM GARY, indust. eng., Harris Methodist -Fort Worth, Fort Worth, TX '68 (MGMT)
RIVES, C. WILSON, dir. pers. serv., Southside Regional Medical Center, Petersburg, VA '69 (PERS)
RIVEST, JEFFREY A., adm., Children Medical and Surgical Center, Johns Hopkins Hospital, Baltimore, MD '77
RIVET, JEANNINE M., RN, vice-pres., Peak Health Plan and Costguard, Colorado Springs, CO '83 (NURS)
RIVET, SUSAN K., RN, coor. cent. serv., St. Joseph Hospital, Providence, RI '86 (CS)
RIVETT, GWENDOLYN D., coor. vol., Commonwealth Hospital, Fairfax, VA '86 (VOL)
RIVIR, VALERIE L., coor. dev., Children's Psychiatric Hospital, Covington, KY '87 (PR)
RIVKIN, WILLIAM B., physicist and tech. dir. nuclear med., Jackson Park Hospital, Chicago, IL '77
RIXEY, GARY R., dir. eng. serv., Sierra Vista Hospital, Truth Or Consequences, NM '78 (ENG)
RIZAN, JANET W., dir. emer. and prompt care, Georgia Baptist Medical Center, Atlanta, GA '87 (AMB)
RIZK, DAVID W., sr. meth. analyst, University of Massachusetts Medical Center, Worcester, MA '86 (MGMT)
RIZK, MARY STUART, assoc. dir. commun. rel., Capitol Hill Hospital, Washington, DC '85 (PR)
RIZZI, JAMES, dir. fin. serv., Sisters of St. Mary, St. Louis, MO '78
RIZZO, ANTHONY, asst. vice-pres. plant oper., Good Samaritan Hospital, West Islip, NY '69 (ENG)
RIZZO, MARYANN G., asst. dir. pur., South Shore Hospital, South Weymouth, MA '86 (PUR)
RIZZO, ROBERT F. JR., adm. mgr. surg., New England Medical Center, Boston, MA '79
RIZZO, THERESA M., dir. vol. serv., Beth Israel Medical Center, New York, NY '87 (VOL)
RIZZOLO, FRANCIS J., exec. dir., Shirley Frank Foundation, New Haven, CT '84
ROACH, DANIEL T., atty., Millard Fillmore Hospital, Buffalo, NY '79 (ATTY)
ROACH, DAVID R., dir. clin. eng., St. Francis Hospital, Blue Island, IL '83 (ENG)
ROACH, DONNA SOKOLIS, health care res. assoc., Heidrick and Struggles, Chicago, IL '84
ROACH, GERALD F., atty., Our Lady of Lourdes Health Center, Pasco, WA '86 (ATTY)
ROACH, JEAN, asst. dir., College of St. Francis, Joliet, IL '83
ROACH, KAY L., RN, dir. nrsg. staff dev., Bethesda Hospital, Zanesville, OH '86 (NURS)
ROACH, MARGARET E., dir. diet., Evergreen Hospital Medical Center, Kirkland, WA '80 (FOOD)
ROACH, MARY, student, Loyola University of Chicago, Chicago, IL '84 (RISK)
ROACH, NANCY K., dir. vol. serv., Lexington Memorial Hospital, Lexington, NC '86 (VOL)
ROACH, WILLIAM H. JR., vice-pres. legal affairs, Rush-Presbyterian-St. Luke's Medical Center, Chicago, IL '76 (ATTY)
ROACHE, ROBERT F., dir. eng. and maint., Albert Einstein Medical Center, Northern Division, Philadelphia, PA '76 (ENG)
ROARK, BOBBY J., coor. commun., Charter Community Hospital of Cleveland, Cleveland, TX '83 (PR)
ROARK, J. PAUL, dir. mgt. syst., Nashville Memorial Hospital, Madison, TN '71 (MGMT)
ROARK, ROBERT R., dir. pers., Laughlin Memorial Hospital, Greeneville, TN '80 (PERS)
ROBB, BEVERLY J., mgr. pub. rel., Saint Joseph Hospital, Fort Worth, TX '84 (PR)
ROBB, CHARLES A., (ret.), Charleston, SC '54 (LIFE)
ROBB, DUNCAN C., dir. soc. serv., Central Vermont Medical Center, Berlin, VT '73 (SOC)
ROBB, PETER E., asst. adm., Straub Clinic and Hospital, Honolulu, HI '86 (PERS)
ROBBINS, CARLA S., dir. pers., HCA Regional Hospital of Jackson, Jackson, TN '82 (PERS)
ROBBINS, CHARLES R., sr. consult., Ernst and Whinney, Richmond, VA '81 (MGMT)
ROBBINS, CHARLIE K., dir. mktg., North Arkansas Medical Center, Harrison, AR '86 (PR)
ROBBINS, DELORIS A., supv. hskpg. and ldry., Hi-Plains Health Center, Burlington, CO '86 (ENVIRON)
ROBBINS, GARY D., pur. agt., Apple River Hospital, Amery, WI '81 (PUR)
ROBBINS, GRETCHEN S., dir. pub. rel., Lutheran Hospital of Fort Wayne, Fort Wayne, IN '86 (PR)
ROBBINS, HAROLD, dir. phys. plant and facil., Parma Community General Hospital, Parma, OH '74 (ENG)
ROBBINS, JUDY A., pers. asst., HCA Regional Hospital -Livingston, Livingston, TN '82 (PERS)
ROBBINS, KAREN L., dir. info. syst., Cook Children's Hospital, Fort Worth, TX '86 (MGMT)
ROBBINS, KENNETH C., atty., Illinois Hospital Association, Naperville, IL '76 (ATTY)
ROBBINS, LAUREN, dir. nrsg. and surg. serv., Good Samaritan Hospital, Cincinnati, OH '84 (AMB)
ROBBINS, MICHAEL A., atty., Bedford Medical Center, Bedford, IN '79 (ATTY)
ROBBINS, PATRICIA B., Dobbs Ferry, NY '81
ROBBINS, RONALD D., supv. eng. and maint., Highlands Hospital and Health Center, Connellsville, PA '87 (ENG)
ROBBINS, STEPHEN A., atty., Sisters of Mercy Health Corporation, Lansing, MI '79 (ATTY)
ROBBINS, TOM, supv. distrib. serv., University of Virginia Hospitals, Charlottesville, VA '86 (ENVIRON)
ROBBINS, VINCENT, dir. sup., proc., and distrib., Temple University Hospital, Philadelphia, PA '86 (PUR)
ROBBINS, WILLIAM T. W., vice-pres. mgt. serv., Texas Hospital Association, Austin, TX '76 (MGMT)
ROBE, KENNETH K., dir. food serv., Allen Memorial Hospital, Waterloo, IA '77 (FOOD)
ROBERDS, SHIRLEY L., RN, vice-pres. nrsg. serv., Mobile Infirmary Medical Center, Mobile, AL '83 (NURS)
ROBERS, MARDI, dir. prog. serv., Cancer Care, Inc., Los Angeles, CA '86 (SOC)
ROBERSON, ANNE, soc. worker, Watertown Memorial Hospital, Watertown, WI '86 (SOC)
ROBERSON, CAROLYN G., coor. commun. rel., William N. Wishard Memorial Hospital, Indianapolis, IN '85 (PR)
ROBERSON, L. A., dir. eng., Nash General Hospital, Rocky Mount, NC '75 (ENG)
ROBERSON, LARRY, exec. dir. pers., Union Medical Center, El Dorado, AR '87 (PERS)
ROBERSON, OLEN, dir. food serv., St. Luke's Medical Center, Phoenix, AZ '77 (FOOD)
ROBERSON, WAYNE, dir. eng., Barton Memorial Hospital, South Lake Tahoe, CA '87 (ENG)
ROBERTS, SR. AGNES ANNE, Sisters of the Holy Cross, Notre Dame, IN '70 (FOOD)
ROBERTS, BEATRICE, RN, nrsg. consult., University of Alabama Hospital, Birmingham, AL '45 (LIFE)
ROBERTS, BRADY W., dir. educ. and trng., Peninsula General Hospital Medical Center, Salisbury, MD '68 (EDUC)

ROBERTS, BRENDA S., RN, dir. nrsg., Hamilton Memorial Hospital, McLeansboro, IL '84 (NURS)
ROBERTS, CAROLINE E., dir. soc. serv., HCA North Beach Hospital, Fort Lauderdale, FL '83 (SOC)
ROBERTS, CAROLYN C., pres., Copley Hospital, Morrisville, VT '81 (RISK)
ROBERTS, CELIA A., coor. qual. assur., Orlando Regional Medical Center, Orlando, FL '83
ROBERTS, CHARLES L., pres., Rehabilitation Centers of America, Inc., Pensacola, FL '84
ROBERTS, CHARLES R., chief soc. work serv., Veterans Administration Wadsworth Medical Center, Los Angeles, CA '83 (SOC)
ROBERTS, CHRISILA LEONA, assoc. dir. risk mgt. and qual. control, Metropolitan Hospital Center, New York, NY '78 (RISK)
ROBERTS, CLAUDETTE L., dir. maternal and child health nrsg., Illinois Masonic Medical Center, Chicago, IL '85 (RISK)
ROBERTS, DAVID C., dir. plng. and mktg., Good Samaritan Medical Center, Phoenix, AZ '74 (PLNG)
ROBERTS, DERRETH C., RN, asst. dir. nrsg. serv. and educ., York Hospital, York, ME '83 (NURS)
ROBERTS, EDWARD J. JR., adm. pub. rel. and vol. serv., Allentown Osteopathic Medical Center, Allentown, PA '80 (PR)
ROBERTS, GERALDINE H., RN, dir. nrsg., Transylvania Community Hospital, Brevard, NC '82 (NURS)
ROBERTS, HUGH O., (ret.), Bethlehem, PA '52 (LIFE)
ROBERTS, IVON E., chief soc. work serv., Veterans Administration Medical Center, Perry Point, MD '72 (SOC)
ROBERTS, JAMES S., MD, asst. vice-pres., Joint Commission on Accreditation of Hospitals, Chicago, IL '80
ROBERTS, JAMES, risk mgr., Swedish American Hospital, Rockford, IL '85 (RISK)
ROBERTS, JANICE ELAINE, pat. rep., Shady Grove Adventist Hospital, Rockville, MD '84 (PAT)
ROBERTS, JAY A., dir. clin. practice affairs, State University of New York, Health Science Center of Brooklyn, Brooklyn, NY '87 (AMB)
ROBERTS, JEAN, dir. soc. serv., Mercy Hospital, Tiffin, OH '86 (SOC)
ROBERTS, JEWELL L., adm. asst. and dir. vol. serv., Newnan Hospital, Newnan, GA '85 (VOL)
ROBERTS, JIM L., dir. pub. rel., Liberty Hospital, Liberty, MO '85 (PR)
ROBERTS, JOHN E., dir. matl. mgt., Northwestern Medical Center, St. Albans, VT '85 (PUR)
ROBERTS, MAJ. JOHN E. JR., MSC USA, oper. trng. off., 30th Hospital Center, Fort Sheridan, IL '84
ROBERTS, JOHN EVAN, Annandale, VA '69
ROBERTS, JOHN L., vice-pres. health care serv., Marriott Corporation, Washington, DC '73 (FOOD)
ROBERTS, JOYCE, dir. vol. serv., Baptist Medical Center, Jacksonville, FL '80 (VOL)
ROBERTS, KAREN R., asst. dir. vol. serv., Mary Hitchcock Memorial Hospital, Hanover, NH '85 (VOL)
ROBERTS, KEITH C., mgr. med. staff rel., Hospital Corporation of America, Nashville, TN '77 (PERS)
ROBERTS, KIM K., dist. dir. plng., Tri-City Medical Center, Oceanside, CA '85 (PR) (PLNG)
ROBERTS, LANA M., RN, vice-pres., Florida Hospital Medical Center, Orlando, FL '80 (NURS)
ROBERTS, LARRY K., dir. bldg. and grds., Putnam County Hospital, Greencastle, IN '75 (ENG)
ROBERTS, LOIS, dir. soc. serv., Cheshire Medical Center, Keene, NH '84 (SOC)
ROBERTS, LOUIS S., dir. maint., Delta Medical Center, Greenville, MS '84 (ENG)
ROBERTS, MARGARET V., dir. soc. serv., Good Samaritan Medical Center, Zanesville, OH '82 (SOC)
ROBERTS, MARLENE L., mktg. and plng. asst., Methodist Hospital of Southern California, Arcadia, CA '86 (PLNG)
ROBERTS, MARY K., RN, dir. nrsg., Meadowview Regional Hospital, Maysville, KY '79 (NURS)
ROBERTS, NANCY L., staff consult., Ernst and Whinney, St. Louis, MO '85
ROBERTS, NORMAN B., (ret.), Houston, TX '39 (LIFE)
ROBERTS, PAMELA J., North Carolina Hospital Association Trust Fund, Raleigh, NC '75 (RISK)
ROBERTS, PATRICIA B., dir., Voluntary Hospitals of America Management Services, Inc., Tampa, FL '75 (PUR)
ROBERTS, PHILIP G., dir. med. eng., Bristol Memorial Hospital, Bristol, TN '85 (ENG)
ROBERTS, RANDALL L., mgr. matl., Methodist Hospital of Kentucky, Pikeville, KY '83 (PUR)(PR)
ROBERTS, RICHARD, pur. agt., Newington Children's Hospital, Newington, CT '76 (PUR)
ROBERTS, RICKY E., nrsg. in-service educ., Medical Center Hospital, Chillicothe, OH '85 (EDUC)
ROBERTS, ROBERT E., mech. proj. eng., Presbyterian Hospital in the City of New York, New York, NY '84 (ENG)
ROBERTS, SALLY, dir. res. and plng., West Virginia Hospital Association, Charleston, WV '87 (PLNG)
ROBERTS, TED R., adm., Keokuk Convalescent Center, Keokuk, IA '59
ROBERTS, TIMOTHY L., student, Wayland Baptist University, Honolulu, HI '85
ROBERTS, WILLIAM E., atty., Indiana Hospital Association, Indianapolis, IN '74 (ATTY)
ROBERTS, LT. WILLIAM HADYN, MSC USA, Naval Postgraduate School, Monterey, CA '80 (PUR)
ROBERTSON, BRENDA S., dir. pat. affairs, U. S. Air Force Hospital Tinker, Tinker AFB, OK '82
ROBERTSON, COLLEEN L., dir. commun. rel., Rappahannock General Hospital, Kilmarnock, VA '86 (PR)
ROBERTSON, EMMETT Y. JR., dir. human res., Cabarrus Memorial Hospital, Concord, NC '73 (PERS)
ROBERTSON, GIL J., mgr. pur., University of Texas M. D. Anderson Hospital and Tumor Institute at Houston, Houston, TX '85 (PUR)
ROBERTSON, GLORIA D., assoc. dir. vol. serv., Camden-Clark Memorial Hospital, Parkersburg, WV '83 (VOL)
ROBERTSON, H. STEWART, dir. mgt. eng., St. Joseph's Hospital, Stockton, CA '81 (MGMT)
ROBERTSON, HERBERT R., vice-pres., Basic Fore, Toledo, OH '70 (FOOD)
ROBERTSON, JAMES E., dir. pers., Granville C. Morton Cancer and Research Hospital, Wadley Research Institute, Dallas, TX '76 (PERS)
ROBERTSON, JAMES O., dir. food serv., Children's Memorial Hospital, Chicago, IL '83 (FOOD)
ROBERTSON, JERRY A., adm. res., Ottawa County Riverview Nursing Home, Oak Harbor, OH '82
ROBERTSON, JOHN M., dir. pers., South Coast Medical Center, South Laguna, CA '83 (PERS)
ROBERTSON, JOHN, dir. environ., John Muir Memorial Hospital, Walnut Creek, CA '86 (ENVIRON)
ROBERTSON, LAURA ELLEN, pat. serv. spec., Group Health, Inc., St. Paul, MN '85 (PAT)
ROBERTSON, LINDA J., dir. commun. rel., HCA Riveredge Hospital, Forest Park, IL '84 (PR)
ROBERTSON, PATRICIA A., RN, vice-pres. pat. care serv., Methodist Hospital, St. Louis Park, MN '76 (NURS)
ROBERTSON, R. KAE, RN, asst. vice-pres. nrsg., Highland Hospital of Rochester, Rochester, NY '86 (NURS)(AMB)
ROBERTSON, RON E., asst. dir. vol. serv., Los Robles Regional Medical Center, Thousand Oaks, CA '83 (VOL)
ROBERTSON, THOMAS L., pres., Roanoke Memorial Hospitals, Roanoke, VA '70
ROBESON, HAROLD J., dir. environ. serv., Jefferson Regional Medical Center, Pine Bluff, AR '86 (ENVIRON)
ROBFOGEL, SUSAN S., atty., Genesee Hospital, Rochester, NY '78 (ATTY)
ROBIDA, DONALD G., dir. biomedical eng. serv., Health Central Metropolitan Hospitals, Minneapolis, MN '81 (ENG)
ROBILIO, JANE, mgr. storeroom, Baptist Memorial Hospital, Memphis, TN '87 (FOOD)
ROBILOTTI, GERARD D., exec. vice-pres. and chief oper. off., Danbury Hospital, Danbury, CT '69
ROBINETT, JOYCE D., coor. adm. serv., Memorial Southeast Hospital, Houston, TX '68 (VOL)
ROBINETTE, JANICE M., RN, coor. nrsg. educ., Abbott-Northwestern Hospital, Minneapolis, MN '83 (EDUC)
ROBINETTE, PAMELA T., atty., Methodist Hospital of Kentucky, Pikeville, KY '83 (ATTY)
ROBINETTE, PATRICK H., dir. soc. serv., Fairview General Hospital, Cleveland, OH '71 (SOC)
ROBINOW, LAWRENCE, vice-pres., Cigna Hospital of Los Angeles, Los Angeles, CA '74
ROBINS, ANITA, dir. pub. rel., Louis A. Weiss Memorial Hospital, Chicago, IL '78 (PR)
ROBINSON-SMITH, LESLIE E., mktg. analyst, NKC Hospitals, Louisville, KY '86 (PLNG)
ROBINSON, A. KEITH, eng., Lakeview Hospital, Bountiful, UT '76 (ENG)
ROBINSON, ANGELA S., dir. soc. serv., South Community Hospital, Oklahoma City, OK '81 (SOC)
ROBINSON, BARBARA ANN, pat. rep., Charleston General Hospital, Charleston, WV '86 (PAT)
ROBINSON, BETTY, asst. adm., Childrens Hospital of Orange County, Orange, CA '83 (PUR)
ROBINSON, CALVIN R., adm., Kenneth W. Clement Center for Family Health Care, Cleveland, OH '76
ROBINSON, CATHERINE A., exec. dir., Western Network for Education in Health Administration, Berkeley, CA '80
ROBINSON, CHERYL A., dir. food serv., Doctors Hospital of Lakewood, Lakewood, CA '82 (FOOD)
ROBINSON, CHRIS C., asst. adm., Memorial Hospital of San Gorgonio Pass, Banning, CA '82
ROBINSON, COLLEEN M., dir. pers., St. Mary Hospital, Philadelphia, PA '85 (PERS)
ROBINSON, CORRINE K., sr. staff soc. worker, Naval Hospital, Orlando, FL '82 (SOC)
ROBINSON, CRAWFORD U. JR., dir. biomedical eng., All Saints Episcopal Hospital, Fort Worth, TX '84 (ENG)
ROBINSON, D. L., dir. environ. serv., North Carolina Baptist Hospital, Winston-Salem, NC '86 (ENVIRON)
ROBINSON, DANIEL J., dir. pers. mgt., Stanford University Hospital, Stanford, CA '84 (PERS)
ROBINSON, DEBBIE CECIL, dir. pers. and pub. rel., Ohio County Hospital, Hartford, KY '87 (PERS)
ROBINSON, DEBORAH J., atty., Harper Hospital, Detroit, MI '81 (ATTY)
ROBINSON, DONNA M., dir. vol., Eastern Idaho Regional Medical Center, Idaho Falls, ID '82 (VOL)
ROBINSON, EDWARD E., atty., Adventist Health Systems North, Hinsdale, IL '77 (ATTY)
ROBINSON, ELIZABETH, dir. vol., Baptist Hospital East, Louisville, KY '79 (VOL)
ROBINSON, EULA COLSTON, coor. pat. rel., University Hospital, Newark, NJ '85 (PAT)
ROBINSON, FLOYD W. JR., asst. dir., University of Texas M. D. Anderson Hospital and Tumor Institute at Houston, Houston, TX '83 (CS)
ROBINSON, FRANKLIN R., mgr. matl., Twin Rivers Regional Medical Center, Kennett, MO '82 (PUR)
ROBINSON, GARY, mgr. hosp. acct., Maritz Motivation, Dallas, TX '78
ROBINSON, GAYLE VERNON, dir. qual. assur. and risk mgt., City of Hope National Medical Center, Duarte, CA '86 (RISK)
ROBINSON, MAJ. GEORGE SHACKLEFORD, MSC USA, prin. investigator, field med. serv., Usambrdl, Fort Detrick, MD '82
ROBINSON, GERALD B., dir. matl. mgt., Providence Hospital, Oakland, CA '81 (PUR)
ROBINSON, GERALD S., asst. chief bldg. mgt., Veterans Administration Medical Center, Minneapolis, MN '87 (ENVIRON)
ROBINSON, GLENN A., reg. dir. mktg., Humana Inc., Mobile, AL '85 (PR) (PLNG)
ROBINSON, GWENN G., chief vol. serv., Veterans Administration Outpatient Clinic, Los Angeles, CA '84 (VOL)
ROBINSON, J. SCOTT, atty., Chippenham Hospital, Richmond, VA '86 (ATTY)
ROBINSON, JAMES E., dir. educ. serv., Our Lady of Lourdes Medical Center, Camden, NJ '85 (EDUC)
ROBINSON, JAMES M. SR., asst. reg. dir., American Hospital Association, Irving, TX '67
ROBINSON, JEAN M., dir. soc. work, University of Michigan Hospitals, Ann Arbor, MI '72 (SOC)
ROBINSON, JOHN E., dir. risk mgt. and mgr. commun., Doctors Memorial Hospital, Atlanta, GA '72 (ENG)
ROBINSON, JOHN L., pat. rep., Memorial Hospital, Colorado Springs, CO '84 (PAT)
ROBINSON, JULIE MARR, asst. dir. pub. rel., Kent County Memorial Hospital, Warwick, RI '86 (PR)
ROBINSON, KAY, RN, dir. nrsg., Baptist Regional Health Center, Miami, OK '86 (NURS)
ROBINSON, KEITH R., supv. maint., Calais Regional Hospital, Calais, ME '82 (ENG)
ROBINSON, KENNETH D., dir. biomedical eng., Johnson County Memorial Hospital, Franklin, IN '86 (ENG)
ROBINSON, LARRY B., asst. eng. constr., Cottonwood Hospital Medical Center, Murray, UT '87 (ENG)
ROBINSON, LINDSAY, vice-pres. health affairs, Empire Blue Cross and Blue Shield, Albany Division, Albany, NY '79 (PLNG)
ROBINSON, M. CHARLENE, asst. adm., Los Alamitos Medical Center, Los Alamitos, CA '80 (RISK)
ROBINSON, M. KAY, dir. human res. dev., Methodist Medical Center of Illinois, Peoria, IL '86 (EDUC)
ROBINSON, MARGARET ANNE, dir. nrsg., Prince Henry's Hospital, Melbourne, Australia '80 (NURS)
ROBINSON, MARGARET, RN, vice-pres. nrsg. serv., Herrick Hospital and Health Center, Berkeley, CA '84 (NURS)
ROBINSON, MARY C., RN, mgr. sup. proc. center, Gaston Memorial Hospital, Gastonia, NC '77 (CS)
ROBINSON, MICHAEL DAVID, adm. res., Richmond Memorial Hospital, Richmond, VA '84
ROBINSON, MICHAELENE H., dir. vol. serv., Spalding Rehabilitation Hospital, Denver, CO '82 (VOL)
ROBINSON, NORMAN E., dir. diet., St. Mark's Hospital, Salt Lake City, UT '68 (FOOD)
ROBINSON, PETER E., dir. sales, AMI Presbyterian-St. Luke's Medical Center, Denver, CO '85
ROBINSON, RALPH E., adm., St. Joseph Hospital, Augusta, GA '87 (AMB)
ROBINSON, RICHARD D., atty., Parkview Memorial Hospital, Fort Wayne, IN '82 (ATTY)
ROBINSON, RONALD P., vice-pres. pers., Medina Community Hospital, Medina, OH '86 (PERS)
ROBINSON, STEWART P., dir. cent. serv., Chambersburg Hospital, Chambersburg, PA '82 (CS)
ROBINSON, TAMERA K., vice-pres. and chief fin. off., Greene Memorial Hospital, Xenia, OH '86 (PLNG)
ROBINSON, TINA A., dir. soc. serv., Tanner Medical Center, Carrollton, GA '82 (SOC)
ROBINSON, VICTORIA JO, RN, dir. nrsg., Ssm Rehabilitation Institute, St. Louis, MO '80 (NURS)
ROBINSON, WENDELL, dir. bldg. serv., Saint Francis Hospital, Tulsa, OK '77 (ENG)
ROBISON, ANNE L., sr. consult., Kurt Salmon Associates, Inc., Atlanta, GA '81 (MGMT)(PLNG)
ROBISON, G. AUSTIN III, asst. adm. mktg. and human res., West Shore Hospital, Manistee, MI '78 (PR) (PLNG)
ROBISON, JACK H., atty., Pocatello Regional Medical Center, Pocatello, ID '86 (ATTY)
ROBISON, JUDY, coor. soc. serv., Willamette Falls Hospital, Oregon City, OR '86 (SOC)
ROBITAILLE, MARK E., chief exec. off. and adm., West Orange Memorial Hospital, Winter Garden, FL '80
ROBLE, DANIEL T., atty., New England Medical Center, Boston, MA '84 (ATTY)
ROBLEE, BRENDA, student, State University of New York, Brockport, NY '87
ROBLES-ARCHULETA, ELVIRA, dir. soc. serv., White Memorial Medical Center, Los Angeles, CA '85 (SOC)
ROBOTTI, JUDITH M., dir. cent. sterile sup., Hartford Hospital, Hartford, CT '83 (CS)
ROBRECHT, SR. ROSARIA, health affairs consult., St. Francis Hospital, Charleston, WV '65
ROCCO, LOUIS J., asst. dir. pur., Lawrence Memorial Hospital of Medford, Medford, MA '86 (PUR)
ROCHA, KIMBERLY J., adm. dir. oper., Lifeplus Foundation-Healthwest, North Hollywood, CA '87 (PLNG)
ROCHE-LEON, HUMBERTO, partner, Pannell Kerr Forster, Hato Rey, P.R. '84 (PLNG)
ROCHE, ELEANOR B., dir. vol., Los Robles Regional Medical Center, Thousand Oaks, CA '81 (VOL)
ROCHE, JOHN M., stationary eng., Rehabilitation Institute of Chicago, Chicago, IL '86 (ENG)
ROCHE, MARCIA F., vice-pres. plng., General Health, Inc., Baton Rouge, LA '82 (PLNG)
ROCHE, PATRICK F., pres., St. Francis Medical Center, Trenton, NJ '65
ROCHEFORT, PEARL, mgr. cent. serv., New York University Medical Center, New York, NY '80 (CS)
ROCHELLE, BARBARA, mgr., The Gracie Company, Atlanta, GA '86 (ENG)
ROCHELLE, FRANCIS R., dir. plans and oper., Metropolitan Nashville General Hospital, Nashville, TN '78 (PLNG)(RISK)
ROCHESTER, JANE A., RN, exec. dir. nrsg., Oral Surgical Institute, Martin-Hill-Carter Professional Corporation, Nashville, TN '87 (NURS)
ROCHFORD, DOLORES, mgr. cent. sup., Southside Hospital, Bay Shore, NY '78 (CS)
ROCHMAN, ESTELLE, dir. soc. work, Normandy Osteopathic Hospital-South, St. Louis, MO '85 (SOC)
ROCHON, SR. DOLORE, RN, vice-pres. pat. serv., St. Joseph's Hospital, St. Paul, MN '77 (NURS)

ROCK, BARRY D., dir. soc. work, Long Island Jewish Medical Center, New York, NY '81 (SOC)
ROCK, ELLEN PENNY, dir. soc. serv., Chilton Memorial Hospital, Pompton Plains, NJ '81 (SOC)
ROCK, K. C. JR., (ret.), Littleton, CO '75 (ENG)
ROCK, MARTIN W., dir. matl. mgt., St. Joseph Hospital, Baltimore, MD '76 (PUR)
ROCK, ROBERT B. JR., dir. prof. rel., Johnson and Johnson Baby Products Company, Skillman, NJ '72 (EDUC)
ROCKAFELLOW, ELIZABETH H., RN, dir. nrsg., All Saints' Rehabilitation Hospital, Wyndmoor, PA '85 (NURS)
ROCKAFELLOW, SANDRA L., dir. soc. serv., McKennan Hospital, Sioux Falls, SD '85 (SOC)
ROCKE, CATHY, reimbursement consult., Coopers and Lybrand, Boston, MA '82
ROCKE, KENNETH E., dir. eng., Indian River Memorial Hospital, Vero Beach, FL '82 (ENG)
ROCKER, SUSAN J., coor. mktg., Archbishop Bergan Mercy Hospital, Omaha, NE '85 (PLNG)
ROCKLIN, CAROL, dir. soc. serv., White Plains Hospital Medical Center, White Plains, NY '77 (SOC)
ROCKMAN, JAY F., vice-pres. health care, Urs Company, Cleveland, OH '74 (PLNG)
ROCKOWITZ, RUTH MESSINGER, chief soc. worker-ped., Strong Memorial Hospital Rochester University, Rochester, NY '86 (SOC)
ROCKS, JEAN A., mgt. eng., Western Reserve Care System, Youngstown, OH '87 (MGMT)
ROCKWELL, CAROLYN K., vice-pres. commun. rel. and dev., Lowell General Hospital, Lowell, MA '75 (PR)
ROCKWELL, DONNA L., RN, clin. dir. nrsg., St. Anthony Hospital, Oklahoma City, OK '84 (NURS)
ROCKWELL, FORBES, mgr. energy, Lawrence General Hospital, Lawrence, MA '79 (ENG)
ROCKWELL, TED R., supv. maint., Oconto Memorial Hospital, Oconto, WI '84 (ENG)
ROD, JOYCE H., dir. vol., Cabrini Medical Center, New York, NY '82 (VOL)
RODAITIS, CECELIA M., RN, asst. adm., Shadyside Hospital, Pittsburgh, PA '82 (NURS)
RODDE, HERBERT RICHARD, exec. dir., Sisters of the Third Order of St. Francis, Peoria, IL '63
RODDY, VIRGINIA D., dir. med. legal affairs, Yale-New Haven Hospital, New Haven, CT '84 (RISK)
RODEBAUGH, BARBARA F., RN, clin. dir., Washington Hospital, Washington, PA '86 (NURS)
RODECKER, DEBORAH LEWIS, atty., Belington Community Medical Services, Charleston, WV '74 (ATTY)
RODEN, JOHN J., mgr. maint., N. T. Enloe Memorial Hospital, Chico, CA '85 (ENG)
RODEN, RAYMOND P., dir. adm., New Britain General Hospital, New Britain, CT '76 (PAT)
RODENBAECK, ANITA MCCORMICK, dir. vol., Children's Hospital of San Francisco, San Francisco, CA '70 (VOL)
RODENBAUGH, PHILIP J., dir. plant oper., Cardinal Glennon Children Hospital, St. Louis, MO '75 (ENG)
RODER, ERLA BETH, RN, dir. nrsg. serv., Cavalier County Memorial Hospital, Langdon, ND '75 (NURS)
RODERER, RICHARD A., sr. vice-pres., Deaconess Hospital, Cincinnati, OH '69
RODERICK, GLENN E., Cleveland, OH '66 (SOC)
RODERICK, WILLARD P., dir. plant oper., Barberton Citizens Hospital, Barberton, OH '82 (ENG)
RODGER, CASSANDRA Z., coor. qual. assur.-adm., Children's Hospital of Michigan, Detroit, MI '80 (RISK)
RODGER, GINETTE L., exec. dir., Canadian Nurses Association, Ottawa, Ont., Canada '82
RODGERS, ALBERT GEORGE, consult., Seventh-Day Adventist Hospital Systems, National Headquarters, Oshawa, Ont., Canada '56 (LIFE)
RODGERS, ANTHONY EDWIN, dir. environ. serv., Ingleside Hospital, Rosemead, CA '85 (ENG)
RODGERS, CLEVELAND, Tulsa, OK '84 (LIFE)
RODGERS, DANIEL J., adm., Norfolk Surgical Group, Ltd., Norfolk, VA '87 (AMB)
RODGERS, GERAL K., dir. diet. serv., Virginia Mason Hospital, Seattle, WA '79 (FOOD)
RODGERS, GERTRUDE L., RN, asst. adm. and dir. nrsg., Fairfax Hospital, Falls Church, VA '73 (NURS)
RODGERS, JOAN, mgr. soc. work, Henry County Health Center, Mount Pleasant, IA '86 (SOC)
RODGERS, KIMBERLEY S., plng. asst., Lee Memorial Hospital, Fort Myers, FL '86 (PLNG)
RODGERS, LEOLA, student, Program in Public Health, University of Alabama at Birmingham, Birmingham, AL '85
RODGERS, NANCY M., dir. pat. and family serv., Halifax Memorial Hospital, Roanoke Rapids, NC '84 (SOC)
RODGERS, SR. ROBERTA MARIE, pat. rep., Mount San Rafael Hospital, Trinidad, CO '79 (PAT)
RODGERS, SALLY J., prog. assoc., University of Iowa College of Medicine, Iowa City, IA '84 (PLNG)
RODGERS, SHEILA M., RN, coor. nrsg. educ., Mississippi State Hospital, Whitfield, MS '86 (EDUC)
RODGERS, LCDR SIDNEY D., MSC USN, health syst. planner, Office of the Assist. Secretary of Defense and Health Affairs, Then Pentagon, Washington, Washington, DC '82
RODGERS, WILLIAM E., coor. telecommun., Menorah Medical Center, Kansas City, MO '85 (ENG)
RODGERS, WILLIAM J., consult. educ. serv., Deaconess Hospital, Evansville, IN '85 (EDUC)
RODINE, MARILYN K., RN, pat. rep. and qual. assur. nrs., Poudre Valley Hospital, Fort Collins, CO '86 (PAT)
RODMAN, LT. COL. TERRAL L., MSC USA, insp. gen., Fitzsimons Army Medical Center, Aurora, CO '72
RODRIGUES, FRANK A., dir. matl. mgt., Danbury Hospital, Danbury, CT '84 (PUR)(CS)
RODRIGUEZ, ALICE J., consult. and instr. media, Education Communication, Costa Mesa, CA '82 (EDUC)
RODRIGUEZ, DENIS, chief eng., State Insurance Fund, San Juan, P.R. '78 (ENG)
RODRIGUEZ, FRANCISCO, maint. eng., Ryder Memorial Hospital, Humacao, P.R. '81 (ENG)
RODRIGUEZ, JORGE, dir. spec. proj., Miami Children's Hospital, Miami, FL '87 (PR)
RODRIGUEZ, KAY, dir., Health Sciences News and Information Services, University of Washington, Seattle, WA '85 (PR)
RODRIGUEZ, LINDA C., dir. soc. serv., Queen of Angels Medical Center, Los Angeles, CA '84 (SOC)
RODRIGUEZ, RICARDO, elec. eng., Clinical Center National Institute of Health, Bethesda, MD '82 (ENG)
RODRIGUEZ, RITA JO, supv. cent. sup., Holy Cross Hospital, Mission Hills, CA '83 (CS)
RODRIGUEZ, ROBERT, arch., Brown Leary Architecture and Planning, San Diego, CA '85 (ENG)
RODRIGUEZ, RUBY M., pers. asst., Illini Community Hospital, Pittsfield, IL '85 (PERS)
RODRIQUEZ, AGNES B., student, Program in Health Systems, Georgia Institute of Technology, Atlanta, GA '87 (MGMT)
RODWAN, BRUCE A., atty., St. Joseph Hospitals, Mount Clemens, MI '84 (ATTY)
ROE, CAROLYN J., RN, vice-pres., Holmes Regional Medical Center, Melbourne, FL '79 (NURS)
ROE, CHARLES W., pres., Baptist Health Services, Gadsden, AL '69
ROE, KENNETH E., Alspach Drug Company, Yuma, AZ '81 (ENG)
ROE, LINDA, RN, dir. nrsg., Portage View Hospital, Hancock, MI '78 (NURS)
ROEBER, BARBARA A., RN, dir. pat. care serv., Mercy Hospital, Valley City, ND '83 (NURS)
ROEBUCK, VINCENT A., mgr. plant oper., Wooster Community Hospital, Wooster, OH '79 (ENG)
ROEDEL, DAVID H., supv. eng., Newberg Community Hospital, Newberg, OR '84 (ENG)
ROEDER, DIANE M., student, Program in Health Administration, University of Massachusetts, Amherst, MA '86
ROEDER, JAMES L., sr. consult., Hamilton Associates, Inc., Richardson, TX '69 (PLNG)
ROEDER, KIM H., atty., Northside Hospital, Atlanta, GA '82 (ATTY)
ROEDER, PENELOPE C., dir. corp. plng., American Medical International, Beverly Hills, CA '82 (PLNG)
ROEDER, ROBERT C., sr. consult., William M. Mercer-Meidinger, Cincinnati, OH '85 (PERS)
ROEDL, MADALENE R., RN, asst. dir. nrsg. critical care area, South Community Hospital, Oklahoma City, OK '82 (NURS)
ROEGER, CECILE A., RN, coor. staff serv., Memorial Care Management, Houston, TX '84 (NURS)
ROEHRICH, JEFF, dir. pur., Memorial Hospital of Sweetwater County, Rock Springs, WY '84 (PUR)
ROEHRICH, THOMAS M., vice-pres. human res., Hillcrest Hospital, Mayfield Heights, OH '86 (PERS)
ROELLER, JEAN C., mgr. cent. serv., Baylor University Medical Center, Dallas, TX '85 (CS)
ROELOFS, EUGENE D., chief eng., Paul Oliver Memorial Hospital, Frankfort, MI '79 (ENG)
ROELOFS, PAUL F., pres., Mediatec, Inc., La Canada, CA '84 (EDUC)
ROEMER, JILL E., RN, assoc. dir. nrsg., St. Joseph Medical Center, Joliet, IL '85 (NURS)
ROEMER, MARY A., RN, clin. dir. maternal and child health, Mount Auburn Hospital, Cambridge, MA '86 (NURS)
ROEPKE, DOLORES M., dir. vol., Scottsdale Memorial Hospital, Scottsdale, AZ '76 (VOL)
ROESER, ANNE ELIZABETH, mgr., Deloitte, Haskins and Sells, Costa Mesa, CA '80 (MGMT)
ROESSLER, JEAN W., dir. vol. serv., Fairview Deaconess Hospital, Burnsville, MN '82 (VOL)
ROETHLER, ERMA, RN, clin. dir., Allen Memorial Hospital, Waterloo, IA '86 (NURS)
ROETTELE, STEPHEN G., asst. exec. dir., St. Francis Hospital, Blue Island, IL '77 (PLNG)
ROETTGER, KEITH O., dir. emp. rel., St. Joseph Mercy Hospital, Pontiac, MI '80 (PERS)
ROGAN, CHARLES FRED, asst. dir. pers., University of Alabama Hospital, Birmingham, AL '83 (PERS)
ROGAN, JAMES C., dir. maint. and eng., Hillcrest Hospital, Mayfield Heights, OH '81 (ENG)
ROGATZ, PETER, MD, vice-pres. med. affairs, Visiting Nurse Service of New York, New York, NY '58
ROGERS, ANN WARD, vice-pres. pub. info., Texas Hospital Association, Austin, TX '82 (PR)
ROGERS, ANNETTE E., Strongsville, OH '86 (MGMT)
ROGERS, ARTHUR M., Scovill Manufacturing Company, Waterbury, CT '71 (HON)
ROGERS, BARBARA A., adm. of med., Sinai Hospital of Baltimore, Baltimore, MD '84
ROGERS, BOBBY G., dir. environ. serv., Sparks Regional Medical Center, Fort Smith, AR '86 (ENVIRON)
ROGERS, BONNIE, assoc. dir. commun., City of Hope, Los Angeles, CA '75 (PR)
ROGERS, BRYAN ALLEN, adm., Toledo Hospital, Toledo, OH '52 (LIFE)
ROGERS, CAROL L., RN, asst. exec. dir. pat. care serv., Kelsey Memorial Hospital, Lakeview, MI '80 (NURS)
ROGERS, CAROLYN F., coor. vol., Ohio Valley Hospital, Steubenville, OH '85 (VOL)
ROGERS, CHARLES JOE JR., asst. adm. pers., Scott and White Memorial Hospital, Temple, TX '83 (PERS)
ROGERS, CHARLES W., dir. mktg., Charter Retreat Hospital and Recovery Center, Decatur, AL '83 (PR)
ROGERS, CINDY JEAN, dir. soc. serv., St. Francis Medical Center, Monroe, LA '84 (SOC)
ROGERS, DANIEL J., staff asst. grants, Toledo Hospital, Toledo, OH '78
ROGERS, DAVID E., MD, distinguished prof. of medicine, New York Hospital-Cornell Medical Center, New York, NY '76 (HON)
ROGERS, DAVID L., atty., Henry Ford Hospital, Detroit, MI '87 (ATTY)
ROGERS, DAVID, dir. emp. rel., Saginaw General Hospital, Saginaw, MI '84 (PERS)
ROGERS, DONALD R., dir. commun. rel. and dev., Bannock Regional Medical Center, Pocatello, ID '84 (PR)
ROGERS, DONNA G., dir. pers., HCA Santa Rosa Medical Center, Milton, FL '85 (PERS)
ROGERS, DOROTHY D., dir. pat. rep., University of Iowa Hospitals and Clinics, Iowa City, IA '74 (PAT)
ROGERS, ERNESTINE D., adm. pers., Rahway Hospital, Rahway, NJ '75 (PERS)
ROGERS, EVERETT R., pur. agt., Morton Hospital and Medical Center, Taunton, MA '79 (PUR)
ROGERS, FRED M., pres., Family Communications, Pittsburgh, PA '75 (HON)
ROGERS, HARVEY W., environ. eng., Clinical Center, National Institutes of Health, Bethesda, MD '85 (ENG)
ROGERS, ILA M., RN, dir. nrsg. serv., Willis-Knighton Medical Center, Shreveport, LA '82 (NURS)
ROGERS, JAMES H., asst. adm., HCA Northwest Regional Hospital, Margate, FL '86
ROGERS, JEFFREY K., vice-pres., St. Joseph's Hospital and Medical Center, Phoenix, AZ '79 (PERS)
ROGERS, JEFFREY W., atty., Sisters of Providence, Seattle, WA '81 (ATTY)
ROGERS, JOHN J., Evergreen Park, IL '86
ROGERS, KARILON L., dir. commun. rel., St. Joseph Riverside Hospital, Warren, OH '85 (PR)
ROGERS, KATHERINE SQUIRES, coor. guest rel., Osteopathic Hospital of Maine, Portland, ME '85 (PAT)
ROGERS, KENNETH A., vice-pres. plng., Millard Fillmore Hospital, Buffalo, NY '84 (PLNG)
ROGERS, LESLIE A., RN, asst. adm., St. Luke's Lutheran Hospital, San Antonio, TX '84 (NURS)
ROGERS, LESTER J., (ret.), Lacey, WA '74 (FOOD)
ROGERS, LULA B., chief diet., St. Elizabeth Hospital, Houston, TX '76 (FOOD)
ROGERS, LYNN D., vice-pres. med. staff affairs, Pomona Valley Community Hospital, Pomona, CA '76 (PR)
ROGERS, MADELINE BARBARA, pat. rep., Sunnybrook Hospital, Toronto, Ont., Canada '85 (PAT)
ROGERS, MARJORIE D., adm. sec. pers., Gibson General Hospital, Princeton, IN '85 (PERS)
ROGERS, MELANIE S., actg. dir. food serv., Kennestone Hospital, Marietta, GA '87 (FOOD)
ROGERS, NANCY, coor. risk mgt., Peninsula Hospital and Medical Center, Burlingame, CA '86 (RISK)
ROGERS, REBECCA B., asst. dir. mktg. commun. and pub. affairs, University Hospital, Augusta, GA '86 (PR)
ROGERS, RICHARD KENNETH, mgr. pers., St. Mary's Hospital, Saginaw, MI '77 (PERS)
ROGERS, SALLY J., dir. commun., United Hospital Fund of New York, New York, NY '83 (PR)
ROGERS, SANDRA G., dir. vol., Skagit Valley Hospital and Health Center, Mount Vernon, WA '80 (VOL)
ROGERS, SUZANNE J., RN, asst. vice-pres. pat. care serv., Methodist Hospital of Indiana, Indianapolis, IN '84 (NURS)
ROGERS, SYLVIA F., dir. soc. serv., Porter Memorial Hospital, Denver, CO '73 (SOC)
ROGERS, TERRIE H., mgr. corp. serv., Baxter Travenol, Romulus, MI '86 (PLNG)
ROGERS, WILLIAM E., dir. risk mgt. serv., The Gleason Agency, Johnstown, PA '80 (RISK)
ROGERS, WILSON D. JR., atty., St. Margaret's Hospital for Women, Boston, MA '73 (ATTY)
ROGGE, WALTER C., dir. hskpg., Wayne General Hospital, Wayne, NJ '86 (ENVIRON)
ROGGENSTEIN, ANGELA P., mgt. eng., Waterbury Hospital Health Center, Waterbury, CT '83 (MGMT)
ROGGERO, ROLAND V., dir. facil. mgt., Weingam Rehabilitation Center, Los Angeles, CA '74 (ENG)
ROGGI, ELIZABETH, sterile proc. tech., Manchester Memorial Hospital, Manchester, CT '86 (CS)
ROGLER, DIANE L., proj. off., Health Care Financing Administration, Baltimore, MD '77
ROGOFF, DAVID P., dir., Voluntary Hospitals of America Management Services, Tampa, FL '73 (PLNG)
ROGOFF, FRAN, dir. clin. soc. work, Valley Hospital Medical Center, Van Nuys, CA '86 (SOC)
ROGOVIN, MITCHELL, atty., Houston Northwest Medical Center, Houston, TX '84 (ATTY)
ROHDE, JUDITH M., asst. dir. neuroscience nrsg., Johns Hopkins Hospital, Baltimore, MD '86 (NURS)
ROHE, DUKE KENNETH, mgt. eng., St. Luke's Episcopal Hospital, Houston, TX '77 (MGMT)
ROHLING, CHARLES L., sr. mgr., SunHealth Corporation, Charlotte, NC '77 (MGMT)
ROHLING, DONALD R., dir. soc. serv., Providence Hospital, Cincinnati, OH '75 (SOC)
ROHN, WILLIAM J., sr. mgr., Group Health Association, Washington, DC '82
ROHR, KATHERINE W., chief diet., Daniel Freeman Memorial Hospital, Inglewood, CA '69 (FOOD)
ROHR, TOM R., dir. pub. rel. and mktg., St. Joseph's Medical Center, Brainerd, MN '83 (PR)
ROHRBACH, JANE CARLISLE, (ret.), Middlefield, OH '46 (EDUC)(LIFE)
ROHRBAUGH, HELEN M., dir. soc. work, Newman Memorial County Hospital, Emporia, KS '81 (SOC)
ROHRE, STEPHEN D., dir. eng., Trinity Medical Center, Carrollton, TX '87 (ENG)
ROHRER, JOHN E., exec. dir., Valley Community Hospital, Dallas, OR '68
ROHRICH, JOHN, dir. educ., Elmhurst Memorial Hospital, Elmhurst, IL '80 (EDUC)
ROHRICH, WILLIAM G., dir. plant serv., Glendale Heights Community Hospital, Glendale Heights, IL '84 (ENG)
ROHWER, BETSY, dir. vol. serv., Oakwood Hospital, Dearborn, MI '86 (VOL)
ROKITA, BRIAN S., dir. nutr. serv., Scottsdale Pueblo Norte, Scottsdale, AZ '84 (FOOD)

ROLAND, ARLENE E., RN, chief nrsg. serv., Veterans Administration Medical Center, Lincoln, NE '85 (NURS)
ROLAND, DAVID H., atty., Reading Hospital and Medical Center, Reading, PA '70 (ATTY)
ROLAND, DEBORAH L., mgr., Peat, Marwick, Mitchell and Company, New York, NY '81 (PLNG)
ROLAND, NORMAN L., chief eng., Orthopaedic Hospital of Charlotte, Charlotte, NC '84 (ENG)
ROLAND, ROBERT L., atty., Baton Rouge General Medical Center, Baton Rouge, LA '70 (ATTY)
ROLEN, NANCY H., coor. vol., Morehead Memorial Hospital, Eden, NC '85 (VOL)
ROLFHUS, ROBERT O., dir. food serv., Wausau Hospital Center, Wausau, WI '75 (FOOD)
ROLFSON, ROALD J., dir. soc. serv., Hebrew Rehabilitation Center for Aged, Boston, MA '77 (SOC)
ROLING, NANCY J., mgr. cent. sterilization, Mercy Health Center, Dubuque, IA '81 (CS)
ROLLE, ANNETTE, asst. mgr., Cedars Medical Center, Miami, FL '83 (CS)
ROLLE, CHRISTOPHER D., atty., Holland and Knight, Bradenton, FL '83
ROLLINGS, HARVEY, atty., Cape Coral Hospital, Cape Coral, FL '80 (ATTY)
ROLLINS, BRENDA E., mgt. eng., Candler General Hospital, Savannah, GA '87 (MGMT)
ROLLINS, FRANK E., dir. support serv., Maryview Hospital, Portsmouth, VA '76 (PUR)
ROLLINS, MARSHALL LEE, telecommun. tech., Gaston Memorial Hospital, Gastonia, NC '86 (ENG)
ROLLMAN, TRENA BAKER, mgr. soc. serv., AMI St. Jude Medical Center, Kenner, LA '79 (SOC)
ROLOFF, MARY A., RN, supv. sup., proc. and distrib., Comanche County Memorial Hospital, Lawton, OK '86 (CS)
ROMAN, CHARLES J., chief bio-med. eng., Mercy Catholic Medical Center, Darby, PA '79 (ENG)
ROMAN, PAMELA L., asst. dir., Foster G. McGaw Hospital, Loyola University of Chicago, Maywood, IL '81
ROMAN, PAUL T., vice-pres. fin., Mercy Hospital of Pittsburgh, Pittsburgh, PA '86
ROMAN, SAL, mng. dir. eng. serv., Sharp Memorial Hospital, San Diego, CA '73 (ENG)
ROMANO, ANNETTA L., RN, (ret.), East Boston, MA '78 (CS)
ROMANO, ANTHONY M., dir. pers., Erie County Medical Center, Buffalo, NY '86 (PERS)
ROMANO, HELEN L., RN, vice-pres. nrsg., Washington Hospital, Washington, PA '85 (NURS)
ROMANO, JAMES D., mgr. bldg. serv., Saratoga Hospital, Saratoga Springs, NY '87 (ENG)
ROMANO, JOHN P., mgr. prod., Maine Medical Center, Portland, ME '81 (FOOD)
ROMANO, MARY D., dir. soc. work, National Rehabilitation Hospital, Washington, DC '81 (SOC)
ROMANO, STEPHANY J., pat. rep. emergency medicine, York Hospital, York, PA '86 (PAT)
ROMANOSKI, FRANK T., dir. syst. support, Mediq Information Systems, Inc., Feasterville, PA '85 (MGMT)
ROMANS, GREG L., dir. mktg., St. Vincent's Hospital, Birmingham, AL '82 (PLNG)
ROMANS, PATRICIA E., dir. commun. rel. and vol. serv., North Iowa Medical Center, Mason City, IA '82 (PR)
ROMANSKY, MICHAEL A., atty., McDermott, Will and Emery, Washington, DC '87 (AMB)
ROMEO, MARY ANN, dir. soc. work, Veterans Administration Medical Center, Albany, NY '85 (SOC)
ROMER, WARD L., dir. med. rec., Tompkins Community Hospital, Ithaca, NY '84
ROMERO, ALEX I., dir. eng., Dauterive Hospital, New Iberia, LA '83 (ENG)
ROMEY, SHAYA, asst. dir. matl. mgt., General Hospital of Everett, Everett, WA '83 (CS)
ROMEYN, CAPT. THOMAS N., MSC USAF, chief med. equip. repair, Wiesbaden Regional Medical Center, APO New York, NY '85 (ENG)
ROMINE, JANICE M., dir. educ., St. John's Hospital, Salina, KS '87 (EDUC)
ROMINE, JULIA J., asst. to vice-pres. fiscal and support serv., Methodist Hospital of Indiana, Inc., Indianapolis, IN '85
ROMING, PETER P., dir. pub. rel., HCA Vista Hills Medical Center, El Paso, TX '85 (PR)
ROMONOSKY, ROBERT A., coor. data proc., Oak Forest Hospital of Cook County, Oak Forest, IL '83 (MGMT)
ROMOT, GEORGE E., dir. pers., Orlando General Hospital, Orlando, FL '82 (PERS)
ROMRIELL, STEVEN R., asst. dir. plant serv., Scripps Memorial Hospital-Chula Vista, Chula Vista, CA '80 (ENG)
ROMUALD, SR. MARY, dir. soc. serv., St. Joseph Hospital, Bangor, ME '74 (SOC)
RONAI, STEPHEN E., atty., Milford Hospital, Milford, CT '68 (ATTY)
RONAN, BETTY, (ret.), Orlando, FL '68 (FOOD)
RONAN, CAPT. MARGARET M., MSC USAF, chief mental health clin., U. S. Air Force Space Division Clinic, El Segundo, CA '84 (SOC)
RONE, ALTONA M., dir. soc. serv., Michigan Osteopathic Medical Center, Detroit, MI '77 (SOC)
RONEY, M. CANDACE, dir. mktg. commun., Health Dimensions, Inc., San Jose, CA '81 (PR)
RONEY, ROBERT R., asst. vice-pres. environ. serv., South Side Hospital of Pittsburgh, Pittsburgh, PA '79 (ENG)
RONEY, RUTH, RN, vice-pres. nrsg., Frederick Memorial Hospital, Frederick, MD '78 (NURS)
RONFELDT, RUTH H., assoc. exec. dir., St. Luke's Hospital, Kansas City, MO '75 (VOL)(PR)
RONHOVDE, LORIE, dir. hskpg., Multicare Medical Center, Tacoma, WA '86 (ENVIRON)
RONIS, ANITA L., meth. analyst, University of Massachusetts Medical Center, Worcester, MA '86 (MGMT)
RONKIN, CHARLES F., adm., Monterey Nursing Inn, Grove City, OH '69
RONNENKAMP, SUE A., alternative delivery syst. spec., Northwestern National Life Insurance Company, Minneapolis, MN '82
RONNING, PHILIP L., vice-pres., St. Vincent Medical Center, Los Angeles, CA '77
RONSEN, KURT C., vice-pres. emp. serv., Mercy Medical Center, Denver, CO '85 (RISK)(PERS)
RONSHAUGEN, NANCY L., mgr. soc. serv., Prairie Lakes Health Care System, Watertown, SD '86 (SOC)
RONTAL, ROBYN A., dir. plng., Botsford General Hospital, Farmington Hills, MI '84 (PLNG)
ROOF, BETTY J., assoc. dir. nrsg., Baptist Medical Center, Columbia, SC '82 (EDUC)
ROOK, BENJAMIN THOMAS, pres., Odell Associates, Inc., Greenville, SC '77
ROOKS, JAN W., sr. budget analyst, Neuro Psychiatric Institute Hospitals and Clinics, Los Angeles, CA '81 (MGMT)
ROONEY, ELIZABETH T., RN, dir. nrsg. serv., Mount St. Mary's Hospital, Lewiston, NY '83 (NURS)
ROONEY, LITA G., coor. vol. serv., Pendleton Memorial Methodist Hospital, New Orleans, LA '85 (VOL)
ROONEY, PATRICK J., mgr. educ. dev., St. Joseph's Medical Center, South Bend, IN '77 (EDUC)
ROONEY, SUSAN, RN, asst. adm., Mercy Hospital of Sacramento, Sacramento, CA '82 (NURS)
ROOS, CARL L. JR., sr. staff consult., Don Rowe Associates, Inc., Cincinnati, OH '80 (MGMT)
ROOS, MARY LOU, asst. mgr. educ., Geisinger Wyoming Valley Medical Center, Wilkes-Barre, PA '85 (EDUC)
ROOSEVELT, JAMES JR., atty., Cape Cod Hospital, Hyannis, MA '84 (ATTY)
ROOSMA, LAURIE, student, Andrews University, Berrien Springs, MI '87 (AMB)
ROOT, ADITA L., RN, adm. spec. serv., Memorial Hospital System, Houston, TX '82 (NURS)
ROOT, DONNA GREENBERG, dir. pub. rel., Abington Memorial Hospital, Abington, PA '86 (PR)
ROOT, GEORGE L. JR., atty., Weissburg and Aronson, Inc., San Diego, CA '77 (ATTY)
ROOT, HARRY M., dir. phys. oper., Woods Psychiatric Institute, Abilene, TX '86 (ENG)
ROOT, JAMES M., mng. dir., J. M. Root and Associates, Woodbury, CT '84 (PLNG)
ROOT, JANE A., dir. human res., plng. and dev., St. Vincent Hospital and Health Center, Indianapolis, IN '74 (EDUC)
ROOT, VERNON T., Kalamazoo, MI '31 (LIFE)
ROOTS, WILLIAM W., dir. pub. info., St. Vincent's Medical Center, Bridgeport, CT '86 (PR)
ROOVER, JOAN E., dir. soc. serv., Charlton Memorial Hospital, Fall River, MA '81 (SOC)
ROPELLA, LORETTA M., asst. prof. soc. work, University of Wisconsin-Milwaukee, Milwaukee, WI '82 (SOC)
ROPER, CAROLE R., dir. media rel., Medical College of Virginia Hospitals, Virginia Commonwealth University, Richmond, VA '83 (PR)
ROPER, DIANE L., RN, asst. vice-pres., Methodist Hospitals of Gary, Gary, IN '81 (NURS)
ROPER, M. BRIAN, adm., University Children's Hospital at Hermann, Houston, TX '85
ROPER, PAUL H., adm., Baptist Memorial Hospital, San Antonio, TX '56 (LIFE)
ROPER, WAYNE J., atty., Froedtert Memorial Lutheran Hospital, Milwaukee, WI '79 (ATTY)
ROREM, C. RUFUS, (ret.), Cherry Hill, NJ '31 (LIFE)
RORRIE, COLIN C. JR., PhD, exec. dir., American College of Emergency Physicians, Irving, TX '64
ROSA, CAROLYN, asst. dir. pub. rel., Booth Memorial Medical Center, Flushing, NY '86 (PR)
ROSA, SUSAN M., dir. soc. serv., Knoxville Area Community Hospital, Knoxville, IA '86 (SOC)
ROSADO, JOSEPH, coor. trng., Presbyterian Hospital in the City of New York, New York, NY '84 (EDUC)
ROSANDER, LCDR R. R., clin. dir., Naval Branch Clinic, Kaneohe Bay, HI '79
ROSARIO, ROSA M., adm. util. review and qual. assur., Joint Diseases North General Hospital, New York, NY '86 (RISK)
ROSASCO, CAROL F., asst. dir., Mount Sinai Medical Center, Miami Beach, FL '87 (AMB)
ROSASCO, EDWARD J., pres. and chief exec. off., Mercy Hospital, Miami, FL '64
ROSASRIO, SR. ALTAGRACIA, RN, dir. nrsg., Hospital de Damas, Ponce, P.R. '78 (NURS)
ROSATO, GARY L., dir. phys. plant and grds., Itasca Memorial Hospital, Grand Rapids, MN '85 (ENG)
ROSATO, J. RONALD, dir. pur., Pendleton Memorial Methodist Hospital, New Orleans, LA '76 (PUR)
ROSATO, ROBERT E., pres., Brotherston Medical Supply, Philadelphia, PA '85 (PUR)
ROSATONE, COLLEEN E., instr., Divine Providence Hospital, Pittsburgh, PA '86 (EDUC)
ROSATTI, ALBERT C., dir. risk mgt., Westmoreland Hospital, Greensburg, PA '83 (RISK)
ROSBOROUGH, BRADLEY J., sr. consult., Arthur Young and Company, Los Angeles, CA '84
ROSCH, RENEE A., atty., Saratoga Hospital, Saratoga Springs, NY '86 (ATTY)
ROSCHE, BRYCE S., vice-pres. mktg., Port Huron Hospital, Port Huron, MI '84 (PLNG)
ROSCOE, RICK W., mgt. eng., Mount Sinai Medical Center, Cleveland, OH '86 (MGMT)
ROSCOW, LOYD J., coor. maint., Asc Health System, Red Bud, IL '75 (ENG)
ROSE, ARCHER RIDDICK, exec. dir., Rockdale Hospital, Conyers, GA '68
ROSE, AVIS A., coor. cent. sup., Illinois Valley Community Hospital, Peru, IL '81 (CS)
ROSE, BARBARA D., mgt. eng., Washoe Medical Center, Reno, NV '86 (MGMT)
ROSE, BARRY, dir. strategic plng., 3c's Corporate Health Group, Chicago, IL '79 (PLNG)
ROSE, C. ALEX, atty., NKC Hospitals, Louisville, KY '79 (ATTY)
ROSE, CAROL J., vice-pres. commun. rel. and mktg., Traverse City Osteopathic Hospital, Traverse City, MI '85 (PR)
ROSE, CAROLYN S., mgr. corp. pub., Intermountain Health Care, Inc., Salt Lake City, UT '86 (PR)
ROSE, EDWARD F., dir. vol. serv., Veterans Administration, Department of Medicine and Surgery, Washington, DC '81 (VOL)
ROSE, EILEEN D. M., RN, (ret.), London, Ont., Canada '71 (CS)
ROSE, ELIZABETH J., assoc. dir. plng., Stanford University Hospital, Stanford, CA '84 (ENG)
ROSE, FRANK A. JR., pres. and adm., Ppo-Mobile, Inc., Mobile, AL '84 (PLNG)
ROSE, JAMES C., dir. nutr., diet. and food serv., Harris Methodist -Fort Worth, Fort Worth, TX '77 (FOOD)
ROSE, JEWELL, dir. matl. mgt., Central Florida Regional Hospital, Sanford, FL '70 (PUR)
ROSE, JULIE A., RN, shift supv., Santa Clara Valley Medical Center, San Jose, CA '87 (NURS)
ROSE, KATHLEEN F., RN, dir. nrsg., Martha's Vineyard Hospital, Oak Bluffs, MA '82 (NURS)
ROSE, MICHAEL S., vice-pres., Western Pennsylvania Hospital, Pittsburgh, PA '74 (PLNG)
ROSE, PATRICIA H., U. S. Department of Energy-Institutional Conservation and Solar Energy Program, Washington, DC '86 (ENG)
ROSE, RUTH W., dir. nutr. serv., Mercy Medical Center, Nampa, ID '76 (FOOD)
ROSE, STEVEN A., RN, vice-pres. nrsg. serv., Holy Redeemer Hospital and Medical Center, Meadowbrook, PA '82 (NURS)
ROSE, THOMAS A., pres., North Carolina Blue Cross and Blue Shield, Inc., Durham, NC '64
ROSE, WALTER T. JR., atty., Cape Canaveral Hospital, Cocoa Beach, FL '81 (ATTY)
ROSE, WILLIAM P., vice-pres., Kaiser Health Plan, Oakland, CA '68
ROSE, WILMA, assoc. dir. soc. work serv., University Hospital, Stony Brook, NY '83 (SOC)
ROSECKY, SR. MARY DE PORRES, dir. soc. serv., St. Francis Hospital, Milwaukee, WI '77 (SOC)
ROSEFIELD, LAURENCE D., assoc. dir., Montefiore Medical Center, Bronx, NY '76
ROSELLI, JOANNE P., rep. referring physicians, Temple University Hospital, Philadelphia, PA '85 (PR)
ROSEN, C. DOUGLAS, adm., Warren Memorial Hospital, Front Royal, VA '75 (PLNG)
ROSEN, JERRY, vice-pres. mktg. and pub. affairs, Overlook Hospital, Summit, NJ '84 (PR)
ROSEN, LAWRENCE JAY, vice-pres. outpatient serv., Ridgeview Institute, Smyrna, GA '74
ROSEN, MARCIA N., adm. coor. med., New York Medical College, Lincoln Medical and Mental Health Center, Bronx, NY '83
ROSEN, MICHAEL N., atty., Mount Sinai Medical Center, New York, NY '82 (ATTY)
ROSEN, MORRIS D., atty., Medical Center of Medical University of South Carolina, Charleston, SC '77 (ATTY)
ROSEN, NANCY, adm. ped., Montefiore Medical Center, Bronx, NY '77
ROSEN, RAYMOND, adm. med. affairs, York Hospital, York, PA '75
ROSEN, SUZANNE, dir. vol. serv., Coney Island Hospital, Brooklyn, NY '66 (VOL)
ROSENBALM, EDWARD F. SR., supv. plant eng., Michiana Community Hospital, South Bend, IN '86 (ENG)
ROSENBAUM, MARCIA F., atty., Perry, Goldstein, Fialkowski and Perry, Philadelphia, PA '77
ROSENBECK, PAUL D., actg. asst. dir. food serv., Medical College of Ohio Hospital, Toledo, OH '82 (FOOD)
ROSENBEK, SUSAN, asst. dir. surg. serv., Meriter Hospital, Madison, WI '87 (AMB)
ROSENBERG, ARTHUR H., atty. and civil rights off., McLean Hospital, Belmont, MA '82 (ATTY)(PAT)
ROSENBERG, DOUGLAS O., pres. and chief oper. off., Glenbrook Hospital, Glenview, IL '76
ROSENBERG, GARY A., atty., New England Medical Center, Boston, MA '84 (ATTY)
ROSENBERG, GARY, PhD, dir. soc. work serv., Mount Sinai Medical Center, New York, NY '71 (SOC)(PERS)
ROSENBERG, LEONARD M., atty., Brookhaven Memorial Hospital Medical Center, Patchogue, NY '85 (ATTY)
ROSENBERG, LESTER A., vice-pres., Daniel, Mann, Johnson and Mendenhall, Los Angeles, CA '83 (ENG)
ROSENBERG, NEVA, Port Jefferson, NY '86 (PLNG)
ROSENBERG, PAUL M., assoc. dir. fiscal and adm. serv., Strong Memorial Hospital Rochester University, Rochester, NY '83 (RISK)
ROSENBERG, RICHELLE A., mgr. media rel., Hermann Hospital, Houston, TX '86 (PR)
ROSENBERG, THEODORE, assoc. adm., Florida Medical Center Hospital, Fort Lauderdale, FL '63
ROSENBERGER, DONALD MARKLEY, pres., Donald M. Rosenberger and Associates, Raymond, ME '39 (LIFE)
ROSENBLEETH, COL. MILTON H., MSC USA, asst. chief of staff, Walter Reed Army Medical Center, Washington, DC '70
ROSENBLOOM, AL, prin., A. and R. Consultants, Chicago, IL '86 (PLNG)
ROSENBLOOM, ALAN G., atty., Thomas Jefferson University Hospital, Philadelphia, PA '86 (ATTY)
ROSENBLOOM, E. SCOTT, MD, dir. emer. serv., Lodi Memorial Hospital, Lodi, CA '87 (AMB)
ROSENBLUM, ARNOLD E., pres., LaGuardia Hospital, Flushing, NY '63 (ATTY)
ROSENBLUM, JAMES, atty., Wilson, Elser, Moskowitz, Edelman and Dicker, New York, NY '87 (RISK)
ROSENBLUT, ALAN H., adm., Morrisania Neighborhood Family Care Center, Bronx, NY '69
ROSENDALE, CRAIG F., asst. dir. matl. mgt., Union Memorial Hospital, Baltimore, MD '84 (PUR)

ROSENE, EFFIE M., adm., Memorial Northwest Hospital, Houston, TX '82
ROSENFELD, EUGENE D., MD, pres., E. D. Rosenfeld Associates, Inc., Roslyn Heights, NY '47 (LIFE)
ROSENFELD, JO ANN, dir., MacNeal Hospital, Berwyn, IL '83 (AMB)
ROSENFELD, NORMAN, prin., Norman Rosenfeld Architects, New York, NY '78
ROSENFELD, ROBIN M., health care consult., Research and Planning Consultants, Austin, TX '86 (PLNG)
ROSENFELD, SUSAN CAROL, atty., Memorial Hospital for Cancer and Allied Diseases, New York, NY '76 (ATTY)
ROSENFIELD, FRAYNE, reg. health educ. spec., Southern California Kaiser Permanente, Pasadena, CA '86 (EDUC)
ROSENFIELD, MAJ. JAMES B., MSC USAF, dir. in-patient soc. work, Malcolm Grow U. S. Air Force Medical Center, Camp Springs, MD '86 (SOC)
ROSENFIELD, ROBERT H., atty., California Association of Hospitals and Health Systems, Sacramento, CA '78 (ATTY)
ROSENKRANTZ, JACOB A., MD, (ret.), Delray Beach, FL '48 (LIFE)
ROSENKRANZ, STANLEY W., atty., Tampa General Hospital, Tampa, FL '85 (ATTY)
ROSENMAN, HARRIET, RN, assoc. adm. nrsg., Hempstead General Hospital Medical Center, Hempstead, NY '85 (NURS)
ROSENSWIKE, CAPT. JAMES T., MSC USAF, dir. med. logistics mgt., 23rd Tactical Fighter Hospital, England AFB, LA '78
ROSENTHAL, DANIEL I., Deloitte Hoskins and Sells, Miami, FL '86 (PLNG)
ROSENTRATER, BRENDA M., dir. soc. serv., Goleta Valley Community Hospital, Santa Barbara, CA '81 (SOC)
ROSENVOLD, RICHARD C., adm. constr., plng., and design, Office of Licensure and Certification, State of Florida, Jacksonville, FL '86 (ENG)
ROSENZWEIG, HARRY, adm., Health & Human Services, Public Health Service, Bureau of Health Facilities, Hyattsville, MD '65
ROSENZWEIG, MICHAEL A., dir. eng., Calvary Hospital, Bronx, NY '84 (ENG)
ROSENZWEIG, PHYLLIS, supv. soc. work, Morristown Memorial Hospital, Morristown, NJ '86 (SOC)
ROSEQUIST, RONALD V., atty., Peralta Hospital, Oakland, CA '79 (ATTY)
ROSGONY, JOAN L., RN, adm. acute care nrsg., South Hills Health System, Pittsburgh, PA '85 (NURS)
ROSIER, NANCIANN, mgr. educ., Lancaster-Fairfield Community Hospital, Lancaster, OH '86 (EDUC)
ROSILLO, RUDY, student, Southern Illinois University, Carbondale, IL '83
ROSINI, SUSAN B., dir. mktg. and pub. rel., Delray Community Hospital, Delray Beach, FL '84 (PR)
ROSITO, ANNAGRACE R., student, Thomas A. Edison State College, Trenton, NJ '86 (FOOD)
ROSKELLY, JAMES, dir. corp. plng. and dev., Moses H. Cone Memorial Hospital, Greensboro, NC '86 (PLNG)
ROSKO, MICHAEL D., asst. prof., Widener College, Chester, PA '72
ROSKOS, RICHARD G., chief eng., Greene Memorial Hospital, Xenia, OH '74 (ENG)
ROSKOSKI, MARGARET JEANETTE, mgr. diet. serv., Virginia Regional Medical Center, Virginia, MN '68 (FOOD)
ROSMAN, BRIAN M., mgr. plng., AMI Diagnostic Services, Inc., Beverly Hills, CA '85
ROSNER, LAWRENCE, dir. human res., Union Hospital, Union, NJ '84 (PERS)
ROSNIK, BARBARA M., coor. vol. serv., Lansing General Hospital, Lansing, MI '84 (VOL)
ROSOWITZ, WILLIAM C., mgr. diet., Community Hospital Medical Center, Phoenix, AZ '84 (FOOD)
ROSS, ARTHUR M., dir. food serv., Bishop Glen Life Care Center, Holly Hill, FL '86 (FOOD)
ROSS, AUSTIN JR., vice-pres., Virginia Mason Medical Center, Seattle, WA '67
ROSS, BARBARA S., dir. vol. serv., Trinity Lutheran Hospital, Kansas City, MO '84 (VOL)
ROSS, BARBARA, RN, coor. pat. educ., St. Luke's Regional Medical Center, Boise, ID '84 (EDUC)
ROSS, BARRY T., assoc. vice-pres., St. Luke's-Roosevelt Hospital Center, New York, NY '71 (MGMT)
ROSS, BERNARD H., exec. dir. natl. serv. for health care, Touche Ross and Company, Chicago, IL '70
ROSS, BETSY, dir., Saint Michael's Medical Center, Newark, NJ '86
ROSS, CHRISTINE D., dir. commun. rel. and dev., John E. Fogarty Memorial Hospital, North Smithfield, RI '83 (PR)
ROSS, DAVID ALLAN, dir. nutr. serv., Lorain Community Hospital, Lorain, OH '74 (FOOD)
ROSS, DAVID E., sr. mng. assoc., Ross Associates, Coudersport, PA '79 (PLNG)
ROSS, DAVID HARVEY, MD, med. dir., Nassau County Department of Health, Mineola, NY '43 (LIFE)
ROSS, DAVID L., atty., Medical College of Virginia, Health Sciences Division, Virginia Commonwealth University, Richmond, VA '77 (ATTY)
ROSS, DEBRA A., dir. diet., Haverford Community Hospital, Havertown, PA '86 (FOOD)
ROSS, DOROTHY M., dir. mktg., New England Deaconess Hospital, Boston, MA '84 (PR) (PLNG)
ROSS, EDWARD J., dir. maint., Miners Hospital Northern Cambria, Spangler, PA '83 (ENG)
ROSS, EDWIN S., asst. vice-pres., American Medical International, Beverly Hills, CA '77 (CS)
ROSS, ELLEN M., RN, vice-pres. nrsg. serv., Port Huron Hospital, Port Huron, MI '86 (NURS)
ROSS, GEORGIA A., dir. soc. serv., St. Francis Hospital of New Castle, New Castle, PA '77 (SOC)
ROSS, HARVEY D., adm. res., Muskogee Regional Medical Center, Muskogee, OK '83
ROSS, J. M., exec. dir., Fairmont Clinic, Fairmont, WV '85
ROSS, JAMES E., dir. prof. serv., St. Joseph Hospital, Lancaster, PA '78 (MGMT)
ROSS, JAMES L., dir. pur. and stores, North Carolina Memorial Hospital, Chapel Hill, NC '79 (PUR)
ROSS, JOAN A., atty., Geisinger Medical Center, Danville, PA '86 (ATTY)
ROSS, JOHN E., dir. pers., St. Francis Hospital Center, Beech Grove, IN '81 (PERS)
ROSS, JOHN J., atty., Children's Hospital National Medical Center, Washington, DC '70 (ATTY)
ROSS, JOYCE, vice-pres. mktg., Baylor University Medical Center, Dallas, TX '80 (PR) (PLNG)
ROSS, JUDITH C., RN, assoc. exec. dir. nrsg., Beaumont Medical Surgical Hospital, Beaumont, TX '86 (NURS)
ROSS, JUDITH N., dir. vol. serv., St. Luke's Memorial Hospital, Spokane, WA '85 (VOL)
ROSS, KATALINA, RN, dir. nrs., Centro Medico Paitilla, Panama, Panama '86 (NURS)
ROSS, KATHRYN W., RN, vice-pres. pat. care serv., Mercy Medical Center, Durango, CO '81 (NURS)
ROSS, KENNETH L. JR., prin., The Falick-Klein Partnership, Inc., Houston, TX '77 (PLNG)
ROSS, KEVIN M., asst. adm., Nesbitt Memorial Hospital, Kingston, PA '84
ROSS, LAURA M., consult., Telecommunications Management, Inc., Houston, TX '84 (ENG)
ROSS, LIZ, pat. rep., Hillcrest Medical Center, Tulsa, OK '81 (PAT)
ROSS, MARTHA F., RN, chairperson nrsg. and pat. care mgt., North Carolina Memorial Hospital, Chapel Hill, NC '85 (NURS)
ROSS, MARTIN B., PhD, vice-pres., Korn-Ferry International, Los Angeles, CA '84
ROSS, MARY E., vice-pres. nrsg., Greater Baltimore Medical Center, Baltimore, MD '80 (NURS)
ROSS, MARY TAFURI, dir. plng., Westerly Hospital, Westerly, RI '83 (PLNG)
ROSS, MURRAY WILLIAM, exec. dir., Alberta Hospital Association, Edmonton, Alta., Canada '50 (LIFE)
ROSS, PATRICIA F., dir. soc. serv., Olean General Hospital, Olean, NY '87 (SOC)
ROSS, PETER W., dir. plant oper., Franklin Memorial Hospital, Farmington, ME '85 (ENG)
ROSS, R. EUGENE, vice-pres. human res., Memorial Care Systems, Houston, TX '86 (PERS)
ROSS, RICHARD A., supt. plant, Walla Walla General Hospital, Walla Walla, WA '75 (ENG)
ROSS, RONI M., mgr. pers., Mount Carmel Hospital, Colville, WA '86 (PERS)
ROSS, TERRY L., supv. maint., plumbing and painting, Memorial Medical Center, Long Beach, CA '83 (ENG)
ROSS, THOMAS L., sr. vice-pres. pat. rel. and serv., Memorial Hospital, Pawtucket, RI '80
ROSS, ZEFF, asst. exec. dir., Humana Hospital -Biscayne, Miami, FL '79
ROSSA, LCDR PETER, coor. qual. assur., Naval Medical Clinic, Portsmouth, NH '87 (RISK)
ROSSATE, DAVID S., dir. emp. rel., Mercy Hospital, Cedar Rapids, IA '78 (PERS)
ROSSELLI, VIRGINIA REGAN, mgr. and ombudsman emp. rel., Cleveland Clinic Hospital, Cleveland, OH '85 (PAT)
ROSSER, DEENA L., RN, chief nrsg. serv., William Jennings Bryan Dorn Veterans Hospital, Columbia, SC '82 (NURS)
ROSSER, JANE W., Duncan, OK '83 (VOL)
ROSSI, CAROLE, pat. rep., Western Pennsylvania Hospital, Pittsburgh, PA '80 (PAT)
ROSSI, CONSTANCE, RN, supv. cent. serv. sup., Lankenau Hospital, Philadelphia, PA '85 (CS)
ROSSI, FRANK J., vice-pres., Leigh Memorial Hospital, Norfolk, VA '77 (PERS)
ROSSI, JOHN A., syst. eng., Harvard Community Health Plan, Brookline Village, MA '81 (MGMT)
ROSSI, JOSEPH J. JR., chief exec. off., St. Francis Hospital, Milwaukee, WI '59
ROSSI, LINDA J., field vice-pres., American General Corporation, Sacramento, CA '86
ROSSI, LOUIS A., dir. eng., Mercy Hospital, Springfield, MA '79 (ENG)
ROSSI, ROBERT A., pres., Robert, Nickerson, McCreery and Sitzenstock, Inc., Toledo, OH '86 (ENG)
ROSSI, THOM, dir. human res., Riddle Memorial Hospital, Media, PA '79 (PERS)
ROSSITER, LILLIAN, RN, tech. consult., Bishop Clarkson Memorial Hospital, Omaha, NE '74 (EDUC)
ROSSITER, PAUL, dir. environ. serv., Chesapeake General Hospital, Chesapeake, VA '87 (ENVIRON)
ROSSITER, WARD, vice-pres. support serv., Deaconess Hospital, Cincinnati, OH '85 (ENG)(RISK)
ROSSMAN, CHRIS, atty., Michigan Hospital Association Service Corporation, Lansing, MI '78 (ATTY)
ROSSMAN, JOHN CHARLES, vice-pres. econ. and policy dev., Hospital Association of New York State, Albany, NY '59
ROSSMANN, DUANE K., adm., HCA Doctors Hospital, Conroe, TX '78
ROSSMEISSL, JAMES M., vice-pres., Oscar J. Boldt Construction Company, Appleton, WI '83
ROSSTON, RICHARD M., atty., Charter Medical Corporation, Macon, GA '83 (ATTY)
ROSTEN, PAULINE J., mgr. hskpg., Vail Valley Medical Center, Vail, CO '86 (ENVIRON)
ROSZKOWSKI, JOSEPH J., atty., John E. Fogarty Memorial Hospital, North Smithfield, RI '79 (ATTY)
ROSZKOWSKI, MARY A., FPO New York, NY '86 (EDUC)
ROTAR, ROBERT A., adm. human res., United Health Services, Inc., Grand Forks, ND '85 (PERS)
ROTAR, STEPHEN J., asst. dir. plant serv., St. Marys Hospital Medical Center, Madison, WI '84 (ENG)
ROTH, ANDREW B., atty., Beekman Downtown Hospital, New York, NY '77 (ATTY)
ROTH, BARRY HOWARD, pres., Forbes Health System, Pittsburgh, PA '72
ROTH, BILL, plant eng., St. Luke's Hospital, Aberdeen, SD '78 (ENG)
ROTH, CAROLYN, student, Program in Hospital and Health Care Administration, St. Louis University School of Law, St. Louis, MO '86 (RISK)
ROTH, CLARA G., RN, asst. adm. nrsg. serv., Skagit Valley Hospital and Health Center, Mount Vernon, WA '81 (NURS)
ROTH, EDWARD J. III, dir. matl. mgt., Aultman Hospital, Canton, OH '86 (PUR)
ROTH, ERLO, MD, chief pathologists, Suburban Hospital and Sanitarium-Cook County, Hinsdale, IL '85
ROTH, FRANK J., dir. pur. and stores, Christ Hospital, Cincinnati, OH '71 (PUR)
ROTH, IRVING, asst. dir., Kingsbrook Jewish Medical Center, Brooklyn, NY '80 (RISK)
ROTH, JOHN K., dir. mgt. serv., Nexus Healthcare Corporation, Mount Holly, NJ '77 (MGMT)
ROTH, KARLA M., dir. vol. serv., Concord Hospital, Concord, NH '84 (VOL)
ROTH, MARY E., RN, dir. nrs. specialty care areas, Memorial Hospital at Gulfport, Gulfport, MS '86 (NURS)
ROTH, MICHAEL D., atty., Capitol Hill Hospital, Washington, DC '79 (ATTY)
ROTH, NORMAN G., asst. vice-pres., Veterans Administration Medical Center, West Haven, CT '75
ROTH, PATRICIA A., Milway Corporation, Radnor, PA '80 (RISK)
ROTH, RAMSAY, mgt. eng., Medical College of Virginia Hospitals, Virginia Commonwealth University, Richmond, VA '83 (MGMT)
ROTH, RICHARD A., mgt. eng., Sierra Medical Center, El Paso, TX '84 (MGMT)
ROTH, ROLAND W., mgr. matl., Community Health Center of Branch County, Coldwater, MI '82 (PUR)
ROTH, ROSEMARY A., RN, asst. dir. nrsg. practice, oper. room and amb. surg. unit, Genesee Hospital, Rochester, NY '87 (NURS)
ROTH, SARAH J., adm. diet. and food supv., West Nebraska General Hospital, Scottsbluff, NE '85 (FOOD)
ROTH, WILLIAM S., pres., Baptist Medical Centers, Birmingham, AL '69 (PR)
ROTHENBERG, JOAN R., dir. info. serv., South Baltimore General Hospital, Baltimore, MD '85 (MGMT)
ROTHENBERG, LESLIE STEVEN, atty., Los Angeles, CA '80 (ATTY)
ROTHENBERGER, DALE L., dir. food serv., Wuesthoff Memorial Hospital, Rockledge, FL '76 (FOOD)
ROTHENBERGER, GARY L., Veterans Administration Medical Center, Marion, IL '76 (SOC)
ROTHENBUEHLER, GARY LEE, supt. plant, Sioux Valley Hospital, Sioux Falls, SD '79 (ENG)
ROTHENHAUSLER, SHIRLEY A., dir. pers., Terrace Plaza Medical Center, Baldwin Park, CA '86 (PERS)
ROTHERMEL, JANE, dir. amb. care, Wake Medical Center, Raleigh, NC '83 (AMB)
ROTHERMICH, JOANN, dir. med. rec., Medical Care Group, St. Louis, MO '84 (RISK)
ROTHGEB, RICHARD PRICE, dir. pers., Retreat Hospital, Richmond, VA '77 (PERS)
ROTHMAN, DENISE E., dir. plng. and govt. rel., Vassar Brothers Hospital, Poughkeepsie, NY '80 (PLNG)
ROTHMAN, ELLIOT PAUL, dir., Martha L. Rothman and Elliot Paul Rothman, Inc., Boston, MA '84
ROTHMAN, IRA J., sr. mgr., Ernst and Whinney, Chicago, IL '86 (MGMT)
ROTHMAN, WILLIAM ARTHUR, exec. vice-pres., Gaylord Hospital, Wallingford, CT '55 (LIFE)
ROTHROCK, CLIFFORD D., dir. pers. and labor rel., Metropolitan Hospital and Health Centers, Detroit, MI '77 (PERS)
ROTHSCHILD, LINDA M., RN, dir. med. and surg. nrsg., Chestnut Hill Hospital, Philadelphia, PA '83 (NURS)
ROTHWELL, LORI LYNN, pat. rep., AMI Presbyterian Aurora Hospital, Aurora, CO '86 (PAT)
ROTKOVITCH, RACHEL, RN, Yale-New Haven Hospital, New Haven, CT '68 (NURS)
ROTONDO, DANTE M., asst. vice-pres. human res., Oakwood Hospital, Dearborn, MI '80 (PERS)
ROTONDO, GIL M., dir. human res., Mercy Hospital, Springfield, MA '83 (PERS)
ROTTACH, ANNA T., pat. rep., Winter Park Memorial Hospital, Winter Park, FL '84 (PAT)
ROUBAL, CAROLINE A., chief diet., Eastern New Mexico Medical Center, Roswell, NM '80 (FOOD)
ROUDABUSH, MICHAEL O., sr. mgt. eng., St. Joseph Hospital, Flint, MI '84 (MGMT)
ROULAND, MARY A., RN, adm. supv., Westside Hospital, Los Angeles, CA '77 (NURS)
ROUNDS, PEARL, risk and qual. assur. mgr., Little Company of Mary Hospital, Torrance, CA '86 (RISK)
ROUNDS, ROBERT J., mgr. telecommun. and electronics, Wausau Hospital Center, Wausau, WI '86 (ENG)
ROUNDS, THOMAS W., dir. matl. and sup. serv., St. Marys Hospital Medical Center, Madison, WI '87 (PUR)
ROURKE, ANTHONY J. J. JR., pres., Anthony J. J. Rourke, Inc., Harrison, NY '85 (MGMT)
ROURKE, MARY P., student, Program in Health Systems Management, University of Connecticut, Storrs, CT '86 (MGMT)
ROUSE, DANIEL R., asst. dir. plant serv., University Hospital, Jacksonville, FL '86 (ENG)
ROUSE, LUCY C., RN, asst. vice-pres. nrsg., Riverside Methodist Hospitals, Columbus, OH '87 (NURS)
ROUSE, RICHARD P., dir. matl. mgt., Central DuPage Hospital, Winfield, IL '80 (PUR)
ROUSSEAU, CHRIS P., eng., Newcomb and Boyd Consulting Engineers, Atlanta, GA '84 (ENG)
ROUSSEAU, HUGHETTE, pat. rep., Centre Hospitalier Universitaire de Sherbrooke, Sherbrooke, Que., Canada '75 (PAT)
ROUSSEAU, ISABELLE MARY, RN, vice-pres. nrsg., Catholic Medical Center, Manchester, NH '67 (NURS)

ROUSSEAU, JEANIE A., dir. vol., South Community Hospital, Oklahoma City, OK '84 (VOL)
ROUSSEAU, MICHAEL L., dir. eng., St. Bernardine Medical Center, San Bernardino, CA '76 (ENG)
ROUSSEAU, ROBERTA, atty., Wilkes-Barre General Hospital, Wilkes-Barre, PA '80 (ATTY)
ROUSSIN, ROBERT D., mgr. matl., Indian River Memorial Hospital, Vero Beach, FL '83 (PUR)
ROUTH, BILLIE, dir. staff dev., Community General Hospital, Thomasville, NC '82 (EDUC)
ROUTH, JANET L., RN, mgr. pat. care serv., Mercy Hospital of Pittsburgh, Pittsburgh, PA '86 (NURS)
ROUTH, ROBERT, asst. vice-pres. bldg. serv., Palisades General Hospital, North Bergen, NJ '80 (ENG)
ROUTLEDGE, JOHN J., dir. pub. rel., Newark Beth Israel Medical Center, Newark, NJ '81 (PR)
ROUTSON, THOMAS C., dir. loss prevention, Georgia Baptist Medical Center, Atlanta, GA '83 (RISK)
ROUTT, BRENDA K., RN, Grand Prairie, TX '86 (NURS)
ROVERE, CARLA LISA, dir. soc. work, Newton Memorial Hospital, Newton, NJ '86 (SOC)
ROVINSKY, MICHAEL, staff consult., Ernst and Whinney, Washington, DC '85
ROVNAK, STEPHANIE MARY, pat. rep., Wheeling Hospital, Wheeling, WV '85 (PAT)
ROVNER, STEVEN P., dir. pur., Frankford Hospital, Philadelphia, PA '81 (PUR)
ROW, CONSTANCE F., pres., Calvert Memorial Hospital, Prince Frederick, MD '83 (PLNG)
ROWAN, BRIAN ANTHONY, mgt. trainee, Bethesda Hospital, Inc., Cincinnati, OH '83
ROWAN, DOROTHY J., coor. educ., Southwest Washington Hospitals, Vancouver, WA '85 (EDUC)
ROWAN, GILBERT R., MD, dir. emer. medicine, Greenwich Hospital, Greenwich, CT '86 (AMB)
ROWAN, JOHN R., dir., Veterans Administration Medical Center, Lexington, KY '57 (LIFE)
ROWAN, MARGARET, asst. vice-pres. and risk mgr., Kuakini Medical Center, Honolulu, HI '86 (RISK)
ROWAN, MICHAEL TERRANCE, asst. vice-pres., St. Vincent Medical Center, Toledo, OH '81 (AMB)
ROWE, CARMEN W., mgr. plant eng. and maint., Waynesboro Hospital, Waynesboro, PA '85 (ENG)
ROWE, DAVID E., pres., David Rowe and Associates, Hinsdale, IL '85
ROWE, DAVID W., mgr. bldg., Lutheran Hospital of Fort Wayne, Fort Wayne, IN '78 (ENG)
ROWE, GEORGE M., mgr. ldry., St. Mary's Hospital, Enid, OK '86 (ENVIRON)
ROWE, KIM G., atty., Washoe Medical Center, Reno, NV '86 (ATTY)
ROWE, MARGARET S., mgr. natl. diet. syst., American Hospital Supply Corporation, McGaw Park, IL '83 (FOOD)
ROWE, RONALD, adm., Rocky Mountain Hospital, Denver, CO '86 (RISK)
ROWELL, BRADFORD V., dir. pub. affairs, Bay State Health Care, Cambridge, MA '85 (PR)
ROWELL, JAMES H., dir. matl. mgt., Polk General Hospital, Bartow, FL '77 (PUR)
ROWELL, JIMMY H., dir. pers., Rutherford Hospital, Rutherfordton, NC '84 (PERS)
ROWELL, PATRICIA O'BRIEN, dir. vol., Massachusetts General Hospital, Boston, MA '80 (VOL)
ROWELL, ROBIN, dir. environ. serv., Mission Community Hospital, Mission Viejo, CA '86 (ENVIRON)
ROWELL, TIMOTHY J., mgt. eng., Deaconess Hospital of Cleveland, Cleveland, OH '83 (MGMT)
ROWELL, VALERIE G., mgt. eng., Fresno Community Hospital and Medical Center, Fresno, CA '85 (MGMT)
ROWETT, NANCY G., dir. pub. rel., Rhode Island Hospital, Providence, RI '75 (PR)
ROWLAND, JEANNE C., dir. human res., Franciscan Medical Center, Rock Island, IL '85 (PERS)
ROWLAND, JOHN A., pres., St. John and West Shore Hospital, Westlake, OH '85 (PLNG)
ROWLAND, PAUL J., dir. plng., Mercy Hospital, Rockville Centre, NY '82 (PLNG)
ROWLETT, LAURA, mgr. bus. off., AMI Nacogdoches Medical Center Hospital, Nacogdoches, TX '85
ROWLETTE, LT. COL. LEMUEL A., MSC USA, chief directorate pat. adm., Fitzsimons Army Medical Center, Aurora, CO '76
ROWLEY, GEORGE W., coor. educ., Restorative Services, Inc., Hobart, IN '86 (EDUC)
ROWLEY, MAVIS, asst. adm., Swedish Hospital Medical Center, Seattle, WA '84 (PLNG)
ROWLEY, PAUL W., adm., Central Laboratories, Timonium, MD '79
ROWLEY, PENNY Y., dir. nutr. and food serv., Saint Francis Hospital, Tulsa, OK '78 (FOOD)
ROWLEY, VICTOR C., Rowley Associates, Rochester, NY '65 (PR) (PLNG)
ROWSE, MARGARET B., supv. cent. serv., Sturdy Memorial Hospital, Attleboro, MA '86 (CS)
ROWTON, HILDE R., dir. soc. serv., Jess Parrish Memorial Hospital, Titusville, FL '81 (SOC)
ROY, ARTHUR P., atty., North Colorado Medical Center, Greeley, CO '86 (ATTY)
ROY, FRANCES R., RN, vice-pres. nrsg. affairs, Mid-Maine Medical Center, Waterville, ME '84 (NURS)
ROY, GAIL F., mgr. sales and prof. rel., St. Joseph Hospital, Orange, CA '85 (PLNG)
ROY, GEORGE R., dir. matl. and prop. mgt., John E. Fogarty Memorial Hospital, North Smithfield, RI '81 (ENG)
ROY, JAMES M. JR., atty., Springdale Memorial Hospital, Springdale, AR '76 (ATTY)
ROY, ROBERT E., risk mgr., Sturdy Memorial Hospital, Attleboro, MA '83 (RISK)
ROY, VIC, sr. mgt. eng., University of Cincinnati Hospital, Cincinnati, OH '86 (MGMT)
ROYAL, DELORES C., dir. pub. affairs and dev., University Hospital, Augusta, GA '82 (PR)
ROYALS, ALVIN WRAY, dir. mgt. eng., Dallas County Hospital District, Dallas, TX '86 (MGMT)
ROYBAL, CHARLOTTE, dir. plng. and dev., St. Vincent Hospital, Santa Fe, NM '85 (PLNG)
ROYSTER, CHERYL LYNN, dir. soc. serv., Fayette County Memorial Hospital, Washington Court House, OH '78 (SOC)
ROZAS, SIDNEY J., MD, pres., AMI Doctors' Hospital of Opelousas, Opelousas, LA '45 (LIFE)
ROZBORIL, APRIL, RN, vice-pres. nrsg., Charles S. Wilson Memorial Hospital, Johnson City, NY '82 (NURS)
ROZMAREK, ROSALYN I., RN, dir. nrsg. serv., Sandwich Community Hospital, Sandwich, IL '73 (NURS)
ROZMUS, MICHAEL J., sr. consult., Price Waterhouse, Pittsburgh, PA '84 (MGMT)
ROZOVSKY, FAY A., assoc. prof. gerontology, Mount St. Vincent University, Halifax, N.S., Canada '78 (ATTY)(RISK)
ROZRAN, ANDREA R., prin., Diversified Health Resources, Inc., Chicago, IL '79 (PLNG)
ROZWADOWSKI, THOMAS A., dir. eng., Frisbie Memorial Hospital, Rochester, NH '84 (ENG)
RUA, PATRICIA PAYER, dir. diet., Mary Greeley Medical Center, Ames, IA '74 (FOOD)
RUANE, BARBARA ANN, vice-pres. nrsg., East Orange General Hospital, East Orange, NJ '81 (NURS)
RUANE, MARILOUISE AGNONE, dir. pub. rel., Community Medical Center, Scranton, PA '77 (PR)
RUBARTH, HANS H., chief productivity improvement prog., Department of National Health and Welfare, Ottawa, Ont., Canada '86 (MGMT)
RUBEL, ERIC, USA, student, Army-Baylor University Program in Health Care Administration, Fort Sam Houston, TX '84
RUBEL, JUDITH D., asst. dir. pub. rel., Lahey Clinic Hospital, Burlington, MA '86 (PR)
RUBENDALL, PATRICIA, dir. pub. rel., St. Joseph Hospital, Mitchell, SD '78 (PR)
RUBENSTEIN, A. DANIEL, MD, consult., Massachusetts Department of Public Health, Bureau of Hospital Facilities, Lynn, MA '48 (LIFE)
RUBESCH, BETTY C., dir. pat. serv., Bridgeport Hospital, Bridgeport, CT '85 (PAT)
RUBIN, MICHAEL S., mgr. institutional audit, Blue Cross and Blue Shield, Miami, FL '82
RUBIN, MURRAY J., assoc. exec. dir., St. John's Riverside Hospital, Yonkers, NY '80
RUBIN, VALERIE K., dir. mktg. and commun. rel., South Miami Hospital, South Miami, FL '81 (PR)
RUBINGER, MARC, vice-pres., The Peabody Group, San Francisco, CA '76
RUBINSTEIN, DOUGLAS, pres., Douglas Group, Inc., Avon, CT '83
RUBINSTEIN, MORRIS, soc. work consult., Veterans Administration Hospital, Hines, IL '69
RUBINSTEIN, WALTER L., mgr., Ernst and Whinney, Los Angeles, CA '82 (MGMT)
RUBLE, VIRGINIA C., asst. adm. anes., Tyler Memorial Hospital, Tunkhannock, PA '70 (PERS)
RUBOTZKY, ALICEBELLE, RN, chief nrsg. serv., Veterans Administration Medical Center, Brooklyn, NY '84 (NURS)
RUBY, ELLEN, Ruby and Cuyjet, Associates, Southampton, NY '84 (SOC)
RUCH, BARBARA J., coor. cent. sup., Marianjoy Rehabilitation Center, Wheaton, IL '85 (CS)
RUCH, SHIRLEY M., RN, dir. maternal and child health nrsg., Polyclinic Medical Center, Harrisburg, PA '86 (NURS)
RUCHLIN, HIRSCH S., health econ., Society of the New York Hospital, New York, NY '85
RUCK, KATHRYN M., dir. pub. rel., Presbyterian-University of Pennsylvania Medical Center, Philadelphia, PA '81 (PR)
RUCKDESCHEL, MARY L., supv. soc. work, Barnes Hospital, St. Louis, MO '83 (SOC)
RUCKER, CHARLES MARTIN, dir. soc. serv., St. Elizabeth Hospital, Appleton, WI '86 (SOC)
RUCKER, ROBERT L., dir. pur., Gottlieb Memorial Hospital, Melrose Park, IL '76 (PUR)
RUCKER, WOMACK H. JR., exec. asst. to pres., Meharry Medical College, Nashville, TN '76 (PLNG)
RUDD, NICHOLAS V., dir. eng. and grds., Primary Children's Medical Center, Salt Lake City, UT '84 (ENG)
RUDDELL, CHARLES A., adm. stores br. and food mgt., Naval Hospital, San Diego, CA '84 (FOOD)
RUDDELL, JANE, atty., Lankenau Hospital, Philadelphia, PA '85 (ATTY)
RUDDER, NORMA L., assoc. dir. and risk mgt. off., Queens Hospital Center, Jamaica, NY '82 (RISK)
RUDDICK, STEVEN L., atty., University of Kansas Hospital, Kansas City, KS '84 (ATTY)
RUDDY, MAUREEN, mgt. analyst, Williamsburg Community Hospital, Williamsburg, VA '85 (RISK)
RUDERMAN, RENEE F., RN, vice-pres. nrsg., Northern Westchester Hospital Center, Mount Kisco, NY '81 (NURS)
RUDIN, HY, vice-pres. human res., Abington Memorial Hospital, Abington, PA '78 (PERS)
RUDIN, JOEL, vice-pres. amb. care, Braintree Hospital, Braintree, MA '87 (AMB)
RUDIN, KATHY J., dir. pat. rel., University Hospital, Jacksonville, FL '85 (PAT)
RUDISILL, AUDREY KAY, RN, dir. nrsg., Charlotte Rehabilitation Hospital, Charlotte, NC '80 (NURS)
RUDMAN, JAY, adm. dir. pat. care serv., Cedars of Lebanon Hospital Division, Los Angeles, CA '78 (SOC)
RUDNER, PATSY ESTELLE, coor. commun. rel. and vol. serv., Mount Sinai Hospital Center, Ste-Agathe Des Monts, Que., Canada '86 (PR)
RUDNICKI, LYNN K., RN, dir. nrsg., Grand View Hospital, Ironwood, MI '83 (NURS)
RUDOLPH, BELLE, dir. food serv., Hempstead General Hospital Medical Center, Hempstead, NY '67 (FOOD)
RUDOLPH, JONATHAN M., dir. syst. dev., Baystate Medical Center, Springfield, MA '84 (PLNG)
RUDOLPH, NANCY B., dir. vol. serv., Flower Memorial Hospital, Sylvania, OH '84 (VOL)
RUDOLPH, STEPHEN PAUL, Wisconsin Physicians Service, Madison, WI '77 (PLNG)
RUDOLPHSEN, DON, asst. adm. gen. serv., Rehabilitation Institute of Chicago, Chicago, IL '76 (ENG)(RISK)
RUE, JONATHAN L., atty., South Miami Hospital, South Miami, FL '86 (ATTY)
RUE, NANCY R., dir. educ., Morton F. Plant Hospital, Clearwater, FL '86 (EDUC)
RUECKERT, CARL F., adm. dir. path., Faxton Hospital, Utica, NY '81 (MGMT)
RUECKERT, JOHN E., pres., Medco, Inc., Locust Grove, VA '67 (MGMT)
RUEDIGER, LINDA K., RN, supv. oper. and emer. room, Hermann Area District Hospital, Hermann, MO '85 (CS)
RUELLO, ROBERT A., asst. adm., Mercy Hospital of New Orleans, New Orleans, LA '81 (PERS)
RUEN, CYNTHIA A., dir. pub. rel., Great Plains Regional Medical Center, North Platte, NE '86 (PR)
RUETER, STEVEN, chief oper. off., Health Ad, Orlando, FL '74 (PLNG)
RUF, GEORGIA, RN, adm. nrsg. serv., HCA North Beach Hospital, Fort Lauderdale, FL '84 (NURS)
RUF, KATHY, PhD, asst. prof., Loma Linda University, Riverside, CA '78 (FOOD)
RUFE, GREG, asst. adm., Bexar County Hospital District, San Antonio, TX '80
RUFF, CLARICE J., coor. pat. diagnostic coder, Johns Hopkins Hospital, Baltimore, MD '87
RUFF, GEORGE G. JR., atty., Baptist Medical Center-Montclair, Birmingham, AL '83 (RISK)(ATTY)
RUFF, MICHAEL F., coor. health care fin. res., Hospital Corporation of America Management Company, Newton, MA '79
RUFF, STEPHEN L. SR., atty., Columbus Hospital, Chicago, IL '70 (ATTY)
RUFF, STEPHEN L. JR., atty., Columbus Hospital, Chicago, IL '75 (ATTY)
RUFFIN, EDMUND S. III, atty., Presbyterian-University Hospital, Pittsburgh, PA '73 (ATTY)
RUFFIN, JO, dir. pur., Grand Valley Hospital, Pryor, OK '77 (PUR)
RUFFIN, MARTHA A., pur. agt., Sierra Vista Community Hospital, Sierra Vista, AZ '81 (PUR)
RUFFING, SR. MARY DANIEL, RN, vice-pres. prof. serv., St. Francis Medical Center, Pittsburgh, PA '79 (NURS)
RUFFNER, CURTIS K. JR., head eng., Saint Joseph Hospital, Reading, PA '71 (ENG)
RUFFNER, JAY S., atty., Phoenix Baptist Hospital and Medical Center, Phoenix, AZ '83 (ATTY)
RUFFOLO, ELLEN A., dir. soc. serv., Warren General Hospital, Warren, PA '85 (SOC)
RUFKAHR, SR. DOROTHY C., dir. pers. serv., Sisters of St. Mary, St. Louis, MO '67 (PERS)
RUFLIN, PAUL L., sr. mgr., Ernst and Whinney, Cleveland, OH '85 (MGMT)
RUFO, MARY KATHRYN, EdD, coor. nrsg. res. and dev., Medical College of Georgia, Augusta, GA '85 (EDUC)
RUGG, DEBORAH C., educ. spec., Carle Foundation Hospital, Urbana, IL '86 (EDUC)
RUGG, ROSEANNE M., dir. plng., Cedars Medical Center, Miami, FL '85 (PLNG)
RUGGIERI, RICHARD J., partner, Deloitte Haskins and Sells, Baltimore, MD '84
RUGGLES, ELAINE M., RN, assoc. adm., Harris County Psychiatric Center, Houston, TX '80 (NURS)
RUGGLES, JOSEPH R., dir. cont. educ., Ohio Hospital Association, Columbus, OH '78 (EDUC)
RUGH, JOHN P., consult., St. Luke's Hospital, Newburgh, NY '57 (LIFE)
RUGH, MARTY, dir. pub. rel., St. Vincent Hospital and Health Center, Indianapolis, IN '77 (PR)
RUIZ, NEFTALIE, dir. environ. and ldry. serv., Long Beach Memorial Hospital, Long Beach, NY '86 (ENVIRON)
RUJAN, ADAM J., mgt. eng., Harper Hospital, Detroit, MI '84 (MGMT)
RULE, JACK, proj. eng., Cromwell Firm, Little Rock, AR '86 (ENG)
RULE, JOANNE THOMPSON, asst. dir. soc. work-ped., Johns Hopkins Hospital, Baltimore, MD '86 (SOC)
RULEY, DANIEL A. JR., atty., Camden-Clark Memorial Hospital, Parkersburg, WV '75 (ATTY)
RULISON, ROBERT G., asst. dir., Malden Hospital, Malden, MA '67
RULLI, GENE, asst. dir. plant oper., Niagara Falls Memorial Medical Center, Niagara Falls, NY '86 (ENG)
RULLMAN, STANLEY D., atty., Mercy Hospital, Hamilton, OH '76 (ATTY)
RULLO, MARIA MICHELE, atty., Newport Harbor Psychiatric Institute, Newport Beach, CA '80 (ATTY)
RUMA, SAM R., pres., Davenport Medical Center, Davenport, IA '72
RUMBAUGH, ROY, adm., Mimbres Memorial Hospital, Deming, NM '75
RUMER, KATHLEEN M., RN, dir. nrsg., Memorial Hospital, Cumberland, MD '81 (NURS)
RUMERY, MICHAEL W., assoc. dir. adm. serv., Middlesex Memorial Hospital, Middletown, CT '86 (RISK)
RUMPZA, PATRICIA A., RN, asst. adm. nrsg., Salinas Valley Memorial Hospital, Salinas, CA '86 (NURS)
RUMRILL, H. FRANCES, pur. agt., A. Lindsey and O. B. O'Connor Hospital, Delhi, NY '82 (PUR)
RUNDELL, ABE, mgr. fin. syst., Cook County Hospital, Chicago, IL '79 (MGMT)
RUNESTRAND, WAYNE R., proj. mgr., Valley Memorial Hospital, Livermore, CA '81 (ENG)
RUNGE, CHARLES W., dir. plng., Toledo Hospital, Toledo, OH '82 (PLNG)
RUNNELLS, GLENN A., spec. oper. room aseptic practice, Superior Surgical Manufacturing, Inc., Seminole, FL '80 (CS)
RUNNELS, LAURES J., RN, asst. dir. nrsg., AMI Presbyterian-Denver Hospital, Denver, CO '82 (NURS)

RUNNING, RUSSELL A., dir. commun., Winter Haven Hospital, Winter Haven, FL '85 (ENG)
RUNNING, SUSAN M., student, Concordia College, Moorhead, MN '86
RUNOLFSON, ELOISE M., chief diet., Washington Hospital, Fremont, CA '81 (FOOD)
RUNYEN, BARBARA, chief oper. off., Frank Cuneo Memorial Hospital, Chicago, IL '86
RUPP, JOHN A., atty., Department of Mental Health, Richmond, VA '85 (ATTY)
RUPP, JOHN P., dir. spec. proj., Sacred Heart General Hospital, Eugene, OR '80 (MGMT)
RUPP, JONNIE S., spec. asst. dir., Veterans Administration Medical Center, Palo Alto, CA '83
RUPP, JOSEPHINE C., asst. to pres., Montgomery Hospital, Norristown, PA '83 (PLNG)
RUPP, LORALLE BUTLER, mgt. eng., William Beaumont Hospital Corporation, Southfield, MI '84 (MGMT)
RUPP, MAJ. THOMAS A., MSC USAF, air force fellow, Joint Commission on Accreditation of Hospitals, Chicago, IL '79
RUPPE, JOHN P., MD, (ret.), Bay Shore, NY '31 (LIFE)
RUPPEL, RONALD W., partner, Price Waterhouse, Miami, FL '83
RUPPERT, LORETTA M., RN, dir. nrsg. prof. affairs, St. Anne's Hospital, Chicago, IL '77 (NURS)
RUSCH, LINDA M., RN, dir. nrsg. serv., Carrier Foundation, Belle Mead, NJ '83 (EDUC)(NURS)
RUSCHIN, DORIS R., RN, dir. nrs., Watsonville Community Hospital, Watsonville, CA '68 (NURS)
RUSCIO, JOSEPH P. DI, adm., Lompoc District Hospital, Lompoc, CA '85 (PLNG)
RUSE, WILLIAM E., pres., Blanchard Valley Hospital, Findlay, OH '61 (ATTY)
RUSH, DANIEL T., atty., Millinocket Regional Hospital, Millinocket, ME '85 (ATTY)
RUSH, JIMMY L., coor. pat. rel., Froedtert Memorial Lutheran Hospital, Milwaukee, WI '84 (PAT)
RUSH, LINWOOD R., dir. nutr. serv., St. Vincent Hospital and Medical Center, Portland, OR '78 (FOOD)
RUSH, RAYMOND J. JR., chief sup., proc. and distrib., Veterans Administration Medical Center, Manchester, NH '83 (CS)
RUSH, ROBIN J., asst. dir. food serv. adm., Broward General Medical Center, Fort Lauderdale, FL '86 (FOOD)
RUSH, TERRI R., dir. commun. rel., Franklin Memorial Hospital, Rocky Mount, VA '86 (PR)
RUSH, WILLIAM H., pres., American Eye Institute, Inc., Gold Beach, OR '75
RUSHING, DEBBIE S., RN, loss prevention spec., Memorial Hospital, Hollywood, FL '85 (RISK)
RUSHING, JAN O., exec. vice-pres., Adventist Health Systems-Sunbelt, Collegedale, TN '82
RUSHING, PAT C., pers. asst., Bruce Hospital, Florence, SC '85 (PERS)
RUSHTON, CYNTHIA M., student, Oakland University, Rochester, MI '87 (PR)
RUSK, CAROLYN S., coor. vol. serv., W. A. Foote Memorial Hospital, Jackson, MI '85
RUSK, HOWARD A., MD, dir., Howard A. Rusk Institute of Rehabilitation Medicine, New York, NY '55 (HON)
RUSK, MARTHA J., assoc. dir. matl. serv., Baylor University Medical Center, Dallas, TX '67 (PUR)
RUSKIN, MELVYN B., atty., Long Island Jewish-Hillside Medical Center, New York, NY '71 (ATTY)
RUSKO, LEONARD J., facil. designer, St. Vincent Charity Hospital, Cleveland, OH '83 (ENG)
RUSNAK, JAMES E., dir. data, California Medical Review, Inc., San Francisco, CA '81 (MGMT)
RUSNOCK, MAUREEN, RN, sr. vice-pres. nrsg., Presbyterian-University Hospital, Pittsburgh, PA '74 (NURS)
RUSSELL, A. YVONNE, MD PhD, assoc. dean commun. affairs, Office of the Dean of Medicine, University of Texas Medical Branch, Galveston, TX '83 (RISK)
RUSSELL, ANN LABREE, atty., University of Minnesota Hospital and Clinic, Minneapolis, MN '87 (ATTY)
RUSSELL, CAPT. BARBARA A., MSC USAF, analyst cost contr., U. S. Air Force Base, Holloman AFB, NM '84
RUSSELL, BETTY SUE, dir. procurement, St. Luke's Episcopal-Texas Children's Hospitals, Houston, TX '85 (PUR)
RUSSELL, C. EDWARD JR., atty., Portsmouth General Hospital, Portsmouth, VA '78 (ATTY)
RUSSELL, DANIEL F., pres., Eastern Mercy Health System, Philadelphia, PA '65
RUSSELL, DONNA A., dir. mktg. and pub. rel., Baptist Hospital East, Louisville, KY '86 (PR)
RUSSELL, DORSYE, RN, vice-pres. health affairs, Mary Washington Hospital, Fredericksburg, VA '68 (NURS)
RUSSELL, ESTHER E., dir. soc. serv., DeKalb General Hospital, Decatur, GA '79 (SOC)
RUSSELL, GAIL DEMPSEY, vice-pres. nrsg., Potomac Hospital, Woodbridge, VA '82 (NURS)
RUSSELL, GAIL E., RN, dir. nrsg., New England Sinai Hospital, Stoughton, MA '80 (NURS)
RUSSELL, GEORGE G., atty., Holy Cross Hospital, Merrill, WI '68 (ATTY)
RUSSELL, JACK R., dir. pers., Wadley Regional Medical Center, Texarkana, TX '74 (PERS)
RUSSELL, JAMES D. M., adm., St. Mary's Hospital, Pierre, SD '59
RUSSELL, JAN M., dir. cont. prof. educ., University of Kansas College of Health Sciences and Bell Memorial Hospital, Kansas City, MO '85 (EDUC)
RUSSELL, JOHN P., dir. matl. mgt., Providence Hospital, Mobile, AL '82 (PUR)
RUSSELL, JOYCE E., dir. educ., Lawrence General Hospital, Lawrence, MA '82 (EDUC)
RUSSELL, KAREN D., actg. dir. pub. rel. and mktg., Richmond Community Hospital, Richmond, VA '86 (PR)
RUSSELL, LINDA B., assoc. exec. dir., Humana Hospital -Baytown, Baytown, TX '85
RUSSELL, LOUISE H., dir. pat. rel., Children's Hospital, Boston, MA '82 (PAT)
RUSSELL, MARK GERALD, dir. soc. serv., Heritage Hospital, Taylor, MI '80 (SOC)
RUSSELL, MARK RICHARDS, sr. vice-pres., Kennedy Memorial Hospital, Stratford, NJ '72
RUSSELL, MAURICE V., EdD, dir. soc. serv., New York University Medical Center, New York, NY '66 (SOC)
RUSSELL, NANCY, dir. environ. serv., Thomas Jefferson University Hospital, Philadelphia, PA '87 (ENVIRON)
RUSSELL, PHYLLIS A., mgr. trng. and dev., University of Massachusetts Medical School and Teaching Hospital, Worcester, MA '75 (EDUC)
RUSSELL, R. TERRY, PhD, dir. bus. plng., Methodist Health Systems, Memphis, TN '80
RUSSELL, ROBERT, asst. dir. human res., Health Sciences Centre, Winnipeg, Man., Canada '86 (EDUC)
RUSSELL, ROLLAND F., dir. plant oper., Monsour Medical Center, Jeannette, PA '86 (ENG)
RUSSELL, ROSEMARY, RN, chief nrsg. serv., Veterans Administration Medical Center, Lebanon, PA '82 (NURS)
RUSSELL, RUSSEL, asst. adm., Skaggs Community Hospital, Branson, MO '86 (RISK)
RUSSELL, SALLY K., adm., Illinois Masonic Medical Center, Chicago, IL '87 (AMB)
RUSSELL, SUSAN E., dir. soc. serv., Bristol Memorial Hospital, Bristol, TN '76 (SOC)
RUSSELL, SUZAN D., vice-pres. pub. affairs, Methodist Hospital, Houston, TX '81 (PR)
RUSSELL, LT. COL. SYDNEY S. III, MSC USAF, dir. health mgt. serv., Air Force Command, Surgeon's Office, Colorado Springs, CO '68
RUSSLER, THOMAS I., adm. asst., City Hospital, Martinsburg, WV '85 (ENG)
RUSSO, BETTY E., RN, spec. asst. to adm., Children's Hospital of Alabama, Birmingham, AL '77 (PAT)
RUSSO, CATHERINE R., mgr. soc. serv., Eden Hospital Medical Center, Castro Valley, CA '85 (SOC)
RUSSO, DIANE M., coor. telecommun., Children's Hospital of Michigan, Detroit, MI '86 (ENG)
RUSSO, DONALD J., dir. plng., Merle West Medical Center, Klamath Falls, OR '86 (PLNG)
RUSSO, DONALD, atty., Southwest Washington Hospitals, Vancouver, WA '85 (ATTY)
RUSSO, DONALD, asst. dir. matl. mgt., St. Vincent's Medical Center, Bridgeport, CT '79 (PUR)
RUSSO, JOAN M., RN, asst. adm. nrsg., University Hospital, Boston, MA '83 (NURS)
RUSSO, JOSEPHINE C., RN, dir. nrsg., Franklin General Hospital, Valley Stream, NY '87 (EDUC)
RUSSO, MARY ANN, United Appeal and Community Chest, Cincinnati, OH '85 (PR)
RUSSO, MATTHEW M., assoc. adm. fiscal serv., Booth Memorial Medical Center, Flushing, NY '84
RUSSO, SALVATORE J., atty., Maimonides Medical Center, Brooklyn, NY '82 (ATTY)
RUSSO, VIVAN, pres. and dir., Clinical Information Management Service, Brooklyn, NY '86
RUST, CAROLE D., exec. dir., Deaconess Healthcare Partners, Evansville, IN '83 (PLNG)
RUST, GRETCHEN L., RN, adm. nrsg. serv., Moritz Community Hospital, Sun Valley, ID '85 (NURS)
RUST, TAMARA J., mgr. commun., Lutheran Hospitals and Home Society, Fargo, ND '85 (PR) (PLNG)
RUST, VICTORIA, mgr. soc. work, Memorial Hospital System, Houston, TX '84 (SOC)
RUST, WILLIAM T., gen. mgr., United Medical Plan of Arizona, Tocson, AZ '83
RUSTAD, PATRICIA M., dir. vol. serv., Royal Victoria Hospital, Montreal, Que., Canada '85 (VOL)
RUSTER, PAMELA L., mgr. soc. serv., Bartholomew County Hospital, Columbus, IN '83 (SOC)
RUSTOW, JANET, asst. dir. soc. work and cont. care, Newton-Wellesley Hospital, Newton, MA '86 (SOC)
RUTH, ALMA L., dir. vol. serv., Hackettstown Community Hospital, Hackettstown, NJ '81 (VOL)
RUTH, JAMES A., dir. food and nutr. serv., Munroe Regional Medical Center, Ocala, FL '77 (FOOD)
RUTH, SAM, pres., Baycrest Centre Foundation, Toronto, Ont., Canada '50 (LIFE)
RUTHART, JAMES S., student, Graduate School of Business, Wayland Baptist University, Plainview, TX '86
RUTHEMEYER, THOMAS JAMES, sr. vice-pres. and treas., Clermont Mercy Hospital, Batavia, OH '74
RUTHERFORD, BEVERLY A., dir. pub. rel., Medical Center Hospital of Vermont, Burlington, VT '81 (PR)
RUTHERFORD, CLARA W., chm., Doctors Hospital, Detroit, MI '85 (PR)
RUTHERFORD, MELVIN L., risk mg:., Children's Hospital Medical Center, Cincinnati, OH '80 (RISK)
RUTHERFORD, RICHARD C., asst. dir. bldg. and grds., Harper Hospital, Detroit, MI '85 (ENG)
RUTHERFORD, SANDRA A., asst. mgr. cent. serv., Beth Israel Hospital, Boston, MA '80 (CS)
RUTHERFORD, THOMAS S., atty., Carrollwood Community Hospital, Tampa, FL '85 (ATTY)
RUTHERFORD, THOMAS, chief eng., Boca Raton Community Hospital, Boca Raton, FL '78 (ENG)
RUTHERFORD, WARREN L., sr. vice-pres., Methodist Hospitals of Dallas, Dallas, TX '68
RUTHERFORD, WILLIAM D., vice-pres. and arch., Clemons, Rutherford and Associates, Inc., Tallahassee, FL '85 (ENG)
RUTISHAUSER, KATHLEEN T., dir. plng., James Cox Associates, Inc., Chicago, IL '86 (PLNG)
RUTKOWSKI, CECILIA, dir. pers., Community General Hospital, Harris, NY '81 (PERS)
RUTLEDGE, BELINDA C., RN, assoc. dir. nrsg., Baptist Medical Center, Columbia, SC '82 (NURS)
RUTLEDGE, FRED D., dir. environ. serv., Jersey Shore Medical Center, Neptune, NJ '87 (ENVIRON)
RUTT, DANIEL A., vice-pres. human res., Queen's Medical Center, Honolulu, HI '86 (PERS)
RUTT, JOHN S., dir. plant oper., Wausau Hospital Center, Wausau, WI '84 (ENG)
RUTTER, STEVEN, asst. dir. soc. work, Queens Hospital Center, Jamaica, NY '87 (SOC)
RUTZKY, JULIUS, MD, corp. med. dir., William Beaumont Hospital, Royal Oak, MI '85
RUVOLO, FRANCES M., student, Program in Healthcare Administration, St. John's University, Jamaica, NY '85
RUXTON, CHRISTINA T., RN, assoc. adm. and dir. pat. serv., Thunderbird Samaritan Hospital, Glendale, AZ '83 (NURS)
RUZICKA, GREGORY A., dir. matl. mgt., Fairfax Hospital, Falls Church, VA '86 (PUR)
RUZICKI, DOROTHY A., PhD RN, coor. pat. educ., Sacred Heart Medical Center, Spokane, WA '84 (EDUC)
RUZUMNA, JANICE M., dir. hosp. info. syst., McPherson Community Health Center, Howell, MI '83 (MGMT)
RYAN, ALICE B., RN, dir. syst. and staff serv.-nrsg., Saint Vincent Health Center, Erie, PA '84 (NURS)
RYAN, CHRISTINA NORDSTROM, coor. adm. and health educ., John Hancock Life Insurance Company, Boston, MA '83 (EDUC)
RYAN, CONSTANCE M., dir. vol., Bridgeton Hospital, Bridgeton, NJ '85 (VOL)
RYAN, CYNTHIA K., mgr. matl., North Kansas City Hospital, North Kansas City, MO '86 (PUR)
RYAN, DOROTHY M., dir. pub. rel. and vol. serv., Hammond-Henry Hospital, Geneseo, IL '77 (VOL)(PR)
RYAN, SR. ELISE MARY, pat. rep., Schumpert Medical Center, Shreveport, LA '84 (PAT)
RYAN, EVELYN M., RN, supv. sup., proc., distrib. and stores, St. Mary Medical Center, Hobart, IN '87 (CS)
RYAN, FRANCIS JOSEPH, (ret.), Jacksonville, AR '58
RYAN, GEORGE B., dir. pub. rel., United Hospital, St. Paul, MN '78 (PR)
RYAN, HOWARD, vice-pres. support serv., Ellis Hospital, Schenectady, NY '79 (ENG)
RYAN, J. BRUCE, exec. vice-pres., Jennings, Ryan, Fedela and Company, Atlanta, GA '86 (PLNG)
RYAN, JACK, MD, pres., Detroit-Macomb Hospital Corporation, Detroit, MI '79 (PLNG)
RYAN, JAMES R., exec. dir., Milwaukee Regional Medical Center, Milwaukee, WI '84
RYAN, JANE L., diet. consult., HCA Gulf Coast Hospital, Panama City, FL '86 (FOOD)
RYAN, JEAN M., dir. vol. serv., Berkshire Medical Center, Pittsfield, MA '80 (VOL)
RYAN, JOSEPH E., prod. mgr., HBO and Company, Atlanta, GA '76 (MGMT)
RYAN, KAREN E., RN, mgr. sup., proc. and distrib., Mercy San Juan Hospital, Carmichael, CA '80 (CS)
RYAN, LONNIE R., dir. sup., proc. and distrib., Tampa General Hospital, Tampa, FL '85 (CS)
RYAN, LORRAINE, risk mgr., Beth Israel Medical Center, New York, NY '85 (RISK)
RYAN, MARGARET J., RN, nrsg. consult., Ryan Associates, Arvada, CO '68 (CS)
RYAN, MARGARET, asst. dir. cent. proc., Good Samaritan Hospital and Health Center, Dayton, OH '85 (CS)
RYAN, MARILYN P., adm. diet., Vanderbilt University Hospital, Nashville, TN '79 (FOOD)
RYAN, MARY C., exec. assoc. med. serv., Saint Thomas Medical Center, Akron, OH '86
RYAN, MARY JANE, adm. asst. pat. care serv., South Shore Hospital, Chicago, IL '69 (PLNG)
RYAN, MICHAEL G., RN, dir. surg. nrsg., Scripps Memorial Hospital, La Jolla, CA '83 (NURS)
RYAN, OLIVE MEGGISON, dir. soc. serv., New England Rehabilitation Hospital, Woburn, MA '77 (SOC)
RYAN, PATRICIA A., RN, dir. nrsg., St. Anthony's Hospital, St. Petersburg, FL '74 (NURS)
RYAN, PATRICK R., dir. food serv. and exec. chef, Doctors Hospital of Pinole, Pinole, CA '86 (FOOD)
RYAN, RICHARD G., chaplain and dir. pub. rel., Sid Peterson Memorial Hospital, Kerrville, TX '85 (PR)
RYAN, RICHARD J., dir. procurement, University Hospital, Cincinnati, OH '81 (PUR)
RYAN, RITA, dir. pub. info., St. Luke's Regional Medical Center, Boise, ID '79 (PR)
RYAN, ROBERT J., atty., Franklin Square Hospital, Baltimore, MD '78 (ATTY)
RYAN, ROBERT L., account exec., Sullivan, Kelly and Associates, Inc., Los Angeles, CA '80 (RISK)
RYAN, STEPHEN A., atty., Post and Schell, Philadelphia, PA '80 (RISK)
RYAN, TIMOTHY F., atty., Merle West Medical Center, Klamath Falls, OR '82 (ATTY)
RYAN, W. PATRICK, atty., St. Joseph Medical Center, Stamford, CT '80 (ATTY)
RYAN, WAYNE P., dir. eng. serv., Champlain Valley Physicians Hospital Medical Center, Plattsburgh, NY '83 (ENG)
RYAN, WILLIAM F., dir. risk mgt., University of Michigan, Ann Arbor, MI '80 (RISK)
RYAN, WILLIAM PATRICK JR., pres., Franciscan Health Care Corporation of Colorado Springs, Colorado Springs, CO '57 (LIFE)
RYANS, DONNA, asst. dir. nrsg., Salem Hospital, Salem, MA '87 (AMB)
RYBA, THOMAS L., asst. adm., HCA Red River Hospital, Wichita Falls, TX '82
RYBERG, JOYCE L., RN, dir. nrsg., Midlands Community Hospital, Papillion, NE '84 (NURS)
RYBERG, MARY-LOU F., RN, vice-pres. nrsg., Good Samaritan Hospital, Lexington, KY '86 (NURS)
RYCHCIK, CHET, dir. nutr. serv., Verdugo Hills Hospital, Glendale, CA '80 (FOOD)
RYCHTARIK, PEGGY J., ins. mgr., Alexian Brothers Health Systems Inc., Elk Grove Village, IL '86 (RISK)
RYDANT, LINDA L., dir. food serv., Kingston Hospital, Kingston, NY '71 (FOOD)
RYDELL, MARJORIE M., dir. soc. serv., Mesa Vista Hospital, San Diego, CA '68 (SOC)

RYDELL, RICHARD L., dir. mgt. syst., Baystate Health Systems, Inc., Springfield, MA '75 (MGMT)
RYDER, JOHN E., mgt. eng., Borgess Medical Center, Kalamazoo, MI '82 (MGMT)
RYDER, ROSS R., atty., Kaiser Foundation Hospitals, Oakland, CA '86 (ATTY)
RYDGREN, BARBARA, asst. vice-pres. support serv., Saint John's Hospital and Health Center, Santa Monica, CA '85 (ENG)
RYE, DOROTHEA S., RN, sr. vice-pres. oper., Miami Valley Hospital, Dayton, OH '76 (NURS)
RYE, DOROTHY C., dir. vol. serv., Salvation Army William Booth Memorial Hospital, Florence, KY '86 (VOL)
RYERSON, PETER J., mgr. health care consulting, Peat, Marwick, Mitchell and Company, Cleveland, OH '76 (MGMT)
RYKER, JOSEPH F., dir. cent. sup., John F. Kennedy Memorial, Turnersville, NJ '83 (CS)
RYMAN, EDITH M., dir. vol. serv., University of Oregon Health Sciences Center, Portland, OR '80 (VOL)
RYNNE, TERRENCE J., pres., Rynne Marketing Group, Chicago, IL '79 (PR) (PLNG)
RYON, CHRISTOPHER M., sr. fixed income analyst, Vanguard Group of Investment Companies, Valley Forge, PA '85
RYZINSKI, TONY, dir. pub. rel., Graduate Hospital, Philadelphia, PA '86 (PR)
RZEMINSKI, PETER J., asst. exec. dir., St. Francis Hospital, Blue Island, IL '75 (PERS)

S

SAAL, RONALD, exec. assoc., Saint Thomas Medical Center, Akron, OH '80 (RISK)
SAARINEN, CLAIRE M., coor. staff dev., Laurentian Hospital, Sudbury, Ont., Canada '84 (EDUC)
SABALLUS, DORIEL, dir. environ. serv., St. Francis Medical Center, Honolulu, HI '86 (ENVIRON)
SABATINO, KATHRYN M., RN, clin. dir. surg. serv., Easton Hospital, Easton, PA '86 (NURS)
SABEL, PATRICK W., dir., Snohomish County Hospital Biomedical Cooperative, Everett, WA '83 (ENG)
SABIC, MARIN I., dir. health care facil. plng. and design, Lbc and W. Architects-Engineers-Planners, Alexandria, VA '79
SABIN, PAUL EDGAR, dir. soc. serv., Methodist Hospital, Jacksonville, FL '81 (SOC)
SABIN, SANDY, RN, pres., The Business of Health, Orangevale, CA '85
SABLE, ERNEST M., adm., Century City Hospital, Los Angeles, CA '47 (LIFE)
SABLES, JAN G., dir. vol., St. John's Hospital, Springfield, IL '83 (VOL)
SABLOWSKY, RICHARD B., atty., Sibley Memorial Hospital, Washington, DC '74 (ATTY)
SABO, LESLIE A., dir. safety, Hillcrest Hospital, Mayfield Heights, OH '85 (ENG)
SABOTA, WILLIAM F., vice-pres. human res., University Hospital, Newark, NJ '86 (PERS)
SABULA, GARY D., mgt. eng., Miriam Hospital, Providence, RI '78 (MGMT)
SACCHETTI, JAMES VINCENT, MD, Dorchester, MA '40 (LIFE)
SACCI, MARTHA L., RN, vice-pres. nrsg., Johns Hopkins Hospital, Baltimore, MD '67 (NURS)
SACCO, FRANK V., chief oper. serv., Memorial Hospital, Hollywood, FL '78 (RISK)
SACCO, PAMELA, rec. adm., Practice Management Consulting, Hendersonville, NC '77
SACCO, SANTO M., asst. dir., Newark Beth Israel Medical Center, Newark, NJ '74 (PERS)
SACCONE, ANNA M., adm. mgr., Children's Hospital, Boston, MA '83
SACERDOTE, DONNA LEVE, dir. food serv., Northern Ocean Hospital System, Point Pleasant, NJ '85 (FOOD)
SACHDEV, NEENA K., consult., Arthur Andersen and Company, Chicago, IL '86
SACHRISON, KATHRYN L., RN, vice-pres. nrsg., Morton F. Plant Hospital, Clearwater, FL '76 (NURS)
SACHS, MICHAEL ALBERT, pres., Strategic Decision Associates, Inc., Chicago, IL '76 (PLNG)
SACIA, JOAN M., chief soc. serv., Visiting Nurse Association, Portland, OR '81 (SOC)
SACK, BILLIE E., asst. adm. nrsg. serv., Kadlec Medical Center, Richland, WA '85 (NURS)
SACKRISON, JEFFREY N., RN, vice-pres. nrsg. serv., Hazleton-St. Joseph Medical Center, Hazleton, PA '86
SACKS, CATHY E., psych. in-patient adm., St. Vincent's Hospital and Medical Center, New York, NY '77
SACKS, DORINDA R., dir. cent. sup., Orlando Regional Medical Center, Orlando, FL '86 (CS)
SACKS, SEYMOUR, atty., Scottsdale Memorial Hospital, Scottsdale, AZ '71 (ATTY)
SACOPULOS, GUS, atty., Terre Haute Regional Hospital, Terre Haute, IN '80 (ATTY)
SADAUSKAS, THOMAS C., dir. med. plans and readiness, U. S. Air Force Medical Center, Scott AFB, IL '86
SADENWATER, SUSAN, coor. risk mgt., Midland Hospital Center, Midland, MI '85 (RISK)
SADLEMYER, JAMES F., vice-pres. fin., St. Michael's Hospital, Stevens Point, WI '81 (PLNG)
SADLER, JANE A., dir. risk mgt., Hutcheson Medical Center, Fort Oglethorpe, GA '80 (RISK)
SADLER, JUDY P., RN, vice-pres. pat. serv., Elliott White Springs Memorial Hospital, Lancaster, SC '82 (NURS)
SADLER, SIDNEY H., mgr. pur., St. Luke Hospital, Fort Thomas, KY '80 (PUR)
SADOWSKI, FRANK G., dir. food serv., Methodist Medical Center of Illinois, Peoria, IL '79 (FOOD)
SADOWSKY, ALICE A., dir. food serv., Anoka-Metropolitan Regional Treatment Center, Anoka, MN '80 (FOOD)
SADOWY, HAROLD S., PhD, vice-pres. plng., mktg. and corp. commun., Pmh Health Resources Inc., Phoenix, AZ '81 (PLNG)
SAEGER, FLORENCE R., instr., Barnes Hospital, St. Louis, MO '85 (EDUC)
SAENZ, GEORGE T., supv. soc. worker, Veterans Administration Medical Center, Houston, TX '84 (SOC)
SAENZ, PATRICK H., RN, pat. advocate, Travelers Insurance Company, San Diego, CA '83
SAFER, BRIAN M., meth. analyst, Presbyterian-University Hospital, Pittsburgh, PA '86 (MGMT)
SAFFELL, MICHAEL H., dir. constr. and bldg. mgt., Freeman Health Services, Inglewood, CA '83
SAFFER, MARK B., MD, pres. clin. mgt. serv., Harper-Grace Hospitals, Detroit, MI '86
SAFFER, VALERI K., vice-pres., Conemaugh Valley Memorial Hospital, Johnstown, PA '80 (PLNG)
SAFIAN, KEITH F., adm., St. John's Episcopal Hospital-South Shore, Far Rockaway, NY '73
SAFRIET, MARIAN L., dir. vol. and auditing, Annie Penn Memorial Hospital, Reidsville, NC '85 (VOL)
SAGAERT, BARBARA L., RN, asst. adm. pat. care serv., Saratoga Community Hospital, Detroit, MI '83 (EDUC)(NURS)
SAGAN, DANIEL S., prin., Schmidt, Garden and Erickson, Inc., Sarasota, FL '86 (ENG)
SAGAR, JOHN F., M. and R. Services, Inc., Hyannis, MA '80 (PUR)
SAGE, DAVID R., vice-pres. staff rel. and dev., Memorial Hospital, South Bend, IN '80 (PERS)
SAGE, ROBERT M., dir. info. syst., Royal Victoria Hospital, Montreal, Que., Canada '86 (MGMT)
SAGER, BERT, atty., Plantation General Hospital, Plantation, FL '68 (ATTY)
SAGHY, RUSSELL J., dir. plant serv., Richmond Heights General Hospital, Cleveland, OH '85 (ENG)
SAHNEY, VINOD K., PhD, adm. corp. plng. and mgt. serv., Henry Ford Hospital, Detroit, MI '77 (MGMT)(PLNG)
SAHRMANN-GROVES, JOAN M., sr. mgr., Ernst and Whinney, Los Angeles, CA '87 (MGMT)
SAINI, SUNITA, dir. soc. work, Peninsula Hospital Center, Far Rockaway, NY '80 (SOC)
SAKAI, ABE, adm., Convalescent Center of Honolulu, Honolulu, HI '86 (ENG)
SAKAI, SUE, dir. soc. serv., Good Samaritan Hospital and Medical Center, Portland, OR '75 (SOC)
SAKATIS, FOTIOS, sr. buyer, New York University Medical Center, New York, NY '86 (PUR)
SAKOVITZ-DALE, JANE, dir. health care, Cone and Company, Boston, MA '84 (PR)
SAKRAN, DONNIS P., asst. vice-pres. pat. serv., Forsyth Memorial Hospital, Winston-Salem, NC '67 (PAT)
SAKS, ROCHELLE G., Montefiore Medical Center, Bronx, NY '85
SALA, RAY M., dir. commun. rel., Philhaven Hospital, Mount Gretna, PA '81 (PR)
SALAKA, KATHLEEN A., dir. vol. serv., Western Reserve Care System, Youngstown, OH '85 (VOL)
SALAMONE, PATRICIA M., dir. pat. commun. and asst. to the pres., Brigham and Women's Hospital, Boston, MA '83 (PAT)
SALANDRA, JOHN A., dir. fin. oper., Catholic Medical Center of Brooklyn and Queens, Woodhaven Queens, NY '85
SALAS, CLARA M., dir. vol. serv., Manhattan Psychiatric Center-Ward's Island, New York, NY '84 (VOL)
SALAS, SANDRA J., dir. vol. serv., Santa Rosa Memorial Hospital, Santa Rosa, CA '86 (VOL)
SALAZAR, AUDREY, sec. cent. serv., Methodist Medical Center, Dallas, TX '86 (CS)
SALAZAR, MICHELLE R., vice-pres. mktg., American Healthcare Management, Inc., Dallas, TX '85 (PLNG)
SALAZAR, REG, mgr. bldg., Los Angeles County-University of Southern California Medical Center, Los Angeles, CA '81 (ENG)
SALCEDO, COL. JOSE R., MSC USA, med. consult., U. S. Army Physical Disability Appeal Board, Washington, DC '71
SALCMAN, ILENE, sr. vice-pres., Franklin Square Hospital, Baltimore, MD '84 (PLNG)
SALE, WILLIAM B., dir. res. and plng., Illinois Foundation for Medical Review, Chicago, IL '77
SALEEBA, SANDRA F., vice-pres. mktg. and plng., Choate-Symmes Health Services, Inc., Arlington, MA '85 (PLNG)
SALEM, CHRISTINA, student, Georgia State University, Institute of Health Administration, Atlanta, GA '83
SALEM, DAVID S., atty., Sutter Community Hospitals, Sacramento, CA '86 (ATTY)
SALEMAN, LAURA LEE, mgr. soc. serv., South Suburban Hospital, Hazel Crest, IL '85 (SOC)
SALEMME, MITZI J., dir. pub. affairs and mktg., Parkside Human Services Corporation, Park Ridge, IL '86 (PR) (PLNG)
SALENKO, CATHY D., atty., Sutter Community Hospitals, Sacramento, CA '86 (ATTY)
SALERNO, GARY, adm. rad., Montefiore Medical Center, Bronx, NY '86
SALESSES, BETH ANN, dir. pub. rel., St. Joseph Hospital, Providence, RI '87 (PR)
SALGUERO, OTTO R., sr. mgr., Ernst and Whinney, Miami, FL '79 (MGMT)
SALHOOT, JOYCE TESTA, asst. adm. clin. serv., Institute for Rehabilitation and Research, Houston, TX '86 (SOC)
SALIBA, GEORGENE, risk mgr., Lehigh Valley Hospital Center, Allentown, PA '85 (RISK)
SALINE, WALTER M., dir. bldg. serv., Providence Hospital, Everett, WA '80 (ENG)
SALINES, JOANNE M., RN, dir. nrsg. info. syst., Brigham and Women's Hospital, Boston, MA '86 (NURS)
SALINSKY, DIANE M., dir. soc. serv., Bruce Hospital, Florence, SC '86 (SOC)
SALISBURY, DAVID W., assoc. adm., Henry Ford Hospital, Detroit, MI '79 (ENG)
SALISBURY, JOHN E., dir. facil., Erlanger Medical Center, Chattanooga, TN '76 (ENG)
SALITROS, PATRICIA H., RN, dir. transitional infant care, Magee-Womens Hospital, Pittsburgh, PA '77 (NURS)
SALKAS, TONI, dir. soc. serv., Rancho Park Hospital, El Cajon, CA '86 (SOC)
SALKIND, HAROLD M., Englewood, NJ '43 (LIFE)
SALLEE, KATHRYN FERN, dir. cent. serv., Bedford Medical Center, Bedford, IN '74 (CS)
SALLEY, WALTER SR., asst. dir., Pennsylvania Hospital, Philadelphia, PA '87 (ENVIRON)
SALMAN, STEVEN L., atty., Sisters of Charity Health Care System, Inc., Cincinnati, OH '80 (RISK)(ATTY)
SALMEN, SHARYN H., RN, dir. nrsg. serv., Poudre Valley Hospital, Fort Collins, CO '78 (NURS)
SALMON, HAROLD W., (ret.), Green Valley, AZ '49 (LIFE)
SALMON, HOWARD W., sr. vice-pres., Magliaro and McHaney, La Jolla, CA '76 (AMB)
SALMON, ROBERT B., coor. natl. healthcare, Crss, Inc., Denver, CO '86 (ENG)
SALMONS, DIANE F., supv. cent. serv., Southern Ocean County Hospital, Manahawkin, NJ '77 (CS)
SALMONS, JOAN, RN, sr. vice-pres., Florida Hospital Medical Center, Orlando, FL '79 (NURS)
SALNESS, JOHN D., adm., Union Hospital, Mayville, ND '86 (PLNG)
SALOMONE, LINDA S., RN, asst. adm. nrsg., Iowa Lutheran Hospital, Des Moines, IA '81 (NURS)
SALPETER, SUSAN, risk control consult., Victor O. Schinnerer, Chicago, IL '86 (RISK)
SALSER, WILLIAM L., student, Southwest Texas State University, San Marcos, TX '86
SALTARELLI, RICHARD, mgr. plant oper., St. John Hospital, Nassau Bay, TX '84 (ENG)
SALTER, BEN, dir. commun. rel. and vol. serv., Shawnee Medical Center Hospital, Shawnee, OK '79 (PR)
SALTER, GILBERT, asst. adm., St. Anthony Medical Center, Louisville, KY '86 (RISK)
SALTER, VERA, PhD, vice-pres. plng. and mktg., Forbes Health System, Pittsburgh, PA '82 (PLNG)
SALTONSTALL, PETER L., vice-pres. dev. and pub. rel., Brigham and Women's Hospital, Boston, MA '87 (PR)
SALTSMAN, LT. ROBERT R., MSC USN, staff civil eng. and head facil. mgt., Naval Hospital, Jacksonville, FL '86 (ENG)
SALTZ, CONSTANCE CORLEY, PhD, consult., Veterans Administration Medical Center, Hampton, VA '86 (SOC)
SALTZMAN, LAURA, dir. soc. work, Church Hospital Corporation, Baltimore, MD '86 (SOC)
SALTZMAN, ROBERT M., atty., Los Angeles County Harbor-University of California at Los Angeles Medical Center, Torrance, CA '86 (ATTY)
SALTZSTEIN, LESLIE K., RN, dir. nrsg., St. Francis Hospital, Milwaukee, WI '82 (NURS)
SALUTE, DIANE C., dir. vol. serv., Reading Hospital and Medical Center, Reading, PA '86 (VOL)
SALVATI, CATHERINE T., pat. rep., West Jersey Hospital-Eastern Division, Voorhees, NJ '81 (PAT)
SALVATO, ROSANNE, student, Program in Public and Health Administration, C. W. Post-Long Island University, Greenvale, NY '85
SALVEKAR, ARVIND MAHADEO, dir. mgt. eng., University of Cincinnati Hospital, Cincinnati, OH '77 (MGMT)
SALVO, STEPHEN F., dir. pers., Anna Jaques Hospital, Newburyport, MA '85 (PERS)
SALYARDS, JEAN, head nrs., Mercy Hospital, Altoona, PA '87 (AMB)
SALYER, DON E., chief eng., Memorial Hospital Medical Center, Modesto, CA '86 (ENG)
SALZMAN, EDYTHE, dir. plng., Nashoba Community Hospital, Ayer, MA '75 (PLNG)
SAMARITAN, GEORGETTE, risk mgr., Shepherd Spinal Center, Atlanta, GA '87 (RISK)
SAMAT, RAMKISHIN K., dir. oper. analyst, Thomas Jefferson University Hospital, Philadelphia, PA '82 (MGMT)
SAMET, DEAN H., staff eng., Joint Commission on Accreditation of Hospitals, Chicago, IL '84 (ENG)
SAMET, KENNETH A., dir. dev., Medlantic Healthcare Group, Washington, DC '81
SAMLUT, RAFAEL, dir. food serv., Bon Secours Hospital, North Miami, FL '79 (FOOD)
SAMMON, MARJORIE I., RN, exec. asst. nrsg., La Grange Memorial Hospital, La Grange, IL '81 (NURS)
SAMMONS, JAMES H., MD, exec. vice-pres., American Medical Association, Chicago, IL '77 (LIFE)
SAMMONS, JUDITH A., RN, dir. nrsg., Henry County Health Center, Mount Pleasant, IA '85 (NURS)
SAMOFF, JAY L., atty., Kingston Hospital, Kingston, NY '85 (ATTY)
SAMOJLOWICZ, ADRIAN A., PhD, pres., Community Medical Center, Scranton, PA '67
SAMPLE, SALLY ANN, Ann Arbor, MI '67 (NURS)
SAMPLEY, MARILYN, student, Program in Hospital Administration, Trinity University, San Antonio, TX '87
SAMPSON, ARTHUR J., vice-pres., Newport Hospital, Newport, RI '74
SAMPSON, CAPT. DONALD, MSC USAF, dir. pat. affairs, U. S. Air Force Hospital, Lubbock, TX '85
SAMPSON, WILLIAM G., head facil. maint., Methodist Hospital of Indiana, Indianapolis, IN '83 (ENG)
SAMRA, MARY M., pat. rep., New England Medical Center, Boston, MA '77 (PAT)
SAMRA, S. MARIA, mgr. facil., HBO and Company, San Mateo, CA '83 (MGMT)
SAMS, BEVERLY A., mgr. matl., Brownwood Regional Hospital, Brownwood, TX '80 (CS)(PUR)
SAMS, PATSY M., dir. diet. serv., Golden Triangle Regional Medical Center, Columbus, MS '84 (FOOD)

SAMS, VERNELL J., dir. vol., St. Louis Regional Medical Center, St. Louis, MO '86 (VOL)
SAMTMANN, CHARLES, assoc. exec. dir., Northwest Institute of Psychiatry, Fort Washington, PA '81
SAMU, GARY A., dir. safety, Alhambra Community Hospital, Alhambra, CA '82 (FOOD)(RISK)
SAMUEL, ELIZABETH A., assoc. exec. dir. nrsg. serv., Kings County Hospital Center, Brooklyn, NY '85 (NURS)
SAMUEL, LAURENCE L., dir. risk mgt. off., Robert Wood Johnson University Hospital, New Brunswick, NJ '81 (RISK)
SAMUEL, MRS. SAMELE, dir. vol. serv., Mount Zion Hospital and Medical Center, San Francisco, CA '74 (VOL)
SAMUELS, BENNETT S., chief soc. work br., U. S. Naval Hospital, FPO New York, NY '84 (SOC)
SAMUELS, CLIFTON E., dir. pers., St. Mark's Hospital, Salt Lake City, UT '71 (PERS)
SAMUELS, LAWRENCE WILLIAM, dir. nutr. and food serv., Walls Regional Hospital, Cleburne, TX '76 (FOOD)
SAMUELS, MARY L., prog. coor., University of Minnesota Hospital and Clinic, Minneapolis, MN '85 (EDUC)
SAMUELS, PHILLIP W., sr. mgt. eng., Indiana University Hospitals, Indianapolis, IN '87 (MGMT)
SAMUELSON, MICHAEL, exec. dir., National Center of Health Promotion, Ann Arbor, MI '86 (EDUC)
SAMUELSON, ROGER B., adm., Newman Memorial County Hospital, Emporia, KS '48 (LIFE)
SANBORN, ALBERT BECKWITH, atty., Holy Cross Health System Corporation, South Bend, IN '82 (ATTY)
SANCHEZ, FREDDIE T. JR., asst. dir. matl. mgt., Medical Center Hospital, Tyler, TX '87 (PUR)
SANCHEZ, LEOPOLDO, mgr. food prod., St. Vincent Hospital, Santa Fe, NM '84 (FOOD)
SANCHEZ, ROSA E., (ret.), Charlotte Amalie, Virgin Islands '67 (FOOD)
SANCHIONI, JOSEPH P., dir. eng., St. Joseph Medical Center, Stamford, CT '81 (ENG)
SANCHO, ROBERT, vice-pres. commun. rel., Bronx-Lebanon Hospital Center, Bronx, NY '83 (PR)
SAND, NORMAN A., atty., Palm Springs General Hospital, Hialeah, FL '68 (ATTY)
SAND, RAYMOND, plng. assoc., Western Wisconsin Health Planning, La Crosse, WI '74
SANDBERG, HAROLD ANTON, mgr. mktg., National Electronic Information Corporation, Secaucus, NJ '72 (MGMT)
SANDBERG, MARGUERITE M., fire safety tech., Orlando Regional Medical Center, Orlando, FL '83 (ENG)
SANDEL, DAN, pres., Devon Industries, Inc., Chatsworth, CA '85 (CS)
SANDEL, PHYLLIS T., corp. dir. human res. dev., Evangelical Health Systems, Oak Brook, IL '83 (EDUC)
SANDELL, CARMEN J., RN, supv. cent. serv., Bryan Memorial Hospital, Lincoln, NE '81 (CS)
SANDER, EDWARD J., dir. mgt. eng., St. John Hospital, Detroit, MI '72 (MGMT)
SANDER, ROBERTA E., dir. vol. serv., Central DuPage Hospital, Winfield, IL '81 (VOL)
SANDERS-WOOLEY, SHAN, med. soc. worker, Spring Hill, TN '86 (SOC)
SANDERS, B. DEE, RN, dir. nrsg., Fort Sanders Regional Medical Center, Knoxville, TN '82 (NURS)
SANDERS, BARBARA B., dir. proj. serv., Hospital Corporation of America, Nashville, TN '83 (PLNG)
SANDERS, CHARLES C., chief eng., Chino Community Hospital, Chino, CA '81 (ENG)
SANDERS, CHARLES M., exec. dir., Memorial Hospital of Sweetwater County, Rock Springs, WY '51 (LIFE)
SANDERS, CYNTHIA E., dir. pers., Terre Haute Regional Hospital, Terre Haute, IN '81 (PERS)
SANDERS, DAVIS A., reg. mgr., Department of Health and Human Services, Office for Civil Rights, Dallas, TX '85
SANDERS, DORIS S., RN, Rocky Mount, NC '81 (NURS)
SANDERS, ELDON L., (ret.), College Station, TX '53 (PUR)(LIFE)
SANDERS, HAL W., dir. adm. and rehab. serv., Candler General Hospital, Savannah, GA '81 (MGMT)
SANDERS, JAMES P. JR., asst. vice-pres. environ. serv., Methodist Hospital, Jacksonville, FL '85 (ENG)
SANDERS, JO A., coor. cont. med. educ., St. Francis Regional Medical Center, Wichita, KS '86 (EDUC)
SANDERS, JOHN G. JR., dir. diet., Portsmouth Psychiatric Center, Portsmouth, VA '81 (FOOD)
SANDERS, JOY, dir. vol. serv. and mgr. lifeline prog., Stillwater Medical Center, Stillwater, OK '78 (VOL)
SANDERS, JUDITH BROWN, RN, dir. nrsg. serv., Brattleboro Retreat, Brattleboro, VT '86 (NURS)
SANDERS, KAY, dir. pub. rel., Southern Baptist Hospital, New Orleans, LA '72 (PR)
SANDERS, MARCY C., dir. vol. serv., Hospital of the University of Pennsylvania, Philadelphia, PA '84 (VOL)
SANDERS, MERLENE, dir. qual. assessment and risk mgt., Utah Valley Regional Medical Center, Provo, UT '86 (RISK)
SANDERS, MYRA K., dir. pers., St. Peters Community Hospital, St. Peters, MO '85 (PERS)
SANDERS, NANCE I., dir. pub. rel. and advertising, Orlando Regional Medical Center, Orlando, FL '86 (PR)
SANDERS, RAYMOND L., dir. plant oper., Wilson Memorial Hospital, Sidney, OH '81 (ENG)
SANDERS, RICHARD H., atty., American College of Surgeons, Chicago, IL '77 (ATTY)
SANDERS, ROBERT N., dir. bldg. serv. and ldry., Sacred Heart Hospital, Norristown, PA '86 (ENVIRON)
SANDERS, RON, supv. biomedical, DePaul Health Center, Bridgeton, MO '82 (ENG)
SANDERS, STEVE, vice-pres., Memorial Baptist Hospital, Southeast, Houston, TX '84
SANDERS, T. IRENE, pres., Sanders and Company, Washington, DC '85 (PR)
SANDERS, THOMAS J., reg. health planner, Veterans Administration Medical Center, St. Louis, MO '86 (PLNG)
SANDERS, TOMMY JOE, vice-pres. shared serv., Baptist Medical Centers, Birmingham, AL '75 (PLNG)
SANDERSON, AILEEN J., med. sup. clerk, Veterans Administration Medical Center, Reno, NV '86 (CS)
SANDERSON, DENNIS J., mgr. matl., Defiance Hospital, Defiance, OH '82 (PUR)
SANDERSON, JEFFREY C., asst. adm., Anne Arundel General Hospital, Annapolis, MD '83 (PLNG)
SANDERSON, JOHN D., adm. asst., St. Elizabeth Hospital Medical Center, Lafayette, IN '83 (PLNG)
SANDERSON, STEPHANIE S., mgr. cent. sup., proc. and distrib., Providence Hospital, Columbia, SC '87 (CS)
SANDGREN, KENT A., asst. dir. facil. eng., St. Marys Hospital of Rochester, Rochester, MN '82 (ENG)
SANDIDGE, SHARON, RN, coor. in-service, St. Mary Hospital, Quincy, IL '77 (EDUC)
SANDIFER, MARK M., Franklin, TN '80 (MGMT)
SANDLEBACK, EUGENE J., dir. assoc. serv., Healthcare Financial Management Association, Oakbrook, IL '71
SANDLER, ROBERT L., Connecticut Hospital Association, Wallingford, CT '70 (MGMT)
SANDLER, SEYMOUR, pur. agt., St. Joseph Medical Center, Stamford, CT '86 (PUR)
SANDLIN, CATHERINE, dir. vol. serv., HCA South Arlington Medical Center, Arlington, TX '84 (VOL)
SANDMAN, JOHN B., pres., St. Ann's Hospital of Columbus, Westerville, OH '72
SANDMEIER, HARRIET H., dir. commun. rel. and plng., Cornwall Hospital, Cornwall, NY '82 (PR) (PLNG)
SANDOVAL, CIRILO C., dir. soc. serv., Las Vegas Medical Center, Las Vegas, NM '86 (SOC)
SANDOVAL, JOE R., coor. soc. serv., Valley Medical Center of Fresno, Fresno, CA '72 (SOC)
SANDOVAL, R. J., asst. vice-pres., All Saints Episcopal Hospital, Fort Worth, TX '84 (PLNG)
SANDOZ, JOLI A., dir. mktg., Monticello Medical Center, Longview, WA '86 (PR) (PLNG)
SANDRIDGE, KATHARINE C., asst. dir., University of Virginia Hospitals, Charlottesville, VA '86 (VOL)
SANDS, ALAN L., dir. ldry. and linen, Santa Rosa Medical Center, San Antonio, TX '86 (ENVIRON)
SANDS, EDWARD J., pur. agt., Montgomery County Memorial Hospital, Red Oak, IA '85 (PUR)
SANDS, JOHN W., adm., The Hospital, Sidney, NY '63
SANDSMARK, MICHAEL S., dir. human res., St. Luke's Hospital, Aberdeen, SD '81 (PERS)
SANDVIG, STACY J., sr. assoc., G. E. Dantona and Associates, Phoenix, AZ '84 (PLNG)
SANDWELL, ANITA A., coor. educ., St. John's Regional Health Center, Springfield, MO '86 (EDUC)
SANETRA, DAVID C., asst. dir. food serv., Resurrection Hospital, Chicago, IL '81 (FOOD)
SANFORD, DOROTHY C., RN, assoc. dir. nrsg. serv., Carraway Methodist Medical Center, Birmingham, AL '82 (NURS)
SANFORD, FRANCES W., dir. pers., St. Mary's Hospital, Orange, NJ '86 (PERS)
SANFORD, JANE L., asst. dir. pat. and food serv., Lutheran Medical Center, Wheat Ridge, CO '82 (FOOD)
SANFORD, JOHN W. III, supv. clin. eng., Mary Imogene Bassett Hospital, Cooperstown, NY '86 (ENG)
SANFORD, KATHLEEN D., RN, vice-pres. nrsg., Harrison Memorial Hospital, Bremerton, WA '86 (NURS)
SANFORD, SARAH J., RN, vice-pres. nrsg. serv., Overlake Hospital Medical Center, Bellevue, WA '82 (NURS)
SANFORD, LTJG VERNON R., MSC USN, Naval Hospital, Bethesda, MD '84
SANGER, JAMES M., sr. vice-pres. oper., Good Samaritan Hospital and Medical Center, Portland, OR '85
SANGSTER, TOM R., vice-pres. indust. rel., Colorado Hospital Association, Denver, CO '67 (PERS)
SANSAM, PHILIP G., adm., Alleghany Regional Hospital, Low Moor, VA '70
SANSBURY, DONALD G., dir. hskpg., New Hanover Memorial Hospital, Wilmington, NC '86 (ENVIRON)
SANSBURY, VICTORIA E., dir. mktg., Good Samaritan Hospital, Cincinnati, OH '86 (PR) (PLNG)
SANSEVIRO, JOSEPH, dir. pur., Huntington Hospital, Huntington, NY '85 (PUR)
SANSKY, ROBERT, dir. eng., HCA Sun City Hospital, Sun City Center, FL '85 (ENG)
SANSPREE, MARY JEAN, dir. educ., Eye Foundation Hospital, Birmingham, AL '87 (EDUC)
SANTAMARIA, ELISA, Newton, NJ '86 (PLNG)
SANTANA, ANA, mgr. telecommun., Saint James Hospital, Newark, NJ '86 (ENG)
SANTANA, MILDRED, asst. clin. coor. surg. center, Milford Hospital, Milford, CT '87 (AMB)
SANTIAGO, JOANN M., student, Southern Illinois University, School of Technical Careers, Carbondale, IL '86
SANTICH, RICHARD J., pres., Sms Communications, Inc., Cleveland, OH '85 (EDUC)
SANTILLANES, JOE L., dir. environ. serv., St. John's Regional Medical Center, Oxnard, CA '86 (ENVIRON)
SANTILO, CHARLES J., asst. dir. eng. and maint., Ellwood City Hospital, Ellwood City, PA '86 (ENG)
SANTIN, CARMEN, RN, dir. nrsg. serv., Lutheran Medical Center, Cleveland, OH '76 (NURS)
SANTO, DONNA L., sr. res. analyst, Market Opinion Research, Detroit, MI '86 (PLNG)
SANTOLI, DENNIS R., pres., Hfic Management Company, Inc., Vienna, VA '84 (RISK)
SANTOPOALO, ROCHELLE D., RN, Evanston, IL '84 (NURS)
SANTORO, MONICA, dir. risk mgt., Presbyterian Hospital in the City of New York, New York, NY '86 (RISK)
SANTORO, THOMAS A., asst. vice-pres. plng., Ellis Hospital, Schenectady, NY '80 (PLNG)
SANTOS, CHERYL A., mktg. consult., Scottish Rite Children's Hospital, Atlanta, GA '83 (PR)
SANTOS, JOSE, dir. matl. mgt., Miami General Hospital, Miami, FL '86 (PUR)
SANTOS, KAREN L., supv. cent. serv., Newington Children's Hospital, Newington, CT '83 (CS)
SANTOS, LUIS, supv. cent. sup., St. Mary Hospital, Hoboken, NJ '85 (CS)
SANTY, MARSHALL O. JR., dir. gen. serv., Androscoggin Valley Hospital, Berlin, NH '79 (FOOD)
SANZ, PABLO, dir. plant, Highland Park Hospital, Miami, FL '86 (ENG)
SANZO, ANTHONY MICHAEL, sr. vice-pres., Allegheny General Hospital, Pittsburgh, PA '77
SANZONE, RAYMOND DAVID, dir., Brookline Hospital, Brookline, MA '69
SAPHIER, MICHAEL D., atty., Saphier and Heller, Los Angeles, CA '76 (ATTY)
SAPHIRE-BERNSTEIN, INGER M., dir. plng., Health Care Management, Inc., Oak Park, IL '83 (PLNG)
SAPIEN, PAUL, dir. biomedical eng., St. Francis Hospital, Evanston, IL '86 (ENG)
SAPOLSKY, JEROME R., adm., Radiation Oncology Associates, Providence, RI '55 (PR)
SAPP, CAROL S., consulting mgr., Christian Hospitals Northeast-Northwest, St. Louis, MO '84 (FOOD)
SAPP, MARY JANE, mgr. telecommun., St. John's Healthcare Corporation, Anderson, IN '83 (ENG)
SARA, SHARON, asst. dir. cent. serv., Somerset Medical Center, Somerville, NJ '86 (CS)
SARANDOS, PETER T., vice-pres. human res., Voluntary Hospitals of America, Irving, TX '86 (PERS)
SARASIN, ARTHUR E., asst. dir. diet., Metropolitan Calgary, Rural and General Hospital, District 93, Calgary, Alta., Canada '82 (FOOD)
SARDARO, JANET L., dir. vol. serv., Sacred Heart Hospital, Norristown, PA '84 (VOL)
SARDELLI, RICHARD M., dir. ins. and risk mgt., Horizon Health Systems, Oak Park, MI '83 (RISK)
SARDON, NANCY J., asst. adm., Lodi Memorial Hospital, Lodi, CA '79
SARDONE, FRANK J., vice-pres. mktg., Ephraim McDowell Regional Medical Center, Danville, KY '85 (PR) (PLNG)
SARENPA, DIANE H., dir. commun., Fairview Southdale Hospital, Minneapolis, MN '85 (ENG)
SARGENT-LEONARD, CARLENE, dir. soc. serv., Milford-Whitinsville Regional Hospital, Milford, MA '85 (SOC)
SARGENT, CHARLOTTE B., dir. vol. serv., Southeast Missouri Hospital, Cape Girardeau, MO '83 (VOL)
SARGENT, FLORENCE BURGLY, chief food serv., Womack Army Community Hospital, Fort Bragg, NC '77 (FOOD)
SARGENT, JOYCE H., dir. vol. serv., Loudoun Memorial Hospital, Leesburg, VA '84 (VOL)
SARGUS, PEARSON C., dir. vol. serv., Ohio Valley Medical Center, Wheeling, WV '85 (VOL)
SARIES, SHIRLEY L., RN, asst. adm. pat. care, Tuality Community Hospital, Hillsboro, OR '86 (NURS)
SARKAR, GEORGE A., PhD, exec. dir., Manhattan Eye, Ear and Throat Hospital, New York, NY '71
SARKIS, GEORGE R., atty., Saint Thomas Medical Center, Akron, OH '87 (ATTY)
SARNA, KIMBERLEY J., mgr. commun. and media rel., Alexian Brothers Medical Center, Elk Grove Village, IL '84 (PR)
SAROSDY, SUSAN D., consult., Cresap, McCormick and Paget, Atlanta, GA '87 (PLNG)
SARRA, JANE B., RN, dir. amb. care, Eye and Ear Hospital of Pittsburgh, Pittsburgh, PA '87 (AMB)
SARRATT, WILLIAM DAVID, mgr. eng., Shriners Hospital for Crippled Children, Greenville, SC '87 (ENG)
SARREL, BERNARD M., dir. plng. and mgt. serv., College of Medicine and Dentistry of New Jersey-College Hospital, Newark, NJ '63
SARSFIELD, HELEN L., RN, vice-pres. pat. care, Silver Cross Hospital, Joliet, IL '78 (NURS)
SARSFIELD, STEPHEN R., asst. dir. risk mgt., Saint Vincent Health Center, Erie, PA '82 (RISK)
SARTAIN, JENDEAN, coor. qual. assur. and med. staff, Navapache Hospital, Show Low, AZ '86 (RISK)
SARTINI, IRENE, mgr. qual. assessment, Charlton Memorial Hospital, Fall River, MA '86
SARTINI, MARLENE M., dir. outpat serv., Ashtabula County Medical Center, Ashtabula, OH '87 (AMB)
SARTOR, JAMES M., dir. cent. serv., St. Vincent Hospital and Medical Center, Portland, OR '78 (CS)
SARTOR, REGINA G., risk mgr. and coor. qual. assur., Northside Hospital, Atlanta, GA '82 (RISK)
SARTORIS, LAURENS, atty., Virginia Hospital Association, Richmond, VA '77 (ATTY)
SASAO, FRANCES, media spec., United Hospital, Port Chester, NY '80 (EDUC)
SASLAW, KAREN L., pres., Saslaw Group, Columbus, OH '86 (PLNG)
SASNETT, GENEVA H., coor. commun. rel., United General Hospital, Sedro Woolley, WA '82 (PR)
SASS, JULAINE J., RN, dir. nrsg., Dakota Midland Hospital, Aberdeen, SD '80 (NURS)
SASS, M. KIM, dir. corp. commun., Albany General Hospital-Cascade West Health Systems, Inc., Albany, OR '81 (PR)
SASS, WANDA L., RN, dir. nrsg. serv., Sheboygan Memorial Medical Center, Sheboygan, WI '83 (NURS)
SASSO, LEONARD A., dir. food serv., Scripps Memorial Hospital, La Jolla, CA '78 (FOOD)
SASSO, MITZI, dir. matl. mgt., French Hospital Medical Center, San Luis Obispo, CA '80 (PUR)
SASSO, RON, mgr. plant oper., Providence-St. Margaret Health Center, Kansas City, KS '80 (ENG)
SATCHELL, ROBERT M., dir. eng., Johnston-Willis Hospital, Richmond, VA '85 (ENG)
SATCHWILL, KATHERINE K., dir. mktg. and commun., Willingway Hospital, Statesboro, GA '82 (PR)
SATEY, FELIX S. JR., asst. adm., Halifax Hospital Medical Center, Daytona Beach, FL '76 (PERS)
SATHER, CARL B., sr. vice-pres. mktg. and plng., Baptist Medical Centers, Birmingham, AL '78 (PLNG)
SATHER, DAVID J., dir. soc. work, Rice Memorial Hospital, Willmar, MN '85 (SOC)

SATIANI, HARESH S., reg. dir., Medical Instrumentation Systems, Cuyahoga Falls, OH '86 (ENG)
SATO, JACOB N., dir. plant oper. and maint., Kuakini Medical Center, Honolulu, HI '84 (ENG)
SATRAPE, VICTORIA J., dir. commun., Franklin Regional Medical Center, Franklin, PA '87 (PR)
SATTAZAHN, CDR MARY D., RN MSC USA, sr. policy analyst-qual. assur., Office of the Assistant Secretary of Defense, Washington, DC '85 (NURS)
SATTERFIELD, MARGARET BUNDY, pat. rep., Baptist Medical Center of Oklahoma, Oklahoma City, OK '86 (PAT)
SATTERFIELD, SHIRLEY B., RN, clin. dir. med. and surg. nrsg., Northwest Texas Hospital, Amarillo, TX '86 (NURS)
SATTERLEE, CRAIG BAUMAN, reg. vice-pres., Hospital Corporation of America, Atlanta, GA '73
SATTERTHWAITE, MARILYN S., RN, dir. supportive nrsg. serv., Lutheran General Hospital, Park Ridge, IL '85 (NURS)
SATTERWHITE, JERRY L., chief soc. work serv., Veterans Administration Medical Center, Birmingham, AL '73 (SOC)
SATTERWHITE, NANCY L., dir. diet., Gordon Crowell Memorial Hospital, Lincolnton, NC '81 (FOOD)
SATURLEY, JOHN W., (ret.), Yucaipa, CA '56 (ENG)(LIFE)
SAUCIER, CINDI S., dir. human res., F. Edward Hebert Hospital, New Orleans, LA '83 (PERS)
SAUCIER, STEPHEN J., vice-pres., Haricomp, Inc., Providence, RI '75 (MGMT)
SAUER, GERALDINE, dir. cent. serv., Southwest Medical Center, Liberal, KS '85 (CS)
SAUER, JAMES E. JR., adm., St. Joseph Medical Center, Burbank, CA '67
SAUER, LAWRENCE M., dir. legislation, Dept. of HHS, Health Resources and Services Administration, Rockville, MD '75
SAUER, ROBERT L., dir. pers., Doylestown Hospital, Doylestown, PA '79 (PERS)
SAUER, VIRGINIA G., coor. educ., Aspen Valley Hospital District, Aspen, CO '84 (EDUC)
SAUERMAN, DONALD M., dir. plant oper., Harrisburg Hospital, Harrisburg, PA '71 (ENG)
SAUERS, SR. FELICE, RN, consult., Mercy Health System, Burlingame, CA '72 (EDUC)
SAUERS, ROBERT J., vice-pres. environ. serv., Unicare Health Facilities, Inc., Milwaukee, WI '79 (ENG)
SAUERTEIG, PAUL J., atty., Lutheran Hospital of Fort Wayne, Fort Wayne, IN '74 (ATTY)
SAUERWEIN, ARTHUR L., dir. plant oper. and maint., Salvation Army Booth Memorial Hospital, Florence, KY '75 (ENG)
SAUERWEIN, LINDA D., coor. vol., Thomas Jefferson University Hospital, Philadelphia, PA '81 (VOL)
SAUM, ROBERT W. JR., RN, clin. nrs. spec., University of California San Francisco Hospitals and Clinics, San Francisco, CA '85 (NURS)
SAUNDERS, CANDICE L., RN, actg. vice-pres. pat. serv., Bethesda Memorial Hospital, Boynton Beach, FL '85 (NURS)
SAUNDERS, CAROL S., dir. pub. rel., Rockford Memorial Hospital, Rockford, IL '81 (PR)
SAUNDERS, CONNIE P., dir. staff dev., Richmond Memorial Hospital, Rockingham, NC '84 (EDUC)
SAUNDERS, DICKSON M., atty., St. John Medical Center, Tulsa, OK '78 (ATTY)
SAUNDERS, DONALD F., exec. dir., Androscoggin Valley Hospital, Berlin, NH '84 (PLNG)
SAUNDERS, DOW W., Holzer Medical Center, Gallipolis, OH '81 (SOC)
SAUNDERS, FREDA I., supv. cent. sup., Community Hospital of Sacramento, Sacramento, CA '82 (CS)
SAUNDERS, FREDERICK L. JR., Wichita, KS '74 (PUR)
SAUNDERS, JANET E., pat. care rep., Massachusetts General Hospital, Boston, MA '82 (PAT)
SAUNDERS, JOLINE HALL, dir. diet., Methodist Hospital, Madison, WI '68 (FOOD)
SAUNDERS, JOSEPH A., atty., St. Mary Medical Center, Long Beach, CA '73 (ATTY)
SAUNDERS, JOSEPH J. JR., dir. matl. mgt., Presbyterian-University of Pennsylvania Medical Center, Philadelphia, PA '77 (PUR)
SAUNDERS, KATHARIN GAY, dir. mktg. and commun. rel., Lakeview Hospital, Bountiful, UT '82 (PR) (PLNG)
SAUNDERS, KATHLEEN, supv. cent. proc., St. Joseph Hospital West, Mount Clemens, MI '85 (CS)
SAUNDERS, LESLIE M., sr. med. facil. planner, Bohm Nbbj, Columbus, OH '83 (PLNG)
SAUNDERS, MARIE E., instr., Fox Valley Technical Institute, Appleton, WI '85 (EDUC)
SAUNDERS, MICHAEL W., syst. mgr., Acute Care Affiliates, Oakland, CA '85 (PUR)
SAUNDERS, NINFA M., RN, dir. human res. and prog. dev., Emory University Hospital, Atlanta, GA '86 (NURS)
SAUNDERS, TRACY E., ed., Tulane University Medical Center, New Orleans, LA '86 (PR)
SAURENMANN, JAMES R., corp. syst. coor., American Medical International, Beverly Hills, CA '82 (MGMT)
SAUT, DORIS, dir. vol., Chippenham Hospital, Richmond, VA '73 (VOL)
SAUTER, JOHN, dir. food serv., Sparks Regional Medical Center, Fort Smith, AR '73 (FOOD)
SAUTER, LT. COL. JOSEPH G., MSC USA, nrsg. meth. analyst, U. S. Army Community Hospital, Fort Carson, CO '85
SAUVE, GUY GERARD, pres., G. Sauve and Associates, Toronto, Ont., Canada '83 (FOOD)
SAVAGE, CAROL S., dir. pub. rel., North Shore Children's Hospital, Salem, MA '85 (PR)
SAVAGE, CRAIG M., vice-pres. plng. and mktg., Memorial Mission Hospital, Asheville, NC '78 (PLNG)
SAVAGE, DENNIS M., mgr. sup., proc., distrib. and ldry., Griffin Hospital, Derby, CT '86 (CS)
SAVAGE, DONALD R., Hewlett-Packard Company, Thousand Oaks, CA '80
SAVAGE, JAMES R., dir. pat. acct., Aultman Hospital, Canton, OH '86 (PAT)
SAVAGE, LANA R., RN, dir. nrsg., Down East Community Hospital, Machias, ME '81 (NURS)
SAVAGE, MARY LEA, RN, assoc. dir. nrsg., Jess Parrish Memorial Hospital, Titusville, FL '84 (NURS)
SAVAGE, NITA I., reg. health care consult., Equitable Life Assurance Society, Chicago, IL '85
SAVAGE, PHILIP M. III, atty., St. Bernardine Medical Center, San Bernardino, CA '71 (ATTY)
SAVAGE, ROBERT L., assoc. adm., United Hospital Center, Clarksburg, WV '74
SAVAGE, WILLIAM M., dir. soc. work, St. Joseph's Hospital, Elmira, NY '73 (SOC)
SAVAGLIO, FRED J., Everett, WA '76 (ENG)
SAVALA, SHEILA M., RN, chief nrsg. serv., Veterans Administration Center, Cheyenne, WY '84 (NURS)
SAVARD, HOMER J., chief eng., St. Mary's Medical Center, Racine, WI '78 (ENG)
SAVCHUK, DANIEL P., prog. mgr. matl. serv., Monitoba Health Organizations, Inc., Winnipeg, Man., Canada '80 (PUR)
SAVERY, JONAN C., dir. risk mgt. and environ. serv., Virginia Beach General Hospital, Virginia Beach, VA '73 (RISK)
SAVETTIERE, GENE, vice-pres. mktg., Scallop Thermal Management, Inc., Edison, NJ '85
SAVIA, JANET S., mgr. consult. rel., Burroughs Healthcare Services, Brisbane, CA '82
SAVING, PETER E., proj. dir., American Medical Buildings, Marietta, GA '85 (PLNG)
SAVISKI, CATHY A., dir. soc. serv., Shelby Medical Center, Alabaster, AL '80 (SOC)
SAVITCH, LANE A., adm., Valley General Hospital, Monroe, WA '79 (PR) (PLNG)
SAVITZ, LAWRENCE, adm. asst. support serv., Jeanes Hospital, Philadelphia, PA '75 (FOOD)
SAWALHA, TAREK S., chief adm., Hafr Al-Batin General Hospital, Hafr Al-Batin, Saudi Arabia '86 (MGMT)
SAWARYNSKI, JACK G., mgr. eng. and maint., AMI Saint Joseph Hospital, Omaha, NE '81 (ENG)
SAWAYA, JANINE A., RN, assoc. exec. dir. nrsg., Humana Hospital -Sunrise, Las Vegas, NV '86 (NURS)
SAWCHUK, PETER L., MD, pres., Emergency Medical Associates, Livingston, NJ '87 (AMB)
SAWDEY, MARION, dir. eng., Hillsdale Community Health Center, Hillsdale, MI '80 (ENG)
SAWHILL, VICTORIA E., RN, coor. in-service educ., West Shore Hospital, Manistee, MI '79 (EDUC)
SAWICKI, GARY, adm. asst. nrsg., John F. Kennedy Medical Center, Edison, NJ '83
SAWIN, POLLY D., RN, dir. nrsg., Sutter Memorial Hospital, Sacramento, CA '84 (NURS)
SAWYER, ANDREA, coor. amb. care, AMI Park Place Hospital, Port Arthur, TX '87 (AMB)
SAWYER, CLIFFORD G., (ret.), Syosset, NY '39 (LIFE)
SAWYER, ED, safety eng., AMI Saint Joseph Hospital, Omaha, NE '80 (ENG)
SAWYER, FRANK H., dir. matl., South Florida Baptist Hospital, Plant City, FL '82 (PUR)
SAWYER, LAURALEE, dir. pub. rel., Providence Hospital, Cincinnati, OH '77 (PR)
SAWYER, MARY-JO P., dir. food serv., Metropolitan Hospital, Richmond, VA '86 (FOOD)
SAWYER, MAUREEN C., dir. soc. serv., Allentown Hospital, Allentown, PA '81 (SOC)
SAWYER, RICHARD E., vice-pres., Hamilton Associates, Inc., Minneapolis, MN '57 (LIFE)
SAWYER, ROBERT C. JR., sr. vice-pres. mktg., Massamont Insurance Agency, Greenfield, MA '86 (RISK)
SAWYER, STEPHEN J., sr. vice-pres., Anderson Debartolo Pan, Inc., Tucson, AZ '79
SAWYER, SUZANNE H., dir. vol. serv., Shands Hospital, Gainesville, FL '86 (VOL)
SAWYER, THOMAS HARRY, pres., General Health, Baton Rouge, LA '69
SAWYES, ROLAND W., assoc. syst. support, HBO and Company, San Mateo, CA '86
SAX, ARLENE J., asst. dir. diet.-prod., St. Luke's Hospitals, Fargo, ND '81 (FOOD)
SAXON, FLOYD E., dir. plant oper., AMI Mission Bay Hospital, San Diego, CA '85 (ENG)
SAXON, JULIANE M., student, Program in Health Care Management, Concordia College, Moorhead, MN '87
SAXON, NANCY JANE, adm. asst. trauma center, Hermann Hospital, Houston, TX '80
SAXON, SAMUEL B., dir. pers., Self Memorial Hospital, Greenwood, SC '83 (PERS)
SAXTON, MARY J., RN, div. dir. nrsg. serv., Boulder Community Hospital, Boulder, CO '84 (NURS)
SAXTON, ROEZANNE M., pur. agt., Palo Alto County Hospital, Emmetsburg, IA '86 (PUR)
SAXTON, THOMAS P., pres., Wilkes-Barre General Hospital, Wilkes-Barre, PA '69
SAY, BRIAN A., dir. mgt. info. serv., Harper-Grace Hospitals, Detroit, MI '82 (MGMT)
SAYER, HENRY D., exec. vice-pres., Pennell and Wiltberger, Inc., Philadelphia, PA '75 (PLNG)
SAYERS, BRUCE E., atty., Hodges, Davis, Gruenberg, Compton and Sayers, Merrillville, IN '83 (ATTY)
SAYERS, ELFRIEDE, mgr. telecommun., Burdette Tomlin Memorial Hospital, Cape May Court House, NJ '86 (ENG)
SAYFORD, NELSON F., dir. mgt. eng., University Hospital, Augusta, GA '83 (MGMT)
SAYLES, MYRNA, dir. soc. serv., HCA North Florida Regional Medical Center, Gainesville, FL '86 (SOC)
SAYLOR, BRENDA C., risk mgr., Christian Hospitals Northeast-Northwest, St. Louis, MO '83 (RISK)
SAYLOR, RICHARD C., dir. eng., Lewistown Hospital, Lewistown, PA '84 (ENG)
SAYRE, LEE F., area vice-pres., SunHealth Inc., Columbia, SC '64
SAYRE, ROBERT W., atty., Bryn Mawr Hospital, Bryn Mawr, PA '75 (ATTY)
SAYVETZ, ANN, atty., Children's Hospital, Denver, CO '84 (ATTY)
SAYWELL, ROBERT MORSE JR., PhD, assoc. prof., Graduate Program in Health Administration, School of Medicine, Indiana University, Indianapolis, IN '78
SAZAMA, GERALD F., atty., St. Joseph's Hospital, Chippewa Falls, WI '86 (ATTY)
SCACCIA, GABRIELLE M., dir. med. rec., Victory Memorial Hospital, Waukegan, IL '80
SCADDAN, GEOFFREY RONALD, exec. dir., King Edward VII Memorial Hospital, Hamilton Hmdx, Bermuda '74
SCALES, GERALD S., RN, adm. nrsg., Rockland Psychiatric Center, Orangeburg, NY '80 (NURS)
SCALES, HOWARD V., dir. plant oper., Seton Medical Center, Austin, TX '63 (ENG)
SCALES, RONALD W., dir. matl. mgt., Memorial Medical Center, Savannah, GA '85 (PUR)
SCALFANI, JOHN J., dir. matl. mgt., Hinsdale Hospital, Hinsdale, IL '83 (PUR)
SCALISE, GREGORY, dir. matl. mgt., Beloit Memorial Hospital, Beloit, WI '79 (PUR)
SCALZI, CYNTHIA C., PhD RN, assoc. prof. nrsg., University of Texas at Austin, School of Nursing, Austin, TX '83 (NURS)
SCALZO, JANET E., dir. mktg., Rushmore National Health Systems, Rapid City, SD '86 (PR)
SCAMMELL, CHARLES, mgt. consult., Coopers and Lybrand, New York City, NY '86 (PLNG)
SCANDLYN, KATHIE D., RN, coor. educ. serv., HCA Coliseum Medical Centers, Macon, GA '83 (EDUC)
SCANLAN, KEVIN P., dir. human res., Christ Hospital and Medical Center, Oak Lawn, IL '83 (PERS)
SCANLAN, LAURA J., sr. consult., Ernst and Whinney, Chicago, IL '80
SCANLAN, MARCIA L., RN, dir. med. and surg. nrsg., Northwestern Memorial Hospital, Chicago, IL '83 (NURS)
SCANLAN, SHARON N., dir. u.-care prog., University of Arkansas Medical Sciences, Little Rock, AR '86 (PR)
SCANLON, MARGARET E., mgr. trng. and dev., Riverside Hospital, Jacksonville, FL '83 (EDUC)
SCANLON, WILLIAM E., asst. adm., Burke Rehabilitation Center, White Plains, NY '71 (ENG)
SCANTLEBURY, VERONICA, vice-pres., Johnson and Higgins, Chicago, IL '87 (AMB)
SCARANO, BARBARA A., coor. vol. serv., J. E. Runnells Hospital-Union County, Berkeley Heights, NJ '84 (VOL)
SCARBOROUGH, CHARLES D., dir. matl. mgt., West Jefferson Medical Center, Marrero, LA '82 (PUR)
SCARBROUGH, ALVA W., vice-pres. human resources, Sioux Valley Hospital, Sioux Falls, SD '67 (PERS)
SCARBROUGH, KATHLEEN J. M., dir. vol., Piqua Memorial Medical Center, Piqua, OH '78 (VOL)
SCARDAVILLE, THOMAS C., corp. dir. mktg., Sch Health Care System, Houston, TX '86 (PR) (PLNG)
SCARDINA, ARALEE J., mgr. hskpg. serv., St. Luke's Hospital, Milwaukee, WI '84 (ENG)(ENVIRON)
SCARFONE, JOHN A., vice-pres., Lenox Hill Hospital, New York, NY '79
SCARPA, CATHERINE M., RN, adm. nrs., University of California San Francisco, San Francisco, CA '84 (NURS)
SCATES, ROBERT F., sr. vice-pres., Baptist Memorial Hospital, Memphis, TN '53 (EDUC)(LIFE)
SCAVONE, ROBERT A., assoc. dir. matl. mgt., Henry Ford Hospital, Detroit, MI '78 (PUR)
SCAVONE, SUSAN R., dir. pers., Noble Hospital, Westfield, MA '86 (PERS)
SCELZI, GERALD J., dir. food serv., Holy Name Hospital, Teaneck, NJ '75 (FOOD)
SCESNY, ALICE M., assoc. dir., Cleveland Clinic Foundation, Cleveland, OH '81 (SOC)
SCEUSA, MICHAEL, dir. corp. pur., Glenbeigh, Inc., Jupiter, FL '86 (RISK)
SCHAAF, BARBARA B., dir. vol. serv., Children's Hospital Medical Center of California, Oakland, CA '85 (VOL)
SCHAAG, HELEN A., RN, clin. dir. critical and spec. care, Saint Joseph Health Center Kansas, Kansas City, MO '87 (AMB)
SCHAAL, LOIS M., dir. diet. serv., University of Cincinnati Hospital, Cincinnati, OH '73 (FOOD)
SCHACHAT, RENE S., dir. soc. serv., Elliot Hospital, Manchester, NH '75 (SOC)
SCHACHER, ROBERT C., atty., Oklahoma Hospital Association, Oklahoma City, OK '73 (ATTY)
SCHACHINGER, EDWARD A., pres., Lerch Bates Hospital Group, Inc., Fairfax, VA '80 (PUR)
SCHACHT, MARSHA C., dir. soc. work serv., Mercy Hospital, Urbana, IL '85 (SOC)
SCHACHTER, MILTON J., adm., Health First Medical Group, Memphis, TN '78
SCHADE, RUDOLF G. JR., atty., John F. Kennedy Medical Center, Chicago, IL '75 (ATTY)
SCHADEN, DANIEL F., assoc. vice-pres., Sinai Hospital of Baltimore, Baltimore, MD '75 (MGMT)
SCHAEDLER, PHILLIP A., atty., Memorial Hospital, Owosso, MI '85 (ATTY)(RISK)
SCHAEFER, ANN ELAINE ARMSTRONG, RN, Mount Clemens, MI '77 (NURS)
SCHAEFER, CAROL C., RN, adm. nrsg., St. Joseph's Hospital of Arcadia, Arcadia, WI '81 (NURS)
SCHAEFER, CHRISTOPHER A., asst. vice-pres., Toledo Hospital, Toledo, OH '81 (PLNG)
SCHAEFER, DANIEL E., Mayo Clinic, Rochester, MN '82 (PLNG)
SCHAEFER, DAVID H., vice-pres. mktg. and plng., Mount Zion Hospital and Medical Center, San Francisco, CA '84 (PLNG)
SCHAEFER, LYNN L., food serv. consult., Daughters of Charity Health Systems-West Central, St. Louis, MO '75 (FOOD)

SCHAEFER, MICHELE, asst. adm., Spelman Memorial Hospital, Smithville, MO '78
SCHAEFER, NORMA F., pur. agt., Richland Hospital, Mansfield, OH '83 (PUR)
SCHAEFER, PAMELA J., dir. plng., St. Luke's Hospitals, Fargo, ND '84 (PLNG)
SCHAEFER, WILLIAM, dir. diet. serv., Albany County Nursing Home, Albany, NY '86 (FOOD)
SCHAEFFER, DAVID H., vice-pres. mgt. support, Pacific Health Resources, Los Angeles, CA '84
SCHAEFFER, KAREN A., RN, asst. adm. and dir. nrsg., Westlake Pavilion, Franklin Park, IL '86 (NURS)
SCHAEFFER, SR. M. JOSEPHA, RN, asst. adm. pat. care serv., Hospital Sisters Health System, Springfield, IL '68 (NURS)
SCHAEFFER, MARY ANN, coor. nutr., Catholic Family Services, Nutrition Program for the Elderly, Scotia, NY '80 (FOOD)
SCHAEFFER, WILLIAM J., dir. support serv., Medical College of Virginia Hospital, Virginia Commonwealth University, Richmond, VA '82
SCHAEFFLER, GRACIELA E., RN, adm. pat. care, White Memorial Medical Center, Los Angeles, CA '76 (NURS)
SCHAER, GARY W., assoc. dir. pers., Saint Francis Medical Center, Peoria, IL '72 (PERS)
SCHAFER, DAVID E., dir. pers., St. Francis Hospital Center, Beech Grove, IN '67 (PERS)
SCHAFER, HANS, dir. facil. plng. and mgt., Medical Plaza Hospital, Fort Worth, TX '83 (PLNG)
SCHAFER, ROBERT P., partner, Arthur Young and Company, Detroit, MI '85
SCHAFER, SEYMOUR J., atty., Hospital Council of Western Pennsylvania, Pittsburgh, PA '70 (ATTY)
SCHAFER, SHIRLEY L., dir. vol., William N. Wishard Memorial Hospital, Indianapolis, IN '84 (VOL)
SCHAFF, BRIAN BROOK, student, Program in Health Administration, Temple University, Philadelphia, PA '85
SCHAFF, DAVID J. VANDER, proj. mgr., Allied Research Associates, Chicago, IL '83 (PLNG)
SCHAFF, THERESA A., asst. dir. environ. serv., Valley Presbyterian Hospital, Van Nuys, CA '86 (ENVIRON)
SCHAFFARCZYK, EDGAR, sr. eng. syst. analyst, Kaiser Permanente Medical Care Program, Oakland, CA '83 (PLNG)
SCHAFFER, GAIL M., atty., Marymount Hospital, Garfield Heights, OH '83 (ATTY)
SCHAFFER, GERALDING L., dir. vol. serv., West Jersey Hospital-Eastern Division, Voorhees, NJ '85 (VOL)
SCHAFFER, JAY, exec. dir. qual. assur. and room serv., Caronia Corporation, Houston, TX '86 (RISK)
SCHAFFER, LINDA K., off. in charge pat. referral off., Ehrling Bergquist U. S. Air Force Regional Hospital, Omaha, NE '86
SCHAFFER, REGINALD R., assoc. dir. bldg. and grd., Harper-Grace Hospitals, Detroit, MI '80 (ENG)
SCHAFFER, S. ANDREW, atty., New York University Medical Center, New York, NY '78 (ATTY)
SCHAFFNER, LESLIE J., adm. dir., St. Vincent's Medical Center, Jacksonville, FL '78
SCHAFFNER, LINDA D., RN, asst. vice-pres., Bethesda North Hospital, Cincinnati, OH '80 (NURS)
SCHAFFNER, MARY MARTIN, atty., St. Thomas Hospital, Nashville, TN '85 (ATTY)
SCHAIBLE, CALVIN L., student, Concordia College, St. Paul, MN '82
SCHAIBLE, JOHN A., PhD, dir. pub. rel., Madison Community Hospital, Madison Heights, MI '81 (PR)
SCHAID, BECKY, dir. pub. rel., Baptist Health Systems, Kansas City, MO '86 (PR)
SCHAIER, BETH F., prog. analyst, St. Clare's -Riverside Medical Center, Denville, NJ '86 (PLNG)
SCHAIN, ERIC H., dir. food serv., Concord Hospital, Concord, NH '85 (FOOD)
SCHALICH, RICHARD H., mgr. ldry. and linen serv., Thomas Jefferson University Hospital, Philadelphia, PA '86 (ENVIRON)
SCHALL, DENNIS WAYNE, oper. analyst, Hinsdale Hospital, Hinsdale, IL '79 (MGMT)
SCHALLERT, STEVEN G., dir. info. serv., Sarah Bush Lincoln Health Center, Mattoon, IL '86 (MGMT)
SCHALM, RUTH A., dir. soc. serv., Lapeer General Hospital, LaPeer, MI '79 (SOC)
SCHAMADAN, JAMES L., MD, pres. and chief exec. off., Scottsdale Memorial Hospital, Scottsdale, AZ '87
SCHAMADAN, WILLIAM E., MD, vice-pres. med. affairs, Mansfield General Hospital, Mansfield, OH '84
SCHAMERLOH, LARRY L., dir. info. syst., Parkview Memorial Hospital, Fort Wayne, IN '87 (MGMT)
SCHANDING, DAVID LOUIS, asst. dir., Lake County Health Department, Waukegan, IL '80
SCHANES, JOSEPH M., chief plant oper., Louis A. Weiss Memorial Hospital, Chicago, IL '72 (ENG)
SCHANKER, NATALIE, dir. consumer rel., Cedars Medical Center, Miami, FL '80 (PAT)
SCHANTZ, THOMAS E., mgt. eng., Magee-Womens Hospital, Pittsburgh, PA '86 (MGMT)
SCHAP, JAMES J., dir. pers., Keswick-Home for Incurables, Baltimore, MD '77 (PERS)
SCHAPER, JOHN H., asst. adm., Kadlec Medical Center, Richland, WA '84 (PLNG)
SCHAPMANN, GERRY, market mgr., Bell South Services, Birmingham, AL '86
SCHAPPI, JOHN V., assoc. ed. labor serv., Bureau of National Affairs, Inc., Washington, DC '83 (EDUC)(PERS)
SCHARENBERG, CHARLES, dir. behavioral medicine serv., Ancilla Systems, Inc., Elk Grove Village, IL '72
SCHARF, LINDA M., RN, asst. adm. nrsg., Millard Fillmore Suburban Hospital, Williamsville, NY '87 (NURS)
SCHARFF, HILLEL, sr. consult., Healthscope, Mount Vernon, NY '86 (PLNG)
SCHARICH, JEANNETTE M., coor. guest rel., Sonoma Valley Hospital, Sonoma, CA '86 (PAT)
SCHARLAU, JAN L., RN, dir. med. surg. serv., Morton F. Plant Hospital, Clearwater, FL '79 (NURS)
SCHARNITZ, NANCY A., dir. pers. serv., Roxborough Memorial Hospital, Philadelphia, PA '81 (PERS)
SCHARRE, PHILIP C., student, University of Tennessee, Knoxville, TN '86 (PLNG)
SCHATSCHNEIDER, ELROY O., dir. hosp. sales, F. Dohmen Company, Germantown, WI '83
SCHATTENBERG, MARY, student, Program in Health Care Administration, University of Minnesota, Minneapolis, MN '86
SCHATZ, BARRY A., sr. asst. dir., F. G. McGaw Hospital, Loyola University, Maywood, IL '79
SCHATZ, GORDON B., atty., Health Industry Manufacturers Association, Washington, DC '84 (ATTY)
SCHATZ, HOWARD L., dir. food serv., Freehold Area Hospital, Freehold, NJ '69 (FOOD)
SCHATZ, JOAN, dir. pat. and family serv., Holy Cross Hospital, Mission Hills, CA '82 (SOC)
SCHATZ, SALLY, RN, dir. nrsg. serv., Bonner General Hospital, Sandpoint, ID '86 (NURS)
SCHATZLE, DOROTHY C., RN, dir. cent. serv., St. Mary's Hospital of Troy, Troy, NY '82 (CS)
SCHAUB, CYNTHIA STRAUFF, vice-pres. human res., Wake Medical Center, Raleigh, NC '80 (RISK)
SCHAUM, KATHLEEN D., dir. food and nutr. serv., AMI Southeastern Medical Center, North Miami Beach, FL '77 (FOOD)
SCHEAR, WILLIAM A., MD, med. dir. qual. assur. and risk mgt., Saint Francis Hospital and Medical Center, Hartford, CT '82 (RISK)
SCHEDER, WILLIAM DAVID, dir. human res., Hospital for Joint Diseases Orthopaedic Institute, New York, NY '65 (PERS)
SCHEELE, LEONARD A., MD, consult., Washington, DC '51 (HON)
SCHEER, STEVEN, mgr. sales and mktg. adm., Huntington Laboratories, Inc., Huntington, IN '87 (ENVIRON)
SCHEERLE, P. K., RN, pres. and chief exec. off., American Nursing Services, Inc., Metairie, LA '85 (NURS)
SCHEFE, JAMES R., dir. plng., Rocky Mountain Child Health Services, Denver, CO '80 (PLNG)
SCHEFF, DEBORAH M., RN, asst. adm. nrsg. serv., Lutheran Medical Center, St. Louis, MO '85 (NURS)
SCHEFF, STARLA K., coor. pub. rel. and mktg., Lynchburg General Hospital, Lynchburg, VA '87 (PR)
SCHEFFER, RICHARD H., pres., Wing Memorial Hospital and Medical Centers, Palmer, MA '65 (AMB)
SCHEFFING, JON, dir. food serv., Saint Joseph Hospital, Denver, CO '73 (FOOD)
SCHEFFLER, ERIC K., mgr. food serv., Anon Anew at Boca Raton, Inc., Boca Raton, FL '79 (FOOD)
SCHEFLOW, RICHARD S., atty., Sherman Hospital, Elgin, IL '74 (ATTY)
SCHEIB, ROBERT A., vice-pres. corp. affairs, Port Huron Hospital, Port Huron, MI '74 (RISK)
SCHEIBE, STEPHEN D., dir. plant oper., Children's Hospital and Medical Center, Seattle, WA '83 (ENG)
SCHEIBER, STEVEN L., mgr. pers., Seaway Hospital, Trenton, MI '82 (PERS)
SCHEIDERMAN, KENNETH B., pres. correspondence div., California College for Respiratory Therapy, National City, CA '81 (EDUC)
SCHEIN, AMY J., Irvington, NY '83 (PLNG)
SCHELBERG, JANE S., atty., Henry Ford Hospital, Detroit, MI '82 (ATTY)
SCHELL, DAVID L., adm., Resthaven Patrons, Inc., Holland, MI '84
SCHELL, PAULINE J., head nrs. cent. serv. and oper. room, Lewis County General Hospital, Lowville, NY '81 (CS)
SCHELL, WILLIAM W., sr. mgt. eng., Thomas Jefferson University Hospital, Philadelphia, PA '81 (MGMT)
SCHELLER, SHARON R., EdD, dir. pers. and emp. trng. and educ., Craig Hospital, Englewood, CO '83 (PERS)(EDUC)
SCHELLER, THOMAS M., dir. environ. serv., Sherman Hospital, Elgin, IL '86 (ENVIRON)
SCHELLHAAS, EDWARD R., vice-pres., Community Hospital of Springfield and Clark County, Springfield, OH '70 (PERS)
SCHELSTRATE, MICHAEL J., mgr. prog. dev., Heritage National Healthplan, Davenport, IA '86
SCHENARTS, ELIZABETH A., mgr. soc. serv., Charlotte Hungerford Hospital, Torrington, CT '84 (SOC)
SCHENARTS, RICHARD L., dir. matl. mgt. and support serv., Danbury Hospital, Danbury, CT '84 (PUR)
SCHENKEIN, GEORGE, Parker, CO '77 (PR)
SCHENKEL, LOUIS I., asst. dir., Hospital of the Albert Einstein College of Medicine, Bronx, NY '79
SCHENKEL, RICHARD BRUCE, reg. sales dir., ARA Services, Inc.-Hospital Food Management, Philadelphia, PA '75 (FOOD)
SCHENKEN, JERALD R., MD, dir. path., Methodist Hospital, Omaha, NE '79
SCHEPS, ALAN T., adm., Wilmer Institute, Johns Hopkins Hospital, Baltimore, MD '68
SCHER, ROBERT E., atty., Kingsbrook Jewish Medical Center, Brooklyn, NY '78 (ATTY)
SCHERBERT, DALE, mgr. plant, Community Memorial Hospital, Menomonee Falls, WI '78 (ENG)
SCHERER, ROBERT C., dir. mktg. and commun., Appleton Medical Center, Appleton, WI '85 (PLNG)
SCHERER, THERESA, asst. adm. in-patient serv., Northeastern Hospital of Philadelphia, Philadelphia, PA '86 (RISK)
SCHERESKY, GRACE D., RN, vice-pres. nrsg., Adventist Health System-North, Hinsdale, IL '69 (NURS)
SCHERGER, KAREN L., supv. corp. commun., AMI Presbyterian-St. Luke's Medical Center, Denver, CO '83 (PR)
SCHERMER, BETH J., atty., Good Samaritan Medical Center, Phoenix, AZ '81 (ATTY)
SCHERMER, RHODA, dir. plng. and mktg., Holy Name Hospital, Teaneck, NJ '80 (PLNG)
SCHERR, MORRIS L., adm., Taylor Manor Hospital, Ellicott City, MD '82 (PLNG)
SCHERR, ROBIN N., consult., Eide Helmeke and Company, Fargo, ND '84 (MGMT)
SCHEUBER, WILLIAM FREDERICK, asst. adm., Botsford General Hospital, Farmington Hills, MI '77
SCHEUER, RUTH, atty., Montefiore Medical Center, Bronx, NY '86 (ATTY)
SCHEUERMAN, JANET L., prin., Herman Smith Associates, Hinsdale, IL '77 (PLNG)
SCHEUERMAN, LINDA C., atty., Hertzberg, Jacob and Weingarten, Detroit, MI '86 (ATTY)
SCHEUFELE, STEPHEN, mgr. biomedical eng., Saint Vincent Hospital, Worcester, MA '80 (ENG)
SCHEURER, JEANNE PEPERA, dir. nutr. serv., Cleveland Metropolitan General Hospital, Cleveland, OH '86 (PUR)
SCHEURING, JO, dir. environ. serv., Christ Hospital, Jersey City, NJ '86 (ENVIRON)
SCHEUTZOW, SUSAN O., atty., Hillcrest Hospital, Mayfield Heights, OH '85 (ATTY)
SCHEXNAYDER, JACKIE G., dir. pers., Lakewood Hospital, Morgan City, LA '86 (PERS)
SCHEXNAYDER, SUZANNE MARIE, RN, dir. matl. mgt., Ochsner Foundation Hospital, New Orleans, LA '83 (CS)(PUR)
SCHEYE, LILLI, dir. bus. strategy serv., Blue Cross and Blue Shield Association, Chicago, IL '85 (PLNG)
SCHIAPPA, GENE P., dir. eng. syst., St. Francis Hospital, Roslyn, NY '85 (ENG)
SCHIAVO, DONNA M., student, Holy Cross, Worcester, MA '85 (PLNG)
SCHICK, D'ANNE, pres., Schick and Affiliates, Washington, DC '72 (MGMT)
SCHICK, IDA C., asst. vice-pres. plng. and mktg., Good Samaritan Hospital, Cincinnati, OH '81 (PLNG)
SCHICK, MARY ELLEN, RN, dir. cent. serv., Allegheny Valley Hospital, Natrona Heights, PA '83 (CS)
SCHIEB, CHARLES EARL, adm. spec. serv., South Hills Health System, Pittsburgh, PA '79 (MGMT)
SCHIEFELBEIN, DAVID J., mgr. food prod., Saga Corporation, Milwaukee, WI '86 (FOOD)
SCHIEFER, SR. CLARE CHRISTI, RN, asst. dir., Pennsylvania Catholic Conference, Harrisburg, PA '81
SCHIEFKE, ELIZABETH A., dir. pur., St. Charles Hospital and Rehabilitation Center, Port Jefferson, NY '86 (PUR)
SCHIEK, JERALYN, dir. pat. acct., Winter Park Memorial Hospital, Winter Park, FL '86
SCHIFF, BARRY L., vice-pres. oper., Wyckoff Heights Hospital, Brooklyn, NY '79
SCHIFFER, LINDA S., dir. pub. affairs, Medical Center of Delaware, Wilmington, DE '77 (PR)
SCHILD, DAVID I., supv. vol., Metropolitan Jewish Geriatric Center, Brooklyn, NY '86 (VOL)
SCHILLACI, MARGARET, RN, dir. nrsg., Children's Hospital, Boston, MA '85 (NURS)
SCHILLER, JAMES E., dir. eng., Bethesda Memorial Hospital, Boynton Beach, FL '81 (ENG)
SCHILLING, MARK A., mgr. maint., Tulane University Hospital and Clinics, New Orleans, LA '85 (ENG)
SCHIMMEL, ROBERT E., partner, Peat, Marwick, Mitchell and Company, Chicago, IL '86
SCHIMMEL, ROBERT S., dir. consulting serv., Park Nicollet Medical Center, Minneapolis, MN '81 (MGMT)
SCHIMMEL, VICTOR E., vice-pres., Amherst Associates, Inc., San Francisco, CA '83
SCHIMSCHEINER, SR. MARY JOEL, adm., Kenmore Mercy Hospital, Kenmore, NY '76
SCHINDEL, LESTER P., vice-pres. corp. serv., St. Mary's Hospital of Troy, Troy, NY '85 (PLNG)
SCHINDERLE, DAVID R., dir. oper. serv., Newport Harbor Psychiatric Institute, Newport Beach, CA '74 (MGMT)
SCHINDLER, BONNIE K., adm. asst. external affairs, East Jefferson General Hospital, Metairie, LA '85 (PLNG)
SCHINDLER, LARRY A., dir. plng. and mktg., Providence-St. Margaret Health Center, Kansas City, KS '78 (PLNG)
SCHINER, WILMA B., RN, dir. trng. and educ., Kapiolani Hospital, Honolulu, HI '75 (EDUC)
SCHINGS, EUGENE P., dir. facil. adm., Swedish Covenant Hospital, Chicago, IL '86 (ENG)
SCHIPPER, MICHAEL, dir. human res., Marlborough Hospital, Marlborough, MA '78 (PERS)
SCHIPPER, NORMAN H., atty., Baycrest Centre-Geriatric Care, Toronto, Ont., Canada '75 (ATTY)
SCHIPPER, W. THOMAS, reg. dir. plant, tech. and safety mgt., Kaiser Regional Hospital Administration, Pasadena, CA '80 (ENG)
SCHIRALLI, LISA M., dir. food and nutr. serv., Hamilton General Hospital, Hamilton, Ont., Canada '81 (FOOD)
SCHIRG, GLENN R., dir. nutr. serv., Vanderbilt University Hospital, Nashville, TN '80 (FOOD)
SCHIRM, SUSAN L., RN, dir. adm. nrsg., Marian Health Center, Sioux City, IA '86 (NURS)
SCHIRO, TERI, dir. commun., Holy Family Hospital, Des Plaines, IL '79 (ENG)
SCHISLER, SALLIE C., asst. adm. commun. rel., Mercy Hospital, Portsmouth, OH '84 (PR)
SCHLABOWSKE, BONNIE, adm. asst., Elmbrook Memorial Hospital, Brookfield, WI '87 (RISK)
SCHLACHTA, LORETTA, dir. amb. care, Santa Rosa Medical Center, San Antonio, TX '87 (AMB)
SCHLADE, TERRY M., atty., American Hospital Association, Chicago, IL '79 (ATTY)
SCHLAEFER, EDWARD V., network dev. spec., SunHealth Corporation, Charlotte, NC '85 (MGMT)
SCHLAEPPI, LT. COL. LLOYD A., MSC USA, chief pat. adm., Army-Baylor University Program in Health Care Administration, Fort Sam Houston, TX '72
SCHLAG, DARWIN W. JR., partner, Laventhol and Horwath, Chicago, IL '71
SCHLAG, JOYCE A., dir. soc. serv., D. T. Watson Rehabilitation Hospital, Sewickley, PA '82 (SOC)
SCHLAG, MARGUERITE K., dir. nrsg. educ. and dev., Robert Wood Johnson University Hospital, New Brunswick, NJ '87 (EDUC)

SCHLAM, ARON, asst. dir., Newark Beth Israel Medical Center, Newark, NJ '74
SCHLEFF, TOM, vice-pres. mktg., Professional Research Consultants, Inc., Omaha, NE '82 (PLNG)
SCHLEGEL, H. JOHN, dir. pers., Children's Hospital, Denver, CO '80 (PERS)
SCHLEGEL, ROBERT J., dir. matl. mgt., Good Samaritan Hospital, Lebanon, PA '86 (PUR)
SCHLEGEL, ROSEMARIE T., dir. vol. serv., Jeanes Hospital, Philadelphia, PA '80 (VOL)
SCHLEICHER, JOSEPH R., dir. primary network serv., Saint Joseph's Care Group, Inc., South Bend, IN '87 (AMB)
SCHLEIF, JOHN V., exec. vice-pres. and chief oper. off., Queen's Medical Center, Honolulu, HI '76
SCHLEIFER, ROBERTA D., doctoral student, University of Illinois at Chicago, Chicago, IL '81 (PLNG)
SCHLEMMER, DAVID L., dir. matl. mgt., Florida Medical Center Hospital, Fort Lauderdale, FL '84 (PUR)
SCHLEMMER, ROBERT N., atty., Dettmer Hospital, Troy, OH '74 (ATTY)
SCHLENKER, JOHN M., supv. maint., St. Tammany Parish Hospital, Covington, LA '71 (ENG)
SCHLESINGER, A. DAVID, (ret.), Chicago, IL '70 (SOC)
SCHLESINGER, GWEN, adm. res., Veterans Administration Medical Center, Cincinnati, OH '84
SCHLESINGER, PAUL K. J., dir. pers., South Chicago Community Hospital, Chicago, IL '86 (PERS)
SCHLETKER, JUDITH M., RN, head nrs. outpatient, Salvation Army William Booth Memorial Hospital, Florence, KY '87 (AMB)
SCHLEY, NANCY A., RN, assoc. dir. nrsg., Lancaster General Hospital, Lancaster, PA '86 (NURS)
SCHLEZINGER, IRA H., vice-pres. plng. and mktg., Hillcrest Medical Center, Tulsa, OK '76 (PLNG)
SCHLICHTING, JAMES J., atty., Naeve Hospital, Albert Lea, MN '80 (ATTY)
SCHLICHTING, NANCY MARGARET, exec. vice-pres., Akron City Hospital, Akron, OH '78
SCHLIEBE, ERIC, chief diet. serv., Veterans Administration Medical Center, Durham, NC '78 (FOOD)
SCHLIEMANN, ANN, mgt. eng., HBO and Company, Houston, TX '86 (MGMT)
SCHLIESSER, JOHN, dir. health facil. plng., Hospital Corporation of America, Nashville, TN '79 (PLNG)
SCHLINKERT, ANN, RN, asst. vice-pres. nrsg., St. Francis-St. George Hospital, Cincinnati, OH '81 (NURS)
SCHLOEMER, MARGARET M., RN, (ret.), Green Valley, AZ '44 (LIFE)
SCHLOEMER, NANCY F., RN, dir. nrsg., Stony Lodge Hospital, Ossining, NY '87 (NURS)
SCHLOMER, JUDY, dir. commun. rel., Deaconess Medical Center, Spokane, WA '78 (PR)
SCHLONECKER, GERALD L., asst. dir. food serv., Allentown Hospital, Allentown, PA '75 (FOOD)
SCHLOSNAGLE, CAROL A., vice-pres. commun., Group Health Cooperative of Puget Sound, Seattle, WA '82 (PR)
SCHLOSS, EUGENE M. JR., atty., Rolling Hills Hospital, Wyndmoor, PA '76 (ATTY)
SCHLOSS, ROBERT A., chm. health careers, Lorain County Community College, Elyria, OH '73 (EDUC)
SCHLOSSBERG, MARILYN F., dir. soc. serv., Miriam Hospital, Providence, RI '74 (SOC)
SCHLOSSER, JOHN ROLLAND JR., exec. vice-pres. and chief exec. off., Clinishare, Chatsworth, CA '74
SCHLOSSER, MARK F., dir. food serv., Memorial Hospital of Michigan City, Michigan City, IN '86 (FOOD)
SCHLOTMAN, ROBERT S., sr. mgr. prod. mktg., HBO and Company, Atlanta, GA '79
SCHLUSSEL, MARK E., atty., Monsignor Clement Kern Hospital for Special Surgery, Warren, MI '74 (ATTY)
SCHMADER, ALICE A., dir. vol. serv., Memorial Hospital, Charleston, WV '84 (VOL)
SCHMEKEL, GARY JAMES, student, Ferris State College, Big Rapids, MI '85
SCHMELING, WINIFRED H., PhD, exec. vice-pres., Management of America, Inc., Tallahassee, FL '83 (PLNG)
SCHMERTZ, BERNIE R., dir. info. syst., University of Utah Health Sciences Center, Salt Lake City, UT '84 (MGMT)
SCHMICKING, KENNETH I., dir. matl. mgt., Rutherford Hospital, Rutherfordton, NC '83 (PUR)
SCHMID, SR. STELLA, RN, dir. nrsg. serv., St. Joseph Riverside Hospital, Warren, OH '82 (NURS)
SCHMIDT, ALBERT F., field rep., Joint Commission on Accreditation of Hospitals, Chicago, IL '63
SCHMIDT, ALICE J., RN, assoc. vice-pres. nrsg., Mount Sinai Hospital, Minneapolis, MN '82 (NURS)
SCHMIDT, CAROL S., RN, vice-pres. pat. care, Boulder Memorial Hospital, Boulder, CO '84 (NURS)
SCHMIDT, CURTIS, risk mgr. and dir. safety and security, Leigh Memorial Hospital, Norfolk, VA '84 (RISK)
SCHMIDT, DANIEL PATRICK, exec. dir., Dean Medical Center, Madison, WI '75
SCHMIDT, DAVID H., exec. asst., Diclemente-Siegel Engineers, Inc., Southfield, MI '85 (ENG)
SCHMIDT, DAVID J., dir. soc. serv., St. Mary's Hospital Medical Center, Green Bay, WI '86 (SOC)
SCHMIDT, DEBORAH J., mgr. mgt. info. syst., St. Joseph Hospital, Bangor, ME '85 (MGMT)
SCHMIDT, DEBORAH M., vice-pres. prof. serv., Mercy Hospital of Watertown, Watertown, NY '87 (AMB)
SCHMIDT, DIANE M., vice-pres. and dir. amb. care, St. Paul-Ramsey Medical Center, St. Paul, MN '87 (AMB)
SCHMIDT, DOLORES, dir. human res., Denver Health and Hospitals, Denver, CO '86 (PERS)
SCHMIDT, DOROTHY P., pat. rep., Louis A. Weiss Memorial Hospital, Chicago, IL '79 (PAT)
SCHMIDT, EDWARD A., microbiologist, Servicemaster Industries, Inc., Downers Grove, IL '78
SCHMIDT, FREDERICK L., atty., Bellin Memorial Hospital, Green Bay, WI '85 (ATTY)
SCHMIDT, JACOB A., corp. dir. matl. acctg., Willis-Knighton Medical Center, Shreveport, LA '70 (PUR)
SCHMIDT, JOHN C., staff mgt. eng., University of California at Los Angeles Medical Center, Management Sciences, Los Angeles, CA '86 (MGMT)
SCHMIDT, JOHN D., coor. rehab. medicine, Coler Memorial Hospital, New York, NY '73
SCHMIDT, LEDLEY K., constr. eng., Allegheny General Hospital, Pittsburgh, PA '86 (ENG)
SCHMIDT, LINDA FAY, RN, dir. cent. sup., Bulloch Memorial Hospital, Statesboro, GA '81 (CS)
SCHMIDT, LINDA R., coor. commun. rel., West Jersey Hospital Garden State, Marlton, NJ '83 (VOL)
SCHMIDT, LOLITA, dir. pers. and pub. rel., Indianhead Medical Center, Shell Lake, WI '82 (PERS)
SCHMIDT, LOUIS D., supv. maint., Trinity Hospital, Erin, TN '81 (ENG)
SCHMIDT, LYSLE E., adm., Mercer County Community Hospital, Coldwater, OH '78
SCHMIDT, MARY L., RN, dir. nrsg., Chestnut Lodge Hospital, Rockville, MD '86 (NURS)
SCHMIDT, MARY LOU J., RN, dir. nrsg. in-service educ., Memorial Hospital at Oconomowoc, Oconomowoc, WI '75 (EDUC)
SCHMIDT, MARY, dir. mktg., Annson Systems, Travenol Laboratories, Inc., Northbrook, IL '86 (PLNG)
SCHMIDT, MELVA M., RN, dir. nrsg. serv. and asst. adm., Kittitas Valley Community Hospital, Ellensburg, WA '81 (NURS)
SCHMIDT, MICHAEL, RN, coor. staff dev., Wheeler Hospital, Gilroy, CA '86 (EDUC)
SCHMIDT, NANCY, adm. amb. care serv., Kingsbrook Jewish Medical Center, Brooklyn, NY '87 (AMB)
SCHMIDT, NORMA P., dir. food serv., Chicago Lakeshore Hospital, Chicago, IL '86 (FOOD)
SCHMIDT, ORVILLE, chief eng., Northfield Hospital, Northfield, MN '79 (ENG)
SCHMIDT, RICHARD O. JR., pres. and chief exec. off., Kenosha Hospital and Medical Center, Kenosha, WI '85 (ATTY)
SCHMIDT, ROGER L., dir. maint. and eng., Butler Memorial Hospital, Butler, PA '80 (ENG)
SCHMIDT, RONALD E., dir. phys. plant oper., Autumn Woods Health Care Facilities, Warren, MI '84 (ENG)
SCHMIDT, TRACY C., adm. asst., Kaiser Foundation Hospital, Panorama City, CA '83
SCHMIDT, WILLIAM A., sr. mgt. eng., Parkview Memorial Hospital, Fort Wayne, IN '82 (MGMT)
SCHMIDT, WILLIAM ARTHUR, consult., Bowie, MD '86 (ENG)
SCHMIDT, WONONA A., Loma Linda, CA '83 (PAT)
SCHMIED, ELSIE ANN, RN, vice-pres. pat. serv., Southern Baptist Hospital, New Orleans, LA '75 (NURS)
SCHMIEDING, JANET L., Grayslake, IL '75
SCHMIERER, MARY ELLEN, supv. cent. sterile reprocessing, Lafayette Home Hospital, Lafayette, IN '81 (CS)
SCHMITT, JOHN P., pres., Medirisk, Inc., Atlanta, GA '82 (RISK)
SCHMITT, MICHAEL K., atty., Hiawatha Community Hospital, Hiawatha, KS '87 (ATTY)
SCHMITT, NANCY H., dir. vol. serv., Huntington Memorial Hospital, Pasadena, CA '86 (VOL)
SCHMITT, ROBYN, RN, mgr. sup., proc. and distrib., Midland Memorial Hospital, Midland, TX '86 (CS)
SCHMITT, S. F., prod. spec., Nalco Chemical Company, Oak Brook, IL '86 (ENG)
SCHMITT, WENDEL J., pres., Newton Memorial Hospital, Newton, NJ '62
SCHMITT, WILLIAM A., atty., Memorial Hospital, Belleville, IL '86 (ATTY)
SCHMITZ, DARLENE T., dir. corp. diet. serv., Adventist Health System, Shawnee Mission, KS '87 (FOOD)
SCHMITZ, HOMER H., sr. vice-pres. mgt. res., Deaconess Hospital, St. Louis, MO '71 (MGMT)
SCHMITZ, JOYCE H., mgr. matl., St. Joseph Hospital, Eureka, CA '83 (CS)
SCHMITZ, LESLEY M., dir. vol., Providence Milwaukie Hospital, Milwaukie, OR '85 (VOL)
SCHMITZ, MARY ELLEN, dir. hskpg., Ottumwa Regional Health Center, Ottumwa, IA '87 (ENVIRON)
SCHMOLL, JON F., atty., Porter Memorial Hospital, Valparaiso, IN '87 (ATTY)
SCHMUCKER, CHAD C., atty., Berrien General Hospital, Berrien Center, MI '80 (ATTY)
SCHMUCKER, KATHRYN LYNN, RN, asst. dir. nrsg. serv., Major Hospital, Shelbyville, IN '82 (NURS)
SCHNABLEGGER, FABIAN, dir. plant oper., Livingston Memorial Hospital, Livingston, MT '84 (ENG)
SCHNACKY, CAROL A., dir. pers., Oakwood Lutheran Homes Associates, Madison, WI '82 (PERS)
SCHNALL, SUSAN M., assoc. dir. and risk mgr., Coler Memorial Hospital, New York, NY '85 (RISK)
SCHNAUFER, MICHAEL, pres., Pro-Lease, Colorado Springs, CO '83
SCHNEBELE, VENITA, asst. vice-pres., Johnson and Higgins, Minneapolis, MN '87 (RISK)
SCHNEBERGER, M. SUSAN, dir. soc. serv., McLaren General Hospital, Flint, MI '77 (SOC)
SCHNECK, FRANK X., dir. soc. serv., Medical Center at Princeton, Princeton, NJ '77 (SOC)
SCHNEDLER, LISA WAGNER, plng. asst., Barnes Hospital, St. Louis, MO '85
SCHNEER, ERROL C., vice-pres., Bronx-Lebanon Hospital Center, Bronx, NY '79 (PR) (PLNG)
SCHNEIDER, CAROLE A., coor. vol., Our Lady of Mercy Hospital, Cincinnati, OH '83 (VOL)
SCHNEIDER, CHARLES M., asst. adm. med. serv., Mary Hitchcock Memorial Hospital, Hanover, NH '84 (MGMT)
SCHNEIDER, EDITH, dir. vol. serv., Elizabeth General Medical Center, Elizabeth, NJ '80 (VOL)
SCHNEIDER, ELEANOR, supv. commun., St. Margaret Hospital, Hammond, IN '81 (ENG)
SCHNEIDER, FREDERIC N., atty., Hillcrest Medical Center, Tulsa, OK '85 (ATTY)
SCHNEIDER, GARY STEVEN, mgr. policy eval., Health Industrial Manufacturers Association, Washington, DC '84
SCHNEIDER, GEORGE A., CPA, chief fin. off., Healthamerica Alabama, Birmingham, AL '86
SCHNEIDER, HAROLD A., exec. dir., Kingsbrook Jewish Medical Center, Brooklyn, NY '52 (LIFE)
SCHNEIDER, HARRY W., dir. pur., Brookdale Hospital Medical Center, Brooklyn, NY '74 (PUR)
SCHNEIDER, HENRY F., dir. maint., Moss Rehabilitation Hospital, Philadelphia, PA '80 (ENG)
SCHNEIDER, HOWARD, supv. maint., University of Washington Hospitals, Seattle, WA '86 (ENG)
SCHNEIDER, JAMES R., pres., James R. Schneider and Associates, Scottsdale, AZ '84 (ENG)
SCHNEIDER, MARGARET, dir. soc. serv., North Memorial Medical Center, Robbinsdale, MN '83 (SOC)
SCHNEIDER, MARJORIE A., dir. commun. and pub. rel., Putnam Hospital Center, Carmel, NY '85 (PR)
SCHNEIDER, SR. MARY GEORGE, staff asst., St. Elizabeth Medical Center, Granite City, IL '84 (RISK)
SCHNEIDER, ORVILLE, dir. eng., Lehigh Valley Hospital Center, Allentown, PA '78 (ENG)
SCHNEIDER, PENNY S., dir. vol. serv., Christ Hospital, Cincinnati, OH '86 (VOL)
SCHNEIDER, PHILLIP L., vice-pres. corp. commun., Medlantic Healthcare Group, Washington, DC '86 (PR)
SCHNEIDER, RAY, dir. maint., Mercy Hospital Medical Center, Des Moines, IA '78 (ENG)
SCHNEIDER, RICHARD L., dir. matl. mgt., North Pennsylvania Hospital, Lansdale, PA '80 (PUR)
SCHNEIDER, ROBERT E., mgt. eng., Methodist Hospital, Omaha, NE '82 (PLNG)(MGMT)
SCHNEIDER, RONALD, dir. matl. mgt., St. Joseph Hospital, Chicago, IL '86 (PUR)
SCHNEIDER, RUSSELL DEAN, adm., San Jacinto Methodist Hospital, Baytown, TX '79
SCHNEIDER, SAMUEL, dir. food serv., Maimonides Medical Center, Brooklyn, NY '68 (FOOD)
SCHNEIDER, SHARON S., dir. food serv., Mercy Hospital, Cadillac, MI '86 (FOOD)
SCHNEIDER, TERRENCE P., dir. matl. mgt., Methodist Hospital, St. Louis Park, MN '86 (PUR)
SCHNEIDER, TOD G., dir. mgt. eng., Bethesda Memorial Hospital, Boynton Beach, FL '86 (MGMT)
SCHNEIDER, VINCENT A. JR., adm., St. Charles Clinic, St. Charles, MO '58
SCHNEIDER, WILLIAM R., asst. reg. adm., Kaiser Medical Centers, Oakland, CA '74 (ENG)
SCHNELLER, LOURDES M., soc. worker, Coral Reef Hospital, Miami, FL '85 (SOC)
SCHNEPPLE, GREGG R., chief exec. off., Mercy San Juan Hospital, Carmichael, CA '74
SCHNETTLER, MARILYN, RN, chief nrsg. serv., Veterans Administration Medical Center, Milwaukee, WI '86 (NURS)
SCHNIBBE, ROBERT, Tomkins Cove, NY '71 (ENG)
SCHNIEDERS, BILL, dir. security and telecommun., Providence-St. Margaret Health Center, Kansas City, KS '85 (ENG)
SCHNIEDMAN, ROSE B., RN, dir. health care serv., Medical Personnel Pool-Miami, Miami, FL '81 (EDUC)
SCHNIER, STEVEN VAUGHAN, atty., Hospital Council of Northern California, San Bruno, CA '79 (ATTY)
SCHNITZER, MARTIN J., atty., Centinela Hospital Medical Center, Inglewood, CA '82 (ATTY)
SCHNITZER, ROBERT M., (ret.), Bradenton, FL '40 (LIFE)
SCHNOEBELEN, MICHAEL, atty., St. Joseph Medical Center, Burbank, CA '68 (ATTY)
SCHOAF, SHEILA M., dir. vol., Goddard Memorial Hospital, Stoughton, MA '74 (VOL)
SCHOBER, EDWARD J., dir. human res. and dev., Kettering Medical Center, Kettering, OH '86 (EDUC)
SCHOBORG, MARY B., student, Program in Health Service Administration, Florida International University, Miami, FL '85
SCHOCH, KURT W., trng. and dev. spec., Community Hospitals of Indiana, Indianapolis, IN '84 (EDUC)
SCHOCHET, BARRY P., sr. vice-pres., National Medical Enterprises, Tampa, FL '83
SCHODOWSKI, LEONARD M., asst. vice-pres. pub. affairs, Hutzel Hospital, Detroit, MI '81 (PR)
SCHODTLER, DARLENE M., mgr. phys. rel., Gottlieb Memorial Hospital, Melrose Park, IL '86 (PLNG)
SCHOELLER, GUNTER H., PhD, dir. eng. and facil., Peralta Hospital, Oakland, CA '78 (ENG)(PLNG)
SCHOELLER, VALMAI C., Jackson, MS '84 (FOOD)
SCHOEMAN, MILTON E. F., PhD, sr. vice-pres., John Short and Associates, Inc., Atlanta, GA '83 (PLNG)
SCHOENBECK, DONALD R., prin., Raymond F. Mickus and Associates, Inc., Bannockburn, IL '83 (PERS)
SCHOENEWEIS, BARBARA J., vice-pres., Amicus, Inc., Radnor, PA '86 (PLNG)
SCHOENFELD, HARVEY, mgt. consult., Harvey Schoenfeld and Associates, Paterson, NJ '51 (PLNG)(LIFE)
SCHOENFELDER, JAMES E., vice-pres. plng. and dev., Home Nursing Agency Affiliates, Altoona, PA '86 (PR) (PLNG)
SCHOENHERR, TYLER B., adm., Moline Public Hospital, Moline, IL '71
SCHOENROCK, LOIS, RN, dir. nrsg., Mounds Park Hospital, St. Paul, MN '85 (NURS)
SCHOEPLEIN, KEVIN D., adm., Saint Anthony Medical Center, Rockford, IL '82 (PLNG)
SCHOESSOW, KAREN L., vice-pres. mktg., Fairfax Hospital Association, Springfield, VA '86 (PR)
SCHOFIELD, GERALD K., dep. dir. adm., Roswell Park Memorial Institute, Buffalo, NY '62
SCHOFIELD, VICKI M., RN, vice-pres. nrsg. serv., Providence Hospital, Holyoke, MA '84 (NURS)
SCHOLL, LINDA, pat. rep., Community Hospital of Springfield and Clark County, Springfield, OH '85 (RISK)
SCHOLL, SR. SUSAN KAY, RN, asst. exec. dir. nrsg. serv., St. Mary's Hospital, Kansas City, MO '86 (NURS)
SCHOLLE, BARBARA A., RN, asst. adm. nrsg., Divine Providence Hospital, Pittsburgh, PA '81 (NURS)
SCHOLTE-IOVINE, JANE, soc. work consult., Granada Hills Community Hospital, Granada Hills, CA '83 (SOC)

SCHOLTZ, SR. KATHERINE, RN, vice-pres. health care serv., Presentation Shared Health Services, Inc., Sioux Falls, SD '77 (NURS)
SCHOLZ, CHARLES A., atty., St. Mary Hospital, Quincy, IL '79 (ATTY)
SCHOLZE, ROBERTA J., RN, dir. surg. and trauma serv., Burnham Hospital, Champaign, IL '84 (NURS)
SCHOMBURG, CHARLES J., dir. bldg. and grds., St. Luke's Episcopal Hospital, Houston, TX '86 (ENG)
SCHONBERG, NANETTE G., dir. vol. serv., Holy Family Hospital, Des Plaines, IL '84 (VOL)
SCHONFELD, PETER J., chief exec. off., McPherson Community Health Center, Howell, MI '76
SCHOOLER, FRANK, asst. adm. mktg. and plng., St. Francis Hospital Center, Beech Grove, IN '85 (PLNG)
SCHOONEMAN, JACQUES, arch., Thonon-Les-Bains, France '70
SCHOONOVER, D. SCOTT, dir. matl. mgt., Marion Memorial Hospital, Marion, SC '80 (PUR)
SCHOPIERAY, JOAN M., student, Program in Health Systems Management, Ferris State College, Big Rapids, MI '86
SCHORI, MICHELLE M., vice-pres. prof. serv., Memorial Hospital, Owosso, MI '86
SCHOTT, EDWARD C., dist. vice-pres., Hospital Corporation of America, Management Company, Overland Park, KS '70
SCHOTTENFELS, JODY W., health planner, Michigan Health Care Corporation, Detroit, MI '81 (PLNG)
SCHOTTINGER, MARK, exec. dir., Arms Acres, Carmel, NY '86 (PR)
SCHOWENGERDT, DANIEL E., vice-pres., Methodist Hospital, St. Louis Park, MN '86 (MGMT)
SCHOWENGERDT, ROWLAND, dir. environ. serv., Hiawatha Community Hospital, Hiawatha, KS '81 (ENG)
SCHRADER, ARLINE D., dir. pers., Grady Memorial Hospital, Atlanta, GA '50 (PERS)(LIFE)
SCHRADER, MICHAEL E., pres., Bridgeport Hospital, Bridgeport, CT '79 (PLNG)
SCHRAFFENBERGER, LOU ANN, dir. prof. practices, American Medical Record Association, Chicago, IL '85
SCHRAFFENBERGER, LUELLA K., RN, adm. dir., South Shore Hospital, Chicago, IL '74 (NURS)
SCHRAGE, CORA B., dir. vol., St. Mary Hospital, Quincy, IL '84 (VOL)
SCHRAGER, LEONARD, dir., Southern New Jersey Hospital Council, Berlin, NJ '58 (PLNG)
SCHRAGGER, BRUCE M., atty., St. Francis Medical Center, Trenton, NJ '84 (ATTY)
SCHRAM, JOHN P., dir. human res. dev., Highland Park Hospital, Highland Park, IL '87 (EDUC)
SCHRAM, RONALD B., atty., Morton Hospital and Medical Center, Taunton, MA '77 (ATTY)
SCHRAMM, CINDY, supv. cent. serv., Holy Family Medical Center, Manitowoc, WI '84 (CS)
SCHRAMM, GEORGE R., asst. dir. eng. and maint., Williamsport Hospital and Medical Center, Williamsport, PA '84 (ENG)
SCHRAMM, WILLIAM R. JR., dir. oper. analyst, Henry Ford Hospital, Detroit, MI '79 (MGMT)
SCHREEG, TIMOTHY M., dir. pers., Jasper County Hospital, Rensselaer, IN '81 (PERS)
SCHREFFLER, ALICE R., coor. qual. assur., Warren Hospital, Phillipsburg, NJ '81 (RISK)
SCHREFFLER, MICHAEL D., dir. vol. serv., Meadville Medical Center, Meadville, PA '86 (VOL)
SCHREIBER, DAPHNE A., dir. plng., Charleston Area Medical Center, Charleston, WV '85 (PLNG)
SCHREIBER, HANITA Z., dir. soc. work, Washington Adventist Hospital, Takoma Park, MD '77 (SOC)
SCHREIBER, MARY P., RN, asst. adm., Saint Francis Hospital, Tulsa, OK '70 (NURS)
SCHREIBER, STUART M., vice-pres. human res., University Hospitals of Cleveland, Cleveland, OH '86 (PERS)
SCHREIDER, BONNIE, clin. analyst risk mgt., St. Joseph Mercy Hospital, Ann Arbor, MI '85 (RISK)
SCHREIER, JOHN J., bus. mgr. surg. serv., St. Alexius Medical Center, Bismarck, ND '87 (PUR)
SCHREIER, SARAH J., matl. mgt. asst., Midland Hospital Center, Midland, MI '82
SCHREIFELS, DEBORAH, dir. commun. affairs, Goldwater Memorial Hospital, New York, NY '86 (PR)
SCHREINER, KENNETH V., exec. vice-pres., Holy Family Hospital, Des Plaines, IL '70
SCHREINER, PAUL A., dir. eng. serv., Rochester St. Mary's Hospital, Rochester, NY '79 (ENG)
SCHRETZMAN, BILLIE, chm. vol. prog., St. Charles Hospital and Rehabilitation Center, Port Jefferson, NY '86 (VOL)
SCHRIER, LINDA L., commun. spec., Blue Cross and Blue Shield of Rhode Island, Providence, RI '85 (PR)
SCHRIEWER, CHARLES R., mgr. cent. serv., Baylor University Medical Center, Dallas, TX '81 (CS)
SCHRIMPER, E. PAULINE, coor. pat. educ., Methodist Hospital-Central Unit, Memphis, TN '84 (EDUC)
SCHRINER, JANET G., RN, dir. maternal nrsg., St. Joseph Hospital, Houston, TX '84 (NURS)
SCHRINER, JOYCE, dir. hskpg. and ldry., Soldiers and Sailors Memorial Hospital, Wellsboro, PA '86 (ENVIRON)
SCHROCK, RICHARD D., sr. vice-pres. fin. and treas., Lutheran Hospitals and Home Society, Fargo, ND '86
SCHRODER, HILARY A., Dunedin, FL '40 (LIFE)
SCHRODER, JACK SPALDING JR., atty., Grady Memorial Hospital, Atlanta, GA '76 (ATTY)
SCHRODER, KATHY E., asst. dir. human res., Hebrew Home and Hospital, Hartford, CT '86 (PERS)
SCHROECK, MARY ANNE, pat. rep., Bethesda Hospital, Inc., Cincinnati, OH '85 (PAT)
SCHROEDER, BARBARA J., coor. pat. educ., Rochester Methodist Hospital, Rochester, MN '86 (EDUC)
SCHROEDER, BRENT W., mgr. food prod., Wesley Manor, Frankfort, IN '85 (FOOD)
SCHROEDER, DANIEL J., mgt. serv. consult., Hospital Corporation of America, Dallas, TX '82 (MGMT)
SCHROEDER, DONNA, supv. cent. sup., Immanuel-St. Joseph's Hospital, Mankato, MN '86 (CS)
SCHROEDER, E. WAYNE, atty., Decatur Memorial Hospital, Decatur, IL '75 (ATTY)
SCHROEDER, JOANNE, dir. diet., St. Anthony's Medical Center, St. Louis, MO '74 (FOOD)
SCHROEDER, JOHN A. II, mgr. biomedical, Hotel Dieu Hospital, New Orleans, LA '86 (ENG)
SCHROEDER, LARRY J., student, Program and Bureau of Hospital Administration, University of Michigan, Ann Arbor, MI '84
SCHROEDER, LOU, RN, vice-pres., Immanuel-St. Joseph's Hospital, Mankato, MN '74 (EDUC)(NURS)
SCHROEDER, PAUL J. JR., atty., Hospital Association of Metropolitan St. Louis, St. Louis, MO '77 (ATTY)
SCHROEDER, SYLVESTER JAMES, (ret.), Orland Park, IL '48 (LIFE)
SCHROEDER, WALTER C., atty., St. Joseph Mercy Hospital, Mason City, IA '68 (ATTY)
SCHROER, RICHARD F., dir. safety and security, Missouri Baptist Hospital, St. Louis, MO '79 (ENG)
SCHROETER, JOAN T., dir. soc. work, Rutland Regional Medical Center, Rutland, VT '84 (SOC)
SCHRON, SPENCER R., prog. analyst, Dept. of HHS, Bureau of Quality Assurance, Health Services Administration, Rockville, MD '69
SCHROT, STEPHEN R., dir. matl. mgt., Winona Memorial Hospital, Indianapolis, IN '86 (PUR)
SCHRULL, JOHN A., dir., Wesley Long Community Hospital, Greensboro, NC '74
SCHRUM, WILLIAM R., dir. human res., Hospital Corporation of America, Nashville, TN '86 (PERS)
SCHUBERT, ANN J., pat. rep., Fawcett Memorial Hospital, Port Charlotte, FL '83 (PAT)
SCHUBERT, ARTHUR J., (ret.), Chicago, IL '80 (ENG)
SCHUBERT, CARL H., safety off., University of California at Los Angeles Medical Center, Los Angeles, CA '86 (ENG)
SCHUBERT, JOAN E., rep. pub. rel., Mendota Community Hospital, Mendota, IL '85 (PR)
SCHUBERT, MARY RODGERS, RN, nrs. recruiter, Western Pennsylvania Hospital, Pittsburgh, PA '85 (NURS)
SCHUBERT, WARREN, dir. food serv., Gouverneur Hospital, New York, NY '81 (FOOD)
SCHUDER, JOSEPH J., dir. fiscal affairs, Millard Fillmore Hospital, Buffalo, NY '65
SCHUELKE, ROBERT R., dir. soc. work, Waukesha Memorial Hospital, Waukesha, WI '85 (SOC)
SCHUELKE, WILFRED KENNETH, asst. adm. pers., Saratoga Community Hospital, Detroit, MI '77 (PERS)
SCHUELLER, SANDRA, coor. pat. serv., Dialysis Associates, Stamford, CT '80 (PAT)
SCHUENGEL, SHIRLEE M., dir. vol., Methodist Evangelical Hospital, Louisville, KY '78 (VOL)
SCHUESSLER, JAMES P., pres. and chief exec. off., Community Memorial Hospital, Toms River, NJ '83 (PLNG)
SCHUESSLER, KENNETH J., atty., Memorial Hospital, Belleville, IL '74 (ATTY)
SCHUETTE, MARGARET W., coor. pur., Mount Vernon Hospital, Alexandria, VA '81 (PUR)
SCHUETZ, BRUCE W., dir. matl. mgt., Huntington Memorial Hospital, Pasadena, CA '86 (PUR)
SCHUETZ, CHARLES D., dir., St. Joseph Hospital, Houston, TX '84
SCHUH, CARL M., mgr. med. sales, Transamerica Delaval Medical Products, Pasadena, CA '85
SCHUH, CHARLES E. III, mgr. cent. serv., Salem Hospital, Salem, OR '86 (ENG)
SCHUH, RONALD A., mgr. cent. proc., St. Michael Hospital, Milwaukee, WI '75 (CS)
SCHUHART, JODY A., vice-pres., Strategic Decision Associates, Chicago, IL '85 (PLNG)
SCHULER, CHARLES P., dir. pers. serv., Phoenix General Hospital, Phoenix, AZ '79 (PERS)
SCHULER, ELROY N., dir. mktg. res. and info., Humana Inc., Louisville, KY '84 (PLNG)
SCHULER, RICHARD A., dir. info. syst., Deaconess Hospital, Evansville, IN '84 (MGMT)
SCHULLER, ELLEN, dir. mktg. commun., Fairview Riverside Hospital, Minneapolis, MN '79 (PR)
SCHULLER, JAMES E., dir. soc. serv., Hennepin County Medical Center, Minneapolis, MN '85 (SOC)
SCHULLER, SR. N. SYLVIA, chief exec. off., St. Francis Medical Center, Pittsburgh, PA '63
SCHULMAN, BEVERLY M., vice-pres., Horizon Health Systems, Inc., Boulder, CO '79 (PR) (PLNG)
SCHULMAN, BEVERLY, sr. consult., Horizon Health Systems, Boulder, CO '87 (AMB)
SCHULMAN, RONALD JAY, dir. plng. and dev. spec., Kaiser Permanente, Pasadena, CA '79 (MGMT)
SCHULMAN, WINIFRED A., mgr. food prod., Greenwich Hospital, Greenwich, CT '75 (FOOD)
SCHULTE, PATRICIA A., student, Ferris State College, Big Rapids, MI '86
SCHULTE, RUTH KOCH, dir. soc. work, Hospital for Sick Children, Toronto, Ont., Canada '82 (SOC)
SCHULTE, WILLIAM A., dir. pur., Okmulgee Memorial Hospital Authority, Okmulgee, OK '81 (PUR)
SCHULTER, KEN M., prin. mgt. eng., Children's Hospital, Denver, CO '85 (MGMT)
SCHULTZ, CHRISTINE G., mgr. pers., Adventist Health Systems, Arlington, TX '86 (PERS)
SCHULTZ, DALE L., dir. risk mgt., Daughters of Charity Health Systems, St. Louis, MO '81 (RISK)
SCHULTZ, DELORES E., RN, dir. nrsg., Superior Memorial Hospital, Superior, WI '81 (NURS)
SCHULTZ, DUANE J., sr. vice-pres., Perkins and Will Group, Inc., Chicago, IL '80 (PLNG)
SCHULTZ, ELIANA C., adm. diet., St. Francis Memorial Hospital, San Francisco, CA '85 (FOOD)
SCHULTZ, JAMES P., vice-pres. human res., Fairview Hospital and Healthcare Service, Minneapolis, MN '85 (PERS)
SCHULTZ, JANET K., mgr. prof. serv., American V. Mueller, Division of Baxter Travenol Laboratories, Chicago, IL '81 (CS)
SCHULTZ, LEA S., inst. eng., University of Virginia Hospitals, Charlottesville, VA '76 (ENG)
SCHULTZ, MARY LOU, RN, head nrs. surg. and cent. sup., Bellevue Hospital, Bellevue, OH '87 (CS)
SCHULTZ, PATRICIA, RN, asst. adm. prof. serv., Lake Shore Hospital, Irving, NY '79 (NURS)
SCHULTZ, ROBERT B., dir. matl. mgt., St. Margaret Hospital, Hammond, IN '75 (PUR)
SCHULTZ, S. ROBERT, asst. dir. pat. acctg., Queen of the Valley Hospital, Napa, CA '73 (MGMT)
SCHULTZ, STEVEN J., dir. amb. serv., Waukesha Memorial Hospital, Waukesha, WI '87 (AMB)
SCHULTZ, THOMAS W., sr. mgr., Price Waterhouse, Birmingham, AL '81 (PLNG)
SCHULTZE, PHYLLIS E., RN, dir. nrsg., Prince William Hospital, Manassas, VA '81 (NURS)
SCHULTZE, ROBERT L., sr. vice-pres. fin., Cleveland Metropolitan General Hospital, Cleveland, OH '68
SCHULZ, ROCKWELL IRWIN, PhD, dir., Program in Health Care Administration, University of Wisconsin, Madison, WI '53 (LIFE)
SCHULZE, ANN LOWE, sr. dir. serv., Methodist Health Systems, Memphis, TN '77
SCHUMACHER, BARBARA B., dir. pers., Hartford Memorial Hospital, Hartford, WI '85 (PERS)
SCHUMACHER, EDWARD J., PhD, sr. consult., Oberfest Associates, Inc., Philadelphia, PA '84 (PLNG)
SCHUMACHER, ELDON L., dir. fin. plng. and reimbursement, Great Plains Health Alliance, Inc., Wichita, KS '84
SCHUMACHER, FLORENCE S., dir. mktg., Milford-Whitinsville Regional Hospital, Milford, MA '85 (PR) (PLNG)
SCHUMACHER, JUDITH, dir. plng. and mktg., Noble Hospital, Westfield, MA '86 (PR) (PLNG)
SCHUMACHER, RON M., atty., Lea Regional Hospital, Hobbs, NM '85 (ATTY)
SCHUMACHER, WILLIAM A., (ret.), Winter Park, FL '68 (EDUC)
SCHUMAKER, CLARENCE J. JR., PhD, health serv. adm. staff off., Office of the Surgeon General-U. S. Air Force, Washington, DC '63
SCHUMANN-OUSLEY, ANN, dir. mktg., Greenleaf Psychiatric Hospital, Bryan, TX '86 (PR)
SCHUMANN, RICHARD E., dir. plant oper., St. Charles Hospital and Rehabilitation Center, Port Jefferson, NY '81 (ENG)
SCHUMANN, RICHARD H., dir. support serv., St. Vincent Charity Hospital, Cleveland, OH '75 (MGMT)
SCHUMER, SR. M. FRANCES, vice-pres. pub. rel., Servantcor, Kankakee, IL '86 (PR)
SCHUNKEWITZ, ALBERT, pres., Albert Schunkewitz Architect, New York, NY '66
SCHUPACK, STEPHEN W., atty., Wesson Memorial Hospital, Springfield, MA '73 (ATTY)
SCHUPBACH, CHERYL D., dir. food serv., Mesquite Community Hospital, Mesquite, TX '82 (FOOD)
SCHUR, DOUGLAS A., atty., California Assn. of Hospitals & Health Systems, Sacramento, CA '86 (ATTY)
SCHUR, JANET R., RN, dir. in-service, Rockingham Nursing Home, Epping, NH '80 (EDUC)
SCHURGIN, WILLIAM P., atty., Northwestern Memorial Hospital, Chicago, IL '83 (ATTY)
SCHURING, DAVE, dir. plng. serv., Borgess Medical Center, Kalamazoo, MI '79 (PLNG)
SCHURMAN, BRUCE A., pres., Marianjoy Rehabilitation Center, Wheaton, IL '74 (PLNG)
SCHUSSLER, DOROTHY, dir. cent. sup. room, Victory Memorial Hospital, Brooklyn, NY '80 (CS)
SCHUSTER, EDITH E., student, Department of Health Care Administration, George Washington University, Washington, DC '86
SCHUSTER, JAMES R., dir. gen. serv., Theda Clark Regional Medical Center, Neenah, WI '86 (ENVIRON)
SCHUSTER, LYNN, coor. risk mgt., St. Mary's Hospital, Milwaukee, WI '84 (RISK)
SCHUSTER, MARLA R., educ., St. Mary's Hospital, Reno, NV '82 (EDUC)
SCHUSTER, RICHARD D., dir. biomedical serv., Jefferson Memorial Hospital, Crystal City, MO '86 (ENG)
SCHUSTER, STEPHEN M. JR., atty., Samuelson, Portnow, Little and Schuster, Reston, VA '77 (ATTY)
SCHUTTA, ALVIN M., mktg. consult. rep., Health One-Amma, St. Paul, MN '67 (CS)
SCHUTTER, LAURIN W., atty., St. John's Hospital, Salina, KS '84 (ATTY)
SCHUWEILER, ROBERT C., actg. dir. matl. mgt. serv., Fairfax Memorial Hospital, Fairfax, OK '86 (PUR)
SCHWAB, PAULA C., dir. pub. affairs, Greater Dayton Area Hospital Association, Dayton, OH '85 (PR)
SCHWAB, RICHARD P., dir. diet. serv., Northern Dutchess Hospital, Rhinebeck, NY '81 (FOOD)
SCHWABE, SCOTT A., mgt. and info. analyst, Highland Hospital of Rochester, Rochester, NY '86 (MGMT)
SCHWABE, WILLIAM J., dir. pers., Albert Einstein Medical Center, Northern Division, Philadelphia, PA '64 (PERS)
SCHWAGER, PETER EMIL, clin. diet., St. Joseph Hospital, Memphis, TN '81 (FOOD)
SCHWAGER, VIRGINIA, pres., Michigan Catholic Health Association, Lansing, MI '77
SCHWALENSTOCKER, ELLEN S., med. econ. analyst, Kaiser Permanente Health Plan, Washington, DC '85 (PLNG)
SCHWAM, ETHEL, dir. diet., Long Island Jewish-Hillside Medical Center, New York, NY '67 (FOOD)
SCHWAN, WALTER F., consult., American Hospital Association, Chicago, IL '54 (LIFE)
SCHWANKE, MICHEL A., dir., Fairview Riverside Hospital, Minneapolis, MN '84 (ENG)
SCHWARBERG, CLIFFORD F., chief exec. off., Mmi Companies, Inc., San Rafael, CA '81

SCHWARTZ, ALAN J., adm. ob.-gyn., University of Michigan Women's Hospitals, Ann Arbor, MI '83
SCHWARTZ, ANNA MARIE, mgr. pat. rep., Northeast Georgia Medical Center, Gainesville, GA '86 (PAT)
SCHWARTZ, DANIEL H., PhD, spec. asst. to pres., Montefiore Medical Center, Bronx, NY '59 (RISK)
SCHWARTZ, HAROLD W., dir. adm. serv., Devereux Foundation, Devon, PA '86 (PUR)
SCHWARTZ, JEFFREY B., atty., Hospital Association of Pennsylvania, Camp Hill, PA '79 (ATTY)
SCHWARTZ, LARRY P., sr. vice-pres. and chief oper. off., Mercy Alternative, Ann Arbor, MI '87 (AMB)
SCHWARTZ, MARILYN C., chief soc. worker, Massachusetts General Hospital, Boston, MA '77 (SOC)
SCHWARTZ, PAUL J., mgr. plant oper., Orlando Regional Medical Center, St. Cloud, FL '84 (ENG)
SCHWARTZ, RICK G., decision analyst, Applied Decision Analysis, Inc., Menlo Park, CA '86 (MGMT)
SCHWARTZ, ROBERT H., atty., Raymond and Dillon, Detroit, MI '85
SCHWARTZ, ROBERT K., consult., New York State Department of Health, White Plains Regional Office, White Plains, NY '57 (LIFE)
SCHWARTZ, ROBERT L., atty., Evanston, IL '82 (ATTY)
SCHWARTZ, ROBERTA, dir. soc. serv., Huntington Hospital, Huntington, NY '82 (SOC)
SCHWARTZ, RONALD A., adm., Doctors Hospital, Columbus, GA '79 (PLNG)
SCHWARTZ, SHARON, dir. day surg., Wausau Hospital Center, Wausau, WI '86 (AMB)
SCHWARTZ, STEPHEN M., dir. mgt. serv., SunHealth Inc., Sun City, AZ '78 (MGMT)
SCHWARTZER, DIANE E., coor. educ., Medical Center at Princeton, Princeton, NJ '87 (EDUC)
SCHWARTZKOPF, DAVID, exec. vice-pres., Penobscot Bay Medical Center, Rockport, ME '83 (PLNG)
SCHWARTZMAN, ARLINE, bd. mem., Robert Wood Johnson University Hospital, New Brunswick, NJ '69
SCHWARZ, CAROLINE M., student, Program in Health Administration and Planning, Washington University School of Medicine, St. Louis, MO '87 (PLNG)
SCHWARZ, GEORGE E., dir. plng., Saint Joseph Hospital, Denver, CO '68 (PLNG)
SCHWARZ, JOHN L., dir. syst. dev., St. Luke's Samaritan Health Care, Inc., Milwaukee, WI '83 (MGMT)
SCHWARZ, PATRICIA A., pat. rep., Huntsville Hospital, Huntsville, AL '82 (PAT)
SCHWARZ, ROBERT RUSSELL, mgr. mgt. eng., United Health Services, Johnson City, NY '68 (MGMT)
SCHWARZ, STEPHEN W., dir. matl. mgt., St. Luke's Hospital West, Chesterfield, MO '77 (PUR)
SCHWARZBACK, SHIRLEY G., RN, clin. dir. amb. spec. care serv., Easton Hospital, Easton, PA '86 (NURS)
SCHWARZSCHILD, PATRICIA M., atty., Charter Westbrook Hospital, Richmond, VA '84 (ATTY)
SCHWEBEL, ROBERT J., dir. risk mgt., Healthcare International, Inc., Austin, TX '82 (RISK)
SCHWEERS, SR. ROSE MARGARET, coor. aux., St. Joseph Hospital, Augusta, GA '83 (VOL)
SCHWEGEL, RICHARD WILLIAM, dir. diet., St. Cloud Hospital, St. Cloud, MN '78 (FOOD)
SCHWEGEL, STEPHEN F., assoc. dir. gen. serv., Bayley Seton Hospital, Staten Island, NY '82 (PLNG)
SCHWEID, PAUL, chm., Victor Kramer Company, Inc., New York, NY '70
SCHWEIGER, KAREN, RN, asst. vice-pres. nrsg., St. Peter's Medical Center, New Brunswick, NJ '77 (NURS)
SCHWEITZER, BETTY H., RN, asst. adm. nrsg. serv., Anne Arundel General Hospital, Annapolis, MD '82 (NURS)
SCHWEITZER, FRANK J. III, hosp. mgt. consult., Bradley, AR '50 (LIFE)
SCHWEITZER, JANET M., dir. commun. rel. and dev., Whidden Memorial Hospital, Everett, MA '85 (PR)
SCHWEITZER, STEVEN J., dir. rec. mgt. serv., Covenant Medical Center-Schoitz, Waterloo, IA '83 (RISK)
SCHWEIZER, M. GERTRUDE, coor. med.-surg., Bon Secours Hospital of Methuen, Methuen, MA '77 (NURS)
SCHWEM, JACK J., pres., La Crosse Lutheran Hospital, La Crosse, WI '63
SCHWENDINGER, ROBERT G., atty., Lake of the Ozarks General Hospital, Osage Beach, MO '80 (ATTY)
SCHWENK, SR. GERTRUDE DOLORES, RN, vice-pres. pat. care serv., St. Joseph's Medical Center, South Bend, IN '71 (NURS)
SCHWENN, W. C., atty., Tuality Community Hospital, Hillsboro, OR '80 (ATTY)
SCHWERING, BETTY T., pat. rep., Clinical Center, National Institutes of Health, Bethesda, MD '85 (PAT)
SCHWERMIN, FRANK J., Highland Park, IL '52 (PLNG)(LIFE)
SCHWERTFEGER, RICK, coor. commun. health educ., Valley Regional Hospital, Claremont, NH '87 (EDUC)
SCHWICKERATH, SR. M. PAUL, rep. pat. serv., St. Jude Hospital and Rehabilitation Center, Fullerton, CA '73 (PAT)
SCHWIE, MICHAEL J., vice-pres. health care group, Morgan Keegan and Company, Inc., Memphis, TN '84
SCHWIND, JAMES W., supv. soc. serv., Mary Rutan Hospital, Bellefontaine, OH '83 (SOC)
SCHWING, CAROL, vice-pres. mktg., Sparrow, Inc., Lansing, MI '84 (PR) (PLNG)
SCHWINN, DAVID E., plant eng., Newman Memorial Hospital, Shattuck, OK '84 (ENG)
SCHWIRIAN, BARBARA A., dir. food and nutr. serv., Mease Health Care, Safety Harbor, FL '86 (FOOD)
SCIACCA, IRIS R., dir., LaGuardia Hospital, New York, NY '84 (RISK)
SCIACCA, WILLIAM W. SR., dir. food serv., Tulane University Hospital and Clinics, New Orleans, LA '78 (FOOD)
SCIGLIANO, ANNE R., dir. commun. rel., Winchester Hospital, Winchester, MA '79 (PR)
SCIORTINO, JOHN E., assoc. dir., New York Hospital, New York, NY '79
SCIPIONE, ADRIAN W., adm., Children's Hospital of Philadelphia, Philadelphia, PA '87 (AMB)
SCIRPO, JOANNE E., supv. cent. serv., St. John and West Shore Hospital, Westlake, OH '82 (CS)
SCIULLO, SUSAN G., vice-pres. fin., Memorial Medical Center, Savannah, GA '87
SCOFIELD, BETTY K., dir. vol. and aux., Research Medical Center, Kansas City, MO '84 (VOL)
SCOFIELD, GILES R. III, atty., Albert Einstein Medical Center, Philadelphia, PA '83 (ATTY)
SCOFIELD, LESLIE JR., risk mgr., Walker Memorial Hospital, Avon Park, FL '87 (RISK)
SCOFIELD, LYNNETTE M., dir. vol. serv., Tompkins Community Hospital, Ithaca, NY '84 (VOL)
SCOGGINS, FRANK M., risk mgt. analyst, Ancilla Systems, Inc., Elk Grove Village, IL '85 (RISK)
SCOGGINS, LINDA G., atty., Hospital Corporation of America, Nashville, TN '86 (ATTY)
SCONYERS, JEFFREY M., atty., Davis Wright and Jones, Seattle, WA '83 (ATTY)
SCONZO, ANDY J., dir. food serv., Army Residence Community, San Antonio, TX '86 (FOOD)
SCOPAC, PAUL A., sr. vice-pres. oper., Hospital of Saint Raphael, New Haven, CT '81 (RISK)
SCOTT, ALEX M., exec. vice-pres., Architects Plus-Atlanta, Inc., Norcross, GA '82
SCOTT, ANITA R., dir. educ. serv., Northeast Georgia Medical Center, Gainesville, GA '86 (EDUC)
SCOTT, ANN L., instr. staff dev., Aultman Hospital, Canton, OH '84 (EDUC)
SCOTT, BARBARA D., RN, vice-pres. nrsg. serv., Edward Hospital, Naperville, IL '80 (NURS)
SCOTT, BERNICE L., dir. educ., Medical Center at Princeton, Princeton, NJ '84 (EDUC)
SCOTT, BERYL H., chief eng., Delnor Hospital, St. Charles, IL '76 (ENG)
SCOTT, BEVAN B., pres., Crothall American, Inc., Newark, DE '84
SCOTT, BOB, dir. plant oper., Passavant Area Hospital, Jacksonville, IL '80 (ENG)
SCOTT, CANDACE L., mgr. pers., Northampton-Accomack Memorial Hospital, Nassawadox, VA '83 (PERS)
SCOTT, CHARLES FRANCIS, vice-pres., St. Joseph's Hospital, Tampa, FL '75
SCOTT, CYNTHIA, Jackson, MS '84
SCOTT, DANIEL S., adm., St. Joseph Health Care Corporation, Albuquerque, NM '63
SCOTT, DAVID R., dir. plant, Northwest Hospital, Seattle, WA '73 (ENG)
SCOTT, DENISE S., coor. mktg. and dev., Duke University Hospital, Durham, NC '86 (PR)
SCOTT, E. DYSON JR., vice-pres. plng. and mktg., St. Francis Xavier Hospital, Charleston, SC '80 (PLNG)
SCOTT, E. JOHN, asst. dir., University of Chicago Hospitals, Chicago, IL '75
SCOTT, EILEEN M., RN, dir. outpatient, Children's Hospital and Health Center, San Diego, CA '87 (AMB)
SCOTT, ELIZABETH L., adm. dir. dev. and commun. rel., St. Joseph Hospital and Health Center, Bryan, TX '81 (PR)
SCOTT, GERALDINE M., mgr. commun., Christ Hospital and Medical Center, Oak Lawn, IL '85 (ENG)
SCOTT, GLENN, adm., Southern Colorado Clinic, Pueblo, CO '87 (AMB)
SCOTT, HAZEL, coor. vol., Cancer Institute-Peter MacCallum Hospital, Melbourne, Australia '85 (VOL)
SCOTT, HELEN C., dir. vol., Holy Cross Hospital, Silver Spring, MD '79 (VOL)
SCOTT, JAMES L., vice-pres. human res., Jewish Hospital of Cincinnati, Cincinnati, OH '86 (PERS)
SCOTT, JAMES R., dir. pers., All Children's Hospital, St. Petersburg, FL '79 (PERS)
SCOTT, JEAN C., dir. cent. serv., Tuomey Hospital, Sumter, SC '85 (CS)
SCOTT, JERRY B., pres., Rushmore National Health Systems, Rapid City, SD '64 (PR)
SCOTT, JOHN G., vice-pres. mktg. and pub. affairs, Southern Baptist Hospital, New Orleans, LA '84 (PLNG)
SCOTT, JOYCE L., dir. diet. serv., Shadyside Hospital, Pittsburgh, PA '82 (FOOD)
SCOTT, JUDITH R., dir. pers., Regina Medical Complex, Hastings, MN '80 (PERS)(PR)
SCOTT, KAREN A., RN, dir. acute care nrsg., Saratoga Hospital, Saratoga Springs, NY '85 (NURS)
SCOTT, KARIN W., dir. commun. rel., Humana Hospital -East Montgomery, Montgomery, AL '82 (PR)(VOL)
SCOTT, KURT M., dir. pers., Hotel Dieu Hospital, New Orleans, LA '84 (PERS)
SCOTT, LAURIE S., dir. food and nutr. serv., Capistrano By the Sea Hospital, Dana Point, CA '86 (FOOD)
SCOTT, LAURIE, RN, risk mgr., Palos Community Hospital, Palos Heights, IL '86 (RISK)
SCOTT, LELAMAE SEELEY, RN, nrsg. consult., SunHealth Corporation, Charlotte, NC '68 (NURS)
SCOTT, LONNIE, dir. matl. mgt., Doctors Regional Medical Center, Poplar Bluff, MO '84 (PUR)
SCOTT, M. GLENN, dir. commun. rel. and mktg., AMI South Bay Hospital, Redondo Beach, CA '81 (PR) (PLNG)
SCOTT, MADISON H., vice-pres. pers. serv., Ohio State University, Columbus, OH '81 (PERS)
SCOTT, MARY JO, dir. vol. serv., St. Joseph's Hospital Medical Center, Bloomington, IL '84 (VOL)
SCOTT, MICHAEL P., staff asst. human res., Ohio State University Hospitals, Columbus, OH '87 (PERS)
SCOTT, PAMELA S., dir. pub. rel., Mountainside Hospital, Montclair, NJ '86 (PR)
SCOTT, RICHARD E., vice-pres., Hillcrest Baptist Medical Center, Waco, TX '72 (PERS)
SCOTT, RICHARD G., asst. to adm., LDS Hospital, Salt Lake City, UT '81 (RISK)
SCOTT, RICHARD L., atty., Republic Health Corporation, Dallas, TX '85 (ATTY)
SCOTT, ROLAND A., (ret.), Galesburg, IL '39 (LIFE)
SCOTT, SHARON I., dir. telecommun., Providence Hospital, Southfield, MI '83 (ENG)
SCOTT, SHARON R., dir. plng. and mktg., Watsonville Community Hospital, Watsonville, CA '85 (PLNG)
SCOTT, SHIRLEY LA DENE, student, Program in Health Administration, California State University, Northridge, CA '85
SCOTT, STACY B., dir. vol. serv., Sarasota Memorial Hospital, Sarasota, FL '85 (VOL)
SCOTT, SUE A., RN, adm. nrsg., Beltway Community Hospital, Pasadena, TX '82 (NURS)
SCOTT, SUSAN I., oper. analyst, Henry Ford Hospital, Detroit, MI '85 (MGMT)
SCOTT, SUSAN R., dir. and mgr. food serv., Holy Family Hospital, Spokane, WA '83 (FOOD)
SCOTT, SUSAN Z., dir. soc. serv., Licking Memorial Hospital, Newark, OH '86 (SOC)
SCOTT, TERRY M., dir. environ. serv., San Jacinto Methodist Hospital, Baytown, TX '86 (ENVIRON)
SCOTT, TIMOTHY G., dir. commun. rel., Nyack Hospital, Nyack, NY '85 (PR)
SCOTT, WANDA R., dir. vol., Tacoma General Hospital, Tacoma, WA '80 (VOL)
SCOTT, WELLINGTON FRIEND, atty., Walthamweston Hospital and Medical Center, Waltham, MA '68 (ATTY)
SCOULAR, DAVID N., dir. plng., Baylor College of Medicine, Houston, TX '73
SCOUMPERDIS, KRIS H., dir. human res. mgt., Good Samaritan Hospital and Medical Center, Portland, OR '85 (PERS)
SCOVIL, MILDRED G., RN, dir. med. and surg. units, Central Washington Hospital, Wenatchee, WA '83 (NURS)
SCRENCI, LOUIS WILLIAM, vice-pres. proj. mgt., Mediq, Inc., Pennsauken, NJ '77 (ENG)
SCRIBANO, ROBERT A., student, Iowa State University, Ames, IA '86 (MGMT)
SCRIMGER, TED R., dir. matl. mgt., Humana Hospital -Medical City Dallas, Dallas, TX '76 (PUR)
SCRIVEN, EDWIN E., mgr. admit., Poudre Valley Hospital, Fort Collins, CO '82 (ENG)
SCRIVNER, MEREDITH, dir. pat. serv., Community Health Services, Milwaukee, WI '87 (AMB)
SCROGGS, HOWARD R., assoc. prof. mktg., Army-Baylor University Program in Health Care Administration, Waco, TX '49 (LIFE)
SCRUGGS, SERENE, RN, dir. emer. serv., Lodi Memorial Hospital, Lodi, CA '87 (AMB)
SCULL, STEPHEN W., dir. pers., Rapides General Hospital, Alexandria, LA '78 (PERS)
SCULLY, PATRICIA, RN, dir. risk mgt. and atty., Tucson Medical Center, Tucson, AZ '82 (RISK)(ATTY)
SCURLOCK, CHARLES W., pres., Scurlock, Lorenz and Roosen-Runge, Seattle, WA '80
SCURTI, ADAM E., atty., St. John Medical Center, Steubenville, OH '74 (ATTY)
SEABOLD, BARBARA MUNSCHAUER, RN, vice-pres., Geisinger Medical Center, Danville, PA '79 (NURS)
SEABORN, SCOTT B., dir. human res., Northern Illinois Medical Center, McHenry, IL '81 (PERS)
SEABURY, A. DUANE JR., adm., Shriners Hospitals for Crippled Children, St. Louis, MO '78
SEABURY, WILLIAM L., vice-pres. human res., Memorial Hospitals Association, Modesto, CA '75 (PERS)
SEAGRAVE, RICHARD E., asst. exec. dir., Phoenixville Hospital, Phoenixville, PA '84
SEAGRAVES, DAVID H., asst. adm. fin., Springhill Memorial Hospital, Mobile, AL '86
SEAGRAVES, JANICE L., asst. dir., Medical Center of Central Georgia, Macon, GA '86 (FOOD)
SEAGROVE, WILLIAM D., dir. pers., University Hospital, Jackson, MS '86 (PERS)
SEAL, DAVID, exec. dir., Halifax Health Network, Daytona Beach, FL '83
SEALE, DARRYL A., sr. mktg. analyst, Geisinger Medical Center, Danville, PA '86 (PLNG)
SEALS, CATHERINE M., supv. cent. serv., Heartland Hospital East, St. Joseph, MO '80 (CS)
SEALY, EDWIN J., acct. exec., Insurance Management Service, Inc., Cleveland, OH '86 (RISK)
SEALY, ROGER L., exec. coor., Pee Dee Area Health Education Center, Florence, SC '78 (EDUC)
SEAMAN, COLEEN ANITA, pat. rep., Baptist Medical Center of Oklahoma, Oklahoma City, OK '86 (PAT)
SEAMAN, GARY R., matl. analyst and storeroom mgr., Sturdy Memorial Hospital, Attleboro, MA '84 (PUR)
SEAMEN, REENA A., dir. mktg. and commun. rel., Spohn Kleberg Memorial Hospital, Kingsville, TX '86 (PR)
SEAQUIST, DORINE, RN, asst. adm. and dir. nrsg., University of Cincinnati Hospital, Cincinnati, OH '76 (NURS)
SEARCY, LINDA M., asst. dir. educ., Tri-City Medical Center, Oceanside, CA '86 (EDUC)
SEARCY, MARGOT W., bus. mgr. amb. care, North Carolina Baptist Hospital, Winston-Salem, NC '87 (AMB)
SEARER, CHARLES H., dir. plant oper. and maint., Servicemaster Management Services, Irvine, CA '87 (MGMT)
SEARLES, KATHLEEN E., mgr. diet., Northeastern Vermont Regional Hospital, St. Johnsbury, VT '83 (FOOD)
SEARS, ANDY, dir. plng., Baptist Hospital East, Louisville, KY '80 (PLNG)
SEARS, RICHARD E., dir. eng., California Medical Center-Los Angeles, Los Angeles, CA '80 (ENG)
SEARS, WAYNE V., dir. info. serv., Rochester General Hospital, Rochester, NY '87 (MGMT)
SEASHOLTZ, JOANNE M., PhD RN, asst. dir. nrsg., North Hills Passavant Hospital, Pittsburgh, PA '86 (NURS)
SEASY, MICHAEL, mgr. soc. serv., Susan B. Allen Memorial Hospital, El Dorado, KS '85 (SOC)
SEAVER, FRANK A. III, vice-pres. human res., Detroit-Macomb Hospital Corporation, Detroit, MI '77 (PERS)

SEAVER, RAY JR., student, Program in Hospital Administration, University of Minnesota, Minneapolis, MN '85
SEAVERS, NORMAN R., dir. educ., Cedars Medical Center, Miami, FL '85 (EDUC)
SEAY, AUDREY B., exec. dir., Health Emergency Medical Services, Inc., Westland, MI '77
SEBALY, JON M., atty., Western Ohio Health Care Corporation, Dayton, OH '84 (ATTY)
SEBASTIAN, MARY E., mgt. eng., SunHealth, Inc., Richmond, VA '85 (MGMT)
SEBASTIANELLI, JOSEPH T., atty., Hospital Association of Pennsylvania, Camp Hill, PA '82 (ATTY)
SEBRANEK, WENDY M., meth. and proc. analyst, Medical College of Virginia Hospitals, Richmond, VA '84 (MGMT)
SEBREE, JACK R., adm. matl., Le Bonheur Children's Medical Center, Memphis, TN '79 (PUR)
SECHRIST, GAIL, adm. asst., Cortland Memorial Hospital, Cortland, NY '86 (RISK)
SECKETA, VONNIE M., dir. food serv., Westview Nursing Home, Racine, WI '86 (FOOD)
SECKINGTON, YVONNE E., mgr. pub. rel., North Kansas City Hospital, North Kansas City, MO '84 (PR)
SECKLER, MARGARET L., dir. pers., Smyrna Hospital, Smyrna, GA '85 (PERS)
SECKLER, NAOMI K., labor rel. rep., Mount Sinai Medical Center, New York, NY '84 (PERS)
SECKMAN, DARYL B., dir. plant oper., eng. and plng., East Liverpool City Hospital, East Liverpool, OH '81 (ENG)(PLNG)
SECORD, CHARLES L., arch., Ranon and Partners, Inc., Tampa, FL '86 (ENG)
SECORD, LAURA J., student, Program in Hospital Administration, University of Minnesota, Minneapolis, MN '83
SECORD, LLOYD DOUGLAS, adm., Sussex Health Centre, Sussex, N.B., Canada '81 (PLNG)
SECREST, VICKIE L., RN, asst. chief nrsg. serv., Veterans Administration Medical Center, Shreveport, LA '83 (NURS)
SEDAY, JOYCE H., RN, dir. nrsg., St. Michael Hospital, Texarkana, AR '86 (NURS)
SEDEKUM, JUDY R., student, College of Saint Francis, Joliet, IL '87 (AMB)
SEDERSTROM, CHARLES V. JR., atty., Immanuel Deaconess Institute, Omaha, NE '69 (ATTY)
SEDGWICK, SARA E., atty., Vanderbilt University Hospital, Nashville, TN '83 (ATTY)
SEDLAK, THOMAS L., mgr. pulmonary care, Meadville Medical Center, Meadville, PA '87 (AMB)
SEDMAN, TOBY L., dir. human res., Jewish Memorial Hospital, Boston, MA '86 (PERS)
SEDWICK, JEANNIE, risk mgr., Wake Medical Center, Raleigh, NC '86 (RISK)
SEDZIOL, POLLYANNA, pat. rep., St. Francis-St. George Hospital, Cincinnati, OH '83 (PAT)
SEECOF, DONNA LEE, RN, Arcadia, CA '82 (NURS)
SEED, HARRIS W., atty., Goleta Valley Community Hospital, Santa Barbara, CA '70 (ATTY)
SEEFRIED, SUSAN E., coor. phys. mktg., Medlantic Healthcare Group, Washington, DC '86 (PLNG)
SEELE, SHIRLEY A., asst. vice-pres., Jewish Hospital of St. Louis, St. Louis, MO '81 (PLNG)
SEEMAN, DIANNE M., dir. risk mgt., Health Central Metropolitan Hospitals, Minneapolis, MN '82 (RISK)
SEERMON, LYNN T., consult., Ernst and Whinney, Chicago, IL '83
SEERVELD, VALERIE G., coor. pat. rel., Montgomery Hospital, Norristown, PA '84 (PAT)
SEESE, LLOYD D., partner, Ernst and Whinney, Phoenix, AZ '86 (MGMT)
SEESOCK, LYNN L., dir. commun., Grant Medical Center, Columbus, OH '83 (ENG)
SEEVER, SAMUEL, gen. counsel, Harris Laboratories, Inc., Lincoln, NE '86 (RISK)
SEEWALD, RONALD J., dir. diet. serv., Mercy Hospital of Pittsburgh, Pittsburgh, PA '82 (FOOD)
SEEWER, DENNIS W., mgr. matl., Joint Township District Memorial Hospital, St. Marys, OH '87 (PUR)
SEFF, FRED IVAN, asst. adm., Skokie Valley Hospital, Skokie, IL '68
SEGAL, JEFFREY D., atty., Los Angeles, CA '83
SEGAL, MARSHALL B., MD, atty., Chicago, IL '77 (ATTY)
SEGAL, STANLEY J., adm., Ashton Hall Nursing Home, Philadelphia, PA '85
SEGAR, GEOFFREY, atty., Community Hospitals of Indiana, Indianapolis, IN '68 (ATTY)
SEGEBARTT, KATHY S., nrsg. instr., Fort Scott Community College, Fort Scott, KS '85 (EDUC)
SEGEL, DAVID L., atty., Ancilla Systems, Inc., Elk Grove Village, IL '69 (ATTY)
SEGEL, PATRICIA A., dir. human res., HCA Riveredge Hospital, Forest Park, IL '86 (PERS)
SEGER, PATRICIA E., dir. mktg. and pub. rel., Jewish Hospital of Cincinnati, Cincinnati, OH '85 (PR)
SEGER, THOMAS M., atty., St. Joseph Hospital and Health Center, Lorain, OH '83 (ATTY)
SEGIL, DEBORAH S., vice-pres. mktg., Healthnet, Inc., Salem, MA '84 (PLNG)
SEGRIST, JOHN W., dir. plant and prop., Good Samaritan Hospital, Cincinnati, OH '83 (ENG)
SEGURA, ALBERTO, MD, dir. emer. serv., Brookhaven Memorial Hospital Medical Center, Patchogue, NY '87 (AMB)
SEGURA, CARLOS, dir. plant oper. and maint., San Gabriel Valley Medical Center, San Gabriel, CA '78 (ENG)
SEGURA, PERRY, pres., Perry Segura Investments, New Iberia, LA '80
SEIBERT, CHRISTINE D., asst. adm. mktg. and pub. rel., Parma Community General Hospital, Parma, OH '84 (PR) (PLNG)
SEIBERT, KATHLEEN F., RN, dir. nrsg. serv., Regina Medical Complex, Hastings, MN '86 (NURS)
SEIBERT, MICHAEL J., supv. util., Shore Memorial Hospital, Somers Point, NJ '86 (ENG)
SEIBOLD, SHARON B., pat. rep., Shawnee Mission Medical Center, Shawnee Mission, KS '79 (PAT)
SEID, JEANETTE L., pur. agt., Baraga County Memorial Hospital, L'Anse, MI '81 (PUR)
SEIDEN, KAREN, dir. risk mgt. and pat. rel., Newark Beth Israel Medical Center, Newark, NJ '86 (RISK)
SEIDL, CARL J., vice-pres. prof. serv., Reading Hospital and Medical Center, Reading, PA '80 (MGMT)
SEIF, MARGUERITE L., RN, (ret.), Galion, OH '69 (NURS)
SEIFERT, HELEN R., RN, coor. pat. educ., Allentown Hospital, Allentown, PA '85 (EDUC)
SEIFERT, RICHARD FRANCIS, adm., Lee Hospital, Johnstown, PA '48 (LIFE)
SEIFERT, THOMAS R., pur. agt., United Hospital District, Blue Earth, MN '82 (PUR)
SEIGEL, SANDRA W., RN, assoc. dir. nrsg., United Hospital, Port Chester, NY '86 (NURS)
SEIGLER, CAROLINE N., RN, vice-pres., Baptist Medical Center, Columbia, SC '77 (NURS)
SEILAND, JOHN O., atty., Baltimore County General Hospital, Randallstown, MD '68 (ATTY)
SEILER, MAJ. GLENN, Morrisville, PA '61
SEILER, JOHN G. JR., sr. vice-pres., Liberty National Bank and Trust Company, Louisville, KY '81
SEILER, RICH, supv. mgt. serv., St. Joseph's Hospital and Medical Center, Phoenix, AZ '86 (MGMT)
SEILER, STEVEN L., sr. vice-pres., Voluntary Hospitals of America, Park Ridge, IL '64
SEITCHIK, MICHAEL, mgr. org. dev., Thomas Jefferson University Hospital, Philadelphia, PA '83 (EDUC)
SEITER, THEODORE J., vice-pres. fin. and mgt. serv., St. Francis Hospital, Roslyn, NY '81
SEITZ, MICHAEL JAMES, dir. safety, security and risk mgt., Abbott-Northwestern Hospital, Minneapolis, MN '82 (RISK)
SEITZ, SUE L., atty., Iowa Methodist Medical Center, Des Moines, IA '83 (ATTY)
SEIZYK, JANET M., RN, dir. nrsg. in-patient serv., St. Joseph's Hospital, Milwaukee, WI '83 (NURS)
SEJDA, MARY LOUISE, RN, dir. nrsg., St. Frances Cabrini Hospital, Alexandria, LA '84 (NURS)
SEJMAN, MICHAEL H., dir. eng., HCA Northeast Community Hospital, Bedford, TX '84 (ENG)
SEJNOST, RICHARD L., exec. vice-pres., Detroit Medical Center Corporation, Detroit, MI '53 (LIFE)
SEKHAR, CHANDRA R., dir. biomedical eng., Michael Reese Hospital and Medical Center, Chicago, IL '84 (ENG)
SEKHAR, MRIDU D., PhD, assoc. dir., University of Chicago Hospitals, Chicago, IL '82
SELBST, PAUL L., assoc. prof., New School for Social Research, New York, NY '60
SELBY, JUDY S., dir. plng. and mktg., Trident Regional Medical Center, Charleston, SC '85 (PLNG)
SELBY, SANDRA K., dir. vol. serv., Ball Memorial Hospital, Muncie, IN '86 (VOL)
SELCOE, THERESA L., pres., Applied Leadership Technologies, Inc., Bloomfield, NJ '64 (PERS)
SELDERS, NORMA J., RN, vice-pres. nrsg., Medina Community Hospital, Medina, OH '86 (NURS)
SELF, CARL E., dir. plant oper., Richmond Memorial Hospital, Richmond, VA '83 (ENG)
SELF, CHARLES H. JR., atty., University of Alabama Hospital, Birmingham, AL '82 (ATTY)
SELF, DOUGLAS S., dir. environ. serv., Gulf Oaks Hospital and Clinic, Biloxi, MS '85 (ENG)
SELF, GLENDA G., adm., Hermann Hospital, Houston, TX '85
SELF, JERRY D., mgr. plant oper., Shelby Medical Center, Alabaster, AL '86 (ENG)
SELF, JOHN G., sr. vice-pres., Affiliated Hospital Systems, Houston, TX '76 (PR)
SELF, SARAH B., asst. dir. soc. work, University Hospital, Jackson, MS '81 (SOC)
SELGREN, MARILYN C., supv. cent. serv., Beloit Memorial Hospital, Beloit, WI '81 (CS)
SELIG, JOSEPH, asst. dir., Staten Island Hospital, Staten Island, NY '79 (MGMT)
SELIGMAN, JANICE, (ret.), New York, NY '40 (LIFE)
SELIGMAN, SIDNEY D., atty., Long Island College Hospital, Brooklyn, NY '79 (PERS)(ATTY)
SELIGSON, DOREEN M., mgr. emp. rel., Mount Sinai Medical Center, New York, NY '84 (PERS)
SELKOWITZ, DAVID, mgr. matl. mgt., University of California at Los Angeles Medical Center, Los Angeles, CA '86 (PUR)
SELL, STEPHEN A., Acton Sell Associates, Detroit, MI '82
SELL, SUSAN M., pat. rep., Methodist Hospital, St. Louis Park, MN '86 (PAT)
SELLARDS, MICHAEL G., exec. dir., Pleasant Valley Hospital, Point Pleasant, WV '82 (PLNG)
SELLARO, DAWN L., asst. vice-pres. corp. plng., Saint Vincent Health Center, Erie, PA '83 (PLNG)
SELLARO, LOUISE, student, Kent State University, Graduate School of Business, Kent, OH '84
SELLARS, ROBERT L., atty., Jupiter Hospital, Jupiter, FL '87 (ATTY)
SELLECK, JANET H., DeWitt Community Hospital, De Witt, IA '83 (PERS)
SELLENTIN, JERRY L., dir. human resources, Bryan Memorial Hospital, Lincoln, NE '70 (PERS)
SELLERS, DOROTHY B., asst. dir. nutr. serv., Kettering Medical Center, Kettering, OH '81 (FOOD)
SELLERS, FRANCES FELTS, RN, dir. nrsg. serv., Kissimmee Memorial Hospital, Kissimmee, FL '68
SELMAN, LT. COL. SHERLEY A., MSC USA, dir. nutr. care, William Beaumont Army Medical Center, El Paso, TX '84 (FOOD)
SELTMAN, KENT, dir. pub. rel., Florida Hospital Medical Center, Orlando, FL '85 (PR)
SELTZER, MARY ANN, coor. nrsg. educ., Shawnee Mission Medical Center, Shawnee Mission, KS '81 (EDUC)
SELTZER, MICHAEL A., dir. oper., Cigna Healthplan of Florida, Inc., Tampa, FL '76 (MGMT)
SELTZER, NATALIE R., prof. and dir. soc. work, University of Illinois, Chicago, IL '85 (SOC)
SELTZER, STEPHEN M., mgt. eng., Grossmont District Hospital, La Mesa, CA '78 (MGMT)
SELTZER, WILLIAM BERNARD, (ret.), Fort Wayne, IN '25 (LIFE)
SELVAGGIO, LINDA J., dir. plng. and mktg., Memorial Hospital of Salem County, Salem, NJ '86 (PR)
SELVIDGE, JO ANN, dir. vol., West Florida Hospital, Pensacola, FL '81 (VOL)
SEMILAN, FAISAL HASSAN, adm., King Fahd Armed Forces Hospital, Jeddah, Saudi Arabia '83
SEMINGSON, HOWARD JOHN, Minot, ND '67
SEMON, ADRIENNE L., mgt. eng., Scripps Memorial Hospital-La Jolla, La Jolla, CA '82 (MGMT)
SEMON, REGINA E., vice-pres., Medco, Inc., Warminster, PA '77 (MGMT)
SEMPLE, RICHARD E., dir. plng. and mktg., Brookhaven Memorial Hospital Medical Center, Patchogue, NY '79 (PR) (PLNG)
SENA, KATHY S., dir. pers., Northeastern Regional Hospital, Las Vegas, NM '86 (PERS)
SENALDI, DARIA LYNN, student, Program in Health Care Administration, Baruch College Mount Sinai School of Medicine, New York, NY '86
SENDROWSKI, MAUREEN P., dir. staff dev. and pat. educ., Leominster Hospital, Leominster, MA '85 (EDUC)
SENGSTOCK, RETTA, dir. clin. serv., Medical Sterilization, Inc., Syosset, NY '78 (CS)
SENKER, THOMAS J., pres. and chief exec. off., Monongalia General Hospital, Morgantown, WV '71
SENNE, JERRY, asst. dir., Orlando Regional Medical Center, Orlando, FL '83
SENNEFF, WILLIAM P., asst. adm., Vermillion County Hospital, Clinton, IN '87 (PLNG)
SENSENBRENNER, F. JOSEPH, atty., Theda Clark Regional Medical Center, Neenah, WI '68 (ATTY)
SENSENIG, LANA SMITH, atty., Piedmont Hospital, Atlanta, GA '86 (ATTY)
SENSION, MARITA MCSHERRY, instr. staff dev., Mennonite Hospital, Bloomington, IL '84 (EDUC)
SENTER, SANDRA IRENE, RN, assoc. adm. pat. serv., Medical Center Hospital, Chillicothe, OH '81 (NURS)
SENYSHYN, LINDA K., coor. vol., University of California San Diego Medical Center, San Diego, CA '83 (VOL)
SEPANIAK, STEPHEN G., atty., Morristown Memorial Hospital, Morristown, NJ '79 (ATTY)
SEPIELLI, RONALD J., dir. mgt. dev. and trng., North Broward Hospital District, Fort Lauderdale, FL '86 (EDUC)
SEPKO, THOMAS RICHARD, dir. soc. serv., St. Jude Hospital-Fullerton, Fullerton, CA '78 (SOC)
SEPP, HOWARD W. JR., sr. vice-pres. mktg. and plng., Memorial Hospital, Chattanooga, TN '81 (PLNG)
SEPSTEAD, KATHRYN, RN, asst. dir. nrsg. med. and surg., St. Nicholas Hospital, Sheboygan, WI '78 (NURS)
SERAFIN-DICKSON, FRANCINE J., RN, asst. dir. cardiovascular nrsg., St. Luke's Episcopal Hospital, Houston, TX '86 (NURS)
SERAFIN, DEBORAH J., dir. pers., St. Francis Hospital of Buffalo, Buffalo, NY '82 (EDUC)
SERAFINI, JOHN R., atty., Salem Hospital, Salem, MA '75 (ATTY)
SERAFINI, MARTHA ANNE, sr. pat. rep., Bronson Methodist Hospital, Kalamazoo, MI '85 (PAT)
SERAG, ADELAIDA V., asst. dir. food serv., Brooklyn Hospital-Caledonian Hospital, Brooklyn, NY '73 (FOOD)
SERBAROLI, FRANCIS J., atty., Westchester County Medical Center, Valhalla, NY '81 (ATTY)
SEREMETA, BARBARA C., dir. educ., St. Luke's General Hospital, Bellingham, WA '79 (EDUC)
SERENTILL, RAMON H., supv. maint., Fawcett Memorial Hospital, Port Charlotte, FL '86 (ENG)
SERFLING, G. AUBREY, dir. fin. plng., Pacific Presbyterian Hospital, San Francisco, CA '75
SERILLA, MICHAEL, asst. adm., Bon Secours Hospital, Grosse Pointe, MI '79 (PUR)
SERIO, M. ELIZABETH, asst. dir. plng., Shands Hospital at the University of Florida, Gainesville, FL '83 (PLNG)
SERIO, THOMAS G., planner and analyst, Orlando Regional Medical Center, Orlando, FL '84 (PLNG)
SERLE, JOHN S., mgr. emp., Kettering Medical Center, Kettering, OH '85 (PERS)
SERLUCO, RICHARD J., Holmdel, NJ '73
SEROKA, MARY ELLEN, RN, New Ringgold, PA '78
SEROSKI, THERESA A., RN, vice-pres. nrsg. serv., Columbia Hospital, Columbia, PA '77 (NURS)
SEROTKIN, MARVA, vice-pres., Carney Hospital, Boston, MA '76
SEROWKA, JUANITA D., RN, dir. nrsg., Margaret Mary Community Hospital, Batesville, IN '81 (NURS)
SERPENTO, S. THOMAS, dir. pers., West Virginia University, Morgantown, WV '83 (PERS)
SERRA, ELAINE J., RN, assoc. dir. nrsg. and human res., University of California Irvine Medical Center, Orange, CA '86 (NURS)
SERTICH, CHRIS M., consult., Pannell, Kerr and Forster, Atlanta, GA '86 (PLNG)
SERVA, ANGELO, dir. pers., Soldiers and Sailors Memorial Hospital, Wellsboro, PA '82 (PERS)
SERVICE, THOMAS J., dir. maint., Euclid General Hospital, Euclid, OH '69 (ENG)
SERVICK, PEGGY, dir. vol. serv., Saint Francis Hospital and Medical Center, Hartford, CT '78 (VOL)
SERVIOLO, WILLIAM J. JR., dir. food serv., Abington Memorial Hospital, Abington, PA '67 (FOOD)
SERWAY, GAY DOREEN, prin., Management Engineer Consultants, South Pasadena, CA '72 (MGMT)
SESSA, BEVERLEY E., dir. med. and clin. soc. serv., Fhp Health Maintenance Organization, Long Beach, CA '86 (SOC)

SETH, ANAND KUMAR, mgr. facil. eng., Massachusetts General Hospital, Boston, MA '80 (ENG)

SETH, ARTHUR W., dir. food serv., St. Frances Xavier Cabrini Hospital, Chicago, IL '80 (FOOD)

SETH, WAYNE E., dir. clin. eng., Indiana University Hospitals, Indianapolis, IN '84 (ENG)

SETHER, ELIZABETH A., RN, dir. nrsg., St. Francis Home, Breckenridge, MN '84 (NURS)

SETSER, HENRY R., atty., Erickson and Sederstrom, Omaha, NE '85

SETTLE, BRIAN C. G., dir. pers., Methodist Medical Center of Illinois, Peoria, IL '81 (PERS)

SETTLEMYRE, JEAN T., RN, group vice-pres., American Medical International, Houston, TX '83 (NURS)

SETZER, ANN L., prog. adm. and prof. of educ., Boehringer Mannheim Corporation, Indianapolis, IN '86 (EDUC)

SEUFERT, GERARD E., mgr., Technician Data Systems Corporation, Rockville, MD '81 (MGMT)

SEVER, BARBARA, RN, vice-pres. pat. serv. and dir. nrsg., St. Anthony Medical Center, Crown Point, IN '86 (NURS)

SEVERN, GARY A., dir. diet., Henry Ford Hospital, Detroit, MI '79 (FOOD)

SEVERNS, DONALD E., dir. maint., Marion General Hospital, Marion, OH '81 (ENG)

SEVERS, DIANA L., Price Waterhouse, Columbus, OH '80 (MGMT)

SEVERSON, GARY A., atty., Houlton Regional Hospital, Houlton, ME '76 (ATTY)

SEVERSON, LAYTON C., risk mgr., Doctors Hospital, Columbus, OH '80 (RISK)

SEVERSON, RALPH A., dir. eng., Midway Hospital, St. Paul, MN '85 (ENG)

SEVERSON, RALPH H., dir. food serv., Humana Hospital -Sunrise, Las Vegas, NV '86 (FOOD)

SEVERYN, BETTY J., RN, (ret.), Chattanooga, TN '79 (NURS)

SEVILLE, CARLTON M., dir. matl., Memorial Hospital at Gulfport, Gulfport, MS '82 (PUR)

SEVY, JOAN M., RN, vice-pres. nrsg., Flower Memorial Hospital, Sylvania, OH '86 (NURS)

SEWALT, PATRICIA, coor. risk mgt. and qual. assur., Garland Memorial Hospital, Garland, TX '86 (RISK)

SEWARD, BARRY L., sr. vice-pres. mktg., Research Health Services, Kansas City, MO '83 (PR)

SEWARD, DIANNE B., supv. sup., proc. and distrib., Henrietta D. Goodall Hospital, Sanford, ME '80 (CS)

SEWARD, RUTH O., dir. soc. serv., Presbyterian-University of Pennsylvania Medical Center, Philadelphia, PA '75 (SOC)

SEWARD, SANDRA JEAN, coor. pat. rel. prog., St. Elizabeth Medical Center, Yakima, WA '86 (PAT)

SEWELL, BRENDA J., dir. pub. rel., King's Daughters Hospital, Brookhaven, MS '83 (PR)

SEWELL, GREGORY KEITH, mgr. eng., Lansing General Hospital, Lansing, MI '78 (ENG)

SEWELL, HYBART D., RN, dir. nrsg. serv., Monroe County Hospital, Monroeville, AL '82 (NURS)

SEWELL, JON SELBY, dir. oper. analyst, Oakwood Hospital, Dearborn, MI '82 (MGMT)

SEWELL, RAY H., dir. pers., Boulder Memorial Hospital, Boulder, CO '85 (PERS)

SEWICK, BONNIE G., adm. food serv., Northern Illinois University, DeKalb, IL '67 (FOOD)

SEXAUER, BRADLEY L., vice-pres. corp. plng., Ingalls Health Systems, Harvey, IL '81 (PLNG)

SEXTON, BARBARA L., cent. serv. inventory control spec., Boca Raton Community Hospital, Boca Raton, FL '86 (CS)

SEXTON, JAMES A., dir. computenance, Servicemaster Industries, Inc., Downers Grove, IL '75 (ENG)

SEXTON, JAMES J., pres., St. Agnes Hospital, Fond Du Lac, WI '72

SEXTON, JOAN, asst. adm. plng., Our Lady of Lourdes Memorial Hospital, Binghamton, NY '80 (PLNG)

SEXTON, JUDITH E., RN, dir. nrsg., Holy Name of Jesus Medical Center, Gadsden, AL '83 (NURS)

SEXTON, SUSAN W., dir. pers., Shriners Hospital for Crippled Children, Minneapolis, MN '86 (PERS)

SEYADI, YOUSEF A., exec. vice-pres., Abdulia Fouad Hospital, Dammam, Saudi Arabia '80

SEYDA, MARY JEAN, Cypress, CA '86 (PAT)

SEYFARTH, DAN R., dir. info. syst., Central Michigan Community Hospital, Mount Pleasant, MI '86 (MGMT)

SEYMORE, J. DAVID, PhD, dir. mktg., plng. and dev., Charter Lakeside Hospital, Memphis, TN '86 (PR) (PLNG)

SEYMOUR, DONALD D., dir. commun., Iowa Methodist Medical Center, Des Moines, IA '84 (ENG)

SEYMOUR, DONALD W., sr. assoc., Cambridge Research Institute, Cambridge, MA '81 (PLNG)

SEYMOUR, JAMES A., vice-pres., AMI Great Plains Division, Omaha, NE '66 (PUR)

SEYMOUR, JOHN R., atty., Parkridge Medical Center, Chattanooga, TN '75 (ATTY)

SEYMOUR, MARTHA D., RN, asst. vice-pres. nrsg., Baptist Medical Center-Montclair, Birmingham, AL '83 (NURS)

SEYMOUR, MARY E., dir. educ., Choate-Symmes Hospitals, Woburn, MA '85 (EDUC)

SEYMOUR, STUART BRANTLEY, sr. mgt. eng., SunHealth Corporation, Charlotte, NC '76 (MGMT)

SFEKAS, STEPHEN J., atty., Miles and Stockbridge, Baltimore, MD '83 (ATTY)

SGANGA, FRED S., adm. amb. care, Jamaica Hospital, Jamaica, NY '82

SGANGA, JOHN P., student, New York University, New York, NY '83

SHA, CAPT. SAMUEL C. H., MSC USN, CO, Naval Hospital Penghu, Makung, Republic of China '82

SHAABAN, TAHA MOSTAFA, adm. dir., Nile Badrawi Hospital, Cairo, United Arab Republic '83

SHABBIR, MAHNAZ M., market res. analyst, Saint Joseph Health Center Kansas, Kansas City, MO '84 (PLNG)

SHACKELFORD, RICHARD L., atty., Charter Suburban Hospital, Mesquite, TX '82 (ATTY)

SHACKELFORD, ROBERT E., dir. matl. mgt., St. Francis Regional Medical Center, Wichita, KS '81 (PUR)

SHACKELFORD, SANDRA D., dir. pub. rel., Shriners Burns Institute, Cincinnati, OH '84 (PR)

SHACKELFORD, W. LARRY, dir. plant serv., St. Francis Hospital, Maryville, MO '76 (ENG)

SHADE, DAVID M., partner, Ernst and Whinney, Chicago, IL '86

SHAFER, BARBARA SPORT, consult., Coopers and Lybrand, Boston, MA '80 (MGMT)

SHAFER, EDWARD A., dir. eng., Ephrata Community Hospital, Ephrata, PA '85 (ENG)

SHAFER, EDWIN M., dir. dev. and pub. rel., Bryan Memorial Hospital, Lincoln, NE '72 (PR)

SHAFER, FRANCIS A., dir. human res., Community Hospital, McCook, NE '79 (PERS)(PR)

SHAFER, JANE B., dir. pat. and commun. health educ., Hunterdon Medical Center, Flemington, NJ '81 (EDUC)

SHAFER, KRISTI L., dir. soc. serv., Muhlenberg Hospital Center, Bethlehem, PA '81 (SOC)

SHAFER, NANCY B., dir. vol. serv., Iowa Lutheran Hospital, Des Moines, IA '79 (VOL)

SHAFFER, ANNE P., vice-pres. ancillary serv., Memorial Hospital, York, PA '80

SHAFFER, DEAN A., dir. matl. mgt., Shelby Memorial Hospital, Shelby, OH '84 (PUR)

SHAFFER, FRANKLIN A., dir. cont. educ. serv., National League for Nursing, Inc., New York, NY '73

SHAFFER, JOHN D., dir. info. serv., Children's Hospital and Health Center, San Diego, CA '87 (MGMT)

SHAFFER, JUDY, chief sup., proc. and distrib., Veterans Administration Medical Center, Salem, VA '85 (CS)

SHAFFER, LARRY K., sr. vice-pres., Kansas Hospital Association, Topeka, KS '86 (PERS)

SHAFFER, MARGARET ANN, dir. nrsg., North Hills Passavant Hospital, Pittsburgh, PA '73 (NURS)

SHAFFER, MICHAEL G., dir. soc. serv., Swedish Medical Center, Englewood, CO '78 (SOC)

SHAFFER, PETER L., arch., Huygens and Dimella, Inc., Boston, MA '81

SHAFFER, ROBERT B., coor. staff dev., University of Iowa Hospitals and Clinics, Iowa City, IA '76 (EDUC)

SHAFFER, RONALD M., asst. eng., Memorial Hospital, York, PA '83 (ENG)

SHAFFER, SHARON K., RN, asst. adm., Marquette General Hospital, Marquette, MI '76 (NURS)

SHAFFER, SUZANNE, coor. in-service, Medical Center Hospital, Tyler, TX '78 (EDUC)

SHAFFNER, WILLIAM G., atty., Eye and Ear Hospital of Pittsburgh, Pittsburgh, PA '86 (ATTY)

SHAH, ANWAR, MD, dir. retina inst., St. Mary's Health Center, St. Louis, MO '75

SHAH, MUKESH C., mgt. eng., Swedish American Hospital, Rockford, IL '85 (MGMT)

SHAHEEN, MICHELLE R., soc. worker, Central Kansas Medical Center, Great Bend, KS '80 (SOC)

SHAHZAD, NADEEM, PhD, vice-pres. human res., Interfaith Medical Center, Brooklyn, NY '75 (PERS)(EDUC)

SHAKESPEARE, WALTER S., Red Bank, NJ '61

SHAKIN, REINA, adm. nrsg. serv., Beth Israel Medical Center, New York, NY '78

SHAKNO, ROBERT J., pres. and chief exec. off., MT. Sinai Medical Center, Cleveland, OH '61

SHALOM, REBECA, dir. soc. serv., Rehabilitation Institute of West Florida, Pensacola, FL '81 (SOC)

SHALOWITZ, NANCY LEE, adm., Northwest Surgicare, Arlington Heights, IL '79

SHAMBLIN, PAMELA R., dir. food serv., Coronado Hospital, Coronado, CA '84 (FOOD)

SHAMBROOK, VIOLA L., supv. cent. sup. serv., Gibson Community Hospital, Gibson City, IL '81 (CS)

SHAMES, JOAN K., pat. rep., Children's Hospital of Pittsburgh, Pittsburgh, PA '81 (PAT)

SHANAHAN, DENISE A., RN, asst. adm. and dir. nrsg., Waterbury Hospital, Waterbury, CT '77 (NURS)

SHANAHAN, SR. MARY ESTELLE, RN, pat. rep., Schumpert Medical Center, Shreveport, LA '79 (PAT)

SHANAHAN, REBECCA M., atty., Community Hospitals of Indiana, Indianapolis, IN '86 (ATTY)

SHANAMAN, JANE A., vice-pres. mktg. and fund dev., Multicare Medical Center, Tacoma, WA '85 (PLNG)

SHANAVER, BARBARA, supv. commun., South Miami Hospital, South Miami, FL '82 (ENG)

SHANDE, GIDEON G., gen. sec., Christian Health Association of Nigeria, Lagos, Nigeria '80 (MGMT)

SHANDERA, NELVA M., RN, asst. dir., Providence Medical Center, Portland, OR '86 (NURS)

SHANE, DAVID W., dir. soc. serv., McDonough District Hospital, Macomb, IL '82 (SOC)

SHANER, KARL L., DrPH, vice-pres. res. and info. serv., Texas Hospital Association, Austin, TX '79 (PLNG)

SHANIKA, GREGORY R., vice-pres., Venice Hospital, Venice, FL '73 (PLNG)

SHANK, RONALD G., dir. matl. mgt., Community Hospital of Lancaster, Lancaster, PA '80 (PUR)

SHANK, SUZANNE, atty., Employers Reinsurance Corporation, Overland Park, KS '83 (ATTY)

SHANKLIN, CAROL W., chm. nutr. and food sci. dept., Texas Woman's University, Denton, TX '86 (FOOD)

SHANKLIN, STEVEN B., dir. soc. serv., Emanuel Hospital and Health Center, Portland, OR '74 (SOC)

SHANKMAN, JAY, dir. safety and fire prevention, Brookdale Hospital Medical Center, Brooklyn, NY '84 (ENG)

SHANLEY, BETTY L., dir. vol. serv., Hospital of Saint Raphael, New Haven, CT '68 (VOL)

SHANNON, DAVID T., vice-pres. adm., North Penn Hospital, Lansdale, PA '82 (PLNG)

SHANNON, JAMES AUGUSTINE, MD, adjunct prof., Rockefeller University, New York, NY '66 (HON)

SHANNON, JOHN E. JR., atty., St. Michael's Hospital, Stevens Point, WI '74 (ATTY)

SHANNON, LT. COL. MICHAEL A., MSC USA, asst. chief pat. adm., Department of the Army, Office of the Surgeon General, Washington, DC '78 (EDUC)

SHANNON, PETER M. JR., atty., Mercy Hospital and Medical Center, Chicago, IL '83 (ATTY)

SHANNON, THOMAS F., dir. pers., St. Mary's Hospital, Amsterdam, NY '83 (PERS)

SHANNON, YOLANDA D., adm. dir., Oak Forest Hospital of Cook County, Oak Forest, IL '87 (AMB)

SHAPCOTT, ELAINE, supv. sterile sup., Middle Tennessee Medical Center, Murfreesboro, TN '86 (CS)

SHAPIRO, BERNARD, pres., North Adams Regional Hospital, North Adams, MA '75

SHAPIRO, DIANE, vice-pres. mktg. and commun., Raritan Bay Health Services Corporation, Perth Amboy, NJ '80 (PR)

SHAPIRO, ELAINE T., RN, dir. trng., West Park Hospital, Philadelphia, PA '84 (EDUC)

SHAPIRO, ENID A., dir. soc. serv., Jewish Memorial Hospital, Boston, MA '81 (SOC)

SHAPIRO, HARVEY M., exec. dir., AMI Doctors Hospital, Tulsa, OK '70

SHAPIRO, IRWIN, exec. vice-pres., Catholic Medical Center, Jamaica, NY '76

SHAPIRO, ISADORE, atty., St. Luke's Hospital, Newburgh, NY '70 (ATTY)

SHAPIRO, JONATHAN B., vice-pres., The Medical Center, Beaver, PA '87 (AMB)

SHAPIRO, JOSHUA E., Robert D. Lynn Associates, Philadelphia, PA '85 (PLNG)

SHAPIRO, MARILYN, atty., Charter Suburban Hospital, Mesquite, TX '86 (ATTY)

SHAPIRO, MARTIN CARL, mgr. clin. eng. serv., Norwalk Hospital, Norwalk, CT '85 (ENG)

SHAPIRO, MARTIN I., supv. biomedical eng., Walter O. Boswell Memorial Hospital, Sun City, AZ '81 (ENG)

SHAPIRO, RHETA, pat. rep., Michael Reese Hospital and Medical Center, Chicago, IL '80 (PAT)

SHAPLEY, SR. MARLENE, dir. amb. care serv., St. Anthony Hospital, Michigan City, IN '87 (AMB)

SHAPS, JACQUELINE H., spec. asst. to chief of staff, Veterans Administration Medical Center, Wayland, MA '86

SHARIFI, MICHAEL, supv. matl. mgt., Georgetown University Medical Center, Washington, DC '86

SHARKEY, LOIS, asst. risk mgr., Atchley Pavilion, New York, NY '84 (RISK)

SHARKEY, MARY, chief soc. worker, Sir Charles Gairdner Hospital, Nedlands, Australia '84 (SOC)

SHARKEY, ROBERT, tech. cent. serv., Mercy Catholic Medical Center, Philadelphia, PA '85 (CS)

SHARLOW, JACQUELINE D., student, University of Connecticut, Storrs, CT '86 (MGMT)

SHARMA, ANAND M., mgt. eng., St. John's Hospital, Springfield, IL '86 (MGMT)

SHARMA, FRANCES, RN, asst. dir. nrsg., University of California at Los Angeles Neuropsychiatric Hospital, Los Angeles, CA '86 (NURS)

SHARMA, SUNIL K., vice-pres., Mei, Inc., Houston, TX '76 (MGMT)

SHARP, DONNA S., RN, dir. nrsg., AMI Garden Park Community Hospital, Gulfport, MS '85 (NURS)

SHARP, E. D., mgr. matl., Shriners Hospital for Crippled Children, Portland, OR '86 (PUR)

SHARP, H. RAY, dir. plant oper., Saint Joseph Hospital, Fort Worth, TX '72 (ENG)

SHARP, JOAN L., dir. diet., Ohio State University Hospitals, Columbus, OH '68 (FOOD)

SHARP, MARI-ELLEN, RN, coor. outpatient, Shriners Hospitals for Crippled Children, St. Louis, MO '87 (AMB)

SHARP, ROBERT A., chief food mgt. serv., Naval Hospital, Corpus Christi, TX '81 (FOOD)

SHARP, THOMAS H. JR., atty., Southwest General Hospital, San Antonio, TX '83 (ATTY)

SHARPE, CHARLES MCRAE, dir. res. and dev., Methodist Medical Center of Oak Ridge, Oak Ridge, TN '82 (PLNG)

SHARPE, GARY L., pres., Health Care Logistics, Inc., Circleville, OH '79

SHARPE, JUDY A., mgr. soc. serv., Providence Hospital, Anchorage, AK '85 (SOC)

SHARPE, MARY P., dir. pub. rel. and mktg. serv., St. Mary's Medical Center, Knoxville, TN '83 (PR)

SHARPE, SAM D., asst. adm. gen. serv., East Tennessee Children's Hospital, Knoxville, TN '82 (PERS)

SHARPE, SUSAN K., asst. adm. mktg., St. Joseph Hospital, Bellingham, WA '86 (PR)

SHARPNACK, PATRICIA A., RN, vice-pres. oper., Huron Road Hospital, Cleveland, OH '84 (NURS)

SHARPY, DAVID A., mgr. pur., Sacred Heart General Hospital, Eugene, OR '81 (PUR)

SHASHINKA, NANCY L., dir. nutr. serv., Holleb and Company, Bensenville, IL '83 (FOOD)

SHATTES, WAYNE SICHLER, vice-pres., John T. Mather Memorial Hospital of Port Jefferson, Port Jefferson, NY '83

SHATTUCK, C. JONATHAN, vice-pres. prov. affairs, Blue Cross-Blue Shield, Chicago, IL '62

SHATZ, ENS WILLIAM B., MSC USN, asst. contr., Naval Hospital, San Diego, CA '81 (PUR)

SHAUB, JOYCE A., coor. vol., Brookside Hospital, San Pablo, CA '80 (VOL)

SHAUB, LINDA, dir. advertising and commun., Cedars Medical Center, Miami, FL '85

SHAUGHNESSY, SR. M. ETHEL, dir. diet., St. Mary's Medical Center, Knoxville, TN '70 (FOOD)

SHAUL, ROGER LOUIS JR., pres., Preferred Medical Marketing Corporation, Charlotte, NC '73

SHAUM, ADA C., dir. soc. serv., St. Francis Hospital Center, Beech Grove, IN '82 (SOC)

SHAVE, PAMELA A., dir. food serv., Florida Living Nursing Center, Apopka, FL '85 (FOOD)

SHAVE, SANDRA L., dir. nutr. serv., St. Michael's Hospital, Stevens Point, WI '81 (FOOD)

SHAVER, ALLEN J., plng. and telecommun. eng., Kaiser Permanente, Pasadena, CA '86 (ENG)

SHAVER, GERALDINE M., RN, assoc. dir. nrsg. serv., Virginia Mason Hospital, Seattle, WA '79 (NURS)

SHAVER, MARY LOUISE, vice-pres. plng. and mktg., Franciscan Health Care, Inc., Milwaukee, WI '82 (PR) (PLNG)
SHAVIN, BARRY R., mgr. logistics, New York University Medical Center, New York, NY '76
SHAW, BENJAMIN T., vice-pres. human res., Medical Center of Delaware, Wilmington, DE '78 (PERS)
SHAW, BEVERLY C., mgr. mktg. and pub. rel., Boulder Community Hospital, Boulder, CO '81 (PR) (PLNG)
SHAW, CONNIE, RN, dir. nrsg., Community Health Center of Branch County, Coldwater, MI '76 (NURS)
SHAW, DAVID R., assoc. adm. plng., University of Alabama Hospital, Birmingham, AL '67 (MGMT)(PLNG)
SHAW, DONALD M., Hamilton, Ksa, Fairfax, VA '72
SHAW, DONNA SUE, consult., Ernst and Whinney, Chicago, IL '85
SHAW, GEORGE PHIL, adm., AMI Central Carolina Hospital, Sanford, NC '80
SHAW, HAL M., asst. dir. eng., Brownwood Regional Hospital, Brownwood, TX '85 (ENG)
SHAW, JOANN, dir. pers., Children's Memorial Hospital, Chicago, IL '86 (PERS)
SHAW, JOHN G., atty., Cumberland County Hospital System, Fayetteville, NC '82 (ATTY)
SHAW, JOHN M., Wylie, TX '52 (LIFE)
SHAW, KATHLEEN F., dir. nrs. recruitment, St. Vincent's Hospital and Medical Center, New York, NY '85 (PERS)
SHAW, MARJORIE A., RN, dir. med. and surg. nrsg., Providence Hospital, Holyoke, MA '86 (NURS)
SHAW, MARY ALICE, dir. educ. serv., Sudbury Algoma Sanatorium, Sudbury, Ont., Canada '84 (EDUC)
SHAW, MICHAEL A., chief eng. and supv. maint., Jefferson General Hospital, Port Townsend, WA '82 (ENG)
SHAW, ROBERT C., pres. and chief exec. off., Robert F. Kennedy Medical Center, Hawthorne, CA '69
SHAW, ROBERT N., vice-pres. reg. oper., Memorial Hospital System, Houston, TX '70
SHAW, RUTH D., supv. cent. sup., Truman Medical Center-West, Kansas City, MO '75 (CS)
SHAW, WALTER R., dir. nutr., St. Francis Medical Center, Lynwood, CA '78 (FOOD)
SHAW, WILLIAM E., dir. plant oper., Welborn Memorial Baptist Hospital, Evansville, IN '82 (ENG)
SHAW, WILLIAM M., gen. mgr., Whittaker Health Services, Chicago, IL '75
SHAWCROFT, HELEN M., dir. plng., University Hospital, Seattle, WA '81 (PLNG)
SHAWN, RITA E., dir. soc. work serv., Binghamton Psychiatric Center, Binghamton, NY '82 (SOC)
SHAWVER, DEBORAH G., dir. pub. rel., St. Peter Hospital, Olympia, WA '81 (PR)
SHAY, CONNIE, in-service instr., HCA Grand Strand General Hospital, Myrtle Beach, SC '85 (EDUC)
SHAY, EDWARD F., atty., Rehabilitation Hospital in Mechanicsburg, Mechanicsburg, PA '80 (ATTY)
SHAY, MARTIN E., asst. dir. eng., Cabrini Medical Center, New York, NY '87 (ENG)
SHAYNAK, ROBERT J., pres., Preiss, Breismeister, Shaynak, New York, NY '81
SHEA, ANNE K., dir. pers., Chestnut Lodge Hospital, Rockville, MD '85 (PERS)
SHEA, FRANCIS L. III, mgr. plant oper., Servicemaster Industries, Inc., Winooskigrove, VT '86 (ENG)
SHEA, HAROLD F. JR., vice-pres., Lawrence General Hospital, Lawrence, MA '81 (ENG)
SHEA, JEAN M., dir. soc. serv., St. Joseph's Hospital, Lowell, MA '72 (SOC)
SHEA, KATHLEEN M., dir. pub. rel. and dev., Warren Hospital, Phillipsburg, NJ '81 (PR)
SHEA, LORETTA, dir. soc. serv., Community Hospital and Rehabilitation Center, Los Gatos, CA '86 (SOC)
SHEA, MIRIAM C., food serv. consult., Minneapolis, MN '67 (FOOD)
SHEA, NANCY E., dir. vol., Houlton Regional Hospital, Houlton, ME '85 (VOL)
SHEAGREN, CRAIG, sr. vice-pres. fin., McDonough District Hospital, Macomb, IL '86 (RISK)
SHEAHAN, GARY C., mgr. hskpg., South Suburban Hospital, Hazel Crest, IL '86 (ENVIRON)
SHEAR, BRUCE A., pres., American International Health Service, Inc., Woburn, MA '86
SHEARER, CAROLYN, atty., Albany Medical Center Hospital, Albany, NY '85 (ATTY)
SHEARER, LINDA, supv. med. soc. work, Arkansas Rehabilitation Institute, Little Rock, AR '82 (SOC)
SHEARER, MARGARET L., dir. vol. serv., Good Samaritan Hospital and Medical Center, Portland, OR '65 (VOL)
SHEARON, SHARON O. M., coor. vol. serv., Houston Medical Center, Warner Robins, GA '85 (VOL)
SHEARS, DONALD H., dir. pat. serv., Genesee Hospital, Rochester, NY '75 (PAT)
SHEATS, KATHLEEN M., RN, clin. dir. nrsg., Maryvale Samaritan Hospital, Phoenix, AZ '86 (NURS)
SHEATS, WILLIAM L., sr. assoc., Voluntary Hospitals of America Management Services, Tampa, FL '81 (MGMT)
SHEBL, JAMES M., PhD, dir. commun. rel., St. Joseph's Hospital, Stockton, CA '84 (PR)
SHECHTNAN, BARBARA R., dir. human res. dev., Cooper Hospital-University Medical Center, Camden, NJ '83 (VOL)
SHECTER, GEORGE O., PhD, pres., Health and Hospital Consultants, Tarzana, CA '53 (LIFE)
SHEDNO, JAMES R., exec. vice-pres., Our Lady of Lourdes Memorial Hospital, Binghamton, NY '74 (PLNG)
SHEEDY, SUSAN, RN, vice-pres. nrsg., Baptist Medical Center-Princeton, Birmingham, AL '80 (NURS)
SHEEHAN, DANIEL F., adm., Marcum and Wallace Memorial Hospital, Irvine, KY '84
SHEEHAN, ELIZABETH E., RN, vice-pres. pat. care serv., Leonard Morse Hospital, Natick, MA '84 (NURS)
SHEEHAN, JOHN C., vice-pres. oper., St. Mary-Corwin Hospital Center, Pueblo, CO '84
SHEEHAN, CAPT. L. ANITA, MSC USN, asst. dir. nrs., U. S. Navy Nurse Corps, Washington, DC '84 (NURS)
SHEEHAN, M. PATRICIA, RN, vice-pres. pat. care serv., Lawrence General Hospital, Lawrence, MA '76 (NURS)
SHEEHAN, MARY C., dir. pub. rel., Goddard Memorial Hospital, Stoughton, MA '86 (PR)
SHEEHAN, MARY F., mgt. eng., Thomas Jefferson University Hospital, Philadelphia, PA '86 (MGMT)
SHEEHAN, RICHARD A., dir. pub. rel., Palos Community Hospital, Palos Heights, IL '84 (PR)
SHEEHAN, SANDRA S., RN, dir. nrsg.-acute care, Memorial Hospital of Dodge County, Fremont, NE '83 (NURS)
SHEEHAN, THOMAS A. III, atty., Tallahassee Community Hospital, Tallahassee, FL '83 (ATTY)
SHEEHAN, THOMAS J., vice-pres. pur., Good Samaritan Medical Center, Milwaukee, WI '71 (PUR)
SHEEHAN, WILLIAM B., pres., Goddard Memorial Hospital, Stoughton, MA '65 (PLNG)
SHEEHE, JAMES S. JR., dir. soc. serv., Memorial Hospital, Cumberland, MD '75 (SOC)
SHEEHY, DAVID J., pres., Sheehy Associates, Pittsburgh, PA '64
SHEEHY, SR. M. MAURICE, dir. nrsg. educ., St. Joseph Mercy School of Nursing, Sioux City, IA '30 (LIFE)
SHEEHY, PATRICK D., dir. commun. rel., St. Joseph Regional Medical Center, Lewiston, ID '83 (PR)
SHEEKEY, R. W., consult., Encom Information Systems, Inc., Markham, Ont., Canada '80 (MGMT)
SHEEN, MAO TING, student, Graduate Program in Hospital Administration, China Medical College, Taichung, Republic of China '86 (PERS)
SHEERAN, KEVIN G., dir. mgt. eng., Magee-Womens Hospital, Pittsburgh, PA '81 (MGMT)
SHEETER, PATRICIA ANN, coor. soc. serv., Clinton Memorial Hospital, Wilmington, OH '85 (SOC)
SHEETS, DAVID A., chief eng., Memorial Hospital, Chester, IL '84 (ENG)
SHEFFER, EVELYN, head vol., Takoma Adventist Hospital, Greeneville, TN '80 (VOL)
SHEFFER, CDR JEANETTE, MSC USN, coor. risk mgt., Naval Hospital, San Diego, CA '86 (RISK)
SHEFFER, STEVEN C., supv. telecommun., Harrisburg Hospital, Harrisburg, PA '85 (ENG)
SHEFFIELD, DENNI, consult., Peat, Marwick, Mitchell, Rochester, NY '81
SHEFFIELD, JERRY W., sr. vice-pres. clin. support, Basic American Medical, Inc., Fort Myers, FL '83 (ENG)
SHEFFIELD, SUSAN G., RN, vice-pres. pat. care serv., St. Vincent's Hospital, Birmingham, AL '84 (NURS)
SHEFFS, FRED A., asst. vice-pres., Bristol Hospital, Bristol, CT '81 (ENG)
SHEHEE, ANNE M., dir. nrsg. educ. and staff dev., Presbyterian Hospital, Dallas, TX '86 (EDUC)
SHEHORN, JOHN L., Deloitte Haskins and Sells, Saginaw, MI '78
SHEIL, PATRICK M., dir. human res., Manhattan Eye, Ear and Throat Hospital, New York, NY '86 (PERS)
SHEIN, LOIS, coor. psych. soc. work prog., Mount Sinai Medical Center, New York, NY '84 (SOC)
SHELBY, A. KAREEN, coor. util. review and qual. assur., Holy Rosary Hospital, Ontario, OR '86 (RISK)
SHELBY, DENNIS R., dir. soc. serv., Kaweah Delta District Hospital, Visalia, CA '79 (SOC)
SHELDON, ANITA R., RN, dir. soc. serv., North Miami Medical Center, North Miami, FL '82 (SOC)
SHELDON, JAMES A., sr. supv. plant oper., St. John's Regional Medical Center, Joplin, MO '80 (ENG)
SHELDON, LYLE ERNEST, asst. adm., Palms of Pasadena Hospital, St. Petersburg, FL '80
SHELDON, MARK L., dir. food serv., Winsted Memorial Hospital, Winsted, CT '84 (FOOD)
SHELDON, MARVIN L., mgr. pur. serv., Robert Packer Hospital, Sayre, PA '82 (PUR)
SHELDON, MICHAEL J., dir. food serv., Arden Hill Hospital, Goshen, NY '82 (FOOD)
SHELL, MARY KATHRYN, (ret.), Fayette, MO '64 (PR)
SHELLEMAN, JOYCE M., student, Graduate School of Public Health, University of Pittsburgh, Pittsburgh, PA '82 (PLNG)
SHELLENBARGER, MELANIE T., Denver, CO '85 (PLNG)
SHELLEY, BETTY B., dir. educ. serv., East Tennessee Baptist Hospital, Knoxville, TN '86 (EDUC)
SHELLEY, SANDRA, RN, dir. nrsg. serv., DePaul Health Center, Bridgeton, MO '86 (NURS)
SHELNUTT, JASON, mgr., Pannell, Kerr and Forster, Atlanta, GA '87 (AMB)
SHELOR, KATHLEEN, coor. risk mgt., University of Maryland Medical Systems, Baltimore, MD '87 (RISK)
SHELTON, DAVID T., dir. pers., El Centro Regional Medical Center, El Centro, CA '86 (PERS)
SHELTON, DONNA SUE, asst. adm., Memorial Hospital, Danville, VA '86 (AMB)
SHELTON, HERSHEL W., sr. vice-pres. and atty., Alta Bates Corporation, Berkeley, CA '82 (ATTY)
SHELTON, JAYNE B., dir. soc. work, Presbyterian-University Hospital, Pittsburgh, PA '66 (SOC)
SHELTON, JOHN L., adm. dir. cardiology and pulmonary serv., St. Joseph Mercy Hospital, Ann Arbor, MI '83
SHELTON, MAX, atty., Baptist Memorial Hospital, Memphis, TN '70 (ATTY)
SHELTON, PAUL S., dir. health educ., Lafayette Home Hospital, Lafayette, IN '82 (EDUC)
SHELTON, RICHARD D., dir. eng., Brokaw Hospital, Normal, IL '80 (ENG)
SHELTON, ROBERT E., pres., Blue Cross Hospital Service, Inc., of Missouri, St. Louis, MO '74
SHELTON, ROBERT M., (ret.), Glen Ellyn, IL '84
SHELTON, SHARON, dir. vol. serv., Georgia Baptist Medical Center, Atlanta, GA '80 (VOL)
SHELTON, WANDA J., dir. soc. work serv., New England Memorial Hospital, Stoneham, MA '86 (SOC)
SHELUB, ELAINE, dir. soc. serv., Kaiser Foundation Hospital, South San Francisco, CA '84 (SOC)
SHEMAK, DIANE K., dir. vol. serv., St. Vincent Medical Center, Toledo, OH '75 (VOL)
SHEMANEK, LEROY C., dir. pers., Walker Methodist Health Center, Inc., Minneapolis, MN '85 (PERS)
SHENE, WILLIAM R., vice-pres. and gen. mgr., Monaghan Medical Corporation, Plattsburgh, NY '86
SHENFELD, MICHELE G., assoc. dir. adm., Bellevue Hospital Center, New York, NY '74
SHENKMAN, JERROLD, Pound Ridge, NY '74 (ATTY)
SHENNUM, MARY, RN, assoc. dir., AMI Saint Joseph Hospital, Omaha, NE '80 (NURS)
SHEPARD, DAISY J., dir. pub. rel., Barnes Hospital, St. Louis, MO '81 (PR)
SHEPARD, J. TATE, vice-pres. human res., St. Francis-St. George Hospital, Cincinnati, OH '85 (PERS)
SHEPARD, JAMES M., dir. human res. info. syst., Detroit Medical Center Corporation, Detroit, MI '81 (PERS)
SHEPARD, JOHN R., adm., Appleton Medical Center, Appleton, WI '54 (LIFE)
SHEPARD, LEONARD G. JR., dir. matl. mgt., Plantation General Hospital, Plantation, FL '77 (PUR)
SHEPARD, MARIE I., RN, dir. nrsg., Orange Memorial Hospital, Orange, TX '86 (NURS)
SHEPARD, MICK, chief eng., Columbia Memorial Hospital, Astoria, OR '81 (ENG)
SHEPARD, STANLEY W., pres. and chief exec. off., New Britain General Hospital, New Britain, CT '49 (LIFE)
SHEPARD, STANLEY, vice-pres. adm., Kessler Institute for Rehabilitation, East Orange, NJ '81
SHEPARDSON, W. PHILIP JR., atty., University of Cincinnati Hospital, Cincinnati, OH '79 (ATTY)
SHEPERD, DENNIS F., dir. nutr. serv., St. Luke's Hospital, Racine, WI '87 (FOOD)
SHEPHARD, THOMAS J. SR., atty., St. Joseph's Hospital, Stockton, CA '86 (ATTY)
SHEPHERD, BENNY, dir. pers., Roanoke Valley Psychiatric Center, Salem, VA '86 (PERS)
SHEPHERD, DOROTHY M., RN, dir. nrsg. serv. and asst. adm., St. Francis Medical Center, Honolulu, HI '85 (NURS)
SHEPHERD, DOUGLAS, adm., National Rehabilitation Hospital, Washington, DC '69
SHEPHERD, GENE, eng., Axtell Christian Hospital, Newton, KS '80 (ENG)
SHEPHERD, JAMES H. JR., risk mgr., Miriam Hospital, Providence, RI '69 (RISK)
SHEPHERD, JOHN C., atty., Hospital Association of Metropolitan St. Louis, St. Louis, MO '77 (ATTY)
SHEPHERD, MARVIN, supv. electro environ. safety, University of California San Francisco, San Francisco, CA '77 (ENG)
SHEPHERD, RICHARD W., pres., Shepherd Company, Oklahoma City, OK '79
SHEPHERD, ROBERT GLENN, dir. eng., Baptist Memorial Hospital-Forrest City, Forrest City, AR '86 (ENG)
SHEPHERD, STEPHEN C., asst. adm., Fairview Park Hospital, Dublin, GA '82
SHEPPARD, CARL F., dir. pers. mgt., Hospital of the University of Pennsylvania, Philadelphia, PA '80 (PERS)
SHEPPARD, DEE J., risk mgr., Our Lady of Lourdes Memorial Hospital, Binghamton, NY '81 (RISK)
SHEPPARD, PETER, exec. vice-pres., Braintree Hospital, Braintree, MA '77
SHEPPARD, SHIRLEY A., RN, sr. vice-pres., Winter Park Memorial Hospital, Winter Park, FL '75 (NURS)
SHER, JULIE A., student, Program in Hospital Administration, University of Minnesota, Minneapolis, MN '86
SHERAW, THOMAS, eng., Monsour Medical Center, Jeannette, PA '86 (ENG)
SHERIDAN, DONNA R., RN, mgt. dev. consult., Stanford University Hospital, Stanford, CA '82 (NURS)
SHERIDAN, ELIZABETH A., RN, assoc. dir. nrsg., Bergen Pines County Hospital, Paramus, NJ '84 (NURS)
SHERIDAN, PATRICK W., mgr., Ernst and Whinney, Cleveland, OH '86 (MGMT)
SHERLOCK, LEA, RN, dir. educ. serv., Memorial Hospital of Dodge County, Fremont, NE '78 (EDUC)
SHERMAN, AMY BETH, dir. pat. rel., St. Francis Hospital, Miami Beach, FL '87 (PAT)
SHERMAN, BARBARA A., RN, vice-pres. nrsg., Allentown Hospital, Allentown, PA '82 (NURS)
SHERMAN, DIANE W., dir. pub. and commun. rel., HCA Brotman Medical Center, Culver City, CA '83 (PR)
SHERMAN, FRANCES, risk mgr., St. Vincent's Medical Center, Staten Island, NY '85 (RISK)
SHERMAN, GILBERT W. II, dist. mgr., Barnes Hospital, St. Louis, MO '77 (FOOD)
SHERMAN, GLENN B., asst. dir. matl. mgt., Beth Israel Medical Center, New York, NY '86 (PUR)
SHERMAN, HAROLD S., vice-pres. corp. dev., St. Francis Medical Center, Trenton, NJ '72 (PLNG)
SHERMAN, HARRIET, asst. chief soc. work serv., Veterans Administration Medical Center, Brooklyn, NY '86 (SOC)
SHERMAN, JOAN L., dir. vol. serv., St. Vincent's Hospital, Harrison, NY '81 (VOL)
SHERMAN, JOHN, atty., Hayt, Hayt and Landau, Great Neck, NY '73 (ATTY)
SHERMAN, JONATHAN ADAM SMITH, student, Yale University School of Medicine, New Haven, CT '86
SHERMAN, LAWRENCE A., Puritan Finance Corporation, Chicago, IL '84 (LIFE)
SHERMAN, RICHARD R., Beverly Hospital, Beverly, MA '83 (PLNG)
SHERMAN, ROGER, Akron, OH '46 (LIFE)
SHERMAN, RONALD B., atty., Staten Island Hospital, Staten Island, NY '84 (ATTY)
SHERMAN, ZAUNIA R., instr. nrsg. educ., Wooster Community Hospital, Wooster, OH '84 (EDUC)
SHERMER, JANET EILEEN, health prog. analyst, Technassociates, Inc., Rockville, MD '78
SHERRATT, MARY J., RN, dir. vol. and adm. asst., Our Lady of Fatima Hospital, North Providence, RI '82 (VOL)
SHERRILL, BLANCHE A., dir. vol. serv., Self Memorial Hospital, Greenwood, SC '80 (VOL)

SHERRILL, CINDI, dir. soc. serv., Hartselle Hospital, Hartselle, AL '78 (SOC)
SHERRILL, LANETTE C., RN, dir. med. nrsg., University of Alabama Hospital, Birmingham, AL '83 (NURS)
SHERRILL, LAURA DELL, coor. pat. rel., Kapiolani Women's and Children's Medical Center, Honolulu, HI '85 (PAT)
SHERRILL, MARILYN W., dir. pers., C. J. Harris Community Hospital, Sylva, NC '82 (PERS)
SHERRILL, PARKER, mgr. state govt. rel., Hospital Corporation of America, Nashville, TN '81
SHERRITON-BARNETT, J., pres., Health Management Consultants, Inc., Hollywood, FL '87 (EDUC)
SHERROD, CHARLES D., dir. eng., Roy H. Laird Memorial Hospital, Kilgore, TX '85 (ENG)
SHERRY, HENRY I., pres., Henry Sherry Associates, Inc., Atlanta, GA '86 (PLNG)
SHERWOOD, GARY A., dir. corp. affairs, Good Samaritan Hospital and Medical Center, Portland, OR '84
SHERWOOD, JANE E., RN, dir. nrsg. serv., Kapiolani Women's and Children's Medical Center, Honolulu, HI '80 (NURS)
SHERWOOD, JOHN M., exec. dir., Wayne County Memorial Hospital, Honesdale, PA '72
SHERWOOD, ROBERT D., dir. pers., Brandywine Hospital, Caln Township, PA '86 (PERS)
SHERWOOD, THOMAS A., RN, chief nrsg. serv., Veterans Administration Medical Center, Philadelphia, PA '75 (NURS)
SHERWOOD, WARREN E., chief soc. work serv., Veterans Administration Medical Center, East Orange, NJ '72 (SOC)
SHERWOOD, WILLIAM A., atty., Humana, Inc., Louisville, KY '86 (ATTY)
SHETLER, CHARLES L., asst. dir. fiscal serv., St. Luke's Hospital, Jacksonville, FL '77
SHETTY, RAVI, student, Program in Hospital and Health Service Management, Kellogg Graduate School of Management, Evanston, IL '84 (PLNG)
SHEVCHUK, JOHN B., health care consult., American Medical International, Houston, TX '74
SHEVIN, ARNOLD D., atty., Coral Reef Hospital, Miami, FL '84 (ATTY)
SHEVLIN, KATHLEEN MARY, PhD, dir. soc. work, Georgetown University Medical Center, Washington, DC '68 (SOC)
SHIBELSKI, PAUL R., vice-pres. human res., National Hospital for Orthopaedics and Rehabilitation, Arlington, VA '82 (PERS)
SHICKICH, BARBARA ALLAN, atty., Group Health Cooperative of Puget Sound, Seattle, WA '83 (ATTY)
SHIDAKER, THOMAS J., adm. asst., Memorial Hospital, Hollywood, FL '85
SHIEBLER, EDWARD R. JR., dir. pub. rel. and dev., Good Samaritan Hospital, West Islip, NY '85 (PR)
SHIELDS, CHARLES A. JR., vice-pres. educ., Canadian College of Health Services Executives, Ottawa, Ont., Canada '80 (EDUC)
SHIELDS, DONALD, health syst. analyst, Air Force Medical System Division, Brooks AFB, TX '80
SHIELDS, JIM, mgr. eng. maint., North Kansas City Hospital, North Kansas City, MO '80 (ENG)
SHIELDS, JOSEPH E., asst. dir. mktg., Osteopathic Hospital of Maine, Portland, ME '83 (PR)
SHIELDS, KAREN, dir. amb. care, Kino Community Hospital, Tucson, AZ '87 (AMB)
SHIELDS, LENA L., RN, asst. adm., Bethany Hospital, Chicago, IL '83
SHIELDS, MARTIN T., assoc. dir. human res., Staten Island Hospital, Staten Island, NY '65 (PERS)
SHIELDS, MAUREEN V., dir. mktg. and pub. rel., Highsmith-Rainey Memorial Hospital, Fayetteville, NC '84 (PR)
SHIELDS, MICHAEL S., asst. adm., Brighton Hospital, Brighton, MI '81 (PERS)
SHIELDS, RALPH G., head maint., Illinois Valley Community Hospital, Peru, IL '79 (ENG)
SHIELDS, SARAH M., dir. vol. serv., Mobile Infirmary Medical Center, Mobile, AL '83 (VOL)
SHIELDS, THOMAS C., atty., Alexian Brothers Medical Center, Elk Grove Village, IL '72 (ATTY)
SHIELS, JAMES H., vice-pres. commun. rel., Meriden-Wallingford Hospital, Meriden, CT '86 (PR)
SHIELS, ROB, adm., Mary Shiels Hospital, Dallas, TX '86 (AMB)
SHIER, DWIGHT W., dir. pers., William Beaumont Hospital-Troy, Troy, MI '80 (PERS)
SHIESLEY, RICHARD, asst. dir. emp. rel., Park Ridge Hospital, Rochester, NY '86 (PERS)
SHIFFER, BRENDA A., RN, dir. nrsg., Hoag Memorial Hospital Presbyterian, Newport Beach, CA '86 (NURS)
SHIFFER, JUDY A., RN, dir. nrsg., Community Hospital of Ottawa, Ottawa, IL '82 (NURS)
SHIFFERD, MARILYN H., exec. dir., Palm Beach Regional Visiting Nurse Association, West Palm Beach, FL '83 (EDUC)
SHILBY, MICHAEL W., dir. vol. serv., Suburban Hospital, Bethesda, MD '81 (VOL)
SHILLING, MARY E., RN, assoc. adm., Greenville General Hospital, Greenville, SC '73 (NURS)
SHIMER, ROBERT TIMOTHY, vice-pres. plng. and bus. dev., Community Home Health Services of Philadelphia, Philadelphia, PA '84 (PLNG)
SHIMITZ, RENEE, mgr. loss control and qual. mgt., Health Central Metropolitan Hospitals, Minneapolis, MN '84 (RISK)
SHIN, CECILIA YOUNG, mgt. eng., Presbyterian-University of Pennsylvania Medical Center, Philadelphia, PA '85 (MGMT)
SHIN, YOUNG SOO, MD, assoc. prof. and dep. dir. inst. hosp. serv., Institute of Hospital Services, Seoul National University Hospital, Seoul, South Korea '78
SHINAL, DIANE J., RN, prof. serv. rep., Nesbitt Memorial Hospital, Kingston, PA '84 (PR)
SHINGAI, BARBARA K., dir. pers., Watsonville Community Hospital, Watsonville, CA '82 (PERS)
SHINN, DAVID B., pres., Shinn and Associates, Haslett, MI '86 (EDUC)
SHINNERS, ANN, dir. soc. serv., St. Joseph's Hospital, Tampa, FL '79 (SOC)
SHINNICK, SR. MARY, corp. treas., Franciscan Sisters Health Care Corporation, Mokena, IL '79
SHINODA, MAKIKO, asst. exec. diet., Fairmont Hospital, San Leandro, CA '80 (FOOD)
SHIPLEY, CHARLES W., acct. exec., Nelson-Padberg Communications, Phoenix, AZ '79 (PLNG)
SHIPLEY, LISA P., Bath Memorial Hospital, Bath, ME '86 (SOC)
SHIPMAN, E. WILLIAM S., atty., Michigan Osteopathic Medical Center, Detroit, MI '87 (ATTY)
SHIPP, EMMA, pat. rep., St. Luke Hospital, Fort Thomas, KY '84 (PAT)
SHIPSEY, S. MADELINE, Quincy, MA '66 (SOC)
SHIRCLIFF, ROBERT LEE, vice-pres., Jewish Hospital, Louisville, KY '79
SHIREY, BRENDA M., dir. emp. rel., St. John's Health and Hospital Center, Pittsburgh, PA '81 (PERS)
SHIREY, JUDITH A., dir. vol. serv., HCA Northeast Community Hospital, Bedford, TX '84 (PR)
SHIREY, RICHARD T., dir. med. decision support syst., Rush-Presbyterian-St. Luke's Medical Center, Chicago, IL '87 (MGMT)
SHIRILLA, PAUL M., atty., Sisters of Mercy Health Corporation, Farmington Hills, MI '82 (ATTY)
SHIRLEY, E. ALAN, atty., Dallas County Hospital, Perry, IA '86 (ATTY)
SHIRLEY, EILEEN, med. lib., Park Ridge Hospital, Rochester, NY '80 (EDUC)
SHIRLEY, ELIZABETH SNIDER, dir. soc. serv., Fauquier Hospital, Warrenton, VA '76 (SOC)
SHIRLEY, JACK W., dir. facil. plng., Methodist Hospital, Lubbock, TX '86 (ENG)
SHIRRIFF, DORIS M., contr. and dir. pers., Penetanguishene General Hospital, Penetanguishene, Ont., Canada '77 (PERS)
SHIVERS, SUSAN MONICA, coor. mktg. and pub. rel., St. Vincent Memorial Hospital, Taylorville, IL '87 (PR)
SHIVERS, VIRGINIA I., RN, dir. spec. care, St. Margaret's Hospital, Montgomery, AL '82 (NURS)
SHIVES, JAMES, asst. supt., Western Maryland Center, Hagerstown, MD '86 (RISK)
SHIVINSKY, STEVEN M., dir. pub. rel., Millard Fillmore Hospital, Buffalo, NY '85 (PR)
SHLALA, THOMAS J., RN, mgr. natl. health care, Coopers and Lybrand, New York, NY '85 (NURS)(RISK)
SHNIPPER, JOAN SHELLEY, dir. pub. affairs, University of Maryland Medical Systems, Baltimore, MD '82 (PR)
SHOBAKEN, BARBARA A., asst. dir. pers., Mount Sinai Medical Center, Miami Beach, FL '78 (PERS)
SHOBERG, HARVEY F., dir. soc. serv., Douglas County Hospital, Omaha, NE '71 (SOC)
SHOCKLEY, ED, asst. adm. plant serv., Department of Health and Hospitals, Denver, CO '86 (ENG)
SHOCKLEY, LORI, mgr. pub. rel., Riddle Memorial Hospital, Media, PA '81 (PR)
SHOCKNEY, JOHN NEAL, dir. pers., Tipton County Memorial Hospital, Tipton, IN '77 (PERS)
SHOE, RUTH M., supv. cent. sterile sup., High Point Regional Hospital, High Point, NC '85 (CS)
SHOEMAKER, JAMES A., dir. plant oper., Deborah Heart and Lung Center, Browns Mills, NJ '81 (ENG)
SHOEMAKER, JERRY R., asst. mgr. matl., HCA Greenview Hospital, Bowling Green, KY '84 (PUR)
SHOEMAKER, KATHRYN, RN, coor. nrsg. educ., Phoebe Putney Memorial Hospital, Albany, GA '85 (EDUC)
SHOEMAKER, ROBERT F., mgr. cent. serv., Methodist Evangelical Hospital, Louisville, KY '73 (CS)
SHOEMAKER, ROSE MARIE, dir. commun. rel., Tawas St. Joseph Hospital, Tawas City, MI '82 (PR)
SHOEMAKER, RUTH ELLEN, RN, asst. vice-pres. nrsg., Hamot Medical Center, Erie, PA '83 (NURS)
SHOFNER, SHIRLEY A., RN, asst. vice-pres., Baylor Health Care System, Dallas, TX '82 (NURS)
SHOGREN, LOUISE A., dir. soc. work serv., St. Joseph's Hospital, Milwaukee, WI '74 (SOC)
SHOHEN, SAUNDRA A., assoc. dir. pub. rel., St. Luke's Roosevelt Hospital Center, New York, NY '81 (PR)
SHOLMAN, VIOLET, dir. vol., Illini Community Hospital, Pittsfield, IL '83 (VOL)
SHONTZ, L. ALLAN, pres., Telcon Associates of St. Louis, Inc., St. Louis, MO '86 (ENG)
SHOOK, DONALD D., vice-pres. dev., Children's Hospital Medical Center, Akron, OH '81
SHOOK, ELEANOR C., risk mgr., Candler General Hospital, Savannah, GA '81 (RISK)
SHOOK, RANDY R., mgr. pub. info., St. Anthony Hospital Systems, Denver, CO '84 (PR)
SHOOTER, ROGER J., actg. dir. soc. serv., Riverside Methodist Hospitals, Columbus, OH '87 (SOC)
SHOPE, RALPH D., asst. adm., Owensboro-Daviess County Hospital, Owensboro, KY '76 (PUR)
SHOPTAW, M. SUE, RN, dir. nrsg., Mississippi Baptist Medical Center, Jackson, MS '83 (NURS)
SHOR, DAVID H., dir. sales and mktg., Pentamation Enterprises, Inc., Sparks, MD '82
SHORE, HERBERT H., exec. dir., Dallas Home and Hospital for Jewish Aged, Dallas, TX '59
SHOREYS, MARGARET LOUISE, dir. vol., Our Lady of Lourdes Medical Center, Camden, NJ '83 (VOL)
SHORNEY, ROGER D., dir. pur., Missouri Rehabilitation Center, Mount Vernon, MO '86 (PUR)
SHOROSKY, ANITA M., asst. adm., U. S. Air Force Hospital Altus, Altus, OK '83
SHORR, ARTHUR SIDNEY, pres., Arthur S. Shorr and Associates, Tarzana, CA '68
SHORS, JOHN D., atty., Iowa Health Systems Agency, Inc., Des Moines, IA '79 (ATTY)
SHORT, BARBARA F., coor. pat. educ., Texas Scottish Rite Hospital, Dallas, TX '86 (EDUC)
SHORT, JOANNE C., RN, coor. risk mgt., Mercy Community Hospital, Port Jervis, NY '70 (RISK)
SHORT, JOHN J., adm. mgr. cardiology, Rush-Presbyterian-St. Luke's Medical Center, Chicago, IL '83
SHORT, MICHAEL, dir. eng. and maint., Gottlieb Memorial Hospital, Melrose Park, IL '86 (ENG)
SHORT, NANCY E., dir. vol., Licking Memorial Hospital, Newark, OH '86 (VOL)
SHORT, TRACY K., dir. mktg. and plng., Sisters of the Sorrowful Mother-Ministry Corporation, Milwaukee, WI '86 (PLNG)
SHORT, VAL T., mgr. commun. rel., Halifax Memorial Hospital, Roanoke Rapids, NC '86 (PR)
SHORTLIFFE, ERNEST CARL, MD, Hamilton, NY '56 (LIFE)
SHOUGH, LINDA R., clin. instr., Community Health Center of Branch County, Coldwater, MI '85 (EDUC)
SHOUGH, RITA D., dir. pers., Lewis-Gale Hospital, Salem, VA '85 (PERS)
SHOULDERS, PATRICK A., atty., St. Mary's Medical Center, Evansville, IN '86 (ATTY)
SHOULDICE, ROSEMARY H., coor. mktg., St. Vincent de Paul Community Stewardship, Jacksonville, FL '86 (PR)
SHOUP, CHARLES, mgr. maint., Holy Cross Hospital, Salt Lake City, UT '83 (ENG)
SHOUP, DAVID N., dir. pat. acct., Good Shepherd Medical Center, Longview, TX '85 (ENG)
SHOUP, ROBERTA LEE, dir. vol. serv., HCA West Paces Ferry Hospital, Atlanta, GA '79 (VOL)
SHOVE, GREGORY A., MD, chm. risk mgt., Racine Medical Center, Racine, WI '86 (RISK)
SHOVELIN, WAYNE F., pres., Gaston Memorial Hospital, Gastonia, NC '72
SHOVLIN, RUTH B., dir. vol. serv., Elmcrest Psychiatric Institute, Portland, CT '85 (VOL)
SHOW, ELLEN VASEY, RN, asst. exec. dir., Westmoreland Hospital, Greensburg, PA '86 (NURS)
SHOWALTER, ANNE HUNTER, dir. soc. work, Fairfax Hospital, Falls Church, VA '80 (SOC)
SHOWALTER, CHARLES L., Slidell, LA '50 (LIFE)
SHOWALTER, GARY L., sr. consult., Peat, Marwick, Mitchell, Cleveland, OH '82 (PLNG)
SHOWALTER, J. STUART, dir. legal serv., Catholic Health Association of the U. S., St. Louis, MO '80 (ATTY)
SHOWALTER, LEE, dir. plant oper., Howard Community Hospital, Kokomo, IN '75 (ENG)
SHOWELL, GINA R., adm. outpatient serv., St. Elizabeth Medical Center, Dayton, OH '87 (AMB)
SHOYS, MICHAEL R., vice-pres., Wisconsin Hospital Association-Shared Services Program, Madison, WI '81 (ENG)
SHRADER, BETTY G., dir. pers., Bluefield Community Hospital, Bluefield, WV '84 (PERS)
SHRAGO, HARRY D., vice-pres. plng. and fin., Voluntary Hospitals of America, Atlanta, GA '82 (PLNG)
SHRECK, JEANNE, dir. vol. serv., Freehold Area Hospital, Freehold, NJ '74 (VOL)
SHREVE, ANN, dir. vol. serv., Bass Memorial Baptist Hospital, Enid, OK '77 (VOL)
SHREVE, KENDIL M., dir. matl. mgt., Frederick Memorial Hospital, Frederick, MD '82 (PUR)
SHREVE, RICHARD B., dir. biomedical serv., Good Samaritan Hospital, Lebanon, PA '82 (ENG)
SHRIDE, STEPHEN E., RN, vice-pres. pat. serv., Cabell Huntington Hospital, Huntington, WV '70 (NURS)
SHRODE, JACK W., (ret.), Vian, OK '47 (LIFE)
SHROPSHIRE, CAROL O., mgr. educ., North Colorado Medical Center, Greeley, CO '82 (EDUC)
SHROPSHIRE, DONALD G., pres. and chief exec. off., Tucson Medical Center, Tucson, AZ '58
SHRYOCK, MINDY, rep. pat. serv., Grandview Hospital and Medical Center, Dayton, OH '78 (PAT)
SHUART, TODD W., dir. environ. eng., Bladen County Hospital, Elizabethtown, NC '86 (ENG)
SHUBBUCK, THOMAS J., dir. eng., Manchester Memorial Hospital, Manchester, CT '82 (ENG)
SHUBIN, HARRY, MD, staff phys. int. medicine, Graduate Hospital, Philadelphia, PA '69
SHUBIN, LETA R., dir. soc. serv., Warminster General Hospital, Warminster, PA '85 (SOC)
SHUBLOM, JENNIE L., dir. soc. serv., Asbury Hospital, Salina, KS '82 (SOC)
SHUCK, DANIEL R., dir. matl. mgt., Community Hospital of Williams County, Bryan, OH '84 (PUR)
SHUE, PATRICIA D., RN, asst. dir. nrsg., York Hospital, York, PA '82 (NURS)
SHUFFITT, MARGARET K., dir. vol., Columbus Hospital, Chicago, IL '71 (VOL)
SHUGARMAN, MARK DAVID, vice-pres. plng. and prof. serv., St. Mary's Medical Center, Racine, WI '77 (PLNG)(RISK)
SHUGARTS, LINDA A., RN, dir. nrsg., St. Joseph Hospital, Lancaster, PA '77 (NURS)
SHULER, CAPT. DONALD E., MSC USN, vice cmdr., Naval Medical Command, Washington, DC '58
SHULINS, SUSAN, commun., mktg. and pub. affs spec., Tampa General Hospital, Tampa, FL '86
SHULKIN, RANDALL S., dir. spec. proj., Southern Maine Medical Center, Biddeford, ME '85 (PLNG)
SHULL, ELIZABETH MAY, coor. pat. rep., Roosevelt Hospital, New York, NY '85 (PAT)
SHULL, GARY W., contr., Grace Hospital, Morganton, NC '83 (PLNG)
SHULMAN, HARRY, atty., Hospital Council of Northern California, San Bruno, CA '79 (ATTY)
SHULMAN, LAUREN, dir. mktg. and pub. rel., Southern Maine Medical Center, Biddeford, ME '86 (PR)
SHULMAN, LAWRENCE C., assoc. vice-pres., Roosevelt Hospital, New York, NY '67 (SOC)
SHULMAN, LEAH, coor. pat. org., Sheppard and Enoch Pratt Hospital, Baltimore, MD '83 (PAT)

SHULMAN, MARTIN L., prog. mgr., Ohio Hospital Management Services, Columbus, OH '77 (MGMT)
SHULMAN, NORMA, dir. pat. rep. and vol. serv., Mount Sinai Medical Center, Cleveland, OH '79 (PAT)(VOL)
SHULSKI, ROY ROBERT, corp. dir. matl. serv., Prince George's General Hospital and Medical Center, Cheverly, MD '79 (PUR)
SHULTZ, EDWARD J., dir. eng., St. Margaret Hospital, Hammond, IN '80 (ENG)
SHULTZ, WALTER R., facil. eng., Geisinger Medical Center, Danville, PA '73 (ENG)
SHUM, NORINE, asst. to chm. oper. room and surg. nrsg., Rush-Presbyterian-St. Luke's Medical Center, Chicago, IL '85
SHUMAKE, JAMES A., dir. plant serv., Flint Osteopathic Hospital, Flint, MI '62 (ENG)
SHUMAN, JOHN D., dir. cent. sup., proc. and distrib., Memorial Hospital, Cumberland, MD '79 (PUR)
SHUMAN, JOHN F., chief eng., Keokuk Area Hospital, Keokuk, IA '82 (ENG)
SHUMAN, LARRY J., prof. eng., University of Pittsburgh, Department of Industrial Engineering, Pittsburgh, PA '71 (MGMT)
SHUMILOFF, PATRICIA A., mgt. eng., Western Reserve Care System, Youngstown, OH '86 (MGMT)
SHUMLAS, ALICE WARNER, dir. food serv., Mayview State Hospital, Bridgeville, PA '80 (FOOD)
SHUMWAY, BARBARA L., dir. pers., North Big Horn Hospital, Lovell, WY '84 (PERS)
SHUMWAY, SANDRA S., RN, dir. prog. dev. and nrsg., Cleveland Clinic Hospital, Cleveland, OH '86 (NURS)
SHUPAK, BARBARA, assoc. dir., St. Vincent's Medical Center, Staten Island, NY '80
SHUPE, ROBERT K., dir. eng., Richardson Medical Center, Richardson, TX '84 (ENG)
SHUR, JUDITH, mgr. risk analysis, University of Texas M. D. Anderson Hospital and Tumor Institute at Houston, Houston, TX '85 (RISK)
SHURRUM, DAVID A., dir. mgt. eng., O'Connor Health Services, San Jose, CA '78 (MGMT)
SHUSTER, SANDRA G., acct. rep., Physicians Health Services, Trumbell, CT '82
SHUTE, JUDITH A., instr., St. John's Mercy Medical Center, St. Louis, MO '86 (EDUC)
SHUTER, MARK H., RN, vice-pres. pat. care serv., Scioto Memorial Hospital, Portsmouth, OH '83 (NURS)
SHUTTLEWORTH, ANNE CRENSHAW, dir. customer serv., Greenville Memorial Hospital, Greenville, SC '80 (PAT)
SHUTTLEWORTH, EMOGENE, dir. food serv., Our Lady of Lake Regional Medical Center, Baton Rouge, LA '73 (FOOD)
SHYDLER, DANIEL H., asst. adm., University of California San Francisco Hospitals and Clinics, San Francisco, CA '82
SIBBEN, MARK T., sr. mgr., Ernst and Whinney, Charlotte, NC '80 (PLNG)
SIBBERNSEN, BEV, dir. soc. serv., Beatrice Community Hospital and Health Center, Beatrice, NE '86 (SOC)
SIBERY, D. EUGENE, pres., Blue Cross of Iowa, Des Moines, IA '59
SIBOLE, WAYNE R., vice-pres. plng. and mktg., Morton F. Plant Hospital, Clearwater, FL '79 (PLNG)
SICHER, CHARLES M., PhD, dir. kellogg proj., Sisters of Mercy Health Corporation, Farmington Hills, MI '85 (RISK)
SICK, JOHN K., dir. pers., Lake Forest Hospital, Lake Forest, IL '67 (PERS)
SICLARI, MARGIE, RN, dir. nrsg., Deepdale General Hospital, Little Neck, NY '81 (NURS)
SIDEL, LARRY D., adm. adv., Montreal General Hospital, Montreal, Que., Canada '81 (CS)
SIDELL, NANCY L., dir. soc. serv., Medical College of Ohio Hospital, Toledo, OH '81 (SOC)
SIDES, LARRY E., pres., Sides and Associates, Inc., Lafayette, LA '78 (PR)
SIDES, MARIAN B., RN, assoc. dir. nrsg. serv., University of Chicago Hospitals, Chicago, IL '86 (NURS)
SIDNEY, GAIL, dir. pub. rel., Santa Monica Hospital Medical Center, Santa Monica, CA '86 (PR)
SIDON, MICHAEL, dir. matl. mgt., York-Finch General Hospital, Downsview, Ont., Canada '86 (PUR)
SIDWELL, LESLIE A., mgr. maint., Ephraim McDowell Regional Medical Center, Danville, KY '85 (ENG)
SIEBENALLER, JACQUELINE, exec. diet., Botsford General Hospital, Farmington Hills, MI '80 (FOOD)
SIEBENBRUNER, JOYCE E., supv. cent. proc. and distrib., Immanuel-St. Joseph's Hospital, Mankato, MN '81 (CS)
SIEBER, EDWARD JR., chief exec. off., Lewis County General Hospital, Lowville, NY '85
SIEBER, EVA J., dir. sup., proc. distrib., Children's Hospital, Columbus, OH '85 (PUR)
SIEBERS, ZADA M., RN, dir. nrs., St. Elizabeth Hospital, Appleton, WI '77 (NURS)
SIEBERT, ROSE A., head nrs., Jewish Hospital of St. Louis, St. Louis, MO '87 (AMB)
SIEDLINSKI, JOHN E., dir. matl. mgt., Copley Memorial Hospital, Aurora, IL '86 (PUR)
SIEFERT, LARAINE W., mgt. eng., Hospital of Saint Raphael, New Haven, CT '83 (MGMT)
SIEG, DONALD J., student, Xavier University, Graduate Program in Hospital and Health Administration, Cincinnati, OH '85 (PLNG)
SIEGAL, BONNIE E., asst. adm. oper. and dir. nrsg., Childrens Hospital of Los Angeles, Los Angeles, CA '83 (NURS)
SIEGAL, DAVID L., MD, Brooklyn, NY '75
SIEGAL, STEPHEN M., exec. vice-pres., Continental Metal Products Company, Inc., Woburn, MA '84
SIEGEL, JANET E., vice-pres., Powercon Corporation, Severn, MD '81 (PLNG)
SIEGEL, KURT W., chief eng., Good Shepherd Hospital, Barrington, IL '86 (ENG)
SIEGEL, RUTH M., atty., Harrisburg Hospital, Harrisburg, PA '84 (ATTY)
SIEGEL, SOLOMON L., mgt. consult., Boca Raton, FL '53 (LIFE)
SIEGERT, LENA M., dir. nutr. and matl. serv., Community Memorial Hospital, Menomonee Falls, WI '78 (FOOD)(PUR)
SIEGERT, MARY T., staff assoc. plng. and prof. serv., Delaware Valley Hospital Council, Philadelphia, PA '82
SIEGLE, DONALD J., vice-pres., Hospital Shared Services Western Pennsylvania, Warrendale, PA '68 (PUR)
SIEGLITZ, MINNIE A., pres. aux. vol., Wuesthoff Memorial Hospital, Rockledge, FL '86 (VOL)
SIEJA, JUDITH A., asst. pub. rel. and dev., Richardson Medical Center, Richardson, TX '86 (PR)
SIEJA, KATHLEEN S., acct. exec., Barkin, Herman, Solochek and Paulsen, Inc., Milwaukee, WI '85 (PR)
SIEMBIEDA, MARGARET S., dir. educ. and trng., Mease Health Care, Dunedin, FL '85 (EDUC)
SIEMER, ROBERT E., atty., Memorial Medical Center, Long Beach, CA '78 (ATTY)
SIEMON, JAMES E., vice-pres., Holy Cross Hospital, Mission Hills, CA '84 (MGMT)
SIEMONSEN, FREDERIC M., Kingston, Ont., Canada '84 (ENG)
SIERACKI, MICAELA M., mgr. lab., DePaul Hospital, Norfolk, VA '85
SIERZEGA, JANET A., dir. soc. work, Somerset Medical Center, Somerville, NJ '85 (SOC)
SIETSEMA, MARGARET R., RN, asst. dir. nrsg. serv., Rice Memorial Hospital, Willmar, MN '86 (NURS)
SIEVERT, PAULA V., pers. adm., New York City Department of Transportation, New York, NY '82 (VOL)
SIEVERTS, STEVEN, vice-pres. health care fin., Blue Cross and Blue Shield of the National Capital Area, Washington, DC '63
SIEWERTSEN, WILLIAM F., dir. risk mgt., St. Joseph Hospital, Flint, MI '85 (RISK)
SIFFORD, HAROLD H., asst. dir. food serv., St. Joseph's Hospital, Tampa, FL '84 (FOOD)
SIGETI, ELIZABETH J., RN, asst. vice-pres. nrsg., Sisters of Charity Hospital, Buffalo, NY '87 (NURS)
SIGG, LORRAINE, dir. risk mgt. and pat. rep., Dickinson County Hospitals, Iron Mountain, MI '85 (RISK)
SIGMOND, ROBERT M., scholar-in-residence, Temple University, Philadelphia, PA '53 (PLNG)(LIFE)
SIGNARINO, RICHARD J., natl. exec. dir., Medical Discount Services, West Hempstead, NY '82 (PERS)
SIGNORACCI, DIANE M., atty., Riverside Methodist Hospitals, Columbus, OH '86 (ATTY)
SIGNORELLI, ANDREW J., MD, exec. med. dir., Faith Hospital, St. Louis, MO '37 (LIFE)
SIGSWORTH, BARBARA R., coor. dev., Lake Wales Hospital, Lake Wales, FL '81 (PR)
SIHLER, HERBERT A. JR., pres., Windsor Hospital, Chagrin Falls, OH '78
SIIRO, KENNETH E., mgr. sup., proc. and distrib., St. Luke's Hospital, Duluth, MN '76 (CS)
SIJAK, JELENA, supv. sterile sup., Richardson Medical Center, Richardson, TX '87 (CS)
SIKES, BARBARA A., dir. vol. serv., Harris Methodist -Fort Worth, Fort Worth, TX '87 (VOL)
SIKES, CHARLES R., reg. mgr., Mra, Inc., Marietta, GA '64 (EDUC)
SIKORA, ALBIN J., vice-pres. emp. rel., Ingalls Memorial Hospital, Harvey, IL '74 (PERS)
SIKORA, ANN, RN, asst. adm. nrsg., Brazosport Memorial Hospital, Lake Jackson, TX '82 (NURS)
SIKORA, PATRICIA A., dir. soc. work, Bon Secours Hospital, Grosse Pointe, MI '74 (SOC)
SIKORSKI, DIANNE L., student, Georgia State University, Institute of Health Administration, Atlanta, GA '84
SIKORSKI, RICHARD A. SR., plant eng., Heritage Hospital, Taylor, MI '74 (ENG)
SIKORYAK, JOHN, dir. pers., Long Beach Memorial Hospital, Long Beach, NY '80 (PERS)
SILAS, DELPHINE, mgr. sterile proc., Bethany Hospital, Chicago, IL '85 (CS)
SILBER, ROBERT W. JR., acct. exec. health care, Bell Telephone of Pennsylvania, Bala Cynwyd, PA '87 (ENG)
SILBERG, NANCY, vice-pres. plng., Pacific Medical Center, Seattle, WA '83 (PLNG)
SILBERGER, PHYLLIS, dir. pers., City Hospital Center at Elmhurst, Flushing, NY '77 (PERS)
SILBERMAN, LORETTA, RN, vice-pres. prof. rel., National Medical Enterprises, Los Angeles, CA '73 (NURS)
SILBERMANN, BARRY D., atty., Cedars-Sinai Medical Center, Los Angeles, CA '80 (ATTY)
SILCOTT, ERNIE JUNE, dir. soc. serv., Touro Infirmary, New Orleans, LA '86 (SOC)
SILER, EDIE L., coor. pat. educ., National Jewish Center, Denver, CO '86 (EDUC)
SILER, JOHN P., atty., McLaren General Hospital, Flint, MI '75 (ATTY)
SILHAN, CAROL J., dir. vol. serv., St. Francis Hospital, Blue Island, IL '81 (VOL)
SILL, GERALD M., vice-pres. legal affairs, Missouri Hospital Association, Jefferson, MO '81 (ATTY)
SILLIMAN, SCOTT E., dir. clin. eng., St. John's Hospital, Springfield, IL '78 (ENG)
SILLING, C. E., (ret.), Charleston, WV '48 (LIFE)
SILLO, TERRY, dir. pers., San Gabriel Valley Medical Center, San Gabriel, CA '83 (PERS)
SILLUP, RAYMOND M., dir. contr. and reimbursment, Western Psychiatric Institute and Clinic, Pittsburgh, PA '83
SILSBY, BRADFORD H., dir. plng., Beverly Hospital, Beverly, MA '73 (PLNG)
SILVA, BEVERLY D., dir. vol. serv., St. Luke's Regional Medical Center, Boise, ID '85 (VOL)
SILVA, JUDY C., RN, vice-pres., Tennessee Christian Medical Center, Madison, TN '80 (NURS)
SILVA, LAWRENCE J., dir. matl. mgt., St. Anne's Hospital, Fall River, MA '82 (CS)(PUR)
SILVA, MARY, dir. pub. affairs, University of Cincinnati Hospital, Cincinnati, OH '86 (PR)
SILVAGNI, KATHLEEN, RN, asst. adm. nrsg., Delaware County Memorial Hospital, Drexel Hill, PA '77 (NURS)
SILVASY, RAYMOND P., dir. risk mgt., South Hills Health System, Pittsburgh, PA '80 (RISK)
SILVER-SMITH, BOBBIE J., pat. rel. rep., Metropolitan Hospital, Richmond, VA '86 (PAT)
SILVER, ARNOLD P., fin. counsel, Samaritan Health Service, Phoenix, AZ '75
SILVER, CLEO M., RN, sr. vice-pres. pat. serv. and plng., McLaren General Hospital, Flint, MI '77 (NURS)(PLNG)
SILVER, CLIFF ROBERT, adm. coor., Mercy Catholic Medical Center, Darby, PA '83
SILVER, HARRISON E., MD, trustee, Riverside General Hospital-University Medical Center, Riverside, CA '71
SILVER, KAREN A., RN, Tampa, FL '82 (NURS)
SILVER, LOUIS, exec. dir., Workmen's Circle Home and Infirmary Foundation for the Aged, Bronx, NY '67
SILVER, MARY ANN, pat. rep., St. Francis Xavier Hospital, Charleston, SC '72 (PAT)
SILVER, MIKE, mgr. matl., North Colorado Medical Center, Greeley, CO '80 (PUR)
SILVERA, MARKETTA M., vice-pres. sales, Granite Systems, Lafayette, CA '86 (FOOD)
SILVERBERG, LEON J., dep. dir. health and safety, New York City Department of Sanitation, New York, NY '73
SILVERBERG, MARTA CUELLAR, asst. adm., Hospital of the Medical College of Pennsylvania, Philadelphia, PA '83 (RISK)
SILVERBERG, YVONNE M., RN, vice-pres. nrsg. serv., St. Clair Memorial Hospital, Pittsburgh, PA '86 (NURS)
SILVERIO, RONALD, asst. environ. serv., Massachusetts General Hospital, Boston, MA '86 (ENVIRON)
SILVERMAN, CHARLES A., dir. adm. serv., St. Joseph's Medical Center, Yonkers, NY '85
SILVERMAN, FRED, pres., Bronx-Lebanon Hospital Center, Bronx, NY '64
SILVERMAN, JILL K., asst. vice-pres., American Health Systems, San Francisco, CA '84 (RISK)(AMB)
SILVERMAN, RICHARD J., dir. human res., Desert Springs Hospital, Las Vegas, NV '85 (PERS)
SILVERS, DIANE JACQUELINE, coor. guest rel., California Medical Center-Los Angeles, Los Angeles, CA '86 (PAT)
SILVERS, J. B., treuhaft prof. mgt., Case Western Reserve University, Cleveland, OH '80
SILVERSTEIN, CAROL KAUFFMAN, atty., Wake Medical Center, Raleigh, NC '74 (ATTY)
SILVERSTEIN, CHARLES M., mgr. editorial serv. pub. rel., Northwestern Memorial Hospital, Chicago, IL '86 (PR)
SILVERSTEIN, ELLEN, mng. coor. pat. and family serv., Sharp Cabrillo Hospital, San Diego, CA '86 (SOC)
SILVERSTEIN, GARY H., vice-pres. oper. and plng., Rockingham Memorial Hospital, Harrisonburg, VA '79 (PLNG)
SILVERSTEIN, SUSAN G., consult. corp. human res., Faulkner Hospital, Boston, MA '86 (PERS)
SILVERSTONE, JEFFREY R., dir. mktg. and prog. dev., Medlantic Healthcare Group, Washington, DC '86 (PR) (PLNG)
SILVESTRI, FRANK, dir. matl. mgt., Sharon General Hospital, Sharon, PA '80 (PUR)
SILVESTRO, JOHN P., assoc. exec. dir., City Hospital Center at Elmhurst, Flushing, NY '72
SILVEY, ANDREA B., RN, vice-pres., Community Hospital of Roanoke Valley, Roanoke, VA '84 (NURS)
SILVIA, ALFRED JR., dir. matl. mgt. and pharm. serv., Morton Hospital and Medical Center, Taunton, MA '86
SILVIN, RICHARD R., group vice-pres., AMI Switzerland, Ltd., Lausanne, Switzerland '78
SIMAK, MELVIN J., exec. dir., Jewish Hospital of Hope, Montreal, Que., Canada '60
SIMANSKI, ROBERT E., dir. commun. and ed., Contractors Association International, Fairfax, VA '86 (ENG)
SIMANSKY, MARY ANN, RN, coor. pat. care, Humana Hospital -Tacoma, Tacoma, WA '84 (PAT)
SIMARD, JOAN J., RN, dir. med. and surg. nrsg., St. Clare's -Riverside Medical Center, Denville, NJ '86 (NURS)
SIMCHUK, CATHY J., RN, exec. dir. outpatient nrsg., Holy Family Hospital, Spokane, WA '84 (NURS)
SIMCO, MARY JANE, RN, dir. nrsg. serv. and surg., Trumbull Memorial Hospital, Warren, OH '83 (NURS)
SIMEK, FRANKLIN E., pres., Lafayette Home Hospital, Lafayette, IN '81 (PLNG)
SIMENSEN, KIMBERLY O'GRADY, assoc., Dain Bosworth, Inc., Minneapolis, MN '80
SIMENZ, SHEILA, vice-pres. pat. serv., Sheboygan Memorial Medical Center, Sheboygan, WI '87 (AMB)
SIMEONIDIS, STEVE, dir. plant oper., St. Vincent's Medical Center, Bridgeport, CT '83 (ENG)
SIMINGTON, NANCY, dir. pub. rel., Booth Memorial Medical Center, Flushing, NY '86 (PR)
SIMIONE, MARY M., RN, dir. amb. pat. serv., Lawrence Memorial Hospital of Medford, Medford, MA '87 (AMB)
SIMKO, RAYMOND E., contr., A. M. McGregor Home, East Cleveland, OH '84 (MGMT)
SIMMONS, ADRIENNE C., asst. adm. plng. serv., St. Vincent Hospital and Medical Center, Portland, OR '82 (PLNG)
SIMMONS, ARLENE P., dir. pub. rel., Millcreek Community Hospital, Erie, PA '84 (PR)
SIMMONS, BEVERLY K., exec. vice-pres., Mid-America Health Network, Kansas City, MO '85 (PLNG)
SIMMONS, BILLY J., dir. cent. serv., Carraway Methodist Medical Center, Birmingham, AL '71 (CS)
SIMMONS, CHERYL A., dir. in-service, Saint James Hospital, Pontiac, IL '82 (EDUC)
SIMMONS, CLARA S., head med. soc. work serv., Kaiser Foundation Hospital-Cleveland, Cleveland, OH '86 (SOC)
SIMMONS, CONSTANCE L., vice-pres. mktg. serv., Health Management Services, Inc., Columbus, OH '83 (PLNG)
SIMMONS, CYRUS, risk mgr., Battle Creek Adventist Hospital, Battle Creek, MI '82 (RISK)

SIMMONS, DAVID A., ScD, pres., Fairfax Hospital, Falls Church, VA '72 (ENG)
SIMMONS, DAVID E., (ret.), Shaker Heights, OH '56 (MGMT)(LIFE)
SIMMONS, DONALD R., dir. facil. plng., Bronson Methodist Hospital, Kalamazoo, MI '83 (PLNG)
SIMMONS, ELAINE M., dir. commun., Glenbrook Hospital, Glenview, IL '86 (ENG)
SIMMONS, EMILY B., dir. soc. work, Wilson Memorial Hospital, Wilson, NC '72 (SOC)
SIMMONS, FATIE G., adm. dir. vol. serv., Our Lady of Lake Regional Medical Center, Baton Rouge, LA '77 (VOL)
SIMMONS, FRANK L., dir. pers., Memorial Hospital, Colorado Springs, CO '86 (PERS)
SIMMONS, G. SCOTT, acct. exec., Hpn, Inc., Fort Wayne, IN '87 (PR)
SIMMONS, GERALD P., dir. matl. mgt., Grace Hospital, Detroit, MI '81 (PUR)(CS)
SIMMONS, HELEN, supv. cent. sup., Albion Community Hospital, Albion, MI '69 (CS)
SIMMONS, J. BRYAN, asst. vice-pres. plng., Waterbury Hospital, Waterbury, CT '85 (PLNG)
SIMMONS, JACQUELINE E., assoc. dir. soc. serv., Georgetown University Medical Center, Washington, DC '86 (SOC)
SIMMONS, JANICE, asst. vice-pres. mktg. and pub. rel., Pontiac General Hospital, Pontiac, MI '86 (PR)
SIMMONS, JEAN D., dir. pers., Memorial Hospital, North Conway, NH '86 (PERS)
SIMMONS, JOHN C., dir. soc. work, Vanderbilt University Hospital, Nashville, TN '72 (SOC)
SIMMONS, JOSEPH M., dir. matl. mgt., Wentzville Community Hospital, Wentzville, MO '86 (PUR)
SIMMONS, JUDITH A., dir. vol. serv., Carolina Eye Associates, Southern Pines, NC '87 (VOL)
SIMMONS, JUDY D., dir. pub. rel., Val Verde Memorial Hospital, Del Rio, TX '85 (PR)
SIMMONS, JUNE P., RN, dir. nrsg. serv., Southside Regional Medical Center, Petersburg, VA '83 (NURS)
SIMMONS, MORRIS, dir. biomedical eng., St. Bernard's Regional Medical Center, Jonesboro, AR '83 (ENG)
SIMMONS, PATRICIA, vice-pres. qual. mgt. serv., Forsyth Memorial Hospital, Winston-Salem, NC '86 (RISK)
SIMMONS, PAUL M., mgt. eng., Cleveland Clinic Hospital, Cleveland, OH '77 (MGMT)
SIMMONS, RICHARD J., atty., National Medical Enterprises, Los Angeles, CA '84 (ATTY)
SIMMONS, ROBERT R., mgr. food serv., Baptist Memorial Hospital, Memphis, TN '87 (FOOD)
SIMMONS, SHARON, asst. to vice-pres. rehab. serv., Iowa Methodist Medical Center, Des Moines, IA '83
SIMMONS, STEVEN R., vice-pres. human res., Winter Park Memorial Hospital, Winter Park, FL '86 (PERS)
SIMMONS, SUZANNE E., adm. asst., Health Care Plan, Inc., West Seneca, NY '85 (PAT)
SIMMONS, VICKIE, cent. serv. tech., St. Anthony Hospital, Michigan City, IN '86 (CS)
SIMMONS, W. JUNE, dir. pat. care serv., Huntington Memorial Hospital, Pasadena, CA '72 (SOC)
SIMMONS, WINONA T., adm. asst., Lewistown Hospital, Lewistown, PA '83 (ENG)
SIMMS, ALLEN B., coor. safety, Ohio Valley Medical Center, Wheeling, WV '84 (ENG)
SIMMS, CATHERINE W., dir. pers., Fish Memorial Hospital at DeLand, De Land, FL '82 (PERS)
SIMMS, FULTON, adm. asst., The Methodist Hospital, Houston, TX '81 (ENG)
SIMMS, JANETTE, dir. plng., Winthrop-University Hospital, Mineola, NY '86 (PLNG)
SIMMS, LILLIAN M., RN, assoc. dir. nrsg., University of Michigan Hospitals, Ann Arbor, MI '81 (NURS)
SIMMS, MILDRED, mgr. cent. proc., Booth Memorial Medical Center, Flushing, NY '82 (CS)
SIMMS, SUSAN F., RN, vice-pres., Arlington Hospital, Arlington, VA '70 (NURS)
SIMMS, THERESA, mgr. cont. educ., Humana Inc., Louisville, KY '71 (EDUC)
SIMON, DEBORAH R., RN, sr. dir. nrsg., Methodist Medical Center of Illinois, Peoria, IL '81 (NURS)
SIMON, ELLEN PERLMAN, dir. soc. serv., Beth Abraham Hospital, Bronx, NY '82 (SOC)
SIMON, ELLIOT J., assoc. adm., Astoria General Hospital, Long Island City, NY '62 (PLNG)
SIMON, ESTHER, adm. food, Rockland Psychiatric Center, Orangeburg, NY '78 (FOOD)
SIMON, FRANCES B., mgr. media and publications, Tulane Medical Center, New Orleans, LA '86 (PR)
SIMON, HARVEY ALLEN, adm., Florence Nightingale Nursing Home, New York, NY '77
SIMON, JAMES K., pres., Triune Corporation, Gibbsboro, NJ '63
SIMON, JAMES LEO, atty., Ravenswood Hospital Medical Center, Chicago, IL '79 (ATTY)
SIMON, JANET W., asst. dir. food serv., Mease Health Care, Dunedin, FL '82 (FOOD)
SIMON, LINDA A., dir. mktg. and plng., Franciscan Sisters Health Care Corporation, Mokena, IL '76 (PLNG)
SIMON, LINDA L., exec. dir. support serv., St. Joseph Hospital, Orange, CA '82 (PUR)
SIMON, MARION E., dir. spec. serv., Michael Reese Hospital and Medical Center, Chicago, IL '74 (PAT)
SIMON, MYRTLE H., dir. vol., Harlem Hospital Center, New York, NY '73 (VOL)
SIMON, OTTO J., RN, dir. nrsg. serv. and asst. adm., Foster G. McGaw Hospital, Loyola University, Maywood, IL '72 (NURS)
SIMON, ROSALYN W., dir. soc. serv., Coral Springs Medical Center, Coral Springs, FL '76 (SOC)
SIMON, SHARRON L., RN, unit dir. emer. serv., Porter Memorial Hospital, Valparaiso, IN '87 (AMB)
SIMONDS, WARREN W., vice-pres., Pitts Management Associates, Inc., Baton Rouge, LA '83
SIMONETTI, GERALDINE, RN, dir. nrsg., Clearfield Hospital, Clearfield, PA '87 (NURS)
SIMONIAN, ALICE, RN, mgr. cent. sup. and matl., Valley Medical Center of Fresno, Fresno, CA '86 (PUR)
SIMONIAN, DEBRA LYN, dir. diet. serv., Valley Children's Hospital, Fresno, CA '84 (FOOD)
SIMONICH, DEAN M., dir. market plng., Los Medanos Community Hospital, Pittsburg, CA '81 (PLNG)
SIMONIS, IRIS C., RN, asst. adm. nrsg., Woman's Hospital of Texas, Houston, TX '86 (NURS)
SIMONS, ARCHIE JR., vice-pres. health serv., Vista Health Plan, Inc., King of Prussia, PA '85
SIMONS, BARBARA J., RN, assoc. adm., Richland Memorial Hospital, Columbia, SC '86 (NURS)
SIMONS, BETTY J., dir. pers., Lakeview Hospital, Bountiful, UT '82 (PERS)
SIMONS, CALVIN, MD, dir. amb. care and commun. medicine, Bronx-Lebanon Hospital Center, Bronx, NY '87 (AMB)
SIMONS, GEORGE N., plant eng., Rockville General Hospital, Rockville, CT '83 (ENG)
SIMONS, JOANNE E., RN, instr. staff dev., Elliot Hospital, Manchester, NH '85 (EDUC)
SIMONSON, DONALD W., dir. plng. and mktg., Community Healthcare Network, Marion, OH '84 (PR) (PLNG)
SIMONSON, PATRICK, asst. to adm., National Rehabilitation Hospital, Washington, DC '84
SIMONSON, PAUL C., dir. pers., Trinity Medical Center, Minot, ND '79 (PERS)
SIMONSON, SUSAN K., dir. soc. serv., Yakima Valley Memorial Hospital, Yakima, WA '82 (SOC)
SIMPSON, BERYL, consult. health care, New York City Health and Hospitals Corporation, New York, NY '74 (CS)
SIMPSON, CALBRIETH L., assoc. exec. dir., D. C. Hospital Association, Washington, DC '82
SIMPSON, CHARLENE L., dir. vol. serv., St. Mark's Hospital, Salt Lake City, UT '83 (VOL)
SIMPSON, DAVID H., dir. soc. work serv., Moss Rehabilitation Hospital, Philadelphia, PA '68 (SOC)
SIMPSON, DELPHINE M., dir. environ. serv., Oakwood Hospital, Dearborn, MI '86 (ENVIRON)
SIMPSON, DONALD K., dir. adm. serv., Navden Clinic, FPO Miami, FL '84
SIMPSON, DOUGLAS, gen. mgr., Productivity Development Systems, Memphis, TN '76 (EDUC)
SIMPSON, GEORGE WHITMORE, adm., Stringfellow Memorial Hospital, Anniston, AL '70
SIMPSON, MAJ. GLENN C., MSC USA, Winn Army Community Hospital, Fort Stewart, GA '83
SIMPSON, GLENN, risk mgr., Shriners Hospital for Crippled Children, Tampa, FL '86 (RISK)
SIMPSON, HAROLD H. II, atty., Baptist Medical Center, Little Rock, AR '76 (ATTY)
SIMPSON, CAPT. JACK RAYMOND, USAF MSC, Medical College of Virginia, School of Health Administration, Richmond, VA '85
SIMPSON, KARIN L., div. mgr., Muhlenberg Regional Medical Center, Plainfield, NJ '77
SIMPSON, LETRELL, corp. vice-pres. mktg., Northeast Georgia Medical Center, Gainesville, GA '72 (PR) (PLNG)
SIMPSON, MARK A., dir. risk mgt., Harriman City Hospital, Harriman, TN '84 (ENG)(RISK)
SIMPSON, MARY J., RN, dir. clin. nrsg., St. Mary's Medical Center, Evansville, IN '82 (NURS)
SIMPSON, MICHAEL, dir. soc. serv., Glendale Adventist Medical Center, Glendale, CA '77 (SOC)
SIMPSON, NANCY A., coor. pat. educ., Mississauga Hospital, Mississauga, Ont., Canada '84 (EDUC)
SIMPSON, NED J., sr. mgr., Peat, Marwick, Mitchell and Company, New York, NY '77 (MGMT)
SIMPSON, PATRICIA M., RN, dir. spec. serv., Park City Hospital, Bridgeport, CT '85 (NURS)
SIMPSON, ROBERT A., asst. vice-pres. matl. mgt., Neponset Valley Health System, Norwood, MA '85 (PUR)
SIMPSON, ROBERT G., atty., Good Samaritan Hospital and Medical Center, Portland, OR '68 (ATTY)
SIMPSON, ROGER A., dir. pers., Union Memorial Hospital, Monroe, NC '82 (PERS)
SIMPSON, RONALD E., dir. pers., Friends Hospital, Philadelphia, PA '73 (PERS)
SIMPSON, ROY L., RN, dir. info. syst., Hospital Corporation of America, Nashville, TN '81 (NURS)
SIMPSON, SANDRA K., dir. mktg., Charter Hospital of Sugarland, Sugarland, TX '84 (PR)
SIMPSON, VANCE, dir. plant oper., Mercy Medical Center, Durango, CO '85 (ENG)
SIMPSON, WILLIAM C. JR., coor. matl. syst., Gulfstream Aerospace Corporation, Savannah, GA '83 (MGMT)
SIMPSON, WILLIAM R., asst. dir. plant serv., Glendale Adventist Medical Center, Glendale, CA '85 (ENG)
SIMS, CHRISTOPHER D., dir. plng. and bus. dev., Baptist Hospital of Miami, Miami, FL '82 (PR) (PLNG)
SIMS, E. ALLEN, dir. mgt. eng., Saginaw General Hospital, Saginaw, MI '70 (MGMT)
SIMS, EVERETT, dir. phys. plant oper., King's Daughters Hospital, Greenville, MS '85 (ENG)
SIMS, HOWELL L., asst. chief eng., Lloyd Noland Hospital and Health Centers, Birmingham, AL '80 (ENG)
SIMS, JANET H., coor. vol., Cross Cancer Institute, Edmonton, Alta., Canada '86 (VOL)
SIMS, JOE, atty., Hospital Corporation of America, Nashville, TN '83 (ATTY)
SIMS, L. M., dir. educ. serv., Medical Center East, Birmingham, AL '83 (EDUC)
SIMS, LINDA C., dir. mktg. proj., ARA Services, Atlanta, GA '84 (FOOD)
SIMS, LINDA KAY, RN, assoc. dir. nrsg. serv., Ochsner Foundation Hospital, New Orleans, LA '80 (NURS)
SIMS, MARION A., dir. diet., Sarasota Memorial Hospital, Sarasota, FL '83 (FOOD)
SIMS, ROSALIND R., supv. soc. serv., Baystate Medical Center, Springfield, MA '84 (SOC)
SIMS, STANLEY LAWRENCE, (ret.), La Crosse, WI '37 (LIFE)
SIMS, THOMAS D., asst. vice-pres. strategic plng. and mktg., Hospital Corporation of America, Nashville, TN '78 (PLNG)
SIMS, WINIFRED T., dir. food serv., Sun Belt Regional Medical Center, Houston, TX '69 (FOOD)
SIMSON, MARY TURK, vice-pres., Colex Weber, Los Angeles, CA '82 (PR)
SINAON, FELINA S., RN, dir. nrsg., Hall-Brooke Hospital, Westport, CT '86 (NURS)
SINCLAIR, ROBERT, dir. risk and ins. mgt., Vanderbilt University Hospital, Nashville, TN '83 (RISK)
SINCLAIR, SARAH E., RN, dir. nrsg. serv., Memorial Hospital at Easton Maryland, Easton, MD '83 (NURS)
SINCLAIR, T. J., atty., Saint Francis Hospital, Tulsa, OK '69 (ATTY)
SINDELAR, FRANK C., asst. dir. matl. mgt., Plantation General Hospital, Plantation, FL '83 (PUR)
SINDONI, JOHN E., dir. pers. mgt. and emp. rel., Jersey Shore Medical Center, Neptune, NJ '80 (PERS)
SINE, DAVID M., pres., David M. Sine and Associates, Essex, CT '86 (ENG)
SINGER, ALISON, mgr. soc. serv., Little Company of Mary Hospital, Torrance, CA '85 (SOC)
SINGER, CHARLES, mktg. consult., Gerber Alley and Company, Norcross, GA '86
SINGER, GARY, dir. hosp. affairs, Maryland Medical Laboratory, Inc., Baltimore, MD '85
SINGER, KARY ANN, vice-pres. pat. serv., Oklahoma Osteopathic Hospital, Tulsa, OK '83 (NURS)
SINGER, STEPHANIE A., asst. mgr. food serv., Dominican Santa Cruz Hospital, Santa Cruz, CA '80 (FOOD)
SINGER, THERESA B., RN, dir. home care, St. Barnabas Medical Center, Livingston, NJ '87 (AMB)
SINGH, MANILLA R., RN, Long Beach, CA '84 (NURS)
SINGH, PRAMILA, RN, asst. adm., Burnham Hospital, Champaign, IL '80 (NURS)
SINGLETON, BARRY W., MD, chief oper. off., Charity Hospital at New Orleans, New Orleans, LA '86 (PERS)
SINGLETON, COLLEEN TAEKO, dir. matl. mgt., Castle Medical Center, Kailua, HI '85 (RISK)(PAT)(PUR)
SINGLETON, EWELL D., adm., Citizens Medical Center, Columbia, LA '83
SINGLETON, J. VERNE, assoc. dir., University Medical Center, Tucson, AZ '78 (MGMT)
SINGLEY, MARSHA B., mgr. telecommun. proj., Hospital Communications Consultants, Nashville, TN '85 (ENG)
SINIORIS, MARIE E., spec. consult. president's off., Rush-Presbyterian-St. Luke's Medical Center, Chicago, IL '77 (PLNG)
SINK, JULIE J., media spec. mktg., Kettering Medical Center, Kettering, OH '82 (PR)
SINKEVICH, DORIS A., RN, dir. nrsg., Quincy City Hospital, Quincy, MA '83 (NURS)
SINKO, JEANNIE B., dir. cent. sterile, Humana Hospital -Augusta, Augusta, GA '82 (CS)
SINNI, RICHARD J., asst. dir., Bellevue Hospital Center, New York, NY '76
SINNOTT, LYNN A., vice-pres., Copley Memorial Hospital, Aurora, IL '81 (PLNG)
SINNOTT, MARGARET A., RN, asst. dir. nrsg.-spec. proj., Mercy Catholic Medical Center, Darby, PA '86 (NURS)
SINNWELL, LINDA E., mgr. soc. work cont. care, St. Luke's Medical Center, Phoenix, AZ '86 (SOC)
SINTIC, DONALD P., RN, mgr. cent. sup., Geauga Hospital, Chardon, OH '82 (CS)
SINYKIN, GORDON, atty., Methodist Hospital, Madison, WI '82 (ATTY)
SIPARI, ORAZIO, atty., Richmond Heights General Hospital, Cleveland, OH '84 (ATTY)
SIPARI, SANDRA A., dir. human res. serv., North Broward Hospital District, Fort Lauderdale, FL '86 (PERS)
SIPE, CAROL J., supv. sup., proc. and distrib., Lewistown Hospital, Lewistown, PA '82 (CS)
SIPP, RICHARD C., sr. asst. dir., Medical College of Ohio Hospital, Toledo, OH '85 (PLNG)
SIPPEL, PHYLLIS M., RN, dir. nrsg., Mease Health Care, Dunedin, FL '83 (NURS)
SIPPEL, WILLIAM H. JR., pres., Deeter Ritchey Sippel Associates, Pittsburgh, PA '75
SIPPY, ROSE ANN Q., dir. diet., University of Iowa Hospitals and Clinics, Iowa City, IA '82 (FOOD)
SIRL, WILLIAM R., vice-pres., St. Joseph Hospital, Flint, MI '68
SIRMANS, TRACY L., student, Georgia State University-Institute of Health Administration, Atlanta, GA '86 (PR)
SIRNEY, ROBERT A., dir. maint. and eng., North Hills Passavant Hospital, Pittsburgh, PA '85 (ENG)
SIROIS, JEROME W., dir. food serv., Sacred Heart Hospital, Norristown, PA '82 (FOOD)
SIROTT, JACK, atty., Lower Bucks Hospital, Bristol, PA '82 (ATTY)
SISEMORE, ROXIE, RN, vice-pres. pat. serv., St. Mary Medical Center, Walla Walla, WA '80 (NURS)
SISK, CATHERINE, mgr. cent. serv. and stores, Children's Hospital and Medical Center, Seattle, WA '86 (CS)
SISK, TERRY STEINER, dir., Metropolitan Hospital, Philadelphia, PA '86 (PR)
SISSELMAN, JEFFREY P., assoc. dir., Coler Memorial Hospital, New York, NY '86 (PLNG)
SISSELMAN, MILTON H., vice-pres. prof. serv., Mount Sinai Medical Center, New York, NY '52 (LIFE)
SISSON, FRAN, RN, dir. nrsg.-acute care, Children's Hospital and Medical Center, Seattle, WA '85 (NURS)
SISTY, JOHN R., chief eng. serv., Veterans Administration Medical Center, Augusta, GA '82 (ENG)
SITES, RICHARD L., dir. risk mgt. and environ. serv., Ohio Hospital Association, Columbus, OH '86 (RISK)
SITES, SARAH K., dir. diet. serv., Ephrata Community Hospital, Ephrata, PA '84 (FOOD)
SITES, WILLIAM G., dir. internal audits, Temple University, Philadelphia, PA '71 (MGMT)

SITKIN, RUTH, dir. vol., Louis A. Weiss Memorial Hospital, Chicago, IL '73 (VOL)

SITRON, HOWARD S., dir. vol. serv., Moss Rehabilitation Hospital, Philadelphia, PA '84 (VOL)

SITTA, SALLY, dir. vol., Naples Community Hospital, Naples, FL '73 (VOL)

SITTASON, KAREN CURRY, dir. educ. serv., St. Francis-St. George Hospital, Cincinnati, OH '79 (EDUC)

SITTERLEY, HAROLD C. JR., mgr. matl., Lee Hospital, Johnstown, PA '81 (PUR)

SITTERLY, TONI S., dir. plng., Thunderbird Samaritan Hospital, Glendale, AZ '82 (PLNG)

SITTERSON, T. B., vice-pres. med. affairs, Pitt County Memorial Hospital, Greenville, NC '80 (RISK)

SITTIG, WILLIAM R. JR., atty., South Side Hospital of Pittsburgh, Pittsburgh, PA '85 (ATTY)

SIVELLY, EDWARD L., adm., Wilkes-Barre General Hospital, Wilkes-Barre, PA '83 (MGMT)

SIVERLY, ANITA J., dir. food and nutr. care, Memorial Hospital Medical Center of Long Beach, Long Beach, CA '80 (FOOD)

SIVERSON, NEIL W., dir. environ. serv., Canby Community Hospital District One, Canby, MN '84 (ENG)(ENVIRON)

SIVILS, CASIE, dir. mktg., Swope Ridge Rehabilitation Hospital, Kansas City, MO '86 (PR)

SIX, ALBERTENA, (ret.), Venice, CA '27 (LIFE)

SIXTA, CONSTANCE S., RN, dir. nrsg., Methodist Hospital, Omaha, NE '85 (NURS)

SIZEMORE, BARBARA A., pat. rep., Careunit Hospital of Cincinnati, Cincinnati, OH '86 (PAT)

SIZEMORE, HELEN, dir. vol., Reid Memorial Hospital, Richmond, IN '73 (VOL)

SJOBERG, DAVID W., vice-pres. plng., Baptist Hospital, Pensacola, FL '80 (PLNG)

SJOBERG, MARYELLEN K., dir. nutr. serv., Harding Hospital, Worthington, OH '80 (FOOD)

SKAGGS, BARBARA WELCH, atty., Harper-Grace Hospitals, Detroit, MI '86 (ATTY)

SKAGGS, LIONEL C., asst. vice-pres. pers. adm., University of Alabama in Birmingham, Birmingham, AL '73 (PERS)

SKAGGS, RONALD L., exec. vice-pres., Harwood K. Smith and Partners, Dallas, TX '73

SKALA, ROGER D., dir. matl. mgt., Bryan Memorial Hospital, Lincoln, NE '72 (PUR)

SKALKA, SUSAN B., dir. nutr. serv., West Boca Medical Center, Boca Raton, FL '80 (FOOD)

SKALLA, ANGELA R., RN, assoc. dir. nrsg., MacNeal Hospital, Berwyn, IL '82 (NURS)

SKANE, SR. JAMES, vice-pres. adm. support serv., Columbus Hospital, Chicago, IL '74

SKANTZ, RONALD J., Adventist Health System-Sunbelt Health Care Corporation, Orlando, FL '82 (PLNG)

SKAPURA, CHRISTOPHER, mgt. eng., Mediflex Systems Corporation, Akron, OH '84 (MGMT)

SKARUPA, JACK A., pres., Greenville Hospital System, Greenville, SC '54 (PLNG)(LIFE)

SKARZYNSKI, PETER C., student, Graduate Program in School of Business, University of Chicago, Chicago, IL '85

SKARZYNSKI, RONALD W., vice-pres. fin., Little Company of Mary Hospital, Evergreen Park, IL '86

SKARZYNSKI, SUSAN M., student, DePaul University, School of Business, Chicago, IL '86

SKEAN, DAVID L., dir. plant oper. and maint., Perry Memorial Hospital, Princeton, IL '80 (ENG)

SKELTON, MARILYN BROCK, pres., Brock Skelton Consulting, Glendale, CA '85

SKENES, ROBERT E., PhD, dir. human res. dev., Alexandria Hospital, Alexandria, VA '87 (EDUC)

SKERMONT, JAMIE M., supv. clin. eng., South Chicago Community Hospital, Chicago, IL '85 (ENG)

SKERTIC, JAMES E., dir. matl. mgt., St. Vincent Medical Center, Toledo, OH '77 (PUR)

SKIBICKI, VERONICA L., asst. dir. info. syst., Hamot Medical Center, Erie, PA '85 (MGMT)

SKIBINSKI, JOHN, McLean, VA '85

SKIDMORE, CYNTHIA A., student, Georgia State University-Institute of Health Administration, Atlanta, GA '82

SKIDMORE, GERALD E., dir. ldry. and linen, Florida Hospital, Forest City, FL '86 (ENVIRON)

SKIDMORE, LINDA D., dir. vol., Hotel Dieu Hospital, New Orleans, LA '83 (VOL)

SKIDMORE, MARY ANN, dir. soc. serv., Charter Peachford Hospital, Atlanta, GA '85 (SOC)

SKILES, PETER H., dir. plng., Blodgett Memorial Medical Center, Grand Rapids, MI '83 (PLNG)

SKILLIN, JUDITH F., dir. vol. serv., Children's Hospital, Richmond, VA '85 (VOL)

SKILLINGS, IRMA L., RN, dir. nrsg. serv., Annie Penn Memorial Hospital, Reidsville, NC '78 (NURS)

SKILLMAN, SALLY, dir. pers., Shriners Hospital for Crippled Children, Shriners Burns Institute Cincinnati, Cincinnati, OH '85 (PERS)

SKINNER, CHERYL, pres. and chief exec. off., Vns Health Services, Inc., Santa Fe, NM '87 (AMB)

SKINNER, ERNESTINE, assoc. dir. diet., North Shore University Hospital, Manhasset, NY '85 (FOOD)

SKINNER, EVAN REICHLIN, Allentown, PA '77 (PERS)

SKINNER, JANE E., mktg. spec., Blue Cross and Blue Shield of Indiana, Indianapolis, IN '86 (PR)

SKINNER, JOHN A., asst. exec. dir., Soldiers and Sailors Memorial Hospital, Wellsboro, PA '78

SKINNER, WESLEY H., dir. pers., Central Michigan Community Hospital, Mount Pleasant, MI '81 (PERS)

SKIPPER, LEN, coor. cent. sup. and equip., Baptist Medical Center-Princeton, Birmingham, AL '84 (CS)

SKIPPER, P. K., dir. plng. and mktg., Midland Memorial Hospital, Midland, TX '85 (PLNG)

SKLAR-JACKSON, ISABEL, assoc. dir. soc. work, Beth Israel Medical Center, New York, NY '85 (SOC)

SKLOOT, RICHARD R., student, Iowa State University, Ames, IA '86 (MGMT)

SKOCIR, MARGARET A., RN, dir. nrsg. critical care and med., St. Michael Hospital, Milwaukee, WI '83 (NURS)

SKODACK, NANCY K., dir. food and nutr. serv., Humana Hospital -Medical City Dallas, Dallas, TX '85 (FOOD)

SKODRAS, DAN P., partner, Crowe, Chizek and Company, South Bend, IN '87 (MGMT)

SKOGEN, LEANNA I., RN, supv. health occup., Aurora Public Schools Tech Center, Aurora, CO '81 (EDUC)

SKOGLUND, CARLA, RN, dir. oper. serv., Muskegon General Hospital, Muskegon, MI '87 (AMB)

SKOGLUND, ROBERT W., supt. constr., Oklahoma Osteopathic Hospital, Tulsa, OK '85 (ENG)

SKOGSBERGH, JAMES H., vice-pres., Memorial Health System, South Bend, IN '82

SKOGSBERGH, NANCY J., RN, assoc. dir. pat. care serv., St. Luke's Methodist Hospital, Cedar Rapids, IA '87 (NURS)

SKOLER, MARTIN E., atty., Wesson Memorial Hospital, Springfield, MA '69 (ATTY)

SKOLLAR, THEODORO M., dir. vol. serv., Amsterdam House, New York, NY '86 (VOL)

SKOLNICK, FRANCES M., student, University of Chicago, Chicago, IL '87

SKOLNICK, SUZANNE, risk mgr. and coor. qual. assur., Glover Memorial Hospital, Needham, MA '86 (RISK)

SKOLROOD, ROBERT K., atty., City of Faith Hospital, Tulsa, OK '82 (ATTY)

SKOMASA, JOHN W., dir. facil. mgt., Alexian Brothers Medical Center, Elk Grove Village, IL '73 (ENG)

SKORCZ, STEPHEN, pres., Capital Area Health Consortium, Newington, CT '85

SKORCZESKI, THOMAS L., St. Paul, MN '77

SKOWLUND, KATHLEEN R., RN, vice-pres. nrsg., Milwaukee Psychiatric Hospital, Milwaukee, WI '83 (NURS)

SKRADZINSKI, MARIE, asst. dir. pur., Riddle Memorial Hospital, Media, PA '75 (PUR)

SKRAJEWSKI, DENNIS J., mgr. clin. res. util., Charlton Memorial Hospital, Fall River, MA '85 (RISK)

SKRETNY, HAROLD, dir. pur., Louis A. Weiss Memorial Hospital, Chicago, IL '77 (PUR)

SKRETVEDT, CLAYTON L., dir. soc. serv., St. Cloud Hospital, St. Cloud, MN '74 (SOC)

SKRIDULIS, EILEEN A., pat. rep., South Suburban Hospital, Hazel Crest, IL '72 (PAT)

SKROS, EDWARD S., adm. res., Frankford Hospital of the City of Philadelphia, Philadelphia, PA '84

SKRUBER, BARBARA, asst. dir. and pat. serv., Cedars Medical Center, Miami, FL '86

SKVERSKY, ARLEEN I., supv. soc. serv., Taylor Hospital, Ridley Park, PA '81 (SOC)

SKYBERG, DONNA M., dir. pers., Jamestown Hospital, Jamestown, ND '85 (PERS)

SLABODNICK, DAVID D., asst. adm., Elyria Memorial Hospital, Elyria, OH '76

SLABY, ANDREW EDMUND, MD PhD, med. dir., Fair Oaks Hospital, Summit, NJ '79

SLACK, CHRISTINE B., RN, supv. cent. serv. and clin., Atascadero State Hospital, Atascadero, CA '85 (CS)

SLACK, GARY D., mgr., Medical Instrumentation Systems-Hospital Shared Engineering Services, Inc., Springfield, OH '79 (ENG)

SLACK, MINDY N., dir. vol. serv. and pat. rel., Mercy Hospital, Urbana, IL '84 (VOL)(PAT)

SLACK, RICHARD S., mgr., Coopers and Lybrand, Minneapolis, MN '80 (PLNG)

SLADE, LOREN D., vice-pres., Des Moines General Hospital, Des Moines, IA '80 (PLNG)

SLADE, MARILYN R., mgr. pat. rel., Hillcrest Hospital, Mayfield Heights, OH '86 (PAT)

SLADEK, JUDY, assoc. adm. pat. serv., Kino Community Hospital, Tucson, AZ '87 (AMB)

SLAGLE, THOMAS F., mgr. pur. and matl., West Georgia Medical Center, La Grange, GA '82 (PUR)

SLARSKY, SANDRA L., dir. mktg., Walthamweston Hospital and Medical Center, Waltham, MA '84 (PR) (PLNG)

SLATE, ALICE JEAN, dir. pat. rel., Sinai Hospital of Detroit, Detroit, MI '73 (PAT)

SLATER, AUDREY S., RN, vice-pres. nrsg., Lancaster General Hospital, Lancaster, PA '85 (NURS)

SLATER, DEVONA J., bus. mgr., Alm, Inc., Leawood, KS '87 (AMB)

SLATER, DOROTHEA L., dir. diet. serv., Columbia Hospital for Women, Washington, DC '79 (FOOD)

SLATER, JULIE, coor. curriculum, Pontiac General Hospital, Pontiac, MI '86

SLATER, RANDALL R., Kaiser Foundation Health Plan, Denver, CO '81 (MGMT)

SLATER, SANDI I., dir. qual. assur., Corning Hospital, Corning, NY '84 (RISK)

SLATER, THOMAS M., Seattle, WA '85 (ENG)

SLATTEN, BETTYANN, dir. vol., Children's Hospital, St. Louis, MO '80 (VOL)

SLAUBAUGH, D. RAY, sr. vice-pres., Graham Hospital, Canton, IL '80 (PR)

SLAUGHTER, CHERYL A., client serv. rep., Commission on Professional and Hospital Activities, Ann Arbor, MI '86 (PLNG)

SLAVEN, TERRENCE M., atty., Good Samaritan Medical Center, Phoenix, AZ '78 (ATTY)

SLAVIC, BEVERLY J., dir. med. mktg., Graduate Hospital, Philadelphia, PA '85 (PLNG)

SLAVIK, LEONARD C., head diet., Bay Medical Center, Bay City, MI '73 (FOOD)

SLAVIK, NELSON S., asst. prof., University of Illinois, Champaign, IL '84 (ENG)

SLAVIN, JOSEPH F., vice-pres. plng., New Jersey Hospital Association, Princeton, NJ '81 (PLNG)

SLAVIN, LARRY, coor. accounts receivable, Memorial Hospital for Cancer and Allied Diseases, New York, NY '80

SLAYBAUGH, MELANIE L., dir. soc. serv., Johnston-Willis Hospital, Richmond, VA '86 (SOC)

SLAYMAKER, DENNIS, dir. plant oper., Spencer Municipal Hospital, Spencer, IA '78 (ENG)

SLAYMAKER, DOUGLAS G., dir. soc. serv., Pascack Valley Hospital, Westwood, NJ '78 (SOC)

SLAYTON, PATRICIA L., dir. mktg. res., Pacific Presbyterian Medical Center, San Francisco, CA '86 (PLNG)

SLAYTON, SASHA E., dir. staff dev., Kennewick General Hospital, Kennewick, WA '84 (EDUC)

SLECHTA, RICHARD C., St. James Hospital Medical Center, Chicago Heights, IL '83 (PLNG)

SLEDGE, ALINDA, dir. soc. serv., Bolivar County Hospital, Cleveland, MS '80 (SOC)

SLEDGE, JANET R., adm. urology, Montefiore Medical Center, Bronx, NY '76

SLEDGE, JOE W. JR., dir. hosp. facil. standards, University of Alabama Hospitals, Birmingham, AL '84 (ENG)

SLEE, VERGIL, MD, pres., Slee and Associates, Brevard, NC '56 (LIFE)

SLEEKER, SHIRLEY S., RN, clin. dir. nrsg., Saint Joseph Health Center Kansas, Kansas City, MO '86 (NURS)

SLEETH, JACQUIE, supv. cent. serv. and infection control, Kennewick General Hospital, Kennewick, WA '83 (CS)

SLEIGHT, GREGORY R., dir. plant serv., St. Joseph's Hospital, Chippewa Falls, WI '82 (ENG)

SLEIGHT, ROBERT E., (ret.), Sun City, AZ '51 (LIFE)

SLEPIAN, FLORENCE W., dir. soc. serv., Brigham and Women's Hospital, Boston, MA '77 (SOC)

SLEVIN, ROSEMARIE A., coor. pat. educ., Memorial Hospital for Cancer and Allied Diseases, New York, NY '85 (EDUC)

SLEWITZKE, COL. CONNIE L., RN, chief nrs. corps., Department of the Army, Office of the Surgeon General, Washington, DC '79 (NURS)

SLIPIEC, STEWART W., dir. mgt. eng., St. Joseph Hospitals, Mount Clemens, MI '85 (MGMT)

SLIWINSKI, EDWARD F., dir. pers., Eastern Long Island Hospital, Greenport, NY '86 (PERS)

SLIWINSKI, RONALD T., asst. adm., Mary Hitchcock Memorial Hospital, Hanover, NH '83 (MGMT)

SLOAN, CATHERINE, asst. dir. nrs., Riverside General Hospital, Secaucus, NJ '86 (NURS)

SLOAN, CHRISTIE J., dir. pers., Tallahassee Memorial Regional Medical Center, Tallahassee, FL '86 (PERS)

SLOAN, CYRUS T. III, atty., Marion Memorial Hospital, Marion, SC '85 (ATTY)

SLOAN, ELIZABETH J., mgr. pub. rel., Health Northeast, Manchester, NH '82 (PR)

SLOAN, JEANNE A., dir. educ. serv., Martin Memorial Hospital, Stuart, FL '80 (EDUC)

SLOAN, JERRY W., vice-pres., Mary Greeley Medical Center, Ames, IA '85

SLOAN, JOSEPH F., adm., Decatur Community Hospital, Decatur, TX '80

SLOAN, JUDITH B., dir. pub. rel., Brawner Psychiatric Institute, Smyrna, GA '85 (PR)

SLOAN, RAYMOND P., assoc. prof., Columbia University School of Public Health and Administrative Medicine, New York, NY '33 (HON)

SLOANE, DEAN L., pres., C. P. Rehabilitation Corporation, New York, NY '80

SLOANE, ROBERT M., chief exec. off., Anaheim Memorial Hospital, Anaheim, CA '61

SLOANE, TATYANA P., dir. soc. serv., Whidden Memorial Hospital, Everett, MA '87 (SOC)

SLOAT, MARCIA L., asst. adm. and dir. human res. serv., Yonkers General Hospital, Yonkers, NY '83 (PERS)

SLOATE, STEVEN G., dir. plng., Shands Hospital, Gainesville, FL '83 (PLNG)

SLOBODA, MARY A., asst. vice-pres. matl. mgt., Overlook Hospital, Summit, NJ '82 (PUR)

SLOBODA, WALTER J., dir. pers., Frisbie Memorial Hospital, Rochester, NH '75 (PERS)

SLOCUM, BRIAN D., mgr., Medical Management, Inc., Seattle, WA '80 (AMB)

SLOHM, NATALIE F., dir. pub. rel., Mary McClellan Hospital, Cambridge, NY '87 (PR)

SLONE, EMMALY, supv. sup., proc. and distrib., Johnson City Medical Center Hospital, Johnson City, TN '83 (CS)

SLONECKER, MICHAEL, vice-pres., Mercy Hospital, Owensboro, KY '87 (AMB)

SLOTTER, JAMES ROLLIN, sr. market analyst, General Health Management, Inc., East Hartford, CT '79 (PLNG)

SLOTTOW, RICHARD, dir. commun. rel., mktg. and dev., St. Francis Memorial Hospital, San Francisco, CA '86 (PR)

SLOWEY, THOMAS W., pres., K. and S. Associates, Inc., Nashville, TN '82 (ENG)

SLOWN, E. DON, div. mgr. environ. serv., Marcus J. Lawrence Memorial Hospital, Cottonwood, AZ '75 (ENG)

SLUBOWSKI, MICHAEL A., vice-pres. satellite and prepayment prog., Henry Ford Hospital, Detroit, MI '87 (AMB)

SLUYS, KATHY M., dir. vol. serv., Montana Deaconess Medical Center, Great Falls, MT '84 (VOL)

SLYE, WANDA B., dir. pers., Wichita General Hospital, Wichita Falls, TX '83 (PERS)

SLYMAN, COL. GEORGE L., MSC USA, dir. indust. oper., Walter Reed Army Medical Center, Washington, DC '70

SMAHA, JEANNE M., dir. amb. care, St. Joseph Hospital, Bangor, ME '87 (AMB)

SMALL, ALFONSO A., dir. pers., Portland Adventist Medical Center, Portland, OR '83 (PERS)

SMALL, ARTHUR H., Department of Surgery, Albany Medical College, Albany, NY '58

SMALL, CINDY L., dir. pub. rel., Carlisle Hospital, Carlisle, PA '85 (PR)

SMALL, KAREN E., supv. human res., Yavapai Regional Medical Center, Prescott, AZ '86 (PERS)

SMALL, LARRY A., dir. media resource, Memorial Medical Center, Springfield, IL '85 (EDUC)

SMALL, MARY L., dir. commun. and pub. rel., Abbott-Northwestern Hospital, Minneapolis, MN '82 (PR)

SMALL, MURRAY JOHNSON, sr. vice-pres., Coastal Emergency Service, Inc., Durham, NC '52 (LIFE)

SMALL, SANDRA K., dir. critical care, Baptist Medical Center, Little Rock, AR '85 (NURS)

SMALL, WILLIAM G., asst. vice-pres. adm. and risk mgt., Oakland University, Rochester, MI '77 (ATTY)

SMALLEY, HAROLD E., PhD, Georgia Institute of Technology, Program in Health Systems, Atlanta, GA '67 (MGMT)

SMALLEY, JOHN A., exec. dir., Lawrence County General Hospital, Ironton, OH '75

SMALLHORN, LT. JOHN P., MSC USN, adm. off., Naval Regional Medical Clinic, Annapolis, MD '80

SMALLWOOD, DOLORES M., mgr. cent. serv., Children's Hospital of Wisconsin, Milwaukee, WI '78 (CS)

SMALLWOOD, DONNA, asst. adm., Orthopedic Cente, Lake Worth, FL '87 (AMB)

SMALLWOOD, KAREN, health res. spec., Blue Cross and Blue Shield of Oklahoma, Tulsa, OK '87 (AMB)

SMEAL, ANGELINE J., RN, dir. nrsg. serv., Conemaugh Valley Memorial Hospital, Johnstown, PA '81 (NURS)

SMEDEROVAC, DAN D., coor. risk mgt. serv., St. Luke's Health System, Phoenix, AZ '80 (RISK)

SMEDSTAD, SARAH E., assoc. dir., University of Texas M. D. Anderson and Tumor Institute at Houston, Houston, TX '86 (FOOD)

SMEED, NICHOLAS, St. Louis, MO '84 (PERS)

SMELTER, RICHARD W., supv. sup., proc. and distrib., Community Memorial Hospital, Menomonee Falls, WI '83 (CS)

SMELTZER, CAROLYN H., EdD RN, sr. assoc. dir., University Medical Center, Tucson, AZ '84 (NURS)

SMELTZER, EARL T., supt. plant, Lock Haven Hospital and Extended Care Unit, Lock Haven, PA '71 (ENG)

SMETHERS, MARILYN J., dir. vol. serv., St. Francis Hospital Center, Beech Grove, IN '84 (VOL)

SMETTZ, ROY L., dir. environ. serv., Lewistown Hospital, Lewistown, PA '73 (ENG)

SMIALEK, ALFRED J., dir., Middlesex County Hospital, Waltham, MA '86

SMIALEK, SR. MARY LAETISSIMA, RN, pat. rep., St. Francis Hospital, Milwaukee, WI '79 (PAT)

SMIKAHL, WILLIAM E., adm., Fallbrook Hospital District, Fallbrook, CA '55 (LIFE)

SMILEY, CHARLES, mgt. eng., University Hospital, Augusta, GA '84

SMILEY, MICHAEL S., mgr. corp. commun., Western Reserve Care System, Youngstown, OH '80 (PR)

SMILEY, VIRGINIA S., dir. vol., Raleigh General Hospital, Beckley, WV '79 (VOL)

SMISKO, SUSAN, dir. commun. rel., Montclair Community Hospital, Montclair, NJ '85 (PR)

SMITH, ADRIENNE C., student, Georgia Institute of Technology, Atlanta, GA '84 (MGMT)

SMITH, ALEX W., atty., Southwest Hospital and Medical Center, Atlanta, GA '69 (ATTY)

SMITH, ALICE A., dir. cent. serv., Methodist Hospital, Sacramento, CA '85 (CS)

SMITH, AMY CAROL, dir. educ. serv., St. Mary-Rogers Memorial Hospital, Rogers, AR '85 (EDUC)

SMITH, ANITA A., dir. dev. and commun. rel., Little Falls Hospital, Little Falls, NY '81 (PR)

SMITH, ANITA T., dir. mktg., Smith County Memorial Hospital, Carthage, TN '81 (PR)

SMITH, ANN G., coor. qual. assur. and accreditation, University of Texas Medical Branch Hospitals, Galveston, TX '83 (RISK)

SMITH, ANN M., dir. pers., Beauregard Memorial Hospital, De Ridder, LA '82 (PERS)

SMITH, ANN PAULINE, RN, dir. nrsg. serv., HCA North Florida Regional Medical Center, Gainesville, FL '80 (NURS)

SMITH, ANNETTE H., dir. vol. serv., Cape Fear Valley Medical Center, Fayetteville, NC '84 (VOL)

SMITH, ARTHUR L., supv. cent. serv. and med. sup., Methodist Hospital, Hattiesburg, MS '85 (CS)

SMITH, ARTHUR R., adm., Smith Hospital, Hahira, GA '74 (MGMT)

SMITH, ASTRID W., dir. risk control, Methodist Health Systems, Inc., Memphis, TN '85 (RISK)

SMITH, B. JANE, mgr. cent. sup., St. Vincent Memorial Hospital, Taylorville, IL '70 (CS)

SMITH, B. WARD, atty., Cozadd, Shangle and Smith, Dearborn, MI '68 (ATTY)

SMITH, BARBARA G., coor. pat. educ., Holy Cross Hospital, Fort Lauderdale, FL '82 (EDUC)

SMITH, LT. COL. BARBARA J., RN, asst. chief nrsg., Womack Army Community Hospital, Fort Bragg, NC '86 (NURS)

SMITH, BARBARA S., dir. soc. serv., Tobey Hospital, Wareham, MA '86 (SOC)

SMITH, BARBARA, pers. dir., Lexington Memorial Hospital, Lexington, NC '86 (PERS)

SMITH, BARBARA, asst. vice-pres., Cooper Hospital-University Medical Center, Camden, NJ '86 (RISK)

SMITH, BARRY R., atty., Northwestern Memorial Hospital, Chicago, IL '76 (ATTY)

SMITH, BERNIE, coor. pat. rel., Queen's Medical Center, Honolulu, HI '86 (PAT)

SMITH, BETTINA F., dir. pub. rel., Holy Cross Hospital, Chicago, IL '85 (PR)

SMITH, BETTYLU, dir. pub. rel., Providence Hospital, Oakland, CA '82 (PR)

SMITH, BILL R., dir. bldg. serv., Mercy Hospital of New Orleans, New Orleans, LA '83 (ENG)

SMITH, BONNIE M., RN, dir. outpatient serv., Allentown Hospital, Allentown, PA '87 (AMB)

SMITH, BRUCE ALLEN, chief exec. off., St. Mary Hospital, Hoboken, NJ '69

SMITH, BRUCE L., atty., Riverside Hospital, Toledo, OH '80 (ATTY)

SMITH, C. GARY, dir. soc. serv. and pers., Baptist Memorial Hospital-Tipton, Covington, TN '77 (SOC)(PERS)

SMITH, C. MICHAEL, eng. consult., Memphis, TN '78 (ENG)

SMITH, C. THOMAS, pres., Yale-New Haven Hospital, New Haven, CT '61

SMITH, CARL EDWARD, vice-pres. pub. affairs, Alta Bates Corporation, Berkeley, CA '84

SMITH, CAROL A., RN, Western Reserve Systems-Northside, Youngstown, OH '77 (NURS)

SMITH, CAROL G., RN, asst. vice-pres., Riverside Hospital, Newport News, VA '83 (NURS)

SMITH, CAROLYN H., mgr. vol. serv., Gaston Memorial Hospital, Gastonia, NC '85 (VOL)

SMITH, CAROLYN, exec. hskpr., Howard University Hospital, Washington, DC '86 (ENVIRON)

SMITH, CATHERINE A., dir. qual. assur., Winona Memorial Hospital, Indianapolis, IN '76 (EDUC)

SMITH, CATHERINE ANNE, mgr. info. unit, Health Insurance Plan, New York, NY '86 (PAT)

SMITH, CATHERINE L., RN, dir. nrsg. serv., D. W. McMillan Memorial Hospital, Brewton, AL '80 (NURS)

SMITH, CATHERINE, dir. pat. care and prog., Bloorview Children's Hospital, Willowdale, Ont., Canada '87 (RISK)

SMITH, CHADWICK H., atty., Montana Hospital Association, Helena, MT '69 (ATTY)

SMITH, CHARLES J., chm.-dept. of anes., Lake District Hospital, Lakeview, OR '84

SMITH, CHARLES L. III, atty., Community Memorial Hospital, Missouri Valley, IA '79 (ATTY)

SMITH, CHARLES W. JR., vice-pres. oper., Prof. Health Care Management Service, Portsmouth, VA '76

SMITH, CHERYL L., RN, asst. adm. pat. serv., Highline Community Hospital, Seattle, WA '86 (NURS)

SMITH, CHESTER S. JR., mgt. eng., Presbyterian Medical Center, Dallas, TX '72 (MGMT)

SMITH, CHRISTOPHER EARL, asst. dir. plant serv., Shawnee Mission Medical Center, Shawnee Mission, KS '83 (ENG)

SMITH, CHUCK, mgr. facil., Good Samaritan Hospital, Downers Grove, IL '86 (ENG)

SMITH, CINDY M., dir. telecommun., Iowa Lutheran Hospital, Des Moines, IA '83 (ENG)

SMITH, CLARENCE L., mgt. rep., Servicemaster Industries, Inc., Downers Grove, IL '81

SMITH, CONNIE L., supv. matl. distrib., Waynesboro Hospital, Waynesboro, PA '85 (CS)

SMITH, CORNELIUS M., bd. chm., Will, Folsom and Smith, Inc., Babylon, NY '30 (LIFE)

SMITH, CRAIG L., pres., Smith Parke and Company, Inc., Sarasota, FL '82 (PLNG)

SMITH, CYNTHIA K., RN, mgr. risk and nrsg. qual. assur., Freeport Memorial Hospital, Freeport, IL '86 (RISK)

SMITH, D. RICHARD, dir. vol. serv., Hermann Hospital, Houston, TX '84 (VOL)

SMITH, DALE A., assoc. adm., St. Mary Hospital, Port Arthur, TX '72

SMITH, DAN M., dir. eng., Grady Memorial Hospital, Chickasha, OK '86 (ENG)

SMITH, DANIEL M. III, pres., Presbyterian Medical Services, Sante Fe, NM '71

SMITH, DANIEL, dir. spec. serv. and risk mgr., Bay Area Hospital, Coos Bay, OR '86 (RISK)

SMITH, DANNETTE ROSE, mgr. soc. serv., Hyde Park Hospital, Chicago, IL '87 (SOC)

SMITH, DANNY K., vice-pres. environ. serv., Candler General Hospital, Savannah, GA '83 (ENG)

SMITH, DARLENE, dir. mktg., Charter Lakeside Hospital, Memphis, TN '86 (PR) (PLNG)

SMITH, DAVID A., dir. pers., St. Vincent Hospital and Health Center, Indianapolis, IN '69 (PERS)

SMITH, DAVID E., consult., Coopers and Lybrand, Boston, MA '84 (PUR)

SMITH, DAVID G., chief adm. off., St. Mary's Hospital, Decatur, IL '73

SMITH, DAVID SCOTT, dir. safety, George Washington University Medical Center, Washington, DC '80 (RISK)

SMITH, DAVID W., atty., St. Clare's Hospital and Health Center, New York, NY '86 (ATTY)

SMITH, DEAN A., asst. dir. plant oper., Queen of the Valley Hospital, Napa, CA '83 (ENG)

SMITH, DEBBE LYNN, RN, asst. dir. nrsg., Lancaster General Hospital, Lancaster, PA '84 (NURS)

SMITH, DEBORAH E., atty., Colorado Hospital Association, Denver, CO '87 (ATTY)

SMITH, DEBORAH J., dir. pub. rel. and mktg., South Amboy Memorial Hospital and Community Mental Health Center, South Amboy, NJ '81 (PR)

SMITH, DEBORAH L., mktg. rep., Good Samaritan Hospital, Cincinnati, OH '86 (PR)

SMITH, DENNIS L., RN, dir. nrsg., Hiawatha Community Hospital, Hiawatha, KS '83 (NURS)

SMITH, DEWEY M., assoc. dir. plant oper., Bristol Memorial Hospital, Bristol, TN '81 (ENG)

SMITH, MAJ. DONALD B., MSC USA, student, Army-Baylor University Program in Health Care Administration, Fort Sam Houston, TX '84

SMITH, DONALD B., asst. adm., La Crosse Lutheran Hospital, La Crosse, WI '73 (MGMT)

SMITH, DONALD L. SR., chief eng., Northern Cumberland Memorial Hospital, Bridgton, ME '84 (ENG)

SMITH, DONALD L., dir. bldg. serv., Baptist Hospital, Pensacola, FL '83 (ENG)

SMITH, DONALD N., MSC USA, fiscal off., U. S. Navy Dental Clinic, Charleston, SC '77

SMITH, DONNA K., RN, asst. vice-pres. nrsg., Newark-Wayne Community Hospital, Newark, NY '86 (NURS)

SMITH, DOUGLAS G., sr. consult., Baird, Kurtz and Dobson, Kansas City, MO '85 (MGMT)

SMITH, DOUGLAS MALCOLM, dir. soc. serv., Grossmont District Hospital, La Mesa, CA '76 (SOC)

SMITH, DYANN, dir. pat. rel., Sioux Valley Hospital, Sioux Falls, SD '80 (PAT)

SMITH, E. KENDRICK, atty., Southwest Hospital and Medical Center, Atlanta, GA '85 (ATTY)

SMITH, E. WATSON, atty., Mobile Infirmary Medical Center, Mobile, AL '74 (ATTY)

SMITH, EDDIE, dir. cent. sup., St. Anthony Hospital, Oklahoma City, OK '81 (CS)

SMITH, EDDIE, dir. biomedical elec., St. Francis Hospital Systems, Colorado Springs, CO '80 (ENG)

SMITH, EDWARD A. JR., dir. clin. serv., University of Virginia Hospitals, Charlottesville, VA '63

SMITH, EDWARD P., mgr. cent. serv., St. Margaret Memorial Hospital, Pittsburgh, PA '71 (CS)

SMITH, EDWARD T., Greater Southeast Community Hospital, Washington, DC '82

SMITH, EILEEN M., asst. supt., University of Wisconsin Hospital and Clinics, Madison, WI '77 (RISK)

SMITH, ELEASE M., dir. vol. serv., Baptist Medical Center-Princeton, Birmingham, AL '81 (VOL)

SMITH, ELIZABETH B., dir. mktg. and pub. rel., HCA Santa Rosa Medical Center, Milton, FL '85 (PR)

SMITH, ELIZABETH DORSEY, RN, dir. maternal-child health and asst. dir. nrsg., Mount Sinai Medical Center, New York, NY '86 (NURS)

SMITH, ELIZABETH M., dir. pub. rel., Robert Packer Hospital, Sayre, PA '74 (PR)

SMITH, ELYSE, dir. matl. mgt., Evanston Hospital, Evanston, IL '79 (PUR)

SMITH, ERNEST W., atty., Clark County Memorial Hospital, Jeffersonville, IN '76 (ATTY)

SMITH, ETHEL, supv. ldry., Waukesha Memorial Hospital, Waukesha, WI '86 (ENVIRON)

SMITH, FRANCES M., RN, dir. prof. dev., St. Vincent Charity Hospital, Cleveland, OH '77 (NURS)

SMITH, FRANCES P., med. lib., Arnold Library, Honolulu, HI '86

SMITH, FRED C. JR., reg. adm., Manhattan Medical Group, New York, NY '87 (AMB)

SMITH, FRED D., contr., St. James Hospital Medical Center, Chicago Heights, IL '82 (MGMT)

SMITH, FRED H., pres. and adm., Warner Brown Hospital, El Dorado, AR '84

SMITH, FREDERICK J., dir. plant oper., HCA North Beach Hospital, Fort Lauderdale, FL '86 (ENG)

SMITH, FROSTENIA M., RN, clin. dir. critical care nrsg., Moses H. Cone Memorial Hospital, Greensboro, NC '86 (NURS)

SMITH, GABRIELLE YEZOVIT, dir. soc. serv., St. Elizabeth Medical Center-North, Covington, KY '82 (SOC)

SMITH, GEORGE R., dir. human res., Fort Wayne State Hospital and Training Center, Fort Wayne, IN '82 (PERS)

SMITH, GEORGE R., health care loss control spec., Cigna Loss Control Services, Gainesville, FL '83 (RISK)

SMITH, GEORGIA R., assoc. dir. pat. and staff educ., Methodist Hospital of Chicago, Chicago, IL '80 (EDUC)

SMITH, GERALD W., mgr. phys. plant, Oakwood Hospital, Dearborn, MI '79 (ENG)

SMITH, GERALD, dir. matl. mgt., Hospital Center at Orange, Orange, NJ '86 (PUR)

SMITH, GERARD K., dir. plant oper. and eng., St. James Mercy Hospital, Hornell, NY '69 (ENG)

SMITH, GERI, health care consult., Life Care Continuum, Stuart, FL '78 (SOC)

SMITH, GLORIA W., dir. diet. serv., Tuomey Hospital, Sumter, SC '75 (FOOD)

SMITH, GREGORY A., dir. mktg., Franciscan Health Care, Inc., Milwaukee, WI '84 (PLNG)

SMITH, GREGORY E. SR., dir. matl. mgt., St. John and West Shore Hospital, Westlake, OH '82 (PUR)

SMITH, GREGORY P., mgr. compensation, St. Vincent Hospital and Health Center, Indianapolis, IN '85 (PERS)

SMITH, HARLAN JAMES, assoc. dir., William W. Backus Hospital, Norwich, CT '76 (RISK)

SMITH, HELEN M., dir. pers., Jefferson Memorial Hospital, Ranson, WV '78 (PERS)

SMITH, HELEN MARIE, dir. soc. serv., Fort Hamilton-Hughes Memorial Hospital, Hamilton, OH '85 (SOC)

SMITH, HENRY J., sr. vice-pres. fin., Magee-Womens Hospital, Pittsburgh, PA '71

SMITH, HMC GERALD LAUREL, MSC USN, student, Southern Illinois University, School of Technical Careers, Carbondale, IL '85

SMITH, HUGH R., dir. soc. serv., St. Mary Hospital, Quincy, IL '79 (SOC)

SMITH, IRIS, adm. asst. cent. sup., South Georgia Medical Center, Valdosta, GA '76 (CS)

SMITH, J. TROY, atty., Carteret General Hospital, Morehead City, NC '85 (ATTY)

SMITH, JACK L. JR., surveyor health facil., Los Angeles County Health Department, Los Angeles, CA '69

SMITH, JACK L., atty., Memorial Hospital, Colorado Springs, CO '78 (ATTY)

SMITH, JAMES E., pur. agt., Saint Joseph Hospital, Denver, CO '83 (PUR)

SMITH, JAMES E. JR., dir. plant oper., Caylor-Nickel Hospital, Bluffton, IN '75 (ENG)

SMITH, JAMES F. SR., prin., Heery Architects and Engineers, Inc., Cupertino, CA '71 (MGMT)

SMITH, JAMES G., atty., Sinai Hospital of Detroit, Detroit, MI '83 (ATTY)

SMITH, JAMES L. III, dir. mgt. eng., Richland Memorial Hospital, Columbia, SC '78 (MGMT)

SMITH, CAPT. JAMES L., MSC USN, asst. chief staff-logistics, Naval Medical Command, Oakland, CA '77

SMITH, JAMES P., dir. federal govern rel., Hospital Corporation of America, Arlington, VA '83

SMITH, JAMES R., exec. dir., Northwestern Pennsylvania Surgical Center, Inc., Erie, PA '87 (AMB)

SMITH, JANE A., RN, asst. adm. nrsg. serv., St. Vincent Hospital and Medical Center, Portland, OR '78 (NURS)

SMITH, JANICE FOSS, student, Department of Health Services Administration, George Washington University, Washington, DC '83

SMITH, JANICE M., dir. sup., proc. and distrib., St. Patrick Hospital, Lake Charles, LA '81 (CS)(PUR)

SMITH, JEAN A., dir. commun. rel., Madison County Hospital, London, OH '76 (VOL)

SMITH, SR. JEAN ANN, dir. vol. serv., Mount Carmel East Hospital, Columbus, OH '85 (VOL)
SMITH, JEANNIE, risk mgt. consult., St. Paul Fire and Marine Company, Atlanta, GA '82 (RISK)
SMITH, JEFFREY L., dir. pur., Cleveland Clinic Hospital, Cleveland, OH '75 (PUR)
SMITH, JEFFREY P., atty., Ballard Community Hospital, Seattle, WA '84 (ATTY)
SMITH, JENNIFER P., dir. pub. rel., Saint Vincent Hospital and Health Center, Billings, MT '84 (PR)
SMITH, JEROME M., atty., Kelsey Memorial Hospital, Lakeview, MI '74 (ATTY)
SMITH, JERRY A., dir. maint., eng. and grds., James Lawrence Kernan Hospital, Baltimore, MD '83 (ENG)
SMITH, JERRY R., dir. plant oper., Southwest Florida Regional Medical Center, Fort Myers, FL '81 (ENG)
SMITH, JERRY W., mgt. eng., North Carolina Baptist Hospital, Winston-Salem, NC '82 (MGMT)
SMITH, JESSE G. III, div. dir., HCA Physicians Services Company, Atlanta, GA '74 (MGMT)
SMITH, JIM, supv. maint. and elec., Desert Hospital, Palm Springs, CA '86 (ENG)
SMITH, JOAN M., RN, asst. dir. nrsg.-adm. serv., East Orange General Hospital, East Orange, NJ '83 (NURS)
SMITH, JOAN M., RN, dir. clin. nrsg., Valley Hospital, Ridgewood, NJ '86 (NURS)
SMITH, JOAN PETERSEN, RN, dir. nrsg. serv., Marin General Hospital, San Rafael, CA '80 (NURS)
SMITH, JOHN ALAN, dir. eng., St. Joseph Hospital, Memphis, TN '84 (ENG)
SMITH, JOHN D., dir. soc. work serv., St. Mary's Hospital, Huntington, WV '85 (SOC)
SMITH, JOHN DANA, dir. info. serv., Lourdes Hospital, Paducah, KY '86 (MGMT)
SMITH, JOHN MCPHEETERS, dir. food serv., St. Peter Hospital, Olympia, WA '70 (FOOD)
SMITH, JOHN N., asst. dir. plant serv., Community Medical Center, Scranton, PA '76 (ENG)
SMITH, JOHN, vice-pres., Booz, Allen and Hamilton, Inc., Atlanta, GA '81 (PLNG)
SMITH, JOHNSON, adm., Conway County Hospital, Morrilton, AR '86 (RISK)
SMITH, JOSEPH B., asst. adm., Houston Medical Center, Warner Robins, GA '81 (MGMT)(RISK)
SMITH, JUANITA M., RN, asst. coor. educ., Campbell County Memorial Hospital, Gillette, WY '86 (EDUC)
SMITH, JUDITH A., mgr. commun. rel., St. Joseph Hospital, Bellingham, WA '83 (PR)
SMITH, JUDITH COTCHETT, pub. rel. off., Emory University Hospital, Atlanta, GA '80 (PR)
SMITH, JUDITH M., educ. dev. spec., Lovelace Medical Center, Albuquerque, NM '82 (EDUC)
SMITH, KARIN M., dir. pub. rel. and mktg., HCA Largo Medical Center Hospital, Largo, FL '85 (PR)
SMITH, KATHLEEN A., dir. cent. serv., Humana Hospital -Huntsville, Huntsville, AL '85 (CS)
SMITH, KATHLEEN A., RN, dir. surg. serv., Kennestone Hospital, Marietta, GA '86 (NURS)
SMITH, KATHRYN FORD, mgt. eng., Emory University Hospital, Atlanta, GA '75 (MGMT)
SMITH, KATHY, coor. eng., Southwest Community Health Services, Albuquerque, NM '86 (ENG)
SMITH, KEVIN J., sr. consult., Price Waterhouse, Chicago, IL '86 (MGMT)
SMITH, KIRBY H. JR., exec. dir., Southside Regional Medical Center, Petersburg, VA '62
SMITH, KOVEN W., dir. eng., Shands Teaching Hospital and Clinics, Gainesville, FL '76 (ENG)
SMITH, LADELL, mgr. nrs. surg., Wayne Memorial Hospital, Goldsboro, NC '87 (AMB)
SMITH, LADELLE, coor. prof. rel. and commun., Presbyterian Hospital, Dallas, TX '87 (PLNG)
SMITH, LARRY A., atty., Kettering Medical Center, Kettering, OH '81 (ATTY)
SMITH, LARRY M., vice-pres. plng. and mktg., St. Francis Medical Center, Cape Girardeau, MO '85 (PLNG)
SMITH, LARRY R., dir. maint., Yakima Valley Memorial Hospital, Yakima, WA '77 (ENG)
SMITH, LAURA C., supv. food serv., Orthopaedic Hospital of Charlotte, Charlotte, NC '75 (FOOD)
SMITH, LAURA J., student, Program in Hospital and Health Care Administration, St. Louis University, St. Louis, MO '84
SMITH, LAURAMAE, mgr. info. serv., McKinsey and Company, Inc., Chicago, IL '84
SMITH, LAVERNE L., RN, chief nrsg. serv., Veterans Administration Medical Center, Philadelphia, PA '78 (NURS)
SMITH, LEO E., dir. bldg. and grds., St. Joseph's Hospital, Tampa, FL '79 (ENG)
SMITH, LESTER H., vice-pres., Smith Seckman Reid, Inc., Nashville, TN '86 (ENG)
SMITH, LILLIAN M., RN, Paradise Valley Hospital, National City, CA '83 (NURS)
SMITH, LINDA K., dir. in-service vol., Hardin Memorial Hospital, Kenton, OH '85 (VOL)
SMITH, LINDA M., asst. adm., Los Angeles County-University of Southern California Medical Center, Los Angeles, CA '83
SMITH, LINDA W., RN, dir. nrsg., John D. Archbold Memorial Hospital, Thomasville, GA '86 (NURS)
SMITH, LISA A., dir. educ., South Seminole Community Hospital, Longwood, FL '84 (EDUC)
SMITH, LISA H., pres., Stratecon, Inc., Claremont, CA '86 (PLNG)
SMITH, LOUIS H., dir. pers., Cornwall Hospital, Cornwall, NY '79 (PERS)
SMITH, LOY I., mgr. cent. sterile sup., Shands Hospital, Gainesville, FL '86 (CS)
SMITH, LUANN GERMAN, dir. food serv., Frances E. Parker Memorial Home, Piscataway, NJ '86 (FOOD)
SMITH, LYNELLE QUINNAM, dir. dev. and pub. rel., Leland Memorial Hospital, Riverdale, MD '81 (PR)
SMITH, MALCOLM, asst. soc. bd. dir., Richmond Memorial Hospital and Health Center, Staten Island, NY '50 (LIFE)
SMITH, MARGARET ELIZABETH, vice-pres. commun. rel., Leila Hospital and Health Center, Battle Creek, MI '84
SMITH, MARGARET J., sr. mgt. syst. analyst, Calgary District Hospital Group, Calgary, Alta., Canada '83 (MGMT)
SMITH, MARIE A., RN, asst. dir. nrsg., Sea View Hospital and Home, Staten Island, NY '84 (NURS)
SMITH, MARIE E., RN, dir. clin. serv., Mount Zion Hospital and Medical Center, San Francisco, CA '84 (NURS)
SMITH, MARION LEIGH, dir. vol. serv., Henry Ford Hospital, Detroit, MI '77 (VOL)
SMITH, MARK A., dir. pers., Holy Cross Hospital of Silver Spring, Silver Spring, MD '66 (PERS)
SMITH, MARK A., mgt. eng., HBO and Company, Houston, TX '86 (MGMT)
SMITH, MARK W., staff spec., Hospital Corporation of America, Management Corporation, Nashville, TN '82 (MGMT)
SMITH, MARTA M., dir. organizational dev. and healthcare serv., Southwest Community Health Services, Albuquerque, NM '86 (PLNG)
SMITH, MARTIN B. JR., pres., Equimed, Inc., Lenexa, KS '80
SMITH, MARTY, supv. cent. sup., South Highlands Hospital, Birmingham, AL '80 (CS)
SMITH, MARY A., RN, adm., Heart Institute of Nevada, Las Vegas, NV '87 (AMB)
SMITH, MARY CAROLYN, field agt., South Carolina Insurance Reserve Fund, Columbia, SC '86 (RISK)
SMITH, MARY ELLEN, asst. dir. food serv., Anne Arundel General Hospital, Annapolis, MD '86 (FOOD)
SMITH, MARY L., RN, dir. nrsg. serv., Saint Joseph Hospital, Fort Worth, TX '83 (NURS)
SMITH, MARY LOU, consult.-benefits and util. practices, Blue Cross and Blue Shield Association, Chicago, IL '87 (AMB)
SMITH, MAUREEN D., risk mgr., St. Vincent's Hospital and Medical Center, New York, NY '82 (RISK)
SMITH, MELVIN DENNIS, head food mgt., Naval Hospital, Long Beach, CA '86 (FOOD)
SMITH, MERLIN W., supv. facil. eng., Shawnee Mission Medical Center, Shawnee Mission, KS '86 (ENG)
SMITH, MICHAEL J., pat. adm., Winn Army Community Hospital, Fort Stewart, GA '80
SMITH, MITCHELL B., exec. dir., Humana Hospital -Sebastian, Sebastian, FL '72
SMITH, NANCY B., dir. vol. serv., Christ Hospital, Jersey City, NJ '70 (VOL)
SMITH, NANCY DOYLE, RN, dir. nrsg. serv., Regional Memorial Hospital, Brunswick, ME '78 (NURS)
SMITH, NANCY K., dir. commun. rel. and educ., Mount St. Mary's Hospital, Lewiston, NY '71 (PR)
SMITH, NANCY, dir. qual. assessment, San Pedro Peninsula Hospital, San Pedro, CA '85 (RISK)
SMITH, OSCAR M., atty., Floyd Medical Center, Rome, GA '72 (ATTY)
SMITH, PAMELA K., asst. adm., Garland Memorial Hospital, Garland, TX '82
SMITH, PATRICIA A., mgr. cent. sterile sup., Edward W. Sparrow Hospital, Lansing, MI '86 (CS)
SMITH, PATRICIA F., RN, dir. pat. serv., Rankin General Hospital, Brandon, MS '85 (NURS)
SMITH, PATRICIA L., asst. dir., University of Chicago Hospitals, Chicago, IL '82 (FOOD)
SMITH, PATRICK R., dir. pur., Centenary Hospital, Scarborough, Ont., Canada '86 (PUR)
SMITH, PATRIZIA D., dir. pat. rel., Kennedy Memorial Hospitals Saddle Brook, Saddle Brook, NJ '86 (PAT)
SMITH, PATTON P. JR., student, Georgia State University-Institute of Health Administration, Atlanta, GA '87
SMITH, PAUL E., asst. dir. eng., Howard University Hospital, Washington, DC '86 (ENG)
SMITH, PAUL ENGLISH, atty., Cabell Huntington Hospital, Huntington, WV '85 (ATTY)
SMITH, PAUL S., dir. support serv., Penobscot Valley Hospital, Lincoln, ME '86 (ENG)
SMITH, PAUL, vice-pres. amb. care, Providence Hospital, Washington, DC '87 (AMB)
SMITH, PAULA E., dir. vol. serv., San Pedro Peninsula Hospital, San Pedro, CA '85 (VOL)
SMITH, PAULA FUSCO, info. syst. analyst, Oakwood Hospital, Dearborn, MI '84 (MGMT)
SMITH, PAULA G., dir. risk mgt., Good Samaritan Hospital and Health Center, Dayton, OH '82 (RISK)
SMITH, PAULA M., RN, asst. dir. nrsg., Childrens Hospital of Los Angeles, Los Angeles, CA '82 (NURS)
SMITH, PENNIE J., dir. mktg. and pub. rel., Wuesthoff Memorial Hospital, Rockledge, FL '86 (PR)
SMITH, PHILIP E., dir. pers., Pendleton Memorial Methodist Hospital, New Orleans, LA '74 (PERS)
SMITH, PHILIP G., dir. maint., St. Francis Hospital, Olean, NY '84 (ENG)
SMITH, PHYLLIS, dir. qual. assur. and risk prevention, Henry Ford Hospital, Detroit, MI '84 (RISK)
SMITH, R. ASHTON, North Andover, MA '48 (LIFE)
SMITH, R. REBECCA, supv. pat. serv., Good Shepherd Hospital, Barrington, IL '85 (FOOD)
SMITH, R. SEYMOUR, vice-pres. commun. rel., Niagara Falls Memorial Medical Center, Niagara Falls, NY '84 (PR) (PLNG)
SMITH, RACHEL W., RN, assoc. dir. nrsg., District of Columbia General Hospital, Washington, DC '86 (NURS)
SMITH, RAYMOND E., sr. rep., Blue Cross of Southern California, San Diego, CA '66
SMITH, REGINA, atty., Harper-Grace Hospitals, Detroit, MI '84 (ATTY)
SMITH, REGINALD D., dir. syst. mgt., Florida Hospital Medical Center, Orlando, FL '84 (MGMT)
SMITH, RICHARD C., mgr. info. serv. plng., Massachusetts General Hospital, Boston, MA '82 (MGMT)
SMITH, RICHARD G., clin. eng., University Medical Center, Tucson, AZ '84 (ENG)
SMITH, RICHARD J., adm. dir. commun. rel., Blessing Hospital, Quincy, IL '85 (PR)
SMITH, RICHARD JAMES, dir. pers., pub. rel. and mktg., Memorial Hospital, Manchester, KY '81 (PR)(PERS)
SMITH, RICHARD L., PhD, dir. qual. assur., Loretto Hospital, Chicago, IL '72 (MGMT)
SMITH, RICK C., dir. food serv., St. Augustine General Hospital, St. Augustine, FL '81 (FOOD)
SMITH, ROBERT J., vice-pres., Sherman Hospital, Elgin, IL '85 (PR) (PLNG)
SMITH, ROBERT M., partner, Touche Ross and Company, Miami, FL '77
SMITH, ROBERT R., atty., Georgia Baptist Medical Center, Atlanta, GA '85 (ATTY)
SMITH, ROBERT R., vice-pres., National Medical Enterprises, Inc., Dallas, TX '86
SMITH, ROBERT, student, New School for Social Research, New York, NY '85
SMITH, ROBIN ANN, dir. soc. work serv., Doctors' Hospital, Shreveport, LA '86 (SOC)
SMITH, ROBIN, student, University of Connecticut, Hartford, CT '84 (MGMT)
SMITH, RODNEY R., adm., Humboldt Cedar Crest Hospital, Humboldt, TN '78 (MGMT)
SMITH, ROLAND E., buyer, Good Samaritan Community Healthcare, Puyallup, WA '85 (PUR)
SMITH, ROSE A., assoc. dir. nrsg. and in-service, Garfield Medical Center, Monterey Park, CA '86 (EDUC)
SMITH, MAJ. ROSS C., MSC USAF, dir. med. logistics mgt., U. S. Air Force Hospital Elmendorf, Anchorage, AK '77 (PUR)
SMITH, ROY H. JR., dir. food serv., Martin Luther Hospital Medical Center, Anaheim, CA '69 (FOOD)
SMITH, ROY MCBEE, atty., Spartanburg Regional Medical Center, Spartanburg, SC '71 (ATTY)
SMITH, RT REV MSGR GEORGE LEWIS, dir. hosp., Diocese of Charleston, Aiken, SC '41 (LIFE)
SMITH, RUTH BERNISS, dir. soc. serv., Joseph P. Kennedy Jr. Memorial Hospital, Boston, MA '77 (SOC)
SMITH, S. DOUGLAS, reg. vice-pres., Hospital Corporation of America, Nashville, TN '68
SMITH, SALLY, RN, dir. sup., proc. and distrib., St. Luke's Medical Center, Phoenix, AZ '85 (CS)
SMITH, SANDER V., MD, (ret.), West Palm Beach, FL '40 (LIFE)
SMITH, SANDRA H., RN, dir. clin. serv., Woman's Hospital, Baton Rouge, LA '79 (NURS)
SMITH, SANDRA L., RN, nrsg. adm. support serv., Pitt County Memorial Hospital, Greenville, NC '86 (NURS)
SMITH, SARAH, supv. consumer rel. rep., Comprehensive Health Services of Detroit, Detroit, MI '81 (PAT)
SMITH, SCOTT, mgr. soc. serv., Geisinger Wyoming Valley Medical Center, Wilkes-Barre, PA '81 (SOC)
SMITH, SHARON A., RN, assoc. dir. nrsg., Mount Auburn Hospital, Cambridge, MA '81 (NURS)
SMITH, SHARON, RN, dir. learning resources, Gaston Memorial Hospital, Gastonia, NC '78 (EDUC)
SMITH, SHEILA D., dir. plng., Maryview Hospital, Portsmouth, VA '87 (PLNG)
SMITH, SHIRLEY C., RN, dir. nrsg., Saint Joseph Hospital, Elgin, IL '80 (NURS)
SMITH, SONJA L., RN, supv. outpatient pavilion and recovery room, St. Margaret Memorial Hospital, Pittsburgh, PA '87 (AMB)
SMITH, STEVE A., supv. maint., Charter Community Hospital of Cleveland, Cleveland, TX '86 (ENG)
SMITH, STEVEN R., atty., Prince George's Hospital Center, Cheverly, MD '85 (ATTY)
SMITH, STUART LEROY, vice-pres. oper., North Shore Medical Center, Miami, FL '74
SMITH, SUSAN H., dir. educ., Clayton General Hospital, Riverdale, GA '86 (EDUC)
SMITH, SUSAN K., dir. soc. serv., Central Michigan Community Hospital, Mount Pleasant, MI '85 (SOC)
SMITH, SUSAN, risk mgr., Methodist Hospital of Indiana, Indianapolis, IN '86 (RISK)
SMITH, SUZETTE A., RN, asst. dir. in-patient nrsg. serv., St. Joseph's Hospital, Milwaukee, WI '82 (NURS)
SMITH, T. WAYNE, mgr. maint. and constr., Utah Valley Regional Medical Center, Provo, UT '87 (ENG)
SMITH, TABATHIA, mgr., Chandler Family Health Center, Detroit, MI '81
SMITH, TAMARA A., market analyst, Medlantic Healthcare Group, Washington, DC '86 (PLNG)
SMITH, TAMMIE R., dir. pub. rel., Woodward Hospital and Health Center, Woodward, OK '87 (PR)
SMITH, TED, dir. pers., HCA Wysong Medical Center, McKinney, TX '86 (PERS)
SMITH, TERRI LEE, dir. diet. internship, Beth Israel Hospital, Boston, MA '77 (FOOD)
SMITH, THERESA E., dir. mktg. and commun. rel., Valley Medical Center of Fresno, Fresno, CA '85 (PR)
SMITH, THOMAS B., atty., St. Thomas Hospital, Nashville, TN '85 (ATTY)
SMITH, THOMAS D., RN, actg. dir. nrsg., Department of Health and Hospitals, Boston, MA '86 (NURS)
SMITH, THOMAS G., dir. pers., Moberly Regional Medical Center, Moberly, MO '86 (PERS)
SMITH, THOMAS W., div. mgr., HBO and Company, Rolling Meadows, IL '73 (MGMT)
SMITH, THOMAS W., dir. bldg. and grds., Palomar Memorial Hospital, Escondido, CA '80 (ENG)
SMITH, CAPT. TIMOTHY Z., Walkersville, MD '83 (ENG)
SMITH, TOM B., atty., Cross County Hospital, Wynne, AR '81 (ATTY)
SMITH, TOMMY A., contr., Health Management Association, Inc., Paintsville, KY '86
SMITH, TRACEY A., student, Yale University, New Haven, CT '85 (PLNG)
SMITH, TRENT C., pres., Pediatrics Services, Inc., Omaha, NE '86 (AMB)

SMITH, VAUGHAN A., pres., American Association of Healthcare Consultants, Arlington, VA '83 (PR) (PLNG)
SMITH, VENETA M., RN, asst. adm. and dir. nrsg. serv., Jay County Hospital, Portland, IN '80 (NURS)
SMITH, W. ALLEN, asst. dir. food and nutr. serv., Poudre Valley Hospital, Fort Collins, CO '86 (FOOD)
SMITH, W. MASON III, vice-pres. and dir., Shepley, Bulfinch, Richardson and Abbott, Boston, MA '79
SMITH, W. STUART, dir. oper., Medical University Hospital of the Medical University of South Carolina, Charleston, SC '86
SMITH, WALLACE E., PhD, dir. soc. serv., Parkview Episcopal Medical Center, Pueblo, CO '74 (SOC)
SMITH, WALLACE WILLIAM, pres., Lakes Region General Hospital, Laconia, NH '65
SMITH, WILBERT L., dir. commun. rel., South Shore Hospital, Chicago, IL '77 (PR)
SMITH, WILLIAM D., dir. pers., William W. Backus Hospital, Norwich, CT '84 (PERS)
SMITH, WILLIAM F. SR., (ret.), Dayton, OH '74
SMITH, WINSTON, dir. bldg. serv., Park City Hospital, Bridgeport, CT '86 (ENVIRON)
SMITHER, JOHN B. III, risk mgr., Lourdes Hospital, Paducah, KY '81 (RISK)
SMITHERMAN, FRANK JR., dir. pur., Memorial Medical Center of Jacksonville, Jacksonville, FL '70 (PUR)
SMITHWICK, MARY M., RN, asst. adm. nrsg., El Camino Hospital, Mountain View, CA '81 (NURS)
SMITS, PAUL E., chief soc. work serv., Veterans Administration Medical Center, Cincinnati, OH '85 (SOC)
SMOAK, JAMES D., adm. food and nutr. serv., St. Anthony's Hospital, St. Petersburg, FL '83 (FOOD)
SMOAKE, PATRICIA P., vice-pres. pub. rel., South Carolina Hospital Association, West Columbia, SC '85 (PR)
SMOCK, E. WILLIAM, assoc., The Stuck Associates, Inc., Jonesboro, AR '84
SMOLDER, A. ANDREW, asst. adm., Eye and Ear Clinic of Charleston, Charleston, WV '85 (PERS)
SMOLDT, ROBERT K., chm. plng. and pub. affairs, Mayo Clinic, Rochester, MN '82 (PLNG)
SMOLEN, ROBERTA S., asst. dir. vol. serv., Society of the New York Hospital, New York, NY '86 (VOL)
SMOLLAR, MARILYN M., chief diet., Grand View Hospital, Ironwood, MI '72 (FOOD)
SMOOT, KENNETH H., dir. emp. rel., Hyde Park Hospital, Chicago, IL '83 (PERS)
SMOUSE, ERIC M., dir. bldg. serv., Memorial Hospital of Bedford County, Everett, PA '83 (ENG)
SMOUT, JAY C., student, University of North Carolina, Chapel Hill, NC '57 (LIFE)
SMRT, STEVE, dir. bldg. and grds., Shriners Hospitals for Crippled Children, Chicago, IL '80 (ENG)
SMUCK, MIKE, mgr. plant oper., Mary Greeley Medical Center, Ames, IA '78 (ENG)
SMYTH, JUSTICE D. III, atty., Baptist Medical Center-Princeton, Birmingham, AL '83 (ATTY)
SMYTH, LIBBY, dir. vol. serv., St. Michael Hospital, Milwaukee, WI '80 (VOL)
SMYTH, NORA ANN, mgr., General Electric Credit Corporation, Stanford, CT '84 (PLNG)
SMYTH, RICHARD J., dir. human resources, Hospital Shared Services Western Pennsylvania, Warrendale, PA '71 (PERS)
SMYTHE, SHEILA M., health care mgt. and fin. consult., Washinton, DC '63
SNAPP, KENT, atty., Medical Center of Independence, Independence, MO '77 (ATTY)
SNAPP, NANCY S., RN, sr. vice-pres. nrsg., Presbyterian Hospital, Charlotte, NC '76 (NURS)
SNAPP, WILLIAM R. III, asst. dir. prof. serv., Naples Community Hospital, Naples, FL '76
SNEAD, L. R., dir. matl. mgt., Lynchburg General Hospital, Lynchburg, VA '86 (CS)(PUR)
SNECINSKI, JANE, dir. environ. serv., Baptist Hospital of Miami, Miami, FL '86 (ENVIRON)
SNEIDER, ALISON, dir. pub. rel., New England Deaconess Hospital, Boston, MA '82 (PR)
SNEIDER, RICHARD M., PhD, pres., Richard M. Sneider and Associates Ltd., Waban, MA '85 (MGMT)
SNELL, FRANCES L., dir. allied health serv., St. John's Healthcare Corporation, Anderson, IN '70 (SOC)
SNELL, ROBERT E., dir. soc. serv., Providence Medical Center, Seattle, WA '78 (SOC)
SNETSELAAR, GARY R., oper. analyst, University of Iowa Hospitals and Clinics, Iowa City, IA '86 (MGMT)
SNEZEK, BARBARA J., RN, mgr. matl. mgt., Lorain Community Hospital, Lorain, OH '86 (CS)
SNIDE, MAJ. WILLIAM H., MSC USA, dir. pers., 455th General Hospital, Providence, RI '85 (PR)
SNIDER, ALAN, indust. eng., Memorial Medical Center of East Texas, Lufkin, TX '86 (MGMT)
SNIDER, GEORGE A. JR., dir. pers., Lincoln General Hospital, Lincoln, NE '79 (PERS)
SNIDER, HOPE H., MD, assoc. chief staff educ., Veterans Administration Medical Center, Cleveland, OH '80 (EDUC)
SNIDER, IRA L., DO, Bloomfield Hills, MI '81
SNIDER, JOHN RICHARD, vice-pres. human res., Beverly Enterprises, Atlanta, GA '73 (PERS)
SNIDER, MARGO DONALDSON, RN, chief nrsg. serv., Veterans Administration Medical Center, Houston, TX '79 (NURS)
SNIDER, MARIE A., dir. commun., Prairie View Mental Health Center, Newton, KS '86 (PR)
SNIDER, PAULA M., consult., Ernst and Whinney, Columbus, OH '87 (MGMT)
SNIDER, ROBERTA, RN, asst. dir. nrsg., Community Hospital of Chula Vista, Chula Vista, CA '82 (NURS)
SNIDERMAN, HOWARD D., mgr. strategic plng., Doctors Hospital, Columbus, OH '86 (PLNG)
SNIEGOCKI, MARK A., dir. mktg. and pub. rel., Reynolds Memorial Hospital, Glen Dale, WV '86 (PR)
SNIFFEN, MICHAEL J., assoc. dir., Society of the New York Hospital, New York, NY '79 (PLNG)
SNIPES, LUCAS ARTHUR, sr. vice-pres., Roanoke Memorial Hospitals, Roanoke, VA '74
SNODGRASS, LARRY B., risk mgr., Fort Sanders Regional Medical Center, Knoxville, TN '84 (RISK)
SNODGRASS, STANLEY B., pres., Healthcare Association of Hawaii, Honolulu, HI '80
SNODGRASS, SUSAN K., asst. to pres., Kapiolani Women's and Children's Medical Center, Honolulu, HI '85 (PLNG)
SNOKE, ALBERT W., MD, Hamden, CT '46 (LIFE)
SNOOK, ERIC L., dir., Center for Continuing Health Education, Chadron State College, Chadron, NE '83 (EDUC)
SNOOK, I. DONALD, pres., Presbyterian-University of Pennsylvania Medical Center, Philadelphia, PA '67
SNOOK, LINDA D., dir. vol. and pub. rel., Sumner Memorial Hospital, Gallatin, TN '79 (VOL)
SNOW, DANIEL M., atty., Pierce, Atwood, Scribner, Allen, Smith and Lancaster, Portland, ME '86 (ATTY)
SNOW, ELMINA L., (ret.), South Lake Memorial Hospital, Clermont, FL '43 (LIFE)
SNOW, MARK J., dir. mktg. and commun. rel., Doylestown Hospital, Doylestown, PA '83 (PLNG)
SNOW, PETER J., vice-pres. policy and plng., Southwest Community Health Services, Albuquerque, NM '84 (PLNG)
SNOW, THEODORE R., dir. maint., Olean General Hospital, Olean, NY '84 (ENG)
SNOWBARGER, JOYCE A., dir. plng., Good Samaritan Hospital, San Jose, CA '82 (PLNG)
SNOWBARGER, VINCENT K., atty., Olathe Medical Center, Olathe, KS '81 (ATTY)
SNOWDALL, ROGER J., mgr. risk and qual. assur., Baptist Medical Center, Kansas City, MO '81 (ENG)
SNOWDEN, DOROTHY G., mgr. plng., Methodist Evangelical Hospital, Louisville, KY '84 (PLNG)
SNOWDEN, JEANNE Y., dir. nutr. serv., Trinity Regional Hospital, Fort Dodge, IA '84 (FOOD)
SNOWDEN, WILLIS T., plant eng., Grady General Hospital, Cairo, GA '81 (ENG)
SNYDER, AILEEN M., dir. diet., Candler General Hospital, Savannah, GA '86 (FOOD)
SNYDER, ALBERT A., partner, Ernst and Whinney, Baltimore, MD '77
SNYDER, ALLEN D., preventive maint. planner, Presbyterian-University Hospital, Pittsburgh, PA '81 (ENG)
SNYDER, LT. COL. ALLEN T., MSC USAF, Department of Air Force Medical Service, Bolling AFB, DC '79
SNYDER, BARBARA L., dir. vol., Sacred Heart Hospital of Pensacola, Pensacola, FL '78 (VOL)
SNYDER, BELLE, dir. soc. serv., St. Elizabeth's Hospital, Chicago, IL '78 (SOC)
SNYDER, CARROLL E., atty., Lakeview Medical Center, Danville, IL '80 (ATTY)
SNYDER, CHARLES W. JR., sr. vice-pres., Adventist Health System-North, Hinsdale, IL '79 (PLNG)
SNYDER, CHARLES, dir. info. syst., South Hills Health System, Homestead, PA '86
SNYDER, DARRYL W., mgr. biomedical eng., Methodist Hospital-Central Unit, Memphis, TN '85 (ENG)
SNYDER, DAVID W. W., adm., Wellington Community Hospital, Wellington, OH '63
SNYDER, DONNA, mgr. soc. serv. and home care, Exeter Hospital, Exeter, NH '86 (SOC)
SNYDER, DOUGLAS C., dir. telecommun. plng., Hospital Corporation of America, Nashville, TN '85 (ENG)
SNYDER, DREW A., exec. vice-pres., St. Vincent's Medical Center, Jacksonville, FL '82
SNYDER, ED L., mgr. plant eng., Lancaster-Fairfield Community Hospital, Lancaster, OH '83 (ENG)
SNYDER, EDWARD H., mgt. eng. analyst, Kaiser Permanente, Washington, DC '86 (MGMT)
SNYDER, GARY L., dir. mktg. and plng., Salvation Army William Booth Memorial Hospital, Florence, KY '82 (PLNG)
SNYDER, GAYLORD M., RN, vice-pres. pat. care serv., St. Mary's Hospital, West Palm Beach, FL '85 (NURS)
SNYDER, GEORGE T., Schofield, WI '82
SNYDER, HARVEY D. D., mgr. trng., George Washington University, Washington, DC '80 (EDUC)
SNYDER, HOWARD J., asst. dir. matl. mgt., St. Marys Hospital of Rochester, Rochester, MN '75 (PUR)
SNYDER, IRA R., mgr., Pannell, Kerr and Forster, Los Angeles, CA '75 (MGMT)
SNYDER, JANE PETERS, vice-pres. pub. rel. and educ., Delaware Valley Hospital Council, Philadelphia, PA '69 (PR)
SNYDER, JANET K., dir. soc. serv., St. Anthony's Medical Center, St. Louis, MO '84 (SOC)
SNYDER, JO, dir. matl. mgt., Queen of the Valley Hospital, West Covina, CA '86 (PUR)
SNYDER, JOHN T., pres., Hospital Association of Central Ohio, Dublin, OH '86 (PLNG)
SNYDER, JUDITH K., pat. rep., Lancaster-Fairfield Community Hospital, Lancaster, OH '82 (PAT)
SNYDER, LINDA G., dir. soc. serv., Bergen Pines County Hospital, Paramus, NJ '82 (SOC)
SNYDER, LYNN SHAPIRO, atty., Epstein, Becker, Borsody Et Al, Washington, DC '86 (ATTY)
SNYDER, MARGARET H., dir. vol. serv., Children's Hospital Medical Center, Cincinnati, OH '83 (VOL)
SNYDER, MARILYN, RN, educator, San Pedro Peninsula Hospital, San Pedro, CA '86 (EDUC)
SNYDER, MARY E., diet., Montrose Memorial Hospital, Montrose, CO '80 (FOOD)
SNYDER, NORMA R., dir. diet., Littleton Hospital, Littleton, NH '72 (FOOD)
SNYDER, PATRICIA R., RN, dir. nrsg., Dominion Hospital, Falls Church, VA '87 (NURS)
SNYDER, PHYLLIS J., asst. dir. nrsg., Moses Taylor Hospital, Scranton, PA '79 (EDUC)
SNYDER, RICHARD H., dir. commun. affairs, Elko General Hospital, Elko, NV '86 (PR)
SNYDER, ROBERT L. II, vice-pres., Johnson and Higgins of Texas, Inc., Houston, TX '84 (RISK)
SNYDER, SONYA, asst. dir. human resources, Palos Community Hospital, Palos Heights, IL '75 (PERS)
SNYDER, SUSAN, Munster, IN '83 (PUR)
SNYDER, SUZANNE, coor. qual. assur. and risk mgt., Burdette Tomlin Memorial Hospital, Cape May Court House, NJ '87 (RISK)
SNYDER, THOMAS L., atty., St. Margaret Memorial Hospital, Pittsburgh, PA '82 (ATTY)
SNYDER, TIMOTHY D., asst. dir. eng. and maint., Grand View Hospital, Sellersville, PA '85 (ENG)
SOARS, SUSAN W., dir. vol. serv., Muncy Valley Hospital, Muncy, PA '85 (VOL)
SOBASKY, SCARLET M., dir. pers., McCray Memorial Hospital, Kendallville, IN '86 (PERS)
SOBCZAK, CASIMER, dir. bldg. and grds., Harper Hospital, Detroit, MI '86 (ENG)
SOBEHRAD, SUSAN J., coor. pub. rel. and mktg., Tomball Regional Hospital, Tomball, TX '85 (PR)
SOBEL, JULES, elec. eng., Tilden, Lobnitz and Cooper, Inc., Orlando, FL '83 (ENG)
SOBIERAJ, JACOB L., atty., St. Mary Hospital, Livonia, MI '77 (ATTY)
SOBIERAY, RICHARD JOSEPH, pres., Boyd Sobieray Associates, Inc., Indianapolis, IN '76 (PLNG)
SOBOL, THEODORE J., vice-pres., Reid Memorial Hospital, Richmond, IN '74 (PERS)
SOBOLIK, DENNIS C., adm. plant serv., Denver Health and Hospitals, Denver, CO '83 (ENG)
SOBOTA, RICHARD E., vice-pres. corp. plng., Detroit Medical Center Corporation, Detroit, MI '85 (PLNG)
SOBSON, DEBORAH A., mgt. eng., Harper-Grace Hospitals, Detroit, MI '86 (MGMT)
SOCHA, RONALD R., dir. mktg., Vanderbilt University Hospital, Nashville, TN '84 (PLNG)
SOCOL, DONNA KANER, atty., Michael Reese Hospital and Medical Center, Chicago, IL '85 (ATTY)
SODA, GEORGINA, mgr. qual. assur., Wyckoff Heights Hospital, Brooklyn, NY '86 (RISK)
SODERBERG, BONNIE L., dir. mgt. syst., budget and staff, New Britain General Hospital, New Britain, CT '82 (MGMT)
SODERHOLM, JOHN C., exec. vice-pres., Ingham Medical Center, Lansing, MI '73 (PLNG)
SODERLUND, TERESA B., RN, vice-pres. nrsg., Cape Canaveral Hospital, Cocoa Beach, FL '85 (NURS)
SODERQUIST, D. LOIS, RN, adm. nrsg., Olympic Memorial Hospital, Port Angeles, WA '82 (NURS)
SOEFFING, ELEANOR H., mgr. amb. syst., Children's Hospital, Boston, MA '80 (MGMT)
SOELLERS, CHARLES E., facil. eng., U. S. Public Health Service Indian Hospital, Tuba City, AZ '87 (ENG)
SOENEN, LYNN E., dir. diet. serv., Sinai Hospital of Detroit, Detroit, MI '75 (FOOD)
SOERRIES, MARY ANN, dir. soc. serv., St. John's Regional Medical Center, Joplin, MO '80 (SOC)
SOFALY, LYNN F., student, Duke University, Department of Health Administration, Durham, NC '83
SOFFERIN, SAMUEL L. JR., dir. food serv., Lakeland Regional Medical Center, Lakeland, FL '67 (FOOD)
SOFFIN, DANIEL B., assoc. plng., United Hospitals, Inc., Cheltenham, PA '82
SOFIO, MARTHA M., RN, corp. dir. of women's serv., Fairview Riverside Hospital, Minneapolis, MN '83 (NURS)
SOHMER, SHIRLEY F., RN, dir. psych. nrsg. serv. and neurosciences, Johns Hopkins Hospital, Baltimore, MD '85 (NURS)
SOIFER, PHILIP, dir. environ. serv., Chilton Memorial Hospital, Pompton Plains, NJ '86 (ENVIRON)
SOINE, TERI L., actg. dir. strategic plng., Queen's Medical Center, Honolulu, HI '84 (PR) (PLNG)
SOKATCH, SEYMOUR A., dir. pers., Children's Hospital Medical Center, Cincinnati, OH '80 (PERS)
SOKOL, MICHAEL, mech. shop foreman, Montefiore Hospital, Pittsburgh, PA '85 (ENG)
SOKOL, STEPHEN, dir. food serv., ARA Services, Hospital Food Management, Environmental Service, Inc., Baltimore, MD '83 (FOOD)
SOKOL, WILLIAM M., atty., Mary Washington Hospital, Fredericksburg, VA '82 (ATTY)
SOKOLOW, ARLENE R., dir. med. soc. work, Bon Secours Hospital, North Miami, FL '85 (SOC)
SOKOLY, LEAH M., RN, asst. adm. nrsg., Gulf Coast Hospital, Baytown, TX '83 (NURS)
SOKUP, JAMES G., vice-pres. plng., Luther Hospital, Eau Claire, WI '85 (PLNG)
SOL, NEIL, PhD, dir. health promotion, Methodist Hospital-Central Unit, Memphis, TN '84 (EDUC)
SOLARSKI, THEODORE J., dir. eng., Memorial Hospital of Burlington County, Mount Holly, NJ '81 (ENG)
SOLBERG, BILL, dir. soc. serv., St. Mary's Hospital, Milwaukee, WI '80 (SOC)
SOLBERG, BRADLEY V., student, Program in Hospital Administration, Concordia College, Moorhead, MN '85
SOLBERG, CAROL A., RN, dir. nrsg., Alfred I. Dupont Institute, Wilmington, DE '86 (NURS)
SOLETHER, RICHALENE, RN, supv. sterile proc. and cent. sup., Knapp Medical Center, Weslaco, TX '80 (CS)
SOLEY, JAMES T. SR., dir., Pennsylvania Hospital, Philadelphia, PA '87 (ENVIRON)
SOLFISBURG, ROY J., partner, Holabird and Root, Chicago, IL '80 (ENG)
SOLIVAN, JESS, vice-pres. pers., New York University Medical Center, New York, NY '73 (PERS)
SOLOMEN, JACK, pres., The Solomen Agency, Inc., Sherman Oaks, CA '81 (PR)
SOLOMON, ELISABETH F. S., exec. dir., Hall-Brooke Hospital, Division of Hall-Brooke Foundation, Westport, CT '65
SOLOMON, HENRY PETER, health policy analyst, Dept. of HHS, Office of Assistant Secretary for Health Policy, Rockville, MD '64
SOLOMON, JOEL C., staff consult., City of New York, Office of Management and Budget, New York, NY '85 (RISK)

SOLOMON, JUDITH M., dir. pur., Nemours Children's Hospital, Jacksonville, FL '81 (PUR)
SOLOMON, MICHAEL R., dir. health care syst. design, Microproducts, Inc., Boca Raton, FL '77
SOLOMON, MILTON, RN, chief nrsg. serv., Veterans Administration Medical Center, Dayton, OH '84 (NURS)
SOLOMON, RONNI P., atty., Emergency Care Research Institute, Plymouth Meeting, PA '84 (ATTY)
SOLOMON, STEVEN P., adm., Hudson Valley Eye Surgeons, Fishkill, NY '85
SOLOMON, STEVEN, assoc. exec. dir., Coney Island Hospital, Brooklyn, NY '86 (RISK)
SOLOVY, ALDEN T., assoc., Health Facilities Corporation, Northfield, IL '86 (PLNG)
SOLSMAN, JAMES A., dir. eng. and plng., Children's Hospital Medical Center, Cincinnati, OH '69 (ENG)
SOLTIS, MARGARET F., coor. qual. assur., Arabian American Oil Company, Dhahran, Saudi Arabia '84 (RISK)
SOLTIS, MARTHA A. C., sr. assoc., Voluntary Hospitals of America Management Services, Tampa, FL '84 (MGMT)
SOLTIS, SAMUEL L., adm. off., Wilkes-Barre General Hospital, Wilkes-Barre, PA '85 (PLNG)
SOLTIS, STEVE J., exec. dir., St. Mary's Hospital, Huntington, WV '58
SOLTOFF, CHARLES, dir. acct. serv., Albert Einstein Medical Center, Philadelphia, PA '87 (PLNG)
SOLTON, LOUIS, consult., Solton Advisory Consultants, Food Service Industry, Auburn, CA '72 (FOOD)
SOMERBY, CHARLES I., prod. support analyst, Hospital Corporation of America, Nashville, TN '78 (MGMT)
SOMERS, CHERYL A., RN, dir. nrsg., Greater Community Hospital, Creston, IA '82 (NURS)
SOMERS, HERMAN M., prof., Woodrow Wilson School, Princeton, NJ '73 (LIFE)
SOMERS, ORVILLE H., dir. info. syst., St. Joseph Mercy Hospital, Ann Arbor, MI '76
SOMERS, PETER A., atty., Elizabeth General Medical Center, Elizabeth, NJ '77 (ATTY)
SOMERVILLE, CHESTER R., blood serv. oper. assoc., American Red Cross, Washington, DC '85
SOMERVILLE, ROBERT S., chief eng., Culpeper Memorial Hospital, Culpeper, VA '62 (ENG)
SOMMA, EDNA, dir. satellite prog., Spaulding Rehabilitation Hospital, Boston, MA '87 (AMB)
SOMMER, SHERYL A., dir. food serv., Richardson Medical Center, Richardson, TX '85 (FOOD)
SOMMER, THOMAS W., coor. plng. and mktg., Madison County Hospital, London, OH '83 (PLNG)
SOMMERNESS, WILLIAM D., atty., St. Luke's Hospital, Duluth, MN '80 (ATTY)
SOMMERS, PAUL A., PhD, chief adm. off., Ramsey Clinic, St. Paul, MN '86 (PR) (PLNG)
SOMMERVILLE, BONNIE L., RN, vice-pres. nrsg., Children's Medical Center, Dayton, OH '84 (NURS)
SOMMERVILLE, JERRY D., sr. vice-pres., Medical Center Hospital, Punta Gorda, FL '86
SOMOZA, PAUL P., vice-pres. plng. and mktg., New England Deaconess Hospital, Boston, MA '66 (PLNG)
SONDER, CONNIE, RN, assoc. exec. dir. pat. care serv., Metropolitan Hospital-Springfield Division, Springfield, PA '86 (NURS)
SONDLEY, S. L. JR., dir. maint., Baptist Memorial Hospital System, San Antonio, TX '86
SONDUCK, ALLAN C., pres. and chief exec. off., Spohn Kleberg Memorial Hospital, Kingsville, TX '84
SONGER, SARA H., coor. educ. and trng., Centre Community Hospital, State College, PA '82 (EDUC)
SONNANSTINE, MILDRED M., coor. vol., Marion General Hospital, Marion, OH '69 (VOL)
SONNEBORN, JAMES E., dep. dir. pub. affairs, U. S. Army Health Services Command, Fort Sam Houston, TX '72 (PR)
SONNEVILLE, LOUIS E., asst. dir. eng. and maint., Mercy Hospital, Davenport, IA '86 (ENG)
SONNHALTER, MARY ALICE, dir. vol. serv., Saint Thomas Medical Center, Akron, OH '86 (VOL)
SONSTEGARD, LOIS J., student, Program in Hospital and Health Care Administration, University of Minnesota, Minneapolis, MN '81
SOOKY, JUDITH, dir. soc. serv., Cuyahoga Falls General Hospital, Cuyahoga Falls, OH '80 (SOC)
SOONG, ELLIOTT, dir. soc. serv., Mount Ascutney Hospital and Health Center, Windsor, VT '87 (SOC)
SOONTIT, ELENA K., vice-pres. pat. care serv., Palisades General Hospital, North Bergen, NJ '85 (NURS)
SOPER, GEORGE E., vice-pres., Memorial Hospital, South Bend, IN '80
SOPER, KENNETH J., assoc. dir. telecommun. serv., George Washington University, Washington, DC '76 (ENG)
SOPER, LAURA, RN, dir. nrsg. serv., Traverse City Osteopathic Hospital, Traverse City, MI '79 (NURS)
SOPHIE, JILL M., RN, asst. dir. nrsg., Northeast Medical Center Hospital, Humble, TX '86 (NURS)
SOPKOWSKI, JEAN A., RN, dir. surg. serv., Poudre Valley Hospital, Fort Collins, CO '87 (AMB)
SORENSEN, JEROLD G., dir. pub. rel., Utah Valley Regional Medical Center, Provo, UT '80 (PR)
SORENSEN, LT. COL. WAYNE B., MSC USA, chief health care adm. br., Army-Baylor University Program in Health Care Administration, Fort Sam Houston, TX '76
SORENSON, JEAN L., adm. dir., Norfolk General Hospital, Norfolk, VA '87 (AMB)
SORENSON, LUANNE T., dir. mktg. commun., La Crosse Lutheran Hospital, La Crosse, WI '82 (PR)
SORENSON, PATSY L., RN, dir. nrsg. serv., Kootenai Medical Center, Coeur D'Alene, ID '82 (NURS)
SORGE, ANNIE L., atty. and asst. adm., Carraway Methodist Medical Center, Birmingham, AL '75 (ATTY)
SORIANO, WILLIAM J., asst. vice-pres. dev. and pub. rel., St. Charles Hospital and Rehabilitation Center, Port Jefferson, NY '78 (PR)
SOROCHTY, BARBARA L., dir. corp. commun., Wesley Medical Center, Wichita, KS '86 (PR)
SORRELLS-JONES, JEAN, RN, chm. ped. nrsg., Rush-Presbyterian-St. Luke's Medical Center, Chicago, IL '84 (NURS)
SORRELS, DONALD E., dir. eng. and energy prog., Hospital Shared Services of Colorado, Inc., Denver, CO '85 (ENG)
SORRENTI, DAN, dir. pub. rel., St. Vincent's Hospital and Medical Center, New York, NY '84 (PLNG)
SORRENTINO, ELEANOR M., student, Program in Health Care Administration, Baruch College, New York, NY '86
SORRENTINO, MATTHEW R., atty., Muhlenberg Hospital Center, Bethlehem, PA '84 (ATTY)
SORRENTO, JOANNE M., RN, dir. nrsg. serv., Westerly Hospital, Westerly, RI '79 (NURS)
SORTINO, FRED, dir. bldg. serv., Good Samaritan Hospital, Suffern, NY '79 (ENG)
SORTINO, LINDA S., RN, clin. dir. maternal and child nrsg., Shands Hospital, Gainesville, FL '86 (NURS)
SOSEBEE, VIRGIL D., first vice-pres. and dir. healthcare financing, Robinson-Humphrey Company, Inc., Atlanta, GA '82 (PLNG)
SOTTONG, JOAN, RN, dir. nrsg. serv., Saint Joseph Hospital and Health Center, Kokomo, IN '76 (NURS)
SOUCIE, CLARA FRASER SAN, dir. pers., Richmond Eye and Ear Hospital, Richmond, VA '83 (PERS)
SOUDER, HAROLD J., dir. matl. and distrib., Fairview General Hospital, Cleveland, OH '80 (PUR)
SOUDERS, BETTY L., RN, St. Louis, MO '77 (NURS)
SOUDERS, JAMES FRANK, vice-pres., SunHealth Corporation, Charlotte, NC '80
SOUDERS, JOSEPH C., dir. plng., Piqua Memorial Medical Center, Piqua, OH '87 (PLNG)
SOULE, SHIRLEY M., dir. soc. serv., Missouri Baptist Hospital, St. Louis, MO '73 (SOC)
SOUTER, GARY L., dir. pers., Jefferson Regional Medical Center, Pine Bluff, AR '86 (PERS)
SOUTHALL, ANTHONY C., MD, chief emer. medicine, St. John Hospital, Detroit, MI '86 (AMB)
SOUTHARD, GORDON P., dir. biomedical eng., Corning Hospital, Corning, NY '84 (ENG)
SOUTHER, NANCY C., coor. vol. serv., McMinnville Community Hospital, McMinnville, OR '86 (VOL)
SOUTHERLAND, LOUIS F., partner, Page, Southerland and Page, Austin, TX '48 (LIFE)
SOUTHWAY, JAMES W., dir. food serv., Cottage Hospital of Grosse Pointe, Grosse Pointe Farms, MI '78 (FOOD)
SOUTHWICK, ARTHUR F., prof., Graduate School of Business, University of Michigan, Ann Arbor, MI '68 (ATTY)
SOUTHWICK, JAY D., adm., Alta View Hospital, Sandy, UT '78
SOUZA, ELLEN C., mgr. fin. analyst and asst. to chief fin. off., New England Deaconess Hospital, Boston, MA '80
SOUZA, GREGORY J., dir. pers., Kaiser Foundation Hospital, South San Francisco, CA '81 (PERS)
SOUZA, MICHAEL G., consult., Touche Ross and Company, Boston, MA '86 (MGMT)
SOUZA, RUTH T., dir. vol., Valley Children's Hospital, Fresno, CA '82 (VOL)
SOVIE, MARGARET D., PhD RN, assoc. dean nrsg. practice, Strong Memorial Hospital of the University of Rochester, Rochester, NY '79 (NURS)
SOVITZKY, RICK, dir. hosp. info. syst., Luther Hospital, Eau Claire, WI '87 (MGMT)
SOVOCOOL, SCOTT R., mgr. biomedical eng., Providence Memorial Hospital, El Paso, TX '86 (ENG)
SOWA, DIANE C., dir. soc. work, Loretto Hospital, Chicago, IL '85 (SOC)
SOWA, WANDA MARIE, mgr. matl. serv., Los Angeles County-University of Southern California Medical Center, Los Angeles, CA '85 (PUR)
SOWADA, BARBARA J., dir. educ., St. Mary's Hospital and Medical Center, Grand Junction, CO '82 (EDUC)
SOWADA, LINDA C., dir. vol. serv., Memorial Hospital, Craig, CO '84 (VOL)
SOWELL, JOHN D., asst. chief eng., Tri-City Medical Center, Oceanside, CA '73 (ENG)
SOWELL, COL. LEWIS C. JR., MSC USA, mgr. phys. plant and asst. dir. bus. and plant serv. mgt., University of Colorado Health Sciences Center, Denver, CO '83 (ENG)
SOWELL, LINDA A. JACKSON, dir., St. Vincent Charity Hospital, Cleveland, OH '85 (PR)
SOWELS, NORMAN GERALD, dir. matl. mgt., Memorial Hospital, Belleville, IL '78 (PUR)
SOWERS, CAPT. HUBERT H. JR., MSC USN, Naval Medical Clinic, San Francisco, CA '68
SOWERS, LINDA M., dir. soc. serv., Fulton County Medical Center, McConnellsburg, PA '77 (SOC)
SOWULESKI, VINCENT, dir. commun., Baystate Medical Center, Springfield, MA '84 (ENG)
SOX, FREDDY KYLE SR., dir. matl. mgt. and pharm. serv., Lexington County Hospital, West Columbia, SC '85 (PUR)
SOYKA, MICHAEL W., assoc., Hayward and Pakan Associates, Poughkeepsie, NY '82 (ENG)
SPACKMAN, DONALD J., dir. eng., Centre Community Hospital, State College, PA '82 (ENG)
SPACKMAN, RICHARD G., vice-pres. human res., Swedish Medical Center, Englewood, CO '86 (PERS)
SPADONI, REYNOLD G., student, Boston University Health Management Programs, Boston, MA '86 (PLNG)
SPADT, BARBARA, adm., Palmerton Hospital, Palmerton, PA '82 (PLNG)
SPADT, SUSAN K., instr. staff dev., Bryn Mawr Hospital, Bryn Mawr, PA '87 (EDUC)
SPAETH, LOUIS P., vice-pres. fin., St. Elizabeth Medical Center, Dayton, OH '72
SPAETH, RONALD G., pres. and chief exec. off., Highland Park Hospital, Highland Park, IL '81 (PLNG)
SPAGNA, LUCREZIA C., mgr. sup., proc. and distrib., St. Christopher's Hospital, Philadelphia, PA '87 (PUR)
SPAHN, FREDERICK A., dir. eng., Desert Hospital, Palm Springs, CA '77 (ENG)
SPAID, LARRY K., pres., Southern Chester County Medical Center, West Grove, PA '71
SPAIN, FREDERICK G., asst. dir. facil. plng., St. Joseph's Hospital and Medical Center, Paterson, NJ '78 (ENG)
SPAIN, MELANIE B., mgr. pub. info., Carle Foundation Hospital, Urbana, IL '85 (PR)
SPAINHOUR, W. ERWIN, atty., Cabarrus Memorial Hospital, Concord, NC '83 (ATTY)
SPALDING, DAVID J., facil. eng., Institute of Living, Hartford, CT '87 (ENG)
SPALDING, DONALD W., pres., Sewickley Valley Hospital, Sewickley, PA '58
SPALLINA, JOSEPH M., sr. consult., CHI Systems, Inc., Ann Arbor, MI '78 (PLNG)
SPANGENBERG, NANCY, RN, dir. nrsg., Passavant Area Hospital, Jacksonville, IL '79 (NURS)
SPANGLER, CHARLOTTE J., unit mgr. oper. room, Conemaugh Valley Memorial Hospital, Johnstown, PA '79
SPANGLER, HUSTON K., MD, (ret.), Rockville, MD '36 (LIFE)
SPANGLER, JAN, adm., Star Lodge Hospital, Scotts Valley, CA '86 (RISK)
SPANGLER, PATRICIA A., mgr. value improvement prog., William Beaumont Hospital, Royal Oak, MI '87 (MGMT)
SPANKO, DOLORES, dir. vol. serv., Central General Hospital, Plainview, NY '80 (VOL)
SPANN, VALERIA T., asst. dir. soc. work serv., Presbyterian Hospital in the City of New York, New York, NY '83 (SOC)
SPANO-SZEKELY, LAURAINE, health care consult., Peat, Marwick, Mitchell and Company, New York, NY '86
SPANO, ROBERT M., prof. and dir., University of Minnesota Hospital and Clinic, Minneapolis, MN '73 (SOC)
SPARAGNA, ANGELO III, MD, dir. med. affairs, Shore Memorial Hospital, Somers Point, NJ '86 (RISK)
SPARKS, BETH, educ. consult., Bishop Clarkson Memorial Hospital, Omaha, NE '80 (EDUC)
SPARKS, BETTY H., mgr. matl., Humana Hospital -Russellville, Russellville, AL '86 (PUR)
SPARKS, CDR BUDDY TOM, MSC USN, cmdr., Naval Supply Systems Command, Washington, DC '73
SPARKS, J. MARTIN, RN, asst. adm. nrsg. serv., Athens Regional Medical Center, Athens, GA '85 (NURS)
SPARKS, JOHN R., atty., Mount Zion Hospital and Medical Center, San Francisco, CA '78 (ATTY)
SPARKS, TOM, consult., Providence Hospital, Washington, DC '86
SPARROW, ELIZABETH G., asst. mgr. food serv., Bayfront Medical Center, St. Petersburg, FL '85 (FOOD)
SPARSO, NORMA M., RN, vice-pres. pat. care, Charlotte Hungerford Hospital, Torrington, CT '81 (NURS)
SPARTZ, M. EDWARD, asst. vice-pres., Bronson Methodist Hospital, Kalamazoo, MI '82 (PUR)
SPARY, WAYNE ALEXANDER, asst. vice-pres. eng., Bethesda Hospital, Inc., Cincinnati, OH '73 (ENG)
SPATA, MARY R., mgr. heart sta., Lutheran General Hospital, Park Ridge, IL '83
SPATER, ANITA, asst. dir. med. rec., Manhattan Eye, Ear and Throat Hospital, New York, NY '78
SPATES, BARBARA J., asst. dir. food serv., Our Lady of Lourdes Medical Center, Camden, NJ '81 (FOOD)
SPATH, BARBARA G., RN, asst. dir. nrsg. critical care, Albany Medical Center Hospital, Albany, NY '86 (NURS)
SPATOLA, JOSEPHINE, supv. pat. rel., Cigna Health Plan of Arizona, Mesa, AZ '84 (PAT)
SPATZ, BETH A., Loudonville, NY '82
SPAULDING, GENE R., dir. environ. serv., St. Luke's Hospital, Chesterfield, MO '86 (ENVIRON)
SPAULDING, GERTRUDE E., (ret.), Royal Oak, MI '42 (LIFE)
SPAULDING, LORI B., dir. pub. rel., St. Francis Hospital Systems, Colorado Springs, CO '86 (PR)
SPAULDING, P. WHITNEY, spec. proj. off., Sisters of Mercy Health Corporation, Farmington Hills, MI '59 (PLNG)
SPAYDE, DANIEL R., dir. soc. serv., Mansfield General Hospital, Mansfield, OH '78 (SOC)
SPAZIANO, ROBERT A., dir. data proc., Huntington Memorial Hospital, Pasadena, CA '72 (MGMT)
SPEAKES, WILFRED SR., supv. hskpg., Abington Memorial Hospital, Abington, PA '87 (ENVIRON)
SPEAKMAN, ANNE, dir. mktg., New England Medical Center, Boston, MA '85 (PR)
SPEAKS, JEFFREY, mgr. support serv., St. Anthony Hospital, Michigan City, IN '86 (ENG)
SPEAR, STELLA Y., dir. prog. dev., Maryland Hospital Education Institute, Lutherville, MD '86 (EDUC)
SPEARE, BERTRAM, sr. vice-pres., Crozer-Chester Medical Center, Chester, PA '69
SPEARS, JEFFRY S., atty., Northern Illinois Medical Center, McHenry, IL '86 (ATTY)
SPEARS, JEWELL, RN, vice-pres. nrsg., Reid Memorial Hospital, Richmond, IN '77 (NURS)
SPEARS, JOHN W., mgr. pur. and asst. dir. matl. serv., Saint Francis Hospital, Tulsa, OK '81 (PUR)
SPEARS, PATRICK F., vice-pres. plng. and mktg., Harris Methodist Health System, Fort Worth, TX '85 (PR) (PLNG)
SPEARS, RAY M. JR., prof. liability rep., Insurance Reserve Funds, Spartanburg, SC '86 (RISK)
SPEARS, WILLIAM R., dir. pat. rel. and risk mgt., Our Lady of Mercy Hospital, Cincinnati, OH '86 (PAT)
SPECHT, KATHERINE R., RN, asst. adm., Susan B. Allen Memorial Hospital, El Dorado, KS '83 (NURS)
SPECHT, ROGER, vice-pres. plng. and prog. dev., Dakota Hospital, Fargo, ND '81 (PLNG)
SPECK, JOSEPH M., mgr. food serv., Wood County Hospital, Bowling Green, OH '68 (FOOD)
SPECK, KATHY, dir. soc. serv., Methodist Hospital, Madison, WI '79 (SOC)
SPECKEN, JACQUELINE I., coor. vol., Cross Cancer Institute, Edmonton, Alta., Canada '86 (VOL)
SPECTOR, LT. NORMAN BENNETT, MSC USAF, dir. pers. and adm. serv., U. S. Air Force Hospital, Tucson, AZ '76
SPECTOR, STANLEY, Staten Island, NY '80
SPEER, JOHNNIE L., supv. food serv., Brazos Psychiatric Hospital, Waco, TX '86 (FOOD)
SPEER, MICHAEL N., vice-pres. human res., Northern Michigan Hospitals, Petoskey, MI '85 (PERS)

SPEER, STEVEN FRANKLIN, mgr. mgt. eng., St. Vincent Hospital and Health Center, Indianapolis, IN '74 (MGMT)
SPEER, WILLIAM L., chief adm., Headquarters Seventh Medical Command, APO New York, NY '75
SPEESE, GEORGE E., pres., Right Moves, Delaware, OH '71 (PERS)
SPEIGHT, VERNON H., mgr. matl., Baldwin County Hospital, Milledgeville, GA '83 (PUR)(CS)
SPELLINGS, JACK D., dir. environ. serv., St. Joseph Hospital, Memphis, TN '86 (ENVIRON)
SPELLMAN, HARRY, partner, Coopers and Lybrand, Pittsburgh, PA '80
SPELLMAN, MARY C., dir. risk mgt., Suburban Hospital, Bethesda, MD '84 (RISK)
SPELMAN, RUTH E., pat. rep., Metropolitan Hospital and Health Centers, Detroit, MI '77 (PAT)
SPENCE, JOHN H., dir. distrib., Sinai Hospital of Baltimore, Baltimore, MD '84 (PUR)
SPENCER, ANA B., coor. pat. rel., Memorial General Hospital, Las Cruces, NM '83 (PAT)
SPENCER, LCDR CHARLES A., MSC USN, dir. info. syst. and plans and analysis div., dent. care oper., Naval Medical Command, Washington, DC '76
SPENCER, DAWN M., vice-pres. human res., Highland Park Hospital, Highland Park, IL '86 (PERS)
SPENCER, FRED L., dir. plant oper., Sioux Valley Hospital, New Ulm, MN '82 (ENG)
SPENCER, GARY C., dir. plant oper., Memorial Hospital, Carthage, IL '84 (ENG)
SPENCER, GREGORY J., asst. adm. human res., LDS Hospital, Salt Lake City, UT '86 (PERS)
SPENCER, JERRY L., dir. maint., Memorial Hospital of Martinsville, Martinsville, VA '84 (ENG)
SPENCER, JOHN E., dir. eng. and maint., Montana Deaconess Medical Center, Great Falls, MT '81 (ENG)
SPENCER, CAPT. LANTA V., USA MSC, health serv. matl. off., U. S. Army Information Systems Selection and Acquistion Agency, Alexandria, VA '82 (PUR)
SPENCER, LORRAINE H., atty., Emory University Hospital, Atlanta, GA '86 (ATTY)
SPENCER, MARY, consult., The Wyatt Company, Atlanta, GA '87 (PERS)
SPENCER, MICHAEL D., State Nursing Services, San Francisco, CA '77
SPENCER, NOLAN, partner, Coopers and Lybrand, Los Angeles, CA '80
SPENCER, RICHARD A., dir. info. mgt., Jewish Hospital, Louisville, KY '84 (MGMT)
SPENCER, RICHARD L. JR., oper. analyst, Scott and White Memorial Hospital, Temple, TX '83 (MGMT)
SPENCER, SHARON M., mgr. mktg. serv., St. Francis Hospital, Evanston, IL '86 (PR)
SPENCER, SHELDON P., adm. dir. matl. mgt., Washington Adventist Hospital, Takoma Park, MD '85 (PUR)
SPENCER, STEVEN H., adm., Waupun Memorial Hospital, Waupun, WI '78
SPENCER, WILLIAM E., dir. matl. mgt., Mennonite Hospital, Bloomington, IL '83 (PUR)
SPENZOS, THOMAS, dir. sup. serv., Hospital for Joint Diseases, New York, NY '81 (FOOD)
SPERANZA, INEZ F., chm. nutr. and food serv., Greater Pittsburgh Guild for the Blind, Bridgeville, PA '76 (FOOD)
SPERBECK, MICHAEL J., vice-pres. fin., Health Dimensions, Inc., San Jose, CA '76 (PLNG)
SPERL, SR. AUGUSTA, dir. pastoral care and pat. adv., Sacred Heart Hospital, Eau Claire, WI '83 (PAT)
SPERO, JEANNETTE R., RN, dean, College of Nursing and Health, University of Cincinnati, Cincinnati, OH '81 (NURS)
SPEROFF, CLAUDIA L., asst. adm. human res. and support serv., Palo Verde Hospital, Tucson, AZ '83 (RISK)
SPEROS, CAROLYN I., dir. pat. educ., Methodist Hospital-Central Unit, Memphis, TN '82 (EDUC)
SPERRY, CHARLES E., exec. vice-pres., Baring Industries, Inc., Miami, FL '76
SPETNAGEL, MAGGIE, dir. commun., Lutheran Medical Center, Wheat Ridge, CO '86 (ENG)
SPEYRER, GARY N., proj. eng., Veterans Administration Medical Center, Newington, CT '85 (ENG)
SPHATT, THOMAS R., assoc. adm., Parma Community General Hospital, Parma, OH '74
SPIAK, JOSEPH A., vice-pres., Merrill Lynch Capital Markets, New York, NY '73
SPIAK, ROBERT R., assoc. adm., Mercy Hospital, Buffalo, NY '82 (PLNG)
SPICE, DONALD R., pres., Braun and Spice Inc., Architects, Middlebug Heights, OH '84
SPICER, MARY B., dir. food and nutr. serv., AMI Doctors' Hospital, Lanham, MD '77 (FOOD)
SPIEGEL, KEVIN M., student, Adelphi University, Program in Medical Service Administration, Garden City, NY '84
SPIEGEL, RHONDA T., spec. asst. to dir., University of California at Los Angeles Medical Center, Los Angeles, CA '87 (AMB)
SPIEGEL, VIRGINIA A., RN, vice-pres. nrsg. serv., Zurbrugg Memorial Hospital, Willingboro, NJ '84 (NURS)
SPIEKER, DAVID P., dir. pers. and pub. rel., St. Mary's Health Center, Jefferson City, MO '72 (PERS)
SPIELER, MARILYN, dir. vol., Mercy Center for Health Care Services, Aurora, IL '72 (VOL)
SPIELMANN, RICHARD G., asst. adm. dir. food serv., Palisades General Hospital, North Bergen, NJ '82 (FOOD)
SPIES, ARTHUR JOHN II, vice-pres., Iowa Hospital Association, Des Moines, IA '77 (PLNG)
SPIES, DEANNA J., RN, mgr. outpat serv., Danbury Hospital, Danbury, CT '87 (AMB)
SPIETH, GREGG, dir. sales, Gates, McDonald and Company, Columbus, OH '86 (RISK)
SPIKE, CAROL B., supv. cent. sup., Chelsea Community Hospital, Chelsea, MI '73 (CS)
SPIKER, DONDA D., dir. pub. rel., Kuakini Medical Center, Honolulu, HI '85 (PR)
SPIKER, ELLWYN DWAYNE, sr. consult. and dir. reg. res. center dev., Healtheast, Inc., Allentown, PA '57 (LIFE)
SPIKER, MICHAEL I., atty., Hospital Corporation of America, Nashville, TN '87 (ATTY)
SPILDE, DUANE, dir. pat. and family serv., The Hospital, Sidney, NY '85 (SOC)
SPILKER, CHRIS, product spec., Siemens Medical System, Iselin, NJ '86 (MGMT)
SPILKER, MARY F., dir. telecommun., Christian Hospitals Northeast-Northwest, St. Louis, MO '83 (ENG)
SPINDLER, IRENE ASEKOFF, dir. plng., St. Joseph's Medical Center, Fort Wayne, IN '76 (PLNG)
SPINDLER, LANCE A., sr. mgt. eng., Acute Care Affiliates, Berkeley, CA '84 (MGMT)
SPINELLA, JUDY L., RN, assoc. adm. in-patient serv., San Francisco General Hospital Medical Center, San Francisco, CA '84 (NURS)
SPINELLA, NICHOLAS A., atty., St. Mary's Hospital, Richmond, VA '69 (ATTY)
SPINELLI, KAREN L., mgr. pers., St. Joseph Hospital, Orange, CA '82 (PERS)
SPINELLI, ROBERT J., adm., Bloomsburg Hospital, Bloomsburg, PA '85
SPINELLO, RICHARD J., br. mgr., Caronia Corporation, Santa Ana, CA '84 (RISK)
SPINK, ANNE M., dir. pub. rel., Fairbanks Memorial Hospital, Fairbanks, AK '82 (PR)
SPINOSI, SHERRY, dir. cent. serv., West Jersey Hospital, Northern Division, Camden, NJ '86 (CS)
SPITZE, GAIL A., dir. soc. serv., Mercy Medical Center, Roseburg, OR '84 (SOC)
SPITZER, ROXANE, RN, dir. nrs., Cedars-Sinai Medical Center, Los Angeles, CA '76 (NURS)
SPITZER, SYLVIA N., Hollywood, FL '82
SPITZER, WILLIAM J., PhD, dir. soc. work serv., Oregon Health Sciences University Hospital, Portland, OR '82 (SOC)
SPITZFADEN, WERNER, dir. soc. serv. and discharge plng., Coastal Communities Hospital, Santa Ana, CA '87 (SOC)
SPIVACK, DAVID, dir. plng., Mount Sinai Medical Center, Miami Beach, FL '81 (PLNG)
SPIVACK, JULIUS, prin., Mitchell Fein, Inc., Rochester, NY '67 (MGMT)
SPIVACK, SAUL M., vice-pres. plng., University Hospital of Brooklyn-Suny Center, Brooklyn, NY '76 (PLNG)
SPLEEN, MICHAEL A., dir. biomedical eng., Lehigh Valley Hospital Center, Allentown, PA '84 (ENG)
SPLICHAL, VELMA L., coor. pat. serv., Illini Hospital, Silvis, IL '73
SPOERL, ALBERTA C., RN, dir. nrsg. serv., Mercy Hospital, Hamilton, OH '83 (NURS)
SPOFFORD, DANIEL D., dir. diet., Mississippi Baptist Medical Center, Jackson, MS '85 (FOOD)
SPOFFORD, JO ANN, RN, mgr. cent. serv., Candler General Hospital, Savannah, GA '82 (CS)
SPOHN, KAREN S., dir. vol., Bethany Medical Center, Kansas City, KS '83 (VOL)
SPOHNHOLTZ, PATRICIA L., RN, dir. critical care and psych. nrsg., Hinsdale Hospital, Hinsdale, IL '84 (NURS)
SPOHRER, GEORGE A. JR., eng., Crowe, Chizek and Company, South Bend, IN '85 (MGMT)
SPOLYAR, WILLIAM PETER, pres., Mid-Maine Medical Center, Waterville, ME '65
SPONHOLZ, JANE K., vice-pres., Cybertec Consulting Group, New York, NY '80 (PLNG)
SPONSELLER, ARTHUR A., vice-pres. human res. mgt. serv., Hospital Council of Southern California, Center of Health Resources, Los Angeles, CA '84 (PERS)
SPONSELLER, KATHLEEN M., mgr. telecommun., Akron City Hospital, Akron, OH '85 (ENG)
SPOON, DOROTHY J., dir. food and nutr. serv., St. John's Regional Medical Center, Joplin, MO '82 (FOOD)
SPOON, EUGENE E., dir. med. commun., Washoe Medical Center, Reno, NV '84 (ENG)
SPOON, KENNETH R., pres., Reid Memorial Hospital, Richmond, IN '76
SPOONER, MARY M., asst. dir., Archdiocese of Chicago Food Service Program, Chicago, IL '85 (FOOD)
SPOONER, WILLIAM A., dir. info. syst., Sharp Memorial Hospital, San Diego, CA '82 (PLNG)(MGMT)
SPORN, CATHERINE D., dir. qual. assur., Washington Hospital Center, Washington, DC '83 (PAT)
SPOSATO, MARY BELLE, dir. pat. rel., Indian River Memorial Hospital, Vero Beach, FL '75 (PAT)
SPOTILA, SR. LORETTA J., RN, asst. vice-pres. nrsg., St. John Hospital, Cleveland, OH '83 (NURS)
SPOTTS, DONNA C., dir. pers., Hackettstown Community Hospital, Hackettstown, NJ '81 (PERS)
SPOTTS, LAWANDA V., dir. food and nutr. serv., York Hospital, York, PA '78 (FOOD)
SPOTTS, PHYLLIS L., dir. soc. serv., Jewish Hospital, Louisville, KY '77 (SOC)
SPOTTS, RICHARD L., vice-pres. support serv., Hackettstown Community Hospital, Hackettstown, NJ '75 (PUR)
SPRAGENS, KATHRYN W., dir. soc. work serv., University of Kansas Hospital, Kansas City, KS '84 (SOC)
SPRAGUE, CAROLINE S., mgr. vol. serv., Central Vermont Medical Center, Berlin, VT '84 (VOL)
SPRAGUE, CHARLES D., dir. bldg. and grds., Labette County Medical Center, Parsons, KS '81 (ENG)
SPRAGUE, GARY RUSSELL, dir., Health Facility Systems, Santa Monica, CA '68 (PLNG)
SPRAGUE, GERRILYNN A., dir. soc. work, North Shore Medical Center, Miami, FL '86 (SOC)
SPRAGUE, JOSEPH G., dir. health facil., Harwood K. Smith and Partners, Inc., Dallas, TX '85 (ENG)
SPRAGUE, STACEY J., student, Program in Health Services Administration, College of Allied Health, University of Kentucky, Lexington, KY '86
SPRAGUE, STEWART A., exec. eng., Hartford Hospital, Hartford, CT '62 (ENG)
SPRAKER, VIRGINIA B., dir. vol. serv., Buchanan General Hospital, Grundy, VA '82 (VOL)
SPRAMELLI, FRANK J., dir. plng. and mktg., Chambersburg Hospital, Chambersburg, PA '85 (PR) (PLNG)
SPRANDEL, RALPH H., dir. matl. mgt. and pharm., Martha Washington Hospital, Chicago, IL '86 (PUR)
SPRANGER, MARCIA J., exec. dir., Spranger and Associates, Santa Barbara, CA '86 (PLNG)
SPRATT, CHRISTINE, dir. soc. serv., Broward General Medical Center, Fort Lauderdale, FL '84 (SOC)
SPRAUER, CONSTANCE D., atty., Bronson Methodist Hospital, Kalamazoo, MI '87 (ATTY)
SPRECHER, A. GRANT, atty., Children's Rehabilitation Hospital, Philadelphia, PA '77 (ATTY)
SPRECHER, JONATHAN E., RN, asst. dir. nrsg., Greater El Monte Community Hospital, South El Monte, CA '84 (NURS)
SPRENGER, DIAN, sr. vice-pres., Missouri Hospital Association, Jefferson City, MO '73 (PR)(PERS)
SPRENGER, FRANZ A., dir. human res., Sarasota Memorial Hospital, Sarasota, FL '77 (PERS)(EDUC)
SPRENGER, KAREN A., dir. environ. serv., Charter Woods Hospital, Dothan, AL '86 (ENVIRON)
SPRENGER, MARJORY S., RN, coor. qual. assur. and in-service, Bruce Hospital, Florence, SC '84 (EDUC)
SPRIDIK, ROSE ANN, adm. rehab. serv., Church Hospital Corporation, Baltimore, MD '85
SPRIGGS, PHYLLIS A., coor. wage and salary, Muskogee Regional Medical Center, Muskogee, OK '85 (PERS)
SPRING, ALLYSON E., prog. mgr., Maine Hospital Association, Augusta, ME '85 (EDUC)
SPRING, DONALD L., mgr. claim dept., John P. Pearl and Associates Ltd., Peoria, IL '85
SPRING, JOHN M., vice-pres. human res., Grant Medical Center, Columbus, OH '75 (PERS)
SPRINGBORG, LOUIS, supv. bldg. and grds., Waseca Area Memorial Hospital, Waseca, MN '81 (ENG)
SPRINGER, C. SPENCER, dir. emp. rel., Rockford Memorial Hospital, Rockford, IL '64 (PERS)
SPRINGER, DANIEL I., mgr. vascular product, Fisher Imaging Corporation, Denver, CO '86
SPRINGER, ERIC W., Horty, Springer and Mattern, Pittsburgh, PA '68 (ATTY)
SPRINGER, EUGENE C., dir. dev., Suburban General Hospital, Pittsburgh, PA '85 (PR)
SPRINGER, EVELYN W., RN, sr. vice-pres. nrsg., Baptist Hospital, Nashville, TN '82 (NURS)
SPRINGER, EVERETT W., coor. expansion prog., Memorial Hospital, Belleville, IL '69 (ENG)
SPRINGER, HOWARD CAMPBELL JR., dir. soc. work, CPC Fairfax Hospital, Kirkland, WA '85 (SOC)
SPRINGER, JOHN KELLEY, pres. and exec. dir., Hartford Hospital, Hartford, CT '60
SPRINGER, MARTHA J., head food mgt., Naval Hospital, Bethesda, MD '85 (FOOD)
SPRINGER, W. BRUCE, atty., Deaconess Hospital, St. Louis, MO '86 (ATTY)
SPRINGER, WILLIAM H., mgr. eng. serv., Memorial Hospital of Greene County, Catskill, NY '82 (ENG)
SPRINGMEIER, ROBERT W., vice-pres. risk mgt. and governmental affairs, Christian Health Services Development Corporation, St. Louis, MO '79 (RISK)
SPRINKER, ROBERT A., dir. eng., The Medical Center, Beaver, PA '81 (ENG)
SPRINKLE, JACKIE C., dir. pub. and commun. rel., Fayette County Hospital, Fayette, AL '86 (PR)
SPRINT, STEPHEN C., vice-pres. human res., Carondelet Community Hospitals, Minneapolis, MN '79 (PERS)
SPRISSLER, FREDERICK P., dir. matl. mgt., St. Luke's Hospital, Bethlehem, PA '84 (PUR)
SPROUL, KENNETH L., vice-pres. fin., Riverview Medical Center, Red Bank, NJ '86
SPROW, RICHARD A., mng. dir. arch., Urs Company, Montvale, NJ '87 (ENG)
SPRUYT, KATHLEEN T., dir. soc. serv., St. John's Queens Hospital, Flushing, NY '78 (SOC)
SPRY, V. TRACY, dir. bldg. and grd., St. Michael's Hospital, Stevens Point, WI '72 (ENG)
SPURGEON, SUNNY, dir. pub. rel., Ball Memorial Hospital, Muncie, IN '77 (PR)
SPUT, MURRAY, pres., Gonchor and Sput Architects and Plnrs, New York, NY '87
SQUARE, REGINA VENITA, student, Texas Women's University, Houston, TX '84
SQUATTRITO, MARIE, RN, asst. adm., Smith House Residence, Stamford, CT '76 (NURS)
SQUIER, RUTH S., RN, vice-pres. nrsg. adm., Portland Adventist Medical Center, Portland, OR '86 (NURS)
SQUIRE, CHARLOTTE C., vice-pres. clin. serv., Mary Immaculate Hospital, Newport News, VA '82 (AMB)
SQUIRE, RICHARD C. II, vice-pres., Deaconess Hospital of Cleveland, Cleveland, OH '71
SQUIRES, LT. COL. DARRELL R., (ret.), Universal City, TX '72
SRIVASTAVA, PINKI P., student, Rensselaer Polytechnic Institute, Troy, NY '86 (MGMT)
SROCK, TIMOTHY G., dir. human res., Harrison Community Hospital, Mount Clemens, MI '85 (PERS)
SROCZYNSKI, MAUREEN A., RN, dir. nrsg., Rhode Island Hospital, Providence, RI '85 (NURS)
ST. ANDRE, CHRISTINE, assoc. adm., George Washington University Hospital, Washington, DC '76 (RISK)
ST. CHARLES, CAROLYN, RN, dir. med. surg. nrsg., Overlake Hospital Medical Center, Bellevue, WA '82 (NURS)
ST. CLAIR, CATHERINE KINLEY, dir. soc. serv., Forbes Metropolitan Health Center, Pittsburgh, PA '80 (SOC)
ST. CLAIR, NELSON LEWIS JR., pres., Riverside Hospital, Newport News, VA '59
ST. DENIS, FRANK H., vice-pres. human res., Healthwest Medical Centers, Chatsworth, CA '66 (PERS)
ST. DENIS, SCOTT P., proj. plan analyst, Kaiser Foundation Health Plan, Pasadena, CA '82 (PLNG)

ST. GEORGE, GEORGE H., adm. and chief exec. off., Mercy Community Hospital, Port Jervis, NY '73 (PLNG)
ST. GEORGE, LORETTA A., Edwards, CA '85 (EDUC)
ST. GEORGE, SANDRA, coor. pub. rel., Milford-Whitinsville Regional Hospital, Milford, MA '86 (PR)
ST. LAWRENCE, CANDACE A., dir. qual. syst. mgt., Decatur Memorial Hospital, Decatur, IL '83 (RISK)
ST. MARY, RANDALL L., atty., Providence Hospital, Everett, WA '77 (ATTY)
ST. MICHEL, CARRIE G., vice-pres. mktg., Summit Health, Ltd., Los Angeles, CA '86 (PR)
ST. PIERRE, CAROLE, coor. self ins. and risk mgr., Manatee Memorial Hospital, Bradenton, FL '80 (RISK)
STAAB, MICHAEL, dir. qual. assur. and educ. serv., Illini Hospital, Silvis, IL '86 (RISK)
STAATS, LORRAINE G., dir. diet., Clayton General Hospital, Riverdale, GA '79 (FOOD)
STACK, BRIAN KENT, Hadley Regional Medical Center, Hays, KS '84
STACK, SR. JEANNE M., dir. educ. serv., Franciscan Services Corporation, Sylvania, OH '86 (EDUC)
STACK, R. TIMOTHY, pres., South Side Healthcare Systems, Inc., Pittsburgh, PA '76 (PLNG)
STACKPOLE, IRVING L., consult., Reading, MA '87 (PLNG)
STACY, JAY, dir. plant oper., Dallas Rehabilitation Institute, Dallas, TX '85 (ENG)
STACY, RICHARD DAVID, mgr. emp. rel., Fairfax Hospital, Falls Church, VA '78 (EDUC)
STADE, ALAN H., chief soc. work serv., Veterans Administration Center, Fargo, ND '85 (SOC)
STADEL, WILLIAM W., MD, med. dir., San Diego County Mental Health Service, San Diego, CA '49 (LIFE)
STADER, BILL N., maint. eng., Moritz Community Hospital, Sun Valley, ID '85 (ENG)
STADLER, BARBARA, dir. vol., Glendale Adventist Medical Center, Glendale, CA '79 (VOL)
STADLER, MARK, atty., Mercy Hospital of Johnstown, Johnstown, PA '86 (ATTY)
STADNIK, WILLIAM J., gen. mgr., Biomedical Electronics Services and Technologies, Lombard, IL '84 (ENG)
STADNYK, JOHN, dir. resp. ther., George Washington University Hospital, Washington, DC '84
STAEHLE, COL. WILLIAM, MSC USA, U. S. Army Dental Activity, Fort Bragg, NC '69
STAEPEL, CARMEN E., client serv. rep., Camden County Health Services Center, Blackwood, NJ '86 (PAT)
STAFF, FRANK, dir. maint., Humana Hospital -Phoenix, Phoenix, AZ '85 (ENG)
STAFF, MELISSA L., student, Program in Industrial Engineering, University of Pittsburgh, Pittsburgh, PA '84 (MGMT)
STAFFORD, ANN S., RN, dir. nrsg. acute care, Memorial Medical Center, Savannah, GA '84 (NURS)
STAFFORD, RICHARD A., mgr. matl., Humana Hospital -Bennett, Plantation, FL '83 (PUR)
STAFFORD, SUSANNE ZIELINSKI, dir. soc. serv., Riverside Methodist Hospitals, Columbus, OH '77 (SOC)
STAFFORD, T. HENRY, exec. dir., St. Luke's Hospital, Kansas City, MO '86 (PR)
STAFFORD, TOM, student, University of Florida, Gainesville, FL '86 (PLNG)
STAFFORD, WILLA M., mgr. benefits and compensation, Bethany Medical Center, Kansas City, KS '86 (PERS)
STAFFORD, WILLIAM L., adm. sales, Marquette Electronics, Inc., Milwaukee, WI '82
STAFVERFELDT, ULF, mgr. matl., The Swedish Planning and Rationalizing Institute of the Health and Social Services, Stockholm, Sweden '86 (PUR)
STAGER, DIANA F., health planner, New Jersey Hospital Association, Princeton, NJ '86 (PLNG)
STAGG, PAUL L., MD, chrman, Baystate Medical Center, Springfield, MA '87 (AMB)
STAGL, JOHN M., Glenview, IL '53 (LIFE)
STAHL, JEAN E., coor. vol. serv., Walter O. Boswell Memorial Hospital, Sun City, AZ '86 (VOL)
STAHL, WALTER C., asst. dir. remodeling and constr., Childrens Hospital of Los Angeles, Los Angeles, CA '84 (ENG)
STAHLER, CONSTANCE A., RN, dir. adm. and med. staff serv., Franciscan Medical Center, Rock Island, IL '79 (RISK)
STAHLER, JANICE E., dir. pat. educ., Lehigh Valley Hospital Center, Allentown, PA '86 (EDUC)
STAHLNECKER, BETTY J., RN, mgr. cent. serv., Mercy Hospital, Council Bluffs, IA '80 (CS)
STAHURA, BARBARA D., coor. emp. educ., Aultman Hospital, Canton, OH '86 (EDUC)
STAIANO, GLORIA, RN, dir. nrsg., Syosset Community Hospital, Syosset, NY '83 (NURS)
STAIB, DONALD R., mgr. natl. architectural sales, Four Seasons Solar Products, Corporation, Holbrook, NY '87
STAINBACK, ERWIN R., adm. dir. anes., Baylor University Medical Center, Dallas, TX '82
STAIR, CHARLES W., group pres., Servicemaster Industries, Inc., Downers Grove, IL '71
STAKELY, CHARLES A., atty., Jackson Hospital and Clinic, Montgomery, AL '79 (ATTY)
STALBERGER, CAROL, dir. vol., Mercy Hospital, Cedar Rapids, IA '79 (VOL)
STALDER, PAM, dir. soc. serv., Lane Memorial Hospital, Zachary, LA '86 (SOC)
STALEY, GAYLE L., RN, coor. pat. educ., Saint Vincent Hospital, Billings, MT '85 (EDUC)
STALEY, JOHN H., sr. asst. dir., University of Iowa Hospitals and Clinics, Iowa City, IA '71
STALEY, RICHARD M., asst. dir. eng. serv., Providence Medical Center, Portland, OR '86 (ENG)
STALLINGS, OLIVIA, chief soc. work, Veterans Administration Medical Center, Allen Park, MI '80 (SOC)
STALNAKER, WANDA LEE, dir. qual. assur. and risk mgt., AMI Palmetto General Hospital, Hialeah, FL '80 (RISK)
STALOCH, LORI A., mgt. eng., Medical College of Virginia Hospitals, Richmond, VA '86 (MGMT)
STALZER, JOHN R., exec. dir., Intertech Corporation, Great Neck, NY '85
STAM, DEBRA L., assoc. dir. educ. serv., Parkview Memorial Hospital, Fort Wayne, IN '86 (EDUC)
STAMATACOS, HELEN, adm. asst., Bon Secours Health System, Inc., Columbia, MD '84
STAMBAUGH, STEWART J., exec. vice-pres., Servicemaster East Management Services, Inc., Wayne, PA '69
STAMEY, ARTHUR W., chief eng. serv., Veterans Administration Medical Center, Reno, NV '86 (ENG)
STAMM, KATHLEEN M., adm. analyst, Group Health Cooperative, Seattle, WA '81 (MGMT)
STAMM, SCOTT C., asst. adm., Kennedy Memorial Hospitals University Medical Center, Stratford, NJ '86 (PLNG)
STAMMER, ANNE, RN, adm., Peter Longmeed General Hospital, Calgary, Alta., Canada '77 (MGMT)
STAMOULIS, CHRYSANTHE H., RN, dir. surg. nrsg. serv., Rhode Island Hospital, Providence, RI '84 (NURS)
STAMPER, RANDALL L., atty., Deaconess Medical Center-Spokane, Spokane, WA '78 (ATTY)
STANCIL, BILL, mgr. pub. rel., Nash General Hospital, Rocky Mount, NC '80 (PR)
STANCOMBE, SHIRLEY, coor. vol. serv., Ridgecliff Hospital, Willoughby, OH '81 (VOL)
STANDLEY, BURGESS P., dir. plng., Massachusetts General Hospital, Boston, MA '80 (PLNG)
STANDLEY, IDA C., dir. vol., Lake Forest Hospital, Lake Forest, IL '72 (VOL)
STANDLEY, STEVEN D., dir. matl. mgt., Firelands Community Hospital, Sandusky, OH '84 (PUR)
STANELLE, MILDRED E., RN, asst. dir. nrsg., Mount Sinai Medical Center, Milwaukee, WI '86 (NURS)
STANEWICK, BARBARA B., RN, nrs. consult., American Sterilizer Company, Erie, PA '85 (CS)
STANFIELD, R. H., dir. ldry. and linen, Jefferson Regional Medical Center, Pine Bluff, AR '86 (ENVIRON)
STANFORD, BETTY J., vice-pres. human res., St. Peter's Medical Center, New Brunswick, NJ '74 (PERS)
STANFORD, GENE A., dir. matl. mgt., Baptist Medical Center of Oklahoma, Oklahoma City, OK '84 (PUR)
STANFORD, GENE, dir. human serv., Arkansas Children's Hospital, Little Rock, AR '82 (PAT)
STANG, HARRY R., atty., Hospital Council of Southern California, Los Angeles, CA '76 (ATTY)
STANG, JOSEPH A., dir. soc. serv., Riverside Medical Center, Kankakee, IL '79 (SOC)
STANGER, LINLEY M., RN, prof. serv. consult., Brim and Associates, Inc., Portland, OR '85 (NURS)
STANGL, LEONARD, sr. vice-pres. corp. affairs, Our Lady of Mercy Hospital, Dyer, IN '68 (PLNG)
STANGO, JOSEPH, mgr. plant oper., St. Joseph Medical Center, Burbank, CA '85 (ENG)
STANGO, MARTY R., chief exec. off., Health Options, Inc., Jacksonville, FL '84
STANISH, THOMAS J., dir. plant oper., Providence-St. Margaret Health Center, Kansas City, KS '84 (ENG)
STANISLAUS, SR. HELEN, RN, adm. asst., Holy Name of Jesus Medical Center, Gadsden, AL '73 (NURS)
STANK, BARBARA J., mgr. bldg. serv., New England Deaconess Hospital, Boston, MA '86 (ENVIRON)
STANK, THOMAS D., mgr. plant oper., Appleton Medical Center, Appleton, WI '76 (ENG)
STANKO, AMBER, RN, asst. adm., Shadyside Hospital, Pittsburgh, PA '82 (NURS)
STANKOVSKY, CHARLES D., dir. mgt. eng., Meriter Hospital, Madison, WI '77 (MGMT)
STANLEY, BONNIE L., RN, vice-pres. nrsg., Hancock Memorial Hospital, Greenfield, IN '86 (NURS)
STANLEY, CHARLOTTE HARDMAN, dir. soc. serv., Helen Hayes Hospital, West Haverstraw, NY '73 (SOC)
STANLEY, FREDERICK F., asst. dir. mgt. eng., Cleveland Clinic Hospital, Cleveland, OH '81 (MGMT)
STANLEY, JAMES, dir. pub. rel., Rehabilitation Institute of Santa Barbara, Santa Barbara, CA '85 (PR)
STANLEY, JOSEPHINE M., dir. vol. serv., Middle Tennessee Mental Health Institute, Nashville, TN '85 (VOL)
STANLEY, RUTH ELLEN, pat. rep., Hardin Memorial Hospital, Elizabethtown, KY '74 (PAT)
STANLEY, SHERYL L., coor. pub. rel., Lea Regional Hospital, Hobbs, NM '85 (PR)
STANLEY, VANETTA L., mgr. pat. assistance, Kaiser Foundation Hospital, Santa Clara, CA '87 (PAT)
STANLEY, WARREN, chief eng., Beaufort Memorial Hospital, Beaufort, SC '85 (ENG)
STANSHINE, ISABEL, RN, assoc. dir. nrsg. serv., Bryn Mawr Hospital, Bryn Mawr, PA '82 (NURS)
STANTON, ADRIAN R., asst. dir. mktg., Suburban Hospital, Bethesda, MD '86 (PLNG)
STANTON, JOHN F., health care planner, Ferrenz Taylor Clark and Associates, Inc., New York, NY '79 (PLNG)
STANTON, JUDY, dir. pub. rel., Mount Sinai Medical Center, Miami Beach, FL '78 (PR)
STANTON, SR. MARGARET MARY, coor. pat. rel., Mercy Catholic Medical Center, Fitzgerald Mercy Division, Darby, PA '73 (PAT)
STANTON, MARY GRACE P., dir. vol., Muhlenberg Hospital Center, Bethlehem, PA '70 (VOL)
STANTON, ROBERT D., atty., Mecosta County General Hospital, Big Rapids, MI '80 (ATTY)
STANTON, RUTH A., RN, dir. nrsg., Brownsville General Hospital, Brownsville, PA '86 (NURS)
STANTON, WILLIAM CLARK, atty., Hospital Council of Southern California, Los Angeles, CA '85 (ATTY)
STANUSH, SHARON M., vice-pres. mktg. and standards, San Antonio Children's Center, San Antonio, TX '86 (PLNG)
STANZIONE, RICHARD W., dir. soc. serv., Washington County Hospital, Hagerstown, MD '84 (SOC)
STAPF, MARY ANN L., RN, asst. coor. cent. sup. room, St. Luke's Hospital, Kansas City, MO '80 (CS)
STAPLES, JANET MARTENS, dir. mktg., Osteopathic Hospital of Maine, Portland, ME '82 (PR) (PLNG)
STAPLES, JANET W., mgr. pers., Jones County Community Hospital, Laurel, MS '85 (PERS)
STAPLES, KEITH JOSEPH, paramedic, Hays Memorial Hospital, San Marcos, TX '82
STAPLES, PAUL L., biomedical eng., Charleston Memorial Hospital, Charleston, SC '87 (ENG)
STAPLETON, DONALD F., dir. telecommun., St. Joseph Hospital, Flint, MI '85 (ENG)
STAPP, GARY L., mgr. bldg. craft, Los Angeles County-University of Southern California Medical Center, Los Angeles, CA '85 (ENG)
STAPP, THOMAS D., mgr. maint., Children's Hospital, St. Louis, MO '81 (ENG)
STARACE, JULIET, dir. soc. serv., St. Joseph's Medical Center, Yonkers, NY '79 (SOC)
STARBIRD, LIFE, mgr. sup., proc. and distrib., St. Francis Hospital and Medical Center, Topeka, KS '86 (CS)
STARBUCK, CHARLES E., atty., Bronson Healthcare Group, Inc., Kalamazoo, MI '83 (ATTY)
STARBUCK, MARY ANN, dir. commun. serv., Hudson Headwaters Health Network, Warrensburg, NY '87 (AMB)
STARCHMAN, LEON, dir. commun. rel., Schick Shadel Hospital, Santa Barbara, CA '85 (PR) (PLNG)
STARESNICK, MICHAEL J., asst. dir., Indiana University Northwest, Gary, IN '82 (PLNG)
STARK, COLETTE R., supv. telecommun., Community Hospital, Munster, IN '83 (ENG)
STARK, GRETCHEN K., RN, dir. nrsg., Boone County Hospital, Boone, IA '82 (NURS)
STARK, J. D., adm. asst. and pur. agt., King's Daughters Hospital, Greenville, MS '81 (PUR)
STARK, JEAN K., RN, dir. cent. sup., Swedish Medical Center, Englewood, CO '83 (CS)
STARK, JOHN C., atty., Southwest Florida Regional Medical Center, Fort Myers, FL '74 (ATTY)
STARK, MARILYN S., prog. serv. rep., Venzke Service Company, Southfield, MI '86 (RISK)
STARK, NATHAN J., atty., Kominers, Fort, Et Al, Washington, DC '68 (ATTY)(HON)
STARK, RANDY L., mgr. emp. rel., St. Clare's Hospital of Schenectady, Schenectady, NY '83 (PERS)
STARK, ROBERT G., asst. adm. eng. and plant oper., Memorial Hospital, Albany, NY '70 (ENG)
STARK, SEYMOUR, dir. commun. rel. and dev., John T. Mather Memorial Hospital, Port Jefferson, NY '74 (PR) (PLNG)
STARK, TALBOT A., student, University of Wisconsin, Madison, WI '87 (MGMT)
STARKEY, BERNARD H., dir. diet., Henry Ford Hospital, Detroit, MI '80 (FOOD)
STARKEY, GENEVIEVE, dir. vol., Memorial Hospital, St. Joseph, MI '70 (VOL)
STARKEY, RHONDA E., plng. and mktg. spec., Southwest Health System, Greensburg, PA '82 (PLNG)
STARKEY, ROBERT L., dir. human res., North Charles Hospital, Baltimore, MD '66 (PERS)
STARKEY, VESTA, (ret.), Albuquerque, NM '82 (SOC)
STARKS, RANDOLPH C., loss prevention spec., Kentucky Hospital Service Corporation, Louisville, KY '83 (RISK)
STARKWEATHER, RICHARD A., dir. trng. and dev., Providence Hospital, Southfield, MI '82 (EDUC)
STARN, D. D., dir. ldry., Marshalltown Medical and Surgical Center, Marshalltown, IA '86 (ENVIRON)
STARN, ROGER R., consult., United Hospital, St. Paul, MN '53 (LIFE)
STARNES, DEBORAH, RN, coor. nrsg. educ., William Beaumont Hospital, Royal Oak, MI '84 (EDUC)
STARNES, JUANITA, dir. vol. serv., Holston Valley Hospital and Medical Center, Kingsport, TN '80 (VOL)
STARNES, KEN, chief eng., HCA Sun Towers Hospital, El Paso, TX '87 (ENG)
STARR-KNECHT, DEBRA, dir. pat. rel., San Gabriel Valley Medical Center, San Gabriel, CA '85 (PAT)
STARR, CONNIE J., dir. commun. rel., Terre Haute Regional Hospital, Terre Haute, IN '84 (PR)
STARR, GROVER L., prin., Neptune and Thomas Associates, San Diego, CA '85 (ENG)
STARR, ROBERT, mgr. matl., Potters Medical Center, East Liverpool, OH '84 (PUR)
STARR, SAM, partner, Jansen and Rogan, New York, NY '81 (ENG)
STARRETT, CLIFFORD W., atty., Morristown Memorial Hospital, Morristown, NJ '79 (ATTY)
STARRETT, FRANCIS M., mgr. path., Bellevue Hospital Center, New York, NY '82
STARRETT, H. GEORGE JR., chief eng., North Pennsylvania Hospital, Lansdale, PA '82 (ENG)
STARRETT, LOYD M., atty., Modern Health Care Services, Inc., North Miami Beach, FL '73 (ATTY)
STARRICK, KATHLEEN PERRIN, dir. hosp. rel., Four Winds Hospital, Katonah, NY '86 (PR)
STARZENSKI, ANN FAIRCHILD, vice-pres., Washington Hospital, Washington, PA '76
STARZYNSKI, MIDGE, RN, dir. nrs., Bethesda Hospital and Community Mental Health Center, Denver, CO '77 (NURS)
STASHOWER, EMILY R., coor. plng., Union Memorial Hospital, Baltimore, MD '83 (PLNG)
STASIOWSKI, SHIRLEY ANN, RN, vice-pres. adm., Richland Memorial Hospital, Columbia, SC '77 (NURS)
STASKO, RUTH B., mgr. pers., West Oaks-Psychiatric Institute Houston, Houston, TX '82 (PERS)
STATES, ELIZABETH R., dir. pers., Charleston Memorial Hospital, Charleston, SC '86 (PERS)
STATHOS, HELEN, dir. food serv., Martha Washington Hospital, Chicago, IL '71 (FOOD)
STATON, JAMES H., assoc. adm., Women and Infants Hospital of Rhode Island, Providence, RI '83
STATZER, MAJ. FRED C., MSC USAF, chief trng. eval. div., School of Health Care Sciences, Sheppard AFB, TX '75
STAUB, JOHN F., pres., St. Clair Ambulatory Care Corporation, Detroit, MI '87 (AMB)
STAUBER, FRANCOISE D., risk mgr., West Virginia University Hospital, Morgantown, WV '84 (RISK)

STAUDER, STEPHANIE C., dir. food serv., Parkside Medical Services Corporation, Park Ridge, IL '86 (FOOD)
STAUFFER, BECKY, dir. outpatient serv., Wyoming Medical Center, Casper, WY '87 (AMB)
STAULCUP, RALPH, assoc. exec. dir., Bronx Municipal Hospital Center, Bronx, NY '73 (PERS)
STAUM, BARRY, MD, mng. partner, Janzen, Johnston and Rockwell, Marina Del Rey, CA '87 (RISK)
STAUNCH, LINDA J., dir. pub. rel., Craven County Hospital, New Bern, NC '86 (PR)
STAVIG, GERALDINE, supv. sup., proc. and distrib., North Memorial Medical Center, Robbinsdale, MN '83 (CS)
STAVRAKAS, SPYROS T., mgr. syst. dev., Travenol Laboratories, Deerfield, IL '84 (PLNG)
STAVRINOU, ANDREW, asst. chief eng., Boca Raton Community Hospital, Boca Raton, FL '84 (ENG)
STAVROS, WILLIAM A., adm. food serv., Quincy City Hospital, Quincy, MA '84 (FOOD)
STAY, GARY E., planner, Intermountain Health Care, Inc.-Northern Region, Ogden, UT '82 (PLNG)
STAY, KAREN J., dir. vol., St. Joseph Hospital and Health Care Center, Tacoma, WA '82 (VOL)
STEACY, JAMES F., exec. vice-pres., Marian Medical Center, Santa Maria, CA '53 (LIFE)
STEADHAM, MARK B., adm. asst., St. Joseph Medical Center, Wichita, KS '83
STEADMAN, CLAYTON D., atty., Medical College of Georgia Hospital and Clinic, Augusta, GA '86 (ATTY)
STEAGALL, DIANE L., dir. commun., Tampa General Hospital, Tampa, FL '86 (ENG)
STEARN, ROBIN R., asst. planner, Providence Hospital, Southfield, MI '80 (PLNG)
STEARNS, CHARLES BALDWIN, exec. vice-pres., Health Management Services, Inc., Columbus, OH '63
STEARNS, GERRY, pres., Care Communications, Inc., Chicago, IL '79
STEARNS, GRETCHEN L., mgr. human syst. res., Saint Vincent Health Center, Erie, PA '86 (MGMT)
STEARNS, HARRIS L., dir. matl. mgt., Jameson Memorial Hospital, New Castle, PA '83 (CS)
STEARNS, NAOMI M., dir. soc. work, Charles A. Dana Hospital of Sidney Farber Cancer Institute, Boston, MA '80 (SOC)
STEBBINS, DEBORAH E., exec. vice-pres. amb. serv., Alta Bates Hospital, Berkeley, CA '81 (PLNG)
STECHER, JO A., pat. educator, Long Island College Hospital, Brooklyn, NY '86 (EDUC)
STECHSCHULTE, EDITH M., RN, dir. nrsg., Lansing General Hospital, Lansing, MI '83 (NURS)
STECK, HANS W., atty., Bingham, Summers, Welch and Spilman, Beech Grove, IN '86 (ATTY)
STECK, JANICE K., RN, coor. cont. educ., Methodist Medical Center of Illinois, Peoria, IL '86 (EDUC)
STECKEL, EVE, dir. vol. serv., Hollywood Medical Center, Hollywood, FL '79 (VOL)
STECKELBERG, ANN M., dir. in-service, Lutheran Community Hospital, Norfolk, NE '86 (EDUC)
STECKER, ALICE F., RN, dir. nrsg., Baker Hospital, North Charleston, SC '86 (NURS)
STECKMAN, DORAL E., plant eng., Medicine Lodge Memorial Hospital, Medicine Lodge, KS '84 (ENG)
STECKROAT, ROBERT W., chief eng., Dakota Hospital, Fargo, ND '73 (ENG)
STEDMAN, EDWIN W., dir. security and telecommun., University Hospital, Boston, MA '86 (ENG)
STEDMAN, HUGH T., atty., Blue Cross and Blue Shield of Georgia-Atlanta, Atlanta, GA '86 (ATTY)
STEDMAN, JULIAN A., dir. biomedical tech., University of Alberta Hospitals, Edmonton, Alta., Canada '81 (ENG)
STEED, ROBERT A., adm., Willamette Falls Hospital, Oregon City, OR '84
STEED, THOMAS W. JR., atty., Rex Hospital, Raleigh, NC '73 (ATTY)
STEEL, LOUISE D., dir. vol. serv. and pat. activ., St. Margaret Memorial Hospital, Pittsburgh, PA '82 (VOL)
STEEL, STEFANIE, dir. pub. affairs and commun., Doctors Hospital, New York, NY '79 (PR)
STEELE, BARBARA S., RN, vice-pres. nrsg., W. A. Foote Memorial Hospital, Jackson, MI '84 (NURS)
STEELE, CHERYL A., RN, head nrs. amb. care, Forbes Regional Health Center, Monroeville, PA '87 (AMB)
STEELE, ELLIOTT SPERO, dir. diet. serv., University Community Hospital, Tampa, FL '86 (FOOD)
STEELE, FRIDAY, pat. serv. rep., Singing River Hospital System, Pascagoula, MS '84 (PAT)
STEELE, GERALD L., dir. plant oper., Wuesthoff Memorial Hospital, Rockledge, FL '83 (ENG)
STEELE, JEANNE ROGGE, consult. pub. rel. and mktg., Northland Health Group, Bangor, ME '84 (PR)
STEELE, KENNETH B., mgt. eng., Yale-New Haven Hospital, New Haven, CT '77 (MGMT)
STEELE, KIM, mgr. hskpg. and safety, Deaconess Medical Center-Spokane, Spokane, WA '86 (ENVIRON)
STEELE, LARRY W., supv. acct. serv., Edmonds Packett Group, Roanoke, VA '85 (PR)
STEELE, MARGARET M., chief diet. serv., Veterans Administration Medical Center, Tucson, AZ '75 (FOOD)
STEELE, MARIAN C., RN, nrs. mgr., Rapid City Regional Hospital, Rapid City, SD '84 (NURS)
STEELE, MARTHA FAYE, dir. pat. rep., Nashville Memorial Hospital, Madison, TN '83 (PAT)
STEELE, MARY H., head nrs. cent. sup., St. Francis Hospital, Columbus, GA '82 (CS)
STEELE, MYRON T., atty., Kent General Hospital, Dover, DE '83 (ATTY)
STEELE, NORMAN J., dir. educ. serv., Children's Hospital of Michigan, Detroit, MI '86 (EDUC)
STEELE, RICHARD J., vice-pres., Birch and Davis Associates, Inc., Silver Spring, MD '80
STEELE, SUSAN E., asst. dir. educ., St. Anthony's Hospital, St. Petersburg, FL '85 (EDUC)
STEELMAN, H. JESS, dir. safety and occup. health, North Broward Hospital District, Fort Lauderdale, FL '86 (ENG)
STEENBLIK, GLEN R., dir. counseling serv., Cottonwood Hospital Medical Center, Murray, UT '86 (SOC)
STEFAN, JUDY C., dir. pers., AMI Anclote Manor Psychiatric Hospital, Tarpon Springs, FL '82 (PERS)
STEFANELLI, LOUISE KATHRYN, dir. soc. serv., Columbus Hospital, Newark, NJ '66 (SOC)
STEFANIDES, CHRISTINE M., RN, asst. adm. and dir. nrsg., Physicians Memorial Hospital, La Plata, MD '86 (NURS)
STEFANO, ELEANOR F., RN, asst. dir. nrsg., Western Pennsylvania Hospital, Pittsburgh, PA '86 (NURS)
STEFANSKY, STEVE, vice-pres. facil. and sup. serv., Mount Sinai Hospital Medical Center of Chicago, Chicago, IL '67 (ENG)
STEFANSON, RANDOLPH E., atty., St. Ansgar Hospital, Moorhead, MN '72 (ATTY)
STEFFEE, SAM L., exec. vice-pres., The Methodist Hospital, Houston, TX '64
STEFFEL, CHARLES R., supv. clin. eng. and elec., St. Paul-Ramsey Medical Center, St. Paul, MN '86 (ENG)
STEFFEL, PATRICIA E., RN, dir. nrsg., Highland View Hospital, Cleveland, OH '67 (NURS)
STEFFEN, KAREN K., RN, asst. adm. nrsg. serv., Good Samaritan Hospital, Kearney, NE '84 (NURS)
STEFFEN, KEITH EMANUEL, asst. adm., Saint Francis Medical Center, Peoria, IL '79
STEFFEN, NATHAN E., dir. plant oper., Saint Joseph Hospital, Elgin, IL '74 (ENG)
STEGER, BYRON L., (ret.), San Antonio, TX '49 (LIFE)
STEGER, WILLIAM G., dir. mktg., Highland Hospital of Rochester, Rochester, NY '86 (PR) (PLNG)
STEGGEMAN, JAMES J., adm. res., Riverside Methodist Hospitals, Columbus, OH '84
STEGMAN, SANDRA, student, University of Dayton, Dayton, OH '87 (AMB)
STEGNER, JOEL R., dir. res. serv., Lifespan, Inc., Minneapolis, MN '81 (PLNG)
STEHLE, EMILY L., commun. spec., Tampa General Hospital, Tampa, FL '86
STEHMAN, CAROL H., asst. dir. food serv., Montgomery Hospital, Norristown, PA '86 (FOOD)
STEIB, CHARLES H., pres., Major Catholic Hospital Alliance, St. Louis, MO '76 (ATTY)(AMB)
STEIBER, STEVEN R., chief exec. off., SRI Gallup, Chicago, IL '86 (PLNG)
STEIERT, LYNWOOD L., facil. eng., Immanuel-St. Joseph's Hospital, St. Joseph's Unit, Mankato, MN '68 (ENG)
STEIGELMAN, LUCIA KAMM, RN, dir. nrs., St. Mary's Health Services, Grand Rapids, MI '83 (NURS)
STEIGER, LT. COL. C. L., MSC USAF, U. S. Air Force Clinic, APO New York, NY '73
STEIGER, DALE L., dir. plng. and mgt. serv., Bon Secours Hospital, Grosse Pointe, MI '69 (PLNG)
STEIGER, MICHAEL W., adm. dir., Joint Township District Memorial Hospital, St. Marys, OH '84 (RISK)
STEIGMAN, WILLIAM F., atty., Spector, Cohen, Gadon and Rosen, Philadelphia, PA '78 (ATTY)
STEIGMEYER, CONNIE L., supv. educ. serv., Terre Haute Regional Hospital, Terre Haute, IN '87 (EDUC)
STEIMLE, EDMUND A. JR., vice-pres., New England Baptist Hospital, Boston, MA '76
STEIN, BARBARA C., dir. vol. serv., Philadelphia Psychiatric Center, Philadelphia, PA '86 (VOL)
STEIN, BARBARA, asst. dir. amb. serv., Children's Hospital, Boston, MA '87 (AMB)
STEIN, DAVID S., PhD, dir. educ. and trng., Ohio State University Hospitals, Columbus, OH '75 (EDUC)
STEIN, ERIC D., asst. adm., Las Encinas Hospital, Pasadena, CA '76 (PERS)
STEIN, ERIC H., vice-pres. mktg. &plng, Ellis Hospital, Schenectady, NY '87 (PR) (PLNG)
STEIN, FLORENCE T., (ret.), Jamesburg, NJ '72 (SOC)
STEIN, GARY A., mgt. eng., Southern Baptist Hospital, New Orleans, LA '80 (MGMT)
STEIN, GERALD L., dir. soc. serv., Theda Clark Regional Medical Center, Neenah, WI '85 (SOC)
STEIN, HARRIET SUSAN, coor. pat. rel., Frankford Hospital, Philadelphia, PA '86 (PAT)
STEIN, M. AUDREY, mgr. sup., proc. and distrib., Community Hospitals of Indiana, Indianapolis, IN '72 (CS)
STEIN, MARTIN, vice-pres. fin., Mount Sinai Hospital, Toronto, Ont., Canada '84 (RISK)
STEIN, ROBERT G., dir. mktg. and mem. rel., Associates of Western Hospitals, San Francisco, CA '81
STEIN, SUSAN C., Rumford, RI '79
STEIN, SUSAN, Chicago, IL '86 (SOC)
STEINBECK, BARBARA A., prod. dev. analyst, Health Systems International, New Haven, CT '86
STEINBERG, CAREN G., dir. mgt. eng., Holy Cross Hospital, Mission Hills, CA '86 (MGMT)
STEINBERG, CECILE G., dir. sales, Carle Foundation Hospital, Urbana, IL '84
STEINBERG, GARY ALAN, asst. dir., Presbyterian-University of Pennsylvania Medical Center, Philadelphia, PA '71
STEINBERG, GERALD M., pres., Gerald M. Steinberg and Associates, Nokesville, VA '82 (ENG)
STEINBERG, ROBERT A., bd. mem., Sinai Hospital of Detroit, Detroit, MI '80 (RISK)
STEINBERG, SAMUEL H., vice-pres. plng. and mktg., Hahnemann University Hospital, Philadelphia, PA '77 (PLNG)
STEINBINDER, AMY, mgr. nrsg. educ., St. Joseph's Hospital and Medical Center, Phoenix, AZ '86 (EDUC)
STEINBRUECKER, SUSAN RUSSLER, mgr. soc. serv., Appleton Medical Center, Appleton, WI '79 (SOC)
STEINEMAN, JAMES J., dir. human res. mgt., St. Francis Memorial Hospital, San Francisco, CA '85 (PERS)
STEINER, SR. AGNES, coor. cont. health educ., Sisters of Charity, Leavenworth, KS '71 (EDUC)
STEINER, BARBARA C., planner, Henry Ford Hospital, Detroit, MI '80 (PLNG)
STEINER, EDWARD F., dir. pers., Covenant Medical Center-Schoitz, Waterloo, IA '74 (PERS)
STEINER, JULIUS MICHAEL, atty., Van Buren Community Hospital, Van Buren, ME '76 (ATTY)
STEINER, MATHEW W., pres., The Steiner Company, Ann Arbor, MI '67 (MGMT)
STEINER, MICHAEL S., mgr. proj. dev., Mount Sinai Medical Center, New York, NY '83
STEINER, SUSAN M., assoc. chief nrsg. serv., Veterans Administration Medical Center, Sepulveda, CA '78
STEINERT, JEFF H., pres., Steinert Healthcare Systems, Inc., Charlotte, NC '76
STEINES, PHILIP A., RN, asst. adm. nrsg., Perry Memorial Hospital, Princeton, IL '83 (NURS)
STEINFADT, DOUGLAS L., dir. matl. mgt., Sioux Valley Hospital, Sioux Falls, SD '75 (PUR)
STEINFELD, JOEL, vice-pres. pers., Hunterdon Medical Center, Flemington, NJ '82 (PERS)
STEINHAUER, GORDON L., adm. stress reduction, St. Lawrence Hospital Dimondale Center, Dimondale, MI '84
STEINHAUER, IVINS JR., dir. cardiopulmonary tech. serv., Martin Memorial Hospital, Stuart, FL '87 (AMB)
STEINHOLTZ, SAMUEL, MD, (ret.), Silver Spring, MD '31 (LIFE)
STEINKE, JANE, RN, mgr. cent. sup., Dearborn County Hospital, Lawrenceburg, IN '85 (CS)
STEINKULLER, ANDREA L., coor. market res., Glendale Heights Community Hospital, Glendale Heights, IL '85 (PLNG)
STEINLE, NANETTE I., dir. food and nutr. serv., King Khaled Eye Specialist Hospital, Riyadh, Saudi Arabia '86 (FOOD)
STEINLY, BEVERLY J., mgr. cent. proc., Children's Hospital, Columbus, OH '86 (PUR)(CS)
STEINMAN, DIANE L., asst. vice-pres., Hospital of the Good Samaritan, Los Angeles, CA '81 (PLNG)
STEINMAN, JAMES F., dir. mktg., Froedtert Memorial Lutheran Hospital, Milwaukee, WI '85 (PLNG)
STEINMETZ, DOLORES, coor. fiscal serv., Children's Mercy Hospital, Kansas City, MO '85 (RISK)
STEISKAL, MARGARET E., mgr. nutr. serv., Riverside Methodist Hospitals, Columbus, OH '75 (FOOD)
STEITZ, ROBIN W., asst. dir. long range plng., Hermann Hospital, Houston, TX '85 (PLNG)
STEJBACH, NANCY A., dir. soc. serv., Sacred Heart-St. Mary's Hospitals, Rhinelander, WI '83 (SOC)
STELL, WAYNE D., supv. sup., proc. and distrib., St. Joseph's Hospital and Health Care Center, Tucson, AZ '85 (CS)
STELMACK, SR. ELIZABETH, pat. rep., St. Vincent's Hospital, Harrison, NY '87 (PAT)
STELSON, JAMES M., mgr. energy and staff eng., Fort Sanders Regional Medical Center, Knoxville, TN '82 (ENG)
STELTER, WILLIS L., arch., Foss Associates, Fargo, ND '83
STELZLE, CHARLES JOSEPH, pat. rep., Good Samaritan Hospital, Cincinnati, OH '87 (PAT)
STEMPHOSKI, RONALD L., vice-pres. human res., Our Lady of Lourdes Memorial Hospital, Binghamton, NY '83 (PERS)
STEMPLE, NATALIE, RN, dir. critical care nrsg. div., Akron City Hospital, Akron, OH '86 (NURS)
STENCE, FRANCES L., RN, vice-pres. pat. serv., Chambersburg Hospital, Chambersburg, PA '75 (NURS)
STENDER, MONICA D., dir. nutr. serv., Baylor Institute for Rehabilitation, Dallas, TX '85 (FOOD)
STENNER, JOHN MARTIN, head mgt. info., Naval Dental Clinic, Jacksonville, FL '82
STENNER, RICHARD H., adm., North Colorado Medical Center, Greeley, CO '69
STENNETT, LEROY B., mgr. matl., Princeton Community Hospital, Princeton, WV '74 (PUR)
STENSEL, ALICE, head diet., Wheelock Memorial Hospital, Goodrich, MI '77 (FOOD)
STENSON, RICHARD VINCENT, adm., Straub Clinic and Hospital, Honolulu, HI '71
STENSRUD, KAREN L., RN, asst. adm. and dir. nrsg. serv., McKay-Dee Hospital Center, Ogden, UT '81 (NURS)
STEPANEK, ROBERT, dir. soc. work, Foster G. McGaw Hospital, Loyola University, Maywood, IL '70 (SOC)
STEPELEVICH, DAVID A., dir. plant oper., Fairmount Institute, Philadelphia, PA '86 (ENG)
STEPHAN, KAREN L., dir. pers., Northwest General Hospital, Milwaukee, WI '85 (PERS)
STEPHANI, MARY S., New Berlin, WI '77 (FOOD)
STEPHEN, RICHARD J. JR., Pembroke Pines, FL '77 (MGMT)
STEPHENS, ANN, dir. pub. rel., Southeastern General Hospital, Lumberton, NC '86 (PR)
STEPHENS, BETSY A., mgt. eng., Bronson Methodist Hospital, Kalamazoo, MI '80 (MGMT)
STEPHENS, CYNTHIA MARIE, pat. rep. off., U. S. Army Hospital, Heidelberg, Germany '87 (PAT)
STEPHENS, GLEN E., atty., Parkview Community Hospital, Riverside, CA '73 (ATTY)
STEPHENS, GREG J., consult., Ross Laboratories, Columbus, OH '84 (FOOD)
STEPHENS, JAMES H., pres. and chief exec. off., St. John's Healthcare Corporation, Anderson, IN '72
STEPHENS, JEAN L., dir. vol. serv., Memorial Medical Center, Savannah, GA '85 (VOL)
STEPHENS, KATHY E., asst. dir. clin. nutr., Harris Methodist -Fort Worth, Fort Worth, TX '82 (FOOD)
STEPHENS, LEWIS C., asst. adm., St. Mary's Hospital, Galesburg, IL '83 (RISK)
STEPHENS, LINDA D., mgt. eng., William Beaumont Hospital, Royal Oak, MI '84 (MGMT)
STEPHENS, MARK A., dir. pub. rel., Mercy Hospital, Wilkes-Barre, PA '80 (PR)
STEPHENS, MARY E., RN, dir. oper. room and cent. serv., St. Luke's Hospital, Milwaukee, WI '80 (NURS)
STEPHENS, MARYLIN, RN, assoc. adm. pat. care, HCA Brotman Medical Center, Culver City, CA '80 (NURS)
STEPHENS, PERRY L., dir. pers., DeKalb General Hospital, Decatur, GA '79 (PERS)
STEPHENS, PHILIP C., dir. environ. serv., Southside Regional Medical Center, Petersburg, VA '75 (ENG)
STEPHENS, ROBERT J., books ed., Catholic Health Association, St. Louis, MO '86 (PR)

STEPHENS, ROBERT L., sr. serv. mgr. matl. mgt., Yale-New Haven Hospital, New Haven, CT '86 (PUR)
STEPHENS, ROBERT R., dir. food serv., Hillcrest Medical Center, Tulsa, OK '73 (FOOD)
STEPHENS, ROGER K., dir. soc. work, Graduate Hospital, Philadelphia, PA '80 (SOC)
STEPHENS, SHEILA A., RN, div. mgr. nrsg. serv., St. Joseph's Hospital, Stockton, CA '82 (NURS)
STEPHENSON, BETTY ANN, asst. mgr. food serv., Scottsdale Memorial Hospital, Scottsdale, AZ '78 (FOOD)
STEPHENSON, DARLENE GILLIKIN, supv. soc. serv., Hampton General Hospital, Hampton, VA '86 (SOC)
STEPHENSON, DAVID, dir. plant oper., Charter Hospital of Long Beach, Long Beach, CA '81 (ENG)
STEPHENSON, JEANNE M., RN, assoc. adm. and dir. nrsg., Phoenix Children's Hospital, Phoenix, AZ '85 (NURS)
STEPHENSON, KENNA, consult., Pitts Management Associates, Inc., Baton Rouge, LA '78
STEPHENSON, LEON M., eng., Clinton Regional Hospital, Clinton, OK '76 (ENG)
STEPHENSON, LINDA KAY, RN, Florence, SC '85 (NURS)
STEPHENSON, RAMONA, RN, head nrs. amb. care unit, Lykes Memorial Hospital, Brooksville, FL '87 (AMB)
STEPLER, SANDRA K., writer and consult., Sandra Stepler and Associates, Valparaiso, IN '86 (PR) (PLNG)
STEPLETON, SANDRA S., dir. nrsg. educ., St. Joseph Health Care Corporation, Albuquerque, NM '84 (EDUC)
STEPNOWSKI, CHARLES J., pres., E. S. P., Inc., Glastonbury, CT '79 (PERS)
STEPOWANY, MARY ELLEN, dir. qual. and risk mgt., Maryland Hospital Education Institute, Lutherville, MD '86 (RISK)
STEPURA, BARBARA A., RN, dir. adm. serv. nrsg., Alexandria Hospital, Alexandria, VA '86 (NURS)
STERGIS, ANN L., chief tech., Berkshire Medical Center, Pittsfield, MA '82 (CS)
STERLING, ALAN W., student, Brigham Young University, Salt Lake City, UT '86 (PLNG)
STERLING, DALLAS E., dir. plant oper., Tampa General Hospital, Tampa, FL '86 (ENG)
STERLING, HENRY P. JR., asst. adm., Chestnut Lodge Hospital, Rockville, MD '82 (PERS)(ENG)
STERLING, SUSAN E., student, Program in Health Services Administration, Indiana University, Indianapolis, IN '82
STERMER, LEA M., asst. dir. food serv., Mercy Hospital Medical Center, Des Moines, IA '80 (FOOD)
STERN, ANN L. L., RN, Wichita, KS '79 (NURS)
STERN, DANIEL, pres., Daniel Stern and Associates, Pittsburgh, PA '83
STERN, IRIS, RN, pat. care rep., Lakeside Hospital, Metairie, LA '85 (PAT)
STERN, JO, dir. commun. rel. and vol. serv., Nesbitt Memorial Hospital, Kingston, PA '84 (PR)
STERN, MELANIE, adm. res., Johns Hopkins University, Baltimore, MD '81
STERN, MERYL C., adm. and med. soc. worker, Associated Social Resources, Beverly Hills, CA '86 (SOC)
STERN, MYRA, student, National College, Evanston, IL '85
STERN, RON, adm., Nesbitt Memorial Hospital, Kingston, PA '74
STERN, SUSAN A., supv. nrsg., Veterans Administration Medical Center, Phoenix, AZ '86 (RISK)
STERNBERG, MERLE T., dir. soc. serv., Bayonne Hospital, Bayonne, NJ '82 (SOC)
STERNDALE, ELIZABETH A., RN, assoc. dir. health and temperance, General Conference of Seventh-Day Adventists, Washington, DC '82 (NURS)
STERNE, GARNET, RN, Lake Charles, LA '86 (NURS)
STERNER, BARBARA BOND, asst. dir. vol., Greater Baltimore Medical Center, Baltimore, MD '84 (VOL)(PAT)
STERNES, DAVID M., dir. soc. serv., Kingsbrook Jewish Medical Center, Brooklyn, NY '85 (SOC)
STERNITZKE, MARK S., mgt. eng., Texas Hospital Association, Richardson, TX '84 (MGMT)
STERNLOF, PAUL W., pres. and chief exec. off., Sharon Hospital, Sharon, CT '55 (LIFE)
STERTMANN, EDWARD A., dir. eng. and maint., Jefferson Regional Medical Center, Pine Bluff, AR '85 (ENG)
STETLER, CHERYL B., RN PhD, chm. staff educ. and nrsg. studies, Massachusetts General Hospital, Boston, MA '86 (EDUC)
STETSON, ROBERT L., asst. vice-pres., St. Luke's Samaritan Health Care, Inc., Milwaukee, WI '85 (PR)
STETT, GREGORY J., dir. biomedical eng., Schumpert Medical Center, Shreveport, LA '80 (ENG)
STETTES, KIM S., dir. commun. rel., St. Anthony's Medical Center, St. Louis, MO '80 (PR)
STETTLER, SHERRY K., RN, dir. educ., Ashley Valley Medical Center, Vernal, UT '85 (EDUC)
STEUSLOFF, KAY M., mgr. health center, Samaritan Health Center, Detroit, MI '82
STEUVER, PATRICIA J., RN, vice-pres. nrsg., St. Elizabeth Medical Center-South, Edgewood, KY '80 (NURS)
STEVELMAN, DANIEL, unit mgr., Brookdale Hospital Medical Center, Brooklyn, NY '77
STEVEN, JAMES D. R., exec. vice-pres., Bethany Enterprises, Inc., Phoenix, AZ '85 (PLNG)
STEVENS, ANITA KAY, mgr. data proc., Logan County Health Center, Guthrie, OK '85 (MGMT)
STEVENS, APRIL A., RN, asst. exec. dir., Forbes Metropolitan Health Center, Pittsburgh, PA '86 (NURS)
STEVENS, LT. COL. CHARLES GREGORY, MSC USA, asst. insp. gen., Fifth Mash, 44th Medical Brigade, Fort Bragg, NC '75
STEVENS, CLARENCE JIM, asst. dir. maint., Bronson Methodist Hospital, Kalamazoo, MI '81 (ENG)
STEVENS, COURTNEY M., RN, asst. dir. pat. serv., Saint Joseph Hospital, Reading, PA '84 (NURS)
STEVENS, DIANA, head nrs., Grady Memorial Hospital, Delaware, OH '87 (AMB)
STEVENS, DONALD M. JR., dir. facil. mgt., Mary Imogene Bassett Hospital, Cooperstown, NY '83 (ENG)
STEVENS, CAPT. EDWARD P., MSC USA, off. med. oper., 18th Airborne Corps Artillery, Fort Bragg, NC '81
STEVENS, ERIC E., bus. mgr. facil. serv., Good Samaritan Hospital and Medical Center, Portland, OR '82 (ENG)
STEVENS, EVERETT J., dir. plant oper., Memorial Hospital, Nacogdoches, TX '81 (ENG)
STEVENS, GAIL DOVE, dir. rehab. proj., Pitt County Memorial Hospital, Greenville, NC '86 (PERS)
STEVENS, GLENDA, dir. matl. mgt., Harris Methodist -Stephenville, Stephenville, TX '85 (PUR)
STEVENS, HENRY, dir. pers., Humana Hospital -Biscayne, Miami, FL '78 (PERS)
STEVENS, JAMES C., dir. matl. mgt., Cortland Memorial Hospital, Cortland, NY '79 (PUR)
STEVENS, JAMES D., adm. asst., HCA Edgefield Hospital, Nashville, TN '80 (RISK)
STEVENS, JAMES G., dir. human resources, Holy Cross Hospital, Fort Lauderdale, FL '73 (PERS)
STEVENS, JEANNE B., dir. pat. rel., Southeastern General Hospital, Lumberton, NC '85 (PAT)
STEVENS, JOYCE M., mgr. matl., Willamette Falls Hospital, Oregon City, OR '83 (PUR)(CS)
STEVENS, KATHLEEN A., coor. plng. and mktg. syst., Katherine Shaw Bethea Hospital, Dixon, IL '86 (PR)
STEVENS, KATHRYN R., dir. soc. work, Grant Hospital of Chicago, Chicago, IL '79 (SOC)
STEVENS, LAWRENCE K., pat. rep., Loma Linda University Medical Center, Loma Linda, CA '86 (PAT)
STEVENS, MARK D., supv. environ., Hospital Center at Orange, Orange, NJ '87 (ENVIRON)
STEVENS, MARVIN L., dir. eng., Cushing Memorial Hospital, Leavenworth, KS '85
STEVENS, MELINDA S., dir. pers., Dallas County Hospital District-Parkland Memorial Hospital, Dallas, TX '85 (PERS)
STEVENS, NANCY, pat. rep., Lehigh Valley Hospital Center, Allentown, PA '76 (PAT)
STEVENS, PATRICIA A., RN, supv. cent. sup., Samaritan Hospital, Troy, NY '83 (CS)
STEVENS, PEGGY D., dir. educ., LDS Hospital, Salt Lake City, UT '84 (EDUC)
STEVENS, PENELOPE L., RN, dir. pat. care serv., Penobscot Valley Hospital, Lincoln, ME '85 (NURS)
STEVENS, RAY O., dir. ldry. and linen serv., Alexandria Hospital, Alexandria, VA '86 (ENVIRON)
STEVENS, ROBERT E., pur. agt., Holy Family Hospital, Estherville, IA '80 (PUR)
STEVENS, ROBERT J., vice-pres. mktg. and sales, Gaston Health Care, Inc., Gastonia, NC '84 (PLNG)
STEVENS, ROBERT M., pres., Rms Associates, Port Washington, NY '84 (PUR)
STEVENS, WILLIAM O., dir. pur., North Penn Hospital, Lansdale, PA '80 (PUR)
STEVENSON-MILLARD, LINDA, dir. soc. serv., Ketchikan General Hospital, Ketchikan, AK '85 (SOC)
STEVENSON, ALICE, dir. soc. work, Detroit Receiving Hospital and University Health Center, Detroit, MI '85 (SOC)(PAT)
STEVENSON, CAROL A., RN, dir. nrsg., Barlow Hospital, Los Angeles, CA '86 (NURS)
STEVENSON, DIANE R., RN, assoc. dir. nrsg., Meriden-Wallingford Hospital, Meriden, CT '86 (NURS)
STEVENSON, G. BARNES III, mgr., Arthur Andersen and Company, Stamford, CT '86
STEVENSON, GERALD K., dir. maint. and eng., Cabell Huntington Hospital, Huntington, WV '78 (ENG)
STEVENSON, GUS, adm., Hauch Medical Clinic, Inc., Pomona, CA '73 (CS)
STEVENSON, RICHARD D., dir. plant serv., Community Memorial Hospital, Monmouth, IL '66 (ENG)
STEVENSON, SUSAN L., adm. asst. orthopaedic surg., Long Island Jewish Medical Center, New York, NY '86
STEVER, BERNARD G., vice-pres. mktg. and food serv. group, Hussmann Corporation, St. Louis, MO '82 (FOOD)
STEVER, M. EDWIN, vice-pres., Magliaro and McHaney, Inc., La Jolla, CA '86
STEVERSON, L. NEIL, atty., St. Mary's Hospital, Richmond, VA '82 (ATTY)
STEWARD, CLIFFORD A., dir. commun. rel., Southside Hospital, Bay Shore, NY '86 (PR)
STEWARD, WILLARD, asst. dir. eng., Lehigh Valley Hospital Center, Allentown, PA '86 (ENG)
STEWART, BETTY, coor. vol. serv., McKenzie-Willamette Hospital, Springfield, OR '85 (VOL)
STEWART, CATHERINE M., dir. vol. serv., New Berlin Memorial Hospital, New Berlin, WI '86 (VOL)
STEWART, CHARLES C., pres., Mercer Medical Center, Trenton, NJ '48 (LIFE)
STEWART, CHARLES J., dir. diet. serv., St. Joseph's Medical Center, Yonkers, NY '81 (FOOD)
STEWART, CHRISTINA M., adm. dir., St. Paul Medical Center, Dallas, TX '87 (AMB)
STEWART, CINDY A., dir. vol. serv., Jewish Hospital, Louisville, KY '81 (VOL)
STEWART, DAVID W., pres., Blue Cross and Blue Shield of the Rochester Area, Rochester, NY '85 (LIFE)
STEWART, DONNA DICOLA, coor. pat. educ., Cedars-Sinai Medical Center, Los Angeles, CA '83 (EDUC)
STEWART, EDGAR A., atty., Selma Medical Center, Selma, AL '68 (ATTY)
STEWART, ELIZABETH H., student, University of Dallas, Irving, TX '84 (PR)
STEWART, ELLEN A., adm. res., HCA West Paces Ferry Hospital, Atlanta, GA '83
STEWART, ELLEN ELIZABETH, atty., Gorsuch, Kirgis, Campbell, Walker and Grover, Denver, CO '85 (ATTY)
STEWART, SR. ESTHER, mgr. cent. sup. serv., St. Joseph Hospital and Health Care Center, Tacoma, WA '82 (CS)
STEWART, FRANCES A., ombudsman, Mount Carmel Medical Center, Columbus, OH '79 (PAT)
STEWART, H. FRANCIS, atty., Tennessee Christian Medical Center, Madison, TN '79 (ATTY)
STEWART, HAL S. R., exec. dir. foundation-pub. rel., Martha Washington Hospital, Chicago, IL '86 (PR)
STEWART, HOLLY D., mgr. sup., proc. and distrib., St. Luke's Hospital, Davenport, IA '80 (CS)
STEWART, JAMES A., vice-pres., Mercy Hospital Medical Center, Des Moines, IA '87 (ENG)
STEWART, JAMES A., assoc. dir. cent. sup., proc. and distrib., Thomas Jefferson University Hospital, Philadelphia, PA '77 (CS)(PUR)
STEWART, JAMES H., mgr. indust. affairs, Syntex Laboratories, Inc., Palo Alto, CA '85
STEWART, JAMES J., asst. dir. eng., Saddleback Community Hospital, Laguna Hills, CA '84 (ENG)
STEWART, JANET M., sr. mgt. eng., Akron City Hospital, Akron, OH '85 (MGMT)
STEWART, JIMMY T., pres., Medicus, Evanston, IL '84 (MGMT)
STEWART, JOAN B., dir. vol. and commun. rel., Community Hospital, Watervliet, MI '85 (VOL)
STEWART, JOHN P., dir. dev., St. Joseph's Hospital Medical Center, Bloomington, IL '86 (PR)
STEWART, JOHN, supv. cent. sup., Lawrence and Memorial Hospital, New London, CT '79 (CS)
STEWART, JOSEPHINE H., dir. psych. soc. work, The Methodist Hospital, Houston, TX '75 (SOC)
STEWART, KATHRYN K., dir. pat. and vol. serv., Welborn Memorial Baptist Hospital, Evansville, IN '84 (PAT)(VOL)
STEWART, KATHRYN W., dir. pers., Mercy Center for Health Care Services, Aurora, IL '85 (PERS)
STEWART, KENNETH P., atty., Wesley Medical Center, Wichita, KS '68 (ATTY)
STEWART, KENNETH, dir. risk mgt., Saint Vincent Hospital, Worcester, MA '80 (RISK)
STEWART, LAWRENCE D., pres., Weatherby Health Care, Inc., Norwalk, CT '76
STEWART, LEARLENE B., dir. food serv., Gottlieb Memorial Hospital, Melrose Park, IL '82 (FOOD)
STEWART, LOUANN, educ. spec., Samaritan Health Center, Detroit, MI '85 (EDUC)
STEWART, LYN S., div. mgr., Sheppard and Enoch Pratt Hospital, Baltimore, MD '80 (RISK)
STEWART, MARY L., coor. vol. serv., Ontario Hospital Association, Don Mills, Ont., Canada '82 (VOL)
STEWART, MICHAEL R., atty., Grinnell General Hospital, Grinnell, IA '78 (ATTY)
STEWART, NANCY J., Family Home Care, Spokane, WA '80 (EDUC)
STEWART, NOEL J., buyer, Champlain Valley Physicians Hospital Medical Center, Plattsburgh, NY '77 (PUR)
STEWART, PATRICIA L., San Antonio, TX '75
STEWART, PEGGY B., RN, chief nrsg. serv., Jerry L. Pettis Memorial Veterans Hospital, Loma Linda, CA '82 (NURS)
STEWART, PETER G., atty., Health Corporation of Archdiocese of New Jersey, Newark, NJ '81 (ATTY)
STEWART, PHYLLIS E., dir. commun., University of Minnesota Hospital and Clinic, Minneapolis, MN '74 (ENG)
STEWART, ROBERT P., dir. soc. work, Timberlawn Psychiatric Hospital, Dallas, TX '76 (SOC)
STEWART, ROBERTA L., dir. plng. and mktg., Medical Center Hospital, Chillicothe, OH '83 (PLNG)
STEWART, SHERI L., coor. prog. dev., Roseville Community Hospital, Roseville, CA '87 (PR) (PLNG)
STEWART, SUSAN C., dir. commun., University of Connecticut Health Center, John Dempsey Hospital, Farmington, CT '84 (ENG)
STEWART, SUSAN H., RN, dir. nrsg. serv., Our Lady of the Way Hospital, Martin, KY '86 (NURS)
STEWART, SUSAN K., student, Program in Industrial Engineering, Iowa State University, Ames, IA '86 (MGMT)
STEWART, SUSAN PHILLIPPE, dir. plng. and mktg. res., Saint Joseph's Care Group, Inc., South Bend, IN '82 (PLNG)
STEWART, THOMAS L., dir. eng. and maint., Memorial Hospital, Carbondale, IL '77 (ENG)
STEWART, TINA, dir. soc. serv., St. John Medical Center, Steubenville, OH '81 (SOC)
STEWART, VICTORIA A., mgr. commun., Robert Packer Hospital, Sayre, PA '85 (ENG)
STEWART, WAYNE CHARLES, student, Temple University, Department of Health Administration, Philadelphia, PA '85
STEWART, WILHELMINA C., RN, vice-pres. pat. and critical care serv., Emanuel Hospital and Health Center, Portland, OR '86 (NURS)
STEWART, WILLIAM H., MD, chancellor, Louisiana State University Medical Center, New Orleans, LA '67 (HON)
STEWART, WILLIAM J., atty., Indian River Memorial Hospital, Vero Beach, FL '73 (ATTY)
STEWERT, MARY ANN, asst. mgt. serv., Children's Hospital National Medical Center, Washington, DC '80
STIBBARDS, J. E., pres. and chief exec. off., Children's Hospital, Buffalo, NY '85
STICH, WILLIAM L., dir. matl. mgt., Kettering Medical Center, Kettering, OH '81 (PUR)
STICHMAN, JOYCE, vice-pres., Memorial Hospital for Cancer and Allied Diseases, New York, NY '87 (PR) (PLNG)
STICHTER, ALVERTA, sr. vice-pres., Lehigh Valley Hospital Center, Allentown, PA '86
STICKEN, JANET M., asst. adm. med. serv., Hills and Dales General Hospital, Cass City, MI '79 (PAT)
STICKLER, K. BRUCE, atty., Wood, Lucksinger and Epstein, Chicago, IL '76 (ATTY)
STIEBER, GEORGE L., dir. plant oper., Saint Mary Hospital, Langhorne, PA '81 (ENG)
STIER, RICHARD D., vice-pres. mktg., Porter Memorial Hospital, Denver, CO '82 (PR) (PLNG)
STIEREN, PATRICIA L., coor. pat. educ. and instr. nrsg., Memorial Medical Center, Springfield, IL '83 (EDUC)
STILES, ALBERT R. SR., risk mgr., Brookhaven Memorial Hospital Medical Center, Patchogue, NY '83 (RISK)
STILES, BILL H., chm., Stiles-Bradley, Chattanooga, TN '79 (PR)

STILES, MICHAEL D., dir. educ. serv., St. Luke's Regional Medical Center, Sioux City, IA '81 (EDUC)
STILGENBAUER, NANCY K., dir. pur., Memorial Hospital, McPherson, KS '80 (PUR)
STILL, KAREN CYNTHIA, plng. analyst, St. Paul Medical Center, Dallas, TX '85 (PLNG)
STILLER, JENNIFER A., atty., St. Joseph's Hospital, Philadelphia, PA '79 (ATTY)
STILLMAN, DONALD, supv. acct., Brian Keith Advertising, Health Care Mktg Division, Oak Brook, IL '84 (PLNG)
STILLMAN, PAUL, dir. plng. and mktg., Manchester Memorial Hospital, Manchester, CT '82 (PLNG)
STILLMAN, ROBBIE R., dir. vol. serv., Akron General Medical Center, Akron, OH '86 (VOL)
STILLWELL, JUDITH W., asst. dir. mktg., Children's Hospital, Columbus, OH '86 (PR)
STILO, PATRICIA C., dir. vol. serv., Muhlenberg Regional Medical Center, Plainfield, NJ '81 (VOL)
STILWILL, MICHAEL K., dir. pers., Mercy Health Center, Dubuque, IA '75 (PERS)
STIMMEL, BARRY E., vice-pres. human rel., Washington Adventist Hospital, Takoma Park, MD '78 (PERS)
STIMSON, DIANNE M., exec. vice-pres. and chief oper. off., Saint Joseph Hospital, Fort Worth, TX '81
STIMSON, RUTH H., assoc. prof., School of Public Health, University of California, Berkeley, CA '57 (LIFE)
STINETORF, MICHAEL E., proj. arch., Kaplan, McLaughlin and Diaz Architects and Planners, San Francisco, CA '86 (ENG)
STINNETT, LOGAN WAYNE, oper. mgr. mktg., Memorial Northwest Hospital, Houston, TX '85 (PLNG)
STINNETT, WILSON M., Longview, TX '76
STINSON, ANTHONY J., dir. support serv., James C. Giuffre Medical Center, Philadelphia, PA '86 (ENVIRON)
STINSON, CATHY CIMINO, dir. human res., Charter Hospital of Tampa Bay, Tampa, FL '86 (PERS)
STINSON, DONNA H., atty., Tallahassee Community Hospital, Tallahassee, FL '83 (ATTY)
STINSON, JAMES A., asst. adm. dir., Duke University Hospital, Durham, NC '77 (MGMT)
STINSON, KARL R., U. S. Army Hospital, Dugway, UT '80
STIPANOVICH, ALICE V., dir. diet., St. Joseph Hospital and Health Center, Lorain, OH '77 (FOOD)
STIPE, SALLY W., pat. rep., St. Elizabeth's Hospital, Chicago, IL '78 (VOL)(PAT)
STIREMAN, LINDA B., dir. mktg. and pub. rel., George L. Mee Memorial Hospital, King City, CA '86 (PR)
STIREWALT, GENE, mgr. plant eng. serv., Rowan Memorial Hospital, Salisbury, NC '86 (ENG)
STIRLEN, ANNE O., dir. soc. work, Norwalk Hospital, Norwalk, CT '86 (SOC)
STITELER, NORMAN A., mgr. cost analysis, Hamot Medical Center, Erie, PA '81 (MGMT)
STITELY, DORIS M., RN, dir. nrsg. serv., Ohio Valley General Hospital, McKees Rocks, PA '77 (NURS)
STITES, ELIZABETH B., dir. corp. commun. and pub. rel., Health East, St. Paul, MN '86 (PR)
STIVER, ALAN W., commun. tech., Western Reserve Health Systems-Southside Medical Center, Youngstown, OH '85 (ENG)
STIWARD, ALICE THOMAS, dir. human res., Charity Hospital of Louisiana at New Orleans, New Orleans, LA '84 (PERS)
STOAKES, JAMES RUSSELL, dir. eng., Lafayette Home Hospital, Lafayette, IN '71 (ENG)
STOCK, DAVID D., vice-pres. plng. and dev., Institute for Rehabilitation and Research, Houston, TX '86 (AMB)
STOCK, KATHLEEN A., mgr. pers., Watertown Memorial Hospital, Watertown, WI '82 (PERS)
STOCK, RICHARD G., vice-pres. corp. serv., Royal Victoria Hospital, Montreal, Que., Canada '81 (PLNG)
STOCKDALE, DANIEL R., Stow, OH '84 (PLNG)
STOCKDALE, MARTHA L., assoc., Ohio Hospital Management Services, Columbus, OH '81 (MGMT)
STOCKEL, CRAIG E., dir. commun. rel. and mktg., Saint James Hospital, Pontiac, IL '86 (PR)
STOCKER, THOMAS A., consult., Price Waterhouse, Denver, CO '86 (MGMT)
STOCKMAN, EPHRIAM B., dir. food serv., Indian River Memorial Hospital, Vero Beach, FL '82 (FOOD)
STOCKMAN, MELANIE A., RN, dir. amb. nrsg., Rhode Island Hospital, Providence, RI '85 (NURS)
STOCKS, GLORIA J., RN, coor. cent. proc. and distrib., Winona Memorial Hospital, Indianapolis, IN '75 (CS)
STOCKS, MARJORIE L., coor. pat. educ., Pacific Presbyterian Medical Center, San Francisco, CA '85 (EDUC)
STOCKTON, PATRICK F., mgr. plant oper., Ottumwa Regional Health Center, Ottumwa, IA '85 (ENG)
STOCKTON, ROBERT L., dir. plant oper. and environ. serv., Coral Reef Hospital, Miami, FL '84 (ENG)
STOCKWELL, DON, mgr. environ. serv., Mercy Hospital of Sacramento, Sacramento, CA '86 (ENVIRON)
STOCKWELL, JOHN FARRINGTON, consult., Center Sandwich, NH '52 (PR)(LIFE)
STODD, JAMES T., dir. pers., Brokaw Hospital, Normal, IL '82 (PERS)
STODDARD, MARK R., adm., Central Valley Medical Center, Nephi, UT '84
STODDARD, WILLIAM D. II, dir. pat., fiscal and admit. serv., University of Iowa Hospitals and Clinics, Iowa City, IA '68
STODDART, TOM D., risk mgr., Orlando Regional Medical Center, Orlando, FL '84 (RISK)
STOECKLIN, D. C., dir. environ. serv., Henry Ford Hospital, Detroit, MI '86 (ENVIRON)
STOEHNER, DORIS J., RN, asst. adm. nrsg. serv., Christian Hospitals Northeast-Northwest, St. Louis, MO '73 (NURS)
STOESSNER, DOROTHY L., dir. vol. serv., Robinson Memorial Hospital, Ravenna, OH '78 (VOL)
STOEVEN, PEGGY A., asst. dir. nrsg., Olympia Fields Osteopathic Medical Center, Olympia Fields, IL '84 (NURS)
STOFFAN, PHILIP M., vice-pres. advancement, St. Lawrence Hospital, Lansing, MI '79 (PR)
STOFFERSON, TERRY L., contr., Lafayette General Medical Center, Lafayette, LA '85
STOGLIN, CORINNE E., RN, assoc. dir. nrsg., Lutheran Medical Center, Wheat Ridge, CO '81 (NURS)
STOGNER, MARCELL C., dir. pers., Riverside Medical Center, Franklinton, LA '86 (PERS)
STOKELY, SHEILA R., dir. pat. rep., University Hospital, Augusta, GA '76 (PAT)
STOKES, ALFRED C., mgr. cent. distrib., Pitt County Memorial Hospital, Greenville, NC '84 (PUR)
STOKES, BILLY M., dir. environ. serv., Humana Hospital -San Antonio, San Antonio, TX '86 (ENVIRON)
STOKES, DONNA J., adm. dir. pub. rel. and mktg., Bay Medical Center, Panama City, FL '85 (PR) (PLNG)
STOKES, GARY L., adm., University Park Hospital, Tyler, TX '75
STOKES, GRADY H., adm., Haywood County Hospital, Clyde, NC '81 (PLNG)
STOKES, JOHN W., dir. institutional rel., North Carolina Memorial Hospital, Chapel Hill, NC '76 (PR)
STOKES, JUDY FORD, pres., Judy Ford Stokes and Associates, Atlanta, GA '84 (FOOD)
STOLAR, ANNE PAXTON, adm., Illinois Cancer Council, Chicago, IL '79
STOLL, CAROLYN I., mgr. pers., Grossmont District Hospital, La Mesa, CA '84 (PERS)
STOLL, CAROLYN P., RN, vice-pres. nrsg. serv., Children's Hospital Medical Center, Cincinnati, OH '78 (NURS)
STOLL, CHRISTINE L., med. dir., Parkside Associates, Inc., Park Ridge, IL '86 (PLNG)
STOLL, RANDELL K., vice-pres. adm., Pomona Valley Community Hospital, Pomona, CA '79 (PLNG)
STOLLE, DAN, dir. human res. dev., Oak Forest Hospital of Cook County, Oak Forest, IL '85 (EDUC)
STOLLER, HELEN E., student, Bowling Green State University, Bowling Green, OH '85 (PLNG)
STOLP-SMITH, STEVEN CALVIN, asst. adm., University of Michigan Hospitals, Ann Arbor, MI '79
STOLPE, SUZANNE M., commun. rel. spec., Providence Hospital, Anchorage, AK '86 (PR)
STOLTZ, KATHRYN R., dir. food and nutr. serv., Slidell Memorial Hospital, Slidell, LA '86 (FOOD)
STOLTZFUS, WARREN L., exec. vice-pres. and chief oper. off., Methodist Evangelical Hospital, Louisville, KY '77
STOLUSKY, WARREN G., atty., Psychiatric Institutes of America, Washington, DC '74 (ATTY)
STONE, ANITA, dir. vol. serv., Kingsbrook Jewish Medical Center, Brooklyn, NY '81 (VOL)
STONE, BARBARA T., dir. vol., Memorial Hospital Southwest, Houston, TX '74 (VOL)
STONE, CLAIRE K., RN, dir. cent. proc., Memorial Hospital, Belleville, IL '78 (CS)
STONE, DAVID, dir. cent. sup., City Hospital Center at Elmhurst, Flushing, NY '83 (CS)
STONE, DONALD R., bus. mgr., Mallincrrodt Institute of Radiology, St. Louis, MO '81
STONE, FRED LYNDON, dir. pers., Citrus Memorial Hospital, Inverness, FL '75 (PERS)
STONE, HARRY J., dir. eng. and maint., Mount Vernon Hospital, Mount Vernon, NY '81 (ENG)
STONE, JACK S., sr. hosp. planner, Hillsborough County Hospital, Tampa, FL '86 (PLNG)
STONE, JEAN, atty., Holy Cross Hospital, Mission Hills, CA '83 (ATTY)
STONE, JEFF, dir. environ. serv., Boaz-Albertville Medical Center, Boaz, AL '86 (ENVIRON)
STONE, JOHN F., atty., Methodist Hospital, St. Louis Park, MN '77 (ATTY)
STONE, JOHN THOMAS JR., sr. vice-pres., Maryview Hospital, Portsmouth, VA '77 (PR) (PLNG)
STONE, JOSEPH MARTIN, exec. dir., Illinois Academy of Family Physicians, Oak Brook, IL '79
STONE, JUDITH T., RN, vice-pres. nrsg., Maine Medical Center, Portland, ME '80 (NURS)
STONE, KENNETH L., supv. maint., Johnston-Willis Hospital, Richmond, VA '86 (ENG)
STONE, LYNDSEY, RN, vice-pres. oper. and nrsg., Presbyterian Hospital, Oklahoma City, OK '79 (NURS)
STONE, MARILYN G., dir. vol. serv., Mount Carmel Medical Center, Columbus, OH '79 (VOL)
STONE, MARSHALL E., mgt. eng., SunHealth Enterprises, Inc., West Columbia, SC '85 (MGMT)
STONE, MARTHA F., dir. vol., Memorial Hospital of Martinsville, Martinsville, VA '86 (VOL)
STONE, MARY JANE, dir. soc. work and coor. discharge plng., Genesee Hospital, Rochester, NY '85 (SOC)
STONE, MARY LOUISE, pat. rep., Medical College of Virginia Hospitals, Richmond, VA '79 (PAT)
STONE, MELISSA WITZLER, dir. clin. soc. work, University of New Mexico Hospital, Albuquerque, NM '80 (SOC)
STONE, PATRICIA A., asst. dir. mktg. and prog. dev., Stanford University Hospital, Stanford, CA '81 (PLNG)
STONE, PATRICK L., sr. mgr. pub. affairs, Humana Inc., Louisville, KY '83 (PR)
STONE, PAULA G., dir. human res., Brunswick Hospital, Supply, NC '86 (PERS)
STONE, PAULA M., dir. human res., Apt General Partnership, Dallas, TX '83 (PERS)
STONE, PHILLIP C., atty., Rockingham Memorial Hospital, Harrisonburg, VA '80 (ATTY)
STONE, RAYMOND E., dir. consumer affairs, Marriott Corporation, Washington, DC '84 (PAT)
STONE, ROBERT E., vice-pres. dev., American Healthcorp, Inc., Nashville, TN '69
STONE, RONNIE C., eng., Veterans Administration Medical Center, Shreveport, LA '85 (ENG)
STONE, SHERWIN J., atty., Central Community Hospital, Chicago, IL '68 (ATTY)
STONE, STEPHANIE L., dir. pub. rel., Crawford Long Hospital Emory University, Atlanta, GA '83 (PR)
STONEBREAKER, MILAN F., dir. bldg. serv., Mainland Center Hospital, Texas City, TX '85 (ENG)
STONEBRIDGE, RAYMOND M., dir. eng., United Hospital, Port Chester, NY '71 (ENG)
STONECIPHER, REILLY L., atty., Pendleton Memorial Methodist Hospital, New Orleans, LA '86 (ATTY)
STONECIPHER, ROBERT L., mgr. facil. eng., Massillon Community Hospital, Massillon, OH '86 (ENG)
STONEHILL, ERIC, atty., Rochester General Hospital, Rochester, NY '81 (ATTY)
STONER, DONALD A., dir. pers., Hutzel Hospital, Detroit, MI '80 (PERS)
STONER, JOYCE, telecommun. spec., Oregon Health Sciences University Hospital, Portland, OR '85 (ENG)
STONER, TERRI J., mgr. cent. sterilizing, University of Iowa Hospitals and Clinics, Iowa City, IA '76 (CS)
STONITSCH, JOHN E., mgr. soc. work, Our Lady of Compassion Care Center, Anchorage, AK '86 (SOC)
STOOPS, JOYCE M., RN, vice-pres. nrsg. serv., Grant Hospital of Chicago, Chicago, IL '83 (NURS)
STORAD, CAROL A., RN, vice-pres. and dir. nrsg., Barberton Citizens Hospital, Barberton, OH '86 (NURS)
STORCH, FAITH COLLEEN, RN, asst. exec. dir. nrsg., St. Marys Hospital Medical Center, Madison, WI '86 (NURS)
STORCH, TRACY F., Gouverneur, NY '50 (LIFE)
STORCZ, KATHLEEN D., mgr. pat. rel., Cigna Healthplan of Arizona, Inc., Phoenix, AZ '82 (PAT)
STORER, RUBY E., RN, supv. cent. serv., Frederick Memorial Hospital, Frederick, MD '83 (CS)
STOREY, STEPHEN D., supv. bldg. and grds., The Hospital, Sidney, NY '82 (ENG)
STORIE, WILLIAM, vice-pres., Fred S. James and Company of Illinois, Chicago, IL '86 (RISK)
STORM, KENNETH E., dir. facil., Portage View Hospital, Hancock, MI '83 (ENG)
STORMENT, LCDR JOHN, (ret.), Roseburg, OR '72
STORMS, ELTING L., atty., Holmes Regional Medical Center, Melbourne, FL '71 (ATTY)
STORMS, PAUL, res. mgr. eng., Logan Memorial Hospital, Russellville, KY '82 (ENG)
STORNANT, BARBARA, dir. pub. rel., AMI North Ridge Medical Center, Fort Lauderdale, FL '80 (PR)
STORTS, RICHARD A., dir. pers., Murray-Calloway County Hospital, Murray, KY '81 (PERS)
STORY, DON P. III, consult., Health Systems Management, Baton Rouge, LA '84 (MGMT)
STORY, COL. JACK P. JR., (ret.), Young Harris, GA '67
STORY, KIRK, asst. adm., Princeton Community Hospital, Princeton, WV '81 (RISK)
STOTEN, SHARON E., RN, dir. nrsg., Indiana University Medical Center, Department of Medicine, Indianapolis, IN '82 (NURS)
STOTHARD, AL, dir. plant oper., Tolfree Memorial Hospital, West Branch, MI '87 (ENG)
STOTT, WILLIAM D., dir. plant oper., Underwood-Memorial Hospital, Woodbury, NJ '82 (ENG)
STOUFFER, CHRISTOPHER, atty., American Oncologic Hospital, Philadelphia, PA '86 (ATTY)
STOUGHTENGER, JEANNE, supv. cent. serv., Mile Bluff Medical Center, Mauston, WI '83 (CS)
STOUP, FRANK L., vice-pres., ARA Maintenance Management Systems, Inc., Arlington, VA '86 (ENG)
STOUT, BETTE J., dir. vol. serv., Duncan Regional Hospital, Duncan, OK '87 (VOL)
STOUT, DAVID H., dir. soc. work serv., Texoma Medical Center, Denison, TX '85 (SOC)
STOUT, GAIL A., dir. diet. serv., Spelman Memorial Hospital, Smithville, MO '84 (FOOD)
STOUT, LARRY R., coor. ldry. serv., St. Luke's Hospital, Kansas City, MO '86 (ENVIRON)
STOUT, LARRY R., atty., Peninsula Medical Center, Ormond Beach, FL '79 (ATTY)
STOUT, MARY A., dir. vol. serv., Pekin Memorial Hospital, Pekin, IL '85 (VOL)
STOUT, MURRAY B., dir. pers. and trng., Blodgett Memorial Medical Center, Grand Rapids, MI '67 (PERS)
STOUT, NAN, Annandale, VA '77 (EDUC)
STOUT, NANCY A., coor. educ., Kessler Institute for Rehabilitation, West Orange, NJ '86 (EDUC)
STOUT, PEARL, (ret.), Webster, NY '27 (LIFE)
STOUT, ROBERT D., pres., Southwestern Vermont Medical Center, Bennington, VT '51 (LIFE)
STOUT, SHERRY L., RN, dir. acute care nrsg., Metropolitan Medical Center, Minneapolis, MN '86 (NURS)
STOUT, SUSAN K., RN, vice-pres. nrsg., Baptist Hospital East, Louisville, KY '80 (NURS)
STOUT, WILLIAM F., consult., Hunter Consulting Group, Atlanta, GA '80 (PLNG)
STOVALL, WILLIAM M., adm. assoc., St. Jude Children's Research Hospital, Memphis, TN '75
STOVER, HAROLD JR., actg. dir. plant, St. Mary's Hospital, Centralia, IL '86 (ENG)
STOVER, W. RICHARD, mgr. clin. eng., Geisinger Medical Center, Danville, PA '78 (ENG)
STOVKA, LESS, dir. diet., West Volusia Memorial Hospital, De Land, FL '77 (FOOD)
STOYANOVICH, PETE, chief eng., Torrance Memorial Hospital Medical Center, Torrance, CA '86 (ENG)
STRACH, JULIE SANFORD, dir. plng. and mktg., Hackley Hospital, Muskegon, MI '80 (PLNG)
STRACHAN, BRIDGIT E., dir. staff dev., Northbay Medical Center, Fairfield, CA '84 (EDUC)
STRACHAN, MARY V., RN, dir. nrs., Boulder City Hospital, Boulder City, NV '73 (NURS)
STRACK, J. GARY, pres. and chief exec. off., Orlando Regional Medical Center, Orlando, FL '71
STRACK, JOHN, adm. amb. care serv., Good Samaritan Medical Center, Phoenix, AZ '84 (MGMT)(AMB)
STRACKE, JEROME, mgr. matl. serv., Evanston Hospital, Evanston, IL '82
STRADER, JUDITH Y., coor. vol., Providence Hospital, Cincinnati, OH '79 (VOL)
STRAHINIC, JOAN, asst. exec. dir. nrsg. serv., St. Mary's Health Center, St. Louis, MO '85 (NURS)

STRAHL, RANDALL LEE, student, Program in Health Service Administration, School of Health Professions, Governors State University, Park Forest South, IL '86
STRAIGHT, ROBERT C., loss control mgr., Hospital Underwriters Mutual Insurance Company, Albany, NY '54 (RISK)(LIFE)
STRAIN, DAVID LEO, proj. mgr., Kroeschell Engineering Company, Chicago, IL '86 (ENG)
STRAIN, GEORGE L., atty., Arkansas Valley Regional Medical Center, La Junta, CO '75 (ATTY)
STRAIN, MERCEDES M., vice-pres., Montana Deaconess Medical Center, Great Falls, MT '76 (PAT)
STRAINER, WILLIAM A., dir. educ., Marymount Hospital, Garfield Heights, OH '82 (EDUC)
STRALEY, ROSE F., City Hospital, Martinsburg, WV '84 (VOL)
STRAMA, BRENDA T., atty., The Methodist Hospital, Houston, TX '86 (ATTY)
STRAMECKY, PATRICK J., vice-pres. mgt. info. syst., Bay Medical Center-General Division, Bay City, MI '86 (MGMT)(AMB)
STRANCKMEYER, EDWARD C., adm. coor. eng., Blessing Hospital, Quincy, IL '69 (ENG)
STRAND, BONNIE, RN, supv. emer., Porter Medical Center, Middlebury, VT '87 (AMB)
STRAND, DAVID L., med. equip. repair foreman, Federal Medical Center, Rochester, MN '80 (ENG)
STRAND, DENNIS E., vice-pres. bus. dev., Affiliated Hospital Systems, Houston, TX '84 (PLNG)
STRAND, ERIC, biomedical eng. tech., Immanuel-St. Joseph's Hospital, Mankato, MN '81 (ENG)
STRAND, MICHAEL W., dir. emp. res. mgt., Washington Hospital Center, Washington, DC '83 (PERS)
STRANG, GEORGIANNA, RN, dir. staff educ., Trumbull Memorial Hospital, Warren, OH '71 (EDUC)
STRANG, SUSAN S., dir. soc. serv., Choate-Symmes Hospitals, Woburn, MA '83 (SOC)
STRANGE, DONALD E., reg. vice-pres., Hospital Corporation of America, Newton, MA '70
STRANSKY, CHRISTINE A., RN, mgr. cent. serv., Columbia Hospital, Milwaukee, WI '80 (CS)
STRASEN, LEANN L., RN, dir. nrsg. critical care serv., Santa Monica Hospital Medical Center, Santa Monica, CA '83 (NURS)
STRASSER, CHRISTOPHER B., dir. matl. mgt., Lehigh Valley Hospital Center, Allentown, PA '83 (PUR)
STRATMAN, PAUL L., dir. pur. serv., Holy Family Hospital, Des Plaines, IL '77 (CS)
STRATMANN, LARRY A., dir. pers., North Arundel Hospital, Glen Burnie, MD '82 (PERS)
STRATMANN, WILLIAM C., PhD, vice-pres., Gordon S. Black Corporation, Rochester, NY '83 (PR)
STRATTON, REBECCA, consult. soc. serv., Fayette Memorial Hospital, Connersville, IN '86 (SOC)
STRATTON, RUSSELL R., sr. mgt. eng., Baystate Health Management Service, Enfield, CT '82 (MGMT)
STRATTON, WAYNE T., atty., Stormont-Vail Regional Medical Center, Topeka, KS '68 (ATTY)
STRAUCH, DANIEL W., adm. fellow, Forbes Health System, Pittsburgh, PA '87
STRAUCH, MARY JANE, San Antonio, TX '80
STRAUCH, PAULETTE J., dir. amb. care, Fox Chase Cancer Center, Philadelphia, PA '87 (AMB)
STRAUGHN, BOB D., chief eng., Central Texas Medical Center, Hearne, TX '87 (ENG)
STRAUS, JANET H., asst. dir., Lubbock County Hospital District-Lubbock General Hospital, Lubbock, TX '82 (ENG)
STRAUS, MRS. ROGER W., New York, NY '20 (LIFE)
STRAUSS, BONNIE E., adm. psych., Johns Hopkins Hospital, Baltimore, MD '76
STRAUSS, CYNTHIA F., atty., Virginia Mason Hospital, Seattle, WA '85 (ATTY)
STRAUSS, ELIZABETH C., Albany, CA '78 (MGMT)
STRAUSS, JOHN H., sr. assoc., Herman Smith Associates, Hinsdale, IL '85 (PLNG)
STRAUSS, MAJ. LAWRENCE I., MSC USA, shc soc. work serv., Walson Army Community Hospital, Fort Dix, NJ '76 (SOC)
STRAUSS, PHIL J., dir. food serv., Baycrest Centre-Geriatric Care, Toronto, Ont., Canada '82 (FOOD)
STRAUSS, RICHARD, pres., Balston, Inc., Lexington, MA '81 (CS)
STRAUSS, ROLAND W., asst. dir. eng., Albert Einstein Medical Center, Philadelphia, PA '83 (ENG)
STRAWHUN, SANDRA L., RN, dir. nrsg., NKC Hospitals, Louisville, KY '79 (NURS)
STRAWHUN, VELMA L., vice-pres. adm., St. Anthony Medical Center, Crown Point, IN '80 (PLNG)
STRAWMYER, STEVE, supv. maint., Witham Memorial Hospital, Lebanon, IN '86 (ENG)
STRAWN, BEN F., dir. bldg. serv., St. Luke's Regional Medical Center, Boise, ID '67 (ENG)
STRAWN, JOEL T., atty., Bethesda Memorial Hospital, Boynton Beach, FL '79 (ATTY)
STRAWN, SHARRON REEVES, mgr. commun. rel., Willis-Knighton Medical Center, Shreveport, LA '83 (PR)
STRAWSER, CHARLES O., mgr. plant oper., Saint Joseph Hospital, Fort Worth, TX '86 (ENG)
STRAWSER, L. LARRY, vice-pres. human res., Lafayette Home Hospital, Lafayette, IN '83 (PERS)
STRAZIS, CYNTHIA, RN, vice-pres. nrsg., Lee Memorial Hospital, Fort Myers, FL '80 (NURS)
STREAM, PATRICIA A., RN, vice-pres., Health Connection, Falls Church, VA '75 (EDUC)
STREAMER, CHARLES W. JR., dir., Intermountain Health Care Tech Service, Murray, UT '79
STRECK, WILLIAM F., MD, pres., Mary Imogene Bassett Hospital, Cooperstown, NY '84
STRECKER, DAVID L., RN, supv. cent. serv., Louis A. Weiss Memorial Hospital, Chicago, IL '84 (CS)
STREED, JAMES G., dir. pub. rel., Trinity Memorial Hospital, Cudahy, WI '85 (PR)
STREEM, RONALD M., exec. dir., St. Joseph Hospital and Health Center, Lorain, OH '59
STREET, EFFIE H., mgr. food serv., Mid-South Hospital, Memphis, TN '78 (FOOD)
STREET, JAMES V., asst. dir. diet., Harper Hospital, Detroit, MI '84 (FOOD)
STREET, JOHN J., mgr. maint., Medcenter Hospital, Marion, OH '85 (ENG)
STREET, RICHARD W., mgr. maint. and oper., Bethany Medical Center, Kansas City, KS '86 (ENG)
STREETER, ALAN W., dir. fin., Kennewick General Hospital, Kennewick, WA '86 (MGMT)
STREETER, ANNE, coor. spec. proj., Baptist Hospital of Miami, Miami, FL '85 (PR)
STREETER, BERNARD A. JR., vice-pres., St. John's Hospital, Lowell, MA '68 (PR)
STREETER, DONNA, asst. adm. pat. serv. and qual. assur., F. Edward Hebert Hospital, New Orleans, LA '86 (RISK)
STREETER, JANICE B., dir. vol. serv., St. John's Hospital, Lowell, MA '78 (VOL)
STREIT, KIM, dir. loan adm., Florida Hospital Association, Orlando, FL '84
STREJC, IRENE, RN, vice-pres. pat. care serv., Glendale Heights Community Hospital, Glendale Heights, IL '86 (NURS)
STRELLA, EVE G., mgt. eng., Park Ridge Hospital, Rochester, NY '86 (MGMT)
STREMBA, JULES E., mgr. matl., Geisinger Wyoming Valley Medical Center, Wilkes-Barre, PA '84 (PUR)
STREMLAU, VIVIAN, dir. in-service, Mercy Hospital, Bakersfield, CA '77 (EDUC)
STRENKO, DOLORES, dir. diet. serv., Southwest Community Health System and Hospital, Middleburg Heights, OH '77 (FOOD)
STRENTZSCH, LT. COL. ALFRED I. JR., (ret.), Portland, TX '70
STRESEN-REUTER, LEA F., RN, vice-pres. nrsg. serv., Memorial Hospital, Fremont, OH '86 (NURS)
STRETCH, SHIRLEY K., dir. pers., Newport Hospital, Newport, RI '80 (PERS)
STRHARSKY, JOHN A., asst. dir. plant oper., Truman Medical Center-West, Kansas City, MO '78 (ENG)
STRICKER, RAMSAE C., dir. environ. serv., St. Joseph's Hospital, Highland, IL '82 (ENG)
STRICKER, SHARON, dir. plng., Roper Hospital, Charleston, SC '84 (PLNG)
STRICKLAND, CECIL G., dir. matl. mgt., Hughston Sports Medicine Hospital, Columbus, GA '82 (PUR)
STRICKLAND, CHERIE A., RN, asst. dir. nrsg., Mount Sinai Medical Center, New York, NY '86 (NURS)
STRICKLAND, EDWIN A., atty., Cooper Green Hospital, Birmingham, AL '76 (ATTY)
STRICKLAND, GLENN, asst. dir. plant eng., Tallahassee Memorial Regional Medical Center, Tallahassee, FL '84 (ENG)
STRICKLAND, JOHN E., adm., HCA Aiken Regional Medical Center, Aiken, SC '71
STRICKLAND, KILBY, adm. asst., Baptist Hospital of Miami, Miami, FL '77 (RISK)
STRICKLAND, NANCY, atty., Cook-Fort Worth Children Medical Center, Fort Worth, TX '86 (RISK)
STRICKLAND, STAN R., mgr. plant oper., Emanuel Medical Center, Turlock, CA '84 (ENG)
STRICKLER, MATTHEW M., atty., Temple University Hospital, Philadelphia, PA '71 (ATTY)
STRICKLIN, NILDA F., RN, dir. in-service, Arab Hospital, Arab, AL '86 (NURS)
STRIEN, M. JANE, diet., Saint James Hospital, Pontiac, IL '81 (FOOD)
STRIEPER, COL. GERALD E., RN MSC USA, chief nrs., U. S. Army Hospital, Atlanta, GA '86 (NURS)
STRIFFLER, PAUL J., dir. facil. mgt., Maryland General Hospital, Baltimore, MD '85 (ENG)
STRIMLING, RICHARD B., vice-pres., Janik, Strimling and Associates, Inc., Chicago, IL '86 (FOOD)
STRINGER, FRANCES K., dir. diet., Forrest County General Hospital, Hattiesburg, MS '70 (FOOD)
STRINGER, PEGGY H., dir. pers., Morehouse General Hospital, Bastrop, LA '84 (PERS)
STRITIKUS, JOY H., vice-pres. outreach, Baptist Medical Center, Montgomery, AL '83 (PLNG)
STRITMATTER, PAUL L., atty., Grays Harbor Community Hospital, Aberdeen, WA '79 (ATTY)
STRITZEL, MARY M., RN, vice-pres. nrsg., Manatee Memorial Hospital, Bradenton, FL '82 (NURS)
STROBEL, LT. COL. FRED H., MSC USA, 68th Medical Group, APO New York, NY '72
STROBEL, JUDITH M., dir. pub. rel., Carondelet Community Hospitals, Minneapolis, MN '86 (PR)
STROBLE, MICHAEL D., dir. mgt. syst., Hendrick Medical Center, Abilene, TX '84 (MGMT)
STRODE, KRISTI A., mgr. commun., Waukesha Hospital Systems, Inc., Waukesha, WI '85 (PR)
STROEBEL, JAMES K., chief exec. off., Margaret Mary Community Hospital, Batesville, IN '73
STROESSER, PIERRE A., dir. food serv., Ravenswood Hospital Medical Center, Chicago, IL '68 (FOOD)
STROH, ALFRED JR., dir. plant oper. and constr., Northwestern Memorial Hospital, Chicago, IL '77 (ENG)
STROH, JOHN J., atty., Hamot Medical Center, Erie, PA '78 (ATTY)
STROHL, BARBARA A., RN, asst. dir. corp. nrsg., Harper-Grace Hospitals, Detroit, MI '85 (NURS)
STROHL, GEORGE R. JR., pres., Community General Osteopathic Hospital, Harrisburg, PA '72
STROHL, W. GARLAND, chief exec. off., Shelby Memorial Hospital, Shelbyville, IL '87 (AMB)
STROHM, LINDA B., dir. food serv., Children's Hospital and Health Center, San Diego, CA '78 (FOOD)
STROHM, PETER R., atty., Kimball Medical Center, Lakewood, NJ '76 (ATTY)
STROHMENGER, WILLIAM R., dir. emp. educ., serv. and mgt. dev., Aultman Hospital, Canton, OH '84 (EDUC)
STROM, NOLA J., dir. food serv., Athol Memorial Hospital, Athol, MA '80 (FOOD)
STROM, PAUL E., dir. adm. support serv., Paracelsus Healthcare, Pasadena, CA '74 (MGMT)
STROM, SHEREE, coor. soc. serv., South Lake Memorial Hospital, Clermont, FL '85 (SOC)
STROM, STEPHEN E., atty., Southeast Missouri Hospital, Cape Girardeau, MO '76 (ATTY)
STROMAN, NEIL, vice-pres. clin. serv., Choate Symmes Health Services, Woburn, MA '72
STROMBACH, BRUCE M., adm. res., Jane Phillips Episcopal-Memorial Medical Center, Bartlesville, OK '81
STROMBERG, ARLAN, adm., Lincoln General Hospital, Lincoln, NE '77
STROMBERG, CLIFFORD D., atty., George Washington University Hospital, Washington, DC '84 (ATTY)
STROMBERG, MARY JANE P., RN, assoc. exec. dir. nrsg., Humana Hospital -Biscayne, Miami, FL '76 (NURS)
STROMBERG, ROSS E., atty., Epstein, Becker, Borsody, Stromberg and Green, San Francisco, CA '68 (ATTY)(PLNG)
STROMBERG, WALLIS S., atty., Humana Hospital -Aurora, Aurora, CO '84 (ATTY)
STROMBOM, KATHIE D., dir. vol. serv., Children's Hospital of Wisconsin, Milwaukee, WI '86 (VOL)
STROMECKI, AMELIA H., RN, dir. clin. prac., Methodist Hospital, Brooklyn, NY '80 (NURS)
STROMSTAD-BOE, DARLENE, dir. serv. dev., Medcenter One, Bismarck, ND '85 (PLNG)
STRONG, ALLEN D., arch., Dreyfuss and Blackford, Sacramento, CA '81
STRONG, CORWIN, dir. safety, Clinical Center, National Institute of Health, Bethesda, MD '79 (ENG)
STRONG, DAVID M., dir. matl. mgt., Providence Memorial Hospital, El Paso, TX '80 (PUR)
STRONG, GARY B., bus. planner clin. serv., Erlanger Medical Center, Chattanooga, TN '85 (PLNG)
STRONG, JOHN W., vice-pres. matl. mgt., Parkside Associates, Inc., Park Ridge, IL '75 (PUR)
STRONG, M. JOAN, dir. pers., Southern Oregon Medical Center, Grants Pass, OR '86 (PERS)
STROUD, BRENDA J., mgr. cent. region human res., Group Health Cooperative of Puget Sound, Seattle, WA '86 (PERS)
STROUD, GERALDINE G., atty., Group Health Association, Inc., Washington, DC '74 (ATTY)(RISK)
STROUD, JIM, assoc. dir. human res., Children's Hospital of the King's Daughters, Norfolk, VA '86 (PERS)
STROUD, LARRY, dir. facil. serv., Iredell Memorial Hospital, Statesville, NC '86 (ENG)
STROUP, SUZANNE, dir. vol. serv., Alliance Community Hospital, Alliance, OH '78 (VOL)
STROUSE, JOAN, pat. rep., Skokie Valley Hospital, Skokie, IL '79 (PAT)
STROWGER, RICHARD J., partner, Price Waterhouse, Detroit, MI '70
STROYZK, JENNIFER L., dir. commun. rel., St. Helen Hospital, Chehalis, WA '83 (PR)
STRUBLES, SHIRLEY F., RN, mgr. nrs., Rapid City Regional Hospital, Rapid City, SD '85 (NURS)
STRUCK, MARY DOWD, RN, vice-pres. pat. care serv., Women and Infants Hospital of Rhode Island, Providence, RI '80 (NURS)
STRUM, DENNIS W., vice-pres. plng. dev., Lutheran Hospital Society, Los Angeles, CA '84 (PLNG)
STRUMPF, LAWRENCE G., dir. food and nutr. serv., St. Luke's-Roosevelt Hospital Center, New York, NY '76 (FOOD)
STRUMPF, VICTOR, dir. mgt. eng., Helene Fuld Medical Center, Trenton, NJ '72 (MGMT)
STRUNIN, MARK A., coor. human res., Summit Health, Ltd., Los Angeles, CA '85 (EDUC)
STRUTHERS, MARGO S., atty., Methodist Hospital, St. Louis Park, MN '76 (ATTY)
STRUWE, LARISSA C., dir. diet. serv., Idaho Elks Rehabilitation Hospital, Boise, ID '85 (FOOD)
STRUXNESS, RONALD E., Evangelical Health Systems, Oak Brook, IL '65
STRYCHARSKI, FRANK, dir. plant, Whidbey General Hospital, Coupeville, WA '80 (ENG)
STRYCHARZ, ALICE LOREEN, asst. dir. nrsg., St. Francis Hospital, Wilmington, DE '79 (NURS)
STRYCHAZ, FRANCES M., dir., West Bay Hospital Conference, San Mateo, CA '82 (PLNG)
STRZELECKI, SARAH, asst. dir. nrsg., Phoenixville Hospital, Phoenixville, PA '79 (EDUC)
STUARDI, A. E. JR., dir. pers., Providence Hospital, Mobile, AL '70 (PERS)
STUART, ANNE PASLEY, dir. pers., Mercy Medical Center, Nampa, ID '83 (PERS)
STUART, BARBARA K., corp. planner, St. Anthony Hospital Systems, Denver, CO '82 (MGMT)
STUART, BOBBIE J., dir. cent. serv., Saint Joseph's Hospital, Atlanta, GA '82 (CS)
STUART, CHRISTINE N., asst. adm., St. John's Episcopal Hospital, Smithtown, NY '85 (PLNG)
STUART, DEAN L., pres., Hospital Purchasing Service of Michigan, Middleville, MI '74 (PUR)
STUART, H. WINSTON JR., dir. info. syst., Peninsula General Hospital Medical Center, Salisbury, MD '85 (MGMT)
STUART, HELEN A., RN, sr. assoc. dir., Community General Hospital of Sullivan County, Harris, NY '68 (NURS)
STUART, RICHARD B., MD, head phys., Ochsner Clinic-New Orleans East, New Orleans, LA '68
STUBBS, DONALD H., vice-pres. human res., St. Joseph's Hospital, Asheville, NC '78 (PERS)
STUBBS, JOHN M., vice-pres., Tillinghast, Nelson and Warren, Inc., Dallas, TX '84 (RISK)
STUBBS, MARY D., adm. res., University of Texas Medical Branch Hospitals, Galveston, TX '85
STUBBS, SR. MARY LOUISE, RN, vice-pres., Hotel Dieu Hospital, New Orleans, LA '85 (NURS)
STUBBS, TISH PRESTON, mgr. educ. and trng., St. Joseph Hospital, Flint, MI '81 (EDUC)

STUCK, BYRON, assoc. adm., Group Health Eastside Hospital, Redmond, WA '74 (MGMT)
STUCKLER, ERNEST M. III, dir. mktg., South Hills Health System, Pittsburgh, PA '86 (PR) (PLNG)
STUDDARD, ELMO T. JR., dir. eng., Brownwood Regional Hospital, Brownwood, TX '84 (ENG)
STUDIN, IRA, dir. health serv. dev., Empire Blue Cross and Blue Shield, New York, NY '82 (PLNG)
STUDNICKI, JAMES, ScD, vice-pres. gen. mgt. and corp. dev., St. Joseph Hospital, Baltimore, MD '65
STUDSRUD, JOHN S., adm., St. Joseph's Hospital and Health Center, Dickinson, ND '76 (PLNG)(MGMT)
STUDSTILL, PEGGY, dir. soc. serv., Clayton General Hospital, Riverdale, GA '75 (SOC)
STUEHLER, GEORGE JR., ScD, sr. vice-pres., John Short and Associates, Inc., Columbia, MD '70 (PLNG)
STUEMKE, MARK O., adm. fellow, Oklahoma Osteopathic Hospital, Tulsa, OK '85
STUENCKEL, ELTON E., dir. commun. rel. and dev., Shore Memorial Hospital, Somers Point, NJ '78 (PR) (PLNG)
STUESSY, ANNE M., dir. commun., Southwest Health Center, Platteville, WI '85 (PR)
STUHMER, PAUL R., mgr. res. and dev., Michigan Physicians Mutual Liability Company, East Lansing, MI '85 (RISK)
STUKES, THOMAS E., atty., Moses H. Cone Memorial Hospital, Greensboro, NC '84 (ATTY)
STULL, GARY L., dir. automated bldg. syst., Metropolitan Medical Center, Minneapolis, MN '81 (ENG)
STULL, JOHN W. JR., dir. cent. serv., Memorial Hospital, Carbondale, IL '82 (CS)
STULTS, DAVID A., dir. pub. rel., Mercy Medical Center, Roseburg, OR '84 (PR)
STULTZ, HAROLD L. JR., dir. pur., Carroll County General Hospital, Westminster, MD '78 (PUR)
STULTZ, JAMES R., dir. pers., Ohio Valley Medical Center, Wheeling, WV '73 (PERS)
STUMACHER, MARTIN, bus. mgr. anesthesiology, Presbyterian Hospital in the City of New York, New York, NY '71
STUMBO, SHARON LEA, dir. plng., Central Baptist Hospital, Lexington, KY '80 (PLNG)
STUMP, BARRY E., vice-pres. human res., St. Luke's Methodist Hospital, Cedar Rapids, IA '76 (PERS)
STUMP, BREVITT D., dir. strategic plng. serv., Community Hospitals of Indiana, Indianapolis, IN '80 (PLNG)
STUMP, FRANK A., dir. pers. serv., Baptist Hospital of Miami, Miami, FL '61 (PERS)
STUMP, JEANNE R., risk mgr., Cape Coral Hospital, Cape Coral, FL '84 (RISK)
STUMP, WALTER A., dir. soc. work, Wernersville State Hospital, Wernersville, PA '83 (SOC)
STUMPF, BARBARA R., RN, asst. dir. nrsg., University of California San Francisco, San Francisco, CA '83 (NURS)
STUMPF, CHARLES F., pres., Worcester Hahnemann Hospital, Worcester, MA '52 (LIFE)
STUMPFEL, JAMES G., mng. partner, Health Consortium, Inc., San Diego, CA '86
STUNKARD, M. E., chief maint. eng., Saint Francis Hospital, Tulsa, OK '80 (ENG)
STUPAK, DENNIS R., pres., Renshaw-Heilman and Associates, Inc., Columbia, SC '85 (ENG)
STUPKA, ANDREA L., clin. spec., Baptist Hospital, Nashville, TN '86 (EDUC)
STURDAVANT, DENNIS R., facil. eng., Queen's Medical Center, Honolulu, HI '85 (ENG)
STURDAVANT, MADELYNE, (ret.), Rochester, MN '43 (MGMT)(LIFE)
STURDEVANT, PHILLIP P., dir. matl. mgt., Lutheran Hospital, Moline, IL '77 (PUR)
STURIALE, JO ANNE, student, University of Wisconsin, Madison, WI '82 (PR)
STURM, JUDITH A., asst. dir. mgt., East Jefferson General Hospital, Metairie, LA '86 (MGMT)
STURM, ROBERT C., dir. facil., Health Central Management Resources, Minneapolis, MN '84
STURMS, IVARS, supv. biomedical, St. Elizabeth's Hospital, Belleville, IL '79 (ENG)
STUTES, RONALD W., chief oper. off., Hermann Hospital, Houston, TX '82
STUTHEIT, BRIAN K., atty., Hospital Corporation of America, Nashville, TN '86 (ATTY)
STUTZ, ROBERT V., vice-pres. and gen. dir., Albert Einstein Medical Center, Philadelphia, PA '83
STUTZINGETZ, RITA K., RN, dir. in-service, Dakota Hospital, Fargo, ND '85 (EDUC)
STUTZMAN, VERNON, spec. consult., United Methodist Church, Division of Health and Welfare, New York, NY '48 (LIFE)
STYBERG, JEROME C., dir. rehabilitative serv., Children's Hospital of Wisconsin, Milwaukee, WI '81 (PLNG)
STYLES, MARGRETTA M., RN, assoc. dir. nrsg., prof. and dean, University of California San Francisco, San Francisco, CA '82 (NURS)
STYMIEST, STEPHEN G., risk mgr., Gencon Risk Management Services, Takoma Park, MD '84 (RISK)
STYRON, CYD, dir. pub. rel. and mktg., Flaget Memorial Hospital, Bardstown, KY '86 (PR)
SUARES, SUSAN A., University of Connecticut, Program in Health Systems Management, Stamford, CT '84 (MGMT)
SUAZO, BESSY J., coor. cent. sup., Lakeshore Hospital, Birmingham, AL '85 (CS)
SUBER, ROBERTA, exec. dir. oper., Healthwest, Chatsworth, CA '72 (SOC)
SUCH, RUSSELL L., vice-pres., St. Barnabas Hospital, Bronx, NY '63 (ENG)
SUCHER, CYNTHIA C., vice-pres. mktg., Winter Park Memorial Hospital, Winter Park, FL '85 (PLNG)
SUCHER, THERESE ORLANDO, RN, clin. dir. nrsg., Fairview General Hospital, Cleveland, OH '86 (NURS)(AMB)
SUCHMAN, CORY C., dir. soc. serv., Kanakanak Hospital, Dillingham, AK '86 (SOC)
SUCHOFF, ANITA, dir. pat. rel., St. John's Episcopal Hospital, Far Rockaway, NY '79 (PAT)
SUCIU, LARRY W., atty., Yuma Regional Medical Center, Yuma, AZ '82 (ATTY)
SUCKIEL, DONALD B., dir. pers., Wayne General Hospital, Wayne, NJ '73 (PERS)
SUCOV, MILDRED, dir. vol. serv. and commun. educ., Western Psychiatric Institute and Clinic, Pittsburgh, PA '84 (VOL)
SUCOV, MILLIE, dir. internal commun. and vol. serv., Western Psychiatric Institute and Clinic, Pittsburgh, PA '87 (PR)
SUDANO, FRANK, Queens Village, NY '71 (ENG)
SUDBURY, J. GRAHAM, atty., Mississippi County Hospitals, Blytheville, AR '68 (ATTY)
SUDBURY, JOAN C., risk mgr., Crump Special Services, Inc., Altamonte Springs, FL '81 (RISK)
SUDRANSKI, L. L., adm. asst., St. Joseph Riverside Hospital, Warren, OH '85 (ENG)
SUEHIRO, RICHARD Y., vice-pres., Kuakini Medical Center, Honolulu, HI '85 (PLNG)
SUGARMAN, GERALD I., MD, Los Feliz Medical Group, Glendale, CA '86 (RISK)
SUGARMAN, H. ARTHUR, adm., Heritage Hospital, Taylor, MI '58
SUGERMAN, RUTH A., dir. vol. serv., Carrier Foundation, Belle Mead, NJ '82 (VOL)
SUGG, WILLIAM TURNEY, vice-pres., Nashville Memorial Hospital, Madison, TN '83
SUGHRUE, TIMOTHY H., vice-pres. plng. and mktg., Rushmore National Health Systems, Inc., Rapid City, SD '87 (PLNG)
SUGRUE, MARY JOAN, atty., United Hospitals Medical Center, Newark, NJ '78 (ATTY)
SUHAY, MARY, dir. vol. serv., Colorado State Hospital, Pueblo, CO '85 (VOL)
SUHRLAND, CAROL S., student, Program in Hospital Administration, University of Minnesota, Minneapolis, MN '83
SUIRE, WILSON J., asst. mgr. and supv. sup., proc. and distrib., Lafayette General Medical Center, Lafayette, LA '87 (CS)
SUITS, MARGARET C., dir. commun., Spartanburg Regional Medical Center, Spartanburg, SC '79 (ENG)
SUKAY, LAWRENCE D., risk mgt. consult., Crawford Risk Management Services, Carlsbad, CA '82 (RISK)
SULDS, VIVIENNE F., dir. vol. serv., Jewish Home and Hospital for Aged-Kingsbridge Center, Bronx, NY '71 (VOL)
SULL, KENNETH J., adm. off., Naval Regional Medical Clinic, Pearl Harbor, HI '82
SULLIVAN-KULL, JULIE, coor. vol. serv., St. Joseph's Hospital and Medical Center, Phoenix, AZ '85 (VOL)
SULLIVAN, ARTHUR J. F., dir. indust. eng., Atlanticare Medical Center, Lynn, MA '72 (MGMT)
SULLIVAN, AUDREY N., dir. diet. prog., Hospital Council of Southern California, Los Angeles, CA '77 (FOOD)
SULLIVAN, BARBARA A., skill bldg. spec. educ. serv., Georgetown University Medical Center, Washington, DC '71 (EDUC)
SULLIVAN, BRIAN R., adm. asst., Hospital Center at Orange, Orange, NJ '84
SULLIVAN, C. CHRISTOPHER, consult., Hospital Corporation of America, Nashville, TN '82 (PLNG)
SULLIVAN, CAROL J., RN, dir. nrsg., Gerald Champion Memorial Hospital, Alamogordo, NM '85 (NURS)
SULLIVAN, CAROL, dir. pub. rel. and dev., St. Elizabeth Hospital, Utica, NY '83 (PR)
SULLIVAN, CHARLES B., exec. vice-pres., Reading Hospital and Medical Center, Reading, PA '71
SULLIVAN, DANIEL L., mgr. mktg., Startel Corporation, Irvine, CA '86 (ENG)
SULLIVAN, DAVID K., regional health planner, Veterans Administration Regional Iv, Hines, IL '83 (PLNG)
SULLIVAN, DEANNA, RN, dir. nrsg., Salvation Army William Booth Memorial Hospital, Florence, KY '84 (NURS)
SULLIVAN, DOLORES M., RN, supv. cent. serv., Westmoreland Hospital, Greensburg, PA '85 (CS)
SULLIVAN, DONA J., dir. nrsg. serv., York General Hospital, York, NE '81 (NURS)
SULLIVAN, EDWARD J. JR., vice-pres., St. Joseph Medical Center, Wichita, KS '73
SULLIVAN, EDWARD, atty., Kennedy Memorial Hospital, Stratford, NJ '80 (ATTY)
SULLIVAN, FRANCIS J., vice-pres. plng. and eng., Beth Israel Hospital, Boston, MA '68 (MGMT)(PLNG)
SULLIVAN, FRANCIS J., (ret.), Tucson, AZ '56 (LIFE)
SULLIVAN, GERALD J., chief exec. off., Sullivan, Kelly and Associates, Inc., Los Angeles, CA '80 (RISK)
SULLIVAN, HERB, dir. risk mgt., Tanner Medical Center, Carrollton, GA '86 (RISK)
SULLIVAN, IDA M., dir. qual. and risk mgt., Montgomery General Hospital, Olney, MD '86 (RISK)
SULLIVAN, JAMES F., clin. eng., Entech, Phoenix, AZ '86 (ENG)
SULLIVAN, JAMES G., partner, Deloitte Haskins and Sells, Boston, MA '81
SULLIVAN, JENNIFER A., atty., Seton Medical Center, Austin, TX '85 (ATTY)
SULLIVAN, JOHN E., Salem, OR '80 (LIFE)
SULLIVAN, JOHN L. JR., dir. facil. mgt., St. Joseph Medical Center, Burbank, CA '80 (ENG)
SULLIVAN, JOHN LOUIS, pres., Lourdes Hospital, Paducah, KY '74
SULLIVAN, JOHN P., dir. human res., Thomas Jefferson University Hospital, Philadelphia, PA '85 (PERS)
SULLIVAN, JOSEPH F., vice-pres. eng. and environ. control, Clara Maass Medical Center, Belleville, NJ '68 (ENG)
SULLIVAN, JOSEPH M., dir. diet. serv., Antelope Valley Hospital Medical Center, Lancaster, CA '82 (FOOD)
SULLIVAN, KATHLEEN M., pub. info. off.-mktg., Edgewater Hospital, Chicago, IL '85 (PR)
SULLIVAN, LAVONA N., RN, asst. adm., Bannock Regional Medical Center, Pocatello, ID '81 (NURS)
SULLIVAN, LUCINE M., atty., Georgetown University Medical Center, Washington, DC '86 (ATTY)
SULLIVAN, SR. M. JOHNETTE, mgr. matl., Mercy Hospital, Portland, ME '59 (PUR)
SULLIVAN, MARY HALL, dir. vol. serv., Sacred Heart Rehabilitation Hospital, Milwaukee, WI '85 (VOL)
SULLIVAN, MARY L., exec. mktg., Wilcox Marketing Group, Inc., Wauwatosa, WI '86 (PR)
SULLIVAN, MAUREEN A., dir. pub. rel., The Arbour, Boston, MA '84 (PR) (PLNG)
SULLIVAN, MAUREEN, pat. rep., University of Minnesota Hospital and Clinic, Minneapolis, MN '86 (PAT)
SULLIVAN, MICHAEL F., mgt. eng., Southwest Community Health Services, Albuquerque, NM '85 (MGMT)
SULLIVAN, NANCY S., health care diet., The Cbord Group, Inc., Ithaca, NY '85 (FOOD)
SULLIVAN, PATRICIA A., ScD, asst. prof., University of Maryland, Baltimore, MD '84 (NURS)
SULLIVAN, RALPH G., assoc. adm., Montgomery General Hospital, Montgomery, WV '79 (PERS)
SULLIVAN, ROBERT E., atty., North Detroit General Hospital, Detroit, MI '80 (ATTY)
SULLIVAN, RONALD M., atty., Owensboro-Daviess County Hospital, Owensboro, KY '82 (ATTY)
SULLIVAN, RUSSELL E., pres., Sullivan and Associates, Consulting Engineers, Houston, TX '84 (ENG)
SULLIVAN, SHARON, dir. util. and risk mgt., Rosewood Medical Center, Houston, TX '86 (RISK)
SULLIVAN, STEPHEN M., atty., Southern Baptist Hospital, New Orleans, LA '79 (ATTY)
SULLIVAN, SUSAN M., supv. soc. serv., Christian Hospital Northwest, Florissant, MO '85 (SOC)
SULLIVAN, SUZANNE E., adm. amb. care, Illinois Masonic Medical Center, Chicago, IL '87 (AMB)
SULLIVAN, THOMAS H., syst. analyst, University Hospital, Jackson, MS '86 (PERS)
SULLIVAN, TONY L., dir. commun., Marianjoy Rehabilitation Center, Wheaton, IL '84 (PR)
SULTAN, MOHAMED, pres., Kuala Lumpur Medical Centre, Kuala Lumpur, Malaysia '81
SULTON, LARRY D., PhD, dir. res. and educ., Marianjoy Rehabilitation Center, Wheaton, IL '85 (EDUC)
SUMMA, ROBERT J., pres., Charlotte Hungerford Hospital, Torrington, CT '79 (PLNG)
SUMMER, STEVEN J., vice-pres. prof. activ., Maryland Hospital Association, Lutherville-Timonium, MD '73
SUMMERELL, PAUL C., student, Graduate Program in Health Administration, Duke University, Durham, NC '86
SUMMERS, BRENDA GAIL, RN, dir. nrsg., Florence General Hospital, Florence, SC '85 (NURS)
SUMMERS, JIM, PhD, vice-pres. serv., Interhealth Corporation, Giddings, TX '77
SUMMERS, MAUREEN, RN, dir. rehab. serv., Henrietta D. Goodall Hospital, Sanford, ME '78
SUMMERS, PATTY A., RN, asst. prof. nrsg., University of Evansville, Evansville, IN '79 (NURS)
SUMMERS, SUZANNE, dir. mktg. and dev., Magic Valley Regional Medical Center, Twin Falls, ID '80 (PR)
SUMMERS, WILLIAM L., dir. facil. and eng., Children's Hospital of Wisconsin, Milwaukee, WI '66 (ENG)
SUMMERSETT, JAMES A. III, exec. dir., Baylor Medical Center at Gilmer, Gilmer, TX '79
SUMMERVILLE, JANE S., asst. vice-pres. corp. commun., Toledo Hospital, Toledo, OH '75 (PR)
SUMNER, GLENN D., reg. mgr., SunHealth, Inc., Marietta, GA '77 (MGMT)
SUMNER, LORI W., dir. amb. nrsg. serv., Baptist Medical Center-Montclair, Birmingham, AL '86 (AMB)
SUMNER, MERCEDES J., RN, dir. med. and surg. int. serv., Tucson Medical Center, Tucson, AZ '84 (NURS)
SUMRALL, BRENDA CRAMPTON, dir. soc. work, University Hospital, Jackson, MS '85 (SOC)
SUNDE, THOMAS L., dir. mktg. commun., Santa Rosa Medical Center, San Antonio, TX '76 (PR)
SUNDQUIST, HELEN, RN, dir. nrs., St. Gabriel's Hospital, Little Falls, MN '77 (NURS)
SUNDSTROM, PHYLLIS, asst. educ., Kelowna General Hospital, Kelowna, B.C., Canada '86 (EDUC)
SUNGA, LUZ, RN, asst. dir. nrsg., St. Francis Hospital, Blue Island, IL '82 (NURS)
SUNNY, MARGARET N., asst. mgr. food serv., Desert Hospital, Palm Springs, CA '82 (FOOD)
SUNQUIST, JOANNE M., RN, New York, NY '84 (NURS)
SUPINGER, SANDY B., coor. pat. serv. and dir. vol., River Oaks Hospital, Jackson, MS '82 (PAT)(VOL)
SUPPLEE, GEORGE H., assoc. adm. facil. eng., Alfred I. Dupont Institute, Wilmington, DE '85 (ENG)
SURANYI, GEORGE, mgr. plant eng. and maint., St. Peter's Medical Center, New Brunswick, NJ '85 (ENG)
SURDOVAL, NANCY J., atty., Mercy Hospital of Pittsburgh, Pittsburgh, PA '86 (ATTY)
SURFUS, MARJORIE DIANNE, RN, adm. nrsg., Wells Community Hospital, Bluffton, IN '80 (NURS)
SUROVICK, LAURIE A., sr. mgt. eng., Harper-Grace Hospitals, Detroit, MI '86 (MGMT)
SURPIN, JO A., pres., Alpha Health Consultants, Pennsauken, NJ '85
SURRATT, MARTHA J., dir. vol. serv., Eliza Coffee Memorial Hospital, Florence, AL '85 (VOL)
SURSO, JOAN A. MCLAUGHLIN, dir. ohio health choice plan, Timken Mercy Medical Center, Canton, OH '83
SURY, ALICE B., dir. adm. serv., Irvington General Hospital, Irvington, NJ '81 (RISK)
SUSALIS, DIANE J., staff mgr., At&t Information Systems, Morristowndge, NJ '86 (PUR)
SUSI, JEFFREY L., Catherine McAuley Health Center, Ann Arbor, MI '77
SUSKIN, JEFFREY, vice-pres. human res., Palisades General Hospital, North Bergen, NJ '86 (PERS)
SUSKOWSKI, GEOFFREY J., pres., Magee-Womens Hospital, Pittsburgh, PA '68 (MGMT)(ENG)

SUSLAVICH, ANN M., mktg. commun. spec., Carlecare, Inc., Urbana, IL '86 (PR)
SUSMAN, MARY E., dir. food serv., Greenleaf Center, Fort Oglethorpe, GA '85 (FOOD)
SUSNJARA, MARY A., asst. dir. vol. serv., Bellevue Hospital Center, New York, NY '85 (VOL)
SUSSILLO, JOSEPH M., atty., Lutheran Medical Center, Brooklyn, NY '75 (ATTY)
SUSSMAN, ANN, dir. vol. serv., Francis Scott Key Medical Center, Baltimore, MD '86 (VOL)
SUSSMAN, JASON H., Ernst and Whinney, Chicago, IL '80
SUSSMAN, MARC E., St. Vincent's Hospital, Birmingham, AL '82
SUSSMAN, RICHARD, dir. matl. mgt., Cooper Hospital-University Medical Center, Camden, NJ '83 (PUR)
SUSTR, STAN, dir. pers., AMI Eastway General Hospital, Houston, TX '86 (PERS)
SUSZEK, WILLIAM J., mgr. phys. plant, Sherman Hospital, Elgin, IL '84 (ENG)
SUSZKO, MARK STEPHEN, asst. matl. mgt., Healthwest Medical Centers, Chatsworth, CA '86 (PUR)
SUTCH, POLLY, dir. vol. serv., Montgomery Hospital, Norristown, PA '80 (VOL)
SUTER, STEPHEN D., facil. eng., Stanford University Medical Center, Stanford, CA '84 (ENG)
SUTHERIN, RUTH, dir. diet., The Medical Center, Beaver, PA '77 (FOOD)
SUTHERLAND, DEBORAH M., coor. nrsg. educ., University Community Hospital, Tampa, FL '80 (EDUC)
SUTHERLAND, EDWARD, dir. matl. mgt., Martin Luther Hospital Medical Center, Anaheim, CA '86 (PUR)
SUTHERLAND, HOLLY A., coor. pub. rel., Emerson Hospital, Concord, MA '86 (PR)
SUTHERLAND, MARY S., assoc. prof., Florida State University, Tallahassee, FL '83 (EDUC)
SUTHERLAND, ROBERT L., mgr. facil., Department of Institutions, Denver, CO '74 (ENG)
SUTPHIN, BRUCE A., atty., Leonard Hospital, Troy, NY '85 (ATTY)
SUTT, IRENE M., RN, Nanticoke, PA '71 (EDUC)
SUTTER, EDWARD P., mgr. telephone equip., Hospital of the University of Pennsylvania, Philadelphia, PA '79 (ENG)
SUTTINGER, JOHN W., dir. soc. work, Toledo Hospital, Toledo, OH '78 (SOC)
SUTTINGER, SARAH JANE, student, University of Michigan Program in Hospital Administration, Ann Arbor, MI '83
SUTTLES, HATTIE, dir. sterile proc., Raritan Bay Medical Center, Perth Amboy, NJ '87 (CS)
SUTTON, ALLEN I., dir. hskpg. and ldry., Brownwood Regional Hospital, Brownwood, TX '86 (ENVIRON)
SUTTON, BEVERLY A., RN, dir. nrsg., Alton Memorial Hospital, Alton, IL '86 (NURS)(AMB)
SUTTON, BUD, mgr. matl., Ft Sanders-Sevier Medical Center, Sevierville, TN '86 (PUR)
SUTTON, CLYDE C., corp. dir. food serv., Zurbrugg Memorial Hospital -Riverside, Riverside, NJ '77 (FOOD)
SUTTON, FRANK C., MD, consult., Dayton, OH '42 (LIFE)
SUTTON, GWEN, RN, nrs. outpatient surg., Twin Cities Hospital, Niceville, FL '87 (AMB)
SUTTON, L. LAVON, dir. vol. serv., AMI South Bay Hospital, Redondo Beach, CA '85 (VOL)
SUTTON, LEWIS R., dir. pers., Sacred Heart Medical Center, Spokane, WA '84 (PERS)
SUTTON, M. BROOKS, RN, dir. maternal and child serv., St. Joseph Hospitals, Mount Clemens, MI '86 (NURS)
SUTTON, MARK F., mgr. pers., Memorial Hospital and Health Care Center, Jasper, IN '81 (PERS)
SUTTON, MARY C., dir. food serv., Gibson General Hospital, Trenton, TN '80 (FOOD)
SUTTON, MARY PATRICIA, dir. soc. serv., Central Suffolk Hospital, Riverhead, NY '86 (SOC)
SUTTON, MINNIE, New York, NY '77 (FOOD)
SUTTON, PAMELA D., vice-pres. human res., Rehabilitation Institute of Chicago, Chicago, IL '81 (PERS)
SUTTON, PATRICIA A., dir. clin. and support serv., Dearborn County Hospital, Lawrenceburg, IN '86 (PERS)
SUTTON, R. RONALD, assoc. adm., Memorial Hospital, Danville, VA '67
SUTTON, RICHARD A., dir. risk mgt. and security, Saint Joseph Hospital, Elgin, IL '84 (RISK)
SUTTON, RICHARD D., coor. spec. proj., Indiana University Hospitals, Indianapolis, IN '84 (ENG)
SUTTON, RICHARD J., dir. serv. and matl., Kaweah Delta District Hospital, Visalia, CA '80 (PUR)
SUTTON, RICHARD O., dir. eng., Tennessee Christian Medical Center, Madison, TN '83 (ENG)
SUTTON, ROBERT E., vice-pres., Riddle Memorial Hospital, Media, PA '83 (PLNG)
SUVAJIAN, JANE M., media spec., Women and Infants Hospital of Rhode Island, Providence, RI '82 (EDUC)
SUVER, JAMES D., dir. and prof., Program in Health Services Administration, University of Colorado at Denver College of Business and Administration, Denver, CO '85
SUWAY, BERNESS, (ret.), Waltham, MA '71 (SOC)
SUWINSKI, CRAIG STEVEN, adm. dir., Watson Clinic, Lakeland, FL '79 (ATTY)
SUYDAM, JERRY M., dir. matl. mgt., Proctor Community Hospital, Peoria, IL '79 (PUR)
SUYDAM, PETER R., div. mgr. biomedical and clin. eng., Christian Health Care Systems, Inc., St. Louis, MO '86 (ENG)
SUZUKI, CARROL, mgr. educ. serv., University Hospital, London, Ont., Canada '79 (EDUC)
SVANDA, CONNIE, RN, dir. nrsg. serv., St. Michael's Hospital, Tyndall, SD '80 (NURS)
SVEC, JOSEPH THOMAS, student, Program in Hospital Administration, Governors State University, Park Forest South, IL '85
SVENDSEN, DON F., exec. eng., Miriam Hospital, Providence, RI '86 (ENG)
SVENDSON, GERALDINE A., RN, assoc. dir., R. E. Thomason General Hospital, El Paso, TX '83 (NURS)(RISK)
SVENINGSON, SHARON A., dir. diet., Scripps Memorial Hospital-Chula Vista, Chula Vista, CA '80 (FOOD)
SVENNINGSEN, KAREN L., dir. pers., Methodist Hospitals of Gary, Gary, IN '78 (PERS)
SVENSSON, MARY L., RN, clin. dir. nrsg., Fairview Southdale Hospital, Minneapolis, MN '84 (NURS)
SVENSSON, PAUL F., asst. dir., Montefiore Medical Center, Bronx, NY '78 (PUR)
SVERHA, JOHN PAUL, adm., Arlington Hospital, Arlington, VA '71
SVETLIK, MAJ. MARY ANNE, MSC USA, student, Graduate Program in Hospital and Health Administration, University of Iowa, Iowa City, IA '81
SWAAN, WIM A., dir. health care facil. plng. and prin., Hellmuth, Obata and Kassabaum, New York, NY '81 (PLNG)
SWADISH, PATRICIA M., RN, vice-pres. pat. care, Highland Park Hospital, Highland Park, IL '81 (NURS)
SWAFFORD, ROGER C., dir. corp. commun., Menorah Medical Center, Kansas City, MO '81 (PR)
SWAGLER, PATIENCE CORNELL, coor. nrsg. educ., Los Robles Regional Medical Center, Thousand Oaks, CA '86 (EDUC)
SWAIN, ANN E., coor. educ., Dallas County Hospital District-Parkland Memorial Hospital, Dallas, TX '82 (EDUC)
SWAIN, ESTELLE G., adm. food serv., John E. Fogarty Memorial Hospital, North Smithfield, RI '70 (FOOD)
SWAIN, JAMES B., pur. agt., Fauquier Hospital, Warrenton, VA '74 (PUR)
SWAIN, RALPH W., assoc. dir. health syst. res., University of Florida, Gainesville, FL '81 (MGMT)
SWALLOW, LILA L., coor. vol., Porter Memorial Hospital, Denver, CO '74 (VOL)
SWAMIDOSS, PONNUSWAMY, asst. adm., Howard University Hospital, Washington, DC '72 (EDUC)(MGMT)
SWAN, DENNIS A., vice-pres., Edward W. Sparrow Hospital, Lansing, MI '85 (PLNG)
SWAN, JAMES, plant eng., Indianhead Medical Center, Shell Lake, WI '78 (ENG)
SWAN, MARY ELIZABETH, supv. cent. serv., Castle Medical Center, Kailua, HI '86 (CS)
SWAN, RICHARD A., vice-pres. corp. dev., St. Vincent Medical Center, Los Angeles, CA '72 (PLNG)
SWANDOLLAR-HOOKS, MARY, dir. mktg., Beaumont Neurological Hospital, Beaumont, TX '86 (PLNG)
SWANENBURG, RICHARD, dir. bldgs. and grds., Eastern State Hospital, Williamsburg, VA '80 (ENG)
SWANEY, ANDREW, dir. environ. serv., Brazos Psychiatric Hospital, Waco, TX '86 (ENG)
SWANGO, MARGARET B., dir. soc. serv., Midwest City Memorial Hospital, Midwest City, OK '85 (SOC)
SWANK, MARY ALICE, dir. nrsg., Licking Memorial Hospital, Newark, OH '86 (NURS)
SWANK, THOMAS L., dir. matl. mgt., Rockford Memorial Hospital, Rockford, IL '84 (PUR)
SWANKOSKI, MICHALINE A., RN, vice-pres. pat. care serv., Lock Haven Hospital and Extended Care Unit, Lock Haven, PA '76 (NURS)
SWANN, JEFFREY C., supv. maint., Ashtabula County Medical Center, Ashtabula, OH '85 (ENG)
SWANN, L. HAMPTON, exec. eng., Baptist Medical Center-Montclair, Birmingham, AL '66 (ENG)
SWANN, SUE, RN, supt. cent. serv., Hilo Hospital, Hilo, HI '77 (CS)
SWANN, WAYNE L., dir. pers., Children's Hospital National Medical Center, Washington, DC '82 (PERS)
SWANSBURG, RUSSELL C., RN PhD, prof. nrsg. adm., Auburn University at Montgomery, School of Nursing, Montgomery, AL '81 (NURS)
SWANSON, BLANCHE B., in-service educ., Unity Medical Center, Fridley, MN '86 (EDUC)
SWANSON, CHARLES H., mgr. data proc., Ferguson Hospital, Grand Rapids, MI '85
SWANSON, CLETA M., dir. vol. serv., Petaluma Valley Hospital, Petaluma, CA '86 (VOL)
SWANSON, CURTIS C., atty., Meriter Hospital, Madison, WI '80 (ATTY)
SWANSON, DAN T., Multicare Medical Center, Tacoma, WA '83 (ENG)
SWANSON, DONALD W., dir. pur., Rochester Methodist Hospital, Rochester, MN '81 (PUR)
SWANSON, DUANE A., exec. vice-pres. oper., C. F. Menninger Memorial Hospital, Topeka, KS '82 (PLNG)
SWANSON, ELAINE H., mgr. vol. serv., Westlake Community Hospital, Melrose Park, IL '86 (VOL)
SWANSON, GERRY, dir. soc. serv., Vista Sandia Hospital, Albuquerque, NM '85 (SOC)
SWANSON, JEANNE C., dir. vol. serv., St. Clare's Hospital of Schenectady, Schenectady, NY '73 (VOL)
SWANSON, JO, RN, instr. staff dev., University of Kansas Hospital, Kansas City, KS '80 (EDUC)
SWANSON, JUDITH M., asst. adm., Tulane University Hospital and Clinics, New Orleans, LA '82
SWANSON, LEON C., adm., North Country Hospital, Bemidji, MN '85
SWANSON, PHYLLIS, dir. vol., Lutheran Medical Center, Wheat Ridge, CO '70 (VOL)
SWANSON, RICHARD A., dir. eng., Memorial Hospital, South Bend, IN '81 (ENG)
SWANSON, RONALD M., pers. asst., Tucson Medical Center, Tucson, AZ '77 (PERS)
SWANSTON, LOIS J., RN, asst. dir. and dir. nrsg., Foster G. McGaw Hospital, Loyola University of Chicago, Maywood, IL '82 (NURS)
SWARO, JOSEPH ERIC SR., mgr. plant oper., Clinton Memorial Hospital, Wilmington, OH '74 (ENG)
SWARTWOUT, JOHN A., assoc. adm., Saint Joseph Hospital, Elgin, IL '69
SWARTZ, CHARLES E., dir. eng. and bldg., Casa Colina Hospital for Rehabilitative Medicine, Pomona, CA '75 (ENG)
SWARTZ, LINDA K., dir. pub. rel. and mktg., Fish Memorial Hospital at DeLand, De Land, FL '84 (PR) (PLNG)
SWARTZ, MARTHA S., atty., Hahnemann University Hospital, Philadelphia, PA '86 (ATTY)
SWARTZ, MARTIN, corp. plng. analyst, Mercy Health Center of Central Iowa, Des Moines, IA '86 (PLNG)
SWARTZ, PETER F., dir. eng., Nathan Littauer Hospital, Gloversville, NY '81 (ENG)
SWARTZ, SHERRI LYNN, supv. pat. rep., Kaiser Permanente, Raleigh, NC '87 (PAT)
SWARTZ, THOMAS J. III, vice-pres. municipal res., E. F. Hutton and Company, Inc., New York, NY '86
SWARZKOPF, JOHN, dir. eng., Foothill Presbyterian Hospital-Morris L. Johnston Memorial, Glendora, CA '85 (ENG)
SWARZMAN, MICHAEL A., assoc. adm., Illinois Masonic Medical Center, Chicago, IL '77 (PUR)
SWASKO, PAUL ALLEN, dir. soc. work, St. Joseph's Hospital and Health Center, Paris, TX '78 (SOC)
SWATECK, STEVEN J., asst. dir. matl. mgt., Copley Memorial Hospital, Aurora, IL '86 (PUR)
SWATH, PEG, dir. diet., Colorado State Hospital, Pueblo, CO '79 (FOOD)
SWAYZE, RICHARD H., dir. plant serv., Lapeer General Hospital, LaPeer, MI '67 (ENG)
SWEAT, CHARLES J., pres., Victoria Hospital, Miami, FL '62
SWEATT, LOIS ANNE, Etna, NH '76 (NURS)
SWEDA, BARBARA, RN, pres. and exec. dir., Home Health Outreach, Inc., Oxford, MI '78 (NURS)
SWEENEY, DOROTHY, coor. risk mgt. and qual. assur., Human Resource Institute, Brookline, MA '83 (RISK)
SWEENEY, FRANCIS J. JR., MD, vice-pres. prof. affairs and med. dir., Mercy Catholic Medical Center, Darby, PA '67
SWEENEY, JANE M., pat. rep., St. Vincent Hospital and Health Center, Indianapolis, IN '81 (PAT)
SWEENEY, JOHN E., (ret.), St. Paul, MN '71 (ENG)
SWEENEY, KATHLEEN N., dir. pers. serv., Melrose-Wakefield Hospital, Melrose, MA '80 (PERS)
SWEENEY, M. MILTON, atty., Tennessee Christian Medical Center, Madison, TN '86 (ATTY)
SWEENEY, MARILYN K., dir. pers., Whitley County Memorial Hospital, Columbia City, IN '81 (PERS)
SWEENEY, MARY T., dir. plng. and mktg., Quincy City Hospital, Quincy, MA '84 (PLNG)
SWEENEY, SHARON LYNNE, student, Duke University, Durham, NC '86
SWEENEY, THOMAS E., atty., Franciscan Health System, Chadds Ford, PA '80 (ATTY)
SWEENY, EDWARD P., exec. dir., West Shore Medical Care Foundation, Lakewood, OH '86 (AMB)
SWEENY, VIRGINIA K., RN, vice-pres. nrsg., St. Vincent's Hospital and Medical Center of New York, New York, NY '79 (NURS)
SWEERIS, CHARLES L., atty., Catherine McAuley Health Center, Ann Arbor, MI '87 (ATTY)
SWEET, E. C., (ret.), Phoenix, AZ '63 (ENG)
SWEET, J. EDWARD JR., pres., Alexandria Hospital, Alexandria, VA '56 (LIFE)
SWEET, JANET H., RN, dir. nrsg. serv., Daviess County Hospital, Washington, IN '74 (NURS)
SWEET, NORMA G., RN, dir. nrsg. serv., Firelands Community Hospital, Sandusky, OH '86 (NURS)
SWEETLAND, KAREN E., asst. adm., Mary Hitchcock Memorial Hospital, Hanover, NH '80
SWEETNICH, M. EDWARD, dir. pers. serv., Good Samaritan Hospital and Health Center, Dayton, OH '86 (PERS)
SWEIGART, SALLY, coor. health educ., Boca Raton Community Hospital, Boca Raton, FL '83 (EDUC)
SWEIKAR, MARY KAY, dir. mktg. and commun., St. Elizabeth Hospital, Danville, IL '78 (PR) (PLNG)
SWENCKY, LAVERNE MARIE, pat. rep., Parma Community General Hospital, Parma, OH '87 (PAT)
SWENSON, DONNA M., mgr. sup. mgt. and proc., Rockford Memorial Hospital, Rockford, IL '81 (CS)
SWENSON, JANELLE F., dir. soc. serv., Trinity Regional Hospital, Fort Dodge, IA '82 (SOC)
SWENSON, STEPHEN R., student, Concordia College, St. Paul, MN '83
SWENSON, VIRGINIA B., dir. and coor. pat. rel., Western Medical Center, Santa Ana, CA '87 (PAT)
SWETONIC, CAPT. MARJORIE A., MSC USN RN, dir. nrsg. serv., Naval Hospital, Philadelphia, PA '77 (NURS)
SWETT, DANIEL R., atty., Michael Reese Hospital and Medical Center, Chicago, IL '74 (ATTY)
SWETT, JONATHAN N., mgt. consult., Voluntary Hospitals of America, Irving, TX '73
SWETZ, MARY L., supv. cent. sup., Frederick Ferris Thompson Hospital, Canandaigua, NY '84 (CS)
SWETZ, SHARON M., asst. vice-pres. and dir. matl. mgt., Southwestern Vermont Medical Center, Bennington, VT '83 (PUR)
SWICEGOOD, HENRY A., Columbus, NC '54 (LIFE)
SWICHAR, LINDA T., dir. soc. serv., North Pennsylvania Hospital, Lansdale, PA '83 (SOC)
SWIDERSKI, EDWARD, Providence Hospital, Washington, DC '84 (PLNG)
SWIER, DONALD WAYNE, dir. phys. plant, Memorial Medical Center of West Michigan, Ludington, MI '75 (ENG)
SWIFT, E., RN, dir. nrsg. prac. and serv., Cuba Memorial Hospital, Cuba, NY '77 (NURS)
SWIFT, EDSON E., exec. dir., St. Elizabeth's Hospital, Hannibal, MO '73
SWIFT, HOWARD G., asst. vice-pres., Midland Hospital Center, Midland, MI '85
SWIFT, LAURENCE B., dir. plant oper., HCA Northwest Regional Hospital, Margate, FL '84 (ENG)
SWIFT, MARY C., dir. diet., Parma Community General Hospital, Parma, OH '67 (FOOD)
SWIFT, PAM, dist. trng. off., St. James University Hospital, Leeds, England '82 (EDUC)
SWIFT, RICHARD B., dir. pers., St. Joseph Hospital, Augusta, GA '73 (PERS)

SWIGER, EDWARD D., dir. ldry., Saints Mary and Elizabeth Hospital, Louisville, KY '86 (ENVIRON)
SWIHART, JOHN B., atty., Dwight D. Eisenhower Army Medical Center, Fort Gordon, GA '86 (ATTY)
SWILLEY, SIDNEY N., chief eng., Shallowford Community Hospital, Chamblee, GA '85 (ENG)
SWIM, C. T. JR., chief eng., Princeton Community Hospital, Princeton, WV '85 (ENG)
SWIM, J. MURRAY, vice-pres. human res., Good Samaritan Hospital, Pottsville, PA '85 (PERS)
SWINDALL, VICTOR A., Indian Head Park, IL '79
SWINEA, MARILYN H., coor. nrsg. educ., Nashville Memorial Hospital, Madison, TN '75 (EDUC)
SWINEHART, FRANK V., vice-pres. plng. and mktg., Grant Medical Center, Columbus, OH '86 (PR) (PLNG)
SWINFORD, RACHEL L. B., pres., Swinford and Associates, Marietta, GA '86 (PLNG)
SWINGLER, ERIC H. III, supv. storeroom and receiving, Helene Fuld Medical Center, Trenton, NJ '86 (CS)
SWINK, JULIA R., RN, assoc. vice-pres. nrsg., The Medical Center, Beaver, PA '86 (NURS)
SWINNEA, JAMES W. JR., asst. vice-pres. adm., University of Texas Medical Branch, Galveston, TX '83 (RISK)
SWINNEY, ALVIS R., vice-pres. mktg. and strategy mgt., Baylor Health Care System, Dallas, TX '86 (PR) (PLNG)
SWIP, JO ANN, coor. allied health prog., Institute for Continuing Education Clarkson Education Center, Ballwin, MO '79 (EDUC)
SWISHER, AMY H., pub. info. off., Southwestern Vermont Medical Center, Bennington, VT '82 (PR)
SWISHER, CATHARINE A., reg. diet. consult., Care Enterprises, Redd Bluff, CA '84 (FOOD)
SWISHER, ELAINE M., RN, vice-pres. pat. serv., Valley Hospital and Medical Center, Spokane, WA '82 (NURS)
SWISHER, KAREN N., atty., Retreat Hospital, Richmond, VA '86 (ATTY)
SWISHER, LOUISE DUNCAN, assoc. exec. dir., Kendrick Memorial Hospital, Mooresville, IN '79 (MGMT)
SWISHER, LT. RAYMOND J., MSC USA, head plng. br., Naval Medical Command, Washington, DC '84 (MGMT)(ENG)
SWITZER, MICHAEL T., proj. mgr., Research Medical Center, Kansas City, MO '83 (ENG)
SWORD, RUSS D., adm., Arh Regional Medical Center, Hazard, KY '72
SWORDS, DENISE, RN, dir. nrsg., Scottish Rite Children's Hospital, Atlanta, GA '86 (NURS)
SY, THOMAS A., asst. plng. and mktg., Health Northeast, Manchester, NH '83 (PLNG)
SYBELDON, JADY R., dir. biomedical eng., R. E. Thomason General Hospital, El Paso, TX '86 (ENG)
SYBROWSKY, CAROL L., staff assoc., Family Health Program, Fountain Valley, CA '87 (PLNG)
SYCAMORE, HUBERT D., asst. dir., New England Deaconess Hospital, Boston, MA '68
SYDNES, ALLEN D., Newton, IA '84
SYER, RONALD M., dir. matl. mgt., Kershaw County Memorial Hospital, Camden, SC '83 (PUR)
SYKES, MELINDA M., sr. consult., SunHealth Corporation, Charlotte, NC '80 (MGMT)
SYLVESTER, AVIS, (ret.), Dallas, TX '77 (EDUC)
SYLVESTER, CORWIN L., supv. oper., Charter Rivers Hospital, West Columbia, SC '86 (ENG)
SYLVESTRI, DONNA P., dir. util., Maxicare New York, Inc., New York, NY '86
SYME, DORIS E., dir. plng. and prog. dev., Huntington Memorial Hospital, Pasadena, CA '85 (PLNG)
SYMES, DALE R., assoc. adm. fin., Lovelace Medical Center, Albuquerque, NM '83 (PLNG)
SYMINGTON, RALPH E., mgr. clin. eng., Salem Hospital, Salem, MA '84 (ENG)
SYMONDS, ANN L., dir. support serv., Valley Medical Center, Renton, WA '83 (CS)
SYMONDS, PATRICIA, RN, dir. nrsg. serv., Belle Fourche Health Care Center, Belle Fourche, SD '81 (NURS)
SYPERT, NANCY R., RN, clin. dir. surg. nrsg., Shands Hospital, Gainesville, FL '86 (NURS)
SYRON, MAJ. EDWARD P., MSC USAF, dep. chief qual. assur., Office of the U. S. Air Force Surgeon General, Bolling AFB, DC '75
SZABIET, SUSAN M., mgt. eng., Sinai Hospital of Detroit, Detroit, MI '87 (MGMT)
SZABO, CHARLEEN R., health syst. spec. and facil. planner, Veterans Administration Medical Center, Washington, DC '87
SZABO, PETER A. JR., adm., Hinsdale Surgical Center, Hinsdale, IL '87 (AMB)
SZANDZIK, DAVID J., sr. bus. analyst, Radius Health Care System, Inc., Oak Park, MI '85 (MGMT)
SZCZECHOWSKI, WALTER P., vice-pres. adm., Wyandotte General Hospital, Wyandotte, MI '69 (MGMT)
SZCZEPANSKI, WARREN J., dir. bldg. serv., Germantown Hospital and Medical Center, Philadelphia, PA '86 (ENVIRON)
SZERLAG, CHESTER T., adm. dir. rad., University of Chicago Hospitals, Chicago, IL '82 (MGMT)
SZEWCZUK, JEANNE M., RN, dir. home care, Crozer-Chester Medical Center, Chester, PA '87 (AMB)
SZKOTNICKI, GERALD M., asst. dir., Community Hospital of Bedford, Bedford, OH '80
SZPAK, CAROLE A., dir. pub. info., Psychiatric Institute of Montgomery County, Rockville, MD '82 (PR)
SZUCHY, STEPHEN J., vice-pres., Miriam Hospital, Providence, RI '79
SZUKALSKI, DICK, dir. environ. serv., Charlotte Memorial Hospital and Medical Center, Charlotte, NC '86 (ENVIRON)
SZUMSKI, JOANNE B., coor. vol. prog., Marian Medical Center, Santa Maria, CA '84 (VOL)
SZYDLOW, WERNER, vice-pres. and dir. health care facil., Wallace and Watson Associates, Allentown, PA '82
SZYMOKOWSKI, RICHARD W., assoc. adm. fin., Greenville Regional Hospital, Greenville, PA '74 (MGMT)
SZYSZKIEWICZ, WALTER, dir. matl. mgt., Harrington Memorial Hospital, Southbridge, MA '85 (PUR)

T

TAASAAS, CARL C., dir. environ. serv., St. Luke's Hospitals, Fargo, ND '86 (ENVIRON)
TABACCO, EDWARD V., dir. gen. serv., Washington Hospital, Fremont, CA '85 (ENG)
TABAK, HARLEY LAIRD, adm., Annaburg Manor Nursing Home, Manassas, VA '78
TABAKA, A. V., asst. adm., Metropolitan Hospital, Detroit, MI '66 (ATTY)
TABAS, ALLAN M., atty., Thomas Jefferson University Hospital, Philadelphia, PA '82 (ATTY)
TABB, LEONARD, dir. cent. serv., North Hills Passavant Hospital, Pittsburgh, PA '79 (CS)
TABER, JOAN M., student, University of New Haven, New Haven, CT '85 (MGMT)
TABER, RUTH J., RN, asst. adm., Sparks Family Hospital, Sparks, NV '80 (NURS)
TABER, STEPHEN L., atty., Hospital Council of Northern California, San Bruno, CA '79 (ATTY)
TABOR, KATHLEEN M., RN, dir. nrsg. serv., Northwestern Medical Center, St. Albans, VT '85 (NURS)
TABOR, SHERRY RUSH, dir. soc. serv. and pat. rep., T. J. Samson Community Hospital, Glasgow, KY '81 (PAT)
TABOR, STEPHEN E., Palisades General Hospital, North Bergen, NJ '83 (PUR)
TABRAH, FRANK, prof. commun. health, University of Hawaii School of Medicine, Honolulu, HI '85 (RISK)
TACCOGNA, RONALD C., supv. cent. serv., Elizabeth General Medical Center, Elizabeth, NJ '81 (CS)
TACHAU, HANS, dir. pers. serv., Western Pennsylvania Hospital, Pittsburgh, PA '80 (PERS)
TACKEL, PHILIP, Brookline, MA '78 (MGMT)
TADMAN, HUGH F., exec. dir., Sisters of Chartiy Grey Nuns of Alberta, Edmonton, Alta., Canada '81 (PR)(PAT)
TAFT, JOHN A. JR., adm. and ceo, Grace Hospital, Morganton, NC '57 (LIFE)
TAFT, LAURIE, dir. vol. serv., Phoenix General Hospital, Phoenix, AZ '81 (VOL)
TAGLIARENI, JOHN C., asst. adm., Martin Memorial Hospital, Stuart, FL '82
TAGUE, KARL R., pres. and chief exec. off., Miami Valley Hospital, Dayton, OH '71
TAICHERT, ROBERT D., atty., Southwest Community Health Services, Albuquerque, NM '76 (ATTY)
TAINTER, LORRIE A., RN, proj. dir. and dir. support syst., St. Vincent Hospital, Santa Fe, NM '86 (NURS)
TAINTOR, FREDERICK G., atty., Central Maine Medical Center, Lewiston, ME '74 (ATTY)
TAIT, IRVING G., dir. maint., Louis Smith Memorial Hospital, Lakeland, GA '82 (ENG)
TAKACH, ALDENA M., student, Program in Health Care Management, Southern Illinois University, Carbondale, IL '86
TAKACH, MARY JO, pub. rel. spec., Fitzgerald and Company, Inc., Cranston, RI '81 (PR)
TAKACH, MARY, RN, dir. nrsg., St. Margaret Memorial Hospital, Pittsburgh, PA '80 (NURS)
TAKAHASHI, SHIRLEY K., RN, mgr. nrsg. serv., Kula Hospital, Kula, HI '77 (EDUC)(NURS)
TAKALA, JANE A., dir. cent. serv. room, King Faisal Specialist Hospital, Riyadh, Saudi Arabia '83 (CS)
TALAFER, JANAN V., newswriter and coor., Yale-New Haven Hospital, New Haven, CT '85 (PR)
TALAMO, JOSEPH J., dir. hskpg. and ldry., The Medical Center, Beaver, PA '86 (ENVIRON)
TALBERT, ANDREW MARC JR., adm. res., Veterans Administration Medical Center, Baltimore, MD '86
TALBERT, D. VANBUREN, dir. plng., Winter Park Memorial Hospital, Winter Park, FL '73 (PLNG)
TALBERT, JAMES LEE, Santa Clara, CA '67 (FOOD)
TALBIRD, NELL W., RN, vice-pres. pat. serv., St. Luke's Hospital, Jacksonville, FL '86 (NURS)
TALBOT, ANTHONY E., dir. telecommun., St. John's Hospital and Health Center, Santa Monica, CA '86 (ENG)
TALBOT, LITA M., chairperson soc. serv., University of Maryland Medical Systems, Baltimore, MD '75 (SOC)
TALBOTT, J. ERIC, reg. hosp. mgr.-atlantic area, Ciba-Geigy Corporation, Parsippany, NJ '85
TALBOTT, KAREN L., exec. vice-pres., Visiting Nurse Service, Inc., Akron, OH '87 (AMB)
TALBOTT, RICHARD E., atty., Emanuel Hospital and Health Center, Portland, OR '80 (ATTY)
TALIAFERRO, JAMES G. JR., chief eng., Humana Hospital -Brentwood, Shreveport, LA '78 (ENG)
TALIAFERRO, JAMES T., risk mgr., Wilson Rehabilitation Center, Fishersville, VA '86 (RISK)
TALKINGTON, DOUGLAS R., dir. matl. mgt., Firelands Community Hospital, Sandusky, OH '84 (PUR)
TALLARICO, VINCENT J., corp. planner, Healtheast, Inc., Allentown, PA '81 (PLNG)
TALLERDAY, WILMA M., hosp. rep. risk mgt. serv., St. Paul Fire and Marine Insurance Company, Aurora, CO '83 (RISK)
TALLEY, JAMES C. II, DeWitt Shepard Company, Knoxville, TN '52 (LIFE)
TALLEY, JAMES R., chief eng., Halifax Memorial Hospital, Roanoke Rapids, NC '84 (ENG)
TALLEY, THOMAS A., mgr. prod. and tech. plng., E. I. Du Pont de Nemours and Company, Wilmington, DE '86 (PR)
TALLY, PATRICIA A., dir. soc. work, Presbyterian Hospital, Dallas, TX '85 (SOC)
TALMANIS, CATHARINE A., coor. clin. prog., Burnaby Hospital, Burnaby, B.C., Canada '87 (EDUC)
TALONE, CARIN HUNT, dir. plng., Suburban General Hospital, Norristown, PA '85 (PR) (PLNG)
TALONE, NICHOLAS, vice-pres. gen. adm., Marshal Hale Memorial Hospital, San Francisco, CA '80
TALSMA, HELEN, supv. sup., proc. and distrib., Desert Samaritan Hospital, Mesa, AZ '86 (CS)
TALUCCI, GINNY, acct. exec., Fred S. James and Company, San Francisco, CA '87 (RISK)
TALVACCHIA, MARY LYNN, prog. coor. health educ., Lankenau Hospital, Philadelphia, PA '81 (EDUC)
TALVACCHIO, JOSEPH A., dir. prof. serv., Ewing Cole Cherry Parsky, Philadelphia, PA '86 (ENG)
TAM, LAURINE, med. soc. worker, Shriners Hospital for Crippled Children, Honolulu, HI '84 (SOC)
TAMBORLANE, THEODOSIA A., atty., Robert Wood Johnson University Hospital, New Brunswick, NJ '86 (ATTY)
TAMBURINI, STEVEN R., pur. agt., Dr. John Warner Hospital, Clinton, IL '80 (PUR)
TAMKIN, JEFFREY H., bd. mem., Cedars-Sinai Medical Center, Los Angeles, CA '83
TAMM, KATHERYNE B., RN, clin. dir. psych. nrsg., Yale-New Haven Hospital, New Haven, CT '86 (NURS)
TAMM, TOOMAS, partner, Bregman and Hamann, Don Mills, Ont., Canada '84
TAMME, RUTH G., dir. soc. serv., Ephraim McDowell Regional Medical Center, Danville, KY '85 (SOC)
TAMMELLEO, A. DAVID, atty., St. Joseph Hospital, Nashua, NH '84 (ATTY)
TAMRAZ, JANE C., dir. pub. rel., Bronson Methodist Hospital, Kalamazoo, MI '85 (PR)
TAMURA, DUANE T., supv. emp. and benefits, West Valley Medical Center, Caldwell, ID '86 (PERS)
TAMURA, ELAINE G., asst. dir. food mgt., St. Agnes Hospital and Medical Center, Fresno, CA '83 (FOOD)
TAN, MARVA, loss prevention, Risk Management Foundation, Cambridge, MA '86 (RISK)
TANAKA, IRENE K., coor. qual. assur. and risk mgr., Tripler Army Medical Center, Honolulu, HI '84 (RISK)
TANAKA, KATHLEEN P., coor. soc. serv., Jeannette District Memorial Hospital, Jeannette, PA '75 (SOC)
TANASCHUK, MARION, RN, nrs. outpatient, Doctors Hospital, Detroit, MI '87 (AMB)
TANASSE, DORRE LEON, pat. rep., St. Elizabeth Medical Center, Yakima, WA '86 (PAT)
TANDESKI, SHIRLEY A., dir. soc. serv., Rolla Community Hospital, Rolla, ND '80 (SOC)
TANDY, WILLIAM C. JR., dir. info. syst., St. John's Eastside Hospital, St. Paul, MN '84 (MGMT)
TANG, AIMEE, dir. group pur., Medical Shared Service of Hawaii, Inc., Honolulu, HI '85 (PUR)
TANG, RAYMOND C. P., Russell Reynolds Associates, Inc., Hong Kong, Hong Kong '80
TANGEN, DOROTHY M., supv. cent. serv., Mercy Medical Center, Coon Rapids, MN '82 (CS)
TANIGUCHI, RONALD T., asst. dir. pharm. serv., Kaiser Foundation Hospital, Honolulu, HI '84 (PUR)
TANK, DARRYL, asst. dir. eng. serv., Emory University Hospital, Atlanta, GA '86 (ENG)
TANKERSLEY, LARRY L., dir. food serv., Providence Hospital, Anchorage, AK '80 (FOOD)
TANKERSLEY, LOIS B., risk mgr. and coor. qual. assur., Nemours Children's Hospital, Jacksonville, FL '81 (RISK)
TANNACHION, JUDITH G., mgr. matl., Lake Shore Hospital, Lake City, FL '86 (PUR)
TANNEN, ARNOLD I., assoc. adm., Schneider Children's Hospital of Long Island Jewish-Hillside Medical Center, New Hyde Park, NY '70 (PLNG)
TANNEN, SUSAN C., mgr. mktg., Shared Services, New York, NY '86 (PLNG)
TANNENHOLZ, DAVID, asst. dir., Coney Island Hospital, Brooklyn, NY '87 (AMB)
TANNER, BUZZ, dir. pub. rel. and mktg., Jones County Community Hospital, Laurel, MS '83 (PR)
TANNER, DAVID J., consult., Marketing Corporation of America, Westport, CT '87 (AMB)(PLNG)
TANNER, DOUGLAS N., asst. adm., Gulf Health, Inc., Mobile, AL '84
TANNER, JUDITH M., mgr. pers., Appleton Medical Center, Appleton, WI '86 (PERS)
TANNER, LAURENCE A., pres. and chief exec. off., New Britain General Hospital, New Britain, CT '78
TANNER, MOIR P., (ret.), Buffalo, NY '29 (LIFE)
TANNER, ROBERT M., Cocke Phillips International, Inc., Washington, DC '84 (ENG)
TANQUARY, CONNIE, dir. nrsg. and qual. assur., Santa Monica Hospital Medical Center, Santa Monica, CA '86 (RISK)
TANTILLO, THOMAS J., dir. soc. serv., Doylestown Hospital, Doylestown, PA '85 (SOC)
TANVERDI, CENGIZ, dir. mgt. eng., Healtheast, Inc., Ronoake, VA '79 (MGMT)
TAPANES, NANCY F., dir. soc. work, North Gables Hospital, Coral Gables, FL '86 (SOC)
TAPANI, DUANE E., supv. power plant, Metropolitan Medical Center, Minneapolis, MN '86 (ENG)
TAPOLCAI, THOMAS J., proj. mgr., Memorial Hospital, South Bend, IN '86 (ENG)
TAPPE, BRUCE V., dir. diet., Beyer Memorial Hospital, Ypsilanti, MI '72 (FOOD)
TAPPER, ANNE P., RN, coor. educ., Children's Seashore House, Philadelphia, PA '85 (EDUC)
TAPPER, JOY RENEE, proj. spec.-plng. and mktg., St. Joseph's Hospital, Milwaukee, WI '86 (PLNG)
TARANGIOLI, JOAN, dir. pub. rel., St. John's Riverside Hospital, Yonkers, NY '86 (PR)
TARASCHI, ROSARIA, consult., American Hospital Resources, Downingtown, PA '85 (PAT)
TARCOLA, ALBERT D., asst. dir. phys. res., University Medical Center, Tucson, AZ '82 (ENG)
TARKE, LINDA H., dir. med. soc. serv., Children's Hospital and Health Center, San Diego, CA '80 (SOC)
TARKETT, MARILEE C., RN, asst. vice-pres. nrsg., Covenant Medical Center -St. Francis, Waterloo, IA '83 (NURS)

TARNOFF, LAWRENCE R., vice-pres. mktg. and dev., Mount Sinai Medical Center, Milwaukee, WI '80 (PR)
TARNOSKY, PAUL E., dir. plant oper., Divine Providence Hospital, Pittsburgh, PA '79 (ENG)
TARNOWSKI, MARILYN J., dir. pub. rel., DePaul Hospital, Norfolk, VA '85 (PR)
TARPLEE, SUE C., mgr., Ernst and Whinney, Indianapolis, IN '87 (MGMT)
TARQUINI, JOSEPH T., pres., The Tarquini Organization, Camden, NJ '78
TARR, DOROTHY A., pat. rep. and risk mgr., Hackettstown Community Hospital, Hackettstown, NJ '83 (PAT)
TARR, SUSANNE M., RN, asst. exec. dir. nrsg., Adams County Memorial Hospital, Decatur, IN '80 (NURS)
TARRANT, JAMES R., exec. vice-pres., Michigan Health Council, East Lansing, MI '79 (EDUC)
TARRANT, MAUREEN, dir. mktg., Porter Memorial Hospital, Denver, CO '85 (PR) (PLNG)
TARRANT, SUSAN NEVARRE, dir. pat. rep., University of Massachusetts Medical Center, Worcester, MA '80 (PAT)
TARTE, JEFFERY P., prin., Arthur Young and Company, Washington, DC '86 (MGMT)(CS)(PLNG)
TARULIS, SEAVER A., dir. facil. mgt., Chicago Osteopathic Health Systems, Inc., Olympia Fields, IL '79 (ENG)
TARULLI, DONNA M., RN, assoc. dir. risk mgt., Cedars-Sinai Medical Center, Los Angeles, CA '82 (RISK)
TARVIN, GLORIA A., dir. soc. work, Rehabilitation Institute of Chicago, Chicago, IL '80 (SOC)
TARVIN, KATHERINE M., RN, dir. nrsg. serv., Mason District Hospital, Havana, IL '81 (NURS)
TARWATER, DAN, dir. pers. serv., St. Rose de Lima Hospital, Henderson, NV '79 (PERS)
TASAKA, MASAICHI, pres., Kuakini Medical Center, Honolulu, HI '53 (LIFE)
TASENS, CRAIG J., pres., Tasens Associates, Inc., Alexandria, VA '87 (PUR)
TASMAN, DOROTHY R., RN, dir. maternal-child health, Mansfield General Hospital, Mansfield, OH '83 (NURS)
TASSANI, SALLY M., pres., St. Francis Hospital, Evanston, IL '86 (PR)
TASSIA, MARIE C., RN, asst. dir. nrsg. serv., York Hospital, York, PA '77 (NURS)
TASSO, CAROL A., RN, chief nrsg. serv., Veterans Administration Medical Center, Brooklyn, NY '76 (NURS)
TATARSKY, MARY R., plng. analyst, Pacific Medical Center, Seattle, WA '87 (PLNG)
TATE, BARBARA ANN, vice-pres. risk mgt., Nexus Healthcare Corporation, Mount Holly, NJ '80 (RISK)
TATE, BONNIE W., dir. pub. rel., Lynchburg General-Marshall Lodge Hospital, Lynchburg, VA '83 (PR)
TATE, CAROLYN E., dir. commun. rel., St. Albans Psychiatric Hospital, Radford, VA '85 (PR)
TATE, EDWARD R., PhD, mgr. market surveillance, Department of Food and Drug Administration, Washington, DC '78 (FOOD)
TATE, EVELYN M., dir. food serv., Navarro Regional Hospital, Corsicana, TX '85 (FOOD)
TATE, JOEL W., adm., Watonga Municipal Hospital, Watonga, OK '82 (PR)
TATE, LYNN M., dir. educ., Providence Hospital, Mobile, AL '80 (EDUC)
TATE, MARY, dir. soc. serv., Community Hospital of Lancaster, Lancaster, PA '77 (SOC)
TATE, PATRICIA L., coor. pur., Eastwood Hospital, Memphis, TN '84 (PUR)
TATEL, LESLIE G., mktg. analyst, Presbyterian Hospital, Dallas, TX '86 (PLNG)
TATHEVOSSIAN, AREK M., sr. plng. assoc., Health Central System, Minneapolis, MN '78 (PLNG)
TATMAN, THOMAS A., dir. matl. mgt., St. Mary's Hospital, Decatur, IL '79 (PUR)
TATNALL, ANDREW W., dir. plng. serv., Kennestone Regional Health Care Systems, Marietta, GA '83 (PLNG)
TATUM, CHARLIE G., dir. eng., Brooklyn Hospital-Caledonian Hospital, Brooklyn, NY '84 (ENG)
TATUM, WILBUR P., adm., Southern California Permanente Medical Group, Los Angeles, CA '85
TAUB, LINDA S., dir. diet., Danbury Hospital, Danbury, CT '75 (FOOD)
TAUB, MARJORIE, dir. soc. work, Jersey City Medical Center, Jersey City, NJ '71 (SOC)
TAURASI, A. RAYMOND, dir. cent. proc., Beth Israel Hospital, Boston, MA '82 (CS)
TAVARES, JOHN M., mgr. telephone syst. mktg., Rca Service Company, Cherry Hill, NJ '86 (ENG)
TAVERNARO, JOSEPH P., supv. cent. serv., Mount Carmel Medical Center, Pittsburg, KS '80 (CS)
TAVOSO, SERENE, dir. soc. serv., Warren Memorial Hospital, Front Royal, VA '83 (SOC)
TAWWATER, JOHN C., dir. risk mgt., Amarillo Hospital District, Amarillo, TX '84 (RISK)
TAXSON, HOWARD P., dir. food serv., Westchester Square Medical Center, Bronx, NY '85 (FOOD)
TAYLOE, BEVERLY C., pat. rep., Glynn-Brunswick Memorial Hospital, Brunswick, GA '82 (PAT)
TAYLOR-WHITNEY, MARIE, dir. soc. serv., Mariners Hospital, Tavernier, FL '85 (SOC)
TAYLOR, ABBIE G., RN, dir. nrs., Matagorda General Hospital, Bay City, TX '81 (NURS)
TAYLOR, ALONZO, assoc. dir. diet., Christiana Hospital, Newark, DE '77 (FOOD)
TAYLOR, ANNA M., RN, vice-pres. nrsg., Lutheran Hospital of Fort Wayne, Fort Wayne, IN '84 (NURS)
TAYLOR, BETTY Y., vice-pres. vol. serv., Tallahassee Memorial Regional Medical Center, Tallahassee, FL '86 (VOL)
TAYLOR, BRIDGETT, spec. asst. govt. rel., Hermann Hospital, Houston, TX '86
TAYLOR, CAL, dir. hskpg., Marshalltown Medical and Surgical Center, Marshalltown, IA '86 (ENVIRON)
TAYLOR, CAROLYN JEAN, dir. educ., Medical Center of Independence, Independence, MO '83 (EDUC)
TAYLOR, CHARLES, dir. nutr. serv., Sumner Memorial Hospital, Gallatin, TN '74 (FOOD)
TAYLOR, CHELLIS EUGENE, atty., Graham Hospital, Canton, IL '68 (ATTY)
TAYLOR, CYNTHIA ANN, pat. rep. and educ. spec., HCA Woodland Heights Medical Center, Lufkin, TX '86 (PAT)
TAYLOR, CYNTHIA M., RN, asst. adm., Suburban Hospital, Bethesda, MD '86 (NURS)
TAYLOR, DAVID J., supv. eng., Kaiser Foundation Hospital, San Francisco, CA '86 (ENG)
TAYLOR, DAVID, dir. plng., Mount Diablo Hospital Medical Center, Concord, CA '81 (PLNG)
TAYLOR, DAVID, head pur. and matl. mgt., Allied Medical Group, Riyadh, Saudi Arabia '81 (PUR)
TAYLOR, DAWSON, atty., Sisters of Providence, Seattle, WA '86 (ATTY)
TAYLOR, DEBRA B., planner and prog. developer, Leonard Morse Hospital, Natick, MA '86 (PLNG)
TAYLOR, DEENI, dir. pharm., St. Joseph Hospital, Augusta, GA '87 (AMB)
TAYLOR, DENNIS W., dir. risk mgt., Hospital Sisters Health System, Springfield, IL '82 (RISK)
TAYLOR, DONALD A., dir. food serv., HCA Edward White Hospital, St. Petersburg, FL '83 (FOOD)
TAYLOR, DONALD D., asst. dir. hskpg., St. Joseph Hospital, Flint, MI '87 (ENVIRON)
TAYLOR, DONALD R., adm., Elyria Memorial Hospital, Elyria, OH '70
TAYLOR, DOROTHY E., RN, dir. nrsg., Greenwich Hospital, Greenwich, CT '84 (NURS)
TAYLOR, DOROTHY, supv. cent. sup. and distrib., Newport Hospital, Newport, RI '82 (CS)
TAYLOR, EDWIN L., (ret.), , West Chester, PA '48 (LIFE)
TAYLOR, ELEANOR J., pat. rep. coor., The Medical Center, Beaver, PA '67 (PAT)
TAYLOR, ELEANOR L., dir. diet. serv., St. Anthony Medical Center, Columbus, OH '73 (FOOD)
TAYLOR, EMILENE, dir. health promotion, Queen of the Valley Hospital, West Covina, CA '86 (EDUC)
TAYLOR, ETHEL Y., compensation mgr., Deaconess Hospital, Evansville, IN '83 (PERS)
TAYLOR, FRANCES J., vice-pres. pers. and educ. res., Methodist Hospitals of Gary, Gary, IN '81 (PERS)
TAYLOR, FRANK L., pres., Frank L. Taylor and Associates, Boiling Springs, PA '74 (MGMT)
TAYLOR, FRANK, dir. cent. serv., United Hospital Center, Clarksburg, WV '80 (CS)
TAYLOR, G. KENT, atty., Magic Valley Regional Medical Center, Twin Falls, ID '86 (ATTY)
TAYLOR, GEORGE M. JR., asst. chief soc. work serv., Veterans Administration Medical Center Brentwood, Los Angeles, CA '82 (SOC)
TAYLOR, GILBERT O., dir. human res. dev., Memorial Medical Center, Long Beach, CA '77 (PERS)
TAYLOR, HANK, vice-pres. mktg., Mercy Hospital, Columbus, OH '86 (PR)
TAYLOR, HAROLD W., dir. maint., Doctors Memorial Hospital, Atlanta, GA '86 (ENG)
TAYLOR, HENRY, dir. pat. rep., Northwestern Memorial Hospital, Chicago, IL '84 (PAT)
TAYLOR, HOWARD R., consult., Salem, SC '48 (LIFE)
TAYLOR, J. M., assoc. dir. pub. affairs, Beth Israel Hospital, Boston, MA '86 (PR)
TAYLOR, JACQUELINE DELORIS, RN, assoc. adm., Valley Hospital Medical Center, Las Vegas, NV '85 (NURS)
TAYLOR, LT. JAMES A., MSC USN, adm. off., USS Tarawa Lha1 Medical, FPO San Francisco, CA '80
TAYLOR, JAMES D., assoc. adm., Scott and White, Temple, TX '73 (PLNG)
TAYLOR, JAMES H., reg. dir., Blue Cross of Western Pennsylvania, Erie, PA '84
TAYLOR, JAMES L., asst. vice-pres. human res., Christ Hospital, Cincinnati, OH '79 (PERS)
TAYLOR, JAMES M., dir. info. resource serv., Samaritan Health Center, Detroit, MI '85 (MGMT)
TAYLOR, JAMES R., asst. vice-pres., Horizon Management Services, Asheville, NC '80 (PLNG)
TAYLOR, MAJ. JAMES WILLIAM JR., MSC USA, Headquarters, U. S. Army Dental Activity, Fort Knox, KY '81
TAYLOR, JAN C., chief exec. off., Daniel Drake Memorial Hospital, Cincinnati, OH '64
TAYLOR, JAN LIPTHRATT, dir. mktg. and pub. rel., Cobb General Hospital, Austell, GA '86 (PR)
TAYLOR, JANE L., mgt. consult., Adult and Pediatric Urology Group, Morristown, NJ '84
TAYLOR, JANET, vice-pres. nrsg., Mercy Hospital, Owensboro, KY '81 (NURS)
TAYLOR, JENNIFER L., coor. educ., Phillips County Hospital, Phillipsburg, KS '86 (EDUC)
TAYLOR, JESS H., pres. and chief exec. off., Pegasus, Erie, PA '82 (ENG)
TAYLOR, JO, dir. cent. sup., St. Francis Hospital Systems, Colorado Springs, CO '81 (CS)
TAYLOR, JOANNE F., dir. vol. serv., Children's Hospital, Columbus, OH '76 (VOL)
TAYLOR, JODY L., sr. vice-pres. med. plng., 3d International, Houston, TX '79 (PLNG)
TAYLOR, JOHN MITCHELL II, dir. pers., Douglas County Hospital, Omaha, NE '80 (PERS)
TAYLOR, JOHN S., plant eng., St. Vincent's Hospital, Birmingham, AL '85 (ENG)
TAYLOR, JOHN, dir. eng., Baptist Memorial Hospital-Lauderdale, Ripley, TN '87 (ENG)
TAYLOR, JULIE A., adm. asst., Northern Michigan Hospitals, Petoskey, MI '86 (PAT)
TAYLOR, KATHY K., dir. human res., Charter Hospital of Augusta, Augusta, GA '85 (PERS)
TAYLOR, KATHY LEE, coor. guest rel., Bon Secours Hospital, Grosse Pointe, MI '86 (PAT)
TAYLOR, KEITH O., prof. emeritus, School of Public Health, University of California, Berkeley, CA '40 (LIFE)
TAYLOR, LOUETTA B., RN, asst. chairperson nrsg., U. S. Air Force Medical Center Keesler, Biloxi, MS '86 (NURS)
TAYLOR, SR. M. DOLORA, vice-pres. matl. and facil. mgt., St. Mary Hospital, Philadelphia, PA '86 (PUR)
TAYLOR, MADELINE E., coor. pers., St. Jude Hospital-Fullerton, Fullerton, CA '86 (PERS)
TAYLOR, MAE F., asst. mgr. cent. serv., Calvary Hospital, Bronx, NY '82 (CS)
TAYLOR, MARGARET M., RN, dir. cent. serv., Memorial Medical Center of Jacksonville, Jacksonville, FL '75 (CS)
TAYLOR, MARION B., dir. vol. serv., Washington Hospital Center, Washington, DC '83 (VOL)
TAYLOR, MARY ZABAWA, atty., Oak Park, IL '86 (RISK)
TAYLOR, MELVIN C., dir. matl. mgt., Union Memorial Hospital, Baltimore, MD '83 (PUR)
TAYLOR, MICHAEL L., dir. human res., Sam Houston Memorial Hospital, Houston, TX '66 (PERS)
TAYLOR, MICHAEL L., asst. vice-pres.-prog. dev., Oakwood Hospital, Dearborn, MI '86
TAYLOR, NANCY, pres., Nanco Health Care and Management Consultant, Fruitland Park, FL '80
TAYLOR, PAMELA A., dir. soc. serv., Maine Medical Center, Portland, ME '81 (SOC)
TAYLOR, PAT A., dir. pub. rel., coor. educ. and dir. activ. ther., Sierra Vista Hospital, Truth Or Consequences, NM '81 (EDUC)(PR)
TAYLOR, PATRICIA G., dir. vol. serv., St. Luke's Hospital, San Francisco, CA '78 (VOL)
TAYLOR, PAUL D., mgr. plant, Brockton Hospital, Brockton, MA '71 (ENG)
TAYLOR, PAUL J., vice-pres., Saint Raphael Corporation, New Haven, CT '73 (PR)
TAYLOR, PAULA J., RN, actg. adm. nrsg. serv., Marietta Memorial Hospital, Marietta, OH '85 (NURS)
TAYLOR, PHILIP J., Coopers and Lybrand, Philadelphia, PA '65
TAYLOR, RICHARD L., exec. vice-pres., Lutheran Medical Center, Wheat Ridge, CO '84
TAYLOR, RICHARD R., mgr. emp., Deaconess Hospital, St. Louis, MO '84 (PERS)
TAYLOR, RICHARD, mgr. gen. serv., Beverly Hospital, Montebello, CA '69 (ENG)
TAYLOR, ROBERT E., eng., Munroe Regional Medical Center, Ocala, FL '78 (ENG)
TAYLOR, ROBERT F. JR., chief soc. worker, Strong Memorial Hospital of the University of Rochester, Rochester, NY '77 (SOC)
TAYLOR, ROBERT J., Robert Taylor and Associates, Edwards, CO '71
TAYLOR, ROBERT W. III, dir. matl. mgt., Rice Memorial Hospital, Willmar, MN '84 (PUR)
TAYLOR, ROY GLENDON, mgr. syst., Hamilton Civic Hospitals, Hamilton, Ont., Canada '67 (MGMT)
TAYLOR, SHARON L., dir. commun. affairs and educ., Burgess Memorial Hospital, Onawa, IA '85 (PR)
TAYLOR, STEVE A., dir. educ. and trng., Baptist Medical Center of Oklahoma, Oklahoma City, OK '86 (EDUC)
TAYLOR, LT. STEVEN A., MSC USN, head outpatient serv., Naval Hospital, Great Lakes, IL '86
TAYLOR, STEVEN, dir. pers., Parkridge Medical Center, Chattanooga, TN '79 (PERS)
TAYLOR, THOMAS C. JR., dir. eng., Union Medical Center, El Dorado, AR '79 (ENG)
TAYLOR, THOMAS W., sr. biomedical tech., Riverside Community Hospital, Riverside, CA '81 (ENG)
TAYLOR, TOMMY R., supv. clin. eng. serv., Wyandotte General Hospital, Wyandotte, MI '85 (ENG)
TAYLOR, TRENTON, dir. phys. plant, Jacksonville Medical Center, Jacksonville, FL '86 (ENG)
TAYLOR, VICTOR W., dir. risk mgt., Adventist Health System, Arlington, TX '83 (RISK)
TAYLOR, WARREN E., adm. corp. lab. serv., Roche Biomedical Laboratory, Inc., Burlington, NC '86
TAYLOR, WAYNE L., sr. policy analyst, Department of Health Care Financing Administration, Washington, DC '80
TAYLOR, WILLIAM F. C., dir. pers., Dana-Farber Cancer Institute, Boston, MA '80 (PERS)
TAYNTOR, GINGER M., dir. vol. serv., Holzer Medical Center, Gallipolis, OH '84 (VOL)
TEACHMAN, NAEA M., dir. vol. serv., Bethany General Hospital, Bethany, OK '86 (VOL)
TEAFORD, SCOTT W., dir. admit. and commun., St. John's Regional Medical Center, Joplin, MO '79 (ENG)
TEAGUE, MARGARET ANN, dir. cont. educ., Baylor University Medical Center, Dallas, TX '77 (EDUC)
TEANO-CONLEY, VENETTA, pur. agt., Mount Washington Pediatric Hospital, Baltimore, MD '85 (PUR)
TEAS, THOMAS C., atty., North Iowa Medical Center, Mason City, IA '78 (ATTY)
TEASLEY, DEBORAH J., assoc. exec. dir., West Jersey Health System, Camden, NJ '86 (NURS)
TEATE, JOHN A., eng. and dir. safety, Polk General Hospital, Bartow, FL '76 (ENG)
TEBBITT, BARBARA VOLK, RN, sr. assoc. dir. and dir. nrsg., University of Minnesota Hospital and Clinic, Minneapolis, MN '78 (NURS)
TEBO, CAROLYN H., dir. cent. serv., Watsonville Community Hospital, Watsonville, CA '85 (CS)
TECSON, JOSEPH A., atty., MacNeal Hospital, Berwyn, IL '81 (ATTY)
TEDDER, CHLOE J., dir. vol. serv., Sparks Regional Medical Center, Fort Smith, AR '73 (VOL)
TEDDER, JEAN O., RN, dir. surg. nrsg., Commonwealth Hospital, Fairfax, VA '86 (NURS)
TEDDER, PAULINE A., RN, dir. nrs., Wilkes General Hospital, North Wilkesboro, NC '82 (NURS)
TEDESCHI, MARGARET M., sr. emp. rep., Memorial Hospital for Cancer and Allied Diseases, New York, NY '83 (PERS)
TEDESCHI, PHILIP J., asst. res. sci., University of Michigan, Program and Bureau of Hospital Administration, Ann Arbor, MI '82 (MGMT)

TEDESCO, DAVID M., dir. emp. rel., New England Sinai Hospital, Stoughton, MA '82 (PERS)
TEDESCO, WALTER R., coor. constr. and facil. mgt., Emerson Hospital, Concord, MA '85 (ENG)
TEDFORD, LARRY V., asst. vice-pres. prof. serv., St. Anthony's Hospital, Amarillo, TX '84 (PUR)
TEDJESKE, DONALD, dir. maint., Lee Hospital, Johnstown, PA '75 (ENG)
TEECE, DONALD P., assoc. adm., Memorial Hospital for Cancer and Allied Diseases, New York, NY '59
TEEHAN, TIMOTHY J., RN, dir. psych. nrsg., Baystate Medical Center, Springfield, MA '84 (NURS)
TEER, CLAUDE E., dir. pur., Memorial Hospital, Colorado Springs, CO '74 (PUR)
TEER, JANET, dir. safety, Dch Regional Medical Center, Tuscaloosa, AL '80 (RISK)
TEETER, JAMES R., assoc. exec. dir., Arkansas Hospital Association, Little Rock, AR '71 (EDUC)
TEHADA, JUDITH A., clin. nrs. educ., Kaiser Foundation Hospital, Hayward, CA '83 (EDUC)
TEHAN, CYNTHIA C., vice-pres. plng., The Church Charity Foundation of Long Island, Hempstead, NY '82 (PLNG)
TEICH, PHYLLIS, adm. rehab. medicine, University Hospital of Brooklyn-Suny Center, Brooklyn, NY '86
TEIG, CAROL D., dir. plng., Jewish Hospital of St. Louis, St. Louis, MO '84 (PLNG)
TEITELBAUM, CAROL, atty., Jewish Hospital, Louisville, KY '83 (ATTY)
TEITELBAUM, KAREN C., mgr. plng., res. and dev., Parkside Human Services, Park Ridge, IL '86 (PLNG)
TEITELL, CONRAD, atty., Mount Sinai Medical Center, New York, NY '73 (ATTY)
TELA, LTJG STEPHEN D., adm. res., Naval Hospital, Pensacola, FL '85
TELECKY, DUANE J., dir. plant oper., Washoe Medical Center, Reno, NV '81 (ENG)
TELEGA, CRAIG W., RN, dir. med. and critical care serv., Stormont-Vail Regional Medical Center, Topeka, KS '84 (NURS)
TELEKY, ROBERT D., mgr. emp. serv., Johns Hopkins Hospital, Baltimore, MD '86 (PERS)
TELFORD, STEPHEN M., student, St. Louis University, St. Louis, MO '86
TELL, ROBERT, dep. exec. dir., Greater Detroit Area Health Council, Inc., Detroit, MI '85 (PLNG)
TELLEM, SUSAN M., pres., Grody Tellem Communications, Inc., Los Angeles, CA '79 (PR)
TELLER, JEROME S., atty., Jewish Hospital of Cincinnati, Cincinnati, OH '76 (ATTY)
TELLISH, PATRICIA A., RN, coor. in-service educ., Aliquippa Hospital, Aliquippa, PA '82 (EDUC)
TELTHORSTER, MARCIA MILLER, dir. vol. serv., Doylestown Hospital, Doylestown, PA '85 (VOL)
TEMOS, CATHY A., supv. sup., proc. and distrib., Lehigh Valley Hospital Center, Allentown, PA '82 (CS)
TEMPLE, EDWARD O. JR., dir. chaplaincy and soc. serv., Lynchburg General-Marsh Lodge Hospital, Lynchburg, VA '77 (SOC)
TEMPLE, ROBERT T., dir. pur., Western Reserve Systems-Southside, Youngstown, OH '86 (PUR)
TEMPLETON, DAVE, dir. prof. serv., Total Business Systems, Inc., Albuquerque, NM '80
TEMPLETON, GEORGE H., chief soc. work serv., Veterans Administration Medical Center, Washington, DC '78 (SOC)
TEMPLIN, JOHN L., dir. prod. improvement div., Applied Leadership Technologies, Greenfield, NY '77 (MGMT)
TEN-EYCK, ROBIN, registrant amb. serv., Lenox Hill Hospital, New York, NY '85
TENAGLIA, RALPH, asst. adm., Hunt Memorial Hospital, Danvers, MA '80 (ENG)
TENAGLIA, SHARLENE, mgr. prop. and casualties, Daughters of Charity Health Systems, St. Louis, MO '82 (RISK)
TENCZAR, SUSAN M., student, Program in Health Service Administration, School of Health Professions, Governors State University, Park Forest South, IL '86
TENDICK, RONALD L., dir. pub. rel., Passavant Area Hospital, Jacksonville, IL '85 (PR)
TENER, EDGAR KENNETH LEON, foreman bldg. and maint., Nevada Mental Health Institution, Sparks, NV '86 (ENG)
TENEROVICZ, THOMAS J., dir. pers. rel., Community General Hospital of Greater Svracuse, Syracuse, NY '79 (PERS)
TENG, CLARENCE, exec. vice-pres., Samaritan Health Service, Phoenix, AZ '79 (PLNG)
TENNANT, ELLEN, dir. spec. events serv., Memorial Hospital Medical Center of Long Beach, Long Beach, CA '75 (VOL)
TENNARO, SONJA, RN, assoc. adm. nrsg. serv., Englewood Hospital, Englewood, NJ '84 (NURS)
TENNEY, BARBARA LEIGH, asst. adm., Scottish Rite Hospital for Crippled Children, Atlanta, GA '78 (ENG)
TENNEY, DOROTHEA A., RN, asst. adm. and dir. nrsg., Fairview Southdale Hospital, Minneapolis, MN '69 (NURS)
TENNEY, MARY T., adm. dir. human res., Long Beach Community Hospital, Long Beach, CA '78 (PERS)
TENNIS, SHARON A., RN, dir. nrsg., Rochester Methodist Hospital, Rochester, MN '82 (NURS)
TENZER, FLORENCE, dir. educ., AMI Parkway Regional Medical Center, North Miami Beach, FL '78 (EDUC)
TENZER, SANDRA, dir. pat. syst., St. Clare's -Riverside Medical Center, Denville, NJ '87 (RISK)
TEPEDINO, GENEVIEVE, RN, dir. nrsg., United Hospital, Port Chester, NY '78 (NURS)
TEPLITZKY, NORMAN, dir. eng., St. Luke's-Roosevelt Hospital Center, New York, NY '79 (ENG)
TEPLITZKY, SANFORD V., atty., Florida Medical Center Hospital, Fort Lauderdale, FL '80 (ATTY)
TEPLY, NANCY A., dir. vol. svcs, Archbishop Bergan Mercy Hospital, Omaha, NE '86 (VOL)
TEPPER, DENNIS J., assoc. dir., Veterans Administration Medical Center, Hampton, VA '77 (MGMT)
TEPPER, SHARON A., dir. pat. and family serv., Memorial Hospital, Colorado Springs, CO '85 (SOC)
TEPPERT, LAURIE S., atty., Elmhurst Memorial Hospital, Elmhurst, IL '85 (ATTY)
TEPPING, MARK ALLEN, dir. mgt. eng., Yale-New Haven Hospital, New Haven, CT '73 (MGMT)
TEREFENCKO, JANE-MARIE, inst. diet. consult., Department of Public Welfare, Institute Services, Harrisburg, PA '85 (FOOD)
TERENZIO, JOSEPH V., pres., United Hospital Fund of New York, New York, NY '54 (ATTY)(LIFE)
TERENZIO, PETER B., (ret.), Naples, FL '48 (ATTY)(LIFE)
TERESI, MARK A., staff analyst, Dallas County Hospital District, Dallas, TX '83
TERHAAR, MARILYN A., RN, dir. nrsg. serv., Silverton Hospital, Silverton, OR '83 (NURS)
TERPENING, WILLIAM L. SR., dir. phys. plant, Garza Memorial Hospital, Post, TX '70 (ENG)
TERRACE, BARBARA A., supv. diet., Gulf Pines Hospital, Port St. Joe, FL '84 (FOOD)
TERRANO, CINDY, dir. acctg., Hillcrest Hospital, Mayfield Heights, OH '86
TERRELL, ROBERT L. JR., adm., St. Albans Psychiatric Hospital, Radford, VA '84
TERRERI, LOUIS E., vice-pres. facil., Mountainside Hospital, Montclair, NJ '79 (ENG)
TERRILL, MARJORIE L., med. lib., Menorah Medical Center, Kansas City, MO '84
TERRILL, ROBERT C., assoc. prof. and coor., Program in Health Service Administration, University of Massachusetts, Boston, MA '78 (EDUC)
TERRILL, TERI, dir. soc. and psych. serv., Kenosha Hospital and Medical Center, Kenosha, WI '86 (SOC)
TERRY, BARBARA J., RN, dir. nrsg. serv., Frick Community Health Center, Mount Pleasant, PA '86 (NURS)
TERRY, GENE S., atty., Texas Scottish Rite Hospital, Dallas, TX '83 (ATTY)
TERRY, JAMES E., dir. environ. serv., Grossmont District Hospital, La Mesa, CA '83 (ENG)
TERRY, JARON M., dir. commun., Mount Carmel Medical Center, Columbus, OH '81 (PR) (PLNG)
TERRY, JEAN E., dir. educ. serv., Freehold Area Hospital, Freehold, NJ '78 (EDUC)
TERRY, ROBERT L., dir. human res., Erlanger Medical Center, Chattanooga, TN '85 (PERS)
TERRY, SUSAN C., RN, asst. dir. nrsg., Brattleboro Memorial Hospital, Brattleboro, VT '84 (NURS)
TERRY, THELMA J., syst. eng., T. J. Terry Health Care Systems Consultant, DeLand, FL '80 (MGMT)
TERRY, THOMAS, dir. matl. mgt., Glens Falls Hospital, Glens Falls, NY '86 (PUR)
TERSCHLUSE, DENNIS R., chief eng., St. John's Mercy Hospital, Washington, MO '73 (ENG)
TERSEN, GLORIA, RN, dir. pat. care resources, St. Luke's Hospital, Milwaukee, WI '77 (NURS)
TERTELL, KAREN L., dir. vol. serv., Johnston R. Bowman Health Center, Chicago, IL '82 (VOL)
TERWILLIGER, CHARLOTTE, dir. soc. work, Geneva General Hospital, Geneva, NY '82 (SOC)
TESELLE, GWEN, RN, asst. adm. clin. serv., Sutter Solano Medical Center, Vallejo, CA '86 (NURS)
TESHIMA, KEN T., dir. plant oper., G. N. Wilcox Memorial Hospital, Lihue, HI '83 (ENG)
TESIK, KATHLEEN M., mgt. eng., Memorial Hospital, Pawtucket, RI '83 (MGMT)
TESMER, MICHAEL G., asst. vice-pres. plng. and qual. assur., St. Elizabeth Hospital, Appleton, WI '83 (PLNG)
TESSIER, CLAUDE, dir. vol. serv., Institut de Readaptation de Montreal, Montreal, Que., Canada '86 (VOL)
TESSIER, ROSEMARIE, dir. vol., Desert Hospital, Palm Springs, CA '83 (VOL)
TEST, RUSSELL A., vice-pres. facil. plng. and mgt., Phoenix General Hospital, Phoenix, AZ '77 (ENG)
TESTA, CLAUDIA J., dir. support serv., Albany General Hospital, Albany, OR '80 (PUR)
TESTON, DIANA DRIVER, dir. soc. serv., St. Joseph's Hospital, Savannah, GA '74 (SOC)
TETRICK, ANNE PAULA, dir. human serv., Worcester Memorial Hospital, Worcester, MA '78 (SOC)
TEUTSCH, ANDREW L., student, Program in Health Service Administration, School of Health Professions, Governors State University, Park Forest South, IL '84
TEUTSCH, WILLIAM J., dir. adm., Association of Surgical Technologists, Littleton, CO '86 (EDUC)
TEWKSBURY, DONNA M., dir. soc. work, St. Vincent Hospital and Medical Center, Portland, OR '82 (SOC)
TEWS, ESTHER, dir. vol. serv., Warren Hospital, Phillipsburg, NJ '78 (PAT)(VOL)
THACKER, ACEL KENT, area mgr. and chemistry supv., LDS Hospital, Salt Lake City, UT '80
THADEIO, ROBERT J., dir. matl. mgt., Walthamweston Hospital and Medical Center, Waltham, MA '81 (PUR)
THALER, CATHY, dir. pub. rel., Mary Immaculate Hospital, Newport News, VA '87 (PR)
THALER, DONNA T., RN, vice-pres. nrsg., Miami Children's Hospital, Miami, FL '77 (NURS)
THALHEIMER, LESLIE A., dir. soc. serv., Middletown Regional Hospital, Middletown, OH '85 (SOC)
THAMAN, AUDREY M., PhD, dir. soc. serv., St. Louis County Hospital, Clayton, MO '77 (SOC)
THAMES, DEBBY D., mktg. rep., Methodist Hospital, Lubbock, TX '86 (PLNG)
THAMES, GLADYS, RN, dir. educ. and trng., John D. Archbold Memorial Hospital, Thomasville, GA '71 (EDUC)
THANE, JEREMY G., atty., St. Patrick Hospital, Missoula, MT '73 (ATTY)
THANEY, KATHLEEN M., RN, chief cancer nrsg. serv., Clinical Center National Institute of Health, Bethesda, MD '86 (NURS)
THARAYIL, PENNAMMA THOMAS, dir. diet., Edgewater Hospital, Chicago, IL '68 (FOOD)
THARP, CHARLOTTE S., dir. media rel., NKC, Inc., Louisville, KY '85 (PR)
THARP, PAUL RUSSELL, vice-pres., White Memorial Medical Center, Los Angeles, CA '77 (PR) (PLNG)
THATCHER, ANDREA, dir. vol., Peralta Hospital, Oakland, CA '73 (VOL)
THATE, MARK E., dir. human res., St. Anthony Medical Center, Crown Point, IN '76 (PERS)
THAXTON, KEITH R., mgr. plant eng., El Camino Hospital, Mountain View, CA '79 (ENG)
THAYER, EDNA L., RN, dir. pat. care serv., Rice County District One Hospital, Faribault, MN '83 (NURS)
THEBEAU, ROBERT S., Colorado Springs, CO '81
THEILER, CAROL RAINER, dir. mktg. and pub. rel., Spartanburg Regional Medical Center, Spartanburg, SC '85 (PR) (PLNG)
THEIMER, THOMAS J., dir. mgt. eng. serv., Northbay Medical Center, Fairfield, CA '86 (MGMT)
THEIN, JAMES T., dir. constr., University of Minnesota Hospital and Clinic, Minneapolis, MN '87 (ENG)
THEIS, ANNE M., dir. commun., Franciscan Sisters Health Care, Little Falls, MN '83 (PR)
THEIS, DAVID W., adm. health serv., Health Management Associates, Pine Bluff, AR '78
THEIS, MONICA L., consult. diet., University of Wisconsin Hospital and Clinics, Madison, WI '86 (FOOD)
THEIS, VAL H., supv. plant, St. Francis Regional Medical Center, Shakopee, MN '85 (ENG)
THEISMAN, NORMAN A., dir. pers., St. Elizabeth's Hospital, Belleville, IL '75 (PERS)
THEISS, BETTY E., RN, chief nrsg. serv., Veterans Administration Medical Center, Minneapolis, MN '80 (NURS)
THELLMAN, ELAINE, RN, vice-pres., Sparks Regional Medical Center, Fort Smith, AR '80 (NURS)
THENELL, CATHY L., coor. commun. rel., Mount Hood Medical Center, Gresham, OR '86 (PR)
THEOBALD, SANDRA, coor. claims, Good Samaritan Hospital, Downers Grove, IL '85 (RISK)
THEODORE, KAREN D., asst. adm., Doctors Hospital, New York, NY '86 (RISK)
THEODOROU, DANNY, pres., Medi Health Management, Inc., Willowdale, Ont., Canada '86
THERIAULT, JOSEPHINE, RN, dir. nrsg., Bradley Memorial Hospital, Southington, CT '78 (NURS)
THEROUX, THOMAS A., dir. plng., Sturdy Memorial Hospital, Attleboro, MA '80 (PLNG)
THESMAN, JEFF, dir. plant serv., Sonora Community Hospital, Sonora, CA '85 (ENG)
THEUS, W. WANDA, RN, assoc. adm. pat. care, Jefferson Regional Medical Center, Pine Bluff, AR '83 (NURS)
THIBEAU, NANCY C., dir. pers., Kennebec Valley Medical Center, Augusta, ME '83 (PERS)
THIBEAULT, JAMES S., dir. mgt. eng., Hospital of Saint Raphael, New Haven, CT '80 (MGMT)
THIBEAULT, LORRAINE E., RN, dir. maternal-child health, Little Company of Mary Hospital, Evergreen Park, IL '85 (NURS)
THIBODEAU, LEONARD J. M., dir. plant oper., Henrietta D. Goodall Hospital, Sanford, ME '85 (ENG)
THIBODEAUX, CHARLENE RITA, coor. pat. rep., East Jefferson General Hospital, Metairie, LA '86 (PAT)
THIBODEAUX, SR. MARIE CHERIE, RN, dir. nrsg., Mercy Hospital, Bakersfield, CA '84 (NURS)
THICKEL, NANCY C., dir. pub. rel., Grandview Hospital and Medical Center, Dayton, OH '81 (PR)
THIEBEN, WILLIAM H., dir. support serv., Kewanee Public Hospital, Kewanee, IL '79 (PERS)(PR)(RISK)
THIEL, NORMAN, dir. environ. serv., Forbes Regional Health Center, Monroeville, PA '86 (ENVIRON)
THIELEMANN, DORIS E., dir. soc. serv., Los Alamos Medical Center, Los Alamos, NM '83 (SOC)
THIELEN, CLAIRE M., supv. indust. eng., Kaiser Permanente Medical Care Program, Oakland, CA '86 (MGMT)
THIEME, CARL W., pres., Cambridge Research Institutes, Inc., Cambridge, MA '86
THIESEN, WALTER, asst. chief eng., Bethel Deaconess Hospital, Newton, KS '83 (ENG)
THIESS, TRUDY M., dir. pub. rel. and mktg., Medical Center of Lake County-Condell Memorial Hospital, Libertyville, IL '82 (PR)
THIESSEN, JO C., spec. proj. consult., Huntington Memorial Hospital, Pasadena, CA '85 (PLNG)
THIFFAULT, GEORGE F., pres., Marketing Plus, Inc., Portland, CT '77 (PR) (PLNG)
THIGPEN, WILLIAM H., atty., Northwestern University Medical School, Evanston, IL '76 (ATTY)
THIRY, MARC T., dir. matl. mgt., Peralta Hospital, Oakland, CA '75 (PUR)
THISTEL, CARL I., dir. soc. work, Sheppard and Enoch Pratt Hospital, Baltimore, MD '86 (SOC)
THOENNES, LINDA LU, dir. diet., Charter Suburban Hospital, Mesquite, TX '79 (FOOD)
THOENNES, LORRAINE, RN, asst. dir. nrsg., Resurrection Hospital, Chicago, IL '83 (NURS)
THOM, MARGARET E., dir. vol. serv., Coral Springs Medical Center, Coral Springs, FL '85 (VOL)
THOMA, GWEN S., dir. educ., Southeast Missouri Hospital, Cape Girardeau, MO '87 (EDUC)
THOMAS, AARON L., pres., Thomas Architects, Inc., Waco, TX '85 (ENG)
THOMAS, ADELAIDE A., RN, dir. nrsg., Elkhart General Hospital, Elkhart, IN '84 (NURS)
THOMAS, ALEXANDER A., pres., Health Center Communicorp, Inc., Pittsburgh, PA '85 (ENG)
THOMAS, ANN H., coor. cont. educ., Marion General Hospital, Marion, OH '78 (EDUC)
THOMAS, BETTY J., RN, dir. house bd. and cabinet affairs, American Nurses Association, Kansas City, MO '81 (NURS)
THOMAS, BEVERLY D., dir. pub. rel., Grady Memorial Hospital, Atlanta, GA '83 (PR)
THOMAS, BONITA LOUISE, pat. rep., Meriter Hospital, Madison, WI '86 (PAT)
THOMAS, CAROLYN M., RN, dir. med. and surg. nrsg., DePaul Health Center, Bridgeton, MO '87 (NURS)

THOMAS, CARROLL J., adm., Lower Bucks Hospital, Bristol, PA '69

THOMAS, CHARLENE R., vice-pres., Georgia Baptist Medical Center, Atlanta, GA '83 (PUR)

THOMAS, CHARLES F., atty., Saint Anthony Medical Center, Rockford, IL '81 (ATTY)

THOMAS, CHARLES S., dir. commun. rel., St. Joseph's Hospital, Tampa, FL '74 (PR)

THOMAS, CONNIE, dir. pub. rel., HCA Donelson Hospital, Nashville, TN '80 (PR)

THOMAS, CONSTANCE S., consult., Peat, Marwick, Mitchell and Company, Atlanta, GA '82 (MGMT)

THOMAS, CYNTHIA, atty., Safecare Company, Inc., Seattle, WA '87 (ATTY)

THOMAS, DALE E., Deloitte Haskins and Sells, Cincinnati, OH '84 (MGMT)

THOMAS, DANIEL P., atty., Hillside Hospital, Warren, OH '76 (ATTY)

THOMAS, DANNY, mgr. telecommun., Owensboro-Daviess County Hospital, Owensboro, KY '85 (ENG)

THOMAS, DAVID J., risk mgr., Medical Mutual Liability Insurance Society of Maryland, Towson, MD '86 (RISK)

THOMAS, DEBORAH D., dir. human res. dev., Eastern Maine Medical Center, Bangor, ME '83 (EDUC)

THOMAS, DEBORAH KAYE, coor. pat. rel., Firelands Community Hospital, Sandusky, OH '85 (PAT)

THOMAS, DIANE B., dir. soc. serv., Union County General Hospital, New Albany, MS '81 (SOC)

THOMAS, DONALD, dir. maint., Alexian Brothers Hospital, St. Louis, MO '85 (ENG)

THOMAS, DOROTHY N., RN, adm., Home Health Services of Louisiana, Division of National Medical Enterprises, New Orleans, LA '87 (AMB)

THOMAS, DREW J., assoc. consult., Earle Nicklas, Inc., Gloversville, NY '54 (LIFE)

THOMAS, EDWARD S., pres., Detroit Receiving Hospital and University Health Center, Detroit, MI '71

THOMAS, EDWARD W., assoc. dir. food serv., Hospital of Saint Raphael, New Haven, CT '81 (FOOD)

THOMAS, ELIZABETH S., dir. vol., East Tennessee Children's Hospital, Knoxville, TN '85 (VOL)

THOMAS, ELLEN JEAN, adm. res., Catholic Medical Center, Manchester, NH '86

THOMAS, ELLEN M., dir. pers. serv., Catholic Medical Center, Manchester, NH '82 (PERS)

THOMAS, FRANCES J., dir. soc. serv., DePaul Hospital, Bridgeton, MO '77 (SOC)

THOMAS, GEORGE L., dir. plant oper. and facil., Hospital Center at Orange, Orange, NJ '80 (ENG)

THOMAS, GEORGE R., vice-pres. plant and facil., Mercy Medical Center, Oshkosh, WI '74 (ENG)

THOMAS, GEORGE RAYMOND, dir. soc. serv., Bothwell Regional Health Center, Sedalia, MO '74 (SOC)

THOMAS, GUY M., dir. med. center plng., Research Health Services, Kansas City, MO '82 (PLNG)

THOMAS, JACK N., atty., Gilmore Memorial Hospital, Amory, MS '83 (ATTY)

THOMAS, JAMES ROGERS, adm., Charter By-the-Sea Hospital, St. Simons Island, GA '78

THOMAS, JANET L., dir. diet., Western Pennsylvania Hospital, Pittsburgh, PA '72 (FOOD)

THOMAS, JANETTE, prog. dir., Alfred State College, Alfred, NY '86

THOMAS, JEAN C., RN, buyer matl. mgt., St. Francis Hospital, Greenville, SC '83 (P [illegible]R)

THOMAS, JEANETTE P., adm. mg[illegible] [illegible]mary care serv., St. John's Primary Health Center, Pittsburgh, PA '85 (PLNG)

THOMAS, JOAN M., vice-pres. mktg., St. Elizabeth Medical Center, Dayton, OH '84

THOMAS, JOANNE, coor. guest rel., Rosewood Medical Center, Houston, TX '80 (PAT)

THOMAS, JOHN C., vice-pres., Voluntary Hospital of America, Tampa, FL '86

THOMAS, KAREN A., RN, vice-pres. pat. care, St. Clare Hospital of Monroe, Monroe, WI '78 (NURS)

THOMAS, KARI A., dir. pers., Pioneer Valley Hospital, West Valley City, UT '86 (PERS)

THOMAS, LAURIE, dir. pub. rel., Humana Hospital -Phoenix, Phoenix, AZ '86 (PR)

THOMAS, LAURITA, mgr. human resource dev., University of Michigan Medical Center, Ann Arbor, MI '85 (EDUC)

THOMAS, LORA L., dir. soc. serv., Desert Samaritan Hospital, Mesa, AZ '84 (SOC)

THOMAS, LOY D., dir. vol. serv., Rush-Presbyterian-St. Luke's Medical Center, Chicago, IL '80 (VOL)

THOMAS, MARCIA M., dir. lib., Cleveland Chiropractic College, Kansas City, MO '84 (PAT)

THOMAS, MARJORIE O., risk mgr., Administrators for the Professions, Inc., Manhasset, NY '85 (RISK)

THOMAS, MARK R., dir. pers., Oklahoma Osteopathic Hospital, Tulsa, OK '77 (PERS)

THOMAS, MARTHA J., dir. lab. serv., Lebanon Valley General Hospital, Lebanon, PA '86 (MGMT)

THOMAS, SR. MARY, pres., Mercy Hospital, Baltimore, MD '51 (LIFE)

THOMAS, MYRA H., RN, dir. nrsg. res., St. Paul Medical Center, Dallas, TX '82 (NURS)

THOMAS, NANCY L., dir. human res., Jenkins Community Hospital, Jenkins, KY '86 (PERS)

THOMAS, NINA J., RN, vice-pres., Nashville Memorial Hospital, Madison, TN '69 (NURS)

THOMAS, OPAL D., dir. pub. rel. and vol. serv., HCA North Clark Community Hospital, Charlestown, IN '83 (PR)

THOMAS, OWEN L., dir. pub. rel. and dev., Bishop Clarkson Memorial Hospital, Omaha, NE '79 (PR) (PLNG)

THOMAS, PATRICIA M. PIGGOTT, soc. worker, Gorgas Army Hospital, APO Miami, FL '76 (SOC)

THOMAS, PAUL A., pres. and chief exec. off., Memorial Hospitals Association, Modesto, CA '73

THOMAS, R. ZACH JR., exec. dir., Charlotte-Mecklenburg Hospital Authority, Charlotte, NC '46 (LIFE)

THOMAS, R. ZACH, Charlotte, NC '82 (LIFE)

THOMAS, RICHARD ALLEN, dir. pers., Western Baptist Hospital, Paducah, KY '76 (PERS)

THOMAS, ROBERT C., risk mgr., Erlanger Medical Center, Chattanooga, TN '80 (RISK)

THOMAS, ROBERT H., exec. dir., Virginia Council on Uniform Hospital Accounting, Richmond, VA '44 (LIFE)

THOMAS, ROBERT L. JR., dir. soc. serv., Burlington Medical Center, Burlington, IA '85 (SOC)

THOMAS, ROBERT, supv. maint., Kino Community Hospital, Tucson, AZ '86

THOMAS, ROBERTA M., RN, asst. dir. nrsg., Somerset Medical Center, Somerville, NJ '82 (NURS)

THOMAS, ROBIN ELAINE, student, Program and Bureau of Hospital Administration, University of Michigan, Ann Arbor, MI '80 (MGMT)

THOMAS, ROGER MICHAEL, dir. pub. rel. and mktg., Methodist Hospital, Omaha, NE '78 (PR)

THOMAS, RONALD C., dir. matl. mgt., Bay Medical Center, Panama City, FL '83 (PUR)

THOMAS, ROSIE M., pat. rep., St. Mary Medical Center, Gary, IN '86 (PAT)

THOMAS, REV. ROYCE, dir. catholic hosp., Diocese of Little Rock, Little Rock, AR '85

THOMAS, RUTH A., dir. environ. serv., Huguley Memorial Hospital, Fort Worth, TX '81

THOMAS, SARAH B., dir. mktg. and pub. rel., HCA Medical Center of Plano, Plano, TX '83 (PR)

THOMAS, SHARRON A., dir. soc. serv., Martin Memorial Hospital, Stuart, FL '86 (SOC)

THOMAS, STEPHEN L., assoc. dir. human res., Cape Fear Valley Medical Center, Fayetteville, NC '87 (PERS)

THOMAS, STUART JAMES, dir. educ., Mercy Hospital, Urbana, IL '74 (EDUC)

THOMAS, SUE ANN, mgr. cent. and environ. serv., Little Company of Mary Hospital, Torrance, CA '86 (CS)

THOMAS, SUSAN V., dir. soc. serv., Northridge Hospital Medical Center, Northridge, CA '81 (SOC)

THOMAS, T. L., adm., G. R. Baker Memorial Hospital, Quesnel, B.C., Canada '85 (CS)

THOMAS, TELFORD W., exec. vice-pres., Washington Hospital, Washington, PA '72

THOMAS, TERRY A. J., student, Ferris State College, Big Rapids, MI '82

THOMAS, THEO M., RN, dir. nrsg., University of South Alabama Medical Center, Mobile, AL '81 (NURS)

THOMAS, THOMAS EDWARD, mgr. health care serv., Southern California Edison, Rosamead, CA '79

THOMAS, THOMAS S., vice-pres. prog. dev. and mktg., Boone Hospital Center, Columbia, MO '85 (PLNG)

THOMAS, VENTRYCE B., RN, assoc. dir. nrsg. serv., Beth Israel Medical Center, New York, NY '86 (NURS)

THOMAS, SR. VINCENT, pat. adv., Hotel Dieu Hospital, New Orleans, LA '84 (PAT)

THOMAS, VIRGINIA M., dir. aux. activ., Fairview General Hospital, Cleveland, OH '69 (VOL)

THOMAS, WENDELL, supv. maint., Twin Oaks Medical Center, Fort Worth, TX '83 (ENG)

THOMAS, WICKIE M., assoc. dir. mktg., Riley Memorial Hospital, Meridian, MS '85 (PLNG)

THOMAS, WILLIAM J., dir. bldg. serv., Yale-New Haven Hospital, New Haven, CT '86 (ENVIRON)

THOMAS, WILMA JEAN, dir. soc. serv., Good Samaritan Hospital, Lexington, KY '87 (SOC)

THOMASHAUER, ROBIN, area adm., Kaiser Permanente Health Plan, Baltimore, MD '75

THOMASON, S. KEITH, dir. mktg. serv., Lexington County Hospital, West Columbia, SC '81 (PR)

THOMASSEN, PATRICIA A., dir. in-service orientation, McKenzie-Willamette Memorial Hospital, Springfield, OR '85 (EDUC)

THOMASSON, W. ALAN, dir. pers., Catawba Memorial Hospital, Hickory, NC '82 (PERS)

THOMASSY, CAROLE S., coor. educ. serv., Westmoreland Hospital, Greensburg, PA '86 (EDUC)

THOME, DIANE D., dir. alternative delivery syst., Little Company of Mary Hospital, Evergreen Park, IL '85 (PLNG)

THOMERSON, JAMES M., dir. eng., Humana Women's Hospital, Indianapolis, IN '86 (ENG)

THOMPSON, ADRIENNE B., coor. and counselor mental health and retardation, Genetic Screening and Counseling Service, West Texas Rehabilitation Center, Abilene, TX '83 (SOC)

THOMPSON, BRENT D., dir. matl. mgt., Holy Cross Hospital, Salt Lake City, UT '84 (PUR)

THOMPSON, BRUCE JR., assoc. dir. oper., University of Virginia Hospitals, Charlottesville, VA '68

THOMPSON, BRUNELDA C., pat. rep., Borgess Medical Center, Kalamazoo, MI '82 (PAT)

THOMPSON, C. J., dir. aux. serv., Bluefield Community Hospital, Bluefield, WV '83

THOMPSON, CINDY L., RN, assoc. adm. nrsg., Midway Hospital, St. Paul, MN '86 (NURS)

THOMPSON, CYD DENISE, student, Webster University, St. Louis, MO '86

THOMPSON, CYNTHIA EDWENA, syst. mgr.-fin., Memorial Medical Center, Savannah, GA '80 (MGMT)

THOMPSON, DAVE, dir. data qual. review, Provider Reimbursement Consultant, Inc., Jacksonville, FL '83 (RISK)

THOMPSON, DAVID DUVALL, MD, dir., Society of the New York Hospital, New York, NY '67

THOMPSON, DAVID R., dir. client serv., Center for Health Affairs, Princeton, NJ '82 (PR)

THOMPSON, DON R., dir. plant oper., Holy Cross Hospital, Salt Lake City, UT '81 (ENG)

THOMPSON, EDWARD T., MD, (ret.), Front Royal, VA '28 (LIFE)

THOMPSON, EGBERT H., chief soc. work serv., Veterans Administration Medical Center, Miami, FL '83 (SOC)

THOMPSON, ELNORA D., mgr. pat. and family serv., Amsterdam Memorial Hospital, Amsterdam, NY '81 (SOC)

THOMPSON, EVELYN C., dir. med. soc. work, Los Angeles County-University of Southern California Medical Center, Los Angeles, CA '76 (SOC)

THOMPSON, G. BYRON, pres., Executive Resource Group, Inc., Miami, FL '82

THOMPSON, GERALDINE, dir. plng., Beth Abraham Hospital, Bronx, NY '79 (PLNG)

THOMPSON, HARRIET A., RN, asst. adm. and dir. nrsg., Hancock County Memorial Hospital, Britt, IA '85 (NURS)

THOMPSON, HARRY J., dir. eng., Doctors Hospital, New York, NY '85 (ENG)

THOMPSON, HELEN M., dir. med. data serv., St. Luke's Hospital, Saginaw, MI '87 (PR) (PLNG)

THOMPSON, J. BRENT, vice-pres. and dir. health facil. design, Cromwell, Truemper, Levy, Parker and Woodsmall, Inc., Little Rock, AR '82

THOMPSON, JACQUELYN A., RN, vice-pres. nrsg., Community Hospital, Geneva, IL '76 (NURS)

THOMPSON, JAMES W., dir. maint., Catawba Memorial Hospital, Hickory, NC '83 (ENG)

THOMPSON, JANET R., Albuquerque, NM '86 (PR)

THOMPSON, JANICE B., coor. pat. rep. lifeline, Lee's Summit Community Hospital, Lees Summit, MO '87 (PAT)

THOMPSON, JEFFREY J., mgr., Blue Cross and Blue Shield of Michigan, Detroit, MI '87 (AMB)

THOMPSON, JO, asst. vice-pres. pat. care, Methodist Hospital of Indiana, Indianapolis, IN '85 (NURS)

THOMPSON, JOAN E., assoc. dir., Children's Hospital, Boston, MA '77 (RISK)

THOMPSON, JOAN LEE, dir. soc. serv., AMI Lucy Lee Hospital, Poplar Bluff, MO '78 (SOC)

THOMPSON, JOBY, dir. pub. affairs, Valley Hospital, Ridgewood, NJ '81 (PR)

THOMPSON, JOHN F., dir. educ., Christian Hospital Northeast-Northwest, St. Louis, St. Louis, MO '72 (EDUC)

THOMPSON, JOHN L., exec. vice-pres. and chief exec. off., Lindsay Hospital Medical Center, Lindsay, CA '84

THOMPSON, JOHN R. JR., MD, (ret.), Jackson, TN '67

THOMPSON, JOHN R., Cape Coral, FL '80 (ENG)

THOMPSON, JON M., dir. mktg. res., Carondelet Rehabilitation Center, Talahassee, FL '86 (PLNG)

THOMPSON, JOYCE O., mgr., Arthur Young and Company, Los Angeles, CA '84 (MGMT)(AMB)

THOMPSON, KATHLEEN K., adm. res., Potomac Hospital, Woodbridge, VA '84

THOMPSON, KAY E., dir. food serv., Lubbock County Hospital District-Lubbock General Hospital, Lubbock, TX '74 (FOOD)

THOMPSON, KENNETH E., dir. eng., St. Barnabas Medical Center, Livingston, NJ '78 (ENG)

THOMPSON, KYLA T., pres., Kyla Thompson and Associates, Denver, CO '78 (PR)

THOMPSON, LANA Y., dir. qual. assur., North Mississippi Medical Center, Tupelo, MS '81 (EDUC)

THOMPSON, LARRY B., supv. plant oper., Sisters of Charity Hospital, Buffalo, NY '84 (ENG)

THOMPSON, LAUREN C., asst. to dir. defense med. syst. support center, Office of the Secretary of Defense, Health Affairs, Arlington, VA '84 (MGMT)

THOMPSON, LAVERNE, dir. soc. serv., Wadley Regional Medical Center, Texarkana, TX '86 (SOC)

THOMPSON, LEE D., dir. emp. rel., Hebrew Rehabilitation Center for Aged, Boston, MA '78 (PERS)

THOMPSON, MRS. LEE J., supv. cent. serv., Riverview Medical Center, Red Bank, NJ '74 (CS)

THOMPSON, LINDA A., RN, vice-pres. nrsg., Theda Clark Regional Medical Center, Neenah, WI '86 (NURS)

THOMPSON, LOIS E., RN, dir. nrsg.-hand surg., Jewish Hospital, Louisville, KY '84 (NURS)

THOMPSON, MARGARET T., RN, pat. rep., Memorial Hospital of Burlington County, Mount Holly, NJ '76 (PAT)

THOMPSON, MARIANN J., dir. risk mgt. serv., Michigan Osteopathic Medical Center, Detroit, MI '84 (RISK)

THOMPSON, MARILYN J., adm., Karen Ann Quinlan Center of Hope Hospice, Newton, NJ '86 (AMB)

THOMPSON, MARY B., asst. dir. nrsg., evaluative and educ. res., Worcester Memorial Hospital, Worcester, MA '85 (EDUC)

THOMPSON, MARY D., RN, (ret.), Silver Spring, MD '80 (NURS)

THOMPSON, MARY LASCHELLE, assoc. adm., Sharpstown General Hospital, Houston, TX '81 (NURS)

THOMPSON, MARY LOU, assoc. dir. pat. care mgt., North Carolina Memorial Hospital, Chapel Hill, NC '78

THOMPSON, MICHAEL L., vice-pres., Baptist Medical Centers, Birmingham, AL '85 (MGMT)

THOMPSON, MICHAL C., RN, vice-pres. nrsg., St. Vincent Charity Hospital and Health Center, Cleveland, OH '86 (NURS)

THOMPSON, PATRICIA A., vice-pres. corp. dev., Deaconess Medical Center-Spokane, Spokane, WA '85 (PLNG)

THOMPSON, PATTE, mgr. pur. serv., St. Mary's Hospital of Kankakee, Kankakee, IL '86 (PUR)

THOMPSON, PAUL, vice-pres. bond analysis, L. F. Rothschild, Unterberg and Towbin, New York, NY '80 (PLNG)

THOMPSON, PETER C., dir. ldry. serv., Harrisburg Hospital, Harrisburg, PA '86 (ENVIRON)

THOMPSON, RAINEY L., Chamblee, GA '85

THOMPSON, RAY, assoc. dir., Mother Frances Hospital Regional Center, Tyler, TX '79

THOMPSON, RICHARD W., PhD, sr. vice-pres., Alabama Hospital Association Birmingham Regional Office, Birmingham, AL '82 (PLNG)

THOMPSON, ROBERT C., mgr. human res., Borgess Medical Center, Kalamazoo, MI '85 (PERS)

THOMPSON, ROBERT E., vice-pres. plng., Lifespan, Inc., Minneapolis, MN '79 (PLNG)

THOMPSON, S. ASHLEY, dir. vol. serv., Manchester Memorial Hospital, Manchester, CT '86 (VOL)

THOMPSON, SAM L., coor. preventive maint., Saint Francis Hospital, Tulsa, OK '80 (ENG)

THOMPSON, SANDRA SYDNOR, mgr. inst. dev., Burger King Corporation, Miami, FL '85 (FOOD)
THOMPSON, SARAH A., atty., Detroit-Macomb Hospital Corporation, Detroit, MI '82 (ATTY)
THOMPSON, SHERENE S., dir. human res., Bay Medical Center, Panama City, FL '86 (PERS)
THOMPSON, SHERRILL W., pat. rep., Atlantic City Medical Center, Atlantic City, NJ '78 (PAT)
THOMPSON, SHERRY L., dir. pers., Humana Hospital -Brentwood, Shreveport, LA '83 (PERS)
THOMPSON, SUSAN M., mgr. cent. serv. room, Mount Clemens General Hospital, Mount Clemens, MI '85 (CS)
THOMPSON, SUSAN, mgr. sup., proc. and distrib., Brockton Hospital, Brockton, MA '85 (CS)
THOMPSON, TED M., coor. safety and security, St. Joseph's Hospital, Parkersburg, WV '77 (ENG)
THOMPSON, TERENCE W., atty., Chandler Community Hospital, Chandler, AZ '86 (ATTY)
THOMPSON, THOMAS A., corp. dir. matl., Samaritan Health Service, Phoenix, AZ '81
THOMPSON, THOMAS D., dir. cent. med. sup., Louisiana State University Hospital, Shreveport, LA '87 (CS)
THOMPSON, THOMAS R., assoc. med. dir. corp. adm. activ., William Beaumont Hospital, Royal Oak, MI '85 (PLNG)
THOMPSON, WESLEY B., vice-pres., Intermountain Health Care Professional Services, Inc., Salt Lake City, UT '79 (PLNG)
THOMPSON, WILLIAM D., pres., Underwood-Memorial Hospital, Woodbury, NJ '57 (LIFE)
THOMSON, FRANCIS S. JR., coor. facil., North Shore Children's Hospital, Salem, MA '85 (ENG)
THOMSON, J. CHRIS, vice-pres., St. John's Regional Health Center, Springfield, MO '79 (PLNG)
THOMSON, JEANE P., producer and acct. exec., Alexander and Alexander of Michigan, Inc., Detroit, MI '85 (RISK)
THOMSON, LICIA, pub. rel. spec., Good Samaritan Hospital, San Jose, CA '81 (PR)
THOMSON, MARY A., vice-pres. adm., Chester County Hospital, West Chester, PA '82 (PR)
THONE, MARTIN V. JR., risk mgr., Bristol Hospital, Bristol, CT '84 (ENG)
THONGCHAI, NUNTAVIT, dir. matl. mgt., University of Chicago Hospitals, Chicago, IL '80 (PUR)
THORBURN, CINDY S., commun. rel. asst. and coor. vol., Rockdale Hospital, Conyers, GA '86 (VOL)
THORDARSON, MARILYN, dir. pub. rel., Sacred Heart Medical Center, Spokane, WA '78 (PR)
THORESON, DONALD L., atty., Saint Cabrini Hospital of Seattle, Seattle, WA '75 (ATTY)
THORESON, SCOTT, student, Concordia College, Moorhead, MN '83
THORN, ALLAN R., chief soc. work serv., Veterans Administration Medical Center, Baltimore, MD '80 (SOC)
THORN, EDWIN CHARLES, adm., Shriners Hospital for Crippled Children, Springfield, MA '66
THORN, LAURLEE, asst. adm., Southwest Texas Methodist Hospital, San Antonio, TX '77
THORN, ROBERT, vice chm. and br. mem., Vista Hill Hospital, Chula Vista, CA '68 (ATTY)
THORN, WILLIAM E., dir. environ. serv., Alexian Brothers Hospital, St. Louis, MO '87 (ENVIRON)
THORNBURG, ANN M., partner, Coopers and Lybrand, Boston, MA '83
THORNBURG, VIRGIL P., dir. matl. mgt., Blanchard Valley Hospital, Findlay, OH '81 (PUR)
THORNE-HENDERSON, MARGARET LORRAINE, dir. in-service and commun. educ., HSA Gulf Coast Hospital, Fort Walton Beach, FL '86 (EDUC)
THORNE, CONRAD H., vice-pres. mktg. and commun. rel., Lincoln Health Resources, Phoenix, AZ '82 (PR)
THORNE, MARILYN G., mgr. food serv., Utah Valley Regional Medical Center, Provo, UT '69 (FOOD)
THORNSBERRY, C. CRAIG, dir. syst. human res. mgt., Voluntary Hospitals of America, Irving, TX '86 (PERS)
THORNTON, BETTY, adm., Group Health Cooperative of Puget Sound, Seattle, WA '87 (AMB)
THORNTON, MAJ. DALE E., MSC USA, Dwight D. Eisenhower Army Medical Center, Fort Gordon, GA '78
THORNTON, DAVID L., National Medical Enterprises, Marietta, GA '81 (ENG)
THORNTON, DONALD E., dir. gen. serv., Harrison Memorial Hospital, Bremerton, WA '85 (RISK)
THORNTON, JAMES A. JR., info. analyst, Jewish Hospital, Louisville, KY '86 (MGMT)
THORNTON, JEFFREY J., chief fin. off., Ephraim McDowell Regional Medical Center, Danville, KY '84 (PLNG)
THORNTON, LETA M., RN, vice-pres. adm., United Hospital, St. Paul, MN '77 (NURS)
THORNTON, MADELINE M., dir. food serv., United Hospital Center, Clarksburg, WV '83 (FOOD)
THORNTON, CAPT. MICHAEL DEWAYNE, MSC USAF, off., U. S. Air Force Department of Defense, Falls Church, VA '79
THORNTON, SARAH A., coor. pers., Memorial Hospital of Carbon County, Rawlins, WY '83 (PERS)
THORNTON, WILLIAM M., sr. vice-pres. oper., Grandview Hospital and Medical Center, Dayton, OH '75
THORP, RONALD E., dir. maint. and eng., Hospital Corporation of America, Las Vegas, NV '87 (ENG)
THORP, STEPHANIE E., student, Program in Hospital and Health Service Management, Kellogg Graduate School of Management, Northwestern University, Evanston, IL '83
THORPE, AMY W., mgt. eng., St. Joseph Hospital, Houston, TX '86 (MGMT)
THORPE, CARMEN R., RN, dir. nrsg. serv., Centro Espanol Memorial Hospital, Tampa, FL '85 (NURS)
THORPE, DARRELL P., MD, vice-pres. corp. plng., Tucson Medical Center, Tucson, AZ '81 (PLNG)
THORPE, TERESA S., nrsg. educ. spec., Children's Medical Center, Dayton, OH '85 (EDUC)
THORPE, WARREN R., dir. corp. eng., Numed, Inc., Encino, CA '69 (ENG)
THORSEN, JOHN S., chief facil. dev. sect., District of Columbia General Hospital, Washington, DC '84 (ENG)
THORSFELDT, HARRIET, RN, dir. matl. mgt., Holladay Park Medical Center, Portland, OR '76 (CS)
THORSNESS, JULIA M., coor. pub. rel., Our Lady of Compassion Care Center, Anchorage, AK '86 (PR)
THORSON, ANONA, RN, dir. nrsg. serv., Canton-Inwood Memorial Hospital, Canton, SD '83 (NURS)
THORSON, JUDY R., coor. emp. dev., University Hospital-University of Nebraska, Omaha, NE '83 (EDUC)
THORSON, NANCY A., mgr. corp. sales, MedAmerica Health Systems, Dayton, OH '80 (PR) (PLNG)
THORSTEINSON, KAY K., dir. soc. serv., Southwestern Vermont Medical Center, Bennington, VT '81 (SOC)
THORSTEN, JON B., mgr. rad. serv., Peninsula General Hospital Medical Center, Salisbury, MD '84
THRASH, ROXANNE, pat. rep., Humana Hospital -Springhill, Springhill, LA '80 (PAT)
THRASHER, DENNIS M., asst. adm. pers. serv., North Detroit General Hospital, Detroit, MI '80 (PERS)
THRASHER, JACQUELYN A., coor. med. staffing, Pri-Medical, Inc., Memphis, TN '81 (PR)
THRELKEL, LEON E., dir. bldg. and grds., Swedish Medical Center, Englewood, CO '81 (ENG)
THRELKELD, KAY L., pres., Forward Concepts Group, Walnut, CA '75 (PR)
THROCKMORTON, ROBERT B., atty., Broadlawns Polk County Hospital, Des Moines, IA '68 (ATTY)
THRONE, MORRIS N., (ret.), Baltimore, MD '48 (LIFE)
THROWER, DOROTHY A., dir. pat. rel., Cigna Healthplan of Arizona, Phoenix, AZ '86 (PAT)
THROWER, SAMUEL SCOTT, student, Program in Hospital Administration, Georgia State University, Atlanta, GA '85
THUDIUM, VERN F., assoc. dir., William Beaumont Hospital, Royal Oak, MI '77
THUM, SR. DOROTHY M., Oregon, OH '69 (FOOD)
THUNHOLM, ROBERT S., dir. human res., Redlands Community Hospital, Redlands, CA '79 (PERS)
THURBER, JAMES A., vice-pres. human res., New England Medical Center, Boston, MA '86 (PERS)
THURINGER, MARK, chief eng., Northern Hills General Hospital, Deadwood, SD '87 (ENG)
THURM, LORRAINE N., dir. vol. serv., St. Francis Medical Center, Trenton, NJ '82 (VOL)
THURM, TERRIE H., RN, dir. nrsg., Ellsworth Municipal Hospital, Iowa Falls, IA '86 (NURS)
THURMAN, ANDREW E., atty., Newman Memorial Hospital, Shattuck, OK '81 (ATTY)
THURMAN, DOROTHY, dir. pur., Lee's Summit Community Hospital, Lees Summit, MO '86 (PUR)
THURMOND, SANDRA BARKER, student, Program in Public Health, University of Alabama at Birmingham, Birmingham, AL '86
THUROW, EVELYN L., RN, adm. dir. substance abuse, Lansing General Hospital, Lansing, MI '83 (NURS)
THURSTON, BENJAMIN E., div. eng., Crothall American, Inc., San Diego, CA '78 (ENG)
THWAITES, BETH BRADFIELD, dir. pub. rel., Redmond Park Hospital, Rome, GA '81 (PR)
THWEATT, ALBERT A., partner, Gresham and Smith, Nashville, TN '79 (PLNG)
THWING, ALICE J., dir. plng., St. Peter Hospital, Olympia, WA '79 (PLNG)
TIANEN, BRUCE J., acct. exec., HBO and Company, Evanston, IL '76 (MGMT)
TIANO, JUDITH W., RN, dir. nrsg., United Hospital Center, Clarksburg, WV '71 (NURS)
TIBBITS, BETTY J., dir. vol. serv., Presbyterian Hospital, Oklahoma City, OK '84 (VOL)
TIBBITTS, SAMUEL J., pres., Lutheran Hospital Society of Southern California, Los Angeles, CA '73 (LIFE)
TIBBOTT, JAMES JOSEPH, student, Temple University, Department of Health Administration, Philadelphia, PA '85
TIBBY, ELLEN, pat. rep., University of Massachusetts Medical Center, Worcester, MA '80 (PAT)
TICE, KIRK C., asst. dir. clin. serv., Rahway Hospital, Rahway, NJ '82
TICHACEK, PATRICIA, supv. commun., Palos Community Hospital, Palos Heights, IL '84 (ENG)
TICHACEK, PEG A., dir. plng., Barnes Hospital, St. Louis, MO '81 (PLNG)
TICHENOR, ROSE MARY, dir. soc. serv., Eye, Ear, Nose and Throat Hospital, New Orleans, LA '84 (SOC)
TICHENOR, SHERRY S., RN, asst. dir. nrsg., St. Joseph Hospital, Lexington, KY '84 (NURS)
TIDWELL, CAROL J., asst. gen. counsel, HealthOne Corporation, Minneapolis, MN '85 (RISK)
TIDWELL, JANET T., RN, dir. nrsg., Germantown Community Hospital, Germantown, TN '86 (NURS)
TIEDEKEN, KATHLEEN H., assoc. exec. dir. nrsg., West Jersey Hospital-Eastern Division, Voorhees, NJ '85 (NURS)
TIEDEMANN, H. FRANK, vice-pres. mktg., Borgess Medical Center, Kalamazoo, MI '79 (PLNG)
TIEMAN, LINDA, RN, vice-pres. nrsg., Mount Carmel Medical Center, Columbus, OH '82 (NURS)
TIEMEYER, SHERYL LYNN, pat. rep., Jackson County Schneck Memorial Hospital, Seymour, IN '81 (PAT)
TIENOR, CYNTHIA A., dir. food mgt. and nutr. serv., St. Luke's Hospital, Milwaukee, WI '86 (FOOD)
TIERNAN, CLAIRE K., RN, vice-pres. nrsg., Bristol Hospital, Bristol, CT '84 (NURS)
TIERNAN, TERESA L., asst. dir. food serv., St. Anne's Hospital, Fall River, MA '86 (FOOD)
TIERNEY, BERARD, dir. educ. serv., Georgetown University Medical Center, Washington, DC '85 (EDUC)
TIERNEY, CAROL F., dir. commun. rel., St. Luke's Hospital, Duluth, MN '85 (PR) (PLNG)
TIERNEY, JEAN K., dir. commun. rel., Community Memorial Hospital, Toms River, NJ '79 (PR)
TIERNEY, JOANNE, coor. soc. serv., Sacred Heart Hospital, Norristown, PA '84 (SOC)
TIERNEY, MARK, assoc. dir. fin. serv., Saint Thomas Medical Center, Akron, OH '86
TIERNO, MICHAEL, dir. food serv., Long Beach Community Hospital, Long Beach, CA '81 (FOOD)
TIERSON, LINDA E., RN, dir. nrsg., Jackson County Memorial Hospital, Altus, OK '82 (NURS)
TIETJEN, WILLIAM R., dir. pat. serv., Meriter Hospital, Madison, WI '75 (SOC)
TIFFANY, KATHLEEN Z., market res. analyst, St. Agnes Hospital and Medical Center, Fresno, CA '84 (PLNG)
TIFFT, ROSABELLE M., dir. commun. rel. and dev., Anna Jaques Hospital, Newburyport, MA '67 (PR)
TIGER, DEBORAH L., asst. dir. food serv., Hendrick Medical Center, Abilene, TX '85 (FOOD)
TIGHE, ALVIN JOHN JR., asst. dir., Grady Memorial Hospital, Atlanta, GA '69 (MGMT)
TIGHE, JOHN J. JR., dir. pers., Barnes Hospital, St. Louis, MO '79 (PERS)
TIGHE, MAUREEN A., dir. plng., New Rochelle Hospital Medical Center, New Rochelle, NY '79 (PLNG)
TIGHE, SR. MOIRA, dir. diet., St. Marys Hospital of Rochester, Rochester, MN '77 (FOOD)
TIGHE, THOMAS J. G. JR., asst. dir., Central Maine Medical Center, Lewiston, ME '69 (PLNG)
TILBURY, MARY S., RN, vice-pres. nrsg. and support serv., Alexandria Hospital, Alexandria, VA '86 (NURS)
TILBY, LINDA, RN, asst. adm. pat. serv., St. Joseph Hospital, Augusta, GA '80 (NURS)
TILDEN, IDA L., dir. cont. educ., Academy of Health Profession, Kansas City, MO '83 (EDUC)
TILDEN, NELSON A., pres., The Furst Group, Medical Search Consulting Division, Overland Park, KS '68
TILL, L. T., assoc. adm. rad., Emory University Hospital, Atlanta, GA '86
TILLERY, LUIZA INGBORG, RN, adm. clin. serv., Memorial Care System, Houston, TX '84 (NURS)
TILLERY, WALTER L., dir. maint., D. T. Watson Rehabilitation Hospital, Sewickley, PA '83 (ENG)
TILLEY, BARBARA D., dir. vol. serv., Atlantic City Medical Center, Mainland Division, Pomona, NJ '76 (VOL)
TILLEY, GARY B., dir. pur., Radford Community Hospital, Radford, VA '84 (PUR)
TILLINGHAST, R. AVERY, dev. consult., Tillinghast Associates, South Windham, CT '70 (PR)
TILLIS, GEORGIANNA S., coor. vol. serv., Pleasant Valley Hospital, Point Pleasant, WV '86 (VOL)
TILLMAN, BOBBIE, dir. mktg., Gulf Coast Hospital, Fort Walton Beach, FL '81 (PR)
TILLMAN, EUGENE, atty., Illinois Hospital Association, Oak Brook, IL '82 (ATTY)
TILLMAN, JANET, dir. soc. work, Baptist Medical Center-Montclair, Birmingham, AL '79 (SOC)
TILLMAN, MICHAEL C., RN, assoc. dir. nrsg., George Washington University Hospital, Washington, DC '86 (NURS)
TILLMAN, TERRILL L., dir. constr., St. Paul-Ramsey Medical Center, St. Paul, MN '83 (ENG)
TILSCHNER, NANCY L., mgr. vol. serv., General Hospital of Everett, Everett, WA '86 (VOL)
TILSON, GERALD ROBERT, plant eng., Beyer Memorial Hospital, Ypsilanti, MI '78 (ENG)
TILSON, JOHN Q., atty., Connecticut Hospital Association, Wallingford, CT '69 (ATTY)
TIMBLIN, MARY E., RN, dir. matl. mgt., Lakewood Hospital, Tacoma, WA '77 (CS)
TIMCHAK, JOAN R., RN, dir. nrsg., Providence Hospital, Washington, DC '78 (NURS)
TIMLIN, MOLLY, dir. pub. rel., Crozer-Chester Medical Center, Chester, PA '83 (PR)
TIMMER, JAN MARIE, mgr. pub. rel., St. Lawrence Hospital, Lansing, MI '86 (PR)
TIMMINS, LAWRENCE E., dir. food serv., Resurrection Hospital, Chicago, IL '69 (FOOD)
TIMMONS, DALE L., dir. pub. rel., Long Island College Hospital, Brooklyn, NY '75 (PR)
TIMMONS, MARILYN, dir. vol. serv., St. Mary's Medical Center, Evansville, IN '80 (VOL)
TIMMS, GEORGE, dir. soc. work serv., Fairfield Memorial Hospital, Winnsboro, SC '86 (SOC)
TIMMS, RANDALL, dir. matl. mgt., Sacred Heart Rehabilitation Hospital, Milwaukee, WI '86 (PUR)
TIMPE-BRENNAN, ANN, atty., Houston, TX '86 (ATTY)
TIMPER, SUZANNE E., dir. vol. serv., Hebrew Hospital for Chronic Sick, Bronx, NY '83 (VOL)
TIMPKO, ANASTASIA, co-dir. educ., Griffin Hospital, Derby, CT '85 (EDUC)
TIMS, HUBERT H., dir. hskpg., Southern Baptist Hospital, New Orleans, LA '86 (ENVIRON)
TINCHER, JACK E., supt. constr., Kettering Medical Center, Kettering, OH '82 (ENG)
TINCHER, TALMADGE, dir. bldg. and grds., Clark County Memorial Hospital, Jeffersonville, IN '80 (ENG)
TINCKNELL, LESLIE D., pres., Wigen, Tincknell, Meyer and Associates, Inc., Saginaw, MI '83
TINDALL, CRAIG JOHNSON, student, George State University, Institute of Health Administration, Atlanta, GA '86
TINDALL, JAMES R., pres., Healthcare Management Services, Marietta, GA '77 (MGMT)
TINDLE, JEFF A., exec. dir., Association of Independent Hospitals, Kansas City, MO '80
TINGLEY, LINDA MCLELLAN, dir. soc. serv., Houlton Regional Hospital, Houlton, ME '82 (SOC)
TINGLEY, TERRY, mgr. cent. serv., University Hospital, Jacksonville, FL '76
TINGSTAD, PHYLLIS F., pres., Tingstad Associates, Inc., Lake Bluff, IL '74 (EDUC)
TINIOS, GREGORY C., dir. food and nutr. serv., Church Hospital Corporation, Baltimore, MD '86 (FOOD)
TINKEN, WILLIE, dir. soc. serv., Tulane University Hospital and Clinics, New Orleans, LA '76 (SOC)
TINKER, A. JAMES, adm., Mercy Hospital, Cedar Rapids, IA '66

TINKER, CAROLYN R., dir. pub. affairs, University of New Mexico Medical Center, Albuquerque, NM '81 (PR)
TINNEY, TIMOTHY R., dir. eng., St. Luke's Hospital, Saginaw, MI '85 (ENG)
TINNIN, ROBERT P. JR., atty., Presbyterian Hospital, Albuquerque, NM '79 (ATTY)
TINSLEY, MARCIA L., coor. soc. serv., St. Mary Medical Center, Gary, IN '85 (SOC)
TINTLE, KEITH D., assoc. adm., Utah Valley Regional Medical Center, Provo, UT '81
TIPPENS, ROBERT M., asst. adm. med. rec., Scott and White Memorial Hospital, Temple, TX '76
TIPPLE, JANE E., coor. pat. educ., Chippenham Hospital, Richmond, VA '83 (EDUC)
TIPTON, ANN J., atty., Holston Valley Hospital and Medical Center, Kingsport, TN '86 (ATTY)(RISK)
TIPTON, CARL K., dir. pub. rel., dev. and pers., Jefferson Memorial Hospital, Jefferson City, TN '84 (PR)
TIPTON, DON, dist. mgr., ARA, Hospital Food Management, El Segundo, CA '81 (FOOD)
TIPTON, GARY D., adm., Harrison Community Hospital, Cadiz, OH '82 (PERS)
TIPTON, TERRI L., dir. commun. rel., Northeast Medical Center Hospital, Humble, TX '86 (PR)
TIRPACK, HENRIETTA M., RN, supv. cent. serv., Decatur General Hospital, Decatur, AL '82 (CS)
TISCH, RONALD I., atty., Memel, Jacobs and Ellingsworth, Washington, DC '84 (ATTY)
TISCHLER, MARLA D., chief soc. work serv., Veterans Administration Lakeside Medical Center, Chicago, IL '81 (SOC)
TISDALE, BRUCE J., adm. dir. human res., Lutheran Hospital of Fort Wayne, Fort Wayne, IN '82 (PERS)
TISDALE, DIANE L., mgr. hskpg., Leominster Hospital, Leominster, MA '86 (ENVIRON)
TISHBERG, LEONARD H., dir. matl. mgt., Sherman Hospital, Elgin, IL '74 (PUR)
TISHKEVICH, EDWARD G., dir. matl. mgt., St. John's Hospital, Lowell, MA '70 (PUR)
TISSOT, ROBERT H., mgr. ins., Cabrini Medical Center, New York, NY '85 (RISK)
TISSUE, GAYLE L., exec. vice-pres. corp. affairs, Children's Hospital of Pittsburgh, Pittsburgh, PA '86 (PLNG)
TITLE, MONROE M., adm., North Detroit General Hospital, Detroit, MI '54 (LIFE)
TITMAN, BETTY L., dir. commun., Children's Hospital National Medical Center, Washington, DC '82 (ENG)
TITUS-LASSWELL, RUTH, diet. consult., Crawford County Hospital District One, Girard, KS '85 (FOOD)
TITUS, GARY L., productivity coor., Lansing General Hospital, Lansing, MI '85 (MGMT)
TITUS, SUSAN E., health care planner, Washington Healthcare Corporation, Washington, DC '81 (PLNG)
TKACZUK, IRENE OLENA, student, Program in Health Systems Management, Rush University, Chicago, IL '85
TLASEK, PATRICIA C., dir. diet. serv., Union Memorial Hospital, Baltimore, MD '77 (FOOD)
TOBACK, SANDY, mem. serv. rep., Community Health Program-Queens-Nassau, New Hyde Park, NY '86 (PAT)
TOBACMAN, KENNETH I., dir. biomedical eng., Grant Hospital of Chicago, Chicago, IL '79 (ENG)
TOBALSKI, JIM, vice-pres. mktg., St. Agnes Hospital, Fond Du Lac, WI '80 (PR)
TOBIAS, BEN, adm., St. Jude Hospital, Brenham, TX '52 (LIFE)
TOBIAS, RICHARD D., dir. plant and facil., William Beaumont Hospital-Troy, Troy, MI '85 (ENG)
TOBIN, ANNE CHRISTINE, RN, dir. nrsg. serv., Deborah Heart and Lung Center, Browns Mills, NJ '83 (NURS)
TOBIN, BENTLEY, atty., Woonsocket Hospital, Woonsocket, RI '68 (ATTY)
TOBIN, CALVIN JAY, vice-pres., Loebl, Schlossman and Hackl, Chicago, IL '77
TOBIN, ELLEN, pres., Health Surveys and Marketing, Inc., Columbia, MD '86 (PAT)
TOBIN, GLORIA J., RN, adm. asst. nrsg., Memorial Hospital System, Houston, TX '84 (NURS)
TOBIN, JOHN H., pres., Waterbury Hospital, Waterbury, CT '82
TOBIN, JOHN H. JR., pres., Hospital Corporation of America, Nashville, TN '78
TOBIN, PHILIP J., vice-pres. natl. acct. mktg.-hosp. prod. div., Abbott Laboratories, North Chicago, IL '85
TOBIN, RONALD GEORGE, dir. eng. and facil., Children's Hospital National Medical Center, Washington, DC '77 (ENG)
TOBLER, TERRI, dir. food serv., Providence Memorial Hospital, El Paso, TX '79 (FOOD)
TOBOLA, LOGIC II, partner, Pierce Goodwin Alexander-Architect, Houston, TX '78
TOBOZ, CAROL, RN, supv. cent. sup. serv., St. Joseph Riverside Hospital, Warren, OH '79 (CS)
TOCI, MARIA A., mgr. pub. rel., Kennedy Memorial Hospitals-University Medical Center, Stratford Division, Stratford, NJ '85 (PR)
TOCMAN, SANDRA S., RN, assoc. exec. dir. and dir. nrsg. serv., Winthrop Hospital, Winthrop, MA '84 (NURS)
TODD, ELIZABETH S., mgr. matl., Northwest Mississippi Regional Medical Center, Clarksdale, MS '83 (PUR)
TODD, KATHY, RN, asst. dir. nrsg., University of California Irvine Medical Center, Orange, CA '86 (NURS)
TODD, MICHAEL J., asst. mgr. adm., Huntington Memorial Hospital, Pasadena, CA '86 (ENG)
TODD, RICHARD K., vice-pres. facil. plng., Interhealth Corporation, Whittier, CA '80 (ENG)
TODD, THOMAS J., asst. vice-pres. human res., University Hospital, Jacksonville, FL '87 (PERS)
TODD, WARREN E., vice-pres. mktg., Monmouth Medical Center, Long Branch, NJ '86 (PR) (PLNG)
TODD, WILLIAM T. JR., info. syst. analyst, Cigna Healthplan of Georgia, Inc., Atlanta, GA '84 (MGMT)
TODER, RICHARD H., prin., Richard Toder Mechanical Consultants, New York, NY '83 (ENG)
TODHUNTER, NEIL E., exec. dir., Oil City Hospital and Skilled Nursing Facility, Oil City, PA '73
TOERNER, G. T., dir. matl. mgt., Tarpon Springs General Hospital, Tarpon Springs, FL '81 (PUR)
TOFANELLI, CAPT. DAVE E., MSC USAF, fin. mgt. fellow, Department of Air Force Medical Service, Bolling AFB, DC '80
TOFT, PAMELA A. GRAY, vice-pres., Methodist Hospital of Indiana, Indianapolis, IN '82 (PERS)
TOGA, ANDREW E., dir. matl. mgt., St. Peter's Hospital, Albany, NY '87 (PUR)
TOGNAZZINI, NANCY L., coor. guest rel., Good Samaritan Hospital, San Jose, CA '86 (PAT)
TOHER, CYNTHIA L., RN, mgr. nrsg., Mercy Hospital, Portland, ME '87 (AMB)
TOJE, MATTHEW D., student, Program in Health Care Administration, Central Michigan University, Mount Pleasant, MI '84
TOKARZ, PATRICIA ANN, RN, dir. nrsg. res. and syst. dev., Mount Sinai Medical Center, Cleveland, OH '82 (NURS)
TOKHEIM, MARIAN D., coor. in-service educ., Jane Lamb Health Center, Clinton, IA '87 (EDUC)
TOKHEIM, ROD J., dir. plng., Lutheran Hospital, Moline, IL '86 (PLNG)
TOLAND, DREXEL, pres., Drexel Toland and Associates, Inc., Memphis, TN '53 (AMB)(LIFE)
TOLAND, JACK R., dir. biomedical eng., Christian Hospital Northwest, Florissant, MO '76 (ENG)
TOLBERT, GAITHER K., dir. vol. serv., Catawba Memorial Hospital, Hickory, NC '85 (VOL)
TOLBERT, SAMUEL H., asst. vice-pres. plng., Self Memorial Hospital, Greenwood, SC '86 (PLNG)
TOLEDO, SERGIO O., dir. environ. serv., Northridge Hospital Medical Center, Northridge, CA '86 (ENVIRON)
TOLER, VERN ELMER, (ret.), Capitola, CA '68 (ENG)
TOLIVER, GARY C., vice-pres. fin., Missouri Hospital Association, Jefferson City, MO '82 (PLNG)
TOLIVER, THELMA J., supv. cent. serv., St. Mary's Hospital, Enid, OK '83 (CS)
TOLL, CELIA-ANN, dir. human res., South Suburban Hospital, Hazel Crest, IL '80 (PERS)
TOLL, LARRY N., dir. food serv., Naval Hospital, Portsmouth, VA '69 (FOOD)
TOLL, SIDNEY A., assoc. adm., North Country Hospital and Health Center, Newport, VT '77
TOLLESON, JOHN LEWIS, adm. food serv., Washington Hospital Center, Washington, DC '77 (FOOD)
TOLLIVER, MARSHA V., coor. pub. info., Hartford Hospital, Hartford, CT '86 (PR)
TOLMIE, EDWARD A., chief eng., Heartland Hospital East, St. Joseph, MO '75 (ENG)
TOLMIE, JOHN KERR, asst. adm., Mount Vernon Hospital, Alexandria, VA '80
TOLSON, SHARON P., dir. mktg., Doctors Hospital of Jefferson, Metairie, LA '85 (PR)
TOM, JUANITA Y. M., chief soc. serv., Leahi Hospital, Honolulu, HI '81 (SOC)
TOM, LINDA, RN, dir. nrsg., Marshall County Memorial Hospital, Britton, SD '80 (NURS)
TOMANDL, TONY, mgr., Arthur Andersen and Company, Kansas City, MO '84
TOMARAS, MARYANDA J., mgr. diet., Alta View Hospital, Sandy, UT '84 (FOOD)
TOMASI, THERESA A., dir. pers., New Britain Memorial Hospital, New Britain, CT '86 (PERS)
TOMASI, THERESA, dir. soc. work, Medical Center Hospital of Vermont, Burlington, VT '85 (SOC)
TOMASIAK, MARY L., dir. matl. mgt., Indianhead Medical Center, Shell Lake, WI '80 (PUR)
TOMASZEWSKI, JAMES A., assoc. vice-pres., Christ Hospital, Cincinnati, OH '79 (RISK)
TOMBERLIN, DON E., asst. vice-pres. med. adm., Memorial Medical Center, Savannah, GA '84 (RISK)
TOMCHO, CAROLYN R., adm. coor. prof. standard review, St. Joseph Hospital and Health Center, Lorain, OH '84 (FOOD)
TOMCIK, HELEN, nrsg. oper. analyst, Western Pennsylvania Hospital, Pittsburgh, PA '86 (MGMT)
TOMIYAMA, ALAN S., dir. pub. rel., St. Mary's Hospital and Medical Center, San Francisco, CA '85 (PR)
TOMKINSON, BARBARA JOAN, dir. nutr., St. Joseph's Health Centre, Toronto, Ont., Canada '82 (FOOD)
TOMKINSON, DAVID S., dir. vol. serv., Salem Hospital, Salem, MA '76 (VOL)
TOMLIN, M. SUE, coor. staff dev., Good Samaritan Hospital and Medical Center, Portland, OR '81 (EDUC)
TOMLIN, MARSHA, coor. educ. res., Clinton Memorial Hospital, Wilmington, OH '82 (EDUC)
TOMLINSON, JUNE H., RN, dir. nrsg. serv., Doctors Hospital of Prince George's County, Lanham, MD '75 (NURS)
TOMLINSON, THELMA S. CHEESEMAN, asst. dir., Wright-Bendel Clinic, Monroe, LA '44 (LIFE)
TOMLINSON, WILLIAM M., pres., Paoli Memorial Hospital, Paoli, PA '70 (PLNG)
TOMME, STEPHEN R., dir. mktg., Kaiser Permanente Medical Care, Denver, CO '84
TOMPKINS, DAVID, mgr. directors and officers liability dept., G. J. Sullivan Company, Los Angeles, CA '85 (RISK)
TOMPKINS, GARY R., RN, dir. nrs., HCA South Austin Medical Center, Austin, TX '85 (NURS)
TOMPKINS, HARRY M., dir. educ., Amsco American Sterilizer Company, Erie, PA '78 (CS)
TOMPKINS, JAMES E., pres. and arch., Tompkins Professional Service, Kansas City, MO '82
TOMPKINS, RICHARD F., vice-pres. and chief info. off., West Virginia University Hospital, Morgantown, WV '86 (PLNG)
TOMS, GLEASON D. JR., dir. matl. mgt., Martha Jefferson Hospital, Charlottesville, VA '81 (PUR)
TOMSHACK, RAMONA A., instr. qual. assur., Sarah Bush Lincoln Health Center, Mattoon, IL '84 (EDUC)
TOMSON, ELIZABETH, dir. risk mgt., North Shore University Hospital, Manhasset, NY '85 (RISK)
TONDERA, BONNIE, RN, vice-pres. nrsg., Huntsville Hospital, Huntsville, AL '79 (NURS)
TONDU, EUGENIO L., asst. chief eng., Beth Abraham Hospital, Bronx, NY '83 (ENG)
TONELLI, ENRICO C., asst. adm., Southside Regional Medical Center, Petersburg, VA '82
TONER, JEFFREY M., dir. pers., Henrietta D. Goodall Hospital, Sanford, ME '79 (PERS)
TONEY, KATHLEEN, coor. cent. proc., Saint Vincent Hospital, Billings, MT '86 (CS)
TONEY, MICHELLE I., coor. pers., Marion General Hospital, Marion, OH '86 (PERS)
TONGES, MARY CRABTREE, RN, vice-pres. nrsg., Clara Maass Medical Center, Belleville, NJ '79 (NURS)
TONKIN, JOHN B. JR., mgr. matl., Metropolitan Hospital-Parkview Division, Philadelphia, PA '85 (PUR)
TONKINS, HARRIET, RN, supv. cent. sup. room, St. Luke's Hospital, Bethlehem, PA '84 (CS)
TONNA, PATRICK R., dir. eng., Alexian Brothers Hospital San Jose, San Jose, CA '85 (ENG)
TONZI, LAWRENCE J., RN, dir. nrsg., Houlton Regional Hospital, Houlton, ME '86 (NURS)
TOOLE, GILES P., mgr. pers., St. Francis Xavier Hospital, Charleston, SC '80 (PERS)
TOOLEY, JOSEPHINE J., cent. serv. tech., St. Anthony Hospital, Michigan City, IN '86 (CS)
TOOMEY, BRIAN, dir. soc. work, Martha's Vineyard Hospital, Oak Bluffs, MA '87 (SOC)
TOOMEY, CONSTANCE, dir. vol. serv., Henry Mayo Newhall Memorial Hospital, Valencia, CA '85 (VOL)
TOOMEY, DAVID F. JR., atty., Holy Name Hospital, Teaneck, NJ '70 (ATTY)
TOOMEY, RICHARD KIRK, mgr., Amherst Associates, Tampa, FL '78 (PLNG)
TOOMEY, ROBERT E., pres., Medcorp Health Systems, Inc., Columbia, SC '72 (PLNG)(LIFE)
TOOMEY, TIMOTHY C., atty., Little Company of Mary Hospital, Evergreen Park, IL '68 (ATTY)
TOOTLE, WILLIAM K., asst. dir. eng., Beverly Hills Medical Center, Los Angeles, CA '85 (ENG)
TOPHAM, ALVIN STANLEY, exec. vice-pres. and chief oper. off., South Shore Hospital, South Weymouth, MA '62 (PLNG)
TOPJIAN, ELKE I., dir. admit. and info., Oakwood Hospital, Dearborn, MI '80
TOPOLESKI, JACK W., exec. dir., Massillon Community Hospital, Massillon, OH '85 (PLNG)
TOPOLOSKY, BRUCE M., pres., Barnert Memorial Hospital Center, Paterson, NJ '84
TOPOR, ROBERT S., dir. mktg. promotion, Sharp Healthcare, San Diego, CA '84 (PR)
TOPPING, TRACY T., atty., Mercy Hospital, Wilkes-Barre, PA '86 (ATTY)
TOPPINS, J. DAVID, asst. dir. diet., St. Mary's Medical Center, Knoxville, TN '79 (FOOD)
TORCH, MARY S., dir. mktg., Holmes Regional Medical Center, Melbourne, FL '87 (PR) (PLNG)
TORCZON, BONNIE, RN, dir. educ. serv., Columbus Community Hospital, Columbus, NE '77 (EDUC)
TORGAN, HAROLD D., atty., Bethesda Hospital and Community Mental Health Center, Denver, CO '71 (ATTY)
TORGERSON, LOIS G., dir. diet., Sacred Heart Medical Center, Spokane, WA '74 (FOOD)
TORGERSON, PAUL M., atty., Fairview Hospital and Healthcare Service, Minneapolis, MN '82 (ATTY)
TORGERUD, KIM, mgt. eng., Lutheran Hospital -LaCrosse, La Crosse, WI '87
TORIAN, JOHN G. II, atty., Our Lady of Lourdes Medical Center, Lafayette, LA '77 (ATTY)
TORIGOE, EILEEN E., dir. human res., Kuakini Health System, Honolulu, HI '82 (PERS)
TORIN, BETH S., North Central Bronx Hospital, Bronx, NY '84 (FOOD)
TORINA, MARY, dir. food serv., Suburban General Hospital, Pittsburgh, PA '72 (FOOD)
TORKELSON, EVELYN M., vice-pres. pat. care serv., Deaconess Medical Center-Spokane, Spokane, WA '83 (NURS)
TORMA, MARY D., dir. oper. and bus. dev., Medisyst, Lorain, OH '81 (MGMT)
TORNATORE, JOHN H., dir. pers., Memorial Hospital of Bedford County, Everett, PA '82 (PERS)
TORPEY, ELIZABETH, coor. mktg., Health Management Strategic, Inc., Washington, DC '86 (PLNG)
TORQUATO, THOMAS M., atty., Lewistown Hospital, Lewistown, PA '82 (ATTY)
TORRADO, ELVIRA, dir. environ. serv., North Shore University Hospital, Manhasset, NY '86 (ENVIRON)
TORRELLAS, RUDY R., sr. sales rep., Vestal Laboratories, Inc., Guaynabo, P.R. '86 (ENVIRON)
TORRENCE, WILLIAM E., adm., Bradley County Memorial Hospital, Cleveland, TN '63
TORRES, CHRISTINE M., supv. sup., proc. and distrib., Pennsylvania Hospital, Philadelphia, PA '86 (CS)
TORRES, EDWARD F., dir., Ahl Torres International, Inc., San Antonio, TX '85 (ENG)
TORRES, SAMUEL, pres., Franciscan Health System, Chadds Ford, PA '68
TORREY, GENE, sr. dir. facil. plng., Abbott-Northwestern Hospital, Minneapolis, MN '78 (ENG)
TORREY, MARY BETH, pat. rep., Abbott-Northwestern Hospital, Minneapolis, MN '86 (PAT)
TORREZ, SR. MARY RACHEL, RN, dir. nrsg., Sonoma Valley Hospital, Sonoma, CA '79 (NURS)
TORREZ, RITA M., dir. pat. serv., St. Clair Memorial Hospital, Pittsburgh, PA '85 (SOC)
TORRIS, ANTHONY R., pres., Health Facilities Planning Consultants, Garland, TX '62 (PLNG)
TORTI, FRANGESCO L., dir. mgt. eng., Sinai Hospital of Detroit, Detroit, MI '84 (MGMT)
TORTORELLA, FRANK ROGERS, asst. adm. oper., Illinois Masonic Medical Center, Chicago, IL '86

TORTORICE, PETER A., mgt. eng., Columbus Hospital, Chicago, IL '85 (MGMT)
TORUNIAN, ANTON, dir. fin., Jewish General Hospital, Montreal, Que., Canada '63
TORVIK, BERNARD, pres., Amtel Communications, Inc., McFarland, WI '86 (ENG)
TOSH, JULIANE, asst. dir. nutr. serv., Irving Community Hospital, Irving, TX '86 (FOOD)
TOSSING, LT. COL. ROSANNE K., RN MSC USA, chief nrsg. serv., U. S. Air Force Hospital Mountain Home, Mountain Home AFB, ID '79 (NURS)
TOSTO, JACQUELINE MARIE, coor. vol., Normandy Osteopathic Medical Center, St. Louis, MO '83 (VOL)
TOTH, CYNTHIA M., student, Graduate Program in Business and Hospital Administration, University of Florida College of Business and Health Related Professions, Gainesville, FL '86
TOTH, FRANCIS B., chief eng., Ohio Valley Hospital, Steubenville, OH '68 (ENG)
TOTH, MARY ANN, dir. plng., Mount Sinai Medical Center, Cleveland, OH '86 (PLNG)
TOTH, NATALIE, coor. pat. rep., Swedish Medical Center, Englewood, CO '77 (PAT)
TOTH, ROBERT C., consult., Holden Hospital, Holden, MA '74 (FOOD)
TOTH, ROBERT G., St. Vincent Charity Hospital and Health Center, Cleveland, OH '84 (PLNG)
TOTH, SUSAN HOLLAND, pat. rep., Cedar Springs Psychiatric Hospital, Colorado Springs, CO '85 (PAT)
TOTTENHAM, TERRY O., atty., Memorial Hospital System, Houston, TX '81 (ATTY)
TOUCHETTE, GEORGETTE, dir. vol., Notre Dame Hospital, Montreal, Que., Canada '79 (VOL)
TOUCHETTE, KATHLEEN S., assoc., Voluntary Hospitals of America Consulting Services, Inc., Tampa, FL '86 (PR)
TOULSTER, BARBARA ANN, coor. vol., Normandy Osteopathic Hospital-South, St. Louis, MO '84 (VOL)
TOUNGATE, CHRISTINE, RN, mgr. sterile proc., St. David's Community Hospital, Austin, TX '84 (CS)
TOURIKIS, EILEEN, RN, supv. cent. proc., St. James Community Hospital, Butte, MT '85 (CS)
TOURTUAL, CHARLES J., dir. soc. work serv., United Health Services, Johnson City, NY '84 (SOC)
TOURVILLE, SHARON, RN, Fairview Riverside Hospital, Minneapolis, MN '83 (NURS)
TOUSEY, LOUANN H., RN, dir. nrsg. serv., Langlade Memorial Hospital, Antigo, WI '83 (NURS)
TOUSIGNANT, ANN K., asst. vice-pres., Faulkner Hospital, Boston, MA '81 (PLNG)
TOUSINAU, DAN L., asst. dir. pers., Schumpert Medical Center, Shreveport, LA '86 (PERS)
TOUSLEE, ESTHER M., RN, dir. nrsg. serv., Citizens Medical Center, Colby, KS '86 (NURS)
TOUSLEY, MARTHA M., RN, dir. educ., Fair Oaks Hospital, Summit, NJ '81 (EDUC)
TOUSSAINT, JACK L., sr. vice-pres., St. Luke's Methodist Hospital, Cedar Rapids, IA '53 (LIFE)
TOVEY, MYRNA W., RN, dir. nrsg. serv., Oneida Hospital, Malad City, ID '84 (NURS)
TOWBER, ALICE P., dir. plng. and risk mgt., Western Baptist Hospital, Paducah, KY '81 (RISK)(PLNG)
TOWER, CATHERINE, RN, vice-pres. nrsg., Worcester Hahnemann Hospital, Worcester, MA '67 (NURS)
TOWER, JOYCE B., asst. dir., New England Deaconess Hospital, Boston, MA '85
TOWER, ROBERT B., pres., Tower, Pinkster and Titus Associates, Inc., Ralamazoo, MI '84
TOWERS, MARGARET M., risk mgr., White Plains Hospital Medical Center, White Plains, NY '84 (RISK)
TOWERS, VELMA L., dir. vol. serv., HCA Doctors Hospital, Lake Worth, FL '86 (VOL)
TOWLE, WILLIAM F., vice-pres., George Kaludis Associates, Inc., Nashville, TN '61 (PLNG)
TOWLER, MARTHA D., mgr. matl., Southside Community Hospital, Farmville, VA '86 (PUR)
TOWLES, LOIS W., pur. agt., Halifax Memorial Hospital, Roanoke Rapids, NC '84 (PUR)
TOWNE-MERRITT, MARY J., asst. dir. nutr. and food serv., Sierra Community Hospital, Fresno, CA '85 (FOOD)
TOWNE, JOAN L., asst. adm. support serv., Perry Memorial Hospital, Princeton, IL '73 (PUR)
TOWNE, THOMAS C., dir. diet., St. Joseph Mercy Hospital, Pontiac, MI '82 (FOOD)
TOWNLEY, BETTY L., vice-pres. mktg., Piqua Memorial Medical Center, Piqua, OH '84 (PR)
TOWNLEY, NANCY C., RN, asst. vice-pres. nrsg. serv., St. Anthony's Hospital, Amarillo, TX '86 (NURS)
TOWNS, FREDERICK B., vice-pres. mktg. and pub. rel., St. Joseph Hospital West, Mount Clemens, MI '67 (PR)
TOWNSEND, CAROL S., asst. dir. human res., La Grange Memorial Hospital, La Grange, IL '86 (PERS)
TOWNSEND, CHARLES L., sr. syst. analyst, Mary Hitchcock Memorial Hospital, Hanover, NH '85 (MGMT)
TOWNSEND, GARY L., oper. analyst, Henry Ford Hospital, Detroit, MI '84 (MGMT)
TOWNSEND, LARRY, dir. risk mgt., St. Thomas Hospital, Nashville, TN '81 (RISK)
TOWNSEND, PAULINE, RN, dir. cent. serv., Somerset Medical Center, Somerville, NJ '77 (CS)
TOWNSEND, RONALD S., dir. pur., Community Hospital of Lancaster, Lancaster, PA '77 (PUR)
TOWNSEND, THEODORE E. JR., vice-pres. pub. affairs, Geisinger Medical Center, Danville, PA '81 (PR)
TOWSON, DOROTHY B., pres., Developmental Strategies, Inc., Satellite Beach, FL '82 (EDUC)
TOWSON, MARILYNN, RN, assoc. chm. nrsg., New England Medical Center, Boston, MA '71 (NURS)
TOYAMA, IRENE, mgr. educ., Riverside Community Hospital, Riverside, CA '86 (EDUC)
TOZZI, LOUIS F., dir. food serv., Bayonne Hospital, Bayonne, NJ '76 (FOOD)
TRACEY, KENNETH J., dir. pur., St. Mary's Hospital-Ozaukee, Port Washington, WI '73 (PUR)
TRACHTENBERG, JUDITH, dir. soc. work, New York Hospital, New York, NY '80 (SOC)
TRACHTENBERG, ROBIN, student, Program in Health Care Administration, Baruch College Mount Sinai School of Medicine, New York, NY '86
TRACY, JAMES E., dir. educ. serv., Meriter Hospital, Madison, WI '71 (EDUC)
TRACY, ROGER D., dir., University of Iowa Medical Center, Iowa City, IA '85 (PLNG)
TRADER, FRED W., (ret.), Fresno, CA '56 (LIFE)
TRAEGER, BARBARA S., asst. vice-pres. pub. rel., Evanston Hospital Corporation, Evanston, IL '68 (PR)
TRAFFAS, SR. M. VINCETTA, assoc. dir. health care, Sisters of St. Francis Health Services, Mishawaka, IN '73
TRAFFORD, MEL L., dir. sup. serv., Salvation Army Residential Treatment Facilities for Children and Youth, Honolulu, HI '86 (ENG)
TRAFTON, BARBARA M., vice-pres. corp. dev., Sisters of Charity Health Systems, Lewiston, ME '81 (PR)
TRAGER, KAY, RN, dir. nrsg. educ., Memorial Hospital of Southern Oklahoma, Ardmore, OK '86 (EDUC)
TRAHAN, JERRY L., med. adm., USS Peleliu, Lha-Five, FPO San Francisco, CA '82
TRAINOR, SR. AILEEN M., adm. asst. risk mgt., Sacred Heart General Hospital, Eugene, OR '83 (RISK)
TRAINOR, VIRGINIA C., mgr. mktg. serv., University Hospital, Boston, MA '86 (PR)
TRAITOR, PATRICIA J., dir. qual. assur. and risk mgt., Wood River Township Hospital, Wood River, IL '84 (RISK)
TRAMO, JOSEPH G., asst. dir., Temple University Hospital, Philadelphia, PA '82 (SOC)
TRANBARGER, RUSSELL E., RN, adm. nrsg., Moses H. Cone Memorial Hospital, Greensboro, NC '72 (NURS)
TRANEL, LT. COL. DAVID A., RN, asst. chief nrsg., Noble Army Community Hospital, Fort McClellan, AL '84 (NURS)
TRANER, DAN, (ret.), Carefree, AZ '28 (LIFE)
TRANKEL, SUSAN K., RN, clin. dir., St. Marys Hospital of Rochester, Rochester, MN '85 (NURS)
TRASOFF, NINA J., dir. news-commun., University Medical Center, Tucson, AZ '85 (PR)
TRAUGER, BYRON R., atty., Tennessee Christian Medical Center, Madison, TN '85 (ATTY)
TRAUGER, EUGENE W., dir. plant oper., Valley View Hospital, Glenwood Springs, CO '77 (ENG)
TRAULSEN, CAROLINE, ombudsman, Northwest Community Hospital, Arlington Heights, IL '78 (PAT)
TRAUM, THEODORE J., sr. vice-pres., Facilities Engineering and Design Consultants, Inc., Rockledge, PA '85 (ENG)
TRAUNTVEIN, HELEN D., RN, asst. adm. nrsg., Primary Children's Medical Center, Salt Lake City, UT '86 (NURS)
TRAUTSCH, SUSAN S., dir. pub. rel., Tuomey Hospital, Sumter, SC '82 (PR)
TRAVERS, BARBARA A., dir. environ. serv., Spaulding Rehabilitation Hospital, Boston, MA '86 (ENVIRON)
TRAVERS, JOHN EDWARD, RN, pres., Emmaus Consultants, Lynchburg, VA '80 (NURS)
TRAVIS, BARBARA A., dir. cont. educ.-health prof., Moraine Valley Community College, Palos Hills, IL '85 (EDUC)
TRAVIS, NORTON L., atty., United Hospital, Port Chester, NY '78 (ATTY)
TRAVIS, ROBERT CHARLES, vice-pres. mktg. and prog. dev., O'Connor Hospital, San Jose, CA '83 (PLNG)
TRAVIS, RONALD D., dir. environ. serv., Muscatine General Hospital, Muscatine, IA '87 (ENVIRON)
TRAVIS, ROSEMARY MCCABE, dir. vol. serv., Terre Haute Regional Hospital, Terre Haute, IN '85 (VOL)
TRAVIS, SHIRLEY, dir. nrsg. and risk mgr., Lincoln General Hospital, Lincoln, NE '85 (RISK)
TRAWICK, JAMES R., dir. matl. mgt., John D. Archbold Memorial Hospital, Thomasville, GA '82 (PUR)
TRAWICK, WALTER S., dir. pers., American Red Cross, Birmingham, AL '84 (PERS)
TRAWICKI, JOSEPH E., vice-pres. matl. mgt., Sunflower Hospital Alliance for Resources Economy, Inc., Topeka, KS '80 (PUR)
TRAYLOR, BARBARA C., dir. pub. affairs, St. Vincent's Hospital, Birmingham, AL '71 (PR)
TRAYNER, RONALD G., atty., McDermott and Trayner, Pasadena, CA '73 (ATTY)
TRAYNOR, ELIZABETH A., RN, dir. nrsg. and assoc. exec. dir., Worcester Memorial Hospital, Worcester, MA '79 (NURS)
TRAYNOR, JUDITH M., mgr. press rel. and spec. events, Mercy Hospital and Medical Center, Chicago, IL '84 (PR)
TRAYNOR, PHILIP M., dir., St. Agnes Hospital and Medical Center, Fresno, CA '87 (AMB)
TREACY, LINDA J., supv. cent. serv., Milford-Whitinsville Regional Hospital, Milford, MA '82 (CS)
TREADAWAY, DEBRA D., dir. pers., Woodward Hospital and Health Center, Woodward, OK '82 (PERS)
TREADGOLD, STEPHEN F., atty., Sharp Memorial Hospital, San Diego, CA '85 (ATTY)
TREADWAY, EARL G., vice-pres. govt. rel., Florida Hospital Associates, Inc., Orlando, FL '76
TREADWAY, GENE M., dir. vol., Baptist Hospital, Pensacola, FL '80 (VOL)
TREADWAY, JOANNE, coor. infection control, pat. educ., nrsg. qual. assur., Palm Drive Hospital, Sebastopol, CA '86 (EDUC)
TRECARTIN, MARY ANN, RN, client serv. consult., Advanced Management Information Services, Lewiston, ME '83 (EDUC)
TRECO, SHERRY, acct. supv., Ketchum Public Relations, Atlanta, GA '81 (PR)
TREECE, MICHAEL L., supv. maint., Paulding County Hospital, Paulding, OH '80 (ENG)
TREFFTZS, S. LANE, dir. maint. and eng., Lutheran Hospital, Moline, IL '84 (ENG)
TREFRY, BETSY, dir. mktg. and health educ., Holy Family Hospital, Spokane, WA '86 (PLNG)
TREFRY, ROBERT J., exec. vice-pres. and chief exec. off., St. Agnes Hospital, White Plains, NY '73
TREGURTHA, JAMES D., dir. plant eng., St. John's Hospital and Health Center, Santa Monica, CA '81 (ENG)
TREHARNE, JACK, dir. bldg., grds. and constr., Houston Northwest Medical Center, Houston, TX '85 (ENG)
TREICHLER, ROBERT L., dir. soc. serv., Rhode Island Hospital, Providence, RI '70 (SOC)
TREJO, ANNE F., account exec., Methodist Health Systems, Memphis, TN '83 (PR)
TRELEASE, JOAN WALSH, RN, dir. nrsg., Cranston General Hospital Osteopathic, Cranston, RI '86 (NURS)
TRELEVEN, RONALD P., sr. rep. pub. rel., Kaiser Foundation Hospital, Oakland, CA '84 (PR)
TREMAIN, CHRISTINE A., dir. soc. serv., Central Montana Hospital, Lewistown, MT '81 (SOC)
TREMAYNE, CLARA T., chm. pat. rep. prog., Barnes Hospital, St. Louis, MO '86 (PAT)
TREMBATH, DOUGLAS R., pres., Luther Hospital, Eau Claire, WI '74
TREMBLAY, EDMOND P. JR., Somerset, MA '76 (MGMT)
TREMBLAY, KATE, mgt. asst. ins., Children's Hospital and Health Center, San Diego, CA '87 (RISK)
TREMBLAY, PETER D., student, Rensselaer Polytechnic Institute, Troy, NY '80 (MGMT)
TREMBLAY, WILLIAM G., dir. matl. mgt., Bonnabel Hospital, Metairie, LA '82 (PUR)
TRENT, EDWARD H., dir. commun. rel., Indian River Memorial Hospital, Vero Beach, FL '80 (PR)
TRENT, HERMAN RADFORD, dir. gen. serv., Halifax-South Boston Community Hospital, South Boston, VA '65 (PUR)
TRENT, KEITH E., dir. matl. mgt., Community Hospital, Anderson, IN '82 (PUR)
TRENT, VIRGINIA R., vice-pres. mktg. and pub. rel., Children's Hospital, St. Louis, MO '80 (PR)
TRENTHAM, B. ALAN, mgt. eng., Tampa General Hospital, Tampa, FL '87 (MGMT)
TRESTER, KENNETH G., dir. plng. and mktg., University of Michigan Medical Center, Ann Arbor, MI '70 (PR)
TREVATHAN, RON, supv. plant oper., Memorial Hospital of Carbon County, Rawlins, WY '87 (ENG)
TREVELYAN, EOIN W., lecturer-mgt., Harvard University, Boston, MA '82 (PLNG)
TREVISON, JUDY, dir. vol. serv., Rockville General Hospital, Rockville, CT '80 (VOL)(PAT)
TREWILER, LOIS E., RN, dir. nrsg. serv., Coshocton County Memorial Hospital, Coshocton, OH '78 (NURS)
TREXLER, DAVID V., exec. dir., Decatur County Memorial Hospital, Greensburg, IN '64
TREXLER, PATRICIA, supv. cent. serv., Lutheran Home at Topton, Topton, PA '79 (CS)
TREZEK, JOAN, vice-pres. pub. affairs, John Muir Memorial Hospital, Walnut Creek, CA '81 (PR)
TREZISE, BARBARA S., coor. soc. serv., Memorial Hospital, Owosso, MI '85 (SOC)
TRIBECK, ROBERT E., adm., Rehabilitation Hospital for Special Services of Nittany Valley, Bellofonte, PA '84
TRIBULSKI, JEAN A., dir. nrsg. educ., Overlook Hospital, Summit, NJ '83 (EDUC)
TRICE, GLENDA A., dir. mktg. and pub. rel., Cumberland Medical Center, Crossville, TN '85 (PR)
TRICE, LARRY F., vice-pres. mktg. and acquisitions, Springhill Memorial Hospital, Mobile, AL '86
TRICK, CHRISTOPHER E., dir. pub. rel., Jefferson Memorial Hospital, Alexandria, VA '85 (PR)
TRICKEL, WILLIAM JR., atty., Florida Hospital Medical Center, Orlando, FL '69 (ATTY)
TRICKLER, BETTY J., LaPorte, IN '83 (NURS)
TRIEBES, DAVID GLENN, adm., Charter Community Hospital, Des Moines, IA '79 (PERS)
TRIEFENBACH, RUTH, RN, vice-pres. nrsg., Deaconess Hospital, St. Louis, MO '75 (NURS)
TRIFARI, LEOPOLD M., MD, (ret.), Boynton Beach, FL '73
TRIGLIA, CHRISTYN N., asst. dir. vol. serv., St. Joseph Hospital, Orange, CA '85 (VOL)
TRILLING, HELEN R., atty., New York University Medical Center, New York, NY '85 (ATTY)
TRIMARCO, PHILIP ANTHONY, oper. asst., American Medical International, Irving, TX '76
TRIMBLE, RUSSELL L., dir. res. and dev., Puritan-Bennett Corporation, Lenexa, KS '76 (ENG)(AMB)
TRIMBLE, TAMARA L., atty., Adventist Health System-Sunbelt, Orlando, FL '82 (ATTY)
TRIMIGLIOZZI, VIRGINIA R., syst. analyst asst., Jersey Shore Medical Center, Neptune, NJ '85 (MGMT)
TRIMM, JERRY M., dir. mgt. eng., Baptist Medical Centers, Birmingham, AL '80 (MGMT)
TRINDER, LT. DOUGLAS W., MSC USN, staff civil eng. and head facil. mgt., Naval Hospital, Camp Pendleton, CA '85 (ENG)
TRINKLE, PENNY S., mgr., McAuley Health Plan, Ann Arbor, MI '87 (PAT)
TRINKLEIN, JOAN KAY, RN, vice-pres. nrsg., Saginaw General Hospital, Saginaw, MI '79 (NURS)
TRIOLO, EILEEN, asst. dir. nrsg. and staff dev., Hospital for Special Surgery, New York, NY '83 (EDUC)
TRIPLETT, JANET B., mgr. vol. serv., Watertown Memorial Hospital, Watertown, WI '77 (VOL)
TRIPLETT, ROBERT E., mgr. info. syst., Forsyth Memorial Hospital, Winston-Salem, NC '86 (MGMT)
TRIPLETT, THOMAS M., atty., Good Samaritan Hospital and Medical Center, Portland, OR '82 (ATTY)
TRIPP, JOHN W., dir. plant oper., Humana Hospital -Medical City Dallas, Dallas, TX '85 (ENG)
TRIPP, LYNNE D., mgr. pub. rel., Mercy Hospital, Muskegon, MI '85 (PR)
TRIPP, PERRY D. JR., dir. eng., Greenville Hospital System, Greenville, SC '78 (ENG)
TRIPP, VIRGINIA A., supv. and chief dispatcher, Salvation Army William Booth Memorial Hospital, Florence, KY '85 (CS)
TRISDALE, VICKI R., vice-pres., Shared Services for Southern Hospitals, Inc., Orlando, FL '86 (PUR)
TRISSEL, RONALD L., Saints Mary and Elizabeth Hospital, Louisville, KY '70 (FOOD)

TRITCHLER, DIANA M., coor. health promotion, U. S. Air Force Hospital, Cheyenne, WY '85 (EDUC)
TRITSCH, WALTER, dir. plant oper. and maint., Riverside Hospital, Wichita, KS '83 (ENG)
TRIULZI, ANTHONY R., chief exec. off., Kingston Hospital, Kingston, NY '59
TRKULA, MELVIN, adm. facil. plng. and mgt., South Hills Health System, Pittsburgh, PA '80 (ENG)
TROELLER, LAURENCE C., eng. consult., Brunswick General Hospital, Amityville, NY '85 (ENG)
TROFINO, JOAN, RN, vice-pres. pat. care serv., Riverview Medical Center, Red Bank, NJ '79 (NURS)
TROIANO, CHRISTIAN L., assoc., Lammers and Gershon, Associates, Reston, VA '79 (PUR)
TROISI, ANGELO J., chief adm. serv., U. S. Army Medical Command, Washington, DC '67
TROMBLEY, DENNIS, chief eng., Granada Hills Community Hospital, Granada Hills, CA '83 (ENG)
TROMBLEY, MARIANNE C., dir. pub. rel. and vol., Soldiers and Sailors Memorial Hospital, Penn Yan, NY '85 (PR)
TROMBLY, CAROL A., dir. commun. rel., Lakes Region General Hospital, Laconia, NH '84 (PR)
TROMBLY, EDGAR GENE, Gibbstown, NJ '75 (ENG)
TROMBLY, SUZANNE M., mgr. educ., Dominican Santa Cruz Hospital, Santa Cruz, CA '82 (EDUC)
TROMPETER, SR. M. DAVID, dir. soc. serv., Saint James Hospital, Pontiac, IL '77 (SOC)
TRONDSEN, ELLIE HARMS, RN, vice-pres. pat. care, San Jose Hospital, San Jose, CA '86 (NURS)
TRONNES, HANS F., chief exec. off., Hans Tronnes Associates, St. Louis Park, MN '65 (PLNG)
TROOP, SHERRY SMITH, dir. pat. rel., North Carolina Baptist Hospital, Winston-Salem, NC '84 (PAT)
TROPIANO, MICHAEL, dir. maint. and plant oper., Thomas Jefferson University Hospital, Philadelphia, PA '85 (ENG)
TROSTY, R. STEPHEN, dir. risk mgt., Lutheran Hospitals and Home Society, Fargo, ND '83 (RISK)
TROTT, WIN, dir. matl. mgt., Children's Hospital of the King's Daughters, Norfolk, VA '83 (PUR)
TROTTER, JAMIE LEE, adm. pat. rep., Doctors Regional Medical Center, Poplar Bluff, MO '86 (PAT)
TROUE, J. PAUL, atty., Leonard Hospital, Troy, NY '69 (ATTY)
TROUT, KENNETH L., MSC USAF, dir. med. logistics mgt., U. S. Air Force Clinic Bentwaters, APO New York, NY '86
TROUTMAN, A. KEVIN, mgr. pers. and mktg., Humana Hospital -Lake Charles, Lake Charles, LA '86 (PR)
TROUTMAN, AUDREY J., mgr. vol., Frick Community Health Center, Mount Pleasant, PA '84 (VOL)
TROW, SUZANNE, assoc. dir., Halifax Health Network, Daytona Beach, FL '86
TROWBRIDGE, FLORENCE, supv. hskpg., Tyler Memorial Hospital, Tunkhannock, PA '86 (ENVIRON)
TROWBRIDGE, PATRICK H., mgr. cent. proc., Saint Francis Hospital, Tulsa, OK '84 (CS)
TROWBRIDGE, VERN H., asst. adm., Children's Hospital of the King's Daughters, Norfolk, VA '80 (ENG)(MGMT)
TROWNSELL, MARILYN, assoc. dir. food serv., Abbott-Northwestern Hospital, Minneapolis, MN '82 (FOOD)
TROXLER, KAY K., mgr. pers., Dch Regional Medical Center, Tuscaloosa, AL '86 (PERS)
TROY, JOAN S., dir. vol. serv., Kimball Medical Center, Lakewood, NJ '85 (VOL)
TROY, PATRICK J., RN, asst. chief nrsg. serv., Veterans Administration Medical Center, Washington, DC '83 (NURS)
TROY, SHIRLEY A., coor. soc. serv., HCA Medical Center of Port St. Lucie, Port St. Lucie, FL '86 (SOC)
TROY, THOMAS J., adm., Central Washington Hospital, Wenatchee, WA '71
TROYER, GLENN T., atty., William N. Wishard Memorial Hospital, Indianapolis, IN '79 (RISK)(ATTY)
TROYER, JEFF, dir. matl. mgt., Moberly Regional Medical Center, Moberly, MO '86 (PUR)
TRUAX, SHELDON K., pres., Truax Associates, Laramie, WY '80
TRUBOFF, CHARLES, dir. soc. serv., Winthrop Hospital, Winthrop, MA '79 (SOC)
TRUDEAU, TERRY W., Ochsner Foundation Hospital, New Orleans, LA '80 (MGMT)
TRUDELL, THOMAS J., pres. and chief exec. off., Marymount Hospital, Garfield Heights, OH '78 (PLNG)
TRUE, ROBERT MERLE, dir. food serv., Columbus Hospital, Chicago, IL '79 (FOOD)
TRUESDELL, JEANIE F., asst. dir. pers., Baptist Medical System, Little Rock, AR '83 (PERS)
TRUETT, WALTER K., chief contracting br., Brooke Army Medical Center, San Antonio, TX '85 (PUR)
TRUITT, GARY R., vice-pres. and atty., Blue Cross of Western Pennsylvania, Pittsburgh, PA '85 (ATTY)
TRUITT, K. RAY, vice-pres. plng. and mktg., Bethany Medical Center, Kansas City, KS '86 (PLNG)
TRUITT, MARSHA A., coor. vol., Vermillion County Hospital, Clinton, IN '86 (VOL)
TRUITT, SONNY, dir. pur., Wilson County Hospital, Neodesha, KS '84 (PUR)
TRUJILLO, CAROL V., dir. staff dev., Lakewood Hospital, Tacoma, WA '84 (EDUC)
TRUJILLO, SANDRA M., pat. rep., Beth Israel Hospital, Denver, CO '85 (PAT)
TRULL, DAVID J., exec. vice-pres., New England Medical Center, Boston, MA '74
TRULLI, ALPHONSO A., adm. eng., St. Elizabeth's Hospital of Boston, Boston, MA '86 (ENG)
TRULUCK, ROGER S., asst. dir. maint., Shands Hospital, Gainesville, FL '85 (ENG)
TRUMAN, GEORGE HAROLD JR., sr. adm. food serv., Center General Hospital, Howard, RI '84
TRUMBO, CLIFFORD R., dir. gen. serv., Good Shepherd Rehabilitation Hospital, Allentown, PA '84 (PUR)
TRUMBORE, MICHAEL D., dir. clin. eng., Charlotte Memorial Hospital and Medical Center, Charlotte, NC '85 (ENG)
TRUMBULL, ALICE I., coor. claims mgt., Society of the New York Hospital, New York, NY '82 (RISK)
TRUMP, JOAN B., sr. soc. worker, Children's Hospital, Buffalo, NY '86 (SOC)
TRUOG, NICHOLAS F., supt. bldg. and grds., Kaiser Foundation Hospital-San Rafael, San Rafael, CA '79 (ENG)
TRUSKOWSKI, FAYE K., RN, dir. nrsg., Auburn General Hospital, Auburn, WA '71 (NURS)
TRUSTEM, DAN C., asst. vice-pres. mgt. info. syst., St. Joseph's Hospital, Marshfield, WI '86 (MGMT)
TRYON, ALINE ELLEN, RN, vice-pres. pat. care serv., Hackettstown Community Hospital, Hackettstown, NJ '86 (NURS)
TRYON, GEOFFREY P., adm. asst., Silver Cross Hospital, Joliet, IL '81
TSAHAKIS, GEORGE JOHN, dir. primary care serv., Baptist Medical Centers, Birmingham, AL '78
TSAI, MARGARET KAN, adm. diet., St. Vincent Medical Center, Los Angeles, CA '79 (FOOD)
TSAI, YIN-FENG THOMAS, student, Program in Hospital Administration, China Medical College, Taichung City Taiwan, Republic of China '87 (PERS)
TSCHETTER, BARBARA R., coor. pat. educ., Huron Regional Medical Center, Huron, SD '85 (EDUC)
TSCHETTER, STAN, dir. eng., St. Anthony Medical Center, Crown Point, IN '84 (ENG)
TSENG, SIMONE, dir. mktg., University of Chicago Medical Center, Chicago, IL '80 (PLNG)
TSUE, ROBERT, assoc. vice-pres., St. Luke's-Roosevelt Hospital Center, New York, NY '84 (MGMT)
TUBB, MARILYN L., dir. mktg. and commun., HCA North Florida Regional Medical Center, Gainesville, FL '81 (PR)(PLNG)
TUBIASH, HOLLY E., sr. consult., CHI Systems, Inc., Philadelphia, PA '84 (PLNG)
TUCCI, BARBARA V., RN, dir. nrsg. serv., El Dorado Hospital and Medical Center, Tucson, AZ '75 (NURS)
TUCK, ELEANOR E., exec. dir., Edna Gladney Home, Fort Worth, TX '82 (SOC)
TUCKER, ALICE, dir. vol. serv., Rehabilitation Hospital of the Pacific, Honolulu, HI '80 (VOL)
TUCKER, CHARLES E., proj. arch. med. div., Haldeman Miller Bregman Hamann, Dallas, TX '86
TUCKER, DAVID A., New Boston, NH '71
TUCKER, DAVID CHRISTOPHER, dir. pers., Jesse Holman Jones Hospital, Springfield, TN '79 (PERS)
TUCKER, DENNIS L., dir. mktg., Holy Family Hospital, Des Plaines, IL '83 (PLNG)
TUCKER, EASTER G., RN, asst. dir. nrsg., Rochester General Hospital, Rochester, NY '82 (NURS)
TUCKER, EDGAR, mgr. plant maint., St. Joseph's Hospital and Medical Center, Phoenix, AZ '86 (ENG)
TUCKER, FORD II, soc. worker, Cleveland Clinic Hospital, Cleveland, OH '75 (SOC)
TUCKER, GAYLE S., dir. pub. rel., Bristol Hospital, Bristol, CT '86 (PR)
TUCKER, GAYLE S., dir. educ. and qual. assur., Forrest County General Hospital, Hattiesburg, MS '86 (EDUC)
TUCKER, J. HOUSTON JR., dir. pers. and pub. rel., Carteret General Hospital, Morehead City, NC '85 (PR)
TUCKER, JACQUELINE W., RN, coor. staff dev., St. Joseph Hospital, Kirkwood, MO '76 (EDUC)
TUCKER, JERRY, chief eng., Tuolumne General Hospital, Sonora, CA '85 (ENG)
TUCKER, LAWRENCE J., health syst. spec., Veterans Administration Medical Center, Dayton, OH '76 (MGMT)
TUCKER, LINDA, asst. adm. pub. affairs and dev., Piedmont Hospital, Atlanta, GA '80 (RISK)(PR)
TUCKER, MELODY SUE, plng. analyst, Community Hospitals of Central California, Fresno, CA '86 (PLNG)
TUCKER, PAUL J., sr. consult., The Marketing Works, Boston, TX '86 (PLNG)
TUCKER, RICHARD D., dir. pers., Wabash County Hospital, Wabash, IN '74 (PERS)
TUCKER, RUTH H., dir. commun. rel., Lapeer General Hospital, LaPeer, MI '77 (PR)
TUCKER, STEPHEN L., prof., Department of Health Care Administration, Trinity University, San Antonio, TX '71 (PLNG)
TUCKER, SUSAN E., student, Ferris State College, Big Rapids, MI '86
TUCKER, WILLIAM P., atty., Church Charity Foundation of Long Island, Hempstead, NY '83 (ATTY)
TUCKETT, ROBERT B., dir. eng., Cannon St. Louis, Inc., St. Louis, MO '86 (ENG)
TUCKMAN, ERIC, vice-pres. legal affairs, Centinela Hospital Medical Center, Inglewood, CA '80 (ATTY)
TUCKNOTT, ROSELLA R., Minnetonka, MN '57 (PUR)(LIFE)
TUDOR, LT. COL. JAMES H. III, MSC USA, chief res. mgt., Army-Baylor Program in Health Administration, Fort Sam Houston, TX '76
TUE, KATHLEEN A., health care analyst, Veterans Administration Medical Center, Minneapolis, MN '82 (PLNG)
TUELL, HENRY O. III, pers. assignment off., Department of the Army, Office of the Surgeon General, Washington, DC '80
TUETKEN, JINNY, dir. pub. rel., St. Elizabeth Medical Center, Granite City, IL '81 (PR)
TUFTS, THOMAS C., pres., Tufts and Wenzel, Architects, Inc., Cleveland, OH '78
TUGGLE, PAUL K., Norcross, GA '86 (RISK)
TUKE, JAY R., adm. asst., Louis A. Weiss Memorial Hospital, Chicago, IL '80
TULIANO, GERALD A., dir. plant oper., Glades General Hospital, Belle Glade, FL '80 (ENG)
TULL, LEONA B., dir. in-service, Nanticoke Memorial Hospital, Seaford, DE '77 (EDUC)
TULLER, EDWIN, vice-pres. corp. plng., American Hospital Association, Chicago, IL '84 (PLNG)
TULLIN, JHAN PATRICIA, dir. soc. serv., Kaiser Foundation Hospital, Martinez, CA '85 (SOC)
TULLIUS, VICTORIA L., dir. soc. serv., N. T. Enloe Memorial Hospital, Chico, CA '82 (SOC)
TULLOCH, THOMAS J., asst. dir. eng. serv., Baptist Hospital of Miami, Miami, FL '83 (ENG)
TULLY-CINTRON, MICHAEL, adm. asst., Kaiser Foundation Hospital, Martinez, CA '87 (RISK)
TULLY, SALLY A., mgr. hlthquest, Virginia Beach General Hospital, Virginia Beach, VA '86 (EDUC)
TUMEY, LINCOLN E., dir. support serv., Southwest Florida Regional Medical Center, Fort Myers, FL '79
TUMULTY, GAIL, RN, asst. dir. nrsg.-med. and surg. areas, Ochsner Foundation Hospital, New Orleans, LA '85 (NURS)
TUNESI, ANGELO J., mgr. bldg., Mount Carmel Mercy Hospital and Medical Center, Detroit, MI '65 (ENG)
TUNNO, ELIZABETH CHRISTINE, pat. rep., Broward General Medical Center, Fort Lauderdale, FL '87 (PAT)
TUNNO, RICHARD H., dir. educ., Winter Park Memorial Hospital, Winter Park, FL '82 (EDUC)
TUNTLAND, CRAIG A., dir. pub. rel., Silver Cross Hospital, Joliet, IL '86 (PR)
TURBENSON, THOMAS J., student, Concordia College, Moorhead, MN '85
TURBIE, MARIE A., RN, vice-pres. pat. care serv., St. Vincent's Medical Center, Bridgeport, CT '70 (NURS)
TURCO, CAPT. RONALD FISHER, MSC USN, head health care operation, Office of Chief of Naval Operations, Washington, DC '77
TUREK, ELAINE, student, College of Lake County, Grayslake, IL '86
TURENNE, VIOLET, RN, nrs. adm., Rochelle Community Hospital, Rochelle, IL '68 (NURS)
TURK, ALICE M., RN, dir. nrsg., Deckerville Community Hospital, Deckerville, MI '81 (NURS)
TURK, J. STANLEY, consult., Ohio Valley Medical Center, Wheeling, WV '28 (LIFE)
TURK, MARY L., atty., Alexian Brothers Medical Center, Elk Grove Village, IL '85 (ATTY)
TURK, PAMELA N., RN, vice-pres. nrsg., Sherman Hospital, Elgin, IL '86 (NURS)
TURK, PATRICIA R., info. syst. analyst and programmer, Baylor Enterprises Group, Dallas, TX '84 (MGMT)
TURKE, KATHLEEN M., dir. soc. serv., Southwood Community Hospital, Norfolk, MA '84 (SOC)
TURLEY, GAIL N., RN, asst. dir. nrsg., Crozer-Chester Medical Center, Chester, PA '86 (NURS)
TURNBACH, SR. ANN, vice-pres. prof. serv., Sacred Heart Hospital, Allentown, PA '85
TURNBULL, JIM, sr. vice-pres., Red Deer Regional Hospital Centre, Red Deer, Alta., Canada '77 (MGMT)
TURNBULL, JOANNE, head psych. soc. work, Duke University Hospital, Durham, NC '85 (SOC)
TURNBULL, SHELBY, facil. energy mgt. eng., Moberly Regional Medical Center, Moberly, MO '85 (ENG)
TURNER-HINER, FLORIDA LILLIAN, exec. diet., Illinois Children's School and Rehabilitation Center, Chicago, IL '87 (FOOD)
TURNER, BARBARA A., RN, dir. qual. assur., Hunterdon Medical Center, Flemington, NJ '77 (RISK)
TURNER, BERTHA L., dir. soc. serv., Vicksburg Medical Center, Vicksburg, MS '86 (SOC)
TURNER, BETTYE H., asst. dir. soc. serv., Presbyterian-University of Pennsylvania Medical Center, Philadelphia, PA '85 (SOC)
TURNER, CAROLYN C., clin. nrs. spec., Memorial Medical Center, Long Beach, CA '84 (EDUC)
TURNER, CHARLENE S., coor. nrsg. educ., Asbury Hospital, Salina, KS '87 (EDUC)
TURNER, CHARLENE, dir. soc. serv., Grady Memorial Hospital, Atlanta, GA '74 (SOC)
TURNER, CHARLES A. III, exec. dir., Coalition for Cost Effective Health Services, Columbus, OH '79 (PLNG)
TURNER, CHERRYL A., mgt. eng., Grady Memorial Hospital, Atlanta, GA '81 (MGMT)
TURNER, DAVID W., dir. matl. mgt., Methodist Hospital, Hattiesburg, MS '82 (PUR)
TURNER, DEBORAH D., dir. commun. rel., Chickasawba Hospital, Mississippi County Hospitals, Blytheville, AR '82 (PR)
TURNER, DOROTHY L., RN, dir. nrsg., Department of Health and Hospitals, Boston, MA '86 (NURS)
TURNER, FRANK J. JR., dir. plant serv. and eng., Miami Valley Hospital, Dayton, OH '75 (ENG)
TURNER, GLADYS T., coor. outpatient and consult. educ. serv., Daymont West Community Mental Health Center, Dayton, OH '72 (SOC)
TURNER, GLORIA A., dir. pat. rel., New York City Health and Hospitals Corporation, New York, NY '75 (PAT)
TURNER, GREGORY W., pres., Lima Memorial Hospital, Lima, OH '82
TURNER, JAMES C., assoc. vice-pres. corp. dev., Fallston General Hospital, Fallston, MD '84 (PLNG)
TURNER, JAMES R., assoc. dean adm., University of North Carolina at Chapel Hill, School of Medicine, Chapel Hill, NC '71
TURNER, JEFFREY, adm., Bexar County Hospital District, San Antonio, TX '78
TURNER, JOHN G., dir. phys. plant, Northwest Community Hospital, Arlington Heights, IL '80 (ENG)
TURNER, JOHN L., mgr. eng., Amsterdam Memorial Hospital, Amsterdam, NY '87 (ENG)
TURNER, JOSEPHINE V., dir. soc. serv., University of Connecticut Health Center, John Dempsey Hospital, Farmington, CT '66 (SOC)
TURNER, JULIA A., RN, vice-pres., St. Anthony Medical Center, Columbus, OH '76 (NURS)
TURNER, KENNETH G., sr. vice-pres., Sacred Heart Hospital, Allentown, PA '75
TURNER, LINDA COFFEY, dir. vol. serv., St. Anthony Medical Center, Columbus, OH '78 (VOL)
TURNER, LORETTA F., asst. dir. nrsg., Winchester Medical Center, Winchester, VA '86 (EDUC)

TURNER, M. KENT, prin., Pearce Corporation, St. Louis, MO '85 (ENG)
TURNER, MARGARET ROBERTSON, pat. advocate, Marquette General Hospital, Marquette, MI '87 (PAT)
TURNER, MARILYN A., RN, dir. nrsg., Bethany General Hospital, Bethany, OK '85 (NURS)
TURNER, MARY M., coor. vol., Harding Hospital, Worthington, OH '78 (VOL)
TURNER, MICHAEL G., serv. adm. dept. of psych., Strong Memorial Hospital, Rochester, NY '86
TURNER, NAN, dir. registration and commun., Commonwealth Hospital, Fairfax, VA '86 (ENG)
TURNER, PATRICK, mgr. strategic plng., Providence Hospital, Cincinnati, OH '82 (PLNG)
TURNER, PAULETA ANN, dir. diet., Memorial Hospital, Colorado Springs, CO '74 (FOOD)
TURNER, PHILIP L., dir. matl. mgt., Mercy Catholic Medical Center, Darby, PA '83 (PUR)
TURNER, R. J., asst. dir., North Hills Passavant Hospital, Pittsburgh, PA '75
TURNER, RHONA L., mgr. pat. food serv., Chedoke-McMaster Hospitals, Hamilton, Ont., Canada '83 (FOOD)
TURNER, RICHARD W., dir. util. mgt., Medical Center of Central Georgia, Macon, GA '81
TURNER, SPENCER MORGAN, staff asst. eng., Hurley Medical Center, Flint, MI '86 (ENG)
TURNER, STEPHANIE A., pat. rep., Memorial Hospital, Charleston, WV '84 (PAT)
TURNER, TERRY T., mgr. plng. and syst., Boca Raton Community Hospital, Boca Raton, FL '82 (MGMT)
TURNER, WILLIAM K., pres., Newport Hospital, Newport, RI '46 (LIFE)
TURNER, WILLIAM W., field rep., Joint Commission on Accreditation of Hospitals, Chicago, IL '52 (LIFE)
TURNER, WILLIAM, chief biomedical eng., King Khalid Eye Specialist Hospital, Riyadh, Saudi Arabia '86 (ENG)
TURNER, WOODROW W. JR., atty., Loudoun Memorial Hospital, Leesburg, VA '79 (ATTY)
TURNEY, A. WARREN, MD, pres., Surgicenters of Michiana, Wolcottville, IN '87 (AMB)
TURNIS, RUTH M., RN, dir. pat., Mercy Health Center, Dubuque, IA '82 (NURS)
TURNLEY, PAUL D., adm., Preventive Medicine Institute, Strang Clinic, New York, NY '81
TURPIN, JUDITH M., buyer, Memorial Hospital, Belleville, IL '86 (PUR)
TURPIN, WILLIAM D., asst. adm., Providence Hospital, Southfield, MI '79 (MGMT)
TURRI, JAMES, vice-pres. ancillary serv., Hazleton-St. Joseph Medical Center, Hazleton, PA '86
TURRIGIANO, ROSEMARIE, pat. rep. and ombudsman, Mendocino Coast District Hospital, Fort Bragg, CA '79 (PAT)
TURUNJIAN, PAULA B., dir. risk mgt., Daniel Freeman Memorial Hospital, Inglewood, CA '82 (RISK)
TURZA, DALE CHAKARIAN, atty., Rogers and Wells, Washington, DC '82 (ATTY)
TUSCHER, ELIZABETH ANN, dir. pur., Little Company of Mary Hospital, Evergreen Park, IL '83 (PUR)
TUSSEY, FREDA B., supv. cent. serv., Highlands Regional Medical Center, Prestonsburg, KY '74 (CS)
TUSTIN, WILLIAM C., dir. matl. mgt., Washington Hospital, Washington, PA '74 (PUR)
TUTAJ, GEORGE A., EdD, assoc. chief bldg. mgt., Veterans Administration Medical Center, Buffalo, NY '81 (MGMT)
TUTEN, ARTHUR A., vice-pres. pers., North Carolina Baptist Hospital, Winston-Salem, NC '80 (PERS)
TUTEN, E. ALLEN, asst. adm., Lincoln General Hospital, Ruston, LA '70
TUTHILL, ESTELLE L., atty., Baptist Medical Centers Corporate Office, Birmingham, AL '82 (ATTY)
TUTHILL, ROBERT C., dir. human res., Middlesex Memorial Hospital, Middletown, CT '86 (PERS)
TUTTLE, BARBARA, dir. soc. work, Rockville General Hospital, Rockville, CT '81 (SOC)
TUTTLE, BETTY, RN, dir. in-service, Memorial Hospital, Carthage, IL '76 (EDUC)
TUTTLE, EMILY J., nrsg. consult., Southwest Community Health Services, Albuquerque, NM '68 (NURS)
TUTTLE, PHYLLIS C., dir. plng., Memorial Hospitals Association, Modesto, CA '85 (PLNG)
TUTTLE, RUSSELL J., dir. commun. rel., Botsford General Hospital, Farmington Hills, MI '86 (PR)
TUVESON, ROBERT F., pres., Health Care Management Studies and Services, Inc., Ponte Vedra Beach, FL '51 (LIFE)
TWARDOS, JOHN J., adm. asst., John F. Kennedy Medical Center, Chicago, IL '83
TWARYNSKI, ANGIE, dir. staff dev., Santa Monica Hospital Medical Center, Santa Monica, CA '75 (EDUC)
TWIGG, JAMES C., adm. asst. plant and grds., Sacred Heart Hospital, Cumberland, MD '76 (ENG)
TWILLEY, JOSEPHINE GRAY, RN, coor. pat. rep. prog., Pitt County Memorial Hospital, Greenville, NC '81 (PAT)
TWILLEY, STEVEN N., dir. dev. and pub. rel., Children's Hospital, Baltimore, MD '79 (PR)
TWITTY, H. R., dir. pur. serv., Memorial Hospital, Chattanooga, TN '78 (PUR)
TWOMEY, GERRI L., atty., Lutheran Hospitals and Home Society, Fargo, ND '81 (ATTY)
TWOMEY, RONALD D., vice-pres. human res., Parkview Memorial Hospital, Fort Wayne, IN '64 (PERS)
TWOMEY, TIM T., dir. pur. serv., Washington Hospital, Fremont, CA '77 (PUR)
TWYON, SANDRA P., chm. nrsg., New England Medical Center, Boston, MA '77 (NURS)
TYE, W. RANDALL, atty., Smyrna Hospital, Smyrna, GA '85 (ATTY)
TYJEWSKI, PAUL G., RN, dir. surg. serv., Mercy Hospital, Muskegon, MI '84 (NURS)
TYLER, GEORGE T., atty., St. Agnes Hospital of the City of Baltimore, Baltimore, MD '68 (ATTY)
TYLER, J. LARRY, pres., Tyler and Company, Atlanta, GA '86
TYLER, JAMES, atty., Skiff Medical Center, Newton, IA '68 (ATTY)
TYLER, MARION H., sr. coor. discharge plng., Rex Hospital, Raleigh, NC '86 (SOC)
TYLER, MARY L., dir. soc. serv., Scottsdale Camelback Hospital, Scottsdale, AZ '85 (SOC)
TYLER, MARY L., RN, adm. nrsg., United Hospital, St. Paul, MN '79 (NURS)
TYLER, PATRICIA D., RN, asst. vice-pres. nrsg., Memorial Hospital, North Little Rock, AR '77 (NURS)
TYLUS, F. KEVIN, mgr., Touche Ross and Company, Newark, NJ '84
TYNAN, JUDY L., mgr. advertising and commun., Olin Water Services, Overland Park, KS '85 (ENG)
TYNAN, THOMAS J., mgr. soc. work serv., Christ Hospital and Medical Center, Oak Lawn, IL '83 (SOC)
TYNDALL, EARL H. JR., exec. dir., Medical Park Hospital, Winston-Salem, NC '84 (RISK)
TYNE, MICHAEL D., exec. vice-pres., Karlsberger Companies, Columbus, OH '68
TYNES, ANNA GRAHAM, dir. soc. serv., Singing River Hospital System, Pascagoula, MS '86 (SOC)
TYRA, HOWARD D., dir. plant oper., Carraway Methodist Medical Center, Birmingham, AL '73 (ENG)
TYRE, JANIE, student, University of Southern California, Sacramento, CA '84 (PLNG)
TYREE, LISA D., dir. vol. serv., Cabell Huntington Hospital, Huntington, WV '85 (VOL)
TYREE, SHERRELL H., corp. dir. pers., Truman Medical Center-West, Kansas City, MO '86 (PERS)
TYSMAN, LEWIS W., coor. commun. rel., Borgess Medical Center, Kalamazoo, MI '84 (PR)
TYSON, CHARLES E., pres., Dannemiller Tyson, Inc., Ann Arbor, MI '86 (PERS)
TYSON, SHIRLEY A., RN, asst. adm., Northern Columbiana County Community Hospital, Salem, OH '73 (NURS)
TYTLER, LINN J., dir. mktg., St. Joseph Health Care Corporation, Albuquerque, NM '85 (PLNG)

U

UBOLDI, MICHAEL J., RN, dir. critical care and med. div., Good Samaritan Hospital and Medical Center, Portland, OR '83 (NURS)
UBSDELL, KENNETH W., mgr. mgt. and info. serv., Kaiser Permanente Medical Care, Walnut Creek, CA '86 (MGMT)
UCHI, THERESA I., sr. mgt. eng., University of California at Los Angeles Medical Center, Los Angeles, CA '84 (MGMT)
UDKOFF, LEORA B., assoc. dir. plng., Cedars-Sinai Medical Center, Los Angeles, CA '82 (PLNG)
UDOVICH, G. WILLIAM, adm., Frostburg Community Hospital, Frostburg, MD '82 (PERS)
UEBELHER, WILLIAM J., dir. educ., Saint Joseph Hospital, Denver, CO '82 (EDUC)
UEMURA, COL. EDWARD H., MSC USA, dep. cmdr. adm., MEDDAC, Fort Meade, MD '69
UFFINGER, TONI SMERAGLIA, dir. soc. work serv., Baptist Medical Center-Princeton, Birmingham, AL '78 (SOC)
UGWUEKE, MICHAEL O., planner, Georgia Baptist Medical Center, Atlanta, GA '86 (PLNG)
UHL, DEBRA L., asst. adm., Vanderbilt University Hospital, Nashville, TN '79
UHLMAN, LARRY, dir. plant oper., Millcreek Community Hospital, Erie, PA '81 (ENG)
UHR, BERNARD, dir. food serv., Medical Center for Aging, Doylestown, PA '81 (FOOD)
UHRICH, BRUCE A., coor. health educ., Doylestown Hospital, Doylestown, PA '87 (EDUC)
UKRIN, DAWN, mgr. cent. sterile proc., Edward Hospital, Naperville, IL '85 (CS)
ULAN, MARTIN S., trustee, York Hospital, York, ME '53 (LIFE)
ULATOWSKI, ADRIAN T., atty., St. Mary's Hospital Medical Center, Green Bay, WI '84 (ATTY)
ULATOWSKI, KENNETH F., dir. mgt. eng., Memorial Medical Center of Jacksonville, Jacksonville, FL '82 (MGMT)
ULFELDER, THOMAS H., Lincoln, MA '85
ULITT, LILLY R., Coronado, CA '80 (FOOD)
ULLERY, JEANETTE DONEY, dir. educ., St. Luke's Regional Medical Center, Boise, ID '85 (EDUC)
ULLMAN, CURTIS, atty., John C. Lincoln Hospital and Health Center, Phoenix, AZ '85 (ATTY)
ULMER, DEBORAH L., dir. in-service educ., Chippenham Hospital, Richmond, VA '78 (EDUC)
ULMER, HARRIET GLASS, dir. plng. and mktg., Hospital of the Good Samaritan, Los Angeles, CA '81 (PLNG)
ULMER, JOAN H., RN, asst. vice-pres. nrsg., Allegheny General Hospital, Pittsburgh, PA '86 (NURS)
ULREY, WALTER D., dir. matl. mgt., Woman's Hospital, Jackson, MS '85 (PUR)
ULRICH, BETH B., dir. soc. serv., Virginia Baptist Hospital, Lynchburg, VA '82 (SOC)
ULRICH, BETH T., RN, dir. renal serv. and nrsg. res. and dev., Hermann Hospital, Houston, TX '86 (NURS)
ULRICH, DOLORES, risk mgr. asst., Mercy Hospital, Port Huron, MI '86 (RISK)
ULRICH, LOIS M., dir. vol. serv., Masonic Home and Charity Fund, Burlington, NJ '86 (VOL)
ULRICH, RICK P., mktg. res. analyst, St. Vincent Medical Center, Toledo, OH '85 (PLNG)
UMANSKY, PAUL, dir. commun. rel., Sinai Hospital of Baltimore, Baltimore, MD '76 (PR)
UMBDENSTOCK, RICHARD J., pres. bd. dir., Group Health Cooperative of Puget Sound, Spokane, WA '85
UMBECK, JOHN A., corp. dir. pur., Evangelical Health Systems, Oak Brook, IL '78 (PUR)
UMBS, JOAN M., cent. serv. tech., New Berlin Memorial Hospital, New Berlin, WI '86 (CS)
UMEDA, JANE S., dir. diet. serv., Kuakini Medical Center, Honolulu, HI '81 (FOOD)
UMFRID, KATHY K., div. mgr. clin. support serv., Deaconess Medical Center, Billings, MT '85 (NURS)
UMMEL, STEPHEN L., pres., Memorial Hospital of South Bend, South Bend, IN '74
UMPHRESS, BETTY L., mgr. cent. sup. and surg. tech., Bear Valley Community Hospital, Big Bear Lake, CA '83 (CS)
UMSCHEID, RODNEY, dir. risk mgt. and safety, University of California, Berkeley, CA '85 (RISK)
UNDERHILL, SR. PATRICIA, exec. vice-pres. oper., Catholic Health Corporation, Omaha, NE '82 (PR) (PLNG)
UNDERHILL, SANDRA, coor. qual. assur. and risk mgt., U. S. Army MEDDAC, Fort Lee, VA '84 (RISK)
UNDERLY, NANCY, RN, adm. pat. care, Tucson Medical Center, Tucson, AZ '78 (NURS)
UNDERRINER, L. J., eng. consult., Eastern Cooperative Services Daughters of Charity, Baltimore, MD '68 (ENG)
UNDERWOOD, DAPHINE L., mgr. matl. mgt., Duke University Hospital, Durham, NC '85 (PUR)
UNDERWOOD, DON T., mgr. eng., Utah Valley Regional Medical Center, Provo, UT '77 (ENG)
UNDERWOOD, FRANCES, supv. cent. serv., Southern Baptist Hospital, New Orleans, LA '80 (CS)
UNDERWOOD, GARY L., dir. clin. serv., Methodist Medical Center of Illinois, Peoria, IL '72
UNDERWOOD, HERBERT G., atty., United Hospital Center, Clarksburg, WV '81 (ATTY)
UNDERWOOD, MARSHA L., dir. spec. proj.-nrsg., Antelope Valley Hospital Medical Center, Lancaster, CA '85 (MGMT)
UNDERWOOD, ROBERT F., sr. consult., Parkside Human Services Corporation, Park Ridge, IL '78 (FOOD)
UNDERWOOD, STEPHANIE J., commun. and commun. rel. asst., Methodist Health System Foundation, New Orleans, LA '85 (PR) (PLNG)
UNGAR, JOHN F., exec. vice-pres., Comsul Limited, San Francisco, CA '86 (ENG)
UNGAR, JOHN W., pres., Lee Hospital, Johnstown, PA '69
UNGER-SMITH, DAVID L., vice-pres., Franklin Square Hospital, Baltimore, MD '82 (PLNG)
UNGER, BERTHA, RN, dir. nrsg. serv., University of California at Los Angeles Neuropsychiatric Hospital, Los Angeles, CA '75 (NURS)
UNGER, CLAIRE, dir. pub. rel., Chilton Memorial Hospital, Pompton Plains, NJ '76 (PR)
UNGER, JUDITH M., dir. soc. serv., Burnham Hospital, Champaign, IL '73 (SOC)
UNGER, KENNETH N., dir. plant improvement, Elmhurst Memorial Hospital, Elmhurst, IL '79 (ENG)
UNGER, MARK, dir. info. res. center, Catholic Health Association of the United States, St. Louis, MO '81
UNHJEM, MICHAEL B., vice-pres., Blue Cross of North Dakota, Fargo, ND '85 (ATTY)
UNITES, LEIGH M., adm. asst., Putnam General Hospital, Hurricane, WV '86 (PERS)(VOL)
UNRATH, AMY J. HEYRMAN, dir. pers., St. Mary's Hospital Medical Center, Green Bay, WI '81 (PERS)
UNRAU, JAMES R., vice-pres. sales, United Health Services, Scottsdale, AZ '83 (MGMT)
UNRUE, BETSY DEVOL, dir. soc. serv., Southwestern Michigan Rehabilitation Hospital, Battle Creek, MI '66 (SOC)
UNSER, BONNIE A., mgr. pub. rel., Glens Falls Hospital, Glens Falls, NY '86 (PR)
UNSER, DANIEL P., dir. matl. mgt., Candler General Hospital, Savannah, GA '74 (PUR)
UNTERBERGER, SUSAN M., atty., Hospital Association of Rhode Island, Providence, RI '86 (ATTY)
UPCHURCH, CHARLES E., dir. eng., Highsmith-Rainey Memorial Hospital, Fayetteville, NC '81 (ENG)
UPDEGROVE, LOYAL R., maint. eng., Ohio Valley Medical Center, Wheeling, WV '80 (ENG)
UPHAM, RONALD T., mgr., McGladrey, Hendrickson and Pullen, Minneapolis, MN '69 (MGMT)
UPP, WILLIAM R., dir. plant oper., Campbell County Memorial Hospital, Gillette, WY '82 (ENG)
UPSHAW, JOAN K., soc. worker, Shawnee Mission Medical Center, Shawnee Mission, KS '74 (SOC)
UPTON, LT. COL. CHARLES RHEA, MSC USAF, adm., Ehrling Bergquist U. S. Air Force Regional Hospital, Omaha, NE '73
UPTON, HARRY F., pres., H. F. Upton Associates, Inc., Darian, CT '83
UPTON, JACK H., assoc. dir. support serv., Moses H. Cone Memorial Hospital, Greensboro, NC '86
UPTON, W. WARREN, atty., Thomas Memorial Hospital, South Charleston, WV '78 (ATTY)
URBAN, ANN B., coor. vol., Christ Hospital, Cincinnati, OH '81 (VOL)
URBAN, EDMUND G., atty., South Suburban Hospital, Hazel Crest, IL '70 (ATTY)
URBAN, JOHN, pres., Preferred Care, Rochester, NY '86
URBAN, NANCY M., RN, dir. nrsg., Pulaski Memorial Hospital, Winamac, IN '86 (NURS)
URBAN, PATRICIA A., dir. vol. serv., Modesto City Hospital, Modesto, CA '85 (VOL)
URBAN, ROSE M., atty., Columbus-Cuneo-Cabrini Medical Center, Chicago, IL '85 (ATTY)
URBAN, STANLEY T., sr. vice-pres. corp. dev., Franciscan Health System, Chadds Ford, PA '69
URBAN, TERRIE, supv. oper. room, Montgomery County Memorial Hospital, Red Oak, IA '84 (CS)(AMB)
URBANOWICZ, LEO A., dir. pub. rel., Rehabilitation Institute of Pittsburgh, Pittsburgh, PA '86 (PR)
URBINE, SR. FLORENCE, RN, bd. chm., Seton Medical Center, Daly City, CA '71
URDANG, MERYL S., pres., Analytics, San Francisco, CA '87 (PLNG)
URDEN, LINDA D., coor. staff dev., Children's Hospital and Health Center, San Diego, CA '85 (EDUC)
URENDA, DANIEL J., dir. human res., St. Mary's Hospital, Enid, OK '86 (PERS)

URIDGE, THOMAS, vice-pres. human res., Ingham Medical Center, Lansing, MI '74 (PERS)

URLAUB, CHARLES J., vice-pres. oper., Rochester St. Mary's Hospital, Rochester, NY '80 (MGMT)

URMY, NORMAN B., dir., Vanderbilt University Hospital, Nashville, TN '82

URNER, THEODORE G., dir. plant oper., Phoenixville Hospital, Phoenixville, PA '82 (ENG)

UROFSKY, MICHELE L., vice-pres., Frankford Hospital, Philadelphia, PA '87 (AMB)

URQUHART, M. LESLEY, risk mgr., St. Vincent Hospital, Santa Fe, NM '84 (RISK)

URQUHART, PAUL J. III, dir. soc. serv., Memorial Mission Hospital, Asheville, NC '81 (SOC)

URSO, LUCY A., supv. commun., Westlake Community Hospital, Melrose Park, IL '85 (ENG)

URTON, PEGGY C., RN, vice-pres. nrsg., Methodist Hospital, Lubbock, TX '87 (NURS)

URVATER, LISA R., dir. advertising and pub. rel., Missouri Baptist Hospital, St. Louis, MO '85 (PR)

USELMAN, JOSEPH, supv. bldg. and grds., Watertown Memorial Hospital, Watertown, WI '80 (ENG)

USHAK, BOHDAN E., mgr. data proc., New York Eye and Ear Infirmary, New York, NY '85 (MGMT)

USHER, CAROL, RN, clin. dir., Allen Memorial Hospital, Waterloo, IA '86 (NURS)

USHER, EDITH M., coor. soc. serv., Bessemer Carraway Medical Center, Bessemer, AL '79 (SOC)

USHER, LINDA M., dir. matl. mgt., Metropolitan Hospital, Richmond, VA '75 (PUR)

USNER, PATRICIA MCMULLEN, dir. pub. rel., Children's Hospital of Philadelphia, Philadelphia, PA '78 (PR)

USSAK, MICHAEL H., dir. admit., Staten Island Hospital, Staten Island, NY '86

UTBERG-HOOD, DONALD L., dir. shared biomedical serv., Harris Methodist Health Service, Fort Worth, TX '84 (ENG)

UTLEY, DONNA L., dir. human res., St. Elizabeth Medical Center, Yakima, WA '81 (PERS)

UTLEY, PHILIP A., Antioch, TN '85 (ENG)

UTNE, EVE M., dir. mktg. commun., American Red Cross, Philadelphia, PA '86 (PR)

UTT, LISHA NORRIS, student, Medical College of Virginia, Virginia Commonwealth University, Department of Health Administration, Richmond, VA '83

UTTER, MARLENE J., dir. commun. rel., Bay Area Medical Center-Menominee, Menominee, MI '83 (PR)

UTZ, JUDITH L., dir. educ. serv., Independence Regional Health Center, Independence, MO '85 (EDUC)

UYEDA, KAREN S., pat. rep., St. Francis Medical Center, Honolulu, HI '86 (PAT)

UZIEL, GLORIA L., RN, asst. adm., Porter Memorial Hospital, Valparaiso, IN '80 (NURS)

UZUANIS, RICHARD A., reg. mgr., American Medical International-Professional Hospital Services, Schaumburg, IL '87

V

VACANTI, CAROLYN M., RN, Rochester, NY '77 (NURS)

VADEN, ALLENE, PhD, dean, University of Southern Mississippi, Hattiesburg, MS '73 (FOOD)

VADEN, H. TAYLOR, pres., Vaden Communications and Marketing, Malvern, PA '86 (PR)

VAGLIA, JUDITH M., RN, assoc. vice-pres. critical care nrsg., Presbyterian-University Hospital, Pittsburgh, PA '86 (NURS)

VAHLBERG, ROBERT J., dir. plng. and prog. dev., Norman Regional Hospital, Norman, OK '86 (PLNG)

VAHLE, LOIS H., RN, instr. educ. and trng., Barnes Hospital, St. Louis, MO '84 (EDUC)

VAIL, ROBERT S., sr. vice-pres., Holy Family Hospital, Spokane, WA '85 (RISK)

VAILE, CHARLES WILLIAM, dir. risk mgt., Memorial Medical Center, Springfield, IL '80 (RISK)

VAITENAS, RAMINTA E., mgr. oper., University of Chicago Hospitals, Chicago, IL '87 (AMB)

VALANCY, ABRAHAM, dir. eng., Brookdale Hospital Medical Center, Brooklyn, NY '72 (ENG)

VALANTINAS, BERNICE, assoc. dir. vol. serv., Evanston Hospital, Evanston, IL '74 (VOL)

VALASEK, ROBERT L., asst. exec. dir., Western Pennsylvania Hospital, Pittsburgh, PA '85 (PERS)

VALDERA-ROBINSON, TRUMMELL, actg. sr. dir. human res., Johns Hopkins Hospital, Baltimore, MD '86 (PERS)

VALDESPINO, MARIA J., supv. pers., Kaiser Foundation Health Plan, Inc., Oakland, CA '84 (PERS)

VALDEZ, GRACIE, risk mgr., Rio Grande Regional Hospital, McAllen, TX '86 (RISK)

VALDEZ, JOE R., RN, adm. res., Bexar County Hospital District, San Antonio, TX '81

VALDEZ, JOY L., coor. vol., HCA Medical Center of Plano, Plano, TX '85 (VOL)

VALDEZ, JUDY, pat. rep., Oakwood Hospital, Dearborn, MI '82 (PAT)

VALDEZ, KAREN E., dir. pers., St. Vincent General Hospital, Leadville, CO '87 (PERS)

VALEK, RAYMOND J., mktg. commun. spec., University of Chicago Hospitals, Chicago, IL '86 (PR)

VALENCE, PHILIP F., George B. H. Mocomber, Boston, MA '82 (ENG)

VALENCIC, NANCY R., RN, asst. dir. nrsg. serv. educ., Lutheran Medical Center, Cleveland, OH '84 (EDUC)(NURS)

VALENTA, ANNETTE LISA, Chicago, IL '78 (PLNG)

VALENTA, CHRISTINE, dir. home health serv., John C. Lincoln Hospital and Health Center, Phoenix, AZ '86 (AMB)

VALENTI, FRANCINE S., RN, charge nrs. recovery room and cent. sup., Francis A. Bell Memorial Hospital, Ishpeming, MI '87 (CS)

VALENTI, LAWRENCE S., proj. mgr., Metrolina Medical Foundation, Charlotte, NC '80

VALENTI, SALVATORE NATHAN, dir. soc. serv., Reading Rehabilitation Hospital, Reading, PA '68 (SOC)

VALENTIN, CARMELO GALINDEZ, dir. health facil., Medical Service Administration of Puerto Rico, Santurce, P.R. '83 (ENG)

VALENTINE, ARTHUR, Fort Worth Children's Hospital, Fort Worth, TX '78

VALENTINE, HOWARD, dir. pur., Dch Regional Medical Center, Tuscaloosa, AL '82 (PUR)

VALENTINE, JUDITH K., pat. rep., White Plains Hospital Medical Center, White Plains, NY '85 (PAT)

VALENTINE, LORENE R., sr. vice-pres. and chief oper. off., St. Francis Health Corporation, Wichita, KS '83 (PR)

VALENTINE, NANCY M., RN, adm. nrsg., McLean Hospital, Belmont, MA '85 (NURS)

VALENTINE, STEVEN T., vice-pres., Amherst Associates, Los Angeles, CA '80 (PLNG)

VALENTINE, WILLIAM E., dir. soc. work, Children's Hospital of San Francisco, San Francisco, CA '84 (SOC)

VALENTINO, JOHN A., mgr. facil., Malcolm Grow U. S. Air Force Medical Center, Washington, DC '86 (ENG)

VALENZANO, GERALD, dir. matl. mgt., St. Elizabeth Hospital, Danville, IL '84 (PUR)

VALENZUELA, MANUEL A., dir. nutr. serv., Holy Cross Hospital and Health Center, Nogales, AZ '86 (FOOD)

VALENZUELA, RODOLFO M., mgt. eng., St. Luke's-Roosevelt Hospital Center, New York, NY '86 (MGMT)

VALERI, MARYANN, mktg. analyst, Atlanticare Medical Center, Lynn, MA '86 (PLNG)

VALEYKO, JAMES F., Ernst and Whinney, Richmond, VA '79

VALINS, SARA, RN, dir. nrsg. serv., St. James Community Hospital, Butte, MT '86 (NURS)

VALLA, RICHARD DELLA, dir. maint. and eng., Roxborough Memorial Hospital, Philadelphia, PA '81 (ENG)

VALLAS, ALEX J., mgr. matl., Magee-Womens Hospital, Pittsburgh, PA '66 (PUR)

VALLERA, MARK W., mgr. cent. distrib., Children's Hospital, Columbus, OH '86 (PUR)

VALLEY, ELIZABETH H., dir. health horizons, Providence Hospital, Mobile, AL '85 (EDUC)

VALLIERE, PAUL I., vice-pres. sales and mktg., Brintech Corporation, Brand-Rex Telecommunication Division, Willimantic, CT '86 (ENG)

VALLONE, CAROLYN A., vice-pres., St. Joseph's Hospital, Tampa, FL '83 (NURS)

VALLONE, FRANK JR., dir. eng., Lydia E. Hall Hospital, Freeport, NY '78 (ENG)

VALO, MARTHA A., dir. diet. serv., Kennedy Memorial Hospital, Stratford, NJ '85 (FOOD)

VALOIS, GWEN A., dir. educ. serv., Houston Northwest Medical Center, Houston, TX '86 (EDUC)

VALOIS, MARIE, counselor, Association Des Hopitaux Du Quebec, Montreal, Que., Canada '85 (MGMT)

VALOON, PATRICIA L., RN, assoc. dir. nrsg., New York University Medical Center, New York, NY '79 (NURS)

VALORE, CARL J., atty., Burdette Tomlin Memorial Hospital, Cape May Court House, NJ '81 (ATTY)

VALORZ, JOHN V., partner, Coopers and Lybrand, Boston, MA '77

VAN ABEL, JOHN P., atty., Aultman Hospital, Canton, OH '68 (ATTY)

VAN AMBURGH, PATRICIA, dir. pat. rel., Providence Medical Center, Seattle, WA '76 (PAT)

VAN ANTWERP, HOWARD III, atty., King's Daughters' Medical Center, Ashland, KY '74 (ATTY)

VAN ARSDALE, DONALD T., dir. pur., St. Elizabeth Medical Center, Dayton, OH '77 (PUR)

VAN ATTA, ELLEN M., mgt. eng., Magee-Womens Hospital, Pittsburgh, PA '84 (MGMT)

VAN BECKUM, LISSA A., coor. pub. rel., Milwaukee Regional Medical Center, Milwaukee, WI '86 (PR) (PLNG)

VAN BOURGONDIEN, KAREN, student, Capital University Law School, Columbus, OH '85 (RISK)

VAN BUSKIRK, DIXIE, risk mgr. and pat. rep., St. Joseph Hospital and Health Care Center, Tacoma, WA '86 (RISK)

VAN BUTSEL, SHARON J., mgr. soc. work, AMI Saint Joseph Hospital, Omaha, NE '86 (SOC)

VAN COUR, PATRICIA J., RN, vice-pres. nrsg., Stoughton Hospital Association, Stoughton, WI '81 (NURS)

VAN CROMBRUGGHE, PHYLLIS, RN, adm. pat. care serv., AMI Rancho Encino Hospital, Encino, CA '86 (NURS)

VAN DAM, RIKA R., sr. mgt. eng., Pacific Health Resources, Los Angeles, CA '81 (MGMT)

VAN DAMME, AGNES P., RN, dir. in-service, Sydenham District Hospital, Wallaceburg, Ont., Canada '84 (EDUC)

VAN DEKERKHOVE, PETER C., chief info. and oper. analyst, Henry Ford Hospital, Detroit, MI '82 (MGMT)

VAN DERWERKEN, JOSEPH B., assoc. dir. matl. mgt., Glens Falls Hospital, Glens Falls, NY '74 (CS)(PUR)

VAN DESAND, PAUL C., dir. plant serv., St. Marys Hospital Medical Center, Madison, WI '80 (ENG)

VAN DEUREN, JAMES M., dir. gen. serv., Community Memorial Hospital, Cheboygan, MI '81 (ENG)

VAN DINE, HENRY I., qual. assur. and reliability eng., Graphic Controls Corporation, Buffalo, NY '84 (ENG)

VAN DOVER, ELAINE M., RN, dir. nrsg. serv., St. Luke's Hospital, Aberdeen, SD '81 (NURS)

VAN DUSEN, DUNCAN W., adm. phys. medicine and rehab., University of Pennsylvania School of Medicine, Philadelphia, PA '68

VAN DUSER, MAUREEN N., asst. vice-pres., Crouse-Irving Memorial Hospital, Syracuse, NY '82 (PERS)

VAN DUYN, SALLY L., dir. educ., Medical Center Hospital, Conroe, TX '86 (EDUC)

VAN DYK, FRANK, Richardson, TX '73 (LIFE)

VAN DYK, ROBERT, exec. dir., Christian Health Care Center, Wyckoff, NJ '77

VAN ECK, MARY JOYCE, dir. vol. serv., Chester County Hospital, West Chester, PA '80 (VOL)

VAN EIMEREN, DIANTHA, RN, dir. nrsg. serv., Berlin Hospital Association, Berlin, WI '86 (NURS)

VAN EPPS, MICHELE L., dir. vol. serv., H. Lee Moffitt Cancer Center, Tampa, FL '86 (VOL)

VAN ERON, MERIAM J., RN, dir. nrsg. support syst., Georgetown University Medical Center, Washington, DC '85 (NURS)

VAN EVERY, PATRICIA J., dir. vol., Casa Colina Hospital for Rehabilitative Medicine, Pomona, CA '84 (VOL)

VAN FRANK, RICHARD N., prin., Jones Mah Gaskill Rhodes, Inc., Memphis, TN '71

VAN GELDER, KAREN, dir. hskpg. serv., Sutter General Hospital, Sacramento, CA '86 (ENVIRON)

VAN GORDER, CHRIS D., vice-pres., Anaheim Memorial Hospital, Anaheim, CA '86

VAN GROOTHEEST, TERRY L., proj. eng., University Hospital-University of Nebraska, Omaha, NE '86 (MGMT)

VAN HEININGEN, PRISCILLA D., dir. emp. rel., Park City Hospital, Bridgeport, CT '81 (PERS)

VAN HEININGEN, ROBERT H., dir. pers. and commun. rel., Charlotte Hungerford Hospital, Torrington, CT '77 (PERS)

VAN HESE, MARILYN, RN, dir. nrsg. serv., St. Luke's Hospital, Davenport, IA '70 (NURS)

VAN HOFF, ANN M., dir. trng., University of Nebraska, School of Nursing, Omaha, NE '71 (EDUC)

VAN HOOK, ALAN F., dir. food serv., Yavapai Regional Medical Center, Prescott, AZ '79 (FOOD)

VAN HOOK, CONNIE, risk mgr. and coor. qual. assessment, St. Benedict's Hospital, Ogden, UT '86 (RISK)

VAN HOOK, THOMAS, programmer health facil., U. S. Army Health Facilities Planning Agency, Washington, DC '80

VAN HOOSE, LAWRENCE K., dir. mktg., Mercy Health Center, Oklahoma City, OK '79 (PR)

VAN HORNE, GRANT, atty., DeKalb Memorial Hospital, Auburn, IN '78 (ATTY)

VAN LIEW, DENNIS J. JR., sr. consult., Deloitte Haskins and Sells, Minneapolis, MN '83 (MGMT)

VAN MOURIK, ROBERT J. A., dir. facil., Holy Cross Hospital, Mission Hills, CA '83 (ENG)

VAN NOSTRAND, GARY K., asst. vice-pres., Medical Center at Princeton, Princeton, NJ '84 (PLNG)

VAN OSTENBERG, PAUL R., exec. dir., American Association of Hospital Dentists, Chicago, IL '84

VAN PELT, KENNETH R., adm. med. staff affairs, Mountainside Hospital, Montclair, NJ '73

VAN REESE, WILLIAM, adm. off., Naval Dental Research Institute, Great Lakes, IL '80

VAN RENSSELAER, JERRE L., dir. food serv., Norfolk General Hospital, Norfolk, VA '76 (FOOD)

VAN SCOY, HOWARD W., exec. dir., Aliquippa Hospital, Aliquippa, PA '56 (LIFE)

VAN SHEA, HELEN, RN, sr. assoc. dir. and dir. nrsg., Society of the New York Hospital, New York, NY '83 (NURS)

VAN SICKLE, PATRICIA A., dir. vol. serv., National Rehabilitation Hospital, Washington, DC '86 (VOL)

VAN SLYKE, ROBERT E., vice-pres. oper., Methodist Hospital, Lubbock, TX '76

VAN SPLINTER, MICHAEL D., dir. environ. serv., Norwood Hospital, Norwood, MA '86 (ENVIRON)

VAN SUMEREN, MARK A., sr. mgt. eng., Ernst and Whinney, Milwaukee, WI '81 (MGMT)

VAN TILBURG, LORIE, supv. soc. work serv., Mercy Hospital and Medical Center, San Diego, CA '86 (SOC)

VAN VELSIR, GREGORY, mgt. syst. analyst, Antelope Valley Hospital Medical Center, Lancaster, CA '87 (MGMT)

VAN VOORHIS, JEAN, asst. dir. nrsg., Westlake Community Hospital, Melrose Park, IL '86 (RISK)

VAN VORST, CHARLES BRIAN, pres. and chief exec. off., Carle Foundation Hospital, Urbana, IL '67

VAN WAGNER, KAREN, PhD, vice-pres. oper., Harris Methodist -Fort Worth, Fort Worth, TX '80 (PLNG)

VAN WINKLE, JAMES O., chief eng. and dir. bldg. and grds., Community Methodist Hospital, Henderson, KY '72 (ENG)

VAN WINKLE, PATRICIA, dir. pers., St. James Mercy Hospital, Hornell, NY '86 (PERS)

VAN WINKLE, SHERYL, cent. serv. tech., St. Michael's Hospital, Tyndall, SD '85 (CS)

VAN ZANDT, RICHARD N., mgr. mktg., Ethicon, Inc., Somerville, NJ '87 (AMB)

VAN ZANTEN, JACK F., sr. vice-pres., Stone, Marraccini and Patterson, San Francisco, CA '77 (PLNG)

VAN ZUILEN, STERLING, dir. eng., Milford Health Care Center, Inc., Milford, CT '75 (ENG)

VAN, GEORGE P., chief exec. off., Columbia Corporation, Nashville, TN '77

VANAGUNAS, AUDREY, dir. risk mgt., Chicago Hospital Risk Pooling Program, Chicago, IL '80 (RISK)

VANASSE, ROBERT T., dir. soc. serv., Greenwich Hospital, Greenwich, CT '85 (SOC)

VANBOKKELEN, WILLIAM R., exec. vice-pres., Christian Hospitals Northeast-Northwest, St. Louis, MO '73

VANBOXTEL, CAROL A., coor. educ., St. Elizabeth Hospital, Appleton, WI '86 (EDUC)

VANCE, DONALD E., dir. plant serv., Luther Hospital, Eau Claire, WI '69 (ENG)

VANCE, DON D., consult., Don Vance Management Engineering Services, Johnston, IA '77 (MGMT)

VANCE, H. BERNARD JR., mgr. pers., Heritage Hospital, Taylor, MI '82 (PERS)

VANCE, MARIE J., dir. diet., Memorial Hospital, Albany, NY '76 (FOOD)

VANCE, ROBERT J., assoc. adm., St. John's Episcopal Hospital-Smithtown, Smithtown, NY '76

VANCRONKHITE, DAVID, vice-pres. sales, Gerber Alley and Company, Norcross, GA '86

VANCURA, BARBARA, RN, instr. staff educ., Chicago Wesley Memorial Hospital, Chicago, IL '77 (EDUC)

VANDE ERVE, ANITA C., adm. dir. pers., Charleston Memorial Hospital, Charleston, SC '85 (PERS)

VANDELICHT, MAVIS J., coor. nrsg. educ., Douglas Community Hospital, Roseburg, OR '85 (EDUC)
VANDEMOORTEL, VICTOR, asst. to corp. dir.-info. syst., Sisters of Mercy Health Corporation, Farmington Hills, MI '78 (MGMT)
VANDENBERG, BERNARD, dir. facil. serv., Holland Community Hospital, Holland, MI '79 (ENG)
VANDENBOSCH, WILLIAM V., adm., Blue Cross and Blue Shield of Arizona, Phoenix, AZ '83 (PLNG)
VANDENBROEK, DEBORAH S., student, University of Michigan Program in Hospital Administration, Ann Arbor, MI '82
VANDENBROEK, DEBORAH S., adm. assoc., Catherine McAuley Health Center, Ann Arbor, MI '87 (PLNG)
VANDENBURG, DUB, asst. dir. eng., Presbyterian Hospital, Oklahoma City, OK '86 (ENG)
VANDENBURGH, HENRY W., coor. med. prog., Center for Continuing Medical Education, Torrance, CA '86 (EDUC)
VANDERBROEK, CHARLES, clin. supv. pat. and family counseling, Holland Community Hospital, Holland, MI '85 (SOC)
VANDERBURG, B. WILLIAM, pres., Voluntary Hospitals of America-New England, Portland, ME '85 (PLNG)
VANDERGRIFT, DON E., vice-pres. human resources, Community Hospitals of Indiana, Indianapolis, IN '68 (PERS)
VANDERGRIFT, LOIS J., dir. soc. serv., Noble Hospital, Westfield, MA '85 (SOC)
VANDERHEOF, FRANCES A., RN, vice-pres. pat. serv., Park City Hospital, Bridgeport, CT '73 (NURS)
VANDERKLISH, JOHN E., (ret.), Newton Center, MA '47 (LIFE)
VANDERLOOP, EDWARD J., dir. risk mgt. and qual. assur., Ellis Hospital, Schenectady, NY '81 (RISK)
VANDERMEY, ROBERTA, coor. pat.-staff rel., University of Michigan Hospitals, Ann Arbor, MI '83 (RISK)
VANDERMOLEN, RICHARD, Parchment, MI '76 (ENG)
VANDERSLICE, JOHN A., dir. diet., Jewish Home and Hospital for Aged at Pittsburgh, Pittsburgh, PA '68 (FOOD)
VANDERSTAY, OTTO R., dir. elec. eng., Childrens Hospital of Los Angeles, Los Angeles, CA '81 (ENG)
VANDERVEEN, JAMES R., vice-pres. and dir. mktg., Mercy Hospital, Miami, FL '85 (PR)
VANDERVORT, HAROLD C., dir. clin. eng., Rush-Presbyterian-St. Luke's Medical Center, Chicago, IL '82 (ENG)
VANDEVERE, EARL DAVID, plant eng., Community Hospital Association, Battle Creek, MI '73 (ENG)
VANDISH, PAUL, risk mgr., Oswego Hospital, Oswego, NY '87 (RISK)
VANDIVER, PATSY DIANNE, RN, asst. dir. nrsg. and maternity, Cooper Green Hospital, Birmingham, AL '80 (NURS)
VANGEWEGE, MITZI, RN, dir. nrsg., St. Peter Hospital, Olympia, WA '83 (NURS)
VANGUNDY, KEN E., dir. plant oper., Havenwyck Hospital, Auburn Hills, MI '82 (ENG)
VANHORN, ELIZABETH, asst. chief soc. work serv., Veterans Administration Medical Center, Milwaukee, WI '86 (SOC)
VANHORN, JEAN, coor. vol. resources, Friends Hospital, Philadelphia, PA '78 (VOL)
VANHORN, MICHAEL W., dir. plant oper., Cuyuna Range District Hospital, Crosby, MN '85 (ENG)
VANKURAN, LAWRENCE, dir. mgt. eng. off. syst., Kaiser Permanente Medical Care Program, Pasadena, CA '82 (MGMT)
VANLANDINGHAM, TED LEE, asst. chief pat. affairs, Naval Hospital, Great Lakes, IL '83
VANLOAN, EUGENE M. III, atty., Concord Hospital, Concord, NH '79 (ATTY)
VANNATTA, GRETCHEN A., dir. educ., Prucare-North Care Medical Group, Oak Park, IL '84 (EDUC)
VANNI, VINCE, dir. commun. rel., HCA Oak Hill Hospital, Spring Hill, FL '86 (PR)
VANOVER, HEADLY, dir. plant oper., Bristol Memorial Hospital, Bristol, TN '83 (ENG)
VANPATTEN, MICHAEL S., dir., Healthcare Communications, Inc., Reston, VA '85 (MGMT)
VANPORTFLEET, WILLIAM J., asst. dir. plant oper., Butterworth Hospital, Grand Rapids, MI '85 (ENG)
VANSALISBURY, ARTHUR E., asst. dir. eng., Booth Memorial Medical Center, Flushing, NY '84 (ENG)
VANSCHOICK, DONALD C., dir. food and nutr., Glenwood Regional Medical Center, West Monroe, LA '85 (FOOD)
VANSICE, SHERRY, rep. emp. rel., Bethesda Hospital, Inc., Cincinnati, OH '86 (PERS)
VANSLYCK, ANN, RN, pres., Avs and Associates, Inc., Phoenix, AZ '84
VANTU, HOANG, mgr. biomedical eng., St. Mary's Hospital, Richmond, VA '86 (ENG)
VANVALIN, LAURA E., asst. dir. diet., Haverford Community Hospital, Havertown, PA '86 (FOOD)
VANWIE, DONALD J., asst. supv. plant, Suburban Hospital and Sanitarium-Cook County, Hinsdale, IL '82 (ENG)
VANZANDT, LYLE W., dir. phys. resources, Marshall Browning Hospital, Du Quoin, IL '75 (PUR)
VANZANT, BETTY L., pat. rep., Research Medical Center, Kansas City, MO '77 (PAT)
VARADIAN, MICHAEL S., exec. vice-pres. and chief oper. off., McLean Health Services, Belmont, MA '76
VARCOE, STEPHEN R., dir. pers., Sioux Valley Hospital, Sioux Falls, SD '78 (PERS)
VAREL, JAMES A., adm. asst. and dir. mgt. eng., St. Mary's Health Center, St. Louis, MO '75 (MGMT)
VARGA, NINA, mgr. matl., St. Mary's Hospital, Orange, NJ '70 (CS)
VARGAS, FRANCES R., RN, pat. serv. rep., St. Jude Hospital-Fullerton, Fullerton, CA '83 (PAT)
VARGAS, JANE, mgr. cent. sup., St. John's Hospital, Salina, KS '81 (CS)
VARGAS, LEEANN G., student, Southern Illinois University, Carbondale, IL '86
VARGASON, ANNE M., dir. soc. serv., Auburn Memorial Hospital, Auburn, NY '86 (SOC)
VARGO, DORIS C., commun. rel. spec., Hillcrest Hospital, Mayfield Heights, OH '86 (PR)
VARHOLAK, DOROTHY M., RN, vice-pres. nrsg. serv., Hebrew Home and Hospital, Hartford, CT '82 (NURS)
VARNADO, JOHN A., dir. diet., East Jefferson General Hospital, Metairie, LA '86 (FOOD)
VARNELL, LESTER J. JR., atty., Palo Pinto General Hospital, Mineral Wells, TX '72 (ATTY)
VARNER, CHARLOTTE F., RN, adm. nrsg. serv., Newark-Wayne Community Hospital, Newark, NY '83 (NURS)
VARNER, JANE A., atty., Hendrick Medical Center, Abilene, TX '86 (ATTY)
VARNER, JOAN L., RN, dir. nrsg. serv., Lawnwood Regional Medical Center, Fort Pierce, FL '80 (EDUC)(NURS)
VARNER, STEVE, mgt. eng., Professional Htlh Care Management, Portsmouth, VA '87 (MGMT)
VARNEY, BONNIE S., dir. educ., Cape Canaveral Hospital, Cocoa Beach, FL '86 (EDUC)
VARNEY, MAJ. RICHARD A., MSC USA, instr., U. S. Army Academy of Health Sciences, Fort Sam Houston, TX '81
VARNUM, DANIEL L., mgt. syst. eng., Iowa Methodist Medical Center, Des Moines, IA '86 (MGMT)
VARNUM, JAMES W., pres., Mary Hitchcock Memorial Hospital, Hanover, NH '82 (PLNG)
VARTAN, KAREN S. HOFMANN, dir. educ. res., North American Foodservice Company, Inc., Chicago, IL '78 (FOOD)
VARTANIAN, MARIE, dir. educ., Leonard Morse Hospital, Natick, MA '75 (EDUC)
VASILAKIS, SUSAN TILLMAN, student, Program in Health Administration, Trinity University, San Antonio, TX '84
VASILIW, ALYCE, mgr. vol. serv., South Suburban Hospital, Hazel Crest, IL '83 (VOL)
VASQUEZ, JOSEPH R., dir. plant serv., College Hospital, Cerritos, CA '84 (ENG)
VASSALLO, JACK, sr. soc. dev. planner, City of Detroit Employment and Training Department, Detroit, MI '75 (PR)(MGMT)
VASSALO, LISA, student, Duke University, Department of Health Administration, Durham, NC '86
VASSE, GREGORY J., vice-pres., Cottage Hospital of Grosse Pointe, Grosse Pointe Farms, MI '82 (PLNG)
VATCHER, JO-ANN, RN, actg. dir. staff dev., Frisbie Memorial Hospital, Rochester, NH '81 (EDUC)
VAUDO, KENNETH A., asst. adm., Eye Foundation Hospital, Birmingham, AL '77
VAUGHAN, CHARLES R., atty., St. Elizabeth Hospital Medical Center, Lafayette, IN '78 (ATTY)
VAUGHAN, JAN, coor. mktg., Houston Community Hospital, Houston, MS '85 (SOC)
VAUGHAN, JOHN S., pres., Dietary Management Advisory, Inc., Rosemont, PA '68 (FOOD)
VAUGHAN, PATRICK, vice-pres. human res., Pennock Hospital, Hastings, MI '71 (PERS)
VAUGHAN, ROBERT G. III, mgt. consult., MacLeod Associates, Baltimore, MD '78 (MGMT)
VAUGHN-CAIN, JERRILYNN, asst. dir. human res., Lutheran Medical Center, Wheat Ridge, CO '85 (PERS)
VAUGHN, CLAIRE A., dir. health promotion and counseling serv., Queen of the Valley Hospital, Napa, CA '76 (SOC)(EDUC)
VAUGHN, DONALD W., mgr. pers., Baltimore County General Hospital, Randallstown, MD '86 (PERS)
VAUGHN, EDGAR D., exec. vice-pres., Intermountain Health Care, Inc., Salt Lake City, UT '69
VAUGHN, FRED E. II, supv. eng., Kingman Community Hospital, Kingman, KS '82 (ENG)
VAUGHN, FREDERICK W., mgt. eng., Cleveland Clinic Hospital, Cleveland, OH '80 (MGMT)
VAUGHN, JAMES D., Davie, FL '85 (PUR)
VAUGHN, LARRY J., dir. pers., Oak Ridge Hospital of the United Methodist Church, Oak Ridge, TN '77 (PERS)
VAUGHN, LYNN, RN, asst. adm. nrsg., Liberty Hospital, Liberty, MO '80 (NURS)
VAUGHN, PAULETTE B., dir. vol. serv., Twin County Community Hospital, Galax, VA '86 (VOL)
VAUGHN, SANDRA S., dir. soc. work, Rush Foundation Hospital, Meridian, MS '78 (VOL)(SOC)
VAUGHT, LOU C., adm., Jennings Community Hospital, North Vernon, IN '76
VAUTIER, ALICE F., RN, vice-pres. pat. serv., Cabell Huntington Hospital, Huntington, WV '85 (NURS)
VAVRECK, SR. BARBARA ANN, mgr. food serv., Saint Vincent Health Center, Erie, PA '81 (FOOD)
VAVREK, GEORGE T., vice-pres. and gen. mgr. health care, Linbeck Construction Company, Dallas, TX '86
VAVROCH, MARY W., atty., Linn County Health Department, Cedars Rapid, IA '87 (ATTY)
VAWTER, ROBERT R. JR., atty., Hospital Corporation of America, Tampa, FL '85 (ATTY)
VAY, DAPHNE, dir. diet., Puget Sound Hospital, Tacoma, WA '77 (FOOD)
VAYDA, VIRGINIA CONYERS, dir. soc. serv., Latrobe Area Hospital, Latrobe, PA '79 (SOC)
VAZQUEZ, JERRY J., adm., Hillsborough County Crisis Center, Inc., Tampa, FL '78
VAZQUEZ, JESUS, legal counsel, bus. mgr. and chm. risk mgt. committee, University of Puerto Rico School of Medicine, Department of Anesthesiology, San Juan, P.R. '86 (RISK)
VEACH, DAVID C., chief eng., Bradley County Memorial Hospital, Cleveland, TN '84 (ENG)
VEALE, FRANK H. III, SunHealth Corporation, Charlotte, NC '83 (MGMT)
VEAR, MARJORIE E., RN, dir. nrsg., Milford-Whitinsville Regional Hospital, Milford, MA '74 (NURS)
VEATCH, DAWN, RN, dir. psych. nrsg., Northwestern Memorial Hospital, Chicago, IL '78 (NURS)
VECOLI, JILL C., pat. serv. spec., Group Health, Inc., Spring Lake Park, MN '85 (PAT)
VEGA, MARY J., dir. vol. serv., St. Francis Hospital, Milwaukee, WI '85 (VOL)
VEITH, MARY C., dir. soc. serv., St. Agnes Medical Center, Philadelphia, PA '85 (SOC)
VELARDE, ROBERT M., RN, dir. nrsg. serv., Centro Espanol Memorial Hospital, Tampa, FL '76 (NURS)
VELASCO, MARY, dir. cent. sterile serv., Botsford General Hospital-Osteopathic, Farmington Hills, MI '85 (CS)
VELCHECK, ROSEMARY P., vice-pres., Missouri Baptist Hospital, St. Louis, MO '84 (RISK)
VELDE, JAMES VANDER, vice-pres. nrsg., Somerset Medical Center, Somerville, NJ '79 (NURS)
VELDE, THOMAS, mgr. matl., Kino Community Hospital, Tucson, AZ '83 (CS)
VELDMAN, HENRY, (ret.), North Attleboro, MA '54 (LIFE)
VELER, JAMES L., asst. dir. plant serv., St. Mary's Hospital and Medical Center, San Francisco, CA '84 (ENG)
VELEY, FRANCES L., mgr. telecommun., Northside Hospital, Atlanta, GA '83 (ENG)
VELEZ, JOSEFINA G., asst. dir. diet. serv., Saint Michael's Medical Center, Newark, NJ '86 (FOOD)
VELGHE, JAMES C., pres., Management Science Associates, Inc., Kansas City, MO '72 (PERS)
VELICK, STEPHEN H., clin. adm., Henry Ford Hospital, Detroit, MI '87 (AMB)
VELTEN, ALICE J., RN, asst. adm. nrsg., St. Anthony Hospital, Oklahoma City, OK '83 (NURS)
VELTMAN, REBECCA W., atty., O'Connor Hospital, San Jose, CA '84 (ATTY)
VELUCHAMY, SAMY, vice-pres. biomedical mgt. serv., Mount Carmel Medical Center, Columbus, OH '86 (ENG)
VEMUGANTI, P. R. RAO, adm. tech. prog., Texas Department of Mental Health and Mental Retardation, Austin, TX '82 (FOOD)
VENABLE, GLEN WALLACE, Engineer Services, Chicago, IL '69 (ENG)
VENABLE, LARRY E., mgr. clin. eng., Middletown Regional Hospital, Middletown, OH '85 (ENG)
VENEMAN, GERARD H., supv. pat. and family serv., Penrose Hospitals, Colorado Springs, CO '80 (SOC)
VENGRIN, SUSAN E., vice-pres. mktg. and plng., Radford Community Hospital, Radford, VA '74 (PR)
VENGROSKI, STELLA, RN, consult. nrsg., Professional Resources for Nursing, New York, NY '72 (NURS)
VENINO, RICHARD O., atty., Northern Ocean Hospital System, Point Pleasant, NJ '70 (ATTY)
VENNE, PHILLIP W., Louisville, KY '85 (PERS)
VENNEMAN, F. CRAIG, dir. pers., Christian Hospitals Northeast-Northwest, St. Louis, MO '84 (PERS)
VENNEY, ROBERT E., atty., Pan American Hospital, Miami, FL '73 (ATTY)
VENOVIC, JOHN A., dir. eng. serv., Rockford Memorial Hospital, Rockford, IL '71 (ENG)
VENTO, RICHARD M., mgr. prof. liability mktg., Enco Insurance, Houston, TX '81 (RISK)
VENTURA, BEVERLY A., RN, dir. nrsg., Mercy Hospital, Springfield, MA '80 (NURS)
VENTURA, CAROL E., RN, dir. surg. nrsg., Theda Clark Regional Medical Center, Neenah, WI '86 (NURS)
VENTURA, LINDA J., dir. psycho soc. work, Daniel Freeman Marina Hospital, Marina Del Rey, CA '83 (SOC)
VENTURA, N. LAWRENCE, vice-pres. oper., St. Joseph Hospital, Bangor, ME '72 (PLNG)
VENTURA, SUSAN C., RN, dir. nrsg., Kenosha Hospital and Medical Center, Kenosha, WI '86 (NURS)
VENZEL, JACQUELINE, dir. commun., Academy of Medicine, Toledo, OH '81 (PR)
VERA, GLORIA LEE, atty., Brackenridge Hospital, Austin, TX '83 (ATTY)
VERA, JOSEPHINE, asst. vice-pres. nrsg. educ., St. Joseph Medical Center, Wichita, KS '71 (EDUC)
VERA, RICHARD F., dir. plant oper., Rosewood Medical Center, Houston, TX '75 (ENG)
VERBEECK, JOHN R., dir. soc. serv., Brunswick General Hospital, Amityville, NY '74 (SOC)
VERCHOTA, ROBERT P., dir. pers., St. Mary's Medical Center, Duluth, MN '84 (PERS)
VERCILLO, MARYJO, student, Program in Health Care Administration, Baruch College Mount Sinai School of Medicine, New York, NY '86
VERDON, GEORGE L., adm. facil. and mgt. serv., Medical Center Hospital of Vermont, Burlington, VT '75 (MGMT)(PLNG)
VERDUYN, TERI L., mgr., Deloitte Haskins and Sells, Minneapolis, MN '85 (NURS)
VERGALES, ANN C., dir. soc. serv., Mount Carmel Medical Center, Columbus, OH '86 (SOC)
VERGAMINI, STEPHEN J., atty., Doctors Hospital, Columbus, OH '79 (ATTY)
VERGON, ADELAIDE B., coor. vol. serv., Galion Community Hospital, Galion, OH '70 (VOL)
VERGOTZ, SR. MARY JANE, supv. soc. work, Saint Vincent Health Center, Erie, PA '86 (SOC)
VERGOWE, WAYNE J., sr. asst. dir., Foster G. McGaw Hospital, Loyola University of Chicago, Maywood, IL '79
VERLEY, JIM D., CO-owner, Hill Music Company, Laramie, WY '85 (PR)
VERMIGLIO, JANICE A., RN, dir. nrsg., Scottsdale Camelback Hospital, Scottsdale, AZ '82 (NURS)
VERMILLION, AUTHER WAYNE, chief eng., Corpus Christi Osteopathic Hospital, Corpus Christi, TX '74 (ENG)
VERNAVA, ALVAH W., dir. soc. serv., Kent County Memorial Hospital, Warwick, RI '68 (SOC)
VERNEGAARD, NIELS P., assoc. exec. dir., Humana Hospital -Biscayne, Miami, FL '80
VERNIER, THOMAS C., dir. mktg., St. Elizabeth's Hospital, Belleville, IL '81 (EDUC)(PR)
VERNON, MARK J., adm. dir. lab. serv., West Jersey Hospital, Eastern Division, Voorhees, NJ '82
VERNON, PAULETTE J., asst. dir. nrsg. spec. serv., Lawnwood Regional Medical Center, Fort Pierce, FL '87 (AMB)

VERNOTZY, LARRY H., chief eng., Sierra Community Hospital, Fresno, CA '84 (ENG)
VERONA, DAVID A., atty., Hinshaw, Culbertson, Et Al, Chicago, IL '81 (ATTY)
VERONICA, SR. ANNE, adm. asst., Good Samaritan Hospital, Suffern, NY '82 (RISK)
VERRATTI, JAMES P., elec. foreman, Montefiore Hospital, Pittsburgh, PA '84 (ENG)
VERRICCHIA, ANTHONY JOSEPH, dir. facil., Durham County General Hospital, Durham, NC '68 (ENG)
VERRIER, GERI, pur. agt., Symmes Hospital, Arlington, MA '86 (PUR)
VERTIN, MICHAEL J., mgr., Ernst and Whinney, Detroit, MI '86 (MGMT)
VERVACK, ANNA CHESTEEN, mgr. cent. serv., Sparks Regional Medical Center, Fort Smith, AR '78 (CS)
VERVENA, LT. COL. ANTHONY H., MSC USAF, Malcolm Grow U. S. Air Force Medical Center, Andrews AFB, MD '68
VESEY, PETER E., New York, NY '52 (LIFE)
VESPOLI, JOSEPH, dir. maint., Brunswick General Hospital, Amityville, NY '82 (ENG)
VEST, MICHELLE, coor. qual. assessment and risk mgt., Pan American Hospital, Miami, FL '86 (RISK)
VESTAL, EARL L., dir. food serv., San Bernardino County Medical Center, San Bernardino, CA '81 (FOOD)
VETRANO, FRANK, exec. dir., Hotel Dieu Hospital, St. Catharines, Ont., Canada '81 (PLNG)
VETRINI, ROBERT J., dir. matl., Christ Hospital, Jersey City, NJ '76 (PUR)
VETROVEC, KENNETH A., dir. mktg. and commun. rel., St. Mary's Medical Center, Racine, WI '79 (PR)
VETTE, WALLY E., dir. food serv., Memorial General Hospital, Las Cruces, NM '84 (FOOD)
VETTRAINO, ANTHONY P., supv. prin. med. soc. work, Boston City Hospital, Boston, MA '77 (SOC)
VEVLE, RICHARD R., pres., Richard R. Vevle Associates, Inc., Birmingham, AL '74 (PLNG)
VIA, ROBERT L., exec. vice-pres., Monongalia General Hospital, Morgantown, WV '73
VIALPANDO, JOAN F., dir. vol., Parkview Episcopal Medical Center, Pueblo, CO '85 (VOL)
VIARENGO, MARILYN, mgr. matl., Mercy Hospital, Bakersfield, CA '86 (PUR)
VIBBERTS, JOHN D., dir. matl. mgt., Jordan Hospital, Plymouth, MA '86 (PUR)
VICCELLIO, CHARLES D., atty., Lake Charles Memorial Hospital, Lake Charles, LA '80 (ATTY)
VICCINELLI, KATHY J., coor. vol. serv., Big Spring State Hospital, Big Spring, TX '83 (VOL)
VICENTE, MARIA C., dir. soc. serv., St. Luke's Hospital, San Francisco, CA '80 (SOC)
VICENZI, GERALD J., vice-pres. info. syst., Mount Sinai Medical Center, Cleveland, OH '73 (MGMT)
VICHURAS, SR. MARY EVELYN, RN, dir. nrsg. serv., Holy Cross Hospital, Chicago, IL '78 (NURS)
VICIK, JOHN J., mgr. mktg. and trng., Personal and Professional Development, Inc., Wheeling, IL '79 (PERS)
VICK, CATHERINE G., dir. commun. serv., HCA Heritage Hospital, Tarboro, NC '85 (VOL)
VICK, RICHARD W., dir. biomedical elec., Winter Haven Hospital, Winter Haven, FL '85 (ENG)
VICK, RUTH W., dir. pers. and labor rel., Queens Hospital Center, Jamaica, NY '80 (PERS)
VICKERS, LEON H., med. dir.-middle east area, McDermott International, Inc., Dubai, Saudi Arabia '85 (RISK)
VICKERS, LEON J., med. dir., McDermott International, Inc., New Orleans, LA '85 (MGMT)
VICKERS, ROHN W., dir. diet. serv., Christ Hospital, Cincinnati, OH '82 (FOOD)
VICKERSTAFF, HUGH, dir., Veterans Administration Medical Center, Birmingham, AL '50 (LIFE)
VICKLUND, RICHARD COLES, sr. vice-pres. plng. and mktg., Heartland Health System, Inc., St. Joseph, MO '78 (PLNG)
VICTORY, SR. ANNE, RN, adm. nrsg. serv., St. Joseph Hospital and Health Center, Lorain, OH '83 (NURS)
VIDAKOVICH, KATHERINE, vice-pres., St. Margaret Memorial Hospital, Pittsburgh, PA '85 (NURS)(AMB)
VIDAL, JOHN, dir. maint., Montefiore Medical Center, Bronx, NY '81
VIDOVIC, LAWRENCE A., dir. soc. work, Oakwood Hospital, Dearborn, MI '83 (SOC)
VIEIRA, ELIZABETH K., dir. mktg. and plng., Jess Parrish Memorial Hospital, Titusville, FL '82 (PR) (PLNG)
VIEIRA, JOSEPH, mgr. pur., St. Luke's Hospital of New Bedford, New Bedford, MA '80 (PUR)
VIELHABER, DAVID P., dir. soc. serv., University Hospitals of Cleveland, Cleveland, OH '74 (SOC)
VIELHAUER, WAYNE S., student, Program in Hospital and Health Administration, University of Alabama, Birmingham, AL '85
VIENS, RICHARD A., dir. facil., North Adams Regional Hospital, North Adams, MA '78 (ENG)
VIERA, JOSEPH GEORGE, supt. bldg. and grds., Santa Teresa Community Hospital, San Jose, CA '74 (ENG)
VIERELA, PHILIP R., asst. adm., Richmond Memorial Hospital, Richmond, VA '75 (ENG)
VIERRA, EUGENE J., atty., Los Banos Community Hospital, Los Banos, CA '84 (ATTY)
VIETORIS, LAURA L., vice-pres. corp. serv., Parkside Home Health Service, Inc., Park Ridge, IL '84
VIETS, HILARY P., dir. new venture dev., Pontiac General Hospital, Pontiac, MI '85 (PLNG)
VIFIAN, KAY R., dir. commun. rel., Guttenberg Municipal Hospital, Guttenberg, IA '84 (PR)
VIGER, KATHLEEN A., RN, dir. surg. nrsg., Maine Medical Center, Portland, ME '84 (NURS)
VIGILIS, JAMES J., dir. plant and maint., St. John's Riverside Hospital, Yonkers, NY '87 (ENG)
VIGNA, MAJ. JOHN, MSC USA, chief pat. adm., DeWitt Army Community Hospital, Fort Belvoir, VA '80
VIGNOLA, MARGO L., Salomon Brothers, Inc., New York, NY '83
VIJIL, CHARLOTTE, supv. pat. rel., St. Francis Medical Center, Lynwood, CA '85 (PAT)
VILANOVA, SANTOS M., dir. pers., Hospital de La Concepcion, San German, P.R. '86 (PERS)
VILLA, MARTHA, supv. med. sup. tech., Veterans Administration Medical Center, Phoenix, AZ '86 (CS)
VILLAFUERTE, RICHARD C., dir. safety and security, University of New Mexico Hospital, Albuquerque, NM '86 (ENG)
VILLAMIN, LETICIA C., Satellite Beach, FL '76 (FOOD)
VILLANUEVA, ALICE A., dir. human res., Riverside Community Hospital, Riverside, CA '86 (PERS)
VILLANUEVA, JUAN E., asst. exec. dir. human res., Bella Vista Hospital, Mayaguez, P.R. '83 (PERS)
VILLEGAS, JEAN M., asst. mgr. sup., proc. and distrib., Providence Memorial Hospital, El Paso, TX '86 (CS)
VILLEGAS, ROSE H., dir. vol. serv., St. Joseph Hospital, Chicago, IL '85 (VOL)
VILLELLA, LYNN BUCKINGHAM, dir. pub. rel. and publicity, Presbyterian Healthcare Services, Albuquerque, NM '83 (PR)
VILLIER, ROBERT L., dir. pub. rel., Temple University Health Sciences Center, Philadelphia, PA '80 (PR)
VILLINES, SHARON L., dir. mktg., Virginia Beach General Hospital, Virginia Beach, VA '84 (PLNG)
VILMONT, SALLY J., RN, mgr., Bishop Clarkson Memorial Hospital, Omaha, NE '84 (NURS)
VILNIT, WILLIAM F., dir. matl. mgt., Day Kimball Hospital, Putnam, CT '79 (CS)(PUR)
VILOTTI, THOMAS W., chief eng., Ukiah General Hospital, Ukiah, CA '79 (ENG)
VILUMS, JANIS JR., dir. health care design, Henningson, Durham and Richardson, San Francisco, CA '70
VINARDI, GREGORY B., adm., St. Francis Hospital, Maryville, MO '69
VINCENT-MOSHER, KAY E., risk mgr., Mount Carmel Mercy Hospital, Detroit, MI '82 (RISK)
VINCENT, DORIS, head nrs., Ellis Hospital, Schenectady, NY '87 (AMB)
VINCENT, JOHN R., dir. soc. work, Our Lady of Lourdes Medical Center, Camden, NJ '86 (SOC)
VINCENT, MARJORIE ELAINE, adm., Bon Secours Ambulatory Surgery Center, Ellicott City, MD '85 (NURS)
VINCENT, MARTHA S., dir. vol. serv., Harper Hospital, Detroit, MI '83 (VOL)
VINCENT, PATRICIA T., dir. soc. serv., St. Joseph's Hospital, Parkersburg, WV '72 (SOC)
VINCENT, VICKI LYNN, pat. rep., Abbeville General Hospital, Abbeville, LA '86 (PAT)
VINCENT, WILLIAM G., dir. eng., Edward W. Sparrow Hospital, Lansing, MI '84 (ENG)
VINCENTI, MARY H., dir. food serv., HCA Deer Park Hospital, Deer Park, TX '80 (FOOD)
VINCI, LINDA M., qual. assur. consult., St. Peter's Medical Center, New Brunswick, NJ '84 (EDUC)
VINEHOUT, KATHLEEN A., asst. prof., Sangamon State University, Springfield, IL '85
VINES, GRACIE MEBANE, chief pat. and family serv., Pitt County Memorial Hospital, Greenville, NC '81 (SOC)
VINES, JAY, adm., HCA Oak Hill Hospital, Spring Hill, FL '79
VINING, KURT E., vice-pres. human res., Sinai Hospital of Detroit, Detroit, MI '73 (PERS)
VINK, JASPER, chief off. and adm., Friendship Services, Gallup, NM '84
VINOPAL, STEVE, supv. environ., Mile Bluff Center, Mauston, WI '76 (ENG)
VINSEL, DOUGLAS B., exec. vice-pres., Wake Medical Center, Raleigh, NC '73
VINSON, ELIZABETH J., dir. food serv., Stamford Hospital, Stamford, CT '86 (FOOD)
VINSON, FAYE R., dir. vol. serv., Bethany Hospital, Chicago, IL '86 (VOL)
VINSON, JERRY W., mgr. maint., Barstow Community Hospital, Barstow, CA '86 (ENG)
VINTON, KENDRA J., med. tech., Walter Reed Army Medical Center, Washington, DC '83
VINYARD, SAM, dir. matl. mgt., Springhill Memorial Hospital, Mobile, AL '83 (PUR)
VIPOND, JONATHAN III, atty., Sacred Heart Hospital, Allentown, PA '85 (ATTY)
VIRAG, DAVID P., chief vol. serv., Veterans Administration Medical Center, Butler, PA '85 (VOL)
VIRDEN, MARK A., asst. vice-pres., Stormont-Vail Regional Medical Center, Topeka, KS '87 (PLNG)
VIRGIL, PHYLLIS M., coor. spec. proj., Hospital Corporation of America, Nashville, TN '81
VIRGILIO, MAJ. BENJAMIN WAYNE, MSC USAF, facil. mgr., U. S. Air Force Medical Center Keesler, Biloxi, MS '84 (ENG)
VIRGINIE, SR. ANNE, pres., Saint Raphael Corporation, New Haven, CT '77
VIRGO, JOHN M., chief exec. off., International Health Economics and Management Institute, Southern Illinois University at Edwardsville, Edwardsville, IL '84
VIRGONA, PATRICIA M., dir. diet., Wyckoff Heights Hospital, Brooklyn, NY '67 (FOOD)
VIRNOCHE-BROWN, KAREN M., support staff, Servicemaster Industries, Inc., Downers Grove, IL '85 (FOOD)
VISLOSKY, CAPT. H. MICHELLE, student, Usamma, Fort Detrick, MD '85 (PUR)
VISSCHER, PATRICIA A., RN, mgr. clin., Bay Medical Center, Bay City, MI '86 (NURS)
VISSERS, SR. M. FIDELIS, pat. rep., St. Nicholas Hospital, Sheboygan, WI '78 (PAT)
VITA, MARGARET R., dir. vol. serv., L. W. Blake Memorial Hospital, Bradenton, FL '84 (VOL)
VITA, PATRICIA, dir. vol. serv., Gaylord Hospital, Wallingford, CT '77 (VOL)
VITALE, ANTHONY F., dir. sup. and serv., Mountainside Hospital, Montclair, NJ '78 (PUR)
VITALE, CHRISTINE M., asst. vice-pres., Roxborough Memorial Hospital, Philadelphia, PA '80
VITALE, ELLEN C., dir. pers., Memorial Hospital, Meriden, CT '86 (PERS)
VITALE, FRANK RALPH, partner, Herman Smith Associates, Redwood City, CA '67
VITALE, JOSEPH A., chief eng., Columbus Hospital, Newark, NJ '85 (ENG)
VITI, ANN S., pat. rep., Kissimmee Memorial Hospital, Kissimmee, FL '86 (PAT)
VITO, MICKI, coor. vol., Community Hospital of Chula Vista, Chula Vista, CA '81 (VOL)
VITOUS, JAMES P., mgt. eng., University of California at Los Angeles Medical Center, Los Angeles, CA '86 (MGMT)
VIVAS, JOSE GUILLERMO, atty., Hospital de Damas, Ponce, P.R. '78 (ATTY)
VIVENS, SOLANGES, RN, dir. nrsg., Washington Home, Washington, DC '82 (NURS)
VIVENZIO, ELIZABETH J., freelancer, Maywood, NJ '86 (PR)
VIVENZIO, JOHN VINCENT, dir. matl. mgt., Barnert Memorial Hospital Center, Paterson, NJ '86 (PUR)
VLAJKOVIC, JOHN, adm. dir. lab., St. Francis Hospital, Evanston, IL '86
VLASIS, VICKI, dir. vol. serv., Christ Hospital, Oak Lawn, IL '70 (VOL)
VLISMAS, DIMITRIA, mgr. food serv., University of California at Los Angeles Medical Center, Los Angeles, CA '86 (FOOD)
VOBORIL, EILEEN, coor. pat. care, Memorial Hospital, Schuyler, NE '86 (EDUC)
VOCKE, CECILIA ANN, pat. rep., Miami Valley Hospital, Dayton, OH '85 (PAT)
VOCKER, MARILYN JOAN, mgr. clin. soc. work, Glenbrook Hospital, Glenview, IL '86 (SOC)
VODENICKER, JOHNETTE L., RN, asst. adm. nrsg., Memorial Hospital, Ormond Beach, FL '85 (NURS)
VODENLIC, IVAN, dir. pur., St. Luke's Hospital, Racine, WI '70 (PUR)
VOELZ, MARY LYNN, dir. commun. rel., Cleveland Community Hospital, Cleveland, TN '86 (PR)
VOGEL, CHARLES R., chief eng., Elmer Community Hospital, Elmer, NJ '71 (ENG)
VOGEL, CHESTER T., eng. consult., White Plains, NY '79 (ENG)
VOGEL, DAVID E., pres., David E. Vogel and Associates, Albuquerque, NM '71
VOGEL, JOHN A. JR., dir. pur., Reading Hospital and Medical Center, Reading, PA '83 (PUR)
VOGEL, JOSEPH F., mgr. pur., Sheppard and Enoch Pratt Hospital, Baltimore, MD '85 (PUR)
VOGEL, LISA R., student, Moorhead State University, Minneapolis, MN '84
VOGEL, LOIS L., RN, dir. nrsg. serv., Skiff Medical Center, Newton, IA '82 (NURS)
VOGEL, MARY LOU, dir. clin. soc. serv., Los Robles Regional Medical Center, Thousand Oaks, CA '83 (SOC)
VOGEL, NANCY A., RN, asst. dir. nrsg., Parma Community General Hospital, Parma, OH '85 (NURS)
VOGELER, BOYD E., dir. mgt. eng., Intermountain Health Care, Inc., Salt Lake City, UT '73 (MGMT)
VOGELGESANG, PHILIP E., sr. vice-pres. corp. serv., Holy Cross Hospital, Fort Lauderdale, FL '85 (PR) (PLNG)
VOGELSANG, JOHN, asst. dir. hskpg., Saint Francis Medical Center, Peoria, IL '87 (ENVIRON)
VOGL, MIKE, mgr. commun., Poudre Valley Hospital, Fort Collins, CO '81 (PR)
VOGLER, JERRY, exec. vice-pres., St. Joseph Health Systems, Flint, MI '75
VOGT, CARL WILLIAM, atty., Duke University Medical Center, Durham, NC '70 (ATTY)
VOGT, J. GAIL, dir. food and nutr. serv., H. Lee Moffitt Hospital and Cancer Research Institute at the University of South Florida, Tampa, FL '85 (FOOD)
VOGT, PATRICIA LYNN, dir. pers., Maryland General Hospital, Baltimore, MD '85 (PERS)
VOGT, THOMAS M., atty., Immanuel-St. Joseph's Hospital, Mankato, MN '77 (ATTY)
VOIGT, CHRISTINE V., risk mgt. asst., Hospital of Saint Raphael, New Haven, CT '83 (RISK)
VOIGT, KEVIN C., dir. pur., Memorial Medical Center, Springfield, IL '80 (PUR)
VOIGT, LOUELLA, dir. counselor soc. serv., Worthington Regional Hospital, Worthington, MN '83 (SOC)
VOILAND, BONITA S., dir. pub. rel., Park Ridge Hospital, Rochester, NY '81 (PR)
VOISIN, ELVIRA D., dir. food serv., Methodist Hospital South-J. R. Flippin Hospital, Memphis, TN '78 (FOOD)
VOITA, ROCHELLE A., parent rep., Children's Hospital, St. Paul, MN '84 (PAT)
VOKES, ROBERT W. H., dir. mktg. and dev., St. Mary's Medical Center, Duluth, MN '81 (PLNG)
VOLD, HENRY J., dir. gen. serv., North Country Hospital, Bemidji, MN '79 (ENG)
VOLGER, THOMAS K., exec. dir., Sisters of St. Mary Data Center, St. Louis, MO '84
VOLK, DAVID L., atty., California Association of Hospitals and Health Systems, Sacramento, CA '80 (ATTY)
VOLKMAN, JUDITH M., dir. vol., University Hospital, Denver, CO '85 (VOL)
VOLKMAR, LARRY E., RN, vice-pres. pat. serv., Jane Lamb Health Center, Clinton, IA '84 (NURS)
VOLLAND, PATRICIA J., sr. dir. pat. serv., Johns Hopkins Hospital, Baltimore, MD '72 (SOC)
VOLPE, BUDDY, dir. learning center, Lutheran General Hospital, San Antonio, TX '86 (EDUC)
VOLPE, TIMOTHY E., dir. soc. work, Northwestern Memorial Hospital, Chicago, IL '84 (SOC)
VOLPICELLI, KATHLEEN M., dir. fin. plng. and reimbursement, Mercy Hospital, Wilkes-Barre, PA '83
VOMVORIS, WILLIAM G., dir. food serv., Presbyterian Hospital in the City of New York, New York, NY '79 (FOOD)
VON BLUECHER, ALEXANDRA, dir. cent. serv., La Crosse Lutheran Hospital, La Crosse, WI '83 (CS)

VON DAMBROWSKI, MICHELE, writer, Rye, NY '84
VON EHREN, WARREN R., (ret.), Madison, WI '54 (LIFE)
VON GUNDEN, HAROLD, consult., Clearfield Hospital, Clearfield, PA '67
VON GUNTEN, GARY L., mgr. oper., Hamot Medical Center, Erie, PA '85 (MGMT)
VON HANDORF, JERRY, dir. eng. and maint., St. Elizabeth Medical Center-South, Edgewood, KY '81 (ENG)
VON HUSEN, MARCY, coor. risk mgt., Mills Memorial Hospital, San Mateo, CA '86 (RISK)
VON KROHN, REX J., (ret.), Vancouver, WA '47 (LIFE)
VON RICHTER, FRANK C., vice-pres., Boston Biomedical Consultants, Waltham, MA '68
VON SCHAVEN, HOWARD, partner, Coopers and Lybrand, Pittsburgh, PA '80
VONDERHAAR, SHARON, adm. dir. amb. care, Christ Hospital and Medical Center, Oak Lawn, IL '87 (AMB)
VONDERHEID, ARDA E., RN, asst. adm. nrsg., Kaiser Foundation Hospital, San Francisco, CA '81 (NURS)
VONDERHEIDT, LEO CHARLES, (ret.), Aurora, IL '16 (LIFE)
VONDERLINDT, ELAINE, assoc. dir. soc. work, University Hospital of Brooklyn-Suny Center, Brooklyn, NY '78 (SOC)
VONHOLTEN, BARBARA J., pat. rep. and coor. vol., Medical Center of Independence, Independence, MO '82 (PAT)(VOL)
VONLINDENBERG, JAN M., dir. human res., Fallston General Hospital, Fallston, MD '83 (PERS)
VOORHEES, CHRISTINE, supv. cent. serv., Hunterdon Medical Center, Flemington, NJ '85 (CS)
VOORHEES, LEE R. JR., atty., Stevens Memorial Hospital, Edmonds, WA '74 (ATTY)
VOORSANGER, ESTHER L., RN, consult. nrsg. adm., Sun City, AZ '71 (EDUC)(NURS)
VORDERER, LAWRENCE HENRY, asst. prof., College of St. Scholastra, Superior, WI '75
VOREES, GEORGE E., chief eng., Lanier Park Hospital, Gainesville, GA '84 (ENG)
VORNBROCK, JOHN G., assoc. adm., Yakima Valley Memorial Hospital, Yakima, WA '74 (MGMT)
VORSETH, DUANE RICHARD, adm., Sartori Memorial Hospital, Cedar Falls, IA '65 (PR)
VOS, DALE, eng., Pella Community Hospital, Pella, IA '73 (ENG)
VOSBURGH, DEBORAH C., dir. soc. serv., Lake Region Hospital and Nursing Home, Fergus Falls, MN '79 (SOC)
VOSE, ANN B., RN, (ret.), Los Lunas, NM '70 (NURS)
VOSS, HENRY D., dir. pers., Memorial Hospital, Cambridge, MN '73 (PERS)
VOSS, SR. M. SARAH, St. Paul's Priory, St. Paul, MN '84
VOSS, RANDALL G., dir. diet., American Fork Hospital, American Fork, UT '82 (FOOD)
VOSS, RUTH ANN, asst. dir. nrsg., St. Marys Hospital of Rochester, Rochester, MN '86 (NURS)
VOSS, WILLMA D., supv. cent. serv., San Bernardino County Medical Center, San Bernardino, CA '83 (CS)
VOSSLER, SR. M. VINCENTIA, coor., Hospitals of Sisters of Mercy, Buffalo Diocese, Buffalo, NY '48 (LIFE)
VOTAW, JANE D., RN, chief nrsg. serv., Veterans Administration Medical Center, Sheridan, WY '82 (NURS)
VOTH, ROY H., dir. soc. work, St. Joseph Medical Center, Wichita, KS '80 (SOC)
VOYLES, DOTTIE, mgr. food serv., Medical Center Hospital, Tyler, TX '68 (FOOD)
VOYTKO, ANDREA J., mgr. pub. rel., mktg. and dev., Memorial Hospital, North Conway, NH '86 (PLNG)
VOYVODICH, MARC E., vice-pres., Northland Health Group, Portland, ME '80
VRACIU, ROBERT A., pres. center for health studies, Hospital Corporation of America, Nashville, TN '81 (PLNG)
VRANEKOVIC, CHARLES E., assoc. dir. bus. affairs, Mental Health Service of Lorain County, Inc., Lorain, OH '86 (MGMT)
VRAVICK, VIRGINIA, prod. mgr., Baxter Travenol Laboratories, Deerfield, IL '86
VRBANICH, DAVID A., mgt. eng., United Hospital, Grand Forks, ND '80 (PLNG)
VREATT, MARY C., RN, dir. pat. rel., Grace Hospital, Detroit, MI '71 (PAT)
VREELAND, JAMES C., dir., Memorial Hospital of Bedford County, Everett, PA '63
VRH, SUSAN A., dir. pub. rel., Modesto City Hospital, Modesto, CA '85 (PR)
VRIESMAN, D. W., pres., St. John's Lutheran Care Center, Mars, PA '79 (PLNG)
VROLIJK, JACOBUS P., tech. consult., American International Group, Inc., New York, NY '82 (ENG)
VROOM, JAMES R., vice-pres., Wake Medical Center, Raleigh, NC '77
VROOMAN, WILLIAM P., coor. adm. syst., Hospital Corporation of America, Nashville, TN '78 (MGMT)
VUKICH, SUSAN C., dir. vol., Northwest Hospital, Seattle, WA '74 (VOL)
VUNCANNON, EILEEN J., dir. pers., Magnolia Hospital, Corinth, MS '82 (PERS)
VYHNALEK, LEONARD P., atty., Great Plains Regional Medical Center, North Platte, NE '78 (ATTY)

W

WAACK, KATHERINE E., dir. vol. serv. and coor. pat. rel., Methodist Hospital, Madison, WI '79 (VOL)(PAT)
WAAGE, MARY A., coor. pat. educ. and amb. care unit, St. Jude Children's Research Hospital, Memphis, TN '86 (EDUC)
WACHS, FRANCESCA L., Long Beach, CA '82
WACHS, MOSES, exec. dir., M. J. G. Nursing Home, Brooklyn, NY '44 (LIFE)
WACHS, NANCY NEIR, ombudsman, Children's Memorial Hospital, Chicago, IL '72 (PAT)
WACHTER, VELMA J., RN, dir. nrsg. serv., St. John's Mercy Hospital, Washington, MO '85 (NURS)
WACKER, DAVID EDWARD, loss control consult., Health Care Insurance Company, Bernardsville, NJ '79 (ENG)
WADACH, CYNTHIA J., dir. vol. serv., Carney Hospital, Boston, MA '87 (VOL)
WADDEL, MAJ. KATHLEEN P., MSC USA, chief ncd, U. S. Army MEDDAC, Nbg, APO New York, NY '84 (FOOD)
WADDELL, ELAINE, asst. to dir., Veterans Administration Medical Center, Bay Pines, FL '74
WADDELL, KAREN VINYARD, group vice-pres., Hospital Corporation of America, Oklahoma City, OK '78 (PR)
WADDELL, KENNETH L., exec. dir., Twin County Community Hospital, Galax, VA '57 (LIFE)
WADE, CLARE L., asst. dir. pub. rel., Holy Family Hospital, Des Plaines, IL '86 (PR)
WADE, CYNTHIA L., dir. commun. rel., St. Joseph's Hospital Medical Center, Bloomington, IL '86 (PR)
WADE, DIANA P., dir. qual. assur. and risk mgt., St. Mary's Hospital, Galveston, TX '80 (RISK)
WADE, G. WAYNE, dir. maint., Decatur County Memorial Hospital, Greensburg, IN '81 (ENG)
WADE, IDA D., RN, asst. chief nrsg., Veterans Administration Medical Center, Spokane, WA '82 (NURS)
WADE, LEO, dir. environ. health and safety, University of Texas Medical Branch Hospitals, Galveston, TX '83 (RISK)
WADE, MARY SANDERS, RN, dir. nrsg. serv., Salem Hospital, Memorial Unit, Salem, OR '76 (NURS)
WADE, RICHARD H., vice-pres. commun., Maryland Hospital Association, Lutherville, MD '79 (PR)
WADE, RONALD D., vice-pres., Ohio Hospital Insurance Company, Columbus, OH '84 (RISK)
WADE, VICKI, risk mgr., Waterman Medical Center, Eustis, FL '86 (RISK)
WADEWITZ, W. MARTIN, asst. dir. bus. off., Margaret R. Pardee Memorial Hospital, Hendersonville, NC '85 (PUR)
WADHWANI, SUNIL T., pres., Campion Health Corporation, Pittsburgh, PA '86 (PLNG)
WADLE, DONALD, asst. adm., Porter Memorial Hospital, Valparaiso, IN '80
WADLEY, ALDOW, chief eng., Charter Suburban Hospital, Mesquite, TX '80 (ENG)
WADNIK, JEAN E., dir. staff dev., Warren Hospital, Phillipsburg, NJ '82 (EDUC)
WADSACK, DEBORAH G., dir. commun. and prof. rel., Humana Hospital -Brentwood, Shreveport, LA '82 (PR)
WADSWORTH, BEVERLY A., coor. vol., Kaiser Foundation Hospital, Hayward, CA '85 (VOL)
WADZINSKI, KATHERINE J., supv. cent. serv., John F. Kennedy Medical Center, Chicago, IL '82 (CS)
WAELTZ, DOLORES, dir. matl. mgt., St. Elizabeth Medical Center, Granite City, IL '84 (PUR)
WAETZMAN, RONALD, chief fin. off., Western Pennsylvania Hospital, Pittsburgh, PA '79
WAGAR, MARK L., pres., The Emerald Health Network, Inc., Cleveland, OH '79
WAGEMAN, JAN, mgr. pur., Lansing General Hospital, Lansing, MI '84 (PUR)
WAGEMAN, RONALD A., chief eng., Good Samaritan Hospital and Medical Center, Portland, OR '85 (ENG)
WAGENAAR, MARTHA ROACH, dir. pat. rel., North Carolina Memorial Hospital, Chapel Hill, NC '83 (PAT)
WAGES, ROBBIE J., dir. pers., Doctors Hospital, Tucker, GA '80 (PERS)
WAGGONER, ANNELIESE K., dir. educ. serv., St. Vincent Hospital, Green Bay, WI '81 (EDUC)
WAGGONER, JAN LISA, student, University of Alabama, Birmingham, AL '87
WAGGONER, JOHN W., asst. dir. eng. and maint., Ochsner Foundation Hospital, New Orleans, LA '84 (ENG)
WAGNER, SR. ANNELLA, St. Scholastica Priory, Duluth, MN '67 (FOOD)
WAGNER, BARBARA, RN, dir. in-service educ., St. Clement Hospital, Red Bud, IL '76 (EDUC)
WAGNER, BARRY LEE, dir. mgt. eng., St. Mary's Hospital and Medical Center, San Francisco, CA '79 (MGMT)
WAGNER, BEVERLY S., dir. vol. and pat. adv., Mid-Island Hospital, Bethpage, NY '83 (VOL)
WAGNER, BUDD G., dir. pub. rel., Saint Cabrini Hospital of Seattle, Seattle, WA '85 (PR)
WAGNER, CAROL ANN, student, University of Houston at Clear Lake City, Houston, TX '81
WAGNER, CAROLYN A., dir. pur., Fairfax Nursing Center, Fairfax, VA '86 (PUR)
WAGNER, CATHERINE BRADFORD, head soc. serv., Allegheny General Hospital, Pittsburgh, PA '79 (SOC)
WAGNER, DAVID A., vice-pres. plng., Trimark Corporation, West Orange, NJ '83 (PLNG)
WAGNER, BRIG. GEN. DONALD B., (ret.), Sugarland, TX '58
WAGNER, DOUGLAS, dir. sterile, proc., distrib. and cent. serv., St. Anthony's Medical Center, St. Louis, MO '85 (CS)
WAGNER, EILEEN C., instr. staff dev., Greater Baltimore Medical Center, Baltimore, MD '86 (EDUC)
WAGNER, ELEANOR R., atty., Joint Commission on Accreditation of Hospitals, Chicago, IL '76 (ATTY)
WAGNER, GAIL K., RN, vice-pres. nrsg., St. Luke's Hospital, Chesterfield, MO '85 (NURS)
WAGNER, GERALD W., assoc. adm., Hinds General Hospital, Jackson, MS '86
WAGNER, GLENN N., vice-pres. municipal res., L. F. Rothschild, Unterberg and Towbin, New York, NY '87
WAGNER, HENRY C., pres., Jewish Hospital, Louisville, KY '68
WAGNER, JAMES A. JR., adm. maternal and infant care, Grady Memorial Hospital, Atlanta, GA '75
WAGNER, JANET A., assoc. dir. mktg., Cape Fear Valley Medical Center, Fayetteville, NC '87 (PR)
WAGNER, JOHN P., atty., Community Hospital of Sacramento, Sacramento, CA '84 (ATTY)
WAGNER, KATHLEEN A., dir. soc. serv., Reading Hospital and Medical Center, Reading, PA '77 (SOC)
WAGNER, KATHY J., RN, vice-pres. nrsg. serv., Kishwaukee Community Hospital, De Kalb, IL '82 (NURS)
WAGNER, LAWRENCE GLENN, risk mgr., Medical Center Hospital, Odessa, TX '86 (RISK)
WAGNER, MARGARET E., dir. educ. serv., Humber Memorial Hospital, Toronto, Ont., Canada '83 (EDUC)
WAGNER, MEREDITH B., head vol. serv., Melrose-Wakefield Hospital, Melrose, MA '70 (VOL)
WAGNER, NICHOLAS D., mgr. food serv., Northwestern Memorial Hospital, Chicago, IL '79 (FOOD)
WAGNER, PATRICIA H., atty., University Hospital, Seattle, WA '76 (ATTY)
WAGNER, PEGGY G., dir. pers., Poplar Springs Hospital, Petersburg, VA '84 (PERS)
WAGNER, PHILLIP W., dir. facil., Lourdes Hospital, Paducah, KY '84 (ENG)
WAGNER, RICHARD A., vice-pres. med. adm., Cigna Health Plan, Inc., Dallas, TX '83
WAGNER, RICHARD F., dir. maint., Munson Medical Center, Traverse City, MI '81 (ENG)
WAGNER, RONALD E., atty., Children's Hospital of Michigan, Detroit, MI '85 (ATTY)
WAGNER, SANDRA M., RN, asst. dir. nrsg. serv., Riddle Memorial Hospital, Media, PA '81 (NURS)
WAGNER, URSULA, dir. soc. serv., Palos Community Hospital, Palos Heights, IL '85 (SOC)
WAGNER, WILLIAM J., dir. mktg. commun., Hamot Medical Center, Erie, PA '86 (PR)
WAGONER, FRANCES F., dir. vol. serv., Greenwich Hospital, Greenwich, CT '84 (VOL)
WAGSTAFF, LISA O., student, Department of Health Service Administration, George Washington University, Washington, DC '86 (MGMT)
WAGSTAFF, THOMAS A., actg. asst. dir. diet. serv., Miriam Hospital, Providence, RI '86 (FOOD)
WAHA, ROGER A., dir. pub., Oakwood Hospital, Dearborn, MI '82 (PR)
WAHL, GISELA A., asst. matl. mgr., Aspen Valley Hospital District, Aspen, CO '81 (CS)
WAHL, JANE SEIDL, RN, assoc. dir., Flushing Hospital and Medical Center, Flushing, NY '80 (RISK)
WAHL, KARENN A., adm. asst. and chief exec. off. staff serv., The Methodist Hospital, Houston, TX '84
WAHLSTROM, MARLENE F., atty., Meriter Hospital, Madison, WI '85 (ATTY)
WAHOSKE, JANA L., mgr. mktg., plng. and dev., North Memorial Medical Center, Robbinsdale, MN '85 (PLNG)
WAHRMAN, JUDITH P., student, Bowling Green State University, Bowling Green, OH '79 (MGMT)
WAIFE, MITCHELL M., exec. vice-pres., Jewish Home and Hospital for Aged, New York, NY '47 (LIFE)
WAINWRIGHT, ALICE K., RN, asst. dir. nrsg., Crozer-Chester Medical Center, Chester, PA '86 (NURS)
WAINWRIGHT, GEORGE L., atty., Goddard Memorial Hospital, Stoughton, MA '68 (ATTY)
WAITE, DOROTHY A., RN, dir. nrsg., Dakota Hospital, Fargo, ND '72 (NURS)
WAITE, DOUGLAS D., vice-pres. fin., Borgess Medical Center, Kalamazoo, MI '81
WAITE, RICHARD A., dir. pub. rel. and fund dev., Gifford Memorial Hospital, Randolph, VT '86 (PR)
WAITE, SUZANNE J., student, Rush University, Chicago, IL '86
WAITER, PATRICIA FINAN, vice-pres. adm., Clinton Memorial Hospital, Wilmington, OH '86
WAITERS, AUGUSTUS JR., asst. chief soc. serv., Veterans Administration Medical Center, Philadelphia, PA '71 (SOC)
WAITS, EMMETT MOORE, chaplain and dir. soc. serv., Gaston Episcopal Hospital, Dallas, TX '75 (SOC)
WAITZ, JUNE C., dir. outpatient care, Jewish Hospital, Louisville, KY '85 (NURS)
WAKAL, WILLIAM, dir. eng., Starke Memorial Hospital, Knox, IN '80 (ENG)
WAKEFIELD, A. R., sr. vice-pres., St. John's Healthcare Corporation, Anderson, IN '83
WAKEFIELD, BRETT A., vice-pres. plng. and mktg., Gottlieb Memorial Hospital, Melrose Park, IL '78 (PLNG)
WAKEFORD, JEFFREY D., dir. biomedical eng., Memorial Hospital, Colorado Springs, CO '86 (ENG)
WALANDER, GARY ARTHUR, clin. eng. and supv. biomedical instrumentation, Bishop Clarkson Memorial Hospital, Omaha, NE '77 (ENG)
WALB, WILLIAM R., vice-pres. oper., Hanover General Hospital, Hanover, PA '87 (RISK)
WALBERG, SHARON L., adm. pat. care, Monticello-Big Lake Community Hospital, Monticello, MN '81 (NURS)
WALBRECQ, JANET S., vice-pres. human res., Tawas St. Joseph Hospital, Tawas City, MI '85 (PERS)
WALCHEK, COL. DENNIS E., RN, asst. chief nrsg., Tripler Army Medical Center, Honolulu, HI '82 (NURS)
WALCHENBACH, DONALD E., (ret.), Grand Rapids, MI '51 (LIFE)
WALCZAK, DAVID M., biomedical eng., Kent General Hospital, Dover, DE '80 (ENG)
WALCZAK, MARK F., dir. mgt. eng., South Hills Health System, Pittsburgh, PA '84 (MGMT)
WALCZAK, REGINA, corp. dir. qual. mgt., National Medical Enterprises, Los Angeles, CA '84 (RISK)
WALCZUK, CAROL A., dir. matl. mgt., Jersey City Medical Center, Jersey City, NJ '86 (PUR)
WALD, ALVIN S., tech. dir. anes., Presbyterian Hospital in the City of New York, New York, NY '85 (ENG)
WALD, ROBERT A., dir. market res., Melrose-Wakefield Hospital, Melrose, MA '84 (PLNG)
WALDECK, JANE, dir. human res., Borgess Medical Center, Kalamazoo, MI '78 (PERS)
WALDEN, ALYCE L., RN, dir. nrsg., Wood County Hospital, Bowling Green, OH '82 (NURS)
WALDEN, CLARKE, atty., Memorial Hospital, Hollywood, FL '81 (ATTY)

WALDEN, IDA B., RN, asst. adm. pat. care serv., Delta County Memorial Hospital, Delta, CO '82 (NURS)
WALDEN, JANE, dir. vol. serv., Community General Hospital, Thomasville, NC '86 (VOL)
WALDEN, JUDITH, exec. dir., Hospital Home Health Care, Inc., Albuquerque, NM '80
WALDHAUSER, TAMAR, dir. rad. serv., Bellevue Hospital Center, New York, NY '69
WALDMAN, BART, atty., Valley Medical Center, Renton, WA '83 (ATTY)
WALDMAN, HILDA R. GLAZER, asst. prof., Allied Health Education, University of Texas Health Science Center, Dallas, TX '83 (EDUC)
WALDNER, LYNN, asst. dir. nutr. serv., United Hospital, St. Paul, MN '80 (FOOD)
WALDO, SHARI C., med. soc. worker, Otsego Memorial Hospital, Gaylord, MI '82 (SOC)
WALDON, DENNIS C., atty., American Hospital Association, Chicago, IL '79 (ATTY)
WALDRON, JAMES A., atty., St. Francis Medical Center, Trenton, NJ '81 (ATTY)
WALDRON, ROBERT E., evening supv. sup., proc. and distrib., Good Samaritan Medical Center, Phoenix, AZ '86 (CS)
WALDROP, DAVID H., dir. soc. serv., Greenville Memorial Hospital, Greenville, SC '79 (SOC)
WALDROP, JOAN M., dir. commun. rel., St. Mary's Hospital, Amsterdam, NY '84 (PR) (PLNG)
WALDROP, KAREN M., dir. commun. and cont. educ., Carraway Methodist Medical Center, Birmingham, AL '84 (EDUC)
WALDROP, REINETTA T., syst. coor., Grady Memorial Hospital, Atlanta, GA '83 (MGMT)
WALDSMITH, JUDY, dir. soc. serv. and rehab. counseling, St. Francis Rehabilitation Hospital and Nursing Home, Green Springs, OH '85 (SOC)
WALEKO, KATHLEEN M., MD, asst. vice-pres. support serv., Magee-Womens Hospital, Pittsburgh, PA '80
WALERIUS, ROBERT J., atty., Providence Medical Center, Seattle, WA '73 (ATTY)
WALES, KAREN S., dir. emp. serv., DePaul Health Center, Bridgeton, MO '87 (PERS)
WALKER, ARCHIE L., chief diet. serv., Veterans Administration Medical Center, St. Louis, MO '74 (FOOD)
WALKER, DANIEL J., atty., Terrebonne General Medical Center, Houma, LA '80 (ATTY)
WALKER, DENISE A., asst. dir. food and nutr. serv., Yale-New Haven Hospital, New Haven, CT '83 (FOOD)
WALKER, DENISE R., dir. commun. rel., Muscatine General Hospital, Muscatine, IA '86 (PR)
WALKER, DENISE S., adm. diet., Amsterdam Memorial Hospital, Amsterdam, NY '81 (FOOD)
WALKER, DENNIS, dir. eng., St. Joseph Hospital, Port Charlotte, FL '81 (ENG)
WALKER, DERRY, vice-pres. plng. and mktg., Moore Regional Hospital, Pinehurst, NC '85 (PR)
WALKER, DUANE D., RN, vice-pres. pat. serv., Queen's Medical Center, Honolulu, HI '72 (NURS)
WALKER, 1ST LT. EDWARD YANCEY III, MSC USAF, liaison off., Ochampus, Aurora, CO '78
WALKER, EDWIN LEE II, coor. facil., University Hospital, Lexington, KY '85 (ENG)
WALKER, EUGENE L., dir. plant oper., Schumpert Medical Center, Shreveport, LA '83 (ENG)
WALKER, GARTH, assoc., Herman Smith Associates, Hinsdale, IL '51
WALKER, GAYLE, dir. soc. serv., Douglas Community Hospital, Roseburg, OR '86 (SOC)
WALKER, GEORGIA-RUTH, asst. dir. diet. adm., Sacred Heart Medical Center, Spokane, WA '84 (FOOD)
WALKER, GORDON J., atty., William Beaumont Hospital, Royal Oak, MI '86 (ATTY)
WALKER, HAROLD EUGENE, dir. eng., University Community Hospital, Tampa, FL '76 (ENG)
WALKER, HAROLD, eng., Levi Arthritis Hospital, Hot Springs National Park, AR '83 (ENG)
WALKER, IRA W., dir. facil. design and construction, Christian Health Services Development Corporation, St. Louis, MO '86 (ENG)
WALKER, JACK R., chief nrs., 9th Aeromedical Evacuation Squadron, APO San Francisco, CA '68 (NURS)
WALKER, JAMES C., chief maint. eng., St. Mary's Hospital, Galesburg, IL '81 (ENG)
WALKER, JAMES E., adm. dir. plant oper. and constr., Proctor Community Hospital, Peoria, IL '85 (ENG)
WALKER, JOEL H., pres., Central Vermont Medical Center, Berlin, VT '51 (LIFE)
WALKER, JOHN B., mgr. indust. segmentation, Gte Service Corporation, Stamford, CT '86 (ENG)
WALKER, JOHN H., dir. risk, University of Alabama in Birmingham, Birmingham, AL '80 (RISK)
WALKER, JOSEPHINE R., dir. pur., Methodist Hospital of Southern California, Arcadia, CA '65 (PUR)
WALKER, JUDITH ANN, RN, nrs. spec. coronary care, Chamberlain Memorial Hospital, Rockwood, TN '74 (EDUC)
WALKER, KAREN E., coor. pub. rel., Deaconess Hospital, Evansville, IN '83 (PR)
WALKER, KAYE, dir. pub. rel., Baptist Medical Center-Montclair, Birmingham, AL '77 (PR)
WALKER, KENNETH D., mgr. sup., proc. and distrib., Park City Hospital, Bridgeport, CT '82 (CS)
WALKER, KENNETH M., dir. pers., Utah Valley Regional Medical Center, Provo, UT '80 (PERS)
WALKER, LINDA F., mgr. telecommun., Providence Hospital, Anchorage, AK '86 (ENG)
WALKER, LULA B., dir. food serv., Jefferson State Vocational School, Louisville, KY '69 (FOOD)
WALKER, MARILYN A., chief nutr. medicine serv., Ehrling Bergquist U. S. Air Force Regional Hospital, Omaha, NE '81 (FOOD)
WALKER, MARILYN R., RN, dir. nrsg., Memorial Hospital, Carthage, IL '73 (NURS)
WALKER, MARY E., coor. new prod., St. Francis-St. George Hospital, Cincinnati, OH '87 (PLNG)
WALKER, MELANIE, dir. soc. serv., Franklin Hospital, Benton, IL '86 (SOC)
WALKER, MYRA HAMILTON, dir. commun., Jo Ellen Smith Medical Center, New Orleans, LA '85 (ENG)
WALKER, OLIVER P., student, University of Alabama at Birmingham, School of Community and Allied Health, Birmingham, AL '87
WALKER, PHYLLIS, dir. vol., Charlotte Hungerford Hospital, Torrington, CT '72 (VOL)
WALKER, RAYMOND C., pres., Chedoke-McMaster Hospital, Hamilton, Ont., Canada '59
WALKER, ROBERT A., field eng., Wilford Hall U. S. Air Force Medical Center, Lackland AFB, TX '86 (ENG)
WALKER, ROBERT J., vice-pres., Walla Walla General Hospital, Walla Walla, WA '83 (PERS)
WALKER, ROBERT J., dir. soc. serv., East Liverpool City Hospital, East Liverpool, OH '80 (SOC)
WALKER, ROBERT R., pres., Intermountain Health Care, Inc., Salt Lake City, UT '82
WALKER, ROBIN L., dir. phys. search, Tyler and Company, Atlanta, GA '85
WALKER, STEPHEN R., atty., Security Pacific Capital Markets Group, Los Angeles, CA '78 (ATTY)
WALKER, SUSAN ALLRED, dir. food mgt., St. Agnes Hospital and Medical Center, Fresno, CA '78 (FOOD)
WALKER, SYLVIA M., dir. comunication serv., El Camino Hospital, Mountain View, CA '83 (PR)
WALKER, THOMAS D., dir. plant oper., Ellsworth Municipal Hospital, Iowa Falls, IA '86 (ENG)
WALKER, THOMAS G., dir. plant oper., AMI Medical Center of Garden Grove, Garden Grove, CA '83 (ENG)
WALKER, WILLIAM P., supv. nuclear medicine and radiation safety, Guernsey Memorial Hospital, Cambridge, OH '86 (ENG)
WALKER, WILLIAM T., atty., Akron General Medical Center, Akron, OH '73 (ATTY)
WALKINSHAW, WALTER, atty., Washington State Hospital Association, Seattle, WA '69 (ATTY)
WALKO, JOHN S., consult. health care, Ernst and Whinney, Pittsburgh, PA '84
WALKO, MARY ANN, RN, adm. dir. amb. clin., Western Reserve Systems-Southside, Youngstown, OH '87 (AMB)
WALKOWIAK, JACK J., dir. bldgs. and grds., Milwaukee Psychiatric Hospital, Milwaukee, WI '84 (ENG)
WALKUSH, RICHARD J., dir. pur., Marshfield Clinic, Marshfield, WI '77 (PUR)
WALL, BARBARA, RN, coor. mktg., Inter Plan, Opi Corporation, Milwaukee, WI '79 (PLNG)
WALL, DEBORAH J., dir. food serv., Childrens Hospital of Orange County, Orange, CA '77 (FOOD)
WALL, DORRIS S., dir. food serv., Kennestone Hospital, Marietta, GA '77 (FOOD)
WALL, GLORIA L., dir. nutr. serv., Huntington Memorial Hospital, Huntington, IN '78 (FOOD)
WALL, HARRIETT A., mktg. analyst, Transition Systems, Inc., Boston, MA '86 (MGMT)(PR) (PLNG)
WALL, HENRY J. JR., atty., Catholic Medical Center of Brooklyn and Queens, Jamaica, NY '73 (ATTY)
WALL, L. LOUISE P., RN, dir. nrsg., nrs. recruitment, retention and staff educ., St. Anthony Hospital, Oklahoma City, OK '87 (NURS)
WALL, LORETTA Y., dir. soc. work, University of Maryland Medical Systems, Baltimore, MD '80 (SOC)
WALL, MATTHEW T., atty., Texas Hospital Association, Austin, TX '86 (ATTY)
WALL, PATRICIA J., planner, Sisters of Providence Health Systems, Seattle, WA '81 (PLNG)
WALLACE-SHAHAN, THOMAS, dir. psych. and soc. serv., Yavapai Regional Medical Center, Prescott, AZ '85 (SOC)
WALLACE, AUDIE E. JR., vice-pres. mech. eng., Vft-Division of Coffman Engineers, Seattle, WA '85 (ENG)
WALLACE, CAROL A., dir. educ., Navarro Regional Hospital, Corsicana, TX '86 (EDUC)
WALLACE, CAROL C., dir. mktg. commun., Children's Hospital Medical Center, Akron, OH '86 (PR)
WALLACE, DEAN E., dir. hskpg., McLeod Regional Medical Center, Florence, SC '86 (ENVIRON)
WALLACE, HARRY N., mgr. cent. serv., St. Mary's Hospital, West Palm Beach, FL '85 (CS)
WALLACE, HELEN M., dir. soc. work, Hamilton Memorial Hospital, McLeansboro, IL '79 (SOC)
WALLACE, JAMES A. III, bus. dev. rep., M. B. Kahn Construction Company, Columbia, SC '87 (PLNG)
WALLACE, JAMES JR., dir. facil. mgt., St. Luke's Hospital, Maumee, OH '80 (ENG)
WALLACE, JEAN A., dir. adm. serv., U. S. Air Force Hospital Whiteman, Whiteman AFB, MO '83 (PLNG)
WALLACE, JEFFREY R., Montgomery, AL '86 (ENG)
WALLACE, JIM, assoc. dir. food serv., West Virginia University Hospital, Morgantown, WV '86 (FOOD)
WALLACE, JO LYNN D., dir. nrsg. educ., Rapides General Hospital, Alexandria, LA '83 (EDUC)
WALLACE, JOHN K. II, MD, (ret.), Jefferson City, MO '55 (LIFE)
WALLACE, LILLIAN C., dir. pur., Kings County Hospital Center, Brooklyn, NY '82 (PUR)
WALLACE, LLOYD E., vice-pres. clin. serv., Valdese General Hospital, Valdese, NC '82 (PLNG)
WALLACE, MARGARET, asst. dir. risk mgt. and loss control, Brigham and Women's Hospital, Boston, MA '86 (RISK)
WALLACE, MARK A., vice-pres., The Methodist Hospital, Houston, TX '81
WALLACE, MILDRED, supv. cent. sup., Braddock General Hospital, Braddock, PA '79 (CS)
WALLACE, PATRICIA W., dir. vol., Methodist Hospital of Southern California, Arcadia, CA '83 (VOL)
WALLACE, PAUL E. JR., Winston-Salem, NC '80
WALLACE, RICHARD A., supv. clin. and indust. eng., Grace Hospital, Detroit, MI '82 (ENG)
WALLACE, RICHARD B., adm., Rabun County Memorial Hospital, Clayton, GA '77
WALLACE, RITA J., dir. vol. serv., Truman Medical Center-East, Kansas City, MO '84 (VOL)
WALLACE, ROBERT C., dir. risk mgt., Williamsport Hospital and Medical Center, Williamsport, PA '80 (RISK)
WALLACE, ROBERT F., exec. dir. affiliate serv., Little Company of Mary Hospital, Burbank, IL '86 (AMB)
WALLACE, ROSE H., dir. pers., Anson County Hospital, Wadesboro, NC '86 (PERS)
WALLACE, RUDY L., dir. diet., Southwest Mississippi Regional Medical Center, McComb, MS '85 (FOOD)
WALLACE, RUTH L., RN, chief nrs., Veterans Administration Medical Center, Oklahoma City, OK '80 (NURS)
WALLACE, SHIRLEY A., coor. staff dev. nrsg., St. Peter's Hospital, Albany, NY '80 (EDUC)
WALLACE, STERLING JR., pat. rep., Veterans Administration Medical Center, Cleveland, OH '80 (PAT)
WALLACE, TRACY T., pub. rel. rep., Phoebe Putney Memorial Hospital, Albany, GA '85 (PR)
WALLACE, YVONNE, dir. med. soc. serv., Newnan Hospital, Newnan, GA '80 (SOC)
WALLAKER, JANICE E., RN, dir. nrsg. serv., Lake Area Hospital, Webster, SD '74 (NURS)
WALLEN, ARLEEN E. R., dir. food serv., Temple University Hospital, Philadelphia, PA '80 (FOOD)
WALLEN, MIRIAM N., Salem, NH '76
WALLER, ADELE A., atty., Rush-Presbyterian-St. Luke Medical Center, Chicago, IL '86 (ATTY)
WALLER, CHARLES D., student, Program in Hospital and Health Administration, University of Alabama, Birmingham, AL '85
WALLER, DANIEL T., pur. agt., Onslow Memorial Hospital, Jacksonville, NC '79 (PUR)
WALLER, HILDA L., Cushing Regional Hospital, Cushing, OK '79 (PAT)
WALLER, JAMES M., microbiologist, Smith-Kline Bioscience Laboratory, St. Louis, MO '84 (MGMT)
WALLER, MICHAEL M., atty., Whidbey General Hospital, Coupeville, WA '78 (ATTY)
WALLEY, JAMES A., dir. eng., Pungo District Hospital, Belhaven, NC '85 (ENG)
WALLEY, KEITH W., atty., vice-pres. plng. and corp. dev., Queen of the Valley Hospital, West Covina, CA '78 (ATTY)(PLNG)
WALLICK, SANDRA A., dir. commun. rel., University Hospital, St. Louis, MO '85 (PR)
WALLIN, BRIAN L., dir. corp. and mktg. commun., Salem Hospital, Salem, MA '80 (PR)
WALLING, JOHN ROBERT, exec. vice-pres. and chief oper. off., Lafayette Home Hospital, Lafayette, IN '74 (PLNG)
WALLIS, STEPHEN R., proj. asst. pur., Lee Memorial Hospital, Fort Myers, FL '84 (PUR)
WALLMAN, GEORGE J., dir. food serv., Montefiore Hospital, Pittsburgh, PA '68 (FOOD)
WALLMAN, GERALD H., adm., Charter Beacon Hospital, Fort Wayne, IN '71
WALLRAFF, NANCY M., dir. commun. rel., Chisago Lakes Hospital and Convalescent and Nursing Care Unit, Chisago City, MN '83 (PR)
WALLS, BETTE JOANN, RN, dir. surg. div., Akron City Hospital, Akron, OH '86 (NURS)
WALLS, JANET E., dir. qual. assur., St. Joseph's Medical Center, Yonkers, NY '73
WALLS, LON G., mgr. media rel., mktg. and pub. rel., Fairfax Hospital, Falls Church, VA '84 (PR)
WALLS, COL. NEAL H., MSC USA, chief staff, Dwight David Eisenhower Army Medical Center, Fort Gordon, GA '68
WALLS, THOMAS R., dir. oper. analyst, Samaritan Health Service, Phoenix, AZ '78 (MGMT)
WALLWORTH, JOHN W., dir. pub. rel., Levi Arthritis Hospital, Hot Springs National Park, AR '82 (PR)
WALMSLEY-AULT, SUSAN, dir. plng., Muhlenberg Regional Medical Center, Plainfield, NJ '80 (PLNG)
WALMSLEY, MARIAN, vice-pres., Sarasota Memorial Hospital, Sarasota, FL '85 (RISK)
WALMUS, ADAM C., health syst. spec. and facil. planner, Veterans Administration Medical Center, Houston, TX '83 (PLNG)
WALN, WILLIAM E., chief pat. affairs serv., Naval Hospital, Great Lakes, IL '80
WALSDORF, THEODORE J., (ret.), Fremont, CA '73 (FOOD)
WALSH, ANNE MARIE ENOCH, mgr. hskpg., Fox Chase Cancer Center, Philadelphia, PA '86 (ENVIRON)
WALSH, ANNE, adm. ped., Medical College of Pennsylvania, Philadelphia, PA '85
WALSH, CAROL JEAN, dir. soc. work, South Charleston Community Hospital, South Charleston, WV '79 (SOC)
WALSH, CATHERINE D., vice-pres. adm. affairs, St. Mary's Hospital, Orange, NJ '82 (RISK)
WALSH, CINDY K., dir. commun., Lakeland Regional Medical Center, Lakeland, FL '86 (PR)
WALSH, DANIEL P., dir. mgt. info. syst., Mercy Catholic Medical Center, Darby, PA '85 (MGMT)
WALSH, DANIEL P., pres., Good Samaritan Hospital, West Islip, NY '75
WALSH, ETTA M., pub. rel. assoc., Worcester Memorial Hospital, Worcester, MA '86 (PR)
WALSH, INEZ C., coor. vol., Essex County Hospital Center, Cedar Grove, NJ '75 (VOL)
WALSH, IRENE, vice-pres. mktg. and plng., Atlanticare Corporation, Lynn, MA '83 (PLNG)
WALSH, J. RUSSELL, assoc. adm., Sacred Heart Hospital, Norristown, PA '72
WALSH, JAMES T., chief eng. serv., Veterans Administration Medical Center, New York, NY '87 (ENG)
WALSH, JEAN M., RN, vice-pres., Allegheny General Hospital, Pittsburgh, PA '77 (NURS)
WALSH, KATHLEEN, RN, adm., Mercy Medical Center, Denver, CO '81 (NURS)
WALSH, LAWRENCE F., asst. adm. human res., Hemet Valley Hospital District, Hemet, CA '83 (PERS)
WALSH, LEE, adm. pat. rel., Riverside Hospital, Boonton, NJ '82 (PAT)

WALSH, LEONARD, adm., Montefiore Health Services, East Elmhurst, NY '84

WALSH, MARCIA S., RN, dir. nrsg. serv., Community Hospital -Onaga, Onaga, KS '86 (NURS)

WALSH, MARIAN, dir. educ. serv., Silver Cross Hospital, Joliet, IL '84 (EDUC)

WALSH, MARILYN, vice-pres. human res., Women and Infants Hospital of Rhode Island, Providence, RI '84 (PERS)

WALSH, MARK, dir. plant oper., Deaconess Hospital of Cleveland, Cleveland, OH '81 (ENG)

WALSH, MARY B., RN, dir. support serv., Brandywine Hospital, Caln Township, PA '82

WALSH, NANCY L., student, Boston University, Boston, MA '86 (PLNG)

WALSH, SR. NORA MARIE, pres., Incarnate Word Health Services, San Antonio, TX '85

WALSH, PAMELA S., assoc. prog. dir.-affordable health care, Greater Detroit Area Health Council, Detroit, MI '87 (PLNG)

WALSH, PATRICIA T., vice-pres. external affairs and sr. vice-pres., Muhlenberg Regional Medical Center, Plainfield, NJ '78 (PR)

WALSH, PATRICK M., vice-pres. corp. dev. and plng., Health Care Corporation of the Sisters of St. Joseph of Carondelet, St. Louis, MO '79 (PLNG)

WALSH, PATRICK S., sr. assoc., Herman Smith Associates, Hinsdale, IL '80 (PUR)

WALSH, RAYMOND, dir. plant facil., King Khaled Eye Specialst Hospital, Riyadh, Saudi Arabia '85 (ENG)

WALSH, RICHARD A., MD, chm. emer. medicine, Maricopa Medical Center, Phoenix, AZ '87 (AMB)

WALSH, RICHARD J., atty., Waynesboro Hospital, Waynesboro, PA '83 (ATTY)

WALSH, ROBERT J., asst. vice-pres. commun. rel., Lutheran Medical Center, Brooklyn, NY '82 (PR)

WALSH, ROSALIE L., pat. rep., St. Francis Hospital, Memphis, TN '79 (PAT)

WALSH, SANDRA JEAN, pat. rep., Presbyterian Hospital in the City of New York, New York, NY '85 (PAT)

WALSH, THOMAS B., dir. mgt. syst. eng., Shands Hospital, Gainesville, FL '70 (MGMT)

WALSH, WILLIAM J., vice-pres. strategic plng. and mktg., Mercy Health System, Omaha, NE '81 (PLNG)

WALTER, BRUNO, mgr. cent. sup., St. Luke's-Roosevelt Hospital Center, New York, NY '81 (CS)

WALTER, DONNA L., dir. pers., Jeannette District Memorial Hospital, Jeannette, PA '87 (PERS)

WALTER, JACK T., dir. plng., Southeastern Indiana Health Management, Inc., Columbus, IN '72 (MGMT)(PLNG)

WALTER, RONALD E., dir. pers., Iowa Methodist Medical Center, Des Moines, IA '80 (PERS)

WALTER, ROSEMARY L., RN, assoc. dir. nrsg., St. Francis Hospital Center, Beech Grove, IN '81 (NURS)

WALTER, WILLIAM LEE, mgr. health care org., Hoechst-Roussel Pharmacuetical, Somerville, NJ '87 (AMB)

WALTER, WILLIAM R., adm., Maury County Hospital, Columbia, TN '66

WALTERMIRC, MARLENE K., RN, in-service instr., Valley Hospital and Medical Center, Spokane, WA '80 (EDUC)

WALTERS, CONSTANCE R., mgr. food and nutr. serv., St. John's Regional Medical Center, Joplin, MO '86 (FOOD)

WALTERS, CYNTHIA J., dir. educ., Baptist Medical Center, Columbia, SC '86 (EDUC)

WALTERS, DARRELL MARVIN, mgr. emp., St. Luke's Methodist Hospital, Cedar Rapids, IA '69 (PERS)

WALTERS, DAVID W., dir. vol. serv., St. Joseph Hospital, Flint, MI '79 (VOL)

WALTERS, DEANNA, coor. qual. assur., Loma Linda University Medical Center, Loma Linda, CA '86 (RISK)

WALTERS, DOROTHY A., RN, dir. nrsg. serv., Casa Grande Regional Medical Center, Casa Grande, AZ '79 (NURS)

WALTERS, FRED M., (ret.), Palacios, TX '44 (LIFE)

WALTERS, GREGORY A., adm. res., Anderson Memorial Hospital, Anderson, SC '86

WALTERS, JAMES MICHAEL, atty., Lake Charles Memorial Hospital, Lake Charles, LA '80 (ATTY)

WALTERS, JAN JORDAN, pat. satisfaction coor., Healthplan Southeast, Inc., Tallahassee, FL '83 (PAT)

WALTERS, JAYNE R., asst. dir. diet.-adm., Harper Hospital, Detroit, MI '80 (FOOD)

WALTERS, JEAN A., asst. vice-pres. qual. assur., Froedtert Memorial Lutheran Hospital, Milwaukee, WI '85 (EDUC)

WALTERS, JEANNE M., dir. pers., River Oaks Hospital, New Orleans, LA '84 (PERS)

WALTERS, JEFF, dir. oper. and prov. rel., Cigna Healthplan of Ohio, Inc., Columbus, OH '87 (AMB)

WALTERS, KAREN A., RN, dir. nrs., Peachtree Patient Center, Atlanta, GA '86 (NURS)

WALTERS, KATHRYN M., dir. soc. serv., St. Anthony Center, Houston, TX '85 (SOC)

WALTERS, MARGARET A., RN, dir. nrsg., Jeannette District Memorial Hospital, Jeannette, PA '86 (NURS)

WALTERS, MERTON, vice-pres., Greater Cleveland Hospital Association, Cleveland, OH '84

WALTERS, MICHAEL J., PhD, vice-pres. mktg. and strategic plng., St. Elizabeth Medical Center-North, Covington, KY '84 (PR)

WALTERS, MONA L., dir. pub. rel., Wake Medical Center, Raleigh, NC '83 (PR)

WALTERS, N. SUE, dir. soc. serv., HCA Regional Hospital -Livingston, Livingston, TN '85 (SOC)

WALTERS, PAMELA J., dir. soc. serv., Wetzel County Hospital, New Martinsville, WV '85 (SOC)

WALTERS, PATRICIA J., supv. sup., proc. and distrib., Mesa Lutheran Hospital, Mesa, AZ '86 (CS)

WALTERS, REGINA G., syst. analyst, St. Francis Hospital Center, Beech Grove, IN '87 (MGMT)

WALTERS, ROBERT A., dir. matl. mgt., Self Memorial Hospital, Greenwood, SC '83 (PUR)

WALTERS, THEODORE R., vice-pres. human res., Timken Mercy Medical Center, Canton, OH '73 (PERS)

WALTHER, TERRY, vice-pres., Memorial Hospital, Belleville, IL '80 (RISK)

WALTHER, VIRGINIA N., asst. dir. soc. work serv., Mount Sinai Medical Center, New York, NY '85 (SOC)

WALTMAN, ENDER, dir. environ. serv., Mobile Infirmary Medical Center, Mobile, AL '86 (ENVIRON)

WALTON, CHARLES E., dir. pers., St. Mary's Hospital, Leonardtown, MD '75 (PERS)

WALTON, FRED M., chief eng., HCA Coliseum Medical Centers, Macon, GA '80 (ENG)

WALTON, GENE C., atty., Memorial General Hospital, Las Cruces, NM '84 (ATTY)

WALTON, GREGORY S., sr. mgr., Ernst and Whinney, Cleveland, OH '86 (MGMT)

WALTON, H. RICHARD, partner, Peat, Marwick, Mitchell and Company, Houston, TX '80

WALTON, MARGARET E., dir. vol. serv., St. Joseph's Hospital, Asheville, NC '79 (VOL)

WALTON, MICHAEL W., assoc. dir., Veterans Administration Medical Center, Charleston, SC '74

WALTON, ROSEMARY HULL, dir. soc. work, Mecosta County General Hospital, Big Rapids, MI '87 (SOC)

WALTON, TERRY, dir. eng. serv., Mid-Columbia Medical Center, The Dalles, OR '81 (ENG)

WALTON, VIVIAN W., dir. soc. serv., Norfolk Community Hospital, Norfolk, VA '77 (SOC)

WALTON, WESLEY S., atty., Holy Cross Hospital, Chicago, IL '75 (ATTY)

WALTON, WILLIAM G., dir. human res., Saint Francis Hospital and Medical Center, Hartford, CT '84 (PERS)

WALTS, LYNN, RN, dir. nrsg., Lake Livingston Medical Center, Livingston, TX '85 (NURS)

WALTUCH, WILLIAM, consult., Medco, Inc., Langhorne, PA '83 (MGMT)

WAMPLER, ATLEE W. III, atty., Watson Clinic, Lakeland, FL '82 (ATTY)

WANDEL, DAVID I., dir. human res., St. Mary's Hospital, Centralia, IL '75 (PERS)

WANDEL, HARALD, asst. vice-pres. plant oper., Morristown Memorial Hospital, Morristown, NJ '85 (ENG)

WANG, KATHARINE C., soc. work consult., Department of Health, Bureau of Hospital Affairs, Suffolk County, Hauppauge, NY '74 (SOC)

WANG, MEI-SHAN L., mgr. clin. diet., Good Samaritan Hospital and Medical Center, Portland, OR '83 (FOOD)

WANG, NAI-CHEN, dir. mgt. eng., Harrisburg Hospital, Harrisburg, PA '81 (MGMT)

WANGELIN, JAMES D., atty., Children's Memorial Hospital, Chicago, IL '81 (ATTY)

WANGLER, RANDALL G., dir. mgt. info. serv., Franciscan Services Corporation, Sylvania, OH '86 (PLNG)

WANNER, JOHN, dir. soc. work, HCA Riveredge Hospital, Forest Park, IL '75 (SOC)

WANTA, STEVE, dir. plant oper., St. Francis Hospital, Wilmington, DE '86 (ENG)

WANTO, GEORGE R., dir. cent. instrumentation center, Montefiore Hospital, Pittsburgh, PA '86 (ENG)

WANTUCK, RICHARD L., pur. agt., Visiting Nurse Association, Pittsburgh, PA '86 (PUR)

WANUCHA, MARY ANN, dir. soc. serv., Bayfront Medical Center, St. Petersburg, FL '81 (SOC)

WARD-GARY, JACQUELINE ANN, RN, vice-pres. nrsg., Venice Hospital, Venice, FL '81 (NURS)

WARD, BOB-AMNDIH, sr. assoc., Health Systems Consultants, Minneapolis, MN '86 (EDUC)

WARD, BONNIE T., soc. worker and coor. util. review, Florence General Hospital, Florence, SC '86 (SOC)

WARD, BRYAN, dir. commun. rel., St. Joseph Medical Center, Stamford, CT '84 (PR)

WARD, CHARLENE, dir. qual. mgt., Sandwich Community Hospital, Sandwich, IL '86 (RISK)

WARD, CHERYL Y., sr. vice-pres. mktg., Providence Hospital, Mobile, AL '85 (PR) (PLNG)

WARD, COLLEEN A., RN, asst. vice-pres. nrsg. serv., Zurbrugg Memorial Hospital, Willingboro, NJ '86 (NURS)

WARD, DICK J., asst. adm., Christian Hospitals Northeast-Northwest, St. Louis, MO '80 (ENG)

WARD, EMILY L., dir. pub. rel., Scenic Mountain Medical Center, Big Spring, TX '82 (PR)

WARD, EMILY T., dir. mktg. and commun. rel., Dominion Hospital, Falls Church, VA '84 (PR)

WARD, FRANCIS PAUL JR., head pat. adm., Naval Hospital, Patuxent River, MD '85

WARD, FRANK E., dir. data proc., Methodist Hospital, Lubbock, TX '86 (MGMT)

WARD, GRACE, dir. pub. rel., HCA Heritage Hospital, Tarboro, NC '86 (PR)

WARD, HOWARD N., atty., Stormont-Vail Regional Medical Center, Topeka, KS '82 (ATTY)

WARD, JEANNE, RN, asst. adm. pat. care, Oconee Memorial Hospital, Seneca, SC '77 (NURS)

WARD, JOANNE, dir. soc. serv., New York Eye and Ear Infirmary, New York, NY '75 (SOC)

WARD, JOHN M., dir. commun., Minneapolis Children's Medical Center, Minneapolis, MN '83 (PR)

WARD, KATHLEEN J., supv. cent. serv., Redlands Community Hospital, Redlands, CA '82 (CS)

WARD, KATHLEEN J., dir. soc. serv., Saint Vincent Health Center, Erie, PA '80 (SOC)

WARD, KEVIN D., dir. pers., Marshalltown Medical and Surgical Center, Marshalltown, IA '81 (PERS)

WARD, LYLE E., dir. soc. work, Cottage Hospital of Grosse Pointe, Grosse Pointe Farms, MI '85 (SOC)

WARD, M. EMMETT, atty., Vicksburg Medical Center, Vicksburg, MS '69 (ATTY)

WARD, MARK THOMAS, student, Program in Hospital Administration, University of Minnesota, Minneapolis, MN '85

WARD, MICHAEL T., vice-pres., Sacred Heart Medical Center, Spokane, WA '82 (PLNG)

WARD, MOZELLE C., coor. pat. rel., Wake Medical Center, Raleigh, NC '78 (PAT)

WARD, PATRICK J., dir., Voluntary Hospitals of America, Tampa, FL '75 (MGMT)

WARD, RICHARD T., adm., Hurley Medical Center, Flint, MI '80 (MGMT)

WARD, ROSIE, dir. pers., Holzer Medical Center, Gallipolis, OH '80 (PERS)

WARD, STEPHEN C., dir. pub. rel. and mktg., St. Mary's Hospital and Medical Center, Grand Junction, CO '85 (PR)

WARD, SUSAN LAWSON, dir. commun. rel., Wallace Thomson Hospital, Union, SC '84 (PR)

WARD, THEODORE D., atty., St. John and West Shore Hospital, Westlake, OH '86 (ATTY)

WARDELL, DORIS ERWAY, RN, vice-pres. nrsg., Chestnut Hill Hospital, Philadelphia, PA '80 (NURS)

WARDELL, HAL, dir. gen. serv., San Antonio Community Hospital, Upland, CA '84

WARDELL, KEVIN S., sr. vice-pres. and chief oper. off., Miami Valley Hospital, Dayton, OH '74

WARDELL, PATRICK R., chief oper. off., Calvary Hospital, Bronx, NY '78 (PLNG)

WARDEN, MARTHA C., dir. nrsg. serv., Baltimore County General Hospital, Randallstown, MD '84 (NURS)

WARDEN, SHAWN, asst. dir. pub. rel., Hospital of Englewood, Chicago, IL '86 (PR)

WARDER, NAOMI R., dir. soc. serv., DePaul Hospital, Norfolk, VA '68 (SOC)

WARDROPE, KAY-FRANCES, soc. worker, Plastic Reconstruction and Cosmetic Associates of Augusta, Augusta, GA '85 (SOC)

WARDRUM, EARL ROY, arch. and health facil. planner, Health Facilities Planning, Shaker Heights, OH '72

WARE, MARY W., dir. med. soc. serv., Memorial Regional Rehabilitation Center, Jacksonville, FL '81 (SOC)

WARE, NANCY L., dir. plng. and outreach, Community Hospital of Springfield and Clark County, Springfield, OH '81 (PLNG)

WARE, ROBERT A., pres., Servicemaster Industries, Inc., Capitol Division, Fredericksburg, VA '78

WARE, SCOTT T., asst. adm. mktg. and pub. rel., Jefferson Regional Medical Center, Pine Bluff, AR '86 (PR) (PLNG)

WAREING, COLLEEN, student, Widener University, Chester, PA '86

WARES, CHERRYL E., dir. vol. serv., Tom Baker Cancer Centre, Calgary, Alta., Canada '85 (VOL)

WARFEL, WILLIAM M., RN, asst. gen. dir. and dir. nrsg. serv., Albert Einstein Medical Center, Northern Division, Philadelphia, PA '81 (NURS)

WARFIELD, MIMI H., asst. dir. food and nutr. serv., West Florida Hospital, Pensacola, FL '85 (FOOD)

WARFORD, ANN M., dir. educ., Sacred Heart General Hospital, Eugene, OR '85 (EDUC)

WARGO, EDWARD J., assoc. vice-pres., Suburban General Hospital, Norristown, PA '79 (PLNG)

WARING, CAROLE D., adm. asst. qual. assur. and risk mgt., Sibley Memorial Hospital, Washington, DC '85 (RISK)

WARING, RICHARD H., dir. human res., Visiting Nursing Association Group, Inc., Buffalo, NY '65 (PERS)

WARLICK, ALEX JR., atty., Onslow Memorial Hospital, Jacksonville, NC '74 (ATTY)

WARLICK, DAN H., dir. plant eng. and constr., HCA West Paces Ferry Hospital, Atlanta, GA '85 (ENG)

WARMACK, DANIEL R., RN, asst. exec. dir. nrsg., St. Joseph's Medical Center, Fort Wayne, IN '79 (NURS)

WARMAN, HAROLD C. JR., vice-pres. adm., Our Lady of Bellefonte Hospital, Ashland, KY '84

WARMATH, WILLIAM T., dir. pat. rel., Wesley Long Community Hospital, Greensboro, NC '83 (PAT)

WARMENHOVEN, GEORGE R., dir. dev. resources, Fairfax Hospital Association, Springfield, VA '82 (PLNG)

WARMUTH, JUDITH F., PhD, dir. nrsg. staff educ., Methodist Hospital, Madison, WI '84 (EDUC)

WARNER-HANDELSMAN, JOANNE, RN, dir. prog. dev., Amicare Home Health Services, Inc., Ann Arbor, MI '80 (NURS)

WARNER, ANNE R., dir. pub. rel., Lenox Hill Hospital, New York, NY '79 (PR)

WARNER, BARBARA H., RN, adm. nrsg. serv., Ohio State University Hospitals, Columbus, OH '86 (NURS)

WARNER, BONNIE D., dir. pur., St. Vincent Hospital and Medical Center, Portland, OR '86 (PUR)

WARNER, CHARLES C., dir. soc. serv., Elmhurst Memorial Hospital, Elmhurst, IL '82 (SOC)

WARNER, CHARLES W., pres., Charles W. Warner Company, Glastonbury, CT '85 (PERS)

WARNER, DEBORAH K., dir. soc. serv., Lakeland Hospital, Elkhorn, WI '85 (SOC)

WARNER, DONALD T., atty., Sharon Hospital, Sharon, CT '75 (ATTY)

WARNER, EDWARD W., atty., Alexian Brothers Hospital, St. Louis, MO '70 (ATTY)

WARNER, EDWIN R., vice-pres., Bayfront Medical Center, St. Petersburg, FL '80

WARNER, GAIL S., dir., Voluntary Hospitals of America, Park Ridge, IL '85 (PLNG)

WARNER, GERARD H. JR., exec. dir., Northwestern Institute of Psychiatry, Fort Washington, PA '69

WARNER, JOHN B. JR., pres., Warner Health Services, St. Louis, MO '63

WARNER, JOSEPH A., dir. commun., St. John's Hospital, Salina, KS '76 (PR)

WARNER, LORA HANSON, student, Medical College of Virginia, Richmond, VA '85 (PLNG)

WARNER, MARY M., RN, field rep., Joint Commission on Accreditation of Hospitals, Chicago, IL '82 (NURS)

WARNER, PATRICIA A., assoc. adm. amb. care serv., University of Michigan Hospitals, Ann Arbor, MI '78 (PLNG)(AMB)

WARNER, RICHARD G., pres., Concord Hospital, Concord, NH '62 (PLNG)

WARNER, SGT. RICHARD L., MSC USAF, adm. supv., Fitzsimons Army Medical Center, Aurora, CO '86

WARNER, SUSAN, Mirin and Warner, Philadelphia, PA '84 (PERS)

WARNER, TIM J., dir. mktg., Meriter Hospital, Madison, WI '82 (PR)
WARNICA, MARJORIE K., RN, coor. sup., proc. and distrib., Maryvale Samaritan Hospital, Phoenix, AZ '85 (CS)
WARNICK, CHARLES J., plng. spec., Regional Medical Center, Madisonville, KY '86 (PLNG)
WARNICK, MYRNA, RN, vice-pres. pat. care serv., California Medical Center-Los Angeles, Los Angeles, CA '76 (NURS)
WARNKE, DELAINE D., coor. staff dev., Trinity Regional Hospital, Fort Dodge, IA '86 (EDUC)
WARNKE, PHILIP K., dir. food serv., Marian Health Center, Sioux City, IA '83 (FOOD)
WARNOCK, MARY R., dir. food serv., McDonough District Hospital, Macomb, IL '79 (FOOD)
WARNOCK, WILLIAM R., vice-pres. pers., Crittenden Memorial Hospital, West Memphis, AR '85 (PERS)
WARREN, ANTHONY W., vice-pres., St. Luke's Hospital, Davenport, IA '83 (PR) (PLNG)
WARREN, BARBARA G., adm. corp. dev., Blue Cross of Lehigh Valley, Allentown, PA '81
WARREN, CHARLES H., adm., Mount Clemens General Hospital, Mount Clemens, MI '81 (PLNG)
WARREN, DAVID G., atty., Duke University Hospital, Durham, NC '76 (ATTY)
WARREN, DEBORAH A., Wethersfield, CT '84 (PLNG)
WARREN, DONALD M., dir. educ., Glendale Adventist Medical Center, Glendale, CA '83 (EDUC)
WARREN, E. THEODORE, coor. staff dev., Stormont-Vail Regional Medical Center, Topeka, KS '77 (EDUC)
WARREN, GEORGE W. JR., dir. matl. mgt., Sisters of Charity Health Care System, Inc., Cincinnati, OH '82 (PUR)
WARREN, JAMES W., (ret.), Toccoa, GA '53 (PR)(LIFE)
WARREN, JANE WHEELER, (ret.), Lakeside, MI '68 (VOL)
WARREN, JANICE H., mgr. tech. trng., Dynamic Control, Longwood, FL '86 (EDUC)
WARREN, MARY, benefits coor., St. Mary's Hospital, West Palm Beach, FL '80 (PERS)
WARREN, MICHAEL D., dir. mktg. and pub. rel., Good Samaritan Hospital, Mount Vernon, IL '85 (PR)
WARREN, MICHAEL JOHN, dir. support serv., Charter Beacon Hospital, Fort Wayne, IN '87 (ENG)
WARREN, PAMELA S., dir. soc. serv., Sherman Oaks Community Hospital, Sherman Oaks, CA '85 (SOC)
WARREN, R. C., (ret.), Pine Bluff, AR '46 (LIFE)
WARREN, RICHARD S., chief exec. off., Nicholas H. Noyes Memorial Hospital, Dansville, NY '58
WARREN, TED, dir. educ. serv., Stormont-Vail Regional Medical Center, Topeka, KS '87 (EDUC)
WARREN, TERRY W., vice-pres., Research and Planning Consultants, Inc., Austin, TX '75 (PLNG)(MGMT)
WARREN, THOMAS G., dist. mgr., Marriott Corporation, Washington, DC '83 (FOOD)
WARREN, WAYNE L., environ. care spec., Veterans Administration, Department of Medicine and Surgery, Washington, DC '86 (ENVIRON)
WARRICK, CHARLES E., dir. linen serv., Methodist Evangelical Hospital, Louisville, KY '86 (ENVIRON)
WARYAS, FRANCES S., vice-pres. pat. care serv., Holy Family Hospital, Spokane, WA '79 (NURS)
WASCHITSCH, WENDIE J., dir. commun. serv., Reading Hospital and Medical Center, Reading, PA '83 (PR)
WASDEN, LT. WAYNE W., dep. dir. qual. assur., Navy Medical Command, Washington, DC '82 (PLNG)
WASE, GORDON M., mgr. health care consult. group, Coopers and Lybrand, Philadelphia, PA '68 (MGMT)
WASEK, ARTHUR A., dir. pers., St. Luke's Hospital, Saginaw, MI '82 (PERS)
WASHAM, DOROTHY L., dir. vol., Kaiser Foundation Hospital, Santa Clara, CA '85 (VOL)
WASHBURN, HERB C., tech. cent. serv., Eden Hospital Medical Center, Castro Valley, CA '72 (CS)
WASHBURN, JOANN, supv. in-patient and outpatient surg., Tolfree Memorial Hospital, West Branch, MI '87 (AMB)
WASHBURN, JULIANE S., dir. diet., Bay Area Medical Center, Marinette, WI '86 (FOOD)
WASHBURN, KENT G., chief amb. care, Letterman Army Medical Center, San Francisco, CA '78
WASHBURN, LINDA C., dir. risk mgt. and qual. assur., Kaiser Foundation Hospital, Los Angeles, CA '78 (RISK)
WASHINGTON, ALISA R., dir. vol. serv., Kaiser Foundation Hospital, Los Angeles, CA '86 (VOL)
WASHINGTON, CAROLYN S., cent. serv. tech., St. Elizabeth Hospital, Beaumont, TX '86 (CS)
WASHINGTON, ERIC A., asst. planner, Methodist Hospitals of Gary, Gary, IN '84 (PLNG)
WASHINGTON, FRED G., asst. to dir., Veterans Administration Medical Center, Marlin, TX '78
WASHINGTON, JOSEPHINE, supv. sup., proc. and distrib., Ochsner Foundation Hospital, New Orleans, LA '79 (CS)
WASHINGTON, KENNETH L., vice-pres. corp. dev., Mercy Medical Center, Roseburg, OR '83 (PLNG)
WASHINGTON, RICHARD B., student, Southern Illinois University, Carbondale, IL '86
WASHINGTON, SHERYL L., student, National University, San Diego, CA '86
WASIURA, JAMES M., dir. matl. mgt., Roswell Park Memorial Institute, Buffalo, NY '86 (PUR)
WASKEY, ANN M., dist. mgr., ARA Healthcare Nutrition Service, San Francisco, CA '86 (FOOD)
WASKO, ALEX E., pur. spec., Metropolitan Dade County, Miami, FL '66 (PUR)
WASSELL, JOSEPH A., McLean, VA '77
WASSER-BERLIN, LISA J., dir. commun. rel., East Orange General Hospital, East Orange, NJ '86 (PR)
WASSER, CHAS MARTIN, dir. plng. and mktg., Ohio Valley Medical Center, Wheeling, WV '81 (PLNG)
WASSERMAN, AGGIE, dir. vol. serv., Cedars-Sinai Medical Center, Los Angeles, CA '80 (VOL)
WASSERMAN, LINDA I., RN, prog. coor., Palms of Pasadena Hospital, St. Petersburg, FL '87 (AMB)
WASSERMAN, MICHAEL E., vice-pres. mktg., Pawating Hospital, Niles, MI '84 (PLNG)
WASSERMAN, MITCHELL, student, Case Western Reserve University, Weather Head School of Management, Cleveland, OH '85 (MGMT)
WASSERMAN, RUTH, RN, Covina, CA '69 (NURS)
WASSERMAN, WILLIAM, dir. mmtp, Montefiore Medical Center, Bronx, NY '83
WASSERMAN, YALE, lib. and ed., National Dental Advisory Service, West Allis, WI '87
WASSILCHALK, DANIEL M., student, Department of Health Care Administration, George Washington University, Washington, DC '84
WASSON, CHRISTINE A., dir. soc. serv., Nanticoke Memorial Hospital, Seaford, DE '84 (SOC)
WASZAK, JOHN J., dir. human res., Charter Beacon Hospital, Fort Wayne, IN '86 (PERS)
WATANABE, MARION K., asst. dir. diet., Virginia Mason Hospital, Seattle, WA '75 (FOOD)
WATANABE, N. BRIAN, vice-pres., St. Joseph's Hospital and Medical Center, Phoenix, AZ '86 (RISK)
WATERBROOK, KEITH J., dir. and vice chancellor, University of Massachusetts Medical School and Teaching Hospital, Worcester, MA '73
WATERCUTTER, WILLIAM E., syst. analyst, Upper Valley Center, Piqua, OH '83 (MGMT)
WATERMAN, JAMES B., atty., Valley Medical Center of Fresno, Fresno, CA '86 (ATTY)
WATERMAN, ROBERT V. P., atty., St. Luke's Hospital, Davenport, IA '78 (ATTY)
WATERMAN, THOMAS C., vice-pres., Medicus Systems Corporation, Houston, TX '72 (MGMT)
WATERS, ALICE B., dir. food serv., St. John Hospital, Detroit, MI '75 (FOOD)
WATERS, ANNETTE, RN, vice-pres. nrsg., St. Francis Hospital, Evanston, IL '77 (NURS)
WATERS, COL. GEORGE A. JR., MSC USA, chief sup. oper., Defense Personnel Support Center, Philadelphia, PA '71
WATERS, GLENN D., asst. adm., Riverside Hospital, Newport News, VA '85
WATERS, J. SCOTT, IV, atty., Voluntary Hospitals of America, Irving, TX '86 (ATTY)
WATERS, JEAN B., dir. commun. rel. and educ., Community Health Center of Branch County, Coldwater, MI '82 (PR)
WATERS, KAREN G., coor. vol., University Hospital and Ambulatory Care Center, Little Rock, AR '85 (VOL)
WATERS, TERRY L., dir. plng., Methodist Health Services Corporation, Peoria, IL '85 (PLNG)
WATERS, WILLIAM J., PhD, asst. dir. health policy, Rhode Island Department of Health, Providence, RI '82 (PLNG)
WATHNE, CARL N., pres. and chief exec. off., Leominster Hospital, Leominster, MA '56 (PLNG)(LIFE)
WATKINS, B. GORDON JR., vice-pres., Wiley and Wilson Architects, Lynchburg, VA '86 (ENG)
WATKINS, BARBARA L., vice-pres. pub. affairs and human serv., Dallas County Hospital District, Dallas, TX '84
WATKINS, CHARLOTTE H., coor. soc. work serv., Georgia Regional Hospital at Augusta, Augusta, GA '85 (SOC)
WATKINS, ELAINE J., RN, vice-pres. nrsg., Deaconess Medical Center, Billings, MT '83 (NURS)
WATKINS, JACK L., EdD, dir. educ., Wesley Long Community Hospital, Greensboro, NC '77 (EDUC)
WATKINS, JAMES A., vice-pres., Touchstone Medical Systems, San Antonio, TX '86
WATKINS, JUDITH A., dir. commun. rel., Meadville Medical Center, Meadville, PA '81 (PR)
WATKINS, MARY ANN, dir. matl. mgt., Rehabilitation Institute, Detroit, MI '80 (PUR)
WATKINS, MELANIE WILSON, dir. soc. serv., St. Joseph Hospital, Kirkwood, MO '83 (SOC)
WATKINS, MYRNA L., dir. vol. serv., Texas Scottish Rite Hospital for Crippled Children, Dallas, TX '83 (VOL)
WATKINS, PHIL, atty., Southwest Texas Methodist Hospital, San Antonio, TX '86 (ATTY)
WATKINS, REGINALD W., actg. chief fin. off., North Broward Medical Center, Pompano Beach, FL '86
WATKINS, RONALD D., dir. bldg. serv., John F. Kennedy Medical Center, Edison, NJ '75 (ENG)
WATKINS, SALLY M., RN, assoc. dir. nrsg. specialty serv., University of Utah Health Sciences Center, Salt Lake City, UT '86 (NURS)
WATKINS, SUE CANTWELL, dir. pers., Eastland Memorial Hospital, Eastland, TX '84 (PERS)
WATKINS, THOMAS D., atty., Heartland Hospital West, St. Joseph, MO '86 (ATTY)
WATKINS, W. D., dir. pers., Valley View Regional Hospital, Ada, OK '69 (PERS)
WATKINS, W. DAVID, atty., Venice Hospital, Venice, FL '86 (ATTY)
WATROUS, ELIZABETH D., RN, clin. mgr., Bay Medical Center, Bay City, MI '82 (NURS)
WATSON, ANITA FENNESSEY, atty., Henry Ford Hospital, Detroit, MI '78 (ATTY)
WATSON, ANITA M., lab. adm. fin. analyst, Stanford University Hospital, Stanford, CA '85 (PLNG)
WATSON, ARLEENE, dir. food serv., Hillcrest Hospital, Simpsonville, SC '80 (FOOD)
WATSON, BARBARA J., supv. diet., Gowanda Psychiatric Center, Helmuth, NY '83 (FOOD)
WATSON, CLAIRE L., head nrs. cent. sup., Goddard Memorial Hospital, Stoughton, MA '83 (CS)
WATSON, CONNIE B., RN, dir. nrsg., Lee's Summit Community Hospital, Lees Summit, MO '85 (NURS)
WATSON, DAVID B., chief eng., Community Health Center of Branch County, Coldwater, MI '84 (ENG)
WATSON, DENNIS D., atty., Hutcheson Medical Center, Fort Oglethorpe, GA '83 (ATTY)
WATSON, DONNA M., staff assoc., Massachusetts Hospital Association, Applied Management Systems, Burlington, MA '81 (MGMT)
WATSON, EDWIN, dir. pur., St. Vincent Infirmary, Little Rock, AR '75 (PUR)
WATSON, ELDEEN A., RN, dir. nrsg., Community Memorial Hospital, Marysville, KS '84 (NURS)
WATSON, FLOELLA, dir. scheduling and word proc., Rehabilitation Institute of Chicago, Chicago, IL '82 (MGMT)
WATSON, J. BRENT, dir. pers., Sacred Heart Hospital of Pensacola, Pensacola, FL '72 (PERS)
WATSON, JOANNE, RN, mgr. cent. serv., Hollywood Presbyterian Medical Center, Los Angeles, CA '83 (CS)
WATSON, KAY, supv. sterile proc., North Colorado Medical Center, Greeley, CO '85 (CS)
WATSON, MELVIN R., dir. plant oper., West Georgia Medical Center, La Grange, GA '84 (ENG)
WATSON, MAJ. MONTE R., MSC USA, William Beaumont Army Medical Center, El Paso, TX '84
WATSON, NANINE J., coor. vol. serv., Providence Hospital, Oakland, CA '84 (VOL)
WATSON, PATRICIA A., coor. commun. rel., St. Francis Hospital, Marceline, MO '85 (PR)
WATSON, PAUL J., vice-pres., Centerra Construction, Inc., Omaha, NE '81 (PLNG)
WATSON, REID, dir. plant serv., Methodist Hospital, Hattiesburg, MS '86 (ENG)
WATSON, RENEE' B., dir. pub. rel. and mktg., St. Francis Hospital, Greenville, SC '86 (PR)
WATSON, RICHARD A., atty., New York Infirmary, New York, NY '79 (ATTY)
WATSON, RITA SULLIVAN, assoc. vice-pres. nrsg., St. Joseph Hospital, Chicago, IL '84 (NURS)
WATSON, ROBERT J., Longwood, FL '80
WATSON, ROBERT, dir. health facil., Howard, Neddles, Tammen and Bergendoff, Kansas City, MO '86
WATSON, RONALD A., mgr. natl. acct., Medtronic, Inc., Minneapolis, MN '82
WATSON, SARA C., dir. food serv., Southeastern General Hospital, Lumberton, NC '78 (FOOD)
WATSON, WESLEY JR., atty., American Health Group International, Inc., Kirkland, WA '84 (ATTY)
WATT, NANCY A., RN, assoc. adm., Irving Community Hospital, Irving, TX '82 (NURS)(AMB)
WATTENGEL, JERALD A., atty., Mount St. Mary's Hospital of Niagara Falls, Lewiston, NY '69 (ATTY)
WATTERS, B. JEAN, RN, dir. risk mgt., Citizens Medical Center, Colby, KS '86 (RISK)
WATTERS, MICHAEL J., supv. eng. and plant serv., Southwest Washington Hospital, Inc., Vancouver, WA '86 (ENG)
WATTERS, RICHARD D., atty., St. Louis Regional Medical Center, St. Louis, MO '78 (ATTY)
WATTERSON, E. MICHAEL, dir. environ. serv., St. Elizabeth's Hospital, Chicago, IL '86 (ENVIRON)
WATTERSON, EDWARD M., dir. plant serv., St. Elizabeth's Hospital, Chicago, IL '79 (ENG)
WATTS, DEBORAH S., RN, adm. nrsg. serv., East Ascension General Hospital, Gonzales, LA '86 (NURS)
WATTS, EMMA, RN, dir. nrsg. serv., Doctors Hospital of Mobile, Mobile, AL '78 (NURS)
WATTS, GREGORY W., dir. environ. serv., Bridgeton Hospital, Bridgeton, NJ '86 (ENVIRON)
WATTS, JERRY L., arch. consult., Baton Rouge General Medical Center, Baton Rouge, LA '81
WATTS, JIM E., dir. mgt. eng., Methodist Hospital of Southern California, Arcadia, CA '81 (MGMT)
WATTS, KATHLEEN A., RN, dir. nrsg. serv., Charter Hospital of Long Beach, Long Beach, CA '82 (NURS)
WATTS, LILLIAN C., RN, adm. coor. cent. sterile sup., Quincy City Hospital, Quincy, MA '83 (CS)
WATTS, LYNETTE K., RN, asst. adm., Los Medanos Community Hospital, Pittsburg, CA '76 (NURS)
WATTS, PEGGY J., corp. planner, Mercy Hospital Medical Center, Des Moines, IA '86 (PLNG)
WATTS, RICHARD A., dir. food serv., HCA West Paces Ferry Hospital, Atlanta, GA '84 (FOOD)
WATTS, RICHARD K., chief eng., West Valley Medical Center, Caldwell, ID '85 (ENG)
WATTS, SUSAN P., dir. commun. and pub. rel., St. Vincent Hospital, Green Bay, WI '82 (PR)
WATTS, WILLIAM B., adm., Huerfano Memorial Hospital, Walsenburg, CO '72 (PERS)
WAUGH, DAVID K. JR., atty., Christian Hospitals Northeast-Northwest, St. Louis, MO '74 (ATTY)
WAUGH, EVELYN C., RN, vice-pres. nrsg. serv., Northeast Georgia Medical Center, Gainesville, GA '83 (NURS)
WAUGH, JENNIE S., RN, dir. nrsg. serv., Jackson General Hospital, Ripley, WV '76 (NURS)
WAUGH, WILLIAM M. JR., prin., A. S. Hansen, Inc., Dallas, TX '85 (PERS)
WAULTERS, DARLIS, asst. dir. amb. care serv., Harrisburg Hospital, Harrisburg, PA '87 (AMB)
WAUNEKA, ANNIE DODGE, PhD, counselor, Navajo Health Authority, Window Rock, AZ '75 (HON)
WAX, JOHN H., chief soc. work serv., Veterans Administration Medical Center, Palo Alto, CA '72 (SOC)
WAXMAN, CLIVE R., exec. dir., Security Forlay Hospital, Riyadh, Saudi Arabia '58
WAXMAN, J. MARK, atty., Weissburg and Aronson, Inc., Los Angeles, CA '82 (ATTY)
WAXMAN, MARC, dir. plng., Arlington Hospital, Arlington, VA '83 (PLNG)
WAY, GEORGE T. C., MD, Poughkeepsie, NY '81
WAY, MICHAEL S., dir. pur., Bronson Methodist Hospital, Kalamazoo, MI '85 (PUR)
WAYMACK, PAMELA M., adm. family medicine, University of Maryland Medical Systems, Baltimore, MD '85
WAYMIRE, DONALD L., adm. asst., St. John's Healthcare Corporation, Anderson, IN '80 (PUR)
WAYNE, MARGARET A., dir. soc. serv., Memorial Hospital, Belleville, IL '79 (SOC)
WAZNIA, ANITA, dir. educ., Nesbitt Memorial Hospital, Kingston, PA '79 (EDUC)
WEAGLE, CYRIL H. JR., asst. adm., N. T. Enloe Memorial Hospital, Chico, CA '62
WEAGLY, SUSAN, atty., Franklin Regional Hospital, Franklin, NH '77 (ATTY)

WEAR, JAMES O., PhD, dir. eng. trng., Veterans Administration Hospital, North Little Rock, AR '75 (ENG)
WEARRING, VIRGINIA M., actg. dir. soc. work, Cook County Hospital, Chicago, IL '85 (SOC)
WEATHERFORD, ANTHONY L., dir. pers., Bristol Hospital, Bristol, CT '85 (PERS)
WEATHERFORD, BARBARA, RN, vice-pres. nrsg. serv., Johnson Memorial Hospital, Stafford Springs, CT '82 (NURS)
WEATHERLY, KATHLEEN, RN, dir. nrsg., Bates Memorial Hospital, Bentonville, AR '76 (NURS)
WEATHERS, CAROLYN R., asst. mgr. cent. sup., Eugene Talmadge Hospitals and Clinics-Medical College of Georgia, Augusta, GA '82 (CS)
WEATHERS, PATRICIA, risk mgr., Lexington County Hospital, West Columbia, SC '85 (RISK)
WEAVER, ANN M., dir. human res., AMI St. Mary's Hospital, Russellville, AR '86 (PERS)
WEAVER, CARL O., vice-pres., Charlton Health System, Inc., Fall River, MA '73 (MGMT)(PLNG)
WEAVER, CHRISTINE R., dir. oper. mgt., Western Pennsylvania Hospital, Pittsburgh, PA '86 (MGMT)
WEAVER, DIANA J., RN, assoc. dir. and dir. nrsg., University Hospital, Lexington, KY '85 (NURS)
WEAVER, FRANK J., dir. pub. affairs, Cleveland Clinic Foundation, Cleveland, OH '81 (PR)
WEAVER, HARRY J., dir. matl., Oil City Area Health Center, Oil City, PA '57 (PUR)(LIFE)
WEAVER, HELEN, coor. vol., Woman's Christian Association Hospital, Jamestown, NY '73 (VOL)
WEAVER, JAMES L., dir. maint. and eng., St. Joseph Hospital, Concordia, KS '74 (ENG)
WEAVER, JOAN, dir., St. Anthony Hospital, Chicago, IL '72 (SOC)(PAT)
WEAVER, JUDY, mgr. sup., proc. and distrib., Western Reserve Systems-Northside, Youngstown, OH '84 (CS)
WEAVER, JULIE L., data base spec., Michigan Hospital Association Service Corporation, Lansing, MI '85 (MGMT)
WEAVER, MARK A., mgr. pur., St. Vincent Memorial Hospital, Taylorville, IL '85 (PUR)
WEAVER, MARY E., RN, dir. nrsg., Mary Breckinridge Hospital, Hyden, KY '83 (NURS)
WEAVER, NANCY F., dir. pers., Cass County Memorial Hospital, Atlantic, IA '87 (PERS)
WEAVER, RICHARD A., environ. serv. consult., Littleton, CO '86 (ENVIRON)
WEAVER, SANDI, dir. risk mgt., Phoebe Putney Memorial Hospital, Albany, GA '80 (RISK)
WEAVER, SHEILA JANE, pat. rep., St. David's Community Hospital, Austin, TX '86 (PAT)
WEAVER, WALDA, dir. food serv., Grand Valley Hospital, Pryor, OK '70 (FOOD)
WEAVERLING, DEE, mgr. matl., AMI Southeastern Medical Center, North Miami Beach, FL '81 (PUR)
WEBB, BARBARA, coor. vol., University of Medicine and Dentistry of New Jersey, University Hospital, Newark, NJ '86 (VOL)
WEBB, BEVERLY E., mgr. med. review serv., Conserv Company, Tampa, FL '86
WEBB, BRUCE R., vice-pres. mktg., Memorial Hospitals Association, Modesto, CA '86 (PR)
WEBB, CAROLYN, dir. spec. educ., Hinds General Hospital, Jackson, MS '86 (EDUC)
WEBB, DELLA W., dir. soc. serv., Prince William Hospital, Manassas, VA '85 (SOC)
WEBB, DOROTHEA L., dir. pers., Greensville Memorial Hospital, Emporia, VA '78 (PERS)
WEBB, DOUGLAS C., dir. pers., John F. Kennedy Memorial Hospital, Philadelphia, PA '83 (PERS)
WEBB, GEORGE N., (ret.), Baltimore, MD '73 (ENG)
WEBB, GREGORY S., adm. mgr., William Beaumont Hospital, Royal Oak, MI '86
WEBB, JAMES R., dir. pur., St. Clair Memorial Hospital, Pittsburgh, PA '82 (PUR)
WEBB, JANE, dir. vol. serv., Henrietta D. Goodall Hospital, Sanford, ME '80 (VOL)
WEBB, JANET L., coor. vol., Blessing Hospital, Quincy, IL '83 (VOL)
WEBB, JOHN R. JR., fiscal and sup. off., Naval Regional Dental Center, Great Lakes, IL '80 (PUR)
WEBB, KATHARINE M., dir. plng., Virginia Hospital Association, Richmond, VA '84
WEBB, MARION L., dir. soc. serv. and pat. rep., Soldiers and Sailors Memorial Hospital, Wellsboro, PA '75 (PAT)(SOC)
WEBB, MILDRED, RN, dir. educ. and trng., Grossmont District Hospital, La Mesa, CA '78 (EDUC)
WEBB, MILLICENT I., vice-pres. mktg. commun., Bed-Check Corporation, Germantown, TN '84 (RISK)
WEBB, NORMAN F. II, pres., Pekin Memorial Hospital, Pekin, IL '77 (PLNG)
WEBB, PAMELA J., mgr. pub. rel., Euclid General Hospital, Euclid, OH '85 (PR)
WEBB, PEGGY, chief adm. diet., Hospital for Special Surgery, New York, NY '72 (FOOD)
WEBB, RAYMOND M., dir. food serv., Latrobe Area Hospital, Latrobe, PA '74 (FOOD)
WEBB, REESA, plng. and mktg. consult., Lutheran Hospitals and Home Society, Englewood, CO '82 (PLNG)
WEBB, ROBERT E., health care info. syst. adv., Ernst and Whinney, Coeur D'Alene, ID '87 (MGMT)
WEBB, RUSSELL M. JR., atty., Hendricks County Hospital, Danville, IN '80 (ATTY)
WEBB, SANDRA M., asst. to chief exec. off.-pat. rel., Good Samaritan Medical Center, Phoenix, AZ '80 (PAT)
WEBB, STEPHEN A., pub. rel. rep., Memorial Medical Center, Long Beach, CA '84 (PR)
WEBB, SUZANNE R., dir. vol. serv., University Hospital, Jacksonville, FL '85 (VOL)
WEBB, THOMAS J., dir., Applied Management Systems, Inc., Burlington, MA '75 (MGMT)
WEBBER, BEVERLY, RN, asst. dir. nrsg., Pacific Presbyterian Medical Center, San Francisco, CA '83 (EDUC)
WEBBER, IRENE, dir. soc. work, Jersey Shore Medical Center, Neptune, NJ '82 (SOC)
WEBBER, JAMES B., pres., James B. Webber, Inc., Lexington, MA '77 (PLNG)
WEBBER, JANE T., assoc. dir. nutr. serv., Baylor University Medical Center, Dallas, TX '71 (FOOD)
WEBBER, MARGARET E. R., dir. vol. serv., Montefiore Medical Center, Bronx, NY '82 (VOL)
WEBBER, STEPHEN W., student, Department of Health Care Administration, George Washington University, Washington, DC '82
WEBBER, VIRGINIA WISE, dir. commun. health and pat. advocate, Addison Gilbert Hospital, Gloucester, MA '86 (PAT)
WEBER, DOROTHY, RN, vice-pres. pat. care serv., Winona Memorial Hospital, Indianapolis, IN '80 (NURS)
WEBER, ERIC R., vice-pres., Timken Mercy Medical Center, Canton, OH '78
WEBER, GEORGE L., mgr. util. review proj., Blue Cross and Blue Shield of Michigan, Detroit, MI '79
WEBER, IAN, dir. pers., Alameda Hospital, Alameda, CA '86 (PERS)
WEBER, JAMES, partner, Ringler Associates, Inc., Detroit, MI '85 (RISK)
WEBER, JEROME J., dir. house serv., Mercy Medical Center, Oshkosh, WI '86 (ENVIRON)
WEBER, LOUISE A., prof. and chairperson, med. rec. adm. prog., Kean College of New Jersey, Union, NJ '81
WEBER, LYNN, dir. soc. serv., Family Hospital, Milwaukee, WI '86 (SOC)
WEBER, SR. MARY J., dir. pat. rel. and advocacy, Our Lady of Mercy Medical Center, Bronx, NY '81 (PAT)
WEBER, MARY, risk mgr., Graham Hospital, Canton, IL '85 (RISK)
WEBER, PHYLLIS, dir. risk mgt., Glendale Adventist Medical Center, Glendale, CA '86 (RISK)
WEBER, RALPH M., vice-pres. plng., Northwestern Memorial Group, Chicago, IL '79 (PLNG)
WEBER, REBECCA J., dir. mktg., Community Hospital, Watervliet, MI '85 (PLNG)
WEBER, RICHARD H., dir. diet. serv., Hackensack Medical Center, Hackensack, NJ '86
WEBER, RONALD JOHN, counselor and trainer, Wellness Centre, Salisbury, NC '83 (EDUC)
WEBER, SCOTT, asst. dir. med. rec., Salinas Valley Memorial Hospital, Salinas, CA '87
WEBER, SHARON THORNTON, dir. soc. serv., Cuero Community Hospital, Cuero, TX '85 (SOC)
WEBER, SHELTON R., atty., NKC Hospitals, Louisville, KY '84 (ATTY)
WEBER, WILLIAM R., atty., St. Peters Community Hospital, St. Peters, MO '82 (ATTY)
WEBRE, THOMAS PAUL, clin. eng., Our Lady of Lake Regional Medical Center, Baton Rouge, LA '85 (ENG)
WEBSTER, BENJAMIN F., exec. vice-pres., Blue Cross of Central Ohio, Columbus, OH '61
WEBSTER, CLARENCE L., supt. elec., Good Samaritan Medical Center, Phoenix, AZ '80 (ENG)
WEBSTER, DANIEL L., supv. clin. eng., Christ Hospital, Cincinnati, OH '86 (ENG)
WEBSTER, DAVID R., med. adm., New York State Office of Health Systems Management, Syracuse, NY '75
WEBSTER, GLENDA J., supv. cent. serv., Ingham Medical Center, Lansing, MI '82 (CS)
WEBSTER, GWENDOLYN YVONNE, dir. nrsg., Howard University Hospital, Washington, DC '77 (NURS)
WEBSTER, HARRY E. III, dir. matl. mgt., Soldiers and Sailors Memorial Hospital, Wellsboro, PA '86 (PUR)
WEBSTER, JAMES W., dir. hskpg. serv., Glens Falls Hospital, Glens Falls, NY '84 (ENG)(ENVIRON)
WEBSTER, PATRICIA A., RN, dir. nrsg., Northbay Medical Center, Fairfield, CA '86 (NURS)
WEBSTER, PATRICIA S., dir. pub. rel., Stillwater Medical Center, Stillwater, OK '81 (PR)
WEBSTER, PHYLLIS E., dir. pub. rel., Dallas-Fort Worth Medical Center, Grand Prairie, TX '84 (PR)
WECHT, CYRIL H., MD, atty., Central Medical Center and Hospital, Pittsburgh, PA '69 (ATTY)
WECKWERTH, VERNON E., assoc. prof., Program in Hospital Administration, University of Minnesota, Minneapolis, MN '65
WEDA, KENNETH A., pres., Good Samaritan Hospital, West Palm Beach, FL '68
WEDDLE, TIMOTHY E., dir. mgt. syst. eng., F. G. McGaw Hospital, Loyola University, Maywood, IL '78 (MGMT)(PLNG)
WEDEEN, MARVIN M., vice-pres., Sewickley Valley Hospital, Sewickley, PA '69 (PLNG)
WEDEL, PAUL GEORGE, pres., Lancaster General Hospital, Lancaster, PA '52 (LIFE)
WEDGE, ROBERT E., partner, Hayes, Large, Suckling, Fruth and Wedge, Altoona, PA '83 (PLNG)
WEDIG, NANCY K., dir. pub. rel., St. Luke's Hospital West, Chesterfield, MO '81 (PR)
WEDMAN, DENNIS J., asst. dir. human res., Saint Alphonsus Regional Medical Center, Boise, ID '86 (PERS)
WEDMORE, BARBARA L., pat. advocate, John Dempsey Hospital-University of Connecticut Health Center, Farmington, CT '81 (PAT)
WEDMORE, TERRY L., dir. safety serv., St. Joseph Mercy Hospital, Mason City, IA '80 (RISK)
WEDRAL, WILLIAM R., chief exec. off., Putnam Hospital Center, Carmel, NY '68
WEDZEL, PATRICIA A., RN, dir. nrsg., Beyer Memorial Hospital, Ypsilanti, MI '85 (NURS)
WEE, MARYANN, risk mgt. consult., Mississippi Hospital Association, Jackson, MS '86 (RISK)
WEED, KATHERINE S., atty., University of Alabama at Birmingham, Birmingham, AL '86 (ATTY)
WEED, WARREN, dir. human res., Riley Memorial Hospital, Meridian, MS '86 (PERS)
WEEDA, NORMA L., dir. educ., Hackley Hospital, Muskegon, MI '82 (EDUC)
WEEDEN, NANCY L., dir. pat. and family serv., Community Hospital of Ottawa, Ottawa, IL '85 (SOC)
WEEDON, ISOBEL LYDIA, hostess, Tri-City Medical Center, Oceanside, CA '85 (PAT)
WEEKES, DAVID H., dir. mktg. and dev., Kennedy Institute for Handicapped, Baltimore, MD '86 (PR)
WEEKS, JAMES M., dir. telecommun., Greenwich Hospital, Greenwich, CT '83 (ENG)
WEEKS, LEWIS E., consult., Ann Arbor, MI '64
WEEKS, RANDALL, atty., Children's Hospital, Denver, CO '73 (ATTY)
WEEKS, SHARON L., soc. worker, Redbud Community Hospital, Clearlake, CA '83 (SOC)
WEEMS, JAMES P., vice-pres. and chief exec. off., Mercy Hospital, Portsmouth, OH '81
WEGER, JANICE L., dir. educ., St. Joseph Mercy Hospital, Mason City, IA '83 (EDUC)
WEGHORST, ROGER A., owner, Roger A. Weghorst Company, Denver, CO '82
WEGMANN, DEBORAH J., RN, assoc. exec. dir. nrsg., Lake Medical Center, Leesburg, FL '86 (NURS)
WEGMENN, CYNTHIA CONNOR, RN, div. dir. surg. nrsg., Pendleton Memorial Methodist Hospital, New Orleans, LA '83 (NURS)
WEGMILLER, DONALD C., pres. and chief exec. off., Health Central Corporation, Minneapolis, MN '85 (PLNG)
WEGNER, GERT E., dir. food serv., Putnam Hospital Center, Carmel, NY '77 (FOOD)
WEGNER, JEFFREY, dir. plant oper., St. Clare Hospital, Baraboo, WI '85 (ENG)
WEGNER, JUNAMAE, dir. vol., Leland Memorial Hospital, Riverdale, MD '85 (VOL)
WEHKING, WILLIAM E., dir. plng., Jewish Hospital of Cincinnati, Cincinnati, OH '76 (PLNG)
WEHLER, RICHARD H., atty., Community Hospital of Springfield and Clark County, Springfield, OH '68 (ATTY)
WEHNER, SR. EMILENE, dir. dev., Divine Providence Hospital, Williamsport, PA '67
WEHR, FREDERICK T., dir. dev. and pub. rel., Church Hospital Corporation, Baltimore, MD '86 (PR) (PLNG)
WEHR, LOIS W., spec. asst. to the exec. vice-pres., Church Hospital Corporation, Baltimore, MD '85 (PAT)
WEHRUNG, H. CRAIG, sr. mgt. eng., Vanderbilt University Hospital, Nashville, TN '81 (MGMT)
WEI, KANG C., partner, Page Southerland Page, Dallas, TX '85 (ENG)
WEIBENER, MARVIN F., supv. soc. serv., City of Faith Hospital, Tulsa, OK '82 (SOC)
WEIDEL, LYNNE C., pres., Weidel and Associates, Lake Oswego, OR '75 (PLNG)
WEIDEN, MICHAEL S., atty., St. Marys Hospital Medical Center, Madison, WI '82 (ATTY)
WEIDMAN, ANNE R., coor. vol., Wyoming County Community Hospital, Warsaw, NY '85 (VOL)
WEIDNER, ROBERT E., vice-pres. adm., Bryn Mawr Hospital, Bryn Mawr, PA '81 (RISK)
WEIGAND, AL J., dir. strategic plng., Baptist Medical Center, Jacksonville, FL '81 (PR) (PLNG)
WEIGERS, KIMBERLY A., adm. res., Veterans Administration Medical Center, Dallas, TX '83
WEIHRAUCH, ROBERTA C., dir. vol. serv., Immanuel-St. Joseph's Hospital, Mankato, MN '87 (VOL)
WEIKEL, M. KEITH, PhD, exec. vice-pres. and chief oper. off., Manor Healthcare, Silver Springs, MD '79 (PLNG)
WEIL, JOSEPH F., dir. plant eng., International Correspondence School, Scranton, PA '86 (ENG)
WEIL, LISA, assoc. dir. prog. coor., Dept. of HHS, National Institute on Alcohol Abuse and Alcoholism, Rockville, MD '68 (MGMT)
WEIL, LOIS, coor. vol., Kaiser Foundation Hospital, Oakland, CA '76 (VOL)
WEIL, NITA, dir. vol. serv., Institute for Rehabilitation and Research, Houston, TX '84 (VOL)
WEIL, SHIRLY, dir. soc. serv., St. Barnabas Medical Center, Livingston, NJ '75 (SOC)
WEIL, THOMAS P., PhD, pres., Bedford Health Associates, Inc., Asheville, NC '56 (LIFE)
WEILAND, JUDITH K., dir. educ. serv., St. Francis Hospital, Blue Island, IL '81 (EDUC)
WEILAND, LINDA, adm. dir. med. info. serv., Providence Hospital, Everett, WA '86 (RISK)
WEIMER, ED, Dallas, TX '86 (LIFE)
WEIMER, PAUL J., dir. info. syst., St. Anthony Medical Center, Columbus, OH '81 (MGMT)
WEIMER, SHARON S., coor. soc. serv., Monongalia General Hospital, Morgantown, WV '81 (SOC)
WEIMER, WILLIAM C., vice-pres. pers. serv., Ohio Hospital Association, Columbus, OH '83 (PERS)
WEIMERSKIRCH, TED, dir. soc. serv., Lutheran Hospital of Fort Wayne, Fort Wayne, IN '86 (SOC)
WEIN, CHARLOTTE EPSTEIN, student, Brooklyn College, Brooklyn, NY '85
WEINANDT, MAURITA A., RN, dir. nrsg. serv., Canoga Park Hospital, Canoga Park, CA '78 (NURS)
WEINANDY, JAMES E., dir. plant oper., Mercy Hospital, Tiffin, OH '75 (ENG)
WEINBERG, DEE, mgr. pub. affairs, Forbes Health System, Pittsburgh, PA '86 (PR)
WEINBERG, HOWARD, dir. hosp. oper., New York City Health and Hospitals Corporation, New York, NY '85
WEINBERG, MARK, sr. mgt. consult., Touche Ross and Company, Chicago, IL '86 (PUR)
WEINBERGER, GERALDINE, pat. rep., Beth Abraham Hospital, Bronx, NY '82 (PAT)
WEINBERGER, STANLEY R., atty., Illinois Health Facilities Authority, Chicago, IL '76 (ATTY)
WEINER, ALAN R., dir. mktg., Southwest Detroit Hospital Corporation, Detroit, MI '63 (PR)

WEINER, DAVID STEPHEN, pres., Children's Hospital, Boston, MA '67
WEINER, EILEEN J., atty., University of Maryland Medical Systems, Baltimore, MD '87 (ATTY)
WEINER, ELAINE, dir., Circulating Nurses, Inc., Malden, MA '84
WEINER, HOWARD D., dir. plant oper., Kaiser Foundation Hospital, Parma, OH '82 (ENG)
WEINER, JACK, pres., Mount Clemens General Hospital, Mount Clemens, MI '84 (PLNG)
WEINER, JAMIE DONNA, coor. trng., Friedman Hospital of the Home for the Jewish Aged, Philadelphia, PA '86 (EDUC)
WEINER, JAYNE, clin. analyst risk mgt., Medical Mutual Liability Insurance Society of Maryland, Towson, MD '85 (RISK)
WEINER, JONATHAN, atty., Albert Einstein Foundation, Philadelphia, PA '86 (ATTY)
WEINER, KATHLEEN QUINT, consult. health res. serv., Virginia Mason Hospital, Seattle, WA '83 (PLNG)
WEINER, MARC VINCENT, chief fin. off., Cottage Hospital of Grosse Pointe, Grosse Pointe Farms, MI '75
WEINER, SARI D., vice-pres. external affairs, Hollywood Presbyterian Medical Center, Los Angeles, CA '85 (PR)
WEINER, STEVEN ALAN, exec. asst., University of Chicago Hospitals, Chicago, IL '79
WEINER, STEVEN I., dir. food and nutr. serv., Kaiser Foundation Hospital, Panorama City, CA '77 (FOOD)
WEINFIELD, DEBRA E., atty., Michael Reese Hospital and Medical Center, Chicago, IL '86 (ATTY)
WEINFIELD, MICHAEL J., adm., Beth Abraham Hospital, Bronx, NY '69
WEINGARDNER, WILLIAM, dir. bldg. maint. and grds., Columbus Hospital, Newark, NJ '86 (ENG)
WEINGART, SR. LORETTA AGNES, pat. rep., St. Joseph's Hospital and Medical Center, Paterson, NJ '68 (PAT)
WEINGARTEN, NANCY, asst. exec. and dir. plng., Waterville Osteopathic Hospital, Waterville, ME '85 (PLNG)
WEINHANDL, RICHARD, asst. mgr. eng., United Hospital, St. Paul, MN '85 (ENG)
WEINHOLD, PENNY L., dir. med. serv., Datacom Systems Corporation, Washington, DC '84
WEINK, JUDY A., coor. commun. health educ., St. Jude Hospital and Rehabilitation Center, Fullerton, CA '86 (EDUC)
WEINPER, LAURIE, pat. rep., Mount Sinai Hospital, Toronto, Ont., Canada '87 (PAT)
WEINRIB, CAROL, vice-pres., Children's Medical Center, Boston, MA '86 (PR) (PLNG)
WEINSTEIN, BERNARD M., comr., Westchester County Medical Center, Valhalla, NY '77
WEINSTEIN, BRUCE J., dir. cent. serv., Daniel Freeman Memorial Hospital, Inglewood, CA '85 (CS)
WEINSTEIN, CYNTHIA ALTMAN, MD, exec. dir. strategic plng., Grand View Hospital, Sellersville, PA '86
WEINSTEIN, GARY B., planner, Washington Hospital, Washington, PA '82 (PLNG)
WEINSTEIN, ISADORE, vice-pres. pub. affairs, Healthwest Medical Centers, Chatsworth, CA '63
WEINSTEIN, JUNE T., pat. rep., Methodist Hospital, Philadelphia, PA '78 (PAT)(RISK)
WEINSTEIN, LEWIS J., atty., Irvington General Hospital, Irvington, NJ '71 (ATTY)
WEINSTEIN, LOIS, dir. prog. plng., Memorial Hospital for Cancer and Allied Diseases, New York, NY '81 (SOC)
WEINSTEIN, CAPT. MARK S., MSC USAF, dir. pat. affairs and med. logistics, U. S. Air Force Clinic Geilenkirchen, APO New York, NY '84
WEINSTEIN, MICHAEL, chief exec. off., AMI Medical Center of North Hollywood, North Hollywood, CA '75
WEINSTEIN, NANCY, RN, assoc. adm., Pembroke Pines General Hospital, Pembroke Pines, FL '83 (NURS)
WEINSTEIN, RONNI JANE, mgr. soc. serv., Highland Park Hospital, Highland Park, IL '81 (SOC)
WEINSTEIN, SHARON M., adm. dir., Robert R. McCormick University Clinics, University Health Sciences-Chicago Medical School, North Chicago, IL '87 (AMB)
WEINSTEIN, STEPHEN, chief exec. off., Lincoln West Hospital, Chicago, IL '86 (PR)
WEINTRAUB, ARNOLD F., dir. food serv., Community General Hospital, Harris, NY '83 (FOOD)
WEINTRAUB, FRANCES C., dir. vol. serv., Wyman Park Medical Center, Baltimore, MD '85 (VOL)
WEIR, ELLIOTT H. JR., exec. vice-pres., Healthcare International, Inc., Austin, TX '79
WEIR, H. PATRICK, atty., Dakota Hospital, Fargo, ND '73 (ATTY)
WEIR, HOLLY E. K., assoc. mktg., South Baltimore General Hospital, Baltimore, MD '86 (PLNG)
WEIR, JEAN H., dir. vol. serv., Forsyth Memorial Hospital, Winston-Salem, NC '80 (VOL)
WEIR, PAULETTE A., mgr. pub. rel., Centinela Hospital Medical Center, Inglewood, CA '84 (PR)
WEIR, SUSAN C., exec. dir., Weir and Associates, Inc., Birmingham, AL '72 (PLNG)
WEIS, ERIC E., asst. vice-pres. and contr., Harrisburg Hospital, Harrisburg, PA '83
WEIS, HENRY LEE, dir. eng. and maint., Ochsner Foundation Hospital, New Orleans, LA '72 (ENG)
WEIS, JOHN N., dir. mktg., Lansing General Hospital, Lansing, MI '82 (PR) (PLNG)
WEIS, JOHN R., assoc. adm., Walter Reed Army Medical Center, Washington, DC '85
WEISBAND, BARRY, mgr. client serv., Forbes Vantage Group, Pittsburgh, PA '86
WEISBAUER, CECILIA, dir. diet. serv., Beth Abraham Hospital, Bronx, NY '80 (FOOD)
WEISBERG, DIANE G., dir. bus. analysis, Integrated Ionics, Inc., Princeton, NJ '85
WEISE, HARRY N., dir. eng. and maint., Dover General Hospital and Medical Center, Dover, NJ '81 (ENG)
WEISENBERG, JANE, dir. human res., Joslin Diabetes Center, Boston, MA '80 (PERS)
WEISENBURGER, DIANE L., supv. pers., Harborview Medical Center, Seattle, WA '81 (PERS)
WEISENSEL, BRUCE C., dir. plng., St. Lawrence Hospital, Lansing, MI '81 (PLNG)
WEISER, STEPHEN J., atty., Ross and Hardies, Chicago, IL '83 (ATTY)
WEISHAAR, GARY L., chief res. mgt., Headquarter Fifth Air Force, APO New York, NY '82 (PLNG)
WEISMAN, DAVID J., mgr. prov. rel., Health Options, Miami, FL '82
WEISMAN, NANCY E., asst. gen. counsel, Rush-Presbyterian-St. Luke's Medical Center, Chicago, IL '83 (ATTY)
WEISS, ALVIN L., atty., Pottstown Memorial Medical Center, Pottstown, PA '82 (ATTY)
WEISS, BARRY J., exec. dir., College Hospital, Cerritos, CA '81 (PLNG)
WEISS, BARRY RICHARD, atty., Pepper, Hamilton and Scheetz, Los Angeles, CA '68 (ATTY)
WEISS, DORIAN, pres., Innovative Risk and Insurance Service, Inc., Chesterfield, MO '86 (RISK)
WEISS, ELLEN COVNER, atty., Hospital of the University of Pennsylvania, Philadelphia, PA '80 (ATTY)(RISK)
WEISS, JACQUE, dir. vol. serv., St. Clare's Hospital, Denville, NJ '79 (VOL)
WEISS, JOSEPH G., vice-pres. eng., Health Corporation of the Archdiocese of Newark, Newark, NJ '74 (ENG)
WEISS, LESTER I., dir. soc. serv., Altoona Hospital, Altoona, PA '83 (SOC)
WEISS, MARCIA A., asst. dir. soc. work, National Rehabilitation Hospital, Washington, DC '78 (SOC)
WEISS, MARY J., dir. food serv., Kenosha Hospital and Medical Center, Kenosha, WI '85 (FOOD)
WEISS, PATRICIA H., RN, supv. cent. serv. room, Southampton Hospital, Southampton, NY '80 (CS)
WEISS, RHODA ELAINE, asst. adm. prog. mktg. and commun. rel., St. Joseph Medical Center, Burbank, CA '80 (PR)
WEISS, RICHARD C., mgr. hosp. affairs, Du Pont Pharmaceuticals, Wilmington, DE '84
WEISS, RICHARD E., chief eng., Mary Lanning Memorial Hospital, Hastings, NE '73 (ENG)
WEISS, ROBERT J., vice-pres. human res., Community Hospital, Anderson, IN '84 (PERS)
WEISS, SANDRA J., atty., Bridgeport Hospital, Bridgeport, CT '87 (ATTY)
WEISS, STUART ALLEN, dir. sup. serv., St. Francis Hospital, Poughkeepsie, NY '70 (PUR)
WEISS, THOMAS M., adm., Hamilton Medical Center Hospital, Lafayette, LA '80
WEISS, WENDY A., dir. soc. serv., Fair Oaks Hospital, Summit, NJ '79 (SOC)
WEISSBERG, LENORE G., dir. soc. work, Deepdale General Hospital, Flushing, NY '85 (SOC)
WEISSBURG, CARL IVAN, exec. dir., United Hospital Association, Los Angeles, CA '68 (ATTY)
WEISSHAAR, ROBIN C., dir. soc. serv., St. Joseph Regional Medical Center, Lewiston, ID '85 (SOC)
WEISSMAN, ANDREW, PhD, dir. soc. work oper. and asst. prof. commun. medicine, Mount Sinai School of Medicine, New York, NY '80 (SOC)
WEISSMAN, CHARLOTTE L., dir. mktg., Panorama Community Hospital, Panorama City, CA '81 (PR) (PLNG)
WEISSMAN, GAIL, RN, dir. nrsg., Mount Sinai Medical Center, New York, NY '71 (NURS)
WEISSMAN, MARIE, dir. soc. serv., Lehigh Valley Hospital Center, Allentown, PA '80 (SOC)
WEISZHAAR, LYLE G., adm. dir. matl. mgt., Dakota Midland Hospital, Aberdeen, SD '83 (PUR)
WEITER, ELIZABETH GREEN, RN, vice-pres. nrsg., Memorial Hospital, Owosso, MI '86 (NURS)
WEITZ, JEAN C., dir. vol. serv., Poudre Valley Hospital, Fort Collins, CO '79 (VOL)
WEITZ, RONALD WAYNE, vice-pres. corp. dev., Prince George's Hospital Center, Cheverly, MD '78 (PLNG)
WEITZEL, HELEN M., dir. vol., Emanuel Hospital and Health Center, Portland, OR '72 (VOL)
WEITZMAN, ELAINE R., dir. plng., North Central Bronx Hospital, Bronx, NY '85 (PLNG)
WEITZMAN, JEFFREY A., clin. eng., LaGuardia Hospital, Flushing, NY '81 (ENG)
WEIZMANN, JANE K., mgr. direct compensation, Thomas Jefferson University Hospital, Philadelphia, PA '86 (PERS)
WEKLAR, MARY ANN, sr. planner, Abington Memorial Hospital, Abington, PA '85 (PLNG)
WELBY, JAMES T., eng. designer, Lovelace Medical Center, Albuquerque, NM '86 (ENG)
WELCH, BEE, dir. vol. serv., Western Pennsylvania Hospital, Pittsburgh, PA '83 (VOL)
WELCH, BERNADETTE E., asst. dir. pers., Suburban Hospital, Bethesda, MD '82 (PERS)
WELCH, BUCK, asst. dir. food serv., Children's Hospital, Denver, CO '79 (FOOD)
WELCH, CAROL A., asst. dir. pat. and family counseling, Mercy Hospital and Medical Center, Chicago, IL '79 (SOC)
WELCH, CHRISTINE I., dir. soc. serv., United Hospital, St. Paul, MN '85 (SOC)
WELCH, DAVID S., dir. matl. mgt., HCA Greenview Hospital, Bowling Green, KY '83 (PUR)
WELCH, ELIZABETH D., coor. health info. syst., AMI Brookwood Medical Center, Birmingham, AL '82 (PLNG)
WELCH, ELIZABETH, RN, dir. nrsg. serv., Owensboro-Daviess County Hospital, Owensboro, KY '78 (NURS)
WELCH, GARY W., chm. anesthesiology, University of Massachusetts Medical Center, Worcester, MA '86 (PLNG)
WELCH, JO, dir. pat. rel., Florida Hospital Medical Center, Orlando, FL '80 (PAT)
WELCH, MARY F., RN, dir. nrsg. serv., Enid Memorial Hospital, Enid, OK '80 (NURS)
WELCH, REYNOLD R., assoc. vice-pres., Maine Medical Center, Portland, ME '72
WELCH, RUTH A., dir. food serv., Jacksonville Medical Center, Jacksonville, FL '86 (FOOD)
WELCKER, JEANNE MARIE, RN, New Orleans, LA '80 (CS)
WELD, ANITA D., dir. pub. rel., Henry Mayo Newhall Memorial Hospital, Valencia, CA '85 (PR)
WELDON, BILL W., assoc. dir., Hermann Hospital, Houston, TX '79
WELDON, JANE W., vice-pres. data serv. and commun., Greater Cincinnati Hospital Council, Cincinnati, OH '86 (PLNG)
WELDON, JOHN B. JR., atty., St. Joseph's Hospital and Medical Center, Phoenix, AZ '82 (ATTY)
WELDY, CHARLES RICHARD, eng., Veterans Administration Medical Center, Leavenworth, KS '65 (ENG)
WELIVER, HOWARD R., Tarkenton Insurance Group, Houston, TX '82 (PERS)
WELLBORN, JOHN L., asst. vice-pres. mktg., Hospital Corporation of America, Nashville, TN '86 (PLNG)
WELLENDORF, ANN C., pat. rep., Michael Reese Hospital and Medical Center, Chicago, IL '81 (PAT)
WELLENDORF, SHARON, RN, coor. educ., Horn Memorial Hospital, Ida Grove, IA '86 (EDUC)
WELLENKAMP, CONRAD, dir. cent. serv., St. Joseph Hospital, Kirkwood, MO '80 (CS)
WELLER, CHARLES D., atty., Hospital Corporation of America, Nashville, TN '86 (ATTY)
WELLER, DONALD M., pur. agt., Margaret Mary Community Hospital, Batesville, IN '86 (PUR)
WELLER, LARRY WOODROW, asst. off., Veterans Administration Medical Center, Bay Pines, FL '73
WELLET, F. LINN, dir. pers., Community Health Center of Branch County, Coldwater, MI '81 (PERS)
WELLINGER, SR. M. ROSITA, exec. vice-pres. and chief oper. off., St. Francis Medical Center, Pittsburgh, PA '66
WELLIVER, CHARLES H., vice-pres. and chief exec. off., Thunderbird Samaritan Hospital and Health Center, Glendale, AZ '80
WELLMAN, JOHN W., atty., Crozer-Chester Medical Center, Chester, PA '74 (ATTY)
WELLMAN, WILLIAM L., mgt. eng., Rush-Presbyterian-St. Luke's Medical Center, Chicago, IL '78 (MGMT)
WELLS, BARBARA L., dir. soc. serv., St. Mary's Hospital of Blue Springs, Blue Springs, MO '86 (SOC)
WELLS, COLEEN, RN, coor. qual. assur., Auburn Faith Community Hospital, Auburn, CA '81 (EDUC)(RISK)
WELLS, MAJ. DAWN L., MSC USA, asst. chief design br., Department of the Army, Office of the Surgeon General, Washington, DC '82
WELLS, EMILY L., dir. mktg. and commun., Theda Clark Regional Medical Center, Neenah, WI '86 (PR)
WELLS, HAROLD W., Gadsden, AL '84 (PR)
WELLS, JACK E., student, Program in Hospital and Health Service Management, Kellogg Graduate School of Management, Northwestern University, Evanston, IL '85
WELLS, JACQUELINE E., atty., Mount Vernon Hospital, Alexandria, VA '86 (ATTY)
WELLS, JAMES BRIAN, partner, Touche Ross and Company, Dallas, TX '78
WELLS, JEAN, coor. pat. serv., Union Medical Center, El Dorado, AR '86 (SOC)
WELLS, JOANNE, mgr. matl., Pembroke Pines General Hospital, Pembroke Pines, FL '80 (PUR)
WELLS, JUNE E., dir. pub. rel., Naeve Health Care Corporation, Albert Lea, MN '81 (PR)
WELLS, LEWIS T., dir. soc. work, Children's Rehabilitation Hospital, Philadelphia, PA '83 (SOC)
WELLS, LINDA O., dir. mktg., Havenwyck Hospital, Auburn Hills, MI '85 (PLNG)
WELLS, MARY ELLEN, asst. to dir., University of Minnesota Hospital and Clinic, Minneapolis, MN '82
WELLS, MARY S., Orlando Regional Medical Center, Orlando, FL '85 (MGMT)
WELLS, MICHAEL, vice-pres. group prog., Alabama Hospital Association, Montgomery, AL '80 (PUR)
WELLS, PAULA B., PhD, bd. chm. and chief exec. off., Wells Engineer, Inc., Omaha, NE '85
WELLS, PEARL, mgr. matl., Memorial Hospital of Carbon County, Rawlins, WY '84 (PUR)
WELLS, ROGER EUGENE, asst. adm., St. Marys Hospital of Rochester, Rochester, MN '68
WELLS, WALLACE R., mgr. plant oper., Valley Hospital Association, Palmer, AK '85 (ENG)
WELLS, WENDY M., assoc. adm., St. Luke's Hospital, Chesterfield, MO '76
WELNER, HAL, adm. reg. serv., Children's Hospital Medical Center of Akron, Akron, OH '85 (PLNG)
WELNER, WILLIAM F., asst. chief eng. serv., Veterans Administration Medical Center, San Francisco, CA '78 (ENG)
WELSER, TIA, RN, coor. pat. care, River District Hospital, St. Clair, MI '83 (PAT)
WELSH, JERRY L., vice-pres. agreements, Hospital Purchasing Service, Middleville, MI '81 (PUR)
WELSH, JOHN H., adm., Woodward Hospital and Health Center, Woodward, OK '70
WELSH, JOHN, vice-pres., Healthcare Marketing Systems, Inc., Minneapolis, MN '85
WELSH, LARRY D., adm., Buena Vista County Hospital, Storm Lake, IA '77
WELSH, LYNN M., dir. diet. serv., St. Joseph's Hospital, Highland, IL '83 (FOOD)
WELSH, ROBERTA M., asst. adm. pat. care serv., Lakeland Hospital, Elkhorn, WI '82 (NURS)
WELSHANS, LAURIE C., mgr. mktg. commun., St. Joseph Hospital, Flint, MI '86 (PR)
WELTE, M. CARMELA, coor. commun. rel., Torrance Memorial Hospital Medical Center, Torrance, CA '84 (PR)
WELTE, VERNA, RN, vice-pres. nrsg. serv., Marian Health Center, Sioux City, IA '82 (NURS)
WEMPLE, TIMOTHY D., adm. dir. med. staff dev., Martin Luther Hospital Medical Center, Anaheim, CA '81
WENBERG, MARCIA LYNN, supv. soc. serv., Memorial Medical Center, Springfield, IL '86 (SOC)

WENDELL, MONA D., RN, dir. educ., Deaconess Hospital of Cleveland, Cleveland, OH '83 (EDUC)
WENDLING, JEFFREY T., sr. vice-pres., Northern Michigan Hospitals, Petoskey, MI '78
WENDORF, CARL E., San Francisco, CA '86
WENDT, LINDA J., prin., Tribrook Group, Inc., Oak Brook, IL '75 (PLNG)
WENDT, RICHARD A., atty., Albion Community Hospital, Albion, MI '78 (ATTY)
WENELL, DUANE R., dir. mktg., Universal Hospital Services, Inc., Bloomington, MN '79 (PLNG)
WENGEL, SHELDON, dir. pub. rel. and dev., Franklin Square Hospital, Baltimore, MD '65 (PR)
WENGER, JILL D., dir. pers., Hiawatha Community Hospital, Hiawatha, KS '86 (PERS)
WENGER, STEVEN L., dir. mktg., Menorah Medical Center, Kansas City, MO '85 (PLNG)
WENGERD, NORMAN W., dir. corp. dev., Sisters of Charity of St. Augustine, Richfield, OH '84 (PLNG)
WENNEN, GINNY, coor. pub. info., Virginia Regional Medical Center, Virginia, MN '82 (PR)
WENNER, CHARLES H., dir. plant oper. and maint., Harrison Community Hospital, Cadiz, OH '81 (ENG)
WENNERMARK, JON R., dir. mgt. eng., Indiana University Hospitals, Indianapolis, IN '73 (MGMT)
WENRICH, KENNETH N., vice-pres. oper., Open Door Estates, Springhouse, PA '61
WENTE, BARBARA A., dir. food serv., Waveny Care Center, New Canaan, CT '82 (FOOD)
WENTE, JAMES J., assoc. adm., Charleston Area Medical Center, Charleston, WV '85
WENTE, THOMAS E., vice-pres., Marian Health Center, Sioux City, IA '65 (PUR)
WENTLAND, SR. MARY A., RN, coor. nrsg. and pat. care serv., St. Francis Medical Center, Breckenridge, MN '83 (NURS)
WENTWORTH, PHILIP MONTGOMERY, exec. vice-pres., Presbyterian Hospital, Dallas, TX '72
WENTWORTH, RITA A., dir. vol., Sacred Heart Hospital, Yankton, SD '84 (VOL)
WENTZ, CHARLOTTE D., dir. vol. serv., Wilkes-Barre General Hospital, Wilkes-Barre, PA '76 (VOL)
WENTZ, JULIA, atty., Christian Hospital Northeast, St. Louis, MO '85 (ATTY)
WENTZ, LYNNE, student, Program in Health Service Administration, School of Health Professions, Governors State University, Park Forest South, IL '87 (AMB)
WENZ, PAUL F., chief exec. off., Iroquois Memorial Hospital, Watseka, IL '63 (PLNG)
WENZEL, CAROL J., dir. commun., Montefiore Hospital, Pittsburgh, PA '86 (ENG)
WENZING, ELEANOR C., RN, supv. cent. sup., Mercy Hospital, Baltimore, MD '86 (CS)
WENZLAFF, DUANE, maint. eng., Sacred Heart Hospital, Yankton, SD '78 (ENG)
WERBELOW, JUDSON, atty., Ingham Medical Center, Lansing, MI '77 (ATTY)
WERBELOW, LOUISE B., chm. vol. serv. com., Edward W. Sparrow Hospital, Lansing, MI '86 (VOL)
WERBINSKI, FRANK J., vice-pres. plant oper., Cheshire Medical Center, Keene, NH '79 (ENG)
WERDEL, WILLIAM A., (ret.), Grand Blanc, MI '54 (LIFE)
WERGIN, MARY E., dir. matl. mgt., Shady Grove Adventist Hospital, Rockville, MD '83 (PUR)
WERIER, HARRY G., actg. supv. med. soc. work, Lac-High Desert Hospital, Lancaster, CA '82 (SOC)
WERKHOVEN, KATHRYN R., RN, dir. nrsg., St. Francis Hospital, Memphis, TN '84 (NURS)
WERLAU, PATRICIA A., dir. soc. serv., United Hospital, Port Chester, NY '78 (SOC)
WERLING, JACQUELINE S., RN, dir. nrsg. amb. serv., N. T. Enloe Memorial Hospital, Chico, CA '87 (AMB)
WERLING, VICKI L., oper. analyst, Medical College of Ohio Hospital, Toledo, OH '86 (MGMT)
WERME, CAROL A., coor. cent. sup. room, Fish Memorial Hospital, New Smyrna Beach, FL '84 (CS)
WERNECKE, HARRY J., adm., Shawano Community Hospital, Shawano, WI '59 (PLNG)
WERNER, ALAN B., dir. food serv., Memorial Hospital, Belleville, IL '83 (FOOD)
WERNER, DANIEL J., vice-pres., St. Mary's Hospital, Reno, NV '81
WERNER, DARLENE J., RN, vice-pres. nrsg. adm., Methodist Hospital of Southern California, Arcadia, CA '80 (NURS)
WERNER, DENNY, Tampa, FL '82 (PUR)
WERNER, JOHN P., dir. mgt. serv., Hahnemann University Hospital, Philadelphia, PA '80 (MGMT)(PLNG)
WERNER, JUNE, RN, chm. nrsg., Evanston Hospital, Evanston, IL '72 (NURS)
WERNER, KENT R., dir. facil. maint., Brockton Hospital, Brockton, MA '81 (PLNG)
WERNER, NICKI B., asst. mgr. cent. proc. and distrib., Appleton Medical Center, Appleton, WI '80 (CS)
WERNER, ROBERT J., atty., Lovelace Medical Center, Albuquerque, NM '73 (ATTY)
WERNER, VALERIE R., Tampa, FL '82 (EDUC)
WERNER, WILLIAM L., dir. operational audit, Toledo Hospital, Toledo, OH '74
WERRY, WILLA MAE, assoc. dir. pers., Florida Hospital Medical Center, Orlando, FL '77 (PERS)
WERTHEIM, ROBYN, dir. compensation, Long Island Jewish Hospital, New Hyde Park, NY '85 (PERS)
WERTS, JOHN F., dir. med. soc. serv., Home Care of Northeastern Pennsylvania, Inc., Wilkes-Barre, PA '84 (SOC)
WERTZ, E. RANDALL, dir. human res., Clark County Hospital, Winchester, KY '86 (PERS)
WESBECHER, ANN, coor. qual. assur., St. Mary Hospital, Quincy, IL '85 (RISK)
WESBURY, STUART A. JR., PhD, pres., American College of Hospital Administrators, Chicago, IL '59 (MGMT)
WESCOTT, JOVETA, student, Program in Health Care Administration, Trinity University, San Antonio, TX '86
WESCOTT, LLOYD, bd. mem., Hunterdon Medical Center, Flemington, NJ '73 (LIFE)
WESELI, ROGER W., pres., Good Samaritan Hospital, Cincinnati, OH '69 (PLNG)
WESENBERG, CAROLINE JOAN, RN, chief oper. off., Health Partners International, Miami, FL '77 (NURS)
WESLEY, ERMA R., dir. soc. serv., University of Alabama Hospital, Birmingham, AL '78 (SOC)
WESLEY, JAMES E., vice-pres. human res., Ochsner Foundation Hospital, New Orleans, LA '73 (PERS)
WESLEY, JOHN A., plant eng., Community Hospital of Anderson and Madison County, Anderson, IN '85 (ENG)
WESLEY, MARY M., dir. soc. serv., Davis Community Hospital, Statesville, NC '79 (SOC)
WESLEY, PHYLLIS F., coor. nrsg. proj., Sarasota Memorial Hospital, Sarasota, FL '84 (MGMT)
WESNER, MARILYN M., risk mgr., Saint Joseph Hospital, Reading, PA '83 (RISK)
WESSEL, ALLAN W., chief mech. eng., Ellerbe Architects, Inc., Bloomington, MN '86 (ENG)
WESSELHOFT, JOCELYN M., dir. pat. serv. and commun. educ., San Jacinto Methodist Hospital, Baytown, TX '85 (SOC)
WESSELS, ROGER W., exec. dir., Garfield Medical Center, Monterey Park, CA '71
WESSLUND, RICHARD, vice-pres. bus. dev., Mercy Services Corporation, San Diego, CA '80 (PLNG)
WESSNER, K. T., chm., Servicemaster Industries, Inc., Downers Grove, IL '72
WESSON, WENDY, Waitsfield, VT '79 (ENG)
WEST, BILLIE R., corp. dir. mgt. trng., Basic American Medical, Inc., Fort Myers, FL '85
WEST, BRYAN C., dir. biomedical inst. serv., Providence Medical Center, Seattle, WA '83 (ENG)
WEST, C. H. JR., supv. oper., Cedars-Sinai Medical Center, Los Angeles, CA '83 (ENG)
WEST, CLYDE, maint. eng., B. J. Workman Memorial Hospital, Woodruff, SC '76 (ENG)
WEST, DANIEL J. JR., PhD, adm., Lackawanna Medical Group, Scranton, PA '80 (AMB)
WEST, DANIEL ROBERT, sr. assoc. exec. dir., Presbyterian Hospital, Dallas, TX '78 (AMB)
WEST, DAVID A., dir. eng. serv., St. Jude Hospital and Rehabilitation Center, Fullerton, CA '73 (ENG)
WEST, DAVID, dir. pers., Albert Einstein Medical Center, Philadelphia, PA '83 (PERS)
WEST, DEBORA H., mgr. pat. rel., Cookeville General Hospital, Cookeville, TN '86 (VOL)(PAT)
WEST, DUANNE, asst. dir. lab. serv., Carraway Methodist Medical Center, Birmingham, AL '87 (MGMT)
WEST, EVELYN S., pat. rep., Redmond Park Hospital, Rome, GA '82 (PAT)
WEST, FRANCES M., RN, assoc. dir. nrsg., Champlain Valley Physicians Hospital Medical Center, Plattsburgh, NY '85 (NURS)
WEST, GEORGE W., pres., Medical Ancillary Services, Inc., Grand Prairie, TX '83
WEST, GROVER L., dir. ldry. serv., St. Paul Medical Center, Dallas, TX '80 (PUR)(ENVIRON)
WEST, HAROLD J., dir. human res., Detroit Osteopathic Hospital, Highland Park, MI '83 (PERS)
WEST, HOWARD P., atty., Richland Memorial Hospital, Columbia, SC '82 (ATTY)
WEST, JAMES W. JR., mgr. matl., Haywood County Hospital, Clyde, NC '80 (PUR)
WEST, JAMES, vice chairperson risk mgt., Allegan General Hospital, Allegan, MI '86 (RISK)
WEST, JAN E., dir. soc. work, Charter Community Hospital of Cleveland, Cleveland, TX '78 (SOC)
WEST, JOHN W., dir. matl. mgt., Holland Community Hospital, Holland, MI '85 (PUR)
WEST, KAY G., atty., American Healthcare Management, Inc., Encino, CA '85 (ATTY)
WEST, LOUISE K., risk mgr., Lawnwood Regional Medical Center, Fort Pierce, FL '80 (RISK)
WEST, MARIE, cent. sup. sr. tech., Orlando Regional Medical Center, Orlando, FL '86 (CS)
WEST, MARION E., dir. vol. serv., Queen's Medical Center, Honolulu, HI '85 (VOL)
WEST, MARY ELLEN, supv. csr, Harrison Community Hospital, Mount Clemens, MI '87 (CS)
WEST, MARY K., hosp. planner, Good Samaritan Hospital and Health Center, Dayton, OH '82 (PLNG)
WEST, SANDRA L., dir. soc. serv., Memorial Hospital of Southern Oklahoma, Ardmore, OK '82 (SOC)
WEST, SHIRLEY CECELIA, dir. nrsg., Morristown-Hamblen Hospital, Morristown, TN '84 (NURS)
WEST, STEVEN J., exec. vice-pres., Galesburg Cottage Hospital, Galesburg, IL '78 (PLNG)
WEST, SUZANNE F., atty., San Antonio Community Hospital, Upland, CA '82 (ATTY)
WEST, W. STEVEN, assoc. dir. and atty., Methodist Health Systems, Inc., Memphis, TN '79 (ATTY)
WEST, WILLIAM, dir. matl. mgt., Ivinson Memorial Hospital, Laramie, WY '84 (PUR)
WESTALL, JAMES, mgr. plant, San Joaquin General Hospital, Stockton, CA '85 (ENG)
WESTALL, PATRICIA T., vice-pres. mktg., Georgia Baptist Medical Center, Atlanta, GA '82 (PLNG)
WESTBROOK, ANITA S., dir. mktg., Clovis High Plains Hospital, Clovis, NM '85 (PR) (PLNG)
WESTBROOK, RANDALL J., dir. pers., South Highlands Hospital, Birmingham, AL '80 (PERS)
WESTCOTT, JOHN A., vice-pres. facil. and eng., Northwestern Memorial Hospital, Chicago, IL '86 (ENG)
WESTCOTT, PAMELA, mktg. asst., Childrens Hospital of Orange County, Orange, CA '85 (PR)
WESTENBERGER, ROBERT ALAN, mgr. bldgs. oper., St. Clare's -Riverside Medical Center, Denville, NJ '86 (ENG)
WESTER, JAN, nrs. educator, St. Joseph Health Care Corporation, Albuquerque, NM '86 (EDUC)
WESTEREN, BERNT A., dir. bldg. and grds., Fairview Riverside Hospital, Minneapolis, MN '70 (ENG)
WESTERGAARD, NEAL M., dir. soc. serv., Des Moines General Hospital, Des Moines, IA '86 (SOC)
WESTERLING, CLIFFORD G., vice-pres. hosp. rel., Canton-Potsdam Hospital, Potsdam, NY '82 (PR)
WESTERMAN, MARJORIE M., RN, dir. nrsg. serv., St. Lawrence Rehabilitation Center, Lawrenceville, NJ '82 (NURS)
WESTERMAN, ROSEMARY, assoc. chief nrsg. serv. and educ., Veterans Administration Medical Center, Chillicothe, OH '85 (EDUC)
WESTERMAN, SHIRLEY A., dir. staff serv., Southwest Florida Regional Medical Center, Fort Myers, FL '81 (RISK)
WESTGATE, KAREN L., planner facil. plng. and dev., Kaiser Permanente Regional Office, Oakland, CA '82
WESTHAUSER, WALTER C., dir. pur., West Allis Memorial Hospital, West Allis, WI '73 (PUR)
WESTHOFEN, RICHARD C., pres., Fisher-Titus Medical Center, Norwalk, OH '64
WESTLAND, EDWARD H., mgr. health facil., Turner Construction Company, Costa Mesa, CA '84 (PLNG)
WESTMAN, NOELENE R., chairperson nrsg. educ., South Miami Hospital, South Miami, FL '86 (EDUC)
WESTMAN, ROBERT T., atty., Jess Parrish Memorial Hospital, Titusville, FL '86 (ATTY)
WESTMORELAND, DON, risk mgr., New Hanover Memorial Hospital, Wilmington, NC '85 (RISK)
WESTMORELAND, J. LOFTON, atty., Sacred Heart Hospital of Pensacola, Pensacola, FL '76 (ATTY)
WESTON, ALAN G., RN, dir. nrsg. serv., Henrietta D. Goodall Hospital, Sanford, ME '76 (NURS)
WESTON, ANN, pat. rep., Fort Hamilton-Hughes Memorial Hospital, Hamilton, OH '81 (PAT)
WESTON, DOROTHY R., dir. pub. rel., Pasadena Bayshore Medical Center, Pasadena, TX '83 (PR)
WESTON, GARY L., dir. matl. mgt., Logan County Hospital, Sterling, CO '86 (PUR)
WESTON, JUDITH JOHNSTON, vice-pres. pub. and governmental affairs, Hospital Council of Northern California, San Mateo, CA '86 (PLNG)
WESTON, JUDY D., coor. wellness, St. Francis Medical Center, Trenton, NJ '87 (EDUC)
WESTPHAL, F. W., dir. eng., Harris Methodist -Fort Worth, Fort Worth, TX '75 (ENG)
WESTRA, SAM, chief eng., Denver Health and Hospitals, Denver, CO '82 (ENG)
WESTREICH, HENRY, adm., Roxbury Medical Group, Pennsylvania, Succasunna, NJ '75
WESTRICK, PAUL R., dir. plng., Methodist Health Service, Inc., Madison, WI '84 (PLNG)
WESTROPE, R. ANN, RN, vice-pres. nrsg., Middletown Regional Hospital, Middletown, OH '83 (NURS)
WESTWOOD, DONNA K., coor. pub. affairs, Miners Hospital Northern Cambria, Spangler, PA '86 (PR)
WETHERILL, BENJAMIN A., dir. soc. serv., Children's Medical Center, Tulsa, OK '68 (SOC)
WETHLY, RICHARD A., dir. pers., Masonic Hospital, Wallingford, CT '74 (PERS)
WETJEN, JOHN M., dir. corp. syst., Fairfax Hospital Association, Springfield, VA '73 (MGMT)
WETSCH, PEGGY A., dir. educ. serv., AMI Medical Center of Garden Grove, Garden Grove, CA '85 (EDUC)
WETSEL, JOHN E. JR., atty., Winchester Medical Center, Winchester, VA '86 (ATTY)
WETSTONE, HOWARD J., MD, vice-pres. critical med. affairs, Hartford Hospital, Hartford, CT '82
WETTELAND, JOANN E., RN, vice-pres. nrsg., Kettering Medical Center, Kettering, OH '86 (NURS)
WETTENGEL, SHARON WALL, dir. soc. serv., Mercy Health Center, Oklahoma City, OK '85 (SOC)
WETTERMAN, LANA M., dir. commun. rel. and dev., Memorial Hospital of Union County, Marysville, OH '84 (PR)
WETZEL, E. THOMAS II, dir. pub. rel., HCA Huntington Hospital, Huntington, WV '81 (PR)
WETZEL, GERRY HAWKINS, sr. vice-pres., Raritan Bay Healthcare Foundation, Perth Amboy, NJ '63 (PLNG)
WETZEL, TERESA, coor. risk mgt., Barnes Hospital, St. Louis, MO '86 (RISK)
WETZEL, THOMAS KEITH, acct. analyst, Blue Cross and Blue Shield of New York, New York, NY '86
WEXLER, BARBARA, dir. mktg. and pub. rel., Granada Hills Community Hospital, Granada Hills, CA '85 (PR) (PLNG)
WEXLER, MELVIN J., corp. dir. mktg., Good Samaritan Hospital and Medical Center, Portland, OR '85 (PR)
WEYHING, ROBERT L. III, atty., Cottage Hospital of Grosse Pointe, Grosse Pointe Farms, MI '82 (ATTY)
WEYHMULLER, GARY J., dir. pers., Fox Chase Cancer Center, Philadelphia, PA '86 (PERS)
WEYLANDT, STEPHEN E., sr. consult., Robert Douglass Associates, Houston, TX '83
WEYMOUTH, THOMAS F., adm. amb. serv., Medical Center of Delaware, Wilmington, DE '86 (AMB)
WEZENSKY, JOHN, vice-pres. guest rel., Central Michigan Community Hospital, Mount Pleasant, MI '78 (PUR)
WHALEN, CHRISTINE M., coor. pub. rel., Deborah Heart and Lung Center, Deborah Hospital Foundation, North Lauderdale, FL '86 (PR)
WHALEN, DONIS L., dir. soc. serv., Winneshiek County Memorial Hospital, Decorah, IA '85 (SOC)
WHALEN, KATHERINE, RN, dir. emer. serv., Kent County Memorial Hospital, Warwick, RI '79 (AMB)
WHALEN, PATRICK J., dir. sales and promotion, Baptist Medical Center, Kansas City, MO '82 (PR) (PLNG)
WHALEN, PAUL W., sr. asst. adm., Montefiore Hospital and Medical Center, Bronx, NY '77
WHALEN, THOMAS C., dir. pers., Miami Children's Hospital, Miami, FL '77 (PERS)
WHALEY, DORIS E., RN, vice-pres. pat. serv., Lancaster-Fairfield Community Hospital, Lancaster, OH '79 (NURS)

WHALL, JOSEPH J., dir. food serv., St. John's Hospital, Lowell, MA '74 (FOOD)
WHAM, SHARON, supv. distrib., Deaconess Medical Center, Billings, MT '77 (CS)
WHARTON, SHARON K., dir. vol. serv., Wilson N. Jones Memorial Hospital, Sherman, TX '84 (VOL)
WHARTON, SHIRLEY G., RN, vice-pres. nrsg., Norfolk General Hospital, Norfolk, VA '81 (NURS)
WHARTON, WILLIAM L., dir. eng., Southland Medical Center, Darlington, SC '84 (ENG)
WHATLEY, GARY, asst. adm., Memorial Medical Center of East Texas, Lufkin, TX '86 (RISK)
WHEAT, MARTHA G., mgr. cent. serv., Arnot-Ogden Memorial Hospital, Elmira, NY '83 (CS)
WHEATCROFT, VIRGINIA, coor. pat. rep. serv., St. Luke's Hospital, Kansas City, MO '74 (PAT)
WHEATLEY, BARBARA, risk mgr., Good Samaritan Hospital and Medical Center, Portland, OR '86 (RISK)
WHEATLEY, JACK B. JR., exec. dir., Humana Hospital -Sun Bay, St. Petersburg, FL '86
WHEATON, JAMES W., dir. plng., Riverside Methodist Hospitals, Columbus, OH '82 (PLNG)
WHEATON, LOIS H., dir. cent. dispatch, St. John's Hospital, Lowell, MA '86 (CS)
WHEDBEE, DOROTHY C., RN, clin. dir. med. nrsg. serv., Moses H. Cone Memorial Hospital, Greensboro, NC '86 (NURS)
WHEELER, ANN, dir. commun., American Medical International Houston Region, Houston, TX '86 (PR)
WHEELER, BARBARA, buyer, Providence Medical Center, Portland, OR '86 (PUR)
WHEELER, C. B., atty., Wadley Regional Medical Center, Texarkana, TX '70 (ATTY)
WHEELER, D. LAMAR, asst. adm., University Hospital, Augusta, GA '70 (PUR)
WHEELER, DAYNON W., supv. plant oper., Research Medical Center, Kansas City, MO '84 (ENG)
WHEELER, DIXIE, supv. cent. serv., Lakes Region General Hospital, Laconia, NH '87 (CS)
WHEELER, ELAINE C., coor. educ., Saint Joseph's Hospital, Atlanta, GA '83 (EDUC)
WHEELER, ELMER, dir. environ. serv., Charter Springs Hospital, Ocala, FL '86 (ENG)
WHEELER, GLORIA A., asst. dir. sterile proc., Long Island College Hospital, Brooklyn, NY '86 (CS)
WHEELER, JO, RN, dir. outpatient serv, Bromenn Healthcare, Bloomington, IL '87 (AMB)
WHEELER, JOAN I., RN, dir. nrsg., St. Elizabeth Hospital, Elizabeth, NJ '82 (NURS)
WHEELER, JOHN R., exec. dir. path. lab., Frisbie Memorial Hospital, Rochester, NH '74
WHEELER, JOHN, dir. plant serv., Graham Hospital, Canton, IL '87 (ENG)
WHEELER, JOSEPH DREW, dir. plant oper., St. Anthony Medical Center, Louisville, KY '76 (ENG)
WHEELER, LAVERN, dir. pur., Pekin Memorial Hospital, Pekin, IL '65 (PUR)
WHEELER, LDCR DAVID L., MSC USN, off. in charge, Branch Medical Clinic, Subase Bangor, Subase Bangor, WA '85 (PERS)
WHEELER, MARGARET M., dir. soc. serv., Methodist Hospital of Indiana, Indianapolis, IN '84 (SOC)
WHEELER, MARK S., adm., Wayne County Hospital, Corydon, IA '85
WHEELER, MARY E., RN, Charlottesville, VA '76 (NURS)
WHEELER, MARY R., dir. nrsg. serv., North Orange Memorial Hospital, Apopka, FL '86 (NURS)
WHEELER, REX A., adm., Joel Pomerene Memorial Hospital, Millersburg, OH '81
WHEELER, WALTER S., adm., Heritage Hospital, Taylor, MI '52 (LIFE)
WHEELER, WINDELL, dir. maint., Grady Memorial Hospital, Delaware, OH '79 (ENG)
WHEELOCK, KAREN L., RN, dir. nrsg., St. Olaf Hospital, Austin, MN '81 (NURS)
WHELAN, JOAN D., rep. pat. serv., Long Beach Community Hospital, Long Beach, CA '79 (PAT)
WHELAN, MARY HELEN, pat. rep., Mercy Medical Center, Denver, CO '86 (PAT)
WHELAN, MERVYN RICHARD, MD, dir. emer. serv. and trng. prog., Geneva General Hospital, Geneva, NY '87 (AMB)
WHELAN, MICHAEL F., University of Massachusetts Medical Center, Worcester, MA '79 (ENG)
WHELAN, RICHARD V. JR., atty., Lutheran Medical Center, Cleveland, OH '80 (ATTY)
WHELAN, SALLIE, dir. info. and publications, Pitt County Memorial Hospital, Greenville, NC '86 (PR)
WHELAN, SHARON A., RN, dir. pat. care serv., Health Central of Owatonna, Owatonna, MN '85 (NURS)
WHELESS, SUSAN F., asst. adm., Annie Pennsylvania Memorial Hospital, Reidsville, NC '83
WHELPLY, FREDERICK G., exec. vice-pres., Bayonne Hospital, Bayonne, NJ '48 (LIFE)
WHETSELL, GEORGE W., prin., Ernst and Whinney, Baltimore, MD '76 (MGMT)
WHICHARD, JAMES W., dir. matl., Rex Hospital, Raleigh, NC '82 (PUR)
WHICHELLO, ROBERT G., dir. pers., Doctors Medical Center, Modesto, CA '83 (PERS)
WHIDDEN, DEBRA F., RN, mgr. critical care and med. serv., Deaconess Medical Center, Billings, MT '86 (NURS)
WHIDDEN, KATHERINE E., dir. pers., Mount Auburn Hospital, Cambridge, MA '86 (PERS)
WHINNERY, DALE E., vice-pres., HealthOne Corporation, Minneapolis, MN '83
WHIPPLE, BEA, mgr. pat. reservations and info., Harper Hospital, Detroit, MI '85
WHIPPLE, DAVID ALLEN, dir. mgt. eng., Methodist Health Systems, Memphis, TN '78 (MGMT)
WHIPPLE, DEFOREST T., (ret.), Delmar, NY '49 (LIFE)
WHIPPLE, INGRID L., asst. vice-pres.-oper., Oakwood Hospital, Dearborn, MI '86
WHIPPLE, RONALD DAVID, head pat. adm., Naval Hospital, Orlando, FL '85 (PAT)
WHISENANT, BETTY E., asst. adm., Cobb General Hospital, Austell, GA '86 (RISK)
WHISMAN, LANA J., coor. soc. serv., Athens Community Hospital, Athens, TN '87 (SOC)
WHISMAN, PHILLIP R., supv. maint., Clark County Hospital, Winchester, KY '85 (ENG)
WHISTON-FOX, SHEILA K., mgr. mgt. productivity, Wesley Medical Center, Wichita, KS '86 (EDUC)
WHITACRE, LT. AUDRY, nrs., U.S. Air Force Regional Hospital, Riverside, CA '87 (MGMT)
WHITAKER, ALFRED E., asst. dir. food serv., Columbus Hospital, Great Falls, MT '86 (FOOD)
WHITAKER, BRUCE B., vice-pres. plng. and mktg., Mercy Hospital, Baltimore, MD '76 (PR) (PLNG)
WHITAKER, CHARLOTTE J., RN, asst. dir. nrsg., Michael Reese Hospital and Medical Center, Chicago, IL '86 (NURS)
WHITAKER, J. RICHARD, dir. soc. serv., St. Charles Hospital, Oregon, OH '83 (SOC)
WHITAKER, MARIAN KRAMER, adm. res., University Hospital, Stony Brook, NY '81
WHITAKER, MEADE JR., atty., South Highlands Hospital, Birmingham, AL '79 (ATTY)
WHITAKER, PHYLLIS, dir. soc. work, Lenoir Memorial Hospital, Kinston, NC '73 (SOC)
WHITBY, CHARLES L. JR., mgt. eng., Medical Center of Central Georgia, Macon, GA '75 (MGMT)
WHITCOMB, MARY LOU, dir. vol. serv., Pacific Presbyterian Medical Center, San Francisco, CA '81 (VOL)
WHITE, ADRIENNE, atty., New York University Medical Center, New York, NY '82 (ATTY)(RISK)
WHITE, ADRIENNE, assoc. dir. plng., Kings County Hospital Center, Brooklyn, NY '87 (AMB)
WHITE, AILEEN D., partner, White, Kirby and Whyte Health Care Communications, Philadelphia, PA '80 (PR)
WHITE, ALICE H., dir. vol. serv., Glens Falls Hospital, Glens Falls, NY '72 (VOL)
WHITE, ANN E., RN, asst. dir. nrsg., United Hospital Center, Clarksburg, WV '82 (NURS)
WHITE, ANN E., RN, dir. nrsg., Dana-Farber Cancer Institute, Boston, MA '80 (NURS)
WHITE, B. J., dir. food serv., Des Moines General Hospital, Des Moines, IA '75 (FOOD)
WHITE, BARBARA H., dir. transportation and commun., Mary Hitchcock Memorial Hospital, Hanover, NH '80 (ENG)
WHITE, BARRY B., atty., North Miami Medical Center, North Miami, FL '73 (ATTY)
WHITE, BELINDA A., emp. rep., Antelope Valley Hospital Medical Center, Lancaster, CA '85 (PERS)
WHITE, CALVIN, dir. pur., North Mississippi Medical Center, Tupelo, MS '87 (PUR)
WHITE, CARLYNE B., RN, dir. surg. serv., AMI Presbyterian-Denver Hospital, Denver, CO '84 (NURS)
WHITE, CAROL F., dir. teleconference prog., Georgia Hospital Association, Atlanta, GA '86 (EDUC)
WHITE, CAROL M., asst. vice-pres., corp. dir. mktg. and pub. rel., American Medical International, Beverly Hills, CA '81 (PR)
WHITE, CAROLIE P., RN, asst. dir. nrsg., Tulane University Hospital and Clinics, New Orleans, LA '83 (NURS)
WHITE, CHRISTOPHER A., atty., Beaches Hospital, Jacksonville Beach, FL '83 (ATTY)
WHITE, CLARENCE H., assoc. adm., Howard University Hospital, Washington, DC '84
WHITE, DANEEN A., dir. vol. serv., Memorial Hospital, Fremont, OH '76 (VOL)
WHITE, DANNY E., dir. plant eng., Amarillo Hospital District, Amarillo, TX '79 (ENG)
WHITE, DENISE, dir. nrsg.-critical care, Metropolitan Medical Center, Minneapolis, MN '85 (NURS)
WHITE, DENNIS A., dir. shared serv., Hospital Shared Services, Charleston, WV '81 (PUR)
WHITE, DOUG, asst. adm., HCA Vista Hills Medical Center, El Paso, TX '86 (RISK)
WHITE, EDDIE T., exec. dir. phys. plant, University of Texas Medical Branch, Galveston, TX '76 (ENG)
WHITE, ELINOR, dir. vol., Emerson Hospital, Concord, MA '72 (VOL)
WHITE, ELISABETH A. M., dir. pers. serv., University of Minnesota Hospital and Clinic, Minneapolis, MN '73 (PERS)
WHITE, ELLIOTT NEAL, assoc. adm., Liberty Medical Center, Baltimore, MD '77
WHITE, FREDERICK EBENER, mgr. indust. eng., St. Luke's Hospital, Kansas City, MO '75 (MGMT)
WHITE, FREDERICK THOMAS JR., dir. plant serv., St. Luke's Hospital, Jacksonville, FL '74 (ENG)
WHITE, GARY H., dir. plant oper., West Houston Medical Center, Houston, TX '85 (ENG)
WHITE, GAYLE, LDS Hospital, Salt Lake City, UT '85 (PAT)
WHITE, GEORGIANA K., coor. medicolegal studies, Harvard School of Public Health, Boston, MA '81 (PAT)
WHITE, HARRIET A., dir. pers. serv., Memorial Hospital of Topeka, Topeka, KS '85 (PERS)(EDUC)
WHITE, HARRY W., atty., City Hospital, Bellaire, OH '76 (ATTY)
WHITE, HELEN A., RN, vice-pres. nrsg., Winchester Medical Center, Winchester, VA '82 (NURS)
WHITE, HERMAN J., dir. human resources, East Orange General Hospital, East Orange, NJ '76 (PERS)
WHITE, J. AUSTIN, pres., Hamilton Hospital, Hamilton, NJ '54 (PLNG)(LIFE)
WHITE, J. PHIL, dir. amb. surg., Intermountain Health Care, Inc., Salt Lake City, UT '86 (AMB)
WHITE, JAMES A., risk mgr., Carle Foundation Hospital, Urbana, IL '80 (RISK)
WHITE, JAMES M. JR., atty., Beverly Hospital, Beverly, MA '76 (ATTY)
WHITE, JANET D., dir. mktg., Meadowview Regional Hospital, Maysville, KY '84 (PR)
WHITE, JANET L., dir. vol. serv., University Community Hospital, Tampa, FL '79 (VOL)
WHITE, JIMMY L., dir. pur., Lafayette Home Hospital, Lafayette, IN '66 (PUR)
WHITE, JOAN, RN, dir. nrsg., Crittenden County Hospital, Marion, KY '87 (NURS)
WHITE, JOHN A., adm., Manor Oaks, Inc., Fort Lauderdale, FL '86
WHITE, JOHN O., student, School of Public Health, Department of Medical Cure Organization, University of Michigan, Ann Arbor, MI '85
WHITE, JOHN P., assoc. dir., Haricomp Group Purchasing, Providence, RI '75 (PUR)
WHITE, JOYCE A., coor. prog. serv., Sisters of Mercy Health Corporation, Farmington Hills, MI '83 (RISK)
WHITE, KAREN M., dir. commun. rel., Independence Regional Health Center, Independence, MO '86 (PR)
WHITE, KATIE M., dir. mktg., Fairview-Ridges Hospital, Minneapolis, MN '84 (PLNG)
WHITE, KENNETH S., atty., Virginia Baptist Hospital, Lynchburg, VA '77 (ATTY)
WHITE, KRISTIN N., dir. risk mgt. serv., Idaho Hospital Association, Boise, ID '86 (RISK)
WHITE, LEE T., atty., Jennie Stuart Medical Center, Hopkinsville, KY '78 (ATTY)
WHITE, LELAND ELWOOD, adm., Deaconess Hospital, Cincinnati, OH '64
WHITE, LELAND I., vice-pres. health serv. and exec. dir., Hospital of the Medical College of Pennsylvania, Philadelphia, PA '71
WHITE, LEWIS A., mgr. matl., Val Verde Memorial Hospital, Del Rio, TX '83 (PUR)
WHITE, LINDA A., coor. nrsg. educ., South Macomb Hospital, Warren, MI '86 (EDUC)
WHITE, LINDA E., RN, vice-pres. nrsg., Deaconess Hospital, Evansville, IN '86 (NURS)
WHITE, MARGUERITE W., RN, assoc. dir. nrsg., Lake Taylor City Hospital, Norfolk, VA '80 (NURS)
WHITE, MARSHA, Dallas, TX '80 (RISK)
WHITE, MARTHA B., adm. diet., Iowa Lutheran Hospital, Des Moines, IA '83 (FOOD)
WHITE, MARY N., student, Department of Health Care Administration, George Washington University, Washington, DC '82
WHITE, MAURICE BUD, dir. maint., Alliance Community Hospital, Alliance, OH '85 (ENG)
WHITE, MICHAEL W., dir. matl. mgt., American International Hospital, Zion, IL '82 (PUR)
WHITE, NANCY J., assoc. dir. diet., Oakwood Hospital, Dearborn, MI '83 (FOOD)
WHITE, OPAL P., dir. pers. and emp. rel., Bexar County Hospital District, San Antonio, TX '83 (PERS)
WHITE, SR. PAMELA, media coor., Sacred Heart Medical Center, Spokane, WA '83 (EDUC)
WHITE, PATRICIA, supv. sup., proc. and distrib., St. Mary Medical Center, Gary, IN '83 (CS)
WHITE, PETER, dir. med. staff affairs and qual. assur., San Gabriel Valley Medical Center, San Gabriel, CA '86 (RISK)
WHITE, R. DOUG, asst. adm., HCA Vista Hills Medical Center, El Paso, TX '83
WHITE, REBECCA E., dir. vol. serv., St. Luke's Hospital, Newburgh, NY '79 (VOL)
WHITE, RICHARD E., mgr. mech. syst., Henry Ford Hospital, Detroit, MI '79 (ENG)
WHITE, RICHARD T., vice-pres., Sandy Corporation, Troy, MI '74
WHITE, ROBERT A., atty., Medical Center at Princeton, Princeton, NJ '78 (ATTY)
WHITE, ROBERT C., dir. matl. mgt., Monticello Medical Center, Longview, WA '85 (CS)(PUR)
WHITE, ROBERT JORDAN, vice-pres., Total Health, Inc., Wilmington, DE '77
WHITE, ROBERT R., asst. vice-pres. amb. serv., Seton Medical Center, Austin, TX '86 (AMB)
WHITE, RON H., dir. food serv., Sam Houston Memorial Hospital, Houston, TX '80 (FOOD)
WHITE, RONALD E., dir. pers. rel., Suburban Community Hospital, Warrensville Heights, OH '86 (PERS)
WHITE, RUSSELL B., dir. emp. rel., Community Medical Center, Scranton, PA '80 (PERS)
WHITE, RUTH M., RN, dir. nrsg. serv., West Nebraska General Hospital, Scottsbluff, NE '81 (NURS)
WHITE, SANDRA L., asst. dir. vol. serv., Kennestone Hospital, Marietta, GA '81 (VOL)
WHITE, SANDY, dir. vol. serv., Medical Center of Los Angeles Mirada, La Mirada, CA '86 (VOL)
WHITE, SELMON T., dir. pers., Westland Medical Center, Westland, MI '85 (PERS)
WHITE, SHARON M., dir. nutr. and food serv., Newton-Wellesley Hospital, Newton, MA '84 (FOOD)
WHITE, SHERI J., coor. nrsg. and pat. educ., Halifax Hospital Medical Center, Daytona Beach, FL '86 (EDUC)
WHITE, MAJ. STEPHEN L., MSC USA, adm. health prog., Office of the Surgeon General, Falls Church, VA '82
WHITE, STEVEN Y., RN, vice-pres. nrsg., Mercy Hospital, Charlotte, NC '87 (NURS)
WHITE, SUZANNE K., RN, dir. critical care serv., Gwinnett Hospital System, Lawrenceville, GA '86 (NURS)
WHITE, T. KAY, RN, dir. nrsg., Armstrong County Memorial Hospital, Kittanning, PA '72 (NURS)
WHITE, THOMAS A., assoc. eng., St. Joseph's Hospital, Savannah, GA '82 (ENG)
WHITE, THOMAS M., exec. dir., Valley Hospital and Medical Center, Spokane, WA '78
WHITE, THOMAS, pres., Jameson Memorial Hospital, New Castle, PA '71
WHITE, WILLIAM H., adm. eng., Framingham Union Hospital, Framingham, MA '67 (ENG)
WHITE, WILLIAM MICHAEL, vice-pres., Children's Hospital, Santa Rosa Medical Center, San Antonio, TX '76
WHITED, MICHAEL, asst. dir. educ., Shawnee Mission Medical Center, Shawnee Mission, KS '83 (EDUC)

WHITEFORD, PATRICIA COOLEY, pat. rep., Mary Greeley Medical Center, Ames, IA '86 (PAT)
WHITEHEAD, BARBARA P., RN, assoc. dir. nrsg., Mid-Maine Medical Center, Waterville, ME '86 (NURS)
WHITEHEAD, CHARLES P., dir. eng., St. Mary's Hospital of Troy, Troy, NY '71 (ENG)
WHITEHEAD, DANIEL G., dir. mktg., Provider Automated Services, Inc., Jacksonville, FL '85
WHITEHEAD, DAVID E., RN, asst. adm., St. Alexius Medical Center, Bismarck, ND '83 (NURS)
WHITEHEAD, DEBORAH AGRILLO, adm. mgr. lab. and diagnostic serv., Brigham and Women's Hospital, Boston, MA '82
WHITEHEAD, E. SLOANE, dir. pers., Milford Hospital, Milford, CT '80 (PERS)
WHITEHEAD, JUDY M., coor. pub. rel., West Oaks-Psychiatric Institute Houston, Houston, TX '86 (PR)
WHITEHEAD, LEWIS H., mgr., Marketing Assistance, Beverly Shores, IN '86
WHITEHEAD, MARTHA H., vice-pres. resource dev., Good Shepherd Medical Center, Longview, TX '83 (PR)
WHITEHEAD, PATRICIA, pat. rep., Baptist Medical Center-Montclair, Birmingham, AL '80 (PAT)
WHITEHILL, AUSTIN R., mgr. consult., Arthur Andersen and Company, Washington, DC '81 (MGMT)
WHITEHOUSE, DOROTHY, RN, assoc. dir. nrsg., NKC Hospitals, Louisville, KY '81 (NURS)
WHITEHOUSE, LYNDA G., RN, dir. nrs., Mission Community Hospital, Mission Viejo, CA '84 (NURS)
WHITEHURST-SULLIVAN, ANN T., vice-pres. foundation and commun., St. Agnes Hospital and Medical Center, Fresno, CA '85 (PR)
WHITEHURST, PEGGY E., dir. vol. serv., Medical Center Hospitals, Norfolk General Hospital Division, Norfolk, VA '71 (VOL)
WHITEHURST, ZEB M. III, mgr. emp., Wilson Memorial Hospital, Wilson, NC '81 (PERS)
WHITELAW, PEPPER, dir. pub. rel., Children's Hospital of Michigan, Detroit, MI '80 (PR)
WHITELY, JOHN J., dir. pub. info., Christ Hospital, Jersey City, NJ '84 (PR)
WHITEMAN, CECILLE C., dir. commun. rel., Normandy Osteopathic Medical Center, St. Louis, MO '85 (PR)
WHITEMAN, PATRICIA, coor. vol., El Dorado Hospital and Medical Center, Tucson, AZ '80 (VOL)
WHITESIDE, KATHLEEN S., corp. dir. human res., Harper Hospital, Detroit, MI '86 (PERS)
WHITESIDES, MARY E., dir. pub. rel., Patrick Henry Healthcare Center, Newport News, VA '86 (PR)
WHITFIELD, CHARLES H. JR., asst. adm., Laughlin Memorial Hospital, Greeneville, TN '82
WHITFIELD, D. J., RN, asst. dir. pat. serv., Rowan Memorial Hospital, Salisbury, NC '76 (NURS)
WHITFIELD, VANCE B., vice-pres. pub. rel., Roanoke Memorial Hospitals, Roanoke, VA '80 (PR) (PLNG)
WHITFORD, BYRON NELSON, Hazel Crest, IL '53 (LIFE)
WHITING, DAVID B., chief eng., St. Mary's Hospital Medical Center, Green Bay, WI '85 (ENG)
WHITING, ELSIE L., asst. dir. nrsg., Albany Medical Center Hospital, Albany, NY '85 (NURS)
WHITING, JOSEPH K., asst. vice-pres., Glenbrook Hospital, Glenview, IL '81 (ENG)
WHITING, MICHAEL D., vice-pres. plng. and dev., Lincoln Health Resources, Phoenix, AZ '77 (PLNG)
WHITING, SUSAN H., dir. pub. rel. and dev., St. Luke's Hospital, Maumee, OH '81 (PR)
WHITKANACK, DEL L., dir. bldg. serv., La Grange Memorial Hospital, La Grange, IL '83 (ENG)
WHITLATCH, JAMES L., atty., Bloomington Hospital, Bloomington, IN '86 (ATTY)
WHITLEY, ELIZABETH, RN, dir. maternal and child prog., Lutheran Medical Center, Wheat Ridge, CO '86 (NURS)
WHITLEY, COL. HELEN BEAUCHAMP, dir. nrsg., U. S. Air Force Regional Hospital, Eglin AFB, FL '83 (NURS)
WHITLEY, NANCY L., coor. health educ., Allegan General Hospital, Allegan, MI '84 (EDUC)
WHITLEY, ODUS V., dir., Bethesda Hospital, Inc., Cincinnati, OH '81 (ENG)
WHITLOCK, CHARLES L., vice-pres. human resources, Saint Joseph's Hospital, Atlanta, GA '76 (PERS)
WHITLOW, CHRISTIE M., RN, supv. cent. serv., Bradford Hospital, Bradford, PA '82 (CS)
WHITMAN, ALLAN, vice-pres. mgt. consult. serv., Presbyterian-University Hospital, Pittsburgh, PA '79 (MGMT)
WHITMAN, CAROL L., supv. food serv., Fairmont Community Hospital, Fairmont, MN '79 (FOOD)
WHITMAN, MARK A., mgt. eng., Christ Hospital, Cincinnati, OH '87 (PLNG)
WHITMAN, PATRICIA E., dir., Hospital Association of New York State, Albany, NY '81 (MGMT)
WHITMAN, RUSSELL E., dir. commun. rel., Calumet Public Hospital, Laurium, MI '85 (PR)
WHITMER, AENOS E. JR., dir. food serv., Indian Path Hospital, Kingsport, TN '80 (FOOD)
WHITMER, TRACY J., dir. med. soc. serv., Jamestown Hospital, Jamestown, ND '81 (SOC)
WHITMIRE, DENNIS L., sr. syst. eng., University of Massachusetts Medical Center, Worcester, MA '74 (MGMT)
WHITMORE, BARBARA, student, Park College, Fort Bliss, TX '86 (RISK)
WHITNEY, BETTY V., dir. food serv., Primary Children's Medical Center, Salt Lake City, UT '76 (FOOD)
WHITNEY, CHRISTINE C., atty., Blue Cross and Blue Shield of Florida, Inc., Jacksonville, FL '84 (ATTY)
WHITNEY, HARRY EUGENE, dir. pers., St. Francis Mercy Hospital, Washington, MO '79 (PERS)
WHITNEY, JOHN H., atty., Grossmont District Hospital, La Mesa, CA '74 (ATTY)
WHITNEY, JOHN R., proj. mgr., Cuh2a, Princeton, NJ '86
WHITNEY, MARTY J., dir. vol. serv., Simi Valley Adventist Hospital, Simi Valley, CA '86 (VOL)
WHITNEY, RICHARD A., dir. eng., Fountain Valley Regional Hospital Medical Center, Fountain Valley, CA '83 (ENG)
WHITNEY, WILLIAM E., atty., North Shore Medical Center, Miami, FL '84 (ATTY)
WHITSETT, CHARLES K., dir. plant oper., Mercer County Joint Township Community Hospital, Coldwater, OH '75 (ENG)
WHITSON, ELIZABETH ANNE, adm. res., University of Houston, Clearlake, TX '86
WHITSON, STEVEN K., student, Program in Health Administration and Planning, Washington University School of Medicine, St. Louis, MO '85
WHITT, KENNETH L., dir. info. serv., University of Texas Health Center, Tyler, TX '85 (PR)
WHITT, LARRY, asst. adm. eng. and plant maint., St. Vincent Infirmary, Little Rock, AR '82 (ENG)
WHITT, PATRICIA BOYLSTON, Grafton, VA '76
WHITT, SHEILA D., dir. soc. serv., Parkway Medical Center Hospital, Decatur, AL '82 (SOC)
WHITTAKER, REBECCA J., RN, coor. cont. educ., Methodist Medical Center of Illinois, Peoria, IL '86 (EDUC)
WHITTEMORE, TERRANCE E., dir. plant oper. and maint., Henry Heywood Memorial Hospital, Gardner, MA '86
WHITTEN, DAVID G., asst. dir., Taubman Center, Ann Arbor, MI '85
WHITTEN, F. DALE, vice-pres. strategic plng. and dev., Daughters of Charity National Health Systems, St. Louis, MO '66 (PLNG)
WHITTEN, LAWRENCE R. JR., mgr. maint., Brookville Hospital, Brookville, PA '82 (ENG)
WHITTEN, NANCY, dir. vol. serv., North Mississippi Medical Center, Tupelo, MS '80 (VOL)
WHITTENBERG, JOAN T., consult., J. Associates, Louisville, KY '74 (PAT)
WHITTENBURG, JAMES D., asst. mgt. eng., Jewish Hospital, Louisville, KY '86 (MGMT)
WHITTINGTON, CATHERINE, cent. serv. tech., St. Elizabeth Hospital, Beaumont, TX '86 (CS)
WHITTINGTON, CATHY BROWN, coor. guest rel., Portsmouth General Hospital, Portsmouth, VA '86 (PAT)
WHITTLETON, DALE H., dir. matl. mgt., St. Vincent Hospital, Santa Fe, NM '84 (PUR)
WHITTON, JEFFREY H., planner, Fort Sanders Regional Alliance, Knoxville, TN '85 (PLNG)
WHITWELL, THELMA A., dir. vol., Valley View Regional Hospital, Ada, OK '70 (VOL)
WHITWORTH, DENI, coor. federal syst., McDonnell Douglas Health Information Systems Company, Hazelwood, MO '86 (FOOD)
WIARD, ANN C., RN, asst. adm. nrsg., St. Anthony Medical Center, Louisville, KY '86 (NURS)
WIBLITZHOUSER, KENNETH F., dir. human res., Rex Hospital, Raleigh, NC '78
WICAL, ROBERT L., dir. pur., Loma Linda University Medical Center, Loma Linda, CA '86 (PUR)
WICHTERMAN, MARY L., mgr. pers., Minneapolis Medical Research, Regional Kidney Disease Program, Minneapolis, MN '80 (PERS)
WICK, NORMAN D., dir. food and nutr. serv., Holy Family Medical Center, Manitowoc, WI '71 (FOOD)
WICKARD, REGINA, risk mgr., W. A. Foote Memorial Hospital, Jackson, MI '86 (RISK)
WICKER, EVELYN B., RN, dir. nrsg. serv., Duke University Hospital, Durham, NC '81 (NURS)
WICKLINE, ROBERT C., dir. plant serv., El Centro Regional Medical Center, El Centro, CA '85 (ENG)(ENVIRON)
WICKLUND, LEONARD S., treas., O'Donnell Wicklund Pigozzi and Peterson Architects, Inc., Deerfield, IL '81
WICKNICK, AGNES E., pur. agt., Providence Medical Center, Portland, OR '86 (PUR)
WICKOWSKI, REV. LEROY A., rep., Archdiocese of Chicago, Chicago, IL '79
WICKS, DEE K., dir. soc. serv., Thayer County Memorial Hospital, Hebron, NE '86 (SOC)
WICKWAR, WILLIAM HARDY, plng. consult., Richland Memorial Hospital, Columbia, SC '82 (PLNG)
WICKWARE, KATHYRN F., RN, asst. adm., Lincoln County Medical Center, Ruidoso, NM '86 (NURS)
WIDAWSKI, NANCY J., nrsg. applications spec., Poudre Valley Hospital, Fort Collins, CO '86 (ENG)
WIDEN, BARRY J., vice-pres. oper., Meridian Healthcare, Towson, MD '75
WIDJESKOG, DONALD J., mgr. eng. serv., St. Peter's Hospital, Albany, NY '85 (ENG)
WIDMAN, JERRY PAUL, vice-pres. fin., Daughters of Charity Health Systems, St. Louis, MO '77
WIDMAN, PAUL E., dir. oper., Cleveland Clinic Hospital, Cleveland, OH '53 (PUR)(LIFE)
WIDMAR, BERNICE R., dir. vol., Norwegian-American Hospital, Chicago, IL '85 (VOL)
WIDMER, THOMAS G., vice-pres. commun. affairs, Marianjoy Rehabilitation Center, Wheaton, IL '84 (PLNG)
WIEBE, WANDA, dir. phys. and pat. serv., Trinity Lutheran Hospital, Kansas City, MO '81 (PAT)
WIEBELHAUS, DONNA JEANNE, coor. vol., King's Daughters Hospital, Temple, TX '81 (VOL)
WIECKING, DAVID K., MD, atty., Medical College of Virginia Hospitals, Virginia Commonwealth University, Richmond, VA '77 (ATTY)
WIECZOREK, CASIMER M., Acme Park, PA '69
WIECZOREK, ELIZABETH, vice-pres. pur. serv., Presentation Shared Health Services, Sioux Falls, SD '84 (PUR)
WIECZOREK, SUSAN M., dir. pub. rel., Meyersdale Community Hospital, Meyersdale, PA '86 (PR)
WIEDEMAN, L. D., asst. adm. fiscal affairs, Lafayette Home Hospital, Lafayette, IN '80
WIEDEN, CLIFFORD O. T., dir. pub. info., Sturdy Memorial Hospital, Attleboro, MA '78 (PR)
WIEDER, GREGORY J., dir. pur., Wentworth-Douglass Hospital, Dover, NH '84 (PUR)
WIEDERHIRN, VIRGINIA, RN, vice-pres. nrsg., St. Elizabeth Hospital, Danville, IL '78 (NURS)(AMB)
WIEDERHOLT, GERALDINE M., dir. med. adm. serv., St. Francis Hospital, Maryville, MO '86
WIEDITZ, RUTH M., RN, dir. nrsg. serv., Edwin Shaw Hospital, Akron, OH '84 (NURS)
WIEDLE, ALVA L., RN, dir. nrsg. serv., St. Luke's Hospital-West, Chesterfield, MO '73 (RISK)
WIEGAND, KENNETH A., dir. mgt. info. serv., Delaware County Memorial Hospital, Drexel Hill, PA '85 (MGMT)
WIEGAND, THEODORE F., vice-pres., Doctors Hospital, New York, NY '76
WIEHL, JAMES G., atty., Barnes Hospital, St. Louis, MO '83 (ATTY)
WIEKER, CHERYL ROBINSON, mgr. soc. work, Johns Hopkins Hospital, Baltimore, MD '86 (PAT)
WIELAND, CATHERINE H., asst. vice-pres., Evanston Hospital, Evanston, IL '72 (FOOD)
WIELAND, JAMES B., atty., Western Pennsylvania Hospital, Pittsburgh, PA '84 (ATTY)
WIELAND, WILLIAM DEAN, dir., Voluntary Hospitals of American Management Service, Tampa, FL '73 (MGMT)(PLNG)
WIEMAN, JOANNE K., chief soc. serv., St. Mary Medical Center, Walla Walla, WA '84 (SOC)
WIEMAN, NANCY L., mgr. qual. assur. and risk mgt., Norristown State Hospital, Norristown, PA '85 (RISK)
WIENCEK, MELVIN R., dir. eng., St. Joseph Medical Center, Joliet, IL '80 (ENG)
WIENER, ABRAHAM B., sr. vice-pres., American Hospital Management Corporation, Miami, FL '83 (MGMT)
WIENER, JAMES W., dir. plant oper., Rose Medical Center, Denver, CO '86 (ENG)
WIENER, MARK S., vice-pres. clin. serv., Research Medical Center, Kansas City, MO '80
WIENS, LORNA MAE, dir. educ., United District Hospital and Home, Staples, MN '84 (EDUC)
WIER, CAROLYN R., student, Columbia University, New York, NY '83
WIER, LANNY, dir. plant oper., Charter Winds Hospital, Athens, GA '87 (ENG)
WIERENGA, PETER, asst. chief eng., Sheboygan Memorial Medical Center, Sheboygan, WI '80 (ENG)
WIESE, CHARLES K., sr. vice-pres., California Health Management Systems, Los Angeles, CA '67 (MGMT)
WIESE, DENNIS, asst. vice-pres., Methodist Hospitals of Gary, Gary, IN '86 (ENG)
WIESE, KATHLEEN F., RN, dir. pat. serv., Mandan Hospital, Mandan, ND '86 (NURS)
WIESE, KAYE JAMISON, asst. adm. nrsg. serv., Heartland Centre, St. Joseph, MO '86 (NURS)
WIESNER, GARY A., dir. matl. mgt., Providence Hospital, Medford, OR '80 (PUR)
WIESNER, HENRY, dir. maint. and eng., St. Joseph's Hospital and Medical Center, Paterson, NJ '77 (ENG)
WIESSNER, CHERYL K., mgr. food serv., Scottsdale Memorial Hospital, Scottsdale, AZ '86 (FOOD)
WIET, MITCHELL J., atty., Northwestern Memorial Hospital, Chicago, IL '83 (ATTY)
WIETECHA, MARK, sr. consult., Hamilton-Ksa, Atlanta, GA '87 (PLNG)
WIETSTOCK, LESLIE J., adm. asst., Community Memorial Hospital, Hettinger, ND '86 (PR)
WIGGERS, D. EUGENE, RN, prof. nrsg., Ricks College, Rexburg, ID '86 (EDUC)
WIGGIN, HARVEY B., dir. qual. assur. and risk mgt., Parkland Medical Center, Derry, NH '84 (RISK)
WIGGINS, BETTI J., dir. food and nutr. serv., Detroit Osteopathic Hospital, Highland Park, MI '78 (FOOD)
WIGGINS, MARJORIE, student, Health Administration and Planning, School of Health Studies, University of New Hampshire, Durham, NH '86 (AMB)
WIGGINS, RODNEY L., dir. mgt. eng., Cleveland Clinic Hospital, Cleveland, OH '80 (MGMT)
WIGGS, BUDDY L., exec. vice-pres., Christ Hospital, Cincinnati, OH '62
WIGGS, JAMES S., tech. oper. room and sterile sup., Oregon Health Sciences University Hospital, Portland, OR '85 (CS)
WIGGY, KARRIE K., dir. vol., Hillcrest Health Center, Oklahoma City, OK '86 (VOL)
WIGHTMAN, DARWIN D., pres., Dakota Hospital, Fargo, ND '53 (LIFE)
WIGLEG, MARGARET CAROL, pat. rep., Mississippi Baptist Medical Center, Jackson, MS '86 (PAT)
WIGNESS, MARILYN E., RN, asst. adm. and dir. nrsg., Northwest Medical Center, Thief River Falls, MN '84 (NURS)
WIIG, TRUDY K., RN, dir. nrsg., Metropolitan Hospital, Dallas, TX '86 (NURS)
WIINAMAKI, ALLAN M., student, Oral Roberts University, Tulsa, OK '86 (MGMT)
WIITALA, EARL R., dir. matl. serv., Healthlink, Portland, OR '85 (PUR)
WIKANDER, NORA E., supv. cent. serv., Wayne General Hospital, Wayne, NJ '86 (CS)
WIKOFF, DANIEL J. SR., dir. maint., Lawrence County General Hospital, Ironton, OH '85 (ENG)
WILBER, CAROL A., dir. pers., Northwestern Medical Center, St. Albans, VT '86 (PERS)
WILBER, MARGARET F., dir. soc. serv., Lakes Region General Hospital, Laconia, NH '80 (SOC)
WILBERG, JOHN, dir. food serv., Alpena General Hospital, Alpena, MI '78 (FOOD)
WILBERTON, ROBERT JR., insp. eng., New Jersey Manufacturers Insurance Company, West Trenton, NJ '83 (ENG)
WILBUR, MARJORIE A., planner, Franciscan Health Care, Inc., Milwaukee, WI '82 (PLNG)
WILBUR, MARY M., plng. asst., West Suburban Hospital Medical Center, Oak Park, IL '85 (PLNG)
WILCHINSKI, SALLY, dir. vol. serv., Kent General Hospital, Dover, DE '76 (VOL)
WILCOX, BARBARA A., RN, dir. nrsg., William W. Backus Hospital, Norwich, CT '83 (NURS)
WILCOX, CATHERINE P., dir. pur., Sharon Hospital, Sharon, CT '74 (PUR)

WILCOX, DONALD P., atty., Texas Medical Association, Austin, TX '73 (ATTY)
WILCOX, FRANCES, RN, mgr. cent. sterile sup., William W. Backus Hospital, Norwich, CT '86 (CS)
WILCOX, GEORGE, dir. plant oper., Charter Grove Hospital, Corona, CA '85 (ENG)
WILCOX, JANICE H., coor. pub. rel. and marketing, DeKalb Memorial Hospital, Auburn, IN '86 (PR) (PLNG)
WILCOX, JOANN C., RN, vice-pres. nrsg., Pontiac General Hospital, Pontiac, MI '82 (NURS)
WILCOX, JOHN F., atty., Sacred Heart Hospital, Eau Claire, WI '80 (ATTY)
WILCOX, LORETTA M., supv. cent. serv., St. Marys Hospital Medical Center, Madison, WI '80 (CS)
WILCOX, PAMELA A., mgr., Ernst and Whinney, Atlanta, GA '79 (MGMT)
WILCOX, WARREN B., dir. plng. and commun. rel., Hospital Home Health Care Agency of California, Torrance, CA '86 (PR)
WILCOX, WILLARD P., dir. health care res., Market Trends, Inc., Bellevue, WA '86 (PLNG)
WILCOXEN, JAY A., dir. cent. serv. and transportation, Rehabilitation Institute of Chicago, Chicago, IL '82 (CS)
WILCOXSON, JACKLYN E., RN, dir. nrsg. serv., Immanuel Medical Center, Omaha, NE '83 (NURS)
WILCZYNSKI, JEROME B., assoc. adm., Children's Hospital of Michigan, Detroit, MI '70 (MGMT)
WILCZYNSKI, JOSEPH, elec. eng., Mercy Hospital and Medical Center, Chicago, IL '81 (ENG)
WILD, ROBERT ANDREW, atty., Hospital for Joint Diseases and Medical Center, New York, NY '71 (ATTY)
WILDASINN, SUE, dir. vol. serv., Miami Valley Hospital, Dayton, OH '80 (VOL)
WILDAY, JEFFERY M., atty., Memorial Medical Center, Springfield, IL '84 (ATTY)
WILDBERGER, EILEEN T., RN, assoc. exec. dir. nrsg., Humana Hospital -Desert Valley, Phoenix, AZ '86 (NURS)
WILDE, GLADYS M., dir. diet., Bethesda Memorial Hospital, Boynton Beach, FL '83 (FOOD)
WILDE, JANA S., rehab. liaison, Marianjoy Rehabilitation Center, Wheaton, IL '86 (PR)
WILDE, JOYCE L., dir. human res., Fairview Riverside Hospital, Minneapolis, MN '86 (PERS)
WILDER, BARBARA, dir. qual. assur., Methodist Hospital of Indiana, Indianapolis, IN '86 (RISK)
WILDER, BESSIE ANN, dir. vol. serv. and commun. res., University Medical Center, Tucson, AZ '79 (VOL)
WILDER, CYNTHIA L., dir. soc. work, Presbyterian Association on Aging, Oakmont, PA '85 (SOC)
WILDER, JOAN K., PhD, prof., University of Detroit, Detroit, MI '84 (EDUC)
WILDER, MARY D., RN, asst. adm. nrsg., Sibley Memorial Hospital, Washington, DC '82 (NURS)
WILDER, PAMELA W., dir. soc. serv., South Florida Baptist Hospital, Plant City, FL '79 (SOC)
WILDER, PAUL, dir. eng., George H. Lanier Memorial Hospital, Valley, AL '86 (ENG)
WILDER, STEVEN S., dir. safety, security and risk mgt., St. Mary's Hospital of Kankakee, Kankakee, IL '85 (RISK)
WILDES, JAY, assoc. adm., West Georgia Medical Center, La Grange, GA '76
WILDFEUER, HENRY, pres., Hix-Lite Chemicals Company, Inc., Garfield, NJ '86 (ENVIRON)
WILDMAN, DURWARD B. JR., vice-pres., Hinsdale Hospital, Hinsdale, IL '68 (PERS)
WILDZUNAS, RICHARD P., vice-pres., Riverview Medical Center, Red Bank, NJ '76
WILE, RUTH E., RN, asst. dir. nrsg. serv., Goddard Memorial Hospital, Stoughton, MA '78 (NURS)
WILENSKY, LLOYD B., dir. corp. plng., Community Hospitals of Central California, Fresno, CA '80 (PLNG)
WILES, ALLEN L., eng., Memorial Hospital, Danville, VA '77 (ENG)
WILES, ANN, sr. mgt. eng., William Beaumont Hospital, Royal Oak, MI '80 (MGMT)
WILES, CATHERINE B., dir. pub. rel. and vol. serv., Citizens General Hospital, New Kensington, PA '70 (VOL)(PR)
WILEY, CHARLES E., RN, asst. dir. nrsg., Jackson Hospital and Clinic, Montgomery, AL '77
WILEY, INGE, pat. rep. and dir. vol. serv., University Community Hospital, Tamarac, FL '83 (PAT)(VOL)
WILEY, JAN, dir. cent. serv., Humana Hospital -Lucerne, Orlando, FL '86 (CS)
WILEY, JOHN WILLIAM, dir. soc. serv., Trumbull Memorial Hospital, Warren, OH '76 (SOC)
WILEY, KAREN L., pat. rep., Providence Hospital, Southfield, MI '82 (PAT)
WILEY, LORRAINE, dir. vol. serv. and commun. rel., Onslow Memorial Hospital, Jacksonville, NC '81 (VOL)(PR)
WILEY, WILLIAM B., atty., West Volusia Memorial Hospital, De Land, FL '81 (ATTY)
WILFONG, HUGH C. II, atty., The Methodist Hospital, Houston, TX '79 (ATTY)
WILFORD, DAN SEWELL, pres., Memorial Care Systems, Houston, TX '68
WILFROM, JAMIE A., buyer, St. Joseph Intercommunity Hospital, Cheektowaga, NY '83 (FOOD)
WILGARDE, RALPH L., adm., Cottage Hospital of Grosse Pointe, Grosse Pointe Farms, MI '57 (LIFE)
WILGUS, LYNDA LOY, dir. soc. serv., Saint Anthony Medical Center, Rockford, IL '86 (SOC)
WILHARM, BECKY, dir. commun. rel., Knoxville Area Community Hospital, Knoxville, IA '85 (PR)
WILHELM, COL. BRUCE D., adm., U. S. Air Force Medical Center Wright-Patterson, Dayton, OH '63
WILHELM, FAYE W., coor. guest rel., Baptist Medical Center, Columbia, SC '74 (PAT)
WILHELM, NORBERT A., MD, (ret.), La Jolla, CA '31 (LIFE)
WILHELM, SHARON D., coor. vol., Good Samaritan Mental Health Center, Puyallup, WA '82 (VOL)
WILHELMI, SR. MARY MARCIA, RN, vice-pres., St. Joseph Mercy Hospital, Mason City, IA '82 (NURS)
WILHIDE, MARGARET W., dir. vol. serv., Bethesda North Hospital, Cincinnati, OH '84 (VOL)
WILHITE, NANCY K., dir. soc. serv., San Juan Regional Medical Center, Farmington, NM '77 (SOC)
WILK, LEONARD E., dir. prod. line serv., St. Joseph Hospital, Chicago, IL '79 (PLNG)
WILK, S. MICHAEL, atty., Kenosha Hospital and Medical Center, Kenosha, WI '73 (ATTY)
WILKE, DANA A., partner, Philo Architects, Houston, TX '80
WILKE, DARLENE, RN, dir. nrsg. serv., Bon Secours Hospital, North Miami, FL '85 (NURS)
WILKEN, LINDA I., dir. diet., Joint Township District Memorial Hospital, St. Marys, OH '81 (FOOD)
WILKENS, GARY R., biomedical supv., Heartland Hospital West, St. Joseph, MO '79 (ENG)
WILKERSON, CARRIE J., Rochester Hills, MI '84 (EDUC)(PERS)
WILKERSON, CORALEAN, supv. blood bank and hematology, Hillcrest Medical Center, Tulsa, OK '86 (ENG)
WILKERSON, LAWSON E., chief eng., Desert Springs Hospital, Las Vegas, NV '84 (ENG)
WILKERSON, LOIS A., RN, supv. nrs. consult., Naval Hospital, Orlando, FL '85 (CS)
WILKERSON, R. W. III, pres. and dir. health care plng., Wilkerson Moose Associates, Inc., Charlotte, NC '68 (PLNG)
WILKERSON, WILLIAM C., dir. gen. stores, Highlands Regional Medical Center, Prestonsburg, KY '84
WILKES, DOLORES R., RN, dir. nrsg., Magic Valley Regional Medical Center, Twin Falls, ID '86 (NURS)
WILKES, LAURIE K., dir. pers., Humana Hospital-Mountain View, Thornton, CO '86 (PERS)
WILKES, LORRIE, RN, dir. nrsg., Magic Valley Regional Medical Center, Twin Falls, ID '86 (NURS)
WILKES, ROGGIE V., dir. diet., University Hospital, Augusta, GA '70 (FOOD)
WILKIN, DOUGLAS, dir. maint., Pawating Hospital, Niles, MI '81 (ENG)
WILKINS, CHARLES BOYD, dir. environ. serv., Nashville Memorial Hospital, Madison, TN '86 (ENVIRON)
WILKINS, CURTIS P., dir. soc. work serv., Lutheran Medical Center, Wheat Ridge, CO '79 (SOC)
WILKINS, DICK, asst. chief eng., Valley Presbyterian Hospital, Van Nuys, CA '80 (ENG)
WILKINS, JEANNINE W., PhD, asst. adm. plng. and mktg., Sierra Nevada Memorial Hospital, Grass Valley, CA '85 (PR) (PLNG)
WILKINS, JOHN G. JR., chief med. facil. constr., Georgia Department of Human Resources, Division of Physical) Health, Atlanta, GA '56 (ENG)(LIFE
WILKINS, LEWIETTE, RN, dir. pat. care serv., Dominguez Medical Center, Long Beach, CA '81 (NURS)
WILKINS, MARTHA J., dir. vol. serv., Monongalia General Hospital, Morgantown, WV '85 (VOL)
WILKINS, RANDY D., asst. dir. environ., Mercy Center for Health Care Services, Aurora, IL '86 (ENVIRON)
WILKINS, RONALD S., mgr. matl., Memorial Hospital, Bainbridge, GA '86 (PUR)
WILKINS, SANDRA, dir. pub. rel., Primary Children's Medical Center, Salt Lake City, UT '78 (PR)
WILKINS, STEPHEN T., Honolulu, HI '86 (PLNG)
WILKINSON, B. CURTIS, atty., Union Hospital, Terre Haute, IN '87 (ATTY)
WILKINSON, BETH M., student, Concordia College, Moorhead, MN '87
WILKINSON, CLINTON B., dir. phys. plant, Shriners Hospital for Crippled Children, Portland, OR '87 (ENG)
WILKINSON, DANIEL A., dir. food serv., Chenango Memorial Hospital, Norwich, NY '81 (FOOD)
WILKINSON, DONALD, exec. liaison, Government Programs, Pittsburgh, PA '82 (PLNG)
WILKINSON, GREGORY A., student, Program in Health Systems Management, University of Connecticut, Storrs, CT '85 (MGMT)
WILKINSON, JAMES A., atty., Shadyside Hospital, Pittsburgh, PA '86 (ATTY)
WILKINSON, JANIE R., mgr. matl., routing and distrib., Medical Center Hospital, Tyler, TX '87 (PUR)
WILKINSON, JERRY M., biomedical eng., McClellan Memorial Veterans Hospital, Little Rock, AR '79 (ENG)
WILKINSON, KEITH, dir. educ. serv., Shaughnessy Hospital, Vancouver, B.C., Canada '83 (EDUC)
WILKINSON, MICHAEL C., assoc. dir., Mississippi Baptist Medical Center, Jackson, MS '68 (ATTY)
WILKINSON, PATRICIA C., dir. soc. serv., New England Sinai Hospital, Stoughton, MA '80 (SOC)
WILKINSON, TIMOTHY E., dir. environ. serv., Jackson-Madison County General Hospital, Jackson, TN '86 (ENVIRON)
WILKINSON, VIRGINIA, dir. hskpg., Douglas Community Hospital, Roseburg, OR '86 (ENVIRON)
WILKS, MAE B., dir. vol. serv., Rhd Memorial Medical Center, Dallas, TX '82 (VOL)
WILL, DICK, dir. diet. serv., St. John's Regional Medical Center, Oxnard, CA '68 (FOOD)
WILLAERT, RICHARD J., dir. matl. mgt., Katherine Shaw Bethea Hospital, Dixon, IL '85 (PUR)
WILLAFORD, PAUL CHRISTIAN, dir. matl. mgt., Rappahannock General Hospital, Kilmarnock, VA '85 (MGMT)
WILLARD, JAMES D., pres., Lutheran Medical Center, Wheat Ridge, CO '77
WILLARD, ZARIFA, dir. pat. and phys. serv., Robert F. Kennedy Medical Center, Hawthorne, CA '87 (PAT)
WILLAUER, LT. COL. GLENN R., MSC USA, assoc. adm., U. S. Air Force Regional Hospital, Eglin AFB, FL '72
WILLDEN, DEE, dir. diet., St. Mary's Hospital, Milwaukee, WI '80 (FOOD)
WILLE, NYLA L., dir. soc. serv., Rice County District One Hospital, Faribault, MN '78 (SOC)
WILLEMSEN, RONALD K., dir. plant oper., St. Mary's Hospital, West Palm Beach, FL '86 (ENG)
WILLEN, PHILIP, pres., Philip Willen Associates, Inc., Baltimore, MD '70 (PR)
WILLETS, JOHN W., PhD, assoc. adm., Burnham Hospital, Champaign, IL '79 (MGMT)
WILLETT, LEE L., asst. dir. pers., Nashville Metropolitan Bordeaux Hospital, Nashville, TN '85 (PERS)
WILLETT, ROBERT LEE, pres., Kettering Medical Center, Kettering, OH '66
WILLETTS, DAVID A., mgr. acctg., Natkin Energy Management, Englewood, CO '86 (ENG)
WILLEY, MICKEY, dir. vol. serv., Union Hospital, Terre Haute, IN '85 (VOL)
WILLHITE, CANDY, RN, dir. critical care nrsg. and res. teams, Children's Memorial Hospital, Chicago, IL '84 (NURS)
WILLIAMS-PARR, ADA, dir. med. soc. serv., Milwaukee County Medical Complex, Milwaukee, WI '85 (SOC)
WILLIAMS, ALICE M., dir. soc. work, Waterbury Hospital, Waterbury, CT '71 (SOC)
WILLIAMS, ANN M., dir. commun. affairs, Cape Cod Hospital, Hyannis, MA '81 (PR)
WILLIAMS, ANNE H., dir. pat. and family serv., Craven County Hospital, New Bern, NC '86 (SOC)
WILLIAMS, BARBARA G., exec. dir., Medi-Share, San Jose, CA '79 (PUR)
WILLIAMS, BERT R. III, asst. to pres., Rupp and Bowman Company, Farmington Hills, MI '85 (PLNG)
WILLIAMS, BRAD L., dir. soc. serv., Methodist Hospital, Lubbock, TX '85 (SOC)
WILLIAMS, BRENDA C., dir. soc. work, Mother Frances Hospital Regional Center, Tyler, TX '77 (SOC)
WILLIAMS, BRENDA LILLIAN, asst. adm., Orangeburg-Calhoun Regional Hospital, Orangeburg, SC '74 (RISK)(PLNG)
WILLIAMS, CAROL A., mgr. matl., Muhlenberg Regional Medical Center, Plainfield, NJ '86 (PUR)
WILLIAMS, CHARLES G., coor. media rel., Good Samaritan Hospital and Medical Center, Portland, OR '85 (PR)
WILLIAMS, CINDY, RN, dir. nrsg., St. Margaret's Hospital, Montgomery, AL '80 (NURS)
WILLIAMS, CLAY, mgt. eng., Desert Springs Hospital, Las Vegas, NV '73 (MGMT)
WILLIAMS, DANA C., reg. dir. oper., Diabetes Treatment Centers, Nashville, TN '79
WILLIAMS, DAVID R., adm. asst., Broward General Medical Center, Fort Lauderdale, FL '81
WILLIAMS, DAVID, risk mgr., Memorial Medical Center, Savannah, GA '87 (RISK)
WILLIAMS, DEBORAH A., asst. dir. cent. serv., Crawford Long Hospital Emory University, Atlanta, GA '87 (CS)
WILLIAMS, DONALD L., dir. pers., San Joaquin Community Hospital, Bakersfield, CA '86 (PERS)
WILLIAMS, DONNA F., dir. dev. and pub. rel., Centre Community Hospital, State College, PA '86 (PR)
WILLIAMS, DOROTHY V., RN, dir. nrsg., West Florida Hospital, Pensacola, FL '81 (NURS)
WILLIAMS, EDWARD A., dir. plant oper., Johnson County Memorial Hospital, Franklin, IN '70 (ENG)
WILLIAMS, EDWARD L., corp. dir. matl. mgt., Mount Carmel Medical Center, Columbus, OH '71 (PUR)
WILLIAMS, EDWARD T., dir. eng., Bryce Hospital, Tuscaloosa, AL '84 (ENG)
WILLIAMS, EILEEN E., dir. food serv., Doctors Hospital of Dallas, Dallas, TX '81 (FOOD)
WILLIAMS, ELIZABETH J., RN, assoc. adm. and dir. nrsg., University Hospital, Denver, CO '83 (NURS)
WILLIAMS, ELIZABETH A., dir. soc. serv., Highland Hospital of Rochester, Rochester, NY '77 (SOC)
WILLIAMS, ELLEN H., chief diet. serv., Veterans Administration Medical Center Brentwood, Los Angeles, CA '67 (FOOD)
WILLIAMS, ELTON L. JR., exec. dir., Lake Charles Memorial Hospital, Lake Charles, LA '82 (PLNG)
WILLIAMS, ERNAMARIE T., dir. pub. rel. and commun., Parkview Episcopal Medical Center, Pueblo, CO '81 (PR)
WILLIAMS, ESTHER L., sec. and chief serv., U. S. Air Force Hospital, Holloman AFB, NM '85
WILLIAMS, EUNICE E., dir. soc. work, Shepherd Spinal Center, Atlanta, GA '86 (SOC)
WILLIAMS, FAYE A., coor. commun. health educ., H. Lee Moffitt Cancer Center, Tampa, FL '86 (EDUC)
WILLIAMS, GAIL C., coor. mktg., St. Luke's Hospital of Kansas City, Kansas City, MO '84 (PLNG)
WILLIAMS, GARNER D., cent. sup. tech., Burke Rehabilitation Center, White Plains, NY '83 (CS)
WILLIAMS, GARY L., dir. pers., Sacred Heart Rehabilitation Center, Inc., Detroit, MI '85 (PERS)
WILLIAMS, GENE, chief eng., W. A. Howe Development Center, Tinley Park, IL '86 (ENG)
WILLIAMS, GEORGE E., mgr. clin. equip. proj., Servicemaster Industries, Inc., Downers Grove, IL '76 (ENG)
WILLIAMS, GEORGE H., dir. plng. and bldg. dev., St. Mary Hospital, Livonia, MI '82 (PLNG)
WILLIAMS, GEORGE P., PhD, vice-pres. support serv., Samaritan Health Service, Phoenix, AZ '78
WILLIAMS, GERALD A., dir. human res., Bi-County Community Hospital, Warren, MI '85 (PERS)
WILLIAMS, GORDON C., sr. vice-pres., Miami Valley Hospital, Dayton, OH '87 (AMB)
WILLIAMS, GRAEME A. W., MD, asst. med. dir. and risk mgr., Lac-King-Drew Medical Center, Los Angeles, CA '86 (RISK)
WILLIAMS, IRA W., dir. pub. rel., High Plains Baptist Hospital, Amarillo, TX '87 (PR)
WILLIAMS, JAMES A., atty., Eastwood Hospital, Memphis, TN '82 (ATTY)
WILLIAMS, JAMES A., atty., Garland Clinic and Hospital, Garland, TX '68 (ATTY)
WILLIAMS, JAMES A., dir. environ. serv., Fairhavens Center, Miami Springs, FL '87 (ENVIRON)
WILLIAMS, JAMES F., sr. vice-pres., Roanoke Memorial Hospitals, Roanoke, VA '62
WILLIAMS, JAMES G., dir. mktg. and commun. rel., Sheboygan Memorial Medical Center, Sheboygan, WI '82 (PLNG)

WILLIAMS, JAMES H., healthcare risk consult., Marsh and McLennan, Chicago, IL '86 (RISK)
WILLIAMS, JANET I., mktg. commun. spec., Highland Park Hospital, Highland Park, IL '85 (PR)
WILLIAMS, JAYNE M., vice-pres. mktg. and plng., St. John's Regional Medical Center, Oxnard, CA '85 (PLNG)
WILLIAMS, JEROME J., tech. bio-med. eng., St. Joseph Health Center, St. Charles, MO '79 (ENG)
WILLIAMS, JESSIE R., dir. matl. mgt., Western Missouri Medical Center, Warrensburg, MO '71 (PUR)
WILLIAMS, JOAN H., dir. pers., Francis Scott Key Medical Center, Baltimore, MD '81 (PERS)
WILLIAMS, JODY N., corp. dir. pub. rel., Sisters of St. Mary Health Care Systems, St. Louis, MO '83 (PR)
WILLIAMS, LT. COL. JOHN A., MSC USA, student, Army-Baylor University Program in Health Care Administration, Fort Sam Houston, TX '80
WILLIAMS, JOHN R., exec. dir., Children's Hospital at Stanford, Palo Alto, CA '64
WILLIAMS, JOHN W. JR., dir. pers., Fort Sanders Regional Medical Center, Knoxville, TN '83 (PERS)
WILLIAMS, JON D., dir. nrsg., Ellis Hospital, Schenectady, NY '87 (AMB)
WILLIAMS, JONI B., mgr. pers., Scottish Rite Children's Hospital, Atlanta, GA '86 (PERS)
WILLIAMS, JOSEPH A., assoc., Dalton, Dalton and Newport, Shaker Heights, OH '80 (ENG)
WILLIAMS, JUDITH H., consult., Stockton, CA '83 (PR) (PLNG)
WILLIAMS, JUDY J., dir. pers., Our Lady of Lourdes Health Center, Pasco, WA '83 (PERS)
WILLIAMS, K. NELSON, dir. environ. serv., Memorial Hospital, Nacogdoches, TX '86 (ENVIRON)
WILLIAMS, KENNETH R., coor. facil. dev., St. Luke's Hospital, Kansas City, MO '82 (ENG)
WILLIAMS, LATHAM, atty., Rush-Presbyterian-St. Luke's Medical Center, Chicago, IL '84 (ATTY)
WILLIAMS, LAURA K., student, University of Illinois, Urbana, IL '87
WILLIAMS, LAUREL J., dir. cont. educ., Scripps Memorial Hospital, La Jolla, CA '85 (EDUC)
WILLIAMS, LAVERN C., asst. chief eng., Theda Clark Regional Medical Center, Neenah, WI '81 (ENG)
WILLIAMS, LESLIE J., adm., Lafayette County Memorial Hospital, Lewisville, AR '85
WILLIAMS, LETHA D., dir. mktg. promotion, Michigan Health Systems, Ann Arbor, MI '83 (PR)
WILLIAMS, LINCOLN, vice-pres. strategic plng., Leominster Hospital, Leominster, MA '85 (PLNG)
WILLIAMS, LISL KING, atty., University Hospital, St. Louis University Center, St. Louis, MO '85 (ATTY)
WILLIAMS, LUCIA ANNE, RN, risk mgr. analyst, Temple University Hospital, Philadelphia, PA '84 (RISK)
WILLIAMS, LULA M., RN, assoc. chief nrsg. serv.-med. and long term care, Veterans Administration Medical Center, Perry Point, MD '86 (NURS)
WILLIAMS, M. ADELE, RN, pat. rep., United Hospital, Grand Forks, ND '68 (PAT)
WILLIAMS, MALA CHHIBBER, pat. liaison, Memorial Hospital, York, PA '86 (PAT)
WILLIAMS, MARGARET M., dir. hskpg. serv., Montgomery General Hospital, Olney, MD '86 (ENVIRON)
WILLIAMS, MARILYN, coor. corp. plng., CPHA, Ann Arbor, MI '82 (PLNG)
WILLIAMS, MARILYN, RN, adm. nrsg. serv., DeKalb Memorial Hospital, Auburn, IN '81 (NURS)
WILLIAMS, MARK S., adm. dir., Saginaw Cooperative Hospitals, Inc., Saginaw, MI '85
WILLIAMS, MARK T., vice-pres. mktg. and dev., Boulder Memorial Hospital, Boulder, CO '85 (PLNG)
WILLIAMS, MARY E., coor. vol., St. Francis Hospital, Charleston, WV '84 (VOL)
WILLIAMS, MARY L., RN, supv. cent., proc. and distrib., Geisinger Wyoming Valley Medical Center, Wilkes-Barre, PA '85 (CS)
WILLIAMS, MELONY J., student, Program in Health Care Administration, Trinity University, San Antonio, TX '85 (PLNG)
WILLIAMS, MICHAEL DALE, vice-pres., Baylor University Medical Center, Dallas, TX '80
WILLIAMS, MICHAEL L., vice-pres., Saint Joseph Hospital and Health Center, Kokomo, IN '80 (PERS)
WILLIAMS, NOAH A., dir. eng., AMI National Park Medical Center, Hot Springs, AR '85 (ENG)
WILLIAMS, NOEL DENISE, adm. res., Little Company of Mary Hospital, Torrance, CA '82
WILLIAMS, NORMA S., RN, supv. cent. serv., St. Francis Xavier Hospital, Charleston, SC '73 (CS)
WILLIAMS, PAMELA R., chief diet., North Canterbury Hospital Board, Christ Church, New Zealand '84 (FOOD)
WILLIAMS, COL. PATRICIA L., MSC USAF, Headquarters Air Force, Sgpc, Bolling AFB, DC '78
WILLIAMS, PATSY M., RN, mgr. nrsg. syst., Hospital Corporation of America, Nashville, TN '80 (NURS)
WILLIAMS, PATTY B., dir. pers., Tallahassee Community Hospital, Tallahassee, FL '85 (PERS)
WILLIAMS, PAULA, dir. nutr. serv., St. Mary's Hospital and Health Center, Tucson, AZ '86 (FOOD)
WILLIAMS, PEGGY A., dir. commun., Alexian Brothers Health System Inc., Elk Grove Village, IL '86 (PR)
WILLIAMS, PEGGY JEAN, pat. rep. and comm. rel., Riverview Medical Center, Red Bank, NJ '86 (PAT)
WILLIAMS, RALPH S., chief eng., Doctors Hospital, Tucker, GA '81 (ENG)
WILLIAMS, RALPH T., dir. emp. rel., Ft Sanders-Sevier Medical Center, Sevierville, TN '77 (PERS)
WILLIAMS, RAY C., prin., Williams Associates, San Francisco, CA '74 (PLNG)
WILLIAMS, CAPT. RAYMOND, MSC USAF III, adm., U. S. Air Force Hospital, Wichita, KS '84
WILLIAMS, REBECCA F., RN, head nrs. cent. serv., Eisenhower Medical Center, Rancho Mirage, CA '82 (CS)
WILLIAMS, REGINA C., atty., Health Central System, Minneapolis, MN '85 (ATTY)
WILLIAMS, RICHARD L., atty., Wyoming Medical Center, Casper, WY '81 (ATTY)
WILLIAMS, ROBERT E., sr. consult., Technicon Data Systems Corporation, Santa Clara, CA '80 (MGMT)
WILLIAMS, ROBERT E., coor. qual. assur., Methodist Medical Center of Illinois, Peoria, IL '80 (RISK)
WILLIAMS, ROBERT L., dir. plant serv., Kaiser Hospital, Woodland Hills, CA '84 (ENG)
WILLIAMS, ROBERT M., MD, dir., Rmw Management, Inc., Petoskey, MI '80
WILLIAMS, ROBERT P., chief bioelectronics, Metropolitan Medical Center, Minneapolis, MN '78 (ENG)
WILLIAMS, ROBERT, chief eng., Rest Haven, Roxbury, MA '69 (ENG)
WILLIAMS, ROBIN LORD, asst. dir. and adm. diet., Mary Black Memorial Hospital, Spartanburg, SC '85 (FOOD)
WILLIAMS, LT. ROGER S., MSC USAF, head mgt. info., Naval Hospital, Charleston, SC '80 (MGMT)
WILLIAMS, RONALD R., sr. vice-pres., Hellmuth, Obata and Kassabaum, Inc., St. Louis, MO '84 (PLNG)
WILLIAMS, RONALD, dir. eng., Long Island College Hospital, Brooklyn, NY '85 (ENG)
WILLIAMS, ROSE B., pat. rep., Queens Hospital Center, Jamaica, NY '83 (PAT)
WILLIAMS, ROY C., atty., Singing River Hospital System, Pascagoula, MS '72 (ATTY)
WILLIAMS, RUTH E., RN, asst. exec. dir., St. Anne's Hospital, Chicago, IL '84 (NURS)
WILLIAMS, SALLY W., vice-pres. client serv., Prep Risk Management Company, Spring House, PA '86 (RISK)
WILLIAMS, SARA JAYNE, vice-pres., St. Thomas Hospital, Nashville, TN '86 (AMB)
WILLIAMS, SARAH J., course supv., School of Health Care Sciences U. S. Air Force, Sheppard AFB, TX '81 (EDUC)
WILLIAMS, SCOTT R., dir. soc. serv., AMI Heights Hospital, Houston, TX '81 (SOC)
WILLIAMS, SHARON L., student, Temple University, Philadelphia, PA '82
WILLIAMS, SMITH JAMES JR., mgr. and dir. trng., American Association of Management, Inc., Baltimore, MD '85 (CS)
WILLIAMS, SUSAN MARGARET, asst. dir. soc. work, Mercy Hospital, Davenport, IA '78 (SOC)
WILLIAMS, SUZANNE M., adm. diet. and asst. dir. food serv., Scottish Rite Children's Hospital, Atlanta, GA '87 (FOOD)
WILLIAMS, SYBIL F., RN, dir. nrsg. serv., Waterman Medical Center, Eustis, FL '86 (NURS)
WILLIAMS, TERESA LUCILE, dir. soc. work, St. Dominic-Jackson Memorial Hospital, Jackson, MS '86 (SOC)
WILLIAMS, THOMAS J., dir. plng., Adventist Health System-North, Hinsdale, IL '84 (PLNG)
WILLIAMS, THOMAS R., dir. matl. mgt., Charlotte Memorial Hospital and Medical Center, Charlotte, NC '84 (PUR)
WILLIAMS, TRACY E., RN, adm. nrsg., Henrico Doctor's Hospital, Richmond, VA '84 (NURS)
WILLIAMS, VALENA M. JR., corp. dir. trng. and educ., Samuel Merritt Hospital, Oakland, CA '86 (EDUC)
WILLIAMS, WALTER A. JR., adm. asst., Baptist Memorial Hospital, Gadsden, AL '79 (RISK)
WILLIAMS, WALTER E., div. dir., Sheppard and Enoch Pratt Hospital, Baltimore, MD '63 (ENG)
WILLIAMS, WAYNE A., proj. mgr., Children's Hospital Medical Center, Cincinnati, OH '84 (ENG)
WILLIAMS, WILLIAM A., dir. maint., Haywood Park General Hospital, Brownsville, TN '84 (ENG)
WILLIAMS, WILLIAM C., dir. biomedical, Carlisle Hospital, Carlisle, PA '85 (ENG)
WILLIAMS, WILLIAM E., atty., Amerihealth, Inc., Atlanta, GA '85 (ATTY)
WILLIAMS, WILLIAM J., chief eng., Memorial Hospital, Charleston, WV '75 (ENG)
WILLIAMSON, ANDREW G., atty., Scotland Memorial Hospital, Laurinburg, NC '84 (ATTY)
WILLIAMSON, DON J., head clin. nutr., Naval Hospital, Bethesda, MD '83 (FOOD)
WILLIAMSON, E. EUGENE, West Palm Beach, FL '68
WILLIAMSON, ERNEST, mgr. eng., Spring Branch Memorial Hospital, Houston, TX '87 (ENG)
WILLIAMSON, HELEN M., dir. gerontoloty serv., Harper-Grace Hospitals, Detroit, MI '81 (PLNG)
WILLIAMSON, JOSEPH A., pres., Delaware Valley Hospital Council, Philadelphia, PA '56 (LIFE)
WILLIAMSON, KAREN A., legal asst., Albert Einstein Hlthcare Foundation, Philadelphia, PA '86 (RISK)
WILLIAMSON, KAY H., RN, asst. adm. nrsg. serv., Memorial City Medical Center, Houston, TX '77 (NURS)
WILLIAMSON, KENNETH, Francis, McGinnis and Rees, Inc., Washington, DC '72 (LIFE)
WILLIAMSON, MARCELLA, pub. info. off., West Virginia University Hospital, Morgantown, WV '85 (PR)
WILLIAMSON, RICHARD W., dir. human res., Memorial Medical Center of Jacksonville, Jacksonville, FL '76 (PERS)
WILLIAMSON, ROBERT E., Miami, FL '47 (LIFE)
WILLIAMSON, STANLEY G., vice-pres. facil. dev., Willis-Knighton Medical Center, Shreveport, LA '74
WILLIAMSON, THOMAS J., mgr. human res., Kaiser Foundation Health Plan, Portland, OR '82 (PERS)
WILLIAMSON, TRACY A., dir. commun. and prof. rel., Oconee Memorial Hospital, Seneca, SC '85 (PR)
WILLIAMSON, W. JOSEPH, dir. mgt. eng., Community Hospital of Anderson and Madison County, Anderson, IN '85 (MGMT)
WILLIFORD, FRANK G., dir. plng. and pers., Alabama Hospital Association, Montgomery, AL '82 (PLNG)
WILLIFORD, MONTEEN H., supv. cent. sup., Highsmith-Rainey Memorial Hospital, Fayetteville, NC '85 (CS)
WILLINGHAM, CHARLES BERNARD, (ret.), West Palm Beach, FL '59
WILLINGHAM, DEEPA B., adm. med. tech., Santa Barbara Cottage Hospital, Santa Barbara, CA '82
WILLINGHAM, PATRICK, exec. vice-pres., Community Health Systems, Jasper, AL '81
WILLIS, DANIEL R., mgr. food serv. and hskpg., Oakville-Trafalgar Memorial Hospital, Oakville, Ont., Canada '83 (FOOD)
WILLIS, DAVID C., assoc. gen. dir., Albert Einstein Medical Center, Philadelphia, PA '72
WILLIS, HAROLD J., atty., Dameron Hospital, Stockton, CA '75 (ATTY)
WILLIS, IRENE R., supv., Hotel Dieu Medical Center, El Paso, TX '80 (CS)
WILLIS, JAMES R., trustee, St. Joseph Regional Medical Center -Oklahoma, Ponca City, OK '86 (ENG)
WILLIS, JANET WHEELER, field rep., Joint Comission on Accreditation of Hospitals, Chicago, IL '65
WILLIS, JOHN R., assoc. adm., Dallas County Hospital District, Dallas, TX '61
WILLIS, MICHAEL K., asst. adm., Bradley County Memorial Hospital, Cleveland, TN '84 (PERS)
WILLIS, MICHAEL R., dir. human res.-data mgt., Florida Hospital Association, Orlando, FL '81 (NURS)(PERS)
WILLIS, MONA M., dir. pers., Woonsocket Hospital, Woonsocket, RI '85 (PERS)
WILLIS, RICHARD, dir. risk mgt., Rochester Methodist Hospital, Rochester, MN '87 (RISK)
WILLIS, SUSAN F., mgr. human res., Tarrant County Hospital District, Fort Worth, TX '86 (PERS)
WILLIS, W. EARL, sr. adv., Virginia Beach General Hospital, Virginia Beach, VA '87
WILLIS, WILLIAM R. JR., atty., Nashville Memorial Hospital, Madison, TN '68 (ATTY)
WILLIS, WILLIAM VAIL, student, Duke University, Department of Health Administration, Durham, NC '86
WILLITS, EILEEN M., RN, vice-pres. nrsg., Emma L. Bixby Hospital, Adrian, MI '86 (NURS)
WILLMAN, DAVID D., partner, Ernst and Whinney, Los Angeles, CA '85
WILLMANN, FRANCES C., vice-pres. human res., Health America Corporation of Texas, San Antonio, TX '82 (EDUC)
WILLMANN, JAY L., sr. partner, Page Southerland Page, Austin, TX '84
WILLMANN, RUTH, RN, dir. nrsg., Mercer County Community Hospital, Coldwater, OH '79 (NURS)
WILLMARTH, RONALD, vice-pres., Michigan Hospital Association Service Corporation, Lansing, MI '86 (RISK)
WILLMORTH, F. M., prin., Willmorth Engineering, Boise, ID '83 (ENG)
WILLMOT, LORRAINE M., dir. pub. rel., Illinois Valley Community Hospital, Peru, IL '82 (PR)
WILLMOTT, JAN D., asst. dir., St. Joseph's Hospital, Asheville, NC '84 (PR)
WILLMS, VICTORIA J., RN, asst. dir. nrsg., Pacific Presbyterian Hospital, San Francisco, CA '81 (NURS)
WILLNER, ROBERT F., pres., United Methodist Association of Health and Welfare Ministries, Lebanon, OH '64
WILLOTT, MARGARET J., dir. pub. rel., Hotel Dieu Hospital, Kingston, Ont., Canada '81 (PR)
WILLOUGHBY, JUDITH G., dir. soc. work, Pulaski Community Hospital, Pulaski, VA '80 (SOC)
WILLOUGHBY, PAMELA, dir. pub. rel., DeKalb General Hospital, Decatur, GA '85 (PR)
WILLOUR, BYRON J., arch., Henningson, Durham and Richardson, Omaha, NE '70
WILLOW, GERALD R., dir. safety and mgr. biomedical eng., Scottsdale Memorial Hospital, Scottsdale, AZ '78 (ENG)
WILLS, CHERYL, dir. soc. serv., Doctors Hospital of Stark County, Massillon, OH '85 (SOC)
WILLS, DAVID HOWARD, dir. matl. mgt., El Dorado Hospital and Medical Center, Tucson, AZ '79 (CS)
WILLS, JEAN, dir. vol., Humana Hospital -Lexington, Lexington, KY '78 (VOL)
WILLS, JOHN H., dir. food and nutr. serv., Morton F. Plant Hospital, Clearwater, FL '76 (FOOD)
WILLS, KATHLEEN, RN, dir. nrsg. adm., Mary Free Bed Hospital and Rehabilitation Center, Grand Rapids, MI '79 (NURS)
WILLS, ROBERT A., vice-pres. oper., Hospital Dietary Service, Farmington Hills, MI '82
WILLSHIER, JAMES J. JR., dir. plng. and dev., St. Joseph Hospital, Lancaster, PA '78
WILLSON, CHARLES R., dir. pharm., Youngstown Hospital Association-Southside Hospital, Youngstown, OH '71
WILLSON, MARY ANNE, dir. plng., Medical University Hospital of the Medical University of South Carolina, Charleston, SC '74 (PLNG)
WILMARTH, HELEN E., RN, dir. med.-surg. and critical care serv., Holy Cross Hospital, Silver Spring, MD '84 (NURS)
WILMARTH, JOAN G., asst. vice-pres. mktg., Cooper Hospital-University Medical Center, Camden, NJ '86 (PR)
WILMOT, DAVID M., United States Air Force, APO New York, NY '76
WILMOT, IRVIN G., exec. vice-pres. and chief oper. off., Montefiore Medical Center, Bronx, NY '61
WILMOT, ROBERT A., atty., St. Michael Hospital, Milwaukee, WI '83 (ATTY)
WILNER, DONNA I., RN, asst. adm. and dir. nrsg., Hickory Memorial Hospital, Hickory, NC '86 (NURS)
WILNER, MARK, qual. assur. eng., Labthermics Techonology, Inc., Champaign, IL '80 (ENG)
WILSON, ARLENE E., RN, dir. nrsg. serv., Kanabec Hospital, Mora, MN '79 (NURS)
WILSON, BARRY P., vice-pres. pub. affairs, Blue Cross and Blue Shield of National Capital Area, Washington, DC '67 (PR)
WILSON, BILL D., adm., Northwest Kansas Regional Medical Center, Goodland, KS '81 (PLNG)
WILSON, CAROL M., RN, asst. dir. nrsg. and health serv. adm., University Hospital-University of Nebraska, Omaha, NE '86 (NURS)

WILSON, CAROLE, dir. risk mgt., Alta Bates Hospital, Berkeley, CA '83 (RISK)
WILSON, CHARLES N., PhD, adm., Shriners Hospitals for Crippled Children-Burns Institute-Galveston Unit, Galveston, TX '68
WILSON, CHARLES R., asst. dir. pers., Mercy Hospital of Sacramento, Sacramento, CA '82 (PERS)
WILSON, CHARLOTTE A., pat. rep., University of Iowa Hospitals and Clinics, Iowa City, IA '79 (PAT)
WILSON, CHERYL A., dir. pub. rel., Brownwood Regional Hospital, Brownwood, TX '81 (PR)
WILSON, CHERYL S., partner, Coopers and Lybrand, Chicago, IL '75
WILSON, CHRISTINE M., dir. health commun. and mktg., Fox Chase Cancer Center, Philadelphia, PA '85 (PLNG)
WILSON, D. JEANETTE, mgr. human res., HSA Riverwood Hospital, Provo, UT '87 (PERS)
WILSON, DAVID B., MD, Jackson, MS '68 (LIFE)
WILSON, DAVID K., Sherlock, Smith and Adams, Inc., Montgomery, AL '78 (ENG)
WILSON, DAVID, consult., Construction Consulting Service, New York City, NY '86 (PUR)
WILSON, DON D., vice-pres., Adventist Health System-Sunbelt, Orlando, FL '86 (PLNG)
WILSON, DONALD G., arch., Wilson Johnson Associates, Overland Park, KS '77
WILSON, DONALD J., dir. eng. and plant oper., Brownsville General Hospital, Brownsville, PA '79 (ENG)
WILSON, DONNA E., vice-pres., John C. Lincoln Hospital and Health Center, Phoenix, AZ '83 (RISK)
WILSON, DORIS A., pat. rep., AMI Presbyterian-St. Luke's Medical Center, Denver, CO '76 (PAT)
WILSON, DORIS J., dir. food serv., Presbyterian Hospital, Dallas, TX '67 (FOOD)
WILSON, DOUGLAS G. JR., exec. dir., Healthcare Medical Center of Tustin, Tustin, CA '77
WILSON, DOUGLAS H., dir. plng., Peninsula General Hospital Medical Center, Salisbury, MD '84 (PLNG)
WILSON, EDMOND CARL, vice-pres. human res., Emma L. Bixby Hospital, Adrian, MI '80 (PERS)
WILSON, ELIZABETH ANN, soc. worker and pat. rep., Tulare District Hospital, Tulare, CA '86 (PAT)
WILSON, ELIZABETH J., dir. food serv., Osteopathic Hospital of Maine, Portland, ME '79 (FOOD)
WILSON, EVELYN, dir. pat. rel., Winter Haven Hospital, Winter Haven, FL '72 (PAT)
WILSON, G. RONALD, dir. educ., Altoona Hospital, Altoona, PA '82 (EDUC)
WILSON, GINA K., dir. food and nutr. serv., Longmont United Hospital, Longmont, CO '84 (FOOD)
WILSON, GUINEVERE, mgr. cent. serv., Cook County Hospital, Chicago, IL '74 (CS)
WILSON, JAMES E., dir. maint., Waynesboro Community Hospital, Waynesboro, VA '85 (ENG)
WILSON, JAMES M., vice-pres. oper., Nexus Healthcare Corporation, Mount Holly, NJ '77
WILSON, JASON A., dir. bldg. serv., Auburn Faith Community Hospital, Auburn, CA '85 (ENG)(ENVIRON)
WILSON, JEANMARIE, RN, dir. nrsg., Wyandotte General Hospital, Wyandotte, MI '86 (NURS)
WILSON, JOELLA M., cent. serv. tech., Grays Harbor Community Hospital, Aberdeen, WA '84 (CS)
WILSON, JOHN D., dir. eng., Owensboro-Daviess County Hospital, Owensboro, KY '78 (ENG)
WILSON, JOHN M., sr. consult., Arthur Andersen and Company, Washington, DC '86
WILSON, JUDITH I., dir. vol. serv., Kapiolani Medical Center for Women and Children, Honolulu, HI '84 (VOL)
WILSON, JUDY L., RN, exec. dir., St. Barnabas Outpatient Center, West Orange, NJ '84 (PLNG)(AMB)
WILSON, KAREN C., dir. pub. rel. and mktg., Rolling Hill Hospital, Elkins Park, PA '83 (PR)
WILSON, KAREN HENRIKSEN, dir. pat. rel., Springhill Memorial Hospital, Mobile, AL '86 (PAT)
WILSON, KATHERINE REEVES, dir. commun. and vol. serv., Good Shepherd Medical Center, Longview, TX '81 (VOL)
WILSON, L. BARRICK JR., vice-pres. corp. commun., St. Joseph Medical Center, Wichita, KS '86 (PR)
WILSON, LARRY Y., exec. vice-pres., Mercy Health System, Burlingame, CA '85 (PLNG)
WILSON, LAWRENCE L., exec. dir., Metropolitan-Edmonton Hospital District 106, Edmonton, Alta., Canada '63
WILSON, LINDA L., asst. vice-pres. human res., West Jersey Hospital, Northern Division, Camden, NJ '86 (PERS)
WILSON, LINDA S., arch., Garikes and Partners Architects, Inc., Birmingham, AL '81 (PLNG)
WILSON, LUCIUS R., MD, (ret.), Fort Stockton, TX '22 (LIFE)
WILSON, MARGARET A., RN, dir. nrsg. serv., St. Mary's Hospital, Galesburg, IL '79 (NURS)
WILSON, MARGARET ANN, dir. vol., Providence Hospital, Everett, WA '72 (VOL)
WILSON, MARGARET E., RN, dir. surg., recovery and cent. sup., Union Medical Center, El Dorado, AR '85 (CS)
WILSON, MARTHA R., RN, asst. adm. nrsg., Katherine Shaw Bethea Hospital, Dixon, IL '73 (NURS)
WILSON, MARY D., coor. vol., Joint Township District Memorial Hospital, St. Marys, OH '81 (VOL)
WILSON, MARY E., adm. asst., McKeesport Hospital, McKeesport, PA '84
WILSON, NANCY E., dir. pub. rel. and mktg. commun., Barberton Citizens Hospital, Barberton, OH '87 (PR)
WILSON, NORMA, RN, dir. qual. assur. and risk mgr., Martha Washington Hospital, Chicago, IL '81 (RISK)
WILSON, PAT, RN, coor. staff dev., University of Oregon Health Sciences Center, Portland, OR '77 (EDUC)
WILSON, PATRICIA ELAINE, RN, dir. cent. serv., Nashville Memorial Hospital, Madison, TN '83 (CS)
WILSON, PATRICIA K., RN, coor. in-service educ., Richmond Community Hospital, Richmond, VA '80 (EDUC)
WILSON, PATRICK J., atty., Munson Medical Center, Traverse City, MI '73 (ATTY)
WILSON, PATTY L., asst. dir. pers., Tuomey Hospital, Sumter, SC '85 (PERS)
WILSON, ROBERT E., consult., Wsi, Charlotte, NC '85 (ENG)
WILSON, ROBERT G., adm., Hinds General Hospital, Jackson, MS '65
WILSON, ROBERT L., atty., Bay Harbor Hospital, Harbor City, CA '77 (ATTY)
WILSON, ROBERT T., bd. mem., Walker Regional Medical Center, Jasper, AL '81
WILSON, RODNEY D., instr., U. S. Air Force School of Health Care Scis, Sheppard AFB, TX '81 (PERS)
WILSON, RONALD C., dir. emp. rel., Barnes Hospital, St. Louis, MO '83 (PERS)
WILSON, RUSSELL W., dir. nutr. and diet., University of California San Diego Medical Center, San Diego, CA '82 (FOOD)
WILSON, RUTH, pat. fin. serv., St. Joseph Hospital East, Mount Clemens, MI '85 (MGMT)
WILSON, SAM, Commonwealth Wilson, Inc., Aurora, CO '85 (MGMT)
WILSON, STEPHANY S., atty., Lovelace Medical Center, Albuquerque, NM '86 (ATTY)
WILSON, STEPHEN K., adm., Memorial Regional Rehabilitation Center, Jacksonville, FL '60
WILSON, STEVEN E., dir. mktg. and pub. rel., HCA Sun Towers Hospital, El Paso, TX '86 (PR)
WILSON, SUMMITT E., Rockville, MD '76 (PUR)
WILSON, SUSAN, dir. soc. serv. and qual. assessment, Baystate Medical Center, Springfield, MA '87 (SOC)
WILSON, THOMAS A., atty., St. Elizabeth Hospital, Appleton, WI '86 (ATTY)
WILSON, THOMAS E., dir. pur., Central Blood Bank of Pittsburgh, Pittsburgh, PA '83 (PUR)
WILSON, THOMAS E., dir., Cambridge Research Institute, Cambridge, MA '86 (PLNG)
WILSON, VERONA L., dir. telecommun., Swedish Hospital Medical Center, Seattle, WA '85 (ENG)
WILSON, VICTORIA, vice-pres. prof. serv., St. Anthony's Hospital, Amarillo, TX '82
WILSON, W. LESTER, dir. plant oper., Memorial Hospital of Salem County, Salem, NJ '78 (ENG)
WILSON, WAYNE R., dir. mktg. and commun., AMI Valley Medical Center, El Cajon, CA '85 (PR)
WILSON, WILLIAM F. JR., asst. mgr. info. res., Deaconess Hospital, Oklahoma City, OK '85
WILSON, WILLIAM L., (ret.), Lyme, NH '39 (LIFE)
WILSON, WILLIE E., dir. support serv., Charter Hospital of Long Beach, Long Beach, CA '83 (RISK)
WILT, CHESTER F. JR., adm. matl. mgt., St. Joseph's Hospital and Medical Center, Phoenix, AZ '84 (PUR)
WILTSE, BONNIE, RN, dir. pat. care, St. Luke's Regional Medical Center, Sioux City, IA '79 (NURS)
WILTSE, PATRICIA M., dir. matl. mgt. serv., Coral Springs Medical Center, Coral Springs, FL '81 (PUR)
WILTSHIRE, CHERYL, dir. util. review and cost containment, Blue Cross and Blue Shield of Virginia, Richmond, VA '84
WILTSHIRE, GLENDA L., mktg. assoc., National Jewish Center for Immunology and Respiratory Medicine, Denver, CO '85 (PLNG)
WILTZ, TONI D., mgr. diet. serv., Memorial Care Systems, Houston, TX '86 (FOOD)
WIMAN, JACK L., eng., Dept. of HHS, U. S. Food and Drug Administration, Fort Collins, CO '78 (ENG)
WIMBERLEY, EDWARD T., PhD, dir. soc. serv., University of Texas Medical Branch Hospitals, Galveston, TX '83 (SOC)
WIMBERLY, JAMES W., dir. plant eng., Lutheran Medical Center, Cleveland, OH '82 (ENG)
WIMER, DARYL R., mgr., Southwestern Bell Telephone Company, St. Louis, MO '84
WIMPFHEIMER, PAUL M., adm., Shaare Zedek Medical Center, Jerusalem, Israel '81 (MGMT)
WIMSATT, ANN, student, University of Florida, Gainesville, FL '84
WINANS, PAMELA A., dir. soc. serv., Union Hospital, Terre Haute, IN '79 (SOC)
WINANS, PATRICIA A., coor. spec. proj., St. Lawrence Hospital, Lansing, MI '76 (VOL)
WINCHEL, GERALD GEORGE, chief eng., Greene County Medical Center, Jefferson, IA '75 (ENG)
WINCHELL, RICHARD, pres., Communicaide, Oakville, Ont., Canada '83 (PR)
WINCHESTER, BRIAN T., dir. biomedical eng., Ottawa Civic Hospital, Ottawa, Ont., Canada '80 (ENG)
WINCHESTER, TOM, dir. plant oper., Jackson County Memorial Hospital, Altus, OK '80 (ENG)
WINDEMUTH, DONNA S., dir. amb. care, Hospital for Special Surgery, New York, NY '85
WINDHAM, GINGER K., RN, dir. maternal and child health, Riverside Hospital, Newport News, VA '83 (NURS)
WINDHAM, ROBERT CHARLES, consulting eng., Baltimore, MD '77 (ENG)
WINDLE, FRANK, dir. plant oper., Philadelphia Psychiatric Center, Philadelphia, PA '85 (ENG)
WINDLE, JANE W., RN, dir. nrsg. serv., Columbus Hospital, Columbus, MS '82 (NURS)
WINDLEY, RODNEY D., pres., Medical-Care, Inc., Atlanta, GA '85
WINDSOR, ROSEMARY G., RN, vice-pres. nrsg. serv., Nanticoke Memorial Hospital, Seaford, DE '81 (NURS)
WINEGARD, DEBORAH J., atty., Charter Medical Corporation, Macon, GA '86 (ATTY)
WINELAND, ELIZABETH M., dir. vol., University of Cincinnati Hospital, Cincinnati, OH '71 (VOL)
WINER-SMITH, ELAINE, pres., Elaine Winer Public Relations, Inc., Whittier, CA '86 (PR)
WINER, BURTON, bd. pres., Franklin Medical Center, Greenfield, MA '71 (ATTY)
WINES, MARY BETH, pat. rep., St. Charles Hospital, Oregon, OH '87 (PAT)
WINESDORFER, JO ANN, pat. rep., Harrison Memorial Hospital, Bremerton, WA '82 (PAT)
WINFREE, CATHY, adm., Valdez Community Hospital, Valdez, AK '86 (RISK)
WINFREE, KEITH F., pres., Keith Winfree and Company, Louisville, KY '86 (MGMT)
WINFREY, GEORGE R., supv. diet., Baptist Memorial Hospital, Memphis, TN '84 (FOOD)
WINFREY, HELGA M., dir. surg. serv., Waterman Medical Center, Eustis, FL '87 (AMB)
WINGARDNER, THOMAS STACK JR., exec. vice-pres., Newington Children's Hospital, Newington, CT '75
WINGERATH, MICHAEL F., asst. chief eng., Alta Bates Hospital, Berkeley, CA '82 (ENG)
WINGERTER, GEORGE J. JR., vice-pres. mktg., Healthcorp Affiliates, Naperville, IL '85 (PLNG)
WINGFIELD, MARGARET J., dir. cent. serv., Brown Schools-Ranch Treatment Center, Austin, TX '86 (CS)
WINGLER, LUCILLE K., RN, dir. nrsg. serv., Clark County Memorial Hospital, Jeffersonville, IN '85 (NURS)
WINGO, KENNETH JOHN, mgr. storeroom, Franklin Square Hospital, Baltimore, MD '86 (PUR)
WINHOLTZ, HOWARD M., asst. prof., St. Mary's College of Winona, Rochester, MN '85
WINICK, JOSEPH M., asst. vice-pres. plng. and dev., American Healthcare Management, Inc., Dallas, TX '75 (PLNG)
WINKLEMAN, LAURIE S., instr. staff dev., Aultman Hospital, Canton, OH '84 (EDUC)
WINKLER, SR. JOAN, pres., Catholic Health Association of Wisconsin, Madison, WI '78
WINKLER, JUNE DAUBERT, dir. vol. serv., Howard County General Hospital, Columbia, MD '83 (VOL)(PAT)
WINKLER, KURT RUNYAN, corp. budget off., Providence Memorial Hospital, El Paso, TX '84
WINKLER, MARTHA E., dir. plng. and mktg., Desert Samaritan Hospital, Mesa, AZ '82 (PLNG)
WINKLER, RODNEY A., dir. food serv., Graham Hospital, Canton, IL '82 (FOOD)
WINKLER, STEVEN ROBERT, vice-pres. oper., Baton Rouge General Medical Center, Baton Rouge, LA '77 (RISK)
WINKLES, SAMUEL G., RN, dir. nrs., Artesia General Hospital, Artesia, NM '85 (NURS)
WINN, AL, dir. soc. serv., Reading Rehabilitation Hospital, Reading, PA '86 (SOC)
WINN, AMY, actg. dir. pub. rel. and mktg., Humana Hospital -Augusta, Augusta, GA '86 (PR)
WINN, JOAN, RN, supv. cent. serv., St. Mary Hospital, Philadelphia, PA '86 (CS)
WINN, ROGER E., vice-pres. human resources, Morton F. Plant Hospital, Clearwater, FL '70 (PERS)
WINN, SANDRA P., Hypoluxo, FL '82
WINN, W. THOMAS, reg. vice-pres., SunHealth Corporation, Charlotte, NC '72 (MGMT)
WINNEY, WAYNE O., market analyst, University of Utah Health Sciences Center, Salt Lake City, UT '85 (PLNG)
WINNING, JANE HAGADORN, RN, dir. nrsg., Emanuel Medical Center, Turlock, CA '80 (NURS)
WINSEY, JOSEPH K., dir. plant oper., Cabarrus Memorial Hospital, Concord, NC '85 (ENG)
WINSLOW, LEE N., dir. biomedical eng., Saint Vincent Health Center, Erie, PA '85 (ENG)
WINSLOW, MARK V., dir. eng. and security, Chalmette General Hospital, Chalmette, LA '84 (ENG)
WINSTON, CHRISTINE J., dir. qual. assur., Holy Cross Hospital, Austin, TX '81 (RISK)
WINSTON, MARGARET A., pers. spec., Jackson Park Hospital, Chicago, IL '85 (PERS)
WINSTON, PAUL K., exec. dir., Health Care Personnel Services, Van Nuys, CA '75 (PERS)
WINSTON, WILLIAM J., dean, Golden Gate University, San Francisco, CA '85 (PR) (PLNG)
WINTER, GAY, RN, facilitator cont. educ., Woodside Medical, Pontiac, MI '78 (EDUC)
WINTER, PEGGI, mgr. educ. serv., St. Anthony's Medical Center, St. Louis, MO '82 (EDUC)
WINTER, WILLIAM EDWARD, adm., Forest Grove Community Hospital, Forest Grove, OR '75
WINTERS-EVERLY, VERONICA S., dir. pub. rel., St. Ann's Hospital of Columbus, Westerville, OH '86 (PR)
WINTERS, BETTY J., RN, vice-pres. prof. serv., Numed, Inc., Encino, CA '85 (NURS)
WINTERS, CURTIS D., dir. matl. mgt., Beauregard Memorial Hospital, De Ridder, LA '83 (PUR)
WINTERS, JOYCE D., mgr. sterile proc. and distrib., University Medical Center Southern Nevada, Las Vegas, NV '83 (CS)
WINTERS, SR. MARY PATRICIA, RN, vice-pres. nrsg., St. Vincent's Medical Center, Jacksonville, FL '82 (NURS)
WINTERS, ROBERT G., atty., Chesapeake Hospital Authority, Chesapeake, VA '78 (ATTY)
WINTERS, SHIRLEY J., dir. pers., Grinnell General Hospital, Grinnell, IA '87 (PERS)
WINTERS, VICKI L., dir. matl. mgt., Grandview Hospital and Medical Center, Dayton, OH '82 (PUR)
WINTERSON, SR. JANE, dir. plng. serv., Sisters of Mercy Province of St. Louis Management and Consulting Office, St. Louis, MO '81 (PLNG)
WION, RICK, mgr. food serv., Mount Sinai Hospital Medical Center, Chicago, IL '80 (FOOD)
WIPPERFURTH, KAY E., RN, vice-pres. pat. serv., Fort Atkinson Memorial Hospital, Fort Atkinson, WI '86 (NURS)
WIPPLE, KENNETH J., pres., Detroit Medical Center Corporation, Detroit, MI '80
WIRE, GEORGE W., asst. dir. food serv., Hoag Memorial Hospital Presbyterian, Newport Beach, CA '68 (FOOD)
WIRE, KATHRYN K., risk mgr., Barnes Hospital, St. Louis, MO '84 (RISK)
WIRTH, BARBARA, risk mgr., Medical Enterprise Development Company, Inc., Baltimore, MD '86 (RISK)
WIRTH, CAROL L., RN, asst. dir. pat. serv., Swedish American Hospital, Rockford, IL '82 (NURS)
WIRTS, CATHLEEN A., student, Program in Industrial and Health Systems Engineer, University of Wisconsin, Madison, WI '86 (MGMT)
WIRTZ, CHERYL L., dir. phys. support, Doctors Hospital of Stark County, Massillon, OH '85 (PR) (PLNG)
WIRTZ, HOWARD L., dir. commun., Brookdale Hospital Medical Center, Brooklyn, NY '78 (ENG)

WIRTZ, VIRGINIA H., RN, mgt. consult., Presbyterian Hospital, Oklahoma City, OK '80 (NURS)
WISCHOW, HEIDI S., dir. educ., Parkview Episcopal Medical Center, Pueblo, CO '86 (EDUC)
WISDOM, PHILIP L., Mansfield, OH '52 (LIFE)
WISE-MARCUSE, PEGGY JO, pat. commun., William Beaumont Hospital, Royal Oak, MI '79 (PAT)
WISE, AMANDA N., dir. vol., Bristol Memorial Hospital, Bristol, TN '79 (VOL)
WISE, CARLA, pat. rep., Sinai Hospital of Detroit, Detroit, MI '80 (PAT)
WISE, CLARENCE H. JR., asst. vice-pres. amb. serv., Self Memorial Hospital, Greenwood, SC '85 (PR) (PLNG)(AMB)
WISE, DELORES, dir. environ. serv., Park Ridge Hospital, Rochester, NY '86 (ENVIRON)
WISE, DOROTHY, dir. pur., Miami Heart Institute, Miami Beach, FL '83 (PUR)
WISE, ERIN, RN, dir. prof. serv., Georgia Hospital Association, Atlanta, GA '82 (NURS)
WISE, JOYCE H., dir. vol. serv., Williamsport Hospital and Medical Center, Williamsport, PA '77 (VOL)(PAT)
WISE, MARK E., vice-pres. human res., Evanston Hospital, Evanston, IL '80 (PERS)
WISE, MARY J., dir. soc. serv., Saint Joseph's Hospital, Atlanta, GA '82 (SOC)
WISE, PHILLIP J., Sumter Regional Hospital, Americus, GA '57 (ENG)(LIFE)
WISE, RONALD L., dir. pub. rel., Cedars-Sinai Medical Center, Los Angeles, CA '81 (PR)
WISE, RONALD L., dir. pers., Memorial Hospital, Hollywood, FL '81 (PERS)
WISE, WILLIAM C., dir. qual. assur., Mary Greeley Medical Center, Ames, IA '86 (ENG)
WISE, WILLIAM D., dir. maint., Glynn-Brunswick Memorial Hospital, Brunswick, GA '64 (ENG)
WISE, WILLIAM DOUGLAS, atty., Carraway Methodist Medical Center, Birmingham, AL '78 (ATTY)
WISEMAN, ANN L., dir. qual. assur. and risk mgt. prog., Columbia Hospital for Women, Washington, DC '83 (RISK)
WISEMAN, BONNIE, vice-pres. and dir., A. T. Kearney, Inc., Chicago, IL '81
WISEMAN, LYNN D., dir. pub. rel., Central Baptist Hospital, Lexington, KY '81 (PR)
WISEMAN, PATRICIA, pat. rep., Clare Community Hospital, Clare, MI '87 (PAT)
WISEMAN, THOMAS G., dir. pers., Clinton Memorial Hospital, St. Johns, MI '82 (PERS)
WISENER, MAUREEN M., asst. pub. rel., Park Ridge Hospital, Fletcher, NC '84 (PR)
WISHAM, HERSCHEL, chief eng., Sumter Regional Hospital, Americus, GA '82 (ENG)
WISHARD, JOE C., supv. plng., St. Vincent Infirmary, Little Rock, AR '86 (ENG)
WISHINSKY, JILL, assoc. plng. and mktg., Staten Island Hospital, Staten Island, NY '86
WISKOWSKI, DOROTHY, mgr. corp. plng., Intermountain Health Care, Inc., Salt Lake City, UT '84 (PLNG)
WISKOWSKI, EUGENE J., vice-pres. fin., West Suburban Hospital Medical Center, Oak Park, IL '79
WISNIEW, RONALD J., vice-pres. emp. rel., Ball Memorial Hospital, Muncie, IN '79 (PERS)
WISNIEWSKI, MARION, RN, dir. educ. and trng., Faxton Hospital, Utica, NY '79 (EDUC)
WISNIOWSKI, JOSEPH JOHN, sr. mgt. eng., Cleveland Clinic Hospital, Cleveland, OH '79 (MGMT)
WISNOM, BARBARA, loss control consult., Hospital Underwriters Mutual Insurance Company, Tarrytown, NY '85 (RISK)
WISNOSKI, RICHARD M., dir. matl. mgt., Easton Hospital, Easton, PA '82 (PUR)
WISS, GAIL R., dir. vol. serv., St. Vincent Charity Hospital, Cleveland, OH '86 (VOL)
WISSER, NAT R., (ret.), Bloomington, MN '74
WISSINK, ANN L., RN, clin. dir. psych. nrsg., Mount Auburn Hospital, Cambridge, MA '82 (NURS)
WISSINK, GERALD L., pres., Manatee Memorial Hospital, Bradenton, FL '86
WISSMAN, PAULA S., RN, dir. nrsg. serv., Driscoll Foundation Children's Hospital, Corpus Christi, TX '80 (NURS)
WISZ, PATRICIA M., RN, dir. nrsg., St. Margaret Hospital, Hammond, IN '85 (NURS)
WITALIS, ROGER W., pres., Witalis and Company, Lafayette, CA '79
WITCHER, CHAD RYAN, pat. rep., Outer Drive Hospital, Lincoln Park, MI '85 (PAT)
WITCHER, KEN, dir. tech. support serv., American Medical International, Beverly Hills, CA '80 (ENG)
WITHAM, BARBARA A., dir. external affairs, Suburban Community Hospital, Warrensville Heights, OH '84 (PLNG)
WITHERELL, DENNIS P., atty., Mercy Hospital, Toledo, OH '80 (ATTY)
WITHERILL, LISTON A., sr. vice-pres., Numed, Encino, CA '55 (PLNG)(LIFE)
WITHERS, KATHLEEN M., student, Program in Health Care Administration, Texas Woman's University, Houston, TX '85
WITHERS, MARY ALICE, RN, vice-pres. nrsg., Valdese General Hospital, Valdese, NC '84 (NURS)
WITHERSPOON, JERE W., asst. exec. dir., Duke Endowment, Charlotte, NC '59
WITKINS, 2ND LT. ALBERT R., MSC USAF, Morton Grove, IL '84
WITMER, JAMES A., dir. mgt. support serv., St. Joseph's Medical Center, Fort Wayne, IN '79 (MGMT)
WITMER, MARK H., asst. dir. support serv., Wilson Memorial Hospital, Wilson, NC '84 (ENG)
WITSBERGER, LYNN M., dir. soc. work, Montefiore Hospital, Pittsburgh, PA '81 (SOC)
WITT, DRENDA WILLIAMS, mgr. pub. rel. and dev., Tarrant County Hospital District, Fort Worth, TX '84 (PR) (PLNG)
WITT, FRANK H., dir. eng., Brazosport Memorial Hospital, Lake Jackson, TX '79 (ENG)
WITT, JOHN A., national adv., Witt Associates Inc., Oak Brook, IL '70
WITT, KENNETH R., dir. eng., Community Hospital of Springfield, Springfield, OH '85 (ENG)
WITT, MARJORIE, RN, assoc. exec. dir. nrsg., Bellevue Hospital Center, New York, NY '77 (NURS)
WITTE, ANITA, dir. environ. serv., Elmhurst Memorial Hospital, Elmhurst, IL '86 (ENVIRON)
WITTE, LAWRENCE MARK, vice-pres. oper., St. Francis Hospital, Poughkeepsie, NY '68
WITTEN, JOHN P., atty., Murphy, Young and Smith, Columbus, OH '86 (ATTY)
WITTENBERG, JODY L., atty., Alexian Brothers Health Systems Inc., Elk Grove Village, IL '85 (ATTY)
WITTENBRINK, BONIFACE, dir. soc. serv., Chicago Osteopathic Medical Center, Chicago, IL '85 (SOC)
WITTENBROOK, JANET B., student, Georgia State University, Institute of Health Administration, Atlanta, GA '86
WITTHUHN, PEGGY L., asst. mgr. pur., Appleton Medical Center, Appleton, WI '87
WITTISH, LINDA G., mgr. pub. rel. and commun., Memorial Medical Center, Savannah, GA '83 (PR)
WITTKOP, JUDY A., asst. dir., Floyd Valley Hospital, Le Mars, IA '84 (PR)
WITTLINGER, DIANNE, RN, clin. dir. nrsg. serv., Fairview General Hospital, Cleveland, OH '86 (NURS)
WITTMAN, GERALD P., dir. soc. serv., Holy Cross Hospital, Merrill, WI '85 (SOC)
WITTMAN, JOEL, vice-pres. health care serv., Staff Builders, Inc., New York, NY '79
WITTMEYER, LYNDA T., vice-pres. adm. mktg., Saint Thomas Medical Center, Akron, OH '87 (PLNG)
WITTNER, STEVEN A., asst. to vice-pres., St. Barnabas Hospital, Bronx, NY '87
WITTRUP, RICHARD D., vice-pres. prof. affairs, Herman Smith Associates International, Jeddah, Saudi Arabia '53
WITTSTOCK, VELDA T., RN, assoc. dir. nrsg. and dir. critical care, St. Joseph Hospital, Orange, CA '85 (NURS)
WIVELL, J. EARL, pres., Medco, Inc., Willow Grove, PA '71 (MGMT)
WIZEMAN, PATRICIA, prin. analyst, University of California San Francisco, San Francisco, CA '80 (PAT)
WIZNER, GEORGELYN, dir. soc. work serv., Northeast Rehabilitation Hospital, Salem, NH '86 (SOC)
WNUK, ALBERT GEORGE, consult. bd. trustee, St. Francis Hospital-Beacon, Beacon, NY '52 (LIFE)
WOCHER, LCDR JOHN CARL, MSC USN, med. dept. placement off., Naval Military Personnel Command, Washington, DC '81
WODEK, CAROL E., adm. asst., Pocatello Regional Medical Center, Pocatello, ID '85 (PLNG)(RISK)
WODINSKY, HAROLD B., adm. and chief oper. off., Toronto-Bayview Regional Cancer Center, Toronto, Ont., Canada '87 (AMB)
WOEHR, BETTY J., dir. vol. serv., Riverview Medical Center, Red Bank, NJ '83 (VOL)
WOELBER, TWILA, Sioux Falls, SD '86 (CS)
WOELHKE, PAUL HAMMOND, vice-pres., Lima Memorial Hospital, Lima, OH '69
WOERLY, JOHN A., dir. pat. registration and telecommun., Methodist Medical Center of Illinois, Peoria, IL '83 (ENG)
WOERNER, ELDON H., dir. eng., Sisters of the Third Order of St. Francis, Peoria, IL '66 (ENG)
WOERTZ, DARRELL H., vice-pres., Simi Valley Adventist Hospital, Simi Valley, CA '81 (PR)
WOFFARD, CHESTER A. III, RN, dir. nrsg., Institute of Living, Hartford, CT '81 (NURS)
WOHL, CHARLES S., adm., Jay County Hospital, Portland, IN '85
WOHLEB, BERNADETTE M., dir. allied health and emp. educ., Scott and White Memorial Hospital, Temple, TX '86 (EDUC)
WOHLFORD, BARBARA A., RN, asst. adm. nrsg., Eisenhower Medical Center, Rancho Mirage, CA '76 (NURS)(EDUC)
WOJACK, MARY ANN, sr. pub. rel. off., St. Clair Health Corporation, Detroit, MI '86 (PR)
WOJEWUCZKI, JOHN T., dir. matl. mgt., Hollywood Medical Center, Hollywood, FL '80 (PUR)
WOJTKOWSKI, DONALD E., group mgr. and chief shared serv., Christian Hospitals Northeast-Northwest, St. Louis, MO '75 (ENG)
WOJTOWICZ, ROGER, chief eng., Lake Forest Hospital, Lake Forest, IL '86 (ENG)
WOLARSKY, JOEL M., vice-pres. plng. and corp. dev., Miriam Hospital, Providence, RI '74 (PLNG)
WOLCHIK, BARBARA J., dir. educ. serv., Hamot Medical Center, Erie, PA '82 (EDUC)
WOLCHUCK-SHER, KAREN S., mgr. consulting serv., Amherst Associates, Tampa, FL '85 (PR) (PLNG)
WOLDUM, KARYL M., RN, assoc. chm. nrsg., New England Medical Center, Boston, MA '82 (NURS)
WOLETZ, JUDITH A., coor. pat. care and mgr. surg., Luther Hospital, Eau Claire, WI '87 (AMB)
WOLF, BETH H., oper. analyst, Mary Hitchcock Memorial Hospital, Hanover, NH '86 (MGMT)
WOLF, DARRYL A., mgr. plant oper., American Medical International, Commerce City, CO '84 (ENG)
WOLF, GAIL A., RN, vice-pres., Shadyside Hospital, Pittsburgh, PA '82 (NURS)
WOLF, JOHN R., vice-pres. human res., Miami Valley Hospital, Dayton, OH '73 (PERS)
WOLF, KARL P., vice-pres. human res., Lakeland Regional Medical Center, Lakeland, FL '82 (PERS)
WOLF, SR. LAURA J., atty., Health Advisory Services, Holy Family Convent of Franciscan Sisters of Christian Charity, Manitowoc, WI '82 (ATTY)
WOLF, MELVIN L., asst. dir. info. serv., Travenol-Compucare, Minneapolis, MN '87 (MGMT)
WOLF, ROGER N., dir. diet., Seton Medical Center, Austin, TX '82 (FOOD)
WOLF, STUART, vice-pres., Specialty Services Group, Bala-Cynwyd, PA '77
WOLF, SUSAN E., acct. exec., Wheelock Associates, Inc., Hanover, NH '85 (PR)
WOLF, TERRY G., mktg. consult., St. Peters, MO '86 (PR) (PLNG)
WOLF, THOMAS A., dir. soc. work and cont. care, Atlanticare Medical Center, Lynn, MA '81 (SOC)
WOLF, WILLIAM JOHN JR., dist. mgr., ARA Services, Riverside Food Production Center, Newport News, VA '85 (FOOD)
WOLFE, DUANE L., coor. facil., Central Nebraska Comprehensive Health Planning Council, Grand Island, NE '74
WOLFE, HARVEY, PhD, prof., University of Pittsburgh, Department of Industrial Engineering, Pittsburgh, PA '69 (MGMT)
WOLFE, JOHN D. JR., mgt. eng., SunHealth Corporation, Charlotte, NC '84 (MGMT)
WOLFER, M. BARBARA, dir. nrsg., Aga Khan University Hospital, Karachi, Pakistan '85 (NURS)
WOLFER, SARA E., RN, asst. adm. nrsg., Memorial Hospital, Hollywood, FL '70 (NURS)
WOLFF, BETTY A., dir. contracting and client serv., corp. mktg., Pacific Presbyterian Medical Center, San Francisco, CA '84 (PLNG)
WOLFF, BETTY J., RN, dir. nrsg. serv., Community Hospital, Elk City, OK '85 (NURS)
WOLFF, BRUCE S., atty., Mount Sinai Medical Center, New York, NY '80 (ATTY)
WOLFF, CAROL R., exec. dir., Area Health Education Center, Camden, NJ '86 (EDUC)
WOLFF, EDWARD C., supv. eng., Imperial Point Medical Center, Fort Lauderdale, FL '86 (ENG)
WOLFF, ELIZABETH F., coor. pub. rel., Moline Public Hospital, Moline, IL '86 (PR)
WOLFF, JANA, dir. mktg., Samaritan Hospital, Troy, NY '86 (PR) (PLNG)
WOLFF, NORA J., coor. vol., AMI Park Plaza Hospital, Houston, TX '84 (VOL)
WOLFF, PETER A., student, Program in Public Health and Hospital Administration, Indiana University, Bloomington, IN '87
WOLFFBRANDT, JAMES, dir. environ. serv., Episcopal Hospital, Philadelphia, PA '86 (ENVIRON)
WOLFGANG, PAUL R., proj. leader, Mount Sinai Medical Center, New York, NY '80 (MGMT)
WOLFGRAM, DONALD G., dir. bldg. and grds., St. Joseph's Hospital, Marshfield, WI '79 (ENG)
WOLFLA, LYMAN H. II, exec. vice-pres., Voluntary Enterprises, Indianapolis, IN '76 (ENG)
WOLFLEY, EUGENE W., dir. matl. mgt., Servicemaster Industries, Inc., Kingsville, TX '80 (PUR)
WOLFMAN, BARRY A., asst. adm., Palms of Pasadena Hospital, St. Petersburg, FL '82
WOLFMEYER, PATRICIA A., dir. plng., AMI Parkway Regional Medical Center, North Miami Beach, FL '82 (PLNG)
WOLFORD, G. RODNEY, pres., Healthlink, Portland, OR '75
WOLFRED, KAREN L., assoc., Laventhol and Horwath, Los Angeles, CA '87 (PR)
WOLFSON, FREDERICK S., atty., Good Samaritan Hospital, Lebanon, PA '80 (ATTY)
WOLFSON, PAMELA, asst. dir. pers., Cabrini Medical Center, New York, NY '85 (PERS)
WOLFSON, RUDOLPH A., pres., Wolfson, Leavitt and Associates, Inc., Chicago, IL '81 (ENG)
WOLINSKY, EUGENE H., pres., Association of Delaware Hospitals, Dover, DE '56 (LIFE)
WOLKE, EUGENE A., dir. qual. assur. and risk mgt., Fort Hamilton-Hughes Memorial Hospital, Hamilton, OH '83 (RISK)
WOLKSTEIN, ANDREW I., dir. facil. matl. mgt., Community Hospital and Health Care System, Cheverly, MD '82 (CS)(PUR)
WOLL, PATRICIA B., dir. emp. rel., Jeanes Hospital, Philadelphia, PA '82 (MGMT)
WOLLARD, DOUGLAS K., dep. mgr. support serv., Department of Health and Hospitals, Denver, CO '76
WOLLETT, PRESTON E., consult., Baltimore, MD '75 (ENG)
WOLLIARD, ANGELA M., RN, vice-pres. pat. care, St. Francis Hospital, Poughkeepsie, NY '75 (NURS)
WOLLMANN, RALPH D., dir. cent. proc. and distrib., St. Luke's Hospitals, Fargo, ND '77 (CS)
WOLLMERING, LAWERENCE E., dir. educ., North Country Hospital, Bemidji, MN '86 (EDUC)
WOLNY, SOPHIE, RN, Chicago Heights, IL '77 (NURS)
WOLOSCHEK, MARY ANN, exec. hskpg. and ldry. mgr., Eagle River Memorial Hospital, Eagle River, WI '86 (ENVIRON)
WOLOSZYN, CLAUDIA T., RN, nrs. counselor, University Hospitals of Cleveland, Cleveland, OH '87 (EDUC)
WOLOZEN, JOHN J. JR., supv. med. auditor, St. Francis Hospital, Jersey City, NJ '76
WOLSCHINA, STEVEN G., atty., Underwood-Memorial Hospital, Woodbury, NJ '85 (ATTY)
WOLSKI, MARY L., pat. advocate, Hurley Medical Center, Flint, MI '85 (PAT)
WOLTZ, CLAUDE C. JR., prod. mgr. med. and sterilant gases, Union Carbide Corporation, Somerset, NJ '85 (CS)
WOLVERTON, GARY C., dir. pers., Morton F. Plant Hospital, Clearwater, FL '78 (PERS)
WOLVERTON, GERRIE, asst. to pres. and pat. rep., Bay Medical Center, Bay City, MI '84 (PAT)(PLNG)
WOLVERTON, MARY K., atty., St. Luke's Hospital, Milwaukee, WI '85 (ATTY)
WOLZ, KENNETH E., New Brighton, MN '49 (LIFE)
WOMACK, CONRAD, dir. plant oper., Hospital Shared Services of Colorado, Denver, CO '81 (ENG)
WOMACK, JO ANNE, mgr. cent. serv., Wake Medical Center, Raleigh, NC '80 (CS)
WOMACK, JUDY, RN, vice-pres. nrsg. serv., Good Samaritan Hospital and Health Center, Dayton, OH '77 (NURS)
WOMACK, TOM, dir. matl. mgt., Rapides General Hospital, Alexandria, LA '86 (PUR)

WOMBLE, BILL R., atty., Doctors Hospital of Dallas, Dallas, TX '84 (ATTY)
WOMBLE, JOHN B., dist. mgr., ARA Services, Hospital Food Management, Environmental Service, Inc., Cleveland, OH '70 (FOOD)
WOMER, CHARLES B., Woodbridge, CT '52 (LIFE)
WONG, ANNA M., med. rec. consult., Natividad Medical Center, Salinas, CA '84
WONG, EDMUND, mgr. eng., University of California San Francisco, San Francisco, CA '79 (ENG)
WONG, EUGENE, chief eng. and maint., St. Elizabeths Hospital, Washington, DC '85 (ENG)
WONG, GEORGE, dir. soc. serv., John F. Kennedy Medical Center, Chicago, IL '84 (SOC)
WONG, MARY, mgr., Arthur Andersen and Company, Oakland, CA '79 (PLNG)
WONG, MELANIE S., dir. plng., Bay Pacific Health Corporation, San Bruno, CA '82 (MGMT)
WONG, OLIVER K., dir. plant oper., Kapiolani Medical Center for Women and Children, Honolulu, HI '87 (ENG)
WONNACOTT, CLARENCE E., (ret.), Salt Lake City, UT '51 (LIFE)
WOO, ALICE C., dir. soc. work, Hospital for Special Surgery, New York, NY '74 (SOC)
WOO, DENNIS, mgr. cent. serv., St. Mary's Hospital of Kankakee, Kankakee, IL '81 (CS)
WOO, PAUL J. JR., sr. vice-pres., Health East, Roanoke, VA '74 (MGMT)
WOOD-WILSON, DORIS, RN, assoc. dir. and nrs. consult., New York City Health and Hospitals Corporation, New York, NY '86 (NURS)
WOOD, ANDREW M., mgr. prog. strategy, Fresno Community Hospital and Medical Center, Fresno, CA '86 (PLNG)
WOOD, BONNIE K., risk mgr., HCA Northeast Community Hospital, Bedford, TX '84 (RISK)
WOOD, CHARLES A., dir. mgt. info. serv., Joslin Diabetes Center, Boston, MA '86 (MGMT)
WOOD, CHARLES T., sr. assoc., Management Systems Institute, Burlington, MA '54 (LIFE)
WOOD, CYNTHIA M., qual. assur. proj. spec.-nrsg., University of Maryland Medical Systems, Baltimore, MD '85 (RISK)
WOOD, DALE ROBERT, vice-pres. oper., Baton Rouge General Medical Center, Baton Rouge, LA '80
WOOD, DARYL, dir. environ. serv., Mecosta County General Hospital, Big Rapids, MI '79 (ENG)
WOOD, DEBORAH D., pat. rep., Lenoir Memorial Hospital, Kinston, NC '81 (PAT)
WOOD, EILEEN, sr. soc. worker, Townsville General Hospital, Queensland, Australia '81 (SOC)
WOOD, EUGENE CHARLES, exec. dir. amb. serv., University of Texas Medical Branch Hospitals, Galveston, TX '85
WOOD, GERARD A., supv. commun., Mount Carmel Mercy Hospital, Detroit, MI '84 (ENG)
WOOD, GREGORY C., vice-pres. adm., Potomac Hospital, Woodbridge, VA '85
WOOD, HILARY A., dir. nrsg., University Hospital, Lexington, KY '85 (NURS)
WOOD, IVAN JR., atty., Sisters of Charity, Houston, TX '77 (ATTY)
WOOD, JACK C., atty., Sisters of Charity Health Care Systems, Houston, TX '68 (ATTY)
WOOD, JAMES ARTHUR, dir. environ. control and safety, St. Joseph's Hospital, Savannah, GA '85 (ENG)
WOOD, JAMES B., adm., Southland Medical Center, Darlington, SC '86
WOOD, JAMES RALPH, pres., Maryland General Hospital, Baltimore, MD '73
WOOD, JANET S. DENNIS, adm. diet., University of Cincinnati Hospital-University Hospital, Cincinnati, OH '86 (FOOD)
WOOD, JEANETTE R., RN, dir. nrsg. serv., Ste Genevieve County Memorial Hospital, Ste Genevieve, MO '84 (NURS)
WOOD, KATHRYN, dir. mktg., Catholic Medical Center of Brooklyn and Queens, Jamaica, NY '85 (PR)
WOOD, CAPT. LESLIE M., MSC USAF, chief clin. eng. and facil., Office of Command Surgeon, Hickam AFB, HI '85 (ENG)
WOOD, LEWIS A. JR., corp. dir. commun. mgt., Ancilla Systems, Inc., Elk Grove Village, IL '78 (PR)
WOOD, LORITA BERRYMAN, exec. vice-pres., Virginia Beach General Hospital, Virginia Beach, VA '74
WOOD, LUCILE A., RN, Omaha, NE '75 (NURS)(RISK)
WOOD, MARK D., mgr. med. serv. and risk mgt., St. Paul Companies, St. Paul, MN '86 (RISK)
WOOD, MARTHA C., asst. dir. dent. health, Massachusetts Department of Public Health, Boston, MA '81 (PR)
WOOD, MARY R., RN, City Island, NY '85 (RISK)
WOOD, MARY S., assoc. tech., University Hospital-University of Nebraska, Omaha, NE '86 (CS)
WOOD, MARY, dir. vol., Vassar Brothers Hospital, Poughkeepsie, NY '79 (VOL)
WOOD, MICHAEL J., pres., Voluntary Hospitals of America, Grand Rapids, MI '76
WOOD, MICHAEL JOSEPH, pres., Mike Wood, Inc., Ponte Vedra Beach, FL '55 (PLNG)(LIFE)
WOOD, PAMELA J., sec. vol. serv., Peninsula General Hospital Medical Center, Salisbury, MD '87 (VOL)
WOOD, PETER W., exec. dir., Clifton Springs Hospital and Clinic, Clifton Springs, NY '78
WOOD, PETER, gen. mgr. commun., Ontario Hospital Association, Don Mills, Ont., Canada '64 (PR)
WOOD, QUIMBY E., Littletown, CO '72 (ENG)
WOOD, REID M., adm., Marcus J. Lawrence Memorial Hospital, Cottonwood, AZ '79
WOOD, RICHARD E., supv. dispatch and distrib., Providence Medical Center, Portland, OR '86 (PUR)
WOOD, ROBERT C., vice-pres., Self Memorial Hospital, Greenwood, SC '70
WOOD, RONALD O., chief fin. off., AMI Doctors' Hospital, Lanham, MD '77
WOOD, ROY C., dir. plant eng., Truman Medical Center-West, Kansas City, MO '84 (ENG)
WOOD, W. CARSON, Fort Myers, FL '82
WOOD, WILLIAM H., atty., Harrisburg Hospital, Harrisburg, PA '76 (ATTY)
WOOD, WILLIAM J., atty., Westview Hospital, Indianapolis, IN '75 (ATTY)
WOOD, WILLIAM K., dir. eng., Corning Hospital, Corning, NY '76 (ENG)
WOOD, WILLIAM W., partner, H. A. Williams and Associates, Columbus, OH '78 (ENG)
WOOD, WILLIAM, dir. risk mgt., Western Reserve Care System, Youngstown, OH '86 (RISK)
WOODALL, HUGH S., dir. soc. serv., Good Samaritan Hospital, Cincinnati, OH '67 (SOC)
WOODALL, J. MARTIN, MD, Jamaica Plain, MA '36 (LIFE)
WOODALL, SHEILA, dir. soc. serv., Paulding Memorial Medical Center, Dallas, GA '86 (SOC)
WOODARD, BARBARA C., RN, asst. adm. nrsg., Presbyterian Hospital, Dallas, TX '82 (NURS)
WOODARD, BARBARA W., meth. coor., Trinity Lutheran Hospital, Kansas City, MO '76 (MGMT)
WOODBURN, CLYDE D., dir. matl. mgt., Menorah Medical Center, Kansas City, MO '86 (PUR)
WOODBURY, SUSAN M., dir. area food serv., Kaiser Sunnyside Medical Center, Clackamas, OR '85 (FOOD)
WOODCOCK, DAVID C., mgr. data proc., Yavapai Regional Medical Center, Prescott, AZ '86 (MGMT)
WOODCOCK, JOHN A. JR., atty., Eastern Maine Medical Center, Bangor, ME '78 (ATTY)
WOODCOCK, SHERRY L., buyer, Yale-New Haven Hospital, New Haven, CT '86 (PUR)
WOODEN, JULIA M., mgt. syst. spec., Maine Medical Center, Portland, ME '82 (MGMT)
WOODERSON, LOUISE, asst. dir. human res., Mid-Columbia Medical Center, The Dalles, OR '86 (PERS)
WOODFORD, JOYCE L., dir. vol., Daniel Freeman Marina Hospital, Marina Del Rey, CA '83 (VOL)
WOODHAM, RAY, pres. emeritus, Presbyterian Hospital, Albuquerque, NM '51 (LIFE)
WOODIN, ERNEST D., mgt. eng. analyst, Mary Imogene Bassett Hospital, Cooperstown, NY '85 (MGMT)
WOODKEY, DONNA L., RN, asst. adm. nrsg., St. Elizabeth Medical Center, Yakima, WA '83 (NURS)
WOODLAND, WILLIAM A., atty., Concord Hospital, Concord, NH '86 (ATTY)
WOODLEY, MILTON B., chief biomedical, Saint Michael's Medical Center, Newark, NJ '85 (ENG)
WOODRING, JEAN, soc. worker, Hardin Memorial Hospital, Elizabethtown, KY '80 (SOC)
WOODROW, RICHARD DAVID, assoc. dir. field work, Columbia University, School of Social Work, New York, NY '84 (SOC)
WOODRUFF, BRUCE E., atty., Christian Hospitals Northeast-Northwest, St. Louis, MO '71 (ATTY)
WOODRUFF, KEVIN J., assoc. mgr., Genesee Hospital, Rochester, NY '84 (FOOD)
WOODS, ADRIANA M., RN, supv. cent. serv., St. Vincent's Hospital and Medical Center, New York, NY '87 (CS)
WOODS, ANN M., soc. worker and coor. admissions, Castle Rest Nursing Home, Syracuse, NY '72 (SOC)
WOODS, BETTY LOU, vice-pres. nrsg. serv., Lewistown Hospital, Lewistown, PA '75 (NURS)
WOODS, BRENDA G., RN, coor. nrsg., Newport News General Hospital, Newport News, VA '87 (NURS)
WOODS, CHERYL Y., asst. dir. bus., St. John Medical Center, Tulsa, OK '82
WOODS, DANIEL J., adm., St. Mary of Nazareth Hospital Center, Chicago, IL '82
WOODS, GERALD D., dir. constr. and licensing, Missouri Division of Health, Jefferson City, MO '53 (LIFE)
WOODS, GERALD W., atty., Medical College of Georgia, Augusta, GA '78 (ATTY)
WOODS, LORENE, cent. sterile tech., Perry Memorial Hospital, Linden, TN '85 (CS)
WOODS, NANCY J., dir. soc. serv., Geisinger Medical Center, Danville, PA '66 (SOC)
WOODS, PATRICIA A., RN, assoc. dir. nrsg., Long Island Jewish Medical Center, New York, NY '80 (NURS)
WOODS, PAULA LOUISE, vice-pres. bus. plng. and prog. dev., National Medical Enterprises, Santa Monica, CA '84 (PLNG)
WOODS, ROBERT A., chief mgt. info. syst., Washington Hospital, Fremont, CA '84 (MGMT)
WOODS, SALLY ANN, RN, dir. allied health serv., Frank Cuneo Memorial Hospital, Chicago, IL '76 (NURS)
WOODS, COL. WILLIAM BENSON, MSC USA, med. coor., Fitzsimons Army Medical Center, Aurora, CO '69
WOODSHANK, MARY ANN, RN, dir. nrsg., St. Margaret's Hospital, Spring Valley, IL '75 (NURS)
WOODSIDE, FRANK C. III, atty., Children's Hospital Medical Center, Cincinnati, OH '76 (ATTY)
WOODSON, DIANNE L., RN, assoc. nrs. adm., Grossmont District Hospital, La Mesa, CA '81 (CS)(NURS)
WOODSON, WILLIAM B., dir. pur., St. Francis Hospital, Charleston, WV '85 (PUR)
WOODWARD, ANITA B., mgr. pat. info., Cleveland Metropolitan General Hospital, Cleveland, OH '84 (PAT)
WOODWARD, CYNTHIA B., dir. commun. rel., Eliza Coffee Memorial Hospital, Florence, AL '86 (PAT)
WOODWARD, ELAINE M., RN, dir. nrsg., Albion Community Hospital, Albion, MI '84 (NURS)
WOODWARD, GERALDINE F., supv. cent. sup., Monongahela Valley Hospital, Monongahela, PA '82 (CS)
WOODWARD, GILBERT L., asst. dir. commun. affairs, Metropolitan Hospital Center, New York, NY '86 (PR)
WOODWARD, JANE, RN, assoc. adm., Framingham Union Hospital, Framingham, MA '68 (NURS)(EDUC)
WOODWARD, KELSEY R., dir. vol. serv., Mary Hitchcock Memorial Hospital, Hanover, NH '84 (VOL)
WOODWARD, MARILYNN E., dir. pur., St. Mary Desert Valley Hospital, Apple Valley, CA '82 (PUR)
WOODWARD, ROBERT L., adm., St. Vincent General Hospital, Leadville, CO '66
WOODY, MARY F., RN, assoc. dir. and dir. nrsg., Emory University Hospital, Atlanta, GA '86 (NURS)
WOODY, PENELOPE, RN, asst. dir. nrsg., Cape Cod Hospital, Hyannis, MA '84 (NURS)
WOOLARD, CHARLES T., mgr. safety, Heartland Hospital West, St. Joseph, MO '72 (ENG)
WOOLARD, WILLIAM H., Demorest, GA '81 (PLNG)
WOOLDRIDGE, MARK, atty., Cooper County Memorial Hospital, Boonville, MO '80 (ATTY)
WOOLE, BILLIE V. JR., dir. prod. mgt., Critikon, Inc., Tampa, FL '84 (PLNG)
WOOLEY, WAYNE BERNARD, asst. mgr. hskpg., Shallowford Community Hospital, Chamblee, GA '86
WOOLLEY, LEWIS E., AMI Doctors' Hospital, Lanham, MD '85 (ENG)
WOOLMAN, LARRY M., dir. bus. off., HCA Deer Park Hospital, Deer Park, TX '84
WOOLWINE, FAY ANNE, dir. vol. serv., AMI Doctors' Hospital, Lanham, MD '86 (VOL)
WOOTEN, GILBERT, risk mgr., Memorial Hospital, Ormond Beach, FL '82 (RISK)
WOOTTEN, WANDA L., dir. environ. serv., Rebsamen Regional Medical Center, Jacksonville, AR '86 (ENVIRON)
WOOTTON, CLYDE A., atty., Blue Cross and Blue Shield of North Carolina, Durham, NC '80 (ATTY)
WOOTTON, RICHARD H., atty., St. Joseph's Regional Health Center, Hot Springs National Park, AR '83 (ATTY)
WORBETZ, PAUL, dir. maint., Carrier Foundation, Belle Mead, NJ '81 (ENG)
WORD, LINDA S., dir. educ. and commun. serv., Missouri Baptist Hospital, St. Louis, MO '86 (EDUC)
WORDAL, MILTON O., atty., Montana Deaconess Medical Center, Great Falls, MT '80 (ATTY)
WORGUL, DOUGLAS R., dir. mktg. serv., Bronson Methodist Hospital, Kalamazoo, MI '84 (PR) (PLNG)
WORK, DOROTHY D., asst. vice-pres. mktg., Methodist Hospitals of Memphis, Memphis, TN '83 (PR)
WORKMAN, DONNA J., supv. cent. sup., Western Medical Center, Santa Ana, CA '77 (CS)
WORKMAN, JOHN R., dir. prof. serv., Erlanger Medical Center, Chattanooga, TN '86
WORKMAN, SUSAN K., health plng. consult., Michigan Hospital Association Service Corporation, Lansing, MI '83 (PLNG)
WORKS, PHILLIS A., mgr. emp., Jefferson Regional Medical Center, Pine Bluff, AR '85 (PERS)
WORLEY, JOHN DAVID JR., adm., Mary Greeley Medical Center, Ames, IA '57 (LIFE)
WORLEY, JUANITA JEAN, RN, dir. in-patient and outpatient surg. serv., Cabell Huntington Hospital, Huntington, WV '85 (NURS)
WORRAL, STEVEN F., asst. adm., St. Helen Hospital, Chehalis, WA '81 (PLNG)
WORRELL, GARY L., adm., Black Hills Community Hospital, Olympia, WA '72
WORRELL, RODNEY A., vice-pres., Mulhauser-McCleary Associates, Inc., Dallas, TX '82 (FOOD)
WORRILOW, LEE S., dir. pub. rel., Bryn Mawr Hospital, Bryn Mawr, PA '69 (PR)
WORTH, JANET CLARK, pat. rep., Hamilton County Nursing Home, Chattanooga, TN '86 (PAT)
WORTH, KAREN, dir. matl. serv., St. Elizabeth Community Health Center, Lincoln, NE '77 (PUR)
WORTHAM, ELIZABETH DYER, assoc. dir. nrsg. educ., Le Bonheur Children's Medical Center, Memphis, TN '81 (EDUC)
WORTHEN, JEFFREY S., asst. adm. amb. serv., Alta View Hospital, Sandy, UT '82 (AMB)
WORTHEN, LEE KENT, chief environ., Veterans Administration, Department of Medicine and Surgery, Washington, DC '74 (ENVIRON)
WORTHEN, PATRICIA A., dir. soc. serv., Hospital of the Good Samaritan, Los Angeles, CA '86 (SOC)
WORTHINGTON, CAROLYN H., dir. educ. and pub. rel., Dorminy Medical Center, Fitzgerald, GA '84 (EDUC)(PR)
WORTHY, SHIRLEY A., Chicago, IL '78 (ATTY)
WORTLEY, MITCHEL L., vice-pres., Watkins Carter Hamilton Architects, Bellaire, TX '86 (ENG)
WORTLEY, NEIL C., adm. emeritus, Lester E. Cox Medical Centers, Springfield, MO '52 (PLNG)(LIFE)
WOTTOWA, PEGGY A., coor. nrsg. educ., Memorial Hospital, Belleville, IL '82 (EDUC)
WOULFIN, ARNOLD C., asst. adm., Bayonne Hospital, Bayonne, NJ '84
WOYNA, SUSAN J., atty., Children's Hospital and Medical Center, Seattle, WA '85 (ATTY)
WOZNIAK, GLORIA, mgr. emp. and emp. rel., Danbury Hospital, Danbury, CT '73 (PERS)
WOZNIAK, KATHLEEN A., asst. chief eng., Veterans Administration Medical Center, Hampton, VA '83 (ENG)
WOZNIAK, LOIS M., coor. pat. educ., St. Charles Hospital, Oregon, OH '84 (EDUC)
WOZNIAK, PAUL R., pres., Little Company of Mary Hospital, Evergreen Park, IL '56 (PLNG)(LIFE)
WOZNIAK, SUE A., buyer, Lapeer General Hospital, LaPeer, MI '82 (PUR)
WOZNISKY, JOHN M., vice-pres. mktg., Graduate Hospital, Philadelphia, PA '81 (PR)
WRABL, CAROL A., RN, vice-pres. pat. care serv., St. John's Regional Medical Center, Joplin, MO '83 (NURS)
WRAY, BRUCE J., dir. pers., Gratiot Community Hospital, Alma, MI '83 (PERS)
WREN, BETTY J., coor. cent. serv., Baptist Medical Center-Princeton, Birmingham, AL '81 (CS)
WREN, GEORGE R., PhD, (ret.), Clarkston, GA '51 (MGMT)(LIFE)
WRIGHT, ALBERT J., Trw Medical Electronics, San Diego, CA '83 (ENG)
WRIGHT, ARTHUR M., atty., Kent and Queen Anne's Hospital, Chestertown, MD '82 (ATTY)
WRIGHT, BARBARA J., RN, vice-pres. nrsg., Camden-Clark Memorial Hospital, Parkersburg, WV '82 (NURS)
WRIGHT, BARBARA SUE, mgr. distrib., St. Mary-Corwin Hospital Regional Medical and Health Center, Pueblo, CO '85 (CS)

WRIGHT, BARRY L., dir. emp. rel., Touro Infirmary, New Orleans, LA '74 (PERS)

WRIGHT, BETTY, dir. pur., Whidden Memorial Hospital, Everett, MA '77 (PUR)

WRIGHT, CARMEN G., dir. soc. serv., Children's Mercy Hospital, Kansas City, MO '86 (SOC)

WRIGHT, CARNEY W., adm., Memorial Hospital, Clarksville, TN '52 (LIFE)

WRIGHT, CAROLE A., dir. telecommun., Centinela Hospital Medical Center, Inglewood, CA '86 (ENG)

WRIGHT, CAROLYN J., RN, asst. adm. nrsg. serv., Madison Memorial Hospital, Rexburg, ID '82 (NURS)

WRIGHT, CATHERINE A., dir. commun. affairs, Community Hospital of Bedford, Bedford, OH '84 (PR)

WRIGHT, CATHERINE P., dir. pub. rel., Riverview Hospital Association, Crookston, MN '80 (PR)

WRIGHT, CYNTHIA ANN, dir. soc. serv., Humana Hospital -Lucerne, Orlando, FL '80 (SOC)

WRIGHT, DAVID B., atty., Salem Hospital, Salem, MA '78 (ATTY)

WRIGHT, DONALD A., dir. eng., Daniel Freeman Memorial Hospital, Inglewood, CA '86 (ENG)

WRIGHT, DOUGLAS E., dir. matl. mgt., Franklin Regional Hospital, Franklin, NH '76 (PUR)

WRIGHT, E. T. JR., dir. plant oper., Spring Shadows Glen, Houston, TX '87 (ENG)

WRIGHT, ELAHVONNE, pers. asst., St. Joseph's Mercy Hospital, Centerville, IA '78 (PAT)

WRIGHT, ELDON S., atty., Western Reserve Care System, Youngstown, OH '77 (ATTY)

WRIGHT, GORDON L., dir. pers. rel., Texas Hospital Association, Austin, TX '70 (PERS)

WRIGHT, HARRY S., Network, Inc., Chester, NJ '81

WRIGHT, JAMES N., dir. risk mgt. and qual. assur., Farmers Insurance Group, Los Angeles, CA '80 (RISK)

WRIGHT, JAMES P., chief eng., Humana Hospital -Springfield, Springfield, IL '85 (ENG)

WRIGHT, JAMES S., sr. partner, Page Southerland Page, Dallas, TX '69

WRIGHT, JANE E., dir. pur., Kimball Medical Center, Lakewood, NJ '80 (PUR)

WRIGHT, JEAN A., dir. pub. rel., Fairbanks Hospital, Indianapolis, IN '85 (PR)

WRIGHT, JENETTE, RN, consult., Ashen and Allen, San Francisco, CA '86

WRIGHT, KEVIN W., owner, Kevin Wright, Inc., Memphis, TN '86 (ENG)

WRIGHT, KITT, dir. cent. serv., St. Anthony's Hospital, Amarillo, TX '83 (CS)

WRIGHT, LARRY K., dir. food serv., Rogue Valley Medical Center, Medford, OR '82 (FOOD)

WRIGHT, LEIGH S., RN, dir. educ., AMI Brookwood Community Hospital, Orlando, FL '84 (EDUC)

WRIGHT, M. RICHARD, PhD, asst. vice-pres. plng., Alexian Brothers Health Systems Inc., Elk Grove Village, IL '77 (PLNG)

WRIGHT, MARJORIE R., RN, asst. prof., University of Texas School of Nursing, Arlington, TX '81 (NURS)

WRIGHT, MELISSA L., dir. commun. rel., Muhlenberg Hospital Center, Bethlehem, PA '84 (PR)

WRIGHT, MOLLY L., clin. coor., Medical College of Virginia Hospitals, Virginia Commonwealth University-Department of Rehabilitation, Richmond, VA '86 (SOC)

WRIGHT, NANCY, risk mgr., Mount Sinai Hospital Medical Center, Chicago, IL '86 (RISK)

WRIGHT, PAT, dir. pat. rep., Baptist Medical Center of Oklahoma, Oklahoma City, OK '78 (PAT)

WRIGHT, PATRICIA A., asst. dir. pers. serv., Merced Community Medical Center, Merced, CA '86 (PERS)

WRIGHT, PATRICIA ANN, dir. matl. mgt., Brookhaven Memorial Hospital Medical Center, Patchogue, NY '62 (PUR)

WRIGHT, PATRICIA F., dir. pat. and family serv., Sacred Heart Hospital, Cumberland, MD '77 (SOC)

WRIGHT, PEGGY B., dir. vol. serv., Good Samaritan Medical Center, Phoenix, AZ '82 (VOL)

WRIGHT, RHEY, dir. plng. and mktg., Poudre Valley Hospital, Fort Collins, CO '84 (PLNG)

WRIGHT, RICHARD A., vice-pres., Johnson and Johnson Hospital Services, New Brunswick, NJ '87 (AMB)

WRIGHT, RICHARD E., adm. dir. risk mgt. serv., Geisinger Medical Center, Danville, PA '79 (RISK)

WRIGHT, RICHARD L., dir. plant oper., Coast Plaza Medical Center, Norwalk, CA '84 (ENG)

WRIGHT, ROBERT A., coor. med. dist., Veterans Administration Medical Center, Memphis, TN '79

WRIGHT, ROBERT E., vice-pres., Mercy Health Center, Oklahoma City, OK '79 (PLNG)

WRIGHT, ROBERT ROY, exec. dir., Healthchoice, Orlando, FL '84 (PLNG)

WRIGHT, STEPHEN A., dir. hskpg., Providence Medical Center, Portland, OR '86 (ENVIRON)

WRIGHT, SUSAN D., dir. soc. serv., Silver Cross Hospital, Joliet, IL '79 (SOC)

WRIGHT, TARLENE, supv. cent. serv., Evergreen Hospital Medical Center, Kirkland, WA '82 (CS)

WRIGHT, VIRGINIA M., mgr. health serv. plng., Intermountain Health Care, Inc., Salt Lake City, UT '82 (PLNG)

WRIGHT, WILLIAM, eng., Children's Hospital, Boston, MA '76 (ENG)

WRIGHTSON, BARBARA S. C., assoc. plng., Melrose-Wakefield Hospital, Melrose, MA '87 (PLNG)

WRIGLEY, SUSAN R., coor. productivity, Glens Falls Hospital, Glens Falls, NY '86 (MGMT)

WRITT, PETER M., dir. pharm. and cent. serv., Bay Area Medical Center, Marinette, WI '80 (CS)

WROBLEWSKI, BONITA, dir. diet. serv., St. Anthony Hospital, Milwaukee, WI '87 (FOOD)

WROBLEWSKI, DANIEL, mgr. matl. mgt., Christ Hospital and Medical Center, Oak Lawn, IL '84 (PUR)

WRONSKI, MICHAEL S., dir. pub. rel., Saint Vincent Hospital, Worcester, MA '83 (PR)

WU, DAVID T., bus. mgr., Outer Drive Hospital, Lincoln Park, MI '80

WU, DELIA L., dir. pers. serv., Methodist Hospital of Southern California, Arcadia, CA '84 (PERS)

WUENSCHE, DORIS J., dir. nrsg. in-service, Citizens Medical Center, Victoria, TX '84 (EDUC)

WULF, MICHAEL E., reg. mgr., Radius Health Care System, Inc., Bettendorf, IA '84 (MGMT)

WULFF, KAREN S., RN, asst. adm., University Hospital, Seattle, WA '83 (NURS)

WUNSCH, LEE R., Gulf State Advertising Agency, Houston, TX '84 (PR)

WURM, ALBERT J., adm. dir. commun. mental health center, Divine Providence Hospital, Williamsport, PA '82

WURST, BOBBIJEAN, supv. cent. sup., Watertown Memorial Hospital, Watertown, WI '78 (CS)

WURST, ROGER L., dir. food serv., Deaconess Medical Center, Billings, MT '85 (FOOD)

WURSTNER, JUDY P., RN, Humana Hospital -Medical City Dallas, Dallas, TX '81 (NURS)

WURTH, MARIE V., dir. human and commun. res., Sierra Vista Community Hospital, Sierra Vista, AZ '85 (PLNG)

WURTZEL, HAROLD A., exec. vice-pres., Pacific Health Resources, Los Angeles, CA '81 (PLNG)

WYAND, JOHN E., dir. plng., St. Vincent Hospital and Health Center, Indianapolis, IN '84 (PLNG)

WYATT, BLAINE R., dir. plng., St. Francis Regional Medical Center, Wichita, KS '82 (PLNG)

WYATT, CHERYL L., consult., Ernst and Whinney, Richmond, VA '83 (MGMT)

WYATT, KATHY, dir. telecommun., Baptist Medical Center of Oklahoma, Oklahoma City, OK '87 (ENG)

WYATT, LANDON D., actg. dir. facil. mgt., Moses H. Cone Memorial Hospital, Greensboro, NC '84 (ENG)

WYATT, LYNN, dir. soc. serv., HCA Bourbon General Hospital, Paris, KY '86 (SOC)

WYATT, ROBERT W., RN, dir. nrsg., HCA Regional Hospital of Jackson, Jackson, TN '84 (NURS)

WYATT, SHERRY ANN, coor. guest rel., Maryview Hospital, Portsmouth, VA '85 (PAT)

WYATT, SONNY, dir. ldry. and linen serv., Greenville Hospital System, Greenville, SC '86 (ENVIRON)

WYCHE, EVERETT H. JR., dir. safety and risk mgt., St. Mary's Hospital and Health Center, Tucson, AZ '83 (RISK)

WYCKOFF, CLARENCE R., asst. plant mgr., Memorial Hospital of Burlington County, Mount Holly, NJ '82 (ENG)

WYCKOFF, ELAINE C., RN, pat. rep., St. Francis Hospital, Roslyn, NY '82 (PAT)

WYCKOFF, JOHN W., unit adm., Terrell State Hospital, Terrell, TX '85

WYCKOFF, MARK A., student, Iowa State University, Ames, IA '86 (MGMT)

WYDICK, GAY C., dir. matl. mgt., Ohio County Hospital, Hartford, KY '82 (PUR)

WYDICK, KAREN, dir. diet. serv., Heartland Hospital West, St. Joseph, MO '77 (FOOD)

WYERS, RICHARD, owner, Consolidated Healthcare Service, Inc., Birmingham, AL '87

WYLIE, LT. COL. JOHN VINCENT, San Antonio, TX '75

WYLIE, LARRY G., dir. environ. serv., Baylor Medical Center at Waxahachie, Waxahachie, TX '85 (ENG)

WYLIE, LAWRENCE G., vice-pres., Fred S. James and Company, Inc., Short Hills, NJ '85 (RISK)

WYLIE, MARCIA A., asst. dir. eng., Cecil H. and Ida M. Green Hospital of Scripps Clinic, La Jolla, CA '84 (ENG)

WYLIE, SHEILA M., sr. mgt. eng., Mount Sinai Medical Center, Miami Beach, FL '85 (MGMT)

WYMAN, ALAN, coor. mktg., Atlanticare Medical Center, Lynn, MA '86 (PLNG)

WYMAN, EVELYN, student, Suffolk University, Boston, MA '77 (EDUC)

WYMER, JOHN FRANCIS JR., adm. emeritus, Good Samaritan Hospital, West Palm Beach, FL '48 (LIFE)

WYNN, ROBERT L. III, atty., Mary Black Memorial Hospital, Spartanburg, SC '76 (ATTY)

WYNSTRA, NANCY A., sr. vice-pres. and gen. council, Allegheny General Hospital, Pittsburgh, PA '79 (ATTY)

WYSE, NANCY L., mgr. matl., Midland Hospital Center, Midland, MI '81 (CS)

WYSOCKI, THERESA GRZYB, RN, New Orleans, LA '82 (NURS)

WYTHE, KATHY PORTER, coor. commun. rel., Medical Center Hospital, Odessa, TX '84 (PR)

WYVOCKI, JUDY, supv. oper. room serv., St. Luke's Hospital, Davenport, IA '87 (AMB)

X

XAVIER, KAREN, dir. family serv., Shriners Hospital for Crippled Children, San Francisco, CA '86 (SOC)

Y

YABLON, MARSHALL S., chm., Diversified Health Resources, Inc., Chicago, IL '67

YABLONKA, ERIC B., mgr. date commun., William Beaumont Hospital-Troy, Troy, MI '84 (ENG)

YABLONSKI, PEGGY G., dir. vol., Community Medical Center, Scranton, PA '80 (VOL)

YABROUDY, JANET E., asst. to dir. pur., New York Eye and Ear Infirmary, New York, NY '85 (PUR)

YACONE, FRANK R., Indianapolis, IN '83

YACOS, NADINE A., asst. vice-pres. nrsg. educ. and res., Children's Medical Center, Dayton, OH '85 (EDUC)

YADGOOD, MAUREEN CIRBEE, Melrose, MA '86 (NURS)

YAEGE, GLEN B., student, School of Health Care Sciences, U. S. Air Force, Sheppard AFB, TX '80

YAEGER, PAUL M., vice-pres. plng., Cedars-Sinai Medical Center, Los Angeles, CA '85 (PLNG)

YAEGER, THERESA J., dir. compensation, Providence Hospital, Southfield, MI '86 (PERS)

YAFFE, HARRY, pres. and chief exec. off., Beth Israel Hospital, Denver, CO '57 (LIFE)

YAGER, BERTA, dir. vol. serv., University Psychiatric Serivces, Omaha, NE '75 (VOL)

YAGER, MARY ELIZABETH, (ret.), St. Petersburg, FL '19 (LIFE)

YAGERLENER, WILLIAM G., dir. commun. rel. and dev., Brighton Hospital, Brighton, MI '85 (PR)

YAHN, JAMES F., dir. sup., proc. and distrib., Methodist Hospital of Southern California, Arcadia, CA '85 (PUR)

YAHNER, CAPT. ANN S., RN, head amb. nrsg., Naval Hospital, Bethesda, MD '87 (AMB)

YAHNKE, MARY A., mgr. matl., Redlands Community Hospital, Redlands, CA '78 (PUR)

YAHRAUS, DALE A., mgr. matl., Kaiser Foundation Hospital, Sacramento, CA '86 (PUR)

YALE-MADURA, KATHRYN A., dir. soc. serv., Quakertown Community Hospital, Quakertown, PA '85 (SOC)

YAMAGUCHI, JANE L., coor. soc. serv., St. Agnes Hospital and Medical Center, Fresno, CA '85 (SOC)

YAMAMOTO, AIMEE K. SUZUKI, dir. soc. work, G. N. Wilcox Memorial Hospital, Lihue, HI '81 (SOC)

YAMAMOTO, MARGARET, dir. pub. rel., Lawrence General Hospital, Lawrence, MA '85 (PR)

YAMANE, AILEEN A., dir. vol., Kuakini Medical Center, Honolulu, HI '82 (VOL)

YAMANISHI, KEI, asst. dir. commun., University of California at Los Angeles Medical Center, Los Angeles, CA '86 (ENG)

YAMANOUCHI, KENNETH K., vice-pres. med. oper., Cigna Health Plan of Arizona, Phoenix, AZ '72

YAMASAKI, BARBARA LEE, supv. cent. serv., emer. room and oper. room, Navy Medical Clinic, Pearl Harbor, HI '78 (CS)

YAMAZAKI, MARY H., dir. pur., Adventist Health System-North, Hinsdale, IL '80 (PUR)

YANCER, DEBORAH A., RN, Heartland Hospital West, St. Joseph, MO '81 (NURS)

YANCEY, STEVE, asst. adm. dir., Sycamore Hospital, Miamisburg, OH '80 (ENG)

YANCOSKIE, TOM, student, Southern Illinois University, School of Technical Careers, Carbondale, IL '86

YANCY, ISAIAH A., acct. mgr., Maritz Motivation Company, Preoductivity Division, Atlanta, GA '86 (MGMT)(PERS)

YANDEL, LAURENCE C., dir. educ., St. Joseph's Hospital and Medical Center, Phoenix, AZ '83 (EDUC)

YANDELL, LLOYD W., dir. bldg. and grds., Kaiser Foundation Hospital, San Francisco, CA '86 (ENG)

YANDRIC, RICHARD A., mgt. eng., Sinai Hospital of Detroit, Detroit, MI '85 (MGMT)

YANEZ, LUIS M., asst. dir. mgt. syst., Stanford University Hospital, Palo Alto, CA '84 (MGMT)

YANG, JIUNHONG, mgt. eng., Mount Sinai Medical Center, Miami Beach, FL '84 (MGMT)

YANG, SHENG TSAN, student, Graduate Program in Hospital Administration, China Medical College, Taichung City Taiwan, Republic of China '86 (PERS)

YANG, THOMAS C., asst. dir. maint., Southern Baptist Hospital, New Orleans, LA '79 (ENG)

YANICH, GEORGE M., sr. mgr., Ernst and Whinney, Cleveland, OH '85 (MGMT)

YANIGLOS, JANET, plng analyst and asst. to pres., Our Lady of Mercy Hospital, Dyer, IN '80 (PLNG)

YANISH, JOSEPH J., adm. off. surg., Veterans Administration Medical Center, Brooklyn, NY '85

YANK, GREGORY F., exec. dir., Western Catholic Health Collaborative, Oakland, CA '75

YANKOUSKI, LOWELL D., dir. matl. mgt., Wausau Hospital Center, Wausau, WI '74 (PUR)

YANKOVIC, OLIVE B., dir. environ. serv., Robinson Memorial Hospital, Ravenna, OH '86 (ENVIRON)

YANKOVICH, JOHN J., vice-pres. pers., Hutcheson Medical Center, Fort Oglethorpe, GA '83 (PERS)

YANNA, DAN D., plant eng., Reading Rehabilitation Hospital, Reading, PA '83 (ENG)

YANNITELLI, PETER F., dir. syst. eng., Samaritan Health Service, Phoenix, AZ '78 (MGMT)

YANOSKY, JOSEPH JR., supv. syst., Ochsner Foundation Hospital, New Orleans, LA '80 (ENG)

YAP, ESTHER, mgt. eng., Kaiser Permanente Medical Care Program, Los Angeles, CA '80 (MGMT)

YAPUNDICH, ROSE M., dir. soc. serv., Anne Arundel General Hospital, Annapolis, MD '85 (SOC)

YARBOROUGH, NEWELL D. JR., dir. plng. and government rel., Georgia Hospital Association, Atlanta, GA '85 (PLNG)

YARBOROUGH, RICHARD F. JR., atty., Marion County General Hospital, Columbia, MS '84 (ATTY)

YARBROUGH, JAMES R., dir. food serv., Hotel Dieu Hospital, New Orleans, LA '69 (FOOD)

YARBROUGH, MARY G., RN, chief oper. off., Mercy Hospital and Medical Center, San Diego, CA '81 (NURS)

YARISH, JOHN A., dir. plant oper. and maint., Louis A. Weiss Memorial Hospital, Chicago, IL '82 (ENG)

YARMEL, JOHN, pur. agt., Nesbitt Memorial Hospital, Kingston, PA '83 (PUR)

YARNO, JANET, supv. cent. sup., Riverside Medical Center, Kankakee, IL '83 (CS)

YARNOLD, MARK S., dir. soc. work, Monmouth Medical Center, Long Branch, NJ '74 (SOC)

YAROCH, W. STEPHEN, supt. maint., Camden County Health Services Center, Blackwood, NJ '85 (ENG)

YARSAWICH, JEAN M., diet. syst. spec., Lifeline Systems, Inc., Watertown, MA '78 (FOOD)

YAST, HELEN T., Oak Park, IL '75 (LIFE)
YATES, BRENDA C., dir. pers., Buchanan General Hospital, Grundy, VA '80 (PERS)
YATES, CAROLYN JOHNSTON, coor. vol. serv., AMI Saint Joseph Hospital, Omaha, NE '76 (VOL)
YATES, COLIN DAVID, exec. dir., Armed Forces Hospital, Jubail, Saudi Arabia '86
YATES, DOROTHY J., RN, supv. cent. proc., Charter Northside Community Hospital, Macon, GA '85 (CS)
YATES, JANE H., vice-pres. consumer affairs and pub. rel., Johnson and Johnson, New Brunswick, NJ '85 (PAT)
YATES, JOHN EARL, dir. hskpg. serv., Hot Spring County Memorial Hospital, Malvern, AR '77 (PERS)(ENVIRON)
YATES, LINDA L., soc. worker, United Hospital, Grand Forks, ND '74 (SOC)
YATES, MARY E., RN, clin. mgr., Bay Medical Center, Bay City, MI '85 (NURS)
YATES, ROBERT H. JR., mgr. matl., Doctors Hospital, Columbus, GA '82 (PUR)
YATES, STEVEN L., sr. mgt. eng., University Hospital-University of Nebraska, Omaha, NE '87 (MGMT)
YAUGER, JOHN THOMAS, vice-pres., M. D. Search, Inc., Norcross, GA '84 (PR)
YAVITZ, RANDALL S., atty., Hospital Corporation of America, Nashville, TN '86 (ATTY)
YAVOROSKY, FRANK E., dir. matl. mgt., Henry Heywood Memorial Hospital, Gardner, MA '81 (PUR)
YAW, RONALD D., (ret.), Port Royal, SC '47 (LIFE)
YAWN, BUDDY, pur. agt., AMI Brookwood Community Hospital, Orlando, FL '83 (PUR)
YAWNEY, B. ANN, dir. soc. serv., Fanny Allen Hospital, Winooski, VT '73 (SOC)
YBARRA, ANTHONY M., mgr. matl., American Healthcare Management, Inc., Dallas, TX '80 (PUR)
YBARRA, CAPT. ROMAN JR., MSC USAF, dir. med. plans and readiness, U. S. Air Force Hospital Elmendorf, Anchorage, AK '78
YEAGER, MARY F., RN, assoc. dir. nrsg., University of Virginia Hospitals, Charlottesville, VA '81 (NURS)
YEAGER, R. BRUCE, vice-pres., Hospital Billing Analysis, Inc., Pasadena, CA '86
YEAKEL, MARGARET K., student, Georgia State University-Institute of Health Administration, Atlanta, GA '86
YEARGAIN, EVE W., vice-pres., The Marketing Works, Austin, TX '82 (PLNG)
YEARICK, ALLEN F. JR., assoc. adm., Abbott-Northwestern Hospital, Minneapolis, MN '81
YEATON, CECELIA E., dir. risk mgt., Hillcrest Hospital, Pittsfield, MA '81 (RISK)
YEDOR, DAVID C., dir. eng., Anaheim Memorial Hospital, Anaheim, CA '85 (ENG)
YEDVAB, JAY OKUN, exec. dir., Bergen Pines County Hospital, Paramus, NJ '61
YEE, ALAN MICHAEL, mgt. eng., West Virginia University Hospitals, Morgantown, WV '83
YEE, JUNE, dir. soc. work, Colonel Belcher Hospital, Calgary, Alta., Canada '81 (SOC)
YEE, YIM CHING, dir. pur. and sup., Gouverneur Hospital, New York, NY '86 (PUR)
YELDELL, SHARON E., dir. educ., Cooper Green Hospital, Birmingham, AL '86 (EDUC)
YELLAN, ROBERT J., vice-pres. govt. and regulatory affairs, Detroit Medical Center, Lansing, MI '84 (PLNG)
YELLON, JUDITH ERIKA, dir. soc. serv., Baltimore County General Hospital, Randallstown, MD '78 (SOC)
YELTON, MICHAEL L., dir. educ. serv., Providence Hospital, Columbia, SC '81 (EDUC)
YEMM, DONNA J., staff dev., Decatur Memorial Hospital, Decatur, IL '86 (EDUC)
YEOMAN, HOWARD, dir. mktg. serv., North Colorado Medical Center, Greeley, CO '86 (PLNG)
YEOMANS, RICHARD C., MSC USAF, adm. and risk mgr., U. S. Air Force Regional Hospital, Sheppard AFB, TX '65 (RISK)
YERDEN, THOMAS R., gen. mgr., Anesthesia Service Medical Grp, Outpat Service, Inc., San Diego, CA '87 (AMB)
YERKES, WILLIAM S., dir. environ. serv., North Shore Medical Center, Miami, FL '86 (ENVIRON)
YESSO, JOHN M., oper. res. analyst, Ohio Medical Indemnity Mutual Corporation, Worthington, OH '84 (MGMT)
YESTER, HENRY RICHARD, dir. matl. mgt., North Hills Passavant Hospital, Pittsburgh, PA '62 (PUR)
YETTER, SR. MARIE, dir. educ., Sacred Heart Hospital, Cumberland, MD '83 (EDUC)
YIELDING, RONALD E., assoc. adm., Lac-King-Drew Medical Center, Los Angeles, CA '68
YINGLING, ROBERT JAMES, asst. dean adm., Rockford School of Medicine, Rockford, IL '68 (PERS)
YINGST, 2ND LT. THOMAS E. III, MSC USAF, dir. med. res. mgt., U. S. Air Force Hospital, Oscoda, MI '83
YISRAEL, WILDA MOORE, mgr. matl., St. Charles General Hospital, New Orleans, LA '79 (PUR)
YOCHUM, RICHARD E., vice-pres. adm., Pomona Valley Community Hospital, Pomona, CA '75
YODER, ANNA F., RN, dir. amb. nrsg. serv., Beth Israel Hospital, Boston, MA '79 (NURS)
YODER, CYNTHIA K., dir. nutr. serv., Washington County Hospital, Hagerstown, MD '82 (FOOD)
YODER, DALE M., Kenosha, WI '86 (ENVIRON)
YOHONN, DONNA M., dir. soc. work serv., New London Hospital, New London, NH '85 (SOC)
YONALLY, BRENDA S., RN, dir. nrsg., Howard Community Hospital, Kokomo, IN '81 (NURS)
YONGUE, MICKEY G., dir. pub. rel., Athens Regional Medical Center, Athens, GA '83 (PR)
YONKOSKI, RONALD P., dir. food serv., Chelsea Community Hospital, Chelsea, MI '82 (FOOD)
YONKSTELTER, W. DENNIS, prin., Innovative Health Association, Los Angeles, CA '86 (PLNG)
YORDY, ALAN R., dir. commun. rel., Sacred Heart General Hospital, Eugene, OR '85 (PR)
YORK, BART, vice-pres., Methodist Hospital of Indiana, Indianapolis, IN '79 (ENG)
YORK, CHARLES M., dir. site support, Oklahoma Memorial Hospital and Clinics, Oklahoma City, OK '64 (ENG)
YORK, FRAN, dir. vol. league, St. Anthony Hospital, Oklahoma City, OK '68 (VOL)
YORK, JAMES MICHAEL, assoc. dir. eng. and comptr, Mount Sinai Medical Center, New York, NY '86 (ENG)
YORK, KARL H., (ret.), Racine, WI '46 (LIFE)
YORK, LAWRENCE R., pres., Larry York and Associates, Inc., Portland, OR '76
YORK, M. KEITH, atty., Habersham County Medical Center, Demorest, GA '82 (ATTY)
YORK, NORMAN, supv. cent. sup., Santa Barbara Cottage Hospital, Santa Barbara, CA '82 (CS)
YORLANO, JOHN C., corp. vice-pres., Center for Health Affairs, Princeton, NJ '86 (PLNG)
YOSHIDA, KEN, PhD, University of Calgary, Department of Community Health Sciences, Faculty of Medicine, Calgary, Alta., Canada '84 (ENG)
YOST, JOHN H., asst. dir. food serv., St. Francis Hospital, Wilmington, DE '83 (FOOD)
YOST, KAREN E., RN, assoc. adm. nrsg., Pocono Hospital, East Stroudsburg, PA '84 (NURS)
YOST, LEONARD W., asst. dir. fin., Illinois Masonic Medical Center, Chicago, IL '80 (RISK)
YOUNCE, JAMES E., dir. clin. eng., Providence Hospital, Mobile, AL '81 (ENG)
YOUNG-DREXLER, JUDY, asst. dir. mgt., American College of Emergency Physicians, Dallas, TX '86 (RISK)
YOUNG-MCKENZIE, IVA C., RN, assoc. dir. nrsg., Howard University Hospital, Washington, DC '83 (NURS)
YOUNG, ALMA T., asst. dir. soc. work serv., Mount Sinai Medical Center, New York, NY '76 (SOC)
YOUNG, ANITA H., dir. commun. rel., Plantation General Hospital, Plantation, FL '80 (PR)
YOUNG, ANN E., dir. vol., Lowell General Hospital, Lowell, MA '83 (VOL)
YOUNG, ANN YAEGER, atty., Memorial Mission Hospital, Asheville, NC '80 (ATTY)
YOUNG, ANNA MAY, RN, dir. nrsg., Delaware Valley Medical Center, Langhorne, PA '79 (NURS)
YOUNG, ARLENE, coor. risk mgt., Franklin General Hospital, Valley Stream, NY '80 (RISK)
YOUNG, BARBARA E., mgr. matl., Hunt Memorial Hospital, Danvers, MA '80 (PUR)
YOUNG, BRENDA, dir. soc. work, William Beaumont Hospital, Royal Oak, MI '84 (SOC)
YOUNG, BRETT M., dir. clin. eng., Marquette General Hospital, Marquette, MI '84 (ENG)
YOUNG, CATHY, supv. soc. serv., St. Anthony Medical Center, Columbus, OH '85 (SOC)
YOUNG, CHARLES T., adm. gen. serv., Polyclinic Medical Center of Harrisburg, Harrisburg, PA '85
YOUNG, CONSTANCE M., RN, dir. nrsg., Good Samaritan Hospital, Baltimore, MD '85 (NURS)
YOUNG, DALE, supv. maint., Decatur County Hospital, Leon, IA '85 (ENG)
YOUNG, DAVID J., atty., Murphey, Young and Smith, Columbus, OH '81 (ATTY)
YOUNG, DAVID M., vice-pres. matl. and support serv., St. Paul Medical Center, Dallas, TX '82 (PUR)
YOUNG, DEAN W., dir. food serv., Bryan Memorial Hospital, Lincoln, NE '84 (FOOD)
YOUNG, EDWIN F., dir. matl. mgt., St. Mary-Corwin Hospital Center, Pueblo, CO '77 (MGMT)
YOUNG, FRANCENE, mgr. support serv., Sch Health Care System, Houston, TX '84 (PERS)
YOUNG, FREDERICK A., chief soc. serv., Center General Hospital, Howard, RI '79 (SOC)
YOUNG, FREDERICK C. JR., exec. vice-pres., Pendleton Memorial Methodist Hospital, New Orleans, LA '79
YOUNG, FREDERICK N., atty., Children's Medical Center, Dayton, OH '73 (ATTY)
YOUNG, GAYLEN W., dir. health care coalitions, American Hospital Association, Chicago, IL '70
YOUNG, HANSFORD L., vice-pres. gen. serv., Providence Hospital, Washington, DC '87 (ENG)
YOUNG, HELEN M., mgr. food serv., Palms West Hospital, Loxahatchee, FL '86 (FOOD)
YOUNG, JACK T., asst. vice-pres. adm. serv., Regional Medical Center at Memphis, Memphis, TN '83 (PUR)
YOUNG, JANE A., dir. vol. serv., HCA Santa Rosa Medical Center, Milton, FL '78 (VOL)
YOUNG, JEAN L., dir. mktg. and clin. serv., Camden-Clark Memorial Hospital, Parkersburg, WV '77 (PR)
YOUNG, JEFFREY D., asst. dir. cafeteria, Ohio Valley Medical Center, Wheeling, WV '84 (FOOD)
YOUNG, JOHN F., dir. plant oper., Mesquite Community Hospital, Mesquite, TX '85 (ENG)
YOUNG, JOHN H., supv. constr., St. Vincent Charity Hospital, Cleveland, OH '86 (ENG)
YOUNG, JUDITH A., RN, asst. dir. nrsg.-fin., St. Elizabeth's Hospital of Boston, Boston, MA '86 (NURS)
YOUNG, JULIE B., asst. dir. pub. rel., Jackson Hospital and Clinic, Montgomery, AL '83 (PR)
YOUNG, KATHY, dir. vol. serv., Hamilton Medical Center, Dalton, GA '78 (VOL)
YOUNG, LAMAR W., vice-pres., Adventist Health System-Eastern and Middle America, Shawnee Mission, KS '71 (PERS)
YOUNG, LAURA C., RN, dir. critical care, Baptist Medical Center-Montclair, Birmingham, AL '84 (NURS)
YOUNG, LESLIE C., dir. prog. dev., HCA Brotman Medical Center, Culver City, CA '86 (PLNG)
YOUNG, LINDA R., RN, asst. dir. nrsg. staff, St. Luke's Hospital, Bethlehem, PA '84 (NURS)
YOUNG, LUCY A., mgr., Grace Hospital, Detroit, MI '85 (MGMT)
YOUNG, MARILYN J., supv. media prod., Memorial Hospital for Cancer and Allied Diseases, New York, NY '85 (EDUC)
YOUNG, MARTHA, tech. serv. eng., 3M, St. Paul, MN '82 (CS)
YOUNG, MARTIN L., asst. supv. distrib., Johnson City Medical Center Hospital, Johnson City, TN '83 (CS)
YOUNG, MARY ANN, adm. nrsg., Utah Valley Regional Medical Center, Provo, UT '86 (NURS)
YOUNG, MARY JOAN, dir. vol. serv., St. Mary's Hospital, Milwaukee, WI '81 (VOL)
YOUNG, MARY L., dir. soc. serv., Children's Specialized Hospital, Mountainside, NJ '85 (SOC)
YOUNG, MARY LEE, risk mgr., Methodist Medical Center of Oak Ridge, Oak Ridge, TN '81 (RISK)
YOUNG, MICHAEL A., asst. adm. and risk mgr., Shadyside Hospital, Pittsburgh, PA '83 (RISK)
YOUNG, MICHAEL G., atty., Texas Medical Association, Austin, TX '84 (ATTY)
YOUNG, NANCY E., RN, asst. adm. nrsg. serv., Memorial Hospital, Albany, NY '80 (NURS)
YOUNG, PATRICIA, RN, risk mgr. and nrs. epidemiologist, Dallas County Hospital, Perry, IA '86 (RISK)
YOUNG, RAY, dir. human res., St. Anthony Hospital, Oklahoma City, OK '86 (PERS)
YOUNG, RICHARD B., mgr., Ernst and Whinney, Kansas City, MO '87 (MGMT)
YOUNG, COL. ROBERT M., MSC USAF, adm., Wilford Hall U. S. Air Force Medical Center, Lackland AFB, TX '70
YOUNG, ROBERT W., pres., R. W. Young Mangement Group, Salt Lake City, UT '85
YOUNG, ROLAND F. III, atty., New Britain General Hospital, New Britain, CT '86 (ATTY)
YOUNG, RONALD J., exec. vice-pres., Lutheran Hospital Society of Southern California, Los Angeles, CA '78
YOUNG, RUTH C., dir. soc. serv., Spaulding Rehabilitation Hospital, Boston, MA '76 (SOC)
YOUNG, SALLY BENJAMIN, mgr. media rel. and spec. proj., Memorial Hospital for Cancer and Allied Diseases, New York, NY '86 (PR)
YOUNG, SAMUEL A., RN, mgr. nrsg. adm., Mercy Hospital of Pittsburgh, Pittsburgh, PA '86 (NURS)
YOUNG, STEPHEN ROBERT, pres., Elmbrook Memorial Hospital, Brookfield, WI '68
YOUNG, STEVEN R., consult., Minneapolis, MN '87 (PLNG)
YOUNG, THOMAS L., atty., Nash General Hospital, Rocky Mount, NC '78 (ATTY)
YOUNG, THOMAS N., adm., Brackenridge Hospital, Austin, TX '71
YOUNG, THOMAS P., dir. plant oper., Western Reserve Systems-Northside, Youngstown, OH '78 (ENG)
YOUNG, WANDA W., vice-pres. health care res., Blue Cross of Western Pennsylvania, Pittsburgh, PA '76
YOUNG, WILLIAM A., dir. pat. and family counselor, Tucson Medical Center, Tucson, AZ '86 (SOC)
YOUNG, WILLIAM J. JR., dir. matl. mgt., Anna Jaques Hospital, Newburyport, MA '84 (PUR)
YOUNGBLOOD, JAMES R., vice-pres. syst., Iowa Methodist Medical Center, Des Moines, IA '87 (MGMT)
YOUNGBLOOD, WILLIAM B., asst. adm., Montefiore Hospital, Pittsburgh, PA '73 (MGMT)
YOUNGDAHL, PAUL DAVID, pres. and chief exec. off., Saint Luke's Hospital, Cleveland, OH '51 (LIFE)
YOUNGER, BRIAN E., sr. consult., Arthur Andersen and Company, Minneapolis, MN '84 (MGMT)
YOUNGER, CATHY A., dir. pers., HCA Bayonet Point-Hudson Regional Medical Center, Hudson, FL '86 (PERS)
YOUNGER, K. JANE, vice-pres., Jewish Hospital, Louisville, KY '78 (NURS)
YOUNGER, LARRY L., USN, head med. serv., Navy Recruiting Command, Arlington, VA '79
YOUNGQUIST, C. ROBERT, (ret.), Butler, PA '45 (LIFE)
YOUNGQUIST, JANE E., dir. vol. serv., Galesburg Cottage Hospital, Galesburg, IL '84 (VOL)
YOUNGSTEIN, EFROM, dir. plng., Kings County Hospital Center, Brooklyn, NY '67 (PLNG)
YOUNIS, DANA J., sterile prep lead tech., Mercy Medical Center, Roseburg, OR '86 (CS)
YOUNKER, NORMAN A., atty., Intermountain Health Care, Inc., Salt Lake City, UT '86 (ATTY)
YOUNKIN, FLORENCE A., dir. nrsg. educ., Horton Memorial Hospital, Middletown, NY '86 (EDUC)
YOUREE, JAMES H., adm., Natividad Medical Center, Salinas, CA '84
YOVINO, ANGELA M., dir. diet. serv., Good Samaritan Hospital, West Islip, NY '84 (FOOD)
YOW, KEVIN B., atty., North Carolina Hospital Association, Raleigh, NC '86 (ATTY)
YU, FREDERICK Y., atty., Humana Hospital -Aurora, Aurora, CO '83 (ATTY)
YUAN, ANNA, gerontologist, Yuan and Associates, La Grange, IL '86
YUN, SUE C., RN, chief trng., dev., pers. and manpower div., District of Columbia General Hospital, Washington, DC '81 (EDUC)
YUNC, KIM W., dir. environ. serv., Methodist Hospital, Philadelphia, PA '87 (ENVIRON)
YUNCK, MYRNA C., RN, dir. nrsg. serv., North Valley Hospital, Whitefish, MT '85 (NURS)
YUNKER, JUNE, supv. prep and sterile, Providence Hospital, Cincinnati, OH '85 (CS)
YURISH, THOMAS, dir. pers., Hazleton-St. Joseph Medical Center, Hazleton, PA '86 (PERS)
YURKO, ROGER M., vice-pres. prof. serv., Mercy Hospital, Port Huron, MI '85
YURKOW, MARY ELLEN, dir. food serv., Toronto Western Hospital, Toronto, Ont., Canada '83 (FOOD)
YUROW, HANK R., vice-pres., North Charles Hospital, Baltimore, MD '79
YURUSH, DOLORES, supv. telephone serv., Metropolitan Hospital and Health Centers, Detroit, MI '83 (ENG)
YUTER, SHEILA M., dir. plng., St. Joseph's Hospital of Stockton, Stockton, CA '82 (PLNG)

Z

ZABKA, JOHN R., dir., Hospital Compensation Service, Hawthorne, NJ '85
ZABRANSKY, SALLY J., coor. mktg., St. Luke's Samaritan Health Care, Inc., Milwaukee, WI '86 (PLNG)
ZACCAGNINO, JOSEPH A., exec. vice-pres., Yale-New Haven Hospital, New Haven, CT '74
ZACHARIAS, BARBARA LEE, dir. soc. work, Hermann Hospital, Houston, TX '79 (SOC)
ZACHARIE, SUSAN H., dir. diet. serv., Natchaug Hospital, Mansfield Center, CT '83 (FOOD)
ZACHARY, BETH, dir. advertising and commun., Adventist Health System-West, Roseville, CA '84 (PR) (PLNG)
ZACHARY, JAMIE L., supv. clin., St. Vincent's Medical Center, Jacksonville, FL '87 (SOC)
ZACHWIEJA, TED T., br. mgr., Boyd-Sobieray Associates, Inc., Charleston, WV '86 (ENG)
ZACK, RITA, asst. pub. rel., St. Luke's Medical Center, Phoenix, AZ '86 (PR)
ZACK, ROBERT A., atty., William Beaumont Hospital, Royal Oak, MI '84 (ATTY)
ZACKS, DAVID M., atty., University Hospital, Augusta, GA '81 (ATTY)
ZAFEREO, CAROLYN S., pat. rel. rep., Memorial Hospital Systems, Southeast Unit, Houston, TX '82 (PAT)
ZAFRON, LEO SEYMOUR, dir. pur., Mercy Hospital, Buffalo, NY '66 (PUR)
ZAGACKI, MARY, RN, vice-pres. and dir. nrsg., St. Francis Hospital, Miami Beach, FL '86 (NURS)
ZAGAMI, MATTHEW ANTHONY, dir. matl. mgt. and pharm., Southside Hospital, Bay Shore, NY '80 (PUR)
ZAGAMI, ROSS, asst. dir. food serv., Sancta Maria Hospital, Cambridge, MA '84 (FOOD)
ZAGARLICK, MARGARET A., RN, Reno, NV '78
ZAGOZEN, JOSEPH J., asst. adm., St. Nicholas Hospital, Sheboygan, WI '86 (RISK)
ZAHLER, FRANCES, coor. oper. res. nrsg., Hospital for Joint Diseases-Orthopaedic Institute, New York, NY '76 (RISK)
ZAHN, EUGENE H. JR., dir. food serv., Columbus Hospital, Chicago, IL '80 (FOOD)
ZAHND, JAMES M., vice-pres. commun. affairs, Iowa Methodist Health System, Des Moines, IA '84 (PR)
ZAHORSKY, THOMAS A., dir. plant oper., AMI Danforth Hospital, Texas City, TX '85 (ENG)
ZAHRANI, CAPT. ALI M., MSC USAF, dir., Armed Forces Hospital, Jubail, Saudi Arabia '87
ZAIKOWSKI, RICHARD A., mgr. matl. mgt., Geisinger System Services, Danville, PA '83 (PUR)
ZAJAC, THOMAS H., mgr. fin. syst., Thomas Jefferson University Hospital, Philadelphia, PA '84 (MGMT)
ZAK, EDWARD J., natl. dir. health care computer serv., Arthur Young and Company, Denver, CO '83 (MGMT)
ZAK, GLORIA, RN, adm. nrsg., United Hospital, Grand Forks, ND '80 (NURS)
ZAKOS, MARGARET E., nrs. consult., Kingston, Ont., Canada '83
ZALAR, KARL JR., dir. satellite oper., Lima Memorial Hospital, Lima, OH '87 (AMB)
ZALEWSKI, WALTER S., chief eng., Overlook Hospital, Summit, NJ '78 (ENG)
ZALOUDEK, JAMES J., dir. plant oper., Church Hospital Corporation, Baltimore, MD '84 (ENG)
ZALUCKY, MICHAEL E., dir. pers., Amsterdam House, New York, NY '86 (PERS)
ZAMAN, ELLEN ROSSMAN, dir. pat. and family serv., Childrens Hospital of Los Angeles, Los Angeles, CA '82 (SOC)
ZAMBONI, GEOFFREY, dir. matl. mgt., H. Lee Moffitt Hospital and Cancer Research Institute at the University of South Florida, Tampa, FL '85 (PUR)
ZAMEN, ROBERT JOSEPH, vice-pres., Texas Hospital Association, Austin, TX '71 (MGMT)
ZAMMIT, JOSEPH, dir. eng., Cabrini Medical Center, New York, NY '86 (ENG)
ZAMORA, SARA ANA, asst. dir. pat. and family rel., Miami Children's Hospital, Miami, FL '86 (PAT)
ZAMORA, THERESA M., mgr. pers., Northside Presbyterian Hospital, Albuquerque, NM '86 (PERS)
ZAMPEDRO, VELMA L., RN, dir. nrsg., Grace Hospital, Morganton, NC '71 (NURS)
ZAMSKY, STEVEN A., atty., Merle West Medical Center, Klamath Falls, OR '74 (ATTY)
ZANARDELLI, JOHN J., exec. vice-pres., Oil City Area Health Center, Oil City, PA '82
ZANE, JOSEPHINE W., dir. pers., Raleigh Community Hospital, Raleigh, NC '80 (PERS)
ZANER, C. LOUISE, asst. dir. food serv., Wabash General Hospital District, Mount Carmel, IL '81 (FOOD)
ZANG, EDWINA H., dir. vol., Children's Medical Center, Tulsa, OK '83 (VOL)
ZANG, FREDERICK W., dir. soc. serv., Truman Medical Center-East, Kansas City, MO '85 (SOC)
ZANG, PAUL R., mgr. soc. serv., Lansing General Hospital, Lansing, MI '81 (SOC)
ZANGARA, ALEXANDER, mgr. pur. and matl. mgt., St. Joseph Mercy Hospital, Ann Arbor, MI '84 (PUR)
ZANGHI, JOHN S., vice-pres. fin., Marymount Hospital, Garfield Heights, OH '81 (PLNG)
ZANGHI, JOSEPH A., dir. pers., Jamestown General Hospital, Jamestown, NY '82 (PERS)
ZANON, JOHN A., dir. matl. mgt., Gottlieb Memorial Hospital, Melrose Park, IL '86 (PUR)
ZANONI, PIER-GEORGE, eng. consult., Michigan Hospital Association Service Corporation, Lansing, MI '86 (ENG)
ZANUCCOLI, ALAN R., asst. dir. matl. mgt., Beverly Hospital, Beverly, MA '85 (PUR)
ZANYLO, KATHY M., dir. soc. serv., Canonsburg General Hospital, Canonsburg, PA '81 (SOC)
ZANZOLA, DONNA, dir. vol. serv., Silver Cross Hospital, Joliet, IL '86 (VOL)
ZAPP, JILL M., dir. plng. serv., Hospital Council of Southern California, Los Angeles, CA '80 (PLNG)
ZAPP, JULIA, reimbursment mgr., Medtronic, Fridley, MN '86
ZAPP, MICHAEL A., sec. and treas., Lauterbach and Eilber, Inc., Columbus, OH '81 (RISK)
ZAPPEN, EDWARD F., atty., St. Joseph's Hospital, Marshfield, WI '68 (ATTY)
ZARA, GEORGE A., chief exec. off. and vice-pres., Desert Samaritan Hospital, Mesa, AZ '78
ZARATE, JUAN M., MD, dir. emer., Mid-Island Hospital, Bethpage, NY '87 (AMB)
ZARDA, DONALD W., maint. eng., Shawano Community Hospital, Shawano, WI '81 (ENG)
ZAREMSKI, MILES J., atty., Northwestern Memorial Hospital, Chicago, IL '83 (ATTY)
ZARILLO, JOSEPH G., dir. mgt. serv., John F. Kennedy Medical Center, Edison, NJ '75 (MGMT)
ZARMIN, GERALD J., vice-pres. fin. oper., Chicago Osteopathic Medical Center, Chicago, IL '81 (PLNG)
ZARNICK, FLORENCE A., RN, dir. nrsg. serv., St. Vincent's Medical Center of Richmond, Staten Island, NY '71 (NURS)
ZARRELLA, EDWARD G., Woodridge, IL '80 (RISK)
ZARRETT, STUART, dir. food serv., Florida Medical Center Hospital, Fort Lauderdale, FL '81 (FOOD)
ZARTMAN, JOSEPH, asst. dir. emp. rel., Providence Hospital, Cincinnati, OH '86 (PERS)
ZARVIS, JOHN P., dir. maint., Providence Hospital, Sandusky, OH '85 (ENG)
ZASTOCKI, DEBORAH K., RN, dir. specialty nrsg., St. Clare's Hospital, Denville, NJ '81 (EDUC)
ZASTROW, PATRICIA J., RN, asst. dir. nrsg., Gottlieb Memorial Hospital, Melrose Park, IL '84 (NURS)
ZATZKE, ROBERT L., dir. maint., Bozeman Deaconess Hospital, Bozeman, MT '85 (ENG)
ZAUGRA, SUSAN, RN, dir. clin. nrsg., Hackley Hospital, Muskegon, MI '84 (NURS)
ZAUTKE, PAULINE J., dir. diet., Phoenix Memorial Hospital, Phoenix, AZ '87 (FOOD)
ZAVIER, AMY M., sr. consult., Blue Cross and Blue Shield of Michigan, Detroit, MI '86 (PLNG)
ZAVODNICK, LESLIE S., sr. consult., Peat, Marwick, Mitchell and Company, Philadelphia, PA '86 (PLNG)
ZAWADSKI, TED F., vice-pres. and gen. council, Cuyahoga County Hospitals, Cleveland, OH '80 (ATTY)
ZAWORSKI, MADELINE R., RN, asst. exec. dir. nrsg. serv., Lorain Community Hospital, Lorain, OH '85 (NURS)
ZAYACHEK, MARY K., asst. to adm.-qual. assur., Mountainside Hospital, Montclair, NJ '84 (RISK)
ZAZO, E., coor. matl. mgt., St. Luke's Hospital, Saginaw, MI '86 (CS)
ZBOROWSKI, JEANNE V., clin. lab. scientist, Washington Hospital, Washington, PA '85
ZBRYSKI, JON, supv. clin. eng., Elkhart General Hospital, Elkhart, IN '85 (ENG)
ZEALLEY, HAROLD A., consult., Elyria Memorial Hospital, Elyria, OH '49 (LIFE)
ZEB, JAHAN, mgt. eng., Health Ventures Corporation, Omaha, NE '86 (MGMT)
ZEBARJADI, SOHEIL, dir. spec. prog. and proj. analyst, Abbott-Northwestern Hospital, Minneapolis, MN '83
ZEBROWSKI, MARTHA, sr. asst. adm., Queens Hospital Center, Jamaica, NY '81
ZEC, GLORIA X., mgr., Ernst and Whinney, Detroit, MI '86 (MGMT)
ZECHMAN, EDWIN K. JR., chief exec. off., Children's Hospital of Pittsburgh, Pittsburgh, PA '85
ZEEGERS, DONNA L., atty., Augusta, ME '82 (ATTY)
ZEEMAN, LAMAR, area serv. coor., Utah Valley Regional Medical Center, Provo, UT '85 (ENG)
ZEGLIN, CHRISTINE M., dir. pers., Greater Laurel Beltsville Hospital, Laurel, MD '86 (PERS)
ZEHR, BENJAMIN D., dir. commun., Methodist Hospital of Indiana, Indianapolis, IN '79 (ENG)
ZEIGLER, SR. MARY CATHERINE, dir. pat. rel., St. Rita's Medical Center, Lima, OH '79 (PAT)
ZEIHER, BERNHARDT A., adm., Parkview Hospital, Toledo, OH '53 (LIFE)
ZEILER, JOY, adm. quailty assur., Penobscot Bay Medical Center, Rockport, ME '80 (RISK)
ZEISMER, NAOMI, mgr. sup., proc. and distrib., Kettering Medical Center, Kettering, OH '72 (CS)
ZEISSER, CHARLES G., dir. pers., St. Marys Hospital Medical Center, Madison, WI '75 (PERS)
ZEITLER, DANIEL R., mgt. eng., Borgess Medical Center, Kalamazoo, MI '81 (MGMT)
ZELANES, ROBERT T., dir. clin. soc. work, AMI Presbyterian-Denver Hospital, Denver, CO '82 (SOC)
ZELLER, ELDON, adm. phys. plant, United Hospital, Grand Forks, ND '79 (ENG)(ENVIRON)
ZELLER, MICHAEL JAY, assoc. dir. pat. accounts, Memorial Hospital for Cancer and Allied Diseases, New York, NY '77
ZELLER, WAYNE D., treas., Western Pennsylvania Hospital, Pittsburgh, PA '52 (LIFE)
ZELLERS, BILLY B., consult., Riverside, CA '51 (LIFE)
ZELLS, ESTHER, risk mgr., North Charles Hospital, Baltimore, MD '87 (RISK)
ZELMAN, MARVIN S., atty., St. Alexis Hospital, Cleveland, OH '77 (ATTY)
ZELONIS, JALOO I., RN, nrs. educator, U. S. Public Health Service Indian Hospital, Whiteriver, AZ '83 (EDUC)
ZELSMAN, ROBERT F., coor. eng. serv., Page Southerland Page, Austin, TX '84 (ENG)
ZEM, JOSEPH L., adm., St. Luke's Hospital, San Francisco, CA '53 (LIFE)
ZEMA, MARLISSA K., dir. food serv., Ira Davenport Memorial Hospital, Bath, NY '86 (FOOD)
ZEMANEK, ALJEANETTE D., dir. pur., Bayonne Hospital, Bayonne, NJ '82 (PUR)
ZEMANICK, MARIE, RN, dir. nrsg., Nesbitt Memorial Hospital, Kingston, PA '78 (NURS)
ZEMANS, JON R., pres., Rochester United Methodist Homes, Rochester, NY '64
ZEMROCK, BEVERLY J., dir. soc. serv., Wooster Community Hospital, Wooster, OH '80 (SOC)
ZENDIAN, ANNE G., dir. educ. serv., Mercy Hospital, Wilkes-Barre, PA '78 (PR) (PLNG)
ZENNIE, CAROL A., dir. commun. rel., Fort Hamilton-Hughes Memorial Hospital, Hamilton, OH '86 (PR)
ZENTMYER, CAPT. ROBERT K., MSC USN, CO, U. S. Naval Hospital, FPO San Francisco, CA '65
ZENTY, THOMAS F. III, chief adm. off., St. Francis Hospital, Jersey City, NJ '79
ZENTZ, ROBERT, RN, vice-pres. nrsg. serv., Sacred Heart Hospital, Allentown, PA '71 (NURS)
ZENUS, JOSEPH R., dir. pur., New England Baptist Hospital, Boston, MA '86 (PUR)
ZENZEN, PAULA M., RN, asst. dir. med. nrsg., Albany Medical Center Hospital, Albany, NY '86 (NURS)
ZEPP, BEVERLY V., dir. vol., Mary Washington Hospital, Fredericksburg, VA '83 (VOL)
ZEPP, STEPHEN M., mgt. eng., Saint Luke's Hospital, Cleveland, OH '85 (MGMT)
ZERBY, GLORIA C., dir. vol. serv., Richmond Heights General Hospital, Cleveland, OH '86 (VOL)
ZERCHER, ANN LEE, RN, assoc. dir. and dir. nrsg. serv., University of Chicago Hospitals, Chicago, IL '85 (NURS)
ZERR, SARAH, dir. vol. serv., Brandywine Hospital, Caln Township, PA '80 (VOL)
ZERWAS, SR. MARY EDWINA, dir. nutr. and diet. serv., St. Mary's Hospital, Huntington, WV '83 (FOOD)
ZESK, EDWARD W., vice-pres., Hospital Association of Rhode Island, Providence, RI '79 (PR)(PERS)
ZICCARDI, GAYLE M., dir. commun., Magee-Womens Hospital, Pittsburgh, PA '82 (ENG)
ZICHY, KATHLEEN H., vice-pres. mktg., Mercy Catholic Medical Center, Darby, PA '86 (PLNG)
ZICKEFOOSE, TED R., gen. mgr., El Camino Insurance Exchange, Mountain View, CA '82 (RISK)
ZID, KATHLEEN, student, Program in Hospital Administration, Ohio State University, Columbus, OH '86
ZIDLE, SEYMOUR R., dir. adm., Manitoba School for Retardates, Portage La Prairie, Man., Canada '64 (MGMT)
ZIDO, VICTORIA C., asst. dir. plng. and mktg., Shadyside Hospital, Pittsburgh, PA '85 (PLNG)
ZIEG, PATRICIA A., atty., AMI Saint Joseph Hospital, Omaha, NE '82 (ATTY)
ZIEGLER, CONNIE, mgr. matl., McMinnville Community Hospital, McMinnville, OR '83 (PUR)
ZIEGWEID, JEAN L., asst. dir. matl. mgt., Holy Family Hospital, Spokane, WA '82 (CS)
ZIELASKIEWICZ, MICHAEL E., RN, vice-pres. nrsg. serv., Horton Memorial Hospital, Middletown, NY '81 (NURS)
ZIELINSKI, CHARLES L., assoc. dir. food serv., Baptist Hospital of Miami, Miami, FL '82 (FOOD)
ZIEM, MARILYN R., asst. dir. nutr. serv., St. Joseph's Hospital, Milwaukee, WI '86 (FOOD)
ZIEMER, LINDA K., adm. mgr. rad. serv., Bethesda Hospital, Inc., Cincinnati, OH '81
ZIEROTH, MARTIN B. JR., dir. plant oper., Lakeview Medical Center, Rice Lake, WI '82 (ENG)
ZIFF, ANNE F., dir. mktg. commun., Bridgeport Hospital, Bridgeport, CT '83 (PR)
ZILL, SHARON, student, University of Houston-Clearlake, Spring, TX '85
ZILLMAN, JUDITH, dir. amb. serv., Good Samaritan Medical Center, Milwaukee, WI '87 (AMB)
ZILLMAN, MARCUS P., exec. dir., Naples Research and Counseling Center, Naples, FL '84 (PR) (PLNG)
ZILLMER, BING G., mgr. constr. eng. serv., La Crosse Lutheran Hospital, La Crosse, WI '84 (ENG)
ZILM, FRANK, Kansas City, MO '79 (PLNG)
ZIMBA, DAVID M., student, Program in Hospital and Health Care Administration, University of Minnesota, Minneapolis, MN '85
ZIMDARS, PETREA, dir. soc. serv., Deaconess Medical Center, Billings, MT '75 (SOC)
ZIMLINGHAUS, ANN M., supv. cent. serv., Harlem Valley Psychiatric Center, Wingdale, NY '82 (CS)
ZIMMANCK, RICHARD A., asst. adm. fin., South Haven Community Hospital, South Haven, MI '81 (PLNG)
ZIMMARO, LISA, risk mgr., Rolling Hill Hospital, Elkins Park, PA '86 (RISK)
ZIMMEL, ROBERT P., dir. recruitment and trng., St. Luke's Hospital, Bethlehem, PA '86 (PERS)
ZIMMER, JAY A., dir. health educ., Atlantic City Medical Center, Atlantic City, NJ '84 (EDUC)
ZIMMER, RICHARD O., mgr., Cooper and Lybrand, St. Louis, MO '70 (MGMT)
ZIMMERLY, PHILIP N., oper. auditor, Florida Medical Center Hospital, Fort Lauderdale, FL '83 (MGMT)
ZIMMERMAN, ALMA C., asst. adm. prof. serv., St. Luke's Hospital, Duluth, MN '65 (PERS)
ZIMMERMAN, BARBARA U., dir. vol. serv., Underwood-Memorial Hospital, Woodbury, NJ '78 (VOL)
ZIMMERMAN, DOROTHY A., RN, adm. asst. pat. serv., Beatrice Community Hospital and Health Center, Beatrice, NE '81 (NURS)
ZIMMERMAN, ELAINE, adm. plng. and human resource dev., Baycrest Centre-Geriatric Care, North York, Ont., Canada '77 (PLNG)
ZIMMERMAN, FREDERICK H., pres., Zimmerman Public Relations, Columbus, OH '86 (PR)
ZIMMERMAN, GREGORY, dir. educ., St. Joseph Hospital, Chicago, IL '76 (EDUC)

ZIMMERMAN, ILISE, adm. clin. res. serv., Mount Sinai Medical Center, New York, NY '81

ZIMMERMAN, JOYCE L., dir. vol. serv., Lewistown Hospital, Lewistown, PA '85 (VOL)

ZIMMERMAN, JULIET G., pres., Strategic Marketing Corporation, Bala Cynwyd, PA '84 (PLNG)

ZIMMERMAN, KARLA A., asst. dir. food and nutr. serv., St. Michael Hospital, Milwaukee, WI '85 (FOOD)

ZIMMERMAN, KATHRYN A., student, Department of Health Care Administration, George Washington University, Washington, DC '84

ZIMMERMAN, KEITH L., chief eng., Sandwich Community Hospital, Sandwich, IL '77 (ENG)

ZIMMERMAN, KENNETH D., mktg. planner, McDonald Davis and Associates, Milwaukee, WI '78 (PR)

ZIMMERMAN, MORTIMER W., (ret.), Boca Raton, FL '51 (LIFE)

ZIMMERMAN, PAUL M., dir. pers., AMI North Ridge Medical Center, Fort Lauderdale, FL '83 (PERS)

ZIMMERMAN, ROBERT J., atty., Rush-Presbyterian-St. Luke's Medical Center, Chicago, IL '78 (ATTY)

ZIMMERMAN, RONALD S., dir. plant oper., Bartholomew County Hospital, Columbus, IN '86 (ENG)

ZIMMERMAN, THOMAS J., risk mgr. and coor., Burlington Medical Center, Burlington, IA '83 (RISK)

ZIMMERMAN, WANNA E., dir. pers., Deaton Hospital and Medical Center, Baltimore, MD '86 (PERS)

ZIMMERMAN, WAYNE A., dir. biomedical, City Hospital Center at Elmhurst, Flushing, NY '84 (ENG)

ZIMMERMANN, ALICE E., dir. vol., Metropolitan Hospital-Springfield Division, Springfield, PA '80 (VOL)

ZIMMERMANN, HANS H., dir. food serv., Waukesha Memorial Hospital, Waukesha, WI '74 (FOOD)

ZIMMERMANN, WALTER J., dir. pur., Greenwich Hospital, Greenwich, CT '86 (PUR)

ZIMMERMANN, WILLIAM R., dir. eng. and maint., Samaritan Hospital, Troy, NY '77 (ENG)

ZINER, ANTHONY J., vice-pres., Northside Hospital, Atlanta, GA '77

ZINGMAN, EDGAR A., atty., Kentucky Hospital Association, Louisville, KY '75 (ATTY)

ZINI, ALDO, prin. consult., Blue Cross of Western Pennsylvania, Pittsburgh, PA '86 (MGMT)

ZINK, ANNA DOROTHY, coor. human resources dev., Baltimore County General Hospital, Randallstown, MD '71 (EDUC)

ZINK, ELIZABETH L., RN, dir. nrsg., Valley View Hospital, Glenwood Springs, CO '83 (NURS)

ZINK, HERMAN, vice-pres., Providence Milwaukie Hospital, Milwaukie, OR '82 (ENG)

ZINN, JACQUELINE, planner, Hospital of the University of Pennsylvania, Philadelphia, PA '80 (PLNG)

ZINN, NOEL L., mgr. pat. and commun. serv., Los Medanos Community Hospital, Pittsburg, CA '86 (SOC)

ZINN, WENDY S., dir. hosp. serv., The Peabody Group, Beachwood, OH '86

ZINNI, IRENA, pat. rel. consumer, Richmond Heights General Hospital, Cleveland, OH '87 (PAT)

ZINSER, KATHERINE E., (ret.), Danbury, CT '22 (LIFE)

ZINSMEISTER, GINA S., pat. rep., Decatur General Hospital, Decatur, AL '83 (PAT)

ZIOBRO, DANIEL, dir. cent. serv., Mercy Hospital, Scranton, PA '77 (CS)

ZIOLKOWSKI, WALTER B., dir. risk mgt. and pat. rel., MacNeal Hospital, Berwyn, IL '80 (RISK)

ZION, SANDRA, RN, nrs.-in-chief and vice-pres., Rhode Island Hospital, Providence, RI '78 (NURS)

ZIONTS, NANCY DRAZNER, mktg. assoc., Healthmark Corporation, Pittsburgh, PA '85 (PLNG)

ZIPF, RITA L., coor. staff educ. and dev., Milton Medical Center, Milton, MA '84 (EDUC)

ZIPIN, MELINDA L., consult., CHI Systems, Inc., Philadelphia, PA '86 (PLNG)

ZIPPRICH, JOHN L. II, atty., Sch Health Care System, Houston, TX '74 (ATTY)

ZIPRICK, ROBERT H., atty., Loma Linda University Medical Center, Loma Linda, CA '83 (ATTY)

ZIPRICK, WILLIAM F., atty., Loma Linda University Medical Center, Loma Linda, CA '85 (ATTY)

ZISKIND, DAVID MILES, partner, Gruzen and Partners Architects-Planners, New York, NY '80

ZISS, ALEXANDER, assoc. dir., Children's Hospital, Boston, MA '73

ZITSMAN, ROBERT D., dir. mktg., Sisters of St. Mary Rehabilitation Institute, St. Louis, MO '84 (PR) (PLNG)

ZITZELBER, ROBERT J., chief eng., St. Vincent Medical Center, Toledo, OH '82 (ENG)

ZLOTNICK, MARIA C., mgr. commun., George Washington University Hospital, Washington, DC '85 (ENG)

ZOCHOLL, JOHN R., mgt. eng., Lutheran Medical Center, Wheat Ridge, CO '86 (MGMT)

ZOELLICK, RAYMOND, assoc. exec. dir., Swedish Hospital Medical Center, Seattle, WA '86 (RISK)

ZOET, ELIZABETH YOUNG, pat. rep., Metropolitan Medical Center, Minneapolis, MN '77 (PAT)

ZOLBER, KATHLEEN K., PhD, dir. nutr. serv., Loma Linda University Medical Center, Loma Linda, CA '67 (FOOD)

ZOLETA, ZENAIDA SULIT, RN, supv. cent. serv., Queen of Angels Medical Center, Los Angeles, CA '83 (CS)

ZOLLAR, CAROLYN, gen. counsel, National Association of Rehabilitation Facilities, Washington, DC '86

ZOLLE, MARK A., mgt. serv. off., University of California at Los Angeles Hospital and Clinics, Los Angeles, CA '86 (PLNG)

ZOLPER, PATRICIA R., dir. vol. serv., Chilton Memorial Hospital, Pompton Plains, NJ '80 (VOL)

ZOLTAK, DAVID A., dir. maint., St. Francis Hospital, Milwaukee, WI '81 (ENG)

ZOMOK, ROBERT J., vice-pres. human res., Butler Memorial Hospital, Butler, PA '81 (PERS)

ZOMPA, DOLORES L., dir. emp. serv., Haricomp, Inc., Providence, RI '85 (PERS)

ZOOK, KAY M., RN, vice-pres., Saint Joseph Hospital, Denver, CO '78 (NURS)

ZORN, JILL B., asst. dir. plng., Mount Sinai Hospital, Hartford, CT '86 (PLNG)

ZOTTER, JEFFREY L., chief fin. off., Slate Belt Medical Center, Bangor, PA '83

ZOUHARY, KATHLEEN MAHER, atty., St. Luke's Hospital, Maumee, OH '80 (ATTY)

ZOWADA, PEG, dir. risk prevention and loss contr., Hospital of Saint Raphael, New Haven, CT '80 (RISK)

ZRELAK, JOHN T. JR., dir. matl. mgt., Midway Hospital Medical Center, Los Angeles, CA '86 (PUR)

ZUBA, JOHN J., contr., Miriam Hospital, Providence, RI '80

ZUBA, MARILYN J., vice-pres. human res., Kenosha Hospital and Medical Center, Kenosha, WI '84 (PERS)

ZUBACK, STEVEN J., mgr. emp. rel., Thomas Jefferson University Hospital, Philadelphia, PA '84 (PERS)

ZUBECK, JOHN J., dir. plant serv., St. Mary's Hospital of Blue Springs, Blue Springs, MO '69 (ENG)

ZUBECK, ROBERT J., dir. plant oper., St. Mary's Hospital, Kansas City, MO '84 (ENG)

ZUBIA, LUIS, mgr. hskpg. serv., Providence Memorial Hospital, El Paso, TX '86 (ENVIRON)

ZUBKOFF, BARBARA S., asst. adm. and dir. pers., South Shore Hospital and Medical Center, Miami Beach, FL '86 (PERS)

ZUBOW, DEBORAH A., asst. vice-pres., Pontiac General Hospital, Pontiac, MI '87 (AMB)

ZUCCARELLI, ANNE-MARIE, dir. pub. rel., Saint Joseph Hospital, Denver, CO '79 (PR)

ZUCCO, GREGORY S., cent. sup. tech., N. T. Enloe Memorial Hospital, Chico, CA '82 (CS)

ZUCK, LYNN E., Virginia, IL '84 (SOC)

ZUCKER, DOUGLAS S., adm. dir. emp. rel., Palisades General Hospital, North Bergen, NJ '86 (PERS)

ZUCKER, LEON W., vice-pres. fin., Public Health Trust of Dade County, Miami, FL '69

ZUCKER, LESLIE A., asst. site coor. mgt. info. syst., St. John's Episcopal Hospital, Smithtown, NY '85 (PLNG)

ZUCKER, RICHARD PAUL, dir. pub. interest, Presbyterian Hospital in the City of New York, New York, NY '80 (PR)

ZUCKER, ROBERT L., vice-pres. and dir. dev., Massillon City Hospital, Massillon, OH '44 (LIFE)

ZUCKERMAN, ALAN M., sr. vice-pres., CHI Systems, Inc., Philadelphia, PA '83 (PLNG)

ZUCKERMAN, JAY, vice-pres., Southside Hospital, Bay Shore, NY '84 (RISK)

ZUERCHER, MARY E., dir. vol. serv., Preston Memorial Hospital, Kingwood, WV '86 (VOL)

ZUFALL, DOROTHY L., coor. educ., Somerset Medical Center, Somerville, NJ '76 (EDUC)

ZUGHAYB, FADY ELIAS, plant eng., American University of Beirut, New York, NY '87 (ENG)

ZUHARS, BETTY H., dir. vol., Doctors Hospital, Columbus, OH '73 (VOL)

ZULKIE, SHARON, Glencoe, IL '76 (FOOD)

ZUMDAHL, MARK E., atty., Community General Hospital, Sterling, IL '84 (ATTY)

ZUNZ, EDWARD A. JR., atty., East Orange General Hospital, East Orange, NJ '76 (ATTY)

ZUPANCIC, NANCY J., asst. adm., Shadyside Hospital, Pittsburgh, PA '85 (NURS)

ZURITIS, JEAN, RN, dir. nrsg. and child care serv., Children's Seashore House, Atlantic City, NJ '73 (NURS)

ZUVEKAS, ANN, prin., Lewin and Associates, Washington, DC '81 (PLNG)

ZUZA, DAVID J., dir. corp. plng., Mid-Michigan Health Care Systems, Inc., Midland, MI '80 (PLNG)

ZUZEK, SUSAN, RN, dir. nrsg., Vassar Brothers Hospital, Poughkeepsie, NY '85 (NURS)

ZVEITEL, HERBERT, dir. plant oper., Northwest Institute of Psychiatry, Fort Washington, PA '81 (ENG)

ZWAHLEN, G. WAYNE, vice-pres. plng., Magee-Womens Hospital, Pittsburgh, PA '78 (PLNG)

ZWALD, PATRICIA R., chief vol. serv., Veterans Administration Medical Center, Nashville, TN '86 (VOL)

ZWAR, RONALD P., mgr. mktg., Mercy-Memorial Medical Center-Mercy Hospital Division, Benton Harbor, MI '86 (PR)

ZWEIBEL, MARK B., Hamden, CT '79

ZWEIG, RAYMOND X., atty., Botsford General Hospital, Farmington Hills, MI '85 (ATTY)

ZWETSCH, NANCY LYNN WALLACE, dir. soc. serv., Frederick Ferris Thompson Hospital, Canandaigua, NY '80 (SOC)

ZWICK, SANDRA E., asst. adm. prof. serv., St. John Hospital, Nassau Bay, TX '83

ZWIESLER, MELANIE L., RN, dir. nrsg. serv., Grandview Hospital and Medical Center, Dayton, OH '86 (NURS)

ZWILLINGER, LAWRENCE, asst. dir. amb. care, Bayley Seton Hospital, Staten Island, NY '81

ZWIREN, STANLEY C., asst. vice-pres. environ. serv., Bronx-Lebanon Hospital Center, Bronx, NY '79 (ENG)

ZWIRN, LESLIE, dir. strategic plng., Methodist Hospital of Indiana, Indianapolis, IN '79 (PLNG)

ZYLKA, MICHAEL J., asst. dir. bldg. oper., Milwaukee County Medical Complex, Milwaukee, WI '86 (ENG)

ZYLSTRA, PETER D., RN, asst. adm. nrsg., Bulloch Memorial Hospital, Statesboro, GA '75 (NURS)(CS)

ZYROLL, THOMAS C., Avanti Health Systems, Kingwood, TX '76

ZYSKOWSKI, STANLEY, steward, Western Massachusetts Hospital, Westfield, MA '57 (LIFE)

ZYTROSKEE, ADRIAN, dir. strategic plng. and health promotion, Adventist Health System-West, Roseville, CA '84 (PLNG)

E Health Organizations, Agencies and Providers

Description of Lists

This section was compiled to provide a directory of information useful to persons in the health field.

International, National, and Regional Organizations

The international, national, and regional list includes many types of voluntary groups concerned with matters of interest to the health field. The information given includes address, telephone number, and the president, director, or secretary. For organizations that maintain permanent offices, office addresses and telephone numbers are given. For organizations not maintaining offices, the addresses and telephone numbers given are those of their corresponding secretaries. The information was obtained directly from the organizations.

Organizations are listed alphabetically by their full names; consult the index under the key word in the organization's name or under the discipline or geographical area that is the focus of the organization if the full designation is unknown.

We present this list simply as a convenient directory. Inclusion or omission of any organization's name indicates neither approval nor disapproval by the American Hospital Association.

United States Government Agencies

National agencies concerned with health-related matters are listed by the major department of government under which the different functions fall.

State and Provincial Organizations and Agencies

The lists of organizations in states, associated areas, and provinces include Blue Cross-Blue Shield plans, health systems agencies, hospital associations and councils, hospital licensure agencies, medical and nursing licensure agencies, peer review organizations, state health planning and development agencies, and statewide health coordinating councils.

There are many active local organizations that do not fall within these categories; contact the hospital association of the state or province for information about such additional groups. The hospital associations and councils listed have offices with full-time executives.

The selected state and provincial government agencies include those within state departments of health and welfare, and other agencies such as comprehensive health planning, crippled children's services, maternal and child health, mental health, and vocational rehabilitation.

The list of health care coalitions contains information obtained from the annual survey of coalitions conducted by the AHA's Office of Health Coalitions and Private Sector Initiatives.

Health Care Providers

Lists of Health Maintenance Organizations, Preferred Provider Organizations, Freestanding Ambulatory Surgery Centers and Hospices are provided in this section. The lists were developed from information provided by state agencies. Following each of these lists is a directory of state agencies from which one can request further information.

As with the list of International, National, and Regional Organizations, these lists are provided simply as a convenient directory. Inclusion or omission of any organization name indicates neither approval nor disapproval by the American Hospital Association.

International, National, and Regional Organizations

A

ACADEMY FOR HEALTH SERVICES MARKETING, (AMERICAN MARKETING ASSOCIATION). Carla Windhorst, exec. dir.; 250 S. Wacker Dr., Suite 200, Chicago, IL 60606; tel. 312/648-0536

ACADEMY FOR IMPLANTS AND TRANSPLANTS. Anthony J. Viscido, D.D.S., exec. dir.; P.O. Box 223, Springfield, VA 22150; tel. 703/451-0001

ACADEMY OF DENTISTRY FOR THE HANDICAPPED. Dr. Paul Van Ostenberg, exec. dir.; 211 East Chicago Ave., Suite 2133, Flr. 16, Chicago, IL 60611; tel. 312/440-2660

ACADEMY OF DENTURE PROSTHETICS. Dr. Charles C. Swoope, sec.-treas.; 8255 N.E. 26th St., Bellevue, WA 98004

ACADEMY OF GENERAL DENTISTRY. Harold E. Donnell Jr., exec. dir.; 211 E. Chicago Ave., Chicago, IL 60611; tel. 312/440-4300

ACADEMY OF ORAL DYNAMICS. Joseph P. Skellchock, D.D.S., sec.; 2363 Philadelphia Ave., Chambersburg, PA 17201; tel. 717/263-2451

ACCREDITATION ASSOCIATION FOR AMBULATORY HEALTH CARE, INC. Ronald S. Moen, exec. dir.; 9933 Lawler Ave., Skokie, IL 60077-3702; tel. 312/676-9610

AEROSPACE MEDICAL ASSOCIATION. R. R. Hessberg, M.D., exec. vice-pres.; Washington National Airport, Washington, DC 20001-4977; tel. 703/892-2240

ALEXANDER GRAHAM BELL ASSOCIATION FOR THE DEAF, INC. Donna McCord Dickman, Ph.D., exec. dir.; 3417 Volta Pl., N.W., Washington, DC 20007; tel. 202/337-5220 (Voice/TTY)

ALLERGY TESTING LABORATORY. Herman Hirschfeld, M.D.; 133 E. 58th St., New York, NY 10022; tel. 212/355-1005

AMBULATORY PEDIATRIC ASSOCIATION. Marge Degnon, exec. sec.; 1311A Dolley Madison Blvd., McLean, VA 22101; tel. 703/556-9222

AMERICAN ACADEMY FOR CEREBRAL PALSY AND DEVELOPMENTAL MEDICINE. John Hinckley, exec. dir.; Box 11083, 2315 Westwood Ave., Richmond, VA 23230; tel. 804/355-0147

AMERICAN ACADEMY OF ALLERGY AND IMMUNOLOGY. Donald L. McNeil, exec. dir.; 611 E. Wells St., Milwaukee, WI 53202; tel. 414/272-6071

AMERICAN ACADEMY OF CHILD & ADOLESCENT PSYCHIATRY. Virginia Q. Anthony, exec. dir.; 3615 Wisconsin Ave., N.W., Washington, DC 20016; tel. 202/966-7300

AMERICAN ACADEMY OF DENTAL ELECTROSURGERY. Maurice J. Oringer, D.D.S., exec. sec.; P.O. Box 374, Planetarium Station, New York, NY 10024; tel. 212/595-1925

AMERICAN ACADEMY OF DENTAL PRACTICE ADMINISTRATION. Linda Doll, exec. sec.; 6134 Cheena, Houston, TX 77096; tel. 713/771-2477

AMERICAN ACADEMY OF DERMATOLOGY. Bradford W. Claxton, exec. dir.; 1567 Maple Ave., Evanston, IL 60201; tel. 312/869-3954

AMERICAN ACADEMY OF FACIAL PLASTIC AND RECONSTRUCTIVE SURGERY, INC. Lee VanBremen, Ph.D., exec. vice-pres.; 1101 Vermont Ave., N.W., Suite 404, Washington, DC 20005; tel. 202/842-4500

AMERICAN ACADEMY OF FAMILY PHYSICIANS. R. Michael Miller, vice-pres.; Socioeconomic and Legal Affairs, 1740 W. 92nd St., Kansas City, MO 64114; tel. 816/333-9700

AMERICAN ACADEMY OF HOSPITAL ATTORNEYS (AHA). Shirley A. Worthy, dir.; 840 N. Lake Shore Dr., Chicago, IL 60611; tel. 312/280-6600

AMERICAN ACADEMY OF IMPLANT DENTISTRY. John P. Winiewicz, exec. dir.; 515 Washington St., Box 2002, Abington, MA 02351; tel. 617/878-7990

AMERICAN ACADEMY OF MEDICAL ADMINISTRATORS. Thomas R. O'Donovan, Ph.D., pres.; 30555 Southfield Rd., Suite 150, Southfield, MI 48076; tel. 313/540-4310

AMERICAN ACADEMY OF MEDICAL DIRECTORS. Roger S. Schenke, dir.; 4830 W. Kennedy Blvd., Suite 648, Tampa, FL 33609-2517; tel. 813/873-2000

AMERICAN ACADEMY OF NEUROLOGY. Jan W. Kolehmainen, exec. dir.; 2221 University Ave., S.E., Suite 335, Minneapolis, MN 55414; tel. 612/623-8115

AMERICAN ACADEMY OF OCCUPATIONAL MEDICINE. Donald L. Hoops, exec. dir.; 2340 S. Arlington Heights Rd., Suite 400, Arlington Heights, IL 60005; tel. 312/228-6850

AMERICAN ACADEMY OF OPHTHALMOLOGY. Bruce E. Spivey, M.D., exec. vice-pres.; 655 Beach St., P.O. Box 7424, San Francisco, CA 94120; tel. 415/561-8500

AMERICAN ACADEMY OF OPTOMETRY. David Lewis, adm.; 5530 Wisconsin Ave., N.W., Suite 917, Washington, DC 20815; tel. 301/652-0905

AMERICAN ACADEMY OF ORAL MEDICINE. Gunter Schmidt, D.D.S., sec.; 222 S. Bemiston, Clayton, MO 63105; tel. 314/721-3753

AMERICAN ACADEMY OF ORTHODONTICS FOR THE GENERAL PRACTITIONER. Jane Taylor, exec. sec.; 3953 N. 76th, Milwaukee, WI 53222; tel. 414/464-7870

AMERICAN ACADEMY OF ORTHOPAEDIC SURGEONS. Thomas C. Nelson, exec. dir.; 222 S. Prospect Ave., Park Ridge, IL 60068; tel. 312/823-7186

AMERICAN ACADEMY OF OTOLARYNGIC ALLERGY. Sandra L. May, exec. dir.; 1101 Vermont Ave., N.W., Suite 302, Washington, DC 20005; tel. 202/682-0456

AMERICAN ACADEMY OF OTOLARYNGOLOGY—HEAD AND NECK SURGERY, INC. Jerome C. Goldstein, M.D., exec. vice-pres.; 1101 Vermont Ave., N.W., Suite 302, Washington, DC 20005; tel. 202/289-4607

AMERICAN ACADEMY OF PEDIATRIC DENTISTRY. Dr. John A. Bogert, exec. dir.; 211 E. Chicago Ave., no. 1036, Chicago, IL 60611; tel. 312/337-2169

AMERICAN ACADEMY OF PEDIATRICS. M. Harry Jennison, M.D., exec. dir.; 1801 Hinman Ave., Evanston, IL 60204; tel. 312/869-4255

AMERICAN ACADEMY OF PHYSICAL MEDICINE AND REHABILITATION. Ike A. Mayeda, exec. dir.; 122 S. Michigan Ave., Suite 1300, Chicago, IL 60603-6107; tel. 312/922-9366

AMERICAN ACADEMY OF PHYSICIAN ASSISTANTS. F. Lynn May, exec. dir.; 1117 N. 19th St., Suite 300, Arlington, VA 22209; tel. 703/525-4200

AMERICAN ACADEMY OF PHYSIOLOGIC DENTISTRY. Dr. William Kopperud, sec.; 567 S. Washington St., Naperville, IL 60540; tel. 312/355-2625

AMERICAN ACADEMY OF PSYCHOANALYSIS. Vivian Mendelsohn, exec. dir.; 30 E. 40th St., Suite 608, New York, NY 10016; tel. 212/679-4105

AMERICAN ACADEMY OF RESTORATIVE DENTISTRY. Harold W. Fountain, D.D.S., sec.-treas.; 435 Whitcomb St., Kalamazoo, MI 49001; tel. 616/344-7259

AMERICAN AGING ASSOCIATION. Denham Harman, M.D., exec. dir.; 42nd and Dewey Ave., Omaha, NE 68105; tel. 402/559-4416

AMERICAN ALLIANCE FOR HEALTH, PHYSICAL EDUCATION, RECREATION, AND DANCE. F. Hal Haywood, actg. exec. vice-pres.; 1900 Association Dr., Reston, VA 22091; tel. 703/476-3400

AMERICAN AMBULANCE ASSOCIATION. Charles S. Clark, exec. vice-pres.; 3814 Auburn Blvd., Suite 70, Sacramento, CA 95821; tel. 916/483-3827

AMERICAN ART THERAPY ASSOCIATION. Edward J. Stygar, Jr., exec. dir.; 505 E. Hawley St., Mundelein, IL 60060; tel. 312/949-6064

AMERICAN ASSEMBLY FOR MEN IN NURSING. Frederick E. May, pres.; Rush University, 600 S. Paulina, 474-H, Chicago, IL 60612; tel. 312/942-7117

AMERICAN ASSOCIATION FOR ACCREDITATION OF LABORATORY ANIMAL CARE (AAALAC). Dr. Albert E. New, exec. dir.; 9650 Rockville Pike, Bethesda, MD 20814; tel. 301/571-1850

AMERICAN ASSOCIATION FOR ADULT AND CONTINUING EDUCATION. Judith Koloski, exec. dir.; 1201 16th St., N.W., Suite 230, Washington, DC 20036; tel. 202/822-7866

AMERICAN ASSOCIATION FOR AUTOMOTIVE MEDICINE. Elaine Petrucelli, exec. dir.; 2350 East Devon Ave., Suite 205, Des Plaines, IL 60016; tel. 312/390-8927

AMERICAN ASSOCIATION FOR CLINICAL CHEMISTRY, INC. Ronald E. Whorton, M.P.H., exec. vice-pres.; 1725 K St., N.W., Suite 1010, Washington, DC 20006; tel. 202/857-0717

AMERICAN ASSOCIATION FOR HOSPITAL PLANNING (See THE FORUM FOR HEALTH PLANNING).

AMERICAN ASSOCIATION FOR LABORATORY ANIMAL SCIENCE. Donald W. Keene, exec. dir.; 70 Timber Creek Dr., Suite 5, Cordova, TN 38018; tel. 901/754-8620

AMERICAN ASSOCIATION FOR RESPIRATORY CARE. Sam P. Giordano, exec. dir.; 1720 Regal Row, Suite 112, Dallas, TX 75235; tel. 214/630-3540

AMERICAN ASSOCIATION FOR THE ADVANCEMENT OF SCIENCE. William D. Carey, exec. off.; 1333 H St., N.W., Washington, DC 20005; tel. 202/326-6400

AMERICAN ASSOCIATION FOR THE STUDY OF HEADACHE. P.O. Box 25152, Chicago, IL 60625; tel. 312/878-8977

AMERICAN ASSOCIATION FOR THE STUDY OF NEOPLASTIC DISEASES. Robert H. Jackson, M.D., pres.; 10607 Miles Ave., Cleveland, OH 44105; tel. 216/341-4335

AMERICAN ASSOCIATION FOR THE SURGERY OF TRAUMA. Jane A. Sylvia, Dept. of Surgery, Rhode Island Hospital, 593 Eddy St., Providence, RI 02902; tel. 401/277-8590

AMERICAN ASSOCIATION OF ANATOMISTS. William P. Jollie, sec.-treas.; Box 101, MCV Station, Richmond, VA 23298;

AMERICAN ASSOCIATION OF BIOANALYSTS. David Birenbaum, adm.; Suite 918, 818 Olive St., St. Louis, MO 63101; tel. 314/241-1445

AMERICAN ASSOCIATION OF BLOOD BANKS. Gilbert M. Clark, exec. dir.; 1117 N. 19th St., Suite 600, Arlington, VA 22209; tel. 703/528-8200

AMERICAN ASSOCIATION OF CERTIFIED ORTHOPTISTS. Barbara Cassin, pres.; Eye Clinic, Shands Teaching Hospital, Gainesville, FL 32610; tel. 904/392-3111

AMERICAN ASSOCIATION OF COLLEGES OF NURSING. Barbara K. Redman, Ph.D., exec. dir.; 1 Dupont Circle, Suite 530, Washington, DC 20036; tel. 202/463-6930

AMERICAN ASSOCIATION OF COLLEGES OF PHARMACY. Carl E. Trinca, Ph.D., exec. dir.; 1426 Prince Street, Alexandria, VA 22314; tel. 703/739-2330

AMERICAN ASSOCIATION OF COLLEGES OF PODIATRIC MEDICINE. Anthony J. McNevin, CAE, pres.; 6110 Executive Blvd., Suite 204, Rockville, MD 20852; tel. 301/984-9350

AMERICAN ASSOCIATION OF CRITICAL-CARE NURSES. Sandra J. Edson, exec. dir.; 1 Civic Plaza, Newport Beach, CA 92660; tel. 714/644-9310

AMERICAN ASSOCIATION OF DENTAL SCHOOLS. Richard D. Mumma, exec. dir.; 1625 Massachusetts Ave., N.W., Washington, DC 20036; tel. 202/667-9433

AMERICAN ASSOCIATION OF ENDODONTISTS. Irma S. Kudo, exec. dir.; 211 E. Chicago Ave., Suite 1501, Chicago, IL 60611; tel. 312/266-7255

AMERICAN ASSOCIATION OF FUND-RAISING COUNSEL, INC. John J. Schwartz, pres.; Rm. 1519, 25 W. 43 St., New York, NY 10036; tel. 212/354-5799

AMERICAN ASSOCIATION OF HEALTH DATA SYSTEMS. William H. Kincaid, exec. dir.; 3550 Woodland Rd., Ann Arbor, MI 48104; tel. 313/971-9492

AMERICAN ASSOCIATION OF HOMES FOR THE AGING. Sheldon L. Goldberg, exec. vice-pres.; 1129 20th St., N.W., Suite 400, Washington, DC 20036; tel. 202/296-5960

AMERICAN ASSOCIATION OF HEALTHCARE CONSULTANTS. Vaughan A. Smith, pres.; 1235 Jefferson Davis Hwy., Suite 602, Arlington, VA 22202; tel. 703/979-3180

AMERICAN ASSOCIATION OF HOSPITAL DENTISTS, INC. Paul Van Ostenberg, D.D.S., M.S., exec. dir.; 211 East Chicago Ave., Chicago, IL 60611; tel. 312/440-2661

AMERICAN ASSOCIATION OF IMMUNOLOGISTS. Dr. Joseph F. Saunders, exec. off.; 9650 Rockville Pike, Bethesda, MD 20814; tel. 301/530-7178

AMERICAN ASSOCIATION OF MEDICAL ASSISTANTS. Ina L. Yenerich, exec. dir.; 20 N. Wacker Dr., Suite 1575, Chicago, IL 60606; tel. 312/899-1500

AMERICAN ASSOCIATION OF MENTAL DEFICIENCY. Albert Berkowitz, Ed.D., exec. dir.; 1719 Kalorama Rd., N.W., Washington, DC 20009; tel. 800/424-3688

AMERICAN ASSOCIATION OF NEUROSCIENCE NURSES. J. Roger Detweiler, exec. dir.; 218 N. Jefferson, Suite 204, Chicago, IL 60606; tel. 312/993-0043

AMERICAN ASSOCIATION OF NURSE ANESTHETISTS. John F. Garde, CRNA, exec. dir.; 216 Higgins Rd., Park Ridge, IL 60068-5790; tel. 312/692-7050

AMERICAN ASSOCIATION OF OCCUPATIONAL HEALTH NURSES. Matilda A. Babbitz, R.N., exec. dir.; 50 Lenox Pointe, Atlanta, GA 30324; tel. 404/262-1162

AMERICAN ASSOCIATION OF ORAL AND MAXILLOFACIAL SURGEONS. Bernard J. Degen, II, exec. dir.; 211 E. Chicago Ave., Suite 930, Chicago, IL 60611; tel. 312/642-6446

AMERICAN ASSOCIATION OF ORTHODONTISTS. Robert L. Wagner, exec. dir.; 460 N. Lindbergh Blvd., St. Louis, MO 63141; tel. 314/993-1700

AMERICAN ASSOCIATION OF PASTORAL COUNSELORS. James W. Ewing, Ph.D., exec. dir.; 9508 A Lee Hwy., Fairfax, VA 22031; tel. 703/385-6967

AMERICAN ASSOCIATION OF PATHOLOGISTS. Harold Waters, Ph.D., exec. off.; 9650 Rockville Pike, Bethesda, MD 20814; tel. 301/530-7130

AMERICAN ASSOCIATION OF PHYSICISTS IN MEDICINE. Elaine Pevar Osterman, exec. off.; 335 E. 45th St., New York, NY 10017; tel. 212/661-9404

AMERICAN ASSOCIATION OF PLASTIC SURGEONS. John E. Hoopes, M.D., sec.; Harvey 811, The Johns Hopkins Hospital, 600 N. Wolfe Street, Baltimore, MD 21205; tel. 301/955-6897

AMERICAN ASSOCIATION OF POISON CONTROL CENTERS. Gary M. Oderda, Pharm.D., M.P.H., University of Maryland School of Pharmacy; 20 N. Pine St., Baltimore, MD 21201; tel. 301/528-7604

AMERICAN ASSOCIATION OF PUBLIC HEALTH DENTISTRY. Joseph M. Doherty, pres.; AAPHD National Office, 10619 Jousting Lane, Richmond, VA 23235; tel. 804/272-8344

AMERICAN ASSOCIATION OF PUBLIC HEALTH PHYSICIANS. Norman Schell, M.D., sec.-treas.; 240 Old Country Road, Mineola, L.I., NY 11501; tel. 516/535-4922

AMERICAN BAPTIST HOMES AND HOSPITALS ASSOCIATION. Kenneth L. George, exec. dir.; P.O. Box 851, Valley Forge, PA 19482-0851; tel. 215/768-2382

AMERICAN BLOOD COMMISSION. Nancy R. Holland, exec. dir.; 1117 N. 19th St., Suite 501, Arlington, VA 22209; tel. 703/522-8414

AMERICAN BOARD OF ALLERGY AND IMMUNOLOGY, A Conjoint Board of the American Board of Internal Medicine and the American Board of Pediatrics. Herbert C. Mansmann Jr., M.D., exec. dir.; University City Science Center, 3624 Market St., Philadelphia, PA 19104; tel. 215/349-9466

AMERICAN BOARD OF ANESTHESIOLOGY. Alan D. Sessler, M.D., sec.; 100 Constitution Plaza, Hartford, CT 06103; tel. 203/522-9857

AMERICAN BOARD OF CARDIOVASCULAR PERFUSION. Beth A. Richmond, Ph.D., co-exec. dir.; Mark G. Richmond, Ed.D., co-exec. dir.; 109 S. 27th Ave., Suite 209, Hattiesburg, MS 39401; tel. 601/264-4491

AMERICAN BOARD OF COLON AND RECTAL SURGERY. Herand Abcarian, M.D., exec. dir.; 615 Griswold, Suite 1717, Detroit, MI 48226; tel. 313/961-7880

AMERICAN BOARD OF DERMATOLOGY, INC. Clarence S. Livingood, M.D., exec. dir.; Henry Ford Hospital, 2799 W. Grand Blvd., Detroit, MI 48202; tel. 313/871-8739

AMERICAN BOARD OF EMERGENCY MEDICINE. Benson S. Munger, Ph.D., exec. dir.; 200 Woodland Pass, Suite D, East Lansing, MI 48823; tel. 517/332-4800

AMERICAN BOARD OF FAMILY PRACTICE. Nicholas J. Pisacano, M.D., exec. dir. and sec.; 2228 Young Dr., Lexington, KY 40505; tel. 606/269-5626

AMERICAN BOARD OF INTERNAL MEDICINE. John A. Benson Jr., M.D., pres.; 3624 Market St., Philadelphia, PA 19104; tel. 215/243-1500

AMERICAN BOARD OF MEDICAL SPECIALTIES. Donald G. Langsley, M.D., exec. vice-pres.; 1 American Plaza, Suite 805, Evanston, IL 60201; tel. 312/491-9091

AMERICAN BOARD OF NEUROLOGICAL SURGERY. M. Stephen Mahaley, Jr., M.D., sec.-treas.; Post Office Box 4056, Chapel Hill, NC 27515-4056; tel. 919/966-3047

AMERICAN BOARD OF NUCLEAR MEDICINE. Joseph F. Ross, M.D., pres.; 900 Veteran Ave., Los Angeles, CA 90024; tel. 213/825-6787

AMERICAN BOARD OF OBSTETRICS AND GYNECOLOGY, INC. James A. Merrill, M.D., exec. dir.; 4507 University Way, N.E., Suite 204, Seattle, WA 98105; tel. 206/547-4884

AMERICAN BOARD OF OPHTHALMOLOGY. William H. Spencer, M.D., exec. dir.; 111 Presidential Blvd., Suite 241, Bala Cynwyd, PA 19004; tel. 215/664-1175

AMERICAN BOARD OF ORAL AND MAXILLOFACIAL SURGERY. Bobbi Leggett, exec. dir.; 211 E. Chicago Ave., Suite 836, Chicago, IL 60611; tel. 312/642-0070

AMERICAN BOARD OF ORTHOPAEDIC SURGERY, INC. Donald B. Kettelkamp, M.D., exec. dir.; 444 N. Michigan Ave., Suite 2970, Chicago, IL 60611; tel. 312/822-9572

AMERICAN BOARD OF OTOLARYNGOLOGY. Bobby R. Alford, M.D., exec. vice-pres.; 5615 Kirby Drive, Suite 936, Houston, TX 77005; tel. 713/528-6200

AMERICAN BOARD OF PATHOLOGY. M. R. Abell, M.D., exec. dir.; Lincoln Center, 5401 W. Kennedy Blvd., P.O. Box 25915, Tampa, FL 33622; tel. 813/879-4864

AMERICAN BOARD OF PEDIATRICS, INC. Robert C. Brownlee, M.D., exec. sec.; 111 Silver Cedar Ct., Chapel Hill, NC 27514; tel. 919/929-0461

AMERICAN BOARD OF PEDIATRIC DENTISTRY. James R. Roche, D.D.S., exec. sec.; Indiana University, School of Dentistry, 1121 W. Michigan St., Indianapolis, IN 46202; tel. 317/274-7868

AMERICAN BOARD OF PHYSICAL MEDICINE AND REHABILITATION. Gordon M. Martin, M.D., exec. dir.; Suite 674, Norwest Center, 21 First St., S.W., Rochester, MN 55902; tel. 507/282-1776

AMERICAN BOARD OF PLASTIC SURGERY, INC. Virginia Milewski, corres. sec.; 1617 John F. Kennedy Blvd., Suite 1561, Philadelphia, PA 19103; tel. 215/568-4000

AMERICAN BOARD OF PREVENTIVE MEDICINE, INC. Stanley R. Mohler, M.D., sec.-treas.; Wright State University, School of Medicine, P.O. Box 927, Dayton, OH 45401; tel. 513/278-6915

AMERICAN BOARD OF PROSTHODONTICS. Douglas C. Wendt, D.D.S., sec.-treas., 4707 Olley Ln., Fairfax, VA 22032; tel. 703/273-7323

AMERICAN BOARD OF PSYCHIATRY AND NEUROLOGY, INC. Stephen C. Scheiber, M.D., exec. sec.; One American Plaza, Suite 808, Evanston, IL 60201; tel. 312/864-0830

AMERICAN BOARD OF RADIOLOGY, INC. Kenneth L. Krabbenhoft, M.D., sec.; 300 Park, Suite 440, Birmingham, MI 48009; tel. 313/645-0600

AMERICAN BOARD OF SCIENCE IN NUCLEAR MEDICINE. Eugene Vinciguerra, Sc.D., admin.; 145 W. 58th St., New York, NY 10019; tel. 212/757-0520

AMERICAN BOARD OF SURGERY, INC. Ward O. Griffen Jr., M.D., exec. dir.; 1617 John F. Kennedy Blvd., Philadelphia, PA 19103; tel. 215/568-4000

AMERICAN BOARD OF THORACIC SURGERY. James V. Maloney, Jr., M.D., sec.; One American Plaza, Suite 803, Evanston, IL 60201; tel. 312/475-1520

AMERICAN BOARD OF UROLOGY, INC. David C. Utz, M.D., exec. sec.; Norwest Ctr., Suite 520, 21 First St., S.W., Rochester, MN 55902; tel. 507/282-6500

AMERICAN BRONCHO-ESOPHAGOLOGICAL ASSOCIATION. Lauren D. Holinger, M.D., sec.; 155 N. Michigan Ave., Chicago, IL. 60601; tel. 312/938-1990

AMERICAN BURN ASSOCIATION. Thomas L. Wachtel, M.D., sec.; 1130 E. McDowell Rd., B-2, Phoenix, AZ 85006; tel. 602/239-2391

AMERICAN CANCER SOCIETY, INC. Nicholas Bottiglieri, M.D., vice-pres., professional education; 777 Third Ave., New York, NY 10017; tel. 212/371-2900

AMERICAN CARDIOLOGY TECHNOLOGISTS' ASSOCIATION. George M. Cate, exec. dir.; 1980 Isaac Newton Square, S., Reston, VA 22090; tel. 703/435-9466

AMERICAN CENTER FOR THE ALEXANDER TECHNIQUE, INC. Barbara Kent, dir., Teacher Training Program; Abraham Goodman House, 129 W. 67 St., New York, NY 10023; tel. 212/799-0468

AMERICAN CHIROPRACTIC ASSOCIATION. Gerald M. Brassard, D.C., exec. vice-pres.; 1701 Clarendon Blvd., Arlington, VA 22209; tel. 703/276-8800

AMERICAN CLEFT PALATE ASSOCIATION. Jane Angelone Graminski, M.B.A., exec. dir.; 331 Salk Hall, University of Pittsburgh, Pittsburgh, PA 15261; tel. 412/681-9620

AMERICAN COLLEGE HEALTH ASSOCIATION. Stephen D. Blom, exec. dir.; 15879 Crabbs Branch Way, Rockville, MD 20855; tel. 301/963-1100

AMERICAN COLLEGE OF ADDICTION TREATMENT ADMINISTRATORS. Laurie Poul, exec. dir; 840 N. Lake Shore Dr., Suite 1103W, Chicago, IL 60611; tel. 312/943-0544

AMERICAN COLLEGE OF ALLERGISTS, INC. James R. Slawny, exec. dir.; 800 E. Northwest Hwy., Suite 101, Mount Prospect, IL 60056; tel. 312/255-0380

AMERICAN COLLEGE OF APOTHECARIES. D. C. Huffman Jr., Ph.D., exec. vice-pres.; 874 Union Ave., Memphis, TN 38163; tel. 901/528-6037

AMERICAN COLLEGE OF CARDIOLOGY. William D. Nelligan, exec. vice-pres.; 9111 Old Georgetown Rd., Bethesda, MD 20814; tel. 301/897-5400

AMERICAN COLLEGE OF CHEMOSURGERY. Michael Thompson, staff coor.; 1567 Maple Ave., Evanston, IL 60201; tel. 312/869-3954

AMERICAN COLLEGE OF CHEST PHYSICIANS. Alfred Soffer, M.D., exec. dir.; 911 Busse Hwy., Park Ridge, IL 60068-2375; tel. 312/698-2200

AMERICAN COLLEGE OF DENTISTS. Gordon H. Rovelstad, D.D.S.; 7315 Wisconsin Ave., Suite 352-N, Bethesda, MD 20814-3304; tel. 301/986-0555

AMERICAN COLLEGE OF EMERGENCY PHYSICIANS. Colin C. Rorrie Jr., Ph.D., exec. dir.; P.O. Box 619911, Dallas, TX 75261-9911; tel. 214/550-0911

AMERICAN COLLEGE OF GASTROENTEROLOGY. Thomas F. Fise, exec. dir.; 13 Elm St., Manchester, MA 01944; tel. 617/927-8330

AMERICAN COLLEGE OF HEALTH CARE ADMINISTRATORS. K. M. Griffin, Ph.D., C.A.E., exec. vice-pres.; 8120 Woodmont Ave., Suite 200, Bethesda, MD 20814; tel. 301/652-8384

AMERICAN COLLEGE OF HEALTHCARE EXECUTIVES. Stuart A. Wesbury Jr., Ph.D., pres.; 840 N. Lake Shore Dr., 1100 West, Chicago, IL 60611; tel. 312/943-0544

AMERICAN COLLEGE OF LEGAL MEDICINE. Thomas W. Teal, exec. sec.; P.O. Box 190, Maple Glen, PA 19002; tel. 215/646-6800

AMERICAN COLLEGE OF MEDICINE. Virginia Kendall, asst. dir.; 233 E. Erie St., Chicago, IL 60611; tel. 312/951-1400

AMERICAN COLLEGE OF NURSE-MIDWIVES. Mary Rita Prah, exec. dir.; 1522 K St., Suite 1120, Washington, DC 20005; tel. 202/347-5445

AMERICAN COLLEGE OF OBSTETRICIANS AND GYNECOLOGISTS. Warren H. Pearse, M.D., exec. dir.; 600 Maryland Ave., S.W., Washington, DC 20024; tel. 202/638-5577

AMERICAN COLLEGE OF PHYSICIAN EXECUTIVES. Roger S. Schenke, dir.; 4830 W. Kennedy Blvd., Suite 648, Tampa, FL 33609-2517; tel. 813/873-2000

AMERICAN COLLEGE OF PHYSICIANS. John R. Ball, M.D., JD, exec. vice-pres.; 4200 Pine St., Philadelphia, PA 19104; tel. 215/243-1200

AMERICAN COLLEGE OF PREVENTIVE MEDICINE. William M. Kane, Ph.D., exec. dir.; 1015 15th St., N.W., Washington, DC 20005; tel. 202/789-0003

AMERICAN COLLEGE OF RADIOLOGY. John J. Curry, exec. dir.; 1891 Preston White Dr., Reston, VA 22091; tel. 703/648-8900

AMERICAN COLLEGE OF SURGEONS. Paul A. Ebert, M.D., FACS., dir.; 55 E. Erie St., Chicago, IL 60611; tel. 312/664-4050

AMERICAN CONGRESS OF REHABILITATION MEDICINE. Ike A. Mayeda, exec. dir.; 130 S. Michigan Ave., Suite 1310, Chicago, IL 60603-6110; tel. 312/922-9368

AMERICAN CORRECTIVE THERAPY ASSOCIATION. David Ser, exec. dir.; 259-08 148th Rd., Rosedale, NY 11422; tel. 718/276-0721

AMERICAN COUNCIL ON PHARMACEUTICAL EDUCATION, INC. Daniel A. Nona, Ph.D., exec. dir.; 311 W. Superior St., Suite 512, Chicago, IL 60610; tel. 312/664-3575

AMERICAN DEAFNESS AND REHABILITATION ASSOCIATION. Steve Sligar, pres.; P.O. Box 55369, Little Rock, AR 72225; tel. 501/663-4617

AMERICAN DENTAL ASSISTANTS ASSOCIATION. John C. Thiel, exec. dir.; 666 N. Lake Shore Dr., Suite 1130, Chicago, IL 60611; tel. 312/664-3327

AMERICAN DENTAL ASSOCIATION. Thomas J. Ginley, Ph.D., exec. dir.; 211 E. Chicago Ave., Chicago, IL 60611; tel. 312/440-2500

AMERICAN DENTAL SOCIETY OF ANESTHESIOLOGY, INC. Peter C. Goulding, exec. dir.; 211 E. Chicago Ave., Suite 948, Chicago, IL 60611; tel. 312/664-8270

AMERICAN DIABETES ASSOCIATION, INC. Robert S. Bolan, Ph.D., exec. vice-pres.; 1660 Duke St., Alexandria, VA 22314; tel. 703/549-1500

AMERICAN DIETETIC ASSOCIATION. Julian Haynes, Ph.D., exec. dir.; 430 N. Michigan Ave., Chicago, IL 60611; tel. 312/280-5000

AMERICAN ELECTROENCEPHALOGRAPHIC SOCIETY. Fay S. Tyner, exec. dir.; 2579 Melinda Dr., N.E., Atlanta, GA 30345; tel. 404/320-1746

AMERICAN EPILEPSY SOCIETY. Priscilla S. Bourgeois, exec. dir.; 33 Hickory Hill, Southington, CT 06489; tel. 203/246-6566

AMERICAN FEDERATION FOR CLINICAL RESEARCH. Charles B. Slack, exec. sec.; 6900 Grove Rd., Thorofare, NJ 08086; tel. 609/848-1000

AMERICAN FERTILITY SOCIETY. Herbert H. Thomas, M.D., exec. dir.; 2131 Magnolia Ave., Suite 201, Birmingham, AL 35256; tel. 205/251-9764

AMERICAN FOUNDATION FOR THE BLIND, INC. William F. Gallagher, exec. dir. ;15 W. 16th St., New York, NY 10011; tel. 212/620-2000

AMERICAN FRACTURE ASSOCIATION. Barbara Dehority, exec. sec.; P.O. Box 668, Bloomington, IL 61701; tel. 309/663-6272

AMERICAN GERIATRICS SOCIETY. Linda Hiddemen Barondess, exec. vice-pres.; 770 Lexington Ave., Suite 400, New York, NY 10021; tel. 212/308-1414

AMERICAN GROUP PRACTICE ASSOCIATION. Donald W. Fisher, Ph.D., exec. vice-pres.; 1422 Duke St., Alexandria, VA 22314; tel. 703/838-0033

AMERICAN GROUP PSYCHOTHERAPY ASSOCIATION, INC. Marsha A. Block, chief exec. off.; 25 E. 21st St., 6th Flr., New York, NY 10010; tel. 212/477-2677

AMERICAN GUILD OF PATIENT ACCOUNT MANAGERS. Carolyn Gostomski, natl. mbrshp. dir.; c/o Hamot Medical Center, 1319 W. 38th St., Erie, PA 16508; tel. 814/866-2687

AMERICAN GYNECOLOGICAL AND OBSTETRICAL SOCIETY. Henry A. Thiede, M.D., sec.; University of Rochester, 601 Elmwood Ave., Box 668, Rochester, NY 14642; tel. 716/275-5201

AMERICAN HEALTH CARE ASSOCIATION. Paul A. Willging, exec. vice-pres.; 1200 15th St., N.W., Washington, DC 20005; tel. 202/833-2050

AMERICAN HEALTH FOUNDATION. Jerry A. Raskin. contr.; 320 E. 43rd St., New York, NY 10017; tel. 212/953-1900

AMERICAN HEALTH PLANNING ASSOCIATION. James O'Donnell, exec. dir.; 1110 Vermont Ave., N.W., Suite 950, Washington, DC 20005; tel. 202/861-1200

AMERICAN HEALTHCARE RADIOLOGY ADMINISTRATORS. Terry Cryan, off. adm.; P.O. Box 334, Sudbury, MA 01776; tel. 617/443-7591

AMERICAN HEART ASSOCIATION, INC. Mary Jane Jesse, M.D., sen. vice-pres.; Office of Scientific Affairs, 7320 Greenville Ave., Dallas, TX 75231; tel. 214/706-1446

AMERICAN HOSPITAL ASSOCIATION. Carol M. McCarthy, Ph.D., J.D., pres.; 840 N. Lake Shore Dr., Chicago, IL 60611; tel. 312/280-6000. REGION 1: John L. Quigley, dir.; John F. Barry, asst. dir.; 5 New England Executive Park, Burlington, MA 01803-5006; tel. 617/272-0787. REGION 2: William Christenson, dir.; Center for Health Affairs, 760 Alexander Rd., CN-1, Princeton, NJ 08543-0001; tel. 609/452-9270. REGION 3: Podge Reed, Jr., dir.; 444 N. Capitol St., N.W., Suite 500, Washington, DC 20001; tel. 202/638-7368. REGION 4: Frank Meisamer, dir.; 15 Dunwoody Pk., Suite 128, Atlanta, GA 30338; tel. 404/394-9510. REGION 5: Nancy S. Shlaes, dir.; Peter O'Neill, asst. dir.; 840 N. Lake Shore Dr., Chicago, IL 60611; tel. 312/280-6661. REGION 6: John Zang, dir.; One Ward Pkwy., Suite 105, Kansas City, MO 64112; tel. 816/561-0501. REGION 7: Sister Marybelle, dir.; 1431 Greenway Dr., Suite 325, Irving, TX 75038; tel. 214/550-1520. REGION 8: Marcia Desmond, dir.; 2140 S. Holly St., Denver, CO 80222; tel. 303/758-2161. REGION 9: Dwight "Speed" Geduldig, dir.; 1023 12th St., Sacramento, CA 95814; tel. 916/447-7262. WASHINGTON OFFICE: Jack W. Owen, exec. vice-pres.; Capitol Pl. No. III, 50 F St., NW, Washington, DC 20001; tel. 202/638-1100.

AMERICAN INSTITUTE OF ARCHITECTS. COMMITTEE ON ARCHITECTURE FOR HEALTH. Michael D. Cohn, dir. hlth. facil. prog.; 1735 New York Ave., N.W., Washington, DC 20006; tel. 202/626-7366

AMERICAN INSTITUTE OF LAUNDERING. (See International Fabricare Institute).

AMERICAN LARYNGOLOGICAL ASSOCIATION, INC. Eugene N. Myers, M.D., sec.; Eye-Ear Hospital, 230 Lothrop St., Rm. 1115, Pittsburgh, PA 15213; tel. 412/647-2110

AMERICAN LARYNGOLOGICAL, RHINOLOGICAL, AND OTOLOGICAL SOCIETY, INC. (THE TRIOLOGICAL SOCIETY). Ann and Bob Holm, section meeting adm.; 2954 Dorman Rd., Broomall, PA 19008; tel. 215/356-8348; Lilibet Coe, adm. asst.; P.O. Box 155, East Greenville, PA 18041; tel. 215/679-7180

AMERICAN LIBRARY ASSOCIATION. Thomas J. Galvin, exec. dir.; 50 E. Huron St., Chicago, IL 60611; tel. 312/944-6780

AMERICAN LUNG ASSOCIATION. James A. Swomley, mng. dir.; 1740 Broadway, New York, NY 10019-4374; tel. 212/315-8700

AMERICAN LUNG ASSOCIATION OF THE MIAMI VALLEY. Fred M. Nathanson, exec. dir.; P.O. Box 902, Dayton, OH 45401; tel. 513/222-8391

AMERICAN MEDICAL ASSOCIATION. James H. Sammons, M.D., exec. vice-pres.; 535 N. Dearborn St., Chicago, IL 60610; tel. 312/645-5000

AMERICAN MEDICAL ASSOCIATION AUXILIARY. Hazel J. Lewis, exec. dir.; 535 N. Dearborn St., Chicago, IL 60610; tel. 312/645-4470

AMERICAN MEDICAL CARE AND REVIEW ASSOCIATION (AMCRA). 5410 Grosvenor Lane, Suite 210, Bethesda, MD 20814; tel. 301/493-9552

AMERICAN MEDICAL PEER REVIEW ORGANIZATION. Andrew Webber, exec. vice-pres;. 440 First St., N.W., Suite 510, Washington, DC 20001; tel. 202/623-1853

AMERICAN MEDICAL RECORD ASSOCIATION. Rita Finnegan, exec. dir.; 875 N. Michigan Ave., Suite 1850, Chicago, IL 60611; tel. 312/787-2672

AMERICAN MEDICAL STUDENT ASSOCIATION/FOUNDATION. Paul R. Wright, exec. dir.; 1890 Preston White Drive, Reston, VA 22091; tel. 703/620-6600

AMERICAN MEDICAL TECHNOLOGISTS. Chester B. Dziekonski, exec. dir.; 710 Higgins Rd., Park Ridge, IL 60068; tel. 312/823-5169

AMERICAN MEDICAL WOMEN'S ASSOCIATION, INC. Carol Davis-Grossman, exec. dir.; 465 Grand St., New York, NY 10002; tel. 212/477-3788

AMERICAN MEDICAL WRITERS' ASSOCIATION. Lillian Sablack, exec. dir.; 5272 River Rd., Suite 410, Bethesda, MD 20816; tel. 301/986-9119

AMERICAN NATIONAL STANDARDS INSTITUTE. Donald L. Peyton, pres.; 1430 Broadway, New York, NY 10018; tel. 212/354-3300

AMERICAN NEPHROLOGY NURSES' ASSOCIATION. Ron P. Brady, exec. dir.; North Woodbury Rd., Box 56, Pitman, NJ 08071; tel. 609/589-2187

AMERICAN NEUROLOGICAL ASSOCIATION. Maura L. McCune, asst. exec dir.; P.O. Box 14730, Minneapolis, MN 55414; tel. 612/378-3290

AMERICAN NURSES' ASSOCIATION. Judith A. Ryan, Ph.D., R.N., exec. dir.; 2420 Pershing Rd., Kansas City, MO 64108; tel. 816/474-5720

AMERICAN NURSES' FOUNDATION, INC. Judith A. Ryan, Ph.D., R.N., exec. dir.; 2420 Pershing Rd., Kansas City, MO 64108; tel. 816/474-5720

AMERICAN OCCUPATIONAL MEDICAL ASSOCIATION. (Includes AOMA Research and Education Fund). Donald L. Hoops, Ph.D., exec. dir.; 2340 S. Arlington Heights Rd., Arlington Heights, IL 60005; tel. 312/228-6850

AMERICAN OCCUPATIONAL THERAPY ASSOCIATION, INC. James J. Garibaldi, exec. dir.; P.O. Box 1725, 1383 Piccard Dr., Suite 300, Rockville, MD 20850-4375; tel. 301/948-9626

AMERICAN OPHTHALMOLOGICAL SOCIETY. Thomas P. Kearns, M.D., sec.-treas.; Mayo Clinic, 200 First St., S.W., Rochester, MN 55905; tel. 507/284-3726

AMERICAN OPTOMETRIC ASSOCIATION. O. Gordon Banks, C.A.E., exec. dir.; 243 N. Lindbergh Blvd., St. Louis, MO 63141; tel. 314/991-4100

AMERICAN ORGANIZATION OF NURSE EXECUTIVES (AHA) Health Care Management & Patient Services. Connie R. Curran, R.N., Ed. D, vice-pres.; 840 N. Lake Shore Dr., Chicago, IL 60611; tel. 312/280-3553

AMERICAN ORTHOPAEDIC ASSOCIATION. Lois Stratemeier, exec. sec.; 222 S. Prospect Ave., Park Ridge, IL 60068; tel. 312/823-7186

AMERICAN ORTHOPSYCHIATRIC ASSOCIATION, INC. Marion F. Langer, Ph.D., exec. dir.; 19 W. 44th St., Suite 1616, New York, NY 10036; tel. 212/354-5770

AMERICAN ORTHOPTIC COUNCIL. Leslie France, adm.; 3914 Nakoma Rd., Madison, WI 53711; tel. 608/233-5383

AMERICAN OSTEOPATHIC ASSOCIATION. John P. Perrin, exec. dir.; 212 E. Ohio St., Chicago, IL 60611; tel. 312/280-5800

AMERICAN OSTEOPATHIC HOSPITAL ASSOCIATION. Richard A. Strano, pres.; 55 W. Seegers Rd., Arlington Heights, IL 60005; tel. 312/952-8900

AMERICAN OTOLOGICAL SOCIETY, INC. D. Thane Cody, M.D., sec.-treas.; Mayo Clinic Jacksonville, 4500 San Pablo Rd., Jacksonville, FL 32224; tel. 904/223-2146

AMERICAN PARKINSON DISEASE ASSOCIATION. 116 John St., rm. 417, New York, NY 10038; tel. 212/732-9550

AMERICAN PEDIATRIC SOCIETY, INC. Audrey Brown, M.D., sec.-treas.; 450 Clarkson Ave., Box 49, Brooklyn, NY 11203; tel. 718/270-1692

AMERICAN PHARMACEUTICAL ASSOCIATION. Dr. John F. Schlegel, pres.; 2215 Constitution Ave., N.W., Washington, DC 20037; tel. 202/628-4410

AMERICAN PHYSICAL THERAPY ASSOCIATION. William D. Zoughlan, exec. vice pres. & chf. exec. off.; 1111 N. Fairfax St., Alexandria, VA 22314; tel. 703/684-2782

AMERICAN PHYSIOLOGICAL SOCIETY. Martin Frank, Ph.D., exec. sec.-treas.; 9650 Rockville Pike, Bethesda, MD 20814; tel. 301/530-7164

AMERICAN PODIATRIC MEDICAL ASSOCIATION. Norman Klombers, D.P.M., exec. dir.; 20 Chevy Chase Circle, N.W., Washington, DC 20015; tel. 202/537-4900

AMERICAN PROTESTANT HEALTH ASSOCIATION. Charles D. Phillips, Ed.D., pres.; 1701 E. Woodfield Rd., Suite 311, Schaumburg, IL 60195; tel. 312/843-2701

AMERICAN PSYCHIATRIC ASSOCIATION. Melvin Sabshin, M.D., med. dir.; 1400 K St., N.W., Washington, DC 20005; tel. 202/682-6000

AMERICAN PSYCHOANALYTIC ASSOCIATION. Helen Fischer, adm. dir.; 309 East 49th St., New York, NY 10017; tel. 212/752-0450

AMERICAN PSYCHOLOGICAL ASSOCIATION. Beverly Jackson, dir. pub. aff.; 1200 17th St., N.W., Washington, DC 20036; tel. 202/955-7710

AMERICAN PSYCHOSOMATIC SOCIETY, INC. George K. Degnon, exec. dir.; 1311A Dolley Madison Blvd., McLean, VA 22101; tel. 703/556-9222

AMERICAN PUBLIC HEALTH ASSOCIATION. William H. McBeath, M.D., exec. dir., 1015 15th St., N.W., Washington, DC 20005; tel. 202/789-5600

AMERICAN PUBLIC WELFARE ASSOCIATION. A. Sidney Johnson III; 1125 15th St., N.W., Suite 300, Washington, DC 20005; tel. 202/293-7550

AMERICAN RED CROSS. 17th and D Sts., N.W., Washington, DC 20006; tel. 202/639-3122

AMERICAN REGISTRY OF CLINICAL RADIOGRAPHY TECHNOLOGISTS. William A. McNeil, exec. dir.; 1616 South Blvd., Edmond, OK 73013; tel. 405/348-5071

AMERICAN REGISTRY OF MEDICAL ASSISTANTS. Annette H. Heyman, dir.; 59½ Southwick Rd., Westfield, MA 01085; tel. 413/562-7336

AMERICAN REGISTRY OF RADIOLOGIC TECHNOLOGISTS. Roland C. McGowan, exec. dir.; 2600 Wayzata Blvd., Minneapolis, MN 55405; tel. 612/377-8416

AMERICAN RHEUMATISM ASSOCIATION. Lynn Bonfiglio, exec. sec.; 1314 Spring St., N.W., Atlanta, GA 30309; tel. 404/266-0795

AMERICAN RHINOLOGIC SOCIETY. Pat A. Barelli, M.D., sec.; 2929 Baltimore, Suite 105, Kansas City, MO 64108; tel. 816/561-4423

AMERICAN ROENTGEN RAY SOCIETY. Phillip Schaper, contr.; American College of Radiology, 1891 Preston White Dr., Reston, VA 22091; tel. 703/648-8941

AMERICAN SCHOOL HEALTH ASSOCIATION. Dana A. Davis, exec. dir.; Box 708, Kent, OH 44240; tel. 216/678-1601

AMERICAN SOCIETY FOR ADOLESCENT PSYCHIATRY. Mary D. Staples, exec. sec.; 24 Green Valley Rd., Wallingford, PA 19086; tel. 215/566-1054

AMERICAN SOCIETY FOR CLINICAL PHARMACOLOGY AND THERAPEUTICS. Elaine Galasso, exec. sec.; 1718 Gallagher Rd., Norristown, PA 19401; tel. 215/825-3838

AMERICAN SOCIETY FOR CYTOTECHNOLOGY. Elsie V. Carruthers, sec.-tres.; 10480 Gregory Circle, Cypress, CA 90630; tel. 714/828-0621

AMERICAN SOCIETY FOR HEAD AND NECK SURGERY. Willard E. Fee, Jr., M.D., sec.; Div. of Otolaryngology/Head and Neck Surgery, Stanford University Medical Center, Stanford, CA 94305; tel. 415/725-6500

AMERICAN SOCIETY FOR HEALTHCARE CENTRAL SERVICE PERSONNEL (AHA). Clarence Daly, dir.; 840 N. Lake Shore Dr., Chicago, IL 60611; tel. 312/280-6160

AMERICAN SOCIETY FOR HEALTHCARE EDUCATION AND TRAINING (AHA). James B. Gantenberg, dir.; 840 N. Lake Shore Dr., Chicago, IL 60611; tel. 312/280-6113

AMERICAN SOCIETY FOR HEALTHCARE HUMAN RESOURCES ADMINISTRATION (AHA). V. Brandon Melton, dir.; 840 N. Lake Shore Dr., Chicago, IL 60611; tel. 312/280-6111

AMERICAN SOCIETY FOR HEALTHCARE RISK MANAGEMENT (AHA). David Meyers, dir.; 840 N. Lake Shore Dr., Chicago, IL 60611; tel. 312/280-6425

AMERICAN SOCIETY FOR HOSPITAL ENGINEERING (AHA). James McLarney, dir.; 840 N. Lake Shore Dr., Chicago, IL 60611; tel. 312/280-6144

AMERICAN SOCIETY FOR HOSPITAL FOOD SERVICE ADMINISTRATORS (AHA). Kathleen Pontius, dir.; 840 N. Lake Shore Dr., Chicago, IL 60611; tel. 312/280-6416

AMERICAN SOCIETY FOR HOSPITAL MARKETING AND PUBLIC RELATIONS (AHA). Lauren Barnett, dir.; 840 N. Lake Shore Dr., Chicago, IL 60611; tel. 312/280-6359

AMERICAN SOCIETY FOR HOSPITAL MATERIALS MANAGEMENT (AHA). Marcie Anthony, dir.; 840 N. Lake Shore Dr., Chicago, IL 60611; tel. 312/280-6137

AMERICAN SOCIETY FOR MEDICAL TECHNOLOGY. Lynn Podell, exec. dir.; 3 Metro Center, Suite 750, Bethesda, MD 20814; tel. 301/961-1931

AMERICAN SOCIETY FOR MICROBIOLOGY. Michael I. Goldberg, Ph.D., exec. dir.; 1913 I St., N.W., Washington, DC 20006; tel. 202/833-9680

AMERICAN SOCIETY FOR PHARMACOLOGY AND EXPERIMENTAL THERAPEUTICS, INC. Kay A. Croker, exec. off.; 9650 Rockville Pike, Bethesda, MD 20814; tel. 301/530-7060

AMERICAN SOCIETY FOR PSYCHOPROPHYLAXIS IN OBSTETRICS, INC (ASPO/LAMAZE). Robert H. Moran, exec. dir.; 1840 Wilson Blvd., Suite 204, Arlington, VA 22201; tel. 703/524-7802

AMERICAN SOCIETY FOR PUBLIC ADMINISTRATION. Keith Mulrooney, exec. dir.; 1120 G St., N.W., Suite 500, Washington, DC 20005; tel. 202/393-7878

AMERICAN SOCIETY FOR TESTING AND MATERIALS. Peter G. Brown, vice-pres.; Finance and Administration, 1916 Race St., Philadelphia, PA 19103; tel. 215/299-5530

AMERICAN SOCIETY FOR THE ADVANCEMENT OF ANESTHESIA IN DENTISTRY. Antonio Reyes-Guerra Jr., D.D.S., exec. sec.; 475 White Plains Rd., Eastchester, NY 10709; tel. 914/961-8136

AMERICAN SOCIETY FOR TRAINING AND DEVELOPMENT. Anthony P. Carnevale, chf. econ., vice-pres. natl. aff.; 1630 Duke St., Box 1443, Alexandria, VA 22313; tel. 703/683-8152

AMERICAN SOCIETY OF ALLIED HEALTH PROFESSIONS. Carolyn M. Del Polito, Ph.D., exec. dir.; Suite 700, 1101 Connecticut Ave., N.W., Washington, DC 20036; tel. 202/857-1150

AMERICAN SOCIETY OF ANESTHESIOLOGISTS. John W. Andes, exec. sec.; 515 Busse Hwy., Park Ridge, IL 60068; tel. 312/825-5586

AMERICAN SOCIETY OF BIOLOGICAL CHEMISTS. Charles C. Hancock, exec. off.; 9650 Rockville Pike, Bethesda, MD 20814; tel. 301/530-7145

AMERICAN SOCIETY OF CLINICAL PATHOLOGISTS. (Includes Board of Registry), Robert A. Dietrich, M.D., chf. of staff; 2100 W. Harrison St.; Chicago, IL 60612; tel. 312/738-1336

AMERICAN SOCIETY OF COLON AND RECTAL SURGEONS. Harriette Gibson, exec. dir.; 615 Griswold, Suite 1717, Detroit, MI 48226; tel. 313/961-7880

AMERICAN SOCIETY OF CONSULTANT PHARMACISTS. R. Timothy Webster, exec. dir.; 2300 9th St., S., Arlington, VA 22204; tel. 703/920-8492

AMERICAN SOCIETY OF CONTEMPORARY MEDICINE AND SURGERY. John G. Bellows, M.D., Ph. D., dir.; 233 E. Erie St., Suite 710, Chicago, IL 60611; tel. 312/951-1400

AMERICAN SOCIETY OF CONTEMPORARY OPHTHALMOLOGY. Randall T. Bellows, M.D., dir.; 233 E. Erie St., Suite 710, Chicago, IL 60611; tel. 312/951-1400

AMERICAN SOCIETY OF CYTOLOGY. Lenore L. Strigari, exec. sec.; 1015 Chestnut St., Suite 1518, Philadelphia, PA 19107; tel. 215/922-3880

AMERICAN SOCIETY OF DENTISTRY FOR CHILDREN. George Teuscher, D.D.S., exec. off.; 211 E. Chicago Ave., Chicago, IL 60611; tel. 312/943-1244

AMERICAN SOCIETY OF DIRECTORS OF VOLUNTEER SERVICES (AHA). Betty Lyon Dudley, dir.; 840 N. Lake Shore Dr., Chicago, IL 60611; tel. 312/280-6110

AMERICAN SOCIETY OF ELECTRONEURODIAGNOSTIC TECHNOLOGISTS, INC. M. Fran Pedelty, exec. dir.; Sixth at Quint, Carroll, IA 51401; tel. 712/792-2978

AMERICAN SOCIETY OF EXTRA-CORPOREAL TECHNOLOGY, INC. George M. Cate, exec. dir.; 1980 Isaac Newton Sq., S., Reston, VA 22090; tel. 703/435-8556

AMERICAN SOCIETY OF HOSPITAL PHARMACISTS. Joseph A. Oddis, exec. vice-pres.; 4630 Montgomery Ave., Bethesda, MD 20814; tel. 301/657-3000

AMERICAN SOCIETY OF INTERNAL MEDICINE. Joseph F. Boyle, M.D., exec. vice-pres.; 1101 Vermont Ave., N.W., Suite 500, Washington, DC 20005; tel. 202/289-1700

AMERICAN SOCIETY OF LAW AND MEDICINE. Lawrence O. Gostin, J.D., exec. dir.; 765 Commonwealth Ave., Boston, MA 02215; tel. 617/262-4990

AMERICAN SOCIETY OF MAXILLOFACIAL SURGEONS. Lousanne Lofgren, 233 N. Michigan Ave., Chicago, IL 60601; tel. 312/856-1818

AMERICAN SOCIETY OF PLASTIC AND RECONSTRUCTIVE SURGEONS, INC. Thomas R. Schedler, CAE, exec. dir.; 233 N. Michigan Ave., Suite 1900, Chicago, IL 60601; tel. 312/856-1818

AMERICAN SOCIETY OF RADIOLOGIC TECHNOLOGISTS. Ward M. Keller, exec. dir.; 15000 Central Ave., S.E., Albuquerque, NM 87123; tel. 505/298-4500

AMERICAN SOCIETY OF THERAPEUTIC RADIOLOGISTS. Fran Glica, exec. sec., Sheila Aubin, mtg. dir.; 1891 Preston White Drive, Reston, VA 22091; tel. 703/648-8900

AMERICAN SPEECH-LANGUAGE-HEARING ASSOCIATION. (Formerly American Speech and Hearing Association.). Frederick T. Spahr, Ph.D., exec. dir.; 10801 Rockville Pike, Rockville, MD 20852; tel. 301/897-5700

AMERICAN SURGICAL ASSOCIATION. Hiram C. Polk Jr., M.D., chm.; Department of Surgery, University of Louisville, Louisville, Ky 40292; tel. 502/588-5585

AMERICAN THORACIC SOCIETY. S. R. Iannotta, exec. dir.; 1740 Broadway, New York, NY 10019-4374; tel. 212/315-8700

AMERICAN THYROID ASSOCIATION, INC. Colum A. Gorman, sec.; Mayo Clinic, 200 First St., S.W., Rochester, MN 55905; tel. 507/284-4738

AMERICAN TRAUMA SOCIETY. Sandra Lillicropp, exec. dir.; P.O. Box 13526, Baltimore, MD 21203; tel. 1-800-556-7890, 301/328-6304

AMERICAN UROLOGICAL ASSOCIATION, INC. Richard J. Hannigan, exec. sec.; 1120 N. Charles St., Baltimore, MD 21201; tel. 301/727-1100

AMTSRAADSFORENINGEN I DANMARK. (National Committee for Danish Hospitals). Johanne Louise Dithmer, head of dept.; Landemaerket 10, DK 1119 Copenhagen K, Denmark; tel. 011 45 11 2161

ARTHRITIS FOUNDATION. Clifford M. Clarke, CAE, pres.; 1314 Spring St., N.W., Atlanta, GA 30309; tel. 404/872-7100

ARTHRITIS SOCIETY. S. L. McConnell, assoc. mng. dir., Suite 401, 250 Bloor St., E. Toronto, Ont. M4W 3P2, Canada; tel. 416/967-1414

ASOCIACIÓN COLOMBIANA DE HOSPITALES. Dr. Augusto Buenda Ferro, exec. sec.; Carrera 17, Nos. 39-15, Apartado Aéreo 29121, Bogotá D.E., Colombia; tel. 32-52-15

ASOCIACIÓN COSTARRICENSE DE HOSPITALES. Apartado Postal 267-1005, San José, Costa Rica, Central America; tel.; tel. 21-49-19

ASOCIACIÓN MEXICANA DE HOSPITALES. Dr. Jorge Ruiz de Esparza, pres.; Queretaro 210, Mexico 7, D.F.; tel. 5-74-01-28

ASOCIACIÓN PERUANA DE HOSPITALES. Arturo Vasi Paez, pres.; Elena Zambrano Sanchez, sec.; Av. Salaverry N. 2409 Block B-2415, of. 206, San Isidro, Lima 27, Peru

ASOCIACIÓN VENEZOLANA DE HOSPITALES. Apartado Postal 4888, Caracas 1010-A Venezuela, South America; tel. 979-91-79

ASSEMBLY OF HOSPITAL SCHOOLS OF NURSING (AHA). Carol M. Sullivan, R.N., dir.; 840 N. Lake Shore Dr., Chicago, IL 60611; tel. 312/280-6432

ASSOCIACAO BRASILEIRA DE HOSPITAIS. Rua Dos Andradas 96, Sobreloja 02, Rio de Janeiro, Brazil CEP 20051

ASSOCIATION DES ETABLISSEMENTS PUBLICS DE SOINS, a.s.b.l. L. Oleffe-van Dierdonck, staff contact Rue des Guildes 9-11, 1040 Bruxelles, Belgium; tel. 02/230.03.65

ASSOCIATION DES MEDECINS DE LANGUE FRANCAISE DU CANADA. M. André de Sève, dir. adm.; 1440 Ste.-Catherine W., 510 Montreal, Que. H3G 2P9; tel. 514/866-2053

ASSOCIATION FOR CLINICAL PASTORAL EDUCATION, INC. Duane Parker, exec. dir.; 1549 Clairmont Rd., Suite 103, Decatur, GA 30033; tel. 404/320-1472

ASSOCIATION FOR EDUCATION AND REHABILITATION OF THE BLIND AND VISUALLY IMPAIRED. Kathleen Megivern, exec. dir.; 206 N. Washington St., Alexandria, VA 22314; tel. 703/836-6060

ASSOCIATION FOR HEALTHCARE QUALITY. William H. Kincaid, exec. dir.; 3550 Woodland Rd., Ann Arbor, MI 48104; tel. 313/971-9492

ASSOCIATION FOR HOSPITAL MEDICAL EDUCATION. Donna F. Cantor, 1101 Connecticut Ave., N.W., Suite 700, Washington, DC 20036; tel. 202/857-1196

ASSOCIATION FOR PRACTITIONERS IN INFECTION CONTROL. Robert B. Willis, exec. dir; 505 E. Hawley St., Mundelein, IL 60060; tel. 312/949-6052

ASSOCIATION FOR RESEARCH IN VISION AND OPHTHALMOLOGY, INC. Janice V. Henkind, adm.; Box C-1002, Wykagyl Station, New Rochelle, NY 10804; tel. 914/636-2154

ASSOCIATION FOR RETARDED CITIZENS. Al Abeson, Ed.D., exec. dir.; 2501 Avenue J, Box 6109, Arlington, TX 76006; tel. 817/640-0204

ASSOCIATION FOR THE ADVANCEMENT OF MEDICAL INSTRUMENTATION. Michael J. Miller, J.D., exec. dir.; 1901 N. Fort Myer Dr., Suite 602, Arlington, VA 22209; tel. 703/525-4890

ASSOCIATION FOR THE CARE OF CHILDREN'S HEALTH. Beverley Johnson, exec. dir.; 3615 Wisconsin Ave., N.W., Washington, DC 20016; tel. 202/244-1801

ASSOCIATION FOR VOLUNTARY SURGICAL CONTRACEPTION, INC. Hugo Hoogenboom, exec. dir.; 122 E. 42nd St., New York, NY 10168; tel. 212/351-2500

ASSOCIATION FOR VOLUNTEER ADMINISTRATION. Jacqueline A. Callahan, exec. dir.; P.O. Box 4584, Boulder, CO 80306; tel. 303/497-0238

ASSOCIATION OF AMERICAN MEDICAL COLLEGES. (See also Council of Teaching Hospitals.). Richard M. Knapp, Ph.D., dir.; Department of Teaching Hospitals, One Dupont Circle, N.W., Suite 200, Washington, DC 20036; tel. 202/828-0490

ASSOCIATION OF AMERICAN PHYSICIANS. Stuart Kornfeld, M.D., sec.; Dept. of Medicine, Washington University School of Medicine, 660 S. Euclid Ave., St. Louis, MO 63110; tel. 314/362-8803

ASSOCIATION OF AMERICAN PHYSICIANS AND SURGEONS, INC. E. Sue Ackley, exec. sec.; 9203 Lake Braddock Drive, Burke, VA 22015; tel. 703/425-6300

ASSOCIATION OF COMMUNITY CANCER CENTERS. Lee E. Mortenson, exec. dir.; 11600 Nebel St., Suite 201, Rockville, MD 20852; tel. 301/984-9496

ASSOCIATION OF LIFE INSURANCE MEDICAL DIRECTORS OF AMERICA. Joseph R. Jurkoic, M.D., sec.; One Tower Sq., Hartford, CT 06183-1030; tel. 203/277-4193

ASSOCIATION OF MEDICAL ILLUSTRATORS. Margaret H. Henry, exec. dir.; 2692 Huguenot Springs Rd., Midlothian, VA 23113; tel. 804/794-2908

ASSOCIATION OF MENTAL HEALTH ADMINISTRATORS. Laurie Poul, exec. dir.; 840 N. Lake Shore Dr., Suite 1103W, Chicago, IL 60611; tel. 312/943-2751

ASSOCIATION OF MENTAL HEALTH CLERGY, INC. George E. Doebler, exec. dir.; 12320 River Oaks Point, Knoxville, TN 37922; tel. 615/544-9717

ASSOCIATION OF MILITARY SURGEONS OF THE U.S. Lt. General Max B. Bralliar, USAF MC Ret., exec. dir.; P.O. Box 104, Kensington, MD 20895; tel. 301/933-2801

ASSOCIATION OF OPERATING ROOM NURSES, INC. Clifford H. Jordan, R.N., Ed.D., F.A.A.N., exec. dir.; 10170 E. Mississippi Ave., Denver, CO 80231; tel. 303/755-6300

ASSOCIATION OF SCHOOLS OF PUBLIC HEALTH, INC. Michael K. Gemmell, exec. dir.; 1015 Fifteenth St., N.W., Suite 404, Washington, DC 20005; tel. 202/842-4668

ASSOCIATION OF SPECIALIZED AND COOPERATIVE LIBRARY AGENCIES. Evelyn Shaevel, interim exec. dir.; 50 E. Huron St., Chicago, IL 60611; tel. 312/944-6780

ASSOCIATION OF STATE AND TERRITORIAL HEALTH OFFICIALS. (Includes Association of Health Facility Licensure and Certification Directors.) George K. Degnon, exec. dir.; 1311A Dolley Madison Blvd., Suite 3A, McLean, VA 22101; tel. 703/556-9222

ASSOCIATION OF SURGICAL TECHNOLOGISTS INC. Sandra L. Wilkins, exec. dir.; 8307 Shaffer Parkway, Littleton, CO 80127; tel. 303/978-9010

ASSOCIATION OF UNIVERSITY ANESTHETISTS. Edward D. Miller Jr., M.D., Department of Anesthesia, Box 238, University of Virginia M.C., Charlottesville, VA 22908;

ASSOCIATION OF UNIVERSITY PROGRAMS IN HEALTH ADMINISTRATION. Gary L. Filerman, Ph.D., pres.; 1911 N. Fort Myer Dr., Suite 503, Arlington, VA 22209; tel. 703/524-5500

ASSOCIATION OF VOLUNTEER BUREAUS. (This Association is deleted since it is no longer in existence.)

ASSOCIATION OF WESTERN HOSPITALS. Kathryn E. Johnson, pres./CEO; 830 Market St., San Francisco, CA 94102; tel. 415/421-8810

ASTHMA & ALLERGY FOUNDATION OF AMERICA. T. J. Schmidt Dunlap, natl. dir.; 1835 K St., N.W., Suite P-900, Washington, DC 20006; tel. 202/293-2950

AUSTRALIAN HOSPITAL ASSOCIATION. E. N. Pickering, exec. dir.; 35 Clarence St., Sydney, New South Wales 2000, Australia; tel. (02) 290-3366

B

BCS FINANCIAL CORPORATION. William E. Ryan, pres.; 676 N. St. Clair, Chicago, IL 60611; tel. 312/951-7700

BIOFEEDBACK SOCIETY OF AMERICA. Francine Butler, Ph.D.; 10200 W. 44th Ave., Suite 304, Wheat Ridge, CO 80033; tel. 303/422-8436

BIOLOGICAL PHOTOGRAPHIC ASSOCIATION, INC. Thomas P. Hurtgen, exec. dir.; 115 Stoneridge Dr., Chapel Hill, NC 27514; tel. 919/967-8247

BIOLOGICAL STAIN COMMISSION, INC. Eric A. Schenk, M.D., sec.; University of Rochester Medical Center, Rochester, NY 14642; tel. 716/275-3197

BLINDED VETERANS ASSOCIATION. Ronald L. Miller, Ph.D., exec. dir.; 1726 M St., N.W., Washington, DC 20036; tel. 202/223-3066

BLIND SERVICE ASSOCIATION, INC. Beatrice Fredman, exec. dir.; 22 W. Monroe St., 11th Flr., Chicago, IL 60603-2501; tel. 312/236-0808

BLUE CROSS AND BLUE SHIELD ASSOCIATION. B. R. Tresnowski, pres.; 676 N. St. Clair, Chicago, IL 60611; tel. 312/440-6000

BRITISH MEDICAL ASSOCIATION. J. D. J. Havard, M.A., M.D., L.L.M., sec.; B.M.A. House Tavistock Square, London, WC1H 9JP England; tel. 01-387-4499

BUNDESKANZLERANT SEKTION VI: VOLKSGESUNDHEIT (Federal Chancellary Department VI: Public Health), Radetzkystrasse 2 1031 Wien, Austria; tel. 0222/75 56 86

C

CANADIAN ANAESTHETISTS' SOCIETY. Lloyd H. Mayeda, exec. dir.; 187 Gerrard St., E., Toronto, Ont. M5A 2E5; tel. 416/923-1449

CANADIAN ASSOCIATION OF MEDICAL RADIATION TECHNOLOGISTS. Daniel F. Steinwald, exec. dir.; 280 Metcalfe St., Suite 410, Ottawa, Ont. K2P 1R7; tel. 613/234-0012 or 234-0441

CANADIAN ASSOCIATION OF PATHOLOGISTS. Dr. M.D.D. McNeely, sec. treas.; 4489 Viewmont Ave., Victoria, B.C. V8Z 5K8; tel. 604/479-7676

CANADIAN ASSOCIATION OF RADIOLOGISTS. Mrs. Alva Ekstrand-Pentecost, exec. dir.; 1440 Ste., Catherine St. W. Suite 506, Montreal, Que. H3G 1R8; tel. 514/866-2035

CANADIAN ASSOCIATION OF SOCIAL WORKERS. Mary Hegan, M.S.W., exec. dir.; 55 Parkdale Ave., Ottawa, Ont. K1Y 1E5; tel. 613/728-1865

CANADIAN ASSOCIATION OF THE DEAF. Suite 311, 271 Spadina Rd., Toronto, Ont. M5R 2V3; tel. 416/928-1350

CANADIAN CANCER SOCIETY. Douglas H. Barr, chief exec. ofr.; 77 Bloor St. W., Suite 1702, Toronto, Ont. M5S 3A1; tel. 416/961-7223

CANADIAN CARDIOVASCULAR SOCIETY. Mrs. D. Lourenco, exec. sec.; 360 Victoria Ave., Rm. 401, Westmount, Que. H3Z 2N4; tel. 514/482-3407

CANADIAN COLLEGE OF HEALTH RECORD ADMINISTRATORS/HEALTH RECORD ASSOCIATION. Patricia A. Hewes, exec. dir.; 1185 Eglinton Ave., E., Suite 301, Don Mills, Ont. M3C 3C6; tel. 416/429-5835

CANADIAN COUNCIL OF BLUE CROSS PLANS. H. D. Russel, 150 Ferrand Dr., Don Mills Ont. M3C 1H6; tel. 416/429-2661

CANADIAN COUNCIL OF THE BLIND. Bruce R. Clark, exec. dir.; 220 Dundas St., Suite 510, London, Ont. N6A 1H3; tel. 519/433-3946

CANADIAN COUNCIL ON HOSPITAL ACCREDITATION. Jennifer Jackman, M.D., interim exec. dir.; 1815 Alta Vista Dr., Ottawa, Ont. K1G 3Y6; tel. 613/523-9154

CANADIAN COUNCIL ON SOCIAL DEVELOPMENT. Terrance M. Hunsley, exec. dir.; 55 Parkdale Ave., Box 3505, Station C, Ottawa, Ont. K1Y 4G1; tel. 613/728-1865

CANADIAN DENTAL ASSOCIATION. Linda Teteruck, dir. commun.; 1815 Alta Vista Dr., Ottawa, Ont. K1G 3Y6; tel. 613/523-1770

CANADIAN DIETETIC ASSOCIATION. Marsha Sharp, exec. dir.; 480 University Ave., Suite 604, Toronto, Ont. M5G 1V2; tel. 416/596-0857

CANADIAN HEARING SOCIETY. Denis Morrice, exec. dir.; 271 Spadina Rd., Toronto, Ont. M5R 2V3; tel. 416/964-9595

CANADIAN HEART FOUNDATION. E. McDonald, exec. dir.; One Nicholas St., Suite 1200, Ottawa, Ont. K1N 7B7; tel. 613/237-4361

CANADIAN HOSPITAL ASSOCIATION/Association des hopitaux du Canada. Jean-Claude Martin, pres.; 17 York St., Suite 100, Ottawa, Ont. K1N 9J6; tel. 613/238-8005

CANADIAN LUNG ASSOCIATION. 75 Albert, Suite 908, Ottawa, Ont. K1P 5E7; tel. 613/237-1208

CANADIAN MEDICAL ASSOCIATION. Leo-Paul Landry, M.D., sec. gen.; Box 8650, Ottawa, Ont. K1G 0G8; tel. 613/731-9331

CANADIAN MEDICAL ENGINEERING CONSULTANTS. A. M. Dolan, pres.; Belfountain, Ont. L0N 1B0; tel. 519/927-3286

CANADIAN MENTAL HEALTH ASSOCIATION. George Rohn, gen. dir.; 2160 Yonge St., Toronto, Ont. M4S 2Z3; tel. 416/484-7750

CANADIAN NATIONAL INSTITUTE FOR THE BLIND. Euclid J. Herie, mng. dir.; 1931 Bayview Ave., Toronto, Ont. M4G 4C8; tel. 416/486-2537

CANADIAN NURSES ASSOCIATION. Ginette Rodger, exec. dir.; 50 The Driveway, Ottawa, Ont. K2P 1E2; tel. 613/237-2133

CANADIAN ORTHOPAEDIC ASSOCIATION. Reginald H. Tabsley, M.D., sec.; 1117 Ste. Catherine St., W., Suite 223, Montreal, Que. H3B 1H9; tel. 514/844-9818

CANADIAN PHARMACEUTICAL ASSOCIATION. Leroy C. Fevang, exec. dir.; 1785 Alta Vista Dr., 2nd floor, Ottawa, Ont. K1G 3Y6; tel. 613/523-7877

CANADIAN PHYSIOTHERAPY ASSOCIATION. Nancy Christie, exec. dir.; 44 Eglinton Ave., W., Suite 201, Toronto, Ont. M4R 1A1; tel. 416/485-1139

CANADIAN PSYCHIATRIC ASSOCIATION. Lea C. Metivier, chf. adm. off.; 225 Lisgar St., Suite 103, Ottawa, Ont. K2P 0C6; tel. 613/234-2815

CANADIAN PUBLIC HEALTH ASSOCIATION. Gerald H. Dafoe, M.H.A., exec. dir.; 1335 Carling Ave., Suite 210, Ottawa, Ont. K1Z 8N8; tel. 613/725-3769

CANADIAN RED CROSS SOCIETY. G. Weber, sec. gen.; The Canadian Red Cross Society, 1800 Alta Vista Dr., Ottawa, Canada K1G 4J5; tel. 613/738-0257

CANADIAN REHABILITATION COUNCIL FOR THE DISABLED. J. R. Sarney, natl. exec. dir.; 1 Yonge St., Suite 2110, Toronto, Ont. M5E 1E5; tel. 416/862-0340

CANADIAN SOCIETY OF HOSPITAL PHARMACISTS. Irene Nicoll, actg. exec. dir.; 123 Edward St., Suite 603, Toronto, Ont. M5G 1E2; tel. 416/979-2049

CANADIAN SOCIETY OF LABORATORY TECHNOLOGISTS. E. Valerie Booth, exec. dir.; Box 830, Hamilton, Ont. L8N 3N8; tel. 416/528-8642

CATHOLIC HEALTH ASSOCIATION OF CANADA. Everett MacNeil, pres.; 1247 Kilborn Avenue, Ottawa, Ontario K1H 6K9; tel. 613/731-7148

CATHOLIC HEALTH ASSOCIATION OF THE UNITED STATES. (Formerly Catholic Hospital Association). John E. Curley Jr., pres./CEO; 4455 Woodson Rd., St. Louis, MO 63134; tel. 314/427-2500

CENTER FOR HEALTH ADMINISTRATION STUDIES. Ronald Andersen, Ph.D., dir.; University of Chicago, 1101 E. 58th St., Chicago, IL 60637; tel. 312/702-7104

CENTRAL NEUROPSYCHIATRIC ASSOCIATION. Claresa F. M. Armstrong, M.D., sec.-treas.; 1301 Astor St., Chicago, IL 60610; tel. 312/427-1257

CENTRAL SOCIETY FOR CLINICAL RESEARCH, INC. John P. Phair, M.D., sec.-treas.; Department of Medicine, Northwestern University Medical School, 303 E. Chicago Ave., Chicago, IL 60611; tel. 312/951-5610

CENTRAL SURGICAL ASSOCIATION. Larry Carey, M.D., sec.; Dept. of Surgery, Ohio State University, 410 W. 10th Ave., Columbus, OH 43210

CHRISTIAN RECORD BRAILLE FOUNDATION. Vernon L. Bretsch, pres.; 4444 S. 52nd St., Lincoln, NE 68516; tel. 402/488-0981

COLLEGE OF AMERICAN PATHOLOGISTS. Howard E. Cartwright, chf. exec. off.; 5202 Old Orchard Rd., Skokie, IL 60077; tel. 312/966-5700

COLLEGE OF FAMILY PHYSICIANS OF CANADA. Reg. L. Perkin, M.D., exec. dir.; 4000 Leslie St., Willowdale, Ont. M2K 2R9; tel. 416/493-7513

COLLEGE OF PHYSICIANS AND SURGEONS OF NEW BRUNSWICK. Victor D. McLaughlin, M.D., FRCSC Regstr.; 10 Prince Edward St., Saint John, NB Canada E2L 4M5; tel. 506/652-5221

COMMISSION ON ACCREDITATION OF REHABILITATION FACILITIES. Alan H. Toppel, exec. dir.; 2500 N. Pantano Rd., Tucson, AZ 85715; tel. 602/886-8575

COMMISSION ON PROFESSIONAL AND HOSPITAL ACTIVITIES. Jean Chenoweth, pres., P.O. Box 1809, Ann Arbor, MI 48106; tel. 313/769-6511

COMMITTEE OF INTERNS AND RESIDENTS. Jonathan House, M.D., exec. dir.; 386 Park Ave., S., New York, NY 10016; tel. 212/725-5500

CONFEDERACIÓN ARGENTINA DE CLINICAS, SANATARIOS Y HOSPITALES PRIVADOS. Tucuman 1668-2 Piso, 1050, Buenos Aires, Argentina

COOLEY'S ANEMIA FOUNDATION, INC. Michael DiFilippo, natl. exec. dir.; 105 E. 22nd St., Suite 911, New York, NY 10010; tel. 212/598-0911, 800/221-3571

CORPORATION PROFESSIONNELLE DES MEDECINS DU QUEBEC. Augustin Roy, M.D., pres.; 1440 W. Ste. Catherine, Suite 914, Montreal, Quebec, H3G 1S5; tel. 514/878-4441

COUNCIL OF COMMUNITY BLOOD CENTERS. James L. MacPherson, exec. dir.; Old Brick House Square, 113 Rowell Court, Falls Church, VA 22046; tel. 703/237-0833

COUNCIL OF JEWISH FEDERATIONS, INC. Mr. Carmi Schwartz, exec. vice-pres.; 730 Broadway, New York, NY 10003; tel. 212/475-5000

COUNCIL OF MEDICAL SPECIALTY SOCIETIES. Richard S. Wilbur, M.D., exec. vice-pres.; Box 70, Lake Forest, IL 60045; tel. 312/295-3456

COUNCIL OF STATE ADMINISTRATORS OF VOCATIONAL REHABILITATION. Joseph H. Owens, exec. dir.; 1055 Thomas Jefferson, N.W., Suite 410, Washington, DC 20005; tel. 202/638-4634

COUNCIL OF TEACHING HOSPITALS OF THE ASSOCIATION OF AMERICAN MEDICAL COLLEGES. James D. Bentley, Ph.D., vice-pres. for Clinical Services; One Dupont Circle, N.W., Suite 200, Washington, DC 20036; tel. 202/828-0490

COUNCIL ON COMMUNITY HEALTH, HOSPITAL, INSTITUTIONAL AND MEDICAL AFFAIRS OF THE AMERICAN DENTAL ASSOCIATION. John S. Klyop, sec.; 211 E. Chicago Ave., Chicago, IL 60611; tel. 312/440-2860

COUNCIL ON EDUCATION FOR PUBLIC HEALTH. Patricia P. Evans, exec. dir.; 1015 Fifteenth St., N.W., Washington, DC 20005; tel. 202/789-1050

COUNCIL ON POSTSECONDARY ACCREDITATION, INC. Richard M. Millard, Ph.D., pres.; Suite 305, One Dupont Circle, N.W., Washington, DC 20036; tel. 202/452-1433

COUNCIL ON SOCIAL WORK EDUCATION. Eunice Shatz, Ph.D., exec. dir.; 1744 R St., N.W., Washington, DC 20009; tel. 202/667-2300

CYSTIC FIBROSIS FOUNDATION. Robert J. Beall, Ph.D., exec. vice-pres. med. aff.; 6931 Arlington Rd., Bethesda, MD 20814; tel. 1-800-FIGHT-CF, 301/951-4422

D

DAMIEN DUTTON SOCIETY FOR LEPROSY AID, INC. Howard E. Crouch, pres.; 616 Bedford Ave., Bellmore, NY 11710; tel. 516/221-5829

DELTA DENTAL PLANS ASSOCIATION. James Bonk, exec. vice-pres.; 211 E. Chicago Ave., Suite 1010, Chicago, IL 60611; tel. 312/337-4707

DERMATOLOGY FOUNDATION Sandra Rahn Goldman, exec. dir.; 1563 Maple Ave., Evanston, IL 60201; tel. 312/328-2256

DEUTSCHE KRANKENHAUSGESELLSCHAFT (German Hospital Association). Hans-Werner Muller, M.D., dir. gen.; Tersteegenstrasse 9, D-4000 Düsseldorf 30, W. Germany; tel. Dusseldorf (0211) 45 47 30

DIETARY MANAGERS ASSN. William St. John, exec. dir.; 4410 W. Roosevelt Rd., Hillside, IL 60162; tel. 312/449-2770

DUKE ENDOWMENT, THE. Billy G. McCall, dep. exec. dir.; 200 S. Tryon St., Suite 1100, Charlotte, NC 28202; tel. 704/376-0291

DYSAUTONOMIA FOUNDATION, INC. Lenore F. Roseman, exec. dir.; 370 Lexington Ave., New York, NY 10017; tel. 212/889-5222

E

EASTERN ORTHOPAEDIC ASSOCIATION. Elizabeth F. Capella, assn. exec.; Suite 3F, 301 S. 8th St., Philadelphia, PA 19106-4072; tel. 215/923-9173

ECRI. Joel J. Nobel, M.D., pres.; 5200 Butler Pike, Plymouth Meeting, PA 19462; tel. 215/825-6000

EDUCATIONAL COMMISSION FOR FOREIGN MEDICAL GRADUATES. Thomas W. Mou, M.D. pres.; 3624 Market St., Philadelphia, PA 19104-2685; tel. 215/386-5900

EGYPTIAN HOSPITAL ASSOCIATION. Yousef S. Raafat, M.D., vice-pres. and sec.; Dar el Hekma, 42 Kasr el Ainy St., Cairo, Egypt; tel.

EMERGENCY NURSES ASSOCIATION. Torry M. Sansone, exec. dir.; 230 East Ohio, Suite 600, Chicago, IL 60611; tel. 312/649-0297

ENDOCRINE SOCIETY, THE. Nettie C. Karpin, exec. dir.; 9650 Rockville Pike, Bethesda, MD 20814; tel. 301/530-9660

ENVIRONMENTAL MANAGEMENT ASSOCIATION. Harold C. Rowe, Ph.D., pres.; 1019 Highland Ave., Largo, FL 33540; tel. 813/586-5710

EPILEPSY FOUNDATION OF AMERICA. William M. McLin, exec. vice-pres.; 4351 Garden City Pkwy. Landover, MD 20785; tel. 301/459-3700

EPISCOPAL GUILD FOR THE BLIND. Rev. Harry J. Sutcliffe; 561 Pacific St., Brooklyn, NY 11217; tel. 718/625-4886

EYE-BANK FOR SIGHT-RESTORATION, INC. Mary Jane O'Neill, exec. dir.; 210 E. 64th St., New York, NY 10021; tel. 212/980-6700

F

FAMILY SERVICE AMERICA. Geneva B. Johnson, pres. and chf. exec. off.; 11700 W. Lake Park Dr., Milwaukee, WI 53224; tel. 414/359-2111

FEDERACAO BRASILEIRA DE HOSPITALS. Rua Anfilofio de Carvalho 29, cob. 01, 20000 Rio de Janeira, Brazil

FEDERACION LATINOAMERICANA DE HOSPITALES. Dr. Guillermo Fajardo, dir.; Sur 75 #4352, Col. Viaducto Piedad, Mexico, D.F 08200; tel. 5-30-79-63

FEDERATION HOSPITALIERE DE FRANCE. Philippe Cadene, exec. dir.; 33 Avenue d'Italie, 75013 Paris, France; tel. 584-32-50

FEDERATION OF AMERICAN HEALTH SYSTEMS. Michael D. Bromberg, exec. dir.; 1111 19th St., N.W., Suite 402, Washington, DC 20036; tel. 202/833-3090

FEDERATION OF STATE MEDICAL BOARDS OF THE UNITED STATES, INC. Bryant L. Galusha, M.D., exec. vice-pres.; 2630 W. Freeway, Suite 138, Fort Worth, TX 76102; tel. 817/335-1141

FEDERAZIONE ITALIANA ASSOCIAZIONI REGIONALI OSPEDALIERE (FIARO). Diodato Lanni, pres.; Via dei Prefetti 46, 00186, Rome, Italy; tel. 48-48-09

FINANCIAL ACCOUNTING STANDARDS BOARD. Michael O. Alexander, dir. res. and tech. activities; High Ridge Park Stamford, CT 06905; tel. 203/329-8401

FIREMAN RED CHILD SAFETY FOUNDATION. Howard P. Schock, exec. dir.; P.O. Box 1360, Evergreen, CO 80439-1360; tel. 303/674-7253

FORUM FOR HEALTHCARE PLANNING (formerly American Association For Hospital Planning). Carol A. Lively, exec. dir.; 1101 Connecticut Ave., N.W., Suite 700, Washington, DC 20036; tel. 202/857-1162

FOUNDATION FOR CHIROPRACTIC EDUCATION AND RESEARCH. Brian E. Cartier, exec. dir.; 1701 Clarendon Blvd., Arlington, VA 22209; tel. 703/276-7445

G

GAUCHER'S DISEASE REGISTRY. Marylin Kattan, dir.; 4642 E. Chapman Ave., #139, Orange, CA 92669; tel. 714/ 532-2212

THE GERONTOLOGICAL SOCIETY OF AMERICA. John M. Cornman, exec. dir.; 1411 K St., N.W., Suite 300, Washington, DC 20005; tel. 202/393-1411

GESELLSCHAFT KRANKENHAUSWESEN DER DEUTSCHEN DEMOKRATISCHEN REPUBLIK. Staedtisches Krankenhaus in Friedrichshain, Leninalle 49, Berlin 1017, German Democratic Republic; tel. 4361160

GREAT PLAINS HEALTH ALLIANCE, INC. Curtis C. Erickson, pres. and chf. exec. off.; 625 Third St., Box 366, Phillipsburg, KS 67661; tel. 913/543-2111

GREATER FLINT AREA HOSPITAL ASSEMBLY. David Seaman, exec. dir.; 702 S. Ballenger Hwy., Flint, MI 48504

GROUP HEALTH ASSOCIATION OF AMERICA, INC. James F. Doherty, pres.and CEO.; 1129 20th St., N.W., Suite 600, Washington, DC 20036; tel. 202/778-3200

GUIDE DOG USERS, INC. Phyllis Stern, pres.; 1178 S. Kenilworth, Oak Park, IL 60304; tel. 312/848-6191

H

HEALTH AND EDUCATION RESOURCES, INC. Dallas Johnson, pres.; 4733 Bethesda Ave., Suite 735, Bethesda, MD 20814; tel. 301/656-3178

HEALTH INDUSTRY DISTRIBUTORS ASSOCIATION. Paul B. Simmons, pres.; Emmon S. Rogers, vice-pres. adm.; Suzanne Respess, vice-pres. mem. serv.; Elizabeth Beck, vice-pres. commun.; 1701 Pennsylvania Ave., N.W., Suite 470, Washington, D.C. 20006; tel. 202/659-0050

HEALTH INDUSTRY MANUFACTURERS ASSOCIATION. Frank E. Samuel, Jr., pres.; 1030 15th St., N.W., Suite 1100, Washington, DC 20005; tel. 202/452-8240

HEALTH INSURANCE ASSOCIATION OF AMERICA. James L. Moorefield, pres.; 1025 Connecticut Ave., N.W., Suite 1200, Washington, DC 20036; tel. 202/223-7780

HEALTH INSURANCE ASSOCIATION OF AMERICA. Shirley M. Nagelschmidt, vice-pres. of pub. rel.; 1001 Pennsylvania Ave., N.W., Suite 500, Washington, DC 20004-2505; tel. 202/624-2000

HEALTHCARE FINANCIAL MANAGEMENT ASSOCIATION. Richard L. Clarke, FHFMA, pres.; 1900 Spring Rd., Suite 500, Oak Brook, IL 60521; tel. 312/571-4700

HEALTHCARE INFORMATION & MANAGEMENT SYSTEMS SOCIETY (AHA). Richard Covert, Ph.D., dir.; 840 N. Lake Shore Dr., Chicago, IL 60611; tel. 312/280-6023

HEAR CENTER. Josephine Wilson, exec. dir.; 301 E. Del Mar Blvd., Pasadena, CA 91101; tel. 213/681-4641

HISTOCHEMICAL SOCIETY, INC. Stanley L. Erlandsen, Ph.D., Dept. of Anatomy, 4-135 Jackson Hall, University of Minnesota, Minneapolis, MN 55455; tel. 612/624-1491

HOCKENBURY SYSTEM, INC. Francis R. Grady, pres.; 101 Erford Rd., Camp Hill, PA 17011; tel. 717/761-3047

HOSPITAL ASSOCIATION OF THE REPUBLIC OF CHINA. 10th floor, No. 27, Pao King Road, Taipei, Taiwan; tel. 02/331-5632

HOSPITAL BOARDS' ASSOCIATION OF NEW ZEALAND, INC. P.O. Box 714, Wellington 1 New Zealand; tel. 64-04-736181

HOSPITAL RESEARCH AND EDUCATIONAL TRUST. Bruce McPherson, pres.; 840 N. Lake Shore Dr., Chicago, IL 60611; tel. 312/280-6489

HUNTINGTON'S DISEASE FOUNDATION OF AMERICA, INC. Gary Wallach, exec. dir.; 140 W. 22nd St., 6th floor, New York, NY 10011; tel. 212/242-1968

I

ILLINOIS ASSOCIATION OF HMO'S (IAHMO). 500 N. Dearborn, Rm. 402, Chicago, IL 60610; 312/321-0343

INDONESIA HOSPITAL ASSOCIATION (PERSI). Mrs. H. E. Subagyo, sec.; Pertamina Central Hospital, Jalan Kyai Maja 2-6, Kebayoran Baru, Jakarta-Selatan, Indonesia Telf 775890; tel. 021-357833

INSTITUTE FOR REHABILITATION AND RESEARCH. Linda Pickle, dir.; Public Relations Dept., 1333 Moursund, Houston, TX 77030; tel. 713/797-1440

INSTITUTE FOR THE ACHIEVEMENT OF HUMAN POTENTIAL. Roselise H. Wilkinson, M.D., med. dir.; 8801 Stenton Ave., Philadelphia, PA 19118; tel. 215/233-2050

INSTITUTE OF HEALTH SERVICES MANAGEMENT (BRITISH). Maureen Dixon, Ph.D., dir.; 75 Portland Pl., London, W1N 4AN, England; tel. 01-580-5041

INSTITUTO NACIONAL DE LA SALUD. Calle Alcalá no. 56, Madrid C.P. 28071, Spain; tel. 221.92.90

INTERNATIONAL ACADEMY OF CYTOLOGY. Claude Gompel, sec.-treas.; 1050 Chemin Ste-Foy, Quebec, Canada G1S 4L8; tel. 418/682-8033

INTERNATIONAL ASSOCIATION FOR DENTAL RESEARCH. John A. Gray, Ph.D., exec. dir.; 1111 14th St., N.W., Suite 1000, Washington, DC 20005; tel. 202/898-1050

INTERNATIONAL ASSOCIATION OF OCULAR SURGEONS. John G. Bellows, M.D., Ph.D., dir.; 233 E. Erie St., Chicago, IL 60611; tel. 312/951-1400

INTERNATIONAL CHILDBIRTH EDUCATION ASSOCIATION, INC. P.O. Box 20048, Minneapolis, MN 55420-0048; tel. 612/854-8660

INTERNATIONAL COLLEGE OF SURGEONS/UNITED STATES SECTION. Robert T. Shirley, exec. dir.; 1516 N. Lake Shore Dr., Chicago, IL 60610; tel. 312/787-6274

INTERNATIONAL COUNCIL FOR HEALTH, PHYSICAL EDUCATION, AND RECREATION. Carl A. Troester Jr., Ed.D., sec. gen.; 1900 Association Dr., Reston, VA 22091; tel. 703/476-3486

INTERNATIONAL COUNCIL ON SOCIAL WELFARE/U.S. COMMITTEE. Benjamin O. Hendrick, exec. dir.; 1744 R Street, N.W., Washington, DC 20009; tel. 202/667-2300

INTERNATIONAL EYE FOUNDATION. R. Douglass Arbuckle, adm. dir.; 7801 Norfolk Ave., Bethesda, MD 20814; tel. 301/986-1830

INTERNATIONAL GLAUCOMA CONGRESS. John G. Bellows, M.D., Ph.D., dir.; 233 E. Erie St., Chicago, IL 60611; tel. 312/951-1400

INTERNATIONAL HOSPITAL FEDERATION. International Office, Dr. Errol N. Pickering, dir.-gen.; 2 St. Andrew's Place, London NW1 4LB, England tel. 01-935-9487 Washington Office, Jack W. Owen, dir.; Capitol Place, Building 3, 50 F Street, N. W., Suite 1100, Washington, DC 20001; tel. 202/638-1100

INTERNATIONAL SOCIETY FOR CLINICAL LABORATORY TECHNOLOGY. David Birenbaum, adm.; Suite 918, 818 Olive, St. Louis, MO 63101; tel. 314/241-1445

J

JOHN MILTON SOCIETY FOR THE BLIND. Rev. Chenoweth J. Watson, dir.; 475 Riverside Dr., Rm. 249, New York, NY 10115; tel. 212/870-3335

JOINT COMMISSION ON ACCREDITATION OF HOSPITALS. Dennis S. O'Leary, M.D., pres.; 875 N. Michigan Ave., Suite 2000, Chicago, IL 60611; tel. 312/642-6061

JOSLIN DIABETES CENTER, INC. Robert F. Bradley, M.D., pres.; One Joslin Place, Boston, MA 02215; tel. 617/732-2470

JUVENILE DIABETES FOUNDATION. Gloria Pennington, exec. dir.; 432 Park Avenue South, New York, NY 10016; tel. 212/889-7575

K

KING EDWARD'S HOSPITAL FUND FOR LONDON. R. J. Maxwell, sec.; 14 Palace Ct., London, W2 4HT England; tel. 01-727-0581

KOREAN HOSPITAL ASSOCIATION. Ho Uk Ha, sec. gen.; (Mapo Hyun Dai Bldg.) 35-1, Mapo-dong, Mapo-gu, Seoul 121, Korea; tel. 718-7521-2, cable address: KORHOSPA

L

LAAKINTOHALLITUS (National Board of Health). Siltasaarenkatu 18A, P.O. Box 220, SF-00531, Helsinki 53, Finland; tel. 358-0-77231

LEUKEMIA SOCIETY OF AMERICA, INC. Peter N. Cakridas, exec. dir.; 733 Third Ave., New York, NY 10017; tel. 212/573-8484

LUTHERAN HOSPITAL ASSOCIATION OF AMERICA. James Anderson, pres.; Hqrs.: Lutheran Hospital, 501 Tenth Ave., Moline, IL 61265; tel. 309/757-2611

LUTHERAN HOSPITALS AND HOMES SOCIETY OF AMERICA. Box 2087, 1202 Westrac Dr., Fargo, ND 58107; tel. 701/293-9053

M

MAGYAR KORHAZSZOVETSEG. Frankel Leo utca 17-19, Budapest 11, Hungary

MANITOBA HEALTH AUXILIARY ASSOCIATION. Betty E. Stephen, pres.; 213 McLeod Ave., W., Dauphin, Manitoba R7N 0H4 Canada; tel. 204/638-4994

MARCH OF DIMES BIRTH DEFECTS FOUNDATION. Charles L. Massey, pres.; 1275 Mamaroneck Ave., White Plains, NY 10605; tel. 914/428-7100

MARITIME HOSPITAL ASSOCIATION. Vernon R. Olive, sec.-treas.; 142 Golf Club Rd., Fredericton, NB E3B 5M6 Canada; tel. 506/455-6079

MARYLAND HOSPITAL ASSOCIATION. Richard J. Davidson, pres.; 1301 York Rd., Suite 800, Lutherville, MD 21093-6087; tel. 301/321-6200

MATERNITY CENTER ASSOCIATION. Ruth Watson Lubic, Ed.D., gen. dir.; 48 E. 92nd St., New York, NY 10128; tel. 212/369-7300

MEDIC ALERT FOUNDATION, INTERNATIONAL. K.W. Harms, pres.; 2323 Colorado Ave., P.O. Box 1009, Turlock, CA 95381; tel. 209/668-3333

MEDICAL GROUP MANAGEMENT ASSOCIATION. Richard V. Grant, Ph.D., exec. dir.; 1355 S. Colorado Blvd., Suite 900, Denver, CO 80222; tel. 303/753-1111

MEDICAL LIBRARY ASSOCIATION. Raymond A. Palmer, exec. dir.; 919 N. Michigan Ave., Suite 3208, Chicago, IL 60611; tel. 312/266-2456

MENDED HEARTS, INC. 7320 Greenville Ave., Dallas, TX 75231

MENTAL HEALTH INSTITUTE. David J. Scurr, supt.; 1200 E. Washington St., Mount Pleasant, IA 52641; tel. 319/385-7231

MIDDLE ATLANTIC HEALTH CONGRESS. Lisa Heher, convention mgr.; Center for Health Affairs, 760 Alexander Rd., CN-1, Princeton, NJ 08543-0001; tel. 609/924-0049

MID-WEST HEALTH CONGRESS. Janice M. Estell, exec. dir.; 4635 Wyandotte, Suite 205, Kansas City, MO 64112; tel. 816/561-6202

MILBANK MEMORIAL FUND. Sidney S. Lee, M.D., pres.; 1 E. 75th St., New York, NY 10021; tel. 212/570-4805

MINNESOTA HEALTHCARE CONFERENCE. Susan Clark, mgr.; 2221 University Ave., S.E., Suite 425, Minneapolis, MN 55414; tel. 612/331-5571

MULTIPLE SCLEROSIS SOCIETY OF CANADA. Alistair M. Fraser, exec. dir.; 250 Bloor St., E., Suite 820, Toronto, Ont. M4W 3P9; tel. 416/922-6065

MUSCULAR DYSTROPHY ASSOCIATION. Robert Ross, vice-pres. and exec. dir.; 810 Seventh Ave., New York, NY 10019; tel. 212/586-0808

N

NATIONAL ACADEMY OF SCIENCES. Alvin G. Lazen, Ph.D., exec. dir.; Institute of Medicine, 2101 Constitution Ave., N.W., NAS 343, Washington, DC 20418; tel. 202/334-2500

NATIONAL ACCREDITATION COUNCIL FOR AGENCIES SERVING THE BLIND AND VISUALLY HANDICAPPED. Dennis L. Hartenstine, exec. dir.; 15 W. 65th St., 9th Flr., New York, NY 10023; tel. 212/496-5880

NATIONAL ACCREDITING AGENCY FOR CLINICAL LABORATORY SCIENCES. Jacqueline N. Parochka, Ed.D., exec. dir.; Suite 608, 547 W. Jackson Blvd., Chicago, IL 60606; tel. 312/461-0333

NATIONAL ALLIANCE FOR THE MENTALLY ILL. Laurie Flynn, exec. dir.; 1901 N. Fort Myer Dr., Suite 500, Arlington, VA 22209; tel. 703/524-7600

NATIONAL ASSEMBLY OF NATIONAL VOLUNTARY HEALTH AND SOCIAL WELFARE ORGANIZATIONS. Leonard W. Stern, exec. dir.; 1319 F St., N.W., Suite 601, Washington, DC 20004; tel. 202/347-2080

NATIONAL ASSOCIATION FOR HEARING AND SPEECH ACTION. Russell L. Malone, Ph.D., exec. dir.; 10801 Rockville Pike, Rockville, MD 20852; tel. 301/897-8682

NATIONAL ASSOCIATION FOR HOME CARE. Val J. Halamandaris, pres.; 519 C St., N.E., Stanton Park, Washington, DC 20002; tel. 202/547-7424

NATIONAL ASSOCIATION FOR HOSPITAL DEVELOPMENT. William C. McGinly, pres.; 112-B E. Broad St., Falls Church, VA 22046; tel. 703/532-6243

NATIONAL ASSOCIATION FOR MEDICAL STAFF SERVICES. P.O. Box 909, Burbank, CA 91503; tel. 818/246-3826

NATIONAL ASSOCIATION FOR MUSIC THERAPY, INC. Edward L. Norwood, RMT, exec. dir.; 1133 Fifteenth St., N.W., Suite 1000, Washington, DC 20005; tel. 202/429-9440

NATIONAL ASSOCIATION FOR PRACTICAL NURSE EDUCATION AND SERVICE. Helen M. Larsen, L.P.N., exec. dir.; 10801 Pear Tree Lane, Suite 151, St. Ann, MO 63074; tel. 314/426-2662

NATIONAL ASSOCIATION FOR SOUTH AFRICAN PROVINCIAL HOSPITALS. Hospital Services Section, P.O. Box 517, Bloemfontein, Orange Free State, South Africa

NATIONAL ASSOCIATION MEDICAL STAFF SERVICES. P.O. Box 909, Burbank, CA 91503-0909

NATIONAL ASSOCIATION OF BOARDS OF PHARMACY. Fred T. Mahaffey, Pharm. D., exec. dir.; 1300 Higgins Rd., Suite 103, Park Ridge, Il 60068; tel. 312/698-6227

NATIONAL ASSOCIATION OF CHILDREN'S HOSPITALS AND RELATED INSTITUTIONS, INC. Robert H. Sweeney, pres.; 401 Wythe St., Alexandria, VA 22314; tel. 703/684-1355

NATIONAL ASSOCIATION OF DENTAL ASSISTANTS. Joseph Salta, pres.; 900 South Washington, Suite G3, Falls Church, VA 22046; tel. 703/237-8616

NATIONAL ASSOCIATION OF DENTAL LABORATORIES. (Includes National Board for Certification in Dental Laboratory Technology). Robert W. Stanley, exec. dir.; 3801 Mt. Vernon Ave., Alexandria, VA 22305; tel. 703/683-5263

NATIONAL ASSOCIATION OF INSTITUTIONAL LAUNDRY MANAGERS. Robert J. Conard, exec. sec.; 781 Twin Oaks Ave., Chula Vista, CA 92010; tel. 714/426-6651

NATIONAL ASSOCIATION OF MEDICAL EQUIPMENT SUPPLIERS. 625 Slaters Lane, Alexandria, VA 22314; tel. 703/836-6263

NATIONAL ASSOCIATION OF PATIENTS ON HEMODIALYSIS AND TRANSPLANTATION, INC. Stuart Kaufer, exec. dir.; 211 E. 43rd St., #301, New York, NY 10017; tel. 212/867-4486

NATIONAL ASSOCIATION OF PHYSICAL THERAPISTS, INC. Shela Denton, sec. and exec. dir.; P.O. Box 367, West Covina, CA 91793; tel. 818/919-7836 or 818/332-7755

NATIONAL ASSOCIATION OF PRIVATE PSYCHIATRIC HOSPITALS. Robert L. Thomas, exec. dir.; 1319 F St., N.W., Suite 1000, Washington, DC 20004; tel. 202/393-6700

NATIONAL ASSOCIATION OF REHABILITATION FACILITIES. James Allen Cox Jr., exec. dir., 5530 Wisconsin Ave., Suite 955, Washington, DC 20015; tel. 301/654-5882

NATIONAL ASSOCIATION OF SOCIAL WORKERS, INC. Betsy S. Vourlekis, Ph.D., ACSW, staff dir. for hlth. & mental hlth.; 7981 Eastern Ave., Silver Spring, MD 20910; tel. 301/565-0333

NATIONAL ASSOCIATION OF STATE MENTAL HEALTH PROGRAM DIRECTORS. Harry C. Schnibbe, exec. dir.; 1101 King St., Suite 160, Alexandria, VA 22314; tel. 202/554-7807

NATIONAL BOARD FOR RESPIRATORY CARE. Steven K. Bryant, exec. dir.; 11015 W. 75th Terr., Shawnee Mission, KS 66214; tel. 913/268-4050

NATIONAL BOARD OF MEDICAL EXAMINERS. Robert L. Volle, Ph.D., pres.; 3930 Chestnut St., Philadelphia, PA 19104; tel. 215/349-6400

NATIONAL BRAILLE ASSOCIATION, INC. Angela P. Coffaro, off. mgr.; 1290 University Ave., Rochester, NY 14607; tel. 716/473-0900

NATIONAL CANCER INSTITUTE OF CANADA. Douglas H. Barr, chf. exec. off.; 77 Bloor St. W., Suite 1702, Toronto, Ont. M5S 3A1; tel. 416/961-7223

NATIONAL CHILDREN'S EYE CARE FOUNDATION. Judith A. Walker, exec. dir.; 1101 Connecticut Ave., N.W., Suite 700, Washington, DC 20036; tel. 202/857-1185

NATIONAL COMMISSION ON CERTIFICATION OF PHYSICIAN'S ASSISTANTS. David L. Glazer, exec. pres.; 2845 Henderson Mill Rd., N.E., Atlanta, GA 30341; tel. 404/493-9100

NATIONAL COMMITTEE FOR CAREERS IN THE MEDICAL LABORATORY. (See Health and Education Resources, Inc.)

NATIONAL COMMITTEE FOR DANISH HOSPITALS. Johanne L. Dithmer, hd. of dept.; Amtsraadsforeningen i Denmark Landemaarket 10, DK 119, Copenhagen K., Denmark; tel. 011 45 11 21 61

NATIONAL CONFERENCE ON SOCIAL WELFARE. Joyce M. Black, pres.; 1730 M St., N.W., Suite 911, Washington, DC 20036; tel. 202/785-0817

NATIONAL COUNCIL ON ALCOHOLISM, INC. Thomas V. Seessel, exec. dir.; 12 W. 21st St., 7th Flr., New York, NY 10010; tel. 212/206-6770

NATIONAL COUNCIL ON RADIATION PROTECTION AND MEASUREMENTS. W. Roger Ney, J.D., exec. dir.; Suite 1016, 7910 Woodmont Ave., Bethesda, MD 20814; tel. 301/657-2652

NATIONAL COUNCIL ON THE AGING, INC. Jack Ossofsky, pres.; 600 Maryland Ave., S.W., West Wing 100, Washington, DC 20024; tel. 202/479-1200

NATIONAL DENTAL ASSOCIATION. 5506 Connecticut Ave., N.W., Suite 24-25, Washington, DC 20015; tel. 202/244-7555

NATIONAL EASTER SEAL SOCIETY. John R. Garrison, exec. dir.; 2023 W. Ogden Ave., Chicago, IL 60612; tel. 312/243-8400

NATIONAL ENVIRONMENTAL HEALTH ASSOCIATION. Nelson Fabian, exec. dir.; 720 S. Colorado Blvd., South Tower, Suite 970, Denver, CO 80222; tel. 303/756-9090

NATIONAL EXECUTIVE HOUSEKEEPERS ASSOCIATION, INC. James H. Powell, exec. dir.; 1001 Eastwind Dr., Suite 301, Westerville, OH 43081; tel. 614/895-7166

NATIONAL FEDERATION OF CATHOLIC PHYSICIANS' GUILDS. Robert H. Herzog, exec. dir.; 850 Elm Grove Rd., Elm Grove, WI 53122; tel. 414/784-3435

NATIONAL FEDERATION OF LICENSED PRACTICAL NURSES. Sammy Griffin, exec. dir.; 214 S. Driver, Durham, NC 27703; tel. 919/596-9609

NATIONAL FIRE PROTECTION ASSOCIATION. Burton R. Klein, hlth. care fire protection eng.; Batterymarch Park, Quincy, MA 02269; tel. 617/770-3000

NATIONAL FOUNDATION FOR ASTHMA, INC. Marion E. Chiara, exec. dir.; P.O. Box 30069, Tucson, AZ 85751-0069; tel. 602/323-6046

NATIONAL FOUNDATION FOR ILEITIS AND COLITIS, INC. George J. Theobald Jr., exec. dir.; 444 Park Ave. S., New York, NY 10016-7374; tel. 212/685-3440

NATIONAL GERIATRICS SOCIETY. Thomas J. Bergen, J.D., exec. dir.; 212 W. Wisconsin Ave., Milwaukee, WI 53203; tel. 414/272-4130

NATIONAL HEADACHE FOUNDATION. Seymour Diamond, M.D., exec. dir.; 5252 N. Western Ave., Chicago, IL 60625; tel. 312/878-7715, toll-free 1-800/523-8858 (in IL), 1-800/843-2256 (outside IL)

NATIONAL HEALTH COUNCIL, INC. Edward Van Ness, exec. vice-pres.; 622 Third Ave., 34th floor, New York, NY 10017-6765; tel. 212/972-2700

NATIONAL HEALTH LAWYERS ASSOCIATION. David J. Greenburg, Esq., exec. dir.; 522 21st St., N.W., Suite 120, Washington, DC 20006; tel. 202/833-1100

NATIONAL HEMOPHILIA FOUNDATION. Allan Brownstein, exec. dir., 19 W. 34th St., Suite 1204, New York, NY 10011; tel. 212/563-0211

NATIONAL HOMECARING COUNCIL. Lila Rosenthal, exec. dir., 235 Park Ave., S., New York, NY 10003; tel. 212/674-4990

NATIONAL HORMONE AND PITUITARY PROGRAM. Salvatore Raiti, M.D., dir., 210 W. Fayette St., Baltimore, MD 21201; tel. 301/837-2552

NATIONAL HOSPITAL INSURANCE FUND. P.O. Box 30443, Nairobi, Kenya

NATIONAL INTRAVENOUS THERAPY ASSOCIATION INC. Mary Larkin, R.N., CRNI, exec. dir.; 87 Blanchard Rd., Cambridge, MA 02138; tel. 617/576-1282

NATIONAL KIDNEY FOUNDATION. John Davis, exec. dir.; 2 Park Ave., New York, NY 10016; tel. 212/889-2210

NATIONAL LEAGUE FOR NURSING. Pamela J. Maraldo, Ph.D., R.N., FAAN, exec. dir.; 10 Columbus Circle, New York, NY 10019; tel. 212/582-1022

NATIONAL MEDICAL ASSOCIATION AND AUXILIARY. Mr. William C. Garrett, exec. vice-pres.; 1012 10th St., N.W., Washington, DC 20001; tel. 202/347-1895

NATIONAL MENTAL HEALTH ASSOCIATION, INC. Preston J. Garrison, exec. dir.; 1021 Prince St., Alexandria, VA 22314-2971; tel. 703/684-7722

NATIONAL MULTIPLE SCLEROSIS SOCIETY. Robert J. Slater, M.D., vice-pres. and dir. med. and comm. serv.; 205 E. 42nd St., New York, NY 10017; tel. 212/986-3240

NATIONAL NUTRITION CONSORTIUM, INC. Betty B. Blouin, R.D., exec. dir.; 24 Third St., N.E., Suite 200, Washington, DC 20002; tel. 202/547-4819

NATIONAL PARKINSON FOUNDATION, INC. Martin J. Fisher, adm.; 1501 N.W. Ninth Ave., Miami, FL 33136; tel. 305/547-6666

NATIONAL PERINATAL ASSOCIATION. George K. Degnon, exec. dir.; 1311A Dolley Madison Blvd., Suite 3A, McLean, VA 22101; tel. 703/556-9222

NATIONAL PHARMACEUTICAL ASSOCIATION. James N. Tyson, exec. dir.; Howard University, P.O Box 934, Washington, DC 20059; tel. 202/328-9229

NATIONAL RECREATION AND PARK ASSOCIATION. (Includes National Therapeutic Recreation Society.). John H. Davis, exec. dir.; 3101 Park Center Dr., Alexandria, VA 22302; tel. 703/820-4940

NATIONAL REGISTRY IN CLINICAL CHEMISTRY. Donald G. Vorhis, exec. dir.; 1155 16th St., N.W., Washington, DC 20036; tel. 202/659-9660

NATIONAL REGISTRY OF EMERGENCY MEDICAL TECHNICIANS. Rocco V. Morando, exec. dir.; 6610 Busch Blvd., P.O. Box 29233, Columbus, OH 43229; tel. 614/888-4484

NATIONAL REHABILITATION ASSOCIATION. (Includes National Rehabilitation Counseling Association.). David L. Mills, exec., dir.; 633 S. Washington St., Alexandria, VA 22314; tel. 703/836-0850

NATIONAL RENAL ADMINISTRATORS ASSOCIATION. Gloria Smith Justice, natl. headquarters dir.; P.O. Box 129, 1115 Rawlins St., Port Huron, MI 48061; tel. 313/987-3625

NATIONAL RESIDENT MATCHING PROGRAM. John S. Graettinger, M.D., exec. vice-pres.; One American Plaza, Suite 807, Evanston, IL 60201; tel. 312/328-3440

NATIONAL RURAL HEALTH ASSOCIATION. Robert van Hook, exec. dir.; 301 East Armour Blvd., Suite 420, Kansas City, MO 64111; tel. 816/756-3140

NATIONAL SAFETY COUNCIL. 444 N. Michigan Ave., Chicago, IL 60611; tel. 312/527-4800

NATIONAL SANITATION FOUNDATION. Nina I. McClelland, Ph.D., pres.; P.O. Box 1468, 3475 Plymouth Rd., Ann Arbor, MI 48106; tel. 313/769-8010

NATIONAL SOCIETY FOR CARDIOVASCULAR & PULMONARY TECHNOLOGY. Brian Cassedy, exec. dir.; 1133 15th St., Suite 1000, Washington, DC 20005; tel. 202/293-5933

NATIONAL SOCIETY FOR MEDICAL RESEARCH. Suite 700, 1029 Vermont Ave., N.W., Washington, DC 20005; tel. 202/347-9565

NATIONAL SOCIETY OF PATIENT REPRESENTATIVES (AHA). Alexandra B. Gekas, dir.; 840 N. Lake Shore Dr., Chicago, IL 60611,; tel. 312/280-6424

NATIONAL SOCIETY TO PREVENT BLINDNESS. Michael L. Weamer, exec. dir.; 500 East Remington Rd., Schaumburg, IL 60173; tel. 312/843-2020

NATIONAL SPINAL CORD INJURY ASSOCIATION. Speed Davis, dir. of prog. oper.; 149 California St., Newton, MA 02158; tel. 617/964-0521 (in MA only), 800/962-9629 (outside MA)

NATIONAL STUDENT NURSES' ASSOCIATION, INC. Robert Piemonte, Ed.D., R.N., exec. dir.; 555 W 57th St., Rm. 1325, New York, NY 10019; tel. 212/581-2211

NATIONAL TAY-SACHS AND ALLIED DISEASES ASSOCIATION. Steven G. Laver, Esq., nat'l. pres.; 385 Elliot St., Newton, MA 02164; tel. 617/964-5508

NATIONALE ZIEKENHUISRAAD. drs C.M. Beumer, sec.; Postbus 9696, 3506 GR Utrecht, The Netherlands; tel. 030-739911

NEUROSURGICAL SOCIETY OF AMERICA. Donald P. Becker, M.D., sec.; Medical College of Virginia, Box 508, Richmond, VA 23298; tel. 804/786-2176

NEUROTICS ANONYMOUS. Grover Boydston; 3636 16th St., N.W., Apt. B911, Washington, DC 20010; tel. 202/232-0414

NEW ENGLAND GERONTOLOGICAL ASSOCIATION. Eugene E. Tillock, Ed.D., exec. dir.; 1 Cutts Rd., Durham, NH 03824; tel. 617/374-0707

NEW ENGLAND HOSPITAL ASSEMBLY, INC. John L. Quigley, exec. dir.; P.O. Box 736, Osterville, MA 02655; tel. 617/428-7807

NUFFIELD PROVINCIAL HOSPITALS TRUST. Dr. Michael Ashley-Miller, sec.; 3 Prince Albert Rd., London NW1 7SP, England; tel. 01-485-6632

NAACOG:THE ORGANIZATION FOR OBSTETRIC, GYNECOLOGIC, AND NEONATAL NURSES. Judith L. Serevino, dir. of comm.; 600 Maryland Ave., S.W., Suite 200, Washington, DC 20024; tel. 202/638-0026

NUTRITION TODAY SOCIETY. Cortez F. Enloe Jr., M.D., exec. vice-pres.; 111 Chinguapir Rd., P.O. Box 1829, Annapolis, MD 21404; tel. 301/267-8616

O

OTOSCLEROSIS STUDY GROUP. H.A. Ted Bailey, Jr., M.D., sec.-treas.; 1200 Medical Towers Bldg., Little Rock, Ark. 72205

P

PAN AMERICAN HEALTH ORGANIZATION. Carlyle Guerra de Macedo, M.D., dir.; 525 23rd St., N.W., Washington, DC 20037; tel. 202/861-3200

PATHOLOGY PRACTICE ASSOCIATION. J. Michael Allen, exec. sec.; 1225 8th St., Suite 590, Sacramento, CA 95814; tel. 916/446-2651

PHILIPPINE HOSPITAL ASSOCIATION. Juan V. Komiya, M.D., pres.; 14 Kamias Rd., Quezon City, Metro Manila, Philippines; tel. nos. 921-2219, 922-7674, 922-7675; cable address "PHILHOSA" 3008

PHYSICIAN EXECUTIVE MANAGEMENT CENTER. David R. Kirschman, pres.; 4830 W. Kennedy Blvd., Suite 648, Tampa, FL 33609-9990; tel. 813/873-1800

PILOT DOGS, INC. John J. Gray, exec. dir.; 625 W. Town St., Columbus, OH 43215; tel. 614/221-6367

PUBLIC RELATIONS SOCIETY OF AMERICA. Elizabeth Ann Kovacs, CAE, exec. vice-pres.; 845 Third Ave., New York, NY 10022; tel. 212/826-1750

PUERTO RICO HOSPITAL ASSOCIATION. Juan Rivera Rivera, chf. exec. off.; Villa Nevarez Professional Center, Suite 101, Rio Piedras, Puerto Rico 00927; tel. 764-0290, 764-0987

R

RADIOLOGICAL SOCIETY OF NORTH AMERICA, INC. Mary Ann Tuft, CAE, exec. dir.; 1415 W. 22nd St., Tower B, Oak Brook, IL 60521; tel. 312/571-2670

RD FOUNDATION FIGHTING BLINDNESS. Robert M. Gray, exec. dir.; 1401 Mt. Royal Ave., 4th flr. Baltimore, MD 21217; tel. 301/225-9400

RECORDING FOR THE BLIND, INC. Stuart Carothers, exec. dir.; 20 Roszel Rd., Princeton, NJ 08540; tel. 609/452-0606

REHABILITATION INTERNATIONAL U.S.A. Philip F. Puleio, Ph.D., exec. dir.; 1123 Broadway, New York, NY 10010; tel. 212/620-4040

RENAL PHYSICIANS ASSOCIATION. 1101 Vermont Ave., N.W., Suite 500, Washington, DC 20005-3547; tel. 202/898-1562

ROBERT WOOD JOHNSON FOUNDATION. P.O. Box 2316, Princeton, NJ 08543-2316; tel. 609/452-8701

ROCHESTER REGIONAL HOSPITAL ASSOCIATION. John E. Flood, pres.; P.O. Box 23239, Rochester, NY 14692; tel. 716/427-2820

ROYAL COLLEGE OF PHYSICIANS AND SURGEONS OF CANADA. James H. Darragh, M.D., exec. dir. and chf. exec. off.; 74 Stanley Ave., Ottawa, Ont. K1M 1P4; tel. 613/746-8177

S

SAIRAALALIITTO. Toinen linja 14, SF-00530 Helsinki, Finland; tel. 358-0-7711

SALVATION ARMY. Comr. Andrew S. Miller, natl. cdr.; 799 Bloomfield Ave., Verona, NJ 07044; tel. 201/239-0606

SEEING EYE, INC. Paula Pursley, vice-pres.; Box 375, Morristown, NJ 07960; tel. 201/539-4425

SHRINERS HOSPITALS FOR CRIPPLED CHILDREN. Jack D. Hoard, exec. adm.; Box 25356, Tampa, FL 33622; tel. 813/885-2575

SICKLE CELL DISEASE FOUNDATION OF GREATER NEW YORK. Dick Campbell, exec. dir.; 209 W. 125th St., Suite 208, New York, NY 10027; tel. 212/865-1201

SOCIETY FOR ADOLESCENT MEDICINE, INC. Edie Moore, adm. dir.; P.O. Box 3462, Granada Hills, CA 91344; tel. 818/368-5996

SOCIETY FOR HOSPITAL PLANNING AND MARKETING (AHA). Judith Neiman, dir.; 840 N. Lake Shore Dr., Chicago, IL 60611; tel. 312/280-6086

SOCIETY FOR HOSPITAL SOCIAL WORK DIRECTORS (AHA). Carolyn Hatzis, dir.; 840 N. Lake Shore Dr., Chicago, IL 60611; tel. 312/280-6415

SOCIETY OF CLINICAL SURGERY. John A. Collins, M.D.; Dept. of Surgery, Stanford University School of Medicine, Stanford, CA 94305; tel. 415/723-6618

SOCIETY OF CRITICAL CARE MEDICINE. Norma J. Shoemaker, exec. dir.; 251 E. Imperial Hwy., Suite 480, Fullerton, CA 92635; tel. 714/870-5243

SOCIETY OF NEUROLOGICAL SURGEONS. Phanor L. Perot Jr., M.D., Ph.D., sec.; Dept. of Neurosurgery, Medical University of South Carolina, 171 Ashley Ave., Charleston, SC 29425,; tel. 803/792-2421

SOCIETY OF NUCLEAR MEDICINE. Henry L. Ernstthal, exec. dir.; 136 Madison Ave., New York, NY 10016; tel. 212/889-0717

SOCIETY OF UNIVERSITY OTOLARYNGOLOGISTS—HEAD AND NECK SURGEONS. Gary L. Schechter, M.D., sec.-treas.; Eastern Virginia Medical School, Dept. of Otolaryngology—Head and Neck Surgery, 825 Fairfax Ave., Norfolk, VA 23507; tel. 804/446-5934

SOCIETY OF UNIVERSITY SURGEONS. Alden H. Harken, M.D., sec.; Dept. of Surgery, University of Pennsylvania, 3400 Spruce St., Philadelphia, PA 19104; tel. 215/662-2007

SOUTHEASTERN HOSPITAL CONFERENCE. James B. Hulett, pres.; 3031 Carter Hill Rd., P.O. Box 11105, Montgomery, AL 36111; tel. 205/832-4130

SOUTHEASTERN SURGICAL CONGRESS. Roger Sherman, M.D., sec.-dir.; 69 Butler St., S.E., Suite 314, Atlanta, GA 30303; tel. 404/221-0570

SOUTHERN MEDICAL ASSOCIATION. William J. Ranieri, exec. vice-pres.; P.O. Box 2446, 2601 Highland Ave., Birmingham, AL 35201; tel. 205/323-4400

SOUTHERN SURGICAL ASSOCIATION. John L. Sawyers, M.D., pres.; Dept. of Surgery, Vanderbilt University Hospital, Nashville, TN 37232; tel. 615/322-2363

SOUTHWEST MICHIGAN HEALTH COORDINATING COUNCIL. Judith Rayman, exec. dir.; 5228 Lovers Lane, Kalamazoo, MI 49002; tel. 616/343-1590

SOUTHWESTERN SURGICAL CONGRESS. Jack A. Barney, M.D., sec.-treas.; 111 East Wacker Drive, Chicago, IL 60601; tel. 312/644-6610

STICHTING HET NEDERLANDSE ZIEKENHUISWEZEN. (See Nationale Ziekenhuisraad.)

SVENSKA SJUKHUSFORENINGEN. (Swedish Hospital Association.). Karl-Eric Wictorson, exec. sec.; Box 27310, S-102 54, Stockholm, Sweden; tel. 08-630560

SWISS HOSPITAL ASSOCIATION. (See Vereinigung Schweizerischer Krankenhauser)

SYGEHUSFORENINGEN I DANMARK. (See Amtsradsforeningen I Danmark.)

T

TECHNOLOGIST SECTION, SOCIETY OF NUCLEAR MEDICINE. Virginia M. Pappas, adm.; 136 Madison Ave., New York, NY 10016; tel. 212/889-0717

TRI-STATE HOSPITAL ASSOCIATION. Brian McCagh, pres.; 7100 Contee Rd., Laurel, MD 20707; tel. 301/725-4300

U

UNION OF THE SOCIETIES FOR MEDICAL SCIENCES. 10, Progresul Street, 70754 Bucharest, Romania

UNITED CANCER COUNCIL, INC. Ellen K. Annala, exec. dir.; 1803 N. Meridian St., Rm. 202, Indianapolis, IN 46202; tel. 317/923-6490

UNITED CEREBRAL PALSY ASSOCIATIONS, INC. Alan Proudfoot, exec. dir.; 66 E. 34th St., New York, NY 10016; tel. 212/481-6300

UNITED HOSPITAL ASSOCIATION. Carl Weissburg, Esq., exec. dir. and legal counsel; 2049 Century Pk., E., 32nd flr., Los Angeles, CA 90067; tel. 213/277-7123

UNITED METHODIST ASSOCIATION OF HEALTH AND WELFARE MINISTRIES. 601 West Riverview Ave., Dayton, OH 45406; tel. 513/227-9494

UNITED OSTOMY ASSOCIATION, INC. Donald P. Binder, natl. dir.; 2001 W. Beverly Blvd., Los Angeles, CA 90057; tel. 213/413-5510

UNITED PARKINSON FOUNDATION. Judy Rosner, exec. dir.; 220 S. State St., Rm. 1806-08, Chicago, IL 60604; tel. 312/922-9734

UNITED STATES OF AMERICA STANDARDS INSTITUTE. (See American National Standards Institute.)

UNITED STATES PHARMACOPEIAL CONVENTION, INC. William M. Heller, Ph.D., exec. dir.; 12601 Twinbrook Pkwy., Rockville, MD 20852; tel. 301/881-0666

UNITED WAY OF AMERICA. William Aramony, pres.; 701 N. Fairfax St., Alexandria, VA 22314-2045; tel. 703/836-7100

UNIVERSITY ASSOCIATION FOR EMERGENCY MEDICINE. Mary Ann Schropp, exec. dir.; 900 W. Ottawa, Lansing, MI 48915; tel. 517/485-5484

V

VERBOND DER VERZORGINGSINSTELLINGEN V.Z.W., Kris Schutyser, gen. dir.; 1, Guimardstraat, 1040 Brussels, Belgium; tel. 02/511-79-23

VEREINIGUNG SCHWEIZERISCHER KRANKENHAUSER. (VESKA—Swiss Hospital Association.). Mr. N. Undritz, sec. gen.; Box 689, Rain 32, CH-5001 Aarau, Switzerland; tel. 064/24-12-22

VERENIGING VAN KATHOLIEKE ZIEKENHUIZEN—INTERNATIONAL CATHOLIC CONFEDERATION OF HOSPITALS. (See Nationale Ziekenhuisraad.)

VOLUNTEER: THE NATIONAL CENTER. 1111 N. 19th St., Suite 500, Arlington, VA 22209; tel. 703/276-0542

W

W. K. KELLOGG FOUNDATION. Robert A. DeVries, prog. dir.; 400 North Ave., Battle Creek, MI 49017-3398; tel. 616/968-1611

WESTERN ORTHOPAEDIC ASSOCIATION. H. Jacqueline Martin, exec. dir.; 2975 Treat Blvd., Bldg. E5, Concord, CA 94518; tel. 415/671-2164

WESTERN SURGICAL ASSOCIATION. John Glover, M.D., sec.; Dept. of Surgery, 3601 W. 13 Mile Rd., Royal Oak, MI 48072; tel. 313/288-2665

WORLD FEDERATION OF HEMOPHILIA. Frank Schnabel, pres.; Suite 1517, 1155 Dorchester Blvd. West, Montreal, Canada H3B 2J6; tel. 514/866-0442

WORLD FEDERATION OF PUBLIC HEALTH ASSOCIATIONS. Susi Kessler, M.D., M.P.H., exec. sec.; c/o APHA, 1015 15th St., N.W., Washington, DC 20005; tel. 202/789-5691

WORLD HEALTH ORGANIZATION. H. Mahler, M.D., dir. gen.; CH-1211, Geneva 27, Switzerland; tel. 022/91-21-11, Telex 27821

WORLD MEDICAL ASSOCIATION. Angel Orozco, exec. dir.; 28 Ave. des Alpes, 01210 Ferney-Voltaire, France; tel. 50/40-75-75

U.S. Government Agencies

Specific addresses have been omitted because of the many changes presently occurring and scheduled for the future among federal agencies. The telephone numbers given are general public information numbers, unless specifically identified with the officials listed.
For more information about U.S. government agencies, consult the U.S. Government Manual, *available from the Office of the* Federal Register, *National Archives and Records Service, Washington, DC 20408. A telephone directory of the U.S. Department of Health and Human Services is available from the Superintendent of Documents, Government Printing Office, Washington, DC 20402. Additional assistance may be obtained by contacting the American Hospital Association's Washington office, 444 N. Capitol St., N.W., Suite 500, Washington, DC 20001; telephone 202/638-1100.*

Executive Office of the President tel. 202/456-1414

Counsel to the President: Arthur B. Culvahouse; 202/456-2632
Chief of Staff: Howard H. Baker, Jr.; 202/456-6797
Assistant to the President for Policy Development: Charles Hobbs; 202/456-6515
Deputy Assistant to the President and Director of Public Liaison: Mari Maseng; 202/456-2270

COUNCIL OF ECONOMIC ADVISORS
Chairman: Beryl W. Sprinkel; 202/395-5042

OFFICE OF MANAGEMENT AND BUDGET
Director: James Miller; 202/395-4840

Department of Agriculture tel. 202/447-8732

Secretary: Richard E. Lyng; 202/447-3631

Department of Commerce tel. 202/377-2000

Secretary: Malcolm Baldridge; 202/377-2112
BUREAU OF ECONOMIC ANALYSIS
Director: Allan Young; 202/523-0693
ECONOMIC DEVELOPMENT ADMINISTRATION
Assistant Secretary: Orson G. Swindle III; 202/377-5081
NATIONAL BUREAU OF STANDARDS
Director: Dr. Ernest Ambler; 301/975-2411

Department of Defense tel. 202/545-6700

Secretary: Caspar W. Weinberger; 202/695-5261
Assistant Secretary of Defense (Health Affairs): Dr. William Mayer; 202/697-2111
CIVILIAN HEALTH AND MEDICAL PROGRAMS OF THE UNIFORMED SERVICES (CHAMPUS) (Denver, CO)
Director: Jimmy Helton; 303/361-8606
UNIFORMED SERVICES UNIVERSITY OF THE HEALTH SCIENCES
President: J. P. Sanford; 301/295-3013
DEPARTMENT OF THE AIR FORCE
Surgeon General: Lt. Gen. Murphy A. Chesney; 202/767-4343
DEPARTMENT OF THE ARMY
Surgeon General: Lt. Gen. Quinn H. Becker; 202/756-0000
DEPARTMENT OF THE NAVY
Surgeon General of the Navy and Director of Navy Medicine: VADM Lewis Seaton; 202/697-0587
Commander, Naval Medical Command: Rear Admiral J. S. Cassells; 202/653-1144

Department of Education tel. 202/245-3192

Secretary: William J. Bennett; 202/732-3000

Department of Health and Human Services tel. 202/475-0257

Secretary: Otis R. Bowen; 202/245-7000
General Counsel: Ronald E. Robertson; 202/245-7741
MANAGEMENT AND BUDGET
Assistant Secretary: S. Anthony McCann; 202/245-6396
HEALTH
Assistant Secretary: Robert Windom; 202/245-7694
HUMAN DEVELOPMENT SERVICES
Assistant Secretary: Jean K. Elder, Ph.D.; 202/245-7246
LEGISLATION
Assistant Secretary: Ronald Docksai; 202/245-7627
PLANNING AND EVALUATION
Assistant Secretary: Robert B. Helms, Ph.D.; 202/245-1858
PUBLIC AFFAIRS
Assistant Secretary: Stephanie Lee-Miller; 202/245-1850

PUBLIC HEALTH SERVICE
Surgeon General: C. Everett Koop, M.D.; 202/245-6467
Alcohol, Drug Abuse, and Mental Health Administration, Rockville, MD
Administrator: Donald I. Macdonald, M.D.; 301/443-4797
Centers for Disease Control, Atlanta 30333
Deputy Director: Donald R. Hopkins, M.D.; 404/329-3291
Food and Drug Administration, Rockville, MD 20857
Commissioner: Frank Young, M.D., Ph.D.; 301/443-2410
Health Resources and Services Administration, Hyattsville, MD 20782
Administrator: David N. Sundwall, M.D.; 301/443-2216
National Institutes of Health, Bethesda, MD 20014
Director: James B. Wyngaarden, M.D.; 301/496-2433

HEALTH CARE FINANCING ADMINISTRATION
Administrator: William L. Roper, M.D.; 202/245-6726

SOCIAL SECURITY ADMINISTRATION: Baltimore, MD 21235
Commissioner: Dorcas R. Hardy; 301/594-3120
Regional Directors:
(1) Boston
Robert C. Green; 617/227-2400
(2) New York
Bernard M. Kilbourn, D.D.S.; 212/264-4600
(3) Philadelphia
Linda Z. Marston; 215/596-6492
(4) Atlanta
Gordon Sherman; 404/881-9600
(5) Chicago
Marlene M. Moleski; 312/353-4247
(6) Dallas
John A. Daeley; 214/767-3301
(7) Kansas City
Robert McClernan; 816/374-2821
(8) Denver
Leza Gooden; 303/844-2388
(9) San Francisco
Donald N. Mings; 415/556-4910
(10) Seattle - Acting Director
Robert Dunn; 206/442-0417

Department of Housing and Urban Development tel. 202/755-5111

Secretary: Samuel R. Pierce; 202/755-6417

Department of Justice tel. 202/633-2000

Attorney General: Edwin Meese III; 202/633-2001
DRUG ENFORCEMENT ADMINISTRATION
Administrator: John C. Lawn; 202/633-1337

Department of Labor tel. 202/523-6666

Secretary: William E. Brock; 202/523-8271
BUREAU OF LABOR STATISTICS
Commissioner: Janet L. Norwood; 202/523-1092
EMPLOYMENT AND TRAINING ADMINISTRATION
Assistant Secretary: Roger D. Semerad; 202/523-6050
OCCUPATIONAL SAFETY AND HEALTH ADMINISTRATION
Assistant Secretary: John Pendergrass; 202/523-6091

Department of State tel. 202/647-4000

Secretary: George P. Schultz; 202/647-4910
AGENCY FOR INTERNATIONAL DEVELOPMENT
Administrator: M. Peter McPherson; 202/647-9620

Independent Agencies

COMMISSION ON CIVIL RIGHTS
Chairman: Clarence M. Pendleton, Jr.; 619/235-6903
CONSUMER PRODUCT SAFETY COMMISSION
Chairman: Carol Dawson; 202/634-7790
ENVIRONMENTAL PROTECTION AGENCY
Administrator: Lee M. Thomas; 202/382-4700
EQUAL EMPLOYMENT OPPORTUNITY COMMISSION
Chairman: Clarence Thomas; 202/634-6700
FEDERAL EMERGENCY MANAGEMENT AGENCY
Director: Julius W. Becton, Jr.; 202/646-3923

Government-Related Groups *Federally aided corporations and quasi-official agencies, such as American National Red Cross, National Academy of Sciences, and World Health Organization, are listed with International, National, and Regional Organizations beginning on page E3.*

State and Provincial Organizations and Agencies

The following list of Blue Cross and Blue Shield Plans is based on the Number 2, 1986 edition of the Directory of Members of Blue Cross and Blue Shield Association, 676 N. St. Clair, Chicago, IL 60611; tel. 312/440-6000. When addressing mail to a plan, use the post office box number.

Blue Cross-Blue Shield Plans

United States

ALABAMA: Blue Cross and Blue Shield of Alabama, Box 995, Birmingham 35298; 450 Riverchase Pkwy., E., Birmingham 35298; tel. 205/988-2100; William H. Mandy, pres.

ALASKA: Blue Cross of Washington and Alaska, Blue Shield in North Central Washington, Box 327, Seattle, WA 98111; 15700 Dayton Ave., N., Seattle, WA 98133; tel. 206/361-3000; Donald A. Lockwood, pres./chf. exec. off.

ARIZONA: Blue Cross and Blue Shield of Arizona, Inc., Box 13466, Phoenix 85002; 2444 W. Las Palmaritas Dr., Phoenix, 85021; tel. 602/864-4100; Robert B. Bulla, pres.

ARKANSAS: Arkansas Blue Cross and Blue Shield, A Mutual Insurance Company, Box 2181, Little Rock 72203; 601 Gaines St., Little Rock 72201; tel. 501/378-2000; George K. Mitchell, M.D., pres./chf. exec. off.

CALIFORNIA: Blue Cross of California, Box 70000, Van Nuys 91470; 21555 Oxnard St., Woodland Hills 91367; tel. 818/703-2345; Leonard D. Schaeffer, pres.
Blue Shield of California (California Physicians' Service Corporation), Box 7168, San Francisco 94120; Two North Point, San Francisco 94133; tel. 415/445-5000; Thomas C. Paton, pres./chf. exec. off.

COLORADO: Blue Cross and Blue Shield of Colorado (Rocky Mountain Hospital and Medical Service), 700 Broadway, Denver 80273; tel. 303/831-2131; Jerome H. Lynch, chm./chf. exec. off.

CONNECTICUT: Blue Cross and Blue Shield of Connecticut, Inc., Box 504, North Haven 06473; 370 Bassett Rd., North Haven 06473; tel. 203/239-4911; John F. Croweak, pres./chf. exec. off.

DELAWARE: Blue Cross and Blue Shield of Delaware, Inc., Box 1991, Wilmington 19899; One Brandywine Gateway, Wilmington 19801; tel. 302/421-3000; Robert C. Cole Jr., pres./chf. exec. off.

DISTRICT OF COLUMBIA: Blue Cross and Blue Shield of the National Capital Area (Group Hospitalization and Medical Services, Inc.), 550 12th St., S.W., Washington 20065; tel. 202/479-8000; J. P. Gamble, pres., exec. div./chf. exec. off.

FLORIDA: Blue Cross and Blue Shield of Florida, Inc., Box 1798, Jacksonville 32231-0014; Box 60729, Jacksonville 32236-2729; 532 Riverside Ave., Jacksonville 32202; tel. 904/791-6111; William E. Flaherty, pres.

GEORGIA: Blue Cross and Blue Shield of Georgia/Atlanta, Inc., Box 4445, Atlanta 30302-4445; 3348 Peachtree Rd., N.E., Atlanta 30326; tel. 404/262-8200
Blue Cross and Blue Shield of Georgia/Columbus, Inc., Box 7368, Columbus 31908-7368; 2357 Warm Springs Rd., Columbus 31904; tel. 404/571-5371; Thomas Kinser, pres./chf. exec. off.

HAWAII: Hawaii Medical Service Association, Box 860, Honolulu 96808; 818 Keeaumoku St., Honolulu 96814; tel. 808/944-2110; Marvin B. Hall, pres.

IDAHO: Blue Cross of Idaho Health Service, Inc., Box 7408; Boise 83707; 1501 Federal Way, Boise 83705; tel. 208/345-4550; Dan L. Duncan, pres.
Blue Shield of Idaho (Medical Service Bureau of Idaho, Inc.), Box 1106, Lewiston 83501; 1602 21st Ave., Lewiston 83501; tel. 208/746-2671; Wayne Olin, pres.

ILLINOIS: Blue Cross and Blue Shield of Illinois (Health Care Service Corporation), Box 1364, Chicago 60690; 233 N. Michigan Ave., Chicago 60601; tel. 312/938-6000; S. Martin Hickman, pres./chf. exec. off.

INDIANA: Blue Cross and Blue Shield of Indiana (Associated Insurance Companies, Inc.), 120 W. Market St., Indianapolis 46204; tel. 317/263-8000; Lloyd J. Banks, chm./chf. exec. off.

IOWA: Blue Cross of Iowa, 636 Grand Ave., Des Moines 50309; tel. 515/245-4500; D. Eugene Sibery, pres.
Blue Cross of Western Iowa and South Dakota, Box 1677, Sioux City 51102; Hamilton Blvd. & I-29, Sioux City 51102; tel. 712/277-3081; Harris W. Feldick, pres.
Blue Shield of Iowa, 636 Grand Ave., Des Moines 50309; tel. 515/245-4500; D. Eugene Sibery, pres.

KANSAS: Blue Cross and Blue Shield of Kansas, Inc., Box 239, Topeka 66629; 1133 Topeka Ave., Topeka 66629; tel. 913/232-1000; G. Wayne Johnston, pres.

KENTUCKY: Blue Cross and Blue Shield of Kentucky, Inc., 9901 Linn Station Rd., Louisville 40223; tel. 502/423-2011; G. Douglas Sutherland, pres.

LOUISIANA: Blue Cross and Blue Shield of Louisiana (Louisiana Health Service and Indemnity Co.), Box 15699, Baton Rouge 70895-5699; 10225 Florida Blvd., Baton Rouge 70815; tel. 504/922-1700; John B. Johnson, Jr., CLU, pres./chf. exec. off.

MAINE: Blue Cross and Blue Shield of Maine (Associated Hospital Service of Maine), 110 Free St., Portland 04101; tel. 207/775-3536; George E. McLean, pres.

MARYLAND: Blue Cross and Blue Shield of Maryland, Inc., Box 9836, Baltimore 21204; 700 E. Joppa Rd., Baltimore 21204; tel. 301/494-5555; Carl J. Sardegna, pres./chf. exec. off.

MASSACHUSETTS: Blue Cross of Massachusetts, Inc., 100 Summer St., Boston 02110; tel. 617/956-2000; David W. Frost, pres.
Blue Shield of Massachusetts, Inc., 100 Summer St., Boston 02110; tel. 617/956-2000; John Larkin Thompson, pres.

MICHIGAN: Blue Cross and Blue Shield of Michigan, 600 Lafayette E., Detroit 48226; tel. 313/225-9000; John C. McCabe, chm./chf. exec. off.

MINNESOTA: Blue Cross and Blue Shield of Minnesota, Box 64560; St. Paul 55164; 3535 Blue Cross Rd., St. Paul 55122; tel. 612/456-8000; Andrew P. Czajkowski, pres./chf. exec. off.

MISSISSIPPI: Blue Cross and Blue Shield of Mississippi, Inc., Box 1043, Jackson 39205; Lakeland Dr.— E. at Flynt, Jackson 39208; tel. 601/932-3704; W. C. Mosley, chm./chf. exec. off., Aaron J. Johnston, pres./chief oper. off.

MISSOURI: Blue Cross and Blue Shield of Kansas City, Box 419169, Kansas City 64141-6169; 3637 Broadway, Kansas City 64141; tel. 816/561-2300; Richard P. Krecker, pres./chf. exec. off.
Blue Cross and Blue Shield of Missouri, 4444 Forest Park Blvd., St. Louis 63108; tel. 314/658-4444; Roy R. Heimburger, pres./chf. exec. off.

MONTANA: Blue Cross and Blue Shield of Montana/Great Falls, Box 5004, Great Falls 59403; 3360 10th Ave. S., Great Falls 59405; tel. 406/761-7310
Blue Cross and Blue Shield of Montana/Helena, Box 4309, Helena 59604; 404 Fuller Ave., Helena 59601; tel. 406/444-8200; Alan F. Cain, pres./chf. exec. off.

NEBRASKA: Blue Cross and Blue Shield of Nebraska, Box 3248, Main P.O. Sta., Omaha 68180; 7261 Mercy Rd., Omaha 68180; tel. 402/390-1800; William H. Heavey, pres./chm.

NEVADA: Blue Cross and Blue Shield of Nevada, Box 10330, Reno 89520-0330; 4600 Kietzke Lane, Bldg. O, Reno 89502; tel. 702/825-0350; Leonard D. Schaeffer, pres.

NEW HAMPSHIRE: Blue Cross and Blue Shield of New Hampshire-Vermont (New Hampshire-Vermont Health Service), Two Pillsbury St., Concord 03306; tel. 603/224-9511; Frank Jillson, pres.

NEW JERSEY: Blue Cross and Blue Shield of New Jersey, Inc., Box 420, Newark 07102; 33 Washington St., Newark 07102; tel. 201/593-2000; Duane E. Minard Jr., chm./chf. exec. off.

NEW MEXICO: New Mexico Blue Cross and Blue Shield, Inc., 12800 Indian School Rd., N.E., Albuquerque 87112; tel. 505/291-3500; Thomas A. Levin, pres./chf. exec. off.

NEW YORK: Blue Cross and Blue Shield of Central New York, Inc., Box 4809, Syracuse 13221-4809; 344 S. Warren St., Syracuse 13202; tel. 315/424-3700; Albert F. Antonini, pres./chf. exec. off.
Blue Cross and Blue Shield of Greater Utica, Inc., 245 Genesee St., Utica 13501; tel. 315/798-4200; John J. Porn, pres.
Blue Cross and Blue Shield of the Rochester Area (Genesee Valley Medical Care, Inc.), 150 E. Main St., Rochester 14647; tel. 716/454-1700; Howard J. Berman, pres./chf. exec. off.
Blue Cross and Blue Shield of the Rochester Area (Rochester Hospital Service Corporation), 150 E. Main St., Rochester 14647; tel. 716/454-1700; Howard J. Berman, pres./chf. exec. off.
Blue Cross of Western New York, Inc., Box 80, Buffalo 14240; 298 Main St., Buffalo 14202; tel. 716/849-6900; Charles E. Rath, pres.
Blue Shield of Northeastern New York, Inc., Box 15013, Albany 12212; 1873 Western Ave., Albany 12203; tel. 518/456-7400; Henry F. Becker, chf. exec. off.
Blue Shield of Western New York, Inc., Box 80, Buffalo 14240; 298 Main St., Buffalo 14202; tel. 716/849-6900; John T. Manyon, pres.
Empire Blue Cross and Blue Shield/Albany, Box 8650, Albany 12208; 1251 New Scotland Ave., Slingerlands 12159; tel. 518/475-2525; Edwin R. Werner, chm./chf. exec. off.
Empire Blue Cross and Blue Shield/New York, Box 345, Grand Central Sta., New York 10017; 622 Third Ave., New York 10017; tel. 212/490-4567; Edwin R. Werner, chm./chf. exec. off.
Hospital Service Corporation of Jefferson County, Box 570, Watertown 13601; 158 Stone St., Watertown 13601; tel. 315/782-2800; James M. Harrington, pres.

NORTH CAROLINA: Blue Cross and Blue Shield of North Carolina, Box 2291, Durham 27702; 5901 Chapel Hill-Durham Blvd., Durham 27707; tel. 919/489-7431; Thomas A. Rose, pres.

NORTH DAKOTA: Blue Cross and Blue Shield of North Dakota, 4510 13th Ave., S.W., Fargo 58121-0001; tel. 701/282-1100; Mayo Christianson, pres.

OHIO: Blue Cross and Blue Shield Mutual of Northern Ohio, 2060 E. Ninth St., Cleveland 44115; tel. 216/687-7000; John Burry Jr., pres./chf. exec. off.
Blue Cross and Blue Shield Mutual of Northern Ohio, Box 943, Toledo 43656; 3737 Sylvania Ave., Toledo 43623; tel. 419/473-7100; Dennis E. McClung, chm.
Central Benefits Mutual Insurance Company, Box 16526, Columbus 43216; 255 E. Main St., Columbus 43215; tel. 614/464-5711; John B. Reinhardt, Jr., pres.
The Community Mutual Insurance Company/Canton, Box 8590, Canton 44711; 4150 Belden Village St., N.W., Canton 44718; tel. 216/492-2151
The Community Mutual Insurance Company/Cincinnati, 1351 William Howard Taft Rd., Cincinnati 45206; tel. 513/872-8100
The Community Mutual Insurance Company/Lima, Box 1046, Lima 45802; 50 Town Square, Lima 45802; tel. 419/228-3457
The Community Mutual Insurance Company/Worthington, 6740 N. High St., Worthington 43085; tel. 614/438-3500; Michael J. Ketchum, chm.
The Community Mutual Insurance Company/Youngstown, 2400 Market St., Youngstown 44507; tel. 216/783-9800
The Community Mutual Insurance Company (executive office), Atrium Two Building, 221 East Fourth St., Suite 2600, Cincinnati 45202; tel. 513/977-8801; Dwane R. Houser, pres./chf. exec. off.

OKLAHOMA: Blue Cross and Blue Shield of Oklahoma (Group Health Service of Oklahoma, Inc.), Box 3283, Tulsa 74102; 1215 S. Boulder Ave., Tulsa 74119; tel. 918/583-0861; Ralph S. Rhoades, pres./chf. exec. off.

OREGON: Blue Cross and Blue Shield of Oregon, Box 1271, Portland 97207; 100 S.W. Market St., Portland 97201; tel. 503/225-5221; Solomon D. Menashe, chm./chf. exec. off.

PENNSYLVANIA: Blue Cross of Greater Philadelphia, 1333 Chestnut St., Philadelphia 19107; tel. 215/448-5000; David S. Markson, pres./chf. exec. off.

Blue Cross of Northeastern Pennsylvania (Hospital Service Association of Northeastern Pennsylvania), 70 N. Main St., Wilkes-Barre 18711; tel. 717/829-6011; Gilbert D. Tough, CAM, pres./chf. exec. off.

Blue Cross of Western Pennsylvania, One Smithfield St., Pittsburgh 15222; tel. 412/255-7000; Eugene J. Barone, pres.

Capital Blue Cross, 100 Pine St., Harrisburg 17101; tel. 717/255-6000, James M. Mead, pres.

Pennsylvania Blue Shield (Medical Service Association of Pennsylvania), 1800 Center St., Camp Hill 17011; tel. 717/763-3151; Leroy K. Mann, pres.

RHODE ISLAND: Blue Cross and Blue Shield of Rhode Island, 444 Westminster Mall, Providence 02901; tel. 401/272-8500; Douglas J. McIntosh, pres.

SOUTH CAROLINA: Blue Cross and Blue Shield of South Carolina, I-20 East at Alpine Rd., Columbia 29219; tel. 803/788-3860; Joseph F. Sullivan, pres.

SOUTH DAKOTA: Blue Cross of Western Iowa and South Dakota, Box 1677, Sioux City, IA 51102; Hamilton Blvd. & I-29, Sioux City, IA 51102; tel. 712/277-3081; Harris W. Feldick, pres.

South Dakota Blue Shield (South Dakota Medical Service, Inc.), 1601 W. Madison St., Sioux Falls 57104; tel. 605/336-1976; Ben R. Johnson, pres.

TENNESSEE: Blue Cross and Blue Shield of Tennessee, 801 Pine St., Chattanooga 37402; tel. 615/755-5600; J. Robert McGuff, pres.

Blue Cross and Blue Shield of Memphis (Memphis Hospital Service and Surgical Association, Inc.), Box 98, Memphis 38101; 85 N. Danny Thomas Blvd., Memphis 38103; tel. 901/529-3111; Arthur P. Waymire, pres.

TEXAS: Blue Cross and Blue Shield of Texas, Inc., Box 665730, Dallas 75265-5730; 901 S. Central Expwy, Richardson 75080; tel. 214/669-6900; John D. Melton, pres.

UTAH: Blue Cross and Blue Shield of Utah, Box 30270, Salt Lake City 84130-0270; 2455 Parley's Way, Salt Lake City 84130-0270; tel. 801/487-6441; Jed H. Pitcher, pres./chm.

VERMONT: Vermont Health Service Corporation, Box 186, Montpelier 05602; Granger Rd., Berlin 05641; tel. 802/223-6131; Timothy F. Meehan, pres./chf. exec. off.

VIRGINIA: Blue Cross and Blue Shield of Virginia, Box 27401, Richmond 23279; 2015 Staples Mill Rd., Richmond 23230; tel. 804/359-7000

Blue Cross and Blue Shield of Virginia, Box 13047, Roanoke 24045; 602 S. Jefferson St., Roanoke 24011; tel. 703/985-5000; I. Lee Chapman, III, pres.

WASHINGTON: Blue Cross of Washington and Alaska, Box 327, Seattle 98111; 15700 Dayton Ave., N., Seattle 98133; tel. 206/361-3000, Donald A. Lockwood, pres./chf. exec. off.

Blue Shield in North Central Washington, Box 327, Seattle 98111; 15700 Dayton Ave., N., Seattle 98133; tel. 206/361-3000, Donald A. Lockwood, pres./chf. exec. off.

King County Medical Blue Shield, Box 21267, Seattle 98111; 1800 Terry Ave., Seattle 98101; tel. 206/464-3600; Winlock W. Pickering, pres.

Medical Service Corporation of Eastern Washington, Box 3048, Spokane 99220; E. 3900 Sprague Ave., Spokane 99202; tel. 509/536-4700; Fred A. Jacot, pres./chf. exec. off.

Pierce County Medical Bureau, Inc., 1114 Broadway Plaza, Tacoma 98402; tel. 206/597-6500; Donald P. Sacco, pres.

Washington Physicians Service, Fourth and Battery Bldg., Suite 600, 2401 4th Ave., Seattle 98121; tel. 206/441-9370; J. W. C. Heath, pres.

WEST VIRGINIA: Blue Cross and Blue Shield of West Virginia, Inc., Box 1353, Charleston 25325; 200 Kanawha Blvd. E., Charleston 25301; tel. 304/347-7600; James W. Heaton, pres.

Blue Cross and Blue Shield of West Central West Virginia, Inc., Box 1948, Parkersburg 26102; 700 Market Sq., Parkersburg 26101; tel. 304/424-7700; Thomas D. Farson, pres.

WISCONSIN: Blue Cross and Blue Shield United of Wisconsin, Box 2025, Milwaukee 53201; 401 W. Michigan St., Milwaukee 53201; tel. 414/226-5000; Thomas R. Hefty, pres./chf. exec. off.

WYOMING: Blue Cross and Blue Shield of Wyoming, Box 2266, Cheyenne 82003-2266; 4000 House Ave., Cheyenne 82003-2266; tel. 307/634-1393; C. E. Chapman, pres.

U.S. Associated Areas

PUERTO RICO: Blue Cross of Puerto Rico (La Cruz Azul de Puerto Rico), Box 6068-G, San Juan 00936; Ave. Pinero Esq. Cesar Gonzalez, Hato Rey 00918; tel. 809/759-9898; José Julian Alvarez, exec. dir.

Seguros de Servicio de Salud de Puerto Rico, Inc., Box G 3628, San Juan 00936; Ponce de León Ave. #431, San Juan 00919; tel. 809/759-9191; Frank W. Fournier, pres.

Canada

ALBERTA: Alberta Blue Cross Plan, 10025-108th St., Edmonton T5J 1K9; tel. 403/423-5221; Frank D. Huntington, pres.

BRITISH COLUMBIA: Medical Services Association, Box 9300, Vancouver V6B 4G3; tel. 604/654-2311; John D. Seney, exec. dir.

MANITOBA: Manitoba Blue Cross (United Health Services Corporation), Box 1046, Winnipeg R3C 2X7; 100A Polo Park Centre, 1485 Portage Ave., Winnipeg R3G 0W4; tel. 204/775-0161; Kerry V. Bittner, pres.

NEW BRUNSWICK: Blue Cross of Atlantic Canada, Box 220, Moncton E1C 8L3; 110 MacBeath Ave., Moncton E1C 6Z4; tel. 506/853-1811; Leon R. Furlong, pres.

NOVA SCOTIA: Maritime Medical Care Incorporated, Box 2200, Halifax B3J 3C6; 5675 Spring Garden Rd., Halifax B3J 1H1; tel. 902/429-9700; David L. McAvoy, gen. mgr.

ONTARIO: Ontario Blue Cross, 150 Ferrand Dr., Toronto M3C 1H6; tel. 416/429-2661; H. Dunbar Russel, pres.

QUEBEC: Quebec Blue Cross (Quebec Hospital Service Association), 550 Sherbrooke St., W., Montréal H3A 1B9; tel. 514/286-8400; Claude Ferron, C.A., pres.

SASKATCHEWAN: Blue Cross MSI (Medical Services Incorporated), Box 4030, Saskatoon S7K 3T2; 516 2nd Ave., N., Saskatoon S7K 2C5; tel. 306/244-1192; Marvin M. Cooney, pres.

Group Medical Services, 1942 Hamilton St., Regina S4P 2C6; tel. 306/352-7638; H. Hoffman, exec. dir.

Health Systems Agencies

The following is a list of federally funded Health Systems Agencies. The information was obtained directly from the agencies. States not listed do not have HSAs. For information about other local agencies and organizations that fulfill similar functions, contact the state or metropolitan hospital associations; see also the list of health planning agencies in section D, AHA Membership.

ALASKA: Northern Alaska Health Resources Association, Inc., 529 Fifth Ave., Suite 8, Fairbanks 99701; tel. 907/456-2553; Sherry McWhorter, exec. dir.
South Central Health Planning and Development Inc., 1135 W. Eighth Ave., Suite 1, Anchorage 99501; tel. 907/278-3631; S. Maureen Aakre, exec. dir.
Southeast Alaska Health Systems Agency, 215 Main St., Suite 203, Ketchikan 99901; tel. 907/225-9681; Jodi Perlmutter, dir.

ARIZONA: Central Arizona Health Systems Agency, 4414 N. 19th Ave., Ste. S, Phoenix 85015; tel. 602/266-7651; Marlene K. Mariani, exec. dir.
Health Systems Agency of Southeastern Arizona, 149 N. Stone Ave., Suite 404, Tucson 85701; tel. 602/623-5733; Phillip M. Lopes, exec. dir.
Navajo Health Systems Agency, Navajo Tribal Council, P.O. Box 604, Window Rock 86515; tel. 602/871-6886, 871-6742; Genevieve Notah, exec. dir.
Western Arizona Health Systems Agency, 219 S. 2nd Ave., #B, Yuma 85364; tel. 602/783-7863; Lenore L. Stuart, exec. dir.

ARKANSAS: Delta-Hills Health Systems Agency, Inc., P.O. Box 701, Newport 72112; tel. 501/523-8973 Frances Flener, exec. dir.
South Arkansas Health Systems Agency, Inc., 1920 N. College St., P.O. Box 1917, El Dorado 71730; tel. 501/862-7951; Bernays B. Malin, Jr., exec. dir.
West Arkansas Health Systems Agency, Inc., Dwr. H, Russellville 72801; tel. 501/968-2229; Robert Hettinga, exec. dir.

CALIFORNIA: Bay Area Health Resources Center, 235 W. MacArthur Blvd., Suite 465, Oakland 94611, tel. 415/652-5566; Gilbert Ojeda, exec. dir.
Central California Health Systems Agency, 208 W. Main St., 2nd Flr., Visalia 93291; tel. 209/733-8676; Sarah A. Sharp, exec. dir.
Golden Empire Health Systems Agency, 2100 21st St., Sacramento 95818; tel. 916/731-5050; Mark Hemmings, exec. dir.
Health Systems Agency of San Diego and Imperial Counties, 2404 F St., San Diego, 92102; tel. 619/237-1001; Virginia M. Reynolds, exec. dir.
Inland Counties Health Systems Agency, 1600 Chicago Ave., Suite R-1, P.O. Box 5950, Riverside 92517; tel. 714/825-7510; Eric G. Beacham, exec. dir.
Mid-Coast Health Systems Agency, 205 17th St., P.O. Box 51002, Pacific Grove 93950-6002; tel. 408/373-7751; David Wright, exec. dir.
North Bay Health Systems Agency, 55 Maria Dr., Suite 837, Petaluma 94952; tel. 707/762-4591; E. Feighery-Ross, actg. exec. dir.
Northern California Health Systems Agency, 813 E. 5th Ave., Chico 95926; tel. 916/895-4461; Patricia Jakobi, exec. dir.
Orange County Health Planning Council, 202 Fashion Lane, Suite 219, Tustin 92680; tel. 714/832-1841; Richard E. Butler, exec. dir.
Ventura-Santa Barbara Health Systems Agency, 3212 Loma Vista Rd., Suite 210, Box 3966, Ventura 93006; tel. 805/648-7939; Samuale Negash, int. exec. dir.

COLORADO: Southeastern Colorado Health Systems Agency, 130 E. Kiowa, Colorado Springs 80903; tel. 303/475-9395; Nancy Sanford, exec. dir.

CONNECTICUT: Health Systems Agency of Eastern Connecticut, Inc., 257 Main St., Suite 509, Norwich 06360; tel. 203/886-1996; Mercedes Primer, dir.
Health Systems Agency of North Central Connecticut, 999 Asylum Ave., Hartford 06105; tel. 203/249-7581; Ralph S. Pollock, pres.
Health Systems Agency of South Central Connecticut, Inc., 131 Bradley Rd., Woodbridge 06525; tel. 203/397-5400; John Huettner, exec. dir.
Northwest Connecticut Health Systems Agency, 20 E. Main St., Rm. 324, Waterbury 06702; tel. 203/757-9601; Christina A. Fishbein, exec. dir.

DELAWARE: Delaware Health Council, Inc., 1925 Lovering Ave., Wilmington 19806; tel. 302/654-8991; Carol Gausz-Mandelberg, exec. dir.

GEORGIA: Appalachian Georgia Health Systems Agency, P.O. Box 829, Cartersville 30120; tel. 404/386-2431; Richard K. Parks, exec. dir.
East Central Georgia Health Systems Agency, Inc., Georgia Railroad Bank Bldg., Suite 1114, 699 Broad St., Augusta 30901; tel. 404/724-9927; William T. McKettrick, exec. dir.
Health Systems Agency of Central Georgia, Inc., Box 2305, Warner Robins 31099; tel. 912/922-2215; Marvin A. Noles, exec. dir.

IDAHO: Idaho Health Systems Agency, Inc., P.O. Box 8868, Boise 83707; tel. 208/336-1660; Mary Anne Saunders, exec. dir.

ILLINOIS: City of Chicago Health Systems Agency, 500 N. Peshtigo Ct., 4th Flr., Chicago 60611; tel. 312/744-8660; Susan Weed, exec. dir.
Comprehensive Health Planning of Northwest Illinois, 206 W. State St., Suite 1008, Rockford 61101; tel. 815/968-0720; Joel B. Cowen, exec. dir.
Comprehensive Health Planning in Southern Illinois, Inc., Box 3698, Carbondale 62902-3698; tel. 618/549-2161; Martin Anderson, exec. dir.
East Central Illinois Health Systems Agency, 302 E. John St., Suite 1707, Champaign 61820; tel. 217/333-3987; Allen Wann, exec. dir.
Health Systems Agency for Kane, Lake, and McHenry Counties, Inc., 188 S. Northwest Hwy., Cary 60013; tel. 312/639-0061; Richard Janishewski, exec. dir.
Iowa-Illinois Health Care Alliance, 1705 2nd Ave., Ste. 607, Rock Island 61201; tel. 309/793-4107; Ruth J. Lee, exec. dir.
Region 9 Health Systems Agency, Inc., 1 E. Doris, Rm. 204, Joliet 60433; tel. 815/726-2232; Mary Pasholk, actg. exec. dir.
Suburban Cook/DuPage Health Systems Agency, Inc., 1010 Lake St., Oak Park 60301; tel. 312/524-9700; Richard Sewell, exec. dir.
West Central Illinois Health Systems Agency, Inc., 412 Myers Bldg., Springfield 62701; tel. 217/544-3412; Roger Ricketts, exec. dir.

IOWA: Health Policy Corporation of Iowa, Ste. 330, Two Ruan Ctr., Des Moines 50309; tel. 515/244-1211; Paul Pietzsch, pres.
Iowa-Illinois Health Care Alliance, 1705 2nd Ave., Ste. 607, Rock Island 61201; tel. 309/793-4107; Ruth J. Lee, exec. dir.

KANSAS: Health Systems Agency of Northeast Kansas, Inc., P.O. Box 781627, Wichita 67278; tel. 316/689-3280 ext. 28; Guillermo Barreto-Vega, exec. dir.
Health Systems Agency of Southeast Kansas, Inc., 407 S. Oliver, Wichita 67218; tel. 316/683-3711; Betty Arnold, exec. dir.

MARYLAND: Central Maryland Health Systems Agency, 501 St. Paul Pl., Suite 1000, Baltimore 21202; tel. 301/752-3500; Marshall Spurlock, exec. dir.
Health Planning Council of the Eastern Shore, Inc., Box 776, Cambridge 21613; tel. 301/228-8911; Fred Dierks, exec. dir.
Montgomery County Health Planning Commission, 50 Monroe St., 3rd flr., Rockville 20850; tel. 301/424-0545; John C. Osborne, exec. dir.
Southern Maryland Health Systems Agency, P.O. Box 85, 9131 Piscataway Rd., Clinton 20735; tel. 301/868-6206; Audrey K. Murawski, actg. exec. dir.
Western Maryland Health Systems Agency, 153 Baltimore St., Cumberland 21502; tel. 301/724-1616; Kery C. Hummel, exec. dir.

MASSACHUSETTS: Central Massachusetts Health Systems Agency, 415 Boston Turnpike, Shrewsbury 01545; tel. 617/845-1066; Mara H. Yerow, exec. dir.
Health Planning Council for Greater Boston, 294 Washington St., Suite 640, Boston 02108; tel. 617/426-2022; Charles Donahue, Jr., exec. dir.
Merrimack Valley Health Planning Council, Inc., 350 Common Street, Lawrence 01840; tel. 617/686-1621; Edmond A. Perregaux, Jr., exec. dir.
North Shore Health Planning Council, 29 Lowell St., Peabody 01960; tel. 617/531-7006; Edward Marakovitz, exec. dir.
Southeastern Massachusetts Health Planning, and Development, Inc., 49 N. Main St., P.O. Box 70, Middleboro 02346; tel. 617/947-6300; John H. Nay, exec. dir.
Western Massachusetts Health Planning Council, 59 Interstate Dr., West Springfield 01089; tel. 413/781-2845; Herbert J. Hooven, exec. dir.

MICHIGAN: East Central Michigan Health Systems Agency, 1230 S. Washington, Suite 301, Saginaw 48601; tel. 517/754-0421; Raymond P. Bauley, exec. dir.
Genesee, Lapeer, and Shiawassee Health Systems, Inc., Walter Reuther Center, Rm. 325, 708 Root St., Flint 48503; tel. 313/238-0650; Stephen F. Davie, exec. dir.
Michigan Mid-South Health Systems Agency, Inc., 528 Mason Plaza, Mason 48854; tel. 517/676-4046; Ronald Parsons, exec. dir.
Northern Michigan Health Systems Agency, 325 E. Lake St., Hollywood Bldg., Petoskey 49770-2488; tel. 616/347-7772; Robert P. Trautman, exec. dir.
Upper Peninsula Health Systems Agency, 308 Pewabic Street, Laurium 49913; tel. 906/337-0703; Gary M. Wenberg, Ph.D., exec. dir.
West Michigan Health Systems Agency, 72 Monroe Ctr., Ste. 200, Grand Rapids 49503; tel. 616/459-1323; Philip Van Heest, pres.

MINNESOTA: Agassiz Health Systems Agency, 31 S. 3rd, Grand Forks, ND 58206; tel. 701/746-0441; Mary Ellen Preston, exec. dir.
Central Minnesota Health Systems Agency, 113 Division St., Sauk Rapids 56379; tel. 612/253-2930; Mary Schmid, exec. dir.
Health Systems Agency of Western Lake Superior, Inc., 202 Ordean Bldg., 424 W. Superior St., Duluth 55802; tel. 218/726-4762; Wende Nelson, exec. dir.
Health Planning Board of Metropolitan Council, 300 Metro Square Bldg., Seventh & Robert Sts., St. Paul 55101, tel. 612/291-6351; Malcolm Mitchell, exec. dir.

MISSISSIPPI: Mississippi Health Systems Agency, Inc., Watkins Bldg., Suite 400, 510 George St., Jackson 39201; tel. 601/948-8905; Philip W. Laird, exec. dir.

MONTANA: Montana Health Systems Agency, Gold Block, 2nd Flr., Helena 59601; tel. 406/443-5965; James H. Foley, exec. dir.

NEVADA: Clark County Coalition Health Systems Agency, 1455 E. Tropicana, Suite 530, Las Vegas 89119; tel. 702/798-1033; Lawrence Matheis, exec. dir.
Greater Nevada Health Systems Agency, 308 N. Curry St., # 205, Carson City 89701; tel. 702/883-7863; Milton Gan, exec. dir.

NEW JERSEY: Bergen-Passaic Health Systems Agency, 15-01 Broadway, Fairlawn 07410; tel. 201/794-8640; Marvin H. Burton, exec. dir.
Central Jersey Health Planning Council, Inc., 451 Wall St., Research Park, Princeton 08540; tel. 609/921-0894; Edward J. Peloquin, exec. dir.
Hudson Health Systems Agency, 871 Bergen Ave., Jersey City 07306; tel. 201/451-5024; Jesse T. S. Huang, exec. dir.
Regional Health Planning Council, 8 Park Place, Newark 07102; tel. 201/622-3280; Martin L. Parker, exec. dir.
Southern New Jersey Health Systems Agency, KOR-Center East, P.O. Box 637, Interstate Business Park, Bellmawr 08031; tel. 609/933-0641; Daniel R. Apostolu, exec. dir.

NEW MEXICO: Navajo Health Systems Agency, Navajo Tribal Council, P.O. Box 604, Window Rock, AZ 86515; tel. 602/871-6886, 871-6742; Genevieve Notah, exec. dir.
New Mexico Health Systems Agency, 120 Vassar S.E., Suite 4A, Albuquerque 87106; tel. 505/265-6789; Richard Brusuelas, exec. dir.

NEW YORK: Central New York Health Systems Agency, 840 James St., Syracuse 13203; tel. 315/478-0984; John Caezza, Ed.D., exec. dir.
Fingerlakes Health Systems Agency, 145 College Ave., Rochester 14607; tel. 716/461-3520; Claire R. Lovinski, exec. dir.
Health Systems Agency of New York City, 275 7th Ave., 27th Flr., New York 10001; tel. 212/741-8880; Daniel T. McGowan, exec. dir.
Health Systems Agency of Northeastern New York, Inc., Pine West Plaza, Washington Ave. Extension, Albany 12205; tel. 518/452-3300; Bruce Stanley, exec. dir.
Health Systems Agency of Western New York, Inc., 2070 Sheridan Dr., Buffalo 14223; tel. 716/876-7131; Brian G. McBride, Ph.D., exec. dir.
Hudson Valley Health Systems Agency, Sterling Lake Rd., Box 696, Tuxedo 10987; tel. 914/351-5146; Regina M. Kelly, exec. dir.
Nassau-Suffolk Health Systems Agency, 1537 Old Country Rd., Plainview 11803; tel. 516/293-5740; Deborah A. Gray, exec. dir.
NY-Penn Health Systems Agency, 306 Press Bldg., 19 Chenango St., Binghamton 13901; tel. 607/722-3445; Denise Murray, exec. dir.

NORTH CAROLINA: Capital Health Systems Agency, Inc., 800 N. Mangum St., Durham 27701; tel. 919/682-3900; Elmer M. Johnson, exec. dir.
Cardinal Health Agency, Inc., 401 E. 11th St., Lumberton 28358; tel. 919/738-9316; Larry Crumbliss, exec. dir.
Eastern Carolina Health Systems Agency, Suite 306, Minges Bldg., 301 S. Evans St., Greenville 27834; tel. 919/758-1372; Roy Selby, exec. dir.
Piedmont Health Systems Agency, Inc., 2120 Pinecroft Rd., Greensboro 27407; tel. 919/294-5831; Gloria Haynes, exec. dir.
Southern Piedmont Health Systems Agency, 1 Charlottetown Center, 1300 Baxter St., Suite 425, Box 35588, Charlotte 28235; tel. 704/372-8494; Eugene Goeller, exec. dir.
Western North Carolina Health Systems Agency, 565 West Fleming Drive, Morganton 28655; tel. 704/433-1636; Charles F. Moeller, exec. dir.

NORTH DAKOTA: Agassiz Health Systems Agency, 31 S. 3rd, Grand Forks 58206; tel. 701/746-0441; Mary Ellen Preston, exec. dir.

OHIO: Community Health Research Group, 55 Shiawassee Ave., Ste. A, Akron 44313; tel. 216/836-0602; James T. Suter, exec. dir.
Health Planning and Resource Development Association of the Central Ohio River Valley, 35 E. Seventh St., Suite 608, Cincinnati 45202; tel. 513/621-2434; James F. Sandmann, pres.
Health Planning Development Council, 4119 Whipple Ave., N.W., Canton 44718; tel. 216/492-7589; Harry Fisher, dir.
Health Systems Agency of Eastern Ohio, Youngstown 44515; Chester A. Amedia, pres.
Health Systems Agency of North Central Ohio, 1501 Euclid Ave., Rm. 319, Cleveland 44115; tel. 216/771-6814; Stephen F. Sears, exec. dir.
Health Systems Association, 50 Town Sq., Lima 45801; tel. 419/227-8361; Martin C. Dodrill, pres.
Northwest Ohio Health Planning, Inc., 635 N. Erie St., Toledo 43624; tel. 419/255-1190; David G. Pollick, exec. dir.
Ohio Hills Health Planning Agency, Inc., 216 Putnam St., Marietta 45750; tel. 614/374-4009; Thomas A. Closser, pres.; Susan W. Isaac, exec. dir.
Scioto Valley Health Systems Agency, 285 E. Main St., Columbus 43215; tel. 614/221-4801; Susan Ewing-Ramsay, exec. dir.

OKLAHOMA: (no health systems agency)

OREGON: Eastern Oregon Health Systems Agency, P.O. Box 7618, Bend 97708; tel. 503/388-0250; Donald J. Ptaenik, actg. exec. dir.
Pacific Health Policy Research, Inc., 1220 S.W. Morrison Ave., Suite 620, Portland 97205; tel. 503/228-8851
Western Oregon Health Systems Agency, 99 W. 10th St., Suite 377B, Eugene 97401; tel. 503/484-9311; Kathleen W. Howard, exec. dir.

PENNSYLVANIA: Health Resources Planning and Development, Inc., Suite 4, Bldg. 1, 2213 Forest Hills Dr., Harrisburg, 17112; tel. 717/652-9371; Ambrose Potrzebowski, exec. dir.
Health Systems Agency of Northeast Pennsylvania, Inc., Warm Bldg., Avoca 18641; tel. 717/655-3703; Eugene Nugent, exec. dir.
Health Systems Agency of Southwestern Pennsylvania, Inc., 11th flr., Convention Tower, 960 Penn Ave., Pittsburgh 15222; tel. 412/562-1800; John W. Clem, exec. dir.
Health Systems Agency of Southeastern Pennsylvania, 230 S. Broad St., 16th flr., Philadelphia 19102; tel. 215/546-1616; Gerald R. Gill, exec. dir.
Keystone Health Systems Agency, P.O. Box 98, Duncansville 16635-0098; tel. 814/696-4003; John J. Schraff, exec. dir.
New York-Pennsylvania Health Systems Agency, 306 Press Bldg., 19 Chenango St., Binghamton, NY 13901; tel. 607/722-3445; Denise Murray, exec. dir.

SOUTH CAROLINA: East Central Georgia Health Systems Agency, Inc., Georgia Railroad Bank Bldg., 699 Broad St., Suite 1114; Augusta, GA 30901; tel. 404/724-9927; William T. McKettrick, exec. dir.
Palmetto-Lowcountry Health Systems Agency, Inc., 107 West 6th North St., P.O. Dwr. 1946, Summerville 29484; tel. 803/871-0350; Katherine H. Duffy, exec. dir.
Pee Dee Regional Health Systems Agency, Inc., 109 W. Laurel St., P.O. Box 13118, Florence 29504-1118; tel. 803/669-1347; Glenn C. Lane, exec. dir.
South Carolina Appalachian Health Council, 211 Century Dr., Bldg. D, Box 6708, Greenville 29606; tel. 803/242-1895; James F. Keasler, exec. dir.
Three Rivers Health Systems Agency, Inc., 3700 Forest Dr., Suite 204, Columbia 29204; tel. 803/782-4787; Gary Thibault, exec. dir.

SOUTH DAKOTA: South Dakota Health Systems Agency, 200 W. Main, Vermillion 57069; tel. 605/624-4446; Walton H. Springall, Jr., exec. dir.

TENNESSEE: ARCHA Health Systems Agency, Box 600, Johnson City 37601; tel. 615/929-0193; David Parker, exec. dir.
Health Resources Development Corp., 814 Jefferson, Memphis 38105; tel. 901/454-6022; Gordon Smith, exec. dir.

UTAH: Navajo Health Systems Agency, Navajo Tribal Council, P.O. Box 604, Window Rock, AZ 86515; tel. 608/871-6886/6742; Genevieve Notah, exec. dir.
Utah Health Systems Agency, 136 E. South Temple, University Club Bldg., Suite 2160, Salt Lake City 84111; tel. 801/581-3476; Stephen Bonney, exec. dir.

VERMONT: Vermont Health Policy Corporation, Waterbury State Office Complex, 103 S. Main St., Waterbury 05676; tel. 802/241-2920; Paul H. Wallace-Brodeur, exec. dir.

VIRGINIA: ARCHA Health Systems Agency, Box 600, Johnson City, TN 37601; tel. 615/929-0193; David Parker, exec. dir.
Central Virginia Health Systems Agency, 908 N. Thompson St., Richmond 23230-3697; tel. 804/355-5723
Eastern Virginia Health Systems Agency, 11 Koger Executive Center, Suite 203, Norfolk 23502; tel. 804/461-1236; Paul M. Boynton, exec. dir.
Health Systems Agency of Northern Virginia, Inc., 7245 Arlington Blvd., Suite 300, Falls Church 22042; tel. 703/573-3100; Dean Montgomery, exec. dir.
Northwestern Virginia Health Systems Agency, Inc., Blue Ridge Hospital, Charlottesville 22901; tel. 804/977-6010; Margaret P. King, exec. dir.
Southwest Virginia Health Systems Agency, Inc., P.O. Box 11844, Roanoke 24022-1844; tel. 703/982-2304; Pamela Corcoran, exec. dir.

WASHINGTON: Central Washington Health Systems Agency, 32 N. 3rd St., Suite 310, Yakima 98901; tel. 509/248-4220; Douglas L. Flow, Ph.D., dir.
Eastern Washington Health Systems Agency, D.S.H.S. Bldg., 121 S. Arthur, Suite A, Spokane 99202; tel. 509/536-1547; SCAN 584-1547; Nick Beamer, exec. dir.
Puget Sound Health Systems Agency, 601 Valley St., Seattle 98109; tel. 206/464-6143; Larry Thompson, exec. dir.

WISCONSIN: Community Health Council, 408 3rd St., Ste. 202, Wausau 54401; tel. 715/845-3107; George Snyder, exec. dir.
Health Systems Agency of Western Lake Superior, Inc., 202 Ordean Bldg., 424 W. Superior St., Duluth, MN 55802; tel. 218/726-4762; Joanne Axtell, exec. dir.
Southeastern Wisconsin Health Systems Agency, Inc., 735 N. Fifth St., Milwaukee 53203; tel. 414/271-9788; Kipton Kaplan, exec. dir.
Western Wisconsin Health Systems Agency, 907 Main St., La Crosse 54601; tel. 608/785-9352; Val Chilsen, exec. dir.

Hospital Associations

The following list of state and metropolitan hospital associations is derived from the American Hospital Association's 1987 Directory of Hospital Associations. National and regional hospital associations are cited in the list beginning on page E3.

United States

ALABAMA: Alabama Hospital Association, 500 N. East Blvd., P.O. Box 17059, East Sta., Montgomery 36193; tel. 205/272-8781; Tommy R. McDougal, pres.

ALASKA: Health Association of Alaska, 319 Seward St., Juneau 99801; tel. 907/586-1790; Dale C. Shirk, exec. dir.

ARIZONA: Arizona Hospital Association, 2411 W. 14th St., Suite 410, Tempe 85281-6943; tel. 602/968-1083; John R. Rivers, pres.

ARKANSAS: Arkansas Hospital Association, 1501 N. University Ave., Prospect Bldg., Suite 400, Little Rock 72207; tel. 501/664-7870; Roger M. Busfield Jr., Ph.D., pres.

CALIFORNIA: California Association of Hospitals and Health Systems, 1023 12th St., P.O. Box 1100, Sacramento 95805-1100; tel. 916/443-7401; C. Duane Dauner, pres.
Hospital Council of Central California, 5771 N. Fresno St., Suite 110, Fresno 93710; tel. 209/435-5076; J. Michael Gallagher, pres.
Hospital Council of Northern California, 1825 S. Grant, Suite 820, San Mateo 94402; tel. 415/572-0330; Sheldon Gulinson, pres.
Hospital Council of San Diego and Imperial Counties, 8305 Vickers St., Suite T, San Diego 92111; tel. 619/292-7074; Dewey Baggett, pres.
Hospital Council of Southern California, 201 N. Figueroa St., 4th flr., Los Angeles 90012; tel. 213/250-5600; Stephen W. Gamble, pres.

COLORADO: Colorado Hospital Association, 2140 S. Holly St., Denver 80222; tel. 303/758-1630; Larry Wall, pres.

CONNECTICUT: Connecticut Hospital Association, 110 Barnes Rd., P.O. Box 90, Wallingford 06492; tel. 203/265-7611; Dennis P. May, pres.

DELAWARE: Association of Delaware Hospitals, Bank of Delaware Bldg., P.O. Box 471, Dover 19901; tel. 302/674-2853; Eugene H. Wolinsky, pres.

DISTRICT OF COLUMBIA: District of Columbia Hospital Association, 1250 Eye St., N.W., Suite 700, Washington 20005; tel. 202/682-1581; Howard T. Jessamy, pres.
Hospital Council of the National Capital Area, Inc., 1250 Eye St., N.W., #700, Washington 20005-3922; tel. 202/789-1500; Anthony J. Monaco, exec. vice-pres. and dir.

FLORIDA: Bay Area Hospital Council, 7200 66th St., N., Pinellas Park 33565; tel. 813/545-3222; Constance C. Smith, exec. dir.
Florida Hospital Association, 307 Park Lake Circle, P.O. Box 6905, Orlando 32853-6905; tel. 305/841-6230; John M. McBryde, pres.
Greater Jacksonville Area Hospital Council, P.O. Box 120, Ponte Vedra Beach 32082; tel. 904/285-4738; Michael J. Wood, exec. dir.
South Florida Hospital Association, Inc., Koger Executive Center, Cleveland Bldg., 8245 N.W. 53rd St., Suite 200, Miami 33166-4609; tel. 305/591-8020; George R. Berch, pres.
Tampa Area Hospital Council, 4023 N. Armenia Ave., Suite 311, Tampa 33607; tel. 813/875-6753; Leo Matti, exec. dir.

GEORGIA: Georgia Hospital Association, North by Northwest Office Park, Atlanta 30339; tel. 404/955-0324; Joseph A. Parker, pres.

HAWAII: Healthcare Association of Hawaii, 932 Ward Ave., Suite 430, Honolulu 96814; tel. 808/521-8961; Stanley B. Snodgrass, pres., CEO

IDAHO: Idaho Hospital Association, 6520 Norwood Dr., P.O. Box 7482, Boise 83707; tel. 208/377-2211; John D. Hutchison, pres.

ILLINOIS: Illinois Hospital Association, Center for Health Affairs, 1151 E. Warrenville Rd., Naperville 60566; tel. 312/357-9370; Kenneth C. Robbins, pres.
Metropolitan Chicago Healthcare Council, 222 S. Riverside Plaza, 17th Flr., Chicago 60606; tel. 312/906-6000; Earl C. Bird, pres.

INDIANA: Indiana Hospital Association, One American Square, P.O. Box 82063, Indianapolis 46282; tel. 317/633-4870; Kenneth G. Stella, pres.

IOWA: Hospital Association of Greater Des Moines, 1980 Financial Center, 666 Walnut, Des Moines 50309; tel. 515/243-8077; H. Mel Willits, pres.
The Iowa Hospital Association, Inc., 100 E. Grand Ave., Des Moines 50309; tel. 515/288-1955; Donald W. Dunn, pres.

KANSAS: Kansas Hospital Association, 1263 Topeka Ave., P.O. Box 2308, Topeka 66601; tel. 913/233-7436; Donald A. Wilson, pres.

KENTUCKY: Kentucky Hospital Association, 1302 Clear Spring Trace, P.O. Box 24163, Louisville 40224; tel. 502/426-6220; William S. Conn Jr., pres.

LOUISIANA: Louisiana Hospital Association, 9521 Brookline Ave., P.O. Box 80720, Baton Rouge 70898-0720; tel. 504/928-0026; Robert Merkel, pres.
Metropolitan Hospital Council of New Orleans, 3340 Severn Ave., Suite 206, Metairie 70005; tel. 504/454-2950; John J. Finn, Ph.D., pres.

MAINE: Maine Hospital Association, 151 Capitol St., Augusta 04330; tel. 207/622-4794; James R. Castle, pres.

MARYLAND: The Maryland Hospital Association, Inc., 1301 York Rd., Suite 800, Lutherville 21093-6087; tel. 301/321-6200; Richard J. Davidson, pres.

MASSACHUSETTS: Massachusetts Hospital Association, 5 New England Executive Park, Burlington 01803; tel. 617/272-8000; Stephen J. Hegarty, pres.
New England Health Network, Inc., 801 Main St., Concord 01742; tel. 617/890-6550; Joel P. Davidsen, pres.

MICHIGAN: Greater Flint Area Hospital Assembly, 702 S. Ballenger Hwy., Flint 48502; tel. 313/238-1230; David A. Seaman, exec. dir.
Hospital Council of East Central Michigan, 141 Harrow Ln., Suite 11, Saginaw 48603; tel. 517/792-1725; Judith Clevey, pres.
Hospital Council of Western and Central Michigan, One VandenBerg Center, Suite 480, Grand Rapids 49503; tel. 616/774-2024; Edward A. Rode, pres.
The Michigan Hospital Association, 6215 W. St. Joseph Hwy., Lansing 48917; tel. 517/323-3443; Spencer C. Johnson, pres.
South Central Michigan Hospital Council, 6215 W. St. Joseph Hwy., Lansing 48917; tel. 517/323-3443; David A. Seaman, pres.
Southeast Michigan Hospital Council of the Michigan Hospital Association, 24725 W. Twelve Mile Rd., Suite 104, Southfield 48034; tel. 313/358-2950; Donald P. Potter, pres.
Southwestern Michigan Hospital Council, 6215 W. St. Joseph Hwy., Lansing 48917; tel. 517/323-3443; David A. Seaman, pres.

MINNESOTA: Council of Community Hospitals, 2550 University Ave., W., Suite 221, St. Paul 55114; tel. 612/641-1121; Allan N. Johnson, pres.
Minnesota Hospital Association, Health Associations Center, 2221 University Ave., S.E., Suite 425, Minneapolis 55414; tel. 612/331-5571; Stephen Rogness, pres.

MISSISSIPPI: Mississippi Hospital Association, 4880 McWillie Circle, P.O. Box 16444, Jackson 39236-0444; tel. 601/982-3251; Samuel W. Cameron, pres.

MISSOURI: Hospital Association of Metropolitan St. Louis, 720 Olive St., 29th Fl., St. Louis 63101; tel. 314/421-3415; Stephen E. Dorn, F.A.C.H.E., pres.
Kansas City Area Hospital Association, Mark Twain Bank Bldg., 10401 Holmes, Suite 430, Kansas City 64131; tel. 816/941-3800; Cheryl L. Jernigan, pres.
Missouri Hospital Association, 4713 Highway 50 West, P.O. Box 60, Jefferson City 65102; tel. 314/893-3700; Charles L. Bowman, pres.

MONTANA: Montana Hospital Association, P.O. Box 5119, 1720 Ninth Ave., Helena 59601; tel. 406/442-1911; James F. Ahrens, pres.

NEBRASKA: Nebraska Hospital Association, 1335 L St., P.O. Box 94833, Lincoln 68509; tel. 402/476-0141; Harlan M. Heald, Ph.D., pres.
Omaha-Council Bluffs Hospital Association, 1335 L St., Lincoln 68508; tel. 402/476-0141; Arnold R. Thomas Jr., exec. dir.

NEVADA: Nevada Hospital Association, 4600 Kietzke Lane, Suite H-184, Reno 89502; tel. 702/827-0184; Fred L. Hillerby, pres.

NEW HAMPSHIRE: New Hampshire Hospital Association, 125 Airport Rd., Concord 03301-5388; tel. 603/225-0900; Gary S. Carter, pres.

NEW JERSEY: New Jersey Hospital Association, Center for Health Affairs, 746-760 Alexander Rd., CN-1, Princeton 08540-0001; tel. 609/275-4000; Louis P. Scibetta, pres.

NEW MEXICO: New Mexico Hospital Association, 5200 Copper, N.E., P.O. Box 8735, Albuquerque 87108; tel. 505/265-3686; Howard M. Shaver, pres.

NEW YORK: Central New York Hospital Association, Inc., 5793 Widewaters Pkwy., Syracuse 13214; tel. 315/445-1851; Richard E. Benoit, pres.
Greater New York Hospital Association, One Harkness Pl., 61 W. 62nd St., New York 10023; tel. 212/246-7100; Kenneth E. Raske, pres.
Hospital Association of New York State, Center for Health Initiatives, 74 North Pearl St., Albany 12207; tel. 518/434-7600; Daniel Sisto, pres.
League of Voluntary Hospitals and Homes of New York, 60 E. 42nd St., New York 10165; tel. 212/687-3347; William J. Abelow, pres. and counsel
Nassau-Suffolk Hospital Council, Inc., 700 Veterans Memorial Hwy., Hauppauge 11788; tel. 516/361-6700; Robert Lord, exec. vice-pres.
Northeastern New York Hospital Association, One Executive Park Dr., Albany 12203; tel. 518/438-2828; Randolph C. Knack, Jr., pres.
Northern Metropolitan Hospital Association, 419 Route 9 W. North, Newburgh 12550; tel. 914/562-7520; Arthur E. Weintraub, pres.
Rochester Regional Hospital Association, P.O. Box 23239, Rochester 14692; tel. 716/427-2820; (vacant), pres.
Western New York Hospital Association, 875 Hopkins Rd., Williamsville 14221; tel. 716/688-0365; John M. Apostolakos, pres.

NORTH CAROLINA: North Carolina Hospital Association, 112 Cox Ave., P.O. Box 10937, Raleigh 27605; tel. 919/832-9550; C. Edward McCauley, pres.

NORTH DAKOTA: North Dakota Hospital Association, Suite 307-315, 312 First Bank of North Dakota Bldg., 401 De Mers, P.O. Box 669, Grand Forks 58206-0669; tel. 701/772-4129; Harvey C. Hanson, pres.

OHIO: Akron Regional Hospital Association, 300 Locust St., Suite B90, Akron 44308-1821; tel. 216/379-8989; Susan L. Fraley, exec. coord.
The Center for Health Affairs, Greater Cleveland Hospital Association, 1226 Huron Rd., Playhouse Square, Cleveland 44115; tel. 216/696-6900; C. Wayne Rice, Ph.D., pres.
Greater Cincinnati Hospital Council, 1811 Losantiville Ave., Suite 450, Cincinnati 45237; tel. 513/531-0200; Lynn R. Olman, pres.
Greater Dayton Area Hospital Association, 32 N. Main St., Suite 1201, Dayton 45402; tel. 513/228-1000; Sarah A. Grim, pres.
Hospital Association of Central Ohio, 425 Metro Pl. N., Suite 120, Dublin 43017; tel. 614/766-2202; John T. Snyder, pres.
Hospital Council of Northwest Ohio, 5515 Southwyck Blvd., Suite 203, Toledo 43614; tel. 419/865-1274; W. Scott Fry, pres. & CEO
Ohio Hospital Association, 21 W. Broad St., Columbus 43215; tel. 614/221-7614; Donald R. Newkirk, pres.

OKLAHOMA: Oklahoma Hospital Association, 777 Northwest Grand Blvd., Suite 112, Oklahoma City 73118; tel. 405/843-9537; John C. Coffey, pres.

OREGON: Farwest Council of Hospitals, 1257 High St., Suite 5, Eugene 97401; tel. 503/345-3299; Peter Ask, exec. dir.
Northwest Oregon Council of Hospitals, 4000 Kruse Way Pl., Bldg. 2, Suite 100, Lake Oswego 97034-2543; tel. 503/636-2204; Jeff E. Poutinen, pres.
Oregon Association of Hospitals, 4000 Kruse Way Place, Bldg. 2, Suite 100, Lake Oswego 97034-2543; tel. 503/636-2204; P. D. Fleissner, pres.

PENNSYLVANIA: The Delaware Valley Hospital Council, Inc., 1315 Walnut St., Philadelphia 19107; tel. 215/735-9695; Charles Pierce, Jr., pres.
The Hospital Association of Pennsylvania, P.O. Box 608, 1200 Camp Hill Bypass, Camp Hill 17011; tel. 717/763-7053; John A. Russell, pres., CEO
Hospital Association of Pennsylvania Northeast Regional Council, One Montage Mountain Rd., Moosic 18507; tel. 717/344-1196; Joseph M. Krella, reg. dir.

The Hospital Council of Eastern Pennsylvania of the Hospital Association of Pennsylvania, 1200 Camp Hill Bypass, P.O. Box 608, Camp Hill 17011; tel. 717/763-7053; Joseph S. Anderson, reg. dir.
Hospital Council of Western Pennsylvania, 500 Commonwealth Dr., Warrendale 15086; tel. 412/776-6400; Jack C. Robinette, pres.

RHODE ISLAND: Hospital Association of Rhode Island, P.O. Box 9627, Providence 02940; tel. 401/421-7100; Calvin Pierson, pres.

SOUTH CAROLINA: South Carolina Hospital Association, 101 Medical Circle, P.O. Box 6009, West Columbia 29171-6009; tel. 803/796-3080; William L. Yates, pres.

SOUTH DAKOTA: South Dakota Hospital Association, 3708 Brooks Place, Suite 1, Sioux Falls 57106; tel. 605/361-2281; Frank M. Drew, pres.

TENNESSEE: Tennessee Hospital Association, 500 Interstate Blvd., S., Nashville 37210; tel. 615/256-8240; Ira M. Lane Jr., pres.

TEXAS: Dallas-Fort Worth Hospital Council, Embassy Bldg., 1431 Greenway Dr., Suite 300, Irving 75038-2417; tel. 214/550-1262; John C. Gavras, pres.
Greater Houston Hospital Council, P.O. Box 66962, Houston 77266-6962 (mailing address); 3333 Eastside, Suite 130, Houston 77098; tel. 713/526-9031; Garrett R. Graham, pres.
Texas Hospital Association, 6225 U.S. Hwy. 290, E., P.O. Box 15587, Austin 78761; tel. 512/453-7204; Terry Townsend, pres.

UTAH: Utah Hospital Association, 515 S. 7th, E., Suite 2-F, Salt Lake City 84102; tel. 801/364-1515; Eugene C. Beck, pres.

VERMONT: Vermont Hospital Association, 148 Main St., Montpelier 05602; tel. 802/223-3461; Norman E. Wright, pres.

VIRGINIA: Virginia Hospital Association, P.O. Box 31394; Richmond 23294; tel. 804/747-8600; Stuart D. Ogren, pres.

WASHINGTON: Seattle Area Hospital Council, 190 Queen Anne Ave., N., 3rd Floor, Seattle 98109; tel. 206/281-8989; James L. Nell, pres.
Washington State Hospital Association, 190 Queen Anne Ave., N., Seattle 98109; tel. 206/281-7211; Leo F. Greenawalt, pres. & CEO

WEST VIRGINIA: West Virginia Hospital Association, 3422 Pennsylvania Ave., Charleston 25302; tel. 304/345-9842; Kenneth M. Rutledge, pres.

WISCONSIN: Hospital Council of Greater Milwaukee Area, 2300 N. Mayfair Rd., Milwaukee 53226; tel. 414/258-9610; Marvin F. Neely Jr., pres.
Wisconsin Hospital Association, 5721 Odana Rd., Madison 53719-1289; tel. 608/274-1820; Robert Taylor, pres.

WYOMING: Wyoming Hospital Association, 2015 S. Greeley Hwy., P.O. Box 5539, Cheyenne 82003; tel. 307/632-9344; Robert C. Kidd II, pres.

U.S. Associated Areas

PUERTO RICO: Puerto Rico Hospital Association, Oficina 101, Villa Nevarez Professional Center, Centro Comercial Villa Nevarez, Rio Piedras 00927; tel. 809/764-0290; Juan Rivera, exec. dir.

Canada

ALBERTA: Alberta Hospital Association, 10025 108th St., Edmonton T5J 1K9; tel. 403/423-1776; Donald A. MacGregor, pres.

BRITISH COLUMBIA: British Columbia Health Association, 500-1985 W. Broadway, Vancouver V6J 4Y3; tel. 604/734-2423; Herman A. Crewson, pres.

MANITOBA: Manitoba Health Organizations, Inc., 600-360 Broadway, Winnipeg R3C 4G6; tel. 204/942-6591; Jeffrey C. Lozon, exec. dir.

NEW BRUNSWICK: New Brunswick Hospital Association, 861 Woodstock Rd., Fredericton E3B 4X4; tel. 506/455-8626; Michel J. Poirier, exec. dir.

NEWFOUNDLAND: Newfoundland Hospital Association, P.O. Box 8234, Post Sta. A., St. John's A1B 3N4; tel. 709/364-7701; Robin J. Burnell, exec. dir.

NORTHWEST TERRITORIES: Northwest Territories Hospital Association, P.O. Box 10, Yellowknife X1A 2N1; tel. 403/920-4111; Lawrence E. Todd, exec. dir.

NOVA SCOTIA: Nova Scotia Association of Health Organizations, 5614 Fenwick St., Halifax B3H 1P9; tel. 902/429-4020; J. F. Ingram, exec. dir.

ONTARIO: Ontario Hospital Association, 150 Ferrand Dr., Don Mills M3C 1H6; tel. 416/429-2661; Gordon R. Cunningham, pres.

PRINCE EDWARD ISLAND: Hospital Association of Prince Edward Island, 57 Queen St., P.O. Box 490, Charlottetown C1A 7L1; tel. 902/892-7030; Dr. Gustave Gingras, pres.

QUEBEC: Association of Hospitals of the Province of Quebec, 505 W. Maisonneuve Blvd., Suite 400, Montreal H3A 3C2; tel. 514/842-4861; Jacques A. Nadeau, exec. v-pres. & exec. dir.

SASKATCHEWAN: Saskatchewan Health-Care Association, 1445 Park St., Regina S4N 4C5; tel. 306/525-2741; Dave Schappert, pres.

Hospital Licensure Agencies

Information for the following list of state hospital licensure agencies was obtained directly from the agencies.

United States

ALABAMA: State Hospital Licensure Agency, Division of Licensure and Certification, Alabama Department of Public Health, 654 State Office Bldg., Montgomery 36130; tel. 205/261-5113; Carroll S. Nason, dir.

ALASKA: Health Facilities Licensing and Certification, 4041 B St., #101, Anchorage 99503; tel. 907/561-2171; Karen Martz, supr.

ARIZONA: Office of Health Care Institution Licensure, Arizona Department of Health Services, 411 N. 24th St., Phoenix 85008; tel. 602/220-6407; Hazel E. Chandler, chf.

ARKANSAS: Division of Health Facility Services, Arkansas Dept. of Health—Area 2300, 4815 W. Markham St., Little Rock 72205; tel. 501/661-2201; Rayburn C. Allen, dir.

CALIFORNIA: Licensing and Certification, Department of Health Services, 714 P St., Rm. 823, Sacramento 95814; tel. 916/445-3054; Virgil J. Toney, Jr., dep. dir.

COLORADO: Division of Health Facilities Regulation, Colorado Department of Health, 4210 E. 11th Ave., Denver 80220; tel. 303/331-4930; Mildred Simmons, dir.

CONNECTICUT: Hospital and Medical Care Division, Connecticut State Department of Health Services, 150 Washington St., Hartford 06106; tel. 203/566-1073; Elizabeth M. Burns, R.N., M.S., dir.

DELAWARE: Office of Health Facilities Licensing and Certification, Department of Health and Social Services, 3000 Newport Gap Pike, Wilmington 19808; tel. 302/571-3499; James E. Harvey, dir.

DISTRICT OF COLUMBIA: Service Facility Regulation Administration, 614 H St., N.W., Washington 20001; tel. 202/727-7190; Francis A. Bowie, adm.

FLORIDA: Office of Licensure and Certification, Department of Health and Rehabilitation Services, 2727 Mahan Dr., Tallahassee 32308; tel. 904/487-2527; Amy M. Jones, dir.

GEORGIA: Standards and Licensure Section, Department of Human Resources, 878 Peachtree St., N.E., Suite 803, Atlanta 30309; tel. 404/894-5137; Phillip A. Arnold, dir.

HAWAII: State Health Planning and Development Agency, P.O. Box 3378, Honolulu 96801; tel. 808/548-2048; Dr. Ben Lambiotte, chf.
Medical Health Services Division, Hospital and Medical Facilities, Licensing Branch, Hawaii Department of Health

IDAHO: Facility Standards Program, Dept. of Health and Welfare, 420 W. Washington St., Boise 83720; tel. 208/334-4169; Jean Schoonover, R.N., prog. supv.

ILLINOIS: Hospital Licensing Section, Division of Health Facilities Standards, Department of Public Health, 525 W. Jefferson, Springfield 62761; tel. 217/782-4977; Joseph L. Voss, adm.

INDIANA: Division of Acute Care Services, Indiana State Board of Health, 1330 W. Michigan St., Indianapolis 46206; tel. 317/633-8486; Harry T. Haver, dir.

IOWA: Division of Health Facilities, Iowa State Department of Inspections and Appeals, Lucas State Office Bldg., Des Moines 50319; tel. 515/281-4115; Dana Petrowsky, adm.

KANSAS: Hospital Program, Bureau of Adult and Child Care Facilities, Kansas Department of Health and Environment, Forbes Field, Bldg. 740, Topeka 66620, tel. 913/296-1240; Greg Reser, med. facil. cert. adm.

KENTUCKY: Division of Licensing and Regulation, Cabinet for Human Resources, Human Resources Bldg., 275 E. Main St., 4th flr. East, Frankfort 40621; tel. 502/564-2800; Woody Dunn, dir.

LOUISIANA: Division of Licensing and Certification, Louisiana Department of Health and Human Resources, Box 3767, Baton Rouge 70821; tel. 504/342-5774; Steve Phillips, dir.

MAINE: Division of Licensing and Certification, Department of Human Services, State House, Station 11, Augusta 04333; tel. 207/289-2606; Louis Dorogi, dir.

MARYLAND: Department of Health and Mental Hygiene, 201 W. Preston St., Baltimore 21201; tel. 301/383-6197; Joseph R. Noll, dir. reg. serv.

MASSACHUSETTS: Division of Health Care Quality, Massachusetts Department of Public Health, 80 Boylston St., Rm. 1125, Boston 02116; tel. 617/727-5860; Irene R. McManus, dir.

MICHIGAN: Bureau of Health Facilities, Michigan Department of Public Health, 3500 N. Logan, Box 30035, Lansing 48909; tel. 517/335-8500; Raj Wiener, chf.

MINNESOTA: Health Resources Division, Minnesota Department of Health, 717 Delaware St., S.E., Minneapolis 55440; tel. 612/623-5440; Janet G. Brodahl, dir.

MISSISSIPPI: Division of Health Facilities Licensure and Certification, Mississippi State Department of Health, 2688 Insurance Center Dr., Jackson 39216; tel. 601/981-6880; Mendal G. Kemp, chf.

MISSOURI: Bureau of Hospital Licensing and Certification, Missouri Department of Health, Box 570, Jefferson City 65102; tel. 314/751-6302; Charles R. Gillilan, chf.

MONTANA: Health Services Division, State Department of Health and Environmental Sciences, Cogswell Bldg., Helena 59620; tel. 406/444-2037; George Fenner, adm.

NEBRASKA: Division of Licensure and Standards, State Department of Health, 301 Centennial Mall, S. Lincoln 68509; tel. 402/471-2946; William H. Page, dir.

NEVADA: Bureau of Regulatory Health Services, Nevada State Division of Health, 505 E. King St., Carson City 89710; tel. 702/885-4475, William C. Schneider, chf.

NEW HAMPSHIRE: Bureau of Health Facilities Administration, Division of Public Health Services, Health & Human Services Bldg., 6 Hazen Dr., Concord, 03301; tel. 603/271-4592; Charles Ferguson, chf.

NEW JERSEY: Licensing, Certification, and Standards, New Jersey State Department of Health, Division of Health Facilities Evaluation, CN 367, Trenton 08625; tel. 609/292-5764; Solomon Goldberg, D.D.S., dir.

NEW MEXICO: Health Services Division, Federal Program Certification Section, Health and Environment Department, 1190 St. Francis Dr., Box 968, Santa Fe 87504; tel. 505/827-2416; Sue K. Morris, sup.

NEW YORK: Bureau of Project Management, Office of Health Systems Management, Department of Health, Empire State Plaza, Albany 12237; tel. 518/473-7915; David R. Collins, dir.

NORTH CAROLINA: Division of Facility Services, Department of Human Resources, 701 Barbour Dr., Raleigh 27603; tel. 919/733-2342; Ira O. Wilkerson Jr., dir.

NORTH DAKOTA: Health Resources Section, State Department of Health, State Capitol, Bismarck 58505; tel. 701/224-2352; Joseph Pratschner, chf.

OHIO:(no licensing agency)

OKLAHOMA: State Department of Health, 1000 N.E. 10th, Oklahoma City 73152; tel. 405/271-4200; Joan K. Leavitt, M.D., comr.

OREGON: Health Facilities Section, Office of Environment and Health Systems, Box 231; Portland 97207; tel. 503/229-5686; Maureen Whitman, mgr.

PENNSYLVANIA: Division of Hospitals, Bureau of Quality Assurance, Health and Welfare Bldg., Harrisburg 17120; tel. 717/783-8980; William W. Walker, dir.

RHODE ISLAND: Department of Health, 75 Davis St., Providence 02908; tel. 401/277-2231; H. Denman Scott, M.D., dir.

SOUTH CAROLINA: Office of Health Licensing, Division of Health Licensing and Certification, South Carolina Department of Health and Environmental Control, 2600 Bull St., Columbia 29201; tel. 803/734-4680; Alan Samuels, dir.

SOUTH DAKOTA: Licensure and Certification Program, State Department of Health, Joe Foss Bldg., 523 E. Capitol, Pierre 57501; tel. 605/773-3364; C. Sue Lydic, dir.

TENNESSEE: Division of Health Care Facilities, Tennessee Department of Health and Environment, 283 Plus Park Blvd., Nashville 37219; tel. 615/367-6303; Polly T. Darnall, dir.

TEXAS: Hospital and Professional Licensure Division, Texas Department of Health, 1100 W. 49th St., Austin 78756; tel. 512/458-7512; Gerald Guthrie, dir.

UTAH: Utah State Department of Health, Bureau of Health Facility Licensure, P.O. Box 16660, Salt Lake City 84116; tel. 801/538-6152; James B. Fisher, dir.

VERMONT: Medical Care Regulation Division, Vermont Department of Health, 60 Main St., P.O. Box 70, Burlington 05402; tel. 802/863-7272; Robert Aiken, dir.

VIRGINIA: Division of Licensure and Certification, Virginia Department of Health, 109 Governor St., Richmond 23219; tel. 804/786-2081; Mary V. Francis, dir.

WASHINGTON: Health Facilities Survey Section, DSHS, Division of Health, ET-31, Olympia 98504; tel. 206/753-5851; Kenneth R. Lewis, supr.

WEST VIRGINIA: Health Facilities Licensure and Certification Section, West Virginia Department of Health, 1800 Washington St., E., Charleston 25305; tel. 304/348-0050; John J. Jarrell, dir.

WISCONSIN: Bureau of Quality Compliance, Division of Health, Department of Health and Social Services, 1 W. Wilson St., Box 309, Madison 53701; tel. 608/267-7185; Larry Tainter, dir.

WYOMING: Department of Health and Social Services, Division of Health and Medical Facilities, Hathaway Bldg., Cheyenne 82002; tel. 307/777-7121; Larry Meuli

Medical and Nursing Licensure Agencies

Information for the following list of state medical and nursing licensure agencies was obtained directly from the agencies. States not listed do not license medical and nursing personnel.

United States

ALABAMA
NURSING: Alabama Board of Nursing, One East Building, Suite 203, 500 Eastern Blvd., Montgomery 36117; tel. 205/261-4060; Shirley J. Dykes, R.N., M.S.N., exec. off.

ALASKA
MEDICAL: Alaska Medical Board, Department of Commerce and Economic Development, Division of Occupational Licensing, P.O. Box D-Lic, Juneau 99811; tel. 907/465-2541; Kurt D. West, lic. exam.

NURSING: Alaska Board of Nursing, 3601 C St., Suite 722, Anchorage 99503; tel. 907/561-2878; Gail M. McGuill, R.N., exec. sec.

ARIZONA
MEDICAL: Arizona Board of Medical Examiners, 1990 W. Camelback Rd., Suite 401, Phoenix 85015; tel. 602/255-3751; Douglas N. Cerf, exec. dir.

NURSING: Arizona State Board of Nursing, 5050 N. 19th Ave., Suite 103, Phoenix 85015; tel. 602/255-5092; Edith B. Summerlin, R.N., Ph.D., exec. dir.

ARKANSAS
NURSING: Arkansas State Board of Nursing, 4120 W. Markham St., Suite 308, Little Rock 72205; tel. 501/371-2751; June Garner, R.N., M.N., exec. dir.

CALIFORNIA
MEDICAL: California Board of Medical Quality Assurance, 1430 Howe Ave., Sacramento 95825; tel. 916/920-6411; Kenneth J. Wagstaff, exec. dir.

NURSING: Board of Registered Nursing, 1030 - 13th St., Ste. 200, Sacramento 95814; tel. 916/322-3350; Catherine M. Puri, R.N., Ph.D., exec. off.
Board of Vocational Nurse and Psychiatric Technician Examiners, 1020 N St., Rm. 406, Sacramento 95814; tel. 916/445-0793; Billie Haynes, R.N., M.Ed.D., exec. off.

COLORADO
MEDICAL: Colorado Board of Medical Examiners, 1525 Sherman St., No. 132, Denver 80203; tel. 303/866-2468; Bruce Douglas, dir.

CONNECTICUT
MEDICAL: Department of Health Services, Division of Medical Quality Assurance, Physician Licensure, 150 Washington St., Hartford 06106; tel. 203/566-7398; Stanley Peck, dir.

NURSING: Connecticut Board of Examiners for Nursing, Department of Health Services, Division of Medical Quality Assurance, 150 Washington St., Hartford 06106; tel. 203/566-1032; Marie Hillard, exec. off.

DELAWARE
MEDICAL: Board of Medical Practice of Delaware, Margaret O'Neill Bldg., 2nd flr., Dover 19903; tel. 302/736-4522; Rosemarie S. Perez, adm. asst.

NURSING: Delaware Board of Nursing, Margaret O'Neill Bldg., 2nd flr., Dover 19901; tel. 302/736-4522; Rosalee J. Seymour, R.N., M.S., exec. dir.

DISTRICT OF COLUMBIA
MEDICAL AND NURSING: Occupational and Professional Licensing Administration, P.O. Box 37200, Rm. 904, Washington 20013; tel. 202/727-7465; Valarie Barry, adm.

FLORIDA
MEDICAL: Florida Board of Medicine, 130 N. Monroe St., Tallahassee 32399; tel. 904/488-0595; Dorothy J. Faircloth, exec. dir.

NURSING: Board of Nursing, 111 Coast Line Dr., E., Suite 504, Jacksonville 32202; tel. 904/359-6331; Judie K. Ritter, R.N., exec. dir.

GEORGIA
MEDICAL: Composite State Board of Medical Examiners, 166 Pryor St., S.W., Atlanta 30303; tel. 404/656-3913; Andrew Watry, exec. dir.

NURSING: Georgia Board of Nursing, 166 Pryor St., S.W., Atlanta 30303; tel. 404/656-3943; Carolyn Hutcherson, exec. dir.

HAWAII
MEDICAL: Board of Medical Examiners, Department of Commerce and Consumer Affairs, P.O. Box 3469; Honolulu 96809; tel. 808/548-4392; John M. Tamashiro, exec. sec.

NURSING: Board of Nursing, P.O. Box 3469, Honolulu 96801; tel. 808/548-3086; Jerold H. Sakoda, exec. sec.

IDAHO
MEDICAL: Idaho State Board of Medicine, 650 W. State, Boise 83720; tel. 208/334-2822; Donald L. Deleski, exec. dir.

NURSING: Idaho State Board of Nursing, 700 W. State St., Boise 83720; tel. 208/334-3110; Phyllis T. Sheridan, R.N., M.S., exec. dir.

ILLINOIS
MEDICAL AND NURSING: Department of Registration and Education, 320 W. Washington, Springfield 62786; tel. 217/785-0800; Gary L. Clayton, dir.

INDIANA
MEDICAL: Health Professions Bureau, Medical Licensing Board of Indiana, P.O. Box 82067, One American Sq., Suite 1020, Indianapolis 46282-0004; tel. 317/232-2960; Mary Gaughan, bd. adm.

NURSING: Indiana State Board of Nursing, Health Professions Bureau, P.O. Box 82067, One American Sq., Suite 1020, Indianapolis 46282; tel. 317/232-2960; Mary Gaughan, adm.

IOWA
MEDICAL: Iowa State Board of Medical Examiners, State Capitol Complex, Executive Hills West, Des Moines 50319; tel. 515/281-5171; William S. Vanderpool, exec. dir.

NURSING: Iowa Board of Nursing, State Capitol Complex, 1223 E. Court Ave., Des Moines 50319; tel. 515/281-3255; Ann E. Mowery, R.N., M.N., exec. dir.

KANSAS
MEDICAL: Kansas State Board of Healing Arts, Landon State Office Building, 900 S.W. Jackson, Suite 553, Topeka 66612; tel. 913/296-7413; Charlene K. Abbott, exec. sec.

NURSING: Kansas State Board of Nursing, Landon State Office Bldg., 900 S.W. Jackson, Suite 551-S, Topeka 66612; tel. 913/296-4929; Lois Rich Sciebetta, R.N., Ph.D., exec. adm.

KENTUCKY
NURSING: Kentucky Board of Nursing, 4010 Dupont Circle, Suite 430, Louisville 40207; tel. 502/897-5143; Sharon M. Weisenbeck, M.S., R.N., exec. dir.

LOUISIANA
MEDICAL: Louisiana State Board of Medical Examiners, 830 Union St., Suite 100, New Orleans 70112; tel. 504/524-6763; Richard M. Nunnally, M.D., pres.

NURSING: Louisiana State Board of Nursing, 907 Pere Marquette Bldg., 150 Baronne St., New Orleans 70112; tel. 504/568-5464; Merlyn Maillian, R.N., exec. dir.
Louisiana State Board of Practical Nurse Examiners, Tidewater Pl., 1440 Canal St., Ste. 2010, New Orleans 70112; tel. 504/568-6480; Terry L. De Marcay, R.N., exec. dir.

MAINE
MEDICAL: Board of Registration in Medicine (State of Maine), RFD 3, Box 461, Waterville 04901; tel. 207/873-2184; Edward Bradley, Jr., chm.

NURSING: Maine State Board of Nursing, 295 Water St., Augusta 04330; tel. 207/289-5324; Jean C. Caron, R.N., exec. dir.

MARYLAND
MEDICAL: Board of Medical Examiners of Maryland, 201 W. Preston St., Baltimore 21201; tel. 301/225-5900; C. Earl Hill, M.D., pres.

NURSING: Maryland State Board of Examiners of Nurses, 201 W. Preston St., Baltimore 21201; tel. 301/225-5880; Donna M. Dorsey, R.N., M.N., exec. dir.

MASSACHUSETTS
MEDICAL: Board of Registration in Medicine, Commonwealth of Massachusetts, Ten West St., Boston 02111; tel. 617/727-3086; Dr. Ralph Deterling, chm.

NURSING: Board of Registration in Nursing, 100 Cambridge St., Rm. 1519, Boston 02202; tel. 617/727-7393; Mary H. Snodgrass, R.N., exec. sec.

MICHIGAN
MEDICAL: Michigan Board of Medicine, 611 W. Ottawa St., Box 30018, Lansing 48909; tel. 517/373-6873; Herman Fishman, lic. exec.

NURSING: Michigan Board of Nursing, Department of Licensing and Regulation, Box 30018, Lansing 48909; tel. 517/373-6873; Herman Fishman, lic. exec.

MINNESOTA
MEDICAL: Minnesota Board of Medical Examiners, 2700 University Ave., West, Ste. 106, St. Paul 55114; tel. 612/642-0538; David M. Ziegenhagen, exec. dir.

NURSING: Minnesota Board of Nursing, 2700 University Ave., West, #108, St. Paul 55114; tel. 612/642-0567; Joyce M. Schowalter, exec. dir.

MISSISSIPPI
NURSING: Mississippi Board of Nursing, 135 Bounds St., Jackson 39206; tel. 601/354-7349; Marcella L. McKay, R.N., M.S.N., exec. dir.

MISSOURI
MEDICAL: Missouri State Board of Registration for the Healing Arts, Box 4, Jefferson City 65102; tel. 314/751-2334; Gary R. Clark, exec. sec.

MONTANA
NURSING: Montana State Board of Nursing, 1424 9th Ave., Helena 59620; tel. 406/444-4279; Phyllis M. McDonald, R.N., M.E., exec. sec.

NEBRASKA
NURSING: Bureau of Examining Boards, 301 Centennial Mall, S., Box 95007, Lincoln 68509; tel. 402/471-2115; Helen L. Meeks, dir.

NEVADA
MEDICAL: Nevada State Board of Medical Examiners, P.O. Box 7238, Reno 89510; tel. 702/329-2559; Kathleen Lewis, exec. dir.

NURSING: Nevada State Board of Nursing, 1281 Terminal Way, Rm. 116, Reno 89502; tel. 702/786-2778; Lonna Burress, R.N., exec. dir.

NEW HAMPSHIRE
MEDICAL: New Hampshire Board of Registration in Medicine, Health and Welfare Bldg., 6 Hazen Dr., Concord 03301; tel. 603/271-4502; William T. Wallace, Jr., M.D., M.P.H., exec. sec.

NURSING: New Hampshire Board of Nursing Education and Nurse Registration, State Office Park, S., 101 Pleasant St., Concord 03301; tel. 603/271-2323; (vacant)

NEW JERSEY
MEDICAL: State Board of Medical Examiners of New Jersey, 28 W. State St., Trenton 08608; tel. 609/292-4843; Charles A. Janousek, exec. sec.

NURSING: New Jersey Board of Nursing, 1100 Raymond Blvd., Newark 07102; tel. 201/648-2490; Sr. Teresa L. Harris, exec. sec.

NEW MEXICO
MEDICAL: New Mexico Board of Medical Examiners, P.O. Box 1388, Santa Fe 87504; tel. 505/827-9933; Christina Romero, bur. chf.

NURSING: State of New Mexico Board of Nursing, 4125 Carlisle, N.E., Albuquerque 87107; tel. 505/841-6524; Nancy Twig, dir.

NEW YORK
MEDICAL: New York State Board for Medicine, Cultural Education Center, Albany 12230; tel. 518/474-3841; Thomas J. Monahan, actg. exec. sec.

NURSING: State Board for Nursing, State Education Department, Cultural Education Center, Room 3013, Albany 12230; tel. 518/474-3843; Milene A. Megel, R.N., Ph.D., exec. sec.

NORTH CAROLINA
MEDICAL: North Carolina Board of Medical Examiners, 222 N. Person St., Suite 214, Raleigh 27601; tel. 919/833-5321; Bryant D. Paris Jr., exec. sec.

NURSING: North Carolina Board of Nursing, Box 2129, Raleigh 27602; tel. 919/828-0740; Carol A. Osman, R.N., exec. dir.

NORTH DAKOTA
MEDICAL: North Dakota State Board of Medical Examiners, 418 E. Broadway Ave., Suite C-10, Bismarck 58501; tel. 701/223-9485; Rolf P. Sletten, exec. sec. and treas.

NURSING: North Dakota Board of Nursing, Kirkwood Office Tower, Ste. 504, Bismarck 58501; tel. 701/224-2974; Karen MacDonald, R.N., exec. dir.

OHIO
MEDICAL: State Medical Board of Ohio, Suite 510, 65 S. Front St., Columbus 43266; tel. 614/466-3934; Ray Q. Bumgarner, exec. dir.

NURSING: State of Ohio Board of Nursing Education and Nurse Registration, 65 S. Front St., Rm. 509, Columbus 43266; tel. 614/466-3947; Rosa Lee Weinert, R.N., exec. sec.

OKLAHOMA
MEDICAL: Oklahoma State Board of Medical Examiners, 5104 N. Francis, Suite C, Oklahoma City 73118; tel. 405/848-6841; Mark R. Johnson, M.D., sec.

NURSING: Oklahoma Board of Nurse Registration and Nursing Education, 2915 N. Classen Blvd., Suite 524, Oklahoma City 73106; tel. 405/525-2076; Sulinda Moffett, R.N., exec. dir.

OREGON
MEDICAL: Oregon Board of Medical Examiners, 1002 Loyalty Bldg., 317 S.W. Alder St., Portland 97204; tel. 503/229-5770; John J. Ulwelling, exec. sec.

NURSING: Oregon State Board of Nursing, 1400 S.W. 5th, Rm. 904, Portland 97201; tel. 503/229-5653; Dorothy J. Davy, R.N., exec. dir.

PENNSYLVANIA
MEDICAL: Pennsylvania State Board of Medicine, P.O. Box 2649, Harrisburg 17105; tel. 717/787-2381; Loretta M. Frank, adm. asst.

NURSING: State Board of Nursing, Department of State, P.O. Box 2649, Harrisburg 17105; tel. 717/783-7142; Miriam H. Limo, exec. sec.

RHODE ISLAND
MEDICAL: Division of Professional Regulation, Rhode Island Department of Health, 104 Cannon Bldg., 75 Davis St., Providence 02908; tel. 401/277-2827; Robert W. McClanaghan, adm.

SOUTH CAROLINA
MEDICAL: State Board of Medical Examiners of South Carolina, 1315 Blanding St., Columbia 29201; tel. 803/734-8901; Stephen S. Seeling, exec dir.

NURSING: State Board of Nursing for South Carolina, 1777 St. Julian Pl., Suite 102, Columbia 29204; tel. 803/737-6594; Renatta S. Loquist, R.N., exec. dir.

SOUTH DAKOTA
MEDICAL: South Dakota State Board of Medical and Osteopathic Examiners, 1323 Minnesota Ave., Sioux Falls 57105; tel. 605/336-1965; Robert D. Johnson, exec. sec.

TENNESSEE
MEDICAL: Tennessee Board of Medical Examiners, 283 Plus Park Blvd., Nashville 37219; tel. 615/367-6231; Louise B. Blair, reg. bds. adm.

NURSING: Tennessee Board of Nursing, 283 Plus Park Blvd., Nashville 37219; tel. 615/367-6232; Elizabeth J. Lund, R.N., exec. dir.

TEXAS
NURSING: Board of Nurse Examiners for the State of Texas, 1300 E. Anderson Ln., Bldg. C, Suite 225, Austin 78752; tel. 512/835-4880; Dr. Louise Sanders, R.N., Ph.D., exec. sec.
Texas Board of Vocational Nurse Examiners, 1300 E. Anderson Ln., Bldg. C, Suite 285, Austin 78752; tel. 512/835-2071; Joyce A. Hammer, R.N., M.S., exec. dir.

UTAH
MEDICAL AND NURSING: Division of Occupational and Professional Licensing, P.O. Box 45802, 160 East 300 South, Salt Lake City 84145; tel. 801/530-6628; David E. Robinson, dir.

VERMONT
NURSING: Vermont State Board of Nursing, 26 Terrace St., Montpelier 05602; tel. 802/828-2396, Lynn B. Hardee, R.N., M.S.N., M., exec. dir.

VIRGINIA
MEDICAL: Virginia State Board of Medicine, 1601 Rolling Hills Dr., Surry Bldg., 2nd flr., Richmond 23229; tel. 804/662-9908; Hilary Connor, M.D., exec. dir.

WASHINGTON
MEDICAL: Licensing Division, Box 9649, Olympia 98504; tel. 206/586-4561; Rolland Runion, adm.

NURSING: Washington State Board of Nursing, Licensing Division, Box 9649, Olympia 98504; tel. 206/753-2686; Constance E. Roth, R.N., Ed.D., exec. sec.
Washington State Board of Practical Nursing, Department of Licensing, Division of Professional Licensing, Box 9649, Olympia 98504; tel. 206/753-3728; Virginia Renz, R.N., actg. exec. sec.

WEST VIRGINIA
MEDICAL: West Virginia Board of Medicine, 100 Dee Dr., Ste. 104, Charleston 25311; tel. 304/348-2921; Ronald D. Walton, exec. dir.

NURSING: West Virginia Board of Examiners for Registered Professional Nurses, Embleton Bldg., 922 Quarrier St., Suite 309, Charleston 25301; tel. 304/348-3728; Garnette Thorne, M.S., R.N., exec. sec.
West Virginia State Board of Examiners for Licensed Practical Nurses, Embleton Bldg., 922 Quarrier St., Suite 506, Charleston 25301; tel. 304/348-3572; Nancy R. Wilson, R.N., exec. sec.

WISCONSIN
MEDICAL: Wisconsin Medical Examining Board, 1400 E. Washington Ave., Madison 53702; tel. 608/266-2811; Deanna Zychowski, adm. asst.

NURSING: Bureau of Health Service Professions, Department of Regulation and Licensing, P.O. Box 8935, 1400 E. Washington Ave., Rm. 174, Madison 53708; tel. 608/266-3735; Ramona Weakland Warden, dir.

WYOMING
MEDICAL: Wyoming Board of Medical Examiners, Hathaway Bldg., 4th flr., Cheyenne 82002; tel. 307/777-6463; Lawrence J. Cohen, M.D., exec. sec.

NURSING: Wyoming State Board of Nursing, Barrett Bldg., 4th flr., 2301 Central Ave., Cheyenne 82002; tel. 307/777-7601; Joan C. Bouchard, R.N., M.N., exec. dir.

U.S. Associated Areas

GUAM
NURSING: Guam Board of Nurse Examiners, Box 2816, Agana 96910; tel. 734-2783; Teofila P. Cruz, nurse exam. adm.

PUERTO RICO
MEDICAL AND NURSING: Office of Regulation and Certification of Professionals Health, Call Box 10200, Santurce 00908; tel. 809/725-7506; Irza Torres Aguiar, exec. dir.

VIRGIN ISLANDS
MEDICAL: Virgin Islands Department of Health, Box 7309; St. Thomas 00801, tel. 809/774-0117; Roy L. Schneider, M.D., comr. of health

NURSING: Virgin Islands Board of Nurse Licensure, Knud-Hansen Complex Hospital Ground, St. Thomas 00801; tel. 809/774-9000 ext. 132; Juanita Molloy, R.N., exec. dir.

Canada

ALBERTA
MEDICAL: College of Physicians and Surgeons of Alberta, 9901 108th St., Edmonton T5K 1G9; tel. 403/423-4764; L. H. le Riche, M.B., CH.B., registrar

MANITOBA
MEDICAL: College of Physicians and Surgeons of Manitoba, 1410-155 Carlton St., Winnipeg R3C 3H8; tel. 204/947-1694; J. B. Morison, M.D., registrar

NEW BRUNSWICK
MEDICAL: College of Physicians and Surgeons of New Brunswick, 10 Prince Edward St., Saint John E2L 4M5

NOVA SCOTIA
MEDICAL: Provincial Medical Board of Nova Scotia, Lord Nelson Hotel, Suite 3050, 1515 S. Park St., Halifax B3J 2L2; tel. 902/422-5823; M. R. Macdonald, M.D., reg.-sec.

PRINCE EDWARD ISLAND
MEDICAL: Medical Council of Prince Edward Island, 206 Spring Park Rd., Charlottetown C1A 3Y9; tel. 902/894-5316; Stewart MacDonald, M.D., registrar

QUEBEC
MEDICAL: Corporation Professionnelle des Medecins du Quebec, 1440 Ste. Catherine St. W., Suite 914, Montreal H3G 1S5; tel. 514/878-4441; Augustin Roy, M.D., pres.-sec. gen.

SASKATCHEWAN
MEDICAL: College of Physicians and Surgeons of Saskatchewan, 211 4th Ave., S., Saskatoon S7K 1N1; tel. 244-7355; D. A. Kendel, M.D., registrar

Peer Review Organizations

The following list of PROs was obtained from the Office of Medical Review, Division of Program Operation, HCFA. For more information, contact the office at 301/594-9208.

United States

ALABAMA: Alabama Quality Assurance Foundation, 236 Goodwin Crest Dr., Suite 300, Twin Towers E. Bldg., Birmingham 35206; tel. 205/942-0785; John W. Miller, exec. dir.

ALASKA: Professional Review Organization for Washington, 2150 N. 107th St., Suite 200, Seattle 98133; tel. 206/364-9700; John Daise, exec. dir.

ARIZONA: Health Services Advisory Group, Inc., P.O. Box 16731, 301 E. Bethany Home Rd., Suite B-157, Phoenix 85012; tel. 602/264-6382; Debra L. Nixon, R.N., exec. dir.

ARKANSAS: Arkansas Foundation for Medical Care, Inc., P.O. Box 1508, 809 Garrison Ave., Fort Smith 72902; tel. 501/785-2471; Jim L. Williams, exec. dir.

CALIFORNIA: California Medical Review, Inc., 1388 Sutter St., Suite 1100, San Francisco 94109; tel. 415/923-2000; Jo Ellen H. Ross, exec. dir.

COLORADO: Colorado Foundation for Medical Care, Suite 400, Bldg. 2, 6825 E. Tennessee Ave., Denver 80224; tel. 303/321-8642; Arja Adair, exec. dir.

CONNECTICUT: Connecticut Peer Review Organization, Inc., 384 Pratt St., Meriden 06450; tel. 203/237-2773; Marcia K. Petrillo, exec. dir.

DELAWARE: West Virginia Medical Institute, Inc., 3412 Chesterfield Ave., S.E., Charleston 25304; tel. 304/925-0461; Betty C. Kirkwood, exec. dir. (located in WV)

DISTRICT OF COLUMBIA: Delmarva Foundation for Medical Care, Inc., 341 B N. Aurora St., Easton 21601; tel. 301/822-0697; Linda Clark, exec. dir.

FLORIDA: Professional Foundation for Health Care, Inc., 2907 Bay to Bay Blvd., Suite 100, Tampa 33629; tel. 813/831-6273; Susanne Snyder, R.N., exec. dir.

GEORGIA: Georgia Medical Care Foundation, 4 Executive Park Dr., N.W., Suite 1300, Atlanta 30329; tel. 404/881-5600; Tom Williams, exec. dir.

HAWAII: Hawaii Medical Services Association, P.O. Box 860, 818 Keeaumoku St., Honolulu 96808; tel. 808/944-3581; Bernard Ho, sen. v.p.

IDAHO: Professional Review Organization for Washington, 2150 N. 107th St., Suite 200, Seattle 98133; tel. 206/364-9700; John Daise, exec. dir. (located in WA)

ILLINOIS: Crescent Counties Foundation for Medical Care, 350 Shuman Blvd., Suite 240, Naperville 60540; tel. 312/357-8770; Thomas R. Hyngstrom, Ph.D., exec. dir.

INDIANA: Peerview, Inc., 501 Congressional Blvd., Suite 200, Carmel 46032; tel. 317/573-6888; Thomas Hanstrom, exec. v.p.

IOWA: Iowa Foundation for Medical Care, 3737 Woodland Ave., Suite 500, W. Des Moines 50265; tel. 515/223-2900; Fred Ferree, exec. v.p.

KANSAS: The Kansas Foundation for Medical Care, Inc., 2947 S.W. Wanamaker Dr., Topeka 66614; tel. 913/273-2552; Larry W. Pitman, exec. dir.

KENTUCKY: Peerview, Inc., 501 Congressional Blvd., Suite 200, Carmel 46032; tel. 317/573-6888; Tom Hanstrom, exec. dir. (located in IN)

LOUISIANA: Louisiana Health Care Review, 1458 Carter Ave., Baton Rouge 70806; tel. 504/928-9817; Leo Stanley, chf. exec. off.

MAINE: Health Care Review, Inc., The Weld Building, 345 Blackstone Blvd., Providence 02906; tel. 401/331-6661

MARYLAND: Delmarva Foundation for Medical Care, Inc., 341 B, N. Aurora St., Easton 21601; tel. 301/822-0697; Linda Clark, dir.

MASSACHUSETTS: Massachusetts Peer Review Organization, Inc., 300 Bearhill Rd., Waltham 02254; tel. 617/890-0011; Tera S. Younger, exec. dir.

MICHIGAN: Michigan Peer Review Organization, 40500 Ann Arbor Rd., Suite 200, Plymouth 48170; tel. 313/459-0900; Gary Horvat, exec. dir.

MINNESOTA: Foundation for Health Care Evaluation, Health Associations Center, FHCE, One Appletree Sq., Suite 700, Minneapolis 54420; tel. 612/854-3306; Julie A. Sanderson, proj. dir.

MISSISSIPPI: Mississippi Foundation for Medical Care, Inc., 1900 N.W. St., P.O. Box 4665, Jackson 39216; tel. 601/948-8894; Fred A. Parish, exec. dir.

MISSOURI: Missouri Patient Care Review Foundation, 311 A Ellis Blvd., Jefferson City 65101; tel. 314/634-4441; MoHammad N. Akhter, M.D., exec. v.p.

MONTANA: Montana-Wyoming Foundation for Medical Care, P.O. Box 5117, 21 N. Main, Helena 59604; tel. 406/443-4020; Janice Connors, exec. dir.

NEBRASKA: Iowa Foundation for Medical Care, Inc., 3737 Woodland Ave., Colony Park Bldg., Suite 500, W. Des Moines 50265; tel. 515/223-2900; Richard L. McMaster, exec. dir. (located in IA)

NEVADA: Nevada Physicians Review Organization, 4600 Kietzke Lane, Bldg. A, Suite 108, Reno 89502; tel. 702/826-1996; Robert Wright, exec. dir.

NEW HAMPSHIRE: New Hampshire Foundation for Medical Care, Box 578, 110 Locust St., Dover 03820; tel. 603/749-1641; Robert A. Aurilio, exec. dir.

NEW JERSEY: The Peer Review Organization of New Jersey, Inc., Central Division, Brier Hill Court, Bldg. J, East Brunswick 08816; tel. 201/238-5570; Martin P. Margolies, exec. dir.

NEW MEXICO: New Mexico Medical Review Association, P.O. Box 9900, 707 Broadway, N.E., Suite 200, Albuquerque 87119-9900; tel. 505/842-6236; Ernest D. Cuaron, chf. oper. off.

NEW YORK: Empire State Medical Scientific and Educational Foundation, Inc., 420 Lakeville Rd., P.O. Box 5434, Lake Success 11042; tel. 516/437-8134; John Q. Podesta, exec. dir.

NORTH CAROLINA: Medical Review of North Carolina, Inc., P.O. Box 37309; 1011 Schaub Dr., Suite 200, Raleigh 27627; tel. 919/851-2955; Charles J. Riddick, exec. dir.

NORTH DAKOTA: North Dakota Health Care Review, Inc., 900 N. Broadway, Suite 212, Minot 58701; tel. 701/852-4231; David Remillard, exec. dir.

OHIO: Peer Review Systems, Inc., 3720-J Olentangy River Rd., Columbus 43214; tel. 614/451-3600; Robert P. Stone, Ph.D., exec. dir.

OKLAHOMA: Oklahoma Foundation for Peer Review, 5801 Broadway Extension, Suite 400, Oklahoma City 73118; tel. 405/840-2891; Neal Thrift, exec. dir.

OREGON: Oregon Medical Professional Review Organization (OMPRO), 1220 Southwest Morrison, Suite 300, Portland 97205; tel. 503/243-1151; Robert A. Berry, pres.

PENNSYLVANIA: Keystone Peer Review Organization, Inc., 645 N. 12th St., P.O. Box 618, Lemoyne 17043-0618; tel. 717/975-9600; Robert R. Weiser, exec. dir.

RHODE ISLAND: Health Care Review, Inc., The Weld Bldg., 345 Blackstone Blvd., Providence 02906; tel. 401/331-6661; Edward J. Lynch, exec. v.p.

SOUTH CAROLINA: South Carolina Professional Review Organization Metrolina, A Division of Metrolina Medical Foundation, 1 Charlotte Center, Suite 150; tel. 704/373-1545; Dan Carrigan, proj. dir.

SOUTH DAKOTA: South Dakota Foundation for Medical Care, 608 W. Ave., N., Sioux Falls 57104; tel. 605/336-3505; Robert D. Johnson, exec. dir.

TENNESSEE: Mid-South Foundation for Medical Care, 6401 Poplar Ave., Suite 400, Memphis 38119; tel. 901/682-0381; Leon J. Swatzell, exec. dir.

TEXAS: Texas Medical Foundation, Barton Oaks Plaza, 2, 901 Mopac Expwy. S., Suite 200, Austin 78746; tel. 512/329-6610; Robert L. King, Jr., exec. dir.

UTAH: Utah Professional Standards Review Organization, 540 E. 5th S. St., Suite 200, Salt Lake City 84102-2707; tel. 801/532-7545; David Buchanan, exec. dir.

VERMONT: New Hampshire Foundation for Medical Care, P.O. Box 578, 110 Locust St., Dover 03820; tel. 603/749-1641; Robert A. Aurilio, exec. dir.

VIRGINIA: Medical Society of Virginia Review Organization, 1904 Byrd Ave., Rm. 120, Richmond 23230; tel. 804/289-5320; Freedman Vaughn, exec. dir.

WASHINGTON: Professional Review Organization for Washington, 2150 N. 107th St., Suite 200, Seattle 98133; tel. 206/364-9700; John Daise, exec. dir.

WEST VIRGINIA: West Virginia Medical Institute, Inc., 3412 Chesterfield Ave., S.E., Charleston 25304; tel. 304/925-0461; Betty C. Kirkwood, exec. dir.

WISCONSIN: Wisconsin Peer Review Organization, 2001 W. Beltline Hwy., Madison 53713; tel. 608/274-1940; Greg E. Simmons, exec. dir.

WYOMING: Montana-Wyoming Foundation for Medical Care, 21 N. Main, Box 5117, Helena 59604; tel. 406/443-4020; Janice Connors, exec. dir.

U.S. Associated Areas

AMERICAN SAMOA-GUAM: Hawaii Medical Services Association, P.O. Box 860, 818 Keeaumoku St., Honolulu 96808; tel. 808/944-3581; Bernard Ho, sen. v.p. (located in HI)

PUERTO RICO: Puerto Rico Foundation for Medical Care, Mercantile Plaza, Suite 605, Hato Ray 00918; tel. 809/753-6805; José Robles, dir.

VIRGIN ISLANDS: Virgin Islands Medical Institute, P.O. Box 1556, Christiansted, St. Croix 00820; tel. 809/778-6470; Patrick Peterson, med. dir.

State Health Planning and Development Agencies

The following is a list of federally funded state health planning and development agencies. The information was obtained from the U.S. Department of Health and Human Services, Public Health Service, Health Resources and Services Administration, Office of Health Planning. For information about other state agencies and organizations that fulfill many of the same functions, contact the state or metropolitan hospital associations.

United States

ALABAMA: State Health Planning Agency, 125 6th St., North Montgomery 36104; tel. 205/261-4107; Michael O. Emfinger, exec. dir.

ALASKA: Division of Planning, Department of Health and Social Services, P.O. Box H 01A, Juneau 99811; tel. 907/465-3037; Dave W. Williams, actg. dir.

ARIZONA: Office of Planning and Budget Development, Arizona Department of Health Services, 1740 W. Adams St., Rm. 407, Phoenix 85007; tel. 602/255-1024; Ted Williams, dir.

ARKANSAS: Arkansas State Health Planning and Development Agency, 4815 W. Markham St., Little Rock 72201; tel. 501/661-2196; Orson Berry, dir.

CALIFORNIA: Office of Statewide Health Planning and Development, 1600 9th St., Room 433, Sacramento 95814; tel. 916/322-5834; Larry G. Meeks, dir.

COLORADO: Colorado State Health Planning and Development Agency, 4210 E. 11th Ave., Room 227, Denver 80220; tel. 303/331-4907; Kristin Paulson, dir.

CONNECTICUT: Office of Policy and Communications, Health Policy, Planning and Statistics Division, Connecticut State Dept. of Health, 150 Washington St., Hartford 06106; tel. 203/566-7886; Richard Grube, dir.

DELAWARE: Bureau of Health Planning and Resource Development, Department of Health and Social Services, 802 Silver Lake Blvd., Robbins Bldg., P.O. Box 637, Dover 19903; tel. 302/736-4776; Amos Burke, dir.

DISTRICT OF COLUMBIA: D.C. State Health Planning and Development Agency, 1331 H St., N.W., 7th flr., Washington 20005; tel. 202/727-0744; Carlessia A. Hussein, Dr. P.H., dir.

FLORIDA: Office of Regulation and Health Facilities, Florida Dept. of Health and Rehabilitative Services, Fort Knox Executive Office Center, 2727 Mahan Drive, Tallahassee 32308; tel. 904/487-2513; Marta V. Hardy, dir.

GEORGIA: State Health Planning Agency, 4 Executive Park Dr., N.E., Suite 2100, Atlanta 30329; tel. 404/633-5247; C. Annette Maxey, exec. dir.

HAWAII: Hawaii State Health Planning and Development Agency, State Department of Health, P.O. Box 3378, Honolulu 96801; tel. 808/548-4050; Patrick J. Boland, actg. adm.

IDAHO: disbanded

ILLINOIS: State Health Planning and Development Agency, Illinois Department of Public Health, 535 W. Jefferson St., Springfield 62761; tel. 217/785-2040; Jaquetta Ellinger, assoc. dir.

INDIANA: Division of Health Planning, Indiana State Board of Health, 1330 W. Michigan St., Indianapolis 46206; tel. 317/633-8512; James K. Ladd, dir.

IOWA: Division of Health Planning and Development, Iowa State Dept. of Public Health, Lucas State Office Bldg., 4th flr., Des Moines 50319; tel. 515/281-4346; Betty Grandquist, div. dir.

KANSAS: Office of Health and Environmental Planning, Kansas Department of Health and Environment, Forbes Field, Bldg. 321, Topeka 66620; tel. 913/862-9360

KENTUCKY: Division of Health Policy and Resource Development, Dept. for Health Services, Cabinet for Human Resources, 275 E. Main St., Frankfort 40621; tel. 502/564-8966; Greg Lawther, dir.

LOUISIANA: Louisiana State Health Planning and Development Agency, Department of Health and Human Resources, 200 Lafayette St., Suite 406, Baton Rouge 70801; tel. 504/342-2001; Bonnie W. Smith, dir., bur. hlth. plng.

MAINE: Bureau of Medical Services, Department of Human Services, State House, Statn. 11, Augusta 04333; tel. 207/289-2716; Trish Riley, dir.

MARYLAND: Maryland Health Resources Planning Community, 201 W. Preston St., Room 115, Baltimore 21201; tel. 301/225-5141; James R. Stanton, exec. dir.

MASSACHUSETTS: State Health Planning and Development Agency, Department of Human Services, One Ashburton Pl., Rm. 1109, Boston 02108; tel. 617/727-8042; Mark Coven, actg. dir.

MICHIGAN: State Health Planning and Development Agency, Office of Health and Medical Affairs, Lewis Cass Bldg., Box 30026, Lansing 48909; tel. 517/373-8155; Patience A. Drake, dir.

MINNESOTA: State Health Planning and Development Agency, 200 Capitol Square Bldg., 550 Cedar St., St. Paul 55101; tel. 612/296-2407; John Dilley, dir.

MISSISSIPPI: Mississippi Health Care Commission, 2688 Insurance Center Dr., Jackson 39216; tel. 601/981-6880; George W. Jobe, exec. dir.

MISSOURI: State Health Planning and Development Agency, Department of Health, 1738 East Elm St., Jefferson City 65101; tel. 314/751-6403; Thomas R. Piper, dir.

MONTANA: Bureau of Health Planning and Resource Development, State Department of Health and Environmental Sciences, Division of Health Services and Medical Facilities, Cogswell Bldg., Helena 59620; tel. 406/444-3121; George M. Fenner, adm.

NEBRASKA: State Health Planning and Development Agency, Nebraska State Department of Health, 301 Centennial Mall, S., Box 95007; Lincoln 68509; tel. 402/471-2337; David Palm, Ph.D., dir.

NEVADA: Division of Health Resources and Cost Review, 505 E. King St., Rm. 603, Carson City 89710; tel. 702/885-4716; Daniel O'Donnell, adm.

NEW HAMPSHIRE: State Department of Health and Human Services, Office of Planning and Policy Development, 6 Hazen Drive, Concord 03301-6524; tel. 603/271-4602; Kathleen G. Sgambati, dir.

NEW JERSEY: Division of Health Planning and Resource Development, New Jersey Department of Health, Trenton 08625; tel. 609/292-7837; Molly J. Coye, M.D., M.P.H., state comr. of hlth.

NEW MEXICO: Health Planning and Development Division, New Mexico Health and Environment Dept., P.O. Box 968, Santa Fe 87504-0968; tel. 505/827-2721; Dale Patrick Curtis, dir., hlth. plng. and dev. div.

NEW YORK: Planning, Policy and Resource Development, New York State Department of Health, Tower Bldg., Rm. 1683, Albany 12237; tel. 518/473-7541; David Abernathy, dep. comr.

NORTH CAROLINA: Health Resource Development State Health Planning, Division of Facility Services, Department of Human Resources, 701 Barbour Dr., Raleigh 27603; tel. 919/733-4130; Jim Berstein, actg. chf.

NORTH DAKOTA: Division of Health Planning, State Department of Health, State Capitol Bldg., Bismarck 58505; tel. 701/224-2894; Gary Garland, dir.

OHIO: State Health Planning and Development Agency, Ohio Department of Health, 246 N. High St., P.O. Box 118, Columbus 43266-0118; tel. 614/466-5364; Frances Williamson, coord.

OKLAHOMA: Oklahoma Health Planning Commission, 1000 N.E. 10th St. and Stonewall, Room 1106, P.O. Box 53551, Oklahoma City 73152; tel. 405/271-5161; Suzanne W. Nichols, dir.

OREGON: State Health Planning and Development Agency, 3886 Beverly Ave., N.E., Suite 19, Salem 97305-1389; tel. 503/378-4684; Richard H. Grant, dir.

PENNSYLVANIA: Bureau of Planning, PA Department of Health, Box 90, Harrisburg 17108; tel. 717/783-3865; Katherine Marconi, Ph.D., dir.

RHODE ISLAND: Health Planning and Resource Development, Rhode Island State Department of Health, 75 Davis St., Providence 02908; tel. 401/277-2231; John T. Tierney, dep. dir.

SOUTH CAROLINA: State Health Planning and Development Agency, South Carolina Health and Human Services Finance Commission, P.O. Box 8206, Columbia 29201-8206; tel. 803/758-0370; Linda S. Sugimoto, div. dir.

SOUTH DAKOTA: Center for Health Policy and Statistics, State Department of Health, Joe Foss Bldg., 523 East Capitol, Pierre 57501; tel. 605/773-3693; Jan Smith, dir.

TENNESSEE: Department of Heath and Environment, State of Tennessee, 287 Plus Park Blvd., Nashville 37219-5407; tel. 615/367-6336; Lee Majure, dir.

TEXAS: Bureau of State Health Planning and Resources Development, Texas Department of Health, 1100 W. 49th St., Austin 78756; tel. 512/458-7261; Carol Daniels, bur. chf.

UTAH: Utah Department of Health, Bureau of Planning and Policy Development, 288 N. 1460 West, P.O. Box 16700, Salt Lake City 84116-0700; tel. 801/538-6122; Gar T. Elison, dir.

VERMONT: State Health Planning and Development Agency, Vermont Department of Health, 60 Main St., P.O. Box 70, Burlington 05402; tel. 802/863-7272; Robert Aiken, dir.

VIRGINIA: Office of Health Planning and Resources Development, Virginia State Department of Health, 109 Governor St., Room 1010, Richmond 23219; tel. 804/786-6970; Raymond O. Perry, asst. comr.

WASHINGTON: Department of Social and Health Services, State Health Coordinating Council, Mail Stop OB-38, 12th and Franklin Streets, Olympia 98504; tel. 206/753-9659; Verne A. Gibbs, exec. dir.

WEST VIRGINIA: State Health and Development Agency, 100 Dee Drive, Charleston 25311; tel. 304/343-3701; Walter J. Dale, chm.

WISCONSIN: State Health Planning and Development Agency, Division of Health, P.O. Box 309, Madison 53701-0309; tel. 608/266-7384; Judith Fryback, dir.

WYOMING: State Health Planning and Development Agency, Department of Health and Social Services, Division of Health and Medical Services, Hathaway Bldg., Cheyenne 82002; tel. 307/777-7121; L. J. Cohen, M.D., adm.

U.S. Associated Areas

AMERICAN SAMOA: American Samoa Health Planning and Development Agency, Department of Health, L.B.J. Tropical Medical Center, Pago Pago, American Samoa 96799; tel. 633-4559 (intl. oper. 160 + 684); Aneterea Puletasi, dir.

GUAM: Guam Health Planning and Development Agency, 212 W. Aspinall Ave., Rm. 155, Agana 96910; tel. 472-6831 (intl. oper. 160 + 671); Dr. Aida Z. Fernandez, actg. adm.

MARIANA ISLANDS: Commonwealth Health Planning and Development Agency, Office of the Governor, Government of Northern Mariana Islands; P.O. Box 570, Saipan, Mariana Islands 96950-7122; (intl. oper. 160 + 671); Mariano R. Bermudes, exec. dir.

PUERTO RICO: Office of Planning, Evaluation and Reports, Dept. of Health, P.O. Box 9342, Santurce 00908, tel. 809/722-8105; José A. Saliceti, dir.

TRUST TERRITORY: Trust Territory of the Pacific Islands, Office of the High Commissioner, Saipan, Mariana Islands 96950; tel. 9355 (intl. oper. 160+671); Masao Ueda, chf.

VIRGIN ISLANDS: Health, Research, Planning and Education, Department of Health, St. Thomas 00801; tel. 809/774-1734; Keith E. Callwood, dep. comm.

State and Provincial Government Agencies

The following list includes state departments of health and welfare and their subagencies as well as such independent agencies as those for crippled children's services, maternal and child health, mental health, and vocational rehabilitation. The information was obtained directly from the agencies.

United States

ALABAMA

The Honorable Guy Hunt, Governor, 205/261-2500.

HEALTH: Department of Public Health, State Office Bldg., Rm. 381, Montgomery 36130; tel. 205/261-5052; Claude Earl Fox, M.D., M.P.H., state hlth. off.
Includes:
Division of Licensure and Certification; tel. 205/261-5113; Carroll S. Nason, dir.
Division of Family Health Services, Doris Barnette, actg. dir.

WELFARE: Alabama Medicaid Agency, 2500 Fairlane Dr., Montgomery 36130; tel. 205/277-2710; James Michael Horsley, comr.
Department of Human Resources, 64 N. Union St., Montgomery 36130; tel. 205/261-3190; Andy Hornsby, comr.

INSURANCE: Department of Insurance, 135 S. Union St., Montgomery 36130; tel. 205/269-3550; John S. Greeno, comr.

OTHER: State Department of Mental Health, 200 Interstate Park Dr., Montgomery 36193; tel. 205/271-9207; Bill McFarland, comr.
Alabama Board of Nursing, One East Building, Suite 203, 500 Eastern Blvd., Montgomery 36117; tel. 205/261-4060; Shirley J. Dykes, R.N., M.S.N., exec. off.
State Department of Education, State Office Bldg., Rm. 481, Montgomery 36130; tel. 205/261-5156; Wayne Teague, supt.
Includes:
Division of Rehabilitation and Crippled Children Service, 2129 E. South Blvd., Montgomery 36111; tel. 205/281-8780; Lamona Lucas, dir.

ALASKA

The Honorable Steve Cowper, Governor, 907/465-2111

HEALTH: Department of Health and Social Services, P.O. Box H-0601, Juneau 99811; tel. 907/465-3030; Myra M. Munson, J.D., M.S.W., comr.
Includes:
Deputy Commissioner for Social Services, Blanche Brunk.
Division of Family and Youth Services; tel. 907/465-3170; Yvonne Chase, dir.
Division of Budget and Finance; tel. 907/465-3082; Frank Hickey, dir.
Division of Mental Health and Developmental Disabilities; tel. 907/465-3370; Melbourne Henry, Ph.D., dir.
Division of Public Assistance; tel. 907/465-3347; John Taber, dir.
Division of Public Health; tel. 907/465-3090; Elizabeth Ward, R.N., M.P.H., dir.
Office of Alcoholism and Drug Abuse; tel. 907/586-6201; Matt Felix, coor.
Assistant Commissioner for Administration, Karen Perdue.
Medicaid Rate Commission, P.O. Box 240249, Anchorage 99524; tel. 907/562-1996
Division of Medical Assistance; tel. 907/465-3355; Kimberly Busch, actg. dir.
Includes:
Health Facilities Licensing and Certification Section, 4041 B. St., Suite 101, Anchorage 99503; tel. 907/561-2171; Karen Martz, supr.

OTHER: Department of Commerce and Economic Development, Division of Occupational Licensing, Alaska Medical Board, P.O. Box D-Lic., Juneau 99811; tel. 907/465-2541; Kurt D. West, lic. exam.
Alaska Board of Nursing, 3601 C St., Suite 722, Anchorage 99503; tel. 907/561-2878; Gail M. McGuill, R.N., exec. sec.
Department of Education, 801 W. 10th St., P.O. Box F, Juneau 99811; tel. 907/465-2800
Includes:
Division of Vocational Rehabilitation, Pouch F, Juneau 99811; tel. 907/465-2814; Michael C. Morgan, dir.

ARIZONA

The Honorable Evan Mecham, Governor, 602/255-4900.

HEALTH: Arizona Department of Health Services, 1740 W. Adams St., Phoenix 85007; tel. 602/255-1024; Ted Williams, dir.
Includes:
Division of Disease Prevention, 431 N. 24th St., Phoenix 85008; tel.602/255-1181; Glyn Caldwell, M.D., asst. dir.
Division of Environmental Health, 2005 N. Central Ave., Phoenix 85004; tel. 602/257-2300; Ron Miller, actg. asst. dir.
Division of Behavioral Health Services, 701 E. Jefferson, Phoenix 85034; tel. 602/255-1213; Thomas Bittker, M.D., asst. dir.
Division of Family Health Services, 1740 W. Adams St., Rm 202, Phoenix 85007; tel. 602/255-1223; Stephen E. Saunders, M.D., M.P.H., asst. dir.
Includes:
Children's Rehabilitative Services, Administrative Offices, 1740 W. Adams St., Rm. 205, Phoenix 85007; tel. 602/255-1860; W. Sundin Applegate, M.D., M.P.H., mgr.
Emergency Medical Services, Health Care Facilities, 411 N. 24th St., Phoenix 85008; tel. 602/220-6423; Hazel Chandler, actg. asst. dir.
Includes:
Office of Health Care Institution Licensure, Medical Facilities Section, Birch Hall, 411 N. 24th St., Phoenix 85008; tel. 602/220-6407; Hazel E. Chandler, chf.

WELFARE: Department of Economic Security, Site Code 010A, P.O. Box 6123, Phoenix 85005; tel. 602/255-5678; Dr. Eddie F. Brown, dir.
Includes:
Division of Employment and Rehabilitation Services, Rehabilitation Services Administration, 1300 W. Washington, Rm. 105, Phoenix 85007; tel. 602/255-3332; James B. Griffith, adm.

INSURANCE: Department of Insurance, 801 E. Jefferson, Phoenix 85034; tel. 602/255-5400

OTHER: Arizona Board of Medical Examiners, 1990 W. Camelback Rd., Suite 401, Phoenix 85015; tel. 602/255-3751; Douglas N. Cerf, exec. dir.
Arizona State Board of Nursing, 5050 N. 19th Ave., Suite 103, Phoenix 85015; tel. 602/255-5092; Edith B. Summerlin, R.N., Ph.D., exec. dir.

ARKANSAS

The Honorable William Clinton, Governor, 501/371-3000

HEALTH: Department of Health, State Health Bldg., Little Rock 72205; tel. 501/661-2111; Ben N. Saltzman, M.D., dir.
Includes:
Bureau of Administrative Support; tel. 501/661-2252; Tom Butler, dir.
Bureau of Environmental Health Services; tel. 501/661-2574; Jerry Hill, dir.
Bureau of Public Health Programs; tel. 501/661-2528; Charles McGrew, dir.
Bureau of Health Resources; tel. 501/661-2242; Stuart Fitzhugh, M.D., dir.
Bureau of Community Health Services; tel. 501/661-2388; Nancy Kirsch, dir.
Division of Health Facility Services, 4815 W. Markham St., Little Rock 72205; tel. 501/661-2201; Rayburn C. Allen, dir.

WELFARE: Department of Human Services; tel. 501/371-1001; Roy Scott, dir.
Includes:
Division of Aging and Adult Services, 1417 Donaghey Building, 7th & Main, Little Rock 72201; tel. 501/371-2441; Herb Sanderson, dep. dir.
Office on Alcohol & Drug Abuse Prevention, 1515 W. 7th St., Suite 310, Little Rock 72201; tel. 501/371-2604
Arkansas Rehabilitation Services, 1401 Brookwood Dr., Box 3781; Little Rock 72203; tel. 501/371-2571; E. Russell Baxter, comr.
State Mental Health Division, Little Rock State Hospital, 4313 W. Markham, Little Rock 72205; tel. 501/664-4500; Herman Harley, dpty. dir. mental health.
Division of Economic and Medical Services, Donaghey Bldg., Seventh & Main Sts., P.O. Box 1437, Little Rock 72203; tel. 501/371-2521; Walt Patterson, dpty.dir.
Includes:
Crippled Children's Section, G.A. Buchanan, M.D., med. dir.
Office of Long-Term Care, Jim Brown, asst. dep. dir.
Office of Medical Services, Ray Hanley, asst. dep. dir.

INSURANCE: Department of Insurance, 400-18 University Tower Bldg., Little Rock, 72204; tel. 501/371-1325

OTHER: Arkansas State Board of Nursing, 4120 W. Markham St., Suite 308, Little Rock 72205; tel. 501/371-2751; June Garner, R.N., M.N., exec. dir.

CALIFORNIA

The Honorable George Deukmejian, Governor, 916/322-9900

HEALTH: Department of Health Services, 714 P. St., Rm. 1253, Sacramento 95814; tel. 916/445-1248; Kenneth W. Kizer, M.D., M.P.H., dir.
Includes:
Licensing and Certification Division, 714 P St., Rm. 823, Sacramento 95814; tel. 916/445-3054; Virgil J. Toney, Jr., dep. dir.

WELFARE: Health and Welfare Agency, Office of the Secretary, 1600 Ninth St., Rm. 450, Sacramento 95814; tel. 916/445-6951; Clifford L. Allenby, sec.
Includes:
Department of Alcohol and Drug Programs, 111 Capitol Mall, Ste. 450, Sacramento 95814; tel. 916/445-1940; Chauncey L. Veatch III, dir.
Department of Developmental Services, 1600 Ninth St., 2nd Flr. NW, Sacramento 95814; tel. 916/322-8154; Gary D. Macomber, dir.
Department of Mental Health, 1600 Ninth St., Ist Flr., Sacramento 95814; tel. 916/323-8173; D. Michael O'Connor, M.D., dir.
Department of Social Services, 744 P St., MS 17-11, Sacramento 95814; tel. 916/445-2077; Linda S. McMahon, dir.
Department of Rehabilitation, 830 K St. Mall, Sacramento 95814; tel. 916/323-0318; P. Cecie Fontanoza, dir.
Includes:
Division of Community Resources Development; tel. 916/323-0390; Joseph Klier, chf. of div.

OTHER: California Board of Medical Quality Assurance, 1430 Howe Ave., Sacramento 95825; tel. 916/920-6411; Kenneth J. Wagstaff, exec. dir.
Board of Registered Nursing, 1030 13th St., Suite 200, Sacramento 95814; tel. 916/322-3350; Catherine M. Puri, R.N., Ph.D., exec. off.
Department of Corporations, Health Care Service Plans Division, 600 S. Commonwealth Ave., Los Angeles 90005; tel. 213/736-3131; 1107 9th St., 8th Flr., Sacramento 95814; tel. 916/324-9028
Board of Vocational Nurse and Psychiatric Technician Examiners, 1020 N St., Rm. 406, Sacramento 95814; tel. 916/445-0793; Billie Haynes, R.N., M.Ed.D., exec. off.

COLORADO

The Honorable Roy Romer, Governor, 303/866-5000

HEALTH: Colorado Department of Health, 4210 E. 11th Ave., Denver 80220; tel. 303/320-8333; Thomas M. Vernon, M.D., exec. dir.
Includes:
Alcohol and Drug Abuse Division, 4210 E. 11th Ave., Denver 80220;tel. 303/331-8201; Robert Aukerman, dir.
Family Health Services Division; tel. 303/331-8360; Daniel Gossert, dir.
Division of Health Facilities Regulation, 4210 E. 11th Ave., Denver 80220; tel. 303/331-4930; Mildred Simmons, dir.

WELFARE: State Department of Social Services, 717 17th St., 12th Flr., Denver 80218; tel. 303/294-5800; Irene M. Ibarra, exec. dir.
Includes:
Aging and Adult Services Division, 717 17th St., 11th Flr., P.O. Box 181000, Denver 80218; tel. 303/294-5905; Bill Hanna, dir.
Division of Rehabilitation, State Department of Social Services, 717 17th St., P.O. Box 181000, Denver 80218-0899; tel. 303/294-2804; Mark Litvin, Ph.D., dir.

OTHER: Colorado Board of Medical Examiners, 1525 Sherman St., No. 132, Denver 80203; tel. 303/866-2468; Bruce Douglas, dir.
Department of Regulatory Agencies, 1525 Sherman, Rm. 110, Denver 80203; tel. 303/866-3304; Henry Salano, exec. dir.
Includes:
Division of Insurance, 303 W. Colfax, 5th Flr., Denver 80204; tel. 303/866-3201; John Kezer, comr.
Includes:

Financial Examination Section; tel. 303/866-3217; Chad H. Collier, chf. ins. examiner.
Department of Institutions, 3520 W. Oxford Ave., Denver 80236; tel. 303/762-4410; (vacant)
Includes:
Division of Mental Health; tel. 303/762-4088; Robert W. Glover, Ph.D., dir.

CONNECTICUT

The Honorable William A. O'Neill, Governor, 203/566-2211

HEALTH: Department of Health Services, 150 Washington St., Hartford 06106; tel. 203/566-4800; Frederik G. Adams, D.D.S., comr.
Includes:
Bureau of Health Promotion; tel. 203/566-5475; Peter Galbraith, D.M.D., bur. chf.
Bureau of Health System Regulation; tel. 203/566-3207; Stephen A. Harriman, bur. chf.
Includes:
Division of Hospital and Medical Care, 150 Washington St., Hartford 06106; tel. 203/566-1073; Elizabeth M. Burns, R.N., M.S., dir.
Division of Medical Quality Assurance; tel. 203/566-7398; Stanley Peck, dir.
Includes:
Licensure and Registration, Hartford 06106; tel. 203/566-4068; Elise Gaulin-Kramer, Ph.D., sect. chf.

WELFARE: Department of Human Resources, 1049 Asylum Ave., Hartford 06105; tel. 203/566-3318; Elliot A. Ginsberg, comr.
Department of Income Maintenance, 110 Bartholomew Ave., Hartford 06106; tel. 203/566-2008; Stephen B. Heintz, comr.

INSURANCE: Department of Insurance, 165 Capital Ave., Hartford 06106; tel; 203/566-5275; Peter W. Gillies, comr.

OTHER: Connecticut Board of Examiners for Nursing; tel. 203/566-1032; Marie Hillard, exec. off.
Department of Aging, 175 Main St., Hartford 06106; tel. 203/566-3238; Mary Ellen Klinck, comr.
State Department of Mental Health, 90 Washington St., Hartford 06106; tel. 203/566-3652; Deborah J. Carr, actg. comr.
Department of Education, 165 Capitol Ave., Hartford 06145; tel. 203/566-5497; Gerald N. Tirozzi, comr.
Includes:
Division of Rehabilitation Services, 600 Asylum Ave., Hartford 06105; tel. 203/566-4440; Marilyn A. Campbell, Ph.D., dir.
Includes:
Bureau of Organizational Support; tel. 203/566-3317; B. Joyce O'Reilly, chf.

DELAWARE

The Honorable Michael Castle, Governor, 302/736-4000

HEALTH: Department of Health and Social Services, 1901 N. DuPont Hwy., New Castle 19720; tel. 302/421-6705; Thomas P. Eichler, sec.
Includes:
Division of Aging, 1901 N. DuPont Hwy., New Castle 19720; tel. 302/421-6791; Eleanor Cain, dir.
Division of Economic Services, Medical Assistance Unit, Biggs Bldg., Box 906, New Castle 19720; tel. 302/421-6734; Phyllis Hazel, dir.
Division of Public Health, Robbins Bldg., 802 Silver Lake Plaza, Dover 19901; tel. 302/736-4701; Lyman J. Olsen, M.D., dir.
Includes:
Emergency Medical Services, Robbins Building, 802 Silver Lake Plaza, Dover 19901; tel. 302/736-4710
Office of Laboratories, 178 N. Legislature, Dover 19901; tel. 302/736-4714; Dr. Mahadeo P. Verma, Ph.D., dir.
Bureau of Personal Health Service; tel. 302/736-4768; John A. J. Forest, M.D.
Includes:
Office of Maternal and Child Health; tel. 302/736-4785; Mari Helen Barrett, R.N., M.S.N., dir.
Office of Handicapped Children; tel. 302/736-4735; Jack Fisher, dir.
Office of Health Facilities Licensing and Certification, 3000 Newport Gap Pike, Wilmington 19808; tel. 302/571-3499; James E. Harvey, dir.

OTHER: Board of Medical Practice of Delaware, Margaret O'Neill Bldg., 2nd Flr., Dover 19903; tel. 302/736-4522; Rosemarie S. Perez, adm. asst.
Delaware Board of Nursing, Margaret O'Neill Bldg., 2nd Flr., Dover 19901; tel. 302/736-4522; Rosalee J. Seymour, R.N., M.S., exec. dir.
Delaware State Hospital, Division of Alcoholism, Drug Abuse & Mental Health, New Castle 19720; tel. 302/421-6441; Robert Davidson, hosp. dir.
Department of Labor, Division of Vocational Rehabilitation, 321 E. 11th St., Wilmington 19801; tel. 302/571-2851; Tony Sokolowski, dir.

DISTRICT OF COLUMBIA

202/727-1000

HEALTH: Department of Human Services, 801 N. Capitol St., Washington 20009; tel. 202/727-0310; Byron C. Marshall, actg. dir.
Includes:
Rehabilitation Services Administration, 605 G St., N.W., Washington 20001; tel. 202/727-3211
Includes:
D.C. Commission of Public Health, 1875 Connecticut Ave., N.W., Washington 20009; tel. 202/673-6700; Reed V. Tuckson, M.D., comr.
Includes:
Bureau of Maternal and Child Health Services, 1875 Connecticut Ave., N.W., Washington 20009; tel. 202/673-6665; Harry Lynch, adm.
Long-Term Care; tel. 202/673-3597; Sue Brown, adm.
Ambulatory Health Care; tel. 202/673-6670; Marlene Kelley, M.D., adm.
Alcohol and Drug Abuse Services; tel. 202/727-0740; Donald C. Brooks, actg. adm.
Preventive Health Services; tel. 202/673-6756; Martin E. Levy, M.D., adm.

WELFARE: Commission on Social Services, Randall School, First and I Sts., S.W., Washington 20024; tel. 202/727-5930; Audrey Rowe, comr. of social services.

OTHER: Department of Consumer and Regulatory Affairs, 614 H St., N.W., Suite 1014, Washington 20001; tel. 202/727-7190; Don Murray, dir.
Includes:
Service Facility Regulation Administration; tel. 202/727-7190; Francis Bowie, adm.
Occupational and Professional Licensing Administration, P.O. Box 37200, Washington 20013; tel. 202/727-7465; Valerie Barry, adm.
Mental Health Services; tel. 202/673-6720; Robert Washington, adm.

FLORIDA

The Honorable Bob Martinez, Governor, 904/488-1234

HEALTH: State Health Office, 1323 Winewood Blvd., Tallahassee 32301; tel. 904/487-2705; E. Charlton Prathers, M.D., M.P.H., actg. dir.

WELFARE: Department of Health and Rehabilitative Services, 1317 Winewood Blvd., Bldg. 6, Rm. 233, Tallahassee 32301; tel. 904/488-7721; Gregory L. Coler, sec.
Includes:
Ambulatory Centers: Office of Regulations and Health Facility; tel. 904/487-2513; Marta Hardy, dir.
Aging and Adult Services, 1321 Winewood Blvd., Bldg. 2, Rm. 321, Tallahassee 32301; tel. 904/488-2881; Margaret Lynn Duggar, prog. staff dir.
Children's Medical Services, 1311 Winewood Blvd., Tallahassee 32399; tel. 904/487-2690; W. W. Ausbon, M.D., prog. dir.
Community Medical Facilities, Office of Health Planning and Development, 1317 Winewood Blvd., Bldg. 2., Rm. 256, Tallahassee 32301; tel. 904/488-8673; Robert Maryanski, dir.
Alcohol, Drug Abuse and Mental Health Program Office, 1317 Winewood Blvd., Tallahassee 32301; tel. 904/488-8304; A. Stephen Hill, Ph.D., staff dir.
Office of Licensure and Certification, 2727 Mahan Dr., Tallahassee 32308; tel. 904/487-2527; Amy M. Jones, dir.

INSURANCE: Department of Insurance, Bureau of Allied Lines, 637 Larson Building, 200 E. Gaines St., Tallahassee 32399; tel. 904/488-6766; Robert Johnson, chf.

OTHER: Florida Board of Medicine, 130 N. Monroe, Tallahassee 32399; tel. 904/488-0595; Dorothy J. Faircloth, exec. dir.
Board of Nursing, 111 Coast Line Dr., E., Suite 504, Jacksonville 32202; tel 904/359-6331; Judie K. Ritter, R.N., exec. dir.
Department of Labor, 2590 Executive Center Circle, East, Tallahassee 32399; tel. 904/488-4398; Hugo D. Menendez, sec.
Includes:
Division of Vocational Rehabilitation, 1709-A Mahan Dr., Tallahassee 32399; tel. 904/488-6210; Calvin Melton, Ph.D., dir.

GEORGIA

The Honorable Joe Frank Harris, Governor, 404/656-2000

HEALTH-WELFARE: Department of Human Resources, Health Bldg., 47 Trinity Ave., S.W., Rm. 522H, Atlanta 30334; tel. 404/656-5680; James G. Ledbetter, Ph.D., comr.
Includes:
Division of Rehabilitation Services, 878 Peachtree St., N.E., Rm. 706, Atlanta 30309; tel. 404/894-6670; Tom Gaines, dir.
Division of Mental Health, Mental Retardation and Substance Abuse, 878 Peachtree St., N.E., Atlanta 30309; tel. 404/894-6300; John Gates, Ph.D., dir.
Division of Public Health, 878 Peachtree St., N.E., Atlanta 30309; tel. 404/894-7505; James W. Alley, M.D., M.P.H., dir.
Division of Administrative Services; tel. 404/656-6395; Andy Carden, dir.
Includes:
Office of Regulatory Services, 878 Peachtree St., N.E., Atlanta 30309; tel. 404/894-5144; Marty Rotter, dir.
Includes:
Compliance Monitoring Section; tel. 404/894-2753; John Lee, dir.
Day Care Licensing Section; tel. 404/894-4719; Jo Cato, dir.
Laboratory Licensure and Development Section; tel. 404/894-5841; Ralph Alford, dir.
Radiological Health Section; tel. 404/894-5795; Bobby Rutledge, actg., dir.
Standards and Licensure Section; tel. 404/894-5137; Phillip A. Arnold, dir.

INSURANCE: Department of Insurance, 700 West Tower, Floyd Building, 2 Martin Luther King, Jr. Dr., Atlanta 30334; tel. 404/656-2056; Warren D. Evans, comr.

OTHER: Composite State Board of Medical Examiners, 166 Pryor St., S.W., Atlanta 30303; tel. 404/656-3913; Andrew Watry, exec. dir.
Georgia Board of Nursing, 166 Pryor St., S.W., Atlanta 30303; tel. 404/656-3943; Carolyn Hutcherson, exec. dir.
State Health Planning Agency, 43A Executive Park Dr., N.E., Atlanta 30329; tel. 404/894-4899; C. Annette Maxey, dir.

HAWAII

The Honorable John Waihee, Governor, 808/548-2211

HEALTH: Hawaii Department of Health, Box 3378, Honolulu 96801; tel. 808/548-6505; John C. Lewin, M.D., dir.
Includes:
Communicable Disease Division, Arthur Liang, M.D., chf.
Dental Health, Manuel C. W. Kau, D.D.S., chf.
Environmental Health, Shinji Soneda, chf.
Family Health Services, Frances Riggs, M.D., chf.
State Health Planning and Development Agency; tel. 808/548-2048; Patrick Boland, actg. adm.
Mental Health Division; tel. 808/548-6333
Includes:
Alcohol and Drug Abuse Branch; tel. 808/548-4280; Joyce Ingram-Chinn, chf.
Medical Health Services Division; tel. 808/548-6510; Elizabeth K. Anderson, M.D., chf.
Includes:
Hospital and Medical Facilities, Licensing Branch; tel. 808/548-5935; Dr. Ben Lambiotte, chf.

WELFARE: Department of Social Services and Housing, 1390 Miller St., Box 339, Honolulu 96809; tel. 808/548-6260; Winona E. Rubin, dir.
Includes:
Medicaid, 1390 Miller St., Box 339, Honolulu 96809; tel. 808/548-3855; Earl S. Motooka, actg. adm.
Vocational Rehabilitation, 1000 Bishop St., Box 339, Honolulu 96809; tel. 808/548-4769; Toshio Nishioka, adm.

OTHER: Department of Commerce and Consumer Affairs, Board of Medical Examiners, P.O. Box 3469, Honolulu 96801; tel. 808/548-4392; John M. Tamashiro, exec. sec.
Department of Commerce and Consumer Affairs, Board of Nursing, P.O. Box 3469, Honolulu 96801; tel. 808/548-3086; Jerold H. Sakoda, exec. sec.
Department of Labor and Industrial Relations; tel. 808/548-7821.
Includes:
Division of Disability Compensation, P.O. Box 3769, Honolulu 96812
Includes:
Plans Branch, 830 Punch Bowl St., Rm. 210, Honolulu 96813; tel. 808/548-5415

IDAHO

The Honorable Cecil Andrus, Governor, 208/334-2411

HEALTH-WELFARE: Idaho Department of Health and Welfare, 450 W. State, Boise 83720; tel. 208/334-4079; Rose Bowman, dir.
Includes:
Division of Field Operations Substance Abuse Section, 450 W. State, Boise 83720; tel. 208/334-5700; Ray Winterowd, bur. chf.
Division of Health; tel. 208/334-5945; Richard Schultz, adm.
Includes:
Bureau of Child Health; tel. 208/334-5967; Z. Koppanyl, M.D., chf.
Bureau of Emergency Medical Services; tel. 208/334-5994; Paul Anderson, chf.

Bureau of Laboratories, 2220 Old Penitentiary Rd., Boise 83712; tel. 208/334-2235; Darrell W. Brock, chf.
Bureau of Preventive Medicine; tel. 208/334-5932; Fritz Dixon, M.D., chf.
Bureau of Vital Statistics, Standards, and Local Health Services; tel. 208/334-5976; Bee Biggs, R.N., chf.
Includes:
Facility Standards Program, 420 W. Washington St., Boise 83720; tel. 208/334-4169; Jean Schoonover, R.N., prog. supr.
Includes:
Licensing and Certification; tel. 208/334-5325; Loyal Perry, supr.

INSURANCE: Department of Insurance, Division of Examinations, 700 W. State St., Boise 83720; tel. 208/334-2250; Larry Cross, chf. examiner.

OTHER: Idaho State Board of Medicine, 650 W. State St., Boise 83720; tel. 208/334-2822; Donald L. Deleski, exec. dir.
Idaho State Board of Nursing, 700 W. State St., Boise 83720; tel. 208/334-3110; Phyllis T. Sheridan, R.N., M.S., exec. dir.
Vocational Rehabilitation, Len B. Jordan Bldg., Rm. 150, 650 W. State, Boise 83720; tel. 208/334-3390; George J. Pelletier, Jr., adm.

ILLINOIS

The Honorable James R. Thompson, Governor, 217/782-2000

HEALTH: Illinois Department of Public Health, 535 W. Jefferson St., Springfield 62761; tel. 217/782-4977; Bernard J. Turnock, M.D., M.P.H., dir.
Includes:
Division of Laboratories; tel. 217/782-6562; David Carpenter, dir.
Division of Health Facilities Standards; tel. 217/782-7412; Rebecca Friedman, chf.
Includes:
Office of Health Policy and Planning; tel. 217/785-2040; Jackie Ellinger, assoc. dir.
Office of Health Regulation; tel. 217/782-2913; John Lumpkin, M.D., assoc. dir.
Office of Health Services; tel. 217/782-5945; Shirley Randolph, assoc. dir.
Office of Administrative Services; tel. 217/785-2033; Gary Robinson, assoc., dir.
Office of Health Protection; tel. 217/782-3985; Byron Francis, M.D., assoc. dir.
Hospital Licensing Section, 525 W. Jefferson St., Springfield 62761; tel. 217/782-4977; Joseph L. Voss, adm.
Ambulatory Health Programs; tel. 217/785-2080

WELFARE: Department of Public Aid, 100 S. Grand Ave., E., Springfield 62762; tel. 217/782-6716; Edward T. Duffy, dir.

INSURANCE: Department of Insurance, 320 W. Washington St., 4th Flr., Springfield 62767; tel. 217/782-1771; John E. Washburn, dir.

OTHER: Department of Registration and Education, 320 W. Washington St., Springfield 62768; tel. 217/785-0800; Gary L. Clayton, dir.
Department of Rehabilitation Services, 623 E. Adams St., Box 19429, Springfield 62794; tel. 217/782-2093; Susan S. Suter, dir.
Division of Services for Crippled Children, 2040 Hill Meadows Drive, Ste. A., Springfield 62702; tel. 217/793-2350; Edward F. Lis, M.D., dir.
Illinois Department of Mental Health and Developmental Disabilities, William G. Stratton Bldg., Rm. 401, Springfield 62706; tel. 217/782-2753; Ann M. Kiley, dir.

INDIANA

The Honorable Robert D. Orr, Governor, 317/232-3140

HEALTH: State Board of Health, 1330 W. Michigan St., Box 1964, Indianapolis 46206; tel. 317/633-0100; Woodrow A. Myers, Jr., M.D., state hlth. comr.
Includes:
Division of Health Facilities; tel. 317/633-0442; Frances H. Safford, dir.
Division of Hospital and Institutional Services; tel. 317/633-8507; James L. White, dir.
Maternal and Child Health; tel. 317/633-8447; T.S. Danielson, Jr., M.D., dir.
Division of Acute Care Services; tel. 317/633-8486; Harry T. Haver, dir.

WELFARE: Department of Public Welfare, State Office Bldg., Rm. 701, 100 N. Senate Ave., Indianapolis 46204; tel. 317/232-4705; Donald L. Blinzinger, adm.
Includes:
Services for Crippled Children Division, 141 S. Meridian St., 6th Flr., Indianapolis 46225; tel. 317/232-4283; Joseph M. Daly, M.D., dir.

INSURANCE: Department of Insurance, 311 W. Washington St., Suite 300, Indianapolis 46204; tel. 317/232-2386; Harry E. Eakins, comr.

OTHER: Department on Aging and Community Services, 251 N. Illinois St., P.O. Box 7083, Indianapolis 46207; tel. 317/232-7000; Jean Merritt, exec. dir.
Medical Licensing Board of Indiana, Health Professionals Bureau, One American Sq., Suite 1020, P O Box 82067, Indianapolis 46282; tel. 317/232-2960; Mary Gaughan, adm.
State Board of Nursing, Health Professionals Bureau, One American Sq., Suite 1020, P.O. Box 82067, Indianapolis 46204; tel. 317/232-2960; Larry Sage, adm.
State Department of Mental Health, 117 E. Washington, Indianapolis 46204; tel. 317/232-7844; Dennis R. Jones, comr.
Department of Rehabilitation, 251 N. Illinois, Indianapolis 46207; tel. 317/232-1139; Jean Merritt, dir.
Includes:
Division of Vocational Rehabilitation, Indiana Rehabilitation Services; tel. 317/232-1304; Mike Neese, dir.

IOWA

The Honorable Terry E. Branstad, Governor, 515/281-5011

HEALTH: Department of Public Health, Lucas State Office Bldg., 3rd & 4th Flrs., Des Moines 50319; tel. 515/281-5605; Mary L. Ellis, dir.
Includes:
Division of Family and Community Health; tel. 515/281-3931; Ronald D. Eckoff, M.D., dir.
Division of Disease Prevention; tel. 515/281-5643; John R. Kelly, dir.
Division of Health Planning and Development; tel. 515/281-4066; Betty Grandquist, dir.
Division of Substance Abuse and Health Promotion; tel. 515/281-3641; Janet Zwick, dir.
Governor's Alliance on Substance Abuse; tel. 515/281-4518; Almo Hawkins, dir.

WELFARE: Department of Human Services, Hoover State Office Building, Des Moines 50319; tel. 515/281-3147; Nancy Norman, comr.
Includes:
Division of Mental Health/Mental Retardation/Developmental Disabilities; tel. 515/281-5874; Charles Palmer, dep. comr.

INSURANCE: Department of Commerce, Division of Insurance, Lucas State Office Bldg., Des Moines 50319; tel. 515/281-5705; William D. Hager, comr.

OTHER: Department of Education, Division of Vocational Rehabilitation Services, 510 E. 12th St., Des Moines 50319; tel. 515/281-4156; Jerry L. Starkweather, adm.
Department of Inspection and Appeals, Division of Health Facilities, Lucas State Office Bldg., Des Moines 50319; tel. 515/281-4115; Dana Petrowsky, adm.
Iowa State Board of Medical Examiners, State Capital Complex, Executive Hills West, Des Moines 50319; tel. 515/281-5171; William S. Vanderpool, exec. dir.
Iowa Board of Nursing, State Capital Complex, 1223 E. Court Ave., Des Moines 50319; tel. 515/281-3255; Ann E. Mowery, R.N., M.N., exec. dir.
Child Health Specialty Clinic, University of Iowa, 246 Hospital School Building, Iowa City 52242; tel. 319/353-4250; Richard Nelson, M.D., dir.
Department of Elder Affairs, 236 Jewett Building, Des Moines 50319; tel. 515/281-5187; Karen Kynef, exec. dir.

KANSAS

The Honorable Mike Hayden, Governor, 913/296-0111

HEALTH: Kansas Department of Health and Environment, Forbes Field Bldg. 740, Topeka 66620; tel. 913/862-9360; Barbara J. Sabol, actg. dir. hlth.
Includes:
Bureau of Adult and Child Care Facilities; tel. 913/296-1240; Greg Reser, med. facil. cert. adm.

WELFARE: State Department of Social and Rehabilitation Services, Docking State Office Bldg., Rm. 603 N, Topeka 66612; tel. 913/296-3271; Robert C. Horder, sec.
Includes:
Mental Health and Retardation Services, State Office Bldg., Topeka 66612; tel. 913/296-3774; Gerald T. Hannah, Ph.D., comr.
Income Maintenance and Medical Services, State Office Bldg., Topeka 66612; tel. 913/296-3271; John Schneider, comr.
Rehabilitation Services, Biddle Bldg., 2700 W. 6th St., Topeka 66606; tel. 913/296-3911; Joan Watson, comr.

INSURANCE: Insurance Department, 420 S.W. 9th, Topeka 66612; tel. 913/296-3071; Fletcher Bell, comr.
Includes:
Accident and Health Division, Rich Huncker, supr.

OTHER State Board of Healing Arts, Landon State Office Building, 900 S.W. Jackson, Suite 553, Topeka 66612; tel. 913/296-7413; Charlene K. Abbott, exec. sec.
Kansas State Board of Nursing, Landon State Office Bldg., Suite 551S, 900 S.W. Jackson, Topeka 66612; tel. 913/296-4929; Lois Rich Sciebetta, R.N., Ph.D., exec. adm.

KENTUCKY

The Honorable Martha Layne Collins, Governor, 502/564-2500

HEALTH: Department for Health Services, Cabinet for Human Resources, 275 E. Main St., Frankfort 40621; tel. 502/564-3970; C. Hernandez, M.D., comr.
Includes:
Division of Licensing and Regulation; tel. 502/564-2800; Woody Dunn, dir.
Division of Health Policy and Resource Development; tel. 502/564-8948, Greg Lawther, dir.
Includes:
Health Policy Analysis Branch, Robert Nelson, mgr.

WELFARE: Department for Social Insurance, 275 E. Main St., Frankfort 40621; tel. 502/564-3703; Mike Robinson, comr.

INSURANCE: Department of Insurance, Life and Health Division, P.O. Box 517, 229 W. Main St., Frankfort 40602; tel. 502/564-3630; Matthew Johnson, dir.

OTHER: Kentucky Board of Nursing, 4010 Dupont Circle, Suite 430, Louisville 40207; tel. 502/897-5143; Sharon M. Weisenbeck, M.S., R.N., exec. dir.
Department For Mental Health/Mental Retardation Services, 275 E. Main St., Frankfort 40621; tel. 502-564-4527; Dennis Boyd, cmr.
Department for Medicaid Services, 275 E. Main St., Frankfort 40621; tel. 502/564-4321; R. Hughes Walker, cmr.
Office of Vocational Rehabilitation, Capital Plaza Tower, 9th Flr., Frankfort 40601; tel. 502/564-4440; Don Fightmaster, assoc. supt.
Commission for Handicapped Children, 982 Eastern Parkway, Louisville 40217; tel. 502/588-3264; William D. Minix, exec. dir.
Commission for Health Economics Control, 275 E. Main St., Frankfort 40621; tel. 502/564-6620; Jack S. Lesshafft, Sr., chm.

LOUISIANA

The Honorable Edwin W. Edwards, Governor, 504/342-6600

HEALTH: Louisiana Department of Health and Human Resources, Box 3776, Baton Rouge 70821; tel. 504/342-6711, Sandra L. Robinson, M.D., M.P.H., sec.
Includes:
Office of Mental Retardation/Developmental Disabilities, 721 Government St., 3rd Flr., Baton Rouge 70802; tel. 504/342-6811; Cecil Colwell, asst. sec.
Office of Preventive and Public Health Services, Box 60630, New Orleans 70160; tel. 504/568-5051; Daneta D. Bardsley, asst. sec.
Office for Prevention and Recovery from Alcohol and Drug Abuse, P.O. Box 53129, Baton Rouge 70892; tel. 504/922-0730; Vern Ridgeway, asst. sec.
Office of Charity Hospital at New Orleans, 1532 Tulane Ave., New Orleans 70140; tel. 504/568-3201; Elliott Roberts, asst. sec.
Office of Family Security, P.O. Box 94065, Baton Rouge 70804; tel. 504/342-3950; Marjorie Stewart, asst. sec.
Office of Hospitals, 200 Lafayette St., 7th Flr., Baton Rouge 70801; tel. 504/342-2595; John King, asst. sec.
Office of Human Development, Box 44367, Baton Rouge 70804; tel. 504/342-4000; Wayne C. Heap, asst. sec.
Office of Management and Finance, Box 3776, Baton Rouge 70821; tel. 504/342-6715; Melvin Meyers, Jr., undersec.
Includes:
Division of Licensing and Certification, Box 3767, Baton Rouge 70821; tel. 504/342-5774; Steve Phillips, dir.
Office of Mental Health, P.O. Box 4049, Baton Rouge 70821; tel. 504/342-2544; James W. Loe, asst. sec.

INSURANCE: Department of Insurance, P.O. Box 94214, Baton Rouge 70804; tel. 504/342-5900; Sherman A. Bernard, comr.

OTHER: Louisiana State Board of Medical Examiners, 830 Union St., Suite 100, New Orleans 70112; tel. 504/524-6763; Richard M. Nunnally M.D., pres.
Louisiana State Board of Nursing, 907 Pere Marquette Bldg., 150 Baronne St., New Orleans 70112; tel. 504/568-5464; Merlyn Maillian, R.N., exec. dir.

Louisiana State Board of Practical Nurse Examiners, Tidewater Pl., 1440 Canal St., Ste. 2010, New Orleans 70112; tel. 504/568-6480; Terry L. De Marcay, R.N., exec. dir.

MAINE

The Honorable John R. McKernan, Jr., Governor, 207/289-1110

HEALTH: Maine Department of Human Services, State House, Station 11, Augusta 04333; tel. 207/289-3707; Rollin Ives, comr.
Includes:
Bureau of Health; tel. 207/289-3201; Phillip Haines, Ph.D., acctg. dir.
Child Health; tel. 207/289-3311; John Serrage, M.D., dir.
Bureau of the Elderly; tel. 207/289-2561; Gail Wright, dir.
Bureau of Medical Services; tel. 207/289-2674; Patricia Riley, dir.
Includes:
Division of Licensing and Certification, tel. 207/289-2606; Louis Dorogi, dir.

INSURANCE: Department of Professional and Financial Regulation, State House, Station 35, Augusta 04333; tel. 207/289-3915; Susan Collins, comr.
Includes:
Bureau of Insurance, Station 34, Augusta 04333; tel. 207/289-3101; Everard Steven, actg. supt.

OTHER: Board of Registration in Medicine, RFD #3, Box 461, Waterville 04901; tel. 207/873-2184; Edward Bradley, Jr., chm.
Maine State Board of Nursing, 295 Water St., Augusta 04330; tel. 207/289-5324; Jean C. Caron, R.N., exec. dir.
Bureau of Rehabilitation, 32 Winthrop St., Augusta 04330; tel. 207/289-2266; Diana C. Scully, dir.
Includes:
Division of Deafness; tel. 207/289-3484; Norman Perrin, dir.
Division of Eye Care, tel. 207/289-3484, Harold Lewis, dir.
Department of Mental Health and Mental Retardation, Station No. 40, 411 State Office Bldg., Augusta 04333; tel. 207/289-4200; Ronald Welsh, actg. dir.
Includes:
Bureau of Mental Health, (vacant)

MARYLAND

The Honorable William Donald Schaefer, Governor, 301/269-6200

HEALTH: Department of Health and Mental Hygiene, 201 W. Preston St., Baltimore 21201; tel. 301/225-6500; Adele Wilzack, R.N., M.S., sec.
Includes:
Aged and Chronically Ill Services Administration; tel. 301/225-5736; Patricia Smith, M.D., dir.
Alcoholism Control Administration; tel. 301/225-6541; John Bland, dir.
Drug Abuse Administration; tel. 301/225-6925; Howard B. Silverman, actg. dir.
Environmental Health Programs; tel. 301/225-6520; William Eichbaum, asst. sec.
Juvenile Services Administration; tel. 301/225-5055; Richard Hamilton
Laboratories Administration; tel; 301/225-6100; J. Mehsen Joseph, Ph.D., dir.
Licensing and Certification; tel. 301/225-5430; Henry Schwartz, chf.
Local Health Administration; tel. 301/225-5300; Ruth H. Singer, M.D., dir.
Medical Care Programs Administration; tel. 301/225-6538; Douglas H. Morgan, asst. sec.
Mental Hygiene Administration; tel. 301/225-6611; Dr. Henry Harbin
Mental Retardation and Developmental Disabilities Administration; tel. 301/225-5600; Lois M. Meszarus, Ph.D., actg. dir.
Office of Planning; tel. 301/225-6816; Elizabeth G. Barnard, dir.
Preventive Medicine Administration; tel. 301/225-6743; Eric Fine, M.D., actg. dir.
Office of Health Regulation, tel. 301/225-6530; Ron Bialek, actg. dir.

WELFARE: Social Services Administration, 300 W. Preston St., Baltimore 21201; tel. 301/576-5200; Frank Blanton, actg. dir.

INSURANCE: Department of Licensing and Regulation, Insurance Division, 501 St. Paul Place, Baltimore 21202; tel. 301/333-6300; Edward J. Muhl, comr.

OTHER: Board of Medical Examiners of Maryland, 201 W. Preston St., Baltimore 21201; tel. 301/225-5900; C. Earl Hill, M.D., pres.
Maryland State Board of Examiners of Nurses, 201 W. Preston St., Baltimore 21201; tel. 301/225-5880; Donna M. Dorsey, R.N., M.N., exec. dir.
Department of Education, 200 W. Baltimore St., Baltimore 21201; tel. 301/333-2000; David W. Hornbeck, supt. of schools
Includes:
Division of Vocational Rehabilitation, tel. 301/333-2294; Richard A. Batterton, asst. state supt.

MASSACHUSETTS

The Honorable Michael Dukakis, Governor, 617/727-2121

HEALTH: Massachusetts Department of Public Health, 150 Tremont St., Boston 02108; tel. 617/727-2700; Bailus Walker, Jr., Ph.D., M.P.H., comr., Vivien Li, exec. asst.
Includes:
Division of Health Care Systems; tel. 617-727-9660; James Divver, asst. comr.
Division of Environmental Health; tel. 617/727-7099; Gerald Parker, asst. comr.
Division of Health Statistics and Research; tel. 617/727-6452; Daniel Friedman, Ph.D., dir.
Office of Emergency Medical Services; tel. 617/451-3433; Frank Keslof, dir.
Division of Health Care Quality, 80 Boylston St., Boston 02116; tel. 617/727-5860; Irene R. McManus, dir.

WELFARE: Department of Public Welfare, 180 Tremont St., Boston 02111; tel. 617/574-0100; Charles M. Atkins, comr.

INSURANCE: Division of Insurance, 100 Cambridge St., Boston 02202; tel. 617/727-3333; Peter Hiam, comr.

OTHER: Board of Registration in Medicine, Commonwealth of Massachusetts, Ten West St., Boston 02111; tel. 617-727-3086; Dr. Ralph Deterling, chm.
Board of Registration in Nursing, 100 Cambridge St., Rm. 1519, Boston 02202; tel. 617/727-7393; Mary H. Snodgrass, R.N., exec. sec.
Divisions of Alcoholism and Drug Rehabilitation, 150 Tremont St., 6th Flr., Boston 02111; tel. 617/727-1960; David Mulligan, dir.
Massachusetts Department of Mental Health, 160 N. Washington St., Boston 02114; tel. 617/727-5600; Edward M. Murphy, comr.
Massachusetts Rehabilitation Commission, 20 Providence St., Boston 02116; tel. 617/727-2172; Elmer C. Bartels, comr.
Commission for the Blind, 110 Tremart St., Boston 02108; tel. 617/727-5550; Charles Crawford, comr.

MICHIGAN

The Honorable James J. Blanchard, Governor, 517/373-1837

HEALTH: Michigan Department of Public Health, 3500 N. Logan St., Lansing 48909; tel. 517/335-8000; Gloria R. Smith, Ph.D., dir.
Includes:
Division of Licensing and Certification; tel. 517/335-8505; Nancy Graham, supr.
Center for Environmental Health Services; tel. 517/335-8350; Lawrence Chadzynski, chf.
Office of Substance Abuse Services; tel. 517/335-8809; Robert C. Brook, adm.
Division for Laboratory Improvement; Bureau of Laboratory and Epidemiological Services; tel. 517/335-8050; Kenneth Wilcox, chf.
Bureau of Community Services; tel. 517/335-8955; Denise Holmes, chf.
Bureau of Health Facilities, 517/335-8500; Raj Wiener, chf.
Includes:
Division of HMO Services; tel. 517/335-8503
Center for Health Promotion; tel. 517/335-8368; Jean Chabut, chf.

WELFARE: Michigan Department of Social Services, 300 S. Capitol Ave., P.O. Box 30037, Lansing 48909; tel 517/373-2035; C. Patrick Babcock, dir.
Includes:
Medical Services Administration, tel. 517/335-7262; Kevin Seitz, dir.

INSURANCE: Department of Licensing and Regulation, Insurance Bureau, P.O. Box 30220, Lansing 48909; tel. 517/373-0220; Herman W. Coleman, comr.

OTHER: Department of Licensing and Regulation, Box 30018, Lansing 48909; tel. 517/373-1870; Raymond Hood, dir.
Includes:
Bureau of Health Services; C. William Howe, dir.
Includes:
Michigan Board of Medicine, 611 W. Ottowa St., Box 30018, Lansing 48909; tel. 517/373-6873; Herman Fishman, lic. exec.
Michigan Board of Nursing; tel. 517/373-6873; Herman Fishman, lic. exec.
Office of Services to the Aging, P.O. Box 30026, Lansing 48909; tel. 517/373-8230; Olivia Maynard, dir.
Department of Education, Box 30008, Lansing 48909; tel. 517/373-3324; (vacant)
Includes:
Bureau of Rehabilitation and Disability Determination, Box 30010; tel. 517/373-3390; Ivan L. Cotman, assoc. supt.
Office of Health and Medical Affairs, Lewis Cass Bldg., Box 30026, Lansing 48909; tel. 517/373-9650; Patience A. Drake, dir.
Michigan Department of Mental Health, Lewis Cass Bldg., 320 N. Walnut, 6th Flr., Lansing 48913; tel. 517/373-3740; Thomas D. Watkins, Jr., actg. dir.

MINNESOTA

The Honorable Rudy Perpich, Governor, 612/296-6013

HEALTH: Department of Health, 717 S.E. Delaware St., Box 9441, Minneapolis 55440; tel. 612/623-5000; Sr. Mary Madonna Ashton, comr.
Includes:
Division of Disease Prevention and Health Promotion; tel. 612/623-5363; Michael Moen, dir.
Division of Environmental Health; tel. 612/623-5320; Raymond Thron, Ph.D., dir.
Division of Health Resources; tel. 612/623-5440; Janet Brodahl, dir.
Includes:
Survey and Compliance Section; tel. 612/623-5420; Clarice Suefert, chf.
Division of Public Health Laboratories; tel. 612/623-5210; Robert Lindner, M.D., dir.
Division of Maternal and Child Health; tel. 612/623-5265; Carolyn McKay, M.D., dir.
Division of Community Services; tel. 612/623-5480; James Parker, dir.
Bureau of Administration; tel. 612/623-5465; Thomas Maloy, asst. comr.
Alternative Delivery Systems; tel. 612/623-5365; Kathleen Burek, dir.

WELFARE: Department of Human Services, Centennial Bldg., 658 Cedar St., 4th Flr. St. Paul 55155; tel. 612/296-6117; Sandra Gardebring, comr.

OTHER: Minnesota Board of Medical Examiners, 2700 University Ave., West., Suite 106, St. Paul 55114; tel. 612/642-0538; David M. Ziegenhagen, exec. dir.
Minnesota Board of Nursing, 2700 University Ave., West, #108, St. Paul 55114; tel. 612/642-0567; Joyce M. Showalter, exec. dir.
Department of Administration, 50 Sherburne Ave., St. Paul 55155
Includes:
Documents Division; tel. 612/297-3000; Stephen Ordahl, dir.
Department of Commerce, 500 Metro, Square Bldg., St. Paul 55101; tel. 612/296-4026; Michael A. Hatch, comr.
Division of Rehabilitation Services, 5th Flr., 390 N. Robert St., St. Paul 55101; tel. 612/296-5616; William Niederloh, asst. comr.

MISSISSIPPI

The Honorable Bill Allain, Governor, 601/359-1000

HEALTH: Department of Health, Felix J. Underwood State Board of Health Bldg., Box 1700, Jackson 32915; tel. 601/960-7400; Alton B. Cobb, M.D., M.P.H., State Health Off.
Includes:
Bureau of Health Services; tel. 601/960-7463; Terry Beck, dir.
Children's Medical Program; tel. 601/960-7613; Sam Valentine, dir.
Bureau of Environmental Health; tel. 601/960-7518; Joe Brown, dir.
Technical Services; tel. 601/960-7873; Betty Jane Phillips, Ph.D., dir.
State Epidemiologist; tel. 601/960-7725; F.E. Thompson, M.D.
Public Health Statistics; tel. 601/960-7960; David Lohrisch, Ph.D., dir.
Health Planning and Resources Development; tel. 601/960-7874; George Jobe, dir.
Division of Health Facility Licensure and Certification, P.O. Box 1700, Jackson 39215; tel. 601/960-7769; Mendal G. Kemp, dir.

WELFARE: Department of Public Welfare, Box 352, Jackson 39205; tel. 601/354-0341; Thomas Brittain, Ph.D., comr.

OTHER: Mississippi Board of Nursing, 135 Bounds St., Jackson 39206; tel. 601/354-7349; Marcella L. McKay, R.N., M.S.N., exec. dir.
Department of Mental Health, 1500 Woolfolk Bldg., Jackson 39201; tel. 601/359-1288, Randy Hendrix, Ph.D., dir.
State Department of Rehabilitation Services, P.O. Box 22806, Jackson 39225; tel. 601/354-6100; John W. Cook, comr.

MISSOURI

The Honorable John Ashcroft, Governor, 314/751-2151.

HEALTH: Department of Health, Box 570, Jefferson City 65102; tel. 314/751-6400; Robert G. Harmon, M.D., M.P.H., dir.
Includes:
Division of Health Resources; tel. 314/751-6272; Garland H. Land, dir.
Bureau of Hospital Licensing and Certification; tel. 314/751-6302; Charles R. Gillilan, chf.

INSURANCE: Division of Insurance, P.O. Box 690, Jefferson City 65102; tel. 314/751-4126; Lewis Crist, dir.

Includes:
Life and Health and Review Section; tel. 314/751-4363; James W. Casey, supr.

OTHER: Missouri State Board of Registration for the Healing Arts, Box 4, Jefferson City 65102; tel. 314/751-2334; Gary R. Clark, exec. sec.
Department of Mental Health, 1915 Southridge, P.O. Box 687, Jefferson City 65102; tel. 314/751-4122; Keith Schafer, Ed.D., dir.
Division of Personal Health Services; 1730 E. Elm, Box 570, Jefferson City 65102; tel. 314/751-6174; Deanna Severance, dir.
Includes:
Missouri Crippled Children's Service, 1730 E. Elm, Box 570, Jefferson City 65102; tel. 314/751-6246; Jack L. Garrett, bur. chf.
Department of Education, 205 Jefferson, Jefferson City 65102; tel. 314/751-4446; Dr. Arthur Mallory
Includes:
Vocational Rehabilitation, 2401 E. McCarty, Jefferson City 65101; tel. 314/751-3251; Don L. Gann, asst. comr.

MONTANA

The Honorable Ted Schwinden, Governor, 406/444-2511.

HEALTH: State Department of Health and Environmental Sciences, W. F. Cogswell Bldg., Helena 59620; tel. 406/444-2544; John J. Drynan, M.D., dir.
Includes:
Health Services Division; tel. 406/444-2037; George Fenner, adm.
Includes:
Bureau of Licensing and Certification; Jacqueline McKnight, chf.
Family and Maternal and Child Health Services Bureau, Sidney Pratt, M.D., chf.
Preventive Health Services Bureau; Dr. Donald Espelin

WELFARE: Department of Social and Rehabilitation Services, Box 4210, 111 Sanders St., Helena 59604; tel. 406/444-5622; Dave Lewis, dir.
Includes:
Rehabilitative Services Division/Visual Service Division, Box 4210, Helena 59604; tel. 406/444-2590; Maggie Bullock, adm.
Community Services Division; tel. 406/444-3865; Norma Harris, adm.
Includes:
Unit on Aging, Montana Information Network, Rm. 308, P.O. Box 4210, Helena 55604; tel. 406/444-3865; Robert E. Bartholomew, supr.

OTHER: Montana State Board of Nursing, 1424 9th Ave., Helena 59620; tel. 406/444-4279; Phyllis M. McDonald, R.N., M.E., exec. sec.

NEBRASKA

The Honorable Kay Orr, Governor, 402/471-2311

HEALTH: State Department of Health, 301 Centennial Mall, S., Lincoln 68509; tel. 402/471-2133; Gregg F. Wright, M.D., M.Ed., dir.
Includes:
Division of Health Systems Planning; tel. 402/471-2337; David Palm, Ph.D., dir.
Division of Licensure and Standards; tel. 402/471-2946, William H. Page, dir.
Division of Maternal and Child Health and Nutrition; tel. 402/471-2907; Georgia Bihr, dir.
Division of Radiological Health; tel. 402/471-2168; Harold Borchert, dir.
Section of Hospitals and Medical Facilities; tel. 402/471-2105; Charlene Gondring, dir.

WELFARE: Nebraska State Department of Social Services, 301 Centennial Mall, S., P.O. Box 95026, Lincoln 68509; tel. 402/471-3121; Kermit McMurray, dir.
Includes:
Medical Services Division; tel. 402/471-9330; Robert Seiffert, adm.
Special Services for Children and Adults; tel. 402/471-9345; Mary Jo Iwan, adm.

INSURANCE: Department of Insurance, Box 94699, Lincoln 68509; tel. 402/471-2201; William H. McCartney, dir.

OTHER: Bureau of Examining Boards, 301 Centennial Mall, S., Box 95007, Lincoln 68509; tel. 402/471-2115; Helen L. Meeks, dir.
Department of Education, Division of Rehabilitation Services, 301 Centennial Mall, S., P.O. Box 94987, Lincoln 68509; tel. 402/471-2961; Jason Andrew, Ph.D., dir.

NEVADA

The Honorable Richard Bryan, Governor, 702/885-5000.

HEALTH-WELFARE: Department of Human Resources, Kinkead Bldg., 505 E. King, Rm. 600, Carson City 89710; tel. 702/885-4400; Jerry Griepentrog, dir.
Includes:
Division of Health; tel. 702/885-4740; Larry Matheis, adm.
Includes:
Bureau of Regulatory Health Services; tel. 702/885-4475; William C. Schneider, chf.
Community Health Services Bureau; tel. 702/885-4885
Includes:
Crippled Children's Services
Division of Rehabilitation; tel. 702/885-4440; Del Frost, adm.
Mental Hygiene and Mental Retardation Division, 1001 N. Mountain St., Gilbert Bldg., Ste. 1-H, Carson City 89710; Tel. 702/885-5943; Dan Payne, Ph.D., adm.
Health Resources and Cost Review, 505 E. King Street, Rm. 603, Carson City 89710; tel. 702/885-4176; Daniel J. O'Donnell, adm.
Welfare Division, 2527 N. Carson St., Carson City 89710; tel. 702/885-4770; Linda Ryan, adm.
Medicaid; tel. 702/885-4698; Keith W. McDonald, dep. adm.

INSURANCE: Department of Commerce, 201 S. Fall St., Carson City 89710; tel. 702/885-4250; Larry Strube, dir.
Includes:
Insurance Division; David G. Gates, comr.

OTHER: Nevada State Board of Medical Examiners, P.O. Box 7238, Reno 89510; tel. 702/329-2559; Kathleen Lewis, exec. dir.
Nevada State Board of Nursing, 1281 Terminal Way, Rm. 116, Reno 89502; tel. 702/786-2778; Lonna Burress, R.N., exec. dir.

NEW HAMPSHIRE

The Honorable John Sununu, Governor, 603/271-1110.

HEALTH-WELFARE: Department of Health and Human Services, 6 Hazen Dr., Concord 03301; tel. 603/271-4685; M. Mary Mongan, comr.
Includes:
Division of Mental Health and Developmental Services, 6 Hazen Dr., Concord 03301; tel. 603/271-4304; Donald L. Shumway, dir.
Division of Public Health Services, 6 Hazen Dr., Concord 03301; tel. 603/271-4501; William T. Wallace, Jr., M.D., M.P.H., dir.
Includes:
Office of Family and Community Health; tel. 603/271-4547; Roger Taillefer, asst. dir.
Office of Health Protection; tel. 603/271-4472; George Morse, asst. dir.
Bureau of Health Facilities Administration; tel. 603/271-4592; Charles Ferguson, chf.
Office of Disease Prevention and Control; tel. 603/271-4671; Richard DiPentima, asst. dir.
Division of Human Services, 6 Hazen Dr., Concord 03301-6521; tel. 603/271-4321; Clifton H. Stickney, actg. dir.

INSURANCE: Department of Insurance, 169 Manchester St., Concord 03301; tel. 603/271-2661; Louis E. Bergeron, comr.
Includes:
Examination Division; tel. 603/271-2241; Robert M. Solitro, dir.

OTHER: Department of Environmental Services, 6 Hazen Dr., Concord 03301; tel. 603/271-3503; Alden H. Howard, comr.
New Hampshire Board of Registration in Medicine, Health and Welfare Bldg., 6 Hazen Dr., Concord 03301; tel. 603/271-4502; William T. Wallace, Jr., M.D., M.P.H., exec. sec.
New Hampshire Board of Nursing Education and Nurse Registration, State Office Park, S., 101 Pleasant St., Concord 03301; tel. 603/271-2323; (vacant)
Department of Education, 101 Pleasant St., Concord 03301; tel. 603/271-3494; John T. MacDonald, Ph.D., comr.
Includes:
Vocational Rehabilitation Division; tel. 603/271-3121; Bruce A. Archambault, chf.

NEW JERSEY

The Honorable Thomas H. Kean, Governor, 609/292-2121.

HEALTH: State Department of Health, CN-360, Trenton 08625; tel. 609/292-7834; Mollie Joel Coye, M.D., M.P.H., comr.
Includes:
Division of Health Planning and Resource Development; tel. 609/292-8772; Joseph Morris, asst. comr.
Includes:
Alternative Health Systems; tel. 609/984-5054; Edwin V. Kelleher, chf.
Division of Local and Community Health Services; tel. 609/292-4043; Leah Z. Ziskin, M.D., asst. comr.
Includes:
Maternal and Child Health Program; Amy Meltzer, M.D., coord.
Division of Health Facilities Evaluation, Paul R. Langevin, Jr., asst. comr.
Includes:
Licensing, Certification and Standards Program, CN 367, Trenton 08625; tel. 609/292-5764, Solomon Goldberg, D.D.S., dir.
Health Facilities Construction; Leonard D. Dileo, dir.
Health Facilities Inspection; tel. 609/292-4304; (vacant)

WELFARE: Division of Public Welfare, CN-716, Hamilton Township 08625; tel. 609/588-2000; Audrey Harris, dir.

OTHER: New Jersey Board of Nursing, 1100 Raymond Blvd., Newark 07102; tel. 201/648-2490; Sr. Teresa L. Harris, exec. sec.
Department of Law and Public Safety, 25 Market St., Trenton 08625; tel. 609/292-4925; W. Cary Edwards, attorney gen.
Includes:
Division of Consumer Affairs, 1100 Raymond Blvd., Newark 07102; tel. 201/648-3537; James J. Barry, dir.
Includes:
Board of Medical Examiners, 28 W. State St., Trenton 08608; tel. 609/292-4843; Charles Janousek, exec. sec.

NEW MEXICO

The Honorable Garrey Carruthers, Governor, 505/827-4011

HEALTH: Department of Health and Environment, 1190 St. Francis Dr., P.O. Box 968, Santa Fe 87504; tel. 505/827-0020; Larry Gordon, sec.
Includes:
Division of Health Services; tel. 505/827-2389; Mary Lou Martinez, dir.
Includes:
Federal Program Certification Section; tel. 505/827-2416; Sue K. Morris, supr.

WELFARE: Human Services Department, Box 2348, Santa Fe 87503; tel. 505/827-4065; Lou Gallegos, sec.
Includes:
Income Support Division; tel. 505/827-4254; Bob Beardsley, dir.
Social Services Division; tel. 505/827-4372; Jack Callaghan, dir.

INSURANCE: State Corporation Commission, P.O. Drawer 1269, Santa Fe 87504; tel. 505/827-4529; Eric Serna, chm.
Includes:
Department of Insurance; tel. 505/827-4500; Vincente B. Jasso, supt.

OTHER: New Mexico Board of Medical Examiners, P.O. Drawer 1388, Santa Fe 87504; tel. 505/827-9933, Christina Romero, bur. chf.
State of New Mexico Board of Nursing, 4125 Carlisle, N.E., Albuquerque 87107; tel. 505/841-6524; Nancy Twig, dir.
Department of Education, Education Bldg., Santa Fe 87501; tel. 505/827-6635; Alan D. Morgan, supt.
Includes:
Division of Vocational Rehabilitation, 604 W. San Mateo, Santa Fe 87503; tel. 505/827-3511; Tres McCleskey, actg. dir.

NEW YORK

The Honorable Mario M. Cuomo, Governor, 518/474-2121.

HEALTH: State Department of Health, Tower Bldg., Empire State Plaza, Albany 12237; tel. 518/474-2011; David Axelrod, M.D., comr.
Includes:
Office of Health Systems Management; tel. 518/474-7028; Raymond Sweeney, dir.
Includes:
Bureau of Project Management; tel. 518/473-7915; David R. Collins, dir.
Bureau of Home Health Care; tel. 518/474-2006; Dr. Nancy Barhydt, dir.
Bureau of Alternative Delivery Systems; tel. 518/474-5515; Joyce Gallimore, dir.
Wadsworth Center for Laboratories and Research, Clinical Lab Evaluation; tel. 518/474-7592; Dr. Herbert W. Dickermen, M.D., Ph.D., dir.
Office of Public Health; tel. 518/474-0180; Linda Randolph, M.D., dir.

WELFARE: New York State Department of Social Services, 40 N. Pearl St., Albany 12243; tel. 518/474-9003; Cesar A. Perales, comr.

OTHER: Department of Education, Rm. III, Main Education Bldg., 89 Washington, Albany 12234; tel. 518/474-5844;
Includes:
New York State Board for Medicine, Cultural Education Center, Albany 12230; tel. 518/474-3841; Thomas J. Monahan, assoc. exec. sec.
State Board for Nursing, Cultural Education Center, Albany 12230; tel. 518/474-3843; Milene A. Megel, R.N., Ph.D., exec. sec.
Office of Vocational Rehabilitation, One Commerce Plaza, Albany 12234; tel. 518/474-2714; Richard M. Switzer, dep. comr.
Office of Mental Retardation and Developmental Disabilities, 44 Holland Ave., Albany 12229; tel. 518/473-1997; Arthur Y. Webb, comr.
Division of Substance Abuse, P.O. Box 8200, Executive Park South, Albany 12203; tel. 518/457-2061; Julio A. Martinez

New York State Office of Mental Health, 44 Holland Ave., Albany 12229; tel. 518/474-4403; Steven E. Katz, M.D., comr.

NORTH CAROLINA

The Honorable James G. Martin, Governor, 919/733-1110.

HEALTH-WELFARE: Department of Human Resources, 325 N. Salisbury St., Raleigh 27611; tel. 919/733-4534; Paul T. Kayye, M.D., interim sec.
Includes:
Division of Facility Services, 701 Barbour Dr., Raleigh 27603; tel. 919/733-2342; Ira O. Wilkerson, Jr., dir.
Division of Mental Health, Mental Retardation, and Substance Abuse Services, 325 N. Salisbury St., Raleigh 27611; tel. 919/733-7011; R.J. Blackley, M.D., interim dir.
Division of Vocational Rehabilitation Services, 620 N. West St., Raleigh 27611; tel. 919/733-3364; Claude A. Myer, dir.
Division of Health Services, Cooper Memorial Bldg., 225 N. McDowell, Raleigh 27602; tel. 919/733-3446; Ronald H. Levine, M.D., M.Ph., dir.

WELFARE: Division of Medical Assistance, 1985 Umstead Dr., Raleigh 27603; tel. 919/733-2060; Barbara D. Matula, dir.

INSURANCE: Department of Insurance, P.O. Box 26387, Raleigh 27611; tel. 919/733-7343; James E. Long, comr.

OTHER: North Carolina Board of Medical Examiners, Suite 214, 222 N. Pearson St. Raleigh 27601; tel. 919/833-5321; Bryant D. Paris, Jr., exec. sec.
North Carolina Board of Nursing, Box 2129, Raleigh 27602; tel. 919/828-0740; Carol A. Osman, R.N., exec. dir.

NORTH DAKOTA

The Honorable George D. Sinner, Governor, 701/224-2000

HEALTH: State Department of Health, State Capitol, Bismarck 58505; tel. 701/224-2372; Robert M. Wentz, M.D., state hlth. off.
Includes:
Division of Maternal and Child Health; tel. 701/224-2493; Dr. Steve McDonough, dir.
Health Resources Section; tel. 701/224-2352; Joseph Pratschner, chf.
Includes:
Division of Health Facilities; tel. 701/224-2352; Fred Gladden, dir.

WELFARE: Department of Human Services, State Capitol, Bismarck 58505; tel. 701/224-2310; John Graham, exec. dir.
Includes:
Division of Economic Assistance; tel.701/224-2332; Donald K. Johnson, dir.
Medical Services Division; tel. 701/224-2321; , Richard Myatt, dir.
Division of Vocational Rehabilitation; tel. 701/224-2907; James O. Fine, div. dir.
Office of Human Services; tel. 701/224-2318; Yvonne Smith, dir.
Includes:
Crippled Childrens Services; tel. 701/224-2436; Robert Nelson, adm.
Developmental Disabilities; tel. 701/224-2768; Darvin Hirsch, dir.
Mental Health Services; tel. 701/224-2766; Samih Ismir, dir.
Division of Drug Abuse and Alcoholism; tel. 701/224-2769; John Allen, adm.

INSURANCE: Department of Insurance, State Capitol, Bismarck 58505; tel. 701/224-2440; Earl R. Pomeroy, comr.

OTHER: North Dakota State Board of Medical Examiners, City Center Plaza, 418 E. Broadway Ave., Suite C-10, Bismarck 58501; tel. 701/223-9485; Rolf P. Sletten, exec. sec. and treas.
Director of Institutions; tel. 701/224-2471; Richard Rayl, dir.
North Dakota Board of Nursing, Kirkwood Office Tower, Suite 504, Bismarck 58501; tel. 701/224-2974; Karen MacDonald, R.N., exec. dir.

OHIO

The Honorable Richard F. Celeste, Governor, 614/466-2000.

HEALTH: Ohio Department of Health, 246 N. High St., Columbus 43266; tel. 614/466-3543; Thomas J. Halpin, M.D., M.P.H., actg. dir.
Includes:
Bureau of Medical Services; tel. 614/466-7857; Joe Sanderell, chf.
Division of Maternal and Child Health; tel. 614/466-3263; James Quilty, M.D., chf.
Division of Nursing; Joya Neff, R.N., chf.
Office of Resource Development; tel. 614/466-3325; Louis Pomerantz, chf.
Division of Licensure and Certification; tel. 614/466-2070; Paul Ritter, chf.
Bureau on Alcoholism, 170 N. High St., 3rd Flr., Columbus 43215; tel. 614/466-3445; Wayne Lindstrom, chf.

WELFARE: Ohio Department of Human Services, 30 E. Broad St., 32nd Flr., Columbus 43266; tel. 614/466-6282; Patricia Barry, dir.
Includes:
Division of Medical Assistance, 31st Flr.; tel. 614/466-2365; John Boyle, chf.
Medicaid Administration, 31st Flr.; tel. 614/466-3196; Paul Offner, dep. dir.

INSURANCE: Department of Insurance, 2100 Stella Ct., Columbus 43266; tel. 614/481-5735; George Fabe, dir.
Includes:
HMO Division; tel. 614/481-5738; Phyllis Wise, sec.

OTHER: State Medical Board of Ohio, Suite 510, 65 S. Front St. Columbus 43266; tel. 614/466-3934; Ray Q. Bumgarner, exec. dir.
State of Ohio Board of Nursing Education and Nurse Registration, 65 S. Front St., Rm. 509, Columbus 43266; tel. 614/466-3947; Rosa Lee Weinert, R.N., exec. sec.
Department of Mental Health, Suite 1180, 30 E. Broad St., Columbus 43215; tel. 614/466-2596; Pamela Hyde, dir.
Department of Mental Retardation and Developmental Disabilities, Suite 1280, 30 E. Broad St., Columbus 43215; tel. 614/466-5214; Robert E. Brown, dir.
Rehabilitation Services Commission, 4656 Heaton Rd., Columbus 43229; tel. 614/438-1210; Robert L. Rabe, adm.
Includes:
Bureau of Disability Determination, 1944 Morse Rd., Columbus 43229; tel. 614/438-1500; Leonard F. Herman, dir.
Bureau of Services for the Visually Impaired, tel. 614/438-1255; Doris E. Barcomb, dir.
Bureau of Vocational Rehabilitation; tel. 614/438-1250; Lowell Morris, dir.
Bureau of Program Support, tel. 614/438-1220; Terry D. Etling, dir.

OKLAHOMA

The Honorable Henry Bellmon, Governor, 405/521-2011.

HEALTH: State Department of Health, 1000 N.E. 10th, Oklahoma City 73152; tel. 405/271-4200; Joan K. Leavitt, M.D., comr.
Includes:
Dental Services; tel. 405/271-5502; Michael L. Morgan, D.D.S., chf.
Institutional Services; tel. 405/271-6868; Robert Warner, chf.
Maternal and Child Health Services; tel. 405/271-4476; Sara R. DePersio, M.D., dir.
Nursing Service; tel. 405/271-5183; Carol Swink, R.M., Ph.D., chf.
Personal Health Services; tel. 405/271-4200; Jerry Nida, M.D., dep. comr.
Public Health Laboratory Services; tel. 405/271-5070; Garry McKee, Ph.D., chf.

WELFARE: Department of Human Services, Box 25352, Oklahoma City 73125; tel. 405/521-3646; Robert Fulton, dir.
Includes:
Crippled Children's Unit; tel. 405/557-2525; Charles Brodt, actg. asst. dir.
Don H. O'Donoghue Rehabilitation Institute; tel. 405/271-6955; William G. Thurman, M.D., chf. of staff
Medical Services Division; tel. 405/557-2539; Charles Brodt, actg. asst. dir.
Oklahoma Children's Memorial Hospital; tel. 405/271-6165; J. Andrew Sullivan, M.D., int. chf. of staff
Oklahoma Memorial Hospital; tel. 405/271-6644; D. Robert McCaffree, M.D., chf. of staff
State of Oklahoma Teaching Hospitals; tel.. 405/271-5656; Antonio Padilla, chf. exec. off.
Rehabilitation Services; tel. 405/424-4311; Jerry Dunlap, dep. dir.
Aging Services, 312 N.E. 28th, Oklahoma City 73105; tel. 405/521-2327; Hannah Atkins, dep. dir.

OTHER: Oklahoma State Board of Medical Examiners, 5104 N. Francis, Suite C, Oklahoma City 73118; tel. 405/848-6841; Mark R. Johnson, M.D., sec.
Oklahoma Board of Nurse Registration and Nursing Education, 2915 N. Classen Blvd., Suite 524, Oklahoma City 73106; tel. 405/525-2076; Sulinda Moffett, R.N., exec. dir.
Department of Mental Health, Programs Division, P.O. Box 53277, Capitol Station, Oklahoma City 73152
Health Planning Commission, 1000 N.E. 10th St., Box 53551, Oklahoma City 73152; tel. 405/271-5161; Suzanne W. Nichols, dir.

OREGON

The Honorable Neil Goldschmidt, Governor, 503/378-3131.

HEALTH: Oregon State Health Division, 1400 S.W. Fifth Ave., Portland 97201; tel. 503/229-5032; Kristine Gebbie, adm.
Includes:
Public Health Laboratory, 1717 S.W. 10th Ave., P.O. Box 275, Portland 97207; tel. 503/229-5882; Dr. Mike Skeels, dir.
Office of Environment and Health Systems; tel. 503/229-6300; Steve Boedigheimer, chf.
Includes:
Health Facilities Section, Box 231; Portland 97207; tel. 503/229-5686; Maureen Whitman, mgr.

WELFARE: Adult and Family Services Division, 417 Public Service Bldg., Salem 97310; tel. 503/378-3680; Freddye Webb-Pettet, adm.

INSURANCE: Department of Commerce; tel. 503/378-4100; Stanton Long, dir.
Includes:
Division of Insurance, Commerce Bldg., 158 12th St. N.E., Salem 97310; tel. 503/378-4271; Theodore R. Kulongoski, comr.

OTHER: Oregon State Board of Medical Examiners, 1002 Loyalty Bldg., 317 S. W. Alder St., Portland 97204; tel. 503/229-5770; John J. Ulwelling, exec. sec.
Oregon State Board of Nursing, 1400 S.W. 5th, Room 904, Portland 97201; tel. 503/229-5653; Dorothy J. Davy, R.N., exec. dir.
Office of Alcohol and Drug Abuse Programs, 301 Public Service Bldg., Salem 97310; tel. 503/378-2163; Jeffrey N. Kushner, dir.
Crippled Children's Division, Oregon Health Sciences University, Box 574, Portland 97207; tel. 503/225-8362; David McFarlane, M.D., dir.
Division of Vocational Rehabilitation, 2045 Silverton Rd., N.E., Salem 97310; tel. 503/378-3830, Joil A. Southwell, adm.
Mental Health Division, 2575 Bittern St., N.E., Salem 97310; tel. 503/378-2671; Joseph E. Murray, adm.

PENNSYLVANIA

The Honorable Bob Casey, Governor, 717/787-2121.

HEALTH: Pennsylvania Department of Health, Rm. 802, Health and Welfare Bldg., Harrisburg 17120; tel. 717/787-6436; N. Mark Richards, M.D., sec.
Includes:
Bureau of Laboratories, Pickering Way and Welsh Pool Rd., Lionville 19353; tel. 215/363-8500; Dr. Vern Pidcoe, dir.
Administration; tel. 717/783-8770; Maria A. Keating, dep. sec.
Community Health; tel 717/787-4366; Alexander B. Rakow, D.O., dep. sec.
Drug and Alcohol Programs; tel. 717/787-9857; Luceille Fleming, dep. sec.
Public Health Programs; tel. 717/783-8804; Donald Reid, M.D., dep. sec.
Planning and Quality Assurance; tel. 717/783-1078; Jennifer Riseon, dep. sec.
Includes:
Primary Care & Home Health Services, 1032A Health & Welfare Building, Harrisburg, 17120; tel. 717/787-1379; Curtis Jennings, dir.
Bureau of Quality Assurance; tel. 717/787-8015; Andrew Major, dir.
Includes:
Division of Hospitals; tel. 717/783-8980; William Walker, dir.

WELFARE: Pennsylvania Department of Public Welfare, Health and Welfare Bldg., Harrisburg 17120; tel. 717/787-2600; John F. White, Jr., sec.
Includes:
Children, Youth, and Families; tel. 717/787-4756; Shirley Walker, dep. sec.
Income Maintenance; tel. 717/783-3063; Patricia Jacobs, dep. sec.
Medical Assistance; tel.717/787-1870
Mental Health; tel. 717/787-6443; Bob Haigh, dep. sec.
Mental Retardation; tel. 717/787-3700; Joseph J. Scartelli, Ph.D., dep. sec.

INSURANCE: Department of Insurance, 1311 Strawberry Square, Harrisburg 17120; tel. 717/787-2317; Constance B. Foster, actg. comr.
Includes:
Division of Company Licensing; tel. 717/783-2142; Ronald E. Chronister, dep. ins. comr.

OTHER: State Board of Medicine, Box 2649, Harrisburg 17105; tel. 717/787-2381; Loretta M. Frank, adm. asst.
State Board of Nursing, Box 2649, Harrisburg 17105; tel. 717/783-7142; Miriam H. Limo, exec. sec.
Division of Laboratory Improvement, Clinical Lab Bureau, P.O. Box 500, Exton 19341; tel. 215/363-8500; Josephine Bertola, dir.
Office of Vocational Rehabilitation, Labor and Industry Bldg., Seventh & Forster Sts., Harrisburg 17120; tel. 717/787-5244; George Lowe, exec. dir.

RHODE ISLAND

The Honorable Edward D. DiPrete, Governor, 401/277-2000.

HEALTH: Department of Health, 75 Davis St., Providence 02908; tel. 401/277-2231; H. Denman Scott, M.D., dir.
Includes:
Division of Family Health; tel. 401/277-2312; William H. Hollinshead, M.D., dir.
Health Planning and Resources Development; tel.401/277-2233; John T. Tierney, assoc. dir.
Rhode Island Department of Mental Health, Retardation and Hospitals, Aime J. Forand Bldg., 600 New London Ave., Cranston 02920; tel. 401/464-3201; Thomas D. Romeo, dir.
Division of Professional Regulation, 104 Cannon Bldg.; tel. 401/277-2827; Robert W. McClanaghan, adm.
Division of Medical Care Standards; tel. 401/277-2788; Donald C. William, chf.
Division of Facilities Regulation; tel. 401/277-2566; Robert DiCenso, chf.

INSURANCE: Department of Business Regulation, 100 N. Main St., Providence 02903; tel. 401/277-2246; Mark A. Pfeiffer, dir.
Includes:
Division of Insurance; tel. 401/277-2223; Samuel L. Torman, asst. dir.

OTHER: Department of Human Services, 600 New London Ave., Cranston 02920; tel. 401/464-3361; Nancy V. Bordeleau, dir.
Includes:
Division of Medical Services, tel. 401/464-3575; Anthony Barile, assoc. dir.
Vocational Rehabilitation, 40 Fountain St., Providence 02903; tel. 401/421-7005; Sherry J. Campanelli, adm.

SOUTH CAROLINA

The Honorable Carroll Campbell, Governor, 803/734-1000

HEALTH: Department of Health and Environmental Control, 2600 Bull St., Columbia 29201; tel. 803/734-4880; Michael D. Jarrett, comr.
Includes:
Bureau of Chronic Disease, Richard Parker, D.V.M., chf.
Bureau of Drug Control; tel. 803/734-4710; T.D. Wyatt Jr., chf.
Bureau of Environmental Sanitation; tel. 803/734-5071; E.C. Fox Jr., chf.
Bureau of Home Health Services; tel. 803/734-5040; Michael Byrd, chf.
Bureau of Laboratories; tel. 803/737-7001; Arthur F. DiSalvo, M.D., chf.
Bureau of Maternal and Child Care; tel. 803/734-4670; Marie Meglen, M.S., C.N.M.
Division of Health Licensing and Certification, Office of Health Licensing, 2600 Bull St., Columbia 29201; tel. 803/734-4680; Alan Samuels, dir.

WELFARE: South Carolina Department of Social Services, Box 1520, Columbia 29202; tel. 803/734-5768; James L. Solomon, Jr., comr.

OTHER: State Board of Medical Examiners of South Carolina, 1315 Blanding, St., Columbia 29201; tel. 803/734-8901; Stephen S. Seeling, exec. dir.
State Board of Nursing for South Carolina, 1777 St. Julian Pl., Suite 102, Columbia 29204; tel. 803/737-6594; Renatta S. Loquist, R.N., exec. dir.
Commission on Alcohol and Drug Abuse, 3700 Forest Drive, Suite 300, Columbia 29204; tel. 803/734-9520; William J. McCord, dir.
Commission on Aging, 915 Main St., Columbia 29201; tel. 803/734-3203; Ruth Q. Seigler, exec. dir.
Commission for the Blind, 1430 Confederate Ave., Columbia 29201; tel. 803/734-7520; William K. James, comr.
Health and Human Service Finance Commission, 1801 Main Street, P.O. Box 8206, Columbia 29202; tel. 803/253-6100; Dennis Caldwell, exec. dir.
Department of Mental Retardation, 2712 Middleburg Drive, P.O. Box 4706, Columbia 29240; tel. 803/737-6444; Charles D. Barnett, Ph.D., comr.
State Department of Mental Health, 2414 Bull St., Box 485, Columbia 29202; tel. 803/734-7780; Joseph J. Bevilacqua, Ph.D., comr.
Vocational Rehabilitation Department, 1410 Boston Ave., P.O. Box 15, West Columbia 29171-0015; tel. 803/734-3500; J.S. Dusenbury, comr.

SOUTH DAKOTA

The Honorable George S. Mickelson, Governor, 605/773-3011.

HEALTH: Department of Health, 523 East Capitol, Joe Foss Bldg., Pierre 57501; tel. 605/773-3361; Katherine A. Kinsman, sec. of hlth.
Includes:
Division of Health Services; tel. 605/773-3757; John N. Jones, dir.
Center for Health Policy and Statistics; tel. 605/773-3693; Jan Smith, dir.
Division of Alcohol and Drug Abuse; tel. 605/773-3123; Robert Anderson, dir.
Division of Public Health; tel. 605/773-3364; Ken Senger, dir.
Includes:
Licensure and Certification Program, tel. 605/773-3364; C. Sue Lydic, dir.

WELFARE: Department of Social Services, 700 Governor's Dr., Pierre 57501; tel. 605/773-3165; James W. Ellenbecker, sec.
Includes:
Office of Medical Services; tel. 605/773-3495; Ervin Schumacher, prog. adm.
Office of Developmental Disabilities and Mental Health; tel. 605/773-3438; Tom Scheinost, prog. adm.

OTHER: State Board of Medical and Osteopathic Examiners, 1323 Minnesota Ave., Sioux Falls 57105; tel. 605/336-1965; Robert D. Johnson, exec. sec.
Department of Vocational Rehabilitation, Richard F. Kneip Bldg., 700 Governor's Dr., Pierre 57501; tel. 605/773-3195; John Madigan, sec.

TENNESSEE

The Honorable Ned Ray McWherter, Governor, 615/741-3011.

HEALTH: Department of Health and Environment, 344 Cordell Hull Bldg., Nashville 37219; tel. 615/741-3111; James E. Word, comr.
Includes:
Office of Administrative Services; tel. 615/741-3824; Robert G. Maxwell, asst. comr.
Bureau of Environment, TERRA Bldg., 150 Ninth Ave., North, Nashville 37219; tel. 615/741-3657; M. T. Bruner, asst. comr.
Bureau of Health Services, 100 9th Ave., North, Nashville 37219; tel. 615/741-7305; Manny Martins, asst. comr.
Medicaid, 729 Church St., Nashville 37219; tel. 605/741-0213; Ray D. Wilson, asst. comr.
Bureau of Manpower and Facilities, 283 Plus Park Blvd., Nashville 37219; tel. 615/367-6204; Sherryl Midgett, asst. comr.
Includes:
Division of Health Care Facilities, 283 Plus Park Blvd.; Nashville 37219; tel. 615/367-6303; Polly T. Darnall, dir.
Includes:
Board of Licensing Health Care Facilities; tel. 615/367-6317; Leslie A. Brown, dir.
Laboratory Licensing Service, 287 Plus Park Blvd., Nashville 37217; tel. 615/367-6287; Jerry Duke, dir.

WELFARE: State Department of Human Services, 400 Deaderick St., Nashville 37219; tel. 615/741-3241; Nancy-Ann E. Min, comr.
Includes:
Family Assistance; tel. 615/741-5463; Michael O'Hara, asst. comr.
Social Services; tel. 615/741-5924; Rachel Touchton, asst. comr.
Division of Rehabilitation Services, Citizens Plaza Bank Bldg., 15th Flr., 400 Deaderick St., Nashville 37219; tel. 615/741-2019; Patsy Matthews, asst. comr.
Tennessee Rehabilitation Center, 9th and C St., Smyrna 37167; tel. 615/741-2095; Joe DiDomenico, asst. comr.

OTHER: Tennessee Board of Medical Examiners, 283 Plus Park Blvd., Nashville 37219; tel. 615/367-6231; Louise B. Blair, adm.
Tennessee Board of Nursing; 283 Plus Park Blvd., Nashville 37219; tel. 615/367-6232; Elizabeth J. Lund, R.N., exec. dir.
Tennessee Department of Mental Health and Mental Retardation, 6th Flr., 706 Church St., Nashville 37219; tel. 615/741-3107; Eric B. Taylor, comr.
Includes:
Division of Alcoholism and Drug Abuse; tel. 615/741-1921; Bob Currie, asst. comr.
Tennessee Commission on Aging, Suite 715, Tennessee Building, 535 Church St., Nashville 37219; tel. 615/741-2056; Emily Wiseman, dir.

TEXAS

The Honorable Bill Clements, Governor, 512/463-4630

HEALTH: Department of Health, 1100 W. 49th St., Austin 78756; tel. 512/458-7111; Robert Bernstein, M.D., comr.
Includes:
Bureau of Crippled Children's Services; tel. 512/465-2666; Janet S. Barkley-Booher, chf.
Bureau of Licensing and Certification; tel. 512/458-7538; Maurice Shaw, chf.
Bureau of Maternal and Child Health; tel. 512/458-7700; Walter P. Peter Jr., M.D., chf.
Bureau of State Health Planning and Resource Development; tel. 512/458-7261; Carol Daniels, chf.
Health Facility, Licensure, and Certification Division, 1100 W. 49th St., Austin 78756; tel. 512/458-7245; Juanita Carroll, dir.
Hospital and Professional Licensure Division; tel. 512/458-7512; Gerald Guthrie, dir.

WELFARE: Texas Department of Human Services, Box 2960, 701 W. 51st St., Austin 78769; tel. 512/450-3011; Marlin W. Johnston, comr.

INSURANCE: State Board of Insurance, 1110 San Jacinto, Austin 78701; tel; 512/463-6169; Lyndon Olsen, Jr., chm.

OTHER: Board of Nurse Examiners for the State of Texas, 1300 E. Anderson Ln., Bldg. C, Suite 225, Austin 78752; tel. 512/835-4880; Dr. Louise Sanders, R.N., Ph.D., exec. sec.
Texas Board of Vocational Nurse Examiners, 1300 E. Anderson Ln., Bldg. C, Suite 285, Austin 78752; tel. 512/835-2071; Joyce A. Hammer, R.N., M.S., exec. dir.
Texas Department of Mental Health and Mental Retardation, Box 12668, Capitol Sta., Austin 78711; tel. 512/454-3761; Gary E. Miller, M.D., comr.

UTAH

The Honorable Norman H. Bangerter, Governor, 801/533-4000.

HEALTH: Utah Department of Health, P.O. Box 16700, Salt Lake City 84116; tel. 801/538-6101; Suzanne Dandoy, M.D., exec. dir.
Includes:
Environmental Health Division; tel. 801/538-6121; Kenneth Alkema, dir.
Administration and Planning Office; tel. 801/538-6930; Sheldon B. Elman, dir.
Health Care Financing Division; tel. 801/538-6151; Roderick L. Betit, dir.
Family Health Services Division; tel. 801/538-6161; Peter C. Van Dyck, M.D., dir.
State Health Laboratory; tel. 801/538-6131; Francis Urry, Ph.D., dir.
Medical Examiners Office; tel. 801/533-5848; Edwin J. Sweeney, M.D., dir.
Division of Community Health Services, P.O. Box 16660, Salt Lake City 84116; tel. 801/538-6129; J. Brett Lazor, M.D., dir.
Includes:
Bureau of Local & Rural Health Systems; tel. 801/538-6113; Robert W. Sherwood, Jr., dir.
Bureau of Health Facility Licensure; tel. 801/538-6152; James B. Fisher, dir.

INSURANCE: Insurance Department, Heber Wells Building, 160 East 300 South, 2nd Flr., Salt Lake City 84111; tel. 801/530-6408; Harold C. Yancey, comr.

OTHER: Division of Occupational & Professional Licensing, 160 East 300 South, P.O. Box 45802, Salt Lake City 84145; tel. 801/530-6628; David E. Robinson, dir.
State Office of Education; 250 E., 500 S., Salt Lake City 84111; tel. 801/533-5431; James R. Moss, supt.
Includes:
Division of Rehabilitation Services; tel. 801/533-5991; Judy Ann Buffmire, Ph.D., dir.
Department of Social Services, P.O. Box 45500, Salt Lake City, 84145; tel. 801/533-7009; Norman G. Angus, exec. dir.
Includes:
Division of Alcoholism and Drugs, P.O. Box 45000, Salt Lake City 84145; tel. 801/533-6532; F. Leon Povey, dir.
Aging and Adult Services; tel. 801/533-6422; Robert Ward, dir.
Family Services; tel. 801/533-5094; Jean Nielsen, dir.
Mental Health; tel. 801/533-5783; Keith Stroud, dir.
Services to the Handicapped; tel. 801/533-4940; Gary Nakao, dir.
Youth Corrections; tel. 801/533-5290; Ron Stromberg, dir.

VERMONT

The Honorable Madeleine N. Kunin, Governor, 802/828-1110.

HEALTH: Vermont Department of Health, 60 Main St., Box 70, Burlington 05402; tel. 802/863-7200; Roberta R. Coffin, M.D., comr.
Includes:
Environmental Health Division; tel. 802/863-7223; Ken Stone, dir.
Epidemiology Division; tel. 802/863-7240; Richard Vogt, M.D., dir.
Medical Services Division; tel. 802/863-7330; Richard Aronson, M.D., dir.
Public Health Laboratory; tel. 802/863-7335; Katherine Kelley, dir.
Public Health Statistics; tel. 802/863-7300; Mary Anne Freedman, dir.
Medical Care Regulation Division; tel. 802/863-7272; Robert Aiken, dir.

WELFARE: Agency of Human Services, 103 S. Main St., Waterbury 05676; tel. 802/241-2220; Gretchen Morse, sec.
Includes:
Department of Mental Health; tel. 802/241-2610; William A. Dalton, comr.
Office of Alcohol and Drug Abuse Programs; tel. 802/241-2170; Richard Powell, dir.

Office on Aging; tel. 802/241-2400; Joel Cook, dir.
Department of Social Welfare; tel. 802/241-2853; Veronica H. Celani, comr.
Includes:
Division of Medicaid Services; tel. 802/241-2880; Elmo Sassarossi, dir.
Department of Social and Rehabilitation Services; tel. 802/241-2100; William M. Young, comr.
Includes:
Vocational Rehabilitation Division, Osgood Bldg., 103 S. Main St., Waterbury 05676; tel. 802/241-2189; Richard C. Douglas, dir.
Vermont Health Policy Corporation; tel. 802/241-2920; Alan Hark, chm.

INSURANCE: Department of Banking and Insurance, 120 State St., Montpelier 05602; tel. 802/828-3301; Thomas P. Menson, comr.

OTHER: Vermont State Board of Nursing, 26 Terrace St., Montpelier 05602; tel. 802/828-2396, Lynn B. Hardee, R.N., M.S.N., exec. dir.

VIRGINIA

The Honorable Gerald L. Baliles, Governor, 804/786-0000.

HEALTH: State Department of Health, 109 Governor St., Room 400, Richmond 23219; tel. 804/786-3561; C.M.G. Buttery, M.D., comr.
Includes:
Division of Handicapped Children; tel. 804/786-3691; W. R. Ferguson, M.D., dir.
Division of Maternal and Child Health; tel. 804/786-7367; Alice Linyear, M.D., dir.
Division of Licensure and Certification, Rm. 1013; tel.804/786-2081; Mary V. Francis, dir.

WELFARE: State Department of Social Services, 8007 Discovery Dr., Richmond 23229; tel. 804/281-9204; William Lukhard, comr.

INSURANCE: State Corporation Commission, Box 1157, Richmond 23209; tel. 804/786-8967; Steven Foster, comr.
Includes:
Bureau of Insurance; tel. 804/786-7694
Includes:
Company Licensing and Regulatory Compliance Section; tel. 804/786-3636; Alfred Gross, supr.

OTHER: State Board of Medicine, 1601 Rolling Hills Dr., Surry Bldg., 2nd Flr., Richmond 23229; tel. 804/662-9908; Dr. Hilary Connor, exec. dir.
Department for the Aging, 101 N. 14th St., 18th Flr., Richmond 23219; tel. 804/225-2271; Wilda Ferguson, comr.
Department of Medical Assistance Services, 600 E. Broad St., Suite 1300, Richmond 23219; tel. 804/786-7933; Ray T. Sorrell, dir.
Department of Mental Health and Mental Retardation, Box 1797, Richmond 23214; tel. 804/786-3921; Howard M. Cullum, comr.
Department of Rehabilitative Services, 4901 Fitzhugh Ave., Box 11045, Richmond 23230; tel. 804/257-0316; Altamont Dickerson, Jr., comr.

WASHINGTON

The Honorable Booth Gardner, Governor, 206/753-5000.

HEALTH-WELFARE: State Department of Social and Health Services, OB-44, Olympia 98504; tel. 206/753-4010; Jule Sugarman, sec.
Includes:
Division of Vocational Rehabilitation; tel. 206/753-2544; Sharon Stewart Johnson, dir.
Bureau of Alcohol and Substance Abuse, Mail Stop OB-44W, Olympia 98504; tel. 206/753-5866; Glen Miller, dir.
Health Policy Planning Section, Mail Stop OB-33; tel. 206/753-2246; Verne A. Gibbs, exec. dir.
Division of Medical Assistance, Mail Stop HB-41, 623 - 8th Ave., S.E., Olympia 98504; tel. 206/753-1777; Ron Kero, dir.
Includes:
Office of Medical and Program Policy; tel. 206/753-5839; Guthrie Turner, M.D., med. dir.
Division of Health, Mail Stop ET-21; tel. 206/753-5871; Les James, actg. dir.
Includes:
Health Facilities Survey Section, ET-31, Olympia 98504; tel. 206/753-5851; Kenneth R. Lewis, supr.

INSURANCE: Office of the Insurance Commissioner, Insurance Bldg., Mail Stop AQ-21, Olympia 98504; tel. 206/753-7300; Dick Marquardt, comr.

OTHER: Licensing Divison, Box 9649, Olympia 98504; tel. 206/586-4561; Rolland Runion, adm.
Program Management Division, Box 9649, Olympia 98504; tel. 206/586-1923; Chris Robert Rose, actg. adm.
Includes:
Washington State Board of Nursing; tel. 206/753-2686; Constance E. Roth; R.N., Ed. D., exec. sec.
Washington State Board of Practical Nursing, Box 9649, Olympia 98504; tel. 206/753-3728; Virginia Renz, R.N. actg. exec. sec.

WEST VIRGINIA

The Honorable Arch A. Moore, Jr., Governor, 304/348-3456

HEALTH: State Department of Health, State Office Bldg. No. 3, 1800 Washington St., E., Charleston 25305; tel. 304/348-2971; David K. Heydinger, M.D., dir.
Includes:
Office of Chief Medical Examiner, Irvin Sopher, M.D., dir.
Office of Environmental Health, Robert Wheeler, actg. dir.
Office of Health Planning and Evaluation, Desmond Byrne, dir.
Office of Behavioral Health Services, George W. Lilley, Jr., Ed. D., dep. dir.
Includes:
Alcoholism Division; Jack Clohan, Jr., dir.
Office of Administration and Oversight; tel. 304/348-0120; Jack Hartley, dir.
Includes:
Health Facilities Licensure and Certification Section; tel. 304/348-0050; John J. Jarrell, dir.
Health Standards Planning and Evaluation; tel. 304/348-0530
Office of Community Services, Nancy J. Tolliver, dir.
Includes:
Primary Care and Recruitment Division; tel. 304/348-4007; Jill Hutchinson, actg. dir.

WELFARE: Dept. of Human Services, 1900 E. Washington St., Charleston 25305; tel. 304/348-2400; Regina S. Lipscomb, comr.
Includes:
Division of Handicapped Children's Services, 1116 Quarrier St., Charleston 25301; tel. 304/348-3071; Janet E. Lucas, adm. dir.
Division of Medical Services; tel. 304/348-8990; Helen Condry, dir.

INSURANCE: Insurance Commissioners Office, 2100 Washington St., E., Charleston 25305; tel. 304/348-3354; Fred E. Wright, comr.
Includes:
Financial Conditions Division; tel. 304/348-2100; John Collins, dir. and chf. examiner

OTHER: West Virginia Board of Medicine, 100 Dee Dr., Suite #104, Charleston 25311; tel. 304/348-2921; Ronald D. Walton, exec. dir.
West Virginia Board of Examiners for Registered Professional Nurses, Suite 309, Embleton Bldg., 922 Quarrier St., Charleston 25301; tel. 304/348-3728; Garnette Thorne, M.S., R.N., exec. sec.
West Virginia State Board of Examiners for Licensed Practical Nurses, Suite 506, Embleton Bldg., 922 Quarrier St., Charleston 25301; tel. 304/348-3572; Nancy R. Wilson, R.N., exec. sec.
State Board of Vocational Education, State Capitol, Charleston 25305; tel. 304/348-3660; Kendall Hall, Pres.
Includes:
Division of Vocational Rehabilitation; tel. 304/766-4601; Earl W. Wolfe, dir.

WISCONSIN

The Honorable Tommy Thompson, Governor, 608/266-2211.

HEALTH-WELFARE: Department of Health and Social Services, P.O. Box 7850, Madison 53707; tel. 608/266-3681; Timothy F. Cullen, sec.
Includes:
Division of Community Services; tel. 608/266-2701; James R. Meier, adm.
Division of Vocational Rehabilitation, 1 W. Wilson St., Rm. 850, Box 7852, Madison 53707; tel. 608/266-1281; Judy Norman-Nunnery, adm.
Division of Health, P.O. Box 309, Madison 53701; tel. 608/266-1511; John Torphy, adm.
Includes:
Bureau of Community Health and Prevention; tel. 608/266-1251; Ivan Imm, dir.
Bureau of Environmental Health; tel. 608/266-2593; Lloyd Riddle, dir.
Bureau of Health Care Financing; tel. 608/266-2522; Tina Nye, dir.
Bureau of Health Statistics; tel. 608/266-1334; Ray Nashold, dir.
Bureau of Correctional Health Services; tel. 608/267-7170; Barbara Whitmore, dir.
Bureau of Planning and Development; tel. 608/266-7384; Judy Fryback, dir.
Bureau of Quality Compliance; tel. 608/267-7185; Larry Tainter, dir.
Includes:
Healthcare Survey Section; tel. 608/266-2460; Kenneth Bjorklund, dir.

INSURANCE: Office of the Commissioner of Insurance, P.O. Box 7873, Madison 53707; tel. 608/266-3585; Thomas P. Fox, comr.

OTHER: Wisconsin Medical Examining Board, 1400 E. Washington Ave., Madison 53702; tel. 608/266-2811; Deanna Zychowski, adm. asst.
Department of Regulation and Licensing, 1400 E. Washington Ave., Rm. 174, P.O. Box 8935, Madison 53708; tel. 608/266-8609; Marlene A. Cummings. sec.
Includes:
Bureau of Health Service Professions; tel. 608/266-3735; Romona Weakland Warden, dir.
State Department of Public Instruction, 125 S. Webster St., P.O. Box 7841, Madison 53707; tel. 608/266-1771; Herbert J. Grover, supt.
Includes:
Division for Handicapped Children and Public Services; tel. 608/266-1649; Victor J. Contrucci, asst. supt.

WYOMING

The Honorable Mike Sullivan, Governor, 307/777-7220.

HEALTH: Department of Health and Social Services, Hathaway Bldg., 2300 Capitol Ave., Cheyenne 82002; tel. 307/777-7656; Sherri Lovercheck, dir.
Includes:
Division of Health and Medical Services; tel. 307/777-7121; Larry Meuli, M.D., adm.
Maternal and Child Health; tel. 307/777-7941; Larry Meuli, M.D., dir.
Crippled Children's Services; tel. 307/777-7948; Stanley Bercich, prog. dir.
Medical Assistance; tel. 307/777-7531; John Harper, dir.
Medical Facilities Services; tel. 307/777-7121; Fred S. Kellow, asst. adm.
Preventive Medicine; tel. 307/777-7951; Harry C. Crawford, M.D., dir.
Division of Health and Medical Facilities; tel. 307/777-7121; Larry Meuli, M.D., dir.

WELFARE: Divison of Public Assistance and Social Services, Hathaway Bldg., Third Flr., Cheyenne 82002; tel. 307/777-7561; Julia Robinson, adm.

OTHER: Wyoming Board of Medical Examiners, Hathaway Bldg., 4th Flr., Cheyenne 82002; tel. 307/777-6463; Lawrence J. Cohen, M.D., exec. sec.
Wyoming State Board of Nursing, Barrett Bldg., 4th Flr., 2301 Central Ave., Cheyenne 82002; tel. 307/777-7601; Joan C. Bouchard, R.N., M.N., exec. dir.
Division of Community Programs, Hathaway Bldg., Cheyenne 82002; tel. 307/777-7115; Steve Zimmerman, adm.
Division of Vocational Rehabilitation, 326 Hathaway Bldg., Cheyenne 82002; tel. 307/777-7385; Robert W. Dingwall, Ed.D., dir.
Wyoming Commission on Aging, Hathaway Bldg., Rm. 139, Cheyenne 82002; tel. 307/777-7986; E. Scott Sessions, dir.

U.S. Associated Areas

GUAM

HEALTH: Department of Public Health and Social Services, Box 2816, Agana 96910; tel. 011-671/734-2083; Leticia V. Espaldon, M.D.
Health Planning and Development Agency, Administration Bldg., Rm. 155, 212 W. Aspinall Ave., Agana 96910; tel. 011-671/472-6831; Aida Z. Fernandez, actg. adm.

WELFARE: Division of Social Services, Box 2816, Agana 96910; tel. 011-671/734-4626; Catherine Illarmo, adm.

OTHER: Department of Vocational Rehabilitation, P.O. Box 2113, Agana 96910; tel. 011-671/646-9468; Angel Luis Jiménez, asst. sec.

PUERTO RICO

HEALTH: Puerto Rico Department of Health, Bldg. A—Medical Center, Call Box 70184, San Juan 00936; Luiz Izquierdo-Mora, sec. hlth.
Includes:
Dental Health, Lourdes Melendez, D.M.O., dir.
Environmental Health, Lic. R. Mayoral, asst. sec.
Family Health, Dr. Castellanos, int. dir.
Administration, Carmen M. Dávila, dir.
Legal Services, Ramon Cancel Negrón, Esq., dir.
Mental Health, Efrén Ramirez, M.D., int. dir.
U.S. Public Health, Anibal Marin, M.D., dir.

WELFARE: Department of Social Services, Box 11398—Fernandez Juncos Sta., San Juan 00910; tel. 809/724-7400; Carmen Sonia Zayas, sec.

OTHER: Vocational Rehabilitation Program, Department of Social Services, Box 1118, Hato Rey 00919; tel. 809/725-1792; Sr. Angel Luis Jiménez, asst. sec.

VIRGIN ISLANDS

HEALTH: Virgin Islands Department of Health, Box 7309, Charlotte Amalie, St. Thomas 00801; tel. 809/774-0117; Roy L. Schneider, M.D., comr.

Includes:

Division of Ambulatory Services, Cora Christian, M.D., asst. comr.

Division of Environmental Health, David Chinnery, field sup.

Division of Hospitals and Medical Services, Lloyd Austin, dep. comr.

Division of Management, Dorothy E. M. Penn, dep. comr.

Division of Mental Health, Alcoholism, and Drug Dependency Services, Patricia A. Todman, Ph.D., dir.

Division of Maternal and Child Health Services, Patricia Adams, dir.

WELFARE: Department of Social Welfare, Box 550, St. Thomas 00801; tel. 809/774-1166; Norman L. Johansen, comr.

OTHER: Vocational Rehabilitation, Department of Social Welfare, Box 550, St. Thomas 00801; tel. 809/774-0930; Sedonie Halbert, dir.

Canada

ALBERTA

HEALTH: Department of Social Services, 424 Legislature Bldg., 109 St. and 97 Ave., Edmonton T5K 2B6; tel. 403/427-2606; Hon. C. E. Osterman

BRITISH COLUMBIA

HEALTH: Ministry of Health, Parliament Bldgs., Victoria V8V 1X4; tel. 604/387-5394; Hon. Peter A. Dueck, min.

MANITOBA

HEALTH: Department of Health, 175 Hargrave St., 7th Flr., Winnipeg R3C 3R8; tel. 204/944-3731; Hon. Laurent Desjardins, min.

OTHER: Department of Manitoba Community Services, Rm. 302, Legislative Bldg., 450 Broadway, Winnipeg R3C 0V8; tel. 204/945-3048; Hon. Muriel Smith, min.

NEW BRUNSWICK

HEALTH: Department of Health and Community Services, Box 5100, Fredericton E3B 5G8; tel. 506/453-2581; Hon. Nancy Clark Teed, min.

NEWFOUNDLAND

HEALTH: Department of Health, Confederation Bldg., St. John's A1C 5T7; tel. 709/576-3124; Hon. Dr. Hugh Twomey, min.

NOVA SCOTIA

HEALTH: Department of Health, Box 488, Halifax B3J 2R8; tel. 902/424-4310; Hon. Ronald S. Russell, C.D.

PRINCE EDWARD ISLAND

HEALTH: Department of Health and Social Services, Sullivan Bldg., 2nd Flr., Box 2000, Charlottetown C1A 7N8; tel. 902/894-4567; Hon. K. Milligan, min.

QUEBEC

HEALTH: Ministry of Health and Social Services, Ministère de la Santé et des Services Sociaux, 1075 Chemin Ste-Foy, 15e étage, Quebec G1S 2M1; tel. 418/643-3160; Madame Therese Lavoie-Roux, min.

SASKATCHEWAN

HEALTH: Department of Health, T. C. Douglas Bldg., 3475 Albert St., Regina S4S 5X5; tel. 306/787-3041; Hon. George McLeod, min.

Statewide Health Coordinating Councils

The following is a list of chairpersons of federally funded statewide health coordinating councils and is accurate as of February, 1987. The information was obtained from the U.S. Department of Health and Human Services, Public Health Service, Health Resources and Services Administration, Office of Health Planning. For information about other state agencies and organizations that fulfill many of the same functions, contact the state or metropolitan hospital associations.

United States

ALABAMA: SHCC, Thurman Turner, chairman, 1320 19th St. S., Birmingham 35205; tel. 205/272-8781

ALASKA: disbanded

ARIZONA: SHCC, Jane Canby, chairperson, 1740 W. Adams, Rm. 312, Phoenix 85007; tel. 602/255-1216

ARKANSAS: SHCC, Orson Berry, director, Arkansas State Health Planning and Development Agency, 4815 W. Markham St., Little Rock 72205; tel. 501/661-2509

CALIFORNIA: disbanded

COLORADO: SHCC, c/o State Health Planning and Development Agency, Patricia Barnett, R.N., chairperson, 4210 E. 11th Ave., Rm. 227, Denver 80220, Attn: Susan Rehak; tel. 303/331-4908

CONNECTICUT: SHCC, John A. Barone, chairman, c/o Dept. of Health Services, Division of Health Planning, 150 Washington St., Hartford 06106; tel. 203/566-7886

DELAWARE: SHCC, State Health Planning and Development Agency, Bureau of Health Planning and Resource Development, Henry S. Redmile, chairperson, 802 Silver Lake Blvd., Robbins Bldg., P.O. Box 637, Dover 19011; tel. 302/736-4776

DISTRICT OF COLUMBIA: SHCC, c/o State Health Planning and Development Agency, Douglas Gentry, chairman, 1331 H St., N.W., Washington 20005; tel. 202/727-0744

FLORIDA: SHCC, George A. Schmidt, staff director, 2723 Blairstone Lane, Tallahassee 32301; tel. 902/487-3706

GEORGIA: State Health Policy, Douglas Skelton, M.D., chairman, 4 Executive Park Dr., N.E., Suite 2100, Atlanta 30329; tel. 404/325-8939

HAWAII: SHCC, c/o State Health Planning and Development Agency, Patrick J. Boland, chairman, P.O. Box 3378, Honolulu 96801; tel. 808/548-4050

IDAHO: disbanded

ILLINOIS: Office of Health Planning, B. Smith Hopkins, M.D., 535 W. Jefferson St., Springfield 62761

INDIANA: disbanded

IOWA: SHCC, Edward R. Lynn, chairman, Jennie Edmundson Hospital, 933 E. Pierce St., Council Bluffs 51501; tel. 712/328-6222

KANSAS: disbanded

KENTUCKY: SHCC, Robert O. Miller, chairman, 201 S. 5th St., Murray 42071; tel. 502/753-3312

LOUISIANA: SHCC, c/o Bureau of Health Planning, Fran Bussie, chairperson, 200 Lafayette St., Suite 406, Baton Rouge 70801; tel. 504/342-2001

MAINE: Statewide Health Coordinating Council, Maine State Health Coordinating Council, c/o Office of Health Planning and Development, Daniel Willett, chairperson, 151 Capitol St., Augusta 04333; tel. 207/289-2716

MARYLAND: SHCC, c/o Maryland Health Resources Planning Commission, James Stanton, exec. dir., 201 West Preston St., Baltimore 21201; tel. 301/225-5141

MASSACHUSETTS: SHCC, Executive Office of Human Services, Office of Health Policy, Steven Gringale, chairman, One Ashburton Pl., Rm. 1109, Boston 02108; tel. 517/335-1545

MICHIGAN: SHCC, Office of Health and Medical Affairs, Sandra Miner, chairperson, Lewis Cass Building, P.O. Box 30026, Lansing 48909; tel. 517/335-1545

MINNESOTA: SHCC, State Square Bldg., 550 Cedar St., Rm. 200, St. Paul 55101

MISSISSIPPI: SHCC, Helen Barnes, M.D., chairperson, P.O. Box 1700, Jackson 39215-1700

MISSOURI: SHCC, c/o State Health Planning and Development Agency, Bill Wilson, chairman, 1738 E. Elm St., Jefferson City 65101

MONTANA: SHCC, Mark B. Listeurd, M.D., chairman, P.O. Box 937, Wolf Point 59201; tel. 406/444-3121

NEBRASKA: SHCC, Floyd Vrtiska, chairman, P.O. Box 194, Table Rock 68447; tel. 402/471-2337

NEVADA: Marvin Sedway, O.D., 505 King St., Rm. 605, Carson City 89710

NEW HAMPSHIRE: disbanded

NEW JERSEY: SHCC, New Jersey State Department of Health, Health/Agriculture Bldg., Ralph Dean, chairman, C.N. 360, Trenton 08625; tel. 609/292-9382

NEW MEXICO: SHCC, Sandy Shauer, chairperson, P.O. Box 1054, Los Lunas 87031; tel. 505/865-9420

NEW YORK: SHCC, c/o State Health Planning and Development Agency, Ralph Rohrdanz, chairman, New York State Dept. of Health Tower Bldg., Rm. 1614, Empire State Plaza, Albany 12237; tel. 518/474-3192

NORTH CAROLINA: SHCC, Howard Strawcutter, M.D., chairman, Vice-President of Medical Affairs, Southeastern General Hospital, P.O. Box 1408, 300 W. 27th St., Lumberton 28359; tel. 919/738-6444, ext. 7289

NORTH DAKOTA: disbanded

OHIO: SHCC, Don Brezine, chairman, Office of Planning and Information, 7th flr., 246 N. High St., P.O. Box 118, Columbus 43266-0118; tel. 512/458-7261

OKLAHOMA: disbanded

OREGON: Oregon Health Council, Dr. Dorin Daniels, chairman, 1980 Calaggett, Ontario 97914; tel. 503/889-9121

PENNSYLVANIA: SHCC, c/o Division of Planning and Technical Assistance, Rm. 1020, P.O. Box 90, Harrisburg 17108; tel. 717/783-1410

RHODE ISLAND: disbanded

SOUTH CAROLINA: SHCC, Edwin R. Mohrmann, chairman, P.O. Box 8206, 1801 Main St., Columbia 29202

SOUTH DAKOTA: disbanded

TENNESSEE: disbanded

TEXAS: SHCC, Dr. Marion Zetzman, chairperson, Texas Dept. of Health, 1100 W. 49th St., Austin 78756; tel. 512/458-7261

UTAH: SHCC, John Florez, chairperson, 207 Park Building, University of Utah, Salt Lake City 84112; tel. 801/581-8365

VERMONT: SHCC, Alan Hark, chairman, P.O. Box 61, Hyde Park 05655; tel. 802/223-6377

VIRGINIA: SHCC, Ronald A. Allison, chairperson, P.O. Box 810, Cedar Bluff 24609; tel. 703/964-6702

WASHINGTON: State Health Coordinating Council, Dan Rubin, actg. exec. dir., 12th & Franklin OB-38, Olympia 98504-0095; tel. 206/753-9659

WEST VIRGINIA: SHCC, State Health Planning and Development Agency, Robert Hall, Ph.D., chairman, 100 Dee Drive, Charleston 25311; tel. 304/343-3701

WISCONSIN: Governor's Health Policy Council, Harold C. Ristow, chairperson, P.O. Box 309, Madison 53701; tel. 608/267-2173

WYOMING: SHCC, Dr. James A. Boucher, O.D., chairperson, P.O. Box 927, Laramie 82070; tel. 307/742-8159

U.S. Associated Areas

AMERICAN SAMOA: Tagoai Matagiese Tunoa, L.B.J. Charles McCludin, hospital-exec. dir., Tropical Medical Center, Pago Pago 96799; tel. 684/633-5743

GUAM: Carmen L. G. Pearson, Administration Bldg., #155, 212 W. Aspinall, Agana 96910

NORTHERN MARIANA ISLANDS: Jose Villagomex, O.F.M., exec. dir., Box 570, Saipan 96950; tel. 234/7122/23

PUERTO RICO: Frank Fornier, Department of Health, Edificio A. Hospital De Psiquiatria, Rio Piedras 00936

TRUST TERRITORY: Minoru Ueki, M.O., Office of the High Commissioner, Trust Territory of the Pacific Islands, Saipan, Mariana Islands 96950

VIRGIN ISLANDS: Leona Bryant, Virgin Islands State Agency, Department of Health, Box 1442, Charlotte Amalie 00801

Health Care Coalitions

The following list of health care coalitions is correct as of April 1986. The information was obtained from the annual survey of coalitions conducted by the American Hospital Association's Office of Health Coalitions and Private Sector Initiatives on behalf of the Group of Six. The Group of Six is comprised of the American Federation of Labor–Congress of Industrial Organizations, American Hospital Association, American Medical Association, Blue Cross and Blue Shield Association, Business Roundtable, Health Insurance Association of America.

ALABAMA: Birmingham Business Coalition, c/o Commerce Center, 2027 1st Avenue North, P.O. Box 10127, Birmingham 35202; tel. 205/945-6500; Keith Carder, chm.
Madison County Medical Society Health/Industry Coalition, 2325 Pansy Street, Suite F, Huntsville 35801; tel. 205/539-7670; Sue Kaczmarek, adm. asst.
Mobile Business Group on Health, c/o Teledyne Continental Motors, P.O. Box 90, Mobile 36601; tel. 205/438-3411 x204; Ken C. Oehler, chm.
Alabama Association to Control Medical Cost, P.O. Box 366, Montgomery 36101; tel. 205/262-6832; Fred C. Crawford, pres.

ALASKA: Alaska Health Cost Management Coalition, 200 West 34th Avenue, Suite 410, Anchorage 99503; tel. 907/276-4334; Richard D. Rubin, pres.

ARIZONA: Greater Phoenix Affordable Health Care Foundation, 326 East Coronado, Suite 201, Phoenix 85004; tel. 602/252-5890; Carol Lockhart, exec. dir.
Tucson Program for Affordable Health Care, 149 North Stone, Suite 404, Tucson 85745; tel. 602/623-5733; Phillip M. Lopes, staff

ARKANSAS: Arkansas Business Health Coalition, 15 Nob View Circle, Little Rock 72205; tel. 501/568-4010 x314; Joe C. Slater, actg. pres.

CALIFORNIA: Kern Coalition for Health Care Cost Containment, P.O. Box 259, Bakersfield 93302; tel. 805/327-5981; Mary Jo Pasek, pres.
San Diego Employers Health Cost Coalition, c/o Rohr Industries, P.O. Box 878, Chula Vista 92012; tel. 619/691-2923; Susan Ebel, chm.
Contra Costa Health Coalition, P.O. Box 6417, Concord 94524; tel. 415/687-8663; Barbara Branson, vice-pres.
Diablo Valley Health Cost Alliance, P.O. Box M, Concord 94524; tel. 415/827-6696; Dennis Kohlmeyer, chm.
Fresno Coalition for Health Care Cost Containment, 2650 West Shaw, Suite 102, Fresno 93711; tel. 209/436-1133; James A. Kelley, former pres.
Employers Health Care Coalition of Greater Los Angeles, One Space Park, Building E, Room 4000, Redondo Beach 90278; tel. 213/536-4013; Patricia Dempster, chm.
Inland Empire Health Care Coalition, c/o Bourns, Inc., P.O. Box 5100, Riverside 92517; tel. 714/781-5060; Shelley Morgan
Health Policy Committee, California Chamber of Commerce, P.O. Box 1736, Sacramento 95808; tel. 415/444-6670; Nancy J. Sullivan, mgr., Insur. & Empl. Ben.
Community Care Network/San Diego Community Healthcare Alliance, 9265 Skypark Court, Suite 200, San Diego 92123; tel. 619/278-CARE; George Murphy, pres.
California Council of Employer Health Care Coalitions, c/o Bank of America, 180 Montgomery St., 24th Flr., San Francisco 94104; tel. 415/622-1113; Clark E. Kerr, pres.
San Francisco Bay Area Employers Group on Health, c/o Shaklee Corp T-311, 444 Market Street, San Francisco 94111; 415/954-2574; Allison Witzel, chm.
Santa Clara County Manufacturing Group Health Cost Containment Committee, 2900 Semiconductor Drive, M.S. 30-110, Santa Clara 95051; tel. 408/749-7557; Les R. Schlaegel, sec./treas.
Tulare County Coalition, Education Building, Visalia 93291; tel. 209/733-6601; Ken Hochnadel, pres.

COLORADO: Colorado Business Coalition for Health, 3300 East First Avenue, Suite 490, Denver 80206; tel. 303/333-7300; Winfred O. Jacobs, pres.
Northern Colorado Health Care Coalition, P.O. Box 1519, Fort Collins 80522; tel. 303/482-5811; Arvid R. Bloom, pres.

CONNECTICUT: South Central Connecticut Health Care Coalition, c/o Embart Corporation, 225 Episcopal Road, Berlin 06037; tel. 203/225-7411 x449; Raymond W. Neiman, sec./treas.
Fairfield/Westchester Business Group on Health, 280 Railroad Avenue, Greenwich 06830; tel. 203/629-1050; Joan Troy, exec. dir.
Business Coalition on Health, 999 Asylum Avenue, Hartford 06105; tel. 203/247-9753; Ralph S. Pollock, exec. dir.

DELAWARE: Delaware Health Care Coalition, P.O. Box 4297, Wilmington 19807; tel. 302/674-6499; Patrick C. Donahue, chm.

DISTRICT OF COLUMBIA: Illinois Health Care Coalition, c/o HIAA, 1025 Connecticut Avenue, N.W., Washington 20036; tel. 202/223-7836; Joel E. Miller, dir.
National Capital Area Health Care Coalition, Suite 500, 1201 Pennsylvania Avenue, N.W., Washington 20006; tel. 202/626-6813; Dindy K. Weinstein, exec. dir.

FLORIDA: North Central Florida Business/Health Care Coalition, 11 West University Avenue, Suite 7, Gainesville 32601; tel. 904/377-4404; Carol Brady, coord.
Jacksonville Health Care Cost Containment Coalition, c/o Chamber of Commerce, P.O. Box 329, Jacksonville 32201; tel. 904/353-0300; James Saffell
Employers Health Care Group of Polk County, P.O. Box 6665, Lakeland 33807; tel. 813/647-1712; David Kribs, adm.
Florida Health Coalition (formerly South Florida Health Action Coalition), 7925 N.W. 12th Street, Suite 330, Miami 33126; tel. 305/592-4936; Stephen White, Ph.D., exec. dir.
Central Florida Health Care Coalition, 223 Pasadena Place, Orlando 32803; tel. 305/648-4657; Marilyn Bell, exec. dir.
Northwest Florida Management Coalition for Health Care Cost Containment, c/o John Appleyard Agency, Inc., P.O. Box 1902, Pensacola 32589; tel. 904/432-8396; John Appleyard
West Coast Healthcare Coalition, 6637 Superior Ave., Suite C, Sarasota 33581; tel. 813/923-1697; Eugene S. Piatek, DPA, exec. dir.
Bay Area Group on Health, P.O. Box 1049, St. Petersburg 33731; tel. 813/576-7772; Steven H. Newhouse, pres.
Florida Business-Health Coalitions Assn., P.O. Box 3449, Tampa 33679; tel. 813/273-0252; Frank M. Brocato, actg. pres.
Hillsborough Coalition for Health, P.O. Box 3449, Tampa 33629; tel. 813/273-0252; Frank M. Brocato, exec. dir.

GEORGIA: Medical/Business Coalition, c/o Chamber of Commerce, Albany 31706; tel. 912/883-6900; Sally Anderson
Greater Atlanta Coalition on Health Care, Suite 552, 1718 Peachtree Street, N.W., Atlanta 30309-2405; tel. 404/875-5300; Walker McCune, exec. dir.
Columbus (Georgia) Health Care Coalition, P.O. Box 1995, Columbus 31902; tel. 404/322-8297; Claude N. Kent, consult.
Hall County Area Health Care Alliance, c/o Fleming Weaver, Chicopee, P.O. Box 2537, Gainesville 30503; tel. 404/532-3161; R. Fleming Weaver, chm.
LaGrange Area Health Care Coalition, c/o Hanes Hosiery, 120 Cooley Industrial Way, LaGrange 30240; tel. 404/884-2700; Roger Orange, chm.
Macon Area Employers Health Care Coalition Limited, P.O. Box 4288, Macon 31213; tel. 912/781-6661; Gary Hinebaugh, pres.
Rome Area Health Care Coalition, c/o Georgia Kraft Company, P.O. Box 1551, Rome 30161; tel. 404/291-6920; L. Frank Thomson, exec. dir.
Association of Georgia Health Care Coalitions, 214 East Factors Walk, Savannah 31401; tel. 912/232-3346; Ewing Barnett
Savannah Business Group on Health Care Cost Management, 214 East Factors Walk, Savannah 31401; tel. 912/232-3346; E. S. Barnett

HAWAII: Hawaii Business Health Council, P.O. Box 3440, Honolulu 96801; tel. 808/525-6684; Fred Fleischmann, chm.

IDAHO: Employer's Health Coalition of Idaho (formerly Treasure Valley Health Care), P.O. Box 8868, Boise 83707; tel. 208/336-1660; Jim Rand, chm.
Major Employers Health Cost Containment Coalition, c/o FMC, P.O. Box 4111, Pocatello 83202; tel. 208/236-8253; Richard M. Scott, chm.

ILLINOIS: Chicago Health Economics Council, Suite 320A, 6160 North Cicero, Chicago 60646; tel. 312/282-8313; Joseph N. Mohr, exec. dir.
Metropolitan Chicago Labor Health Care Council, 201 North Wells Street, Suite 1730, Chicago 60606; tel. 312/236-5511; Ray Kull, pres.
Midwest Business Group on Health, 8303 West Higgins Road, Suite 200, Chicago 60631; tel. 312/380-9090; James D. Mortimer, pres.
Business Health Roundtable, P.O. Box 1031, Decatur 62525; tel. 217/422-2200; R. Joan Stewart, chamber liaison
Joliet Area Health Care Coalition, 3033 North Jefferson Street, Joliet 60434; tel. 815/744-5676; Ronald W. Batozech
Employers' Health Care Group of Lake County, P.O. Box 655, Mundelein 60060; tel. 312/949-7730; Arthur F. Vyse III, exec. dir.
Central Illinois Coalition on Healthcare, 5407 North University, Peoria 61614; tel. 309/692-7666; Larry Newell, pres.
Iowa-Illinois Health Care Alliance, 1702 2nd Avenue, Plaza Office Building, Ste. 607, Rock Island 61201; tel. 309/793-4107; Ruth J. Lee, exec. dir.
Rockford Council for Affordable Health Care, 5732 East Riverside Boulevard, Rockford 61111; tel. 815/654-0210; Johanna M. Lund, pres. & exec. dir.
Sangamon County Health Care Coalition, c/o WCIHSA, 412 Myers Bldg., Springfield 62701; tel. 217/544-3412; Roger Ricketts

INDIANA: Anderson Chamber of Commerce/Health Care Coalition, P.O. Box 469, Anderson 46015; tel. 317/642-0264; George D. Dohertye, coalition chm.
Evansville Area Health Care Coalition, 123 Northwest 4th, 417, Evansville 47708; tel. 812/424-8397, Linda G. Owen, dir.
Northeast Indiana Business Group on Health, P.O. Box 11825, Fort Wayne 46861; tel. 219/744-3476, Herman J. Rutkowski, sec. & exec. dir.
Three Rivers Health Planning Coalition, P.O. Box 11828, Fort Wayne 46861; tel. 219/637-5294; Paul Schirmeyer, exec. dir.
Northwest Indiana Business Group on Health, 8149 Kennedy Avenue, Highland 46322; tel. 219/838-3280, Robert E. Montgomery II, staff coord.
Central Indiana Business Group on Health, c/o Shirley Bales, 307 North Pennsylvania, Indianapolis 46204; tel. 317/633-9302; Shirley A. Bales, pres.
Indiana Business-Medicine Coalition, 3935 North Meridian, Indianapolis 46208; tel. 317/925-7545; Michael Huntley, staff
Marion County Medical Society, Medicine/Business Coalition, Suite 202, 211 North Delaware Street, Indianapolis 46204; tel. 317/639-3406; Lori A. Norris, asst. exec. dir.
Greater Lafayette Health Care Cost Group, c/o Arnett Clinic, 2600 Greenbush Street, Lafayette 47902; tel. 317/448-8000; Richard T. McPherson, M.D., chm., Exec. Comm.
Delaware-Blackford County Chapter, Indiana Business/Medicine Coalition, 223 North Cole Street, Muncie 47303; tel. 317/282-7595; Jack Moore, M.D.

IOWA: Employers Health Association, P.O. Box 2936, Cedar Rapids 52406; tel. 319/395-2147; Larry F. Milroy, chm.
Central Iowa Health Association, Suite 330, Two Ruan Center, Des Moines 50265; tel. 515/244-12ll; coord.
Health Policy Corporation of Iowa, Suite 330, Two Ruan Center, Des Moines 50265; tel. 515/244-1211; Paul M. Pietzsch, pres.
Iowa Business Labor Coalition on Health, c/o Health Policy Corp., Suite 330, Two Ruan Center, Des Moines 50265; tel. 515/244-1211; coord.

KANSAS: Community Programs for Affordable Health Care (CPAHC), 1500 SW Tenth Avenue, Topeka 66604; tel. 913/354-5845; Scott Buckley, asst. dir.
Health Care Cost Containment, 4101 Southgate Drive, P.O. Box 5168, Topeka 66605; tel. 816/361-1212; Fred J. Atchity, treas.
Kansas Employer Coalition on Health, 1271 Harrison Street, Topeka 66612; tel. 913/233-0351; Jim Schwartz, cnsltg. dir.
The Sedgwick County Health Care Cost Containment Roundtable, 929 N. St. Francis, Wichita 67214; tel. 316/268-5118; Bruce Carmichael, chm.

LOUISIANA: Greater Baton Rouge Health Care Alliance, 5215 Essen Lane, Suite 6, Baton Rouge 70809; 504/766-7767; Kerry Everitt, exec. dir.
Health Care Coalition-Monroe-West, P.O. Box 2884, Monroe 71207; tel. 318/388-1292; Phala M. Wright, dir.
Southeast Louisiana Health Cost Management (SLHCM), 1440 Canal Street, Suite 1704, New Orleans 70112; tel. 504/529-1116; Linda M. Lambert, exec. dir.

Shreveport Coalition for Medical Cost Containment, P.O. Box 3188, Shreveport 71133; tel. 318/631-7306; David Werner, chm.

MARYLAND: Maryland Health Care Coalition, P.O. Box 148, Oxon Hill 20745; tel. 703/799-4850; Robert H. Davis, Ph.D., mng. dir.

MASSACHUSETTS: Health Action Forum of Greater Boston, c/o Frank B. Hall & Co., 89 Broad Street, Boston 02110; tel. 617/482-3100 x321; James Hooley, pres.

Massachusetts Health Care Coalition, c/o Massachusetts Business Roundtable, 250 Boylston Street, Boston 02116; tel. 617/267-0881; Paula Griswald, dir., Health Care Policy

Merrimack Valley Business Group on Health, c/o Wang Laboratories, Inc., M.S. 011-200, Lowell 01851; tel. 617/967-4034; Frank Gallo, chm.

Southeastern Massachusetts Health Care Coalition, 49 North Main Street, P.O. Box 70, Middleboro 02346; tel. 617/947-6300; John H. Wells, exec. dir.

Greater Springfield Health Care Coalition, 1500 Main Street, 600 Bay State West Plaza, Springfield 01115; tel. 413/567-3727; A. C. Brown, dir.

Central Massachusetts Business Group on Health, c/o Wm. McGovern, Norton Co., 120 Front Street, Worcester 01608-1446; tel. 617/795-5861; William McGovern, The Norton Company, chm.

Worcester Area Systems for Affordable Health Care, 950 Main Street, Worcester 01610; tel. 617/793-7696; Robert Bradbury, Ph.D., exec. dir.

Worcester Medicine—Business Coalition, Mechanics Hall, 321 Main Street, Worcester 01608; tel. 617/753-1579; Charlotte Wilder, exec. sec.

MICHIGAN: West Michigan Business Group on Health, c/o Amway Corporation, 7575 East Fulton Road, Ada 49355; tel. 616/676-6878; Tom Cole

Greater Detroit Area Health Council, 1900 Book Building, Detroit 48226; tel. 313/963-4990; Robert Tell, dpty. exec. dir.

Kalamazoo Employer Health Care Coalition, c/o The Upjohn Company, 7000 Portage Road, Kalamazoo 49001; tel. 616/323-5532; Paul M. Millholland, chm.

MINNESOTA: Minnesota Coalition on Health, Suite 440, 2221 University Avenue, S.E., Minneapolis 55414; tel. 612/623-3384; Carol Hough, exec. sec.

MISSOURI: Mid-America Coalition on Health Care, One West Armour Boulevard, Suite 202, Kansas City 64111; tel. 816/531-6550; Forrest D. Brown, exec. dir.

Mid-Missouri Business Health Coalition, P.O. Box 391, Mexico 65265; tel. 314/682-8284; Blair J. Smith, sec.

Ozarks Medicine/Business Coalition, 1200 East Woodhurst Drive, D-200, Springfield 65804; tel. 417/887-1017; Michael S. Clarke, M.D., chm.

St. Louis Area Business Health Coalition, 77 West Port Plaza, Suite 561, St. Louis 63146; tel. 314/576-4090; James C. Stutz, exec. dir.

Jackson Health Care Coalition, 201 South President Street, Jackson 39201; tel. 601/948-7575; Ellis M. Moffitt, M.D.

MONTANA: Health Care Cost Containment Advisory Council, c/o Governor's Office, State Capitol, Helena 59620; tel. 406/444-3111; J. Michael Pichette, chm.

NEBRASKA: Omaha Cost Containment Coalition, 9001 Arbor, Suite 207, Omaha 68124; tel. 402/633-4647; Wm. G. Woodhams, exec. dir.

NEVADA: Northern Nevada Employers' Health Cost Coalition, P. O. Box 21106, Reno 89515-1106; tel. 702/788-6370; Adeline L. Hageman, pres.

NEW HAMPSHIRE: Health Care Cost Management Committee of BIA, Business and Industry Ass'n., 23 School Street, Concord 03301; tel. 603/224-5388; Yvonne L. Nanasi, prog. mgr.

Valley Health Care Coalition, 127 Mascoma Street, Lebanon 03766; tel. 603/448-3774; Lindsay Huppe, adm.

NEW JERSEY: New Jersey Business Group on Health, 855 Valley Road, Suite 1000, Clifton 07013; tel. 201/472-0780; Allison A. Alkire, pres.

NEW MEXICO: Medicine/Business Coalition of New Mexico, 2400 Louisiana NE., Bldg. 1, Suite 306, Albuquerque 87110; tel. 505/884-2747; Robert J. Hoffman, exec. dir.

NEW YORK: Tri-County Business Roundtable, c/o NY-Penn Health Systems Agency, 306 Press Bldg., 19 Chenango Street, Binghamton 13905; tel. 607/722-3445; Ann Bachrach, tech. asst.

Two Rivers Health Management Association, c/o John Riley, 14 McNamara Avenue, Binghamton 13903; tel. 607/723-2818; John Riley, pres.

Southern Tier Health Management Corp., 175 Grand Central Avenue, Elmira Heights 14903; tel. 607/734-1574; Linda Couchon, asst. dir., J.E.T.

Finger Lakes Area Hospitals' Corporation, One Franklin Square, Geneva 14456; tel. 315/789-7633; James R. Furey, exec. dir.

Medicine/Business Coalition of New York State, 420 Lakeville Road, P.O. Box 5404, Lake Success 11042; tel. 516/488-6100 x237; Ed Hynes, staff dir.

New York Business Group on Health, 622 Third Avenue, 34th Floor, New York 10017; tel. 212/808-0550; Leon J. Warshaw, M.D., exec. dir.

New York City Committee for Affordable Health Care, 61 West 62nd Street, New York 10024; tel. 212/246-7100; Holly Michaels Fisher, prog. dir.

Rochester Area Hospitals Corporation, 220 Alexander Street, Suite 608, Rochester 14607; tel. 716/546-3280; Sara E. Hartman, vice-pres., Planning

Health Care Action Council, c/o Metro. Development Assn., 1900 State Tower Building, Syracuse 13202; tel. 315/422-8284; Albert A. Bingham, chm.

Mohawk Valley Business and Industry Health Care Coalition, P.O. Box 524, Utica 13501; tel. 315/793-7492; Edward D. Peterson, pres.

NORTH CAROLINA: Council on Health Costs, Suite 906, 1012 Kings Drive, Charlotte 28283; tel. 704/334-7656; George M. Stiles, Jr., exec. dir.

Business/Medical Coalition, Durham Chamber of Commerce, 4019 N. Roxboro, Durham 27704; tel. 919/479-5612; Wallace E. Cole, liasion

Guilford County Health Care Coalition, Cone Mills Corp., 1201 Maple Street, Greensboro 27410; tel. 719/379-6173; H. F. Butler, chm.

Pitt-Greenville Health Care Coalition, East Carolina University School of Medicine, Department of Pediatrics, Greenville 27834; tel. 919/757-2540; Jon B. Tingelstad, M.D., co-chm.

Unifour Business Medical Coalition, P.O. Box 3584, Hickory 28603-3584; tel. 704/324-9716; Charles N. Burger, exec. dir.

Scotland County Business Health Care Coalition, c/o Cardinal Health Agency, 401 East 11th Street, East, Lumberton 28358; tel. 919/738-9316; Glenn Parriash, chm.

Committee on Cost Effective Medical Care, P.O. Box 27167, Raleigh 27611; tel. 919/833-3836; Harriet Kestenbaum

Forsyth Medicine/Business Coalition, 1401-D Old Mill Circle, Winston-Salem 27103; tel. 919/760-1234; James T. Robinson, exec. dir.

NORTH DAKOTA: North Dakota Employer Health Care Group, P. O. Box 1951, Fargo 58107; tel. 701/237-4787; Lloyd Jackson, member (coord. member)

OHIO: Ashtabula County Health Action Council, 1315 West 47th Street, P.O. Box 675, Ashtabula 44004; tel. 216/997-5851; Doy Gillespie, chm.

Stark County Health Care Coalition, 1700 Gateway Boulevard, S.E., Canton 44707; tel. 216/453-4677; Martha L. DuShaw, Ph.D., exec. dir.

Greater Cincinnati Health Care Coalition, c/o General Electric Company, C-63, 1 Neuman Way, P.O. Box 156301, Cincinnati 45215; tel. 513/243-6188; Charles T. Ohmer, pres.

Greater Cleveland Coalition on Health Care Cost Effectiveness, 2828 Euclid Avenue, Cleveland 44115; tel. 216/781-6547; Alberta Johnson, chm.

Health Action Council of Northeast Ohio, P.O. Box 39008, Cleveland 44139; tel. 216/248-2559; Donald C. Flagg, actg. exec. dir.

Coalition for Cost Effective Health Services, 285 East Main Street, Columbus 43215; tel. 614/221-1381; Grant A. Drennen, int. exec. dir.

Ohio Health Action Council, c/o Ohio Manufacturer's Assn., 100 East Broad Street, Columbus 43215; tel. 614/224-1722; Mark W. Uher

Miami Valley Health Care Coalition, 40 South Perry Street, Suite 107, Dayton 45402; tel. 513/461-0541; Robert M. Whalen, exec. dir.

Mad River Valley Health Care Coalition, 406 BancOhio Building, 4 West Main Street, Springfield 45502; tel. 513/323-6313; Faye M. Flack, exec. dir.

Toledo Business Coalition on Health Care, 136 North Summit Street, Fort Industry Square, Toledo 43604; tel. 419/244-0036; Dick Hanley, consult./adv.

OKLAHOMA: Tulsa Business Health Group, 616 South Boston, Tulsa 74119; tel. 918/585-1201; Donald W. Underwood, exec. dir.

OREGON: Greater Portland Business Group on Health, 221 NW 2nd Avenue, Portland 97209; tel. 503/228-9411; Richard A. Rix, exec. dir.

Oregon Business Health Care Coalition, P.O. Box 974, Salem 97308; tel. 503/623-8321, Gloria English, pres.

PENNSYLVANIA: Northeast Pennsylvania Business Council on Health Care, WARM Building, Avoca 18641; tel. 717/457-5406; George E. Kauffman, exec. dir.

Erie Business Coalition for Health Care Cost Containment, 3537 West 12th Street, Erie 16505; tel. 814/838-8383; Arlene P. Simmons, exec. dir.

Johnstown Business Council on Health Care, 567 Central Avenue, Johnstown 15902; tel. 814/536-4167; Robert D. Krizner, adm. mgr.

Lancaster County Business Group on Health, P.O. Box 1558, Lancaster 17603; tel. 717/397-3531; Sally Halbleib, coord.

Lehigh Valley Business Conference on Health Care, P.O. Box 6001, Lehigh Valley 18001; tel. 215/868-0990; Charles K. MacKay, pres.

Health Care Alliance, P.O. Box 714, New Cumberland 17070; tel. 717/272-1840; Thomas S. Longenecker, exec. dir.

Joint Health Cost Containment Program/PENJERDEL, 1346 Chestnut Street, Suite 800, Philadelphia 19107; tel. 215/545-1234; Gerald Gleeson

Philadelphia Area Committee on Health Care Costs, 1333 Chestnut Street, Philadelphia 19107; tel. 215/448-5707; Thomas McElvogue, staff

Task Force on Health Care Coalitions, c/o Philadelphia County Medical Society, 2100 Spring Garden Street, Philadelphia 19038; tel. 215/563-5343; John Trevi, exec. dir.

Pittsburgh Business Group on Health, c/o Allegheny Conference on Comm. Dvlpmt., 600 Grant Street, Suite 4444, Pittsburgh 15219; tel. 412/281-1890; Richard D. Ekstrom, chm.

Pittsburgh Program for Affordable Health Care, Suite 4444, 600 Grant Street, Pittsburgh 15219; tel. 412/281-1890; Charles C. Robb, prog. mgr.

RHODE ISLAND: Rhode Island Business Group on Health, 222 Richmond Street, Suite 235, Providence 02903; tel. 401/751-7170; F. Richard Burdett, exec. dir.

SOUTH CAROLINA: Midlands Employer Health Council, Suite 2392, 989 Knox Abbott Drive, Columbia 29202; tel. 803/794-5208; Betty McWhorter, exec. dir.

Coastal Plains Business Group on Health, P.O. Box 5353, Florence 29502; tel. 803/669-1347; Glenn Lane, vol. staff

Florence Area Industry-Health Care Coalition/McLeod Regional Medical Center, P.O. Box F-8700, Florence 29501; tel. 803/667-2297; Charles H. Frenzel, chm.

Catawba Employer's Health Council, P.O. Box 70, Fort Mill 29715; tel. 803/547-2901 x404; J. Kevin Gill, chm.

Southern Piedmont Employers Health Council, c/o Spring Industries, Inc., P.O. Box 70, Fort Mill 29715; tel. 803/547-2901; Kevin Gill, actg. chm.

Piedmont Region Business Group on Health, P.O. Box 6708, Greenville 29606; tel. 803/242-1895; James F. Keasler, staff

Upper Savannah Businessmen's Group on Health Care, Box 3516, Greenwood 29648; tel. 803/229-2744; Donald E. Matthieu, sec.

Orangeburg Area Coalition on Health, 3000 Saint Matthews Road, Orangeburg 29115; tel. 803/533-2463; Robert E. Waters, coord.

Piedmont Medical Center Health Care Coalition, 222 South Herlong Road, Rock Hill 29730; tel. 803/329-1234; Morris Maple, chm.

Trident Industrial Health Coalition, P.O. Drawer 1946, Summerville 29484; tel. 803/871-0350; Phyllis Malchano, vol. staff

TENNESSEE: Chattanooga Area Healthcare Coalition, 1103 Maclellan Building, Chattanooga 37402; tel. 615/265-1044; Harold H. Winters, exec. dir.

Chattanooga Task Force on Health Care Costs, c/o Provident Life & Accident, Fountain Square, Chattanooga 37402; tel. 615/755-1836; Sanford M. Barth, resource/staff

Cleveland Associated Industries, P.O. Box 212, Cleveland 37364-0212; tel. 615/472-1566; David Germain, mng. dir.

Sumner County Health Care Coalition, c/o Donnelley Printing Co., 801 Steam Plant Road, Gallatin 37066; tel. 615/452-5170; Dwight Leimenstoll, chm.

Kingsport Area Business Council on Health Care, P.O. Box 3786, Kingsport 37664; tel. 615/229-6575; Rob Johnson, chm., Cost Containment Comm.

Knox Area Health Care Committee, c/o Greater Knoxville C.C., 301 Church Avenue, Knoxville 37902; tel. 615/632-4550; David R. Evans, chm.

Blount Health Care Coalition, 309 South Washington Street, Maryville 37801; tel. 615/983-2241; Bobbie Householder, sec./treas.

Memphis Business Group on Health, 2714 Union Extended, Suite 200, Memphis 38112; tel. 901/323-1808; Gordon C. Smith, exec. dir.

Memphis Health Care Coalition, 6264 Poplar, Memphis 38119; tel. 901/761-0200; Michael Cates, staff

Morristown Health Services Association, 1600 East Andrew Johnson Hwy., Suite 4, Morristown 37814; tel. 616/584-4422; Debra C. Sudheimer, exec. dir.

Tennessee Business Healthcare Coalition, 500 Interstate Blvd., South, Nashville 37210; tel. 615/256-8240; Lamar F. Jackson, Jr., staff liaison

TEXAS: Amarillo Business/Medicine Health Care Coalition, P.O. Box 1261, Amarillo 79170; tel. 806/378-2916; Larry Higgins, chm.

Austin Area Coalition for Health Action, P.O. Box 9948, Austin 78766; tel. 512/454-4797; James L. Grey, pres.

Texas Business Group on Health, P.O. Box 619616, MD3L47, DFW Airport 75261; tel. 815/355-3480; Barbara Channell

Golden Triangle Business Group on Health, P.O. Box 5827, Beaumount 77706; tel. 409/839-3300; D. A. Schelp, pres.

Dallas Business Group on Health, c/o Texas Instruments, P.O. Box 225474, M.S. 217, Dallas 75265; tel. 214/995-5263; Raymond L. Brooks, pres.

Tarrant Employers Health Action Group, c/o Gearhart Industries, P.O. Box 1936, Fort Worth 76101; tel. 817/293-1300; Anita Dale, pres.

Houston Area Health Care Coalition, 1535 W. Loop South, Suite 322, Houston 77027; tel. 713/963-8983; Sandra S. Person, exec. dir.

San Antonio Employers Alliance for Employee Benefits, P.O. Box 28510, San Antonio 78284; tel. 512/522-2962; Lorraine Eubanks, pres.

Smith County Business/Medicine Coalition, P.O. Box 130848, Tyler 75701-0848; tel. 214/593-7058; Louree Alexander, staff

Crossroads Health Care Coalition, c/o E. I. DuPont, P.O. Box 2626, Victoria 77902; tel. 512/572-1217; Janet Kutchka, state rep.

UTAH: Personnel Association of Central Utah/Utah Valley Advisory Coalition for Health, P.O. Box 390, Provo 84603; tel. 801/379-7204; Chris Coons, bd. member

Utah Health Cost Management Foundation, 10 South Main, P.O. Box 45530, Salt Lake City 84145; tel. 801/533-3460; Evan J. Schelin, exec. dir.

VERMONT: Vermont Coalition for Health, 93 South Main Street, Waterbury 05676; tel. 802/244-5693; Patricia F. Novotny, exec. dir.

VIRGINIA: Lynchburg Health Care Coalition, P.O. Box 11108, Lynchburg 24506; tel. 804/528-7296; Shirley Floyd, sec./treas.

Peninsula Medical-Business Coalition, P.O. Box 38, Newport News 23607; tel. 804/244-8800; Elizabeth Kinney, co-chm.

Tidewater Health Coalition, c/o Health Management Associates, 870 World Trade Center, Norfolk 23510; tel. 804/622-5294; Gregory J. Mertz, consult.

Richmond Area Business Group on Health, P.O. Box 14631, Richmond 23221; tel. 804/359-2774; Ann Strader, exec. dir.

Richmond Program for Affordable Health Care, P.O. Box 27401, Richmond 23279; tel. 804/359-7359; Cynthia M. Martin, prog. dir.

Roanoke Valley Health Care Coalition, 40 Franklin Road, P.O. Box 2021, Roanoke 24022; tel. 703/985-2300; John Larew, sec.

WASHINGTON: North Olympic Health Care Cost Coalition, P.O. Box 1150, Port Angeles 98362; tel. 206/457-0411; Rob Orton, past pres.

Health Care Purchasers Association of Puget Sound, Court in the Square, 401 Second Ave. South, Ste. 630, Seattle 98104; tel. 206/343-5856; Andrea B. Castell, exec. dir.

Spokane Area Medicine/Business Coalition, Suite 370 W. 101 College, Spokane 99201; tel. 509/328-3955; Dorothy Oaks, sec./treas., coord.

WISCONSIN: Fox Cities Employers Health Cost Management Coalition, P.O. Box 2163, Appleton 54913; Marty Myse, bd. member

Milwaukee Construction Industry Health Care Coalition, c/o ACEA Health Fund, 180 N. Executive Dr., Ste. 306, Brookfield 53226; tel. 414/785-1430; Henry Hunt, chm.

Green Bay Employers Coalition on Health Care Management, P.O. Box 19001, Green Bay 54307-9001; tel. 414/433-1066; William R. Dagneau, pres.

Medicine, Business & Industry Committee of the Brown County Medical Society, P.O. Box 1700, Green Bay 54305; tel. 414/433-3653; Stephen Hathaway, M.D., chm.

Kenosha Manufacturers & Employers Association Health Care Coalition, P.O. Box 518, Kenosha 53141; tel. 414/654-2196

Sheboygan County Physician/Business Health Coalition, P.O. Box 1, Kohler 53044; John P. Hermann, M.D., pres.

Greater Milwaukee Business Group on Health (GMBGH), 735 West Wisconsin Avenue, Suite 600, Milwaukee 53233; tel. 414/271-9788; Richard Wagner, staff rep.

Greater Milwaukee Committee Joint Health Care Task Force, c/o Assn. of Commerce, 135 West Wells St., Suite 608, Milwaukee 53203; tel. 414/276-3337; Dennis Conta, hlth. care conslt./prog. dir.

Midwest Business Group on Health-Racine, 300 5th Street, Racine 53403; tel. 414/634-1931; Roger Caron, sec.

WYOMING: Wyoming Coalition for Health, P.O. Box 5539, Cheyenne 82003; tel. 307/632-9344; Robert C. Kidd II, dir.

Health Maintenance Organizations

The following is a list of Health Maintenance Organizations developed from information provided by state and federal agencies. The list is current as of January 1, 1987.

We present this list simply as a convenient directory. Inclusion or omission of any organization indicates neither approval nor disapproval by the American Hospital Association.

United States

ALABAMA

Alabama Health Plan, 530 Beacon Parkway West, Suite 400-E, Birmingham 35209; tel. 205/945-1003; William J. Goss, President

Amicare Advantage Plan, Inc., AMI Building, Suite 600, 22 Inverness Center Parkway, Birmingham 35243; tel. 205/991-2525; Jay Stuman, Executive Director

CMP Blue Cross/Blue Shield of Alabama, 450 Riverchase Parkway East, Birmingham 35298; tel. 205/988-2116

Complete Health, Inc., The Complete Health Building, 2160 Highland Avenue, Suite 100, Birmingham 35205; tel. 205/933-7661; William Featheringill, President and CEO

Health Advantage Plans, Inc., 701 Ridgeway Road, Fairfield 35064; tel. 205/783-5106; Pam Nichols, Acting Director

Health Maintenance Group of Birmingham, 936 S. 19th Street, Birmingham, 35205; tel. 205/985-5590; Ann F. Cobb, Director

HealthAmerica Alabama - Birmingham, 300 Century Park South, Suite 200, Birmingham 35226; tel. 205/979-8300; Jack Walker, Executive Director

Humana Health Plan of Alabama, Inc., 500 Lowell Drive, Suite F, Huntsville 35801; tel. 205/534-8411; Thomas Harbuck, Executive Director

Maxicare - Alabama - Mobile, 1110 Montlimar Drive, Suite 850, Mobile 36609; tel. 205/343-1827; Max H. Berns, M.D.

Mobile Health Plan d/b/a Prime Health, 124 University Blvd., Mobile 36608; tel. 205/342-0022; Becky S. Holliman

PARTNERS National Health Plans of Alabama, Inc., 600 Beacon Parkway West, Suite 280, Birmingham 35209; tel. 205/942-5787; Robert R. Vogel, Chief Executive Officer

Southeast Health Plan Inc., 2100 SouthBridge Parkway, Suite 395, Birmingham 35209; tel. 205/871-2600; George Salem, CEO

West Alabama Health Services, Inc., 607 Wilson Avenue, Eutaw 35462; tel. 205/372-4770; James W. Coleman, Director

Westworld Community Healthplans, Inc. c/o Livingston-Tombigbee Regional Medical Center, P. O. Drawer AA, Livingston 35470; tel. 205/652-9511; Paul E. Majors, Jr., Administrator

ARIZONA

Arizona Private Practice Plan, Inc., 4909 East Broadway, Suite 290, Tucson 85711; Bert B. Wagener, President

CIGNA Healthplan of Arizona, Phoenix, 11001 North Black Canyon Highway, Suite 400, Phoenix 85029; tel. 602/371-2500; Bert Wagener, President

CIGNA Healthplan of Arizona, Inc., Tucson, 4907 East Broadway, Suite 100, Tucson 85711; tel. 602/571-6500; Kris Kreutz, Vice President, General Manager

FHP, Inc., 1600 West Broadway, Suite 245, Tempe 85282; tel. 602/966-6773; Robert J. Abrams, Associate Regional Vice President

First Health of Arizona, Inc., 830 South Main Street, Cottonwood 86326; tel. 602/634-2216; Reid M. Wood, President

Health Advantage, Inc., 326 East Coronado Road, Phoenix 85004; tel. 602/252-3846; Hal L. Hupp, CEO

Health Dimensions of Arizona, Inc., 9201 North 25th Avenue, Suite 180, Phoenix 85021; tel. 602/861-0033; Maurice N. Echales, President

Health Horizons Plan, 4747 N. 7th Street Suite 202, Phoenix 85014; tel. 602/277-3300; Charles J. Meler, President

HealthAmerica Corporation of Tucson, Inc., 3737 N. 7th Street, #201, Phoenix 85014; tel. 602/279-1991; Michael J. Harris, President

Humana Insurance Company, Humana Care Plus - Phoenix, Camelhead Square, 3033 North 44th Street, Suite 220, Phoenix 85018; tel. 602/840-1851; Joe Blanford, Executive Director

Intergroup of Arizona, Inc., 707 North Alveron Way, Suite 300, Tucson 85711; tel. 602/326-4357; Rick Barrett, President

Liberty Care, 8777 E. Via De Ventura, Suite 200, Scottsdale 85260; tel. 602/951-6100

Maxicare Arizona, Inc., 300 West Clarendon Avenue, Suite 450, Phoenix 85013; tel. 602/265-1866; Candice Yeager, Executive Director

Medmark Healthplan of Arizona, Inc., 4745 North 7th Street, Suite 427, Phoenix 85014; tel. 602/277-4277; Conrad V. Schmitt, President

Neighborhood Health Care Plan, 839 West Congress, Tucson 85705; tel. 602/792-9890

Partners In Health Maintenance of Arizona, Inc., 4201 North 24th Street, Suite 100, Phoenix 85016; tel. 602/224-0847; John M. Hanretty, Chief Operating Officer

Patient's Choice, Inc., 222 North Central Avenue, Suite 550, Phoenix 85004; tel. 602/254-8808; Ruth A. Eckelmann, President

Physicians Health Plan of Arizona, 711 East Missouri, Suite 101, Phoenix 85014; tel. 602/265-5700; T. Stevens Spruth

The Samaritan Health Plan, Inc., 5300 North Central Avenue, Suite 220, Phoenix 85012; tel. 602/230-1555; Thomas J. Groves, M.D., President

Summit Healthplan of Arizona, Inc., 1800 Avenue of the Stars, Los Angeles 90067; tel. 213/201-4000; William L. Pierpoint, President

United Medical Plan of Arizona, Inc., 4041 North Central Avenue, Building B, Phoenix 85012; tel. 602/264-4057; Stanley I. Aronovitch, President

University Famli-Care, Inc., 1650 East Fort Lowell, Suite 208, Tucson 85719; tel. 602/327-5555; Rubin Bressler, M.D., President

ARKANSAS

American Dental Providers, Inc., 617 Boyle Bldg., Little Rock 72201; tel. 501/376-0660; Robert Iriana

American HMO/American Health Care Providers, Inc., 2228 Cottonale Lane, Little Rock 72202; tel. 501/666-7600; Daniel R. Schuh, Vice President

Baptist Medical System HMO, Inc., 1501 N. University, Suite 530, Little Rock 72207; tel. 501/663-2747; Gerald Blouin, Executive Director

Bull Shoals Community Hospital and Clinic, Inc., P. O. Box 356, Bull Shoals 72619; tel. 501/445-4292; Abija Hughes

HMO Arkansas, 601 Gaines, Little Rock 72201; tel. 501/378-2571; David Bridges, Executive Director

Health Care Plus, Three Financial Centre, 900 S. Shackleford, Suite 509, Little Rock 72211; tel. 501/221-3435; G. F. Tim McCleary, Jr., Executive Director

HealthAmerica - Little Rock, 6209 West 12th Street, Little Rock 72204; tel. 501/663-6638

Maxicare Arkansas, 5000 Rogers, Suite 400, Ft. Smith 72903; tel. 501/484-5130; Bob Moody, Executive Dir.

CALIFORNIA

AV-MED of California, 1524 McHenry Avenue, Suite 425, Modesto 95350; tel. 209/527-3350; Clive Riddle, Vice President and General Manager

Advanced Dental Systems, Inc., 3162 Newberry Drive, San Jose 95118

Aetna Dental Care for Groups, Inc., 15260 Ventura Blvd., #2100, Sherman Oaks 91403; tel. 818/995-1140

Aetna Healthcare Programs of California, Inc., 101 West Broadway, #1060, San Diego 92101; tel. 612/231-4145

Allstate Vision Plans, 165 DuBois Street, Santa Cruz 95060; tel. 408/425-0989

AmeriMed, 303 N. Glenoaks Boulevard, Suite 900, Burbank 91502; tel. 818/956-5500

American Healthguard Corporation, 7335 Topanga Canyon, Suite 111, Canoga Park 91303; tel. 818/992-6929

Amicare Advantage Plan, Inc., 9665 Wilshire Blvd., Suite 200, Beverly Hills 90212; tel. 213/205-6700; Dr. Marvin Dunn, Executive Director

Apple Health and Dental Plan, Inc., 1101 South Winchester Blvd., #173-G, San Jose 95128; tel. 408/241-3350

Bay Area Vision Centers, 715 Bryant Street, San Francisco 94107; tel. 415/391-2020

Bay Pacific Health Plan - San Francisco Bay Area, 1111 Bayhill Drive, Suite 300, San Bruno 94066; tel. 415/952-2005

CIGNA Dental Health of California, Inc., 6701 Center Drive W. Suite 655, Los Angeles 90045; tel. 213/215-9917

CIGNA Health Plans of California, 505 N. Brand Blvd. Suite 400, Glendale 91203; tel. 818/500-6262; G. Michael Sheley, President

CIGNA Healthplans of CA - San Diego, 5703 Oberlin Drive, Suite 302, San Diego 92121; tel. 619/457-5402; Don Triano, Sr. Vice President

CIGNA Healthplans of Southern California, 1711 West Temple Street, Los Angeles 90026; tel. 213/413-1313

California Dental Care, Inc., 213 Kenroy Lane #5, Roseville 95678; tel. 916/969-2273; James J. Ashen, D.D.S., President

California Dental Health Plan, 14471 Chambers Road, #100, Tustin 92680; tel. 714/731-6133

California Medical Plans, Inc., 109 East Lexington, El Cajon 92020; tel. 619/447-5055

California Physicians' Service, Two Northpoint, San Francisco 94133; tel. 415/445-5222

California Psychological Health Plan, 3600 Wilshire Boulevard, #900, Los Angeles 90010; tel. 213/381-6285

California Vision Service, 100 Howe Avenue, Sacramento 95825; tel. 916/481-8720

California Wellness Plan, 2800 28th Street, Santa Monica 90405; tel. 213/450-6623

CareAmerica - Southern California, Inc., 20520 Nordhoff, Chatsworth 91311, tel. 818/407-2222; Larry Gray, President/CEO

Central Coast Dental Service, 601 East Ocean Avenue, Lompoc 93436; tel. 805/736-8686

Central Valley Health Plan, 6700 North First Street, Suite 124, Fresno 93710; tel. 209/435-8366

Children's Hospital Health Plan, 3700 California St., San Francisco 94118; tel. 415/668-8211; Charles Cross, Acting Chief Executive Officer

Choice Healthcare Plan, 101 West Broadway, Suite 1060, San Diego 92101; tel. 619/231-4145; Jeanette W. Flood, Executive Director

City of San Jose, 801 North First Street, Room 215, San Jose 95110; tel. 408/277-4380; Frances A. Galloni, Director of Personnel

Community Dental Services, 2235 Sepulveda Boulevard, Torrance 90501; tel. 213/328-3310

Community Dentalplan, Inc., 2217 East First Street, Los Angeles 90033

Community Health Group, 4004 Beyer Boulevard, San Ysidro 92073; tel. 619/428-4463

Consolidated Health Service, Inc., 9845 Erma Road, #203, San Diego 92131; tel. 619/578-2775

ConsumerHealth, Inc., 1401 Dove Street, Suite 209, Newport Beach 92660; tel. 714/752-8522; Dennis R. Fratt, President

Continental Dental Plan, 60 Brookhollow, Santa Ana 92705; tel. 714/850-1244

Contra Costa Health Plan, 20 Allen Street, Martinez 94553; tel. 415/372-4653; Milton Camhi, Executive Director

County of L.A., 313 North Figueroa Street, Los Angeles 90012; tel. 213/974-7711

Delta Dental Plan of California, 1235 Mission Street, San Francisco 94103; tel. 415/864-9800; John Weaver, Director, Personnel and Corporate Services

Dental Benefit Providers of California, Inc., 4305 Hacienda Drive, Tower B-500, Pleasanton 94566

Dental Benefit Systems, Inc., 2021 The Alameda, Suite 150, San Jose 95126; tel. 408/241-9292

Dental Health Services, 3833 Atlantic Avenue, Long Beach 90807; tel. 213/595-6000; Godfrey Pernell, D.D.S., President

Eyecare USA of California, Inc., 9610 Ridgehaven Court, San Diego 92123; tel. 619/560-6667

FHP, Inc., 9900 Talbert Avenue, Fountain Valley 92728; tel. 714/963-7233; Robert Gumbiner, M.D., President

Family Health Foundation of Alviso, 1621 Gold Street, Alviso 95002; tel. 408/262-7944; James M. Clayton, President & Chief Executive Officer

Family Health Services, Inc., 701 South Parker Street, Orange 92668

Foundation Health Plan, 2600 V. Street, Sacramento 95818; tel. 916/456-7000; George Deubel, President & Chief Executive Officer

Foundation for Medical Care of Sonoma County, 3033 Cleveland Avenue, Santa Rosa 95401; tel. 707/544-2010

French Health Plan, 4131 Geary Blvd., San Francisco 94118; tel. 415/666-8800; Leslie Smith, Chief Executive Officer

General Med, 5200 West Century Boulevard, Los Angeles 90045; tel. 213/568-9000; Chan Wheeler, Regional Vice President

General Med, 701 South Parker, Suite 5000, Orange 92668; tel. 714/541-9300

Golden Pacific Dental Health Plan, 5405 Arrow Highway, Montclair 91763; tel. 714/946-4549; Robert L. Kerman, President

Golden West Health Plan, 888 West Ventura Boulevard #7, Camarillo 93010; tel. 805/987-8941

The following is a list of Health Maintenance Organizations developed from information provided by state and federal agencies. The list is current as of January 1, 1987.

We present this list simply as a convenient directory. Inclusion or omission of any organization indicates neither approval nor disapproval by the American Hospital Association.

Greater California Dental Plan, 7009 Owensmouth Ave. Suite #200, Canoga Park 91303; tel. 818/348-1500
Greater San Diego Health Plan, 3702 Ruffin Road, San Diego 92123; tel. 619/571-3102; Douglas C. Werner
Group Dental Service, 14260 Ventura Boulevard, Suite 201, Sherman Oaks 91423; tel. 818/907-1971
Group Health Service Plan, 1801 'I' Street, Sacramento 95814; tel. 916/444-9160; Lawrence J. O'Brien, Executive Director
Heals, The Personal Care Physician Health Plan, 5801 Christie Avenue, Sixth Floor, Emeryville 94608; tel. 415/420-0800
Health Benefits Incorporated, 1234 West Oak Street, Stockton 95201; tel. 209/948-1046
Health Plan of America - Greater Bay, 3260 Blume Drive, Suite 120, Richmond 94806; tel. 415/223-9580
The Health Plan of America, 505 South Main Street, Suite 300, Orange 92668; tel. 714/972-9200; Lawrence N. Kugelman, President
Health Plan of the Redwoods, 3033 Cleveland Avenue, Santa Rosa 95401; tel. 707/544-2010; Philip J. Schrefer, Executive Director
Healthamerica Corp., 828 San Pablo Avenue, Albany 94706; tel. 415/527-2020
Healthdent of California, Inc., 2856 Arden Way, #104, Sacramento 95825; tel. 916/486-0749
Healthgroup International (EQUICOR), 5000 Van Nuys Boulevard, Suite 200, Sherman Oaks 91403; tel. 818/907-0800; Joseph P. Radigan, President
Holman Professional Counseling Centers, 6900 Owensmouth Avenue, Canoga Park 91303; tel. 818/704-1444
Hygeia, Inc., 1251 South Atlantic Boulevard, Los Angeles 90022; tel. 213/268-3514
IPM Health Plan, 100 Corporate Place, Suite C, Vallejo 94590; tel. 707/557-3110; L. Jerome Ashford, President
Inland Health Plan, P. O. Box 50035, San Bernardino 92412; tel. 714/824-1860; Robert Mack, Chief Executive Officer
Inter Valley Health Plan, Inc., 300 S. Park Ave., Suite 300, Pomona 91766; tel. 714/623-6333
Janus Dental Services, Inc., 17660 Lakewood Boulevard, Bellflower 90706
Kaiser Foundation Health Plan, Inc., 1 Kaiser Plaza, Oakland 94612; tel. 415/271-5910
Lakewood Dental Plan, 1715 South Bascom Avenue, Campbell 95008
Laurel Dental Plan, Inc., 5451 Laurel Canon Blvd., #109, North Hollywood 91607
Lifeguard, Inc., 1715 South Bascom Avenue, Campbell 95008; tel. 408/371-9611
Maxicare Health Plans, Inc., 5200 W. Century Blvd., Los Angeles 90045; tel. 231/568-9000; Stephen R. Casey, Vice President, Government Relations
Mediq Orthodontic Care Services, Inc., 23441 Madison Street #300, Torrance 90505; tel. 213/373-9101
Mercy Expanded Care, 4077 Fifth Avenue, San Diego 92103; tel. 619/294-8111
MetLife HealthCare Network of Southern California, Inc., 4500 E. Pacific Coast Hwy., #600, Long Beach 90804; tel. 213/597-9932; David L. Slade, President/CEO
Modern Health Care Systems, 5200 South San Gabriel Place, Suite A, Pico Rivera 90660; tel. 213/948-1511
National Health Care Systems of California, Inc., 18662 MacArthur Blvd., #101, Irvine 92715; tel. 714/833-1900; Robert Y. Kim
North-East San Diego Health Plan, Inc., 342-C Rancheros Drive, San Marcos 92069; tel. 619/471-0985
OMNI Dent of California, 130 Ryan Court, Suite 201, San Ramon 94583
Optometric Services of California, Inc., 714 West Olympic Blvd., Los Angeles 90015; tel. 213/749-0528
Oral Health Services, Inc., 15720 Ventura Boulevard, Suite 222, Encino 91436; tel. 818/990-6725; Dr. Jack D. Schulman, President and CEO
Orange Plan Healthcare, 13800 Arizona Street, Westminster 92683; tel. 714/891-2104; M. Gomez, Vice President/Adm.
Orthodontic Smile Center, Inc., 1371 North Euclid Avenue, Anaheim 92801
PacifiCare of California, 5995 Plaza Drive, Cypress 90630; tel. 714/952-1121; David L. Mauss, President
Pacific Union Dental, Inc., 5801 Christie Avenue, #555, Emeryville 94608; tel. 415/547-8227
Palomar Pomerado Health Network, 215 South Hickory Street, #326, Escondido 92025; tel. 619/489-4660; Michael P. Lance, Chief Executive Officer
Peak Health Plan of California, 2655 Camino del Rio North, Suite 300, San Diego 92108; tel. 619/299-6464; Jeffrey M. Folick, President, Chief Executive Officer
Plan for Health, Inc., 5252 Balboa Avenue, #701, San Diego 92117; tel. 619/484-8600
Preferred Health Plan, Inc., 4034 Park Boulevard, P. O. Box 33688, San Diego 92103; tel. 619/297-6670
Private Medical Care, Inc., 5122 Katelia Avenue, #206, Los Alamitos 90720; tel. 213/493-6661
Professional Dental Services, Inc., 4700 Von Karman, Newport Beach 92660; tel. 714/476-2366
Psychology Systems Health Plan, 615 South Main Street, Milpitas 95035; tel. 408/263-8046
Ross-Loos Medical Group, Inc., 505 N. Brand Boulevard, Glendale 91203; tel. 818/500-6262
Safeguard Health Plans, P. O. Box 3210, Anaheim 92803; tel. 714/778-1005; Steven J. Baileys, D.D.S., Chief Operating Officer
Scan Health Plan, 521 East 4th Street, Long Beach 90802; tel. 213/435-0380; Sam L. Ervin, President and Chief Executive Officer
Summa Health Plan, 3425 North First Street, Fresno 92707; tel. 209/224-1426
Supplemental Dental Plans, Inc. d/b/a Dental Coverage & Care of Southern California, 1020 West Olympic Boulevard, Los Angeles 90015; tel. 213/276-0204
TakeCare Corporation, 2101 Webster Street, K-15, Oakland 94659; tel. 415/645-3120; Thomas F. Wagner, Acting Executive Director
Travelers Health Network, 2600 Michelson, Suite 600, Irvine 92715; tel. 714/553-9444; Stephen M. Crane, Vice President
UCSD Health Plan, P.O. Box 880237, San Diego 92108; tel. 619/294-5450
United Health Plan, 3405 W. Imperial Highway, Inglewood 90303; tel. 213/671-3465; Clyde W. Oden, OD, MPH, President & Chief Executive Officer
Universal Care, 2360 Pacific Avenue, Suite E, Long Beach 90806; tel. 213/424-6200
VIP Health Plan, P. O. Box 832, Oxnard 93202; tel. 805/487-8541; John Harris, General Manager
ValuCare, 6700 North 1st Street, Suite 124, Fresno 93710; tel. 209/435-8366; John Cronin, President
Watts Health Foundation, 10300 Compton Avenue, Los Angeles 90002; tel. 213/564-4331
Western Dental Services, Inc., 4000 MacArthur Blvd., #700 East, Newport Beach 92660; tel. 714/955-1439
Westworld Community Healthplan Inc., 23072 Lake Center Drive, Suite 200, Lake Forest 92630; tel. 714/768-2981
Whittaker Health Services of Southern California, 10800 Wilshire Boulevard, #600, Los Angeles 90024; 213/475-9411

COLORADO
CIGNA Healthplan of Colorado, Inc., 950 South Cherry Street, Suite 1414, Denver 80222; tel. 303/782-9109; James M. Cameron, Vice President and General Manager
Comprecare, P. O. Box 441170, Aurora 80044; tel. 303/695-6685; Eric D. Sipf, Chief Executive Officer
HMO Colorado, 700 Broadway, Suite 612, Denver 80203; tel. 303/831-3369; Judd Jessup, President
HMO Health Plans, Inc., 216 Victoria Avenue, Alamosa 81101; tel. 303/589-3601; Robert Otts, Chief Executive Officer
Health Dimensions of Colorado, 669 Citadel Drive East, Colorado Springs 80909; tel. 303/597-8400; Dr. George Goldstein, President
Health Network of Colorado Springs, Inc., 1400 East Boulder Street, Colorado Springs 80909; tel. 303/475-5110; Ron Burnside, Chief Executive Officer
Healthcare United, P. O. Box 340, Englewood 80151; tel. 303/788-6776; Karen Pederson, Vice President, Health Services
Humana Insurance Company, Humana Care Plus - Denver, Stanford Place 2, 7979 East Tufts Ave. Pkwy., Suite 304, Denver 80237; tel. 303/741-5500; Jim Franklin, Executive Director
Kaiser Fdn. Health Plan of CO, Colorado Permanente Medical Group, P.C., 2045 Franklin, Denver 80205; tel. 303/861-3264; Dr. Toby Cole, Executive Medical Director
MetLife HealthCare Network of Colorado, Inc., 534 Commons Drive, Golden 80401; tel. 303/526-9121; Charlie Stark, CEO
Peak Health Plan, LTD., North Creek I, 5725 Mark Dabling Boulevard, Colorado Springs 80919; tel. 303/548-8700; Jeannine Rivet, Senior Vice President
Prudential Health Care Plan, Inc. dba Prucare of Colorado, Inc., 4643 South Ulster Street, Suite 1000, Denver 80237; tel. 303/796-6100
Qual-Med, Inc., 719 Main Street, Alamosa 81101; tel. 303/589-9033
Rocky Mountain HMO, 2784 CrossRoad Blvd., Grand Junction 81506; tel. 303/243-7050; Michael Weber, Executive Director
Share Health Plan of Colorado, 5575 Tech Center Drive, Suite 200, Colorado Springs 80919; tel. 303/598-3334; Richard M. Jackson, Chief Executive Officer
Southern Colorado Health Plan, Inc., 201 W. 8th Street Suite 200, Pueblo 81003; tel. 303/545-6272

CONNECTICUT
CIGNA Healthplan of CT., Inc., 2 Riverview Square, East Hartford 06108; tel. 203/289-6088; Thomas G. Boyajy, Executive Director
Community Health Care Plan, 221 Whitney Avenue, New Haven 06511; tel. 203/773-8398; John Nelson, President
ConnectiCare, Inc., 999 Asylum Avenue, Suite 600, Hartford 06105; tel. 203/549-0022
Constitution Health Network, 20-30 Beaver Road, Wethersfield 06109; tel. 203/721-7784
HealthCare, Inc., 127 Washington Avenue, North Haven 06473; tel. 203/393-0470; Steven Beloff, President/Chief Executive Officer
Kasier Foundation Health Plan of CT; Kaiser Permanente Northeast Region, 60 Washington Street, Hartford 06106; tel. 203/280-1200; Daniel A. Gregorie, Regional Medical Director
Liberty Health Plans, Inc., 1183 New Haven Road, Naugatuck 06770; tel. 203/723-4451
Oxford Health Plans, Inc., 23 Old Kings Highway South, Darien 06820; tel. 203/656-1442; Stephen Wiggins, Chief Executive Officer
Physicians Health Services of Connecticut, Inc., 120 Hawley Lane, Trumbull 06611; tel. 203/373-7700; Michael E. Herbert, President
Yale University Health Plan, 17 Hillhouse Avenue, New Haven 06520; tel. 203/436-3298

DELAWARE
CIGNA Healthplan of Delaware, Inc., 1 Beaver Valley Road, Wilmington 19803; tel. 302/792-6635; Steve J. Schulman, President
Delaware Valley HMO, P. O. Box 7358, Wilmington 19803; tel. 302/652-6500; Alfred E. Meyer, Executive Director
HMO of Delaware, Inc., 200 Hygeia Drive, Newark 19714; tel. 302/454-3466; Virginia Davis, Vice President
Health Plan of Delaware, Ltd., Christiana Executive Campus, 200 Continental Drive, Suite 115, Newark 19713; tel. 302/368-2090; Robert J. Greczyn, Jr., Chief Executive Officer
Healthcare Delaware, Inc., Seventh & Clayton Streets, Wilmington 19805; tel. 302/421-4166; Andrew A. Zampini, Executive Director
Total Health Plus and DentaHealth Plus, One Brandywine Gateway, P. O. Box 8792, Wilmington 19899; tel. 302/421-3034; Robert J. White, Vice President and General Manager

DISTRICT OF COLUMBIA
ANI, 1901 Pennsylvania Avenue, Suite 600, Washington 20006; tel. 202/676-5883; Ronald K. Davy
George Washington University Health Plan, 1901 Pennsylvania Avenue N.W., Washington 20006; tel. 202/676-5583; Robert Hubbard, Chief Executive Officer
Group Health Association, 4301 Connecticut Avenue N.W., Washington 20008; tel. 202/364-2002; Robert Pfotenhaver, Director
Kaiser Foundation Health Plan of the Mid-Atlantic States, Inc., Kaiser Permanente, 4200 Wisconsin Ave. N.W. Suite 300, Washington 20016; tel. 202/364-3410; Alan J. Silverstone, Vice President & Regional Manager

FLORIDA
AV-Med Health Plan, Inc., 9400 South Dadeland Boulevard, Suite 200, Miami 33156; tel. 305/665-5437; Edward C. Peddie, President
AmeriPlan Health Services, 515 Lomax Street, Jacksonville 32204; tel. 904/355-2952; Mike MacKay, Executive Director
Association I.N.E.D., Inc., 770 West 29th Street, Hialeah 33012; tel. 305/885-8511; Eduardo E. Gonzalez, President and Medical Director
CAC Health Plan, Inc., 2850 Douglas Road, Coral Gables 33134; tel. 305/441-1140; Benjamin Leon, Jr., Administrator
CIGNA HealthPlan of Florida, Inc., P. O. Box 24203, Tampa 33623; tel. 813/884-2400; Bradley C. Arms, Executive Vice President and General Manager

The following is a list of Health Maintenance Organizations developed from information provided by state and federal agencies. The list is current as of January 1, 1987.

We present this list simply as a convenient directory. Inclusion or omission of any organization indicates neither approval nor disapproval by the American Hospital Association.

CIGNA Healthplan of South Florida, 6301 N.W. 5th Way, Suite 4100, Ft. Lauderdale 33309; tel. 305/493-5400; Allan Boshell, Vice President
Capital Health Plan, 2140 Centerville Place, Tallahassee 32308; tel. 904/386-3161; John Hogan, Administrative Director
Central Florida Physicians Health Plan, 701 Altaloma Avenue, Suite C, Orlando 32803; tel. 305/896-3105; Wallace M. Philips, Jr., M.D., President
Clinica Fatima, 1454 SW First Street, Miami 33135; tel. 305/643-4133; Bruno Barreiro, President
Clinica Las Mercedes, Inc., 1479 NW 27th Avenue, Miami 33135; tel. 305/633-3776; Antonio Ramirez, M. D., President
Comprehensive American Care, Inc., 708 LeJune Road, Suite 517, Miami 33127; tel. 305/441-1140; Benjamin Leon, Jr., Administrator
Doctor's Care, Inc., 2850 Douglas Road, Coral Gables 33134; tel. 305/444-2255; Richard Richter, Administrator
Finlay Medical Centers HMO Corp., 1401 Brickell Avenue, Suite 603, Miami 33131; tel. 305/374-8400; Louis A. Raventos, President
Florida 1st Health Plan, Inc., P. O. Box 9126, Winter Haven 33883; tel. 813/293-0785; Robert P. Hebert, Executive Director
Florida Health Care Plan, 350 N. Clyde Morris Blvd., Daytona Beach 32014; tel. 904/255-8451; William Moore, Executive Director
Gables Health Plan, Inc., 951 S.W. SR 42nd Avenue, Miami 33134; tel. 305/443-1639; S. Hernandez
Greater Miami Health Care Center, 506 West Flagler Street, Miami 33130; tel. 305/545-9292; Sylvia Urlich, Executive Director
HMO America, Inc., 314 North Gadsden Street, Tallahassee 32301; tel. 904/224-8863; Janegale Boyd, Administrator
Health Alliance Plan, Inc., 1430 Lakeland Hills Blvd., Suite 400, Lakeland 33805; tel. 813/682-2193
Health Options of South Florida, 3900 N.W. 79th Avenue, Suite 475, Miami 33166; tel. 305/591-9955; Richard Smith, Executive Director
Health Options, Inc., P. O. Box 2210, Jacksonville 32203; tel. 904/791-6086; Harvey J. Matoren, President
HealthAmerica Florida, 5701 West Sunrise Blvd., Plantation 33313; tel. 305/581-5000; Dr. Jacob Lazarovic, Medical Director
HealthWin, 2170 State Road 434 W., Suite 170, Longwood 32779; tel. 305/788-1455; Ken Hoverman, General Manager
Healthplan Southeast, 3375 I Capital Circle N.E., Suite 2, Tallahassee 32308; tel. 904/385-0100; Bonnie C. Bailey, Chief Operating Officer
Healthwin/HMO of Florida, 7785 Baymeadows Way, Suite 100, Jacksonville 32216; tel. 904/739-2338; Ken Sellers, Vice President
Heritage Health Plan of South Florida, 8325 N.W. 53rd Street, Suite 100, Miami 33166; tel. 305/591-3311; James F. H. Henry, President
Humana Health Plan of Florida, Inc., 1 Corporate Dr., Suite 105, Clearwater 33520; tel. 813/576-7376; Marilyn Doughman
International Medical Centers, 178 N.W. 54th Street, Miami 33127; tel. 305/795-7922; Arleen Richards, Medical Director
International Medical Clinic, Inc., 1505 N.W. 167th Street, Miami 33169; tel. 305/623-2625; Miguel Recarey
Jackson Memorial Hospital Health Plan, 1611 N.W. 12th Avenue, Miami 33136; tel. 305/549-6502; Ramon Rivera, Administrator
Medical Center Health Plan, Inc., 8333 North Davis Highway, Pensacola 32514; tel. 904/474-8237; John Torti, Executive Director
MetLife HealthCare Network of Florida, Inc., 851 Trafalgar Court, Suite 243, Maitland 32751; tel. 305/660-0444; John A. Bradley, President and Chief Executive Officer
Miami Age Organization Center, Inc., 510 S.W. 22nd Avenue, Miami 33135; tel. 305/642-2400; William Diaz
Network Health Care, Inc., 1895 West Commercial Blvd., Suite 120, Ft. Lauderdale 33309; tel. 305/491-9055; Jack Kronfled, Acting CEO
Pasteur Health Plan HMO, Inc., 3233 Palm Avenue, Hialeah 33012; tel. 305/885-8222; Ismael Hernandez, M.D., President
Physicians Health Plan of FL., Inc., 3816 West Linebaugh Avenue, Suite 300, Tampa 33624; tel. 813/968-9342; Thor Anderson, Executive Director
Prudential Health Care of Florida, Inc., 2301 Lucien Way, Suite 230, Maitland 32751; tel. 305/660-7001; David A. George, Vice President
SunCare HMO, Inc., 6622 Southpoint Dr. South, Suite 401, Jacksonville 32216; tel. 904/733-8159; David E. Harrell, President
Suncoast Health Plan, Inc., 1605 Main Street, Suite 1105, Sarasota 33577; tel. 813/952-1903; Richard S. Morse, M.D., President
Sunshine Health Plan, P. O. Box 4009, South Daytona 32021; tel. 904/756-4616; Henry Duke, Executive Director
Tampa Bay Health Plan, 9800 - 4th Street, N., Suite 400, St. Petersburg 33702; tel. 813/576-9226; William Norsworthy, Managing Director
Travelers Health Network of Florida, Inc., 6100 Hollywood Boulevard, Suite 610, Hollywood 33024; tel. 305/981-6667; Raul J. Medina, Executive Director
United American Healthcare, Inc., 6415 Lake Worth Road, Lake Worth 33463; tel. 305/439-0001; Ira A. Falk, President
Well Care HMO, Inc., 7626 Massachusetts Ave., New Port Richey 33552; tel. 813/842-9998; Paul Lukowski, Adm.

GEORGIA
Ameriplan Health Services, Ltd., 2839 Paces Ferry Road, Suite 500, Atlanta 30339; tel. 404/433-9342; Thomas A. Killila, Executive Director
CIGNA Healthplan of Georgia, Inc., 1360 Peachtree St., NE, Midtown Plaza II, Suite 1300, Atlanta 30309; tel. 404/881-9779; Mary Gannon, Vice President and General Manager
EQUICOR Health Plan, Inc., 5820 Hamilton Road, Suite 209, Columbus 31904; tel. 404/576-4183; Robert B. Thompson, Plan Manager
Georgia Health Network, 938 Peachtree Street NE, Atlanta 30309; tel. 404/876-1439; S. William Clark, Jr., M.D., President and Chairman of the Board
HCA Care of Georgia, Inc., 5820 Hamilton Rd., Suite 209, Columbus 31904; tel. 404/576-4183; Robert B. Thompson, Plan Manager
HMO Georgia, Inc., 3340 Peachtree Road, NE, Tower Place, Suite 350, Atlanta 30326; tel. 404/365-7150; Robert W. Maynard, President
Health 1st, Inc., 950 East Paces Ferry Road, NE, Suite 975, Atlanta 30326; tel. 404/364-8800; Joseph Barber, Chief Executive Officer
Humana Health Plan of Georgia, Inc., Humana Care Plus, 414 Wheeler Executive Center, Wheeler Road, Augusta 30309; tel. 404/736-7200; Gwen Butler, Operations Manager
Kaiser Foundation Health Plan of Georgia, Inc., 3355 Lenox Road, N. E., Suite 1000, Atlanta 30326; tel. 404/233-0555; Edgar T. Carlson, Regional Manager
Maxicare/HealthAmerica Georgia - Atlanta, 990 Hammond Drive, Suite 500, Atlanta 30328; tel. 404/396-9222; David E. Record, Jr., Executive Director
MedCenters Health Plan, 300 Interstate North Parkway, Suite 630, Atlanta 30339; tel. 404/951-9515; Valerie Schneider, Executive Director
PruCare of Atlanta, 2849 Paces Ferry Road, Suite 400, Atlanta 30339; tel. 404/436-0842; Herbert Romig, Director, Health Care Management

HAWAII
HMO Health Services/ Hawaii Medical Service Association, P. O. Box 860, Honolulu 96808; tel. 808/944-2411; Paul Yamashita, Director
Health Plan Hawaii, P. O. Box 860, Honolulu 96808; tel. 808/944-2808
Island Care and Best Care, P. O. Box 37549, Honolulu 96837; tel. 808/943-1127; Gary Taylor, President, Chief Executive Officer
Kaiser Fdn. Health Plan/HI Reg., 677 Ala Moana Blvd., Honolulu 96813; tel. 808/529-5301; Ronald Wyatt, Vice President
Straub Health Plan, 88 S. King Street, Honolulu 96813; tel. 808/523-2311

IDAHO
Peak Health Plan - Idaho, 1513 Tyrell Lane, Boise 83706; tel. 208/343-3330; T. Stevens Spruth, President

ILLINOIS
ANCHOR Organization for Health Maintenance, 310 South Michigan Avenue, Suite 600, Chicago 60604; tel. 312/347-3434; William E. Gold, Ph.D., President and Chief Executive Officer
Access Health, Inc., 310 South Michigan Avenue, Suite 2300, Chicago 60604; tel. 312/922-9338; Edward J. Sandrick, Director, Administration and Planning
Aetna Healthcare Systems, Inc. "CHOICE Healthcare Plan", 1400 East Touhy, Touhy Office Plaza, Suite G1, Des Plaines 60018; tel. 312/299-8470; Thomas C. Handy, Executive Director
American HMO, 19740 Governors Highway, P. O. Box 160, Flossmoor 60422; tel. 312/957-2550; Asif Sayeed, President
American Health Care Providers, 18141 Dixie Highway, Suite 115, Homewood 60430; tel. 312/957-2550
CIGNA Health Plan of Illinois, Inc., 1700 Higgins Road, Suite 600, Des Plaines 60018; tel. 312/699-5600; Robert Harris, Vice President and General Manager
COMPASS Health Care Plans, 310 S. Michigan, Suite 1810, Chicago 60604; tel. 312/294-0200; Henry F. Keaton, President
CarleCare, 602 University Avenue, Urbana 61801; tel. 217/337-3469; Harlan J. Failor, President
Chicago Care, Inc., 1101 West Lake Street, Suite 304, Oak Park 60301; tel. 312/524-1010; Joseph Dannon, M.D., President
Chicago HMO Ltd., 540 North LaSalle Street, Chicago 60610; tel. 312/751-7700; Judith K. Brown, Executive Director
Chicago HMO Plus Ltd., 540 North LaSalle St., Chicago 60610; tel. 312/751-4460; Melvin K. Roseman, M.D., Executive Director
CliniCare, 7124 Windsor Lake Pkwy., Rockford 61111; tel. 815/654-3600; Robert Vaupell, President/CEO
Complete Health Care Corporation, 201 North Joliet, P.O. Box 2487, Corner of Cass & Joliet Streets, Joliet 60634; tel. 815/727-4448; Spurgeon Green, Jr., M.D., President
Cooperative Health Plan, Inc., 1100 Jorie Boulevard Suite 343, Oak Brook 60521; tel. 312/990-2300; Jon Jaeger, Executive Director
Dreyer HMO, 1 Constitution Drive, Aurora 60506; tel. 312/859-0400; Robert S. Pietrusiak, Executive Director
Firemans Fund Employers Insurance, 5999 New Wilke Road, Suite 212, Rolling Meadows 60008; tel. 312/439-4400; Janet A. Fast, Regional Sales Director
Foundation for Medical Care/Central Ill., 2600 Farragut, Springfield 62704; tel. 217/787-2002; Diane Riddle, Executive Director
HMO Great Lakes/HealthWin, One Trans Am Plaza Drive, Oak Brook Terrace 60148; tel. 312/953-1690; Edward A. Dulik, Chief Operating Officer
HMO Illinois (Blue Cross-Blue Shield), 233 North Michigan Avenue, Chicago 60601; tel. 312/938-7491; Lisa Dietmier, Director
Health Care Services Corp., 233 North Michigan Avenue, Chicago 60601; tel. 312/938-6359; Donald A. Pebworth, J.D.
Health Plan of Central Illinois, Inc., 207 Main Street, Peoria 61602; tel. 309/676-2300; David W. Meister, Jr., President
HealthChicago, 950 Warrenville Road, Lisle 60532; tel. 312/964-6200; Thomas S. Johnson, President and Chief Executive Officer
Hospital Sisters HMO Corp. of Illinois, 444 North Northwest Highway, Suite 330, Park Ridge 60068; tel. 312/692-9550; Michael S. Sherman, Chief Executive Officer
Humana Insurance Company, Humana Care Plus - Chicago, One Pierce Place, Suite 1220, Itasca 60143; tel. 312/250-0055; Molly Miceli, Executive Director
Illinois Masonic Community Health Plan, 836 Wellington, Chicago 60657; tel. 312/883-7014; Gerald Mungerson, President
Maxicare Illinois, Inc., 310 South Michigan Avenue, Suite 1730, Chicago 60604; tel. 312/786-9830; William Carr, Executive Director
Med Care HMO, 1515 North Harlem Avenue, Oak Park 60302; tel. 312/524-8200; Sondra L. Rafferty, President
Metlife Healthcare Network of Illinois, Inc., 1375 East Woodfield Road, Suite 100, Schaumburg 60173; tel. 312/882-4470; Thomas O. Maxfield, III, President/Chief Executive Officer
Metrocare, 1033 West Van Buren, Chicago 60607; tel. 312/421-3098; Evan Freund, Executive Director
Michael Reese Health Plan, 2545 S. King Dr., Chicago 60616; tel. 312/808-3810; Barry Averill, President & Chief Executive Officer
Mile Square Health Plan of Illinois, 2045 W. Washington, Chicago 60612; tel. 312/942-3879; Robert L. Williams, Vice President, Health Plan Operations
MultiCare HMO, 400 West Erie St. Suite 400, Chicago 60610; tel. 312/664-0035; Richard A. Lutz, Executive Director
NOWCARE Corporation, 60 Revere Drive, Suite 900, Northbrook 60062; tel. 312/291-0100; Edward J. Smith, President
NorthCare Medical Group, S.C., 1350 East Touhy Avenue, Des Plaines 60018; tel. 312/299-9800; Dr. Arnold L. Widen, Medical Director
Personal Care HMO, Inc., 510 Devonshire Dr. Suite G, Champaign 61820; tel. 217/351-1226; Alan L. Mytty

The following is a list of Health Maintenance Organizations developed from information provided by state and federal agencies. The list is current as of January 1, 1987.

We present this list simply as a convenient directory. Inclusion or omission of any organization indicates neither approval nor disapproval by the American Hospital Association.

Professional Care, Inc. (ProHealth Illinois), 520 North 4th Street, Suite 201A, Springfield 62702; tel. 217/528-2288; Michael D. Burchardt, Executive Director

Safeguard Health Plans, Inc., 980 North Michigan Avenue, Suite 1400, Chicago 60611; tel. 312/266-6371; Peter D. Connolly, Vice President

Share Health Plan of Illinois, Inc., Hamilton Lakes, One Pierce Place, Suite 600, Itasca 60143; tel. 312/250-3200; John G. Ruther, President and Chief Executive Officer

Total Health Care, Inc., 650 West Noleman Street, Centralia 62801; tel. 618/533-5400; William A. Costello, Chief Operating Officer

Travelers Health Network, 120 South Riverside Plaza, Chicago 60606; tel. 312/930-9797; William M. Shaw, Director of Sales and Marketing

Union Health Service, 1634 West Polk, Chicago 60612; tel. 312/829-4224; Brendan Stewart, Executive Director

University of Illinois HMO, 1740 West Taylor Street, Suite 1400 (M/C 693), Chicago 60612; tel. 312/996-0028; Darren T. Horndasch, Acting Director

INDIANA

1st Care Health Plan of Indiana, Inc., 211 North Delaware Street, Suite 300, Indianapolis 46204; tel. 317/635-7112; Hal Hefner, Executive Vice President

American Eye Vision Care, Inc., Farmers Citizens Bank Building, P. O. Box 485, Salem 47167; tel. 812/883-4171; Larry Anders

Arnett HMO, Inc., Purdue National Bank, Suite 901, Lafayette 47901; tel. 317/448-8000; Mike Wolff

CompDent of Indiana, Inc., 8395 Keystone Crossing, Suite 204, Indianapolis 46240; tel. 317/253-7081; Jeffrey B. Goodwin

HMO America - Indiana, Inc., 540 North LaSalle Street, Chicago 60610; tel. 219/738-2786; Judith K. Brown, Executive Director

Health Maintenance of Indiana, 333 North Alabama, Suite 300, Indianapolis 46204; tel. 317/262-4501; Ronald Zingaro

HealthPlus, HMO, Inc., 1099 North Meridian Street, Suite 800, Indianapolis 46204; tel. 317/630-3500; Robert Finnegan

Indiana Vision Services, Inc., P. O. Box 657, Shelbyville 47176; tel. 317/398-0233; Douglas Stacy

MaxiCare, 9480 Priority Way West Drive, Indianapolis 46240; tel. 317/844-5775; John Pearce, Regional Vice President

Maxicare Indiana, Inc., 4755 Kingsway Drive, Suite 200, Indianapolis 46205; tel. 317/257-6510; Vicki F. Perry

MetLife HealthCare Network of Indiana, Inc., 3921 N. Meridian St., P.O. Box 680, Indianapolis 46208; tel. 317/923-2400; Robert E. Ivancevich, Chief Executive Officer

Metro Health, Inc., 9480 Priority Way West Drive, Indianapolis 46240; tel. 317/844-5775; John Pierce

Partners National Health Plans of Indiana, Inc., 1 Michiana Square, 100 East Wayne, #502, South Bend 46624; tel. 219/233-4677; R. J. Wurzburg, Chief Executive Officer

Physicians Choice of Northwest Indiana, Inc., 100 East 90th Drive, Merrillville 46410; tel. 219/769-7264; Vincent Portelli

Physicians Health Plan of Northern Indiana, Inc., 1415 Magnavox Way, Fort Wayne 46804; tel. 219/432-6690; Ron Musilli

Physicians Health Plan of Southern Indiana, Corporation, One Riverfront Place, Suite 400, Evansville 47708; tel. 812/465-4000; Daniel E. Horrell, Chief Executive Officer

Physicians Health Services, Incorporated, One Riverfront Place - Suite 400, P. O. Box 3357, Evansville 47732; tel. 812/465-6000; Daniel E. Horrell, Chief Executive Officer

Welborn HMO, Inc., 19 N.W. Fourth Street Suite 600, Evansville 47708; tel. 812/425-3939; Jim Klesack

IOWA

Cedar Valley Health Plan, 2705 University Avenue, Waterloo 50701; tel. 319/235-4330; G. Michael Hammes, Executive Director

Des Moines Health Plan, Inc., One Corporate Place, 1501 42nd Street, Suite 380, West Des Moines 50265; tel. 515/223-5005; Robert A. Meller, Plan Director

Family Health Plan, 2900 Westown Parkway, Suite D, West Des Moines 50265; tel. 515/223-6566; Robert A. Meller, Director of Marketing

HMO Iowa, 1002 First Interstate Bank Bldg., Locust at 6th, Des Moines 50309; tel. 515/244-6300; Jack Davis, President

Heartland Health Network, Inc., Box 1677, Hamilton Blvd. and I-29, Sioux City 51102; tel. 712/277-3081

Heritage National Healthplan, Inc., 11 Corporate East, 1910 East Kimberly Road, Davenport 52807; tel. 309/752-4445; Lloyd F. Mathwick, President

Medical Associates HMO (Clinic Health Plan), One CyCare Plaza, Suite 230, Dubuque 52001; tel. 319/556-8070; Larry Cremer, Vice President

Quad-City Health Plan, 11 Corporate East, 1910 East Kimberly Road, Davenport 52807; tel. 319/344-4401; G. Michael Hammes, Executive Director

Share Health Plan of Iowa, Century Building, Suite 200, 2700 Westown Parkway, West Des Moines 50265; tel. 515/225-1234; Marc Dahlquist, President

Total Health Network of Iowa, P. O. Box 7270, Station 74, Des Moines 50309; tel. 515/245-4591; Mike Stoll, Executive Director

University Health Care Plan of Iowa, 2150 Grand Avenue, Des Moines 50312; tel. 515/243-8701; John Bergman, Chief Executive Officer

KANSAS

CIGNA Healthplan of Kansas City, Inc., 32 Corporate Woods, Suite 700, 9225 Indian Creek Parkway, Overland Park 66210; tel. 913/451-9388; Richard F. Henderson, Vice President and General Manager

EQUICOR Health Plan, Inc., P. O. Box 780008, 2959 N. Rock Road, Wichita 67226; tel. 316/681-1152; Robert A. Vohs, President

Family Health Plan Corporation, 120 West Sixth Street, Box 886, Newton 67114; tel. 316/283-5880; Walter D. Rogers, Chief Executive

HMO Kansas, Inc., P. O. Box 110, Topeka 66601; tel. 913/233-2751; G. Wayne Johnston, President

Humana Health Plan of Kansas, Inc., 10955 Lowell, Suite 505, Overland Park 66210; tel. 913/451-6000; Harry J. Werronen, President

Kaiser Foundation Health Plan of Kansas City, Inc., 6900 Squibb Road, Suite 201, Shawnee Mission 66202; tel. 913/384-9090; Andrew W. Dubill, Vice President

Medplan, Inc., 10551 Barkley, Suite 120, Overland Park 66212; tel. 913/648-6670; Donald B. Bletz, M.D., President

MetLife HealthCare Network of Kansas City, Inc., 32 Corporate Woods, Suite 1000, 9225 Indian Creek Pkwy., Overland Park 66210; tel. 913/451-5656; Robert W. Jacobs, President and Chief Executive Officer

Physicians Health Plan of Kansas, Inc., 400 SW 8th Street, Suite 100, Topeka 66603; tel. 913/233-4870; Jim E. Agin, President and Chief Executive Officer

Total Health Care, Inc., 3637 Broadway, P. O. Box 23163, Kansas City 64141; tel. 816/561-2300; Richard P. Krecker, President

KENTUCKY

ChoiceCare of Kentucky, 3043 Dixie Highway, Edgewood 41017; tel. 606/341-6600

HMO Kentucky, Inc., 9901 Linn Station Road, Louisville 40223; tel. 502/423-2520; Michael P. McDonald, Executive Director

HealthAmerica of Kentucky, Inc., 303 N. Hurstbourne Lane, Suite 200, P. O. Box 34098, Louisville 40222; tel. 502/429-4600; Robert A. Gormley, M.D., Chief Executive Officer

HealthWise of Kentucky, Ltd., 489 East Main Street, Lexington 40507; tel. 606/259-1771; Steven M. Barney, Executive Director

Humana Health Plan, Inc., 500 West Main Street, Box 1438, Louisville 40201; tel. 502/580-2713; Wayne T. Smith, President

Humana Health Plan, Inc., Humana Care Plus - Louisville, 9300 Shelbyville Road, Suite 700, Louisville 40222; tel. 502/423-1355; Karen Sholtis, Executive Director

Independence Health Plan, 870 Corporate Drive, Suite 402, Lexington 40503; tel. 606/223-4554; Robert W. Young, M.D., Chief Operating Officer

Maxicare Kentucky, Inc., 870 Corporate Drive, Suite 402, Lexington 40503; tel. 606/223-4554; Robert W. Young, M.D., M.H.P., Executive Director

MediPlan Health Maintenance Organization, Inc., 10101 Linn Station Road, Suite 900, Louisville 40223; tel. 502/425-4440; Paul B. Osborne, Chief Executive Officer

MetLife HealthCare Network of Kentucky, Inc., 10509 Timberwood Circle, Suite 200, Louisville 40223; tel. 502/423-3900; Steve Linehan, President

Mountain Trails Health Plan, Inc., Drawer C, 108 Cumberland Avenue, Harlan 40831; tel. 606/573-5658; Ron S. Spatafora, Director

Partners In Health Maintenance, 850 Barrett Avenue, Suite 205, Louisville 40204; tel. 502/582-1153; John T. Byrd, Chief Executive Officer

Southeastern United Medigroup, Inc., 9901 Linn Station Road, Louisville 40223; tel. 502/423-2800; William R. Newsom, Executive Vice President

LOUISIANA

Av-Med of Louisiana, Inc. Health Maintenance Organization, 2900 Ridgelake Drive, 2nd Floor, Metairie 70002; tel. 504/834-0840; Bradley E. Balles, Vice President - General Manager

CIGNA Healthplan of Baton Rouge, Inc., 2 United Plaza, Suite 310, 8550 United Plaza Blvd., Baton Rouge 70809; tel. 504/922-4260

CIGNA Healthplan of North Louisiana, 3007 Knight Street, Suite 250, Shreveport 71105; tel. 318/861-9330; Charles Neff, General Manager

EQUICOR Health Plan, Equitable - HCA Corporation, 17050 Medical Center Drive, Suite 307, Baton Rouge 70816; tel. 504/295-1553

Gulf South Health Plans, Inc., 5615 Corporate Blvd., Suite 5A, Baton Rouge 70808; tel. 504/927-7212

HMO Louisiana, Inc., P.O. Box 95041, Baton Rouge 70895; tel. 504/922-1886; J. B. Manry, Jr., Executive Director

Healthamerica Partners Louisiana, Inc., 3323 West End Avenue, Nashville, TN 37203; 615/385-7300

Healthamerica Lousiana Partners, L. P. of New Orleans, Louisiana, 4150 One Shell Square, New Orleans tel. 504/529-4561

Lousiana Health Service and Indemnity Company, 10225 Florida Blvd., Baton Rouge 70815; tel. 504/922-1700

Maxicare Louisiana, Inc., 3850 North Causeway Blvd., Suite 990, Metairie 70002; tel. 504/836-2022; Ron Varbrough, Executive Director

Ochsner Health Plan, 1516 Jefferson Highway, New Orleans 70121; tel. 504/838-3901; William H. Townsend, President

Physicians' Health Plan, Inc., 920 Pierremont Rd. Suite 505, Shreveport 71106; tel. 318/869-4915

Travelers Health Network of LA, Inc., 1 Poydras Plaza, 639 Loyola Ave., Suite 1320, New Orleans 70113; tel. 504/529-4596; Ernest Sylvester, Vice President, Executive Director

MAINE

HMO Maine, P. O. Box 8883, Portland 04104; tel. 207/775-4050; Thomas Gorham, Director

Healthsource Maine, Inc., 30 U.S. Route 1, Yarmouth 04096; tel. 207/846-6430; Richard White, Chief Executive Director

WellCare of New England, Inc., 39 Darling Avenue, South Portland 04106; tel. 207/773-6994; David C. Gaynor, Chief Executive Officer

MARYLAND

Chesapeake Health Plan, Inc., P. O. Box 8838, Baltimore 21224; tel. 301/282-8622; Joseph LaAsmar, President

Clinical Associates, P.A., Kenilworth West, 660 Kenilworth Drive, Towson 21204; tel. 301/296-5300

Columbia Medical Plan, Inc., Two Knoll North Drive, Columbia 21045; tel. 301/997-8500; James E. Jordan, M.D., President, Medical Director

Constant Care Community Health Center, Inc., 1501 Division Street, Baltimore 21217; tel. 301/383-8300; Harvey Webb, Jr., DDS, Executive Director

Delmarva Health Care Plan, Inc., 108 North Harrison Street, Easton 21601; tel. 301/822-7223; Peter J. Borchardt, Executive Director

Free State Health Plan, Inc., 2205 York Road, Timonium 21093; tel. 301/683-0100; Brian A. Krisak, General Manager

The Johns Hopkins Health Plan, 1000 E. Eager Street, Baltimore 21202; tel. 301/522-9900; Ms. Barbara B. Hill, President

HealthAmerica Maryland, L.P., 1 S. Calvert Street, Suite 1100, Baltimore 21202; tel. 301/234-0670; Ms. Marcia C. Cohen, Chief Executive Officer

HealthCare Corporation of the Mid-Atlantic, 7939 Honeygo Boulevard, Building A, Baltimore 21236; tel. 301/529-2500; David Wolf, President

HealthPlus, 6611 Kenilworth Avenue, Suite 300, Riverdale 20737; tel. 301/277-6520; Barrett Toan, Executive Director

Healthamerica Maryland L.P., One South Calvert Street, Suite 1100, Baltimore 21202; tel. 301/234-0670

MD-Individual Practice Association, Inc., 451 Hungerford Drive, Suite 700, Rockville 20850; tel. 301/762-8205; Leon Kaplan, Chief Operating Officer

PHN-HMO, Inc., 5700 Executive Dr., Suite 104, Baltimore 21228; tel. 301/747-9060

The following is a list of Health Maintenance Organizations developed from information provided by state and federal agencies. The list is current as of January 1, 1987.

We present this list simply as a convenient directory. Inclusion or omission of any organization indicates neither approval nor disapproval by the American Hospital Association.

West Baltimore Health Care Corporation, 1850 West Baltimore Street, Baltimore 21223; tel. 301/566-8700; Michael Rashid, Executive Director

MASSACHUSETTS

Bay State HealthCare, 101 Main Street, Cambridge 02142; tel. 617/868-7000; Lionelle D. Wells, M.D., Chairman & Chief Executive Officer

Berkshire Health Plan, 725 North Street, Pittsfield 01201; tel. 413/499-4009; Robert H. Booz, Executive Director

Central Massachusetts Health Care, Inc., 300 Mechanics Tower, Worcester 01608; tel. 617/798-8667; James M. Scoggins, President and Chief Executive Officer

CIGNA Health Plan of Massachusetts, Bank of Boston Building, 1350 Main Street, Springfield 01103; tel. 413/733-1177; Richard Kaplan, Executive Director

Commonwealth Physicians Health Plan, 1030 President Avenue, Fall River 02720; tel. 617/675-2500; Robert Renga, Executive Vice President

Fallon Community Health Plan, 425 Lake Avenue North, Worcester 01605; tel. 617/852-7085; Christy W. Bell, Executive Director

Family Health Plan, One Speen Street, Framingham 01701; tel. 617/879-4500; Priscilla Kimball, Chief Executive Officer

Harvard Community Health Plan, Post Office Box 9100, Hearthstone Plaza Offices, Brookline Village 02147; tel. 617/731-8240; Thomas Pyle, Chief Executive Officer

Harvard University Group Health Program, 75 Mt. Auburn Street, Cambridge 02138; tel. 617/495-2010; Warren E. C. Wacker, M.D., Director

Health New England, Bay Tower, Springfield 01115; tel. 413/787-4000; Richard Belloff, President

Healthway Medical Plan, Inc., 1 Pearl Street, Brockton 02401; tel. 617-586-5600; John Parker, Executive Director

Kaiser Foundation Health Plan of Massachusetts, 100 University Drive, Amherst 01002; tel. 413/256-0151; Frederick Q. Rice, Area Manager

Lahey Clinic - BC/BS HMP, 41 Mall Road, Burlington 01805; tel. 617/273-5100; Dr. Robert E. Wise, Chief Executive Officer

MIT Health Plan, Medical Dept.-MIT, 77 Mass Avenue, Cambridge 02139; tel. 617/253-4487; Dr. Arnold N. Weinberg, M.D., Medical Director

Medical East Community Health Plan, 325 Wood Road, Braintree 02184; tel. 617/849-3061; William A. Schlag, Executive Director

Medical West Community Health Plan, 444 Montgomery Street, Chicopee 01020; tel. 413/594-3111; Ronald Hemmelgarn, Regional Executive Director

MetLife HealthCare Network of Massachusetts, Blue Hills Office Park, 150 Royall Street, Suite 170, Canton 02021; tel. 617/821-2620; Robert C. Ritter, President

Metlife HealthCare Network of RI, Inc., Blue Hills Office Park, Suite 170, 150 Royall Street, Canton 02021; tel. 617/821-2620; Terry Nimnicht, President

Metro West Health Plan, 1 Cranberry Hill, Lexington 02173; tel. 617/863-1880; Susan DeAmicis

Montachusett Health Plan, Leominster Plaza, 285 Central Street, Leominster 01453; tel. 617/534-4100; Glenn Young, Executive Director

Multigroup Health Plan, 27 Mica Lane, Wellesley 02181; tel. 617/431-1070; Daniel Kaplan, Executive Director

Neighborhood Health Plan, 1 Fields Corner, Dorchester 02122; tel. 617/288-1293; Jay Harrington, Chief Executive Officer

North Shore Health Plan, 27 Centennial Drive, Peabody 01960; tel. 617/532-1063; Rita Berkson, Executive Director

Pilgrim Health Care, Inc., P. O. Box 200, 10 Accord Executive Drive, Norwell 02061; tel. 617/871-3950; Allan Greenberg, Chief Executive Officer

Tufts Associated Health Plan, 400-2 Totten Pond Road, Waltham 02254; tel. 617/466-9400; Dr. Harris Berman, President

MICHIGAN

Butterworth HMO, 220 Raybrook, Suite 300, Grand Rapids 49506; tel. 616/942-0954; Vic Turvey, Chief Executive Officer

Comprehensive Health Services of Detroit, Inc., 6500 John C. Lodge, Detroit 48202; tel. 313/875-4200; Ellis J. Bonner, President, Chief Executive Officer

Delta Dental Plan of Michigan, Inc., P. O. Box 30416, Lansing 48909; tel. 517/349-6000; Patrick P. Gribben, Jr., President

Grand Valley Health Plan, 4550 Cascade Road, S.E., Grand Rapids 49506; tel. 616/949-2410; Ron Palmer, President, Executive Director

Great Lakes Health Care, 1769 S. Garfield Avenue, Traverse City 49684; tel. 616/941-7823; Sharon Carlin, Executive Director

Greater Flint HMO, G-3245 Beecher Road, Flint 48504; tel. 313/733-9500; Donald Roseberry, Executive Director

Group Health Service of Michigan, Inc., 4200 Fashion Square Blvd., Saginaw 48603; tel. 517/791-3200; James Hayden, Executive Director

HMO West, 67 West Michigan Mall, Suite 608, Battle Creek 49017; tel. 616/963-9156; Diane D. Giannunzio, Executive Director

Health Alliance Plan of Michigan, Inc., 2850 West Grand Blvd., Detroit 48202; tel. 313/872-8100; James Walworth, President

Health Care Network, 26900 West 11 Mile, P. O. Box 5043, Southfield 48086; tel. 313/354-7450; Charles Zech, Executive Director

Health Central, 1401 S. Creyts Road, Lansing 48917; tel. 517/627-1111; Lee J. Lich, Executive Director

Health Central, 2316 South Cedar Street, Lansing 48910; tel. 517/322/4000; D. Bonta Hiscoe, M.D., Medical Director

Health Circle, 3624 South Westnedge, Kalamazoo 49008; tel. 616/388-9500; Bob Smedes, Executive Director

HealthAmerica of Michigan/LOI c/o Geo. A. Dean, M.D., 18900 West Ten Mile Road, Southfield 48075; tel. 313/424-8340; Edward J. Maszak, Executive Director

HealthPlus of Michigan, 2050 South Linden Road, Flint 48504; tel. 313/733-6100; Michael A. Mark, President

LakeShore HMO, Inc., 68 West 8th Street, Suite 140, Holland 49423; tel. 616/392-6401; Ronald Harms, President

M-Care, 3601 Plymouth Rd., Ann Arbor 48105; tel. 313/747-8700; Sandra Billingslea, President

Maxicare's Independence Health Plan, 15565 Northland Drive, Suite 700E, Southfield 48075; tel. 313/424-8904; William Alvin, Executive Director

McAuley Health Plan, Inc., 555 Briarwood Circle, P. O. Box 1308, Ann Arbor 48106; tel. 313/747-7200; John Zilavy, Executive Director

MedExtend, 363 West Big Beaver, Troy 48084; tel. 313/524-8130; D. Michael Elliott, President

Mercy Alternative Care Choices - Michigan and Iowa, 2000 Hogback Road, Suite 15, Ann Arbor 48105; tel. 313/971-7667; Marianne Udow, Vice President

Michigan HMO, 7650 Second Avenue, Detroit 48202; tel. 313/873-2800; Ronald R. Dobbins, President, Chief Executive Officer

NorthMed Associates, Inc., 109 E. Front Street, Suite 309, Traverse City 49684; tel. 616/941-1690; Gene Tang, M.D.

NuVision, Inc., 2284 S. Ballenger Highway, P. O. Box 2600, Flint 48501; tel. 313/767-0900; Eli Shapiro, O.D., President

Physicians Health Plan, Inc., One Michigan Avenue, Suite 700, Lansing 48933; tel. 517/372-7400; James Savage, President

Preferred Health Plan, 2850 West Grand Boulevard, Detroit 48202; tel. 313/876-3203; Robert Asmussen, President

Total Health Care, Inc., 3455 Woodward Avenue, Detroit 48201; tel. 313/833-8800; Kenneth Rimmer, Executive Director

West Michigan Health Care Network, 611 Cascade W. Parkway S.E., Grand Rapids 49506; tel. 616/957-5057; Hugh Hufnagel, Executive Director

MINNESOTA

Central Minnesota Group Health Plan, 1245 - 15th Street N., St. Cloud 56301; tel. 612/253-5348; Neil White, Executive Director

Community Health Center, 4th Street at 11th Avenue, Two Harbors 55616; tel. 218/834-2171

Coordinated Health Care, 17 West Exchange Street, Suite 220, St. Paul 55102; tel. 612/292-0860; Ingrid Sundgaard, Executive Director

First Plan HMO, Fourth Street at 11th Avenue, Two Harbors 55616; tel. 218/834-2171; John Bjorum, Executive Director

Group Health, Inc., 2829 University Avenue, S.E., Minneapolis 55414; tel. 612/623-8400; George C. Halvorson, President and Chief Executive Officer

HMO Minnesota, 3535 Blue Cross Road, P. O. Box 43179, St. Paul 55164; tel. 612/456-8433; Mary Brainerd, Chief Operating Officer

Health Partners, 6600 Citywest Parkway, Eden Prairie 55344; tel. 612/829-1600; Chester A. Anderson, M.D., President and Chairman of the Board

MAYO Health Plan, 21 First Street S.W., Suite 401, Rochester 55902; tel. 507/284-3541; A. Schilmoeller, Administrator

MORE HMO Plan, Inc., 802 North 9th Street, Suite 108, Virginia 55792; tel. 218/749-5890; Mike Laukka, Executive Director

Medcenters Health Plan, 4951 Excelsior Blvd., St. Louis Park 55416; tel. 612/927-3908; Sheila Leatherman, Executive Director

Metropolitan Health Plan, Hennepin County Bureau of Health, Administrative Offices, 822 S. 3rd St., Suite 140, Minneapolis 55415; tel. 612/347-8557; Joan Delich, Administrator

Metropolitan Health Plan Hennepin County Bureau of Health, 701 Park Avenue, Minneapolis 55415; tel. 612/347-2340; John Bluford, Director

Physicians Health Plan, 5601 Smetana Drive, P. O. Box 1587, Minnetonka 55343; tel. 612/936-1200; Richard Burke, Chief Executive Officer

Senior Health Plan, 1295 Bandana Blvd. No., Suite 220, St. Paul 55108; tel. 612/647-1313; Jim Lauer, President

Share Health Plan, 3600 West 80th Street, Suite 700, Bloomington 55431; tel. 612/830-3166; Brian D. Kovalchuk, President and CEO

MISSOURI

CIGNA Healthplan of Kansas City, Inc., 9225 Indian Creek Parkway, #700, Overland Park 66210; tel. 913/451-9388

CIGNA Healthplan of St. Louis, Inc., 1807 Park 270 Drive, Suite 426, St. Louis 63146; tel. 314/878-2866

Care+Plus of Missouri, Inc., East Tenth Street, P. O. Box 8, Rolla 65401; tel. 314/364-0900; Charles A. James, Ph.D., Chief Executive Officer

Group Health Plan, Inc., 11475 Olde Cabin Road, St. Louis 63141; tel. 314/993-5955; Ron Lodder, President and Chairman of the Board

Health Plan of Mid-America, P. O. Box 410604, Kansas City 64141; tel. 816/941-3030; Linda Laitner, Executive Vice President, Chief Executive Officer

Humana Health Plan of Missouri, Inc., 500 W. Main St., Louisville, KY 40201; tel. 502/580-2016

Kansas City Health Care, Inc., 6900 Squibb Road, Suite 200, Shawnee Mission KS 66202; tel. 913/384-9090

Labor Health Institute of St. Louis, 300 South Grand, St. Louis 63103; tel. 314/658-5621; Dr. Edward J. Berger, Medical Director

Maxicare Missouri, 500 N.W. Plaza, Suite 1050, St. Ann 63074; tel. 314/344-9972; Greg Stobbe, Executive Director

Metlife HealthCare Network of St. Louis, Inc., 8670 Big Bend, St. Louis 63119; tel. 314/968-0277; Dan M. DeGood, CEO

Physicians Health Plan of Greater St. Louis, Inc., 1807 Park 270 Drive, Suite 224, St. Louis 63146; tel. 314/275-7000

Prime Health Kansas City, Inc., 6801 E. 117th Street, Kansas City 64134; tel. 816/765-6200; Robert F. Rasmussen, President and Chief Executive Officer

PruCare Prudential Health Care Plan, Inc., 1300 East 104th St. Suite 320, Kansas City 64131; tel. 816/941-4500; John Kennedy

Prudential Health Care Plan, Inc., 10845 Olive Blvd., Creve Coeur 63141; tel. 314/567-1100

Sanus Health Plan, Inc., 500 Northwest Plaza, St. Ann 63074; tel. 314/739-7755; Barrett Toan, Executive Director

Total Health Care, P. O. Box 413163, Kansas City 64141; tel. 816/561-2300; Dennis McCart, Director

NEBRASKA

Amicare Advantage Plan, Inc., One First National Center, 1620 Dodge Street, Suite 1600, Omaha 68102; tel. 402/341-7500; Tom Gage, Marketing Director

HMO Nebraska, Inc., 2421 South 73rd Street, Omaha 68124; tel. 402/392-2800; Roger Mason, Executive Director

Maxicare/HealthAmerica Nebraska, Inc., 17th and N Street, Lincoln 68508; tel. 402/475-7000

Maxicare/HealthAmerica Nebraska L.P., 10506 Burt Circle, Omaha 68114; tel. 402/493-1500; Paul D. Kadavy, Executive Director

Personal Health Care, 10810 Farnam Drive, Suite 325, Omaha 68154; tel. 402/333-3400; David Roberts, Chief Executive Officer

Physicians Health Plan of Nebraska, 1123 Davenport, Suite 104, Omaha 68154; tel. 402/333-5800

Share Health Plan of Nebraska, Inc., 300 Blackstone Center, 302 South 36th Street, Omaha 68131; tel. 402/345-9900; John Braasch, Chief Executive Officer

The following is a list of Health Maintenance Organizations developed from information provided by state and federal agencies. The list is current as of January 1, 1987.

We present this list simply as a convenient directory. Inclusion or omission of any organization indicates neither approval nor disapproval by the American Hospital Association.

Share Health Plan of Nebraska, 302 South 36th Street, Omaha 68131; tel. 402/345-9900; John M. Braasch, Chief Executive Officer

NEVADA

ChoiceCare Nevada, Ltd. Partnership, 4045 S. Spencer, Suite 210, Las Vegas 89119; tel. 702/732-4200; James Merritt, Chief Executive Officer

Foundation Health Plan, P. O. Box 7138, Reno 89510; tel. 702/329-3555; Ernest Givani, Vice President

Health Plan of Nevada, Inc., 888 South Rancho Drive, P. O. Box 15645, Las Vegas 89114; tel. 702/646-8100; Anthony M. Marlon, M.D., Chief Executive Officer

Humana Medical Plan of Nevada, Inc., 3101 South Maryland Parkway, Las Vegas 89109; tel. 702/737-7211; Jerry Anderson, Executive Director

Maxicare/UHS Nevada, Inc., 1850 East Flamingo Road, Suite 120, Las Vegas 89119; tel. 702/732-1920; Sandy Snell, Executive Director

Total Life Care, 3121 South Maryland Parkway, Suite 220, Las Vegas 89109; tel. 702/731-0053; Saul O. Sobol, M.D., Chief Executive Officer

Western Health Plans of Nevada, Inc., 1105 Terminal Way, Suite 210, Reno 89502; tel. 702/329-2070; Richard Lohmeyer, Chief Executive Officer

NEW HAMPSHIRE

Beacon Health, Inc., 336 Portsmouth Avenue, Greenland 03840; tel. 603/431-1511; Robert Vaccaro, Executive Director

Good Health Network Blue Cross/Blue Shield of NH, 2 Pillsbury Street, Concord 03306; tel. 603/224-9511; Armand Francoeur, Senior Director

Healthsource N.H., P. O. Box 2041, Concord 03301; tel. 603/225-5077; Sally Crawford, Chief Executive Officer

Matthew Thronton Health Plan, Inc., 589 West Hollis Street, CS 2028, Nashua 03061; tel. 603/883-2800; Martha H. Marsh, President & Chief Executive Officer

Nashua Alternative Health Plan, Two Pillsbury Street, Concord 03306; tel. 603/224-9511

WellCare of New England, Inc., 228 Maple Street, P. O. Box 5820, Manchester 03108; tel. 603/622-2599; David C. Gaynor, Regional Executive Director

NEW JERSEY

CIGNA Healthplan of New Jersey, 1000 Lenola Road, Moorestown 08057; tel. 609/778-5800; Franz Herpok, Vice President and General Manager

CoMed, 3 Stewart Court, Denville 07834; tel. 201/361-3444; Barry Goldberg, Chief Executive Officer

Foundation Health Plan, 748 Morris Turnpike, Short Hills 07078; tel. 201/564-8511; Robert A. Clemente, Chief Operating Officer

HIP of Greater New Jersey, 1 Sears Drive, Paramus 07652; tel. 201/599-4800; Mary Conroy, Administrator

HIP of New Jersey, Inc., 165 Old Marlton Pike, Rt. #70, East, Medford 08055; tel. 609/654-6600; Elizabeth Bayardi, President

HMO-NJ/US Health Care, South 61 Paramus Road, Paramus tel. 201/843-6200; Robert Normyle, Vice President Marketing

Medigroup Central Inc., 416 Bellevue Avenue, Trenton 08618; tel. 609/396-4600; Sharon J. Hayman, President & Chief Operating Officer

Medigroup-Metro, Inc., 341 Roseville Avenue, Newark 07107; tel. 201/481-0004; David Dintenfass, Executive Director

Medigroup-North, Inc., 111 Howard Boulevard, Suite 105, Mt. Arlington 07856; tel. 201/398-6700; Lawrence Tyson, Executive Director

Medigroup-Shoreline, Inc., 223 Monmouth Road, West Long Branch 07764; tel. 201/229-8600; Dr. Stephen Kardos, President

Medigroup-South, Inc., 4 Greentree Center, Marlton 08053; tel. 609/983-8808; Carol Thomas, Executive Director

OMNICARE/The HMO, 1138 East Chestnut Avenue, Building 3, Vineland 08360; tel. 609/696-8009; Dr. Dominic DeCencio, President

Oxford Health Plans of New Jersey, 1050 Wall St. West, Lyndhurst 07071; tel. 201/939-0333; Stephen Wiggins, Chief Executive Officer

PruCare of New Jersey, 600 Fire Road, Pleasantville 08232; tel. 609/641-6200; Rhonda Stock, Director

Rutgers Community Health Plan, Inc., One Worlds Fair Drive, Somerset 08873; tel. 201/469-4300; Roger W. Birnbaum, President & Chief Executive Officer

US Healthcare, 287 Northern Boulevard, Suite 109, Great Neck 11021; tel. 516/466-8870; Michael Stocker, M.D., President

NEW MEXICO

Firstsource, 12800 Indian School Road NE, Albuquerque 87112; tel. 505/291-3573; Mark S. Hawkins, Executive Director

Health Dimensions, Inc., 1720 Louisiana Avenue, N.E., Suite 200, Albuquerque 87110; tel. 505/265-5967

Health Plus of New Mexico, 6100 Pan American Freeway, Suite 190, Albuquerque 87109; tel. 505/823-8311

Lovelace Health Plan, Inc., P. O. Box 27107, Albuquerque 87125-7107; tel. 505/262-7363; J. T. Michelson, Vice President and Chief Operating Officer

New Mexico Health Plan, Inc., 4501 Indian School Road, Suite B, Albuquerque 87110; tel. 505/265-8600; Douglas L. Flow, Vice President and Chief Operating Officer

NEW YORK

BlueCare Plus, Box 4310, 258 Genesee Street, Utica 13504; tel. 315/797-0104; Joseph C. Guereschi, Chief Executive Officer

Capital Area Community H/P, 1201 Troy-Schenectady Road, Latham 12110; tel. 518/783-3110; Warren Paley, President

Capital District Physician's Health Plan, Inc., 3 Washington Square, Albany 12205; tel. 518/452-1921; Fred Vorys, Acting Plan Manager

ChoiceCare Long Island, 50 Charles Lindbergh Blvd., Uniondale 11553; tel. 516/222-1460; David S. Reynolds, Ph.D., Executive Director

Community Blue The HMO of Blue Cross of Western New York, Inc., 237 Main Street, Buffalo 14203; tel. 716/847-2790; Richard A. Villari, Vice President

Elderplan, Inc., 1276 - 50th Street, Brooklyn 11219; tel. 718/438-2600; Dennis Kodner, General Director

Empire Blue Cross and Blue Shield HealthNet, P. O. Box 8650, Albany 12208; tel. 518/436-3200; John J. Hoefs, Divisional Vice President, Alternate Delivery Systems

Foundation Health Plan (FHP), 4513 Old Vestal Road, Box 897, Binghamton 13902; tel. 607/729-9318; Frederick F. Yanni, Jr., President

Genesee Valley Group Health Association, 150 E. Main Street, Rochester 14647; tel. 716/454-1700; Raymond Savage, President

Health Care Plan, 900 Guaranty Bldg., Buffalo 14202; tel. 716/847-1480; Dr. Arthur Goshin, President

Health Insurance Plan/Greater NY, 220 West 58th Street, New York 10019; tel. 212/956-8000; Robert L. Biblo, President

HealthWays of New York, Inc., 555 White Plains Road, Tarrytown 10591; tel. 914/631-8400; Patricia T. Akellian, President and Chief Operating Officer

Independent Health Association, Inc., 4510 Main Street, Buffalo 14226; tel. 716/839-2932; Frank Colantuono, President

Kaiser Foundation Health Plan of the Northeast, 7-11 S. Broadway, White Plains 10601; tel. 914/682-7720; Michael M. Dudley, Regional Manager

Maxicare New York, Inc., 300 Park Avenue South, 12th Floor, New York 10010; tel. 212/529-5533; Steven Karten, Executive Director

Metropolitan Health Plan Metropolitan Hospital Center, 1901 First Avenue, New York 10029; tel. 212/230-6016; Barbara Lusen, Executive Director

Mid-Hudson Health Plan, 138 Pine Street, Kingston 12401; tel. 914/338-0202; Edward Ullmann, Executive Director

Mohawk Valley Phys. Health Plan, Inc., 108 Union Street, Schenctady 12305; tel. 518/370-4793; David Oliker, President

Oxford Health Plans of New York, 212 Fifth Avenue, 17th Floor, New York 10010; tel. 212/696-5520; Stephen F. Wiggins, Chief Executive Officer

Patients' Choice, Inc., 250 Harrison Street, Syracuse 13202; tel. 315/476-0874; Edwin J. Curran, Acting Chief Executive Officer

Physicians Health Services of New York, Inc., 200 Central Park Avenue, Hartsdale 10530; tel. 914/682-8006; Richard Walker, President

Preferred Care, 259 Monroe Avenue, Suite A, Rochester 14607; tel. 716/325-3920; John Urban, President

Prepaid Health Plans a/k/a Health Services Medical Corp. of Central N.Y., 8278 Willett Parkway, Baldwinsville 13027; tel. 315/638-2133; Frederick F. Yanni, Jr., President

Rochester Health Network, 349 W. Commercial St., Suite 2900, E. Rochester 14445; tel. 716/381-5500; Richard Greene, President

Rochester Hospital Service Corp. a/k/a Blue Choice, Gateway Centre, 150 E. Main Street, Rochester 14647; tel. 716/454-1700; Nancy Boyer, Vice President

Sanus Health Plan of Greater New York, 271 Madison Ave., New York 10016; tel. 212/683-7799; Victor Botnick, Executive Director

Total Health HMO, 1010 Northern Boulevard, Suite 324, Great Neck 11021; tel. 516/466-1000; Peter Strassberg, M.D., President

Travelers Health Network of New York, Inc. Metropolitan Division, 650 Fifth Avenue, 3rd Floor, New York 10019; tel. 212/757-1067; David Friedman, Executive Director

U. S. Healthcare, Inc., 287 Northern Boulevard, Suite 109, Great Neck 11021; tel. 516/466-8870; Michael A. Stocken, MD, President

WellCare of New York, Inc., 300 Stony Brook Court, Newburgh 12550; tel. 914/561-5028; Robert Goff, Executive Director

NORTH CAROLINA

Blue Cross & Blue Shield of N.C., P. O. Box 2291, Durham 27702; tel. 919/489-7431; Ken M. Davenport, Director

Carolina Medical Care, 1012 Kings Drive, Suite 100, Charlotte 28283; tel. 704/377-4100

Central Carolina Physicians Health Plan, Inc., 4020 West Chase Center Blvd., Suite 450, Raleigh 27607; tel. 919/833-8000; Randall N. H. Madry, Chief Executive Officer

Dental Concepts of America, P. O. Box 34621, Charlotte 28234; tel. 704/375-6915

EQUICOR Health Plan of North Carolina, Inc., P. O. Box 10187, Raleigh 27605; tel. 919/828-5711; Sandra P. Babb, Plan Manager

Kaiser Foundation Health Plan of NC, 2900 Highwoods Boulevard, Raleigh 27604; tel. 919/878-9870; Alvin W. Washington, Vice President and Regional Manager

Maxicare/HealthAmerica North Carolina, Inc., 5511 Capital Center Drive, Suite 400, Raleigh 27606; tel. 919/859-3700; Dr. Samuel Warburton, Executive Director (Acting) Vice President, Medical Affairs

Partners National Health Plans of NC, Inc., P. O. Box 24907, Winston-Salem 27114; tel. 919/760-4844; John Jones, Chief Executive Officer

Personal Care Plan of N.C., Inc., P. O. Box 30004, Durham 27702; tel. 919/489-7431

Physicians Health Plan of NC., Inc., 2307 West Cone Boulevard, Suite 200, Greensboro 27408; tel. 919/282-0900; Frank Mascia, Chief Executive Officer

PruCare of Charlotte, 2100 Rexford Road, Suite 314, Charlotte 28211; tel. 704/365-6070; Jerry Sykora, Director, Health Care Management

Wake Health Services, P. O. Box 10155, Raleigh 27605; tel. 919/755-1888

Winston-Salem Health Care Plan, 250 Charlois Blvd., Winston-Salem 27103; tel. 919/768-4730; Clifford R. Guy, M.D., Vice President, Medical Director

NORTH DAKOTA

CapCare, P. O. Box 489, Bismarck 58501; tel. 701/222-8754; James J. Smid, Jr.

Care Plan HMO Blue Cross/Blue Shield, 4510 - 13th Ave. S.W., Fargo 58121; tel. 701/282-1113; Jim Austin, Executive Director

Heart of America HMO Human Service Center, Rugby 58368; tel. 701/776-5848; Paul Orth, Executive Director

MedCenters of North Dakota, Inc., 45 South Fourth Street, Fargo 58126; tel. 701/293-5452; Steffen Christensen, M.D.

TeamCare HMO, Inc., P. O. Box 2043, Minot 58702; tel. 701/282-1100; Tyrone Langager

West River HMO, 4510 - 13th Ave. S.W., Fargo 58121; tel. 701/282-1113; Jim Austin, Executive Director

OHIO

CIGNA Healthplan of Ohio, Inc., 2500 Corporate Exchange Drive, Suite 200, Columbus 43229; tel. 614/890-5531; Joseph Rochester, Vice President and General Manager

CMP - Comm. Mutual Ins. Co./ Health Maint. Plan, 1351 William H. Taft Road, Cincinnati 45206; tel. 513/872-8441

Capital Area Community Health Plan, Inc. dba Community Health Plan of Ohio, 817-C Eastgate South Drive, Cincinnati 45245; tel. 513/752-0500; Kenneth C. Page, Regional Administrator

CliniCare Inc., 1040 Delaware Avenue, Marion 43302; tel. 614/383-1112; Thomas Bishop, President

ChoiceCare, 441 Vine St., Suite 1200, Carew Tower, Cincinnati 45202; tel. 513/784-5200

The following is a list of Health Maintenance Organizations developed from information provided by state and federal agencies. The list is current as of January 1, 1987.

We present this list simply as a convenient directory. Inclusion or omission of any organization indicates neither approval nor disapproval by the American Hospital Association.

Day-Med HM Plan, 2728 West 3rd Street, P. O. Box 80, Mid City Station, Dayton 45402; tel. 513/268-4400; Jeanette Prear, Chief Executive Officer

Dayton Area Health Plan, One Prestige Place, Suite 750, Miamisburg 45342; tel. 513/439-0096; Pamela B. Morris, Chief Executive Officer

Family HealthNet of Ohio, 560 East Town Street, Columbus 43215; tel. 614/461-9900; Patrick A. Talley, Executive Vice President

Family Health Plan, 11 East Bancroft Street, Toledo 43620; tel. 419/241-6501; Robert Campbell, President

HMO Health Ohio Blue Cross and Blue Shield of Ohio, 2060 East Ninth Street, Cleveland 44115; tel. 216/687-6264; Vincent R. Kaval, Vice President, Alternative Delivery Systems

Health Maintenance Plan/Community Mutual Blue Cross and Blue Shield, 4665 Cornell Road, Suite 300, Cincinnati 45241; tel. 513/530-8600; Anthony A. Fata, Vice President

Health Maintenance Plan/Community Mutual Insurance Company, 221 East Fourth Street, Suite 2600, Cincinnati 45202; tel. 513/977-8855; Wendell Brown, General Manager

Health Management System, 3000 Guernsey Street, Bellaire 43906; tel. 614/676-4623; Adrian Kutska, Chief Executive Officer

Health Ohio, Inc., 372 East Center Street, Marion 43302; tel. 614/387-6355; Dr. Frank Murphy, Executive Director

Health One, 4885 Olentangy River Road, Columbus 43214; tel. 614/451-1551; Dr. William Hamelberg, Medical Director

Health One, 255 East Main Street, Columbus 43215; tel. 614/462-4555; James Barlow, Executive Director

Health Options, 14 South Paint Street, Chilicothe 45601; tel. 614/775-8181; Ms. Mary Ann Hanson, Chief Executive Officer

Health Plan of the Upper OH Valley, 52160 National Road East, St. Clairsville 43950; tel. 614/695-3585; John Pollack, President

Health Power of Dayton, Inc., 560 E. Town Street, Columbus 43215; tel. 614/461-9900; Glenn R. Sperry, President

HealthSphere, 1873 Tamarack Road, Newark 43055; tel. 614/522-8511; Ms. Kathie Davis, Plan Manager

Holzer health Plan d/b/a Advacare, 385 Jackson Pike, Gallipolis 45631; tel. 614/446-5281; John B. Reinhardt

Hometown Hosptial Health Plan, 830 Amherst Road NE, P. O. Box 552, Massillon 44648; tel. 216/837-6880; Jack W. Topoleski, Chief Executive Officer

Hospital Choice Health Plan, Inc., 96 Northwoods Blvd., Worthington 43085; tel. 614/888-3929; Bradley C. Engel, President & Chief Executive Officer

Humana Health Plan, Inc., 700 Ackerman Place, Suite 340, Columbus 43202; tel. 614/262-8575; Walt Simmers

Independent Medical Plan, Inc., 430 Grant Street, Akron 44311; tel. 216/434-1921; Barbara Barber, Executive Secretary

Kaiser Foundation Health Plan of Ohio, P. O. Box 5508, Cleveland 44101; tel. 216/621-5600; Kathryn R. Paul, Vice President and Regional Manager

Licking Memorial Hospital Health Plan, 1320 West Main Street, Suite HP, Newark 43055; tel. 614/366-0533; William Andrews, Chief Executive Officer

MagnaCare Health Plan, 2133 Luray Avenue, Cincinnati 45206; tel. 513/961-4300; Robert Quirk, President and Chief Executive Officer

Maxicare Ohio, Inc., 801-B West Eighth Street, Suite 111, Cincinnati 45203; tel. 513/381-5775; Bruce Ardis, Executive Director

Maxicare/HealthAmerica Corporation of Ohio-Cleveland, 1375 East 9th Street, Suite 1400, Cleveland 44114; tel. 216/579-9100; James Tye, Acting Chief Executive Officer

MedCare Health Plan, 333 North Main Street, Columbiana 44408; tel. 216/747-3113; Dr. Paul Wm. Weiss, President

MedChoice, 3737 Sylvania Avenue, P. O. Box 385, Toledo 43691; tel. 419/473-7373; William H. Kincaid, Executive Director

MedPlan, P. O. Box 2695, Columbus 43216; tel. 614/442-7256; Ms. Barbara Lockhart, Executive Director

Medical Value Plan, Fort Industry Square, 136 North Summit Street, Toledo 43604; tel. 419/244-2902; David Smith, Chief Operating Officer

MetLife HealthCare Network of Cleveland, Inc., Four Commerce Park Square, Suite 400, 23200 Chagrin Boulevard, Beechwood 44122; Mel Dettra, President and CEO

MetLife HealthCare Network of Greater Columbus, Inc., 4900 Blazer Memorial Pkwy., Dublin 43017; tel. 614/761-8777; David Parsons, CEO

MetLife Healthcare Network of Cincinnati, Inc., Northmark III, Suite 100, 4501 Erskine Road, Cincinnati 45242; tel. 513/745-9700; John W. O'Neil, CEO

Peak Health Plan of Ohio, 11260 Chester Road, Suite 800, Cincinnati 45246; tel. 513/772-7325; Robert Sheehy, President

Personal Physician Care of Ohio, Inc., 2475 East 22nd Street, Suite 611, Cleveland 44115; tel. 216/687-0015; Richard E. Jenkins, M.B.A., Executive Director

Physicians Health Plan of Ohio, 3650 Olentangy River Rd., Columbus 43214; tel. 614/764-4884; Richard Cornett, Senior Vice President

Premier Health Plan, Inc., 3900 East Market Street, Warren 44484; tel. 216/856-7831; Richard A. Bisconti, President

PruCare of Central Ohio, 100 E. Campus View Blvd., Suite 350, Columbus 43085; tel. 614/431-5601; Alexandra L. Lukawsky, Manager, Health Care Services

Share Health Plan, First Federal Plaza, Suite 909, 701 Adams Street, Toledo 43624; tel. 419/241-8245; David Edwards, Chief Executive Officer

The Toledo Health Plan, Inc., 4 Sea Gate, Suite 605, Toledo 43604; tel. 419/249-7950; James W. Eppel, Jr., President

Total Health Care Plan, Inc., 8300 Hough Avenue, Cleveland 44103; tel. 216/231-1200; James G. Turner, President and Chief Executive Officer

United Health Plan, Inc., 1865 Fountain Square Court, Suite 106, Columbus 43224; tel. 614/268-5308; Jeanne Thimons, Administrator

University Health Plan, 2055 Reading Road, Cincinnati 45202; tel. 513/721-3388; Hirsh J. Cohen, Executive Director

WellCare Health Plan, 6874 Strimbu Drive, Brookfield 44403; tel. 216/448-0100; Keith Strassner, Executive Director

Western Ohio Health Care Plan, 1 Prestige Place, Suite 650, Miamisburg 45342; tel. 513/439-0050; David Shafer, Chief Operating Officer

Western Reserve Health Plan, 19201 Villaview, Cleveland 44119; tel. 216/486-0152; Michael Keresman, Chief Executive Officer

OKLAHOMA

Aetna Choice Healthcare Plan, Two Memorial Place, 8023 E. 63rd Place, Suite 210, Tulsa 74133; tel. 918/250-6171; Jack Armstrong, President/Chief Executive Officer

Dental Plan of America, Inc., 523 West Main Street, Oklahoma City 73102; tel. 405/236-3762

EQUICOR Health Plan, Inc., 2601 N.W. Expressway, Suite 200 West, Oklahoma City 73112; tel. 405/848-1653; J. Randall Linaman, President

HMO of Oklahoma, 8181 South Lewis, Tulsa 74137; tel. 918/493-8060; Richard L. Bonwell, Executive Director

Health Accord of Oklahoma, 4200 E. Skelly Drive, Suite 520, Tulsa 74135; tel. 918/481-6411; Robert S. Hughes, Chief Executive Officer

MultiMed Health Plan, 515 Central Park Drive, Central Park 2, Suite 306, Oklahoma City 73105; tel. 405/557-0208; William Tatum, M.D., Medical Director

PacifiCare of Oklahoma, 7134 South Yale Avenue, Suite 500, Tulsa 74136; tel. 918/496-1200; David Hallock, President

Physicians Health Plan of Oklahoma, 6506 South Lewis, Suite 208, Tulsa 74136; tel. 918/747-9473; Ms. Betsey Barnes, Director of Medical Services

PruCare of Oklahoma, 3330 NW 56th, Suite 500, Oklahoma City 73112; tel. 405/942-6687; Mark Shaughnessy, Vice President

PruCare of Tulsa, 7912 E. 31st Court, Tulsa 74145; tel. 918/624-4664; Ed Muldoon, Vice President

TAKECARE Prepaid Health Service of Oklahoma, 1437 S. Boulder, Tulsa 74119; tel. 918/584-4800; Ronald F. King, Executive Vice President

TAKECARE Prepaid Health Service of Oklahoma, Inc., 3401 N.W. 63rd Street, Oklahoma City 73116; tel. 405/843-3610; Tom P. Hadley, Jr., Vice President & Executive Director

OREGON

BestCare, 9400 S.W. Barnes Road, Suite 307, Portland 97225; tel. 503/297-1046; Sanford Weisenburg, Executive Director

Capitol Health Care, Inc., P. O. Box 12625, Salem 97309; tel. 503/364-4868; Roger B. Lyman

Eugene Clinic Health Plan, P. O. Box 10727, Eugene 97440; tel. 503/687-6206; Hugh Prichard, Executive Director

Good Health Plan T/N, 500 N.E. Multnomah, Suite 700, Portland 97232; tel. 503/231-8098; Mrs. Mary McWilliams, Executive Director

Kaiser Foundation Health Plan of the NW, 3600 North Interstate Avenue, Portland 97227; tel. 503/280-2050; Michael Katcher, Regional Manager, Sr. Vice President

Northwest AmeriCare Health Plan, 4800 S.W. Macadam Avenue, Suite 305, Portland 97201; tel. 503/222-5217; Tom Heerhartz, Chief Executive Officer

Pacificare of Oregon, 7360 S.W. Hunziker Rd., Suite 200, Tigard 97223; tel. 503/620-9324; Stephen L. Bennett

Phys. Assn. of Clackamas County, P. O. Box 286, Gladstone 97027; tel. 502/659-4212; Thomas Bechtol

Selectcare, Healthguard Services, Inc., 488 East 11th Avenue, Eugene 97401; tel. 503/485-1850; Howard W. Kriz, Jr.

Sisters of Providence Good Health Plan of Oregon, 500 N.E. Multnomah, Suite 700, Portland 97232; tel. 503/231-8098; Mary O. McWilliams, Executive Director

Willamette Health Service, Inc., 1933 SW Jefferson Street, Portland 97201; tel. 503/228-7556; Gerald L. Cogan

PENNSYLVANIA

Central Medical Health Plan, 1200 Center Avenue, Pittsburgh 15219; tel. 412/562-3301; Thomas Gallagher, President

Comprehensive Health Services Plan, Inc., 3450 North 17th Street, Philadelphia 19140

Delaware Valley HMO, P. O. Box 1111, Concordville 19331; tel. 215/358-5650; Alfred F. Meyer, President

Freedom Health Care, Inc., 150 Strafford Avenue, Wayne 19087; tel. 215/293-9338; Robert A. Zelten, Chief Executive Officer

Geisinger Health Plan, Geisinger Office Building, Danville 17822; tel. 717/271-8761; Howard G. Hughes, M.D., President

The HMO Alliance, Inc., 1709 Blvd. of Allies, Pittsburgh 15219; tel. 412/553-6400

HMO of Pennsylvania, 980 Jolly Road, P. O. Box 1109, Blue Bell 19422; tel. 215/628-4800

HMO of Western Pa, Inc. Harmar Health Center, 701 Russellton Road, Cheswick 15024; tel. 412/274-4400; Julian Eligator, M.D., Executive Director

HealthGuard of Lancaster, Inc., 40 East Grant, Lancaster 17602; tel. 717/291-9321; James Godfrey, President

Healthamerica Corporation of Philadelphia, Public Ledger Building, Room 101, 6th & Chestnut Streets, Philadelphia 19106

Healthwin, Inc., 980 Jolly Road, P. O. Box 1109, Blue Bell 19422; tel. 215/283-6789; Dan Nolen

Heritage Health Plan of Southeastern Pennsylvania, 2570 Boulevard of the Generals, Building 200, Norristown 19403; Emanuel W. Sandberg, President

Independent Health of Pennsylvania, Inc., 150 East 8th Street, Erie 16501; tel. 814/453-5090; Geraldine Zurn, Executive Director

John Hancock Healthplan of Pennsylvania, Inc., 3550 Market Street, Philadelphia 19104; tel. 215/823-8600; R. Lynne Morgan, Chief Executive Officer

Keystone Health Plan Central, Inc., P. O. Box 8812, Camp Hill 17011; tel. 717/975-7458; Thomas Bickman, President and Chief Executive Officer

Maxicare/HealthAmerica of Pennsylvania, 5 Gateway Center, 2nd Floor, Pittsburgh 15222; tel. 412/553-7300

Omni Health Plan, Inc., 434 Lackawanna Avenue, Scranton 18503; tel. 717/343-6466

PARTNERS National Health Plans, 150 Monument Road, Suite 106, Bala Cynwyd 19004; tel. 215/668-1440

Physicians Health Plan of W. Pennsylvania, Inc., P. O. Box 101769, Pittsburgh 15237; tel. 412/366-9000; Larry Rambo, Chief Executive Officer

Riverside Health Plan, Inc., 701 Sharon Road, Beaver 15009; tel. 412/775-4404; Ronald P. Kocent, Chief Executive Officer

Silver Spring Health Plan, 1 Phico Drive, Mechanicsburg 17055; tel. 717/691-1777; Donald Steffes, President

Travelers Health Network of Pennsylvania, Inc., 3 Gateway Center, 6 South, Pittsburgh 15222; tel. 412/765-0500; Ms. Debra A. Trachy, Vice President and Executive Director

Vista Health Plan, Inc., 2002 Renaissance Blvd., Suite 220, King of Prussia 19406; tel. 215/277-4800; Tom Minugh, President and Chief Executive Officer

The following is a list of Health Maintenance Organizations developed from information provided by state and federal agencies. The list is current as of January 1, 1987.

We present this list simply as a convenient directory. Inclusion or omission of any organization indicates neither approval nor disapproval by the American Hospital Association.

RHODE ISLAND

Commonwealth Physicians H/P c/o Metro Center, 475 Kilvert St., Warwick 02886; tel. 401/737-6900; Robert Renga, Chief Executive Officer

HMO Rhode Island, Inc., 30 Chestnut Street, Providence 02903; tel. 401/274-6674; Michael C. Gerhardt, President

Ocean State Physicians H/P, Metro Center, 475 Kilvert Street, Warwick 02886; tel. 401/737-6900; Blair S. Suellentrop, CEO

RI Group Health Assn., 2 Davol Square, Providence 02903; tel. 401/421-4410; Bruce Bradley, President

SOUTH CAROLINA

Anderson Health Plan, 800 North Fant Street, Anderson 29621; tel. 803/261-1686; William T. Manson, III, Executive Director

Companion HealthCare Corporation, P. O. Box 6170, Columbia 29260; tel. 803/786-8466; Earl W. Robertson, Sr. Vice President

Equicor Healthplan of South Carolina, Inc., 9304 Medical Plaza Drive, Charleston 29418; tel. 803/572-0800; J. B. Richardson, Executive Director

Humana Health Plan of South Carolina, Inc., 533 Georgia Avenue, North Augusta 29841; tel. 404/868-5000; Don Murphree, Chairman, Executive Committee

Maxicare/Health America South Carolina, Inc., 2320 East North Street, P. O. Box 17009, Greenville 29606; tel. 803/233-7437; William E. Martin, Executive Director

Patient's Choice, Inc., 175 Dunbar Street, Spartanburg 29301; tel. 803/582-9909; W. Thomas Maynard, President and Chief Executive Officer

Physicians Health Plan of SC, 4700 Forest Drive, Suite 104, Columbia 29204; tel. 803/787-6066; Thomas M. Robertson, Chief Executive Officer

Travelers Health Network of SC, Inc., 24 Market Street, Suite 210, Charleston 29401; tel. 803/723-7835; Bill Martin, Executive Director

SOUTH DAKOTA

South Dakota Physicians Health Group (Dakotacare), 1323 South Minnesota Avenue, Sioux Falls 57105; tel. 605/334-4000

TENNESSEE

First Choice Health Plan, Inc., P. O. Box 110845, Nashville 37220; tel. 615/834-3995; Thomas S. Fillebrown

HCA Care of Tennessee, Inc., P. O. Box 550, Nashville 37202; tel. 615/327-9951; Linda West

HealthStream Corp., 3920 Dayton Boulevard, P. O. Box 15249, Chatanooga 37415; tel. 615/870-4931; Michael M. Aiken, M.D.

Heritage National Healthplan of Tennessee, 1016 Weisgarber Road, Suite 259, Knoxville 37909; tel. 615/584-1127; Cynthia A. Winker, Operations Manager

Humana Health Plan of Tennessee, Inc., Osborne Office Center, Suite 510, Chattanooga 37411; tel. 615/899-5291; Vicky Hatfield, Executive Director

Physicians Health Plan, Ltd. Health Master, 4535 Harding Road, Suite 310, Nashville 37205; tel. 615/298-9990; John L. Wolf

Prudential Health Care Plan, Inc., 227 French Landing Drive, Suite 200, Nashville 37228; tel. 615/248-7100; P. A. Butcher

Southern Health Plan, Inc. d/b/a IPA Apple Plan and d/b/a Medicare & More, P. O. Box 97, Memphis 38101; tel. 901/529-9696; Tim Hogan, Executive Director

Tennessee First Health Plan, 912 South Gay Street, Suite 800, Knoxville 37902; tel. 615/546-2529; John Coyle, Executive Director

Tennessee Health Care Network, Inc. Care Choice, 801 Pine Street, Chattanooga 37402; tel. 615/755-5744; Wayne E. Willison

Tennessee Health Plan, Inc., 16 Brentshire Square, Jackson 38305; tel. 901/668-6900; Rob Dunning, Plan Administrator

Traveler's Health Network of TN-Knoxville, 408 Ceder Bluff Road, Suite 500, Knoxville 37923; tel. 615/690-6767; Dr. David England, Medical Director

TEXAS

Alliance Health Plan, Inc., 2600 North Loop West, P.O. Box 922009, Houston 77292; tel. 713/923-7231; Elliott Wolf, Chief Executive Officer

CIGNA Health Network, Inc., 12222 Merit Drive, Suite 650, Dallas 75251; tel. 214/788-0616; Mark O. Johnson, General Manager

Central Texas Health Plan, Inc. d/b/a South Texas Health Plan, 8202 N. Pan Am Expressway, Suite 300, San Antonio 78239; tel. 512/650-0841; Herb Springall, Chief Operations Officer

Central Texas Health Plan, Inc. d/b/a Mid-Texas Health Plan, 2402 H.K. Dodgen Loop, Suite 207, Temple 76501; tel. 817/778-4202; Dennis Simmons, Executive Vice President and General Manager

Cigna Healthplan of Texas - Dallas, P. O. Box 202575, Dallas 75220; tel. 214/964-2041; Dr. Joel Bettigole, Vice President, General Manager

Cigna Healthplan of Texas - Houston, 1360 Post Oak Blvd., Houston 77056; tel. 713/266-4418; Dr. Donald Gessler, General Manager, Vice President

Coastal Bend Health Plan, P. O. Box 3457, Corpus Christi 78404; tel. 512/887-0101; Tom Dwyer, Executive Director

East Texas Health Plan, 3800 Paluxy, Suite 590, Tyler 75703; tel. 214/581-0922; Brent Casey, Executive Director

Greater Amarillo Health Plan, Inc. d/b/a FIRSTCARE, 1901 Medi-Park Place, Suite 2000, Amarillo 79106; tel. 806/353-2131; Mike Autrey, Executive Director

Harris Health Plan, Inc., 1325 Pennsylvania Ave. 4th Floor, Fort Worth 76104; tel. 817/878-5800; Bill Richards, Interim Executive Director

Humana Health Plan of Texas, Inc., Humana Health Plan of Dallas, 1603 LBJ Freeway at Luna, Suite 820, Dallas 75234; tel. 214/247-6992; Maurice Trimm, Operations Manager

Humana Health Plan of Texas, Inc., Humana Health Plan of Corpus Christi, 3301 South Alameda, Suite 506, Corpus Christi 78411; tel. 512/854-8955; Jim Salver, Executive Director

Humana Health Plan of Texas, Inc., Humana Health Plan of San Antonio, 70 Northeast Loop 410, Suite 410, San Antonio 78216; tel. 512/366-4502; Ernest B. Paliszewski, Executive Director

Humana Health Plan of Texas, Inc., Humana Health Plan of Houston, Renaissance Plaza, 2616 South Loop West, Suite 270, Houston 77054; tel. 713/661-6858; Sally Imig, Operations Manager

Kaiser Fdn. Health Plan of Tx., 12720 Hillcrest, Suite 600, Dallas 75230; tel. 214/458-5000; Ms. Margaret Jordan, Vice President, Regional Manager

Maxicare North Texas, Inc., 122 W. Carpenter Freeway, Suite 200, Irving 75039; tel. 214/252-1001; Chris Wing, Executive Director

Maxicare San Antonio, Inc., 4499 Medical Drive, Suite 383, San Antonio 78229; tel. 512/696-6306; Ms. Frances Willmann, Executive Director

Maxicare Texas, Inc., 6900 Fannin, Suite 1000, Houston 77030; tel. 713/797-0123; Alex Slabosky, Executive Director

MetLife HealthCare Network of Texas, Inc., 1320 Greenway Dr., Suite 1000, Irving 75038; Fran Prescott, CEO

Mid-Texas Health Plan, P. O. Box 6127, Temple 76503; tel. 817/778-5233; Chuck Gardner, Interim Executive Vice President & General Manager

Pacificare of Texas, Inc., 8000 IH-10 West, Suite 335, San Antonio 78230; tel. 512/525-9127; Steve Bennett, President

Prudential Health Care Plan, Inc., P. O. Box 2884, Houston 77001; tel. 713/993-9440; Vince Contorno, Vice President

Prudential Health Care Plan, Inc. d/b/a PruCare of Austin, P. O. Box 26725, Austin 78755; tel. 512/465-6666; Mo Keathley, Vice President

Prudential Health Care Plan, Inc. d/b/a PruCare of San Antonio, 613 N.W. Loop 410, Suite 600, San Antonio 78216; tel. 512/366-1921; Ken Bates, Vice President

Prudential Health Care Plan, Inc. d/b/a PruCare of North Texas, 6060 N. Central Expressway, Suite 230, Dallas 75206; tel. 214/369-8480; Russell H. Folk, Vice President & CEO

Rio Grande HMO, Inc., 4150 Pinnacle, Suite 203, El Paso 79902; tel. 915/542-1547; Larry Bowermon, Chief Executive Officer

Sanus Texas Health Plan, Inc., 3800 Buffalo Speedway, Suite 230, Houston 77098; tel. 713/993-9520; E. E. Horn, Executive Director

Sanus Texas Health Plan, Inc., 8600 Freeport Parkway, Suite 3040, Irving 75063; tel. 214/929-0376; Stan Alekna, Executive Director

Scott & White Health Plan, 2401 South 31st Street, Temple 76508; tel. 817/774-3000; Deny Radefeld, Executive Director

Share Health Plan of Texas, 3520 Executive Center Drive, Suite 100, Austin 78731; tel. 512/477-4273; Diana Tchida, President and Chief Executive Officer

Southwest Health Plan, Inc., 3310 Live Oak, Suite 300, LB16, Dallas 75204; tel. 214/821-6622; Martin Q. Dale, President and Chief Executive Officer

Texas Health Plans, Inc., 3307 Northland Drive, Suite 300, Austin 78731; tel. 512/454-6771; W. Lee Smith, Dr. P.H., President and Chief Executive Officer

Travelers Health Network of Texas, Inc. San Antonio Division, 9901 IH 10 West, Suite 300, San Antonio 78230; tel. 512/699-6060; Thomas C. Jackson, Executive Director and Vice President

Travelers Health Network of Texas, Inc., 433 E. Las Colinas Blvd., Suite 750, Irving 75039; tel. 214/506-0000; Linda F. James, Ph.D., Executive Director

Travelers Health Network of Texas, Inc. - Houston Division, Post Oak Central One, 2000 Post Oak Blvd., Suite 1650, Houston 77056; tel. 713/622-6667; Jerry H. Brazil, Executive Director

United Dental Care of Texas, Inc., 15851 Dallas Parkway, Suite 755, Dallas 75248; tel. 214/458-7474; James B. Kingston, President

United Medical Plan, 1300 Post Oak Blvd., Suite 1500, Houston 77056; tel. 713/623-0244; Ms. Kathleen Cartwright, President

UTAH

Deseret Healthcare, 10 South Main Street, Salt Lake City 84101; tel. 801/533-8793; Merwin U. Stewart, President

EQUICOR Equitable HCA Corporation, 5295 South 300 West, Suite 280, Murray 84107; tel. 801/265-2777; Kim P. Vance

Educators Health Care, 875 E. 5180 S., Murray 84107; tel. 801/262-7476; Donald W. Ulmer, President

FHP Health Plan, Inc., 35 West Broadway, Salt Lake City 84101; tel. 801/355-1234; Elden R. Mitchell, Regional Vice President

HCA Care of Utah, Inc., 4052 W. Pioneer Parkway, West Valley 84120; tel. 801/964-0444; Kim P. Vance

HealthWise, 2505 Parley's Way, Salt Lake City 84109; tel. 801/481-6177; C. David Kikumoto, President

IHC Care, Inc., 36 South State, 22nd Floor, Salt Lake City 84111; tel. 801/530-3587; William H. Nelson, President

Maxicare Utah, Inc., 675 East 500 South #330, Salt Lake City 84102; tel. 801/532-5743; Fred W. Wasserman, Chairman

Physicians Health Plan of Utah, 1121 East 3900 South, Suite 220, Salt Lake City 84124; tel. 801/268-1475; Colin Gardner, Chief Executive Officer

VERMONT

Community Health Plan - Bennington Health Center, 655 Main Street, Bennington 05201; tel. 802/447-2343

VIRGINIA

AETNA/CHOICE Healthcare Plan, 8615 Westwood Center Drive, Suite 101, Vienna 22180; tel. 703/790-5020; F. Kenneth Wood

CapitalCare, Inc., 1235 Jefferson Davis Highway, Suite 1105, Arlington 22202; tel. 703/685-5028; David Metz, President

Choice Healthcare Plan, 8615 Westwood Center Dr. Suite 101, Vienna 22180; tel. 703/790-5020

EQUICOR Health Plan, Inc., 4050 Innslake Drive, Glen Allen 23060; tel. 804/273-1100; Gordon L. Church, Regional Vice President

Health Plan of Virginia, Inc. d/b/a Travelers Health Network, 100 West Plume Street, Suite 720, Norfolk 23510; tel. 804/622-6711; Dr. Claude A. Smith, Executive Vice President

Healthkeepers/HMO Plus (an affiliate of Blue Cross/Blue Shield of Virginia, 602 South Jefferson, Box 13808, Roanoke 24037; tel. 804/985-5000

Maxicare Virginia, L.P., The Halifax Building, Suite 320, 6161 Kempsville Circle, Norfolk 23502; tel. 804/466-0712; David P. Hunsaker, Executive Director

Network Health Plan Corporation, 8550 Lee Highway, Fairfax 22031; tel. 703/849-8800; Mrs. Virginia Dollard, Executive Director

Optima Health Plan, 18 Koger Ex. Center, Suite 118, Norfolk 23502; tel. 804/466-6400; Jack McNamara, President

Physicians Health Plan, Inc., 1700 North Moore Street, Suite 1500, Arlington 22209; tel. 703/525-0602; Richard Friedman

PruCare of Richmond, 1000 Chinaberry Blvd., Richmond 23225; tel. 804/323-0900; Jim Brittian, Vice President

The following is a list of Health Maintenance Organizations developed from information provided by state and federal agencies. The list is current as of January 1, 1987.

We present this list simply as a convenient directory. Inclusion or omission of any organization indicates neither approval nor disapproval by the American Hospital Association.

Southern Health Services, 2812 Emerywood Parkway, Richmond 23229; tel. 804/282-2500; Howard J. Newman, President

Virginia HMO, Inc. (d/b/a HMO Plus), P. O. Box 26623, Richmond 23220; tel. 804/254-3855; Gail Howerton

WASHINGTON

AmeriCare of WA, P. O. Box 3387, Bellevue 98009; tel. 206/451-8063; Ms. Mary Fowler, Chief Executive Officer

CIGNA Healthplan of Washington, Inc., 701 5th Avenue, 29th Floor Columbia Center, Seattle 98104; tel. 206/625-8880; Richard O. Danielson, Vice President and General Manager

Group Health Coop. of Puget Sound, 300 Elliott Avenue West, Seattle 98119; tel. 206/326-6845; Mr. Gail Warden, President and Chief Executive Officer

Group Health Northwest, P. O. Box 204, Spokane 99210; tel. 509/838-9100; Henry Berman, President and Chief Executive Officer

Group Health of WA, 300 Elliott Avenue W., Seattle 98119; tel. 206/326-6262; Henry Berman, M.D.

HMO Washington, 4010 Lake Washington Blvd. N.E., Suite 300, Kirkland 98033; tel. 206/828-9200; Jerry R. Hansen, President and Chief Executive Officer

HealthPlus, P. O. Box 2113, Seattle 98111; tel. 206/775-6502; Jeff Blancett, Executive Vice President

Humana Health Plan of Washington, Inc., One Pacific Building, 621 Pacific Avenue, Suite 5, Tacoma 98402; tel. 206/272-5335; Keith Macumber, Market Sales Manager

Maxicare of Washington, 5750 Columbia Center, Seattle 98104; tel. 206/624-5333; Stephen H. Moore, M.D., Executive Director

Pacific Health, 401 - 2nd Avenue South, Suite 300, Seattle 98104; tel. 206/326-4645; Ms. Nancy Silberg, President

Thurston County Health Maintenance Organization, 520 East Union, Olympia 98501; tel. 206/352-7611; B. J. Mabry, Executive Manager

Virginia Mason MedCenters, Inc., 1919 IBM Building, 1200 - 5th Avenue, Seattle 98101; tel. 206/223-8844; Kevin Roberg, President

WEST VIRGINIA

Mountaineer Med Plan, Inc., 1200 J.D. Anderson Drive, Morgantown 26505; tel. 304/624-2332; Dawn Newell

The Health Plan of The Upper Ohio Valley, Inc., Riley Building, Suite 900, Wheeling 26003; tel. 304/232-1063; John Pollack, President

WISCONSIN

Aetna Healthcare Asssurance Programs of Wisconsin, Inc., 3077 North Mayfair Road, Milwaukee 53222; tel. 414/257-3636; Sam Ours, Acting Executive Director

Community Choice Health Plan, Inc., 115 East Waldo Blvd., Manitowoc 54220; tel. 414/684-4447; William L. Mineau

CompCare Health Services Ins. Corp., 401 W. Michigan Street, Milwaukee 53201; tel. 414/226-6744; George Collentine, M.D., Medical Director

DeanCare HMO, 6515 Grand Teton Plaza, Madison 53719; tel. 608/833-7300; John Turcott, President

Eau Claire Chippewa Health Protection Plan, 400 Westwood Drive, Wausau 54401; tel. 715/847-8244

Employers Health Insurance Company, WEG Boulevard, Green Bay 54344; tel. 800/558-4444; Gregory M. Devine

Family Health Plan, 12500 West Bluemound road, Elm Grove 53122; tel. 414/786-3338; Conrad Sobczak, Executive Director

Greater LaCrosse Health Plans, Inc., 815 South 10th Street, LaCrosse 54601; tel. 608/785-2644; Steven Kunes, Marketing Director

Group Health Coop. of Eau Claire, 1030 Regis Court, Eau Claire 54701; tel. 715/836-8552; Mr. Claire Johnson, General Manager

Group Health Cooperative of South Central Wisconsin, One South Park Street, Madison 53715; tel. 608/257-9700; Patrick R. Brady, Executive Director

Gunderson Clinic/Wisconsin Physicians Service Q Care Plan, 1836 South Avenue, La Crosse 54601; tel. 608/782-7300

HMO Midwest, 502 Second Street, Hudson 54016; tel. 612/456-8433; Mary K. Brainerd

HMO of Wisconsin, 576 - 3rd Street, Prairie du Sac 53578; tel. 608/643-2491; Devon W. Barrix, Chief Executive Officer

Health Protection Plan c/o Wausau Insurance Company, 2000 Westwood Drive, Wausau 54401; tel. 715/845-5211; Jeffrey Zriny

Health Reach, 2266 N. Prospect, Suite 612, Milwaukee 53202; tel. 414/271-7123; Ray P. Madina, Executive Director

Hospital Health Plan of Northweastern Wisconsin, Inc., 744 South Webster Avenue, P. O. Box 1700, Green Bay 54305; tel. 414/433-3796; Patrick Hawley

Hospital Sisters Health Insurance Corporation of Wisconsin, Unity Health Plan, 402 Graham Avenue, Suite 330, Eau Clair 54701; tel. 715/839-7272; Carol Ebel

Lake Winnebago Area Health Protection Plan, 2000 Westwood Drive, Wausau 54401; tel. 715/847-8666

Maxicare Health Insurance Company, 733 N. Van Buren 4th Floor, Milwaukee 53202; tel. 414/271-6371; Max Kenyon, Executive Director

MetLife HealthCare Network of Wisconsin, Inc., 1 Park Plaza, Park Place, Suite 170, Milwaukee 53224; Mike Silgen, CEO

Midelfort HealthPlan, 2620 Stein Boulevard, Eau Claire 54701; tel. 715/832-3235; LMs. Kathryn R. Teeters, Director

Milwaukee Health Prot. Plan, 6620 West Capital Drive, Milwaukee 53216; tel. 414/463-2800; Bill Warner, Administrator

Network Health Plan, Inc., 411 Lincoln Drive, Neenah 54956; tel. 414/727-2700; Mark Moody, Executive Director

Network Health Plan, Inc., Appleton Center Office Building, 100 West Lawrence Street, Appleton 54911; tel. 414/738-4000; Mark Moody, Executive Director

Nicolet Health Plan, 878 Airport Road, Menasha 54952; tel. 414/725-6833

North Central Health Protection Plan, P. O. Box 969, Wausau 54401; tel. 715/847-8866; Jeffrey Zriny

Physicians Plus HMO, 345 West Washington Avenue, Madison 53703; tel. 608/257-7587; Peggy Ann Smelser, Executive Director

Portage County HealthGuard, P. O. Box 250, Stevens Point 54481; tel. 715/346-8134; Rollie Diehl, Acting Executive Director

PrimeCare Health Plan of WI, 1233 North Mayfair Road, Milwaukee 53226; tel. 414/453-9070; John McGinnis, President

Q Care c/o Wisconsin Physicians Service, P. O. Box 8190, Madison 53708; tel. 608/221-4711; Martin Timmins

Samaritan Health Plan Insurance Corporation, 1101 North Market Street, Suite 200, Milwaukee 53202; tel. 414/277-9000

Security Health Plan of Wisconsin, Inc. Marshfield Clinic, 1000 North Oak Avenue, Marshfield 54449; tel. 715/387-5679; Robert J. DeVita

SelecCare c/o Wisconsin Physicians Service, P. O. Box 8190, Madison 53708; tel. 608/221-5076; Dennis Fahey

St. Francis Health Maintenance Organization, Inc., 3237 South 16th Street, Milwaukee 53215; tel. 414/647-5000; Julie Jacobson, Director of Operations

TotalCare Health Plan, Inc., 2040 West Wisconsin Avenue, Milwaukee 53233; tel. 414/937-8340; Robert W. Timberlake, Executive Director

Trane Health Protection Plan, 2000 Westwood Drive, Wausau 54401; tel. 715/842-6815; Mike Egan, Administrator

Wisconsin Health Org. Ins. Corp., 2350 West Villard Avenue, Milwaukee 53209; tel. 414/527-9950; Kipton Kaplan, President and Chief Executive Officer

WYOMING

Blue Cross and Blue Shield of Wyoming d/b/a HMO Wyoming, P. O. Box 2375, Cheyenne 82003; tel. 307/637-4466; Lloyd B. Wilder, Senior Director

U.S. Associated Areas

GUAM

FHP, Inc. (Guam), P. O. Box 6690-C, Tamunig 96911; tel. 671/646-7826

PUERTO RICO

Caribbean Medical Services, Inc., Calle 2 E-13, Urb. Santa Cruz, Bayamon 00619; tel. 809/780-6536

Cooperativo de Servicios de Salud Castaner, Apartado 245, Castaner 00631; tel. 809/829-5770

Gastronomical Workers Union Local 610 Metropolitan Hotel Association Health & Welfare Fund, Calle Monserrate 608 Pda. 15-1/2, Santurce 00907; tel. 809/724-8856

Group Health Management, Inc., Ave. Ponce de Leon 69 Altos, Apartado 3333, Hato Rey 00919; tel. 809/758-7022; Edwin Mariota, Vice President

Group Sales & Service of Puerto Rico, Inc., Calle Ing. Fernando Calder #463, Urb. Eleonar Roosevelt, Hato Rey 00918; tel. 809/764-5792; Luis A. Salgado-Torres, President

H.M.O. Medical System Corp., San Patricio Plaza Suite 194, Caparra Heights 00920; tel. 809/725-9555

Health Plus, Inc., Royal Bank Center, Suite A-285, Hato Rey 00917; tel. 809/766-2800

Island Healthcare, Inc., Apartado 3310, Hato Rey 00919; tel. 809/726-6582

Medic Plan, Inc., Calle Tanca 252, Apartado 4268, San Juan 00905; tel. 809/724-6295

Mennonite General Hospital, Inc., Calle Jose G. Vazquez, Apartado 1379, Aibonito 00609

Plan Comprensivo de Salud, Inc., Avenida Ponce de Leon 328, Avenida de Diego 301 - Pda. 22, Santurce 00909; tel. 809/724-0190

Plan Familiar de Salud, Inc., Avenida Ponce de Leon 156, Puerta de Tierra, San Juan 00901; tel. 809/721-7733

Plan Medico Doctor Gubern, Inc., Calle General Valero Num. 267, Apartado 846, Fajardo 00648; tel. 809/863-0924; Montserrat J. de Garcia, Chief Executive Officer

Plan San Carlos de Servicios de Salud, Inc., Calle Dufresne #11, Apartado 639, Humacao 00661; tel. 809/852-4444

Plan de Salud Doctores Perea, Inc., Edif. Radio Centro 305-B, Apartado 3087 - Est. Marina, Mayaguez 00709; tel. 809/833-5179

Plan de Salud Hospital Metropolitano, Inc., Apartado EH - Caparra Heights, San Juan 00922; tel. 809/783-2600

Plan de Salud Hospital de la Concepcion, Inc., Calle Luna Num. 41, Apartado 285, San German 00753; tel. 809/892-1860

Plan de Salud de la Federacion de los Maestros de Puerto Rico, Inc., Edif. La Electronica, Inc. - Ofic. 301, Rio Piedras 00936; tel. 809/758-5610

Police Medical Services, Inc., Avenida Domenech Num. 385, Hato Rey 00918; tel. 809/751-2400

Puerto Rico HMO, Inc., Edif. Caso - Ofic. 701, Ave. Ponce de Leon 1225 - Parada 18, Santurce 00907; tel. 809/721-3450

Ryder Health Plan, Inc., Call Box 859, Humacao 00661; tel. 809/852-0846; Francisco Rivera Santiago, Administrator

Servi Medical, Inc. c/o Dr. Bernadette Tariak, Ave. Munoz Rivera 402, Parada 31, Hato Rey 00917; tel. 809/758-5555

Servicios Medicos Integrados, Inc., Monte Mall 2do. Piso Suite 19B, Ave. Munoz Rivera, Hato Rey 00918; tel. 809/758-1870; Jose Ramos, President

Servicios Medicos Rodmar, Inc., Ave. Fernandez Juncos 1826, Santurce 00910; tel. 809/728-4525

Servicios de Salud de Diego, Ave. de Diego 310 - Pda. 22, Santurce 00940; tel. 809/725-0450

Health Maintenance Organization Agencies

Information for the following list was obtained directly from the agencies.

ALABAMA: Department of Insurance, 135 S. Union St., Montgomery 36130; tel. 205/269-3550; John S. Greeno, comr.

ARIZONA: Department of Insurance, 801 E. Jefferson, Phoenix 85034; tel. 602/255-5400

ARKANSAS: Department of Insurance, 400-18 University Tower Bldg., Little Rock, 72204; tel. 501/371-1325

CALIFORNIA: Department of Corporations, Health Care Service Plans Division, 600 S. Commonwealth Ave., Los Angeles 90005; tel. 213/736-3131: 1107 9th St., 8th Flr., Sacramento 95814; 916/324-9028

COLORADO: Department of Regulatory Agencies, Division of Insurance, Financial Examination Section, 303 W. Colfax, 5th Flr., Denver 80204; tel. 303/866-3201; John Kezer, comr.

CONNECTICUT: Department of Insurance, 165 Capital Ave., Hartford 06106; tel. 203/566-5275; Peter W. Gillies, comr.

DELAWARE: Department of Health and Social Services, Division of Public Health, Office of Health Facilities Licensing and Certification, 3000 Newport Gap Pike, Wilmington 19808; tel. 302/571-3499; James E. Harvey, dir.

FLORIDA: Department of Insurance, Bureau of Allied Lines, 637 Larson Building, 200 E. Gaines St., Tallahassee 32399; tel. 904/488-6766; Robert Johnson, chf.

GEORGIA: Department of Insurance, 700 West Tower, Floyd Building, 2 Martin Luther King, Jr., Dr., Atlanta 30334; tel. 404/656-2056; Warren D. Evans, comr.

HAWAII: Department of Labor and Industrial Relations, Division of Disability Compensation, Plans Branch, 830 Punchbowl St., Rm 210, Honolulu 96813; tel. 808/548-5415

IDAHO: Department of Insurance, Division of Examinations, 700 W. State St., Boise 83720; tel. 208/334-2250; Larry Cross, chf. examiner

ILLINOIS: Department of Insurance, 320 W. Washington St., 4th Flr., Springfield 62767; tel. 217/782-1771; John E. Washburn, dir.

INDIANA: Department of Insurance, 311 W. Washington St., Suite 300, Indianapolis 46204; tel. 317/232-2385

IOWA: Dept. of Commerce, Division of Insurance, Lucas State Office Bldg., Des Moines 50319; tel. 515/281-5705; William D. Hager, comr.

KANSAS: Insurance Department, Accident and Health Division, 420 S.W. 9th, Topeka 66612; tel. 913/296-3071; Fletcher Bell, comr.

KENTUCKY: Department of Insurance, Life and Health Division, P.O. Box 517, 229 W. Main St., Frankfort 40602; tel. 502/564-3630; Matthew Johnson, dir.

LOUISIANA: Department of Insurance, P.O. Box 94214, Baton Rouge 70804; tel. 504/342-5900; Sherman A. Bernard, comr.

MAINE: Department of Professional and Financial Regulation, Bureau of Insurance, State House, Station 34, Augusta 04333; tel. 207/289-3101; Everard Steven, actg. supt.

MARYLAND: Department of Licensing and Regulation, Insurance Division, 501 St. Paul Place, Baltimore 21202; tel. 301/333-6300; Edward J. Muhl, comr.

MASSACHUSETTS: Division of Insurance, 100 Cambridge St., Boston 02202; tel. 617/727-3333; Peter Hiam, comr.

MICHIGAN: Department of Public Health, Bureau of Health Facilities, Division of HMO Services, 3500 N. Logan, Lansing 48909; tel; 517/335-8500; Raj Wiener, chf.

MINNESOTA: Department of Health, Alternative Delivery Systems, 717 S.E. Delaware St. P.O. Box 9441, Minneapolis 55440; tel. 612/623-5365; Kathleen Burek, dir.

MISSOURI: Division of Insurance, Life and Health and Review Section, P.O. Box 690, Jefferson City 65102; tel. 314/751-4126; James W. Casey, supr.

NEBRASKA: Department of Insurance, Box 94699, Lincoln 68509; tel. 402/471-2201; William H. McCartney, dir.

NEW YORK: Department of Health, Office of Health Systems Management, Bureau of Alternative Delivery Systems, Empire State Plaza, Corning Tower Building, Albany 12237; tel. 518/474-5515; Joyce Gallimore, dir.

NEVADA: Department of Commerce, Insurance Divison, 201 S. Fall St., Carson City 89710; tel. 702/885-4270; David A. Gates, comr.

NEW HAMPSHIRE: Department of Insurance, Examination Division, 169 Manchester St., Concord 03301; tel. 603/271-2241; Robert M. Solitro, dir.

NEW JERSEY: Department of Health, Division of Health Planning and Resource Development, Alternative Health Systems, CN 360, Trenton 08625; tel. 609/984-5054; Edwin V. Kelleher, chf.

NEW MEXICO: State Corporation Commission, Department of Insurance, P.O. Drawer 1269, Santa Fe 87504; tel. 505/827-4500; Vicente B. Jasso, supt.

NORTH CAROLINA: Department of Insurance, P.O. Box 26387, Raleigh 27611; tel. 919/733-7343; James E. Long, comr.

NORTH DAKOTA: Department of Insurance, State Capitol, Bismarck 58505; tel. 701/224-2440; Earl R. Pomeroy, comr.

OHIO: Department of Insurance, HMO Division, 2100 Stella Ct., Columbus 43266; tel. 614/481-5738; Phyllis Wise, sec.

OKLAHOMA: Health Planning Commission, P.O. Box 53551, 1000 N.E. 10th St., Oklahoma City 73152; tel. 405/271-3960; Suzanne W. Nichols, dir.

OREGON: Department of Commerce, Division of Insurance, Commerce Bldg., 158 12th St. N.E., Salem 97310; tel. 503/378-4271; Theodore R. Kulongoski, comr.

PENNSYLVANIA: Department of Insurance, Division of Company Licensing, 1311 Strawberry Square, Harrisburg 17120; tel. 717/783-2142; Ronald E. Chronister, dep. ins. comr.

RHODE ISLAND: Department of Business Regulation, Division of Insurance, 100 N. Main St., Providence 02903; tel. 401/277-2223; Samuel L. Torman, asst. dir.

SOUTH CAROLINA: Department of Health and Environmental Control, Division of Health Licensing and Certification, Office of Health Licensing, 2600 Bull St., Columbia 29201; tel. 803/734-4680; Alan Samuels, dir.

SOUTH DAKOTA: Department of Health, Center for Health Policy and Statistics, 523 East Capitol, Pierre 57501; tel. 605/773-3693; Jan Smith, dir.

TENNESSEE: Department of Health and Environment, Bureau of Manpower and Facilities, 283 Plus Park Blvd., Nashville 37219; tel. 615/367-6204; Sherryl Midgett, asst. comr.

TEXAS: State Board of Insurance, 1110 San Jacinto, Austin 78701; tel; 512/463-6169; Lyndon Olsen, Jr., chm.

UTAH: Insurance Department, Heber Wells Building, 160 East 300 South, 2nd flr., Salt Lake City 84111; tel. 801/530-6408; Harold C. Yancey, comr.

VERMONT: Department of Banking and Insurance, 120 State St., Montpelier 05602; tel. 802/828-3301; Thomas P. Menson, comr.

VIRGINIA: State Corporation Commission, Bureau of Insurance, Company Licensing and Regulatory Compliance Section, Box 1157, Richmond 23209; tel. 804/786-3636; Alfred Gross, supr.

WASHINGTON: Office of the Insurance Commissioner, Insurance Building, Mail Stop Aq-21, Olympia 98504; tel. 206/753-7300; Dick Marquardt, comr.

WEST VIRGINIA: Insurance Commissioner's Office, Financial Conditions Division, 2100 Washington St., E., Charleston 25305; tel. 304/348-2100; John Collins, dir. & chf. examiner

WISCONSIN: Office of the Commissioner of Insurance, P.O. Box 7873, Madison 53707; tel. 608/266-3585; Thomas P. Fox, comr.

WYOMING: Department of Insurance, Herschler Building, 122 West 25th Street; tel. 307/777-7401; Gordon W. Taylor, Jr., ins. comr.

Freestanding Ambulatory Surgery Centers

The following list of freestanding ambulatory surgery centers was developed from information provided by state agencies. It is current as of January 1, 1987.

The AHA Guide contains two types of ambulatory surgery center listings: those that are hospital based and those that are freestanding. Hospital based ambulatory surgery centers are listed in section A of the AHA Guide and are identified by Facility Code F1. Please refer to that section for information on the over 5,000 hospital based ambulatory surgery centers.

Those freestanding ambulatory surgery centers accredited by the Joint Commission on Accreditation of Hospitals (JCAH) are identified by a hollow square (□). These surgery centers have been found to be in substantial compliance with the Joint Commission standards for ambulatory health care facilities, as found in the Ambulatory Health Care Standards Manual.

We present this list simply as a convenient directory. Inclusion or omission of any organization's name indicates neither approval nor disapproval by the American Hospital Association.

United States

ALABAMA

Baptist Medical Center - Montclair, 800 Montclair Road, Birmingham 35213; tel. 205/592-1225; Dennis A. Hall

Baptist Surgery Center, 2035 East South Boulevard, Montgomery 36111; tel. 205/288-2030; Faye Wimberly, RN

Birmingham Outpatient Surgical Center, Inc., 2720 University Boulevard, Birmingham 35205; tel. 205/323-7500; William O. Fitzpatrick, III, M.D.

Day Surgery of Huntsville, 911 Big Cove Road, Huntsville 35801; tel. 205/532-5600; John E. Hornbeak

Day Surgery of Muscle Shoals, 201 Avalon Avenue, Muscle Shoals 35661; tel. 205/386-1601; Charles Stokes

Decatur Med-Surg Center, Inc., 2828 Highway 31, South, Decatur 35603; tel. 205/353-2000; Bradford W. Dykes

Gadsden Surgery Center, 418 South Fifth Street, Gadsden 35901; tel. 205/543-1253; Scott Hardee

Holy Name of Jesus Ambulatory Surgical Center, Moragne Park, Gadsden 35902; tel. 205/543-5200; Bill Drinkard, Executive Director

Huntsville Surgery Center, 721 Madison Street, Huntsville 35801; tel. 205/533-4888; Bobbye H. Riggs

MediVision of Dothan, 2802 Ross Clark Circle, Southwest, Dothan 36301; tel. 205/793-3411; Leonard D. Canalejo, Director of Nursing

Mobile Eye Surgery Institute, 2882 Dauphin Street, Mobile 36606; tel. 205/473-2020; Sandy Bunch

Mobile Surgery Center, 1721 Springhill Avenue, Mobile 36608; tel. 205/438-3614; Stephen E. Cochran

Montgomery Surgical Center, Inc., 855 East South Boulevard, Montgomery 36116; tel. 205/284-9600; Trice C. Nichols

Outpatient Services East, Ltd., 52 Medical Plaza Drive, East, Suite 401, Birmingham 35235; tel. 205/838-3998; James E. Stidham, Chief Operating Officer

Springhill Surgery Center, 1725 Springhill Avenue, Mobile 36608; tel. 205/433-3445; Jeffery M. St. Clair

Surgicenter of Dothan, 1450 Ross Clark Circle, Southeast, Dothan 36301; tel. 205/793-3442; Krystal Cosby, Executive Director

Tuscaloosa Surgical Center, 1400 McFarland Blvd. N., Tuscaloosa 35406; tel. 205/345-5500; W. Omar Smith, M.D., Director

ALASKA

Alaska Surgery Center, 4001 Laurel Street, Anchorage 99508; tel. 907/563-3327; Louise Bjornstad, Executive Director

Alaska Women's Health Services, 2740 Lake Otis Parkway, Anchorage 99508; tel. 907/258-6162

Geneva Woods Surgical Center, 3730 Rhone Circle, Anchorage 99058; tel. 907/561-1170

ARIZONA

16th Street EmergiCenter John C. Lincoln Hospital & Medical Center, 6245 North 16th Street, Phoenix 85018

Academy Eye Surgery Center, 310 North Wilmot, Suite 106, Tucson 85711; tel. 602/885-6783; Joseph L. McCready, M.D.

Academy Surgical Center, 310 North Wilmot Road, Suite 309, Tucson 85711; tel. 602/296-7080; Janet R. Pelczynski, Operations Manager

Ambulatory Surgical Center, 605 West 10th Street, Mesa 85201; tel. 602/839-8880; M. Kent Moore, M.D.

Arizona Foot Institute, P.C., 2440 East Indian School Road, Phoenix 85014; tel. 602/954-6224; Alfred J. D'Angelo, D.P.M.

Arizona Foot Institute, P.C., 1901 West Glendale Avenue, Phoenix 85021; tel. 602/246-0816; B. R. Kaplan, D.P.M.

Arizona Medical Plaza Surgery, 1728 West Glendale Avenue, Phoenix 85021; tel. 602/995-0729; Susan J. Griffin, R.N., Administrator

Arizona Podiatry Surgical Center, 129 West Catalina Drive, Phoenix 85013; tel. 602/274-4100; Alexander Borgeas, D.P.M.

Bell-West Urgent Care Center Phoenix General Hospital, 4344 West Bell Road, Phoenix 85023; tel. 602/978-3088

Boswell Eye Institute, 10541 Thunderbird Road, Sun City 85351; tel. 602/933-3402; Kristi De Witt, Administrator

Center for Cataract Surgery, Ltd., 2916 North 3rd Street, Phoenix 85012; Sheldon Zinn, M.D.

Cigna Health Plan of Arizona, Inc. - Ambulatory Surgery, 2720 East Camelback Road, Phoenix 85016; tel. 602/957-0700; Bert B. Wagener

Deer Valley Physicians Emergicenter, 2525 West Greenway Road, Phoenix 85023

Desert Foothills Medical Center, Box 2150, Carefree 85377; tel. 602/488-9220

Dulaney Eye Clinic, Ltd. The Cataract Institute, 9425 West Bell Road, Sun City 85351; tel. 602/974-3613; David D. Dulaney, M.D.

East Valley Eye Institute, 2150 South Dobson, Suite 5, Mesa 85202; tel. 602/839-1717; Dr. Bluth

East Valley Health Service Center Samaritan Health Services, 11015 Apache Trail, Apache Junction 85220

Eye Institute of So. Arizona, 5632 East 5th Street, Tucson 85711; tel. 602/790-8888; Arline Deal, Administrator

Eye Surgery Center at Mesa, 6553 East Baywood, Mesa 85206; tel. 602/969-1349; Ronald W. Barnet, M.D.

Eye Surgery Center at Sun City, 13203 North 103rd Avenue, Sun City 85351; tel. 602/933-2594; Ronald W. Barnet, M.D.

Eye Surgery Center of Arizona, 636 West Southern Avenue, Mesa 85202; tel. 602/969-1349; Lorin M. Swagel, M.D.

Footcare SurgiCenter, 12250 North 111th Avenue, Youngtown 85363; tel. 602/979-4466; Gary N. Friedlander, D.P.M.

Gary Hall Eye Surgery Institute, P.C., 2501 North 32nd Street, Phoenix 85008; tel. 602/957-6799; Gerald Burbach, Administrator

Green Valley Emergency Center St. Mary's Hospital & Health Center, 100 West Esperanza Boulevard, Green Valley 85614; tel. 602/791-2069

Havasu Foot and Ankle Surgi-Center, 90 Riviera Drive, Lake Havasu 86403; tel. 602/855-7800; Robert Novack, D.P.M.

Havasu Outpatient Surgery Center, 151 Riviera Drive, Lake Havasu City 86403; tel. 602/855-9477; Dave Chapman, Administrator

Heatherbrae Ambulatory Surgical Center The Center for Outpatient Surgery, 1950 West Heatherbrae Drive, Suite 5, Phoenix 85015; tel. 602/230-0437; Sandara L. Dina, Administrator/Director

Jesse Owens Memorial Medical Center Phoenix Memorial Hospital, 325 East Baseline Road, Phoenix 85040; tel. 602/243-4251

The Lear Surgery Clinic - Scottsdale, a subsidiary of The Lear Eye Clinic, Ltd., 7351 East Osborn #104, Scottsdale 85251; tel. 602/990-9400; Samuel L. Pallin, M.D., F.A.C.S.

The Lear Surgery Clinic, a subsidiary of The Lear Eye Clinic, Ltd., 10615 West Thunderbird, A-100, Sun City 85351; tel. 602/974-9375; Samuel L. Pallin, M.D., F.A.C.S.

Lincoln Metro EmergiCenter John C. Lincoln Hospital, 3131 West Peoria Avenue, Phoenix 85029; tel. 602/866-8250

Maryvale Urgent Care Center, 8260 West Indian School, Phoenix 85033; tel. 602/849-3232

Medical Surgical Systems, Inc., Virginia Medical Park, 333 E. Virginia Ave., Suite 110, Phoenix 85004; tel. 602/252-9082; Alfred William Ferry

Medical Village Ambulatory Surgical Center, 11361 North 99th Avenue #105, Peoria 85345; tel. 602/974-0522; Brad Hayman, D.P.M.

Mesa Eye Surgeons, P.C. Cataract Surgery Clinic, 140 South Power Road, Mesa 85206; tel. 602/981-1345; Robert P. Gervais, M.D.

Metro Ambulatory Surgery, Inc., 3131 West Peoria Avenue, Phoenix 85029; tel. 602/375-1083; Kevin William Cleary, D.O., President, Board of Directors

Mohave Valley Medical Center, 1225 East Hancock Road, Riviera 85442; tel. 602/758-3931; James R. Harrell, Executive Director

Morenci Healthcare Center, Burro Valley and Coronado Alley, Morenci 85540; tel. 602/865-4511; Eddie W. Arnold, Administrator

Nogales Medical Clinic, 711 Morley Avenue, Nogales 85621; tel. 602/287-2726; Imogene A. Ball

Northern Arizona Eyeclinic Cataract and Ocular Surgery Institute, 900 North San Francisco Street, Flagstaff 86001; tel. 602/774-1888; J. Charles Casebeer, M.D.

Northwest Emergency Center Tucson General Hospital, 1601 West Ina Road, Tucson 85704; tel. 602/742-1101

Outpatient Surgical Care Ltd., 1530 West Glendale, Suite 105, Phoenix 85021; tel. 602/995-3395; Stephen Garber, M.D.

Phoenix Surgical Facility, Ltd., 1010 East McDowell Road, Suite 301, Phoenix 85006; tel. 602/271-9510; Wallace A. Reed, M.D.

Policlinica San Xavier, 809 East Washington Street, Phoenix 85007; tel. 602/238-3560; Peter Martin, Senior Vice President and Chief Executive Officer

Prescott Outpatient Surgical Center, 815 Ainsworth Drive, Prescott 86301; tel. 602/778-9770; Ruth B. White, Director

Ramar Medical Center A.S.C., 1555 East Ramar Road, Bullhead City 86442; tel. 602/763-8700; Roger Scott

Santa Cruz Surgical Center, 699 West Ajo Way, Tucson 85713; Richard Edward Quint

Scottsdale Memorial Hospital Outpatient Surgical Center, 3604 Wells Fargo Avenue, Suite N, Scottsdale 85251; tel. 602/481-4349; Anita Finch, R.N.

Southwest Eye Association, 801 - 20th Avenue, Safford 85546; tel. 602/428-6930; James F. Holder, O.D.

Southwestern Eye Center, 4760 Falcon Drive, Mesa 85205; tel. 602/985-7400; L. Lothaire Bluth, M.D., Medical Director

Southwestern Eye Center, 1515 E. Florence Blvd., Casa Grande 85222; tel. 602/985-7400; L. Lothaire Bluth, M.D., Medical Director

Southwestern Eye Center, 1375 W. 16th St., Yuma 85364; tel. 602/985-7400; L. Lothaire Bluth, M.D., Medical Director

Southwestern Eye Center d/b/a East Valley Eye Institute, 2150 S. Dobson, Mesa 85202; tel. 602/985-7400; L. Lothaire Bluth, M.D., Medical Director

Southwestern Eye Center Surgicenter, Ltd., Desert Professional Center, 1515 East Florence Boulevard, Casa Grande 85222; ; tel. 602/426-9224; Barbara Currier

Sun City Surgical Center, 13260 North 94th Drive, Peoria 85345; tel. 602/277-0619; H. William Reese, D.P.M.

Surgi-Tech Centers, 3271 North Civic Center Plaza, Scottsdale 85251; tel. 602/994-5977; Richard Jacoby, D.P.M.

SurgiCenter of Glendale, 5757 West Thurnderbird Road, Glendale 85306; tel. 602/843-1900; Wallace A. Reed, M.D., Executive Director

SurgiCenter, Inc., 1040 East McDowell Road, Phoenix 85006; tel. 602/258-1521; Wallace A. Reed, M.D.

SurgiSite, Inc., 10599 North Tatum Blvd., Suite F-150, Paradise Valley 85253; tel. 602/998-3263; Barbara Nicholich

The following list of freestanding ambulatory surgery centers was developed from information provided by state agencies. It is current as of January 1, 1987.

The AHA Guide *contains two types of ambulatory surgery center listings: those that are hospital based and those that are freestanding. Hospital based ambulatory surgery centers are listed in section A of the* AHA Guide *and are identified by Facility Code F1. Please refer to that section for information on the over 5,000 hospital based ambulatory surgery centers.*

Those freestanding ambulatory surgery centers accredited by the Joint Commission on Accreditation of Hospitals (JCAH) are identified by a hollow square (□). These surgery centers have been found to be in substantial compliance with the Joint Commission standards for ambulatory health care facilities, as found in the Ambulatory Health Care Standards Manual.

We present this list simply as a convenient directory. Inclusion or omission of any organization's name indicates neither approval nor disapproval by the American Hospital Association.

Surgical Eye Center of Arizona, Inc., 555 West Catalina Drive, Phoenix 85013; tel. 602/277-7997; Donald Miles, M.D.
TMC Family Medical Center, 1460 West Valencia Road, Tucson 85706; tel. 602/294-3131; David Colwell, Manager
Tempe Surgical Center, Inc., 2000 East Southern Avenue, Suite 101, Tempe 85282; tel. 602/838-9313; Wilson T. Shill, M.D.
Thomas-Davis Medical Centers d/b/a Thomas-Davis Surgi-Center, 750 N. Alvernon, P. O. Box 12650, Tucson 85732; tel. 602/881-6985; James J. Vitali
Thunderbird Urgent Care Center, 720 East Thunderbird Road, Phoenix 85022; tel. 602/863-2854
Valley Outpatient Surgery Center, 160 West University Drive, Mesa 85201; tel. 602/835-7373; Craig R. Cassidy, D.O.
West Valley Emergency Center, 1580 North Litchfield Road, Goodyear 85338; tel. 602/932-5701
Williams Emergency & Surgical Center Flagstaff Hosp. & Medical Center of No. Arizona, Inc., 301 South 7th Street, Williams 86046
Yuma Outpatient Surgery Center, 2475 Avenue A, Suite B, Yuma 85364; tel. 602/726-6910; Ronald F. Jones

ARKANSAS

Arkansas Ear, Nose and Throat Clinic, P.A., Ambulatory Surgery Center, 960 Medical Tower Building, Little Rock 72205; tel. 501/227-8501; Janelle Green, RN
Arkansas Surgery Center, 10 Hospital Circle, Batesville 72501; tel. 501/793-4040; Fredric J. Sloan, M.D.
Central Arkansas Surgery Center, Inc., 1024 North University Avenue, Little Rock 72207; tel. 501/663-0158; Jeanne Crews, Administrator
Cosmetic Facial Surgery, #2 Lile Court, Little Rock 72205; tel. 501/224-1044; Ellery C. Gay, M.D., President and Director
□ **(The) Ear and Nose-Throat Clinic, P.A. Outpatient Surgery Center,** 1200 Medical Towers Building, Little Rock 72205; tel. 501/227-5050; Joseph R. Phillips, RN, BS
Freeway Surgery Center, 5800 West Tenth Street, Suite 205, Little Rock 72204; tel. 501/663-7166; Pamela J. Hooper
Hot Springs Outpatient Surgery, P.A., 100 Ridgeway, Suite 7, Hot Springs 71901; tel. 501/624-4464; Othella Brogan, Director
Lowery Medical/Surgical Eye Center, P.A., 105 Central Avenue, Searcy 72143; tel. 501/268-7154; Benjamin R. Lowery, M.D.
Northeast Arkansas Surgery Center, Inc., 505 East Matthews, Jonesboro 72401; tel. 501/972-1723; William R. Tarver, Administrator
South Arkansas Outpatient Surgi-Center, 4800 South Hazel, Suite B, Pine Bluff 71603; tel. 501/536-0798; Lila M. King, COA

CALIFORNIA

Arcadia Outpatient Surgery, Inc., 614 West Duarte Road, Arcadia 91006; tel. 818/445-4714
Bay Area Surgery Centers (Sutter), 450 Sutter Street, 6th Floor, San Francisco 94108; tel. 415/981-1666; Ken Newcomb, Regional Director, Administrator
Beverly Surgical Center, 105 West Beverly Boulevard, Montebello 90640; tel. 213/728-5400; James G. Ovieda, Administrator
Community Family Planning Clinic, 4101 Long Beach Boulevard, Long Beach 90807; tel. 213/595-5277
Doctors Surgical Center, Inc., 9461 Grindlay Street, Suite 102, Cypress 90630; tel. 714/995-3001
Escondido Surgery Center, 343 East Second Avenue, Escondido 92025; tel. 619/480-6606
Good Samaritan Outpatient Surgery Center, 1245 Wilshire Boulevard, Ground Floor, Los Angeles 90017; tel. 213/977-2525; Norma M. Haynes, R.N., Manager
Granada Hills Surgical Center, Inc., 10339 Balboa Boulevard, Granada Hills 91334; tel. 818/366-3717
Greater Sacramento Surgery Center, 3201 Del Paso Boulevard, Sacramento 95815; tel. 916/929-7229; Susan Brunone, MHS, Administrator
Grossmont Surgery Center, 8881 Fletcher Parkway, La Mesa 92041; tel. 619/698-0930
McHenry Surgery Center, 1524 McHenry Avenue, Suite 240, Modesto 95350; tel. 209/576-2900; Helen Huston, RN, Director
Mercy San Juan Surgery Center, 6660 Coyle Avenue, Suite 100, Carmichael 95608; tel. 916/965-1936; Carl J. Conli, Administrator
Out-Patient Surgery Center, 17752 Beach Boulevard, Huntington Beach 92647; tel. 714/842-1426
Plasticenter, Inc., 3003 Salisbury Lane, Santa Cruz 95065; tel. 408/462-1000
Sacramento Plastic Surgery Center, 95 Scripps Drive, Sacramento 95825; tel. 916/929-1833
San Diego Outpatient Surgical Center, Inc., 770 Washington Street, San Diego 92103; tel. 619/299-9530
San Joaquin Surgical Center, Inc., 2828 Fresno Street, Fresno 93721; tel. 209/441-7004; Joan Growdon, Administrator
South Bay Ambulatory Surgical Center, 251 Landis Street, Chula Vista 92010; tel. 619/585-1020
Southwest Surgical Clinic, 4201 Torrance Boulevard, #240, Torrance 90503; tel. 213/540-7803; Dr. Otto Munchow, Administrator
Surgecenter of Palo Alto, 400 Forest Avenue, Palo Alto 94301; tel. 415/324-1832; Margo Mynderse-Isola, Executive Director
Surgicenter of South Bay, 23500 Madison Street, Torrance 90505; tel. 213/539-5120; D. Timothy Paulson, Executive Director
Sutter Surgery Center, 75 Scripps Drive, Sacramento 95825; tel. 916/929-9431; Marc Jones, Administrative Director
Walnut Creek Ambulatory Surgery, Inc., 2021 Ygnacio Valley Road, Building H Suite 102, Walnut Creek 94598; tel. 415/933-0290; Lori Fried, Administrator

COLORADO

□ **Ambulatory Surgery, Ltd.,** 320 East Fontanero, Suite 101, Colorado Springs 80907; tel. 303/634-8878
Boulder Surgery Center, 2525 - 4th Street, Boulder 80302; tel. 303/441-0570
Cherry Creek Eye Surgery Center Division of Rose Medical Center, 4999 East Kentucky Avenue, Denver 80222; tel. 303/692-0903
Colorado Outpatient Eye Surgical Center, 2480 South Downing, Denver 80210; tel. 303/777-7303
Colorado Springs Eye Surgery Center, Inc., 2920 North Cascade Avenue, Colorado Springs 80907; tel. 303/636-3352; Charles Mercers, Chief Executive Officer
Colorado Springs Medical Center Ambulatory Surgery Unit, 209 South Nevada Avenue, Colorado Springs 80903; tel. 303/475-7700; Hugh Servis, M.D., Medical Director
DTC Eye Surgery Center, 8400 East Prentice Avenue, Suite 1200, Englewood 80111; tel. 303/793-3000
Denver Eye Surgery Center, 13722 Denver West Parkway, Suite 120, Golden 80401; tel. 303/279-6600
Evergreen Eye Surgical Center, 28577 Buffalo Park Road, Evergreen 80439; tel. 303/674-4285
Eye Surgery Center of Colorado, P.C., 8403 Bryant Street, Westminster 80030; tel. 303/426-4810
Lakewood Surgical Center, 2201 Wadsworth Blvd., Lakewood 80215; tel. 303/234-0445; Connie Emmerich, Administrator
Medivision of South Denver, 8381 Southpark Lane, Littleton 80120; tel. 303/730-0404
North Denver Surgical Center, Ltd., 10001 North Washington, Thornton 80229; tel. 303/252-0083
Porter South SurgiCenter, 7730 South Broadway, Littleton 80122; tel. 303/798-8431
□ **Rocky Mountain Surgery Center, Ltd.,** 2405 Broadway, Boulder 80302; tel. 303/449-2020; Nathan W. Stiewig, Executive Director
St. Luke's Hospital ASC, 601 East 19th Avenue, Denver 80205; tel. 303/839-7777

CONNECTICUT

Bridgeport Surgical Center, 4920 Main Street, Bridgeport 06606; tel. 203/374-1515; Bernard A. Kershner, President
Connecticut Surgical Center, 81 Gillett Street, Hartford 06106; tel. 247-5555; Margaret Rubino
Danbury Surgical Center, 73 Sandpit Road, Suite 101, Danbury 06810; tel. 203/743-2400; Bernard A. Kershner, President
Hartford Surgical Center, 100 Retreat Avenue, Suite 100, Hartford 06106; tel. 203/549-7970; Bernard A. Kershner, President
Johnson Ambulatory Surgery Center, 148 Hazard Avenue, P. O. Box 909, Enfield 06082; tel. 203/749-8365; Anthony T. Valente
Naugatuck Valley Surgical Center, 160 Robbins Street, Waterbury 06708; tel. 203/755-6663; Bernard A. Kershner, President
Temple Surgical Center, 60 Temple Street, New Haven 06510; tel. 203/624-6008; Bernard A. Kershner, President

FLORIDA

AMI Single Day Surgery, 6629 Beach Boulevard, Jacksonville 32216; tel. 904/721-3096
□ **AMI Single Day Surgery,** 2589 North State Road 7, Lauderhill 33313; tel. 305/485-6400
AMI Single Day Surgery, 6950 West 20th Avenue, Hialeah 33016; tel. 305/821-0079
AMI Single Day Surgery, 1885 South Andrews Avenue, Ft. Lauderdale 33315; tel. 305/462-6366; Ross S. Ackerman, Executive Director
□ **AMI Single Day Surgery,** 1001 N.W. 13th Street, Boca Raton 33432; tel. 305/394-0022
□ **AMI Single Day Surgery,** 1130 Ponce DeLeon Blvd., Clearwater 33516; tel. 813/581-4800; Patricia L. Metcalf, Executive Director
□ **AMI Single Day Surgery,** 1500 Charles Street, New Port Richey 33522; tel. 813/848-0446
□ **AMI Single Day Surgery,** 1661 Phillips Road, Tallahassee 32308; tel. 904/878-5165
Ambulatory Centre of Miami, 8700 North Kendall Drive, Miami 33176; tel. 305/595-9511
Ambulatory Surgery Center, 4500 East Fletcher Avenue, Tampa 33613; tel. 813/977-8550; Larry Cyment, Administrator
Ambulatory Surgery Center/Bradenton, 5817 21st Avenue W., Bradenton 33529
Ambulatory Surgical Center of Central Florida, Inc., 801 North Stone Street, Deland 32720
Ambulatory Surgical Facility, 4470 Sheridan Street, Hollywood 33021; tel. 305/962-3210; Rosine G. Levy, Acting Executive Director
Bay Eye and Surgical Center, 1600 Jenks Avenue, Panama City 32405; tel. 904/763-6666
Cape Surgery Center, 1700 Waldemere, Sarasota 33579; tel. 813/953-1900
East Coast Hospital Inc. d/b/a Community Health Services of Crescent City, 1125 North Summit Street, Crescent City 32012; tel. 904/698-2791
Florida Eye Clinic Ambulatory Surgical Center, 160 Boston Avenue, Altamonte Springs 32701; tel. 305/834-7776; Julia C. Lewis, Chief Executive Officer
□ **Florida Surgical Center,** 2001 SW 13th Street, Gainesville 32608; tel. 904/375-7373; Russell Kenwood, Executive Director
Institute for Plastic & Reconstructive Surgery, Inc., 820 Arthur Godfrey Road, Miami Beach 33140; tel. 305/673-6164
Island Clinic Ambulatory Surgi Center, 2330 North Roosevelt Boulevard, Key West 33040
Medivision of Orange County, Inc., 116 W. Sturtevant St., Orlando 32806; tel. 305/423-4090; Eric Kriss, Chief Executive Officer

The following list of freestanding ambulatory surgery centers was developed from information provided by state agencies. It is current as of January 1, 1987.

The AHA Guide *contains two types of ambulatory surgery center listings: those that are hospital based and those that are freestanding. Hospital based ambulatory surgery centers are listed in section A of the* AHA Guide *and are identified by Facility Code F1. Please refer to that section for information on the over 5,000 hospital based ambulatory surgery centers.*

Those freestanding ambulatory surgery centers accredited by the Joint Commission on Accreditation of Hospitals (JCAH) are identified by a hollow square (□). These surgery centers have been found to be in substantial compliance with the Joint Commission standards for ambulatory health care facilities, as found in the Ambulatory Health Care Standards Manual.

We present this list simply as a convenient directory. Inclusion or omission of any organization's name indicates neither approval nor disapproval by the American Hospital Association.

The Ophthalmology Center Lake Worth, 2889 Tenth Avenue No., Lake Worth 33461

Out-Patient Surgical Facility of Venice, Inc., 600 Nokomis Avenue, S., P. O. Box 2047, Venice 33595; tel. 813/484-9773

Sarasota Surgery Center, 983 South Beneva Road, Sarasota 33582; tel. 813/365-5355; William Hamburg, Executive Director

Southwest Florida Institute of Ambulatory Surgery, Inc., 3700 Central Avenue, Suite 2, Ft. Myers 33901; tel. 813/275-0665

St. Luke's Surgical Center, 1570 U.S. Highway 19 No., Tarpon Springs 33589; tel. 813/938-9737

St. Petersburg Surgery Center, 539 Pasadena Ave., South, St. Petersburg 33707; tel. 813/345-8337; Pam Wiseman, Administrator

□ **Surgical Services of Ft. Myers, Inc. d/b/a AMI Single Day Surgery,** 4035 Evans Avenue, Ft. Myers 33901; tel. 813/939-7375

□ **Surgical Services of Tampa, Inc. d/b/a AMI Single Day Surgery,** 5013 N. Armenia Avenue, Tampa 33603; tel. 813/875-0562

Surgicare Center, 4101 Evans Avenue, Ft. Myers 33901; tel. 813/936-8212

Surgicare of Charlotte County, 21297 Olean Boulevard, Port Charlotte 33592; tel. 813/625-2300; Jose Flynn, Executive Director

Surgicenter of the Palm Beaches, 2808 Australian Avenue, West Palm Beach 33407; tel. 305/848-5700; Laurence Kustin, Managing Director

Venice Same Day Surgery, 950 Cooper Street, Venice 33595

GEORGIA

Ambulatory Surgical Facility of Brunswick, 8 Tower Medical Park, 3215 Shrine Road, Brunswick 31520; tel. 912/264-4882; Jimmy L. Dixon, Administrator

Atlanta Outpatient Surgery Center, 993 Johnson Ferry Road, Suite 300, Atlanta 30342; tel. 404/252-3074; Janie Ellison, Administrator

Atlanta Surgi-Center, Inc., 1113 Spring Street, N.W., Atlanta 30309; tel. 404/892-8608; Elizabeth Petzelt, Administrator

Atlanta Women's Medical Center, Inc., 3316 Piedmont Road, N.E., Suite 220, Atlanta 30305; tel. 404/262-3920

Augusta Surgical Center, 915 Russell Street, Augusta 30904; tel. 404/738-4925; Beryl Barrett, Administrator

Coliseum Same Day Surgery, 310 Hospital Drive, Macon 31208; tel. 912/742-1403; John Greer, Administrator

Columbus Women's Health Organization, Inc., 1226 Third Avenue, Columbus 31901; tel. 404/323-8363; Ms. Ann McCrory, Administrator

Dunwoody Outpatient Surgicenter, Inc., 4553 North Shallowford Road, Suite 60-C, Atlanta 30338; tel. 404/457-6303; Lauretta Mink, Administrator

Emory Clinic Ambulatory Surgery Center, 1327 Clifton Road, N.E., Atlanta 30322; tel. 404/321-0111; J. Lee Tribble, Administrator

Feminist Women's Health Center, 500 - 14th Street, N.W., Atlanta 30318; tel. 404/874-7551; Ms. Lynn Thogerson, Administrator

Gwinnett Ambulatory Surgical Center, 2131 Fountain Drive, Snellville 30278; tel. 404/979-8200; Dianne Barbaris, Administrator

Hillcrest Clinic of Atlanta, 384 Peachtree Street, N.E., Atlanta 30308; tel. 404/522-6200; Ms. Teresa Blake, Administrator

Marietta Surgical Center, 796 Church Street, Marietta 30060; tel. 404/422-1579; Ms. Charlotte Bellantoni, Administrator

Medical Eye Associates, Inc., 1429 Oglethorpe Street, Macon 31201; tel. 912/743-7061; David L. King, Administrator

Northlake-Tucker Ambulatory Surgical Center, 4915 LaVista Road, Tucker 30084; tel. 404/934-1984; R. B. Keene, Administrator

Northside Outpatient Surgery Center, 5675 Peachtree-Dunwoody Road, Suite 410, Atlanta 30342; tel. 404/256-2250; Ms. Marilyn Epstein, Administrator

Northside Women's Clinic, Inc., 3543 Chamblee-Dunwoody Road, Atlanta 30341; tel. 404/455-4210; James W. Gay, M.D., Administrator

Planned Parenthood of East Central Georgia, 1289 Broad Street, Augusta 30901; tel. 404/724-5557; Colonel Arnaldo Correa, Administrator

Savannah Medical Clinic, 803 East 34th Street, Savannah 31401; tel. 912/236-1603; Ms. Robin Fenn, Administrator

Surgi Center, Inc., 5675 Peachtree-Dunwoody Road, #602C, Atlanta 30342; tel. 404/257-1009; Ms. Doris B. Boye-Mintz, Administrator

Surgicare of Augusta, 915 Russell St., Augusta 30904; tel. 404/738-4925; Beryl Barrett, Administrator

HAWAII

Aloha Eye Clinic, 239 Wakea Avenue, Kahului, Maui 96732; tel. 808/877-3984; Russell T. Stodd, M.D.

Cataract and Retina Center of Hawaii, 1712 Liliha Street, Suite 400, Honolulu 96817; tel. 808/524-1010; Worldster Lee, M.D.

Faulkner Institute for Eye Care and Surgery, 1100 Ward Avenue, Suite 1001, Honolulu 96814; tel. 808/521-2305; Gerald D. Faulkner, M.D., President

Hawaiian Eye Surgicenter, 606 Kilani Avenue, Wahiawa 96786; tel. 808/621-8448; John M. Corboy, M.D., Director

The Honolulu Medical Group, 550 South Beretania Street, Honolulu 96813; Victor Hay-Roe, M.D.

Professional Plaza ASC, 1520 Liliha Street, Suite 302, Honolulu 96817; Alan Inouye, M.D., Medical Director

Surgicare of Hawaii, Inc., 226 North Kuakini Street, Suite 200, Honolulu 96817; tel. 808/528-2511; Allen B. Richardson, President

IDAHO

Idaho Ambucare Center, Inc., 211 West Iowa, Nampa 83651; tel. 208/467-4222; Gregory N. Schaefer, M.D., President

Idaho Eye Surgicenter, Inc., 2025 East 17th Street, Idaho Falls 83401; tel. 208/529-1922; Kenneth Turley, M.D., Medical Director

□ **Idaho Falls Surgical Center,** 1945 East 17th Street, Idaho Falls 83401; tel. 208/529-1945; James A. Haney, M.D., Medical Director

Magic Valley Ear, Nose and Throat Associates, Magic Valley Surgery Center, 570 Shoup Avenue West, Twin Falls 83301; tel. 208/733-1662; Thomas G. Samter, Administrator

North Idaho Day Surgery Center, Inc., 2205 North Ironwood Place, Coeur d'Alene 83814; tel. 208/664-0543; Michael P. Christensen, M.D., President

Twin Falls Clinic Hospital, Inc., 666 Shoshone Street East, Twin Falls 83301; tel. 208/733-3700; Marley Jackman, Administrator

ILLINOIS

Albany Medical-Surgical Center, 5086 North Elston, Chicago 60630; tel. 312/725-0200; Louis Myers, M.D., Medical Director

Ambulatory Surgical Center of Northwestern University, 240 East Huron Street, Chicago 60611; tel. 312/908-5221; Bernard C. Pecaro, D.D.S., M.D., Administrator

American Eye Institute, Inc., New Route 13, West, Marion 62959; tel. 618/997-1816; Dennis L. Ryll, M.D., Administrator

□ **Amsurg,** 330 North Madison Street, Joliet 60435; tel. 815/744-3000; Jo Ann Karpel, Administrator

Biogenetics, 520 North Michigan Avenue, 11th Floor, Chicago 60611; tel. 312/266-1235; Clifford Josefik, Administrator

Carbondale Clinic, 2601 West Main Street, Carbondale 62901; tel. 618/549-5361; Wayne Given, Administrator

Chang's Medical Arts Building, 923 North Center, Maryville 62062; tel. 618/345-7004; Shih-Chung Chang, M.D., Administrator

□ **Concord Medical Center,** 17 West Grand, Chicago 60610; tel. 312/467-6555; Mrs. Sherry Walker, Administrator

□ **Concord West,** 530 North Cass Avenue, Westmont 60559; tel. 312/963-2500; Nader Bozorgi, M.D., Medical Director

Day Surgery Facilities, Inc., 4211 North Cicero Avenue, Chicago 60641; tel. 312/794-1000; Andrew Cameron, Administrator

Desnick Eye Center, 3101 North Harlem Avenue, Chicago 60634; tel. 312/282-6840; Tom Quirck, Administrator

Doctors Surgicenter, 1045 East Mc Cord, Centralia 62801; tel. 618/532-3110; Charles K. Fischer, M.D., Administrator

Du Page Surgi-Center, Inc., 837 South Westmore Avenue, Lombard 60148; tel. 312/495-9788; K. Jafari, M.D., Administrator

Hawthorn Place Surgical Center, 1900 Hollister Drive, Libertyville 60048; tel. 312/367-8100; Mary Fogel, RN, Administrator

Hedd Surgicenter, 6020 South Halsted, Chicago 60621; tel. 312/651-9200; Ester M. Pimentel, M.D., Medical Director and Administrator

Hinsdale Surgical Center Inc., 40 South Clay Street, Hinsdale 60521; tel. 312/325-5035; Peter A. Szabo, Jr., Administrator

The Hope Clinic for Women, 1602 - 21st Street, Granite City 62040; tel. 618/451-5722; Laura Moody, RN, MBA, Executive Director

Horizons AMB Surgical Center, 630 Locust Street, Carthage 62321; tel. 217/357-3685; James E. Coeur, M.D., Administrator/Owner

Hugar Surgery Center, 1614 North Harlem Avenue, Elmwood Park 60635; tel. 312/452-6100; Donald W. Hugar, DPM, FACFS, Executive Director

Ingalls Same Day Surgery, 6701 West 159th Street, Tinley Park 60477; tel. 312/429-0222; Joseph J. Maschek, Administrator

Lincoln Ambulatory Surgical Center, 15643 South Lincoln Avenue, Harvey 60426; tel. 312/339-7000; Frederick Weiss, M.D., Medical Director

Loyola University/Mulcahy O-P Center, 2160 South First Avenue, Maywood 60153; tel. 312/531-3000; Joseph R. Eraci, M.D., Administrator

Metro Surgical Center, 201 North Wells Street, Chicago 60606; tel. 312/263-5300; Nasiruddin Rana, M.D., Administrator

Michigan Avenue Medical Center, 30 South Michigan Avenue, Chicago 60603; tel. 312/726-2105; Regalodo S. Florendo, M.D., Administrator

Midwest Center for Day Surgery, 3811 Highland Avenue, Downers Grove 60515; tel. 312/852-9300; Barbara Hemmerling, Administrator

Northwest Surgicare, 1100 West Central Road, Arlington Heights 60005; tel. 312/259-3080; Nancy L. Shalowitz., Administrator

Notre Dame Hills Surgical Center, 6401 West Main Street, Belleville 62223; tel. 618/398-5705; Kathleen Ferguson, RN, Administrator

One Day Surgery Center, 325 West Lincoln Avenue, Belleville 62221; tel. 618/235-4373; L. P. Maun, M.D., Administrator

Park Medical Center, 2814 West Peterson, Chicago 60659; tel. 312/465-0434; Eileen Adams, Administrator

Paulina Surgi-Center, Inc., 7616 North Paulina, Chicago 60626; tel. 312/761-0500; Sheldon Schecter, Administrator

Planned Parenthood Midwest Center, 100 East Ohio, Chicago 60611; tel. 312/664-3410; Amy Dienesch, Executive Director

Suburban Otolaryngology S. Ctr., 3340 South Oak Park Avenue, Berwyn 60402; tel. 312/749-3070; Edward A. Razim, M.D., Administrator

Suite Nine Twenty Five West, 845 North Michigan Avenue, Chicago 60611; tel. 312/642-4619; E. V. Tanski, M.D., Administrator

Surgicare Center Inc., 333 Dixie Highway, Chicago Heights 60411; tel. 312/754-4890; M. J. Crowe, Administrator

The following list of freestanding ambulatory surgery centers was developed from information provided by state agencies. It is current as of January 1, 1987.

The AHA Guide *contains two types of ambulatory surgery center listings: those that are hospital based and those that are freestanding. Hospital based ambulatory surgery centers are listed in section A of the* AHA Guide *and are identified by Facility Code F1. Please refer to that section for information on the over 5,000 hospital based ambulatory surgery centers.*

Those freestanding ambulatory surgery centers accredited by the Joint Commission on Accreditation of Hospitals (JCAH) are identified by a hollow square (□). These surgery centers have been found to be in substantial compliance with the Joint Commission standards for ambulatory health care facilities, as found in the Ambulatory Health Care Standards Manual.

We present this list simply as a convenient directory. Inclusion or omission of any organization's name indicates neither approval nor disapproval by the American Hospital Association.

□ **Urban Health Services, L.T.D.,** 18 South Michigan Avenue, Chicago 60603; tel. 312/726-2002; Regalado S. Florendo, M.D., Owner

INDIANA

Akin Medical Center, 2019 State Street, New Albany 47150; tel. 812/945-3557; Ms. Nancy Crumbo, B.S.N., RN, Administrator

American Surgery Center (North), 8651 North Township Line Road, Indianapolis 46260; tel. 317/876-2090; Kate Cancel, President

American Surgery Center of Indianapolis, 2007 North Capitol Avenue, Indianapolis 46202; tel. 317/926-4359; Rick S. Mohler, President

Calumet Surgery Center, 7847 Calumet Avenue, Munster 46321; tel. 219/836-5102; Fred A. Portney, M.D., Chief Administrative Officer

Evansville Surgery Center Associates, 1212 Lincoln Avenue, P. O. Box 1195, Evansville 47714; tel. 812/428-0810; William Hamburg, Administrator

Fairfield Surgical Center, Inc., 2828 Fairfield Avenue, Ft. Wayne 46807; tel. 219/744-8232; George W. Bowers, M.D., Administrator

Fort Wayne Ophthalmic Surgical Center, 321 East Wayne Street, Ft. Wayne 46802; tel. 219/422-5976; J. Rex Parent, M.D., Administrator

Fort Wayne Surgical Center, Inc., 1333 Maycrest Drive, Ft. Wayne 46805; tel. 219/423-3339; Edward D. Miller, B.S., M.D., Administrator

Indiana Eye Clinic, 30 North Emerson Avenue, Greenwood 46142; tel. 317/881-3937; B. H. Draffen, Executive Director

MHC Surgical Center, Inc., 6111 Harrison Street, Merrillville 46410; tel. 219/980-6000; Janyce Buchelt, RN, Executive Director

MediVision of Jeffersonville, Inc., 1305 Wall Street, Suite 101, Jeffersonville 47130; tel. 812/288-9674; Maurice E. John, Jr., M.D., President

South Bend Clinic Surgicenter, 211 North Eddy Street, Box 4061, South Bend 46634; tel. 219/234-8161; Eugene Ladewski, Executive Officer

SurgiCare Center, 1203 Hadley Road, Mooresville 46158; tel. 317/831-1160; Charles D. Swisher, Executive Director

Surgical Care Center, Inc., 8103 Clearvista Parkway, Indianapolis 46256; tel. 317/842-8666; Dr. Richard B. Rich, Executive Director

Surgical Center of Indiana, 209 Sparks Avenue, Jeffersonville 47130; tel. 812/282-2440; Ms. Gail Arora Fawbush, Administrator

Surgical Center of New Albany, 2201 Green Valley Road, New Albany 47150; tel. 812/949-1223; Mrs. Irene M. Fox, RN, Administrator

IOWA

Surgery Center of East Des Moines, 1301 Pennsylvania Avenue, #100, Des Moines 50316; tel. 515/266-3140; Alsie Sydness, RN, Administrator

Surgery Center of West Des Moines, 974-73rd, Suite 9, Des Moines 50312; tel. 515/224-1984; Alsie Sydness, Administrator

KANSAS

Hospital Surgical Center of Topeka, 830 Lane, Topeka 66606; tel. 913/233-1451; Charles E. Beall

Magna-Care, Inc., 11111 Nall Avenue, Leawood 66211; tel. 913/491-3999; David Waldman

Microsurgery, Inc., 920 Washburn, Topeka 66606; tel. 913/233-3939; Adrienne V. Prokop

Newman-Young Clinic, 710 West 8th Street, Fort Scott 66701; tel. 316/223-3100; Thomas W. Smith, Business Manager

Surgi-Care, Inc., 4401 West 109th Street, Overland Park 66211; tel. 913/345-1444; Adele Hughey

Surgicare of Wichita, Inc., 810 North Lorraine, Wichita 67214; tel. 316/685-2207; Margaret Orman, Administrator

KENTUCKY

Aaron Surgicenter, 300 Bomar Heights, Columbia 42728; tel. 502/384-4764; Art Norlin, Administrator

American Surgery Center of Louisville, 614 East Chestnut Street, Louisville 40202; tel. 502/589-9488; Stanley Litts, President

EMW Women's Surgical Center, 410 W. Chestnut St. Suite 900, Louisville 40202; tel. 502/589-2124; Dona F. Wells

King's Daughters Memorial Hospital, King's Daughters Drive, Frankfort 40601; tel. 502/875-5240; Ronald T. Tyrer

Lexington Surgery Center, 1725 Harrodsburg Road, Lexington 40504; tel. 606/276-2525; Janice C. Kincaid

The McPeak Center for Eye Care, Bravo Boulevard, Glasgow 42141; tel. 502/651-2181; Phyllis Skipworth, Administrator

Outpatient Care Center of Jewish Hospital, 225 Abraham Flexner Way, Louisville 40202; tel. 502/587-4709; Joanne Berryman, Administrator

Outpatient Surgical Care Facility, 4414 Churchman Avenue, Louisville 40215; tel. 502/366-9525; Calvin Harding, M.D.

Owensboro Ambulatory Surgical Facility, 1100 Walnut Street, Owensboro 42301; tel. 502/683-2751; Glenn D. Higdon

Paintsville Eye Institute, 191 Euclid Avenue, Paintsville 41240; tel. 606/789-3717; Marcus Minix

Pikeville Surgical Center, 261 Town Mountain Road, Pikeville 41501; tel. 606/432-0356; Erlindo Valera, M.D.

Same Day Surgery Center, 1801 Ashley Circle, Bowling Green 42101; tel. 502/781-4330; James Barnett

Surgecenter of Louisville, 4005 Dupont Circle, Louisville 40207; tel. 502/897-7401; Stephen D. Stewart, Administrator

Surgical Center of Elizabethtown, 708 Westport Road, P. O. Box 2085, Elizabethtown 42701; tel. 502/737-5200; Debra K. Myers

Walk In and Out Surgery Center, 353 Bogle Street, Somerset 42501; tel. 606/679-9322; Jim Bentley

LOUISIANA

Baton Rouge Ambulatory Surgicare Services (B.R.A.S.S.), 5328 Didesse Drive, Baton Rouge 70809; tel. 504/766-1718; Laura Cronin, Administrator

Baton Rouge Ambulatory Surgicare Services East (B.R.A.S.S. East), 505 East Airport, Baton Rouge 70806; tel. 504/925-2031; Laura Cronin, Administrator

□ **Covington Surgery Center,** 725 West 11th Avenue, Covington 70433; tel. 504/893-5925; Ruth Miller, R.N., B.S., Administrative Director

Surgicare Outpatient Center of Lake Charles, 214 South Ryan, Lake Charles 70601; tel. 318/436-6941; Janet Hagan, Administrator

MAINE

E.W. Dixon Medical Center under Maine Coast Memorial Hospital, HCR 60, P. O. Box 52, West Gouldsboro 04607; tel. 207/963-7462; Richard P. Fredericks, Chief Executive Officer

MARYLAND

Annapolis Plastic Surgery, 1300 Ritchie Highway, Arnold 21012; tel. 301/544-0707; Dr. Jack Frost

Baltimore Washington Eye Center of Paul A. Kohlhepp, M.D., P.A., 200 Hospital Drive, Suite 406, Glen Burnie 21061; tel. 301/761-1267

Bon Secours Ambulatory Surgical Center, 2850 Health Park Drive, Ellicott City 21043; tel. 301/461-1600

Dubroff Eye Center, 8905 Fairview Road, Silver Spring 20910; tel. 301/585-4122

Greater Dundalk Medical Center, 2112 Dundalk Avenue, Dundalk 21222; tel. 301/288-4800

Klatsky Plastic Surgery Facility, 122 Slade Avenue, Pikesville 21208; tel. 301/484-0400; Stanley A. Klatsky, M.D., Director

□ **Montgomery Surgery Center,** 46 West Gude Drive, Rockville 20850; tel. 301/424-6901

Peninsula Obstetrics & Gynecology, P.A., 314 West Carroll Street, Salisbury 21801; tel. 301/546-3125; Joseph H. Cutchin, Jr., M.D., President

Rotunda ASC, 711 West 40th Street, Suite 410, Baltimore 21211; tel. 301/889-4885

Towson ASC, 920 Providence Road, Suite 103, Towson 21204; tel. 301/583-8637

MASSACHUSETTS

Andover Surgical Day Care Clinic, Inc., 138 Haverhill Street, Andover 01810; tel. 617/475-2880

Bay State Health Care Center - South Shore, 780 Main Street, South Weymouth 02190; tel. 617/331-9300; Greger C. Anderson, Chief Executive Officer

Boston Center for Ambulatory Surgery, Inc., 170 Commonwealth Avenue, Boston 02116; tel. 617/267-0710

Eye Specialists of New England, 1350 Main Street, 12th Floor, Springfield 01103; tel. 413/734-5606; Jean Hirsch, R.N., Chief Executive

Greater New Bedford Surgicenter, Inc., 540 Hawthorn Street, North Dartmouth 02747; tel. 617/997-1271

Maple Surgery Center, 130 Maple Street, Springfield 01103; tel. 413/739-9668

New England Eye Surgical Center, 696 Main Street, Weymouth 02190; tel. 617/331-3820; Kenneth Camerota, Chief Executive Officer

□ **Same Day SurgiClinic,** 272 Stanley Street, Fall River 02720; tel. 617/672-2290; Dr. John Harries, Chief Executive Officer

MICHIGAN

Bronson Outpatient Surgery/Crosstown, 150 E. Crosstown Parkway - Suite 110, Kalamazoo 49007; tel. 616/345-6006; Ruth Allen, Director

Community Surgical Center, 30671 Stephenson Highway, Madison Heights 48071; tel. 303/588-8000

Feminine Health Care Clinic, 2032 South Saginaw, Flint 48503; tel. 313/232-8071

Henry Ford Hospital-Fairlane Center, 19401 Hubbard Drive, Dearborn 48126; tel. 313/336-2100

Henry Ford Hospital - West Bloomfield, 6777 West Maple Road, West Bloomfield 48033; tel. 313/661-4100

Holland Eye Clinic, 999 South Washington, Holland 49423; tel. 616/396-2316

Hutzel Health Center - Warren, 4050 East 12 Mile Road, Warren 48092; tel. 313/573-3140; Melva Parks, Clinical Director

John V. Balian, M.D., P.C. Balian Eye Center, 432 W. University, Rochester 48063; tel. 313/651-6122

Lawrence D. Castleman, M.D., PC. Castleman Eye Center, 14050 Dix-Toledo Road, Southgate 48195; tel. 313/283-0500

Lee Eye Center, 750 Stewart Road, Monroe 48161; tel. 313/241-1106

Mercy Hospital of South County, 8166 Douglas Road, Lambertville 48144; tel. 313/947-0567

Metropolitan Eye Center, 21711 Greater Mack, St. Clair Shores 48080; tel. 313/774-6820

Michigan Center for Ocular Surgery, 330080 Utica Road, P.O. Box 26010, Fraser 48026; tel. 313/296-7250; Norbert P. Czajkowski, M.D., P.C.

Midwestern Health Center, 5050 Schaefer Avenue, Dearborn 48126; tel. 313/581-2600

The New Clinic for Women, Inc., 320 East Fulton, Grand Rapids 49503; tel. 616/456-5727

Planned Parenthood of Mid-Michigan, 3100 Professional Drive, P. O. Box 3673, Ann Arbor 48104; tel. 313/973-0710

Providence Hospital, Surgical Center of Southfield, 29877 Telegraph Road, Suite 208, Southfield 48034; tel. 313/424-3013

Reproductive Health Care Center of South Central Michigan, 420 West Michigan Avenue, Kalamazoo 49007; tel. 616/372-1200

□ **St. Lukes Surgicare Center,** 800 Cooper Street, Saginaw 48602; tel. 517/771-6602; Marjorie R. O'Dell, Administrator

The following list of freestanding ambulatory surgery centers was developed from information provided by state agencies. It is current as of January 1, 1987.

The AHA Guide contains two types of ambulatory surgery center listings: those that are hospital based and those that are freestanding. Hospital based ambulatory surgery centers are listed in section A of the AHA Guide and are identified by Facility Code F1. Please refer to that section for information on the over 5,000 hospital based ambulatory surgery centers.

Those freestanding ambulatory surgery centers accredited by the Joint Commission on Accreditation of Hospitals (JCAH) are identified by a hollow square (□). These surgery centers have been found to be in substantial compliance with the Joint Commission standards for ambulatory health care facilities, as found in the Ambulatory Health Care Standards Manual.

We present this list simply as a convenient directory. Inclusion or omission of any organization's name indicates neither approval nor disapproval by the American Hospital Association.

Summit Medical Center, 15800 West McNichols, Detroit 48235; tel. 313/272-8450
Troy Obstetrics & Gynecology, P.C., 1565 West Big Beaver Road, Building F, Troy 48084; tel. 313/643-7775; Reza S. Mohajer, M.D., Administrator
Walrose Reconstructive Surgery Center, Inc., 125 West Walnut, Kalamazoo 49007; tel. 616/343-1381; Dr. Frank J. Newman, Medical Director
West Oakland Ambulatory Care Center, 1885 North Pontiac Trail, Walled Lake 48088; tel. 313/624-6635; John Kolozsvary, Administrator
□ **Western Michigan Ambulatory Surgical Center,** 1000 East Paris, Suite 100, Grand Rapids 49506; tel. 616/949-9121; Janice Hoeksema, Director
Women's Counseling Center, 13000 West Seven Mile Road, Detroit 48235; tel. 313/861-3939

MINNESOTA
MN Surgery Center at St. Marys, 701 - 25th Avenue South, Minneapolis 55454; tel. 612/338-3778
Maplewood Surgery Center, 1655 Beam Avenue, Maplewood 55109; tel. 612/779-4300
Midwest Surgicenter, 393 North Dunlap Street, Suite 900, St. Paul 55104; tel. 612/642-9199
Minneapolis Single Day Surgery, 6701 Country Club Drive, Golden Valley 55427; tel. 612/544-7022; Frank F. Coffey
Northway Surgicenter, Inc., 1555 Northway Drive, St. Cloud 56301; tel. 612/259-4150; Penny Dykstra, RN, Unit Coordinator
Ridgedale Surgery Center, 2000 Plymouth Avenue South, Minnetonka 55343; tel. 612/541-1045
St. Cloud Surgical Center, 1401 St. Germain Street, St. Cloud 56301; tel. 612/251-8385; Edward D. Stack, Administrator
St. Paul Surgical Center, 409 North Dunlap, Suite 900, St. Paul 55104; tel. 612/647-0116
Surgicare of Minneapolis, 6525 Barrie Road, Minneapolis 55435; tel. 612/920-9100; Ed Stack, Vice President, Administrator
Willmar Surgery Center, 1320 South First Street, P. O. Box 2002, Willmar 56201; tel. 612/235-6506; Lynn Freeman, Administrator

MISSISSIPPI
Biloxi Outpatient, 127 Lameuse Street, Biloxi 39530; tel. 601/374-2130; John B. Edwards, M.D., Administrator
Gulf South Outpatient Center, 31st Avenue, P. O. Box 1778, Gulfport 39501; tel. 601/864-0008; Thomas A. Graves, M.D., Administrator
Gulfport Outpatient Surgical Center, 1240 Broad Avenue, Gulfport 39501; tel. 601/868-1120; L. V. Johnston, Administrator
Outpatient Surgery Facility Lowery A. Woodall, Sr., 105 South 28th Avenue, Hattiesburg 39401; tel. 601/264-1072; Lowery A. Woodall, Sr., Administrator
Surgicare of Jackson, 766 Lakeland Drive, Jackson 39216; tel. 601/362-8700; Sheila Grillis, RN, Administrator

MISSOURI
Ambulatory Surgery Center of St. Luke's, 215 West 43rd Street, Kansas City 64111; tel. 816/932-3200; Charles C. Lindstrom
Broadway Surgical Center, 4177 Broadway, Kansas City 64111; tel. 816/561-1414; Frederick J. McCoy, M.D.
Cataract Surgery Center of St. Joseph, 3201 Ashland, St. Joseph 64506; tel. 816/279-0079; Nancy Moore, RN, CNOR
Cataract Surgery Center of St. Louis, 900 North Highway 67 (Lindberg), Florissant 63031; tel. 314/838-3021; William Waugh
Cataract and Glaucoma Outpatient Surgicenter, 7220 Watson Road, St. Louis 63119; tel. 314/352-5515; Stanley C. Becker, M.D.
Cave Springs Surgery Center, 4203 South Cloverleaf Drive, St. Charles 63303; tel. 314/928-0087; Norman Constable, MA
Center for Eye Surgery, 6650 Troost, Suite 301, Kansas City 64131; tel. 816/276-7757; Richard B. Klein
Community Surgical Center, 7700 Florissant Road, Normandy 63121; tel. 314/382-6660; Alberta Trautman, RN
□ **DaySurg of Independence,** 2311 Redwood Avenue, Independence 64057; tel. 816/373-9312; Jan Holsten, Director
Doctors Surgical Center, 6401 Front Street, P. O. Box 25468, Kansas City 64119; tel. 816/241-5652; Maurice Miller
Doctors' Park Surgery, 30 Doctors' Park, Cape Girardeau 63701; tel. 314/334-9606; Ronald G. Wittmer
Freeman Hospital DaySurg, 1102 West 32nd, Joplin 64804-3599; tel. 417/782-8700; Richard E. Long, President
Kansas City Outpatient Cataract Surgery Center, 2900 Baltimore, Kansas City 64018; tel. 816/753-6511; Elpidio Q. Fahel
Outpatient Surgery Center at Lerwick Clinic, 4th and Pine, St. Louis 63102; tel. 314/241-8181; Jay S. Van Tilburg
Outpatient Surgery Center, Inc., 450 North New Ballas Road, St. Louis 63141; tel. 314/991-0776; Linda Drohlich, Administrator
St. John's Surgery Center, 11700 Studt Avenue, Creve Coeur 63141; tel. 314/997-0047; Dianne Latta, Administrator
Surgery Center of Springfield, 1350 East Woodhurst Drive, Springfield 65804; tel. 417/887-5243; Betty Fisher
Surgicenter of Kansas City, 1800 East Meyer Boulevard, Kansas City 64132; tel. 816/523-0100; Marge McMillen
The Tobin Eye Institute, 3902 Sherman, St. Joseph 64506; tel. 816/279-1363; W. Ken Spalding

MONTANA
The Eye Surgicenter, 1600 Poly Drive, Billings 59102; tel. 406/252-6608
Flathead Outpatient Surgical Center, 66 Claremont Street, Kalispell 59901; 406/752-8484
Gallatin Outpatient Clinic, Inc., 300 N. Willson, Bozeman 59715; tel. 406/586-1956
Highland View Outpatient Surgical Center, Inc., 840 South Montana, Butte 59701; tel. 406/782-2391
Northern Rockies Surgicenter, Inc., 1020 No. 27th Street, Billings 59101; tel. 406/248-7186
WEB Properties, Inc., Eye Surgical Center, 1221 North 26th Street, Billings 59102; tel. 406/252-5681
Yellowstone Eye Surgicenter, 1145 North 29th Street, Suite 403, Billings 59101; tel. 406/248-3121

NEBRASKA
Bergan Mercy Outpatient Surgery Bergan Mercy Hospital, 7710 Mercy Road, Omaha 68124; tel. 402/398-6816; Mary Alexander, Director
□ **Omaha Surgical Center Center Healthcare, Inc.,** 8051 West Center Road, Omaha 68124; tel. 402/391-3333; G. Randy Boldt

NEVADA
Aesthetic Associates Day Surgery Center, 1580 East Desert Inn Road, Las Vegas 89109; tel. 702/735-6755; Charles A. Vinnik, M.D.
Carson Ambulatory Surgery Center, 1299 Mountain Street, Carson City 89701; tel. 702/883-1700; Joan P. Smith, R.N.
Eye Surgery Center of Nevada, 3839 North Carson Street, Carson City 89701; tel. 702/882-3950; Michael J. Fischer, M.D., Administrator
Las Vegas Surgicare, 850 South Rancho Drive, Las Vegas 89106; tel. 702/870-2090; Teida Clark, Administrator
Northern Nevada Plastic Surgery Associates, 932 Ryland Street, Reno 89502; tel. 702/322-3446; Audrey M. DeMars
Rancho Surgical Plaza, 888 South Rancho Drive, Las Vegas 89106; tel. 702/877-8660; S. M. Doubrava, M.D.
Red Rock Surgical Center, Inc., 5701 W. Charleston Blvd. - Suite 102, Las Vegas 89102; tel. 702/870-1814; Donna M. Onofre, Administrator
Reno Medical Plaza Ambulatory Surgical Center, 2005 Silverada Blvd., Reno 89520; tel. 702/359-0212; Susan Petrinovich
Reno Procedure Center, 350 West Sixth Street, Suite 3D, Reno 89503; tel. 702/322-7133; Michael J. Glass, M.D.
Sahara-Lindell Surgery Center, 2575 Lindell Road, Las Vegas 89102; tel. 702/367-7874; Elizabeth Timonen, Office Manager
Shepherd Eye Surgicenter, 3196 South Maryland Parkway, Las Vegas 89109; tel. 702/731-2088; John R. Shepherd, M.D.
University Medical Center of Southern Nevada, 1800 West Charleston Boulevard, Las Vegas 89102; tel. 702/383-2000; Richard J. Couglin, Administrator

NEW HAMPSHIRE
Concord Feminist Health Center, 38 South Main Street, Concord 03301; tel. 603/225-2739; Judith Popkin
Nashua Eye Surgery Center, 5 Coliseum Avenue, Nashua 03063; tel. 603/882-9800; Paul O'Leary, Administrator
New Hampshire Eye Surgicenter, Bedford Commons, Bedford 03102; tel. 603/622-5953; Paul Pender, M.D.
NorthEast 1 Day Surgery Center, 445 Cypress Street, Manchester 03103; tel. 603/627-4889; Stephen Earnhart, Director
Partial Hospitalization Program, 69 Willard Street, Berlin 03570; tel. 603/752-7404; Richard Anderson, Ph.D
Salem Health Center, 32 Stiles Road, Salem 03079; tel. 603/898-4000; Stephen Earnhart

NEW JERSEY
A.H.R./A.H.C., Illinois & Marmora Avenues, Atlantic City 08401; tel. 609/347-0988
A.H.R./A.H.C., 323 Madison Avenue, Atlantic City 08401; tel. 609/347-0008
Bergen Lanning Health Center, Clinton and West Streets, Canden 08104; tel. 609/757-7653; Joseph Surowiec
Bernard W. Gimble Multiple Sclerosis Comprehensive Care and Holy Name Hospital, 718 Teaneck Road, Teaneck 07666; tel. 201/837-0727; Maureen McMahon
Burlington County Health Department Deborah Heart and Lung Center, Browns Mills 08015; tel. 609/267-0631; Walter Trommelen
Burlington County Health Department Zurbrugg Memorial Hospital, Taylor Street, Riverside 08075; tel. 609/265-5548; Walter Trommelen
Calvary Baptist Community Health Center, 227 Broadway, Paterson 07501; tel. 201/345-6789; Thomas L. Curry, Executive Director
Camcare Health Corporation, Sixth and Stevens Street, Camden 08103; tel. 609/541-3270; Michael LaDeau
Cape May County Public Health Center Crest Haven Complex - DN 601, Garden State Parkway, Cape May Court House 08210; tel. 609/465-1187; Louis J. Lamanna, M.A.H.O., Public Health Coordinator
Cumberland County Health Department Pre Natal/Postpartum Clinic, Temporarily c/o Bridgeton Hospital, Bridgeton 08302; tel. 609/451-0708; Anne McGuigan
Cumberland Family Medicine Associates, 7 Bacon Street, Port Norris 08349; tel. 609/785-1150; Dr. Mortensen
East Orange General Hospital, 300 Central Avenue, East Orange 07019; tel. 201/672-8400; Laurence M. Merlis
Health Services of Hudson County, 706-714 Bergen Avenue, Jersey City 07306; tel. 201/451-5555; Marilyn Bennett
Med/Mark Same Day Surgery Center, 101 Old Short Hills Road, West Orange 07052; tel. 201/325-6565; Sheila Bloom
Medical Care Center at Woodbridge, 1500 Route 9 North, Woodbridge 07095; tel. 201/636-CARE
Metropolitan Comprehensive Health Group, 194 Clinton Avenue, Newark 07108; tel. 201/242-2300; Marie Reale

The following list of freestanding ambulatory surgery centers was developed from information provided by state agencies. It is current as of January 1, 1987.

The AHA Guide *contains two types of ambulatory surgery center listings: those that are hospital based and those that are freestanding. Hospital based ambulatory surgery centers are listed in section A of the* AHA Guide *and are identified by Facility Code F1. Please refer to that section for information on the over 5,000 hospital based ambulatory surgery centers.*

Those freestanding ambulatory surgery centers accredited by the Joint Commission on Accreditation of Hospitals (JCAH) are identified by a hollow square (□). These surgery centers have been found to be in substantial compliance with the Joint Commission standards for ambulatory health care facilities, as found in the Ambulatory Health Care Standards Manual.

We present this list simply as a convenient directory. Inclusion or omission of any organization's name indicates neither approval nor disapproval by the American Hospital Association.

Mountainside Family Practice Associates, 799 Bloomfield Avenue, Verona 07044; tel. 201/239-6966; Sofia H. Anthony, M.D., Director

N.Y.S.A.I.L.A. Medical Center of Newark, 123 - 131 Clifford Street, Newark 07105; tel. 201/344-8890; Paul Copolla

Newark Day Center Geriatric Health Service, 43 Hill Street, Newark 07102; tel. 201/643-5710; Trish Morris

Newark Mini-Surgi Site, Inc., 145 Roseville Avenue, Newark 07107; tel. 201/485-3300; Alice Barnett

North Camden Health Center, 6th and Erie Streets, Camden 08102; tel. 609/757-7253; Lawrence DeVaro

North Jersey Women's Medical Center, Inc., 6000 Kennedy Boulevard, West New York 07093; tel. 201/869-9293; Saul Luchs, M.D.

North Newark Health Services Corp., 741 Broadway, Newark 07104; tel. 201/483-0700; Edgar Dudley

Osborn Family Health Center Our Lady of Lourdes Medical Center, 1601 Haddon Avenue, Camden 08103; tel. 609/757-3700; Margaret Carr Cofsky

Pilgrim Medical Group, 393 Bloomfield Avenue, Montclair 07042; tel. 201/746-1500; Janice Darmstatter and Judith Cohen, Administrators

Plainfield Health Care Center, 609 West Fourth Street, Plainfield 07060; tel. 201/753-6401; Julane W. Miller

Planned Parenthood of Monmouth County, Inc., 69 East Newman Springs Road, Shrewsbury 07701; tel. 201/842-9300; Ms. Phyllis Kinsler, Executive Director

Planned Parenthood of Northwest New Jersey, 196 Speedwell Avenue, Morristown 07960; tel. 201/539-8980; Ms. Carole Harper, Director of Clinical Services

Pleasantville Ambulatory Health Care Center, 119 West Bayview Avenue, Pleasantville 08232; tel. 609/641-5111

Princeton Ambulatory Surgery, Inc., 281 Witherspoon Street, Princeton 08542; tel. 609/734-4601; Dennis Doody

Roseland Surgical Center, 556 Eagle Rock Avenue, Roseland 07068; tel. 201/226-1717; Gene D'Allessandro

St. Joseph's Hospital/Family Health Center, 160 Market Street, Paterson 07505; tel. 201/977-2447; Roy Brown, M.D., M.P.H.

Summit Surgical Center at West Jersey, Carnie Boulevard & Evesham Road, Voorhees 08043; tel. 609/770-5813; Maureen A. Miller, Vice President

SurgiCare of Central Jersey, Inc., 40 Stirling Road, Watchung 07060; tel. 201/769-8000; Ruth Kruger, R.N.

Wallkill Valley General Hospital Health Care Center, 19 Hospital Road, Franklin 07416; tel. 201/827-9121; Mary Ann Kellar, RN, Health Center Supervisor

NEW MEXICO

Alamogordo Eye Clinic, Inc., 1124 Tenth Street, Alamogordo 88310; tel. 505/434-1200; Donald J. Ham, M.D., F.A.C.S.

Ambulatory Surgical Center of Santa Fe, 102 Faithway, Santa Fe 87501; tel. 505/982-6317; John D. Gundzik, M.D.

Presbyterian Day Surgery Center, 301 Cedar, SE, Albuquerque 87102; tel. 505/841-1012

St. Joseph Day Surgery, 1720 Wyoming Bouleveard, NE, Albuquerque 87112; tel. 505/292-9200

St. Vincent Hospital Ambulatory Surgery Center, 455 St. Michaels Drive, Santa Fe 87501; tel. 505/983-3361

NEW YORK

Capital Area Community Health Plan, 1201 Troy-Schenectady Road, Latham 12110; tel. 518/783-3110; Warren Paley, President

Harrison Center for Outpatient Surgery, Inc., 550 Harrison Center, Syracuse 13202; David G. Murray, M.D., Chief Executive

□ **Huntington Surgery Center,** 380 Park Avenue, Huntington 11743; tel. 516/673-5122; Dr. M. Mamakos, Director

Hurley Avenue Surgical Center, Inc., 40 Hurley Avenue, Kingston 12401; tel. 914/338-4777; C. Alexander Howard, Administrator

□ **Long Island Plastic Surgical Group,** 110 Willis Avenue, Mineola 11501; tel. 516/742-3404; Jerry Lorenzo, Business Manager

New York Institute for Ambulatory Surgery, 99 Dutch Hill Plaza, Orangeburg 10963; tel. 914/359-7272

North Medical Outpatient Surgery, Inc., 5100 West Taft Road, 5th Floor, Liverpool 13088; tel. 315/458-2828; A. John Merola, M.D., CEO; Thomas D. Minicucci, Administrator

NORTH CAROLINA

Asheville Hand Ambulatory Surgery Center, 34 Granby Street, P.O. Box 2089, Asheville 28802; tel. 704/258-0962; E. Brown Crosby, M.D., Executive Officer

Blue Ridge Day Surgery Center, 2501 North Street, Suite 150, Raleigh 27607; tel. 919/781-4311; Ms. Margaret Buffaloe, Director

Brinton Surgical Center, P.A., 603 East Center Avenue, P. O. Box 550, Mooresville 28115; tel. 704/664-1414; Dr. Lewis F. Brinton, Executive Officer

Carolina Clinic, Inc., 1700 South Tarboro Street, Wilson 27893; tel. 919/291-1300; Benjamin B. Brockwell, Executive Vice President

Chapel Hill Surgical Center, 109 Conner Drive, Suite 1201, Chapel Hill 27514; tel. 919/968-0611; Dr. Gary S. Berger, Chief Executive Officer

Charlotte Surgery Center, Ltd., 2825 Randolph Road, Charlotte 28211; tel. 704/377-1647; Ms. Margaret Slattery, Executive Officer

Crist Clinic for Women, 200 Memorial Drive, Jacksonville 28540; tel. 919/353-2115; Dr. Takey Crist, Executive Officer

Durham Ambulatory Surgical Center, 120 Carver Street, P. O. Box 15727, Durham 27704; tel. 919/477-9677; Joseph T. Jordan, Jr., Administrator/Director

Eastern Carolina Surgical Center, Inc., 102 Bethesda Drive, Greenville 27834; tel. 919/752-0672; Ms. Joyce G. Dixon, Executive Director

Eye Surgery and Laser Clinic, 500 Lake Concord Road, NE, Concord 28025; tel. 704/782-1127; Dr. William J. Burchfield, Administrator

FEMCARE, 62 Orange Street, Asheville 28801; tel. 704/255-8400; Arthur S. Morris, Jr., M.D., Executive Officer

Fayetteville Ambulatory Surgical Center, 1781 Metromedical Drive, Fayetteville 28304; tel. 919/323-1647; Dr. John T. Henley, Jr., Director

The Fleming Center, Inc., 3613 Haworth Drive, Raleigh 27609; tel. 919/781-5550; Dr. Paul A. Fleming, Executive Officer

Gaston Ambulatory Surgery, 2511 Court Drive, Gastonia 28054; tel. 704/866-7775; John G. Yeatman, Operations Officer

□ **Hawthorne Surgical Center,** 1999 South Hawthorne Road, Winston-Salem 27103; tel. 919/760-3880; Dale R. Pinilis, Executive Officer

Hickory Eye Care Center, P.A. Outpatient Surgical Center, 27 Thirteenth Avenue, NE, Hickory 28601; tel. 704/322-6040; Dr. Richard M. Griffin, Administrator

Lexington Clinic for Women, P.A., 7 Medical Park Drive, Lexington 27292; tel. 704/243-2431; Lloyd D. Lohr, Executive Director

MediVision of Charlotte, Inc., 2200 East Seventh Street, Charlotte 28204; tel. 704/334-4318; Bill Owens, Admnistrator

MediVision of Greensboro, Inc., 3312 Battleground Avenue, Greensboro 27410; tel. 919/282-8330; William Owen, Regional Manager

MediVision of North Carolina, 2170 Midland Road, Southern Pines 28387; tel. 919/295-2100; William E. Owen, Administrator

□ **Moore Ambulatory Surgery Center,** 325 Page Road, Pinehurst 28374; tel. 919/295-1008; Peter D. Mertzanis, Chief Operating Officer

New Bern Outpatient Surgery Center, Inc., 801 College Court, New Bern 28560; tel. 919/633-2000; Danny Jackson, Executive Officer

The Outpatient Surgical Center, Inc., 522 North Elam Avenue, Greensboro 27403; tel. 919/294-1833; Dr. L. L. Patseavouras, President

Pinewest OB-GYN Inc., Surgicenter, 405 Gatewood Avenue, High Point 27260; tel. 919/885-0901; Dr. Carl M. Hoffman, Medical Director

Plastic Surgery Center of N.C., Inc., 2901 Maplewood Avenue, Winston-Salem 27103; tel. 919/768-6210; Dr. John A. Fagg, Executive Officer

Raleigh Plastic Surgery Center, Inc., 1112 Dresser Court, Raleigh 27609; tel. 919/872-2616; W. Blake Garside, Executive Officer

Raleigh Women's Health Organization, Inc., 917 West Morgan Street, Raleigh 27603; tel. 919/832-0535; Ms. Susan Hill, Vice President

Rex Hospital, Inc. Same Day Surgery, 4420 Lake Boone Trail, Raleigh 27607; tel. 919/755-3193; Donna Kanich, Director of Same Day Surgery

SameDay Surgery Center at Presbyterian, 1800 East Fourth Street, Charlotte 28204; tel. 704/371-4200; Richard T. Howerton, III, FACHE, Executive Vice President

Surgical Center of Greensboro, Inc., 1211 Virginia Street, Greensboro 27401; tel. 919/272-0012; Dr. Donald E. Linder, Executive Officer

Wilson Outpatient Surgical Center, 1704 South Tarboro Street, Wilson 27893; tel. 919/237-5649; Ms. Alva J. Morris, Executive Officer

Woman Care, 712 North Elm Street, High Point 27262; tel. 919/889-3646; Dr. Robert C. Crawford, Executive Officer

NORTH DAKOTA

Centennial Medical Center, 1500 - 24th Avenue SW, P. O. Box 40, Minot 58702; tel. 701/852-0777; Dr. MacDonald

Fargo Clinic/Same Day Surgery, 321 Eighth Avenue North, Fargo 58102; tel. 701/234-6400; Lloyd Smith

R & G Medical and Surgical Center, 109 Seventh Street West, Dickinson 58601; tel. 701/255-6017; Dick Hushka

Western Dakota Medical Group/WD Day Surgery, 1102 Main - P. O. Box 1206, Williston 58801; tel. 701/572-7711; Mrs. K. Johnson, Clinical Nurse - Director

OHIO

□ **Aultman Center for One Day,** 4715 Whipple Avenue, N.W., Canton 44718; tel. 216/492-3050; David Huffman, Administrator

Austintown Ambulatory Surgery Center, 45 North Canfield, Niles Road, Youngstown 44515; tel. 216/792-2722; James M. Conti, Chief Executive Officer

Braver Memorial Ambulatory Surgery Center, 88 South Portage Path, Akron 44303; tel. 216/864-4179

Mercy Ambulatory Surgery Center, 2990 Mack Road, Fairfield 45014; tel. 513/874-6440; Eric L. Myers, Director

Northwest Coast Health Services, Inc. Ambulatory Surgery Center, 1600 Superior Street, Toledo 43604

Sandusky Surgeons, Inc., 1221 Hayes Avenue, Sandusky 44870; tel. 419/625-1374

□ **St. Francis-St. George Surgical Center,** 2841 Boudinot Avenue, Cincinnati 45238; tel. 513/389-5900; William Copeland, Chief Executive Officer

Surgery Center for Ambulatory Care, 16480 St. Clair Ave., East Liverpool 43920; tel. 216/386-9000; Joann Bradfield, Chief Executive Officer

□ **The Surgery Center,** 19250 East Bagley Road, Cleveland 44130; tel. 216/826-3240; Barbara A. Peris, Administrator

Toledo Clinic and Outpatient Surgery Center, 4235 Secor Road, Toledo 43623; tel. 419/473-3561; Robert Campbell, Administrator

□ **The Wright Surgery Center,** 1611 South Green Road, Cleveland 44121; tel. 216/382-1868; Douglas Eastwood, M.D., Medical Director

The following list of freestanding ambulatory surgery centers was developed from information provided by state agencies. It is current as of January 1, 1987.

The AHA Guide contains two types of ambulatory surgery center listings: those that are hospital based and those that are freestanding. Hospital based ambulatory surgery centers are listed in section A of the AHA Guide and are identified by Facility Code F1. Please refer to that section for information on the over 5,000 hospital based ambulatory surgery centers.

Those freestanding ambulatory surgery centers accredited by the Joint Commission on Accreditation of Hospitals (JCAH) are identified by a hollow square (☐). These surgery centers have been found to be in substantial compliance with the Joint Commission standards for ambulatory health care facilities, as found in the Ambulatory Health Care Standards Manual.

We present this list simply as a convenient directory. Inclusion or omission of any organization's name indicates neither approval nor disapproval by the American Hospital Association.

OKLAHOMA

Center for Ambulatory Surgery of Oklahoma, Inc., 818 Northwest 12th Street, Oklahoma City 73106; tel. 405/235-4525; Robert A. Bryan, Director

Central Oklahoma Ambulatory Surgical Center, 3301 Northwest 63rd Street, Oklahoma City 73116; tel. 405/842-9732; W. Edward Dalton, M.D., Paul Silverstein, M.D., J. Michael Kelly, M.D.

Heritage Eye Surgicenter of Oklahoma, 104 Heritage Building, 6922 South Western, Oklahoma City 73139; tel. 405/636-1508; Edward D. Glinski, D.O.

M.D. Physicians Outpatient Surgical Center, 8121 National Avenue, Suite 108, Midwest City 73110; tel. 405/732-7905; Bill Beaman, Director

Oklahoma Ambulatory Surgical Center, 6908 East Reno, Midwest City 73110; tel. 405/737-6871; Richard E. Doner, M.D.

Oklahoma Surgicare, 13313 North Meridian, Oklahoma City 73120; tel. 405/755-6240; Lee Youngblood, Administrator

Orthopedic Associates, 3301 Northwest 50th Street, Oklahoma City 73112; tel. 405/947-0911; David R. Brown, M.D.

Osteopathic Surgicenter, 744 West 7th Street, Tulsa 74127; tel. 918/584-1060; D. A. Nunneley, D.O.

Outpatient Surgical Center of Ponca City, Inc., 400 Fairview, Ponca City 74601; tel. 405/762-0695; Ms. Karen McConnell, R.N.

Physicians Surgical Center, 805 East Robinson, Norman 73071; tel. 405/364-9789; J. J. Beller, M.D., President

Southern Oklahoma Surgical Center, Inc., 2412 North Commerce, Ardmore 73401; tel. 405/226-5000; Ms. Ann Willis, R.N., Facility Coordinator

Southern Plains Medical Center, Inc., 2222 Iowa Avenue, Chickasha 73018; tel. 405/224-4853; James W. Loy

Surgicare of Tulsa, 4415 South Harvard Avenue, Suite 100, Tulsa 74135; tel. 918/742-2502; Ms. Carla K. Cartwright

OREGON

Lovejoy Surgicenter, Inc., 933 NW 25th Avenue, Portland 97210; tel. 503/221-1870; Allene Klass

North Bend Medical Center, Inc., 1900 Woodland Drive, Coos Bay 97420; tel. 503/267-5151; Philip J. Keizer, M.D.

Northbank Surgical Center (Capitol Health Care), 700 Bellevue Street SE #300, Salem 97301; tel. 503/362-3704; Roger Lyman, President

Northwest Eye Center, 1700 Valley River Drive, Eugene 97401; tel. 503/343-3900; Jim Heath, Administrator

☐ **Oregon Surgery Center,** 9200 S.W. Oleson Road, Portland 97223; tel. 503/246-4903; Tasker K. Robinette, MHA, FACHE

The Portland Clinic Surgical Center, 800 S.W. 13th Avenue, Portland 97205; tel. 503/221-0161; J. Michael Schwab

Schmiesing Eye Surgery Center, 2925 Siskiyou Boulevard, Medford 97504; tel. 503/779-2020; Don C. Schmiesing, M.D., Administrator

PENNSYLVANIA

Allegheny Outpatient Surgery Center, 320 East North Avenue, Pittsburgh 15212; tel. 412/321-5900; Georgia E. Demas, CRNA, MS, Director of Operations

Center for Ambulatory Surgery, Adams and Mulberry Streets, Scranton 18510; tel. 717/348-1114

Chestnut Hills Hospital Outpatient Surgical Center, 8815 Germantown Ave., Suite 100, Philadelphia 19118; tel. 215/242-5353; Dennis Zamojski, Administrator

Day Surgery Center, 145 North Sixth Street, Reading 19601; tel. 215/378-8321; Richard L. Bitner, M.D., Medical Director

Dermatologic SurgiCenter, 1200 Locust Street, Philadelphia 19107; tel. 215/546-3666; Anthony V. Benedetto, DO, FACP, Medical Director

Drs. Cohen-Demos Plastic Surgery, Ltd. North Shore Ambulatory Surgery Center, Two Allegheny Center, Suite 636, Pittsburgh 15212; tel. 412/231-1700

Esper Medical Center ASC, 5050 West Ridge Road, Erie 16506; tel. 814/833-8800

Eye Clinic Ambulatory Surgical Center, 601-605 Wyoming Avenue, Kingston 18704; tel. 717/288-7405

Eye Surgery Center, 558 East Lancaster Avenue, Radnor 19087; tel. 215/688-9333; Linsa Wassman, Administrator

Graduate Surgi-Center, 1829 Pine Street, Philadelphia 19103; tel. 215/893-0300

Lancaster Surgery Center, 217 Harrisburg Avenue, Lancaster 17603; tel. 717/295-2500; Shelvy J. Thompson, R.N., Administrative Director

Memorial Eye Institute/Pennsylvania Eye Surgery Center, 4100 Linglestown Road, Harrisburg 17112; tel. 717/657-2020

NEI Ambulatory Surgical Center, 204 Mifflin Avenue, Scranton 18503; tel. 717/342-3145

Pennsylvania College of Podiatric Medicine, 8th and Race Streets, Philadelphia 19107; tel. 215/629-0300; James E. Bates, D.P.M., President

Southwestern Ambulatory Surgery Center, 500 Lewis Run Road, Pittsburgh 15236; tel. 412/466-0600

United Surgi-Center, 205 Newtown Road, Warminister 18974; tel. 215/672-7600

RHODE ISLAND

Blackstone Valley Surgicare, Inc., 333 School Street, Pawtucket 02860; tel. 401/728-3800; Frances Caprera, Administrator

Kent County Memorial Hospital, 455 Tollgate Road, Warwick 02886; tel. 401/737-7000; John J. Hynes, Administrator

Planned Parenthood of Rhode Island, 187 Westminster Mall, Providence 02903; tel. 401/421-9620; Ms. Mary Ann Sorrentino, Executive Director

Women's Medical Center, 100 Highland Avenue, Providence 02906; tel. 800/441-7711; Ms. Joyce Costabile, Administrator

SOUTH CAROLINA

Bay Microsurgical Unit, Inc., P. O. Drawer L, Georgetown 29442; tel. 803/546-8421; Angela A. Moses, Executive Director

Carolina Eye ASF, 210 University Parkway, Suite 1500 B, Aiken 29801; tel. 803/649-3952; Stephen K. VanDeVliet, M.D.

Charleston Plastic Surgery Center, 159 Rutledge Avenue, Charleston 29403; tel. 803/722-1985; Barbara Hagerty, Administrator

Greenville Surgery Center, 5 Memorial Medical Court, Greenville 29605; tel. 803/295-3067; Vicki Stephens, Administrator

MicroSurgery Center, 1655 East Greenville Street, Anderson 29621; tel. 803/224-6375; C. C. Hyde, Business Administrator

Pee Dee Ambulatory Surgery Center, 604 East Cheves Street, Florence 29501; tel. 803/669-3822; Leonard Ford, Administrator

St. Andrews Day Hospital At Medical Park, 7035 St. Andrews Road, Irmo 29063; tel. 803/749-0924; Shirley P. Padgett, Administrator

SOUTH DAKOTA

Black Hills Regional Eye Institute, 2800 South Third Street, Rapid City 57701; tel. 605/341-4100; Richard C. Hanafin, Director

Great Plains Eye Surgery Center, Inc., 501 West 25th Street, Sioux Falls 57105; tel. 605/334-7715; Thomas C. White, President

Memorial Medical Center, ASC, 420 Fourth Street, NE, Watertown 57201; Edmond L. Weiland, Administrator

Sioux Falls Surgical Center, 910 East 20th Street, Sioux Falls 57105; Donald Schellpfeffer, Medical Director

SurgiClinic, 1010 - 9th Street, Rapid City 57701; Chris G. Jaeger, Administrator

TENNESSEE

Ambulatory Surgical Treatment Center, 408 State of Franklin Road, Johnson City 37604; tel. 615/461-6166

Appalachian Ambulatory Surgical Center, 106 Rogosin Drive, Elizabethton 37643; tel. 615/543-5888

Arrowsmith Eye Surgery Center, 210 - 25th Avenue, North, Parkview Tower, Ninth Floor, Nashville 37203; tel. 615/327-2244

The Birth Center at North Park Hospital, 2051 Hamill Road, Hixson 37343; tel. 615/870-2676; William Adams, Administrator

Brentwood Outpatient Surgical Center, 5111 Maryland Way, Suite 105, Brentwood 37027; tel. 615/377-8105

Bristol Surgery Center, 305 Blountville Highway, Bristol 37620; tel. 615/968-2223; N. D. Presley, Administrator

Charlotte Avenue Medical Clinic, Inc., 4407 Charlotte Avenue, Nashville 37209; tel. 615/298-4491

Chattanooga Surgery Center, 400 North Holtzclaw Avenue, Chattanooga 37404; tel. 615/698-6871

Chattanooga Women's Clinic, 6230 Vance Road, Chattanooga 37421; tel. 615/899-1637

East Tennessee Women's Clinic, Inc., 1501 West Clinch Avenue, Knoxville 37916; tel. 615/637-4240

Family Planning Clinic for Reproductive Health, 210 19th Avenue, North, Nashville 37203; tel. 615/320-1292

John Wilson Eye Clinic, 118 East Watauga Avenue, Johnson City 37601; tel. 615/929-8193; David M. Wilson, Chief Executive

Knoxville Center for Reproductive Health, Inc., 1547 West Clinch Avenue, Knoxville 37916; tel. 615/637-3861; Robert L. Mueller, M.D., Medical Director

Memphis Area Medical Center for Women, 29 South Bellevue Boulevard, Memphis 38104; tel. 901/722-8050

Memphis Center for Reproductive Health, 1462 Poplar Avenue, Memphis 38104; tel. 901/274-3550; Carolyn R. Stone, Executive Director

Memphis Eye and Cataract Ambulatory Surgery Center, 6485 Poplar Avenue, Memphis 38119; tel. 901/767-4014

Memphis Surgery Center, 1044 Cresthaven Road, Memphis 38119; tel. 901/682-1516

Monroe Maternity Center, Inc., Lost Sea Pike - New Highway 68, P. O. Box 115, Madisonville 37354; tel. 615/442-6624; Dr. Barbara Lewin, Chief Executive Officer

Ophthalmic Ambulatory Surgical Center, P.C., 2001 Hayes Street, Nashville 37203; tel. 615/327-2001

☐ **Parkside Surgery Center,** 340 - 23rd Avenue, North, P. O. Box 23557, Nashville 37203; tel. 615/327-1123; Debby McMillin, RN, Administrator

Parkside Surgery Center, 637 Skyline Drive, Jackson 38301; tel. 901/424-1211

Planned Parenthood Association of Nashville, 112 - 21st Avenue South, Nashville 37203; tel. 615/327-1095

Planned Parenthood Center of Memphis, 1407 Union Avenue, 3rd Floor, Memphis 38104; tel. 901/725-1717

Plaza Surgery Center c/o Plaza Ambulatory Care Center, 979 East Third Street, Chattanooga 37403; tel. 615/778-3192

Rivergate Surgery Center, 647 Myatt Drive, Madison 37115; tel. 615/868-8942

Shea Clinic, 6133 Poplar Pike at Ridgeway, Memphis 38119; tel. 901/761-9720; Dr. John J. Shea, Jr., President and Medical Director

Surgical Affiliates, Inc., 4515 Harding Road, Suite 300, Nashville 37207; tel. 615/384-3541; Andrew W. Miller, President and Chief Executive Officer

The Surgery Center, 2761 Sullins Street, Knoxville 37919; tel. 615/522-2949; Carolyn Liles, R.N., Executive Director

Urology Surgery Center, Inc., 2011 Church Street, Nashville 37203; tel. 615/329-7700; Tom E. Nesbitt, Sr., M.D., President

Volunteer Medical Clinic, 313 Concord Street, Knoxville 37919; tel. 615/522-5173

The following list of freestanding ambulatory surgery centers was developed from information provided by state agencies. It is current as of January 1, 1987.

The AHA Guide *contains two types of ambulatory surgery center listings: those that are hospital based and those that are freestanding. Hospital based ambulatory surgery centers are listed in section A of the* AHA Guide *and are identified by Facility Code F1. Please refer to that section for information on the over 5,000 hospital based ambulatory surgery centers.*

Those freestanding ambulatory surgery centers accredited by the Joint Commission on Accreditation of Hospitals (JCAH) are identified by a hollow square (☐). These surgery centers have been found to be in substantial compliance with the Joint Commission standards for ambulatory health care facilities, as found in the Ambulatory Health Care Standards Manual.

We present this list simply as a convenient directory. Inclusion or omission of any organization's name indicates neither approval nor disapproval by the American Hospital Association.

Wesberry Eye and Dental Institute and Surgery Ct., 2900 South Perkins Road, Memphis 38118; tel. 901/362-3100

TEXAS

Ambulatory Urological Surgery Center, Inc., 1149 Ambler, Abilene 79601; tel. 915/676-3557

Arlington Day Surgery, 918 North Davis Drive, Arlington 76012; tel. 817/860-9933; Beverly Maurer, Administrator

Austin Surgery Center, 4207 James Casey, Suite 203, Austin 78745; tel. 512/440-7894; Dorothy Bishop, Administrator

Bailey Square Surgical Center, Ltd., 1111 West 34th Street, Austin 78705; tel. 512/454-6753

Bay Area Surgicare Center - Houston, 200 Medical Center Blvd., Suite 106, Webster 77598; tel. 713/332-2433; Donna P. Smith, Administrator

Baylor SurgiCare, 3920 Worth Street, Dallas 75246; tel. 214/820-2581

Brazosport Eye Institute, 103 Parking Way, Lake Jackson 77566; tel. 409/297-2961; Frank J. Grady, MD, Ph.D., FACS, Director

The Cataract Center of East Texas, Inc., 802 Turtle Creek Drive, Tyler 75701; tel. 214/595-4333

☐ **Cataract Surgery Center, P.A.,** 2801 Lemmon Avenue West, Dallas 75204; tel. 214/528-4195

Coastal Bend Ambulatory Surgical Center, 900 Morgan, Corpus Christi 78404; tel. 512/888-4288; Jack A. Sahadi, M.D., Medical Director

Dallas Eye Surgicenter, 720 S. Cedar Ridge Road, Duncanville 75137; tel. 214/296-6634

Dallas Surgery Center, Inc., 5744 LBJ Freeway, Dallas 75240; tel. 214/788-5080; David E. Rose, Administrator

The Day Surgery Center, 9830 Memorial Blvd., Humble 77338; tel. 713/446-5780

DeHaven Ambulatory Surgical Center, 1424 East Front Street, Tyler 75702; tel. 214/595-4144

Denton Ambulatory Surgery Center, 2515 Scripture, Suite 200, Denton 76201; tel. 817/566-4900

Duncanville Surgery Center, 1018 E. Wheatland Road, Duncanville 75116; tel. 214/296-6912

Eye Surgery Center, 2001 Ed Carey Drive, Suite 3, Harlingen 78550; tel. 512/423-2100; Michael Laney, C.O.M.T., Administrator

Eye Surgery Center, P.A., 1817 S.W. Dodgen Loop, Temple 76502; tel. 817/773-7785

☐ **Eyes of Texas, Inc.,** 155 E. Loop 338, Suite A, Mail: Rt. 1, Box 210A, Odessa 79762; tel. 915/367-3906

Facial Plastic and Cosmetic Surgical Center, 6300 Humana Plaza, Suite 475, Abilene 79606; tel. 915/695-3630

Greenpark Surgery Center, 7515 South Main Street, Suite 800, Houston 77030; tel. 713/796-9666; Pat Schmidt, Administrator

Greenville Surgery Center, 7150 Greenville Avenue, Suite 200, Dallas 75231; tel. 214/891-0466

Hermann Outpatient Surgery Center, 2727 Gramercy, Houston 77025; tel. 713/660-6900; Shirley Schoener, RN, Director

The Houston Institute of Cosmetic, Plastic, and Reconstructive Surgery, P.A., 1200 Binz, Suite 720, Houston 77004; tel. 713/526-0515

Houston MicroSurgical Center/Houston Eye Clinic, 1200 Binz, Suite 1000, Houston 77004; tel. 713/526-1600

Humana Day Surgery - Bryan, 2800 East 29th Street, Bryan 77802; tel. 409/776-4300

Hurst Day Surgery Centers, Inc., 1717 Precinct Line Road, Hurst 76054; tel. 817/498-9211

Institute of Eye Surgery, Houston, Inc., 6699 Chimney Rock, Second Floor, Houston 77081; tel. 713/665-1406

Medi-Plex of Houston Surgicare, Inc., 15201 East Freeway, Channelview 77530; tel. 713/457-1000

MediVision of Northwest Houston, 427 W. 20th Street, First Floor, Houston 77008; tel. 713/868-3641

Mid-Cities Surgicenter An Outpatient Center of AlternaCare Corp., 2012 Plaza Drive, Bedford 76021; tel. 817/283-5994

North Texas Surgi-Center, 917 Midwestern Parkway East, Wichita Falls 76302; tel. 817/767-7273

One-Day Surgery Center, 1001 Haskell Street, Mail: 1001 Montgomery St. Suite 200, Fort Worth 76107; tel. 817/735-3555

Physicians Daysurgery Center, 3930 Crutcher St., Dallas 75246; tel. 214/827-0760; Susan W. Akins, RN, MSN, Director

Port Arthur Day Surgery Center, 3449 Gates Blvd., Port Arthur 77642; tel. 409/983-6144

Promenade Surgicare, 2105 Promenade Center, Richardson 75080; tel. 214/699-9944; Lynn Warren, Administrator

San Antonio Eye Surgicenter, 800 McCullough, San Antonio 78215; tel. 512/226-6169

South Texas Eye Surgicenter, Inc., 4406 N. Laurent, Victoria 77901; tel. 512/578-0107

South Texas Institute of Eye Surgery, 7810 Louis Pasteur, Suite 101, San Antonio 78229; tel. 512/692-0218; Robert H. Poirier, M.D., Medical Director

South Texas Surgical Institute, Inc., 5756 South Staples, Corpus Christi 78413; tel. 512/993-2450

South Texas Surgicare Center, 1327 Third Street, Corpus Christi 78404; tel. 512/882-3204; Alicia Sandoval, Administrator

St. Mary's Surgicenter, St. Mary of the Plains Hospital, 2301 Quaker, Lubbock 79410; tel. 806/793-8801; Charles E. Roberts, Administrator/Vice President

Surgery Center of Fort Worth, 2001 West Rosedale, Fort Worth 76104; tel. 817/877-4777

Surgi-Med, 3810 Hughes Court, Dickinson 77539; tel. 713/337-7001; Carlos R. Bolano, M.D., Administrator

Surgical Center of El Paso, 1815 North Stanton, El Paso 79902; tel. 915/533-8412

Surgical Center of Southeast Texas, 3127 College Avenue, Beaumont 77701; tel. 409/835-2607

Surgicare Outpatient Center of Victoria, 1903 E. Sabine, Victoria 77901; tel. 512/576-4105; M. Margaret Coleman, Administrator

Surgicare of Central San Antonio, 1008 Brooklyn Avenue, San Antonio 78215; tel. 512/225-0496; Dennis Solheim, Regional Director, Administrator

Surgicare, Ltd., 3534 Vista, Pasadena 77504; tel. 713/947-0330

Surgicenter of San Antonio, Inc., 7902 Ewing Halsell Drive, San Antonio 78229; tel. 512/696-7742

Surgicenter of Southeast Texas, 233 Interstate 45 North, P. O. Box 3091, Conroe 77305; tel. 713/353-7684

Texas Outpatient Surgicare (T.O.P.S.), 17080 Red Oak Drive, Houston 77090; tel. 713/444-0065; Karen Cox, Administrator

Texoma Eye Institute, 1020 Hwy. 75 N., P. O. Box 1039, Denison 75020; tel. 214/465-7311

☐ **Travis Centre Outpatient Surgery,** 6655 Travis, Suite 200, Houston 77030; tel. 713/526-5100; Steve Smith, Executive Director

Tyler Square Ambulatory Services Center, 415 South Fleishel, P. O. Box 7817, Tyler 75711; tel. 214/595-0141; Susi Harper, RN, Director

Valley Eye Clinic and Outpatient Surgery Center, P.A., 1515 North Ed Carey Drive, Harlingen 78550; tel. 512/423-2772; Dr. Charles C. Denton

Valley Surgical Medical Clinic, Inc., 8061 Alameda, El Paso 79915; tel. 915/858-5333

West Houston Surgicare, 970 Campbell Road, Houston 77024; tel. 713/461-3547

Wilson Surgicenter, 4315 28th Street, Lubbock 79410; tel. 806/792-2104; Bill H. Wilson, M.D., Chief Executive

UTAH

FHP Medical Center, 1525 West 2100 South, Salt Lake City 84119; tel. 801/973-9999; Elden Mitchell, Regional Vice President

Intermountain Surgical Center, 359 - 8th Avenue, Salt Lake City 84103; tel. 801/575-8823; Joan W. Lelis

McKay-Dee Surgical Center, 3903 Harrison Boulevard, Ogden 84409; tel. 801/625-2809; Suzanne Richins

Provo Surgical Center, 585 North 500, West, Provo 84601; tel. 801/375-0983; Gary Ashby, Administrator

Salt Lake Surgical Center, 617 East 3900 South, Salt Lake City 84107; tel. 801/261-3141; Marjorie D. Kimes, R.N.

VIRGINIA

Ambulatory Surgical Center, 844 Kempsville Road, Norfolk 23502; tel. 804/466-6900; Richard A. Hanson, Administrator

Fairfax Surgical Center, 10730 Main Street, Fairfax 22030; tel. 703/691-0670; Sharon B. Jonnson, RN, Administrator

Hampton General Outpatient Emergency Center, 300 Marcella Road, Hampton 23666; tel. 804/727-7456; Roger M. Eitelman, Administrator

Lewis-Gale Clinic, Inc. Same Day Surgery, 1802 Braeburn Drive, Salem 24153; tel. 703/772-3670; Darrell D. Whitt, Executive Vice President

Surgi-Center of Winchester, Inc., 1860 Amherst Street, Winchester 22601; tel. 703/665-5300; Randolph M. Jackson, M.D., Medical Director

Urosurgical Center of Richmond, Inc., 5224 Monument Avenue, Richmond 23226; tel. 804/285-9980; C. M. Kinloch Nelson, M.D., President

☐ **Virginia Ambulatory Surgery Center,** 337 - 15th Street, SW, Charlottesville 22903; tel. 804/295-4800; Michael J. Cordell, Administrator

Virginia Heart Institute, 205 North Hamilton Street, Richmond 23221; tel. 804/359-9265; Charles L. Baird, Jr., M.D., Director

WASHINGTON

Bellingham Surgery Center, 2980 Squalicum Parkway, Bellingham 98225; tel. 206/671-6933; Thomas W. Friedland, M.D.

Everett Surgical Center, Inc., 3025 Rucker Avenue, Everett 98201; tel. 206/339-2464; Rita Sweeney, R.N., Administrator

Evergreen Surgical Center, 12034 Northeast 130th Lane, Kirkland 98034; tel. 206/821-3131; Ronald E. Abrams, M.D.

Eyecare Associates Institute, 3915 Talbot Road, Suite 309, Renton 98055; tel. 206/235-9911; Robert Bockoven, M.D., Administrator

Green River Surgical Center, 126 Auburn Avenue, Auburn 98002; Kenneth Newcomb, Manager

M. C. Corporation of Washington, 1051 - 116th Avenue NE, Bellevue 98004; tel. 206/454-2018; Hershell H. Boyd, M.D.

☐ **Mid-Columbia Surgical,** Williams Boulevard, Suite 471, Richland 99352; tel. 509/943-1134; Dr. Luckey

North Kitsap Ambulatory Surgical Center, 20696 Bond Road, NE, Poulsbo 98370; tel. 206/779-2020; Thomas D. Case, M.D.

Northwest Eye Surgery Center, 1560 North 115th, Suite 102, Seattle 98133; tel. 206/365-7332; Charles T. Heaney, Ph.D., Administrator

Olympic Ambulatory Surgery Center, Inc., 2601 Cherry, Bremerton 98310; tel. 206/479-5990; Donald Talcott, M.D.

Pacific Cataract and Laser Institute, 2517 N.E. Kresky, Chehalis 98532; tel. 206/748-8632; Wayne Carlson, Administrator

Physicians Eye Surgery Center, 3930 Hoyt Avenue, Everett 98206; tel. 206/259-2020; Hugh Minor, M.D.

Plastic Surgeons Northwest Ambulatory Plastic Surgery, 1002 South Tenth, Tacoma 98405; tel. 206/627-0818; Thomas J. Irish, M.D.

Plastic SurgiCenter of Olympia, 4 Olympia Professional Park, 400 Lilly Road NE, Olympia 98506; tel. 206/456-4400; Wayne Dickason, M.D.

Plastic and Reconstructive Surgeons, 17930 Talbot Road South, Renton 98055; tel. 206/228-3187; Mack Rickey, M.D.

Seattle Microsurgical Eyecare, 5300 - 17th Northwest, Seattle 98107; tel. 206/783-3929; Jack C. Bunn, M.D.

Sequim Diagnostic Services, 933 North 5th Avenue, Sequim 98382; tel. 206/683-1101; Everyl A. Beavon, Administrator

Skagit Ear, Nose, Throat, Facial Surgery, 111 South 13th Street, Mount Vernon 98273; tel. 206/336-2178; Gary K. Johnson, M.D.

The following list of freestanding ambulatory surgery centers was developed from information provided by state agencies. It is current as of January 1, 1987.

The AHA Guide contains two types of ambulatory surgery center listings: those that are hospital based and those that are freestanding. Hospital based ambulatory surgery centers are listed in section A of the AHA Guide and are identified by Facility Code F1. Please refer to that section for information on the over 5,000 hospital based ambulatory surgery centers.

Those freestanding ambulatory surgery centers accredited by the Joint Commission on Accreditation of Hospitals (JCAH) are identified by a hollow square (□). These surgery centers have been found to be in substantial compliance with the Joint Commission standards for ambulatory health care facilities, as found in the Ambulatory Health Care Standards Manual.

We present this list simply as a convenient directory. Inclusion or omission of any organization's name indicates neither approval nor disapproval by the American Hospital Association.

Spokane Eye Surgery Center, ASC., W. 208 Fifth Street, Spokane 99204; tel. 509/456-8150; Bruce Ellingsen, M.D., Medical Director

Spokane Surgery Center, North 1120 Pines Road, Spokane 99206; tel. 509/924-3235; Craig O. Jacobs, D.P.M.

Tacoma Ambulatory Surgery Center, 915 - 6th Avenue, Suite Three, Tacoma 98405; tel. 206/272-3916; Albert W. Edmonds, M.D., Medical Director

Wenatchee Surgical Center, 600 Orondo Street, Wenatchee 98801; tel. 509/662-8956; Glen Howard, Administrator

WEST VIRGINIA

Cabell-Huntington Surgery Center, 1201 Hal Greer Boulevard, Huntington 25701; tel. 304/523-1885; Ann Allen, Facility Director

Harrison Medical Services, Inc., 1370 Johnson Avenue, Bridgeport 26330; tel. 304/624-6328; Mark C. Clement, Executive Director

Jerry N. Black, M.D., Surgical Suite, 10 Amalia Drive, Buckhannon 26201; tel. 304/472-2100; Jerry N. Black, M.D., Owner

Summersville Ambulatory Surgery Center, 818 Arbuckle Road, Summersville 26651; tel. 304/872-3226; Y. Don Joo, M.D., President

SurgiCare, 3200 MacCorkle Avenue, SE, Charleston 25304; tel. 304/348-9556; Larry E. Robertson, President

WISCONSIN

Doctors SurgiCenter, Oshkosh, 501 Doctors Court, Oshkosh 54901; tel. 414/233-1233; Sherry Lynch, RN, Clinical Director

Eau Claire Surgery Center, 950 West Clairemont Avenue, Eau Claire 54701; tel. 715/839-9339; Nedra J. Moran, Chief Executive Officer

Marshfield Clinic, 1000 North Oak Avenue, Marshfield 54449; tel. 715/387-5123; Frederick J. Wenzel, Executive Director

Nicolet Clinic, Neenah, 411 Lincoln Street, Neenah 54956; tel. 414/727-4200; Michael A. Wilson, Executive Vice President

□ **St. Luke's Surgery,** 4570 South 27th Street, Milwaukee 53221; tel. 414/281-8760; Phyllis Smith, Clinical Coordinator

WYOMING

Casper Surgical Center, 245 South Fenway St., Casper 82601; tel. 307/577-8778; J. Phil White, Director

Information for the following list was obtained directly from the agencies.

Free Standing Ambulatory Surgery Center Agencies

ALABAMA: Department of Public Health, Division of Licensure and Certification, State Office Building, Montgomery 36130; tel. 205/261-5113; Carroll S. Nason, dir.

ALASKA: Division of Medical Assistance, Licensing and Certification Section, 4041 B St., Suite 101, Anchorage 99503; tel. 907/561-2171; Karen Martz, supr.

ARIZONA: Department of Health Services, Emergency Medical Services, Health Care Facilities, Office of Health Care Institution Licensure, Medical Facilities Section, Birch Hall, 411 N. 24th St., Phoenix 85008; tel. 602/220-6407; Hazel E. Chandler, chf.

ARKANSAS: Department of Health, Division of Health Facility Services, 4815 W. Markham St., Little Rock 72205; tel. 501/661-2201; Rayburn C. Allen, dir.

CALIFORNIA: Department of Health Services, Licensing and Certification Division, 714 P St., Rm. 823, Sacramento 95814; tel. 916/445-3054; Virgil J. Toney, Jr., dep. dir.

COLORADO: Department of Health, Division of Health Facilities Regulation, 4210 E. 11th Ave., Denver 80220; tel. 303/331-4930; Mildred Simmons, dir.

CONNECTICUT: Department of Health Services, Bureau of Health System Regulation, Division of Hospital and Medical Care, 150 Washington St., Hartford 06106; tel. 203/566-1073; Elizabeth M. Burns, R.N., M.S., dir.

DELAWARE: Department of Health and Social Services, Division of Public Health, Office of Health Facilities Licensing and Certification, 3000 Newport Gap Pike, Wilmington 19808; tel. 302/571-3499; James E. Harvey, dir.

DISTRICT OF COLUMBIA: Department of Consumer and Regulatory Affairs, Service Facility Regulation Administration, 614 H St., N.W., Suite 1014, Washington 20001, tel. 202/727-7000; Don Murray, dir.

FLORIDA: Department of Health and Rehabilitation Services, Office of Licensure and Certification, Office of Regulations and Health Facility, 2727 Mahan Dr., Tallahassee 32308; tel. 904/487-2513; Marta Hardy, dir.

GEORGIA: Department of Human Services, Division of Administrative Services, Office of Regulatory Services, Standards and Licensure Section, 878 Peachtree St., N.E., Atlanta 30309; tel. 404/894-5137; Phillip A. Arnold, dir.

HAWAII: Department of Health, Medical Health Services Division, Hospital and Medical Facilities Licensing Branch, P.O. Box 3378, Honolulu 96801; tel. 808/548-5935; Dr. Ben Lambiotte, chf.

IDAHO: Department of Health and Welfare, Facility Standards Program, Licensing and Certification, 420 W. Washington St., Boise 83720; tel. 208/334-5325; Loyal Perry, supr.

ILLINOIS: Department of Public Health, Division of Health Facilities Standards, Hospital Licensing Section, 525 W. Jefferson St., Springfield 62761; tel. 217/782-4977; Joseph L. Voss, adm.

INDIANA: State Board of Health, Division of Acute Care Services, 1330 W. Michigan St., P.O. Box 1964, Indianapolis 46206; tel. 317/633-8486; Harry T. Haver, dir.

IOWA: Department of Inspection and Appeals, Division of Health Facilities, Lucas State Office Bldg., Des Moines 50319; tel. 515/281-4115; Dana L. Petrowsky, adm.

KANSAS: Department of Health and Environment, Bureau of Adult and Child Care Facilities, 740 Forbes Field Bldg., Topeka 66620; tel. 913/296-1240; Greg Reser, med. facil. cert. adm.

KENTUCKY: Cabinet for Human Resources, Department for Health Services, Division of Licensing and Regulation, C.H.R. Bldg., 275 E. Main St., Frankfort 40621; tel. 502/564-2800; Woody Dunn, dir.

MAINE: Department of Human Services, Bureau of Medical Services, Division of Licensing and Certification, State House 11, Augusta 04333; tel. 207/289-2606; Louis Dorogi, dir.

MARYLAND: Department of Health and Mental Hygiene, Office of Health Regulation, 201 W. Preston St., Baltimore 21201; tel. 301/225-6530; Ron Bialek, actg. dir.

MASSACHUSETTS: Department of Public Health, Division of Health Care Quality, 80 Boylston St., Boston 02116; tel. 617/727-5860; Irene McManus, dir.

MICHIGAN: Department of Public Health, Division of Licensing and Certification, 3500 N. Logan, Lansing 48909; tel. 517/335-8505; Nancy Graham, supr.

MINNESOTA: Department of Health, Division of Health Resources, Survey and Compliance Section, 717 Delaware St., S.E., Minneapolis 55440; tel. 612/623-5420; Clarice Suefert, chf.

MISSISSIPPI: Department of Health, Division of Licensure and Certification, P.O. Box 1700, Jackson 39215; tel. 601/960-7769; Mendal G. Kemp, dir.

MISSOURI: Department of Health, Bureau of Hospital Licensing and Certification, P.O. Box 570, Jefferson City 65102; tel. 314/751-6302; Charles R. Gillilan, chf.

MONTANA: Department of Health and Environmental Sciences, Bureau of Licensing and Certification, Cogswell Bldg., Helena 59620; tel. 406/444-2037; Jacqueline McKnight, chf.

NEBRASKA: Department of Health, Division of Licensure and Standards, 301 Centennial Mall, S., Lincoln 68509; tel. 402/471-2946; William H. Page, dir.

NEW YORK: Department of Health, Office of Health Systems Management, Bureau of Alternative Delivery Systems, Empire State Plaza, Corning Tower Building, Albany 12237; tel. 518/474-5515; Joyce Gallimore, dir.

NEVADA: Department of Human Resources, Division of Health,, Bureau of Regulatory Health Services, 505 E. King St., Carson City 89710; tel. 702/885-4475; William C. Schneider, chf.

NEW HAMPSHIRE: Department of Health and Human Services, Bureau of Health Facilities Administration, 6 Hazen Dr., Concord 03301; tel. 603/271-4592; Charles Ferguson, chf.

NEW JERSEY: Division of Health Facilities Evaluation, Licensing, Certification and Standards Program, CN 367, Trenton 08625; tel. 609/292-5764; Solomon Goldberg, D.D.S., dir.

NEW MEXICO: Department of Health and Environment, Federal Program Certification Section, P.O. Box 968, Santa Fe 87504; tel. 505/827-2416; Sue K. Morris, supr.

NORTH CAROLINA: Department of Human Resources, Division of Facility Services, 701 Barbour Dr. Raleigh 27603; tel. 919/733-2342; Ira O. Wilkerson, Jr., dir.

NORTH DAKOTA: Department of Health, Health Resources Section, Division of Health Facilities, State Capitol, Bismarck 58505; tel. 701/224-2352; Joe Pratschner, chf.

OHIO: Department of Health, Division of Licensure and Certification, 246 N. High St., P.O. Box 118, Columbus 43266; tel. 614/466-2070; Paul Ritter, chf.

OKLAHOMA: Department of Health, Division of Medical Facilities Institutional Services, 1000 Northeast 10th St., P.O. Box 53551, Oklahoma City 73152; Robert Warner, chf. adm. serv.

OREGON: Division of Health, Health Facilities Section, 1400 S.W. 5th Ave., Portland 97207; tel. 503/229-5686; Maureen Whitman, mgr.

PENNSYLVANIA: Bureau of Quality Assurance, Division of Hospitals, Health and Welfare Bldg., Harrisburg 17120; tel. 717/783-8980; William Walker, dir.

RHODE ISLAND: Department of Health, Division of Medical Care Standards, 75 Davis St., Providence 02908; tel. 401/277-2788; Donald C. William, chf.

SOUTH CAROLINA: Department of Health and Environmental Control, Division of Health Licensing and Certification, Office of Health Licensing, 2600 Bull St., Columbia 29201; tel. 803/734-4680; Alan Samuels, dir.

SOUTH DAKOTA: Department of Health, Division of Public Health, Licensure and Certification Program, 523 E. Capitol, Pierre 57501; tel. 605/773-3364; C. Sue Lydic, dir.

TENNESSEE: Department of Health and Environment, Bureau of Manpower and Facilities, Division of Health Care Facilities, Board of Licensing Health Care Facilities, 283 Plus Park Blvd, Nashville 37217; tel. 615/367-6317; Leslie A. Brown, dir.

TEXAS: Department of Health, Health Facility Licensure and Certification Division, 1100 W. 49th St., Austin 78756; tel. 512/458-7245; Juanita Carroll, dir.

UTAH: Utah Department of Health, Division of Community Health Services, Bureau of Health Facility Licensure, P.O. Box 16660, Salt Lake City 84116; tel. 801/538-6152; James B. Fisher, dir.

VIRGINIA: Department of Health, Division of Licensure and Certification, 1013, 109 Governor St., Richmond 23219; tel. 804/786-2081; Mary V. Francis, dir.

WASHINGTON: Department of Social and Health Services, Division of Health, Health Facilities Survey Section, ET-31, Olympia 98504; tel. 206/753-5851; Kenneth R. Lewis, supr.

WEST VIRGINIA: Department of Health, Office of Health Standards Planning and Evaluation, Health Facilities Licensure and Certification Section, 1800 Washington St., East, Charleston 25305; tel. 304/348-0050; John J. Jarrell, dir.

WISCONSIN: Department of Health and Social Services, Division of Health, Bureau of Quality Compliance, Healthcare Survey Section, P.O. Box 309, Madison 53701; tel. 608/266-2460; Kenneth Bjorklund, dir.

WYOMING: Department of Health and Social Services, Division of Health and Medical Services, Division of Health and Medical Facilities, 4th flr., Hathaway Bldg., 2300 Capitol Ave., Cheyenne 82002; tel. 307/777-7121; Larry Meuli, adm.

Hospices

The following is a list of freestanding hospices developed from information provided by state agencies. The list is current as of January 1, 1987. For a complete list of hospital based hospice programs please refer to Section A. In Section A, over 700 hospitals with a hospice program are identified by Facility Code F21.

Those hospices accredited by the Joint Commission on Accreditation of Hospitals (JCAH) are identified by a hollow square (□). These hospices have been found to be in substantial compliance with the Joint Commission standards for hospices, as found in the Hospice Standards Manual.

We present this list simply as a convenient directory. Inclusion or omission of any organization's name indicates neither approval nor disapproval by the American Hospital Association.

United States

ALABAMA

Baptist Hospice, 2105 East South Boulevard, Montgomery 36116; tel. 205/286-3199; W. Taylor Morrow

□ **Baptist Medical Center-Montclair Hospice,** 800 Montclair Road, Birmingham 35213; tel. 205/592-1000; Dennis A. Hall

Etowah County Hospice Organization, 901 Goodyear Avenue, Gadsden 35903; tel. 205/543-4031; Donna B. Hedgspeth, RN, ECHO Director

Heritage Hospice, 2300 Airport Boulevard, Mobile 36606; tel. 205/479-8921; Henry B. Fulgham

Villa Mercy, Inc. (Hospice), 101 Villa Drive, P. O. Box 1096, Daphne 36526; tel. 205/626-2694; Sister Mary Eileen Wilhelm

ALASKA

Hospice of Juneau, Building D, Suite 15, Juneau 99801; tel. 907/780-6530

ARIZONA

Hospice of the Valley, 214 E. Willetta, Phoenix 85004; tel. 602/258-1572; Joan P. Lowell, Administrator

Hospice of Yuma, 281 W. 24th Street, Suite 120, Yuma 85364; tel. 602/343-2222; Phyllis K. Swanson, Administrator

Lawrence Memorial Hospice, 202 S. Willard Street, Cottonwood 86326; tel. 602/634-2251; L. Ann Coen, R.N., Administrator

St. Mary's Hospice, 1601 W. St. Mary's Road, Tucson 85703; tel. 602/886-8263; Anne O. Hubbert, R.N., Administrator

ARKANSAS

Area Agency on Aging Home Health and Hospice, 115 North Tenth, Suite H119, Post Office Box 1724, Fort Smith 72902; tel. 501/783-4500; Jim Medley, Executive Director

Baptist Medical Center Hospice, 9601 Interstate 630, Exit 7, Little Rock 72205; tel. 501/227-1070; Mary J. Dickson, Vice President for Nursing

Heart of the Lake Hospice, Inc., Post Office Box 314, Greers Ferry 72067; tel. 501/723-8169; Jane A. Beall

Hospice of Cherokee Village, Inc., 13 Minentonka, Post Office Box 986, Cherokee Village 72525; tel. 501/257-3108; Sally Lindemood

Hospice of the Ozarks, 906 South Baker Street, Mountain Home 72653; tel. 501/425-2797; Phillip A. Thompson, Executive Director

Washington Regional Medical Center Hospice, 1125 North College, Fayetteville 72703; tel. 501/442-1099; Jim McDonald, Hospice Director

CALIFORNIA

Alta Bates Hospice, 5232 Claremont Avenue, Oakland 94618; tel. 415/654-8420

□ **Community Hospice Inc.,** 601 McHenry Ave., Suite C, Modesto 95350; tel. 209/577-0615; Jane Merrill

Comprehensive Comm. HHA, 50 Florence Street, Daly City 94014; tel. 415/994-9100

Home Health Services Hospice, 11266 Washington Boulevard, Culver City 90230; tel. 213/390-7454

Home Hospice of Sanoma County, 1811 - Fourth Street, Santa Rosa 95404; tel. 707/542-5045; Bruce Fortin, Executive Director

□ **Hope Hospice, Inc.,** 4750 First Street, Room 4, Pleasonton 94566; tel. 415/462-9353; Patricia A. Gilchrest

Horizon Hospice, 12709 Poway Road, Suite 102, Poway 92064; tel. 619/748-3030; Karen D. Cline, Director

□ **Hospice of Contra Costa,** 140 Mayhew Way, Suite 606, Pleasant Hill 94523; tel. 415/932-8229; Lars Egede-Nissen

Hospice of Marin, 77 Mark Drive, Suite 17, San Rafael 94903; tel. 415/472-6240; Mary Taverna, Executive Director

□ **Hospice of San Joaquin,** 430 East Park Street, Stockton 95201; tel. 209/466-0690; Barbara Tognoli

Hospice of the Monterey Peninsula, 8900 Carmel Valley Road, Carmel 93923; tel. 408/625-0441; Judith C. Herrmann, President

Hospice of the Valley, 1150 South Bascom Avenue, Suite 7A, San Jose 95128; tel. 408/947-1233

□ **Hospital Home Health Care,** 23456 Hawthorne Blvd., #120, Torrance 90505; tel. 213/373-6373; G. Lorain Brault

Kaiser Permanente Hospice Program, 9961 Sierra Avenue, Fontana 92335; tel. 714/829-2459; C. Marshall, RN, Program Director

Livingston Memorial VNA Hospice, 1996 Eastman Avenue, Suite 101; Ventura 93003; tel. 714/879-5480

Loma Linda Hospice, 11275 B Mountain View Avenue, Loma Linda 92354; tel. 714/824-4744

□ **San Diego Hospice Corporation,** 3840 Calle Fortunada, San Diego 92123; tel. 619/560-0302

San Pedro Peninsula Home Care and Hospice, 1386 B West 7th Street, San Pedro 90732; tel. 213/514-5390

VNA Home Health Care, Hospice, 2216 The Alameda, Santa Clara 95050; tel. 408/244-1280; Sharon Miller, RN, MSN, Hospice Program Manager

Vesper Hospice, 311 MacArthur Boulevard, San Leandro 94577; tel. 415/632-4390; Iris L. Preece, M.S.W., Director

Visiting Nurse Association of Los Angeles, Inc. Hospice in the Home Program, 3755 Beverly Boulevard, Los Angeles 90004; tel. 213/667-1050; Fran Zonfrillo, PHN, Director of Hospice

COLORADO

Arkansas Valley Hospice, P.O. Box 434, 1100 Carson, LaJunta 81050; tel. 303/384-8827; Jean Rickman

Boulder County Hospice, Inc., 2825 Marine, Boulder 80303; tel. 303/449-7740; Martin Schaefer

Bristlecone Hospice, P.O. Box 1327, 101 W. Main Street, Frisco 80443; tel. 303/668-5604; Shirley Kelley

Denver Catholic Commun. Svcs. Hospice of Peace, 200 Josephine, Denver 80206; tel. 303/388-4411; Ann Luke

Grand River Home Health Care Hospice, 701 East 5th, Rifle 81650; tel. 303/625-1510; Linda Sours

Hilltop Hospice, (Hilltop Rehab. Hosp. & Hspc. Program), 1100 Patterson Road, Grand Junction 81506; tel. 303/241-6395; Barb Hocking

Hospice Del Valle, Inc., P.O. Box 1554, 421 Hunt, Alamosa 81101; tel. 303/589-9019; Judi Lamb

Hospice, Inc. of Larimer County, P.O. Box 8901, 5205 South College Avenue, Fort Collins 80525; tel. 303/266-6533; Char Loberg

Hospice, Inc. of Weld County, 1801 16th Street, Greeley 80631; tel. 303/352-8487; Cheryl Rademacher

Hospice of Memorial Hospital, 311 Mapleton Avenue, Boulder 80302; tel. 303/443-0230; Joan Massaro

Hospice of Metro Denver, Inc., 450 Lincoln Street, Denver 80203; tel. 303/778-1010; Kathryn W. Johnson

Hospice of St. John, 1320 Everett Court, Lakewood 80215; tel. 303/232-7900; David Wood

Hospice of The Eastern Plains, P.O. Box 997, 790 Main Street, Limon 80828; tel. 303/775-2367; Marcee Morris

Lamar Area Hospice Association, Inc., P.O. Box 843, 610 West Elm, Lamar 81052; tel. 303/336-2100; M. McClain

□ **Lutheran Hospice Care,** 8300 West 38th Avenue, Wheatridge 80033; tel. 303/425-8000; Diana Woodhouse

Mount Evans Hospice, Inc., P.O. Box 2770, 3709 South Colo. Highway 74, Evergreen 80439; tel. 303/674-6400; Louisa Walthers

Pikes Peak Hospice, Inc., 601 North Tejon, Colorado Springs 80903; tel. 303/633-3400; Moira Reinhardt

Porter Home Hospice (Porter Memorial Hospital), 850 East Harvard, Suite G55, Denver 80210; tel. 303/778-5672; Jo Anne Glover

St. Mary's Hospice Care, 2525 North 7th, Grand Junction 81502; tel. 303/244-2341; Pat Means

St. Thomas More Hospice, 1019 Sheridan, Canon City 81212; tel. 303/275-3381; Sr. M. Judith Kuhn

Sangre De Cristo Hospice, 102 West Orman, Pueblo 81004; tel. 303/542-0032; Joni Fair

San Juan Hospice, Inc., 375 East Park Avenue, Durango 81301; tel. 303/247-4311; Christy Whitney

CONNECTICUT

□ **Hospice Care Inc.,** 461 Atlantic Street, Stamford 06901; tel. 203/324-2592; Janice Casey, R.N., M.S.

DELAWARE

Delaware Hospice - Central Division, 637 S. Governors Avenue, Dover 19901; tel. 302/674-7359; Laura Voras, R.N., PPC

Delaware Hospice - Northern Division, 100 Ridgely Building, 3519 Silverside Road, Wilmington 19810; tel. 302/478-5707; Ms. Virginia Wagner, Executive Director

Delaware Hospice, Inc. - Southern Division-Lewes, 1632 Savannah Road, Suite 5, Lewes 19958; tel. 302/645-5455; Sandy Keck, R.N., PCC

Delaware Hospice, Inc. Southern Division-Seaford, 701 Middleford Road, Nanticoke Professional Building, Seaford 19973; tel. 302/629-4983

DISTRICT OF COLUMBIA

□ **Hospice Care of District of Columbia,** 1749 St. Matthew's Court, N.W., Washington, D.C. 20036; tel. 202/347-1700; Anne Towne, Administrator

Hospice of Washington, 3720 Upton St., N.W., Washington, D.C. 20016; tel. 202/966-3720; Monica Kashuta, M.S.N., R.N., Administrator

FLORIDA

Big Bend Hospice, Inc., 1315 Hodges Drive, Tallahassee 32308; tel. 904/878-5310

Brevard Hospice, Inc., 110 Longwood Avenue, P.O. Box 6, Rockledge 32955; tel. 305/636-2211

Good Shepherd Hospice of Polk Co. Inc., P.O. Box 1183, Winter Haven 33882; tel. 813/293-6737

Hernando-Pasco Hospice Inc., 13825 U.S. 19, Suite 404, Hudson 33567; tel. 813/863-7971

Hope Hospice, 3949 Evans Ave., Suite 300, Ft. Myers 33901; tel. 813/936-1157

Hospice by the Sea Inc., 1580 N.W. 2nd Ave., Suite #6, Boca Raton 33432; tel. 305/395-5031

Hospice Care Inc., 3400 70th Ave., North, Pinellas Park 33565; tel. 813/521-1199

Hospice Care of Broward Co. Inc., 309 S.E. 18th Street, Ft. Lauderdale 33316; tel. 305/467-7423

Hospice Inc., 2331 N. State Road 7, Suite 211, Lauderhill 33313; tel. 305/486-4085

□ **Hospice of Central Fla. Inc.,** P.O. Box 449, Winter Park 32790; tel. 305/875-0028

Hospice of Charlotte, 3109 Tamiami Trail Units 243, Port Charlotte 33952; tel. 813/625-9992

Hospice of Citrus County, 504 W. Grace Street, P.O. Box 368, Inverness 32651; tel. 904/344-5055

Hospice of Florida Keys, P.O. Box 190, Key West 33040; tel. 305/294-8812

Hospice of Gold Coast HHS, 911 E. Atlantic Blvd., #200, Pompano Beach 33060; tel. 305/785-2990

Hospice of Hillsborough, Inc., 6400 North 15th Street, P.O. Box 9375, Tampa 33674; tel. 813/237-1356

Hospice of Indian River County, 2400 15th Avenue, Vero Beach 32960; tel. 305/569-1444

□ **Hospice of Martin Inc.,** 925 Lincoln Ave., Stuart 33497; tel. 305/287-7860

Hospice of N.E. Florida, Inc., 3599 University Blvd. S., Suite 3, Jacksonville 32216; tel. 904/398-4724

Hospice of N.W. Florida, Inc., 2001 N. Palafox Street, Suite E, Pensacola 32501; tel. 904/433-2155

Hospice of Naples, Inc., 850 6th Avenue N., Naples 33940; tel. 813/261-4404

□ **Hospice of Palm Beach County,** 444 Bunker Road, West Palm Beach 33405; tel. 305/582-2205

Hospice of Saint Francis, P.O. Box 5563, Titusville 32780; tel. 305/269-4240

Hospice of Sarasota Co., Inc., 2344 Bee Ridge Road, Sarasota 33579; tel. 813/922-0755

Hospice of South Brevard, Inc., 1350 South Hickory Street, Melbourne 32901; tel. 305/676-7233

Hospice of the Treasure Coast, P.O. Box 1742, Ft. Pierce 33454; tel. 305/465-0504

The following is a list of freestanding hospices developed from information provided by state agencies. The list is current as of January 1, 1987. For a complete list of hospital based hospice programs please refer to Section A. In Section A, over 700 hospitals with a hospice program are identified by Facility Code F21.

Those hospices accredited by the Joint Commission on Accreditation of Hospitals (JCAH) are identified by a hollow square (☐). These hospices have been found to be in substantial compliance with the Joint Commission standards for hospices, as found in the Hospice Standards Manual.

We present this list simply as a convenient directory. Inclusion or omission of any organization's name indicates neither approval nor disapproval by the American Hospital Association.

Hospice of Volusia, 303 N. Clyde Morris Blvd., P.O. Box 1990, Daytona Beach 32015; tel. 904/254-4237

Lake Hospice, Inc., 222 East 4th Avenue, Mount Dora 32757; tel. 904/383-0794

Methodist Hospice, 580 West 8th Street, Jacksonville 32209; tel. 904/798-8340

North Central Florida Hospice Inc., 801 S.W. Second Ave., Gainesville 32602; tel. 904/338-2121

Ocala Hospice Inc., 1229 S.E. Fort King St., P.O. Box 271, Ocala 32678; tel. 904/351-4610

GEORGIA

Albany Community Hospice, 417 Third Avenue, Albany 31703; tel. 912/888-4047; Tricia Helms, RN, Director

American Hospice, 102 West Mimosa Street, Jonesboro 30236; tel. 404/471-2914; Pat Sanders

Columbus Hospice, Inc., Medical Arts Building, Suite 207, 1310 Thirteenth Avenue, Columbus 31901; tel. 404/327-5153; Joel Anderson

Comfort Care, 312 Hospital Drive, Thomson 30824; tel. 404/595-5115; William Rawlings, Jr.

☐ **Family Life Enrichment Centers,** 3450 New High Shoals Road, High Shoals 30645; tel. 404/769-7738; Magda D. Bennett

☐ **Grady Memorial Hospital Hospice Program,** 80 Butler Street, S.E., Atlanta 30325; tel. 404/589-4307; J. W. Pinkston

The Greatest Gift, A Hospice, 604 Battlefield Parkway, Ft. Oglethorpe 30742; tel. 404/866-9854; Jerry Sue McConathy

☐ **Hamilton Medical Center Hospice,** P. O. Box 1168, Dalton 30720; tel. 404/278-2105; Reynolds Jennings

Hospice Atlanta, 100 Edgewood Avenue, N.E., Atlanta 30303; tel. 404/577-6989; Kathy Ziegler

Hospice of Athens, Inc., 320 N. Milledge Avenue, Athens 30601; tel. 404/548-8923; Dr. Stephen Lucas

Hospice of Central GA., 1043 Walnut Street, Macon 31201; tel. 912/742-2115; Nancy White

☐ **Hospice of Georgia, Inc.,** Box 37-A, High Shoals 30645; tel. 404/769-7738; Magda D. Bennett

Hospice of Houston Co., Inc., P. O. Box 1023, Warner Robins 31099; tel. 912/922-1777; Jackie Connors

☐ **Hospice of the Golden Isles, Inc.,** 2228 Starling Street, Brunswick 31520; tel. 912/265-4735; Karen S. Catlin, Executive Director

Hospice Savannah, Inc., 3025 Bull Street, P. O. Box 23015, Savannah 31403; tel. 912/236-1182; Anne K. Stewart, Executive Director

☐ **Kennestone Regional Hospice,** P. O. Box 1208, Marietta 30061; tel. 404/426-3131; M. Sharon Smith, Ed.D.

☐ **Northside Hospice,** 1000 Johnson Ferry Road, Atlanta 30342; tel. 404/252-2708; W. Chris Clark

Peachtree Hospice, 3123 Presidential Drive, Altanta 30340; tel. 404/457-0700; Joan Lipovsky

St. Joseph Hospice, 2260 Wrightsboro Road, Augusta 30910; tel. 404/737-7648; Ralph E. Robinson

St. Joseph Hospital Home Health Care & Hospice, 3108B Wrightsboro Rd., Augusta 30909; tel. 404/737-7490; Janet Berhang Doggett, RN, MSN, Director

Southwest Christian Hospice, 7225 Lester Road, Union City 30291; tel. 404/969-8354; Janice H. Weaver, Director

☐ **Taylor Memorial Hospice,** Macon Highway, Hawkinsvile 31036; tel. 912/783-0200; Patricia Holland

☐ **West Georgia Medical Center,** 1514 Vernon Road, LaGrange 30204; tel. 404/882-141; Charles L. Foster, Jr.

HAWAII

Hospice Hawaii, 310 Paoakalani Ave., Suite 204, Honolulu 96815; tel. 808/924-9255; Evelyn Char, RN, MS, Executive Director

☐ **St. Francis Medical Center Hospice Program,** 2230 Liliha Street, Honolulu 96817; tel. 808/547-6011; Sister Maureen Keleher, FACHE, Chief Executive Officer

Samuel Mahelona Memorial Hospital Hospice Program, 4800 Kawaihau Road, Kapaa, Kauai 96746; tel. 808/822-4961; John M. English, Administrator

IDAHO

Good Samaritan Hospice, Idaho Falls 83401; tel. 208/523-4795; Marilyn Watts, Coordinator

Hospice of North Idaho, 2003 Lincoln Way, Coeur d'Alene 83814; tel. 208/667-4537; Ms. Kay McGruder, Administrator

Hospice of the Palouse, P. O. Box 9461, Moscow 83843; tel. 208/882-1228; Ms. Connie Simonsmeier, Administrator

MSTI - Hospice of Boise, 151 E. Bannock, Boise 83712; tel. 208/386-2711; Eugene G. Gunderson, Administrator

Magic Valley Regional Medical Center Home Hospice Services, 650 Addison Avenue West, Twin Falls 83301; tel. 208/737-2500; Ms. Mary Detienne, RN, BSN, Director

Magic Valley Staffing Service, Inc., 219 - 2nd Street North, Twin Falls 83301; tel. 208/734-0600; Gary L. Thietten, RN, Administrator

Mercy Hospice c/o Mercy Medical Center, 1512 - 12th Avenue Road, Nampa 83651; tel. 208/467-1171; C. Kregg Hanson, President/CEO

ILLINOIS

Alexian Brothers Medical Center - Hospice, 800 West Biesterfield Road, Elk Grove Village 60007; tel. 312/437-5500; Brother Philip Kennedy, C.F.A.

Belleville Hospice, Inc., 315 North Church Street, Belleville 62220; tel. 618/235-1703; John B. Lee

BroMenn Hospice, 807 North Main Street, Bloomington 61701; tel. 309/827-4321; Donna L. Boyd, Director

Cancer Home Health Service of Decatur Memorial Hospital, 2300 North Edward, Decatur 62526; tel. 217/877-8121; Don Gent, President

Care for the Terminally Ill McDonough District Hospital, 525 East Grant Street, Macomb 61455; tel. 309/833-4101; David W. Shane

Chicago Area Jewish Hospice Association, 2901 West Touhy, Chicago 60645; tel. 312/508-4321; Aida Berenson, Executive Director

Columbus-Cuneo-Cabrini Medical Center for Hospice Services, 2520 North Lakeview Avenue, Chicago 60614; tel. 312/833-7300; Robert J. O'Mara, Ph.D.

Community Hospice, Inc., Ottawa Branch, 507 Clinton, Ottawa 61350; tel. 815/434-0673; Nancy Strezo, RN

Community Hospice, Inc., Spring Valley Branch, 600 E. First Street, Spring Valley 61362; tel. 815/664-5311; Lois Getty, R.N.

☐ **Community Nursing Service,** 330 E. Avenue, Bellwood 60104; tel. 312/681-3000; Saundra Spilotro, R.N., M.P.H.

Community Nursing Service of Oak Park and River Forest Home Hospice Care, 124 South Marion, Oak Park 60302; tel. 312/383-1719; Jo Ann Lingle

DeKalb County Hospice, 615 North First Street #206, DeKalb 60115; tel. 815/756-3000; Karen Hagen, R.N., M.S.N., Executive Director

East St. Louis Volunteer Hospice Program (St. Marys Hospital), 129 North 8th Street, East St. Louis 62201; tel. 618/274-1905; Sr. Janet Sue Smith, A.S.C.

☐ **Four Fountains Hospice,** 201 South Belt West, Belleville 62220; tel. 618/277-1800; Marcia Buchs

Fox Valley Hospice, 113 East Wilson Street, Batavia 60510; tel. 312/879-6064; Vivian J. Nimmo, Executive Director

Grundy Community Hospice, 1340 Edwards Street, Morris 60450; tel. 815/942-8525; Linda Popidinski

Home Health and Hospice of Illinois Masonic Medical Center, 836 West Wellington, Chicago 60657; tel. 312/833-7048; Kathleen Woods, Director

Home Hospice, VNA North, 2008 Dempster, Evanston 60202; tel. 312/328-1900; Catherine B. Carey

Home Hospice Nursing, Inc., 808 South Catherine, LaGrange 60525; tel. 312/482-4550; Ruth Hadwen

Horizon Hospice, Inc., 2800 North Sheridan, Chicago 60657; tel. 312/871-3658; Elizabeth Deyermond, Executive Director

Hospice Care Inc., P.O. Box 109, Carbondale 62903; tel. 618/457-5525; Lisa Popov, Executive Director

Hospice for McHenry County, P. O. Box 835, Woodstock 60098; tel. 815/338-5450; Jacqueline Charles

Hospice of Adams County, 1005 Broadway, Quincy 62301; tel. 217/223-5811; John Tripp

Hospice of DuPage, Inc., 600 S. Lambert Road, Building M Suite 117, Glen Ellyn 60137; tel. 312/469-5556

Hospice of Highland Park Hospital, 718 Glenview Avenue, Highland Park 60035; tel. 312/480-3858; Sr. Elizabeth McWilliams

Hospice of Kankakee Valley, Inc., 162-1/2 East Court Street, P. O. Box 202, Kankakee 60901; tel. 815/939-4141; Sarah Hertz

Hospice of Lincolnland, 100 Professional Plaza, P. O. Box 825, Mattoon 61938; tel. 217/234-4044; Carolyn Bruce

Hospice of Lincolnland - 1, 252 West Wood, Paris 61944; tel. 217/466-2430; Carolyn Bruce

Hospice of Lincolnland - 2, 102 East North Central, Tuscola 61953; tel. 217/253-3804; Carolyn Bruce

Hospice of Lincolnland - 3, 103 South Central, P. O. Box 352, Casey 62420; tel. 217/932-4942; Carolyn Bruce

Hospice of Little Co. of Mary Hospital, 2800 West 95th Street, Evergreen Park 60642; tel. 312/422-6200; Marilyn German, Director

Hospice of Madison County, 2100 Madison Avenue, Granite City 62040; tel. 618/798-3399; Janet Smith, RN, BSN, Program Director

Hospice of Northeastern Illinois, , P. O. Box 622, Barrington 60011; tel. 312/381-5599; Rick R. Space, Executive Director

Hospice of Northwest Illinois, Inc., 155 W. Front Street, P.O. Box 185, Stockton 61085; tel. 815/947-3260; Ralph D. Krubeck

☐ **Hospice of Proviso - Leyden,** 330 Eastern Avenue, Bellwood 60104; tel. 312/547-5480; Judy Wilson

Hospice of the Good Samaritan, 605 North 12th Street, Mt.Vernon 62864; tel. 618/242-4600; Marilyn Fowler

Hospice of the North Shore, 615 Locust Road, Wilmette 60091; tel. 312/256-4601; Ralph T. Schwab, Executive Director

Hospice Suburban South, 3543 Ionia Avenue, Olympia Fields 60461; tel. 312/748-1070; Joan Coogan

Joliet Area Community Hospice, 2112 West Jefferson Street, Suite 254, Joliet 60435; tel. 815/744-4104; Mary Jo Smith, Executive Director

La Grange Colonial Manor Hospice Program, 339 Ninth Avenue, La Grange 60525; tel. 312/554-4660; Lisa Rozwat, Hospice Coordinator

Lake Forest Hospital Hospice Program, 660 North Westmoreland Road, Lake Forest 60045; tel. 312/234-5600; William G. Ries, President

Lakeview Medical Center Hospice, 812 North Logan Avenue, Danville 61832; tel. 217/443-5000; Rebecca Hawkins

Mercy Hospice Care Program, 1400 West Park, Urbana 61801; tel. 217/337-2470; Jan Shepardson

Meridian Hospice, 5445 South Ingleside Avenue, Chicago 60615; tel. 312/955-5529; Rosemary Crowley

The Methodist Medical Center of Illinois Hospice Services, 221 N.E. Glen Oak, Peoria 61636; tel. 309/672-5746; Vickie Lannie

Northern Illinois Hospice Association, 845 N. Church Street, Rockford 61103; tel. 815/964-0230; Judith A. Carra

Northwest Comm. Hospital Home Hospice, 800 West Central Road, Arlington Heights 60005; tel. 312/577-4047; Nancy Hartshorn, MSN

☐ **Northwestern Memorial Hospital Hospice Program,** 303 East Superior Street, 9E Passavant Pavillion, Chicago 60611; tel. 312/908-7476; Jeanne Martinez, RN, MPH, Clinical Manager

Ogle County Hospice Association, 822 North 2nd Street, Rochelle 61068; tel. 815/562-2400; Kathleen M. Espe, Executive Director

Parkside Home Health Services, 1460 Renaissance Dr., Park Ridge 60068; tel. 312/297-1090; Barbe Creagh, M.S.W.

Pathway Hospice, 501 Tenth Avenue, Moline 61265; tel. 309/757-2031; Maxine Duhm/Loralyn Anderson

Pekin Memorial Hospital Hospice, Court and 14th Streets, Pekin 61554; tel. 309/353-0356; Norman F. Webb, II, President

The following is a list of freestanding hospices developed from information provided by state agencies. The list is current as of January 1, 1987. For a complete list of hospital based hospice programs please refer to Section A. In Section A, over 700 hospitals with a hospice program are identified by Facility Code F21.

Those hospices accredited by the Joint Commission on Accreditation of Hospitals (JCAH) are identified by a hollow square (□). These hospices have been found to be in substantial compliance with the Joint Commission standards for hospices, as found in the Hospice Standards Manual.

We present this list simply as a convenient directory. Inclusion or omission of any organization's name indicates neither approval nor disapproval by the American Hospital Association.

Pike County Health Dept. Hospice Care, 113 East Jefferson Street, Pittsfield 62363; tel. 217/285-4407; Martha Lowry, R.N.
QLS Massac County Volunteer Hospice, 213 West Fifth Street, P. O. Bldg., 2nd Floor, Metropolis 62960; tel. 618/524-3717; Jean Dorsett-Robinson, Chief Executive Officer
Rainbow Hospice, Inc., P. O. Box 4027, 1040 Thacker Street, Des Plaines 60016; tel. 312/699-6023; Christine M. Koza, Executive Director
Saint Anthony's Hospital Home Health Care/Hospice, Saint Anthony's Way, Alton 62002; tel. 618/465-2571; Cynthia Murphy
St. Elizabeth Hospital Hospice, 600 Sager Avenue, Danville 61832; tel. 217/442-6300; H. Dolores Connelly
St. John's Hospital Hospice Program, 800 East Carpenter, Springfield 62769; tel. 217/544-6464; Mr. Allison C. Laabs, Administrator
St. Thomas Hospice, Inc., 7 Salt Creek Lane, Hinsdale 60521; tel. 312/920-8300; Raymond Brockill
Sauk Valley Hospice, P. O. Box 82, Dixon 61021; tel. 815/288-3673; Cheryl Price
Spoon River Hospice Association, 210 West Walnut, Canton 61520; tel. 309/647-5353; Charlotte Van Sickle
Star Hospice Saint Therese Medical Center, 2615 Washington Street, Waukegan 60085; tel. 312/360-2220; Carole Weber, R.N.
West Towns Visiting Nursing Service, Inc./Hospice, 2140 South Wesley, Berwyn 60402; tel. 312/749-7171; Sandra Kubik, RN, MPH, Executive Director
Whiteside County Hospice Association, P. O. Box 918, Rock Falls 61071; tel. 815/626-9242; Marilyn Williams, Executive Director
Wood River Township Hospital Hospice, Edwardsville Road, Wood River 62095; tel. 618/254-3821; W. Eugene Cowsert

INDIANA
□ **Ball Memorial Hospital,** 2401 University Avenue, Muncie 47303; tel. 317/747-4273; Ruth Anne Tolle, Nurse Coordinator
Bartholomew County Area Hospice, 2400 East 17th Street, Columbus 47201; tel. 812/376-5813; Sandy Anderson, Administrator
Bedford Medical Center, 2900 West 16th Street, Bedford 47421; tel. 812/279-3581; Joy E. Hamme, Hospice Coordinator
Cameron Memorial Community Hospital, 416 East Maumee Street, Angola 46703; tel. 219/665-2141; JoAnn Engber, Hospice Coordinator
Elkhart Community Hospice, 600 East Blvd., Elkhart 46514; tel. 219/294-2621; Jan Yoder
Family Care Home Health Agency, 1000 East Main Street, Danville 46122; tel. 317/745-5417; Maura Fox, RN
Goshen General's Cooperative, 200 High Park, Goshen 46526; tel. 219/533-2141; Pam Kuhns, Patient Care Coordinator, Administrator
Holy Cross Parkview Hospital, 1401 North Michigan Street, Plymouth 46563; tel. 219/936-3181; Dorothy Steinke
Home Health Care Services of Kosciusko Co., Inc., 827 South Union, Warsaw 46580; tel. 219/267-3683; Robert Blauvelt, Executive Director
Hospice of Bloomington, Inc. Care Of Bloomington Hospital, P. O. Box 1149, Bloomington 47402; tel. 812/336-5595; Martha Lloyd, Executive Director
Hospice of Grant Co., Inc., P. O. Box 1004, Marion 46952; tel. 317/662-3540; Martha Ferguson
Hospice of Huntington, 1215 Etna Avenue, Huntington 46750; tel. 219/356-3000; Marcia Brown / Cindy MacDonald
Hospice of North West Indiana, 9104 Columbia Avenue, Munster 46321; tel. 219/836-2164; Donna Excell, Executive Director
Hospice of Southern Indiana, 1850 State Street, New Albany 47150; tel. 812/945-4596
Hospice of St. Joseph County, 902 East Cedar Street, South Bend 46617; tel. 219/237-7837; Thomas Burzynski, Executive Director
Hospice of Wabash Valley, 612 Merchants Bank Bldg., Terre Haute 47807; tel. 812/232-6311; Jacquelyn Fox
King's Daughters', 112 Presbyterian Avenue, P. O. Box 447, Madison 47250; tel. 812/265-5211; Rich Reuss, R.P.T.
Lawrence County Area Hospice Dunn Memorial Hospital, 1600 23rd Street, Bedford 47421; tel. 812/275-3331
Lincoln Trail Hospice, 1206 Ritterskamp, Vincennes 47591; tel. 812/882-7435; Mrs. Janine Curry, RN
Memorial Hospital, 1101 Michigan Avenue, Logansport 46947; tel. 219/753-7541; Marilyn Minich
Methodist Hospital Hospice, 1604 North Capitol Avenue, Indianapolis 46202; tel. 317/924-6411; Marcia Tracey / Neil Irick, M.D.
Mother Theresa Hospice Crown Point, Indiana, Main at Franciscan, Crown Point 46307; tel. 219/738-2100; Paul C. Poparad
Noble County Home Health Care/Hospice, 1030 Lakepark Drive, Kendallville 46755; tel. 219/347-1100; Marilyn Allgood
Ohio Valley Hospice, P. O. Box 3402, Evansville 47733; tel. 812/422-2596; Elizabeth Freed, Director
Pike County Hospice, 125 Peterburg, Petersburg 47567; tel. 812/354-6844; Dotty Weisman, Coordinator
Porter Memorial Hospice, 814 LaPorte Avenue, Valparaiso 46383; tel. 219/464-8611; Barbara Boise
Reid Memorial Hospital Hospice/Home Care, 1401 Chester Blvd., Richmond 47374; tel. 317/983-3000; Doug Tweddale
River Valley Hospice, 600 Wilson Creek Road, Lawrenceburg 47025; tel. 812/537-1010; Susan Block
St. John's Hospice of Madison County, 2015 Jackson Street, Anderson 46014; tel. 317/646-8334; Beth Furnish
St. Joseph Memorial Hospital, 1907 West Sycamore, Kokomo 46901; tel. 317/456-5417; Polly Jones, Director of Outreach Services
St. Vincent's Hospital and Stress Center, 8401 Harcourt Road, Indianapolis 46260; tel. 317/875-4671; Margie Pile
V.N.A. LaPorte County Hospice Program, 2466 North Street Road 39, LaPorte 46350; tel. 219/362-5914; Mary Ann Smith, Hospice Coordinator
V.N.S. & Hospice, Inc., 227 East Washington Blvd., Fort Wayne 46802; tel. 219/422-2451; Hazel Etzler / Steve Arter
Visiting Nurse Health Care, Inc., P. O. Box 2340, Anderson 46018; tel. 317/643-7371
Wells County Hospice Wells Community Hospital, 1100 South Main Street, Blufton 46714; tel. 219/824-3210; Roronda Mahon

IOWA
Amicare Home Health Services, Siouxland, Inc. dba/Hospice of Siouxland, 50011th Street, Sioux City 51105; tel. 712/233-1137; Trudy Pfeiffer, RN, Administrator
□ **Cedar Valley Hospice,** Kimball and Ridgeway, Waterloo 50702; tel. 319/234-5705; Cheryl A. Hoerner, Executive Director
Holy Family Hospice, 826 North 8th Street, Esterville 51334; tel. 712/362-2631; Judy Hanson, Director
□ **Hospice of Central Iowa,** 2116 Grand Avenue, Des Moines 50312; tel. 515/243-4235; Kate Colburn, Executive Director
□ **Hospice of Cerro Gordo,** 810 - 12th Street NW, Mason City 50401; tel. 515/423-3508; Ann MacGregor, Executive Director
Iowa River Hospice, Inc., 3 South 4th Avenue, P. O. Box 981, Marshalltown 50158; tel. 515/753-7704; Pat Rittscher, RN, Executive Director
Mercy Hospital Medical Center, 1055 6th Street, Des Moines 50314; tel. 515/247-8383; Pat McDermott, RN, Executive Director

KANSAS
Abilene Area Hospice, Inc. Memorial Hospital, 511 N.E. 10th Street, Abilene 67410; tel. 913/263-2100; Jan Konrade, Director
Cowley County Hospice, Inc., P. O. Box 344, Winfield 67156; tel. 316/221-7130; JoAnne Vonderbrink, RN, Coordinator
Harvey County Hospice, Inc., P. O. Box 632, Newton 67114; tel. 316/283-4989; Carole Hull, Administrative Director
Hospice Care in Douglas Co., 336 Missouri - Lower Level, Lawrence 66044; tel. 913/749-5006; Anne Benjamin, Director
Hospice Care, Inc., 2803 Claflin Road, Manhattan 66502; tel. 913/539-2273; Lois Deyoe, Director
Hospice Inc. of Decatur County Decatur County Hospital, P. O. Box 268, Oberlin 67749; tel. 913/475-2208; Amelia Suzman, Director
Hospice of Ellsworth County, Inc. Ellsworth Memorial Hospital, Room #205, Ellsworth 67439; tel. 913/472-5159; Susan Mehler, RN, Director
Hospice of Hope, Hoxie 67740; tel. 913/675-3281; Kathleen Cooper, Administrative Director
Hospice of NCK, Inc., P. O. Box 165, Belleville 66935; tel. 913/527-5201; Loren Hedstrom, Director
Hospice of Olathe Medical Center, 215 West 151st Street, Olathe 66061; tel. 913/791-4315; Linda Welter, BSN, Administrative Director
Hospice of Ottawa County c/o Ottawa County Health Department, Courthouse, Minneapolis 67467; tel. 913/392-2822; June Clark, RN, Director
Hospice of Reno County, Inc., 1701 East 23rd, Hutchinson 67502; tel. 316/665-2473; Ardith Alexander, Director
Hospice of Salina, P. O. Box 1937, Salina 67402; tel. 913/827-4411; Kaye Pogue, RN, Director
Hospice of Southwest Kansas, P. O. Box 1970, Liberal 67901; tel. 316/624-2469; Dr. John Loucks, Director
Hospice of the Flint Hills, P. O. Box 102, Emporia 66801; tel. 316/342-2240; Alan Henke
Hospice of the Plains, Inc., 507 Elm Street, Hays 67601; tel. 913/625-1139; Karen Crow, Administrator
Hospice of the Prairie, Inc., Box 788, Dodge City 67801; tel. 316/227-8133; Cleda Dodge, Director
Hospice of Trego County, P. O. Box 314, Wakeeney 67672; tel. 913/743-2182; Alice Ochs, Administrative Director
Hospice of Wichita, Inc., 1831 Woodrow, Wichita 67203; tel. 316/265-9441; John G. Carney, Executive Director
Jeanne R. Corley Hospice, 608 North 5th, Garden City 67846; tel. 316/275-2156; Janice Weiser, Coordinator
Leavenworth Hospice-Cushing Memorial Hospital, 623 Marshall Street, Leavenworth 66048; tel. 913/682-8000; Gayle Edwards, Administrative Director
McPherson County Hospice, Inc., P. O. Box 37, 1000 Hospital Drive, McPherson 67460; tel. 316/241-6677; Chris Anderson, Administrative Director
Mobile Agency for Southwest Hospice, 617 North Main, Garden City 67846; tel. 316/275-4077; Angela P. Miller, Coordinator
Pawnee County Home Health Hospice, 715 Broadway, Courthouse, Larned 67750; tel. 316/285-6963; Barbara Hammond, ARNPC, Administrative Director
Phillips County Area Hospice, Box 607, Phillipsburg 67661; tel. 913/543-5226; Genny Robben, Coordinator
Serenity Hospice of Golden Belt Home Health Service, P. O. Box 937, Great Bend 67530; tel. 316/792-8171; Sr. Dominic Haug, Administrator
Smith County Hospice, P. O. Box 324, Smith Center 66967; tel. 913/282-3506; Debra Evangelidis, Administrative Director
Solomon Valley Hospice, P. O. Box 217, Beloit 67420; tel. 913/738-2266; Barbara Cashatt, RN, Administrative Director
Sumner County Hospice, Inc., P. O. Box 121, Wellington 67152; tel. 316/326-5016; Jim & Doris Barber, Administrators
Topeka Hospice/Topeka Shawnee County Health Department, 824 Washburn, Topeka 66606; tel. 913/235-5476; Connie Wood, RN, Administrative Director
Trinity Association of Southwest Kansas, 107 Layton, P. O. Box 788, Dodge City 67801; tel. 316/227-8133; Carolyn Eichman, Administrative Director

KENTUCKY
Ashland Community Hospice, 2026 Winchester Avenue, Ashland 41101; tel. 606/329-1890; Carolyn S. Rickey, Administrator
Elizabethtown Area Hospice, P. O. Box 368, Elizabethtown 42701; tel. 502/737-6300; Julie Henahan, Executive Director

The following is a list of freestanding hospices developed from information provided by state agencies. The list is current as of January 1, 1987. For a complete list of hospital based hospice programs please refer to Section A. In Section A, over 700 hospitals with a hospice program are identified by Facility Code F21.

Those hospices accredited by the Joint Commission on Accreditation of Hospitals (JCAH) are identified by a hollow square (☐). These hospices have been found to be in substantial compliance with the Joint Commission standards for hospices, as found in the Hospice Standards Manual.

We present this list simply as a convenient directory. Inclusion or omission of any organization's name indicates neither approval nor disapproval by the American Hospital Association.

Glasgow Area Hospice, South Liberty Street, P. O. Box 551, Glasgow 42141; tel. 502/651-3553; Ethel Fant, Administrator

Harlan County Community Hospice, Inc., P. O. Box 189, Harlan 40831; tel. 606/573-6111; Elaine C. Smith, MSW, Executive Director

Hazard-Perry County Community Hospice, P. O. Box 1234, Hazard 41701; tel. 606/439-2111; Sister Virginia M. Farrell, Administrator

Lourdes Hospice Program, 1530 Lone Oak Road, Paducah 42001; tel. 502/444-2262; Deborah Burnette, Administrator

Madison County Hospice, Fifth Street Offices, Room 406, Richmond 40475; tel. 606/623-4486; Janet Brandenburg, Administrator

Murray-Calloway County Hospital Hospice Program, 803 Poplar Street, Murray 42071; tel. 502/753-5131; Nancy Rose, Director

Pennyroyal Hospice, 1605 South Virginia Street, Hopkinsville 42240; tel. 502/886-8171; Linda Clouse, RN, Administrator

Regional Medical Center of Hopkins County, Hospital Drive, Madisonville 42431; tel. 502/825-5100; John Svoboda, Administrator

St. Anthony's Hospice of Henderson County, 700 North Elm, P. O. Box 351, Henderson 42420; tel. 502/826-2326; Rebecca S. Curry, Administrator

☐ **St. Claire Medical Center,** 222 Medical Circle, Morehead 40351; tel. 606/784-6661; Sister Mary Jeannette, S.N.D., Administrator

☐ **St. Elizabeth Medical Center Home Health Agency/Hospice,** 401 East 20th Street, Covington 41014; tel. 606/292-4256; Patricia Furnish, RN, Administrator

MARYLAND

☐ **Coastal Hospice, Inc.,** Bateman and Wayne Streets, Salisbury 21801; tel. 301/742-8732; Marion F. Keenan

☐ **Harford Home Health Agency/Hospice,** 52 East Broadway, Bel Air 21014; tel. 301/838-1244

Jewish Social Services Agency of Metropolitan Washington, 6123 Montrose Rd., Rockville 20852; tel. 301/881-3700; Mary Frances Grieshaber, Administrator

The Joseph Richey House, Inc., 820 North Eutaw Street, Baltimore 21201; tel. 301/523-2150

Montgomery Hospice Society, 6701 Wisconsin Avenue, Chevy Chase 20815; tel. 301/951-9009; Ann E. O'Neil, RN, MSN, Executive Director

MASSACHUSETTS

Burbank Hospital Hospice, Nichols Road, Fitchburg 01420; tel. 617/343-5000; Cynthia Childs

Cranberry Area Hospice, P. O. Box 928, Plymouth 02360; tel. 617/747-3716; Marion Wilson, Executive Director

Hospice Association of Cape Cod, Inc., 66 School St., Hyannis 02601; tel. 617/778-5037; Mary E. McCarthy, RN, Executive Director

Hospice at Home, Inc., 83 Boston Post Road, Sudbury 01776; tel. 617/443-8150; Laureeann Lerner, Executive Director

Hospice Care, Inc., 39 Hospital Road, Arlington 02174; tel. 617/648-3172; Ed Dolan, Executive Director

☐ **Hospice Care at Southwood Community Hospital,** 111 Dedham Street, Norfolk 02056; tel. 617/668-0385; Ethel C. Slate, RN

Hospice Care of Greater Taunton, Inc., 88 Washington Street, Taunton 02780; tel. 617/823-5528; Sister M. Thomas More, O.P.

Hospice Community Services VNA, Inc., 1100 High Street, Dedham 02026; tel. 617/329-8603; Kathy Wisnieski, Hospice Case Manager

Hospice in Franklin County, 164 High Street, Greenfield 01301; tel. 413/772-0211; Susie Krock

Hospice of Cambridge, 186 Alewife Brook Parkway, Suite 206, Cambridge 02138; tel. 617/547-2620; Kristina Snyder

Hospice of Community Health Agency, Inc., 141 Park Street, Attleboro 02703; tel. 617/222-0118; Mary Luby, RN, Hospice Director

☐ **Hospice of Hampshire County, Inc.,** P. O. Box 1204, 7 Denniston Place, Northampton 01061; tel. 413/586-8288; Joan Keochakian

Hospice of Northern Berkshire, Inc., P. O. Box 171, North Adams 01247; tel. 413/663-5146; Laura Aiello, MSW

Hospice of South Berkshire, P. O. Box 428, Great Barrington 01230; tel. 413/528-4786; Stephanie Boszko, Coordinator

Hospice of the Good Shepherd, 2042 Beacon St., Newton 02168; tel. 617/969-6130; Ellen Rudikoff, Ph.D.

Hospice of the North Shore, Inc., 3 Winter Street, Beverly 01915; tel. 617/927-7075; Marah Ren

Hospice of the South Shore, Inc., 400 Franklin Street, Braintree 02184; tel. 617/849-1710; Susan DiStasic

Hospice Outreach, Inc., 243 Forest Street, Fall River 02721; tel. 671/673-1589; Linda Valley

Hospice Program Emerson Hospital, Old Road to Nine Acre Corner, Concord 01742; tel. 617/369-1400; Paul Montgomery, Hospice Coordinator

Hospice WEST, Inc., 254 South Street, Waltham 02154; tel. 617/894-1100; J. Donald Schumacher, Psy.D., Chief Operating Officer

Massachusetts General Hospital Chelsea Memorial Health Center, 100 Bellingham Street, Chelsea 02150; tel. 617/884-8300; J. Andrew Billings, M.D.

☐ **Metrowest Hospice,** 50 Lawrence Street, Framingham 01701; tel. 617/875-3511; Joan B. Gray

Nashoba Palliative Care Service, Central Avenue, Ayer 01432; tel. 617/772-3336; Rachel R. Gallant, RN

Old Colony Hospice, Inc., P. O. Box 647, Stoughton 02072; tel. 617/364-4850; Carol L. Holden

Shared Caring Hospice, Inc., P. O. Box 565, Newburyport 01950; tel. 617/462-1210; Jean Garnett

VNA Home Care Hospice Division, 451 Andover Street, North Andover 01845; tel. 617/686-1010; Constance Carroll, Hospice Director

VNA of North Shore Hospice, 5 Hutchison Drive, Danvers 01923; tel. 617/777-6100; Susan H. Comparone, Executive Director

☐ **Visiting Nurse Association,** 50 Lawrence Street, Framingham 01701; tel. 617/875-3511; Helen Siegel

Visiting Nurse Association of Boston, 100 Boylston Street, Boston 02116; tel. 617/426-5555; Eileen M. Freitag, Executive Director

☐ **Visiting Nurse Association of Central Massachusetts Hospice,** 120 Thomas Street, Worcester 01608; tel. 617/756-7176; June Grace

Visiting Nurse Association of Springfield, Inc., 600 Berkshire Avenue, Springfield 01109; tel. 413/781-5070; Maureen Skipper, President

Visiting Nurse of Greater Lowell, 150 Middlesex Street, Box 1965; Lowell 01853; tel. 617/459-9343; Shirley Cyronis, Executive Director

☐ **Wareham Area Hospice,** 166 Main Street, Wareham 02571; tel. 617/295-8544

MICHIGAN

Andy Schollett Memorial Hospice, P. O. Box 587, Atlanta 49709; tel. 517/785-3134

Angela Hospice Home Care, 14501 Levan Road, Livonia 48154; tel. 313/591-5157; Sister Giovanni, RN, MSA, Executive Director

Barry Community Hospice, 911 W. Green St., P. O. Box 102; Hastings 49058; tel. 616/948-8452; Susan Corkwell, Director

Bay de Noc Hospice, 1019 Ludington St., Escanaba 49829; tel. 906/786-3915

Bay Valley Community Hospice, 100 S. Dort Hwy., Flint 48503; tel. 313/762-7500

Beth Eden Hospice, P. O. Box 2216, Dearborn 48123; tel. 313/277-6889; Mercedes Watson, RN

Blue Water Hospices, Inc., 2601 Electric Ave., Port Huron 48060; tel. 313/985-1591; Linda D. Howard, Executive Director

Cass County Hospice, Inc., 24010 Hospital Road, Cassopolis 49031; tel. 616/445-8654

Charlevoix County Hospice, P.O. Box 233, Boyne City 49712; tel. 616/536-2842; Margaret Lasater, Executive Director

Citizens for Hospice, 27 E. Chicago St., Coldwater 49028; tel. 517/278-5903; Pat Reed, Administrative Assistant

Complete Hospice Care, 23100 Providence Drive, Ste. 400, Southfield 48075; tel. 313/559-4530; Frances J. Holthus, RN, Administrator

Cottage Hospice, 159 Kercheval, Grosse Pointe Farms 48236; tel. 313/884-8600; Sonora L. Seely, Director

Cranbrook Hospice Care, 1669 W. Maple Road, Birmingham 48009; tel. 313/644-6116; Patricia J. Johnson, RN, Executive Director

Dansville Hospice, Inc., 1134 Dakin Road, Dansville 48819; tel. 517/623-6477

Downriver Hospice, Inc., P. O. Box 312, Trenton 48183; tel. 313/671-6343

Eaton Community Hospice, P. O. Box 636, Charlotte 48813; tel. 517/543-5310

Good Samaritan Hospice Care, Inc., 450 North Ave., Battle Creek 49017; tel. 616/965-1391; Jo Cunningham, Executive Director

H.O.M.E. Life, 4063 E. Huron Dr., Ann Arbor 48104; tel. 313/434-4663

Hiawatha Hospice, Inc., 1022 Shannon Dr., Munising 49862; tel. 906/387-4969; Earlene E. Ingraham, Coordinator

Home Hospice, Inc., 21685 Northland Dr., Paris 49338; tel. 616/796-7371; Kathleen Babbin, Director

Hospice at Home, Inc., 610 Ship Street, Box 675; St. Joseph 49085; tel. 616/983-0402; Stephen S. Towns, Director

Hospice Care, Inc., 110 S. Clay, Sturgis 49091; tel. 616/651-6255; Debbie M. Allen, Executive Director

Hospice for Clinton County/Clinton Memorial Hospital Home Care Program, 805 S. Oakland St., St. Johns 48879; tel. 517/224-6881; Paul McNamara, Chief Executive Officer

Hospice for Communities, 135 S. Leroy, Fenton 49430; tel. 313/750-0280; Donna Lloyd, Executive Director

Hospice for Presque Isle County, 123 South Third St., Rogers City 49779; tel. 517/730-7200

Hospice of Alpena, P. O. Box 566, Alpena 49707; tel. 517/354-5258; Pamela S. Paquette, Program Coordinator

Hospice of Bay County, 1503 Kosciuszko, Bay City 48708; tel. 517/893-7471; Christine Chesny, Administrator

Hospice of Central Michigan, Inc., 1012 West High Street, Mt. Pleasant 48858; tel. 517/773-6137; Mary Ellen Grenier, Director

Hospice of Clare, P.O. Box 664, 185 W. Main, Harrison 48625; tel. 517/539-5320; Dorothy Penner, Administrator

Hospice of Gladwin Area, 211 E. Cedar St., Gladwin 48624; tel. 517/426-9943; Pastor Roger Hardy, President of Board of Directors

Hospice of Greater Grand Rapids, 1901 Robinson Rd., S.E., Grand Rapids 49506; tel. 616/454-1426; Marsha Zandbergen, Executive Director

Hospice of Greater Kalamazoo, Inc., 301 Cedar St., Kalamazoo 49007; tel. 616/345-0273

Hospice of Helping Hands, P. O. Box 71, West Branch 48661; tel. 517/345-3660; Jan Ehanger

Hospice of Hillsdale County, Hillsdale Community Health Center, Hillsdale 49242; tel. 517/437-4451

Hospice of Holland, Inc., 280 E. Eighth St., Holland 49423; tel. 616/396-2972

Hospice of Huron Shores, Inc., 200 Hemlock St., Tawas City 48764; tel. 517/362-3411; Rose Shoemaker, Director

Hospice of Jackson, 437 Fern Ave., Jackson 49202; tel. 517/783-2648; Julie Schaefer, Executive Director

Hospice of Kalkaska County, Inc., P. O. Box 1087, Kalkaska 49646; tel. 616/258-5286; Pamela Luce, Executive Director

Hospice of Lansing, 1210 W. Saginaw, Lansing 48915; tel. 517/485-8350

Hospice of Lenawee, 204 E. Church St., Adrian 49221; tel. 517/263-2323; Susan Engle, Administrator

Hospice of Mason County, 10 Atkinson Dr. Suite 3, P. O. Box 715, Ludington 48431; tel. 616/845-0321; Maureen K. Smith, RN, Director

Hospice of Midland, 1122 Eastman Road, Midland 48640; tel. 517/631-7510

Hospice of Muskegon County, 313 W. Webster, Muskegon 49440; tel. 616/728-3442

Hospice of North Ottawa Community, Inc., 1309 Sheldon Rd., Grand Haven 49417; tel. 616/846-2015; Betsy Walter, Executive Director

The following is a list of freestanding hospices developed from information provided by state agencies. The list is current as of January 1, 1987. For a complete list of hospital based hospice programs please refer to Section A. In Section A, over 700 hospitals with a hospice program are identified by Facility Code F21.

Those hospices accredited by the Joint Commission on Accreditation of Hospitals (JCAH) are identified by a hollow square (☐). These hospices have been found to be in substantial compliance with the Joint Commission standards for hospices, as found in the Hospice Standards Manual.

We present this list simply as a convenient directory. Inclusion or omission of any organization's name indicates neither approval nor disapproval by the American Hospital Association.

Hospice of Petoskey, Inc., 116 W. Mitchell, Petoskey 49770; tel. 616/347-9700
Hospice of Saginaw, 3037 Davenport, Saginaw 48602; tel. 517/799-6020; S. J. Schultz, BSN, MS, Executive Director
☐ **Hospice of Southeastern Michigan,** 22401 Foster Winter Dr., Southfield 48075; tel. 313/559-9209; Paul T. Werner, MD, Executive Director
Hospice of the North, Inc., P. O. Box 846, Gaylord 49735; tel. 517/732-9458; Carol Schultz, Executive Director
Hospice of the Straits, 748 S. Main St., Cheboygan 49721; tel. 616/627-5601; Rosemary Maurice, Executive Director
Hospice of Washtenaw, 3765 Plaza Dr., Ann Arbor 48108; tel. 313/995-1995; Patricia Roggenbeck, RN, Hospice Program Director
Hospice of Wexford-Missaukee, Oak and Hobart St., Cadillac 49601; tel. 616/779-7352
Hospice Services of Western Wayne County, Inc., 6701 Harrison St., Garden City 48135; tel. 313/522-4244; Nora J. Anderson, Executive Director
Ionia Area Hospice, 117 N. Depot St., Ionia 48846; tel. 616/527-0681; Bernice Falsetta, Executive Administrator
Iron County Hospice, Inc., 1400 West Ice Lake Road, Iron River 49935; tel. 906/265-6121
Lake Superior Hospice Association, 425 W. Fisher Street, Marquette 49855; tel. 906/226-2646
Lapeer Area Hospice, Inc., 544 N. Main, Lapeer 48446; tel. 313/667-0042; Kim Sangster, Executive Director
Livingston Community Hospice, Inc., 317 Fowler St., Howell 48843; tel. 517/548-4344; E. Anne Aldrich, Executive Director
Loryce M. Dyer Hospice, 220 Burdette St., St. Ignace 49781; tel. 906/643-8585
Manistee Area Hospice, Inc., P. O. Box 293, Manistee 49660; tel. 616/723-6064; Janet Stroup, Executive Director
Marinette-Menominee County Hospice, 1708 Seventh Street, Menominee 49858; tel. 906/863-6331
Marlette Community Hospital Hospice Program, 2770 Main St., Marlette 48453; tel. 517/635-7491
The Memorial Hospice, 800 East Boulevard, Kingsford 49801; tel. 906/774-1313
Memorial Hospital - Hospice Program, 826 W. King St., Owosso 48867; tel. 517/725-8101
Michigan Home Health Care, Inc., 955 E. Commerce Dr., Traverse City 49684; tel. 616/943-8450; Lilo Hoelzel-Seipp, RN, Ph.D., Chief Executive Officer
Michigan Home Health Care, Terminal Care, 6861 Wilson Rd., Indian River 49749; tel. 616/238-8971
Montcalm Area Hospice, P. O. Box 641, Stanton 48888; tel. 517/831-4014; Mildred Denslow, Patient Care Coordinator
Munson Medical Center - Hospice Program, Sixth and Madison Sts., Traverse City 49684; tel. 616/922-9395; Mary Raymer, A.C.S.W., Manager
Northern Lights Hospice, 205 Osceola, Laurium 49913; tel. 906/337-1033
Oceana County Hospice, P. O. Box 5, New Era 49446; tel. 616/873-2131
Portage Lake Hospice, 201 Isle Royale, Houghton 49931; tel. 906/482-2490
R. P. Hicks Memorial Hospice, Inc., 502 W. Harrie, Newberry 49868; tel. 906/293-5181; Theresa Shifflet, RN, MSN, Lois Michelin, Co-Directors
Ross Common County Home Hospice with Loving Care, Ross Common 48653; tel. 517/275-8967
St. Mary's Hospital Hospice Care Program, 830 S. Jefferson, Saginaw 48601; tel. 517/776-8567; Audrey Machul, Director of Hospice
Sault Area Community Hospice, Inc., 125 Arlington, Sault Ste. Marie 49783; tel. 906/632-2202
Schoolcraft Area Hospice, Inc., 315 Walnut Street, Manistique 49854; tel. 906/341-5027; Shirley Swanson, President
South Haven Area Hospice, 955 S. Bailey Ave., South Haven 49090; tel. 616/637-5271; Janine Glupker, RN, Hospice Director
United Caring Service, 119 E. Sanilac - Eastgate Plaza #5, Sandusky 48471; tel. 313/648-2670
Wings of Hope Hospice, Inc. of Allegan County, 407 Naomi St., Plainwell 49080; tel. 616/685-1645

MINNESOTA
Hospice St. Paul of Bethesda, 559 Capital Blvd., St. Paul 55103; tel. 612/221-2612; Donald Mills, CEO
☐ **Immanuel - St. Josephs Hospice,** 325 Garden Boulevard, Mankato 56001; tel. 507/625-4031; Alice Weydt, Director
Pope County Hospice, 10 S.E. 4th Ave., Glenwood 56334; tel. 612/634-4521; Sharon Larson, Hospice Supervisor
St. Cloud Hospital Hospice, 1406 6th Ave. No., St. Cloud 56301; tel. 612/255-5610; Judith K. Muyres, Assistant Manager

MISSISSIPPI
Gulf Coast Community Hospice, 4642 West Beach Boulevard, Biloxi 39531; tel. 601/388-6711; Hal D. Bishop, M.D., Medical Director
Home Health Agency Multi-County, P. O. Box 17167, Hattiesburg 39404; tel. 601/583-2665; Frances Steele, Executive Director
☐ **North Mississippi Medical Center Home Health Agency,** 1030 South Gloster, Tupelo 38801; tel. 601/841-3607; Bob Corban

MISSOURI
☐ **Kansas City Hospice, Inc.,** 8800 Blue Ridge Blvd., Kansas City 64138; tel. 816/765-8023; Andrew T. Parker, Jr.
☐ **VNA of Greater Kansas City Hospice,** 527 West 39th Street, Kansas City 64111; tel. 816/531-1200; Kathy J. Thomas, MNRN, Administration Director

MONTANA
Anaconda Pintler Hospice, 112 Oak, P. O. Box 596, Anaconda 59711; tel. 406/563-5422; Ruth Laslovich, Director
Big Sky Hospice, 1006 North 29th, Billings 59101; tel. 406/248-7442; Roxlyn Woosley, RN, BSN, Executive Director
☐ **Columbus Hospital - Hospice/Home Care,** 500 - 15th Avenue South, P. O. Box 5013, Great Falls 59403; tel. 406/727-3333; William J. Downer, Jr., Chief Executive Officer
Dillon Hospice, 1260 South Atlantic, Dillon 59725; tel. 406/683-2324
The Flathead Hospice, Inc., 723 - 5th Avenue East, Kalispell 59901; tel. 406/752-8667; Robin Riley, RN, Director
Gallatin Hospice, P. O. Box 1934, Bozeman 59715; tel. 406/587-5683
Gateway Hospice, Inc., P. O. Box 709, Livingston 59047; tel. 406/222-8144; Julia Jardine, Program Coordinator
Helping Hands Hospice, 921 - 3rd Street West, Roundup 59072; tel. 406/323-2784
Highlands Hospice, Inc., 25 West Front Street, P. O. Box 267, Butte 59703; tel. 406/782-6776; Gerry Green Varcoe, Director
Hospice of St. Peter's Community Hospital, 2475 Broadway Street East, Helena 59601; tel. 406/444-2195
Hospice of the Bitterroot, P. O. Box 1343, Hamilton 59840; tel. 406/363-1437
Kootenai Volunteer Hospice, P. O. Box 781, Libby 59923; tel. 406/293-6764
Mountain West Hospice Care, 715 Kensington, Suite 15; Missoula 59801; tel. 406/728-8848; James M. Beers, Director
☐ **St. Joseph Mission Mountain Hospice,** P. O. Box 1010, Polson 59860; tel. 406/883-5377; Sheila Gapay

NEBRASKA
Family Hospice, 7500 Mercy Road, Omaha 68124; tel. 402/398-6119; Carolyn Geiger, Administrator
Good Samaritan Hospice, 31st and Central Avenue, Kearney 68848; tel. 308/234-7900; David Glover, Senior Vice President

NEW JERSEY
☐ **The Hospice, Inc.,** 34 Label Street, Montclair 07042; tel. 201/783-7879; Loraine A. Sciara
☐ **Passaic Valley Hospice,** 738 Riverview Dr., Totowa 07511; tel. 201/256-4636; Nancy Murray
☐ **Samaritan Hospice,** 214 West Second Street, Morrestown 08057; tel. 609/778-8181; Clark D. Dingman

NEW MEXICO
Carlsbad Hospice, Inc., 1003 West Riverside, P. O. Drawer PP, Carlsbad 88220; tel. 505/885-8257; Nancy Flanagan, RN, Coordinator
Hospital Home Care-Hospice, 405 Grand, N.E., Albuquerque 87102; tel. 505/842-7100; Patricia Finnegan, M.A., Director
Mesilla Valley Hospice, 2906 Hillrise, P. O. Box 15146, Las Cruces 88004; tel. 505/522-4400; Kathleen Russell, RN, Executive Director
St. Mary's Hospice, South Main and Chisum Street, Roswell 88201; tel. 505/622-1110; George Macko, Chief Executive Officer
Visiting Nurse Service Hospice, 1316 Apache Avenue, Santa Fe 87501; tel. 505/471-9201; Bette Betts, Hospice Direcotr

NEW YORK
☐ **Beth Abraham Hospital,** 612 Allerton Avenue, Bronx 10467; tel. 212/920-5881; Roberta Gill
The Brooklyn Hospice, 4915 Tenth Avenue, Brooklyn 11219; tel. 718/851-5900
Cabrini Hospice, 227 East 19th Street, New York 10003; tel. 212/725-6480; Mary A. Cooke, RN, MA, Director
Hospice Buffalo, Inc., 2929 Main Street, Buffalo 14214; tel. 716/838-4438; Charlotte N. Shedd, R.N., M.N., Executive Director
Hospice of Schenectady, 514 McClellan Street, Schenectady 12304; tel. 518/377-8846
☐ **Ritter-Scheuer Hospice of Beth Abraham Hospital,** 612 Allerton AVenue, Bronx 10467; tel. 212/920-5945
St. Peters Hospital Hospice, 315 South Manning Blvd., Albany 12208; tel. 518/454-1686
United Hospital Hospice, 406 Boston Post Road, Port Chester 10573; tel. 914/939-7000

NORTH CAROLINA
Albermarle Home Care/Hospice, P.O. Box 189, 400 S. Road St., Elizabeth City 27909; tel. 919/338-4066; Kay Whedebee, R.N., Supervisor
Alexander County Home Health Agency, 322 First Avenue, S.W., Taylorsville 28681; tel. 704/632-9704; Chris Moretz, R.N., Supervisor
Appalachian District Health Department, Route 5, Box 199, Bamboo Rd., Boone 28607; tel. 704/372-8813; Carl D. Tuttle, Administrator
Caldwell County Hospice, Inc., 902 Kirkwood St., Lenoir 28645; tel. 704/754-0101; Gibbie Harris, Executive Director
Columbus County Hospice, Inc., P.O. Box 810, 304 Jefferson St., Whiteville 28472; tel. 919/642-9051; Ann L. Fox, Executive Director
Craven County Home Health - Hospice Agency, P.O. Box 1390, 2102 Neuse Blvd., New Bern 28560; tel. 919/633-2605; Elizabeth Joyner, M.P.H., Health Director
Dare Hospice, P.O. Box 2511, 1706 Bayview Dr., Kill Devil Hills 27948; tel. 919/441-6111; Priscilla Small, President
Duplin Home Care and Hospice, Inc., P.O. Box 235, Kenansville 28349; tel. 919/296-0819; Lynn S. Hardy, Administrator
Eastern Carolina Home Health Hospice Services, 614 East 12th St., Washington 27889; tel. 919/946-7145; Janet D. Sasnett, Administrator
Halifax Co. Hm. Hlth./Hospice Agency, P.O. Box 10, Halifax 27839; tel. 919/583-5021; Virgil A. Cook, Administrator
Health Horizon, Inc., 300 W. 27th St., P.O. Box 1408, Lumberton 28359; tel. 919/738-5882; Miriam Edwards, R.N., Director
Home Health Services of Cumberland County, Inc., 711 Executive Place, P.O. Box 53324, Fayetteville 28305; tel. 919/483-3489; Elizabeth A. Hudspeth, Administrator
Hospice at Charlotte, Inc., 1331 The Plaza, Charlotte 28205; tel. 704/375-0100; Janet Fortner, Executive Director
Hospice at Greensboro, Inc., 706 N. Greene St., Greensboro 27401; tel. 919/274-4592; Pamela Barrett, Director
Hospice of Alamance County, Inc., 1713 Edgewood Avenue, Burlington 27215; tel. 919/229-2691; Sandra Marshall, R.N., Director
Hospice of Alexander County, Inc., 324 1st Avenue, S.W., Taylorsville 28681; tel. 704/632-5026; Ruth Taylor, R.N., Executive Director

The following is a list of freestanding hospices developed from information provided by state agencies. The list is current as of January 1, 1987. For a complete list of hospital based hospice programs please refer to Section A. In Section A, over 700 hospitals with a hospice program are identified by Facility Code F21.

Those hospices accredited by the Joint Commission on Accreditation of Hospitals (JCAH) are identified by a hollow square (□). These hospices have been found to be in substantial compliance with the Joint Commission standards for hospices, as found in the Hospice Standards Manual.

We present this list simply as a convenient directory. Inclusion or omission of any organization's name indicates neither approval nor disapproval by the American Hospital Association.

Hospice of Avery County, Inc., P.O. Box 221, Newland 28657; tel. 704/733-9269; Mary Howk, Executive Director
Hospice of Burke County, Inc., 232 Enola Rd., P.O. Box 2107, Morganton 28655; tel. 704/433-8842; A. Malanie Price, Executive Director
Hospice of Cabarrus County, Inc., P.O. Box 1235, 920 Church St., Concord 28026; tel. 704/788-9434; Jodi Kiser, Acting Executive Director
Hospice of Carteret County, Inc., P.O. Box 3598, 107 South 9th St., Morehead City 28557; tel. 919/247-2808; William Holt, Administrator
Hospice of Catawba Valley, Inc., 237 Second St., N.W., Hickory 28601; tel. 704/328-4200; Angela Corn, Executive Director
Hospice of Chatham County, Inc., P.O. Box 1077, Pittsboro 27312; tel. 919/542-5545; Susan H. Edelstein, Executive Director
Hospice of Cleveland County, Inc., 201 W. Marion St., Suite 306, Shelby 28150; tel. 704/487-4677; Evelyn West, Director
Hospice of Davidson County, Inc., P.O. Box 1941; 206-D West Center St., Lexington 27292; tel. 704/246-6185; Nancy B. Ratledge, R.N., Director
Hospice of Davie County, 210 Hospital St., P.O. Box 665, Mocksville 27028; tel. 704/634-5881; Connie L. Stafford, Administrator
Hospice of Fayetteville VA Med. Ctr., 23 Ramsey Street, Fayetteville 28301; tel. 919/488-2120; Minnie Howie
Hospice of Gaston Co., Inc., 990 Robinwood Rd., Gastonia 28054; tel. 704/861-8405; Eleanor Beasley, Director
Hospice of Harnett Co., 111A North Ellis St., Dunn 28334; tel. 919/892-1213; Grace Tart, Director
Hospice of Haywood County, Inc., P.O. Box 163, Lake Junaluska 28745; tel. 704/627-3383; Rev. Ron Hicks, Executive Director
Hospice of Henderson County, P.O. Box 2395, 790 N. Grove St., Hendersonville 28793; tel. 704/692-6178; Mary Cleary, Executive Director
Hospice of Iredell County, Inc., P.O. Box 822, Statesville 28677; tel. 704/873-4719; Catherine Burgess, Director
Hospice of Lee County, Inc., 1135 Carthage St., Sanford 27330; tel. 919/774-4100, ext. 221; Peggy Wilcox, R.N., Director
Hospice of Macon County, Inc., P.O. Box 1594, Franklin 28734; tel. 704/369-6641; William Spooner, Director
Hospice of Mitchell County, Inc., P.O. Box 156, 114 Oak Avenue, Spruce Pine 28777; tel. 704/765-2189; Kymra Fowler-Stewart, Director/President
Hospice of Pamlico County, Inc., P.O. Box 42, Oriental 28571; tel. 919/249-2111; Fran Deaton, Ph.D., Director
Hospice of Polk County, Inc., P.O. Box 722, Tryon 28782; tel. 704/894-3638; Elizabeth Schulman, Executive Director
Hospice of Randolph, Inc., P.O. Box 9, 379 S. Cox St., Asheboro 27204; tel. 919/629-9300; Billie Vuncannon, Executive Director
Hospice of Rowan County, Inc., P.O. Box 1603, 130 N. Merritt Avenue, Salisbury 28145; tel. 704/637-7645; Lynette Y. Wilson, Director
Hospice of Rutherford County, Inc., P.O. Box 336, Forest City 28043; tel. 704/245-0095; Lucille Nanney, Executive Director
Hospice of Scotland County, Inc., P.O. Box 1033, 600 West Church St., Laurenburg 28352; tel. 919/276-7176; Linda McQueen, Director
Hospice of Surry County, Inc., P.O. Box 1034, 615 N. Main St., Mt. Airy 27030; tel. 919/789-2922; Shirley Furches, Coordinator
Hospice of the Piedmont, Inc., 323 Blvd., High Point 27262; tel. 919/889-8446; Kitty T. Boone, Administrator
Hospice of Union County, Inc., P.O. Box 1306, 211-E N. Main St., Monroe 28110; tel. 704/289-3133; Cynthia M. Simpson, Executive Director
Hospice of Wake County, Inc., 619 Oberlin Rd., P.O. Box 12043, Raleigh 27605; tel. 919/833-0161; Beth C. McAllister, Executive Director
Hospice of Wilkes, Inc., P.O. Box 609, West D. St., North Wilkesboro 28659; tel. 919/651-8107; Jane Sowden, R.N., Executive Director
Hospice of Wilson, Inc., P.O. Box 3793, 1705 South Tarboro St., Wilson 27893; tel. 919/243-5147; Patti Lotts, Director
Hospice of Winston-Salem/Forsyth Co., Inc., 3333 Silas Creek Parkway, Winston-Salem 27103; tel. 919/768-3972; Linda Scherl, Director
Hospice of Yancey County, Inc., P.O. Box 471, 314 W. Main St., Burnsville 28714; tel. 704/682-9675; Gwendolyn Green, R.N., Administrative Director
Housecalls Home Health Care, Inc., P.O. Box 339, 108 N. Fayetteville St., Liberty 27298; tel. 919/622-3071; Terry J. Ward, Director
Johnston County Health Center, 618 North Eighth St., Smithfield 27577; tel. 919/934-4168; Helen M. Ray, Director
Lower Cape Fear Hospice, Inc., 5221 Wrightsville Avenue, Wilmington 28403; tel. 919/392-4313; Eloise Thomas, Executive Director
Mountain Area Hospice, Inc., P.O. Box 16, 40 Church St., Asheville 28802; tel. 704/255-0231; Judith Noth, Executive Director
Onslow Hospice, Inc., 328 Mildred Avenue, Jacksonville 28540; tel. 919/347-6266; Judith Brown, Administrator
Richmond County Hospice, Inc., P.O. Box 2136, 110 South Hancock St., Rockingham 28379; tel. 919/997-4464; Carole Venable, Director
Roanoke-Chowan Hospice, Inc., P.O. Box 272, 404 Colony Ave., Ahoskie 27910; tel. 919/332-3392; Nolie Jenkins, Director
Roanoke Home Care, P.O. Box 396, Plymouth 27962; tel. 919/793-3023; Judith C. Wright, Health Director
St. Joseph of the Pines, Inc., 295 Pinehurst Avenue, Southern Pines 28387; tel. 919/692-2212, ext. 117; Lorena Maree, Director
Sandhills Hospice, Inc., P.O. Box 1913; Pinehurst 28374; tel. 919/295-7246; Mary McKinsey, Administrator
Stanly County Hospice, Inc., P.O. Box 55, 301 Yadkin St., Albermarle 28002; tel. 704/983-4216; Audrey Plyler, Executive Director
Triangle Hospice, Inc., 1202 Broad St., Durham 27705; tel. 919/286-9199; Patricia Soenksen, Administrator
Tri-County Visiting Nurses, Inc., 1204 The Plaza, Charlotte 28205; tel. 704/372-2294; Martha Cochran, Executive Director
Yadkin County Hospice, P.O. Box 457, Yadkinville 27055; tel. 919/679-2026; Leonard Wood, Administrator

NORTH DAKOTA
Hospice of the Red River Valley, 1325 South Eleventh Street, Fargo 58103; tel. 701/237-4629; Edith Lohr, Administrator

OHIO
Carriage Inn Hospice, Inc., 1 Ross Park, Steubenville 43952; tel. 614/283-7487; Karen Nichols
□ **Hospice of Lake County,** 5976 Heisley Road, Mentor 44060; tel. 216/357-5833; David A. Simpson

OKLAHOMA
Cross Timbers Hospice, P. O. Box 2514-73402, 4 - 8th Street NE; Ardmore 73401; tel. 405/223-0655
Eastern Oklahoma Hospice, 300 Rockefeller Drive, Muskogee 74401; tel. 918/683-1192
Garfield County Hospice Association, 208 West Maple, Suite 612; Enid 73701; tel. 405/234-2273; Sharon Doty, Executive Director
Hospice of Central Oklahoma, Inc., 4215 NW 23rd, Suite 101; Oklahoma City 73107; tel. 405/947-5300; Mary Ellen Baker, RN, Director
Hospice of Lawton Area, Inc., P. O. Box 2074, 1011 SW "C" Avenue, Suite 6; Lawton 73502; tel. 405/248-5885; Kathryn A. Sarvak, RN, Director
Hospice of Ponca City, Inc., P. O. Box 2525, Plaza 14, 2128 N. 14th St.; Ponca City 74602; tel. 405/762-9102
Hospice of Pontotoc, Inc., 117 North Broadway, Suite 105; Ada 74820; tel. 405/436-6535
Hospice of Rogers County, Inc., 127 West Blue Starr, Claremore 74017; tel. 918/341-1606
Hospice of Washington County, Inc., 3807 Silverlake View, Bartlesville 74006; tel. 918/333-5338
Hospice of Western Oklahoma, P. O. Box 634, 600 North 13th Street; Clinton 73601; tel. 405/323-6875
Judith Karman Hospice, Inc., 720 South Husband, Suite 10; Stillwater 74074; tel. 405/377-8012
Seminole Hospice Program, Inc., P. O. Box 1622, Seminole 74868; tel. 405/382-3458

OREGON
Mt. Hood Hospice, P.O. Box 835, Sandy 97055; tel. 503/668-5545; Judith Wesley, Director

PENNSYLVANIA
Centre Hospice (A program of Centre Homecare, Inc.), 221 West High Street, Bellefonte 16823; tel. 814/355-2273; Fran Gustkey, Supervisor of Hospice
□ **Chandler Hall Hospice,** Buck Road & Barclay Street, Newtown 18940; tel. 215/860-4000; Jane W. Fox, Executive Director
□ **Family Hospice of Indiana County,** 121 Airport Office & Professional Center, Indiana 15701; tel. 412/463-8711; Michele Rega, BSN, Director of Hospice Services
Forbes Hospice - Forbes Health System, 6655 Frankstown Avenue, Pittsburgh 15206; tel. 412/665-3301; Maryanne Fello, Director
Holy Redeemer Hospice Program of Holy Redeemer Visiting Nurse & Home Health Agency, 12265 Townsend Rd., Philadelphia 19154; tel. 215/671-9200
Home Hospice Agency of St. Francis, S. Mercer & Phillips Street, New Castle 16101; tel. 412/658-3511
Home Nursing Agency/Visiting Nurse Association Hospice Program, 201 Chestnut Avenue, P. O. Box 392, Altoona 16603; tel. 800/445-6262
Hospice - Albert Einstein Medical Center, York and Tabor Roads, Philadelphia 19141; tel. 215/456-7155
Hospice of Chester County, 121 West Union Street, West Grove 19390; tel. 215/696-6574
□ **Hospice of Lancaster County,** 717 Fountain Avenue, Lancaster 17601; tel. 717/394-1575
Hospice of PA., Inc., 916 Wyoming Avenue, Scranton 18509; tel. 717/961-0725
Hospice Saint John, 383 Wyoming Avenue, Kingston 18704; tel. 717/288-5428; Patricia Savage, M.S.W., Executive Director
□ **Hospice Services of Visiting Nurses Association of Butler County, Inc.,** 154 Hindman Road, Butler 16001; tel. 412/282-6806; Brenda E. Yeadon, Vice President/Director
McKean County Visiting Nurse Association Hospice Program, P. O. Box 465, 195 Pleasant Street; Bradford 16701; tel. 814/362-7466; Francie Ambuske, RN, Executive Director
Northern Chester County Community Nursing Services Hospice Program, 301 Gay Street, Phoenixville 19460; tel. 215/933-1263; Mrs. Shirley S. Weinstein, RN, Executive Director
Professional Home Health Care Agency Hospice Program, 325 North Second Street, Wormleysburg 17043; tel. 717/761-2181
Regional Home Health Services, 1202 Clayton Avenue, Williamsport 17701; tel. 717/323-9891; Joan Lynch, RN, CNA, Executive Director
Sacred Heart Medical Center Hospice, Ninth and Wilson Streets, Chester 19013; tel. 215/494-0700
□ **Wissahickon Hospice,** 8835 Germantown Avenue, Philadelphia 19118; tel. 215/247-0277; Priscilla D. Kissick, RN, MN, Executive Director

RHODE ISLAND
Hospice Care of Rhode Island, 345 Blackstone Boulevard, Providence 02906; tel. 401/272-4900; Robert J. Canny
Northern Rhode Island Hospice, Marquette Plaza, Woonsocket 02895; tel. 401/769-5670; Ms. Ruth D. Cooke, RN
VNA, Inc. (Hospice), 157 Waterman Street, Providence 02906; tel. 401/331-8842; Ms. Diane Jansson, Administrator

SOUTH CAROLINA
□ **Baptist Medical Ctr. - Columbia HHA Hospice,** 1333 Taylor St., Columbia 29220; tel. 803/771-5002; Joanne T. Myers, Interim Director

The following is a list of freestanding hospices developed from information provided by state agencies. The list is current as of January 1, 1987. For a complete list of hospital based hospice programs please refer to Section A. In Section A, over 700 hospitals with a hospice program are identified by Facility Code F21.

Those hospices accredited by the Joint Commission on Accreditation of Hospitals (JCAH) are identified by a hollow square (☐). These hospices have been found to be in substantial compliance with the Joint Commission standards for hospices, as found in the Hospice Standards Manual.

We present this list simply as a convenient directory. Inclusion or omission of any organization's name indicates neither approval nor disapproval by the American Hospital Association.

Caroline Hospice of Beaufort, Inc., 706 Bay Street, Beaufort 29902; tel. 803/525-6257; Veronica Tovey, Administrator
Elliott White Springs Memorial Hospital Hospice, 800 Meeting Street, Lancaster 29720; tel. 803/286-1472; Carolina Doster, RN, Director
Greenville Hospital System Hospice, 701 Grove Road, Greenville 29605; tel. 803/242-8020; David H. Waldrop, Director
Hospice of Charleston, Inc., P. O. Box 1125, Charleston 29402; tel. 803/763-0350; Roberta H. Frank, Executive Director
Hospice of Georgetown County, Inc., P. O. Box 1436, Georgetown 29442; tel. 803/546-3410; Brenda Stroup, RN, Executive Director
Hospice of Greenwood, Spring Street, Greenwood 29646; tel. 803/227-4111; Nancy Garrett, Director
Hospice of the Pee Dee, 555 E. Cheves Street, Florence 29503; tel. 803/667-2565; Virginia Swaggard, Director
Hospice Volunteers of Hilton Head, P. O. Box 7092, Hilton Head Island 29938; tel. 803/842-4112; Carole Klein, Director
Mercy Hospice of Horry County, 1101 5th Avenue, Conway 29526; tel. 803/248-7323; Charles L. Brown, Executive Director
Spartanburg General Hospital Hospice, 101 East Wood Street, Spartanburg 29303; tel. 803/591-6785; Ann S. Orsban, RN, BSN, MBA, Interim Director
York County Hospice, Inc., 523 Saluda Street, Rock Hill 29731; tel. 803/329-4663; Len Anderson, MSW, Director

TEXAS

Bay Area Nursing Service, 535 Bayshore Drive, La Porte 77571; tel. 713/471-8445
☐ **Chrysalis Home Care and Hospice, Inc.,** 3300 W. Mockingbird, Suite LL132, Dallas 75235; tel. 214/956-7977
Community Hospice of St. Joseph, 1401 South Main Street, Fort Worth 76104; tel. 817/336-9371, ext. 8950
Dallas Hospice Care, Inc., 5740 Prospect, Suite 2004, Dallas 75206; tel. 214/823-2891
Ella C. McFadden Hospice, 820 Clarksville, P.O. Box 70, Paris 75360; tel. 214/785-4521
Family Service Hospice, Inc., 1424 Hemphill, Fort Worth 76104; tel. 817/927-8884
Galveston Hospice Group, Inc., 111 36th Street, P.O. Box 2448, Galveston 77550; tel. 409/762-5113
Hillcrest Baptist Medical Center Home Health Services, 3000 Herring Avenue, P.O. Box 5100, Waco 76708; tel. 817/756-8607
Home Hospice of Grayson County, 812 N. Travis, P.O. Box 2283, Sherman 75090; tel. 214/668-9315
Hospice of Abilene, Inc., 1917 South 6th Street, Abilene 79602; tel. 915/677-8516
Hospice of East Texas, 766 S. Beckham, Tyler 75701; tel. 214/593-2171
Hospice of El Paso, Inc., 3901 North Mesa, Suite 310, El Paso 79902; tel. 915/532-5699
Hospice of Odessa, 300 North Jackson, P.O. Box 11091, Odessa 79760; tel. 915/332-1431
Hospice of the Plains, Inc., 2601 Dimmitt Road, Plainview 79072; tel. 806/296-5531, ext. 5234
Hospice of San Angelo, Inc., 203 East Harris, San Angelo 76903; tel. 915/658-6524
Hospice San Antonio, Inc., 8207 Callaghan, Suite 355, San Antonio 78230; tel. 512/377-3882
Hospice of Texarkana, Inc., 600 West 16th Street, Texarkana 75501; tel. 214/794-4263
Hospice of VNA, 3100 Timmons, Suite 200, Houston 77027; tel. 713/840-7744
Hospice of Wichita Falls, Inc., P.O. Box 1736, Wichita Falls 76307; tel. 817/322-8268
Houston Hospice, 8707 Katy Freeway, Suite 208, Houston 77024; tel. 713/468-2441
King William Hospice, 323 E. Johnson Street, San Antonio 78204; tel. 512/222-0171
☐ **New Age Hospice of Houston,** 7 Chelsea Place, Houston 77021; tel. 713/748-5021; Cherry Hershberger
Nolan County Hospice, Inc., 300 East Arizona, P.O. Box 1653, Sweetwater 79556; tel. 915/235-1448
☐ **St. Anthony's Hospital,** 200 N.W. 7th Street, Amarillo 79107; tel. 806/378-5028
South Texas Home Health and Hospice Services, Inc., Route 3, Box 21 Capri Road, Alice 78332; tel. 1-800/242-3063
The Southeast Texas Hospice, Inc., 912 West Cherry, P.O. Box 2385, Orange 77630; tel. 713/886-0622
Spohn Hospice, 600 Elizabeth Street, Corpus Christi 78404; tel. 512/881-3159
Valley Baptist Medical Center Home Health/Hospice, 2101 Pease Street, P.O. Drawer 2588, Harlingen 78550; tel. 512/421-1999
Visiting Nurses Association of Brazoria County, Inc., P.O. Box 1386, Angleton 77515; tel. 409/849-6476
The Visiting Nurse Association of Texas, 8200 Brookriver Drive, Suite 200-N, Dallas 75247; tel. 214/689-0000
Visiting Nurse Association of Texas, 8200 Brookriver Drive, Suite 200-N, Dallas 75247; tel. 214/639-2637
Visiting Nurse Association of Texas Home Hospice, 8200 Brookriver Drive, Suite 200-N, Dallas 75247; tel. 214/689-0648

VIRGINIA

☐ **Hospice of Northern Virginia, Inc.,** 4715 North 15th Street, Arlington 22205; tel. 703/525-7070; Mary L. Stone, Administrator
Maryview Wellspring Home Care, 3636 High Street, Portsmouth 23707; tel. 804/398-2338; Cheryl B. Samuels, RN, CNA, Administrative Director
Medical College of Virginia Hospital's Continuing Care Program (Hospice), Ground Floor, North Hospital, MCV, Box 30, MCV Station; Richmond 23298; tel. 804/786-9901; Susan J. Mellette, M.D., Director
Norfolk General Hospital Oncology Special Care Unit/Hospice, 600 Gresham Drive, Norfolk 23507; tel. 804/628-3602

WASHINGTON

Community Hospice, 1035 - 11th Avenue, Longview 98632; tel. 206/425-8510; Lorraine Berndt, Executive Director
Community Hospice - Community Home Health Care, 100 West Harrison - South Tower, Seattle 98119; tel. 206/282-5048; Margaret Z. Shepherd, Executive Director
Good Samaritan Hospice, 407 - 14th Avenue SE, Puyallup 98372; tel. 206/848-6661; Linda Paulson, RN, MBA, Administrative Director
Hospice of Clark County, 316 East 4th Plain Blvd., Vancouver 98663; tel. 206/693-6441
Hospice of Seattle, 500 - 17th Avenue, P. O. Box C-34008, Seattle 98124; tel. 206/326-5969
Hospice of Snohomish County, 1010 SE Everett Mall Way, Suite 105; Everett 98208; tel. 206/355-8855; Tina Jordan, MSN, Executive Director
☐ **Hospice of Spokane,** 412 South Bernard, Spokane 99210; tel. 509/624-0840
☐ **Hospice of Tacoma,** 750 Market Street, Tacoma 98402; tel. 206/383-1788; Eileen M. Ales, Chief Executive Officer
Hospice of Whatcom County, 1111 Cornwall Suite 205, Bellingham 98225; tel. 206/734-9210
Hospice Southwest - Southwest Washington Hospitals, P. O. Box 1600, Vancouver 98668; tel. 206/696-5055; Ron Deisher, Director
Tri-Cities Chaplaincy - Hospice Program, 7514 West Yellowstone, Kennewick 99336; tel. 509/783-7416

WEST VIRGINIA

Hospice Association of Greater Parkersburg Area, Inc., P. O. Box 1465, Parkersburg 26102; tel. 304/422-7225; Steve McNew
Hospice of Huntington, Inc., P. O. Box 464, Huntington 25701; tel. 304/529-4217; Charlene Farrell, Executive Director
Hospice of Preston County, Inc., P. O. Box 229, Kingwood 26537; tel. 304/329-1161; Mary R. Furbee
Hospice of Putman, Inc., P. O. Box 352, Hurricane 25528; tel. 304/562-2056; Mary Pat Harper
Hospice of the Panhandle, Inc., P. O. Box 1418, CHI Room 232; Martinsburg 25401; tel. 304/263-8971; Mary Jo Gibbs, Director
Kanawha Hospice Care, Inc., P. O. Box 2013, Charleston 25327; tel. 304/348-9506; Patricia Kepler, Executive Director
Morgantown Hospice, Inc., P. O. Box 4222, Morgantown 26505; tel. 304/598-3424; Margaret M. Kearney
People's Hospice, Inc., P. O. Box 382, Clarksburg 26301; tel. 304/623-0524; Susan Watkins
Raleigh County Hospice Care, Inc., 311 Dry Hill Rd., Beckley 25801; tel. 304/253-6080; Betty Perry, Patient Care Coordinator

WISCONSIN

Appleton Community Hospice, 120 West Franklin, P. O. Box 1074, Appleton 54912; tel. 414/733-8562; Mary Runge, RN, Executive Director
☐ **Bellin Memorial Hospital,** 744 South Webster Avenue, Green Bay 54303; tel. 414/433-3500; JoAnn Johnson, Vice President
Dr. Kate-Lakeland Hospice, P. O. Box 829, Woodruff 54568; tel. 715/356-8805; Michael Girard
HospiceCare, Inc., 303 Lathrop Street, Madison 53705; tel. 608/238-3399; Wally Kelley, Executive Director
Jefferson Home Health and Hospice, 1203 8th Street, Baraboo 53913; tel. 608/356-7570; Evelyn Hayes, M.S.W., Coordinator
☐ **Kenosha Hospice Alliance,** 5159 - 6th Avenue, Kenosha 53140; tel. 414/658-8344; Carol Peltier
Milwaukee Hospice Home Care, 1022 North 9th Street, Milwaukee 53233; tel. 414/271-3686; James M. Ewens, Executive Director
☐ **Mount Sinai Hospice,** 6925 N. Port Washington Road, Glendale 53217; tel. 414/352-3300; Daniel A. Kane
North End Drug Hospice, 2 North 8th Street, Manitowoc 54220; tel. 414/684-8237; Lynn Seidl, RN
St. Francis Hospice, 620 South 11th Street, LaCrosse 54601; tel. 608/782-4050; Joseph Kruse
Seton Health Care, 2243 North Prospect Avenue, Milwaukee 53202; tel. 414/225-8150; Deb Mulrain, RN

Hospice Agencies

Information for the following list was obtained directly from the agencies.

ALABAMA: Department of Public Health, Division of Licensure and Certification, State Office Bldg., Montgomery 36130; tel. 205/261-5113; Carroll S. Nason, dir.

ALASKA: Division of Medical Assistance, Health Facilities Licensing and Certification Section, 4041 B St., Suite 101, Anchorage 99503; tel. 907/561-2171; Karen Martz, supr.

ARIZONA: Department of Health Services, Emergency Medical Services, Health Care Facilities, Office of Health Care Institution Licensure, Medical Facilities Section, Birch Hall, 411 N. 24th St., Phoenix 85008; tel. 602/220-6407; Hazel E. Chandler, chf.

ARKANSAS: Department of Health, Division of Health Facility Services, 4815 W. Markham St., Little Rock 72205; tel. 501/661-2201; Rayburn C. Allen, dir.

CALIFORNIA: Department of Health Services, Licensing and Certification Division, 714 P St., Rm. 823, Sacramento 95814; tel. 916/445-3054; Virgil J. Toney, Jr., dep. dir.

COLORADO: Department of Health, Division of Health Facilities Regulation, 4210 E. 11th Ave., Denver 80220; tel. 303/331-4930; Mildred Simmons, dir.

CONNECTICUT: Department of Health Services, Bureau of Health System Regulation, Division of Hospital and Medical Care, 150 Washington St., Hartford 06106; tel. 203/566-1073; Elizabeth M. Burns, R.N., M.S., Dir.

DELAWARE: Department of Health and Social Services, Division of Public Health, Office of Health Facilities Licensing and Certification, 3000 Newport Gap Pike, Wilmington 19808; tel. 302/571-3499; James E. Harvey, dir.

DISTRICT OF COLUMBIA: Department of Consumer and Regulatory Affairs, Service Facility Regulation Administration, 614 H St., N.W., Suite 1014, Washington 20001; tel. 202/727-7000; Don Murray, dir.

FLORIDA: Office of Licensure and Certification, 2727 Mahan Dr., Tallahassee 32308; tel. 904/487-2527; Amy Jones, dir.

GEORGIA: Department of Human Services, Division of Administrative Services, Office of Regulatory Services, Standards and Licensure Section, 878 Peachtree St., N.E., Atlanta 30309; tel. 404/894-5137; Phillip A. Arnold, dir.

HAWAII: Department of Health, Medical Services Division, Hospital and Medical Facilities Licensing Branch, P.O. Box 3378, Honolulu 96801; tel. 808/548-5935; Dr. Ben Lambiotte, chf.

IDAHO: Department of Health and Welfare, Facility Standards Program, 420 W. Washington St., Boise 83720; tel. 208/334-5325; Jean Schoonover, R.N., prog. supr.

ILLINOIS: Department of Public Health, Division of Health Facilities Standards, Ambulatory Health Programs, 535 W. Jefferson St., Springfield 62761; tel. 217/785-2080

INDIANA: State Board of Health, Division of Acute Care Services, 1330 W. Michigan St., Indianapolis 46206; tel. 317/633-8486; Harry T. Haver, dir.

IOWA: Department of Inspection and Appeals, Division of Health Facilities, Lucas State Office Bldg., Des Moines 50319; tel. 515/281-4115; Dana Petrowsky, adm.

KANSAS: Department of Health and Environment, Bureau of Adult and Child Care Facilities, 740 Forbes Field Building, Topeka 66620; tel. 913/296-1240; Greg Reser, med. facil. cert. adm.

LOUISIANA: Department of Health and Human Resources, Office of Management and Finances, Division of Licensing and Certification, Box 3767, Baton Rouge 70821; tel. 504/342-5774; Steve Phillips, dir.

MAINE: Department of Human Services, Bureau of Medical Services, Division of Licensing and Certification, State House, Station 11, Augusta 04333; tel. 207/289-2606; Louis Dorogi, dir.

MARYLAND: Department of Health and Mental Hygiene, Office of Health Regulation, 201 W. Preston St., Baltimore 21201; tel. 301/225-6530; Ron Bialek, actg. dir.

MASSACHUSETTS: Department of Public Health, Division Of Health Care Quality, 80 Boylston St., Boston 02116, tel. 617/727-5860; Irene McManus, dir.

MICHIGAN: Department of Public Health, Division of Licensing and Certification, 3500 N. Logan, Lansing 48909; tel. 517/335-8505; Nancy Graham, supr.

MINNESOTA: Department of Health, Division of Health Resources, Survey and Compliance Section, 717 Delaware St., S.E., Minneapolis 55440; tel. 612/623-5420; Clarice Suefert, chf.

MISSISSIPPI: Department of Health, Division of Licensure and Certification, P.O. Box 1700, Jackson 39215; tel. 601/960-7769, Mendal G. Kemp, dir.

MISSOURI: Department of Health, Bureau of Hospital Licensing and Certification, P.O. Box 570, Jefferson City 65102; tel. 314/751-6302; Charles R. Gillilan, chf.

MONTANA: Department of Health and Environmental Sciences, Bureau of Licensing and Certification, Cogswell Bldg. Helena 59620; tel. 406/444-2037; Jacqueline McKnight, chf.

NEBRASKA: Department of Health, Division of Licensure and Standards, 301 Centennial Mall, S., Lincoln 68509; tel. 402/471-2946; William H. Page, dir.

NEW YORK: Department of Health, Office of Health Systems Management, Bureau of Home Health Care, Empire State Plaza, 1970 Corning Tower Building, Albany 12237; tel. 518/474-2006; Dr. Nancy Barhydt, dir.

NEVADA: Department of Human Resources, Division of Health, Bureau of Regulatory Health Services, 505 E. King St., Carson City 89710; tel. 702/885-4475; William C. Schneider chf.

NEW HAMPSHIRE: Department of Health and Human Services, Bureau of Health Facilities Administration, 6 Hazen Dr., Concord 03301; tel. 603/271-4592; Charles Ferguson, chf.

NEW JERSEY: Department of Health, Division of Health Facilities Evaluation, Certification and Standards Program, CN 367, Trenton 08625; tel. 609/292-5764, Dr. Solomon Goldberg, D.D.S. dir.

NEW MEXICO: Department of Health and Environment, Federal Program Certification Section, P.O. Box 968, Santa Fe 87504; tel. 505/827-2416; Sue K. Morris, supr.

NORTH CAROLINA: Department of Human Resources, Division of Facility Services, 701 Barbour Dr., Raleigh 27603; tel. 919/733-2342; Ira O. Wilkerson, Jr., dir.

NORTH DAKOTA: Department of Health, Health Resources Section, Division of Health Facilities, State Capitol, Bismarck 58505; tel. 701/224-2352; Joseph Pratschner, chf.

OHIO: Department of Health, Division of Licensure and Certification, 246 N. High St., P.O. Box 118, Columbus 43266; tel. 614/466-2070; Paul Ritter, chf.

OREGON: State Health Division, Health Facilities Section, 1400 S.W. 5th Ave., Portland 97207; tel. 503/229-5686; Maureen Whitman, mgr.

PENNSYLVANIA: Department of Health, Primary Care and Home Health Services, 1032A Health and Welfare Bldg., Harrisburg 17120; tel. 717/787-1379; Curtis Jennings, dir.

RHODE ISLAND: Department of Health, Division of Medical Care Standards, 75 Davis St., Providence 02908; tel. 401/277-2788; Donald C. William, chf.

SOUTH CAROLINA: Department of Health and Environmental Control, Division of Health Licensing and Certification, Office of Health Licensing, 2600 Bull St., Columbia 29201; tel. 803/734-4680; Alan Samuels, dir.

SOUTH DAKOTA: Department of Health, Division of Public Health, Licensure and Certification Program, 523 East Capitol, Joe Foss Building, Pierre 57501; tel. 605/773-3364; C. Sue Lydic, dir.

TENNESSEE: Department of Health and Environment, Division of Health Care Facilities, Board of Licensing Health Care Facilities, 283 Plus Park Blvd., Nashville 37219; tel. 615/367-6317; Leslie A. Brown, dir.

TEXAS: Department of Health, Health Facility Licensure, and Certification Division, 1100 W. 49th St., Austin 78756; tel. 512/458-7245; Dr. Juanita Carroll, dir.

UTAH: Department of Health, Division of Community Health Services, Bureau of Health Facility Licensure, P.O. Box 16660, Salt Lake City 84116; tel. 801/538-6152; James B. Fisher, dir.

VIRGINIA: Department of Health, Division of Licensure and Certification, 109 Governor St., Rm. 1013, Richmond 23219; tel. 804/786-2081; Mary V. Francis, dir.

WASHINGTON: Department of Social and Health Services, Division of Health, Health Facilities Survey Section, ET-31, Olympia 98504; tel. 206/753-5851; Kenneth R. Lewis, supr.

WEST VIRGINIA: Department of Health, Office of Health Standards Planning and Evaluation, Health Facility Licensure and Certification Section, 1800 Washington St. E., Charleston 25305; tel. 304/348-0050; John J. Jarrell, dir.

WISCONSIN: Department of Health and Social Services, Division of Health, Bureau of Quality Compliance, Healthcare Survey Section, P.O. Box 309, Madison 53701; tel. 608/266-2460; Kenneth Bjorklund, dir.

WYOMING: Department of Health and Social Services, Division of Health and Medical Services, Hathaway Bldg., 2300 Capitol Ave., Cheyenne 82002, tel. 307/777-7121; Larry Meuli, adm.

Accredited Substance Abuse Programs

The substance abuse programs listed have been accredited as of January 1, 1987, by the Joint Commission on Accreditation of Hospitals by decision of the Accreditation Committee of the Board of Commissioners.

The programs listed here have been found to be in substantial compliance with the Joint Commission standards for substance abuse programs, as found in the Consolidated Standards Manual.

Please refer to section A of the AHA Guide for information on hospitals with inpatient and/or outpatient alcohol and chemical dependency services. These hospitals are identified by Approval Codes F48 and F49. In section A, those hospitals identified by Approval Codes 1a and/or 1b are JCAH accredited.

We present this list simply as a convenient directory. Inclusion or omission of any organization's name indicates neither approval nor disapproval by the American Hospital Association.

Alabama

Birmingham

Alcoholism Recovery Services, 2701 Jefferson Avenue, S.W., Birmingham 35211; tel. 205/923-6552; Sarah Harkless

Hill Crest Hospital, 6869 5th Avenue South, Birmingham 35212; tel. 205/833-9000; Gary W. Lang

V.A. Medical Center, 700 S. 19th Street, Birmingham 35233

Daphne

Bradford at Mobile, Highway 98, Daphne 35210; tel. 205/626-6226; Carol Chandler

Decatur

Charter Retreat Hospital, 2205 Beltline Rd., S.W., Decatur 35602; tel. 205/350-1450; Jim R. Johnson

Guntersville

Marshall-Jackson Mental Health, 2409 Homer Clayton Drive, Guntersville 35976; tel. 205/582-4465; Alan Krichev, M.D.

Madison

Bradford/Huntsville, 1600 Browns Ferry Road, Madison 35758; tel. 205/271-1431; Jane Ann Hester

Mobile

Doctors Hospital of Mobile, 1700 Center Street, Mobile 36604; tel. 205/438-4551; Nina Edwards

Pelham

Bradford at Birmingham, County Highway 35 Fungo Hollow Rd., Pelham 35210; tel. 205/664-3460; Dr. Howard Cohen

Prattville

Bradford/Montgomery/Prattville, Route 3, Prattville 36067; tel. 205/365-6949; John Solomon

Warrior

Brookwood Recovery Center, End of Albritton Road, Warrior 35180; tel. 205/647-1945; Morris B. Hamilton, Jr.

Alaska

Anchorage

Charter North Hospital, 2530 De Barr Road, Anchorage 99514; tel. 907/338-7575; R. D. Reynolds

Arizona

Chandler

Valley Hope Alcoholism, 501 North Washington, Chandler 85224; tel. 602/899-3335; William D. Leipold, Ph.D.

Phoenix

St. Lukes Behavioral Health, 1800 East Van Buren, Phoenix 85006; tel. 602/258-7373; Robert Rundio

V.A. Medical Center, 7th Street & Indian School Rd., Phoenix 85012; tel. 602/277-5551; Marty Titus

Scottsdale

Camelback Hospitals, 7441 E. Earll Drive, Scottsdale 85251; tel. 602/941-7500; Dale Rinard

Tucson

3HO Drug & Alcohol Program, 1050 North Cherry Avenue, Tucson 85719; tel. 602/327-1734; Mukta Kaur Khalsa

Cottonwood De Tucson, 4110 Sweetwater Drive, Tucson 85745; tel. 602/743-0411; David J. Briick

Sierra Tucson, 16500 Lago Del Oro, Tucson 85704; tel. 602/624-4000; Bill O'Donnell

Wickenburg

Arc/The Meadows, Highway 89/93, Wickenburg 85358; tel. 602/684-2815; J. P. Mellody

Arkansas

North Little Rock

The Bridgeway, #21 Bridgeway Road, North Little Rock 72118; tel. 501/771-1500; Sharon Stevens

California

Alameda

Source of Service & Ind. Systems of TRT, I516 Oak Street, Suite 213, Alameda 94501; tel. 415/523-5484; Mary Jane Denton, Ph. D.

Bakersfield

Kern View Hospital, Inc., 3600 San Dimas Street, Bakersfield 93301; tel. 805/327-7621; Walter Reid

Cerritos

College Hospital, 10802 College Place, Cerritos 90701; tel. 213/924-9581; Barry Weiss

Chula Vista

Southwood Psychiatric, 950 3rd Avenue, Chula Vista 92011; tel. 619/426-6310; Thomas M. Balestrieri

Vista Hill Hospital, 730 Medical Center Court, Chula Vista 92010; tel. 619/421-6900; Robert J. Neher

Costa Mesa

Starting Point of Orange, 350 West Bay Street, Costa Mesa 92627; Donald J. Beld

Loma Linda

V.A. Medical Center, 11201 Benton Street, Loma Linda 91786; tel. 714/825-7084; Calvin E. Chandler

Los Angeles

Care Unit Hospital of Los Angeles, 5035 Coliseum Street, Los Angeles 90016; tel. 212/295-6441; Gregory L. McAllester

V.A. Medical Center/West Los Angeles, Wilshire & Sawtelle Blvds., Los Angeles 90073; tel. 213/478-3711; James H. Blake

Watts Health Foundation, Inc., 10300 Compton Avenue, Los Angeles 90002; tel. 213/564-4331; Clyde Oden, O.D., M.P.H.

Manhattan Beach

Vista Recovery Center, 1200 Rosecrans Avenue #204, Manhattan Beach 90266; tel. 213/640-7200; William Nathan

Martinez

V.A. Medical Center, 150 Muir Road, Martinez 94520; tel. 415/228-6800; C. H. Nixon

Oakland

E. A. Gladman Memorial Hospital, 2633 E. 27th Street, Oakland 94601; tel. 415/536-8111; Morton Bakar

Orangevale

Starting Point, 8773 Oak Avenue, Orangevale 95666; tel. 916/988-5700; Fred Fix

Pasadena

Impact Drug and Alcohol, 1680 North Fair Oaks Avenue, Pasadena 91103; tel. 213/681-2575; James M. Stillwell

Rancho Mirage

Betty Ford Center, 39000 Bob Hope Drive, Rancho Mirage 92270; tel. 619/340-0033; John T. Schwarzlose

Redwood City

Woodside Women's Hospital, 1600 Gordon Street, Redwood City 94061; tel. 415/368-4134; Jacquelyn Thompson

Sacramento

Starting Point, 1001 Grand Avenue, Sacramento 85662; Jack Sumner, M.S.W.

San Diego

Mesa Vista Hospital, 7850 Vista Hill Ave., San Diego 92123; tel. 619/694-8300; Robert L. Neher, Jr.

Torrance

Del Amo Hospital, 23700 Camino Del Sol, Torrance 90505; tel. 213/530-1151; Gregory A. Miller

Ventura

C.P.C. Vista Del Mar Hospital, 801 Seneca Street, Ventura 93001; tel. 805/653-6434; Dr. Nate Newman

Colorado

Arvada

Cottonwood Hill, Inc., 13455 West 58th Avenue, Arvada 80001; tel. 303/420-1702; Donna Rock

Boulder

Boulder Psychiatric Institute, 777 29th Street, Suite 200, Boulder 80303; tel. 303/499-2233; Robert P. Snead, M.D.

Whole Person Health Center, 999 Alpine Avenue, Boulder 80302; tel. 303/449-4121; Darwin W. Smith, M.D.

The substance abuse programs listed have been accredited as of January 1, 1987, by the Joint Commission on Accreditation of Hospitals by decision of the Accreditation Committee of the Board of Commissioners.

The programs listed here have been found to be in substantial compliance with the Joint Commission standards for substance abuse programs, as found in the Consolidated Standards Manual.

Please refer to section A of the AHA Guide *for information on hospitals with inpatient and/or outpatient alcohol and chemical dependency services. These hospitals are identified by Approval Codes F48 and F49. In section A, those hospitals identified by Approval Codes 1a and/or 1b are JCAH accredited.*

We present this list simply as a convenient directory. Inclusion or omission of any organization's name indicates neither approval nor disapproval by the American Hospital Association.

Denver

A.M.I. Presbyterian/St. Luke's Hospital, 1601 East 19th Avenue, Denver 80203; tel. 303/839-6889; J. Rock Tonkel

The Centre at Porter, 2525 S. Downing Street, Denver 80210; tel. 303/778-5774; Betty Ross

V.A. Medical Center, 1055 Clermont Street, Denver 80220; tel. 303/399-8020; James G. Martin

Durango

Laplata Community Hospital, 3801 North Main Avenue, Durango 81301; tel. 303/259-1110; Tom Galbraith

Estes Park

Harmony Foundation, Inc., 1600 Fish Hatchery Road, Estes Park 80517; tel. 303/586-4491; Howard Clarke, Jr.

Florence

Parkside Lodge of Florence, 521 West 5th Street, Florence 81226; tel. 303/784-4806; Paula Burton

Fort Collins

Larico Center For Youth, 640 West Prospect, Fort Collins 80521; tel. 303/482-1037; Donna Bresee

New Beginnings at Fort Collins, 1225 Redwood, Ft. Collins 80524; tel. 303/493-3389; Cam Pratt

Green Mountain Falls

The Ark, Inc., 10930 Hondo Avenue, Green Mountain Falls 80819; tel. 303/684-9483; Howard L. McFadden

Lakewood

New Beginnings of Denver, 1325 Everett Court, Lakewood 80215; tel. 303/231-9090; William J. McCabe, Ph.D.

Pueblo

Colorado State Hospital, 1600 W. 24th Street, Pueblo 81003; tel. 303/543-1170; Haydee Kort, M.D.

Thornton

Parkside Lodge of Colorado, Inc., 8801 Lipan, Thornton 80221; tel. 303/430-0800; Ronald J. Dreier

Wheat Ridge

Adolescents & Family Institute, 10001 W. 32nd Avenue, Wheat Ridge 80033; tel. 303/238-1231; Alex M. Panio, Jr., Ph.D.

Connecticut

Bridgeport

Greater Bridgeport Community, 1635 Central Avenue, Bridgeport 06610; tel. 203/579-6615; Melodie Peet, M.P.H.

Guenster Rehabilitation Center, 276 Union Avenue, Bridgeport 06607; tel. 203/384-9301; Robert R. Ryan

Hamden

The Children's Center, 1400 Whitney Avenue, Hamden 06517; tel. 203/248-2116; Brian F. Lynch

Hartford

Blue Hills Hospital, 51 Coventry Street, Hartford 06112; tel. 203/566-4405; Stephen A. Glass

New Haven

Shirley Frank Foundation, 659 George Street, New Haven 06511; tel. 203/787-2771; Francis J. Rizzolo

Newtown

Fairfield Hills Hospital, Newtown 06470; tel. 203/426-2531; Dennis Angelini, Ph.D.

North Stonington

Stonington Institute, Swantown Hill Road, North Stonington 06359; tel. 203/535-1010; Michael Angelides

Norwalk

Vitam Center, Inc., 57 West Rocks Rd., Norwalk 06851; tel. 203/846-2091; Leonard A. Kenowitz

Norwich

Norwich Hospital, Laurel Hill Rd., Rte. 12, Norwich 06360; tel. 203/889-7361; Garrell S. Mullaney

Portland

Elmcrest Psychiatric Institute, 25 Marlborough St., Portland 06480; tel. 203/342-0480; John F. McCarthy

Sandy Hook

Eagle Hill Alcoholism, 28 Alberts Hill Road, Sandy Hook 06482; tel. 203/426-8085; William T. Moriarty

Stamford

Liberation Programs, Inc., 119 Main Street, Stamford 06901; tel. 203/359-3134; Doris DeHuff

Westport

Hall Brooke Foundation, 47 Long Lots Rd., Westport 06880; tel. 203/227-1251; Bennett Rosner, M.D.

Delaware

Delaware City

Lower Kensington Environment; Government Bacon Health Center, Delaware City 19706; tel. 302/834-9201; Terence McSherry

Wilmington

Brandywine Counseling, 305 West 12th Street, Wilmington 19801; tel. 302/656-2348; David S. Skinner

District of Columbia

St. Elizabeth's Hospital, 2700 Martin L. King Jr., Ave., S.E., Washington DC 20032; tel. 202/562-4000; William G. Prescott, M.D.

Florida

Avon Park

Florida Alcohol Treatment; 100 West College Dr., Avon Park 33825; tel. 813/453-3151; Glenn E. Rohrer, Ph.D.

Boca Raton

Praxis Addiction Treatment, 1000 N.W. 15th Street, Boca Raton 33432; tel. 305/392-8444; Carl W. Lindner

Bowling Green

Bowling Green Inn, Inc., Bowling Green 33834; tel. 813/375-2218; George F. Furnival

Coral Springs

Careunit of Coral Springs, 3275 N.W. 99th Way, Coral Springs 33065; tel. 305/753-5200; Conrad P. Foss

Daytona Beach

ACT Corporation, 1220 Willis Avenue, Daytona Beach 32104; tel. 904/255-7384; J. Wayne Dreggors

Delray Beach

The Beachcomber, 4493 North Ocean Boulevard, Delray Beach 33444; tel. 305/276-6226; James Bryan

Fair Oaks Hospital at Boca Raton, 5440 Linton Boulevard, Delray Beach 33445; tel. 305/495-1000; Roy M. Chernoff

Fort Lauderdale

Coral Ridge Psychiatric, 4545 North Federal Highway, Fort Lauderdale 33308; tel. 304/771-2711; Michael J. Held

Fort Lauderdale Hospital, 1601 East Las Olas Blvd., Fort Lauderdale 33301; tel. 305/463-4321; Larry M. Parrish

Gulf Breeze

The Friary, Rte. 2, Gulf Breeze 32561; tel. 904/932-9375; Ronald J. Catanzaro, M.D.

Hollywood

Memorial Hospital, 3501 Johnson Street, Hollywood 33021; tel. 305/987-2000; S. A. Mudano

Jacksonville

C.P.C. St. Johns River Hospital, 6300 Beach Boulevard, Jacksonville 32216; tel. 904/724-9202; Patrick G. Kelly

Methodist Hospital, 580 West Eighth Street, Jacksonville 32209; tel. 904/354-2071; Marcus E. Drewa

Oak Psychiatric Center, 2534 Oak Street, Jacksonville 32204; tel. 904/389-2351; Joseph A. Virzi, M.D., P.A.

Jensen Beach

Heritage Jensen Beach, 2065 N.E. Indian River Drive, Jensen Beach 33457; tel. 305/334-5566; James D. Carraway

Kissimmee

Brookwood Recovery Center, Kissimmee 32742; tel. 305/933-5222; Bob Hinds

Lake Worth

Lake Hospital of the Palm, 1710 Fourth Ave., North, Lake Worth 33460; tel. 305/588-7341; Alan T. Penn

Leesburg

Lake/Sumter Community, 404 Webster Street, Leesburg 32748; tel. 904/787-9178; Bert Lacey

Longwood

West Lake Hospital, 589 W. Sanlando Spring, Longwood 32750; tel. 305/834-0900; Irving B. Sawyers, Jr.

The substance abuse programs listed have been accredited as of January 1, 1987, by the Joint Commission on Accreditation of Hospitals by decision of the Accreditation Committee of the Board of Commissioners.

The programs listed here have been found to be in substantial compliance with the Joint Commission standards for substance abuse programs, as found in the Consolidated Standards Manual.

Please refer to section A of the AHA Guide for information on hospitals with inpatient and/or outpatient alcohol and chemical dependency services. These hospitals are identified by Approval Codes F48 and F49. In section A, those hospitals identified by Approval Codes 1a and/or 1b are JCAH accredited.

We present this list simply as a convenient directory. Inclusion or omission of any organization's name indicates neither approval nor disapproval by the American Hospital Association.

Miami

Highland Park General Hospital, 1660 N.W. 7th Court, Miami 33136; tel. 305/324-8111; Jay S. Weinstein

St. Lukes Center, 2693 Biscayne Boulevard, Miami 33137; tel. 305/573-1259; William Kintz, A.C.S.W.

The Village South, Inc., 3180 Biscayne Boulevard, Miami 33137; tel. 305/573-3784; Matthew Gissen, J.D.

West Sands Psychiatric, 11100 N.W. 27th Street, Miami 33172; tel. 305/591-3230; Rea A. Oliver

Ocala

Charter Springs Hospital, 3130 S.W. 27th Avenue, Ocala 32678; tel. 904/237-7293; Gregory A. Williams

Panama City

Crossroads/The Recovery Center, 2121 Lisenby Avenue, Panama City 32405; tel. 904/784-0869; B. Philip Cotton, M.D.

Pensacola

Lakeview Center-C.S.M., 1221 West Lakeview Avenue, Pensacola 32501; tel. 904/432-1222; Morris L. Eaddy, Ph.D.

Pineland

The Cloisters at Pine Island, Waterfront Drive, Pineland 33945; tel. 813/283-1019; Michael G. Doherty, M.H.S., C.A.C.

Sarasota

Anabasis, Inc., 1084 South Briggs Avenue, Sarasota 33577; tel. 813/365-5245; James D. Poage

South Miami

South Miami Hospital Alcohol, 7400 S.W. 62nd Avenue, South Miami 33143; tel. 305/661-4611; Merrill W. Crews

Tampa

A.M.C. Psychiatric Care Center, 1936 West Buffalo Avenue, Tampa 33607; tel. 813/874-0849; Thomas E. Kiernan

Charter Hospital of Tampa, 4004 N. Riverside Dr., Tampa 33603; tel. 813/238-8671; James P. Hackett, Jr.

Care Unit of Tampa, 301 East 7th Avenue, Tampa 33602; tel. 813/273-9427; Daniel T. McMurray

Glenbeigh of Tampa, 3102 East 138th Avenue, Tampa 33612; tel. 813/971-5000; Robert Denson

West Palm Beach

Hanley-Hazelden Center, 1043 45th Street, West Palm Beach 33407; tel. 305/848-1666; Patrick D. Griffin

The Palm Beach Institute, 1014 N. Olive Avenue, West Palm Beach 33401; tel. 305/833-7553; Ronald J. Catanzaro, M.D.

Winter Park

Lynnhaven, 1600 Dodd Road, Winter Park 32792; tel. 305/677-6842; Staples Shearer

Woodville

Disc Village Treatment Center, Natural Bridge Road, Woodville 32362; tel. 904/421-4115; Thomas Oak

Georgia

Atlanta

Charter Peachford Hospital, 2151 Peachford Road, Atlanta 30338; tel. 404/455-3200; James W. Eyler

C.P.C. Parkwood Hospital, 1999 Cliff Valley Way, Atlanta 30329; tel. 404/633-8431; Ronald E. Yates, M.P.H.

Georgia Mental Health Institute, 1256 Briarcliff Rd., N.E., Atlanta 30306; tel. 404/894-5643; B.C. Robbins

Outpatient Addiction Clinic, 4470 Chamblee Dunwoody Rd., Suite 1, Atlanta 30338; tel. 404/451-0358; F. W. Chambers, M.H.A.

Safe Center of Atlanta, Inc., 1605 Chantilly Drive, Suite 200, Atlanta 30324; tel. 404/633-3700; I. Jack Whitworth

Clayton

Woodridge Hospital, Germany Road, Clayton 30525; tel. 404/782-3100; Louise Kuntz

College Park

Anchor of Atlanta, Inc., 5454 Yorktowne Drive, College Park 30349; tel. 404/991-6044; Benjamin H. Underwood

Columbus

The Bradley Center, Inc., 2000 16th Avenue, Columbus 31993; tel. tel. 404/324-4882; John C. Connelly, M.D.

Decatur

Georgia Regional Hospital at Atlanta, 3073 Panthersville Rd., Decatur 30037; tel. 404/243-2110; Richard A. Fields, M.D.

Dublin

Brookwood Recovery Center, 804 Industrial Boulevard, Dublin 31040; tel. 912/275-0353; Harold E. Ward

Fort Oglethorpe

Greenleaf Center, Inc., 500 Greenleaf Circle, Fort Oglethorpe 30742; tel. 404/861-4357; Jimmie W. Harden, F.A.C.H.A.

Macon

Coliseum Psychiatric Hospital, 340 Hospital Drive, Macon 31201; tel. 912/741-1355; Louis A. Valente

Milledgeville

Central State Hospital, Swint Avenue, Milledgeville 31062; tel. 912/453-5562; Myers R. Kurtz

Moultrie

Turning Point Care Center, Inc., 319 Bypass, Moultrie 31768; tel. 912/985-4815; Gary Bulkin

Rome

Northwest Georgia Regional, 1305 Redmond Road, Rome 30161; tel. 404/295-6466; Robert L. Pulliam

Savannah

Georgia Regional Hospital, 1915 Eisenhower Drive, Savannah 31406; tel. 912/356-2034; Galen C. Huffman, M.D.

Smyrna

Ridgeview Institute, 3995 So. Cobb Drive, Smyrna 30080; tel. 404/434-4567; Edward J. Osborne

St. Simons Island

Charter By-The-Sea Hospital, 2927 Demere Rd., St. Simons Island 31522; tel. 912/638-1999; James R. Thomas

Valdosta

Greenleaf Center, Inc., 2209 Pineview Drive, Valdosta 31602; tel. 912/247-4357; Norman M. Davis, Jr.

Idaho

Boise

C.P.C. Intermountain Hospital, 303 N. Allumbaugh, Boise 83704; tel. 208/377-8400; Paul Logan

Coeur D'Alene

St. Benedict's Act Center, 2003 Lincoln Way, Coeur D'Alene 83814; tel. 208/677-9591; George Dimas

Pine Crest Hospital, 2301 N. Ironwood Place, Coeur D'Alene 83814; tel. 208/666-1441; Joseph F. Wofer, Jr.

Pocatello

Aspen Crest Hospital, 797 Hospital Way, Pocatello 83201; tel. 208/234-0797; Michael M. Williams

Illinois

Belleville

Daybreak, 220 West Lincoln, Belleville 62222; tel. 618/235-6532; Gary M. Pippemger

Bloomington

McLean County Alcohol & Drug, 702 W. Chestnut, Bloomington 61701; tel. 309/827-6026; Russell J. Hagen

Bolingbrook

Life Works Chemical Dependency, 420 Medical Center Drive, Bolingbrook 60439; tel. 312/759-5750; Thomas G. McCabe

Chicago

Chicago's Alcoholic Treatment, 3026 S. California Ave., Chicago 60608; tel. 312/254-3680; Richard E. Sherman, Ph.D.

H.C.A. Chicago Lakeshore, 4840 North Marine Drive, Chicago 60640; tel. 312/878-9700; Jerome Kearney

Project C.O.A.T. -Center, 8054 South Western Avenue, Chicago 60620; tel. 312/471-1232; Gertrude Gray

Des Plaines

Forest Hospital, 555 Wilson Lane, Des Plaines 60016; tel. 312/635-4100; Mary Jane Such

Effingham

Effingham County Guidance, 1108 South Willow, Effingham 62401; tel. 217/347-7179; Cheryl Compton, A.C.S.W.

Elgin

Lovellton Residential, 600 Villa Street, Elgin 60120; tel. 312/695-0077; Patricia Macalister

Forest Park

Riveredge Hospital, 8311 West Roosevelt Road, Forest Park 60130; tel. 312/771-7000; Thomas F. Martin

The substance abuse programs listed have been accredited as of January 1, 1987, by the Joint Commission on Accreditation of Hospitals by decision of the Accreditation Committee of the Board of Commissioners.

The programs listed here have been found to be in substantial compliance with the Joint Commission standards for substance abuse programs, as found in the Consolidated Standards Manual.

Please refer to section A of the AHA Guide *for information on hospitals with inpatient and/or outpatient alcohol and chemical dependency services. These hospitals are identified by Approval Codes F48 and F49. In section A, those hospitals identified by Approval Codes 1a and/or 1b are JCAH accredited.*

We present this list simply as a convenient directory. Inclusion or omission of any organization's name indicates neither approval nor disapproval by the American Hospital Association.

Freeport

SoJourn House, Inc., 565 North Turner Ave., Freeport 61032; tel. 815/232-5121; Brenda Bombard

Hoffman Estates

ARC/Chicago, 1776 Moon Lake Boulevard, Hoffman Estates 60194; tel. 312/882-0070; John F. Buckley

Hopedale

Hopedale Medical Complex, Tremont & Second, Hopedale 61747; tel. 309/449-3321; L. H. Rossi, M.D.

Moline

Pathways to Recovery, 555 Sixth Street, Moline 61265; tel. 309/757-2901; Maxine Duhm

Mundelein

Parkside Lodge of Mundelein, 24647 N. Highway 21, Mundelein 60060; tel. 312/634-2020; Carl L. Anderson

Park Ridge

Lutheran Center, 1700 Luther Lane, Park Ridge 60068; tel. 312/696-6017; Rev. Carl Anderson

Rockford

Alcare of Rockford, 1055 East State Street, Rockford 61108; tel. 815/965-8600; Gary Confer, S.A.C.

Skokie

Skokie Valley Hospital, 9600 Gross Point Rd., Skokie 60076; tel. 312/677-9600; Ralph G. Hutchins

Winfield

Alcoholism Treatment Center, 27 W. 751 Shady Way, Winfield 60190; tel. 312/653-4000; Paul Teodo

Indiana

Anderson

Anderson Center of St. John's, 2210 Jackson Street, Anderson 46014; tel. 317/646-8388; George Horaitis

Crestview Center, Inc., 2201 Hillcrest Drive, Anderson 46012; tel. 317/649-1961; Michael B. Erickson

Carmel

Tri-County Mental Health, 11711 N. Meridian St., Suite 600, Carmel 46032; tel. 317/875-4637; Larry L. Burch, A.C.S.W.

Evansville

Evansville State Hospital, 3400 Lincoln Avenue, Evansville 47715; tel. 812/473-2216; John Hedges

Fort Wayne

Charter Beacon Hospital, 1720 Beacon Street, Fort Wayne 46805; tel. 219/423-3651; Gerald Wallman

Indianapolis

Fairbanks Hospital, Inc., 8101 Clearvista Parkway, Indianapolis 46256; tel. 317/849-8222; Thomas W. Brink

Jeffersonville

Lifespring Mental Health, 207 West 13th Street, Jeffersonville 47130; tel. 812/283-4491; Joseph B. Brill, M.D.

Lebanon

Koala Center, 1711 LaFayette Avenue, Lebanon 46052; tel. 317/482-3711; E. Robert Edwards

Madison

Madison State Hospital, Madison 47250; tel. 812/265-2611; Jerry A. Thaden

Marion

Jonah Institute at Wabash, 131 North Washington Street, Marion 46952; tel. 317/664-6225; Donald Osborne, M.A.

V.A. Medical Center, E. 38th Street, Marion 46952; tel. 317/674-3321; A. G. Branch

Iowa

Cherokee

Mental Health Institute, 1200 West Cedar St., Cherokee 51012; tel. 712/225-2594; E. A. Kjenaas, M.D.

Independence

Mental Health Institute, Highway 20W, Independence 50644; tel. 319/334-2583; Bhasker J. Dave, M.D.

Mount Pleasant

Mental Health Institute, 1200 East Washington, Mount Pleasant 52641; tel. 319/385-7231; David J. Scurry

Kansas

Atchison

Valley Hope Alcoholism, 1816 North 2nd, Atchison 66002; tel. 913/367-1618; William D. Leipold, Ph.D.

Kansas City

Keystone Treatment Center, 8919 Parallel Parkway, Ste. 116, Kansas City 66102; tel. 913/299-6838; Robert M. Borgren

Larned

Larned State Hospital, RR3, Larned 67550; tel. 316/285-2131; George W. Getz, M.D.

Norton

Valley Hope Alcoholism, 709 West Holme, Norton 67654; tel. 913/877-5101; William D. Leipold, Ph.D.

Osawatomie

Osawatomie State Hospital, Osawatomie 66064; tel. 913/755-3151; J. Russell Mills

Topeka

C.F. Menninger Memorial Hospital, 5800 S.W. Sixth Avenue, Topeka 66606; tel. 913/273-7500; Edward J. Zoble, Ph.D.

Wichita

St. Joseph Medical Center, 3600 East Harry, Wichita 67218; tel. 316/685-1111; Joseph A. Heeb

Kentucky

Corbin

Cumberland River District, American Greeting Rd., Corbin 40701; tel. 606/528-7010; Roland D. Mullins

Falmouth

St. Luke Hospital, Care Unit, 512 Maple Avenue, Falmouth 41040; tel. 606/572-3100; John D. Hoyle

Lexington

V.A. Medical Center/Lexington, Leestown Road, Lexington 40507; tel. 606/233-4511; John R. Rowan

Louisville

Jefferson Alcohol & Drug Abuse, 600 South Preston Street, Louisville 40202; tel. 502/583-3951; Diane E. Hague, M.S.S.W.

K.M.I. Medical Center, 8521 La Grange Road, Louisville 40222; tel. 502/426-6380; Charles L. Webb, Jr.

Our Lady of Peace Hospital, 2020 Newburg Road, Louisville 40205; tel. 502/451-3330; William T. Dunn

Owensboro

Green River Regional MH-MR, 233 West Ninth Street, Owensboro 43202; tel. 502/684-0696; J. Frank Dearness, A.C.S.W.

Louisiana

Alexandria

Briarwood Hospital, 110 John Eskew Drive, Alexandria 71303; tel. 318/445-5111; James A. Schmidt

Baton Rouge

Chemical Dependency of Baton, 4040 North Blvd., Baton Rouge 70821; tel. 504/387-7900; Chris Barnette

Lafayette

Chemical Dependency Unit, 2520 North University Avenue, Lafayette 70507; tel. 318/234-5614; Ronald E. Weller

Insight of America Hospital, 310 Youngsville Hwy., Lafayette 70508; tel. 318/837-8787; Darryl Wagley

Mandeville

Bowling Green Inn of St. Tamman, 701 Florida Avenue, Mandeville 70448; tel. 504/626-5661; George Rozelle, Ph.D.

Southeast Louisiana Hospital, Highway 190, Mandeville 70448; tel. 504/626-8161; Gary A. Sneed, M.D.

New Orleans

Charity Hospital of Louisiana, 1532 Tulane Avenue, New Orleans 70140; tel. 504/568-3202; Elliott C. Roberts, Sr.

Methodist Psychiatric, 5610 Read Boulevard, New Orleans 70127; tel. 504/244-5661; Sam Katich

New Orleans Adolescent, 210 State Street, New Orleans 70118; tel. 504/897-3400; George C. Daul, Jr., M.D.

The substance abuse programs listed have been accredited as of January 1, 1987, by the Joint Commission on Accreditation of Hospitals by decision of the Accreditation Committee of the Board of Commissioners.

The programs listed here have been found to be in substantial compliance with the Joint Commission standards for substance abuse programs, as found in the Consolidated Standards Manual.

Please refer to section A of the AHA Guide for information on hospitals with inpatient and/or outpatient alcohol and chemical dependency services. These hospitals are identified by Approval Codes F48 and F49. In section A, those hospitals identified by Approval Codes 1a and/or 1b are JCAH accredited.

We present this list simply as a convenient directory. Inclusion or omission of any organization's name indicates neither approval nor disapproval by the American Hospital Association.

Pineville

Central Louisiana State Hospital, Pineville 71361; tel. 318/484-6200; Roy D. Hill, M.D.

Shreveport

Charter Forest Hospital, 9320 Linwood Avenue, Shreveport 71138; tel. 318/688-3930; F. Jeffrey Loker

Slidell

Northshore Psychiatric, Suite C, 104 Medical Center Drive, Slidell 70458; tel. 504/646-5500; James A. Coleman, F.A.C.H.A.

Maine

South Windham

Pinetree Alcoholic Treatment Center, 1040 Main Street, South Windham 04082; tel. 207/892-2192; Griffith C. Matthews

Maryland

Baltimore

Baltimore City Health Dept., 2514-18 Greenmount Avenue, Baltimore 21218; tel. 301/396-6066; Susan Guarneri, M.D., M.P.H.

Francis Scott Key Medical Center, 4940 Eastern Avenue, Baltimore 21224; tel. 301/955-0150; Ronald R. Peterson

Franklin Square Hospital, 9000 Franklin Square Drive, Baltimore 21237; tel. 301/682-7000; Michael R. Merson

Mainstream Associates, Inc., 4900 Wetheredsville Road, Baltimore 21207; tel. 301/448-5700; Lockwood Rush, Ph.D.

Quinn Center, Inc., 8441 Belair Road, Baltimore 21236; tel. 301/529-2880; Joseph F. Quinn

Bel Air

New Beginnings at Hidden Brook, 522 Thomas Run Road, Bel Air 21014; tel. 301/879-1919; Michael Barbieri

Chestertown

A.F. Whitsitt Alcohol, Scheeler Road, Chestertown 21620; tel. 301/778-6800; D. Cherrey Jones, R.N., M.A.

Crownsville

Hope House Alcohol Recovery, Crownsville 21032; tel. 301/987-0242; Arthur M. Harris

Cumberland

Allegany County Health, Willowbrook Road, Cumberland 21502; tel. 301/777-2285; Jane A. Fiscus, M.D.

East New Market

New Beginnings at Warwick, Rte 1, East New Market 21631; tel. 301/943-8108; Breck Stringer

Easton

Talbot County Alcoholism, 100 South Hanson Street, Easton 21601; tel. 301/822-2292; Eugene H. Guthrie, M.D.

Ellicott City

Oakview Treatment Center, 3100 Health Park Drive, Ellicott City 21043; tel. 301/461-9922; Charles J. Hooker III, M.S.M.

Fort Howard

V. A. Medical Center, Fort Howard 21052; tel. 301/477-1800; Robert Haith, Jr.

Gambrills

Meadows Recovery Center, 730 Maryland Route 3, Gambrills 21054; tel. 301/923-6022; Paul A. Brown

Olney

Melwood Farm Incorporated, 19715 Zion Road, Olney 20832; tel. 301/924-5000; Stuart M. Brownell

Poolesville

Seneca House, 13025 Riley's Lock Road, Poolesville 20837; tel. 301/948-2412; Robert C. Roman

Salisbury

Worcester County Health, William H. Hudson Center, Salisbury 21801; tel. 301/742-0151; Donald Harting, M.D., M.P.H.

Silver Spring

Kolmac Clinic, 1003 Spring Street, Silver Spring 20910; tel. 301/589-0255; George Kolodner, M.D.

Suitland

St. Luke Institute, Inc., 2420 Brooks Drive, Suitland 20746; tel. 301/967-3700; Rev. Michael Peterson, M.D.

Towson

Sheppard & Enoch Pratt, 6501 N. Charles Street, Towson 21204; tel. 301/823-8200; Robert W. Gibson, M.D.

Massachusetts

Brookline

Human Resource Institute, 227 Babcock Street, Brookline 02146; tel. 617/731-3200; Joseph W. Nolan

Lynn

Mount Pleasant Hospital, 60 Granite Street, Lynn 01904; tel. 617/581-5600; Dr. Walter Henry

Milford

Valley Adult Counseling, 115 Water Street, Milford 01757; tel. 617/478-0820; Joseph Lo Piccolo

Rutland

Rutland Heights Hospital, Maple Avenue, Rutland 01543; tel. 617/886-4711; Hulot W. Haden

Westboro

Spectrum House, Inc., 155 Oak Street, Westboro 01581; tel. 617/757-8827; Robert P. Galea

Michigan

Ann Arbor

Child & Family Services/Washtenaw, 2301 Platt Road, Ann Arbor 48104; tel. 313/971-6520; William J. Vollano, A.C.S.W.

Washtenaw Council Alcoholism, 2301 Platt Road, Ann Arbor 48104; tel. 313/971-7900; Barry Kistner

Auburn Hills

Eastwood at Auburn Hills, 1360 Doris Road, Auburn Hills 48057; tel. 313/373-2660; Jan Shaw

Baldwin

Regional Health Care, 4967 North Michigan Avenue, Baldwin 49304; tel. 616/745-4624; Joseph C. Baer, R.S., M.P.H.

Battle Creek

Psychological Consultants, 1407 Comerica Bldg., Battle Creek 49017; tel. 616/968-2811; Jeffrey Andert, Ph.D.

Bay City

Bay Area Social Intervention, 1110 Washington Ave., Bay City 48706; tel. 517/895-9861; John R. Jozwiak

Robertson Neuro-Chem. Clinic, P.C., 200 S. Wenona Street, Suite G-25, Bay City 48706; tel. 517/893-6611; Joel C. Robertson, Pharm. D.

Benton Harbor

New Horizons Recovery Center, 960 Agard Street, Benton Harbor 49022; tel. 616/927-5433; Kathleen D. Scarry

Birmingham

Montgomery & Associates, 690 East Maple, Birmingham 48011; tel. 313/642-8042; Gertrude Montgomery

Triad Mental Health Services, 555 S. Woodward, Suite 614, Birmingham 48011; tel. 313/646-6990; David P. Stanislaw, Jr., M.S.W.

Bloomfield Hills

Auro Medical Center, 2515 Woodward Avenue, Suite 250, Bloomfield Hills 48013; tel. 313/335-1130; Yatinder M. Singhal, M.D.

Oakland Psychological Clinic, 2000 N. Woodward Ave., Suite 102, Bloomfield Hills 48013; tel. 313/335-6670; Barry H. Tigay, Ph.D.

Brighton

Brighton Hospital, 12851 E. Grand River Ave., Brighton 48116; tel. 313/227-1211; Ivan C. Harner

Caro

Alcohol Information Counseling, 2266 West Caro Road, Caro 48723; tel. 517/673-8114; Mr. Crolson

Chelsea

Chelsea Community Hospital, 775 South Main Street, Chelsea 48118; tel. 313/475-1311; Willard H. Johnson

Clare

Human Aid Incorporated, 210 West 7th Street, Clare 48617; tel. 517/386-3405; Wayne Charnes

Clarkston

Clinical Resources, Inc., 5885 Ortonville Road, Clarkston 48016; tel. 313/625-8333; Sherwin L. Sokolov, M.A.

Dearborn

S. Bazini, M.D., Psychiatric, 1414 East Parklane Towers, Dearborn 48126; tel. 313/271-5800; S. Bazini, M.D.

The substance abuse programs listed have been accredited as of January 1, 1987, by the Joint Commission on Accreditation of Hospitals by decision of the Accreditation Committee of the Board of Commissioners.

The programs listed here have been found to be in substantial compliance with the Joint Commission standards for substance abuse programs, as found in the Consolidated Standards Manual.

Please refer to section A of the AHA Guide *for information on hospitals with inpatient and/or outpatient alcohol and chemical dependency services. These hospitals are identified by Approval Codes F48 and F49. In section A, those hospitals identified by Approval Codes 1a and/or 1b are JCAH accredited.*

We present this list simply as a convenient directory. Inclusion or omission of any organization's name indicates neither approval nor disapproval by the American Hospital Association.

Dearborn Heights

Dearborn Heights Human Service, 5928 Telegraph Road, Dearborn Heights 48127; tel. 313/277-3293; Phyllis A. Merchant

Detroit

Allied Health Services O.P.C., Inc., 20400 Livernois, Detroit 48221; tel. 313/345-1915; Millicent Dudley, M.D.

Doctors Hospital, 2730 E. Jefferson Ave., Detroit 48207; tel. 313/259-3050; William N. Hettiger

Eastwood Community Clinics, 15085 East 7 Mile Rd., Detroit 48205; tel. 313/526-6000; J. William Sumner

Hutzel Hospital, 4287 Brush Street, Detroit 48201; tel. 313/494-7411; Frank P. Iacobell

Jefferson Medical Industrial Clinic, 23871 W. McNichols Road, Detroit 48219; tel. 313/531-4177; A. S. Patel, M.D.

Metro East Drug Treatment, 15317 E. Warren Avenue, Detroit 48224; tel. 313/824-1110; Leslie B. Carroll, M.S.

Nardin Park Substance Abuse, 9605 Grand River, Detroit 48204; tel. 313/834-5930; Paul Scott

Northeast Guidance Center, 13340 East Warren, Detroit 48215; tel. 313/824-8000; Walter E. Beck, A.C.S.W.

Paul Robeson-Harriet Tubman, 4707 Woodward Avenue, Detroit 48201; tel. 313/831-0750; Dennis S. Evans

Robinwood Clinic LTD., 18820 Woodward Avenue, Detroit 48203; tel. 313/369-1400; Helen L. Pilzner

Sacred Heart Rehabilitation, 569 East Elizabeth Street, Detroit 48201; tel. 313/962-0422; Rev. Vaughan M. Quinn

Salvation Army Harbor Light, 2643 Park, Detroit 48201; tel. 313/964-0577; Captain John MacDonald

Self Help Addiction, 1852 West Grand Blvd., Detroit 48208; tel. 313/894-2410; Allan Bray

East Detroit

Daily Living Counseling Clinic, 22422 Gratiot, East Detroit 48021; tel. 313/445-2212; Dr. Donald E. Rutkowski, M.D.

East Lansing

Meridian Professional, 5031 Park Lake Road, East Lansing 48823; tel. 517/332-0811; Thomas S. Gunnings

Michigan Deaconess Treatment, 704 Abott Road, East Lansing 48823; tel. 517/332-2266; Dan Anderson

Edmore

Tri-County Community Hospital, 1131 East Howard Street, Edmore 48829; tel. 517/427-5116; Darwin Finkbeiner

Farmington Hills

Farmington Area Advisory, 23450 Middlebelt, Farmington Hills 48024; tel. 313/477-6767; Betty G. Arnold

North Point Mental Health, 30840 Northwestern Highway, Suite 100, Farmington Hills 48018; tel. 313/851-2266; Alan A. Rickfelder, Ph.D.

Flint

Choices Unlimited, Inc., 3717 Van Slyke Road, Suite 3, Flint 48507; tel. 313/232-2162; Harold S. Sommerschield, Ph.D.

Hurley Medical Center, One Hurley Plaza, Flint 48502; tel. 313/257-9000; Phillip C. Dutcher

Insight, 2425 South Linden Road, Flint 48504; tel. 313/733-5981; Stephen N. Lebel

Koala Center Day Treatment, 1207 North Ballenger Highway, Flint 48504; tel. 313/767-1190; William M. Trosko

National Council on Alcoholism, 202 E. Boulevard Dr., Suite 350, Flint 48503; tel. 313/767-0350; Clarence L. Childs

Psychotherapy & Training, 400 No. Saginaw, Flint 48502; tel. 313/234-3658; James Earl Sutton

Gaylord

Community, Family & Children, 1665 W. M-32, Building B, Gaylord 49735; tel. 517/732-3581; Clement C. Veeser

Grand Rapids

Alcohol and Chemical Abuse, 3330 Claystone, S.E., Grand Rapids 49506; tel. 616/949-7460; Joseph Merrell III

Alcohol Outpatient Services, 1331 Lake Drive, S.E., Grand Rapids 49506; tel. 616/456-8010; Charles F. Logie, Jr.,

Care Unit of Grand Rapids, 1931 Boston, S.E., Grand Rapids 49506; tel. 616/243-2273; Valerie Costantino

Our Hope Association, 324 Lyon, N.E., Grand Rapids 49503; tel. 616/451-2039; Nancy P. Mueller

River Valley Recovery Center, 1450 Leonard, Northeast, Grand Rapids 49505; tel. 616/776-1199; Leslie Louisell

Hillsdale

Turning Point Treatment Center, 3300 Beck Road, Hillsdale 49242; tel. 517/439-1507; Thomas J. Burke

Howell

McPherson Community Health, 620 Byron Rd., Howell 48843; tel. 517/546-1410; Peter J. Schonfeld

Inkster

Hegira Programs, Inc., 1375 Inkster Road, Inkster 48141; tel. 313/565-7577; Edward L. Forry

Jackson

Bridgeway Center, Inc., 1410 West Ganson Street, Jackson 49202; tel. 517/783-2732; Nancy L. Siegrist

Kalamazoo

Kalamazoo Alcohol & Drug Abuse, 1104 South Westnedge Avenue, Kalamazoo 49008; tel. 616/349-8785; Thomas E. Lucking

Womancare, Inc., 4215 West Main Street, Suite 101, Kalamazoo 49007; tel. 616/388-4477; Judith K. Loudin, M.A.

Lansing

Comprehensive Substance Abuse, 808 Southland, Lansing 48910; tel. 517/393-0150; William Allen

National Council on Alcoholism, 913 W. Holmes, Suite #143, Lansing 48910; tel. 517/482-2028; Stuart C. Lindsay

Lincoln Park

Boniface Community Action Corp., 25050 W. Outer Drive, Suite 201, Lincoln Park 48146; tel. 313/928-8310; Anna L. Wheeler, M.S.W.

Parkside Mental Health, 25700 West Outer Drive, Lincoln Park 48146; tel. 313/386-7810; Marie V. Mayberry, M.A., L.L.P.

Livonia

Community Commission on Health, 13325 Farmington Road, Livonia 48150; tel. 313/261-3760; John Farrar

St. Mary Hospital, 36475 Five Mile Road, Livonia 48154; tel. 313/464-4800; Sister Mary Modesta

Marquette

Marquette General Hospital, 420 W. Magnetic Street, Marquette 49855; tel. 906/228-9440; Robert Neldberg

Project Rehabilitation, 241 Wright Street, Marquette 49855; tel. 906/228-4692; Laurence Ziomkowski

Mason

Sparrow/Fairview Adolescent, 800 East Columbia Avenue, Mason 48854; tel. 517/676-3480; F. Boiten Plasman

Mount Clemens

Catholic Social Services, 235 South Gratiot, Mount Clemens 48043; tel. 313/468-2616; Katherine P. Kenny, A.C.S.W.

Psychiatric Center, 41700 Hayes Road, Mount Clemens 48044; tel. 313/263-0400; Kenneth G. Schooff, M.D.

Mount Pleasant

Mount Pleasant Counseling, 3480 South Isabella Road, Mount Pleasant 48858; tel. 517/773-9655; Marilyn S. Wightman

Owosso

Project Alternative-Counseling, 344½ West Main Street, Owosso 48867; tel. 517/725-8124; Karen L. Arndorfer

Pontiac

Highland Waterford Center, 5770 Highland Road, Pontiac 48054; tel. 313/673-1286; Maurice Kelley

Residents Awareness Program, 1435 North Oakland Blvd., Pontiac 48054; tel. 313/666-2722; Dr. F. Gerald St. Souver

Port Huron

The Center for Human Resources, 1113 Military Street, Port Huron 48060; tel. 313/985-5168; Scott Nill

Rochester

Individual & Group, 139 Walnut, Rochester 48063; tel. 313/652-6133; Gail S. Thomas

Romeo

Community Human Services, Inc., 332 South Main Street, Romeo 48065; tel. 313/752-9696; Patricia A. Gibbs

Royal Oak

Catholic Social Services, 1424 East 11 Mile Road, Royal Oak 48067; tel. 313/548-4044; Margaret A. Huggard, M.S.W.

Saginaw

Insight International, Inc., 1230 S. Washington, Saginaw 48601; tel. 517/755-2173; William Keaton

Tri-County Centers, Inc., 4709 State Street, Saginaw 48603; tel. 517/790-3366; William E. Watters

The substance abuse programs listed have been accredited as of January 1, 1987, by the Joint Commission on Accreditation of Hospitals by decision of the Accreditation Committee of the Board of Commissioners.

The programs listed here have been found to be in substantial compliance with the Joint Commission standards for substance abuse programs, as found in the Consolidated Standards Manual.

Please refer to section A of the AHA Guide for information on hospitals with inpatient and/or outpatient alcohol and chemical dependency services. These hospitals are identified by Approval Codes F48 and F49. In section A, those hospitals identified by Approval Codes 1a and/or 1b are JCAH accredited.

We present this list simply as a convenient directory. Inclusion or omission of any organization's name indicates neither approval nor disapproval by the American Hospital Association.

Southfield

Central Therapeutic Services, 17600 West 8 Mile Rd., Suite #7, Southfield 48075; tel. 313/559-4340; K. G. Thimotheose, Ph.D.

Comprehensive Psychiatric, 21415 Civic Center Drive, Suite 117, Southfield 48076; tel. 313/353-4440; Elliott D. Luby, M.D.

Counseling Associates, 25835 Southfield Road, Suite 101, Southfield 48075; tel. 313/559-0545; Sidney H. Grossberg, Ph.D.

D.I.C. Substance Abuse Services, 20755 Greenfield Road, Southfield 48075; tel. 313/336-2466; Eugene T. Donovan, M.D.

Family Resources, Inc., 28448 Franklin Road, Southfield 48034; tel. 313/354-4580; Charles V. Sears

Innervisions P.C., 26555 Evergreen, Suite 700, Southfield 48076; tel. 313/358-5151; Dr. Newton W. Hoilette

O. Ganesh M.D., P.C., 28165 Greenfield, Southfield 48076; tel. 313/569-6642; Orekonde Ganesh, M.D.

Sturgis

Substance Abuse Council, 900 Myrtle Ave., Sturgis 49091; tel. 616/651-5481; Donald H. Raiche

Taylor

Community Care Services, 8750 Telegraph Rd., Suite 300, Taylor 48180; tel. 313/287-6993; William P. Walsh

Traverse City

Northwestern Michigan Alcoholic, 116 E. Eighth Street, Traverse City 49684; tel. 616/941-2252; David N. Abeel, M.S.W.

Trenton

Seaway Hospital Unit of P.C.N.A., 5450 Fort, Trenton 48183; tel. 313/671-3802; Edward V. Slingerland

Troy

Consortium for Human Services, 755 W. Big Beaver Rd., Suite 2019, Troy 48084; tel. 313/362-4333; James A. Evans

Perspectives of Troy, P.C., 1615 West Big Beaver Rd., Troy 48084; tel. 313/643-0200; Vera A. Sekulov, Ph.D.

Woodland Hills Center, 755 West Big Beaver Rd., Suite 2009, Troy 48084; tel. 313/362-2610; Virginia Jones

Warren

Substance Abuse Center, 29600 Civic Center Blvd., Warren 48081; tel. 313/573-7583; Diane E. Raab

Minnesota

Blaine

Anthony Louis Center, 1000 Paul Parkway, Blaine 55434; tel. 612/757-2906; Jon D. Benson

Brainerd

Brainerd Regional Human, 1777 Highway, 18 East, Brainerd 56401; tel. 218/828-2201; Armond D'Arcangelo, Jr.

Center City

Hazelden Foundation, 15425 Pleasant Valley Road, Center City 55012; tel. 612/257-4010; Harold A. Swift

Fergus Falls

Fergus Falls State Hospital, First & Union Avenues, Fergus Falls 56537; tel. 218/739-7259; O. John Bloom

Minneapolis

Abbott-Northwestern Hospital, 800 E. 28th Street at Chicago Ave., Minneapolis 55407; tel. 612/874-4000; Gordon M. Sprenger

Irene Whitney Center, 4954 Upton Avenue, South, Minneapolis 55410; tel. 612/347-4444; Betty Trivlieai

St. Mary's Hospital, 2414 South Seventh Street, Minneapolis 55454; tel. 612/338-2229; Francis Wiesner

A.R.C.-Parkview Adult, 3705 Park Center Boulevard, Minneapolis 55416; tel. 612/929-5531; John W. Hagen

Minnetonka

Omegon, Inc., 2000 Hopkins Crossroads, Minnetonka 55343; tel. 612/541-4738; Nancy Rosendahl

Moose Lake

Moose Lake Regional Treatment Center, 100 Lakeshore Drive, Moose Lake 55767; tel. 218/485-4411; Frank R. Milczark

Rochester

The Gables, 604-5 Street, Southwest, Rochester 55902; tel. 507/282-2500; Mary Keyes

St. Paul

New Connection Programs, 73 Leech Street, St. Paul 55102; tel. 612/224-4384; William J. Payne

St. Peter

St. Peter Regional Treatment, 100 Freeman Drive, St. Peter 56082; tel. 507/931-7115; Joseph W. Solien

Stillwater

Jamestown, 11550 Jasmine Trail North, Stillwater 55082; tel. 612/429-5307; Carol K. Frisch

Waverly

New Beginnings/Maryville, Route 1, Waverly 55390; tel. 612/658-4811; Gil Gilchrist

Willmar

Willmar Regional Treatment, North Highway 71, Box 1128, Willmar 56201; tel. 612/231-5100; Gregory G. Spartz

Mississippi

Biloxi

Bienville Recovery Center, 401 East Beach Drive, Biloxi 39533; tel. 601/374-2500; Doyle P. Smith, M.D.

Gulf Oaks Hospital and Clinic, 4645 West Beach Blvd., Biloxi 39531; tel. 601/388-0650; Theodore S. Johnson

Gulfport

C.P.C. Sand Hill Hospital, 12222 Highway 49 North, Gulfport 39503; tel. 601/831-1700; Chuck Lecluyse

Missouri

Boonville

Valley Hope Alcoholism, Ashely Road, Boonville 65233; tel. 816/882-6547; William D. Leipold, Ph.D.

Columbia

Mid-Missouri Mental Health, Three Hospital Drive, Columbia 65201; tel. 314/449-2511; A. E. Daniel, M.D.

Ellisville

Horizon Hospital, 1033 Manchester Road, Ellisville 63011; tel. 314/227-4400; Vernon Westrich

Florissant

Christian Hospital Northwest, 1225 Graham Road, Florissant 63031; tel. 314/839-3800; Fred L. Brown

Independence

Comprehensive Mental Health, 10901 Winner Rd., Independence 64052; tel. 816/254-3652; William H. Kyles

Jefferson City

Whispering Oaks Hospital, 1314 West Edgewood Drive, Jefferson City 65102; tel. 314/634-5000; George L. Faler, Jr.

Kansas City

Baptist Medical Center, 6601 Rockhill Road, Kansas City 64131; tel. 816/361-3500; Dan H. Anderson

Community Addictions Programs, 616 E. 63rd Street, Kansas City 64110; tel. 816/333-3440; Diane J. Mnookin

Industrial Rehabilitation, 5811 Truman Road, Kansas City 64108; tel. 816/231-4357; Maurice L. Cummings

Research Psychiatric Center, 2333 East 63rd Street, Kansas City 64132; tel. 816/444-8161; Gail M. Oberta

Lonedell

Koala Center, Highway FF & Mountain Road, Lonedell 63060; tel. 314/629-5100; Michael Gardine

St. Charles

C.P.C. Weldon Spring Hospital, 5931 Highway 94 South, St. Charles 63301; tel. 314/441-7300; Alan Barry, Ph.D.

St. Louis

Behavioral Health Systems, Inc., 5615 Pershing Avenue, Suite 12, St. Louis 63112; tel. 314/727-1666; William W. Clendenin

Care Unit Hospital, 1755 S. Grand Boulevard, St. Louis 63104; tel. 314/771-0500; Vincent B. Sullian

Family/Childrens Services, 2650 Olive Street, St. Louis 63103; tel. 314/521-6464; Paul K. Reed

Parkside Lodge of St. Louis, Inc., 4201 McKibbon Rd., St. Louis 63134; tel. 314/428-4201; Matt McCourt

St. John's Mercy Medical Center, 615 South New Ballas Rd., St. Louis 63141; tel. 314/569-6000; Charles E. Thoele

The substance abuse programs listed have been accredited as of January 1, 1987, by the Joint Commission on Accreditation of Hospitals by decision of the Accreditation Committee of the Board of Commissioners.

The programs listed here have been found to be in substantial compliance with the Joint Commission standards for substance abuse programs, as found in the Consolidated Standards Manual.

Please refer to section A of the AHA Guide *for information on hospitals with inpatient and/or outpatient alcohol and chemical dependency services. These hospitals are identified by Approval Codes F48 and F49. In section A, those hospitals identified by Approval Codes 1a and/or 1b are JCAH accredited.*

We present this list simply as a convenient directory. Inclusion or omission of any organization's name indicates neither approval nor disapproval by the American Hospital Association.

Montana

Billings

Rimrock Foundation, 1231 North 29th, Billings 59107; tel. 406/248-3175; David W. Cunningham

Nebraska

Grand Island

Grand Island Memorial Hospital, 640 North Darr, Grand Island 68801; tel. 308/382-3170; Kenneth Klaasmeyer

O'Neill

Valley Hope Alcoholism, North 10th Street, O'Neill 68763; tel. 402/336-3747; William D. Leipold, Ph.D.

Omaha

Lutheran Medical Center, 515 South 26th Street, Omaha 68103; tel. 402/536-6660; Sandra C. Carson

Nevada

Las Vegas

Care-Unit Hospital of Nevada, 5100 West Sahara, Las Vegas 89102; tel. 702/362-8404; Manley W. Jones

Montevista Centre, 5900 W. Rochelle Avenue, Las Vegas 89126; tel. 702/368-0878; James T. Harper

Reno

Reno Professional Counseling, 400 South Wells, Reno 89502; tel. 702/322-2333; William E. Thornton, M.D.

Truckee Meadows Hospital, 1240 East Ninth Street, Reno 89512; tel. 702/323-0478; Laura J. Thomas

Sparks

Truckee Meadows Hospital-North, 2100 El Rancho Drive, Sparks 89431; tel. 702/323-0478; Laura J. Thomas

New Hampshire

Dover

Seaborne Hospital, Seaborne Drive, Dover 03820; tel. 603/742-9300; Albert C. Charest

Dublin

Beech Hill Hospital, Old Harrisville Rd., Dublin 03444; tel. 603/563-8511; John H. Valentine

Nashua

Nashua Brookside Hospital, 11 Northwest Blvd., Nashua 03063; tel. 603/886-5000; Kenneth F. Courage, Jr.

Spofford

Spofford Hall, Route 9-A, Spofford 03462; tel. 603/363-4545; William Hawthorne, M.D.

New Jersey

Blairstown

The Little Hill Foundation, Ward Road, Blairstown 07825; tel. 201/362-6114; Geraldine O. Delaney

Hammonton

Ancora Psychiatric Hospital, Hammonton 08037; tel. 609/561-1700; Marlene Lopez

Hoboken

The Harbor, 1405 Clinton Street, Hoboken 07030; tel. 201/656-4040; John J. Clancy

Lafayette

Sunrise House Foundation, Inc., Sunset Inn Road, Lafayette 07848; tel. 201/383-6300; Frank L. Clisham

Lakehurst

New Beginnings-Lakehurst, 440 Beckerville Rd., Lakehurst 08733; tel. 201/657-4800; Charles Ward, Sr., C.A.C.

Lakeland

Camden County Center, Collier Dr., Lakeland 08012; tel. 609/228-4200; Michael De Filippo

Long Branch

Monmouth Chemical Dependency, 152 Chelsea Avenue, Long Branch 07740; tel. 201/222-5190; William R. Stender

Lyons

V.A. Medical Center/Lyons, Lyons 07939; tel. 201/647-0180; A. Paul Kidd

Morristown

Parkside Lodge of New Jersey, East Second and Pancoast Ave., Morristown 08057; tel. 609/235-7900; James W. Philbrick

Center for Addictive, 95 Mount Kemble Ave., Morristown 07960; tel. 201/285-4700; Arthur S. McLellan, M.D.

Passaic

Passaic Alcoholism Rehab., 70 Parker Avenue, Passaic 07055; tel. 201/472-0364; Lila E. White

Rancocas

Hampton Hospital, Rancocas Road & 1295, Rancocas 08073; tel. 609/267-7000; Marc Lazarius

Seabrook

Seabrook House, Inc., Polk Lane, Seabrook 08302; tel. 609/455-7575; Jerome J. Diehl, F.A.C.A.T.A.

Stirling

Honesty House, 1272 Long Hill Road, Stirling 07980; tel. 201/647-3211; Vale C. Betts, C.A.C.

Summit

Fair Oaks Hospital, 19 Prospect Street, Summit 07901; tel. 201/277-0143; William A. Howe

New Mexico

Albuquerque

Care-Unit Hospital, 505 High Street, N.E., Albuquerque 87102; tel. 505/848-8088; Judith A. Blanch

Vista Sandia Hospital, 501 Alameda Blvd., N.E., Albuquerque 87113; tel. 505/823-2000; Audrey Worell, M.D.

Santa Fe

Pinon Hills Hospital, 313 Camino Alire, Santa Fe 87501; tel. 505/988-8003; Fred Kotzen, Ph.D.

New York

Albany

Hope House, Inc., 261 North Pearl Street, Albany 12207; tel. 518/465-7879; Lewis F. Krupka

St. Peter's Hospital, 315 South Manning Boulevard, Albany 12208; tel. 518/454-1550; Sister Ellen Lawlor

Bronx

Bronx Alcoholism Treatment Center, 1500 Waters Place, Bronx 10461; tel. 212/931-0600; Ronald B. Lonesome, M.D.

Brooklyn

Kings County Hospital Center, 451 Clarkson Avenue, Brooklyn 11203; tel. 718/735-3131; Ira C. Clark

Buffalo

Bry-Lin Hospitals, Inc., 1263 Delaware Ave., Buffalo 14209; tel. 716/886-8200; Leonard Pleskow

Stutzman Alcoholism Treatment, 360 Forest Avenue, Buffalo 14213; tel. 716/882-4900; Clifton Hutcherson

Carmel

Arms Acres, Inc., Seminary Hill Rd., Carmel 10512; tel. 914/225-3400; Mark Schottinger, M.A.

Freeport

Freeport Hospital, 267 South Ocean Avenue, Freeport 11520; tel. 516/378-0800; James Heckler

Glen Oaks

Hillside Hospital, 75-59 263rd Street, Glen Oaks 11004; tel. 718/470-8000; Robert K. Match, M.D.

Middletown

Middletown Alcoholism, 141 Monahagen Avenue, Middletown 10940; tel. 914/342-5511; Richard C. Ward

New York

Gracie Square Hospital, 420 East 76th Street, New York 10021; tel. 212/988-4400; Robert J. Campbell, M.D.

Manhattan Alcoholism Treatment, 600 E. 125th Street, Ward's Island, New York 10035; tel. 212/369-0703; K. Santiago-Vazques, M.P.S., R.N.

Mount Sinai Hospital, One Gustave Levy Place, New York 10029; 212/650-6500; Barry Freedman

Postgraduate Center for M.H., 124 East 28th Street, New York 10016; tel. 212/689-7700; Harry Sands, Ph.D.

Orangeburg

Russell E. Blaisdell, R.P.C. Campus, Orangeburg 10962; tel. 914/359-8500; Louis R. Brandes, M.D.

Poughkeepsie

Dutchess County Department, 230 North Road, Poughkeepsie 12601; tel. 914/485-9700; Kenneth M. Glatt, Ph.D.

Queens Village

Creedmoor Alcoholism Treatment Center, 80-45 Winchester Boulevard, Queens Village 11427; tel. 718/464-7500; Jose Sarabia

The substance abuse programs listed have been accredited as of January 1, 1987, by the Joint Commission on Accreditation of Hospitals by decision of the Accreditation Committee of the Board of Commissioners.

The programs listed here have been found to be in substantial compliance with the Joint Commission standards for substance abuse programs, as found in the Consolidated Standards Manual.

Please refer to section A of the AHA Guide *for information on hospitals with inpatient and/or outpatient alcohol and chemical dependency services. These hospitals are identified by Approval Codes F48 and F49. In section A, those hospitals identified by Approval Codes 1a and/or 1b are JCAH accredited.*

We present this list simply as a convenient directory. Inclusion or omission of any organization's name indicates neither approval nor disapproval by the American Hospital Association.

Rhinebeck

Rhinebeck Lodge, RD #1 Milan Hollow Road, Rhinebeck 12572; tel. 914/266-3481; Irwin Scheintaub, C.S.W.

Rochester

Alcoholism Treatment Facility, 435 East Henrietta Road, Rochester 14620; tel. 716/461-4114; J. Claude Curtin, Ph.D.

J. L. Norris Alcoholism, 1600 South Avenue, Rochester 14620; tel. 716/461-0410; Alice McDowell

Park Ridge Chemical Dependency, 1565 Long Pond Road, Rochester 14626; tel. 716/227-6505; Patrick J. Madden

Scotia

Conifer Park, Inc., 150 Glenridge Road, Scotia 12302; tel. 518/399-6446; Gail W. Harkness

Syracuse

Syracuse Brick House, 121 Green Street, Syracuse 13203; tel. 315/463-0330; Jerome P. Gilbert

Valhalla

Westchester County Medical, Grasslands Reservation, Valhalla 10595; tel. 914/347-7017; Bernard M. Weinstein

Westhampton Beach

Seafield Center, Inc., #7 Seafield Lane, Westhampton Beach 11978; tel. 516/288-1122; George W. Benedict

North Carolina

Asheville

Highland Hospital, 49 Zillicoa Street, Asheville 28801; tel. 704/254-3201; Jack W. Bonner III, M.D.

Black Mountain

Alcoholic Rehabilitation Center, Old U.S. Highway 70, Black Mountain 28711; tel. 704/669-3417; Arthur Friedman

Brevard

Transylvania Community Center, 4 Lane Asheville Hwy., Brevard 28712; tel. 704/884-9111; Robert Purcell, Sr.

Butner

North Carolina Alcoholic Center, West "E" Street, Butner 27509; tel. 919/575-7928; Robert L. Baucom, M.D.

Charlotte

Charlotte Treatment Center, 1715 Sharon Road West, Charlotte 28224; tel. 704/554-8373; James F. Emmert

Durham

Durham County General Hospital, 3643 North Roxboro Street, Durham 27704; tel. 919/471-3411; Ralph E. Jennings

Greensboro

Fellowship Hall, Inc., Hwy. 29 N. Hicone Rd. Exit, Greensboro 27415; tel. 919/621-3381; Edward C. McMillan

Greenville

W. B. Jones Alcohol Rehab. Center, Route 1, Greenville 27834; tel. 919/758-3151; Thomas L. Reece

Pineville

C.P.C. Cedar Spring Hospital, 19600 Pineville-Matthews Road, Pineville 28134; tel. 714/541-6676; Ervin M. Funderburk, Jr.

Raleigh

Charter Northridge Hospital, 400 Newton Road, Raleigh 27609; tel. 919/847-0008; D. Tony Mobley

North Dakota

Jamestown

North Dakota State Hospital, S.E. of City, Jamestown 58401; tel. 701/252-7733; R. A. Aligada, M.D.

Mandan

Heartview Foundation, 2nd Street, N.W., Mandan 58554; tel. 701/663-2321; Will O. Wells

Ohio

Akron

Interval Brotherhood Home, Inc., 3445 South Main Street, Akron 44319; tel. 216/644-4095; Father Samuel R. Ciccolini

Summit County Community Drug, 513 W. Market St., Suite 1, Akron 44303; tel. 216/434-4141; Theodore Paul Zielgler

Ashtabula

Lake Area Recovery Center, 2801 C. Court, Ashtabula 44004; tel. 216/992-4432; Kathleen Kinney

Canton

Alcohol & Drug Assistance, 1341 Market Avenue, North, Canton 44714; tel. 216/453-8252; Douglas E. Harton

Crisis Intervention Center, 2421 13th Street, N.W., Canton 44708; tel. 216/452-9812; Lori S. Lapp, M.B.A.

Cincinnati

Care Unit Hospital of Cincinnati, 3156 Glenmore Ave., Cincinnati 45211; tel. 513/481-8822; Larry J. Burge

Center for Comprehensive Health, 830 Ezzard Charles Rd., Cincinnati 45214; tel. 513/381-6660; Don Turner

Eden Treatment Center, 206 William Howard Taft Road, Cincinnati 45219; tel. 513/751-3364; Pamela Babcock

Emerson A. North Hospital, 5642 Hamilton Avenue, Cincinnati 45224; tel. 513/541-0135; Marvin E. Phelps

St. Francis-St. George Alcohol, 2852 Boudinot Avenue, Cincinnati 45238; tel. 513/389-5329; William M. Copeland

Cleveland

Alcoholism Services, 3030 Euclid Avenue, Cleveland 44115; tel. 216/391-2300; Myrtle I. Muntz

Glenbeigh Hospital/Cleveland, 18120 Puritas Avenue, Cleveland 44135; tel. 216/476-0222; T. R. Sucher III

Glenwillow

New Directions, Inc., 30245 Pettibone Road, Glenwillow 44139; tel. 216/439-8366; Nikki Babbit, Ph.D.

Mansfield

Richland Hospital, 1451 Lucas Road, Mansfield 44901; tel. 419/589-5511; S. J. Cocuzza

Marysville

Charles B. Mills Center, 715 South Plum Street, Marysville 43040; tel. 513/644-9192; Mary K. Reynolds, A.C.S.W.

Newark

Shepherd Hill, 200 Messimer Drive, Newark 43055; tel. 614/522-8484; Donald H. Boyanowski

Portsmouth

Southern Hills Hospital, 727 8th Street, Portsmouth 45662; tel. 614/354-8651; Earl L. McLane

Rock Creek

Glenbeigh Hospital, Rte. 45, Rock Creek 44084; tel. 216/563-3400; Kenneth C. McArthur

Sandusky

Tri-County Addictions Center, 2020 Hayes Avenue, Sandusky 44870; tel. 419/625-7262; Shirley Gahr

Sylvania

Flower Hospital, 5200 Harroun Rd., Sylvania 43560; tel. 419/885-1444; Dale D. Stoll

Toledo

St. Vincent Medical Center, 2213 Cherry Street, Toledo 43608; tel. 419/259-4098; Allen Johnson

Toledo Hospital, 2124 N. Cove Blvd., Toledo 43606; tel. 419/473-4218; Bryan A. Rogers

Troy

Dettmer Hospital, 3130 North Dixie Highway, Troy 45373; tel. 513/335-7166; Charles H. Bair

Vandalia

Serenity Living, 716 South Dixie Drive, Vandalia 45377; tel. 513/890-2056; Joseph J. Trevino, M.D., C.A.C.

Warren

Chemical Awareness, 1353 East Market, Warren 44483; tel. 216/399-3677; Joseph Sylvester

Trumbull Co. Council, 1296 Tod Place, N.W., Warren 44485; tel. 216/392-2561; Edward M. Mink

Westerville

The Campus, 905 South Sunbury Road, Westerville 43081; tel. 614/895-1000; James Ignelzi

Willoughby

Ridgecliff Hospital, 35900 Euclid Avenue, Willoughby 44094; tel. 216/951-1177; Irene A. Keal, Ph.D.

Xenia

Greene Hall, 1141 N. Monroe Drive, Xenia 45385; tel. 513/372-8011; Herman N. Menapace

Youngstown

Alcoholic Clinic of Youngstown, 2151 Rush Blvd., Youngstown 44507; tel. 216/744-1181; Gerald V. Carter

Psychiatric Care, Inc., 540 Parmalee Ave., Suite 500, Youngstown 44510; tel. 216/747-3126; Douglas C. Darnall, Ph.D.

The substance abuse programs listed have been accredited as of January 1, 1987, by the Joint Commission on Accreditation of Hospitals by decision of the Accreditation Committee of the Board of Commissioners.

The programs listed here have been found to be in substantial compliance with the Joint Commission standards for substance abuse programs, as found in the Consolidated Standards Manual.

Please refer to section A of the AHA Guide *for information on hospitals with inpatient and/or outpatient alcohol and chemical dependency services. These hospitals are identified by Approval Codes F48 and F49. In section A, those hospitals identified by Approval Codes 1a and/or 1b are JCAH accredited.*

We present this list simply as a convenient directory. Inclusion or omission of any organization's name indicates neither approval nor disapproval by the American Hospital Association.

Oklahoma

Broken Arrow

Country View, 12300 E. 91st Street, Broken Arrow 74012; tel. 918/252-2541; William R. Reid, M.D.

Cushing

Valley Hope Alcoholism, 100 South Jones, Cushing 74023; tel. 918/225-1736; William R. Leipold

Fort Supply

Western State Hospital, 1 Mile East on Highway 27, Fort Supply 73841; tel. 405/766-2311; James B. Shackelford, M.D.

Lawton

Great Plains Hospital; 1601 Southwest 82nd, Lawton 73505; tel. 415/248-0580; Bill Vickers

Oklahoma City

Presbyterian Hospital, 700 N.W. Seventh Street, Oklahoma City 73102; tel. 405/271-4119; Harry M. Neer

V.A. Medical Center Oklahoma, 921 Northeast 13th Street, Oklahoma City 73104; tel. 405/272-9876; John H. Steward

Shawnee

Greenleaf Center, Inc., 1601 Gordon Cooper Drive, Shawnee 74801; tel. 405/275-9610; Joel O. Montgomery

Tulsa

Brookhaven Hospital, 201 South Garnett, Tulsa 74128; tel. 918/438-4257; Marilyn Fowler

Parkside Center, 1620 East 12th Street, Tulsa 74120; tel. 918/582-2131; William T. Duncan

Shadow Mountain Institute, 6262 South Sheridan, Tulsa 74133; tel. 918/492-8200; Donald E. Carlson

Oregon

Eugene

Serenity Lane, Inc., 616 E. 16th, Eugene 97401; tel. 403/687-1110; Neil McNaughton

Gresham

Mount Hood Medical Center, 24700 S.E. Stark, Gresham 97030; tel. 503/667-1122; Joseph J. Henery

Riverside Hospital-East, 4101 N.E. Division Street, Gresham 97030; tel. 503/661-0775; Richard Kolbell

Roseburg

V.A. Roseburg Hospital, Roseburg 97470; tel. 503/378-2374; T. Kaye Miyamoto

Salem

Oregon State Hospital, 2600 Center St., N.E., Salem 97310; tel. 503/378-2348; Robert J. Benning, M.S.W.

Pennsylvania

Allenwood

Koala Center, Allenwood 17810; tel. 717/538-2567; Neil Murphy, C.A.C.

Bensalem

Livengrin Foundation, Inc., 4833 Hulmeville Rd., Bensalem 19020; tel. 215/639-2300; Carl W. Illenberger

Blossburg

Endless Mountains Treatment, 520 Ruah Street, Blossburg 16912; tel. 717/638-2948; Frank Tripoli

Centre Hall

Meadows Psychiatric Center, Road #1, Centre Hall 16828; tel. 814/364-2161; James G. Dalzell, M.H.A.

Chester

U.H.S. Keystone Center, 2001 Providence Road, Chester 19013; tel. 215/876-9000; Marcia N. Carlisle

Drexel Hill

Mirmont Alcoholism Treatment, 100 Yearsley Mill Road, Drexel Hill 19037; tel. 215/565-9232; Thomas F. Crane

Eagleville

Eagleville Hospital, 100 Eagleville Road, Eagleville 19408; tel. 215/539-6000; Martha L. Waters

East Stroudsburg

College Hill Medical Center, 329 East Brown Street, East Stroudsburg 18301; tel. 717/421-3740; Richard A. Gale, Sr.

Ephrata

ARC/The Terraces, 1170 South State Street, Ephrata 17522; tel. 717/627-0790; James M. Norton

Erie

Serenity Hall, Inc., 414 West 5th Street, Erie 16507; tel. 814/459-4775; Suzanne C. Mack

Harrisburg

Gaudenzia Common Ground, 2835 North Front Street, Harrisburg 17110; tel. 717/238-5553; Penelope Grodenchik

Hummelstown

Talbot Place, Ltd., Nye Road, Hummelstown 17036; tel. 717/533-8500; Frank J. Deflavia

Kennett Square

Bowling Green Inn-Brandywine, 495 Newark Road, Kennett Square 19348; tel. 215/268-3588; Jeffrey J. Kegley, M.S.W., F.A.C.A.T.A.

Lafayette Hill

Eugenia Hospital, 660 Thomas Road, Lafayette Hill 19444; tel. 215/836-1380; Eugene Wayne

Malvern

Malvern Institute, 940 King Road, Malvern 19355; tel. 215/647-0330; Joseph J. Driscoll, C.A.C., M.B.A.

Norristown

Valley Forge Medical Center, 1033 W. German Town Pike, Norristown 19401; tel. 215/539-8500; Alice K. Hand

Philadelphia

Bridge Therapeutic Center, 8400 Pine Road, Philadelphia 19111; tel. 215/342-5000; John J. Toto

The Fairmount Institute, 561 Fairthorne Ave., Philadelphia 19128; tel. 215/487-4000; Eugene C. Wayne

Pittsburgh

Brighton Woods Treatment Center, 3530 Fleming Avenue, Pittsburgh 15212; tel. 412/734-1010; Gerald F. Vozel

Pottsville

Good Samaritan Hospital, E. Norwegian & Tremont Streets, Pottsville 17901; tel. 717/621-4000; Frederick J. Siembieda

Shippensburg

Roxbury, 601 Roxbury Road, Shippensburg 17257; tel. 717/532-4217; Claire F. Beckwith

Somerset

Twin Lakes Center for Drug, RD #7, Somerset 15501; tel. 814/443-3639; Mark T. Pile, A.C.S.W.

Washington

Greenbriar Treatment Center, 800 Manor Drive, Washington 15301; tel. 412/225-9700; James Vernarsky

Wernersville

Caron Rehabilitation Hospitals, Galen Hall Road, Wernersville 19565; tel. 215/678-2332; Leo C. McLaughlin

Wilkes-Barre

Clear Brook, Inc., Road 10 East Northhampton Street, Wilkes-Barre 18702; tel. 717/823-1171; David Lombard, C.A.C.

Williamsburg

New Beginnings at Cove Forge, RD #1, Williamsburg 16693; tel. 814/832-2131; George Obermeir

Wrightsville

Riverview, Inc., RD #2, Wrightsville 17368; tel. 717/252-3631; Jurgen H. Schwermen

York

York Alcohol & Drug Services, 40 North George Street, York 17401; tel. 717/854-9591; Janice L. Klein, A.C.S.W.

Rhode Island

North Kingstown

High Point Alcoholism, Tower Hill Road, North Kingstown 02852; tel. 401/295-2511; Edward T. Lees, Ph.D.

Greenwich

Good Hope Center, John Potter Road, W. Greenwich 02816; tel. 401/397-5029; Alan Willoughby

South Carolina

Charleston

V.A. Medical Center, 109 Bee Street, Charleston 29403; tel. 803/577-5011; J. Fred Hoefer, Jr.

Johns Island

New Beginnings at Fenwick, 1709 River Road, Johns Island 29455; tel. 803/559-2461; John H. Magill

The substance abuse programs listed have been accredited as of January 1, 1987, by the Joint Commission on Accreditation of Hospitals by decision of the Accreditation Committee of the Board of Commissioners.

The programs listed here have been found to be in substantial compliance with the Joint Commission standards for substance abuse programs, as found in the Consolidated Standards Manual.

Please refer to section A of the AHA Guide for information on hospitals with inpatient and/or outpatient alcohol and chemical dependency services. These hospitals are identified by Approval Codes F48 and F49. In section A, those hospitals identified by Approval Codes 1a and/or 1b are JCAH accredited.

We present this list simply as a convenient directory. Inclusion or omission of any organization's name indicates neither approval nor disapproval by the American Hospital Association.

South Dakota

Canton

Keystone Treatment Center, 1010 East 2nd Street, Canton 57013; tel. 605/987-2751; Mitzi Carroll

Hot Springs

V.A. Medical Center, Hot Springs 57747; tel. 605/745-4101; Thomas F. Wheaton

Sioux Falls

River Park Lodge, 4201 South Minnesota Avenue, Sioux Falls 57105; tel. 605/331-2000; Glenn Jorgenson

Tennessee

Chattanooga

Council for Alcohol & Drug, 207 Spears Avenue, Chattanooga 37405; tel. 615/756-7644; Euel R. Mahoney

The Crossroads, 7444 Min Tom Drive, Chattanooga 37421; tel. 615/899-5400; W. Kenneth Helton

Harrison

Addiction Recovery, 8614 Harrison Bay Road, Harrison 37341; tel. 615/344-3737; Vernon Westrich

Johnson City

Watauga Area Mental Health, 109 West Watauga Avenue, Johnson City 37601; tel. 615/928-6545; G. Robert Owens

Louisville

Peninsula Psychiatric Center, Jones Bend Road, Louisville 37777; tel. 615/970-9800; William C. Greer

Memphis

Charter Lakeside Hospital, 2911 Brunswick Road, Memphis 38134; tel. 901/377-4700; Charles E. Smith

Memphis Mental Health, 865 Poplar Avenue, Memphis 38104; tel. 901/524-1200; Robert D. Fink, M.D.

Methodist Outreach, Inc., 2009 Lamar Avenue, Memphis 38114; tel. 901/276-5401; Janet A. Kirk

Mid-South & Germantown Commission, 135 N. Pauline Street, Memphis 38105; tel. 901/527-5211; Jack G. Olpin

Rivendell Clinic, 210 Jackson, Suite 401, Memphis 38105; tel. 901/527-6035; F. A. Steinberg, Ph.D.

St. Francis Hospital, Inc., 5959 Park Avenue, Memphis 38119; tel. 901/765-1800; M. Rita Schroeder

Nashville

Cumberland Heights, RTE. 2 River Rd., Nashville 37209; tel. 615/352-1757; Jacob K. Albright, Jr.

H.C.A. Park View Medical Center, 2401 Murphy Avenue, Nashville 37203; tel. 615/327-2237; Ernest Bacon

Hubbard Hospital, 1005 Dr. D.B. Todd Blvd., Nashville 37208; tel. 615/327-6111; Dr. Andre L. Lee, D.P.A., F.A.C.H.A.

Koala Adolescent Center, 1220 8th Avenue, South, Nashville 37203; tel. 615/726-1337; Zachary Nelson

Samaritans, Inc., 319 South 4th Street, Nashville 37206; tel. 615/244-4802; Cecilia Mynatt

Oak Ridge

Ridgeview Psychiatric Hospital, 240 W. Tyrone Road, Oak Ridge 37830; tel. 615/482-1076; Ben Bursten, M.D.

Texas

Abilene

Woods Psychiatric Institute; 4225 Woods Place, Abilene 79602; tel. 915/698-2320; David Brown

Argyle

Baylor-Parkside Lodge, Route 1, Argyle 76226; tel. 817/455-2201; Will O. Wells

Arlington

C.P.C. Millwood Hospital, 1011 North Cooper Street, Arlington 76011; tel. 817/261-3121; Harry G. Harrier

Austin

Austin State Hospital, 4110 Guadalupe, Austin 78751; tel. 512/452-0381; H. K. Dudley, Jr.

Parkside Lodge of Austin, 1900 Rio Grande, Austin 78705; tel. 512/482-0075; Obed Nelson

Shoal Creek Hospital, 3501 Mills Ave., Austin 78731; tel. 512/452-0361; R. D. Jones, Jr.

Beaumont

M.H.M.R. of Southeast Texas, 2750 South Eighth Street, Beaumont 77701; tel. 409/838-3003; Roger Pricer, Ph.D.

Big Spring

Big Spring State Hospital, Lamesa Highway, Big Spring 79720; tel. 915/267-8216; A. K. Smith, M.S.H.A.

Center Point

Starlite Village Hospital, Elm Pass Road, Center Point 78010; tel. 512/634-2212; Annabelle Lindner, A.R.T.

Corpus Christi

Bayview A. Psychiatric, 6629 Wooldridge Road, Corpus Christi 78415; tel. 512/993-9700; Sally A. Reagan, Ph.D.

Chemical Dependency Unit, 5517 South Alameda Avenue, Corpus Christi 78412; tel. 512/993-6100; E. P. Williams III, M.D.

Denton

Brookwood Recovery Center, 4601 Interstate 35 North, Denton 76201; tel. 817/565-8100; John Saylor

El Paso

Sun Valley Regional Hospital, 1155 Idaho Street, El Paso 79902; tel. 915/544-4000; Robert Thackston

Houston

Group Plan Clinic/New Spirit, 5005 Woodway Suite 200, Houston 77056; tel. 713/871-0855; Thomas A. Blocker, M.D.

Houston Partial Hospital, 4101 Greenbriar Drive, Suite 240, Houston 77098; tel. 713/529-4350; Harry K. Scharold

Spring Shadows Glen, 2801 Gessner, Houston 77080; tel. 713/462-4200; G. Jerry Mueck

West Oak Psychiatric, 6500 Hornwood, Houston 77074; tel. 713/995-0909; Kay Ellen Peck

Westheimer Psychiatric Day, 5050 Westheimer, Suite 407, Houston 77056; tel. 713/877-8007; Peyton L. Thompson

Hunt

La Hacienda Treatment Center, FM 1340, Hunt 78024; tel. 512/238-4222; John Lacey

Kerrville

Kerrville State Hospital, 721 Thompson Drive, Kerrville 78029; tel. 512/896-2211; Luther W. Ross, M.D.

Liverpool

Parkside Lodge of Chocolate, 638 Harbor Road, Liverpool 77577; tel. 713/393-2023; Don L. Devens

Longview

Meadow Pines Hospital, 22 Bermuda Lane, Longview 75601; tel. 817/274-1366; William E. Stiner

McAllen

Charter Palms Hospital, 1421 East Jackson, McAllen 78502; tel. 512/631-5421; Allan Cross

Midland

Clearview Hospital, 200 South County Road 1233, Midland 79707; tel. 915/697-5200; Philip H. Lundberg

Rosenberg

Orchard Creek Hospital, Rosenberg 77471; tel. 713/342-0010; Jerry C. Wilson

Rusk

Rusk State Hospital, Highway 69, North, Rusk 75785; tel. 214/683-3490; John V. White, M.D.

San Antonio

Brookwood Recovery Center, 14747 Jones Maltsberger Road, San Antonio 78247; tel. 205/877-1835; Kevin G. Cedergren

Colonial Hills Hospital, 4330 Vance Jackson Road, San Antonio 78230; tel. 512/341-5131; James M. Hunt

Patrician Movement, 222 E. Mitchell, San Antonio 78210; tel. 512/532-3126; Rev. Msgr. Dermot N. Brosnan

Temple

V.A. Medical Center, 1901 S. 1st Street, Temple 76501; tel. 817/778-4811; E. A. Borrell

Terrell

Terrell State Hospital, East Brin, Terrell 75160; tel. 214/563-6452; Don A. Gilbert

Tyler

University Park Hospital, 4101 University Boulevard, Tyler 75701; tel. 214/566-8666; Gary Stokes

Vernon

Vernon Center, Highway 70 West, Vernon 76384; tel. 817/552-9901; Jack Barthold

Waco

Brazos Psychiatric Hospital, Waco 76702; tel. 817/772-3500; James L. Legge

V.A. Medical Center, Memorial Drive, Waco 76703; tel. 817/752-6581; Irvin Knoll

Wichita Falls

Red River Hospital, 1505 8th Street, Wichita Falls 76301; tel. 817/322-3171; Thomas L. Ryba

The substance abuse programs listed have been accredited as of January 1, 1987, by the Joint Commission on Accreditation of Hospitals by decision of the Accreditation Committee of the Board of Commissioners.

The programs listed here have been found to be in substantial compliance with the Joint Commission standards for substance abuse programs, as found in the Consolidated Standards Manual.

Please refer to section A of the AHA Guide *for information on hospitals with inpatient and/or outpatient alcohol and chemical dependency services. These hospitals are identified by Approval Codes F48 and F49. In section A, those hospitals identified by Approval Codes 1a and/or 1b are JCAH accredited.*

We present this list simply as a convenient directory. Inclusion or omission of any organization's name indicates neither approval nor disapproval by the American Hospital Association.

Wichita Falls State Hospital, Lake Road, Wichita Falls 76307; tel. 817/692-1220; Richard M. Bruner

Wilmer

Parkside Lodges of Texas, 200 Green Road, Wilmer 75171; tel. 214/988-1503; Frank Fields

Utah

Salt Lake City

C.P.C. Olympus View Hospital, 1430 East 4500 South, Salt Lake City 84117; tel. 801/272-8000; Jerry L. Smith

Highland Ridge Hospital, 4578 Highland Drive, Salt Lake City 84117; tel. 801/272-9851; Richard J. Bell

St. Benedict's Act., 1255 East 3900, South, Salt Lake City 84124; tel. 801/263-1300; H. Lynn Warner, Ph.D.

St. George

Brightway at St. George, 155 West 1470, South, St. George 84770; tel. 801/673-0303; Douglas M. Dinsmore

Virginia

Charlottesville

Charter Hospital, 2101 Arlington Boulevard, Charlottesville 22903; tel. 804/977-1120; Jerome Johnson

Mountain Wood, 500 Old Lynchburg Road, Charlottesville 22905; tel. 804/971-8245; Randall A. Brandt

Chesapeake

New Beginnings/Serenity Lodge, 2097 South Military Highway, Chesapeake 23320; tel. 804/543-6888; John G. Martin

Galax

The Life Center of Galax, 112 Painter Street, Galax 24333; tel. 703/236-2994; Charles A. Speir

Harrisonburg

Arlington Treatment Center, Route 11 North, Harrisonburg 22801; tel. 703/434-7396; Morris A. Hill

Norfolk

C.M.H.C. & Psychiatric Institution, 721 Fairfax Avenue, Norfolk 23501; tel. 804/446-5000; Thomas J. Campbell

Richmond

Charter Westbrook Hospital, 1500 Westbrook Avenue, Richmond 23227; tel. 804/266-9671; Richard V. Woodard

Metropolitan Hospital, 701 West Grace Street, Richmond 23220; tel. 804/775-4184; Thomas G. Honaker

Psychiatric Institute, 3001 Fifth Avenue, Richmond 23222; tel. 804/329-4392; James Mathay

St. John's Hospital, Route 2, Richmond 23233; tel. 804/784-3501; Mark A. Heirholzer

Springfield

Straight, Inc., 5515 Backlick Road, Springfield 22151; tel. 703/642-1980; Page Peary

Staunton

Western State Hospital, Richmond Road, Staunton 24401; tel. 703/885-9207; L. F. Harding

Washington

Bellingham

Olympic Center/Bellingham, 1603 East Illinois Street, Bellingham 98226; tel. 206/733-9111; John W. Rietz, M.Ed., J.D.

Seattle

Seattle Indian Health Board, 1531 13th Avenue, South, Seattle 98114; tel. 206/324-9360; Joann Kauffman

Tacoma

Puyallup Tribal Health, 2209 East 32nd Street, Tacoma 98404; tel. 206/597-6215; Rodney E. Smith

V.A. Medical Center/Tacoma, American Lake, Tacoma 98403; tel. 206/588-2185; William C. Claypool

Yakima

Columbia Hospital, Highland Drive, Yakima 98909; tel. 509/865-2000; Natalie J. Novick

Wisconsin

Janesville

Parkside Lodge of Wisconsin, 320 Lincoln Street, Janesville 53545; tel. 608/754-2264; Ronald Del Ciello

Rock County Health Care Center, Highway 51, North, Janesville 53545; tel. 608/755-2500; Dennis Kirchoff

Kenosha

St. Catherine's Hospital, 3556 7th Avenue, Kenosha 53140; tel. 414/656-3011; Richard W. Berger

La Crosse

La Crosse Lutheran Hospital, 1910 South Avenue, La Crosse 54601; tel. 608/785-0530; John J. Schwen

Milwaukee

DePaul Rehabilitation, 4143 S. 13th Street, Milwaukee 53221; tel. 414/281-4400; A. Bela Maroti

Prescott

River Wood Center, 445 Court Street No., Prescott 54021; tel. 715/262-3286; G. F. Gould

Tomah

V.A. Medical Center/Tomah, Tomah 54660; tel. 608/372-3971; Jon Chisman

Index

Abbreviations Used in AHA Guide

AB, Army base
acad., academy
acct., accountant
acctg., accounting
actg., acting
activ., activities
adj., adjutant
ADM, admiral
adm., administrator; administration; administrative
admit., admitting
adv., adviser; advisory
AEC, Atomic Energy Commission
AFB, Air Force base
aff., affairs
affil., affiliate; affiliation
agen., agencies
agt., agent
AHA, American Hospital Association
AK, Alaska
AL, Alabama
Alta., Alberta
amb., ambulatory
anes., anesthesiology; anesthetist
APO, Army Post Office
arch., architect
AR, Arkansas
A.R.T., accredited record technician
assn., association
assoc., associate
asst., assistant
attend., attending
atty., attorney
auth., authority
aux., auxiliary
Ave., avenue
AZ, Arizona

B.C., British Columbia
bd., board
bd. chm., chairman of the board
bd. mem., board member; member board of trustees
bd. pres., president of the board
bd. sec., secretary of the board
biomed., biomedical
bkpr., bookkeeper
bldg., building(s)
Blvd., boulevard
bnkg., banking
br., branch
Br., brother
Brig., brigadier
bur., bureau
bus., business

CA, California
Capt., captain
CDR, commander, rank
cent., central
cert., certified
chf., chief
chg., charge
chm., chairman
clg., college
clin., clinical; clinic(s)
cmdr., commander, title
cncl., council
CO, Colorado; commanding officer
Col., colonel
com., committee
comdg., commanding
comdt., commandant
comm., community
commun., communications
comp., comprehensive
comr., commissioner
constr., construction
consult., consultant; consulting
cont., continuous; continuation; continuing
contr., controller; comptroller
conv., convalescent
coor., coordinator; coordinating
corp., corporation; corporate
corr., corresponding
C.O.S., chief of staff
counsl., counselor
CPA, certified public accountant
cr., credit
Ct., court
CT, Connecticut
ctr., center
CWO, chief warrant officer

DC, District of Columbia
D.D., doctor of divinity
D.D.S., doctor of dental surgery
DE, Delaware
dent., dental; dentistry
dep., deputy
dept., department
dev., development
diet., dietitian; dietary; dietetics
dir., director
dis., diseases
dist., district
distrib., distribution
div., division
D.O., doctor of osteopathy
Dr., drive
Dr.P.H., doctor of public health
D.Sc., doctor of science
D.V.M., doctor of veterinary medicine
Dwr., drawer

E., east
econ., economist; economics
ed., editor; editorial
Ed.D., doctor of education
educ., education; educational
elec., electrical; electronics
emer., emergency
emp., employee; employment
eng., engineer; engineering
ENS, ensign
environ., environmental
equip., equipment
est., established
exec., executive
Expwy., expressway
ext., extension

facil., facilities
fdn., foundation
fed., federal; federation
fin., finance; financial
FL, Florida
flr., floor
FPO, Fleet Post Office
FT, full-time

GA, Georgia
gen., general
ger., geriatric
govt., government; governmental
grds., grounds

HHS, Department of Health and Human Services
HI, Hawaii
hist., histologic
hlth., health
HM, Helmsman
HMO, health maintenance organization
Hon., honorable; honorary
hosp., hospital(s)
hqrs., headquarters
hshld., household
hskpg., housekeeping
hskpr., housekeeper
Hts., heights
Hwy., highway
hyg., hygiene

IA, Iowa
ID, Idaho
IL, Illinois
IN, Indiana
Inc., incorporated
indust., industrial
info., information
inhal., inhalation
ins., insurance
insp., inspector; inspection
inst., institute(s); institutional
instr., instructor; instruction
int., intern; internal
intl., international

J.D., doctor of law
Jr., junior

KS, Kansas
KY, Kentucky

LA, Louisiana
lab., laboratory; laboratories
ldry., laundry
L.H.D., doctor of humanities
lib., librarian; library
L.P.N., licensed practical nurse
Lt., lieutenant
Ltd., limited
LCDR, lieutenant commander
LL.D., doctor of laws
LT.GEN., lieutenant general
LTJG, lieutenant (junior grade)

MA, Massachusetts
maint., maintenance
Maj., major
Man., Manitoba
matl., material(s)
Matr., matron
mbrshp., membership
M.C., member of Congress
MC, Medical Corps
MD, Maryland; doctor of medicine
ME, Maine
mech., mechanic; mechanical
med., medical; medicine
mem., member
met., metropolitan
meth., method(s)
mgr., manager(s)
mgt., management
MI, Michigan
mil., military
min., minister
mktg., marketing
MN, Minnesota
mng., managing
MO, Missouri
MS, Mississippi
MSC, Medical Service Corps
Msgr., monsignor
MT, Montana
Mt., mount

N., north
natl., national
N.B., New Brunswick
NC, North Carolina
ND, North Dakota
NE, Nebraska
Nfld., Newfoundland
NH, New Hampshire
NJ, New Jersey
NM, New Mexico
nrs., nurse; nurses
nrsg., nursing
N.S., Nova Scotia
nucl., nuclear
nutr., nutrition; nutritional
NV, Nevada
N.W.T., Northwest Territories
NY, New York

ob., obstetrics; obstetrical
occup., occupation; occupational
O.D., doctor of optometry
off., office; officer
OH, Ohio
OK, Oklahoma
Ont., Ontario
oper., operation(s); operational; operating
o.r., operating room
OR, Oregon
orth., orthopedic

PA, Pennsylvania
pat., patient
path., pathologist; pathology
P.E.I., Prince Edward Island
pers., personnel
pharm., pharmacy; pharmacist; pharmaceutical
Ph.D., doctor of philosophy
PHS, Public Health Service
phys., physician; physical
Pkwy., parkway
Pl., place
plng., planning
pp., pages
PR, Puerto Rico
prac., practical
pres., president
prev., preventive
prim., primary
prin., principal; principle
proc., processing; procedures
prod., production
prof., professor; professional
prog., program
proj., project(s)
prop., property
prov., provincial; provisional
PSRO, Professional Standards Review Organization
psych., psychiatric; psychiatrist; psychiatry
psychol., psychological; psychologist; psychology
PT, part-time
pub., public
pur., purchasing

Q.C., Queen's Counsel
Que., Quebec

rad., radiation; radiologist; radiology
RADM, rear admiral
Rd., road
rec., record(s)
reg., registered; region; regional
regstr., registrar
rehab., rehabilitation
rel., relations
rep., representative
res., resident; research
resp., respiratory; respiration
ret., retired
Rev., reverend
R.F.D., rural free delivery
RI, Rhode Island
rm., room
R.N., registered nurse
rot., rotating
R.R.A., registered record administrator
Rt., right
Rte., route

S., south
Sask., Saskatchewan
SC, South Carolina
Sc.D., doctor of science
sci., science; scientific
SD, South Dakota
sec., secretary
sect., section
sen., senior
serv., service(s)
SHCC, statewide health coordinating council
soc., social
spec., special; specialist
Sgt., sergeant
Sq., square
sqdn., squadron
Sr., senior; sister
SS., saints
St., saint; street
Sta., station
stat., statistical; statistician
Ste., sainte
sup., supply(s)
supr., superior
supt., superintendent
supv., supervisor; supervisory
surg., surgeon; surgical
syst., system(s)

tech., technical; technician; technologist
tel., telephone
telecommun., telecommunications
Terr., terrace
ther., therapeutic; therapy
TN, Tennessee
Tpke., turnpike
treas., treasurer
Twp., township
trng., training
TX, Texas

Univ., university
USA, United States Army
USAF, United States Air Force
USMC, United States Marine Corps
USN, United States Navy
USPHS, United States Public Health Service
UT, Utah
util., utility(s); utilization

VA, Virginia
VADM, vice admiral
VI, Virgin Islands
vice-pres., vice-president
vlg., village
vol., volunteer(s)
VT, Vermont

W., west
WA, Washington
welf., welfare
WI, Wisconsin
WV, West Virginia
WY, Wyoming

AHA members $60
Nonmembers $150
Telephone orders 1.800.AHA.2626

AHA Product no. G01-010087
ISSN 0094-8969
ISBN 0-87258-452-6